MW00474138

THE

HOLY BIBLE

CONTAINING THE

OLD AND NEW TESTAMENTS

THE TEXT CAREFULLY PRINTED FROM THE MOST CORRECT COPIES OF THE PRESENT AUTHORIZED TRANSLATION, INCLUDING THE MARGINAL READINGS AND PARALLEL TEXTS

WITH

A COMMENTARY AND CRITICAL NOTES

DESIGNED AS A HELP TO A BETTER UNDERSTANDING OF THE SACRED WRITINGS

BY ADAM CLARKE, LL.D., F.S.A., &c.

A NEW EDITION, WITH THE AUTHOR'S FINAL CORRECTIONS

For whatsoever things were written aforetime were written for our learning, that we through patience and comfort of the Scriptures might have hope.—Rom. xv. 4.

THE OLD TESTAMENT

VOLUME III.—JOB TO SOLOMON'S SONG

ABINGDON
NASHVILLE

ISBN 0-687-09120-9

Printed in the United States of America

PREFACE

TO THE

BOOK OF JOB

THIS is the most singular book in the whole of the Sacred Code: though written by the same inspiration, and in reference to the same end, the salvation of men, it is so different from every other book of the Bible, that it seems to possess nothing in common with them, for even the *language*, in its construction, is dissimilar from that in the *Law*, the *Prophets*, and the *historical books*. But on all hands it is accounted a work that contains "the purest *morality*, the sublimest *philosophy*, the simplest *ritual*, and the most majestic *creed*." Except the *two first chapters* and the *ten last verses*, which are merely *prose*, all the rest of the book is *poetic;* and is every where reducible to the *hemistich* form, in which all the other poetic books of the Bible are written: it is therefore properly called a POEM; but whether it belongs to the *dramatic* or *epic* species has not been decided by learned men. To try it by those *rules* which have been derived from *Aristotle*, and are still applied to ascertain compositions in these departments of poetry, is, in my opinion, as absurd as it is ridiculous. Who ever made a poem on these rules? And is there a poem in the universe worth reading that is strictly conformable to these rules? *Not one.* The rules, it is true, were deduced from compositions of this description:—and although they may be very useful, in assisting poets to methodize their compositions, and to keep the different parts distinct; yet they have often acted as a species of critical trammels, and have cramped genius. Genuine poetry is like a mountain flood: it pours down, resistless, bursts all bounds, scoops out its own channel, carries woods and rocks before it, and spreads itself abroad, both deep and wide, over all the plain. Such, indeed, is the poetry which the reader will meet with in this singular and astonishing book. As to Aristotle himself, although he was a keen-eyed plodder of nature, and a prodigy for his time; yet if we may judge from his *poetics*, he had a soul as incapable of feeling the true *genie createur*, as *Racine* terms the *spirit of poetry*, as he was, by his physics, metaphysics, and analogies, of discovering the true system of the universe.

As to the book of Job, it is most evidently a *poem*, and a *poem* of the highest order; dealing in *subjects* the most grand and sublime; using *imagery* the most chaste and appropriate; described by language the most happy and energetic; conveying *instruction*, both in Divine and human things, the most ennobling and useful; abounding in *precepts* the most pure and exalted, which are enforced by *arguments* the most strong and conclusive, and illustrated by *examples* the most natural and striking.

All these points will appear in the strongest light to every attentive reader of the book; and to such its great *end* will be answered: they will learn from it, that God has way every where: that the *wicked*, though bearing rule for a time, can never be ultimately prosperous and happy; and that the *righteous*, though oppressed with sufferings and calamities, can never be forgotten by Him in whose hands are his saints, and with whom their lives are precious; that in this world neither are the wicked ultimately punished, nor the righteous ultimately rewarded; that God's judgments are a great deep, and his ways past finding out; but the issues of all are to the glory of his wisdom and grace, and to the eternal happiness of those who trust in him. This is the grand design of the book, and this design will be strikingly evident to the simplest and most unlettered reader, whose heart is right with God, and who is seeking instruction, in order that he may glorify his Maker, by receiving and by doing good.

Notwithstanding all this, there is not a book in Scripture on the subject of which more *difficulties* have been started. None, says *Calmet*, has furnished more subjects of doubt and embarrassment; and none has afforded less information for the solution of those doubts. On this subject the great questions which have been agitated refer, principally, 1. To the *person* of Job. 2. To his *existence*. 3. To the *time* in which he lived. 4. To his *country*. 5. To his *stock* or *kindred*. 6. To his *religion*. 7. To the *author* of the book. 8. To its *truth*. 9. To its *authenticity;* and, 10. To the *time* and *occasion* on which it was written.

With respect to the *first* and *second*, several writers of eminent note have denied the *personality* of Job; according to them, no such person ever existed; he is merely *fabulous*, and is like the *Il penseroso*, or *sorrowful man* of Milton; sorrow, distress, affliction, and persecution personified, as the name imports. According to them, he is a mere *ideal being*, created by the genius of the poet; clothed with such attributes, and placed in such circumstances, as gave the poet scope and materials for his work.

Thirdly, as to the *time* in which those place him who receive this as a *true history*, there is great variety. According to some, he flourished in the *patriarchal age;* some make him *contemporary* with *Moses;* that he was in the captivity in Egypt, and that he lived at the time of the *exodus*. Some place him in the time of the Israelitish *judges;* others in the days of *David;* others, in those of *Solomon;* and others, in the time of the *Babylonish captivity*, having been teacher of a school at Tiberias in Palestine, and, with the rest of his countrymen, carried away into Babylon; and that he lived under *Ahasuerus* and *Esther*. *Fourthly*, as to his *country:* some make him an *Arab;* others, an *Egyptian;* others, a *Syrian;* some an *Israelite;* and some, an *Idumean*. *Fifthly*, as to his *origin:* some derive him from *Nachor*, and others from *Esau*, and make him the *fifth* in descent *from Abraham*. *Sixthly*, as to his *religion:* some suppose it to have been *Sabæism;* others, that it was *patriarchal;* and others, that he was bred up in the *Jewish* faith. *Seventhly*, as to the *author* of the work, learned men are greatly divided: some suppose the author to have been *Elihu;* others, *Job;* others, *Job* and *his friends;* others, *Moses;* some, *Solomon;* others, *Isaiah;* and others, *Ezra*, or some *unknown Jew*, posterior to the captivity. *Eighthly*, as to the book: some maintain that it is a history of *fact*, given by one best qualified to record it; and others, that it is an instructive *fiction*—facts, persons, dialogues and all, being supposititious; given, however, by the inspiration of God, in a sort of *parabolic* form, like those employed in the Gospel; and similar to that of the *rich man and Lazarus*. *Ninthly*, as to its *authenticity:* while some, and those not well qualified to judge, have asserted it to be a mere *human production*, of no Divine authority; others have clearly shown that the book itself, whatever questions may arise concerning the *person*, *author*, *time*, *place*, &c., was ever received by the Jewish *Church* and *people* as authentic, genuine, and divinely inspired; and incorporated, with the highest propriety, among the most instructive, sublime, and excellent portions of Divine revelation. *Tenthly*, as to the *occasion* on which it was written, there are considerable differences of opinion: some will have it to be written for the *consolation* of the *Hebrews* in their peregrinations through the *wilderness;* and others, for the comfort and encouragement of the Israelites in the *Babylonish captivity:* these state that *Job* represents *Nehemiah*, and that his three professed friends, but real enemies, *Eliphaz* the *Temanite*, *Bildad* the *Shuhite*, and *Zophar* the *Naamathite*, represent *Sanballat* the *Horonite*, *Tobiah* the *Ammonite*, and *Geshem* the *Arabian!* and that the whole book should be understood and interpreted on this ground; and that, with a little allowance for poetic colouring, all its parts perfectly harmonize, thus understood; showing, in a word, that into whatsoever troubles or persecutions God may permit his people to be brought, yet he will sustain them in the fire, bring them safely through it, and discomfit all their enemies: and that whatsoever is true on this *great scale*, is true also on that which is more *contracted;* as he will equally support, defend, and finally render conqueror, every individual that trusts in him.

I shall not trouble my readers with the arguments which have been used by learned men, *pro* and *con*, relative to the particulars already mentioned: were I to do this, I must transcribe a vast mass of matter, which, though it might display great learning in the authors, would most certainly afford little edification to the great bulk of my readers. My own opinion on those points they may naturally wish to know; and to that opinion they have a right: it is such as I dare avow, and such as I feel no disposition to conceal. I believe Job to have been a *real person*, and his history to be a *statement* of *facts*.

As the preface to this book (I mean the first chapter) states him to have lived in the land of *Uz*, or *Uts*, I believe, with Mr. *Good* and several other learned men, this place to have been "situated in *Arabia Petræa*, on the south-western coast of the lake *Asphaltites*, in a line between Egypt and Philistia, surrounded with Kedar, Teman, and Midian; all of which were districts of Arabia Petræa; situated in Idumea, the land of Edom or Esau; and comprising so large a part of it, that *Idumea* and *Ausitis*, or the land of *Uz*, and the land of *Edom*, were convertible terms, and equally employed to import the same region: thus, Lam. iv. 21: 'Rejoice and be glad, O daughter of Edom, that dwellest in the land of Uz.' " See Mr. *Good's Introductory Dissertation;* who proceeds to observe: "Nothing is clearer than that all the persons introduced into this poem were *Idumeans*, dwelling in Idumea; or, in other words, Edomite Arabs. These characters are, *Job* himself, dwelling in the land of *Uz; Eliphaz* of *Teman*, a district of as much repute as *Uz*, and (upon the joint testimony of *Jer*. xlix. 7, 20; *Ezek*. xxv. 13; *Amos* i. 11, 12, and *Obadiah* ver. 8, 9) a part, and a principal part, of *Idumea; Bildad* of *Shuah*, always mentioned in conjunction with *Sheba* and *Dedan*, all of them being uniformly placed in the vicinity of Idumea; *Zophar* of *Naamah*, a city whose name imports *pleasantness*, which is also stated, in Josh. xv. 21, 41, to have been situated in Idumea, and to have lain in a southern direction towards its coast, or the shores of the Red Sea; and *Elihu* of *Buz*, which as the name of a place occurs but once in sacred writ, but is there (Jer. xxv. 22) mentioned in conjunction with *Teman* and *Dedan;* and hence necessarily, like themselves, a border city upon *Ausitis, Uz*, or *Idumea*. It had a number of names: it was at first called *Horitis*, from the *Horim* or *Horites*, who appear to have first settled there. Among the descendants of these, the most distinguished was *Seir;* and from him the land was known by the name of the *Land of Seir*. This *chief* had a numerous family, and among the most signalized of his grandsons was *Uz*, or *Uts;* and from him, and not from *Uz* the son of Nahor, it seems to have been called *Ausitis*, or the *Land of Uz*. The family of *Hor, Seir*, or *Uz*, were at length dispossessed of the entire region by *Esau*, or *Edom;* who strengthened himself by his marriage with one of the daughters of *Ishmael;* and the conquered territory was denominated *Idumea*, or the land of Edom." I think this is conclusive as to the *country* of Job and his friends. See Mr. *Good* as above.

The *man* and his *country* being thus ascertained, the *time* in which he lived is the point next to be considered.

I feel all the difficulties of the various chronologies of learned men: all that has been offered on the subject is only *opinion* or *probable conjecture;* and, while I differ from many respectable authors, I dare not say that I have more to strengthen my opinion than they have to support theirs.

I do not believe that he lived under the *patriarchal* dispensation; nor in any time *previous* to the *giving of the Law*, or to the *death of Moses*. I have examined the opposite arguments, and they have brought no conviction to my mind. That he lived *after* the giving of the Law appears to me very probable, from what I consider frequent references to the Mosaic institutions occurring in the book, and which I shall notice in their respective places. I know it has been asserted *there are no such references;* and I am astonished at the assertion: the reader will judge whether a plain case is made out where the supposed references occur. An obstinate adherence to a preconceived system is like *prejudice;* it has neither *eyes* nor *ears.*

With this question, that relative to the *author* of the book is nearly connected. Were we to suppose that *Job* himself, or *Elihu,* or *Job* and *his friends,* wrote the work, the question would at once be answered that regards the *time;* but all positive evidence on this point is wanting: and while other suppositions have certain *arguments* to support them, the above claimants who are supported only by critical *conjecture,* must stand where they are for want of evidence. The opinions that appear the most probable, and have plausible arguments to support them, are the following: 1. *Moses* was the author of this book, as many portions of it harmonize with his acknowledged writings. 2. *Solomon* is the most likely author, as many of the sentiments contained in it are precisely the same with those in the Proverbs; and they are delivered often in nearly the same words. 3. The book was written by some *Jew,* in or soon after the time of the Babylonish captivity.

1. That *Moses* was the author has been the opinion of most learned men; and none has set the arguments in support of this opinion in so strong a light as Mr. *Mason Good,* in his *Introductory Dissertation* to his *translation* and *notes* on this book. Mr. G. is a gentleman of great knowledge, great learning, and correct thinking; and whatever he says or writes is entitled to respect. If he have *data,* his deductions are most generally consecutive and solid. He contends, "that the writer of this poem must in his style have been equally master of the *simple* and of the *sublime;* that he must have been minutely and elaborately acquainted with *Astronomy, Natural History,* and the *general science* of his age; that he must have been a *Hebrew* by birth and *native language,* and an *Arabian* by long residence and local study; and, finally, that he must have flourished and composed the work before the exodus." And he thinks that "every one of these features is consummated in *Moses,* and in *Moses* alone; and that the whole of them give us his complete lineaments and portraiture. Instructed in all the learning of Egypt, it appears little doubtful that he composed it during some part of his forty years' residence with the hospitable Jethro, in that district of Idumea which was named Midian." In addition to these external proofs of identity, Mr. *Good* thinks, "a little attention will disclose to us an internal proof, of peculiar force, in the close and striking similarity of diction and idiom which exists between the book of Job and those pieces of poetry which *Moses* is usually admitted to have composed. This point he proceeds to examine; and thinks that the following examples may make some progress toward settling the question, by exhibiting a very singular proof of general *parallelism.*

"The order of creation, as detailed in the first chapter of Genesis, is precisely similar to that described in Job xxxviii. 1–20, the general arrangement that occupied the *first* day;—the formation of the *clouds,* which employed the *second;*—the separation of the *sea,* which took up a part of the *third;*—and the establishment of the *luminaries* in the skies, which characterized the *fourth.*

"In this general description, as given in Genesis, the vapour in the clouds, and the fluid in the sea, are equally denominated *waters:* thus, ver. 5, 6, 7, 'And God said, Let there be a firmament *in the midst of the waters,* and let it divide the *waters from the waters.* And God made the firmament, and divided the *waters which were under* the firmament from the *waters which were above* the firmament.'

"Let us compare this passage with Job xxvi. 8–10:—

> He driveth together the *waters* into His thick clouds;
> And the cloud is not rent under them.—
> He setteth a bow on the face of the *waters,*
> Till the consummation of light and of darkness.

"These are, perhaps, the only instances in the Bible in which the cloudy vapours are denominated *waters,* before they become concentrated into rain; and they offer an identity of thought, which strongly suggests an identity of person. The following is another very striking peculiarity of the same kind, occurring in the same description, and is perhaps still more in point. The combined simplicity and sublimity of Gen. i. 3, 'And God said, Be light! and light was,' has been felt and praised by critics of every age, Pagan and Mohammedan, as well as Jewish and Christian; and has by all of them been regarded as a characteristic feature in the Mosaic style. In the poem before us we have the following proof of identity of manner, chap. xxxvii. 6:—

Behold! He saith to the snow, Be!
On earth then falleth it.
To the rain—and it falleth;—
The rains of his might.

"This can hardly be regarded as an allusion, but as an instance of identity of manner. In the psalmist we have an allusion: and it occurs thus, xxxiii. 9, הוא אמר ויהי *hu amar vaiyehi*, 'He spake, and it existed;' and I copy it that the reader may see the difference. The eulogy of Longinus upon the passage in Genesis is a eulogy also upon that in Job; and the Koran, in verbally copying the psalmist, has bestowed an equal panegyric upon all of them:—

قال كن فيكون

DIXIT, 'ESTO;' ET FUIT.—*He said*, BE THOU; *and it* WAS.

"With reference to the description of the creation, in the book of Genesis, I shall only farther observe, that the same simplicity of style, adapted to so lofty a subject, characteristically distinguishes the writer of the book of Job, who commonly employs a diction peculiarly magnificent, as though trusting to the subject to support itself, without the feeble aid of rhetorical ornaments. Of this the description of the tribunal of the Almighty, given in the first and second chapters of the ensuing poem, is a striking example, as indeed I have already remarked; and that of the midnight apparition in the fourth chapter is no less so.

"The following instances are of a more general nature, and lead, upon a broader principle, to the same conclusion:—

Ch. ver.	JOB	Ch. ver.	EXODUS
xiii. 24.	Wherefore accountest thou me thine enemy? Wouldst thou hunt down the parched stubble?	xv. 7.	Thou sentest forth thy wrath, Consuming them as stubble.
iv. 9.	By the blast of God they perish; And by the breath of His nostrils they are consumed.	8.	And with the blast of thy nostrils The waters were gathered together.
xv. 24.	*Distress* and *anguish* dismay him; They overwhelm him as a king ready for battle.	10.	Thou didst blow with thy wind: The sea covered them.
xx. 26.	Terrors shall be upon him—	16.	Terror and dread shall fall upon them: By the might of thine arm they shall be still as a stone.
26.	Every *horror* treasured up in reserve for him. A fire unblown shall consume him.		

Ch. ver.	JOB	Ch. ver.	DEUTERONOMY
27.	The heavens shall disclose his iniquity, And the earth shall rise up against him.	xxviii. 22.	And Jehovah shall smite thee with a consumption; And with a fever, and with an inflammation, And with an extreme burning.
xviii. 15.	Brimstone shall be rained down upon his dwelling.		
16.	Below shall his root be burnt up, And above shall his branch be cut off.	23.	And the heaven over thy head shall be brass; And the earth under thee, iron.
xii. 17.	Counsellors he leadeth captive, And judges he maketh distracted.	24.	And Jehovah shall make the rain of thy land powder and dust; From heaven shall it come down upon thee, Until thou be destroyed.
24.	He bewildereth the judgment of the leaders of the people of a land, And causeth them to wander in a pathless desert:	28.	Jehovah shall smite thee with destruction, And blindness, and astonishment of heart.

Ch. ver.	Job	Ch. ver.	Deuteronomy
vii. 25.	They grope about in darkness, even without a glimpse; Yea, he maketh them to reel like the drunkard.	xxviii. 29.	And thou shalt grope at noonday, As the blind gropeth in darkness: And thou shalt not prosper in thy ways: And thou shalt only be oppressed. And consumed continually.
viii. 17.	His roots shall be entangled in a rock; With a bed of stones shall he grapple;		
18.	Utterly shall it drink him up from his place; Yea, it shall renounce him, and say, "I never knew thee."	63.	And it shall come to pass, As Jehovah exulted over you, To do you good, and to multiply you, So will Jehovah exult over you, To destroy you, and reduce you to naught.
19.	Behold the Eternal exulting in his course; Even over his dust shall rise up another.		

"In this specimen of comparison it is peculiarly worthy of remark, that not only the same train of ideas is found to recur, but in many instances the same words, where others might have been employed, and perhaps have answered as well; the whole obviously resulting from the habit of thinking upon subjects in the same manner, and by means of the same terms which is common to every one, and which distinguishes original identity from intentional imitation. I will only advert to one instance: the use of the very powerful, but not very common verb שש *sis*, 'to exult,' *exulto, glorior*, γαυριαω, which occurs in the last verse of both the above passages, and is in each instance equally appropriate: ישיש יהוה *yasis Yehovah*—הוא משוש *hu mesos*, ستو سش

"The same term is again employed, Job xxxix. 21, to express the spirited prancing of the high mettled war-horse.

"The above passage from chap. viii. 19 has not been generally understood, and has been given erroneously in the translations." Mr. *Good*, in his notes, p. 101–103, enters at large into a defence of his version of this passage.

Ch. ver.	Job	Ch. ver.	Deuteronomy
viii. 8.	For examine, I beseech thee, the past age; Yea, gird thyself to the study of its forefathers;	xxxii. 7.	Reflect on the days of old; Contemplate the times of ages beyond ages; Inquire of thy father, and he will show thee; Thine elders, *and they will* instruct thee.
10.	Shall not they instruct thee, counsel thee, And swell forth the sayings of their wisdom?		
xx. 17.	He shall not behold the branches of the river, Brooks of honey and butter.—	13.	He gave him to suck honey out of the rock, And oil out of the flinty rock,
xxix. 6.	When my path flowed with butter, And the rock *poured out* for me rivers of oil.	14.	Butter of kine, and milk of sheep.
xv. 27.	Though his face be enveloped with fatness, And heaped up with fatness on his loins.	15.	But Jeshurun waxed fat, and kicked: Thou art waxen fat, thou art grown thick; Thou art *enveloped with* fatness.
vi. 4.	The arrows of the Almighty are within me; Their poison drinketh up my spirit: The *terrors* of God set themselves in array against me;	23.	I will heap mischiefs upon them, I will spend my arrows upon them.
xvi. 13.	His arrows fly around me; He pierceth my reins without mercy.	42.	I will make mine arrows drunk with blood.

"The fine pathetic elegy of the *ninetieth* psalm has been usually ascribed to Moses; and Dathé imagines it was written by him a little before his death.

"Kennicott and Geddes have some doubt upon this point, chiefly because the ultimate period assigned in it to the life of man is fourscore years; while Moses was at his death a hundred and twenty years old, yet 'his eye was not dim, nor his natural force abated;' Deut. xxxiv. 7.

"The following comparison will, perhaps, have a tendency to confirm the general opinion, by rendering it probable that its author and the author of the Book of Job were the same person.

Ch. ver.	Job	Psa. ver.	Psalm
xiv. 2.	He springeth up as a flower, and is cut down; Yea, he fleeth as a shadow, and endureth not.	xc. 5.	They are like the passing grass of the morning;
3.	And dost thou cast thine eyes upon such a one? And wouldst thou bring me into judgment with thyself?	6.	In the morning it springeth up and groweth: In the evening it is cut down and withereth.
16.	Yet now art thou numbering my steps; Thou overlookest nothing of my sins:—	7.	For we are consumed by thine anger, And by thy wrath are we troubled.
18.	And for ever, as the crumbling mountain dissolveth, And the rock mouldereth away from his place,	8.	Thou hast set our iniquities before thee: Our secret sins in the light of thy countenance.
19.	So consumest thou the hope of man, Thou harassest him continually till he perish.	9.	Behold, all our days are passed away in thy wrath, We spend our years as a tale that is told.
vii. 21.	Why wilt thou not turn away from my transgression, And let my calamity pass by?	10.	Their strength is labour and sorrow; It is soon cut off, and we flee away.
xi. 14.	If the iniquity of thy hand thou put away, And let not wickedness dwell in thy tabernacles,	12.	So teach us to number our days That we may apply our hearts unto wisdom.
16.	Lo! then shalt thou forget affliction; As waters passed by shalt thou remember it:	14.	O satisfy us early with thy mercy, That we may rejoice and be glad all our days,
17.	And brighter shall the time be than noontide; Thou shalt shine forth, thou shalt grow vigorous, like the day-spring.	15.	Make us glad according to the days of our affliction, To the years we have seen evil:
		16.	Let thy wonders be shown unto thy servants And thy glory unto their children;
		17.	And let the beauty of Jehovah, our God be upon us, And establish thou the work of our hands.

"The strictly and decidedly acknowledged productions of Moses are but few; and in the above examples I have taken a specimen from by far the greater number. It is, indeed, not a little astonishing that, being so few, they should offer a resemblance in so many points.

"There may at times be some difficulty in determining between the similarity of style and diction resulting from established habit, and that produced by intentional imitation; yet, in the former case, it will commonly, if I mistake not, be found looser, but more general; in the latter, stricter, but more confined to particular words or idioms; the whole of the features not having been equally caught, while those which have been laid hold of are given more minutely than in the case of habit. The *manner* runs carelessly through every part, and is perpetually striking us unawares; the *copy* walks after it with measured but unequal pace, and is restless in courting our attention. The specimens of resemblance now produced are obviously of the former kind: both sides have an equal claim to originality, and seem very powerfully to establish a unity of authorship."

Thus far Mr. Good; who has, on his own side of the question, most certainly exhausted the subject. The case he has made out is a strong one: we shall next examine whether a stronger cannot be made out in behalf of *Solomon*, as the second candidate for the authorship of this most excellent book.

2. That this book was the work of Solomon was the opinion of some early Christian writers, among whom was Gregory Nazianzen; and of several moderns, among whom were Spanheim and Hardouin. The latter has gone so far as to place the death of Job in the *thirty-fifth* year of the reign of David; and he supposes that Solomon wrote the work in question, about the *second* or *third* year of his reign. On this last opinion no stress whatever should be placed.

As the argument for Moses has been supported by supposed *parallelisms* between his acknowledged works and the Book of Job, so has that which attributes the latter to Solomon. That Solomon, from his *vast learning* and *wisdom*, was capable of such a work, none can deny. His knowledge in *astronomy*, *natural history*, *politics*, *theology*, *languages*, and the *general science* of *his* age, must have given him at least equal qualifications to those possessed by Moses. And if *he* was the author of the Book of Canticles, which most men believe, he had certainly a *poetic mind*, equal, if not superior, to all the writers who had existed previously to his time. The Book of Proverbs and that of Ecclesiastes are almost universally attributed to him: now, in the Book of Job, there are a multitude of *sentiments, sentences, terms*, and *modes of speech*, which are almost peculiar to Solomon, as will appear from the whole books.

In both we find the most exalted eulogium of *wisdom*. See Job xxviii. 12; Prov. viii. 11, &c. Job says, "The *fear of the Lord*, that is *wisdom;* and to depart from evil, that is *understanding;*" chap. xxviii. 28. Solomon says, "The *fear of the Lord* is the beginning of *knowledge*, but *fools* despise *wisdom* and *instruction;*" Prov. i. 7.

Job speaks of the *state of the dead* nearly in the same terms as Solomon: compare chap. xxi. 33, xii. 22, xxxvi. 5, with Prov. ix. 18.

Job says, chap. xxvi. 6, "*Hell* is naked before him, and *destruction* hath no covering." Solomon says, Prov. xv. 11, "*Hell* and *destruction* are before the Lord; how much more the hearts of the children of men?" Job says, "Man drinketh iniquity like water;" chap. xv. 16. And *Elihu* charges him with "drinking *up* scorning like water;" chap. xxxiv. 7. The same image occurs in *Solomon*, Prov. xxvi. 6: "He that sendeth a message by the hand of a fool *drinketh* damage."

In Job xv. 34 it is said, "Fire shall consume the tabernacle of *bribery*." The same turn of thought occurs Prov. xv. 27: "He that is greedy of gain troubleth his own house; but he that hateth *gifts* shall live."

Both speak of *weighing the spirits* or *winds*. See Job xxviii. 25; Prov. xvi. But to me the parallelism in these cases is not evident, as both the reason of the saying, and some of the terms in the original, are different. Job tells his friends, "If they would *hold their peace*, it would be their *wisdom;*" chap. xiii. 5. Solomon has the same sentiment in nearly the same words, Prov. xvii. 28: "Even a fool, when he *holdeth his peace*, is counted *wise;* and he that shutteth his lips is esteemed a man of understanding."

Solomon represents the *rephaim* or *giants* as in *hell*, or the *great deep;* Prov. ii. 18; ix. 18, vii. 27. The like sentiment is in Job xxvi. 5. See the Hebrew.

In Job xxvii. 16, 17, it is said that "If the wicked heap up silver as the dust, and prepare raiment as the clay; the just shall put it on, and the innocent shall divide the silver." The like sentiment is found, Prov. xxviii. 8: "He that by usury and unjust gain increaseth his substance, he shall gather for him that will pity the poor." Solomon says, Prov. xvi. 18: "Pride goeth before destruction, and a haughty spirit before a fall:" and, "Before destruction the heart of man is haughty; and before honour is humility;" xviii. 12: and, "A man's pride shall bring him low; but honour shall uphold the humble in spirit." The same sentiment is expressed in Job xxii. 29: "When men are *cast down*, then thou shalt say, There is a *lifting up;* and he shall save the *humble* person."

Both speak nearly in the same way concerning the *creation* of the *earth* and the *sea*. "Where wast thou when I *laid the foundations of the earth?*—Who *shut up the sea* with doors, when it brake forth as if it had issued from the womb?" Job xxxviii. 4–8. This seems a reference to the *flood*. In Prov. vii. 22–29 *Wisdom* says: "The Lord possessed me in the beginning of his way—when as yet he had not *made the earth*—when he gave to the *sea his decree* that the *waters* should not *pass his commandment:* when he *appointed* the *foundations of the earth*." These are precisely the same kind of conceptions, and nearly the same phraseology.

In Job xx. 7 it is said, "The wicked shall *perish* for ever, like his own DUNG." And in Prov. x. 7 it is said, "The name of the wicked shall ROT."

It would not be difficult to enlarge this list of correspondences by a collation of passages in *Job* and in *Proverbs;* but most of them will occur to the attentive reader. There is, however, another *class of evidence* that appears still more forcible, viz.: There are several *terms* used frequently in the Book of Job and in the books of Solomon which are almost *peculiar* to those books, and which argue an *identity* of *authorship*. The noun תושיה *tushiyah*, which may signify *essence, substance, reality, completeness*, occurs in Job and Proverbs. See Job v. 12, vi. 13, xi. 6, xii. 16, xxvi. 3, and xxx. 22; Proverbs ii. 7, iii. 21, viii. 14, and xviii. 1. And it occurs only *twice*, as far as I can recollect, in all the Bible besides; viz., Isa. xxviii. 29, and Mic. vi. 9. The word הוה *havvah*, used in the sense of *misfortune, ruinous downfall, calamity*, occurs Job vi. 2, 30, xxx. 13, and in Prov. x. 3, xi. 6, xvii. 4, and xix. 13. It occurs nowhere else, except once in Ezek. vii. 26, once in Micah vii. 3, and a few times in the Psalms, v. 9, lii. 2, 7, lv. 12, xci. 3, xciv. 20, xxxvii. 12, and lxii. 3.

The word תחבלות *tachbuloth, wise counsels*, occurs only in Job xxxvii. 12, and in Prov. i. 5, xi. 14, xii. 5, xx. 18, and xxiv. 6; and nowhere else in the Bible in this form. And פתה *potheh, the silly one, simpleton, fool*, is used precisely in the same sense in Job v. 2, Prov. xix. 7, and in various other parts of the same book. The word אבדון, *abaddon, destruction*, Job xxvi. 6, xxviii. 22, xxxi. 12, connected sometimes with שאול *sheol, hell*, or the *grave;* and מות *maveth, death*, occurs as above, and in Prov. xv. 11, and xxvii. 20.

Calmet, who refers to several of the above places, adds: It would be easy to collect a great number of similar parallel passages; but it must make a forcible impression in favour of this opinion when we observe in Job and Proverbs the same *principles*, the same sentiments, the same terms, and some that are found only in Job and Solomon. We may add farther, the beauty of the *style*, the sublimity of the *thoughts*, the dignity of the *matter*, the *form* and *order* in which the *materials* of this writer are laid down, the vast *erudition* and astonishing *fecundity* of *genius*, all of which perfectly characterize Solomon.

Besides the above, we find many *forms of expression* in this book which prove that its author had a *knowledge of the law of God*, and *many* which show that he was acquainted with the *Psalms* of David, and a few very like what we find in the *writings of the prophets.* I shall insert a few more:—

Job xv. 27: Because he covereth his face with *fatness.*	Psa. xvii. 10: They are *inclosed* in their own *fat.* lxxiii. 7: Their eyes stand out with *fatness.*
Job xxxiv. 14: If he set his heart upon man, he shall gather unto himself his *spirit* and his *breath.*	Psa. civ. 29: Thou hidest thy face, and they are troubled: thou *takest away* their *breath;* they die, and return to their dust.
Job xxi. 9: Their houses are safe from fear; neither is the rod of God upon them.	Psa. lxxiii. 5: They are not in trouble as other men; neither are they plagued like other men.
Job xxi. 10: Their bull gendereth, and faileth not; their cow calveth, and casteth not her calf.	Psa. cxliv. 13, 14: Let our sheep bring forth thousands;—and our oxen be strong to labour.
Job xxi. 18: They (the wicked) are as *stubble* before the *wind;* and as *chaff* that the storm carrieth away.	Psa. i. 4: The ungodly are like the *chaff* which the *wind* driveth away.
Job xxii. 19: The *righteous see it*, and are *glad;* and the innocent laugh them to scorn.	Psa. lviii. 10: The *righteous shall rejoice* when he seeth the *vengeance;* he shall wash his feet in the blood of the wicked.
Job xxxviii. 41: Who provideth for the *raven his* food? when his *young ones cry unto God.*	Psa. cxlvii. 9: He giveth to the *beast his* food; and to the *young ravens which cry.*
Job xii. 21: *He poureth contempt upon princes*, and weakeneth the strength of the mighty.	Psa. cvii. 40: *He poureth contempt upon princes*, and causeth them to wander in the wilderness.
Job iii. 3: *Let the day perish in which I was born;* and the night in which it was said, There is a man-child conceived. See also chap. x. 18.	Jer. xv. 10: *Wo* is me, my mother, *that thou hast borne me, a man of strife.* xx. 14, 15: *Cursed be the day wherein I was born*—let not the day wherein my mother bare me be blessed.
Job xxi. 7: *Wherefore do the wicked live*, become old, and are *mighty in power?*	Jer. xii. 1, 2: *Wherefore doth the way of the wicked prosper? they grow;* yea, they *bring forth fruit.*
Job xxviii. 12: But where shall *wisdom be found*, and where is the place of *understanding?* 13: Man knoweth not the price thereof; neither is it found in the land of the living.	Collate these verses with *Baruch* iii. 14, 15, 29, and see Prov. i. 20–23, ii. 2–7, iii. 13–18, iv. 5–9, viii. 10–35.

The remarkable sentiment that "God, as Sovereign of the world, does treat the righteous and the wicked, independently of their respective merits, with a similar lot in this life, and that like events often happen to both," is maintained in the Book of Job and the Ecclesiastes of Solomon. Job ix. 22–24: "He *destroyeth* the *perfect* and the *wicked.* If the scourge slay suddenly, he will laugh at the trial of the *innocent.* The *earth* is *given* into the *hand* of the *wicked;* he covereth the faces of the judges thereof; if not, where and who is he?" x. 15: "If I be *wicked,* wo unto me; and if I be *righteous,* yet will I not lift up my head." ix. 15: "*Whom,* though I were *righteous,* yet would I not *answer;* I would make supplication to my Judge." xii. 6: "The tabernacles of *robbers prosper,* and they that *provoke God* are *secure;* into whose hand God bringeth abundantly." xxi. 7–9: "Wherefore do the *wicked live, become old,* yea are *mighty* in *power?* Their *seed* is *established* in their *sight,* and their *offspring before their eyes.* Their *houses* are *safe* from *fear,* neither is the *rod of God upon them.*"

Similar sentiments, with a great similarity of expression, are found in the following passages from *Solomon.* Eccles. vi. 8: "For what hath the *wise* more than the *fool?*" viii. 14: "There be *just men* to whom it happeneth *according* to the *work* of the *wicked.* Again, there be *wicked men* to whom it happeneth *according* to the *work* of the *righteous.*" ix. 2: "*All things come alike to all:* there is *one event to the righteous* and to the *wicked;* to the *good* and to the *clean,* and to the *unclean;* to him that *sacrificeth,* and to him that *sacrificeth not.* As is the *good,* so is the *sinner;* and he that *sweareth,* as he that *feareth* an *oath.*" vii. 15: "There is a *just man* that *perisheth* in his *righteousness;* and there is a *wicked man* that *prolongeth* his life in *his wickedness.*"

I may conclude this with the words of a learned translator of the book of Job, and apply in reference to *Solomon* what he applies to *Moses:* "The specimens of resemblance now produced have an equal claim to originality, and seem very powerfully to establish a unity of authorship." I think the argument much stronger in favour of Solomon as its author than of Moses: and while even here I hesitate, I must enter my protest against the conclusions drawn by others; and especially those who profess to show where *David, Solomon, Isaiah, Jeremiah, Ezekiel,* &c., have *copied* and *borrowed* from Job! Some of them, in all probability, never saw the book; and those who did had an *inspiration, dignity, manner,* and *power* of their own, that rendered it quite unnecessary to borrow from him. Such plagiarism would appear, in common cases, neither requisite nor graceful. I have a high opinion of the book of Job, but God forbid that I should ever bring it on a level with the *compositions* of the *sweet singer of Israel,* the inimitable *threnodies* of *Jeremiah,* or the *ultra-sublime* effusions of the *evangelical prophet.* Let each keep his place, and let God be acknowledged as the inspirer of all.

Thus, by exactly the same process, we come to different conclusions; for the evidence is now as strong *that Job lived posterior to the days of Moses;* that he was acquainted with the *Law* and the *Prophets;* that either he took much from the *Psalms* and *Proverbs,* or that *David* and *Solomon* borrowed much from him; or that *Solomon,* the son of *David,* wrote the history; as it is that he lived in the days of *Moses.*

For my own part, I think the *later date* by far the most probable; and although I think the arguments that go to prove *Solomon* to be the *author* are *weightier* than those so skilfully brought forth by learned men in behalf of *Moses,* yet I think if possible that it was the work of *neither,* but rather of *some learned Idumean,* well acquainted with the Jewish religion and writers; and I still hold the opinion which I formed more than *thirty* years ago, when I read over this book in the *Septuagint,* and afterwards in the *Hebrew,* that it is most probable the work was originally composed in *Arabic,* and afterwards translated into *Hebrew* by a person who either had not the same command of the *Hebrew* as he had of the *Arabic,* or else purposely affected the *Arabic idiom,* retaining many *Arabic words* and *Arabisms;* either because he could not find appropriate expressions in the *Hebrew,* or because he wished to *adorn* and *enrich* the *one language* by borrowing copiously from the other. The *Hebrew* of the book of Job differs as much from the pure Hebrew of *Moses* and the *early prophets,* as the Persian of *Ferdoosy* differs from that of *Saady.* Both these were *Persian poets;* the *former* wrote in the simplicity and purity of his elegant native language, adopting very few *Arabic* words; while *the latter* labours to introduce them at every turn, and has thus produced a language neither *Persian* nor *Arabic*. And so prevalent is this custom become with all Persian writers, both in *prose* and *verse*, that the pure Persian becomes daily more and more corrupted, insomuch that there is reason to fear that in process of time it will be swallowed up in the language of the conquerors of that country, in which it was formerly esteemed the most polished language of Asia. Such influence has the language of a conqueror on the country he has subdued; witness our own, where a paltry *French phraseology*, the remnant of one of the evils brought upon us by our *Norman conqueror* and *tyrant*, has greatly weakened the strong current of our mother tongue; so that, however amalgamated, filed, and polished by eminent authors, we only speak a very tolerable jargon, *enriched*, as we foolishly term it, by the spoils of other tongues. The best specimen of our ancient language exists in the *Lord's prayer*, which is pure *English*, or what is called *Anglo-Saxon*, with the exception of three frenchified words, *trespasses*, *temptation*, and *deliver*.

But to return to the book of Job. The collections of Mr. Good, Dr. Magee, and others, if they do not prove that *Moses was the author of the book*, prove that the author was well acquainted with the Mosaic writings; and prove that he was also acquainted with the ninetieth Psalm; and this last circumstance will go far to prove that he lived *after* the days of *David*, for we have no evidence whatever that the ninetieth Psalm was *published* previously to the collection and publication of the Psalms now generally termed the *Psalms of David*, though many of them were written by other hands, and not a few even *after the Babylonish captivity*. And, as to the *inscription* to this Psalm, תפלה משה איש האלהים *tephillah Mosheh ish haelohim*, "A prayer of Moses, the man of God;" 1. We know not that *Moses* the *Jewish lawgiver* is meant: it might be another person of the same name. 2. And even in that case it does not positively state that this Moses was the *author* of it. 3. The *inscriptions* to the Psalms are of *dubious*, and many of them of *no authority:* some of them evidently *misplaced;* and others either bearing *no relation* to the *matter* of the *Psalms* to which they are prefixed, or evidently contradictory to that matter. Hence our translators have considered these inscriptions as of *no authority;* and have not admitted them, in any case, into the *body* of their respective Psalms. The *parallelism*, therefore, drawn from this Psalm, will not help much to prove that *Moses was the author of the book of Job;* but it will go far to prove, as will be seen in other cases, that the author of this book was acquainted with the *book of Psalms*, as several of the preceding collections testify; and that there is a probability that he had read the *prophets* that lived and wrote in the *time*, and *after* the time, of the *Babylonish captivity*, which appears to me the only thing that shakes the argument in favour of *Solomon;* unless we take the *converse* of the question, and say that *Moses, David, Solomon, Isaiah, Jeremiah*, and *Micah*, all knew and borrowed from the *book of Job*. But this supposition will, in its turn, be shaken by the consideration that there are several things in the book of Job which evidently refer to the *law as already given*, and to some of the *principal occurrences* in the Israelitish history, if such references can be made out. These considerations have led me to think it probable that the book was written *after the captivity* by some unknown but highly eminent and inspired man. We may wonder, indeed, that the author of such an eminent work has not been handed down to posterity; and that the question should be left at the discretion of the whole *limbus* of conjecture; but we find, not only several books in the Bible, but also other works of minor importance and a later date, similarly circumstanced. We have no certain evidence of the *author* of the books of *Judges, Samuel, Kings, Chronicles, Ruth, Ezra, Nehemiah*, or *Esther;* we can, in reference to them, make *probable conjectures*, but this is all. Even in the *New Testament* the author of the *Epistle to the Hebrews* is still unknown; though a pretty general tradition, and strong internal evidence, give it to St. Paul; yet this point is not *so proved* as to exclude all doubt.

The finest poems of heathen antiquity, the *Iliad* and *Odyssey*, cannot be certainly traced to their author. Of the person called *Homer*, to whom they have been attributed, no one knows any thing. He is still, for aught we know, a *fabulous* person; and the relations concerning him are entitled to little more credit than is due to the *Life of Æsop* by *Planudes*. *Seven* different *cities* have claimed the honour of being his birth-place. They are expressed in the following distich:—

Ἑπτα πολεις διεριζουσι περι ριζαν Ὁμηρου,
Σμυρνα, Ῥοδος, Κολοφον, Σαλαμις, Χιος, Αργος, Αθηναι.

Smyrna, Rhodos, Colophon, Salamis, Chios, Argos, Athenæ,
Orbis de Patria certat, HOMERE, *tua.*

Nor have these claims ever been adjusted. Some have gone so far as to attribute the work to *Solomon*, king of Israel, composed *after* his defection from the true religion to idolatry! that the word *Homer*, Ὁμηρος *Homeros*, is merely *Hebrew*, אמרים *omerim*, with a *Greek* termination, signifying the *sayings* or *discourses*, from אמר *amar, he spoke;* the whole work being little more than the *dialogues* or *conversations* of the eminent characters of which it is composed. Even the *battles* of Homer are full of *parleys;* and the principal information conveyed by the poem is through the *conversation* of the respective chiefs.

The *Makamaton*, or *assemblies*, of the celebrated Arabic author *Hariri*, show us how *conversations* were anciently carried on among the *Arabs*, and even in the same country in which the plan of the poem of Job is laid; and were we closely to compare the *sex concessus* of that author, published by *Schultens*, we might find many analogies between them and the turn of conversation in the book of Job. But the *uncertainty* relative to the *author* detracts nothing from the *merit* and *excellency* of the *poem*. As it is the most singular, so it is the best, as a whole, in the *Hebrew* canon. It exhibits a full view of the opinions of the eastern sages on the most important points; not only their *religion* and *system* of *morals* are frequently introduced, but also their philosophy, astronomy, natural history, mineralogy, and *arts* and *sciences* in general; as well those that were *ornamental*, as those which ministered to the comforts and necessities of life. And on a careful examination, we shall probably find that several arts, which are supposed to be the discoveries of the *moderns*, were not unknown to those who lived in a very remote antiquity, and whom it is fashionable to consider as *unlettered* and *uncultivated barbarians*.

As the person, family, time, and descendants of Job are so very uncertain, I shall not trouble my readers with the many *genealogical tables* which have been constructed by chronologists and commentators; yet it might be considered a *defect* were I not to notice what is inserted at the end of the *Greek* and *Arabic* Versions relative to this point; to which I shall add Dr. *Kennicott's* Tables, and the substance of a letter which contains some curious particulars.

"And he (Job) dwelt in the land of *Ausitis*, in the confines of Idumea and Arabia; and his former name was *Jobab*. And he took to wife Arabissa, and begat a son whose name was Ennon. And his (Jobab's) father's name was Zarith, one of the sons of the children of Esau; and his mother's name was Bosora; and thus he was the *fifth* from Abraham."

"And these are the kings who reigned in Edom; which region he also governed; the first was *Balak*, the son of Beor, the name of whose city was Dennaba. And after Balak reigned *Jobab*, who is also called Job. And after him *Assom*, the governor of the country of the Temanites. After him *Adad*, the son of Basad, who cut off Madian in the plain of Moab; and the name of his city was Gethaim."

"The *friends* who came to visit him were *Eliphaz*, son of Sophan, of the children of Esau, king of the Temanites. *Baldad*, the son of Amnon, of Chobar, tyrant of the Sauchites. *Sophar*, king of the Minaites. *Thaiman*, son of Eliphaz, governor of the Idumeans."

"This is translated from the Syriac copy. He dwelt in the land of *Ausitis*, on the borders of the Euphrates; and his former name was *Jobab;* and his father was Zareth, who came from the east." This is verbatim from the *Codex Alexandrinus*.

The *Arabic* is not so circumstantial, but is the same in substance. "And Job dwelt in the land of *Auz*, between the boundaries of Edom and Arabia; and he was at first called *Jobab*. And he married a strange woman, and to her was born a son called *Anun*. But Job was the son of *Zara*, a descendant of the children of *Esau;* his mother's name was *Basra*, and he was the *sixth* from Abraham. Of the kings who reigned in Edom, the first who reigned over that land was *Balak*, the son of Beor, and the name of his city was Danaba. And after him *Jobab*, the same who is called Job. And after Job, he (Assom) who was prince of the land of Teman. And after him (Adad) the son of Barak, he who slew and put to flight Madian, in the plains of Moab; and the name of his city was Jatham. And of the *friends* of Job who visited him was *Eliphaz*, the son of Esau, king of the Temanites."

Dr. Kennicott says, When Job lived seems deducible from his being contemporary with Eliphaz, the Temanite, thus:—

ABRAHAM

ISAAC

1		1
2 Esau.	Jacob.	2
3 Eliphaz.	Levi.	3
4 Teman.	Kohath.	4
5 Eliphaz the Temanite.	Amram—Job.	5
	Moses.	

The late Miss Mary Freeman Shepherd, well known for her strong masculine genius, and knowledge of various languages, sent me the following genealogy and remarks, which she thought would clearly ascertain the time of Job. I faithfully transcribe them from her letter to me, a short time before her death.

"Shem, two years after the flood, begat Arphaxad and Uz, and also Aram	2
Arphaxad begat Salah at	35
Salah begat Eber at	30
Eber begat Peleg at	34
Peleg, in whose time the earth was divided, begat Reu at	30
Reu begat Serug at	32
Serug begat Nahor at	30
Nahor begat Terah at	29
Terah begat Abraham at	70
Abraham begat Ishmael at eighty-six, Israel at	100
Isaac married at forty, soon after, probably at forty-three, Esau and Jacob born	43
Jacob married at forty, had Reuben his first-born, and Levi born of Leah, by the time he was forty-four	44
Levi begat Kohath, suppose at	40
Kohath begat Amram, suppose at	40
Amram begat Moses, suppose at	40
After the deluge	599

"Shem was the father of Aram, who gave his name to the Aramites, *i. e.*, the Syrians; and he was the father of Uz, who gave his name to the *land of Uz*, in which Job *dwelt*, not was *born*, for the text says, *There was a man in the land of Uz, called Job*.

"In Gen. xlvi. 13, one of the sons of Issachar is named *Job*. In the genealogies of Num. xxvi. 24, and in 1 Chron. vii. 1, he is called *Jashub*. It is remarkable that there is no mention in Chronicles of the sons of Jashub, or of any of the sons of Issachar, among the thousands of Israel, sons of Tola, where, might not *Job* be called *Jashub?* Mitzraim, *i. e.*, Egypt, was a son of Ham; Uz and Aram, sons of Shem; Ishmael by Hagar, and Midian by Keturah, both sons to Abram. How well does this account for the nearness of the languages of these people, being scions from the same mother tongue!

"Ishmael, the father of the tribes of Arabia; Arabic was, therefore, not their mother tongue. The roots of these languages germinated from the Hebrew roots, and so a new language sprang up, afterwards formed according to grammatic rules, and enriched as arts and sciences, and cultivated genius, added new inventions. Things new and unknown before gave rise to new words or names. Nouns, and the action, operation, and effects of arts and sciences, produced verbs or roots. Thus the Arabic become so copious and rich, and has roots not in the pure original Hebrew. All this considered, might not Moses have written the book of Job, as parts of Ezra, Nehemiah, and Daniel were written, after the captivity, in a mixed language, in order that it might be the better understood by those for whom it was written; those of the people who, being left in Jerusalem, had retained their native Hebrew; and those who had, by long residence in Babylon, corrupted and mingled it with the Chaldaic, which is a dialect of the Hebrew, like the modern language of Italy when compared with that of ancient Rome, or our modern Latin when compared with that of the Augustan age.

"By the influence of climate upon the organs of speech, the different avocations, usages, diet, turn of mind, and genius of men, the dialects which all streamed from one language, and *pronounced* in one and the same *speech*, confounded, (not annihilated, troubled, but not dried up,) no new language then created, yet so confounded in utterance that they understood not one another's speech. The operation was upon the ear of the heart, as in the day of pentecost: one man spoke, and all, though of different tongues, understood; the ear suggested the various sounds to the tongue, and from thence the varied pronunciations of one and the same language often makes it misunderstood.

"*Shem*, who lived five hundred and two years after the deluge, being still alive, and in the three hundred and ninety-third year of his life, when Abram was born, therefore the Jewish tradition that Shem was the Melchisedek, (my righteous king of Salem,) an epithet, or title of honour and respect, not a proper name, and, as the head and father of his race, Abraham paid tithes to him; this seems to me well founded, and the idea confirmed by these remarkable words, Psalm cx., *Jehovah hath sworn, and will not repent,* אתה כהן לעולם על דברתי מלכי־צדק *attah cohen leolam al dibrathi malki-tsedek.* As if he had said, *Thou*, my only-begotten Son, first-born of many brethren; not according to the *substituted* priesthood of the sons of Levi, who, after the sin of the golden calf, stood up in lieu of all the first-born of Israel, invested with their forfeited rights of primogeniture of king and priest; the Lord hath sworn, and will not repent, (change,) Thou art a priest for ever after the (my order of Melchisedek, my own original primitive) order of primogeniture; even as *Shem* the *man of name*, the *Shem* that stands the *first* and foremost of the sons of Noah. The *righteous prince and priest of the most high God* meets his descendant Abraham after the slaughter of the kings, with refreshments; blessed him as the head and father of his race, and as such, he receives from Abraham the tithe of all the spoil.

"How beautifully does Paul of Tarsus, writing to the Hebrews, point through Melchisedek,—Shem, the head and father of their race, invested in all the original rights of primogeniture, priest of the most high God, blessing Abraham as such, as Levi even had existence, and as such receiving tithe from Abraham, and in him from Levi yet in the loins of his forefathers, when Moses on this great and solemn occasion records simply this: Melchisedek, king of Salem, priest of the most high God, *sine genealogia;* his pedigree not mentioned, but standing, as *Adam* in St. Luke's genealogy, without father and without mother, *Adam of God*, Luke iii., last verse;—how beautifully, I say, doth St. Paul point through Melchisedek to Jehoshua our great High Priest and King, whose eternal generation who shall declare! *Hammashiach*, the Lord's Anointed, Priest, and King, after the order of Melchisedek, only begotten first-born Son! The Levitical priesthood that arose from the sin of the golden calf and the forfeited rights of the first-born, in whose stead stood the sons of Levi, (the reward of their zeal for God, on that sad occasion.) This right of primogeniture, as the streams of Jordan at the presence of God, *conversus est retrorsum*, to its fountain head; and *Judah was his sanctuary*, Psalm cxiv. Reuben forfeited by incest his *excellence;* Simeon and Levi, the right in priority of birth, theirs; and Judah, he to whom his brethren should bow down as their head. From the time of Abraham, who married a sister of Haran, prince of the tribe of Judah, to the time of *Jesus*, the tribes of Levi and Judah intermarried: thus was incorporated the source and streams in one. And the very names of all the sons of the tribes of Israel lost in *one*, that of Jehudah, from which they call themselves Jehudim.

"The *shebit*, tribe, not sceptre, the rod or ensign of the chief of a tribe. 'The *tribe, genealogy,* shall not recede from Jehudah until Shiloh come;' for whose genealogy they subsist. Ten, by the schism of Jeroboam, may be carried away beyond the river, and heard of no more; but Jehudah, Levi, and Benjamin, shall be tribes; and their registers shall be clear and unbroken until the temple and city and all the registers of genealogy are destroyed. The people are one; one people worshipping one God. 'I have prayed,' said Jehoshua Mashiach, 'that ye might be one in me, as I and my Father are one.'

"Ham, the son of Noah, begat Cush, and Cush begat Nimrod, and Saba, and others. Nimrod began a monarchy, and founded Babel. Out of that land went forth Asshur, and builded Nineveh. Nimrod was therefore contemporary with Peleg. Compare Gen. ii. 8, 9, with Gen. ix. 10–25.

"Thus, in about two hundred and ten or twenty years after the deluge, by the confusion of tongues, was the earth divided; as its inhabitants, dispersing no doubt in families together formed themselves into nations, people, and tribes and kindreds, and from thence into *tongues*.

"From the knowledge I have of the Hebrew, I have caught a glance of the genius, spirit, and tone of the general march of the oriental tongues, and even of the expression of their character. To me the book of Job seems to have much of the Chaldee, both in words and idiom, and much of the sublimity and spirit of the writings of Moses. His grand descriptions of the Most High, his wondrous works, his power, wisdom, justice, and truth, all speak the historian of Genesis, the legislator of Israel, the unconsumed fire of the burning bush, the loud thunders of Sinai, and the shinings of the light of God. That pointed exactness and conciseness of narration that distinguish Moses, are also conspicuous in the book of Job. If Moses did indeed write this book, he wrote it for the *nations*, as well as for Israel; and took, as the best vehicle of a general conveyance, a language most generally understood. At this day, for the facilitating of intercourse in the Levant, Mediterranean, Archipelago, &c., there is a language called *Lingua Franca,* the language of the Franks. To Israel Moses conveyed the pure language of their fathers; but rather than the nations should be famished for bread, or die for thirst, he put *manna* in their coarse earthen vessels, and wine in their wooden cups.

"You see, my dear sir, how strong is female obstinacy; I struggle and contend for the body of Moses. I admire Moses; I admire Job. God, by the prophet Ezekiel and the apostle St. James, ascertains the history of Job to be a fact, not a fiction. And thus inspiration sustains its inspiration.

"Will you, dear sir, think it worth while to collect and put together these scattered scraps, as little pegs to better shelves, which you must furbish, smooth, and point;—too hard a work for *Mary* the aged? Blessed are the pure of heart, for they shall see God: and in him see all truth."—*M. F. S.*

Miss Shepherd is a strong auxiliary to Mr. Good; still I remain unconvinced. My readers must choose for themselves.

The history of Job, but strangely disguised, is well known among the Asiatics. He is called by the Arabic and Persian historians ايوب *Ayoub*, which is exactly the same as the *Hebrew* איוב *Ayoub*, which Europeans have strangely metamorphosed into *Job*. In the *Tareekh Muntekheb* his genealogy is given thus: Ayoub the son of Anosh, the son of Razakh, the son of Ais, (Esau,) the son of Isaac. He was a prophet, and was afflicted by a grievous malady *three years*, or according to others, *seven years;* at the end of which, when eighty years of age, he was restored to perfect health, and had a son named *Bash ben Ayoub*. Other writers say he had *five* sons, with whom he made war on a brutal people called *Dsul Kefel,* whom he exterminated because they refused to receive the knowledge of the true God, whom he preached to them. *Khondemir*, who entitles him *Job the patient,* gives us his history in the following manner:—

"*Job*, by his father's side, was descended from *Esau*, and by his mother from *Lot*. *Abou Giaffer al Tabary* relates that God sent him to preach to the inhabitants of *Thaniah*, a people who dwelt between Remla and Damascus; but *three* persons only received the truth. Nevertheless, as he was very zealous in the service of God, he rewarded his faith and obedience by heaping riches upon him, and giving him a numerous family. This excited the envy of the devil, who, presenting himself before God, accused Job as one who was *selfish* in his devotion; and, were it not for the temporal blessings which he received from his Maker, he would not worship even once in the day. God having given Satan permission to spoil Job of his goods, and deprive him of his children, he gave the same proofs of his piety, worshipping God as before, and patiently bearing his great losses. Satan, enraged to be thus baffled, presented himself once more before God, and asserted that Job continued thus faithful because he knew that God would reward his constancy with an equal or even greater portion of earthly blessings: but if he would afflict his *body* by some grievous disease, he would soon abandon his service, and be at the end of his patience. In order fully to show the piety of this exemplary man, God permitted Satan to afflict his body as he pleased, with the exception of his *eyes*, his *ears*, and his *tongue*. The devil, having received this permission, blew up the nostrils of Job such a pestilential heat as immediately turned his whole mass of blood into corruption, so that his whole body became one ulcer, the smell of which was so offensive that his greatest intimates could not approach him; and he was obliged to be carried out of the city, and laid in a distant place entirely by himself. Notwithstanding, Job continued both his patience and piety. His wife, *Rosina*, never forsook him, but continued daily to bring him the necessaries of life. Satan observing this, stole from her the provision she had made for her husband; and when reduced to the lowest ebb, he appeared to her under the form of an old *bald woman*, and told her, that if she would give her the two tresses of hair that hung down on her neck, she would provide her daily with what was necessary for her husband's support. This offer appearing so very advantageous in behalf of her afflicted husband, she accepted the offer, and gave the two tresses to the old woman.

"Satan, overjoyed at the success of his plots, went to Job, told him that his wife had been caught in the act of adultery, and that her tresses had been cut off, and here was the proof of the fact. Job, seeing this, and finding his wife without her tresses, not supposing that he was deceived by the devil, lost his patience, and bound himself by an oath, that if he should ever recover his health he would inflict on her the most exemplary punishment. Satan, supposing he had now gained his end, transformed himself into an *angel of light*, and went throughout the country as a messenger of God, informing the people that Job, who was counted a prophet, had fallen from his piety and brought the wrath of God upon him; that they should no more listen to his preaching, but banish him from among them, lest the curse of God should fall on the whole country.

"Job, coming to understand how the matter stood, had recourse to God by faith and prayer, and said these remarkable words, which are found in the KORAN: 'Distress closes me in on every side: but thou, O Lord, art more merciful than all those who can feel compassion.' On this all his pains and sufferings immediately ceased; for Gabriel, the faithful servant of the Most High, descended from heaven, took Job by the hand, and lifting him up from the place where he lay, stamped on the ground with his foot, and immediately a spring of water rose up from the earth, out of which Job having drunk, and washed his body, he was instantly cleansed of all his ulcers, and restored to perfect health.

"God, having thus restored him, greatly multiplied his goods, so that the rain and the snow which fell around his dwelling were precious; and his riches became so abundant, as if showers of gold had descended upon him."

This is the sum of the account given by the oriental historians, who, forsaking the truth of the sacred history, have blended the story with their own fables. The great facts are however the same in the main; and we find that with them the personality, temptation, and deliverance of Job, are matters of serious credibility. Abul Faragius says that the trial of Job happened in the twenty-fifth year of Nahor, son of Serug; thus making him prior to Abraham. He calls him ايوب الطديق *Ayoub assadeek, Job the righteous.* See *Abul Faragius, Ebn Batric, D'Herbelot,* &c.

Commentators have considered this book as being divided into distinct parts. Mr. Good, who considers it a regular Hebrew epic, divides it into *six parts* or books, which he considers to be its natural division, and unquestionably intended by the author. These six parts are, an *opening* or *exordium*, containing the introductory history or decree concerning Job; *three* distinct series of arguments, in each of which the speakers are regularly allowed their respective turns; the *summing* up of the controversy; and the *close* of the *catastrophe*, consisting of the suffering hero's grand and glorious acquittal, and restoration to prosperity and happiness.

PART I.—*The* TEMPTATION *of Job decreed*

Which contains.—1. A brief narrative of Job. 2. The tribunal of the *Almighty*. 3. His remarks to *Satan* concerning Job's fidelity. 4. Satan's reply. 5. The *Almighty* consents to his temptation. 6. Return of the celestial tribunal. 7. The fidelity of Job proved and declared. 8. *Satan* insinuates that he would not have proved true had the attack been made on his person. 9. The *Almighty* consents to a second trial. 10. The trial made. 11. Job's utter misery. 12. The visit of his three friends to condole with him. Chap. i. and ii.

PART II.—*First Series of Controversy*

1. Exclamation of *Job* on his miserable condition. 2. Speech of *Eliphaz*, accusing him of want of firmness, and suspecting his integrity, on account of the affliction with which he is visited. 3. *Job's* reply, reproaching his friends with cruelty; bewailing the disappointment he had felt in them; calling for death as the termination of his miseries; then longing for life, expostulating with the Almighty, and supplicating his forgiveness. 4. *Bildad* resumes the argument of Eliphaz with great severity; openly accuses Job of hypocrisy; and exhorts him to repentance, in order that he may avoid utter ruin. 5. *Job* in reply longs to plead his cause before God, but is overwhelmed at his majesty. 6. He again desponds, and calls for death as the only refuge from his sorrows. 7. *Zophar* continues the argument on the side of his companions; condemns Job acrimoniously for still daring to assert his innocence; and once more exhorts him to repentance, as the only means of obtaining a restoration to the favour of the *Almighty*. 8. *Job* is stimulated to a still severer reply. 9. Accuses his companions of declaiming on the part of God, with the base hope of propitiating him. 10. Boldly demands his trial at the tribunal of the Almighty; and, realizing the tribunal before him, commences his pleading, in an address variegated on every side by opposite feelings: fear, triumph, humiliation, expostulation, despondency. Chap. iii.–xiv.

PART III.—*Second Series of Controversy*

1. *Eliphaz* commences the discussion in his regular turn; accuses Job of vehemence and vanity; asserts that no man is innocent; and that his own conduct sufficiently proves himself not to be so. 2. *Job* replies; and complains bitterly of the unjust reproaches heaped upon him; and accuses his companions of holding him up to public derision. 3. He pathetically bemoans his lot; and looks forward to the grave with glimmering, through despair, of a resurrection from its ruins. 4. *Bildad* perseveres in his former argument of Job's certain wickedness, from his signal sufferings; and, in a string of lofty traditions, points out the constant attendance of misery upon wickedness. 5. *Job* rises superior to this attack; appeals to the piety and generosity of his friends; asserts the Almighty to have afflicted him for purposes altogether unknown; and then soars to a full and triumphant hope of a

future resurrection, and vindication of his innocence. 6. *Zophar* repeats the former charge; and *Job* replies, by directly controverting his argument, and proving, from a variety of examples, that in the present world the wicked are chiefly prosperous, and the just for the most part subject to affliction. Chap. xv.–xxi.

PART IV.—*Third Series of Controversy*

1. *Eliphaz,* in direct opposition to Job's last remarks, contends that certain and utter ruin is the uniform lot of the wicked; and adduces the instances of the *deluge,* and of Sodom and the other cities of the plain. 2. *Job* supports his position by fresh and still more forcible examples. Though he admits that, in the mystery of Providence, prosperity and adversity are often equally the lot of both the righteous and the wicked; yet he denies that this ought to be held as an argument in favour of the last, whose prosperity is in the utmost degree precarious, and who in calamity are wholly destitute of hope and consolation. 3. *Bildad* replies in a string of lofty but general apophthegms, tending to prove that Job cannot be without sin, since no man is so in the sight of God. 4. *Job* rejoins with indignation; takes a general survey of his life, in the different capacities of a magistrate, a husband, and a master; and challenges his companions to point out a single act of injustice he had committed. Chap. xxii.–xxxi.

PART V.—*The Summing up of the Controversy*

1. *Zophar,* who ought to have concluded the last series, having declined to prosecute the debate any farther, the general argument is summed up by *Elihu,* who has not hitherto spoken, though present from the first. 2. He condemns the subject matter of the opponents of Job, as altogether irrelevant; accuses Job himself, not of suffering for any past impiety, but of speaking irreverently during the controversy. 3. He contests several of Job's positions; asserts that afflictions are often sent by the Almighty for the wisest and most merciful purposes; and that, in every instance, our duty is submission. 4. He closes with describing the Creator as supreme and uncontrollable; and as creating, upholding, and regulating all nature according to his own will and pleasure; incomprehensibly and mysteriously yet ever wisely and benevolently. Chap. xxxii.–xxxvii.

PART VI.—*The Acquittal and Restoration of Job*

1. The *Almighty* appears to pronounce judgment; speaks to Job in a sublime and magnificent address out of a whirlwind. 2. *Job* humbles himself before God, and is accepted. 3. His *friends* are severely reproved for their conduct during the controversy, a sacrifice is demanded of them, and Job is appointed their intercessor. 4. He prays for his friends, and his prayer is accepted. 5. He is restored to his former state of prosperity, and his substance in every instance doubled. Chap. xxxviii.–xlii.

On this plan Mr. Good has constructed his learned translation and excellent observations on this book.

The following *Synopsis* or general view of this book is very intelligible, and may serve as an index to the work:—

I. The Historical Exordium, written in *prose.*—Chap. i., ii.

II. The threefold Series of Controversy, written in *poetry.*—Chap. iii.–xlii. ver. 1–6.

III. The *issue* of Job's trial; restoration to health and prosperity, in *prose.*—Chap. xlii. ver. 7–17.

1. Job's Disputation with his three friends, who came to visit him, in a *threefold* series, chap. iii.–xxxi.; including Job's speech, in which he curses the day of his birth, chap. iii.: this gives rise to the

First Series of Controversy, comprehended in chap. iv.–xiv.

1. With **Eliphaz**, chap. iv.–vii.
   - *a.* The Speech of *Eliphaz,* chap. iv., v.
   - *b.* The Answer of *Job,* chap. vi., vii.
2. With **Bildad**, chap. viii.–x.
   - *a.* The Speech of *Bildad,* chap. viii.
   - *b.* The Answer of *Job,* chap. ix., x.
3. With **Zophar**, chap. xi.–xiv.
   - *a.* The Speech of *Zophar,* chap. xi.
   - *b.* The Answer of *Job,* chap. xii.–xiv.

Second Series of Controversy, included in chap. xv.–xxi.

1. With **Eliphaz**, chap. xv., xvii.
   - *a.* The Speech of *Eliphaz,* chap. xv.
   - *b.* The Answer of *Job,* chap. xvi., xvii.
2. With **Bildad**, chap. xviii., xix.
   - *a.* The Speech of *Bildad,* chap. xviii.
   - *b.* The Answer of *Job,* chap. xix.
3. With **Zophar**, chap. xx., xxi.
   - *a.* *Zophar's* Speech, chap. xx.
   - *b.* The Answer of *Job,* chap. xxi.

Third Series of Controversy, included in chap. xxii.–xxxi.

1. With **Eliphaz**, chap. xxii.–xxiv.
   - *a.* The Speech of *Eliphaz,* chap. xxii.
   - *b.* The Answer of *Job,* chap. xxiii., xxiv.
2. With **Bildad**, chap. xxv.–xxxi.
   - *a.* The Speech of *Bildad,* chap. xxv.
   - *b.* The Answer of *Job,* chap. xxvi.–xxxi.

Elihu's judgment concerning the Controversy, delivered at *four* different intervals, pausing for Job's answer, chap. xxxii.–xxxvii.

- *a.* Elihu's *first* Speech, chap. xxxii., xxxiii.
- *b.* Elihu's *second* Speech, chap. xxxiv.
- *c.* Elihu's *third* Speech, chap. xxxv.
- *d.* Elihu's *fourth* Speech, chap. xxxvi., xxxvii.

The **Almighty** appears, speaks out of a whirlwind, and determines the Controversy, chap. xxxviii.–xli.

- *a.* The first Speech of the *Almighty,* chap. xxxviii., xxxix.
- *b.* The second Speech of the *Almighty,* chap. xl., xli.
- *c.* The Answer and *humiliation* of *Job,* chap. xlii., ver. 1–6.

Historical Narration concerning the restoration of Job to health and great worldly prosperity; with the account of his age and death, chap. xlii., ver. 7–17.

Some have contended that the *whole* of this book is written in *verse;* but I can see no rule or method by which the *two first chapters,* and the *ten last verses* of chap. xlii. can be reduced to poetry or poetic arrangement. They are merely *narrative;* and are utterly destitute of that dignity and pathos everywhere evident in this poem, and in every part of the Hebrew hemistich poetry wherever it occurs. I could almost suppose these places the work of *another hand;* a *Preface* and a *Conclusion* written by some person who was well acquainted with the fact of Job's temptation, and who found such additions necessary to cast light upon the poem. But they are most probably the work of the same hand. There are, in different parts of the body of the poem, *sentences in prose,* which are the *headings* to the different speeches. This is frequent among the Arabic and Persian poets. Such headings are generally in *rubric,* and should here stand by themselves.

THE

BOOK OF JOB

As the time in which Job lived is so very uncertain, (see the *preface*, and the *observations* at the end of the notes on the first chapter,) the date found in our common English Bibles, which is upon the supposition that Moses wrote the book while among the Midianites, about *one thousand five hundred and twenty years* before the commencement of the Christian era, is inserted in the margin, not because it is the most probable, but because it is the most generally received.

CHAPTER I

Character of Job, 1. *His family*, 2. *His substance*, 3. *Care of his family*, 4, 5. *Satan accuses him to God as a selfish person, who served God only for the hope of secular rewards*, 6–11. *Satan is permitted to strip him of all his children and property*, 12–19. *Job's remarkable resignation and patience*, 20–22.

A. M. cir. 2484
B. C. cir. 1520
Ante I. Olymp. cir. 744
Ante U. C. cir. 767

THERE was a man [a]in the land of Uz, whose name *was* [b]Job, and that man was [c]perfect and upright, and one that feared God, and eschewed evil.

2 And there were born unto him seven sons and three daughters.

3 His [d]substance also was seven thousand sheep, and three thousand camels, and five hundred yoke of oxen, and five hundred she-asses, and a very great [e]household; so that this man was the greatest of all the [f]men of the East.

A. M. cir. 2484
B. C. cir. 1520
Ante I. Olymp. cir. 744
Ante U. C. cir. 767

4 And his sons went and feasted in *their* houses, every one his day, and sent and called for their three sisters to eat and to drink with them.

5 And it was so, when the days of *their* feasting were gone about, that Job sent and sanctified them, and rose up early in the morning, [g]and offered burnt-offerings *according* to the number of them all: for Job said, It may

[a]Gen. xxii. 20, 21——[b]Ezek. xiv. 14; James v. 11——[c]Chap. ii. 3——[d]Or, *cattle*——[e]Or, *husbandry*——[f]Heb. *sons of the East*——[g]Gen. viii. 20; chap. xlii. 8

NOTES ON CHAP. I

Verse 1. *In the land of Uz*] This country was situated in Idumea, or the land of *Edom*, in *Arabia Petræa*, of which it comprised a very large district. See the *preface*.

Whose name was *Job*] The original is איוב *Aiyob;* and this orthography is followed by the *Chaldee*, *Syriac*, and *Arabic*. From the *Vulgate* we borrow *Job*, not very dissimilar from the Ιωβ *Iob* of the *Septuagint*. The name signifies *sorrowful*, or *he that weeps*. He is supposed to have been called *Jobab*. See more in the *preface*.

Perfect and upright] תם וישר *tam veyashar;* COMPLETE as to his *mind* and *heart*, and STRAIGHT OR CORRECT as to his *moral deportment*.

Feared God] Had him in continual reverence as the fountain of justice, truth, and goodness.

Eschewed evil.] סר מרע *sar mera*, departing from, or avoiding evil. We have the word *eschew* from the old French *eschever*, which signifies to *avoid*. All *within* was holy, all *without* was righteous; and his whole life was employed in *departing* from *evil*, and *drawing nigh to God*. Coverdale translates **an innocent and vertuous man, soch one as feared God, an eschued evell.** From this translation we retain the word *eschew*.

Verse 3. *His substance also was seven thousand sheep*] *A thousand*, says the Chaldee, *for each of his sons. Three thousand camels: a thousand for each of his daughters. Five hundred yoke of oxen* for *himself. And five hundred she-asses* for his *wife*. Thus the *Targum* divides the substance of this eminent man.

A very great household] עבדה רבה מאד *abuddah rabbah meod*, "a very great estate." The word עבדה *abuddah* refers chiefly to husbandry, including *all manner of labour* in the *field*, with *cattle*, and every description of *servants*.

The greatest of all the men of the East.] He was more eminent than any other person in that region in wisdom, wealth, and piety. He was the chief *emir* of that district.

Verse 4. *Feasted in* their *houses, every one his day*] It is likely that a *birthday festival* is here intended. When the birthday of one arrived, he invited his brothers and sisters to feast with *him;* and each observed the same custom.

Verse 5. *When the days of* their *feasting were gone about*] At the conclusion of the year, when the birthday of each had been celebrated,

A. M. cir. 2484
B. C. cir. 1520
Ante I. Olymp. cir. 744
Ante U. C. cir. 767

be that my sons have sinned, and [h]cursed God in their hearts. Thus did Job [i]continually.

6 Now [k]there was a day [l]when the sons of God came to present themselves before the LORD, and [m]Satan came also [n]among them.

[h]1 Kings xxi. 10, 13——[i]Heb. *all the days*——[k]Chap. ii. 1——[l]1 Kings xxii. 19; chap. xxxviii. 7

[m]Hebrew, *the adversary*, 1 Chron. xxi. 1; Rev. xii. 9, 10
[n]Heb. *in the midst of them*

the pious father appears to have gathered them all together, that the whole family might hold a *feast to the Lord*, offering burnt-offerings in order to make an atonement for sins of all kinds, whether presumptuous or committed through ignorance. This we may consider as a general custom among the godly in those ancient times.

And cursed God in their hearts.] וברכו אלהים *uberechu Elohim.* In this book, according to most interpreters, the verb ברך *barach* signifies both to *bless* and to *curse;* and the noun אלהים *Elohim* signifies the *true God, false gods,* and *great* or *mighty.* The reason why Job offered the burnt-offerings appears to have been this: in a country where idolatry flourished, he thought it possible that his children might, in their festivity, have given way to idolatrous thoughts, or done something prescribed by idolatrous rites; and therefore the words may be rendered thus: *It may be that my children have blessed the gods in their hearts.* Others think that the word ברך *barach* should be understood as implying *farewell, bidding adieu*—lest my children have *bidden adieu* to God, that is, *renounced* him, and *cast off his fear.* To me this is very unlikely. Mr. *Mason Good* contends that the word should be understood in its regular and general sense, *to bless;* and that the conjunction ו *vau* should be translated *nor.* "Peradventure my sons may have sinned, *nor* blessed God in their hearts." This version he supports with great learning. I think the sense given above is more plain, and less embarrassed. They might have been guilty of some species of *idolatry.* This is possible even among those called *Christians,* in their *banquets;* witness their songs to Bacchus, Venus, &c., which are countless in number, and often sung by persons who would think themselves injured, not to be reputed Christians. Coverdale, in his translation, (1535,) renders the passage thus: **Peradventure my sonnes have done some offence, and have been unthankful to God in their hertes.**

Thus did Job continually.] At the end of every year, when all the birthday festivals had gone round.

Verse 6. *There was a day when the sons of God*] All the *versions,* and indeed all the critics, are puzzled with the phrase *sons of God;* בני האלהים *beney haelohim,* literally, *sons of the God,* or *sons of the gods.* The *Vulgate* has simply *filii dei, sons of God.* The *Septuagint,* οἱ αγγελοι του θεου, *the angels of God.* The *Chaldee,* כתי מלאכיא *kittey malachaiya, troops of angels.* The *Syriac* retains the Hebrew words and letters, only leaving out the demonstrative ה *he* in the word האלהים *haelohim,* thus, ܒܢܝ ܐܠܘܗܝܡ *baney Elohim.* The *Arabic* nearly copies the Hebrew also, بنوا الوهيم *banoa Iloheem;* to which, if we give not the literal translation of the *Hebrew,* we may give what translation we please. *Coverdale* (1535) translates it, **servauntes of God.** The *Targum* supposes that this assembly took place on the day of the *great atonement,* which occurred once each year. *And there was a day of judgment in the beginning of the year; and the troops of angels came, that they might stand in judgment before the Lord.* But what are we to make of this whole account? Expositions are endless. That of Mr. *Peters* appears to me to be at once the most simple and the most judicious: "The Scripture speaks of God after the manner of men, for there is a necessity of condescending to our capacities, and of suiting the revelation to our apprehension. As kings, therefore, transact their most important affairs in a *solemn council* or *assembly,* so God is pleased to represent himself as having *his council* likewise; and as passing the decrees of his providence in an *assembly* of his *holy angels.* We have here, in the case of *Job,* the same grand assembly held, as was before in that of *Ahab,* 1 Kings xxii.; the same host of heaven, called here the *sons of God,* presenting themselves *before* Jehovah, as in the vision of *Micaiah* they are said to stand *on his right hand and on his left.* A *wicked spirit* appearing among them, here called *Satan* or the *adversary,* and there *a lying spirit;* both bent on mischief, and ready to do all the hurt they were permitted to do; for both were under the *control* of his power. The *imagery* is just the same; and the only *difference* is in the *manner* of the relation. That mentioned above, Micaiah, as a *prophet,* and in the actual exercise of his prophetic office, delivers, as he received it, in a *vision. I saw the Lord sitting on his throne, and all the* HOST *of* HEAVEN *standing by him, on his right hand and on his left; and there came forth a* LYING SPIRIT, *and stood* BEFORE *the Lord, and said,* 1 Kings xxii. 19-22. The other, as a *historian,* interweaves it with his history; and tells us, in his plain narrative style, *There was a day when the* SONS *of God came to* PRESENT *themselves* BEFORE *the Lord; and* SATAN *came also among them.* And this he delivers in the same manner as he does, *There was a man in the land of Uz, whose name was Job.*

"The things delivered to us by these two inspired writers are the same in substance, equally high, and above the reach of human sight and knowledge; but the *manner* of delivering them is different, each as suited best to his particular purpose. This, then is the prophetical way of representing things, as to the manner of doing them, which, whether done exactly in the same manner, concerns us not to know; but which are really done: and God would have them described as done in this manner, to make the more lively and lasting impression on us. At the same time, it must not be forgotten that representations of this kind are founded in a well-known and established truth, viz., the doctrine of *good and bad angels,* a point revealed from the beginning, and with-

A. M. cir. 2484
B. C. cir. 1520
Ante I. Olymp. cir. 744
Ante U. C. cir. 767

7 And the LORD said unto
Satan, Whence comest thou?
Then Satan answered the LORD,
and said, From °going to and
fro in the earth, and from walking up and
down in it.

8 And the LORD said unto Satan, ᵖHast
thou considered my servant Job, that *there is*
none like him in the earth, a perfect and an
upright man, one that feareth God and escheweth evil?

9 Then Satan answered the
LORD, and said, Doth Job fear
God for naught?

10 Hast not thou made a hedge
about him, and about his house, and about all
that he hath on every side? thou hast blessed the work of his hands, and his [q]substance
is increased in the land.

11 [r]But put forth thine hand now, and
touch all that he hath, [s]and he will curse
thee to thy face.

[o]Chap. ii. 2; Matt. xii. 43; 1 Pet. v. 8——[p]Heb. *Hast thou set thine heart on*

[q]Or, *cattle*——[r]Chap. ii. 5; xix. 21——[s]Heb. *if he curse thee not to thy face*

out a previous knowledge of which, the visions of the prophets could scarcely be intelligible." See Gen. xxviii.

And Satan came also] This word *also* is emphatic in the original, השטן *hassatan, the Satan*, or *the adversary;* translated by the *Septuagint* ὁ Διαβολος. The original word is preserved by the *Chaldee*, *Syriac*, and *Arabic;* indeed, in each of them the word signifies an *adversary*. St. *Peter*, 1st Epist., ch. v., ver. 8, plainly refers to this place; and fully proves that השטן *hassatan*, which he literally translates ὁ αντιδικος, the ADVERSARY, is no other than ὁ Διαβολος, the DEVIL, or chief of bad demons, which he adds to others by way of explanation. There are many δαιμονες, *demons*, mentioned in Scripture; but the word *Satan* or *devil* is never found in the originals of the Old and New Testaments in the *plural* number. Hence we reasonably infer, that all evil spirits are under the government of ONE *chief*, the DEVIL, who is more powerful and more wicked than the rest. From the GREEK Διαβολος comes the LATIN *Diabolus*, the SPANISH *Diablo*, the FRENCH *Diable*, the ITALIAN *Diavolo*, the German **Teuffel**, the DUTCH *Duivel*, the ANGLO-SAXON **deofle**, and the ENGLISH *Devil*, which some would derive from the compound THE-EVIL; ὁ πονηρος, the *evil one*, or *wicked one*.

It is now fashionable to deny the existence of this evil spirit; and this is one of what St. John (Rev. ii. 24) calls τα βαθη του σατανα, *the depths of Satan;* as he well knows that they who deny his being will not be afraid of his power and influence; will not watch against his wiles and devices; will not pray to God for deliverance from the evil one; will not expect him to be trampled down under their feet, who has no existence; and, consequently, they will become an easy and unopposing prey to the enemy of their souls. By leading men to disbelieve and deny his existence, he throws them off their guard; and is then their complete master, and they are led captive by him at his will. It is well known that, among all those who make any profession of religion, those who deny the existence of the devil are they who pray little or none at all; and are, apparently, as careless about the existence of God as they are about the being of a devil. Piety to God is with them out of the question; for those who do not pray, especially in *private*, (and I never met with a devil-denier who did,) have no *religion* of any kind, whatsoever pretensions they may choose to make.

Verse 7. *From going to and fro in the earth*] The translation of the *Septuagint* is curious: Περιελθων την γην και εμπεριπατησας την ὑπ' ουρανον, παρειμι; "Having gone round the earth, and walked over all that is under heaven, I am come hither." The *Chaldee* says, "I am come from going round the earth to examine the works of the children of men; and from walking through it." *Coverdale*, who generally hits the sense, translates thus: **I have gone aboute the londe and walked thorow it.** Mr. *Good* has it, *from roaming round the earth, and walking about it.*

St. Peter, as has been already stated, ver. 6, refers to this: *Be sober, be vigilant; for your* ADVERSARY *the* DEVIL GOETH ABOUT, *as a roaring lion, seeking whom he may devour.* I rather think, with *Coverdale*, that ארץ *arets* here signifies rather that *land*, than the *habitable globe.* The words are exceedingly emphatic; and the latter verb התהלך *hithhallech* being in the *hithpael* conjugation shows how *earnest* and *determined* the devil is in his work: he *sets himself to walk;* he is *busily employed in it;* he is seeking the destruction of men; and while they sleep, he wakes—while they are careless, he is alert. The spirit of this saying is often expressed by the simple inhabitants of the country: when they perceive a man plotting mischief, and frequent in transgression, they say, *The devil is* BUSY *with him.*

Verse 8. *Hast thou considered my servant Job*] Literally, *Hast thou placed thy heart on my servant Job?* Hast thou viewed his conduct with attention, whilst thou wert roaming about, seeking whom thou mightest devour? viz., the careless, prayerless, and profligate in general.

Verse 9. *Doth Job fear God for naught?*] Thou hast made it his interest to be exemplary in his conduct: for this assertion Satan gives his reasons in what immediately follows.

Verse 10. *Hast not thou made a hedge about him*] Thou hast *fortified* him with *spikes* and *spears*. Thou hast defended him as by an unapprochable hedge. He is an object of thy peculiar care; and is not exposed to the common trials of life.

Verse 11. *But put forth thine hand*] Shoot the dart of poverty and affliction against him.

And he will curse thee to thy face.] אם לא על פניך יברכך *im lo al paneycha yebarechecca*, "If he will not bless thee to thy appearances." He will bless thee only in proportion to the temporal good thou bestowest upon him; to the provi-

A. M. cir. 2484
B. C. cir. 1520
Ante I. Olymp. cir. 744
Ante U. C. cir. 767

12 And the LORD said unto
Satan, Behold, all that he hath *is*
in thy [t]power, only upon himself
put not forth thine hand. So
Satan went forth from the presence of the
LORD.
13 And there was a day when his sons and
his daughters *were* eating and drinking wine
in their eldest brother's house:
14 And there came a messenger unto Job,
and said, The oxen were ploughing, and the
asses feeding beside them:
15 And the Sabeans fell *upon them,* and
took them away; yea, they have slain the
servants with the edge of the sword; and I
only am escaped alone to tell thee.
16 While he *was* yet speaking, there came
also another, and said, [u]The fire of God is
fallen from heaven, and hath burned up the
sheep, and the servants, and
consumed them; and I only am
escaped alone to tell thee.

A. M. cir. 2484
B. C. cir. 1520
Ante I. Olymp. cir. 744
Ante U. C. cir. 767

17 While he *was* yet speak-
ing, there came also another, and said, The
Chaldeans made out three bands, and [v]fell
upon the camels, and have carried them away,
yea, and slain the servants with the edge of
the sword; and I only am escaped alone to
tell thee.
18 While he *was* yet speaking, there came
also another, and said, Thy sons and thy
daughters *were* eating and drinking wine in
their eldest brother's house;
19 And behold, there came a great wind
[w]from the wilderness, and smote the four
corners of the house, and it fell upon the
young men, and they are dead; and I only
am escaped alone to tell thee.

[t]Heb. *hand*——[u]Or, *A great fire*

[v]Heb. *rushed*——[w]Heb. *from aside, &c.*

dential and gracious *appearances* or *displays* of thy power in his behalf. If *thou* wilt be gracious, *he* will be pious. The exact maxim of a great statesman, Sir Robert Walpole: *Every man has his price.* "But you have not bought such a one?" "No, because I would not go up to his price. He valued himself at more than I thought him worth; and I could get others cheaper, who, in the general muster, would do as well." No doubt Sir R. met with many such; and the devil many more. But still God has multitudes that will neither sell their souls, their consciences, nor their country, for any price; who, though God should slay them, will nevertheless trust in him; and be honest men, howsoever tempted by the devil and his vicegerents. So did Job; so have done thousands; so will all do, in whose hearts Christ dwells by faith.

Verse 12. *All that he hath* is *in thy power*] Satan cannot deprive a man even of an *ass*, a *sheep*, or a *pig*, but by especial permission of God. His power and malice are ever bounded, and under control.

So Satan went forth] The Targum adds, *with authority from the presence of the Lord.*

Verse 13. *There was a day*] *The first day of the week*, says the *Targum*. It no doubt refers to one of those *birthday festivals* mentioned before.

Verse 14. *The asses feeding beside them*] אתנות *athonoth*, the *she-asses*, which appear to have been more domesticated, as of more worth and use than the others, both for their milk and their work.

Verse 15. *And the Sabeans fell*] The *Vulgate* alone understands this of a *people*. The *Septuagint*, *Syriac*, and *Arabic*, understand it as implying a *marauding party*. The *Chaldee* says, "Lilith, queen of Zamargad, rushed suddenly upon them, and carried them away." The *Sabeans* mentioned here are supposed to have been the same with those who were the descendants of Abraham by Keturah, whose son Jokshan begat Sheba. The sons of Keturah were sent by Abraham into the east, Gen. xxv. 6, and inhabited Arabia Deserta, on the east of the land of Uz. Hordes of predatory banditti were frequent in those countries and continue so to the present day. They made sudden incursions, and carried off *men*, *women*, *children*, *cattle*, and *goods* of every description; and immediately retired to the desert, whither it was in vain to pursue them.

Verse 16. *The fire of God is fallen*] Though *the fire of God* may mean a *great*, a *tremendous* fire, yet it is most natural to suppose *lightning* is meant; for as *thunder* was considered to be the *voice of God*, so *lightning* was the *fire of God.* And as the *prince of the power of the air* was permitted now to arm himself with this dreadful artillery of heaven, he might easily direct the zigzag lightning to every part of the fields where the sheep were feeding, and so destroy the whole in a moment.

Verse 17. *The Chaldeans made out three bands*] The *Chaldeans* inhabited each side of the Euphrates near to Babylon, which was their capital. They were also mixed with the wandering *Arabs*, and lived like them on *rapine*. They were the descendants of *Chesed*, son of Nahor and brother of Huz, from whom they had their name *Casdim*, which we translate *Chaldeans.* They divided themselves into *three bands*, in order the more speedily and effectually to encompass, collect, and drive off the three thousand camels: probably they mounted the camels and rode off.

Verse 19. *A great wind from the wilderness*] Here was another proof of the influence of *the prince of the power of the air*. What mischief might he not do with this tremendous agent, were he not constantly under the control of the Almighty! He seems to have directed four different currents, which, blowing against the four corners or sides of the house, crushed it together, and involved all within in one common ruin.

A. M. cir. 2484
B. C. cir. 1520
Ante I. Olymp. cir. 744
Ante U. C. cir. 767

20 Then Job arose, [x]and rent
his [y]mantle, and shaved his head,
and fell down upon the ground,
and worshipped,
21 And said, [z]Naked came I out of
my mother's womb, and naked shall I
return thither: the LORD gave,
and the LORD hath taken
away; blessed be the name of
the LORD.
22 [a]In all this Job sinned not, nor [b]charged
God foolishly.

[x]Gen. xxxvii. 29; Ezra ix. 3——[y]Or, *robe*——[z]Psa. xlix. 17; Eccles. v. 15; 1 Tim. vi. 7——[a]Chap. ii. 10——[b]Or, *attributed folly to God*

Verse 20. *Rent his mantle*] Tearing the garments, shaving or pulling off the hair of the head, throwing dust or ashes on the head, and sitting on the ground, were acts by which immoderate grief was expressed. Job must have felt the bitterness of anguish when he was told that, in addition to the loss of all his *property,* he was deprived of his *ten children* by a violent death. Had he not felt this most poignantly, he would have been unworthy of the name of *man.*

Worshipped] *Prostrated himself;* lay all along upon the ground, with his face in the dust.

Verse 21. *Naked came I out of my mother's womb*] I had no earthly possessions when I came into the world; I cannot have less going out of it. What I have the *Lord gave:* as it was his *free gift,* he has a right to resume it when he pleases; and I owe him *gratitude* for the time he has permitted me to enjoy this gift.

Naked shall I return thither] Whither? Not to his *mother's womb* surely; nor does he call the *earth* his *mother* in this place. In the first clause of the verse he speaks without a *metaphor,* and in the latter he speaks in reference to the *ground* on which he was about to fall. As I came out of my mother's womb destitute of the earthly possessions, so shall I return שמה *shammah,* THERE; i. e., to the earth on which he was now falling. That *mother earth* was a common expression in different nations, I allow; but I believe no such metaphor was now in the mind of Job.

The Lord gave] The *Chaldee* has, "The WORD of the Lord, מימרא דיי *meymera dayai,* gave; and the WORD of the Lord and the house of his judgment, have taken away!" WORD is used here *personally,* as in many other places of all the *Targums.*

Blessed be the name of the Lord.] The following is a fine praphrase on the sentiment in this verse:—

"*Good* when he *gives, supremely good;*
Nor less when he *denies;*
Afflictions from his sovereign hand,
Are *blessings* in disguise."

Seeing I have lost my temporal goods, and all my domestic comforts, may God alone be all my portion! The *Vulgate, Septuagint,* and *Coverdale,* add, *The Lord hath done as he pleased.*

Verse 22. *In all this Job sinned not*] He did not give way to any action, passion, or expression, offensive to his Maker. He did not charge God with acting unkindly towards him, but felt as perfectly satisfied with the *privation* which the hand of God had occasioned, as he was with the *affluence* and *health* which that hand had bestowed. This is the transaction that gave the strong and vivid colouring to the character of Job; in this, and in *this alone,* he was a *pattern* of *patience* and *resignation.* In this Satan was utterly disappointed; he found a man who loved his God more than his earthly portion. This was a rare case, even in the experience of the devil. He had seen multitudes who bartered their God for money, and their hopes of blessedness in the world to come for secular possessions in the present. He had been so often successful in this kind of temptation, that he made no doubt he should succeed again. He saw many who, when riches increased, set their hearts on them, and forgot God. He saw many also who, when deprived of earthly comforts, blasphemed their Maker. He therefore inferred that Job, in similar circumstances, would act like the others; he was disappointed. Reader, has he, by *riches* or *poverty,* succeeded with thee? Art thou pious when affluent, and patient and contented when in poverty?

THAT Job lived *after* the giving of the law, seems to me clear from many references to the rites and ceremonies instituted by Moses. In chap. i. 5, we are informed that he *sanctified* his children, and *offered burnt-offerings daily in the morning for each of them.* This was a general ordinance of the law, as we may see, Lev. ix. 7: "Moses said unto Aaron, Go unto the altar, and offer thy sin-offering and thy *burnt-offering,* and make an atonement for thyself and for the people." Ver. 22: "And Aaron lifted up his hands towards the people, and blessed them, and came down from offering the *burnt-offering.*"

This sort of offering, we are told above, *Job offered continually;* and this also was according to the law, Exod. xxix. 42: "This shall be a *continual* burnt-offering throughout your generations." See also Num. xxviii. 3, 6, 10, 15, 24, 31.

This custom was observed *after the captivity,* Ezra iii. 5: "They offered the *continual burnt-offering:* and of every one that offered a free-will-offering." See also Neh. x. 33. Ezekiel, who prophesied during the captivity, enjoins this positively, chap. xlvi. 13-15: "Thou shalt daily prepare a *burnt-offering* unto the Lord; thou shalt prepare it *every morning.*"

Job appears to have thought that his children might have *sinned* through *ignorance,* or sinned *privately;* and it was consequently necessary to make the due sacrifices to God in order to prevent his wrath and their punishment; he therefore offered the burnt-offering, which was prescribed by the law in cases of sins committed *through ignorance.* See the ordinances Lev. iv. 1-35; v. 15-19, and particularly Num. xv. 24-29. I think it may be fairly presumed that the offerings which Job made for his children were in reference to these laws.

The *worship* of the *sun, moon,* and *stars,* as being the most prevalent and most seductive idolatry, was very expressly forbidden by the law, Deut. iv. 19: "Take heed, lest thou lift up thine eyes to heaven; and when thou seest the *sun*, and the *moon*, and the *stars*, even all the *host* of *heaven*, shouldest be driven to worship them, and serve them." Job purges himself from this species of idolatry, chap. xxxi. ver. 26-28: "If I beheld the *sun* when it shined, or the *moon* walking in brightness, and my heart hath been secretly enticed, or my mouth hath kissed my hand: this also were an iniquity *to be punished by* the judge; for I should have *denied* the *God* that is *above*."

He clears himself also from *adultery* in reference to the law enacted against that sin, Job xxxi. 9-12: "If mine heart have been deceived by a woman, or if I have laid wait at my neighbour's door; then let my wife grind to another: for this is a heinous crime; yea, it is an iniquity *to be punished by* the judges." See the law against this sin, Exod. xx. 14, 17: "Thou shalt not commit *adultery:* thou shalt not *covet* thy *neighbour's wife*." Lev. xx. 10: "The man that committeth *adultery* with another man's wife shall surely be put to death;" see Deut. xxii. 22. And for the *judge's* office in such cases, see Deut. xvii. 9-12: "Thou shalt come unto the priests and Levites, and unto the *judge* that shall be in those days; and they shall show thee the sentence of *judgment*." 1 Sam. ii. 25: "If one man sin against another, the *judge* shall *judge* him."

The following will, I think, be considered an evident allusion to the *passage of the Red Sea*, and the destruction of the *proud Egyptian king:* Job xxvi. 11, 12: "The pillars of heaven tremble, and are astonished at his reproof. He *divideth* the *sea* with his power; and by his understanding he *smiteth* through the *proud*." These, with several others that might be adduced, are presumptive proofs that the *writer* of this book lived after the giving and establishment of the law, if not much later, let Job himself live when he might. See other proofs in the notes.

CHAPTER II

The sons of God once more present themselves before him; and Satan comes also, accusing Job as a person whose steadfastness would be soon shaken, provided his body were to be subjected to sore afflictions, 1–5. *He receives permission to afflict Job, and smites him with sore boils,* 6–8. *His wife reviles him,* 9. *His pious reproof,* 10. *His three friends come to visit and mourn with him.*

A. M. cir. 2484
B. C. cir. 1520
Ante I. Olymp. cir. 744
Ante U. C. cir. 767

AGAIN [a]there was a day when
the sons of God came to present themselves before the LORD,
and Satan came also among them
to present himself before the LORD.
2 And the LORD said unto Satan, From
whence comest thou? And [b]Satan answered
the LORD, and said, From going to and fro in
the earth, and from walking up and down in it.

3 And the LORD said unto Satan, Hast thou considered my
servant Job, that *there is* none
like him in the earth, [c]a perfect
and an upright man, one that feareth God, and
escheweth evil? and still he [d]holdeth fast his
integrity, although thou movedst me against
him, [e]to [f]destroy him without cause.
4 And Satan answered the LORD, and said,

A. M. cir. 2484
B. C. cir. 1520
Ante I. Olymp. cir. 744
Ante U. C. cir. 767

---

[a]Chap. i. 6——[b]Chap. i. 7——[c]Chap. i. 1, 8——[d]Chap. xxvii. 5, 6——[e]Heb. *to swallow him up*——[f]Chap. ix. 17

NOTES ON CHAP. II

Verse 1. *Again there was a day*] How long this was after the former trial, we know not: probably *one whole year*, when, as the *Targum* intimates, it was the time of the annual atonement; which, if so, must have been at least one whole year after the former; and during which period the patience and resignation of Job had sufficient scope to show themselves. This appearance of the *sons of God* and *Satan* is to be understood metaphorically—there could be nothing *real* in it—but it is intended to instruct us in the doctrine of the existence of good and evil spirits; that Satan pursues man with implacable enmity, and that he can do no man hurt, either in his person or property, but by the especial permission of God; and that God gives him permission only when he purposes to overrule it for the greater manifestation of his own glory, and the greater good of his tempted followers.

Verse 3. *To destroy him without cause.*] Thou wishedst me to permit thee to destroy a man whose sins have not called for so heavy a judgment. This seems to be the meaning of this saying. The original word, לבלעו *leballeo*, signifies to *swallow down* or *devour;* and this word St. Peter had no doubt in view in the place quoted on verse 7 of the preceding chapter: "*Your adversary the devil goeth about as a roaring lion, seeking whom he may* DEVOUR; ζητων, τινα καταπιῃ, *seeking whom he may* SWALLOW or GULP DOWN. See the note on 1 Pet. v. 8.

Verse 4. *Skin for skin*] That is, A man will part with all he has in the world to save his life; and he will part with all by piecemeal, till he has nothing left on earth, and even be thankful, provided his life be spared. Thou hast only destroyed his *property;* thou hast left him his *life* and his health. Thou hast not touched his *flesh* nor his *bone;* therefore he is patient and resigned. Man, through the love of life, will go much farther: he will give up one *member* to save the *rest;* yea, *limb* after *limb*, as long as there is hope that, by such sacrifices, life may be spared or *prolonged*. This is the meaning given to the passage by the *Targum;* and, I believe, the true one; hence, ver. 6, the Lord says, *Save his life.*

A. M. cir. 2484 B. C. cir. 1520 Ante I. Olymp. cir. 744 Ante U. C. cir. 767
Skin for skin, yea, all that a man
hath will he give for his life.
5 [g]But put forth thine hand
now, and touch his [h]bone and
his flesh, and he will curse thee to thy face.
6 [i]And the LORD said unto Satan, Behold,
he *is* in thine hand; [k]but save his life.
7 So went Satan forth from the presence
of the LORD, and smote Job with sore boils
[l]from the sole of his foot unto
his crown.
8 And he took him a potsherd
to scrape himself withal; [m]and
he sat down among the ashes.
9 Then said his wife unto him, [n]Dost thou
still [o]retain thine integrity? curse God, and die.
10 But he said unto her, Thou speakest as
one of the foolish women speaketh. What?

A. M. cir. 2484 B. C. cir. 1520 Ante I. Olymp. cir. 744 Ante U. C. cir. 767

[g]Chap. i. 11——[h]Chap. xix. 20——[i]Chap. i. 12——[k]Or, *only*——[l]Isa. i. 6

[m]2 Sam. xiii. 19; chap. xlii. 6; Ezek. xxvii. 30; Matt. xi. 21——[n]Chap. xxi. 15——[o]Ver. 3

Verse 5. *He will curse thee to thy face.*] Literally, *If he will not bless thee to thy face* or *appearances.* His *piety* to *thee* will be always regulated by thy *bounty* to *him.* See the note on chap. i. 11.

Verse 6. *But save his life.*] His *body* thou shalt have permission to afflict, but against his *life* thou shalt have no power; therefore take care of his life. The original, נפשו שמור *naphsho shemor*, may be translated, *keep his soul;* but the word also signifies *life;* yet in the hands of the destroyer the life of this holy man is placed! How astonishing is the economy of salvation! It is so manged, by the unlimited power and skill of God, that the grand adversary of souls becomes himself, by the order of God, the *preserver* of that which the evil of his nature incessantly prompts him to destroy!

Verse 7. *Sore boils*] בשחין רע *bischin ra*, "with an evil inflammation." What this diabolical disorder was, interpreters are not agreed. Some think it was the *leprosy;* and this is the reason why he dwelt by himself, and had his habitation in an unclean place, *without the city*, (Septuagint, εξω της πωλεως,) or in the open air: and the reason why his friends beheld him *afar off*, ver. 12, was because they knew that the disorder was infectious.

His *scraping* himself with a *potsherd* indicates a disease accompanied with intolerable *itching*, one of the characteristics of the *smallpox. Query*, Was it not this disorder? And in order to save his life (for that he had in especial command) did not Satan himself direct him to the *cool regimen*, without which, humanly speaking, the disease must have proved fatal? In the *elephantiasis* and *leprosy* there is, properly speaking, no boil or *detached inflammation*, or *swelling*, but *one uniform disordered state* of the *whole surface*, so that the whole body is covered with loathsome scales, and the skin appears like that of the *elephant*, thick and wrinkled, from which appearance the disorder has its name. In the *smallpox* it is different; each *pock* or *pustule* is a separate inflammation, tending to suppuration; and during this process, the fever is in general very high, and the anguish and distress of the patient intolerable. When the suppuration is pretty far advanced, the *itching* is extreme; and the hands are often obliged to be confined to prevent the patient from literally *tearing* his own flesh.

Verse 9. *Then said his wife*] To this verse the *Septuagint* adds the following words: "Much time having elapsed, his wife said unto him, How long dost thou stand steadfast, saying, 'Behold, I wait yet a little longer looking for the hope of my salvation?' Behold thy memorial is already blotted out from the earth, together with thy sons and thy daughters, the fruits of my pains and labours, for whom with anxiety I have laboured in vain. Thyself also sittest in the rottenness of worms night and day, while I am a wanderer from place to place, and from house to house, waiting for the setting of the sun, that I may rest from my labours, and from the griefs which oppress me. Speak therefore some word against God, and die." We translate ברך אלהים ומת *barech Elohim vamuth, Curse God, and die.* The verb ברך *barach* is supposed to include in it the ideas of *cursing* and *blessing;* but it is not clear that it has the former meaning in any part of the sacred writings, though we sometimes translate it so.

Here it seems to be a strong *irony. Job* was exceedingly afflicted, and apparently dying through sore disease; yet his soul was filled with gratitude to God. His *wife*, destitute of the salvation which her husband possessed, gave him this *ironical* reproof. *Bless God, and die*—What! bless him for his *goodness*, while he is destroying all that thou hast! bless him for his support, while he is casting thee down and destroying thee! Bless on, and die.

The *Targum* says that Job's wife's name was *Dinah*, and that the words which she spake to him on this occasion were בריך מימרא דיי ומית *berich meymera dayai umith. Bless the word of the Lord, and die.*

Ovid has such an *irony* as I suppose this to have been:—

Quid vos sacra juvant? quid nunc Ægyptia prosunt
Sistra?———
Cum rapiant mala fata bonos, ignoscite fasso,
Sollicitor nullos esse putare deos.
Vive pius, moriere pius; cole sacra, colentem
Mors gravis a templis in cava busta trahet.
AMOR. lib. iii., *Eleg.* ix. ver. 33.

"In vain to gods (if gods there are) we pray,
And needless victims prodigally pay;
Worship their sleeping deities: yet death
Scorns votaries, and stops the praying breath.
To hallow'd shrines intruding fate will come,
And drag you from the altar to the tomb."
STEPNEY.

Verse 10. *Thou speakest as one of the foolish*] Thou speakest like an infidel; like one who has

A. M. cir. 2484
B. C. cir. 1520
Ante I. Olymp. cir. 744
Ante U. C. cir. 767

[p]shall we receive good at the
hand of God, and shall we not
receive evil? [q]In all this did
not Job [r]sin with his lips.
11 Now when Job's three [s]friends heard of
all this evil that was come upon him, they
came every one from his own place; Eliphaz
the [t]Temanite, and Bildad the [u]Shuhite, and
Zophar the Naamathite: for they had made
an appointment together to come [v]to mourn
with him and to comfort him.

A. M. cir. 2484
B. C. cir. 1520
Ante I. Olymp. cir. 744
Ante U. C. cir. 767

12 And when they lifted up
their eyes afar off, and knew
him not, they lifted up their
voice, and wept; and they rent
every one his mantle, and [w]sprinkled dust
upon their heads toward heaven.
13 So they sat down with him upon
the ground [x]seven days and seven nights,
and none spake a word unto him:
for they saw that *his* grief was very
great.

---

[p]Ch. i. 21; Rom. xii. 12; James v. 10, 11——[q]Ch. i. 22——[r]Psa. xxxix. 1——[s]Prov. xvii. 17——[t]Gen. xxxvi. 11; Jer. xlix. 7——[u]Gen. xxv. 2——[v]Ch. xlii. 11; Rom. xii.15——[w]Neh. ix. 1; Lam. ii. 10; Ezek. xxvii. 30——[x]Gen. l. 10

---

no knowledge of God, of religion, or of a future state.

The Targum, who calls this woman *Dinah*, translates thus: "Thou speakest like one of those women who have wrought folly in the house of their father." This is in reference to an ancient rabbinical opinion, that Job lived in the days of the patriarch Jacob, whose daughter Dinah he had married.

Shall we receive good] This we have received in great abundance for many years:—

And shall we not receive evil?] Shall we murmur when He *afflicts* us for a *day*, who has given us *health* for so *many years?* Shall we blaspheme his name for *momentary privations*, who has given us such a *long succession of enjoyments?* His blessings are his own: he never *gave* them to us; they were only *lent*. We have had the long, the free, the unmerited use of them; and shall we be offended at the *Owner*, when he comes to reclaim his own property? This would be foolish, ungrateful, and wicked. So may every one reason who is suffering from adversity. But who, besides Job, reasons thus? Man is naturally discontented and ungrateful.

In all this did not Job sin with his lips.] The Chaldee adds, *But in his heart he thought words.* He had surmisings of heart, though he let nothing escape from his lips.

Verse 11. *Job's three friends*] The first was *Eliphaz the Temanite;* or, as the *Septuagint* has it, Ελιφαζ ὁ Θαιμανων βασιλευς, *Eliphaz the king of the Thaimanites.* Eliphaz was one of the sons of Esau; and Teman, of Eliphaz, Gen. xxxvi, 10, 11. Teman was a city of Edom, Jer. xlix. 7-20; Ezek. xxv. 13; Amos i. 11, 12.

Bildad the Shuhite] Or, as the *Septuagint*, Βαλδαδ ὁ Συχεων τυραννος, *Baldad, tyrant of the Suchites. Shuah* was the son of Abraham by Keturah; and his posterity is reckoned among the Easterns. It is supposed he should be placed with his brother *Midian*, and his brother's sons *Sheba* and *Dedan.* See Gen. xxv. 2, 3. Dedan was a city of Edom, see Jer. xlix. 8, and seems to have been situated in its southern boundary, as Teman was in its western. Ezek. xxv. 13.

Zophar the Naamathite] Or, according to the *Septuagint*, Σωφαρ Μιναιων Βασιλευς, *Sophar king of the Minaites.* He most probably came from that *Naamah*, which was bordering upon the Edomites to the south and fell by lot to the tribe of Judah, Josh. xv. 21-41. These circumstances, which have already been mentioned in the *introduction*, prove that Job must have dwelt in the land of *Edom*, and that all his friends dwelt in *Arabia Petræa*, or in the countries immediately adjacent. That some of those Eastern people were highly *cultivated*, we have at least indirect proof in the case of *the Temanites*, Jer. xlix. 7: *Concerning Edom thus saith the Lord of hosts, Is wisdom no more in Teman? Is counsel perished from the prudent? Is their wisdom vanished?* They are celebrated also in *Baruch*, iii. 22, 23. Speaking of *wisdom* he says: *It hath not been heard of in Chanaan; neither hath it been seen in Theman. The Agarenes that seek wisdom upon earth, the merchants of Meran and of Theman, the expounders of fables, and searchers out of understanding, none of these have known the way of wisdom.* It is evident enough from these quotations that the inhabitants of those districts were celebrated for their knowledge; and the sayings of Job's three friends are proofs that their reputation for wisdom stood on a very solid foundation.

Verse 12. *They rent every one his mantle*] I have already had frequent occasions to point out and illustrate, by quotations from the ancients, the actions that were used in order to express profound grief; such as wrapping themselves in sackcloth, covering the face, strewing dust or ashes upon the head, sitting upon the bare ground, &c., &c.; significant actions which were in use among all nations.

Verse 13. *They sat down with him upon the ground seven days*] They were astonished at the unprecedented change which had taken place in the circumstances of this most eminent man; they could not reconcile his present situation with any thing they had met with in the history of Divine providence. The *seven days* mentioned here were the period appointed for mourning. The Israelites mourned for Jacob *seven days*, Gen. l. 10. And the men of Jabesh mourned so long for the death of Saul, 1 Sam. xxxi. 13; 1 Chron. x. 12. And Ezekiel sat on the ground with the captives at Chebar, and mourned with and for them *seven days.* Ezek. iii. 15. The wise son of Sirach says, "*Seven days* do men mourn for him that is dead;" Ecclus. xxii. 12. So calamitous was the state of Job, that they considered him as a dead man: and went through the prescribed period of mourning for him.

They saw that his *grief was very great.*]

This is the reason why they did *not speak* to him: they believed him to be suffering for heavy crimes, and, seeing him suffer so much, they were not willing to add to his distresses by invectives or reproach. Job himself first broke silence.

CHAPTER III

Job curses the day of his birth, and regrets that he ever saw the light, 1–12. *Describes the empire of death and its inhabitants,* 13–19. *Regrets that he is appointed to live in the midst of sorrows, for the calamities which he feared had overtaken him,* 20–26.

A. M. cir. 2484
B. C. cir. 1520
Ante I. Olymp. cir. 744
A. U. C. cir. 767

AFTER this opened Job his
mouth and cursed his day.
2 And Job [a]spake, and
said,
3 [b]Let the day perish wherein I was
born, and the night *in which* it was
said, There is a man-child conceived.
4 Let that day be darkness;
let not God regard it from above,
neither let the light shine upon it.
5 Let darkness and [c]the shadow of death

[a]Hebrew, *answered*——[b]Chapter x. 18, 19; Jeremiah xv. 10; xx. 14

[c]Chap. x. 21, 22; xvi. 16; xxviii. 3; Psa. xxiii. 4; xliv. 19; cvii. 10, 14; Jer. xiii. 16; Amos v. 8

NOTES ON CHAP. III

Verse 1. *After this opened Job his mouth*] After the *seven days' mourning* was over, there being no prospect of relief, Job is represented as thus *cursing the day of his birth.* Here the *poetic* part of the book *begins;* for most certainly there is nothing in the preceding chapters either in the *form* or *spirit* of *Hebrew poetry.* It is easy indeed to break the sentences into *hemistichs;* but this does not constitute them *poetry:* for, although *Hebrew poetry* is in general in hemistichs, yet it does not follow that the division of *narrative* into hemistichs must necessarily constitute it *poetry.*

In many cases the Asiatic poets introduce their compositions with *prose narrative;* and having in this way prepared the reader for what he is to expect, begin their *deevans, cassidehs, gazels,* &c. This appears to be the plan followed by the author of this book. Those who still think, after examining the structure of those chapters, and comparing them with the undoubted poetic parts of the book, that *they* also, and the *ten* concluding verses, are *poetry,* have my consent, while I take the liberty to believe most decidedly the opposite.

Cursed his day.] That is, the day of his birth; and thus he gave vent to the agonies of his soul, and the distractions of his mind. His execrations have something in them awfully solemn, tremendously deep, and strikingly sublime. But let us not excuse all the things which he said in his haste, and in the bitterness of his soul, because of his former well established character of patience. He bore all his *privations* with becoming resignation to the Divine will and providence: but now, feeling himself the subject of continual sufferings, being in heaviness through manifold temptation, and probably having the light of God withdrawn from his mind, as his consolations most undoubtedly were, he regrets that ever he was born; and in a very high strain of impassioned poetry curses his day. We find a similar execration to this in Jeremiah, chap. xx. 14-18, and in other places; which, by the way, are no proofs that the one borrowed from the other; but that this was the common mode of Asiatic thinking, speaking, and feeling, on such occasions.

Verse 3. *There is a man-child conceived.*] The word הרה *harah* signifies to *conceive;* yet here, it seems, it should be taken in the sense of *being born,* as it is perfectly unlikely that the night of conception should be either distinctly known or published.

Verse 4. *Let that day be darkness*] The meaning is exactly the same with our expression, "Let it be blotted out of the calendar." However distinguished it may have been, as the birthday of a man once celebrated for his possessions, liberality, and piety, let it no longer be thus noted; as he who was thus celebrated is now the sport of adversity, the most impoverished, most afflicted, and most wretched of human beings.

Let not God regard it from above] אל ידרשהו *al yidreshehu,* "Let Him not *require* it"—let Him not consider it essential to the completion of the days of the year; and therefore he adds, *neither let the light shine upon it.* If it must be a part of *duration,* let it not be distinguished by the light of the sun.

Verse 5. *Let darkness and the shadow of death stain it*] יגאלהו *yigaluhu,* "pollute or avenge it," from גאל *gaal,* to *vindicate, avenge, &c.;* hence גאל *goel,* the nearest of kin, whose right it was to *redeem* an inheritance, and *avenge* the death of his relative by slaying the murderer. Let this day be pursued, overtaken, and destroyed. Let natural darkness, the total privation of the solar light, rendered still more intense by death's shadow projected over it, *seize on* and destroy this day, εκλαβοι αυτην, *Septuagint;* alluding, perhaps, says Mr. *Parkhurst,* to the avenger of blood seizing the offender.

Let a cloud dwell upon it] **Let the dymme cloude fall upon it.**—*Coverdale. Let the thickest clouds have there their dwelling-place*—let that be the period of time on which they shall constantly rest, and never be *dispersed.* This seems to be the import of the original, תשכן עליו אננה *tishcan alaiv ananah.* Let it be the

A. M. cir. 2484 B. C. cir. 1520 Ante I. Olymp. cir. 744 Ante U. C. cir. 767

[d]stain it; let a cloud dwell upon
it; [e]let the blackness of the day
terrify it.
6 *As for* that night, let dark-
ness seize upon it; [f]let it not be joined unto
the days of the year, let it not come into the
number of the months.
7 Lo, let that night be solitary,
let no joyful voice come therein.
8 Let them curse it that curse
the day, [g]who are ready to raise
up [h]their mourning.
9 Let the stars of the twilight thereof be
dark; let it look for light, but *have* none;

A. M. cir. 2484 B. C. cir. 1520 Ante I. Olymp. cir. 744 Ante U. C. cir. 767

---

[d]Or, *challenge it*——[e]Or, *let them terrify it, as those* who have *a bitter day;* Amos viii. 10

[f]Or, *let it not rejoice among the days*——[g]Jer. ix. 17, 18 [h]Or, *a leviathan*

---

place in which *clouds* shall be continually *gathered together*, so as to be the storehouse of the densest vapours, still in the act of being increasingly condensed.

Let the blackness of the day terrify it.] **And let it be lapped in with sorrowe.**—*Coverdale.* This is very expressive: *lap* signifies to fold up, or envelope any particular thing with fold upon fold, so as to *cover it everywhere* and *secure it in all points.* Leaving out the semicolon, we had better translate the whole clause thus: "Let the thickest cloud have its dwelling-place upon it, and let the bitterness of a day fill it with terror." *A day* similar to that, says the *Targum,* in which *Jeremiah was distressed for the destruction of the house of the sanctuary;* or like that in which *Jonah was cast into the sea of Tarsis;* such a day as that on which some great or national misfortune has happened: probably in allusion to that in which *the darkness that might be felt* enveloped the whole land of Egypt, and the night in which the destroying angel slew all the first-born in the land.

Verse 6. As for *that night, let darkness seize upon it*] I think the *Targum* has hit the sense of this whole verse: "Let darkness seize upon that night; let it not be reckoned among the annual festivals; in the number of the months of the calendar let it not be computed."

Some understand the word אפל *ophel* as signifying a *dark storm;* hence the Vulgate, *tenebrosus turbo,* "a dark whirlwind." And hence *Coverdale,* **Let the darck storme overcome that night, let it not be reckoned amonge the dayes off the yeare, nor counted in the monethes.** Every thing is here personified; *day, night, darkness, shadow of death, cloud,* &c.; and the same idea of the total extinction of that portion of time, or its being rendered ominous and portentous, is pursued through all these verses, from the *third* to the *ninth,* inclusive. The *imagery* is diversified, the *expressions* varied, but the *idea* is the same.

Verse 7. *Lo, let that night be solitary*] The word הנה *hinneh, behold,* or *lo,* is wanting in one of *De Rossi's* MSS., nor is it expressed in the *Septuagint, Vulgate, Syriac,* or *Arabic.*

The word גלמוד *galmud,* which we translate *solitary,* is properly *Arabic.* From جلم *ghalama* or *jalama,* signifying to *cut off, make bare, amputate,* comes جلمود *jalmud,* a *rock,* a *great stone;* and جلاميدة *jalameedet, weight,* a *burden, trouble,* from which we may gather Job's meaning: "Let that night be grievous, oppressive, as destitute of good as a bare rock is of verdure." The *Targum* gives the sense, *In that night let there be tribulation.*

Let no joyful voice come therein.] Let there be no choirs of singers; no pleasant music heard; no dancing or merriment. The word רננה *renanah* signifies any brisk *movement,* such as the vibration of the rays of light, or the brisk modulation of the voice in a cheerful ditty. The *Targum* has, *Let not the crowing of the rural or wild cock resound in it.* Let all work be intermitted; let there be no sportive exercises; and let all animals be totally silent.

Verse 8. *Let them curse it that curse the day*] This translation is scarcely intelligible. I have waded through a multitude of interpretations, without being able to collect from them such a notion of the verse as could appear to me probable. *Schultens, Rosenmüller,* and after them Mr. *Good,* have laboured much to make it plain. They think the custom of *sorcerers* who had *execrations* for peoples, places, things, days, &c., is here referred to; such as Balaam, Elymas, and many others were: but I cannot think that a man who knew the Divine Being and his sole government of the world so well as Job did, would make such an allusion, who must have known that such *persons* and their *pretensions* were impostors and execrable vanities. I shall give as near a translation as I can of the words, and subjoin a short paraphrase: יקבהו ארריו יום העתידים ערר לויתן *yikkebuhu orerey yom haathidim orer livyathan;* "Let them curse it who detest the day; them who are ready to raise up the leviathan." That is, Let them curse my birthday who hate daylight, such as adulterers, murderers, thieves, and banditti, for whose practices the *night* is more convenient; and let them curse it who, being like me *weary of life,* are desperate enough to provoke the leviathan, the crocodile, to tear them to pieces. This version is nearly the same as that given by *Coverdale.* **Let them that curse the daye give it their curse also, then those that be ready to rayse up leviathan.** By *leviathan* some understand the greatest and most *imminent dangers;* and others, the *devil,* whom the *enchanters* are desperate enough to attempt to raise by their incantations.

Calmet understands the whole to be spoken of the *Atlantes,* a people of *Ethiopia,* who *curse the sun* because it parches their fields and their bodies; and who *fearlessly attack, kill,* and *eat* the *crocodile.* This seems a good sense.

Verse 9. *Let the stars of the twilight thereof*] The stars of the twilight may here refer to the planets *Venus, Jupiter, Mars,* and *Mercury,* as well as to the brighter fixed stars.

Let it look for light] Here the prosopopœia or personification is still carried on. The *darkness* is represented as *waiting* for the lustre of the *evening star,* but is disappointed; and then for the *aurora* or *dawn,* but equally in vain.

A. M. cir. 2484
B. C. cir. 1520
Ante I. Olymp. cir. 744
Ante U. C. cir. 767

neither let it see [l]the dawning
of the day:
10 Because it shut not up the
doors of my *mother's* womb, nor
his sorrow from mine eyes.
11 [k]Why died I not from the womb? *why*
did I *not* give up the ghost when I came out
of the belly?
12 [l]Why did the knees prevent me? or
why the breast that I should suck?
13 For now should I have lain still and
been quiet, I should have slept:
then had I been at rest,
14 With kings and counsellors
of the earth, which [m]built desolate places for themselves;
15 Or with princes that had gold, who filled
their houses with silver.
16 Or [n]as a hidden untimely birth I had
not been; as infants *which* never saw light.
17 There the wicked cease *from* troubling;
and there the [o]weary be at rest.

A. M. cir. 2484
B. C. cir. 1520
Ante I. Olymp. cir. 744
Ante U. C. cir. 767

---

[l]Heb. *the eyelids of the morning*, chap. xli. 18——[k]Chap. x. 18——[l]Gen. xxx. 3; Isa. lxvi. 12

[m]Chapter xv. 28——[n]Psa. lviii. 8——[o]Heb. *wearied in strength*

He had prayed that its *light*, the *sun*, should not shine upon it, ver. 4; and here he prays that its *evening star* may be totally obscured, and that it might never see the *dawning of the day*. Thus his execration comprehends every thing that might *irradiate* or *enliven* it.

Verse 10. *Because it shut not up the doors*] Here is the reason why he curses the day and the night in which he was conceived and born; because, had he never been brought into existence, he would never have seen trouble. It seems, however, very harsh that he should have wished the destruction of his *mother*, in order that his birth might have been prevented; and I rather think Job's execration did not extend thus far. The *Targum* understands the passage as speaking of the *umbilical cord*, by which the fœtus is nourished in its mother's womb: had this been shut up, there must have been a miscarriage, or he must have been *dead born;* and thus *sorrow would have been hidden from his eyes*. This seeming gloss is much nearer the letter and spirit of the Hebrew than is generally imagined. I shall quote the words: כי לא סגר דלתי בטני *ki lo sagar dalthey bitni, because it did not shut up the doors of my belly*. This is much more consistent with the feelings of humanity, than to wish his mother's womb to have been his grave.

Verse 11. *Why died I not from the womb*] As the other circumstance did not take place, why was I not *still-born*, without the possibility of reviviscence? or, as this did not occur, why did I not *die as soon as born?* These *three* things appear to me to be clearly intended here:—1. Dying in the womb, or never coming to maturity, as in the case of an *abortion*. 2. Being still-born, without ever being able to breathe. 3. Or, if born alive, dying within a short time after. And to these states he seems to refer in the following verses.

Verse 12. *Why did the knees prevent me?*] Why was I dandled on the knees? Why was I nourished by the breasts? In either of the above cases I had neither been received into a mother's lap, nor hung upon a mother's breasts.

Verse 13. *For now should I have lain still*] In that case I had been insensible; *quiet*—without these overwhelming agitations; *slept*—unconscious of evil; *been at rest*—been out of the reach of calamity and sorrow.

Verse 14. *With kings and counsellors of the earth*] I believe this translation to be perfectly correct. The *counsellors*, יעצי *yoatsey*, I suppose to mean the privy council, or advisers of kings; those without whose advice kings seldom undertake wars, expeditions, &c. These mighty agitators of the world are at rest in their graves, after the lives of commotion which they have led among men: most of whom indeed have been the troublers of the peace of the globe.

Which built desolate places] Who erect mausoleums, funeral monuments, sepulchral pyramids, &c., to keep their *names* from *perishing*, while their *bodies* are turned to *corruption*. I cannot think, with some learned men, that Job is here referring to those patriotic princes who employed themselves in repairing the ruins and desolations which others had occasioned. His simple idea is, that, had he died from the womb, he would have been equally at rest, neither troubling nor troubled, as those defunct kings and planners of wars and great designs are, who have nothing to keep even their *names* from perishing, but the monuments which they have raised to contain their corrupting flesh, mouldering bones, and dust.

Verse 15. *Or with princes that had gold*] Chief or mighty men, lords of the soil, or fortunate adventurers in merchandise, who got gold in abundance, filled their houses with silver, left all behind, and had nothing reserved for themselves but the *empty places* which they had made for their last dwelling, and where their dust now sleeps, devoid of care, painful journeys, and anxious expectations. He alludes here to the case of the *covetous*, *whom nothing can satisfy*, as an Asiatic writer has observed, *but the dust that fills his mouth when laid in the grave*.—Saady.

Verse 16. *Or as a hidden untimely birth*] An early miscarriage, which was scarcely perceptible by the parent herself; and in this case he *had not been*—he had never had the distinguishable form of a human being, whether *male* or *female*.

As infants] Little ones; those farther advanced in maturity, but miscarried long before the time of birth.

Verse 17. *There the wicked cease*] In the grave the oppressors of men cease from irritating, harassing, and distressing their fellow creatures and dependents.

And there the weary be at rest.] Those who were worn out with the cruelties and tyrannies of the above. The troubles and the troubled, the restless and the submissive, the toils of the

A. M. cir. 2484
B. C. cir. 1520
Ante I. Olymp. cir. 744
Ante U. C. cir. 767

18 *There* the prisoners rest together; [p]they hear not the voice
of the oppressor.
19 The small and great are
there; and the servant *is* free from his master.
20 [q]Wherefore is light given to him that is
in misery, and life unto the [r]bitter *in* soul;
21 Which [s]long [t]for death, but it *cometh* not;
and dig for it more than [u]for hid treasures;
22 Which rejoice exceedingly, *and* are glad,
when they can find the grave?
23 *Why is light given* to a
man whose way is hid, [v]and
whom God hath [w]hedged in?
24 For my sighing cometh [x]be-
fore I eat, and my roarings are poured out
like the waters.
25 For [y]the thing which I greatly feared is
come upon me, and that which I was afraid
of is come unto me.
26 I was not in safety, neither had I rest,
neither was I quiet; yet trouble came.

A. M. cir. 2484
B. C. cir. 1520
Ante I. Olymp. cir. 744
Ante U. C. cir. 767

---

[p]Chapter xxxix. 7——[q]Jeremiah xx. 18——[r]1 Samuel i. 10; 2 Kings iv. 27; Proverbs xxxi. 6——[s]Hebrew, *wait*——[t]Revelation ix. 6——[u]Proverbs ii. 4——[v]Ch. xxix. 8; Lamentations iii. 7——[w]Chapter i. 10——[x]Hebrew, *before my meat*——[y]Hebrew, *I feared a fear, and it came upon me*

---

great and the labours of the slave, are here put in opposition.

Verse 18. *The prisoners rest together*] Those who were slaves, feeling all the troubles, and scarcely tasting any of the pleasures of life, are quiet in the grave together; and the voice of the oppressor, the hard, unrelenting task-master, which was more terrible than death, is heard no more. *They* are free from his exactions, and *his* mouth is silent in the dust. This may be a reference to the Egyptian bondage. The children of Israel cried by reason of their oppressors or task-masters.

Verse 19. *The small and great are there.*] All sorts and conditions of men are equally blended in the grave, and ultimately reduced to one common dust; and between the bond and free there is no difference. The *grave* is

"The appointed place of rendezvous, where all
These travellers meet."

Equality is absolute among the sons of men in their *entrance* into and *exit* from the world: all the intermediate state is *disparity*. All men *begin* and *end life alike;* and there is no difference between the king and the cottager. A contemplation of this should equally humble the *great* and the *small.* The saying is *trite,* but it is *true:*—

Pallida mors æquo pulsat pede pauperum tabernas,
Regumque turres.
Hor. Odar. lib. i., Od. iv., ver. 13.

"With equal pace impartial Fate
Knocks at the palace as the cottage gate."

Death is that state,

"Where they an equal honour share
Who buried or unburied are.
Where *Agamemnon* knows no more
Than *Irus* he contemn'd before.
Where fair *Achilles* and *Thersites* lie,
Equally *naked, poor,* and *dry.*"

And why do not the *living* lay these things to heart?

There is a fine saying in *Seneca ad Marciam,* cap. 20, on this subject, which may serve as a comment on this place: Mors—servitutem invito domino remittit; hæc captivorum catenas levat; hæc e carcere eduxit, quos exire imperium impotens vetuerat. Hæc est in quo nemo humilitatem suam sensit; hæc quæ nulli paruit; hæc quæ nihil quicquam alieno fecit arbitrio. Hæc, ubi res communes fortuna male divisit, et æquo jure genitos alium alii donavit, exæquat omnia. —"Death, in spite of the master, manumits the slave. It loosens the chains of the prisoners. It brings out of the dungeon those whom impotent authority had forbidden to go at large. This is the state in which none is sensible of his humiliation. Death obeys no man. It does nothing according to the will of another. It reduces, by a just law, to a state of equality, all who in their families and circumstances had unequal lots in life."

Verse 20. *Wherefore is light given*] Why is life granted to him who is incapable of enjoying it, or of performing its functions?

Verse 21. *Which long for death*] They look to it as the *end* of all their miseries; and long more for a separation from life, than those who love gold do for a rich mine.

Verse 22. *Which rejoice exceedingly.* Literally, *They rejoice with joy,* and *exult when they find the grave.*

There is a various reading here in one of *Kennicott's* MSS., which gives a different sense. Instead of *who rejoice,* אלי גיל *eley gil,* with joy, it has אלי גל *eley gal, who rejoice at the* tomb, *and exult when they find the grave.*

Verse 23. *To a man whose way is hid*] Who knows not what is before him in either world, but is full of fears and trembling concerning both.

God hath hedged in?] Leaving him no way to escape; and not permitting him to see one step before him.

There is an exact parallel to this passage in Lam. iii. 7, 9: *He hath hedged me about that I cannot get out. He hath inclosed my ways with hewn stone.* Mr. *Good* translates the verse thus: *To the man whose path is broken up, and whose futurity God hath overwhelmed.* But I cannot see any necessity for departing from the common text, which gives both an *easy* and a *natural* sense.

Verse 24. *For my sighing cometh*] Some think that this refers to the *ulcerated state* of Job's *body, mouth, hands,* &c. He longed for food, but was not able to lift it to his mouth with his hands, nor masticate it when brought thither. This is the sense in which *Origen* has taken the words. But perhaps it is most natural to suppose that he means his sighing took away all appetite, and served him in place of meat. There is the same thought in Psa. xlii. 3: *My tears have been my meat day and night;* which place is not an imitation of Job, but more likely *Job* an imitation of it, or, rather, both an imitation of *nature.*

My roarings are poured out] My lamentations are like the noise of the murmuring stream, or the dashings of the overswollen torrent.

Verse 25. *For the thing which I greatly feared*] Literally, *the fear that I feared;* or, *I feared a fear,* as in the *margin.* While I was in prosperity I thought adversity might come, and I had a dread of it. I feared the loss of my family and my property; and both have occurred. I was not lifted up: I knew that what I possessed I had from Divine Providence, and that he who gave might take away. I am not stripped of my all as a punishment for my self-confidence.

Verse 26. *I was not in safety*] If this verse be read *interrogatively,* it will give a good and easy sense: *Was I not in safety? Had I not rest? Was I not in comfort? Yet trouble came.* It is well known that, previously to this attack of Satan, Job was in great prosperity and peace. Mr. *Good* translates, *I had no peace; yea, I had no rest. Yea, I had no respite, as the trouble came on;* and refers the whole to the quick succession of the series of heavy evils by which he was tried. There is a similar thought in the Psalmist: *Deep crieth unto deep at the noise of thy water-spouts; all thy waves and thy billows have gone over me;* Psa. xlii. 7. One evil treads on the heels of another.

In this chapter Job's conflict begins. *Now,* and not *before,* Satan appears to have access to his *mind.* When he deprived him of his *property,* and, what was still dearer, of his *sons* and his *daughters,* the hope of his family, he bore all with the most exemplary patience, and the deepest resignation to the Divine will. When his adversary was permitted to touch his *body,* and afflict it in the most grievous and distressing manner, rendered still more intolerable by his being previously deprived of all the *comforts* and *necessaries* of life; still he held fast his integrity; no complaint, no murmur was heard. From the Lord's hand he received his *temporal good;* and from that hand he received his *temporal evil,* the privation of that good. Satan was, therefore, baffled in all his attempts; Job continued to be *a perfect and upright man, fearing God, and avoiding evil.* This was Job's triumph, or rather the triumph of Divine grace; and Satan's defeat and confusion.

It is indeed very seldom that God permits Satan to waste the *substance* or afflict the *body* of any man; but at all times this malevolent spirit may have access to the *mind* of any man, and inject doubts, fears, diffidence, perplexities, and even *unbelief.* And here is the spiritual conflict. Now, *their wrestling is not with flesh and blood*—with *men* like themselves, nor about *secular* affairs; but they have to contend with *angels, principalities and powers, and the rulers of the darkness of this world, and spiritual wickednesses in heavenly places.* In such cases Satan is often permitted to diffuse *darkness* into the understanding, and envelope the heavens with clouds. Hence are engendered *false views* of God and his providence, of men, of the spiritual world, and particularly of the person's own state and circumstances. Every thing is distorted, and all seen through a false medium. Indescribable distractions and uneasiness are hereby induced; the mind is like a troubled sea, tossed by a tempest that seems to confound both heaven and earth. Strong *temptations* to things which the soul contemplates with abhorrence are injected; and which are followed by immediate *accusations,* as if the injections were the *offspring of the heart itself;* and the trouble and dismay produced are represented as the sense of guilt, from a consciousness of having, in heart, committed these evils. Thus Satan tempts, accuses, and upbraids, in order to perplex the soul, induce skepticism, and destroy the empire of faith. Behold here the *permission* of God, and behold also his *sovereign control:* all this time the grand tempter is not permitted to touch the *heart,* the seat of the affections, nor offer even the slightest violence to the *will.* The soul is cast down, but not destroyed; perplexed, but not in despair. It is on all sides harassed; without are fightings, within are fears: but the *will* is inflexible on the side of God and truth, and the heart, with all its train of affections and passions, follows it. The man does not wickedly depart from his God; the outworks are violently *assailed,* but not *taken;* the city is still safe, and the citadel impregnable. Heaviness may endure for the night, but joy cometh in the morning. Jesus is soon seen walking upon the waters. He speaks peace to the winds and the sea: immediately there is a calm. Satan is bruised down under the feet of the sufferer, the clouds are dispersed, the heavens re-appear, and the soul, to its surprise, finds that the storm, instead of hindering, has driven it nearer to the haven whither it would be.

The reader who closely examines the subject will find that this was the case of Job. The following chapters show the conflict of the soul; the end of the book, God's victory and his exaltation. Satan sifted Job as wheat, but his faith failed not.

CHAPTER IV

Eliphaz answers; and accuses Job of impatience, and of despondence in the time of adversity, 1–6; *asserts that no innocent man ever perished, and that the wicked are afflicted for their sins,* 7–11; *relates a vision that he had,* 12–16, *and what was said to him on the occasion,* 17–21.

A. M. cir. 2484
B. C. cir. 1520
Ante I. Olymp. cir. 744
Ante U. C. cir. 767

THEN Eliphaz the Temanite
answered and said,
2 *If* we assay [a]to commune
with thee, wilt thou be grieved?
but [b]who can withhold himself from speaking?
3 Behold, thou hast instructed many, and
thou [c]hast strengthened the weak hands.
4 Thy words have upholden him that was
falling, and thou [d]hast strengthened [e]the
feeble knees.
5 But now it is come upon thee, and thou
faintest: it toucheth thee, and
thou art troubled.
6 *Is* not *this* [f]thy fear, [g]thy
confidence, thy hope, and the
uprightness of thy ways?
7 Remember, I pray thee, [h]who *ever* perished, being innocent? or where were the
righteous cut off?
8 Even as I have seen, [i]they that plough
iniquity, and sow wickedness, reap the
same.

A. M. cir. 2484
B. C. cir. 1520
Ante I. Olymp. cir. 744
Ante U. C. cir. 767

[a]Heb. *a word*——[b]Heb. *who can refrain from words?* [c]Isa. xxxv. 3——[d]Isa. xxxv. 3——[e]Heb. *the bowing knees;* Heb. xii. 12

[f]Ch. i. 1——[g]Prov. iii. 26——[h]Psalm xxxvii. 25 [i]Psalm vii. 14; Proverbs xxii. 8; Hosea x. 13; Galatians vi. 7, 8

NOTES ON CHAP. IV

Verse 1. *Then Eliphaz the Temanite answered*] For *seven days* this person and his two friends had observed a profound silence, being awed and confounded at the sight of Job's unprecedented affliction. Having now sufficiently contemplated his afflicted state, and heard his bitter complaint, forgetting that he came as a *comforter*, and not as a *reprover*, he loses the feeling of the *friend* in the haughtiness of the *censor*, endeavouring to strip him of his only consolation,—the testimony of his conscience, that in simplicity and godly sincerity, not in fleshly wisdom, but by the grace of God, he had his conversation among men,—by insinuating that if his ways had been upright, he would not have been abandoned to such distress and affliction; and if his heart possessed that righteousness of which he boasted, he would not have been so suddenly cast down by adversity.

Verse 2. If *we assay to commune with thee*] As if he had said, Should I and my friends endeavour to reason with thee ever so mildly, because we shall have many things to say by way of reprehension, thou wilt be grieved and faint; and this we may reasonably infer from the manner in which thou bearest thy present afflictions. Yet as thou hast uttered words which are injurious to thy Maker, who can forbear speaking? It is our duty to rise up on the part of God, though thereby we shall grieve him who is our friend. This was a plausible beginning, and certainly was far from being insincere.

Verse 3. *Thou hast instructed many*] Thou hast seen many in affliction and distress, and thou hast given them such advice as was suitable to their state, and effectual to their relief; and by this means thou hast *strengthened the weak hands*, and *the feeble knees*—the desponding have been encouraged, and the irresolute confirmed and excited to prompt and proper actions, by thy counsel and example.

Verse 5. *But now it is come upon thee*] Now it is thy turn to suffer, and give an example of the efficacy of thy own principles; but instead of this, behold, thou faintest. Either, therefore, thou didst *pretend* to what thou hadst not; or thou art not making a proper use of the principles which thou didst recommend to others.

Verse 6. Is *not* this *thy fear*] I think *Coverdale* hits the true meaning: **Where is now thy feare of God, thy stedfastnesse, thy pacience, and the perfectnesse of thy life?** If these be genuine, surely there is no cause for all this complaint, vexation, and despair. That this is the meaning, the next words show.

Verse 7. *Remember, I pray thee*] Recollect, if thou canst, a single instance where God abandoned an innocent man, or suffered him to perish. Didst thou ever hear of a case in which God abandoned a righteous man to destruction? Wert thou a righteous man, and innocent of all hidden crimes, would God abandon thee thus to the malice of Satan? or let loose the plagues of affliction and adversity against thee?

Verse 8. *They that plough iniquity*] A proverbial form of speech drawn from nature. Whatever seed a man sows in the ground, he reaps the same kind; for every seed produces its like. Thus *Solomon*, Prov. xxii. 8: "He that soweth iniquity shall reap vanity." And St. Paul, Gal. vi. 7, 8: "Be not deceived, God is not mocked; for whatsoever a man soweth, that shall he also reap. For he that soweth to his flesh, shall of the flesh reap corruption; but he who soweth to the Spirit, shall of the Spirit reap life everlasting." And of the same nature is that other saying of the apostle, *He that soweth sparingly, shall reap sparingly*, 2 Cor. ix. 6.

The same figure is employed by the Prophet *Hosea* viii. 7: *They have sown the wind, and they shall reap the whirlwind;* and chap. x. 12, 13: *Sow to yourselves in righteousness; reap in mercy. Ye have ploughed wickedness; ye have reaped iniquity.* The last sentence contains, not only the same *image*, but almost the *same words* as those used by Eliphaz.

Our Lord expresses the same thing, in the following words: Matt. vii. 16-18: *Do men gather grapes of thorns, or figs of thistles? Every good tree bringeth forth good fruit, but a corrupt tree bringeth forth evil fruit.* So the Greeks:—

Ατης αρουρα θανατον εκκαρπιζεται.

ÆSCH. Ἑπτα επι Θηβαις, ver. 607.

"The field of iniquity produces the fruit of death."

Ὑβρις γαρ εξανθους' εκαρπωσε σταχυν
Ατης, ὁθεν παγκλαυτον εξαμᾳ θερος.

IB. Περσαι, ver. 823.

"For oppression, when it springs,
Puts forth the blade of vengeance; and its fruit
Yields a ripe harvest of repentant wo."—POTTER.

The image is common every where, because it is a universal law of nature.

A. M. cir. 2484 B. C. cir. 1520 Ante I. Olymp. cir. 744 Ante U. C. cir. 767

9 By the blast of God they
perish, and [k]by the breath of his
nostrils are they consumed.
10 The roaring of the lion, and
the voice of the fierce lion, and [l]the teeth of
the young lions, are broken.
11 [m]The old lion perisheth for lack of prey,
and the stout lion's whelps are scattered
abroad.
12 Now a thing was [n]secretly brought to
me, and mine ear received a little thereof.
13 [o]In thoughts from the visions of the night, when deep
sleep falleth on men,
14 Fear [p]came upon me, and
[q]trembling, which made [r]all my bones to shake.
15 Then a spirit passed before my face; the
hair of my flesh stood up:
16 It stood still, but I could not discern the
form thereof: an image *was* before mine eyes,
[s]*there was* silence, and I heard a voice, *saying,*
17 [t]Shall mortal man be more just than

---

[k]That is, *by his anger;* as Isa. xxx. 33; see Exod. xv. 8; chap. i. 19; xv. 30; Isa. xi. 4; 2 Thess. ii. 8——[l]Psa. lviii. 6——[m]Psa. xxxiv. 10

[n]Heb. *by stealth*——[o]Chap. xxxiii. 15——[p]Heb. *met me*——[q]Hab. iii. 16——[r]Heb. *the multitude of my bones* [s]Or, *I heard a still voice*——[t]Chap. ix. 2

Verse 9. *By the blast of God they perish*] As the noxious and parching east wind blasts and destroys vegetation, so the wicked perish under the indignation of the Almighty.

Verse 10. *The roaring of the lion*] By the roaring lion, fierce lion, old lion, stout lion, and lion's whelps, tyrannous rulers of all kinds are intended. The design of Eliphaz in using these figures is to show that even those who are possessed of the greatest *authority* and *power*—the *kings, rulers,* and *princes* of the earth—when they become wicked and oppressive to their subjects are cast down, broken to pieces, and destroyed, by the incensed justice of the Lord; and their *whelps*—their children and intended *successors,* scattered without possessions over the face of the earth.

Verse 11. *The old lion perisheth*] In this and the preceding verse the word *lion* occurs *five times;* and in the original the words are all different:—

1. אריה *aryeh,* from ארה *arah,* to tear off. 2. שחל *shachal,* which as it appears to signify *black* or *dark,* may mean the *black lion,* which is said to be found in Ethiopia and India. 3. כפיר *kephir,* a *young lion,* from כפר *caphar, to cover,* because he is said to *hide* himself in order to surprise his prey, which the *old one* does not. 4. ליש *layish,* from לש *lash, to knead, trample upon;* because of his method of seizing his prey. 5. לביא *labi,* from לבא *laba, to suckle with the first milk;* a lioness giving suck; at which time they are peculiarly fierce. All these words may point out some *quality* of the lion; and this was probably the cause why they were originally given: but it is likely that, in process of time, they served only to designate the beast, without any particular reference to any of his properties. We have one and the same idea when we say the *lion,* the *king of beasts,* the *monarch of the forest,* the *most noble of quadrupeds,* &c.

Verse 12. *Now a thing was secretly brought to me*] To give himself the more authority, he professes to have received a vision from God, by which he was taught the secret of the Divine dispensations in providence; and a confirmation of the doctrine which he was now stating to Job; and which he applied in a different way to what was designed in the Divine communication.

Mine ear received a little thereof.] Mr. *Good* translates, "And mine ear received a whisper along with it." The *apparition* was the general subject; and the *words* related ver. 17, &c., were the *whispers* which he heard when the apparition stood still.

Verse 13. *From the visions of the night*] "It is in vain," says Mr. *Good,* "to search through ancient or modern poetry for a description that has any pretensions to rival that upon which we are now entering. Midnight—solitude—the deep sleep of all around—the dreadful chill and horripilation or erection of the hair over the whole body—the shivering, not of the *muscles* only, but of the *bones* themselves—the gliding approach of the spectre—the abruptness of his pause—his undefined and indescribable form—are all powerful and original characters, which have never been given with equal effect by any other writer."

Mr. *Hervey's* illustration is also striking and natural. "'Twas in the *dead of night;* all nature lay shrouded in darkness; every creature was buried in *sleep.* The most *profound silence* reigned through the universe. In these solemn moments Eliphaz, alone, all wakeful and solitary, was musing on sublime subjects. When, lo! an awful being burst into his apartment. *A spirit passed before his face.* Astonishment seized the beholder. His bones shivered within him; his flesh trembled all over him; and the hair of his head stood erect with horror. *Sudden* and *unexpected* was its appearance; not such its departure. *It stood still,* to present itself more fully to his view. It made a solemn pause, to prepare his mind for some momentous message. After which *a voice was heard.* A *voice,* for the importance of its meaning, worthy to be had in everlasting remembrance. It spoke, and these were its words:"

Verse 17. *Shall mortal man*] אנוש *enosh;* Greek βροτος· poor, weak, dying man.

Be more just than God?] Or, האנוש מאלוה יצדק *haenosh meeloah yitsdak;* shall poor, weak, sinful man be justified before God?

Shall a man] גבר *gaber,* shall even the *strong* and *mighty man,* be pure before his Maker? Is any man, considered merely in and of himself, either holy in his conduct, or pure in his heart? No. He must be justified by the mercy of God, through an *atoning sacrifice;* he must be *sanctified* by the Holy Spirit of God, and thus made a partaker of the Divine nature. Then he is justified before God, and pure in the sight of his Maker: and this is a work which God himself alone can do; so the work is not *man's*

A. M. cir. 2484 B. C. cir. 1520 Ante I. Olymp. cir. 744 Ante U. C. cir. 767

God? shall a man be more pure
than his Maker?
18 Behold, he [u]put no trust in
his servants; [v]and his angels he
charged with folly:
19 [w]How much less *in* them that dwell in
[x]houses of clay, whose foundation *is* in the
dust, *which* are crushed before
the moth?
20 [y]They are [z]destroyed from
morning to evening: they perish
for ever without any regarding *it*.
21 [a]Doth not their excellency *which is* in
them go away? [b]they die, even without wisdom.

[u]Chap. xv. 15; xxv. 5; 2 Pet. ii. 4——[v]Or, *nor in his angels* in whom *he put light*——[w]Chap. xv. 16——[x]2 Cor. iv. 7; v. 1——[y]Psa. xc. 5, 6——[z]Heb. *beaten in pieces*——[a]Psa. xxxix. 11; xlix. 14——[b]Ch. xxxvi. 12

work, but God's. It is false to infer, from the words of this spectre, (whether it came from heaven or hell, we know not, for its communication shows and rankles a wound, without providing a cure,) that no man can be justified, and that no man can be purified, when God both justifies the ungodly, and sanctifies the unholy. The meaning can be no more than this: no man can make an atonement for his own sins, nor purify his own heart. Hence all *boasting* is for ever excluded. Of this Eliphaz believed Job to be guilty, as he appeared to talk of his righteousness and purity, as if they had been his own acquisition.

Verse 18. *Behold, he put no trust in his servants*] This verse is generally understood to refer to the fall of angels; for there were some of those heavenly beings *who kept not their first estate:* they did not persevere to the end of their probation, and therefore fell into condemnation, and are *reserved in chains of darkness unto the judgment of the great day;* Jude 6. It is said *he put no trust in them*—he knew that nothing could be *absolutely immutable* but himself; and that no intelligent beings could *subsist* in a state of *purity*, unless continually dependent on himself, and deriving constant supplies of grace, power, and light, from him who gave them their being.

And his angels he charged with folly] Not *chargeth*, as many quote the passage. He *charged* those with folly who kept not their first estate. It does not appear that he is *charging* the others in the same way, who continue steadfast.

The several translations of this verse, both ancient and modern, are different from each other. Here are the chief:—

In angelis suis reperit pravitatem, "In his angels he found perverseness," VULGATE. The SEPTUAGINT is nearly the same. *Il met la lumiere dans ses anges*, "He puts light into his angels," FRENCH BIBLE. Even those pure intelligences have continual need of being irradiated by the Almighty. ܘܒܡܠܐܟܘܗܝ ܢܣܝܡ ܬܡܗܐ *wa-bemalakui neshim temcho*, "And he hath put amazement in his angels," SYRIAC. The ARABIC is the same. *In angelis suis ponet gloriationem*, "In his angels he will put exultation," MONTANUS. The Hebrew is תהלה *toholah, irradiation*, from הלה *halah, to irradiate, glister*, or *shine*. In this place we may consider angels (מלאכים *malachim*) as heavenly or earthly messengers or angels of the Lord; and the *glory, influence*, and *honour* of their office as being *put in them* by the Most High. They are as planets which shine with a *borrowed light*. They have nothing but what they have received. Coverdale translates the whole verse thus: **Beholde he hath founde unfaythfulnesse amonge his owne servaunts and proude disobedience amonge his angels.** The sense is among all these interpreters; and if the *fallen angels* are meant, the passage is plain enough.

Verse 19. *How much less*] Rather, with the VULGATE, *How much more?* If angels may be unstable, how can man arrogate stability to himself who dwells in an earthly tabernacle, and who must shortly return to dust?

Crushed before the moth? The slightest accident oftentimes destroys. "A *fly*, a *grapestone*, or a *hair* can kill." Great men have fallen by all these. This is the general idea in the text; and it is useless to *sift* for meanings.

Verse 20. *They are destroyed from morning to evening*] In almost every moment of time some human being comes into the world, and some one departs from it. Thus are they "destroyed from morning to evening."

They perish for ever] יאבדו *yobedu; peribunt*, they *pass by;* they *go out of sight;* they moulder with the dust, and are soon forgotten. Who regards the past generation now among the dead?

Isaiah has a similar thought, chap. lvii. 1: "The righteous perisheth, and NO MAN LAYETH IT TO HEART: and merciful men are taken away, none considering that the righteous is taken away from the evil to come." Some think that Isaiah borrowed from Job; this will appear possible when it has been *proved*, which has never yet been done, that the writer of this book flourished *before* Isaiah. If, however, he borrowed the above thought, it must be allowed that it has been wondrously improved by coming through his hands.

Verse 21. *Doth not their excellency—go away?*] Personal beauty, corporeal strength, powerful eloquence, and various mental endowments, pass away, or are *plucked up by the roots;* they are no more seen or heard among men, and their memory soon perisheth.

They die, even without wisdom.] If wisdom means *the pursuit of the best end, by the most legitimate and appropriate means*, the great mass of mankind appear to perish without it. But, if we consider the subject more closely, we shall find that all men die in a state of comparative ignorance. With all our boasted science and arts, how little do we know! Do we know any thing to *perfection* that belongs either to the *material* or *spiritual* world? Do we understand even what *matter* is? What is its *essence?* Do we understand what *spirit* is? Then, what is its *essence?* Almost all the phenomena of nature, its grandest operations, and the laws of the heavenly bodies, have been explained on the principle of *gravitation* or *attraction;* but in *what does this consist?* Who can answer? We can traverse every part of the huge and trackless ocean by means of the *compass;* but who understands the nature of *magnetism* on which all this depends? We eat and drink in order to maintain life; but what is *nutrition*, and how is it effected? This has never been explained. Life depends on *respiration* for its continuance; but by what kind of action is it, that *in a moment* the *lungs* separate the *oxygen*, which is friendly to life, from the *nitrogen*, which would destroy it; suddenly absorbing the *one*, and expelling the *other?* Who, among the generation of *hypothesis-framers*, has *guessed* this out? Life is continued by the *circulation of the blood;* but by what power and law does it circulate? Have the *systole* and *diastole* of the heart, on which this circulation depends, ever been satisfactorily explained? Most certainly not. Alas, *we die without wisdom;* and must *die*, to know these, and ten thousand other matters equally unknown, and equally important. To be safe, in reference to eternity, we must know the only true God, and Jesus Christ whom he has sent; whom to know is life eternal. This knowledge, obtained and retained, will entitle us to all the rest in the eternal world.

CHAPTER V

Eliphaz proceeds to show that the wicked are always punished by the justice of God, though they may appear to flourish for a time, 1–8; *extols the providence of God, by which the counsels of the wicked are brought to naught, and the poor fed and supported,* 9–16; *shows the blessedness of being corrected by God, in the excellent fruits that result from it; and exhorts Job to patience and submission, with the promise of all secular prosperity, and a happy death in a mature and comfortable old age,* 17–27.

A. M. cir. 2484
B. C. cir. 1520
Ante I. Olymp. cir. 744
Ante U. C. cir. 767

CALL now, if there be any
that will answer thee; and
to which of the saints wilt thou
[a]turn?
2 For wrath killeth the foolish man, and
[b]envy slayeth the silly one.
3 [c]I have seen the foolish taking root:
but suddenly I cursed his habitation.
4 [d]His children are far from
safety, and they are crushed in
the gate, [e]neither *is there* any to deliver *them*.
5 Whose harvest the hungry eateth up, and
taketh it even out of the thorns, and [f]the

A. M. cir. 2484
B. C. cir. 1520
Ante I. Olymp. cir. 744
Ante U. C. cir. 767

---

[a]Or, *look*——[b]Or, *indignation*——[c]Psa. xxxvii. 35, 36; Jer. xii. 2, 3

[d]Psa. cxix. 155; cxxvii. 5——[e]Psa. cix. 12——[f]Chap. xviii. 9

NOTES ON CHAP. V

Verse 1. *Call now, if there be any*] This appears to be a strong *irony*. From whom among those *whose foundations are in the dust, and who are crushed before the moth*, canst thou expect succour?

To which of the saints wilt thou turn?] To whom among the *holy ones*, (קדשים *kedoshim*,) or among those who are equally dependent on Divine support with thyself, and can do no good but as influenced and directed by God, *canst thou turn* for help? Neither angel nor saint can help any man unless sent especially from God; and all prayers to *them* must be foolish and absurd, not to say impious. Can the *channel* afford me water, if the *fountain* cease to emit it?

Verse 2. *For wrath killeth the foolish man*] *Foolish*, *silly*, and *simple*, are epithets given by *Solomon* to sinners and transgressors of all kinds. Such parallelisms have afforded a presumptive argument that Solomon was the author of this book. See the *preface*. The words of Eliphaz may be considered as a sort of *maxim*, which the wisdom and experience of ages had served to establish; viz., The wrath of God is manifested only against the wicked and impious; and if thou wert not such, God would not thus contend with thee.

Verse 3. *I have seen the foolish taking root*] I have seen wicked men for a time in prosperity, and becoming established in the earth; but I well knew, from God's manner of dealing with men, that they must soon be blasted. I even ventured to *pronounce their doom;* for I knew that, in the order of God's providence, that was inevitable. *I cursed his habitation.*

Verse 4. *His children are far from safety*] His posterity shall not continue in prosperity. *Ill gotten, ill spent;* whatever is got by wrong must have God's curse on it.

They are crushed in the gate] The *Targum* says, *They shall be bruised in the gate of hell, in the day of the great judgment.* There is reference here to a custom which I have often had occasion to notice: viz., that in the Eastern countries the *court-house*, or *tribunal of justice*, was at the GATE *of the city;* here the magistrates attended, and hither the plaintiff and defendant came for justice.

Verse 5. *Whose harvest*] Their possessions, because acquired by unjust means, shall not be under the protection of God's providence; he shall abandon them to be pillaged and detroyed by the wandering *half-starved* hordes of the *desert banditti.* They shall carry it suddenly off; *even the thorns*—grain, weeds, thistles, and all, shall they carry off in their rapacious hurry.

The robber swalloweth us] Or, more properly, the *thirsty*, צמים *tsammim*, as is plain from their *swallowing up* or *gulping down;* opposed to the *hungry* or *half-starved*, mentioned in the preceding clause. The *hungry* shall *eat up* their grain, and the *thirsty* shall *drink down* their wine and oil, here termed חילם *cheylam*, their *strength* or *power*, for the most obvious reasons.

There seem to be *two* allusions in this verse: 1. To the hordes of wandering predatory banditti, or half-starved Arabs of the desert, who have their scanty maintenance by the plunder

A. M. cir. 2484 B. C. cir. 1520 Ante I. Olymp. cir. 744 Ante U. C. cir. 767

robber swalloweth up their substance.
6 Although [g]affliction cometh
not forth of the dust, neither
doth trouble spring out of the ground;
7 Yet man is [h]born unto [i]trouble, as [k]the
sparks fly upward.
8 I would seek unto God, and unto
God would I commit my
cause:
9 [l]Which doeth great things
[m]and unsearchable; marvellous
things [n]without number:
10 [o]Who giveth rain upon the earth, and
sendeth waters upon the [p]fields:
11 [q]To set up on high those that be low;

[g]Or, *iniquity*——[h]Gen. iii. 17, 18, 19; 1 Cor. x. 13——[i]Or, *labour*——[k]Heb. *the sons of the burning coal lift up to fly*——[l]Chap. ix. 10; xxxvii. 5; Psa. xl. 5; lxxii. 18; cxlv. 3; Rom. xi. 33——[m]Heb. *and* there is *no search*——[n]Heb. *till* there be *no number*——[o]Chap. xxviii. 26; Psa. lxv. 9, 10; cxlvii. 8; Jer. v. 24; x. 13; li. 16; Acts xiv. 47——[p]Heb. *out-places*——[q]1 Sam. ii. 7; Psa. cxiii. 7

of others. These descendants of Ishmael have ever had their hands against all men, and live to this day in the same predatory manner in which they have lived for several thousands of years. M. *Volney's* account of them is striking: "These men are smaller, leaner, and blacker, than any of the Bedouins yet discovered. Their wasted legs had only tendons without calves. Their belly was shrunk to their back. They are in general small, lean, and swarthy, and more so in the bosom of the desert than on the borders of the more cultivated country. They are ordinarily about five feet or *five feet two inches* high; they seldom have more than about six ounces of food for the whole day. Six or seven dates, soaked in melted butter, a little milk, or curd, serve a man for twenty-four hours; and he seems happy when he can add a small portion of coarse flour, or a little ball of rice. Their *camels* also, which are their only support, are remarkably meagre, living on the meanest and most scanty provision. *Nature* has given it a small head without ears, at the end of a long neck without flesh. She has taken from its legs and thighs every muscle not immediately requisite for motion; and in short has bestowed on its withered body only the vessels and tendons necessary to connect its frame together. She has furnished it with a strong jaw, that it may grind the hardest aliments; and, lest it should consume too much, she has straitened its stomach, and obliged it to chew the cud." Such is the description given of the Bedouin and his camel, by M. Volney, who, while he denies the true God, finds out a deity which he calls *Nature*, whose works evince the highest providence, wisdom, and design! And where does this most wonderful and intelligent *goddess* dwell? Nowhere but in the creed of the infidel; while the genuine believer knows that *nature* is only the *agent* created and employed by the great and wise God to accomplish, under his direction, the greatest and most stupendous beneficial effects.

The *second allusion* in the verse I suppose to be to the loss Job had sustained of his cattle by the predatory *Sabeans;* and all this Eliphaz introduces for the support of his grand argument, to convict Job of hidden crimes, on which account his enemies were permitted to destroy his property; that property, because of this wickedness, being placed out of the protection of God's providence.

Verse 6. *Affliction cometh not forth of the dust*] If there were not an adequate cause, thou couldst not be so grievously afflicted.

Spring out of the ground] It is not from mere *natural* causes that affliction and trouble come; God's justice inflicts them upon offending man.

Verse 7. *Yet man is born unto trouble*] לעמל *leamal*, to *labour*. He must *toil* and be *careful;* and if in the course of his labour he meet with trials and difficulties, he should rise superior to them, and not *sink* as thou dost.

As the sparks fly upward.] ובני רשף יגביהו עוף *ubeney resheph yagbihu uph; And the sons of the coal lift up their flight*, or *dart upwards.* And who are *the sons of the coal?* Are they not bold, intrepid, ardent, fearless men, who rise superior to all their trials; combat what are termed chance and occurrence; succumb under no difficulties; and rise superior to time, tide, fate, and fortune? I prefer this to all the various meanings of the place with which I have met. *Coverdale* translates, **It is man that is borne unto mysery, like as the byrde for to fle** Most of the ancient *versions* give a similar sense.

Verse 8. *I would seek unto God*] Were I in your place, instead of wasting my time, and irritating my soul with useless complaints, I would apply to my Maker, and, if conscious of my innocence, would confidently commit my cause to him.

Verse 9. *Which doeth great things*] No work, however complicated, is too deep for his counsel to plan; none, however stupendous, is too great for his power to execute. He who is upright is always safe in referring his cause to God, and trusting in him.

Verse 10. *Who giveth rain upon the earth*] The *Chaldee* gives this verse a fine turn: "Who gives rain on the face of the land of *Israel*, and sends waters on the face of the *provinces* of the *people.*" Similar to our Lord's saying, which is expressed in the half of the compass: *Your Father which is in heaven*—SENDETH RAIN ON THE JUST AND ON THE UNJUST; Matt. v. 45.

Sendeth waters upon the fields] The term חוצות *chutsoth*, which we translate *fields*, and generally signifies *streets*, may here mean those *plantations* which are *laid out* in *ridges* or *plats*, in an *orderly*, *regular* manner. God does not only send rain upon the *earth* in a *general* manner, but, by an *especial providence*, waters the *cultivated ground*, so that not one ridge is destitute of its due proportion of fructifying moisture.

Verse 11. *To set up on high those that be low*] He so distributes his providential blessings without partiality, that the land of the *poor man* is as well *sunned* and *watered* as that of the *rich;* so that he is thus set upon a level with the lords of the soil.

A. M. cir. 2484 B. C. cir. 1520 Ante I. Olymp. cir. 744 Ante U. C. cir. 767

that those which mourn may be
exalted to safety.
12 [r]He disappointeth the devices of the crafty, so that the
hands [s]cannot perform *their* enterprise.
13 [t]He taketh the wise in their own craftiness: and the counsel of the froward is carried headlong.
14 [u]They [v]meet with darkness in the day-
time, and grope in the noonday as in the
night.
15 But [w]he saveth the poor from the sword,
from their mouth, and from the
hand of the mighty.
16 [x]So the poor hath hope,
and iniquity stoppeth her mouth.
17 [y]Behold, happy *is* the man whom God
correcteth: therefore despise not thou the
chastening of the Almighty:
18 [z]For he maketh sore, and bindeth up:
he woundeth, and his hands make whole.
19 [a]He shall deliver thee in six troubles:
yea, in seven [b]there shall no evil touch
thee.

A. M. cir. 2484 B. C. cir. 1520 Ante I. Olymp. cir. 744 Ante U. C. cir. 767

---

[r]Neh. iv. 15; Psa. xxxiii. 10; Isa. viii. 10——[s]Or, *cannot perform any thing*——[t]Psa. ix. 15; 1 Cor. iii. 19——[u]Deut. xxviii. 29; Isa. lix. 10; Amos viii. 9——[v]Or, *run into*——[w]Psa. xxxv. 10

[x]1 Sam. ii. 9; Psa. cvii. 42——[y]Psa. xciv. 12; Prov. iii. 11, 12; Heb. xii. 5; James i. 12; Rev. iii. 19——[z]Deut. xxxii. 39; 1 Sam. ii. 6; Isa. xxx. 26; Hos. vi. 1——[a]Psa. xxxiv. 19; xci. 3; Prov. xxiv. 16; 1 Cor. x. 13——[b]Psa. xci. 10

Verse 12. *He disappointeth the devices of the crafty*] All these sayings refer to God's *particular providence*, by which he is ever working for the *good*, and counterworking the plots of the *wicked*. And as various as are the contingent, capricious, and malevolent acts of men, so varied are his providential interferences; disappointing the devices, snares, and plots of the crafy, so that their plans being confounded, and their machinery broken in pieces, *their hands cannot perform their enterprises.*

Verse 13. *He taketh the wise in their own craftiness*] So counterworks them as to cause their feet to be taken in their own snares, and their evil dealings to fall on their own pate. Such frequent proofs has God given of his especial interference in behalf of the innocent, who have been the objects of the plots and evil designs of the wicked, by turning those evil devices against their framers, that *he who digs a pit for his neighbour shall fall into it himself* has become a universal *adage*, and has passed, either in so many words or in sense, into all the languages of all the people of the earth. *Lucretius* expresses it strongly:

> Circumretit enim vis atque injuria quemque,
> Atque, unde exorta est, ad eum plerumque revortit.
> Lucret. lib. v., ver. 1151.

> "For force and wrong entangle the man that uses them;
> And, for the most part, recoil on the head of the contriver."

Verse 14. *They meet with darkness in the daytime*] God confounds them and their measures; and, with all their cunning and dexterity, they are outwitted, and often act on their own projects, planned with care and skill, as if they had been the crudest conceptions of the most disordered minds. They act in *noonday* as if the *sun were extinct*, and their *eyes put out.* Thus does God "abate their pride, assuage their malice, and confound their devices."

Verse 15. *He saveth the poor from the sword, from their mouth*] This is rather a harsh construction. To avoid this, some have proposed to render מחרב *mechereb*, which we translate *from the sword, the persecuted*, but, I am afraid, on very slender authority. Instead of מחרב מפיהם *mechereb mippihem*, "from the sword, from their mouth," *eleven* of *Kennicott* and *De Rossi's* MSS. read מחרב פיהם *mechereb pihem, from the sword of their mouth;* and with these MSS. the *Chaldee*, *Vulgate*, *Syriac*, and *Arabic* agree. The verse, therefore, may be translated thus:—

> He saveth from the sword of their mouth;
> The poor from the hand of the mighty.

Or thus:—

> He saveth from the sword of their mouth;
> And with a strong hand the impoverished.

Verse 16. *So the poor*] דל *dal*, he who is made *thin*, who is *wasted*, *extenuated; hath hope*—he sees what God is accustomed to do, and he expects a repetition of gracious dealings in his own behalf; and because God deals thus with those who trust in him, therefore the *mouth of impiety is stopped.*

Religion is kept alive in the earth, because of God's signal interventions in behalf of the bodies and souls of his followers.

Verse 17. *Behold, happy is the man*] הנה *hinneh behold*, is wanting in *five* of *Kennicott's* and *De Rossi's* MSS., and also in the *Syriac*, *Vulgate*, and *Arabic.*

We have had *fathers of our flesh*, who corrected us for their pleasure, or according to their caprices, and we were subject to them: how much more should we be subject to the *Father of spirits*, and live? for he corrects that we may be partakers of his holiness, in order that we may be rendered fit for his glory. See Heb. xii. 5; James i. 12; and Prov. iii. 12.

Verse 18. *For he maketh sore, and bindeth up*] Thus nervously rendered by *Coverdale*, **For though he make a wounde, he giveth a medicyne agayne; though he smyte, his honde maketh whole agayne.**

Verse 19. *He shall deliver thee in six troubles*] The numbers *six* and *seven* are put here for *many.* Though a number of troubles should come upon thee *all at once*, and there should be no hope, humanly speaking, yet God would rid thee out of them all; for he saves as well from *many* as from *few.* We may also understand the words, He who hath been thy deliverer in past troubles, will not deny his help in those which are to come.

A. M. cir. 2484
B. C. cir. 1520
Ante I. Olymp. cir. 744
Ante U. C. cir. 767

20 [c]In famine he shall redeem
thee from death: and in war
[d]from the power of the sword.
21 [e]Thou shalt be hid [f]from
the scourge of the tongue: neither shalt thou
be afraid of destruction when it cometh.
22 At destruction and famine thou shalt
laugh: [g]neither shalt thou be afraid of the
beasts of the earth.
23 [h]For thou shalt be in league with the
stones of the field: and the beasts of the field
shall be at peace with thee.

[c]Psa. xxxiii. 19; xxxvii. 19——[d]Heb. *from the hands*——[e]Psalm xxxi. 20——[f]Or, *when the tongue scourgeth*——[g]Isa. xi. 9; xxxv. 9; lxv. 25; Ezek. xxxiv. 25——[h]Psa. xci. 12; Hos. ii. 18

24 And thou shalt know [i]that
thy tabernacle *shall be* in peace;
and thou shalt visit thy habitation, and shalt not [k]sin.

A. M. cir. 2484
B. C. cir. 1520
Ante I. Olymp. cir. 744
Ante U. C. cir. 767

25 Thou shalt know also that [l]thy seed
shall be [m]great, and thine offspring [n]as the
grass of the earth.
26 [o]Thou shalt come to *thy* grave in a full
age, like as a shock of corn [p]cometh in his
season.
27 Lo this, we have [q]searched it, so it *is;*
hear it, and know thou *it* [r]for thy good.

[i]Or, *that peace is thy tabernacle*——[k]Or, *err*——[l]Psa. cxii. 2——[m]Or, *much*——[n]Psa. lxxii. 16——[o]Prov. ix. 11; x. 27——[p]Heb. *ascendeth*——[q]Psa. cxi. 2——[r]Heb. *for thyself;* Prov. ix. 12

Verse 20. *In famine he shall redeem thee*] The *Chaldee*, which understands this chapter as speaking of the *troubles and deliverances of the Israelites in Egypt and the wilderness*, renders this verse as follows: "In the famine of Egypt he redeemed thee from death; and in the war of Amalek, from the slaying of the sword."

Verse 21. *Thou shalt be hid from the scourge of the tongue*] The *Targum* refers this to the *incantations of Balaam:* "From injury by the tongue of Balaam thou shalt be hidden in the clouds; and thou shalt not fear from the blasting of the Midianites, when it shall come."

Perhaps no evil is more dreadful than the *scourge of the tongue:* evil-speaking, detraction, backbiting, calumny, slander, tale-bearing, whispering, and scandalizing, are some of the terms which we use when endeavouring to express the baleful influence and effects of that member, which is a *world of fire,* kindled from the nethermost hell. The Scripture abounds with invectives and execrations against it. See Psa. xxxi. 20, lii. 2-4; Prov. xii. 18, xiv. 3; James iii. 5-8.

Neither shalt thou be afraid] "Thou shouldst have such strong confidence in God, that even in the presence of destruction thou shouldst not fear death," the God of life and power being with thee.

Verse 22. *At destruction and famine thou shalt laugh*] This most forcibly expresses the strongest security, and confidence in that security. "In the desolation of Sihon, and in the famine of the desert, thou shalt laugh; and of the camps of Og, who is compared to a wild beast of the earth, thou shalt not be afraid."—*Targum.*

Verse 23. *Thou shalt be in league with the stones of the field*] Instead of אבני *abney, stones,* Mr. *Good* reads בני *beney, sons,* or *produce;* but this reading is not supported by any ancient *version,* nor, as far as I know, by any MS. yet collated. We must, therefore, take up the text as we find it, and make the best we can of the present reading.

The *Chaldee* gives a plausible sense: Thou needest not to fear, "because thy covenant is on tables of stone, which are publicly erected in the field; and the Canaanites, which are compared to the beasts of the field, have made peace with thee."

Perhaps the reference is to those *rocks* or *strong holds,* where banditti secured themselves and their prey, or where the *emirs* or neighbouring *chiefs* had their ordinary residence. Eliphaz may be understood as saying: Instead, then, of taking advantage of thee, as the *Sabeans* have done, the circumjacent chieftains will be confederate with thee; and the very beasts of the field will not be permitted to harm thy flocks.

Coverdale seems to have had an idea of this kind, as we find he translates the verse thus:—

But the castels in the londe shall be confederate with the,
And the beastes of the felde shall gibe the peace.

I believe the above to be the meaning of the place. See the next verse.

Verse 24. *Thou shalt know*] Thou shalt be so fully satisfied of the friendly disposition of all thy neighbours, that thou shalt rest secure in thy bed, and not be afraid of any danger, though sleeping in thy *tent* in the *field;* and when thou returnest from thy country excursions, thou shalt find that thy *habitation* has been preserved in peace and prosperity, and that thou hast *made no mistake* in thy trust, in thy confidence, or in thy confederates.

The word אהלך *oholecha,* "thy tabernacle," means simply a *tent,* or *moveable dwelling,* composed of *poles, pins,* and *cloth,* or *skin,* to be pitched any where in a few moments, and struck again with the same ease.

The word נוך *navecha,* which we properly translate thy *habitation,* signifies a *solid, permanent dwelling-place.* See Josh. xxii. 4, 6, 7, 8; 2 Sam. xviii. 17; xix. 8; 1 Kings xii. 16; Psa. lii. 7; xci. 10; cxxxii. 3; Lam. ii. 4; Mal. ii. 12; and with these passages compare the place in the text.

As to תחטא *techeta,* which we translate *thou shalt* not SIN, it comes from חטא *chata,* to *err,* to *mistake,* to *miss the mark:* hence to *sin, transgress God's laws,* seeking for happiness in forbidden and unlawful things, and therefore *missing the mark,* because in *them* happiness is not to be found: and it is very likely, from the connection above, that to *mistake* or *err* is its meaning in this place. I need not add, that the Arab chiefs, who had their castles or strong holds, frequently in their country excursions lodged in *tents* in the open fields; and that on such occasions a hostile neighbour sometimes took advantage of their absence, attacked and pillaged their houses, and carried off their families and household. See at the end of this chapter.

Verse 25. *Thine offspring as the grass*] Thou shalt have a numerous and permanent issue.

Verse 26. *Thou shalt come to* thy *grave*] Thou shalt not die before thy time; thou shalt depart from life like a full-fed guest; happy in what thou hast known, and in what thou hast enjoyed.

Like as a shock of corn] Thou shalt completely run through the round of the *spring*, *summer*, *autumn*, and *winter* of life; and thou shalt be buried like a wholesome seed in the earth; from which thou shalt again rise up into an eternal *spring!*

Verse 27. *Lo this, we have searched it*] What I have told thee is the sum of our wisdom and experience on these important points. These are established maxims, which universal experience supports. *Know*—understand, and reduce them to practice *for thy good.* Thus ends *Eliphaz*, the *Temanite*, "full of wise saws and ancient instances;" but he miserably perverted them in his application of them to Job's case and character. They contain, however, many wholesome truths, of which the wise in heart may make a very advantageous practical use.

THE predatory excursions referred to in verse 23 were not unfrequent among our own barbarous ancestors. An affecting picture of this kind is drawn by *Shakspeare*, from *Holinshed's Chronicles*, of the case of *Macduff*, whose castle was attacked in his absence by *Macbeth* and his wife and all his children murdered. A similar incident was the ground of the old heroic ballad of *Hardicanute.* When the veteran heard that a host of Norwegians had landed to pillage the country, he armed, and posted to the field to meet the invading foe. He slew the chief in battle, and routed his pillaging banditti. While this was taking place, another party took the advantage of his absence, attacked his castle, and carried off or murdered his lovely wife and family; which, being perceived on his return by the war and age-worn chief, is thus affectingly described by the unknown poet:—

Loud and chill blew the westlin wind,
  Sair beat the heavy showir,
Mirk grew the nicht eir *Hardyknute*
  Wan neir his stately tower:

His tower that us'd with torches bleise
  To shine sae far at nicht,
Seim'd now as black as mourning weid,
  Nae marvel, sair he sich'd.

"Thair's nae light in my lady's bowir,
  Thair's nae light in my hall;
Nae blink shynes round my *Fairly* fair,
  Nor *ward* stands on my wall.

"What bodes it, *Thomas! Robert!* say?"
  Nae answer—speaks their dreid;
"Stand back, my sons, I'll be your gyde;"
  But bye they pass'd with speid.

"As fast I haif sped owr Scotland's foes"—
  There ceis'd his brag of weir.
Sair schamt to mind ocht but his dame,
  And maiden *Fairly* fair.

Black feir he felt; but what to feir
  He wist not yet with dreid;
Sair schook his body, sair his limbs,
  And all the warrior fled.

The ending of this poem is lost; but we here see that the castle of *Hardicanute* was surprised, and his family destroyed, or carried off, while he and his sons had been employed in defeating the invading Norwegians. Thank God! *civilization*, the offspring of the spread of *Christianity*, has put an end to these barbarous practices among us; but in the *East*, where *Christianity* is not, they flourish still. Britons! send out your Bible and your missionaries to tame these barbarians; for whom *heathenism* has done nothing, and the *Koran* next to nothing. *Civilization* itself, without the *Bible*, will do as little; for the civilized Greeks and Romans were barbarians, fell and murderous; living in envy and malice, hateful, hating one another, and offering *hundreds* at a time of *human victims* to their ruthless deities. Nothing but *Christianity* ever did, or even can, cure these evils.

CHAPTER VI

Job answers, and vindicates himself; and shows that the great affliction which he suffered was the cause of his complaining, by which life was rendered burdensome to him, 1–13. *He complains that, whereas he expected consolation from his friends, he had received nothing but the bitterest reproaches, on the assumed ground that he must be a wicked man, else God would not so grievously afflict him,* 14–20. *He shows them that they knew nothing of his case, and that they had no compassion,* 21–23. *And then entreats them, if they can, to show him in what he has offended, as he is ready to acknowledge and correct every trespass,* 24–30.

A. M. cir. 2484
B. C. cir. 1520
Ante I. Olymp. cir. 744
Ante U. C. cir. 767

BUT Job answered and said,
2 O, that my grief were
thoroughly weighed, and my
calamity [a]laid in the balances
together!
3 For now it would be heavier [b]than the
sand of the sea: therefore [c]my words are
swallowed up.
4 [d]For the arrows of the Almighty *are*
within me, the poison whereof drinketh up my
spirit: [e]the terrors of God do set themselves
in array against me.
5 Doth the wild ass bray [f]when he hath
grass? or loweth the ox over his fodder?
6 Can that which is unsavoury
be eaten without salt? or is there
any taste in the white of an
egg?
7 The things *that* my soul refuseth to touch
are as my sorrowful meat.
8 O that I might have my request; and
that God would grant *me* [g]the thing that I
long for!
9 Even [h]that it would please God to destroy me; that he would let loose his hand,
and cut me off!
10 Then should I yet have comfort; yea, I
would harden myself in sorrow: let him not

[a]Heb. *lifted up*——[b]Prov. xxvii. 3——[c]That is, *I want words to express my grief;* Psa. lxxvii. 4——[d]Psa. xxxviii. 2——[e]Psa. lxxxviii. 15, 16——[f]Heb. *at grass*——[g]Heb. *my expectation*——[h]1 Kings xix. 4

NOTES ON CHAP. VI

Verse 2. *O that my grief were thoroughly weighed*] Job wished to be dealt with according to justice; as he was willing that his sins, if they could be proved, should be weighed against his sufferings; and if this could not be done, he wished that his sufferings and his complainings might be weighed together; and it would then be seen that, bitter as his complaint had been, it was little when compared with the distress which occasioned it.

Verse 3. *Heavier than the sand of the sea*] This includes *two ideas:* their *number* was too great to be counted; their *weight* was too great to be estimated.

Verse 4. *The arrows of the Almighty*] There is an evident reference here to *wounds inflicted by poisoned arrows;* and to the burning fever occasioned by such *wounds*, producing such an intense parching thirst as to dry up all the moisture in the system, stop all the salivary ducts, thicken and inflame the blood, induce putrescency, and terminate in raging mania, producing the most terrifying images, from which the patient is relieved only by death. This is strongly expressed in the fine figure: *The* POISON DRINKETH *up my* SPIRIT; *the* TERRORS *of* GOD SET THEMSELVES *in* ARRAY *against me.* That *calamities* are represented among the Eastern writers as the *arrows of the Almighty*, we have abundant proofs. In reference to this, I shall adduce that fine saying attributed to *Aaly*, the son-in-law of *Mohammed*, in the *Toozuki Teemour;* which I have spoken of elsewhere. "It was once demanded of the fourth califf, (*Aaly*,) 'If the canopy of *heaven* were a *bow;* and if the *earth* were the *cord thereof;* and if *calamities* were the *arrows;* if *mankind* were the *mark* for those arrows; and if *Almighty God*, the tremendous and glorious, were the unerring *Archer;* to whom could the sons of Adam flee for protection?' The califf answered, 'The sons of Adam must flee unto the Lord.'" This fine image Job keeps in view in the eighth and ninth verses, wishing that the *unerring marksman* may *let fly* these arrows, *let loose his hand*, to destroy and cut him off.

Verse 5. *Doth the wild ass*] פרא *pere*, translated *onager*, by the *Vulgate*, from the ονος αγριος of the *Septuagint*, which we properly enough, translate *wild ass.* It is the same with the *tame ass;* only in a wild state it grows to a larger size, is stronger, and more fleet. The meaning of Job appears to be this: You condemn me for complaining; do I complain without a cause? The *wild ass* will not *bray*, and the *ox* will not low, unless in *want.* If they have plenty of provender, they are silent. Were I at rest, at ease, and happy, I would not complain.

Verse 6. *Can that which is unsavoury*] Mr. *Good* renders this verse as follows: *Doth insipid food without a mixture of salt, yea, doth the white of the egg give forth pungency?* Which he thus illustrates: "Doth that which hath nothing of seasoning, nothing of a pungent or irritable power within it, produce pungency or irritation? I too should be quiet and complain not, if I had nothing provocative or acrimonious, but, alas! the food I am doomed to partake of is the very calamity which is most acute to my soul—that which I most loathe, and which is most grievous or trying to my palate." Some render the original, *Is there any dependence on the drivel of dreams?*

There have been a great variety of interpretations given of this verse. I could add another; but that of Mr. *Good* is as likely to be correct as that of any other critic.

Verse 8. *O that I might have*] As Job had no hope that he should ever be redeemed from his present helpless state, he earnestly begs God to shorten it by taking away his life.

Verse 9. *Let loose his hand*] A metaphor taken from *an archer drawing his arrow to the head*, and then *loosing his hold*, that *the arrow may fly to the mark.* See on ver. 4.

Verse 10. *Then should I yet have comfort*] Instead of עוד *od*, YET, three of *Kennicott's* and *De Rossi's* MSS. have זאת *zoth*, THIS. *And* THIS *should be my comfort.* The expectation that he will speedily make an end of me would cause me to rejoice with great joy. This reading is supported by the *Vulgate* and the *Chaldee.*

I would harden myself in sorrow] To know that I should shortly have an end put to my miseries would cause me to endure the present with determinate resolution. *Let him not spare*—let him use whatever *means* he chooses, for I will not resist his decree; he is *holy*, and his decrees must be just.

A. M. cir. 2484
B. C. cir. 1520
Ante I. Olymp. cir. 744
Ante U. C. cir. 767

spare; for [l]I have not concealed
the words of [k]the Holy One.
11 What *is* my strength, that I
should hope? and what *is* mine
end, that I should prolong my life?
12 *Is* my strength the strength of stones?
or *is* my flesh [l]of brass?
13 *Is* not my help in me?
and is wisdom driven quite from
me?
14 [m]To [n]him that is afflicted
pity *should be showed* from his friend; but he
forsaketh the fear of the Almighty.
15 [o]My brethren have dealt deceitfully as

[i]Acts xx. 20——[k]Lev. xix. 2; Isa. lvii. 15; Hos. xi. 9
[l]Heb. *brazen*
[m]Heb. *To him that melteth*——[n]Prov. xvii. 17——[o]Psa. xxxviii. 11; xli. 9

Verse 11. *What* is *my strength*] I can never suppose that my strength will be restored; and, were that possible, have I any comfortable prospect of a happy termination of my life? Had I any prospect of *future* happiness, I might well bear my *present* ills; but the state of my *body* and the state of my *circumstances* preclude all hope.

Verse 12. Is *my strength the strength of stones?*] I am neither a *rock*, nor is my flesh *brass*, that I can endure all these calamities. This is a proverbial saying, and exists in all countries. Cicero says, *Non enim est e saxo sculptus, aut e* ROBORE *dolatus* HOMO; *habet corpus, habet animum; movetur mente, movetur sensibus.* "For man is not chiselled out of the *rock*, nor hewn out of the *oak;* he has a body, and he has a soul; the one is actuated by intellect, the other by the senses." Quæst. Acad. iv. 31. So *Homer*, where he represents Apollo urging the Trojans to attack the Greeks:—

Νεμεσησε δ' Απολλων,
Περγαμου εκκατιδων· Τρωεσσι δε κεκλετ' αυσας·
Ορνυσθ', ἱπποδαμοι Τρωες, μηδ' εικετε χαρμης
Αργειοις· επει ου σ φ ι λ ι θ ο ς χρως, ουδε σ ι δ η ρ ο ς,
Χαλκον ανασχεσθαι ταμεσιχροα βαλλομενοισιν.
ILIAD, lib. iv., ver. 507.

But Phœbus now from Ilion's towering height
Shines forth reveal'd, and animates the fight.
Trojans, be bold, and force to force oppose;
Your foaming steeds urge headlong on the foes!
Nor are their bodies ROCKS, nor ribb'd with STEEL;
Your weapons enter, and your strokes they feel.
POPE.

These are almost the same expressions as those in Job.

Verse 13. Is *not my help in me?*] My help is all in myself; and, alas! that is perfect weakness: *and my subsistence,* תושיה *tushiyah,* all that is *real, stable,* and *permanent, is driven quite from me.* My *friends* have forsaken me, and I am abandoned to *myself;* my *property* is all taken away, and I have no *resources* left. I believe Job neither said, nor intended to say, as some interpreters have it, *Reason is utterly driven from me.* Surely there is no mark in this chapter of his being deranged, or at all impaired in his intellect.

Verse 14. *To him that is afflicted pity* should be showed *from his friend; but he forsaketh the fear of the Almighty.*] The *Vulgate* gives a better sense, *Qui tollit ab amico suo misericordiam, timorem Domini dereliquit,* "He who takes away mercy from his friend, hath cast off the fear of the Lord." The word למס *lammas,* which we render *to him who is* AFFLICTED, from מסה *masah, to dissolve,* or *waste away,* is in thirty-two of Dr. *Kennicott's* and *De Rossi's* MSS. למאס *lemoes,* "to him that *despiseth* his friend;" and hence the passage may be read: *To him who despiseth his friend, it is a reproach; and he will forsake the fear of the Almighty:* or, as Mr. *Good* translates,

"Shame to the man who despiseth his friend!
He indeed hath departed from the fear of the Almighty."

Eliphaz had, in effect, *despised* Job; and on this ground had acted any thing but the part of a *friend* towards him; and he well deserved the severe stroke which he here receives. A heathen said, *Amicus certus in re incerta cernitur;* the full sense of which we have in our common adage:—

A FRIEND IN NEED *is a* FRIEND INDEED

Job's *friends*, so called, supported *each other* in their attempts to blacken the character of this worthy man; and their hand became the heavier, because they supposed the hand of God was upon him. To each of them, individually, might be applied the words of another heathen:—

——Absentem qui rodit amicum,
Qui non defendit alio culpante; solutos
Qui captat risus hominum, famamque dicacis,
Fingere qui non visa potest; commissa tacere
Qui nequit; hic niger est; hunc tu, Romane, caveto.
HOR. Satyr. lib. i., s. iv., ver. 81.

He who, malignant, tears an absent friend;
Or, when attack'd by others, don't defend;
Who trivial bursts of laughter strives to raise,
And courts, of prating petulance, the praise;
Of things he never saw who tells his tale,
And friendship's secrets knows not to conceal;—
This man is *vile;* here, Roman, fix your mark;
His *soul's* as *black* as his complexion's dark.
FRANCIS.

Verse 15. *Have dealt deceitfully as a brook*] There is probably an allusion here to those *land torrents* which make a sudden appearance, and as suddenly vanish; being produced by the rains that fall upon the mountains during the rainy season, and are soon absorbed by the thirsty sands over which they run. At first they seem to promise a *permanent stream,* and are noticed with delight by the people, who fill their tanks or reservoirs from their waters; but sometimes they are so large and rapid as to carry every thing before them: and then suddenly fail, so that there is no time to fill the tanks. The approach of Job's friends promised much of sympathy and compassion; his expectations were raised: but their conduct soon con-

A. M. cir. 2484
B. C. cir. 1520
Ante I. Olymp. cir. 744
Ante U. C. cir. 767

a brook, *and* [p]as the stream of
brooks they pass away;
16 Which are blackish by reason of the ice, *and* wherein the
snow is hid:
17 What time they wax warm, [q]they vanish:
[r]when it is hot, they are [s]consumed out of
their place.
18 The paths of their way are turned aside;
they go to nothing, and perish.
19 The troops of [t]Tema looked, the companies of [u]Sheba waited for them.
20 They were [v]confounded because they
had hoped; they came thither, and were
ashamed.
21 [w]For now [x]ye are [y]nothing; ye see
my casting down, and [z]are
afraid.
22 Did I say, Bring unto me?
or, Give a reward for me of your
substance?
23 Or, Deliver me from the enemy's
hand? or, Redeem me from the hand of the
mighty?
24 Teach me, and I will hold my tongue:
and cause me to understand wherein I have
erred.
25 How forcible are right words! but what
doth your arguing reprove?
26 Do ye imagine to reprove words, and
the speeches of one that is desperate, *which
are* as wind?

[p]Jer. xv. 18——[q]Heb. *they are cut off*——[r]Heb. *in the heat thereof*——[s]Heb. *extinguished*——[t]Gen. xxv. 15——[u]1 Kings x. 1; Psa. lxxii. 10; Ezek. xxvii. 22, 23——[v]Jer. xiv. 3

[w]Or, *For now ye are* like *to them;* Hebrew, *to it* [x]Chapter xiii. 4——[y]Hebrew, *not*——[z]Psalm xxxviii. 11

vinced him that they were physicians of no value; therefore he compares them to the *deceitful torrents* that soon *pass away.*

Verse 16. *Blackish by reason of the ice*] He represents the waters as being sometimes suddenly frozen, their foam being turned into the semblance of snow or hoar-frost: when the heat comes, they are speedily liquefied; and the evaporation is so strong from the heat, and the absorption so powerful from the sand, that they soon disappear.

Verse 18. *The paths of their way*] They sometimes forsake their *ancient channels,* which is a frequent case with the river *Ganges;* and, growing smaller and smaller from being divided into numerous streams, *they go to nothing and perish*—are at last utterly lost in the sands.

Verse 19. *The troops of Tema looked*] The *caravans* coming from *Tema* are represented as arriving at those places where it was well known torrents did descend from the mountains, and they were full of expectation that here they could not only slake their thirst, but fill their *girbas* or *water-skins;* but when they arrive, they find the waters totally dissipated and lost. In vain did the caravans of Sheba *wait for them;* they did not reappear: and they *were confounded, because they had hoped* to find here refreshment and rest.

Verse 21. *For now ye are nothing*] Ye are just to me as those deceitful torrents to the caravans of Tema and Sheba; they were *nothing* to them; ye are *nothing* to me.

Ye see my *casting down*] Ye see that I have been hurried from my eminence into want and misery, as the flood from the top of the mountains, which is divided, evaporated, and lost in the desert.

And are afraid.] Ye are terrified at the calamity that has come upon me; and instead of drawing near to comfort me, ye start back at my appearance.

Verse 22. *Did I say, Bring unto me?*] Why do you stand aloof? Have I asked you to bring me any presents? or to supply my wants out of your stores?

Verse 23. *Or, Deliver me*] Did I send to you to come and avenge me of the destroyers of my property, or to rescue my substance out of the hands of my enemies?

Verse 24. *Teach me*] Show me where I am mistaken. Bring proper arguments to convince me of my errors; and you will soon find that I shall gladly receive your counsels, and abandon the errors of which I may be convicted.

Verse 25. *How forcible are right words*] A well-constructed argument, that has truth for its basis, is *irresistible.*

But what doth your arguing reprove?] Your *reasoning* is defective, because your *premises* are false; and your *conclusions* prove nothing, because of the falsity of the premises whence they are drawn. The last clause, literally rendered, is, *What reproof, in a reproof from you?* As you have *proved no fault* you have consequently *reproved* no *vice.* Instead of מה נמרצו *mah nimretsu,* "how forcible," מה נמלצו *mah nimletsu,* "how savoury or pleasant," is the reading of two MSS., the *Chaldee,* and some of the *rabbins.* Both senses are good, but the common reading is to be preferred.

Verse 26. *Do ye imagine to reprove words*] Is it some expressions which in my hurry, and under the pressure of unprecedented affliction, I have uttered, that ye catch at? You can find no flaw in my conduct; would ye *make me an* OFFENDER *for a* WORD? Why endeavour to take such advantage of a man who complains in the bitterness of his heart, through despair of life and happiness?

Verse 27. *Ye overwhelm the fatherless*] Ye see that I am as destitute as the most *miserable orphan;* would ye overwhelm such a one? and would you *dig a pit for your friend*—do ye lay wait for me, and endeavour to entangle me in my talk? I believe this to be the spirit of Job's words.

Verse 28. *Look upon me*] View me; consider my circumstances; compare my words; and you must be convinced that I have spoken nothing but truth.

Verse 29. *Return, I pray you*] *Reconsider the whole subject. Do not be offended. Yea,*

A. M. cir. 2484 B. C. cir. 1520 Ante I. Olymp. cir. 744 Ante U. C. cir. 767

27 Yea, [a]ye overwhelm the fatherless, and ye [b]dig *a pit* for your
friend.
28 Now therefore be content,
look upon me; for *it is* [c]evident unto you
if I lie.

29 [d]Return, I pray you, let it
not be iniquity; yea, return again,
my righteousness *is* [e]in it.
30 Is there iniquity in my
tongue? cannot [f]my taste discern perverse
things?

A. M. cir. 2484 B. C. cir. 1520 Ante I. Olymp. cir. 744 Ante U. C. cir. 767

---

[a]Hebrew, *ye cause to fall upon*——[b]Psa. lvii. 6 [c]Heb. *before your face*——[d]Chap. xvii. 10

[e]That is, *in this matter*——[f]Heb. *my palate*, chap. xii. 11; xxxiv. 3

---

reconsider the subject; my righteousness is in it—my argumentation is a sufficient proof of my innocence.

Verse 30. *Is there iniquity in my tongue?*] Am I not an *honest* man? and if in my haste my tongue had uttered *falsity*, would not my conscience discern it? and do you think that such a man as your friend is would defend what he knew to be wrong?

I HAVE done what I could to make this chapter plain, to preserve the connection, and show the dependence of the several parts on each other; without which many of the sayings would have been very obscure. The whole chapter is an inimitable apology for what he had uttered, and a defence of his conduct. This might have ended the controversy, had not his friends been determined to bring him in guilty. They had prejudged his cause, and assumed a certain position, from which they were determined not to be driven.

CHAPTER VII

Job continues to deplore his helpless and afflicted state, 1–6. *He expostulates with God concerning his afflictions,* 7–12; *describes the disturbed state of his mind by visions in the night season; abhors life,* 13–16; *and, showing that he is unworthy of the notice of God, begs pardon and respite,* 17–21.

A. M. cir. 2484 B. C. cir. 1520 Ante I. Olymp. cir. 744 Ante U. C. cir. 767

IS *there* not [a]an [b]appointed
time to man upon earth? *are*
not his days also like the days
of a hireling?
2 As a servant [c]earnestly desireth the shadow, and as a hireling looketh
for *the reward of* his work:
3 So am I made to possess
[d]months of vanity, and weari-
some nights are appointed to me.

A. M. cir. 2484 B. C. cir. 1520 Ante I. Olymp. cir. 744 Ante U. C. cir. 767

---

[a]Or, *a warfare*——[b]Chap. xiv. 5, 13, 14; Psa. xxxix. 4

[c]Heb. *gapeth after*——[d]See chap. xxix. 2

NOTES ON CHAP. VII

Verse 1. Is there *not an appointed time to man*] The *Hebrew*, with its literal rendering, is as follows: חלא צבא לאנוש עלי ארץ *halo tsaba leenosh aley arets*, "Is there not a warfare to miserable man upon the earth?" And thus most of the *versions* have understood the words. The SEPTUAGINT: Ποτερον ουχι πειρατηριον εστι ὁ βιος ανθρωπου επι της γης; "Is not the life of man a place of trial upon earth?" The VULGATE: *Militia est* vita hominis super terram, "The life of man is a warfare upon earth." The CHALDEE is the same. *N'y a-t-il pas comme un train de guerre ordonnê aux mortels sur la terre?* "Is there not a continual campaign ordained for mortals upon the earth?" FRENCH BIBLE. The GERMAN and DUTCH the same. COVERDALE: **Is not the life off man upon earth a very bataple?** CARMARDEN, Rouen, 1566: **Hath man any certayne tyme upon earth?** SYRIAC and ARABIC: "Now, man has time upon the earth." *Non è egli il tempo determinato â l'huomo sopra la terra?*" "Is there not a determined time to man upon the earth?" BIB. ITAL., 1562. All these are nearer to the true sense than ours; and of a bad translation, worse use has been made by many theologians. I believe the simple sentiment which the writer wished to convey is this: *Human life is a state of probation*; and every day and place is a time and place of *exercise*, to *train us up* for eternal life. *Here* is the *exercise*, and here the *warfare:* we are *enlisted* in the *bands of the Church militant*, and must accomplish our *time of service*, and be honourably *dismissed* from the *warfare*, having *conquered* through the blood of the Lamb; and then receive the *reward* of the heavenly inheritance.

Verse 2. *Earnestly desireth the shadow*] As a man who labours hard in the *heat* of the day earnestly desires to get under a *shade*, or wishes for the *long evening shadows*, that he may rest from his labour, gct his day's wages, retire to his food, and then go to rest. *Night* is probably what is meant by the *shadow;* as in VIRGIL, Æn. iv., ver. 7: Humentemque Aurora *polo dimoverat* UMBRAM. "The morning had removed the humid shadow, i. e., *night*, from the world." Where SERVIUS justly observes: *Nihil interest, utrum* UMBRAM *an* NOCTEM *dicat:* NOX *enim* UMBRA *terræ est*, "It makes no difference whether he says *shadow* or *night;* for night is the *shadow* of the earth."

Verse 3. *So am I made to possess*] But night is no relief to me; it is only a continuance of my anxiety and labour. I am like the *hireling*, I have my *appointed* labour for the *day*. I am like the *soldier* harassed by the enemy: I am obliged to be continually on the watch, always on the look out, with scarcely any rest.

A. M. cir. 2484
B. C. cir. 1520
Ante I. Olymp. cir. 744
Ante U. C. cir. 767

4 [e]When I lie down, I say,
When shall I arise, and [f]the
night be gone? and I am full
of tossings to and fro unto the
dawning of the day.
5 My flesh is [g]clothed with worms and
clods of dust; my skin is broken, and become
loathsome.
6 [h]My days are swifter than
a weaver's shuttle, and are spent
without hope.
7 O remember that [i]my life *is*
wind: mine eye [k]shall no more [l]see good.
8 [m]The eye of him that hath seen me shall
see me no *more:* thine eyes *are* upon me,
[n]and I *am* not.

A. M. cir. 2484
B. C. cir. 1520
Ante I. Olymp. cir. 744
Ante U. C. cir. 767

---

[e]Deut. xxviii. 67; chap. xvii. 12——[f]Heb. *the evening be measured*——[g]Isa. xiv. 11——[h]Chap. ix. 25; xvi. 22; xvii. 14; Psa. xc. 6; cii. 11; ciii. 15; cxliv. 4; Isa. xxxviii. 12; xl. 6; James iv. 14——[i]Psa. lxxviii. 39; lxxxix. 47——[k]Heb. *shall not return*——[l]*To see*, that is, *to enjoy*——[m]Chap. xx. 9——[n]That is, *I can live no longer*

Verse 4. *When I lie down*] I have so little rest, that when I do lie down I long for the return of the light, that I may rise. Nothing can better depict the state of a man under continual afflictions, which afford him no respite, his days and his nights being spent in constant anguish, utterly unable to be in any one posture, so that he is continually changing his position in his bed, finding ease nowhere: thus, as himself expresses it, he is *full of tossings.*

Verse 5. *My flesh is clothed with worms*] This is perhaps no figure, but is literally true: the miserably ulcerated state of his body, exposed to the open air, and in a state of great destitution, was favourable to those insects that sought such places in which to deposit their *ova*, which might have produced the animals in question. But the figure is too horrid to be farther illustrated.

Clods of dust] I believe all the commentators have here missed the sense. I suppose Job to allude to those *incrustations* of indurated or dried *pus*, which are formed on the tops of pustules in a state of decay: such as the *scales* which fall from the pustules of the smallpox, when the patient becomes convalescent. Or, if Job's disease was the *elephantiasis*, it may refer to the *furfuraceous scales* which are continually falling off the body in that disorder. It is well known, that in this disease the *skin* becomes very *rigid*, so as to *crack* across, especially at the different *joints*, out of which fissures a loathsome *ichor* is continually exuding. To something like this the words may refer, *My* SKIN IS BROKEN, and become LOATHSOME.

Verse 6. *Swifter than a weaver's shuttle*] The word ארג *areg* signifies rather the *weaver* than his *shuttle.* And it has been doubted whether any such instrument were in use in the days of Job. Dr. Russell, in his account of Aleppo, shows that though they wove many kinds of curious cloth, yet no *shuttle* was used, as they conducted every thread of the *woof* by their *fingers.* That some such instrument as the *shuttle* was in use from time immemorial, there can be no doubt: and it is certain that such an instrument must have been in the view of Job, without which the figure would lose its expression and force. In almost every nation the whole of human existence has been compared to a *web;* and the principle of life, through the continual succession of moments, hours, days, weeks, months, and years, *to a thread woven through that web.* Hence arose the fable of the *Parcæ* or *Fates*, called also the *Destinies* or *Fatal Sisters.* They were the daughters of *Erebus* and *Nox*, darkness and night; and were *three* in number, and named *Clotho, Lachesis,* and *Atropos.* Clotho held the distaff; Lachesis spun off the thread; and Atropos cut it off with her scissors, when it was determined that life should end. Job represents the *thread of his life* as being *spun out* with great rapidity and tenuity, and about to be *cut off.*

And are spent without hope.] Expectation of future good was at an end; *hope* of the alleviation of his miseries no longer existed. The *hope* of future good is the *balm of life:* where that is not, there is *despair;* where despair is, there is *hell.* The fable above mentioned is referred to by *Virgil*, Ecl. iv., ver. 46, but is there applied to *time:*—

Talia Secla, suis dixerunt, currite, fusis
Concordes stabili fatorum numine Parcæ.

"The FATES, when they this happy *thread* have *spun*
Shall bless the sacred *clue*, and bid it *smoothly run.*" DRYDEN.

Isaiah uses the same figure, chap. xxxviii. 12:—

My *life* is cut off, as by the *weaver:*
He will sever me from the *loom.*
In the course of the day thou wilt finish my *web.* LOWTH.

Coverdale translates thus: **My dayes passe over more spedely then a weaver can weave out his webbe and are gone or I am awarre.**

A fine example of this figure is found in the *Teemour Nameh*, which I shall give in Mr. *Good's* translation:—

"Praise be to God, who hath *woven* the *web* of human affairs in the *loom* of his will and of his wisdom, and hath made *waves of times* and of *seasons* to *flow* from the *fountain* of his *providence* into the *ocean* of his *power.*" The simile is fine, and elegantly expressed.

Verse 7. *My life* is *wind*] Mr. *Good* translates, "O remember that, if my life pass away, mine eye shall turn no more to scenes of goodness;" which he paraphrases thus: "O remember that, if my life pass away, never more shall I witness those scenes of Divine favour, never more adore thee for those proofs of unmerited mercy, which till now have been so perpetually bestowed on me." I think the *common translation* gives a very good sense.

Verse 8. *Shall see me no* more] If I die in my present state, with all this load of undeserved odium which is cast upon me by my friends, I shall never have an opportunity of vindicating my character, and regaining the good opinion of mankind.

Thine eyes are *upon me, and I* am *not.*] Thou canst look me into nothing. Or, Let thine eye

A. M. cir. 2484
B. C. cir. 1520
Ante I. Olymp. cir. 744
Ante U. C. cir. 767

9 *As* the cloud is consumed
and vanisheth away; so [o]he that
goeth down to the grave shall
come up no *more.*
10 He shall return no more to his house,
[p]neither shall his place know him any more.
11 Therefore I will [q]not refrain my mouth;
I will speak in the anguish of my spirit; I
will [r]complain in the bitterness of my soul.
12 *Am* I a sea, or a whale, that thou settest
a watch over me?
13 [s]When I say, My bed shall
comfort me, my couch shall ease
my complaint;
14 Then thou scarest me
with dreams, and terrifiest me through
visions:
15 So that my soul chooseth strangling, *and*
death rather [t]than my life.
16 [u]I loathe *it;* I would not live alway:
[v]let me alone; [w]for my days *are* vanity.
17 [x]What *is* man, that thou shouldest mag-

A. M. cir. 2484
B. C. cir. 1520
Ante I. Olymp. cir. 744
Ante U. C. cir. 767

[o]2 Sam. xii. 23——[p]Chap. viii. 18; xx. 9; Psa. ciii. 16——[q]Psa. xxxix. 1, 9; xl. 9——[r]1 Sam. i. 10; chap. x. 1——[s]Chap. ix. 27

[t]Heb. *than my bones*——[u]Chap. x. 1——[v]Chap. x. 20; xiv. 6; Psa. xxxix. 13——[w]Psa. lxii. 9——[x]Psa. viii. 4; cxliv. 3; Heb. ii. 6

be upon me as judged to death, and I shall immediately cease to live among men.

Verse 9. As *the cloud is consumed*] As the cloud is dissipated, so is the breath of those that go down to the grave. As that cloud shall never return, so shall it be with the dead; they return no more to sojourn with the living. See on the following verses.

Verse 10. *He shall return no more to his house, neither shall his place know him any more.*] He does not mean that he shall be *annihilated*, but that he shall never more become an inhabitant of the earth.

The word שאול, which we properly enough translate *grave*, here signifies also the *state of the dead, hades*, and sometimes any *deep pit*, or even *hell* itself.

Verse 11. *Therefore I will not refrain*] All is hopeless; I will therefore indulge myself in complaining.

Verse 12. Am *I a sea, or a whale*] "Am I condemned as the Egyptians were who were drowned in the Red Sea? or am I as Pharaoh, who was drowned in it in his sins, that thou settest a keeper over me?" *Targum.* Am I as dangerous as the sea, that I should be encompassed about with barriers, lest I should hurt mankind? Am I like an ungovernable *wild beast* or *dragon*, that I must be put under locks and bars? I think our own version less exceptionable than any other hitherto given of this verse. The meaning is sufficiently plain. Job was hedged about and shut in with insuperable difficulties of various kinds; he was entangled as a wild beast in a net; the more he struggled, the more he lost his strength, and the less probability there was of his being extricated from his present situation. The *sea* is shut in with barriers, over which it cannot pass; for God has "placed the sand for the *bound* of the sea by a perpetual decree, that it cannot pass it: and though the waves thereof toss themselves, yet can they not prevail; though they roar, yet can they not pass over it;" Jer. v. 22. "*For* thou hast set a *bound* that they may not pass over; that they turn not again to cover the earth;" Psa. civ. 9. "Or *who* shut up the sea with *doors*, when it brake forth, *as if* it had issued out of the womb? When I made the cloud the *garment* thereof, and thick darkness a *swaddling band* for it, and brake up for it my *decreed place*, and set *bars* and *doors;* and said, Hitherto shalt thou come, but no farther: and here shall thy proud waves be stayed;" chap. xxxviii. 8.

Here then is Job's allusion: the *bounds, doors, garment, swaddling bands, decreed place,* and *bars*, are the *watchers* or *keepers* which God has set to prevent the *sea* from *overflowing the earth;* so Job's *afflictions* and *distresses* were the *bounds* and *bars* which God had apparently set to prevent him from injuring his fellow creatures. At least Job, in his complaint, so takes it. Am I like the *sea*, which thou hast imprisoned within bounds, ready to overwhelm and destroy the country? or am I like a *dragon*, which must be cooped up in the same way, that it may not have the power to kill and destroy? Surely in my prosperity I gave no evidence of such a disposition; therefore should not be treated as a man dangerous to society. In this Job shows that *he will not refrain his mouth.*

Verse 14. *Thou scarest me with dreams*] There is no doubt that Satan was permitted to haunt his *imagination* with dreadful dreams and terrific appearances; so that, as soon as he fell asleep, he was suddenly roused and alarmed by those appalling images. He needed rest by sleep, but was afraid to close his eyes because of the horrid images which were presented to his imagination. Could there be a state more deplorable than this?

Verse 15. *Chooseth strangling*] It is very likely that he felt, in those interrupted and dismal slumbers, an oppression and difficulty of breathing something like the *incubus* or *nightmare;* and, distressing as this was, he would prefer death by this means to any longer life in such miseries.

Verse 16. *I loathe* it; *I would not live alway*] Life, in such circumstances, is hateful to me; and though I wish for long life, yet if length of days were offered to me with the sufferings which I now undergo, I would despise the offer and spurn the boon.

Mr. *Good* is not satisfied with our common version, and has adopted the following, which in his *notes* he endeavours to illustrate and defend:

Verse 15. So that my soul coveteth suffocation,
And death in comparison with my suffering.
16. No longer would I live! O, release me!
How are my days vanity!

Verse 17. *What* is *man that thou shouldest magnify him? and that thou shouldest set thine heart upon him?*] Two different ideas have been drawn from these words:—

1. Man is not worth thy notice; why therefore dost thou contend with him?

A. M. cir. 2484 B. C. cir. 1520 Ante I. Olymp. cir. 744 Ante U. C. cir. 767

nify him? and that thou shouldest set thine heart upon him?
18 And *that* thou shouldest
visit him every morning, *and* try
him every moment?
19 How long wilt thou not depart from me,
nor let me alone till I swallow down my spittle?
20 I have sinned; what shall I do unto
thee, [y]O thou Preserver of men?
why [z]hast thou set me as a mark
against thee, so that I am a burden to myself?
21 And why dost thou not pardon my transgression, and take away mine iniquity? for
now shall I sleep in the dust; and thou shalt
seek me in the morning, but I *shall* not *be*.

---

[y]Psa. xxxvi. 6 — [z]Chap. xvi. 12; Psa. xxi. 12; Lam. iii. 12

---

2. How astonishing is thy kindness that thou shouldest *fix thy heart*—thy strongest affections, on such a poor, base, vile, impotent creature as man, (אנוש *enosh,*) that thou shouldest so highly exalt him beyond all other creatures, and mark him with the most particular notice of thy providence and grace!

The paraphrase of *Calmet* is as follows: "Does man, such as he at present is, merit thy attention! What is man that God should make it his business to examine, try, prove, and afflict him? Is it not doing him too much honour to think thus seriously about him? O Lord! I am not worthy that thou shouldest concern thyself about *me!*"

Verse 19. *Till I swallow down my spittle?*] This is a proverbial expression, and exists among the Arabs to the present day; the very language being nearly the same. It signifies the same as, *Let me draw my breath; give me a moment's space; let me have even the twinkling of an eye.* I am urged by my sufferings to continue my complaint; but my strength is exhausted, my *mouth dry* with speaking. Suspend my sufferings even for so short a space as is necessary to swallow my spittle, that my parched tongue may be moistened, so that I may renew my complaint.

Verse 20. *I have sinned; what shall I do*] Dr. *Kennicott* contends that these words are spoken to *Eliphaz*, and not to God, and would paraphrase them thus: "You say I must have been a sinner. What then? I have not sinned against thee, O thou spy upon mankind! Why hast thou set up *me* as a butt or mark to shoot at? Why am *I* become a burden unto thee? Why not rather overlook my transgression, and pass by mine iniquity? I am now sinking to the dust! To-morrow, perhaps, I shall be sought in vain!" See his vindication of Job at the end of *these notes* on this book. Others consider the address as made to God. Taken in this light, the sense is plain enough.

Those who suppose that the address is made to God, translate the 20th verse thus: "Be it that I have sinned, what injury can I do unto thee, O thou Observer of man? Why hast thou set me up as a mark for thee, and why am I made a burden to thee?" The *Septuagint* is thus: Ει εγω ἡμαρτον, τι δυνησομαι πραξαι, ὁ επισταμενος τον νουν των ανθρωπων; *If I have sinned, what can I do, O thou who knowest the mind of men?* Thou knowest that it is impossible for *me* to make any restitution. I cannot blot out my offences; but whether I have sinned so as to bring all these calamities upon me, thou knowest, who searchest the hearts of men.

Verse 21. *And why dost thou not pardon*] These words are spoken *after the manner of men.* If thou have any design to save me, if I have sinned, why dost thou not pardon my transgression, as thou seest that I am a dying man; and to-morrow morning thou mayest seek me to do me good, but in all probability I shall then be no more, and all thy kind thoughts towards me shall be unavailing? If I have sinned, then why should not I have a part in that mercy that flows so freely to all mankind?

That Job does not criminate himself here, as our text intimates, is evident enough from his own repeated assertions of his innocence. And it is most certain that *Bildad*, who immediately answers, did not consider him as criminating but as *justifying* himself; and this is the very ground on which *he* takes up the subject. Were we to admit the contrary, we should find strange inconsistencies, if not contradictions, in Job's speeches: on such a ground the controversy must have immediately terminated, as he would then have acknowledged that of which his friends accused him; and here the book of Job would have ended.

CHAPTER VIII

Bildad answers, and reproves Job for his justifying himself, 1, 2. *Shows that God is just, and never punishes but for iniquity; and intimates that it was on account of their sins that his children were cut off,* 3, 4. *States that, if Job would humble himself to the Almighty, provided he were innocent, his captivity would soon be turned, and his latter end be abundantly prosperous,* 5–7. *Appeals to the ancients for the truth of what he says; and draws examples from the vegetable world, to show how soon the wicked may be cut off, and the hope of the hypocrite perish,* 8–19. *Asserts that God never did cast off a perfect man nor help the wicked; and that, if Job be innocent, his end shall be crowned with prosperity,* 20–22.

A. M. cir. 2484
B. C. cir. 1520
Ante I. Olymp. cir. 744
Ante U. C. cir. 767

THEN answered Bildad the
Shuhite, and said,
2 How long wilt thou speak
these *things?* and *how long shall*
the words of thy mouth *be like* a strong wind?
3 [a]Doth God pervert judgment? or doth
the Almighty pervert justice?
4 If [b]thy children have sinned against him,
and if he have cast them away [c]for their
transgression;
5 [d]If thou wouldest seek unto God betimes,
and make thy supplication to the Almighty;
6 If thou *wert* pure and up-
right, surely now he would awake
for thee, and make the habitation
of thy righteousness prosperous.
7 Though thy beginning was small, yet thy
latter end should greatly increase.
8 [e]For inquire, I pray thee, of the former
age, and prepare thyself to the search of their
fathers:
9 (For [f]we *are but of* yesterday, and know
[g]nothing, because our days upon earth *are* a
shadow:)

[a]Gen. xviii. 25; Deut. xxxii. 4; 2 Chron. xix. 7; chap. xxxiv. 12, 17; Dan. ix. 14; Rom. iii. 5——[b]Chap. i. 5, 18 [c]Heb. *in the hand of their transgression*——[d]Ch. v. 8; xi. 13; xxii. 23, &c.——[e]Deut. iv. 32; xxxii. 7; ch. xv. 18——[f]Gen. xlvii. 9; 1 Chron. xxix. 15; ch. vii. 6; Psa. xxxix. 5; cii. 11; cxliv. 14——[g]Heb. *not*

NOTES ON CHAP. VIII

Verse 1. *Bildad the Shuhite*] Supposed to be a descendant of *Shuah*, one of the sons of Abraham, by Keturah, who dwelt in Arabia Deserta, called in Scripture the *east country.* See Gen. xxv. 1, 2, 6.

Verse 2. *How long wilt thou speak these things?*] Wilt thou still go on to charge God foolishly? Thy heavy affliction proves that thou art under his wrath; and his wrath, thus manifested, proves that it is for thy sins that he punisheth thee.

Be like *a strong wind?*] The *Arabic*, with which the *Syriac* agrees, is روح العظمة *ruch-olazomati, the spirit of pride.* Wilt thou continue to *breathe forth a tempest of words?* This is more literal.

Verse 3. *Doth God pervert judgment?*] God afflicts thee; can he afflict thee for naught? As he is just, his judgment is just; and he could not inflict punishment unless there be a cause.

Verse 4. *If thy children have sinned*] I know thy children have been cut off by a terrible judgment; but was it not because by transgression they had filled up the measure of their iniquity?

And he have cast them away] *Has sent them off*, says the *Targum, to the place of their transgression*—to that punishment due to their sins.

Verse 5. *If thou wouldest seek unto God*] Though God has so severely afflicted thee, and removed thy children by a terrible judgment; yet if thou wilt now humble thyself before him, and implore his mercy, thou shalt be saved. He cut *them* off in their sins, but he spares *thee;* and this is a proof that he waits to be gracious to thee.

Verse 6. *If thou* wert *pure and upright*] Concerning thy guilt there can be no doubt; for if thou hadst been a holy man, and these calamities had occurred through accident, or merely by the malice of thy enemies, would not God, long ere this, have manifested his power and justice in thy behalf, punished thy enemies, and restored thee to affluence?

The habitation of thy righteousness] Strongly ironical. If thy house had been as a temple of God, in which his worship had been performed, and his commandments obeyed, would it now be in a state of ruin and desolation?

Verse 7. *Though thy beginning was small*] Thy *former state*, compared to that into which God would have brought thee, would be small; for to show his respect for thy piety, because thou hadst, through thy faithful attachment to him, suffered the loss of all things, he would have greatly multiplied thy former prosperity, so that thou shouldest now have vastly more than thou didst ever before possess.

Verse 8. *Inquire—of the former age*] לדור רישון *ledor rishon*, of the *first age;* of the *patriarchs;* the first generation of men that dwelt upon the earth: not of the *age that was just past*, as Mr. *Peters* and several others have imagined, in order to keep up the presumption of Job's high antiquity. *Bildad* most evidently refers to an antiquity exceedingly remote.

Verse 9. *For we* are but of *yesterday, and know nothing*] It is evident that Bildad refers to those times in which human life was protracted to a much *longer date* than that in which Job lived; when men, from the long period of *eight* or *nine hundred years*, had the opportunity of making many observations, and treasuring up a vast fund of knowledge and experience. In comparison with *them*, he considers *that age* as *nothing*, and that generation as being only of *yesterday*, not having had opportunity of laying up knowledge: nor could they expect it, as their days upon earth would be but a *shadow*, compared with that *substantial* time in which the fathers had lived. Perhaps there may be an allusion here to the *shadow* projected by the *gnomon of a dial*, during the time the sun is above the horizon. As is a single *solar day*, so is our *life*. The following beautiful motto I have seen on a sundial: UMBRÆ SUMUS! "We are shadows!" referring to the different shadows by which the gnomon marked the hours, during the course of the day; and all intended to convey this moral lesson to the passengers: Your life is composed of time, marked out by such shadows as these. Such as time *is*, such are *you;* as fleeting, as transitory, as unsubstantial. These *shadows* lost, *time* is lost; *time* lost, *soul* lost! Reader, take heed!

The writer of this book probably had before his eyes these words of David, in his last prayer, 1 Chron. xxix. 15: "For we are strangers before thee, and sojourners, as all our fathers *were;*

A. M. cir. 2484 B. C. cir. 1520 Ante I. Olymp. cir. 744 Ante U. C. cir. 767

10 Shall not they teach thee,
and tell thee, and utter words out
of their heart?
11 Can the rush grow up without mire? can the flag grow without water?
12 [h]Whilst it *is* yet in his greenness, *and*
not cut down, it withereth before any *other* herb.
13 So *are* the paths of all that forget God; and the [i]hypocrite's hope shall perish:
14 Whose hope shall be cut off, and

[h]Psa. cxxix. 6; Jer. xvii. 6——[i]Ch. xi. 20; xviii. 14; xxvii. 8; Psa. cxii. 10; Prov. x. 28

our days upon earth are as a SHADOW, and there is no *expectation.* There is no reason to *hope* that they shall be *prolonged;* for our lives are limited down to *threescore years* and *ten,* as the average of the life even of *old men.*

Verse 10. *Shall not they teach thee*] Wilt thou not treat their maxims with the utmost deference and respect? They *utter words from their heart*—what they say is the fruit of long and careful experience.

Verse 11. *Can the rush grow*] The word גמא *gome,* which we translate *rush,* is, without doubt, the Egyptian flag *papyrus,* on which the ancients *wrote,* and from which our *paper* derives its name. The *Septuagint,* who made their Greek translation in Egypt, (if this book made a part of it,) and knew well the import of each word in both languages, render גמא *gome* by *παπυρος papyrus,* thus: Μη θαλλει παπυρος ανευ ὑδατος; *Can the* PAPYRUS *flourish without water?* Their translation leaves no doubt concerning the meaning of the original. They were probably *writing on* the *very substance* in question, while making their translation. The technical language of no science is so thoroughly barbarous as that of *botany:* the description of this plant by *Linnæus,* shall be a proof. The plant he calls "*Cyperus Papyrus;* CLASS *Triandria;* ORDER *Monogynia;* Culm three-sided, naked; umbel longer than the involucres; involucels three-leaved, setaceous, longer; spikelets in threes.—Egypt, &c. *Involucre* eight-leaved; general *umbel* copious, the rays sheathing at the base; *partial* on very short peduncles; *spikelets* alternate, sessile; *culm* leafy at the base; *leaves* hollow, ensiform."

Hear our plain countryman *John Gerarde,* who describes the same plant: "*Papyrus Nilotica,* Paper Reed, hath many large flaggie leaves, somewhat triangular and smooth, not much unlike those of cats-taile, rising immediately from a tuft of roots, compact of many strings; amongst the which it shooteth up two or three naked stalkes, square, and rising some six or seven cubits high above the water; at the top whereof there stands a tuft or bundle off chaffie threds, set in comely order, resembling a tuft of floures, but barren and void of seed;" GERARDE'S *Herbal,* p. 40. Which of the two descriptions is easiest to be understood by common sense, either with or without a knowledge of the Latin language? This plant grows in the *muddy* banks of the Nile, as it requires an abundance of water for its nourishment.

Can the flag grow without water?] Parkhurst supposes that the word אחו *achu,* which we render *flag,* is the same with that species of *reed* which Mr. *Hasselquist* found growing near the river Nile. He describes it (p. 97) as "having scarcely any branches, but numerous leaves, which are narrow, smooth, channelled on the upper surface; and the plant about eleven feet high. The Egyptians make *ropes* of the leaves. They lay the plant in water, like hemp, and then make good and strong *cables* of them." As אח *ach* signifies to *join, connect, associate,* hence אחי *achi,* a *brother.* אחו *achu* may come from the same root, and have its name from its usefulness in making *ropes, cables,* &c., which are composed of *associated* threads, and serve to *tie, bind together,* &c.

Verse 12. *Whilst it* is *yet in his greenness*] We do not know enough of the natural history of this plant to be able to discern the strength of this allusion; but we learn from it that, although this plant be very succulent, and grow to a great size, yet it is short-lived, and speedily withers; and this we may suppose to be in the *dry season,* or on the retreat of the waters of the Nile. However, *Soon* RIPE, *soon* ROTTEN, is a maxim in horticulture.

Verse 13. *So* are *the paths*] The *papyrus* and the *rush* flourish while they have a plentiful supply of *ooze* and *water;* but take these away, and their prosperity is speedily at an end; so it is with the *wicked* and profane; their prosperity is of short duration, however great it may appear to be in the beginning. Thou also, O thou enemy of God, hast flourished for a time; but the blast of God is come upon thee, and now thou art dried up from the very roots.

The hypocrite's hope shall perish] A *hypocrite,* or rather *profligate,* has no inward religion, for his heart is not right with God; he has only *hope,* and that *perishes* when he gives up the ghost.

This is the first place in which the word *hypocrite* occurs, or the noun חנף *chaneph,* which *rather* conveys the idea of *pollution* and *defilement* than of *hypocrisy.* A *hypocrite* is one who only *carries the mask of godliness,* to serve secular purposes; who wishes to be taken for a religionist, though he is conscious he has *no religion.* Such a person cannot have *hope* of any good, because he knows he is *insincere:* but the person in the text has hope; therefore *hypocrite* cannot be the meaning of the original word. But all the *vile,* the *polluted,* and the *profligate* have *hope;* they hope to end their iniquities before they end life; and they hope to get at last to the kingdom of heaven. *Hypocrite* is a very improper translation of the Hebrew.

Verse 14. *Whose hope shall be cut off*] Such persons, subdued by the strong habits of sin, hope on fruitlessly, till the last thread of the web of life is cut off from the beam; and then they find no more strength in their hope than is in the threads of the spider's web.

Mr. *Good* renders, *Thus shall their support rot away.* The foundation on which they trust is rotten, and by and by the whole superstructure of their confidence shall tumble into ruin.

A. M. cir. 2484
B. C. cir. 1520
Ante I. Olymp. cir. 744
Ante U. C. cir. 767

whose trust *shall be* [k]a spider's
web.
15 [l]He shall lean upon his
house, but it shall not stand:
he shall hold it fast, but it shall not endure.
16 He *is* green before the sun, and his
branch shooteth forth in his garden.
17 His roots are wrapped about the heap,
and seeth the place of stones.
18 [m]If he destroy him from his place, then *it*
shall deny him, *saying,* I have not seen thee.
19 Behold, this *is* the joy of
his way, and [n]out of the earth
shall others grow.
20 Behold, God will not cast
away a perfect *man,* neither will he [o]help the
evil doers:
21 Till he fill thy mouth with laughing,
and thy lips with [p]rejoicing.
22 They that hate thee shall be [q]clothed
with shame; and the dwelling-place of the
wicked [r]shall come to naught.

[k]Heb. *a spider's house;* Isa. lix. 5, 6——[l]Ch. xxvii. 18 [m]Ch. vii. 10; xx. 9; Psa. xxxvii. 36——[n]Psa. cxiii. 7

[o]Heb. *take the ungodly by the hand*——[p]Heb. *shouting for joy*——[q]Psa. xxxv. 26; cix. 29——[r]Heb. *shall not be*

Verse 15. *He shall lean upon his house*] This is an allusion to the spider. When he suspects his *web*, here called his *house*, to be frail or unsure, he leans upon it in different parts, propping himself on his hinder legs, and pulling with his fore claws, to see if all be safe. If he find any part of it injured, he immediately adds new cordage to that part, and attaches it strongly to the wall. When he finds all safe and strong, he retires into his hole at one corner, supposing himself to be in a state of complete security, when in a moment the *brush* or the *besom* sweeps away both himself, his house, and his confidence. This I have several times observed; and it is in this that the strength and *point* of the comparison consist. The *wicked*, whose hope is in his temporal possessions, strengthens and keeps his house in repair; and thus *leans* on his earthly supports; in a moment, as in the case of the *spider*, his house is overwhelmed by the blast of God's judgments, and himself probably buried in its ruins. This is a very fine and expressive metaphor, which not one of the commentators that I have seen has ever discovered.

Verse 16. *He* is *green before the sun*] This is another metaphor. The wicked is represented as a luxuriant plant, in a good soil, with all the advantages of a good situation; well exposed to the sun; the roots intervolving themselves with stones, so as to render the tree more stable; but suddenly a blast comes, and the tree begins to die. The sudden fading of its leaves, &c., shows that its root is become as rottenness, and its vegetable life destroyed. I have often observed sound and healthy trees, which were flourishing in all the pride of vegetative health, suddenly struck by some unknown and incomprehensible blast, begin to die away, and perish from the roots. I have seen also the prosperous wicked, in the inscrutable dispensations of the Divine providence, blasted, stripped, made bare, and despoiled, in the same way.

Verse 18. *If he destroy him from his place*] Is not this a plain reference to the *alienation of his inheritance?* God destroys him from it; it becomes the property of another; and on his revisiting it, the place, by a striking *prosopopœia*, says, "I know thee not; I have never seen thee." This also have I witnessed; I looked on it, felt regret, received instruction, and hasted away.

Verse 19. *Behold this* is *the joy of his way*] A strong irony. Here is the issue of all his mirth, of his sports, games, and pastimes! See the unfeeling, domineering, polluting and polluted scape-grace, levelled with those whom he had despised, a servant of servants, or unable to work through his debaucheries, cringing for a morsel of bread, or ingloriously ending his days in that bane of any well-ordered and civilized state, a *parish workhouse.* This also I have most literally witnessed.

Out of the earth shall others grow.] As in the preceding case, when *one* plant or tree is blasted or cut down, *another* may be planted in the same place; so, when a spendthrift has run through his property, another possesses his inheritance, and grows up from that soil in which he himself might have continued to flourish, had it not been for his extravagance and folly.

This verse Mr. *Good* applies to God *himself*, with no advantage to the argument, nor elucidation of the sense, that I can see. I shall give his translation, and refer to his learned notes for his vindication of the version he has given:—

"Behold the Eternal (הוא) exulting in his course;
Even over his dust shall raise up another."

In this way none of the ancient *versions* have understood the passage. I believe it to be a strong *irony*, similar to that which some think flowed from the pen of the *same writer: Rejoice, O young man, in thy youth; and let thy heart cheer thee in the days of thy youth; and walk in the ways of thine heart, and in the sight of thine eyes. But know thou, that for all these God will bring thee into judgment;* Eccles. xi. 9. These two places illustrate each other.

Verse 20. *Behold, God will not cast away a perfect* man] This is another of the *maxims* of the *ancients*, which Bildad produces: "As sure as he will punish and root out the wicked, so surely will he defend and save the righteous."

Verse 21. *Till he fill thy mouth with laughing*] Perhaps it may be well to translate after Mr. *Good* "*Even yet* may he fill thy mouth with laughter!" The two verses may be read as a *prayer;* and probably they were thus expressed by Bildad, who speaks with less virulence than his predecessor, though with equal positiveness in respect to the grand charge, viz., *If thou wert not a sinner of no mean magnitude, God would not have inflicted such unprecedented calamities upon thee.*

This most exceptionable position, which is so contrary to matter of fact, was founded upon maxims which they derived from the *ancients.* Surely *observation* must have, in numberless instances, corrected this mistake. They must have seen many *worthless men* in high *prosperity*, and many of the *excellent of the earth* in deep *adversity* and *affliction;* but the opposite was an article of their *creed*, and all appearances and facts must take its colouring.

Job's friends must have been acquainted, at least, with the history of the ancient *patriarchs;* and most certainly they contained facts of an opposite nature. Righteous *Abel* was persecuted and murdered by his wicked brother *Cain. Abram* was obliged to leave his own country on account of worshipping the true God; *so* all tradition has said. *Jacob* was persecuted by his brother *Esau; Joseph* was sold into slavery by his brothers; *Moses* was obliged to flee from Egypt, and was variously tried and afflicted, even by his own brethren. Not to mention *David*, and almost all the *prophets.* All these were proofs that the best of men were frequently exposed to sore afflictions and heavy calamities; and it is not by the prosperity or adversity of men in this world, that we are to judge of the approbation or disapprobation of God towards them. In every case our Lord's rule is infallible: *By their fruits ye shall know them.*

CHAPTER IX

Job acknowledges God's justice and man's sinfulness, 1–3. *Celebrates his almighty power as manifested in the earth and in the heavens*, 4–10. *Maintains that God afflicts the innocent as well as the wicked, without any respect to their works: and hath delivered the earth into the hands of the wicked*, 11–24. *Complains of his lot, and maintains his innocence*, 25–35.

A. M. cir. 2484
B. C. cir. 1520
Ante I. Olymp. cir. 744
Ante U. C. cir. 767

THEN Job answered and said,
2 I know *it is* so of a truth:
but how should [a]man be just
[b]with God?
3 If he will contend with him, he cannot
answer him one of a thousand.
4 [c]*He is* wise in heart, and mighty
in strength; who hath hardened *himself*
against him, and hath prospered?
5 Which removeth the mountains, and they know not: which
overturneth them in his anger.
6 Which [d]shaketh the earth out of her
place, and [e]the pillars thereof tremble.
7 Which commandeth the sun, and it

[a]Psa. cxliii. 2; Rom. iii. 20——[b]Or, *before God*——[c]Ch. xxxvi. 5

[d]Isa. ii. 19, 21; Hag. ii. 6, 21; Heb. xii. 26——[e]Chap. xxvi. 11

NOTES ON CHAP. IX

Verse 2. *I know* it is *so of a truth*] I acknowledge the general truth of the maxims you have advanced. God will not ultimately punish a righteous person, nor shall the wicked finally triumph; and though righteous before man, and truly sincere in my piety, yet I know, when compared with the immaculate holiness of God, all my righteousness is nothing.

Verse 3. *If he will contend with him*] God is so holy, and his law so strict, that if he will enter into judgment with his creatures, the most upright of them cannot be justified in his sight.

One of a thousand.] Of a thousand offences of which he may be accused he cannot vindicate himself even in *one.* How little that any man does, even in the way of righteousness, truth, and mercy, can stand the penetrating eye of a just and holy God, when all *motives, feelings*, and *objects*, come to be scrutinized! In his sight, on this ground, no man living can be justified. O, how necessary to fallen, weak, miserable, imperfect and sinful man, is the doctrine of justification by faith, and sanctification through the Divine Spirit, by the sacrificial death and mediation of the Lord Jesus Christ!

Verse 4. He is *wise in heart, and mighty in strength*] By his infinite knowledge he searches out and sees all things, and by his almighty power he can punish all delinquencies. He that rebels against him must be destroyed.

Verse 5. *Removeth the mountains, and they know not*] This seems to refer to earthquakes. By those strong convulsions, mountains, valleys, hills, even whole islands, are removed in an instant; and to this latter circumstance the words, *they know not*, most probably refer. The work is done in the twinkling of an eye; no warning is given; the mountain, that seemed to be as firm as the earth on which it rested, was in the same moment both *visible* and *invisible;* so suddenly was it swallowed up.

Verse 6. *The pillars thereof tremble.*] This also refers to an earthquake, and to that *tremulous motion* which sometimes gives warning of the approaching catastrophe, and from which this violent convulsion of nature has received its name. *Earthquakes*, in Scripture language, signify also violent commotions and disturbances in *states; mountains* often signify *rulers; sun, empires; stars, petty states.* But it is most likely that the expressions here are to be understood literally.

Verse 7. *Which commandeth the sun*] Obscures it either with clouds, with thick darkness, or with an eclipse.

A. M. cir. 2484
B. C. cir. 1520
Ante I. Olymp. cir. 744
Ante U. C. cir. 767

riseth not; and sealeth up the
stars.
8 [f]Which alone spreadeth out
the heavens, and treadeth upon
the [g]waves of the sea.
9 [h]Which maketh [i]Arcturus, Orion, and
Pleiades, and the chambers of the south.
10 [k]Which doeth great things past finding
out; yea, and wonders without
number.
11 [l]Lo, he goeth by me, and
I see *him* not: he passeth on
also, but I perceive him not.
12 [m]Behold, he taketh away, [n]who can
hinder him? who will say unto him, What
dost thou?

[f]Gen. i. 6; Psa. civ. 2, 3——[g]Heb. *heights*——[h]Gen. i. 16; chap. xxxviii. 31, &c.; Amos v. 8——[i]Heb. *Ash, Cesil, and Cimah*

[k]Chap. v. 9; Psa. lxxi. 15——[l]Chap. xiii. 8, 9; xxxv. 14——[m]Isa. xlv. 9; Jer. xviii. 6; Rom. ix. 20——[n]Heb. *who can turn him away?* chap. xi. 10

Sealeth up the stars.] Like the contents of a letter, wrapped up and sealed, so that it cannot be read. Sometimes the heavens become as black as ebony, and no star, figure, or character, in this great book of God can be read.

Verse 8. *And treadeth upon the waves*] This is a very majestic image. God not only walks upon the waters, but, when the sea runs mountains high, he steps from billow to billow in his almighty and essential majesty. There is a similar sentiment in David, Psa. xxix. 10: "The Lord sitteth upon the flood; yea, the Lord sitteth King for ever." But both are far outdone by the Psalmist, Psa. xviii. 9-15, and especially in these words, ver. 10, *He did fly on the wings of the wind.* Job is great, but in every respect David is greater.

Verse 9. *Which maketh Arcturus, Orion, and Pleiades, and the chambers of the south.*] For this translation the original words are עשה עש כסיל וכימה והדרי תמן *oseh ash, kesil, vechimah vehadrey theman*, which are thus rendered by the Septuagint: Ὁ ποιων Πλειαδα, και Ἑσπερον, και Αρκτουρον, και ταμεια νοτου; "Who makes the Pleiades, and Hesperus, and Arcturus, and Orion, and the chambers of the south."

The Vulgate, *Qui facit Arcturum, et Oriona, et Hyadas, et interiora Austri;* "Who maketh Arcturus, and Orion, and the Hyades, and the innermost chambers of the south."

The Targum follows the Hebrew, but paraphrases the latter clause thus: "and the chambers or houses of the planetary domination in the southern hemisphere."

The Syriac and Arabic, "Who maketh the Pleiades, and Arcturus, and the giant, (*Orion* or *Hercules*,) and the boundaries of the south."

Coverdale has, **He maketh the waynes of heaven, the Orions, the vii starres and the secrete places of the south.** And on the *vii starres* he has this marginal note: **some call these seven starres, the clock henne with hir chickens.** See below.

Edmund Becke, in his edition, 1549, follows *Coverdale;* but puts vaynes *of heaven* for *waynes*, which *Carmarden*, in his Bible, Rouen, 1566, mistaking, changes into waves *of heaven.*

Barker's Bible, 1615, reads, "He maketh *the starres* Arcturus, Orion, and Pleiades, and the climates of the south." On which he has this note, "These are the names of certain starres, whereby he meaneth that all starres, both knowen and unknowen, are at His appointment."

Our early translators seem to agree much with the German and Dutch: **Er machet den wagen am himmel, und Orion, und die Glucken, und die Sterne gegen mittag;** "He maketh the wagon of heaven, (*Charles's wain,*) and Orion, and the clucking hen, (*the Pleiades,*) and the stars of the mid-day region." See above, under *Coverdale.*

The *Dutch* version is not much unlike the *German*, from which it is taken: **Die den wagen maecht, den Orion, ende het sevengesternte, end de binnenkameren van't Zuyden.**

The *European* versions, in general, copy one or other of the above, or make a compound translation from the whole; but all are derived ultimately from the *Septuagint* and *Vulgate.*

As to the *Hebrew* words, they might as well have been applied to any of the other constellations of heaven: indeed, it does not appear that *constellations* are at all meant. *Parkhurst* and *Bate* have given, perhaps, the best interpretation of the words, which is as follows:—

"כימה *kimah*, from כמה *camah*, *to be hot* or *warm*, denotes genial heat or warmth, as opposed to עש *ash*, a parching, biting air, on the one side; and כסיל *kesil*, the rigid, contracting *cold*, on the other; and the chambers (thick clouds) of the south." See more in *Parkhurst*, under כמה.

I need scarcely add that these words have been variously translated by critics and commentators. Dr. *Hales* translates *kimah* and *kesil* by *Taurus* and *Scorpio;* and, if this translation were indubitably correct, we might follow him to his conclusions, viz., that Job lived 2337 years before Christ! See at the end of this chapter.

Verse 10. *Great things past finding out*] Great things without end; wonders without number.—*Targum.*

Verse 11. *Lo, he goeth by me, and I see* him *not*] He is incomprehensible in all his ways, and in all his works; and he must be so if he be God, and *work* as God; for his own nature and his operations are past finding out.

Verse 12. *He taketh away*] He never *gives*, but he is ever *lending:* and while the gift is useful or is improved, he permits it to remain; but when it becomes useless or is misused, he recalls it.

Who can hinder him?] Literally, *Who can cause him to restore it?*

What dost thou?] He is supreme, and will give account of none of his matters. He is infinitely wise, and cannot mistake. He is infinitely kind, and can do nothing cruel. He is infinitely good, and can do nothing wrong. No one, therefore, should question either his motives or his operations.

A. M. cir. 2484 B. C. cir. 1520 Ante I. Olymp. cir. 744 Ante U. C. cir. 767

13 *If* God will not withdraw
his anger, [o]the [p]proud helpers
do stoop under him.
14 How much less shall I answer him, *and* choose out my words *to reason* with him?
15 [q]Whom, though I were righteous, *yet* would I not answer, *but* I would make supplication to my Judge.
16 If I had called, and he had answered me; *yet* would I not believe that he had hearkened unto my voice.
17 For he breaketh me with a tempest, and multiplieth my wounds [r]without cause.
18 He will not suffer me to take my breath, but filleth me with bitterness.

[o]Chap. xxvi. 12; Isa. xxx. 7——[p]Heb. *helpers of pride* or *strength*——[q]Chap. x. 15

19 If *I speak* of strength, lo
he is strong: and if of judgment,
who shall set me a time *to*
plead?
20 If I justify myself, mine own mouth shall condemn me: *if I say* I *am* perfect, it shall also prove me perverse.
21 *Though* I *were* perfect, *yet* would I not know my soul: I would despise my life.
22 This *is* one *thing,* therefore I said *it,* [s]He destroyeth the perfect and the wicked.
23 If the scourge slay suddenly, he will laugh at the trial of the innocent.
24 The earth is given into the hand of the wicked: [t]he covereth the faces of the judges thereof; if not, where, *and* who *is* he?

[r]Chap. ii. 3; xxxiv. 6——[s]Eccles. ix. 2, 3; Ezek. xxi. 3
[t]2 Sam. xv. 30; xix. 4; Jer. xiv. 4

Verse 13. If *God will not withdraw his anger*] It is of no use to contend with God; he cannot be successfully resisted; all his opposers must perish.

Verse 14. *How much less shall I answer*] I cannot contend with my Maker. He is the *Lawgiver* and the *Judge.* How shall I stand in judgment before *him?*

Verse 15. *Though I were righteous*] Though clear of all the crimes, public and secret, of which you accuse me, yet I would not dare to stand before his immaculate holiness. Man's holiness may profit man, but in the sight of the infinite purity of God it is nothing. Thus sung an eminent poet:—

"I loathe myself when God I see,
And into nothing fall;
Content that thou exalted be,
And Christ be all in all."

I would make supplication to my Judge.] Though not conscious of any sin, I should not think myself thereby justified; but would, from a conviction of the exceeding breadth of the commandment, and the limited nature of my own perfection, cry out, "Cleanse thou me from secret faults!"

Verse 16. *If I had called, and he had answered*] I could scarcely suppose, such is his majesty and such his holiness, that he could condescend to notice a being so *mean,* and in every respect so infinitely *beneath* his notice. These sentiments sufficiently confuted that slander of his friends, who said he was presumptuous, had not becoming notions of the majesty of God, and used blasphemous expressions against his sovereign authority.

Verse 17. *He breaketh me with a tempest*] The *Targum, Syriac,* and *Arabic* have this sense: *He powerfully smites even every hair of my head, and multiplies my wounds without cause.* That is, There is no reason known to myself, or to any man, why I should be thus most oppressively afflicted. It is, therefore, cruel, and inconsequent to assert that *I suffer for my crimes.*

Verse 18. *He will not suffer me to take my breath*] I have no respite in my afflictions; I suffer continually in my body, and my mind is incessantly harassed.

Verse 19. *If* I speak *of strength, lo,* he is *strong*] Human wisdom, power, and influence avail nothing before him.

Who shall set me a time] מי יועידני *mi yoideni,* "Who would be a witness for me?" or, Who would dare to appear in my behalf? Almost all the *terms* in this part of the speech of Job, from ver. 11 to ver. 24, are *forensic* or *juridical,* and are taken from *legal processes* and *pleadings* in their *gates* or *courts of justice.*

Verse 20. *If I justify myself*] God must have some reason for his conduct towards me; I therefore do not pretend to justify myself; the attempt to do it would be an insult to his majesty and justice. Though I am conscious of none of the crimes of which you accuse me; and know not *why* he contends with me; yet he must have some reason, and that reason he does not choose to explain.

Verse 21. Though *I* were *perfect*] Had I the fullest conviction that, in every thought, word, and deed, I were blameless before him, yet I would not plead this; nor would I think it any security for a life of ease and prosperity, or any proof that my days should be prolonged.

Verse 22. *This* is *one* thing] My own observation shows, that in the course of providence the righteous and the wicked have an equal lot; for when any sudden calamity comes, the *innocent* and the *guilty* fall alike. There may be a few exceptions, but they are very extraordinary, and very rare.

Verse 24. *The earth is given into the hand of the wicked*] Is it not most evident that the worst men possess most of this world's goods, and that the righteous are scarcely ever in power or affluence? This was the case in Job's time; it is the case still. Therefore *prosperity* and *adversity* in this life are no marks either of God's approbation or disapprobation.

He covereth the faces of the judges thereof] Or, *The faces of its decisions he shall cover.* God is often stated in Scripture as *doing* a thing

A. M. cir. 2484
B. C. cir. 1520
Ante I. Olymp. cir. 744
Ante U. C. cir. 767

25 Now [u]my days are swifter
than a post: they flee away, they
see no good.
26 They are passed away as
the [v]swift [w]ships: [x]as the eagle *that* hasteth
to the prey.
27 [y]If I say, I will forget my complaint,
I will leave off my heaviness, and comfort
myself:

28 [z]I am afraid of all my sorrows, I know that thou [a]wilt not
hold me innocent.
29 *If* I be wicked, why then
labour I in vain?
30 [b]If I wash myself with snow water, and
make my hands never so clean;
31 Yet shalt thou plunge me in the ditch,
and mine own clothes shall [c]abhor me.

[u]Chap. vii. 6, 7——[v]Heb. *ships of desire*——[w]Or, *ships of Ebeh*——[x]Hab. i. 8——[y]Chap. vii. 13

[z]Psa. cxix. 120——[a]Exod. xx. 7——[b]Jer. ii. 22——[c]Or, *make me to be abhorred*

which he only *permits* to be done. So he permits the eyes of judgment to be blinded; and hence false decisions. Mr. *Good* translates the verse thus:—

"The earth is given over to the hand of INJUSTICE;
She hoodwinketh the faces of its judges.
Where every one liveth is it not so?"

And vindicates the translation in his learned notes: but I think the Hebrew will not bear this rendering; especially that in the *third* line.

Where, and *who* is *he?*] If this be not the case, *who* is he that acts in this way, and *where* is he to be found? If God does not *permit* these things, who is it that *orders* them?

Coverdale translates, **As for the worlde, he geveth it over into the power of the wicked, such as the rulers be wherof all londes are full. Is it not so? Where is there eny, but he is soch one?** This sense is clear enough, if the original will bear it. The last clause is thus rendered by the *Syriac* and *Arabic, Who can bear his indignation?*

Verse 25. *Swifter than a post*] מני רץ *minni rats, than a runner.* The light-footed messenger or *courier* who carries messages from place to place.

They flee away] The *Chaldee* says, *My days are swifter than the shadow of a flying bird.* So swiftly do they flee away that I cannot discern them; and when past they cannot be recalled. There is a sentiment like this in VIRGIL, *Geor.* lib. iii., ver. 284:—

Sed FUGIT *interea,* FUGIT IRREPARABILE *tempus!*—
"But in the meanwhile time flies! irreparable time flies away!"

Verse 26. *As the swift ships*] אניות אבה *oniyoth ebeh. Ships of desire,* or *ships of Ebeh,* says our *margin;* perhaps more correctly, *inflated ships,* the sails bellying out with a fair brisk wind, tide favourable, and the vessels themselves lightly freighted.

The *Vulgate* has, *Like ships freighted with apples. Ships laden with the best fruits.*—TARGUM. *Ships well adapted for sailing.*—ARABIC. **Shipes that be good under sale.**—COVERDALE. Probably this relates to the light fast-sailing ships on the Nile, which were made of *reeds* or *papyrus.*

Perhaps the idea to be seized is not so much the *swiftness* of the passage, as their leaving *no trace* or *track* behind them. But instead of אבה *ebeh,* איבה *eybah, hostile ships* or the *ships of enemies,* is the reading of *forty-seven* of *Kennicott's* and *De Rossi's* MSS., and of the *Syriac* version. If this be the true reading, what is its sense? My days are gone off like the light vessels of the pirates, having stripped me of my property, and carried all irrecoverably away, under the strongest press of sail, that they may effect their escape, and secure their booty.

The next words, *As the eagle* that *hasteth to the prey,* seem at least to countenance, if not confirm, the above reading: the idea of *robbery* and *spoil, prompt attack* and *sudden retreat,* is preserved in both images.

Verse 27. *I will forget my complaint*] I will *forsake* or *forego* my complaining. *I will leave off my heaviness.* VULGATE, *I will change my countenance*—force myself to smile, and endeavour to assume the *appearance* of *comfort.*

Verse 28. *I am afraid of all my sorrows*] *Coverdale* translates, after the *Vulgate,* **Then am I afrayed of all my workes.** Even were I to cease from complaining, I fear lest not one of my works, however well intentioned, would stand thy scrutiny, or meet with thy approbation.

Thou wilt not hold me innocent.] *Coverdale,* after the *Vulgate,* **For I knowe thou favourest not an evil doer;** but this is not the sense of the original: Thou wilt not acquit me so as to take away my afflictions from me.

Verse 29. If *I be wicked*] If I am the sinner you suppose me to be, in vain should I labour to counterfeit joy, and cease to complain of my sufferings.

Verse 30. *If I wash myself with snow water*] Supposed to have a more detergent quality than common water; and it was certainly preferred to common water by the ancients. Of this we find an example in an elegant but licentious author: *Tandem ergo discubuimus, pueris Alexandrinis* AQUAM *in manus* NIVATAM *infundentibus, aliisque insequentibus ad pedes.*—PETR. *Satyr.,* cap. xxxi. "At length we sat down, and had *snow water* poured on our hands by lads of Alexandria," &c.

Mr. *Good* supposes that there is an allusion here to the ancient rite of *washing the hands* in token of *innocence.* See Psa. xxvi. 6: *I will* WASH *my hands in* INNOCENCY; and lxxiii. 13: *Verily I have cleansed my heart in vain, and* WASHED *my* HANDS IN INNOCENCY. And by this ceremony *Pilate* declared himself *innocent* of the blood of Christ, Matt. xxvii. 24.

Verse 31. *And mine own clothes shall abhor me.*] Such is thine infinite purity, when put in opposition to the purity of man, that it will bear no comparison. Searched and tried by the

A. M. cir. 2484
B. C. cir. 1520
Ante I. Olymp. cir. 744
Ante U. C. cir. 767

32 For [d]*he is* not a man as
I *am, that* I should answer him,
and we should come together in
judgment.
33 [e]Neither is there [f]any [g]day's-man betwixt us, *that* might lay his hand upon us both.
34 [h]Let him take his rod
away from me, and let not his
fear terrify me:
35 *Then* would I speak,
and not fear him; [i]but *it is* not so with
me.

[d]Eccles. vi. 10; Isa. xlv. 9; Jer. xlix. 19; Rom. ix. 20
[e]Ver. 19; 1 Sam. ii. 25——[f]Heb. *one that should argue*
[g]Or, *umpire*——[h]Chap. xiii. 20, 21, 22; xxxiii. 7; Psa. xxxix. 10——[i]Heb. *but I am not so with myself*

eye of God, I should be found as a *leper*, so that my *own clothes* would dread to touch me, for fear of being infected by my corruption. This is a strong and bold figure; and is derived from the corrupted state of his *body*, which his clothes dreaded to touch, because of the contagious nature of his disorder.

Verse 32. *For he is not a man as I am*] I cannot contend with him as with one of my fellows in a court of justice.

Verse 33. *Neither is there any day's-man*] בינינו מוכיח *beyneynu mochiach, a reprover, arguer*, or *umpire between us*. DAY'S-MAN, in our law, means an arbitrator, or umpire between party and party; as it were bestowing a *day*, or certain time on a *certain day*, to decree, judge, or decide a matter.—*Minshieu*. DAY is used in law for the *day of appearance in court*, either originally or upon assignation, for hearing a matter for trial.—*Idem*. But *arbitrator* is the proper meaning of the term here: one who is, by the consent of both parties, to judge between them, and settle their differences.

Instead of לא יש *lo yesh, there is not*, fifteen of *Kennicott's* and *De Rossi's* MSS., with the *Septuagint, Syriac*, and *Arabic*, read לו יש *lu yesh, I wish there were:* or, *O that there were!* Ειθε ην ὁ μεσιτης ἡμων, και ελεγχων και διακουων αναμεσον αμφοτερων; *O that we had a mediator, an advocate, and judge between us both!*—SEPT. Poor Job! He did not yet know the *Mediator* between God and man: the only means by which God and man can be brought together and reconciled. Had St. Paul this in his eye when he wrote 1 Tim. ii. 5, 6? *For there is one God, and one Mediator between God and men, the man Christ Jesus; who gave himself a ransom for all.* Without this *Mediator*, and the *ransom price* which he has laid down, God and man can never be united: and that this union might be made possible, Jesus took the human into conjunction with his Divine nature; and thus *God was manifest in the flesh.*

Verse 34. *Let him take his rod away*] In the Masoretic Bibles, the word שבטו *shibto, his rod*, is written with a large ט *teth*, as above; and as the letter in numerals stands for 9, the *Masora* says the word was thus written to show the *nine calamities* under which Job had suffered, and which he wished God to remove.

As שבט *shebet* signifies, not only *rod*, but also *sceptre* or the *ensign of royalty*, Job might here refer to God sitting in his majesty upon the judgment-seat; and this sight so appalled him, that, filled with terror, he was unable to speak. When a sinful soul sees God in his majesty, terror seizes upon it, and prayer is impossible. We have a beautiful illustration of this, Isa. vi. 1-5: "I saw the Lord sitting upon a throne, high and lifted up, and his train filled the temple. Then said I, Wo is me, for I am undone, because I am a man of unclean lips; for mine eyes have seen the King, the Lord of hosts."

Verse 35. *But it is not so with me.*] I am not in such circumstances as to plead with my Judge. I believe the sense of these words is nearly as *Coverdale* has expressed it:—**For as longe as I am in soch fearfulnesse, I can make no answere.** A natural picture of the state of a penitent soul, which needs no additional colouring.

ON the names of the constellations mentioned ver. 9, and again chap. xxxviii. 31, &c., much has been written, and to little effect. I have already, in the notes, expressed my doubts whether any constellation be intended. Dr. *Hales*, however, finds in these names, as he thinks, astronomical data, by which he ascertains the time of Job. I shall give his words:—

"The cardinal constellations of spring and autumn, in *Job's* time, were *Chimah*, and *Chesil* or *Taurus*, and *Scorpio;* noticed ix. 9, and again, xxxviii. 31, 32; of which the principal stars are, *Aldebaran*, the bull's eye, and *Antares*, the scorpion's heart. Knowing, therefore, the longitudes of these stars, at present, the interval of time from thence to the assumed date of *Job's* trial will give the difference of the longitudes; and ascertain their positions then, with respect to the vernal and autumnal points of intersection of the equinoctial and ecliptic; according to the usual rate of the *precession of the equinoxes*, one degree in 71 years. See that article, vol. i., p. 185.

"The following calculations I owe to the kindness and skill of the respectable *Dr. Brinkley*, *Andrew's* Professor of Astronomy in the University of Dublin.

"In A. D. 1800 *Aldebaran* was in 2 signs, 7 degrees, east longitude. But since the date of *Job's* trial, B. C. 2338, i. e., 4138 years, the precession of the equinoxes amounted to 1 sign, 27 degrees, 53 minutes; which, being subtracted from the former quantity, left *Aldebaran* in only 9 degrees, 7 minutes longitude, or distance from the *vernal* intersection; which, falling within the constellation *Taurus*, consequently rendered it the cardinal constellation of *spring*, as *Pisces* is at present.

"In A. D. 1800 *Antares* was in 8 signs, 6 degrees, 58 minutes, east longitude; or 2 signs, 6 degrees, 58 minutes, east of the *autumnal* intersection: from which subtracting as before the amount of the precession, *Antares* was left only 9 degrees, 5 minutes east. Since then, the autumnal equinox was found within *Scorpio*, this was the cardinal constellation of *autumn*, as *Virgo* is at present.

"Such a combination and coincidence of various rays of evidence, derived from widely different sources, *history*, sacred and profane, *chronology*, and *astronomy*, and all converging to the same focus, tend strongly to establish the time of *Job's* trial, as rightly assigned to the year B. C. 2337, or 818 years after the deluge, 184 years before the birth of Abram; 474 years before the settlement of *Jacob's* family in *Egypt;* and 689 years before their *exode* or departure from thence." *New Analysis of Chronology*, vol. ii., p. 57.

Now all this is specious; and, were the *foundation* sound, we might rely on the permanence of the building, though the rains should descend, the floods come, and the winds blow and beat on that house. But all these deductions and conclusions are founded on the *assumption* that *Chimah* and *Chesil* mean *Taurus* and *Scorpio:* but this is the very point that is to be proved; for proof of this is not offered, nor, indeed, can be offered; and such assumptions are palpably nugatory. That עש *ash* has been generally understood to signify the *Great Bear;* כסיל *Kesil, Orion;* and כימה *Kimah*, the *Pleiades;* may be seen everywhere: but that they do signify these constellations is perfectly uncertain. We have only conjectures concerning their meaning; and on such conjectures no *system* can be built. Genuine *data*, in Dr. *Hales's* hands, are sure to be conducted to legitimate conclusions: but neither he nor any one else can construct an astronomical fabric in the limbus of conjecture. *When* JOB lived is perfectly uncertain: but that this book was written 818 years after the deluge; 184 years before the birth of Abram, and 689 years before the exodus; and that all this is demonstrable from *Chimah* and *Chesil* signifying *Taurus* and *Scorpio*, whence the positions of the equinoxes at the time of Job's trial can be ascertained; can never be proved, and should never be credited.

In what many learned men have written on this subject, I find as much solidity and satisfaction as from what is piously and gravely stated in the *Glossa Ordinaria:—*

Qui facit Arcturum. Diversæ sunt constellationes, varios status *ecclesiæ signantes. Per* Arcturum, *qui semper super orizontem nostrum apparet, significatur status* apostolorum *qui in* episcopis *remanet. Per* Oriona, *qui est tempestatis signum, significatur status* martyrum. *Per* Hyadas, *quæ significant* pluvios, *status* doctorum *doctrinæ pluvium effundentium. Per* interiora austri, *quæ sunt nobis occulta, status* Anachoretarum, *hominum aspectus declinantium.* "These different constellations signify *various states* of the Church. By *Arcturus*, which always appears above our horizon, is signified the *apostolic state*, which still remains in *episcopacy*. By *Orion*, which is a tempestuous sign, is signified the *state* of the *martyrs*. By the *Hyades*, (kids,) which indicate rain, the *state* of the *doctors*, pouring out the rain of doctrine, is signified. And by the *inner chambers of the south*, which are hidden from us, the *state* of the *Anchorets* (hermits) is signified, who always shun the sight of men."

Much more of the same allegorical matter may be found in the same place, the *Glossa Ordinaria* of *Strabus* of *Fulda*, on the ninth chapter of Job. But how unreal and empty are all these things! What an *uncertain* sound do such trumpets give!

CHAPTER X

Job is weary of life, and expostulates with God, 1–6. *He appeals to God for his innocence; and pleads on the weakness of his frame, and the manner of his formation*, 7–13. *Complains of his sufferings, and prays for respite*, 14–20. *Describes the state of the dead*, 21, 22.

A. M. cir. 2484 B. C. cir. 1520 Ante I. Olymp. cir. 744 Ante U. C. cir. 767

MY [a]soul is [b]weary of my
life; I will leave my complaint upon myself; [c]I will
speak in the bitterness of my
soul.
2 I will say unto God, Do not condemn me;
show me wherefore thou contendest with me.
3 *Is it* good unto thee that
thou shouldest oppress, that thou
shouldest despise [d]the work of thine hands,
and shine upon the counsel of the wicked?

A. M. cir. 2484 B. C. cir. 1520 Ante I. Olymp. cir. 744 Ante U. C. cir. 767

[a]1 Kings xix. 4; chap. vii. 16; Jonah iv. 3, 8——[b]Or, *cut off while I live*

[c]Chap. vii. 11——[d]Heb. *the labour of thine hands?* Psa. cxxxviii. 8; Isa. lxiv. 8

NOTES ON CHAP. X

Verse 1. *My soul is weary of my life*] Here is a proof that נפש *nephesh* does not signify the animal life, but the soul or immortal mind, as distinguished from חי *chai*, that animal life; and is a strong proof that Job believed in the distinction between these two principles; was no materialist; but, on the contrary, credited the proper immortality of the soul. This is worthy of observation. See chap. xii. 10.

I will leave my complaint] I will charge myself with the cause of my own calamities; and shall not charge my Maker foolishly: but I must deplore my wretched and forlorn state.

Verse 2. *Do not condemn me*] Let me not be afflicted in thy wrath.

Show me wherefore thou contendest] If I am afflicted because of my sins, show me what that sin is. God never afflicts but for past sin, or to try his followers; or for the greater manifestation of his grace in their support and deliverance.

Verse 3. Is it *good unto thee*] Surely it can be no gratification to thee to distress the children of men, as if thou didst despise the work of thy own hands.

And shine upon the counsel] For by my afflictions the harsh judgments of the wicked will appear to be confirmed: viz., that God regards

A. M. cir. 2484 B. C. cir. 1520 Ante I. Olymp. cir. 744 Ante U. C. cir. 767

4 Hast thou eyes of flesh? or [e]seest thou as man seeth?
5 *Are* thy days as the days of man? *are* thy years as man's days,
6 That thou inquirest after mine iniquity, and searchest after my sin?
7 [f]Thou [g]knowest that I am not wicked; and *there is* none that can deliver out of thine hand.
8 [h]Thine hands [i]have made me and fashioned me together round about; yet thou dost destroy me.
9 Remember, I beseech thee, that [k]thou hast made me as the clay; and wilt thou bring me into dust again?
10 [l]Hast thou not poured me out as milk, and curdled me like cheese?
11 Thou hast clothed me with skin and flesh, and hast [m]fenced me with bones and sinews.
12 Thou hast granted me life and favour, and thy visitation hath preserved my spirit.
13 And these *things* hast thou hid in thine

[e]1 Sam. xvi. 7——[f]Heb. It is *upon thy knowledge* [g]Psa. cxxxix. 1, 2——[h]Psa. cxix. 73

[i]Heb. *took pains about me*——[k]Gen. ii. 7; iii. 19; Isa. lxiv. 8——[l]Psa. cxxxix. 14, 15, 16——[m]Heb. *hedged*

not his most fervent worshippers; and it is no benefit to lead a religious life.

Verse 4. *Hast thou eyes of flesh?*] Dost thou judge as *man* judges? Illustrated by the next clause, *Seest thou as man seeth?*

Verse 5. Are *thy days as the days of man*] אנוש *enosh, wretched, miserable man. Thy years as man's days;* גבר *gaber, the strong man.* Thou art not short-lived, like man in his present imperfect state; nor can the years of the long-lived patriachs be compared with thine. The difference of the phraseology in the original justifies this view of the subject. Man in his *low estate* cannot be likened unto thee; nor can he in his *greatest excellence*, though made in thy own image and likeness, be compared to thee.

Verse 6. *That thou inquirest*] Is it becoming thy infinite dignity to concern thyself so much with the affairs or transgressions of a despicable mortal? A word spoken in the heart of most sinners.

Verse 7. *Thou knowest that I am not wicked*] While thou hast this knowledge of me and my conduct, why appear to be sifting me as if in order to find out sin; and though none can be found, treating me as though I were a transgressor?

Verse 8. *Thine hands have made me*] Thou art well acquainted with human nature, for thou art its author.

And fashioned me together round about] All my powers and faculties have been planned and executed by thyself. It is thou who hast refined the materials out of which I have been formed, and modified them into that excellent symmetry and order in which they are now found; so that the *union* and *harmony* of the different parts, (יחד *yachad,*) and their arrangement and *completion,* (סביב *sabib,*) proclaim equally thy wisdom, skill, power, and goodness.

Yet thou dost destroy me.] ותבלעני *vatteballeeni,* "and thou wilt swallow me up." Men generally care for and prize those works on which they have spent most time, skill, and pains: but, although thou hast formed me with such incredible skill and labour, yet thou art about to destroy me! How dreadful an evil must sin be, when, on its account, God has pronounced the sentence of death on all mankind; and that body, so curiously and skilfully formed, must be decomposed, and reduced to dust!

Verse 9. *Thou hast made me as the clay*] Thou hast fashioned me, according to thy own mind, out of a mass of clay: after so much skill and pains expended, men might naturally suppose they were to have a permanent being; but thou hast decreed to turn them into dust!

Verse 10. *Hast thou not poured me out as milk*] After all that some learned men have said on this subject, in order to confine the images here to simple *nutrition*, I am satisfied that *generation* is the true notion. *Respicit ad* fetus *in* matris utero *primam formationem, quum in embryonem ex* utriusque *parentis* semine *coalescit.—Ex* semine liquido, lac *quodammodo* referente, *me formasti.—In interpretando, inquit Hieronymus, omnino his accedo qui de* genitali semine *accipiunt, quod ipsa tanquam natura* emulget, *ac dein concrescere in utero ac coalescere jubet.* I make no apology for leaving this untranslated.

The different expressions in this and the following verse are very appropriate: *the pouring out like milk*—coagulating, *clothing with skin and flesh, fencing with bones* and *sinews,* are well imagined, and delicately, and at the same time forcibly, expressed.

If I believed that Job referred to *nutrition,* which I do not, I might speak of the *chyle,* the *chylopoietic* organs, the *lacteal* vessels, and the generation of all the solids and fluids from this substance, which itself is derived from the food taken into the *stomach.* But this process, properly speaking, does not take place till the human being is brought into the world, it being previously nourished by the *mother* by means of the *funis umbilicus,* without that action of the *stomach* by which the *chyle* is prepared.

Verse 12. *Thou hast granted me life and favour*] Thou hast brought me from my mother's womb; given me an actual existence among men; by thy favour or mercy thou hast provided me with the means of life; and *thy visitation*—thy continual providential care, has *preserved* me *in life*—has given me the air I breathe, and furnished me with those powers which enable me to respire it as an agent and preserver of life. It is by God's continued visitation or influence that the life of any man is preserved; *in him we live, move, and have our being.*

Verse 13. *And these* things *hast thou hid in thine heart*] Thou hast had many gracious purposes concerning me which thou hast not made known; but thy visitations and mercy are

A. M. cir. 2484
B. C. cir. 1520
Ante I. Olymp. cir. 744
Ante U. C. cir. 767

heart: I know that this *is* with
thee.
14 If I sin, then [n]thou mark-
est me, and thou wilt not acquit
me from mine iniquity.
15 If I be wicked, [o]wo unto me; [p]and *if*
I be righteous, *yet* will I not lift up my head.
I am full of confusion; therefore [q]see thou
mine affliction;
16 For it increaseth. [r]Thou huntest me as
a fierce lion: and again thou showest thyself
marvellous upon me.
17 Thou renewest [s]thy witnesses against
me, and increasest thine indignation upon me;
changes and war *are* against me.

18 [t]Wherefore then hast thou
brought me forth out of the
womb? O that I had given up
the ghost, and no eye had seen me!
19 I should have been as though I had not
been; I should have been carried from the
womb to the grave.
20 [u]*Are* not my days few? [v]cease *then, and*
[w]let me alone, that I may take comfort a little,
21 Before I go *whence* I shall not return,
[x]*even* to the land of darkness [y]and the shadow of death;
22 A land of darkness, as darkness *itself;*
and of the shadow of death, without any
order, and *where* the light *is* as darkness.

[n]Psa. cxxxix. 1——[o]Isa. iii. 11——[p]Chap. ix. 12, 15, 20, 21——[q]Psa. xxv. 18——[r]Isa. xxxviii. 13; Lam. iii. 10 [s]That is, *thy plagues*, Ruth i. 21

[t]Chap. iii. 11——[u]See chap. vii. 6, 16; viii. 9; Psa. xxxix. 5——[v]Psa. xxxix. 13——[w]Chap. vii. 16, 19 [x]Psa. lxxxviii. 12——[y]Psa. xxiii. 4

sufficient proofs of kindness towards me; though for purposes unknown to me thou hast sorely afflicted me, and continuest to treat me as an enemy.

Verse 14. *If I sin*] From thee nothing can be hidden; if I sin, thou takest account of the transgression, and canst not hold me for innocent when thou knowest I am guilty.

Verse 15. *If I be wicked*] I must meet with that punishment that is due to the workers of iniquity.

If *I be righteous*] I am only in the state which my duty to my Creator requires me to be in; and I cannot therefore suppose that on this account I can deserve any thing by way of *favour* from the justice of my Maker.

I am *full of confusion*] I am confounded at my state and circumstances. I know that thou art merciful, and dost not afflict willingly the children of men; I know I have not wickedly departed from thee; and yet I am treated by thee as if I were an apostate from every good. I am therefore full of confusion. See thou to my affliction; and bring me out of it in such a way as shall at once prove my innocence, the righteousness of thy ways, and the mercy of thy nature.

Verse 16. *For it increaseth.*] Probably this refers to the *affliction* mentioned above, which is increased in proportion to its duration. Every day made his escape from such a load of evils less and less probable.

Thou huntest me as a fierce lion] As the hunters attack the king of beasts in the forest, so my friends attack me. They assail me on every side.

Thou showest thyself marvellous] Thy designs, thy ways, thy works, are all incomprehensible to me; thou dost both confound and overpower me. Mr. *Good* translates thus:—

"For uprousing as a ravenous lion dost thou
spring upon me.
And again thou showest over me thy vast
power."

Verse 17. *Thou renewest thy witnesses*] In this speech of Job he is ever referring to *trials in courts of judicature,* and almost all his terms are *forensic.* Thou bringest witnesses in continual succession to confound and convict me.

Changes and war] I am as if attacked by successive troops; one company being wearied, another succeeds to the attack, so that I am harassed by continual warfare.

Verse 18. *Wherefore then*] Why didst thou give me a being, when thou didst foresee I should be exposed to such incredible hardships? See on chap. iii. 10, &c.

Verse 19. *I should have been as though*] Had I given up the ghost as soon as born, as I could not then have been conscious of existence, it would have been, as it respects myself, as though I had never been; being immediately transported from my mother's womb to the grave.

Verse 20. Are *not my days few?*] My life cannot be long; let me have a little respite before I die.

Verse 21. *I shall not return*] I shall not return again from the *dust* to have a dwelling among *men.*

To the land of darkness] See the notes on chap. iii. 5. There are here a crowd of obscure and dislocated terms, admirably expressive of the obscurity and uncertainty of the subject. What do we know of the state of separate spirits? What do we know of the spiritual world? How do souls exist separate from their respective bodies? Of what are they capable, and what is their employment? Who can answer these questions? Perhaps nothing can be said much better of the state than is here said, *a land of obscurity, like darkness.*

The shadow of death] A place where death rules, over which he projects his shadow, intercepting every light of every kind of life.

Without any order, ולא סדרים *velo sedarim,* having no arrangements, no distinctions of inhabitants; the poor and the rich are there, the master and his slave, the king and the beggar, their bodies in equal corruption and disgrace, their souls distinguished only by their moral character. Stripped of their flesh, they stand in their naked simplicity before God in that place.

Verse 22. Where *the light* is *as darkness.*]

A palpable obscure: it is space and place, and has only such light or capability of distinction as renders "darkness visible." The following words of *Sophocles* convey the same idea: Ιω σκοτος εμοι φαος; "Thou darkness be my light." It is, as the *Vulgate* expresses it, *Terra tenebrosa, et operta mortis caligine: Terra miseriæ et tenebrarum, ubi umbra mortis, et nullus ordo, sed sempiternus horror inhabitat:* "A murky land, covered with the thick darkness of death: a land of wretchedness and obscurities, where is the shadow of death, and no order, but sempiternal horror dwells everywhere." Or, as *Coverdale* expresses this last clause, **Whereas is no ordre but terrible feare as in the darknesse.** A *duration* not characterized or measured by any of the attributes of time; where there is *no order* of darkness and light, night and day, heat and cold, summer and winter. It is the *state of the dead!* The *place of separate spirits!* It is *out of time, out of probation, beyond change* or *mutability.* It is on the *confines* of *eternity!* But *what* is THIS? and *where? Eternity!* how can I form any conception of thee? In thee there is no order, no bounds, no substance, no progression, no change, no past, no present, no future! Thou art an indescribable something, to which there is no analogy in the compass of creation. Thou art infinity and incomprehensibility to all finite beings. Thou art what, living, I know not, and what I must die to know; and even then I shall apprehend no more of thee than merely that thou art E-T-E-R-N-I-T-Y!

CHAPTER XI

Zophar answers Job, and reproves him severely for his attempts to justify himself; charges him with secret iniquity, and contends that God inflicts less punishment on him than his iniquities deserve, 1–6. *Shows the knowledge and perfections of God to be unsearchable, and that none can resist his power,* 7–11. *Warns him against vanity of mind, and exhorts him to repentance on the ground that his acceptance with God is still a possible case, and that his latter days may yet become happy and prosperous,* 12–20.

A. M. cir. 2484
B. C. cir. 1520
Ante I. Olymp. cir. 744
Ante U. C. cir. 767

THEN answered Zophar the
Naamathite, and said,
2 Should not the multitude of
words be answered? and should
[a]a man full of talk be justified?
3 Should thy [b]lies make men hold their
peace? and when thou mockest, shall no man
make thee ashamed?
4 For [c]thou hast said, My
doctrine *is* pure, and I am clean
in thine eyes.
5 But O that God would speak,
and open his lips against thee;
6 And that he would show thee the secrets
of wisdom, that *they are* double to that which
is! Know therefore that [d]God exacteth of

[a]Heb. *a man of lips*——[b]Or, *devices*

[c]Chap. vi. 10; x. 7——[d]Ezra ix. 13

NOTES ON CHAP. XI

Verse 1. *Zophar the Naamathite*] Of this man and his friends, see chap. ii. 11. He is the most inveterate of Job's accusers, and generally speaks without feeling or pity. In *sour godliness* he excelled all the rest. This chapter and the twentieth comprehends all that he said. He was too crooked to speak much in measured verse.

Verse 2. *Should not the multitude of words be answered?*] Some translate, "To multiply words profiteth nothing."

And should a man full of talk be justified] איש שפתים *ish sephathayim,* "a man of lips," a proper appellation for a great talker: he is "a man of lips," i. e., his *lips* are the only active parts of his system.

Verse 3. *Should thy lies make men hold their peace?*] This is a very severe reproof, and not justified by the occasion.

And when thou mockest] As thou despisest others, shall no man put thee to scorn? Zophar could never think that the solemn and awful manner in which Job spoke could be called *bubbling,* as some would translate the term לעג *laag.* He might consider Job's speech as *sarcastic* and *severe,* but he could not consider it as *nonsense.*

Verse 4. *My doctrine* is *pure*] לקחי *likchi,* "my assumptions." What I assume or take as right, and just, and true, are so; the precepts which I have formed, and the practice which I have founded on them, are all correct and perfect. Job had not exactly said, *My doctrine* and *way of life are pure,* and *I am clean in thine eyes;* but he had vindicated himself from their charges of *secret sins* and *hypocrisy,* and appealed to God for his general uprightness and sincerity: but Zophar here begs the question, in order that he may have something to say, and room to give vent to his invective.

Verse 5. *But O that God would speak*] How little feeling, humanity, and charity is there in this prayer!

Verse 6. *The secrets of wisdom*] All the depths of his own counsels; the heights, lengths, and breadths, of holiness. *That they are double to that which is.* תושיה *tushiyah,* which we translate *that which is,* is a word frequent in *Job* and in the *Book of Proverbs,* and is one of the evidences brought in favour of *Solomon* as the author of this book. It signifies *substance* or *essence,* and is translated by a great variety of terms; enterprise, completeness, substance, the whole constitution, wisdom, law, sound wisdom, solid complete happiness, solidity of reason and truth, the complete total sum, &c., &c. See Taylor's Hebrew and English Concord., under ישה. In this place the versions are various. *Coverdale,* following the *Vulgate,* translates: **That he might shewe the (out of his secrite wissdome) how manyfolde his lawe is.** The *Septuagint,* ὁτι διπλους εσται των κατα σε, *that*

A. M. cir. 2484
B. C. cir. 1520
Ante I. Olymp. cir. 744
Ante U. C. cir. 767

thee *less* than thine iniquity *deserveth.*
7 [e]Canst thou by searching
find out God? canst thou find out
the Almighty unto perfection?
8 *It is* [f]as high as heaven; what canst thou
do? deeper than hell; what canst thou know?
9 The measure thereof *is* longer than the
earth, and broader than the sea.

10 [g]If he [h]cut off, and shut up,
or gather together, then [i]who can
hinder him?
11 For [k]he knoweth vain men:
he seeth wickedness also; will he not then
consider *it?*
12 For [l]vain [m]man would be wise, though
man be born *like* a wild ass's colt.
13 [n]If thou [o]prepare thine heart, and

A. M. cir. 2484
B. C. cir. 1520
Ante I. Olymp. cir. 744
Ante U. C. cir. 767

---

[e]Eccles. iii. 11; Rom. xi. 33——[f]Heb. *the heights of heaven*——[g]Ch. ix. 12; xii. 14; Rev. iii. 7——[h]Or, *make a change*——[i]Heb. *who can turn him away?* chap. ix. 12

[k]Psa. x. 11, 14; xxxv. 22; xciv. 11——[l]Heb. *empty* [m]Psa. lxxiii. 22; xcii. 6; Eccles. iii. 18; Rom. i. 22 [n]Chap. v. 8; xxii. 21——[o]1 Sam. vii. 3; Psa. lxxviii. 8

---

it is double to what it is with thee. Mr. *Good* translates, "For they are intricacies to INIQUITY." This is a meaning never before given to תושיה *tushiyah*, and a meaning which even his own learned note will not make generally prevalent. Perhaps Zophar is here, in mind, comparing the wisdom which has been *revealed* with the wisdom *not revealed.* The perfection and excellence of the Divine nature and the purity of his law, are, in substance and essence, double or manifold to the revelation already made.

Less *than thine iniquity* deserveth.] Mr. *Good* translates, *And the knowledge hath withdrawn from thee because of thy sins;* and represents Zophar as praying that God would reveal to him the secrets of wisdom, and the knowledge which he had withdrawn from him because of his transgressions. That Zophar intends to insinuate that God afflicted Job because of his iniquities, is evident; and that he thought that God had inflicted less chastisement upon him than his sins deserved, is not less so; and that, therefore, Job's complaining of harsh treatment was not at all well founded.

Verse 7. *Canst thou by searching find out God?*] What is God? A Being self-existent, eternal, infinite, immense, without bounds, incomprehensible either by mind, or time, or space. Who then can find this Being out? Who can fathom his depths, ascend to his heights, extend to his breadths, and comprehend the infinitude of his perfections?

Verse 8. It is *as high as heaven*] High as the heavens, what canst thou work? Deep below *sheol,* (the invisible world,) what canst thou know? Long beyond the earth, and broad beyond the sea, is its measure. These are instances in the immensity of created things, and all out of the reach of human power and knowledge; and if these things are so, how incomprehensible must he be, who designed, created, preserves, and governs the whole!

We find the same thought in Milton:—

"These are thy glorious works, Parent of good!
Almighty! Thine this universal frame:
How wondrous fair! Thyself how wondrous then!"

Verse 10. *If he cut off*] As he is unlimited and almighty, he cannot be *controlled.* He will do whatsoever he pleases; and he is pleased with nothing but what is *right.* Who then will dare to find fault? Perhaps Zophar may refer to Job's former state, his losses and afflictions. *If he cut off,* as he has done, thy children; *if he shut up,* as he has done, thyself by this sore *disease;* or *gather together* hostile bands to invade thy territories and carry away thy property; who can hinder him? He is sovereign, and has a right to dispose of his own property as he pleases.

Verse 11. *He knoweth vain men*] מתי שוא *methey shav,* "men of falsehood."

He seeth wickedness] He sees as well what is *in man,* as what man *does;* and of his actions and propensities he cannot be an indifferent spectator.

Verse 12. *For vain man would be wise*] The original is difficult and uncertain, ואיש נבוב ילבב *veish nabub yillabeb,* "And shall the hollow man assume courage," or "pride himself?" Or, as Mr. *Good* rather paraphrases it, *Will he then accept the hollow-hearted person?* The *Chaldee* gives *two* renderings: *An eloquent man shall become wiser in his heart, and the colt of the wild ass is born as the son of man.* Or, *The wise man shall ponder it; and the refractory youth, who at last becomes prudent, shall make a great man.* *Coverdale:*—**A vayne body exalteth him self; and the son of man is like a wylde asse's foale.** *Houbigant* translates thus:—*A man who hath understanding will become prudent; but he who is as the wild ass hath no heart,* i. e., *sense.* According to this critic, the meaning is this:—A man of sense, should he at any time transgress, will learn wisdom from it; but a man of a brutish mind, uncultivated and unreflecting, will plunge yet deeper into iniquity.

Though man be born like *a wild ass's colt*] Is translated by Mr. *Good, Or shall the wild ass colt assume the man?* This is making a sense, but such as I fear the original will never allow. There is no end to the translations of this verse, and conjectures relative to its meaning. I shall conclude with the *Vulgate:*—*Vir vanus in superbiam erigitur, et tanquam pullum onagri se liberum natum putat,* "Vain man is puffed up with pride; and he supposes himself to be born free like the wild ass's colt." Man is full of self-conceit; and imagines himself born to act as he pleases, to roam at large, to be under no control, and to be accountable to none for his actions.

Verse 13. *If thou prepare thine heart*] Make use of the powers which God has given thee, and be determined to seek him with all thy soul.

And stretch out thine hands toward him] Making fervent prayer and supplication, putting away *iniquity* out of thy *hand,* and not permitting *wickedness to dwell in thy tabernacle;* then

A. M. cir. 2484
B. C. cir. 1520
Ante I. Olymp. cir. 744
Ante U. C. cir. 767

[p]stretch out thine hands toward
him;
14 If iniquity *be* in thine hand,
put it far away, and [q]let not
wickedness dwell in thy tabernacles.
15 [r]For then shalt thou lift up thy face
without spot; yea, thou shalt be steadfast,
and shalt not fear:
16 Because thou shalt [s]forget *thy* misery,
and remember *it* as waters *that* pass
away:
17 And *thine* age [t]shall [u]be clearer than
the noonday; thou shalt shine
forth, thou shalt be as the morning.

A. M. cir. 2484
B. C. cir. 1520
Ante I. Olymp. cir. 744
Ante U. C. cir. 767

18 And thou shalt be secure,
because there is hope; yea, thou shalt dig *about*
thee, and [v]thou shalt take thy rest in safety.
19 Also thou shalt lie down, and none shall
make *thee* afraid; yea, many shall [w]make
suit unto thee.
20 But [x]the eyes of the wicked shall fail,
and [y]they shall not escape, and [z]their hope
shall be as [a]the giving up of the ghost.

---

[p]Psa. lxxxviii. 9; cxliii. 6——[q]Psa. ci. 3——[r]See Gen. iv. 5, 6; chap. xxii. 26; Psa. cxix. 6; 1 John iii. 21——[s]Isa. lxv. 16——[t]Heb. *shall arise above the noonday*——[u]Psa. xxxvii. 6; cxii. 4; Isa. lviii. 8, 10

[v]Lev. xxvi. 5, 6; Psalm iii. 5; iv. 8; Proverbs iii. 24——[w]Heb. *entreat thy face;* Psa. xlv. 12——[x]Lev. xxvi. 16; Deut. xxviii. 65——[y]Heb. *flight shall perish from them*——[z]Ch. viii. 14; xviii. 14; Prov. xi. 7——[a]Or, *a puff of breath*

---

thou shalt *lift up thy face without a blush*, thou wilt become *established*, and *have nothing to fear*, ver. 14, 15.

There is a sentiment in Prov. xvi. 1, very similar to that in the 13th verse, which we translate very improperly:—

לאדם מערכי לב *leadam maarchey leb.*
To man are the preparations of the heart:
ומיהוה מענה לשון *umeyehovah maaneh lashon.*
But from Jehovah is the answer to the tongue.

It is man's duty to pray; it is God's prerogative to answer. Zophar, like all the rest, is true to his principle. Job must be a wicked man, else he had not been afflicted. There must be some iniquity in his hand, and some wickedness tolerated in his family. So they all supposed.

Verse 16. *Because thou shalt forget* thy *misery*] Thou shalt have such long and complete rest, that thou shalt scarcely remember thy *labour*.

As waters that *pass away*] Like as the mountain floods, which sweep every thing before them, houses, tents, cattle, and the produce of the field, and are speedily absorbed by the sandy plains over which they run; so shalt thou remember thy sufferings: they were wasting and ruinous for the time, but were soon over and gone.

Verse 17. Thine *age shall be clearer than the noonday*] The *rest of thy life* shall be unclouded prosperity.

Thou shalt shine forth] Thou shalt be in this unclouded state, as the sun in the firmament of heaven, giving light and heat to all around thee.

Thou shalt be as the morning.] Thus the sun of thy prosperity shall arise, and shine more and more unto the perfect day. This is the image which the sacred writer employs, and it is correct and elegant.

Verse 18. *And thou shalt be secure*] Thou shalt not fear any farther evils to disturb thy prosperity, for thou shalt have a well-grounded *hope* and confidence that thou shalt no more be visited by adversity.

Yea, thou shalt dig] I believe this neither refers to *digging his* grave, nor to *curiously investigating* surrounding circumstances; but to the custom of *digging for water* in the places where they pitched their tents. It was a matter of high importance in Asiatic countries to find good wells of wholesome water; and they were frequently causes of contention among neighbouring chiefs, who sometimes stopped them up, and at other times seized them as their own. Through envy of Isaac's prosperity the Philistines stopped up all the wells which Abraham had digged, Gen. xxvi. 12-16. And we find the herdsmen of Gerar contending with Isaac's servants about the wells which the latter had digged; so that they were obliged to abandon two of the chief of them, and remove to a distance in order to dig and find quiet possession. See Gen. xxxi. 17-22. Zophar, in reference to all these sorts of contentions and petty wars about *wells* and *springs*, tells Job that in the state of prosperity to which he shall be brought by the good providence of God, he shall *dig*—find wells of living water; none shall contend with him; and he shall rest in safety, all the neighbouring chieftains cultivating friendship with him; see on chap. v. 23, 24; and that this is the meaning of the passage the following verse shows: *Thou shalt lie down, and none shall make thee afraid; yea, many shall make suit unto thee.* Thou shalt be in perfect security; no enemy shall molest thee, and many shall seek thy friendship.

Verse 20. *The eyes of the wicked shall fail*] They shall be continually looking out for help and deliverance; but their expectation shall be cut off.

And they shall not escape] They shall receive the punishment due to their deserts; for God has his eye continually upon them. ומנוס אבד מנהם *umanos abad minnehem*, literally, "And escape perishes from them." *Flight* from impending destruction is impossible.

And their hope shall be as *the giving up of the ghost.*] ותקותם מפח נפש *vethikvatham mappach naphesh*, "And their hope an exhalation of breath," or *a mere wish of the mind.* They retain their hope to the last; and the *last breath* they breathe is the final and eternal termination of their hope. They give up their *hope* and their *ghost* together; for a *vain* hope cannot enter into that place where *shadow* and *representation* exist not; all being *substance* and *reality.* And thus endeth Zophar the Naamathite; whose premises were in general good, his conclusions legitimate, but his *application* of them to Job's case totally erroneous; because he still proceeded on the ground that Job was a wicked man, if not *ostensibly*, yet *secretly;* and that the sufferings he was undergoing were the means by which God was unmasking him to the view of men.

But, allowing that Job had been a bad man, the exhortations of Zophar were well calculated to enforce repentance and excite confidence in the Divine mercy. Zophar seems to have had a full conviction of the all-governing providence of God; and that those who served him with an honest and upright heart would be ever distinguished in the distribution of temporal good. He seems however to think that rewards and punishments were distributed in this *life*, and does not refer, at least very evidently, to a *future state*. Probably his information on subjects of divinity did not extend much beyond the grave; and we have much cause to thank God for a clearer dispensation. *Deus nobis hæc otia fecit.* God grant that we may make a good use of it!

CHAPTER XII

Job reproves the boasting of his friends, and shows their uncharitableness towards himself, 1–5; *asserts that even the tabernacles of robbers prosper; and that, notwithstanding, God is the Governor of the world; a truth which is proclaimed by all parts of the creation whether animate of inanimate, and by the revolutions which take place in states,* 6–25.

A. M. cir. 2484
B. C. cir. 1520
Ante I. Olymp. cir. 744
Ante U. C. cir. 767

AND Job answered and said,
2 No doubt but ye *are* the
people, and wisdom shall die
with you.
3 But [a]I have [b]understanding as well as
you; [c]I *am* not inferior to you: yea, [d]who
knoweth not such things as these?
4 [e]I am *as* one mocked of his neighbour,
who [f]calleth upon God, and he answereth
him: the just upright *man is* laughed to scorn.

5 [g]He that is ready to slip
with *his* feet *is as* a lamp despised in the thought of him that
is at ease.
6 [h]The tabernacles of robbers prosper, and
they that provoke God are secure; into whose
hand God bringeth *abundantly.*
7 But ask now the beasts, and they shall
teach thee; and the fowls of the air, and they
shall tell thee:

A. M. cir. 2484
B. C. cir. 1520
Ante I. Olymp. cir. 744
Ante U. C. cir. 767

[a]Chap. xiii. 2——[b]Heb. *a heart*——[c]Heb. *I fall not lower than you*——[d]Heb. *with whom are* not *such as these?*

[e]Ch. xvi. 10; xvii. 2, 6; xxi. 3; xxx. 1——[f]Psa. xci. 15
[g]Prov. xiv. 2——[h]Ch. xxi. 7; Psa. xxxvii. 1, 35; lxxiii. 11, 12; xcii. 7; Jer. xii. 1; Mal. iii. 15

NOTES ON CHAP. XII

Verse 2. *No doubt but ye* are *the people*] Doubtless ye are the wisest men in the world; all wisdom is concentrated in you; and when ye die, there will no more be found on the face of the earth! This is a strong irony.

Verse 3. *I* am *not inferior to you*] I do not fall short of any of you in understanding, wisdom, learning, and experience.

Who knoweth not such things as these?] All your boasted wisdom consists only in *strings of proverbs* which are in every person's mouth, and are no proof of wisdom and experience in them that use them.

Verse 4. *I am* as *one mocked of his neighbour*] Though I am invoking God for help and salvation, yet my friends mock me in this most solemn and sacred work. But God answereth me.

The just upright man is *laughed to scorn*] This is a very difficult verse, on which no two critics seem to be agreed. Mr. *Good* translates the fourth and fifth verses thus:—

"Thus brother is become a laughing-stock to his companions,
While calling upon God that he would succour him.
The just, the perfect man, is a laughing-stock to the proud,
A derision amidst the sunshine of the prosperous,
While ready to slip with his foot."

For a vindication of this version, I must refer to his notes. *Coverdale* gives at least a good sense. **Thus he that calleth upon God, and whom God heareth, is mocked of his neighboure: the godly and innocent man is laughed to scorne. Godlynesse is a light despysed in the hertes of the rich; and is set for them to stomble upon.** The *fifth* verse is thus rendered by Mr. *Parkhurst:* "A torch of contempt, or contemptible link, (see Isa. vii. 4, xl. 2, 3,) לעשתות *leashtoth*, to the splendours of the prosperous (is he who is) ready (נכון *nachon*, Job xv. 23, xviii. 12; Psa. xxxviii. 17) to slip with his foot." The general sense is tolerably plain; but to *emendations* and *conjectures* there is no end.

Verse 6. *The tabernacles of robbers prosper.*] Those who live by the plunder of their neighbours are often found in great secular prosperity; and they that provoke God by impiety and blasphemy live in a state of security and affluence. These are administrations of Providence which cannot be accounted for; yet the Judge of all the earth does right. Therefore prosperity and adversity are no evidences of a man's spiritual state, nor of the place he holds in the approbation or disapprobation of God.

Verse 7. *But ask now the beasts, and they shall teach thee*] Mr. *Good's* paraphrase here is very just: "Why tell ye me that the Almighty hath brought this calamity upon me? Every thing in nature, the beasts of the field, the fowls of the heaven, every inhabitant of earth and sea, and every thing that befalls them, are the

A. M. cir. 2484
B. C. cir. 1520
Ante I. Olymp. cir. 744
Ante U. C. cir. 767

8 Or speak to the earth, and it shall teach thee: and the fishes of the sea shall declare unto thee.

9 Who knoweth not in all these that the hand of the LORD hath wrought this?

10 [i]In whose hand *is* the [k]soul of every living thing, and the breath of [l]all mankind.

11 [m]Doth not the ear try words? and the [n]mouth taste his meat?

12 [o]With the ancient *is* wisdom; and in length of days understanding.

13 [p]With [q]him *is* wisdom and strength, he hath counsel and understanding.

14 Behold, [r]he breaketh down, and it cannot be built again: he [s]shutteth [t]up a man, and there can be no opening.

15 Behold, he [u]withholdeth the waters, and they dry up: also he [v]sendeth them out, and they overturn the earth.

16 [w]With him *is* strength and wisdom: the deceived and the deceiver *are* his.

---

[i]Num. xvi. 22; Dan. v. 23; Acts xvii. 28——[k]Or, *life*——[l]Heb. *all flesh of man*——[m]Chap. xxxiv. 3——[n]Heb. *palate*, chap. vi. 30——[o]Chap. xxxii. 7

[p]That is, *with God*——[q]Ch. ix. 4; xxxvi. 5——[r]Ch. xi. 10——[s]Isa. xxii. 22; Rev. iii. 7——[t]Heb. *upon*——[u]1 Kings viii. 35; xvii. 1——[v]Gen. vii. 11——[w]Ver. 13

---

work of his hands; and every thing feels and acknowledges him to be the universal Creator and Controller. It is the common doctrine of all nature; but to apply it as *ye* would apply it to me, and to assert that I am suffering from being guilty of hypocrisy, is equally impertinent. He ordains every thing in wisdom as well as in power; but why events happen as they happen, why good and evil are promiscuously scattered throughout nature or human life, ye are as ignorant of as myself."

Verse 10. *In whose hand* is *the soul of every living thing*] נפש כל חי *nephesh col chai*, "the soul of all life."

And the breath of all mankind.] ורוח כל בשר *veruach col besar*, "and the spirit or breath of all flesh." Does not the *first* refer to the *immortal soul*, the principle of all *intellectual life;* and the *latter* to the *breath, respiration*, the grand means by which *animal existence* is continued? See chap. x. 1.

Verse 11. *Doth not the ear try words?*] All these are common-place sayings. Ye have advanced nothing new; ye have cast no light upon the dispensations of Providence.

Verse 12. *With the ancient* is *wisdom*] Men who have lived in those primitive times, when the great facts of nature were recent, such as the creation, fall, flood, confusion of tongues, migration of families, and consequent settlement of nations, had much knowledge from those facts; and their *length of days*—the many hundreds of years to which they lived, gave them such an opportunity of accumulating wisdom by *experience*, that they are deservedly considered as oracles.

Verse 13. *With him* is *wisdom and strength*] But all these things come from GOD; he is the Fountain of wisdom and the Source of power. He alone can give us unerring counsel, and understanding to comprehend and act profitably by it. See on ver. 16.

Verse 14. *He breaketh down*] He alone can *create*, and he alone can *destroy*. Nothing can be annihilated but by the same Power that created it. This is a most remarkable fact. No power, skill, or cunning of man can annihilate the smallest particle of matter. Man, by chemical agency, may change its *form;* but to reduce it to *nothing* belongs to God alone. In the course of his providence God breaks down, so that it cannot be built up again. See proofs of this in the total political destruction of *Nineveh, Babylon, Persepolis, Tyre*, and other cities, which have broken down never to be rebuilt; as well as the Assyrian, Babylonian, Grecian, and Roman empires, which have been dismembered and almost annihilated, never more to be regenerated.

He shutteth up a man] He often frustrates the best laid purposes, so that they can never be brought to good effect.

Verse 15. *He withholdeth the waters*] This is, I think, an allusion to the *third* day's work of the creation, Gen. i. 9: *And God said, Let the waters be gathered together unto one place, and let the dry land appear.* Thus the earth was drained, and the waters collected into seas, and bound to their particular places.

Also he sendeth them out] Here is also an allusion to the *flood*, for when he broke up the fountains of the great deep, then the *earth was overturned.*

Verse 16. *With him* is *strength and wisdom*] עז ותושיה *oz vethushiyah, strength and sufficiency.* Strength or power, springing from an exhaustless and infinite source of potency. In the *thirteenth* verse it is said, *With him* is *wisdom and strength;* but the expressions are not the same, חכמה וגבורה *chochmah ugeburah, intelligence* and *fortitude*, or *strength* in *action*, the *wisdom* ever guiding the exertions of *power;* but here is *strength* or *power* in *essence*, and an eternal *potentiality.* With him is every excellence, *in potentia* and *in esse.* He *borrows* nothing, he *derives* nothing. As he is self-existent, so is he self-sufficient. We have had the word *tushiyah* before. See the note on chap. xi. 6.

The deceived and the deceiver are *his.*] Some think this refers to the *fall;* even *Satan* the deceiver or beguiler, and *Adam* and *Eve*, the *deceived* or beguiled, are his. Satan, as this book shows, cannot act without especial *permission;* and *man*, whom the seducer thought to make his own property for ever, is claimed as the *peculium* or especial property of God, for the *seed of the woman* was then appointed to *bruise the head of the serpent;* and Jesus Christ has assumed the nature of man, and thus brought human nature into a *state of fellowship with himself.* Thus *he who sanctifieth and they who are sanctified are all of one, for which cause he is not ashamed to call them brethren;* Heb. ii. 11.

A. M. cir. 2484
B. C. cir. 1520
Ante I. Olymp. cir. 744
Ante U. C. cir. 767

17 He leadeth counsellors away spoiled, and [x]maketh the judges fools.
18 He looseth the bond of kings, and girdeth their loins with a girdle.
19 He leadeth princes away spoiled, and overthroweth the mighty.
20 [y]He removeth away [z]the speech of the trusty, and taketh away the understanding of the aged.

21 [a]He poureth contempt upon princes, and [b]weakeneth the strength of the mighty.
22 [c]He discovereth deep things out of darkness, and bringeth out to light the shadow of death.
23 [d]He increaseth the nations, and destroyeth them: he enlargeth the nations, and [e]straiteneth them *again*.
24 He taketh away the heart of the chief of

[x]2 Sam. xv. 31; xvii. 14, 23; Isa. xix. 12; xxix. 14; 1 Cor. i. 19——[y]Chap. xxxii. 9; Isa. iii. 1, 2, 3——[z]Heb. *the lip of the faithful*——[a]Psa. cvii. 40; Dan. ii. 21

[b]Or, *looseth the girdle of the strong*——[c]Dan. ii. 22; Matt. x. 26; 1 Cor. iv. 5——[d]Psa. cvii. 38; Isa. ix. 3; xxvi. 15——[e]Heb. *leadeth in*

Verse 17. *He leadeth counsellors away spoiled*] The events of *war* are also in his hand. It is he who gives *victory;* through him even the *counsellors*—the great men and chief men, are often led into captivity, and found among the *spoils*.

And maketh the judges fools.] He infatuates the judges. Does this refer to the foolish conduct of some of the *Israelitish judges*, such as *Samson?*

Verse 18. *He looseth the bond of kings*] He takes away their splendid robes, and clothes them with sackcloth; or, he dissolves their authority, permits their subjects to rebel and overthrow the state, to bind them as captives, and despoil them of all power, authority, and liberty. Many proofs of this occur in the Israelitish history and in the history of the principal nations of the earth, and not a few in the history of Britain.

Verse 19. *He leadeth princes away spoiled, and overthroweth the mighty.*] What multitudes of proofs of this does the history of the world present! Even the late disastrous war with the French republic and empire, which began in 1793, and continued without intermission till 1814, was afterwards renewed, and had a catastrophe that went nearly to ruin Europe. How many princes, or rather *priests*, כהנים *cohanim*, have been spoiled of their power, influence, and authority; and how many *mighty men*—captains, generals, admirals, &c., have been overthrown! But supposing that the writer of the Book of Job lived, as some think, *after* the *captivity*, how many *priests* were led away spoiled, both from Israel and Judah; and how many *kings* and *mighty men* were overthrown in the disastrous wars between the Assyrians, Babylonians, and Jews!

Verse 20. *He removeth away the speech of the trusty*] The faithful counsellor and the eloquent orator avail nothing: *Quos Deus vult perdere, prius dementat;* "God infatuates those whom he is determined to destroy." The writer might have had his eyes on Isa. iii. 1-3, which the reader will do well to consult.

The understanding of the aged.] זקנים *zekenim* signifies the same here as our word *elders* or *elder-men;* which includes in itself the two ideas of *seniority*, or considerably advanced age, and *official authority*. These can do no more to save a state which God designs to destroy, notwithstanding their great political wisdom and knowledge, than the child who can neither reason nor speak.

Verse 21. *He poureth contempt upon princes*] נדיבים *nedibim*, "those of royal extraction;" widely different from the כהנים *cohanim* mentioned ver. 19.

Weakeneth the strength of the mighty.] אפיקים *aphikim*, the *compact;* the *well-strung together; the nervous* and *sinewy*. Perhaps there is a reference here to the *crocodile*, as the same term is applied, chap. xl. 13, to the *compactness* of his bones: and as רפה מזיח *rippah meziach*, which we translate *weakeneth the strength*, signifies more properly *looseth the girdle*, as the *margin* has properly rendered it, the reference seems still more pointed; for it is known that "the crocodile, from the shoulders to the extremity of the tail, is covered with large *square scales*, disposed like *parallel girdles, fifty-two* in number. In the middle of each *girdle* are *four protuberances*, which become higher as they approach the end of the tail, and compose *four rows*." See the quotation in *Parkhurst*, under the word אפק *aphak*. What is human strength against this? We may say as the Lord said, Job xl. 19: *He that made him can make his sword to approach* unto him. He alone can *loose the girdles of this mighty one.*

Verse 22. *He discovereth deep things out of darkness*] This may refer either to God's works in the great deep, or to the plots and stratagems of wicked men, conspiracies that were deeply laid, well digested, and about to be produced into existence, when *death*, whose *shadow* had hitherto concealed them, is to glut himself with *carnage*.

Verse 23. *He increaseth the nations*] Mr. *Good* translates, *He letteth the nations grow licentious.* Pride, fulness of bread, with extensive trade and commerce, produce luxury; and this is ever accompanied with profligacy of manners. When, then, the cup of this iniquity is full, God destroys the nation, by bringing or permitting to come against it a nation less pampered, more necessitous, and inured to toil.

He enlargeth the nations] Often permits a nation to acquire an accession of territory, and afterwards shuts them up within their ancient boundaries, and often contracts even those. All these things seem to occur as natural events, and the consequences of state intrigues, and such like causes; but when Divine inspiration comes to pronounce upon them, they are shown to be the consequence of God's acting in his judgment and mercy; for it is by *him* that kings reign; it is *he* who putteth down one and raiseth up another.

Verse 24. *He taketh away the heart of the*

A. M. cir. 2484
B. C. cir. 1520
Ante I. Olymp. cir. 744
Ante U. C. cir. 767

the people of the earth, and [f]causeth them to wander in a wilderness *where there is* no way.

25 [g]They grope in the dark without light, and he maketh them to [h]stagger [i]like *a* drunken *man.*

[f]Psa. cvii. 4, 40——[g]Deut. xxviii. 29; chap. v. 14

[h]Heb. *wonder*——[i]Psa. cvii. 27

chief] Suddenly deprives the leaders of great counsels, or mighty armies of courage; so that, panic-struck, they flee when none pursueth, or are confounded when about to enter on the accomplishment of important designs.

And causeth them to wander in a wilderness] A plain allusion to the journeyings of the Israelites in the deserts of Arabia, on their way to the promised land. Their *chief, Aaron,* had his *courage all taken away* by the clamours of the people; and so made them a molten calf to be the object of their worship, which defection from God was the cause of their wandering nearly *forty* years in the trackless wilderness. The reference is so marked, that it scarcely admits of a doubt; yet *Houbigant* and some others have called it in question, and suppose that those *chiefs* or *heads of families* which led out colonies into distant parts are principally intended. It answers too well to the case of the Israelites in the wilderness to admit of any other interpretation.

Verse 25. *They grope in the dark*] The writer seems to have had his eye on those words of Moses, Deut. xxviii. 28, 29: *The Lord shall smite thee with madness, and blindness, and astonishment of heart; and thou shalt* GROPE AT NOON-DAY, *as the* BLIND GROPETH IN DARKNESS. And this also may refer to the unaccountable errors, transgressions, and judicial blindness of the Israelites in their journeying to the promised land; but it will apply also to the state of wicked nations under judicial blindness. The writer is principally indebted for his *imagery,* and indeed for the *chief expressions* used here, to Psa. cvii. 27: *They reel to and fro, and stagger like a drunken man.* 39, 40: *Again, they are minished and brought low through oppression, affliction, and sorrow. He* POURETH CONTEMPT UPON PRINCES, *and* CAUSETH THEM TO WANDER IN THE WILDERNESS, *where there is* NO WAY.

Mr. *Good* has some judicious reflections on this chapter, particularly on ver. 13-22: "It should be observed," says he, "that the entire passage has a reference to the machinery of a regular and political government; and that its general drift is to imprint on the mind of the hearer the important doctrine that the whole of the constituent principles of such a government, its officers and institutions; its monarchs and princes; its privy-counsellors, judges, and ministers of state; its chieftains, public orators, and assembly of elders; its nobles, or men of hereditary rank; and its stout robust peasantry, as we should express it in the present day; nay, the deep designing villains that plot in secret its destruction;—that the nations themselves. and the heads or sovereigns of the nations, are all and equally in the hands of the Almighty: that with him human pomp is poverty; human excellence, turpitude; human judgment, error; human wisdom, folly; human dignity, contempt; human strength, weakness."

CHAPTER XIII

Job defends himself against the accusations of his friends, and accuses them of endeavouring to pervert truth, 1–8. Threatens them with God's judgments, 9–12. Begs some respite, and expresses strong confidence in God, 13–19. He pleads with God, and deplores his severe trials and sufferings, 20–28.

A. M. cir. 2484
B. C. cir. 1520
Ante I. Olymp. cir. 744
Ante U. C. cir. 767

LO, mine eye hath seen all *this,* mine ear hath heard and understood it.
2 [a]What ye know, *the same* do I know also: I *am* not inferior unto you.
3 [b]Surely I would speak to the Almighty, and I desire to reason with God.
4 But ye *are* forgers of lies, [c]ye *are* all physicians of no value.

[a]Chap. xii. 3——[b]Chap. xxiii. 3; xxxi. 35

[c]Chap. vi. 21; xvi. 2

NOTES ON CHAP. XIII

Verse 1. *Lo, mine eye hath seen all* this] Ye have brought nothing *new* to me; I know those maxims as well as you: nor have you any knowledge of which I am not possessed.

Verse 3. *Surely I would speak to the Almighty*] אולם *ulam, O that:—I wish I could speak to the Almighty!*

I desire to reason with God.] He speaks here in reference to the proceedings in a court of justice. Ye pretend to be advocates for God, but ye are forgers of lies: O that God himself would appear! Before him I could soon prove my innocence of the evils with which ye charge me.

Verse 4. *Ye are forgers of lies*] Ye frame deceitful arguments: ye reason sophistically, and pervert truth and justice, in order to support your cause.

Physicians of no value.] Ye are as feeble in your reasonings as ye are inefficient in your skill. Ye can neither heal the wound of my mind, nor the disease of my body. In ancient times every wise man professed skill in the healing art, and probably Job's friends had tried their skill on his *body* as well as on his *mind.* He therefore had, in his argument

A. M. cir. 2484
B. C. cir. 1520
Ante I. Olymp. cir. 744
Ante U. C. cir. 767

5 O that ye would altogether
hold your peace! and [d]it should
be your wisdom.
6 Hear now my reasoning, and
hearken to the pleadings of my lips.
7 [e]Will ye speak wickedly for God? and
talk deceitfully for him?
8 Will ye accept his person? will ye contend for God?
9 Is it good that he should search you out?
or as one man mocketh another, do ye *so* mock
him?
10 He will surely reprove you,
if ye do secretly accept persons.
11 Shall not his excellency
make you afraid? and his dread
fall upon you?
12 Your remembrances *are* like unto ashes,
your bodies to bodies of clay.
13 [f]Hold your peace, let me alone, that I
may speak, and let come on me what *will*.
14 Wherefore [g]do I take my flesh in my
teeth, and [h]put my life in mine hand?
15 [i]Though he slay me, yet will I trust in

[d]Prov. xvii. 28——[e]Chap. xvii. 5; xxxii. 21; xxxvi. 4
[f]Heb. *be silent from me*

[g]Chap. xviii. 4——[h]1 Sam. xxviii. 21; Psa. cxix. 109
[i]Psa. xxiii. 4; Prov. xiv. 32

against their teaching, a double advantage: Your skill in *divinity* and *physic* is equal: in the former ye are *forgers of lies;* in the latter, ye are *good-for-nothing* physicians. I can see no reason to depart from the general meaning of the original to which the ancient versions adhere. The Chaldee says: "Ye are idle physicians; and, like the mortified flesh which is cut off with the knife, so are the whole of you." The imagery in the former clause is *chirurgical*, and refers to the *sewing together*, or *connecting the divided sides* of wounds; for טפלי *topheley*, which we translate *forgers*, comes from טפל *taphal*, to fasten, tie, connect, sew together. And I question whether טפלי *topheley* here may not as well express SURGEONS, as רפאי *ropheey*, in the latter clause, PHYSICIANS. Ye are CHIRURGEONS of *falsity*, and *worthless* PHYSICIANS.

Verse 5. *Hold your peace! and it should be your wisdom.*] In Prov. xvii. 28 we have the following *apophthegm:* "Even a fool, when he holdeth his peace, is counted wise; and he that shutteth his lips, a man of understanding." There is no reason to say that Solomon quotes from Job: I have already expressed my opinion that the high antiquity attributed to this *book* is perfectly unfounded, and that there is much more evidence that *Solomon* was its *author*, than there is that it was the composition of *Moses*. But, whenever Job lived, whether *before* Abraham or *after* Moses, the book was not written till the time of Solomon, if not later. But as to the saying in question, it is a general apophthegm, and may be found among the wise sayings of all nations.

I may observe here, that a *silent man* is not likely to be a *fool;* for *a fool will be always prating*, or, according to another adage, *a fool's bolt is soon shot*. The Latins have the same proverb: *Vir sapit, qui pauca loquitur*, "A wise man speaks little."

Verse 6. *Hear now my reasoning*] The speeches in this book are conceived as if delivered in a *court of justice*, different counsellors pleading against each other. Hence most of the terms are *forensic*.

Verse 7. *Will ye speak wickedly for God?*] In order to support your own cause, in contradiction to the evidence which the whole of my life bears to the uprightness of my heart, will ye continue to assert that God could not thus afflict me, unless flagrant iniquity were found in my ways; for it is on this ground alone that ye pretend to vindicate the providence of God. Thus ye tell lies for God's sake, and thus ye wickedly contend for your Maker.

Verse 8. *Will ye accept his person?*] Do you think to act by him as you would by a *mortal;* and, by telling lies in his favour, attempt to conciliate his esteem?

Verse 9. *Is it good that he should search you out?*] Would it be to your credit if God should try your hearts, and uncover the motives of your conduct? Were you tried as I am, how would you appear?

Do ye so *mock him?*] Do ye think that you can deceive him; and by flattering speeches bring him to your terms, as you would bring an undiscerning, empty mortal, like yourselves?

Verse 10. *He will surely reprove you*] You may expect, not only his disapprobation, but his hot displeasure.

Verse 11. *His dread fall upon you?*] The very apprehension of his wrath is sufficient to crush you to nothing.

Verse 12. *Your remembrances* are *like unto ashes*] Your *memorable sayings* are *proverbs of dust*. This is properly the meaning of the original: זכרניכם משלי אפר *zichroneycem mishley epher*. This he speaks in reference to the ancient and reputedly wise sayings which they had so copiously quoted against him.

Your bodies to bodies of clay.] This clause is variously translated: *Your swelling heaps* are *swelling heaps of mire*. That is, *Your high-flown speeches* are dark, involved, and incoherent; they are all sound, no sense; great swelling words, either of difficult or no meaning, or of no point as applicable to my case.

Verse 13. *Hold your peace*] You have perverted righteousness and truth, and your pleadings are totally irrelevant to the case; you have travelled out of the road; you have left law and justice behind you; it is high time that you should have done.

Let come on me what will.] I will now defend myself against you, and leave the cause to its issue.

Verse 14. *Wherefore do I take my flesh in my teeth*] A proverbial expression. I risk every thing on the justice of my cause. *I put my life in my hand*, 1 Sam. xxviii. 21. I run all hazards; I am fearless of the consequences.

Verse 15. *Though he slay me*] I have no dependence but God; I trust in him alone. Should

A. M. cir. 2484 B. C. cir. 1520 Ante I. Olymp. cir. 744 Ante U. C. cir. 767

him: [k]but I will [l]maintain mine
own ways before him.
16 He also *shall be* my salvation: for a hypocrite shall not
come before him.
17 Hear diligently my speech, and my declaration with your ears.
18 Behold now, I have ordered *my* cause;
I know that I shall be justified.
19 [m]Who *is* he *that* will plead with me?
for now, if I hold my tongue, I shall give up
the ghost.
20 [n]Only do not two *things* unto me: then
will I not hide myself from thee.
21 [o]Withdraw thine hand far from me:
and let not thy dread make me afraid.
22 Then call thou and I will answer: or let
me speak, and answer thou
me.
23 How many *are* mine iniquities and sins? make me to know
my transgression and my sin.
24 [p]Wherefore hidest thou thy face, and
[q]holdest me for thine enemy?
25 [r]Wilt thou break a leaf driven to and fro?
and wilt thou pursue the dry stubble?
26 For thou writest bitter things against me,
and [s]makest me to possess the iniquities of
my youth.
27 [t]Thou puttest my feet also in the stocks,
and [u]lookest narrowly unto all my paths; thou
settest a print upon the [v]heels of my feet.
28 And he, as a rotten thing, consumeth, as
a garment that is moth-eaten.

---

[k]Chap. xxvii. 5——[l]Heb. *prove* or *argue*——[m]Chap. xxxiii. 6; Isa. l. 8——[n]Chap. ix. 34; xxxiii. 7——[o]Psa. xxxix. 10——[p]Deut. xxxii. 20; Psa. xiii. 1; xliv. 24; lxxxviii. 14; Isa. viii. 17

[q]Deut. xxxii. 42; Ruth i. 21; chap. xvi. 9; xix. 11; xxxiii. 10; Lam. ii. 5——[r]Isa. xlii. 3——[s]Chap. xx. 11; Psa. xxv. 7——[t]Chap. xxxiii. 11——[u]Heb. *observest*
[v]Heb. *roots*

---

he even destroy my life by this affliction, yet will I hope that when he has tried me, I shall come forth as gold. In the common printed Hebrew text we have לא איחל *lo ayachel, I will* NOT *hope;* but the Vulgate, Syriac, Arabic, and Chaldee have read לו *lo,* HIM, instead of לא *lo,* NOT; with *twenty-nine* of Kennicott's and De Rossi's MSS., and the Complutensian and Antwerp Polyglots. Our translators have followed the best reading. Coverdale renders the verse thus: **Lo, there is nether comforte ner hope for me, yf he wil slaye me.**

But I will maintain mine own ways] I am so conscious of my innocence, that I fear not to defend myself from your aspersions, even in the presence of my Maker.

Verse 16. *He also* shall be *my salvation*] He will save me, *because* I trust in him.

A hypocrite] A *wicked man* shall never be able to stand before him. I am conscious of this; and were I, as you suppose, *a secret sinner*, I should not dare to make this appeal.

Verse 18. *Behold now, I have ordered*] I am now ready to come into court, and care not how many I have to contend with, provided they speak truth.

Verse 19. *Who* is *he* that *will plead with me?*] Let my accuser, the *plaintiff*, come forward; I will defend my cause against him.

I shall give up the ghost.] I shall cease to breathe. Defending myself will be as respiration unto me; or, While he is stating his case, I will be *so silent* as scarcely to *appear to breathe.*

Verse 20. *Only do not two* things *unto me*] These *two* things are the following: 1. *Withdraw thine hand far from me*—remove the heavy affliction which thy hand has inflicted. 2. *Let not thy dread make me afraid*—terrify me not with dreadful displays of thy majesty. The *reasons* of this request are sufficiently evident: 1. How can a man stand in a court of justice and plead for his life, when under grievous bodily affliction? *Withdraw thy hand far from me.* 2. Is it to be expected that a man can be sufficiently recollected, and in self-possession, to plead for his life, when he is overwhelmed with the awful appearance of the judge, the splendour of the court, and the various ensigns of justice? *Let not thy dread make me afraid.*

Verse 22. *Then call thou*] Begin thou first to plead, and I will answer for myself; or, I will first state and defend my own case, and then answer *thou* me.

Verse 23. *How many* are *mine iniquities*] Job being permitted to begin first, enters immediately upon the subject; and as it was a fact that he was grievously afflicted, and this his friends asserted was in consequence of grievous iniquities, he first desires to have them specified. What are the *specific* charges in this indictment? To say I must be a *sinner* to be thus afflicted, is saying nothing; tell me *what* are the *sins*, and show me the *proofs.*

Verse 24. *Wherefore hidest thou thy face*] Why is it that I no longer enjoy thy *approbation?*

Holdest me for thine enemy?] Treatest me as if I were the vilest of sinners?

Verse 25. *Wilt thou break a leaf*] Is it becoming thy dignity to concern thyself with a creature so contemptible?

Verse 26. *Thou writest bitter things against me*] The indictment is filled with bitter or grievous charges, which, if proved, would bring me to bitter punishment.

The iniquities of my youth] The levities and indiscretions of my *youth* I acknowledge; but is this a *ground* on which to form charges against a man, the integrity of whose *life* is unimpeachable?

Verse 27. *Thou puttest my feet also in the stocks*] בסד *bassad,* "in a clog," such as was tied to the feet of slaves, to prevent them from running away. This is still used in the West Indies, among *slave-dealers;* and is there called the *pudding*, being a large collar of iron, locked round the ankle of the unfortunate man. Some have had them *twenty* pounds' weight; and, having been condemned to carry them for several years, when released could not walk without them! A case of this kind I knew: The slave had learned to walk well with his *pudding*, but when taken off, if he attempted to walk, he fell down, and was obliged to resume it occasionally, till practice had taught him the proper centre of gravity, which had been so materially altered by wearing so large a weight; the badge at once of *his oppression*, and of the *cruelty* of his *task-masters!*

And lookest narrowly] Thou hast seen all my goings out and comings in; and there is no step I have taken in life with which thou art unacquainted.

Thou settest a print upon the heels of my feet.] Some understand this as the *mark* left on the foot by the clog; or the *owner's mark* indented on this clog; or, Thou hast pursued me as a hound does his game, by the *scent*.

Verse 28. *And he, as a rotten thing*] I am like a *vessel* made of *skin;* rotten, because of old age; or like a *garment* corroded by the *moth*. So the *Septuagint*, *Syriac*, and *Arabic* understood it. The word *he* may refer to himself.

CHAPTER XIV

The shortness, misery, and sinfulness of man's life, 1–4. *The unavoidable necessity of death; and the hope of a general resurrection,* 5–15. *Job deplores his own state, and the general wretchedness of man,* 16–22.

A. M. cir. 2484
B. C. cir. 1520
Ante I. Olymp. cir. 744
Ante U. C. cir. 767

MAN *that is* born of a woman
is [a]of few days, and [b]full
of trouble.
2 [c]He cometh forth like a
flower, and is cut down: he fleeth also as a
shadow, and continueth not.
3 And [d]dost thou open thine eyes upon such
a one, and [e]bringest me into
judgment with thee?
4 [f]Who [g]can bring a clean
thing out of an unclean? not one.
5 [h]Seeing his days *are* determined, the
number of his months *are* with thee, thou hast
appointed his bounds that he cannot pass:

A. M. cir. 2484
B. C. cir. 1520
Ante I. Olymp. cir. 744
Ante U. C. cir. 767

---

[a]Heb. *short of days*——[b]Chapter v. 7; Eccles. ii. 23——[c]Chap. viii. 9; Psa. xc. 5, 6, 9; cii. 11; ciii. 15; cxliv. 4; Isa. xl. 6; James i. 10, 11; iv. 14; 1 Pet. i. 24

[d]Psa. cxliv. 3——[e]Psa. cxliii. 2——[f]Heb. *who will give?*——[g]Gen. v. 3; Psa. li. 5; John iii. 6; Rom. v. 12; Eph. ii. 3——[h]Chap. vii. 1; xxx. 23; Heb. ix. 27

NOTES ON CHAP. XIV

Verse 1. *Man—born of a woman*] There is a delicacy in the original, not often observed: אדם ילוד אשה *Adam yelud ishah*, "Adam born of a woman, few of days, and full of tremor." *Adam*, who did *not* spring from *woman*, but was immediately formed by *God*, had *many days*, for he lived *nine hundred* and *thirty* years; during which time neither sin nor death had multiplied in the earth, as they were found in the days of Job. But the *Adam* who springs *now from woman*, in the way of ordinary generation, has *very few years*. *Seventy*, on an average, being the highest term, may be well said to be *few in days;* and all matter of fact shows that they are full of fears and apprehensions, רגז *rogez*, cares, anxieties, and tremors. He seems born, not indeed to *live*, but to *die;* and, by living, he forfeits the title to life.

Verse 2. *He cometh forth like a flower*] This is a frequent image both in the Old and New Testament writers; I need not quote the places here, as the readers will find them all in the *margin*.

He fleeth also as a shadow] Himself, as he appears among men, is only the *shadow* of his *real*, *substantial*, and *eternal* being. He is here compared to a *vegetable;* he springs up, bears his flower, is often nipped by disease, blasted by afflictions, and at last cut down by death. The bloom of youth, even in the most prosperous state, is only the forerunner of hoary hairs, enfeebled muscles, impaired senses, general debility, anility, and dissolution. All these images are finely embodied, and happily expressed, in the beautiful lines of a very nervous and correct poet, too little known, but whose compositions deserve the *first place* among what may be called the *minor poets* of Britain. See at the end of the chapter.

Verse 3. *Dost thou open thine eyes upon such a one*] The whole of this chapter is directed to God alone; in no part of it does he take any notice of his friends.

Verse 4. *Who can bring a clean* thing] This verse is thus rendered by the *Chaldee:* "Who will produce a clean thing from man, who is polluted with sins, except God, who is one?" By *Coverdale* thus: **Who can make it cleane, that commeth of an uncleane thinge? No body.**

The text refers to man's *original* and corrupt nature. Every man that is born into the world comes into it in a corrupt or sinful state. This is called *original sin;* and is derived from *fallen Adam*, who is the stock, to the utmost ramifications of the human family. Not one human spirit is born into the world without this corruption of nature. All are impure and unholy; and from this principle of depravity all transgression is produced; and from this corruption of nature God alone can save.

The *Septuagint*, in the *Codex Alexandrinus*, reads the verse thus: Τις γαρ εσται καθαρο· απο ῥυπου; ουδε εἱς, εαν και μιας ἡμερας γενηται ὁ βιος αυτου επι της γης; "Who is pure from corruption? Not one, although he had lived but one day upon the earth."

Verse 5. *Seeing his days* are *determined*] The general *term* of human life is fixed by God himself; in vain are all attempts to prolong it beyond this term. Several attempts have been made in all nations to find an *elixir* that would expel all the seeds of disease, and keep men in

A. M. cir. 2484
B. C. cir. 1520
Ante I. Olymp. cir. 744
Ante U. C. cir. 767

6 [l]Turn from him, that he may
[k]rest, till he shall accomplish,
[l]as a hireling, his day.
7 For there is hope of a tree,
if it be cut down, [m]that it will sprout again,
and that the tender branch thereof will not
cease.
8 Though the root thereof wax old in the
earth, and the stock thereof die
in the ground;
9 *Yet* through the scent of
water it will bud, and bring forth
boughs like a plant.
10 But man dieth, and [n]wasteth away: yea,
man giveth up the ghost, and where *is* he?
11 *As* the waters fail from the sea, and

A. M. cir. 2484
B. C. cir. 1520
Ante I. Olymp. cir. 744
Ante U. C. cir. 767

---

[l]Chap. vii. 16, 19; x. 20; Psa. xxxix. 13——[k]Heb. *cease*

[l]Ch. vii. 1——[m]Ver. 14——[n]Heb. *is weakened* or *cut off*

---

continual health; but all these attempts have failed. *Basil, Valentine, Norton, Dastin, Ripley, Sandivogius, Artephius, Geber, Van Helmont, Paracelsus, Philalethes,* and several others. both in Europe and Asia, have written copiously on the subject, and have endeavoured to prove that a *tincture* might be produced, by which all *imperfect metals* may be transmuted into *perfect;* and an *elixir* by which the *human body* may be kept in a state of endless repair and health. And these profess to teach the method by which this *tincture* and this *elixir* may be made! Yet all these are dead; and dead, for aught we know, comparatively young! *Artephius* is, indeed, said to have lived *ninety* years, which is probable; but some of his foolish disciples, to give credit to their thriftless craft, added another *cipher*, and made his age *nine hundred!* Man may endeavour to pass the *bound;* and God may, here and there, produce a *Thomas Parr*, who died in 1635, aged *one hundred* and *fifty-two;* and a *Henry Jenkins*, who died in 1670, aged *one hundred* and *sixty-nine;* but these are rare instances, and do not affect the general *term.* Nor can death be avoided. *Dust thou art, and unto dust thou shalt return,* is the *law;* and that will ever render nugatory all such pretended *tinctures* and *elixirs.*

But, although man *cannot pass his appointed bounds*, yet he may so live as *never to reach them;* for folly and wickedness abridge the term of human life; and therefore the psalmist says, *Bloody and deceitful men shall not live out* HALF *their days*, Psa. lv. 23, for by indolence, intemperance, and disorderly passions, the life of man is shortened in cases innumerable. We are not to understand the *bounds* as applying to *individuals*, but to the *race* in general. Perhaps there is no case in which God has determined absolutely that man's age shall be so long, and shall neither be more nor less. The contrary supposition involves innumerable absurdities.

Verse 6. *Turn from him, that he may rest*] Cease to try him by afflictions and distresses, that he may enjoy some of the comforts of life, before he be removed from it: and thus, like a *hireling*, who is permitted by his master to take a little repose in the heat of the day, from severe labour, I shall also have a breathing time from affliction, before I come to that bound over which I cannot pass. See chap. x. 20, where there is a similar request.

Verse 7. *For there is hope of a tree*] We must not, says *Calmet*, understand this of an *old tree*, the stem and roots of which are *dried up* and *rotted:* but there are some trees which grow from *cuttings;* and some which, though pulled out of the earth, and having had their roots dried and withered by long exposure to the sun and wind, will, on being replanted, take root and resume their verdure. There are also certain trees, the fibres of which are so solid, that if after several years they be steeped in water, they resume their vigour, the tubes dilate, and the blossoms or flowers which were attached to them expand; as I have often witnessed in what is called the *rose of Jericho.* There are few trees which will not send forth new shoots, when the stock is cut down level with the earth.

Verse 9. *Through the scent of water it will bud*] A fine metaphor: the water acts upon the decaying and perishing tree, as strong and powerful odours from musk, otto of roses, ammonia, &c., act on a fainting or swooning person.

Verse 10. *But man dieth*] No human being ever can spring from the dead body of man; *that* wasteth away, corrupts, and is dissolved; for the man dies; and when he breathes out his last breath, and his body is reduced to dust, then, *where is he?* There is a beautiful verse in the Persian poet *Khosroo*, that is not unlike this saying of Job:—

رفتم سوي خطيره و بگريستم بزار
از هجره دوستان كه اسير فنا شدند
گفتم ايشان كجا شدند و خطر
داداز مرا جواب ايشان كجا

"I went towards the burying ground, and wept
To think of the departure of friends which were captives to death;
I said, *Where are they?* and *Fate*
Gave back this answer by *Echo, Where are they?*"

Thus paraphrased by a learned friend:—

Beneath the cypress' solemn shade,
As on surrounding tombs I gazed,
I wept, and thought of friends there laid,
Whose hearts with warmest love had blazed.
Where are those friends my heart doth lack,
Whose words, in grief, gave peace? *Ah, where?*
And *Fate*, by *Echo*, gave me back
This short but just reply, *Ah, where?*

Verse 11. *The waters fail from the sea*] I believe this refers to *evaporation*, and nothing else. As the waters are evaporated from the sea, and the river in passing over the sandy desert is partly exsiccated, and partly absorbed; and yet the waters of the sea are not exhausted, as these vapours, being condensed, fall down in rain, and by means of rivers return again into the sea: so man is imperceptibly removed from

A. M. cir. 2484 B. C. cir. 1520 Ante I. Olymp. cir. 744 Ante U. C. cir. 767

the flood decayeth and drieth
up:
12 So man lieth down, and
riseth not: [o]till the heavens *be*
no more, they shall not awake, nor be raised
out of their sleep.
13 O that thou wouldest hide me in the
grave, that thou wouldest keep me secret, until
thy wrath be past, that thou
wouldest appoint me a set time,
and remember me!
14 If a man die, shall he live
again? all the days of my appointed time
[p]will I wait, [q]till my change come.
15 [r]Thou shalt call, and I will answer thee:
thou wilt have a desire to the work of thine hands.

A. M. cir. 2484 B. C. cir. 1520 Ante I. Olymp. cir. 744 Ante U. C. cir. 767

[o]Psa. cii. 26; Isa. li. 6; lxv. 17; lxvi. 22; Acts iii. 21; Rom. viii. 20; 2 Pet. iii. 7, 10, 11; Rev. xx. 11; xxi. 1

[p]Chap. xiii. 15——[q]Ver. 7; 1 Cor. xv. 51; 2 Cor. iii. 18; Phil. iii. 21——[r]Chap. xiii. 22

his fellows by death and dissolution; yet the human race is still continued, the population of the earth being kept up by perpetual generations.

Verse 12. *So man lieth down*] He falls asleep in his bed of earth.

And riseth not] Men shall not, like cut down trees and plants, reproduce their like; nor shall they arise till the heavens are no more, till the earth and all its works are burnt up, and the general resurrection of human beings shall take place. Surely it would be difficult to twist this passage to the denial of the resurrection of the body. Neither can these expressions be fairly understood as implying Job's belief in the *materiality* of the soul, and that the whole man *sleeps* from the day of his death to the morning of the resurrection. We have already seen that Job makes a distinction between the animal life and rational soul in man; and it is most certain that the doctrine of the *materiality of the soul*, and its *sleep* till the resurrection, has no place in the sacred records. There is a most beautiful passage to the same purpose, and with the same imagery, in Moschus's epitaph on the death of Bion:—

Αι, αι, ται μαλαχαι μεν επαν κατα καπον ολωνται,
Η τα χλωρα σελινα, το τ' ευθαλες ουλον ανηθον,
'Υστερον αυ ζωοντι, και εις ετος αλλο φυοντι·
Αμμες δ', οἱ μεγαλοι, και καρτεροι, η σοφοι ανδρες,
'Οπποτε πρωτα θανωμες, ανακοοι εν χθονι κοιλᾳ
Εὑδομες ευ μαλα μακρον, ατερμονα, νηγρετον ὑπνον.
Idyll. iii., ver. 100.

Alas! alas! the mallows, when they die,
Or garden herbs, and sweet Anethum's pride,
Blooming in vigour, wake again to life,
And flourish beauteous through another year:
But we, the great, the mighty, and the wise,
When once we die, unknown in earth's dark womb
Sleep, long and drear, the endless sleep of death.
J. B. B. C.

A more cold and comfortless philosophy was never invented. The next verse shows that Job did not entertain this view of the subject.

Verse 13. *O that thou wouldest hide me in the grave*] Dreadful as death is to others, I shall esteem it a high privilege; it will be to me a covert from the wind and from the tempest of this affliction and distress.

Keep me secret] Hide my soul with thyself, where my enemies cannot invade my repose; or, as the poet expresses it:—

"My spirit hide with saints above,
My body in the tomb."

Job does not appear to have the *same thing* in view when he entreats God to *hide him in the grave;* and to *keep him secret, until his wrath be past.* The former relates to the *body;* the latter to the *spirit.*

That thou wouldest appoint me a set time] As he had spoken of the death of his body before, and the secreting of his spirit in the invisible world, he must refer here to the *resurrection;* for what else can be said to be an object of desire to one whose body is mingled with the dust?

And remember me!] When my body has paid that debt of death which it owes to thy Divine justice, and the morning of the resurrection is come, when it may be said thy *wrath*, אפך *appecha*, "thy displeasure," against the body is past, it having suffered the sentence denounced by thyself: *Dust thou art, and unto dust thou shalt return,* for *in the day thou eatest thereof thou shalt surely die;* then *remember me*—raise my body, unite my spirit to it, and receive both into thy glory for ever.

Verse 14. *If a man die, shall he live* again?] The *Chaldee* translates, If a wicked man die, can he ever live again? or, *he can never live again.* The *Syriac* and *Arabic* thus: "If a man die, shall he revive? Yea, all the days of his youth he awaits till his old age come." The *Septuagint:* "If a man die, shall he live, having accomplished the days of his life? I will endure till I live again." Here is no doubt, but a strong persuasion, of the certainty of the general resurrection.

All the days of my appointed time] צבאי *tsebai*, "of my warfare;" see on chap. vii. 1. *Will I await till* חליפתי *chaliphathi, my renovation, come.* This word is used to denote the springing again of grass, Psa. xc. 5, 6, after it had once withered, which is in itself a very expressive emblem of the resurrection.

Verse 15. *Thou shalt call*] Thou shalt say, *There shall be time no longer: Awake, ye dead! and come to judgment!*

And I will answer thee] My dissolved frame shall be united at thy call; and body and soul shall be rejoined.

Thou wilt have a desire] תכסף *tichsoph*, "Thou wilt *pant* with desire;" or, "Thou wilt *yearn* over the work of thy hands." God has subjected the creature to vanity, in *hope;* having determined the resurrection. Man is one of the noblest works of God. He has exhibited him as a master-piece of his creative skill, power, and goodness. Nothing less than the strongest call upon justice could have induced him thus to destroy the work of his hands. No wonder that he has an earnest desire towards it; and that although *man dies, and is as water*

A. M. cir. 2484
B. C. cir. 1520
Ante I. Olymp. cir. 744
Ante U. C. cir. 767

16 [s]For now thou numberest
my steps: dost thou not watch
over my sin?
17 [t]My transgression *is* sealed
up in a bag, and thou sewest up mine
iniquity.
18 And surely the mountain falling [u]cometh
to naught, and the rock is removed out of his
place.
19 The waters wear the stones: thou [v]wash-
est away the things which grow *out* of the
dust of the earth; and thou destroyest the [w]hope of man.
20 Thou prevailest for ever
against him, and he passeth: thou
changest his countenance, and sendest him
away.
21 His sons come to honour, and [x]he knoweth *it* not; and they are brought low, but he
perceiveth *it* not of them.
22 But his flesh upon him shall have pain,
and his soul within him shall mourn.

A. M. cir. 2484
B. C. cir. 1520
Ante I. Olymp. cir. 744
Ante U. C. cir. 767

[s]Chapter x. 6, 14; xiii. 27; xxxi. 4; xxxiv. 21; Psalm lvi. 8; cxxxix. 1, 2, 3; Proverbs v. 21; Jeremiah xxxii. 19——[t]Deuteronomy xxxii. 34; Hosea xiii. 12

[u]Hebrew, *fadeth*——[v]Hebrew, *overflowest*——[w]Chapter xi. 20; xxvii. 8——[x]Ecclesiastes ix. 5; Isaiah lxiii. 16

spilt upon the ground that cannot be gathered up again; yet doth he devise means that his banished be not expelled from him. Even God is represented as *earnestly longing* for the ultimate reviviscence of the sleeping dust. He cannot, he will not, forget the work of his hands.

Verse 16. *For now thou numberest my steps*] כי עתה *ki attah*, ALTHOUGH *thou*, &c. Though thou, by thy conduct towards me, seemest bent on my utter destruction, yet thou delightest in mercy, and I shall be saved.

Verse 17. *My transgression* is *sealed up in a bag*] An allusion to the custom of collecting evidence of state transgressions, *sealing them up in a bag*, and presenting them to the judges and officers of state to be examined, in order to trial and judgment. Just at this time (July, 1820) charges of state transgressions, *sealed up in a* GREEN BAG, and presented to the two houses of parliament, for the examination of a secret committee, are making a considerable noise in the land. Some suppose the allusion is to *money sealed up in bags;* which is common in the East. This includes two ideas: 1. Job's transgressions were all *numbered;* not one was passed by. 2. They were sealed up; so that none of them could be lost. These bags were indifferently *sewed* or *sealed*, the two words in the text.

Verse 18. *The mountain falling cometh to naught*] Every thing in nature is exposed to mutability and decay:—even mountains themselves may fall from their bases, and be dashed to pieces; or be suddenly swallowed up by an earthquake; and, by the same means, the strongest and most massive rocks may be removed.

Verse 19. *The waters wear the stones*] Even the common stones are affected in the same way. Were even *earthquakes* and violent concussions of nature wanting, the action of *water*, either *running* over them as a *stream*, or *even falling upon them* in *drops*, will wear these stones. Hence the proverb:—

Gutta cavat lapidem non vi sed sæpe cadendo.

"Constant droppings will make a hole in a flint."

Εκ θαμινης ραθαμιγγος, ὁκως λογος, αιες ιοισας,
Χ' ἁ λιθος ες ρωχμον κοιλαινεται.

"From frequent dropping, as the proverb says, perpetually falling, even a stone is hollowed into a hole."

Thou washest away the things] Alluding to sudden falls of rain occasioning floods, by which the fruits of the earth are swept away; and thus *the hope of man*—the *grain* for his household, and *provender* for his cattle, *is destroyed.*

Verse 20. *Thou prevailest for ever against him*] It is impossible for him to withstand thee: every stroke of thine brings him down.

Thou changest his countenance] Probably an allusion to the custom of *covering the face*, when the person was condemned, and *sending him away* to execution. See the case of Haman, in the note on *Esther*, chap. vii. 8.

Verse 21. *His sons come to honour*] When dead, he is equally indifferent and unconscious whether his children have met with a splendid or oppressive lot in life; for as to this world, when man dies, *in that day all his thoughts perish.*

Verse 22. *But his flesh upon him shall have pain*] The sum of the life of man is this, *pain of body* and *distress of soul;* and he is seldom without the one or the other, and often oppressed by both. Thus ends Job's discourse on the miserable state and condition of man.

THE last verse of the preceding chapter has been differently translated and explained.

Mr. *Good's* version is the following, which he vindicates in a learned note:—

For his flesh shall drop away from him;
And his soul shall become a waste from him.

The *Chaldee* thus: "Nevertheless his flesh, on account of the worms, shall grieve over him; and his soul, in the house of judgment, shall wail over him." In another copy of this version it is thus: "Nevertheless his flesh, before the window is closed over him, shall grieve; and his soul, for seven days of mourning, shall bewail him in the house of his burial." I shall give the *Hebrew:*—

אך בשרו עליו יכאב

Ach besaro alaiv yichab,

ונפשו עליו תאבל׃

Venaphsho alaiv teebal.

Which Mr. *Stock* translates thus, both to the spirit and letter:—

But over him his flesh shall grieve;
And over him his breath shall mourn.

"In the daring spirit of oriental poetry," says he, "the *flesh*, or body, and the *breath*, are made conscious beings; the former lamenting its putrefaction in the grave, the latter mourning over the mouldering clay which it once enlivened."

This version is, in my opinion, the most natural yet offered. The *Syriac* and *Arabic* present nearly the same sense: "But his body shall grieve over him; and his soul be astonished over him."

Coverdale follows the Vulgate: **Whyle he lyveth his flesh must have travayle; and whyle the soul is in him, he must be in sorowe.**

On ver. 2. I have referred to the following beautiful lines, which illustrate these finely figurative texts:—

He cometh forth as a FLOWER, *and is* CUT DOWN; *he fleeth also as a shadow, and continueth not.*

All flesh is GRASS, *and all the goodliness thereof is as the* FLOWER *of the field.*

The GRASS *withereth, the* FLOWER *fadeth; but the word of our God shall stand for ever.*

The morning flowers display their sweets,
And gay their silken leaves unfold;
As careless of the noonday heats,
As fearless of the evening cold.

Nipp'd by the wind's untimely blast,
Parch'd by the sun's directer ray,
The momentary glories waste,
The short-lived beauties die away.

So blooms the human face divine,
When youth its pride of beauty shows;
Fairer than spring the colours shine,
And sweeter than the virgin rose.

Or worn by slowly-rolling years,
Or broke by sickness in a day,
The fading glory disappears,
The short-lived beauties die away.

Yet these, new rising from the tomb,
With lustre brighter far shall shine;
Revive with ever-during bloom,
Safe from diseases and decline.

Let sickness blast, let death devour,
If heaven must recompense our pains:
Perish the grass and fade the flower,
If firm the word of God remains.

See a Collection of Poems on Sundry Occasions, by the Rev. *Samuel Wesley*, Master of *Blundell's* School, *Tiverton*.

CHAPTER XV

Eliphaz charges Job with impiety in attempting to justify himself, 1–13; *asserts the utter corruption and abominable state of man,* 14–16; *and, from his own knowledge and the observations of the ancients, shows the desolation to which the wicked are exposed, and insinuates that Job has such calamities to dread,* 17–35.

A. M. cir. 2484 B. C. cir. 1520 Ante I. Olymp. cir. 744 Ante U. C. cir. 767

THEN answered Eliphaz the
Temanite, and said,
2 Should a wise man utter [a]vain
knowledge, and fill his belly with
the east wind?
3 Should he reason with unprofitable talk?
or with speeches wherewith he
can do no good?
4 Yea, [b]thou castest off fear, and
restrainest [c]prayer before God.
5 For thy mouth [d]uttereth thine iniquity,
and thou choosest the tongue of the crafty.

A. M. cir. 2484 B. C. cir. 1520 Ante I. Olymp. cir. 744 Ante U. C. cir. 767

---

[a]Heb. *knowledge of wind*——[b]Heb. *thou makest void*——[c]Or, *speech*——[d]Heb. *teacheth*

NOTES ON CHAP. XV

Verse 2. *Should a wise man utter vain knowledge*] Or rather, *Should a wise man utter the science of wind?* A science without solidity or certainty.

And fill his belly with the east wind?] בטן *beten*, which we translate *belly*, is used to signify any part of the cavity of the body, whether the region of the *thorax* or *abdomen;* here it evidently refers to the *lungs*, and may include the *cheeks* and *fauces*. The *east wind*, קדים *kadim*, is a very *stormy wind* in the Levant, or the eastern part of the Mediterranean Sea, supposed to be the same with that called by the Greeks ευροκλυδων, *euroclydon*, the *east storm*, mentioned Acts xxvii. 14. Eliphaz, by these words, seems to intimate that Job's speech was a perfect *storm* or *tempest of words*.

Verse 3. *Should he reason with unprofitable talk?*] Should a man talk disrespectfully of his Maker, or speak to him without reverence? and should he suppose that he has *proved* any thing, when he has uttered words of little meaning, and used *sound* instead of *sense?*

Verse 4. *Thou castest off fear*] Thou hast no reverence for God.

And restrainest prayer] Instead of *humbling* thyself, and making *supplication* to thy Judge, thou spendest thy time in arraigning his providence and justifying thyself.

When a man has any doubts whether he has grieved God's Spirit, and his mind feels troubled, it is much better for him to go immediately to God, and ask *forgiveness*, than spend any time in finding excuses for his conduct, or labouring to divest it of its seeming obliquity. *Restraining* or suppressing *prayer*, in order to find excuses or palliations for infirmities, indiscretions, or improprieties of any kind, which appear to trench on the sacred limits of *morality* and *godliness*, may be to a man the worst of evils: humiliation and prayer for *mercy* and *pardon* can never be out of their place to any soul of man who, surrounded with evils, is ever liable to offend.

Verse 5. *For thy mouth uttereth*] In attempting to justify thyself, thou hast added iniquity to sin, and hast endeavoured to impute blame to thy Maker.

The tongue of the crafty.] Thou hast *var-*

A. M. cir. 2484 B. C. cir. 1520 Ante I. Olymp. cir. 744 Ante U. C. cir. 767

6 [e]Thine own mouth condemneth thee, and not I: yea, thine own lips testify against thee.
7 *Art* thou the first man *that* was born? [f]or wast thou made before the hills?
8 [g]Hast thou heard the secret of God? and dost thou restrain wisdom to thyself?
9 [h]What knowest thou, that we know not? *what* understandest thou, which *is* not in us?
10 [i]With us *are* both the gray-headed and very aged men, much elder than thy father.
11 *Are* the consolations of God small with thee? is there any secret thing with thee?
12 Why doth thine heart carry thee away? and what do thy eyes wink at,

A. M. cir. 2484 B. C. cir. 1520 Ante I. Olymp. cir. 744 Ante U. C. cir. 767

[e]Luke xix. 22; Psa. xc. 2——[f]Prov. viii. 25——[g]Rom. xi. 34; 1 Cor. ii. 11——[h]Ch. xiii. 2——[i]Ch. xxxii. 6, 7

nished thy own conduct, and used *sophistical* arguments to defend thyself. Thou resemblest those *cunning persons*, ערומים *arumim*, who derive their *skill* and *dexterity* from the *old serpent*, "the *nachash*, who was ערום *arum*, *subtle*, or *crafty*, beyond all the beasts of the field;" Gen. iii. 1. Thy wisdom is not from *above*, but from *beneath*.

Verse 7. Art *thou the first man* that *was born?*] Literally, "Wert thou born before Adam?" Art thou in the pristine state of purity and innocence? Or art thou like Adam in his *first state?* It does not become the fallen descendant of a fallen parent to talk as thou dost.

Made before the hills?] Did God create thee the beginning of his ways? or wert thou the first intelligent creature which his hands have formed?

Verse 8. *Hast thou heard the secret of God?*] "Hast thou hearkened in God's council?" Wert thou one of the *celestial cabinet*, when God said, *Let* US *make man in* OUR *image, and in* OUR *likeness?*

Dost thou restrain wisdom to thyself?] Dost thou wish us to understand that God's counsels were revealed to none but thyself? And dost thou desire that we should give implicit credence to whatsoever thou art pleased to speak? These are all strong sarcastic questions, and apparently uttered with great contempt.

Verse 9. *What knowest thou*] Is it likely that thy intellect is greater than ours; and that thou hast cultivated it better than we have done ours?

What *understandest thou*] Or, *Dost thou understand* any thing, *and it is not with us?* Show us any point of knowledge possessed by thyself, of which we are ignorant.

Verse 10. *With us* are *both the gray-headed*] One copy of the *Chaldee Targum* paraphrases the verse thus: "Truly Eliphaz the hoary-headed, and Bildad the long-lived, are among us; and Zophar, who in age surpasseth thy father." It is very likely that Eliphaz refers to himself and his friends in this verse, and not either to the old men of their tribes, or to the masters by whom they themselves were instructed. Eliphaz seems to have been the *eldest* of these sages; and, therefore, he takes the lead in each part of this dramatic poem.

Verse 11. Are *the consolations of God small with thee?*] Various are the renderings of this verse. Mr. *Good* translates the verse thus: "Are then the mercies of God of no account with thee?" or, "the addresses of kindness before thee?"

The VULGATE thus:—"Can it be a difficult thing for God to comfort thee? But thou hinderest this by thy intemperate speeches."

The SYRIAC and ARABIC thus:—"Remove from thee the threatenings (*Arabic*, reproaches) of God, and speak tranquilly with thy own spirit."

The SEPTUAGINT thus:—"Thou hast been scourged lightly for the sins which thou hast committed; and thou hast spoken greatly beyond measure; or, with excessive insolence."

Houbigant thus:—"Dost thou not regard the threatenings of God; or, has there been any thing darkly revealed to thee."

Coverdale:—**Dost thou no more regarde the comforte of God? But thy wicked wordes wil not suffre the.**

Scarcely any two translators or interpreters agree in the *translation*, or even *meaning* of this verse. The *sense*, as expressed in the *Vulgate*, or in our own *version*, or that of *Coverdale*, is plain enough:—"Hast thou been so unfaithful to God, that he has withdrawn his consolations from thy heart? And is there any secret thing, any bosom sin, which thou wilt not give up, that has thus provoked thy Maker?" This is the sense of our version: and I believe it to be as near the original as any yet offered. I may just add the *Chaldee:*—"Are the consolations of God few to thee? And has a word in secret been spoken unto thee?" And I shall close all these with the *Hebrew text*, and the literal version of *Arius Montanus:*—

המעט ממך תנחומות אל

hameat mimmecha tanchumoth el.

ודבר לאט עמך׃

vedabar laat immak.

Nonne parum a te consolationes Dei? Et verbum latet tecum?

"Are not the consolations of God small to thee? And does a word (or thing) lie hidden with thee?"

Now, let the reader choose for himself.

Verse 12. *Why doth thine heart carry thee away?*] Why is it that thou dost conceive and entertain such high sentiments of thyself?

And what do thy eyes wink at] With what splendid opinion of thyself is thine eye dazzled? Perhaps there is an allusion here to that *sparkling in the eye* which is excited by sensations of joy and pleasing objects of sight, or to that furious *rolling of the eyes* observed in deranged persons. *Rosenmüller* translates thus:—

Quo te tuus animus rapit?
Quid occuli tui vibrantes?

"Whither does thy soul hurry thee?
What mean thy rolling eyes?"

A. M. cir. 2484
B. C. cir. 1520
Ante I. Olymp. cir. 744
Ante U. C. cir. 767

13 That thou turnest thy
spirit against God, and lettest
such words go out of thy mouth?
14 [k]What *is* man, that he
should be clean? and *he which is* born of a
woman, that he should be righteous?
15 [l]Behold, he putteth no trust in his saints;
yea, the heavens are not clean in his sight.
16 [m]How much more abominable and filthy
is man, [n]which drinketh iniquity like water?
17 I will show thee, hear me; and that *which*
I have seen I will declare;
18 Which wise men have told
[o]from their fathers, and have not
hid *it*:
19 Unto whom alone the earth
was given, and [p]no stranger passed among them.
20 The wicked man travaileth with pain all
his days, [q]and the number of years is hidden
to the oppressor.
21 [r]A dreadful sound *is* in his ears: [s]in
prosperity the destroyer shall come upon him.
22 He believeth not that he shall return out
of darkness, and he is waited for of the sword.

[k]1 Kings viii. 46; 2 Chron. vi. 36; chap. xiv. 4; Psa. xiv. 3; Prov. xx. 9; Eccles. vii. 20; 1 John i. 8, 10 —— [l]Chap. iv. 18; xxv. 5

[m]Ch. iv. 19; Psa. xiv. 3; liii. 3 —— [n]Ch. xxxiv. 7; Prov. xix. 28 —— [o]Chap. viii. 8 —— [p]Joel iii. 17 —— [q]Psa. xc. 12 —— [r]Heb. *a sound of fears* —— [s]1 Thess. v. 3

Thou seemest transported beyond thyself; thou art actuated by a furious spirit. Thou art *beside thyself;* thy *words* and thy *eyes* show it. None but a *madman* could speak and act as thou dost; for *thou turnest thy spirit against God, and lettest such words go out of thy mouth*, ver. 13. This latter sense seems to agree best with the words of the text, and with the context.

Verse 13. *That thou turnest thy spirit against God*] The ideas here seem to be taken from an *archer*, who *turns his eye* and his *spirit*—his *desire*—against the object which he wishes to hit; and then *lets loose* his arrow that it may attain the mark.

Verse 14. *What* is *man, that he should be clean?*] מה אנוש *mah enosh;* what is *weak, sickly, dying, miserable* man, that he should be clean? This is the import of the original word *enosh.*

And—born of a woman, that he should be righteous?] It appears, from many passages in the sacred writings, that *natural birth* was supposed to be a defilement; and that every man born into the world was in a state of moral pollution. Perhaps the word יצדק *yitsdak* should be translated, *that he should justify himself*, and not *that he should be righteous.*

Verse 15. *Behold, he putteth no trust in his saints; yea, the heavens are not clean in his sight.*] The *Vulgate* has, "Behold, among his saints, none is immutable; and the heavens are not clean in his sight."

Coverdale:—**Beholde, he hath found unfaithfulnesse amonge his owne sanctes, yea, the very heavens are unclene in his sight.**

Eliphaz uses the same mode of speech, chap. iv. 17, 18; where see the notes. Nothing is immutable but GOD: *saints* may fall; *angels* may fall; all their goodness is *derived* and *dependent.* The *heavens* themselves have no purity compared with his.

Verse 16. *How much more abominable and filthy* is *man*] As in the preceding verse it is said, *he putteth no trust in his saints*, it has appeared both to translators and commentators that the original words, אף כי *aph ki*, should be rendered *how much* LESS, not *how much* MORE: How much less would he put confidence in man, who is filthy and abominable in his nature, and profligate in his practice, as he *drinks down iniquity like water?* A man who is under the power of sinful propensities commits sin as greedily as the *thirsty man* or *camel* drinks down water. He thinks he can never have enough. This is a finished character of a BAD *man; he hungers and thirsts after* SIN: on the contrary, the GOOD *man hungers and thirsts after* RIGHTEOUSNESS.

Verse 17. *I will show thee, hear me; and that* which *I have seen I will declare*] Eliphaz is now about to quote a whole collection of *wise sayings* from the ancients; all good enough in themselves, but sinfully misapplied to the case of Job.

Verse 19. *Unto whom alone the earth was given*] He very likely refers to the *Israelites*, who got possession of the promised land from God himself; no *stranger* being permitted to dwell in it, as the old inhabitants were to be exterminated. Some think that *Noah* and *his sons* may be intended; as it is certain that the *whole earth* was *given to them*, when there were no *strangers*—no other family of mankind—in being. But, *system* apart, the words seem to apply more clearly to the *Israelites.*

Verse 20. *The wicked man travaileth with pain*] This is a most forcible truth: a life of sin is a life of misery; and he that WILL *sin* MUST *suffer.* One of the *Targums* gives it a strange turn:—"All the days of the ungodly Esau he was expected to repent, but he did not repent; and the number of years was hidden from the sturdy Ishmael." The sense of the original, מתחולל *mithcholel*, is *he torments himself:* he is a true *heautontimoreumenos*, or self-tormentor; and he alone is author of his own sufferings, and of his own ruin.

Verse 21. *A dreadful sound* is *in his ears*] If he be an oppressor or tyrant, he can have no rest; he is full of suspicions that the cruelties he has exercised on others shall be one day exercised on himself; for even in his prosperity he may expect the destroyer to rush upon him.

Verse 22. *That he shall return out of darkness*] If he take but a few steps in the dark, he expects the *dagger* of the assassin. This appears to be the only meaning of the place. Some think the passage should be understood to signify that he has no hope of a *resurrection;* he can never escape from the tomb. This I

A. M. cir. 2484
B. C. cir. 1520
Ante I. Olymp. cir. 744
Ante U. C. cir. 767

23 He [t]wandereth abroad for
bread, *saying,* Where *is it?* he
knoweth that [u]the day of darkness is ready at his hand.
24 Trouble and anguish shall make him
afraid; they shall prevail against him, as a
king ready to the battle.
25 For he stretcheth out his hand against God,
and strengtheneth himself against the Almighty.
26 He runneth upon him, *even* on *his* neck,
upon the thick bosses of his bucklers;
27 [v]Because he covereth his face with his
fatness, and maketh collops of
fat on *his* flanks.
28 And he dwelleth in desolate cities, *and* in houses which
no man inhabiteth, which are ready to become
heaps.
29 He shall not be rich, neither shall his
substance continue, neither shall he prolong
the perfection thereof upon the earth.
30 He shall not depart out of darkness;
the flame shall dry up his branches, and
[w]by the breath of his mouth shall he go
away.

[t]Psa. lix. 15; cix. 10——[u]Chap. xviii. 12

[v]Chap. xvii. 10——[w]Chap. iv. 9

doubt: in the days of the writer of this book, the doctrine of a future judgment was understood in every part of the East where the knowledge of the true God was diffused.

Verse 23. *He wandereth abroad for bread*] He is reduced to a state of the utmost indigence; he who was once in affluence requires a morsel of bread, and can scarcely by begging procure enough to sustain life.

Is ready at his hand.] *Is* בידו *beyado, in his hand*—in his possession. As he cannot get *bread,* he must soon meet *death.*

Verse 24. *Trouble and anguish shall make him afraid*] He shall be in continual fear of death; being now brought down by adversity, and stripped of all the goods which he had got by oppression, his life is a mark for the meanest assassin.

As a king ready to the battle.] The acts of his wickedness and oppression are as numerous as the troops he commands; and when he comes to meet his enemy in the field, he is not only deserted but slain by his troops. How true are the words of the poet:—

Ad generum Cereris sine cæde et vulnere pauci
Descendunt reges, et sicca morte tyranni.
Juv. Sat., ver. 112.

"For few usurpers to the shades descend
By a dry death, or with a quiet end."

Verse 25. *He stretcheth out his hand against God*] While in *power* he thought himself *supreme.* He not only did not acknowledge God, by whom kings reign, but *stretched out his hand*—used his *power,* not to *protect,* but to *oppress* those over whom he had supreme rule; and thus *strengthened himself against the Almighty.*

Verse 26. *He runneth upon him*] *Calmet* has properly observed that this refers to God, who, like a mighty conquering hero, marches against the ungodly, rushes upon him, seizes him by the throat, which the *mail* by which it is encompassed cannot protect; neither his shield nor spear can save him when the *Lord of hosts* comes against him.

Verse 27. *Because he covereth his face*] He has lived in luxury and excess; and like a man overloaded with flesh, he cannot defend himself against the strong gripe of his adversary.

The *Arabic,* for *maketh collops of fat on his flanks,* has وجعل الثريا فوق العيوق *He lays the Pleiades upon the Hyades,* or, *He places Surreea upon aiyuk,* a proverbial expression for, His ambition is boundless; He aspires as high as heaven; His head touches the stars; or, is like the *giants* of old, who were fabled to have attempted to scale heaven by placing one high mountain upon another:—

Ter sunt conati imponere Pelio Ossam
Scilicet, atque Ossæ frondosum involvere Olympum
Ter Pater extructos disjecit fulmine montes.
Virg. Geor. i., ver. 281.

"With mountains piled on mountains, thrice they strove
To scale the steepy battlements of Jove;
And thrice his lightning and red thunder play'd,
And their demolish'd works in ruins laid."
Dryden.

To the lust of power and the schemes of ambition there are no bounds; but see the end of such persons: the haughty spirit precedes a fall; their palaces become desolate; and their heaven is reduced to a chaos.

Verse 28. *He dwelleth in desolate cities*] It is sometimes the fate of a tyrant to be obliged to take up his habitation in some of those cities which have been ruined by his wars, and in a house so ruinous as to be ready to fall into heaps. Ancient and modern history afford abundance of examples to illustrate this.

Verse 29. *He shall not be rich*] The whole of what follows, to the end of the chapter, seems to be directed against Job himself, whom Eliphaz indirectly accuses of having been a *tyrant* and *oppressor.* The threatened evils are, 1. *He shall not be rich,* though he labours greatly to acquire riches. 2. *His substance shall not continue*—God will blast it, and deprive him of *power* to preserve it. 3. *Neither shall he prolong the perfection thereof*—all his works shall perish, for God will blot out his remembrance from under heaven.

Verse 30. *He shall not depart out of darkness*] 4. He shall be in continual afflictions and distress. 5. *The flame shall dry up his branches*—his *children* shall be cut off by sudden judg-

A. M. cir. 2484
B. C. cir. 1520
Ante I. Olymp. cir. 744
Ante U. C. cir. 767

31 Let not him that is deceived [x]trust in vanity: for vanity
shall be his recompense.
32 It shall be [y]accomplished
[z]before his time, and his branch shall not be
green.
33 He shall shake off his unripe grape as
the vine, and shall cast off his
flower as the olive.
34 For the congregation of
hypocrites *shall be* desolate, and
fire shall consume the tabernacles of bribery.
35 [a]They conceive mischief, and bring forth
[b]vanity, and their belly prepareth deceit.

A. M. cir. 2484
B. C. cir. 1520
Ante I. Olymp. cir. 744
Ante U. C. cir. 767

[x]Isa. lix. 4——[y]Or, *cut off*——[z]Ch. xxii. 16; Psa. lv. 23

[a]Psa. vii. 14; Isa. lix. 4; Hos. x. 13——[b]Or, *iniquity*

ments. 6. *He shall pass away by the breath of his mouth;* for by the breath of his mouth doth God slay the wicked.

Verse 31. *Let not him that is deceived*] 7. He has many *vain imaginations* of obtaining wealth, power, pleasure, and happiness; but he is *deceived;* and he finds that he has trusted בשוא *bashshav, in a lie;* and this lie is his recompense.

Verse 32. *It shall be accomplished before his time*] I believe the *Vulgate* gives the true sense: *Antequam dies ejus impleantur, peribit;* "He shall perish before his time; before his days are completed." 8. He shall be removed by a violent death, and not live out half his days. 9. *And his branch shall not be green*—there shall be no *scion* from his roots; all his *posterity* shall fail.

Verse 33. *He shall shake off his unripe grape*] 10. Whatever *children* he may have, they shall never survive him, nor come to mature age. They shall be like *wind-fall grapes* and *blasted olive blossoms.* As the *vine* and *olive,* which are among the most *useful* trees, affording *wine* and *oil,* so necessary for the worship of God and the comfort of man, are mentioned here they may be intended to refer to the hopeful progeny of the oppressor; but who fell, like the untimely grape or the blasted olive flower, without having the opportunity of realizing the public expectation.

Verse 34. *The congregation of hypocrites*] 11. Job is here classed with *hypocrites,* or rather the *impious* of all kinds. The *congregation,* or עדת *adath, society,* of such, shall be *desolate,* or a *barren rock,* גלמוד *galmud.* See this Arabic word explained in the note on chap. iii. 7.

Fire shall consume the tabernacles of bribery.] 12. Another insinuation against Job, that he had perverted justice and judgment, and had taken *bribes.*

Verse 35. *They conceive mischief*] The figure here is both elegant and impressive. The wicked *conceive* mischief, from the seed which Satan sows in their hearts; in producing which they *travail* with many pangs, (for sin is a sore labour,) and at last their *womb* produces *fraud* or *deception.* This is an *accursed* birth, from an *iniquitous* conception. St. *James* gives the figure at full length, most beautifully touched in all its parts: *When lust hath conceived it bringeth forth sin; and sin, when it is finished, bringeth forth death;* James i. 15, where see the note.

Poor Job! what a fight of affliction had he to contend with! His *body* wasted and tortured with sore *disease;* his *mind* harassed by *Satan;* and his *heart* wrung with the unkindness, and false accusations of his *friends.* No wonder he was greatly agitated, often distracted, and sometimes even thrown off his guard. However, all his enemies were chained; and beyond that chain they could not go. God was his unseen Protector, and did not suffer his faithful servant to be greatly moved.

CHAPTER XVI

Job replies to Eliphaz, and through him to all his friends, who, instead of comforting him, had added to his misfortunes; and shows that, had they been in his circumstances, he would have treated them in a different manner, 1–5. *Enters into an affecting detail of his suffering,* 6–16. *Consoles himself with the consciousness of his own innocence, of which he takes God to witness, and patiently expects a termination of all his sufferings by death,* 17–22.

A. M. cir. 2484
B. C. cir. 1520
Ante I. Olymp. cir. 744
Ante U. C. cir. 767

THEN Job answered and said,
2 I have heard many such
things: [a]miserable [b]comforters
are ye all.
3 Shall [c]vain words have an
end? or what emboldeneth thee
that thou answerest?
4 I also could speak as ye *do:*

A. M. cir. 2484
B. C. cir. 1520
Ante I. Olymp. cir. 744
Ante U. C. cir. 767

[a]Or, *troublesome*——[b]Chap. xiii. 4

[c]Heb. *words of wind*

NOTES ON CHAP. XVI

Verse 2. *I have heard many such things*] These sayings of the ancients are not strange to me; but they do not apply to my case: ye see me in affliction; ye should endeavour to console me. This ye do not; and yet ye pretend to do it! *Miserable comforters* are *ye all.*

Verse 3. *Vain words*] Literally, *words of air. What emboldeneth thee*] Thou art totally ignorant of the business; what then can induce thee to take part in this discussion?

Verse 4. *I also could speak*] It is probably better to render some of these *permissives* or *potential verbs* literally in the *future tense,* as in the Hebrew: *I also* WILL *speak.* Mr. *Good* has adopted this mode.

A. M. cir. 2484
B. C. cir. 1520
Ante I. Olymp. cir. 744
Ante U. C. cir. 767

if your soul were in my soul's
stead, I could heap up words
against you, and [d]shake mine
head at you.

5 *But* I would strengthen you with my
mouth, and the moving of my lips should
assuage *your grief*.

6 Though I speak, my grief is not assuaged:
and *though* I forbear, [e]what am I eased?

7 But now he hath made me weary: thou
hast made desolate all my company.

8 And thou hast filled me with wrinkles,
which is a witness *against me:* and my leanness rising up in me beareth witness to my
face.

9 [f]He teareth *me* in his wrath, who hateth
me: he gnasheth upon me with his teeth;
[g]mine enemy sharpeneth his eyes upon me.

10 They have [h]gaped upon me
with their mouth; they [i]have
smitten me upon the cheek re-
proachfully; they have [k]gathered
themselves together against me.

A. M. cir. 2484
B. C. cir. 1520
Ante I. Olymp. cir. 744
Ante U. C. cir. 767

11 God [l]hath [m]delivered me to the ungodly,
and turned me over into the hands of the
wicked.

12 I was at ease, but he hath broken me
asunder: he hath also taken *me* by my neck,
and shaken me to pieces, and [n]set me up for
his mark.

13 His archers compass me round about, he
cleaveth my reins asunder, and doth not spare;
he poureth out my gall upon the ground.

14 He breaketh me with breach upon breach,
he runneth upon me like a giant.

15 I have sewed sackcloth upon my skin,

[d]Psa. xxii. 7; cix. 25; Lam. ii. 15——[e]Heb. *what goeth from me?*——[f]Ch. x. 16, 17——[g]Ch. xiii. 24——[h]Psa. xxii. 13——[i]Lam. iii. 30; Mic. v. 1——[k]Psa. xxxv. 15 [l]Ch. i. 15, 17——[m]Heb. *hath shut me up*——[n]Ch. vii. 20

If your soul were in my soul's stead] If you were in my place, I also could quote many wise sayings that might tend to show that you were hypocrites and wicked men; but would this be fair? Even when I might not choose to go farther in *assertion*, I might *shake my head* by way of *insinuation* that there was much more behind, of which I did not choose to speak; but would this be right? That such sayings are in memory, is no proof that they were either made for me, or apply to my case.

Verse 5. *I would strengthen you with my mouth*] Mr. *Good* translates thus:—

"With my own mouth will I overpower you,
Till the quivering of my lips shall fail;"

for which rendering he contends in his learned notes. This translation is countenanced by the *Septuagint*, *Syriac*, and *Arabic* versions.

Verse 6. *Though I speak*] But it will be of no avail thus to speak; for reprehensions of *your* conduct will not serve to mitigate *my* sufferings.

Verse 7. *But now he hath made me weary*] The *Vulgate* translates thus:—*Nunc autem oppressit me dolor meus; et in nihilum redacti sunt omnes artus mei;* "But now my grief oppresses me, and all my joints are reduced to nothing." Perhaps Job alluded here to his *own afflictions*, and the *desolation of his family*. Thou hast made me weary with continual affliction; my strength is quite exhausted; and thou hast made desolate all my company, not leaving me a single child to continue my name, or to comfort me in sickness or old age. Mr. *Good* translates:—

"Here, indeed, hath he distracted me;
Thou hast struck apart all my witnesses."

Verse 8. *Thou hast filled me with wrinkles*] If Job's disease were the *elephantiasis*, in which the whole skin is *wrinkled* as the skin of the *elephant*, from which this species of leprosy has taken its name, these words would apply most forcibly to it; but the whole passage, through its obscurity, has been variously rendered. *Calmet* unites it with the preceding, and *Houbigant* is not very different. He translates thus:—"For my trouble hath now weakened all my frame, and brought wrinkles over me: he is present as a witness, and ariseth against me, who telleth lies concerning me; he openly contradicts me to my face." Mr. *Good* translates nearly in the same way; others still differently.

Verse 9. *He teareth* me *in his wrath*] Who the person is that is spoken of in this verse, and onward to the end of the *fourteenth*, has been a question on which commentators have greatly differed. Some think God, others Eliphaz, is intended: I think *neither*. Probably God permitted *Satan* to *show* himself to Job, and the *horrible* form which he and his *demons* assumed increased the misery under which Job had already suffered so much. All the expressions, from this to the end of the *fourteenth* verse, may be easily understood on this principle; *e. g.*, ver. 9: "He (*Satan*) gnasheth upon me with his teeth; mine enemy sharpeneth his eyes upon me." Ver. 10: "They (*demons*) have gaped on me with their mouth;—they have gathered themselves together against me." Ver. 11: "God hath delivered me to the ungodly, (עויל *avil*, to the EVIL ONE,) and turned me over into the hands of the wicked." He hath abandoned me to be tortured by the *tempter* and his *host*.

If we consider all these expressions as referring to Job's *three friends*, we must, in that case, acknowledge that the *figures* are all strained to an insufferable height, so as not to be justified by any *figure* of speech.

Verse 13. *His archers compass me*] רביו *rabbaiv* "his great ones." The *Vulgate* and *Septuagint* translate this *his spears;* the *Syriac*, *Arabic*, and *Chaldee*, *his arrows*. On this and the following verse Mr. *Heath* observes: "The metaphor is here taken from huntsmen: first, they surround the beast; then he is shot dead; his entrails are next taken out; and then his body is broken up limb by limb."

Verse 15. *I have sewed sackcloth*] שק *sak*,

A. M. cir. 2484 B. C. cir. 1520 Ante I. Olymp. cir. 744 Ante U. C. cir. 767

and [o]defiled my horn in the
dust.
16 My face is foul with weeping, and on my eyelids *is* the
shadow of death.
17 Not for *any* injustice in mine hands: also
my prayer *is* pure.
18 O earth, cover not thou my blood, and
[p]let my cry have no place.
19 Also now, behold, [q]my witness *is* in heaven, and my record
is on [r]high.
20 My friends [s]scorn me: *but*
mine eye poureth out *tears* unto God.
21 [t]O that one might plead for a man with
God, as a man *pleadeth* for his [u]neighbour!
22 When [v]a few years are come, then I shall
[w]go the way *whence* I shall not return.

---

[o]Chap. xxx. 19; Psa. vii. 5—— [p]Chap. xxvii. 9; Psa. lxvi. 18, 19——[q]Rom. i. 9——[r]Heb. *in the high places* [s]Heb. are *my scorners*

[t]Chap. xxxi. 35; Eccles. vi. 10; Isa. xlv. 9; Rom. ix. 20——[u]Or, *friend*——[v]Hebrew, *years of number* [w]Eccles. xii. 5

---

a word that has passed into almost all languages, as I have already had occasion to notice in other parts of this work.

Defiled my horn in the dust.] The *horn* was an emblem of *power;* and the metaphor was originally taken from beasts, such as the urus, wild ox, *buffalo,* or perhaps the *rhinoceros,* who were perceived to have so much power in their horns. Hence a horn was frequently worn on crowns and helmets, as is evident on ancient coins; and to this day it is an appendage to the diadem of the kings and chiefs of Abyssinia. In the second edition of Mr. Bruce's Travels in Abyssinia, vol. viii., plates 2 and 3, we have engravings of two chiefs, *Kefla Yasous,* and *Woodage Ashahel,* who are represented with this emblem of *power* on their forehead. Mr. Bruce thus describes it: "One thing remarkable in this cavalcade, which I observed, was the head dress of the *governors of provinces.* A large broad fillet was bound upon their forehead, and tied behind their head. In the middle of this was a *horn,* or a conical piece of silver, gilt, about *four* inches in length, much in the shape of our common candle extinguishers. This is called *kirn,* or horn; and is only worn in reviews, or *parades after victory.* This, I apprehend, like all others of their usages, is taken from the Hebrews; and the several allusions made in Scripture to it arise from this practice. 'I said unto the fools, Deal not foolishly; and to the wicked, Lift not up the *horn.*' 'Lift not up your *horn* on high, speak not with a stiff neck; for promotion cometh not,' &c. 'But my *horn* shalt thou *exalt* like the horn of a unicorn.' 'And the *horn* of the righteous shall be *exalted* with honour.' And so in many other places throughout the Psalms." In a note on the same page we have the following observation: "The crooked manner in which they hold their neck when this ornament is on their forehead, for fear it should fall forward, perfectly shows the meaning of 'Speak not with a stiff neck when you hold the horn on high (or erect) like the horn of the unicorn.' "—Bruce's Travels, vol. iv., p. 407.

Defiling or *rolling the horn in the dust,* signifies the disgrace or destruction of power, authority, and eminence.

Mr. *Good* translates, *I have rolled my* turban *in the dust,* which he endeavours to justify in a long note. But in this, I think, this very learned man is mistaken. The Hebrew קרן *keren* is the same as the Æthiopic *kirn,* and both mean exactly, in such connection, what Mr. Bruce has noticed above. The *horn* on the *diadem* is the emblem of power, authority, and eminence.

Verse 16. *On my eyelids* is *the shadow of death*] Death is now *fast approaching* me; already his *shadow* is projected over me.

Verse 17. *Not for* any *injustice*] I must assert, even with my last breath, that the charges of my friends against me are groundless. I am afflicted unto death, but not on account of my iniquities.

Also my prayer is *pure.*] I am no hypocrite, God knoweth.

Verse 18. *O earth, cover not thou my blood*] This is evidently an allusion to the murder of Abel, and the verse has been understood in *two* different ways: 1. Job here calls for justice against his destroyers. His *blood* is his *life,* which he considers as taken away by *violence.* and therefore calls for vengeance. Let my blood cry against my murderers, as the blood of Abel cried against Cain. My innocent life is taken away by violence, as his innocent life was; as therefore the *earth* was not permitted *to cover his blood,* so that his murderer should be concealed, let my death be avenged in the same way. 2. It has been supposed that the passage means that Job considered himself accused of shedding innocent blood; and, conscious of his own perfect innocence, he prays that the earth may not cover any blood shed by him. Thus Mr. Scott:—

"O earth, the blood accusing me reveal;
Its piercing voice in no recess conceal."

And this notion is followed by Mr. *Good.* But, with all deference to these learned men, I do not see that this meaning can be supported by the Hebrew text; nor was the passage so understood by any of the ancient versions. I therefore prefer the first sense, which is sufficiently natural, and quite in the manner of Job in his impassioned querulousness.

Verse 19. *My witness* is *in heaven*] I appeal to God for my innocence.

Verse 20. *My friends scorn me*] They deride and insult me, but my eye is towards God; I look to him to vindicate my cause.

Verse 21. *O that one might plead*] Let me only have liberty to plead with God, as a man hath with his fellow.

Verse 22. *When a few years are come*] I prefer Mr. *Good's* version:—

"But the years numbered to me are come,
And I must go the way whence I shall not return."

Job could not, in his present circumstances, expect *a few years of longer life;* from his own conviction he was expecting death every hour. The next verse, the *first* of the following chapter, should come in here: *My breath is corrupt, &c.*] He felt himself as in the arms of death: he saw the grave as already digged which was to receive his dead body. This verse shows that our translation of the *twenty-second* verse is improper, and vindicates Mr. *Good's* version.

I HAVE said on ver. 9 that a part of Job's sufferings probably arose from appalling representations made to his eye or to his imagination by Satan and his agents. I think this neither irrational nor improbable. That he and his demons have power to make themselves manifest on especial occasions, has been credited in all ages of the world; not by the weak, credulous, and superstitious only, but also by the wisest, the most learned, and the best of men. I am persuaded that many passages in the Book of Job refer to this, and admit of an easy interpretation on this ground.

CHAPTER XVII

Job complains of the injustice of his friends, and compares his present state of want and wo with his former honour and affluence, 1–6. *God's dealings with him will even astonish upright men; yet the righteous shall not be discouraged, but hold on his way,* 7–9. *Asserts that there is not a wise man among his friends, and that he has no expectation but of a speedy death,* 10–16.

A. M. cir. 2484
B. C. cir. 1520
Ante I. Olymp. cir. 744
Ante U. C. cir. 767

MY [a]breath is corrupt, my
days are extinct, [b]the graves
are ready for me.
2 *Are there* not mockers with
me? and doth not mine eye [c]continue in their
[d]provocation?
3 Lay down now, put me in a surety with
thee; who *is* he *that* [e]will strike hands with me?
4 For thou hast hid their heart
from understanding: therefore
shalt thou not exalt *them*.
5 He that speaketh flattery to
his friends, even the eyes of his children
shall fail.
6 He hath made me also a [f]by-word of the
people; and [g]aforetime I was as a tabret.

A. M. cir. 2484
B. C. cir. 1520
Ante I. Olymp. cir. 744
Ante U. C. cir. 767

[a]Or, *spirit is spent*——[b]Psa. lxxxviii. 3, 4——[c]Heb. *lodge*——[d]1 Sam. i. 6, 7——[e]Prov. vi. 1; xvii. 18; xxii. 26——[f]Chap. xxx. 9——[g]Or, *before them*

NOTES ON CHAP. XVII

Verse 1. *My breath is corrupt*] Rather, *My spirit is oppressed,* רוחי חבלה *ruchi chubbalah: My days are extinct, and the sepulchral cells* are ready *for me.*—PARKHURST. There is probably a reference here to cemeteries, where were several niches, in each of which a corpse was deposited. See on ver. 16.

For חבלה *chubbalah, corrupted* or *oppressed,* some MSS. have חלה *chalah, is made weak;* and one has נבלה *is worn down, consumed:* this is agreeable to the *Vulgate, Spiritus meus attenuebatur;* "My spirit is exhausted."

Verse 2. Are there *not mockers with me?*] This has been variously translated. The VULGATE: "I have not sinned, and yet my eye dwells upon afflictions." SEPTUAGINT: "I conjure you, labouring under afflictions, what evil have I done? Yet strangers have robbed me of my substance." Mr. GOOD: "But are not revilers before me? Alas, mine eye penetrateth their rebukes." CALMET thinks the Hebrew might be translated thus: "If I have not been united in friendship with the wicked, why are my eyes in bitterness?" COVERDALE translates both verses thus: **My breth fayleth, my dayes are shortened, I am harde at deathes dore. I have disceaved no man, yet must myne eye continue in hevynesse.** Mr. HEATH: "Were it not so, I have sarcasms enow in store; and I could spend the whole night unmoved at their aggravations." The general meaning is sufficiently plain, and the reader has got translations enough.

Verse 3. *Lay down now*] Deposit a pledge; stake your conduct against mine, and your life and soul on the issue; let the cause come before God; let him try it; and see whether any of you shall be justified by him, while I am condemned.

Verse 4. *For thou hast hid their heart*] This address is to *God;* and here he is represented as *doing* that which in the course of his providence he only *permits* to be done.

Shalt thou not exalt them.] This was exactly fulfilled: not one of Job's friends was exalted; on the contrary, God condemned the whole; and they were not received into the Divine favour till Job sacrificed, and made intercession for them.

Verse 5. *He that speaketh flattery*] There is a great variety of meaning given to the terms in this verse. The general sense is, The man who expects much from his friends will be disappointed: while depending on them his children's eyes may fail in looking for bread.

Verse 6. *He hath made me also a by-word*] My afflictions and calamities have become a subject of general conversation, so that my poverty and affliction are proverbial. *As poor as Job, As afflicted as Job,* are proverbs that have even reached our times and are still in use.

Aforetime I was as a tabret.] This is not the translation of the Hebrew ותפת לפנים אהיה *vethopheth lephanim eheyeh.* Instead of לפנים *lephanim,* I would read לפניהם *liphneyhem,* and then the clause might be translated thus: *I shall be as a furnace,* or *consuming fire* (Topheth) *before them.* They shall have little reason to mock when they see the end of the Lord's dealings with me; my example will be a consuming fire to them, and my false friends

A. M. cir. 2484 B. C. cir. 1520 Ante I. Olymp. cir. 744 Ante U. C. cir. 767

7 [h]Mine eye also is dim by reason of sorrow, and all [i]my members *are* as a shadow.
8 Upright *men* shall be astonied at this, and the innocent shall stir up himself against the hypocrite.
9 The righteous also shall hold on his way, and he that hath [k]clean hands [l]shall be stronger and stronger.
10 But as for you all, [m]do ye return, and come now: for I cannot find *one* wise *man* among you.
11 [n]My days are past, my purposes are broken off, *even* [o]the thoughts of my heart.
12 They change the night into day: the light *is* [p]short because of darkness.
13 If I wait, the grave *is* mine house: I have made my bed in the darkness.
14 I have [q]said to corruption, Thou *art* my father: to the worm, *Thou art* my mother, and my sister.
15 And where *is* now my hope? as for my hope, who shall see it?
16 They shall go down [r]to the bars of the pit, when *our* [s]rest together *is* in the dust.

A. M. cir. 2484 B. C. cir. 1520 Ante I. Olymp. cir. 744 Ante U. C. cir. 767

[h]Psalm vi. 7; xxxi. 9——[i]Or, *my thoughts*——[k]Psalm xxiv. 4——[l]Hebrew, *shall add strength*——[m]Chapter vi. 29——[n]Chapter vii. 6; ix. 25——[o]Hebrew, *the possessions*——[p]Hebrew, *near*——[q]Hebrew, *cried* or *called*——[r]Chapter xviii. 13——[s]Chapter iii. 17, 18, 19

will be confounded. COVERDALE translates thus: **He hath made me as it were a byworde of the comon people. I am his gestinge stocke amonge them.**

Verse 7. *Mine eye also is dim*] Continual weeping impairs the sight; and indeed any affliction that debilitates the frame generally, weakens the *sight* in the same proportion.

All my members are *as a shadow.*] Nothing is left but *skin* and *bone.* I am but the *shadow* of my *former self.*

Verse 8. *Upright* men *shall be astonied*] In several of these verses Job is supposed to speak prophetically of his future restoration, and of the good which religious society should derive from the history of his original affluence, consequent poverty and affliction, and final restoration to health, peace, and prosperity. The *upright* will receive the account with astonishment, and wonder at the dispensations of the Almighty; while *hypocrites,* false professors and the *sour-headed,* godly, shall be unmasked, and *innocent* men, whether in affliction or affluence, shall be known to be favourites of the Almighty.

Verse 9. *The righteous also shall hold on his way*] There shall be no doubt concerning the dispensations of the Divine providence. My case shall illustrate all seemingly intricate displays of God's government. None shall be stumbled at seeing a godly man under oppression, knowing that God never permits any thing of the kind but for the good of the subject, and the manifestation of his own mercy, wisdom, and love. Therefore, whatever occurs to the righteous man, he will take it for granted that all is well and justly managed, and that the end will be glorious.

Shall be stronger and stronger.] He shall take encouragement from my case, stay himself on the Lord, and thus gain strength by every blast of adversity. This is one grand use of the book of Job. It casts much light on seemingly partial displays of Divine providence: and has ever been the great *text-book* of godly men in a state of persecution and affliction. This is what Job seems prophetically to declare.

Verse 10. *But as for you all*] Ye are too proud, and too full of self-importance, to profit by what ye see. *Return*—enter into yourselves, consider your ways, go again to school, get back to your own houses, and endeavour to acquire humility and knowledge; for there is not one wise man among you.

Verse 11. *My days are past*] Job seems to relapse here into his former state of gloom. These *transitions* are very frequent in this poem; and they strongly mark the struggle of piety and resignation with continued affliction, violent temptation, and gloomy providences.

The thoughts of my heart.] All my purposes are interrupted; and all my schemes and plans, in relation to myself and family, are torn asunder, destroyed, and dissipated.

Verse 12. *They change the night into day*] These purposes and thoughts are so very gloomy, that they change day into night.

The light is *short because of darkness.*] אור קרוב מפני חשך *or karob mippeney choshek,* "The light is near from the face of darkness." I have scarcely any light: what is called *light* is so near akin to darkness, that it is scarcely severed from it. There is either *no light,* or merely such as is sufficient to render *darkness visible.* A fine picture of the state of his mind—he was generally in darkness; but had occasional *gleams* of hope.

Verse 13. *The grave* is *mine house*] Let my life be long or short, the grave at last will be my *home.* I expect soon to lie down in darkness—there is my end: I cannot reasonably hope for any thing else.

Verse 14. *I have said to corruption*] I came from a corrupted stock, and I must go to corruption again. The Hebrew might be thus rendered: *To the ditch I have called, Thou* art *my father. To the worm,* Thou art *my mother and my sister.* I am in the nearest state of affinity to *dissolution* and *corruption:* I may well call them my *nearest relations,* as I shall soon be blended with them.

Verse 15. *And where* is *now my hope?*] In the circumstances in which I am found, of what use can *hope* be? Were I to form the expectation of future good, who could ever see it realized? Is it then any wonder that I should complain and bemoan my wretched lot?

Verse 16. *They shall go down to the bars of the pit*] All that I have must descend into the depths of the grave. Thither are we all going; and there alone can I *rest.*

בדי *baddey*, which we translate *bars*, signifies also *branches*, *distended limbs*, or *claws*, and may here refer either to a personification of the grave, a monster who seizes on human bodies, and keeps them fast in his *deadly gripe;* or to the different *branching-off-alleys* in subterranean cemeteries, or catacombs, in which *niches* are made for the reception of different bodies.

When our *rest together* is *in the dust.*] That is, according to some critics, My *hope* and *myself* shall descend together into the grave. It shall never be realized, for the time of my departure is at hand.

In those times what deep shades hung on the state of man after death, and on every thing pertaining to the eternal world! Perplexity and uncertainty were the consequences; and a corresponding gloom often dwelt on the minds of even the best of the Old Testament believers. Job's friends, though learned in all the wisdom of the Arabians, connected with the advantages derivable from the Mosaic writings, and perhaps those of the earlier prophets, had little clear or distinct in their minds relative to all subjects *post mortem*, or of the invisible world. Job himself, though sometimes strongly confident, is often harassed with doubts and fears upon the subject, insomuch that his sayings and experience often appear contradictory. Perhaps it could not be otherwise; the true light was not then come: Jesus alone brought life and immortality to light by his Gospel.

CHAPTER XVIII

Bildad, in a speech of passionate invective, accuses Job of impatience and impiety, 1–4; *shows the fearful end of the wicked and their posterity; and apparently applies the whole to Job, whom he threatens with the most ruinous end,* 5–21.

A. M. cir. 2484
B. C. cir. 1520
Ante I. Olymp. cir. 744
Ante U. C. cir. 767

THEN answered Bildad the
Shuhite, and said,
2 How long *will it be ere*
ye make an end of words?
mark, and afterwards we will speak.
3 Wherefore are we counted
[a]as beasts, *and* reputed vile in
your sight?
4 [b]He teareth [c]himself in his
anger: shall the earth be forsaken for thee?

A. M. cir. 2484
B. C. cir. 1520
Ante I. Olymp. cir. 744
Ante U. C. cir. 767

[a]Psa. lxxiii. 22——[b]Chap. xiii. 14 — [c]Heb. *his soul*

NOTES ON CHAP. XVIII

Verse 1. *Then answered Bildad*] The following analysis of this speech, by Mr. *Heath*, is judicious: "Bildad, irritated to the last degree that Job should treat their advice with so much contempt, is no longer able to keep his passions within the bounds of decency. He proceeds to downright abuse; and finding little attention given by Job to his arguments, he tries to terrify him into a compliance. To that end he draws a yet more terrible picture of the final end of wicked men than any yet preceding, throwing in all the circumstances of Job's calamities, that he might plainly perceive the resemblance; and at the same time insinuating that he had much worse still to expect, unless he prevented it by a speedy change of behaviour. That it was the highest arrogance in him to suppose that he was of consequence enough to be the cause of altering the general rules of Providence, ver. 4. And that it was much more expedient for the good of the whole, that he, by his example, should deter others from treading in the same path of wickedness and folly;" ver. 5-7.

Verse 2. *How long* will it be ere *ye make an end*] It is difficult to say to whom this address is made: being in the *plural* number, it can hardly be supposed to mean Job only. It probably means all present; as if he had said, It is vain to talk with this man, and follow him through all his quibbles: take notice of this, and then let us all deliver our sentiments fully to him, without paying any regard to his self-vindications. It must be owned that this is the plan which Bildad followed; and he amply unburdens a mind that was labouring under the spirit of rancour and abuse. Instead of *How long* will it be ere *ye make an end of words?* Mr. *Good* translates: "*How long will ye plant thorns* (irritating, lacerating, wounding invectives) *among words?*" translating the unusual term קנצי *kintsey, thorns*, instead of *bounds* or *limits*. The word קנצי *kintsey* may be the Chaldee form for קצי *kitsey*, the נ *nun* being inserted by the Chaldeans for the sake of *euphony*, as is frequently done; and it may be considered as the contracted plural from קץ *kats*, a *thorn*, from קץ *kats*, to lacerate, rather than קץ *kets*, an *end*, from קצה *katsah*, to cut off.

Schultens and others have contended that קנץ *kanats*, is an Arabic word, used also in Hebrew; that قنص *kanasa*, signifies to *hunt*, to *lay snares;* and hence مقنص *maknas*, a snare: and that the words should be translated, "How long will you put captious snares in words?" But I prefer קנצי *kintsey*, as being the *Chaldee* form for קצי *kitsey*, whether it be considered as expressing *limits* or *thorns;* as the whole instance is formed after the Chaldee model, as is evident, not only in the word in question, but also in למלין *lemillin, to words*, the Chaldee plural instead of למלים *lemillim*, the Hebrew plural.

Verse 3. *Counted as beasts*] Thou treatest us as if we had neither reason nor understanding.

Verse 4. *He teareth himself in his anger*] Literally, *Rending his own soul in his anger;* as if he had said, Thou art a madman: thy fury has such a sway over thee that thou eatest thy own flesh. While thou treatest us as beasts, we see thee to be a furious maniac, destroying thy own life.

Shall the earth be forsaken for thee?] To say

A. M. cir. 2484 B. C. cir. 1520 Ante I. Olymp. cir. 744 Ante U. C. cir. 767

and shall the rock be removed out of his place?

5 Yea, [d]the light of the wicked shall be put out, and the spark of his fire shall not shine.

6 The light shall be dark in his tabernacle, [e]and his [f]candle shall be put out with him.

7 The steps of his strength shall be straitened, and [g]his own counsel shall cast him down.

8 For [h]he is cast into a net by his own feet, and he walketh upon a snare.

9 The gin shall take *him* by the heel, *and* [i]the robber shall prevail against him.

A. M. cir. 2484 B. C. cir. 1520 Ante I. Olymp. cir. 744 Ante U. C. cir. 767

10 The snare *is* [k]laid for him in the ground, and a trap for him in the way.

11 [l]Terrors shall make him afraid on every side, and shall [m]drive him to his feet.

12 His strength shall be hunger-bitten, and [n]destruction *shall be* ready at his side.

13 It shall devour the [o]strength of his skin: *even* the first-born of death shall devour his strength.

14 [p]His confidence shall be rooted out of

[d]Prov. xiii. 9; xx. 20; xxiv. 20——[e]Ch. xxi. 17; Psa. xviii. 28——[f]Or, *lamp*——[g]Ch. v. 13——[h]Ch. xxii. 10; Psa. ix. 15; xxxv. 8——[i]Ch. v. 5——[k]Heb. *hidden*

[l]Ch. xv. 21; xx. 25; Jer. vi. 25; xx. 3; xlvi. 5; xlix. 29 [m]Heb. *scatter him*——[n]Ch. xv. 23——[o]Heb. *bars* [p]Ch. viii. 14; xi. 20; Psa. cxii. 10; Prov. x. 28

the least, afflictions are the common lot of men. Must God work a miracle in providence, in order to exempt thee from the operation of natural causes? Dost thou wish to engross all the attention and care of providence to thyself alone? What pride and insolence!

Verse 5. *The light of the wicked shall be put out*] Some think it would be better to translate the original, "Let the light of the wicked be extinguished!" Thou art a bad man, and thou hast perverted the understanding which God hath given thee. Let that understanding, that abused gift, be taken away. From this verse to the end of the chapter is a continual invective against Job.

Verse 6. *The light shall be dark in his tabernacle*] His *property* shall be destroyed, his house pillaged, and himself and his family come to an untimely end.

His candle shall be put out] He shall have no *posterity*.

Verse 7. *The steps of his strength*] Even in his greatest prosperity he shall be in straits and difficulties.

His own counsel] He shall be the dupe and the victim of his own airy, ambitious, and impious schemes.

Verse 8. *For he is cast into a net*] His own conduct will infallibly bring him to ruin. He shall be like a wild beast taken in a net; the more he flounces in order to extricate himself, the more he shall be entangled.

He walketh upon a snare.] He is continually walking on the meshes of a net, by which he must soon be entangled and overthrown.

Verse 9. *The gin shall take* him] *Houbigant* reads the *tenth* before the *ninth* verse, thus: "The snare is laid for him in the ground, and a trap for him in the way. The gin shall take him by the heel, and the robber shall prevail against him."

From the beginning of the *seventh* verse to the end of the *thirteenth* there is an allusion to the various arts and methods practised in hunting. 1. A number of persons extend themselves in a forest, and drive the game before them, still straitening the space from a broad base to a narrow point in form of a triangle, so that the farther they go the less room have they on the right and left, the hunters lining each side, while the drovers with their dogs are coming up behind. "The steps of his strength shall be straitened," ver. 7. 2. *Nets, gins,* and *pitfalls*, are laid or formed in different places, so that many are taken before they come to the point where the two lines close. "He is cast into a net, he walketh upon a snare—the trap is laid for him in the way—the snare in the ground," ver. 8, 9, 10. 3. The *howling of the dogs*, with the *shouts* of the *huntsmen*, fill him with dismay, and cause him to run himself beyond his strength and out of breath. "Terrors shall make him afraid on every side, and shall drive him to his feet," ver. 11. 4. While spent with hunger and fatigue, he is entangled in the spread nets; and the huntsman either pierces him with an arrow or spear, or cuts the sinews of his legs, so that he is easily captured and destroyed. "The robbers shall prevail against him," ver. 9. "His strength is hunger-bitten, and destruction is ready at his side," ver. 12. This latter verse is thus paraphrased by the Chaldee: "Let his first-born son be famished; and affliction be prepared for his wife."

Verse 13. *It shall devour the strength of his skin*] This may refer to the *elephant*, or to the *rhinoceros*, whose skin scarcely any dart can pierce: but in the case referred to above, the animal is taken in a pitfall, and then the *first-born of death*—a sudden and *overwhelming stroke*—deprives him of life. See the account of hunting the *elephant* in the East at the end of the chapter. The Chaldee has: "The strength of his skin shall devour his flesh; and the angel of death shall consume his children."

Verse 14. *His confidence shall be rooted out*] His dwelling-place, how well soever fortified, shall now be deemed utterly insecure.

And it shall bring him to the king of terrors.] Or, as Mr. *Good* translates, "And dissolution shall invade him as a monarch." He shall be completely and finally overpowered.

The phrase *king of terrors* has been generally thought to mean *death;* but it is not used in any such way in the text. For למלך בלהות *lemelech ballahoth, to the king of destructions*, one of *De Rossi's* MSS. has כמלך *kemelech*, "as a king;" and one, instead of בלהות *ballahoth*, with ו *vau holem*, to indicate the *plural, terrors* or *destructions*, has בלהות *ballahuth*, with ו *vau shurek*, which is *singular*, and singnifies *terror*,

A. M. cir. 2484
B. C. cir. 1520
Ante I. Olymp. cir. 744
Ante U. C. cir. 767

his tabernacle, and it shall bring
him to the king of terrors.
15 It shall dwell in his tabernacle, because *it is* none of his:
brimstone shall be scattered
upon his habitation.
16 [q]His roots shall be
dried up beneath, and above

A. M. cir. 2484
B. C. cir. 1520
Ante I. Olymp. cir. 744
Ante U. C. cir. 767

[q]Chap. xxix. 19; Isa. v. 24; Amos ii. 9; Mal. iv. 1

destruction. So the Vulgate seems to have read, as it translates, *Et calcet super eum, quasi rex, interitus;* "And shall tread upon him as a king or destroyer. Or as a king who is determined utterly to destroy him." On this verse the bishop of Killala, Dr. Stock, says, "I am sorry to part with a beautiful phrase in our common version, *the king of terrors,* as descriptive of *death;* but there is no authority for it in the Hebrew text."

It may however be stated that death has been denominated by similar epithets both among the Greeks and Romans.

So *Virgil,* Æn. vi., ver. 100.

——Quando hic *inferni* janua *regis*
Dicitur.

"The gates of the *king of hell* are reported to be here."

And Ovid, Metam. lib. v., ver. 356, 359.

Inde tremit tellus: et rex pavit ipse silentum.
Hanc metuens cladem, tenebrosa sede tyrannus
Exierat.

"Earth's inmost bowels quake, and nature groans;
His terrors reach the direful KING of HELL.
Fearing this destruction, the *tyrant* left his *gloomy court.*"

And in Sophocles, (Œdip. Colon., ver. 1628, edit. Johnson.)

Εννυχιων αναξ,
Αιδωνευ.

"O Pluto, *king of shades.*" That is, the invisible demon, who dwells in darkness impenetrable.

Old Coverdale translates: **Very fearfulnesse shall bringe him to the kynge.**

Verse 15. *It shall dwell in his tabernacle*] *Desolation* is here *personified,* and it is said that it shall be the inhabitant, its former owner being destroyed. *Brimstone shall be scattered upon his habitation,* so that, like Sodom and Gomorrah, it may be an everlasting monument of the Divine displeasure.

In the Persian poet *Saady,* we find a couplet which contains a similar sentiment:—

پرده داري ميكند در قصر قيصر عنكبوت
بومي نوبت ميزند بر كنبد افراسياب

Purdeh daree meekund dar keesri Keesar ankeboot
Boomee Noobat meezund ber kumbed Afraseeab.

"The spider holds the veil in the palace of Cæsar;
The owl stands sentinel on the watchtower of Afrasiab."

The palaces of those mighty kings are so desolate that the *spider* is the only *chamberlain,* and the *owl* the only *sentinel.* The *web* of the former is all that remains as a substitute for the *costly veil* furnished by the *chamberlain* in the palace of the *Roman monarch;* and the *hooting* of the latter is the only remaining substitute for the sound of *drums* and *trumpets* by which the *guards* were accustomed *to be relieved* at the watchtower of the *Persian king.*

The word قيصر *Keesur,* the same as Καισαρ or *Cæsar,* is the term which the Asiatics always use when they designate the *Roman emperor.*

Afrasiab was an ancient king who invaded and conquered Persia about *seven hundred* years before the Christian era. After having reigned *twelve* years, he was defeated and slain by *Zalzer* and his son, the famous *Rustem.* The present reigning family of Constantinople claim descent from this ancient monarch.

Brimstone shall be scattered upon his habitation.] This may either refer to the destruction of Sodom and Gomorrah, as has already been intimated, or to an ancient custom of *fumigating houses* with brimstone, in order to *purify* them from defilement. Pliny says, Hist. Nat., lib. xxxv., c. 15, speaking of the uses of sulphur, *Habet et in religionibus locum ad expiandas suffitu domos;* which Dr. *Holland* paraphrases thus: "Moreover brimstone is employed ceremoniously in hallowing of houses; for many are of opinion that the perfume and burning thereof will keep out all enchantments; yea, and drive away foul fiends and evil sprites that do haunt a place."

Ovid refers to the same, *De Arte. Am.,* lib. ii., ver. 329.

Et veniat, quæ *lustret* anus *lectumque locumque:*
Præferat et tremula *sulphur* et ova manu.

This alludes to the ceremony of purifying the *bed* or place in which a sick person was confined; an *old woman* or *nurse* was the operator, and *eggs* and *sulphur* were the instruments of *purification.*

On this and other methods of purgation see an excellent note in Servius on these words of Virgil, Æn. vi., ver. 740.

———— Aliæ panduntur inanes
Suspensæ ad ventos: aliis sub gurgite vasto
Infectum eluitur scelus, aut exuritur igni.

"For this are various penances subjoin'd;
And some are hung to bleach upon the wind;
Some plunged in waters, others, plunged in fires."

Unde etiam, says *Servius,* in sacris Liberi omnibus tres sunt istæ purgationes: nam aut *tæda* purgantur et *sulphure,* aut *aqua* abluuntur, aut *aëre* ventilantur.

"These three kinds of purgation are used in the rites of Bacchus: they are purged by flame and sulphur, or washed in water, or ventilated by the winds."

A. M. cir. 2484 B. C. cir. 1520 Ante I. Olymp. cir. 744 Ante U. C. cir. 767

shall his branch be cut off.
17 [r]His remembrance shall
perish from the earth, and he
shall have no name in the
street.
18 [s]He shall be driven from light into darkness, and chased out of the world.
19 [t]He shall neither have son nor nephew

[r]Psa. xxxiv. 16; cix. 13; Prov. ii. 22; x. 7——[s]Heb. *they shall drive him*——[t]Isa. xiv. 32; Jer. xxii. 30 [u]Psa. xxxvii. 16

among his people, nor any remaining in his dwellings.
20 They that come after *him*
shall be astonied at [u]his day,
as they that [v]went before [w]were affrighted.
21 Surely such *are* the dwellings of the
wicked, and this *is* the place *of him that*
[x]knoweth not God.

A. M. cir. 2484 B. C. cir. 1520 Ante I. Olymp. cir. 744 Ante U. C. cir. 767

[v]Or, *lived with him*——[w]Hebrew, *laid hold on horror* [x]Jeremiah ix. 3; x. 25; 1 Thess. iv. 5; 2 Thess. i. 8; Tit. i. 16

But it is most likely that Bildad, in his usual uncharitable manner, alludes to the destruction of Job's property and family by *winds* and *fire: for the* FIRE OF GOD *fell from heaven and burnt up the sheep and the servants, and* CONSUMED *them; and a great wind*, probably the *sulphureous suffocating simoom, smote the four corners of the house*, where Job's children were feasting, and killed them; see chap. i. 16, 19.

Verse 16. *His roots shall be dried up—his branch be cut off.*] He shall be as utterly destroyed, both in *himself*, his *posterity*, and his *property*, as a tree is whose branches are all lopped off, and whose every root is cut away.

Verse 17. *His remembrance shall perish*] He shall have none to survive him, to continue his name among men.

No name in the street.] He shall never be a man of reputation; after his demise, none shall talk of his *fame*.

Verse 18. *He shall be driven from light*] He shall be taken off by a violent death.

And chased out of the world.] The wicked is DRIVEN AWAY in *his iniquity*. This shows his reluctance to depart from life.

Verse 19. *He shall neither have son nor nephew*] *Coverdale*, following the *Vulgate*, translates thus: **He shal neither haue children ner kynss folk among his people, no ner eny posterite in his countrie: yonge and olde shal be astonyshed at his death.**

Verse 20. *They that come after* him] The *young* shall be struck with astonishment when they hear the relation of the judgments of God upon this wicked man. *As they that went before.* The *aged* who were his contemporaries, and who saw the judgments that fell on him, were affrighted, אחזו שער *achazu saar, seized with horror*—were *horrified;* or, as Mr. *Good* has well expressed it, *were panic-struck.*

Verse 21. *Such* are *the dwellings*] This is the common lot of the wicked; and it shall be particularly the case with him *who knoweth not God*, that is *Job*, for it is evident he alludes to him. Poor Job! hard was thy lot, severe were thy sufferings.

ON the elephant hunt to which I have referred, ver. 13, I shall borrow the following account extracted from Mr. Cordiner's History of Ceylon, by Mr. *Good:*—

"We have a curious description of the elephant hunt, which is pursued in a manner not essentially different from the preceding, except that the snares are pallisadoed with the strongest possible stakes, instead of being netted, and still farther fortified by interlacings. They are numerous, but connected together; every snare or inclosure growing gradually narrower, and opening into each other by a gate or two that will only admit the entrance of a single animal at a time.

"The wood in which elephants are known to abound is first surrounded, excepting at the end where the foremost and widest inclosure is situated, with fires placed on moveable pedestals, which in every direction are drawn closer and closer, and, aided by loud and perpetual shouts, drive the animals forward till they enter into the outer snare. After which the same process is continued, and they are driven by fear into a second, into a third, and into a fourth; till at length the elephants become so much subdivided, that by the aid of cordage fastened carefully round their limbs, and the management of decoy elephants, they are easily capable of being led away one by one, and tamed. A single hunt thus conducted will sometimes occupy not less than two months of unremitting labour; and the entrance of the elephants into the snares is regarded as an amusement or sport of the highest character, and as such is attended by all the principal families of the country." *Account of Ceylon*, p. 218-226.

CHAPTER XIX

Job complains of the cruelty of his friends, 1–5. *Pathetically laments his sufferings*, 6–12. *Complains of his being forsaken by all his domestics, friends, relatives, and even his wife*, 13–19. *Details his sufferings in an affecting manner, calls upon his friends to pity him, and earnestly wishes that his speeches may be recorded*, 20–24. *Expresses his hope in a future resurrection*, 25–27. *And warns his persecutors to desist, lest they fall under God's judgments*, 28, 29.

A. M. cir. 2484
B. C. cir. 1520
Ante I. Olymp. cir. 744
Ante U. C. cir. 767

THEN Job answered and said,
2 How long will ye vex my
soul, and break me in pieces with
words?
3 These [a]ten times have ye reproached me:
ye are not ashamed *that* ye [b]make yourselves
strange to me.
4 And be it indeed *that* I have erred, mine
error remaineth with myself.
5 If indeed ye will [c]magnify *yourselves*
against me, and plead against me my reproach:

[a]Gen. xxxi. 7; Lev. xxvi. 26——[b]Or, *harden yourselves against me*——[c]Psa. xxxviii. 16

6 Know now that God hath
overthrown me, and hath compassed me with his net.
7 Behold, I cry out of [d]wrong,
but I am not heard: I cry aloud, but *there is*
no judgment.
8 [e]He hath fenced up my way that I cannot
pass, and he hath set darkness in my paths.
9 [f]He hath stripped me of my glory, and
taken the crown *from* my head.
10 He hath destroyed me on every side,

A. M. cir. 2484
B. C. cir. 1520
Ante I. Olymp. cir. 744
Ante U. C. cir. 767

[d]Or, *violence*——[e]Chap. iii. 23; Psa. lxxxviii. 8——[f]Psa. lxxxix. 44

NOTES ON CHAP. XIX

Verse 2. *How long will ye vex my soul*] Every thing that was irritating, vexatious, and opprobrious, his friends had recourse to, in order to support their own system, and overwhelm him. Not one of them seems to have been touched with a feeling of tenderness towards him, nor does a kind expression drop at any time from their lips! They were called *friends;* but this term, in reference to them, must be taken in the sense of *cold-blooded acquaintances.* However, there are many in the world that go under the sacred name of *friends,* who, in times of difficulty, act a similar part. Job's friends have been, by the general consent of posterity, consigned to endless infamy. May all those who follow their steps be equally enrolled in the annals of bad fame!

Verse 3. *These ten times*] The exact arithmetical number is not to be regarded; *ten times* being put for many times, as we have already seen. See particularly the note on Gen. xxxi. 7.

Ye make yourselves strange to me.] When I was in affluence and prosperity, ye were my intimates, and appeared to rejoice in my happiness; but now ye scarcely know me, or ye profess to consider me a wicked man because I am in adversity. Of this you had no suspicion when I was in prosperity! Circumstances change men's minds.

Verse 4. *And be it indeed* that *I have erred*] Suppose indeed that I have been mistaken in any thing, that in the simplicity of my heart I have gone astray, and that this matter remains with myself, (for most certainly there is no public stain on my life,) you must grant that this error, whatsoever it is, has hurt no person except myself. Why then do ye treat me as a person whose life has been a general blot, and whose example must be a public curse?

Verse 6. *Know now that God hath overthrown me*] The matter is between him and me, and he has not commissioned *you* to add reproaches to *his* chastisements.

And hath compassed me with his net.] There may be an allusion here to the different modes of *hunting* which have been already referred to in the preceding chapter. But if we take the whole verse together, and read the latter clause before the former, thus, "Know, therefore, that God hath encompassed me with his net, and overthrown me;" the allusion may be to an ancient mode of combat practised among the ancient Persians, ancient Goths, and among the Romans. The custom among the Romans was this: "One of the combatants was armed with a *sword* and *shield,* the other with a *trident* and *net.* The *net* he endeavoured to cast over the head of his adversary, in which, when he succeeded, the entangled person was soon pulled down by a noose that fastened round the neck, and then despatched. The person who carried the *net* and *trident* was called *Retiarius,* and the other who carried the sword and shield was termed *Secutor,* or the *pursuer,* because, when the *Retiarius* missed his throw, he was obliged to run about the ground till he got his net in order for a second throw, while the *Secutor* followed hard to prevent and despatch him." The *Persians* in old times used what was called کمند *kumund, the noose.* It was not a *net,* but a sort of *running loop,* which horsemen endeavoured to cast over the heads of their enemies that they might pull them off their horses.

That the *Goths* used a *hoop net* fastened to a pole, which they endeavoured to throw over the heads of their foes, is attested by *Olaus Magnus, Hist. de Gentibus Septentrionalibus,* Rom. 1555, lib. xi., cap. 13, *De diversis Modis prœliandi Finnorum.* His words are, Quidam restibus instar *retium* ferinorum ductilibus sublimi jactatione utuntur: ubi enim cum hoste congressi sunt, injiciunt eos restes quasi laqueos in caput resistentis, ut equum aut hominem ad se trahant. "Some use elastic ropes, formed like hunting nets, which they throw aloft; and when they come in contact with the enemy, they throw these ropes over the head of their opponent, and by this means they can then drag either man or horse to themselves." At the head of the page he gives a wood-cut representing the *net,* and the manner of throwing it over the head of the enemy. To such a device Job might allude, *God hath encompassed me with his* NET, *and overthrown me.*

Verse 7. *I cry out of wrong*] I complain of violence and of injustice; but no one comes to my help.

Verse 8. *He hath fenced up my way*] This may allude to the mode of hunting the elephant, described at the conclusion of the preceding chapter; or to the operations of an invading army. See under ver. 11.

Verse 9. *He hath stripped me of my glory*] I am reduced to such circumstances, that I have lost all my honour and respect.

Verse 10. *Mine hope hath he removed like a tree.*] There is no more hope of my restoration to affluence, authority, and respect, than there

A. M. cir. 2484 B. C. cir. 1520 Ante I. Olymp. cir. 744 Ante U. C. cir. 767

and I am gone: and mine hope
hath he removed like a tree.
11 He hath also kindled his
wrath against me, and [g]he
counteth me unto him as *one of* his enemies.
12 His troops come together, and [h]raise up
their way against me, and encamp round about
my tabernacle.
13 [i]He hath put my brethren far from me,
and mine acquaintance are verily estranged
from me.
14 My kinsfolk have failed, and my familiar
friends have forgotten me.
15 They that dwell in mine house, and my
maids, count me for a stranger:
I am an alien in their sight.
16 I called my servant, and he
gave *me* no answer; I entreated
him with my mouth.
17 My breath is strange to my wife, though
I entreated for the children's *sake* of [k]mine
own body.
18 Yea, [l]young [m]children despised me; I
arose, and they spake against me.
19 [n]All [o]my inward friends abhorred
me: and they whom I loved are turned
against me.
20 [p]My bone cleaveth to my skin, [q]and to

[g]Chapter xiii. 24; Lam. ii. 5——[h]Chapter xxx. 12
[i]Psalm xxxi. 11; xxxviii. 11; lxix. 8; lxxxviii. 8, 18
[k]Heb. *my belly*——[l]Or, *the wicked*

[m]2 Kings ii. 23——[n]Psalm xli. 9; lv. 13, 14, 20
[o]Hebrew, *the men of my secret*——[p]Chap. xxx. 30; Psa. cii. 5; Lam. iv. 8——[q]Or, *as*

is that a tree shall grow and flourish, whose roots are extracted from the earth. I am pulled up by the roots, withered, and *gone.*

Verse 11. *And he counteth me unto him as* one of *his enemies.*] From the *seventh* to the *thirteenth* verse there seems to be an allusion to a hostile invasion, battles, sieges, &c. 1. A neighbouring chief, *without provocation*, invades his neighbour's territories, and none of his friends will come to his help. "I cry out of wrong, but I am not heard," ver. 7. 2. The foe has seized on all the passes, and he is hemmed up. "He hath fenced up my way that I cannot pass," ver. 8. 3. He has surprised and carried by assault the regal city, seized and possessed the treasures. "He hath stripped me of my glory, and taken the crown from my head," ver. 9. 4. All his armies are routed in the field, and his strong places carried. "He hath destroyed me on every side," ver. 10. 5. The enemy proceeds to the greatest length of outrage, wasting every thing with fire and sword. "He hath kindled his wrath against me, and treateth me like one of his adversaries, ver. 11. 6. He is cooped up in a small camp with the wrecks of his army; and in this he is closely besieged by all the power of his foes, who encompass the place, and *raise forts* against it. "His troops come together, and raise up their way against me, and encamp round about my tabernacle." 7. Not receiving any assistance from friends or neighbours, he abandons all hope of being able to keep the field, escapes with the utmost difficulty, and is despised and neglected by his friends and domestics because he has been unfortunate. "I am escaped with the skin of my teeth," ver. 20. "My kinsfolk have failed—all my intimate friends abhorred me," ver. 14-19.

Verse 14. *My kinsfolk have failed*] Literally, *departed:* they have all left my house now there is no more hope of *gain.*

Verse 15. *They that dwell in mine house*] In this and the following verses the disregard and contempt usually shown to men who have fallen from affluence and authority into poverty and dependence, are very forcibly described: formerly reverenced by *all*, now esteemed by none. Pity to those who have fallen into adversity is rarely shown; the *rich have many friends*, and to him who appears to be gaining worldly substance much court is paid; for *many worship the rising sun, who think little of that which is gone down.* Some are even reproached with that eminence which they have lost, though not culpable for the loss. A *bishop*, perhaps *Bale*, of *Ossory*, being obliged to leave his country and fly for his life, in the days of bloody Queen Mary, and who never regained his bishopric, was met one morning by one like those whom Job describes, who, intending to be witty at the expense of the venerable prelate, accosted him thus: "Good morrow, BISHOP *quondam.*" To which the bishop smartly replied, "Adieu, KNAVE *semper.*"

Verse 17. *Though I entreated for the children's* sake *of mine own body.*] This may imply no more than adjuring her by the tenderest ties, by their affectionate intercourse, and consequently by the *children* which had been the seals of their mutual affection, though these children were no more.

But the mention of his *children* in this place may intimate that he had still some remaining; that there might have been *young ones*, who, not being of a proper age to attend the festival of their elder brothers and sisters, escaped that sad catastrophe. The *Septuagint* have, Προσεκαλουμην δε κολακευων υιους παλλακιδων μου, "I affectionately entreated the *children of my concubines.*" But there is no ground in the Hebrew text for such a strange exceptionable rendering. *Coverdale* has, **I am fayne to speake fayre to the children of myne owne body.**

Verse 19. *My inward friends*] Those who were my greatest *intimates.*

Verse 20. *My bone cleaveth to my skin.*] My flesh is entirely wasted away, and nothing but skin and bone left.

I am escaped with the skin of my teeth.] I have had the most narrow escape. If I still live, it is a thing to be wondered at, my sufferings and privations have been so great. To *escape with the skin of the teeth* seems to have been a proverbial expression, signifying great difficulty. I had as narrow an escape from death, as the thickness of the enamel on the teeth. I was within a hair's breadth of destruction; see on verse 11.

A. M. cir. 2484
B. C. cir. 1520
Ante I. Olymp. cir. 744
Ante U. C. cir. 767

my flesh, and I am escaped with
the skin of my teeth.
21 Have pity upon me, have
pity upon me, O ye my friends;
[r]for the hand of God hath touched me.
22 Why do ye [s]persecute me as God, and
are not satisfied with my flesh?
23 [t]O that my words were
now written! O that they were
printed in a book!
24 That they were graven
with an iron pen and lead in the rock for
ever!
25 For I know *that* my Redeemer liveth, and

A. M. cir. 2484
B. C. cir. 1520
Ante I. Olymp. cir. 744
Ante U. C. cir. 767

---

[r]Chap. i. 11; Psa. xxxviii. 2 —— [s]Psa. lxix. 26 —— [t]Heb. *Who will give*, &c.

Verse 21. *Have pity upon me*] The iteration here strongly indicates the depth of his distress, and that his spirit was worn down with the length and severity of his suffering.

Verse 22. *Why do ye persecute me as God*] Are not the afflictions which God sends enough? Do ye not see that I have as much as I can bear? When the papists were burning Dr. Taylor at Oxford, while wrapped in the flames, one of the true sons of the Church took a stick out of the faggots, and threw it at his head, and split open his face. To whom he calmly said, *Man, why this wrong? Do not I suffer enough?*

And are not satisfied with my flesh?] Will ye persecute my *soul*, while God is persecuting my *body?* Is it not enough that my *body* is destroyed? Why then labour to torment my *mind?*

Verse 23. *O that my words were now written!*] Job introduces the important subject which follows in a manner unusually solemn; and he certainly considers the words which he was about to utter of great moment, and therefore wishes them to be *recorded* in every possible way. All the modes of writing then in use he appears to refer to. As to *printing*, that should be out of the question, as no such art was *then* discovered, nor for nearly *two thousand* years after. Our translators have made a strange mistake by rendering the verb יחקו *yuchaku, printed*, when they should have used *described, traced out*. O that my words were fairly traced out in a book! It is necessary to make this remark, because superficial readers have imagined that the *art of printing* existed in Job's time, and that it was not a discovery of the *fifteenth* century of the Christian era: whereas there is no proof that it ever existed in the world before A. D. 1440, or thereabouts, for the first printed book with a date is a *psalter* printed by *John Fust*, in 1457, and the first *Bible* with a date is that by the same artist in 1460.

Three kinds of writing Job alludes to, as being practised in his time: 1. *Writing in a book*, formed either of the leaves of the *papyrus*, already described, (see on chap. viii. 11,) or on a sort of *linen cloth*. A roll of this kind, with unknown characters, I have seen taken out of the envelopments of an Egyptian mummy. *Denon*, in his travels in Egypt, gives an account of a book of this kind, with an engraved *facsimile*, taken also out of an Egyptian mummy. 2. *Cutting with an iron stile on plates of lead.* 3. *Engraving on large stones* or *rocks*, many of which are still found in different parts of Arabia.

To the present day the *leaves* of the *palm tree* are used in the East instead of *paper*, and a *stile* of brass, silver, iron, &c., with a *steel point*, serves for a pen. By this instrument the letters are cut or engraved on the substance of the leaf, and afterwards some black colouring matter is rubbed in, in order to make the letters apparent. This was probably the oldest mode of writing, and it continues among the Cingalese to the present day. It is worthy of remark that PLINY (*Hist. Nat.*, lib. xiii., c. 11) mentions most of these methods of writing, and states that the *leaves* of the *palm tree* were used before other substances were invented. After showing that *paper* was not used before the conquest of Egypt by Alexander the Great, he proceeds: In palmarum foliis primo scriptitatum; deinde quarundam arborum libris: *postea publica monumenta* plumbeis voluminibus, *mox et privata* linteis *confici cœpta, aut* ceris. "At first men wrote on palm tree leaves, and afterwards on the bark or rind of other trees. In process of time, public monuments were written on *rolls of lead*, and those of a private nature on *linen books*, or tables covered with *wax*."

Pausanias, lib. xii., c. 31, giving an account of the Bœotians, who dwelt near fount Helicon, states the following fact:—Και μοι μολιβδον εδεικνυσαν, ενθα ἡ πηγη, τα πολλα ὑπο του χρονου λελυμασμενον, εγγεγραπται γαρ αυτῳ τα εργα; "They showed me a *leaden table* near to the fountain, on which his works (*Hesiod's*) were written; but a great part had perished by the injuries of time."

Verse 24. *Iron pen and lead*] Some suppose that the meaning of this place is this: the *iron pen* is the *chisel* by which the letters were to be *deeply cut* in the *stone* or *rock;* and the *lead* was melted into those cavities in order to preserve the engraving distinct. But this is not so natural a supposition as what is stated above; that Job refers to the different kinds of writing or perpetuating public events, used in his time: and the quotations from *Pliny* and *Pausanias* confirm the opinion already expressed.

Verse 25. *For I know that my Redeemer liveth*] Any attempt to establish the *true meaning* of this passage is almost hopeless. By learned men and eminent critics the words have been understood very differently; some vehemently contending that they refer to the *resurrection of the body, and the redemption of the human race by Jesus Christ;* while others, with equal vehemence and show of argument, have contended that they refer only *to Job's restoration to health, family comforts, and general prosperity, after the present trial should be ended.* In defence of these two opinions larger treatises have been written than the whole book of Job would amount to, if written even in *capitals*. To discuss the arguments on either side the nature of this work forbids; but my own view of the subject will be reasonably expected by the reader. I shall therefore lay down *one principle*, without which no mode of interpreta-

A. M. cir. 2484 B. C. cir. 1520 Ante I. Olymp. cir. 744 Ante U. C. cir. 767

that he shall stand at the latter
day upon the earth:
26 [u]And *though* after my skin
worms destroy this *body*, yet [v]in
my flesh shall I see God:

27 Whom I shall see for
myself, and mine eyes shall
behold, and not [w]another;
[x]*though* my reins be consumed
[y]within me.

[u]Or, *After I shall awake, though this* body *be destroyed, yet out of my flesh shall I see God*——[v]Psa. xvii. 15; 1 Cor. xiii. 12; 1 John iii. 2

[w]Heb. *a stranger*——[x]Or, *my veins within me are consumed with earnest desire* [for that day]——[y]Heb. *in my bosom*

tion hitherto offered can have any weight. The principle is this: *Job was now under the especial inspiration of the Holy Spirit, and spoke prophetically.*

Now, whether we allow that the passage refers to the *general resurrection* and *the redemption by Christ*, or to Job's *restoration to health, happiness, and prosperity*, this principle is equally necessary. 1. In those times no man could speak so clearly concerning the general resurrection and the redemption by Jesus Christ as Job, by one class of interpreters, is supposed here to do, unless especially inspired for this very purpose. 2. Job's restoration to health and happiness, which, though it did take place, was so totally improbable to himself all the way through, so wholly unexpected, and, in every sense, impossible, except to the almighty power of God, that it could not be *inferred* from any thing that had already taken place, and must be foreshown by direct inspiration. Now, that it was *equally easy* to predict either of these events, will be at once evident, because both were in *futurity*, and both were *previously determined.* Nothing *contingent* could exist in either; with them *man* had nothing to do; and they were equally within the knowledge of Him to whose *ubiquity* there can be neither *past* nor *future time;* in whose *presence absolute and contingent events* subsist in their own *distinctive characters*, and are never resolved into each other.

But another question may arise, *Which was most likely to be the subject of this oracular declaration, the general resurrection and redemption by Christ; or the restoration of Job to health and affluence?*

If we look only to the *general importance* of these things, this question may be soon decided; for the doctrine of human redemption, and the general resurrection to an eternal life, are of infinitely greater importance than any thing that could affect the personal welfare of Job. We may therefore say, of two things which only the power of God can effect, and one of which only shall be done, it is natural to conclude he will do that which is of most importance; and that is of most importance by which a greater measure of glory is secured to himself, and a greater sum of good produced to mankind.

As, therefore, a revelation by which the *whole human race*, in all its successive generations, to the end of time, may be most essentially benefited, is superior in its worth and importance to that by which *one man* only can be benefited, it is natural to conclude here, that the revelation relative to the general resurrection, &c., is that which most likely the text includes.

But to this it may be answered, God does not do always in the first instance that which is most necessary and important *in itself*, as every thing is done in that *order* and in that *time* which seems best to his godly wisdom; therefore, a thing of *less importance* may be done *now*, and a thing of *greater importance* left to a *future time.* So, God made the *earth* before he made *man*, produced *light* before he formed the *celestial luminaries*, and instituted the *Mosaic economy* before the *Christian dispensation.* This is all true, for every thing is done in that *season* in which it may best fulfil the designs of providence and grace. But the question still recurs, Which of the predictions was most congruous to the circumstances of Job, and those of his companions; and which of them was most likely to do most good on that occasion, and to be most useful through the subsequent ages of the world? The subject is now considerably narrowed; and, if this question could be satisfactorily answered, the true meaning of the passage would be at once found out. 1. For the sake of righteousness, justice, and truth, and to vindicate the ways of God with man, it was necessary that Job's *innocence* should be cleared; that the false judgments of his friends should be corrected; and that, as Job was now reduced to a state of the lowest distress, it was worthy the kindness of God to give him some direct intimation that his sufferings should have a happy termination. That such an event *ought* to take place, there can be no question: and that it did take place, is asserted in the book; and that Job's friends *saw* it, were reproved, corrected, and admitted into his favour of whom they *did not speak that which was right*, and who had, in consequence, *God's wrath kindled against them*, are also attested facts. But surely there was no need of *so solemn a revelation* to inform them of what was shortly to take place, when they lived to see it; nor can it be judged essentially necessary to the support of Job, when the ordinary consolations of God's Spirit, and the excitement of a good hope through grace, might have as completely answered the end.

2. On the other hand, to give men, who were the chiefs of their respective tribes, proper notice of a doctrine of which they appear to have had no adequate conception, and which was so necessary to the peace of society, the good government of men, and the control of unruly and wayward passions, which the doctrine of the general resurrection and consequent judgment is well calculated to produce; and to stay and support the suffering godly under the afflictions and calamities of life; were objects worthy the highest regards of infinite philanthropy and justice, and of the most pointed and solemn revelation which could be given on such an occasion. In short, they are the *grounds* on which *all revelation* is given to the sons of men: and the prophecy in question, viewed in this light, was, in that dark age and country, *a light shining in a dark place;* for the doctrine of the gen-

A. M. cir. 2484
B. C. cir. 1520
Ante I. Olymp. cir. 744
Ante U. C. cir. 767

28 But ye should say, [z]Why persecute we him, [a]seeing the root of the matter is found in me?

29 Be ye afraid of the sword: for wrath *bringeth* the punishments of the sword, [b]that ye may know *there is* a judgment.

A. M. cir. 2484
B. C. cir. 1520
Ante I. Olymp cir. 744
Ante U. C. cir. 767

[z]Ver. 22——[a]Or, *and what root of matter is found in me?*——[b]Psa. lviii. 10, 11

eral resurrection, and of future rewards and punishments, existed among the *Arabs* from time immemorial, and was a part of the public creed of the different tribes when Mohammed endeavoured to establish his own views of that resurrection and of future rewards and punishments, by the edge of the sword. I have thus endeavoured dispassionately to view this subject; and having instituted the preceding mode of reasoning, without foreseeing where it would tend, being only desirous to find out truth, I arrive at the conclusion, that the prophecy in question was not designed to point out the *future prosperity of Job;* but rather the *future redemption of mankind by Jesus Christ, and the general resurrection of the human race.*

After what has been stated above, a short paraphrase on the words of the text will be all that is necessary to be added.

I know, ידעתי *yadati,* I have a firm and full persuasion, *that my Redeemer,* גאלי *goali,* my *Kinsman,* he whose right it was among the ancient Hebrews to redeem the forfeited heritages belonging to the family, to vindicate its honour, and to avenge the death of any of his relatives by slaying the murderer; (Lev. xxv. 25; Num. xxxv. 12; Ruth iii. 13;) but here it must refer to *Christ,* who has truly the *right* of redemption, being of the *same kindred,* who was *born of woman, flesh of flesh and bone of our bone.*

Liveth, חי *chai,* is the living One, who has the keys of hell and death: the Creator and Lord of the spirits of all flesh, and the principle and support of all *life.*

And that *he shall stand at the latter* day *upon the earth. The latter day,* אחרון *acharon,* the latter day, or *time,* when God comes to judgment; or *finally,* or *at last,* or *in the last time,* or *latter days,* as the Gospel is termed, he shall be manifested in the flesh.

He shall stand, יקום *yakum, he shall arise,* or *stand up,* i. e., to give sentence in judgment: or he himself shall arise from the dust, as the passage has been understood by some to refer to the resurrection of Christ from the dead.

Upon the earth, על עפר *al aphar,* over the *dead,* or those who are reduced to *dust.* This is the meaning of עפר *aphar* in Psa. xxx. 9: *What profit is there in my blood when I go down to the pit? Shall the* DUST (*i. e.,* the *dead*) *praise thee? He shall arise over the dust* —over them who sleep in the dust, whom he shall also raise up.

Verse 26. *And* though *after my skin* worms *destroy this* body] *My skin,* which is now almost all that remains *of* my former self, except the bones; see ver. 20. *They destroy this*—not body. נקפו זאת *nikkephu zoth, they*—diseases and affliction, destroy THIS wretched composition of misery and corruption.

Yet in my flesh shall I see God] Either, I shall arise from the dead, have a renewed body, and see him with eyes of flesh and blood, though what I have now shall shortly moulder into dust; or, I shall see him *in the flesh;* my *Kinsman,* who shall partake of my flesh and blood, in order that he may ransom the lost inheritance.

Verse 27. *Whom I shall see for myself*] Have a personal interest in the *resurrection,* as I shall have in the *Redeemer.*

And mine eyes shall behold] That very person who shall be the *resurrection,* as he is the *life.*

And not another] ולא זר *velo zar,* and not a *stranger,* one who has *no relation* to human nature; but גאלי *goali,* my redeeming Kinsman.

Though *my reins be consumed within me.*] Though I am now apparently on the brink of death, the thread of life being spun out to extreme tenuity.

This, on the mode of interpretation which I have assumed, appears to be the meaning of this passage. The words may have a somewhat different colouring put on them; but the basis of the interpretation will be the same.

I shall conclude with the version of *Coverdale:*—

For I am sure that my Redeemer liveth;
And that I shal ryse out of the earth in the latter daye;
That I shal be clothed againe with this skynne
And se God in my flesh.
Yee, I myself shal beholde him,
Not with other, but with these same eyes.
My reins are consumed within me, when ye saye,
Why do not we persecute him?
We have founde an occasion against him.

Verse 28. *But ye should say*] Or, *Then ye shall say.*

Why persecute we him] Or, as Mr. *Good,* How did we persecute him! Alas! we are now convinced that we did wrong.

Seeing the root of the matter] A *pure practice,* and a *sound hope,* resting on the solid ground of *sound faith,* received from God himself. Instead of בי *bi, in* ME, בו *bo, in* HIM, is the reading of more than *one hundred* of *Kennicott's* and *De Rossi's* MSS., and in several of the *versions. Seeing the root of the matter is found in* HIM.

Verse 29. *Be ye afraid of the sword*] Of God's judgments.

For wrath bringeth] Such anger as ye have displayed against me God will certainly resent and punish.

That ye may know there is *a judgment.*] That ye may know that God will judge the world; and that the unequal distribution of riches and poverty, afflictions and health, in the present life, is a proof that there must be a future judgment, where evil shall be punished and virtue rewarded.

IT would not be fair, after all the discussion of the preceding verses in reference to the two grand opinions and modes of interpretation instituted by learned men, not to inform the

reader that a *third* method of solving all difficulties has been proposed, viz., that Job refers to a Divine conviction which he had just then received, that God would appear in the most evident manner to vindicate his innocence, and give the fullest proofs to his friends and to the world that his afflictions had not been sent as a scourge for his iniquities. Dr. Kennicott was the proposer of this third mode of solving these difficulties, and I shall give his method in his own words.

"These five verses, though they contain but *twelve* lines, have occasioned controversies without number, as to the general meaning of Job in this place, whether he here expressed his firm belief of a *resurrection to happiness after death*, or of *a restoration to prosperity during the remainder of his life*.

"Each of these positions has found powerful as well as numerous advocates; and the short issue of the whole seems to be, that each party has confuted the opposite opinion, yet without establishing its own. For how could Job here express his conviction of a reverse of things in *this* world, and of a restoration to *temporal prosperity*, at the very time when he strongly asserts that his miseries would soon be terminated by death? See chap. vi. 11; vii. 21; xvii. 11-15; xix. 10, and particularly in chap. vii. 7: *O remember that my life is wind; mine eye shall no more see good.*

"Still less could Job here express *a hope full of immortality*, which sense cannot be extorted from the words without every violence. And as the *possession* of such belief is not to be reconciled with Job's so bitterly cursing the day of his birth in chap. iii., so the declaration of such belief would have solved at once the whole difficulty in dispute.

"But if neither of the preceding and opposite opinions can be admitted, if the words are not meant to express Job's belief either of a *restoration* or of a *resurrection*, what then are we to do? It does not appear to me that any other interpretation has *yet* been proposed by the learned; yet I will now venture to offer a *third* interpretation, different from both the former, and which, whilst it is free from the preceding difficulties, does not seem liable to equal objections.

"The conviction, then, which I suppose Job to express here, is this: That though his dissolution was hastening on amidst the unjust accusations of his pretended friends, and the cruel insults of his hostile relations; and though, whilst he was thus singularly oppressed with anguish of mind, he was also tortured with pains of body, torn by sores and ulcers from head to foot, and sitting upon dust and ashes; yet still, out of that miserable body, in his flesh thus stripped of skin, and nearly dropping into the grave, HE SHOULD SEE GOD, who would *appear in his favour*, and vindicate THE INTEGRITY *of his character*. This opinion may perhaps be fairly and fully supported by the sense of the words themselves, by the context, and by the following remarks.

"We read in chap. ii. 7, that *Job* was smitten with *sore boils from the sole of his foot unto his crown;* and ver. 8, 'He sat down among the *ashes*.' In chap. vii. 5, Job says, 'My flesh is clothed with worms, and clods of *dust;* my skin is broken, and become loathsome.' In chap. xvi. 19: 'Also now, behold, my witness is in heaven, and my record is on high.' Then come the words of Job, chap. xix. 25-29. And then, in opposition to what Job had just said, that God would soon appear to vindicate him, and that even his accusing *friends* would acquit him, Zophar says, chap. xx. 27, that '*the heaven* would reveal his iniquity, and the *earth* would rise up against him.' Lastly, this opinion concerning Job's words, as to God's *vindication* of him, is confirmed strongly at the end of the book, which records the conclusion of Job's history. His firm hope is here supposed to be that, *before his death*, he should, *with his bodily eyes*, see GOD *appearing and vindicating his character*. And from the conclusion we learn that God did thus appear: *Now*, says Job, *mine eye seeth thee.* And then did God most effectually and for ever brighten the glory of Job's fame, by *four* times calling him HIS SERVANT; and, as his anger was kindled against Job's *friends*, by speaking to them in the following words: 'Ye have not spoken of me the thing that is right, as *my servant* Job hath. Go to *my servant* Job,— and *my servant* Job shall pray for you,—in that ye have not spoken of me the thing which is right, like *my servant* Job,' chap. xl. 7, 8."

Dr. K. then gives the common version, and proposes the following as a new version:—

Ver. 25. For I know that my Vindicator liveth,
And he at last shall arise over *this* dust.
26. And after that mine adversaries have mangled *me* thus,
Even in my flesh shall I see God.
27. Whom I shall see on my side;
And mine eyes shall behold, but not estranged *from me:*
All this have I made up in mine own bosom.
28. Verily ye shall say, Why have we persecuted him;
Seeing the truth of the matter is found with him?
29. Tremble for yourselves at the face of the sword;
For the sword waxeth hot against iniquities:
Therefore be assured that judgment will take place.

KENNICOTT'S *Remarks on Select Passages of Scripture*, p. 165.

There is something very plausible in this plan of Dr. Kennicott; and in the conflicting opinions relative to the meaning of this celebrated and much controverted passage, no doubt some will be found who will adopt it as a middle course. The theory, however, is better than some of the arguments by which it is supported. Yet had I not been led, by the evidence mentioned before, to the conclusion there drawn, I should probably have adopted Dr. K.'s opinion with some modification: but as to his *new version*, it is what I am persuaded the Hebrew text can never bear. It is even too loose a paraphrase of the original, as indeed are most of the new versions of this passage. Dr. Kennicott says, that such a confidence as those cause Job to express, who make him speak concerning the *future resurrection*, ill comports with his cursing so bitterly the day of his birth, &c. But this objection has little if any strength, when we consider that it is not at all probable that Job had this confidence any time before the moment in which he uttered it: it was then a *direct revelation*, nothing of which he ever had before, else he had never dropped those words of impatience and irritation which we find in several of his speeches. And this may be safely inferred from the consideration, that *after this time* no such words escaped his lips: he bears the rest of his sufferings with great patience and fortitude; and seems to look forward with steady hope to that day in which all tears shall be wiped away from off all faces, and it be fully proved that the Judge of all the earth has done right.

CHAPTER XX

Zophar answers Job, and largely details the wretchedness of the wicked and the hypocrite; shows that the rejoicing of such is short and transitory, 1–9. *That he is punished in his family and in his person,* 10–14. *That he shall be stripped of his ill-gotten wealth, and shall be in misery, though in the midst of affluence,* 15–23. *He shall at last die a violent death, and his family and property be finally destroyed,* 24–29.

A. M. cir. 2484
B. C. cir. 1520
Ante I. Olymp. cir. 744
Ante U. C. cir. 767

THEN answered Zophar the
Naamathite, and said,
2 Therefore do my thoughts
cause me to answer, and for *this*
[a]I make haste.
3 I have heard the check of my reproach,
and the spirit of my understanding causeth
me to answer.
4 Knowest thou *not* this of old, since man
was placed upon earth,
5 [b]That the triumphing of
the wicked *is* [c]short, and the
joy of the hypocrite *but* for a
moment?
6 [d]Though his excellency mount up to
the heavens, and his head reach unto [e]the
clouds;
7 *Yet* he shall perish for ever [f]like his own
dung: they which have seen him shall say,
Where *is* he?

[a]Hebrew, *my haste* is *in me*——[b]Psalm xxxvii. 35, 36
[c]Heb. *from near*

[d]Isa. xiv. 13, 14; Obad. 3, 4——[e]Heb. *cloud*——[f]Psa. lxxxiii. 10

NOTES ON CHAP. XX

Verse 2. *Therefore do my thoughts*] It has already been observed that Zophar was the most inveterate of all Job's *enemies*, for we really must cease to call them *friends*. He sets no bounds to his invective, and outrages every rule of charity. A man of such a bitter spirit must have been, in general, very unhappy. With him Job is, by insinuation, every thing that is base, vile, and hypocritical. Mr. *Good* translates this verse thus: "Whither would my tumult transport me? And how far my agitation within me?" This is all the modesty that appears in Zophar's discourse. He acknowledges that he is pressed by the impetuosity of his spirit to reply to Job's self-vindication. The original is variously translated, but the sense is as above.

For this *I make haste.*] ובעבור חושי בי *ubaabur chushi bi, there is sensibility in me,* and my *feelings* provoke me to reply.

Verse 3. *I have heard the check of my reproach*] Some suppose that Zophar quotes the words of Job, and that some words should be supplied to indicate this meaning; *e. g.*, "I have heard (sayest thou) the check or charge of my reproach?" Or it may refer to what Job says of Zophar and his companions, chap. xix. 2, 3: *How long will ye vex my soul—these ten times have ye reproached me.* Zophar therefore assumes his old ground, and retracts nothing of what he had said. Like many of his own complexion in the present day, he was determined to believe that *his* judgment was infallible, and that *he* could not err.

Verse 4. *Knowest thou* not *this of old*] This is a maxim as ancient as the world; it began with the first man: A wicked man shall triumph but a short time; God will destroy the proud doer.

Since man was placed upon earth] Literally, *since* ADAM *was placed on the earth;* that is, since the fall, wickedness and hypocrisy have *existed;* but they have never *triumphed* long. Thou hast lately been expressing confidence in reference to a general judgment; but such is thy character, that thou hast little reason to anticipate with any joy the decisions of that day.

Verse 6. *Though his excellency mount up to the heavens*] Probably referring to the original state of Adam, of whose fall he appears to have spoken, ver. 4. He was created in the *image of God;* but by his sin against his Maker he fell into wretchedness, misery, death, and destruction.

Verse 7. *He shall perish for ever*] He is *dust*, and shall return to the dust from which he was taken. Zophar here hints his disbelief in that doctrine, the resurrection of the body, which Job had so solemnly asserted in the preceding chapter. Or he might have been like some in the present day, who believe that the wicked shall be annihilated, and the bodies of the righteous only be raised from the dead; but I know of no scripture by which such a doctrine is confirmed.

Like his own dung] His reputation shall be abominable, and his putrid carcass shall resemble his own excrement. A speech that partakes as much of the malevolence as of the asperity of Zophar's spirit.

A. M. cir. 2484 B. C. cir. 1520 Ante I. Olymp. cir. 744 Ante U. C. cir. 767

8 He shall fly away [g]as a dream, and shall not be found: yea, he shall be chased away as a vision of the night.

9 [h]The eye also *which* saw him shall *see him* no more; neither shall his place any more behold him.

10 [i]His children shall seek to please the poor, and his hands [k]shall restore their goods.

11 His bones are full *of* [l]*the sin* of his youth, [m]which shall lie down with him in the dust.

12 Though wickedness be sweet in his mouth, *though* he hide it under his tongue;

13 *Though* he spare it, and forsake it not; but keep it still [n]within his mouth:

14 *Yet* his meat in his bowels is turned, *it is* the gall of asps within him.

15 He hath swallowed down riches, and he shall vomit them up again: God shall cast them out of his belly.

16 He shall suck the poison of asps: the viper's tongue shall slay him.

17 He shall not see [o]the rivers, [p]the

[g]Psa. lxxiii. 20; xc. 5——[h]Chap. vii. 8, 10; viii. 18; Psa. xxxvii. 36; ciii. 16——[i]Or, *The poor shall oppress his children*——[k]Ver. 18

[l]Chap. xiii. 26; Psa. xxv. 7——[m]Chap. xxi. 26 [n]Heb. *in the midst of his palate*——[o]Psa. xxxvi. 9; Jer. xvii. 6——[p]Or, *streaming brooks*

Verse 8. *He shall fly away as a dream*] Instead of rising again from corruption, as thou hast asserted, (chap. xix. 26,) with a new body, his flesh shall rot in the earth, and his spirit be dissipated like a vapour; and, like a vision of the night, nothing shall remain but the bare impression that such a creature had once existed, but shall appear no more for ever.

Verse 10. *His children shall seek to please the poor*] They shall be reduced to the lowest degree of poverty and want, so as to be obliged to become servants to the poor. *Cursed be Ham, a servant of servants shall he be.* There are cases where the poor actually serve the poor; and this is the lowest or most abject state of poverty.

His hands shall restore their goods.] He shall be obliged to restore the goods that he has taken by violence.

Mr. *Good* translates: *His branches shall be involved in his iniquity;* i. e., his children shall suffer on his account. "His own hands shall render to himself the evil that he has done to others."—*Calmet.* The clause is variously translated.

Verse 11. *His bones are full* of the sin *of his youth*] Our translators have followed the VULGATE, *Ossa ejus implebuntur vitiis adolescentiæ ejus;* "his bones shall be filled with the sins of his youth." The SYRIAC and ARABIC have, *his bones are full of marrow;* and the TARGUM is to the same sense. At first view it might appear that Zophar refers to those infirmities in old age, which are the consequences of youthful vices and irregularities. עלומו *alumav*, which we translate *his youth*, may be rendered *his hidden things;* as if he had said, *his secret vices* bring down his strength to the dust. For this rendering *Rosenmüller* contends, and several other German critics. Mr. *Good* contends for the same.

Verse 12. *Though wickedness be sweet in his mouth*] This seems to refer to the *secret sins* mentioned above.

Hide it under his tongue] This and the *four* following verses contain an allegory; and the reference is to a man who, instead of taking wholesome food, takes what is *poisonous*, and is so delighted with it because it is sweet, that he rolls it under his tongue, and will scarcely let it down into his stomach, he is so delighted with the taste; "he spares it, and forsakes it not, but keeps it still within his mouth," ver. 13. "But when he swallows it, it is turned to the gall of asps within him," ver. 14, which shall corrode and torture his bowels.

Verse 15. *He shall vomit them up again*] This is also an allusion to an effect of most ordinary *poisons;* they occasion a nausea, and often excruciating *vomiting;* nature striving to eject what it knows, if retained, will be its bane.

Verse 16. *He shall suck the poison of asps*] That delicious morsel, that *secret, easily-besetting sin*, so palatable, and so pleasurable, shall act on the life of his soul, as the poison of asps would do on the life of his body.

The poison is called *the gall of asps*, it being anciently supposed that the *poison of serpents* consists in their *gall*, which is thought to be copiously exuded when those animals are *enraged;* as it has been often seen that their bite is *not poisonous* when they are *not angry. Pliny*, in speaking of the various parts of animals, *Hist. Nat.* lib. xi., c. 37, states, from this circumstance, that in the gall the poison of serpents consists; *ne quis miretur id* (fel) *venenum esse serpentum.* And in lib. xxviii., c. 9, he ranks the *gall* of horses among the poisons: *Damnatur* (fel) *equinum tantum inter venena.* We see, therefore, that the *gall* was considered to be the source whence the poison of serpents was generated, not only in Arabia, but also in Italy.

Verse 17. *He shall not see the rivers*] Mr. *Good* has the following judicious note on this passage: "Honey and butter are the common results of a rich, well-watered pasturage, offering a perpetual banquet of grass to kine, and of nectar to bees; and thus loading the possessor with the most luscious luxuries of pastoral life, peculiarly so before the discovery of the means of obtaining *sugar*. The expression appears to have been proverbial; and is certainly used here to denote a very high degree of temporal prosperity." See also chap. xxix. 6. To the Hebrews such expressions were quite familiar. See Exod. iii. 8; xiii. 5; xxxiii. 3; 2 Kings xviii. 32; Deut. xxxi. 20, and elsewhere.

The Greek and Roman writers abound in such images.

A. M. cir. 2484 B. C. cir. 1520 Ante I. Olymp. cir. 744 Ante U. C. cir. 767

floods, the brooks of honey and
butter.
18 That which he laboured for
[q]shall he restore, and shall not
swallow *it* down: [r]according to his
substance *shall* the restitution *be,*
and he shall not rejoice *therein.*
19 Because he hath [s]oppressed

A. M. cir. 2484 B. C. cir. 1520 Ante I. Olymp. cir. 744 Ante U. C. cir. 767

[q]Ver. 10, 15——[r]Heb. *according to the substance of his exchange*——[s]Heb. *crushed*

Milk and honey were such delicacies with the ancients, that *Pindar* compares his song to them for its *smoothness* and *sweetness:*—

Χαιρε
Φιλος. Εγω τοδε τοι
Πεμπω μεμιγμενον μελι λευκῳ
Συν γαλακτι· κιρναμενα δ' εερσ' αμ-
φεπει πομ' αοιδιμον, Αιο-
λισιν εν πνοαισιν αυλων.

PIND. Nem. iii., ver. 133.

"Hail, friend! to thee I tune my song;
For thee its *mingled sweets* prepare;
Mellifluous accents pour along;
Verse, *pure as milk*, to thee I bear;
On all thy actions falls the dew of praise;
Pierian draughts thy thirst of fame assuage,
And breathing flutes thy songs of triumph raise."

J. B. C.

Qui te, Pollio, amat, veniat, quo te quoque gaudet;
Mella fluant illi, ferat et *rubus* asper *amomum.*

VIRG. Ecl. iii., ver. 88.

"Who Pollio loves, and who his muse admires;
Let Pollio's fortune crown his full desires
Let *myrrh*, instead of *thorn*, his fences fill;
And *showers* of *honey* from his *oaks* distil!"

DRYDEN.

OVID, describing the *golden age*, employs the same image:—

Flumina *jam* lactis, *jam* flumina nectaris *ibant;*
Flavaque *de viridi stillabant* ilice mella.

Metam. lib. i., ver. 3.

"*Floods* were with *milk*, and *floods* with *nectar*, fill'd;
And *honey* from the sweating *oak* distill'd."

DRYDEN.

HORACE employs a similar image in nearly the same words:—

Mella *cava manant ex* ilice, *montibus altis;*
Levis crepante lympha desilit pede.

Epod. xvi., ver. 46.

"From hollow *oaks*, where *honey'd streams* distil,
And bounds with noisy foot the pebbled rill."

FRANCIS.

Job employs the same metaphor, chap. xxix. 6:—

When I washed my steps with *butter*,
And the rock poured out to me rivers of *oil*.

Isaiah, also, chap. vii. 22, uses the same when describing the produce of a *heifer* and two *ewes:*—

From the plenty of *milk* that they shall produce,
He shall eat *butter: butter* and *honey* shall he eat,
Whosoever is left in the midst of the land.

And *Joel*, iii. 18:—

And it shall come to pass in that day,
The *mountains* shall drop down *new wine*,
And the hills shall flow with *milk;*
And all the *rivers* of Judah shall flow with waters.

These expressions denote *fertility* and *abundance;* and are often employed to point out the *excellence* of the promised land, which is frequently denominated *a land flowing with milk and honey:* and even the superior blessings of the *Gospel* are thus characterized, Isa. li. 1.

Verse 18. *That which he laboureth for shall he restore*] I prefer here the reading of the *Arabic*, which is also supported by the *Syriac*, and is much nearer to the *Hebrew* text than the common version. *He shall return to labour, but he shall not eat; he shall toil, and not be permitted to enjoy the fruit of his labour.* The whole of this verse Mr. *Good* thus translates:—

"To labour shall he return, but he shall not eat.
A *dearth* his *recompense:* yea, nothing shall he *taste.*"

It may be inquired how Mr. *Good* arrives at this meaning. It is by considering the word יעלס *yaalos*, which we translate *he shall rejoice*, as the Arabic علس *alasa*, "he ate, drank, tasted;" and the word כהיל *kehil*, which we make a compound word, *keeheyl*, "according to substance," to be the pure Arabic word كحل *kahala*, "it was fruitless," applied to a year of *dearth:* hence *kahlan*, "a barren year." Conceiving these two to be pure *Arabic* words, for which he seems to have sufficient authority, he renders תמורתו *temuratho, his recompense*, as in chap. xv. 31, and not *restitution*, as here.

The general meaning is, He shall labour and toil, but shall not reap, for God shall send on his land blasting and mildew. *Houbigant* translates the verse thus: *Reddet labore partum; neque id absumet; copiosæ fuerunt mercaturæ ejus, sed illis non fruetur.* "He shall restore what he gained by labour, nor shall he consume it; his merchandises were abundant, but he shall not enjoy them." O, how doctors disagree! Old *Coverdale* gives a good sense, which is no unfrequent thing with this venerable translator:—

But laboure shal he, and yet have nothinge to eate; great travayle shal he make for riches, but he shal not enjoye them.

Verse 19. *He hath oppressed* and *hath forsaken the poor*] Literally, *He hath broken in pieces the forsaken of the poor;* כי רצץ עזב דלים *ki ritstsats azab dallim.* The poor have fled from famine, and left their children behind them; and this hard-hearted wretch, meaning Job all the while, has suffered them to perish, when he might have saved them alive.

A. M. cir. 2484
B. C. cir. 1520
Ante I. Olymp. cir. 744
Ante U. C. cir. 767

and hath forsaken the poor; *because* he hath violently taken away a house which he builded not;

20 [t]Surely he shall not [u]feel quietness in his belly, he shall not save of that which he desired.

21 [v]There shall none of his meat be left; therefore shall no man look for his goods.

22 In the fulness of his sufficiency he shall be in straits: every hand of the [w]wicked shall come upon him.

23 *When* he is about to fill his belly, *God* shall cast the fury of his wrath upon him, and shall rain *it* upon him [x]while he is eating.

A. M. cir. 2484
B. C. cir. 1520
Ante I. Olymp. cir. 744
Ante U. C. cir. 767

24 [y]He shall flee from the iron weapon, *and* the bow of steel shall strike him through.

25 It is drawn, and cometh out of the body; yea, [z]the glittering sword cometh out of his gall: [a]terrors *are* upon him.

26 All darkness *shall be* hid in his secret places: [b]a fire not blown shall consume him;

[t]Eccles. v. 13, 14——[u]Heb. *know*——[v]Or, *There shall be none left for his meat*——[w]Or, *troublesome*——[x]Num. xi. 33; Psa. lxxviii. 30, 31——[y]Isa. xxiv. 18; Jer. xlviii. 43; Amos v. 19——[z]Chap. xvi. 13——[a]Chap. xviii. 11——[b]Psa. xxi. 9

He hath violently taken away a house which he builded not] Or rather, He hath thrown down a house, and hath not rebuilt it. By neglecting or destroying the forsaken orphans of the poor, mentioned above, he has destroyed a house, (*a family*,) while he might, by helping the wretched, have preserved the family from becoming extinct.

Verse 20. *Surely he shall not feel quietness in his belly*] I have already remarked that the word בטן *beten*, which we translate *belly*, often means in the sacred Scriptures the whole of the human trunk; the regions of the *thorax* and *abdomen*, with their contents; the heart, lungs, liver, &c., and consequently all the *thoughts*, *purposes*, and *inclinations* of the mind, of which those viscera were supposed to be the functionaries. The meaning seems to be, "He shall never be satisfied; he shall have an endless desire after secular good, and shall never be able to obtain what he covets."

Verse 21. *There shall none of his meat be left*] *Coverdale* translates thus: **He devoured so gredily, that he left nothinge behynde, therefore his goodes shal not prospere.** He shall be stripped of every thing.

Verse 22. *In the fulness of his sufficiency he shall be in straits*] This is a fine saying, and few of the menders of Job's text have been able to improve the version. It is literally true of every great, rich, wicked man; he has no God, and anxieties and perplexities torment him, notwithstanding he has his portion in this life.

Every hand of the wicked shall come upon him.] All *kinds* of misery shall be his portion. *Coverdale* translates: **Though he had plenteousnesse of every thinge, yet was he poore; and, therefore, he is but a wretch on every syde.**

Verse 23. When *he is about to fill his belly*] Here seems a plain allusion to the *lustings of the children of Israel in the desert.* God showered down *quails* upon them, and showered down his wrath while the flesh was in their mouth. The allusion is too plain to be mistaken; and this gives some countenance to the bishop of Killala's version of the 20th verse:—

"Because he acknowledged not the *quail* in his stomach,
In the midst of his delight he shall not escape."

That שלו, which we translate *quietness*, means a *quail*, also the history of the Hebrews' lustings, Exod. xvi. 2-11, and Num. xi. 31-35, sufficiently proves. Let the reader mark all the expressions here, from ver. 20 to 23, and compare them with Num. xi. 31-35, and he will probably be of opinion that Zophar has that history immediately in view, which speaks of the Hebrews' murmurings for bread and flesh, and the miraculous *showers* of *manna* and *quails*, and the judgments that fell on them for their murmurings. Let us compare a few passages:—

Verse 20. *He shall not feel quietness*] שלו *selav*, the quail. "He shall not save of that which he desired." Verse 21: "There shall none of his meat be left." Exod. xvi. 19: "Let no man leave of it till the morning."

Verse 22. *In the fulness of his sufficiency, he shall be in straits.*] Exod. xvi. 20: "But some of them left of it until the morning, and it bred worms and stank."

Verse 23. *When he is about to* fill his belly, *God shall cast the* fury of his wrath *upon him, and shall* rain it *upon him while he is eating.*] Num. xi. 33: "And while the flesh was yet between their teeth, ere it was chewed, the wrath of the Lord was kindled against the people, and the Lord smote the people with a very great plague." Psa. lxxviii. 26-30: "He rained flesh upon them as dust, and feathered fowls like as the sand of the sea: so they did eat and were filled—but, while the meat was in their mouth, the wrath of God came upon them," &c. These show to what Zophar refers.

Verse 24. *He shall flee from the iron weapon*] Or, "Though he should flee from the iron armour, the brazen bow should strike him through." **So that yf he fle the yron weapens, he shal be shott with the stele bow.**—*Coverdale.* That is, he shall most certainly perish: all kinds of deaths await him.

Verse 25. *It is drawn, and cometh out*] This refers to *archery:* The arrow is *drawn out* of the sheaf or quiver, and discharged from the bow against its mark, and pierces the vitals, and passes through the body. So *Coverdale:*— **The arowe shal be taken forth, and go out at his backe.**

Verse 26. *A fire not blown shall consume him*] As Zophar is here showing that the wicked cannot escape from the Divine judgments; so he points out the different instruments which God employs for their destruction. The *wrath of God*—any secret or supernatural curse. The *iron weapon*—the spear or such like. The *bow*, and its swift-flying *arrow. Darkness*—deep horror and perplexity. *A fire not blown*—a supernatural fire; *lightning:* such as fell on

A. M. cir. 2484 B. C. cir. 1520 Ante I. Olymp. cir. 744 Ante U. C. cir. 767

it shall go ill with him that is left
in his tabernacle.
27 The heaven shall reveal his
iniquity; and the earth shall rise
up against him.
28 The increase of his house shall depart,
and his goods shall flow away
in the day of his wrath.
29 [c]This *is* the portion
of a wicked man from God,
and the heritage [d]appointed unto him by
God.

[c]Chap. xxvii. 13; xxxi. 2, 3

[d]Heb. *of his decree from God*

Korah, and his company, to whose destruction there is probably here an allusion: hence the words, *It shall go ill with him who is left in his tabernacle.* "And the Lord spake unto Moses and Aaron, Separate yourselves from among this congregation, that I may consume them in a moment. *Get ye up from about the tabernacle* of Korah, Dathan, and Abiram. *Depart* from the *tents* of these wicked men. There came out a fire from the Lord and consumed the two hundred and fifty men that offered incense;" Num. xvi. 20, &c.

Verse 27. *The heaven shall reveal his iniquity; and the earth shall rise up against him.*] Another allusion, if I mistake not, to the destruction of Korah and his company. The heaven revealed their iniquity; God declared out of heaven his judgment of their rebellion. "And the glory of the Lord appeared unto all the congregation;" Num. xvi. 20, &c. And then *the earth rose up against them.* "The ground clave asunder that was under them, and the earth opened her mouth and swallowed them up; and they went down alive into the pit, and the earth closed upon them;" Num. xvi. 31-33.

Verse 28. *The increase of his house shall depart,* and his goods *shall flow away in the day of his wrath.*] A farther allusion to the punishment of the rebellious company of Korah, who not only perished *themselves*, but their *houses* also, and their *goods*. Num. xvi. 32.

These examples were all in point, on the ground assumed by Zophar; and such well-attested facts would not be passed over by him, had he known the record of them; and that he did know it, alludes to it, and quotes the very circumstances, is more than probable.

Verse 29. *This* is *the portion*] As God has dealt with the *murmuring Israelites*, and with the *rebellious sons* of *Korah*, so will he deal with those who *murmur* against the *dispensations* of his *providence*, and rebel against his *authority*. Instead of an *earthly portion*, and an *ecclesiastical heritage*, such as Korah, Dathan, and Abiram sought; they shall have *fire* from God to *scorch them*, and the *earth* to *swallow them up*.

Dr. *Stock*, bishop of Killala, who has noticed the allusion to the *quails*, and for which he has been most unmeritedly ridiculed, gives us the following note on the passage:—

"Here I apprehend is a fresh example of the known usage of Hebrew poets, in adorning their compositions by allusions to facts in the history of their own people. It has escaped all the interpreters; and it is the more important, because it fixes the date of this poem, so far as to prove its having been composed *subsequently* to the transgression of Israel, at Kibroth Hattaavah, recorded in Num. xi. 33, 34. Because the wicked acknowledges not the *quail*, that is, the meat with which God has filled his stomach; but, like the ungrateful Israelites, *crammed*, and *blasphemed his feeder*, as *Milton* finely expresses it, he shall experience the same punishment with them, and be cut off in the midst of his enjoyment, as Moses tells us the people were who lusted."

If I mistake not, I have added considerable strength to the prelate's reasoning, by showing that there is a reference also to the history of the *manna*, and to that which details the *rebellion of Korah* and his company; and if so, (and they may dispute who please,) it is a proof that the Book of Job is not *so old* as, much less *older* than, the *Pentateuch*, as some have endeavoured to prove, but with no evidence of success, at least to my mind: a point which never has been, and I am certain never can be, proved; which has multitudes of presumptions against it, and not one clear incontestable fact for it. Mr. *Good* has done more in this case than any of his predecessors, and yet Mr. *Good* has failed; no wonder then that *others*, unmerciful criticisers of the bishop of Killala, have failed also, who had not a tenth part of Mr. *Good's* learning, nor one-hundredth part of his critical acumen.

It is, however, strange that men cannot suffer others to differ from them on a subject of confessed difficulty and comparatively little importance, without raising up the cry of *heresy* against them, and treating them with superciliousness and contempt! These should know, if they are *clergymen*, whether *dignified* or *not*, that such conduct ill becomes the *sacerdotal* character; and that *ante barbam docet senes* cannot be always spoken to the *teacher's* advantage.

As *a good story is not the worse for being twice told*, the following lines from a clergyman, who, for his *humility* and piety, was as much an honour to his *vocation* as he was to human nature, may not be amiss, in point of advice to all *Warburtonian* spirits:—

"Be *calm* in arguing, for *fierceness* makes
Error a *fault*, and *truth discourtesy*.
Why should I feel another man's mistakes
More than his *sickness* or his *poverty?*
In love I should: but anger is not love
Nor *wisdom* neither; therefore, gently move.
Calmness is great advantage: he that lets
Another chafe, may warm him at *his* fire,
Mark all his wanderings, and enjoy his frets;
As cunning fencers suffer heat to tire.
Truth dwells not in the clouds: the bow that's there
Doth often aim at, never hit, the sphere."

HERBERT.

Dr. *Stock's* work on the Book of Job will stand honourably on the same shelf with the best on this difficult subject.

CHAPTER XXI

Job expresses himself as puzzled by the dispensations of Divine Providence, because of the unequal distribution of temporal goods; he shows that wicked men often live long, prosper in their families, in their flocks, and in all their substance, and yet live in defiance of God and sacred things, 1–16. *At other times their prosperity is suddenly blasted, and they and their families come to ruin,* 17–21. *God, however, is too wise to err; and he deals out various lots to all according to his wisdom: some come sooner, others later, to the grave: the strong and the weak, the prince and the peasant, come to a similar end in this life; but the wicked are reserved for a day of wrath,* 22–33. *He charges his friends with falsehood in their pretended attempts to comfort him,* 34.

A. M. cir. 2484
B. C. cir. 1520
Ante I. Olymp. cir. 744
Ante U. C. cir. 767

BUT Job answered and said,
2 Hear diligently my speech,
and let this be your consolations.
3 Suffer me that I may speak;
and after that I have spoken, [a]mock on.
4 As for me, *is* my complaint to man? and
if *it were so,* why should not my spirit be
[b]troubled?
5 [c]Mark me, and be astonished, [d]and lay
your hand upon *your* mouth.
6 Even when I remember I am afraid, and
trembling taketh hold on my flesh.
7 [e]Wherefore do the wicked live, become old, yea, are mighty in
power?
8 Their seed is established in
their sight with them, and their
offspring before their eyes.
9 Their houses [f]*are* safe from fear, [g]neither
is the rod of God upon them.
10 Their bull gendereth, and faileth not;
their cow calveth, and [h]casteth not her calf.
11 They send forth their little ones like a
flock, and their children dance.
12 They take the timbrel and harp, and rejoice at the sound of the organ.

A. M. cir. 2484
B. C. cir. 1520
Ante I. Olymp. cir. 744
Ante U. C. cir. 767

[a]Chap. xvi. 10; xxvii. 2——[b]Heb. *shortened*——[c]Heb. *look unto me*——[d]Judg. xviii. 19; chap. xxix. 9; xl. 4; Psa. xxxix. 9

[e]Chap. xii. 6; Psa. xvii. 10, 14; lxxiii. 3, 12; Jer. xii. 1; Hab. i. 16——[f]Heb. are *peace from fear*——[g]Psa. lxxiii. 5——[h]Exod. xxiii. 26

NOTES ON CHAP. XXI

Verse 2. *Let this be your consolations.*] ותהי זאת תנחומתיכם *uthehi zoth tanchumotheychem* may be translated, "And let this be your retractations." Let what I am about to say induce you to *retract* what you have said, and to *recall* your false judgments.

נחם *nacham* signifies, not only to *comfort,* but to *change one's mind,* to *repent;* hence the *Vulgate* translates *et agite pœnitentiam,* "and repent," which *Coverdale* follows in his version, **and amende yourselves.** Some suppose the verse to be understood ironically: I am now about to give you consolations for those you have given me. When I have done, then turn them into *mockery* if you please.

Verse 4. *As for me*] האנכי *heanochi,* "Alas for me!" Is it not with a man that I speak? And, if this be the case, why should not my spirit be troubled? I do not reply against my *Maker:* I suffer much from God and man; why then may I not have the privilege of complaining to creatures like myself?

Verse 5. *Mark me, and be astonished*] Consider and compare the state in which I was once, with that in which I am now; and be astonished at the judgments and dispensations of God. You will then be confounded; you will put your hands upon your mouths, and keep silent.

Putting the hand on the mouth, or the *finger on the lips,* was the token of silence. The Egyptian god *Harpocrates,* who was the *god of silence,* is represented with his finger compressing his upper lip.

Verse 6. *I am afraid* I am about to speak of the mysterious workings of Providence; and I tremble at the thought of entering into a detail on such a subject; my very flesh trembles.

Verse 7. *Wherefore do the wicked live*] You have frequently asserted that the wicked are invariably punished in this life; and that the righteous are ever distinguished by the strongest marks of God's providential kindness; how then does it come that many wicked men live long and prosperously, and at last die in peace, without any evidence whatever of God's displeasure? This is a fact that is occurring daily; none can deny it; how then will you reconcile it with your maxims?

Verse 8. *Their seed is established*] They see their own *children* grow up, and become settled in the land; and behold their *children's children* also; so that their generations are not cut off. Even the posterity of the wicked continue.

Verse 9. *Neither* is *the rod of God upon them.*] They are not afflicted as other men.

Verse 10. *Their bull gendereth*] עבר *ibbar, passes over, i. e.,* on the cow, referring to the actions of the bull when coupling with the female. Their flocks multiply greatly, they bring forth in time, and none of them is barren.

Verse 11. *They send forth their little ones*] It is not very clear whether this refers to the *young of the flocks* or to their *children.* The first clause may mean the former, the next clause the latter; while the *young* of their *cattle* are in flocks, their numerous *children* are healthy and vigorous, *and dance for joy.*

Verse 12. *They take the timbrel and harp*] ישאו *yisu,* they *rise up* or *lift themselves up,*

A. M. cir. 2484
B. C. cir. 1520
Ante I. Olymp. cir. 744
Ante U. C. cir. 767

13 They [i]spend their days [k]in wealth, and in a moment go down to the grave.
14 [l]Therefore they say unto God, Depart from us; for we desire not the knowledge of thy ways.
15 [m]What *is* the Almighty, that we should serve him? and [n]what profit should we have, if we pray unto him?
16 Lo, their good *is* not in their hand: [o]the counsel of the wicked is far from me.
17 [p]How oft is the [q]candle of the wicked

[i]Ch. xxxvi. 11——[k]Or, *in mirth*——[l]Ch. xxii. 17 [m]Exod. v. 2; ch. xxxiv. 9——[n]Ch. xxxv. 3; Mal. iii. 14 [o]Ch. xxii. 18; Psa. i. 1; Prov. i. 10; Ezek. xi. 2; Luke xxiii. 51; Acts v. 33——[p]Ch. xviii. 6——[q]Or, *lamp*

probably alluding to the rural exercise of dancing.

תף *toph*, which we translate *timbrel*, means a sort of *drum*, such as the *tom-tom* of the Asiatics.

כנור *kinnor* may mean something of the *harp* kind.

עוגב *ugab*, *organ*, means nothing like the instrument now called the *organ*, though thus translated both by the *Septuagint* and *Vulgate;* it probably means the *syrinx*, composed of several unequal pipes, close at the bottom, which, when blown into at the top, gives a very *shrill* and *lively* sound. To these instruments the youth are represented as *dancing joyfully*. Mr. *Good* translates: "They trip merrily to the sound of the pipe." And illustrates his translation with the following verse:—

"Now pursuing, now retreating,
Now in circling troops they meet;
To brisk notes in cadence beating,
Glance their many twinkling feet."

The original is intended to convey the true notion of the gambols of the rustic nymphs and swains on festival occasions; and let it be observed that this is spoken of the children of those who say unto God, "Depart from us; for we desire not the knowledge of thy ways. What is the Almighty, that we should serve him? and what profit should we have if we pray unto him?" ver. 14, 15. Is it any wonder that the children of such parents should be living to the flesh, and serving the lusts of the flesh? for neither they nor their parents know God, nor pray unto him.

Verse 13. *They spend their days in wealth*] There is a various reading here of some importance. In the text we have יבלו *yeballu, they grow old*, or wear out as with old age, *terent vetustate;* and in the *margin*, יכלו *yechallu, they consume;* and the *Masora* states that this is one of the *eleven* words which are written with ב *beth* and must be read with כ *caph*. Several *editions* have the former word in the *text*, and the latter in the *margin;* the former being what is called the *kethib*, the latter *keri*.

יבלו *yeballu, they grow old*, or *wear out*, is the reading of the *Antwerp*, *Paris*, and *London* Polyglots; יכלו *yechallu, they accomplish* or *spend*, is the reading of the *Complutensian Polyglot*, thirteen of *Kennicott's* and *De Rossi's* MSS., the *Septuagint*, *Chaldee*, *Syriac*, and *Arabic*. The *Vulgate* has *ducunt*, "they lead or spend," from which our translation is borrowed. I incline to the former, as Job's argument derives considerable strength from this circumstance; they not only *spend* their days in faring sumptuously every day; but they even *wear out* so as to *grow old* in it; they are not cut off by any sudden judgment of God. This is fact; therefore your doctrine, that the wicked are cut off suddenly and have but a short time, is far from the truth.

In a moment go down to the grave.] They wear out their years in pleasure; grow old in their gay and giddy life; and die, as in a moment, without previous sickness; or, as Mr. *Good* has it, *They quietly descend into the grave.*

Verse 14. *They say unto God*] This is the language of their *conduct*, though not directly of their *lips*.

Depart from us] Let us alone; we do not trouble thee. Thy ways are painful; we do not like cross-bearing. Thy ways are spiritual; we wish to live after the flesh. We have learned to do our own will; we do not wish to study thine.

Verse 15. *What is the Almighty*] What allegiance do we owe to him? We feel no *obligation* to *obey* him; and what profit can we derive from *prayer?* We are as happy as flesh and blood can make us: our kingdom is of this world; we wish for no other portion than that which we have.

Those who have never prayed as they ought know nothing of the benefits of prayer.

Verse 16. *Their good is not in their hand*] With all their boasting and self-dependence, God only *lends* them his bounty; and though it appears to be their own, yet it is at his disposal. Some of the wicked he permits to live and die in *affluence*, provided it be acquired in the ordinary way of his providence, by trade, commerce, &c. Others he permits to possess it for a *while* only, and then strips them of their illegally procured property.

The counsel of the wicked is far from me.] Some understand the words thus: "Far be it from me to advocate the cause of the wicked." I have nothing in common with them, and am not their apologist. I state a fact: they are often found in continual prosperity. I state another fact: they are often found in wretchedness and misery.

Verse 17. *How oft is the candle of the wicked put out?*] The *candle* or *lamp* is often used, both as the emblem of *prosperity* and of *posterity*. Oftentimes the rejoicing of the wicked is short; and, not unfrequently, his *seed* is cut off from the earth. The *root* is dried up, and the *branch* is withered.

God *distributeth sorrows in his anger.*] He must be incensed against those who refuse to *know*, *serve*, and *pray* unto him. In his anger, therefore, he portions out to each his due share of misery, vexation, and wo.

A. M. cir. 2484
B. C. cir. 1520
Ante I. Olymp. cir. 744
Ante U. C. cir. 767

put out? and *how oft* cometh
their destruction upon them?
God [r]distributeth sorrows in his
anger.
18 [s]They are as stubble before the wind,
and as chaff that the storm [t]carrieth away.
19 God layeth up [u]his iniquity [v]for his children: he rewardeth him, and he shall know *it*.
20 His eyes shall see his destruction, and
[w]he shall drink of the wrath of the Almighty.
21 For what pleasure *hath* he in his house
after him, when the number of his
months is cut off in the midst?
22 [x]Shall *any* teach God
knowledge? seeing he judgeth
those that are high.
23 One dieth [y]in his full strength, being
wholly at ease and quiet.
24 His [z]breasts are full of milk, and his
bones are moistened with marrow.
25 And another dieth in the bitterness of
his soul, and never eateth with pleasure.

A. M. cir. 2484
B. C. cir. 1520
Ante I. Olymp. cir. 744
Ante U. C. cir. 767

---

[r]Luke xii. 46——[s]Psalm i. 4; xxxv. 5; Isaiah xvii. 13; xxix. 5; Hosea xiii. 3——[t]Hebrew, *stealeth away*——[u]That is, *the punishment of his iniquity*——[v]Exodus xx. 5——[w]Psalm lxxv. 8; Isaiah li. 17; Jeremiah xxv. 15; Revelation xiv. 10; xix. 15——[x]Isaiah xl. 13; xlv. 9; Romans xi. 34; 1 Cor. ii. 16——[y]Hebrew, *in his very perfection*, or *in the strength of his perfection*——[z]Or, *milk pails*

Verse 18. *They are as stubble before the wind*] "His fan is in his hand; he will thoroughly cleanse his floor, and the chaff he will burn with unquenchable fire. Therefore the wicked shall not stand in the judgment, but shall be like the *chaff* which the wind driveth away." Were not this a common thought, I should have supposed that the author of this book borrowed it from Psa. i. 4. The original signifies that they shall be *carried away by a furious storm;* and borne off as *booty* is by the swift-riding robbers of the desert, who make a sudden irruption, and then set off at full speed with their prey.

Verse 19. *God layeth up his iniquity for his children*] This is according to the declaration of God, Exod. xx. 5: "Visiting the iniquity of the fathers upon the children, unto the third and fourth generation of them that hate me." This always supposes that the *children*, who are thus visited, have *copied their parents' example;* or that *ill-gotten property* is found in their hands, which has descended to them from their wicked fathers; and of this God, in his judgments, strips them. It is, however, very natural to suppose that children brought up without the fear of God will walk in the sight of their own eyes, and according to the imaginations of their own hearts.

He rewardeth him, and he shall know it.] He shall so visit his transgressions upon him, that he shall at last discern that it is God who hath done it. And thus they will find that there would have been *profit* in *serving* him, and *safety* in *praying* unto him. But this they have neglected, and now it is too late.

Verse 20. *His eyes shall see his destruction*] He shall perceive its approach, and have the double punishment of *fearing* and *feeling; feeling* a THOUSAND deaths in *fearing* ONE.

He shall drink of the wrath] The cup of God's wrath, the cup of trembling, &c., is frequently expressed or referred to in the sacred writings, Deut. xxxii. 33; Isa. li. 17-22; Jer. xxv. 15; Rev. xiv. 8. It appears to be a metaphor taken from those cups of poison which certain criminals were obliged to drink. A *cup* of the *juice of hemlock* was the *wrath* or *punishment* assigned by the Athenian magistrates to the philosopher *Socrates*.

Verse 21. *For what pleasure* hath *he in his house after him*] What may happen to his posterity he neither knows nor cares for, as he is now numbered with the dead, and numbered with them before he had lived out half his years. Some have translated the verse thus: "Behold how speedily God destroys the house of the wicked after him! How he shortens the number of his months!"

Verse 22. *Shall* any *teach God knowledge?*] Who among the sons of men can pretend to teach GOD how to govern the world, who himself teaches *those that are high*—the heavenly inhabitants, that excel us infinitely both in knowledge and wisdom? Neither angels nor men can comprehend the reasons of the Divine providence. It is a depth known only to God.

Verse 23. *One dieth in his full strength*] In this and the three following verses Job shows that the inequality of fortune, goods, health, strength, &c., decides nothing either for or against persons in reference to the approbation or disapprobation of God, as these various lots are no indications of their *wickedness* or *innocence*. One has a *sudden*, another a *lingering* death; but by none of these can their eternal states be determined.

Verse 24. *His breasts are full of milk*] The word עטיניו *atinaiv*, which occurs nowhere else in the Hebrew Bible, is most likely an *Arabic* term, but probably so *provincial* as to be now lost. **عطن** *atana* signifies to macerate hides so as to take off the hair: hence Mr. *Good* thinks it means here, that *sleekness of skin* which is the effect of *fatness* both in man and beast. But as the radical idea signifies to *stink*, as leather does which is thus macerated, I cannot see how this meaning can apply here. Under the root עטן *atan*, Mr. *Parkhurst* gives the following definitions: "עטן occurs, not as a verb, but as a noun masculine plural, in construction, עטיני *atiney, the bowels, intestines;* once Job xxi. 24, עטיניו *atinaiv*, his bowels or intestines, *are full of*, or *abound with*, חלב *chalab, fat*. So the LXX.: Τα δε εγκατα αυτου πληρη στεατος. The VULGATE: Viscera, ejus *plena sunt adipe*, 'his intestines are full of fat.' May not עטינים *atinim* be a noun masculine plural from עטה *atah, to involve*, formed as גליונים *gailyonim, mirrors*, from גלה *galah, to reveal?* And may not the *intestines*, including those fatty parts, the mesentery and omentum, be so called on account of their wonderful *involutions?*" I think

A. M. cir. 2484
B. C. cir. 1520
Ante I. Olymp. cir. 744
Ante U. C. cir. 767

26 They shall [a]lie down alike
in the dust, and the worms shall
cover them.
27 Behold, I know your
thoughts, and the devices *which* ye wrongfully
imagine against me.
28 For ye say, [b]Where *is* the house of the
prince? and where *are* [c]the dwelling-places
of the wicked?
29 Have ye not asked them that go by the
way? and do ye not know their tokens,
30 [d]That the wicked is reserved to the day
of destruction? they shall be
brought forth to [e]the day of wrath.
31 Who shall declare his way
[f]to his face? and who shall repay him *what* he hath done?
32 Yet shall he be brought to the [g]grave
and shall [h]remain in the tomb.
33 The clods of the valley shall be sweet
unto him, and [i]every man shall draw after
him, as *there are* innumerable before him.
34 How then comfort ye me in vain, seeing
in your answers there remaineth [k]falsehood?

[a]Chapter xx. 11; Eccles. ix. 2——[b]Chapter xx. 7
[c]Heb. *the tent of the tabernacles of the wicked*——[d]Prov. xvi. 4; 2 Pet. ii. 9

[e]Heb. *the day of wraths*——[f]Gal. ii. 11——[g]Heb. *graves*——[h]Heb. *watch in the heap*——[i]Heb. ix. 27
[k]Heb. *transgression*

this conjecture to be as likely as any that has yet been formed.

Verse 26. *They shall lie down alike in the dust*] Death levels all distinctions, and the grave makes all equal. There may be a difference in the grave itself; but the human corpse is the same in all. Splendid monuments enshrine *corruption;* but the *sod* must lie close and heavy upon the putrefying carcass, to prevent it from becoming the bane of the living.

Verse 27. *I know your thoughts*] Ye still think that, because I am grievously afflicted, I must therefore be a felonious transgressor.

Verse 28. *For ye say, Where* is *the house of the prince?*] In order to prove your point, ye *ask, Where is the house of the tyrant and oppressor?* Are they not overthrown and destroyed? And is not this a proof that God does not permit the wicked to enjoy prosperity?

Verse 29. *Have ye not asked them that go by the way?*] This appears to be Job's answer. Consult travellers who have gone through different countries; and they will tell you that they have seen both examples—the wicked in great prosperity in some instances, while suddenly destroyed in others. See at the end of the chapter.

Do ye not know their tokens] Mr. *Good* translates the whole verse thus: "Surely thou canst never have inquired of men of travel; or thou couldst not have been ignorant of their tokens. Hadst thou made proper inquiries, thou wouldst have heard of their awful end in a thousand instances. And also of their *prosperity.*" See at the end of this chapter.

Verse 30. *That the wicked is reserved to the day of destruction?*] Though every one can tell that he has seen the wicked in prosperity, and even spend a long life in it; yet this is no proof that God loves him, or that he shall enjoy a prosperous lot in the next world. There, he shall meet with the *day of wrath.* There, the wicked shall be punished, and the just rewarded.

Verse 31. *Who shall declare his way to his face?*] But while the wicked is in power, who shall dare to tell him to his face what his true character is? or, who shall dare to repay him the evil he has done? As such a person cannot have his punishment in this life, he must have it in another; and for this the *day of wrath*—the day of judgment, is prepared.

Verse 32. *Yet shall he be brought to the grave*] He shall die like other men; and the corruption of the grave shall prey upon him. Mr. Carlyle, in his specimens of Arabic poetry, Translations, p. 16, quotes this verse, which he translates and paraphrases, והוא לקברות יובל "He shall be brought to the grave," ועל גדיש ישקוד "And shall *watch upon the high-raised heap.*"

It was the opinion of the pagan Arabs, that upon the death of any person, a bird, by them called *Manah,* issued from the brain, and haunted the sepulchre of the deceased, uttering a lamentable scream. This notion, he adds, is evidently alluded to in Job xxi. 32. Thus *Abusahel,* on the death of his mistress:—

"If her *ghost's* funereal *screech*
Through the earth my grave should reach,
On *that voice* I loved so well
My transported ghost would dwell."

Verse 33. *The clods of the valley shall be sweet unto him*] Perhaps there is an allusion here to the Asiatic mode of interment for princes, saints, and nobles: a well-watered valley was chosen for the tomb, where a perpetual spring might be secured. This was intended to be the emblem of a *resurrection,* or of a *future life;* and to *conceal* as much as possible the disgrace of the rotting carcass.

Every man shall draw after him] There seem to be two allusions intended here: 1. To *death,* the common lot of all. *Millions have gone before him* to the tomb; and כל אדם *col adam, all men, shall follow him:* all past generations have died; all succeeding generations shall die also. 2. To pompous *funeral processions;* multitudes *preceding,* and multitudes *following,* the corpse.

Verse 34. *How then comfort ye me in vain*] Mr. *Good* translates: "How vainly then would ye make me retract!" See the note on ver. 2. I cannot *retract* any thing I have said, as I have proved by fact and testimony that your positions are false and unfounded. Your pretensions to comfort me are as hollow as the arguments you bring in support of your exceptionable doctrines.

THIS chapter may be called Job's triumph over the insinuated calumnies, and specious but false doctrines, of his opponents. The irritability of his temper no longer appears: from the time he got that glorious discovery of his *Redeemer,* and the joyous hope of an *eternal in-*

heritance, chap. xix. 25, &c., we find no more murmurings, nor unsanctified complainings. He is now full master of himself; and reasons conclusively, because he reasons coolly. Impassioned transports no longer carry him away: his mind is serene; his heart, fixed; his hope, steady; and his faith, strong. Zophar the Naamathite is now, in his presence, as an infant in the gripe of a mighty giant. Another of these pretended friends but real enemies comes forward to renew the attack with virulent invective, malevolent insinuation, and unsupported assertion. Him, Job meets, and vanquishes by pious resignation and fervent prayer. Though, at different times after this, Job had his buffetings from his grand adversary, and some seasons of comparative darkness, yet his faith is unshaken, and he stands as a beaten anvil to the stroke. He effectually exculpates himself, and vindicates the dispensations of his Maker.

There appears to be something in the 29th verse which requires to be farther examined: *Have ye not asked them that go by the way? And do ye not know their tokens?* It is probable that this verse may allude to the custom of *burying the dead by the way-side*, and raising up *specious* and *descriptive monuments* over them. Job argues that the lot of outward prosperity fell alike to the just and to the unjust, and that the sepulchral monuments by the way-side were proofs of his assertion; for his friends, as well as himself and others, had noted them, and asked the history of such and such persons, from the nearest inhabitants of the place; and the answers, in a great variety of cases, had been: "*That* monument points out the place where a wicked man lies, who was all his lifetime in prosperity and affluence, yet oppressed the poor, and shut up the bowels of his compassion against the destitute; and *this* belongs to a man who lived only to serve his God, and to do good to man according to his power, yet had not a day of health, nor an hour of prosperity; God having given to the former *his portion in this life*, and reserved the recompense of the latter to a *future state*."

The *Septuagint* render the verse thus:—Ερωτησατε παραπορευμενους ὁδον, και τα σημεια αυτων ουκ απαλλοτριωσατε, "Inquire of those who pass by the way; and their signs [monuments] ye will not alienate." That is, When ye hear the history of these persons, ye will not then assert that the man who lived in prosperity was a genuine worshipper of the true God, and therefore was blessed with temporal good; and that he who lived in adversity was an enemy to God, and was consequently cursed with the want of secular blessings. Of the *former* ye will hear a different account from those who dare now speak the truth, because the prosperous oppressor is no more; and of the *latter* ye shall learn that, though afflicted, destitute, and distressed, he was one of those who acknowledged God in all his ways, and never performed an act of religious service to him in hope of *secular gain;* sought his approbation only, and met death cheerfully, in the hope of being eternally with the Lord.

Neither good nor evil can be known by the occurrences of this life. Every thing argues the certainty of a future state, and the necessity of a day of judgment. They who are in the habit of marking casualties, especially if those whom they love not are the subjects of them, as tokens of Divine displeasure, only show an ignorance of God's dispensations, and a malevolence of mind that would fain arm itself with the celestial thunders, in order to transfix those whom they deem their enemies.

CHAPTER XXII

Eliphaz reproves Job for his attempts to clear his character and establish his innocence, 1–4. *Charges him with innumerable transgressions; with oppressions towards his brethren, cruelty to the poor, hard-heartedness to the needy, and uncharitableness towards the widow and the orphan; and says it is on these accounts that snares and desolations are come upon him*, 5–11. *Speaks of the majesty and justice of God: how he cut off the antediluvians, the inhabitants of Sodom and the cities of the plain*, 12–20. *Exhorts him to repent and acknowledge his sins, and promises him great riches and prosperity*, 21–30.

A. M. cir. 2484
B. C. cir. 1520
Ante I. Olymp. cir. 744
Ante U. C. cir. 767

THEN Eliphaz the Temanite
answered and said,
2 [a]Can a man be profitable
unto God, [b]as he that is wise
may be profitable unto himself?
3 *Is it* any pleasure to the Almighty, that
thou art righteous? or *is it* gain *to him*,
that thou makest thy ways perfect?
4 Will he reprove thee for fear
of thee? will he enter with thee
into judgment?
5 *Is* not thy wickedness great? and thine
iniquities infinite?

[a]Chap. xxxv. 7; Psa. xvi. 2; Luke xvii. 10——[b]Or, *if he may be profitable* doth his *good success* depend *thereon?*

NOTES ON CHAP. XXII

Verse 2. *Can a man be profitable unto God*] God does not afflict thee because thou hast *deprived* him of any excellency. A man may be profitable to a man, but no man can profit his Maker. He has no interest in thy conduct; he does not punish thee because thou hast offended and deprived him of some good. Thy iniquities are against justice, and justice requires thy punishment.

Verse 3. Is it *any pleasure to the Almighty*] Infinite in his perfections, he can neither *gain* nor *lose* by the wickedness or righteousness of men.

A. M. cir. 2484
B. C. cir. 1520
Ante I. Olymp. cir. 744
Ante U. C. cir. 767

6 For thou hast [c]taken a
pledge from thy brother for
naught, and [d]stripped the naked
of their clothing.
7 Thou hast not given water to the weary
to drink, and thou [e]hast withholden bread
from the hungry.
8 But *as for* [f]the mighty man, he had the
earth; and the [g]honourable man dwelt in it.
9 Thou hast sent widows away empty, and
the arms of [h]the fatherless have been broken.

A. M. cir. 2484
B. C. cir. 1520
Ante I. Olymp. cir. 474
Ante U. C. cir. 767

10 Therefore [i]snares *are* round
about thee, and sudden fear troubleth thee;
11 Or darkness, *that* thou canst
not see; and abundance of [k]waters cover thee.
12 *Is* not God in the height of heaven? and
behold [l]the height of the stars, how high they
are!
13 And thou sayest, [m]How [n]doth God know?
can he judge through the dark cloud?
14 [o]Thick clouds *are* a covering to him, that

[c]Exodus xxii. 26, 27; Deuteronomy xxiv. 10, &c.; chap. xxiv. 3, 9; Ezekiel xviii. 12——[d]Hebrew, *stripped the clothes of the naked*——[e]See chap. xxxi. 17; Deuteronomy xv. 7, &c.; Isaiah lviii. 7; Ezekiel xviii. 7, 16; Matt. xxv. 42——[f]Heb. *the man of arm*——[g]Heb. *eminent* or *accepted for countenance*——[h]Chapter xxxi. 21; Isa. x. 2; Ezek. xxii. 7——[i]Chap. xviii. 8, 9, 10; xix. 6——[k]Psalm lxix. 1, 2; cxxiv. 4; Lam. iii. 54——[l]Heb. *the head of the stars*——[m]Or, *What*——[n]Psa. x. 11; lix. 7; lxxiii. 11; xciv. 7——[o]Psa. cxxxix. 11, 12

Verse 4. *For fear of thee?*] Is it because he is afraid that thou wilt do him some *injury*, that he has stripped thee of thy power and wealth?

Verse 5. Is *not thy wickedness great?*] Thy sins are not only *many*, but they are *great;* and of thy continuance in them *there is no end*, אין קץ *ein kets.*

Verse 6. *Thou hast taken a pledge*] Thou hast been vexatious in all thy doings, and hast exacted where nothing was due, so that through thee the poor have been unable to procure their necessary clothing.

Verse 7. *Thou hast not given water*] It was esteemed a great virtue in the East to furnish thirsty travellers with water; especially in the deserts, where scarcely a *stream* was to be found, and where *wells* were very rare. Some of the Indian devotees are accustomed to stand with a *girbah* or skin full of water, on the public roads, to give drink to weary travellers who are parched with thirst.

Verse 8. *But* as for *the mighty man, he had the earth*] איש זרוע *ish zeroa, the man of arm.* Finger, hand, and arm, are all emblems of strength and power. The *man of arm* is not only the *strong man*, but the *man* of *power* and *influence*, the man of *rapine* and *plunder*.

The honourable man] Literally, the man whose *face is accepted*, the respectable man, the man of *wealth.* Thou wert an enemy to the *poor* and *needy*, but thou didst favour and flatter the *rich* and *great*.

Verse 9. *The arms of the fatherless*] Whatever *strength* or *power* or property they had, of that thou hast deprived them. Thou hast been hard-hearted and cruel, and hast enriched thyself with the spoils of the poor and the defenceless.

Verse 10. *Therefore snares*] As thou hast dealt with others, so has God, in his retributive providence, dealt with thee. As thou hast spoiled, so art thou spoiled. Thou art taken in a net from which thou canst not escape. There is an allusion here to the hunting of the elephant: he is driven into an inclosure in the woods, passing from strait to strait, till brought into a narrow point, from which he cannot escape; and then his consternation is great, and his roaring terrible. God hath hunted thee down, as men hunt down those wild and dangerous beasts. See on chap. xviii.

Verse 11. *Or darkness*, that *thou canst not see*] The sense of this passage, in the connection that the particle *or* gives it with the preceding verse, is not easy to be ascertained. To me it seems very probable that a letter has been lost from the first word; and that או *o*, which we translate OR, was originally אור *or*, LIGHT. The copy used by the *Septuagint* had certainly this reading; and therefore they translate the verse thus: Το φως σοι εις σκοτος απεβη; *Thy* LIGHT *is changed into darkness;* that is, Thy *prosperity* is turned into *adversity*.

Houbigant corrects the text thus: instead of או חשך לא תראה *o chosech lo tireh, or darkness thou canst not see*, he reads חשך לא אור תראה *chosech lo or tireh, darkness, not light, shalt thou behold;* that is, Thou shalt dwell in thick darkness. Mr. *Good* translates: "Or darkness which thou canst not penetrate, and a flood of waters shall cover thee." Thou shalt either be enveloped in deep darkness, or overwhelmed with a flood.

The versions all translate differently; and neither they nor the MSS. give any light, except what is afforded by the Septuagint. *Coverdale* is singular: **Shuldest thou then send darcknesse? Shulde not the water floude runne over the?** Perhaps the meaning is: "Thou art so encompassed with darkness, that thou canst not see thy way; and therefore fallest into the snares and traps that are laid for thee."

Verse 12. Is *not God in the height of heaven?*] It appears, from this and the following verses, that Eliphaz was attributing infidel and blasphemous speeches or sentiments to Job. As if he had said: "Thou allowest that there is a God, but thou sayest that he is infinitely exalted above the heavens and the stars, and that there is so much dense ether and thick cloud between his throne and the earth, that he can neither see it nor its inhabitants." These were sentiments which Job never held, and never uttered; but if a man be dressed in a bear's skin, he may be hunted and worried by his own dogs. Job's friends attribute falsities to him, and then dilate upon them, and draw inferences from them injurious to his character. *Polemic writers*, both in *theology* and *politics*, often act in this way.

Verse 14. *He walketh in the circuit of heaven*] He confines himself to those infinitely exalted regions and cares nothing for the inhabitants of the earth.

A. M. cir. 2484
B. C. cir. 1520
Ante I. Olymp. cir. 744
Ante U. C. cir. 767

he seeth not; and he walketh
in the circuit of heaven.
15 Hast thou marked the old
way which wicked men have
trodden?
16 Which [p]were cut down out of time, [q]whose
foundation was overflown with a flood:
17 [r]Which said unto God, Depart from us:
and [s]what can the Almighty do [t]for them?
18 Yet he filled their houses with good
things: but [u]the counsel of the wicked is far
from me.
19 [v]The righteous see *it,* and are glad: and
the innocent laugh them to
scorn.
20 Whereas our [w]substance is
not cut down, but [x]the remnant
of them the fire consumeth.
21 Acquaint now thyself [y]with him, and
[z]be at peace: thereby good shall come unto
thee.
22 Receive, I pray thee, the law from his
mouth, and [a]lay up his words in thine heart.
23 [b]If thou return to the Almighty, thou
shalt be built up, thou shalt put away iniquity
far from thy tabernacles.

A. M. cir. 2484
B. C. cir. 1520
Ante I. Olymp. cir. 744
Ante U. C. cir. 767

---

[p]Ch. xv. 32; Psa. lv. 23; cii. 24; Eccles. vii. 17 —— [q]Heb. *a flood was poured upon their foundation;* Gen. vii. 11; 2 Pet. ii. 5 —— [r]Ch. xxi. 14 —— [s]Psa. iv. 6 —— [t]Or, *to them*

[u]Chap. xxi. 16 —— [v]Psa. lviii. 10; cvii. 42 —— [w]Or, *estate* —— [x]Or, *their excellency* —— [y]That is, *with God* —— [z]Isa. xxvii. 5 —— [a]Psa. cxix. 11 —— [b]Chap. viii. 5, 6; xi. 13, 14

Verse 15. *Hast thou marked the old way*] This is supposed to be another accusation; as if he had said, "Thou followest the same way that the wicked of old have walked in." Here is an evident allusion to the FLOOD, as is particularly noted in the next verse.

Verse 16. *Whose foundation was overflown with a flood*] The unrighteous in the days of Noah, who appear to have had an abundance of all temporal good, (ver. 18,) and who surpassed the deeds of all the former wicked, said in effect to God, *Depart from us.* And when Noah preached unto them the terrors of the Lord, and the necessity of repentance, they rejected his preaching with, *What can the Almighty do for us?* Let him do his worst; we care not for him, ver. 17.

For למו *lamo, to* THEM, the *Septuagint, Syriac,* and *Arabic* have evidently read לנו *lanu, to* US. This reading quotes their *own saying;* the former reading narrates it in *the third person.* The meaning, however, is the same.

Verse 18. *But the counsel of the wicked is far from me.*] Sarcastically quoting Job's words, chap. xxi. 14, 16. Job, having in the preceding chapter described the wicked, who said unto the Almighty, "Depart from us," &c., adds, *But the counsel of the wicked is far from me.* Eliphaz here, having described the impious, among whom he evidently ranks Job, makes use of the same expression, as if he had said, "Thank God, I have no connection with you nor your companions; nor is my mind contaminated by your creed."

Verse 19. *The righteous see* it, *and are glad*] They see God's judgments on the incorrigibly wicked, and know that the Judge of all the earth does right; hence they rejoice in all the dispensations of his providence.

Verse 20. *Whereas our substance is not cut down*] We, who fear the Lord, still continue in health and peace; whereas they who have departed from him are destroyed even to their very remnant.

Mr. *Good* thinks that קימנו *kimanu,* which we translate *our substance,* is the same as the Arabic قومنا *our people* or *tribe;* and hence he translates the clause thus: "For our tribe is not cut off; while even the remnant of these a conflagration consumed." The reference here is supposed to be to the destruction of the men of Sodom and Gomorrah. A judgment by a *flood* took off the world of the ungodly in the days of *Noah.* Their remnant, those who lived in the same ungodly way, were taken off by a judgment of fire, in the days of *Lot.* Eliphaz introduces these two examples in order to terrify Job into a compliance with the exhortation which immediately follows.

Verse 21. *Acquaint now thyself with him*] Perhaps the verb הסכן *hasken* should be translated here, *treasure up,* or *lay up. Lay up* or procure an *interest now with him, and be at peace.* Get the Divine favour, and then thou wilt be at peace with God, and have happiness in thy own soul.

Thereby good shall come unto thee.] בהם *bahem,* "in them," shall good come unto thee. That is, in getting an interest in the Divine favour, and in having thy soul brought into a state of peace with him; thereby, in them, that is, these two things, good will come unto thee. First, thou wilt have an interest in his favour, from which thou mayest expect all blessings; and, secondly, from his peace in thy conscience thou wilt feel unutterable happiness. Get these blessings *now,* for thou knowest not what a day may bring forth. Reader, hast *thou* these blessings?

Verse 22. *Receive, I pray thee, the law from his mouth*] Some, who wish to place Job *before* the law given by Moses, say that this means the *Noahic precepts;* others, that the *law of nature* is intended! Stuff and vanity! The allusion is plainly to the *law* given by God to the children of Israel, called here by way of emphasis, תורה *torah, the* LAW, which contained אמריו *amaraiv, his* WORDS, the *words* or *sayings of God* himself; consequently, it is not the *Noahic precepts,* nor the *law of nature,* neither of which were ever *written* or *registered* as the *words of God's mouth.*

Verse 23. *Thou shalt be built up*] God will restore thee to thy wonted state of prosperity; and thou shalt again have a *household,* not only of *servants,* but of *children* also. So much may be implied in the words, *Thou shalt be* BUILT UP. See my sermon on ver. 21-23.

A. M. cir. 2484
B. C. cir. 1520
Ante I. Olymp. cir. 744
Ante U. C. cir. 767

24 Then shalt thou [c]lay up gold [d]as dust, and the *gold* of Ophir as the stones of the brooks.

25 Yea, the Almighty shall be thy [e]defence, and thou shalt have [f]plenty of silver.

26 For then shalt thou have thy [g]delight in the Almighty, and [h]shalt lift up thy face unto God.

27 [i]Thou shalt make thy prayer unto him, and he shall hear thee, and thou shalt pay thy vows.

28 Thou shalt also decree a thing, and it shall be established unto thee: and the light shall shine upon thy ways.

A. M. cir. 2484
B. C. cir. 1520
Ante I. Olymp. cir. 744
Ante U. C. cir. 767

29 When *men* are cast down, then thou shalt say, *There is* lifting up; and [k]he shall save [l]the humble person.

30 [m]He shall deliver the island of the innocent: and it is delivered by the pureness of thine hands.

---

[c]2 Chron. i. 15——[d]Or, *on the dust*——[e]Or, *gold*
[f]Heb. *silver of strength*——[g]Chap. xxvii. 10; Isa. lviii. 14
[h]Chap. xi. 15——[i]Psa. l. 14, 15; Isa. lviii. 9

[k]Prov. xxix. 23; James iv. 6; 1 Pet. v. 5——[l]Heb. *him that hath low eyes*——[m]Or, *The innocent shall deliver the island*, Gen. xviii. 26, &c.

Verse 24. *Then shalt thou lay up gold as dust*] The original is not fairly rendered in this translation, ושית על עפר בצר *veshith al aphar batser*, which *Montanus* renders: *Et pone super pulverem munitionem*, "And fix a tower upon the dust;" ובצור נחלים אופיר *ubetsur nechalim Ophir*, *et in petra torrentes Ophir*, "and in the rock, the torrents of Ophir."

The *Vulgate* is widely different: *Dabit pro terra silicem, et pro silice torrentes aureos*, "He will give thee flint for earth: and torrents of gold for flint;" which *Calmet* thus paraphrases: "Instead of brick thou shalt build with solid stone; and for ornaments, instead of stone as formerly, thou shalt have massive gold!"

All the versions are different. Mr. *Good* translates: "Then count thou treasure as dust: then shall he make fountains to gush forth amidst the rocks."

Coverdale is different from all: **He shal give the an harvest, which, in plenty and abundance, shal exceade the dust of the earthe, and the golde of Ophir like ryber stones.**

Verse 25. *Thou shalt have plenty of silver.*] Here again the versions and critics vary. The critics may disagree; but the doctrine of Eliphaz is sufficiently plain: "To those whom God loves best he gives the most earthly good. The rich and the great are his high favorites: the poor and the distressed he holds for his enemies."

In the above verses there seems to be a reference to the mode of obtaining the precious metals: 1. Gold in dust; 2. Gold in streams from the hills and mountains; 3. Silver in mines; כסף תועפות *keseph toaphoth*, "silver of giddiness;" of mines so deep as to make one giddy by looking into them. See Mr. *Good*.

Verse 26. *For then shalt thou have thy delight*] Thou shalt know, from thy temporal prosperity, that God favours thee; and for his bounty thou shalt be grateful. How different is this doctrine from that of St. Paul and St. John! "Being justified by faith, we have peace with God, through our Lord Jesus." "Because ye are sons, God hath sent forth the Spirit of his Son into your hearts, crying, Abba, Father!" "The Spirit himself beareth witness with our spirits that we are the children of God." "We glory in tribulation also, knowing that tribulation worketh patience; and patience, experience; and experience, hope: and hope maketh not ashamed, because the love of God is shed abroad in our hearts by the Holy Ghost, which is given unto us." "We love him because he first loved us." *Tribulation* itself was often a mark of God's favour.

Verse 27. *Thou shalt make thy prayer unto him*] תעתיר *tatir*, *thou shalt open* or *unbosom thyself*. And when the *heart* prays, God hears; and the person, being blessed, vows fidelity, prays on, is supported, and enabled to pay his vows.

Verse 28. *Thou shalt also decree a thing*] Whatsoever thou purposest in his strength, thou shalt be enabled to accomplish.

Verse 29. *When* men *are cast down*] There is a great difficulty in this verse; the sense, however, is tolerably evident, and the following is nearly a literal version: *When they shall humble themselves, thou shalt say, Be exalted*, or, there *is exaltation: for the down-cast of eye he will save.* The same sentiment as that of our Lord, "He that exalteth himself shall be abased; but he that humbleth himself shall be exalted."

Verse 3. *He shall deliver the island of the innocent*] The word אי *ai*, which we translate *island*, is most probably the Arabic particle اي *whosoever, whatsoever, any, whosoever he may be*, as اي رجل *ai rajuli, whatsoever man he may be*. And it is most probable that both words are Arabic, اي نقى or اى تقا *any innocent, chaste, pure*, or *holy person;* for the word has the same meaning both in Hebrew and Arabic. The text may therefore be translated, *He shall deliver every innocent person: He*, the innocent person, *shall be delivered by the pureness of thy hands;* i. e., as thou lovest justice, so thou wilt do justice. Instead of כפיך *cappeyca*, *thy hands*, the *Vulgate*, *Syriac*, and *Arabic* have read כפיו *cappaiv*, *his* or their *hands*. Mr. *Good* thinks that אי *ai* signifies *house*, as اي and اوي in Arabic signify *to reside, to have a home*, &c.; and therefore translates the passage thus: "The house of the innocent shall be delivered; and delivered by the pureness of thy hands." The reader may adopt which he pleases; but the word *island* must be given up, as it cannot make any consistent sense.

THUS ends Eliphaz the Temanite, who began with a tissue of the bitterest charges, continued with the most cruel insinuations, and ended with common-place exhortations to repentance, and promises of secular blessings in consequence:

and from his whole speech scarcely can one new or important maxim be derived. Blessed be God for Moses and the prophets! for Jesus, the evangelists, and the apostles! Their trumpet gives no uncertain sound: but by that of Job's friends who can prepare himself for the battle?

CHAPTER XXIII

Job answers; apologizes for his complaining; wishes to plead his cause in the presence of his Maker, from whom he knows he should receive justice; but regrets that he cannot find him, 1–9. *He, however, gives himself and his cause up to God, with the conviction of his own innocence, and God's justice and goodness,* 10–14. *He is, nevertheless, afraid when he considers the majesty of his Maker,* 15–17.

A. M. cir. 2484 B. C. cir. 1520 Ante I. Olymp. cir. 744 Ante U. C. cir. 767

THEN Job answered and said,
2 Even to-day *is* my complaint bitter: [a]my stroke is heavier than my groaning.
3 [b]O that I knew where I might find him! *that* I might come *even* to his seat!
4 I would order *my* cause before him, and fill my mouth with arguments.
5 I would know the words *which* he would answer me, and understand what he would say unto me.
6 [c]Will he plead against me with *his* great power? No; but he would put *strength* in me.
7 There the righteous might dispute with him; so should I be delivered for ever from my judge.
8 [d]Behold, I go forward, but he *is* not *there;* and backward, but I cannot perceive him:
9 On the left hand, where he doth work, but

[a]Heb. *my hand*——[b]Chap. xiii. 3; xvi. 21

[c]Isa. xxvii. 4, 8; lvii. 16——[d]Chap. ix. 11

NOTES ON CHAP. XXIII

Verse 2. *Even to-day* is *my complaint bitter*] Job goes on to maintain his own innocence, and shows that he has derived neither conviction nor consolation from the discourses of his friends. He grants that his complaint is bitter; but states that, loud as it may be, the affliction which he endures is heavier than his complaints are loud.

Mr. *Good* translates: "And still is my complaint rebellion?" Do ye construe my lamentations over my unparalleled sufferings as rebellion against God? This, in fact, they had done from the beginning: and the original will justify the version of Mr. *Good;* for מרי *meri*, which we translate *bitter*, may be derived from מרה *marah*, "he rebelled."

Verse 3. *O that I knew where I might find him!*] This and the following verse may be read thus: "Who will give me the knowledge of God, that I may find him out? I would come to his establishment; (the place or way in which he has promised to communicate himself;) I would exhibit, in detail, my judgment (the cause I wish to be tried) before his face; and my mouth would I fill with convincing or decisive arguments;" arguments drawn from his common method of saving sinners, which I should prove applied fully to my case. Hence the confidence with which he speaks, ver. 6.

Verse 5. *I would know the words* which *he would answer me*] He would speak nothing but what was true, decree nothing that was not righteous, nor utter any thing that I could not comprehend.

Verse 6. *Will he plead against me*] He would not exhibit his majesty and his sovereign authority to strike me dumb, or so overawe me that I could not speak in my own vindication.

No; but he would put strength *in me.*] On the contrary, he would treat me with tenderness, he would rectify my mistakes, he would show me what was in my favour, and would temper the rigid demands of justice by the mild interpretations of equity; and where *law* could not clear me, *mercy* would conduct all to the most favourable issue.

Verse 7. *There the righteous might dispute with him*] נוכח *nochach*, might *argue* or *plead.* To *dispute with God* sounds very harsh.

So should I be delivered for ever] Mr. *Good* translates: "And triumphantly should I escape from my condemnation." The Hebrew word לנצח *lanetsach* may as well be translated *to victory* as *for ever:* and in this sense the *Vulgate* understood the words: *Proponat æquitatem contra me; et perveniat ad victoriam judicium meum.* "He would set up equity against me; and would lead on my cause to victory." *Coverdale* renders thus:—**But let hym gibe me like power to go to lawe, then am I sure to wynne my matter.** Nothing less than the fullest conviction of his own innocence could have led Job to express himself thus to the Judge of quick and dead!

Verse 8. *Behold, I go forward*] These two verses paint in vivid colours the distress and anxiety of a soul in search of the favour of God. No *means* are left *untried*, no *place unexplored*, in order to find the object of his research. This is a true description of the conduct of a genuine penitent.

Verse 9. *On the left hand, where he doth work*] In these two verses Job mentions the four cardinal points of the heavens: the EAST, by the word קדם *kedem*, which signifies *before;* the WEST, by אחור *achor*, which signifies *after*, or the *back part;* the NORTH, by שמאל *semol*, which signifies the *left;* and the SOUTH, by ימין *yamin*, which signifies the *right.* Such is the situation of the world to a man who faces the

A. M. cir. 2484 B. C. cir. 1520 Ante I. Olymp. cir. 744 Ante U. S. cir. 767

I cannot behold *him:* he hideth
himself on the right hand, that
I cannot see *him:*
10 But he [e]knoweth [f]the way
that I take: *when* [g]he hath tried me, I shall
come forth as gold.
11 [h]My foot hath held his steps, his way
have I kept, and not declined.
12 Neither have I gone back from the commandment of his lips; [i]I [k]have
esteemed the words of his mouth
more than [l]my necessary *food.*
13 But he *is* in one *mind,* and
[m]who can turn him? and *what* [n]his soul
desireth, even *that* he doeth.
14 For he performeth *the thing that is* [o]ap-
pointed for me: and many such *things are*
with him.

A. M. cir. 2484 B. C. cir. 1520 Ante I. Olymp. cir. 744 Ante U. C. cir. 767

[e]Psa. cxxxix. 1, 2, 3——[f]Heb. *the way* that is *with me* [g]Psa. xvii. 3; lxvi. 10; James i. 12——[h]Psa. xliv. 18 [i]Heb. *I have hid* or *laid up*

[k]John iv. 32, 34——[l]Or, *my appointed portion* [m]Chap. ix. 12, 13; xii. 14; Rom. ix. 19——[n]Psa. cxv. 3 [o]1 Thess. iii. 3

east; see Gen. xiii. 9, 11, and xxviii. 14. And from this it appears that the Hebrews, Idumeans, and Arabs had the same ideas of these points of the heavens. It is worthy of remark that Job says, *He hideth himself on the right hand,* (the *south,*) *that I cannot see him:* for in fact, the southern point of heaven is not visible in Idumea, where Job was. Hence it comes that when he spake before, chap. ix. 9, of the constellations of the antarctic pole, he terms them the *hidden chambers of the south;* i. e., those compartments of the celestial concave that never appeared above the horizon in that place.—See *Calmet.*

Mr. *Good* translates these verses as follows:—

Behold! I go forward, and he is not there;
And backward, but I cannot perceive him.
On the left hand I feel for him, but trace *him* not:
He enshroudeth the right hand, and I cannot see *him.*

The simple rendering of *Coverdale* is nervous and correct:—

For though I go before, I fynde hym not:
Yf I come behynde, I can get no knowledge of him:
Yf I go on the left syde to pondre his workes,
I cannot attayne unto them:
Agayne, yf I go on the right syde, he hydeth himself,
That I cannot se him.

Verse 10. *But he knoweth the way that I take*] He *approves* of my conduct; my ways *please* him. He tries me: but, like gold, I shall lose nothing in the fire; I shall come forth more pure and luminous. If that which is reputed to be gold is exposed to the action of a strong fire, if it be genuine, it will lose nothing of its *quality,* nor of its *weight.* If it went into the fire *gold,* it will come out *gold;* the strongest fire will neither alter nor destroy it. So Job: he went into this furnace of affliction an innocent, righteous man; he came out the same. His character lost nothing of its *value,* nothing of its *lustre.*

Verse 11. *My foot hath held his steps, his way have I kept*] I have carefully marked his *providential deailngs;* and in his *way*—his pure and undefiled religion—have I walked. I have not only been *generally* but *particularly* religious: I have attended carefully to the *weightier* matters of the law, and have not forgotten its *slightest* injunctions.

Coverdale is curious:—**Neverthels my fete kepe his path, his hye strete have I holden, and not gone out of it.** The **hye strete** is *highway,* the *causeway,* or *raised road;* formed, as they anciently were, by stones in the manner of *pavement.* It has its name from the Latin *strata,* paved, *via* being understood: *via lapidibus strata,* "a way paved with stones:" hence *street,* a raised road or pavement either in town or country. And hence the *four grand Roman* or *British roads* which intersected this kingdom: viz. *Watling street, Icknild* or *Ricknild street, Ermin street,* and *Fosse street.* Some say these *streets* or roads were made by *Bellinus,* a British king.

Fosse street began in Cornwall, passed through Devonshire, Somersetshire, and along by Titbury upon Toteswould, beside Coventry, unto Leicester; and thence by the wide plains to Newark and to Lincoln, where it ends.

Watling street begins at Dover, passes through the middle of Kent, over the Thames by London, running near Westminster, and thence to St. Alban's, Dunstable, Stratford, Towcester, Weden, Lilbourn, Atherston, Wreaken by Severn, Worcester, Stratton, through Wales unto Cardigan, and on to the Irish sea.

Ermin, or *Erminage street,* running from St. David's in Wales, to Southampton.

Ricknild, or *Icknild street,* running by Worcester, Wycomb, Birmingham, Lichfield, Derby, Chesterfield, and by York, into Tynemouth. See *Camden, Holinshed,* and *Minshieu.*

Verse 12. *The commandment of his lips*] The written law that proceeded from his own mouth.

I have esteemed the words of his mouth] Mr. *Good* has given a better version of the original: *In my bosom have I stored up the words of his mouth.* The Asiatics carry every thing precious or valuable in their *bosom,* their handkerchiefs, jewels, purses, &c. Job, therefore, intimates that the words of God's mouth were to him a *most precious treasure.*

Verse 13. *But he* is *in one* mind] The original is והוא באחד *vehu beechad,* and is literally, *But he is in one:* properly rendered by the *Vulgate, Ipse enim solus est, But he is alone.* And not badly rendered by *Coverdale:*—**It is he himself alone.** He has no partner; his designs are his own, they are formed in his infinite wisdom, and none can turn his determinations aside. It is vain, therefore, for man to contend with his Maker. He designs my happiness, and you cannot prevent its accomplishment.

Verse 14. *For he performeth* the thing that is *appointed for me*] *Coverdale* translates:—**He rewardeth me into my bosome, and many other thinges mo doth he, as he maye by his power.** חקי *chukki* may as well be translated *bosom* here as in the 12th verse; but probably it may mean

A. M. cir. 2484 B. C. cir. 1520 Ante I. Olymp. cir. 744 Ante U. C. cir. 767

15 Therefore am I troubled at
his presence: when I consider, I
am afraid of him.
16 For God [p]maketh my heart
soft, and the Almighty troubleth me:
17 Because I was not cut
off before the darkness, *neither*
hath he covered the darkness
from my face.

[p]Psalm xxii. 14

a *portion, lot, sufficiency: For he hath appointed me my lot; and like these there are multitudes with him.* He diversifies human affairs: scarcely any two men have the same lot; nor has the same person the same portion at all times. He has multitudes of resources, expedients, means, &c., which he employs in governing human affairs.

Verse 15. *Therefore am I troubled*] I do not as yet see an end to my afflictions: he has not exhausted his means of trial; therefore, when I consider this, I am afraid of him.

Verse 16. *For God maketh my heart soft*] Prostrates my *strength*, deprives me of *courage*, so that I sink beneath my burden, and I am troubled at the thought of the Almighty, the self-sufficient and eternal Being.

Verse 17. *Because I was not cut off*] "O, why can I not draw darkness over my face? Why may not thick darkness cover my face?"—Mr. *Good.* This verse should be read in connection with the preceding; and then we shall have the following sense. Ver. 16: "The Lord hath beaten down my strength, and my soul has been terrified by his fear." Ver. 17: "For it is not this deep night in which I am enveloped, nor the evils which I suffer, that have overwhelmed me; I sink only through the fear which the presence of his Majesty inspires. This is my greatest affliction; sufferings, diseases, yea, death itself, are nothing in comparison of the terror which my soul feels in the presence of his tremendous holiness and justice."

NOTHING can humble a pious mind so much as Scriptural apprehensions of the majesty of God. It is easy to contemplate his *goodness*, *loving-kindness*, and *mercy;* in all these we have an interest, and from them we expect the greatest good: but to consider his *holiness* and *justice*, the infinite *righteousness* of his nature, under the conviction that we have *sinned*, and *broken the laws* prescribed by his *sovereign Majesty*, and to feel ourselves brought as into the presence of his judgment-seat,—who can bear the thought? If cherubim and seraphim veil their faces before his throne, and the *holiest* soul exclaims,

I loathe myself when God I see,
And into nothing fall;

what must a *sinner* feel, whose conscience is not yet purged from dead works, and who feels the wrath of God abiding on him? And how, without such a mediator and sacrifice as Jesus Christ is, can any human spirit come into the presence of its Judge? Those who can approach him *without terror*, know little of *his* justice, and nothing of *their* sin. When we approach him in prayer, or in any ordinance, should we not feel more *reverence* than we generally do?

CHAPTER XXIV

Job asserts that there are various transgressors whose wickedness is not visited on them in this life; and particularizes the unjust and oppressive, 1–6; *those who are cruel to the poor,* 7–13; *the murderer,* 14; *the adulterer,* 15; *thieves and plunderers,* 16, 17. *Nevertheless they have an accursed portion, and shall die, and their memory perish,* 18–20. *He speaks of the abuse of power, and of the punishment of oppressors,* 21–24; *and asserts that what he has said on these subjects cannot be contradicted,* 25.

A. M. cir. 2484 B. C. cir. 1520 Ante I. Olymp. cir. 744 Ante U. C. cir. 767

WHY, seeing [a]times are not
hidden from the Almighty,
do they that know him not see
his days?
2 *Some* remove the [b]land-
marks; they violently take away
flocks, and [c]feed *thereof*.
3 They drive away the ass of

[a]Acts i. 7——[b]Deut. xix. 14; xxvii. 17; Prov. xxii. 28; xxiii. 10; Hos. v. 10——[c]Or, *feed* them

NOTES ON CHAP. XXIV

Verse 1. *Why, seeing times are not hidden from the Almighty*] Mr. *Good* translates: "Wherefore are not doomsdays kept by the Almighty, so that his offenders may eye their periods?" *Doomsdays* are here used in the same sense as *term times;* and the wish is, that God would appoint such times that the falsely accused might look forward to them with comfort; knowing that, on their arrival, they should have a fair hearing, and their innocence be publicly declared; and their detractors, and the unjust in general, meet with their deserts. But God reserves the knowledge of these things to himself. "The holy patriarch," says Mr. *Good*

A. M. cir. 2484 B. C. cir. 1520 Ante I. Olymp. cir. 744 Ante U. C. cir. 767

the fatherless, they [d]take the
widow's ox for a pledge.
4 They turn the needy out of
the way: [e]the poor of the earth
hide themselves together.
5 Behold, *as* wild asses in the desert, go
they forth to their work; rising betimes for a
prey: the wilderness *yieldeth* food for them
and for *their* children.

[d]Chap. xxii. 6; Deut. xxiv. 6, 10, 12, 17——[e]Prov. xxviii. 28——[f]Heb. *mingled corn* or *dredge*

6 They reap *every one* his [f]corn
in the field: and [g]they gather the
vintage of the wicked.
7 They [h]cause the naked to
lodge without clothing, that *they have* no
covering in the cold.
8 They are wet with the showers of the
mountains, and [i]embrace the rock for want of
a shelter.

A. M. cir. 2484 B. C. cir. 1520 Ante I. Olymp. cir. 744 Ante U. C. cir. 767

[g]Heb. *the wicked gather the vintage*——[h]Exod. xxii. 26, 27; Deut. xxiv. 12, 13; chap. xxii. 6——[i]Lam. iv. 5

"has uniformly admitted that in the aggregate scale of Providence the just are rewarded and the wicked punished for their respective deeds, in some period or other of their lives. But he has contended in various places, and especially in chap. xxi. 7-13, that the exceptions to this general rule are numerous: so numerous, as to be sufficient to render the whole scheme of providential *interposition* perfectly mysterious and incomprehensible, chap. xxiii. 8-12; so in the passage before us: if the retribution ye speak of be universal, and which I am ready to admit to a certain extent to be true and unquestionable, I not only ask, Why do the just ever suffer in the midst of their righteousness? but, Why do not the wicked see such retribution displayed before their eyes by stated judgments, so that they may at one and the same time know and tremble?"

Verse 2. Some *remove the landmarks*] Stones or posts were originally set up to ascertain the bounds of particular estates: and this was necessary in open countries, before *hedges* and *fences* were formed. Wicked and covetous men often removed the landmarks or *termini*, and set them *in* on their neighbours' ground, that, by contracting their boundaries, they might enlarge their own. The law of Moses denounces curses on those who remove their neighbours' landmarks. See Deut. xix. 14, xxvii. 17, and the note on the former place, where the subject is considered at large.

They violently take away flocks, and feed thereof.] Mr. *Good* translates ירעו *yiru, they destroy,* deriving the word, not from רעה *raah,* to *feed,* but from רע *ra,* to *rend,* to *destroy.*

The Septuagint had read רעה *roeh,* a *shepherd;* and therefore have translated ποιμνιον συν ποιμενι ἁρπασαντες, "violently carrying off both the flock and the shepherd."

Verse 4. *They turn the needy out of the way*] They will not permit them to go by the accustomed paths; they oblige them to take circuitous routes. When the Marquis of H. was made ranger of Richmond Park, he thought it his duty to shut up a pathway which had existed for a long time; and those who presumed, after this shutting up, to break the fence, and take that path as formerly, were prosecuted. A *cobbler* near the place entered an action against the marquis: the cause was tried, the marquis cast, and the path ordered to be opened, on the ground that it had, time out of mind, been a public undisputed path. When one asked the *cobbler,* "How he could have the boldness to go to law with the Marquis of H.?" he answered, "Because I did not like to leave the world worse than I found it." All tolerated oppression and voluntary forfeiture of ancient rights, are injurious to society at large, and they who *wink* at them *leave the world worse than they found it.*

Verse 5. *Rising betimes for a prey*] The general sense here seems plain enough. There are some who live a lawless roaming life: make a predatory life their employment; for this purpose, frequent the wilderness, where they seize on and appropriate whatsoever they find, and by this method they and their families are supported.

Mr. *Good* says: "The sense has never yet been understood by any commentator;" and hence he proposes a different division of the words, placing ערבה *arabah,* the *desert* or *wilderness,* in the first hemistich, thus:—

"Rising early for the pillage of the wilderness;
The bread of themselves *and* of their children."

Others think that the words are spoken solely of the poor under the hand of oppression, who are driven away from their homes, and obliged to seek such support as the wilderness can afford. Such was originally the state of the *Bedouins,* and of the wandering Arab hordes in general: the oppression of the tyrannous governors obliged them to seek refuge in the deserts, where they still live in a roaming predatory life.

Verse 6. *They reap* every one *his corn in the field*] This is perfectly characteristic. These wandering hordes often make sudden irruptions, and carry off the harvest of grain, olives, vines, &c., and plunge with it into the wilderness, where none can follow them. The *Chaldee* gives the same sense: "They reap in a field that is not their own, and cut off the vineyard of the wicked."

Verse 7. *They cause the naked to lodge without clothing*] Or rather, *They spend the night naked, without clothing; and without a covering from the cold:* another characteristic of the wandering Arabs. They are *ill-fed, ill-clothed,* and often miserably off, even for *tents.* They can have little household stuff: as they are plunderers, they are often obliged to fly for their lives, and cannot encumber themselves with what is not absolutely needful.

Verse 8. *They are wet with the showers of the mountains*] Mr. *Good* thinks that *torrents,* not *showers,* is the proper translation of the original זרם *zerem;* but I think *showers of the mountain* strictly proper. I have seen many of these in mountainous countries, where the tails of *water-spouts* have been intercepted and broken, and the *outpouring* of them would be

A. M. cir. 2484
B. C. cir. 1520
Ante I. Olymp. cir. 744
Ante U. C. cir. 767

9 They pluck the fatherless
from the breast, and take a
pledge of the poor.
10 They cause *him* to go naked
without clothing, and they take away [k]the
sheaf *from* the hungry;
11 *Which* make oil within their walls, *and*
tread *their* wine-presses, and suffer thirst.
12 Men groan from out
of the city, and the soul of
the wounded crieth out: yet
God layeth not folly *to*
them.
13 They are of those that rebel against the
light; they know not the ways thereof, nor
abide in the paths thereof.

---

[k]Job chap. xxii. 7

---

incredible to those who have never witnessed similar phenomena. The *rain* fell in *torrents*, and produced torrents on the land, carrying away earth and stones and every thing before them, scooping out great gullies in the sides of the mountains. *Mountain torrents* are not produced but by such extraordinary *outpourings of rain*, formed either by *water-spouts*, or by vast *masses of clouds intercepted* and *broken* to pieces by the mountain tops.

And embrace the rock for want of a shelter.] In such cases as that related above, the *firm rock* is the only shelter which can be found, or safely trusted.

Verse 9. *They pluck the fatherless from the breast*] They forcibly take young children in order that they may bring them up in a state of *slavery*. This verse is the commencement of a new paragraph, and points out the arbitrary dealings of oppressors, under despotic governors.

Take a pledge of the poor.] Oppressive landlords who let out their grounds at an exorbitant rent, which the poor labourers, though using the utmost diligence, are unable at all times to pay; and then the unfeeling wretch *sells them up*, as the phrase here is, or takes their *cow*, their *horse*, their *cart*, or their *bed*, in pledge, that the money shall be paid in such a time. This is one of the crying sins of some countries of Europe.

Verse 10. *They cause* him *to go naked*] These cruel, hard-hearted oppressors seize the *cloth* made for the *family wear*, or the *wool* and *flax* out of which such *clothes* should be made.

And they take away the sheaf] Seize the *grain* as soon as it is reaped, that they may pay themselves the exorbitant rent at which they have leased out their land: and thus the *sheaf*—the *thraves* and *ricks*, by which they should have been supported, are taken away from the hungry.

Verse 11. *Make oil within their walls*] Thus stripped of all that on which they depended for *clothing* and *food*, they are obliged to become *vassals* to their lord, labour in the fields on scanty fare, or *tread their wine-presses*, from the produce of which they are not permitted to quench their *thirst*.

Verse 12. *Men groan from out of the city*] This is a new paragraph. After having shown the oppressions carried on in the *country*, he takes a view of those carried on in the *town*. Here the miseries are too numerous to be detailed. The *poor* in such places are often in the most wretched state; they are not only *badly fed*, and *miserably clothed*, but also most *unwholesomely lodged*. I was once appointed with a benevolent gentleman, J. S., Esq., to visit a district in St. Giles's London, to know the real state of the poor. We took the district in *House Row*, and found each dwelling full of people, dirt, and wretchedness. Neither old nor young had the appearance of health: some were *sick*, and others lying *dead*, in the same place! Several beds, if they might be called such, on the floor in the same apartment; and, in one single house, *sixty souls!* These were groaning under various evils; *and the soul of the wounded*, wounded in spirit, and *afflicted* in body, *cried out* to God and man for help! It would have required no subtle investigation to have traced all these miseries to the *doors*, the *hands*, the *lips*, and the *hearts*, of ruthless landlords; or to oppressive systems of public expenditure in the support of ruinous wars, and the stagnation of trade and destruction of commerce occasioned by them: to which must be added the enormous taxation to meet this expenditure.

Yet God layeth not folly to them.] He does not impute their calamities to their own folly. Or, according to the *Vulgate*, *Et Deus inultum abire non patitur;* "And God will not leave (these disorders) unpunished." But the Hebrew may be translated *And God doth not attend to their prayers.* Job's object was to show, in opposition to the mistaken doctrine of his friends, that God did not hastily punish every evil work, nor reward every good one. That *vice* often went long unpunished, and *virtue* unrewarded; and that we must not judge of a man's state either by his *prosperity* or *adversity*. Therefore, there might be cases in which the innocent oppressed poor were crying to God for a redress of their grievances, and were not immediately heard; and in which their oppressors were faring sumptuously every day, without any apparent mark of the Divine displeasure. These sentiments occur frequently.

Verse 13. *They—rebel against the light*] Speaking of wicked men. They rebel against the light of God in their consciences, and his light in his word. They are tyrants *in grain*, and care neither for God nor the poor. *They know not the ways thereof*—they will not learn their duty to God or man. *Nor abide in the paths thereof*—if brought at any time to a better mind, they speedily relapse; and are *steady* only in *cruelty* and *mischief*. This is the character of the oppressors of suffering humanity, and of sinners audacious and hardened.

This whole verse Mr. *Good* translates in the following manner:—

> They are indignant of the light;
> They respect not its progress;
> And will not return to its paths.

They hate good; they regard not its operation; they go out of the way of righteousness, and refuse to return.

A. M. cir. 2484 B. C. cir. 1520 Ante I. Olymp. cir. 744 Ante U. C. cir. 767

14 [l]The murderer rising with
the light killeth the poor and
needy, and in the night is as a
thief.

15 [m]The eye also of the adulterer waiteth
for the twilight, [n]saying, No eye shall see me:
and [o]disguiseth *his* face.

16 In the dark they dig through houses,
which they had marked for themselves in the
daytime: they [p]know not the light.

17 For the morning *is* to them even as the
shadow of death: if *one* know
them, they are in the terrors of
the shadow of death.

18 He *is* swift as the waters;
their portion is cursed in the earth: he beholdeth not the way of the vineyards.

19 Drought and heat [q]consume the snow-waters: *so doth* the grave *those which* have
sinned.

20 The womb shall forget him; the worm
shall feed sweetly on him; [r]he shall be no

[l]Psalm x. 8——[m]Proverbs vii. 9——[n]Psalm x. 11
[o]Heb. *setteth his face in secret*

[p]John iii. 20——[q]Hebrew, *violently take*
[r]Prov. x. 7

Verse 14. *The murderer rising with the light*] Perhaps the words should be read as Mr. *Good* has done:—

> With the daylight ariseth the murderer;
> Poor and needy, he sheddeth blood.

This description is suitable to a *highwayman;* one who robs in daylight, and who has been *impelled* by *poverty* and *distress* to use this most unlawful and perilous mode to get bread; and for fear of being discovered or taken, commits murder, and thus adds crime to crime.

In the night is as a thief.] Having been a *highwayman* in the *daytime*, he turns *footpad* or *housebreaker by night;* and thus goes on from sin to sin.

There have been several instances like the case above, where poverty and distress have induced a man to go to the highway and rob, to repair the ruin of himself and family. I shall introduce an *authentic* story of this kind, which the reader may find at the end of this chapter.

Verse 15. *The eye also of the adulterer*] This is another sin particularly of the city. The *adulterer* has made his *assignation;* he has *marked the house* of her into whose good graces he has *insinuated himself*, called *digging through the house;* he *waits* impatiently *for the dusk;* and then goes forth, having *muffled* or *disguised his face*, and spends a criminal night with the faithless wife of another man. The *morning dawns:* but it is to him *as the shadow of death*, lest he should be detected before he can reach his own home. *And if one know him* —if he happen to be *recognized* in coming out of the forbidden house; *the terrors of death* seize upon him, being afraid that the thing shall be brought to light, or that he shall be called to account, a sanguinary account, by the injured husband.

This seems to be the general sense of the very natural picture which Job draws in the 15th, 16th, and 17th verses.

Verse 16. *In the dark they dig through houses*] Thieves in Bengal very frequently dig through the *mud wall* and under the *clay floors* of houses, and, entering unperceived, plunder them while the inhabitants are asleep.

Mr. *Good's* version of this paragraph I shall lay before the reader:—

> Ver. 15. For the dark too watcheth the eye of the adulterer;
> Exclaiming, No eye shall behold me.
> Then putteth he the muffler on his face;
> Ver. 16. He wormeth into houses amidst the darkness.
> In the daytime they seal themselves up,
> They know not the light:
> Ver. 17. For, the dawn they reckon to themselves as the death-shade;
> The horrors of the death-shade as it returneth.

Verse 18. *He is swift as the waters*] Literally, *Light is he on the face of the waters: and cursed shall be their portion on the earth,* which Mr. *Good* translates:—

> Miserable is this man on the waters:
> Deeply miserable the lot of those on dry land.

He beholdeth not the way of the vineyards.] These no longer flourish or bring forth fruit. The labour of the vintage fails.

Verse 19. *Drought and heat consume the snow-waters*] The public cisterns or large tanks which had been filled with water by the melting of the snow on the mountains, and which water was stored for the irrigation of their lands, had been entirely exhausted by the intensity of the heat, and the long continuance of drought.

So doth *the grave* those which *have sinned.*] For this whole paragraph we have only two words in the original; viz., שאול חטאו *sheol chatau,* "the pit, they have sinned;" which Mr. *Good* translates:—"They fall to their lowest depth."

I believe the meaning to be,—even the deepest tanks, which held most water, and retained it longest, had become exhausted; so that expectation and succour were cut off from this as well as from every other quarter.

I have elsewhere shown that שאול *sheol* signifies, not only *hell* and the *grave*, but any deep *pit;* and, also, that חטא *chata* signifies *to miss the mark.* Mr. *Good*, properly aware of these acceptations of the original words, has translated as above; and it is the only ground on which any consistent meaning can be given to the original.

Verse 20. *The womb shall forget him*] The mother that bare him shall have no affection for him, nor be afflicted at his death. But the word רחם *rechem* signifies *compassion, mercy. Mercy shall be unmindful of him.* How dread-

A. M. cir. 2484 more remembered; and wicked-
B. C. cir. 1520
Ante I. Olymp. ness shall be broken as a tree.
cir. 744
Ante U. C. cir. 21 He evil entreateth the barren
767 *that* beareth not: and doeth not
good to the widow.
22 He draweth also the mighty with his
power: he riseth up, [s]and no *man* is sure
of life.
23 *Though* it be given him *to be* in safety,
whereon he resteth; yet [t]his A. M. cir. 2484
eyes *are* upon their ways. B. C. cir. 1520
Ante I. Olymp.
cir. 744
24 They are exalted for a Ante U. C. cir.
little while, but [u]are gone and 767
brought low; they are [v]taken out of the way
as all *other,* and cut off as the tops of the ears
of corn.
25 And if *it be* not *so* now, who will make
me a liar, and make my speech nothing worth?

[s]Or, *he trusteth not* his own *life*——[t]Psa. xi. 4; Prov. xv. 3——[u]Heb. *are not*——[v]Heb. *closed up*

ful such a state! When mercy itself forgets the sinner, his perdition slumbereth not.

The worm shall feed sweetly on him] The *Chaldee* has, "The cruel, who have neglected to commiserate the poor, shall be sweet to the worms." He shall be brought into a state of the greatest degradation, and shall be no more remembered.

And wickedness shall be broken as a tree.] He shall be as a rotten or decayed tree, easily broken to pieces. If it were clear that עולה *avlah,* here rendered *wickedness,* has the same sense as עלה *aleh,* a *leaf, sucker,* or *shoot,* then we might translate according to the ingenious version of Mr. *Good;* viz., *But the shoot shall be broken off as a tree;* which might, in this case, be supposed to refer to illicit commerce, the *fruit* of the *womb* becoming *abortive.*

Verse 21. *He evil entreateth the barren*] I believe the original word רעה should be translated *he feedeth;* and so the *Vulgate* understood the word: *Pavit enim sterilem.* He has been kind to the barren woman; but he has done no good to the widow. He has shown no mercy to *large families;* he has been an enemy to the procreation of children. Though he may, for particular reasons, have provided for a *barren woman;* yet the *widow* he has not comforted, she being old or infirm, or such as might not suit his purpose.

Verse 22. *He draweth also the mighty*] *Calmet* gives the following version of the original: "He draws with him guards for his defence; he raises himself up, and does not feel assured of his life." In the midst even of his guards he is afraid; and dares not put confidence in any person. This is an admirable delineation of the inquietudes and terrors of a tyrant.

Verse 23. Though *it be given him* to be *in safety*] The *Vulgate* gives this verse a singular turn: *Dedit ei Deus locum pœnitentiæ, et ille abutitur eo in superbiam,* "God gave him space for repentance, but he has abused it through pride." This is by no means conformable to the original. I think the words should be translated thus: "He gives *them* (*i. e.,* the guards) to him for security, and he leans upon them; yet his eyes are upon their ways." Though he have taken the guards, mentioned in the preceding verse, for his personal defence, and for this purpose he uses them; yet he is full of diffidence, and he is continually watching them lest they should be plotting his destruction. The true picture of an Eastern tyrant. *Without* are fightings; *within* are fears.

Verse 24. *They are exalted for a little while*] Such tyrants are exalted for a time, for God putteth down one and raiseth up another; but he turns his hand against them, and they are gone. They are removed by his justice as all of the same character have been and shall be; time and judgment shall mow them down as the grass, and crop them off as the ears of ripe corn. They may flourish for a time, and continue their oppressions; but they shall at last come to an untimely end. Few tyrants ever visit the eternal world *sicca morte,* but by a violent death. All Eastern history is full of this great *fact.*

Verse 25. *And if* it be *not* so *now*] Job has proved by examples that the righteous are often oppressed; that the wicked often triumph over the just; that the impious are always wretched even in the midst of their greatest prosperity; and he defies his friends to show one flaw in his argument, or an error in his illustration of it; and that existing facts are farther proofs of what he has advanced.

In the preceding chapters we find Job's friends having continual recourse to this assertion, which it is the grand object of all their discourses to prove, viz., The righteous are so distinguished in the approbation of God, that they live always in prosperity, and die in peace.

On the other hand, Job contends that the dispensations of Providence are by no means thus equal in this life; that experience shows that the righteous are often in adversity, and the wicked in power and prosperity.

Job's friends had also endeavoured to prove that if a reported good man fell into adversity, it was a proof that his character had been mistaken, that he was an internal sinner and hypocrite; and that God, by these manifest proofs of his disapprobation, unmasked him. Hence they charged Job with hypocrisy and secret sins, because he was now suffering adversity; and that his sins must be of the most heinous nature, because his afflictions were uncommonly great. This Job repels by appeals to numerous facts where there was nothing equivocal in the character; where the *bad* was demonstrably bad, and yet in *prosperity;* and the *good* demonstrably good, and yet in *adversity.* It is strange that none of these could hit on a middle way: viz., The wicked may be in prosperity, but he is ever miserable in his soul: the righteous may be in adversity, but he is ever happy in his God. In these respects, God's ways are always equal.

On ver. 14, I have referred to the case of unfortunate men who, falling into adversity, madly have recourse to plunder to restore their ruined circumstances. The following anecdote is told of the justly celebrated Dr. Sharp, archbishop of York, the grandfather of that highly benevolent, useful, learned, and eminent man, Granville Sharp, Esq., with whom I had for several years the honour of a personal acquaintance.

"Never was any man, as well by the tenderness of his nature as by the impulse of religion, better disposed to succour the distressed, and relieve the necessities of the poor; to which merciful offices he had so strong an inclination that no reasonable solicitations were ever in danger of meeting with a repulse. Nay, he was more prone to seek out proper objects of his bounty, than to reject them when recommended; and so far was his charity from any suspicion of being extorted by importunity, that it appeared rather a delight than uneasiness to him to extend his liberality upon all proper occasions."

For the same reason, a singular anecdote of the archbishop, related in the London Chronicle of Aug. 13, 1785, and always credited by his family, may be thought worth preserving.

"It was his lordship's custom to have a saddle-horse attend his carriage, that in case of fatigue from sitting, he might take the refreshment of a ride. As he was thus going to his episcopal residence, and was got a mile or two before his carriage, a decent, well-looking young man came up with him; and, with a trembling hand and a faltering tongue presented a pistol to his lordship's breast, and demanded his money. The archbishop, with great composure, turned about; and, looking steadfastly at him, desired he would remove that dangerous weapon, and tell him fairly his condition. 'Sir! sir!' with great agitation, cried the youth; 'no words, 'tis not a time; your money instantly.' 'Hear me, young man,' said the archbishop; 'you see I am an old man, and my life is of very little consequence: yours seems far otherwise. I am named Sharp, and am archbishop of York; my carriage and servants are behind. Tell me what money you want, and who you are, and I will not injure you, but prove a friend. Here, take this; and now ingenuously tell me how much you want to make you independent of so destructive a business as you are now engaged in.' 'O sir,' replied the man, 'I detest the business as much as you. I am—but—but—at home there are creditors who will not stay—fifty pounds, my lord, indeed would do what no tongue besides my own can tell.' 'Well, sir, I take it on your word; and, upon my honour, if you will, in a day or two, call on me at ——, what I have now given you shall be made up that sum.' The highwayman looked at him, was silent, and went off; and, at the time appointed, actually waited on the archbishop, and assured his lordship his words had left impressions which nothing could ever destroy.

"Nothing more transpired for a year and a half or more; when one morning a person knocked at his grace's gate, and with peculiar earnestness desired to see him. The archbishop ordered the stranger to be brought in. He entered the room where his lordship was, but had scarce advanced a few steps before his countenance changed, his knees tottered, and he sank almost breathless on the floor. On recovering, he requested an audience in private. The apartment being cleared, 'My lord,' said he, 'you cannot have forgotten the circumstances at such a time and place; gratitude will never suffer them to be obliterated from my mind. In me, my lord, you now behold that once most wretched of mankind; but now, by your inexpressible humanity, rendered equal, perhaps superior, in happiness to millions. O, my lord!' tears for a while preventing his utterance, "tis you, 'tis you that have saved me, body and soul; 'tis you that have saved a dear and much-loved wife, and a little brood of children, whom I tendered dearer than my life. Here are the fifty pounds; but never shall I find language to testify what I feel. Your God is your witness; your deed itself is your glory; and may heaven and all its blessings be your present and everlasting reward! I was the younger son of a wealthy man; your lordship knows him; his name was ——. My marriage alienated his affection; and my brother withdrew his love, and left me to sorrow and penury. A month since my brother died a bachelor and intestate. What was *his*, is become *mine;* and by your astonishing goodness, I am now at once the most penitent, the most grateful, and happiest of my species.'"

See *Prince Hoar's* life of *Granville Sharp, Esq.*, page 13.

I have no doubt there have been several cases of a similar kind, when the *first step* in delinquency was urged by *necessity;* but few of such wretched adventurers have met with an *Archbishop Sharp*. An *early* and *pious education* is the only means under God to prevent such dangerous steps, which generally lead to the most fearful catastrophe. Teach a child, that whom God loveth he chasteneth. Teach him, that God suffers men to hunger, and be in want, that he may try them if they will be faithful, and do them good in their latter end. Teach him, that he who patiently and meekly bears providential afflictions, shall be relieved and exalted in due time. Teach him, that it is no sin to die in the most abject poverty and affliction, brought on in the course of Divine providence; but that any attempts to alter his condition by robbery, knavery, cozening, and fraud, will be distinguished with heavy curses from the Almighty, and necessarily end in perdition and ruin. A child thus educated is not likely to abandon himself to unlawful courses.

CHAPTER XXV

Bildad, the Shuhite, in an irregular speech, shows that God's dominion is supreme, his armies innumerable, and his providence extended over all, 1–3; *that man cannot be justified before God; that even the heavenly bodies cannot be reputed pure in his sight; much less man, who is naturally weak and sinful*, 4–6.

A. M. cir. 2484
B. C. cir. 1520
Ante I. Olymp. cir. 744
Ante U. C. cir. 767

THEN answered Bildad the
Shuhite, and said,
2 Dominion and fear *are* with
him, he maketh peace in his high
places.
3 Is there any number of his armies? and
upon whom doth not [a]his light arise?
4 [b]How then can man be justified with God?
or how can he be clean *that is*
born of a woman?
5 Behold even to the moon,
and it shineth not; yea, the stars
are not pure in his sight.
6 How much less man, *that is* [c]a
worm? and the son of man, *which is* a
worm?

A. M. cir. 2484
B. C. cir. 1520
Ante I. Olymp. cir. 744
Ante U. C. cir. 767

[a]James i. 17——[b]Chap. iv. 17, &c.; xv. 14, &c.; Psa. cxxx. 3; cxliii. 2——[c]Psa. xxii. 6

NOTES ON CHAP. XXV

Verse 1. *Bildad the Shuhite*] This is the last attack on Job; the others felt themselves foiled, though they had not humility enough to acknowledge it, but would not again return to the attack. Bildad has little to say, and that little is very little to the point. He makes a few assertions, particularly in reference to what Job had said in the commencement of the preceding chapter, of his *desire to appear before God, and have his case tried by him, as he had the utmost confidence that his innocence should be fully proved.* For this Bildad reprehends Job with arguments which had been brought forth often in this controversy, and as repeatedly confuted, chap. iv. 18, and xv. 14, 15, 16.

Verse 2. *Dominion and fear* are *with him*] God is an absolute sovereign; his fear is on all the hosts of heaven; and by his sovereignty he establishes and preserves order in the heavens, and among all the inhabitants of the eternal world: how canst thou, therefore, dare to appeal to him, or desire to appear before him?

Verse 3. *Is there any number of his armies?*] He has *troops* innumerable; he can serve himself of all his creatures; every thing may be a means of *help* or *destruction*, according to his Divine will. When he purposes to save, none can destroy; and when he is determined to destroy, none can save. It is vain to trust in his creatures against himself.

Upon whom doth not his light arise?] That is, his *providence* rules over all; he is universal Lord; he causes his sun to arise on the evil and the good, and sends his rain on the just and unjust.

Verse 4. *How then can man be justified?*] Or, ומה *umah, With what, shall a man be justified with God?* Though this is no conclusion from Bildad's premises, yet the question is of the highest importance to man. Neither Bildad nor any of his fellows could answer it; the doctrine of redemption through the *blood of the cross* was then known only through *types* and *shadows.* We, who live in the Gospel dispensation, can readily answer the question, With what shall *miserable man* (אנוש *enosh*) be justified with God?—*Ans.* By bringing forward, by *faith*, to the throne of the Divine justice, the *sacrificial offering of the Lord Jesus Christ;* and confiding absolutely in it, as being a full, sufficient, and complete atonement and sacrifice for his sins, and for the salvation of a lost world.

How, or *with what* (ומה *umah*) shall he be clean that is born of a woman?—*Ans.* By receiving that grace or heavenly influence communicated by the power and energy of the eternal Spirit applying to the heart the efficacy of that blood which cleanses from all unrighteousness. This, and this only, is the way in which a *sinner*, when truly *penitent*, can be *justified before God:* and in which a *believer*, convinced of indwelling sin, can be *sanctified* and cleansed from all unrighteousness. This is the only means of *justification* and *sanctification*, without which there can be no *glorification.* And these two great works, which constitute the whole of *salvation*, have been procured for a lost world by the incarnation, passion, death, and resurrection of the Lord Jesus Christ, who was delivered for our offences, and rose again for our justification; to whom be glory and dominion now and for evermore, Amen!

Verse 5. *Behold even to the moon, and it shineth not*] It is continually *changing* its appearance. It never appears twice in its whole revolution with the *same face:* it is ever *waxing* or *waning;* and its face is variegated with opaque spots. Its changeableness can never be compared with the unchangeable nature of God.

Yea, the stars are not pure in his sight.] Whatever their excellence may be as stars, it is nothing in comparison with him from whom they have derived their being and splendour. See the notes on chap. iv. 18, and xv. 14-16. The *Targum* reads: "Behold, the moon is as yet spotted in her eastern part; the sun shines not; and the stars are not pure in his sight."

Some think that by *stars* are meant those *angels who kept not their first estate:* this may be so, but I cannot see it in the text. It may, however, mean the *heavenly host*, as it is supposed to do, chap. xxviii. 7; but I still must hesitate on the propriety of such applications.

It is probable this speech of Bildad was delivered in the *night-season*, when clouds interrupted the bright shining of the moon. The third verse seems to refer immediately to the *stars*, which to the naked eye are innumerable. The *sun* is not mentioned, because of his absence.

This speech of Bildad is both confused and inconclusive. His reasoning is absurd, and he draws false conclusions from his premises. In the third verse, he says, "Is there any number of his armies? and upon whom does not his light arise?" But how absurd is the conclusion which he draws from his questions:—"How then can a man be justified with God, or he be clean who is born of a woman?"

This has no relation to the premises; still to us the question is not difficult, and has already been answered in the notes: "A man can be justified with God," through the blood of Christ; and "he can be clean who is born of a woman." through the sanctification of the Spirit.

Verse 6. *How much less man*, that is *a worm?*] Or as the *Targum:*—"How much more man, who in his life is a reptile; and the son of man, who in his death is a worm." Almost all the *versions* read, "Truly man is corruption, and the son of man a worm." The *original* is degradingly expressive: "Even because אנוש *enosh, miserable man*, is רמה *rimmah, a crawling worm;* and the son of Adam, who is תולעה *toleah*, a *worm*, or rather *maggot*, from its eating into and dividing certain substances."—*Parkhurst*.

Thus endeth Bildad the Shuhite, who endeavoured to speak on a subject which he did not understand; and, having got on bad ground, was soon confounded in his own mind, spoke incoherently, argued inconclusively, and came abruptly and suddenly to an end. Thus, his three friends being confounded, Job was left to pursue his own way; they trouble him no more; and he proceeds in triumph to the end of the thirty-first chapter.

CHAPTER XXVI

Job, perceiving that his friends could no longer support their arguments on the ground they had assumed, sharply reproves them for their want both of wisdom and feeling, 1–4; *shows that the power and wisdom of God are manifest in the works of creation and providence; gives several proofs; and then adds that these are a small specimen of his infinite skill and unlimited power,* 5–14.

A. M. cir. 2484
B. C. cir. 1520
Ante I. Olymp. cir. 744
Ante U. C. cir. 767

BUT Job answered and said,
2 How hast thou helped
him that is [a]without power?
how savest thou the arm *that*
hath [b]no strength?
3 How hast thou counselled *him that hath*
no wisdom? and *how* hast thou
plentifully declared the thing as
it is?
4 To whom hast thou uttered
words? and whose spirit came from thee?
5 Dead *things* are formed from under the

[a]Neh. v. 5 — [b]1 Sam. ii. 9

NOTES ON CHAP. XXVI

Verse 2. *How hast thou helped* him] This seems a species of irony. How wonderfully hast thou counselled the unskilful and strengthened the weak! Alas for you! ye could not give what ye did not possess! In this way the *Chaldee* understood these verses: "Why hast thou pretended to give succour, when *thou art* without strength? And save, while thy arm is weak? Why hast thou given counsel, when *thou art* without understanding? And supposest that thou hast shown the very essence of wisdom?"

Verse 4. *Whose spirit came from thee?*] Mr. *Good* renders the verse thus: *From whom hast thou pillaged speeches? And whose spirit hath issued forth from thee?* The retort is peculiarly severe; and refers immediately to the proverbial sayings which in several of the preceding answers have been adduced against the irritated sufferer; for which see chap. viii. 11-19, xv. 20-35, some of which he has already complained of, as in chap. xii. 3, and following. I concur most fully therefore with Dr. Stock in regarding the remainder of this chapter as a sample, ironically exhibited by Job, of the harangues on the power and greatness of God which he supposes his friends to have taken out of the mouths of other men, to deck their speeches with borrowed lustre. Only, in descanting on the same subject, he shows how much he himself can go beyond them in eloquence and sublimity.

Job intimates that, whatever *spirit* they had, it was not the Spirit of God, because in their answers falsehood was found.

Verse 5. *Dead* things *are formed from under the waters*] This verse, as it stands in our version, seems to convey no meaning; and the Hebrew is obscure; הרפאים *harephaim*, "the Rephaim," certainly means not *dead things;* nor can there be any propriety in saying that *dead things*, or things without life, *are formed under the waters*, for such things are formed everywhere in the earth, and under the earth, as well as under the waters.

The *Vulgate* translates: *Ecce gigantes gemunt sub aquis, et qui habitant cum eis.* "Behold the giants, and those who dwell with them, groan from under the waters."

The *Septuagint:* Μη γιγαντες μαιωθησονται ὑποκατωθεν ὑδατος, και των γειτονων αυτου; "Are not the giants formed from under the waters, and their neighbours?"

The *Chaldee:* אפשר דגבריא דמתמזמזין יתברין ואנון מלרע למיא ומשריתהון *eposhar degibraiya demithmazmezin yithbareyan veinnun millera lemaiya umashreiyatehon*, "Can the trembling giants be regenerated, when they and their hosts are under the water?"

The *Syriac* and *Arabic:* "Behold, the giants are slain, and are drawn out of the water." None of these appear to give any sense by which the true meaning can be determined.

There is probably here an allusion to the destruction of the earth by the general deluge. Moses, speaking concerning the state of the earth before the flood, says, Gen. vi. 4, "There were giants נפלים *nephilim*, in the earth in those days." Now it is likely that Job means the same by רפאים *rephaim* as Moses does by the *nephilim;* and that both refer to the antediluvians, who were all, for their exceeding great iniquities, overwhelmed by the waters of the deluge. Can those mighty men and their neighbours, all the sinners who have been gath-

A. M. cir. 2484
B. C. cir. 1520
Ante I. Olymp. cir. 744
Ante U. C. cir. 767

waters, [c]and the inhabitants
thereof.
6 [d]Hell *is* naked before him,
and destruction hath no covering.
7 [e]He stretcheth out the north over the
empty place, *and* hangeth the earth upon nothing.
8 [f]He bindeth up the waters in his thick
clouds; and the cloud is not rent
under them.
9 He holdeth back the face of
his throne, *and* spreadeth his
cloud upon it.
10 [g]He hath compassed the waters with
bounds, [h]until the day and night come to an
end.

A. M. cir. 2484
B. C. cir. 1520
Ante I. Olymp. cir. 744
Ante U. C. cir. 767

[c]Or, *with the inhabitants*——[d]Psa. cxxxix. 8, 11; Prov. xv. 11; Hebrews iv. 13——[e]Chap. ix. 8; Psa. xxiv. 2; civ. 2, &c.

[f]Prov. xxx. 4——[g]Chap. xxxviii. 8; Psa. xxxiii. 7; civ. 9; Prov. viii. 29; Jer. v. 22——[h]Heb. *until the end of light with darkness*

ered to them since, be rejected from under the waters, by which they were judicially overwhelmed?

Mr. *Good* thinks the shades of the heroes of former times, the gigantic spectres, the mighty or enormous dead, are meant.

I greatly question whether *sea-monsters* be not intended, such as porpoises, sharks, narwals, grampuses, and whales. We know, however, that an opinion anciently prevailed, that the Titans, a race of men of enormous stature, rebelled against the gods, and endeavoured to scale heaven by placing one mountain on the top of another; and that they and their structure were cast down by the thunder of the deities, and buried under the earth and sea; and that their struggles to arise produce the earthquakes which occur in certain countries. Now although this opinion is supported by the most respectable antiquity among the heathens, it is not to be supposed that in the word of God there can be any countenance given to an opinion at once as absurd as it is monstrous. (But still the poet may use the language of the common people.) I must therefore either refer the passage here to the *antediluvians*, or to the vast *sea-monsters* mentioned above.

Verse 6. *Hell* is *naked before him*] *Sheol*, the *place of the dead*, or of *separate spirits*, is always in his view. *And there is no covering to Abaddon*—the place of the *destroyer*, where *destruction* reigns, and where those dwell who are eternally separated from God. The ancients thought that hell or Tartarus was a vast space in the centre, or at the very bottom of the earth. So Virgil, *Æn.* lib. vi., ver. 577:—

——————— Tum Tartarus ipse
Bis patet in præceps tantum, tenditque sub umbras,
Quantus ad æthereum cœli suspectus Olympum
Hic genus antiquum terræ, Titania pubes,
Fulmine dejecti, fundo volvuntur in imo.

"Full twice as deep the dungeon of the fiends,
The huge Tartarean gloomy gulf, descends
Below these regions, as these regions lie
From the bright realms of yon ethereal sky.
Here roar the *Titan race*, th' *enormous birth;*
The ancient offspring of the teeming earth.
Pierced by the *burning bolts* of old they fell,
And still roll bellowing in the depths of hell."
Pitt.

And some have supposed that there is an allusion to this opinion in the above passage, as well as in several others in the Old Testament; but it is not likely that the sacred writers would countenance an opinion that certainly has nothing in fact or philosophy to support it. Yet still a poet may avail himself of popular opinions.

Verse 7. *He stretcheth out the north over the empty place*] על תהו *al tohu, to the hollow waste.* The same word as is used, Gen. i. 2, *The earth was without form,* תהו *tohu.* The north must here mean the *north pole*, or northern hemisphere; and perhaps what is here stated may refer to the opinion that the earth was a vast extended plain, and the heavens poised upon it, resting on this plain all round the horizon. Of the *south* the inhabitants of Idumea knew nothing; nor could they have any notion of inhabitants in that hemisphere.

Hangeth the earth upon nothing.] The *Chaldee* says: "He lays the earth upon the waters, nothing sustaining it."

Verse 8. *He bindeth up the waters*] Drives the aqueous particles together, which were raised by evaporation, so that, being condensed, they form clouds which float in the atmosphere, till, meeting with strong currents of wind, or by the agency of the electric fluid, they are farther condensed; and then, becoming too heavy to be sustained in the air, fall down in the form of rain, when, in this poetic language, *the cloud is rent under them.*

Verse 9. *He holdeth back the face of his throne*] Though all these are most elegant effects of an omniscient and almighty power, yet the great Agent is not personally discoverable; he dwelleth in light unapproachable, and in mercy hides himself from the view of his creatures. The words, however, may refer to those obscurations of the face of heaven, and the hiding of the body of the sun, when the atmosphere is laden with dense vapours, and the rain begins to be poured down on the earth.

Verse 10. *He hath compassed the waters with bounds*] Perhaps this refers merely to the *circle* of the horizon, the line that terminates light and commences darkness, called here עד תכלית אורעם חשך *ad tachlith or im chosech,* "until the completion of light with darkness." Or, if we take תכלית *tachlith* here to be the same with תכלת *techeleth*, Exod. xxv. 4, and elsewhere, which we translate *blue*, it may mean that sombre sky-blue appearance of the horizon at the time of *twilight*, i. e., between light and darkness; the line where the one is terminating and the other commencing. Or, He so circumscribes the waters, retaining them in their own place, that they shall not be able to overflow the earth until day and night, that is, time itself, come to an end.

A. M. cir. 2484
B. C. cir. 1520
Ante I. Olymp. cir. 744
Ante U. C. cir. 767

11 The pillars of heaven tremble, and are astonished at his reproof.
12 [i]He divideth the sea with his power, and by his understanding he smiteth through [k]the proud.
13 [l]By his Spirit he hath garnished the heavens; his hand hath formed [m]the crooked serpent.
14 Lo, these *are* parts of his ways: but how little a portion is heard of him? but the thunder of his power who can understand?

[i]Exod. xiv. 21; Psa. lxxiv. 13; Isa. li. 15; Jer. xxxi. 35 — [k]Heb. *pride*——[l]Psa. xxxiii. 6——[m]Isa. xxvii. 1

Verse 11. *The pillars of heaven tremble*] This is probably a poetical description either of thunder, or of an earthquake:—

"He shakes creation with his nod;
Earth, sea, and heaven, confess him God."

But there may be an allusion to the *high mountains*, which were anciently esteemed by the common people as the *pillars* on which the *heavens rested;* and when these were shaken with earthquakes, it might be said *the pillars of heaven tremble.* Mount *Atlas* was supposed to be one of those pillars, and this gave rise to the fable of Atlas being a man who bore the heavens on his shoulders. The Greek and Roman poets frequently use this image. Thus SILIUS ITALICUS, lib. i., ver. 202:—

Atlas subducto tracturus vertice cœlum:
Sidera nubiferum fulcit caput, æthereasque
Erigit æternum compages ardua cervix:
Canet barba gelu, frontemque immanibus umbris
Pinea silva premit; vastant cava tempora venti
Nimbosoque ruunt spumantia flumina rictu.

"Atlas' broad *shoulders* prop th' incumbent *skies:*
Around his cloud-girt *head* the *stars* arise.
His towering *neck* supports th' *ethereal way;*
And o'er his *brow* black *woods* their gloom display.
Hoar is his *beard; winds* round his *temples* roar;
And from his *jaws* the rushing *torrents* pour."
J. B. C.

Verse 12. *He divideth the sea with his power*] Here is a manifest allusion to the passage of the Red Sea by the Israelites, and the overthrow of Pharaoh and his host, according to the opinion of the most eminent critics.

He smiteth through the proud.] רהב *Rahab*, the very name by which Egypt is called Isa. li. 9, and elsewhere. *Calmet* remarks: "This appears to refer only to the passage of the Red Sea, and the destruction of Pharaoh. Were we not prepossessed with the opinion that Job died before Moses, every person at the first view of the subject must consider it in this light." I am not thus prepossessed. Let *Job* live when he might, I am satisfied the *Book of Job* was written long after the death of Moses, and not earlier than the days of Solomon, if not later. The farther I go in the work, the more this conviction is deepened; and the opposite sentiment appears to be perfectly gratuitous.

Verse 13. *By his Spirit he hath garnished the heavens*] See the observations below.

Verse 14. *Lo, these* are *parts of his ways*] קצות *ketsoth, the ends* or *extremities*, the *outlines*, an *indistinct sketch*, of his eternal power and Godhead.

How little a portion is heard] שמץ *shemets, a mere whisper;* admirably opposed, as Mr. *Good* has well observed, to רעם *raam, the thunder*, mentioned in the next clause. As the *thunder* is to a *whisper*, so are the *tremendous and infinitely varied works* of God to the *faint outlines* exhibited in the above discourse. Every reader will relish the dignity, propriety, and sense of these expressions. They force themselves on the observation of even the most heedless.

By his Spirit he hath garnished the heavens.—Numerous are the opinions relative to the true meaning of this verse. Some think it refers to the *clearing of the sky* after a storm, such as appears to be described ver. 11, 12; and suppose *his Spirit* means the *wind*, which he directs to sweep and cleanse the face of the sky, by which the splendour of the day or the lustre of the night is restored: and by the *crooked, flying*, or *aerial serpent*, as it is variously rendered, the *ecliptic* is supposed to be meant, as the sun's apparent course in it appears to be *serpentine*, in his approach to and recession from each of the *tropics*. This *tortuous line* may be seen on any terrestrial globe. Many will object to this notion as too refined for the time of Job; but this I could easily admit, as astronomy had a very *early existence* among the *Arabians*, if not its *origin*. But with me the chief objection lies against the *obscurity* of the allusion, if it be one; for it must require no small ingenuity, and almost the spirit of divination, to find out the *sun's oblique path in the zodiac* in the words *His hand hath formed the crooked serpent.* Others have imagined that the allusion is to the *lightning* in that *zigzag form* which it assumes when discharged from one cloud into another during a thunder storm. This is at once a natural and very apparent sense. To *conduct* and *manage* the *lightning* is most certainly a work which requires the *skill* and *omnipotence* of GOD, as much as *garnishing the heavens by his Spirit, dividing the sea by his power*, or causing *the pillars of heaven to tremble by his reproof.* Others think that the *act* of the *creation* of the solar system is intended to be expressed, which is in several parts of the sacred writings attributed to the *Spirit of God;* (Gen. i. 2; Psa. xxxiii. 6;) and that the *crooked serpent* means either *Satan*, who deceived our first parents, or *huge aquatic animals;* for in Isa. xxvii. 1, we find the *leviathan* and *dragon of the sea* called נחש ברח *nachash bariach*, the very terms that are used by Job in this place: "In that day the Lord with his sore and great and strong sword shall punish leviathan, the piercing serpent, (נחש ברח *nachash bariach,*) even leviathan, that crooked serpent, (נחש עקלתון *nachash akallathon,*) and he shall slay the dragon (התנין *hattannin*) that is in the sea." And we know that in Gen. i. 21 התנינם הגדלים

hattanninim haggedolim, which we translate *great whales*, includes all *sea-monsters* or *vast aquatic animals*. *Calmet*, who without hesitation adopts this sentiment, says: "I see no necessity to have recourse to allegory here. After having exhibited the effects of the sovereign power of God in the *heavens*, in the *clouds*, in the vast collection of *waters* in the *sea*, it was natural enough for Job to speak of the production of *fishes*." The intelligent Dr. *Sherlock* gives another interpretation. After strongly expressing his disapprobation of the opinion that Job should descend, after speaking of the *creation of the heavens and their host*, to the *formation of snakes* and *adders*, he supposes "that Job here intended to oppose that grand religious system of *sabæism* which prevailed in his time, and to which, in other parts of this book, he alludes; a system which acknowledged two opposite independent principles by which the universe was governed, and paid Divine adoration to the celestial luminaries. Suppose, therefore, Job to be acquainted with the fall of man, and the part ascribed to the *serpent* of the introduction of evil, see how aptly the parts cohere. In opposition to the idolatrous practice of the time, he asserts God to be the maker of all the host of heaven: *By his Spirit he garnished the heavens*. In opposition to the false notion of two independent principles, he asserts God to be the maker of him who was the author of evil: *His hand hath formed the crooked serpent*. You see how properly the *garnishing of the heavens* and the *forming of the serpent* are joined together. That this is the ancient traditionary explication of this place, we have undeniable evidence from the translation of the *Septuagint*, who render the latter part of this verse, which relates to the serpent, in this manner: Προσταγματι δε εθανατωσε δρακοντα αποστατην. *By a decree he destroyed the apostate dragon*. The *Syriac* and *Arabic* versions are to the same effect: *And his hand slew the flying serpent*.

"These translators apply the place to the *punishment* inflicted on the serpent; and it comes to the same thing, for the *punishing the serpent* is as clear an evidence of God's power over the author of evil as the *creating* him. We need not wonder to see so much concern in this book to maintain the supremacy of God, and to guard it against every false notion; for this was the theme, the business of the author."—Bp. *Sherlock* on Prophecy, Diss. ii.

From the contradictory opinions on this passage, the reader will no doubt feel cautious what mode of interpretation he adopts, and the absolute necessity of admitting no texts of doubtful interpretation as vouchers for the essential doctrines of Christianity. Neither metaphors, allegories, similes, nor figurative expressions of any kind, should ever be adduced or appealed to as proofs of any article in the Christian faith. We have reason to be thankful that this is at present the general opinion of the most rational divines of all sects and parties, and that the *allegory* and *metaphor men* are everywhere vanishing from the meridian and sinking under the horizon of the Church. Scriptural Christianity is prevailing with a strong hand, and going forward with a firm and steady step.

CHAPTER XXVII

Job strongly asserts his innocence; determines to maintain it, and to avoid every evil way, 1–7. *Shows his abhorrence of the hypocrite by describing his infamous character, accumulated miseries, and wretched end*, 8–23.

A. M. cir. 2484 B. C. cir. 1520 Ante I. Olymp. cir. 744 Ante U. C. cir. 767

MOREOVER Job [a]continued
his parable, and said,
2 *As* God liveth, [b]*who* hath
taken away my judgment; and
the Almighty, *who* hath [c]vexed my soul;
3 All the while my breath *is*
in me, and [d]the spirit of God *is*
in my nostrils;
4 My lips shall not speak
wickedness, nor my tongue utter deceit.

[a]Hebrew, *added to take up*——[b]Chapter xxxiv. 5——[c]Hebrew, *made my soul bitter*, Ruth i. 20; 2 Kings iv. 27——[d]That is, *the breath which God gave him*, Gen. ii. 7

NOTES ON CHAP. XXVII

Verse 1. *Continued his parable*] After having delivered the preceding discourse, Job appears to have *paused* to see if any of his friends chose to make any reply; but finding them all silent, he resumed his discourse, which is here called משלו *meshalo, his parable*, his *authoritative weighty discourse;* from משל *mashal, to exercise rule, authority, dominion*, or *power*.—*Parkhurst*. And it must be granted that in this speech he assumes great boldness, exhibits his own unsullied character, and treats his friends with little ceremony.

Verse 2. Who *hath taken away my judgment*] Who has *turned aside my cause*, and has not permitted it to come to a hearing, where I might have justice done to me, but has abandoned me to the harsh and uncharitable judgment of my enemies? There appears to be a great want of reverence in these words of Job; he speaks with a degree of irritation, if not bitterness, which cannot be justified. No man should speak thus of his Maker.

Verse 3. *All the while my breath* is *in me*] As Job appears to allude to the *creation of Adam*, whom God made out of the dust of the earth, *and breathed into his nostrils the breath of life*, so that *he became a living soul*, the whole of Job's assertion may be no more than a periphrasis for *As long as I live and have my understanding*. Indeed נשמתי *nishmathi* may be rendered *my mind* or *understanding*, and רוח אלוה *ruach Eloah, the breath of God, the*

A. M. cir. 2484
B. C. cir. 1520
Ante I. Olymp. cir. 744
Ante U. C. cir. 767

5 God forbid that I should justify you: till I die [e]I will not remove my integrity from me.

6 My righteousness [f]I hold fast, and will not let it go: [g]my heart shall not reproach *me* [h]so long as I live.

7 Let mine enemy be as the wicked, and he that riseth up against me as the unrighteous.

8 [i]For what *is* the hope of the hypocrite, though he hath gained, when God taketh away his soul?

9 [k]Will God hear his cry when trouble cometh upon him?

10 [l]Will he delight himself in the Almighty? will he always call upon God?

11 I will teach you [m]by the hand of God: *that* which *is* with the Almighty will I not conceal.

---

[e]Chap. ii. 9; xiii. 15——[f]Chap. ii. 3——[g]Acts xxiv. 16 [h]Heb. *from my days*——[i]Matt. xvi. 26; Luke xii. 20 [k]Chap. xxxv. 12; Psa. xviii. 41; cix. 7; Prov. i. 28; xxviii. 9; Isa. i. 15; Jer. xiv. 12; Ezek. viii. 18; Mic. iii. 4; John ix. 31; James iv. 3——[l]See chap. xxii. 26, 27——[m]Or, being *in the hand*, &c.

---

principle of animal life, the same that he breathed into Adam; for it is there said, Gen. ii. 7, He breathed into his nostrils, נשמת חיים *nismath chaiyim, the breath of lives*, or that principle from which *animal* and *spiritual* life proceeds; in consequence of which he became לנפש חיה *lenephesh chaiyah, an intelligent* or *rational animal.*

Verse 4. *My lips shall not speak wickedness*] As I have hitherto lived in all good conscience before God, as he knoweth, so will I continue to live.

Verse 5. *God forbid*] חלילה לי *chalilah lli, far be it from me, that I should justify you*—that I should now, by any kind of acknowledgment of wickedness or hypocrisy justify your harsh judgment. You say that God afflicts me for my crimes; I say, and God knows it is truth, that I have not sinned so as to draw down any such judgment upon me. Your judgment, therefore, is pronounced at your own risk.

Verse 6. *My righteousness I hold fast*] I stand firmly on this ground; I have endeavoured to live an upright life, and my afflictions are not the consequence of my sins.

My heart shall not reproach me] I shall take care so to live that I shall have a conscience void of offence before God and man. "Beloved, if our heart condemn us not, then have we confidence toward God;" 1 John iii. 21. This seems to be Job's meaning.

Verse 7. *Let mine enemy be as the wicked*] Let my accuser be proved a lying and perjured man, because he has laid to my charge things which he cannot prove, and which are utterly false.

Verse 8. *What* is *the hope of the hypocrite*] The word חנף *chaneph*, which we translate, most improperly, *hypocrite*, means a *wicked fellow*, a *defiled, polluted wretch*, a *rascal*, a *knave*, a man who sticks at nothing in order to gain his ends. In this verse it means a *dishonest man*, a *rogue*, who by overreaching, cheating, &c., has amassed a fortune.

When God taketh away his soul?] Could he have had any well-grounded hope of eternal blessedness when he was acquiring earthly property by guilt and deceit? And of what avail will this property be when his soul is summoned before the judgment-seat? A righteous man *yields up* his soul to God; the wicked does not, because he is afraid of God, of death, and of eternity. God therefore takes the soul away—forces it out of the body. Mr. *Blair* gives us an affecting picture of the death of a wicked man. Though well known, I shall insert it as a striking comment on this passage:—

"How shocking must thy summons be, O death!
To him that is at ease in his possessions;
Who, counting on long years of pleasures here;
Is quite unfurnished for that world to come!
In that dread moment how the frantic soul
Raves round the walls of her clay tenement;
Runs to each avenue, and shrieks for help,
But shrieks in vain! How wishfully she looks
On all she's leaving, now no longer hers!
A little longer, yet a *little* longer,
O, might she stay, to wash away her stains,
And fit her for her passage! Mournful sight!
Her very eyes weep blood; and every groan
She heaves is big with horror. But the foe,
Like a stanch murderer, steady to his purpose,
Pursues her close, through every lane of life,
Nor misses once the track, but presses on;
Till, forced at last to the tremendous verge,
At once she sinks to everlasting ruin."

THE GRAVE.

The *Chaldee* has, *What can the detractor expect who has gathered together* (ממון דשקר *mamon dishkar, the mammon of unrighteousness*) *when God plucks out his soul?* The *Septuagint:* Τις γαρ εστιν ετι ελπις ασεβει, ὁτι επεχει; Μη πεποιθως επι Κυριον ει ἁρα σωθησεται; "*For what is the hope of the ungodly that he should wait for? shall he, by hoping in the Lord, be therefore saved?*" Mr. *Good* translates differently from all the versions:—

"Yet what is the hope of the wicked that he should prosper,
That God should keep his soul in quiet?"

I believe our version gives as true a sense as any; and the words appear to have been in the eye of our Lord, when he said, "For what is a man profited if he shall gain the whole world, and lose his own soul? or what shall a man give in exchange for his soul?" Matt xvi. 26.

Verse 11. *I will teach you by the hand of God*] Relying on *Divine assistance*, and not speaking out of my own head, or quoting what *others* have said I will teach you what the mind of the Almighty is, and I will conceal nothing. Job felt that the *good hand of his God was upon him*, and that therefore he should make no mistake in his doctrines. In this way the *Chaldee* understood the words, ביד אל *beyad El, by the*

A. M. cir. 2484
B. C. cir. 1520
Ante I. Olymp. cir. 744
Ante U. C. cir. 767

12 Behold, all ye yourselves
have seen *it;* why then are ye
thus altogether vain?
13 ⁿThis *is* the portion of a
wicked man with God, and the heritage of
oppressors, *which* they shall receive of the
Almighty.
14 ᵒIf his children be multiplied, *it is* for
the sword: and his offspring shall not be
satisfied with bread.
15 Those that remain of him
shall be buried in death: and
ᵖhis widows shall not weep.
16 Though he heap up silver
as the dust, and prepare raiment as the clay;
17 He may prepare *it,* but ᵠthe just shall
put *it* on, and the innocent shall divide the
silver.
18 He buildeth his house as a moth, and
ʳas a booth *that* the keeper maketh.

ⁿChap. xx. 29——ᵒDeut. xxviii. 41; Esther ix. 10; Hos. ix. 13——ᵖPsa. lxxviii. 64——ᵠProv. xxviii. 8; Eccles. ii. 26——ʳIsa. i. 8; Lam. ii. 6

hand of God, which it translates בנבואת אלהא *binbuath Elaha, by the prophecy of God.* Those who reject the literal meaning, which conveys a very good sense, may adopt the translation of Mr. *Good,* which has much to recommend it: "I will teach you concerning the *dealings of God.*"

Verse 12. *Ye yourselves have seen* it] Your own experience and observation have shown you that the righteous are frequently in affliction, and the wicked in affluence.

Why then are ye thus altogether vain?] The original is very emphatical: הבל תהבלו *hebel tehbalu,* and well expressed by Mr. *Good:* "Why then should ye thus *babble babblings?*" If our language would allow it, we might say *vanitize vanity.*

Verse 13. *This* is *the portion of a wicked man*] Job now commences his promised teaching; and what follows is a description of the *lot* or *portion* of the *wicked man* and of *tyrants.* And this remuneration shall they have *with God* in general, though the hand of man be not laid upon them. Though he does not at all times show his displeasure against the wicked, by reducing them to a state of poverty and affliction, yet he often does it so that men may see it; and at other times he seems to pass them by, reserving their judgment for *another world,* that men may not forget that there is a day of judgment and perdition for ungodly men, and a future recompense for the righteous.

Verse 14. *If his children be multiplied*] As numerous families were supposed to be a proof of the benediction of the Almighty, Job shows that this is not always the case; for the offspring of the wicked shall be partly cut off by *violent deaths,* and partly reduced to great *poverty.*

Verse 15. *Those that remain of him*] שרידיו *seridaiv, his remains,* whether meaning himself personally, or his family.

Shall be buried in death] Shall come to *utter* and *remediless destruction.* Death shall have his *full conquest* over them, and the *grave* its *complete victory.* These are no common dead. All the *sting,* all the *wound,* and all the *poison* of sin, remains: and so evident are God's judgments in his and their removal, that even *widows* shall not weep for them; the *public* shall not bewail them; for when the wicked perish *there is shouting.*

Mr. *Good,* following the *Chaldee,* translates: *Entombed in corruption,* or *in the pestilence.* But I see no reason why we should desert the literal reading. *Entombed in corruption* gives no nervous sense in my judgment; for in corruption are the high and the low, the wicked and the good, entombed: but *buried in death* is at once nervous and expressive. Death itself is the *place* where he shall lie; he shall have no redemption, no resurrection to life; death shall ever have dominion over him. The expression is very similar to that in Luke xvi. 22, as found in several *versions* and MSS.: *The rich man died, and was buried in hell; and, lifting up his eyes, being in torment, he saw,* &c. See my note there.

Verse 16. *Though he heap up silver*] Though he amass riches in the greatest abundance, he shall not enjoy them. Unsanctified wealth is a curse to its possessor. *Money,* of all earthly possessions, is the most dangerous, as it is the *readiest* agent to do good or evil. He that *perverts* it is doubly cursed, because it affords him the most immediate means of sinful gratification; and he can sin more in an hour through this, than he can in a day or week by any other kind of property. On the other hand, they who use it *aright* have it in their power to do the most *prompt* and *immediate* good. Almost every kind of want may be speedily relieved by it. Hence, he who uses it as he ought is doubly blessed; while he who *abuses* it is doubly cursed.

Verse 17. *The just shall put* it *on*] Money is God's property. "The silver is mine, and the gold is mine, saith the Lord;" and though it may be abused for a time by unrighteous hands, God, in the course of his providence, brings it back to its proper use; and often the righteous possess the inheritance of the wicked.

Verse 18. *He buildeth his house as a moth*] With great skill, great pains, and great industry; but the structure, however skilful, shall be dissolved; and the materials, however costly, shall be brought to corruption. To its owner it shall be only a temporary habitation, like that which the *moth* makes in its *larve* or *caterpillar* state, during its change from a *chrysalis* to a winged insect.

As a booth that *the keeper maketh.*] A *shed* which the *watchman* or *keeper of a vineyard* erects to cover him from the scorching sun, while watching the ripening grapes, that they may be preserved from depredation. Travellers in the East have observed that such *booths* or *sheds* are made of the *lightest* and most *worthless* materials; and after the harvest or vintage is in, they are quite neglected, and by the winter rains, &c., are soon dissolved and destroyed.

A. M. cir. 2484 B. C. cir. 1520 Ante I. Olymp. cir. 744 Ante U. C. cir. 767

19 The rich man shall lie
down, but he shall not be gathered: he openeth his eyes, and
he *is* not.
20 [s]Terrors take hold on him as waters,
a tempest stealeth him away in the night.
21 The east wind carrieth him away, and he
departeth: and as a storm hurl-
eth him out of his place.
22 For *God* shall cast upon
him, and not spare: [t]he would
fain flee out of his hand.
23 *Men* shall clap their hands at him, and
shall hiss him out of his place.

A. M. cir. 2484 B. C. cir. 1520 Ante I. Olymp. cir. 744 Ante U. C. cir. 767

[s]Chap. xviii. 11

[t]Heb. *in fleeing he would flee*

Verse 19. *The rich man shall lie down*] In the grave.

But he shall not be gathered] Neither have a respectable burial among men, nor be gathered with the righteous in the kingdom of God. It may be that Job alludes here to an opinion relative to the state of certain persons after death, prevalent in all nations in ancient times, viz., that those whose funeral rites had not been duly performed, wander about as *ghosts*, and find *no rest*.

He openeth his eyes] In the morning of the resurrection.

And he is *not.*] He is utterly lost and undone for ever. This seems to be the plain sense of the passage; and so all the *versions* appear to have understood it; but *Reiske* and some others, by making יאסף *yeaseph* an *Arabic* word, signifying, not the idea of *gathering*, but *care, anxiety*, &c., have quite altered this sense of the passage; and Mr. *Good*, who copies them, translates thus: *Let the rich man lie down, and care not.* I see no manner of occasion to resort to this interpretation, which, in my judgment, gives a sense inferior to that given above, or to the following: *The rich man shall lie down*—go to his rest, fully persuaded that his property is in perfect safety; *but he shall not be gathered*, or *he shall not gather*—make any farther addition to his stores: *he openeth his eyes in the morning, when he is not*—marauders in the night have stripped him of all his property, as in the case of Job himself; a case quite probable, and not unfrequent in Arabia, when a hostile tribe makes a sudden incursion, and carries off an immense booty. But I prefer the first meaning, as it is obtained without crucifying the text. *Coverdale* translates: **When the rich man dyeth, he carieth nothinge with him: he is gone in the twinckelinge of an eye.**

Verse 20. *Terrors take hold on him as waters*] They come upon him as an irresistible flood; and he is overwhelmed as by a tempest in the night, when darkness partly hides his danger, and deprives him of discerning the way to escape.

Verse 21. *The east wind carrieth him away*] Such as is called by Mr. *Good a levanter*, the *euroclydon*, the *eastern storm* of Acts xxvii. 14.

Verse 22. God *shall cast upon him*] Or, rather, the *storm* mentioned above shall incessantly pelt him, and give him no respite; nor can he by any means escape from its fury.

Verse 23. Men *shall clap their hands at him*] These two verses refer to the storm, which is to sweep away the ungodly; therefore the word *God*, in verse 22, and *men* in this verse, should be omitted. Verse 22: "For it shall fall upon him, and not spare: flying from its power he shall continue to fly. Verse 23. It shall clap its hands against him, and *hiss*, וישרק *veyishrok, shriek*, him out of his place." Here the storm is personified, and the wicked actor is *hissed* and driven by it from off the stage. It seems it was an ancient method to *clap the hands* against and *hiss* a man from any public office, who had acted improperly in it. The populace, in European countries, express their disapprobation of public characters who have not pleased them in the same manner to the present day, by *hisses, groans*, and the like.

CHAPTER XXVIII

Job, in showing the vanity of human pursuits in reference to genuine wisdom, mentions mining for and refining gold and silver, 1; *iron and other minerals*, 2; *the difficulties of mining*, 3, 4; *produce of grain for bread from the earth, and stones of fire from under it*, 5. *He speaks of precious stones and gold dust*, 6; *of the instinct of fowls and wild beasts in finding their way*, 7, 8; *and of the industry and successful attempts of men in mining and other operations*, 9–11: *but shows that with all their industry, skill, and perseverance, they cannot find out true wisdom*, 12; *of which he gives the most exalted character*, 13–22; *and shows that God alone, the fountain of wisdom, knows and can teach it*, 23–27; *and in what this true wisdom consists*, 28.

A. M. cir. 2484 B. C. cir. 1520 Ante I. Olymp. cir. 744 Ante U. C. cir. 767

SURELY there is [a]a vein for
the silver, and a place for
gold *where* they fine *it*.
2 Iron is taken out of the [b]earth,
and brass *is* molten *out of* the stone.
3 He setteth an end to darkness, and
searcheth out all perfection: the [c]stones of
darkness, and the [d]shadow of
death.
4 The flood breaketh out from
the inhabitant; *even the waters*
forgotten of the foot: they are dried up, they
are gone away from men.
5 *As for* the earth, out of it cometh bread,

A. M. cir. 2484 B. C. cir. 1520 Ante I. Olymp. cir. 744 Ante U. C. cir. 767

[a]Or, *a mine*——[b]Or, *dust* [c]Ver. 6——[d]Psa. xxiii. 4

NOTES ON CHAP. XXVIII

Verse 1. *Surely there is a vein for the silver*] This chapter is the oldest and finest piece of *natural history* in the world, and gives us very important information on several curious subjects; and could we ascertain the precise meaning of all the original words, we might, most probably, find out allusions to several useful arts which we are apt to think are of modern, or comparatively modern, invention.

The word מוצא *motsa*, which we here translate *vein*, signifies literally, *a going out;* i. e., a *mine*, or place dug in the earth, whence the silver ore is extracted. And this ore lies generally in *veins* or *loads*, running in certain directions.

A place for gold where *they fine* it.] This should rather be translated, *A place for gold* which *they refine*. Gold ore has also its peculiar mine, and requires to be refined from earthy impurities.

Verse 2. *Iron is taken out of the earth*] This most useful metal is hidden under the earth, and men have found out the method of separating it from its ore.

Brass is *molten* out of *the stone.*] As brass is a factitious metal, *copper* must be the meaning of the Hebrew word נחושה *nechusah:* literally, the stone is poured out for brass. If we retain the common translation, perhaps the process of making brass may be that to which Job refers; for this metal is formed from copper melted with the stone *calamine;* and thus *the stone is poured out* to make *brass*.

Verse 3. *He setteth an end to darkness*] As it is likely Job still refers to mining, the words above may be understood as pointing out the persevering industry of man in penetrating into the bowels of the earth, in order to seek for metals and precious stones. Even the stones that lay hidden in the bowels of the earth he has digged for and brought to light, and has penetrated in directions in which the solar light could not be transmitted; so that he appears to have gone to the regions of the shadow of death. Mr. *Good* translates: "*Man* delveth into *the region* of darkness; and examineth, to the uttermost limit, the stones of darkness and death-shade."

Verse 4. *The flood breaketh out from the inhabitant*] This passage is very difficult. Some think it refers to *mining;* others to *navigation*. If it refer to the former, it may be intended to point out the waters that spring up when the miners have sunk down to a considerable depth, so that the mine is drowned, and they are obliged to give it up. Previously to the invention of the steam-engine this was generally the case: hence ancient mines may be reopened and worked to great advantage, because we have the means now to take off the water which the ancient workers had not. When, therefore, floods break out in those *shafts*, they are abandoned; and thus they are,

Forgotten of the foot] No man treads there any more. The waters increase דלו *dallu, they are elevated*, they rise up to a level with the spring, or till they meet with some fissure by which they can escape; and then מאנוש נעו *meenosh nau, they are moved* or carried away *from men;* the stream is lost in the bowels of the earth.

Mr. *Peters* thinks that both this verse, and ver. 26 of chap. ix., refer to navigation, then in a state of infancy; for the *sea* is not so much as mentioned; but נחל *nachal*, a torrent or flood, some river or arm of the sea perhaps of a few leagues over, which, dividing the several nations, must interrupt their hospitality and commerce with each other, unless by the help of navigation. According to this opinion the verse may be translated and paraphrased thus: *The flood*—rivers and arms of the sea—*separateth from the stranger*, מעם גר *meim gar*, divides different nations and peoples: *they are forgotten of the foot*—they cannot walk over these waters, they must embark in vessels; then *they dwindle away*, דלו *dallu*, from the size of men, that is, in proportion to their departure from the land they lessen on the sight; נעו *nau, they are tossed up and down*, namely, by the action of the waves. This receives some countenance from the psalmist's fine description, Psa. cvii. 26, 27, of a ship in a rough sea: *They mount up to heaven; they go down again to the depths: their soul is melted because of trouble. They reel to and fro*, ינועו *yanuu*, (the same word as above,) *they stagger like a drunken man*. Mr. *Good's* translation is singular:—

He breaketh up the veins from the matrice,
Which, though thought nothing of under the foot,
Are drawn forth, are brandished among mankind.

This learned man thinks that it applies solely to *mining*, of which I cannot doubt; and therefore I adopt the first interpretation: but as to agreement among translators, it will be sought in vain. I shall just add *Coverdale:* **With the ryver of water parteth he a sunder the straunge people, that knoweth no good neighbourheade; such as are rude, unmannerly, and boysterous.**

Verse 5. *The earth, out of it cometh bread*] Or the earth, ממנה *mimmennah, from itself*, by its own vegetative power, *it sends out bread*, or the *corn* of which bread is made.

And under it is turned up as it were fire.] It seems as if this referred to some combustible fossil, similar to our stone coal, which was dug up out of the earth in some places of Arabia. The *Chaldee* gives a translation, conformable to

A. M. cir. 2484 B. C. cir. 1520 Ante I. Olymp. cir. 744 Ante U. C. cir. 767

and under it is turned up as it
were fire.
6 The stones of it *are* the place
of sapphires: and it hath [e]dust
of gold.
7 *There is* a path which no fowl knoweth,
and which the vulture's eye hath not seen:
8 The lion's whelps have not trodden it, nor
the fierce lion passed by it.
9 He putteth forth his hand
upon the [f]rock; he overturneth
the mountains by the roots.
10 He cutteth out rivers among
the rocks; and his eye seeth every precious
thing.
11 He bindeth the floods [g]from overflowing;
and *the thing that is* hid bringeth he forth to
light.

[e]Or, *gold ore*——[f]Or, *flint*

[g]Heb. *from weeping*

a very ancient opinion, which supposed the centre of the earth to be a vast *fire*, and the place called *hell*. "The earth from which food proceeds, and under which is gehenna, whose cold snow is converted into the likeness of fire; and the garden of Eden, which is the place whose stones are sapphires," &c. The *Vulgate* has, "The land from which bread has been produced has been destroyed by fire." If this be the meaning of the original, there is probably an allusion to the destruction of Sodom and Gomorrah; and the seventh and eighth verses may be supposed to refer to that catastrophe, there being no place left tangible or visible where those cities once stood: neither *fowl* nor *beast* could discern a *path* there, the whole land being covered with the lake Asphaltites.

Verse 6. *The stones—the place of sapphires*] In the language of mineralogists, the gangue, matrix, or bed in which the sapphire is found. For a description of this stone, see on ver. 16.

Dust of gold] Or rather, *gold dust.*

Verse 7. There is *a path which no fowl knoweth*] The instinct of birds is most surprising. They traverse vast forests, &c., in search of food, at a great distance from the place which they have chosen for their general residence; and return in all weathers, never missing their track: they also find their own nest without ever mistaking another of the same kind for it. Birds of passage, also, after tarrying in a foreign clime for six or seven months, return to their original abode over kingdoms and oceans, without missing their way, or deviating in the least from the proper direction; not having a single object of sight to direct their peregrinations. In such cases even the keen scent of the vulture, and the quick, piercing sight of the eagle, would be of no use. It is possible that Job may here refer to undiscovered mines and minerals; that notwithstanding man had already discovered much, yet much remained undiscovered, especially in the internal structure and contents of the earth. Since his time innumerable discoveries have been made; and yet how little do we know! Our various conflicting and contradictory *theories* of the earth are full proofs of our ignorance, and strong evidences of our folly. The present dogmatical systems of *geology* itself are almost the *ne plus ultra* of brain-sick visionaries, and system-mad mortals. They talk as confidently of the structure of the globe, and the manner and time in which all was formed, as if they had examined every part from the centre to the circumference; though not a soul of man has ever penetrated two miles in perpendicular depth into the bowels of the earth.

And with this scanty, defective knowledge, they pretend to build systems of the universe, and blaspheme the revelation of God! Poor souls! All these things are to them *a path which no fowl knoweth*, which the *vulture's eye hath not seen*, on which the *lion's whelps have not trodden*, and by which the *fierce lion hath not passed*. The *wisdom* necessary to such investigations is out of *their* reach; and they have not simplicity of heart to seek it where it may be found.

One of the *Chaldee Targums* gives a strange turn to this verse:—"The path of the tree of life Sammael, (Satan,) though flying like a bird, hath not known; nor hath the eye of Eve beheld it. The children of men have not walked in it; nor hath the serpent turned towards it."

Verse 9. *He putteth forth his hand upon the rock*] Still there appears to be a reference to *mining.* Man puts his hand upon the rock, he breaks that to pieces, in order to extract the metals which it contains.

He overturneth the mountains] He excavates, undermines, or digs them away, when in search of the metals contained in them: this is not only poetically, but literally, the case in many instances.

Verse 10. *He cutteth out rivers among the rocks*] He cuts canals, adits, &c., in the rocks, and drives levels under ground, in order to discover *loads* or *veins* of ore. These are often continued a great way under ground; and may be poetically compared to rivers, channels, or canals.

His eye seeth every precious thing.] He sinks those *shafts*, and drives those *levels*, in order to discover where the precious minerals lie, of which he is in pursuit.

Verse 11. *He bindeth the floods*] Prevents the risings of springs from drowning the mines; and conducts rivers and streams from their wonted course, in order to *bring forth to light what was hidden under their beds.* The *binding* or *restraining* the *water*, which, at different depths, annoys the miner, is both difficult and expensive: in some cases it may be drawn off by pipes or canals into neighbouring water courses; in others, it is conducted to one receptacle or reservoir, and thence drawn off. In Europe it is generally done by means of *steam-engines.* What method the ancients had in mining countries, we cannot tell; but they *dug deep* in order to find out the riches of the earth. PLINY says, nervously, *Imus in viscera terræ; et in sede manium opes quærimus.* "We descend into the bowels of the earth; and seek for wealth even in the abodes of departed spirits."—The *manes* or ghosts of the dead, or spirits pre-

A. M. cir. 2484
B. C. cir. 1520
Ante I. Olymp. cir. 744
Ante U. C. cir. 767

12 [h]But where shall wisdom
be found? and where *is* the place
of understanding?
13 Man knoweth not the [i]price
thereof; neither is it found in the land of the
living.

14 [k]The depth saith, It *is* not
in me: and the sea saith, *It is*
not with me.
15 [l]It [m]cannot be gotten for
gold, neither shall silver be weighed *for* the
price thereof.

A. M. cir. 2484
B. C. cir. 1520
Ante I. Olymp. cir. 744
Ante U. C. cir. 767

---

[h]Ver. 20; Eccles. vii. 24——[i]Prov. iii. 15——[k]Ver. 22; Rom. xi. 33, 34

[l]Heb. *fine gold shall not be given for it*——[m]Prov. iii. 13, 14, 15; viii. 10, 11, 19; xvi. 16

---

siding over the dead, were supposed to have their habitation in the centre of the earth; or in the deepest pits and caves. OVID, speaking of the degeneracy of men in the iron age, *Met.* lib. i., ver. 137, says:—

Nec tantum segetes alimentaque debita dives
Poscebatur humus; sed *itum est in viscera terræ:*
Quasque *recondiderat, Stygiisque admoverat umbris,*
Effodiuntur opes, irritamenta malorum.
Jamque nocens ferrum, ferroque nocentius aurum
Prodierat: prodit bellum, quod pugnat utroque;
Sanguineaque manu crepitantia concutit arma.

"Nor was the ground alone required to bear
Her annual income to the crooked share:
But greedy mortals, rummaging her store,
Digg'd from her entrails first the precious ore;
And that alluring ill to sight display'd,
Which, next to hell, the prudent gods had laid.
Thus cursed *steel*, and more accursed *gold*,
Gave mischief birth, and made that mischief bold;
And double death did wretched man invade,
By *steel* assaulted, and by *gold* betray'd."

DRYDEN.

By *binding the floods from overflowing*, some have supposed that there is an allusion to the *flux* and *reflux* of the sea. In its *flowing* it is so *bound*, has its *bounds* assigned by the Most High, that it does not drown the adjacent country; and in its *ebbing* the parts which are ordinarily *covered* with the water are *brought to view.*

Verse 12. *But where shall wisdom be found?*] It is most evident that the terms *wisdom* and *understanding* are used here in a widely different sense from all those arts and sciences which have their relation to man in his animal and social state, and from all that *reason* and *intellect* by which man is distinguished from all other animals. Now as these terms חכמה *chochmah, wisdom*, and בינה *binah, understanding* or *discernment*, are often applied in the sacred writings in their common acceptations, we must have recourse to what Job says of them, to know their meaning in *this place.* In ver. 28, he says, The *fear of the Lord is* WISDOM, *and to depart from evil is* UNDERSTANDING. We know that the *fear of the Lord* is often taken for the whole of that religious reverence and holy obedience which God prescribes to man in his word, and which man owes to his Maker. Hence the *Septuagint* render חכמה *chochmah, wisdom*, by θεοσεβια, *Divine worship;* and as to a *departure from evil*, that is necessarilv implied in a religious life; but it is here properly distinguished, that no man might suppose that a *right faith*, and a proper performance of the rites of religious worship, is the whole of religion. No. They must not only worship God *in the letter*, but also in the *spirit;* they must not only have the *form*, but also the *power* of *godliness:* and this will lead them to worship God in spirit and truth, to walk in his testimonies, and abstain from every appearance of evil; hence they will be truly *happy:* so that *wisdom* is another word for *happiness.* Now these are things which man by study and searching could never find out; they are not of an *earthly origin.* The *spirit of a man*, human understanding, *may know the things of a man*—those which concern him in his animal and social state: *but the Spirit of God* alone *knows the things of God;* and therefore WISDOM—all true religion—must come by Divine revelation, which is the mode of its attainment. *Wisdom* finds out the *thing*, and *understanding* uses and applies the *means;* and then the great *end* is obtained.

Verse 13. *Man knoweth not the price thereof*] It is of infinite value; and is the only science which concerns *both worlds.* Without it, the wisest man is but a beast; with it, the simplest man is next to an angel.

Neither is it found in the land of the living.] The world by wisdom, *its* wisdom, never knew God. True religion came by Divine revelation: that alone gives the true notion of God, his attributes, ways, designs, judgments, providences, &c., whence man came, what is his duty, his nature, and his end. *Literature, science, arts*, &c., &c., can only avail man for the *present life;* nor can they contribute to his true *happiness*, unless tempered and directed by genuine religion.

Verse 14. *The depth saith, It* is *not in me*] Men may dig into the bowels of the earth, and there find gold, silver, and precious stones; but these will not give them true happiness.

The sea saith, It is *not with me.*] Men may explore foreign countries, and by navigation connect as it were the most distant parts of the earth, and multiply the comforts and luxuries of life; but every voyage and every enjoyment proclaim, True happiness is not here.

Verse 15. *It cannot be gotten for gold*] Genuine religion and true happiness are not to be acquired by earthly property. Solomon made gold and silver as plentiful as the stones in Jerusalem, and had all the delights of the sons of men, and yet he was not happy; yea, he had *wisdom*, was the wisest of men, but he had not the wisdom of which Job speaks here, and therefore, to him, all was vanity and vexation of spirit. If Solomon, as some suppose, was the author of this book, the sentiments expressed here are such as we might expect from this deeply experienced and wise man.

A. M. cir. 2484
B. C. cir. 1520
Ante I. Olymp. cir. 744
Ante U. C. cir. 767

16 It cannot be valued with
the gold of Ophir, with the precious onyx, or the sapphire.
17 The gold and the crystal
cannot equal it: and the exchange of it
shall not be for [n]jewels of fine
gold.
18 No mention shall be made
of [o]coral, or of pearls: for the
price of wisdom *is* above rubies.

[n]Or, *vessels of fine gold*

[o]Or, *Ramoth*

Verse 16. *The gold of Ophir*] Gold is *five* times mentioned in this and verses 17 and 19, and *four* of the times in different words. I shall consider them all at once.

1. סגור SEGOR, from סגר *sagar*, to *shut up*. *Gold* in the *mine*, or *shut up* in the *ore; native* gold washed by the streams out of the mountains, &c.; *unwrought gold.*

Verse 16. 2. כתם KETHEM, from כתם *catham*, to *sign* or *stamp: gold* made *current* by being *coined*, or *stamped* with its *weight* or *value;* what we would call *standard* or *sterling* gold.

Verse 17. 3. זהב ZAHAB, from זהב *zahab*, to be *clear*, *bright*, or *resplendent:* the *untarnishing* metal; the only metal that always keeps its lustre. But probably here it means gold *chased*, or that in which precious stones are *set; burnished* gold.

4. פז PAZ, from פז *paz*, to *consolidate*, joined here with כלי *keley*, *vessels*, *ornaments*, *instruments*, &c.: *hammered* or *wrought gold;* gold in the finest *forms*, and most elegant *utensils.* This metal is at once the brightest, most solid, and most precious, of all the *metals* yet discovered, of which we have no less than *forty* in our catalogues.

In these verses there are also *seven* kinds of *precious stones*, &c., mentioned: *onyx*, *sapphire*, *crystal*, *coral*, *pearls*, *rubies*, and *topaz.* These I shall also consider in the order of their occurrence.

Verse 16. 1. שהם *shoham*, the ONYX, from ονυξ, *a man's nail*, *hoof of a horse*, because in *colour* it resembles both. This stone is a species of *chalcedony;* and consists of alternate layers of white and brown *chalcedony*, under which it generally ranges. In the *Vulgate* it is called *sardonyx*, compounded of *sard* and *onyx. Sard* is also a variety of chalcedony, of a deep reddish-brown colour, of which, and alternate layers of *milk-white* chalcedony, the sardonyx consists. A most beautiful block of this mineral sardonyx, from Iceland, now lies before me.

2. ספיר *sappir*, the SAPPHIRE stone, from ספר *saphar*, to *count*, *number;* probably from the number of *golden spots* with which it is said the *sapphire of the ancients* abounded. PLINY says, *Hist. Nat.* lib. xxxvii., cap. 8: Sapphirus *aureis punctis* collucet: cœruleæ et sapphiri, raraque cum purpura: optimæ apud Medos, nusquam tame perlucidæ. "The sapphire glitters with golden spots. Sapphires are sometimes of an azure, never of a purple colour. Those of Media are the best, but there are none transparent." This may mean the *blood stones;* but see below.

What we call the *sapphire* is a variety of the perfect *corundum;* it is in hardness inferior only to the *diamond.* It is of several colours, and from them it has obtained several names. 1. The transparent or translucent is called the *white* sapphire. 2. The *blue* is called the oriental *sapphire.* 3. The *violet blue*, the oriental *amethyst.* 4. The *yellow*, the oriental *topaz.* 5. The *green*, the oriental *emerald.* 6. That with *pearly reflections*, the *opalescent* sapphire. 7. When transparent, with a pale, reddish, or bluish reflection, it is called the *girasol* sapphire. 8. A variety which, when polished, shows a *silvery star* of six rays in a direction perpendicular to the axis, is called *asteria.* When the meaning of the Hebrew word is collated with the description given by *Pliny*, it must be evident that a *spotted opaque* stone is meant, and consequently not what is now known by the name *sapphire.* I conjecture, therefore, that *lapis lazuli*, which is of a *blue colour*, with *golden-like spots*, formed by *pyrites* of iron, must be intended. The *lapis lazuli* is that from which the beautiful and unfading colour called *ultramarine* is obtained.

Verse 17. 3. זכוכית *zechuchith*, CRYSTAL, or *glass*, from זכה *zachah*, to be *pure*, *clear*, *transparent. Crystal* or *crystal of quartz* is a six-sided prism, terminated by six-sided pyramids. It belongs to the *siliceous* class of minerals: it is exceedingly clear and brilliant, insomuch that this property of it has become proverbial, as *clear as crystal.*

Verse 18. 4. ראמות *ramoth*, CORAL, from ראם *raam*, to be *exalted* or *elevated;* probably from this remarkable property of coral, "it always grows from the tops of marine rocky caverns with the head downwards." *Red coral* is found in the Mediterranean, about the isles of Majorca and Minorca, on the African coast, and in the Ethiopic ocean.

5. גביש *gabish*, PEARLS, from גבש *gabash*, in Arabic, to be *smooth*, to *shave off the hair;* and hence גביש *gabish*, the *pearl*, the *smooth round substance;* and also *hail* or *hailstones*, because of their resemblance to *pearls.* The *pearl* is the production of a shell-fish of the *oyster* kind, found chiefly in the East Indies, and called *berberi;* but pearls are occasionally found in the *common oyster*, as I have myself observed, and in the *muscle* also. They are of a brilliant sparkling white, perfectly round in general, and formed of *coats* in the manner of an *onion.* Out of one oyster I once took *six* pearls. When large, fine, and without spots, they are valuable. I have seen one that formed the whole body of a Hindoo idol, *Creeshna*, more than an inch in length, and valued at 300 guineas.

Verse 18. 6. פנינים *peninim*, RUBIES, from פנה *panah*, he *turned*, *looked*, *beheld.* The *oriental ruby* is blood-red, rose-red, or with a tinge of violet. It has occasionally a mixture of *blue*, and is generally in the form of *six-sided prisms.* It is a species of the *sapphire*, and is sometimes *chatoyant* in its appearance, i. e., has a curious kind of reflection, similar to the *cat's eye:* and as this is particularly striking, and *changes* as you *turn* the stone, hence probably the name *peninim*, which you derive from פנה *panah*, to turn, look, behold, &c.

But some learned men are of opinion that the *magnet* or *loadstone* is meant, and it is thus called because of the remarkable property it has

A. M. cir. 2484 B. C. cir. 1520 Ante I. Olymp. cir. 744 Ante U. C. cir. 767

19 The topaz of Ethiopia shall
not equal it, neither shall it be
valued with pure gold.
20 [p]Whence then cometh wis-
dom? and where *is* the place of understanding?
21 Seeing it is hid from the eyes of all living and kept close from the fowls of the [q]air.
22 [r]Destruction and death say, We have
heard the fame thereof with our
ears.
23 God understandeth the way
thereof, and he knoweth the place
thereof.
24 For he looketh to the ends of the earth,
and [s]seeth under the whole heaven;
25 [t]To make the weight for the winds;

[p]Ver. 12——[q]Or, *heaven*——[r]Ver. 14

[s]Prov. xv. 3——[t]Psa. cxxxv. 7

of *turning north* and *south.* And this notion is rendered the more likely, because it agrees with another word in this verse, expressive of a different property of the magnet, viz., its *attractive* influence: for the Hebrew words משך חכמה מפנינים *meshech chochmah mippeninim,* which we render, *The price of wisdom is above rubies,* is literally, *The* ATTRACTION *of wisdom is beyond the peninim,* the *loadstone;* for all the gold, silver, and precious stones, have strong influence on the human heart, attracting all its passions strongly; yet the *attraction of wisdom*—that which insures a man's *happiness* in both worlds—is more powerful and influential, when understood, than all of these, and even than the *loadstone,* for that can only attract *iron;* but, *through desire* of the other, *a man, having separated himself* from all those earthly entanglements, *seeketh and intermeddleth with* ALL WISDOM. The *attractive* property of the loadstone must have been observed from its first discovery; and there is every reason to believe that the *magnet* and its virtues were known in the East long before they were discovered in Europe.

7. פטדה *pitdah, the* TOPAZ. This word occurs only in Exod. xxviii. 17; xxxix. 10; Ezek. xxviii. 13, and in the present place; in all of which, except that of Ezekiel, where the Septuagint is all confusion, the *Septuagint* and *Vulgate* render the word always τοπαζιον, *topazius, the* TOPAZ. This stone is generally found in a prismatic form, sometimes limpid and nearly transparent, or of various *shades* of *yellow, green, blue, lilac,* and *red.*

I have thus given the best account I can of the stones here mentioned, allowing that they answer to the names by which we translate them. But on this point there is great uncertainty, as I have already had occasion to observe in other parts of this work. Beasts, birds, plants, metals, precious stones, unguents, different kinds of grain, &c., are certainly mentioned in the sacred writings; but whether we know what the different Hebrew terms signify, is more than we can certainly affirm. Of some there is little room to doubt; of others *conjecture* must, in the present state of our knowledge, supply the place of *certainty.* See PHILIP'S *Elementary Introduction* to MINERALOGY; an accurate work, which I feel pleasure in recommending to all students in the science.

Verse 19. *The topaz of Ethiopia*] The country called *Cush,* which we call *Ethiopia,* is supposed to be that which extends from the eastern coast of the Red Sea, and stretches towards Lower Egypt. *Diodorus Siculus* says that the topaz was found in great abundance, as his description intimates, in an island in the Red Sea called *Ophiodes,* or the *isle of serpents. Hist.* lib. iii., p. 121. His account is curious, but I greatly doubt its correctness; it seems too much in the form of a legend: yet the reader may consult the place.

Verse 20. *Whence then cometh wisdom?*] Nearly the same words as in verse 12, where see the note.

Verse 22. *Destruction and death say, We have heard the fame thereof*] אבדון ומות *Abaddon vamaveth,* the destroyer, and his offspring death. This is the very name that is given to the *devil* in Greek letters Αβαδδων, Rev. ix. 11, and is rendered by the Greek word Απολλυων, *Apollyon,* a word exactly of the same meaning. No wonder *death* and the *devil* are brought in here as saying *they had heard the fame of wisdom,* seeing ver. 28 defines it to be *the fear of the Lord, and a departure from evil;* things point blank contrary to the interests of Satan, and the extension of the empire of death.

Verse 23. *God understandeth the way thereof*] It can only be taught by a revelation from himself. Instead of הבין *hebin, understandeth,* six MSS. have הכין *hechin, disposed* or *established.* This reading is also supported by the *Septuagint;* Ὁ Θεος εν συνεστησεν αυτης ὁδον, "God hath well established her way:" *falsely* rendered *bene cognovit, hath well known,* in the *Latin version* of the Septuagint in the London Polyglot; but *bene constituit, hath well established,* in the *Complutensian, Antwerp,* and *Paris* Polyglots.

Verse 24. *For he looketh to the ends of the earth*] His knowledge is unlimited, and his power infinite.

Verse 25. *To make the weight for the winds*] God has given an atmosphere to the earth, which, possessing a certain degree of *gravity* perfectly suited to the necessities of all animals, plants, vegetables, and fluids, is the cause in his hand of preserving animal and vegetative life through the creation; for by it the *blood* circulates in the veins of animals, and the *juices* in the tubes of vegetables. Without this *pressure* of the atmosphere, there could be no respiration; and the *elasticity* of the particles of air included in animal and vegetable bodies, without this superincumbent pressure, would rupture the vessels in which they are contained, and destroy both kinds of life. So exactly is this *weight of the winds* or *atmospheric air* proportioned to the necessities of the globe, that we find it in the mean neither too *light* to prevent the undue *expansion* of animal and vegetable tubes, nor too *heavy* to *compress* them so as to prevent due circulation. See at the end of the chapter.

A. M. cir. 2484
B. C. cir. 1520
Ante I. Olymp. cir. 744
Ante U. C. cir. 767

and he weigheth the waters by
measure.
26 When he [u]made a decree
for the rain, and a way for the
lightning of the thunder:
27 Then did he see it, and [v]declare it; he
prepared it, yea, and searched
it out.
28 And unto man he said,
Behold, [w]the fear of the LORD,
that *is* wisdom: and to depart from evil *is*
understanding.

[u]Chap. xxxviii. 25——[v]Or, *number it*——[w]Deut. iv. 6; Psa. cxi. 10; Prov. i. 7; ix. 10; Eccles. xii. 13

And he weigheth the waters by measure.] He has exactly proportioned the *aqueous surface* of the earth to the *terrene parts*, so that there shall be an adequate surface to produce, by *evaporation*, moisture sufficient to be treasured up in the atmosphere for the irrigation of the earth, so that it may produce grass for cattle, and corn for the service of man. It has been found, by a pretty exact calculation, that the aqueous surface of the globe is to the terrene parts as *three* to *one;* or, that *three-fourths* of the surface of the globe is *water*, and about *one-fourth earth.* And other experiments on evaporation, or the quantity of vapours which arise from a given space in a given time, show that it requires such a proportion of *aqueous surface* to afford moisture sufficient for the other proportion of *dry land.* Thus God has given the waters by measure, as he has given the due proportion of *weight* to the *winds.*

Verse 26. *When he made a decree for the rain*] When he determined how that should be *generated;* viz., By the *heat* of the sun *evaporation* is produced: the particles of vapour being lighter than the air on the surface, ascend into the atmosphere, till they come to a region where the air is of their own *density;* there they are formed into *thin clouds*, and become suspended. When, by the sudden passages of *lightning*, or by *winds* strongly *agitating* these clouds, the particles are driven together and condensed, so as to be *weightier* than the *air* in which they float, then they fall down in the form of *rain;* the drops being greater or less according to the *force* or *momentum*, or suddenness, of the agitation by which they are driven together, as well as to the degree of *rarity* in the lower regions of the atmosphere through which they fall.

A way for the lightning of the thunder] ודרך לחזיז קולות *vederech lachaziz koloth.* קול *kol* signifies *voice* of any kind; and *koloth* is the plural, and is taken for the frequent *claps* or *rattlings* of thunder. חז *chaz* signifies to *notch, indentate*, or *serrate*, as in the *edges* of the leaves of trees; חזיז *chaziz* must refer to the *zigzag* form which lightning assumes in passing from one cloud into another. We are informed that "this is a frequent occurrence in hot countries." Undoubtedly it is; for it is frequent in *cold countries* also. I have seen this phenomenon in England in the most distinct manner for hours together, with a few seconds of interval between each flash. Nothing can better express this appearance than the original word.

Verse 27. *Then did he see it, and declare it*] When he had finished all his creative operations, and tried and proved his work, חקרה *chakarah*, investigated and found it to be very good; then he gave the needful revelation to man; for,

Verse 28. *Unto man he said*] לאדם *laadam, unto man*, he said: This probably refers to the revelation of his will which God gave to Adam after his fall. He had before sought for *wisdom* in a *forbidden way.* When he and Eve saw that the tree was pleasant to the eyes, *and a tree to be desired to make one wise*, they took and did eat, Gen. iii. 6. Thus they lost all the *wisdom* that they had, by not setting the *fear of the Lord* before their eyes; and became *foolish, wicked*, and *miserable.* Hear, then, what God prescribes as a proper remedy for this dire disease: The fear of the Lord, that is wisdom; it is thy only wisdom now to set God always before thy eyes, that thou mayest not again transgress.

Depart from evil is understanding.] Depart from the evil *within* thee, and the evil *without* thee; for thy own evil, and the evil that is now, through thee, brought into the world, will conspire together to sink thee into ruin and destruction. Therefore, let it be thy constant employment to shun and avoid that evil which is everywhere diffused through the whole moral world by thy offence; and labour to be *reconciled* to him by the righteousness and true holiness, that thou mayest escape the bitter pains of an eternal death. See the note on verse 12.

FROM what has been observed on verses 25, 26, and from the doctrine of the atmosphere in general, I can safely draw the following conclusions:—

1. From the *gravity* and *elasticity* of the air, we learn that it closely invests the earth, and all bodies upon it, and binds them down with a force equal to 2160 pounds on every square foot. Hence it may properly be termed the *belt* or *girdle* of the globe.

2. It prevents the arterial system of animals and plants from being too much distended by the impetus of the circulating juices, or by the elastic power of the air so plenteously contained in the blood, and in the different vessels both of plants and animals.

3. By its gravity it prevents the blood and juices from oozing through the pores of the vessels in which they are contained; which, were it not for this circumstance, would infallibly take place. Persons who ascend high mountains, through want of a sufficiency of pressure in the atmosphere, become relaxed, and spit blood. Animals, under an exhausted receiver, swell, vomit, and discharge their fæces.

4. It promotes the mixture of contiguous fluids; for when the air is extracted from certain mixtures, a separation takes place, by which their properties, when in combination, are essentially changed.

5. To this principle we owe winds in general, so essential to navigation, and so necessary to the purification of the atmosphere. The air is

put into motion by any alteration of its equilibrium.

6. Vegetation depends entirely on the gravity and elasticity of the air. Various experiments amply prove that plants in vacuo never grow.

7. Without air there could be no evaporation from the sea and rivers; and, consequently, no rain; nor could the clouds be suspended, so necessary to accumulate and preserve, and afterwards to distil, these vapours, in the form of dew, rain, snow, and hail, upon the earth.

8. Without air, all the charms of vocal and instrumental sounds would become extinct; and even language itself would cease.

9. Without it heat could not be evolved, nor could fire exist; hence a universal rigour would invest the whole compass of created nature.

10. Without air, animal life could never have had a being; hence God created the firmament or atmosphere before any animal was produced. And without its continual influence animal life cannot be preserved; for it would require only a few moments of a total privation of the benefits of the atmosphere to destroy every living creature under the whole heaven.

11. It has been found, by repeated *experiments*, that a column or rod of *quicksilver*, about *twenty-nine inches and a half high*, and *one inch* in *diameter*, weighs about *fifteen* pounds; and such a column is suspended in an exhausted tube by the weight of the *atmosphere;* hence it necessarily follows, that a column of *air*, one *square inch* in diameter, and as *high as the atmosphere*, weighs about *fifteen pounds* at a medium. Thus it is evident that the atmosphere presses with the weight of *fifteen pounds* on every *square inch;* and, as a *square foot* contains *one hundred and forty-four* square inches, every such foot must sustain a weight of incumbent atmospheric air equal to *two thousand one hundred and sixty pounds*, as has been before stated. And from this it will follow, that a middle-sized man, whose surface is about *fifteen square feet*, constantly sustains a load of air equal to *thirty-two thousand four hundred pounds!* But this is so completely counterbalanced by the air *pressing equally in all directions*, and by the *elasticity* of the air included in the various cavities of the body, that no person in a pure and healthy state of the atmosphere feels any inconvenience from it; so accurately has God *fitted the weight to the winds.*

It has been suggested that my computation of 15 *square* feet for the surface of a *middle-sized man*, is too *much;* I will, therefore, take it at 14 *square* feet. From this computation, which is within the measure, it is evident that every such person sustains *a weight of air* equal, at a medium, to about 30,240 *lbs.* troy, or 24,882½ *lbs.* avoirdupois, which make 1,777 *stone*, 4 *lbs.* equal to *eleven* TONS, *two* HUNDRED and *eighteen pounds* and *a half.*

12. Though it may appear more *curious* than *useful*, yet from the simple fact which I have completely demonstrated myself by experiment, that *the atmosphere presses with the weight of fifteen pounds on every square inch*, we can tell the *quantum of pressure* on the *whole globe*, and weigh the whole atmosphere to a pound!

The *polar* and *equatorial* circumference of the earth is well known. Without, therefore, entering too much into *detail*, I may state that the surface of the terraqueous globe is known to contain about *five thousand, five hundred, and seventy-five* BILLIONS *of square* FEET; hence, allowing *fifteen pounds to each square inch, and two thousand one hundred and sixty pounds to each square foot*, the whole surface must sustain a pressure from the atmosphere equal to *twelve* TRILLIONS *and forty-two thousand billions of* POUNDS! or *six thousand and twenty-one* BILLIONS *of* TONS! And this weight is the *weight of the whole atmosphere* from its contact with every part of the earth's surface to its utmost highest extent!

Experiments also prove that the air presses *equally in all directions*, whether *upwards, downwards*, or *laterally;* hence the earth is not incommoded with this enormous weight, because its *zenith* and *nadir, north* and *south* pressure, being perfectly equal, *counterbalance* each other! This is also the case with respect to the human body, and to all bodies on the earth's surface.

To make the foregoing calculations more satisfactory, it may be necessary to add the following observations:—

A bulk of atmospheric air, equal to one *quart*, when taken near the level of the sea, at a temperature of 50° Fahrenheit, weighs about 16 *grains*, and the same bulk of *rain water*, taken at the same temperature, weighs about 14,621 *grains:* hence *rain water* is about 914 times specifically heavier than *air.*

I have already shown that the *pressure* of the atmosphere is equal to about 15 *lbs.* troy on every *square inch;* and that this pressure is the same in all directions; and thence shown that on this datum the *whole weight of the atmosphere* may be computed. I shall re-state this from a computation of the earth's surface in *square miles*, which is recommended to me as peculiarly accurate. A square mile contains 27,878,400 square feet. The earth's surface, in round numbers, is 200,000,000, or *two hundred millions*, of square miles. Now, as from the preceding data it appears that there is a pressure of 19,440 *lbs.* troy on every *square yard*, the pressure or *weight* of the *whole atmosphere*, circumfused round the whole surface of the earth, amounts to 12,043,468,800,-000,000,000, or, *twelve* TRILLIONS, *forty-three thousand four hundred and sixty-eight* BILLIONS, *eight hundred thousand* MILLIONS *of pounds.*

Though we cannot tell to what *height* the atmosphere extends, the air growing more and more *rare* as we ascend in it; yet we can ascertain, as above, the quantum of *weight* in the whole of this atmosphere, which the terraqueous globe sustains equally diffused over its surface, as well as over the surfaces of all bodies existing on it. At first view, however, it is difficult for minds not exercised in matters of philosophy to conceive how such an immense pressure can be borne by animal beings. Though this has been already explained, let the reader farther consider that, as *fishes* are surrounded by *water*, and live and move in it, which is a much denser medium than our atmosphere; so all *human beings* and all other animals are surrounded by *air*, and live and move in it. A *fish taken out of the water* will die in a very short time: *a human being*, or any other animal, *taken out of the air*, or put in a place *whence the air is ex-*

tracted, will die in a much shorter time. *Water gravitates* towards the *centre* of the earth, and so does *air*. Hence, as a *fish* is pressed on every side by that fluid, so are all animals on the earth's surface by atmospheric air. And the pressure in both cases, on a given surface, is as has been stated above; the air contained in the vessels and cells of animal bodies being a sufficient counterpoise to the air without.

Having said thus much on the pressure of the atmosphere, as intimated by Job, the reader will permit me to make the following general reflections on the subject, of which he may make what use he may judge best.

It is generally supposed that former times were full of barbaric ignorance; and that the system of philosophy which is at present in repute, and is established by experiments, is quite a modern discovery. But nothing can be more false than this; as the Bible plainly discovers to an attentive reader that the doctrine of *statics*, the *circulation* of the blood, the *rotundity* of the earth, the *motions* of the celestial bodies, the process of *generation*, &c., were all known long before *Pythagoras, Archimedes, Copernicus*, or *Newton* were born.

It is very reasonable to suppose that God implanted the first principles of every science in the mind of his first creature; that *Adam* taught them to his posterity, and that *tradition* continued them for many generations with their proper improvements. But many of them were lost in consequence of wars, captivities, &c. Latter ages have re-discovered many of them, principally by the direct or indirect aid of the Holy Scriptures; and others of them continue hidden, notwithstanding the accurate and persevering researches of the moderns.

CHAPTER XXIX

Job laments his present condition, and gives an affecting account of his former prosperity, having property in abundance, being surrounded by a numerous family, an enjoying every mark of the approbation of God, 1–6. *Speaks of the respect he had from the young,* 7, 8; *and from the nobles,* 9, 10. *Details his conduct as a magistrate and judge in supporting the poor, and repressing the wicked,* 11–17; *his confidence, general prosperity, and respect,* 18–25.

A. M. cir. 2484
B. C. cir. 1520
Ante I. Olymp. cir. 744
Ante U. C. cir. 767

MOREOVER Job [a]continued
his parable, and said,
2 O that I were [b]as *in* months
past, as *in* the days *when* God
preserved me;
3 [c]When his [d]candle shined
upon my head, *and when* by
his light I walked *through* darkness;
4 As I was in the days of my youth, when

A. M. cir. 2484
B. C. cir. 1520
Ante I. Olymp. cir. 744
Ante U. C. cir. 767

[a]Heb. *added to take up*——[b]See chap. vii. 3

[c]Chap. xviii. 6——[d]Or, *lamp;* Psa. xviii. 28

NOTES ON CHAP. XXIX

Verse 2. *O that I were as* in *months past*] Job seems here to make an apology for his complaints, by taking a view of his former prosperity, which was very great, but was now entirely at an end. He shows that it was not removed because of any bad use he had made of it; and describes how he behaved himself before God and man, and how much, for justice, benevolence, and mercy, he was esteemed and honoured by the wise and good.

Preserved me] Kept, guarded, and watched over me.

Verse 3. *When his candle shined upon my head*] Alluding most probably to the custom of illuminating festival or assembly rooms by lamps pendant from the ceiling. These shone literally *on the heads* of the guests.

By his light I walked through *darkness*] His *light*—prosperity and peace—continued to illuminate my way. If adversity came, I had always the light of God to direct me. Almost all the nations of the world have represented their great men as having a *nimbus* or *Divine glory* about their heads, which not only signified the honour they had, but was also an emblem of the inspiration of the Almighty.

Verse 4. *The days of my youth*] The original word rather means *in the days of my winter*, חרפי *charpi*, from חרף *charaph*, "to strip or make bare." Mr. *Harmer* supposes the *rainy season* is intended, when the fields, &c., parched up by long drought, are revived by the *plentiful showers*. Mr. *Good* thinks the word as found in the *Arabic*, which means *top* or *summit*, and which he translates *perfection*, is that which should be preferred. Others think the *autumnal* state is meant, when he was *loaded with prosperity*, as the trees are with *ripe fruit*.

The secret of God was *upon my tabernacle*] בסוד אלוה *besod Eloah*, "the secret assembly of God," meaning probably the same thing that is spoken of in the beginning of this book, *the sons of God, the devout people, presenting themselves before God*. It is not unlikely that such a *secret assembly of God* Job had in his own house; where he tells us, in the next verse, "The Almighty was with him, and his children were about him."

Mr. *Good* translates differently: *When God fortified my tent over me;* supposing that the Hebrew סוד *sod* is the Arabic سد *sud*, "a barrier or fortification." Either will make a good sense.

A. M. cir. 2484
B. C. cir. 1520
Ante I. Olymp. cir. 744
Ante U. C. cir. 767

[e]the secret of God *was* upon my
tabernacle;
5 When the Almighty *was* yet
with me, *when* my children *were*
about me;
6 When [f]I washed my steps with butter,
and [g]the rock poured [h]me out rivers of oil;
7 When I went out to the gate through the
city, *when* I prepared my seat in the street!
8 The young men saw me, and hid themselves: and the aged arose, *and* stood up.
9 The princes refrained talking, and [i]laid
their hand on their mouth.
10 [k]The nobles held their peace, and their
[l]tongue cleaved to the roof of their mouth.
11 When the ear heard *me*, then it blessed me;
and when the eye saw *me*, it gave witness to me:
12 Because [m]I delivered the
poor that cried, and the fatherless, and *him that had* none to
help him.
13 The blessing of him that was ready to
perish came upon me: and I caused the
widow's heart to sing for joy.
14 [n]I put on righteousness, and it clothed
me: my judgment *was* as a robe and a diadem.
15 I was [o]eyes to the blind, and feet *was*
I to the lame.
16 I *was* a father to the poor: and [p]the
cause *which* I knew not I searched out.
17 And I brake [q]the [r]jaws of the wicked,
and [s]plucked the spoil out of his teeth.
18 Then I said, [t]I shall die in my nest, and
I shall multiply *my* days as the sand.

[e]Psa. xxv. 14——[f]Gen. xlix. 11; Deut. xxxii. 13; xxxiii. 24; ch. xx. 17——[g]Psa. lxxxi. 16——[h]Heb. *with me*——[i]Ch. xxi. 5——[k]Heb. *The voice of the nobles was hid*——[l]Psa. cxxxvii. 6——[m]Psa. lxxii. 12; Prov. xxi. 13; xxiv. 11

[n]Deut. xxiv. 13; Psa. cxxxii. 9; Isa. lix. 17; lxi. 10; Ephes. vi. 14, &c.; 1 Thess. v. 8——[o]Num. x. 31 [p]Prov. xxix. 7——[q]Psa. lviii. 6; Prov. xxx. 14——[r]Heb. *the jaw-teeth* or *the grinders*——[s]Heb. *cast*——[t]Psa. xxx. 6

Verse 6. *Washed my steps with butter*] See the note on chap. xx. 17.

Verse 7. *When I went out to the gate*] Courts of justice were held at the gates or entrances of the cities of the East; and Job, being an *emir*, was *supreme magistrate:* and here he speaks of his going to the gate to administer justice.

I prepared my seat in the street] I administered judgment openly, in the most public manner; and none could say that I, in any case, perverted justice. Mr. *Good* translates:—"As I went forth the city rejoiced at me, as I took my seat abroad."

Verse 8. *The young men saw me, and hid themselves*] From all classes of persons I had the most marked respect. The YOUNG, through modesty and bashfulness, shrunk back, and were afraid to meet the eye of their prince; and the AGED *rose from their seats* when I entered the place of judgment. These were the *elders* of the people, who also sat with the judge, and assisted in all legal cases.

Verse 9. *The princes refrained talking*] They never ventured an opinion in opposition to mine; so fully were they persuaded of the justice and integrity of my decision.

Verse 10. *The nobles held their peace*] PRINCES שרים *sarim*, and NOBLES, נגידים *negidim*, must have been *two* different classes of the great men of Idumea. שר *sar*, PRINCE, *director*, or *ruler*, was probably the *head of a township*, or what we would call a *magistrate* of a particular district. נגיד *nagid*, a NOBLE, or one of those who had the privilege of standing *before*, or in the *presence* of, the chief ruler. The participle נגד *neged* is frequently used to signify *before, in the presence of, publicly, openly*. And on this account, it is most likely that the *noun* means one of those nobles or counsellors who were always admitted to the royal presence. Mr. *Good* thinks that *renowned speakers* or *eminent orators* are meant: and others have embraced the same opinion. Job here intimates that his *judgment* was so *sound*, his *decisions* so *accredited*, and his *reasoning power* so *great*, that every person paid him the utmost deference.

Verse 11. *When the ear heard* me] This and the six following verses present us with a fine exhibition of a man full of benevolence and charity, acting up to the highest dictates of those principles, and rendering the miserable of all descriptions happy, by the constant exercise of his unconfined philanthropy.

Verse 12. *Because I delivered the poor that cried*] This appears to be intended as a *refutation* of the charges produced by *Eliphaz*, chap. xxii. 5-10, to confute which Job appeals to *facts*, and to *public testimony*.

Verse 15. *I was eyes to the blind, and feet* was *I to the lame.*] Alluding probably to the difficulty of travelling in the Arabian deserts. *I was eyes to the blind*—those who *did not know the way*, I furnished with *guides. I was feet to the lame*—those who were *worn out*, and *incapable* of walking, I set forward on my *camels*, &c.

Verse 16. *The cause* which *I knew not I searched out.*] When any thing difficult occurred, I did not give it a *slight* consideration; I examined it to the bottom, whatever pain, time, and trouble it cost me, that I might not pronounce a hasty judgment.

Verse 17. *I brake the jaws of the wicked*] A metaphor taken from hunting. A *beast of prey* had entered into the fold, and carried off a *sheep*. "The *huntsman* comes, assails the *wicked* beast, *breaks his jaws*, and *delivers the spoil out of his teeth.* See the case 1 Sam. xvii. 34-37.

Verse 18. *I shall die in my nest*] As I endeavoured to live *soberly* and *temperately, fearing God*, and *departing from evil*, endeavouring *to promote the welfare of all around me*, it was natural for me to conclude that I should live

A. M. cir. 2484 B. C. cir. 1520 Ante I. Olymp. cir. 744 Ante U. C. cir. 767

19 [u]My root *was* [v]spread out
[w]by the waters, and the dew lay
all night upon my branch.
20 My glory *was* [x]fresh in
me, and [y]my bow was [z]renewed in my
hand.
21 Unto me *men* gave ear, and waited, and
kept silence at my counsel.
22 After my words they spake not again;
and my speech dropped upon them.
23 And they waited for me as
for the rain; and they opened
their mouth wide, *as* for [a]the
latter rain.
24 *If* I laughed on them, they believed *it*
not; and the light of my countenance they
cast not down.
25 I chose out their way, and sat chief, and
dwelt as a king in the army, as one *that* comforteth the mourners.

[u]Chap. xviii. 16——[v]Heb. *opened*——[w]Psa. i. 3; Jer. xvii. 8

[x]Heb. *new*——[y]Gen. xlix. 24——[z]Heb. *changed* [a]Zech. x. 1

long, be very prosperous, and see my posterity multiply as the sands on the seashore.

Verse 19. *My root* was *spread out by the waters*] A metaphor taken from a healthy tree growing beside a rivulet where there is plenty of water; which in consequence flourishes in *all seasons;* its leaf does not *wither*, nor its fruit *fall off*. See Psa. i. 3; Jer. xvii. 8.

Verse 20. *My glory* was *fresh in me*] My *vegetative* power was great; my *glory*—my splendid *blossom*, large and *mellow fruit*, was always in season, and in every season.

My bow was renewed] I was never without means to accomplish all my wishes. I had prosperity everywhere.

Verse 21. *Unto me* men *gave ear*] The same idea as in ver. 9-11.

Verse 22. *My speech dropped upon them.*] It descended as *refreshing dew;* they were encouraged, comforted, and strengthened by it.

Verse 23. *They waited for me as for the rain*] The idea continued. They longed as much to hear me speak, to receive my counsel and my decisions, as the thirsty land does for refreshing waters.

They opened their mouth wide] A metaphor taken from ground *chapped* with long drought.

The latter rain.] The rain that falls a little before *harvest*, in order to *fill* and *perfect* the grain. The *former* rain is that which falls about *seed-time*, or in *spring*, in order to impregnate and *swell* the seed, and *moisten* the earth to produce its nourishment.

Verse 24. *I laughed on them, they believed* it *not*] Similar to that expression in the Gospel, Luke xxiv. 41: *And while they believed not for joy, and wondered, he said* ——. Our version is sufficiently perspicuous, and gives the true sense of the original, only it should be read in the *indicative* and not in the *subjunctive* mood: *I laughed on them—they believed it not.* We have a similar phrase: *The news was too good to be true.*

The light of my countenance] This evidence of my benevolence and regard. A *smile* is, metaphorically, *the light of the countenance.*

They cast not down.] They gave me no occasion to change my sentiments or feelings towards them. I could still smile upon them, and they were *then* worthy of my approbation. Their *change* he refers to in the beginning of the next chapter.

Verse 25. *I chose out their way, and sat chief—as a king in the army*] I cannot see, with some learned men, that our version of the original is wrong. I have not seen it mended, and I am sure I cannot improve it. The whole verse seems to me to point out Job in his *civil*, *military*, and *domestic* life.

As *supreme magistrate* he *chose out their way*, adjusted their differences, and *sat chief*, presiding in all their civil assemblies.

As *captain general* he *dwelt as a king in the midst of his troops*, preserving order and discipline, and seeing that his fellow soldiers were provided with requisites for their warfare, and the necessaries of life.

As a *man* he did not think himself superior to the meanest offices in domestic life, to relieve or support his fellow creatures; he went about *comforting the mourners*—visiting the sick and afflicted, and ministering to their wants, and seeing that the *wounded* were properly attended. Noble Job! Look at him, ye *nobles* of the earth, ye lieutenants of counties, ye generals of armies, and ye lords of provinces. Look at JOB! Imitate his active benevolence, and be healthy and happy. Be as guardian angels in your particular districts, blessing all by your example and your bounty. Send your *hunting horses* to the plough, your *game cocks* to the *dunghill;* and at last live like *men* and *Christians.*

CHAPTER XXX

Job proceeds to lament the change of his former condition, and the contempt into which his adversity had brought him, 1–15. *Pathetically describes the afflictions of his body and mind,* 16–31.

A. M. cir. 2484
B. C. cir. 1520
Ante I. Olymp. cir. 744
Ante U. C. cir. 767

BUT now *they that are*
[a]younger than I have me in
derision, whose fathers I would
have disdained to have set with
the dogs of my flock.
2 Yea, whereto *might* the [b]strength of their
hands *profit* me, in whom old age was
perished?
3 For want and famine *they*
were [c]solitary; fleeing into the
wilderness [d]in former time desolate and waste;
4 Who cut up mallows by the bushes, and
juniper roots *for* their meat.
5 They were driven forth from among *men*,
(they cried after them as *after* a thief;)

[a]Heb. *of fewer days than I*——[b]Chap. xii. 21

[c]Or, *dark as the night*——[d]Heb. *yesternight*

NOTES ON CHAP. XXX

Verse 1. *But now* they that are *younger than I have me in derision*] Compare this with chap. xxix. 8, where he speaks of the respect he had from the youth while in the days of his prosperity. Now he is no longer affluent, and they are no longer respectful.

Dogs of my flock.] Persons who were not deemed sufficiently respectable to be trusted with the care of those dogs which were the guardians of my flocks. Not confidential enough to be made shepherds, ass-keepers, or camel-drivers; nor even to have the care of the dogs by which the flocks were guarded. This saying is what we call an expression of *sovereign contempt*.

Verse 2. *The strength of their hands* profit *me*] He is speaking here of the fathers of these young men. What was the strength of their hands to me? Their old age also has perished. The sense of which I believe to be this: I have never esteemed their strength even in their most vigorous youth, nor their conduct nor their counsel even in old age. They were never good for any thing, either young or old. As their youth was without profit, so their old age was without honour. See *Calmet*.

Mr. *Good* contends that the words are Arabic, and should be translated according to the meaning in that language, and the first clause of the third verse joined to the latter clause of the second, without which no good meaning can be elicited so as to keep properly close to the letter. I shall give the Hebrew text, Mr. *Good's* Arabic, and its translation:—

The Hebrew text is this:—

עלימו אבד כלח
aleymo abad calach
בחסר ובכפן גלמוד:
becheser ubechaphan galmud

The Arabic version this:—

عليهم ابدا كلاح
بحصر و جوع جلمود ۞

Which he translates thus:—

"With whom crabbed looks are perpetual,
From hunger and flinty famine."

This translation is very little distant from the import of the present Hebrew text, if it may be called *Hebrew*, when the principal words are pure Arabic, and the others constructively so.

Verse 3. *Fleeing into the wilderness*] Seeking something to sustain life even in the barren desert. This shows the extreme of want, when the desert is supposed to be the only place where any thing to sustain life can possibly be found.

Verse 4. *Who cut up mallows by the bushes*] מלוח *malluach*, which we translate *mallows*, comes from מלח *melach, salt;* some herb or shrub of a salt nature, sea-purslane, or the salsaria, salsola, or saltwort. *Bochart* says it is the ἅλιμος of the Greeks, and the *halimus* of the Romans. Some translate it *nettles*. The *Syriac* and *Arabic* omit the whole verse. The halimus, or *atriplex halimus*, grows near the sea in different countries, and is found in Spain, America, England, and Barbary. The *salsaria*, *salsola*, or *saltwort*, is an extensive genus of plants, several common to Asia, and not a few indigenous to a dry and sandy soil.

And juniper roots for *their meat.*] רתמים *rethamim*. This is variously translated *juniper*, *broom*, *furze*, *gorse*, or *whin*. It is supposed to derive its name from the *toughness* of its twigs, as רתם *ratham* signifies to *bind;* and this answers well enough to the *broom*. *Genista quoque vinculi usum præstat*, "The broom serves for bands," says PLINY, *Hist. Nat.* lib. xxiv., c. 9. But how can it be said that the roots of this shrub were eaten? I do not find any evidence from Asiatic writers that the roots of the juniper tree were an article of food; and some have supposed, because of this want of evidence, that the word לחמם *lachmam, for their bread*, should be understood thus, *to bake their bread*, because it is well known that the wood of the juniper gives an intense heat, and the coals of it endure a long time; and therefore we find *coals of juniper*, גחלי רתמים *gachaley rethamim*, used Psa. cxx. 4 to express severe and enduring punishment. But that the roots of the juniper were used for food in the *northern countries*, among the *Goths*, we have a positive testimony from Olaus Magnus, himself a Goth, and archbishop of Upsal, in lib. vii., c. 4, of his *Hist. de Gentibus Septentrionalibus*. Speaking of the great number of different trees in their woods, he says: "There is a great plenty of beech trees in all the northern parts, the virtue whereof is this: that, being cut between the bark and the wood, they send forth a juice that is good for drink. The fruit of them in famine serves for *bread*, and their bark for clothing. Likewise also the berries of the juniper, yea, even the roots of this tree are eaten for bread, as holy Job testifies, though it is difficult to come at them by reason of their prickles: in these prickles, or thorns, live coals will last a whole year. If the inhabitants do not quench them, when winds arise they set the woods on fire, and destroy all the circumjacent fields." In this account both the properties of the juniper tree, referred to by Job and David, are mentioned by the Gothic prelate. They use its berries and roots for *food*, and its wood for *fire*.

Verse 5. *They were driven forth*] They

A. M. cir. 2484
B. C. cir. 1520
Ante I. Olymp. cir. 744
Ante U. C. cir. 767

6 To dwell in the cliffs of the
valleys, *in* [e]caves of the earth,
and *in* the rocks.
7 Among the bushes they
brayed; under the nettles they were gathered
together.
8 *They were* children of fools, yea, children
of [f]base men: they were viler than the
earth.
9 [g]And now am I their song, yea, I am their
by-word.
10 They abhor me, they flee far from me,
[h]and spare not [i]to spit in my face.
11 Because he [k]hath loosed my cord, and
afflicted me, they have also let
loose the bridle before me.
12 Upon *my* right *hand* rise the
youth: they push away my feet,
and [l]they raise up against me the ways of their
destruction.
13 They mar my path, they set forward my
calamity, they have no helper.
14 They came *upon me* as a wide breaking
in *of waters:* in the desolation they rolled
themselves *upon me.*
15 Terrors are turned upon me: they pursue [m]my soul as the wind; and my welfare
passeth away as a cloud.

[e]Heb. *holes*——[f]Heb. *men of no name*——[g]Chap. xvii. 6; Psa. xxxv. 15; lxix. 12; Lam. iii. 14, 63——[h]Heb. *and withhold not spittle from my face*

[i]Num. xii. 14; Deut. xxv. 9; Isa. l. 6; Matt. xxvi. 67; xxvii. 30——[k]See chap. xii. 18——[l]Chap. xix. 12
[m]Heb. *my principal*

were persons whom no one would employ; they were driven away from the city; and if any of them appeared, the hue and cry was immediately raised up against them. The last clause Mr. *Good* translates, "They slunk away from them like a thief," instead of "They cried after them," &c.

Verse 6. *To dwell in the cliffs of the valleys*] They were obliged to take shelter in the most dangerous, out-of-the-way, and unfrequented places. This is the meaning.

Verse 7. *Among the bushes they brayed*] They cried out among the bushes, seeking for food, as the wild ass when he is in want of provender. Two MSS. read ינאקו *yinaku, they groaned,* instead of ינהקו *yinhaku, they brayed.*

Under the nettles] חרול *charul,* the *briers* or *brambles,* under the brushwood in the thickest parts of the underwood; they huddled together like wild beasts.

Verse 8. *Children of fools*] *Children of nabal; children without a name;* persons of no consideration, and descendants of such.

Viler than the earth.] Rather, *driven out of the land;* persons not fit for civil society.

Verse 9. *Now am I their song*] I am the subject of their mirth, and serve as a proverb or by-word. They use me with every species of indignity.

Verse 10. *They abhor me*] What a state must civil society be in when such indignities were permitted to be offered to the aged and afflicted!

Verse 11. *Because he hath loosed my cord*] Instead of יתרי *yithri, my cord,* which is the keri or marginal reading, יתרו *yithro, his cord,* is the reading of the text in many copies; and this reading directs us to a metaphor taken from an archer, who, observing his butt, sets his arrow on the string, draws it to a proper degree of tension, levels, and then loosing his hold, the arrow flies at the mark. He hath let loose his arrow against me; it has hit me; and I am wounded. The *Vulgate* understood it in this way: *Pharetram enim suam aperuit.* So also the *Septuagint:* Ανοιξας γαρ φαρετραν αυτου; "He hath opened his quiver."

They have also let loose the bridle] When they perceived that God had afflicted me, they then threw off all restraints; like headstrong horses, *swallowed the bit,* got the *reins on their own neck,* and *ran off at full speed.*

Verse 12. *Upon* my *right* hand *rise the youth*] The word פרחח *pirchach,* which we translate *youth,* signifies properly *buds,* or the *buttons* of *trees.* Mr. *Good* has *younglings. Younkers* would be better, were it not too colloquial.

They push away my feet] They trip up my heels, or they in effect trample me under their feet. They rush upon and overwhelm me. They are violently incensed against me. They roll themselves upon me, התגלגלו *hithgalgalu, velut unda impellit undam,* as waves of the sea which wash the sand from under the feet, and then swamp the man to the bottom; see verse 14.

Verse 13. *They mar my path*] They destroy the *way-marks,* so that there is no safety in travelling through the deserts, the *guide-posts* and *way-marks* being gone.

These may be an allusion here to a besieged city: the besiegers strive by every means and way to distress the besieged; *stopping up the fountains, breaking up the road, raising up towers* to project arrows and stones into the city, called here *raising up against it the ways of destruction,* verse 12; preventing all succour and support.

They have no helper.] "There is not an adviser among them."—Mr. *Good.* There is none to give them better instruction.

Verse 14. *They came* upon me *as a wide breaking in*] They *storm* me on every side.

In the desolation they rolled themselves] When they had made the *breach,* they *rolled in* upon me as an *irresistible torrent.* There still appears to be an allusion to a besieged city: the *sap,* the *breach,* the *storm,* the *flight,* the *pursuit,* and the *slaughter.* See the following verse.

Verse 15. *Terrors are turned upon me*] Defence is no longer useful; they have beat down my walls.

They pursue my soul as the wind] I seek safety in flight, my strong holds being no longer tenable; but they pursue me so swiftly, that it

A. M. cir. 2484
B. C. cir. 1520
Ante I. Olymp. cir. 744
Ante U. C. cir. 767

16 [n]And now my soul is poured
out upon me; the days of affliction have taken hold upon me.
17 My bones are pierced in me
in the night season: and my sinews take no
rest.
18 By the great force *of my disease* is my
garment changed: it bindeth me about as the
collar of my coat.
19 He hath cast me into the mire, and I am
become like dust and ashes.
20 I cry unto thee, and thou dost not hear
me: I stand up, and thou regardest me *not*.
21 Thou art [o]become cruel to me: with
[p]thy strong hand thou opposest
thyself against me.
22 Thou liftest me up to the
wind; thou causest me to ride
upon it, and dissolvest my [q]substance.
23 For I know *that* thou wilt bring me *to*
death and *to* the house [r]appointed for all living.
24 Howbeit he will not stretch out *his* hand
to the [s]grave, though they cry in his destruction.
25 [t]Did not I weep [u]for him that was in
trouble? was *not* my soul grieved for the poor?
26 [v]When I looked for good, then evil came
unto me: and when I waited for light, there
came darkness.

A. M. cir. 2484
B. C. cir. 1520
Ante I. Olymp. cir. 744
Ante U. C. cir. 767

[n]Psa. xlii. 4——[o]Heb. *turned to be cruel*——[p]Heb. *the strength of thy hand*——[q]Or, *wisdom*——[r]Heb. ix. 27

[s]Hebrew, *heap*——[t]Psalm xxxv. 13, 14; Rom. xii. 15——[u]Heb. *for him that was hard of day*——[v]Jer. viii. 15

is impossible for me to escape. They follow me like a *whirlwind;* and as *fast* as that drives away the *clouds* before it, so is my prosperity destroyed. The word נדבתי *nedibathi*, which we translate *my soul*, signifies properly *my nobility, my excellence:* they endeavour to destroy both *my reputation* and *my property.*

Verse 18. *Is my garment changed*] There seem to be here plain allusions to the effect of his cruel disease; the whole body being enveloped with a kind of elephantine hide, formed by innumerable incrustations from the ulcerated surface.

It bindeth me about] There is now a new kind of covering to my body, formed by the effects of this disease; and it is not a garment which I can cast off; it is as closely attached to me as the collar of my coat. Or, my disease seizes me as a strong armed man; it *has throttled me, and cast me in the mud.* This is probably an allusion to two persons struggling: the stronger seizes the other by the throat, brings him down, and treads him in the dirt.

Verse 20. *I cry unto thee*] I am persecuted by man, afflicted with sore disease, and apparently forsaken of God.

I stand up] Or, as some translate, "*I persevere*, and thou lookest upon me." Thou seest my desolate, afflicted state; but thine eye doth not affect thy heart. Thou leavest me unsupported to struggle with my adversities.

Verse 21. *Thou art become cruel to me*] Thou appearest to treat me with cruelty. I cry for mercy, trust in thy goodness, and am still permitted to remain under my afflictions.

Thou opposest thyself] Instead of *helping*, thou opposest me; thou appearest as my *enemy.*

Verse 22. *Thou liftest me up to the wind*] Thou hast so completely stripped me of all my substance, that I am like *chaff* lifted up by the wind; or as a *straw*, the sport of every breeze; and at last carried totally away, being *dissipated* into particles by the continued agitation.

Verse 23. *Thou wilt bring me* to *death*] This must be the issue of my present affliction: to God alone it is possible that I should survive it.

To *the house appointed for all living.*] Or to the house, מועד *moed*, the *rendezvous*, the place of general assembly of human beings: the great devourer in whose jaws all that have lived, now live, and shall live, must necessarily meet.

"————O great man-eater!
Whose every day is carnival; not sated yet!
Unheard of epicure! without a fellow!
The veriest gluttons do not always cram!
Some intervals of abstinence are sought
To edge the appetite: thou seekest none.
Methinks the countless swarms thou hast devour'd,
And thousands that each hour thou gobblest up,
This, less than this, might gorge thee to the full.
But O! rapacious still, thou gap'st for more,
Like one, whole days defrauded of his meals,
On whom lank hunger lays her skinny hand,
And whets to keenest eagerness his cravings;
As if diseases, massacres, and poisons,
Famine, and war, were not thy caterers."

THE GRAVE.

Verse 24. *He will not stretch out* his *hand to the grave*] After all that has been said relative to the just *translation* and true *meaning* of this verse, is it not evident that it is in the mouth of Job a *consolatory* reflection? As if he said, Though I suffer *here*, I shall not suffer *hereafter*. Though he add stroke to stroke, so as to destroy my life, yet his displeasure shall not proceed beyond the grave.

Though they cry in his destruction.] Mr. *Good* translates: *Surely there, in its ruin, is freedom.* In the *sepulchre* there is *freedom* from calamity, and rest for the weary.

Verse 25. *Did not I weep for him that was in trouble?*] Mr. *Good* translates much nearer the sense of the original, לקשה יום *liksheh yom.* "Should I not then weep for the *ruthless day?*" May I not lament that my sufferings are only to terminate with my life? Or, Did I not mourn for those who *suffered* by *times of calamity?*

Was not *my soul grieved for the poor?* Did I not relieve the distressed according to my power; and did I not sympathize with the sufferer?

A. M. cir. 2484
B. C. cir. 1520
Ante I. Olymp. cir. 744
Ante U. C. cir. 767

27 My bowels boiled, and rested
not: the days of affliction prevented me.
28 [w]I went mourning without
the sun: I stood up, *and* I cried in the congregation.
29 [x]I am a brother to dragons,
and a companion to [y]owls.
30 [z]My skin is black upon me, and
[a]my bones are burned with heat.
31 My harp also is *turned* to mourning, and
my organ into the voice of them that weep.

[w]Psa. xxxviii. 6; xlii. 9; xliii. 2——[x]Psa. cii. 6; Mic. i. 8

[y]Or, *ostriches*——[z]Psa. cxix. 83; Lam. iv. 8; v. 10
[a]Psa. cii. 3

Verse 27. *My bowels boiled*] This alludes to the strong commotion in the bowels which every humane person feels at the sight of one in misery.

Verse 28. *I went mourning without the sun*] חמה *chammah*, which we here translate *the sun*, comes from a root of the same letters, which signifies to hide, protect, &c., and may be translated, *I went mourning without a protector* or *guardian;* or, the word may be derived from חם *cham*, to be *hot*, and here it may signify fury, rage, anger; and thus it was understood by the *Vulgate: Mœrens incedebam, sine furore*, I went mourning without anger; or, as *Calmet* translates, *Je marchois tout triste, mais sans me laisser aller a l'emportement;* "I walked in deep sadness, but did not give way to an angry spirit." The *Syriac* and *Arabic* understood it in the same way.

Verse 29. *I am a brother to dragons*] By my mournful and continual cry I resemble תנים *tannim*, the *jackals* or *hyenas.*

And a companion to owls.] בנות יענה *benoth yaanah*, to the *daughters of howling:* generally understood to be the *ostrich;* for both the *jackal* and the *female ostrich* are remarkable for their mournful cry, and for their attachment to desolate places.—*Dodd.*

Verse 30. *My skin is black*] By continual exposure to the open air, and parching influence of the sun.

My bones are burned with heat.] A strong expression, to point out the raging fever that was continually preying upon his vitals.

Verse 31. *My harp also is* turned *to mourning*] Instead of the *harp*, my only music is my own *plaintive cries.*

And my organ] What the עגב *uggab* was, we know not; it was most probably some sort of *pipe* or *wind instrument.* His *harp*, כנור *kinnor*, and his *pipe*, עגב *uggab*, were equally mute, or only used for mournful ditties.

This chapter is full of the most painful and pathetic sorrow; but nevertheless tempered with a calmness and humiliation of spirit, which did not appear in Job's lamentations previously to the time in which he had that remarkable revelation mentioned in the nineteenth chapter. After he was assured that his *Redeemer was the living God*, he submitted to his dispensations, kissed the rod, and mourned not without hope, though in deep distress, occasioned by his unremitting sufferings. If the groaning of Job was great, his stroke was certainly heavy.

CHAPTER XXXI

Job makes a solemn protestation of his chastity and integrity, 1–12; *of his humanity,* 13–16; *of his charity and mercy,* 17–23; *of his abhorrence of covetousness and idolatry,* 24–32; *and of his readiness to acknowledge his errors,* 33, 34; *and wishes for a full investigation of his case, being confident that this would issue in the full manifestation of his innocence,* 36–40.

A. M. cir. 2484
B. C. cir. 1520
Ante I. Olymp. cir. 744
Ante U. C. cir. 767

I MADE a covenant with mine
[a]eyes; why then should I
think upon a maid?
2 For what [b]portion of God
is there from above? and *what*
inheritance of the Almighty
from on high?
3 *Is* not destruction to the

[a]Matt. v. 28

[b]Chap. xx. 29; xxvii. 13

NOTES ON CHAP. XXXI

Verse 1. *I made a covenant with mine eyes*] ברית כרתי לעיני *berith carati leeynai:* "I have cut" or divided "the covenant sacrifice with my eyes." My conscience and my eyes are the contracting parties; God is the Judge; and I am therefore bound not to look upon any thing with a delighted or covetous eye, by which my conscience may be defiled, or my God dishonoured.

Why then should I think upon a maid?] ומה אתבונן על בתולה *umah ethbonen al bethulah. And why should I set myself to contemplate*, or *think upon, Bethulah?* That *Bethulah* may here signify an *idol*, is very likely. *Sanchoniatho* observes, that *Ouranos* first introduced *Baithulia* when he erected *animated stones*, or rather, as *Bochart* observes, ANOINTED *stones*, which became representatives of some deity. I suppose that Job purges himself here from this species of idolatry. Probably the *Baithulia* were at first emblems only of the *tabernacle;* בית אלוה *beith Eloah*, "the house

A. M. cir. 2484
B. C. cir. 1520
Ante I. Olymp. cir. 744
Ante U. C. cir. 767

wicked? and a strange *punish-*
ment to the workers of iniquity?
4 [c]Doth not he see my ways,
and count all my steps?
5 If I have walked with vanity, or if my
foot hath hasted to deceit;
6 [d]Let me be weighed in an even balance,
that God may know mine integrity.
7 If my step hath turned out of the way,
and [e]mine heart walked after mine eyes, and
if any blot hath cleaved to mine hands;
8 *Then* [f]let me sow, and let another eat;
yea, let my offspring be rooted out.
9 If mine heart have been deceived by a
woman, or *if* I have laid wait at
my neighbour's door;
10 *Then* let my wife grind
unto [g]another, and let others bow
down upon her.
11 For this *is* a heinous crime; yea, [h]it
is an iniquity *to be punished by* the judges.
12 For it *is* a fire *that* consumeth to destruction, and would root out all mine increase.
13 If I did despise the cause of my man
servant or of my maid-servant, when they contended with me;
14 What then shall I do when [i]God riseth up?
and when he visiteth, what shall I answer him?

[c]2 Chron. xvi. 9; chap. xxxiv. 21; Prov. v. 21; xv. 3; Jer. xxxii. 19——[d]Heb. *Let him weigh me in balances of justice*——[e]See Num. xv. 39; Eccles. xi. 9; Ezek. vi. 9; Matt. v. 29

[f]Lev. xxvi. 16; Deut. xxviii. 30, 38, &c.; Mic. vi. 15——[g]2 Sam. xii. 11; Jer. viii. 10; Amos vii. 17——[h]Gen. xxxviii. 24; Lev. xx. 10; Deut. xxii. 22; see ver. 28——[i]Psa. xliv. 21

of God;" or of that *pillar* set up by Jacob, Gen. xxviii. 18, which he called בית אלהים *beith Elohim*, or *Bethalim;* for idolatry always supposes a pure and holy worship, of which it is the counterfeit. For more on the subject of the *Baithulia*, see the notes on Gen. xxviii.

Verse 2. *For what portion of God* is there *from above?*] Though I have not, in this or in any other respect, wickedly departed from God, yet what reward have I received?

Verse 3. Is *not destruction to the wicked?*] If I had been guilty of such secret hypocritical proceedings, professing faith in the *true God* while in *eye* and *heart* an *idolater*, would not such a worker of iniquity be distinguished by a *strange* and unheard-of punishment?

Verse 4. *Doth not he see my ways*] Can I suppose that I could screen myself from the eye of God while guilty of such iniquities?

Verse 5. *If I have walked with vanity*] If I have been guilty of *idolatry*, or the worshipping of a *false god:* for thus שוא *shav*, which we here translate *vanity*, is used Jer. xviii. 15; (compare with Psa. xxxi. 6; Hos. xii. 11; and Jonah ii. 9;) and it seems evident that the whole of Job's discourse here is a vindication of himself from all idolatrous dispositions and practices.

Verse 6. *Mine integrity.*] תמתי *tummathi*, my perfection; the totality of my unblameable life.

Verse 7. *If my step hath turned out of the way*] I am willing to be sifted to the uttermost—for every *step* of my *foot*, for every *thought* of my *heart*, for every *look* of mine *eye*, and for every *act* of my *hands*.

Verse 8. *Let me sow, and let another eat*] Let me be plagued both in my circumstances and in my family.

My offspring be rooted out.] It has already appeared probable that *all* Job's children were not destroyed in the fall of the house mentioned chap. i. 18, 19.

Verse 9. *If mine heart have been deceived by a woman*] The Septuagint add, ανδρος ἑτερου, *another man's wife.*

Verse 10. *Let my wife grind unto another*] Let her work at the *handmill*, grinding corn; which was the *severe* work of the meanest *slave.* In this sense the passage is understood both by the *Syriac* and *Arabic.* See Exod. xi. 5, and Isa. xlvii. 2; and see at the end of the chapter.

And let others bow down upon her.] Let her be in such a state as to have no command of her own person; her owner disposing of her person as he pleases. In Asiatic countries, slaves were considered so absolutely the property of their owners, that they not only served themselves of them in the way of scortation and concubinage, but they were accustomed to accommodate their guests with them! Job is so conscious of his own innocence, that he is willing it should be put to the utmost proof; and if found guilty, that he may be exposed to the most distressing and humiliating punishment; even to that of being deprived of his goods, bereaved of his children, his wife made a *slave*, and subjected to all indignities in that state.

Verse 11. *For this* is *a heinous crime*] Mr. *Good* translates,

"For this would be a premeditated crime,
And a profligacy of the understanding."

See also ver. 28.

That is, It would not only be a sin against the *individuals* more particularly concerned, but a sin of the first magnitude against *society;* and one of which the *civil magistrate* should take particular cognizance, and punish as justice requires.

Verse 12. *For it* is *a fire*] Nothing is so destructive of domestic peace. Where *jealousy* exists, unmixed misery dwells; and the adulterer and fornicator *waste their substance* on the unlawful objects of their impure affections.

Verse 13. *The cause of my man-servant*] In ancient times *slaves* had no action at law against their owners; they might dispose of them as they did of their cattle, or any other property. The slave might complain; and the owner might hear him if he pleased, but he was not compelled to do so. Job states that he had admitted them to all civil rights; and, far from preventing their case from being heard, he was ready to permit them to complain even against *himself*, if they had a cause of complaint, and to give them all the benefit of the law.

A. M. cir. 2484 B. C. cir. 1520 Ante I. Olymp. cir. 744 Ante U. C. cir. 767

15 [k]Did not he that made me
in the womb make him? and
[l]did not one fashion us in the
womb?
16 If I have withheld the poor from their
desire, or have caused the eyes of the widow
to fail;
17 Or have eaten my morsel myself alone,
and the fatherless hath not eaten thereof;
18 (For from my youth he was brought up
with me, as *with* a father, and I
have guided [m]her from my mother's womb;)
19 [n]If I have seen any perish
for want of clothing, or any poor without
covering;
20 If his loins have not [o]blessed me, and *if* he
were *not* warmed with the fleece of my sheep;
21 If I have lifted up my hand [p]against the
fatherless, when I saw my help in the gate:

[k]Chap. xxxiv. 19; Prov. xiv. 31; xxii. 2; Mal. ii. 10——[l]Or, *did he not fashion us in one womb?*

[m]That is, *the widow*——[n]Ezek. xviii. 7, 16; Matt. xxv. 36——[o]See Deut. xxiv. 13——[p]Chap. xxii. 9

Verse 15. *Did not he that made me—make him?*] I know that God is the Judge of all; that all shall appear before him in that state where the king and his subject, the master and his slave, shall be on an equal footing, all civil distinctions being abolished for ever. If, then, I had treated my slaves with injustice, how could I stand before the judgment-seat of God? I have treated others as I wish to be treated.

Verse 17. *Or have eaten my morsel myself alone*] *Hospitality* was a very prominent virtue among the ancients in almost all nations: friends and strangers were equally welcome to the board of the affluent. The supper was their grand meal: it was then that they saw their friends; the business and fatigues of the day being over, they could then enjoy themselves comfortably together. The *supper* was called *cœna* on this account; or, as *Plutarch* says, Το μεν γαρ δειπνον φασι κοινα δια την κοινωνιαν καλεισθαι· καθ' ἑαυτους γαρ ηριστων επιεικως οἱ παλαι Ῥωμαιοι, συνδειπνουντες τοις φιλοις. "The ancient Romans named *supper* CŒNA, (κοινα,) which signifies *communion* (κοινωνια) or *fellowship;* for, although they *dined alone,* they *supped with their friends.*"—PLUT. *Symp.* lib. viii., prob. 6, p. 687. But Job speaks here of dividing his bread with the hungry: *Or have eaten my morsel myself alone.* And he is a poor despicable caitiff who would eat it alone, while there was another at hand full as hungry as himself.

Verse 18. This is a very difficult verse, and is variously translated. Take the following instances:—For from his youth *he* (the male orphan) was brought up with me as a father. Yea, I have guided *her* (the female orphan) from her mother's womb.—*Heath.*

Nam a pueris educavit me commiseratio; jam inde ab utero matris meæ illa me deduxit. —*Houbigant.*

"For commiseration educated me from my childhood;
And she brought me up even from my mother's womb."

This is agreeable to the *Vulgate.*

"Behold, from my youth calamity hath quickened me;
Even from my mother's womb have I distributed it."

This is Mr. *Good's* version, and is widely different from the above.

For mercy grewe up with me fro my youth,
And compassion fro my mother's wombe.
Coverdale.

Ὁτι εκ νεοτητος μου εξετρεφον ὡς πατηρ, και εκ γαστρος μητρος μου ὡδηγησα.—*Septuagint.* "For from my youth I nourished them as a father; and I was their guide from my mother's womb."

The *Syriac.*—"For from my childhood he educated me in distresses, and from the womb of my mother in groans." The *Arabic* is nearly the same.

The general meaning may be gathered from the above; but who can reconcile such discordant translations?

Verse 20. *If his loins have not blessed me*] This is a very delicate touch: the part that was *cold* and *shivering* is now covered with *warm woollen.* It *feels* the comfort; and by a fine *prosopopœia,* is represented as blessing him who furnished the clothing.

Verse 21. *If I have lifted up my hand against the fatherless*] I have at no time opposed the orphan, nor given, in behalf of the rich and powerful, a decision against the poor, *when I saw my help in the gate*—when I was sitting chief on the throne of judgment, and could have done it without being called to account.

There are sentiments very like these in the poem of *Lebeid,* one of the authors of the *Moallakhat.* I shall quote several verses from the elegant translation of Sir William Jones, in which the character of a charitable and bountiful chief is well described:—

"Oft have I invited a numerous company to the death of a camel bought for slaughter, to be divided with arrows of equal dimensions."

"I invite them to draw lots for a camel without a foal, and for a camel with her young one, whose flesh I distribute to all the neighbours."

"The guest and the stranger admitted to my board seem to have alighted in the sweet vale of *Tebaala,* luxuriant with vernal blossoms."

"The cords of my tent approaches every needy matron, worn with fatigue, like a camel doomed to die at her master's tomb, whose vesture is both scanty and ragged."

"There they crown with meat (while the wintry winds contend with fierce blasts) a dish flowing like a rivulet, into which the famished orphans eagerly plunge."

"He distributes equal shares, he dispenses justice to the tribes, he is indignant when their right is diminished; and, to establish their right, often relinquishes his own."

"He acts with greatness of mind, and nobleness of heart; he sheds the dew of his liberality

A. M. cir. 2484 B. C. cir. 1520 Ante I. Olymp. cir. 744 Ante U. C. cir. 767

22 *Then* let mine arm fall from
my shoulder blade, and mine arm
be broken from [q]the bone.
23 For [r]destruction *from* God
was a terror to me, and by reason of his highness I could not endure.
24 [s]If I have made gold my hope, or have
said to the fine gold, *Thou art* my confidence;
25 [t]If I rejoiced because my wealth *was*
great, and because mine hand had [u]gotten
much;
26 [v]If I beheld [w]the sun when it shined,
or the moon walking [x]*in* brightness;
27 And my heart hath been secretly enticed,
or [y]my mouth hath kissed my hand:
28 This also *were* [z]an iniquity
to be punished by the judge: for
I should have denied the God
that is above.
29 [a]If I rejoiced at the destruction of him
that hated me, or lifted up myself when evil
found him;
30 ([b]Neither have I suffered [c]my mouth to
sin, by wishing a curse to his soul;)
31 If the men of my tabernacle said not, O that
we had of his flesh! we cannot be satisfied.
32 [d]The stranger did not lodge in the street:
but I opened my doors [e]to the traveller.
33 If I covered my transgressions [f]as
[g]Adam, by hiding mine iniquity in my bosom:

[q]Or, *the chanelbone*——[r]Isaiah xiii. 6; Joel i. 15
[s]Mark x. 24; 1 Tim. vi. 17——[t]Psa. lxii. 10; Prov. xi. 28
[u]Heb. *found much*——[v]Deut. iv. 19; xi. 16; xvii. 3; Ezek. viii. 16——[w]Heb. *the light*——[x]Heb. *bright*
[y]Heb. *my hand hath kissed my mouth*

[z]Ver. 11——[a]Prov. xvii. 5——[b]Matt. v. 44; Rom. xii. 14——[c]Heb. *my palate*——[d]Gen. xix. 2, 3; Judg. xix. 20, 21; Rom. xii. 13; Heb. xiii. 2; 1 Pet. iv. 9
[e]Or, *to the way*——[f]Or, *after the manner of men*
[g]Gen. iii. 8, 12; Prov. xxviii. 13; Hos. vi. 7

on those who need his assistance; he scatters around his own gains and precious spoils, the prizes of his valour."—Ver. 73-80.

Verse 22. *Let mine arm fall*] Mr. *Good*, as a medical man, is at home in the translation of this verse:—

"May my shoulder-bone be shivered at the blade,
And mine arm be broken off at the socket."

Let judgment fall particularly on those parts which have either done wrong, or refused to do right when in their power.

Verse 23. *Destruction* from *God* was *a terror*] I have ever been preserved from outward sin, through the fear of God's judgments; I knew his eye was constantly upon me, and I could

"Never in my Judge's eye my Judge's anger dare."

Verse 24. *Gold my hope*] For the meaning of זהב *zahab*, polished gold, and כתם *kethem*, stamped gold, see on chap. xxviii. 15-17.

Verse 26. *If I beheld the sun when it shined*] In this verse Job clears himself of that idolatrous worship which was the most ancient and most consistent with reason of any species of idolatry; viz., *Sabœism*, the worship of the heavenly bodies; particularly the *sun* and *moon, Jupiter* and *Venus;* the two latter being the *morning* and *evening stars*, and the most resplendent of all the heavenly bodies, the sun and moon excepted.

"Job," says *Calmet*, "points out three things here:

"1. The worship of the sun and moon; much used in his time, and very anciently used in every part of the East; and in all probability that from which idolatry took its rise.

"2. The custom of adoring the sun at its rising, and the moon at her change; a superstition which is mentioned in Ezek. viii. 16, and in every part of profane antiquity.

"3. The custom of *kissing the hand;* the form of adoration, and token of sovereign respect."

Adoration, or the religious act of *kissing the hand*, comes to us from the Latin; *ad*, to, and *os, oris*, the mouth. The hand lifted to the mouth, and there saluted by the lips.

Verse 28. *For I should have denied the God* that is *above.*] Had I paid Divine adoration to them, I should have thereby denied the God that made them.

Verse 29. *If I rejoiced*] I did not avenge myself on my enemy; and I neither bore malice nor hatred to him.

Verse 30. *Neither have I suffered my mouth to sin*] I have neither *spoken evil* of him, nor *wished evil* to him. How few of those called *Christians* can speak thus concerning their *enemies;* or those who have done them any mischief!

Verse 31. *If the men of my tabernacle said*] I believe the *Targum* gives the best sense here:—"If the men of my tabernacle have not said, Who hath commanded that we should not be satisfied with his flesh?" My domestics have had all kindness shown them; they have lived like my own children, and have been served with the *same viands* as my family. They have never seen *flesh* come to my table, when they have been obliged to live on *pulse.*

Mr. *Good's* translation is nearly to the same sense:—

"If the men of my tabernacle do not exclaim,
Who hath longed for his meat without fulness?"

"Where is the man that has not been satisfied with his flesh?" i. e., fed to the full with the provisions from his table. See Prov. xxiii. 20; Isa. xxiii. 13, and Dan. x. 3.

Verse 32. *The stranger did not lodge in the street*] My kindness did not extend merely to my family, domestics, and friends; the *stranger* —he who was to me perfectly unknown, and the *traveller*—he who was on his journey to some other district, found my doors ever open to receive them, and were refreshed with my *bed* and my *board.*

Verse 33. *If I covered my transgressions as*

A. M. cir. 2484 B. C. cir. 1520 Ante I. Olymp. cir. 744 Ante U. C. cir. 767

34 Did I fear a great [h]multitude, or did the contempt of families terrify me, that I kept silence, *and* went not out of the door?

35 [i]O that one would hear me! [k]behold, my desire *is*, [l]*that* the Almighty would answer me, and *that* mine adversary had written a book:

36 Surely I would take it upon my shoulder, *and* bind it *as* a crown to me.

37 I would declare unto him the number of my steps; as a prince would I go near unto him.

[h]Exod. xxiii. 2——[i]Ch. xxxiii. 6——[k]Or, *behold my sign is that the Almighty will answer me*——[l]Chap. xiii. 22

Adam] Here is a most evident allusion to the *fall.* Adam *transgressed* the commandment of his Maker, and he endeavoured to *conceal* it; *first*, by *hiding himself* among the trees of the garden: "I heard thy voice, and went and HID myself;" *secondly*, by laying the *blame* on his *wife:* "The woman gave me, and I did eat;" and *thirdly*, by *charging* the whole directly on *God* himself: "The woman which THOU GAVEST ME to be with me, SHE gave me of the tree, and I did eat." And it is very likely that Job refers immediately to the Mosaic account in the Book of *Genesis.* The spirit of this saying is this: When I have departed at any time from the path of rectitude, I have been ready to *acknowledge* my error, and have not sought excuses or palliatives for my sin.

Verse 34. *Did I fear a great multitude*] Was I ever prevented by the voice of the *many* from decreeing and executing what was right? When many *families* or *tribes* espoused a particular cause, which I found, on examination, to be wrong, did they *put me in fear*, so as to prevent me from doing justice to the weak and friendless? Or, in any of these cases, was I ever, *through fear*, self-seeking, or favour, prevented from declaring my mind, or constrained to keep my house, lest I should be obliged to give judgment against my conscience? Mr. *Good* thinks it an imprecation upon himself, if he had done any of the evils which he mentions in the preceding verse. He translates thus:—

"Then let me be confounded before the assembled multitude,
And let the reproach of its families quash me!
Yea, let me be struck dumb! let me never appear abroad!"

I am satisfied that ver. 38, 39, and 40, should come in either here, or immediately after ver. 25; and that Job's words should end with ver. 37, which, if the others were inserted in their proper places, would be ver. 40. See the reasons at the end of the chapter.

Verse 35. *O that one would hear me!*] I wish to have a fair and full hearing: I am grievously accused; and have no proper opportunity of clearing myself, and establishing my own innocence.

Behold, my desire is] Or, הן תוי *hen tavi*, "There is my pledge." I bind myself, on a great penalty, to come into court, and abide the issue.

That *the Almighty would answer me*] That he would call this case immediately *before himself;* and oblige my *adversary* to come into court, to put his accusations into a legal form, that I might have the opportunity of vindicating myself in the presence of a judge who would hear dispassionately my pleadings, and bring the cause to a righteous issue.

And that *mine adversary had written a book*] That he would not indulge himself in vague accusations, but would draw up a proper *bill of indictment*, that I might know to what I had to plead, and find the accusation in a tangible form.

Verse 36. *Surely I would take it upon my shoulder*] I would be contented to stand before the bar as a criminal, bearing upon my shoulder the *board* to which the *accusation* is affixed. In a book of *Chinese punishments* now before me, containing *drawings* representing various criminals brought *to* trial, *in* trial, and *after* trial, charged with different offences; in almost all of them a *board* appears, on which the *accusation* or *crime* of which they are accused, or for which they suffer, is fairly written. Where the punishment is capital, this board appears fastened to the *instrument*, or stuck near the *place* of *punishment.* In one case a large, heavy plank, through which there is a hole to pass the head,—or rather a *hole* fitting the *neck*, like that in the *pillory*,—with the *crime* written upon it, rests on the *criminal's shoulders;* and this he is obliged to carry about for the *weeks* or *months* during which the punishment lasts. It is probable that Job alludes to something of this kind; which he intimates he would *bear about with him* during the *interim* between *accusation* and the *issue* in judgment; and, far from considering this a disgrace, would clasp it as dearly as he would adjust a crown or diadem to his head; being fully assured, from his *innocence*, and the *evidence* of it, which would infallibly appear on the trial, that he would have the *most honourable acquittal.* There may also be an allusion to the manner of receiving a favour from a superior: it is immediately *placed on the head*, as a mark of respect; and if a piece of *cloth* be given at the *temple*, the receiver not only puts it on his *head*, but *binds* it there.

Verse 37. *I would declare unto him the number of my steps*] I would show this adversary the different *stations* I had been in, and the *offices* which I had filled in life, that he might trace me through the whole of my civil, military, and domestic life, in order to get evidence against me.

As a prince would I go near] Though carrying my own accusation, I would go into the presence of my judge as the נגיד *nagid, chief*, or *sovereign commander* and *judge*, of the people and country, and would not shrink from having my conduct investigated by even the meanest of my subjects.

In these *three* verses we may observe the following particulars:—

1. Job wishes to be *brought to trial*, that he might have the opportunity of vindicating himself: *O that I might have a hearing!*

2. That his *adversary*, Eliphaz and his companions, whom he considers as *one party*, and

A. M. cir. 2484
B. C. cir. 1520
Ante I. Olymp. cir. 744
Ante U. C. cir. 767

38 If my land cry against me,
or that the furrows likewise thereof [m]complain;
39 If [n]I have eaten [o]the fruits
thereof without money, or [p]have [q]caused
the owners thereof to lose their
life:
40 Let [r]thistles grow instead
of wheat, and [s]cockle instead of
barley. The words of Job are ended.

A. M. cir. 2484
B. C. cir. 1520
Ante I. Olymp. cir. 744
Ante U. C. cir. 767

[m]Heb. *weep*——[n]James v. 4——[o]Heb. *the strength thereof*——[p]1 Kings xxi. 19

[q]Heb. *caused the soul of the owners thereof to expire* or *breathe out*——[r]Gen. iii. 18——[s]Or, *noisome weed*

joined together *in one*, would *reduce* their vague charges *to writing*, that they might come before the court in a legal form: *O that my adversary would write down the charge!*

3. That the Almighty, שדי *Shaddai*, the *all-sufficient* God, and not *man*, should be the judge, who would not permit his adversaries to attempt, by false evidence, to establish what was false, nor suffer himself to cloak with a hypocritical covering what was iniquitous in his conduct: *O that the Almighty might answer for me*—take notice of or be judge in the cause!

4. To him he purposes cheerfully to confess all his ways, who could at once judge if he prevaricated, or concealed the truth.

5. This would give him the strongest encouragement: he would go *boldly* before him, with the highest persuasion of an honourable acquittal.

Verse 38. *If my land cry*] The most careless reader may see that the introduction of this and the two following verses here, disturbs the connection, and that they are most evidently out of their place. Job seems here to refer to that *law*, Lev. xxv. 1-7, by which the Israelites were obliged to give the *land rest every seventh year*, that the soil might not be too much exhausted by perpetual cultivation, especially in a country which afforded so few advantages to improve the arable ground by manure. He, conscious that he had acted according to this law, states that his *land* could *not cry out against him*, nor its *furrows complain*. He had not broken the law, nor exhausted the soil.

Verse 39. *If I have eaten the fruits thereof without money*] I have never been that *narrow-minded* man who, through a principle of *covetousness*, exhausts his land, putting himself to no *charges*, by *labour* and *manure*, to strengthen it; or defrauds those of their *wages* who were employed under him. *If I have eaten the fruits of it*, I have cultivated it *well* to produce those fruits; and this has not been *without money*, for I have gone to expenses on the soil, and *remunerated* the labourers.

Or have caused the owners thereof to lose their life] Coverdale translates, **Yee yf I have greved eny of the plowmen.** They have not panted in labour without due recompense.

Verse 40. *Let thistles grow instead of wheat*] What the word חוח *choach* means, which we translate *thistles*, we cannot tell: but as חח *chach* seems to mean *to hold, catch as a hook, to hitch*, it must signify some kind of *hooked thorn*, like the brier; and this is possibly its meaning.

And cockle] באשה *bashah*, some *fetid* plant, from באש *baash*, to *stink*. In Isa. v. 2, 4, we translate it *wild grapes;* and Bishop *Lowth*, *poisonous berries:* but *Hasselquist*, a pupil of the famous Linnæus, in his Voyages, p. 289, is inclined to believe that the *solanum incanum*, or *hoary nightshade* is meant, as this is common in Egypt, Palestine, and the East. Others are of opinion that it means the *aconite*, which بيش *beesh*, in Arabic, denotes: this is a poisonous herb, and grows luxuriantly on the sunny hills among the vineyards, according to *Celsus* in *Hieroboticon*. بيش *beesh* is not only the name of an *Indian poisonous* herb, called the *napellus moysis, but* بيش موش *beesh moosh*, or فارة البيش *farut al beesh*, is the name of an *animal*, resembling a mouse, which lives among the roots of this very plant. "May I have a crop of this instead of barley, if I have acted improperly either by my land or my labourers!"

The words of Job are ended.] That is, his defence of himself against the accusations of his *friends*, as they are called. He spoke afterwards, but never to *them;* he only addresses *God*, who came to determine the whole controversy.

These words seem very much like an *addition* by a later hand. They are wanting in many of the MSS. of the Vulgate, two in my own possession; and in the *Editio Princeps* of this version.

I suppose that at first they were inserted in *rubric*, by some scribe, and afterwards taken into the text. In a MS. of my own, of the *twelfth* or *thirteenth* century, these words stand in *rubric*, actually *detached from the text;* while in another MS., of the *fourteenth* century, they form a *part of the text.*

In the Hebrew text they are also *detached:* the hemistichs are complete without them; nor indeed can they be incorporated with them. They appear to me an *addition* of no authority. In the first edition of our Bible, that by Coverdale, 1535, there is a *white line* between these words and the conclusion of the chapter; and they stand, forming no part of the text, thus:—

Here ende the wordes of Job.

Just as we say, in reading the Scriptures, "Here ends such a chapter;" or, "Here ends the first lesson," &c.

On the subject of the *transposition*, mentioned above, I have referred to the *reasons* at the end of the chapter.

Dr. Kennicott, on this subject, observes: "Chapters xxix., xxx., and xxxi., contain Job's animated *self-defence*, which was made necessary by the reiterated accusation of his friends. This defence now concludes with six lines (in the Hebrew text) which declare, that if he had enjoyed his estates *covetously*, or procured them *unjustly*, he wished them to prove *barren* and *unprofitable*. This part, therefore, seems naturally to follow ver. 25, where he speaks of his *gold*, and how *much his hand had gotten*. The remainder of the chapter will then consist of these *four* regular parts, viz.,

"1. His *piety to God*, in his freedom from idolatry, ver. 26-28.

"2. His *benevolence to men*, in his charity both of temper and behaviour, 29-32.

"3. His *solemn assurance* that he did not *conceal* his guilt, from fearing either the *violence* of the *poor*, or the *contempt* of the *rich*, ver. 33, 34.

"4. (Which must have been the last article, because conclusive of the work) he infers that, being *thus secured by his integrity*, he may *appeal safely to God himself*. This appeal he therefore makes boldly, and in such words as, when rightly translated, form an image which perhaps has no parallel. For where is there an image so magnificent or so splendid as this? Job, thus conscious of innocence, wishing even God *himself* to draw up his indictment, [rather his *adversary* Eliphaz and companions to draw up this indictment, the *Almighty* to be *judge*,] that very indictment *he would bind round his head;* and with that indictment as *his crown* of glory, he would, with the dignity of a *prince*, *advance* to his trial! Of this wonderful passage I add a version more just and more intelligible than the present:—

"Ver. 35. O that one would grant me a hearing!
Behold, my desire is that the Almighty would answer me;
And, as plaintiff against me, draw up the indictment.
With what earnestness would I take it on my shoulders!
I would bind it upon me as a diadem.
The number of my steps would I set forth unto Him;
Even as a prince would I approach before Him!"

I have already shown that *Eliphaz* and his *companions*, not GOD, are the *adversary* or *plaintiff* of whom Job speaks. This view makes the whole clear and consistent, and saves Job from the charge of presumptuous rashness. See also Kennicott's Remarks, p. 163.

It would not be right to say that no other interpretation has been given of the first clause of verse 10 than that given above. The manner in which Coverdale has translated the 9th and 10th verses is the way in which they are generally understood: **Yf my hert hath lusted after my neghbour's wife, or yf I have layed wayte at his dore; O then let my wife be another man's harlot, and let other lye with her.**

In this sense the word *grind* is not unfrequently used by the ancients. *Horace* represents the *divine Cato* commending the young men whom he saw frequenting the stews, because they left other men's wives undefiled!

Virtute esto, inquit sententia *dia Catonis*,
Nam simul ac venas inflavit tetra libido,
Huc juvenes *œquum est* descendere, non alienas
Permolere uxores. SAT. lib. i., s. 2., ver. 32.

"When awful Cato saw a noted spark
From a night cellar stealing in the dark:
'Well done, my friend, if lust thy heart inflame,
Indulge it *here*, and spare the married dame.'"
FRANCIS.

Such were the *morals* of the *holiest state* of heathen Rome; and even of *Cato*, the purest and severest *censor* of the public manners! O tempora! O mores!

I may add from a scholiast:—*Molere* vetus verbum est pro *adulterare*, *subagitare*, quo verbo in deponenti significatione utitur alibi *Ausonius*, inquiens, Epigr. vii., ver. 6, de crispa impudica et detestabili:—

Deglubit, fellat, *molitur*, per utramque cavernam.
Qui enim coit, quasi *molere* et terere videtur.

Hinc etiam *molitores* dicti sunt, *subactores*, ut apud eundem, Epigr. xc., ver. 3.

Cum dabit uxori *molitor* tuus, et tibi *adulter*.

Thus the *rabbins* understand what is spoken of *Samson grinding* in the prison-house: quod ad ipsum Palæstini certatim suas uxores adduxerunt, suscipiendæ ex eo prolis causa, ob ipsius robur.

In this sense St. *Jerome* understands *Lam.* v. 13: *They took the young* **men** *to* GRIND. *Adolescentibus ad impudicitiam sunt abusi*, ad concubitum scilicet nefandum. Concerning *grinding of corn*, by portable *millstones*, or *querns*, and that this was the work of *females* alone, and they the *meanest slaves;* see the note on Exod. xi. 5, and on Judg. xvi. 21.

The *Greeks* use μυλλας to signify a *harlot;* and μυλλω, to *grind*, and also *coeo*, *ineo*, in the same sense in which *Horace*, as quoted above, *alienas* PERMOLERE *uxores*.

So *Theocritus*, Idyll. iv., ver. 58.

Ειπ' αγε μοι Κορυδων, *το γεροντιον η ῥ' ετι μυλλει*
Τηναν ταν κυανοφρυν ερωτιδα, τας ποτ' εκνισθη·

Dic age mihi, Corydon, senecio ille num adhuc *molit*,
Illud nigro supercilio *scortillum*, quod olim deperibat?

Hence the Greek *paronomasia*, μυλλαδα μυλλειν, *scortam molere*. I need make no apology for leaving the principal part of this note in a foreign tongue. To those for whom it is designed it will be sufficiently plain. If the above were Job's meaning, how dreadful is the wish or imprecation in verse the *tenth!*

CHAPTER XXXII

Elihu comes forward, and expresses his disapprobation both of Job and his three friends—with the one for justifying himself; and with the others for taking up the subject in a wrong point of view, and not answering satisfactorily—and makes a becoming apology for himself, 1–22.

A. M. cir. 2484
B. C. cir. 1520
Ante I. Olymp. cir. 744
Ante U. C. cir. 767

SO these three men ceased [a]to
answer Job, because he *was*
[b]righteous in his own eyes.
2 Then was kindled the wrath
of Elihu the son of Barachel [c]the Buzite, of
the kindred of Ram: against Job was his
wrath kindled because he justified [d]himself
rather than God.
3 Also against his three friends was his wrath
kindled, because they had found no answer,
and *yet* had condemned Job.
4 Now Elihu had [e]waited till Job had spoken,
because they *were* [f]elder than he.

A. M. cir. 2484
B. C. cir. 1520
Ante I. Olymp. cir. 744
Ante U. C. cir. 767

5 When Elihu saw that *there*
was no answer in the mouth of
these three men, then his wrath
was kindled.
6 And Elihu the son of Barachel the Buzite
answered and said, I *am* [g]young, [h]and ye *are*
very old; wherefore I was afraid, and [i]durst
not show you mine opinion.
7 I said, Days should speak, and multitude
of years should teach wisdom.
8 But *there is* a spirit in man; and [k]the
inspiration of the Almighty giveth them
understanding.

[a]Hebrew, *from answering*——[b]Chapter xxxiii. 9 [c]Genesis xxii. 21——[d]Hebrew, *his soul*——[e]Hebrew, *expected Job in words*——[f]Hebrew, *elder for days* [g]Hebrew, *few of days*

[h]Chapter xv. 10——[i]Hebrew, *feared*——[k]1 Kings iii. 12; iv. 29; chapter xxxv. 11; xxxviii. 36; Proverbs ii. 6; Ecclesiastes ii. 26; Daniel i. 17; ii. 21; Matthew xii. 25; James i. 5

NOTES ON CHAP. XXXII

Verse 1. *These three men ceased to answer Job*] They supposed that it was of no use to attempt to reason any longer with a man who justified himself before God. The truth is, they failed to convince Job of any point, because they argued from false principles; and, as we have seen, Job had the continual advantage of them. There were points on which he might have been successfully assailed; but they did not know them. Elihu, better acquainted both with human nature and the nature of the Divine law, and of God's moral government of the world, steps in, and makes the proper discriminations; acquits Job on the ground of their accusations, but condemns him for his too great self-confidence, and his trusting too much in his external righteousness; and, without duly considering his frailty and imperfections, his incautiously arraigning the providence of God of unkindness in its dealings with him. This was the point on which Job was particularly vulnerable, and which Elihu very properly clears up.

Because he was *righteous in his own eyes.*] The *Septuagint*, *Syriac*, *Arabic*, and *Chaldee*, all read, "Because he was righteous in THEIR eyes;" intimating, that they were now convinced that he was a holy man, and that they had charged him foolishly. The reading of these ancient versions is supported by a MS. of the *thirteenth* century, in Dr. *Kennicott's* collections; which, instead of בעיניו *beeinaiv*, *in* HIS *eyes*, has בעיניהם *beeineyhem*, *in* THEIR *eyes*. This is a reading of considerable importance, but it is not noticed by *De Rossi*. *Symmachus* translates nearly in the same way: *Δια τον αυτον δικαιον φαινεσθαι επ' αυτων*; *Because he appeared more righteous than themselves.*

Verse 2. *Then was kindled the wrath*] This means no more than that Elihu was *greatly excited*, and felt a *strong* and *zealous desire* to vindicate the justice and providence of God, against the aspersions of Job and his friends.

Elihu the son of Barachel the Buzite] Buz was the second son of Nahor, the brother of Abram, Gen. xxii. 21.

Of the kindred of Ram] Kemuel was the third son of Nahor; and is called in Genesis (see above) *the father of Aram*, which is the same as *Ram*. A city of the name of *Buz* is found in Jer. xxv. 23, which probably had its name from this family; and, as it is mentioned with Dedan and Tema, we know it must have been a city in *Idumea*, as the others were in that district. Instead of the *kindred of Ram*, the Chaldee has *of the kindred of Abraham.* But still the question has been asked, *Who was Elihu?* I answer, He was "the son of Barachel the Buzite, of the kindred of Ram:" this is all we know of him. But this Scriptural answer will not satisfy those who are determined to find out mysteries where there are none. Some make him a descendant of Judah; St. Jerome, Bede, Lyranus, and some of the rabbins, make him Balaam the son of Beor, the magician; Bishop Warburton makes him Ezra the scribe; and Dr. Hodges makes him the second person in the glorious Trinity, the Lord Jesus Christ, and supposes that the chief scope of this part of the book was to convict Job of self-righteousness, and to show the necessity of the doctrine of justification by faith! When these points are *proved*, they should be *credited*.

Because he justified himself rather than God.] Literally, *he justified his soul*, נפשו *naphhso, before God*. He defended, not only the *whole of his conduct*, but also his *motives*, *thoughts*, &c.

Verse 3. *They had found no answer*] They had condemned Job; and yet could not answer his arguments on the general subject, and in vindication of himself.

Verse 6. *I am young*] How *young* he was, or how *old* they were, we cannot tell; but there was no doubt a great disparity in their ages; and among the Asiatics the *youth* never spoke in the presence of the *elders*, especially on any subject of controversy.

Verse 7. *Days should speak*] That is, men are to be reputed wise and experienced in proportion to the time they have lived. The Easterns were remarkable for treasuring up wise sayings: indeed, the principal part of their boasted wisdom consisted in *proverbs* and *maxims* on different subjects.

Verse 8. *But* there is *a spirit in man*] Mr. *Good* translates:—

A. M. cir. 2484 B. C. cir. 1520 Ante I. Olymp. cir. 744 Ante U. C. cir. 767

9 [l]Great men are not *always*
wise; neither do the aged understand judgment.
10 Therefore I said, Hearken
to me; I also will show mine opinion.
11 Behold, I waited for your words; I gave
ear to your [m]reasons, whilst ye searched out
[n]what to say.
12 Yea, I attended unto you, and, behold,
there was none of you that convinced Job, *or* that answered his
words:
13 [o]Lest ye should say, We
have found out wisdom: God thrusteth him
down, not man.
14 Now he hath not [p]directed *his* words
against me: neither will I answer him with
your speeches.

A. M. cir. 2484 B. C. cir. 1520 Ante I. Olymp. cir. 744 Ante U. C. cir. 767

[l]1 Cor. i. 26——[m]Heb. *understandings*——[n]Heb. *words*

[o]Jer. ix. 23; 1 Cor. i. 29——[p]Or, *ordered* his *words*

"But surely there is an afflation in mankind,
And the inspiration of the Almighty actuateth them."

Coverdale, thus—

Every man (no doute) hath a mynde; but it is the inspyracion of the Allmightie that geveth understondinge.

I will now offer my own opinion, but first give the original text: רוח היא באנוש ונשמת שדי תבינם *ruach hi beenosh venishmath shaddai tebinem.* "The spirit itself is in miserable man, and the breath of the Almighty causeth them to understand." How true is it that *in God we live, move, and have our being!* The *spirit itself* is in man as the spring or fountain of his animal existence; and by the afflatus of this spirit he becomes capable of understanding and reason, and consequently of discerning Divine truth. The animal and intellectual lives are here stated to be *from God;* and this appears to be an allusion to man's creation, Gen. ii. 7: "And God breathed into man's nostrils the breath of lives," נשמת חיים *nishmath chaiyim,* i. e., animal and intellectual, and thus he became *a living soul,* נפש חיה *nephesh chaiyah,* a *rational animal.*

When man fell from God, the Spirit of God was grieved, and departed from him; but was restored, as the enlightener and corrector, in virtue of the *purposed* incarnation and atonement of our Lord Jesus; hence, he is "the true Light that lighteth every man that cometh into the world," John i. 9. That afflatus is therefore still continued to אנוש *enosh,* man, in his *wretched, fallen state;* and it is by *that Spirit,* the רוח אלהים *Ruach Elohim,* "the Spirit of the merciful or covenant God," that we have any conscience, knowledge of good and evil, judgment in Divine things, and, in a word, *capability of being saved.* And when, through the light of that Spirit, convincing of sin, righteousness, and judgment, the sinner turns to God through Christ, and finds redemption in his blood, the remission of sins; then it is the office of *that same Spirit* to give him *understanding* of the great work that has been done *in* and *for* him; "for *the Spirit itself* (αυτο το Πνευμα, Rom. viii. 16, the same words in *Greek* as the *Hebrew* רוח היא *ruach hi* of Elihu) beareth witness with his spirit that he is a child of God." It is the *same Spirit* which *sanctifies,* the *same Spirit* that *seals,* and the *same Spirit* that *lives* and *works* in the believer, *guiding* him by his *counsel* till it *leads* him *into glory.* In this one saying, independently of the above paraphrase, Elihu spoke more sense and sound doctrine than all Job's friends did in the whole of the controversy.

Verse 9. *Great men are not* always *wise*] This is a true saying, which the experience of every age and every country increasingly verifies. And it is most certain that, in the case before us, the aged did not understand judgment; they had a great many wise and good sayings, which they had collected, but showed neither wisdom nor discretion in applying them.

Verse 11. *I waited for your words; I gave ear to your reasons*] Instead of תבונותיכם *tebunotheychem,* your *reasons,* תכונותיכם *techunotheychem,* your *arguments,* is the reading of *nine* of *Kennicott's* and *De Rossi's* MSS. The sense, however, is nearly the same.

Whilst ye searched out what to say.] עד תחקרון מלין *ad tachkerun millin;* "Whilst ye were searching up and down for words." A fine irony, which they must have felt.

Verse 12. *Yea, I attended unto you*] Instead of ועדיכם *veadeychem, and unto you,* one MS. reads the above letters with *points* that cause it to signify *and your testimonies;* which is the reading of the *Syriac, Arabic,* and *Septuagint.*

Behold, there was *none of you that convinced Job*] *Confuted Job.* They spoke multitudes of *words,* but were unable to overthrow his *arguments.*

Verse 13. *We have found out wisdom*] We, by dint of our own wisdom and understanding, have found out the *true system of God's providence;* and have been able to account for all the sufferings and tribulations of Job. Had they been able to *confute* Job, they would have *triumphed* over him in their own self-sufficiency.

God thrusteth him down, not man.] This is no *accidental* thing that has happened to him: he is suffering under the just judgments of God, and therefore he must be the wicked man which we supposed him to be.

Verse 14. *He hath not directed*] I am no *party* in this controversy; I have no party feeling in it: he has not spoken a word against me, therefore I have no cause of irritation. I shall speak for *truth;* not for *conquest* or *revenge. Neither will I answer him with your speeches;* your passions have been inflamed by contradiction, and you have spoken foolishly with your lips.

A. M. cir. 2484 B. C. cir. 1520 Ante I. Olymp. cir. 744 Ante U. C. cir. 767

15 They were amazed, they answered no more: [q]they left off speaking.

16 When I had waited, (for they spake not, but stood still, *and* answered no more;)

17 *I said,* I will answer also my part, I also will show mine opinion.

18 For I am full of [r]matter, [s]the spirit within me constraineth me.

19 Behold, my belly *is* as wine *which* [t]hath no vent; it is ready to burst like new bottles.

20 I will speak, [u]that I may be refreshed; I will open my lips, and answer.

21 Let me not, I pray you, [v]accept any man's person, neither let me give flattering titles unto man.

22 For I know not to give flattering titles; *in so doing* my Maker would soon take me away.

[q]Hebrew, *they removed speeches from themselves* — [r]Hebrew, *words* — [s]Hebrew, *the spirit of my belly* — [t]Hebrew, *is not opened* — [u]Hebrew, *that I may breathe* — [v]Leviticus xix. 15; Deuteronomy i. 17; xvi. 19; Proverbs xxiv. 23; Matthew xxii. 14; Mark xii. 14; Luke xx. 21

Verse 15. *They were amazed*] Mr. *Good* translates: "They (the *speeches*) are dissipated; they no longer produce effect; the words have flirted away from them." Your words, being without proper reference and point, are scattered into thin air: there is nothing but *sound* in them; they are quite destitute of *sense.* But I prefer the words as spoken of Job's *friends.* They took their several parts in the controversy as long as they could hope to maintain their ground: for a considerable time they had been able to bring nothing *new;* at last, weary of their own *repetitions,* they gave up the contest.

Verse 16. *When I had waited*] I waited to hear if they had any thing to reply to Job; and when I found them in effect speechless, then I ventured to come forward.

Verse 17. *I will answer also my part*] אענה חלקי *aaneh chelki,* "I will recite my portion." We have already seen that the book of Job is a sort of *drama,* in which several persons have their different *parts* to *recite.* Probably the book was used in this way, in ancient times, for the sake of public instruction. Eliphaz, Zophar, and Bildad, had *recited* their *parts,* and Job had *responded* to each: nothing was brought to issue. Elihu, a bystander, perceiving this, comes forward and takes a *part,* when all the rest had expended their materials: yet Elihu, though he spoke well, was incapable of closing the controversy; and God himself appears, and decides the case.

Verse 18. *I am full of matter*] מלים *millim,* "I am full of WORDS," or *sayings;* i. e., wise sentences, and ancient opinions.

The spirit within me constraineth me.] How similar to the words of St. Paul! *The love of Christ constraineth us.* Elihu considered himself *under the influence of that Spirit of God* which gives understanding, and felt anxiously concerned for the welfare both of Job and his friends.

Verse 19. *My belly* is *as wine* which *hath no vent*] New wine in a state of effervescence.

Like new bottles.] *Bottles,* or rather *bags,* made of *goat-skins.* The head and shanks being cut off, the animal is *cased* out of the skin. The skin is then properly dressed; the *anus* and four shank holes properly tied up; and an aperture left at the neck or in some other place for the liquor to be poured in, and drawn out. One of these now lies before me, well tanned, and beautifully ornamented, and capable of holding many gallons. They are used, not only to carry wine and water, but for butter, and also for various *dry goods.* I have mentioned this in another place. When the wine is in a state of fermentation, and the skin has no vent, these bottles or *bags* are ready to *burst;* and if they be *old,* the *new wine* destroys them, breaks the old stitching, or rends the old skin. Our Lord makes use of the same figure, Matt. ix. 17; where see the note.

Verse 20. *I will open my lips and answer.*] In the preceding verse Elihu compares himself to a *skin-bottle,* in which the wine was in a state of *fermentation,* and the *bottle* ready to burst for want of *vent.* He carries on the metaphor in this verse: the bottle must be *opened* to save it from bursting; *I will* OPEN *my mouth.*

Verse 21. *Let me not—accept any man's person*] I will speak the truth without fear or favour.

Neither let me give flattering titles] I will not give epithets to any man that are not descriptive of his true state. I will not beguile him by telling him he *is* what he *is not.* אכנה *acanneh,* from כנה *canah,* is generally supposed to signify to *surname,* to put a name *to* or *upon* a name, as the French word *surnom* implies. It means to give proud titles to persons who are worthless. It is well known that the Arabs make court to their superiors by carefully avoiding to address them by their proper names, instead of which they salute them with some title or epithet expressive of respect.—SCOTT. See below. Titles expressive of *office, ecclesiastical, civil,* or *military,* are always proper, and never forbidden, because they serve for *distinction;* but the Asiatic titles are in general bombastically and sinfully complimentary. The reader will find several specimens at the end of this chapter.

Verse 22. *My Maker would soon take me away.*] Were I to copy this conduct while under the influence which I now feel, God might justly consume me as in a moment. He is my Maker; he made me to *know truth,* to *tell truth,* and to *live* according to *truth;* for he is the *God of truth:* I shall, therefore, through his help, speak *the* TRUTH, *the* WHOLE TRUTH, *and* NOTHING BUT THE TRUTH.

WE find from the above that *vain titles* of ceremony, expressive of the most eminent qualities, were given to *worthless men,* from time immemorial; and no wonder, for *hypocrisy* entered into *man* at the same time that *sin* entered into the *world.*

Of the flattering titles used in the East, I shall give a few specimens from the قواعد السلطنت شاه جهان *Kooayid us Sultanet* SHAH JEHAN, or, "The Rules observed during the Reign of the Mogul Emperor Shah Jehan."

Speaking of the emperor, he is entitled,

"The SUN which illuminates the firmament in the universe of royalty and dominion; the MOON, which irradiates the sky of monarchy and felicity; the King who in pomp resembles *Gem-sheed*. His hand is boundless as the ocean in bestowing bounties, being the key of the gates of kindness and liberality!" Again:—

"The SUN of the heaven of prosperity and empire, the SHADOW OF GOD, the Asylum of the Universe, the splendour of whose instructive front causes light and gladness to the world and to mankind."

"The just and vigilant Monarch; the Asylum of Truth, the Refuge of the World; the Diffuser of Light, the Solver of all human difficulties."

"The Lord of the Age, who is endowed with such perfect excellence, both in internal and external qualifications, that on all occasions he holds fast the thread of good counsel, prudence, and purity of morals."

"The faculty of apprehension is possessed by him in such a degree, that before the matter has scarcely obtained utterance he comprehends the purport, and gives answers with the tongue of inspiration."

Addresses to Persons of Distinction

"Let them convey to the presence of glorious empire, the Sultan, in pomp like Solomon, the centre of the universe, powerful as heaven!"

"Let them who kiss the carpet of the palace, in pomp like heaven, convey this letter to his majesty, whose sight is as creative as alchymy, king of kings, the asylum of the world!"

"To the exalted presence, which gratifies the desires of all people, the most beneficent of the age, the *vizier*, protector of the universe, may the Almighty perpetuate his fortune!"

"May this letter be dignified in the presence of *Naweeb Saheb*, diffuser of benefits, of exalted pomp, the respectable, the discriminator of ranks! May his power increase!"

"Let them convey this to the perusal of his excellency, conversant in realities and mysteries, the support of excellencies, the cream of his contemporaries, and the cherisher of the poor!"

These are a specimen of the *flattering titles* given in the East to persons in eminent stations. Their kings they clothe in all the attributes of the Deity, when both in their public and private character they are corrupt and unholy, rascals in grain, and the ruthless oppressors of suffering humanity.

CHAPTER XXXIII

Elihu offers himself in God's stead to reason with Job in meekness and sincerity, 1–7. *Charges Job with irreverent expressions,* 8–12. *Vindicates the providence of God, and shows the various methods which he uses to bring sinners to himself:—By dreams and visions,* 13–15; *by secret inspirations,* 16–18; *by afflictions,* 19–22; *by messengers of righteousness,* 23; *and by the great atonement,* 24. *How and from what God redeems men, and the blessings which he communicates,* 25–30. *Job is exhorted to listen attentively to Elihu's teaching,* 31–33.

A. M. cir. 2484 B. C. cir. 1520 Ante I. Olymp. cir. 744 Ante U. C. cir. 767

WHEREFORE, Job, I pray
thee, hear my speeches,
and hearken to all my words.
2 Behold, now I have opened
my mouth, my tongue hath spoken in [a]my
mouth.
3 My words *shall be of* the uprightness of my
heart: and my lips shall utter knowledge clearly.
4 [b]The Spirit of God hath made
me, and the breath of the Almighty
mighty hath given me life.
5 If thou canst answer me,
set *thy words* in order before me, stand up.
6 [c]Behold, I *am* [d]according to thy wish in
God's stead: I also am [e]formed out of the
clay.

A. M. cir. 2484 B. C. cir. 1520 Ante I. Olymp. cir. 744 Ante U. C. cir. 767

[a]Heb. *in my palate*——[b]Gen. ii. 7——[c]Chap. ix. 34, 35; xiii. 20, 21; xxxi. 35

[d]Heb. *according to thy mouth*——[e]Heb. *cut out of the clay*

NOTES ON CHAP. XXXIII

Verse 3. *My words* shall be of *the uprightness*] As God has given me his Spirit, from that Spirit alone will I speak; therefore all my words shall be of uprightness, knowledge, and truth.

Knowledge clearly.] דעת ברור *daath barur, pure science.* I shall lay down no *false positions*, and I shall have no false consequences.

Verse 4. *The Spirit of God hath made me*] Another plain allusion to the account of the *creation of man*, Gen. ii. 7, as the words נשמת *nishmath, the breath* or *breathing* of God, and תחיני *techaiyeni, hath given me life,* prove: "He *breathed* into his nostrils the *breath* of *lives*, and he became a *living soul.*"

Verse 6. *I am according to thy wish in God's stead: I also am formed out of the clay.*] Mr. *Good*, and before him none other that I have seen, has most probably hit the true meaning:—

"Behold, I am thy fellow.
I too was formed by God out of the clay."

The word כפיך *kephicha*, which we translate *according to thy wish*, and which, if *Hebrew*, would mean *like to thy mouth;* he considers as pure Arabic, with a Hebrew postfix, كفو *kefoo*, signifying *fellow, equal, like.* Taken in this way, the passage is very plain, only לאל *lael, by* or *through God*, must be added to the *last* clause of the verse instead of the *first*, as Mr. *Good* has properly done.

A. M. cir. 2484 B. C. cir. 1520 Ante I. Olymp. cir. 744 Ante U. C. cir. 767

7 [f]Behold, my terror shall not
make thee afraid, neither shall
my hand be heavy upon thee.
8 Surely thou hast spoken [g]in
mine hearing, and I have heard the voice of
thy words, *saying,*
9 [h]I am clean without transgression, I
am innocent; neither *is there* iniquity in
me.
10 Behold, he findeth occasions against me,
[i]he counteth me for his enemy.
11 [k]He putteth my feet in the stocks, he
marketh all my paths.
12 Behold, *in* this thou art not
just: I will answer thee, that God
is greater than man.
13 Why dost thou [l]strive
against him? for [m]he giveth not account of
any of his matters.
14 [n]For God speaketh once, yea twice, *yet*
man perceiveth it not.
15 [o]In a dream, in a vision of the night,
when deep sleep falleth upon men, in slumberings upon the bed;
16 [p]Then [q]he openeth the ears of men, and
sealeth their instruction,

[f]Chap. ix. 34; xiii. 21——[g]Heb. *in mine ears*——[h]Ch. ix. 17; x. 7; xi. 4; xvi. 17; xxiii. 10, 11; xxvii. 5; xxix. 14; xxxi. 1——[i]Chap. xiii. 24; xvi. 9; xix. 11——[k]Chap. xiii. 27; xiv. 16; xxxi. 4

[l]Isa. xlv. 9——[m]Heb. *he answereth not*——[n]Chap. xl. 5; Psalm. lxii. 11——[o]Numbers xii. 6; chapter iv. 13——[p]Chapter xxxvi. 10, 15——[q]Hebrew, *he revealeth* or *uncovereth*

Verse 7. *My terror shall not make thee afraid*] This is an allusion to what Job had said, chap. ix. 34: "Let him take his rod away from me, and let not his fear terrify me." Being thy *equal*, no fear can impose upon thee so far as to overawe thee; so that thou shouldst not be able to conduct thy own defence. We are on *equal terms;* now prepare to defend thyself.

Verse 8. *Surely thou hast spoken*] What Elihu speaks here, and in the three following verses, contains, in general, simple quotations from Job's own words, or the obvious sense of them, as the reader may see by referring to the *margin*, and also to the notes on those passages.

Verse 11. *He putteth my feet in the stocks*] See the note on chap. xiii. 27.

Verse 12. In *this thou art not just*] Thou hast laid charges against God's dealings, but thou hast not been able to *justify* those charges; and were there nothing else against thee, these irreverent speeches are so many proofs that thou art not *clear* in the sight of God.

Verse 13. *Why dost thou strive against him?*] Is it not useless to contend with God? Can he do any thing that is *not right?* As to his giving thee *any account* of the *reasons why he deals thus and thus* with thee, or any one else, thou needest not expect it; he is sovereign, and is not to be called to the bar of his creatures. It is sufficient for thee to know that "he is too wise to err, and too good to be unkind."

Verse 14. *For God speaketh once*] Though he will not be summoned to the bar of his creatures, nor condescend to detail the reasons of his conduct, which they could not comprehend, yet he so acts, in the main, that the *operation* of his *hand* and the *designs* of his *counsel* may sufficiently appear, provided men had their *eyes* open upon his *ways*, and their *hearts* open to receive his *influence*.

Elihu, having made the general statement that God would not come to the bar of his creatures to give account of his conduct, shows the *general means* which he uses to bring men to an acquaintance with themselves and with him: he states these in the six following *particulars*, which may be collected from ver. 15-24.

Verse 15. I. *In a* DREAM—*when deep sleep falleth upon men*] Many, by such means, have had the most salutary warnings; and to decry *all* such, because there are many *vain dreams*, would be nearly as much wisdom as to deny the Bible, because there are many foolish books, the authors of which supposed they were under a Divine influence while composing them.

II. *In a* VISION *of the night—in slumberings upon the bed*] *Visions* or *images* presented in the *imagination* during slumber, when men are betwixt sleeping and waking, or when, *awake* and in bed, they are wrapt up in deep contemplation, the darkness of the night having shut out all objects from their sight, so that the mind is not diverted by images of earthly things impressed on the senses. Many warnings in this way have come from God; and the impression they made, and the good effect they produced, were the proofs of their Divine origin. To deny this would be to call into doubt the testimony of the best, wisest, and holiest men in all ages of the Church. Of one of these visions we have a remarkable account in chap. iv. of this book, ver. 12-21. And this vision seems to have taken place in the night season, when *Eliphaz* awoke *from a deep sleep.* There is this difference between the accidents of the *dream* and the *vision:* the *former* takes place *when deep sleep falleth upon men;* the *latter*, in the *night, in* or *after* slumberings upon the bed.

Verse 16. *Then he openeth the ears of men, and sealeth, &c.*] III. By *secret* INSPIRATIONS. A dream or a vision simply considered is likely to do no good; it is the *opening of the understanding*, and the *pouring in of the light*, that make men wise to salvation. Serious alarms, holy purposes, penitential pangs for past sins, apprehension of death and judgment, discoveries of God's justice, of Christ's love, of the world's vanity, of heaven's excellence, &c., &c., &c., are often used by the Divine Spirit *to withdraw men from their* evil *purpose, and to hide pride from man*, ver. 17; and of all these openings of the ear of the heart, and sealing instructions upon the conscience, we have numerous examples in the history of the Church, in the experience of good men, and even in the civil and providential history of all nations.

A. M. cir. 2484
B. C. cir. 1520
Ante I. Olymp. cir. 744
Ante U. C. cir. 767

17 That he may withdraw man
from his [r]purpose, and hide pride
from man.
18 He keepeth back his soul
from the pit, and his life [s]from perishing by
the sword.
19 He is chastened also with pain upon his
bed, and the multitude of his bones with
strong *pain:*
20 [t]So that his life abhorreth bread, and his
soul [u]dainty meat.

21 His flesh is consumed away,
that it cannot be seen; and his
bones *that* were not seen stick out.
22 Yea, his soul draweth near
unto the grave, and his life to the destroyer.
23 If there be a messenger with him, an interpreter, one among a thousand, to show unto
man his uprightness:
24 Then he is gracious unto him, and saith,
Deliver him from going down to the pit: I
have found [v]a ransom.

A. M. cir. 2484
B. C. cir. 1520
Ante I. Olymp. cir. 744
Ante U. C. cir. 767

---

[r]Hebrew, *work*——[s]Hebrew, *from passing by the sword*

[t]Psa. cvii. 18——[u]Heb. *meat of desire*——[v]Or, *an atonement*

Verse 18. *He keepeth back his soul from the pit*] By the above means, how many have been snatched from an untimely death! By taking the warning thus given, some have been prevented from perishing by the *pit*—some *sudden accident;* and others from the *sword* of the *assassin* or *nocturnal murderer.* It would be easy to give examples, in all these kinds; but the knowledge of the reader may save this trouble to the commentator.

Verse 19. *He is chastened also with pain upon his bed, &c.*] IV.—AFFLICTIONS are a *fourth* means which God makes use of to awaken and convert sinners. In the hand of God these were the cause of the salvation of *David*, as himself testifies: *Before I was afflicted, I went astray,* Psa. cxix. 67, 71, 75.

The multitude of his bones] By such diseases, especially those of a *rheumatic* kind, when to the patient's apprehension *every bone* is *diseased, broken,* or *out of joint.*

Some render the passage, *When the multitude of his bones is yet strong;* meaning those sudden afflictions which fall upon men when in a state of great firmness and vigour. The original, ורוב עצמיו אתן *verob atsamaiv ethan,* may be translated, *And the strong multitude of his bones.* Even the strong multitude of his bones is chastened with pain upon his bed; the place of rest and ease affording him no peace, quiet, or comfort.

The *bones* may be well termed *multitudinous,* as there are no less than 10 in the *cranium,* or *skull; upper jaw,* 13; *lower jaw,* 1; *teeth,* 32; *tongue,* 1; *vertebræ,* or *back-bone,* 24; *ribs,* 24; *sternum,* or *breast-bone,* 3; *os innominatum,* 1; *scapula,* or *shoulder-blades,* 2; *arms,* 6; *hands,* 54; *thigh-bones,* 2; *knee-bones,* 2; *legs,* 4; *feet,* 54: in all, not less than 233 bones, without reckoning the *ossa sethamoides;* because, though often numerous, they are found only in hard labourers, or elderly persons.

Verse 20. *His life abhorreth bread*] These expressions strongly and naturally point out that general *nausea,* or *loathing* which sick persons feel in almost every species of disorder.

Verse 21. *His flesh is consumed away*] As in atrophy, marasmus, and consumptive complaints in general.

Verse 22. *His soul draweth near unto the grave*] נפש *nephesh, soul,* is here taken for the *immortal spirit,* as it is distinguished from חיה *chaiyah,* the *animal life.* The former draws near to the pit, שחת *shachath, corruption;* perhaps he meant dissipation, considering it merely as the *breath.* The latter draws near לממתים *lamemithim,* to the *dead;* i. e., to those who are *already buried.* Mr. *Good* translates it *the Destinies;* and supposes the same is meant among the HEBREWS by the *Memithim,* as among the GREEKS by their Μοιραι; the LATINS, by their *Parcæ;* the GOTHS, by their *Fatal Sisters;* the SCANDINAVIANS, by their goddess *Hela;* and the ARABIANS, by *Azrael,* or the *angel of death.* I think, however, the signification given above is more natural.

Verse 23. *If there be a messenger with him, an interpreter, &c.*] V.—The MESSENGERS of righteousness; this is a FIFTH *method,* אם יש עליו מלאך מליץ *im yesh alaiv malach melits,* "If there be over him an interpreting or mediatorial angel or messenger." *One among a thousand,* אחד מני אלף *echad minni aleph.* "One from the CHIEF, HEAD, or TEACHER."

To show unto man his uprightness] להגיד לאדם ישרו *lehaggid leadam yoshro,* "to manifest or cause to be declared to man his righteousness:" to show unto *Adam—men in general,* the descendants of the first man—his purity and holiness; to convince him of sin, righteousness, and judgment, that he may be prepared for the discovery of what is next to be exhibited.

Verse 24. *Then he is gracious unto him*] He exercises mercy towards fallen man, and gives command for his respite and pardon.

Deliver him from going down to the pit] Let him who is thus instructed, penitent, and afflicted, and comes to me, find a *pardon;* for—

VI. *I have found a ransom.*] כפר *copher, an atonement. Pay a ransom for him,* פדעהו *pedaehu,* that he may not go down *to the pit*—to corruption or destruction, for *I have found out an atonement.* It is this that gives efficacy to all the preceding means; without which they would be useless, and the salvation of man impossible. I must think that the *redemption of a lost world,* by *Jesus Christ,* is not obscurely signified in ver. 23, 24.

While the whole world lay in the wicked one, and were all hastening to the *bottomless pit,* God so loved the world that he gave his only-begotten Son, that whosoever believeth on him might not perish, but have everlasting life. Jesus Christ, the great sacrifice, and *head* of the Church, commissions his *messengers—apostles* and their *successors—to show men the righteousness of God,* and his displeasure at

A. M. cir. 2484 B. C. cir. 1520 Ante I. Olymp. cir. 744 Ante U. C. cir. 767

25 His flesh shall be fresher
[w]than a child's: he shall return
to the days of his youth:
26 He shall pray unto God,
and he will be favourable unto him: and he
shall see his face with joy: for he will render
unto man his righteousness.
27 [x]He looketh upon men, and *if any* [y]say,
I have sinned, and perverted *that which was*
right, and it [z]profited me not:
28 [a]He will [b]deliver his soul from going
into the pit, and his life shall see the light.

29 Lo, all these *things* worketh God [c]oftentimes with
man,
30 [d]To bring back his soul from
the pit, to be enlightened with the light
of the living.
31 Mark well, O Job, hearken unto me:
hold thy peace, and I will speak.
32 If thou hast any thing to say, answer me:
speak, for I desire to justify thee.
33 If not, [e]hearken unto me: hold thy peace,
and I shall teach thee wisdom.

A. M. cir. 2484 B. C. cir. 1520 Ante I. Olymp. cir. 744 Ante U. C. cir. 767

[w]Heb. *than childhood*——[x]Or, *He shall look upon men, and say, I have sinned,* &c.——[y]2 Sam. xii. 13; Prov. xxviii. 13; Luke xv. 21; 1 John i. 9

[z]Rom. vi. 21——[a]Or, *He hath delivered my soul, &c.; and my life*——[b]Isa. xxxviii. 17——[c]Heb. *twice* and *thrice*——[d]Ver. 28; Psa. lvi. 13——[e]Psa. xxxiv. 11

sin; and at the same time his infinite love, which commands them to proclaim *deliverance* to the captives, and that they who believe on him shall not perish, shall not *go down to the pit* of destruction, for *he has found out an atonement;* and that whoever comes to him, through Christ, shall have everlasting life, in virtue of that atonement or ransom price.

Should it be objected against my interpretation of אלף *aleph,* that it cannot be translated *chief* or *head,* because it is without the *vau shurek,* אלוף *alluph,* which gives it this signification; I would answer, that this form of the word is not *essential* to the signification given above, as it occurs in several places without the *vau shurek,* where it most certainly signifies a *chief,* a *leader, captain,* &c., e. g., Zech. ix. 7; Jer. xiii. 21, and Gen. xxxvi. 30; in the first of which we translate it *governor;* in the second, *captain;* and in the third, *duke.* And although we translate אלוף *alluph* an *ox* or *beeve,* (and it most certainly has this meaning in several places,) yet in this signification it is written without the *vau shurek* in Prov. xiv. 4; Psa. viii. 7; Isa. xxx. 24; and in Deut. vii. 13; xxviii. 4, 18, 51; which all show that this letter is not absolutely necessary to the above signification.

Verse 25. *His flesh shall be fresher than a child's*] He shall be born a *new creature.*

He shall return to the days of his youth] He shall be *born again,* and become a *child of God,* through faith in Christ Jesus.

Verse 26. *He shall pray unto God*] Being now adopted into the heavenly family, and become a *new creature,* he shall have the *spirit of prayer,* which is indeed the very *breath* and *language* of the *new* or *spiritual life.*

He will be favourable unto him] He shall manifest his good will to him; he shall live under the influences of Divine grace.

He shall see his face with joy] He shall know that God is reconciled to him; and this shall fill him with joy, בתרועה *bithruah, with exultation:* for, "being justified by faith, he has peace with God, through our Lord Jesus Christ, by whom he has received the atonement; and REJOICES in the hope of the glory of God."

He will render unto man his righteousness.] So good and gracious is the Lord, that by his grace he will enable this convert to live to his glory, to bring forth all the fruits of the Spirit, and then *reward* him for the work, as if it were done by his own might.

Verse 27. *He looketh upon men*] אנשים *anashim,* wretched, fallen men. He *shines into them,* to convince them of sin; and if any, under this convincing light of God, *say, I have sinned* against *heaven* and before thee, *and perverted the right*—abused the powers, faculties, mercies, and advantages, which thou didst give me, by seeking rest and happiness in the creature, *and it profited me not*—it was all *vanity* and *vexation* of spirit; ולא שוה לי *velo shavah li,* "and it was not equal to me," did not *come up* to my expectation, nor supply my wants:—

Verse 28. *He will deliver his soul*] He will do that to every *individual penitent sinner* which he has promised in his word to do for a lost world—he will deliver his soul from going down to the pit of hell.

And his life shall see the light.] He shall walk in the light, as Christ is in the light; always enjoying a clear sense of his acceptance through the blood of the Lamb. See another mode of paraphrasing these verses at the end of the chapter.

Verse 29. *Lo, all these* things *worketh God*] God frequently uses one, or another, or all of these means, to bring *men,* גבר *gaber,* stout-hearted men, who are far from righteousness, to holiness and heaven.

Oftentimes] פעמים שלש *paamayim shalosh,* "three times over;" or as פעמים *paamayim* is by the *points* in the *dual* number, then it signifies *twice three times,* that is, *again* and *again; very frequently.* Blessed be God!

Verse 30. *To bring back his soul from the pit*] Nearly a repetition of the promise in ver. 28.

To be enlightened with the light of the living.] An echo of Psa. lvi. 13: "Thou hast delivered my soul from death, that I may walk before God in the light of the living;" and probably quoted from it.

Verse 31. *Mark well, O Job*] Pay the deepest attention to what I have said, and to what I shall say.

Verse 32. *If thou hast any thing to say*] If thou hast any objection to make against what I have already stated, now answer, now speak freely; for it is my desire that thou shouldst stand clear of all charges.

Verse 33. *If not*] Then I will proceed:

listen carefully, *keep silence*, and *I will teach thee* what true *wisdom* is.

Job was silent; none of his friends chose to intermeddle farther; and in the next chapter Elihu addresses both Job and them.

THERE are some *various readings* in the MSS. and *versions* on certain words in the concluding verses of this chapter, which it will be necessary to mention, as they, if adopted, will lead to a somewhat different paraphrase to that given, especially of verses 26, 27, and 28.

Verse 26. For צדקתו *tsidkatho*, HIS *righteousness*, one MS. and the *Chaldee* have כצדקתו *ketsidkatho*, ACCORDING *to his righteousness.*

Verse 28. For נפשו *naphsho*, HIS *soul*, which is the *keri* reading, and that which our translation has followed, נפשי MY *soul* is the reading of many MSS., early *editions*, the *Complutensian*, *Antwerp*, and *London Polyglots*, the *Jerusalem Targum*, the *Chaldee*, the *Vulgate*, and *Coverdale.*

For חיתו *chaiyatho*, HIS *life*, many MSS., early *editions*, the *Complutensian*, *Antwerp*, and *London Polyglots*, the *Jerusalem Targum*, *Chaldee*, *Vulgate*, and *Coverdale*, read חיתי *chaiyathi*, MY *life*. Both of these are properly the *kethib* or *textual* readings in the best editions, but are directed by the *Masora* to be changed for the *keri* readings, or those inserted in the *margin.*

For באור תראה *baor tireh*, SHALL SEE *the light*, six of *Kennicott's* and *De Rossi's* MSS. have תהיה *tihyeh*, and *twenty-one* have כאור *caor*, thus כאור תהיה *caor tihiyeh*, SHALL BE AS *the light*. The whole verse, by these various readings, will stand thus:—"He will deliver MY soul from going into the pit, and MY life SHALL BE AS the light." But if, with the *Septuagint*, *Syriac*, and *Arabic*, we read פדה *padah*, in the *imperative* mood, then the verse will read thus:—"DELIVER THOU MY SOUL from going down to the pit, and MY life SHALL BE AS the light."

On the 26th, 27th, 28th, and 29th, verses, the following paraphrase has been recommended.

Verse 26. *He* (Jesus Christ, the *head* and *ransom price*) *shall pray unto God*, (shall make *intercession* for the transgressors, for he is the Mediator between God and man.) *And he* (God the Father) *will be favourable*, (ירצהו *yirtsehu*, will manifest his *good will* towards him.) *And he shall see his face* (פניו *panaiv*, his *faces*, God the Father, Son, and Spirit) *with joy*, (בתרועה *bithruah*, with *exultation* or *triumph*,) *for he will render unto man his righteousness*, (ישב לאנוש צדקתו *yasheb leenosh tsidkatho*, "He will restore to wretched man his righteousness;" i. e., he will create the soul anew, and restore to the fallen spirit that righteousness and true holiness which it has lost, and bring it again to its original state of perfection, through the grand atonement mentioned ver. 24.)

But *when* is it that wretched miserable man shall be brought to this state of salvation? This is answered in

Verse 27. *When God, looking upon men, seeth any of them saying, I have sinned and perverted that which is right, and it hath profited me nothing*—has afforded nothing *equal* to my wishes, and the tribulation which I sustained in seeking happiness in forbidden things. *Redeem my soul from going down to destruction, and my life shall see the light*, or *shall be as the light.* This is the prayer of the penitent, which God has promised to hear.

This is one of the best, the deepest, the most spiritual, and most important chapters which the reader has yet met with in the Book of Job. It is every way important, and full of useful information. It is a grand exhibition of the WAY of salvation as revealed to patriarchs and prophets.

CHAPTER XXXIV

Elihu begins with an exhortation to Job's friends, 1–4; *charges Job with accusing God of acting unrighteously, which he shows is impossible*, 5–12; *points out the power and judgments of the Almighty*, 13–30; *shows how men should address God, and how irreverently Job has acted*, 31–37.

A. M. cir. 2484 B. C. cir. 1520 Ante I. Olymp. cir. 744 Ante U. C. cir. 767

FURTHERMORE Elihu answered and said,

2 Hear my words, O ye wise *men;* and give ear unto me, ye that have knowledge.

3 [a]For the ear trieth words, as the [b]mouth tasteth meat.

4 Let us choose to us judgment: let us know among ourselves what *is* good.

A. M. cir. 2484 B. C. cir. 1520 Ante I. Olymp. cir. 744 Ante U. C. cir. 767

[a]Chap. vi. 30; xii. 11

[b]Heb. *palate*

NOTES ON CHAP. XXXIV

Verse 3. *The ear trieth words*] I do not think, with *Calmet*, that the *inward ear*, or *judgment*, is meant simply. The Asiatics valued themselves on the *nice and harmonious collection of words*, both in speaking and in writing; and perhaps it will be found here that Elihu labours as much for harmonious versification as for pious and weighty sentiments. To connect *sense* with *sound* was an object of general pursuit among the *Hebrew*, *Arabic*, and *Persian* poets; and so fond are the latter of *euphony*, that they often sacrifice both *sense* and *sentiment* to it; and some of the *Greek* poets are not exempt from this fault.

Verse 4. *Let us choose to us judgment*] Let us not seek the applause of men, nor contend

A. M. cir. 2484 B. C. cir. 1520 Ante I. Olymp. cir. 744 Ante U. C. cir. 767

5 For Job hath said, [e]I am
righteous; and [d]God hath taken
away my judgment.
6 [e]Should I lie against my
right? [f]my wound *is* incurable without transgression.
7 What man *is* like Job, [g]*who* drinketh up
scorning like water?
8 Which goeth in company with the workers of iniquity, and walketh with wicked men.
9 For [h]he hath said, It profiteth a man
nothing that he should delight
himself with God.
10 Therefore hearken unto me,
ye [i]men of understanding; [k]far
be it from God, *that he should do* wickedness;
and *from* the Almighty, *that he should commit* iniquity.
11 [l]For the work of a man shall he render
unto him, and cause every man to find according to *his* ways.
12 Yea, surely God will not do wickedly,

A. M. cir. 2484 B. C. cir. 1520 Ante I. Olymp. cir. 744 Ante U. C. cir. 767

[c]Ch. xxxiii. 9——[d]Ch. xxvii. 2——[e]Ch. ix. 17——[f]Heb. *mine arrow;* ch. vi. 4; xvi. 13——[g]Ch. xv. 16——[h]Ch. ix. 22, 23, 30; xxxv. 3; Mal. iii. 14——[i]Heb. *men of heart*——[k]Gen. xviii. 25; Deut. xxxii. 4; 2 Chron. xix. 7; chap. viii. 3; xxxvi. 23; Psa. xcii. 15; Rom. ix. 14——[l]Psa. lxii. 12; Prov. xxiv. 12; Jer. xxxii. 19; Ezek. xxxiii. 20; Matt. xvi. 27; Romans ii. 6; 2 Cor. v. 10; 1 Peter i. 17; Rev. xxii. 12

for victory. Let our aim be to obtain correct views and notions of all things; and let us labour to find out what is good.

Verse 5. *Job hath said, I am righteous*] Job had certainly said the words attributed to him by Elihu, particularly in chap. xxvii. 2, &c., but it was in vindication of his aspersed character that he had asserted his own righteousness, and in a different sense to that in which Elihu appears to take it up. He asserted that he was righteous *quoad* the charges his friends had brought against him. And he never intimated that he had at all times a pure heart, and had never transgressed the laws of his Maker. It is true also that he said, *God hath taken away my judgment;* but he most obviously does not mean to charge God with injustice, but to show that he had dealt with him in a way wholly mysterious, and not according to the ordinary dispensations of his providence; and that he did not interpose in his behalf, while his friends were overwhelming him with obloquy and reproach.

Verse 6. *Should I lie against my right?*] Should I acknowledge myself the sinner which they paint me, and thus lie against my right to assert and maintain my innocence?

My wound is *incurable without transgression.*] If this translation is correct, the meaning of the place is sufficiently evident. In the tribulation which I endure, I am treated as if I were the worst of culprits; and I labour under incurable maladies and privations, though without any *cause* on my part for such treatment. This was all most perfectly true; it is the testimony which God himself gives of Job, that "he was a perfect and upright man, fearing God and eschewing evil;" and that "Satan had moved the Lord against him, to destroy him, WITHOUT A CAUSE." See chap. i. 1, and ii. 3.

The *Chaldee* translates thus:—

"On account of my judgment, I will make the son of man a liar, who sends forth arrows without sin."

Mr. *Good* thus:—

"Concerning my cause I am slandered;
He hath reversed my lot without a trespass."

The latter clause is the most deficient, אנוש חצי בלי פשע; Miss Smith's translation of which is the best I have met with: "A man cut off, without transgression." The word חצי *chitstsi,* which we translate *my wound,* signifies more literally,*my arrow;* and if we take it as a contracted noun, חצי *chitstsey* for חצים *chitstsim,* it means *calamities.* אנוש *anush,* which we translate *incurable,* may be the noun *enosh,* wicked, miserable man; and then the whole may be read thus: "A man of calamities without transgression." I suffer the punishment of an enemy to God, while free from transgression of this kind.

Verse 7. *Drinketh up scorning like water?*] This is a repetition of the charge made against Job by *Eliphaz,* chap. xv. 16. It is a proverbial expression, and seems to be formed, as a metaphor, from a *camel drinking,* who takes in a large draught of water, even the most *turbid,* on its setting out on a journey in a caravan, that it may serve it for a long time. Job deals largely in scorning; he fills his heart with it.

Verse 8. *Which goeth in company with the workers of iniquity*] This is an allusion to a *caravan:* all kinds of persons are found there; but yet a holy and respectable man might be found in that part of the company where profligates assembled. But surely this assertion of Elihu was not strictly true; and the words, literally translated, will bear a less evil meaning: "Job makes a *track* ארח *arach,* to *join fellowship,* לחברה *lechebrah,* with the workers of iniquity;" i. e., Job's present mode of reasoning, when he says, "I am righteous, yet God hath taken away my judgment," is according to the assertion of sinners, who say, "There is no profit in serving God; for, if a man be righteous, he is not benefited by it, for God does not vindicate a just man's cause against his oppressors." By adopting so much of their creed, he intimates that Job is taking the *steps* that lead to *fellowship* with them. See ver. 9.

Verse 10. *Far be it from God*] Rather, *Wickedness, far be that from God; and from iniquity, the Almighty.* The sense is sufficiently evident without the *paraphrase* in our version.

Verse 11. *For the work of a man shall he render*] God ever will do *justice;* the righteous shall never be forsaken, nor shall the wicked ultimately prosper.

A. M. cir. 2484
B. C. cir. 1520
Ante I. Olymp. cir. 744
Ante U. C. cir. 767

neither will the Almighty [m]per-
vert judgment.
13 Who hath given him a
charge over the earth? or who
hath disposed [n]the whole world?
14 If he set his heart [o]upon man, *if* he
[p]gather unto himself his spirit and his breath;
15 [q]All flesh shall perish together, and man
shall turn again unto dust.
16 If now *thou hast* understanding, hear
this: hearken to the voice of my words.
17 [r]Shall even he that hateth right [s]govern?
and wilt thou condemn him that is most just?
18 [t]*Is it fit* to say to a king, *Thou art*
wicked? *and* to princes, *Ye are* ungodly?
19 *How much less to him* that [u]accepteth
not the persons of princes, nor regardeth the
rich more than the poor? for
[v]they all *are* the work of his
hands.
20 In a moment shall they die,
and the people shall be troubled [w]at midnight,
and pass away: and [x]the mighty shall be
taken away without hand.
21 [y]For his eyes *are* upon the ways of man,
and he seeth all his goings.
22 [z]*There is* no darkness, nor shadow of
death, where the workers of iniquity may hide
themselves.
23 For he will not lay upon man more *than
right;* that he should [a]enter into judgment
with God.
24 [b]He shall break in pieces mighty men
[c]without number, and set others in their stead.

A. M. cir. 2484
B. C. cir. 1520
Ante I. Olymp. cir. 744
Ante U. C. cir. 767

---

[m]Ch. viii. 3——[n]Heb. *all of it*——[o]Heb. *upon him* [p]Psa. civ. 29——[q]Gen. iii. 19; Eccles. xii. 7——[r]Gen. xviii. 25; 2 Samuel xxiii. 3——[s]Heb. *bind*——[t]Exodus xxii. 28——[u]Deut. x. 17; 2 Chron. xix. 7; Acts x. 34; Rom. ii. 11; Gal. ii. 6; Ephes. vi. 9; Col. iii. 25; 1 Pet. i. 17

[v]Ch. xxxi. 15——[w]Exod. xii. 29, 30——[x]Heb. *they shall take away the mighty*——[y]2 Chron. xvi. 9; ch. xxxi. 4; Psa. xxxiv. 15; Prov. v. 21; xv. 3; Jer. xvi. 17; xxxii. 19 [z]Psa. cxxxix. 12; Amos ix. 2, 3; Heb. iv. 13——[a]Heb. *go* [b]Dan. ii. 21——[c]Heb. *without searching out*

Verse 13. *Who hath given him a charge*] *Who* is it that governs the world? Is it not God? Who disposes of all things in it? Is it not the Almighty, by his just and merciful providence? The government of the world shows the care, the justice, and the mercy of God.

Verse 14. *If he set his heart upon man*] I think this and the following verse should be read thus:—"If he set his heart upon man, he will gather his soul and breath to himself; *for* all flesh shall perish together, and man shall turn again unto dust." On whomsoever God *sets his heart*, that is, *his love*, though his body shall perish and turn to dust, like the rest of men, yet his *soul* will God gather to himself.

Verse 17. *Shall—he that hateth right govern?*] Or, *Shall he who hateth judgment, lie under obligation?* It is preposterous to suppose that he who lives by no rule, should impose rules upon others. God, who is the *fountain* of all *justice* and *righteousness*, *binds* man by his laws; and wilt thou, therefore, *pretend to condemn him who is the sum of righteousness?*

Verse 18. Is it fit *to say to a king*, Thou art *wicked?*] The sentence is very short, and is thus translated by the VULGATE: *Qui dicit regi, Apostata? Qui vocat duces impios?* "Who says to a king, Apostate? Who calls leaders impious?" Literally, *Who calls a king Belial? Who calls princes wicked?* Civil governors should be treated with respect; no man should speak evil of the ruler of the people. This should never be permitted. Even where the *man* cannot be respected, because his *moral conduct* is improper, even there the *office* is sacred, and should be reverenced. He who permits himself to talk against the *man*, would destroy the *office* and *authority*, if he could.

Verse 19. *That accepteth not*] If it be utterly improper to speak against a king or civil governor, how much more so to speak disrespectfully of God, who is not influenced by human caprices or considerations, and who regards the *rich* and the *poor* alike, being equally his creatures, and equally dependent on his providence and mercy for their support and salvation.

Verse 20. *In a moment shall they die*] Both are equally dependent on the Almighty for their breath and being; the *mighty* as well as the *poor*. If the *great men* of the earth have abused their power, he sometimes cuts them off by the most *sudden* and *unexpected death;* and even at midnight, when in security, and least capable of defence, they are cut off by the people whom they have oppressed, or by the *invisible hand* of the angel of death. This appears to be spoken in reference to *Eastern tyrants*, who seldom die a natural death.

Verse 22. There is *no darkness*] In this life; and *no shadow of death* in the other world—no annihilation *in which the workers of iniquity may hide themselves*, or take refuge.

Verse 23. *For he will not lay upon man*] The meaning appears to be this: He will not call man a second time into judgment; he does not try a cause twice; his decisions are just, and his sentence without appeal.

Mr. *Good* translates:—

"Behold, not to man hath he intrusted the time
Of coming into judgment with God."

Man's time is not in his own hand; nor is his lot cast or ruled by his own wisdom and power. When God thinks best, he will judge for him; and, if oppressed or calumniated, he will bring forth his righteousness as the light, and do him justice on his adversaries.

Verse 24. *He shall break in pieces*] In multitudes of cases God depresses the *proud*, and raises up the *humble* and *meek*. Neither their *strength* nor *number* can afford them security.

A. M. cir. 2484
B. C. cir. 1520
Ante I. Olymp. cir. 744
Ante U. C. cir. 767

25 Therefore he knoweth their
works, and he overturneth *them*
in the night, so that they are
[d]destroyed.
26 He striketh them as wicked men [e]in the
open sight of others;
27 Because they [f]turned back [g]from
him, and [h]would not consider any of his
ways:
28 So that they [i]cause the cry of the poor
to come unto him, and he [k]heareth the cry of the afflicted.
29 When he giveth quietness,
who then can make trouble? and
when he hideth *his* face, who then can behold
him? whether *it be done* against a nation, or
against a man only:
30 That the hypocrite reign not, lest [l]the
people be ensnared.
31 Surely it is meet to be said unto God,

[d]Heb. *crushed*——[e]Heb. *in the place of beholders*——[f]1 Sam. xv. 11——[g]Heb. *from after him*——[h]Psa. xxviii. 5; Isa. v. 12——[i]Chap. xxxv. 9; James v. 4——[k]Exod. xxii. 23——[l]1 Kings xii. 28, 30; 2 Kings xxi. 9

Verse 25. *He knoweth their works*] He knows what they have done, and what they are *plotting* to do.

He overturneth them *in the night*] In the revolution of a single night the plenitude of power on which the day closed is annihilated. See the cases of Belshazzar and Babylon.

Verse 26. *He striketh them as wicked men*] At other times he executes his judgments *more openly;* and they are suddenly destroyed in the *sight of the people.*

Verse 27. *Because they turned back*] This is the reason why he has dealt with them in judgment. They had departed from him in their *hearts,* their *moral conduct,* and their *civil government.* He is speaking of corrupt and tyrannical rulers. And *they did not,* would not, *understand* any of his ways.

Verse 28. *So that they cause the cry of the poor*] They were cruel and oppressive: the poor cried through their distresses, and against their oppressors; and God heard the cry of the poor. Nothing so dreadful appears in the court of heaven against an unfeeling, hard-hearted, and cruel man of power, as the prayers, tears, and groans of the poor.

In times of little liberality, when some men thought they did God service by persecuting those who did not exactly receive *their creed,* nor worship God in *their way,* a certain great man in Scotland grievously persecuted his tenants, because they had religious meetings in private houses out of the order of the establishment; though he never molested them when they spent their time and their money in the alehouse. A holy, simple woman, one of those people, went one morning to the house of the great persecutor, and desired to speak with him. The servant desired to know her message, and he would deliver it; for she could not be admitted. She told him she could deliver her message to none but his master; said it was a matter of great importance, and concerned himself intimately, and alone. The servant having delivered this message, and stated that the woman appeared to have something particular on her mind, his worship condescended to see her. "What is your business with *me?*" said he, in a haughty, overbearing tone. To which she answered, "Sir, we are a hantle o' puir folk at ——, who are strivin' to sairve God accordin' to our ain conscience, and to get our sauls sav'd: yee persecute us; and I am come to beg yee to let us alane; and in ye dinna, we'll pray yee dead." This rhetoric was irresistible. His lordship did not know what influence such people might have in heaven; he did not like to put such prayers to the proof; wisely took the old woman's advice, and *e'en let them alane.* He was safe; they were satisfied; and God had the glory. When the poor refer their cause to God, he is a terrible avenger. Let the potsherds strive with the potsherds of the earth; but wo to the man that contendeth with his Maker.

Verse 29. *When he giveth quietness, who then can make trouble?*] How beautiful is this sentiment, and how true! He ever acts as a sovereign; but his actions are all wise and just. *If he give quietness, who dares to give trouble?* And if he give to every human being the right to worship himself according to their conscience, for the director of which he gives both his *word* and his *Spirit,* who shall dare to say to another, "Thou shalt worship God in my way, or not at all;" or, through a *pretended liberality,* say, "Thou shalt be *tolerated* to worship him so and so;" and even that toleration be shackled and limited?

Reader, thou hast as much right to tolerate another's mode of worship as he has to tolerate thine: or, in other words, neither of you have any such right at all; the pretension is as absurd as it is wicked.

If, however, there be any thing in the religious practice of any particular people that is inimical, by fair construction, to the peace of the country, then the civil power may interfere, as they ought to do in all cases of *insurrection;* but let no such inference be drawn when not most obviously flowing from the practice of the people, and the principles they profess; and when solemnly disclaimed by the persons in question. Whatever converts sinners from the error of their ways must be good to society and profitable to the state.

Whether it be done *against a nation*] He defends and supports nations or individuals, howsoever weak, against their enemies, howsoever numerous and powerful. He destroys nations or individuals who have filled up the measure of their political or moral iniquity, though all other nations and individuals stand up in their support.

Verse 30. *That the hypocrite reign not*] The *Vulgate* translates, *Who causes a wicked man to reign because of the sins of the people.* This was precisely the defence which Hegiage, the oppressive ruler of the Babylonian Irak, under the caliph Abdul Malec, made when he found the people in a state of insurrection. See at the end of the chapter.

Verse 31. *Surely it is meet to be said unto God*] This is Elihu's exhortation to Job:

A. M. cir. 2484
B. C. cir. 1520
Ante I. Olymp. cir. 744
Ante U. C. cir. 767

[m]I have borne *chastisement,* I
will not offend *any more:*
32 *That which* I see not teach
thou me: if I have done iniquity,
I will do no more.
33 [n]*Should it be* according to thy mind? he
will recompense it, whether thou refuse, or
whether thou choose; and not I: therefore
speak what thou knowest.
34 Let men [o]of understanding tell me, and
let a wise man hearken unto
me.
35 [p]Job hath spoken without
knowledge, and his words *were*
without wisdom.
36 [q]My desire *is that* Job may be tried unto
the end, because of *his* answers for wicked men.
37 For he addeth rebellion unto his sin, he
[r]clappeth *his hands* among us, and multiplieth
his words against God.

[m]Dan. ix. 7-14——[n]Heb. Should it be *from with thee?* [o]Heb. *of heart*

[p]Chapter xxxv. 16——[q]Or, *My father, let Job be tried* [r]Isa. lv. 12

Humble thyself before God, and say, "*I have suffered—I will not offend.*"

Verse 32. That which *I see not*] "What I do not know, teach thou me; wherein I have done iniquity, I will do so no more."

Verse 33. *According to thy mind? he will recompense it*] Mr. *Good* renders the whole passage thus:—

"Then in the presence of thy tribes,
According as thou art bruised shall he make it whole.
But it is thine to choose, and not mine;
So, what thou determinest, say."

This may at least be considered a paraphrase on the very obscure original. If thou wilt not thus come unto him, he will act according to justice, whether that be *for* or *against* thee. Choose what part thou wilt take, to humble thyself under the mighty hand of God, or still persist in thy supposed integrity. Speak, therefore; the matter concerns thee, not me; but let me know what thou art determined to do.

Verse 34. *Let men of understanding tell me*] I wish to converse with wise men; and by men of wisdom I wish what I have said to be judged.

Verse 35. *Job hath spoken without knowledge*] There is no good in arguing with a self-willed, self-conceited man. Job has spoken like a man destitute of wisdom and discretion.

Verse 36. *My desire* is that *Job may be tried unto the end*] אבי יבחן איוב *abi yibbachen Aiyob,* "My father, let Job be tried." So the VULGATE, *Pater mi, probetur Job.* But it may be as in the common translation, *I wish Job to be tried;* or, as Mr. *Good* renders it, *Verily, let Job be pursued to conquest for replying like wicked men.*

This is a very harsh wish: but the whole chapter is in the same spirit; nearly destitute of mildness and compassion. Who could suppose that such arguings could come out of the mouth of the loving Saviour of mankind? The reader will recollect that a very pious divine has supposed *Elihu* to be *Jesus Christ!*

Verse 37. *He addeth rebellion unto his sin*] An ill-natured, cruel, and unfounded assertion, borne out by nothing which Job had ever said or intended; and indeed, more severe than the most inveterate of his friends (so called) had ever spoken.

Mr. *Good* makes this virulent conclusion still more virulent and uncharitable, by translating thus:—

"For he would add to his transgressions apostasy;
He would clap his hands in the midst of us:
Yea, he would tempest his words up to God."

There was no need of *adding* a caustic here; the words in the tamest translation are tart enough. Though Elihu began well and tolerantly, he soon got into the spirit, and under the mistake, of those who had preceded him in this "tempest of words."

ON ver. 30 I have referred to the case of Hegiage, governor of the Babylonian Irak, under the caliph Abdul Malec. When Hegiage was informed that the people were in a state of mutiny because of his oppressive government, before they broke out into open acts of hostility, he mounted on an eminence, and thus harangued them:—

"God has given me dominion over you; if I exercise it with severity, think not that by putting me to death your condition will be mended. From the manner in which you live you must be always ill-treated, for God has many executors of his justice; and when I am dead he will send you another, who will probably execute his orders against you with more rigour. Do you wish your prince to be moderate and merciful? Then exercise righteousness, and be obedient to the laws. Consider that your own conduct is the cause of the good or evil treatment which you receive from him. A prince may be compared to a *mirror;* all that you see in him is the reflection of the objects which you present before him."

The people immediately dropped their weapons, and quietly returned to their respective avocations. This man was one of the most valiant, eloquent, and cruel rulers of his time; he lived towards the close of the 7th century of the Christian era. He is said to have put to death 120,000 people; and to have had 50,000 in his prisons at the time of his decease.

Yet this man was capable of *generous actions.* The following anecdote is given by the celebrated Persian poet *Jami,* in his *Baharistan:*—

Hegiage, having been separated from his attendants one day in the chase, came to a place where he found an Arab feeding his camels. The camels starting at his sudden approach, the Arab lifted up his head. and seeing a man splendidly arrayed, became incensed, and said, *Who is this who with his fine clothes comes into the desert to frighten my camels? The curse of God light upon him!* The governor, approaching the Arab, saluted him very civilly, with the *salaam, Peace be unto thee!* The Arab, far from returning the salutation, said, *I wish thee neither peace, nor any other blessing of God.* Hegiage, without seeming to heed what he had said, asked him very civilly "to give him a little water to drink." The Arab, in a surly tone, answered, *If thou desirest to drink, take the pains to alight, and draw for thyself; for I am neither thy companion nor thy slave.* The governor accordingly alighted, and having drank, asked the Arab, "Whom dost thou think the greatest and most excellent of men?" *The prophet sent by God,* said the Arab, *and thou mayest burst with spleen.* "And what thinkest thou of Aaly?" returned Hegiage. *No tongue can declare his excellence,* said the Arab. "What," asked Hegiage, "is thy opinion of the caliph Abdul Malec?" *I believe him to be a very bad prince,* replied the Arab. "For what reason?" said Hegiage. *Because,* said the Arab, *he hath sent us for governor the most execrable wretch under heaven.* Hegiage, finding himself thus characterized, was silent; but his attendants coming up, he rejoined them, and ordered them to bring the Arab with them.

The next day Hegiage ordered him to be set at table with himself, and bade him "eat freely." The Arab, ere he tasted, said his usual grace, "*God grant that the end of this repast may be no worse than the beginning!*" While at meat the governor asked him, "Dost thou recollect the discourse we had together yesterday?" The Arab replied, *God prosper thee in all things! but as to the secret of yesterday, take heed that thou disclose it not to-day.* "I will not," said Hegiage; "but thou must choose one of these two things: either *acknowledge me for thy master,* and I will retain thee about my person; or else *I will send thee to Abdul Malec,* and tell him what thou hast said of him." *There is a third course,* replied the Arab, *preferable to those two.* "Well, what is that?" said the governor. *Why, send me back to the desert, and pray God that we may never see each other's face again.* Cruel and vindictive as Hegiage was, he could not help being pleased with the frankness and courage of the man; and not only forgave him the preceding insults, but ordered him 10,000 pieces of silver, and sent him back to the desert, according to his wish.

CHAPTER XXXV

Elihu accuses Job of impious speeches, 1–4. *No man can affect God by his iniquity, nor profit him by his righteousness,* 5–8. *Many are afflicted and oppressed, but few cry to God for help; and, for want of faith, they continue in affliction,* 9–16.

A. M. cir. 2484
B. C. cir. 1520
Ante I. Olymp. cir. 744
Ante U. C. cir. 767

ELIHU spake moreover, and
said,
2 Thinkest thou this to be
right, *that* thou saidst, My righteousness *is* more than God's?
3 For [a]thou saidst, What advantage will it
be unto thee? *and,* What profit shall I have
[b]*if I be cleansed* from my sin?
4 [c]I will answer thee, and [d]thy companions
with thee.
5 [e]Look unto the heavens, and
see; and behold the clouds *which*
are higher than thou.
6 If thou sinnest, what doest
thou [f]against him? or *if* thy transgressions
be multiplied, what doest thou unto him?
7 [g]If thou be righteous, what givest
thou him? or what receiveth he of thine
hand?
8 Thy wickedness *may hurt* a man as thou

A. M. cir. 2484
B. C. cir. 1520
Ante I. Olymp. cir. 744
Ante U. C. cir. 767

[a]Ch. xxi. 15; xxxiv. 9——[b]Or, by it *more than by my sin*——[c]Heb. *I will return to thee words*——[d]Chap. xxxiv. 8

[e]Chap. xxii. 12——[f]Prov. viii. 36; Jer. vii. 19——[g]Ch. xxii. 2, 3; Psa. xvi. 2; Prov. ix. 12; Rom. xi. 35

NOTES ON CHAP. XXXV

Verse 2. *My righteousness* is *more than God's?*] This would indeed be a blasphemous saying; but Job never said so, neither directly nor constructively: it would be much better to translate the words צדקי מאל *tsidki meel, I am righteous* BEFORE *God.* And Job's meaning most certainly was, "Whatever I am in *your* sight, I know that in the *sight of God* I am a righteous man;" and he had a right to assume this character, because God himself had given it to him.

Verse 3. *What advantage will it be unto thee?*] As if he had said to God, "My righteousness cannot profit thee, nor do I find that it is of any benefit to myself." Or perhaps Elihu makes here a general assertion, which he afterwards endeavours to exemplify: Thou hast been reasoning *how* it may *profit thee,* and thou hast said, "What profit shall I have in righteousness more than in sin?"

Verse 4. *I will answer thee*] I will show thee the evil of a sinful way, and the benefit of righteousness; and supply what thy friends have omitted in their discourses with thee.

Verse 5. *Look unto the heavens*] These heavens, and their host, God has created: the bare sight of them is sufficient to show thee that God is infinitely beyond thee in wisdom and excellence.

Behold the clouds] שחקים *shechakim,* the *ethers,* (Vulgate, *æthera,*) from שחק *shachak,* to *contend, fight together:* the agitated or conflicting air and light; the strong agitation of these producing both light and heat. Look upon these, consider them deeply, and see and acknowledge the perfections of the Maker.

Verse 6. *If thou sinnest*] God is not benefited by thy righteousness, nor injured by thy iniquity, howsoever multiplied it may be.

Verse 8. *Thy wickedness* may hurt] It is better to translate this literally:

A. M. cir. 2484 B. C. cir. 1520 Ante I. Olymp. cir. 744 Ante U. C. cir. 767

art; and thy righteousness *may*
profit the son of man.
9 [h]By reason of the multitude
of oppressions they make *the*
oppressed to cry: they cry out by reason of
the arm of the mighty.
10 But none saith, [i]Where *is* God my
Maker, [k]who giveth songs in the night;
11 Who [l]teacheth us more than the beasts
of the earth, and maketh us wiser than the
fowls of heaven?
12 [m]There they cry, but none giveth answer, because of the pride of evil men.
13 [n]Surely God will not hear
vanity, neither will the Almighty
regard it.
14 [o]Although thou sayest
thou shalt not see him, *yet* judgment
is before him; therefore [p]trust thou in
him.
15 But now, because *it is* not *so,* [q]he hath
[r]visited in his anger; yet [s]he knoweth *it*
not in great extremity:
16 [t]Therefore doth Job open his mouth in
vain; he multiplieth words without knowledge.

A. M. cir. 2484 B. C. cir. 1520 Ante I. Olymp. cir. 744 Ante U. C. cir. 767

[h]Exod. ii. 23, 24; iii. 7, 8, 9, 16, 19; v. 4, 5, 6, &c.; Psa. xii. 5; Eccles. v. 8; Isa. v. 7; chap. xxxiv. 28——[i]Isa. li. 13——[k]Psa. xlii. 8; lxxvii. 6; cxlix. 5; Acts xvi. 25 [l]Psa. xciv. 12——[m]Prov. i. 28

[n]Chap. xxvii. 9; Prov. xv. 29; Isa. i. 15; Jer. xi. 11 [o]Chap. ix. 11——[p]Psa. xxxvii. 5, 6——[q]That is, *God* [r]Psa. lxxxix. 32——[s]That is, *Job*——[t]Chap. xxxiv. 35, 37; xxxviii. 2

To a man like thyself is thy wickedness:
And to the son of man, thy righteousness:

That is—

Thou mayest injure thyself and others by thy wickedness,
And thou mayest benefit both by thy righteousness;
But God thou canst neither hurt nor profit.

Verse 9. *By reason of the multitude*] Or rather, "From among the multitude" the oppressed clamour, יזעיקו *yaziku: they shout,* ישועו *yeshavveu, because of the mighty.*

The wicked rich oppress the wicked poor; these cry aloud because of their oppressors; but they have no relief, because they call not upon God.

Verse 10. *Where* is *God my Maker*] They have no just apprehension of his *being;* they do not consider themselves his *creatures*, or that he who created them still *preserves* them, and would make them *happy* if they would pray unto him.

Who giveth songs in the night] This is variously translated. "Before whom the high angels give praise in the night."—CHALDEE.

"Who sets the night-watches."—SEPTUAGINT.

"Gives meditations in the night."—SYRIAC and ARABIC.

"**And that shyneth upon us that we might prayse him in the night.**"—COVERDALE.

A holy soul has continual communion with God: night and day its happiness is great; and God, from whom it comes, is the continual subject of its songs of praise.

Verse 11. *Who teacheth us more than the beasts*] "The ox knoweth his owner, and the ass his master's crib; but Israel doth not know me, my people do not consider;" Isa. i. 3. *Beasts, birds, fowls,* and in many cases *pondfishes*, know and seem thankful to the hand that feeds them; while man, made much more noble than they, gifted with the greatest powers, privileged with the most important benefits, considers not the Lord, nor discerns the operation of his hand. Quadrupeds, reptiles, and fowls, have more gratitude to their masters than man has to his God.

Verse 12. *There they cry*] They bewail their calamities, but sorrow not for the *cause* of them; they cry against their *oppressors*, but they call not upon God.

Because of the pride of evil men.] Or מפני *mippeney*, from the face, presence, or influence, of the pride of wicked men. They cry for deliverance from the pride of wicked men; but they are not heard, because they cry not to God.

Verse 13. *Surely God will not hear vanity*] He will not attend to such vain cries; they cry *from* their oppressions, but they cry not *to* God.

Verse 14. *Thou sayest thou shalt not see* HIM] Several MSS. have "Thou shalt not see *me*," and the Septuagint, and *one* other, "Thou shalt not see *us;*" but without the points, תשורנו, the original may be read *see* HIM or *see* US, the third person singular, or the first person plural.

Yet *judgment* is *before him*] Rest assured that God has not forgotten either to *punish* or to *save;* therefore trust in him; choose to be a *monument* of his *mercy,* rather than of his *justice.*

Verse 15. *But—because* it is *not* so] Rather, "But now, because he visiteth not in his anger." This is more literal than the versions generally proposed; and the sense of the place appears to be this: Because vengeance is not speedily executed on an evil work, therefore are the hearts of the children of men set in them to do iniquity. This is, in effect, the charge which Elihu brings against Job.

Verse 16. *Therefore doth Job open his mouth in vain*] God will execute vengeance when it may best serve the ends of his justice, providence, and mercy. The delay of judgment is not proof that it shall not be executed; nor is the deferring of mercy any proof that God has forgotten to be gracious.

He multiplieth words without knowledge] However this may apply to Job, it most certainly applies very strongly and generally to the words, not only of Job's three friends, but to those also of Elihu himself. The contest is frequently a *strife of words.*

CHAPTER XXXVI

Elihu vindicates God's justice, and his providential and gracious dealings with men, 1–9. *Promises of God to the obedient, and threatenings to the disobedient; also promises to the poor and afflicted,* 10–16. *Sundry proofs of God's mercy, with suitable exhortations and cautions,* 17–33.

A. M. cir. 2484 B. C. cir. 1520 Ante I. Olymp. cir. 744 Ante U. C. cir. 767

ELIHU also proceeded, and said,
2 Suffer me a little, and I will show thee that [a]*I have* yet to speak on God's behalf.
3 I will fetch my knowledge from afar, and will ascribe righteousness to my Maker.
4 For truly my words *shall* not *be* false: he that is perfect in knowledge *is* with thee.
5 Behold, God *is* mighty, and despiseth not *any:* [b]*he is* mighty in strength *and* [c]wisdom.
6 He preserveth not the life of the wicked: but giveth right to the [d]poor.
7 [e]He withdraweth not his eyes from the

[a]Heb. *that* there are *yet words for God*——[b]Chap. ix. 4; xii. 13, 16; xxxvii. 23; Psa. xcix. 4

[c]Heb. *heart*——[d]Or, *afflicted*——[e]Psa. xxxiii. 18; xxxiv. 15

NOTES ON CHAP. XXXVI

Verse 1. *Elihu also proceeded*] Mr. *Heath* gives a good summary of this chapter. Elihu goes on to lay before Job the impropriety of his behaviour towards God, and desires him to consider how vain it will prove. That God Almighty will never yield the point; that he will administer impartial justice to all men, ver. 2-6. That the general course of his providence is to favour the righteous: and that though he may sometimes correct them in love, yet if they submit patiently to his fatherly corrections, they shall enjoy all manner of prosperity; but if they be stubborn, and will not submit, they will only draw down greater proofs of his displeasure, ver. 7-16. He tells him that, had he followed the former course, he had probably, before now, been restored to his former condition; whereas, by persisting in the latter course, he was in a fair way of becoming a signal example of Divine justice, ver. 17, 18. He therefore warns him to use the present opportunity, lest God should cut him off while he was in a state of rebellion against him; for with God neither wealth, power, nor any other argument that he could use, would be of any avail, ver. 18-26. That God was infinitely powerful; there was no resisting him: and infinitely wise, as sufficiently appeared by his works; there was, therefore, no escaping out of his hands. That his purity was so great that the sun, in his presence, was more dim than the smallest ray of light when compared to that grand luminary; that his holiness was manifest by his aversion to iniquity; and his goodness, in supplying the wants of his creatures.

Verse 2. *That* I have *yet to speak on God's behalf.*] I have other proofs to allege in behalf of God's justice and providence.

Verse 3. *I will fetch my knowledge from afar*] למרחוק *lemerachok,* "from the distant place," meaning probably both *remote antiquity* and *heaven;* see below. I will show thee that all antiquity and experience are on my side. I can bring proofs from the remotest ages and from the most distant countries to demonstrate that God is infinitely WISE, and can do nothing *foolish* or *erroneous;* that he is infinitely POWERFUL, and can bring all the *purposes* of his wisdom to *effect;* that he is infinitely GOOD, and can will nothing, and can do nothing that is not *good* in itself, and well calculated to do *good* to his creatures. And I shall show that his operations in the *heavens* and on the *earth* prove and demonstrate the whole.

And will ascribe righteousness to my Maker.] By proving the above points, the righteous conduct of God, and his gracious government of the world, will be fully established.

That Elihu brings his knowledge *from afar*—from *every part* of the *creation,* as well as from the *Divine nature*—is evident from the end of the chapter. 1. The *omnipotence* of God;—*God is great.* 2. The *eternity* of God;—*We know him not, the number of his years cannot be found out,* ver. 26. 3. From the *economy* of God in the atmosphere, in *dews, rain, vapour,* and the *irrigation* of the earth;—*He maketh small the drops,* &c., ver. 27, 28. 4. In the *thunder* and *lightning,* by which he performs such wonders in the atmosphere, and executes such judgments in the world;—*Also who can understand the noise of his tabernacle? He spreadeth his light upon it. He judgeth the people,* &c., ver. 29-33.

Verse 4. *My words* shall *not* be *false*] My words shall be truth without falsity.

He that is perfect in knowledge is *with thee.*] "The perfection of knowledge is with thee." Thou art a sensible, well-informed man, and will be able to judge of what I say.

Verse 5. *God* is *mighty, and despiseth not* any] He reproaches no man for his want of knowledge. *If any man lack wisdom, he may come to God, who giveth liberally, and upbraideth not.* I prefer this to the *passive* sense, *will not be despised.*

He is *mighty*] Literally, "He is mighty in strength of heart;" he can never be terrified nor alarmed.

Verse 6. *He preserveth not the life*] He will not give *life* to the wicked; all such forfeit life by their transgressions.

But giveth right] Justice will he give to the afflicted or *humble,* עניים *aniyim.*

Verse 7. *He withdraweth not his eyes*] Exactly similar to those words of David, Psa. xxxiv. 15: "The eyes of the Lord are upon the righteous."

But with kings are they *on the throne*] I think the words should be read thus:—"But

A. M. cir. 2484
B. C. cir. 1520
Ante I. Olymp. cir. 744
Ante U. C. cir. 767

righteous: but [f]with kings *are*
they on the throne; yea, he doth
establish them for ever, and they
are exalted.
8 And [g]if *they be* bound in fetters, *and* be
holden in cords of affliction;
9 Then he showeth them their work, and
their transgressions that they have exceeded.
10 [h]He openeth also their ear to discipline,
and commandeth that they return from iniquity.
11 If they obey and serve *him,* they shall
[i]spend their days in prosperity, and their
years in pleasures.
12 But if they obey not, [k]they shall perish
by the sword, and they shall
die without knowledge.
13 But the hypocrites in
heart [l]heap up wrath: they cry
not when he bindeth them.
14 [m]They [n]die in youth, and their life *is*
among the [o]unclean.
15 He delivereth the [p]poor in his affliction,
and openeth their ears in oppression.
16 Even so would he have removed thee
out of the strait [q]*into* a broad place, where
there is no straitness; and [r]that [s]which should
be set on thy table *should be* full of [t]fatness.
17 But thou hast fulfilled the judgment of

[f]Psa. cxiii. 8——[g]Psa. cvii. 10——[h]Ch. xxxiii. 16, 23
[i]Ch. xxi. 13; Isa. i. 19, 20——[k]Heb. *they shall pass away by the sword*——[l]Rom. ii. 5——[m]Chap. xv. 32; xxii. 16; Psa. lv. 23

[n]Heb. *their soul dieth*——[o]Or, *sodomites;* Deut. xxiii. 17——[p]Or, *afflicted*——[q]Psa. xviii. 19; xxxi. 8; cxviii. 5
[r]Heb. *the rest of thy table*——[s]Psalm xxiii. 5——[t]Psalm xxxvi. 8

with kings upon the throne shall he place them; and they shall be exalted for ever." The word וישיבם *vaiyeshibem,* he will *establish* or *place them,* should be added to the first clause, as I have done; and then the sense becomes much clearer. Instead of לנצח *lanetsach, for ever,* perhaps *to victory* would be a better sense: "But with kings upon the throne will he place them; and they shall be exalted or triumph to victory." This is precisely the same idea, and conveyed in nearly the same words, as that of our Lord:—"To him that overcometh will I grant to sit with me in my throne, even as I also overcame, and am set down with my Father in his throne;" Rev. iii. 21. "Unto him that loved us, and washed us from our sins in his own blood, and hath made us kings and priests unto God and his Father, to him be glory," &c.; Rev. i. 5, 6.

Verse 8. *And if* they be *bound in fetters*] These are *means* which God uses, not of *punishment,* but of *correction.*

Verse 9. *He showeth them their work*] He shows them the exceeding sinfulness of sin.

That they have exceeded.] יתגברו *yithgabbaru,* "that they have strengthened themselves," and did not trust in the living God; and therefore they would not help themselves when trouble came.

Verse 10. *He openeth also their ear*] He gives them to *understand* the reason why they are thus corrected, and commands them to *return* from those iniquities which have induced him to visit them with afflictions and distresses.

Verse 11. *If they obey and serve* him] There may appear in the course of Providence to be some exceptions to this *general rule;* but it is most true, that this is literally or spiritually fulfilled to all the genuine followers of God. Every man is happy, in whatsoever circumstances, whose heart is unreservedly dedicated to his Maker.

Verse 12. *But if they obey not*] This also is a *general rule,* from which, in the course of Providence, there are only few, and those only *apparent,* deviations. Instead of *they shall perish by the sword,* the meaning of the Hebrew בשלח יעברו *beshelach yaaboru,* is, "By a dart they shall pass by." They shall be in *continual dangers,* and often *fall* before they have lived out half their days. Mr. *Good* translates: *They pass by as an arrow.* The VULGATE: *Transibunt per gladium.* "They shall pass away by the sword."

Verse 13. *But the hypocrites in heart*] חנפי *chanphey, the profligates, the impious,* those who have neither the *form* nor the *power* of godliness. The *hypocrite* is he who has the *form* but not the *power,* though he wishes to be thought as *inwardly* righteous as he is *outwardly* correct; and he takes up the profession of religion only to serve secular ends. This is not the meaning of the word in the book of Job, where it frequently occurs.

They cry not] "Though he binds them, yet they cry not." They are too *obstinate* to *humble themselves* even under the *mighty hand of God.*

Verse 14. *They die in youth*] Exactly what the psalmist says, "Bloody and deceitful men shall not live out *half their days,*" Psa. lv. 23. Literally, the words of Elihu are, "They shall die in the youth of their soul."

Their life is *among the unclean.*] בקדשים *bakedeshim,* among the whores, harlots, prostitutes, and sodomites. In this sense the word is used, though it also signifies *consecrated persons;* but we know that in idolatry characters of this kind were consecrated to Baal and Ashtaroth, Venus, Priapus, &c. Mr. *Good* translates, *the rabble.* The *Septuagint: Their life shall be wounded by the angels.*

Verse 15. *And openeth their ears in oppression.*] He will let them know for what end they are afflicted, and *why* he permits them to be oppressed. The word יגל *yigel* might be translated *he shall make them exult,* or *sing with joy,* in oppression; like the three Hebrews in the burning fiery furnace.

Verse 16. *Even so would he have removed thee*] If thou hadst turned to, obeyed, and served him, thy present state would have been widely different from what it is.

Verse 17. *But thou hast fulfilled the judg-*

A. M. cir. 2484
B. C. cir. 1520
Ante I. Olymp. cir. 744
Ante U. C. cir. 767

the wicked: [u]judgment and justice take hold *on thee.*
18 Because *there is* wrath,
beware lest he take thee away
with *his* stroke: then [v]a great ransom cannot
[w]deliver thee.
19 [x]Will he esteem thy riches? *no,* not
gold, nor all the forces of strength.
20 Desire not the night, when the people
are cut off in their place.
21 Take heed, [y]regard not iniquity: for
[z]this hast thou chosen rather than affliction.

22 Behold, God exalteth by his
power: [a]who teacheth like him?
23 [b]Who hath enjoined him
his way? or [c]who can say,
Thou hast wrought iniquity?
24 Remember that thou [d]magnify his work,
which men behold.
25 Every man may see it; man may behold
it afar off.
26 Behold, God *is* great, and we [e]know *him*
not, [f]neither can the number of his years be
searched out.
27 For he [g]makes small the drops of water:

---

[u]Or, *judgment and justice should uphold* thee——[v]Psa. xlix. 7——[w]Heb. *turn thee aside*——[x]Prov. xi. 4 [y]Psa. lxvi. 18——[z]See Heb. xi. 25——[a]Isa. xl. 13, 14; Rom. xi. 34; 1 Cor. ii. 16

[b]Chapter xxxiv. 13——[c]Chapter xxxiv. 10——[d]Psa. xcii. 5; Revelation xv. 3——[e]1 Corinthians xiii. 12 [f]Psalm xc. 2; cii. 24, 27; Hebrews i. 12——[g]Psalm cxlvii. 8

---

ment of the wicked] As thou art acting like the wicked, so God deals with thee as he deals with them.

Elihu is not a whit behind Job's other friends. None of them seems to have known any thing of the permission given by God to Satan to afflict and torment an innocent man.

Verse 18. *Because* there is *wrath*] This is a time in which God is punishing the wicked; take heed lest thou be cut off in a moment. Redeem the time; the days are evil.

Then a great ransom] When he determines to *destroy*, who can *save?*

Verse 20. *Desire not the night*] Thou hast wished for *death;* (here called *night;*) desire it not; leave that with God. If he hear thee, and send *death*, thou mayest be cut off in a way at which thy soul would shudder.

Verse 21. *Regard not iniquity*] It is sinful to entertain such wishes; it is an insult to the providence of God. *He* sends affliction; he knows this to be best for thee: but *thou* hast preferred *death* to *affliction*, thereby setting thy wisdom against the wisdom of God. Many in affliction, long for death; and yet they are not prepared to appear before God! What madness is this! If he takes them at their wish, they are ruined for ever. Affliction may be the means of their salvation; the wished-for death, of their eternal destruction.

Verse 22. *God exalteth by his power*] He has brought thee low, but he can raise thee up. Thou art not yet out of the reach of his mercy. Thy affliction is a proof that he acts towards thee as a merciful Parent. He knows what is best to be done; he teaches thee how thou shouldst suffer and improve. Why sin against his kindness? *Who can teach like him?*

Verse 23. *Who hath enjoined him his way*] Has God taken instructions from any man how he shall govern the world?

Thou hast wrought iniquity?] Who can prove, in the whole compass of the creation, that there is one thing *imperfect, superabundant*, or *out of its place?* Who can show that there is, in the course of the Divine providence, one *unrighteous*, cruel, or unwise *act?* All the cunning and wickedness of man have never been able to find out the *smallest flaw* in the work of God.

Verse 24. *Remember that thou magnify his work*] Take this into consideration; instead of fretting against the dispensations of Divine providence, and quarrelling with thy Maker, attentively survey his works; consider the operation of his hands; and see the proofs of his *wisdom* in the *plan* of all, of his *power* in the *production* and *support* of all, and of his *goodness* in the *end* for which all have been made, and to which every operation in *nature* most obviously tends; and then *magnify his work.* Speak of him as thou shalt find; let the visible works of thy Maker prove to thee his eternal power and Godhead, and let *nature* lead thee to the Creator.

Verse 25. *Every man may see it*] He who says he can examine the earth with a philosophic eye, and the heavens with the eye of an astronomer, and yet says he cannot see in them a system of infinite skill and contrivance, must be ignorant of science, or lie against his conscience, and be utterly unworthy of confidence or respect.

Verse 26. *God is great*] He is *omnipotent.*

We know him *not*] He is *unsearchable.*

Neither can the number of his years be searched out.] He is *eternal.*

These three propositions are an ample foundation for endless disquisition. As to paraphrase and comment, they need none in this place; they are too profound, comprehensive, and sublime.

Verse 27. *He maketh small the drops of water*] This appears simply to refer to *evaporation*, and perhaps it would be better to translate יגרע *yegara*, "he exhales;" detaches the smallest particles of the aqueous mass from the surface in order to form *clouds*, as *reservoirs* for the purpose of furnishing *rain* for the watering of the earth. God is seen in *little* things, as well as *great things;* and the *inconceivably little*, as well as the *stupendously great*, are equally the work of *Omnipotence.*

They pour down rain] These exceedingly minute drops or *vapour* become collected in *clouds;* and then, when *agitated by winds*, &c., many particles being united, they become *too heavy* to be sustained by the air in which they before were suspended, and so *fall down* in rain, which is either a *mist*, a *drizzle*, a *shower*,

A. M. cir. 2484
B. C. cir. 1520
Ante I. Olymp. cir. 744
Ante U. C. cir. 767

they pour down rain according
to the vapour thereof:
28 [h]Which the clouds do drop
and distil upon man abundantly.
29 Also can *any* understand the spreadings
of the clouds, *or* the noise of his tabernacle?

30 Behold, he [i]spreadeth his
light upon it, and covereth [k]the
bottom of the sea.
31 For [l]by them judgeth
he the people; he [m]giveth meat in abundance.

[h]Prov. iii. 20——[i]Chap. xxxvii. 3——[k]Heb. *the roots* [l]Chap. xxxvii. 13; xxxviii. 23

[m]Psalm cxxxvi. 25; Acts xiv. 17

a *storm*, or a *waterspout*, according to the influence of different *winds*, or the presence and quantum of the *electric fluid*. And all this is proportioned, לְאֵדוֹ *le-edo*, "to its vapour," to the *quantity of the fluid evaporated* and condensed into clouds.

Verse 28. *Which the clouds do drop*] In proportion to the *evaporation* will be the *clouds* or *masses of volatilized* and *suspended vapour;* and in proportion to this will be the quantum of *rain* which in different forms will fall upon the earth.

There is a remarkable addition to this verse in the *Septuagint*. I shall insert the whole verse: Ῥυησονται παλαιωματα, εσκιασε δε νεφη επι αμυθητῳ βροτῳ· ὡραν εθετο κτηνεσιν, οιδασι δε κοιτης ταξιν· επι τουτοις πασιν ουκ εξισταται σου ἡ διανοια, ουδε διαλλασσεται σου ἡ καρδια απο σωματος; "The rains descend, and the clouds cover with their shadows multitudes of men: he hath appointed to animals to know the order of their dwellings. At the contemplation of these things is not thy mind transported, and thy heart ready to part from thy body?"

Verse 29. *Can* any *understand the spreadings of the clouds*] Though the *vapour* appear to be fortuitously raised, and subject, when suspended in the atmosphere, to innumerable *accidents*, to different winds and currents which might drive it all to the *sandy deserts*, or direct its course so that it should fall again into the *great deep* from which it has been exhaled, without watering and refreshing the earth; yet so does the good and wise providence of God manage this matter, that every part of the arable terrene surface receives an ample supply; and in every place, where requisite, it may be truly said that "The rain cometh down, and the snow from heaven, and water the earth, and cause it to bring forth and bud, that it may minister seed to the sower, and bread to the eater."

In *Egypt*, where there is *little or no rain*, the earth is watered by the annual *inundation of the Nile;* there, because this system of *evaporation* is not necessary, it does not exist. Who can account for this economy? How are these clouds so judiciously and effectually *spread through the atmosphere*, so as to supply the wants of the earth, of men, and of cattle? I ask, with Elihu, "Who can understand the spreadings of these clouds?" And I should like to see that volunteer in the solution of paradoxes who would step forward and say, *I am the man.*

The noise of his tabernacle?] By the *tabernacle* we may understand the whole *firmament* or *atmospheric expansion;* the place where the Almighty seems more particularly to dwell; whence he sends forth the *rain of his strength*, and the *thunder of his power.*

The *noise* must refer to the blowing of winds and tempests, or to the claps, peals, and rattling of thunder, by means of the electric fluid.

Verse 30. *He spreadeth his light upon it*] Or, as Mr. *Good* translates, "He throweth forth from it his flash." These two verses may both have an allusion to the sudden rarefaction of that part of the atmosphere whence the thunder proceeds, by the agency of the electric fluid; the *rushing in of the air* on each side to restore the equilibrium, which the passage of the fire had before destroyed. The noise produced by this sudden rushing in of the air, as well as that occasioned by the *ignition* of the *hydrogen gas*, which is one of the constituents of water, is *the thunder of his tabernacle*, viz., the *atmosphere*, where God appears, in such cases, to be manifesting his presence and his power.

Elihu says that *God spreadeth his light upon it.* This is spoken in reference to the *flashes* and *coruscations* of *lightning* in the time of thunder storms, when, even in a dark night, a *sudden flash* illuminates for a moment the surface of the earth under that place.

And covereth the bottom of the sea.] He doth whatsoever it pleaseth him in the heavens above, in the earth beneath, in the sea, and in all deep places. Yea, the depths of the sea are as much under his control and influence as the atmosphere, and its whole collection of vapours, meteors, and galvanic and electric fluids.

Verse 31. *By them judgeth he the people*] He makes storms, tempests, winds, hurricanes, tornadoes, thunder and lightning, drought and inundation, the instruments of his justice, to punish rebellious nations.

He giveth meat in abundance.] Though by these he punishes offenders, yet through the same, as instruments, he provides for the wants of men and animals in general. Storms, tempests, and hurricanes, agitate the lower regions of the atmosphere, disperse noxious vapours, and thus render it fit for *respiration;* and without these it would soon become a stagnant, putrid, and deadly mass, in which neither animals could live, nor vegetables thrive. And by *dews*, *rains*, *snows*, *frosts*, *winds*, *cold*, and *heat*, he fructifies the earth, and causes it to bring forth abundantly, so that every thing living is filled with plenteousness.

Some critics translate this latter clause thus:—*He passeth sentence amain.* I cannot see this meaning in the original words. Not one of the versions has so understood them; nor does this translation, supposing even that the Hebrew would bear it, give so fine and so elegant an idea as that of the common version. I always feel reluctant to give a sense in any case that is not supported in some of its parts by any of the ancient versions, and more especially when it is contrary to the whole of them; and still more particularly when opposed to the *Arabic*, which in the *Book of Job*, contain-

A. M. cir. 2484
B. C. cir. 1520
Ante I. Olymp. cir. 744
Ante U. C. cir. 767

32 [n]With clouds he covereth the light; and commandeth it not to *shine* by *the cloud* that cometh betwixt.

33 [o]The noise thereof showeth concerning it, the cattle also concerning [p]the vapour.

[n]Psa. cxlvii. 8——[o]1 Kings xviii. 41, 45 [p]Heb. *that which goeth up*

ing so many *Arabisms*, I consider to be of very great importance.

Verse 32. *With clouds he covereth the light.*] This is an extraordinary saying, על כפים כסה אור *al cappayim kissah or*, which Mr. *Good* translates, "He brandisheth the blaze athwart the concave." The *Vulgate*, with which all the other *versions* less or more agree, has, *In manibus abscondit lucem*, "In his hands he hideth the light;" or, more literally, "By the hollow of his hands (כפים *cappayim*) he concealeth the light, (אור *or*,") the *fountain of light*, i. e., the SUN.

And commandeth it not to shine *by* the cloud *that cometh betwixt.*] I am afraid this is no translation of the original. Old *Coverdale* is better:—**And at his commandement it commeth agayne;** which is a near copy of the *Vulgate*. Here again Mr. *Good* departs from all the versions, both ancient and modern, by translating thus:—"And launcheth his penetrating bolt." Dr. Stock, in my opinion, comes nearer the original and the versions in his translation:—

"And giveth charge as to what it shall meet."

The mending of the text by conjecture, to which we should only recur in desperate necessity, has furnished Mr. *Good* and *Reiske* with the above translation. For my own part, I must acknowledge an extreme difficulty both here and in the concluding verse, on which I am unwilling to lay a correcting hand. I think something of the doctrine of *eclipses* is here referred to; the *defect of the solar light*, by the *interposition* of the *moon*. So in the time of an eclipse God is represented as *covering the body of the sun with the hollow of his hand*, and thus obscuring the solar light, and then removing his hand so as to permit it to re-illuminate the earth.

Mr. *Good* gets his translation by dividing the words in a different manner from the present text. I shall give both:—

Hebrew: ויצו עליה במפגיע
Vayetsav aleyha bemaphgia

Mr. *Good:* ויצוע ליהב מפגיע
Veyezvo liahbe mapegio.

Of which he learnedly contends, "And launcheth his penetrating bolt," is the literal sense. The change here made, to produce the above meaning, is not a violent one; and I must leave the reader to judge of its importance.

Verse 33. *The noise thereof showeth concerning it, the cattle also concerning the vapour.*] I think this translation very unhappy. I shall give each hemistich in the original:—

יגיד עליו רעו
Yaggid alaiv reo
מקנה אף על עולה
Mikneh aph al oleh.

I think this may be translated without any violence to any word in the text:—

Its loud noise (or his thunder) shall proclaim
concerning him;
A magazine of wrath against iniquity.

This is literal, and gives, in my opinion, a proper meaning of the passage, and one in strict connection with the context. And it is worthy of remark that every wicked man trembles at the *noise of thunder* and the *flash of lightning*, and considers this a *treasury of Divine wrath*, emphatically called among us *the artillery of the skies;* and whenever the noise is heard, it is considered *the voice of God*. Thus the thunder *declares concerning him*. The next chapter, which is a continuation of the subject here, confirms and illustrates this meaning. For יגיד *yaggid*, Houbigant reads יניד *yanid;* and for מקנה *mikneh*, מקנאת *mikkinath;* and translates thus: "He agitates with himself his thunder, from the indignation of his wrath against iniquity."

CHAPTER XXXVII

Elihu continues to set forth the wisdom and omnipotence of God, as manifested in the thunder and lightning, 1–5; *in the snows and frosts,* 6–8; *in various meteors; and shows the end for which they are sent,* 9–13. *Job is exhorted to consider the wondrous works of God in the light, in the clouds, in the winds, in heat and cold, in the formation of the heavens, and in the changes of the atmosphere,* 14–22. *The perfections of God, and how he should be reverenced by his creatures,* 23, 24.

A. M. cir. 2484
B. C. cir. 1520
Ante I. Olymp. cir. 744
Ante U. C. cir. 767

AT this also my heart trembleth, and is moved out of his place.

2 [a]Hear attentively the noise of his voice, and the sound *that* goeth out of his mouth.

3 He directeth it under the whole heaven, and his [b]lightning unto the [c]ends of the earth.

4 After it [d]a voice roareth: he thundereth with the voice of his excellency; and he will not stay them when his voice is heard.

[a]Heb. *Hear in hearing*——[b]Heb. *light*

[c]Heb. *wings of the earth*——[d]Psa. xxix. 3; lxviii. 33

NOTES ON CHAP. XXXVII

Verse 1. *My heart trembleth*] This is what the *Septuagint* has anticipated; see under ver. 28 of the preceding chapter. A proper consideration of God's majesty in the *thunder* and *lightning* is enough to appal the stoutest heart, confound the wisest mind, and fill all with humility and devotion. This, to the middle of ver. 5, should be added to the preceding chapter, as it is a continuation of the account of the thunder and lightning given at the conclusion of that chapter. Our present division is as absurd as it is unfortunate.

Verse 2. *Hear attentively*] "Hear with hearing." The words seem to intimate that there was *actually at that time* a violent storm of thunder and lightning, and that the successive peals were now breaking over the house, and the lightning flashing before their eyes. The storm *continued* till Elihu had finished, and out of *that storm* the Almighty spoke. See the beginning of the succeeding chapter.

The noise of his voice] The sudden *clap.*

And the sound that *goeth out.*] The *peal* or *continued rattling, pounding,* and *thumping,* to the end of the peal. The whole is represented as the *voice of God* himself, and the *thunder* is immediately *issuing from his mouth.*

Verse 3. *He directeth it under the whole heaven*] He directeth it (*the lightning*) under the whole heaven, in the twinkling of an eye from east to west; *and its light*—the reflection of the flash, not the *lightning, unto the ends of the earth,* so that a whole hemisphere seems to see it at the same instant.

Verse 4. *After it a voice roareth*] After the flash has been seen, the peal is heard; and this will be more or fewer seconds after the peal, in proportion to the distance of the thunder cloud from the ear. Lightning traverses any space without any perceivable succession of time; nothing seems to be any obstacle to its progress. A multitude of persons taking hands, the first and the last connected with the electric machine, all feel the shock in the same instant; and were there a chain as conductor to go round the globe, the last would feel the shock in the same moment as the first. But as *sound* depends on the undulations of the air for its propagation, and is known to travel at the rate of only 1142 feet in a second; consequently, if the flash were only 1142 feet from the spectator, it would be seen in one second, or one swing of the pendulum, *before* the sound could reach the *ear,* though the clap and the flash take place in the same instant, and if twice this distance, two seconds, and so on. It is of some consequence to know that lightning, at a considerable distance, suppose six or eight seconds of time, is never known to burn, kill, or do injury. When the flash and the clap immediately succeed each other, then there is strong ground for apprehension, as the thunder cloud is *near.* If the thunder cloud be a *mile and a half* distant, it is, I believe, never known to kill man or beast, or to do any damage to buildings, either by throwing them down or burning them. Now its distance may be easily known by means of a pendulum clock, or watch that has seconds. When the *flash* is *seen,* count the *seconds* till the *clap* is *heard.* Then compute: If only one second is counted, then the thunder cloud is within 1142 feet, or about 380 yards; if two seconds, then its distance is 2284 feet, or 761 yards; if three seconds, then 3426 feet, or 1142 yards; if four seconds, then the cloud is distant 4568 feet, or 1522 yards; if five seconds, then the distance is 5710 feet, or 1903 yards; if six seconds, then the distance is 6852 feet, or 2284 yards, one mile and nearly one-third; if seven seconds, then the distance of the cloud is 7994 feet, or 2665 yards, or one mile and a half, and 25 yards. Beyond this distance lightning has not been known to do any damage, the fluid being too much diffused, and partially absorbed, in its passage over *electric* bodies, i. e., those which are not fully impregnated by the electric matter, and which receive their full charge when they come within the electric attraction of the lightning. For more on the rain produced by thunder storms, see on chap. xxxviii. 25. This scale may be carried on at pleasure, by adding to the last sum for every second 1142 feet, and reducing to yards and miles as above, allowing 1760 yards to one mile.

He thundereth with the voice of his excellency] גאונו *geono, of his majesty:* nor is there a sound in nature more descriptive of, or more becoming, the majesty of God, than that of THUNDER. We hear the *breeze* in its *rustling,* the *rain* in its *pattering,* the *hail* in its *rattling,* the *wind* in its *hollow howlings,* the *cataract* in its *dash,* the *bull* in his *bellowing,* the *lion* in his *roar;* but we hear GOD, the Almighty, the Omnipresent, in the continuous peal of THUNDER! This sound, and this sound only, becomes the majesty of Jehovah.

And he will not stay them] ולא יעקבם *velo yeahkebem,* and he hath not *limited* or *circumscribed* them. His lightnings light the world; literally, the whole world. The electric fluid is diffused through all nature, and everywhere art can exhibit it to view. To his thunder and lightning, therefore, he has assigned no limits. And when his voice soundeth, when the lightning goes forth, who shall assign its limits, and who can stop its progress? It is, like God, IRRESISTIBLE.

A. M. cir. 2484
B. C. cir. 1520
Ante I. Olymp. cir. 744
Ante U. C. cir. 767

5 God thundereth marvellously
with his voice; [e]great things
doeth he, which we cannot comprehend.
6 For [f]he saith to the snow, Be thou *on*
the earth; [g]likewise to the small
rain, and to the great rain of his
strength.
7 He sealeth up the hand of
every man: [h]that all men may know his work.

A. M. cir. 2484
B. C. cir. 1520
Ante I. Olymp. cir. 744
Ante U. C. cir. 767

[e]Chap. v. 9; ix. 10; xxxvi. 26; Rev. xv. 3——[f]Psa. cxlvii. 16, 17

[g]Heb. *and to the showers of rain, and to the showers of rain of his strength*——[h]Psa. cix. 27

Verse 5. *God thundereth marvellously with his voice*] This is the conclusion of Elihu's description of the lightning and thunder: and here only should chap. xxxvi. have ended. He began, chap. xxxvi. 29, with the *noise of God's tabernacle;* and he ends here with the *marvellous thundering* of Jehovah. Probably the writer of the book of Job had seen the description of a similar thunder storm as given by the psalmist, Psa. lxxvii. 16, 17, 18, 19:—

Ver. 16. The waters saw thee, O God!
The waters saw thee, and were afraid.
Yea, the deeps were affrighted!
Ver. 17. The clouds poured out water;
The ethers sent forth a sound;
Yea, thine arrows went abroad.
Ver. 18. The voice of thy thunder was through the expanse:
The lightnings illumined the globe;
The earth trembled and shook!
Ver. 19. Thy way is in the sea,
And thy paths on many waters;
But thy footsteps are not known.

Great things doeth he] This is the beginning of a new paragraph; and relates particularly to the phenomena which are afterwards mentioned. All of them wondrous things; and, in many respects, to us incomprehensible.

Verse 6. *For he saith to the snow, Be thou on the earth*] SNOW is generally defined, "A well-known meteor, formed by the freezing of the vapours in the atmosphere." We may consider the formation of snow thus:—A cloud of vapours being condensed into drops, these drops, becoming too heavy to be suspended in the atmosphere, descend; and, meeting with a *cold region* of the air, they are frozen, each drop shooting into several points. These still continuing their descent, and meeting with some intermitting gales of a warmer air, are a little thawed, blunted, and again, by falling into colder air, frozen into clusters, or so entangled with each other as to fall down in what we call *flakes.*

Snow differs from *hail* and *hoar-frost* in being *crystallized:* this appears on examining a flake of snow with a magnifying glass; when the whole of it will appear to be composed of fine *spicula* or points diverging like rays from a centre. I have often observed the particles of snow to be of a regular figure, for the most part beautiful stars of *six points* as clear and transparent as ice. On each of these points are other collateral points, set at the same angles as the main points themselves, though some are irregular, the points broken, and some are formed of the fragments of other regular stars. I have observed snow to fall sometimes entirely in the form of separate regular *six-pointed stars,* without either clusters or flakes, and each so large as to be the eighth of an inch in diameter.

The *lightness* of snow is owing to the excess of its *surface,* when compared with the *matter* contained under it.

Its *whiteness* is owing to the small particles into which it is divided: for take *ice,* opaque almost to *blackness,* and pound it fine, and it becomes as white as snow.

The immediate cause of the formation of snow is not well understood: it has been attributed to *electricity;* and *hail* is supposed to owe its more compact form to a more intense electricity, which unites the particles of *hail* more closely than the moderate electricity does those of *snow.* But rain, snow, hail, frost, ice, &c., have all one common origin; they are formed out of the *vapours* which have been exhaled by heat from the surface of the waters.

Snow, in northern countries, is an especial blessing of Providence; for, by covering the earth, it prevents corn and other vegetables from being destroyed by the intense cold of the air in the winter months; and especially preserves them from cold piercing winds. It is not a fact that it possesses in itself any fertilizing quality, such as *nitrous salts,* according to vulgar opinion: its whole use is covering the vegetables from intense cold, and thus preventing the natural heat of the earth from escaping, so that the intense cold cannot freeze the juices in the tender tubes of vegetables, which would *rupture* those tubes, and so destroy the plant.

Mr. *Good* alters the *punctuation* of this verse, and translates thus:—

Behold, he saith to the snow, BE!
On earth then falleth it.
To the rain,—and it falleth:
The rains of his might.

By the *small rain,* we may understand *drizzling showers:* by the *rain of his strength,* sudden *thunder storms,* when the rain descends in *torrents:* or violent rain from dissipating water-spouts.

Verse 7. *He sealeth up the hand of every man*] After all that has been said, and much of it most learnedly, on this verse, I think that the act of *freezing* is probably intended; that when the earth is bound up by intense frost, *the hand,* יד *yad, labour,* of *every man is sealed up;* he can do no more labour in the field, till the *south wind* blow, by which a *thaw* takes place. While the earth is in this state of rigidity, *the beasts go into their dens, and remain in their places,* ver. 8, some of them sleeping out the winter in a state of torpor, and others of them feeding on the stores which they had collected in *autumn.* However, the passage may mean no more than by the severity of the rains beasts are drawn to their covers; and man is obliged to intermit all his labours. The mighty rains are past. Who would have thought that on this verse, as its *Scriptural* foundation, the doctrine of *chiromancy* is built! God has

A. M. cir. 2484
B. C. cir. 1520
Ante I. Olymp. cir. 744
Ante U. C. cir. 767

8 Then the beasts [i]go into
dens, and remain in their places.
9 [k]Out of the south cometh the
whirlwind: and cold out of
the [l]north.
10 [m]By the breath of God frost is given:
and the breadth of the waters is straitened.
11 Also by watering he wearieth the thick
cloud: he scattereth [n]his bright
cloud:
12 And it is turned round
about by his counsels: that they
may [o]do whatsoever he commandeth them
upon the face of the world in the earth.
13 [p]He causeth it to come, whether for
[q]correction, or [r]for his land, or [s]for mercy.

A. M. cir. 2484
B. C. cir. 1520
Ante I. Olymp. cir. 744
Ante U. C. cir. 767

---

[i]Psa. civ. 22——[k]Heb. *out of the chamber*——[l]Heb. *scattering* winds——[m]Chap. xxxviii. 29, 30; Psa. cxlvii. 17, 18——[n]Heb. *the cloud of his light*——[o]Psa. cxlviii. 8

[p]Exod. ix. 18, 23; 1 Sam. xii. 18, 19; Ezra x. 9; chap. xxxvi. 31——[q]Heb. *a rod*——[r]Chap. xxxviii. 26, 27 [s]2 Sam. xxi. 10; 1 Kings xviii. 45

---

so *marked the hand* of every man by the *lines* thereon exhibited, that they tell all the good or bad fortune they shall have during life; and he has done this that all men, by a judicious examination of their hands, *may know his work!* On this *John Taisnier*, a famous mathematician, lawyer, musician, and poet laureate of Cologne, has written a large folio volume, with more *hands* in it than fell to the lot of *Briareus:*—printed at Cologne, 1683.

Verse 9. *Out of the south cometh the whirlwind*] See the note on chap. ix. 9. What is rendered *south* here, is there rendered *chambers.* Mr. *Good* translates here, *the utmost zone.* The *Chaldee:*—"From the supreme chamber the commotion shall come; and from the cataracts of Arcturus the cold." What the *whirlwind,* סופה *suphah,* is, we know not. It might have been a wind peculiar to that district; and it is very possible that it was a scorching wind, something like the *simoom.*

Verse 10. *By the breath of God frost is given*] The *freezing* of water, though it is generally allowed to be the effect of *cold,* and has been carefully examined by the most eminent philosophers, is still involved in much mystery; and is a very proper subject to be produced among the *great things which God doeth,* and which *we cannot comprehend,* ver. 5. Water, when frozen, becomes *solid,* and increases considerably in *bulk.* The expansive power in freezing is so great, that, if water be confined in a *gun-barrel,* it will split the solid metal throughout its whole length. Bombshells have been filled with water, and plugged tight, and exposed to cold air, when they have been rent, though the shell has been nearly two inches thick! Attempts have been made to account for this; but they have not, as yet, been generally successful. The *breath of God freezes the waters;* and that *breath thaws them.* It is the work of Omnipotence, and there, for the present, we must *leave it.*

The breadth of the waters is straitened.] This has been variously translated; מוצק *mutsak,* which we here render *straitened,* we translate ver. 18 *melted.* Mr. *Good* thinks that the idea of a mirror is implied, or something *molten;* and on this ground it may be descriptive of the state of water formed into *ice.* He therefore translates:—

By the blast of God the frost congealeth,
And the expanse of the waters into a mirror.

I have only to observe, that in the act of freezing wind or air is necessary; for it has been observed that water which lay low in ponds did not freeze till some slight current of air fell on and ruffled the surface, when it instantly shot into ice.

Verse 11. *By watering he wearieth the thick cloud*] Perhaps it would be better to say, *The brightness* ברי *beri, dissipates the cloud;* or, if we follow our version, *By watering* the earth *he wearieth,* wearieth out or emptieth, *the thick cloud*—causes it to pour down all its contents upon the earth, that they may cause it to bring forth and bud. The *Vulgate* understood it differently: *Frumentum desiderat nubes; et nubes spargunt lumen suum.* "The grain desireth the clouds; and the clouds scatter abroad their light."

Verse 12. *And it is turned round about by his counsels*] The original is difficult: והוא מסבות מתהפך בתחבולתו *vehu mesibboth mithhappech bethachbulothav;* which has been thus paraphrased: *And he*—the sun, *makes revolutions*—causes the heavenly bodies to revolve round him, *turning round himself*—turning round his own axis, *by his attachments*—his *attractive* and *repulsive* influences, by which the heavenly bodies revolve round him, and by which, as if strongly *tied* to their *centre,* בחבל *bechebel,* with a *cable* or *rope,* they are projected to their proper distances, and prevented from *coming too near,* or *flying off too far.*

That they may do whatsoever he commandeth them] That men may perform his will, availing themselves of the influences of the sun, moon, times, seasons, &c., to cultivate the earth for the sustenance of themselves and their cattle.

Upon the face of the world in the earth.] אל פני תבל ארצה *al peney thebel aretsah, over the surface of the habitable world.* Perhaps the above exposition may appear to be too far-fetched; and possibly the passage refers only to the *revolutions of the seasons,* and the operations connected with them.

Verse 13. *He causeth it to come*] The *Vulgate* translates the text thus: *Sive in una tribu, sive in terra sua, sive in quocunque loco misericordiæ suæ eas jusserit inveniri.* "Whether in one tribe, or whether in his own land, or in whatsoever place of his mercy he has commanded them to come." In the preceding verse it is said that God conducts the clouds according to the orders of his counsels, whithersoever he pleases: and here it is added that, when he designs to heap *favours* upon any land, he commands the clouds to go thither, and pour out on it their fertilizing showers. See *Calmet.*

The *Vulgate* certainly gives a good sense, and our *common version* is also clear and intelligi-

A. M. cir. 2484
B. C. cir. 1520
Ante I. Olymp. cir. 744
Ante U. C. cir. 767

14 Hearken unto this, O Job:
stand still, and [t]consider the
wondrous works of God.
15 Dost thou know when God
disposed them, and caused the light of his
cloud to shine?
16 [u]Dost thou know the balancings of the
clouds, the wondrous works of [v]him which is
perfect in knowledge?
17 How thy garments *are*
warm, when he quieteth the
earth by the south *wind?*
18 Hast thou with him [w]spread
out the sky, *which is* strong, *and* as a molten
looking-glass?
19 Teach us what we shall say unto him?
for we cannot order *our speech* by reason of
darkness.

[t]Psa. cxi. 2——[u]Chap. xxxvi. 29——[v]Chap. xxxvi. 4——[w]Gen. i. 6; Isa. xliv. 24

ble; but there are doubts whether the *Hebrew* will bear this meaning. Here it is stated that God sends the rain either *for correction,* לשבט *leshebet*, which signifies *rod, staff, tribe*, and is here taken as the symbol of *correction;* he sends rain sometimes as a *judgment*, inundating certain lands, and sweeping away their produce by irresistible floods: or *for his land,* לארצו *leartso*, his own land, *Palestine*, the place of his favoured people: or *for mercy,* לחסד *lechesed;* when a particular district has been devoured by *locusts*, or cursed with *drought*, God, in his mercy, sends fertilizing rains to such places to restore the ears which the caterpillars have eaten, and to make the desert blossom like the garden of the Lord. Some think that Job refers to the curse brought upon the *old world* by the *waters of the deluge.* Now, although God has promised that there shall no more be a flood of waters to destroy the whole earth; yet we know he can, very consistently with his promise, inundate any particular district; or, by a superabundance of rain, render the toil of the husbandman in any place vain. Therefore, still his rain may come for judgment, for mercy, or for the especial help of his people or Church.

Verse 14. *Hearken unto this*] Hear what I say on the part of God.

Stand still] Enter into deep contemplation on the subject.

And consider] Weigh every thing; examine separately and collectively; and draw right conclusions from the whole.

The wondrous works of God.] *Endless* in their *variety; stupendous* in their *structure; complicated* in their *parts; indescribable* in their *relations* and *connections;* and *incomprehensible* in the *mode* of their *formation*, in the *cohesion* of their parts, and in the *ends* of their creation.

Verse 15. *Dost thou know when God disposed them*] Dost thou know the laws by which they are governed; and the causes which produce such and such phenomena?

And caused the light of his cloud to shine?] Almost every critic of note understands this of the *rainbow*, which God gave as a sign that the earth should no more be destroyed by water. See Gen. ix. 13, and the note there.

Verse 16. *Dost thou know the balancings of the clouds*] How are the clouds suspended in the atmosphere? Art thou so well acquainted with the nature of *evaporation*, and the *gravity* of the *air* at different heights, to support different *weights* of aqueous vapour, so as to keep them floating for a certain portion of time, and then let them down to water the earth; dost thou know these things so as to determine the laws by which they are regulated?

Wondrous works of him which is perfect in knowledge?] This is a paraphrase. Mr. *Good's* translation is much better:—

"Wonders, perfections of wisdom!"

Verse 17. *How thy garments* are *warm*] What are *warmth* and *cold?* How difficult this question! Is *heat* incontestably a *substance*, and is *cold* none? I am afraid we are in the dark on both these subjects. The existence of *caloric*, as a substance, is supposed to be demonstrated. Much, satisfactorily, has been said on this subject; but is it yet beyond doubt? I fear not. But supposing this question to be set at rest, is it demonstrated that *cold* is only a *quality*, the mere *absence* of *heat?* If it be demonstrated that there is such a substance as *caloric*, is it equally certain that there is *no such substance* as *frigoric?* But *how do our garments keep us warm?* By preventing the too great dissipation of the natural heat. And why is it that certain substances, worked into clothing, keep us warmer than others? Because they are bad conductors of caloric. Some substances conduct off the caloric or natural heat from the body; others do not conduct it at all, or imperfectly; hence those keep us warmest which, being bad conductors of caloric, do not permit the natural heat to be thrown off. In these things we know but little, after endless cares, anxieties, and experiments!

But is the question yet satisfactorily answered, why the north wind brings cold, and the south wind heat? If it be so to my *readers*, it is not so to *me;* yet I know the *reasons* which are alleged.

Verse 18. *Hast thou with him spread out the sky*] Wert thou with him when he made the expanse; fitted the weight to the winds; proportioned the aqueous to the terrene surface of the globe; the solar attraction to the quantum of vapours necessary to be stored up in the clouds, in order to be occasionally deposited in fertilizing showers upon the earth? and then dost thou know how gravity and elasticity should be such essential properties of atmospheric air, that without them and their due proportions, we should neither have animal nor vegetable life?

Strong—as a molten looking-glass?] Like a *molten mirror.* The whole concave of heaven, in a clear day or brilliant night, being like a mass of polished metal, reflecting or transmitting innumerable images.

Verse 19. *Teach us what we shall say unto him?*] Thou pretendest to be so very wise, and to know every thing about God, pray make

A. M. cir. 2484 B. C. cir. 1520 Ante I. Olymp. cir. 744 Ante U. C. cir. 767

20 Shall it be told him that I speak? If a man speak, surely he shall be swallowed up.

21 And now *men* see not the bright light which *is* in the clouds: but the wind passeth, and cleanseth them.

22 [x]Fair weather cometh out of the north: with God *is* terrible majesty.

23 *Touching* the Almighty, [y]we cannot find him out: [z]*he is* excellent in power, and in judgment, and in plenty of justice: he will not afflict.

24 Men do therefore [a]fear him: he respecteth not any *that are* [b]wise of heart.

[x]Heb. *Gold*——[y]1 Tim. vi. 16——[z]Chap. xxxvi. 5

[a]Matt. x. 28——[b]Matt. xi. 25; 1 Cor. i. 26

us as wise as thyself, that we may be able to approach with thy boldness the Sovereign of the world; and maintain our cause with thy confidence before him. As for our parts, we are ignorant; and, on all these subjects, are enveloped with darkness. Mr. *Good* translates:—

"Teach us how we may address him,
When arrayed in robes of darkness."

It is a strong and biting *irony*, however we take it.

Verse 20. *Shall it be told him that I speak?*] Shall I dare to whisper even before God? And suppose any one were to *accuse* me before him for what I have spoken of him, though that has been well intended, how should I be able to stand in his presence? I should be swallowed up in consternation, and consumed with the splendour of his majesty.

But in what state art *thou?* What hast *thou* been doing? *Thou* hast arraigned God for his government of the world; *thou* hast found fault with the dispensations of his providence; *thou* hast even charged him with *cruelty!* What will become of THEE?

Verse 21. *And now* men *see not the bright light*] Mr. *Good* gives the sense clearer:—

"Even now we cannot look at the light
When it is resplendent in the heavens,
And a wind from the north hath passed
along and cleared them."

Elihu seems to refer to the insufferable brightness of the *sun*. Can any man look at the sun shining in his strength, when a clear and strong wind has purged the sky from clouds and vapours? Much less can any gaze on the majesty of God. Every creature must sink before him. What execrably dangerous folly in man to attempt to arraign His conduct!

Verse 22. *Fair weather cometh out of the north*] Is this any version of the original מצפון זהב יאתה *mitstsaphon zahab yeetheh?* which is rendered by almost every version, ancient and modern, thus, or to this effect: "From the north cometh gold." Calmet justly remarks, that in the time of Moses. Job, and Solomon, and for a long time after, gold was obtained from Colchis, Armenia, Phasis, and the land of Ophir, which were all north of Judea and Idumea; and are in the Scriptures ordinarily termed the north country. "But what relation can there be between, *Gold cometh out of the north*, and, *With God is terrible majesty?*" Answer: Each thing has its properties, and proper characteristics, which distinguish it; and each country has its advantages. *Gold*, for instance, comes from the *northern countries;* so praises offered to the Supreme God should be accompanied with fear and trembling: and as this metal is from the north, and northern countries are the places whence it must be procured; so terrible majesty belongs to God, and in him alone such majesty is eternally resident.

As זהב *zahob*, which we translate *gold*, (see chap. xxviii. 16,) comes from a root that signifies to be *clear*, *bright*, *resplendent*, &c.; Mr. *Good* avails himself of the radical idea, and translates it *splendour:*—

"Splendour itself is with God;
Insufferable majesty."

But he alters the text a little to get this meaning, particularly in the word יאתה *yeetheh*, which we translate *cometh*, and which he contends is the pronoun אתה *itself;* the י *yod*, as a performative, here being, as he thinks, an *interpolation*. This makes a very good sense; but none of the ancient versions understood the place thus, and none of the MSS. countenance this very learned critic's emendation.

Verse 23. Touching *the Almighty, we cannot find him out*] This is a very abrupt exclamation, and highly descriptive of the state of mind in which Elihu was at this time; full of solemnity, wonder, and astonishment, at his own contemplation of this "great First Cause, least understood." The ALMIGHTY! we cannot find him out.

Excellent in power and in judgment] We must not pretend to comprehend his being, the mode of his existence, the wisdom of his counsels, nor the mysteries of his conduct.

He will not afflict.] לא יענה *la yeanneh, he will not* ANSWER. He will give account of none of his matters to us. We cannot comprehend his *motives*, nor the *ends* he has in view.

Verse 24. *Men do therefore*] Therefore men, אנשים *anashim*, wretched, miserable, ignorant, sinful men, *should fear him.*

He respecteth not any] No man is valuable in his sight on account of his wisdom; for what is his wisdom when compared with that of the *Omniscient?* Whatever good is in man, God alone is the author of it. Let him, therefore, that glorieth, glory in the Lord.

THUS ends the speech of *Elihu;* a speech of a widely different description, on the whole, from that of the three friends of Job who had spoken so largely before him. In the speeches of Eliphaz, Zophar, and Bildad, there is little besides a tissue of borrowed *wise sayings*, and *ancient proverbs* and *maxims*, relative to the nature of God, and his moral government of the world. In the speech of Elihu every thing appears to be *original;* he speaks from a deep and comprehensive mind, that had profoundly studied the subjects on which he discoursed.

His descriptions of the Divine attributes, and of the wonderful works of God, are correct, splendid, impressive, and inimitable. Elihu, having now come nearly to a close, and knowing that the Almighty would appear and speak for himself, judiciously prepares for and announces his coming by the thunder and lightning of which he has given so terrific and majestic a description in this and the preceding chapter. The evidences of the Divine presence throng on his eyes and mind; the incomprehensible glory and excellency of God confound all his powers of reasoning and description; he cannot arrange his words by reason of darkness; and he concludes with stating, that to poor weak man God must for ever be incomprehensible, and to him a subject of deep religious fear and reverence. Just then the terrible majesty of the Lord appears! Elihu is silent! The rushing mighty wind, for which the description of the thunder and lightning had prepared poor, confounded, astonished Job, proclaims the presence of Jehovah: and out of this whirlwind God answers for and proclaims himself! Reader, canst thou not conceive something of what these men felt? Art thou not astonished, perplexed, confounded, in reading over these descriptions of the thunder of God's power? Prepare, then, to hear the voice of God himself out of this whirlwind.

CHAPTER XXXVIII

The Lord answers Job out of a whirlwind, and challenges him to answer, 1–3. *He convinces him of ignorance and weakness, by an enumeration of some of his mighty works; particularly of the creation of the earth,* 4–7. *The sea and the deeps,* 8–18. *The light,* 19–21. *Snow, hail, thunder, lightning, rain, dew, ice, and hoar-frost,* 22–30. *Different constellations, and the ordinances of heaven influencing the earth,* 31–33. *Shows his own power and wisdom in the atmosphere, particularly in the thunder, lightnings, and rain,* 34–38. *His providence in reference to the brute creation,* 39–41.

A. M. cir. 2484
B. C. cir. 1520
Ante I. Olymp. cir. 744
Ante U. C. cir. 767

THEN the LORD answered
Job [a]out of the whirlwind,
and said,
2 [b]Who *is* this that darkeneth
counsel by [c]words without knowledge?
3 [d]Gird up now thy loins like a man; for I
will demand of thee, and [e]answer thou me.

4 [f]Where wast thou when I laid
the foundations of the earth? declare, [g]if thou hast understanding.
5 Who hath laid the measures
thereof, if thou knowest? or who hath
stretched the line upon it?
6 Whereupon are the [h]foundations thereof

A. M. cir. 2484
B. C. cir. 1520
Ante I. Olymp. cir. 744
Ante U. C. cir. 767

[a]So Exod. xix. 16, 18; 1 Kings xix. 11; Ezek. i. 4; Nah. i. 3——[b]Chap. xxxiv. 35; xlii. 3——[c]1 Tim. i. 7——[d]Chap. xl. 7

[e]Heb. *make me know*——[f]Psa. civ. 5; Prov. viii. 29; xxx. 4——[g]Hebrew, *if thou knowest understanding*——[h]Heb. *sockets*

NOTES ON CHAP. XXXVIII

Verse 1. *The Lord answered Job out of the whirlwind*] It is not סופה *suphah*, as in the preceding chapter, ver. 9; but סערה *searah*, which signifies something turbulent, tumultuous, or violently agitated; and here may signify what we call a *tempest*, and was intended to fill Job's mind with solemnity, and an awful sense of the majesty of God. The *Chaldee* has, *a whirlwind of grief*, making the whole rather *allegorical* than *real;* impressing the scene on Job's *imagination.*

Verse 2. *Who* is *this that darkeneth counsel*] As if he had said, Who art *thou* who pretendest to speak on the deep things of God, and the administration of his justice and providence, which thou canst not comprehend; and leavest my counsels and designs the darker for thy explanation?

Verse 3. *Gird up now thy loins*] I will not confound thee with my terrors; dismiss all fearful apprehensions from thy mind; now act like a man, כגבר *kegeber*, like a hero: stand and vindicate thyself. *For I will demand of thee*—I will ask thee a series of questions more easy of solution than those which thou hast affected to discuss already; and then thou shalt have the opportunity of answering for thyself.

The most impressive and convincing manner of arguing is allowed to be that by *interrogation*, which the Almighty here adopts. The best orations delivered by the ancients were formed after this manner. That celebrated oration of Cicero against Catiline, which is allowed to be his masterpiece, begins with a multitude of short questions, closely pressed upon each other. See the end of the chapter.

Verse 4. *Where wast thou when I laid the foundations of the earth?*] Thou hast a limited and derived being; thou art only of *yesterday;* what canst thou know? Didst thou see me create the world?

Verse 5. *Who hath laid the measures thereof*] Who hath adjusted its polar and equatorial distances from the centre?

Who hath stretched the line] Who hath formed its zones and its great circles, and adjusted the whole of its *magnitude* and *gravity* to the *orbit* in which it was to move, as well as its *distance* from that great centre about which it was to revolve? These questions show the difficulty of the subject; and that there was an unfathomable depth of counsel and design in the formation of the earth.

Verse 6. *Whereupon are the foundations thereof fastened?*] How does it continue to revolve in the immensity of space? What *supports* it? Has it foundations like a *building,*

A. M. cir. 2484 B. C. cir. 1520 Ante I. Olymp. cir. 744 Ante U. C. cir. 767

[i]fastened? or who laid the corner-
stone thereof;
7 When the morning stars sang
together, and all [k]the sons of
God shouted for joy?
8 [l]Or *who* shut up the sea with doors, when
it brake forth, *as if* it had issued out of the
womb?

9 When I made the cloud the
garment thereof, and thick darkness a swaddlingband for it,
10 And [m]brake [n]up for it my
decreed *place*, and set bars and doors,
11 And said, Hitherto shalt thou come, but
no farther: and here shall [o]thy proud waves
[p]be stayed?

[i]Heb. *made to sink*——[k]Chap. i. 6——[l]Gen. i. 9; Psa. xxxiii. 7; civ. 9; Prov. viii. 29; Jer. v. 22

[m]Or, *establish my decree upon it*——[n]Ch. xxvi. 10
[o]Heb. *the pride of thy waves*——[p]Psa. lxxxix. 9; xciii. 4

and is it fastened with a *key-stone*, to keep the mighty fabric in union?

Verse 7. *When the morning stars sang together*] This must refer to some intelligent beings who existed before the creation of the visible heavens and earth: and it is supposed that this and the following clause refer to the same beings; that by the *sons of God*, and the *morning stars*, the angelic host is meant; as they are supposed to be *first*, though perhaps not *chief*, in the order of creation.

For the latter clause the *Chaldee* has, "All the troops of angels." Perhaps their creation may be included in the term *heavens*, Gen. i. 1: "In the beginning God created the heavens and the earth." These witnessed the progress of the creation; and, when God had finished his work, celebrated his wisdom and power in the highest strains.

Verse 8. Who *shut up the sea with doors*] Who *gathered the waters together into one place*, and fixed the sea its limits, so that it cannot overpass them to inundate the earth?

When it brake forth, as if *it had issued out of the womb?*] This is a very fine metaphor. The sea is represented as a newly born infant issuing from the womb of the void and formless chaos; and the delicate circumstance of the *liquor amnii*, which bursts out previously to the birth of the fœtus, alluded to. The allusion to the birth of a child is carried on in the next verse.

Verse 9. *When I made the cloud the garment*] Alluding to the cloth in which the new-born infant is first received. The *cloud* was the same to the newly raised *vapour*, as the above recipient to the new-born child.

And thick darkness a swaddlingband for it] Here is also an allusion to the first dressings of the new-born child: it is *swathed* in order to support the body, too tender to bear even careful handling without some medium between the hand of the nurse and the flesh of the child. "The image," says Mr. *Good*, "is exquisitely maintained: the new-born ocean is represented as issuing from the womb of chaos; and its dress is that of the new-born infant."

There is here an allusion also to the creation, as described in Gen. i. *Darkness* is there said to be *on the face of the* DEEP. Here it is said, the *thick darkness* was a *swaddling-band* for the new-born SEA.

Verse 10. *And brake up for it my decreed* place] This refers to the decree, Gen. i. 9: "Let the waters under the heavens be gathered together unto one place."

And set bars and doors] *And let the dry land appear.* This formed the *bars* and *doors* of the sea; the land being everywhere a barrier against the encroachments and inundations of the sea; and great rivers, bays, creeks, &c., the doors by which it passes into the interior of continents, &c.

Verse 11. *Hitherto shalt thou come*] Thus far shall thy flux and reflux extend. The *tides* are marvellously limited and regulated, not only by the *lunar* and *solar attractions*, but by the quantum of *time* also which is required to remove any part of the earth's surface from under the immediate attractive influence of the sun and moon. And this regulation takes place by means of the *rotation* of the earth round its own axis, which causes *one thousand and forty-two* miles of its equator to pass from under any given point in the heavens in one hour; and about *five hundred and eighty* miles in the latitude of London: so that the *attracted fluid parts* are every moment passing from under the direct attractive influence, and thus the tides cannot generally be raised to any extraordinary height. The attraction of the sun and moon, and the gravitation of its own parts to its own centre, which prevent too great a *flux* on the one hand, and too great a *reflux* on the other; or, in other words, too *high* a *tide*, and too *deep* an *ebb*, are also some of those *bars* and *doors* by which its *proud waves are stayed*, and prevented from *coming farther;* all being regulated by these laws of attraction by the sun and moon, the gravitation of its own parts from the sun and moon, and the diurnal motion round its own axis, by which the fluid parts, easily yielding to the above attraction, are continually moving from under the direct attractive influence. Here a world of wisdom and management was necessary, in order to proportion all these things to each other, so as to procure the great benefits which result from the flux and reflux of the sea, and prevent the evils that must take place, at least occasionally, were not those *bars* and *doors* provided. It is well known that the spring-tides happen at the *change* and *full* of the moon, at which time she is in *conjunction* with and *opposition* to the sun. As these *retire* from their conjunction, the tides *neap* till about three days after the *first quadrature*, when the tides begin again to be more and more elevated, and arrive at their *maximum* about the *third* day after the *opposition*. From this time the tides *neap* as before till the *third* day after the *last quadrature;* and afterwards their daily elevations are continually increased till about the *third* day after the *conjunction*, when they recommence their *neaping;* the principal phenomena of the tides always taking place *at* or *near the same points* of every *lunar synodic* revolution.

A. M. cir. 2484 B. C. cir. 1520 Ante I. Olymp. cir. 744 Ante U. C. cir. 767

12 Hast thou [q]commanded the
morning since thy days; *and*
caused the dayspring to know
his place;
13 That it might take hold of the [r]ends of
the earth, that [s]the wicked might be shaken
out of it?
14 It is turned as clay *to* the
seal; and they stand as a garment.
15 And from the wicked their
[t]light is withholden, and [u]the high arm shall
be broken.
16 Hast thou [v]entered into the springs of the

[q]Psa. lxxiv. 16; cxlviii. 5——[r]Heb. *wings*——[s]Psa. civ. 35——[t]Ch. xviii. 5——[u]Psa. x. 15——[v]Psa. lxxvii. 19

Verse 12. *Hast thou commanded the morning*] This refers to *dawn* or *morning twilight*, occasioned by the *refraction* of the *solar rays* by means of the *atmosphere;* so that we receive the light by *degrees*, which would otherwise burst at once upon our eyes, and injure, if not destroy, our sight; and by which even the body of the sun himself becomes evident several minutes before he rises above the horizon.

Caused the dayspring to know his place] This seems to refer to the different *points* in which *daybreak* appears during the *course of the earth's revolution in its orbit;* and which variety of *points of appearing* depends on this annual revolution. For, as the earth goes round the sun every year in the ecliptic, one half of which is on the north side of the equinoctial, and the other half on its south side, the sun appears to change his place every day. These are matters which the wisdom of God alone could plan, and which his power alone could execute.

It may be just necessary to observe that the dawn does not appear, nor the sun rise exactly in the same point of the horizon, two successive days in the whole year, as he declines *forty-three* degrees north, and *forty-three* degrees south, of east; beginning on the 21st of March, and ending on the 22d of December; which variations not only produce the *places* of *rising* and *setting*, but also the *length of day and night.* And by this declination north and south, or approach to and recession from the tropics of Cancer and Capricorn, the solar light *takes hold of the ends of the earth*, ver. 13,—enlightens the arctic and antarctic circles in such a way as it would not do were it always on the equinoctial line; these tropics taking the sun *twenty-three and a half* degrees north, and as many south, of this line.

Verse 13. *That the wicked might be shaken out of it?*] The meaning appears to be this: as soon as the light begins to dawn upon the earth, thieves, assassins, murderers, and adulterers, who all hate and shun the light, fly like ferocious beasts to their several dens and hiding places; for such do not dare to *come to the light, lest their works be manifest*, which *are not wrought in God.* To this verse the *fifteenth* appears to belong, as it connects immediately with it, which connection the introduction of the *fourteenth* verse disturbs. "And from the wicked," such as are mentioned above, "their light is withholden;" they love darkness rather than light, because their deeds are evil; and as they prowl after their prey in the night-season, they are obliged to *sleep in the day*, and thus its "light is withholden" from them. "And the high arm shall be broken;" or, as Mr. *Good* translates, "The roving of wickedness is broken off." They can no longer pursue their predatory and injurious excursions.

Verse 14. *It is turned as clay* to *the seal*] The earth, like *soft clay*, is capable of modifying itself in endless ways, and assuming infinite forms. As a proof of this, see the astonishing variety of plants, flowers, and fruits, and the infinitely diversified hues, odours, tastes, consistency, and properties, of its vegetable productions.

There seems to be an allusion here to the *sealing of clay*, which I believe *has been*, and *is now*, frequent in the East. *Six* of those *Eastern seals* for *sealing clay*, made of brass, the *figures* and *characters* all in *relief*, the interstices being entirely perforated and cut out, so that the upper side of the seal is the same as the lower, now lie before me. They seem to have been used for stamping *pottery*, as some of the fine clay still appears in the interstices.

And they stand as a garment.] The earth receiving these *impressions* from the solar light and heat, plants and flowers spring up, and *decorate* its surface as the most beautiful *stamped garment* does the person of the most sumptuously dressed female.

Mr. *Good* translates the whole verse thus:—

"Canst thou cause them to bend round as clay to the mould, so that they are made to sit like a garment?"

He supposes that reference is here made to the *rays of light;* but take his own words: "The image, as it appears to me, is taken directly from the art of pottery, an image of very frequent recurrence in Scripture; and in the present instance admirably forcible in painting the ductility with which the new light of the morning bends round like clay to the mould, and accompanies the earth in every part of its shape so as to fit it, as we are expressly told in the ensuing metaphor, like a garment, as the clay fits the mould itself." Mr. *Good* supposes that a *mould* in which the pottery is *formed*, not a *seal* by which it is *impressed*, is referred to here. In this sense I do not see the metaphor consistent, nor the allusion happy. It is well known that the rays of light never *bend.* They may be reflected at particular angles, but they never go out of a *straight course.* A gun might as well be expected to shoot round a corner, as a ray of light to go out of a straight line, or to follow the sinuous or angular windings of a tube, canal, or adit. But if we take in the sun as he advances in his diurnal voyage, or rather the earth, as it turns round its own axis from west to east, the metaphor of Mr. *Good* will be correct enough; but we must leave out *bending* and *ductility*, as every part of the earth's surface will be at least successively *invested* with the light.

Verse 16. *Hast thou entered into the springs*

A. M. cir. 2484
B. C. cir. 1520
Ante I. Olymp. cir. 744
Ante U. C. cir. 767

sea? or hast thou walked in the
search of the depth?
17 Have [w]the gates of death
been opened unto thee? or hast
thou seen the doors of the shadow of death?
18 Hast thou perceived the breadth of the
earth? declare if thou knowest it all.
19 Where *is* the way *where* light dwelleth?
and *as for* darkness, where *is* the place
thereof,
20 That thou shouldest take it
[x]to the bound thereof, and that
thou shouldest know the paths *to*
the house thereof?
21 Knowest thou *it*, because thou wast then
born? or *because* the number of thy days *is*
great?
22 Hast thou entered into [y]the treasures of
the snow? or hast thou seen the treasures of
the hail,

[w]Psa. ix. 13——[x]Or, *at* —— [y]Psa. cxxxv. 7

of the sea? Of these *springs*, *inlets*, or *outlets* of the sea, we know just as much as Job. There was prevalent among philosophers an opinion, that through a *porous bottom* fresh matter was constantly oozing by which the sea was supplied with new materials. But through such pores these materials might as well ooze *out* as ooze *in*.

Walked in the search of the depth?] Hast thou walked from the shallow beach through the great ocean's bed, till thou hast arrived at its profoundest depths? In other words, Dost thou know the depths of the sea? Job, we may presume, did not. No man since him has found them out. In multitudes of places they are unfathomed by any means hitherto used by man.

Verse 17. *Have the gates of death been opened unto thee?* Dost thou know in what the article of *death* consists? This is as inexplicable as the question, What is animal *life?*

The doors of the shadow of death?] צלמות *tsalmaveth, the intermediate state, the openings into the place of separate spirits.* Here *two* places are distinguished: מות *maveth, death*, and צלמות *tsalmaveth, the shadow of death.* It will not do to say, *death* is the *privation of life*, for what then would be the *shadow* of that *privation?*

Verse 18. *The breadth of the earth?*] At that time the circumference of the globe was not known, because the earth itself was supposed to be a vast *extended plain*, bordered all round with the ocean and the sky.

Verse 19. Where *light dwelleth*] What is the *source of light?* Yea, what is *light* itself? It is not in the *sun*, for *light* was before the *sun;* but *what* is *light?* It is no doubt a *substance;* but of what kind? and of what are its *particles?* As to *darkness*, what is IT? Is it philosophical to say, it is the mere *privation of light?* I shall think philosophy has made some advances to general accuracy and perfection when it proves to us what *cold* is, and what *darkness* is, leaving *mere privations* out of the question.

Verse 20. *Shouldest take it to the bound thereof?*] Or, as Mr. *Good*, translates, "That thou shouldest lay hold of it in its boundary." That thou shouldest go to the very spot where *light* commences, and where *darkness* ends; and see the *house* where each dwells. Here *darkness* and *light* are *personified*, each as a real intelligent being, having a separate existence and local dwelling. But poetry animates everything. It is the region of fictitious existence.

I believe this verse should be translated thus:—"For thou canst take US to its boundary; for thou knowest the paths to its house." This is a strong irony, and there are several others in this Divine speech. Job had valued himself too much on his knowledge; and a chief object of this august speech is to humble his "knowing pride," and to cause him to seek true wisdom and humility where they are to be found.

Verse 21. *Knowest thou*] This is another strong and biting irony, and the literal translation proves it: "Thou knowest, because thou was then born; and the number of thy days is great," or *multitudinous*, רבים *rabbim, multitudes.*

Verse 22. *The treasures of the snow*] The places where *snow* is formed, and the cause of that formation. See on chap. xxxvii. 6.

Treasures of the hail] It is more easy to account for the formation of *snow* than of *hail.* Hail, however, is generally supposed to be drops of rain frozen in their passage through cold regions of the air; and the hail is always in proportion to the *size of the raindrop* from which it was formed. But this meteor does not appear to be formed from a *single drop of water*, as it is found to be composed of *many small spherules* frozen together, the centre sometimes *soft* like snow, and at other times formed of a *hard nucleus*, which in some cases has been of a *brown* colour, capable of ignition and explosion. In the description given of snow, chap. xxxvii. 6, it has been stated that both *snow* and *hail* owe their formation to electricity; the hail being formed in the higher regions of the air, where the cold is intense, and the electric matter abundant. By this agency it is supposed that a great number of aqueous particles are brought together and frozen, and in their descent collect other particles, so that the *density* of the substance of the hailstone grows less and less from the centre, this being formed *first* in the higher regions, and the surface being collected in the lower. This theory is not in all cases supported by fact, as in some instances the *centre* has been found *soft* and *snow-like*, when the *surface* has been *hard.*

Hail is the only meteor of this kind, from which no apparent good is derived. *Rain* and *dew* invigorate and give life to the whole vegetable world; *frost*, by expanding the water contained in the earth, pulverizes and renders the soil fertile; *snow* covers and defends vegetables from being destroyed by too severe a frost; but *hail* does none of these. It not only does *no good*, but often *much harm*—always

A. M. cir. 2484 B. C. cir. 1520 Ante I. Olymp. cir. 744 Ante U. C. cir. 767

23 [z]Which I have reserved against the time of trouble, against the day of battle and war?
24 By what way is the light parted, *which* scattereth the east wind upon the earth?
25 Who [a]hath divided a water-course for the overflowing of waters, or a way for the lightning of thunder;
26 To cause it to rain on the earth, *where* no man *is; on* the wilderness, wherein *there is* no man;
27 [b]To satisfy the desolate and waste

[z]Exod. ix. 18; Josh. x. 11; Isa. xxx. 30; Ezek. xiii. 11, 13; Rev. xvi. 21——[a]Chap. xxviii. 26——[b]Psa. cvii. 35

some. It has a chilling, blasting effect in spring and summer, and cuts the tender plants so as to injure or totally destroy them. In short, the *treasures* of hail are not well known; and its *use* in the creation has not yet been ascertained. But *frost* is God's universal *plough*, by which he cultivates the whole earth.

Verse 23. *Reserved against the time of trouble*] לעת צר *leeth tsar*, "to the season of strictness," i. e., the season when the earth is *constringed* or *bound* by the frost.

Against the day of battle and war?] Hailstones being often employed as instruments of God's displeasure against his enemies, and the enemies of his people. There is probably an allusion here to the *plague of hail* sent on the Egyptians. See Exod. ix. 23, and the notes there, for more particulars concerning *hailstones*, remarkable showers of them, &c. There may be also a reference to Josh. x. 10, 11, where a destructive shower of what are called *hailstones* fell upon the Canaanitish kings who fought against Israel. See the note there also.

Verse 24. *By what way is the light parted*] Who can accurately describe the *cause* and *operation* of a *thunder cloud*, the cause, nature, and mode of operation of the *lightning* itself? Is it a *simple element* or *compound substance?* What is its *velocity?* and why not *conductible* by *every kind* of *substance*, as it is known to exist in *all*, and, indeed, to be diffused through every portion of nature? How *is it parted?* How does it take its *zigzag* form? This is the curious, indescribable, and unknown *parting*. Are all the *causes* of *positive* and *negative* electricity found out? What are *its particles*, and how do they *cohere*, and in what *order* are they propagated? Much has been said on all these points, and how little of that much satisfactorily!

Scattereth the east wind upon the earth?] קדים *kadim*, the *eastern storm*, *euroclydon*, or *levanter*.

Verse 25. *Divided a water-course*] The original תעלה *tealah*, from עלה *alah*, *to ascend*, may signify rather a *cloud*, or *clouds* in general, where the waters are *stored up*. I cannot see how the *overflowings* or *torrents* of water can be said to *ascend* any other way than by *evaporation;* and it is by this Divine contrivance that the earth is not only *irrigated*, but even *dried;* and by this means too much moisture is not permitted to lie upon the ground, which would not only be injurious to vegetation, but even destroy it. But *query*, may not a *waterspout* be intended?

A way for the lightning of thunder] "A path for the bolt of thunder." God is represented as directing the course even of the *lightning;* he launches the bolt, and makes the path in which it is to run. To grasp, manage, and dart the thunderbolt or lightning, was a work which heathenism gave to Jupiter, its supreme god. None of the inferior deities were capable of this. But who can thunder with a voice like the Almighty? He is THE THUNDERER.

Verse 26. *To cause it to rain on the earth*] It is well known that *rain* falls copiously in thunder-storms. The *flash* is first seen, the *clap* is next heard, and last the *rain* descends. The *lightning* travels all lengths in no perceivable *succession* of time. *Sound* is propagated at the rate of 1142 feet in a second. *Rain* travels still more slowly, and will be seen *sooner* or *later* according to the weight of the drops, and the *distance* of the cloud from the place of the spectator. Now the *flash*, the *clap*, and the *rain*, take place all in the same moment, but are discernible by us in the *succession* already mentioned, and for the reasons given above; and more at large in the note on chap. xxxvi. 29, &c.

But how are these things formed? The *lightning* is represented as coming immediately from the hand of God. The *clap* is the effect of the *lightning*, which causes a vacuum in that part of the atmosphere through which it passes; the air rushing in to restore the equilibrium may cause much of the noise that is heard in the clap. An easy experiment on the airpump illustrates this: Take a glass receiver open at both ends, over one end tie a piece of sheep's bladder wet, and let it stand till thoroughly dry. Then place the open end on the plate of the airpump, and exhaust the air slowly from under it. The bladder soon becomes *concave*, owing to the pressure of the atmospheric air on it, the supporting air in the receiver being partly thrown out. Carry on the exhaustion, and the air presses at the rate of *fifteen pounds* on every square inch; see on chap. xxviii. The fibres of the bladder, being no longer capable of bearing the pressure of the atmospheric column upon the receiver, are torn to pieces, with a noise equal to the report of a musket, which is occasioned by the air rushing in to restore the equilibrium. Imagine a rapid succession of such experiments, and you have the *peal* of thunder, the rupture of the first bladder being the *clap*. But the *explosion* of the gases (oxygen and hydrogen) of which water is composed will also account for the noise. See below.

But how does the thunder cause rain? By the most accurate and incontestable experiments it is proved that *water* is a composition of *two elastic airs* or *gases* as they are called, *oxygen* and *hydrogen*. In 100 parts of water there are 88¼ of *oxygen*, and 11¾ of *hydrogen*. Pass a succession of electric sparks through

A. M. cir. 2484 B. C. cir. 1520 Ante I. Olymp. cir. 744 Ante U. C. cir. 767

ground; and to cause the bud
of the tender herb to spring forth?
28 [c]Hath the rain a father?
or who hath begotten the drops
of dew?

29 Out of whose womb came the
ice? and the [d]hoary frost of heaven,
who hath gendered it?
30 The waters are hid as *with*
a stone, and the face of the deep [e]is [f]frozen.

[c]Jer. xiv. 22; Psa. cxlvii. 8——[d]Psa. cxlvii. 16

[e]Heb. *is taken*——[f]Chap. xxxvii. 10

water by means of a proper apparatus, and the two gases are produced in the proportions mentioned above.

To decompose water by *galvanism:*—Take a narrow glass tube *three* or *four inches* long; fit *each* end with a cork penetrated by a piece of slender iron wire, and fill the tube with water. Let the ends of the two wires within the tube be distant from each other about *three quarters of an inch*, and let one be made to communicate with the *top*, the other with the bottom of a *galvanic pile* in action. On making this communication, bubbles of air will be formed, and ascend to the top of the tube, the water decreasing as it is decomposed.

The oxygen and hydrogen formed by this experiment may be *recomposed* into the same weight of *water*. Take any quantity of the oxygen and hydrogen gases in the proportions already mentioned; ignite them by the electric spark, and they produce a quantity of *water* equal in weight to the gases employed. Thus, then, we can convert *water* into *air*, and reconvert this air into water; and the proportions hold as above. I have repeatedly seen this done, and assisted in doing it, but cannot, in this place, describe every thing in detail.

Now to the purpose of this note: the *rain* descending after the *flash* and the *peal*. The electric spark or matter of lightning, passing through the atmosphere, ignites and decomposes the *oxygen* and *hydrogen*, which *explode*, and the *water* which was formed of these two falls down in the form of *rain*. The explosion of the gases, as well as the rushing in of the circumambient air to restore the equilibrium, will account for the *clap* and *peal:* as the *decomposition* and *ignition* of them will account for the *water* or *rain* which is the attendant of a thunder storm. Thus by the *lightning of thunder* God *causes it to rain on the earth*. How marvellous and instructive are his ways!

Verse 27. *To satisfy the desolate and waste*] The thunder cloud not only explodes over *inhabited* countries, that the air may be purified, and the rain sent down to fertilize the earth, but it is conducted over *deserts* where there is no human inhabitant; and this to *cause the bud of the tender herb to spring forth:* for there are beasts, fowls, and insects, that inhabit the desert and the wilderness, and must be nourished by the productions of the ground. Every tribe of animals was made by the hand of God, and even the lowest of them is supported by his kind providence.

Verse 28. *Hath the rain a father?*] Or, *Who is the father of the rain?* We have seen above one part of the apparatus by which God produces it; other causes have been mentioned on chap. xxxvi. 27, &c.

The drops of dew?] אגלי *egley*, the sphericles, the small round drops or *globules*. *Dew* is a dense moist vapour, found on the earth in spring and summer mornings, in the form of a mizzling rain. Dr. *Hutton* defines it, "a thin, light, insensible mist or rain, descending with a slow motion, and falling while the sun is below the horizon. It appears to differ from *rain* as *less* from *more*. Its origin and matter are doubtless from the *vapours* and *exhalations* that rise from the earth and water." Various experiments have been instituted to ascertain whether dew *arises* from the *earth*, or *descends* from the *atmosphere;* and those *pro* and *con* have alternately *preponderated*. The question is not yet decided; and we cannot yet tell any more than Job *which hath begotten* the *drops of dew*, the *atmosphere* or the *earth*. Is it *water* deposited from the atmosphere, *when the surface of the ground is colder than the air?*

Verse 29. *Out of whose womb came the ice?*] Ice is a solid, transparent, and brittle body, formed of water by means of cold. Some philosophers suppose that ice is only the re-establishment of water in its *natural state;* that the mere absence of *fire* is sufficient to account for this re-establishment; and that the *fluidity of water* is a *real fusion*, like that of *metals* exposed to the action of *fire;* and differing only in this, that a greater portion of fire is necessary to one than the other. *Ice*, therefore, is supposed to be the *natural state of water;* so that in its natural state water is *solid*, and becomes fluid only by the action of fire, as solid metallic bodies are brought into a state of fusion by the same means.

Ice is *lighter* than water, its specific gravity being to that of water as *eight* to *nine*. This *rarefaction* of ice is supposed to be owing to the *air-bubbles* produced in water by *freezing*, and which, being considerably larger in proportion to the water frozen, render the body so much specifically lighter; hence *ice* always *floats* on water. The air-bubbles, during their production, acquire a great expansive power, so as to burst the containing vessels, be they ever so strong. See examples in the note on chap. xxxvii. 10.

The hoary frost of heaven, who hath gendered it?] *Hoar-frost* is the congelation of *dew*, in frosty mornings, on the grass. It consists of an assemblage of little crystals of ice, which are of various figures, according to the different disposition of the vapours when met and condensed by the cold. Its production is owing to some laws with which we are not yet acquainted. Of this subject, after the lapse and experience of between *two* and *three thousand* years, we know about as much as Job did. And the question, *What hath engendered the hoar-frost of heaven?* is, to this hour, nearly as inexplicable to *us* as it was to *him!* Is it enough to say that hoar-frost is water deposited from the atmosphere at a low temperature, so as to produce *congelation?*

Verse 30. *The waters are hid as* with *a stone*] Here is a reference to *freezing* in the winter, as we may learn from some of the constellations mentioned below, which arise above our horizon, in the winter months.

The word יתחבאו *yithchabbau* is understood by the versions in general as implying *harden-*

A. M. cir. 2484
B. C. cir. 1520
Ante I. Olymp. cir. 744
Ante U. C. cir. 767

31 Canst thou bind the sweet
influences of[g] [h]Pleiades, [i]or
loose the bands of [k]Orion?
32 Canst thou bring forth [l]Maz-
zaroth in his season? or canst thou [m]guide
Arcturus with his sons?
33 Knowest thou [n]the ordinances of heaven? canst thou set the dominion thereof in
the earth?
34 Canst thou lift up thy voice
to the clouds, that abundance of
waters may cover thee?
35 Canst thou send lightnings,
that they may go, and say unto thee, [o]Here
we *are?*
36 [p]Who hath put wisdom in the inward
parts? or who hath given understanding to
the heart?

A. M. cir. 2484
B. C. cir. 1520
Ante I. Olymp. cir. 744
Ante U. C. cir. 767

---

[g]Chap. ix. 9; Amos v. 8——[h]Or, *the seven stars*——[i]Heb. *Cimah*——[k]Heb. *Cesil*——[l]Or, *the twelve signs*

[m]Heb. *guide them*——[n]Jer. xxxi. 35——[o]Heb. *Behold us*
[p]Chap. xxxii. 8; Psa. li. 6; Eccles. ii. 26

---

ing or *congelation;* and we know in some intense frosts the ice becomes as *hard as a stone;* and even the *face of the deep*—the very *seas* themselves, not only in the polar circles, but even in northern countries, *Norway, Sweden, Denmark, Holland,* and parts of *Germany,* are really frozen, and locked up from all the purposes of navigation for several months in winter.

Verse 31. *Canst thou bind the sweet influences of Pleiades*] The *Pleiades* are a constellation in the sign *Taurus.* They consist of *six stars* visible to the naked eye; to a good eye, in a clear night, *seven* are discernible; but with a *telescope* ten times the number may be readily counted. They make their appearance in the *spring. Orion* may be seen in the morning, towards the end of *October*, and is visible through *November, December,* and *January;* and hence, says Mr. *Good,* it becomes a correct and elegant synecdoche for the winter at large. The *Pleiades* are elegantly opposed to *Orion,* as the *vernal* renovation of nature is opposed to its *wintry* destruction; the mild and open benignity of *spring,* to the severe and icy inactivity of *winter.*

I have already expressed my mind on these supposed constellations, and must refer to my notes on chap. ix. 9, &c., and to the learned notes of Doctor *Hales* and Mr. *Mason Good* on these texts. They appear certain, where I am obliged to doubt; and, from their view of the subject, make very useful and important deductions. I find reluctance in departing from the ancient versions. In this case, these learned men follow them; I cannot, because I do not see the evidence of the groundwork; and I dare not draw conclusions from premises which seem to me precarious, or which I do not understand. I wish, therefore, the reader to examine and judge for himself.

Coverdale renders the 31st and 32d verses thus:

Hast thou brought the VII starres together? Or, Art thou able to breake the circle of heaven? Canst thou bringe forth the mornynge starre, or the evenynge starre, at convenient tyme, and conveye them home agayne?

Verse 32. *Mazzaroth in his season?*] This is generally understood to mean the *signs of the zodiac.* מזרות *Mazzaroth,* according to Parkhurst, comes from מזר *mazar,* to *corrupt;* and he supposes it to mean that *pestilential* wind in Arabia, called *simoom,* the *season* of which is the *summer heats.*

Verse 33. *Knowest thou the ordinances of heaven?*] Art thou a thorough astronomer? Art thou acquainted with all the laws of the planetary system? Canst thou account for the difference of their motions, and the influence by which they are retained and revolve in their orbits? And canst thou tell what influence or *dominion* they exercise *on the earth?* Sir Isaac Newton has given us much light on many of these things; but to his system, which is most probably the true one, *gravity* is essential; and yet what this *gravity* is he could neither explain nor comprehend; and his followers are not one whit wiser than he. No man has ever yet fully *found out the ordinances of heaven, and the dominion thereof on the earth.*

Verse 34. *Canst thou lift up thy voice to the clouds*] Canst thou produce *lightning* and *thunder,* that water may be formed, and poured down upon the earth?

Thunder is called קלות *koloth,* voices; for it is considered the voice of God: here then *Job's voice,* קולך *kolecha,* is opposed to the *voice of* JEHOVAH!

Verse 35. *Canst thou send lightnings*] We have already seen that the lightning is supposed to be immediately in the *hand* and under th *management* of God. The great god of the heathen, *Jupiter Brontes,* is represented with the forked lightnings and thunderbolt in his hand. He seems so to grasp the bickering flame that, though it struggles for liberty, it cannot escape from his hold. *Lightnings*—How much like the sound of thunder is the original word: ברקים *Berakim!* Here are both *sense* and *sound.*

Here we are?] Will the winged lightnings be thy messengers, as they are mine?

Verse 36. *Who hath put wisdom in the inward parts?*] Who has given לשכוי *lasechvi,* to the *contemplative* person, *understanding?* Even the most sedulous attention to a subject, and the deepest contemplation, are not sufficient to investigate truth, without the inspiration of the Almighty, which alone can give understanding. But who has given man the *power* to conceive and understand? A power which he knows he has, but which he cannot comprehend. Man knows nothing of his own *mind,* nor of the *mode* of its *operations.* This mind we possess, these operations we perform;—and of either do we know any thing? If we know not *our own spirit,* how can we comprehend that SPIRIT which is *infinite* and *eternal?*

Mr. *Good* thinks that this verse is a continuation of the subject above, relative to the *lightnings,* and therefore translates thus:—

Who putteth understanding into the vollies?
And who giveth to the shafts discernment?

A. M. cir. 2484 B. C. cir. 1520 Ante I. Olymp. cir. 744 Ante U. C. cir. 767

37 Who can number the clouds
in wisdom? or [q]who can stay
the bottles of heaven,
38 [r]When the dust [s]groweth into
hardness, and the clods cleave fast together?
39 [t]Wilt thou hunt the prey for the lion?
or fill [u]the appetite of the young lions,
40 When they [v]couch in *their*
dens, *and* abide in the covert to
lie in wait?
41 [w]Who provideth for the
raven his food? when his young ones
cry unto God, they wander for lack of
meat.

[q]Heb. *who can cause to lie down*——[r]Or, *When the dust is turned into mire*——[s]Heb. *is poured*

[t]Psa. civ. 21; cxlv. 15——[u]Heb. *the life*——[v]Gen. xlix. 9 [w]Psa. cxlvii. 9; Matt. vi. 26

All the *versions*, except the *Septuagint*, which trifles here, understand the place as we do. Either makes a good sense. The *Septuagint* has, "Who hath given the knowledge of weaving to women; or the science of embroidery?" Instead of *understanding to the heart*, the *Vulgate* has, *understanding to the cock;* that it might be able to distinguish and proclaim the watches of the night.

Verse 37. *Who can number the clouds*] Perhaps the word ספר *saphar*, which is commonly rendered to *number*, may here mean, as in Arabic, to *irradiate*, as Mr. *Good* contends; and may refer to those celestial and inimitable tinges which we sometimes behold in the sky.

Bottles of heaven] The clouds: it is an allusion to the *girbahs*, or bottles made of skin, in which they are accustomed to carry their water from *wells* and *tanks*.

Verse 38. *When the dust groweth into hardness*] That is, Who knows how the *dust*—the *elementary particles* of matter, were concreted; and how the *clods*—the several parts of the earth, continue to cohere? What is the principle of *cohesion* among the different particles of matter, in all *metals* and *minerals?* Even *water*, in a solid form, constitutes a part of several gems, called thence *water of crystallization*. Who can solve this question? How is it that 90 parts of *alumine*, 7 of *silex*, and 1.2 of *oxide* of *iron*, constitute the *oriental ruby?* and that 90 parts of *silex*, and 19 of *water*, form the *precious opal?* And how can 46 parts of *silex*, 14 of *alumine*, 28 of *carbonate of lime*, 6.5 of *sulphate of lime*, 3 of *oxide of iron*, and 2 of *water*, enter into the constitution, and form the substance, of the *lapis lazuli?* How do these solids and fluids of such differing natures *grow into hardness*, and form this curious mineral?

Take another example from that beautiful precious stone, the emerald. Its analysis shows it to be composed of *glucine* 13, *silex* 64.5, *alumine* 16, *lime* 1.6, and *oxide of chrome* 3.25. Now how can these *dusts*, utterly worthless in themselves, *grow into hardness*, *combine*, and form one of the most beautiful, and, next to the *diamond*, the most precious, of all the *gems?* The almighty and infinitely wise God has done this in a way only known to and comprehensible by himself.

Verse 39. *Wilt thou hunt the prey for the lion?*] Rather the *lioness*, or *strong lion*. Hast thou his instinct? Dost thou know the *habits* and *haunts* of such animals as he seeks for his food? Thou hast neither his *strength*, his *instinct* nor his *cunning*.

In the best Hebrew Bibles, the *thirty-ninth* chapter begins with this verse, and begins properly, as a new subject now commences, relating to the *natural history* of the *earth*, or the animal kingdom; as the preceding chapter does to *astronomy* and *meteorology*.

Verse 40. *When they couch in* their *dens*] Before they are capable of trusting themselves abroad.

Abide in the covert] Before they are able to hunt down the prey by running. It is a fact that the *young lions*, before they have acquired sufficient strength and swiftness, *lie under cover*, in order to surprise those animals which they have not fleetness enough to overtake in the forest; and from this circumstance the כפירים *kephirim*, "young lions, or lions' whelps," have their name: the root is כפר *caphar*, to *cover* or *hide*. See the note on chap. iv. 11, where *six* different names are given to the lion, all expressing some distinct quality or state.

Verse 41. *Who provideth for the raven*] This bird is chosen, perhaps, for his voracious appetite, and general hunger for prey, beyond most other fowls. He makes a continual cry, and the cry is that of hunger. He dares not frequent the habitations of men, as he is considered a bird of ill omen, and hated by all.

This verse is finely paraphrased by Dr. YOUNG:—

"Fond man! the vision of a moment made!
Dream of a dream, and shadow of a shade!
What worlds hast thou produced, what creatures framed,
What insects cherish'd, that thy God is blamed?
When pain'd with hunger, the wild *raven's* brood
Calls upon God, importunate for food,
Who hears their cry? Who grants their hoarse request,
And stills the clamours of the craving nest?"

On which he has this note:—"The reason given why the raven is particularly mentioned as the care of Providence is, because by her *clamorous* and *importunate voice* she particularly seems always calling upon it; thence κορασσω, α κοραξ, is *to ask earnestly*.—*Ælian*. lib. ii., c. 48. And since there were ravens on the banks of the Nile, more clamorous than the rest of that species, those probably are meant in this place."

THE commencement of Cicero's oration against Catiline, to which I have referred on ver. 3, is the following:—

Quousque tandem abutere, Catilina, patientia **nostra?** Quamdiu etiam furor iste tuus nos eludet? Quem ad finem sese effrenata jactabit audacia? Nihilne te nocturnum præsidium palatii,—nihil urbis vigiliæ,—nihil timor populi,—nihil concursus bonorum omnium,—nihil hic munitissimus habendi senatus locus—nihil horum ora, vultusque moverunt? Patere tua consilia non sentis? Constrictam jam omnium horum conscientia teneri conjurationem tuam non vides? Quid proxima, quid superiore nocte egeris,—ubi fueris,—quos convocaveris,—quid consilii ceperis, quem nostrum ignorare arbitraris? O tempora! O mores! Senatus hæc intelligit,—consul videt; hic tamen vivit! Vivit? immo vero eitam in senatum venit; fit publici consilii particeps; notat et designat oculis ad cædem unumquemque nostrum! Nos autem, viri fortes, satisfacere reipublicæ videmur, si istius furorem ac tela vitemus!

"How long wilt thou, O Catiline, abuse our patience? How long shall thy madness outbrave our justice? To what extremities art thou resolved to push thy unbridled insolence of guilt? Canst thou behold the nocturnal arms that watch the palatium,—the guards of the city,—the consternation of the citizens,—all the wise and worthy clustering into consultation,—the impregnable situation of the seat of the senate,—and the reproachful looks of the fathers of Rome? Canst thou behold all this, and yet remain undaunted and unabashed? Art thou insensible that thy measures are detected? Art thou insensible that this senate, now thoroughly informed, comprehend the whole extent of thy guilt? Show me the senator ignorant of thy practices during the last and preceding night, of the place where you met, the company you summoned, and the crime you concerted. The senate is conscious,—the consul is witness to all this; yet, O how mean and degenerate! the traitor lives! Lives? he mixes with the senate; he shares in our counsels; with a steady eye he surveys us; he anticipates his guilt; he enjoys the murderous thought, and coolly marks us to bleed! Yet we, boldly passive in our country's cause, think we act like Romans, if we can escape his frantic rage!"

The reader will perceive how finely Cicero rushes into this invective, as if the danger had been too immediate to give him leisure for the formality of address and introduction. See *Guthrie's* Orations of Cicero.

Here is eloquence! Here is nature! And in thus speaking her language, the true orator pierces with his lightnings the deepest recesses of the heart. The success of this species of oratory is infallible in the *pulpit*, when the preacher understands how to manage it.

CHAPTER XXXIX

Several animals described: the wild goats and hinds, 1–4. *The wild ass,* 5–8. *The unicorn,* 9–12. *The peacock and ostrich,* 13–18. *The war-horse,* 19–25. *The hawk,* 26. *And the eagle and her brood,* 27–30.

A. M. cir. 2484
B. C. cir. 1520
Ante I. Olymp. cir. 744
Ante U. C. cir. 767

KNOWEST thou the time when the wild goats of the [a]rock bring forth? *or* canst thou mark when [b]the hinds do calve?

2 Canst thou number the months *that* they fulfil? or knowest thou the time when they bring forth?

[a]1 Sam. xxiv. 2; Psa. civ. 18 — [b]Psa. xxix. 9

NOTES ON CHAP. XXXIX

Verse 1. *Knowest thou the time*] To know *time,* &c., only, was easy, and has nothing extraordinary in it; but the meaning of these questions is, to know the *circumstances,* which have something peculiarly expressive of God's providence, and make the questions proper in this place. *Pliny* observes, that the *hind* with young is by instinct directed to a certain herb, named *seselis,* which facilitates the birth. *Thunder,* also, which looks like the more immediate hand of Providence, has the same effect. Psa. xxix. 9: "The VOICE of the Lord maketh the HINDS to CALVE." See Dr. YOUNG. What is called the *wild goat,* יעל *yael,* from עלה *alah, to ascend, go* or *mount up,* is generally understood to be the *ibex* or *mountain goat,* called *yael,* from the wonderful manner in which it *mounts* to the *tops* of the *highest* rocks. It is certain, says *Johnston,* there is no crag of the mountains so *high, prominent* or *steep,* but this animal will *mount* it in a number of *leaps,* provided only it be rough, and have protuberances large enough to receive its hoofs in leaping. This animal is indigenous to Arabia, is of amazing strength and agility, and considerably larger than the common goat. Its *horns* are very long, and often bend back over the whole body of the animal; and it is said to throw itself from the tops of rocks or towers, and light upon its horns, without receiving any damage. It goes five months with young.

When the hinds do calve?] The *hind* is the *female* of the *stag,* or *cervus elaphus,* and goes *eight months* with young. They live to *thirty-five* or *forty* years. Incredible *longevity* has been attributed to some stags. One was taken by Charles VI., in the forest of Senlis, about whose neck was a collar with this inscription, *Cæsar hoc mihi donavit,* which led some to believe that this animal had lived from the days of some one of the *twelve Cæsars,* emperors of Rome.

I have seen the following form of this inscription:

Tempore quo Cæsar Roma dominatus in alta
Aureolo jussit collum signare monili;
Ne depascentem quisquis me gramina lædat.
Cæsaris heu! caussa perituræ parcere vitæ!

Which has been long public in the old English ballad strain, thus:—

"When Julius Cæsar reigned king,
About my neck he put this ring;
That whosoever should me take
Would save my life for Cæsar's sake."

A. M. cir. 2484
B. C. cir. 1520
Ante I. Olymp. cir. 744
Ante U. C. cir. 767

3 They bow themselves, they
bring forth their young ones,
they cast out their sorrows.
4 Their young ones are in good
liking, they grow up with corn; they go forth,
and return not unto them.
5 Who hath sent out the wild ass free? or
who hath loosed the bands of the wild ass?
6 [c]Whose house I have made the wilderness, and the [d]barren land his dwellings.
7 He scorneth the multitude of the city,
neither regardeth he the crying
[e]of the driver.
8 The range of the mountains
is his pasture, and he searcheth
after every green thing.
9 Will the [f]unicorn be willing to serve thee,
or abide by thy crib?
10 Canst thou bind the unicorn with his
band in the furrow? or will he harrow the
valleys after thee?
11 Wilt thou trust him, because his strength

A. M. cir. 2484
B. C. cir. 1520
Ante I. Olymp. cir. 744
Ante U. C. cir. 767

[c]Chap. xxiv. 5; Jeremiah ii. 24; Hos. viii. 9——[d]Heb. *salt places*

[e]Heb. *of the exactor*, chap. iii. 18——[f]Num. xxiii. 22; Deut. xxxiii. 17

Aristotle mentions the longevity of the stag, but thinks it *fabulous*.

Verse 3. *They bow themselves*] In order to bring forth their young ones.

They cast out their sorrows.] חבליהם *chebleyhem;* the *placenta, afterbirth,* or umbilical cord. So this word has been understood.

Verse 4. *In good liking*] After the fawns have sucked for some time, the dam leads them to the pastures, where they feed on different kinds of herbage; but not *on corn,* for they are not born before harvest-time in Arabia and Palestine, and the stag does not feed on corn, but on grass, moss, and the shoots of the *fir, beech,* and other trees: therefore the word בר *bar,* here translated *corn,* should be translated the *open field* or *country.* See *Parkhurst. Their nurslings bound away.*—Mr. *Good.* In a short time they become independent of the mother, leave her, *and return no more.* The spirit of the *questions* in these verses appears to be the following:—Understandest thou the cause of breeding of the mountain goats, &c.? Art thou acquainted with the course and progress of the parturition, and the manner in which the bones grow, and acquire solidity in the womb? See Mr. *Good's* observations.

Houbigant's version appears very correct: (Knowest thou) "how their young ones grow up, increase in the fields, and once departing, return to them no more?"

Verse 5. *Who hath sent out the wild ass free?*] פרא *pere,* which we translate *wild ass,* is the same as the *ονος αγριος* of the Greeks, and the *onager* of the Latins; which must not, says *Buffon,* be confounded with the *zebra,* for this is an animal of a different species from the *ass.* The *wild ass* is not *striped* like the *zebra,* nor so elegantly shaped. There are many of those animals in the deserts of Libya and Numidia: they are of a gray colour; and run so swiftly that no horse but the Arab *barbs* can overtake them. *Wild asses* are found in considerable numbers in East and South Tartary, in Persia, Syria, the islands of the Archipelago, and throughout Mauritania. They differ from *tame* asses only in their independence and liberty, and in their being stronger and more nimble: but in their shape they are the same. See on chap. vi. 5.

The bands of the wild ass?] ערוד *arod,* the *brayer,* the same animal, but called thus because of the frequent and peculiar noise he makes. But Mr. *Good* supposes this to be a different animal from the wild ass, (the *jichta* or *equus hemionus,*) which is distinguished by having solid hoofs, a uniform colour, no cross on the back, and the tail hairy only at the tip. The ears and tail resemble those of the *zebra;* the hoofs and body, those of the *ass;* and the limbs, those of the *horse.* It inhabits Arabia, China, Siberia, and Tartary, in grassy *saline plains* or *salt wastes,* as mentioned in the following verse.

Verse 6. *Whose house*] Habitation, or place of resort.

The barren land] מלחה *melechah,* the *salt land,* or *salt places,* as in the margin. See above.

Verse 7. *He scorneth the multitude*] He is so swift that he cannot be run or hunted down. See the description in ver. 5.

Verse 8. *The range of the mountains*] The mountains and desert places are his peculiar places of pasture; and he lives on any thing that is *green,* or any kind of *vegetable* production.

Verse 9. *Will the unicorn be willing to serve thee?*] The "fine elegant animal like a horse, with one long rich curled horn growing out of his forehead," commonly called the *unicorn,* must be given up as fabulous. The *heralds* must claim him as their own; place him in their armorial bearings as they please, to indicate the unreal actions, fictitious virtues, and unfought martial exploits of mispraised men. It is not to the honour of the royal arms of Great Britain that this fabulous animal should be one of their *supporters.*

The animal in question, called רים *reim,* is undoubtedly the *rhinoceros,* who has the latter name from the *horn* that grows on his *nose.* The rhinoceros is known by the name of *reim* in Arabia to the present day. He is allowed to be a savage animal, showing nothing of the intellect of the elephant. His *horn* enables him to combat the latter with great success; for, by putting his nose under the elephant's belly, he can rip him up. His *skin* is like armour, and so very hard as to resist sabres, javelins, lances, and even musket-balls; the only penetrable parts being the belly, the eyes, and about the ears.

Or abide by thy crib?] These and several of the following expressions are intended to point out his *savage, untameable* nature.

Verse 10. *Canst thou bind the unicorn—in the furrow?*] He will not plough, nor draw in the yoke *with another?* nor canst thou use him *singly,* to harrow the ground.

A. M. cir. 2484 B. C. cir. 1520 Ante I. Olymp. cir. 744 Ante U. C. cir. 767

is great? or wilt thou leave thy
labour to him?
12 Wilt thou believe him, that
he will bring home thy seed, and
gather *it into* thy barn?
13 *Gavest thou* the goodly wings unto the
peacocks? or [g]wings and feathers unto the
ostrich?
14 Which leaveth her eggs in the earth,
and warmeth them in the
dust,
15 And forgetteth that the foot
may crush them, or that the wild
beast may break them.
16 She is [h]hardened against her young ones,
as though *they were* not hers: her [i]labour is
in vain without fear;
17 Because God hath deprived her of wis-

A. M. cir. 2484 B. C. cir. 1520 Ante I. Olymp. cir. 744 Ante U. C. cir. 767

[g]Or, *the feathers of the stork and ostrich*

[h]Lam. iv. 3——[i]Ver. 17

Verse 12. *That he will bring home thy seed*] Thou canst make no domestic nor agricultural use of him.

Verse 13. *The goodly wings unto the peacocks?*] I believe *peacocks* are not intended here; and the Hebrew word רננים *renanim* should be translated *ostriches;* and the term חסידה *chasidah*, which we translate *ostrich*, should be, as it is elsewhere translated, *stork;* and perhaps the word נצה *notsah*, rendered here *feathers*, should be translated *hawk*, or *pelican*.

The *Vulgate* has, *Penna struthionis similis est pennis herodii et accipitris;* "the feather of the ostrich is like to that of the stork and the hawk." The *Chaldee* has, "The wing of the wild cock, who crows and claps his wings, is like to the wing of the stork and the hawk." The *Septuagint*, not knowing what to make of these different terms, have left them all untranslated, so as to make a sentence without sense. Mr. *Good* has come nearest both to the *original* and to the meaning, by translating thus:—

"The wing of the ostrich tribe is for flapping;
But of the stork and falcon for flight."

Though the wings of the ostrich, says he, cannot raise it from the ground; yet by the motion here alluded to, by a *perpetual vibration*, or *flapping*—by perpetually catching or *drinking in* the wind, (as the term נעלסה *neelasah* implies, which we render *goodly*,) they give it a rapidity of running beyond that possessed by any other animal in the world. *Adanson* informs us, that when he was at the factory in Padore, he was in possession of two tame ostriches; and to try their strength, says he, "I made a full-grown negro mount the smallest, and two others the largest. This burden did not seem at all disproportioned to their strength. At first they went a pretty high trot; and, when they were heated a little, they expanded their wings, as if it were *to catch the wind*, and they moved with such fleetness as to seem to be off the ground. And I am satisfied that those ostriches would have distanced the fleetest racehorses that were ever bred in England."

As to נצה *notsah*, here translated *falcon*, Mr. *Good* observes, that the term ناز *naz* is used generally by the Arabian writers to signify both *falcon* and *hawk;* and there can be little doubt that such is the real meaning of the Hebrew word; and that it imports various species of the falcon family, as *jer-falcon*, *gos-hawk*, and *sparrow-hawk*.

"The argument drawn from natural history advances from *quadrupeds* to *birds;* and of birds, those only are selected for description which are most common to the country in which the scene lies, and at the same time are most singular in their properties. Thus the *ostrich* is admirably contrasted with the *stork* and the *eagle*, as affording us an instance of a winged animal totally incapable of flight, but endued with an unrivalled rapidity of running, compared with birds whose flight is proverbially fleet, powerful, and persevering. Let man, in the pride of his wisdom, explain or arraign this difference of construction.

"Again, the *ostrich* is peculiarly opposed to the *stork* and to some species of the *eagle* in another sense, and a sense adverted to in the verses immediately ensuing; for the *ostrich* is well known to take *little* or *no care* of its *eggs*, or of its *young;* while the *stork* ever has been, and ever deserves to be, held in proverbial repute for its *parental tenderness*. The Hebrew word חסידה *chasidah*, imports kindness or affection; and our own term *stork*, if derived from the Greek στοργη, *storgé*, as some pretend, has the same original meaning."—GOOD'S JOB.

Verse 14. *Which leaveth her eggs in the earth*] This want of parental affection in the *ostrich* is almost universally acknowledged. Mr. *Jackson*, in his *Account of Morocco*, observes: "The ostrich, having laid her eggs, goes away, *forgetting* or *forsaking* them: and if some other ostrich discover them, she hatches them as if they were her own, *forgetting* probably whether they are or are not; so deficient is the recollection of this bird." This illustrates verse 15: "And forgetteth that the foot may crush them, or that the wild beast may break them." The poet seems well acquainted with every part of the subject on which he writes; and facts incontestable confirm all he says. For farther illustration, see the account from Dr. *Shaw* at the end of the chapter.

Verse 16. *She is hardened against her young*] See before, and the extracts from Dr. *Shaw* at the end of the chapter. She neglects her little ones, which are often found half starved, straggling, and moaning about, like so many deserted orphans, for their mother.

Verse 17. *God hath deprived her of wisdom*] Of this foolishness we have an account from the ancients; and here follow two instances: "1. It covers its head in the reeds, and thinks itself all out of sight because itself cannot see. So *Claudian*:—

——————'Stat lumine clauso
Ridendum revoluta caput: creditque latere
Quæ non ipsa videt.'

"2. They who hunt them draw the skin of an ostrich's neck on one hand, which proves a suffi-

A. M. cir. 2484 B. C. cir. 1520 Ante I. Olymp. cir. 744 Ante U. C. cir. 767

dom, neither hath he [k]imparted
to her understanding.
18 What time she lifteth up
herself on high, she scorneth the
horse and his rider.
19 Hast thou given the horse strength?
hast thou clothed his neck with
thunder?
20 Canst thou make him
afraid as a grasshopper? the
glory of his nostrils [l]*is* terrible.
21 [m]He paweth in the valley, and rejoiceth

A. M. cir. 2484 B. C. cir. 1520 Ante I. Olymp. cir. 744 Ante U. C. cir. 767

[k]Chap. xxxv. 11——[l]Heb. *terrors*

[m]Or, His feet *dig*

cient lure to take them with the other. They have so little brain that Heliogabalus had *six hundred* heads for his supper. Here we may observe, that our judicious as well as sublime author just touches the great points of distinction in each creature, and then hastens to another. A description is exact when you cannot add but what is common to another thing; nor withdraw, but something peculiarly belonging to the thing described. A likeness is lost in too much description, as a meaning is often in too much illustration."—Dr. Young.

Verse 18. *She lifteth up herself*] *When she raiseth up herself to run away.* Proofs of the fleetness of this bird have already been given. It neither flies nor runs distinctly, but has a motion composed of both; and, using its wings as sails, makes great speed. So *Claudian:*—

Vasta velut Libyæ venantum vocibus ales
Cum premitur, calidas cursu transmittit arenas,
Inque modum veli sinuatis flamine pennis
Pulverulenta volat.

"*Xenophon* says, *Cyrus* had horses that could overtake the goat and the wild ass; but none that could reach this creature. A thousand golden ducats, or a *hundred* camels, was the stated price of a horse that could equal their speed."—Dr. Young.

Verse 19. *Hast thou given the horse strength?*] Before I proceed to any observations, I shall give Mr. *Good's* version of this, perhaps inimitable, description:—

Ver. 19. Hast thou bestowed on the horse mettle?
Hast thou clothed his neck with the thunder flash?
Ver. 20. Hast thou given him to launch forth as an arrow?
Terrible is the pomp of his nostrils.
Ver. 21. He paweth in the valley, and exulteth.
Boldly he advanceth against the clashing host:
Ver. 22. He mocketh at fear, and trembleth not:
Nor turneth he back from the sword.
Ver. 23. Against him rattleth the quiver,
The glittering spear, and the shield:
Ver. 24. With rage and fury he devoureth the ground;
And is impatient when the trumpet soundeth.
Ver. 25. He exclaimeth among the trumpets, Aha!
And scenteth the battle afar off,
The thunder of the chieftains, and the shouting.

In the year 1713, a letter was sent to the Guardian, which makes No. 86 of that work, containing a critique on this description, compared with similar descriptions of *Homer* and *Virgil.* I shall give the substance of it here:—

The great Creator, who accommodated himself to those to whom he vouchsafed to speak, hath put into the mouths of his prophets such sublime sentiments and exalted language as must abash the pride and wisdom of man. In the book of Job, the most ancient poem in the world, we have such paintings and descriptions as I have spoken of in great variety. I shall at present make some remarks on the celebrated description of the *horse,* in that holy book; and compare it with those drawn by *Homer* and *Virgil.*

Homer hath the following similitude of a *horse* twice over in the *Iliad,* which *Virgil* hath copied from him; at least he hath deviated less from *Homer* than Mr. *Dryden* hath from him:—

Ὡς δ' ὁτε τις στατος ἱππος, ακοστησας επι φατνῃ,
Δεσμον απορρῆξας θειει πεδιοιο κροαινων,
Ειωθως λουεσθαι εὐῤῥειος ποταμοιο,
Κυδιοων· ὑψου δε καρη εχει, αμφι δε χαιται
Ωμοις αΐσσονται· ὁ δ' αγλαϊηφι πεποιθως
Ῥιμφα ἑ γουνα φερει μετα τ' ηθεα και νομον ἱππων.
Hom. Il. lib. vi., ver. 506; and lib. xv., ver. 263.

Freed from his keepers, thus with broken reins
The wanton courser prances o'er the plains,
Or in the pride of youth o'erleaps the mound,
And snuffs the female in forbidden ground;
Or seeks his watering in the well-known flood,
To quench his thirst, and cool his fiery blood;
He swims luxuriant in the liquid plain,
And o'er his shoulders flows his waving mane;
He neighs, he snorts, he bears his head on high;
Before his ample chest the frothy waters fly.

Virgil's description is much fuller than the foregoing, which, as I said, is only a simile; whereas *Virgil* professes to treat of the *nature* of the *horse:*—

——Tum, si qua sonum procul arma dedere,
Stare loco nescit: micat auribus, et tremit artus
Collectumque premens volvit sub naribus ignem:
Densa juba, et dextro jactata recumbit in armo.
At duplex agitur per lumbos spina, cavatque
Tellurem, et solido graviter sonat ungula cornu.
Virg. Georg. lib. iii., ver. 83.

Which is thus admirably translated:—

The fiery courser, when he hears from far
The sprightly trumpets, and the shouts of war,
Pricks up his ears; and, trembling with delight,
Shifts pace, and paws, and hopes the promised fight.
On his right shoulder his thick mane reclined,
Ruffles at speed, and dances in the wind.
His horny hoofs are jetty black and round;
His chin is double: starting with a bound,
He turns the turf, and shakes the solid ground.
Fire from his eyes, clouds from his nostrils flow;
He bears his rider headlong on the foe.

Now follows that in the *Book of Job,* which, under all the disadvantages of having been written in a language little understood, of being expressed in phrases peculiar to a part of

A. M. cir. 2484
B. C. cir. 1520
Ante I. Olymp. cir. 744
Ante U. C. cir. 767

in *his* strength: [n]he goeth on
to meet the [o]armed men.
22 He mocketh at fear, and
is not affrighted: neither turneth he back from the sword.
23 The quiver rattleth against
him, the glittering spear and the
shield.
24 He swalloweth the ground
with fierceness and rage: neither believeth

[n]Jer. viii. 6

[o]Heb. *the armour*

the world whose manner of thinking and speaking seems to us very uncouth; and, above all, of appearing in a *prose* translation; is nevertheless so transcendently above the heathen descriptions, that hereby we may perceive how faint and languid the images are which are formed by human authors, when compared with those which are figured, as it were, just as they appear in the eye of the Creator. God, speaking to Job, asks him:—

[To do our translators as much justice as possible, and to help the critic, I shall throw it in the hemistich form, in which it appears in the Hebrew, and in which all Hebrew poetry is written.]

Ver. 19. Hast thou given to the HORSE strength?
Hast thou clothed his neck with thunder?
Ver. 20. Canst thou make him afraid as a grasshopper?
The glory of his nostrils is terrible!
Ver. 21. He paweth in the valley, and rejoiceth in strength:
He goeth on to meet the armed men.
Ver. 22. He mocketh at fear, and is not affrighted:
Neither turneth he back from the sword.
Ver. 23. Against him rattleth the quiver,
The glittering spear and the shield.
Ver. 24. He swalloweth the ground with rage and fierceness:
Nor doth he believe that it is the sound of the trumpet.
Ver. 25. He saith among the trumpets, Heach!
And from afar he scenteth the battle,
The thunder of the captains, and the shouting.

Here are all the great and sprightly images that thought can form of this generous beast, expressed in such force and vigour of style as would have given the great wits of antiquity new laws for the sublime, had they been acquainted with these writings.

I cannot but particularly observe that whereas the classical poets chiefly endeavour to paint the *outward figure, lineaments, and motions*, the *sacred poet* makes all the beauties to flow from an *inward principle* in the creature he describes; and thereby gives great spirit and vivacity to his description. The following phrases and circumstances are singularly remarkable:—

Ver. 19. *Hast thou clothed his neck with thunder?*

Homer and *Virgil* mention nothing about the neck of the horse but his mane. The sacred author, by the bold figure of *thunder*, not only expresses the *shaking* of that remarkable beauty in the horse, and the *flakes of hair*, which naturally suggest the idea of *lightning;* but likewise the *violent agitation* and force of the neck, which in the oriental tongues had been flatly expressed by a metaphor less bold than this.

Ver. 20. *Canst thou make him afraid as a grasshopper?*—There is a twofold beauty in this expression, which not only marks the courage of this beast, by asking if he can be *scared;* but likewise raises a noble image of his *swiftness*, by insinuating that, if he could be frightened, he would *bound away* with the *nimbleness* of a *grasshopper.*

The glory of his nostrils is terrible.] This is more strong and concise than that of Virgil, which yet is the noblest line that was ever written without inspiration:—

Collectumque premens volvit sub naribus ignem.

And in his nostrils rolls collected fire.
GEOR. iii., ver. 85.

Ver. 21. He rejoiceth in his strength.
Ver. 22. He mocketh at fear.
Ver. 24. Neither believeth he that it is the sound of the trumpet.
Ver. 25. He saith among the trumpets, Ha! ha!

These are signs of courage, as I said before, flowing from *an inward principle.* There is a peculiar beauty in his *not believing it is the sound of the trumpet:* that is, he cannot believe it for joy; but when he is sure of it, and is *among the trumpets*, he saith, Ha! ha! He neighs, he rejoices.

His docility is elegantly painted in his being *unmoved at the rattling quiver, the glittering spear, and the shield*, ver. 23, and is well imitated by *Oppian*,—who undoubtedly read Job, as Virgil did,—in his Poem on Hunting:—

Πως μεν γαρ τε μαχαισιν αρηϊος εκλυεν ἱππος
Ηχον εγερσιμοθον δολιχων πολεμηϊον αυλων;
Η πως αντα δεδορκεν ασκαρδαμυκτοισιν οπωπαις
Αιζηοισι λοχον πεπυκασμενον ὁπλιτῃσι;
Και χαλκον σελαγευντα, και αστραπτοντα σιδηρον;
Και μαθεν ευτε μενειν χρειω, ποτε δ' αυτις ορουειν.
OPPIAN CYNEGET, lib. i., ver. 206.

Now firm the managed war-horse keeps his ground,
Nor breaks his order though the trumpet sound!
With fearless eye the glittering host surveys,
And glares directly at the helmet's blaze.
The master's word, the laws of war, he knows;
And when to stop, and when to charge the foes.

He swalloweth the ground, ver. 24, is an expression for *prodigious swiftness* in use among the Arabians, Job's countrymen, to the present day. The Latins have something like it:—

Latumque fuga *consumere campum.*
NEMESIAN.

In flight the extended champaign to consume.

Carpere prata fuga.
VIRG. GEORG. iii., ver. 142.

In flight to crop the meads.

A. M. cir. 2484
B. C. cir. 1520
Ante I. Olymp. cir. 744
Ante U. C. cir. 767

he that it is [p]the sound of the
trumpet.
25 He saith among the trumpets, Ha, ha; and he smelleth
the battle afar off, the thunder
of the captains, and the [q]shout-
ing.
26 Doth the hawk fly by thy

A. M. cir. 2484
B. C. cir. 1520
Ante I. Olymp. cir. 744
Ante U. C. cir. 767

[p]2 Sam. vi. 15; xv. 10

[q]Amos i. 14

————Campumque volatu
Cum rapuere, pedum vestigia quæras.

When, in their flight, the champaign they have snatch'd,
No track is left behind.

It is indeed the boldest and noblest of images for swiftness; nor have I met with any thing that comes so near it as Mr. Pope's, in *Windsor Forest*:—

Th' impatient courser pants in every vein,
And pawing, seems to beat the distant plain;
Hills, vales, and floods, appear already cross'd;
And ere he starts, a thousand steps are lost.

He smelleth the battle afar off, and what follows about the *shouting*, is a circumstance expressed with great spirit by *Lucan*:—

So when the ring with joyful shouts resounds,
With rage and pride th' imprison'd courser bounds;
He frets, he foams, he rends his idle rein,
Springs o'er the fence, and headlong seeks the plain.

This judicious and excellent critique has left me little to say on this sublime description of the horse: I shall add some cursory notes only. In verse 19 we have the singular image, *clothed his neck with thunder*. How *thunder* and the *horse's neck* can be well assimilated to each other, I confess I cannot see. The author of the preceding critique seems to think that the principal part of the allusion belongs to the *shaking* of this remarkable beauty (the *mane*) in a horse; and the *flakes* of *hair*, which naturally suggest the idea of *lightning*. I am satisfied that the *floating mane* is here meant. The original is רעמה *ramah*, which *Bochart* and other learned men translate as above. How much the *mane* of a horse *shaking* and *waving* in the wind adds to his beauty and stateliness, every one is sensible; and the Greek and Latin poets, in their description of the horse, take notice of it. Thus Homer:—

———— Αμφι δε χαιται
Ωμοις αἰσσονται. ILIAD vi., ver. 509.

"His *mane dishevell'd* o'er his shoulders *flies*."

And Virgil:—

Luduntque per colla, per armos.
ÆN. xi., ver. 497.

The verb רעם *raam* signifies to *toss*, to *agitate;* and may very properly be applied to the *mane*, for reasons obvious to all. *Virgil* has seized this characteristic in his fine line, Georg. iii. ver. 86:—

Densa juba, et dextro jactata recumbit in armo.

"His *toss'd* thick mane on his right shoulder falls."

Naturally, the horse is one of the most *timid* of animals; and this may be at once accounted for from his *small quantity of brain*. Perhaps there is no animal of his size that has *so little*. He acquires *courage* only from *discipline;* for naturally he starts with terror and affright at any sudden noise. It requires much discipline to bring him to hear the *noise of drums* and *trumpets*, and especially to bear a pair of kettle drums placed on each side his neck, and beaten there, with the most alarming variety of sounds. Query, Does the sacred text allude to *any thing of this kind?* I have been led to form this thought from the following circumstance. In some ancient MSS. of the *Shah Nameh*, a most eminent heroic poem, by the poet *Ferdoosy*, the Homer of India, in my own collection, adorned with paintings, representing regal interviews, animals, battles, &c., there appear in some places representations of *elephants, horses*, and *camels*, with a pair of drums, something like our kettle drums, hanging on each side of the animal's neck, and beaten, by a person on the saddle, with two plectrums or drumsticks; the *neck* itself being literally *clothed* with the *drums* and the *housings* on which they are fixed. Who is it then that has *framed* the *disposition* of such a *timid* animal, that by proper *discipline* it can bear those *thundering* sounds, which at first would have scared it to the uttermost of distraction? The *capacity* to receive *discipline* and *instruction* is as great a *display* of the *wisdom* of God as the *formation* of the *bodies* of the largest, smallest, or most complex animals is of his *power*. I leave this observation without laying any stress upon it. On such difficult subjects *conjecture* has a lawful range.

Verse 21. *He paweth in the valley*] יחפרו *yachperu*, "*they dig* in the valley," i. e., in his violent galloping, in every pitch of his body, he scoops up sods out of the earth. *Virgil* has seized this idea also, in his *cavat tellurem;* "he scoops out the ground." See before.

Verse 25. *He saith among the trumpets, Ha, ha*] The original is peculiarly emphatical: האח *Heach!* a strong, partly *nasal*, partly *guttural* sound, exactly resembling the first note which the horse emits in *neighing*. The strong, guttural sounds in this hemistich are exceedingly expressive: האח ומרחוק יריח מלחמה *Heach! umerachok yariach milchamah;* "Heach, for from afar he scenteth the battle."

The reader will perceive that Mr. *Good* has given a very different meaning to ver. 20 from that in the present text, *Canst thou make him afraid as a grasshopper?* by translating the Hebrew thus:—

"Hast thou given him to launch forth as an arrow?"

The word ארבה *arbeh*, which we translate *locust* or *grasshopper*, and which he derives from רבה *rabah*, the א *aleph* being merely formative, he says, "may as well mean an *arrow* as it does in chap. xvi. 13, רביו *rabbaiv*, 'His arrows fly around me.'" The verb רעש *raash* in the word התרעישנו *hatharishennu*, "Canst thou make him

A. M. cir. 2484 B. C. cir. 1520 Ante I. Olymp. cir. 744 Ante U. C. cir. 767

wisdom, *and* stretch her wings
toward the south?
27 Doth the eagle mount up
[r]at thy command, and [s]make
her nest on high?
28 She dwelleth and abideth on the rock,
upon the crag of the rock, and
the strong place.
29 From thence she seeketh [t]the
prey, *and* her eyes behold afar off.
30 Her young ones also suck up blood:
and [u]where the slain *are*, there *is* she.

A. M. cir. 2484 B. C. cir. 1520 Ante I. Olymp. cir. 744 Ante U. C. cir. 767

[r]Heb. *by thy mouth*——[s]Jer. xlix. 16; Obad. 4

[t]Chap. ix. 26——[u]Matt. xxiv. 28; Luke xvii. 37

afraid?" he contends, "signifies to *tremble, quiver, rush, launch, dart forth;* and, taken in this sense, it seems to unite the two ideas of *rapidity* and *coruscation.*" This is the *principal* alteration which this learned man has made in the text.

I shall conclude on this subject by giving *Coverdale's* translation: **Hast thou geven the horse his strength, or lerned him to bow down his neck with feare; that he letteth himselfe be dryven forth like a greshopper, where as the stout neyenge that he maketh is fearfull? He breaketh the grounde with the hoffes of his fete chearfully in his strength, and runneth to mete the harnest men. He layeth aside all feare, his stomack is not abated, neither starteth he aback for eny swerde. Though the qyvers rattle upon him, though the speare and shilde glistre: yet russheth he in fearsley, and beateth upon the grounde. He feareth not the noise of the trompettes, but as soone as he heareth the shawmes blowe, Tush (sayeth he) for he smelleth the batell afarre of, the noyse, the captaynes, and the shoutinge.** This is wonderfully nervous, and at the same time accurate.

Verse 26. *Doth the hawk fly by thy wisdom*] The *hawk* is called נץ *nets,* from its swiftness in darting down upon its prey; hence its *Latin* name, *nisus,* which is almost the same as the *Hebrew.* It may very probably mean the *falcon,* oberves Dr. *Shaw.* The flight of a strong falcon is wonderfully swift. A falcon belonging to the Duke of Cleves flew out of Westphalia into Prussia in one day; and in the county of Norfolk, a hawk has made a flight at a woodcock of near *thirty miles* in an *hour. Thuanus* says, "A hawk flew from London to Paris in one night." It was owing to its *swiftness* that the Egyptians in their hieroglyphics made it the emblem of the *wind.*

Stretch her wings toward the south?] Most of the *falcon* tribe pass their spring and summer in cold climates; and wing their way toward warmer regions on the approach of winter. This is what is here meant by *stretching her wings toward the south.* Is it through thy teaching that *this* or any other *bird of passage* knows the precise time for taking flight, and the direction in which she is to go in order to come to a warmer climate? There is much of the *wisdom* and *providence* of God to be seen in the migration of *birds of passage.* This has been remarked before. There is a beautiful passage in *Jeremiah,* chap. viii. 7, on the same subject: "The stork in the heavens knoweth her appointed times; and the turtle, and the crane, and the swallow, observe the time of their coming: but my people know not the judgment of the Lord."

Verse 27. *Doth the eagle mount up*] The eagle is said to be of so acute a sight, that when she is so high in the air that men cannot see her, she can discern a small fish in the water! See on ver. 29.

Verse 28. *Upon the crag of the rock*] שן סלע *shen sela,* the *tooth of the rock,* i. e., some *projecting* part, whither *adventurous man* himself dares not follow her.

And the strong place.] ומצודה *umetsudah.* Mr. *Good* translates this word *ravine,* and joins it to ver. 29, thus: "And thence espieth the ravine: her eyes trace the prey afar off."

Verse 29. *Her eyes behold afar off.*] The *eagle* was proverbial for her strong and clear sight. So *Horace,* lib. i., sat. iii., ver 25:—

Cum tua pervideas oculis mala lippus inunctis,
Cur in amicorum vitiis tam cernis acutum,
Quam aut aquila, aut serpens Epidaurius?

"For wherefore while you carelessly pass by
Your own worst vices with unheeding eye,
Why so sharp-sighted in another's fame,
Strong as an *eagle's ken,* or dragon's beam?"
FRANCIS.

So *Ælian,* lib. i., cap. 42. And *Homer,* Iliad xvii., calls the eagle *οξυτατον ὑπουρανιων πετεηνων,* "The most quick-sighted of all fowls under heaven."

Verse 30. *Her young ones also suck up blood*] The eagle does not feed her young with *carrion,* but with prey *newly* slain, so that they may *suck up blood.*

Where the slain are, *there* is *she.*] These words are quoted by our Lord. "Wheresoever the carcass is, there will the eagles be gathered together," Matt. xxiv. 28. It is likely, however, that this was a proverbial mode of expression; and our Lord adapts it to the circumstances of the Jewish people, who were about to fall a prey to the Romans. See the notes there.

IN the preceding notes I have referred to Dr. *Shaw's* account of the *ostrich* as the most accurate and authentic yet published. With the following description I am sure every intelligent reader will be pleased.

"In commenting therefore upon these texts it may be observed, that when the *ostrich* is full grown, the neck, particularly of the male, which before was almost naked, is now very beautifully covered with red feathers. The plumage likewise upon the shoulders, the back, and some parts of the wings, from being hitherto of a dark grayish colour, becomes now as black as jet, whilst the rest of the feathers retain an exquisite whiteness. They are, as described ver. 13, *the very feathers and plumage of the stork,* i. e., they consist of such black and white feathers as the *stork,* called from thence חסידה *chasidah,* is known to have. But the belly, the thighs, and the breast, do not partake of this covering, being usually naked, and when touched are of the same warmth as the flesh of *quadrupeds.*

"Under the joint of the great pinion, and sometimes under the less, there is a strong pointed excrescence like a cock's spur, with which it is said to prick and stimulate itself, and thereby acquire fresh strength and vigour whenever it is pursued. But nature seems rather to have intended that, in order to prevent the suffocating effects of too great a *plethora*, a loss of blood should be consequent thereupon, especially as the *ostrich* appears to be of a hot constitution, with lungs always confined, and consequently liable to be preternaturally inflamed upon these occasions.

"When these birds are surprised by coming suddenly upon them whilst they are feeding in some valley, or behind some rocky or sandy eminence in the deserts, they will not stay to be curiously viewed and examined. Neither are the *Arabs* ever dexterous enough to overtake them, even when they are mounted upon their *jinse*, or horses, as they are called, of family. *They, when they raise themselves up for flight*, (ver. 18,) *laugh at the horse and his rider*. They afford him an opportunity only of admiring at a distance the extraordinary agility and the stateliness of their motions, the richness of their plumage, and the great propriety there was of ascribing to them (ver. 13) *an expanded quivering wing*. Nothing, certainly, can be more beautiful and entertaining than such a sight! The wings, by their repeated though unwearied vibrations, equally serving them for sails and oars; whilst their feet, no less assisting in conveying them out of sight, are in no degree sensible of fatigue.

"By the repeated accounts which I often had from my conductors, as well as from *Arabs* of different places, I have been informed that the *ostrich* lays from thirty to fifty eggs. *Ælian* mentions more than eighty, but I never heard of so large a number. The first egg is deposited in the centre; the rest are placed as conveniently as possible round about it. In this manner it is said to *lay*—deposit or thrust (ver. 14)—*her eggs in* THE EARTH, and *to warm them in the sand, and forgetteth*, as they are not placed, like those of some other birds, upon trees or in the clefts of rocks, &c., *that the foot* of the traveller *may crush them, or that the wild beasts may break them.*

"Yet notwithstanding the ample provision which is hereby made for a numerous offspring, scarce one quarter of these eggs are ever supposed to be hatched; and of those that are, no small share of the young ones may perish with hunger, from being left too early by their dams to shift for themselves. For in these the most barren and desolate recesses of the *Sahara*, where the *ostrich* chooses to make her nest, it would not be enough to lay eggs and hatch them, unless some proper food was near at hand, and already prepared for their nourishment. And accordingly we are not to consider this large collection of eggs as if they were all intended for a brood; they are, the greatest part of them, reserved for food, which the dam breaks and disposes of according to the number and the cravings of her young ones.

"But yet, for all this, a very little share of that στοργη, or natural affection, which so strongly exerts itself in most other creatures, is observable in the *ostrich*. For, upon the least distant noise or trivial occasion, she forsakes her eggs, or her young ones, to which perhaps she never returns; or if she do, it may be too late either to restore life to the one, or to preserve the lives of the other. Agreeably to this account, the *Arabs* meet sometimes with whole nests of these eggs undisturbed; some of which are sweet and good, others are addle and corrupted, others again have their young ones of different growths, according to the time it may be presumed they have been forsaken by the dam. They oftener meet a few of the little ones, no bigger than well-grown pullets, half starved, straggling, and moaning about, like so many distressed orphans, for their mother. And in this manner the *ostrich* may be said (ver. 16) *to be hardened against her young ones, as though they were not hers; her labour* in hatching and attending them so far *being vain without fear*, or the least concern of what becomes of them afterwards. This want of affection is also recorded, Lam. iv. 3: *The daughter of my people*, says the prophet, *is cruel, like the ostriches in the wilderness.*

"Neither is this the only reproach that may be due to the *ostrich;* she is likewise inconsiderate and foolish in her private capacity; particularly in the choice of food, which is frequently highly detrimental and pernicious to her; for she swallows every thing greedily and indiscriminately, whether it be pieces of rags, leather, wood, stone, or iron. When I was at *Oram*, I saw one of these birds swallow, without any seeming uneasiness or inconveniency, several leaden bullets, as they were thrown upon the floor, scorching hot from the mould; the inner coats of the *œsophagus* and *stomach* being probably better stocked with glands and juices than in other animals with shorter necks. They are particularly fond of their own excrement, which they greedily eat up as soon as it is voided. No less fond are they of the dung of hens and other poultry. It seems as if their *optic* as well as *olfactory* nerves were less adequate and conducive to their safety and preservation than in other creatures. The *Divine providence in this*, no less than in other respects, (ver. 17,) *having deprived them of wisdom, neither hath it imparted to them understanding.*

"Those parts of the *Sahara* which these birds chiefly frequent are destitute of all manner of food and herbage, except it be some few tufts of coarse grass, or else a few other solitary plants of the *laureola*, *apocynum*, and some other kinds; each of which is equally destitute of nourishment; and, in the *psalmist's* phrase, (Psa. cxxix. 6,) *even withereth afore it groweth up.* Yet these herbs, notwithstanding their dryness, and want of moisture in their temperature, will sometimes have both their leaves and their stalks studded all over with a great variety of *land snails*, which may afford them some little refreshment. It is very probable, likewise, that they may sometimes seize upon *lizards*, *serpents*, together with *insects* and *reptiles* of various kinds. Yet still, considering th great voracity and size of this *camel-bird*, it is wonderful, not only how the little ones, after they are weaned from the provisions I have mentioned, should be brought up and nourished, but even how those of fuller growth and much better qualified to look out for themselves, are able to subsist.

"Their organs of digestion, and particularly the gizzards, which, by their strong friction, will wear away iron itself, show them indeed to be *granivorous;* but yet they have scarce ever an opportunity to exercise them in this way, unless when they chance to stray, which is very seldom, towards those parts of the country which are sown and cultivated. For these, as they are much frequented by the *Arabs* at the several seasons of grazing, ploughing, and gathering in the harvest; so they are little visited by, as indeed they would be an improper abode for, this shy, timorous bird; φιλερημος, *a lover of the deserts.* This last circumstance in the behaviour of the *ostrich* is frequently alluded to in the Holy Scriptures; particularly Isa. xiii. 21, and xxxiv. 13, and xliii. 20; Jer. l. 39; where the word, יענה *yaanah,* instead of being rendered the *ostrich,* as it is rightly put in the margin, is called the *owl;* a word used likewise instead of *yaanah* or the *ostrich,* Lev. xi. 16, and Deut. xiv. 15.

"Whilst I was abroad, I had several opportunities of amusing myself with the actions and behaviour of the *ostrich.* It was very diverting to observe with what dexterity and *equipoise* of body it would play and frisk about on all occasions. In the heat of the day, particularly, it would strut along the sunny side of the house with great majesty. It would be perpetually fanning and priding itself with its *quivering expanded wings;* and seem at every turn to admire and be in love with its shadow. Even at other times whether walking about, or resting itself upon the ground, the wings would continue these fanning vibrating motions, as if they were designed to mitigate and assuage that extraordinary heat wherewith their bodies seem to be naturally affected.

"Notwithstanding these *birds* appear tame and tractable to such persons of the family as were more known and familiar to them, yet they were often very rude and fierce to strangers, especially the poorer sort, whom they would not only endeavour to push down by running furiously upon them; but would not cease to peck at them violently with their bills, and to strike them with their feet; whereby they were frequently very mischievous. For the inward claw, or hoof rather as we may call it, of this *avis bisulca,* being exceedingly strong pointed and angular, I once saw an unfortunate person who had his belly ripped open by one of these strokes. Whilst they are engaged in these combats and assaults, they sometimes make a fierce, angry, and hissing noise, with their throats inflated, and their mouths open; at other times, when less resistance is made, they have a chuckling or cackling voice, as in the poultry kind; and thereby seem to rejoice and laugh as it were at the timorousness of their adversary. But during the lonesome part of the night, as if their organs of voice had then attained a quite different tone, they often made a very doleful and hideous noise; which would be sometimes like the roaring of a *lion;* at other times it would bear a near resemblance to the hoarser voices of other *quadrupeds,* particularly of the *bull* and the *ox.* I have often heard them groan, as if they were in the greatest agonies; an action beautifully alluded to by the Prophet *Micah,* i. 8, where it is said, *I will make a mourning like the yaanah* or *ostrich. Yaanah,* therefore, and רננים *renanim,* the names by which the *ostrich* is known in the Holy Scriptures, may very properly be deduced from ענה *anah,* and רנן *ranan,* words which the *lexicographi* explain by *exclamare* or *clamare fortiter;* for the noise made by the *ostrich* being loud and sonorous, *exclamare* or *clamare fortiter* may, with propriety enough, be attributed to it; especially as those words do not seem to denote any certain or determined mode of voice or sound peculiar to any one particular *species* of animals, but such as may be applicable to them all, to *birds* as well as to *quadrupeds* and other creatures."

Shaw's Travels, p. 541, edit. 4to. 1757.

The subjects in this chapter have been so various and important, that I have been obliged to extend the notes and observations to an unusual length; and yet much is left unnoticed which I wished to have inserted. I have made the best selection I could, and must request those readers who wish for more information to consult *zoological* writers.

CHAPTER XL

Job humbles himself before the Lord, 1–5. *And God again challenges him by a display of his power and judgments,* 6–14. *A description of behemoth,* 15–24.

A. M. cir. 2484
B. C. cir. 1520
Ante I. Olymp. cir. 744
Ante U. C. cir. 767

MOREOVER the LORD answered Job, and said,
2 Shall he that [a]contendeth
with the Almighty instruct *him?*
he that reproveth God, let him
answer it.
3 Then Job answered the LORD,
and said,

A. M. cir. 2484
B. C. cir. 1520
Ante I. Olymp. cir. 744
Ante U. C. cir. 767

---

[a]Chap. xxxiii. 13

NOTES ON CHAP. XL

Verse 1. *Moreover the Lord answered*] That is, the Lord continued his discourse with Job. *Answered* does not refer to any thing *said* by Job, or any *question* asked.

I think it very likely that this whole piece, from the beginning of this *first* verse to the end of the *fourteenth,* was originally the *ending* of the poem. Mr. *Heath* has noticed this, and I shall lay his words before the reader: "The former part of this chapter is evidently the conclusion of the poem; the latter part whereof seems to be in great disorder; whether it has happened from the carelessness of the transcriber, or, which appears most probable, from the skins of parchment composing the roll having by some accident changed their places. It is plain from the *seventh* verse of the *forty-second* chapter that Jehovah is the *last* speaker

A. M. cir. 2484
B. C. cir. 1520
Ante I. Olymp. cir. 744
Ante U. C. cir. 767

4 [b]Behold, I am vile; what
shall I answer thee? [c]I will lay
mine hand upon my mouth.
5 Once have I spoken; but I
will not answer; yea, twice; but I will proceed no farther.
6 [d]Then answered the LORD unto Job out
of the whirlwind, and said,
7 [e]Gird up thy loins now like a man: [f]I
will demand of thee, and declare thou unto me.
8 [g]Wilt thou also disannul my judgment?
wilt thou condemn me, that thou mayest be
righteous?
9 Hast thou an arm like God? or canst
thou thunder with [h]a voice like
him?

A. M. cir. 2484
B. C. cir. 1520
Ante I. Olymp. cir. 744
Ante U. C. cir. 767

10 [i]Deck thyself now *with*
majesty and excellency; and
array thyself with glory and beauty.
11 Cast abroad the rage of thy wrath: and
behold every one *that is* proud, and abase him.
12 Look on every one *that is* [k]proud, *and*
bring him low; and tread down the wicked in
their place.
13 Hide them in the dust together; *and*
bind their faces in secret.
14 Then will I also confess unto thee that
thine own right hand can save thee.

---

[b]Ezra ix. 6; chapter xlii. 6; Psalm li. 4——[c]Chapter xxix. 9; Psalm xxxix. 9——[d]Chapter xxxviii. 1——[e]Ch. xxxviii. 3

[f]Chapter xlii. 4——[g]Psalm li. 4; Romans iii. 4——[h]Chapter xxxvii. 4; Psalm xxix. 3, 4——[i]Psalm xciii. 1; civ. 1——[k]Isaiah ii. 12; Daniel iv. 37

---

in the poem. If, then, immediately after the end of the *thirty-ninth* chapter, we subjoin the *fifteenth* verse of the *forty-second* chapter, and place the *fourteen* first verses of the *fortieth* chapter immediately after the *sixth* verse of the *forty-second* chapter, and by that means make them the conclusion of the poem, all will be right; and this *seventh* verse of the *forty-second* chapter will be in its natural order. The action will be complete by the judgment of the Almighty; and the catastrophe of the poem will be grand and solemn." To these reasons of Mr. *Heath*, Dr. *Kennicott* has added others, which the reader may find at the end of the chapter. Without taking any farther notice of the transposition in this place, I will continue the notes in the present order of the verses.

Verse 2. *He that reproveth God, let him answer it.*] Let the man who has made so free with God and his government, answer to what he has now heard.

Verse 4. *Behold, I am vile*] I acknowledge my inward defilement. I cannot answer thee.

I will lay mine hand upon my mouth.] I cannot excuse myself, and I must be dumb before thee.

Verse 5. *Once have I spoken*] See on chap. xlii. 3, &c.

I will proceed no farther.] I shall attempt to justify myself no longer; I have spoken repeatedly; and am confounded at my want of respect for my Maker, and at the high thoughts which I have entertained of my own righteousness. All is impurity in the presence of thy Majesty.

Verse 7. *Gird up thy loins*] See chap. xxxviii. 1-3. Some think that this and the preceding verse have been repeated here from chap. xxxviii. 1-3, and that several of the words *there, here,* and chap. xlii. 3, have been repeated, in after times, to connect some false gatherings of the sheets of parchment, on which the end of this poem was originally written. See on ver. 1, and at the end of the chapter.

Verse 8. *Wilt thou condemn me*] Rather than submit to be thought in the wrong, wilt thou condemn MY conduct, in order to justify *thyself?* Some men will never acknowledge themselves in the wrong. "God may err, but we cannot," seems to be their impious maxim. Unwillingness to acknowledge a fault frequently leads men, directly or indirectly, to this sort of blasphemy. There are *three* words most difficult to be pronounced in all languages,—I AM WRONG.

Verse 9. *Hast thou an arm like God?*] Every word, from this to the end of verse 14, has a wonderful tendency to humble the soul; and it is no wonder that at the conclusion of these sayings Job fell in the dust confounded, and ascribed righteousness to his Maker.

Verse 10. *Deck thyself now* with *majesty*] *Act* like God, seeing thou hast been assuming to thyself perfections that belong to him alone.

Verse 13. *Hide them in the dust together*] Blend the high and the low, the rich and the poor, in one common ruin. Show them that thou art supreme, and canst do whatsoever thou pleasest.

Bind their faces in secret.] This seems to refer to the custom of preserving *mummies:* the whole body is wrapped round with strong swathings of linen or cotton cloth. Not only the limbs, but the very *head, face,* and all, are rolled round with strong filleting, so that not *one feature* can be seen, not even the protuberance of the nose. On the outside of these involutions a human face is ordinarily *painted;* but as to the *real face* itself, it is emphatically *bound in secret,* for those rollers are never intended to be removed.

Verse 14. *Thine own right hand can save thee.*] It is the prerogative of God alone to save the human soul. Nothing less than unlimited power, exerted under the direction and impulse of unbounded mercy, can save a sinner. This is most clearly asserted in this speech of Jehovah: When thou canst extend an arm like God, i. e., an uncontrollable power—when thou canst arm thyself with the lightning of heaven, and thunder with a voice like God—when thou canst deck thyself with the ineffable glory, beauty, and splendour of the supreme majesty of Jehovah—when thou canst dispense thy judgments over all the earth, to abase the proud, and tread down the wicked—when thou

A. M. cir. 2484
B. C. cir. 1520
Ante I. Olymp. cir. 744
Ante U. C. cir. 767

15 Behold now [l]behemoth,
which I made with thee; he
eateth grass as an ox.
16 Lo now, his strength *is* in
his loins, and his force *is* in the
navel of his belly.
17 [m]He moveth his tail
like a cedar: the sinews of

A. M. cir. 2484
B. C. cir. 1520
Ante I. Olymp. cir. 744
Ante U. C. cir. 767

[l]Or, *the elephant*, as some think

[m]Or, *He setteth up*

canst as having the keys of hell and death, blend the high and the low in the dust together; then I will acknowledge to thee that thy own right hand can save thee. In other words: Salvation belongeth unto the Lord; no man can save his own soul by works of righteousness which he *has* done, *is* doing, or *can* possibly do, to all eternity. Without Jesus every human spirit must have perished everlastingly. Glory be to God for his unspeakable gift!

Verse 15. *Behold now behemoth*] The word בהמות *behemoth* is the plural of בהמה *behemah*, which signifies *cattle* in general, or *graminivorous* animals, as distinguished from חיתו *chayetho*, all *wild* or *carnivorous* animals. See Gen. i. 24. The former seems to mean kine, horses, asses, sheep, &c., and all employed in domestic or agricultural matters; the latter, all wild and savage beasts, such as lions, bears, tigers, &c.: but the words are not always taken in these senses.

In this place it has been supposed to mean some animal of the *beeve* kind. The *Vulgate* retains the *Hebrew* name; so do the *Syriac* and *Arabic*. The *Chaldee* is indefinite, translating *creature* or *animal*. And the *Septuagint* is not more explicit, translating by *θηρια*, *beasts* or *wild beasts;* and old *Coverdale*, **the cruell beaste**, perhaps as near to the truth as any of them. From the *name*, therefore, or the understanding had of it by the ancient *versions*, we can derive no assistance relative to the individuality of the animal in question; and can only hope to find what it is by the characteristics it bears in the description here given of it.

These, having been carefully considered and deeply investigated both by critics and naturalists, have led to the conclusion that either the *elephant*, or the *hippopotamus* or *river-horse*, is the animal in question; and on comparing the characteristics between these two, the balance is considerably in favour of the *hippopotamus*. But even here there are still some difficulties, as there are some parts of the description which do not well suit even the *hippopotamus;* and therefore I have my doubts whether *either* of the animals above is that in question, or whether any animal now in existence be that described by the Almighty.

Mr. *Good* supposes, and I am of the same opinion, that the animal here described is now *extinct*. The *skeletons* of three lost genera have actually been found out: these have been termed *palæotherium*, *anoplotherium*, and *mastodon* or *mammoth*. From an actual examination of a part of the skeleton of what is termed the *mammoth*, I have described it in my note on Gen. i. 24.

As I do not believe that either the *elephant* or the *river-horse* is intended here, I shall not take up the reader's time with any detailed description. The elephant is well known; and, though not an inhabitant of these countries, has been so often imported in a tame state, and so frequently occurs in exhibitions of wild beasts, that multitudes, even of the common people, have seen this tremendous, docile, and sagacious animal. Of the *hippopotamus* or *river-horse*, little is generally known but by description, as the habits of this animal will not permit him to be tamed. His amphibious nature prevents his becoming a constant resident on dry land.

The *hippopotamus* inhabits the rivers of *Africa* and the lakes of *Ethiopia:* feeds generally by night; wanders only a few miles from water; feeds on vegetables and roots of trees, but never on *fish;* lays waste whole plantations of the sugar-cane, rice, and other grain. When irritated or wounded, it will attack boats and men with much fury. It moves slowly and heavily: swims dexterously; walks deliberately and leisurely over head into the water; and pursues his way, even on all fours, on the bottom; but cannot remain long under the water without rising to take in air. It sleeps in reedy places; has a tremendous voice, between the *lowing* of an *ox* and the *roaring* of the *elephant*. Its head is large; its mouth, very wide; its skin, thick and almost devoid of hair; and its tail, naked and about a foot long. It is nearly as large as the elephant, and some have been found *seventeen feet* long. Mr. *Good* observes: "Both the *elephant* and *hippopotamus* are naturally quiet animals; and never interfere with the grazing of others of different kinds unless they be irritated. The *behemoth*, on the contrary, is represented as a quadruped of a ferocious nature, and formed for tyranny, if not rapacity; equally lord of the floods and of the mountains; rushing with rapidity of foot, instead of slowness or stateliness; and possessing a rigid and enormous *tail*, like a cedar tree, instead of a short naked tail of about a *foot long*, as the hippopotamus; or a weak, slender, hog-shaped tail, as the elephant."

The *mammoth*, for size, will answer the description in this place, especially ver. 19: *He is the chief of the ways of God.* That to which the part of a skeleton belonged which I examined, must have been, by computation, not less than *twenty-five* feet high, and *sixty* feet in length! The bones of *one toe* I measured, and found them *three feet* in length! One of the very smallest grinders of an animal of this extinct species, full of processes on the surface more than an inch in depth, which shows that the animal had lived on *flesh*, I have just now weighed, and found it, in its very dry state, *four pounds eight ounces*, avoirdupois: the same grinder of an *elephant* I have weighed also, and found it just *two pounds*. The mammoth, therefore, from this proportion, must have been as large as two *elephants* and a quarter. We may judge by this of its size: *elephants* are frequently *ten* and *eleven* feet high; this will make the mammoth at least *twenty-five* or *twenty-six* feet high; and as it appears to have been a *many-toed* animal, the *springs* which such a creature could make must have been almost incredible: nothing by *swift-*

A. M. cir. 2484 B. C. cir. 1520 Ante I. Olymp. cir. 744 Ante U. C. cir. 767

his stones are wrapped together.
18 His bones *are as* strong pieces of brass; his bones *are* like bars of [n]iron.
19 He *is* the chief of the ways of God: he that made him can make his sword to approach *unto him*.
20 Surely the mountains [o]bring him forth food, where all the beasts of the field play.
21 He lieth under the shady trees, in the covert of the reed, and fens.
22 The shady trees cover him *with* their shadow, the willows of the brook compass him about.
23 Behold, [p]he drinketh up a river, *and* hasteth not: he trusteth that he can draw up Jordan into his mouth.
24 [q]He taketh it with his eyes: *his* nose pierceth through snares.

[n]Daniel ii. 40——[o]Psalm civ. 14——[p]Hebrew, *he oppresseth*

[q]Or, *Will* any *take him in his sight*, or *bore* his *nose with a gin?* chap. xli. 1, 2

ness could have escaped its pursuit. God seems to have made it as the proof of his power; and had it been prolific, and not become extinct, it would have depopulated the earth. Creatures of this kind must have been living in the days of Job; the behemoth is referred to here, as if perfectly and commonly known.

He eateth grass as an ox.] This seems to be mentioned as something *remarkable* in this animal: that though from the form of his *teeth* he must have been *carnivorous*, yet he *ate grass as an ox;* he lived both on animal and vegetable food.

Verse 16. *His strength* is *in his loins*] This refers to his great *agility*, notwithstanding his *bulk;* by the *strength of his loins* he was able to take vast *springs*, and make astonishing bounds.

Verse 17. *He moveth his tail like a cedar*] Therefore it was neither the *elephant*, who has a *tail* like that of the *hog*, nor the *hippopotamus*, whose tail is only about a *foot* long.

The sinews of his stones] I translate with Mr. *Good*, and for the same reasons, *the sinews of his haunches*, which is still more characteristic; as the animal must have excelled in *leaping*.

Verse 18. *His bones* are as *strong pieces of brass—bars of iron.*] The tusk I have mentioned above is uncommonly *hard, solid*, and *weighty* for its size.

Verse 19. *He* is *the chief of the ways of God*] The *largest, strongest*, and *swiftest* quadruped that God has formed.

He that made him] No power of *man* or *beast* can overcome him. God alone can overcome him, and God alone could *make his sword* (of *extinction*) *approach to him.*

Verse 20. *The mountains bring him forth food*] It cannot therefore be the *hippopotamus*, as he is seldom found far from the rivers where he has his chief residence.

Where all the beasts of the field play.] He frequents those places where he can have most *prey*. He makes a mock of all the beasts of the field. They can neither resist his *power*, nor escape from his *agility*. All this answers to what we know of the *mammoth*, but not at all to the *hippopotamus.*

Verse 21. *He lieth under the shady trees*] This and the following verses refer to certain *habits* of the *behemoth*, with which we are and must be unacquainted.

Verse 22. *The willows of the brook compass him*] This would agree well enough with the hippopotamus.

Verse 23. *Behold, he drinketh up a river*] A similar mode of expression, and of precisely the same meaning, as that in chap. xxxix. 24: "He swalloweth the ground with fierceness." No river can stop his course: he wades through all; stems every tide and torrent; and *hurries not* as though he were in danger.

He trusteth that he can draw up Jordan] Even when the river overflows its banks, it is no stoppage to him: though the whole impetuosity of its stream rush against his mouth, he is not afraid. Mr. *Good* has seized the true idea in his translation of this verse:—

"If the stream rage, he revileth not:
He is unmoved, though Jordan rush against
his mouth."

From this mention of Jordan it is probable that the behemoth was once an *inhabitant* of the mountains, marshes, and woods, of the land of Palestine.

Verse 24. *He taketh it with his eyes*] He looks at the sweeping tide, and *defies* it.

His *nose pierceth through snares.*] If *fences* of *strong stakes* be made in order to restrain him, or prevent him from passing certain boundaries, he tears them in pieces with his teeth; or, by pressing his nose against them, breaks them off. If other parts of the description would answer, this might well apply to the elephant, the *nose* here meaning the *proboscis*, with which he can *split trees*, or even *tear them up from the roots!*

Thus ends the description of the *behemoth;* what I suppose to be the *mastodon* or *mammoth*, or some creature of this kind, that God made as *the chief of his works*, exhibited in various countries for a time, cut them off from the earth, but by his providence preserved many of their skeletons, that succeeding ages might behold the *mighty power* which produced this *chief of the ways of God*, and admire the *providence* that rendered that race extinct which would otherwise, in all probability, have extinguished every other race of animals!

I am not unapprized of the strong arguments produced by learned men to prove, on the one hand, that *behemoth* is the *elephant;* and, on the other, that he is the *hippopotamus* or *riverhorse;* and I have carefully read all that *Bochart*, that chief of learned men, has said on the subject. But I am convinced that an animal now *extinct*, probably of the kind already mentioned, is the creature pointed out and described by the inspiration of God in this chapter.

On ver. 30 of the preceding chapter we have seen, from Mr. *Heath's* remarks, that the *fourteen* first verses were probably transposed. In the following observations Dr. Kennicott appears to prove the point.

"It will be here objected, that the poem could not possibly end with this question from *Job;* and, among other reasons, for this in particular; because we read in the very next verse, *That after the Lord had spoken these words unto Job*, &c. If, therefore, the last speaker was not *Job*, but *the Lord*, Job could not originally have concluded this poem, as he does at present.

"This objection I hold to be exceedingly important; and, indeed, to prove decisively that the poem must have ended at first with some speech from God.

"And this remark leads directly to a very interesting inquiry: *What* was at first *the conclusion* of this poem? This may, I presume, be pointed out and determined, not by the alteration of any one word, but only by allowing a *dislocation* of the *fourteen* verses which now begin the *fortieth* chapter. Chapters xxxviii., xxxix., xl., and xli., contain a magnificent display of the Divine power and wisdom in the works of the Creator; specifying the *lion, raven, wild goat, wild ass, unicorn, peacock, ostrich, horse, hawk, eagle, behemoth*, and *leviathan.*

"Now, it must have surprised most readers to find that the description of these creatures is strangely *interrupted* at chap. xl. 1, and as strangely *resumed* afterwards at chap. xl. 15; and therefore, if these *fourteen* verses will connect with and regularly follow what now *ends* the poem, we cannot much doubt that these *fourteen verses* have again found their true station, and should be restored to it.

"The greatness of the supposed transposition is no objection: because so *many verses* as would fill *one piece of vellum* in an ancient roll, might be easily sewed in *before* or *after* its proper place. In the case before us, the *twenty-five lines* in the *first fourteen* verses of chapter xl. seem to have been sewed in improperly after chap. xxxix. 30, instead of after chap. xlii. 6. That such large parts have been transposed in rolls, to make which the parts are sewed together, is absolutely certain; and that this has been the case here, is still more probable for the following reason:—

"The lines here supposed to be out of place are *twenty-five*, and contain *ninety-two words;* which might be written on *one piece* or *page* of *vellum*. But the MS. in which these *twenty-five lines* made *one page*, must be supposed to have the same, or nearly the same, number of lines in *each of the pages adjoining*. And it would greatly strengthen this presumption if these *twenty-five* lines would fall in regularly at the end of any other set of lines, nearly of the same number; if they would fall in after the *next* set of *twenty-five*, or the *second* set, or the *third*, or the *fourth*, &c. Now, *this is actually the case here;* for the lines after these *twenty-five*, being *one hundred* or *one hundred and one*, make just *four times twenty-five*. And, therefore, if we consider these *one hundred and twenty-five lines* as written on *five equal pieces* of vellum, it follows that the *fifth* piece *might be* carelessly sewed up *before* the other *four*.

"Let us also observe that present *disorder* of the speeches, which is this. In chapters xxxviii. and xxxix., *God* first speaks to Job. The end of chap. xxxix. is followed by, 'And the Lord answered Job and said,' whilst yet Job had *not* replied. At chap. xl. 3-5, Job answers; but he says, *he had* then *spoken* TWICE, and *he would add no more;* whereas, this was his *first* reply, and he speaks afterwards. From chap. xl. 15 to xli. 34 are now the description of behemoth and leviathan, which would regularly follow the descriptions of the horse, hawk, and eagle. And from chap. xlii. 1 to xlii. 6 is now *Job's* speech, after which we read in ver. 7, 'After the Lord had spoken these words unto Job!'

"Now, all these confusions are removed at once if we only allow that a piece of vellum containing the *twenty-five lines*, (chap. xl. 1-14,) originally followed chap. xlii. 6. For then, after God's *first speech*, ending with *leviathan*, Job replies: then God, to whom Job replies the *second* time, when he *added no more;* and then God addresses him the *third*, when Job is silent, and the *poem* concludes: upon which the *narrative* opens regularly, with saying, 'After the Lord had spoken these words unto Job,' &c.; chap. xlii. 7."—*Kennicott's* Remarks, p. 161.

The reader will find much more satisfaction if he read the places as above directed. Having ended chap. xxxix., proceed immediately to ver. 15 of chap. xl.; go on regularly to the end of ver. 6 of chap. xlii., and immediately after that, add the first *fourteen* verses of chap. xl. We shall find then that the poem has a consistent and proper ending, and that the concluding speech was spoken by JEHOVAH.

CHAPTER XLI

God's great power in the leviathan, of which creature he gives a very circumstantial description, 1–34.

A. M. cir. 2484
B. C. cir. 1520

CANST thou draw out [a]leviathan [b]with a hook? or his tongue with a cord [c]*which* thou lettest down?

[a]That is, *a whale* or *a whirlpool*——[b]Psa. civ. 26; Isa. xxvii. 1——[c]Heb. which *thou drownest*

NOTES ON CHAP. XLI

Verse 1. *Canst thou draw out leviathan*] We come now to a subject not less perplexing than that over which we have passed, and a subject on which learned men are less agreed than on the preceding. What is *leviathan?* The Hebrew word לויתן *livyathan* is retained by

A. M. cir. 2484
B. C. cir. 1520
Ante I. Olymp. cir. 744
Ante U. C. cir. 767

2 Canst thou [d]put a hook into
his nose? or bore his jaw through
with a thorn?
3 Will he make many suppli-
cations unto thee? will he speak soft *words*
unto thee?
4 Will he make a covenant with thee? wilt
thou take him for [e]a servant for ever?
5 Wilt thou [f]play with him as *with* a bird?
or wilt thou bind him for thy
maidens?
6 Shall thy companions make
a banquet of him? shall they part
him among the merchants?
7 Canst thou fill his skin with barbed irons?
or his head with fish spears?
8 Lay thine hand upon him, remember the
battle, do no more.

[d]Isa. xxxvii. 29——[e]Exod. xxi. 1, &c. [f]Psa. civ. 26

the Vulgate and the Chaldee. The Septuagint have, Αξεις δε δρακοντα; "*Canst* thou draw out the DRAGON?" The Syriac and Arabic have the same. A species of *whale* has been supposed to be the creature in question; but the description suits no animal but the *crocodile* or alligator; and it is not necessary to seek elsewhere. The crocodile is a natural inhabitant of the Nile, and other Asiatic and African rivers. It is a creature of enormous voracity and strength, as well as fleetness in swimming. He will attack the largest animals, and even men, with the most daring impetuosity. In proportion to his size he has the largest mouth of all monsters. The upper jaw is armed with *forty* sharp strong teeth, and the under jaw with *thirty-eight*. He is clothed with such a coat of mail as cannot be pierced, and can in every direction resist a musket-ball. The Hebrew לוי *levi* תן *ten* signifies the *coupled dragon;* but what this is we know not, unless the crocodile be meant.

With a hook] That crocodiles were caught with a *baited hook*, at least one species of crocodile, we have the testimony of *Herodotus*, lib. ii., c. 70: Επεαν νωτον συος δελεαση περι αγκιστρον, μετιει ες μεσον τον ποταμον, κ. τ. λ. "They take the back or chine of a swine, and bait a hook with it, and throw it into the midst of the river; and the fisherman stands at some distance on the shore holding a young pig, which he irritates, in order to make it squeak. When the crocodile hears this he immediately makes towards the sound; and, finding the baited hook in his way, swallows it, and is then drawn to land, when they dash mud into his eyes, and blind him; after which he is soon despatched." In this way it seems *leviathan* was *drawn out by a hook:* but it was undoubtedly both *a difficult* and *dangerous* work, and but barely practicable in the way in which *Herodotus* relates the matter.

Or his tongue with a cord] It is probable that, when the animal was taken, they had some method of casting a noose round his *tongue*, when opening his mouth; or piercing it with some barbed instrument. *Thevenot* says that in order to take the crocodile they dig holes on the banks of the river, and cover them with sticks. The crocodiles fall into these, and cannot get out. They leave them there for several days without food, and then let down nooses which they pitch on their jaws, and thus draw them out. This is probably what is meant here.

Verse 2. *Canst thou put a hook into his nose?*] Canst thou put a ring in his nose, and lead him about as thou dost thine ox? In the East they frequently lead the oxen and buffaloes with a ring in their noses. So they do *bulls* and *oxen* in this country.

Bore his jaw through with a thorn?] Some have thought that this means, Canst thou deal with him as with one of those little fish which thou stringest on a rush by means of the thorn at its end? Or perhaps it may refer to those *ornaments* with which they sometimes adorned their horses, mules, camels, &c.

Verse 3. *Will he make many supplications*] There are several allusions in these verses to matters of which we know nothing.

Verse 4. *Will he make a covenant*] Canst thou *hire* him as thou wouldst a servant, who is to be so *attached* to thy family as to have *his ear bored*, that he may abide in thy house for ever? Is not this an allusion to the law, Exod. xxi. 1-6?

Verse 5. *Wilt thou play with him*] Is he such a creature as thou canst tame; and of which thou canst make a *pet*, and give as a plaything to thy little girls? נערותיך *naarotheycha;* probably alluding to the custom of catching birds, tying a string to their legs, and giving them to children to play with; a custom execrable as ancient, and disgraceful as modern.

Verse 6. *Shall thy companions make a banquet*] Canst thou and thy friends feast on him as ye were wont to do on a camel sacrificed for this purpose? Or, canst thou dispose of his flesh to the *merchants*—to buyers, as thou wouldst do that of a camel or an ox? It is certain, according to *Herodotus*, lib. ii. c. 70, that they killed and ate crocodiles at *Apollonople* and *Elephantis*, in Egypt.

Verse 7. *Canst thou fill his skin with barbed irons?*] This refers to some kind of harpoon work, similar to that employed in taking *whales*, and which they might use for some other kinds of animals; for the skin of the crocodile could not be pierced. *Herrera* says that he saw a crocodile defend itself against *thirty* men; and that they fired six balls at it without being able to wound it. It can only be wounded under his belly.

Verse 8. *Lay thine hand upon him?*] Mr. *Heath* translates, "Be sure thou strike home. Mind thy blow: rely not upon a second stroke." Mr. *Good* translates:—

"Make ready thy hand against him.
Dare the contest: be firm."

He is a dangerous animal; when thou attackest him, be sure of thy advantage; if thou miss, thou art ruined. Depend not on other advantages, if thou miss the first. **Kill him** at once, or he will kill thee.

A. M. cir. 2484
B. C. cir. 1520
Ante I. Olymp. cir. 744
Ante U. C. cir. 767

9 Behold, the hope of him is in
vain: shall not *one* be cast down
even at the sight of him?
10 None *is so* fierce that dare
stir him up: who then is able to stand before me?

11 [g]Who hath prevented me, that I should repay *him?* [h]*whatsoever is* under the whole heaven is mine.

12 I will not conceal his parts, nor his power, nor his comely proportion.

13 Who can discover the face of his garment? *or* who can come *to him* [i]with his double bridle?

14 Who can open the doors of his face? his teeth *are* terrible round about.

15 *His* [k]scales *are his* pride, A. M. cir. 2484 B. C. cir. 1520
shut up together *as with* a close Ante I. Olymp. cir. 744
seal. Ante U. C. cir. 767

16 One is so near to another, that no air can come between them.

17 They are joined one to another, they stick together, that they cannot be sundered.

18 By his neesings a light doth shine, and his eyes *are* like the eyelids of the morning.

19 Out of his mouth go burning lamps, *and* sparks of fire leap out.

20 Out of his nostrils goeth smoke, as out of a seething pot or caldron.

21 His breath kindleth coals, and a flame goeth out of his mouth.

---

[g]Rom. xi. 35——[h]Exod. xix. 5; Deut. x. 14; Psa. xxiv. 1; l. 12; 1 Cor. x. 26, 28

[i]Or, *within*——[k]Hebrew, *strong pieces of shields*

Verse 9. *Behold, the hope*] If thou miss thy first advantage, there is no hope afterwards: the very sight of this terrible monster would dissipate thy spirit, if thou hadst not a positive advantage against *his life*, or a place of sure retreat to save *thine own.*

Verse 10. *None* is so *fierce that dare stir him up*] The most courageous of men dare not provoke the crocodile to fight, or even attempt to rouse him, when, sated with fish, he takes his repose among the reeds. The strongest of men cannot match him.

Who then is able] If thou canst not stand against the *crocodile*, one of the *creatures* of my hand, how canst thou resist me, who am his Maker? This is the use which God makes of the formidable description which he has thus far given of this terrible animal.

Verse 11. *Who hath prevented me*] Who is it that hath laid me under obligation to him? Do I need my creatures? All under the heavens is my property.

Verse 12. *I will not conceal his parts*] This is most certainly no just translation of the original. The *Vulgate* is to this effect: *I will not spare him:* nor yield to his *powerful words, framed for the purpose of entreaty.* Mr. *Good* applies it to leviathan:—

"I cannot be confounded at his limbs and
violence;
The strength and structure of his frame."

The Creator cannot be intimidated at the most formidable of his own works: *man* may and should tremble; God cannot.

Verse 13. *Who can discover the face of his garment?*] Who can rip up the hide of this terrible monster? Who can take away his covering, in order to pierce his vitals?

Verse 14. *The doors of his face?*] His jaws; which are most tremendous.

Verse 15. His *scales* are his *pride*] They are impenetrable, as we have already seen.

Verse 16. *One is so near to another*] It has already been stated, that a musket-ball fired at him in *any direction* cannot make a passage through his scales.

Verse 18. *By his neesings a light doth shine*] It is very likely that this may be taken *literally.* When he spurts up the water out of his nostrils, the drops form a sort of *iris* or *rainbow.* We have seen this effect produced when, in certain situations and state of the atmosphere, water was thrown up forcibly, so as to be broken into small drops, which has occasioned an appearance like the *rainbow.*

The eyelids of the morning.] It is said that, under the water, the eyes of the crocodile are exceedingly *dull;* but when he lifts his head above water they *sparkle* with the greatest vivacity. Hence the Egyptians, in their hieroglyphics, made the *eyes* of the *crocodile* the emblem of the *morning.* Ανατολην λεγοντες δυο οφθαλμους κροκοδειλου ζωογραφουσι.—Horapp. Egypt. Ieroglyph., lib. i., c. 65. This is a most remarkable circumstance, casts light on ancient history, and shows the rigid correctness of the picture drawn above.

The same figure is employed by the Greek poets.

Χρυσεας ἡμερας βλεφαρον.

"The *eyelid* of the golden day."
Soph. Antig. ver. 103.

Νυκτος αφεγγες βλεφαρον.

"The darksome *eyelid* of the night."
Eurip. Phœniss. ver. 553.

Verse 19. *Out of his mouth go burning lamps*] Dr. *Young*, in his paraphrase, has a sensible note on this passage:—"This is nearer the truth than at first view may be imagined. The crocodile, according to naturalists, lying long under water, and being there forced to hold its breath, when it emerges, the breath long repressed is hot, and bursts out so violently, that it resembles fire and smoke. The *horse* does not repress his breath by any means so long, neither is he so fierce and animated; yet the most correct of poets ventures to use the same metaphor concerning him, *volvit sub naribus ignem.* By this I would caution against a false opinion of the boldness of Eastern metaphors, from passages ill understood."

A. M. cir. 2484
B. C. cir. 1520
Ante I. Olymp. cir. 744
Ante U. C. cir. 767

22 In his neck remaineth
strength, and [l]sorrow is turned
into joy before him.
23 [m]The flakes of his flesh
are joined together: they are firm in themselves: they cannot be moved.
24 His heart is as firm as a stone; yea, as
hard as a piece of the nether *millstone.*
25 When he raiseth up himself, the mighty
are afraid; by reason of breakings they purify
themselves.
26 The sword of him that layeth at him
cannot hold: the spear, the dart, nor the
[n]habergeon.
27 He esteemeth iron as straw, *and* brass as
rotten wood.

[l]Heb. *sorrow rejoiceth*——[m]Heb. *The fallings*——[n]Or, *breastplate*

28 The arrow cannot make
him flee: sling-stones are turned
with him into stubble.
29 Darts are counted as stubble:
he laugheth at the shaking of a spear.
30 [o]Sharp stones *are* under him: he spreadeth sharp-pointed things upon the mire.
31 He maketh the deep to boil like a
pot: he maketh the sea like a pot of ointment.
32 He maketh a path to shine after him; *one*
would think the deep *to be* hoary.
33 Upon earth there is not his like, [p]who
is made without fear.
34 He beholdeth all high *things:* he *is* a
king over all the children of pride.

A. M. cir. 2484
B. C. cir. 1520
Ante I. Olymp. cir. 744
Ante U. C. cir. 767

[o]Heb. *Sharp pieces of potsherd*——[p]Or, *who behave themselves without fear*

Verse 22. *In his neck remaineth strength*] Literally, "strength has its dwelling in his neck." The *neck* is the seat of strength of most animals; but the *head* and *shoulders* must be here meant, as the crocodile has *no neck*, being shaped nearly like a *lizard*.

And sorrow is turned into joy before him.] ולפניו תדוץ דאבה *ulephanaiv taduts deabah;* "And *destruction* exulteth before him." This is as fine an image as can well be conceived. It is in the true spirit of poetry, the legitimate offspring of the *genie createur.* Our translation is simply *insignificant.*

Verse 23. *The flakes of his flesh*] His muscles are strongly and firmly compacted.

Verse 24. *Hard as a piece of the nether* millstone.] Which is required to be harder than that which runs above.

Verse 25. *By reason of breakings they purify themselves.*] No version, either ancient or modern, appears to have understood this verse; nor is its true sense known. The *Septuagint* have, "When he turns himself, he terrifies all the quadrupeds on the earth." The original is short and obscure: משברים יתחטאו *mishshebarim yithchattau.* Mr. *Good* takes the plural termination ים *im*, from the first word, of which he makes the noun ים *yam, the sea*, and thus translates it, "They are confounded at the tumult of the sea." In this I can find no more light than in our own. Mr. *Heath* has, "For very terror they fall to the ground." The translations of it are as unsatisfactory as they are various. I shall give both the verses from *Coverdale:*—

His herte is as harde as a stone; and as fast as the stythye (anvil) **that the hammer man smyteth upon: when he goeth the mightiest off all are afrayed, and the waives heby.** The dull swell in the waters proclaims his advance; and when this is perceived, the stout-hearted tremble.

Verse 26. *Habergeon.*] The hauberk, the Norman armour for the head, neck, and breast, formed of rings. See on Neh. iv. 16.

Verse 29. *Darts are counted as stubble*] All these verses state that he cannot be *wounded* by any kind of *weapon*, and that he cannot be *resisted* by any human *strength.*

A young crocodile, seen by M. *Maillet, twelve* feet long, and which had not eaten a morsel for *thirty-five* days, its mouth having been tied all that time, was nevertheless so strong, that with a blow of its tail it overturned a bale of coffee, and five or six men, with the utmost imaginable ease! What power then must lodge in one *twenty* feet long, well fed, and in health!

Verse 30. *Sharp stones* are *under him*] So hard and impenetrable are his scales, that splinters of flint are the same to him as the softest reeds.

Verse 31. *He maketh the deep to boil like a pot*] This is occasioned by strongly agitating the waters at or near the bottom; and the froth which arises to the top from this agitation may have the appearance of *ointment.* But several travellers say that the crocodile has a very strong scent of musk, and that he even imparts this *smell* to the *water* through which he passes, and therefore the text may be taken literally. This property of the crocodile has been noticed by several writers.

Verse 32. *He maketh a path to shine after him*] In certain states of the weather a rapid motion through the water disengages many sparks of phosphoric fire. I have seen this at sea; once particularly, on a fine clear night, with a good breeze, in a fast-sailing vessel, I leaned over the stern, and watched this phenomenon for hours. The *wake* of the vessel was like a stream of fire; millions of particles of fire were disengaged by the ship's swift motion through the water, nearly in the same way as by the electric cushion and cylinder; and all continued to be absorbed at a short distance from the vessel. Whether this phenomenon takes place in *fresh water* or in the *Nile*, I have had no opportunity of observing.

The deep to be *hoary.*] By the *frost* and *foam* raised by the rapid passage of the animal through the water.

Verse 33. *Upon earth there is not his like*] There is no creature among terrestrial animals so thoroughly dangerous, so exceedingly strong, and so difficult to be wounded or slain.

Who is made without fear.] Perhaps there is no creature who is at all acquainted with *man*, so totally destitute of fear as the crocodile.

Verse 34. *He is a king over all the children of pride.*] There is no animal in the waters that does not fear and fly from him. Hence the *Chaldee* renders it, *all the offspring of* FISHES.

Calmet says, that by *the children of pride* the Egyptians are meant; that the crocodile is called their *king*, because he was one of their principal divinities; that the kings of Egypt were called *Pharaoh*, which signifies a *crocodile;* and that the Egyptians were proverbial for their *pride*, as may be seen in Ezek. xxxii. 12. And it is very natural to say that Job, wishing to point out a cruel animal, adored by the Egyptians, and considered by them as their chief divinity, should describe him under the name of *king of all the children of pride.*

Houbigant considers the לויתן *livyathan*, the *coupled dragon*, to be emblematical of *Satan:* "He lifts his proud look to God, and aspires to the high heavens; and is king over all the sons of pride." He is, in effect, the governor of every proud, haughty, impious man. What a king! What laws! What subjects!

Others think that MEN are intended by *the sons of pride;* and that it is with the design to abate their pride, and confound them in the high notions they have of their own importance, that God produces and describes an animal of whom they are all afraid, and whom none of them can conquer.

AFTER all, what is *leviathan?* I have strong doubts whether either *whale* or *crocodile* be meant. I think even the *crocodile* overrated by this description. He is too great, too powerful, too important, in this representation. No beast, terrestrial or aquatic, deserves the high character here given, though that character only considers him as unconquerably strong, ferociously cruel, and wonderfully made. Perhaps *leviathan* was some extinct *mammoth* of the *waters*, as *behemoth* was of the *land.* However, I have followed the general opinion by treating him as the *crocodile* throughout these notes; but could not finish without stating my doubts on the subject, though I have nothing better to offer in the place of the animal in behalf of which almost all learned men and critics argue, and concerning which they generally agree. As to its being an emblem either of *Pharaoh* or the *devil*, I can say little more than, *I doubt.* The description is extremely dignified; and were we sure of the animal, I have no doubt we should find it in every instance correct. But after all that has been said, we have yet to learn what leviathan is!

CHAPTER XLII

Job humbles himself before God, 1–6. *God accepts him; censures his three friends; and commands Job to offer sacrifices for them, that he might pardon and accept them, as they had not spoken what was right concerning their Maker*, 7–9. *The Lord turns Job's captivity; and his friends visit him, and bring him presents*, 10, 11. *Job's affluence becomes double to what it was before*, 12. *His family is also increased*, 13–15. *Having lived* one hundred and forty *years after his calamities, he dies*, 16, 17.

A. M. cir. 2484
B. C. cir. 1520
Ante I. Olymp. cir. 744
Ante U. C. cir. 767

THEN Job answered the LORD, and said,
2 I know that thou [a]canst do every *thing*, and *that* [b]no thought can be withholden from thee.
3 [c]Who *is* he that hideth counsel without knowledge? therefore have I uttered that I understood not; [d]things too wonderful for me, which I knew not.
4 Hear, I beseech thee, and I will speak: [e]I will demand of thee, and declare thou unto me.
5 I have heard of thee by the hearing of the ear; but now mine eye seeth thee:

[a]Gen. xviii. 14; Matt. xix. 26; Mark x. 27; xiv. 36; Luke xviii. 27——[b]Or, *no thought of thine can be hindered*

[c]Chap. xxxviii. 2——[d]Psa. xl. 5; cxxxi. 1; cxxxix. 6——[e]Chap. xxxviii. 3; xl. 7

NOTES ON CHAP. XLII

Verse 2. *I know that thou canst do every thing*] Thy power is unlimited; thy wisdom infinite.

Verse 3. *Who is he that hideth counsel*] These are the words of Job, and they are a repetition of what Jehovah said, chap. xxxviii. 2: "Who is this that darkeneth counsel by words without knowledge?" Job now having heard the Almighty's speech, and having received his reproof, echoes back his words: "Who is he that hideth counsel without knowledge?" Alas, *I* am the man; *I have uttered what I understood not; things too wonderful for me, that I knew not.*

God had said, chap. xxxviii. 3: "Gird up now thy loins like a man; I will demand of thee, and answer thou me." In allusion to this, Job exclaims to his Maker, ver. 4: "Hear, I beseech thee, and I will speak: I will ask of THEE, and declare THOU unto ME." I acknowledge my ignorance; I confess my foolishness and presumption; I am ashamed of my conduct; I lament my imperfections; I implore thy mercy; and beg thee to show me thy will, that I may ever think, speak, and do, what is pleasing in thy sight.

Things too wonderful] I have spoken of thy judgments, which I did not comprehend.

Verse 5. *I have heard of thee*] I have now such a discovery of thee as I have never had before. I have only heard of thee by tradition, or from imperfect information; now the eye of my mind clearly perceives thee; and in seeing *thee*, I see *myself;* for the light that discovers

A. M. cir. 2484 B. C. cir. 1520 Ante I. Olymp. cir. 744 Ante U. C. cir. 767

6 Wherefore I [f]abhor *myself,*
and repent in dust and ashes.
7 And it was *so,* that after the
LORD had spoken these words
unto Job, the LORD said to Eliphaz the Temanite, My wrath is kindled against thee, and against thy two friends: for ye have not spoken of me *the thing that is* right, as my servant Job *hath.*

8 Therefore take unto you now [g]seven bullocks and seven rams, and [h]go to my servant Job, and offer up for yourselves a burnt-offering; and my servant Job shall [i]pray for you: for [k]him will I accept: lest I deal with you *after your* folly, in that ye have not spoken of me *the thing which is* right, like my servant Job.

9 So Eliphaz the Temanite and Bildad the Shuhite *and* Zophar the Naamathite went, and did according as the LORD commanded them; the LORD also accepted [l]Job.

10 [m]And the LORD turned the captivity of Job, when he prayed for his friends: also the

[f]Ezra ix. 6; chap. xl. 4——[g]Num. xxiii. 1——[h]Matt. v. 24——[i]Gen. xx. 17; James v. 15, 16; 1 John v. 16

[k]Heb. *his face* or *person;* 1 Sam. xxv. 35; Mal. i. 8 ——[l]Heb. *the face of Job*——[m]Psa. xiv. 7; cxxvi. 1

thy glory and excellence, discovers my meanness and vileness.

Verse 6. *I abhor* myself] Compared with thine, my strength is weakness; my wisdom, folly; and my righteousness, impurity.

"I loathe myself when thee I see;
And into nothing fall."

Repent] I am deeply distressed on account of the *imaginations* of my heart, the *words* of my tongue, and the *acts* of my life. I roll myself in the *dust,* and sprinkle *ashes* upon my head. Job is now sufficiently humbled at the feet of Jehovah; and having earnestly and piously prayed for instruction, the Lord, in a finishing speech, which appears to be contained in the *first fourteen verses* of chap. xl., perfects his teaching on the subject of the late controversy, which is concluded with, "When thou canst act like the Almighty," which is, in effect, what the questions and commands amount to in the preceding verses of that chapter, "then will I also confess unto thee, that thy own right hand can save thee." In the *fifth* verse of the *fortieth* chapter, Job says, "ONCE have I spoken." This must refer to the declaration above, in the beginning of this chapter, (xlii.) And he goes on to state, chap. xl. 5: "Yea, TWICE; but I will proceed no farther." This *second* time is that in which he uses these words: after which he spoke no more; and the Lord concluded with the remaining part of these *fourteen* verses, viz., from ver. 7 to 14, inclusive. Then the thread of the story, in the form of a *narration* is resumed in this chapter (xlii.) at ver. 7.

Verse 7. *After the Lord had spoken these words*] Those recorded at chap. xl. 7-14; he said to Eliphaz, who was the eldest of the three friends, and chief speaker: *Ye have not spoken of me—right.* Mr. *Peters* observes, "It will be difficult to find any thing in the speeches of Eliphaz and his companions which should make the difference here supposed, if we set aside the doctrine of a *future state;* for in this view the others would speak more worthily of God than Job, by endeavouring to vindicate his providence in the exact distribution of good and evil in this life: whereas Job's assertion, chap. ix. 22, 'This is one thing, therefore I said it, *He destroyeth the perfect and the wicked,*' which is the argument on which he all along insists, would, upon this supposition, be directly charging God that he made no distinction between the good and the bad. But now, take the other life into the account, and the thing will appear in quite a contrary light; and we shall easily see the reason why God approves of the sentiments of *Job,* and condemns those of his *friends.* For supposing the friends of Job to argue that the *righteous* are never afflicted *without remedy* here, nor the *wicked prosperous on the whole* in this life, which is a wrong representation of God's providence; and Job to argue, on the other hand, that the righteous are sometimes afflicted here, and that *without remedy,* but shall be *rewarded in the life to come;* and that the *wicked prosper* here, but shall be *punished hereafter,* which is the true representation of the Divine proceedings; and here is a very apparent difference in the drift of the one's discourse, and of the others'. For Job, in this view, speaks worthily of God, and the rest unworthily. The best moral argument that mankind have ever had to believe in *a life to come,* is that which Job insists on—that *good* and *evil* are, for the most part, dealt out *here* promiscuously. On the contrary, the topic urged by his friends, and which they push a great deal too far, that God rewards and punishes in this world, tends, in its consequences, like that other opinion which was held by the stoics in after times, that *virtue is its own reward,* to sap the very foundation of that proof we have, from reason, of another life. No wonder, therefore, that the sentiments of the one are approved, and those of the other condemned."

Verse 8. *Take—seven bullocks and seven rams*] From this it appears that Job was considered a *priest,* not only in his own family, but also for others. For his children he offered burnt-offerings, chap. i. 5; and now he is to make the same kind of *offerings,* accompanied with *intercession,* in behalf of his three friends. This is a full proof of the innocence and integrity of Job: a more decided one could not be given, that the accusations of his friends, and their bitter speeches, were as *untrue* as they were *malevolent.* God thus clears *his* character, and confounds *their* devices.

Verse 10. *The Lord turned the captivity of Job*] The *Vulgate* has: Dominus quoque conversus est ad pœnitentiam Job; "And the LORD turned Job to repentance." The *Chaldee:* "The WORD of the Lord (מימרא דיי *meymera dayai*) turned the captivity of Job." There is a remark which these words suggest, which has been

A. M. cir. 2484 B. C. cir. 1520 Ante I. Olymp. cir. 744 Ante U. C. cir. 767

LORD [n]gave Job [o]twice as much
as he had before.
11 Then came there unto him
[p]all his brethren, and all his
sisters, and all they that had been of his acquaintance before, and did eat bread with him
in his house: and they bemoaned him, and
comforted him over all the evil that the LORD
had brought upon him: every man also gave
him a piece of money, and every one an ear-
ring of gold.

12 So the LORD blessed [q]the
latter end of Job more than his
beginning: for he had [r]fourteen
thousand sheep, and six thousand
camels, and a thousand yoke of oxen, and a
thousand she-asses.
13 [s]He had also seven sons and three
daughters.
14 And he called the name of the first, Jemima; and the name of the second, Kezia;
and the name of the third, Keren-happuch.

A. M. cir. 2484 B. C. cir. 1520 Ante I. Olymp. cir. 744 Ante U. C. cir. 767

[n]Heb. *added all that* had been *to Job unto the double*——[o]Isa. xl. 2——[p]See chap. xix. 13

[q]Chap. viii. 7; James v. 11——[r]See chap. i. 3——[s]Chap. i. 2

rarely, if at all, noticed. It is said that *the Lord turned the captivity of Job* WHEN HE PRAYED FOR HIS FRIENDS. He had suffered much through the unkindness of these friends; they had criticised his conduct without *feeling* or *mercy;* and he had just cause to be irritated against them: and that he had such a feeling towards *them,* several parts of his discourses sufficiently prove. God was now about to show Job his *mercy;* but *mercy* can be shown only to the *merciful;* Job must *forgive* his unfeeling friends, if he would be *forgiven* by the *Lord;* he directs him, therefore, to *pray for them,* ver. 8. He who can *pray* for another cannot entertain *enmity* against him: Job did so; and *when* he prayed for his friends, God turned the captivity of Job. "Forgive, and ye shall be forgiven."

Some suppose that Job, being miraculously restored, armed his servants and remaining friends, and fell upon those who had spoiled him; and not only recovered his own property, but also spoiled the spoilers, and thus his substance became double what it was before. Of this I do not see any intimation in the sacred text.

Verse 11. *Then came there unto him all his brethren*] "Job being restored to his former health and fortunes, the author," says Mr. *Heath,* "presents us with a striking view of *human friendship.* His *brethren,* who, in the time of his affliction, *kept at a distance* from him; his *kinsfolk,* who *ceased to know him;* his *familiar friends,* who had *forgotten* him; and his *acquaintance,* who had *made themselves perfect strangers* to him; those to whom he had *showed kindness,* and who yet had *ungratefully* neglected him, on the return of his prosperity now come and condole with him, desirous of renewing former familiarity; and, according to the custom of the Eastern countries, where there is no approaching a great man without a *present,* each brings him a *kesitah,* each a jewel of gold." See ver. 12.

A piece of money] קשיטה *kesitah* signifies a *lamb;* and it is supposed that this piece of money had a *lamb* stamped on it, as that quantity of gold was generally the current value for a lamb. See my note on Gen. xxxiii. 19, where the subject is largely considered. The *Vulgate, Chaldee, Septuagint, Arabic,* and *Syriac,* have *one lamb* or *sheep;* so it appears that they did not understand the *kesitah* as implying a *piece of money* of any kind, but a *sheep* or a *lamb.*

Earring of gold] Literally, a *nose-jewel.* The *Septuagint* translate, τετραδραχμον χρυσου, a tetradrachm of gold, or *golden daric;* but by adding και ασημου, *unstamped,* they intimate that it was four drachms of uncoined gold.

Verse 12. *The Lord blessed the latter end of Job*] Was it not in consequence of his friends bringing him a *lamb, sheep,* or other kind of *cattle,* and the *quantity of gold* mentioned, that his stock of *sheep* was increased so speedily to 14,000, his *camels* to 6000, his *oxen* to 2000, and his *she-asses* to 1000?

Mr. *Heath* takes the story of the conduct of Job's friends by the worst handle; see ver. 11. Is it not likely that they themselves were the *cause* of his sudden accumulation of property? and that they did not visit him, nor seek his familiarity *because* he *was now prosperous;* but because they saw that *God had turned his captivity,* and miraculously healed him? This gave them full proof of his *innocence,* and they no longer considered him an *anathema,* or *devoted person,* whom they should avoid and detest, but one who had been suffering under a strange dispensation of Divine Providence, and who was now no longer a suspicious character, but a favourite of heaven, to whom they should show every possible kindness. They therefore joined hands with God to make the poor man live, and their *presents* were the cause, under God, of his restoration to *affluence.* This takes the subject by the other handle; and I think, as far as the text is concerned, by the *right* one.

He had fourteen thousand sheep] The reader, by referring to chap. i. 3, will perceive that the whole of Job's property was exactly *doubled.*

Verse 13. *Seven sons and three daughters.*] This was the *same number* as before; and so the Vulgate, Septuagint, Syriac, and Arabic read: but the Chaldee *doubles* the sons, "And he had *fourteen* sons, and three daughters."

Verse 14. *The name of the first Jemima*] ימימה *yemimah, days upon days.*

Kezia] קציעה *ketsiah, cassia,* a well-known aromatic plant. And,

Keren-happuch.] קרן הפוך *keren happuch,* the *inverted* or *flowing horn, cornucopiæ,* the *horn of plenty.* The Chaldee will not permit these names to pass without a *comment,* to show the reason of their imposition: "He called the first *Jemimah,* because she was as *fair* as the *day;* the second *Ketsiah,* because she was as precious as *cassia;* the third *Keren-happuch,* because her face was as splendid as the *emerald.*" Cardmarden's Bible, 1566, has the Hebrew names,

A. M. cir. 2484
B. C. cir. 1520
Ante I. Olymp. cir. 744
Ante U. C. cir. 767

15 And in all the land were no
women found *so* fair as the
daughters of Job: and their
father gave them inheritance
among their brethren.

16 After this [t]lived Job a
hundred and forty years, and saw
his sons, and his sons' sons, *even*
four generations.

17 So Job died, *being* old and [u]full of days.

[t]Chap. v. 28; Prov. iii. 16

[u]Gen. xxv. 8

The Vulgate has, "He called the name of one *Day*, of the second *Cassia*, and of the third *The Horn of Antimony*."

The versions in general preserve these names, only the Septuagint, Syriac, and Arabic translate *Jemimah*, DAY; and the former for *Keren-happuch* has Αμαλθαιας κερας, the *horn of Amalthea*. This refers to an ancient fable. *Amalthea* was the nurse of Jupiter, and fed him with goat's milk when he was young. The goat having by accident her *horn* struck off, Jupiter translated the animal to the heavens, and gave her a place among the *constellations*, which she still holds; and made the *horn* the emblem of *plenty:* hence it is always pictured or described as filled with *fruits, flowers*, and the *necessaries* and *luxuries* of life. It is very strange how this fable got into the Septuagint.

Coverdale is singular: **The first he called Daye, the seconde Poverte, the thirde, All plenteousnes.**

Verse 15. *Gave them inheritance among their brethren.*] This seems to refer to the history of the daughters of *Zelophehad*, given Num. xxviii. 1-8, who appear to have been the *first* who were allowed an *inheritance among their brethren.*

Verse 16. *After this lived Job a hundred and forty years*] How *long* he *had* lived before his afflictions, we cannot tell. If we could rely on the *Septuagint*, all would be plain, who add here, Τα δε παντα ετη εζησεν, διακοσια τεσσαρακοντα; "And all the years that Job lived were two hundred and forty." This makes him *one hundred years of age* when his trial commenced. *Coverdale* has, **After this lyved Job forty yeares**, omitting the *hundred*. So also in *Becke's* Bible, 1549. From the age, as marked down in the *Hebrew text*, we can infer nothing relative to the *time* when Job lived. See the subscription at the end of the Arabic.

Verse 17. *Job died*, being *old and full of days.*] He had seen life in all its varieties; he had *risen higher* than all the men of the East, and *sunk lower* in affliction, poverty, and distress, than any other human being that had existed before, or has lived since. He died when he was *satisfied with this life;* this the word שבע *seba* implies. He knew the *worst* and the *best* of human life; and in himself the whole *history of Providence* was exemplified and illustrated, and many of its *mysteries* unfolded.

We have now seen the end of the *life* of *Job*, and the *end* or *design* which God had in view by his afflictions and trials, in which he has shown us that he is *very pitiful, and of tender mercy*, James v. 11; and to discern this *end of the Lord* should be the object of every person who reads or studies it. *Laus in excelsis Deo!*

Both in the *Arabic* and *Septuagint* there is a considerable and important addition at the end of the *seventeenth* verse, which extends to many lines; of this, with its variations, I have given a translation in the PREFACE.

At the end of the *Syriac* version we have the following subscription:—

"The Book of the righteous and renowned Job is finished, and contains 2553 verses."

At the end of the *Arabic* is the following:—

"It is completed by the assistance of the Most High God. The author of this copy would record that this book has been translated into Arabic from the Syriac language." "Glory be to God, the giver of understanding!" "The Book of Job is completed; and his age was *two hundred and forty* years." "Praise be to God for ever!"

So closely does the *Arabic* translator copy the *Syriac*, that in the Polyglots one *Latin* version serves for both, with the exception of a few marginal readings at the bottom of the column to show where the *Syriac* varies.

Masoretic Notes

Number of verses, *one thousand and seventy. Middle* verse, chap. xxii. 16. *Sections, eight.*

AT the close of a book I have usually endeavoured to give some account of the *author*, or of him who was its chief *subject*. But the Book of Job is so *unique* in its subject and circumstances, that it is almost impossible to say any thing satisfactorily upon it, except in the way of *notes* on the *text*. There has been so much controversy on the *person* and *era* of Job, that he has almost been reduced to an *ideal* being, and the book itself considered rather as a *splendid poem* on an *ethic* subject than a *real history* of the man whose name it bears.

The *author*, as we have already seen in the *preface*, is not known. It has been attributed to *Job* himself; to *Elihu*, one of his friends; to *Moses;* to some *ancient Hebrew*, whose name is unknown; to *Solomon;* to *Isaiah* the prophet; and to *Ezra* the scribe.

The *time* is involved in equal darkness: *before* Moses, in the *time* of the *exodus*, or a *little after;* in the *days of Solomon;* during the *Babylonish captivity*, or even *later;* have all been mentioned as probable *eras.*

How it was originally *written*, and in what *language*, have also been questions on which great and learned men have divided. Some think it was originally written in *prose*, and afterwards reduced to *poetry*, and *the substance* of the different speeches being retained, but much *added* by way of *embellishment. Theodore*, bishop of *Mopsuestia* in *Cilicia*, a writer of the *fourth* century, distinguishes between *Job* and the *author* of the *book* that goes under his name, whom he accuses of a vain ostentation of profane sciences; of writing a *fabulous* and *poetical* history; of making Job speak things inconsistent with his religion and piety, and more proper to give offence than to edify. As *Theodore* had only seen the Book of Job in the *Greek version*, it must be owned that he had too much ground for his severe criticism, as there are in that version several allusions to the *mythology* of the Greeks, some of which are cursorily mentioned in the *notes.* Among these may be reckoned the names of *constellations* in chapters ix. and xxxviii., and the naming one of Job's daughters *Keren-happuch*, the *horn of Amalthea*, chap. xlii. 14.

We need not confound the *time* of Job and the *time* of the *author* of the book that goes under his name. Job may have been the same as *Jobab*, 1 Chron. i. 35-44, and the *fifth* in descent from Abraham; while the *author* or *poet*, who reduced the memoirs into verse, may have lived as late as the *Babylonish captivity.*

As to the *language*, though nervous and elevated, it is rather a *compound* of *dialects* than a *regular language.* Though Hebrew be the basis, yet many of the *words*, and frequently the *idiom*, are pure Arabic, and a Chaldee phraseology is in many places apparent.

Whoever was the *author*, and in whatsoever *time* it may have been written, the Jewish and Christian Church have ever received it as a *canonical book*, recommended by the *inspiration* of the Almighty. It is in many respects an obscure book, because it refers to all the *wisdom of the East.* If we understood all its allusions, I have little doubt that the best judges would not hesitate to declare it *the Idumean Encyclopædia.* It most obviously makes continual references to *sciences* the most exalted and useful, and to *arts* the most difficult and ornamental. Of these the notes have produced frequent proofs.

The *author* was well acquainted with all the wisdom and learning of the ancient world, and of his own times; and as a *poet* he stands next to David and Isaiah: and as his subjects have been more varied than theirs, he knew well how to avail himself of this circumstance; and has pressed into his service all the influence and beauty of his art, to make the four persons, whom he brings upon the stage, keep up each his proper character, and maintain the opinions which they respectively undertook to defend. "The *history*," says *Calmet*, "as to the *substance* and circumstances, is exactly true. The *sentiments, reasons*, and *arguments* of the several persons, are very faithfully expressed; but it is very probable that the *terms* and *turns of expression* are the *poet's*, or the *writer's*, whosoever he may be."

The *authority* of this book has been as much acknowledged as its *Divine inspiration.* The Prophet *Ezekiel* is the first who quotes it, chap. xiv. 14-20, where he mentions Job with Noah and Daniel, in such a way as makes his *identity* equal with *theirs;* and of *their* personal existence no one ever doubted.

The Apostle *James*, chap. v. 11, mentions him also, and celebrates his *patience*, and refers so particularly to the termination and happy issue of his trials, as leaves us no room to doubt that he had seen his history, as here stated, in the book that bears his name.

St. *Paul* seems also to quote him. Compare Rom. ii. 11, "For there is no respect of persons with God," with Job xxxiv. 19, "God accepteth not the person of princes, nor regardeth the rich more than the poor; for they are all the work of his hands."

1 Tim. vi. 7: "For we brought nothing into this world; and it is certain we can carry nothing out." Job i. 21: "Naked came I out of my mother's womb; and naked shall I return thither."

Heb. xii. 5: "My son, despise not thou the chastening of the Lord, nor faint when thou art rebuked of him." Job v. 17: "Happy is the man whom God correcteth; therefore despise not thou the chastening of the Almighty." A similar saying is found Prov. iii. 11, probably all coming from the same source. See the comparisons from the writings of Solomon, in the *preface.*

Job is to be found in the ancient *martyrologies*, with the title of *prophet, saint*, and *martyr;* and the *Greek Church* celebrates a festival in his honour on the *fifth* of May; and the corrupt Churches of *Arabia, Egypt, Ethiopia, Russia*, and *Muscovy*, follow it in their worship of *Saint Job!*

But no Church has proceeded so far both to *honour* and *disgrace* this excellent man as the *Church of Rome.* I shall quote the words of *Dom. Calmet*, one of the most learned and judicious divines that Church could ever boast of. "The *Latins* keep his festival on the *tenth* of May. This, next to the *Maccabees*, brothers and martyrs, is the first saint to whom the western Church has decreed public and religious honours, and we know not of any saint among the patriarchs and prophets to whom *churches* have been consecrated, or *chapels* dedicated in *greater number*, than to this holy man. We see abundance of them, particularly in *Spain* and *Italy.* And he is invoked principally against the *leprosy, itch, foul disease*, and other distempers which relate to *these.*" See *Baillie's* Lives of the Saints.

Calmet goes on to say that "there are several reputable *commentators* who maintain that Job was afflicted with this *scandalous disease;* among whom are *Vatablus, Cyprian Cisterc. Bolducius*, and *Pineda*, in their commentaries on Job; and *Desganges* in *Epist. Medicin. Hist. De Lue Venerea.* The *Latin Church* invokes Saint Job in diseases of this nature; and lazarettos and hospitals, wherein care is taken of persons who have this *scandalous distemper* upon them, are for the most part dedicated to him." See *Calmet's Dissertation sur la maladie de Job*, and his Dictionary, under the article JOB.

The conduct of this Church, relative to this holy man, forms one of the foulest calumnies ever inflicted on the character of either saint or sinner; and to make him the *patron* of every diseased prostitute and debauchee through the whole extent of the papal dominions and influence, is a conduct the most execrable, and little short of blasphemy against the *holiness* of God. As to their *lazarettos, hospitals*, and *chapels*, dedicated to this eminent man on these scandalous grounds, better raze them from their foundations, carry their materials to an unclean place, or transport them to *the valley of the son of Hinnom*, and consume them there; and then openly build others dedicated *ad fornicantem Jovem*, in conjunction with *Baal Peor* and *Ashtaroth*, the *Priapus* and *Venus* of their predecessors!

If those of that communion should think these reflections severe, let them know that the *stroke* is heavier than the *groan;* and let them put away from among them what is a dishonour to God, a disgrace to his saints, and their own ineffable reproach.

Of the *disease* under which Job laboured, enough has been said in the notes. On this head many writers have run into great extravagance. *Bartholinus* and *Calmet* state that he was afflicted with *twelve* several diseases; the latter specifies them. *Pineda* enumerates *thirty-one* or *thirty-two;* and St. *Chrysostom* says he was afflicted with all the maladies of which the human body is capable; that he suffered them in their *utmost extremities;* and, in a word, that on his one body all the maladies of the world were accumulated! How true is the saying, "*Over*-doing is *un*-doing!" It is enough to say, that this great man was afflicted in his *property*, *family*, *body*, and *soul;* and perhaps none, before or since his time, to a greater degree in all these kinds.

On Job's *character* his own words are the best comment. Were we to believe his mistaken and uncharitable *friends*, he, by *assertion* and *inuendo*, was guilty of almost every species of crime; but every charge of this kind is rebutted by his own *defence*, and the character given to him by the God whom he worshipped, frees him from even the *suspicion* of guilt.

His *patience*, *resignation*, and *submission* to the Divine will, are the most prominent parts of his character which are presented to our view. He bore the loss of every thing which a worldly man values without one unsanctified feeling or murmuring word. And it is in this respect that he is recommended to our notice and to our *imitation*. His *wailings* relative to the *mental* agonies through which he passed, do not at all affect this part of his character. He bore the loss of his goods, the total ruin of his extensive and invaluable establishment, and the destruction of his hopes in the awful death of his children, without uttering a reprehensible word, or indulging an irreligious feeling.

If however we carefully examine our translation of this poem, we shall find many things in Job's *speeches* that appear to be blemishes in his *character*. Even his own concessions appear to be heavy taxes on the high reputation he has had for *patience* and humble submission to the Divine will. In several cases these apparent *blemishes* are so contrasted with declarations of the highest *integrity* and *innocence* that they amount nearly to *contradictions*. Dr. *Kennicott* has examined this subject closely, and has thought deeply upon it, and strongly asserts that this *apparent inconsistency* arises from a misapprehension of Job's words in some cases, and mistranslation of them in others.

I shall take a large quotation on this subject from his "Remarks on Select Passages of Scripture."

"The *integrity* or *righteousness* of Job's character being resolutely maintained by Job himself, and the whole poem turning on the *multiplied miseries* of a man *eminently good*, the grand difficulty through the poem seems to be, how these positions can consist with the several passages where Job is now made to own himself *a very grievous sinner*. This matter, as being of great moment, should be carefully examined.

"In chap. vii. 20, 21, he says, 'I have sinned; What shall I do unto thee, O thou Preserver of men? Why dost thou not pardon my transgression, and take away mine iniquity?'

"In chap. ix. 20: 'If I justify myself, mine own mouth shall condemn me: If I say, I am perfect, it shall also prove me perverse. I know that thou wilt not hold me innocent.' 30, 31: 'If I wash myself with snow-water, yet shalt thou plunge me in the ditch, and my own clothes shall abhor me.' Lastly, in xlii. 6: 'I abhor myself, and repent in dust and ashes.'

"Whereas he says, in chap. x. 7, 'Thou knowest that I am not wicked.' xiii. 15: 'I will maintain my own ways before him.' 18. 'I know that I shall be justified.' xxiii. 10: 'He knoweth the way that I take; when he hath tried me, I shall come forth as gold.' 11: 'My foot hath held his steps; his way have I kept, and not declined.' And lastly, in chap. xxvii. 5: 'Till I die I will not remove my integrity from me.' 6: 'My righteousness I hold fast; I will not let it go: my heart shall not reproach me so long as I live.'

"And now if any one, ascribing these contrarieties to Job's inconsistency with himself, should pronounce him *right* in owning himself a *great sinner*, and *wrong* in pleading his own *integrity*, he will soon see it necessary to infer the contrary. Had Job really been, and owned himself to be, a *great sinner*, his *great sufferings* had been then accounted for, agreeably to the maxims of his friends, and all difficulty and dispute had been at an end. But as the whole poem turns on Job's uncommon *goodness*, and yet uncommon *misery*, so this *goodness* or *innocence*, this *righteousness* or *integrity*, is not only insisted upon by *Job*, but expressely admitted by God himself, both in the beginning of this book and at the end of it. See chap. i. 8, 21; ii. 3; and xlii. 7, 8.

"That *Job* did not here plead *guilty*, or contradict the asseveration of his *innocence*, appears farther from the subsequent speeches. So *Bildad*, who spoke next, understood him, chap. viii. 6. So *Zophar* understood him, chap. xi. 4. So *Eliphaz*, to whom he spoke the former words, understood him likewise, chap. xv. 13, 14. And, lastly, *Elihu*, after hearing all the replies of Job to his friends, tells him, (chap. xxxiii. 8, 9,) 'Surely, thou hast spoken in mine hearing, and I have heard the voice of thy words, saying, I am clean, without transgression; I am innocent, neither is there iniquity in me.'

"If therefore this inconsistency in Job's declaration concerning himself cannot have obtained in this book at first, it must arise from some *misrepresentation* of the true sense. And as it relates to Job's *confession of guilt*, expressed in the three chapters, vii., ix., and xlii., on these passages I shall make a few remarks, in hopes of removing one of the greatest general difficulties which now attend this poem.

"As to the first instance, Job appears, at least from our English version of chap. vii. 20, to be confessing his sins to *God*, whereas he is really speaking there in reply to *Eliphaz;* and it is obvious that the same words, applied thus differently, must carry very different ideas. Who does not see the *humility* and *sorrow* with which Job would say, 'I have sinned against thee, O God?' and yet see the resentment and force with which he would say to *Eliphaz, I have sinned*, you say; but, granting this, What is it to YOU? *to* (or against) *thee, O Eliphaz, what crime have I committed?* That Job, in other places, *repeats* ironically, and confutes by *quoting* the sayings of his friends, will appear hereafter.

"*Eliphaz* had been attempting to terrify him by the recital of a *vision*, and the long speech of a *spirit*, chap. iv. 12-21. Job in reply, (chap. vi. 15-27,) complains of the cruel treatment he had begun to experience from his nominal friends, and false brethren; and (chap. vii. 14) particularly complains that he (*Eliphaz*) had terrified him with *dreams* and *visions*, Job then goes on, (chap. vii. 17, &c.,) *What is a miserable man*, like myself, *that thou makest so much of him?* 1 Sam. xxvi. 24: *That thou settest thy heart upon him? that*, with such officious affection, *thou visitest him every morning, and art trying him every moment? How long will it be till thou depart from me; and leave me at liberty to* breathe, and even *swallow* down my spittle? You say, I *must have been a sinner;* what then? I have not sinned against THEE. *O thou spy upon mankind! Why hast thou set up me* as a butt or *mark to shoot at? Why am I become a burden unto thee?* Why not rather *overlook my transgression*, and *pass by mine iniquity? I am now sinking to the dust; to-morrow, perhaps, I shall be sought in vain.*

"As the first part of this difficulty arose from Job's first reply to *Eliphaz*, the second part of the same difficulty arises from Job's first reply to *Bildad*, in chap. ix., when Job is now made to say as follows, (ver. 2 and 4:) 'How shouldst thou be just with God? Who hath hardened himself against him and prospered?' Ver. 20: 'If I justify myself, my own mouth shall condemn me;' with many other self-accusatory observations, which have been already quoted from verses 28, 30, and 31. Now this chapter, which in our present version of it is very unintelligible, will perhaps recover its original meaning, and prove beautifully consistent, upon these two principles: That from ver. 2 to ver. 24, Job is really *exposing his friends*, by ironically quoting some of *their absurd maxims;* and that in verses 28 and 31 he is speaking, *not to God*, but in reply to *Bildad*.

"Thus, in ver. 2, 'I know it is so of a truth;' i. e., Verily I perceive that *with you* the matter stands thus, as, *How shall man be just with God;* and again, *God is omnipotent;* which is granted and enlarged upon.

"Verses 15 and 16 strongly confirm the idea of Job's *irony* on the maxims of his friends, thus: Whom (God) *I am not to answer*, you say, *even though I were righteous; but I am to make supplication to my Judge.* Nay; *If I have called to God, and he hath really answered me, I am not to believe that he hath heard my voice, Because, &c.* So again, as to verses 20-22: *If I justify myself*, then you say, *My own mouth proves me wicked! If I say, I am perfect*, then *it proves me perverse.* And even supposing that *I am perfect and upright, yet am I not to know it.* In short, *my soul loatheth my very life;* i. e., I am almost tired to death with such nonsense.

"Whereas the *one* sole true conclusion is *this, which, therefore*, I resolutely *maintain:* 'God destroyeth the perfect and the wicked.' And as to verses 28 and 31, the whole embarrassment attending them is removed when we consider them as directed to *Bildad;* who, by the vehemence of his speech, hath shown that he would continue to insist upon Job's guilt: 'If I wash myself in snow-water, and make my hands ever so clean; yet wilt thou (Bildad) plunge me in the ditch,' &c.

"Let us proceed, therefore, to the third and last part of this general difficulty, which arises at present from Job's confession in chap. xlii. 5: 'I abhor myself, and repent in dust and ashes.' But *repent* of what? and why *abhor himself?* He was at that instant in the very situation he had been earnestly wishing and often praying for: and was it possible for him not to seize that favourable moment? What he had so often wished was, that God would appear, and permit him to ask the reason for his uncommon sufferings. See chap. x. 2; xiii. 3, and 18 to 23; xix. 7; xxiii. 3-10; xxxi. 35-37, &c. And now when *God* does appear, we see that Job, immediately attentive to this matter, resolves to put the question, and declares this resolution: 'Hear, I beseech thee, and I will speak; I will demand of thee, and declare thou unto me. I have heard of thee by the hearing of the ear; but now mine eye seeth thee.' What now becomes of Job's *question?* Does he put any? Far, at present, are the next words from any such meaning, at least in our present version; for there the verse expresses nothing but *sorrow for sin*, which sets the poem at variance with itself. It also loses all sight of the *question*, for which the poem had been preparing, and which Job himself declares he would now put. Add, that in the first of these two lines the verb does not signify, *I abhor myself;* that the first hemistich is evidently too short, and that the second is not properly IN *dust*, but על *al*, UPON *dust* and *ashes*."

"It is therefore submitted to the learned, whether the restoration of *two letters*, which, at the same time that they lengthen the line, will remove the inconsistency, and give the very question here wanted, be not strongly and effectually recommended by *the exigence of the place.* As על כן *al ken*, is properly *therefore*, and על מה *al mah* (x. 2) is *wherefore*, מה *mah* was easily dropped before כן *ken;* it not being recollected that כן *ken* here is connected, not with the preposition before it, but with the verb after it, and signifies *hoc modo.* The true reading, therefore, and the true sense I humbly conceive to stand thus:—

Hear, I beseech thee, and I will speak;
I will demand of thee, and declare thou unto me.
I have heard of thee by the hearing of the ear;
But now mine eye seeth thee.

WHEREFORE (על מה) am I thus become loathsome
And scorched up, upon dust and ashes?

"See chap. vii. 5: 'My flesh is clothed with worms, and clods of dust; my skin is broken (וימאס) and *become loathsome.*' See also chap. xxx. 30: 'My skin is black upon me, and my bones are *burnt with heat;*' and ii. 8, x. 2, xvi. 15."

So far Dr. *Kennicott* in vindication of Job; and the reader will do justice to his learning and ingenuity. Allowing his general positions to be true, he has, in my opinion, pushed his consequences too far. Job certainly was not a *grievous sinner*, but a most *upright man.* This point is sufficiently proved; but that he accuses himself of *nothing* wrong, of *no inward* evil, is certainly not correct. He thought too highly of himself; he presumed too much on what was without; but when God shone upon his heart, he saw that he was vile, and therefore might most properly *loathe himself.* There are multitudes who are decent and correct in their outward behaviour, whose hearts may be deceitful and desperately wicked. Even the Pharisees made clean the outside of the cup and platter. Job was a very righteous and upright man; but at the time in question, he was not cleansed from all inward sin. This removes all contradiction from what he *asserts*, and from what he *concedes*. With this abatement, Dr. *Kennicott's* criticism may fairly stand. When a man sees himself in the light of God, he sees what, by his own discernment, wisdom, and reason, he had never seen before. His mind might have been previously deeply imbued with the principles of justice, righteousness, and truth, his whole conduct be regulated by them, and he be conscious to himself that he had not wickedly departed from the laws imposed on him by these principles. But when the *light that maketh manifest* shines through the inmost recesses of the heart, and vibrates through the soul, then *spiritual wickedness* becomes evident, and the deceitfulness of the heart is discovered. That light refers every thing to the Divine *standard*, the *holiness of God;* and the man's own righteousness in this comparison is found to be imperfection itself, and little short of impurity. Job appears to have been in this state: he thought himself *rich and increased in goods*, and *to have need of nothing;* but when God shone in upon his heart, he found himself to be *wretched*, and *miserable*, and *poor*, and *blind*, and *naked;* and he was now as ready to confess his great vileness, as he was before to assert and vindicate the unimpeachable righteousness of his *conduct*. Here was no *contradiction*. His friends attacked him on the ground of his being a bad and wicked man: this charge he repels with indignation, and dared them to the proof. They had nothing to allege but their *system* and their *suspicions:* but he who suffers must have sinned. Job, being conscious that this was false as applied to him, knowing his own innocence, boldly requires on their ground to know *why* God contended with him? God answers for himself; humbles the self-confident yet upright man; shines into his heart, and then he sees that he is *vile*. When a beam of the solar light is admitted into an apartment we see ten thousand atoms or motes dancing in that beam. These are no particles of *light*, nor did the light bring them there; they were there before, but there was not light sufficient to make them manifest. Just so when the light of God visits the soul of a sincere man, who has been labouring in all his outward conduct to stand approved of God; he is astonished at his inward impurity, loathes himself, and is ready to think that many devils have *suddenly* entered into him. No: all the evils thou seest were there before, but thou hadst not light sufficient to make them manifest. Shall it be said after this, that the conduct of Divine Providence cannot be vindicated in suffering an upright man to become a butt for the malice of Satan for so long a time, and for no purpose? The greatest, the most important purposes were accomplished by this trial. Job became a much better man than he ever was before; the dispensations of God's providence were illustrated and justified; Satan's devices unmasked; patience crowned and rewarded; and the Church of God greatly enriched by having bequeathed to it the vast treasury of Divine truth which is found in the BOOK OF JOB.

Corrected for a new edition, March 1st, 1829.—A. C.

INTRODUCTION

TO THE

BOOK OF PSALMS

Section I.—On the Names given to this Book

THIS book is termed in Hebrew ספר תהלים *Sepher Tehillim,* which some learned men derive from הל *hal* or הלל *halal,* to *move briskly, irradiate, shine;* and translate, The Book of the Shinings forth, Irradiations, Manifestations, or Displays, namely, of Divine wisdom and love exhibited in God's dealing with his chosen people, or with particular persons, as *figures, for the time being,* of what should be accomplished either in the person of Christ, or in his mystical body the Church. But as *halal* signifies also *to praise,* and praise arises from a sense of gratitude, is the expression of inward joy, and was often exhibited by brisk notes, sprightly music, &c., it may be well denominated *The Book of Praises,* as the major part of the Psalms have for their subject the praises of the Lord.

That the Psalms were sung in the Jewish service, and frequently accompanied by musical instruments, there is no doubt, for the fact is repeatedly mentioned; and hence the most ancient translation we have of the Psalms, viz., the Septuagint, as it stands in what is called the Codex Alexandrinus, is called Ψαλτηριον, *The Psaltery,* which is a species of musical instrument resembling the *harp,* according to the accounts given of it by some of the ancients. From this term came the *Psalterium* of the *Vulgate,* and our word *Psalter,* all of which are deduced from the verb ψαλλω, *to sing,* as the voice no doubt always accompanied this instrument, and by it the key was preserved and the voice sustained.

A *Psalm* is called in Hebrew מזמור *mizmor,* from זמר *zamar, to cut off,* because in singing each word was separated into its component syllables, each syllable answering to a note in the music.

Section II.—General Division of the Book

The Hebrews divide the Psalms into *five books,* and this division is noticed by several of the primitive fathers. The origin of this division is not easily ascertained; but as it was considered a book of great excellence, and compared for its importance to the Pentateuch itself, it was probably divided into five books, as the law was contained in so many volumes. But where the divisions should take place the ancients are not agreed; and some of them divide into *three fifties* rather than into *five parts;* and for all these divisions they assign certain allegorical reasons which merit little attention.

The division of the Hebrews is as follows:—

Book I. From Psalm i. to Psalm xli. inclusive.
Book II. From Psalm xlii. to Psalm lxxii. inclusive.
Book III. From Psalm lxxiii. to Psalm lxxxix. inclusive.
Book IV. From Psalm xc. to Psalm cvi. inclusive.
Book V. From Psalm cvii. to Psalm cl. inclusive.

The *First, Second,* and *Third* Books end with *Amen and Amen;* the *Fourth,* with *Amen and Hallelujah;* the *Fifth,* with *Hallelujah.*

But the Psalms themselves are differently divided in all the VERSIONS, and in many MSS. This is often very embarrassing to the reader, not only in consulting the Polyglots, but also in referring to theological works, whether of the Greek or Latin Church, where the Psalms are quoted; the Greek ecclesiastical writers following the *Septuagint;* and those of the Latin Church, the *Vulgate.* I shall lay a proper table of these variations before the reader, remarking first, that though they differ so much in the division of the Psalms, they all agree in the *number one hundred and fifty.*

A Table of the Differences in dividing the Psalms between the *Hebrew* text and the ancient VERSIONS, *Syriac, Septuagint, Chaldee, Arabic, Æthiopic,* and *Vulgate.*

In the above versions Psalm ix. and x. make only Psalm ix. Hence there is one Psalm *less* in the reckoning as you proceed to

Psalm cxiv., cxv., which make Psalm cxiii. in all those versions. Hence two Psalms are *lost* in the reckoning.

Psalm cxvi. is divided at verse 9, the versions beginning Psalm cxv. at verse 10. Hence one Psalm is *gained* on the above reckoning.

Psalm cxix. makes Psalm cxviii. in all the versions.

Psalm cxlvii. they divide at verse 11, and begin Psalm cxlvii. with verse 12. Here then the reckoning becomes equal, and all end alike with Psalm cl.

In the Syriac, Septuagint, Æthiopic, and Arabic, there is what they call an *extra-numeral* Psalm, said to have been composed by David after his victory over Goliath. A translation of this will be found at the close of these notes.

The Hebrew MSS. agree often with the *versions* in uniting Psalms which the common *Hebrew* text has separated, and thus often support the ancient *versions.* These things shall be considered in the course of the notes.

SECTION III.—ON THE COMPILATION OF THE BOOK, AND THE AUTHORS TO WHOM THE PSALMS HAVE BEEN ATTRIBUTED

After having said so much on the *name* and ancient *divisions* of this important book, it may be necessary to say something in answer to the question, "Who was the author of the Book of Psalms?" If we were to follow the popular opinion, we should rather be surprised at the question, and immediately answer, DAVID, king of Israel! That many of them were composed by *him,* there is no doubt; that several were written long after his time, there is internal evidence to prove; and that many of them were written even by his *contemporaries,* there is much reason to believe.

That the *collection,* as it now stands, was made long after David's death, is a general opinion among learned men; and that *Ezra* was the collector and compiler is commonly believed. Indeed all antiquity is nearly unanimous in giving Ezra the honour of collecting the different writings of Moses and the prophets, and reducing them into that form in which they are now found in the Holy Bible, and consequently the *Psalms* among the rest. See this subject treated at large in the *preface to Ezra,* &c.

In making this collection it does not appear that the compiler paid any attention to *chronological arrangement.* As he was an inspired man, he could judge of the pieces which came by Divine inspiration, and were proper for the general edification of the Church of God.

The writer of the SYNOPSIS, attributed to St. *Athanasius,* says that the friends of King Hezekiah chose *one hundred and fifty* Psalms out of the number of *three thousand* which David had composed, and that they suppressed the rest: he says farther, that this is written in the *Chronicles;* but it is not found in the *Chronicles* which we now have, though it might have been in other Chronicles which that author had seen.

That some Scriptural collections were made under the influence and by the order of Hezekiah, we learn from Prov. xxv. 1: "These are also proverbs of Solomon, which the men of Hezekiah, king of Judah, copied out." But whether these were employed on the writings of the *father,* as they were on those of the *son,* we cannot tell. The above authority is too slender to support any building of magnitude.

The only method we have of judging is from the internal evidence afforded by several of the Psalms themselves, and from the *inscriptions* which many of them bear. As far as *time* and *facts* are concerned, many of them can be traced to the days of David, and the *transactions* which then occurred, and in which he bore so eminent a part. But there are others in which we find no *note* of *time,* and no reference to the *transactions* of David's reign.

As to the *inscriptions,* they are of slender authority; several of them do not agree with the subject of the Psalm to which they are prefixed, and not a few of them appear to be out of their places.

In one of the prologues attributed to St. *Jerome,* but probably of Eusebius, at the end of

Vol. II. of St. Jerome's Works by *Martinay,* we find a *table* in which the whole Book of Psalms is dissected, showing those which have *inscriptions,* those which have *none,* and those to which the *name* of a particular *person,* as author, is prefixed. I shall give these in gross, and then in detail: Psalms without any name prefixed, 17; Psalms with an inscription, 133; in all 150.

These are afterwards divided into those which bear *different kinds* of *titles, without names;* and those which have *names* prefixed. I shall give these from the *Quincuplex Psalterium,* fol. *Paris,* 1513, as being more correct than in the edition of Jerome, by *Martinay.*

Psalms which have no inscription *of any kind:* Psa. i., ii., xxxii., xlii., lxx., xc., xcii., xciii., xciv., xcv., xcvi., xcvii., xcviii., xcix., ciii., cxv., cxxxvi., cxlvii 18

Psalms to which David's *name is prefixed:* Psa. iii., iv., v., vi., vii., viii., ix., x., xi., xii., xiii., xiv., xv., xvi., xvii., xviii., xix., xx., xxi., xxii., xxiii., xxiv., xxv., xxvi., xxvii., xxviii., xxix., xxx., xxxi., xxxiii., xxxiv., xxxv., xxxvi., xxxvii., xxxviii., xxxix., xl., l., li., lii., liii., liv., lv., lvi., lvii., lviii., lix., lx., lxi., lxii., lxiii., lxiv., lxvii., lxviii., lxix., lxxxv., c., cii., cvii., cviii., cix., cxxxiii., cxxxvii., cxxxviii., cxxxix., cxl., cxli., cxlii., cxliii., cxliv., 70

Psalms attributed to Solomon: Psa. lxxi., cxxvi 2

Psalms attributed to the sons of Korah: Psa. xli., xliii., xliv., xlv., xlvi., xlvii., xlviii., lxxxiii., lxxxiv., lxxxvi 10

Psalms with the name of Asaph *prefixed:* Psa. xlix., lxxii., lxxiii., lxxiv., lxxv., xxvi., lxxvii., lxxviii., lxxix., lxxx., lxxxi., lxxxii 12

A Psalm to which the name of Heman *is prefixed:* Psa. lxxxvii 1

A Psalm to which the name of Ethan *is prefixed:* Psa. lxxxviii 1

A Psalm to which the name of Moses *is prefixed:* Psa. lxxxix 1

Psalms with titles without any name *specified:* A Song or Psalm, lxv. A Song or Psalm, lxvi. A Psalm or Song, xci. A Prayer of the Afflicted, ci 4

Hallelujah *Psalms:* Psa. civ., cv., cvi., cx., cxi., cxii., cxiii., cxiv., cxvi., cxvii., cxviii., cxxxiv., cxxxv., cxlv., cxlvi., cxlviii., cxlix., cl 18

Psalms or Songs of Degrees: Psa. cxix., cxx., cxxi., cxxii., cxxiii., cxxiv., cxxv., cxxvii., cxxviii., cxxix., cxxx., cxxxi., cxxxii 13

Sum total of all kinds: Psalms having no inscription, 18. David's, 70. Solomon's, 2. Sons of Korah, 10. Asaph, 12. Heman, 1. Ethan, 1. Moses, 1. Psalms and Songs, 3. Prayer, 1. Hallelujah, 18. Psalms of Degrees, 13.

Grand total 150

Supposing that the *persons* already mentioned are the authors of those Psalms to which their names are prefixed, there are still *fifty-three,* which, as bearing *no proper name,* must be attributed to uncertain authors, though it is very probable that several of them were made by David.

The reader will observe that as the preceding enumeration is taken from the *Vulgate,* consequently it is not exactly the same with ours: but the rules already given at page 200, will enable him to accommodate this division to that in our common Bibles, which is the same with that in the *Hebrew* text.

In order to make the preceding table as correct as possible, I have carefully collated that in the Benedictine edition of St. Jerome's WORKS, with professedly the same table in the Quincuplex Psalter, in both of which there are several errors. In the *Works,* though all the numbers are given at large, as *primus, decimus, centesimus, &c.,* yet the sum total, under each head, rarely agrees with the items above it. This was so notoriously the case in the table in Jerome's Works, that I thought best to follow that in the *Psalter* above mentioned, which had been carefully corrected by Henry Stephens.

After all, this table gives but small satisfaction, when we come to collate it with the Psalms in the Hebrew text, or as they stand in our common English Bibles. That nothing might be wanting, I have made an analysis of the whole from our present text, collating this with the Hebrew where I was in doubt; and by this the reader will see how greatly these tables differ from each other; and that many Psalms must now come under a different arrangement, because of their different titles, from that which they had in St. Jerome's time. For instance, in St. Jerome's time there were *seventy*, or, as in some copies, *seventy-two* Psalms that had the name of David in the inscriptions; at present there are *seventy-three* thus inscribed in the Hebrew text.

Section IV.—Classification of the Psalms as they stand in our common version

Jerome gave two editions of the Latin Psalter, one from the Hebrew, and the other corrected from the Septuagint. Both of these may be found in his Works, and in the Quincuplex Psalter mentioned above. I shall now add a table, on a similar plan with the above, taken from our present authorized text.

A Classified Table of the Psalms taken from the text in common use

Psalms which have no inscription *of any kind:* Psa. i., ii., x., xxxiii., xliii., lxxi., xci., xciii., xciv., xcv., xcvi., xcvii., xcix., civ., cv., cvii., cxiv., cxv., cxvi., cxvii., cxviii., cxix., cxxxvi., cxxxvii 24

Psalms to which David's *name is prefixed:* Psa. iii., iv., v., vi., vii., viii., ix., xi., xii., xiii., xiv., xv., xvi., xvii., xviii., xix., xx., xxi., xxii., xxiii., xxiv., xxv., xxvi., xxvii., xxviii., xxix., xxx., xxxi., xxxii., xxxiv., xxxv., xxxvi., xxxvii., xxxviii., xxxix., xl., xli., li., lii., liii., liv., lv., lvi., lvii., lviii., lix., lx., lxi., lxii., lxiii., lxiv., lxv., lxviii., lxix., lxx., lxxxvi., ci., ciii., cviii., cix., cx., cxxii., cxxiv., cxxxi., cxxxiii., cxxxviii., cxxxix., cxl., cxli., cxlii., cxliii., cxliv., cxlv 73

Psalms attributed to Solomon: Psa. lxxii., cxxvii 2

Psalms attributed to the sons of Korah: Psa. xlii., xliv., xlv., xlvi., xlvii., xlviii., xlix., lxxxiv., lxxxv., lxxxvii 10

Psalms with the name of Asaph *prefixed:* Psa. l., lxxiii., lxxiv., lxxv., lxxvi., lxxvii., lxxviii., lxxix., lxxx., lxxxi., lxxxii., lxxxiii 12

A Psalm to which the name of Heman *is prefixed:* Psa. lxxxix 1

A Psalm to which the name of Ethan *is prefixed:* Psa. lxxxix 1

A Psalm to which the name of Moses *is prefixed:* Psa. xc 1

Psalms with titles without any name *specified:* A Song or Psalm, lxvi. A Psalm or Song, lxvii. A Psalm or Song for the Sabbath day, xcii. A Psalm or Song, xcviii. A Psalm or Song, c. A Prayer of the Afflicted, cii 6

Hallelujah *Psalms:* Psa. cvi., cxi., cxii., cxiii., cxxxv., cxlvi., cxlvii., cxlviii., cxlix., cl. 10

Psalms or Songs of Degrees: Psa. cxx., cxxi., cxxiii., cxxv., cxxvi., cxxviii., cxxix., cxxx., cxxxii., cxxxiv 10

Sum total of all kinds: Psalms having no *inscription*, 24. Psalms having David's name prefixed, 73. Psalms having Solomon's name, 2. Ditto, sons of Korah, 10. Ditto, Asaph, 12. Ditto, Heman, 1. Ditto, Ethan, 1. Psalms and Songs, 6. Hallelujah Psalms, 10. Psalms of Degrees, 10.

Grand total 150

After all that has been done to assign each Psalm to its author, there are few of which we can say positively, *These were composed by David.*

Most commentators, as well as historians of the life and reign of David, have taken great pains to throw some light upon this subject, particularly *Calmet, Delaney, Chandler*, and *Venema.* The former has made *seven divisions* of them, to ascertain the *order* of *time* in which they were written. I shall adopt this plan, and accommodate it to the Psalms as they stand in our present authorized version, after simply remarking that there are several Psalms which appear to be ill-divided, some making *two* or *three*, which in all probability made originally but one; and others, which formerly made *two* or more, now improperly connected.

This has been already noticed in comparing the differences of the numeration between the *versions* and the *Hebrew* text. See p. 201; see also at the end of the following table.

Section V.—Chronological Arrangement of the Book of Psalms

1. Psalms *which contain* no Note *or* Indication *of the* Time *when written*

Psalm i. "Blessed is the man," &c. This is generally considered as a *Preface* to the whole book; supposed by some to have been written by *David:* but others attribute it to *Ezra*, who collected the book of Psalms.

Psalm iv. "Hear me when I call." The evening prayer of a *pious man.*

Psalm viii. "O Lord our Lord." The *privileges* and *dignity* of man.

Psalm xix. "The heavens declare the glory of God." God's glory in the *creation.* The excellence, perfection, and use of the Divine *law.*

Psalm lxxxi. "Sing aloud unto God." Supposed to be a Psalm usually sung at the *Feast of Trumpets*, or the beginning of the *year;* and at the *Feast of Tabernacles.*

Psalm xci. "He that dwelleth in the secret place." The *happiness* of those who trust in the Lord. This Psalm might be placed during or after the *Captivity.*

Psalm cx. "The Lord said unto my Lord." The advent, birth, passion, priesthood, and kingdom of Christ. Probably composed by *David.*

Psalm cxxxix. "O Lord, thou hast searched me." On the *wisdom* and *providence* of God.

Psalm cxlv. "I will extol thee, my God, O King." Thanksgiving for the *general benefits* bestowed by God.

In none of these is there any distinct notation of time.

II. Psalms *composed by* David *while* persecuted *by* Saul

Psalm xi. "In the Lord put I my trust." Composed by David when in the court of Saul, his friends exhorting him to escape for his life from the jealousy and cruelty of Saul.

Psalm xxxi. "In thee, O Lord, do I put my trust." Composed when David was proscribed, and obliged to flee from Saul's court.

Psalm xxxiv. "I will bless the Lord at all times." Supposed to have been composed by David, when, by feigning himself to be mad, he escaped from the court of Achish, king of Gath.

Psalm lvi. "Be merciful unto me, O God." Composed in the *cave* of *Adullam*, after his escape from Achish.

Psalm xvi. "Preserve me, O God." David persecuted by Saul, and obliged to take refuge among the *Moabites* and *Philistines.*

Psalm liv. "Save me, O God, by thy name." David, betrayed by the *Ziphims*, escapes from the hands of Saul.

Psalm lii. "Why boastest thou thyself in mischief." Composed by David when *Doeg* betrayed him to Saul, who, not finding him, slew the priests at *Nob.*

Psalm cix. "Hold not thy peace, O God." An invective against *Doeg*, and the rest of his *enemies.*

Psalm xvii. "Hear the right, O Lord." When Saul carried his persecution to the highest pitch.

Psalm xxii. "My God, my God, why hast thou forsaken me." *Saul's* persecution of *David* an emblem of the persecutions of *Christ* by the *Jews.*

Psalm xxxv. "Plead my cause, O Lord." Against *Saul* and his *courtiers*, who plotted his destruction.

Psalm lvii. "Be merciful unto me, O God." While shut up in the cave of *En-gedi;* 1 Sam. xxiv. 4.

Psalm lviii. "Do ye indeed speak righteousness." Against the wicked *counsellors* of Saul.

Psalm cxiii. "I cried unto the Lord with my voice." David in the cave of *En-gedi*, 1 Sam. xxiv.

Psalm cxl. "Deliver me, O Lord." Under the same persecutions praying for Divine succour.

Psalm cxli. "Lord, I cry unto thee." Same as the preceding.

Psalm vii. "O Lord my God, in thee do I put my trust." When violently persecuted by Saul.

III. Psalms *composed after the Commencement of the reign of* David, *and after the Death of* Saul

Psalm ii. "Why do the heathen rage." Written by David after he had established his throne at Jerusalem, notwithstanding the envy and malice of his enemies. A prophecy of the reign of Christ.

Psalm ix. "I will praise thee, O Lord, with my whole heart." Sung by David on bringing the ark from the house of *Obed-edom.*

Psalm xxiv. "The earth is the Lord's, and the fulness thereof." Sung on the same occasion.

Psalm lxviii. "Let God arise, let his enemies be scattered." Sung on bringing the ark from *Kirjath-jearim* to Jerusalem.

Psalm ci. "I will sing of mercy and judgment." David describes the manner in which he will form his court, his ministers, and confidential servants.

Psalm xxix. "Give unto the Lord, O ye mighty." Composed after the *dearth* which fell on the land because of Saul's unjust persecution of the *Gibeonites;* 2 Sam. xxi.

Psalm xx. "The Lord hear thee in the day of trouble." Composed when David was about to march against the *Ammonites* and *Syrians;* 2 Sam. x. 16.

Psalm xxi. "The king shall joy in thy strength." Thanksgiving to God for the victory over the *Ammonites,* &c.; a continuation of the subject in the preceding.

Psalm xxxviii. "O Lord, rebuke me not in thy wrath." Composed during the time of a grievous *affliction,* after his transgression with *Bath-sheba.* See Psa. vi.

Psalm xxxix. "I said, I will take heed to my ways." A continuation of the same subject.

Psalm xl. "I waited patiently for the Lord." Thanksgiving for his *recovery.*

Psalm xli. "Blessed is he who considereth the poor." A continuation of the preceding subject.

Psalm vi. "O Lord, rebuke me not in thine anger." Supposed to be written in a time of *sickness* after his sin with *Bath-sheba.* See Psa. xxxviii.

Psalm li. "Have mercy upon me, O God." Written after he received the reproof by *Nathan* the prophet; 2 Sam. xii.

Psalm xxxii. "Blessed is he whose transgression is forgiven." Written about the same time, and on the same subject.

Psalm xxxiii. "Rejoice in the Lord, O ye righteous." A continuation of the preceding Psalm.

IV. Psalms *composed during the* rebellion *of* Absalom

Psalm iii. "Lord, how are they increased that trouble me?" When David was driven from Jerusalem by Absalom.

Psalm iv. "Hear me when I call." Composed at the same time.

Psalm lv. "Give ear to my prayer." When he was flying from Jerusalem before Absalom.

Psalm lxii. "Truly my soul waiteth upon God." Exercising faith and patience during Absalom's rebellion.

Psalm lxx. "Make haste, O God, to deliver me." During the same.

Psalm lxxi. "In thee, O Lord, do I put my trust." Continuation of the preceding.

Psalm cxliii. "Hear my prayer, O Lord." Written during the *war* with *Absalom.*

Psalm cxliv. "Blessed be the Lord my strength." Written after the overthrow of *Absalom, Sheba,* and other rebels.

V. Psalms *written between the* Rebellion *of* Absalom, *and the* Babylonish Captivity

Psalm xviii. "I will love thee, O Lord, my strength." Thanksgivings for all the benefits which David had received from God. See 2 Sam. xxii.

Psalm xxx. "I will extol thee, O Lord." Composed at the dedication of the *threshing-floor* of *Ornan;* 2 Sam. xxiv. 25.

Psalm lxxii. "Give the king thy judgments." Composed by David when he invested *Solomon* with the kingdom.

Psalm xlv. "My heart is inditing a good matter." Written by the sons of Korah, for *Solomon's marriage.*

Psalm lxxviii. "Give ear, O my people." Sung by the choir of *Asaph,* on the *victory* gained by *Asa* over *Baasha* king of Israel; 2 Chron. xvi. 4, &c.

Psalm lxxxii. "God standeth in the congregation." Instructions given to the *judges* in the days of *Jehoshaphat,* king of Judah.

Psalm lxxxiii. "Keep not thou silence, O God." Thanksgiving for the *victories* of *Jehoshaphat,* king of Judah, over the *Ammonites, Idumeans,* and others. See 2 Chron. xx. 1, &c.

Psalm lxxvi. "In Judah is God known." Sung by the choir of *Asaph* after the victory over *Sennacherib.*

Psalm lxxiv. "O God, why hast thou cast us off?" Lamentation over the temple destroyed by *Nebuchadnezzar.*

Psalm lxxix. "O God, the heathen are come." On the same subject; composed probably during the captivity.

VI. Psalms *composed during the* Captivity

Psalm x. "Why standeth thou afar off?" Lamentation of the Jews during the captivity.

Psalm xii. "Help, Lord, for the godly man ceaseth." Composed by the captive Jews showing the wickedness of the *Babylonians.*

Psalm xiii. "How long wilt thou forget me." Continuation of the preceding.

Psalm xiv. "The fool hath said in his heart." A prayer of the poor captives for deliverance from their captivity.

Psalm liii. "The fool hath said in his heart, There is no God." This Psalm is almost verbatim with Psalm xiv., and, like it, describes the wickedness of the *Babylonians,* both having been composed during the captivity.

Psalm xv. "Lord, who shall abide in thy tabernacle?" This Psalm was probably intended to point out the *character* of *those* who might expect to return to their own land, and join in the temple service.

Psalm xxv. "Unto thee, O Lord, do I lift up my soul." A prayer of the captives for deliverance.

Psalm xxvi. "Judge me, O Lord." Continuation of the same.

Psalm xxvii. "The Lord is my light and my salvation." The *captives* express their confidence in God.

Psalm xxviii. "Unto thee will I cry." Prayers and thanksgivings of the *captives.*

Psalm xxxvi. "The transgression of the wicked." Complaints of the captives against the Babylonians.

Psalm xxxvii. "Fret not thyself." A Psalm of consolation for the *captives.*

Psalm xlii. "As the hart panteth." Composed by the sons of *Korah* during the *captivity.*

Psalm xliii. "Judge me, O God." Continuation of the same.

Psalm xliv. "We have heard with our ears." Same subject.

Psalm xlix. "Hear this, all ye people." By the sons of *Korah:* comfort for the *captives.*

Psalm l. "The mighty God, even the Lord, hath spoken." God's reprehension of the Jews, showing them the *cause* of their *captivity.*

Psalm lx. "O God, thou hast cast us off." The *captives* express their hope of a speedy restoration.

Psalm lxiv. "Hear my voice, O God." The captives complain of their *oppression* under the *Babylonians.*

Psalm lxix. "Save me, O God." The captive *Levites* complain of the *cruelty* of the *Babylonians.*

Psalm lxxiii. "Truly God is good to Israel." *Asaph* warns the captives against the bad *example* of the *Babylonians,* and against being *envious* at the *prosperity* of the *wicked.* Compare this with Psalm xxxvii.

Psalm lxxv. "Unto thee, O God, do we give thanks." *Asaph* prays for the deliverance of the people.

Psalm lxxvii. "I cried unto God with my voice." *Jeduthun* and *Asaph* complain of the long duration of the *captivity.*

Psalm lxxx. "Give ear, O Shepherd of Israel." *Asaph* prays for the deliverance of the people.

Psalm lxxxiv. "How amiable are thy tabernacles." The sons of *Korah* pray for their release.

Psalm lxxxvi. "Bow down thine ear." The same subject.

Psalm lxxxviii. "O Lord God of my salvation." The same subject.

Psalm lxxxix. "I will sing of the mercies of the Lord." *Ethan* prays for the deliverance of the captive Jews.

Psalm xc. "Lord, thou hast been our dwelling." The *Levites*, the *descendants of Moses*, request their return from captivity.

Psalm xcii. "It is a good thing to give thanks." The same subject, and by the same persons.

Psalm xciii. "The Lord reigneth." The same, by the same persons.

Psalm xcv. "O come, let us sing unto the Lord." The same.

Psalm cxix. "Blessed are the undefiled in the way." A Psalm supposed to have been made by *Daniel*, or some other *captive prophet*, for the instruction of the people.

Psalm cxx. "In my distress I cried." The captives pray for deliverance.

Psalm cxxi. "I will lift up mine eyes." The same subject.

Psalm cxxx. "Out of the depths have I cried." The same.

Psalm cxxxi. "Lord, my heart is not haughty." The *heads* of the *people* pray for their return.

Psalm cxxxii. "Lord, remember David." A prayer of the captive Jews in behalf of the *house of David*.

VII. *Psalms written* after *the Jews were permitted by the edict of* Cyrus *to return to their own land*

Psalm cxxii. "I was glad when they said." A Psalm of thanksgiving when they heard of the *edict of Cyrus*, permitting their return.

Psalm lxi. "Hear my cry, O God." Thanksgivings when the Jews were about to return to Jerusalem.

Psalm lxiii. "O God, thou art my God." A Psalm of the people, now on their return to Judea.

Psalm cxxiv. "If it had not been the Lord, who was on our side." On the same subject.

Psalm xxiii. "The Lord is my shepherd." Thanksgiving to God for their *redemption* from *captivity*.

Psalm lxxxvii. "His foundation is in the holy mountains." Thanksgivings by the sons of Korah for their return from captivity.

Psalm lxxxv. "Lord,thou hast been favourable unto thy land." Thanksgivings for their return.

Psalm xlvi. "God is our refuge and strength." Sung by the sons of *Korah* at the *dedication of the second temple.*

Psalm xlvii. "O clap your hands, all ye people." The same.

Psalm xlviii. "Great is the Lord." A continuation of the preceding.

Psalm xcvi. "O sing unto the Lord a new song." This and the three preceding all sung at the *dedication of the second temple.*

Psalm xcvii. "The Lord reigneth; let the earth rejoice." Thanksgivings of the Jews for their deliverance; sung at the *dedication of the second temple.*

Psalm xcviii. "O sing unto the Lord a new song; for he hath done marvellous things." A continuation of the above.

Psalm xcix. "The Lord reigneth; let the people tremble." Sung on the same occasion.

Psalm c. "Make a joyful noise." On the same occasion.

Psalm cii. "Hear my prayer, O Lord." A description of the *sufferings* of the *captives* while in *Babylon;* and thanksgivings for their *deliverance.*

Psalm ciii. "Bless the Lord, O my soul." On the same subject.

Psalm civ. "Bless the Lord, O my soul. O Lord my God." On the same.

Psalm cv. "O give thanks unto the Lord." Thanksgivings for deliverance from Babylon.

Psalm cvi. "Praise ye the Lord. O give thanks unto the Lord." On the same subject. A recapitulation of what God did for their fathers in *Egypt* and in the *wilderness.*

Psalm cvii. "O give thanks—his mercy endureth for ever." A fine poetical description of the *miseries of the captivity.*

Psalm cviii. "O God, my heart is fixed." The Jews, delivered from captivity, pray for their brethren yet beyond the *Euphrates.*

Psalm cxi. "Praise ye the Lord. I will praise the Lord with my whole heart." Thanksgivings of the Jews *after* their *captivity.*

Psalm cxii. "Praise ye the Lord. Blessed is the man that feareth." A continuation of the same subject.

Psalm cxiii. "Praise ye the Lord. Praise, O ye servants." A continuation of the above.

Psalm cxiv. "When Israel went out of Egypt." The same subject.

Psalm cxvi. "I love the Lord." The same subject.

Psalm cxvii. "O praise the Lord, all ye nations." The same subject.

Psalm cxxvi. "When the Lord turned again our captivity." A prayer for the remnant *still remaining in captivity.*

Psalm cxxxiii. "Behold, how good and how pleasant." Happy union of the *priests* and *Levites* in the service of God, after the *captivity.*

Psalm cxxxiv. "Behold, bless ye the Lord." An exhortation to the priests and Levites properly to discharge their duties in the temple, after they had returned from their captivity.

Psalm cxxxv. "Praise ye the Lord. Praise ye the name of the Lord." Same as the preceding.

Psalm cxxxvi. "O give thanks unto the Lord." Same as before.

Psalm cxxxvii. "By the rivers of Babylon, there we sat down." The Levites on their return, relate how they were insulted in their captivity.

Psalm cxlviii. "Praise ye the Lord. Praise ye the Lord from the heavens." Thanksgiving for deliverance from the captivity; and an invitation to all creatures to celebrate the praise of the Lord.

Psalm cxlix. "Praise ye the Lord. Sing unto the Lord a new song." On the same subject.

Psalm cl. "Praise ye the Lord. Praise God in his sanctuary." A continuation of the preceding Psalms.

Psalm cxlvi. "Praise ye the Lord. Praise the Lord, O my soul." Supposed to have been composed by *Haggai*, and *Zechariah*, to comfort the people when the edict of Cyrus was *revoked.* See the notes on this Psalm.

Psalm cxlvii. "Praise ye the Lord: for it is good." Thanksgiving of the same *prophets* after the long *dearth* mentioned by *Haggai*, chap. i. In the *Vulgate* this Psalm is divided at ver. 12, "Praise the Lord, O Jerusalem;" and is supposed by *Calmet* to have been sung at the dedication of the walls of Jerusalem. The *whole* Psalm is suitable to the occasions mentioned above.

Psalm lix. "Deliver me from mine enemies." Probably sung about the same time. See Neh. iv. and following chapters.

Psalm lxv. "Praise waiteth for thee, O God." Composed by *Haggai* and *Zechariah*, after the Lord had sent the *rain promised by Haggai*, chap. i.; and when they had begun the *repairs* of the *temple.* See Psalm cxlvii.

Psalm lxvi. "Make a joyful noise." A continuation of the above.

Psalm lxvii. "God be merciful unto us." The same subject.

Psalm cxviii. "O give thanks unto the Lord; for he is good." A song of praise after the death of *Cambyses*, or probably after the *dedication of the walls of Jerusalem.* Supposed to have been written by *Nehemiah.*

Psalm cxxv. "They that trust in the Lord." The Jews encouraging each other to resist *Sanballat* and *Tobiah*, and their other enemies.

Psalm cxxvii. "Except the Lord build the house." Composed to encourage the people to labour at the rebuilding of the walls of Jerusalem; and to put their confidence in the Lord.

Psalm cxxviii. "Blessed is every one that feareth the Lord." A continuation of the preceding.

Psalm cxxix. "Many a time have they afflicted me." A description of the peace and comfort enjoyed by the Jews under the reign of Darius.

Psalm cxxxviii. "I will praise thee with my whole heart." A continuation of the same subject.

For the *reasons* of the above *chronological arrangement* the reader may refer to the notes, and see also another table, page 214. This arrangement is better than none; and I hope will in the main be found as correct as can reasonably be expected, and a great help to a proper understanding of the Psalms.

SECTION VI. GENERAL OBSERVATIONS ON THE GREAT DIFFERENCE OF CHARACTER BETWEEN THE HEBREW POETS, AND THOSE OF GREECE AND ITALY

The *Hebrew Psalter* is the most ancient collection of poems in the world; and was composed long before those in which ancient Greece and Rome have gloried. Among all the *heathen* nations *Greece* had the honour of producing not only the *first*, but also the most sublime, of poets: but the subjects on which they employed their talents had, in general, but little tendency to meliorate the moral condition of men. Their subjects were either a *fabulous theology*, a *false and ridiculous religion*, *chimerical wars*, *absurd heroism*, *impure love*, *agriculture*, *national sports*, or *hymns in honour of gods* more corrupt than the most profligate of men. Their writings served only to render vice amiable, to honour superstition, to favour the most dangerous and most degrading passions of men, such as impure love, ambition, pride, and impiety. What is said of the *Greek poets* may be spoken with equal truth of their successors and imitators, the *Latin poets;* out of the whole of whose writings it would be difficult to extract even the *common maxims* of a *decent morality*. I am well aware that fine sentiments, strong and terse expressions, and luminous thoughts, may be found in different parts of their writings; but compared with what is of a different kind, it may be well said of these,—

"Apparent rari nantes in gurgite vasto."

The Hebrew poets, on the contrary, justly boast the highest antiquity: they were men inspired of God, holy in their lives, pure in their hearts, labouring for the good of mankind; proclaiming by their incomparable compositions the infinite perfections, attributes, and unity of the Divine nature; laying down and illustrating the purest rules of the most refined morality, and the most exalted piety. God, his attributes, his works, and the religion which he has given to man, were the grand subjects of their Divinely inspired muse. By their wonderful art, they not only embellished the history of their own people, because connected intimately with the history of God's providence, but they also, by the light of the Spirit of God that was within them, foretold future events of the most unlikely occurrence, at the distance of many hundreds of years, with such exact circumstantiality as has been the wonder and astonishment of considerate minds in all succeeding generations; a fact which, taken in its connection with the holiness and sublimity of their doctrine; the grandeur, boldness, and truth of their imagery; demonstrates minds under the immediate inspiration of that God whose nature is ineffable, who exists in all points of time, and whose wisdom is infinite.

Some of the greatest both of the Greek and Roman poets, were men obscure in their birth, desperate in their fortunes, and of profligate manners; a fact at once proved both by their history and by their works. But the Hebrew poets were among the greatest men of their nation: and among them were found kings of the highest character, judges of the greatest integrity, heroes the most renowned, and lawgivers whose fame has reached every nation of the earth. By means of these men the lamp of true religion has been lighted in the earth; and wherever there is a ray of truth among the sons of men, it is an emanation immediately taken, or indirectly borrowed, from the prophets, poets, and statesmen, of the sons of Jacob.

The chief of the Hebrew *poets* were *Moses*, *David*, *Solomon*, *Job*, or whoever was the author of the book so called, *Isaiah*, *Jeremiah*, and most of the *minor prophets*. Solomon himself wrote *one thousand and five* hymns and poems: yet we know not that we have any of his poetical works, except the *Canticles*, though there may be some *Psalms* of his composition in the book before us.

Several of the *fathers*, both Greek and Latin, maintain that David is the author of the *whole book of Psalms*. And although they allow that several of them speak of times most obviously *posterior* to the days of David, yet they assert that he is the author of these also, and that he spoke of those events by the *spirit of prophecy!* The rabbins assert that the book of Psalms was composed by *ten* different authors, viz. *Adam, Melchizedek, Abraham, Moses,* the *sons of Korah, David, Solomon, Asaph, Jeduthun,* and *Ethan.* But this opinion is slenderly supported.

SECTION VII. OBSERVATIONS ON THE MANNER IN WHICH SEVERAL OF THE PSALMS APPEAR TO HAVE BEEN COMPOSED

That there were *several authors,* and that the Psalms were composed at *different times,* is sufficiently evident from the compositions themselves. The *occasions* also on which they were written are frequently pointed out by their contents; and these things have been kept constantly in view, in the construction of the preceding table.

There is a difficulty which should not be overlooked, and with which almost every reader is puzzled, viz., How is it that in the *same Psalm* we find so many *different states* of mind and circumstances pointed out? These could not be the experience of *one* and the *same person,* at the *same time.* The answer that is commonly given is this: Such Psalms were composed *after* the full termination of the *events* which they celebrate. For instance, David had fallen into distress—his sorrows became multiplied—he was filled with torturing fears. He called earnestly on the Lord for help; he was heard after a long night and fight of afflictions; and he most feelingly and sublimely praises God for his deliverance. Now all these different circumstances he describes *as if then existing,* though considerably *distant* in point of time; *beginning* the Psalm with the language of the *deepest penitential distress,* almost bordering on despair; and *ending* it with the *strongest confidence in God,* and thanksgiving for his *deliverance.* The thirtieth Psalm is a case in point; to the *notes* on which the reader is referred. Now it is possible that the psalmist, having obtained deliverance from sore and oppressive evils, might sit down to compose a hymn of thanksgiving to celebrate God's mercies; and in order to do this the more effectually, might describe the different circumstances enumerated above, as if he *were then passing through them.*

But I own that, to me, this is not a satisfactory solution. I rather suppose that such Psalms, and perhaps most of those called *acrostic,* were composed from *diaries* or *memoranda;* and in forming a Psalm, materials out of *different days,* having little congruity with each other as to the time in which they happened, would necessarily enter into the composition. This supposition will, in my opinion, account for all anomalies of this kind, which we perceive in the book of Psalms.

On this rule we can account for apparent contradictions in several Psalms: taken as metrical compositions formed from memoranda of religious experience for different days, they may well express different states; as the state of the author's mind was not likely to be precisely the same in all those times on which he made the memoranda. I can illustrate what I mean by the following extract from the *Spiritual Diary* of *Doctor John Rutty:*—

"*Seventh month,* 1768, 3d day: Amidst our palpable desolations, matter of some comfort appeared. An inward voice of thanksgiving to God for the gift of his Son, the Lord Jesus Christ, to us Gentiles; the mystery hid from ages, adorable, incomprehensible, unutterable, and unmerited; and if the sweet singer of Israel had occasion to say, 'Awake, sackbut, psaltery, and harp, and praise the Lord;' so had I, so had we, so had every one whose eyes the god of this world had not blinded.

"My native fierceness seemed, in the clear vision, to be the chief sin of my bosom, not yet wholly subdued: good Lord, and God of love, subdue it!

"7th. Soul, awake! the everlasting antitypal Sabbath I trust is at hand, the end of all labours, sufferings, and sins; see and prepare for it by letting the earth now enjoy its Sabbaths, even in a gradual relaxation and holy carelessness in all the special concerns of flesh and blood.

"8th. Protracted my vesper beyond the usual time, by reason of a sweet inspired song of thanksgiving to a gracious and ever adorable Providence.

"10th. Thy work is not yet done; the war in the members is still felt. Patience hath not yet had its perfect work. O my poverty! Lord, help me!

"11th. In the midst of various discouragements I was induced, even from observation, to believe that our late labour had not been wholly in vain; yea, on the 15th and 20th, I was a witness to some effects thereof.

"19th. A silent meeting with a loaded atmosphere; great heaviness, and the holy fire almost but not quite out.

"22d. I am a wonder of God's mercy and bounty. He is, as it were, renewing my youth, and giving, in old age, to enjoy and sweetly apply the labours of my youth, whilst multitudes of my equals and associates are dropping into eternity, or else various ways distressed. Awake, soul, and work; for the eleventh hour is come!

"23d. In a religious view, suffering is my portion. Lord, sustain!

"25th. A sweet song of thanksgiving.

"31st. The tenor of the drawing or proper steerage this day was, to keep carefully the holy medium between a criminal remissness in temporals on the one hand, and an anxiety about them on the other." *Spiritual Diary*, vol. ii, p. 235.

One sentence excepted, which is not relevant, here are the whole memoranda of the eminent man's religious experience for one month, in which we find the following states distinctly marked:

1. Mourning over the small progress of religion in the place where he dwelt, yet receiving encouragement from other quarters, day 3d. 2. Exulting in God for redemption by Christ Jesus, ditto. 3. Humbled on a view of his natural fierceness of spirit, ditto. 4. Rejoicing at the prospect of being soon released from earth, day 7th. 5. Thanksgiving for providential blessings, day 8th. 6. Fighting against inward sin, day 10th. 7. Encouraged in the performance of his duty, days 11th, 15th, 20th. 8. Mourning over the heavenly flame, almost extinct, day 19th. 9. Triumphing in a restoration of mental and bodily vigour, day 22d. 10. Complaining of his suffering lot, day 23d. 11. Happy in his soul, and giving praise to God, day 25th. 12. Forming holy resolutions for the government of his future life, day 31st.

Let us compare this with Psalm xxx., to which I have already referred in this introduction. The Psalm begins with "I will extol thee, O Lord." And we find in it *seven* different states distinctly marked:

1. He had been in great distress, and nearly overwhelmed by his enemies; implied in ver. 1. 2. He extols God for having lifted him up, and preserved him from his adversaries, ver. 1, 3. 3. He is brought into great prosperity, trusts in what he had received, and forgets to depend wholly on the Lord, ver. 4–6. 4. The Lord hides his face from him, and he is brought into great distress, ver. 7: "Thou didst hide thy face, and I was troubled." 5. He makes earnest prayer and supplication, and pleads strongly with the Lord, ver. 8–10. 6. He is restored to the Divine favour, and filled with joy, ver. 11. 7. He purposes to glory in God alone, and trust in him forever, ver. 12.

Now it is impossible that David could have been in all these states when he penned this Psalm: suppose them to be the *memoranda* taken from one week's journal, and dressed in this poetic form; for it is possible that he might have passed through all these states in one *week.* Let us examine the *month's* experience, extracted from the diary of *Dr. Rutty;* and let an able hand clothe that in a poetic dress; and we shall find it as apparently contradictory as the xxxth Psalm. Suppose both formed from *memoranda* of a *diary*, and all is plain.

I have spent the more time on this subject, because it is important to have some *general rule* by which we may account for the apparent inconsistencies often occurring in the same Psalm.

There is another class of Psalms to which this mode of interpretation is not applicable: I mean those composed in the *dialogue* form. There are several of this kind; and as the several interlocutors are not distinguished, it requires considerable attention to find out the different parts which belong to the speakers. I shall give an example of this class.

The *ninety-first* Psalm contains, in general, a description of the happiness of those who trust in the Lord: but is evidently divided among *three* speakers: the *psalmist;* another whom we may call his *friend;* and thirdly, *Jehovah.* I shall endeavour to assign to each his part.

The *psalmist* begins with asserting, in general terms, the happiness of the godly: "He that dwelleth in the secret place of the Most High shall abide under the shadow of the Almighty," ver. 1.

His *friend* states his own experience, and replies, "I will say of the Lord, He is my refuge," &c., ver. 2.

The psalmist answers: "Surely he shall deliver thee," &c., ver. 3; and goes on to enumerate the great privileges of the godly, to ver. 8.

The *friend* then resumes, and shows how blessed the psalmist must be, who has an interest in the same God; and enters into a detail of his privileges, ver. 9–13.

This speech concluded, *Jehovah* speaks, confirms what was said concerning the blessedness of the godly; and to such persons he promises the highest spiritual honours, long life, and endless salvation, ver. 14–16.

Other Psalms of this class, such as the xxth and xxxth, &c., will be particularly pointed out in the course of the notes on this subject.

Section VIII.—On the Use made of the Psalms in the New Testament

Some have imagined that the book of Psalms is to be understood mystically, in reference to the Christian system; and, indeed, on this plan they have been interpreted and applied by many *fathers*, both ancient and modern. To this opinion I cannot subscribe: and therefore cannot frame a commentary in this way. That several of them are quoted, both by our Lord and his apostles, we have the fullest proof; and where they have shown the way, we may safely follow. Bishop *Horne*, who contends for the spiritual sense of this book, gives an interesting view of the principal passages that have been *quoted* in the *New Testament;* and from his *preface* I shall select a few paragraphs on this part of the subject: "No sooner," says he, "have we opened the book, than the *second* Psalm presents itself, to all appearance, as an inauguration hymn composed by David, the anointed of Jehovah; when by him crowned with victory, and placed triumphant on the sacred hill of Sion. But let us turn to Acts iv. 25, and there we find the apostles declaring the Psalm to be descriptive of the exaltation of Jesus Christ, and of the opposition raised against his Gospel, both by Jew and Gentile.

"In the *eighth* Psalm we may imagine the writer to be setting forth the pre-eminence of man in general above the rest of the creation: but by Heb. ii. 6, we are informed that the supremacy conferred on the second Adam, the man Christ Jesus, over all things in heaven and earth, is the subject there treated of.

"St. Peter stands up, Acts ii. 25, and preaches the resurrection of Jesus from the latter part of the *sixteenth* Psalm; and, lo, *three thousand* souls are converted by the sermon.

"Of the *eighteenth* Psalm we are told in the course of the sacred history, 2 Sam. xxii., that 'David spake unto the Lord the words of this song in the day that the Lord had delivered him out of the hand of all his enemies, and out of the hand of Saul:' yet, in Rom. xv. 9, the *ninth* verse of that Psalm is adduced as a proof that the Gentiles should glorify God for his mercy in Christ Jesus: 'As it is written, For this cause I will confess to thee among the Gentiles, and sing unto thy name.'

"In the *nineteenth* Psalm David seems to be speaking of the material heavens and their operations only, when he says: 'Their sound is gone out into all the earth, and their words into the ends of the world.' But St. Paul, Rom. x. 18, quotes the passage to show that the Gospel had been universally published by the apostles.

"The *twenty-second* Psalm Christ appropriated to himself, by beginning it in the midst of his sufferings on the cross: 'My God, my God, why hast thou forsaken me?' Three other verses of it are also applied to him; and the words of the *eighth* verse were actually used by the chief priests when they reviled him: 'He trusted in God,' &c., Matt. xxvii. 43.

"When David says, in the *fortieth* Psalm, 'Sacrifice and offering thou didst not desire—Lo, I come—to do thy will;' we might suppose him only to declare, in his own person, that obedience is better than sacrifice; but, from Heb. x. 5, we learn that Messiah in that place speaks of his advent in the flesh to abolish the legal sacrifices, and to do away sin by the oblation of himself, once for all.

"That tender and pathetic complaint in the *forty-first* Psalm: 'Mine own familiar friend, in whom I trusted, which did eat of my bread, hath lifted up his heel against me,' undoubtedly might be, and probably was, originally uttered by David upon the revolt of his old friend and counsellor Ahithophel, to the party of his rebellious son Absalom. But we are certain, from John xiii. 18, that this scripture was fulfilled when Christ was betrayed by his apostate disciple: 'I speak not of you all; I know whom I have chosen: but that the scripture may be fulfilled, He that eateth bread with me hath lifted up his heel against me.'

"The *forty-fourth* Psalm we must suppose to have been written on occasion of a persecution under which the Church at that time laboured; but a verse of it is cited, Rom. viii. 36, as expressive of what Christians were to suffer on their blessed Master's account: 'As it is written, For thy sake we are killed all the day long; we are accounted as sheep for the slaughter.'

"A quotation from the *forty-fifth* Psalm in Heb. i. 3, certifies us that the whole is addressed to the Son of God, and therefore celebrates his spiritual union with the Church, and the happy fruits of it.

"The *sixty-eighth* Psalm, though apparently conversant about Israelitish victories, the translation of the ark to Sion, and the services of the tabernacle; yet does, under those figures, treat of Christ's resurrection; his going up on high leading captivity captive, pouring out the gifts of the Spirit, erecting his Church in the world, and enlarging it by the accession of the nations to the faith; as will be evident to any one who considers the force and consequence of the apostle's citation from it, Eph. iv. 7, 8: 'Unto every one of us is given grace according to the measure of the gift of Christ. Wherefore he saith, When he ascended up on high, he led captivity captive, and gave gifts unto men.'

"The *sixty-ninth* Psalm is *five* times referred to in the Gospels, as being uttered by the prophet in the person of the Messiah. The *imprecations*, or rather *predictions*, at the latter end of it, are applied, Rom. xi. 9, 10, to the Jews; and to Judas, Acts i. 20, where the *hundred and ninth* Psalm is also cited as prophetical of the sore judgments which should befall that arch traitor, and the wretched nation of which he was an epitome.

"St. Matthew, informing us, chap. xiii. 35, that Jesus spake to the multitude in parables, gives it as one reason why he did so: 'That it might be fulfilled which was spoken by the prophet, Psa. lxxiii. 2, I will utter things which have been kept secret from the foundation of the world.

"The *ninety-first* Psalm was applied by the tempter to the Messiah; nor did our Lord object to the application, but only to the false inference which his adversary suggested from it; Matt. iv. 6, 7.

"The *ninety-fifth* Psalm is explained at large in Heb. iii. and iv., as relative to the state and trials of Christians in the world, and to their attainment of the heavenly rest.

"The *hundred and tenth* Psalm is cited by Christ himself, Matt. xxii. 44, as treating of his exaltation, kingdom, and priesthood.

"The *hundred and seventeenth* Psalm, consisting only of *two verses*, is employed, Rom. xv. 11, to prove that the Gentiles were one day to praise God for the mercies of redemption.

"The twenty-second verse of the *hundred and eighteenth* Psalm: 'The stone which the builders refused,' &c., is quoted *six* different times as spoken of our Saviour. See Matt. xxi. 42; Mark xii. 10; Luke xx. 17; Acts iv. 11.

"And *lastly:* 'the fruit of David's body,' which God is said in the *hundred and thirty-second* Psalm to have promised that he would place upon his *throne*, is asserted, Acts ii. 30, to be 'Jesus Christ.'" Bishop Horne on the Psalms, preface, p. xi.

That several of the above quotations are directly *prophetic*, and were intended to announce and describe the Redeemer of the world and the Gospel state, there is not the slightest reason to doubt; that others of them are *accommodated* to the above subjects, their own historical meaning being different, may be innocently credited: but let it always be remembered, that these accommodations are made by the same Spirit by which the Psalms were originally given; that this Spirit has a right to extend his own meaning, and to adapt his own words to subjects, transactions, and times, to which, from similarity of circumstances, they may be applicable. Many passages of the Old Testament seem to be thus quoted in the New; and often the words a *little altered*, and the meaning *extended*, to make them suitable to existing circumstances. Every writer is at perfect liberty thus to employ his own words, which he might have already used on very different occasions. I need not tell the learned reader that the finest, as well as the oldest, of the heathen writers, *Homer*, is full of quotations *from himself;* and *Virgil*, his imitator, has not unfrequently followed his steps. But still there is a great and weighty difference as the subject respects the Holy Spirit; to his infinite wisdom and knowledge all times and circumstances, whether *past* or *future*, are always laid open; and, as it is one of the perfections of the work of God to produce the *greatest* and most *numerous effects* by the *fewest* and *simplest means*, so it is one of the perfections of the Holy Scriptures to represent things that are not as though they were; and to make the facts which then existed the representatives of those which should afterwards take place. Thus, the Holy Scriptures contain an infinity of meaning: the Old Testament, as it were, included and referred to in the New; as the New refers *back* to the Old, by which it was adumbrated; and refers *forward*, not only to all times and great occurrences during this mortal state, but also to the endless states of the just and the unjust in the eternal world.

Section IX.—On the Subject Matter of the Psalms, and the Method of Applying Them

The late learned Bishop *Horsley*, in his *preface* to the book of Psalms, says: "It is true that many of the Psalms are commemorative of the miraculous interpositions of God in behalf of his chosen people; for, indeed, the history of the Jews is a fundamental part of revealed religion. Many were probably composed upon the occasion of remarkable passages in David's life, his dangers, his afflictions, his deliverances. But of those which relate to the public history of the natural Israel, there are few in which the fortunes of the mystical Israel, the Christian Church, are not adumbrated; and of those which allude to the life of David, there are none in which the *Son of David* is not the principal and immediate subject.

"David's complaints against his enemies are Messiah's complaints, first of the unbelieving Jews, then of the heathen persecutors and the apostate faction in the latter ages. David's afflictions are the Messiah's sufferings; David's penitential supplications are the supplications of Messiah in agony; David's songs of triumph and thanksgiving are Messiah's songs of triumph and thanksgiving for his victory over sin, and death, and hell. In a word, there is not a page of this book of Psalms in which the pious reader will not find his *Saviour*, if he read with a view of finding him; and it was but a just encomium of it (the book of Psalms) that came from the pen of one of the early fathers, that *'it is a complete system of divinity for the use and edification of the common people of the Christian Church.'* "

Of the compilation of this book the above learned writer speaks thus: "The Psalms appear to be compositions of various authors, in various ages; some much more ancient than the time of King David, some of a much later age. Of many, David himself was undoubtedly the author; and that those of *his* composition were *prophetic*, we have David's own authority; for thus King David, at the close of his life, describes himself and his sacred songs: "David the son of Jesse said, and the man who was raised up on high, the anointed of the God of Jacob, and the sweet psalmist of Israel, said, The Spirit of Jehovah spake by me, and his word was in my tongue." It was the word, therefore, of *Jehovah's Spirit* which was uttered by David's tongue.

"The Psalms are all poems of the lyric kind, that is, adapted to music, but with great variety in the style of composition. Some are simply odes. An *ode* is a dignified sort of song, narrative of the facts either of public history or private life, in a highly adorned and figurative style. Some are of the kind called elegiac, which are pathetic compositions upon mournful subjects. Some are ethic, delivering grave maxims of life or the precepts of religion in solemn, but for the most part simple, strains. Some are enigmatic, delivering the doctrines of religion in *enigmas* contrived to strike the imagination forcibly, and yet easy to be understood. In all these the author delivers the whole matter in his own person. But a very great, I believe the far greater, part are a sort of dramatic odes, consisting of *dialogues* between persons sustaining certain characters. In these dialogue Psalms the persons are frequently the *psalmist* himself, or the *chorus of priests and Levites*, or the *leader* of the

Levitical band, opening the ode with a proem, declarative of the subject, and very often closing the whole with a solemn admonition drawn from what the other persons say. The other persons are JEHOVAH, sometimes as one, sometimes as another of the *Three Persons;* CHRIST in his incarnate state sometimes *before,* sometimes *after,* his resurrection; the *human soul* of Christ as distinguished from the *Divine essence.* Christ, in his incarnate state, is personated sometimes as a *Priest,* sometimes as a *King,* sometimes as a *Conqueror.* The resemblance is very remarkable between this *Conqueror* in the book of *Psalms,* and the *Warrior* on the *white horse* in the book of *Revelation,* who goes forth with a *crown* on his head, and a *bow* in his hand, conquering and to conquer. And the conquest in the *Psalms* is followed, like the conquest in the Revelation, by the *marriage* of the Conqueror. These are circumstances of similitude which, to any one versed in the *prophetic style,* prove beyond a doubt that the *mystical Conqueror* is the same personage in both."

There is an opinion relative to the construction of this book, which, though to myself it appear as fanciful as it is singular, yet deserves to be mentioned, especially as so great a man as Dr. *Horsley* supposes, that if it were kept in view, it would conduce much to a right understanding of the book.

The whole collection of the Psalms forms a sort of HEROIC TRAGEDY. The *redemption of man* and the *destruction of Satan,* is the PLOT. The PERSONS OF THE DRAMA are the *Persons* of the GODHEAD; *Christ* united to one of them: *Satan, Judas,* the *apostate Jews,* the *heathen persecutors,* the *apostates* of *latter times.* The ATTENDANTS: *believers, unbelievers, angels.* The SCENES: *heaven, earth, hell.* The TIME of the *action:* from the *fall* to the final overthrow of the *apostate faction,* and the *general judgment.*

SECTION X.—ON THE PARTICULAR SUBJECT AND USE OF EACH PSALM

I have already given different tables relative to the division, chronological arrangement, and supposed authors and occasions on which they were composed. There have been some others made, in which they have been classed according to their subjects, and their uses for the godly and the Christian Church. The most circumstantial that I have seen is that in the *Quintuplex Psalterium,* printed in 1508, already noticed in the beginning of this introduction. The following, from Bishop *Horsley,* may be probably of most general use:—

Services of the Festivals *of the Jewish Church*

For the SABBATH, Psa. xix., civ., and cxviii. For the PASSOVER, Psa. lxxviii., cv., cxiv. For PENTECOST, Psa. cxi., cxxxv., cxxxvi. For the FEAST OF TRUMPETS, Psa. lxxxi. For the FEAST OF TABERNACLES, Psa. lxv., lxvii.

A war song, Psa. cxlix. Thanksgiving for national deliverances, or successful war, Psa. xlviii., lxvi., lxxvi., cxv., cxxiv., cxxv., cxliv. Thanksgiving after a storm, hurricane, or earthquake, Psa. xxix., xlvi. Upon placing the ark in Solomon's temple, Psa. cxxxii. Prayers in seasons of national calamity, Psa. lxxix. Prayers for help in war, Psa. xliv., lx., lxi. Thanksgiving for Hezekiah's recovery, Psa. xxx., cxvi. Prayers in the time of Manasseh's captivity, Psa. lxxix., lxxx. Thanksgiving for Manasseh's return, Psa. lxxxv. Prayers, lamentations, and confessions of the captives, Psa. lxxiv., lxxvii., cii., cvi., cxxxvii. Songs of triumph and thanksgiving of the returned captives, Psa. cvii., cxxvi., cxlvi., cxlvii. A king of Judah's inauguration vow, Psa. ci. Grand chorus for all the voices and all the instruments, Psa. cl. The blessedness of the righteous, and the final perdition of the opposite faction, Psa. i., xxxvi., xxxvii., cxii. The extermination of the religious faction, Psa. xiv., liii. True godliness described as distinct from the ritual, Psa. xv., 1. The believer's scruples arising from the prosperity of the wicked, removed by revealed religion, and the consideration of their latter end, Psa. lxxiii. The pleasures of devotion, Psa. lxxxiv. Divine ænigmata; the subject, the Redeemer's divinity, the immortality of the soul, and a future retribution, Psa. xlix. A mystical prayer of David in the character of the high priest, Psa. xvi. Prayers of believers for protection against the atheistical conspiracy, Psa. iii., iv., x., xii., xiii., xvii., xliii., liv., cxx., cxxiii., cxl. The believer's penitential confessions and deprecations, Psa. vi., xxxii., xxxviii., xxxix., li. Believer's prayer for the promised redemption, Psa. cxxx., cxliii.

Believers lament their afflicted state in this short and evil life, and pray for the resurrection, Psa. xc. Prayers for grace and mercy, Psa. v., xxv., xxvi., cxxxi. Songs of triumph in prospect of the establishment of God's universal kingdom, Psa. xlvii., lxvii., xciii. A believer's general praises and thanksgivings, Psa. viii., xix., xxiii., ciii., cxix. A believer's thanksgiving for the final extirpation of iniquity, and the idolatrous religions and persecuting power, Psa. ix., xi., lii., lxvi. The Church prays for preservation from corruptions, Psa. xxviii., cxli.; for deliverance from the persecution of her enemies, Psa. vii., latter part of xxvii., from ver. 7 to the end, and xxxi., lix.; for Messiah's deliverance and success, Psa. xx. The Church gives thanks for Messiah's victory, Psa. xxi.; for her own final deliverance, Psa. xviii.; for the final extirpation of iniquity and idolatry, Psa. xcii. Messiah's prayers, Psa. xxii., xxxv., xli., lvi., lvii., lxi., lxii., lxiii., lxxxvi., lxxxviii.; in agony. When taken and deserted, Psa. cxlii.; thanksgivings, Psa. xl., cxvii., and cxviii., one Psa. cxxxviii; accusation of the impenitent Jews, his enemies, Psa. lv., lxiv., lxix.; prophetic malediction of the Jewish nation, Psa. cix.; exaltation, Psa. ii., xxiv., xlv., xcv., xcvi., xcvii., xcviii., xcix., c., cx.; comforts of the afflicted Israelites with the promise of the final excision of the idolatrous faction, Psa. xciv., exhorts to holiness and trust in God by the example of his own deliverance, Psa. xxxiv.; predicts the final judgment, Psa. lxxv. God promises the Messiah protection and glory, Psa. xci. God's just judgment foretold upon the unjust judges of our Lord, Psa. lviii., lxxxii. The reign of the king's son, Psa. lxxii. Salvation is of the Jews, Psa. lxxxvii.

Of the Psalms, *six* are alphabetical, xxv., xxxiv., xxxvii., cxi., cxii., cxlv.

Forty-five of the Psalms are called by the Masoretes *Mizmor*, iii., iv., v., vi., viii., ix., xii., xiii., xv., xix., xx., xxi., xxii., xxiii., xxiv., xxix., xxxi., xxxviii., xxxix., xl., xli., xlvii., xlix., l., li., lii., liii., liv., lv., lxiii., lxxvii., lxxix., lxxx., lxxxii., lxxxiv., lxxxv., xcviii., c., ci., cix., cx., cxxxix., cxl., cxli., cxliii.

Six are called *Michtam*, xvi., lvi., lvii., lviii., lix., lx.

Thirteen are called *Maschil*, xxxii., xlii., xliv., xlv., lii., liii., liv., lv., lxxiv., lxxviii., lxxxviii., lxxxix., cxlii.

Seven are called *Mizmor Shir*, xxxi., lxv., lxvii., lxviii., lxxv., lxxvii., xcii.

Five are called *Shir Mizmor*, xlviii., lxvi., lxxxiii., lxxxviii., cviii.

One is called *Shir*, xlvi.

Four are called *Tephillah*, xvii., lxxxvi., xc., cii.

One is called *Tehillah*, cxlv.; *one, Shiggaion*, vii.; *one, Lehazchir*, lxx.

Fifteen are called *Shir Hammaaloth*, or *Songs of Steps*, cxx.–cxxxiv.

Section XI.—On the General Use of the Psalms in the Christian Church

That our blessed Lord used the book of Psalms as he did other books of Scripture, and quoted from it, we have already seen; this stamps it with the highest authority: and that he and his disciples used it as a book of *devotion*, we learn from their singing the *Hillel* at his last supper, which we know was composed of Psalms cxiii., cxiv., cxv., cxvi., cxvii., and cxviii.; see Matt. xxvi. 30, and the notes there: and that they were used by the Christian Church from the earliest times in devotional exercises, especially in praising God, we have the most ample proof. At first what was called *singing* was no more than a *recitativo* or solemn mode of reading or repeating, which in the Jewish Church was accompanied by *instruments of music*, of the nature of which we know nothing. The Christian religion, which delights in *simplicity*, while it retained the Psalms as a book Divinely inspired, and a book of devotion, omitted the instrumental music, which, however, in after times, with other corruptions, crept into the Church, and is continued in many places, with small benefit to the godly, and little edification to the multitude. What good there might have been derived from it has been lost in consequence of the improper persons who generally compose what is commonly called the *choir of singers*. Those whose peculiar office it is to direct and lead the singing in Divine worship, should have clean hands and pure hearts. To see this part of public worship performed by unthinking if not profligate youths of both sexes, fills the serious with pain, and the ungodly with contempt. He who sings not with the *spirit* as well as the *understanding*, offers a sacrifice to God as acceptable as the dog's head and swine's blood would have been under the Mosaic law.

I shall not enter into the question whether the *Psalms* of *David*, or *hymns* formed on New Testament subjects, be the most proper for Christian congregations; *both* I think may be profitably used. Nor will I take up the controversy relative to the adapting the Psalms to express an evangelical meaning in every place. I need only give my opinion, that I consider this a difficult, if not a dangerous, work. Where the Psalms evidently relate to the *Gospel dispensation*, the matter is plain; there it is proper and necessary to give them their full direction and meaning; but to turn those in this way that evidently have no such reference, I consider a temerarious undertaking, and wholly unwarrantable.

But the most difficult task is, throwing them into a *modern poetic form*, especially into *metre;* as in such cases many things are introduced for the sake of the poetry, and the final jingle, which were never spoken by the inspired penman; and it is an awful thing to add to or detract from the word of God, either in *poetry* or *prose*. And how frequently this is done in most metrical versions of the Psalms, need not be pointed out here. Perhaps one of the most faultless in this respect is an almost obsolete one in our own language, viz., that by *Sternhold* and *Hopkins*. Because of its uncouth form, this version has been unjustly vilified, while others, by far its inferiors, have been as unreasonably extolled. The authors of this *version* (for it has been taken directly from the Hebrew text) have sacrificed every thing to the literal sense and meaning. The others, and especially that of *Tate* and *Brady*, which is no version from the original, sacrifice often the literal and true sense to sound and smoothness of numbers; in which, however, they are not always successful.

I shall add only one word on the subject of this very ancient version. I can sing almost every Psalm in the version of *Sternhold* and *Hopkins* AS the *Psalms of David;* I can sing those of the *new version* AS the Psalms of Dr. *Brady* and *Nahum Tate*. Either let one equally *literal*, with a better *versification*, be made; or restore to the people that form of sound words of which they have too long been deprived. But, to serve the purposes of devotion, we want a better translation of the Psalms; a translation in which the *hemistich*, or Hebrew poetic form, shall be carefully preserved; and with a very few expletives, (which should be distinguished by *italics*, or otherwise, in the printing, to bring the lines into those forms, to which our versification or musical measures may extend,) we might sing the whole, without singing any thing in sense or meaning which was not *David's*. Indeed a species of *recitativo* singing would be the most proper for these sacred odes; as it would answer much better the solemn purposes of devotion, than the great mass of those tunes which are commonly employed in Church music, in which the style of singing is rarely adapted to the grand and melting compositions of *the sweet singer of Israel*. Let the plan be copied which is adopted from the Hebrew MSS. in Dr. *Kennicott's* edition; let them be translated line for line, as Dr. *Lowth* has done his version of Isaiah; let a dignified recitativo music be adapted to the words; attend to metre, and be regardless of rhyme; and then the Psalms will be a mighty help to devotion, and truly religious people will sing with the spirit and the understanding also. Were a version of this kind made and substituted for that most inaccurate version in the *Prayerbook*, a stumbling-block would be taken out of the way of some sincere minds, who are pained to find, not only important differences, but even contradictions, between the Psalms which they read in their authorized version, and those which are used in the public service of the Church.

As many persons are greatly at a loss to account for the strange varieties between these two versions, (that in the *Bible*, and that in the Prayerbook,) it may be necessary to give them some information on this head. Properly speaking, the *Psalms* in the *Prayerbook*, called the *reading Psalms*, are rather a *paraphrase* than a *version*. It was never taken immediately from the *Hebrew*, with which it disagrees in places innumerable. In the main it follows the *Septuagint* and the *Vulgate*, but often differs from *them*, even where they *differ* from the *Hebrew*, and yet without following the *latter*. And there are many *words*, *turns of thought*, and varieties of *mood*, *tense*, and *person*, in it which do not appear in any of the above.

In the *prose Psalms* in our *authorized version* our translators have acted very conscientiously, as they have done in all other cases where they have *added* any thing, even the smallest particle, in order to fill up the sense, or accommodate the *Hebrew idiom* to that of the *English;* they have shown this by putting the *expletive* or *supplied* word in the *italic* letter. Thousands of such expletives, many of them utterly unnecessary, are found in the *prose Psalms* in the *Prayerbook;* but they have no such distinguishing mark, and are all printed as if they were the words of the Holy Spirit!

There are some things in this version that are *contradictory* to what is found in the Hebrew text. I shall give one example.

In Psalm cxxv. 3 we have the following words in the Hebrew text: כי לא ינוח שבט הרשע על גורל הצדיקים *ki lo yanuach shebet haresha al goral hatstsaddikim,* which is faithfully translated in our common version, "For the rod of the wicked (*wickedness,* marg.) shall not rest upon the lot of the righteous:" this is rendered in the *prose Psalms* in the *Prayerbook* thus: "For the rod of the ungodly cometh not into the lot of the righteous."

"This," say the objectors, "is neither *Scripture* nor *truth.* 1. It is not *Scripture:* the *Hebrew* is, as our authorized version hath it: 'The rod of the wicked shall not rest.' But your version saith, 'The rod of the ungodly cometh not.' 2. It is not *truth:* 'The rod of the wicked *often* cometh *into* the lot of the righteous;' but here is the difference: though it *may come,* and often *doth come, into the lot of the righteous,* yet God never permitteth it to *rest* there. Here therefore your reading Psalms contradict both *Scripture* and *fact.*"

It may be asked, From what source is this objectionable reading derived? It evidently cannot be derived from the *Hebrew text,* as the reader will at once perceive. It is not in the *Vulgate,* which reads, Quia non relinquet Dominus virgam peccatorum super sortem justorum. "For the Lord will not leave the rod of sinners upon the lot of the righteous." It is not in the *Septuagint,* Ὁτι ουκ αφησει Κυριος την ῥαβδον των ἁμαρτωλων επι τον κληρον των δικαιων, which is precisely the same as the *Vulgate.* Nor does this strange version receive any support from either the *Chaldee, Syriac, Æthiopic,* or *Arabic.*

To attempt to vindicate such a translation will neither serve the interests of the *Church,* nor those of Christianity, especially when we have one so very different and so very faithful put into the hands of the people by the *authority of the Church and the state.* That in the *Prayerbook* should be immediately suppressed, and replaced by that in our *authorized version,* that the people may not have a different version put into their hands on the *Lord's day,* and in times of *public devotion,* from that which they find in their *Bible;* in consequence of which they are often confounded with discrepancies which it is out of their power to reconcile. It is passing strange that the rulers of the Church have slumbered so long over a subject of such vast magnitude and importance.

To be fully satisfied on this subject, I have collated this *Prayerbook version* in many places with the *Hebrew text,* the *Septuagint,* the *Vulgate,* the old *Itala* or *Antehieronymian,* and the *oriental* versions in general; and find much cause of complaint against its general looseness, and frequent inaccuracy; and would give that advice to the rulers of our Church, that the prophet did to the rulers of the Jewish Church, on a subject in which the best interests of the people were concerned: "Go through, go through the *gates;* cast up, cast up the *highway; take up* the *stumbling-block* out of the way of my people; lift up a *standard* for the people;" Isa. lvii. 14; lxii. 10.

With respect to *helps,* I may say in general that I have occasionally consulted, 1. The *Critici Sacri.* 2. *Venema;* whom I should have been glad to have used more particularly, but his plan would have led me into such an extent of comment, as would have far surpassed my limits. 3. *Rosenmüller's* collections were of more use; but neither did his plan quadrate with mine. 4. *Calmet* afforded me most assistance, as he is, in almost all respects, the most judicious of all the commentators. 5. Could I have wholly agreed with the plan of the truly pious *Bishop Horne,* I might have enriched my work with many of those spiritual remarks with which his *commentary* abounds. Where I differ from *his plan* will best appear in a preceding part of this *introduction,* to which I must refer the reader. 6. From the very learned *Bishop Horsley* I have borrowed several useful *notes,* particularly of a critical kind. 7. But the work which I think may be of most use to masters of families, and ministers in general, is that excellent and judicious one by *Dr. Wm. Nicolson,* formerly *bishop of Gloucester,* with the quaint but expressive title, "DAVID'S HARP STRUNG AND TUNED; or an easy ANALYSIS of the whole *book of Psalms,* cast into such method, that the sum of every Psalm may quickly be collected and remembered." In many places I have introduced the whole of the *analysis*, with some corrections, leaving out the *prayers* at the *end of each Psalm;* which, though very useful for the *family*, or for the *closet*, could not properly have a place in a *comment*. This work was *finished* by the author, October 22, 1658. 8. From an old folio MS. on vellum in my own collection, I have extracted some curious notes and renderings. It contains the Vulgate, or more properly the Antehieronymian version, with a translation after each verse in the ancient Scottish dialect, and after that a paraphrase in same language. I have given the eighth Psalm as it stands in this ancient MS., after my notes on that Psalm. Most of my readers will find this at least an *edifying curiosity*. Extracts from it will appear in different parts of the work. I know nothing like the book of Psalms: it contains all the lengths, breadths, depths, and heights of the patriarchal, Mosaic, and Christian dispensations. It is the most useful book in the Bible, and is every way worthy of the wisdom of God.

Reader, may the Spirit of the ever blessed God make this most singular, most excellent, and most exalted of all his works, a present and eternal blessing to thy soul!—Amen.

ADAM CLARKE.

THE BOOK

OF

PSALMS

Chronological Notes relative to the Psalms written by David, upon the supposition that they were all composed in a period of about forty-seven *years. See the* Introduction.

Year from the Creation, 2942–2989.—Year before the birth of Christ, 1058–1011.—Year before the vulgar era of Christ's nativity, 1062–1015.—Year since the Deluge, according to Archbishop Usher, and the English Bible, 1286–1333.—Year from the destruction of Troy, according to Dionysius of Halicarnassus, 123–170.—Year before the first Olympiad, 286–239.—Year before the building of Rome, 309–262.—Year of the Julian Period, 3652–3699.—Year of the Dionysian Period, 460–507.

PSALM I

The blessedness of the righteous shown, in his avoiding every appearance of evil, 1. *In his godly use of the law of the Lord,* 2. *This farther pointed out under the metaphor of a good tree planted in a good well-watered soil,* 3. *The opposite state of the ungodly pointed out, under the metaphor of chaff driven away by the wind,* 4. *The miserable end of sinners, and the final happiness of the godly,* 5, 6.

I. DAY. MORNING PRAYER

BLESSED [b]*is* the man that walketh not
in the counsel of the [c]ungodly, nor standeth in the way of sinners, [d]nor sitteth in the
seat of the scornful.
2 But [e]his delight *is* in the law of the LORD;

[a]Luke xx. 42; Acts i. 20——[b]Prov. iv. 14, 15 [c]Or, *wicked*

[d]Psa. xxvi. 4; Jer. xv. 17——[e]Psa. cxix. 35, 47, 92

NOTES ON PSALM I

Verse 1. *Blessed* is *the man*] This Psalm has no *title*, and has been generally considered, but without especial reason, as a *preface* or *introduction* to the whole book.

The word אשרי *ashrey*, which we translate *blessed*, is properly in the *plural* form, *blessednesses;* or may be considered as an *exclamation* produced by contemplating the state of the man who has taken God for his portion; *O the blessedness of the man!* And the word האיש *haish*, is emphatic: THAT *man;* that *one* among a *thousand* who lives for the accomplishment of the end for which God created him. 1. God made man for happiness. 2. Every man feels a desire to be happy. 3. All human beings abhor misery. 4. Happiness is the grand object of pursuit among all men. 5. But so perverted is the human heart, that it seeks happiness where it cannot be found; and in things which are naturally and morally unfit to communicate it. 6. The true way of obtaining it is here laid down.

That walketh not in the counsel of the ungodly] There is a double CLIMAX in this verse, which it will be proper to note:—

1. There are here *three* characters, each *exceeding* the other in sinfulness. 1. The UNGODLY רשעים *reshaim*, from רשע *rasha*, to be *unjust;* rendering to none his due; withholding from God, society, and himself, what belongs to each. *Ungodly*—he who has not God in him; who is without God in the world. 2. SINNERS, חטאים *chattaim*, from חטא *chata*, "to miss the mark," "to pass over the prohibited limits," "to transgress." This man not only does *no good*, but he *does evil*. The former was *without God*, but not *desperately wicked*. The latter adds *outward transgression* to the *sinfulness* of his heart. 3. SCORNFUL, לצים *letsim*, from לצה *latsah*, "to mock, deride." He who has no religion; lives in the open breach of God's laws; and turns *revelation*, the *immortality of the soul*, and the existence of an *invisible world*, into ridicule. He is at least a *deist*, and endeavours to *dissolve*, as much as he can, the *bonds* of moral obligation in civil society. As the *sinner* exceeds the *ungodly*, so the *scornful* exceeds *both*.

The *second climax* is found in the words, 1. *Walk;* 2. *Stand;* 3. *Sit:* which mark *three different degrees* of evil in the *conduct* of those persons.

Observe, 1. The *ungodly* man—one uninfluenced by God. 2. The *sinner*—he who adds to *ungodliness transgression*. 3. The *scornful*—the deist, atheist, &c., who make a mock of every thing sacred. The UNGODLY man *walks*, the SINNER *stands, and the* SCORNFUL man *sits down* in the way of iniquity.

Mark certain circumstances of their differing characters and conduct. 1. The *ungodly*

and [f]in his law doth he meditate day and night.
3 And he shall be like a tree [g]planted by the rivers of water, that bringeth forth his fruit in his season: his leaf also shall not [h]wither; and whatsoever he doeth shall [i]prosper.

[f]Josh. i. 8; Psa. cxix. 1, 97——[g]Jer. xvii. 8; Ezek. xlvii. 12

[h]Heb. *fade*——[i]Gen. xxxix. 3, 23; Psa. cxxviii. 2; Isa. iii. 10

man has his *counsel;* 2. The *sinner* has his *way;* and, 3. The *scorner* has his *seat.*

The *ungodly man* is unconcerned about religion; he is neither zealous for his own salvation, nor for that of others: and he *counsels* and *advises* those with whom he converses to adopt his plan, and not trouble themselves about praying, reading, repenting, &c., &c.; there is no need for such things; live an honest life, make no fuss about religion, and you will fare well enough at last. Now, "blessed is the man who walks not in this man's counsel;" who does not come into his measures, nor act according to his plan.

The *sinner* has his particular *way* of transgressing; one is a *drunkard,* another *dishonest,* another *unclean.* Few are given to every species of vice. There are many *covetous men* who abhor *drunkenness;* many *drunkards* who abhor *covetousness;* and so of others. Each has his *easily besetting sin;* therefore, says the prophet, *let the wicked* forsake HIS WAY. Now, *blessed is he who stands not in such a man's* WAY.

The *scorner* has brought, in reference to himself, all religion and moral feeling to an end. He has *sat down*—is utterly confirmed in impiety, and makes a mock at sin. His conscience is seared; and he is a believer in all unbelief. Now, *blessed is the man who sits not down in his* SEAT.

See the *correspondent relations* in this account. 1. He who *walks* according to the *counsel* of the *ungodly* will soon, 2. *Stand* to look on the *way* of *sinners;* and thus, being off his guard, he will soon be a partaker in their evil deeds. 3. He who has abandoned himself to transgression will, in all probability, soon become hardened by the deceitfulness of sin; and *sit down* with the *scorner,* and endeavour to turn religion into ridicule.

The last correspondency we find is:—1. The *seat* answers to the *sitting* of the *scornful.* 2. The *way* answers to the *standing* of the *sinner;* and 3, the *counsel* answers to the *walking* of the *ungodly.*

The great lesson to be learned from the whole is, sin is *progressive;* one evil propensity or act leads to another. He who acts by *bad counsel* may soon do *evil deeds;* and he who abandons himself to *evil doings* may end his life in *total apostasy* from God. "When lust has conceived, it brings forth sin; and when sin is finished, it brings forth death." Solomon, the son of David, adds a profitable advice to those words of his father: "Enter not into the path of the wicked, and go not in the way of evil *men;* avoid it, pass not by it, turn from it, and pass away;" Prov. iv. 14, 15.

As the *blessedness* of the man is great who avoids the ways and the workers of iniquity, so his *wretchedness* is great who acts on the *contrary:* to him we must reverse the words of David: "Cursed is the man who walketh in the counsel of the ungodly; who standeth in the way of sinners; and who sitteth in the seat of the scornful." Let him that readeth understand.

Verse 2. *But his delight is in the law of the Lord*] חפצו *chephtso,* his will, desire, affection, every *motive* in his heart, and every *moving principle* in his soul, are on the side of *God* and his *truth.* He takes up *the law of the Lord* as the *rule* of *his life;* he brings all his actions and affections to this holy *standard.* He looketh into the perfect law of liberty; and is not a forgetful hearer, but a doer of the word; and is therefore blessed in his deed. He not only *reads* to gain knowledge from the Divine oracles, but he *meditates* on what he has read, feeds on it; and thus receiving *the sincere milk of the word,* he grows thereby unto eternal life. This is not an *occasional* study to him; it is his work *day and night.* As his *heart* is in it, the *employment* must be *frequent,* and the *disposition* to it *perpetual.*

Verse 3. *Like a tree planted*] Not like one growing wild, however strong or luxuriant it may appear; but one that has been carefully *cultivated;* and for the proper growth of which all the advantages of soil and situation have been chosen. If a child be brought up in the discipline and admonition of the Lord, we have both reason and revelation to encourage us to expect a godly and useful life. Where religious education is neglected, alas! what fruits of righteousness can be expected? An *uncultivated soul* is like an *uncultivated field,* all overgrown with briers, thorns, and thistles.

By the rivers of water] פלגי מים *palgey mayim,* the streams or divisions of the waters. Alluding to the custom of *irrigation* in the eastern countries, where streams are conducted from a canal or river to different parts of the ground, and turned *off* or *on* at pleasure; the person having no more to do than by *his foot* to turn a sod from the side of one stream, to cause it to share its waters with the other parts to which he wishes to direct his course. This is called "watering the land with the foot," Deut. xi. 10, where see the note.

His fruit in his season] In such a case expectation is never disappointed. Fruit is expected, fruit is borne; and it comes also in the time in which it should come. A godly education, under the influences of the Divine Spirit, which can never be withheld where they are earnestly sought, is sure to produce the fruits of righteousness; and he who reads, prays, and meditates, will ever *see* the *work* which God has given him to do; the *power* by which he is to perform it; and the *times, places,* and *opportunities* for doing those things by which God can obtain most glory, his own soul most good, and his neighbour most edification.

His leaf also shall not wither] His *profession* of true religion shall always be regular and unsullied; and his *faith* be ever shown by his *works.* As the *leaves* and the *fruit* are the evidences of the vegetative perfection of the tree; so a zealous religious profession, accompanied with good works, are the evidences of

4 The ungodly *are* not so: but *are* [k]like the chaff which the wind driveth away.

5 Therefore the ungodly [l]shall not stand in the judgment, nor sinners in the congregation of the righteous.

6 For [m]the LORD knoweth the way of the righteous: but the way of the ungodly shall perish.

---

[k]Job xxi. 18; Psa. xxxv. 5; Isa. xvii. 13; xxix. 5; Hos. xiii. 3

[l]Wisd. v. 1——[m]Psa. xxxvii. 18; Nah. i. 7; John x. 14; 2 Tim. ii. 19

---

the soundness of faith in the Christian man. *Rabbi Solomon Jarchi* gives a curious turn to this expression: he considers the *leaves* as expressing those matters of the law that seem to be of no real use, to be quite unimportant, and that apparently neither add nor diminish. But even these things are parts of the Divine revelation, and *all have their use;* so even the apparently indifferent actions or sayings of a truly holy man have their use; and from the *manner* and *spirit* in which they are done or said, have the tendency to bear the observer to something great and good.

Whatsoever he doeth shall prosper] It is always healthy; it is extending its roots, increasing its woody fibres, circulating its nutritive juices, putting forth fruitbuds, blossoms, leaves, or fruit; and all these operations go on, in a healthy tree, in their proper seasons. So the godly man; he is ever taking deeper root, growing stronger in the grace he has already received, increasing in heavenly desires, and, under the continual influence of the Divine Spirit, forming those purposes from which much fruit to the glory and praise of God shall be produced.

Verse 4. *The ungodly* are *not so*] The *Vulgate* and *Septuagint*, and the versions made from them, such as the *Æthiopic* and *Arabic*, double the last negation, and add a clause to the end of the verse, "Not so the ungodly, *not so;* they shall be like the dust which the wind scatters away *from the face of the earth.*" There is nothing solid in the men; there is nothing good in their ways. They are not of God's planting; they are not good grain; they are only *chaff*, and a chaff that shall be separated from the good grain when the fan or shovel of God's power throws them up to the wind of his judgments. The manner of *winnowing* in the eastern countries is nearly the same with that practised in various parts of these kingdoms before the invention of *winnowing machines.* They either throw it up in a place out of doors by a large wooden shovel against the wind; or with their *weights* or *winnowing fans* shake it down leisurely in the wind. The grain falls down nearly perpendicularly; and the chaff, through its lightness, is blown away to a distance from the grain.

An ungodly man is never steady; his purposes are abortive; his conversation light, trifling, and foolish; his professions, friendships, &c., frothy, hollow, and insincere; and both he and his works are carried away to destruction by the wind of God's judgments.

Verse 5. *Therefore the ungodly shall not stand*] This refers to the *winnowing* mentioned in the preceding verse. Some of the versions have, *The ungodly shall not arise in the judgment*—they shall have *no resurrection*, except to shame and everlasting contempt. But probably the meaning is, When they come to be judged, they shall be condemned. They shall have nothing to plead in their behalf. That the impious were never to have any resurrection, but be annihilated, was the opinion of several among the Jews, and of some among Christians. The former believe that only the true Israelites shall be raised again; and that the souls of all others, the Christians not excepted, die with their bodies. Such unfounded opinions are unworthy of refutation.

Verse 6. *The Lord knoweth*] יודע *yodea*, approveth the way, **alloweth the way,** *Coverdale*, of the righteous, צדיקים *tsaddikim*, from צדק *tsadak*, to *give even weight;* the men who give to all their *due;* opposed to רשעים *reshaim*, ver. 1, they who withhold *right* from all; see above. Such holy men are under the continual eye of God's *providence;* he *knows* the way that they take; *approves* of their motives, purposes, and works, because they are all wrought through himself. He *provides* for them in all exigencies, and *defends* them both in body and soul.

The way of the ungodly shall perish.] Their projects, designs, and operations, shall perish; God's curse shall be on all that they *have, do,* and *are.* And in the day of judgment they shall be condemned to everlasting fire in the perdition of ungodly men. *The wicked shall perish at the presence of the Lord.* Reader, take warning!

ANALYSIS OF THE FIRST PSALM

The *το κρινομενον* in this Psalm is, *Who is the happy man?* or, *What may make a man happy?*

I. This question the prophet resolves in the first two verses: 1. *Negatively.* It is he, 1. "That walks not in the counsel of the ungodly." 2. "That stands not in the way of sinners." 3. "That sits not in the seat of the scornful." 2. *Positively.* It is he. 1. "Whose delight is in the law of the Lord." 2. "Who doth meditate in the law day and night."

II. This happiness of the good man is illustrated two ways: 1. By a similitude. 2. By comparing him with a wicked man.

1. The similitude he makes choice of is that of a *tree;* not every *tree* neither, but that which hath these eminences: 1. It is "planted;" it grows not of itself, neither is wild. 2. "Planted by the rivers of water;" it wants not moisture to fructify. 3. It doth fructify; "it brings forth fruit;" it is no *barren* tree. 4. The fruit it brings is seasonable; "it brings forth fruit in its season." 5. It is always green, winter and summer; "the leaves wither not." Clearly, without any trope, *Whatsoever* this good man *doth*, or takes in hand, "it shall prosper."

2. He shows this good man's happiness by comparing him with a wicked man, in whom you shall find all the contrary.

1. In general. *Not so.* As for the ungodly, it is not so with them: *not so* in the plantation; in the place; in the seasonable fruit; in the greenness; in the prosperity. So far from being like a *tree*, that they are like, 1. *Chaff*, a light and empty thing. 2. *Chaff* which the wind whiffles up and down. 3. *Chaff* which the

wind scatters or *driveth away.* 4. And never leaves scattering, till it has driven it from the face of the earth. So the *Vulgate, Septuagint,* and *Arabic.*

2. And that no man may think that their punishment shall extend only to this life; in plain terms he threatens to them, 1. Damnation at the great day: "They shall not stand in judgment;" though some refer this clause to this life. When he is judged by men, *causa cadet,* he shall be condemned. 2. Exclusion from the company of the just: "Sinners shall not stand in the congregation of the righteous."

III. In the close he shows the cause why the godly is happy, the wicked unhappy: 1. Because "the way of the righteous is known to God;" approved by him, and defended. 2. But the way, studies, plots, "counsels of the wicked, shall perish."—DAVID'S HARP STRUNG AND TUNED. See the introduction.

PSALM II

This Psalm treats of the opposition raised, both by Jew and Gentile, against the kingdom of Christ, 1–3. *Christ's victory, and the confusion of his enemies,* 4–6. *The promulgation of the Gospel after his resurrection,* 7–9. *A call to all the potentates and judges of the earth to accept it, because of the destruction that shall fall on those who reject it,* 10–12.

A. M. cir. 2957
B. C. cir. 1047
Ante I. Ol. 271
Anno Davidis, Regis
Israelitarum, 9

WHY [a]do the heathen [b]rage,
and the people [c]imagine
a vain thing?
2 The kings of the earth set
themselves, and the rulers take counsel together, against the LORD, and against his
[d]anointed, *saying,*
3 [e]Let us break their bands
asunder, and cast away their
cords from us.
4 [f]He that sitteth in the heavens [g]shall laugh: the LORD shall have them
in derision.
5 Then shall he speak unto them in his

[a]Psa. xlvi. 6; Acts iv. 25, 26——[b]Or, *tumultuously assemble*——[c]Heb. *meditate*

[d]Psa. xlv. 7; John i. 41——[e]Jer. v. 5; Luke xix. 14
[f]Psa. xi. 4——[g]Psa. xxxvii. 13; lix. 8; Prov. i. 26

NOTES ON PSALM II

Verse 1. *Why do the heathen rage*] It has been supposed that David composed this Psalm after he had taken Jerusalem from the Jebusites, and made it the head of the kingdom; 2 Sam. v. 7-9. The Philistines, hearing this, encamped in the valley of Rephaim, nigh to Jerusalem, and Josephus, Antiq. lib. vii. c. 4, says that all Syria, Phœnicia, and the other circumjacent warlike people, united their armies to those of the Philistines, in order to destroy David before he had strengthened himself in the kingdom. David, having consulted the Lord, 2 Sam. v. 17-19, gave them battle, and totally overthrew the whole of his enemies. In the *first* place, therefore, we may suppose that this Psalm was written to celebrate the taking of Jerusalem, and the overthrow of all the kings and chiefs of the neighbouring nations. In the *second* place we find, from the use made of this Psalm by the apostles, Acts iv. 27, that David typified Jesus Christ; and that the Psalm celebrates the victories of the Gospel over the *Philistine Jews,* and all the confederate power of the *heathen governors* of the Roman empire.

The heathen, גוים *goyim,* the nations; those who are commonly called *the Gentiles.*

Rage, רגשו *rageshu;* the gnashing of teeth, and tumultuously rushing together, of those indignant and cruel people, are well expressed by the *sound* as well as the *meaning* of the original word. *A vain thing.* Vain indeed to prevent the spread of the Gospel in the world. To prevent Jesus Christ, the King of kings, and Lord of lords, from having the empire of his own earth. So vain were their endeavours that every effort only tended to open and enlarge the way for the all-conquering sway of the sceptre of righteousness.

Verse 2. *Against his anointed*] על משיחיה *al Meshichiah,* "Against his *Messiah.*"—*Chaldee.* But as this signifies the *anointed* person, it may refer first to *David,* as it does secondly to *Christ.*

Verse 3. *Let us break their bands*] These are the words of the confederate heathen powers; and here, as Bishop Horne well remarks, "we may see the ground of opposition; namely, the unwillingness of rebellious nature to submit to the obligations of Divine laws, which cross the interests, and lay a restraint on the desires of men. Corrupt affections are the most inveterate enemies of Christ, and their language is, We will not have this man to reign over us. Doctrines would be readily believed if they involved in them no precepts; and the Church may be tolerated in the world if she will only give up her discipline."

Verse 4. *He that sitteth in the heavens*] Whose kingdom ruleth over all, and is *above* all might and power, human and diabolical. *Shall laugh.* Words spoken after the manner of men; shall utterly contemn their puny efforts; shall beat down their pride, assuage their malice, and confound their devices.

Verse 5. *Then shall he speak unto them in his wrath*] He did so to the Jews who rejected the Gospel, and vexed and ruined them by the Roman armies; he did so with the opposing Roman emperors, destroying all the contending factions, till he brought the empire under the dominion of one, and him he converted to Christianity viz., *Constantine* the Great.

A. M. cir. 2957
B. C. cir. 1047
Ante I. Ol. 271
Anno Davidis, Regis
Israelitarum, 9

wrath, and [h]vex them in his sore
displeasure.
6 Yet have I [i]set my king
[k]upon [l]my holy hill of Zion.
7 I will declare [m]the decree: the LORD
hath said unto me, [n]Thou *art*
my Son; this day have I begotten
thee.
8 [o]Ask of me, and I shall
give *thee* the heathen *for* thine inheritance,

A. M. cir. 2957
B. C. cir. 1047
Ante I. Ol. 271
Anno Davidis, Regis
Israelitarum, 9

[h]Or, *trouble*——[i]Heb. *anointed*——[k]Heb. *upon Zion the hill of my holiness*——[l]2 Sam. v. 7——[m]Or, *for a decree*

[n]Acts xiii. 33; Heb. i. 5; v. 5——[o]Psa. xxii. 27; lxxii. 8; lxxxix. 27; Dan. vii. 13, 14; see John xvii. 4, 5; xix. 15

Verse 6. *I set my king upon my holy hill of Zion.*] Here the Gospel shall be first preached; here the kingdom of Christ shall be founded; and from hence shall the doctrine of the Lord go out into all the earth.

Verse 7. *I will declare the decree*] These words are supposed to have been spoken by the Messiah. I will declare to the world the decree, the purpose of God to redeem them by my blood, and to sanctify them by my Spirit. My death shall prove that the required *atonement* has been made; my *resurrection* shall prove that this atonement has been *accepted.*

Thou art *my Son*] Made man, born of a woman by the creative energy of the Holy Ghost, that thou mightest feel and suffer for man, and be the first-born of many brethren.

This day have I begotten thee.] By thy *resurrection* thou art declared to be the Son of God, εν δυναμει, *by miraculous power*, being raised from the dead. Thus by thy wondrous and supernatural *nativity*, most extraordinary *death*, and miraculous *resurrection*, thou art declared to be the Son of God. And as in that Son dwelt all the fulness of the Godhead bodily, all the sufferings and the death of that human nature were stamped with an infinitely meritorious efficacy. We have St. Paul's authority for applying to the *resurrection* of our Lord these words, "Thou art my Son; this day have I begotten thee;"—see Acts xiii. 33; see also Heb. v. 5;—and the man must indeed be a bold interpreter of the Scriptures who would give a different gloss to that of the apostle. It is well known that the words, "Thou art my Son; this day have I begotten thee," have been produced by many as a proof of the *eternal generation of the Son of God.* On the subject itself I have already given my opinion in my note on Luke i. 35, from which I recede not one hair's breadth. Still however it is necessary to spend a few moments on the clause before us. The word היום *haiyom*, TO-DAY, is in no part of the sacred writings used to express *eternity*, or any thing in reference to it; nor can it have any such signification. *To-day* is an absolute designation of the *present*, and equally excludes *time past* and *time future;* and never can, by any figure, or allowable latitude of construction, be applied to express *eternity*. But why then does the Divine Spirit use the word *begotten* in reference to the declaration of the inauguration of the Messiah to his kingdom, and his being seated at the right hand of God? Plainly to show both to Jews and Gentiles that this Man of sorrows, this Outcast from society, this Person who was prosecuted as a blasphemer of God, and crucified as an enemy to the public peace and a traitor to the government, is no less than that *eternal Word*, who *was in the beginning with God*, who *was God*, and *in whom dwelt all the fulness of the Godhead bodily:* that this rejected Person was he for whom in the fulness of time a body was prepared, *begotten* by the exclusive *power* of the *Most High* in the womb of an *unspotted virgin*, which body he gave unto death as a *sin-offering* for the redemption of the world; and having raised it from death, *declared* it to be that *miraculously-begotten Son of God*, and now gave farther proof of this by raising the God-man to *his right hand.*

The word ילדתי *yalidti*, "I have begotten," is here taken in the sense of *manifesting, exhibiting*, or *declaring;* and to this sense of it St. Paul (Rom. i. 3, 4) evidently alludes when speaking of "Jesus Christ, who was made of the seed of David according to the flesh, του ὁρισθεντος Υἱου Θεου εν δυναμει, κατα Πνευμα αγιωσυνης, εξ αναστασεως νεκρων; *and declared* (*exhibited* or *determined*) *to be the Son of God with power*, according to the Spirit of holiness." This very rejected Person I this day, by raising him from the dead, and placing him at my right hand, giving to him all power in heaven and earth, declare to be my Son, the beloved one in whom I am well pleased. Therefore hear *him*, believe on *him*, and obey *him;* for there is no redemption but through *his* blood; no salvation but in *his* name; no resurrection unto eternal life but through *his* resurrection, ascension, and powerful intercession at my right hand. *Thou art my Son; this day have I declared and manifested thee to be such.* It was absolutely necessary to the salvation of men, and the credibility of the Gospel, that the *supernatural* origin of the *humanity* of Jesus Christ should be manifested and demonstrated. Hence we find the inspired writers taking pains to show that he was born of a *woman*, and of that woman by the *sovereign power of the everlasting God.* This vindicated the character of the blessed virgin, showed the human nature of Christ to be immaculate, and that, even in respect to this nature, he was every way qualified to be a proper atoning sacrifice and Mediator between God and man. I need not tell the learned reader that the Hebrew verb ילד *yalad*, *to beget*, is frequently used in reference to *inanimate* things, to signify their *production*, or the *exhibition* of the things produced. In Gen. ii. 4: *These are the generations,* תולדות *toledoth*, of the heavens and the earth; this is the order in which God produced and exhibited them. See *Heb.* and *Eng. Concord.*, *Venema*, &c.

Verse 8. *Ask of me, and I shall give* thee] Here a *second* branch of Christ's office as Saviour of the world is referred to; viz., his *mediatorial* office. Having died as an *atoning sacrifice*, and *risen again* from the dead, he was now to *make intercession* for mankind; and in virtue and on account of what he had done and suffered, he was, *at his request*, to have the *nations for his inheritance, and the uttermost parts of the earth for his possession.* He was to become supreme Lord in the mediatorial

A. M. cir. 2957
B. C. cir. 1047
Ante I. Ol. 271
Anno Davidis, Regis Israelitarum, 9

and the uttermost parts of the
earth *for* thy possession.
9 [p]Thou shalt break them with
a rod of iron; thou shalt dash
them in pieces like a potter's vessel.
10 Be wise now therefore, O ye kings: be
instructed, ye judges of the earth.

11 [q]Serve the LORD with fear,
and rejoice [r]with trembling.
12 [s]Kiss the Son, lest he be
angry, and ye perish *from* the
way, when [t]his wrath is kindled but a little.
[u]Blessed *are* all they that put their trust in
him.

A. M. cir. 2957
B. C. cir. 1047
Ante I. Ol. 271
Anno Davidis, Regis Israelitarum, 9

---

[p]Psa. lxxxix. 23; Rev. ii. 27; xii. 5——[q]Heb. xii. 28——[r]Phil. ii. 12——[s]Gen. xli. 40; 1 Sam. x. 1; John v. 23

[t]Rev. vi. 16, 17——[u]Psa. xxxiv. 8; lxxxiv. 12; Prov. xvi. 20; Isa. xxx. 18; Jer. xvii. 7; Rom. ix. 33; x. 11; 1 Pet. ii. 6

---

kingdom; in consequence of which he sent his apostles throughout the habitable globe to preach the Gospel to every man.

Verse 9. *Thou shalt break them with a rod of iron*] This may refer to the *Jewish nation*, whose final rejection of the Gospel was foreseen, and in whose place the *Gentiles* or *heathen* were brought into the Church of Christ. They were dispossessed of their land, their *city* was razed to its foundations, their *temple* was burnt with fire, and upwards of a *million of themselves* were slaughtered by the Romans! So heavily did the *iron rod* of God's judgments fall upon them for their obstinate unbelief.

Verse 10. *Be wise—O ye kings*] An exhortation of the Gospel to the rulers of all kingdoms, nations, and states, to whom it may be sent. All these should listen to its maxims, be governed by its precepts, and rule their subjects according to its dictates.

Be instructed, ye judges] Rather, *Be ye reformed*—cast away all your idolatrous maxims; and receive the Gospel as the law, or the *basis* of the law, of the land.

Verse 11. *Serve the Lord with fear*] A general direction to all men. *Fear God* with that *reverence* which is due to his supreme *majesty*. *Serve* him as *subjects* should their *sovereign*, and as *servants* should their *master*.

Rejoice with trembling.] If ye serve God aright, ye cannot but be *happy;* but let a *continual filial fear* moderate all your joys. Ye must all stand at last before the judgment-seat of God; watch, pray, believe, work, and keep humble.

Verse 12. *Kiss the Son, lest he be angry*] It is remarkable that the word *son* (בר *bar*, a Chaldee word) is not found in any of the versions except the *Syriac*, nor indeed any thing equivalent to it.

The *Chaldee*, *Vulgate*, *Septuagint*, *Arabic*, and *Æthiopic*, have a term which signifies *doctrine* or *discipline:* "Embrace discipline, lest the Lord be angry with you," &c. This is a remarkable case, and especially that in so pure a piece of Hebrew as this poem is, a *Chaldee* word should have been found; בר *bar*, instead of בן *ben*, which adds nothing to the strength of the expression or the elegance of the poetry. I know it is supposed that בר *bar* is also pure Hebrew, as well as Chaldee; but as it is taken in the former language in the sense of *purifying*, the versions probably understood it so here. *Embrace that which is pure;* namely, the *doctrine* of God.

As all *judgment* is committed to the *Son*, the Jews and others are exhorted to *submit* to him, to be *reconciled* to him, that they might be received into his family, and be acknowledged as his adopted children. Kissing was the token of *subjection* and *friendship*.

Is kindled but a little.] The *slightest stroke* of the *iron rod* of Christ's justice is sufficient to break in pieces a whole rebel world. Every sinner, not yet reconciled to God through Christ, should receive this as a most solemn warning.

Blessed are *all they*] He is only the *inexorable Judge* to them who harden their hearts in their iniquity, and will not come unto him that they may have life. But all they who *trust in him*—who repose all their trust and confidence in him as their *atonement* and as their *Lord*, shall be blessed with *innumerable blessings*. For as the word is the same here as in Psa. i. 1, אשרי *ashrey*, it may be translated the same. "O the blessedness of all them who trust in him!"

This Psalm is remarkable, not only for its subject—the future kingdom of the *Messiah*, its *rise*, *opposition*, and *gradual extent*, but also for the elegant *change* of *person*. In the first verse the *prophet* speaks; in the third, the *adversaries;* in the fourth and fifth, the *prophet answers;* in the sixth, *Jehovah* speaks; in the seventh, the *Messiah;* in the eighth and ninth, *Jehovah answers;* and in the tenth to the twelfth, the *prophet* exhorts the *opponents* to submission and obedience.—Dr. *A. Bayly*.

ANALYSIS OF THE SECOND PSALM

The prime subject of this Psalm is CHRIST; the type, DAVID. The persons we are chiefly to reflect on are *three*, and which make *three parts* of the Psalm: I. The enemies of Christ; II. Christ the Lord; III. The princes and judges of the earth.

I. The enemies of Christ are great men, who are described here, partly from their *wickedness*, and partly from their *weakness*.

First, Their *wickedness* is apparent. 1. They *furiously rage.* 2. They *tumultuously assemble.* 3. They *set themselves*—stand up, *and take counsel, against the Lord and against his anointed.* 4. They encourage themselves in mischief, saying, "Come, and let us cast away their cords from us." All which is sharpened by the interrogatory *Why?*

Secondly, Their *weakness;* in that they shall never be able to bring their plots and conspiracies against Christ and his kingdom to pass; for, 1. What *they imagine is but a vain thing.* 2. "He that sits in heaven shall laugh, and have them in derision." 3. "He shall speak unto them in his wrath, and vex them in his sore displeasure." 4. For, maugre all their plots, "God hath set up his king upon his holy hill of Zion."

II. At ver. 6 begins the exaltation of Christ

to his kingdom, which is the SECOND PART of the Psalm; in which the prophet, by a προσωποποιϊα, or personification, brings in God the Father speaking, and the Son answering.

First, The words of the Father are, "I have set my king;" where we have the inauguration of Christ, or his vocation to the crown.

Secondly, The answer of the Son, "I will preach the law;" which sets forth his willing obedience to publish and proclaim the laws of the kingdom; of which the chief is, "Thou art my Son, this day have I begotten thee."

Thirdly, The reply of the Father, containing the reward that Christ was to have upon the publication of the Gospel; which was, 1. An addition to his empire by the conversion and accession of the Gentiles: "Ask of me, and I will give thee the heathen for thine inheritance," &c. 2. And the confusion of his enemies: "Thou shalt break them," who would not have thee reign, that did rage and stand up against thee, "with a rod of iron; and break them in pieces as a potter's vessel."

III. In the *third part* the prophet descends to his exhortation and admonition, and that very aptly; for, Is Christ a King? Is he a King anointed by God? Is he a great King, a powerful King? So great that the nations are his subjects? So powerful that he will break and batter to pieces his enemies? Besides, Is he the only begotten Son of God? Be wise, therefore, O ye kings. In this we find,

First, The persons to whom this *caveat* is given: *kings* and *judges*.

Secondly, What they are taught. 1. To *know* their duty: "Be wise; be learned." 2. To *do* their duty: "Serve the Lord with fear; rejoice with trembling; kiss the Son."

Thirdly, The time when this is to be done; even *now*. The reason double: 1. Drawn from his wrath, and the consequent punishment: "Lest he be angry, and ye perish from the right way, when his wrath is kindled but a little." 2. From the happy condition of those who learn to know, and fear, and serve, and adore him: "Blessed are all they that put their trust in him." There must be no delay; this is the time of wrath, and the day of salvation.

PSALM III

David complains, in great distress, of the number of his enemies, and the reproaches they cast on him, as one forsaken of God, 1, 2; *is confident, notwithstanding, that God will be his protector*, 3; *mentions his prayers and supplications, and how God heard him*, 4, 5; *derides the impotent malice of his adversaries, and foretells their destruction*, 6, 7; *and ascribes salvation to God*, 8.

A Psalm of David, [a]when he fled from Absalom his son

A. M. 2981 B. C. 1023 Anno Davidis, Regis Israelitarum, 33

LORD, [b]how are they increased that trouble me? many *are*
they that rise up against me.
2 Many *there be* which say of
my soul, [c]*There is* no help for
him in God. Selah.
3 But thou, O LORD, *art* [d]a
shield [e]for me; my glory, and
[f]the lifter up of mine head.

[a]2 Sam. xv., xvi., xvii., xviii.——[b]2 Sam. xv. 12; xvi. 15 [c]2 Sam. xvi. 8; Psa. lxxi. 11

[d]Gen. xv. 1; Psa. xxviii. 7; cxix. 114——[e]Or, *about* [f]Psa. xxvii. 6

NOTES ON PSALM III

This is said to be *A Psalm of David, when he fled from Absalom his son.*] See the account, 2 Sam. xv. 1, &c. And David is supposed to have composed it when obliged to leave Jerusalem, passing by the mount of Olives, weeping, with his clothes rent, and with dust upon his head. This Psalm is suitable enough to these circumstances; and they mutually cast light on each other. If the inscription be correct, this Psalm is a proof that the Psalms are not placed in any chronological order.

The word *Psalm*, מזמור *mizmor*, comes from זמר *zamar*, to *cut*, whether that means to *cut into syllables*, for the purpose of its being adapted to musical tones, or whether its being *cut on wood*, &c., for the direction of the singers; what we would call a Psalm in *score*. This last opinion, however, seems too technical.

Verse 1. *Lord, how are they increased that trouble me?*] We are told that *the hearts of all Israel went after Absalom*, 2 Sam. xv. 13; and David is astonished to find such a *sudden* and *general* revolt. Not only the *common people*, but his *counsellors* also, and many of his chief *captains*. How *publicly* does God take vengeance for the sins which David committed so *privately!* In the horrible rebellion of Absalom we see the adultery of Bath-sheba, and the murder of Uriah. Now the words of Nathan begin to be fulfilled: "The sword shall not depart from thy house."

Verse 2. *No help for him in God.*] These were some of the *reproaches* of his enemies, *Shimei* and others: "He is now down, and he shall never be able to rise. God alone can save him from these his enemies; but God has visibly cast him off." These reproaches deeply affected his heart; and he mentions them with that *note* which so frequently occurs in the Psalms, and which occurs here for the *first* time, סלה *selah*. Much has been said on the meaning of this word; and we have nothing but conjecture to guide us. The *Septuagint* always translate it by Διαψαλμα *diapsalma*, "a pause in the Psalm." The *Chaldee* sometimes translates it by לעלמין *lealmin*, "for ever." The rest of the versions leave it unnoticed. It either comes

A. M. 2981 B. C. 1023 Anno Davidis, Regis Israelitarum, 33

4 I cried unto the LORD with
my voice, and [g]he heard me out
of his [h]holy hill. Selah.
5 [i]I laid me down and slept;
I awaked; for the LORD sustained me.
6 [k]I will not be afraid of ten thousands of
people, that have set *themselves* against me
round about.

7 Arise, O LORD; save me,
O my God: [l]for thou hast smitten all mine enemies *upon* the
cheek bone; thou hast broken
the teeth of the ungodly.
8 [m]Salvation *belongeth* unto the
LORD: thy blessing *is* upon thy people.
Selah.

---

[g]Psalm xxxiv. 4——[h]Psalm ii. 6; xliii. 3; xcix. 9——[i]Leviticus xxvi. 6; Psalm iv. 8; Prov. iii. 24——[k]Psalm xxvii. 3——[l]Job xvi. 10; xxix. 17; Psalm lviii. 6; Lamentations iii. 30——[m]Proverbs xxi. 31; Isaiah xliii. 11; Jeremiah iii. 23; Hosea xiii. 4; Jonah ii. 9; Rev. vii. 10; xix. 1

---

from סל *sal*, to *raise* or *elevate*, and may denote a particular *elevation* in the voices of the performers, which is very observable in the Jewish singing to the present day; or it may come from סלה *salah*, to *strew* or *spread out*, intimating that the subject to which the word is attached should be *spread out*, *meditated on*, and *attentively considered* by the reader. *Fenwick*, *Parkhurst*, and *Dodd*, contend for this meaning; and think "it confirmed by Psa. ix. 16, where the word *higgaion* is put before *selah*, at the end of the verse." Now higgaion certainly signifies *meditation*, or a fit subject for meditation; and so shows *selah* to be really a *nota bene*, *attend to* or *mind this*.

Verse 3. *Thou, O Lord*, art *a shield*] As a *shield* covers and defends the body from the strokes of an adversary, so wilt thou cover and defend me from them that rise up against me.

The lifter up of mine head.] Thou wilt restore me to the *state* from which my enemies have cast me down. This is the meaning of the phrase; and this he speaks *prophetically*. He was satisfied that the deliverance would take place, hence his confidence in prayer; so that we find him, with comparative unconcern, laying himself down in his bed, expecting the sure protection of the Almighty.

Verse 4. *I cried unto the Lord with my voice*] He was exposed to much danger, and therefore he had need of *fervour*.

He heard me] Notwithstanding my enemies said, and my friends feared, that there *was no help for me in my God;* yet *he heard me out of his holy hill. Selah: mark this*, and take encouragement from it. God never forsakes those who trust in him. He never shuts out the prayer of the distressed.

Verse 5. *I laid me down and slept*] He who knows that he has God for his Protector may go quietly and confidently to his bed, not fearing the *violence of the fire*, the *edge of the sword*, the *designs of wicked men*, nor the *influence of malevolent spirits*.

I awaked] Though humanly speaking there was reason to fear I should have been murdered in my bed, as my most confidential servants had been corrupted by my rebellious son; yet God, my shield, protected me. I both slept and awaked; and my life is still whole in me.

Verse 6. *I will not be afraid of ten thousands*] Strength and numbers are nothing against the omnipotence of God. He who has made God his refuge certainly has no cause to fear.

Verse 7. *Arise, O Lord*] Though he knew that God had undertaken his defence, yet he knew that his continued protection depended on his continual prayer and faith. God never ceases to help as long as we pray. When our hands hang down, and we restrain prayer before him, we may then justly fear that our enemies will prevail.

Thou hast smitten] That is, Thou *wilt* smite. He speaks in full confidence of God's interference; and knows as surely that he shall have the victory, as if he had it already. *Breaking the jaws* and *the teeth* are expressions which imply, confounding and destroying an adversary; treating him with extreme contempt; *using him like a dog*, &c.

Verse 8. *Salvation* belongeth *unto the Lord*] It is God alone who saves. He is the fountain whence help and salvation come; and to him alone the praise of all saved souls is due. His blessing is upon his people. Those who are saved from the power and the guilt of sin are his people. His mercy saved them; and it is by his *blessing* being continually upon them, that they continue to be saved. David adds his *selah* here also: *mark this!* 1. Salvation comes from God. 2. Salvation is continued by God. These are great truths; *mark them!*

Analysis of the Third Psalm

The occasion of this Psalm was Absalom's rebellion. David being deserted by his subjects, railed on by Shimei, pursued for his crown and life by his ungracious son, and not finding to whom to make his moan, betakes himself to his God; and before him he expostulates his wrong, confesses his faith, and makes his prayer.

There are *three* strains of this accurate Psalm: I. His complaint. II. The confession of his confidence. III. His petition.

I. He begins with a sad and bitter complaint, amplified,

1. By the number and multitude of his enemies. They were many, very many; they were multiplied and increased: "All Israel was gathered together from Dan to Beer-sheba, as the sand of the sea for multitude;" 2 Sam. xvii. 11.

2. From their malice they came together to do him mischief. They rose up, not *for* him, but *against* him; not to *honour*, but to *trouble* him; not to *defend* him as they ought, but to take away his *crown* and *life;* 2 Sam. xvii. 2.

3. From their insults and sarcasm. It was not *Shimei* only, but many, that said it: "Many—say there is no help for him in his God."

II. The *second* part of the Psalm sets forth David's confidence:—

1. To their *multitude*, he opposeth ONE GOD. But THOU, O LORD!

2. To their malicious insurrection, Jehovah;

who, he believed, 1. Would be a *buckler* to receive all the arrows shot against him. 2. His *glory*, to honour, though they went about to dishonour, him. 3. The *lifter up of his head*, which they wished to lay low enough.

3. To their vain boast of desertion, *There is no help for him in his God*, he opposeth his own experience, "I cried unto the Lord, and he heard me."

4. By whose protection being sustained and secured, he deposes all care and fear, all anxiety and distraction. 1. He sleeps with a quiet mind: "I laid me down and slept; I awoke." 2. He sings a *requiem:* "I will not be afraid of ten thousands of the people, that have set themselves against me round about."

III. In the close, or *third* part, he petitions and prays, notwithstanding his security: "Arise, O Lord; save me, O my God!" To move God to grant his request, he thankfully reminds him of what he had done before:—

1. "Arise and save me, for thou hast smitten all mine enemies." Thou art the same God: do then the same work; be as good to thy servant as ever thou hast been.

2. He inserts an excellent maxim: *Salvation* belongeth *unto the Lord*. As if he had said, It is thy property and prerogative to save. If thou save not, I expect it from none other.

3. Lastly, as a good king should, in his prayers he remembers his subjects. He prayed for those who were using him despitefully: *Thy blessing be upon thy people!* To the same sense, *Coverdale*, in his translation.

PSALM IV

David prays to be heard, 1; *expostulates with the ungodly,* 2; *exhorts them to turn to God, and make their peace with him,* 3–5; *shows the vain pursuits of men in search of happiness, which he asserts exists only in the approbation of God,* 6, 7; *commends himself to the Lord, and then quietly takes his repose,* 8.

To the [a]chief Musician on Neginoth, A Psalm of David

A. M. cir. 2981
B. C. cir. 1023
Anno Davidis, Regis Israelitarum, 33

HEAR me when I call, O God
of my righteousness: thou
hast enlarged me *when I was* in
distress; [b]have mercy upon me,
and hear my prayer.

2 O ye sons of men, how long
will ye turn my glory into shame?
how long will ye love vanity, *and*
seek after leasing? Selah.
3 But know that the [c]LORD hath set
apart him that is godly for himself: the

A. M. cir. 2981
B. C. cir. 1023
Anno Davidis, Regis Israelitarum, 33

[a]Or, *overseer*, Hab. iii. 19——[b]Or, *be gracious unto me*——[c]2 Tim. ii. 19; 2 Pet. ii. 9

NOTES ON PSALM IV

This Psalm seems to have been composed on the same occasion with the preceding, viz., *Absalom's rebellion.* It appears to have been an *evening* hymn, sung by David and his company previously to their going to rest. It is inscribed *to the chief Musician upon Neginoth*, למנצח בנגינות *lamnatstseach binginoth.* Probably the first word comes from נצח *natsach*, to be *over*, or *preside;* and may refer to the *precentor* in the choir. Some suppose that it refers to the *Lord Jesus*, who is the Supreme Governor, or victorious Person; the Giver of *victory. Neginoth* seems to come from נגן *nagan*, to strike; and probably may signify some such instruments as the *cymbal, drum,* &c., and *stringed instruments* in general. But there is no certainty in these things. What they *mean*, or what they *were*, is known to no man.

Verse 1. *Hear me when I call*] No man has a right to expect God to hear him if he do not call. Indeed, how shall he be heard if he *speak* not? There are multitudes who expect the blessings of God as confidently as if they had prayed for them most fervently; and yet such people pray not at all!

God of my righteousness] Whatever pardon, peace, holiness, or truth I possess, has come entirely from thyself. Thou art the *God of my salvation*, as thou art the *God of my life.*

Thou hast enlarged me] I was in *prison;* and thou hast brought me forth *abroad. Have mercy on me*—continue to act in the same way. I shall always *need* thy *help;* I shall never *deserve* to have it; let me have it in the way of *mere mercy*, as thou hast hitherto done.

Verse 2. *O ye sons of men*] בני איש *beney ish*, ye *powerful men*—ye who are now at the head of affairs, or who are leaders of the multitude.

Love vanity] The poor, empty, shallow-brained, pretty-faced Absalom; whose prospects are all *vain*, and whose promises are all *empty!*

Seek after leasing?] This is a Saxon word, from **leasunge**, *falsehood*, from **leasan**, *to lie. Cardmarden* has adopted this word in his translation, Rouen, 1566. It is in none of the Bibles *previously* to that time, nor in any *after*, as far as my own collection affords me evidence; and appears to have been borrowed by King James's translators from the above.

Selah.] Mark this! See what the end will be!

Verse 3. *The Lord hath set apart him that is godly*] חסיד *chasid*, the pious, benevolent man. He has marked such, and put them aside as his own property. "This merciful man, this feeling, tender-hearted man, is my own property; touch not a hair of his head!"

A. M. cir. 2981 B. C. cir. 1023 Anno Davidis, Regis Israelitarum, 33

LORD will hear when I call unto
him.
4 [d]Stand in awe, and sin not:
[e]commune with your own heart
upon your bed, and be still. Selah.
5 Offer [f]the sacrifices of righteousness, and
[g]put your trust in the LORD.
6 *There be* many that say, Who will show us
any good? [h]LORD, lift thou up the
light of thy countenance upon us.
7 Thou hast put [i]gladness in
my heart, more than in the time
that their corn and their wine increased.
8 [k]I will both lay me down in peace, and
sleep: [l]for thou, LORD, only makest me dwell
in safety.

[d]Eph. iv. 26——[e]Psalm lxxvii. 6; 2 Cor. xiii. 5——[f]Deut. xxxiii. 19; Psa. l. 14; li. 19; 2 Sam. xv. 12——[g]Psa. xxxvii. 3; lxii. 8

[h]Num. vi. 26; Psa. lxxx. 3, 7, 19; cxix. 135——[i]Isa. ix. 3——[k]Job xi. 18, 19; Psa. iii. 5——[l]Lev. xxv. 18, 19; xxvi. 5; Deut. xii. 10

Verse 4. *Stand in awe, and sin not*] The *Septuagint*, which is copied by St. *Paul*, Eph. iv. 26, translate this clause, Οργιζεσθε, και μη ἁμαρτανετε; *Be ye angry, and sin not.* The *Vulgate*, *Syriac*, *Æthiopic*, and *Arabic*, give the same reading; and thus the original רגזו *rigzu* might be translated: If ye be angry, and if ye think ye have cause to be angry; do not let your disaffection carry you to acts of rebellion against both God and your king. Consider the subject deeply before you attempt to act. Do nothing rashly; do not justify one evil act by another: sleep on the business; converse *with your own heart upon your bed;* consult your pillow.

And be still.] ודמו *vedommu*, "and be *dumb*." Hold your peace; fear lest ye be found fighting against God. *Selah. Mark this!*

Verse 5. *Offer the sacrifices of righteousness*] Do not attempt to offer a sacrifice to God for prosperity in your present rebellious conduct. Such a sacrifice would be a sin. Turn to God from whom you have revolted; and offer to him a *righteous sacrifice*, such as the *law* prescribes, and such as *he* can receive. Let all hear and consider this saying. No *sacrifice*—no performance of religious duty, will avail any man, if his heart be not right with God. And let all know, that under the Gospel dispensation no sacrifice of any kind will be received but through the all-atoning sacrifice made by Christ.

Because of sin, justice has *stopped every man's mouth;* so that none can have access to God, but through the Mediator. By him only can the *mouth* of a sinner be *opened* to plead with God. Hear this, ye who trust in *yourselves*, and hope for heaven without either faith or dependence on the vicarious sacrifice of Christ.

Verse 6. *Who will show us* any *good?*] This is not a fair translation. The word *any* is not in the text, nor any thing equivalent to it; and not a few have quoted *it*, and preached upon the text, placing the principal emphasis on this illegitimate word.

The place is sufficiently emphatic without this. There are *multitudes who say, Who will show us good?* Man wants *good;* he hates *evil* as evil, because he has *pain, suffering*, and *death* through it; and he wishes to find that *supreme good* which will content his heart, and save him from evil. But men mistake this good. They look for a good that is to gratify their *passions;* they have no notion of any happiness that does not come to them through the *medium of their senses*. Therefore they reject *spiritual good*, and they reject the Supreme God, by whom alone all the powers of the soul of man can be gratified.

Lift thou up the light of thy countenance] This alone, the *light of thy countenance*—thy peace and *approbation*, constitute the *supreme good*. This is what we want, wish, and pray for. The *first* is the *wish* of the *worldling*, the *latter* the wish of the *godly*.

Verse 7. *Thou hast put gladness in my heart*] Thou hast given my soul what it wanted and wished for. I find now a happiness which earthly things could not produce. I have peace of conscience, and joy in the Holy Ghost; such inward happiness as they cannot boast who have got the highest increase of *corn* and *wine;* those TWO THINGS in the abundance of which many suppose happiness to be found.

To *corn* and *wine* all the versions, except the *Chaldee*, add *oil;* for *corn, wine*, and *oil*, were considered the highest blessings of a temporal kind that man could possess.

Verse 8. *I will both lay me down in peace, and sleep*] Most men lie down, and most sleep, daily, for without *rest* and *sleep* life could not be preserved; but alas! how few lie down in *peace!* peace with their own consciences, and peace with God! David had then two great blessings, *rest* by *sleep*, and *peace* in his *soul*. He had a happy soul; and when he lay down on his bed, his body soon enjoyed its repose, as the *conscience* was in *peace*. And he had a *third* blessing, a *confidence* that he should sleep in *safety*. And it was so. No fearful *dreams* disturbed his repose, for he had a mind *tranquillized* by the peace of God. As to his *body*, that enjoyed its due rest, for he had not overloaded *nature* either with *dainties* or *superfluities*. Reader, are not many of thy sleepless hours to be attributed to thy disordered soul—to a sense of guilt on thy conscience, or to a fear of death and hell?

Pray incessantly till thou get the *light of God's countenance*, till his Spirit bear witness with thine that thou art a child of God. Then thy repose will do thee good: and even in thy sleep thy happy soul will be getting forward to heaven.

ANALYSIS OF THE FOURTH PSALM

There are THREE parts in this Psalm:—

I. An entrance, or petition for audience, ver. 1.

II. An *apostrophe* to his enemies, which is, 1. Reprehensive, ver. 2, 3. 2. Admonitory, ver. 4, 5.

III. A *petition* for himself and God's people, ver. 6, 7, 8.

I. He proposes his request and suit for audience. "Hear me when I call;" and this he founds on *four* arguments: 1. God has *promised* to hear me when I call: "Call upon me in trouble, and I will hear thee." I call; hear me, therefore, when I call. 2. His own *innocence:* "Hear me, O God of my righteousness." 3. He requests no more than what God had done for him at other times: *Thou hast enlarged me in trouble*, and why not now? 4. It was *mercy* and *favour* to answer him then; it will be the same to do it again: "Have mercy on me, and hear."

II. His *petition* being thus proposed and ended, he proceeds to the *doctrinal* part; and, turning himself to his enemies, 1. He sharply reproves them; 2. Then warns them, and gives them good counsel.

1. He turns his speech from God to men; the chief but the worst of men. בני איש *beney ish*, "ye eminent men." Not plebeians, but nobles. The charge he lays to them, 1. They "turned his glory into shame." They endeavoured to dishonour him whom God had called and anointed to the kingdom. 2. "They loved vanity." A vain attempt they were in love with. 3. "They sought after falsity." They pursued that which would deceive them; they would find at last that treachery and iniquity lied to itself. 4. That this charge might have the more weight, he figures it with a stinging interrogation, *How long?* Their sin had *malice* and *pertinacity* in it; and he asks them *how long* they intended to act thus.

And that they might, if possible, be drawn from their attempts, he sends them a *noverint, know ye,* which has two clauses: 1. Let them *know* that God hath set apart him that is godly for himself. 2. That God *will hear*, when either he or any good man calls upon him.

2. The reproof being ended, he gives them *good counsel:—*

1. That though they be *angry*, they ought not to let the sun go down upon their wrath.

2. That they *commune with their own hearts* —their conscience. That they do this on their beds, when secluded from all company, when passion and self-interest did not rule; and then they would be the better able to judge whether they were not in an *error*, whether their anger were not *causeless*, and their persecution *unjust?*

3. That they *offer the sacrifice of righteousness*—that they serve and worship God with an honest, sincere, and contrite heart.

4. That they *put their trust in the Lord;* trusting no more to their lies, nor loving their vanities, but relying on God's promises.

III. The *third* part begins with this question, *Who will show us any good?* 1. Who will show us that good which will make us happy? To which David, in effect, returns this answer, that it is not *bona animi*, intellectual gifts; nor *bona fortunæ*, earthly blessings; nor *bona corporis*, corporeal endowments: but *the light of God's countenance.* 2. Therefore he prefers his petition: "Lord, lift thou up the light of thy countenance upon us." God's countenance is his *grace*, his *favour*, his *love;* and the *light of his countenance*, the *exhibition* and *expression* of this grace, favour, and love; in which alone lies all the happiness of man. Of this David expresses two effects, *gladness* and *security:—*

1. *Gladness* and *joy* far beyond that which may be had from any temporal blessings: "Thou hast put gladness in my heart more than in the time that their corn, and wine, and oil increased; gladness beyond the joy in harvest; and this joy is from the *light of God's countenance. Thou puttest.* THOU, by way of eminence.

2. *Security*, expressed under the metaphor of *sleep:* "I will lay me down in peace, and sleep;" just as in a *time of peace*, as if there were no *war* nor preparation for *battle.*

3. To which he adds the reason: "For thou, Lord, alone makest me to dwell in safety." I am safe, because I enjoy the light of thy countenance.

PSALM V

David continues instant in prayer, 1, 2; *makes early application to God,* 3; *and shows the hatred which God bears to the workers of iniquity,* 4–6. *His determination to worship God, and to implore direction and support,* 7, 8. *He points out the wickedness of his enemies,* 9, *and the destruction they may expect,* 10; *and then shows the happiness of those who trust in the Lord,* 11, 12.

To the chief Musician upon Nehiloth, A Psalm of David

GIVE ear to my words, O LORD, consider my meditation.

2 Hearken unto the [a]voice of my cry, my King, and my God: [b]for unto thee will I pray.

[a]Psa. iii. 4

[b]Psa. lxv. 2

NOTES ON PSALM V

This Psalm is inscribed *to the chief Musician upon Nehiloth, A Psalm of David.* As *neginoth* may signify all kinds of instruments struck with a *plectrum*, stringed instruments, those like the drum, cymbals, &c.; so *nechiloth*, from חל *chal*, to be *hollow*, to *bore through*, may signify any kind of *wind* instruments, such as the horn, trumpet, flute, &c. See on the title to the preceding Psalm. The *Septuagint* have, Εις το τελος, ὑπερ της κληρονομουσης, "In favour of her who obtains the inheritance." The *Vulgate* and *Arabic* have a similar reading. The word נחילות *nechiloth* they have derived from נחל *nachal*, to *inherit*. This may either refer to the Israelites who obtained the inheritance of the promised land, or to the Church of Christ which obtains through him, by faith and prayer, the inheritance among the saints in light. This Psalm is, especially, for the whole Church of God.

Verse 1. *Give ear to my words*] This is properly a *morning hymn*, as the preceding was

3 [c]My voice shalt thou hear in the morning,
O LORD; in the morning will I direct *my*
prayer unto thee, and will look up.
4 For thou *art* not a God that hath pleasure
in wickedness: neither shall evil dwell with
thee.
5 [d]The foolish shall not stand [e]in thy sight:
thou hatest all workers of iniquity.
6 [f]Thou shalt destroy them that speak leasing:
[g]the LORD will abhor [h]the bloody and deceitful man.
7 But as for me, I will come *into* thy house

[c]Psa. xxx. 5; lxxxviii. 13; cxxx. 6——[d]Hab. i. 13——[e]Heb. *before thine eyes*

[f]Rev. xxi. 8——[g]Psa. lv. 23——[h]Heb. *the man of blood and deceit*

an *evening hymn.* We have seen from the conclusion of the last Psalm that David was very happy, and lay down and slept in the peace and love of his God. When he opens his eyes on the following morning, he not only remembers but feels the happiness of which he spoke; and with his first recollections he *meditates* on the goodness and mercy of God, and the glorious state of salvation into which he had been brought. He calls on God *to give ear to his words;* probably words of God's *promises* which he had been pleading.

Verse 2. *Hearken unto the voice of my cry*] We may easily find the process through which David's mind was now passing: 1. We have seen from the preceding Psalm that he lay down in a very happy frame of mind, and that he had enjoyed profound repose. 2. As soon as he awakes in the morning, his heart, having a right direction, resumes its work. 3. He meditates on God's goodness; and on his own happy state, though pursued by enemies, and only safe as long as God preserved him by an almighty hand and especial providence. 4. This shows him the need he has of the *continual protection* of the Most High; and therefore he begins to form his *meditation* and the *desires* of his heart into *words*, to which he entreats the Lord to *give ear.* 5. As he was accustomed to have answers to his prayers, he feels the necessity of being *importunate*, and therefore lifts up his *voice.* 6. Seeing the *workers of iniquity, liars,* and *blood-thirsty* men strong to accomplish their own purposes in the destruction of the godly, he becomes greatly in earnest, and *cries* unto the Lord: "Hearken unto the voice of my cry." 7. He knows that, in order to have a *right answer*, he must have a proper *disposition of mind.* He feels his subjection to the supreme authority of the Most High, and is ready to *do* his *will* and *obey* his *laws;* therefore he prays to God as his *King:* "Hearken, my King and my God." I have not only taken thee for my GOD, to *save, defend*, and make me *happy;* but I have taken thee for my KING, to *govern, direct*, and *rule* over me. 8. Knowing the necessity and success of prayer, he purposes to continue in the spirit and practice of it: "Unto thee will I pray." R. S. Jarchi gives this a pretty and pious turn: "When I have power to pray, and to ask for the things I need, then, O Lord, give ear to my *words;* but when I have no power to plead with thee, and fear seizes on my heart, then, O Lord, consider my *meditation!*"

Verse 3. *My voice shalt thou hear in the morning*] We find from this that he had not prayed in vain. He had received a blessed answer; God had *lifted upon him the light of his countenance;* and he therefore determines to be an early applicant at the throne of grace: "My voice shalt thou hear in the morning." He finds it good to *begin* the day with God; to let Divine things occupy the first place in his waking thoughts; as that which first occupies the mind on awaking is most likely to keep possession of the *heart* all the day through.

In the morning will I direct my prayer] Here seems to be a metaphor taken from an archer. He *sees* his *mark;* puts his *arrow in his bow; directs* his shaft to the mark, i. e., takes his aim; lets fly; and then *looks up*, to see if he have hit his mark. Prayers that have a right aim, will have a prompt answer; and he who sends up his petitions to God through Christ, from a warm, affectionate heart, may confidently *look up* for an answer, for it will come. If an immediate answer be not given, let not the upright heart suppose that the prayer is not heard. It has found its way to the throne; and *there* it is registered.

Verse 4. *Neither shall evil dwell with thee.*] As thou art holy, so thou hast pleasure only in holiness; and as to *evil men*, they shall never enter into thy glory; לא יגרך רע *lo yegurecha ra*, "the evil man shall not even *sojourn* with thee."

Verse 5. *The foolish shall not stand*] He is a fool and a madman who is running himself out of breath for no prize, who is fighting against the Almighty; this every wicked man does; therefore is every *wicked* man a *fool* and a *madman.*

Thou hatest all workers of iniquity] Some sin *now* and *then*, others *generally;* some *constantly*, and some *labour* in it with all their might. These are the WORKERS *of iniquity.* Such even the God of infinite love and mercy *hates.* Alas! what a *portion* have the workers *of iniquity!* the hatred of God Almighty!

Verse 6. *That speak leasing*] Falsity, from the Anglo-Saxon **leasunge** *leasunge, a lie, falsity, deceit;* from **leas** *leas, lie*, which is from the verb **leasian** *leasian*, to *lie.* See on Psa. iv. 2.

The Lord will abhor the bloody and deceitful man.] איש דמים *ish damim*, the *man of bloods;* for he who has the *spirit* of a murderer, will rarely end with *one* bloodshedding. So the Jews, who clamoured for the blood of our Lord, added to that, as far and as long as they could, the blood of his disciples.

Verse 7. *In the multitude of thy mercy*] David considered it an inexpressible privilege to be permitted to attend *public worship;* and he knew that it was only through the *multitude of God's mercy* that he, or any man else, could enjoy such a privilege. He knew farther that, from the *multitude of this mercy*, he might receive *innumerable blessings* in his house. In this spirit, and with this dependence, he went to the house of the Lord. He who takes David's views of this subject will never, willingly, be absent from the means of grace.

in the multitude of thy mercy: *and* in thy
fear will I worship [i]toward [k]thy holy temple.
8 [l]Lead me, O LORD, in thy righteousness,
because of [m]mine enemies; make [n]thy way
straight before my face.
9 For *there is* no [o]faithfulness [p]in their
mouth; their inward part *is* [q]very wickedness;
[r]their throat *is* an open sepulchre; [s]they flatter with their tongue.
10 [t]Destroy thou them, O God; [u]let them
fall [v]by their own counsels; cast them out
in the multitude of their transgressions; for
they have rebelled against thee.
11 But let all those that put their trust in
thee [w]rejoice: let them ever shout for joy,
because [x]thou defendest them: let them also
that love thy name be joyful in thee.
12 For thou, LORD, [y]wilt bless the righteous; with favour wilt thou [z]compass him as
with a shield.

---

[i]1 Kings viii. 29, 30, 35, 38; Psa. xxviii. 2; cxxxii. 7; cxxxviii. 2——[k]Heb. *the temple of thy holiness*——[l]Psa. xxv. 5——[m]Heb. *those which observe me;* Psa. xxvii. 11 [n]Psa. xxv. 4; xxvii. 11——[o]Or, *steadfast*——[p]Heb. *in his mouth*, that is, *in the mouth of any of them*

[q]Heb. *wickedness*——[r]Luke xi. 44; Rom. iii. 13 [s]Psa. lxii. 4——[t]Or, *Make them guilty*——[u]2 Sam. xv. 31; xvii. 14, 23——[v]Or, *from their counsels*——[w]Isa. lxv. 13——[x]Heb. *thou coverest over*, or *protectest them* [y]Psa. cxv. 13——[z]Heb. *crown him*

In thy fear] Duly considering the infinite holiness of thy majesty, will I worship, אשתחוה *eshtachaveh*, will I bow and prostrate myself in the deepest self-abasement and humility.

Toward thy holy temple.] If David was the author of this Psalm, as is generally agreed, the *temple* was not built at this time: only the *tabernacle* then existed; and in the preceding clause he speaks of coming into the *house*, by which he must mean the *tabernacle.* But *temple* here may signify the *holy of holies*, *before* which David might prostrate himself while in the *house*, i. e., the court of the tabernacle. Even *in* the *house of God*, there is the *temple of God;* the *place* where the Divine Shechinah dwells. God was in Christ reconciling the world to himself. In him dwelt all the fulness of the Godhead bodily. In all ages and dispensations, Jesus was ever the *temple* where the Supreme Deity was met with and worshipped. The human nature of Jesus was the real temple of the Deity. Nowhere else can God be found.

Verse 8. *Lead me, O Lord, in thy righteousness*] When entered into the *house*, and prostrated before the *temple*, he knew that, unless God continued to *lead* and direct, he was not likely to profit even by such great advantages. We need God not only to bring us to his house, but to keep our feet while we are there.

Because of mine enemies] His conduct was marked; his enemies looked upon and watched him with an evil eye. They would have been glad of his *halting*, that they might have brought a reproach on the good cause which he had espoused. O how cautiously should those walk who make a profession of living to God, of knowing themselves to be in his favour, and of being delivered from all sin in this life!

Make thy way straight] Show me that I must go *right on;* and let thy light always shine on my path, that I may see how to proceed.

Verse 9. *No faithfulness in their mouth*] They make professions of friendship; but all is hollow and deceitful: "They flatter with their tongue."

Very wickedness] Their *heart* is full of all kinds of depravity.

Their throat is *an open sepulchre*] It is continually gaping for the dead; and sends forth effluvia destructive to the living. I fear that this is too true a picture of the whole human race; totally corrupt within, and abominable without. The heart is the *centre* and *spring* of this corruption; and the *words* and *actions* of men, which proceed from this source, will send out incessant streams of various impurity; and thus they continue till the grace of God changes and purifies the heart.

Verse 10. *Destroy thou them, O God*] All these apparently *imprecatory* declarations should be translated in the *future* tense, to which they belong; and which shows them to be *prophetic.* Thou WILT destroy them; thou WILT cast them out, &c.

Verse 11. *Let all those that put their trust in thee rejoice*] Such expressions as these should be translated in the same way, *declaratively* and *prophetically:* "All those who put their trust in thee SHALL rejoice,—SHALL ever shout for joy."

Verse 12. *For thou, Lord, wilt bless the righteous*] A righteous soul is a peculiar object of God's affectionate regards; and therefore will be a subject of continual blessing.

With favour] Literally, *Like a shield, thy favour will crown him.* God loves such; and this love is their defence. In all places, times, and circumstances, it will preserve them. "Keep yourselves," says the apostle, "in the love of God." He who abides in this love need not fear the face of any adversary. Thus ended the morning's devotion of this excellent man: a model by which every Christian may frame his own.

ANALYSIS OF THE FIFTH PSALM

This Psalm consists of FIVE *parts:*—

I. An introduction, in which he petitions to be heard; professes his earnestness about it, ver. 1, 2, 3; and his confidence of audience.

II. He delivers his petition, ver. 8; and the reason of it—his *enemies.*

III. These enemies he circumstantially describes, ver. 9.

IV. He prophesies that God will destroy them, ver. 10.

V. He prays for the Church, that God would preserve it, ver. 11, 12.

I. 1. In the entrance he prays very earnestly for audience; he shows that he meant to be serious and fervent in it; and he chooses a variety of *words* to express the *same thing*, which rise by degrees in the description: 1. He rises from *meditation;* 2. To *words;* 3. From words to a *voice;* 4. From a voice to a *cry.* Then he desires God, 1. To *consider.* 2. To *give ear.* 3.

To *hearken.* 1. He *considers,* who weighs the justice of the cause. 2. He *gives ear,* who would understand what the suppliant means. 3. He attends and *hearkens,* who intends to satisfy the petitioner.

2. The reasons he uses here to beget audience are very considerable:—

1. The relation that was between him and his God: "Thou art my King and my God."

2. That he would sue to none other: "To thee will I pray;" which he illustrates, 1. From the *time.* It is a morning petition. 2. It was a well composed and ordered prayer. 3. He would *lift up his eyes* with it; that is, have all his hope and expectation exercised in it. "My voice shalt thou hear in the morning; I will direct my prayer unto thee, and look up."

3. The *third* reason is taken from the nature of God: whom he *will* and whom he *will not hear.* 1. Persevering sinners God will not regard. 2. To the upright he is ready to look. The sinners whom God will not hear he thus describes: 1. Men who *delighted in wickedness, evil, foolish, workers of iniquity—liars—bloodthirsty* and *deceitful.* Now it was not likely that God should hear such: "For thou art not a God who hast pleasure in wickedness, neither shall evil dwell with thee." These it is said he *hated;* these he would *destroy;* these he did *abhor.* 2. But on the contrary, he who was *faithful;* who *relied on God;* who *feared the Lord;* who *attended the ordinances of his house;* who *worshipped towards his temple;* and who came, not *trusting to himself,* but in the *multitude of God's mercies;* him he would hear.

II. David, having petitioned for audience, and delivered the grounds of his confidence, brings forth his petition that his life may be *holy* and *innocent:*—

1. "Lead me in thy righteousness."

2. "Make thy way straight before me." For which he gives this reason: "Because of mine enemies."

III. These his enemies he circumstantially describes:—

1. By their MOUTH: "There is no faithfulness in their mouth."

2. By their HEART: "Their inward parts are very wickedness."

3. By their THROAT: "Their throat is an open sepulchre."

4. By their TONGUE: "They flatter with their tongue."

IV. Then he proceeds to prophesy against these enemies:—

1. God will *destroy them.*

2. They shall *fall by their own counsels.*

3. They shall *be cast out in the multitude of their transgressions.* For which predictions he gives this reason: *They are rebels.* For *they have rebelled against thee.* Rebels, not against *David,* but against *God.* They have not rejected *me,* but they have rejected *thee.*

V. The *conclusion* contains his prayer for God's people, whom he here describes: 1. They are *righteous.* 2. They *put their trust in God.* 3. They *love his name.*

And he prays for them, that, 1. They may be happy; that they may *shout for joy.* 2. They may be *joyful in God.*

And he expects an answer; because, 1. God *defends them.* 2. He will continue to *bless them.* 3. He will with his *favour compass them as with a shield.*

PSALM VI

This Psalm contains a deprecation of eternal vengeance, 1; *a petition to God for mercy,* 2. *This is enforced from a consideration of the psalmist's sufferings,* 3; *from that of the Divine mercy,* 4; *from that of the praise and glory which God would fail to receive if man were destroyed,* 5; *from that of his humiliation and contrition,* 6, 7. *Being successful in his supplication, he exults in God,* 8, 9; *and predicts the downfall of all his enemies,* 10.

I. DAY. EVENING PRAYER

To the chief Musician on Neginoth [a]upon [b]Sheminith, A Psalm of David

A. M. cir. 2970
B. C. cir. 1034
Davidis, Regis
Israelitarum,
cir. annum
22

O [c]LORD, rebuke me not in thine anger, neither chasten me in thy hot displeasure.

2 [d]Have mercy upon me, O LORD, for I *am* weak: O LORD, [e]heal me; for my bones are vexed.

3 My soul is also sore vexed: but thou, O LORD, [f]how long?

4 Return, O LORD, deliver my soul: O save me for thy mercies' sake.

---

[a]Or, *upon the eighth;* see 1 Chron. xv. 21——[b]Psa. xii. title

[c]Psa. xxxviii 1; Jer. x. 24; xlvi. 28——[d]Psa. xli. 4——[e]Hos. vi. 1——[f]Psa. xc. 13

NOTES ON PSALM VI

This Psalm has the following inscription: *To the chief Musician on Neginoth, upon Sheminith, A Psalm of David;* which the *Chaldee* translates, "To be sung on neginoth, a harp of eight strings." The various interpretations given to this inscription, both by ancients and moderns, show us that nothing is known concerning it. We have already seen that *neginoth* probably signifies all instruments which emitted sounds by *strokes,* or *stringed instruments* in general. This Psalm was to be accompanied with such instruments; but *one* of a particular kind is specified, viz., *sheminith;* so called from its having *eight* strings. The *chief musician* is directed to accompany the recital of this Psalm with the above instrument.

Verse 1. *O Lord, rebuke me not*] This Psalm, which is one of the *seven Penitential Psalms,* is

A. M. cir. 2970
B. C. cir. 1034
Davidis, Regis
Israelitarum,
cir. annum
22

5 [g]For in death *there is* no
remembrance of thee: in the
grave who shall give thee thanks?
6 I am weary with my groan-
ing; [h]all the night make I my bed to swim;
I water my couch with my tears.
7 [i]Mine eye is consumed because of
grief; it waxeth old because of all mine enemies.
8 [k]Depart from me, all ye
workers of iniquity; for the LORD
hath [l]heard the voice of my
weeping.
9 The LORD hath heard my supplication;
the LORD will receive my prayer.
10 Let all mine enemies be ashamed and
sore vexed: let them return *and* be ashamed
suddenly.

A. M. cir. 2970
B. C. cir. 1034
Davidis, Regis
Israelitarum,
cir. annum
22

---

[g]Psa. xxx. 9; lxxxviii. 11; cxv. 17; cxviii. 17; Isa. xxxviii. 18——[h]Or, *every night*——[i]Job xvii. 7; Psa. xxxi. 9; xxxviii. 10; lxxxviii. 9; Lam. v. 17——[k]Psa. cxix. 115; Matt. vii. 23; xxv. 41; Luke xiii. 27——[l]Psa. iii. 4

---

supposed to have been written during some grievous disease with which David was afflicted after his transgression with Bath-sheba. It argues a deep consciousness of sin, and apprehension of the just displeasure of God. It is the very language of a true penitent who is looking around for help, and who sees, as *Bishop Horne* well expresses it, "*above*, an angry God, ready to take vengeance; *beneath*, the fiery gulf, ready to receive him; *without*, a world in flames; *within*, the gnawing worm." Of all these, none so dreadful as an angry God; his wrath he particularly deprecates. God rebukes and chastens him, and he submits; but he prays not to be rebuked *in anger*, nor chastened in *hot displeasure*, because he knows that these must bring him down to total and final *destruction*.

Verse 2. *Have mercy*] I have no *merit*. I deserve all I feel and all I fear.

O Lord, heal me] No earthly physician can cure my malady. *Body* and *soul* are both diseased, and only God can help me.

I am weak] אמלל *umlal*. I am *exceedingly weak;* I cannot take nourishment, and my strength is exhausted.

My bones are vexed.] The disease hath entered into my bones.

Verse 3. *How long?*] How long shall I continue under this malady? How long will it be before thou speak peace to my troubled heart?

Verse 4. *Return, O Lord*] Once I had the light of thy countenance; by sin I have forfeited this; I have provoked thee to depart: O Lord, return! It is an awful thing to be obliged to say, *Return, O Lord*, for this supposes *backsliding;* and yet what a mercy it is that a *backslider may* RETURN to *God*, with the expectation that *God* will *return* to *him!*

Verse 5. *In death* there is *no remembrance of thee*] Man is to glorify thee on earth. The end for which he was born cannot be accomplished in the grave; heal my body, and heal my soul, that I may be rendered capable of loving and serving thee here below. A dead body in the grave can do no good to men, nor bring any glory to thy name!

Verse 7. *Mine eye is consumed*] עששה *asheshah*, is blasted, withered, sunk in my head.

Verse 8. *Depart from me, all ye workers of iniquity*] It seems that while he was suffering grievously through the disease, his enemies had insulted and mocked him;—upbraided him with his transgressions, not to increase his *penitence*, but to cast him into *despair*.

The Lord hath heard the voice of my weeping.] The Lord pitifully beheld the sorrows of his heart, and mercifully forgave his sins.

Verse 10. *Ashamed and sore vexed*] May they as deeply deplore their transgressions as I have done mine! May *they return;* may they be *suddenly converted!* The original will bear this meaning, and it is the most congenial to Christian principles.

ANALYSIS OF THE SIXTH PSALM

The parts of this Psalm are TWO, in general:—

I. A *petition* to God for himself, contained in the first *seven* verses.

II. The account of his *restoration*, contained in the *three* last.

I. The *petition* consists of *two* parts: 1. Deprecation of *evil;* 2. Petition for *good*.

1. He prays to God to *avert* his *wrath:* "O Lord, rebuke me not," &c.

2. He entreats to be partaker of *God's favour:* "Have mercy upon me," &c. 1. To his BODY: "Heal me, O Lord." 2. To his SOUL: "Deliver my soul: O save me!"

He enforces his petition by divers weighty reasons:

1. From the *quantity* and *degrees* of his *calamity*, which he shows to be great from the *effects*. 1. In *general;* he was in a languishing disease: "I am weak." 2. In *particular;* 1. Pains in his *bones:* "My bones are vexed." 2. Trouble in his *soul:* "My *soul* also is troubled."

2. From the *continuance* of it. It was a *long* disease; a lingering sickness; and he found no ease, no, not from his God. The pain I could the better bear if I had comfort from heaven. "But thou, O Lord, how long?" Long hast thou withdrawn the light of thy countenance from thy servant.

3. From the *consequence* that was likely to follow; *death*, and the *event* upon it. It is my intention to celebrate and praise thy name; the *living* only can do this: therefore, let *me live;* for *in death there is no remembrance of thee; in the grave who shall give thee thanks?*

4. And that he was brought now to the *gates of death*, he shows by *three* apparent *symptoms:* 1. *Sighs* and *groans*, which had almost broken his heart; the companions of a perpetual grief: "I am weary of my groaning." 2. The abundance of his *tears* had dried and wasted his body: "He made his bed to swim, and watered his couch with his tears." 3. His *eyes* also *melted away*, and *grew dim*, so that he seemed *old* before his time: "My eye is consumed because of grief; it waxeth old."

5. That which added to his sorrow was, *he had many ill-wishers* who insulted over him:

"Mine eye is waxen old because of mine enemies."

II. But at last receiving comfort and joy, he is enabled to look up; and then he turns upon his enemies, who were longing for his destruction: "Depart from me, all ye workers of iniquity."

He magnifies God's mercy; and mentions its manifestation *thrice* distinctly: 1. "The Lord hath heard the voice of my weeping." 2. "The Lord hath heard my supplication." 3. "The Lord will receive my prayer."

Then follows his prophetic declaration concerning them: 1. Shame and confusion to see their hope frustrated: "They shall be confounded." 2. Vexation, to see the object of their envy restored to health and prosperity: "They shall be sore vexed." 3. They shall return to their companions with *shame*, because their wishes and plots have miscarried. 4. He intimates that this shame and confusion shall be *speedy:* "They shall return, and be ashamed suddenly." Or, possibly, this may be a wish for their conversion, ישבו *yashubu*, let *them be* CONVERTED, רגע *raga, suddenly*, lest sudden destruction from the Lord should fall upon them. Thus the genuine follower of God prays, "That it may please thee to have mercy upon our enemies, persecutors, and slanderers; and to TURN their HEARTS." A *Christian* should take up every thing of this kind in a *Christian* sense.

PSALM VII

The psalmist prays against the malice of his enemies, 1, 2; *protests his own innocence*, 3–5; *prays to God that he would vindicate him, for the edification of his people*, 6–8; *prays against the wickedness of his enemies*, 9; *expresses strong confidence in God*, 10; *threatens transgressors with God's judgments*, 11–13; *shows the conduct and end of the ungodly*, 14–16; *and exults in the mercy and lovingkindness of his Maker*, 17.

[a]Shiggaion of David, which he sang unto the Lord, [b]concerning the [c]words of Cush the Benjamite

A. M. cir. 2943 B. C. cir. 1061 Sauli, Regis Israelitarum, cir. annum 35

O LORD my God, in thee do I put my trust: [d]save me from all them that persecute me, and deliver me:

2 [e]Lest he tear my soul like a lion, [f]rending *it* in pieces, while *there is* [g]none to deliver.

3 O LORD my God, [h]if I have done this; if there be [i]iniquity in my hands;

[a]Hab. iii. 1——[b]2 Samuel xvi.——[c]Or, *business*——[d]Psa. xxxi. 15

[e]Isa. xxxviii. 13——[f]Psa. l. 22——[g]Hebrew, *not a deliverer*——[h]2 Sam. xvi. 7, 8——[i]1 Sam. xxiv. 11

This Psalm is entitled, *Shiggaion of David, which he sang unto the Lord, concerning the words of Cush the Benjamite.* The word שגיון *shiggayon* comes from שגה *shagah*, to *wander*, a wandering song; i. e., a Psalm composed by David in his wanderings, when he was obliged to hide himself from the fury of Saul.

Bishop *Horsley* thinks it may have its name, a *wandering ode*, from its being in different parts, taking up different subjects, in different styles of composition. But he has sometimes thought that *shiggaion* might be an *unpremeditated* song; an *improviso.*

As to *Cush the Benjamite*, he is a person unknown in the Jewish history; the name is probably a name of *disguise;* and by it he may covertly mean *Saul* himself, the *son of Kish*, who was of the *tribe* of *Benjamin.* The subject of the Psalm will better answer to Saul's unjust persecution and David's innocence, than to any other subject in the history of David.

Verse 1. *O Lord my God*] יהוה אלהי *Yehovah Elohai*, words expressive of the strongest confidence the soul can have in the Supreme Being. Thou self-existent, incomprehensible, almighty, and eternal Being, who neither needest nor hatest any thing that thou hast made; thou art my God: God in *covenant* with thy creature man; and my God and portion particularly. Therefore, *in thee do I put my trust*—I repose all my confidence *in thee*, and expect all my good *from thee.*

Save me] Shield me from my persecutors; abate their pride, assuage their malice, and confound their devices!

Deliver me] From the counsels which they have devised, and from the snares and gins they have laid in my path.

Verse 2. *Lest he tear my soul like a lion*] These words seem to answer well to *Saul.* As the *lion* is *king* in the forest; so was *Saul* king over the land. As the *lion*, in his fierceness, seizes at once, and tears his prey in pieces; so David expected to be seized and suddenly destroyed by *Saul.* He had already, in his rage, thrown his javelin at him, intending to have pierced him to the wall with it. As from the *power of the lion* no beast in the forest could deliver any thing; so David knew that *Saul's power* was irresistible, and that none of his friends or well-wishers could save or deliver him out of such hands. "Lest he tear my soul (my life) like a lion, rending it in pieces, while there is none to deliver." All this answers to *Saul*, and to none else.

Verse 3. *If I have done this*] David was accused by Saul of *affecting the kingdom;* and of *waiting* for an opportunity to *take away the life of his king, his patron*, and his *friend.* In his application to God he refers to these charges; meets them with indignation; and clears himself of them by a strong appeal to his Judge; and an imprecation that, if he had meditated or designed any such thing, he might meet with

A. M. cir. 2943
B. C. cir. 1061
Sauli, Regis
Israelitarum,
cir. annum
35

4 If I have rewarded evil unto
him that was at peace with me;
(yea, [k]I have delivered him that
without cause is mine enemy:)
5 Let the enemy persecute my soul, and
take *it;* yea, let him tread down my life upon
the earth, and lay mine honour in the dust.
Selah.
6 Arise, O LORD, in thine anger, [l]lift up
thyself because of the rage of mine enemies:
and [m]awake for me *to* the judgment *that* thou
hast commanded.
7 So shall the congregation of the people compass thee about: for their sakes
therefore return thou on high.
8 The LORD shall judge the
people: judge me, O LORD, [n]ac-
cording to my righteousness, and according to
mine integrity *that is* in me.
9 O let the wickedness of the wicked come
to an end; but establish the just: [o]for the
righteous God trieth the hearts and reins.
10 [p]My defence *is* of God, which saveth
the [q]upright in heart.
11 [r]God judgeth the righteous, and God is
angry *with the wicked* every day.

A. M. cir. 2943
B. C. cir. 1061
Sauli, Regis
Israelitarum,
cir. annum
35

---

[k]1 Samuel xxiv. 7; xxvi. 9——[l]Psa. xciv. 2——[m]Psa. xliv. 23——[n]Psalm xviii. 20; xxxv. 24——[o]1 Samuel xvi. 7; 1 Chronicles xxviii. 9; Psalm cxxxix. 1; Jeremiah xi. 20; xvii. 10; xx. 12; Revelation ii. 23——[p]Hebrew, *My buckler* is *upon God*——[q]Psalm cxxv. 4——[r]Or, *God* is *a righteous Judge*

---

nothing but curse and calamity either from God or man.

Verse 4. *Yea, I have delivered him*] When, in the course of thy providence, thou didst put his life in my hand in the *cave*, I contented myself with cutting off his skirt, merely to show him the danger he had been in, and the spirit of the man whom he accused of designs against his life; and yet even for this my heart smote me, because it appeared to be an indignity offered to him who was the *Lord's anointed*. This fact, and my venturing my life frequently for his good and the safety of the state, sufficiently show the falsity of such accusations, and the innocence of my life.

Verse 5. *Let the enemy persecute my soul*] If I have been guilty of the things laid to my charge, let the worst evils fall upon me.

Verse 6. *Arise, O Lord, in thine anger*] To thee I commit my cause; arise, and sit on the throne of thy judgment in my behalf.

Verse 7. *For their sakes therefore return thou on high.*] Thy own people who compass thy altar, the faithful of the land, are full of gloomy apprehensions. They hear the charges against me; and see how I am persecuted. Their minds are divided; they know not what to think. For *their sakes, return thou on high*—ascend the judgment-seat; and let them see, by the dispensations of thy providence, *who* is *innocent* and *who is guilty*. David feared not to make this appeal to God; for the consciousness of his innocence showed him at once how the discrimination would be made.

Verse 8. *The Lord shall judge the people*] He will execute justice and maintain truth among them. They shall not be as sheep without a shepherd.

Judge me, O Lord] Let my innocence be brought to the light, and my just dealing made clear as the noonday.

Verse 9. *The wickedness of the wicked*] The iniquity of *Saul's* conduct.

But establish the just] Show the people *my* uprightness.

Verse 10. *My defence* is *of God*] I now leave my cause in the hands of my Judge. I have no uneasy or fearful apprehensions, because I know God will save the upright in heart.

Verse 11. *God is angry* with the wicked *every day.*] The *Hebrew* for this sentence is the following: ועל זעם בכל יום *veel zoem becol yom;* which, according to the *points*, is, *And God is angry every day*. Our translation seems to have been borrowed from the *Chaldee*, where the whole verse is as follows: אלהא דינא זכאה ובתקוף רגיז על רשיעי כל יומא: *elaha daiyana zaccaah ubithkoph rageiz al reshiey col yoma:* "God is a righteous Judge; and in strength he is angry against the wicked every day."

The VULGATE: *Deus Judex justus, fortis, et patiens; numquid irascitur per singulos dies?* "God is a Judge righteous, strong, and patient; —will he be angry every day?"

The SEPTUAGINT: Ὁ Θεος Κριτης δικαιος, και ισχυρος, και μακροθυμος, μη οργην επαγων καθ' ἑκαστην ἡμεραν; "God is a righteous Judge, strong and longsuffering; not bringing forth his anger every day."

SYRIAC: "God is the Judge of righteousness; he is not angry every day."

The ARABIC is the same as the *Septuagint*.

The ÆTHIOPIC: "God is a just Judge, and strong and longsuffering; he will not bring forth tribulation daily."

COVERDALE: **God is a righteous judge, and God is ever threateninge.**

KING EDWARD'S Bible by *Becke* 1549, follows this reading.

CARDMARDEN: **God is a righteous judge, [strong and patient] and God is provoked every day.** *Cardmarden* has borrowed *strong and patient* from the *Vulgate* or *Septuagint;* but as he found nothing in the *Hebrew* to express them, he put the words in a *smaller letter*, and included them in *brackets*. This is followed by the *prose version* in our *Prayer Book*.

The GENEVAN *version*, printed by *Barker*, the king's printer, 1615, translates thus: "God judgeth the righteous, and him that contemneth God every day." On which there is this marginal note: "He doth continually call the wicked to repentance, by some signs of his judgments."

My ancient *Scotico-English* MS. *Psalter* only begins with the conclusion of this Psalm.

I have judged it of consequence to trace this verse through all the ancient versions in order to be able to ascertain what is the *true reading*, where the evidence on one side amounts to a

A. M. cir. 2943 B. C. cir. 1061 Sauli, Regis Israelitarum, cir. annum 35

12 If he turn not, he will [s]whet
his sword; he hath bent his bow,
and made it ready.
13 He hath also prepared for
him the instruments of death; [t]he ordaineth
his arrows against the persecutors.
14 [u]Behold, he travaileth with iniquity, and
hath conceived mischief, and brought forth
falsehood.
15 [v]He made a pit, and digged
it, [w]and is fallen into the ditch
which he made.
16 [x]His mischief shall return
upon his own head, and his violent dealing
shall come down upon his own pate.
17 I will praise the [y]LORD according to his
righteousness: and will sing praise to the
name of the LORD most high.

A. M. cir. 2943 B. C. cir. 1061 Sauli, Regis Israelitarum, cir. annum 35

[s]Deut. xxxii. 41——[t]Deut. xxxii. 23, 42; Psa. lxix. 7 [u]Job xv. 35; Isa. xxxiii. 11; lix. 4; James i. 15——[v]Heb. *He hath digged a pit*——[w]Esth. vii. 10; Job iv. 8; Psa. ix. 15; x. 2; xxxv. 8; xciv. 23; cxli. 10; Prov. v. 22; xxvi. 27; Eccles. x. 8——[x]1 Kings ii. 32; Esth. ix. 25 [y]Psa. ix. 1; xxii. 22; xxviii. 7; xxxv. 18; xliii. 4; lii. 9; liv. 6; lvi. 4; lvii. 9; lxix. 30; lxxi. 22; lxxxvi. 12; cviii. 3; cix. 30; cxi. 1, &c.

positive *affirmation*, "God IS angry every day;" and, on the other side, to as positive a *negation*, "He is NOT angry every day." The mass of evidence supports the latter reading. The *Chaldee* first corrupted the text by making the addition, *with the wicked*, which our translators have followed, though they have put the words into *italics*, as not being in the Hebrew text. In the MSS. collated by *Kennicott* and *De Rossi* there is no various reading on this text.

The true sense may be restored thus:—

אֵל *el*, with the vowel point *tsere*, signifies GOD: אַל *al*, the same letters, with the point *pathach*, signifies *not*. Several of the versions have read it in this way: "God judgeth the righteous, and is NOT angry every day." He is not always chiding, nor is he daily punishing, notwithstanding the continual wickedness of men: hence, the ideas of *patience* and *long-suffering* which several of the versions introduce. Were I to take any of the translations in preference to the above, I should feel most inclined to adopt that of *Coverdale*.

Verse 12. *If he turn not*] This clause the *Syriac* adds to the preceding verse. Most of the versions read, "If ye return not." Some contend, and not without a great show of probability, that the two verses should be read in connection, thus: "God is a just Judge; a God who is provoked every day. If (the sinner) turn not, he will whet his sword; he hath bent his bow, and made it ready." This, no doubt, gives the sense of both.

Verse 13. *He hath also prepared for him the instruments of death*] This appears to be all a prophecy of the tragical death of *Saul*. He was wounded by the *arrows* of the *Philistines;* and his own *keen sword*, on which he fell, terminated his woful days!

Verse 14. *He travaileth with iniquity*] All these terms show the pitch of envy, wrath, and malevolence, to which Saul had carried his opposition against David. He *conceived mischief;* he *travailed* with *iniquity;* he *brought forth falsehood*—all his expectations were blasted.

Verse 15. *He made a pit*] He determined the destruction of David. He laid his plans with much artifice; he executed them with zeal and diligence; and when he had, as he supposed, the grave of David digged, he fell into it himself! The metaphor is taken from pits dug in the earth, and slightly covered over with reeds, &c., so as not to be discerned from the solid ground; but the animal steps on them, the surface breaks, and he falls into the pit and is taken. "All the world agrees to acknowledge the equity of that sentence, which inflicts upon the *guilty* the punishment intended by them for the *innocent*."—*Horne*.

Verse 16. *Shall come down upon his own pate.*] Upon his *scalp*, קדקד *kodkod*, the top of the head. It may refer to *knocking the criminal on the head*, in order to deprive him of life. Had *scalping* been known in those days, I should have thought the reference might be to that barbarous custom.

Verse 17. *I will praise the Lord according to his righteousness*] I shall celebrate both his justice and his mercy. I will sing praise to the name of the Lord Most High. The *name* of God is often put for his *perfections*. So here, שם יהוה עליון *shem Yehovah Elyon;* "The perfections of Jehovah, who is above all." My old *Scotico-English* MS., mentioned at the conclusion of the *introduction*, begins at this verse, where are the following words by way of paraphrase: **Sang falles til ioy: and he that synges well that name, his ioy es mare than i kan tell.** Those who are happy may sing; and he who can duly celebrate the name of God, who knows it to be a strong tower into which he can run and find safety, has inexpressible happiness. That is the sense of the above.

ANALYSIS OF THE SEVENTH PSALM

I. His appeal to God by way of *petition*, ver. 1, 2, 6.

II. The *reasons* of this appeal,—set down through the whole Psalm.

III. His doxology or thanksgiving, ver. 17.

I. He begins his appeal with a petition for deliverance from his persecutors: "Save me, and deliver me," ver. 1. In which he desires God to be,

1. *Attentive* to him: 1. Because of the relation between them. For he was *the Lord his God*. 2. He trusted in him: "O Lord my God, I trust in thee," ver. 1.

2. *Benevolent* to him. For he was now in danger of death. He had, 1. Enemies. 2. Many enemies. 3. Persecuting enemies. 4. But one above the rest, a *lion ready to rend him in pieces;* so that if God forsook him, he would do it. "Save me from those that persecute me," &c., ver. 2.

II. And then he gives his reasons why he doth appeal to his God, which are: 1. His own *innocence*. 2. God's *justice*.

1. He makes a protestation of his innocence. He was accused that he lay in wait, and plotted

for Saul's life and kingdom; but he clears himself, shows the impossibility of it, and that with a fearful imprecation. 1. *O Lord—if I have done* any such thing as they object; *if I have rewarded evil to him that was at peace with me*, ver. 3, 4, which was indeed an impossible matter. *For I have delivered him*—as Saul in the *cave*, 1 Sam. xxiv. 2. His imprecation—*Then let mine enemy persecute me*—let him take both my life and my honour, kingdom, property, and whatever thou hast promised me.

2. And, which is the second reason of this appeal, being innocent, he calls for justice. "Arise, O Lord—lift up thyself—awake for me to judgment." For, 1. The rage of my enemies is great. 2. The judgment was thine that chose me to be king of thy people. Awake for me. 3. This will be for thy honour, and the edification of thy Church. "The congregation of thy people shall compass thee about. For their sakes return thou on high." Ascend the tribunal, and do justice.

Now, upon this argument of God's justice, he dwells and insists to the last verse of the Psalm.

1. He avows God to be his Judge.

2. He prays for justice to be done to *him* and to the *wicked*. 1. To *him*, an innocent person: "Judge me, O Lord, according to my righteousness." 2. To the *wicked:* "O let the wickedness of the wicked come to an end!"

3. He prays not only for *himself*, but for all *good men:* "Establish the just." And adds this reason, that as "God trieth the hearts and reins," he is fittest to be judge, in whom is required *knowledge* and *prudence*.

4. The other two properties of a judge are, to *save*, and to *punish;* and the triumph of his faith is, that he knows He will do both. 1. *He will save the just and upright in heart*, and therefore his *defence is in God*. 2. He will *punish the wicked*, for he is *angry with them every day;* and yet even to them he shows much clemency and forbearance. He waits for their conversion. He whets, binds on, and sharpens his instruments of death; but he shoots not till there is no remedy. But, *If they will not return he will whet his sword*, &c.

5. But the Lord's longsuffering had no good effect upon Saul; he grew worse and worse: *He travailed with mischief; conceived iniquity; brought forth falsehood;* and *digged a pit* for his innocent neighbour, into which he fell himself. Thus the righteous God *executed judgment* and *vindicated innocence*.

III. The close of the Psalm is a *doxology*. Thanks that a good and merciful God would judge for the righteous, save those who are true of heart, *establish the just*, and take vengeance upon the wicked. For this, saith David, "I will praise the Lord according to his righteousness, and I will sing praise to the name of the Lord the Most High."

The righteous may be oppressed, but they shall not be forsaken: nor can they lose even by their afflictions, for they shall be turned to their advantage. Every occurrence helps a good man, whether prosperous or adverse; but to the wicked every thing is a curse. By his wickedness, even his blessings are turned to a bane.

PSALM VIII

The glory and excellence of God manifested by his works, 1, 2; *particularly in the starry heavens*, 3; *in man*, 4; *in his formation*, 5; *and in the dominion which God has given him over the earth, the air, the sea, and their inhabitants*, 6, 7, 8: *in consequence of which God's name is celebrated over all the earth*, 9.

To the chief Musician [a]upon Gittith, A Psalm of David

O LORD our Lord, how [b]excellent *is* thy name in all the earth! who [c]hast set thy glory above the heavens.

2 [d]Out of the mouth of babes and sucklings hast thou [e]ordained strength because of thine enemies, that thou mightest still [f]the enemy and the avenger.

[a]Psa. lxxxi., lxxxiv., title——[b]Psa. cxlviii. 13——[c]Psa. cxiii. 4

[d]See Matt. xi. 25; xxi. 16; 1 Cor. i. 27——[e]Heb. *founded* [f]Psa. xliv. 16

NOTES ON PSALM VIII

The inscription to this Psalm is the following: *To the chief Musician upon Gittith, A Psalm of David.* This has been metaphrased, "To the conqueror, concerning the winepresses;" and has been supposed to be a Psalm intended for the time of *vintage:* and as that happened about the time of the year in which it is supposed the world was created, hence there is a general celebration of those works, and of the creation, and the high privileges of man. The *Chaldee* gives it a different turn: "A Psalm of David, to be sung upon the harp, which he brought out of Gath." That the Psalm has respect to our Lord and the time of the Gospel, is evident from the reference made to ver. 2, in Matt. xi. 25, the express quotation of it in Matt. xxi. 16, and another reference to it in 1 Cor. i. 27. The *fourth* and *sixth* verses are quoted Heb. ii. 6-9. See also 1 Cor. xv. 27, and Eph. i. 22. The *first* and *second* ADAM are both referred to, and the first and second creation also; and the glory which God has received, and is to receive, through both. It relates simply to Christ and redemption.

Verse 1. *O Lord our Lord*] יהוה אדנינו *Yehovah Adoneynu; O Jehovah our Prop, our Stay*, or *Support.* אדני *Adonai* is frequently used: sometimes, indeed often, for the word

3 When I [g]consider thy heavens, the work of thy fingers, the moon and the stars, which thou hast ordained;

4 [h]What is man, that thou art mindful of him? and the son of man, that thou visitest him?

[g]Psa. cxi. 2

[h]Job vii. 17; Psa. cxliv. 3; Heb. ii. 6

יהוה *Yehovah* itself. The root דן *dan* signifies *to direct, rule, judge, support.* So *Adonai* is the Director, Ruler, Judge, Supporter of men. It is well joined with *Jehovah;* this showing what God is *in himself;* that, what God is *to man;* and may here very properly refer to our Lord Jesus.

How excellent is *thy name in all the earth!*] How illustrious is the name of Jesus throughout the world! His incarnation, birth, humble and obscure life, preaching, miracles, passion, death, resurrection, and ascension, are celebrated through the whole world. His religion, the gifts and graces of his Spirit, his people—Christians—his Gospel and the preachers of it, are everywhere spoken of. No name is so universal, no power and influence so generally felt, as those of the Saviour of mankind. Amen.

Thy glory above the heavens.] The *heavens* are glorious, the most glorious of all the works of God which the eye of man can reach; but the *glory of God* is infinitely *above* even these. The words also seem to intimate that no power, earthly or diabolical, can *lessen* or injure that glory. The glory and honour which God has by the Gospel shall last through time, and through eternity; and of that glory none shall be able to rob him, to whom majesty and dominion are eternally due. This has been applied by some to the *resurrection* of our Lord. He *rose* from the dead, and *ascended* above all heavens; and by these his glory was sealed, his mission accomplished, and the last proof given to his preceding miracles.

Verse 2. *Out of the mouth of babes and sucklings*] We have seen how our Lord applied this passage to the Jewish children, who, seeing his miracles, cried out in the temple, "Hosanna to the Son of David!" Matt. xxi. 16. And we have seen how the *enemy* and *the avenger*—the *chief priests* and the *scribes*—were offended because of these things; and as the Psalm wholly concerns Jesus Christ, it is most probable that in this act of the Jewish children the prophecy had its *primary* fulfilment; and was left to the Jews as a witness and a sign of the Messiah, which they should have acknowledged when our Lord directed their attention to it.

There is also a very *obvious sense* in which the *mouths of babes and sucklings show forth the praises of God;* viz., the means by which they derive their first nourishment. In order to extract the milk from the breasts of their mothers, they are obliged to *empty their own mouths entirely of air*, that the eternal air, pressing on the breast, may force the milk through its proper canals into the mouth of the child, where there is no resistance, the child having extracted all air from its own mouth, which in this case resembles a perfectly *exhausted receiver* on the plate of an *airpump;* and the *action* of *sucking* is performed on the same principle that the receiver is exhausted by the working of the airpump. Of this curious pneumatic action the child is capable the moment it breathes; and, its strength considered, performs it as perfectly the first hour as it does in any other period of its childhood or infancy. What does all this argue? Why *instinct.* And pray what is *instinct?* You cannot tell. But here is an operation by which the pure *Boylean vacuum* is made; and this by an infant *without any previous teaching!* Do you suppose that this is an *easy operation*, and that it requires little *skill?* You are mistaken. You have done this yourself while an infant, under the sole guidance of God. Can you do it *now?* You are startled! Shall I tell you what appears to you a secret? There is not one in ten thousand *adults*, who have had their first nourishment from the breasts of their mothers, who can perform the same operation again! And those who have had occasion to practise it have found great difficulty *to learn that art* which, in the first moment of their birth, they performed to perfection! Here is the finger of God; and here, *out of the mouths of babes and sucklings*, he *has ordained* such a *strength* of *evidence* and *argument* in favour of his being, his providence, and his goodness, as is sufficient to *still* and *confound* every infidel and atheist in the universe, all the *enemies* of righteousness, and all the *vindicators* of desperate and hopeless causes and systems.

The words may also be applied to the *apostles* and *primitive preachers* of the Gospel; to the *simple* and *comparatively unlearned* followers of Christ, who, through his teaching, were able to confound the *wise* among the *Jews*, and the *mighty* among the *heathens:* and in this sense our Lord uses the term *babes*, Matt. xi. 25: "I thank thee, O Father—because thou hast hid these things from the *wise* and *prudent*, and hast revealed them to *babes.*"

We may also witness, in the *experience* of multitudes of simple people who have been, by the preaching of the Gospel, converted from the error of their ways, such a strength of *testimony* in favour of the work of God in the *heart*, and his effectual teaching in the *mind*, as is calculated to *still*, or reduce to silence, every thing but *bigotry* and *prejudice*, neither of which has either *eyes* or *ears*. This *teaching*, and these *changing* or *converting* influences, come from God. They are not acquired by human *learning;* and those who put this in the place of the Divine teaching never grow wise to salvation. To enter into the kingdom of heaven, a MAN must become as a *little child.*

Verse 3. *When I consider thy heavens*] כי אראה *ki ereh; because I will see.* He had often seen the heavens with astonishment, and he purposes to make them frequent subjects of contemplation; and he could not behold them without being affected with the skill, contrivance, and power, manifested in their formation.

The work of thy fingers] What a view does this give of the majesty of God! The *earth* is nearly *eight thousand* English miles in diameter: but to form an adequate conception of its magnitude, we must consider it in its *superficial* and *solid contents.* Upon the supposition

5 For thou hast made him a little lower than the angels, and hast crowned him with glory and honour.

6 [i]Thou madest him to have dominion over the works of thy hands; [k]thou hast put all *things* under his feet:

---

[i]Gen. i. 26, 28

[k]1 Cor. xv. 27; Heb. ii. 8

---

that the earth's *polar* diameter is *seven thousand nine hundred and forty* miles, and its *equatorial, seven thousand nine hundred and seventy-seven,* (estimates considered to very near approximations to the truth,) the whole superficies of the terraqueous globe will amount to about *one hundred and ninety-eight millions, nine hundred and eighty thousand, seven hundred* square miles; and its solid contents, in *cubic miles,* will be expressed by the following figures: 264,544,857,944, i. e., *two hundred and sixty-four thousand five hundred and forty-four millions, eight hundred and fifty-seven thousand, nine hundred and forty-four.* Great as we have shown the *bulk* of the earth to be, from the most accurate estimates of its diameter, it is but small when compared with the bulks of some of the other bodies in the solar system. The planet *Herschel,* or *Georgium Sidus,* known on the continent of Europe by the name of *Uranus,* is *eighty times and a half* greater than the earth; *Saturn, nine hundred and ninety-five* times greater; *Jupiter, one thousand two hundred and eighty-one* times greater; and the *sun,* the most prodigious body in the system, *one million three hundred and eighty-four thousand, four hundred and sixty-two* times greater. The *circumference* of the sun contains not *fewer* than *two millions seven hundred and seventy-seven thousand* English miles; and a degree of latitude, which on the earth amounts only to *sixty-nine* miles and a *half,* will on the sun (the circle being supposed in both instances to be divided into *three hundred and sixty degrees*) contain not less than about *seven thousand seven hundred* and *forty miles,* a quantity almost equal to the terrestrial axis. But the immense *volume* (in cubic miles) which the solar surface includes amounts to the following most inconceivable quantity: 366,252,-303,118,866,128, i. e., *three hundred and sixty-six thousand two hundred and fifty-two billions, three hundred and three thousand one hundred and eighteen millions, eight hundred and sixty-six thousand, one hundred and twenty-eight.* Notwithstanding the amazing magnitude of the sun, we have abundant reason to believe that some of the fixed stars are much larger; and yet we are told they are *the work of* GOD'S FINGERS! What a *hand,* to move, form, and launch these globes! This expression is much more *sublime* than even that of the prophet: "Who hath measured the waters in the hollow of his hand, and meted out the heavens with a span, and comprehended the dust of the earth in a measure; and weighed the mountains in scales, and the hills in a balance!" Isa. xl. 12. This is *grand;* but the *heavens* being the work of GOD'S FINGERS is yet more sublime.

The moon and the stars] The sun is not mentioned, because the heavens—the moon, planets, and stars—could not have appeared, had *he* been present. Those he wished to introduce because of their immense variety, and astonishing splendour; and, therefore, he skilfully leaves out the sun, which would have afforded him but one object, and one idea. To have mentioned him with the others would have been as ridiculous in *astronomy,* as the exhibition of the top and bottom of a vessel would be in *perspective.* Various critics have endeavoured to restore the *sun* to this place: and even Bishop *Horsley* says, "It is certainly strange that the sun should be omitted, when the moon and the stars are so particularly mentioned." But with great deference to him, and to Dr. *Kennicott,* who both show how the text may be *mended,* I say, it would be most strange had the psalmist introduced the *sun,* for the reasons already assigned. The *Spirit* of God is always right; our *heads* sometimes, our *hearts* seldom so.

Which thou hast ordained] כוננתה *conantah,* which thou hast prepared and established. Made their respective spheres, and fitted them for their places. Space to matter, and matter to space; all adjusted in number, weight, and measure.

Verse 4. *What is man*] מה אנוש *mah enosh,* what is wretched, miserable man; man in his fallen state, full of infirmity, ignorance, and sin?

That thou art mindful of him?] That thou settest thy heart upon him, keepest him continually in thy merciful view.

And the son of man] ובן אדם *uben Adam,* and the son of Adam, the first great rebel; the fallen child of a fallen parent. See the note on Job vii. 17. Some think eminent men are here intended. What is *man* in *common;* what the *most eminent men;* that thou shouldst be mindful of them, or deign to visit them?

That thou visitest him?] By sending thy Holy Spirit to convince him of *sin, righteousness,* and *judgment.* It is by these *visits* that man is preserved in a salvable state. Were God to withhold them, there would be nothing in the soul of man but sin, darkness, hardness, corruption, and death.

Verse 5. *Thou hast made him a little lower than the angels*] The original is certainly very emphatic: ותחסרהו מעט מאלהים *vattechasserchu meat meelohim,* Thou hast lessened him for a little time from God. Or, Thou hast made him less than God for a little time. See these passages explained at large in the notes on Heb. ii. 6, &c., which I need not repeat here.

Verse 6. *Thou madest him to have dominion*] Jesus Christ, who, being in the form of God, and equal with God, *for a time* emptied himself, and made himself of no reputation; was afterwards *highly exalted,* and had a name above every name. See the notes referred to above, and those on Phil. ii. 6-9.

Thou hast put all things *under his feet*] Though the whole of the brute creation was made subject to Adam in his state of innocence; yet it could never be literally said of him, that God had put all things under his feet, or that he had dominion over the work of God's hands; but all this is most literally true of our Lord Jesus; and to him the apostle, Heb. ii. 6, &c., applies all these passages.

7 [l]All sheep and oxen, yea, and the beasts
of the field;

8 The fowl of the air, and the fish of the sea,
and whatsoever passeth through the paths of
the seas.

9 [m]O LORD our Lord, how excellent *is* thy
name in all the earth!

---

[l]Heb. *Flocks and oxen all of them*

[m]Ver. 1

Verse 7. *All sheep and oxen*] All *domestic* animals, and those to be employed in *agriculture.*

Beasts of the field] All *wild beasts*, and inhabitants of the *forest.*

Verse 8. *The fowl of the air*] All these were given to man in the beginning; and he has still a general dominion over them; for thus saith the Lord: "The fear of you, and the dread of you, shall be upon every BEAST of the EARTH, and upon every FOWL of the AIR, and upon all that MOVETH upon the EARTH, and upon all the FISHES of the SEA; into your hand are they delivered;" Gen. ix. 2. To this passage the psalmist most obviously refers.

Verse 9. *O Lord our Lord*] The psalmist concludes as he began. Jehovah, our prop and support! his name is excellent in all the earth. The name of JESUS is celebrated in almost every part of the habitable globe; for his Gospel has been preached, or is in the progress of being preached, through the whole world. *Bibles* and *missionaries* are now carrying his name, and proclaiming his fame, to the utmost nations of the earth.

The whole of this Psalm, and *the seventh and eighth* verses in particular, have been the subject of much *spiritualization* in ancient and modern times. I shall give two examples: one from the pious Bishop *Horne;* the other from the ancient *Latino-Scotico-English* Psalter, mentioned before.

That of Bishop *Horne*, on the 7th and 8th verses, is as follows: "Adam, upon his creation, was invested with sovereign dominion over the creatures, in words of the same import with these, Gen. i. 28, which are therefore here used, and the creatures particularized, to inform us that what the first Adam lost by transgression, the second Adam gained by obedience. That glory which was set above the heavens could not but be over all things on the earth; and accordingly we hear our Lord saying, after his resurrection, 'All power is given unto me in heaven and earth,' Matt. xxviii. 18. Nor is it a speculation unpleasing or unprofitable to consider that he who rules over the material world is Lord also of the intellectual or spiritual creation represented thereby.

"The souls of the faithful, lowly, and harmless, are the *sheep* of his pasture; those who, like *oxen*, are strong to labour in the Church, and who by expounding the word of life tread out the corn for the nourishment of the people, own him for their kind and beneficent Master. Nay, tempers fierce and untractable as the *wild beasts* of the desert, are yet subject to his will. Spirits of the angelic kind, that, like the *birds of the air*, traverse freely the superior region, move at his command; and these evil ones, whose habitation is in the *deep abyss*, even to the great *leviathan* himself, all, all are put under the feet of the King Messiah; who, because he humbled himself, and became obedient to death, was therefore highly exalted, and had a name given him above every name; that at the name of Jesus every knee should bow, whether of things in heaven, or things on earth, or things under the earth; and that every tongue should confess that Jesus is Lord, to the glory of God the Father; Phil. ii. 8, &c." Thus far the pious bishop.

I shall now give, as a singular curiosity, the whole Psalm, with its translation and paraphrase, from the ancient MS. already mentioned; inserting first the *Latin text;* next, the *translation;* and, thirdly, the *paraphrase.* The Latin text seems to be the old *Itala*, or *Antehieronymian;* at least it has readings which have been thought peculiar to that version.

PSALM VIII

Ver. 1. Domine Deus noster, quoniam admirabile est nomen tuum in universa terra.

Trans. **Lord our Lord, qwat thi name es wonderfull in al the Erde.**

Par. The prophete in louing, bygynnes and says: Lord of al, thow ert specialy our Lord that dredes the, loves the. *Thi name* that es the ioy and the fame of thi name Ihesu: for the creaturs that thu hes made and bought qwat it es wonderful. Als so say withouten end: for nane suffis for to knaw al creaturs: in qwilk wonder of the, and that in al the Erd, nought in a party anely.

Quoniam elevata est magnificencia tua super Celos.

Trans. **For lyfted es thi worchyp aboven hevens.**

Par. That es at say, thu ert mare worthy to be loued and wirchepyd than any Aungel or haly Saule may thynk.

Verse 2. Ex ore infancium et lactencium perfecisti laudem, propter inimicos tuos, ut destruas inimicum et ultorem.

Trans. **Of the mouth of nought spekand, and sowkand, thou has made louying, for thin enmys, that thou destroye the enmy and the venger.**

Par. Nought anely thow ert loued of perfite men, bot of the mouthe of barnes that spekes nought: Zit there er tha that kan nought speke the wisdom of this werld: and of soukand, the qwilk gladdely resayves the lare of haly Kyrk theare moder. Thow has made thi luf thug perfyte for thin enmys: fals cristen men, to schame and to schende for thai er wer than er haythen men. That thu destruy the enmy; that es, he that es wyse in his awen eghen; and wil nought be underloute til thi wil: *and the venger:* that es he that defends his Syn; and sais that he synnes nought; or that his syn es les than other mennes.

Ver. 3. Quoniam videbo celos tuos, et opera digitorum tuorum, lunam et stellas quas tu fundasti.

Trans. **For I sal se thi hevens werkes of thi fyngers the mone and the Sternys the qwilk thow groundid.**

Par. Thow destrues al that es contrariand til the; bot i in al thying confourom me to do thi wil; for thi i sal se in lyf withouten end. *Thi hevens*, that es Aungels and Apostels the qwilk er werkes of thi fingers: that es, thai er mode perfyte thurgh the Haly Gost, of qwam es seven gyftes. Of he be bot a Spirit, als mani fyngers er in a hand. And i sal see the *Mone*, that es haly Kyrk: and the sternes that es ilk a ryghtwise man by hym selfe, the qwilk thu groundid in charite.

Ver. 4. Quid est homo quod memor es ejus; aut filius hominis, quoniam visitas eum?

Trans. **Qwat es man that thu ert menand of hym: or son of man for thou visites hym?**

Par. Als it war with despyte, he sais *man*, erdely and synful, qwat es he, that thu has mynd of hym. Als fer sett fra the; at the lest gyfand hym hele and ese of body. Or *son of man:* that es, he that es gastely, and beres the ymage of heven. Qwat es he, for thou visits hym. Als present the qwilk es nere the for clennes of lyf. Or *son of man* he calles Crist, thrugh qwam he visits mannes kynd.

Ver. 5. Minuisti eum paullo minus ab angelis: gloria et honore coronasti eum; et constituisti eum super opera manuum tuarum.

Trans. **Thow lessed hym a littil fra aungels; with ioy and honour thu coround hym: and thu sett him aboven the werkes of thi hend.**

Par. Crist was *lessed fra aungels*, for he was dedely, and mught suffer pyne; but a littel; for in other thyng, es he abouen aungels, thair Kyng and Sychthu thou coround hym with ioy, that es with brighthede of body, na mare sufferand pyne; and honour, for he es honourable til al: and thou sett hym abouen aungels and al creatures.

Ver. 6, 7. Omnia subjecisti sub pedibus ejus: oves et boves insuper et pecora campi.

Trans. **Al thynges thu underkest undyr his fete: schepe and oxen al over that, and the bestes of the feld.**

Par. That undyr hys Lordschyp and hys myght, in has cestyn al thyng: tha er *schepe* that er innocentes, als well aungels als men. *And oxen*, tha er, traveland men gastely, in haly Kyrk, *over that;* and the *bestes of the feld;* thai er lufers of this werld, wonnand, in the feld of fleschly lusts; noght in hillis of vertus; and so be the brode way thai ga til hell.

Ver. 8. Volucres celi et pisces maris qui perambulant semitas maris.

Trans. **Fowls of heven and fysche of the see, that gas the wayes of the see.**

Par. Fowls of heven, er prowde men that wald hee thair setil abouen al other. *Fysches of the see*, er covaytus men, the qwilk in the ground of the werld, sekes erthdly gudes, that all stretes in the see, sone wither oway. Al thir sal be underlout til Crist onther herts in grace, or thare in pine.

Ver. 9. Domine Deus noster, quam admirabile est nomen tuum in universa terra.

Trans. **Lard our Lard qwat thi name is wonderful in al the erth.**

Par. Als he bigan swa he endes, schewand that bygyning and endyng of al gode, is of Gode; and til his louing agh i for to be done.

The reader will no doubt be struck with the remarkable agreement between the pious bishop of Norwich and this ancient translator and paraphrast, particularly on the 7th and 8th verses. The language also is in several respects singular. The participle of the present tense, which we terminate with *ing*, is here almost always terminated with *and*. So *Spekand*, *sowkand*, *gyfand*, *sufferand*, *traveland*, for speaking, sucking, giving, suffering, travelling, &c.

As the participle signifies the *continuance* of the action, the termination *and* seems much more proper than *ing; speak-and*, i. e., *continuing* to speak; *give-and*, *continuing* to give; *suffer-and*, suffer more; *travel-and*, travel on, &c. There are some words in this ancient MS. which I have met nowhere else.

Analysis of the Eighth Psalm

This Psalm begins and ends with a general proposition, figured by an exclamation, which contains an admiration; for he admires what he cannot perfectly comprehend. "O Lord our Lord, how excellent is thy name in all the earth! who hast set thy glory above the heavens." Such is the glory of thy divinity, power, and goodness, that it fills not only the earth, but transcends the very heavens, in which angels and blessed spirits, though they know much more than we on earth, yet cannot comprehend thy Majesty, which fills all and exceeds all.

This general proposition being premised, the prophet descends to some *particular instances*, in which the excellence of God's name particularly appears; and he mentions *three:* I. *Infants.* II. The *heavens*, with the *moon* and *stars.* III. *Man* himself.

I. The excellence of God's power, divinity, and goodness, appears in infants: "Out of the mouth of babes and sucklings thou hast ordained strength." 1. The sucking of babes, and speaking of young children, are evident demonstrations of God's excellent name; for who taught the babe to suck, or the dumb infant to speak, but the *Lord our Governor?* 2. The children that cried "Hosanna!" in the temple, struck with the miracles of our Lord; while the priests, through *envy*, were *dumb.* 3. Or by *babes* may be meant such as the worldly-wise repute no better than *children* and *fools.* By simple *prophets*, ignorant *fishermen*, humble *confessors*, and faithful *martyrs*, hath he *stilled the enemy* and the *avenger;* confounded the wisest philosophers, and stopped the mouths of devils.

II. The next instance in which the glory and excellence of God's name appears is the *heavens*, the *moon* and the *stars:* these are the works of his *fingers*, and therefore called *Thy heavens;* whose amplitude is great, order and orbs wonderful, beauty admirable, matter durable, and motions various yet stable; together with the *stars*, whose multitude is innumerable, magnitude vast and various, order admirable, and influences secret and wonderful. The varying, yet regular and constant course of the *moon*, her changes, phases, and influences on the earth and the waters, on men and other animals. All these have been *ordained* by the all-wise God; and the earth and its inhabitants are receiving continual benefits from them.

When I *consider* these things, then I say to myself:

III. "What is man, that thou art mindful of him? or the son of man, that thou visitest him?" This is the psalmist's *third* instance to manifest the excellence of God's providence and government of the world, in which he reflects upon man in his *baseness* and in his *dignity.*

1. In his baseness, vileness, and misery, signified by the question, *What is man?* As if he should say, What a poor creature? how miserable! What except dust and ashes, as to his body, when he was at the best; for he was *taken from the dust of the ground*, even when his soul was formed *in the image of God.* But now

miserable dust while he lives, and to dust he shall return when he dies. What then is this miserable creature, of what worth, that thou, so great, and so glorious a Being, who art higher than the heavens, shouldst *visit* and *take care* of him!

2. This is his dignity; he can know, love, serve, and enjoy thee for ever; and thou settest thy love upon him above all other creatures. This thou hast showed in the following ways:—

1. In *visiting* him, and in being *mindful* of him: 1. Thou visitest him by conferring on him many temporal blessings. 2. In illuminating his mind by thy Holy Spirit. 3. In sending him thy *law* and thy *Gospel*, by *prophets* and *apostles*. 4. In giving thy *Son* to take upon himself human nature, and to die, the just for the unjust, that thou mightest bring him to thyself, through whom he is to receive remission of sins, and an eternal inheritance among the saints in light. 5. In making him, fallen and wretched as he is, lord of thy creatures; giving him all sheep and oxen, the beasts of the field, the fowls of heaven, and the fish of the sea. 6. But this universal dominion belongs principally to the Lord Jesus, *through* whom and *by* whom all good comes to man, and *to* whom all glory should be given, world without end. Let God's excellent name be exalted throughout all the earth!

PSALM IX

David praises God for the benefits which he has granted to Israel in general, and to himself in particular, 1–6. *He encourages himself in the Lord, knowing that he will ever judge righteously, and be a refuge for the distressed,* 7–10. *He exhorts the people to praise God for his judgments,* 11, 12; *prays for mercy and support; and thanks God for his judgments executed upon the heathen,* 13–16. *He foretells the destruction of the ungodly,* 17; *prays for the poor and needy, and against their oppressors,* 18–20.

II. DAY. MORNING PRAYER

To the chief Musician upon Muth-labben, A Psalm of David

A. M. cir. 2962 B. C. cir. 1042 Davidis, Regis Israelitarum, cir. annum 14

I WILL praise *thee,* O LORD, with my whole heart; I will show forth all thy marvellous works.

2 I will be glad and [a]rejoice in thee: I will sing praise to thy name, O [b]thou Most High.

A. M. cir. 2962 B. C. cir. 1042 Davidis, Regis Israelitarum, cir. annum 14

3 When mine enemies are turned back, they shall fall and perish at thy presence.

---

[a]Psa. v. 11

[b]Psa. lvi. 2; lxxxiii. 18

NOTES ON PSALM IX

The inscription to this Psalm in the HEBREW text is, *To the chief Musician upon Muth-labben, A Psalm of David.* The CHALDEE has, "A Song of David, to be sung concerning the Death of the Strong Man, (or *champion,* דנברא *degabra,*) who went out between the Camps;" that is, Goliath, on account of whose defeat this Psalm has been supposed by many to have been composed. The date in the margin is several years posterior to the death of Goliath. See the *introduction.*

The VULGATE: "A Psalm of David, for the end; concerning the secrets of the Son."

The SEPTUAGINT and ÆTHIOPIC are the same with the *Vulgate.*

The SYRIAC: "A Psalm of David concerning Christ's receiving the throne and the kingdom, and defeating his enemies."

The ARABIC: "Concerning the mysteries of the Son, as to the glory of Christ, his resurrection, and kingdom, and the destruction of all the disobedient."

Houbigant causes the Hebrew title to agree with the *Vulgate, Septuagint,* and *Æthiopic,* by uniting על מות *al muth,* "concerning the death," into the word עלמות *alamoth,* which signifies *secrets* or hidden things. "To the chief musician, or conqueror; secrets concerning the Son: A Psalm of David."

About a hundred MSS. and printed editions unite the words as above. Some translate עלמות *alamoth,* "concerning the youth or infancy; the infancy of the Son." Several of the *fathers* have on this ground interpreted it, "concerning the *incarnation* of our Lord." Indeed, the title and the Psalm have been so variously understood, that it would be as painful as it would be useless to follow the different commentators, both ancient and modern, through all their conjectures.

Verse 1. *I will praise* thee, *O Lord, with my whole heart*] And it is only when the *whole heart* is employed in the work that God can look upon it with acceptance.

I will show forth] אספרה *asapperah,* "I will *number out,* or *reckon up;*" a very difficult task, נפלאותיך *niphleotheycha,* "thy miracles;" supernatural interventions of thy power and goodness. He whose eye is attentive to the operation of God's hand will find many of these. In the Vulgate this Psalm begins with *Confitebor tibi, Domine,* "I will confess unto thee, O Lord," which my old MS. above quoted translates thus: **I sal schrife Lard, til the, in al my hert, I sal tel al thi wonders.** On which we find the following curious *paraphrase:* "Here the prophete spekes agaynes that grucches with ese of il men: and the travel and anguis of gude men. *I sal schrife til the Lard;* that is, I sal lufe the in al my hert, hally gederant it til thi luf: and gyfand

A. M. cir. 2962
B. C. cir. 1042
Davidis, Regis Israelitarum, cir. annum 14

4 For [c]thou hast maintained
my right and my cause; thou
sattest in the throne judging
[d]right.

5 Thou hast rebuked the heathen, thou hast
destroyed the wicked, thou hast [e]put out their
name for ever and ever.

6 [f]O thou enemy, destructions are come to
a perpetual end: and thou hast destroyed
cities; their memorial is perished with them.

7 [g]But the LORD shall endure for ever: he
hath prepared his throne for judgment.

8 And [h]he shall judge the world in righteousness, he shall minister judgment to the
people in uprightness.

9 [i]The LORD also will be [k]a
refuge for the oppressed, a
refuge in times of trouble.

10 And they that [l]know thy
name will put their trust in thee: for thou,
LORD, hast not forsaken them that seek thee.

11 Sing praises to the LORD, which dwelleth
in Zion: [m]declare among the people his doings.

12 [n]When he maketh inquisition for blood,
he remembereth them: he forgetteth not the
cry of the [o]humble.

13 Have mercy upon me, O LORD; consider my trouble *which I suffer* of them that
hate me, thou that liftest me up from the gates
of death:

A. M. cir. 2962
B. C. cir. 1042
Davidis, Regis Israelitarum, cir. annum 14

---

[c]Heb. *thou hast made my judgment*——[d]Heb. *in righteousness*——[e]Deut. ix. 14; Prov. x. 7——[f]Or, *the destructions of the enemy are come to a perpetual end; and* their *cities hast thou destroyed*, &c.

[g]Psa. cii. 12, 26; Heb. i. 11——[h]Psa. xcvi. 13; xcviii. 9——[i]Psa. xxxii. 7; xxxvii. 39; xlvi. 1; xci. 2——[k]Heb. *a high place*——[l]Psa. xci. 14——[m]Psa. cvii. 22——[n]Gen. ix. 5——[o]Or, *afflicted*

---

na party tharof tyl errour, na to covatyse: ne til fleschly luf. A vile errour it is that some men says, that God dose unrightwisly in mani thinges in erthe: for tham thynk that tay sold noght be done. Als I hard say noght lang sythem, of a man of religyon, and of grete fame, that qwen he was in the see, in poynte to peryshe, he said tyl Gode: Lard thu dos unryghtwysly if thou sofyr us to perysch here. God myght haf answered and said, My rightwysnes reches to sofer a beter man than thou ert to perisse here: for I hope, had he ben a ryghtwyse man, he had noght sayd swa: for al ar unryghtwyse, that hopes that any unrightwysnes may be in Godes wylle. Bot I sal luf the in al thi workes; and tel al thy wonders; that is, bathe that er sene, and that ar noght sene; visibels and invisibels."

Verse 2. *I will be glad and rejoice in thee*] I am glad that thou hast heard my prayer, and showed me mercy; and I will rejoice in thee, in having thee as my portion, dwelling and working in my heart.

Verse 3. *When mine enemies are turned back*] It is a sure sign of a nearly approaching complete conquest over sin, when, by resistance to its influences, it begins to lose its power. That is the time to *follow on to know the Lord*.

Verse 5. *Thou hast rebuked the heathen*] We know not what this particularly refers to, but it is most probably to the Canaanitish nations, which God destroyed from off the face of the earth; hence it is said, *Thou hast put out their name for ever and ever*, לעולם ועד *leolam vaed, endlessly*. Here עולם *olam* has its proper signification, *without end*. He who contends it means only *a limited time*, let him tell us *where* the Hivites, Perizzites, Jebusites, &c., now dwell; and *when* it is likely they are to be restored to Canaan.

Verse 6. *Destructions are come to a perpetual end*] Rather, "The enemy is desolated for ever; for thou hast destroyed their cities, and their memory is perished with them." Multitudes of the cities of the Canaanites have perished so utterly that neither name nor vestige remains of them.

Verse 7. *But the Lord shall endure*] All things shall have an end but God and holy spirits.

Verse 8. *He shall judge the world in righteousness*] All the dispensations of God's providence are founded in righteousness and truth.

Verse 9. *A refuge*] משגב *misgab, a high place*, where their enemies can neither *reach* nor *see* them. He who has God for his portion has all safety in him.

Verse 10. *They that know thy name*] Who have an experimental acquaintance with thy mercy, *will put their trust in thee*, from the conviction that *thou never hast forsaken*, and *never will forsake, them that trust in thee*.

Verse 11. *Declare among the people his doings.*] It is the duty of all those who have received the salvation of God, to recommend him and his salvation to the whole circle of their acquaintance, Christians, so called, when they meet, seldom speak about God! Why is this? Because they have nothing to say.

Verse 12. *When he maketh inquisition for blood*] This not only applies to the *Canaanites*, *Moabites*, *Ammonites*, and *Philistines*, who shed the blood of God's people unjustly, but to all the nations of the earth who, to enlarge their territory, increase their wealth, or extend their commerce, have made destructive wars. For the blood which such nations have shed, their blood shall be shed. If *man* should make no inquisition for this iniquitously spilt blood, GOD will do it, for he *remembers them;* and the *cry of the humbled*, distressed people, driven to distraction and ruin by such wars, *is not forgotten before him*.

Verse 13. *Have mercy upon me, O Lord*] David, having laid down the preceding maxims, now claims his part in their truth. I also am in trouble through the unjust dealings of my enemies; I am brought to the *gates of death;* have mercy on *me*, and lift *me* up, that, being saved from the *gates of death*, I may show forth thy praise in *the gates of the daughter of Zion*.

A. M. cir. 2962
B. C. cir. 1042
Davidis, Regis Israelitarum, cir. annum 14

14 That I may show forth all
thy praise in the gates of the
daughter of Zion: I will [p]rejoice
in thy salvation.

15 [q]The heathen are sunk down in the pit
that they made: in the net which they hid
is their own foot taken.

16 The LORD is [r]known *by* the judgment
which he executeth: the wicked is snared in
the work of his own hands. [s]Higgaion.[t]
Selah.

17 The wicked shall be turned
into hell, *and* all the nations [u]that
forget God.

A. M. cir. 2962
B. C. cir. 1042
Davidis, Regis Israelitarum, cir. annum 14

18 [v]For the needy shall not
always be forgotten: [w]the expectation of the
poor shall *not* perish for ever.

19 Arise, O LORD; let not man prevail: let
the heathen be judged in thy sight.

20 Put them in fear, O LORD: *that* the
nations may know themselves *to be but* men.
Selah.

---

[p]Psa. xiii. 5; xx. 5; xxxv. 9——[q]Psa. vii. 15, 16; xxxv. 8; vii. 6; xciv. 23; Prov. v. 22; xxii. 8; xxvi. 27——[r]Exod. vii. 5; xiv. 4, 10, 31

[s]That is, *meditation*——[t]Psa. xix. 14; xcii. 3——[u]Job viii. 13; Psa. l. 22——[v]Ver. 12; Psa. xii. 5——[w]Prov. xxiii. 18; xxiv. 14

The gates of death—an *open grave*, leading to a *yawning hell. The gates of the daughter of Zion*—all the *ordinances* of God, by which the soul is helped forward to heaven.

Verse 15. *The heathen are sunk down in the pit*] See on Psa. vii. 15.

Verse 16. *The Lord is known* by *the judgment*] It is not every *casualty* that can properly be called a *judgment of God.* Judgment is his strange work; but when he executes it, his mind is plainly to be seen. There are no natural causes to which such calamities can be legally attributed.

The wicked is snared in the work of his own hands.] There is nothing that a wicked man does that is not against his own interest. He is continually doing himself harm, and takes more pains to destroy his soul than the righteous man does to get his saved unto eternal life. This is a weighty truth; and the psalmist adds: *Higgaion; Selah.* Meditate on this; mark it well. See on Psa. iii. 3. Some think that it is a direction to the musicians, something like our *Presto, Largo, Vivace, Allegro,* "Play briskly and boldly; beat away; and let *sense* and *sound* accompany each other."

Verse 17. *The wicked shall be turned into hell*] לשאולה *lisholah, headlong into hell, down into hell.* The original is very emphatic.

All the nations that forget God.] They will not live in his fear. There are both *nations* and *individuals* who, though they *know* God, *forget* him, that is, are *unmindful* of him, do not *acknowledge* him in their designs, ways, and works. These are all to *be thrust down into hell.* Reader, art thou forgetful of thy *Maker*, and of HIM who *died* for thee?

Verse 18. *The needy shall not alway be forgotten*] The needy, and the poor, whose expectation is from the Lord, are never forgotten, though sometimes their deliverance is delayed for the greater confusion of their enemies, the greater manifestation of God's mercy, and the greater benefit to themselves.

Verse 19. *Arise, O Lord*] Let this be the time in which thou wilt deliver thy poor people under oppression and persecution.

Verse 20. *Put them in fear*] שיתה יהוה מורה להם *shithah Yehovah morah lahem,* "O Lord, place a teacher among them," that they may know they also are accountable creatures, grow wise unto salvation, and be prepared for a state of blessedness. Several MSS. read מורא *morre, fear;* but *teacher* or *legislator* is the reading of all the *versions* except the *Chaldee. Coverdale* has hit the sense, translating thus: **O Lorde, set a Scholemaster over them**; and the old Psalter, **Sett Lord a brynger of Law abouen tham.**

That *the nations may know themselves* to be but *men*] אנוש *enosh;* Let the Gentiles be taught by the preaching of thy Gospel that they are *weak* and *helpless*, and stand in need of the salvation which Christ has provided for them. This may be the spirit of the petition. And this is marked by the extraordinary note *Selah;* Mark well, take notice. So the term may be understood.

"This whole Psalm," says Dr. Horsley, "seems naturally to divide into three parts. The first *ten* verses make the FIRST part; the *six* following, the SECOND; and the remaining *four* the THIRD.

"The FIRST part is prophetic of the utter extermination of the irreligious persecuting faction. The prophecy is delivered in the form of an Επινικιον, or song of victory, occasioned by the promise given in the *fifteenth* verse of the *tenth* Psalm; and through the whole of this song the psalmist, in the height of a prophetic enthusiasm, speaks of the threatened vengeance as accomplished.

"The SECOND part opens with an exhortation to the people of God to praise him as the Avenger of their wrongs, and the watchful Guardian of the helpless, and, as if the flame of the prophetic joy which the oracular voice had lighted in the psalmist's mind was beginning to die away, the strain is gradually lowered, and the notes of triumph are mixed with supplication and complaint, as if the mind of the psalmist were fluttering between things present and to come, and made itself alternately present to his actual condition and his future hope.

"In the THIRD part the psalmist seems quite returned from the prophetic enthusiasm to his natural state, and closes the whole song with explicit but cool assertions of the future destruction of the wicked, and the deliverance of the persecuted saints, praying for the event."

ANALYSIS OF THE NINTH PSALM

This Psalm consists of *five* chief parts:—

I. David's thanksgiving, ver. 1, 2, amplified and continued till the *tenth* verse.

II. An exhortation to others to do the like, ver. 11, and the reason of it, ver. 12.

III. A petition for himself, ver. 13, and the reason of it, ver. 14.

IV. A remembrance of God's mercy in the overthrow of his enemies, for which he sings a song of triumph, from ver. 15-19.

V. A prayer in the conclusion against the prevalence of the heathen, ver. 19, 20.

I. His profession of praise is set down in the two first verses, in which we may perceive,—

1. The matter of it, with the extent: *All the marvellous works of God.*

2. That he varies the synonyms. *I will praise thee; I will show forth; I will be glad and rejoice in thee; I will sing praise to thy name, O thou Most High!* in which there is a *climax.*

3. The principle whence this praise flowed: 1. Not from the *lips*, but from the *heart.* 2. From the *whole heart:* "I will praise thee with my whole heart."

This he amplifies from the cause, which is double:

1. That which outwardly moved him, and gave him a just occasion to do so; the overthrow of his enemies: "When my enemies are turned back;" who were not overcome by strength or valour, but by the presence and power of God.

2. They shall fall and perish at thy presence. Thou wast the chief cause of this victory; and, therefore, deservest the thanks. Of this the prophet makes a full narrative in the two next verses, setting God as it were upon the bench, and doing the office of Judge. 1. "Thou maintainest my right, and my cause." 2. "Thou sattest on the throne judging right." 3. "Thou hast rebuked the heathen." 4. "Thou hast destroyed the wicked; thou hast put out their name for ever." In a word, Thou art a just Judge, and defendest the innocent, and punishest their oppressors; and *therefore I will praise thee.*

3. And then, upon the confidence of God's justice and power, he exults over his enemies. *O thou enemy, destructions are come to a perpetual end.* Thy power of hurting and destroying is taken away; the fortified cities in which thou dwellest are overthrown; and their memory and thine are perished.

4. Next, to make his assertion clearer; to the enemies' power he opposes that of God; his kingdom to their kingdom. But the Lord, in the administration of his kingdom, is, 1. Eternal: "The Lord shall endure for ever." 2. His office to be Judge: "He hath prepared his throne for judgment." 3. He is a universal Judge: "He shall judge the whole world." 4. He is a just Judge: "He shall judge in righteousness; he shall minister judgment to the people in uprightness." 5. He is a merciful Judge: "For the Lord will be a refuge for the oppressed; a refuge in times of trouble."

5. The effect of this execution of justice. His people are encouraged: who are here described, 1. By their *knowing* him: "They that know thy name." 2. By *trusting* in him: "Will put their trust in thee." 3. By their *seeking* him: "For thou, Lord, hast not forsaken them that seek thee."

II. An exhortation to others to praise God: "Sing praises to the Lord." The reason of this, 1. He *dwells* in Zion. 2. He *works* graciously there: "Sing praises to the Lord that DWELLS in Zion: declare among the people his DOINGS.' 3. That will destroy their oppressors, and avenge their blood: "When he maketh inquisition for blood, he remembereth them; he forgetteth not the cry of the humble."

III. A petition for himself: "Have mercy on me, O Lord; consider my trouble," &c.; for which he gives these reasons:—

1. That "I may show forth thy praise."

2. "ALL thy praise."

3. "In the gates of the daughter of Zion."

4. That I may do it with joyful lips.

5. Which I will do: "I WILL rejoice in thy salvation."

IV. Then he sings forth his song of triumph over his enemies:—

1. The "heathen are sunk down in the pit they have made."

2. "In the net which they hid are their own feet taken."

3. This is the Lord's work. Though wicked men did doubt before of his providence and justice; yet now "the Lord was known by the judgment which he executed."

4. For "the wicked was snared in the work of his own hands. Higgaion, Selah." Which is a thing exceedingly to be meditated upon, and not forgotten.

5. "The wicked shall be turned into hell, and all the people that forget God." 1. Their breath is in their nostrils, and die they must. 2. If they repent not, they shall suffer eternal punishment. 3. However this may be, God's goodness shall be manifested to the innocent: "The expectation of the poor shall not perish for ever."

V. A prayer in the conclusion against the prevalence of the heathen, in which he shows great earnestness and faith:—

1. "Arise, O Lord; let not man prevail."

2. "Let the heathen be judged in thy sight."

3. "Put them in fear, O Lord!" Now they fear nothing, being in their height of prosperity. They are insolent and proud; manifest thy Divine presence to their terror.

4. For then they will know themselves to be but *men*—infirm and mortal creatures; and not insult over thy people, nor glory in their own strength and prosperity.

The original word has been translated *teacher, lawgiver, governor.* Then send them, 1. A *teacher*, who may make them wise unto salvation. 2. A *lawgiver*, who shall rule them in thy fear. 3. A *governor*, that shall tame and reduce to order their fierce and savage nature. Let the nations be converted unto thee. This will be the noblest triumph. Let their hearts be conquered by thy mercy. And thus the Psalm will conclude as it began, *To the Conqueror*, on whose vesture and thigh is the name written, KING OF KINGS, AND LORD OF LORDS.

PSALM X

The psalmist complains to God of the oppressions which the poor suffer from the wicked man, whom he describes as the hater of the poor, 1, 2; *proud*, 3; *one who will not seek God*, 4; *and is regardless of his judgments*, 5; *self-confident*, 6; *blasphemous and deceitful*, 7; *strives by subtlety and treachery to destroy the poor*, 8–10; *and supposes that God is regardless of his conduct*, 11. *The psalmist calls earnestly on God to preserve the poor and humble, and cast down the oppressor*, 12–15. *He foresees that his prayer is heard; that judgment will be executed, and the poor delivered*, 16–18.

A. M. cir. 3559 B. C. cir. 445 Artaxerxis, R. Persarum, cir. annum 20

WHY standest thou afar off,
O LORD? *why* hidest thou
thyself in times of trouble?
2 [a]The wicked in *his* pride
doth persecute the poor: [b]let them be taken
in the devices that they have imagined.
3 For the wicked [c]boasteth of his [d]heart's
desire, and [e]blesseth [f]the covetous, *whom* the
LORD abhorreth.
4 The wicked, through the pride of his countenance, [g]will not seek *after God:* [h]God
is not in all his [i]thoughts.
5 His ways are always grievous: [k]thy judgments *are* far above out of his
sight: *as for* all his enemies,
[l]he puffeth at them.
6 [m]He hath said in his heart,
I shall not be moved: [n]for *I shall* [o]never *be*
in adversity.
7 [p]His mouth is full of cursing, and [q]deceit,
and fraud: [r]under his tongue *is* mischief [s]and
[t]vanity.
8 He sitteth in the lurking places of the villages: [u]in the secret places doth he murder
the innocent: [v]his eyes are [w]privily set against
the poor.

[a]Hebrew, *In the pride of the wicked he doth persecute*——[b]Psalm vii. 16; ix. 15, 16; Proverbs v. 22——[c]Psalm xciv. 4——[d]Heb. *souls*——[e]Prov. xxviii. 4; Rom. i. 32——[f]Or, *the covetous blesseth* himself, *he abhorreth the LORD*——[g]Psa. xiv. 2——[h]Or, *all his thoughts* are There is *no God*——[i]Psa. xiv. 1; lxxiii. 1

[k]Prov. xxiv. 1; Isa. xxvi. 11——[l]Psa. xii. 5——[m]Psa. xxx. 6; Eccles. viii. 11; Isa. lvi. 12——[n]Rev. xviii. 7——[o]Heb. *unto generation and generation*——[p]Rom. iii. 14——[q]Heb. *deceits*——[r]Job xx. 12——[s]Psa. xii. 2——[t]Or, *iniquity*——[u]Hab. iii. 14——[v]Psa. xvii. 11——[w]Heb. *hide themselves*

NOTES ON PSALM X

Verse 1. *Why standest thou afar off, O Lord?*] This Psalm makes a part of the preceding in the *Vulgate* and *Septuagint;* and in four of *Kennicott's* and *De Rossi's* MSS. It seems to belong to the time of the *captivity*, or the *return* of the captives. It was probably made in reference to *Sanballat*, and the other enemies of the Jews. There is a great similarity between this and Psalms xiii., xiv., xxxv., and liii. In these, as *Calmet* remarks, we find the same complaints, the same sentiments, and almost the same expressions.

God is represented here as standing at some distance, beholding the oppression of his people, and yet apparently disregarding it.

Verse 2. *The wicked in* his *pride*] On no principle of *nature* or *reason* can we account for a *wicked man* persecuting a *humble follower of God* because of his *religion*. The devil hates godliness; and the wicked man hates it also, because the devil is in his heart.

Verse 3. *Boasteth of his heart's desire*] Boasts among his fellows how often he has gratified such and such passions, in such and such circumstances. This shows the excess of a depraved and imbruted spirit. He who can boast of his iniquity, is in the broad road to perdition. Should such a one repent and turn to God, it would be equal to any miracle.

Blesseth the covetous, whom *the Lord abhorreth.*] Or, *he blesseth the covetous, he abhorreth the Lord.* Those who are like himself he commends, and with them he associates; and *they abhor the Lord*—they have a mortal hatred against every thing that is holy; and they are under the full influence of that *carnal mind* which is *enmity* to the Lord.

Verse 4. *Will not seek* after God] He is too *proud* to bend his knee before his Judge; he is too haughty to put on sackcloth, and lay himself in the dust; though without deep repentance and humiliation he must without doubt perish everlastingly.

Verse 5. *His ways are always grievous*] Or, *He is travailing in pain* to bring *forth iniquity at all times.* He is full of lust, or *irregular* and *unholy desires;* he *conceives* and *brings forth sin;* and sin being finished, time, place, and opportunity concurring, *death* is *soon brought forth.*

Thy judgments are *far above out of his sight*] He is so blinded with sin, that he cannot see the operations of God's hand.

He puffeth at them.] He whistles at them; insults God, and despises men. He overthrows them with his *breath;* he has only to give orders, and they are destroyed. "Bring me the head of Giaffer," said an Asiatic despot. The head was immediately brought! No trial, no judge, no jury; but the despot's will and caprice.

Verse 6. *I shall not be moved*] I have whatever I covet. I hold whatsoever I have gotten. I have money and goods to procure me every gratification.

Verse 7. *His mouth is full of cursing, and deceit, and fraud*] What a finished character! A blasphemer, a deceitful man, and a knave!

Verse 8. *He sitteth in the lurking places*] In this and the following verse there appears to be an allusion to *espionage*, or setting of *spies* on a man's conduct; or to the conduct of an assassin or private murderer. He sitteth in *lurking* places—in *secret* places; his *eyes*—spies—are *privily set;* he lieth in *wait secretly:* he doth *catch* the poor, when he draweth him into his *net.* He is like a hunter that lays his

A. M. cir. 3559
B. C. cir. 445
Artaxerxis,
R. Persarum,
cir. annum
20

9 He [x]lieth in wait [y]secretly
as a lion in his den: he lieth in
wait to catch the poor: he doth
catch the poor, when he draweth
him into his net.
10 [z]He croucheth, *and* humbleth himself,
that the poor may fall [a]by his strong ones.
11 He hath said in his heart, God hath forgotten: [b]he hideth his face; he will never
see *it.*
12 Arise, O LORD; O God, [c]lift up thine
hand: forget not the [d]humble.
13 Wherefore doth the wicked contemn God?
he hath said in his heart, Thou wilt not require *it.*
14 Thou hast seen *it;* for thou beholdest
mischief and spite, to requite *it*
with thy hand: the poor [e]com-
mitteth [f]himself unto thee; [g]thou
art the helper of the fatherless.
15 [h]Break thou the arm of the wicked and
the evil *man:* seek out his wickedness *till* thou
find none.
16 [i]The LORD *is* King for ever and ever:
the heathen are perished out of his land.
17 LORD, thou hast heard the desire of the
humble: thou wilt [k]prepare [l]their heart, thou
wilt cause thine ear to hear:
18 To [m]judge the fatherless and the oppressed, that the man of the earth may no
more [n]oppress.

[x]Psa. xvii. 12; Mic. vii. 2——[y]Heb. *in the secret places*——[z]Heb. *he breaketh himself*——[a]Or, *into his strong parts*——[b]Job xxii. 13; Psalm. lxxiii. 11; xciv. 7; Ezekiel viii. 12; ix. 9——[c]Micah v. 9——[d]Or, *afflicted* [e]Hebrew, *cleaveth*

[f]2 Tim. i. 12; 1 Pet. iv. 19——[g]Psa. lxviii. 5; Hos. xiv. 3——[h]Psa. xxxvii. 17——[i]Psa. xxix. 10; cxlv. 13; cxlvi. 10; Jer. x. 10; Lam. v. 19; Dan. iv. 34; vi. 26; 1 Tim. i. 17——[k]Or, *establish*——[l]1 Chron. xxix. 18 [m]Psa. lxxxii. 3; Isa. xi. 4——[n]Or, *terrify*

traps and gins, digs his pits, sets his nets; and when the prey falls into them, he destroys its life.

Verse 10. *He croucheth*] Of the scoffing, mocking, insulting, and *insidious* conduct of *Sanballat, Tobiah,* and *Geshem,* the fourth and sixth chapters of *Nehemiah* give abundant proof; and possibly the allusion is to them. The lion squats down and gathers himself together, that he may make the greater spring.

Verse 11. *God hath forgotten*] He hath cast off this people, and he will never more re-establish them. So *Sanballat* thought.

Verse 12. *Arise, O Lord*] Hear their reproaches see their guile, consider thy oppressed people. "Lift up thine hand," *threaten* them, that they may desist and repent. If they repent not let them be punished.

Verse 13. *Wherefore doth the wicked contemn God?*] How is it that the Lord permits such persons to triumph in their iniquity? The longsuffering of God leadeth them to repentance.

Verse 14. *Thou hast seen* it] Nothing can escape thy notice. Thou hast not forgotten thy justice, though judgment is not speedily executed on an evil work. But thou *wilt requite it with thy hand.* By thy *power* thou wilt cast down and destroy the wicked.

The poor committeth himself unto thee] To thee he has given up his body, his soul, and his cause; with the full conviction that thou who art the *helper of fatherless,* will not forget *him.*

Verse 15. *Break thou the arm*] Destroy his *power,* deprive him of his *influence,* that he may be no longer able to oppress.

Seek out his wickedness till *thou find none.*] All his public haunts and private ways shall be investigated; thou wilt bring all his villanies to light, and continue to inflict punishment, while there is a crime to punish. Or, "Continue to judge and punish transgressors, till not one is to be found." This agrees with the following verse.

Verse 16. *The Lord* is *king for ever*] He has, and ever will have, the supreme power.

The heathen are perished out of his land.] They are all either cut off or *converted.* This may refer to the *Canaanites.* What a mercy that we can say this of our own country! Once it was entirely heathen; now not one heathen family in the whole land.

Verse 17. *Lord, thou hast heard*] Thou hast not permitted thy tempted and afflicted followers to pray in vain.

Thou wilt prepare their heart] See the economy of the grace of God: 1. God *prepares* the *heart;* 2. *Suggests the prayer;* 3. *Hears* what is prayed; 4. *Answers* the petition. He who has got a cry in his heart after God, may rest assured that that cry proceeded from a Divine preparation, and that an answer will soon arrive. No man ever had a cry in his heart after salvation, but from God. He who continues to cry shall infallibly be heard.

Verse 18. *That the man of the earth may no more oppress.*] I believe the Hebrew will be better translated thus: "That he may not add any more to drive away the wretched man from the land." Destroy the influence of the tyrant; and let him not have it again in his power to add even one additional act of oppression to those which he has already committed.

How many for the sake of their religion, and because they would serve God with a pure conscience, have, by wicked *lords,* proud and arrogant *land owners,* been driven off their farms, turned out of their houses, deprived of their employments, and exposed to wretchedness! While they served the devil, and were regardless of their souls, they had quiet and peaceable possession; but when they turned to the Lord, and became *sober* and *industrious,* attended the means of grace, read their Bible, and were frequent in prayer, then the *vile man of the earth* drove them from their dwellings! In the sight of such Philistines, piety towards God is the highest of crimes. What a dreadful account must these give *to the Judge of the fatherless and the oppressed!*

Analysis of the Tenth Psalm

This Psalm divides itself into three parts:—

I. A complaint against the enemies of the godly.

II. A narration of the enemies' malice.

III. A petition to be delivered from them.

I. 1. He complains of God's absence, which is quickened by the question, 1. "Why standest thou afar off?" 2. "Why hidest thou myself in times of trouble?" ver. 1.

II. He complains of the enemies: "The wicked in his pride doth persecute the poor."

These he describes by *eight* characters:—

1. *Insolence*, pride, and the effect, persecution of good men. Having acquired dignity, places of honour, and riches, they become persecutors, they conspire to oppress good men. "Let them be taken in their own devices," ver. 2. Amen.

2. The wicked man *glories in mischief*, which is a sign of extreme malice: "The wicked boasteth of his heart's desire," ver. 3.

3. He *applauds* and *encourages* others in their *rapine* and *spoil*, to which they are moved by their *covetousness:* "He blesseth the covetous," ver. 3.

4. He *contemns God* and *man*. 1. Man. He never thinks of being called to an account: God's "judgments are out of his sight, and he puffs at his enemies." 2. God. Him he reverences not: "He will not seek after God; neither is he in all his thoughts," 4, 5.

5. He lives in *profane security:* "He saith in his heart, I shall never be moved; I shall never be in adversity;" I am elevated beyond the reach of misfortune, ver. 6.

6. He is full of falsehood and deceit: "His mouth is full of cursing, deceit, and fraud." He will not stick at an *oath*. He will curse himself; and take God to witness in his exactions, that he is doing nothing but what is right, ver. 7.

7. He is *cruel*. See the 9th and 10th verses, where he is compared to a *thief*, an *archer*, an *assassin*, a *lion*, &c. He is bad in heart, ver. 6; in *tongue*, ver. 7; in *work*, ver. 8, 10:—he is altogether bad.

8. He is a close atheist: "He hath said in his heart, God hath forgotten; he hideth his face, and will never see it:" which is the cause of his cruelty, falsehood, security, &c., ver. 11.

III. The third part is a *petition* to be freed from the wicked man: "Arise, O Lord, lift up thy hand, forget not the humble," ver. 12. To induce God thus to act, he uses two arguments:—

1. That thereby God would assert his own glory. For why should the wicked be suffered thus to blaspheme? "Wherefore doth the wicked contemn God? He hath said in his heart, Thou wilt not require it," ver. 13.

2. The *second* argument is taken from God's *nature* and *work*. 1. In punishing wicked men. 2. In defending the helpless. "Surely thou hast seen it; for thou beholdest michief and spite to requite it," &c., ver. 14.

Then he returns to his prayer, and enforces his *second* argument taken from the *justice* and *office* of God:

1. That he would deprive the wicked of his power and strength: "Break thou the arm of the wicked—seek out his wickedness till thou find none," ver. 15. Let none escape—let them appear no more.

2. That he would *hear* and defend the righteous. Be to thy people what thou hast been in times past. 1. "The Lord is King for ever and ever." 2. He *had expelled the Canaanites* before them: "The heathen are perished out of the land." 3. "Thou hast heard the desire of the humble," ver. 16, 17.

Upon which he concludes with profession of strong confidence:—

1. "Thou wilt prepare the heart of the humble."

2. "Thou wilt cause thine ear to hear." 1. To the safety of the oppressed: "To judge the fatherless and the poor," ver. 18. 2. To the ruin of the oppressor: "That the man of the earth may no more oppress;" that he may have neither power nor influence left by which he may be a plague to the upright, or a supporter of infidelity, ver. 18.

PSALM XI

David's friends advise him to flee to the wilderness from Saul's fury, 1–3. *He answers that, having put his trust in God, knowing that he forsakes not those who confide in him, and that he will punish the ungodly, he is perfectly satisfied that he shall be in safety,* 4–7.

To the chief Musician, *A Psalm* of David

A. M. cir. 2942 B. C. cir. 1062 Sauli, Regis Israelitarum, cir. annum 34

[a]IN the Lord put I my trust: [b]how say ye to my soul, Flee *as* a bird to your mountain?

2 For, lo, [c]the wicked bend *their* bow, [d]they make ready their arrow upon the string, that they may [e]privily shoot at the upright in heart.

A. M. cir. 2942 B. C. cir. 1062 Sauli, Regis Israelitarum, cir. annum 34

[a]Psa. lvi. 11——[b]See 1 Sam. xxvi. 19, 20——[c]Psa. lxiv. 3, 4——[d]Psa. xxi. 12——[e]Heb. *in darkness*

NOTES ON PSALM XI

The inscription is, *To the chief Musician,* A Psalm *of David.* By the *chief musician* we may understand the *master-singer;* the *leader of the band;* the *person* who *directed the choir:* but we know that the word has been translated, *To the Conqueror;* and some deep and mystical senses have been attributed to it, with which I believe the text has nothing to do.

Verse 1. *In the Lord put I my trust: how say ye*] Some of David's friends seem to have

A. M. cir. 2942
B. C. cir. 1062
Sauli, Regis
Israelitarum,
cir. annum
34

3 [f]If the foundations be destroyed, what can the righteous
do?
4 [g]The LORD *is* in his holy
temple, the LORD'S [h]throne *is* in heaven: [i]his
eyes behold, his eyelids try, the children of
men.
5 The LORD [k]trieth the righteous: but the
wicked and him that loveth violence his soul hateth.
6 [l]Upon the wicked he shall
rain [m]snares, fire, and brimstone,
and [n]a horrible tempest: [o]*this shall be* the
portion of their cup.
7 For the righteous LORD [p]loveth righteousness; [q]his countenance doth behold the upright.

A. M. cir. 2942
B. C. cir. 1062
Sauli, Regis
Israelitarum,
cir. annum
34

[f]Psa. lxxxii. 5——[g]Heb. ii. 20——[h]Psa. ii. 4; Isa. lxvi. 1; Matt. v. 34; xxiii. 22; Acts vii. 49; Rev. iv. 2——[i]Psa. xxxiii. 13; xxxiv. 15, 16; lxvi. 7——[k]Gen. xxii. 1; James i. 12——[l]Gen. xix. 24; Ezek. xxxviii. 22

[m]Or, *quick burning coals*——[n]Or, *a burning tempest* [o]See Gen. xliii. 34; 1 Sam. i. 4; ix. 23; Psa. lxxv. 8 [p]Psa. xlv. 7; cxlvi. 8——[q]Job xxxvi. 7; Psa. xxxiii. 18; xxxiv. 15; 1 Pet. iii. 12

given him this advice when they saw Saul bent on his destruction: "Flee *as* a bird to your mountain;" you have not a moment to lose; your ruin is determined; escape for your life; get off as *swiftly* as possible to the hill-country, to some of those inaccessible fortresses best known to yourself; and hide yourself there from the cruelty of Saul. To which advice he answers, "In the Lord put I my trust;" shall I act as if I were conscious of evil, and that my wicked deeds were likely to be discovered? Or shall I act as one who believes he is forsaken of the protection of the Almighty? No: I put my trust in him, and I am sure I shall never be confounded.

Verse 2. *For, lo, the wicked bend* their *bow*] Perhaps these are more of the words of his advisers: Every thing is ready for thy destruction: the arrow that is to pierce thy heart is already set on the bow-string; and the person who hopes to despatch thee is concealed in ambush.

Verse 3. *If the foundations be destroyed*] If Saul, who is the vicegerent of God, has cast aside his fear, and now regards neither truth nor justice, a righteous man has no security for his life. This is at present thy case; therefore flee! They have utterly destroyed the foundations; (of truth and equity;) what can righteousness now effect? *Kimchi* supposes this refers to the *priests* who were murdered by Doeg, at the command of Saul. The priests are destroyed, the preservers of knowledge and truth; the Divine worship is overthrown; and what can the righteous man work? These I think to be also the words of David's advisers. To all of which he answers:—

Verse 4. *The Lord* is *in his holy temple*] He is still to be sought and found in the place where he has registered his name. Though the priests be destroyed, the God in whose worship they were employed still lives, and is to be found in his temple by his upright worshippers. And he tries the heart and the reins of both sinners and saints. Nothing can pass without his notice. I may expect his presence in the *temple;* he has not promised to meet me in the *mountain.*

Verse 5. *The Lord trieth the righteous*] He does not abandon them; he tries them to show their faithfulness, and he afflicts them for their good.

His soul hateth.] The *wicked* man must ever be abhorred of the Lord; and the *violent* man—the destroyer and murderer—*his soul hateth;* an expression of uncommon strength and energy: all the perfections of the Divine nature have such in abomination.

Verse 6. *Upon the wicked he shall rain*] This is a manifest allusion to the destruction of Sodom and Gomorrah.

Snares] Judgments shall fall upon them *suddenly* and *unawares.*

Fire] Such as shall come immediately from *God,* and be *inextinguishable.*

Brimstone] Melted by the fire, for their *drink!* This shall be the portion of their *cup.*

A horrible tempest] רוח זלעפות *ruach zilaphoth,* "the spirit of terrors." Suffering much, and being threatened with more, they shall be filled with confusion and dismay. My old MS. has **gost of stormis**. See at the end. Or, *the blast of destructions.* This may refer to the horribly suffocating Arabian wind, called سموم *Smum.*

Mohammed, in describing his *hell,* says, "The wicked shall drink nothing there but hot stinking water; breathe nothing but burning winds; and eat nothing but the fruit of the tree *zakon,* which shall be in their bellies like *burning pitch.*" Hell enough!

The portion of their cup.] *Cup* is sometimes put for *plenty,* for *abundance;* but here it seems to be used to express the *quantum* of *sorrow* and *misery* which the *wicked* shall have on the earth. See Psa. lxxv. 8; Isa. li. 17, 21, 22, 23; Jer. xxv. 15, xlix. 12; Lam. iv. 21, 22. It is also used in reference to the afflictions of the *righteous,* Matt. xx. 22, xxvi. 39, 42; John xviii. 11.

We find a similar metaphor among the heathens. The following, from *Homer,* Il. xxiv., ver. 525, is in point:—

> *Ὡs γαρ επεκλωσαντο θεοι δειλοισι βροτοισι,*
> *Ζωειν αχνυμενους· αυτοι δε τ' ακηδεες εισι.*
> *Δοιοι γαρ τε πιθοι κατακειαται εν Διος ουδει*
> *Δωρων, οἱα διδωσι, κακων· ἑτερος δε εαων·*
> *Ὡ μεν καμμιξας δῳη Ζευς τερπικεραυνος,*
> *Αλλοτε μεν τε κακῳ ὁγε κυρεται, αλλοτε δ' εσθλῳ.*

Such is, alas! the god's severe decree,
They, only they are *bless'd,* and only free.
Two urns by Jove's high throne have ever stood,
The source of *evil* one, and one of *good.*
From thence the CUP of mortal man he fills:
Blessings to *these;* to *those* distributes *ills.*
To most he mingles *both:* the wretch decreed
To taste the bad *unmix'd,* is curs'd indeed.
—POPE.

Verse 7. *The righteous Lord loveth righteousness*] He loves that which resembles himself. *His countenance*—his face—is ever open and unclouded to the upright. They always enjoy his salvation, and know that he is pleased with them.

The preceding verse my old MS. translates and paraphrases thus:—

He sal rayne on synful, snares, fyre, brimstane, and gost of stormis.

Par.—He sal rayne on synful in this werld, *snares*, that es wiked Lare: *fyre* is covatyse: *brunstane*, that es stynk of il werkes: and *gost of stormis*, that es a stormy though that es withoutyn rest in Ihesu Crist, and ay es traveld with the wynd of the devel. Or *the gast of stormys*, es the last depertyng of synful fra ryghtwis men, and there fyre, brunston, storm, er part of the chalyie of thaim: that es, thai ar thair part in pyne. He cals thair pyne a *Cop*, for ilk dampned man sal drynk of the sorow of Hel, eftir the mesure of hys Syn. Behald the pynes of wikid men: fyrst, God raynes upon thaim *snares*, that es qwen he suffers fals prophetes that comes in clathing of mekenes; and withinnen er wers than wolves, to desayf thaim thurgh errour. Sythen the fyre of lychery, and covatys wastes al the gude that thai haf done: eftirward for stynk of il werkes thai er castyn fra Crist, and al his Halows, and then er in sentence of dome; as in a grete storme, dryven in til a pitte of Hel, to bryn in fyre withoutyn ende. This es the entent of this wers.

Verse 7. **For ryghtwis es Lord; and he lufes ryghtwisnes; evennes saw the face of hym**] Yf ge ask qwy oure lorde yelded pyne to synful? lo here an answere; for he es rightwis. Als so if ge wil witt qwy he gifes ioy til gude men? Lo here an answere; for he lufed ryghtwisnes: that es, ryghtwis men, in the qwilk er many ryghtwisneses: thof ane be the ryghtwisnes of God, in the qwilk al ryghtwise men or parcenel. *Evenes saw his face:* that es, evenes es sene in his knawyng inence, both the partys of gud and il. This es ogayne wryches at sais, If God saf me noght, I dar say he es unryghtwis: bot thof thai say it now, qwen he suffris wryched men errour in thought, and worde and dede; thai sal noght be so hardy to speke a worde qwen he comes to dampne thaire errour. Bot who so lufes here and haldes that na unevenes may be in hym, qwam so he dampnes, or qwam so he saves, he sal have thaire myght to stand and to speke gude space. Now er swilk in a wonderful wodenes, that wenes for grete wordes to get ought of God.

The former part of this Psalm, *Flee* as *a bird*, &c., this ancient author considers as the voice of *heresy* inviting the *true Church* to go away into error; and intimates that those who were separating from *haly kyrk* were very pure, and unblameable in all their conduct; and that *mountain* or *hill*, as he translates it, signifies *eminent virtues*, of which they had an apparently good stock. So it appears that those called *heretics* lived then a holier life than those called *halows* or saints.

Analysis of the Eleventh Psalm

This Psalm is composed dialoguewise, betwixt David and those of his counsellors that persuaded him to fly to some place of safety from Saul's fury; which, if he did not, he was in a desperate condition. The Psalm has *two* parts.

I. He relates his counsellors' words, ver. 1, 2, 3.

II. To which he returns his answer, ver. 1, and confirms it, ver. 4-7.

I. You, my counsellors, whether of good or bad will I know not, tempt me, that, giving up all hope of the kingdom, I go into perpetual banishment. Such, you say, is Saul's fury against me. Thus, then, ye advise, "Flee *as* a bird to your mountain:" and your arguments are,

1. The greatness of the danger I am in: "For, lo, the wicked bend *their* bow."

2. The want of aid; there is no hope of help. For *the foundations are cast down.* Saul has broken all the leagues and covenants he has made with you. He has slain the priests with the sword, has taken thy fortresses, laws subverted. If thou stay, perish thou must: some righteous men, it is true, are left; but *what can the righteous do?*

II. To these their arguments and counsel, David returns his answer in a sharp reprehension. I tell you,

1. "I trust in God: how say you then to my soul." And he gives his reasons for it from the sufficiency and efficiency of God.

1. You say *the foundations are cast down;* yet I despair not, for God is sufficient.

1. *Present in his holy temple;* he can defend.

2. He is a great King, and *his throne is in heaven.*

3. Nothing is hidden from him: "His eyes behold, and his eyelids," &c.

4. He is a just God, and this is seen in his proceedings both to the just and unjust. 1. *He trieth the righteous*, by a fatherly and gentle correction. 2. "But the wicked, and him that loveth violence, his soul hateth."

These two last propositions he expounds severally, and begins with the *wicked.*

1. "Upon the wicked he shall rain snares, fire and brimstone," &c. 1. He shall rain upon them when they least think of it, even in the midst of their jollity, as rain falls on a fair day. 2. Or, he shall *rain down* the vengeance when he sees good, for it *rains not always.* Though he defer it, yet it *will* rain. 3. The punishment shall come to their utter subversion, as the fire on Sodom, &c. 4. This is the portion of their cup, that which they must expect from him.

2. But he does good to the just: "For the righteous Lord loveth righteousness; his countenance doth behold the upright." He bears him good will, and is careful to defend him.

On the whole the Psalm shows, 1. That David had the strongest conviction of his own uprightness. 2. That he had the fullest persuasion that God would protect him from all his enemies, and give him a happy issue out of all his distresses.

PSALM XII

The psalmist, destitute of human comfort, craves help from God, 1; *gives the character of those who surrounded him, and denounces God's judgments against them,* 2–5; *confides in the promises of God, and in his protection of him and all good men,* 6–8.

To the chief Musician [a]upon [b]Sheminith, A Psalm of David

HELP, [c]LORD; for the [d]godly man ceaseth; for the faithful fail from among
the children of men.
2 [e]They speak vanity every one with his
neighbour: [f]*with* flattering lips, *and* with [g]a
double heart do they speak.
3 The LORD shall cut off all flattering lips,
and the tongue that speaketh [h]proud [i]things:
4 Who have said, With our tongue will we prevail; our lips [k]*are* our own: who *is* lord over us?
5 For the oppression of the poor, for the
sighing of the needy, [l]now will I arise, saith
the LORD; I will set *him* in safety *from him*
that [m]puffeth [n]at him.
6 The words of the LORD *are* [o]pure words:
as silver tried in a furnace of earth, purified
seven times.

[a]Or, *upon the eighth*——[b]Psalm vi. title——[c]Or, *Save*——[d]Isaiah lvii. 1; Micah vii. 2——[e]Psalm x. 7——[f]Psalm xxviii. 3; lxii. 4; Jeremiah ix. 8; Romans xvi. 18——[g]Hebrew, *a heart and a heart;* 1 Chronicles xii. 33——[h]1 Samuel ii. 3; Psalm xvii. 10; Daniel vii. 8, 25——[i]Hebrew, *great things*——[k]Hebrew, are *with us*——[l]Exodus iii. 7, 8; Isaiah xxxiii. 10 [m]Or, *would ensnare him*——[n]Psalm x. 5——[o]2 Samuel xxii. 31; Psalm xviii. 30; xix. 8; cxix. 140; Proverbs xxx. 5

NOTES ON PSALM XII

The inscription to this Psalm is: *To the chief Musician upon Sheminith, A Psalm of David.* See on the title of Psa. vi. The *Arabic* has "Concerning the end (of the world which shall happen) on the eighth day. A prophecy relative to the Advent of the Messiah."

Some think that this Psalm was made when Doeg and the Ziphites betrayed David to Saul, see 1 Sam. xxii. and xxiii.; but it is most likely that was written during the Babylonish captivity.

Verse 1. *Help, Lord*] Save me, O Lord; for merciful men fail, and faithful men have passed away from the sons of Adam. **Make safe me, Lord; for haly failed, for lessed es sothfastnes fra sons of men.** OLD MS.

Verse 2. *They speak vanity every one with his neighbour*] They are false and hollow; they say one thing while they mean another; there is no trusting to what they say.

Flattering lips, and *with a double heart do they speak*] בלב ולב *beleb valeb,* "With a heart and a heart." They seem to have *two hearts; one* to speak fair words, and the *other* to invent mischief. The old MS. both translates and paraphrases curiously.

Trans. **Dayn spak ilkan til his neghbur: swykil lippis in hert, and thurgh hert thai spak.**

Par.—Sothfastnes es lessed, and falsed waxes: and al sa vayn spak ilkone to bygyle his neghbur: and many spendes thair tyme in vayne speche withoutyn profyte and gastely frute. And thai er *swyku lippis;* that er jangelers berkand ogaynes sothfastnes. And *swykel,* for *thai speke in hert and thurgh hert;* that es in dubil hert, qwen a fals man thynkes ane, and sais another, to desaif hym that he spekes with.

This homely comment cannot be mended.

Verse 3. *Proud things*] גדלות *gedoloth, great things;* great swelling words, both in their *promises* and in their *commendations.*

Verse 4. *Our lips* are *our own*] Many think, because they have the faculty of speaking, that therefore they may speak what they please.

Old MS.—The qwilk sayd, our toung we sal wyrchip, our lippes er of us, qwas our Lorde? Tha Ypocrites worchepes thair toung; for thai hee tham self janglyng and settes in thaire pouste to do mykil thyng and grete: and thai rose tham that thair lippes that es thair facund and thair wyls er of tham self, nought of God, ne of haly menes lare; for thi thai say *qua es our Lord?* that es, qwat es he to qwas rewle and conversacioun we sal be undir lout? and confourme us til? Als so to say, Thar es none.

Verse 5. *For the oppression of the poor*] This seems to refer best to the tribulations which the poor Israelites suffered while captives in Babylon. The Lord represents himself as looking on and seeing their affliction; and, hearing their cry, he determines to come forward to their help.

Now will I arise] I alone delivered them into the hands of their enemies, because of their transgressions; I alone can and will deliver them from the hands of their enemies; and the manner of their deliverance shall show the power and influence of their God.

From him that *puffeth at him.*] Here is much *interpolation* to make out a sense. Several of the *versions* read, "I will give him an open salvation." My work shall be manifest.

Verse 6. *The words of the Lord* are *pure words*] None of his promises shall fall to the ground; the salvation which he has promised shall be communicated.

Silver tried in a furnace of earth] A reference to the purification of silver by the *cupel.* This is a sort of instrument used in the purification of silver. It may be formed out of a strong iron ring or hoop, adjusted in width and depth to the quantum of silver to be purified, and rammed full of well pulverized calcined bone. The metal to be purified must be mingled with *lead,* and laid on the cupel, and exposed to a strong heat in an air furnace. The impurities of the metal will be partly absorbed, and partly

7 Thou shalt keep them, O LORD, thou shalt preserve [p]them from this generation for ever.

8 The wicked walk on every side, when [q]the vilest men are exalted.

[p]Heb. *him;* that is, *every one of them*

[q]Heb. *the vilest of the sons of men are exalted*

thrown off in fume. The metal will continue in a state of agitation till all the impurities are thrown off; it will then become perfectly *still,* no more *motion* appearing, which is the token that the process is completed, or, according to the words of the text, is *seven times,* that is, perfectly *purified.*

Verse 7. *Thou shalt keep them—thou shalt preserve them*] Instead of the pronoun *them* in these clauses, several MSS., with the *Septuagint,* the *Vulgate,* and the *Arabic,* have *us.* The sense is equally good in both readings. God did bring forth the Israelites from Babylon, according to his word; he separated them from *that generation,* and reinstated them in their own land, according to his word; and most certainly he has *preserved them from generation to generation* to the present day, in a most remarkable manner.

Verse 8. *The wicked walk on every side*] The land is full of them. *When the vilest men are exalted;* rather, *As villany gains ground among the sons of Adam.* See the Hebrew. The *Vulgate* has, "In circuito impii ambulant; secundum altitudinem tuam multiplicasti filios hominum;" which is thus translated and paraphrased in my old MS.:—

Trans. **In umgang wiked gos: eftir thy heenes thu has multiplied the sons of man.**

Par. Us thu kepes; bot wiked gas in umgang; that es, in covatyng of erdley gudes, that turnes with the whele of seven daies: in the qwilk covatys, thai ryn ay aboute; for thai sett nane endyng of thaire syn: and tharfor settes God na terme of thair pyne, but sons of men that lyfs skilwisly and in ryghtwisnes, thu has multiplied, aftir thi heghnes in vertus; aftir the heghnes of thi consayll, thou hast multiplied men bath il and gude; for na man may perfitely witt in erd, qwy God makes so many men, the qwilk he wote well sal be dampned: bot it es the privete of his counsayle, so ryghtwis, that no thyng may be ryghtwiser.

In this we find a number of singular expressions, which, while they elucidate the text, will not be uninteresting to the antiquary. Here, for instance, we see the true etymology of the words *righteous* and *righteousness,* i. e., *right wise* and *right wiseness.* For we have it above as a *noun,* **ryghtwisnes**; as an *adjective,* **ryghtwis**; and as an *adjective* in the *comparative* degree, **rightwiser**: and we should have had it as an *adverb, ryghtwisely,* had not the word **skilwisly** occurred to the author.

Righteousness is *right wiseness,* or that which is according to *true wisdom.* A *righteous* man is one who is *right wise;* properly instructed in *Divine wisdom,* and *acts* according to its dictates; and among them who act *rightwisely,* there are some who act *rightwiser* than others; and nothing can be *rightwiser* than ever to *think* and *act* according to the *principles* of that *wisdom* which comes from above.

Right, **riht** rectus, *straight,* is opposed to *wrong,* from **wrang,** *injury,* and that from **wrangen,** to *twist.* As **rehtan** *rehtan* signifies to *direct,* so **wrangen** *wrangen* signifies to *twist,* or *turn* out of a *straight* or *direct* line. *Right* is *straight,* and *wrong, crooked.* Hence the *righteous* man is one who goes *straight forward,* acts and walks by *line* and *rule;* and the *unrighteous* is he who walks in *crooked paths,* does what is *wrong,* and is never guided by true *wisdom.* Such a person is sometimes termed *wicked,* from the Anglo-Saxon **wiccian,** to act by *witch*-craft, (hence **wicca,** *wicca,* a *witch,*) that is to renounce God and righteousness, and to give one's self to the devil, which is the true character of a *wicked* man. Let him that readeth understand.

The vilest men are exalted] Were we to take this in its obvious sense, it would signify that at that time wickedness was the way to preferment, and that good men were the objects of persecution.

ANALYSIS OF THE TWELFTH PSALM

There are *four* parts in this Psalm:—

I. A *prayer,* and the reason of it; ver. 1, 2.

II. A *prophecy* of the fall of the wicked, ver. 3, whose arrogance he describes, ver. 4.

III. God's *answer* to the petition, with a promise full of comfort, ver. 5; ratified, ver. 6.

IV. A *petitory,* or *affirmative conclusion: Keep them;* or a confident affirmation that God will keep them from the contagion of the wicked, ver. 7, of which there were too many, ver. 8.

I. The *prayer,* which is very short, for he breaks in upon God with one word, הושעה *Hoshiah! Help! Save, Lord!* ver. 1. For which he gives two reasons:—

1. The scarcity of good men: "For the godly man ceaseth," &c. There is neither piety nor fidelity among men.

2. The great abundance of the wicked; the licentious times; the perfidiousness, hypocrisy, and dissimulation of the men among whom he lived. "They speak vanity every one with his neighbour," &c.; ver. 2. They take no care to perform what they promise.

II. The *prophecy.* This shows the end of their dissembling: "The Lord shall cut off all flattering lips;" ver. 3. These are described,

1. As proud boasters: "With our tongues will we prevail," &c.

2. As persons restrained by no authority: "Who is the Lord over us?" ver. 4.

III. God's *answer* to the petition, *Help, Lord!* is it so that the wicked are so numerous, so tyrannous, so proud, and so arrogant?

1. "I will arise, saith the Lord."

2. I will not delay: "Now I will arise;" ver. 5.

3. "I will set him in safety (my followers) from him that puffeth," &c.

4. I am moved to it by his sighs and groans: "For the oppression of the poor, for the sighing of the needy," &c.; ver. 5.

5. And of this let no man doubt: "The words of the Lord are pure words." There is no more fallacy in the words of God than there is impurity in silver seven times refined; ver. 6.

IV. A petitory, or affirmative conclusion: *Thou shalt keep them, O Lord;* or, *O keep them!* The overflowings of wickedness are great.

1. *Keep them.* For unless God keep them they will be infected.

2. *Keep them from this generation.* **For they** are a generation of vipers.

3. *Keep them for ever.* For unless thou enable them to *persevere,* they will fall.

4. *And keep them.* For the power, pride, and influence of these impious men are very great. 1. "The wicked walk on every side." As wolves they seek whom they may devour. 2. And wickedness is the way to preferment: "The vilest men are exalted;" ver. 8.

Thy people call on thee for help; they know thou canst help, and therefore are they confident that thou wilt help, because they know that thou art good.

PSALM XIII

***This Psalm contains the sentiments of an afflicted soul that earnestly desires succour from the Lord. The psalmist complains of delay,* 1–3; *prays for light and comfort, because he finds himself on the brink of death,* 3; *dreads the revilings of his enemies,* 4; *anticipates a favourable answer, and promises thanksgiving,* 5, 6.**

To the [a]chief Musician, A Psalm of David

A. M. cir. 3464
B. C. cir. 540
Ante U. C. cir. 214
Olymp. LX. cir. ann. prim.

HOW long wilt thou forget me, O LORD? for ever? [b]how long wilt thou hide thy face from me?

2 How long shall I take counsel in my soul, *having* sorrow in my heart daily? how long shall mine enemy be exalted over me?

3 Consider *and* hear me, O LORD my God: [c]lighten mine eyes, [d]lest I sleep the *sleep of* death;

4 [e]Lest mine enemy say, I have prevailed against him: *and* those that trouble me, rejoice when I am moved.

5 But I have [f]trusted in thy mercy; my heart shall rejoice in thy salvation.

6 I will sing unto the LORD, because he hath [g]dealt bountifully with me.

[a]Or, *overseer*——[b]Deut. xxxi. 17; Job xiii. 24; Psa. xliv. 24; lxxxviii. 14; lxxxix. 46; Isa. lix. 2

[c]Ezra ix. 8——[d]Jer. li. 39——[e]Psa. xxv. 2; xxxv. 19; xxxviii. 16——[f]Psa. xxxiii. 21——[g]Psa. cxvi. 7; cxix. 17

NOTES ON PSALM XIII

There is nothing particular in the inscription. The Psalm is supposed to have been written during the captivity, and to contain the prayers and supplications of the distressed Israelites, worn out with their long and oppressive bondage.

Verse 1. *How long wilt thou forget me*] The words עד אנה *ad anah, to what length, to what time,* translated here *how long?* are *four* times repeated in the two first verses, and point out at once great dejection and extreme earnestness of soul.

Hide thy face from me?] How long shall I be destitute of a clear sense of thy *approbation?*

Verse 2. *Take counsel in my soul*] I am continually framing ways and means of deliverance; but they all come to naught, because thou comest not to my deliverance. When a soul feels the burden and guilt of sin, it tries innumerable schemes of self-recovery; but they are all useless. None but God can speak peace to a guilty conscience.

Mine enemy be exalted] Satan appears to triumph while the soul lies under the curse of a broken law.

Verse 3. *Consider* and *hear me*] Rather, *answer me.* I have prayed; I am seeking thy face; I am lost without thee; I am in darkness; my life draws nigh to destruction; if I die unforgiven, I die eternally. O Lord my God, *consider* this; hear and answer, for thy name's sake.

Verse 4. *Let mine enemy say*] Satan's ordinary method in temptation is to excite strongly to sin, to blind the understanding and inflame the passions; and when he succeeds, he triumphs by insults and reproaches. None so ready then to tell the poor soul how deeply, disgracefully, and ungratefully it has sinned! Reader, take heed.

When I am moved.] When moved from my steadfastness and overcome by sin. O what desolation is made by the fall of a righteous soul! Itself covered with darkness and desolation, infidels filled with scoffing, the Church clad in mourning, the Spirit of God grieved, and Jesus crucified afresh, and put to an open shame! O God, save the pious reader from such wreck and ruin!

Verse 5. *But I have trusted in thy mercy*] Thou wilt not suffer me to fall; or if I have fallen, wilt thou not, for his sake who died for sinners, once more lift up the light of thy countenance upon me? Wilt thou not cover my sin?

My heart shall rejoice in thy salvation.] There is no true joy but of the heart; and the heart cannot rejoice till all guilt is taken away from the conscience.

Verse 6. *I will sing unto the Lord*] That heart is turned to God's praise which has a clear sense of God's favour.

Because he hath dealt bountifully with me.] כי גמל עלי *ki gamel alai, because he hath recompensed me.* My sorrows were deep, long continued, and oppressive, but in thy favour is life. A moment of this spiritual joy is worth a year of sorrow! O, to what blessedness has this godly sorrow led! He has given me the oil of joy for the spirit of heaviness, and the garments of praise for mourning.

The old MS. Psalter, which I have so frequently mentioned and quoted, was written at least *four hundred* years ago, and written probably in Scotland, as it is in the Scottish dialect. That the writer was not merely a commentator, but a truly religious man, who was well acquainted with the travail of the soul, and that faith in the Lord Jesus Christ which brings peace to the troubled heart, is manifested from various portions of his comment. To prove this I shall, I think I may say, favour the reader with another extract from this Psalm on the words, "How long wilt thou forget me," &c., ver. 1. I have only to observe that with this commentator a true penitent, one who is deeply in earnest for his salvation, is called a *perfyte man;* i. e., one wholly given up to God.

How lang lord for getes thu me in the endyng? How lang o way turnes thou thi face fro me? The voice of haly men that covaytes and yernes the comyng of Iehu Crist, that thai might lyf with hym in ioy; and pleynaund tham of delaying. And sais, *Lord how lang for getes thu me in the endyng?* That I covayte to haf and hald. That es how lang delayes thu me fra the syght of Iehu Crist, that es ryght endyng of myn entent. And how lang turnes thu thi face fra me? that es, qwen wil thu gif me perfyte Knawing of the? This wordes may nane say sothly, bot a perfyte man or woman, that has gedyrd to gydir al the desyres of thair Saule, and with the nayle of luf fested tham in Iehu Crist. Sa tham thynk one hour of the day war our lang to dwel fra hym; for tham langes ay til hym; bot tha that lufs noght so, has no langyng that he come: for thair conscience sais thaim, that thai haf noght lufed hym als thai suld have done.

The language of true Christian experience has been the same in all times and nations. "But he that loveth not knoweth not God; for God is love;" and to such this is strange language.

Analysis of the Thirteenth Psalm

"This Psalm," says Bishop Nicolson, "is a fit prayer for a soul that is sensible of God's desertion."

It has *three* parts:—

I. A heavy and bitter complaint of God's absence, ver. 1, 2.

II. An earnest petition for God's return, ver. 3. The reason, ver. 4.

III. A profession of faith and confidence, with joy in God, accompanied with thanksgiving, ver. 5, 6.

I. He bitterly complains, and aggravates it.

1. That God had forgotten him: "Wilt thou forget me?"

2. That he hid his face from him: "Wilt thou hide thy face?"

3. That he was distracted with many cares, what way to take, and what counsel to follow, to recover God's favour: "I take counsel in my soul, having sorrow in my heart."

4. In the meantime, his *enemy was exalted, triumphed* and *insulted over him.*

5. And, lastly, he complains of the delay, which is quickened by the *erotesis,* (interrogation,) and *anaphora,* (beginning several sentences with the same words,) *How long? How long? How long? What! for ever?*

II. His petition, ver. 3. Of which there are three degrees opposed to the parts of his complaint, ver. 1, 2.

1. *Look upon me,* or *consider me.* Thou hast hitherto seemed to turn away thy face; but once behold me, and give me a proof of thy love.

2. *Hear me.* Thou hast seemed to have forgotten; but now, I pray thee, remember me; and show that thou dost not neglect my prayer.

3. *Lighten my eyes.* I have been vexed in my soul, and agitated various counsels to recover thy favour; but do thou instruct me, and illuminate me, as to what course I shall take.

That his petition might be the sooner heard, he urges many arguments:—

1. From that relation that was between him and God: "O Lord my God, hear me!"

2. From a bitter event that was likely to follow, if God heard him not: "Lest I sleep the sleep of death."

3. From another afflictive consequence—the boasting and insult of his adversaries: "Lest my enemy say, I have prevailed against him; and those that trouble me rejoice when I am moved."

But although the answer was delayed, yet he does not despair—for,

III. In the conclusion, he professes faith, joy, and thankfulness:—

1. His *faith:* "I have trusted in thy mercy."

2. His *joy:* "My heart shall rejoice in thy salvation."

3. His *thankfulness:* "I will sing unto the Lord, because he hath dealt bountifully with me."

According to this scale, this Psalm can neither be read nor paraphrased without profit.

PSALM XIV

The sentiments of atheists and deists, who deny the doctrine of a Divine providence. Their character: they are corrupt, foolish, abominable, and cruel, 1–4. *God fills them with terror,* 5; *reproaches them for their oppression of the poor,* 6. *The psalmist prays for the restoration of Israel,* 7.

To the chief Musician, *A Psalm* of David

A. M. cir. 3440
B. C. cir. 564
Ante U. C. cir. 190
Olymp. LIV. cir. ann. prim.

THE [a]fool hath said in his
heart, *There is* no God.
[b]They are corrupt, they have
done abominable works, *there*
is none that doeth good.
2 [c]The LORD looked down from heaven
upon the children of men, to see if there were
any that did understand, *and* seek God.
3 [d]They are all gone aside, they are *all*
together become [e]filthy: *there*
is none that doeth good, no, not
one.

A. M. cir. 3440
B. C. cir. 564
Ante U. C. cir. 190
Olymp. LIV. cir. ann. prim.

4 Have all the workers of ini-
quity no knowledge? who [f]eat up my people
as they eat bread, and [g]call not upon the
LORD.
5 There [h]were they in great fear: for God
is in the generation of the righteous.
6 Ye have shamed the counsel of the

[a]Psa. x. 4; liii. 1, &c.——[b]Gen. vi. 11, 12; Rom. iii. 10, &c.——[c]Psa. xxxiii. 13; cii. 19——[d]Rom. iii. 10, 11, 12——[e]Heb. *stinking*

[f]Jeremiah x. 25; Amos iii. 4; Micah iii. 3——[g]Psalm lxxix. 6; Isaiah lxiv. 7——[h]Hebrew, *they feared a fear;* Psalm liii. 5

NOTES ON PSALM XIV

There is nothing particular in the *title;* only it is probable that the word לדוד *ledavid, of David,* is improperly prefixed, as it is sufficiently evident, from the construction of the Psalm, that it speaks of the *Babylonish captivity.* The author, whoever he was, (some say Haggai, others Daniel, &c.,) probably lived beyond the Euphrates. He describes here, in fervid colours, the iniquity of the Chaldeans. He predicts their terror and destruction; he consoles himself with the prospect of a speedy return from his exile; and hopes soon to witness the reunion of the tribes of Israel and Judah. It may be applied to *unbelievers* in general.

Verse 1. *The fool hath said in his heart, There is no God.*] נבל *nabal,* which we render *fool,* signifies an *empty fellow,* a *contemptible person,* a *villain.* One who has a muddy head and an unclean heart; and, in his darkness and folly, says in his heart, "There is no God." "And none," says one, "but a *fool* would say so." The word is not to be taken in the strict sense in which we use the term *atheist,* that is, one who denies the *being of a God,* or confounds him with *matter.* 1. There have been some, not many, who have denied the existence of God. 2. There are others who, without absolutely denying the Divine existence, deny his *providence;* that is, they acknowledge a Being of infinite power, &c., but give him nothing to do, and no world to govern. 3. There are others, and they are very numerous, who, while they profess to acknowledge both, deny them in their heart, and live as if they were persuaded there was no God either to punish or reward.

They are corrupt] They are in a state of *putrescency;* and *they have done abominable works*—the corruption of their *hearts* extends itself through all the actions of their *lives.* They are a plague of the most deadly kind; propagate nothing but destruction; and, like their father the devil, spread far and wide the contagion of sin and death. Not *one of them does good.* He cannot, for he has no Divine influence, and he denies that such can be received.

Verse 2. *The Lord looked down from heaven*] Words spoken after the manner of men. From this glorious eminence God is represented as looking down upon the habitable globe, *to see if there were any that did understand* that there was a Supreme Being, the governor and judge of men; and, in consequence, *seek God* for his mercy, support, and defence.

Verse 3. *They are all gone aside*] They will not walk in the *straight* path. They seek *crooked* ways; and they have departed from *truth,* and the God of truth.

They are all *together become filthy*] נאלחו *neelachu.* They are become *sour* and *rancid;* a metaphor taken from milk that has fermented, and turned sour, rancid, and worthless.

There is *none that doeth good, no, not one.*] This is not only the state of heathen Babylon, but the state of the *whole inhabitants of the earth,* till the grace of God changes their heart. By *nature,* and from nature, by *practice,* every man is sinful and corrupt. He *feels* no good; he is *disposed* to no good; he *does* no good. And even God himself, who cannot be deceived, cannot find a single exception to this! Lord, what is man?

The *Vulgate,* the Roman copy of the *Septuagint,* the *Æthiopic,* and the *Arabic,* add those six verses here which are quoted by St. Paul, Rom. iii. 13-18. See the notes on those passages, and see the *observations* at the end of this Psalm.

Verse 4. *Have all the workers of iniquity no knowledge?*] Is there not one of them who takes this dreadful subject into consideration? To their deeply fallen state they add cruelty; they oppress and destroy the poor, without either interest or reason.

Who eat up my people as *they eat bread*] Ye make them an easy and unresisting prey. They have no power to oppose you, and therefore you destroy them. That this is the meaning of the expression, is plain from the speech of Joshua and Caleb relative to the Canaanites, Num. xiv. 9: "Neither fear ye the people of the land; for they are bread for us."

And call not upon the Lord.] They have no *defence,* for they *invoke not the Lord.* They are all either *atheists* or *idolaters.*

Verse 5. *There were they in great fear*] This is a manifest allusion to the history of the *Canaanitish nations;* they were struck with terror at the sight of the Israelites, and by this allusion the psalmist shows that a destruction similar to that which fell upon them, should fall on the Babylonians. Several of the versions add, from Psa. liii. 5, "Where no fear was." They were struck with terror, where no real cause of terror existed. Their fears had magnified their danger.

For God is *in the generation*] They feared the Israelites, because they knew that the Almighty God was among them.

Verse 6. *Ye have shamed the counsel of the*

A. M. cir. 3440
B. C. cir. 564
Ante U. C. cir. 190
Olymp. LIV. cir. ann. prim.

poor, because the LORD *is* his
[i]refuge.
7 [k]O [l]that the salvation of
Israel *were come* out of Zion!
[m]when the LORD bringeth back
the captivity of his people, Jacob
shall rejoice, *and* Israel shall be
glad.

A. M. cir. 3440
B. C. cir. 564
Ante U. C. cir. 190
Olymp. LIV. cir. ann. prim.

[i]Psa. ix. 9; cxlii. 5——[k]Heb. *Who will give*, &c.; see Rom. xi. 26——[l]Psa. liii. 6——[m]Job xlii. 10; Psa. cxxvi. 1

poor] Instead of תבישו *tabishu*, "Ye have shamed," Bishop *Horsley* proposes to read תבישם *tabishem*, and translates the clause thus: "The counsel of the helpless man shall put *them* to shame." But this is not authorized by MS. or *version*. There is no need for any change: the psalmist refers to the *confidence* which the afflicted people professed to have in God for their deliverance, which confidence the Babylonians turned into *ridicule*. The poor people took counsel together to expect help from God, and to wait patiently for it; and this counsel ye derided, because ye did not *know*—did not *consider*, that God was in the congregation of the righteous.

Verse 7. *O that the salvation*] Or, more literally, *Who will give from Zion salvation to Israel?* From Zion the deliverance must come; for God alone can deliver them; but *whom* will he make his instruments?

When the Lord bringeth back] For it is Jehovah alone who can do it. *Jacob shall rejoice*, and *Israel shall be glad*. That is, according to *Calmet*, the remains of the kingdom of Israel, and those of Judah, shall be rejoined, to their mutual satisfaction, and become one people, worshipping the same God; and he has endeavoured to prove, in a dissertation on the subject, that this actually took place after the return from the Babylonish captivity.

Many of the fathers have understood this verse as referring to the *salvation of mankind by Jesus Christ;* and so it is understood by my old MS. Psalter, as the following paraphrase will show: **Qwa sal gyf of Syon hele til Israel? qwen Lord has turned o way the captyfte of his folk, glad sal Jacob, and fayne be Israel.** Qwa bot Crist that ge despyse, qwen ge wil nout do his counsaile of Syon fra heven, sal gyf hele til Israel? that es, sal saf al trew cristen men; noght als ge er that lufs noght God. And qwen our Lord has turned o way the captyfte of his folk: that es, qwen he has dampned the devel, and al his Servaundes, the qwilk tourmentes gude men, and makes tham captyfs in pyne. *Then glade sal Jacob;* that es, al that wirstils o gayns vices and actyf: *and fayne sal be Israel:* that es, al that with the clene egh of thair hert, sees God in contemplatyf lyf. For *Jacob* es als mikil at say als, *Wrestler*, or *suplanter* of *Syn. Israel* es, *man seand God.*

Of the two chief opinions relative to the *design* of this Psalm: 1. That it refers to *Absalom's rebellion*. 2. That it is a complaint of the *captives in Babylon;* I incline to the latter, as by far the most probable.

I have referred, in the note on ver. 3, to that remarkable addition of no less than *six verses*, which is found here in the *Vulgate*, the Vatican copy of the *Septuagint*, the *Æthiopic*, and the *Arabic*, and also in St. *Paul's* Epistle to the Romans, chap. iii. 13-18, which he is supposed to have quoted from this Psalm as it then stood in the Hebrew text; or in the version of the *Seventy*, from which it has been generally thought he borrowed them. That they are not interpolations in the *New Testament* is evident from this, that they are not wanting in any MS. yet discovered; and they exist in all the ancient versions, the *Vulgate*, *Syriac*, *Æthiopic*, and *Arabic*. Yet it has been contended, particularly by St. *Jerome*, that St. Paul did not quote them from this Psalm; but, being intent on showing the corruption and misery of man, he collected from *different parts* several passages that bore upon the subject, and united them here, with his quotation from Psa. xiv. 3, as if they had all belonged to that place: and that succeeding copyists, finding them in *Romans*, as quoted from that Psalm, inserted them into the *Septuagint*, from which it was presumed they had been lost. It does not appear that they made a part of this Psalm in *Origen's Hexapla*. In the portions that still exist of this Psalm there is not a word of these additional verses referred to in that collection, neither here nor in the parallel Psalm liii.

The places from which *Jerome* and others say St. Paul borrowed them are the following:—

Rom. iii. 13: "Their mouth is an open sepulchre; with their tongues they have used deceit." Borrowed from Psa. v. 10.

"The poison of asps is under their lips." From Psa. cxl. 3.

Verse 14: "Whose mouth is full of cursing and bitterness." From Psa. x. 7.

Verse 15: "Their feet are swift to shed blood." From Prov. i. 16, or Isa. lix. 7.

Verses 16, 17, 18: "Destruction and misery are in their ways, the way of peace they have not known, and there is no fear of God before their eyes." From Isa. lix. 7, 8.

When the reader has collated all these passages in the *original*, he will probably feel little satisfaction relative to the probability of the hypothesis they are summoned to support.

These verses are not found in the best copies of the *Vulgate*, though it appears they were in the old *Itala* or *Antehieronymain* version. They are not in the *Codex Alexandrinus* of the *Septuagint;* nor are they in either the *Greek* or *Latin* text of the *Complutensian* Polyglot. They are wanting also in the *Antwerp* and *Parisian* Polyglots. They are neither in the *Chaldee* nor *Syriac* versions. They are not acknowledged as a part of this Psalm by *Theodoret*, *Chrysostom*, *Euthymius*, *Arnobius*, *Apollinaris*, the *Greek Catena*, *Eusebius*, of Cæsarea, nor *Jerome*. The latter, however, acknowledges that they were in his time *read in the churches*. I have seen no Latin MS. without them; and they are quoted by *Justin Martyr* and *Augustine*. They are also in the *Editio Princeps* of the *Vulgate*, and in all the ancient *Psalters* known. They are in that *Psalter* which I have frequently quoted, both in the *Latino-Scotico-English* version and paraphrase.

Of this version the following is a faithful copy, beginning with the *third* verse of the *fourteenth* Psalm:—

Al tha helddid togyder; thai er made unprofytable:
Thar es none that dos gude; thar es none til one.
A grave opynnand, es the throte of tham.
With thaire tunges trycherusly thai wroght
Venym of snakes undir the lippis of tham.
Qwhas mouth es ful of werying and bitternes:
Swyft thaire fete to spil blode.
Brekyng and wikednes in thair waies:
And the way of pees thai knew noght:
The drede of God es noght byfore the eghen of thaim.

There is a good deal of difference between this, and that *version* attributed to *Wiclif*, as it stands in my large MS. Bible, quoted in different parts of the New Testament, particularly in 1 Cor. xiii. 1, &c. I shall give it here line for line with the above.

Alle boweden aweye to gydre; thei ben maad unprofitable:
Ther is not that doith good thing, ther is not til to oon.
A Sepulcre opnyng is the throote of hem:
With her tungis thei diden gylinly; or trecherously:
The venym of eddris, that is clepid Aspis, under her lippis:
The mouth of whom is ful of cursing, or worrying and bittrenesse:
The feet of hem ben swift for to schede out blood:
Contricioun or defouling to God, and infelicite or cursidnesse, the wayes of hem;
And thei knewen not the weyes of pees;
The dreed of God is not bifore her ygen.

The words underlined in the above are added by the translator as explanatory of the preceding terms. It is worthy of remark that *Coverdale* inserts the whole of the addition in this Psalm; and *Cardmarden* has inserted it in his Bible, but in a letter different from the text.

It is now time to state what has been deemed of considerable importance to the authenticity of these verses; viz., that they are found in a *Hebrew* MS., numbered by *Kennicott* in his catalogue 649. It is in the public library at *Leyden;* contains the *Psalms* with a *Latin version* and *Scholia;* and appears to have been written about the end of the *fourteenth* century, and probably by some *Christian*. I shall give the text with a literal *translation*, as it stands in this MS., line for line with the preceding:—

קבר פתוח גרונם
An open sepulchre is their throat;

לשונם יחליקיון
With their tongues they flatter;

חמת עכשוב תחת לשונם
The venom of the asp is under their tongue;

אשר פיהם אלה ומרמה מלא
Whose mouth of cursing and bitterness is full;

קלו רגליהם לשפוך דם:
Swift are their feet to shed blood;

מזל רע ופגע רע בדרכיהם
An evil aspect, and an evil event, in their ways:

ודרך שלום לא ידעו
And the way of peace they know not.

אין פחד אלהים לנגר עיניהם:
No fear of God before their eyes.

It would be easy to criticise upon the Hebrew in this long quotation. I shall content myself with what *Calmet*, who received his information from others that had inspected the Leyden MS., says of this *addition:* "Les sçavans, qui ont examiné ce manuscrit, y ont remarqué un Hebreu barbare en cet endroit; et des façons de parler, qui ne sentent point les siecles où la langue Hebraïque etoit en usage." "Learned men, who have examined this MS., have remarked a barbarous Hebraism in this place, and modes of speech which savour not of those ages in which the Hebrew language was in use."

If this be an interpolation in the Psalm, it is *very ancient;* as we have the testimony of *Jerome*, who was prejudiced against it, that it was read in all the churches in his time, and how long before we cannot tell. And that these verses are a valuable portion of Divine revelation, as they stand in Rom. iii. 13-18, none can successfully deny. See *Rosenmüller*, *Kennicott*, and *De Rossi*.

Analysis of the Fourteenth Psalm

This Psalm is the practical atheist's character, and has two parts:—

I. The description of the practical atheist, from ver. 1 to 7.

II. A petition for the Church, ver. 7.

I. 1. The atheist is here noted to us by different characters:—

1. From his *name*, נבל *nabal*, a *fool*, or rather a *churl;* no natural fool, but a sinful: a *fool* in that in which he should be wise.

2. His hypocrisy or cunning; *he saith*, but he will not have it known, it is to himself, "He saith in his heart." He is a close, politic *fool.*

3. His saying, or his chief and prime principle: "There is no God."

4. From his practice; confessing God in his words for some political advantages, yet in his works denying him. For, 1. His heart is wicked and unregenerate: "They are corrupt." 2. He is a sinner in a high practical degree: "They have done abominable works." 3. He performs no duty: "There is none that doeth good." He *commits* sin; he *omits* duty.

2. The psalmist demonstrates what he said *three* ways; and convinces them,—

1. By the testimony of *God* himself; he is a witness against them. He is, 1. An eyewitness: *he looks on.* 2. He is in heaven, and they are continually under his notice: "He looked down from heaven." 3. He sees *the children of men*, their *hearts* and their *works*. 4. And the object of his looking is to inquire after their *religion:* "To see if there were any that did understand and seek God."

2. And then he gives his testimony in these general terms: "They are all gone aside, they are all together become filthy: there is none that doeth good, no, not one."

3. Next he accuses them of *two sins* of which they were especially guilty. 1. *Injustice:* "They eat up my people as bread." 2. *Impiety:* "They call not upon the Lord."

4. And that his testimony is true, he convinces them, 1. By the light of their own *conscience:* "Have all the workers of iniquity no knowledge?" Does not their own conscience tell them that all this is true? Do they not *know* this? 2. By *fear* and *terror*, the effects of an evil conscience: "There were they in great fear." They said, *There is no God;* but their conscience told them that *God was in the congregation of the righteous*, and that they should grievously answer for their *injustice* and *impiety*. 3. By the *hardness* of their *heart*, and contempt of the good counsels of the godly.

If *he* reproved, *they* mocked. If he said *God was his refuge,* they laughed him to scorn. "Ye have shamed the counsel of the poor, because the Lord is his refuge."

II. The second part of the Psalm contains a petition for the Church:—

1. He prays that God would *send salvation to his people.*

2. That it might be *out of Zion;* because *Christ* was anointed and set a King upon the holy hill of Zion: "O that the salvation of Israel were come out of Zion!"

3. For then the consequence would be the great joy and happiness of all his people for their deliverance from captivity, *spiritual* and *temporal:* "When the Lord bringeth back the captivity of his people, Jacob shall rejoice, and Israel shall be glad."

PSALM XV

The important question answered, Who is a proper member of the Church militant? *and who shall finally join the* Church triumphant? *Ver.* 1 *contains the question; ver.* 2–5, *the answer.*

A Psalm of David

LORD, [a]who shall [b]abide in thy tabernacle? who shall dwell in [c]thy holy hill?

2 [d]He that walketh uprightly, and worketh righteousness, and [e]speaketh the truth in his heart.

[a]Psa. xxiv. 3, &c.——[b]Heb. *sojourn*——[c]Psa. ii. 6; iii. 4

[d]Isa. xxxiii. 15——[e]Zech. viii. 16; Eph. iv. 25

NOTES ON PSALM XV

The *title,* מזמור לדוד *mizmor ledavid, a Psalm of David,* has nothing in it particularly worthy of notice. If it were a Psalm composed during the captivity, relating to their return and settlement in their own land, with the restoration of their temple service and all the ordinances of God, and a description of the persons who should then be considered Israelites indeed, the name of *David* is improperly prefixed. But the subject is of the most general utility, and demands the most solemn and serious attention of all men who profess to believe in the immortality of the soul.

Verse 1. *Lord, who shall abide in thy tabernacle?*] The literal translation of this verse is, "Lord, who shall sojourn in thy tabernacle? who shall dwell in the mountain of thy holiness?" For the proper understanding of this question we must note the following particulars:—

1. The *tabernacle,* which was a kind of *moveable temple,* was a type of the *Church militant,* or the state of the people of God in this world.

2. *Mount Zion,* the *holy mount,* where the temple was built, was the type of the *kingdom of heaven.* There the ark became *stationary,* and was no longer carried about from place to place; and the whole was typical of the *rest* that remains for the people of God.

3. The TABERNACLE was a temporary and frequently-removed building, carried about from place to place, and not long in any one place. Concerning this it is said מי יגור *mi yagur,* "Who shall *lodge,* or *sojourn,*" there? It is not a *residence,* or *dwelling-place,* but a place to *lodge* in for a time.

4. The TEMPLE was a *fixed* and *permanent* building; and here it is inquired, מי ישכן *mi yiscon,* "Who shall *dwell, abide,*" or have his *permanent residence,* there?

5. The *tabernacle* being a migratory temple, carried about on the shoulders of the priests and Levites, there was no *dwelling* there for any; they could but *lodge* or *sojourn.*

6. The *temple* being *fixed,* the priests, Levites, &c., became *permanent occupiers.* There was no *lodging* or *sojourning,* but *permanent residence* for all connected with it.

7. The *tabernacle* is, therefore, a proper type of the *Church militant,* wandering up and down, tossed by various storms and tempests; the followers of God, having here *no continuing city; sojourning* only on earth to get a preparation for eternal glory.

8. The *temple* is also a proper type or emblem of the *Church triumphant* in heaven. "Here the wicked cease from troubling, and the weary are at rest." It is the *dwelling-place,* the *eternal residence,* of all who are faithful unto death, who are made *pillars in that temple of God, to go no more out for ever.*

The questions therefore are,

1. Who can be considered a fit member of the Church of Christ here below? and,

2. Who shall be made partakers of an endless glory? In answer to these questions, the character of what we may term a *true Israelite,* or a *good Christian,* is given in the following particulars:—

Verse 2. *He that walketh uprightly*] הולך תמים *holech tamim,* 1. *He walks perfectly.* Who sets God before his eyes, takes his word for the rule of his conduct, considers himself a *sojourner* on earth, and is continually *walking* to the kingdom of God. He acts according to the *perfections* of God's law; he has respect to all its parts, and feels the weight and importance of all its injunctions.

And worketh righteousness] 2. He is not

3 [f]*He that* backbiteth not with his tongue,
nor doeth evil to his neighbour, [g]nor [h]taketh
up a reproach against his neighbour.
4 [i]In whose eyes a vile person is contemned;
but he honoureth them that fear the LORD.
He that [k]sweareth to *his own* hurt, and changeth not.
5 [l]*He that* putteth not out his money to usury,
[m]nor taketh reward against the innocent. He
that doeth these *things* [n]shall never be moved.

[f]Lev. xix. 16; Psalm xxxiv. 13——[g]Exod. xxiii. 1 [h]Or, *receiveth*, or, *endureth*——[i]Esther iii. 2——[k]Judges xi. 35

[l]Exod. xxii. 25; Lev. xxv. 36; Deut. xxiii. 19; Ezek. xviii. 8; xxii. 12——[m]Exod. xxiii. 8; Deut. xvi. 19 [n]Psa. xvi. 8; 2 Pet. i. 10

satisfied with a *contemplative* life; he has *duties* to perform. The law of *righteousness* has placed him in certain *relations*, and each of these relations has its peculiar duties. פעל צדק *poel tsedek*, the words here used, signify to *give just weight*, to *render* to all their *dues*. 1. As he is the *creature* of GOD, he has duties to perform to *him*. He owes God his heart: *My son, give me thy heart;* and should love him with all his heart, soul, mind, and strength. This is giving GOD *his due*. 2. As a *member of civil society*, he has various duties to perform to his fellows, as they have to him. He is to love them as himself, and do unto all men as he would they should do unto him. 3. There are duties which he owes to *himself*. That his *body* may be in health, vigour, and activity, he should avoid every thing by which it might be injured, particularly all excesses in eating, drinking, sleeping, &c. That his *soul* may be saved, he should avoid all sin; all irregular and disorderly passions. He owes it to his soul to apply to God for that grace which produces repentance, faith, and holiness; and in order to get all these blessings, he should *read, watch, pray, hear the word preached*, and diligently use all the *ordinances of God*. He who acts not thus, *defrauds both his body and soul:* but the person in the text works righteousness—*gives to all their due;* and thus keeps a conscience void of offence, both towards God and man.

And speaketh the truth in his heart.] 3. He is a *true* man; in him there is no *false way*. He is no man of *pretences; speaking one thing*, and *meaning another*. He *professes* nothing but what he *feels* and *intends;* with him there are no *hollow friendships, vain compliments*, nor *empty professions of esteem, love, regard*, or *friendship*. His *mouth* speaks nothing but what his *heart* dictates. His *heart*, his *tongue*, and his *hand*, are all in unison. *Hypocrisy, guile*, and *deceit*, have no place in his soul.

Verse 3. He that *backbiteth not with his tongue*] לא רגל על לשנו *lo ragal al leshono*, "he foots not upon his tongue." 4. He is one who treats his neighbour with respect. He says nothing that might injure him in his *character, person*, or *property;* he *forgets* no calumny, he is *author* of no slander, he *insinuates* nothing by which his neighbour may be injured. The *tongue*, because of its slanderous conversation, is represented in the nervous original as *kicking about* the character of an absent person; a very common vice, and as destructive as it is common: but the man who expects to see God abhors it, and *backbites not with his tongue*. The words *backbite* and *backbiter* come from the Anglo-Saxon bac, *the back*, and **bitan**, *to bite*. How it came to be used in the sense it has in our language, seems at first view unaccountable; but it was intended to convey the treble sense of *knavishness, cowardice*, and *brutality*. He is a *knave*, who would rob you of your *good name;* he is a *coward*, that would speak of you in your *absence* what he dared not to do in your *presence;* and only an ill-conditioned *dog* would fly at and *bite* your *back* when your *face* was *turned*. All these *three ideas* are included in the term; and they all meet in the *detractor* and *calumniator*. His tongue is the tongue of a *knave*, a *coward*, and a *dog*. Such a person, of course, has no right to the privileges of the *Church militant*, and none of his disposition can ever see God.

Nor doeth evil to his neighbour] 5. He not only avoids *evil speaking*, but he avoids also *evil acting* towards his neighbour. He *speaks* no *evil* of him; he *does* no *evil* to him; he does him no *harm;* he occasions him no *wrong*. On the contrary, he *gives him his due*. See under the second particular.

Nor taketh up a reproach against his neighbour.] 6. The word חרפה *cherpah*, which we here translate *a reproach*, comes from חרף *charaph, to strip*, or *make bare*, to *deprive one of his garments;* hence חרף *choreph*, the *winter*, because it *strips the fields* of their *clothing*, and the *trees* of their *foliage*. By this, nature appears to be *dishonoured* and *disgraced*. The application is easy: a man, for instance, of a good character is reported to have done something wrong: the tale is spread, and the slanderers and *backbiters* carry it about; and thus the man is *stripped* of *his fair character*, of his *clothing of righteousness, truth*, and *honesty*. All may be *false;* or the man, in an hour of the power of darkness, may have been tempted and *overcome;* may have been wounded in the cloudy and dark day, and deeply mourns his fall before God. Who that has not the heart of a devil would not strive rather to *cover* than *make bare* the fault? Those *who feed*, as the proverb says, *like the flies, passing over all a man's whole parts to light upon his wounds*, will take up the tale, *and carry it about*. Such, in the course of their diabolic work, carry the story of scandal to the righteous man; to him who loves his God and his neighbour. But what reception has the tale-bearer? The good man *taketh it not up;* לא נשא *lo nasa*, he will not *bear* it; it shall not be propagated from him. He cannot prevent the detractor from *laying it down;* but it is in his power not to *take it up:* and thus the progress of the slander may be arrested. *He taketh not up a reproach against his neighbour;* and the tale-bearer is probably discouraged from carrying it to another door. Reader, drive the slanderer of your neighbour far away from you: ever remembering that in the law of God, as well as in the law of the land, "the *receiver* is as bad as the *thief*."

Verse 4. *In whose eyes a vile person is contemned*] 7. This man judges of others by their conduct; he tries no man's heart. He knows men only by the *fruits* they bear; and thus he gains knowledge of the *principle* from which they proceed. *A vile person,* נמאס *nimas,* the *reprobate,* one abandoned to sin; is *despised,* נבזה *nibzeh,* is *loathsome,* as if he were covered with the *elephantiasis* or *leprosy,* for so the word implies. He may be *rich,* he may be *learned,* he may be a *great man* and *honourable* with his master, in high offices in the state; but if he be a spiritual *leper,* an *infidel,* a *profligate,* the righteous man must despise him, and hold him, because he is an enemy to God and to man, in sovereign contempt. If he be in power, he will not treat him as if *worthy* of his dignity; while he *respects* the *office* he will *detest* the *man.* And this is quite right; for the popular odium should ever be pointed against vice.

Aben Ezra gives a curious turn to this clause, which he translates thus: "He is mean and contemptible in his own eyes;" and it is certain that the original, נבזה בעיניו נמאס *nibzeh beeynaiv nimas,* will bear this translation. His *paraphrase* on it is beautiful: "A pious man, whatever good he may have done, and however concordant to the Divine law he may have walked, considers all this of no worth, compared with what it was his duty to do for the glory of his Creator." A sentiment very like that of our Lord, Luke xvii. 10: "So likewise ye, when ye shall have done all those things which are commanded you, say, We are unprofitable servants; we have done that which was our duty to do."

Taken in this sense, the words intimate, that the man who is truly pious, who is a proper member of the Church *militant,* and is going straight to the *Church triumphant,* is truly *humble;* he knows he *has nothing but what he has received,* he has no *merit,* he trusts not in himself, but in the living God. He renounces his *own righteousness,* and trusts in the *eternal mercy of God* through the *infinitely meritorious atonement* made by Jesus Christ. The language of his heart is,—

"I loathe myself when God I see,
And into nothing fall;
Content that thou exalted be,
And Christ be all in all."

He honoureth them that fear the Lord] 8. This cause is a proof, however just the sentiment, that *Aben Ezra* has mistaken the meaning of the preceding clause. The truly pious man, while he has in contempt the *honourable* and *right honourable* profligate, yet *honours them that fear the Lord,* though found in the most abject poverty; though, with *Job,* on the *dunghill,* or, with *Lazarus,* covered with *sores* at the rich man's gate. Character is the object of his attention; persons and circumstances are of minor importance.

The fear of the Lord is often taken for the *whole of religion;* and sometimes for that *reverence* which a man feels for the *majesty* and *holiness of God,* that induces him to hate and depart from evil. Here it may signify the lowest degree of religion, *repentance whereby we forsake sin.*

Sweareth to his own *hurt, and changeth not.*] 9. If at any time he have bound himself by a solemn engagement to do so and so, and he finds afterwards that to keep his *oath* will be greatly to his *damage;* yet such reverence has he for *God* and for *truth,* that he will not *change,* be the consequences what they may. He is faithful also to his *promises;* his bare word will bind him equally with an *oath.* He that will not be honest *without* an oath will not be honest *with* one.

The *Hebrew* might be thus translated: "He sweareth to afflict himself, and does not change;" and thus the *Chaldee* has rendered this clause. He has promised to the Lord to keep his body under, and bring it into subjection; to deny himself that he may not pamper the flesh, and have the more to give to the poor.

Verse 5. *Putteth not out his money to usury*] 10. As *usury* signifies *unlawful interest,* or that which is got by *taking advantage of the necessity of a distressed neighbour,* no man that fears God can be guilty of it. The word נשך *neshech,* which we translate *usury,* comes from *nashach,* to *bite as a serpent;* and here must signify that *biting* or *devouring usury,* which ruins the man who has it to pay. "The *increase of usury* is called נשך *neshech,* because it resembles the *biting of a serpent.* For as this is so small at first, as scarcely to be perceptible, but the *venom* soon spreads and diffuses itself till it reaches the vitals; so the *increase* of *usury,* which at first is not perceived nor felt, at length grows so much as by degrees to *devour* another's substance." *Middoch's* edition of *Leigh's* Critica Sacra, sub voce נשך.

The Jews ever were, and are still, remarkable for *usury* and *usurious contracts;* and a Jew that is saved from it is in the fair way, charity would suppose, to the kingdom of heaven. The Roman laws condemned the *usurer* to the forfeiture of *four times the sum.* Cato de Rust., lib. i.

Nor taketh reward against the innocent.] 11. He neither gives nor receives a *bribe* in order to pervert justice or injure an innocent man in his cause. The lawyer, who sees a poor man opposed by a rich man, who, though he is convinced in his conscience that the poor man has justice and right on his side, yet takes the *larger fee* from the *rich* man to plead against the poor man, has in fact taken a *bribe against the innocent,* and without the most signal interposition of the mercy of God, is as sure of hell as if he were already there.

He that doeth these things] He in whose character all these excellences meet, though still much more is necessary under the *Christian dispensation, shall never be moved*—he shall stand fast for ever. He is an upright, honest man, and God will ever be his support.

Now we have the important question answered, Who shall go to heaven? The man who to *faith in Christ Jesus* adds those *eleven* moral excellences which have been already enumerated. And only such a character is fit for a place in the Church of Christ.

On this verse there is a singular reading in my old MS. *Psalter,* which I must notice. The clause, *Qui pecuniam suam non dedit ad usuram,* "who putteth not out his money to usury," is thus translated: **He that gaf nout his catel til oker.** Now this intimates that the author had either read *pecudem,* CATTLE, for *pecuniam,* MONEY; or that *catel* was the only *money* current in his time and country. And indeed it has long been the case, that the *Scottish* peasantry paid their rents *in kind;* so many *cows* or *sheep* given to the laird for the usufruct of the ground. That this is no mistake in the *translation* is evident enough from the *paraphrase,* where he repeats the words, with his gloss upon them: **He that gaf nout his Catel till oker** bodyly als covaytus men dos gastly: that he seke naght for his gude dede, na mede of this werld, bot anely of heven.

The very unusual word *oker* signifies *produce* of any kind, whether of *cattle, land, money*, or even the human *offspring.* It is found in the *Anglo-Saxon*, the *Gothic*, the *German*, and the *Danish;* in all which languages it signifies *produce, fruit, offspring, usury*, and the like. Dr. *Jameson* does not show the word in any of its forms, though it is evident that it existed in the ancient *Scottish* language.

The word *catel* may be used here for *chattels, substance* of any kind, moveable or immoveable; but this word itself was originally derived from *cattle*, which were from the beginning the *principal substance* or *riches* of the inhabitants of the country. Indeed the word *pecunia, money*, was derived from *pecus, cattle*, which were no longer used as a medium of commerce when silver and gold came into use. There is a passage in *Chaucer* where *cattel catching* seems to be used for *getting money.* Speaking of the wicked priests of his time, he says:—

> **Some on her churches dwell**
> **Apparailled poorely proud of porte;**
> **The seven Sacramentes thei doen sell,**
> **In Cattel catching is her comfort.**
> **Of each matter thei wollen mell;**
> **And doen hem wrong is her disport.**
> **To affraie the people thei been fell**
> **And hold hem lower than doeth the Lorde.**
>
> *Plowmanne's Tale*, 3d part.

Analysis of the Fifteenth Psalm

A Psalm of doctrine, consisting of *two* parts, in which we have the character of a sound Christian, (rather, an upright Jew.)

I. The *first* part is delivered in the form of a *dialogue* between God and the prophet, from ver. 1-5.

II. The *second* is the *epiphonema*, or moral reflection, in the close of the last verse.

I. 1. The question proposed by the psalmist to God,

1. "Lord, who shall sojourn in thy holy tabernacle?"

2. "Who shall rest upon thy holy hill?" That is, because all are not *Israel* which are *of Israel*, therefore the psalmist asks of God, Who shall *sojourn* as a true member in the *Church militant?* And who shall *rest* in the *Church triumphant?*

2. To which God returns the following answer, containing very remarkable notes of the true character of a member of the Church:—

1. In *general*, he is a man, who is, 1. *Upright* in *thought;* he is an honest man: "He that walketh uprightly." 2. *Just* in his *deed:* "He works righteousness." 3. *True* in his *word:* "He speaks the truth in his heart."

2. In *particular*, he is a man who avoids evil.

1. In himself he is no slanderer: "He backbites not with his tongue."

2. He is no wrong-doer: "Nor doeth evil to his neighbour."

3. He is no reviler, tale-bearer, nor talehearer: "He takes not up a reproach against his neighbour."

4. He is no favourer of sin: "In whose eyes an evil person is contemned."

5. He is no oppressor nor extortioner: *He puts not his money* to his poor brother *to usury.*

6. No briber: "He takes no reward against the innocent."

3. Such a man is he who *honours them that fear the Lord.*

4. "He sweareth to his own hurt, and changeth not." He will surely keep his word; his character is composed of piety and charity.

II. The *epiphonema*, or moral reflection has these *two* parts:—

1. The *party* to whom this privilege belongs: "He that doeth these things;" for the *doers*, not the *hearers*, of the law shall be justified.

2. The *promise* made to him: "He shall never be moved." The life of grace is the way to the life of glory. See the preceding notes.

PSALM XVI

The contents of this Psalm are usually given in the following manner: David, sojourning among idolaters, and being obliged to leave his own country through Saul's persecution, cries to God for help; expresses his abhorrence of idolatry, and his desire to be again united to God's people, 1–4; *and declares his strong confidence in God, who had dealt bountifully with him,* 5–7. *Then follows a remarkable prophecy of the resurrection of Christ,* 8–11.

A. M. cir. 2946
B. C. cir. 1058
Sauli, Regis
Israelitarum,
cir. annum
38

[a]Michtam [b]of David

PRESERVE me, O God:
[c]for in thee do I put my trust.
2 *O my soul,* thou hast said
unto the LORD, Thou *art* my
LORD; [d]my goodness *extendeth*
not to thee;
3 *But* to the saints that *are* in
the earth, and *to* the excellent, in
whom *is* all my delight.

[a]Or, *A golden* Psalm *of David*——[b]So Psa. lvi., lvii., lviii., lix., lx.

[c]Psa. xxv. 20——[d]Job xxii. 2, 3; xxxv. 7, 8; Psa. l. 9; Rom. xi. 35

NOTES ON PSALM XVI

The *title* of this Psalm in the Hebrew is מכתם לדוד *michtam ledavid;* which the *Chaldee* translates, "A straight sculpture of David." The *Septuagint*, Στηλογραφια τῳ Δαυιδ, "The inscription on a pillar to David;" as if the Psalm had been inscribed on a pillar, to keep it in remembrance. As כתם *catham* signifies to *engrave* or *stamp*, this has given rise to the above inscription. מכתם *michtam* also means *pure* or *stamped gold;* and hence it has been supposed that this title was given to it on account of its *excellence: a golden Psalm*, or a Psalm worthy to be *written in letters of gold;* as some of the verses of *Pythagoras* were called *the golden verses*, because of their *excellence*. Gold being the most *excellent* and *precious* of all metals, it has been used to express metaphorically *excellence* and *perfection* of *every kind*. Thus a *golden tongue* or *mouth*, the most *excellent eloquence;* so *Chrysostom* means, this eminent man having had his name from his eloquence;—a *golden book*, one of the *choicest* and *most valuable* of its kind, &c. But I have already sufficiently expressed my doubts concerning the meanings given to these titles. See the note on the title of Psalm lx.

That David was the author there can be no doubt. It is most pointedly attributed to him by St. Peter, Acts ii. 25-31. That its principal parts might have some relation to his circumstances is also probable; but that Jesus Christ is its main scope, not only appears from quotations made by the apostle as above, but from the circumstance that some parts of it never did and never could apply to David. From the most serious and attentive consideration of the whole Psalm, I am convinced that every verse of it belongs to Jesus Christ, and none other: and this, on reference, I find to be the view taken of it by my ancient Psalter. But as he is referred to here as the Redeemer of the world, consequently, as God manifested in the flesh, there are several portions of the Psalm, as well as in the New Testament, where the *Divine* and *human* natures are spoken of *separately:* and if this *distinction* be properly regarded, we shall find, not only no inconsistency, but a beautiful harmony through the whole.

Verse 1. *Preserve me, O God: for in thee do I put my trust.*] On the mode of interpretation which I have hinted at above, I consider this a prayer of the *man* Christ Jesus on his entering on his great atoning work, particularly his *passion* in the garden of Gethsemane. In that passion, Jesus Christ most evidently speaks as *man;* and with the strictest propriety, as it was the *manhood*, not the *Godhead*, that was engaged in the *suffering*.

שמרני *shomreni, keep me—preserve, sustain*, this feeble *humanity*, now about to bear the load of that punishment due to the whole of the human race. *For in thee,* חסיתי *chasithi, have I hoped.* No *human* fortitude, or animal courage, can avail in my circumstances. These are no *common* sufferings; they are not of a *natural* kind; they are not *proportioned* to the strength of a *human* body, or the *energy* of a human spirit; and my *immaculate humanity*, which is subjected to these sufferings, must be dissolved by them, if not upheld by thee, the strong God. It is worthy of remark, that our Lord here uses the term, אל *El*, which signifies the *strong God*, an expression remarkably suited to the *frailty* of that *human nature*, which was now entering upon its vicarious sufferings. It will be seen with what admirable propriety the *Messiah varies the appellations* of the Divine Being in this address; a circumstance which no translation without paraphrase can express.

Verse 2. *Thou hast said unto the Lord, Thou* art *my Lord*] Thou hast said ליהוה *layhovah*, to Jehovah, the supreme, self-existing, and eternal Being; *Thou* art *my Lord,* אדני אתה *adonai attah*, Thou art my *prop, stay*, or *support.* As the Messiah, or Son of God, Jesus derived his being and support from Jehovah; and the man Christ was supported by the eternal Divinity that dwelt within him, without which he could not have sustained the sufferings which he passed through, nor have made an atonement for the sin of the world; it is the suffering Messiah, or the Messiah in prospect of his sufferings, who here speaks.

My goodness extendeth *not to thee*] There are almost endless explanations of this clause; no man can read them without being confounded by them. The SEPTUAGINT read ὁτι των αγαθων μου ου χρειαν εχεις; *Because thou dost not need my goods.* The VULGATE follows the *Septuagint*. The CHALDEE: *My good is given only by thyself.* So the SYRIAC: *My good is from thee.* The ARABIC: *Thou dost not need my good works.* And in this sense, with shades of difference, it has been understood by most commentators and critics.

Bishop *Horsley* translates, *Thou art my good —not besides thee.* Dr. *Kennicott, My goodness is not without thee.*

I think the words should be understood of what the Messiah was doing for men. My goodness, טובתי *tobathi*, "my bounty," is not to thee. What I am doing can add nothing to thy divinity; thou art not providing this astonishing sacrifice because thou canst derive any excellence from it: but this bounty extends *to the saints*—to all the spirits of just men made perfect, whose bodies are still in the earth; and to the excellent, אדירי *addirey*, "the noble or supereminent ones," those who through faith and patience inherit the promises. The saints and illustrious ones not only taste of my goodness, but enjoy my salvation. Perhaps *angels*

A. M. cir. 2946
B. C. cir. 1058
Sauli, Regis Israelitarum, cir. annum 38

4 Their sorrows shall be multiplied *that* [e]hasten *after* another
god: their drink-offerings of
blood will I not offer, [f]nor
take up their names into my
lips.
5 [g]The LORD *is* the portion
of [h]mine inheritance [i]and [k]of

[e]Or, *give gifts to another*——[f]Exodus xxiii. 13; Joshua xxiii. 7; Hosea ii. 16, 17——[g]Deut. xxxii. 9; Psa. lxxiii. 26; cxix. 57; cxlii. 5; Jeremiah x. 16; Lamentations iii. 24——[h]Hebrew, *of my part*——[i]Numbers xvi. 14; Deuteronomy ix. 29——[k]Psalm xi. 6; xxiii. 5; cxvi. 13

themselves may be intended; they are not uninterested in the incarnation, passion, death, and resurrection of our Lord. They *desire to look into these things;* and the victories of the cross in the conversion of sinners cause joy among the angels of God.

The קדושים *kedoshim*, "saints," or consecrated persons, may refer to the *first planters of Christianity, evangelists, apostles*, &c., who were separated from all others, and *consecrated* to the great important work of preaching among the Gentiles the unsearchable riches of Christ. With these was all the *desire*, חפץ *chephets*, the *good will* and *delight* of Christ. In all their ministrations he was both *with* them and *in* them.

The passage, taken as referring to David, intimates that he abhorred the company of the profane and worthless, and delighted to associate with them that excelled in virtue.

On these two verses the translation and paraphrase of my old Psalter must not be forgotten:—

Verse 1. Conserva me, Domine, &c.

Trans. **Kepe me Lord, for I hoped in the; I said til Lord, my God thou ert; for, of my gudes thu has na nede.**

Par.—The voice of Crist in his manhede; prayand til the fader, and sayand: Lord, fader, kepe me imang peplis, for I hoped in the, noght in me. I said til the, my God, thu ert in that, that I am man; for thu has no nede of my godes; bot I haf of the, al that I haf; here is the wil pride of men confounded; that evenes that thai haf ought of tham self bot syn.

Verse 2. Sanctis qui sunt in terra, &c.

Trans. **Til halowes the qwilk er in his land, he selcouthed all my willes in tham.**

Par.—Noght til wiked, bot til halows clene in saule, and depertid fra erdly bysynes, the qwilk er in his land: that es, thai haf fested thair hope in the land of heven; and rotyd in luf: the qwilk hope es als anker in stremys of this werld. He selcouthed al my willes, that of wondirful, he made my willes, of dying and rysing, sett and fulfilled in tham: that es, in thair profete, qware in thai feled qwat it profeted tham my mekenes that wild dye, and my myght to rise.

Verse 4. *Their sorrows shall be multiplied* that *hasten* after *another* god] The Chaldee has: "They multiply their idols, and afterwards hasten that they may offer their gifts." In the Hebrew text there is no word for *God*, and therefore *Messiah* or *Saviour* might be as well substituted; and then the whole will refer to the unbelieving Jews. They would not have the true Christ; they have sought, and are seeking, another Messiah; and how amply fulfilled has the prophetic declaration been in them! Their *sorrows have been multiplied* for more than 1800 years.

The *Vulgate* and *Septuagint*, and after them the *Æthiopic* and *Arabic*, have given this clause a widely different turn: "their afflictions have been multiplied, and afterwards they have run swiftly;" referring to the suffering saints: the more they were afflicted and persecuted, the more fervent and prosperous they became.

Their drink-offerings of blood will I not offer] נסך *nesech* is a *libation*, whether of *wine* or *water*, poured out on the sacrifice. A *drink-offering of blood* is not a correct form of expression; it is rather the *libation on the blood of the sacrifice* already made. Coverdale translates the same; but *Mathewes*, who reformed his text in a few places, has **Their brente offeringes of bloude**, without much mending the text; though by this the exceptionable idea of a *drink-offering of blood* is avoided. As applicable to our Lord, here is an intimation that their libations and sacrifices should cease. None of these should exist under the Christian dispensation; Jesus Christ's offering upon the cross being the accomplishment and termination of all such sacrifices.

Nor take up their names into my lips.] None of those sacrifices shall be mentioned with any kind of respect after the *end* of their institution shall have been accomplished; for sacrifice, offering, burnt-offering, and sacrifice for sin, such as are offered according to the law, God would no longer receive; therefore Jesus said; "Lo, I come to do thy will; a body hast thou prepared me." Since that time all these sacrifices have ceased. The old *Psalter* is curious:—

Verse 4. Multiplicate sunt infirmitates eorum; postea acceleraverunt.

Trans. **Manyfalded er thair sekenes: and sythen thai hasted thaim.**

Par.—That es at say; thai knew that thai war ful seke in body and saule, and sythen thai hasted tham til the Leche; for he that feles him seke, he sekes remedy. Il men wenes that thai er noght seke for thi thai dye in thair syn.

Non congregabo conventicula eroum de sanguinibus, &c.

Trans. **I sal noght gadyr the coventes of tha of blodes; ne I sal be menand of their names thurgh my lippis.**

Par. That est at say, by the coventes of haly men, my servaundes sal nout fleschely, but gastly: for *blode* bytakyns syn and unclenes that thai er in, that folous thair flesche, and the vanites of thair blode; that er comen of grete kyn. Ne I sal by menand of thair names; for thai er chaunged fra syn till ryghtwisnes on domesday, qwen I sal speke thrugh my lippes til thaim that haldes the name of wykednes: sa ye weryed til fyer with outen end.

Verse 5. *The Lord* is *the portion of mine inheritance*] The Messiah speaks. Jehovah is the portion of mine inheritance; I seek no earthly good; I desire to do the will of God, and that only. It is God who has given me this lot—to redeem mankind—to have them for

A. M. cir. 2946
B. C. cir. 1058
Sauli, Regis
Israelitarum,
cir. annum
38

my cup: thou maintainest my
lot.
6 The lines are fallen unto me
in pleasant *places;* yea, I have
a goodly heritage.
7 I will bless the LORD, who hath given me
counsel: [l]my reins also instruct me in the
night seasons.
8 [m]I have set the LORD always
before me: because [n]*he is* at
my right hand, [o]I shall not be
moved.
9 Therefore my heart is glad, [p]and my
glory rejoiceth: my flesh also shall [q]rest in
hope.
10 [r]For thou wilt not leave [s]my soul in

A. M. cir. 2946
B. C. cir. 1058
Sauli, Regis
Israelitarum,
cir. annum
38

[l]Psa. xvii. 3——[m]Acts ii. 25, &c.——[n]Psa. lxxiii. 23; cx. 5; cxxi. 5——[o]Psa. xv. 5——[p]Psa. xxx. 12; lvii. 8

[q]Heb. *dwell confidently*——[r]Psa. xlix. 15; Acts ii. 27, 31; xiii. 35——[s]Lev. xix. 28; Num. vi. 6

mine inheritance. From him I have received the *cup of suffering,* which I shall drink for their sake, through which I shall impart to them the *cup of consolation.* He, by the grace of God, has *tasted death for every man;* and he has instituted the *cup of blessing* to commemorate his passion and death.

Verse 6. *The lines are fallen unto me in pleasant* places] Here is an allusion to the ancient division of the land by lot among the Israelites, the breadth and length being ascertained by lines which were used in measuring. I have got a rich inheritance of immortal spirits; and I myself, as man, shall have a name above every name, and be raised to thy throne, on which I shall sit, and be admired in my saints to all eternity.

I have a goodly heritage.] A Church, an innumerable multitude of saints, partakers of the Divine nature, and filled with all the fulness of God. And these shall dwell with me in the heaven of heavens to all eternity. The old *Psalter:*—

Verse 5. Dominus pars hereditatis mee et calicis mei, &c.

Trans. **Lord es part of myn herytage and of my chalyce; thow ert that sal restore myn herytage til me.**

Par. Lord the fader es part, that es, he es porcioun and mede of myn herytage; that es of haly men, qwam I weld in herytage. Other men cheses tham what tham lyst: my part es God, and he es part of my chalyce: that es, he es my copp of al my delyte and joy. Wereldys men drynkes the venemus lustes, and the drubly delytes of lychery and covatys: I in my halows sal drynk God; for thu ert fadyr that sal restore till me, that es, til my men, myn herytage, that thai lost in Adam: that es thu restores til tham the knawyng of my bryghthede.

Verse 6. Punes ceciderunt michi in preclaris, &c.

Trans. **Strynges fel to me in ful bryght: for qwy, myn herytage is ful bryght til me.**

Par. Strynges, that er merkes of my possessioun, in thi bryghtnes, fel als with cutte; als the possessioun of prestes and dekens in the alde law, was God; for qwy myn herytage, that es haly men es bryght til me of thai seme layth and aute castyng til some of the werld, til me thai er fairer and bryght.

Verse 7. *Who hath given me counsel*] Jesus, as *man,* received all his knowledge and wisdom from God; Luke ii. 40-52. And in him were hidden all the treasures of wisdom and knowledge.

My reins also instruct me] כליותי *kilyothai, reins* or *kidneys,* which from their *retired* situation in the body, says *Parkhurst,* and being *hidden* in fat, are often used in Scripture for the most *secret workings* and *affections of the heart.*

The *kidneys* and their *fat* were always to be burnt in sacrifice, to indicate that the most secret purposes and affections of the soul are to be devoted to God.

In the night seasons.] That is, in the time of my *passion,* my secret purposes and determinations concerning the redemption of man support me. "For the joy that was set before him he endured the cross, despising the shame;" Heb. xii. 2.

Verse 8. *I have set the Lord always before me*] This verse, and all to the end of ver. 11, are applied by St. Peter to the *death and resurrection of Christ.* Acts ii. 25, &c.

In all that our Lord *did, said,* or *suffered,* he kept the glory of the Father and the accomplishment of his purpose constantly in view. He tells us that he did not come down from heaven to do his own will, but the will of the Father who had sent him. See John xvii. 4.

He is *at my right hand*] That is, I have his constant presence, approbation, and support. All this is spoken by Christ as *man.*

I shall not be moved.] Nothing can swerve me from my purpose; nothing can prevent me from fulfilling the Divine counsel, in reference to the salvation of men.

Verse 9. *Therefore my heart is glad*] Unutterably happy in God; always full of the Divine presence; because whatsoever I do pleaseth him. The *man* Christ Jesus must be constantly in communion with God, because he was without spot and blemish.

My glory rejoiceth] My *tongue,* so called by the Hebrews, (see Psa. lvii. 8; xxx. 12,) because it was bestowed on us to glorify God, and because it is our *glory,* being the instrument of expressing our thoughts by words. *See Dodd.* But *soul* bids as fair to be the meaning. See the notes on Acts ii. 25, &c.

My flesh also shall rest in hope.] There is no sense in which these and the following words can be spoken of David. Jesus, even on the cross, and breathing out his soul with his life, saw that his rest in the grave would be very short: just a sufficiency of time to prove the *reality* of his death, but not *long enough* to produce *corruption;* and this is well argued by St. Peter, Acts ii. 31.

Verse 10. *Thine Holy One*] This is in the plural number, חסידיך *chasideycha, thy Holy Ones;* but none of the *versions* translate it in the *plural;* and as it is in the singular number, חסידך *chasidecha,* in several *ancient*

A. M. cir. 2946
B. C. cir. 1058
Sauli, Regis
Israelitarum,
cir. annum
38

hell; neither wilt thou suffer
thine Holy One to see corruption.
11 Thou wilt show me the
[t]path of life: [u]in thy presence
is fulness of joy; [v]at thy right
hand *there are* pleasures for evermore.

A. M. cir. 2946
B. C. cir. 1058
Sauli, Regis
Israelitarum,
cir. annum
38

---

[t]Matt. vii. 14——[u]Psa. xvii. 15; xxi. 6; Matt. v. 8; 1 Cor. xiii. 12; 1 John. iii. 2——[v]Psa. xxxvi. 8

---

editions, among which is the *Complutensian Polyglot*, and no less than *two hundred and sixty-four* of *Kennicott's* and *De Rossi's* MSS., and in the quotation by St. *Peter*, in Acts ii. 27; xiii. 35, we may take it for granted that the present reading is a corruption; or that חסידיך is an emphatic singular.

As to *leaving the soul in hell*, it can only mean permitting the *life* of the Messiah to *continue* under the power of *death;* for שאול *sheol* signifies a *pit*, a *ditch*, the *grave*, or *state of the dead.* See the notes on the parallel places, Acts ii. 25, &c.

See corruption.] All human beings see corruption, because born in sin, and liable to the curse. The human body of Jesus Christ, as being without sin, saw no corruption.

Verse 11. *Thou wilt show me the path of life*] I first shall find the *way out of the regions of death*, to *die no more.* Thus Christ was the *first fruits* of them that slept. Several had before risen from the dead, but they *died again.* Jesus rose from the dead, and is alive for evermore. Jesus Christ's resurrection from the dead was the first entrance out of the grave to eternal life or lives, חיים *chaiyim*, for the word is in the *plural*, and with great propriety too, as this resurrection implies the *life* of the *body*, and the *life* of the *rational soul* also.

In thy presence] פניך *paneycha, thy faces.* Every holy soul has, throughout eternity, the *beatific vision*, i. e., "it sees God as he is," because it is *like him;* 1 John iii. 2. It drinks in beatification from the presence of the Eternal TRINITY.

Thy right hand] The place of honour and dignity; repeatedly used in this sense in the Scriptures.

Pleasures for evermore.] נצח *netzach, onwardly; perpetually, continually*, well expressed by our translation, *ever* and *more;* an eternal progression. Think of *duration* in the most extended and unlimited manner, and there is still *more;* more to be suffered in hell, and more to be enjoyed in heaven. Great God! grant that my readers may have this beatific sight; this eternal progression in unadulterated, unchangeable, and unlimited happiness! Hear this prayer for His sake, who found out the path of life, and who by his blood purchased an entrance into the holiest! Amen and Amen.

For the application of the whole Psalm to David, see the analysis at the end, which is a little altered from *David's Harp Strung and Tuned.*

The remains of this Psalm in the old *Psalter* are worthy to be inserted:—

Verse 7. Benedicam Dominum qui tribuit michi intellectum, &c.

Trans. **I sal blis the Lord that gaf til me undirstandyng; and over that til the nyght, suyled me my neres.**

Par. That es I sal luf the fader that hafs gyfen undyrstandyng til my servauntes, thurgh the qwilk the herytage of heven may be sene and welded; and over that undyrstandyng, in the qwilk I saw, sais Crist, al sothefast thynges and haly. Of that I sal lof him that my nerys that es the Jewis of qwas kynd I toke flesch, that es my kyn snybbed me in wranges and temptaciounis, and passiouns, til the nyght, that es al the dede thai missaid hym, als so oure nerys; that es our fleschely delytes makes us worthy snybbyng til our dede; for perfytely may we noght be with outen syn, qwyles we lyf.

Verse 8. Providebam Dominum in conspectu meo, &c.

Trans. **I pervaide God ay in my syght: for he es at the ryght hand til me, that I be nout styrred.**

Par. And in al thys anguys I for gatt nout God: bot I pervayde hym ay in my syght; that es, I comande o mang passand thynges: I toke nout my nee fra hym that ay es; bot I fested it in hym, so that he was ay in my sight, and he es nout fyled in synnes that assyduely with the ee of his thoght, byhaldes God, for he es at the ryght hand of me: that I be noght styred; that es, he helps me in desyre of endless gudes, that I last stabil in hym, and for thi nane il thyng may haf mayster of me.

Verse 9. Propter hoc, elatum, est cor meum, et exultavit lingua mea, &c.

Trans. **Thar fore gladded es my hert, and my toung joyed over that, and my flesch sal rest in hope.**

Par. This es ful joy that in hert es resayved. and with toung schewed, and over that joy in hert and mouth, my flesch sal rest in hope of rysyng.

Verse 10. Quoniam non derelinques in Inferno animam meam, &c.

Trans. **For thow sal noght lefe my Saule in hell; ne thu sal noght gyf thi Halow to se corrupcioun.**

Par. That es at say, the Saule that I haf als veray man, sal noght be left in hell; and my body that thu haloued, sal noght rote. Here men may knaw that this es goddes word; for other mens bodis rotes.

Verse 11. Notas michi fecisti vias vite, &c.

Trans. **Knawen thu maked til me, the wayes of lyf: thou sal ful fil me of joy with thi face, delytynges in thi ryghth and in til the end.**

Par. Knawen thu maked thurgh me till myne, the wayes of lyf, that es the wayes of mekenes and charite, that men came til heven thurgh mekenes, fra qwethyn thai fel thurgh Pryde: and thow sal ful fil me; that es, my servaundes, of joy with thi face; that es, in the syght of the, apertly; so that thai desyre nothing over, qwen thai af sene the, face til face, and ay til than delytynges til tham in way of this lyf. In thi ryght hand; that es thi favoure, and thi mercy the qwilk delytyngs ledys tham intil the ende; that es, in til perfectioun of endeles Blisfulhede.

I have given the whole of the translation and comment of this Psalm from this ancient Psalter, as a curious specimen of the doctrine and language of our northern neighbours in the *thirteenth* or *fourteenth* century.

Analysis of the Sixteenth Psalm

Michtam David: David's precious jewel, or Psalm of gold; literally to be understood of David, but primarily and principally of Christ, Acts ii., whom he calls חסיד *chasid*, God's Holy One, ver. 10. And foretells his passion, resurrection, and ascension, ver. 9, 10, 11.

This Psalm has *two* parts: I. *Petition*, ver. 1. II. *Thanksgiving*, ver. 7.

I. The *petition* begins the Psalm. It is for *preservation:* "Preserve me, O God." Keep me to the kingdom both temporal and eternal that thou hast promised. Guard me; guide me; keep me. To induce the Lord to do this, he produces his reasons:—

1. His *confidence:* "For in thee I trust." This is a powerful plea; for to trust God is the highest honour we can do him; it acknowledges him as Sovereign.

2. His relation: "O my soul, thou hast said unto the Lord, Thou art my God."

3. For this I would show myself thankful, and return the best of my best. But what can I give, save τα σα εκ των σων, "thy own things from thy own property?" *My goods* or goodness, my beneficence or bounty, *is nothing unto thee.* Sacrifice thou needest not, Psa. l. 8, nor art delighted in them: but mercy thou requirest, Hosea, vi. 6.

4. Then I will seek out thy *receivers:* "Thy saints that are in the earth." The family of the saints were the object of David's bounty, and his delight. But my liberality and charity shall extend *to the saints that are in the earth*, and unto such as are excellent; "in whom is all my delight."

5. But as for the *wicked* men and idolaters, I have no delight in them.

These he points out by two characteristics:—

1. They "hasten after another god," or *endow another god.* They spare no cost, but are lavish in endowing their gods: "Israel, part with thy jewels," &c.

2. They offer their children to Molech: "Their drink-offerings of BLOOD will I not offer." On these accounts:—

1. "Their sorrows shall be multiplied." They shall be grievously punished.

2. I will not participate with them: "Their offerings I will not offer."

3. They are objects of my detestation: "I will not take up their names into my lips."

6. He gives another reason why he should show himself so thankful to God and bountiful to his saints—God's great bounty and liberality to him.

1. That God had given him a satisfactory portion: "The Lord is the portion of mine inheritance, and of my cup."

2. That God defended him in it: "Thou maintainest my lot."

3. That it was a fair portion: "The lines are fallen to me in pleasant places," &c.

II. The *second* part of this Psalm is David's THANKSGIVING. It begins with, "I will bless the Lord," ver. 7, not only for the temporal blessings mentioned before, but for the following spiritual blessings:—

1. For the illumination of his mind; that I may understand the thing that is right: "The Lord hath given me counsel."

2. For the sanctifying influence on his heart: "My reins instruct me in the night seasons." When he was most retired he seemed to hear a voice within him, saying, "This is the way; walk in it."

3. For his *confidence and watchfulness:* "I have set the Lord always before me." I do not forget my God; and he does not forget me.

4. For the *consciousness* he had of the Divine *presence:* "The Lord is at my right hand;" always ready to help and support me.

5. For his *power to preserve:* "I shall not be moved." Satan may stand at my right hand to resist and trouble me; Zech. iii. 1; but God is on my right hand to assist and comfort me; therefore, "I shall not be moved." While David prays and trusts, God supports; and while God supports, Satan cannot conquer.

6. For his *inward* happiness: "Therefore, my heart is glad." Wicked men rejoice in *appearance;* but David rejoiced in *heart.* He was all happy. His heart, glory, flesh, spirit, soul, body—all were overjoyed; and the reason was the prospect of his *resurrection.*

1. "My flesh shall rest or dwell in hope." 1. In this world, as in an *inn;* 2. In the *grave*, as in a *repository;* 3. In *heaven*, as in an endless *mansion.*

2. "Thou wilt not leave my soul in hell." Thou wilt not suffer death to have a final triumph; my flesh shall revive.

3. "Neither wilt thou suffer thy HOLY ONE to see corruption;" meaning the *Messiah*, who should descend from his family. Christ's resurrection is the cause and pledge of ours.

7. He is thankful for the promise of a future life, which is here illustrated:—

1. From the *quantity:* "Fulness of joy."
2. From the *quality:* "Pleasures."
3. From the *honour:* "At thy right hand."
4. From the *perpetuity:* "For evermore."
5. From the *cause:* "Thy presence." The sight of God, the beatific vision. "Thou wilt show me the path of life: in thy presence is fulness of joy; at thy right hand there are pleasures for evermore."

For the application of the whole Psalm to *Christ* alone, see the preceding notes.

PSALM XVII

David implores the succour of God against his enemies; and professes his integrity and determination to live to God's glory, 1. *He prays for support, and expresses strong confidence in God,* 5–9; *describes the malice and cruelty of his enemies, and prays against them,* 10–14; *receives a strong persuasion of support and final victory,* 15.

A Prayer of David

A. M. cir. 2946
B. C. cir. 1058
Sauli, Regis
Israelitarum,
cir. annum
38

HEAR [a]the right, O LORD,
attend unto my cry, give ear
unto my prayer, *that goeth* [b]not
out of feigned lips.
2 Let my sentence come forth from thy presence; let thine eyes behold the things that are
equal.
3 Thou hast proved mine heart; [c]thou hast
visited *me* in the night; [d]thou hast tried me,
and shalt find nothing: I am
purposed *that* my mouth shall
not transgress.
4 Concerning the works of
men, by the word of thy lips I have
kept *me from* the paths of the destroyer.
5 [e]Hold up my goings in thy paths, *that* my
footsteps [f]slip not.
6 [g]I have called upon thee, for thou wilt

A. M. cir. 2946
B. C. cir. 1058
Sauli, Regis
Israelitarum,
cir. annum
38

[a]Heb. *justice*——[b]Heb. *without lips of deceit*——[c]Psa. xvi. 7——[d]Job xxiii. 10; Psa. xxvi. 2; lxvi. 10; cxxxix. 2; Zech. xiii. 9; Mal. iii. 2, 3; 1 Pet. i. 7——[e]Psa. cxix. 133
[f]Heb. *be not moved*——[g]Psa. cxvi. 2

NOTES ON PSALM XVII

The title is, *A prayer of David;* in which there is nothing that requires explanation. David was most probably the author of this Psalm; and it appears to have been written about the time in which Saul had carried his persecution against him to the highest pitch. See 1 Sam. xxvii. The Arabic calls it "A prayer of a perfect man, of Christ himself, or of any one redeemed by him." Dr. *Delaney*, in his life of David, supposes that this poem was written just after parting with Jonathan, when David went into exile.

Verse 1. *Hear the right*] Attend to the justice of my cause, יהוה צדק *Yehovah tsedek*, righteous Jehovah. "O righteous Jehovah, attend unto my cry."

Goeth *not out of feigned lips.*] My supplication is sincere: and the desire of my heart accompanies the words of my lips.

Verse 2. *My sentence come forth from thy presence*] Thou knowest my heart, and my ways; judge me as thou shalt find; let me not fall under the judgment of man.

Let thine eyes behold the things that are equal.] Thou knowest whether I render to all their due, and whether others act justly by me. Thou canst not be deceived: do justice between me and my adversaries.

Verse 3. *Thou hast proved mine heart*] Thou well knowest whether there be any evil way in me. Thou hast given me to see many and sore trials; and yet, through thy mercy, I have preserved my integrity both to thee and to my king. Thou hast seen me in my most *secret* retirements, and knowest whether I have *plotted* mischief against him who now wishes to take away my life.

Thou hast tried me] צרפתני *tseraphtani;* Thou *hast put me to the test*, as they do *metals*, in order to detect their *alloy*, and to *purify* them: well expressed by the *Vulgate*, *Igne me examinasti*, "Thou hast tried me by fire;" and well paraphrased in my old *Psalter*,—*Thu examynd* me the lykkenyng of the fournas, that purges metal, *and imang* al this, wykednes es nout funden in me: that es, *I am funden clene of syn*, and so ryghtwis.—He who is saved from his sin is *right wise;* he has found the *true wisdom.*

My mouth shall not transgress.] This clause is added to the following verse by the *Vulgate* and *Septuagint:* "That my mouth may not speak according to the works of men, I have observed difficult ways because of the words of thy lips." That is, So far from doing any improper *action*, I have even refrained from all *words* that might be counted inflammatory or seditious by my adversaries; for I took thy word for the regulation of my conduct, and prescribed to myself the most painful duties, in order that I might, in every respect, avoid what would give offence either to thee or to man. Among the genuine followers of God, plots and civil broils are never found.

Verse 4. *The paths of the destroyer.*] Some render, *hard* or *difficult paths*, the sense of which is given above. But the passage is exceedingly obscure. My old *Psalter* translates and paraphrases as follows:—

Trans. **That my mouthe speke noght the werkes of men, for the wordes of thi lippes I haf keped hard wayse.**

Par. That es, that nothing passe of my mouthe bot at falles to the louyng of *the; noght til werkes of men*, that dos o gaynes thy wil; als to say, I spak *noght* bot gude; and *for the wordes of thi lippes*, that es, to ful fil the *wordes* that thi prophetes saide; *I kepe hard waies* of verteus and of *tribulacioun*, the qwilk men thynk hard; and for thi thai leve the *hard* way til heven, and takes the soft way til hel; but it es ful hard *at the* end.

Verse 5. *Hold up my goings in thy paths*] David walked in God's ways; but, without Divine assistance, he could not walk *steadily*, even in them. The *words of God's lips* had shown him the steps he was to take, and he implores the strength of God's grace to enable him to walk in those steps. He had been kept from the *paths of the destroyer;* but this was not sufficient; he must *walk in God's paths*—must spend his life in *obedience* to the Divine

A. M. cir. 2946
B. C. cir. 1058
Sauli, Regis
Israelitarum,
cir. annum
38

hear me, O God: incline thine
ear unto me, *and hear* my speech.
7 [h]Show thy marvellous loving-
kindness, O thou [i]that savest by
thy right hand them which put their trust *in*
thee from those that rise up *against them.*
8 [k]Keep me as the apple of the eye, [l]hide
me under the shadow of thy wings,
9 From the wicked [m]that oppress me, *from*
[n]my deadly enemies, *who* compass me about.
10 [o]They are enclosed in their own fat:
with their mouth they [p]speak
proudly.
11 They have now [q]compassed
us in our steps: [r]they have
set their eyes bowing down to the earth;
12 [s]Like as a lion *that* is greedy of his prey,
and as it were a young lion [t]lurking in secret
places.
13 Arise, O LORD, [u]disappoint him, cast
him down: deliver my soul from the wicked,
[v]*which is* [w]thy sword;

A. M. cir. 2946
B. C. cir. 1058
Sauli, Regis
Israelitarum,
cir. annum
38

[h]Psa. xxxi. 21——[i]Or, *that savest them which trust* in thee *from those that rise up against thy right hand* [k]Deut. xxxii. 10; Zech. ii. 8——[l]Ruth ii. 12; Psa. xxxvi. 7; lvii. 1; lxi. 4; lxiii. 7; xci. 1, 4; Matt. xxiii. 37 [m]Heb. *that waste me*——[n]Heb. *my enemies against the soul*

[o]Deut. xxxii. 15; Job xv. 27; Psa. lxxiii. 7; cxix. 70 [p]1 Sam. ii. 3; Psa. xxxi. 18——[q]1 Sam. xxiii. 26——[r]Psa. x. 8, 9, 10——[s]Heb. *The likeness of him* (that is, *of every one of them*) is *as a lion* that *desireth to ravin*——[t]Heb. *sitting*——[u]Heb. *prevent his face*——[v]Isa. x. 5——[w]Or, *by thy sword*

will. Negative holiness can save no man. "Every tree that bringeth not forth good fruit is hewn down, and cast into the fire."

Verse 6. *Incline thine ear unto me*] David prayed from a conviction that God would hear: but he could not be satisfied unless he received an answer. In a believer's mind the petition and the answer should not be separated.

Verse 7. *Show thy marvellous lovingkindness*] David was now exposed to imminent danger; common interpositions of Providence could not save him; if God did not work *miracles* for him, he must fall by the hand of Saul. Yet he lays no *claim* to such miraculous interpositions; he expects all from God's *lovingkindness.*

The common reading here is הפלה חסדיך *haphleh chasadeycha*, "distinguish thy holy ones;" but הפלא *haphle*, "do wonders," is the reading of about *seventy* MSS., some ancient editions, with the *Septuagint*, *Vulgate*, *Chaldee*, *Syriac*, and *Arabic*. The marginal reading of this verse is nearer the original than that of the text.

Verse 8. *Keep me as the apple of the eye*] Or, *as the black of the daughter of eye.* Take as much care to preserve me now by *Divine influence*, as thou hast to preserve my *eye* by thy *good providence.* Thou hast entrenched it deeply in the skull; hast ramparted it with the forehead and cheek-bones; defended it by the eyebrow, eyelids, and eyelashes; and placed it in that situation where the hands can best protect it.

Hide me under the shadow of thy wings] This is a metaphor taken from the *hen* and her *chickens.* See it explained at large in the note on Matt. xxiii. 37. The Lord says of his followers, Zech. ii. 8: "He that toucheth you, toucheth the apple of mine eye." How dear are our eyes to us! how dear must his followers be to God!

Verse 9. From *my deadly enemies*, who *compass me about.*] This is a metaphor taken from huntsmen, who spread themselves around a large track of forest, driving in the deer from every part of the circumference, till they are forced into the nets or traps which they have set for them in some particular narrow passage. The metaphor is carried on in the following verses.

Verse 10. *They are enclosed in their own fat*] Dr. *Kennicott*, Bishop *Horsley*, *Houbigant*, and others, read the passage thus: עלי חבלמו סגרו *alai chablamo sageru*, "They have closed their net upon me." This continues the metaphor which was introduced in the preceding verse, and which is continued in the two following: and requires only that עלי *ali*, "upon me," should *begin* this verse instead of *end* the preceding; and that חלב *cheleb*, which signifies *fat*, should be read חבל *chebel*, which signifies *rope*, *cable*, or *net.* This important reading requires only the *interchange* of *two letters.* The *Syriac* translates it, *shut their mouth:* but the above emendation is most likely to be true.

They speak proudly.] Having compassed the mountain on which I had taken refuge, they now exult, being assured that they will soon be in possession of their prey.

Verse 11. *They have now compassed us in our steps*] Instead of אשרנו *ashshurenu*, "our steps," Dr. *Kennicott* and others recommend אשרינו *ashreynu*, "O lucky we, at last we have compassed him." He cannot now escape; he is sure to fall into our hands.

They have set their eyes bowing down to the earth] All the commentators and critics have missed the very expressive and elegant metaphor contained in this clause. *Kennicott* says, *They drove the hart into toils, and then shot him.* Bishop *Horsley* says, on the clause, *They have set their eyes bowing down to the earth:* "This is the attitude of huntsmen, taking aim at an animal upon the ground." No, it is the attitude of the huntsmen looking for the *slot*, or track of the hart's, hind's, or antelope's foot on the ground. See at the conclusion of the Psalm.

Verse 12. *Like as a lion* that *is greedy of his prey*] I believe the word *lion* is here used to express *Saul* in his strength, kingly power, and fierce rapacity. See the observations at the end of the Psalm.

Verse 13. *Arise, O Lord, disappoint him*] When *he* arises to spring upon and tear me to pieces, arise *thou*, O Lord; disappoint him of his prey; seize him, and cast him down.

Deliver my soul] Save my life.

From the wicked, which is *thy sword*] Saul

A. M. cir. 2946 B. C. cir. 1058 Sauli, Regis Israelitarum, cir. annum 38

14 [x]From men *which are* thy
hand, O LORD, from men of the
world, [y]*which have* their portion
in *this* life, and whose belly thou
fillest with thy hid *treasure:* [z]they are full of
children, and leave the rest of
their *substance* to their babes.
15 As for me, [a]I will behold thy
face in righteousness: [b]I shall
be satisfied, when I awake, with thy likeness.

A. M. cir. 2946 B. C. cir. 1058 Sauli, Regis Israelitarum, cir. annum 38

[x]Or, *From men* by *thine hand*——[y]Psa. lxxiii. 12; Luke xvi. 25; James v. 5

[z]Or, their *children are full*——[a]1 John iii. 2——[b]Psa. iv. 6, 7; xvi. 11; lxv. 4

is still meant, and we may understand the words as either implying the *sword*, the *civil power*, with which God had intrusted him, and which he was now grievously abusing; or, it may mean, *deliver me by* THY *sword*—cut him off who wishes to cut me off. On this ground the next verse should be read *from men*, BY *thy hand.* So the margin. The hand of God not only meaning his *power*, but his *providence*.

Verse 14. *From men of the world,* which have] ממתים מחלד *mimethim mecheled, from mortal men of time;* temporizers; men who shift with the times; who have no fixed principle but one, that of securing their own secular interest: and this agrees with what follows—which have *their portion in this life;* who never seek after any thing *spiritual;* who have bartered heaven for earth, and have got the *portion* they desired; for thou *fillest their belly with thy hid treasure.* Their *belly*—their *sensual appetites*—is their *god;* and, when their animal desires are satisfied, they take their rest without consideration, like the beasts that perish.

Their portion in this *life*] בחיים *bachaiyim, in lives*, probably meaning *heritable lands* and *estates;* for they leave them to their children, they *descend* to *posterity*, and every one has his *life portion* in them. They are *lands of lives.*

They are full of children] Have a numerous offspring, whom they educate in the same principles, and to whom they leave a large earthly patrimony, and who spend it as their fathers have done, and perhaps even more dissolutely. Often *covetous* fathers lay up riches, which *profligate* sons scatter to all the winds of heaven. I have seen many instances of this.

Verse 15. *As for me*] I cannot be satisfied with such a portion.

I will behold thy face] Nothing but an evidence of thy *approbation* can content my soul.

In righteousness] I cannot have thy approbation unless I am *conformed* to thy *will.* I must be *righteous* in order that my *heart* and *life* may please thee.

I shall be satisfied, when I awake, with thy likeness.] Nothing but God can satisfy the wishes of an immortal spirit. He made it with infinite capacities and desires; and he alone, the infinite Good, can meet and gratify these desires, and fill this all-capacious mind. No soul was ever satisfied but by God; and he satisfies the soul only by restoring it to his image, which, by the *fall*, it has lost.

I think there is an allusion here to the *creation of Adam.* When God breathed into him the *breath of lives*, and *he became a living soul*, he would appear as one *suddenly awaked from sleep.* The first object that met his eyes was his *glorious Creator;* and being *made* in his *image* and in his *likeness*, he could converse with him face to face—was capable of the most intimate union with him, because he was filled with holiness and moral perfection. Thus was he *satisfied;* the God of infinite perfection and purity filling all the powers and faculties of his soul. David sees this in the light of the Divine Spirit, and knows that his happiness depends on being *restored to this image* and *likeness;* and he longs for the time when he shall completely arise out of the *sleep* and *death* of sin, and be *created anew after the image of God, in righteousness and true holiness.* I do not think that he refers to the *resurrection* of the *body*, but to the resurrection of the *soul* in this life; to the regaining the image which Adam lost.

The paraphrase in my old *Psalter* understands the whole of this Psalm as referring to the persecution, passion, death, and resurrection of Christ; and so did several of the primitive fathers, particularly St. Jerome and St. Augustine. I shall give a specimen from ver. 11:—

Projicientes me, nunc circumdederunt me: oculos suos statuerunt declinare in terram.

Trans. **Forth castand me now, thai haf umgyfen me: thair eghen thai sette to heelde in the erde.**

Par.—Forth kasten me out of the cite, als the stede had bene fyled of me: now thai haf umgyfen me in the cros hyngand, als folk that gedyrs til a somer gamen: for thai sett thair eghen, that es the entent of thaire hert to heeld in the erde; that es, in erdly thynges to covayte tham, and haf tham. And thai wende qwen thai slew Crist that he had suffird al the ill, and thai nane.

Perhaps some of my readers may think that this needs translating, so far does our present differ from our ancient tongue.

Text.—They have now cast me forth; they have surrounded me: their eyes they set down to the earth.

Par.—They have cast me out of the city, as if the state were to be defiled by me: now they have surrounded me hanging on the cross, as people gathered together at summer games. For they set their eyes, that is, the intent of their heart, down to the earth; that is, earthly things, to covet them and to have them: and they thought, when they slew Christ, that *he* had suffered all the ill, and *they* none.

BY the *slot* or track of the hart on the ground, referred to in ver. 11, experienced huntsmen can discern whether there have been a hart *there*, whether he has been there *lately*, whether the *slot* they see be the track of a *hart* or a *hind*, and whether the animal be *young* or *old.* All these can be discerned by the *slot.* And if the reader have that *scarce book* at hand, *Tuberville on Hunting*, 4to, 1575 or 1611, he will find all this information in chap. xxii., p. 63, entitled, *The Judgment and Knowledge by the Slot of a Hart;* and on the same page a wood-cut, representing a huntsman with *his eyes set, bowing down to the earth*, examining *three slots* which he had just found. The cut is a fine illustration of this clause. Saul and his men were hunting David, and curiously searching every place to find out any *track*, *mark*, or *footstep*, by which they might learn whether he *had been in such a place*, and whether he had been *there lately*. Nothing can more fully display the accuracy and intensity of this search than the metaphor contained in the above clause. He who has been his late Majesty's huntsmen looking for the slot in Windsor Forest will see the strength and propriety of the figure used by the psalmist.

Verse 12. *Like as a lion* that *is greedy of his prey*.—This is the picture of Saul. While his huntsmen were beating every bush, prying into every cave and crevice, and examining every foot of ground to find out a *track*, Saul is ready, whenever the game is started, to spring upon, seize, and destroy it. The metaphors are well connected, well sustained, and strongly expressive of the whole process of this persecution.

In the *ninth* verse the huntsmen beat the forest to raise and drive in the game. In the *tenth* they set their nets, and speak confidently of the expected success. In the *eleventh*, they felicitate themselves on having found the *slot*, the certain indication of the prey being at hand. And in the *twelfth*, the king of the sport is represented as just ready to spring upon the prey; or, as having his bow bent, and his arrow on the string, ready to let fly the moment the prey appears. It is worthy of remark, that *kings* and *queens* were frequently present, and were the *chiefs of the sport;* and it was they who, when he had been killed, *broke up* the deer: 1. Slitting down the brisket with their knife or sword; and, 2. Cutting off the head. And, as *Tuberville* published the first edition of his book in the reign of Queen *Elizabeth*, he gives a large wood-cut, p. 133, representing this princess just alighted from her horse—the stag stretched upon the ground—the huntsman kneeling, holding the fore foot of the animal with his left hand, and with his right presenting a knife to the queen for the purpose of the *breaking up*. As the second edition was published in the reign of *James the First*, the image of the *queen* is taken out and a *whole length of James* introduced in the place.

The same appears in *Tuberville's* Book of *Falconrie*, connected with the above. In p. 81, edition 1575, where the *flight of the hawk at the heron* is represented, the queen is seated on her charger: but in the edition of 1611 King *James* is placed on the same charger, the queen being removed.

The *lion* is the *monarch of the forest;* and is used successfully here to represent *Saul, king of Israel*, endeavouring to *hunt down David; hemming him in* on *every side; searching* for *his footsteps;* and ready to *spring upon him, shoot him* with his *bow*, or *pierce* him with his *javelin*, as soon as he should be obliged to flee from his *last cover*. The whole is finely imagined, and beautifully described.

Analysis of the Seventeenth Psalm

David's appeal to God in justification of himself; and his petition for defence against his enemies.

There are THREE parts in this Psalm:—

I. A *petition*. 1. For audience, ver. 1 and 6. 2. For perseverance in good, ver. 5. 3. For special favour, ver. 7, 8. 4. For immediate deliverance, ver. 13, 14.

II. A *narration;* in which we meet with, 1. His appeal to God, and his own justification, ver. 2, 3, 4. 2. The reasons of it; his enemies and their character, ver. 9 to 14.

III. A *conclusion;* which has two parts. 1. One belonging to this life; and, 2. One belonging to the life to come, ver. 15.

I. 1. He begins with *petition* for audience. And he urges it for two reasons: 1. The justness of his cause: "Hear the right, O Lord." 2. The sincerity of his heart: "That goeth not out of feigned lips."

2. Again, there were other reasons why he desired to be heard: 1. He felt himself prone to slip, and fall from God: "Hold up my goings," &c. 2. He was in great danger, and nothing but a miracle could save him: "Show thy marvellous lovingkindness." 3. His enemies were insolent and mighty, and God's sword only could prevail against them: "Arise, O Lord," ver. 13, 14.

II. *A narration:* His appeal to God. Since a verdict must pass upon him, he desired that God should pronounce it: "Let my sentence come forth from thy presence." I know that thou art a righteous Judge, and canst not be swayed by prejudice: "Let thine eyes behold the thing that is equal," and then I know it must go well with me: "Thou hast proved my heart. Thou hast tried me before on this business, and hast *found nothing*.

1. *Nothing* in my HEART: "Thou hast proved my heart."

2. *Nothing* in my TONGUE: "For I am purposed that my mouth shall not offend."

3. *Nothing* in my HAND: "For, concerning the works of men," which are mischievous; *by the words of thy lips*, I have had so great a regard to thy commandments that "I have kept myself from the paths of the wicked;" of him who, to satisfy his own desires, breaks all laws.

4. He confesses that he was poor and weak, and liable to fall, unless sustained by the grace of God: "Hold up my goings in thy paths."

And this first petition he renews, and takes courage from the assurance that he shall be heard: "I will call upon thee, for thou wilt hear me." And he puts in a special petition, which has two parts:—

1. "Show thy marvellous lovingkindness;" let me have more than ordinary help. And this he urges from the consideration that *God saves them who trust in him from those who rise up against them.*

2. That he would save him with the greatest care and vigilance, as a man would preserve the apple of his eye, or as a hen would guard her young: "Keep me as the apple of the eye; hide me," &c.

And to prevail in this *special petition*, he brings his arguments from his present necessity. He was encompassed with enemies, whom he describes:—

1. They were capital enemies; they hemmed him in on every side.

2. They were powerful, proud, and rich: "Men enclosed in their own fat, speaking proudly with their tongues," ver. 10.

3. Their counsels were fixed, and bent to ruin him: "They set their eyes, bowing down to the earth," ver. 11.

4. They were such enemies as prospered in

their designs, ver. 14. 1. Men of the world. 2. They had their portion in this life, and sought for none other. 3. They fed themselves without fear: "Their bellies were full." 4. They had a numerous offspring, and therefore more to be dreaded because of their family connections. 5. They left much substance behind them, so that their plans might be all continued and brought to effect.

III. The *conclusion*, containing the expectation of David, opposed to his enemies' felicity.

1. In this life: "As for me, I will behold thy face in righteousness."

2. In the life to come: "When I awake," rise from the dead, "after thy likeness, I shall be satisfied with it."

On each of these divisions the reader is referred to the notes.

PSALM XVIII

David's address of thanks to Jehovah, 1–3. *A relation of sufferings undergone, and prayers made for assistance*, 4–6. *A magnificent description of Divine interposition in behalf of the sufferer*, 7–15; *and of the deliverance wrought for him*, 16–19. *That this deliverance was in consideration of his righteousness*, 20–24; *and according to the tenor of God's equitable proceedings*, 25–28. *To Jehovah is ascribed the glory of the victory*, 29–36; *which is represented as complete by the destruction of all his opponents*, 37–42. *On these events the heathen submit*, 43–45. *And for all these things God is glorified*, 46–50.

III. DAY. EVENING PRAYER

To the chief Musician, *A Psalm* of David, [a]the servant of the LORD, who spake unto the LORD the words of [b]this song in the day *that* the LORD delivered him from the hand of all his enemies, and from the hand of Saul: And he said,

A. M. cir. 2986 B. C. cir. 1018 Davidis, Regis Israelitarum, cir. annum 38

I [c]WILL love thee, O LORD,
my strength.
2 The LORD *is* my rock, and
my fortress, and my deliverer;
my God, [d]my strength, [e]in whom
I will trust; my buckler, and the
horn of my salvation, *and* my
high tower.

A. M. cir. 2986 B. C. cir. 1018 Davidis, Regis Israelitarum, cir. annum 38

3 I will call upon the LORD, [f]*who is worthy*
to be praised: so shall I be saved from mine
enemies.
4 [g]The sorrows of death compassed me, and

[a]Psa. xxxvi. title——[b]2 Sam. xxii——[c]Psa. cxliv. 1
[d]Heb. *my rock*

[e]Hebrews ii. 13——[f]Psalm lxxvi. 4——[g]Psalm cxvi. 3

NOTES ON PSALM XVIII

The title: "To the chief Musician, *A Psalm* of David, the servant of the LORD, who spake unto the LORD the words of this song in the day *that* the LORD delivered him from the hand of all his enemies, and from the hand of Saul."

Except the first clause, this title is taken from 2 Sam. xxii. 1. The reader is requested to turn to the notes on 2 Sam. xxii. 1, for some curious information on this Psalm, particularly what is extracted from Dr. *Kennicott.* This learned writer supposes the whole to be a song of the Messiah, and divides it into *five parts*, which he thus introduces:—

"The Messiah's sublime thanksgivings, composed by David when his wars were at an end, towards the conclusion of his life. And in this sacred song the goodness of God is celebrated, 1. For Messiah's resurrection from the dead, with the wonders attending that awful event, and soon following it. 2. For the punishment inflicted on the Jews; particularly by the destruction of Jerusalem. And, 3. For the obedience of the Gentile nations. See Rom. xv. 9; Heb. ii. 13; and Matt. xxviii. 2-4; with xxiv. 7, and 29."

And that the title now prefixed to this hymn here and in 2 Sam. xxii. 1, describes only the *time* of its composition, seems evident; for who can ascribe to David *himself* as the subject, verses 5, 6, 8-17, 21-26, 30, 42, 44, &c.?

In Dr. *Kennicott's* remarks there is a new translation of the whole Psalm, p. 178, &c.

The strong current of commentators and critics apply this Psalm to Christ; and to oppose a whole host of both ancients and moderns would argue great self-confidence. In the *main* I am of the same mind; and on this principle chiefly I shall proceed to its illustration; still however considering that there are many things in it which concern David, and him only. Drs. *Chandler* and *Delaney* have been very successful in their illustration of various passages in it; all the best critics have brought their strongest powers to bear on it; and most of the commentators have laboured it with great success; and Bishop *Horne* has applied the whole of it to Christ. My old Psalter speaks highly in its praise: "This Psalme contenes the sacrement of al chosyn men, the qwilk doand the law of God thurgh the seven fald grace of the Haly Gast fra al temptaciouns, and the pouste of dede and of the devel lesid: this sang thai syng til God; and thankes him and says, *I sal luf the Lord*, noght a day or twa, bot ever mare: *my strength*, thurgh quam I am stalworth in thoght."

Verse 1. *I will love thee*] Love always subsists on motive and reason. The verb רחם *racham* signifies to *love with all the tender feelings of nature.* "From my inmost bowels will I love thee, O Lord!" Why should he love Jehovah? Not merely because he was infinitely great and good, possessed of all possible perfections, but because he was *good to him:* and he here enumerates some of the many blessings he received from him.

My strength.] 1. Thou who hast given me *power* over my adversaries, and hast enabled me to avoid evil and do good.

Verse 2. *The Lord* is *my rock*] 2. I stand

A. M. cir. 2986
B. C. cir. 1018
Davidis, Regis
Israelitarum,
cir. annum
38

the floods of [h]ungodly men made
me afraid.
5 The [i]sorrows of hell compassed me about: the [k]snares
of death prevented me.
6 In my distress I called upon the LORD,
and cried unto my God: he heard
my voice out of his temple, and
my cry came before him, *even*
into his ears.
7 [l]Then the earth shook and trembled; the
foundations also of the hills moved and

A. M. cir. 2986
B. C. cir. 1018
Davidis, Regis
Israelitarum,
cir. annum
38

[h]Heb. *Belial*——[i]Or, *cords*——[k]2 Sam. xxii. 6; Prov. xiii. 14; xiv. 27——[l]Acts iv. 31

on him as my *foundation*, and derive every good from him who is the source of good. The word סלע *sela* signifies those craggy precipices which afford shelter to men and wild animals; where the *bees* often made their nests, and whence honey was collected in great abundance. "He made him to suck honey out of the rock," Deut. xxxii. 13. 3. He was his *fortress;* a place of *strength* and *safety*, fortified by *nature* and *art*, where he could be safe from his enemies. He refers to those inaccessible heights in the rocky, mountainous country of Judea, where he had often found refuge from the pursuit of Saul. What these have been to my body, such has the Lord been to my soul.

Deliverer] 4. מפלטי *mephalleti*, he who causes me to *escape*. This refers to his preservation in straits and difficulties. He was often *almost* surrounded and taken, but still the Lord *made a way for his escape*—made a *way out* as his enemies *got in;* so that, while they got in at one side of his strong hold, he got out of the other, and so *escaped* with his life. These escapes were so narrow and so unlikely that he plainly saw the hand of the Lord was in them. 5. *My God*, אלי *Eli*, my *strong God*, not only the object of my adoration, but he who puts strength in my soul. 6. *My strength*, צורי *tsuri*. This is a different word from that in the first verse. *Rabbi Maimon* has observed that צור *tsur*, when applied to God, signifies *fountain, source, origin*, &c. God is not only the *source* whence my *being* was *derived*, but he is the *fountain* whence I *derive* all my *good; in whom*, says David, *I will trust*. And why? Because he knew him to be an eternal and *inexhaustible fountain* of goodness. This fine idea is lost in our translation; for we render two Hebrew words of widely different meaning, by the same term in English, *strength*. 7. *My buckler*, מגני *maginni*, my *shield*, my *defender*, he who covers my head and my heart, so that I am neither slain nor wounded by the darts of my adversaries. 8. *Horn of my salvation. Horn* was the emblem of power, and power in exercise. This has been already explained; see on 1 Sam. ii. 1. The *horn of salvation* means a *powerful*, an *efficient salvation*. 9. *My high tower;* not only a place of defence, but one from which I can discern the country round about, and always be able to discover danger before it approaches me.

Verse 3. *I will call upon the Lord*] When he was conscious that the object of his worship was such as he has pointed out in the above *nine* particulars, it is no wonder that he resolves to *call upon him;* and no wonder that he expects, in consequence, to be saved from his enemies; for who can destroy him whom such a God undertakes to save?

Verse 4. *The sorrows of death compassed me*] חבלי מות *chebley maveth*, the *cables* or *cords of death*. He was almost taken in those *nets* or *stratagems*, by which, if he had been entangled, he would have lost his life. The stratagems to which he refers were those that were intended for his destruction; hence called *the cables* or *cords of death*.

The floods of ungodly men] Troops of wicked men were rushing upon him like an irresistible torrent; or like the waves of the sea, one impelling another forward in successive ranks; so that, thinking he must be overwhelmed by them, he was for the moment *affrighted;* but God turned the torrent aside, and he escaped.

Verse 5. *The sorrows of hell*] חבלי שאול *chebley sheol*, the *cables* or *cords of the grave*. Is not this a reference to the *cords* or *ropes* with which they *lowered the corpse into the grave?* or the bandages by which the dead were swathed? He was as good as dead.

The snares of death prevented me.] I was just on the point of dropping into the pit which they had digged for me. In short, I was all but a dead man; and nothing less than the immediate *interference* of God could have saved my life.

Verse 6. *In my distress I called*] His enemies had no hope of his destruction unless God should abandon him. They hoped that this was the case, and that therefore they should prevail. But God *heard his cry and came down* to his help; and this interference is most majestically described in the 7th and following verses. Dr. *Dodd* has collected some excellent observations on these verses from *Chandler, Delaney*, and others, which I shall transcribe, as I know not that any thing better can be offered on the subject.

Verse 7. *Then the earth shook and trembled*] "In this and the following verses David describes, by the sublimest expressions and grandest terms, the majesty of God, and the awful manner in which he came to his assistance. The representation of the storm in these verses must be allowed by all skilful and impartial judges to be truly sublime and noble, and in the genuine spirit of poetry. The majesty of God, and the manner in which he is represented as coming to the aid of his favourite king, surrounded with all the powers of nature as his attendants and ministers, and arming (as it were) heaven and earth to fight his battles, and execute his vengeance, is described in the loftiest and most striking terms. The *shaking of the* earth; the trembling of the mountains and pillars of heaven; the *smoke* that drove out of his nostrils; the *flames* of devouring fire that flashed from his mouth; the *heavens bending* down to convey him to the battle; his riding upon a *cherub*, and rapidly

A. M. cir. 2986 B. C. cir. 1018 Davidis, Regis Israelitarum, cir. annum 38

were shaken, because he was
wroth.
8 There went up a smoke
[m]out of his nostrils, and fire out
of his mouth devoured: coals were kindled
by it.

9 [n]He bowed the heavens also,
and came down: and darkness
was under his feet.
10 [o]And he rode upon a cherub,
and did fly: yea, [p]he did fly upon the wings
of the wind.

A. M. cir. 2986 B. C. cir. 1018 Davidis, Regis Israelitarum, cir. annum 38

[m]Heb. *by his*——[n]Psa. cxliv. 5

[o]Psa. xcix. 1——[p]Psa. civ. 3

flying on the *wings of a whirlwind;* his concealing his majesty in the *thick clouds* of heaven; the bursting of the *lightnings* from the *horrid darkness; the uttering of his voice* in *peals* of *thunder;* the *storm* of *fiery hail;* the *melting of the heavens*, and their dissolving into floods of *tempestuous rain;* the *cleaving of the earth*, and disclosing of the bottom of the hills, and the subterraneous channels or torrents of water, by the very breath of the nostrils of the Almighty; are all of them circumstances which create admiration, excite a kind of horror, and exceed every thing of this nature that is to be found in any of the remains of heathen antiquity. See *Longinus* on the Sublime, sec. 9, and *Hesiod's* description of Jupiter fighting against the Titans, which is one of the grandest things in all pagan antiquity; though upon comparison it will be found infinitely short of this description of the *psalmist's;* throughout the whole of which God is represented as a mighty warrior going forth to fight the battles of David, and highly incensed at the opposition his enemies made to his power and authority.

"When he descended to the engagement the very heavens bowed down to render his descent more awful; his *military tent* was *substantial darkness;* the *voice* of his *thunder* was the *warlike alarm* which sounded to the *battle;* the *chariot* in which he rode was the *thick clouds* of heaven, conducted by *cherubs*, and carried on by the irresistible force and rapid wings of an *impetuous tempest;* and the darts and weapons he employed were *thunderbolts, lightnings, fiery hail, deluging rains*, and *stormy winds!*

"No wonder that when God thus arose, all his enemies should be scattered, and those who hated him should flee before him.

"It does not appear from any part of David's history that there was any such storm as is here described, which proved destructive to his enemies, and salutary to himself. There might, indeed, have been such a one, though there is no particular mention of it: unless it may be thought that something of this nature is intimated in the account given of David's second battle with the Philistines, 2 Sam. v. 23, 24. It is undoubted, however, that the storm is represented as real; though David, in describing it, has heightened and embellished it with all the ornaments of poetry. See Chandler, Delaney, and Lowth's ninth Prelection.

"Verse 8. *There went up a smoke out of his nostrils*—Or, 'There ascended into his nostrils a smoke,' as the words, literally rendered, signify. The ancients placed the seat of anger in the *nose*, or nostrils; because when the passions are warm and violent, it discovers itself by the heated vehement breath which proceeds from them. Hence the physiognomists considered open wide nostrils as a sign of an angry, fiery disposition.

"This description of a *smoke* arising into and a *fire* breaking forth from the nostrils of God, denotes, by a poetical figure, the greatness of his anger and indignation.

"*Fire out of his mouth devoured*—means that consuming fire issued out of his mouth. *Coals were kindled by it*, thus we render the next clause; but the words do not mean that fire proceeding from God kindled coals, but that burning coals issued from his mouth; and it should be rendered 'living coals from his mouth burned, and consumed around him.'—*Chandler*.

"Verse 9. *He bowed the heavens also, and came down*—He made the heavens bend under him when he descended to take vengeance on his enemies. The psalmist seems here to express the appearance of the Divine majesty in a glorious cloud, descending from heaven, which underneath was substantially dark, but above, bright, and shining with exceeding lustre; and which, by its gradual approach to the earth, would appear as though the heavens themselves were bending down and approaching towards us.

"Verse 10. *He rode upon a cherub, and did fly*—That is, as it is immediately explained, *Yea, he did fly upon the wings of the wind*. God was in the storm, and by the ministry of angels guided the course of it, and drove it on with such an impetuous force as nothing could withstand. He 'rides in the whirlwind and directs the storm.' Angels are in a peculiar sense the attendants and messengers of the Almighty, whom he employs as his ministers in effecting many of those great events which take place in the administration of his providence; and particularly such as manifest his immediate interposition in the extraordinary judgments which he inflicts for the punishment of sinful nations. See Psa. ciii. 20, civ. 4. The *cherub* is particularly mentioned as an emblem of the Divine presence, and especially as employed in supporting and conveying the chariot of the Almighty, when he is represented as riding in his majesty through the firmament of heaven:—

——Forth rush'd with whirlwind sound
The chariot of paternal Deity;
Flashing thick flames, wheel within wheel undrawn,
Itself instinct with spirit, but convey'd
By four cherubic shapes.
Par. Lost, lib. vi."

This seems to be the image intended to be conveyed in the place before us. "He rode upon a cherub, and did fly; he flew on the wings of the wind," i. e., the cherub supported and led on the tempest, in which the Almighty rode as in his chariot. This is agreeable to the office elsewhere ascribed to the cherubim. Thus

A. M. cir. 2986
B. C. cir. 1018
Davidis, Regis
Israelitarum,
cir. annum
38

11 He made darkness his secret
place; [q]his pavilion round about
him *were* dark waters *and* thick
clouds of the skies.
12 [r]At the brightness *that was* before him
his thick clouds passed; hail-*stones* and coals
of fire.
13 The LORD also thundered in the heavens,
and the Highest gave [s]his
voice; hail-*stones* and coals of
fire.
14 [t]Yea, he sent out his arrows,
and scattered them; and he shot out lightnings,
and discomfited them.
15 [u]Then the channels of waters were seen,
and the foundations of the world were discov-

A. M. cir. 2986
B. C. cir. 1018
Davidis, Regis
Israelitarum,
cir. annum
38

[q]Psa. xcvii. 3——[r]Psa. xcvii. 3——[s]Psalm xxix. 3

[t]Josh. x. 10; Psa. cxliv. 6; Isa. xxx. 30——[u]Exod. xv. 8; Psa. cvi. 9

they supported the mercy-seat, which was peculiarly the throne of God under the Jewish economy. God is expressly said to "make the clouds his chariot," Psa. civ. 3; and to "ride upon a swift cloud," Isa. xix. 1: so that "riding upon a cherub," and "riding upon a swift cloud," is riding in the cloud as his chariot, supported and guided by the ministry of the cherubim. The next clause in the parallel place of Samuel is, "He was seen on the wings of the wind;" ירא *yera*, he *was seen*, being used for ידא *yede*, he *flew*, ד *daleth* being changed into ר *resh*. Either of them may be the true reading, for the MSS. are greatly divided on these places; but on the whole וירא *vaiyera* appears to be the better reading: "And he was *seen* on the wings of the wind."

As the original has been supposed by adequate judges to exhibit a fine specimen of that poetry which, in the choice of its terms, conveys both *sense* and *sound*, I will again lay it before the reader, as I have done in the parallel place, 2 Sam. xxii. 2. The words in *italic* to be read from right to left.

וירכב על כרוב ויעף
vaiyaoph kerub al waiyirkab
And he rode upon a cherub, and did fly!
וידא על כנפי רוח
ruach canphey al waiyede
Yea, he flew on the wings of the wind!

The word רוח *ruach*, in the last line, should be pronounced, not *ruak*, which is no Hebrew word: but as a Scottish man would pronounce it, were it written *ruagh*. With this observation, how astonishingly is the *rushing of the wind* heard in the last word of each hemistich! *Sternhold* and *Hopkins* have succeeded in their version of this place, not only beyond all *they* ever did, but beyond every ancient and modern poet on a similar subject:—

"On cherub and on cherubin
Full royally he rode;
And on the wings of mighty winds
Came flying all abroad."

Even the old *Anglo-Scottish Psalter* has not done amiss:—

**And he steygh aboven cherubyn and he flow;
He flow aboven the fethers of wyndes.**

Verse 11. *He made darkness his secret place*] God is represented as dwelling in the *thick darkness*, Deut. iv. 11, Psa. xcvii. 2. This representation in the place before us is peculiarly proper; as thick heavy clouds deeply charged, and with lowering aspects, are always the forerunners and attendants of a tempest, and greatly heighten the horrors of the appearance: and the representation of them, spread about the Almighty as a tent, is truly grand and poetic.

Dark waters] The vapours strongly condensed into clouds; which, by the stroke of the lightning, are about to be precipitated in torrents of rain. See the next verse.

Verse 12. *At the brightness* that was *before him his thick clouds passed*] The word נגה *nogah* signifies the *lightning*. This *goes before him;* the *flash* is seen before the *thunder* is heard, and before the *rain* descends; and then the *thick cloud passes*. Its contents are precipitated on the earth, and the cloud is entirely dissipated.

Hail-stones *and coals of fire.*] This was the *storm* that followed the *flash* and the *peal;* for it is immediately added—

Verse 13. *The Lord also thundered in the heavens, and the Highest gave his voice*] And then followed the *hail and coals of fire*. The former verse mentioned the *lightning*, with its effects; this gives us the report of the *thunder*, and the increasing *storm of hail and fire* that attended it. Some think the words *hail-stones and coals of fire* are entered here by some careless transcribers from the preceding verse; and it is true that they are wanting in the Septuagint and the Arabic, in the parallel place in 2 Samuel, and in *five* of *Kennicott's* and *De Rossi's* MSS. I should rather, with Bishop *Horsley*, suppose them to be an interpolation in the preceding verse: or in that to have been borrowed from this; for this most certainly is their true place.

Verse 14. *He sent out his arrows—he shot out lightnings*] I believe the latter clause to be an illustration of the former. *He sent out his arrows*—that is, he shot out *lightnings;* for lightnings are the *arrows* of the Lord, and there is something very like the *arrowhead* apparent in the *zigzag* lightning. *Sense* and *sound* are wonderfully combined in the Hebrew of this last clause: וברכים רב ויהמם *uberakim rab vaihummem*, "and thunderings he multiplied and confounded them." Who does not hear the *bursting*, *brattling*, and *pounding* of thunder in these words? See *Delaney?*

Verse 15. *The channels of water were seen*] This must refer to an *earthquake;* for in such cases, the ground being rent, water frequently gushes out at the fissures, and often rises to a tremendous height. Whole rivers were poured out of the chasms made by the earthquake in Jamaica, A. D. 1694; and new lakes of water were formed, covering a *thousand* acres of land!

A. M. cir. 2986 B. C. cir. 1018 Davidis, Regis Israelitarum, cir. annum 38

ered at thy rebuke, O LORD, at the blast of the breath of thy nostrils.

16 [v]He sent from above, he took me, he drew me out of [w]many waters.

17 He delivered me from my strong enemy, and from them which hated me: for they were too strong for me.

18 They prevented me in the day of my calamity: but the LORD was my stay.

19 [x]He brought me forth also into a large place; he delivered me, because he delighted in me.

20 [y]The LORD rewarded me according to my righteousness; according to the cleanness of my hands hath he recompensed me.

21 For I have kept the ways of the LORD, and have not wickedly departed from my God.

22 For all his judgments *were* before me, and I did not put away his statutes from me.

23 I was also upright [z]before him, and I kept myself from mine iniquity.

24 [a]Therefore hath the LORD recompensed me according to my righteousness, according to the cleanness of my hands [b]in his eyesight.

25 [c]With the merciful thou wilt show thyself merciful; with an upright man thou wilt show thyself upright;

26 With the pure thou wilt show thyself

[v]Psa. cxliv. 7——[w]Or, *great waters*——[x]Psa. xxxi. 8; cxviii. 5——[y]1 Sam. xxiv. 20

[z]Heb. *with*——[a]1 Sam. xxvi. 23——[b]Heb. *before his eyes*——[c]1 Kings viii. 32

Verse 16. *He drew me out of many waters.*] Here the allusion is still carried on. The waters thus poured out were sweeping the people away; but God, by a miraculous interference, sent and drew David out. Sometimes *waters* are used to denote *multitudes of people;* and here the word may have that reference; multitudes were gathered together against David, but God delivered him from them all. This seems to be countenanced by the following verse.

Verse 17. *He delivered me from my strong enemy*] Does not this refer to his conflict with Ishbi-benob? "And Ishbi-benob, which *was* of the sons of the giant—thought to have slain David. But Abishai the son of Zeruiah succoured him, and smote the Philistine, and killed him. Then the men of David sware unto him, saying, Thou shalt go no more out with us to battle, that thou quench not the light of Israel;" 2 Sam. xxi. 16, 17. It appears that at this time he was in the most imminent danger of his life, and that he must have fallen by the hands of the giant, if God had not sent Abishai to his assistance. *They were too strong for me.* He was nearly overpowered by the Philistines; and his escape was such as evidently to show it to be supernatural.

Verse 18. *They prevented me in the day of my calamity*] They took advantage of the time in which I was least able to make head against them, and their attack was sudden and powerful. I should have been overthrown, *but the Lord was my stay.* He had been nearly exhausted by the fatigue of the day, when the giant availed himself of this advantage.

Verse 19. *He brought me forth also into a large place*] He enabled me to clear the country of my foes, who had before cooped me up in holes and corners. This appears to be the allusion.

Verse 20. *The Lord rewarded me*] David proceeds to give the reasons why God had so marvellously interposed in his behalf.

According to my righteousness] Instead of being an enemy to Saul, I was his friend. I dealt *righteously* with him while he dealt *unrighteously* with me.

Verse 21. *I have kept the ways of the Lord*] I was neither an *infidel* nor a *profligate;* I trusted in God, and carefully observed all the ordinances of his religion.

Verse 22. *All his judgments* were *before me*] I kept his law before my eyes, that I might see my duty and know how to walk and please God.

Verse 23. *I was also upright*] The times in which David was most afflicted were the times of his greatest uprightness. *Adversity* was always to him a time of spiritual prosperity.

Mine iniquity.] Probably meaning what is generally termed *the easily-besetting sin; the sin of his constitution,* or that to which the *temperament* of his body most powerfully disposed him. What this was, is a subject of useless conjecture.

Verse 25. *With the merciful thou wilt show thyself merciful*] Thou wilt deal with men as they deal with each other. This is the general tenor of God's providential conduct towards mankind; well expressed by Mr. *Pope* in his universal prayer:—

"Teach me to feel another's wo;
To hide the fault I see:
The mercy I to others show,
That mercy show to me."

It is in reference to this that our Lord teaches us to pray: "Forgive us our trespasses, as we forgive them that trespass against us." If we act *feelingly* and *mercifully* towards our fellow creatures, God will act *tenderly* and *compassionately* towards us. The merciful, the upright, and the pure, will ever have the God of mercy, uprightness, and purity, to defend and support them.

Verse 26. *With the froward*] עקש *ikkesh, the perverse man;* he that is crooked in his tempers and ways.

Thou wilt show thyself froward.] תתפתל *tithpattal, thou wilt set thyself to twist, twine, and wrestle.* If *he* contend, *thou* wilt contend with him. Thou wilt follow him through all his windings; thou wilt trace him through all his crooked ways; untwist him in all his cun-

A. M. cir. 2986
B. C. cir. 1018
Davidis, Regis
Israelitarum,
cir. annum
38

pure; and [d]with the froward
thou wilt [e]show thyself froward.
27 For thou wilt save the
afflicted people; but wilt bring
down [f]high looks.
28 [g]For thou wilt light my [h]candle: the LORD
my God will enlighten my darkness.
29 For by thee I have [i]run through a
troop; and by my God have I leaped over a
wall.
30 *As for* God, [k]his way *is* perfect: [l]the
word of the LORD is [m]tried: he *is* a buckler
[n]to all those that trust in
him.
31 [o]For who *is* God save the
LORD? or who *is* a rock save our
God?
32 *It is* God that [p]girdeth me with strength
and maketh my way perfect.
33 [q]He maketh my feet like hinds' *feet,*
and [r]setteth me upon my high places.
34 [s]He teacheth my hands to war, so that a
bow of steel is broken by mine arms.
35 Thou hast also given me the shield of

A. M. cir. 2986
B. C. cir. 1018
Davidis, Regis
Israelitarum,
cir. annum
38

[d]Lev. xxvi. 23, 24, 27, 28; Prov. iii. 34——[e]Or, *wrestle*——[f]Psa. ci. 5; Prov. vi. 17——[g]Job xviii. 6 [h]Or, *lamp*, Job xxix. 3——[i]Or, *broken*——[k]Deut. xxxii. 4; Dan. iv. 37; Rev. xv. 3——[l]Psa. xii. 6; cxix. 140; Prov. xxx. 5

[m]Or, *refined*——[n]Psalm xvii. 7——[o]Deuteronomy xxxii. 31, 39; 1 Sam. ii. 2; Psa. lxxxvi. 8; Isa. xlv. 5 [p]Psalm xci. 2——[q]2 Samuel ii. 18; Habakkuk iii. 19——[r]Deuteronomy xxxii. 13; xxxiii. 29——[s]Psalm cxliv. 1

ning wiles; and defeat all his schemes of stubbornness, fraud, overreaching, and deceit.

My old *Psalter* has, **With the wiked thow sal be wike.** Here the term *wicked* is taken in its *true original* sense, *crooked*, or *perverse*. With the **wiked**, the *perverse*, thou wilt show thyself **wike**, i. e., *perverse;* from **piccan**, to *draw back*, to *slide*. As *he draws back* from thee, thou wilt *draw back* from him. It may, as before intimated, come from **piccian**, to seek for *enchantments; leaving God*, and *going to devils;* to act like a *witch:* but *here* it must *mean* as above. The plain import is, "If thou perversely oppose thy Maker, he will oppose thee: no work or project shall prosper that is not begun in his name, and conducted in his fear."

Verse 27. *For thou wilt save the afflicted*] The afflicted are the *humble;* and those thou hast ever befriended.

Verse 28. *For thou wilt light my candle*] Thou wilt restore me to prosperity, and give me a happy issue out of all my afflictions. By the *lamp of David* the *Messiah* may be meant: thou wilt not suffer my family to become extinct, nor the kingdom which thou hast promised me utterly to fail.

Verse 29. *I have run through a troop*] This may relate to some remarkable victory; and the taking of some fortified place, possibly *Zion*, from the Jebusites. See the account 2 Sam. v. 6-8.

Verse 30. *God, his way* is *perfect*] His conduct is like his nature, absolutely pure.

The word of the Lord is tried] Literally *tried in the fire*. It has stood all tests; and has never failed those who pleaded it before its author.

He is *a buckler*] A sure protection to every simple believing soul. We cannot believe his word too *implicity;* nor trust too *confidently* in him.

Verse 31. *For who* is *God save the Lord?*] "For who is Eloah, except Jehovah?" None is worthy of adoration but the self-existent, eternal, infinitely perfect, and all-merciful Being.

Or who is *a rock*] A *fountain* emitting continual supplies of grace and goodness.

Verse 32. *God—girdeth me with strength*] The girdle was a necessary part of the Eastern dress; it *strengthened* and *supported* the loins; served to *confine* the *garments* close to the body; and in it they tucked them up when journeying. The *strength* of God was to his *soul* what the *girdle* was to the *body*. I need not add, that the *girdle* was also an *ornamental* part of the dress, and from it the sword was suspended.

And maketh my way perfect.] He directs me so that I do not go astray; he blesses me in my undertakings; and by him the issue of my labours is crowned with prosperity.

Verse 33. *My feet like hinds'* feet] Swiftness, or *speed of foot*, was a necessary qualification of an ancient hero. This was of great advantage in pursuing, combating, or escaping from a fallen foe. Ποδας ωκυς Αχιλλευς, "the swift-footed Achilles," is frequently given by *Homer* as a most honourable qualification of his hero.

Upon my high places.] In allusion to the *hinds*, *antelopes*, *mountain goats*, &c., which frequented such places, and in which they found both *food* and *safety*. God frequently preserved the life of David by means of these.

Verse 34. *He teacheth my hands to war*] The success which I have had in my military exercises I owe to the Divine help. How few of the conquerors of mankind can say so! And how few among those who call themselves *Christian warriors* dare to say so! *War* is as contrary to the spirit of Christianity as murder. Nothing can justify Christian nations in shedding each other's blood! All men *should* live in peace; all men *might* live in peace; and the nation that is *first* to break it is under a heavy curse.

A bow of steel is broken by mine arms.] All the *versions* render this: "Thou hast made my arm like a brazen bow." A bow of *steel* is out of the question. In the days of David it is not likely that the method of making *steel* was known. The method of making *brass* out of *copper* was known at a very early period of the world; and the ancients had the art of *hardening* it, so as to work it into the most efficient swords. From his own account David was *swift, courageous*, and *strong*.

Verse 35. *The shield of thy salvation*] In all battles and dangers God defended him. He was constantly safe because he possessed the

A. M. cir. 2986 B. C. cir. 1018 Davidis, Regis Israelitarum, cir. annum 38

thy salvation: and thy right hand
hath holden me up, and [t]thy
gentleness hath made me great.

36 Thou hast enlarged my steps
under me, [u]that [v]my feet did not slip.

37 I have pursued mine enemies, and overtaken them; neither did I turn again till they
were consumed.

38 I have wounded them that they were not
able to rise: they are fallen under my feet.

39 For thou hast girded me with strength
unto the battle: thou hast [w]subdued under
me those that rose up against me.

40 Thou hast also given me the necks of
mine enemies; that I might destroy them that
hate me.

41 They cried, but *there was*
none to save *them:* [x]*even* unto
the LORD, but he answered them
not.

42 Then did I beat them small as the dust
before the wind: I did [y]cast them out as the
dirt in the streets.

43 [z]Thou hast delivered me from the strivings of the people; *and* [a]thou hast made me
the head of the heathen: [b]a people *whom* I
have not known shall serve me.

44 [c]As soon as they hear of me, they shall
obey me: [d]the strangers [e]shall [f]submit
[g]themselves unto me.

45 [h]The strangers shall fade away, and be
afraid out of their close places.

[t]Or, *with thy meekness thou hast multiplied me* [u]Prov. iv. 12——[v]Heb. *mine ankles*——[w]Heb. *caused to bow*——[x]Job xxvii. 9; xxxv. 12; Prov. i. 28; Isa. i. 15; Jer. xi. 11; xiv. 12; Ezek. viii. 18; Mic. iii. 4; Zech. vii. 13——[y]Zech. x. 5

[z]2 Sam. ii. 9, 10; iii. 1——[a]2 Sam. viii——[b]Isa. lii. 15; lv. 5——[c]Heb. *At the hearing of the ear*——[d]Heb. *the sons of the stranger*——[e]Deut. xxxiii. 29; Psa. lxvi. 3; lxxxi. 15——[f]Or, *yield feigned obedience*——[g]Heb. *lie* [h]Mic. vii. 17

salvation of God. Everywhere God protected him. *Thy gentleness*, ענותך *anvathecha*, thy *meekness* or *humility*. Thou hast enabled me to bear and forbear; to behave with courage in adversity, and with humility in prosperity; and thus I am become *great*. By these means thou hast *multiplied* me. The *Vulgate* reads, *Disciplina tua ipsa me docebit;* "And thy discipline itself shall teach me." In this sense it was understood by most of the *versions*. The old *Psalter* paraphrases thus: Thi chastying suffers me noght to erre fra the end to com.

Verse 36. *Enlarged my steps*] See on ver. 19. From the hand of God he had continual prosperity; and while he walked with God no enemy was able to prevail against him. He details his successes in the following verses.

Verse 40. *The necks of mine enemies*] Thou hast made me a complete conqueror. *Treading on the neck* of an enemy was the triumph of the conqueror, and the utmost disgrace of the vanquished.

Verse 41. *They cried*] The Philistines called upon their gods, but there was none to save them.

Even *unto the Lord*] Such as Saul, Ish-bosheth, Absalom, &c., who, professing to worship the true God, *called on him* while in their opposition to David; but God no more heard *them* than their *idols* heard the Philistines.

Verse 42. *Then did I beat them*] God was with *him*, and *they* had only an arm of flesh. No wonder then that his enemies were destroyed.

Small as the dust before the wind] This well expresses the manner in which he treated the Moabites, Ammonites, and the people of Rabbah: "He put them under saws, and under harrows of iron, and under axes of iron; and made them pass through the brick-kiln," &c. See 2 Sam. xii. 31, and the notes there.

Verse 43. *The strivings of the people*] Disaffections and insurrections among my own subjects, as in the revolt of *Absalom*, the *civil war of Abner* in favour of *Ish-bosheth*, &c.

The head of the heathen] ראש גוים *rosh goyim*, "the chief," or "governor, of the nations;" all the circumjacent heathen people; all these were subdued by David, and brought under tribute.

A people whom *I have not known*] The people whom he *knew* were those of the *twelve tribes;* those whom he did *not know* were the Syrians, Philistines, Idumeans, &c. All these *served him*, that is, paid him *tribute*.

Verse 44. *As soon as they hear of me*] His victories were so rapid and splendid over powerful enemies, that they struck a general terror among the people, and several submitted without a contest.

Strangers shall submit themselves unto me.] Some translate this: "The children of the foreign woman have lied unto me." This has been understood *two* ways: My own people, who have sworn fealty to me, have broken their obligation, and followed my rebellious son. Or, The heathens, who have been brought under my yoke, have promised the most cordial obedience, and flattered me with their tongues, while their hearts felt enmity against me and my government. Nevertheless, even in this unwilling subjection I was secure, my police being so efficient, and my kingdom so strong.

Verse 45. *The strangers shall fade away*] בני נכר *beney nechar*, the same persons mentioned above. They shall not be able to effect any thing against me; יבלו *yibbolu*, "they shall fall as the leaves fall off the trees in winter."

And be afraid out of their close places.] Those who have formed themselves into *banditti*, and have taken possession of *rocks* and *fortified places*, shall be so afraid when they hear of my successes, that they shall surrender at discretion, without standing a siege. Perhaps all these verbs should be understood in the *perfect* tense, for David is here evidently speaking of a kingdom at rest, all enemies having *been subdued;* or, as the *title* is, *when the Lord* HAD *delivered him from all his enemies.*

A. M. cir. 2986
B. C. cir. 1018
Davidis, Regis
Israelitarum,
cir. annum
38

46 The LORD liveth, and blessed *be* my Rock: and let the God
of my salvation be exalted.
47 *It is* God that [i]avengeth
me, [k]and [l]subdueth the people under me.
48 He delivereth me from mine enemies:
yea, [m]thou liftest me up above those
that rise up against me: thou hast delivered me from the [n]violent
man.
49 [o]Therefore will I [p]give
thanks unto thee, O LORD, among
the heathen, and sing praises unto thy name.
50 [q]Great deliverance giveth he to his king;
and showeth mercy to his anointed, to David,
and to his seed [r]for evermore.

A. M. cir. 2986
B. C. cir. 1018
Davidis, Regis
Israelitarum,
cir. annum
38

---

[i]Heb. *giveth avengements for me*——[k]Psa. xlvii. 3——[l]Or, *destroyeth*——[m]Psa. lix. 1——[n]Heb. *man of violence*——[o]Rom. xv. 9——[p]Or, *confess*——[q]Psa. cxliv. 10——[r]2 Sam. vii. 13

Verse 46. *The Lord liveth*] By him alone I have gained all my victories; and he *continueth*, and will be my *Rock*, the *Source* whence I may at all times derive help and salvation. May his name be blessed! May his kingdom be exalted!

Verse 47. *God that avengeth me*] The way that I took was after his own heart; therefore he sustained me in it, and did me justice over my enemies.

Subdueth the people under me.] He keeps down the spirits of the disaffected, and weakens their hands. They are subdued, and they continue under me; and this is the Lord's doing.

Verse 48. *He delivereth me*] That is, he *hath delivered* me, and continues to deliver me, from all that rise up against me.

The violent man.] Saul; this applies particularly to him.

Verse 49. *Will I give thanks unto thee—among the heathen*] Quoted by St. Paul, Rom. xv. 9, to prove that the *calling of the Gentiles* was predicted, and that what then took place was the fulfilment of that prediction.

But there is a sense in which it applies particularly to David, well observed by *Theodoret:* "We see," says he, "evidently the fulfilment of this prophecy; for even to the present day David praises the Lord among the Gentiles by the mouth of true believers; seeing there is not a town, village, hamlet, country, nor even a desert, where Christians dwell, in which God is not praised by their singing the Psalms of David."

Verse 50. *Great deliverance giveth he to his king*] David was a king of God's appointment, and was peculiarly favoured by him. Literally, *He is magnifying the salvations of his king.* He not only delivers, but follows up those deliverances with innumerable blessings.

Showeth mercy—to David] I have no *claim* upon his bounty. I *deserve* nothing from him, but he continues to show *mercy.*

To his seed] His *posterity.* So the words זרע *zera* and σπερμα, in the Old and New Testament, should be universally translated. The common translation is totally improper, and *now* more so than formerly, when *anatomy* was less understood.

For evermore.] עד עולם *ad olam, for ever;* through all duration of created worlds. And *more*—the eternity that is beyond time. This shows that another *David* is meant, with another kind of *posterity,* and another sort of *kingdom.* From the *family of David* came the *man Christ Jesus;* his *posterity* are the *genuine Christians;* his *kingdom,* in which they are *subjects,* is *spiritual.* This *government* shall last through all time, for Christianity will continue to prevail till the *end of the world:* and it will be extended through *eternity;* for that is the kingdom of glory in which Jesus reigns on the throne of his Father, and in which his followers shall reign with him for ever and ever.

It has already been remarked that this whole Psalm has been understood as relating to the *passion* and *victories* of CHRIST, and the *success of the Gospel in the earth.* In this way Bishop *Horne* has understood and paraphrased it; and in the same way it is considered by the ancient *Psalter,* so often mentioned. Many of the primitive *fathers* and modern *interpreters* have taken the same view of it. Those passages which I judged to have this meaning I have pointed out, and have only to add that, as David was a *type of Christ,* many things spoken of him *primarily,* refer to our Lord *ultimately;* but much judgment and caution are required in their application. To apply the whole Psalm in this way appears to me very injudicious, and often derogatory from the majesty of Christ. Let this be my excuse for not following the same track in which many of my predecessors have gone.

ANALYSIS OF THE EIGHTEENTH PSALM

David's Επινικιον, or song of triumph after his conquest of all his enemies.

This Psalm may be divided into *four* parts:—

I. David shows what God is to his servants, and the effect it wrought upon him, ver. 1, 2, 3.

II. The great danger in which he was from the power and multitude of his enemies, ver. 4-28.

III. His glorious victories, and their consequences, ver. 29-45.

IV. His thanksgiving for those victories, ver. 46-50.

I. What God is to his servants, and to him especially. 1. *Strength.* 2. *Rock.* 3. *Fortress.* 4. *Deliverer.* 5. *Tower.* 6. *Buckler.* 7. *Horn* of *salvation.* 8. *High tower,* ver. 1, 2. (See the *notes.*)

The *effect* it wrought in him. It produced, 1. *Love:* "I will love the Lord." 2. *Confidence:* "In him will I trust." 3. The *spirit* of *prayer:* "I will call on the Lord." The fruit of all which was his *safety:* "So shall I be saved from mine enemies," ver. 3.

II. The great dangers in which he was, and of his escape.

1. His danger was great; for, 1. He was *encompassed with the sorrows of death.* 2. Was *terrified* with the *floods of ungodly men.* 3. *Surrounded* by the *sorrows of hell.* And, 4. *Prevented* by the *snares of death,* ver. 4, 5.

2. He shows how he *behaved* in these dangers, and from whom he sought for help: 1. "He called upon the Lord." 2. "He cried unto his God."

3. He shows the *goodness* of God to him, and his readiness to help him: 1. "He heard me out of his holy temple." 2. "My cry came into his ears."

4. The *cause* of his escape was the immediate hand of God, who testified his presence by many supernatural signs. 1. EARTHQUAKES: "The earth shook and trembled." 2. HILLS and *mountains* were *moved* from their places: "The hills moved," &c., ver. 7. 3. SMOKE came out of his nostrils. 4. A consuming FIRE came out of his mouth; and became permanent, for *coals were kindled* by it, ver. 8. 5. A THICK DARKNESS announced his presence; and the atmosphere was greatly confused: "He bowed the heavens; darkness was under his feet," ver. 9. 6. There were *mighty winds* and *tempests:* "He flew on the wings of the wind," ver. 10. 7. There were violent inundations, with blackness of the atmosphere, dark waters, thick clouds of the sky, ver. 11. 8. Great THUNDERS: "The Lord thundered; the Highest gave his voice." 9. There was great HAIL, and FIERY METEORS: "Hailstones and coals of fire," ver. 12, 13. 10. *Tremendous* LIGHTNINGS, and *fearful* CHASMS opened in the earth: "He sent out," &c., ver. 14, 15.

5. He reckons up his *deliverances*, with the *manner* and *causes:*—

1. "He took, he drew me out of many waters," ver. 16.

2. He did this in a supernatural way: "He sent from above," ib.

6. He describes his enemies from whom God delivered him. 1. They were very *numerous*, compared to *many waters*, ver. 16: "He drew me out of many waters." 2. They were very *strong*. 3. Full of *malice*. 4. Too *strong for him*. 5. INSIDIOUS and CRUEL: "They prevented me in the day of my calamity," ver. 17, 18.

7. But God was his STAY: and the *causes* which moved God to help him were, 1. His own *good will:* "Because he delighted in me." 2. David's *innocence;* which he declares from ver. 20 to ver. 25.

8. And then, *ab hypothesi*, from his own particular case, he takes occasion to discourse *in thesi*, that this is not only true in David's person, but shall be verified in all that are upright as he was: which he proves from the nature and usual manner of God's proceedings with good and bad men, from ver. 25 to 28.

III. David's *glorious* VICTORIES, and their CONSEQUENCES, from ver. 28 to 46.

1. His victory he expresses and amplifies many ways:—

1. From the opposition which he conquered. Nor *troops* nor *walls* hindered, ver. 29.

2. From God's singular *protection*. He was his *Buckler, his Rock*.

3. From his *armour*. He was made *fleet;* and had military *knowledge, strength*, and *defence*, from God, ver. 33.

4. From his *safety*. He was not wounded in the battle.

5. From his *success*. He routed his enemies; they fled, and he pursued, ver. 37.

6. From the *greatness* of the *victory*. It was a complete conquest; for his enemies were *taken*, or *consumed*, or *wounded*, so as to be *unable* to *rally*. They *fell under his feet;* their *necks* were *brought down*, ver. 38 to 42.

7. From the *cause*. All was of God; he takes nothing to himself. THOU *hast girded me*. THOU *hast subdued*. THOU *hast given me, &c*.

2. The *consequences* of these victories were the propagation and enlargement of David's kingdom:—

1. Before these victories there were murmurings and insurrections among his people: but now, being conqueror, they are all quiet: "Thou hast delivered me from the strivings of the people," ver. 43.

2. He was exalted to be *head of the heathen:* Moabites, Ammonites, &c., *served him*, ver. 44.

3. People whom he had *not known* became tributary to him: "Aliens shall serve me," ver. 44.

4. This, it is true, they did out of *fear*, not *affection*. They *dissembled* in their fidelity; and several *fell off:* but still they were obliged to *submit*, ver. 45.

IV. David's THANKSGIVING. This is the main scope of the Psalm; to celebrate and extol the name and mercy of God for his victories. This has *two* parts: 1. His *present* thanksgiving. 2. His profession for the *future*.

1. He magnifies God: "The Lord liveth; and blessed be my Rock; and let the God of my salvation be exalted;" ver. 46. And to this end, in the two next verses, he makes mention again of his victories, and attributes the whole success to God, ver. 47, 48.

2. He professes still to do it; he will not cease even among the heathen: "Therefore will I give thanks," ver. 49.

3. And he shows how much reason he had to do so: because, 1. He had *great deliverances*. 2. He was the man of God's *choice; his king—his anointed*. 3. This goodness was to survive him, and go to his *posterity:* "To David, and to his seed." 4. It was to have *no end:* it was to be *for evermore*, ver. 50.

Here the *true David* and the *spiritual seed* are referred to; and for this the reader is requested to examine the notes, and the remark before this *analysis*.

PSALM XIX

The heavens and their host proclaim the majesty of God, 2–6; *the excellence and perfection of the Divine law,* 7–10; *its usefulness,* 11. *The psalmist prays for pardon and preservation from sin,* 12, 13; *and that his words and thoughts may be holy,* 14.

IV. DAY. MORNING PRAYER

To the chief Musician, A Psalm of David

THE [a]heavens declare the glory of God; and the firmament showeth his handywork.

2 Day unto day uttereth speech, and night unto night showeth knowledge.

3 *There is* no speech nor language [b]*where* [c]their voice is not heard.

4 [d]Their [e]line is gone out through all the

[a]Gen. i. 6; Isa. xl. 22; Rom. i. 19, 20——[b]Or, *without these their voice is heard*

[c]Heb. *without their voice heard*——[d]Rom. x. 18——[e]Or, *Their rule* or *direction*

NOTES ON PSALM XIX

The *title* of this Psalm has nothing particular in it; but it is not very clear that it was written by David, to whom it is attributed; though some think that he composed it in the wilderness, while persecuted by Saul. For this opinion, however, there is no solid ground. There is no note in the Psalm itself to lead us to know *when*, *where*, or *by whom* it was written. It is a highly finished and beautiful ode.

Verse 1. *The heavens declare the glory of God*] Literally, *The heavens number out the glory of the strong God.* A first view of the starry heavens strikes every beholder with astonishment at the *power* by which they were made, and by which they are supported. To find out the *wisdom* and *skill* displayed in their contrivance requires a measure of *science:* but when the vast *magnitude* of the celestial bodies is considered, we feel increasing astonishment at these works of the *strong God.*

The firmament] The whole *visible expanse;* not only containing the *celestial bodies* above referred to, but also the *air*, *light*, *rains*, *dews*, &c., &c. And when the composition of these principles is examined, and their great utility to the earth and its inhabitants properly understood, they afford matter of astonishment to the wisest mind, and of adoration and gratitude even to the most unfeeling heart.

Verse 2. *Day unto day uttereth speech*] Each day is represented as teaching another relative to some new excellence discovered in these *manifold works* of God. The *nights* also, by the same figure, are represented as giving information to each other of the increase of knowledge already gained.

"The labours of these our instructers know no intermission; but they continue incessantly to lecture us in the science of Divine wisdom. There is one glory of the sun, which shines forth by day; and there are other glories of the moon and of the stars, which become visible by night. And because *day* and *night* interchangeably divide the world between them, they are therefore represented as transmitting, in succession, each to other, the task enjoined them, like the two parts of a choir, chanting forth alternately the praises of God."—Bishop *Horne.*

Verse 3. There is *no speech nor language* where *their voice is not heard.*] Leave out the expletives here, which pervert the sense; and what remains is a tolerable translation of the original:—

אין אמר ואין דברים בלי נשמע קולם׃

Ein omer veein debarim, beli nishma kolam.

"No speech, and no words; their voice without hearing."

בכל הארץ יצא קום ובקצה תבל מליהם

Bechol haarets yatsa kavvam: Ubiktsey thebel milleyhem.

"Into all the earth hath gone out their sound; and to the extremity of the habitable world, their eloquence."

The word קו *kav*, which we translate *line*, is rendered *sonus*, *by the Vulgate*, and *φθογγος*, *sound*, by the *Septuagint;* and St. Paul, Rom. x. 18, uses the same term. Perhaps the idea here is taken from a *stretched cord*, that emits a *sound* on being struck; and hence both ideas may be included in the same word; and קום *kavvam* may be either *their line*, or *cord*, or *their sound.* But I rather think that the Hebrew word originally meant *sound* or *noise;* for in Arabic the verb قوا *kavaha* signifies *he called out, cried, clamavit.* The sense of the whole is this, as Bishop *Horne* has well expressed it:—

"Although the heavens are thus appointed to teach, yet it is not by *articulate sounds* that they do it. They are not endowed, like man, with the faculty of speech; but they address themselves to the mind of the intelligent beholder in another way, and that, when understood, a no less forcible way, the way of picture or representation. The instruction which the heavens spread abroad is as universal as their substance, which extends itself in lines, or *rays.* By this means their words, or rather their *significant actions* or operations, מליהם, are everywhere present; and thereby they preach to all the nations the power and wisdom, the mercy and lovingkindness, of the Lord."

St. Paul applies this as a prophecy relative to the universal spread of the Gospel of Christ, Rom. x. 18; for God designed that the light of the Gospel should be diffused wheresoever the light of the celestial luminaries shone; and be as useful and beneficent, in a *moral* point of view, as that is in a *natural.* All the inhabitants of the earth shall benefit by the Gospel of Christ, as they all benefit by the *solar*, *lunar*, and *stellar light.* And, indeed, all have thus benefited, even where the *words* are not yet come. "Jesus is the true Light that lighteth every man that cometh into the world." His *light*, and the *voice* of his *Spirit*, have already gone through the earth; and his *words*, and the *words of his apostles*, are by means of the *Bible* and *missionaries* going out to all the extremities of the habitable globe.

On these words I shall conclude with the translation of my old *Psalter:*—

Verse 1. **Hevens telles the joy of God; and the werkes of his handes schewis the firmament.**

Verse 2. **Day til day riftes word; and nyght til nyght schewes conyng.**

Verse 3. **Na speches er, ne na wordes, of the qwilk the voyces of thaim be noght herd.**

earth, and their words to the end of the
world. In them hath he set a tabernacle for
the sun,
5 Which *is* as a bridegroom coming out of
his chamber, [f]*and* rejoiceth as a strong man to
run a race.
6 His going forth *is* from the end of the
heaven, and his circuit unto the ends of it: and
there is nothing hid from the heat thereof.
7 [g]The [h]law of the LORD *is* perfect, [i]con-
verting the soul: the testimony of the LORD
is sure, making wise the simple.

[f]Eccles. i. 5——[g]Psa. cxi. 7

[h]Or, *doctrine*——[i]Or, *restoring*

Verse 4. **In al the land yede the soune of tham; and in endes of the wereld thair wordes.**

Verse 5. **In the Soun he sett his tabernacle; and he as a spouse comand forth of his chaumber: he joyed als geaunt at ryn the way.**

Verse 6. **Fra heest heven the gangyng of hym: and his gayne rase til the heest of hym: nane es that hym may hyde fra his hete.**

All the *versions*, except the *Chaldee*, render the last clause of the *fourth* verse thus: "In the sun he hath placed his tabernacle;" as the old *Psalter* likewise does. They supposed that if the Supreme Being had a *local* dwelling, this must be it; as it was to all human appearances the fittest place. But the Hebrew is, "Among them hath he set a tabernacle for the sun." He is the *centre* of the *universe;* all the other heavenly bodies appear to serve him. He is like a *general* in his pavilion, surrounded by his troops, to whom he gives his orders, and by whom he is obeyed. So, the solar influence gives motion, activity, light, and heat to all the planets. To none of the other heavenly bodies does the psalmist assign a *tabernacle*, none is said to have a *fixed dwelling*, but the sun.

Verse 5. *Which* is *as a bridegroom, &c.*] This is a reference to the *rising of the sun*, as the following verse is to the *setting*. He makes his appearance above the horizon with splendour and majesty; every creature seems to rejoice at his approach; and during the whole of his course, through his whole circuit, his apparent revolution from east to west, and from one tropic to the same again, no part of the earth is deprived of its proper proportion of light and heat. The sun is compared to a *bridegroom* in his *ornaments*, because of the *glory* and *splendour* of his *rays;* and to a *giant* or *strong man running a race*, because of the *power* of his *light* and *heat*. The apparent motion of the sun, in his *diurnal* and *annual* progress, are here both referred to. Yet both of these have been demonstrated to be *mere* appearances. The sun's *diurnal* motion arises from the earth's rotation on its axis from west to east in *twenty-three hours, fifty-six minutes*, and *four seconds*, the *mean* or *equal* time which elapses between the two consecutive meridian-transits of the same fixed star. But on account of the sun's apparent ecliptic motion in the *same* direction, the earth must make about the *three hundred and sixty-fifth* part of a *second* revolution on its axis before any given point of the earth's surface can be *again* brought into the same direction with the sun as before: so that the length of a natural day is *twenty-four hours* at a mean rate. The apparent revolution of the sun through the *twelve* constellations of the zodiac in a *sidereal* year, is caused by the earth's making one *complete* revolution in its orbit in the same time. And as the earth's axis makes an angle with the axis of the ecliptic of about *twenty-three degrees* and *twenty-eight minutes*, and always maintains its parallelism, i. e., is always directed to the same point of the starry firmament; from these circumstances are produced the regular *change* of the seasons, and continually differing *lengths* of the days and nights in all parts of the terraqueous globe, except at the *poles* and on the *equator*. When we say that the earth's axis is always directed to the *same* point of the heavens, we mean to be understood only in a *general* sense; for, owing to a *very slow* deviation of the terrestrial axis from its *parallelism*, named the *precession of the equinoctial points*, which becomes sensible in the lapse of some years, and which did not escape the observation of the ancient astronomers, who clearly perceived that it was occasioned by a slow revolution of the celestial poles around the poles of the ecliptic, the complete revolution of the earth in its orbit is *longer* than the *natural* year, or the earth's *tropical* revolution, by a little more than *twenty* minutes; so that in *twenty-five thousand seven hundred and sixty-three* entire terrestrial revolutions round the sun, the seasons will be renewed *twenty-five thousand seven hundred and sixty-four* times. And in *half* this period of *twelve thousand eight hundred and eighty-two* natural years, the points which are *now* the north and south poles of the heavens, around which the whole starry firmament appears to revolve, will describe circles about the *then* north and south poles of the heavens, the semi-diameters of which will be upwards of *forty-seven* degrees.

Coming out of his chamber] מחפתו *mechuppatho*, from under his veil. It was a sort of *canopy* erected on four poles, which four Jews held over the bridegroom's head.

Verse 7. *The law of the Lord*] And here are *two* books of Divine Revelation: 1. The *visible* HEAVENS, and the *works of creation* in general. 2. The BIBLE, or Divinely inspired writings contained in the *Old* and *New Testaments*. These may all be called *the* LAW of *the Lord;* תורה *torah*, from ירה *yarah*, to *instruct*, *direct*, put *straight*, *guide*. It is God's system of *instruction*, by which men are *taught* the knowledge of God and themselves, *directed* how to walk so as to please GOD, redeemed from *crooked* paths, and *guided* in the way everlasting. Some think that תורה *torah* means the *preceptive* part of Revelation. Some of the primitive fathers have mentioned *three* LAWS given by God to man: 1. The *law of nature*, which teaches the knowledge of God, as to his eternal power and Deity, by the visible creation. 2. The *law* given to *Moses* and the *prophets*, which teaches more perfectly the knowledge of God, his *nature*, his *will* and our *duty*. 3. The *law of grace* given by Christ Jesus, which shows the doctrine of the *atonement*, of *purification*, and of the *resurrection* of the body. The *first* is written in *hieroglyphics* in the heavens and the earth.

8 The statutes of the LORD *are* right, rejoicing the heart: [k]the commandment of the LORD *is* pure, [l]enlightening the eyes.

9 The fear of the LORD *is* clean, enduring for ever: the judgments of the LORD *are* [m]true *and* righteous altogether.

10 More to be desired *are they* than gold, [n]yea, than much fine gold: [o]sweeter also than honey, and [p]the honey-comb.

11 Moreover, by them is thy servant warned: *and* [q]in keeping of them *there is* great reward.

---

[k]Psa. xii. 6——[l]Psa. xiii. 3——[m]Heb. *truth*——[n]Psa. cxix. 72, 127; Prov. viii. 10, 11, 19

[o]Psa. cxix. 103——[p]Heb. *the dropping of honey-combs*——[q]Prov. xxix. 18

The *second* was written on *tables* of *stone*, and in many *rites* and *ceremonies*. The *third* is to be written on the *heart* by the *power* of the *Holy Ghost*.

Is *perfect*] תמימה *temimah*, it is perfection. it is perfect in itself as a law, and requires *perfection* in the *hearts* and *lives* of men. This is ITS *character*.

Converting the soul] Turning it back to God. Restoring it to right reason, or to a sound mind; teaching it its own interest in reference to both worlds. This is ITS *use*.

The testimony of the Lord] עדות *eduth*, from עד *ad*, *beyond*, *forward*. The various types and appointments of the law, which *refer* to something *beyond* themselves, and *point forward* to the Lamb of God who takes away the sin of the world. Some understand, the *doctrinal* parts of the law.

Is *sure*] נאמנה *neemanah*, are *faithful;* they point out the things *beyond* them *fairly*, *truly*, and *fully*, and make no vain or *false* report. They all bear testimony to the great atonement. This is THEIR *character*.

Making wise the simple.] The simple is he who has but *one end* in view: who is concerned about his soul, and earnestly inquires, "What shall I do to be saved?" These testimonies point to the atonement, and thus the *simple-hearted* is made wise unto salvation. This is THEIR *use*.

Verse 8. *The statutes of the Lord*] פקודים *pikkudim*, from פקד *pakad*, he visited, *cared*, *took notice of*, *appointed to a charge*. The *appointments*, or *charge delivered* by God to man for his regard and observance.

Are *right*] ישרים *yesharim*, from ישר *yashar*, to make *straight*, *smooth*, *right*, *upright*, opposed to *crookedness* in mind or conduct; showing what the man should be, both *within* and *without*. This is THEIR *character*.

Rejoicing the heart] As they show a man what he is to observe and keep in charge, and how he is to please God, and the Divine help he is to receive from the *visitations* of God, they contribute greatly to the *happiness* of the upright—they *rejoice the heart*. This is THEIR *use*.

The commandment] מצוה *mitsvah*, from צוה *tsavah*, to *command*, *give orders*, *ordain*. What God has *ordered* man to do, or not to do. What he has *commanded*, and what he has *prohibited*.

Is *pure*] From ברה *barah*, to clear, *cleanse*, *purify*. All God's commandments lead to *purity*, *enjoin purity*, and *point* out that *sacrificial offering* by which *cleansing* and *purification* are acquired. This is ITS *character*.

Enlightening the eyes.] Showing men what they should *do*, and what they should *avoid*. It is by God's commandments that we *see* the exceeding *sinfulness of sin*, and the *necessity of redemption*, so that we may love the Lord with all our heart, and our neighbour as ourselves. For this is the end of the commandment, and thus to *enlighten the eyes* is ITS *use*.

Verse 9. *The fear of the Lord*] יראה *yirah*, from ירא *yara*, to *fear*, to *venerate;* often put for the whole of Divine worship. The reverence we owe to the Supreme Being.

Is *clean*] טהורה *tehorah*, from טהר *tahar*, to be *pure*, *clean;* not differing much from ברה *barah*, (see above,) to be *clean* and *bright* as the *heavens;* as purified SILVER. Its object is to purge away all *defilement*, to make a *spotless character*.

Enduring for ever] עומדת לעד *omedeth laad*, *standing up to* PERPETUITY. The *fear* that prevents us from offending God, that causes us to *reverence* him, and is the *beginning* as it is the safeguard of *wisdom*, must be carried all through life. No soul is safe for a moment without it. It prevents departure from God, and keeps that clean which God has purified. This is ITS *use*.

The judgments of the Lord] משפטים *mishpatim*, from שפט *shaphat*, he *judged*, *regulated*, *disposed*, All God's *regulations*, all his *decisions;* what he has *pronounced* to be *right* and proper.

Are *true*] אמת *emeth*, *truth*, from אם *am*, to *support*, *confirm*, *make stable*, and *certain*. This is the *character* of God's *judgments*. They shall all *stand*. All dispensations in providence and grace *confirm* them; they are *certain*, and have a *fixed character*.

And *righteous altogether*.] They are not only according to *truth;* but they are *righteous*, צדקו *tsadeku*, they give to *all their due*. They show what belongs to *God*, to *man*, and to *ourselves*. And hence the word *altogether*, יחדו *yachdav*, *equally*, is added; or *truth and righteousness united*.

Verse 10. *More to be desired* are they *than gold*] This is strictly true; but who believes it? By most men *gold* is preferred both to *God* and his *judgments;* and they will barter every heavenly portion for gold and silver!

Sweeter also than honey] To those whose mental taste is rectified, who have a spiritual discernment.

Honey-comb.] Honey is *sweet;* but honey just out of the *comb* has a sweetness, richness, and flavour, far beyond what it has after it becomes exposed to the *air*. Only those who have eaten of honey from the comb can feel the force of the psalmist's comparison: *it is better than gold*, yea, than *fine gold* in the greatest quantity; it is *sweeter* than *honey*, yea, than *honey* from the *comb*.

Verse 11. *By them is thy servant warned*] נזהר *nizhar*, from זהר *zahar*, to be *clear*, *pellucid*. By these laws, testimonies, &c., thy ser-

12 [r]Who can understand *his* errors? [s]cleanse thou me from [t]secret *faults.*

13 [u]Keep back thy servant also from presumptuous *sins:* [v]let them not have dominion over me: then shall I be upright, and I shall be innocent from [w]the great transgression.

14 [x]Let the words of my mouth, and the meditation of my heart, be acceptable in thy sight, O LORD, [y]my strength, and my [z]redeemer.

[r]Psalm xl. 12——[s]Lev. iv. 2, &c.——[t]Psa. xc. 8——[u]Gen. xx. 6; 1 Sam. xxv. 32, 33, 34, 39——[v]Psa. cxix. 133; Rom. vi. 12, 14

[w]Or, *much*——[x]Psa. li. 15——[y]Heb. *my rock;* Psa. xviii. 1——[z]Isa. xliii. 14; xliv. 6; xlvii. 4; 1 Thess. i. 10

vant is *fully instructed; he sees all clearly;* and he *discerns* that in *keeping of them there is great reward:* every man is wise, holy, and happy, who observes them. All Christian experience confirms this truth. Reader, what says *thine?*

Verse 12. *Who can understand* his *errors?*] It is not possible, without much of the Divine light, to understand all our *deviations* from, not only the *letter*, but the *spirituality*, of the Divine law. Frequent self-examination, and walking in the light, are essentially necessary to the requisite degree of spiritual perfection.

Cleanse thou me from secret faults.] From those which I have committed, and have forgotten; from those for which I have not repented; from those which have been committed in my heart, but have not been brought to act in my life; from those which I have committed without knowing that they were sins, sins of *ignorance;* and from those which I have committed in private, for which I should blush and be confounded were they to be made public.

Verse 13. *From presumptuous* sins] Sins committed not through *frailty* or *surprise*, but those which are the offspring of *thought, purpose*, and *deliberation.* Sins against judgment, light, and conscience. The words might be translated, *Preserve thy servant also from the proud;* from tyrannical governors, i. e., from evil spirits.—Bishop *Horsley*. So most of the *versions* understand the place.

Let them not have dominion over me] Let me never be brought into a *habit* of sinning. He who sins *presumptuously* will soon be *hardened* through the deceitfulness of sin.

Then shall I be upright] Let me be preserved from all the evil that the craft and malice of the devil or man work against me, then shall I continue to walk *uprightly*, and shall be *innocent from the great transgression*—from habitual sinning, from *apostasy*, from my *easily-besetting sin.* He who would be innocent from the great transgression, must take care that he indulge not himself in any. See Bishop *Horne*. Most men have committed some particular sin which they ought to deplore as long as they breathe, and on account of the enormity of which they should for ever be humbled.

Verse 14. *Let the words of my mouth*] He has prayed against practical sin, the sins of the *body;* now, against the *sins* of the *mouth* and of the *heart.* Let my *mouth* speak nothing but what is *true, kind*, and *profitable;* and my *heart* meditate nothing but what is *holy, pure*, and *chaste*.

Acceptable in thy sight] Like a *sacrifice* without spot or blemish, offered up with a perfect heart to God.

O Lord, my strength] צורי *tsuri*, "my fountain, my origin."

My redeemer.] גאלי *goali*, my *kinsman*, he whose right it is to redeem the forfeited inheritance; for so was the word used under the old law. This prayer is properly concluded! he was *weak*, he felt the need of God's *strength.* He had *sinned* and *lost all title to the heavenly inheritance*, and therefore needed the interference of the *Divine kinsman;* of HIM who, because the children were partakers of flesh and blood, also partook of the same. No prayer can be *acceptable* before God which is not offered up in his *strength;* through HIM who took our nature upon him, that he might redeem us unto God, and restore the long-lost inheritance. **Lord my helpar and my byer.**—Old *Psalter*. He who is my only *help*, and he that *bought* me with his blood. This prayer is often, with great propriety, uttered by pious people when they enter a place of worship.

ANALYSIS OF THE NINETEENTH PSALM

I. There are TWO parts in this Psalm. The *first* is *doctrinal;* the *second, penitential.* The doctrinal part has two members:—

1. The first teaches us to know God by *natural reason*, from the *book of creation*, from ver. 1 to ver. 7.

2. But because this way is insufficient to save a soul, therefore in the *second* part we have a better way prescribed, which is the *book of the Scriptures;* the excellences of which are described from ver. 7 to ver. 11.

II. The *penitential* part begins at the *twelfth* verse, for since the reward to be expected proceeds from the keeping of God's law, and David's heart told him he had not kept it, therefore, he begs *pardon* and *grace*, ver. 12 to ver. 14.

I. "The heavens declare," &c. By the *glory of God* we are to understand his goodness, wisdom, power; in a word, all his attributes, of which we have a double declaration:—

1. A testimony from the *creatures*, but especially the *heavens*, whose magnitude, beauty, order, variety, perpetual motion, light, influences, &c., declare that there is an omnipotent, wise, good, and gracious God, who is their Creator; with this David begins: "The heavens declare the glory of God, and the firmament showeth forth," &c.

2. The vicissitude of day and night, proceeding from their motions, declares this also: "Day unto day uttereth speech," &c. 1. The heavens are *diligent* preachers; for they *preach all day* and *all night*, without intermission. 2. They are *learned* preachers, for they preach in all tongues: "There is no speech—where their voice is not heard." 3. They are *universal preachers*, for they preach to the whole world: "Their sound is gone through all the earth," &c.

3. But among all these creatures the SUN, for which God in heaven has set a *throne*,

makes the fairest and clearest evidence, and that in the three following ways:—

1. By his *splendour*, light, and beauty; he riseth as gloriously as a bridegroom coming from under his canopy.

2. By his *wonderful celerity*, not only in revolving round his own axis, which revolution, although he is *one million three hundred and eighty-four thousand four hundred and sixty-two* times bigger than the earth, he performs in *twenty-five* days *fourteen* hours of our time, but also in the *swiftness* with which his light comes to the earth. It travels at the rate of *one hundred and ninety-four thousand one hundred and eighty-eight* miles in a *second* of time; and reaches our earth in *eight minutes* and about *twelve seconds*, a distance of *ninety-five millions five hundred and thirteen thousand seven hundred and ninety-four* English miles, at a mean rate.

3. His strange and miraculous *heat*, from which nothing is *hidden*, and by which every thing is *benefited*.

II. But as the declaration, even from the most glorious of creatures, is not sufficient to make men wise and happy, he has been pleased to declare himself by his WRITTEN WORD, called here the LAW generally; and is commended to us by the following reasons:—

1. From the *author:* It is the "law of Jehovah."

2. From its *sufficiency:* It is "perfect."

3. From its *utility:* "It converts the soul:—gives wisdom to the simple."

4. From its *infallibility:* "The testimony of the Lord is sure."

5. From its *perspicuity:* "The statutes of the Lord are right."

6. From the *effects* it works on the *soul:* "They rejoice the heart." They quiet the troubled conscience; "being justified by faith, we have peace with God."

7. From its *purity:* "The commandment of the Lord is pure." It is opposed to all *bad opinions* and *evil practices.*

8. From its *effects in the understanding:* "It enlightens the eyes." It dispels all darkness and ignorance, all doubts and fears, diffidence, carnal security, false worship, &c., and gives us to see our own *deformities.*

9. From its *uncorruptness:* "The fear of the Lord is clean." Other religions are *polluted* with human inventions, strange ceremonies, uncommanded sacrifices, false gods, &c.

10. From its *perpetuity:* "It endureth for ever." It is an endless law, and an everlasting Gospel.

11. From its *truth and equity:* "It is altogether true and righteous."

From all which David concludes, that it is both *precious* and *delightful.*

1. The *price* of it is beyond the best gold: "More to be desired than gold; yea, than much fine gold."

2. It is *delightful:* "Sweeter than honey and the honey-comb."

3. This he knew by his own *experience:* "Moreover, by them is thy servant illuminated."

4. It is *profitable* to observe them: "For in keeping of them there is, 1. A *reward.* 2. A *great reward.*"

III. But this last consideration sent David to the throne of mercy. What! a reward, a great reward! and only to those who *keep God's law?* My conscience tells me that the reward is not for *me; I* cannot plead this *observance.* David had public sins, secret faults and errors, to deplore. But he had at hand *three* means of help: 1. *Confession of sin.* 2. *Petition* for *grace.* 3. *Faith* in the Divine *mercy*, through the great *Redeemer.*

1. He knew he was an *offender*, but he *knew not how greatly* he had *offended.* He saw that he was *guilty*, and asked *pardon.* He felt that he was *impure*, and asked *cleansing:* "Who can understand his errors? cleanse thou me from my secret faults."

2. He prays that he may be preserved from *presumptuous sins;* that he might not be hardened in transgression: "Keep back also thy servant from presumptuous sins." For which he gives *two* reasons: 1. If he were not *kept back* from them, sin would get the *dominion* over him. Sin would become a king, who would command, rule, and enslave him. 2. If thus kept back, he would be *innocent from the great transgression;* for he that gets under the strong habit of sin may at last deny God himself, renounce the blood of the covenant, and become a castaway.

3. Lastly, that his prayer may be heard, he prays for his prayer: "Let the words of my mouth and the meditation of my heart be acceptable in thy sight." This is *pleading*, or *supplication.*

That prayer and supplication may be successful he acts *faith* in God, whom he,

1. Claims as his *strength;* literally, his *rock*, by whom alone he could resist and overcome.

2. His *redeemer*, through whom alone he could get pardon for the past, and grace to help him in time of need. To this word he adds nothing, as it includes every thing necessary to saint and sinner. See the *notes.*

PSALM XX

A prayer for the king in his enterprises, that his prayers may be heard, his offerings accepted, and his wishes fulfilled, 1–4. *Confidence of victory expressed,* 5, 6. *Vain hopes exposed; and supplication made for the king.*

To the chief Musician, A Psalm of David

A. M. cir. 2968
B. C. cir. 1036
Davidis, Regis
Israelitarum,
cir. annum
20

THE LORD hear thee in the
day of trouble; [a]the name
of the God of Jacob [b]defend
thee.
2 Send [c]thee help from [d]the sanctuary, and
[e]strengthen thee out of Zion.
3 Remember all thy offerings, and [f]accept
thy [g]burnt sacrifice. Selah.
4 [h]Grant thee according to thine own
heart, and fulfil all thy counsel.
5 We will [i]rejoice in thy salvation, and [k]in the name of our
God we will set up *our* banners: the LORD
fulfil all thy petitions.
6 Now know I that the LORD saveth [l]his
anointed; he will hear him [m]from his holy
heaven [n]with the saving strength of his right
hand.

A. M. cir. 2968
B. C. cir. 1036
Davidis, Regis
Israelitarum,
cir. annum
20

---

[a]Prov. xviii. 10——[b]Heb. *set thee on a high place*——[c]Heb. *thy help*——[d]1 Kings vi. 16; 2 Chron. xx. 8; Psa. lxxiii. 17——[e]Heb. *support thee*——[f]Heb. *turn to ashes;* or, *make fat*——[g]Exod. xxx. 9; Lev. i. 9; Num. xxiii. 6; Deut. xxxiii. 10; 2 Sam. xxiv. 22——[h]Psa. xxi. 2——[i]Psa. xix. 4——[k]Exod. xvii. 15; Psa. lx. 4——[l]Psa. ii. 2——[m]Heb. *from the heaven of his holiness*——[n]Heb. *by the strength of the salvation of his right hand*

NOTES ON PSALM XX

It is most likely that this Psalm was penned on the occasion of David's going to war; and most probably with the Ammonites and Syrians, who came with great numbers of *horses* and *chariots* to fight with him. See 2 Sam. x. 6-8; 1 Chron. xix. 7. It is one of the *Dialogue Psalms*, and appears to be thus divided: Previously to his undertaking the war, David comes to the tabernacle to offer sacrifice. This being done, the *people*, in the king's behalf, offer up their prayers; these are included in the *three* first verses: the fourth was probably spoken by the *high priest;* the *fifth*, by *David* and his *attendants;* the last clause, by the high priest; the *sixth*, by the *high priest*, after the victim was consumed; the *seventh* and *eighth*, by *David* and his *men;* and the *ninth*, as a *chorus* by all the *congregation*.

Verse 1. *The Lord hear thee*] David had already offered the *sacrifice* and *prayed*. The *people* implore God to succour him in the day of trouble; of both *personal* and *national* danger.

The name of the God of Jacob] This refers to Jacob's wrestling with the Angel; Gen. xxxii. 24, &c. And who was this Angel? Evidently none other than the *Angel of the Covenant*, the Lord Jesus, in whom was the *name of God*, the *fulness of the Godhead bodily*. He was the *God of Jacob*, who *blessed* Jacob, and gave him a *new name* and a *new nature*. See the *notes* on the above place in Genesis.

Verse 2. *Send thee help from the sanctuary*] This was the *place* where God recorded his name; the place where he was to be sought, and the place where he manifested himself. He dwelt between the *cherubim* over the *mercy-seat*. He is now in Christ, reconciling the world to himself. This is the true sanctuary where God must be sought.

Strengthen thee out of Zion] The *temple* or *tabernacle* where his prayers and sacrifices were to be offered.

Verse 3. *Remember all thy offerings*] The *minchah*, which is here mentioned, was a *gratitude-offering*. It is rarely used to signify a bloody sacrifice.

Burnt sacrifice] The *olah* here mentioned was a *bloody sacrifice*. The blood of the victim was spilt at the altar, and the flesh consumed. One of these offerings implied a *consciousness* of *sin* in the offerer; and this sacrifice he brought as an *atonement:* the other implied a sense of *mercies* already *received*, and was offered in the way of *gratitude*.

David presents himself before the Lord with offerings of both kinds.

This prayer of the *people* is concluded with *Selah*, which we have taken up in the general sense of *so be it. Hear and answer. It will and must be so*, &c.

Verse 4. *Grant thee according to thine own heart*] May God give thee whatsoever thou art setting thy heart upon, and accomplish all *thy desires*! This was probably the prayer of the *high priest*.

Verse 5. *We will rejoice in thy salvation*] We expect help from thee alone; it is in thy cause we engage; and to *thee*, as our war is a just one, we consecrate our banners, inscribed with thy name. It is said that the *Maccabees* had their name from the inscription on their banners; which was taken from Exod. xv. 11, מי כמכה באלם יהוה *mi camochah baelim Yehovah*, "Who is like unto thee, O Lord, among the gods?" The word being formed from the *initial* letters מ M, כ C, ב B, י I, מכבי M*a* C*a* B I, whence *Maccabeus* and *Maccabees*.

The words of this verse were spoken by David and his officers; immediately after which I suppose the high priest to have added, *The Lord fulfil all thy petitions!*

Verse 6. *Now know I that the Lord saveth his anointed*] These are probably the words of the *priest* after the victim had been consumed; and those *signs* had accompanied the offering, which were proofs of God's *acceptance* of the sacrifice; and, consequently, that the campaign would have a successful issue. David is God's *anointed;* therefore, he is under his especial care. *He will hear him.* David must continue to *pray*, and to *depend* on God; else he cannot expect continual salvation. David has vast multitudes of enemies against him; he, therefore, requires supernatural help. Because of this, *God will hear him with the saving strength of his right hand.*

The HAND of God is his *power;* the RIGHT *hand*, his *almighty power;* the STRENGTH *of his right hand*, his almighty power in *action;* the SAVING *strength of his right hand*, the *miraculous effects* wrought by his almighty power brought into *action*. This is what David was to expect; and it was the prospect of this that caused him and his officers to exult as they do in the following verse.

A. M. cir. 2968
B. C. cir. 1036
Davidis, Regis
Israelitarum,
cir. annum
20

7 [o]Some *trust* in chariots, and
some in horses: [p]but we will
remember the name of the LORD
our God.
8 They are brought down and fallen: but
we are risen, and stand upright.
9 Save, LORD: let the king
hear us when we call.

A. M. cir. 2968
B. C. cir. 1036
Davidis, Regis
Israelitarum,
cir. annum
20

[o]Psa. xxxiii. 16, 17; Prov. xxi. 31; Isa. xxxi. 1 — [p]2 Chron. xxxii. 8

Verse 7. *Some* trust *in chariots*] The words of the original are short and emphatic: *These in chariots; and these in horses; but we will record in the name of Jehovah our God.* Or, as the *Septuagint*, μεγαλυνθησομεθα, "we shall be magnified." Or, as the *Vulgate*, *invocabimus*, "we shall invoke the name of the Lord." This and the following verse I suppose to be the words of David and his officers. And the mention of *chariots* and *horses* makes it likely that the war with the *Ammonites* and *Syrians* is that to which reference is made here; for they came against him with vast multitudes of *horsemen* and *chariots*. See 2 Sam. x. 6-8. According to the law, David could neither have chariots nor horses; and those who came against him with cavalry must have a very great advantage; but he saw that Jehovah his God was more than a match for all his foes, and in him he trusts with implicit confidence.

Verse 8. *They are brought down and fallen*] They were so confident of victory that they looked upon it as *already gained*. They who trusted in their *horses* and *chariots* are *bowed down*, and prostrated on the earth: they are all overthrown.

But we are risen] We who have trusted in the *name of Jehovah* are *raised up* from all despondency; and we *stand upright*—we shall conquer, and go on to conquer.

Verse 9. *Save, Lord*] This verse was spoken by all the *congregation*, and was the *chorus* and *conclusion* of the piece.

The verse may be read, *Lord, save the king! He will hear us in the day of our calling.* The *Vulgate*, *Septuagint*, *Æthiopic*, *Arabic*, *Anglo-Saxon*, read the verse thus: *Lord, save the king! and hear us whensoever we shall call upon thee.* The *Syriac* reads differently: *The Lord will save us: and our king will hear us in the day in which we shall call upon him.* This refers all to GOD; while the others refer the latter clause *to* DAVID. *Lord, save David;* and *David will save us.* "If thou preservest *him*, he will be thy minister for good to *us*." This appears to be the easiest sense of the place, and harmonizes with all the rest.

ANALYSIS OF THE TWENTIETH PSALM

This Psalm is a form of prayer delivered by David to the people, to be used by them for the king, when he went out to battle against his enemies.

In this Psalm there are the following parts:—

I. A benediction of the people for their king, ver. 1-4.

II. A congratulation or triumph of the people after the victory, supposed to be already obtained, ver. 5-8.

III. A petition, ver. 9.

I. The benediction directed to David's person. The particulars; that he may have,

1. *Audience* in his necessity: "The Lord hear thee in the day of trouble."

2. *Protection:* "The name of the God of Jacob defend thee," ver. 1.

3. *Help* and *strength* in battle: "Send thee help—strengthen thee;" which is amplified, 1. By the *place:* "Help from the sanctuary;" 2. "Strength out of Zion."

4. *Acceptance* of his *person;* testified by the acceptance of his offerings and sacrifices, ver. 3.

5. *Answers* to his *petitions:* "Grant thee according to thy own heart, and fulfil all thy counsel," ver. 4; which is plainly set down in the next verse: "The Lord fulfil all thy petitions," ver. 5.

This benediction being ended, they persuade themselves that the prayer of it shall be granted, because it will redound to God's glory; and they will be thankful, and honour him for the victory.

1. "We will rejoice in thy salvation." Or, Do this, "that we may rejoice."

2. "In the name of our God will we set up our banners." We will enter the city joyfully, with displayed banners, which we will erect as trophies to the honour of God.

II. Now follow the congratulation and triumph of their faith: for they give thanks as for a victory already obtained; as to their faith it was certain. *Before* they prayed for *audience* and *protection: here* they testify they are certain and secure of both.

1. Of *protection:* "Now know I that the Lord will save," &c.

2. Of *audience:* "He will hear from his holy heaven."

3. Of *help:* "With the saving strength of his right hand," ver. 6.

The certainty they had of this victory proceeded solely from their confidence in God. And this they illustrate by an argument drawn *a dissimili:* they were *not like* others who trust more to their *arms* than to their *prayers;* more to their *numbers* than to *God.*

1. "Some trust in chariots, and some in horses;" as the Ammonites, 2 Sam. x. 6.

2. But we do not so: "We will remember the name of the Lord our God; the Lord of hosts, mighty in battle." Arms may be used by good or bad men; but the difference lies in the *object*, the *end*, and the *confidence*. A bad cause cannot have God's concurrence: a good cause will have his countenance and support.

3. And therefore the *success* was according to the confidence. 1. They who trusted in their arms, &c., *are brought down, and fallen.* 2. We who trusted in the Lord our God, are *risen, and stand upright*, ver. 8.

III. The third part contains a short ejaculation, and is the sum of the Psalm.

1. "Save, Lord!" *Thou* alone canst save us: in *thee*, and in none other, do we put our trust.

2. "Let the king hear us." We propose to continue in prayer and faith; therefore, when we call, *let the king*, the *Messiah*, which *thou hast set on thy holy hill.* Psa. ii. 6, hear us.

Or, according to another arrangement of the words: 1. *Lord, save* our *king.* Make him wise and good, preserve his person, and prosper his government; that we may have peace in our time, and secular prosperity. 2. Hear thou us when we call. Let us have also spiritual prosperity, that we may perfectly love thee, and worthily magnify thy name.—**Eala ðu dryht, gehalne do cyninge.** "O thou Lord, health give the king."—*Anglo-Saxon.*

PSALM XXI

The psalmist returns thanks to God for giving him the victory over his enemies; which victory he had earnestly requested, 1, 2. *He enters into a detail of the blessings that in consequence of the victory he had obtained,* 3–7. *He predicts the destruction of all those who may hereafter rise up against him,* 8–12; *and concludes with praising the power of Jehovah,* 13.

To the chief Musician, A Psalm of David

A. M. cir. 2968
B. C. cir. 1036
Davidis, Regis
Israelitarum,
cir. annum
20

THE king shall joy in thy
strength, O LORD; and [a]in
thy salvation how greatly shall
he rejoice!

2 [b]Thou hast given him his heart's desire,
and hast not withholden the request of his lips.
Selah.

3 For thou preventest him with
the blessings of goodness: thou
[c]settest a crown of pure gold on
his head.

A. M. cir. 2968
B. C. cir. 1036
Davidis, Regis
Israelitarum,
cir. annum
20

4 [d]He asked life of thee, *and* thou gavest
it him, [e]*even* length of days for ever and ever.

5 His glory *is* great in thy salvation: honour and majesty hast thou laid upon him.

---

[a]Psa. xx. 5, 6——[b]Psa. xx. 4, 5——[c]2 Sam. xii. 30; 1 Chron. xx. 2

[d]Psalm lxi. 5, 6——[e]2 Samuel vii. 19; Psa. xci. 16

NOTES ON PSALM XXI

In the *title* of this Psalm there is nothing particularly worthy of remark. The *occasion* of it is variously understood. Some think it was composed to celebrate the victory obtained over *Sennacherib;* others, that it was made on the recovery of *Hezekiah,* and the grant of *fifteen* years of longer life; see ver. 4. Others, and they with most appearance of propriety, consider it a song of rejoicing composed by David for his victory over the *Ammonites,* which ended in the capture of the royal city of *Rabbah,* the crown of whose king David put on his own head, see ver. 3, and to procure which victory David offered the prayers and sacrifices mentioned in the preceding Psalm. Lastly, many think that it is to be wholly referred to the *victories of the Messiah;* and it must be owned that there are several expressions in it which apply better to our Lord than to David, or to any other person; and to him the *Targum* applies it, as does likewise my old *Anglo-Scottish Psalter* in paraphrasing the text.

Verse 1. *The king shall joy*] מלך משיחא *melech Meshicha,* "the King Messiah."—*Targum.* What a difference between ancient and modern heroes! The former acknowledged all to be of God, because they took care to have their quarrel *rightly founded;* the latter sing a *Te Deum,* pro forma, because they well know that their battle is *not* of the Lord. Their own vicious conduct sufficiently proves that they looked no higher than the arm of human strength. God suffers such for a time, but in the end he confounds and brings them to naught.

Verse 2. *Thou hast given him his heart's desire*] This seems to refer to the prayers offered in the preceding Psalm; see especially verses 1-4.

Verse 3. *Thou preventest him*] To *prevent,* from *prævenio,* literally signifies *to go before.* Hence that prayer in the *communion service* of our public Liturgy, "*Prevent* us, O Lord, in all our doings, with thy most gracious favour!" That is, "*Go before us* in thy mercy, make our way plain, and enable us to perform what is right in thy sight!" And this sense of *prevent* is a literal version of the original word תקדמנו *tekademennu.* "For thou shalt go before him with the blessings of goodness."

Our ancestors used *God before* in this sense. So in Henry V.'s speech to the French herald previously to the battle of *Agincourt:*—

"Go therefore; tell thy master, here I am.
My ransom is this frail and worthless trunk;
My army, but a weak and sickly guard:
Yet, *God before,* tell him we will come on,
Though France himself, and such another neighbour,
Stand in our way."

A crown of pure gold] Probably alluding to the crown of the king of Rabbah, which, on the taking of the city, David took and put on his own head. See the history, 2 Sam. xii. 26-30.

Verse 4. *He asked life of thee*] This verse has caused some interpreters to understand the Psalm of *Hezekiah's sickness, recovery,* and the promised *addition to his life of* fifteen *years;* but it may be more literally understood of the *Messiah,* of whom David was the *type,* and in several respects the *representative.*

Verse 5. *His glory is great*] But great as

A. M. cir. 2968
B. C. cir. 1036
Davidis, Regis Israelitarum, cir. annum 20

6 For thou hast made [f]him
most blessed for ever: [g]thou
hast [h]made him exceeding glad
with thy countenance.

7 For the king trusteth in the LORD, and
through the mercy of the Most High he [i]shall
not be moved.

8 Thine hand shall [k]find out all thine enemies: thy right hand shall find out those that
hate thee.

9 [l]Thou shalt make them as a fiery oven
in the time of thine anger: the LORD shall
[m]swallow them up in his wrath, [n]and the fire
shall devour them.

10 [o]Their fruit shalt thou destroy from the earth, and their
seed from among the children of
men.

11 For they intended evil against thee: they
[p]imagined a mischievous device, *which* they
are not able *to perform.*

12 Therefore [q]shalt thou make them turn
their [r]back, *when* thou shalt make ready *thine
arrows* upon thy strings against the face of
them.

13 Be thou exalted, LORD, in thine own
strength: *so* will we sing and praise thy
power.

[f]Heb. *set him* to be *blessings;* Gen. xii. 2; Psa. lxxii. 17 —— [g]Psa. xvi. 11; xlv. 7; Acts ii. 28 —— [h]Heb. *gladded him with joy* —— [i]Psa. xvi. 8 —— [k]1 Sam. xxxi. 3 —— [l]Mal. iv. 1 —— [m]Psa. lvi. 1, 2

[n]Psa. xviii. 8; Isa. xxvi. 11 —— [o]1 Kings xiii. 34; Job xviii. 16, 17, 19; Psa. xxxvii. 28; cix. 13; Isa. xiv. 20 —— [p]Psa. ii. 1 —— [q]Or, *thou shalt set them* as *a butt;* see Job vii. 20; xvi. 12; Lam. iii. 12 —— [r]Heb. *shoulder*

his glory was, it had its greatness from *God's salvation.* There is no true *nobility* but of the soul, and the soul has none but what it receives from the *grace* and *salvation* of God.

Verse 6. *Thou hast made him most blessed for ever*] Literally, "Thou hast set him for blessings for ever." Thou hast made the Messiah the *Source* whence all blessings for time and for eternity shall be derived. He is the Mediator between God and man.

Thou hast made him exceeding glad] Jesus, as Messiah, *for the joy that was set before him,* of redeeming a lost world by his death, *endured the cross, and despised the shame,* and is for ever set down on the right hand of God.

Verse 7. *The king trusteth in the Lord*] It was not by my *skill* or *valour* that I have gained this victory, but by *faith* in the *strong, protecting, and conquering arm of* JEHOVAH.

He shall not be moved.] Perhaps this may be best understood of him who was David's *prototype.* His throne, kingdom, and government, shall remain for ever.

Verse 8. *Thine hand shall find out*] Thy uncontrollable *power* shall find out all thine enemies, wheresoever *hidden* or howsoever *secret.* God knows the secret sinner, and where the workers of iniquity hide themselves.

Verse 9. *Thou shalt make them as a fiery oven*] By thy wrath they shall be burnt up, and they shall be the means of consuming others. One class of sinners shall, in God's judgments, be the means of destroying another class; and at last themselves shall be destroyed.

Verse 10. *Their fruit shalt thou destroy*] Even their *posterity* shall be cut off, and thus their *memorial* shall perish.

Verse 11. *For they intended evil*] Sinners shall not be permitted to do all that *is in their power* against the godly; much less shall they be able to perform all that they *wish.*

Verse 12. *Therefore shalt thou make them turn their back*] God can in a moment strike the most powerful and numerous army, even in the moment of victory, with *panic;* and then even the *lame,* the army which they had nearly routed, shall take the prey, and divide the spoil.

Against the face of them.] Thou shalt cause them to turn their backs and fly, as if a volley of arrows had been discharged in their faces. This seems to be the *sense* of this difficult verse.

Verse 13. *Be thou exalted*] *Exalt thyself, O Lord*—thy creatures cannot exalt thee. *Lift thyself up,* and discomfit thy foes by thine own strength! Thou canst give a victory to thy people over the most formidable enemies, though they strike not one blow in their own defence. God's right hand has often given the victory to his followers, while they stood still to see the salvation of God. How little can the strength of man avail when the Lord *raiseth up himself* to the battle! His children, therefore, may safely trust in him, for the name of the Lord is a strong tower; the righteous flee into it, and are safe.

Praise thy power.] God is to receive praise in reference to that attribute which he has *exhibited* most in the defence or salvation of his followers. Sometimes he *manifests* his *power,* his *mercy,* his *wisdom,* his *longsuffering,* his *fatherly care,* his *good providence,* his *holiness,* his *justice,* his *truth,* &c. Whatever attribute or perfection he exhibits most, *that* should be the chief subject of his children's *praise.* One wants *teaching,* prays for it, and is deeply instructed: he will naturally celebrate the *wisdom* of God. Another feels himself beset with the most *powerful* adversaries, with the *weakest* of whom he is not *able* to cope: he cries to the Almighty God for *strength;* he is heard, and strengthened with strength in his soul. He therefore will naturally magnify the all-conquering *power* of the Lord. Another feels himself lost, condemned, on the brink of hell; he calls for *mercy,* is heard and saved: *mercy,* therefore, will be the *chief subject* of his praise, and the *burden of his song.*

The old Anglo-Scottish Psalter says, We sal make knowen thi wordes in gude wil and gude werk, for he synges well that wirkes well. For thi, sais he twise, we sal syng; ane tyme for the luf of hert; another, for the schewyng of ryghtwisness, til ensampil.

ANALYSIS OF THE TWENTY-FIRST PSALM

This is the people's Επινικιον, or *triumphal song*, after the victory which they prayed for in the former Psalm, when David went out to war. In this they praise God for the conquest which he gave him over his enemies, and for the singular mercies bestowed on himself. It consists of *three* parts:—

I. The general proposition, ver. 1.

II. The narration, which is twofold, from ver. 1-4. 1. An enumeration of the blessings bestowed on David, from ver. 1 to 6. 2. An account how God would deal with his enemies, from ver. 6 to 12.

III. A vow, or acclamation, ver. 13, which is the *epilogue* of the piece.

I. The *sum of the Psalm* is contained in the *first verse:* "The king shall joy; the king shall be exceeding glad." Joy is the affection with which the king and people were transported; for all that follows shows but the rise and causes of it.

I. The rise and object of it: "The strength of God; the salvation of God." 1. His *strength*, by which he subdued his enemies, and contemned dangers. 2. His *salvation*, by which he escaped dangers, and fell not in battle.

II. 1. The *narration* of the goodness of God to David's person, the particulars of which are the following:—

1. God granted to him what his *heart* desired*:* "Thou hast given him his heart's desire;" and what his *lips* requested: "and hast not withholden the request of his lips."

2. He granted him more than he asked: "Thou preventest him with the blessings of goodness."

3. He chose him to be *king:* "Thou hast set a crown of pure gold upon his head." In which God prevented him, and chose him when he thought not of it.

4. When David went to war, "he asked life, and thou gavest him even length of days for ever and ever:" which is most true of Christ, the Son of David. In him his life and kingdom are immortal.

5. A great accession of *glory, honour*, and *majesty.* Though his glory was great, it was *in God's salvation:* "Honour and majesty did God lay upon him."

All which are summed up under the word *blessing* in the next verse. "For thou hast made him most blessed for ever;" and God had added the *crown* of all, a *heart to rejoice* in it: "Thou hast made him exceeding glad with thy countenance."

6. The *continuance* of these blessings, which is *another* favour, with the *cause* of it: "For the king trusteth in the Lord, and through the mercy of the Most High he shall not be moved." Thus far the *first part* of the *narrative*, which concerned David's person particularly.

2. The *effects* of God's goodness to David in *outward* things, and to the whole kingdom, in the overthrow of his enemies, (for without God's protection what kingdom is safe?) form the *second part.*

1. God would make David his *instrument* in delivering Israel by the overthrow of his enemies: "Thine hand."

2. He would certainly do it, for he could *find them out* wheresoever they were: "Thine hand shall find out thine enemies."

3. This was easy to be done, as easy as for fire to consume stubble: "Thou shalt make them as a fiery oven."

4. This destruction should be universal; it should reach even to their *posterity:* "Their fruit shalt thou destroy, and their seed."

5. Their judgment should be fearful and unavoidable. God would set them up as a *mark to shoot at:* "Thou shalt make them turn their back, when thou shalt make ready thine arrows."

At last the *cause* is added for these judgments; of the succour he will afford his afflicted, oppressed people; and the revenge he will take upon their enemies: "They intended evil against thee; they imagined a mischievous device."

III. The vow or acclamation. This is properly the *epilogue*, and has *two parts:* 1. A petition—"Save the king and the people." 2. A profession: "And we will give thanks to thee."

1. "Be thou exalted, O Lord, in thine own strength." Show thyself more powerful in defending thy Church than men and devils are in their attempts to destroy it.

2. We will be a thankful people; we will show that we have not received this grace of God in vain: "So will we sing, and praise thy power."

PSALM XXII

Under great affliction and distress, the psalmist prays unto God, 1–3; *appeals to God's wonted kindness in behalf of his people,* 4, 5; *relates the insults that he received,* 6–8; *mentions the goodness of God to him in his youth, as a reason why he should expect help now,* 9–11; *details his sufferings, and the indignities offered to him,* 12–18; *prays with the confidence of being heard and delivered,* 19–24; *praises God. and foretells the conversion of the nations to the true religion,* 25–31.

IV. DAY. EVENING PRAYER

To the chief Musician upon [a]Aijeleth Shahar, A Psalm of David

A. M. cir. 2946 B. C. cir. 1058 Sauli Regis Israelitarum, cir. annum 38

MY [b]God, my God, why hast thou forsaken me? *why art thou so* far [c]from helping me, *and from* [d]the words of my roaring?

2 O my God, I cry in the day-time, but thou hearest not; and in the night-season, and [e]am not silent.

3 But thou *art* holy, O *thou* that inhabitest the [f]praises of Israel.

[a]Or, *the hind of the morning*——[b]Matt. xxvii. 46; Mark xv. 34——[c]Heb. *from my salvation*

[d]Heb. v. 7——[e]Heb. there is *no silence to me*——[f]Deut. x. 21

NOTES ON PSALM XXII

The title of this Psalm, *To the chief Musician upon Aijeleth Shahar, A Psalm of David*, has given rise to many conjectures. The words אילת השחר *aiyeleth hashshachar* are translated in the margin, "the hind of the morning;" but what was this? Was it the name of a *musical instrument?* or of a tune? or of a *band of music? Calmet* argues for the last, and translates "A Psalm of David, addressed to the Musicmaster who presides over the Band called the Morning Hind." This is more likely than any of the other conjectures I have seen. But *aiyeleth hashshachar* may be the name of the *Psalm* itself, for it was customary among the Asiatics to give names to their poetic compositions which often bore no relation to the subject itself. Mr. *Harmer* and others have collected a few instances from *D' Herbelot's* Bibliotheque Orientale. I could add many more from MSS. in my own collection:—thus *Saady* calls a famous miscellaneous work of his *Gulisstan*, "The Country of Roses," or, "The Rose Garden:" and yet there is nothing relative to such a *country*, nor concerning *roses* nor *rose gardens*, in the book. Another is called *Negaristan*, "The Gallery of Pictures;" yet no *picture gallery* is mentioned. Another *Beharistan*, "The Spring Season;" *Bostan*, "The Garden;" *Anvar Soheely*, "The Light of Canopus;" *Bahar Danush*, "The Garden of Knowledge;" *Tuhfit Almumeneen*, "The Gift of the Faithful," a treatise on *medicine; Kemeea Isadut*, "The Alchymy of Life;" *Mukhzeen ul Asrar*, "The Magazine of Secrets;" *Sulselet al Zahab*, "The Golden Chain;" *Zuhfit al Abrar*, "The Rosary of the Pious;" *Merat ul Asrar*, "The Mirror of Secrets;" *Durj ul Durar*, "The most precious Jewels;" *Deru Majlis*, "The Jewel of the Assembly;" *Al Bordah*, "The Variegated Garment;" a poem written by *Al Basiree*, in praise of the *Mohammedan* religion, in gratitude for a cure which he believed he received from the prophet who appeared to him in a dream. The poem is written in *one hundred and sixty-two couplets*, each of which ends with م *mim*, the *first letter* in the name of *Mohammed*.

Scarcely one of the above *titles*, and their number might be easily trebled, bears any relation to the *subject* of the work to which it is prefixed, no more than *Aijeleth Shahar* bears to the matter contained in the twenty-second Psalm. Such *titles* are of very little importance *in themselves;* and of no farther use to us than as they serve to distinguish the different *books*, *poems*, or *Psalms*, to which they are prefixed. To me, many seem to have spent their time uselessly in the investigation of such subjects. See my note on 2 Sam. i. 18.

On the *subject* of the Psalm itself, there is considerable diversity of opinion: 1. Some referring it all to David; 2. Others referring it all to Christ; and, 3. Some, because of the application of several verses of it to our Lord in his sufferings, take a middle way, and apply it *primarily* to *David*, and in a *secondary* or *accommodated* sense, to *Christ*. Of this opinion was *Theodore* of *Mopsuestia*, who gave a very rational account of his own plan of interpretation; for which he was condemned by the *second* council of Constantinople or *fifth* Œcumenic council. *Grotius* and others have nearly copied his plan; and I think, with a little correction, it is the only safe one. That several parts of it relate to *David, primarily*, there is very little reason to doubt; that several passages may be applied by way of *accommodation* to our *Lord*, though *originally* belonging to and expressing the state of *David*, may be piously believed; and that it contains portions which are *direct prophecies* of our Lord's passion, death, and victory, appears too evident to be safely denied. On this plan I propose to treat it in the following paraphrase; keeping it as near to the Gospel standard as I can. Dr. *Delaney* supposes the Psalm to have been written by David when he was at *Mahaniam*, the very place where God appeared to Jacob in his distress. See Gen. xxii. And on this supposition the *third, fourth*, and *fifth* verses may be easily and strikingly illustrated: *Our fathers trusted in thee;* why may not *I? Thou didst deliver* THEM; why may not *I* expect deliverance also? THEY *cried unto thee, trusted in thee, and were not confounded; I* cry unto thee, trust in thee; and why should *I* be confounded? For thou art the same God, thou changest not; and with thee there is no respect of persons. Thus David encouraged himself in the Lord; and these considerations helped to sustain him in his painful exercises and heavy distresses.

Verse 1. *My God, my God, why hast thou forsaken me?*] Show me the cause why thou hast abandoned me to my enemies; and why thou seemest to disregard my prayers and cries? For a full illustration of this passage, I beg the reader to refer to my note on Matt. xxvii. 46.

The words of my roaring?] שאגתי *shaagathi*, The *Vulgate, Septuagint, Syriac, Æthiopic*, and *Arabic*, with the *Anglo-Saxon*, make use of terms which may be thus translated: "My sins (or foolishness) are the cause why deliverance is so far from me." It appears that these versions have read שגגתי *shegagathi*, "my sin of ignorance," instead of שאגתי *shaagathi*, "my roaring:" but no MS. extant supports this reading.

Verse 2. *I cry in the day-time, and in the night-season*] This seems to be David's own experience; and the words seem to refer to his own case alone. Though I am not heard, and

A. M. cir. 2946
B. C. cir. 1058
Sauli, Regis
Israelitarum,
cir. annum
38

4 Our fathers [g]trusted in thee:
they trusted, and thou didst deliver them.
5 They cried unto thee, and
were delivered: [h]they trusted in thee, and
were not confounded.
6 But I *am* [i]a worm, and no man; [k]a reproach of men, and despised of the people.
7 [l]All they that see me laugh me to scorn:
they [m]shoot out the lip, [n]they shake the head,
saying,
8 [o]He [p]trusted on the LORD *that* he would
deliver him: [q]let him deliver him, [r]seeing
he delighted in him.

9 [s]But thou *art* he that took
me out of the womb: thou
[t]didst make me hope *when I was*
upon my mother's breasts.
10 I was cast upon thee from the womb:
[u]thou *art* my God from my mother's belly.
11 Be not far from me; for trouble *is* near;
for *there is* [v]none to help.
12 [w]Many bulls have compassed me: strong
bulls of Bashan have beset me round.
13 [x]They [y]gaped upon me *with* their
mouths, *as* a ravening and a roaring lion.
14 I am poured out like water, [z]and all my
bones are [a]out of joint: [b]my heart is like

A. M. cir. 2946
B. C. cir. 1058
Sauli, Regis
Israelitarum,
cir. annum
38

[g]2 Kings xviii. 5; Psa. xiii. 5; Dan. iii. 28; Eph. i. 12, 13——[h]Psa. xxv. 2, 3; xxxi. 1; lxxi. 1; Isa. xlix. 23; Rom. ix. 33——[i]Job xxv. 6; Isa. xli. 14——[k]Isa. liii. 3 [l]Matt. xxvii. 39; Mark xv. 29; Luke xxiii. 35——[m]Heb. *open*——[n]Job xvi. 4; Psa. cxix. 25——[o]Matt. xxvii. 43——[p]Heb. *He rolled* himself *on the LORD*——[q]Psa. xci. 14

[r]Or, *if he delight in him*——[s]Psa. lxxi. 6——[t]Or, *keptest me in safety*——[u]Isa. xlvi 3; xlix. 1——[v]Heb. *not a helper*——[w]Deut. xxxii. 14; Psa. lxviii. 30; Ezek. xxxix. 18; Amos iv. 1——[x]Job xvi. 10; Psa. xxxv. 21; Lam. ii. 16; iii. 46——[y]Heb. *opened their mouths against me* [z]Dan. v. 6——[a]Or, *sundered*——[b]Josh. vii. 5; Job xxiii. 16

thou appearest to forget or abandon me; yet I continue to cry both day and night after thy salvation.

Verse 3. *But thou* art *holy*] Though I be not heard, even while I cry earnestly, yet I cannot impute any fault or unkindness to my Maker; for *thou art holy*, and canst do nothing but what is *right*. This is the language of profound resignation, in trials the most difficult to be borne.

Inhabitest the praises of Israel.] Thou dwellest in the *sanctuary* where the praises, thanksgivings, and sacrifices of thy people are continually offered.

Verse 4. *Our fathers trusted in thee*] David is supposed to have been, at the time of composing this Psalm, at *Mahanaim*, where Jacob was once in such great distress; where he wrestled with the angel, and was so signally blessed. David might well allude to this circumstance in order to strengthen his faith in God. I am now in the place where God so signally blessed the *head* and *father* of our *tribes*. I *wrestle* with God, as he did; may I not expect similar success?

Verse 5. *They cried unto thee*] So do *I*. THEY *were delivered;* so may *I*. THEY *trusted in thee; I* also trust in thee. *And were not confounded;* and is it likely that *I* shall be put to confusion?

Verse 6. *But I* am *a worm, and no man*] I can see no sense in which our Lord could use these terms. David might well use them to express his vileness and worthlessness. The old Psalter gives this a remarkable turn: **I am a worme**, that es, I am borne of the mayden with outen manseede; **and nout man** anely, bot god als so: and nevir the latter, **I am reprobe of men**, In spitting, buffetyng, and punging with the thornes **and outkasting of folk**; for thai chesed Barraban the thefe, and nought me.

Verse 7. *Laugh me to scorn*] They utterly despised me; set me at naught; treated me with the utmost contempt. *Laugh to scorn* is so completely antiquated that it should be no longer used; *derided, despised, treated with contempt*, are much more expressive and are still in common use.

They shoot out the lip, they shake the head] This is applied by St. Matthew, chap. xxvii. 39, to the conduct of the Jews towards our Lord, when he hung upon the cross; as is also the following verse. But both are primarily true of the insults which David suffered from Shimei and others during the rebellion of Absalom; and, as the cases were so similar, the evangelist thought proper to express a similar conduct to Jesus Christ by the same expressions. These insults our Lord literally received; no doubt David received the same.

Verse 9. *But thou* art *he that took me out of the womb*] Thou hast made me; and hast guided and defended me from my earliest infancy.

Verse 11. *Be not far from me; for trouble is near*] A present God is a present blessing. We always need the Divine help; but more especially when troubles and trials are at hand.

Verse 12. *Many bulls have compassed me*] The *bull* is the emblem of brutal strength, that gores and tramples down all before it. Such was Absalom, Ahithophel, and others, who rose up in rebellion against David; and such were the Jewish rulers who conspired against Christ.

Strong bulls *of Bashan*] Bashan was a district beyond Jordan, very fertile, where they were accustomed to fatten cattle, which became, in consequence of the excellent pasture, the largest, as well as the fattest, in the country. See *Calmet*. All in whose hands were the chief power and influence became David's enemies; for Absalom had stolen away the hearts of all Israel. Against Christ, the chiefs both of Jews and Gentiles were united.

Verse 13. *They gaped upon me*] They were fiercely and madly bent on my destruction.

Verse 14. *I am poured out like water*] That is, as the old *Psalter:* **Thai rought na mare to sla me than to spil water.**

The images in this verse are strongly descriptive of a person in the deepest distress;

A. M. cir. 2946
B. C. cir. 1058
Sauli, Regis
Israelitarum,
cir. annum
38

wax; it is melted in the midst
of my bowels.
15 [c]My strength is dried up
like a potsherd; and [d]my tongue
cleaveth to my jaws; and thou hast brought
me into the dust of death.
16 For [e]dogs have compassed me: the
assembly of the wicked have enclosed me:
[f]they pierced my hands and my feet.
17 I may tell all my bones:
[g]they look *and* stare upon me.
18 [h]They part my garments
among them, and cast lots upon
my vesture.
19 But be [i]not thou far from me, O LORD:
O my strength, haste thee to help me.
20 Deliver my soul from the sword; [k]my
[l]darling [m]from the power of the [n]dog.

A. M. cir. 2946
B. C. cir. 1058
Sauli, Regis
Israelitarum,
cir. annum
38

---

[c]Prov. xvii. 22——[d]Job xxix. 10; Lam. iv. 4; John xix. 28——[e]Rev. xxii. 15——[f]Matt. xxvii. 35; Mark xv. 24; Luke xxiii. 33; John xix. 23, 37; xx. 25

[g]Luke xxiii. 27, 35——[h]Luke xxiii. 34; John xix. 23, 24——[i]Ver. 11; Psa. x. 1——[k]Psa. xxxv. 17——[l]Heb. *my only one*——[m]Heb. *from the hand*——[n]Ver. 16

---

whose strength, courage, hope, and expectation of succour and relief, had entirely failed.

Our Lord's sufferings were extreme; but I cannot think there is any sound theologic sense in which these things can be spoken of Christ, either in his agony in the garden, or his death upon the cross.

Verse 15. *My strength is dried up*] All these expressions mark a most distressed and hopeless case.

Into the dust of death.] This means only that he was *apparently* brought nigh to the grave, and consequent *corruption;* this latter David saw; but Jesus Christ never saw corruption.

Verse 16. *For dogs have compassed me*] This may refer to the *Gentiles*, the Roman soldiers, and others by whom our Lord was surrounded in his trial, and at his cross.

They pierced my hands and my feet] The other sufferings David, as a type of our Lord, might pass through; but the *piercing of the hands and feet* was peculiar to our Lord; therefore, this verse may pass for a *direct revelation.* Our Lord's hands and feet were pierced when he was nailed to the cross, David's never were pierced.

But there is a various reading here which is of great importance. Instead of כארו *caaru, they pierced*, which is what is called the *kethib*, or *marginal* reading, and which our translators have followed; the *keri* or textual reading is כארי *caari, as a lion.* In support of each reading there are both MSS. and eminent critics. The *Chaldee* has, "Biting as a lion my hands and my feet;" but the *Syriac, Vulgate, Septuagint, Æthiopic*, and *Arabic* read, "*they pierced* or *digged;*" and in the *Anglo-Saxon* the words are, **hi dulfon hande mine and fet mine**; "*They dalve* (digged) *hands mine, and feet mine.*"

The *Complutensian* Polyglot has כארו *caaru, they digged* or *pierced*, in the *text;* for which it gives כרה *carah*, to *cut, dig*, or *penetrate*, in the margin, as the root whence כארו is derived. But the Polyglots of *Potken, Antwerp, Paris*, and *London*, have כארי *caari* in the text; and כארו *caaru* is referred to in the *margin;* and this is the case with the most correct Hebrew Bibles. The whole difference here lies between י *yod* and ו *vau*, which might easily be mistaken for each other; the former making *like a lion;* the latter, *they pierced.* The latter is to me most evidently the true reading.

Verse 17. *I may tell all my bones*] This may refer to the violent *extension* of his body when the whole of its weight hung upon the nails which attached his hands to the transverse beam of the cross. The body being thus extended, the principal bones became prominent, and easily discernible.

Verse 18. *They part my garments*] This could be true in *no sense* of David. The fact took place at the crucifixion of our Lord. The soldiers divided his *upper garment* into four parts, each soldier taking a part; but his *tunic* or *inward vestment* being without seam, woven in one entire piece, they agreed not to divide, but to cast lots *whose* the *whole* should be. Of this scripture the Roman soldiers knew nothing; but they fulfilled it to the letter. This was foreseen by the Spirit of God; and this is a direct revelation concerning Jesus Christ, which impresses the whole account with the broad seal of eternal truth.

Verse 19. *Be not thou far from me*] In the first verse he asks, *Why hast thou forsaken me?* Or, as if astonished at their wickedness, *Into what hands hast thou permitted me to fall?* Now he prays, *Be not far from me.* St. *Jerome* observes here, that it is the *humanity* of our blessed Lord which speaks to his *divinity.* Jesus was *perfect man;* and as *man* he suffered and died. But this *perfect* and *sinless man* could not have sustained those sufferings so as to make them expiatory had he not been supported by the *Divine nature.* All the expressions in this Psalm that indicate any *weakness*, as far as it relates to Christ, (and indeed it relates *principally* to him,) are to be understood of the *human nature;* for, that in him *God* and *man* were united, but not confounded, the whole New Testament to me bears evidence, the *manhood* being a perfect man, the *Godhead* dwelling bodily in that manhood. Jesus, as MAN, was conceived, born, grew up, increased in wisdom, stature, and favour with God and man; hungered, thirsted, suffered, and died. Jesus, as GOD, knew all things, was from the beginning with God, healed the diseased, cleansed the lepers, and raised the dead; calmed the raging of the sea, and laid the tempest by a word; quickened the human nature, raised it from the dead, took it up into heaven, where as the Lamb newly slain, it ever appears in the presence of God for us. These are all Scripture facts. The *man* Christ Jesus could not work those miracles; the *God* in that man could not have *suffered* those sufferings. Yet *one person* appears to do and suffer all; here then is GOD *manifested in the* FLESH.

O my strength] The *divinity* being the power by which the *humanity* was sustained in this dreadful conflict.

Verse 20. *Deliver my soul from the sword*]

A. M. cir. 2946
B. C. cir. 1058
Sauli, Regis Israelitarum, cir. annum 38

21 [o]Save me from the lion's
mouth: [p]for thou hast heard
me from the horns of the unicorns.

22 [q]I will declare thy name unto [r]my brethren: in the midst of the congregation will I
praise thee.

23 [s]Ye that fear the LORD, praise him; all
ye the seed of Jacob, glorify him; and fear
him, all ye the seed of Israel.

24 For he hath not despised nor abhorred
the affliction of the afflicted; neither hath he
hid his face from him; but [t]when he cried
unto him, he heard.

25 [u]My praise *shall be* of thee
in the great congregation: [v]I will
pay my vows before them that
fear him.

26 [w]The meek shall eat and be satisfied:
they shall praise the LORD that seek him:
your heart [x]shall live for ever.

27 [y]All the ends of the world shall remember and turn unto the LORD: [z]and all the
kindreds of the nations shall worship before
thee.

28 [a]For the kingdom *is* the LORD'S: and he
is the governor among the nations.

29 [b]All *they that be* fat upon earth shall

[o]2 Tim. iv. 17——[p]Isa. xxxiv. 7; Acts iv. 27——[q]Heb. ii. 12; Psa. xl. 9——[r]John xx. 17; Rom. viii. 29——[s]Psa. cxxxv. 19, 20——[t]Heb. v. 7——[u]Psa. xxxv. 18; xl. 9, 10; cxi. 1——[v]Psa. lxvi. 13; cxvi. 14; Eccles. v. 4

[w]Lev. vii. 11, 12, 15, 16; Psa. lxix. 32; Isa. lxv. 13——[x]John vi. 51——[y]Psa. ii. 9; lxxii. 11; lxxxvi. 8; xcviii. 3; Isa. xlix. 6——[z]Psa. xcvi. 7——[a]Psa. xlvii. 8; Obad. 21; Zech. xiv. 9; Matt. vi. 13——[b]Psa. xlv. 12

Deliver נפשי *naphshi, my life;* save me alive, or raise me again.

My darling] יחידתי *yechidathi, my only one.* The only human being that was ever produced since the creation, even by the power of God himself, without the agency of man. ADAM the *first* was created out of the dust of the earth; that was his *mother;* God was the *framer.* ADAM the *second* was produced in the womb of the *virgin;* that was his mother. But that which was conceived in her was by the *power of the Holy Ghost;* hence the man Christ Jesus is the ONLY Son of God; God is his Father, and he is his ONLY ONE.

Verse 21. *Save me from the lion's mouth*] Probably our Lord here includes his *Church* with himself. The *lion* may then mean the *Jews;* the *unicorns,* רמים *remim,* (probably the *rhinoceros,*) the *Gentiles.* For the *unicorn,* see the note on Num. xxiii. 22. There is no quadruped or *land animal* with one horn only, except the rhinoceros; but there is a *marine* animal, the *narwall* or *monodon,* a species of *whale,* that has a very fine curled ivory horn, which projects from its snout. One in my own museum measures *seven feet four inches,* and is very beautiful. Some of these animals have struck their horn through the side of a ship; and with it they easily transfix the whale, or any such animal. The old Psalter says, "The unicorn es ane of the prudest best that es, so that he wil dye for dedeyn if he be haldyn ogayn his wil."

Verse 22. *I will declare thy name unto my brethren*] I will make a complete revelation concerning the God of justice and love, to my *disciples;* and I will announce to the Jewish *people* thy merciful design in sending me to be the Saviour of the world.

Verse 23. *Ye that fear the Lord*] This is an exhortation to the *Jews* particularly, to profit by the preaching of the Gospel. Perhaps, by *them that fear him,* the *Gentiles,* and particularly the *proselytes,* may be intended. The *Jews* are mentioned by name: *Glorify him, all ye seed of Jacob; fear him, all ye seed of Israel.*

Verse 24. *For he hath not despised*] It is his property to help and save the poor and the humble; and he rejects not the sighings of a contrite heart. Perhaps it may mean, Though ye have despised *me* in my humiliation, yet God has graciously received me in the character of a sufferer on account of sin; as by that humiliation unto death the great atonement was made for the sin of the world.

Verse 25. *The great congregation*] In ver. 22 he declares that he will *praise God in the midst of the congregation.* Here the *Jews* seem to be intended. In this verse he says *he will praise him in the* GREAT CONGREGATION. Here the *Gentiles* are probably meant. The Jewish nation was but a *small number* in comparison of the *Gentile* world. And those of the former who received the Gospel were very few when compared with those among the Gentiles who received the Divine testimony. The one *was* (for there is scarcely a converted Jew *now*) קהל *kahal,* an *assembly;* the other *was, is,* and *will be* increasingly, קהל רב *kahal rab,* a GREAT ASSEMBLY. Salvation *was* of the *Jews,* it is *now* of the *Gentiles.*

Verse 26. *The meek shall eat*] ענוים *anavim,* the POOR, shall eat. In the true only Sacrifice there shall be such a provision for all believers, that they shall have a fulness of joy. Those who offered the sacrifice, fed on what they offered. Jesus, the true Sacrifice, is the bread that came down from heaven; they who eat of this bread shall never die.

Verse 27. *All the ends of the world*] The Gospel shall be preached to every nation under heaven; and *all the kindred of nations,* משפחות *mishpechoth,* the *families* of the nations: not only the *nations* of the world shall receive the Gospel as a *revelation* from God, but *each family* shall embrace it for their own salvation. *They shall worship before* Jesus the Saviour, and through him shall all their praises be offered unto God.

Verse 28. *The kingdom* is *the Lord's*] That universal sway of the Gospel which in the New Testament is called *the kingdom of God;* in which all men shall be God's subjects; and righteousness, peace, and joy in the Holy Ghost, be *universally* diffused.

Verse 29. *All* they that be *fat upon earth*] The *rich,* the *great,* the *mighty,* even *princes,*

A. M. cir. 2946 B. C. cir. 1058 Sauli, Regis Israelitarum, cir. annum 38

eat and worship: [c]all they that
go down to the dust shall bow
before him: and none can keep
alive his own soul.
30 A seed shall serve him; [d]it shall be accounted to the LORD for a generation.
31 [e]They shall come, and shall
declare his righteousness unto a
people that shall be born, that he hath done *this.*

A. M. cir. 2946 B. C. cir. 1058 Sauli, Regis Israelitarum, cir. annum 38

[c]Isa. xxvi. 10; Phil. ii. 19——[d]Psa. lxxxvii. 6——[e]Psa. lxxviii. 6; lxxxvi. 9; cii. 18; Isa. lx. 3; see Rom. iii. 21, 22

governors, and *kings*, shall embrace the Gospel. They shall count it their greatest honour to be called *Christian;* to join in the assemblies of his people, to commemorate his sacrificial death, to dispense the word of life, to discourage vice, and to encourage the profession and practice of pure and undefiled religion.

That go down to the dust] Every *dying man* shall put his trust in Christ, and shall expect glory only through the great Saviour of mankind.

None can keep alive his own soul.] The *Vulgate* has: Et anima mea illi vivet, et semen meum serviet ipsi; "and my soul shall live to him, and my seed shall serve him." And with this agree the *Syriac*, *Septuagint*, *Æthiopic*, *Arabic*, and *Anglo-Saxon*. The old *Psalter* follows them closely: **And my saule sal lyf til him; and my sede til hym sal serve.** I believe this to be the true reading. Instead of נפשו *naphsho*, HIS *soul*, some MSS., in accordance with the above ancient versions, have נפשי *naphshi*, MY *soul*. And instead of לא *lo*, *not*, two MSS., with the versions, have לו *lo*, *to* HIM. And for חיה *chiyah*, shall *vivify*, some have יחיה *yichyeh*, shall *live*. The text, therefore, should be read, *My soul* (נפשי *napshi*) *shall live* (לו *lo*) *to him: my seed* (זרעי *zari*) *shall serve him*. These may be the words of *David* himself: "I will live to this Saviour while I live; and my spiritual posterity shall serve him through all generations."

Verse 30. *Shall be accounted to the Lord for a generation.*] They shall be called *Christians* after the name of Christ.

Verse 31. *Unto a people that shall be born*] That is, one generation shall continue to announce unto another the true religion of the Lord Jesus; so that it shall be for ever propagated in the earth. Of his kingdom there shall be no end.

ANALYSIS OF THE TWENTY-SECOND PSALM

This Psalm concerns the Messiah, his passion, and his kingdom. Though, in some sense, it, may be applied to David as a *type*, yet *Christ* is the *thing signified*, and therefore it is primarily and principally verified of and in him; for he is brought in here, speaking,

First, Of his *dereliction;* then showing his *passion*, and the *cruelty* of his enemies.

Secondly, *Entreating* ease and *deliverance* from his sufferings.

Thirdly, *Promising thanks* to God; foretelling the preaching of the Gospel, and the enlargement of his kingdom by the accession of all nations.

There are *three* chief parts in this Psalm:—

I. Our Saviour's *complaint*, and the *causes* of it: prophetically expressing his sufferings nearly throughout the whole Psalm.

II. His *petition* and *prayer* that God would not absent himself, but deliver and save him, ver. 3, 4, 5, 9, 10, 11, 19, 20, 21.

III. His *thanksgiving* and *prophetic declaration* concerning the conversion of the Gentiles; from ver. 22 to the end.

I. He begins with a heavy complaint of dereliction in his extremity; and that he was not heard, though he prayed with strong crying and tears: "My God, my God, why hast thou forsaken me?" &c. The words are *repeated* to show the deep anguish of his heart.

2. He shows how well-grounded his complaint was: for God had dealt with him contrary to his usual method; for when his saints called upon him, he heard *them* in *their* distress. Martyres si non eripuit, tum non deseruit. "If he did not deliver the martyrs, yet he did not desert them in their sufferings." His case was more grievous than any that had gone before. Of this he speaks particularly in the three succeeding verses, 3, 4, and 5, by which he reminds God of his promise: "Call on me in the time of trouble, and I will deliver thee." Of this they who went before had experience: and as he was the same God still, why should *this Sufferer* only be deserted? for *they* were heard and comforted.

1. "Thou art holy," propitious and benevolent. "Thou dwellest in the praises of Israel;" thou art continually helping them, and they are continually praising thee for this help.

To prove all this he brings the *example* of the *fathers:*—

2. "Our fathers trusted in thee, and thou didst deliver them."

3. "They cried unto thee—and were not confounded."

But my case is worse than any other: "I am a worm, and am no man."

He then details his sufferings:—

1. The scoffs and scorns cast upon him: "I am become the reproach of men, and the despised among the people."

2. Their contempt is expressed both by *words* and *gestures:* "All they that see me laugh me to scorn: they shoot out the lip—and shake the head."

3. They laboured to deprive him of his God. They uttered this insulting sarcasm: "He trusted in the Lord that he would deliver him; let him deliver him, since he delighted in him."

II. He now breaks off the narration of his sufferings, has immediate recourse to God, refutes their irony, shows his confidence in God, and prays for assistance. This he strengthens by *three arguments* drawn from God's goodness towards him:—

1. His *generation* and *birth:* "Thou—tookest me out of my mother's womb."

2. His *sustenance* and support ever since: "Thou didst make me hope when I was upon my mother's breasts;—thou art my God from my mother's belly." In a word, he was his *Saviour*, *Protector*, and *Preserver*.

3. Trouble is near, and there is none to help. Therefore, "Be not far from me."

Now he returns to the *narration* of his passion, in which he sets forth the *despite, cruelty,* and *rage* of the Jews towards him, whom he compares to *bulls, lions, dogs,* &c., ver. 16.

1. They apprehended him: "Many bulls have compassed me;" &c.

2. They longed to condemn and devour him: "They gaped on me with their mouths, as a ravening and roaring lion."

3. This was the cruelty of the *lions* and *bulls,* the *chief rulers,* and *chief priests;* and now follows the ravin of the *dogs,* the "multitude of the people:" they were the "assembly of the wicked;" and being stirred up by the *priests* and *rulers,* "they compassed him round about."

4. They crucify him. And his passion is foretold, with what he should suffer in body and soul.

1 "I am poured out like water." My blood is poured out freely; and no more account taken of it, than if it were water spilt on the ground.

2. "All my bones (when hung on the cross) are out of joint."

3. "My heart (at the sense of God's hatred to sin) is dissolved *and melted* like wax."

4. "My strength (my animal spirits and muscular energy) is dried up like a potsherd;" or like a *pot,* whose *fluid* is *evaporated* by hanging long over a fierce fire.

5. "My tongue (for thirst) cleaveth to my jaws."

6. "Thou hast brought me to death—to the dust of death:" to the grave.

7. "They pierced my hands and my feet." I am crucified also, and die upon the cross.

8. By my long hanging upon the cross, my bones are so disjointed that they may be easily told: "I may tell all my bones."

9. "They look and stare upon me." They feel no *compassion,* but take pleasure in my agonies. This is an affection which is characteristic only of a devil.

10. "They part my garments among them." They delighted in his destruction for the sake of his *spoils.*

Having thus far described his *sufferings,* and the *malice* of his enemies, he begins again to *pray;* which is, in effect, the same with that ejaculation with which Christ gave up the ghost: "Into thy hands, O Lord, I commend my spirit." "Be not thou far from me, O Lord." "Deliver my soul from the sword, my darling from the power of the dog." "Save me from the lion's mouth," &c.

III. This part, which is a *profession of thanks* for deliverance, contains a clear prophecy of the resurrection of Christ; that, having conquered death and Satan, he was to reign and gather a Church out of all nations, which was to continue for ever. This is amplified,

First, By a public profession of the benefit received from God: "I will declare thy name in the midst of the congregation, I will pay my vows." In which we have,

1. The *propagation, proclamation,* and *preaching* of the *Gospel:* "I will declare thy name;" which is amplified,

(1.) By the notation of the *objects* to whom preached, honoured here by the name of, 1. *Brethren.* 2. Those that *fear the Lord.* 3. The *seed of Jacob,* the *seed of Israel.* 4. The *meek* or *poor.* 5. The *fat*—rich, great, or eminent of the earth. 6. They that go down to the dust.

(2.) By the *place:* "The midst of the congregation"—the *great* congregation, i. e., both among the *Jews* and among the *Gentiles.*

(3.) By the *worship* they were to pay: 1. *Praise.* 2. *Paying of vows.* 3. *Fear,* or religious reverence.

2. An *exhortation* to his brethren, &c., to do this duty; and they must be fit for it, for every one is not fit to take God's name in his mouth. It is, *Ye that fear the Lord—the seed of Jacob—the seed of Israel,* fear him, serve the Lord in fear, rejoice before him with reverence. Give him both external and internal worship.

3. And to *engage* them to this, he gives *two reasons:*

Reason 1. Drawn from God's *goodness,* his acceptance of our worship, hearing our prayers, and affording help when we call: "For the Lord hath not despised nor abhorred the affliction of the afflicted. When he cried to him, he heard him."

Reason 2. The great *good* that should happen to them who would believe and accept the Gospel; whom he calls here *the meek,* that is, the humble, broken-hearted, the penitent, the heavy laden; those who are oppressed with the burden of their sins, and astonished at a sense of God's wrath. To them are made *three* promises of comfort:—

1. "They shall eat, and be satisfied." They shall be fed with the word and ordinances of God.

2. "They shall praise the Lord for his mercy;" seeking his favour in his ordinances, which, under the Gospel, are generally *eucharistical.*

3. "Their heart shall live for ever;" their conscience being quieted and pacified, and freed from a sense of God's wrath.

Secondly, The prophet proceeds, and shows us the amplitude of these benefits; that they belong, not only to the Jews but to the Gentiles, by whose conversion the kingdom of Christ is to be enlarged.

1. "All the ends of the world," being warned, by the preaching of the Gospel, and allured by these promises, shall remember—consider the lamentable condition in which they are, and deplore their former estate, impiety, and idolatry. And the mercy of God being now manifested to them—

2. They shall cast away their gods, *turn* from their evil ways, and seek that God from whom they have been alienated. And being converted—

3. They shall embrace a new form of religion under the Gospel: "All the kindreds of the nations shall worship before thee."

4. Of which the reason is, because Christ is advanced to the throne; all power is given to him: "For the kingdom is the Lord's, and he is governor among the people."

5. He then shows the *two kinds* of *people* who should become subjects of the kingdom; in effect, *rich* and *poor.*

1. "The fat upon the earth." The wealthy, the mighty; kings, princes, great men, are to be called into the kingdom, that they may be partakers of its grace: "All *they that be* fat upon the earth," &c.

2. "They also that go down to the dust." That is, the *poor,* the neglected, who draw out their life in misery, and sit, as it were, in the dust; those who are perpetual mourners, and have, as it were, perpetual dust and ashes upon their heads: "These shall bow before him."

Lastly. He amplifies the greatness of this

benefit by the *perpetuity* of Christ's kingdom. It was not a feast of one hour, it was to continue.

1. "A seed shall serve him." But this and the preceding clause may signify the psalmist's resolution to live to God himself, and to show others the same way. See the *notes*.

This *seed*, however, shall be accounted to the Lord for a generation. It shall be a peculiar people, a royal priesthood, a holy nation, and called by Christ's own name—CHRISTIANS.

2. When *one* generation is past, *another* shall come up to perform this duty, being instructed by their fathers: "They shall come and declare his righteousness to a people that shall be born." *Manebit semper ecclesia;* "the Church is immortal."

3. He concludes with the *cause* of all. Why called, justified, sanctified, saved. He hath done it; the GOD, the Author of all; the Fountain of all grace; the Giver of Jesus Christ, and eternal life through him. For by him, and of him, and through him, are all things; and to him be glory and dominion for ever and ever!

PSALM XXIII

The Lord is the Pastor of his people; therefore it may be inferred that they shall not want, 1. *How he guides, feeds, and protects them,* 2, 3. *Even in the greatest dangers they may be confident of his support,* 4. *His abundant provision for them,* 5. *The confidence they may have of his continual mercy, and their eternal happiness.*

A Psalm of David

A. M. cir. 3468
B. C. cir. 536
Cyri,
R. Persarum,
cir. annum
primum.

THE LORD *is* [a]my shepherd;
[b]I shall not want.
2 [c]He maketh me to lie down
in [d]green pastures; [e]he leadeth me beside the [f]still waters.
3 He restoreth my soul: [g]he
leadeth me in the paths of righteousness for his name's sake.

[a]Isa. xl. 11; Jer. xxiii. 4; Ezek. xxxiv. 11, 12, 23; John x. 11; 1 Peter ii. 25; Revelation vii. 17——[b]Phil. iv. 19——[c]Ezek. xxxiv. 14——[d]Hebrew, *pastures of tender grass*——[e]Revelation vii. 17——[f]Hebrew, *waters of quietness*——[g]Psalm v. 8; xxxi. 3; Prov. viii. 20

NOTES ON PSALM XXIII

There is nothing particular in the *title;* it is simply attributed to *David;* but as it appears to be a thanksgiving of the Israelites for their *redemption from the Babylonish captivity*, it cannot with propriety be attributed to David. Some think it was written by David in his *exile*, which is not likely; others, that he penned it when he was *finally delivered from the persecution of Saul.* I rather incline to the opinion that it was written *after the captivity.* The *Chaldee* seems to suppose that it was written to celebrate the goodness of God to the *Israelites in the desert.* It is a truly beautiful Psalm. Supposing it to have been written *after the captivity*, we see, 1. The redeemed captives giving thanks to God for their liberty. 2. Acknowledging that God had brought back their lives from the grave. 3. They represent themselves in Judea as a flock in an excellent pasture. 4. They declare that from the dangers they have passed through, and from which God had delivered them, they can have no fear of any enemy. 5. They conclude, from what God has done for them, that his goodness and mercy shall follow them all their days. And, 6. That they shall no more be deprived of God's worship, but shall all their days have access to his temple.

Verse 1. *The Lord* is *my shepherd*] There are two *allegories* in this Psalm which are admirably well adapted to the purpose for which they are produced, and supported both with *art* and *elegance*. The *first* is that of a *shepherd;* the *second*, that of a *great feast*, set out by a *host* the most kind and the most liberal. As a *flock*, they have the most excellent *pasture;* as *guests*, they have the most nutritive and abundant *fare*. God condescends to call himself the *Shepherd* of his people, and his followers are considered as a *flock* under his guidance and direction. 1. He leads them out and in, so that they find pasture and safety. 2. He knows where to feed them, and in the course of his grace and providence leads them in the way in which they should go. 3. He watches over them, and keeps them from being destroyed by ravenous beasts. 4. If any have strayed, he brings them back. 5. He brings them to the *shade* in times of scorching heat; in times of persecution and affliction, he finds out an asylum for them. 6. He takes care that they shall lack no manner of thing that is good.

But who are his flock? All real penitents, all true believers; all who obediently *follow* his example, abstaining from every appearance of evil, and in a holy life and conversation showing forth the virtues of Him who called them from darkness into his marvellous light. "My sheep hear my voice, and follow me."

But who are not his flock! Neither the backslider in heart, nor the vile Antinomian, who thinks the more he sins, the more the grace of

A. M. cir. 3468
B. C. cir. 536
Cyri,
R. Persarum,
cir. annum
primum

4 Yea, though I walk through the
valley of [h]the shadow of death,
[i]I will fear no evil: [k]for thou
art with me; thy rod and thy
staff they comfort me.
5 [l]Thou preparest a table before me in the
presence of mine enemies: thou
[m]anointest [n]my head with oil;
my cup runneth over.
6 Surely goodness and mercy
shall follow me all the days of my life: and I
will dwell in the house of the LORD [o]for ever.

A. M. cir. 3468
B. C. cir. 536
Cyri,
R. Persarum,
cir. annum
primum.

[h]Job iii. 5; x. 21, 22; xxiv. 17; Psa. xliv. 19——[i]Psa. iii. 6; xxvii. 1; cxviii. 6——[k]Isa. xliii. 2

[l]Psa. civ. 15——[m]Heb. *makest fat*——[n]Psa. xcii. 10
[o]Heb. *to length of days*

God shall be magnified in saving him; nor those who fondly suppose they are covered with the righteousness of Christ while living in sin; nor the crowd of the *indifferent* and the *careless*, nor the immense herd of *Laodicean loiterers;* nor the fiery bigots who would exclude all from heaven but themselves, and the party who believe as they do. These the Scripture resembles to *swine, dogs, wandering stars, foxes, lions, wells without water*, &c., &c. Let not any of these come forward to *feed on this pasture*, or take of the *children's bread*. Jesus Christ is the *good Shepherd;* the Shepherd who, to save his flock, laid down his own life.

I shall not want.] How can they? He who is their Shepherd has all power in heaven and earth; therefore he *can protect them.* The silver and gold are his, and the cattle on a *thousand* hills; and therefore he can *sustain* them. He has all that they need, and his heart is full of love to mankind; and therefore he will withhold from them no manner of thing that is good. The old *Psalter* both translates and paraphrases this clause well: **Lord governs me, and nathing sal want to me. In stede of pastour thare he me sett.** "The voice of a rightwis man: **Lord** Crist **es my kyng**, and for thi (therefore) **nathyng sal me want**: that es, in hym I sal be siker, and suffisand, for I hope in hymn gastly gude and endles. **And he ledes me in stede of pastoure**, that es, understandyng of his worde, and delyte in his luf. Qwar I am siker to be fild, thar in that stede (place) he sett me, to be nurysht til perfectioun." Who can say more, who need say less, than this?

Verse 2. *He maketh me to lie down in green pastures*] בנאות דשא *binoth deshe*, not *green pastures*, but *cottages of turf* or *sods*, such as the shepherds had in open champaign countries; places in which themselves could repose safely; and *pens* thus constructed where the flock might be safe all the night. They were enclosures, and enclosures where they had *grass* or provender to eat.

Beside the still waters.] *Deep waters*, that the strongest heat could not exhale; not by a *rippling current*, which argues a *shallow* stream. Or perhaps he may here refer to the waters of *Siloam*, or *Shiloah, that go softly*, Isa. viii. 6, compared with the *strong current* of the *Euphrates*. Thou hast brought us from the land of our captivity, from beyond this mighty and turbulent river, to our own country streams, wells, and fountains, where we enjoy peace, tranquillity, and rest.

The old *Psalter gives this a beautiful turn:* **On the water of rehetyng forth he me broght.** On the water of grace er we broght forth, that makes to recover our strengthe that we lost in syn. **And reheteis** (strengthens) us to do gude workes. **My saule he turned**, that es, of a synful wreche, he made it ryghtwis, and waxyng of luf in mekeness. First he turnes our saules til hym; and then he ledes and fedes it. Ten graces he telles in this psalme, the qwilk God gyfs til his lufers, (i. e., them that love him.)

Verse 3. *He restoreth my soul*] Brings back my life from destruction; and converts my soul from sin, that it may not eternally perish. Or, after it has *backslidden* from him, heals its backslidings, and restores it to his favour. See the old paraphrase on this clause in the preceding note.

In the paths of righteousness] במעגלי צדק *bemageley tsedek*, "in the circuits" or "orbits of righteousness." In many places of Scripture man appears to be represented under the notion of a *secondary planet moving round its primary;* or as a planet revolving round the sun, from whom it receives its *power* of *revolving*, with all its *light* and *heat*. Thus man stands in reference to the *Sun of righteousness;* by *his power* alone is he enabled to *walk uprightly;* by his *light* he is *enlightened;* and by his *heat* he is *vivified*, and enabled to bring forth *good fruit*. When he keeps in his proper *orbit*, having the *light* of the glory of God reflected from the face of Jesus Christ, he is enabled to *enlighten* and *strengthen* others. He that is enlightened may enlighten; he that is fed may feed.

For his name's sake.] To display the glory of his grace, and not on account of any *merit* in me. God's motives of conduct towards the children of men are derived from the perfections and goodness of his own nature.

Verse 4. *Yea, though I walk through the valley of the shadow of death*] The reference is still to the *shepherd*. Though I, as one of the *flock*, should walk through the most dismal valley, in the dead of the night, exposed to pitfalls, precipices, devouring beasts, &c., I should fear no evil under the guidance and protection of such a Shepherd. He knows all the *passes*, dangerous defiles, hidden pits, and abrupt precipices in the way; and he will guide me around, about, and through them. See the phrase *shadow of death* explained on Matt. iv. 16. "Thof I ward well and imang tha, that nouther has knowyng of God, ne luf or in myddis of this lyf, that es schadow of ded; for it es blak for myrkenes of syn; and it ledes til dede and il men, imang qwam gude men wones:—I sal nout drede il, pryve nor apert; for thu ert with me in my hert, qwar I fele thu so, that eftir the schadow of dede, I be with the in thi vera lyf."—Old *Psalter*.

For thou art *with me*] He who has his God for a companion need fear no danger; for he can neither *mistake* his way, nor be *injured*.

Thy rod and thy staff] שבטך *shibtecha*, thy *sceptre, rod, ensign* of a *tribe, staff of office;* for so שבט *shebet* signifies in Scripture. *And thy staff*, ומשענתך *umishantecha*, thy *prop* or support. The former may signify the shepherd's crook; the latter, some sort of *rest* or *support*, similar to our *camp stool*, which the shepherds might carry with them as an occasional seat, when the earth was *too wet* to be sat on with safety. With the *rod* or *crook* the shepherd could *defend* his sheep, and with it lay *hold of their horns* or legs to pull them out of *thickets*, *bogs*, *pits*, or *waters*. We are not to suppose that by the rod *correction* is meant: there is no idea of this kind either in the text, or in the original word; nor has it this meaning in any part of Scripture. Besides, *correction* and *chastisement* do not *comfort;* they are not, at least for the present, joyous, but grievous; nor can any person look forward to them with *comfort*. They abuse the text who paraphrase *rod* correction, &c. The other term שען *shaan* signifies *support*, something *to rest on*, as a *staff*, *crutch*, *stave*, or the like. The *Chaldee* translates thus: "Even though I should walk in captivity, in the valley of the shadow of death, I will not fear evil. Seeing thy Word (מימרך *meymerach*, thy personal Word) is my Assistant or Support; thy right word and thy law console me." Here we find that the Word, מימר *meymar*, is distinguished from any thing *spoken*, and even from the *law* itself. I cannot withhold the paraphrase of the *old Psalter*, though it considers the *rod* as signifying correction: "Sothly I sal drede na nylle; for **thy wande**, that es thi lyght disciplyne, that chasties me as thi son: **and thi staf**, that es thi stalworth help, that I lene me til, and haldes me uppe; thai have comforthed me; lerand (*learning, teaching*) me qwat I suld do; and haldand my thaught in the, that es my comforth."

Verse 5. *Thou preparest a table before me*] Here the *second allegory* begins. A magnificent banquet is provided by a most liberal and benevolent host; who has not only the *bounty* to feed me, but *power* to protect me; and, though surrounded by *enemies*, I sit down to this table with confidence, knowing that I shall feast in perfect security. This may refer to the favour God gave the poor captive Israelites in the sight of the Chaldeans who had grievously treated them for *seventy* years; and whose king, Cyrus, had not only permitted them now to return to their own land, but had also furnished them with every thing requisite for their passage, and for repairing the walls of Jerusalem, and rebuilding the temple of the Lord, where the sacrifices were offered as usual, and the people of God *feasted* on them.

Thou anointest my head with oil] Perfumed oil was poured on the heads of distinguished guests, when at the feasts of great personages. The woman in the Gospel, who poured the box of ointment of spikenard on the head of our Lord, (see Matt. xxvi. 6, 7; Mark xiv. 8; Luke vii. 46,) only acted according to the custom of her own country, which the host, who invited our Lord, had shamefully neglected.

My cup runneth over.] Thou hast not only given me abundance of *food*, but hast filled my *cup* with the best *wine*.

Verse 6. *Goodness and mercy shall follow me*] As I pass on through the vale of life, thy goodness and mercy shall follow my every step; as I proceed, so shall they. There seems to be an allusion here to the waters of the rock smitten by the rod of Moses, which followed the Israelites all the way through the wilderness, till they came to the Promised Land. God never leaves his true followers; providential mercies, gracious influences, and miraculous interferences, shall never be wanting when they are necessary. *I will dwell in the house*, ושבתי *veshabti*, "and I shall RETURN to the house of the Lord," *for ever*, לארך ימים *leorech yamim*, "for length of days." During the rest of my life, I shall not be separated from God's house, nor from God's ordinances; and shall at last dwell with him in glory. These two last verses seem to be the language of a priest returned from captivity to live in the temple, and to serve God the rest of his life.

Analysis of the Twenty-third Psalm

The scope of this Psalm is to show the happiness of that man who has God for his protector, and is under his care and tuition.

To illustrate this protection, &c., David proposes *two allegories:* the one of a *shepherd;* the other of a *free-hearted man* given to *hospitality*, and *entertaining* his guests bountifully. It has *two* parts: the *first* sets forth, 1. God's care in providing him with all necessaries, ver. 1-4. 2. His liberality in supplying him with all that he needed, ver. 5.

The *second* part shows his confidence in God's grace, and his thankfulness, ver. 6.

I. He begins the first with this position, "God is my shepherd;" and upon it infers, "Therefore I shall not want." He will do for me what a good shepherd will do for his sheep.

1. He will feed me in *green pastures*, ver. 2.
2. He will there provide for my safety: "He makes me to lie down."
3. He will provide waters of comfort for me.
4. These waters shall be gently-flowing streams, *still waters*—not turbulent and violent.
5. He will take care to preserve me in health; if sick, he will *restore me.*
6. He goes before and leads me, that I may not mistake my way: "He leads me in paths of righteousness," which is his love; for it is "for his name's sake."
7. He *restores*. If I err and go astray, and *walk through the valley of the shadow of death*, (for a sheep is a straggling creature,) *I will fear no evil: for his rod and staff comfort me;* his *law* and his *Gospel* both contribute to my correction and support.

Thus, as a good Shepherd, he supplies me with *necessaries*, that I want nothing: but over and above, as a *bountiful Lord*, he has furnished me *copiously* with *varieties* which may be both for *ornament* and *honour*.

1. He *has prepared a table for me*—and that *in the presence of my enemies.*
2. He *hath anointed my head with oil*, to refresh my spirits, and cheer my countenance.
3. And *my cup runneth over*—with the choicest wine he gladdens my heart.

II. The last verse, 1. Sets out David's confidence that it shall be no worse with him: "Surely goodness and mercy shall follow me all the days of my life."

2. Then he expresses his *thankfulness:* "I will dwell in the house of the Lord for ever." In thy house, among the faithful, I will praise thy name as long as I live.

On each point in this analysis the reader is requested to consult the *notes.*

PSALM XXIV

The Lord is Sovereign Ruler of the universe, 1, 2. *The great question, Who is fit to minister to the Lord in his own temple?* 3–6. *The glory of God in his entrance into his temple,* 7–10.

V. DAY. MORNING PRAYER

A Psalm of David

A. M. cir. 2962
B. C. cir. 1042
Davidis, Regis
Israelitarum,
cir. annum
14

THE [a]earth *is* the LORD'S,
and the fulness thereof; the
world, and they that dwell therein.
2 [b]For he hath founded it upon
the seas, and established it upon the floods.
3 [c]Who shall ascend into the hill of the
LORD? or who shall stand in his holy place?
4 [d]He [e]that hath [f]clean hands, and [g]a pure
heart; who hath not lifted up his
soul unto vanity, nor [h]sworn deceitfully.
5 He shall receive the blessing
from the LORD, and righteousness from the
God of his salvation.
6 This *is* the generation of them that
seek him, that [i]seek thy face, [k]O Jacob.
Selah.
7 [l]Lift up your heads, O ye gates; [m]and be

[a]Exod. ix. 29; xix. 5; Deut. x. 14; Job xli. 11; Psa. l. 12; 1 Cor. x. 26, 28——[b]Gen. i. 9; Job xxxviii. 6; Psa. civ. 5; cxxxvi. 6; 2 Peter iii. 5——[c]Psa. xv. 1——[d]Isaiah xxxiii. 15, 16

[e]Hebrew, *the clean of hands*——[f]Job xvii. 9; 1 Tim. ii. 8——[g]Matt. v. 8——[h]Psa. xv. 4——[i]Psa. xxvii. 8; cv. 4——[k]Or, O God of *Jacob*——[l]Isa. xxvi. 2——[m]Psa. xcvii. 6; Hag. ii. 7; Mal. iii. 1; 1 Cor. ii. 8

NOTES ON PSALM XXIV

It is probable that this Psalm was composed on occasion of bringing the ark from the house of Obed-edom to Mount Sion, and the questions may respect the fitness of the persons who were to minister before this ark: the last verses may refer to the opening of the city gates in order to admit it. As many of the expressions here are nearly the same with those in Psalm xv., I must refer to that place for their particular illustration; though it is most likely that the two Psalms were composed on very different occasions. The first contains a *general question* relative to *who shall be saved?* This is more particular; and refers to the temple and tabernacle service, and who is fit to minister there.

Verse 1. *The earth* is *the Lord's*] He is the Creator and Governor of it; it is his own property. Men may claim districts and kingdoms of it as *their* property, but God is Lord of the soil.

The fulness thereof] "All its creatures."—*Targum.* Every tree, plant, and shrub; the silver and the gold, and the cattle on a thousand hills.

They that dwell therein.] All *human beings.*

Verse 2. *He hath founded it upon the seas*] He not only created the vast *mass,* but separated the land from the waters, so that the mountains, &c., being elevated above the waters, appear to be founded on them, and notwithstanding all the tossings and ragings of the ocean, these waters cannot prevail. It is established upon the floods, and cannot be shaken.

Verse 3. *Who shall ascend*] Who is sufficiently holy to wait in his temple? Who is fit to minister in the holy place?

Verse 4. He that *hath clean hands*] He whose conscience is irreproachable; whose heart is without deceit and uninfluenced by unholy passions.

Who hath not lifted up his soul] Who has no *idolatrous* inclination; whose faith is pure, and who conscientiously fulfils his promises and engagements.

Verse 5. *He shall receive the blessing*] Perhaps alluding to Obed-edom, at whose house the ark had been lodged, and on whom God had poured out especial blessings.

And righteousness] Mercy: every kind of necessary good. It is the mercy of God that crowns the *obedience* and *fidelity* of good men. For what made them *good* and *faithful?* God's mercy. What crowns their fidelity? God's mercy.

Verse 6. *This* is *the generation*] This is the description of people who are such as God can approve of, and delight in.

That seek thy face, O Jacob.] It is most certain that אלהי *Elohey, O God,* has been lost out of the *Hebrew* text in most MSS., but it is preserved in two of *Kennicott's* MSS., and also in the *Syriac, Vulgate, Septuagint, Æthiopic, Arabic,* and *Anglo-Saxon.* "Who seek thy face, O God of Jacob."

Selah.] That is, It is confirmed; it is true. The persons who abstain from every appearance of evil, and seek the approbation of God, are those in whom God will delight.

Verse 7. *Lift up your heads, O ye gates*] The address of those who preceded the ark, the gates being addressed instead of the *keepers* of the gates. Allusion is here made to the triumphal entry of a victorious general into the imperial city.

In the hymn of *Callimachus* to Apollo, there are two lines very much like those in the text; they convey the very same sentiments. The poet represents the god coming into his temple, and calls upon the priests to open the doors, &c.

Αυτοι νυν κατοχηες ανακλινεσθε πυλαων,
Αυται δε κληιδες· ὁ γαρ Θεος ουκ ετι μακραν;

"Fall back, ye bolts; ye pond'rous doors, give way;
For not far distant is the god of day."

Callim. Hymn in Apol., ver. 6, 7.

The whole of this hymn contains excellent sentiments even on the subject of the Psalms.

A. M. cir. 2962
B. C. cir. 1042
Davidis, Regis
Israelitarum,
cir. annum
14

ye lift up, ye everlasting doors;
and the King of glory shall
come in.
8 Who *is* this King of glory?
The LORD strong and mighty, the LORD
mighty in battle.
9 Lift up your heads, O ye
gates: even lift *them* up, ye
everlasting doors: and the King
of glory shall come in.
10 Who is this King of glory? The LORD
of hosts, he *is* the King of glory. Selah.

A. M. cir. 2962
B. C. cir. 1042
Davidis, Regis
Israelitarum,
cir. annum
14

Everlasting doors] There seems to be a reference here to something like our *portcullis*, which hangs by pullies *above* the gate, and can be let down at any time so as to prevent the gate from being forced. In the case to which the psalmist refers, the portcullis is let down, and the persons preceding the ark order it to be raised. When it is lifted up, and appears above the head or top of the gate, then the folding doors are addressed: "Be ye lift up, ye everlasting doors;" let there be no obstruction; and the mighty Conqueror, the King of glory, whose presence is with the ark, and in which the symbol of his glory appears, shall enter. Make due preparations to admit so august and glorious a Personage.

Verse 8. *Who* is *this King of glory?*] This is the answer of those who are *within*. Who is this glorious King, for whom ye demand entrance? To which they reply:—

The Lord strong and mighty, the Lord mighty in battle.] It is *Jehovah*, who is come to set up his abode in his imperial city: He who has conquered his enemies, and brought salvation to Israel. To make the matter still more solemn, and give those *without* an opportunity of describing more particularly this glorious Personage, those *within* hesitate to obey the first summons: and then it is *repeated*, ver. 9—

Lift up your heads, O ye gates; even lift them *up, ye everlasting doors; and the King of glory shall come in.*] To which a more particular question is proposed:—*Who is* HE, THIS *King of glory?* To which an answer is given that admitted of no reply. *The Lord of hosts*—he who is coming with innumerable armies, *He is this King of glory.* On which, we may suppose, the portcullis was lifted up, the gates thrown open, and the whole cavalcade admitted. This verse seems to have been spoken before the ark appeared: Who is this (זה *zeh*) King of glory? when its coming was merely announced. In the *tenth* verse the form is a little altered, because the ark, the symbol of the Divine Presence, had then arrived. Who is He, (מי הוא *mi hu*,) this King of glory? Here He is, to answer for himself. "The Lord is in his holy temple; let all the earth keep silence before him."

Though this Psalm has all the appearance of being an *unfinished piece*, yet there is a vast deal of dignity and majesty in it; and the *demands* from *without*, the *questions* from those *within*, and the *answers* to those questions, partake of the true sublime; where nature, dignity, and simplicity, are very judiciously mingled together. The whole procedure is *natural*, the *language dignified*, and the *questions* and *answers* full of *simplicity* and elevated sentiments.

Several, both among ancients and moderns, have thought this Psalm speaks of the *resurrection of our Lord*, and is thus to be understood. It is easy to apply it in this way: Jesus has conquered sin, Satan, and death, by dying. He now rises from the dead; and, as a mighty Conqueror, claims an entrance into the realms of glory, the kingdom which he has purchased by his blood; there to appear ever in the presence of God for us, to which he purposes to raise finally the innumerable *hosts* of his followers; for in reference to these, He is *the Lord of hosts;* and, in reference to his victory, He is *the Lord mighty in battle.*

ANALYSIS OF THE TWENTY-FOURTH PSALM

The subject of this Psalm is Christ, called the King of glory, ver. 7, and it has *two* parts:—

I. The first concerns Christ's lordship, which is, in general, over the whole world, ver. 1, 2; but in particular, over the Church, ver. 3 to 7.

II. An exhortation to all men to receive Christ for their King.

I. The first part of this Psalm shows that God is King of all the world; but in this kingdom he has two kinds of subjects—

1. Either all men in general: "For the earth is the Lord's, and all that therein is; the compass of the world, and they that dwell therein." And for this he gives a reason, from the creation of it. He ought to have the dominion of it, and all in it: "For he hath founded it upon the seas, and established it upon the floods."

2. But all are not his subjects in the same way. There are a people whom he has called to be his subjects in another manner. There is a mountain which he hath sanctified and chosen above all other hills to make the seat of his kingdom, viz., the *Church;* and over them that live in it he is in a more peculiar manner said to be *Lord*, than of the whole earth; and these are more properly called his servants and subjects. And yet among these there is a difference too, for some only profess to be his servants, and call him *Lord*, as hypocrites; there are some others that are his servants really and truly. And that this difference may be taken notice of, the prophet asks, *Quis?* "WHO shall ascend into the hill of the Lord?" And "WHO shall stand in his holy place?" As if he should say, Not *quisquis;* it is not *every one;* for infidels are not so much as *in* the Church. Hypocrites, howsoever in the Church, are not true members of the mystical Church; and some who come to the hill of the Lord, yet stand not in his holy place; *for many believe only for a season, and few continue faithful unto death.*

3. That it may then be truly known who they are over whom he is truly *Rex gloriæ*, "the King of glory," the prophet gives us their character, and sets down three distinctive notes by which they may be known:—

1. *Cleanness of hands:* "He that hath clean hands;" *à cæde furto, &c.;* is free from all external wicked actions. For the hand is οργανον οργανων, the organ of the organs.

2. *Purity of heart.* For external purity is not enough, except the heart, the fountain of our actions, be clean.

3. *Truth of the tongue.* Is not guilty of lies and perjuries. "He that hath clean hands and

a pure heart; who hath not lifted up his soul unto vanity, nor sworn deceitfully." After the prophet has given the character by which you may know the man, he assigns his reward, and ends with an acclamation. 1. This is he that "shall receive the blessing from the Lord, and righteousness (i. e., justification) from the God of his salvation." 2. "This is the generation of them that seek thee;" that is, these are the people of God: let others boast themselves, and please themselves as they list, yet these are the godly party; these are they "that seek thy face, O God of Jacob."

II. The second part is considered by some as an *exhortation* to all men, especially princes, nobles, and magistrates, that they receive, acknowledge, and worship Christ, as King.

1. *Lift up your heads, O ye gates;* that is, as some understand it—O ye princes that sit in the *gates*, lift up your *heads* and *hearts* to him, that the King of glory may come in.

2. To which good counsel the prophet brings in the princes asking this question: "Who is this King of glory!" to which he answers, "The Lord strong and mighty, the Lord mighty in battle." One who is able to bruise you to atoms with his iron rod, and will do so if you reject him. And that the exhortation may pierce the deeper, he doubles both it and the answer.

After all, the most natural meaning is that which is given in the notes: from which we may infer:—

1. That the regal city is in no state of safety, if it have not the *ark of the Lord*.

2. That the *ark*—even the purest form of sound words in devotion, is nothing, unless they who minister and worship have *clean hands* and *pure hearts*, endeavouring to worship God in spirit and in truth.

3. That where the right faith is professed, and the worshippers act according to its dictates, *there* is the presence and the continual indwelling of God: "Lift up your heads, O ye gates—and the King of glory shall come in."

PSALM XXV

The psalmist, in great distress, calls upon God frequently, 1–5; *prays for pardon with the strong confidence of being heard,* 6–11; *shows the blessedness of the righteous,* 12–14; *again earnestly implores the Divine mercy; and prays for the restoration of Israel,* 15–22.

A Psalm of David

A. M. cir. 3426
B. C. cir. 578
A. U. C. cir. 176
Olymp. L.
cir. annum
tertium

UNTO [a]thee, O LORD, do I lift
up my soul.
2 O my God, I [b]trust in thee:
let me not be ashamed, [c]let not
mine enemies triumph over
me.
3 Yea, let none that wait on
thee be ashamed: let them be
ashamed which transgress without cause.

[a]Psalm lxxxvi. 4; cxliii. 8; Lamentations iii. 41

[b]Psa. xxii. 5; xxxi. 1; xxxiv. 8; Isa. xxviii. 16; xlix. 23; Rom. x. 11——[c]Psa. xiii. 4

NOTES ON PSALM XXV

This Psalm seems to refer to the case of the captives in Babylon, who complain of oppression from their enemies, and earnestly beg the help and mercy of God.

It is the first of those called acrostic Psalms, i. e., Psalms each line of which begins with a several letter of the Hebrew alphabet in their common order. Of acrostic Psalms there are *seven*, viz., xxv., xxxiv., xxxvii., cxi., cxii., cxix., and cxlv. It is fashionable to be violent in encomiums on the Jews for the very *faithful manner* in which they have preserved the Hebrew Scriptures; but these encomiums are, in general, ill placed. Even this Psalm is a proof with what *carelessness* they have watched over the sacred deposit committed to their trust. The letter ו *vau* is wanting in the *fifth* verse, and ק *koph* in the *eighteenth;* the letter ר *resh* being twice inserted, once instead of ק *koph;* and a whole line added at the end, entirely out of the alphabetical series.

Verse 1. *Do I lift up my soul.*] His soul was *cast down*, and by *prayer* and *faith* he endeavours to *lift it up* to God.

Verse 2. *I trust in thee*] I depend upon thy infinite goodness and mercy for my support and salvation.

Let me not be ashamed] Hide my iniquity, and forgive my guilt.

Verse 3. *Let none that wait on thee be ashamed*] Though he had burden enough of *his own*, he felt for *others* in similar circumstances, and became an intercessor in their behalf.

Transgress without cause.] Perhaps בוגדים *bogedim* may here mean *idolatrous persons.* "Let not them that wait upon and worship thee be ashamed: but they shall be ashamed who vainly worship, or trust in false gods." See Mal. ii. 11-16. The Chaldeans have evil en-

A. M. cir. 3426
B. C. cir. 578
A. U. C. cir. 176
Olymp. L.
cir. annum
tertium

4 [d]Show me thy ways, O
LORD; teach me thy paths.
5 Lead me in thy truth, and
teach me: for thou *art* the God
of my salvation; on thee do I wait all the day.
6 Remember, O LORD, [e]thy [f]tender mercies and thy loving-kindnesses; for they *have
been* ever of old.
7 Remember not [g]the sins of my youth, nor
my transgressions: [h]according to thy mercy
remember thou me for thy goodness' sake, O
LORD.
8 [i]Good and upright *is* the
LORD: therefore will he teach
sinners in the way.
9 The meek will he guide
in judgment: and the meek will he teach
his way.
10 All the paths of the LORD *are* mercy and
truth unto such as keep his covenant and his
testimonies.
11 [k]For thy name's sake, O LORD, pardon
mine iniquity; [l]for it *is* great.
12 What man *is* he that feareth the LORD?

A. M. cir. 3426
B. C. cir. 578
A. U. C. cir. 176
Olymp. L.
cir. annum
tertium

---

[d]Exod. xxxiii. 13; Psa. v. 1; xxvii. 11; lxxxvi. 11; cxix. cxliii. 8, 10——[e]Psa. ciii. 17; cvi. 1; cvii. 1; Isa. lxiii. 15; Jer. xxxiii. 11——[f]Heb. *thy bowels*

[g]Job xiii. 26; xx. 11; Jer. iii. 25——[h]Psa. li. 1——[i]Psa lii. 9; liv. 6; lxxiii. 1, &c.——[k]Psa. xxxi. 3; lxxix. 9; cix. 21; cxliii. 11——[l]See Rom. v. 20

---

treated us, and oppressed us: they trust in their idols, let them see the vanity of their idolatry.

Verse 4. *Show me thy ways*] The psalmist wishes to *know* God's *way*, to be taught his *path*, and to be led into his *truth*. He cannot discern this *way* unless God *show* it; he cannot *learn* the *path* unless God *teach* it; and he cannot *walk* in God's *truth* unless God *lead* him: and even then, unless God *continue* to *teach*, he shall never *fully* learn the lessons of his salvation; therefore he adds, "Lead me in thy truth, and teach me;" ver. 5.

That he may get this *showing*, *teaching*, and *leading*, he comes to God, as the "God of his salvation;" and that he may not lose his labour, he "waits on him all the day." Many lose the benefit of their earnest prayers, because they do not *persevere* in them. They pray for *a time;* get remiss or discouraged; restrain prayer; and thus lose all that was already wrought for and in them.

Verse 5. *On thee do I wait*] This is the line in which ו *vau*, the sixth letter in the order of the alphabet, is lost; for the line begins with א *aleph*, אותך *othecha*, "on thee." But four of *Kennicott's* and *De Rossi's* MSS. have ואותך *veothecha*, "AND upon thee." This restores the lost ו *vau*, which signifies "and." The *Septuagint*, *Syriac*, *Vulgate*, *Arabic*, *Æthiopic*, and *Anglo-Saxon*, preserve it.

Verse 6. *Remember, O Lord, thy tender mercies, and thy loving-kindness*] The word רחמים *rachamim*, means the *commiseration* that a man feels in his bowels at the sight of distress. The second word, חסדים *chasadim*, signifies those *kindnesses* which are the offspring of a *profusion of benevolence*.

They have been *ever of old.*] Thou wert ever wont to display thyself as a ceaseless fountain of good to all thy creatures.

Verse 7. *Remember not the sins of my youth*] Those which I have committed through *inconsiderateness*, and *heat of passion*.

According to thy mercy] As it is *worthy of thy mercy* to act according to the measure, the greatness, and general practice of thy mercy; so give me an *abundant pardon, a plentiful salvation.*

For thy goodness' sake] *Goodness* is the nature of God; *mercy* flows from that *goodness.*

Verse 8. *Good and upright* is *the Lord*] He is *good* in his *nature*, and *righteous* in his *conduct.*

Therefore will he teach sinners] Because he is good, he will teach sinners, though they deserve nothing but destruction: and because he is *right*, he will *teach* them the *true way.*

Verse 9. *The meek will he guide*] ענוים *anavim*, the *poor*, the *distressed; he will lead in judgment*—he will direct them in their cause, and bring it to a happy issue, for he will show them the *way* in which they should go.

Verse 10. *All the paths of the Lord*] ארחות *orchoth* signifies the *tracks* or *ruts* made by the *wheels of wagons* by often passing over the same ground. *Mercy* and *truth* are the *paths* in which God *constantly walks* in reference to the children of men; and so *frequently* does he show them *mercy*, and so frequently does he fulfil his *truth*, that his paths are earnestly discerned. How frequent, how deeply indented, and how multiplied are those *tracks* to every *family* and *individual!* Wherever we go, we see that God's mercy and truth have *been there* by the *deep tracks* they have left behind them. But he is more abundantly merciful to those who *keep his covenant and his testimonies;* i. e., those who are conformed, not only to the letter, but to the spirit of his pure religion.

Verse 11. *For thy name's sake, O Lord, pardon*] I have sinned; I need mercy; there is no reason why thou shouldst show it, but what thou drawest from the goodness of thy own nature.

Verse 12. *That feareth the Lord*] Who has a proper apprehension of *his* holiness, justice, and truth; and who, at the same time, sees *himself* a fallen spirit, and a transgressor of God's holy law, and consequently under the curse. That is the person that truly and reverently fears God.

Him shall he teach] Such a person has a *teachable spirit.*

The way that *he shall choose.*] The way that in the course of Providence he has chosen, as the way in which he is to gain things honest in the sight of all men; God will bless him in it, and give him as much earthly prosperity as may be useful to his soul in his secular *vocation.*

A. M. cir. 3426
B. C. cir. 578
A. U. C. cir. 176
Olymp. L.
cir. annum
tertium

[m]him shall he teach in the way
that he shall choose.
13 [n]His soul [o]shall dwell at
ease; and [p]his seed shall inherit
the earth.
14 [q]The secret of the LORD *is* with them
that fear him; [r]and he will show them his
covenant.
15 [s]Mine eyes *are* ever toward the LORD;
for he shall [t]pluck my feet out of the net.
16 [u]Turn thee unto me, and have mercy
upon me; for I *am* desolate and afflicted.
17 The troubles of my heart are enlarged:
O bring thou me out of my
distresses.
18 [v]Look upon mine affliction
and my pain; and forgive all
my sins.
19 Consider mine enemies; for they are
many; and they hate me with [w]cruel hatred.
20 O keep my soul, and deliver me: [x]let me
not be ashamed; for I put my trust in thee.
21 Let integrity and uprightness preserve
me; for I wait on thee.
22 [y]Redeem Israel, O God, out of all his
troubles.

A. M. cir. 3426
B. C. cir. 578
A. U. C. cir. 176
Olymp. L.
cir. annum
tertium

---

[m]Psalm xxxvii. 23——[n]Proverbs xix. 23——[o]Hebrew, *shall lodge in goodness*——[p]Psalm xxxvii. 11, 22, 29——[q]Proverbs iii. 32; see John vii. 17; xv. 15

[r]Or, *and his covenant to make them know it*——[s]Psa. cxli. 8——[t]Heb. *bring forth*——[u]Psa. lxix. 16; lxxxvi. 16 [v]2 Sam. xvi. 12——[w]Heb. *hatred of violence*——[x]Ver. 2 [y]Psa. cxxx. 8

Verse 13. *His soul shall dwell at ease*] בטוב תלין *betob talin*, "shall lodge in goodness;" this is the *marginal* reading in our version; and is preferable to that in the text.

His seed shall inherit] His *posterity* shall be blessed. For them many prayers have been sent up to God by their pious fathers; and God has registered these prayers in their behalf.

Verse 14. *The secret of the Lord* is *with them*] סוד *sod*, the *secret assembly* of the Lord is with them that fear him; many of them have a Church in their own house.

He will show them his covenant.] He will let them see how great blessings he has provided for them that love him. Some refer this to the covenant of redemption by Christ Jesus.

Verse 15. *Mine eyes* are *ever toward the Lord*] All my expectation is from him alone. If I get at any time entangled, he will pluck my feet out of the net.

Verse 16. *Turn thee unto me*] Probably the prayer of the poor captives in Bablyon, which is continued through this and the remaining verses.

Verse 17. *The troubles of my heart are enlarged*] The evils of our captive state, instead of lessening, seem to multiply, and each to be extended.

Verse 18. *Look upon mine affliction*] See my distressed condition, and thy eye will affect thy heart.

Forgive all my sins.] My sins are the *cause* of all my sufferings; forgive these.

This is the verse which should begin with the letter ק *koph;* but, instead of it, we have ר *resh* both here, where it should *not* be, and in the next verse where it should be. Dr. *Kennicott* reads קומה *kumah*, "arise," and *Houbigant*, קצר *ketsar*, "cut short." The word which began with ק *koph* has been long lost out of the verse, as every *version* seems to have read that which now stands in the Hebrew text.

Verse 19. *Consider mine enemies*] Look upon them, and thou wilt see how impossible it is that I should be able to resist and overcome them. They are many, they hate me, and their hatred drives them to acts of *cruelty* against me.

Verse 20. *O keep my soul*] Save me from sin, and keep me alive.

Let me not be ashamed] He ends as he began; see verse 2: "Let me not be confounded, for I put my trust in thee."

Verse 21. *Let integrity and uprightness*] I wish to have a *perfect heart*, and an *upright life*. This seems to be the meaning of these two words.

Verse 22. *Redeem Israel, O God*] The people are prayed for in the preceding verses as if *one person;* now he includes the whole, lest his own personal necessities should narrow his heart, and cause him to forget his fellow sufferers.

This verse stands out of the order of the Psalm; and does not appear to have formed a part of the *alphabetical* arrangement. It is a general prayer for the redemption of Israel from captivity; and may well be applied to those of the true Israel who are seeking for complete redemption from the power, the guilt, and the pollution of sin; and from all the *troubles* that spring from it. And let it be ever known, that God alone can redeem Israel.

Analysis of the Twenty-fifth Psalm

This Psalm is a continued earnest prayer of a man or a people pressed with danger and enemies, and sensible of God's heavy displeasure against sin. It consists of *five petitions*.

I. His *first* petition is, that his "enemies may not triumph over him," ver. 2, 3.

II. His *second* is for *instruction*, ver. 4, 5, which he urges, ver. 8, 9, 10, 12, 13, 14.

III. His *third* is for *mercy* and *forgiveness*, ver. 6, 7, 11.

IV. His *fourth* is a renewal of his first, ver. 15, 16, 17, &c., with many arguments.

V. His *fifth* is for Israel in general, ver. 22.

I. He begins with the profession of his faith and confidence in God, without which there can be no prayer: "Unto thee, O Lord," &c.; he relies not on, nor seeks after, any human help. And upon this living hope, he prays—

1. For this life, that it shame him not, as it does where a man hopes, and is frustrated: "Let me not be ashamed." Make it appear that I hope not in thee in vain.

2. "Let not mine enemies triumph over me." Glorying that I am deserted. This petition he urges by this argument: The example may prove dangerous, if thou send me no help; but it will be to thy glory, if I be relieved. If he were delivered, the faith and hope of others would be confirmed; if deserted, the good would faint and fail, the wicked triumph: therefore he prays, O, let none that wait on thee be ashamed; but let them be ashamed who transgress, that is, they that do me wrong *maliciously, without any cause* being given by *myself.*

II. He petitions for *instruction*, that he may be always guided and governed by the word of God, that he sink not under the cross, but rely on God's promises.

1. "Show me thy ways, and teach me thy paths." Show me that thou often dealest severely with thy best servants: bringest down, before thou exaltest; mortifiest, before thou quickenest; and settest the cross before the crown. *Teach me*—show me, that this is *thy way.*

2. "Lead me in thy truth, and teach me." Cause me to remember that thy promises are firm and true; *yea* and *amen* to those who trust in thee. This makes me hope still: "Thou art the God of my salvation."

III. His third petition is for *mercy.* He prays for mercy, and the removal of the sin that obstructs it.

1. "Remember, O Lord, thy tender mercies, &c., which have been ever of old;" i. e., deal mercifully with me as thou hast ever done with those who flee to thee in their extremity.

2. He prays for the *remission* of the *sins* of his *youth:* "Remember not the sins of my youth." This petition he repeats, ver. 11: "For thy name's sake pardon mine iniquity;" and upon this confession: "For it is great."

The psalmist here breaks off prayer; and, to confirm his confidence, speaks of the nature and person of God. It is necessary sometimes, even in the midst of our prayers, to call to mind the nature of God, and his ways with his people, lest, through a sense of our unworthiness or great unfaithfulness, we should be discouraged. And this course David takes; he says,

1. "Good and upright is the Lord." 1. *Good,* for he receives sinners *gratis.* 2. *Upright*—constant and true in his promises; therefore he will teach sinners in the way.

2. "The meek will he guide in judgment." He will not suffer them to be tempted above their strength; will teach them what to answer; and will not proceed with rigour, but will interpret all in the most favourable sense.

3. In a word, "All the ways of the Lord are mercy and truth." 1. *Mercy,* in that he freely offers the remission of sins, the graces of his Spirit, support in distresses, and at last eternal life, to those who by faith and a good conscience walk before him: "Keep his covenant and his testimonies;" for the words of the *covenant* are: "I will be thy God, and the God of thy seed;" upon which follows: "Walk before me, and be thou perfect."

4. Upon the confidence of which promises and covenant the psalmist repeats his prayer: "O Lord, pardon mine iniquity; for it is great," ver. 11.

The psalmist now admires the happiness of him who trusts in God: "What man is he that feareth the Lord!" This happiness he sets forth by the fruits that follow his piety:—

1. The *first* fruit he shall gather is instruction and direction in his vocation, and private life: "Him shall he teach in the way," &c.

2. The *second* is, that his happiness shall not be *momentary,* but firm and lasting: "His soul shall dwell at ease."

3. The *third* is, that he shall be happy in his *posterity:* "His seed shall inherit the land."

4. The *fourth* is, that the redemption of mankind by Christ Jesus, with all the effects of it, pardon, holiness, &c., which is a secret unknown to the world, shall be revealed and applied to him: "The secret of the Lord is with them that fear him; and he will show them his covenant."

IV. Being confirmed by these promises, and cheered with these fruits, he,

1. Testifies his faith in God for deliverance: "My eyes are ever toward the Lord; he will pluck my feet out of the net."

2. He then renews his former prayer, it being nearly the same as that with which he began. It is conceived in several clauses: 1. "Turn thee unto me." 2. "Have mercy upon me." 3. "O bring me out of my distresses." 4. "Look upon my affliction and trouble, and forgive me all my sins." 5. "Consider mine enemies." 6. "O keep my soul, and deliver me." 7. "Let me not be ashamed." 8. "Let integrity and uprightness preserve me."

Petitioners, and men in misery, think they can never say enough. This makes him often *repeat* the same thing. The sum is, that God would hear and grant him defence and deliverance in his dangers; remission of sins which caused them; and protect, direct, and govern him in his troubles.

3. That he might prevail in his suit, like an excellent orator, he uses many arguments to induce God to be propitious to him:—

1. His faith and trust in his promises: "Mine eyes are ever towards the Lord."

2. The danger he was now in: "His feet were in the net."

3. He was oppressed, alone, and had none to help him: "I am desolate and afflicted."

4. His inward afflictions and pain were grievous: "The troubles of my heart are enlarged."

5. His enemies were many, powerful, merciless, cruel: "Mine enemies are many—and hate me with cruel hatred."

6. And yet I am innocent, and desire to be so; and am thy servant: "Let integrity and uprightness preserve me; for I wait upon thee."

V. The psalmist having thus, through the Psalm, prayed for himself, at last offers up a short but earnest petition for the whole Church; which proceeds from that *fellowship* or *communion* which ought to be among all saints: "Redeem Israel, O God, out of all his troubles!" Turn our captivity, and forgive the sins which have occasioned it.

PSALM XXVI

The psalmist appeals to God for his integrity, and desires to be brought to the Divine test in order to have his innocence proved, 1–3; *shows that he had avoided all fellowship with the wicked, and associated with the upright,* 4–8; *prays that he may not have his final lot with the workers of iniquity,* 9, 10; *purposes to walk uprightly before God,* 11, 12.

A Psalm of David

A. M. cir. 3426
B. C. cir. 578
A. U. C. cir. 176
Olymp. L.
cir. annum
tertium

JUDGE [a]me, O LORD; for I
have [b]walked in mine integrity: [c]I have trusted also in the
LORD; *therefore* I shall not slide.
2 [d]Examine me, O LORD, and prove me;
try my reins and my heart.
3 For thy [e]loving-kindness *is* before mine
eyes: and [f]I have walked in thy truth.
4 [g]I have not sat with vain persons, neither will I go in with dissem-
blers.
5 I have [h]hated the congregation of evil doers; [i]and will
not sit with the wicked.
6 [k]I will wash mine hands in innocency: so
will I compass thine altar, O LORD:
7 That I may publish with the voice of thanksgiving, and tell of all thy wondrous works.
8 LORD, [l]I have loved the habitation of thy

[a]Psalm vii. 8——[b]Verse 11; 2 Kings xx. 3; Proverbs xx. 7——[c]Psalm xxviii. 7; xxxi. 14; Proverbs xxix. 25 [d]Psalm vii. 9; xvii. 3; lxvi. 10; cxxxix. 23; Zechariah xiii. 9——[e]Psalm xvii. 7; xxxvi. 7; xl. 10, 11; li. 1, &c.——[f]2 Kings xx. 3——[g]Psalm i. 1; Jeremiah xv. 17 [h]Psalm xxxi. 6; cxxxix. 21, 22——[i]Psalm i. 1——[k]See Exodus xxx. 19, 20; Psalm lxxiii. 13; 1 Timothy ii. 8 [l]Psa. xxvii. 4

NOTES ON PSALM XXVI

This Psalm, and the two following, are supposed by *Calmet* to be all parts of one ode, and to relate to the time of the captivity, containing the prayers, supplications, complaints, and resolutions of the Israelites in Babylon. This is probable; but we have not evidence enough to authorize us to be nice on such points. See on the following verse.

Verse 1. *Judge me, O Lord*] There are so many strong assertions in this Psalm concerning the innocence and uprightness of its author, that many suppose he wrote it to vindicate himself from some severe reflections on his conduct, or accusations relative to plots, conspiracies, &c. This seems to render the opinion probable that attributes it to David during his exile, when all manner of false accusations were brought against him at the court of Saul.

I have walked in mine integrity] I have never plotted against the life nor property of any man; I have neither coveted nor endeavoured to possess myself of Saul's crown.

I have trusted] Had I acted otherwise, I could not have been prosperous; for thou wouldst not have worked miracles for the preservation of a wicked man.

I shall not slide.] I shall be preserved from swerving from the paths of righteousness and truth.

Verse 2. *Examine me, O Lord*] To thee I appeal; and feel no hesitation in wishing to have all the motives of my heart dissected and exposed to thy view, and to that of the world.

Verse 3. *For thy loving-kindness*] A sense of thy favour and approbation was more to my heart than thrones and sceptres; and in order to retain this blessing, *I have walked in thy truth.*

Verse 4. *I have not sat with vain persons*] מתי שוא *methey shav, men of lies, dissemblers, backbiters,* &c.

Neither will I go in with dissemblers] נעלמים *naalamim,* the *hidden ones,* the *dark designers,* the *secret plotters* and conspirators in the state.

Verse 5. *I have hated the congregation of evil doers*] I have never made one in the crowds of discontented persons; persons who, under pretence of rectifying what was wrong in the *state,* strove to subvert it, to breed general confusion, to overturn the laws, seize on private property, and enrich themselves by the spoils of the country.

Verse 6. *I will wash mine hands in innocency*] Washing the hands was frequent among the Jews, and was sometimes an action by which a man declared his innocence of any base or wicked transaction. This *Pilate* did, to protest his innocence of the mal-treatment and death of Christ. I will maintain that innocence of life in which I have hitherto walked; and take care that nothing shall be found in my heart or life that would prevent me from using the most holy ordinance, or worshipping thee in spirit and truth.

So will I compass thine altar] It is a mark of respect among the Hindoos to *walk* several times *round* a *superior,* and round a *temple.*

Verse 7. *That I may publish*] I have endeavoured to act so as always to keep a conscience void of offence towards thee and towards man. I have made a profession of faith in thee, and salvation from thee, and my *practice* gives no lie to my *profession.*

Verse 8. *Lord, I have loved the habitation of thy house*] I have carefully used thine ordinances, that I might obtain more grace to help me to persevere. And I have not been attentive to those duties, merely because they were *incumbent* on me; but *I have loved the place where thine honour dwelleth;* and my delight in thy ordinances has made my attendance as pleasant as it was profitable. This verse would be better translated, *Jehovah, I have loved the habitation of thy house, and the place of the tabernacle of thy glory.* The *habitation* must mean the *holy of holies,* where the Divine Presence was manifest; and the *place of the tabernacle* must refer to the *mercy-seat,* or the place where the *glory of the Lord* appeared between the cherubim, upon the lid or cover of the ark of the covenant. From his dwelling there, משכן *mishcan,* the *place* and the *appearance* were called שכינה *shechinah;* the dwelling of Jehovah, or that glorious appearance which was the symbol of the Divine Presence.

A. M. cir. 3426 B. C. cir. 578 A. U. C. cir. 176 Olymp. L. cir. annum tertium

house, and the place [m]where
thine honour dwelleth.
9 [n]Gather[o] not my soul with
sinners, nor my life with
[p]bloody men:
10 In whose hands *is* mischief, and their
right hand is [q]full of [r]bribes.
11 But as for me, I will
walk [s]in mine integrity: redeem me and be merciful
unto me.
12 [t]My foot standeth in an [u]even place:
[v]in the congregations will I bless the
LORD.

[m]Heb. *of the tabernacle of thy honour*——[n]Or, *Take not away*——[o]See 1 Sam. xxv. 29; Psa. xxviii. 3 [p]Heb. *men of blood*——[q]Heb. *filled with*

[r]Exod. xxiii. 8; Deut. xvi. 19; 1 Sam. viii. 3; Isa. xxxiii. 15——[s]Ver. 1——[t]Psa. xl. 2——[u]Psa. xxvii. 11 [v]Psa. xxii. 22; cvii. 32; cxi. 1

Verse 9. *Gather not my soul with sinners*] As I have never loved their company, nor followed their practice, let not my eternal lot be cast with them! I neither love them nor their ways; may I never be doomed to spend an eternity with them!

Verse 10. *Their right hand is full of bribes*] He speaks of persons in office, who took bribes to pervert judgment and justice.

Verse 11. *But as for me, I will walk in mine integrity*] Whatever I may have to do with public affairs, shall be done with the strictest attention to truth, justice, and mercy.

Redeem me] From all snares and plots laid against my life and my soul.

And be merciful unto me.] I *deserve* no good, but thou art merciful; deal with me ever in thy mercy.

Verse 12. *My foot standeth in an even place*] On the above principles I have taken my stand: to abhor evil; to cleave to that which is good; to avoid the company of wicked men; to frequent the ordinances of God; to be true and just in all my dealings with men; and to depend for my support and final salvation on the mere mercy of God. He who acts in this way, *his feet stand in an even place.*

I will bless the Lord.] In all my transactions with men, and in all my assemblings with holy people, I will speak good of the name of the Lord, having nothing but good to speak of that name.

ANALYSIS OF THE TWENTY-SIXTH PSALM

There are *four* general parts in this Psalm:—

I. An appeal of David to God to be his Judge, ver. 1, 2.

II. The causes that induced him to make the appeal. His conscious innocence, integrity, &c.

III. A petition, ver. 9, 11.

IV. His gratitude, ver. 12.

I. He begins with his appeal to God, whom he knew to be a *just Judge;* and therefore desires to be dealt with according to law: "Judge me; examine me; prove me; try me; even my reins and my heart."

II. Then he assigns two causes of it; his *integrity* and his *faith.*

1. His *faith* and confidence in God were such that he knew that the Judge of all the world would do him right. "I have trusted in the Lord; therefore, I shall not slide." I will not change my religion, though powerfully tempted to do so.

2. His *integrity:* "I have walked in my integrity." For which he assigns the cause: "Thy loving-kindness is before my eyes; I have walked in thy truth." I follow thy *word,* and the principle it lays down.

Next he sets down his integrity by an injunction of parts, which were two: 1. How he carried himself to men; 2. How he conducted himself towards God.

1. He abstained from all society, confederacy, counsels, and intimacy with wicked men; he did hate and abominate their ways: "I have not sat in counsel with vain persons, neither will I go in with dissemblers. I have hated the congregation of evil doers, and will not sit with the wicked."

2. The other degree of his *integrity* was, his *piety:* "I will wash my hands in innocence," i. e., I will worship thee; and for this end he would keep his hands from blood, oppression, &c., in order that he "might publish with the voice of thanksgiving, and tell of all the wondrous works of the Lord."

3. He mentions a second act of his piety, his *love to God's house,* and the service done in it: "O Lord, I have loved the habitation of thy house, and the place where thy honour dwelleth."

III. Upon which conscientiousness of his integrity he falls to prayer, that God would not suffer him to be polluted with the conversation of wicked men, nor involved in their punishment: "Gather not my soul with sinners."

Observe the many titles he gives to wicked men:—

1. They are *vain persons;* void of the fear of God; irreligious, ver. 4.

2. *Deep, dark men;* saying one thing with their mouth, and another with their heart, ver. 4.

3. *Malignant;* doing all for their own ends, ver. 5.

4. *Impious;* regardless of God and religion, ver. 5.

5. *Sinners;* traders in wickedness, ver. 9.

6. *Blood-thirsty* men; cruel and revengeful. ver. 9.

7. *Mischievous;* ready to execute with their *hands* what they had plotted in their *heart,* ver. 10.

8. *Lovers of bribes;* perverting judgment for the sake of money, ver. 10.

With such David will have nothing to do: "But as for me, I will walk in my integrity." *Redeem me* from such people, *and be merciful to me.*

IV. Lastly. He shows his gratitude. "My foot stands in an even place;" hitherto I am sure I am in the good way. I will *therefore praise the Lord in the congregation;* not only privately, but publicly.

My foot hath hitherto been kept right by thy grace and mercy; therefore, when thou shalt bring me back again to thy temple, I will not be ungrateful, but will sing praises to thy name in and with the great congregation. Amen.

PSALM XXVII

The righteous man's confidence in God, 1–3; *his ardent desire to have the spiritual privilege of worshipping God in his temple, because of the spiritual blessings which he expects to enjoy there,* 4–6; *his prayer to God for continual light and salvation,* 7–9; *his confidence that, though even his own parents might forsake him, yet God would not,* 10. *Therefore he begs to be taught the right way to be delivered from all his enemies, and to see the goodness of the Lord in the land of the living,* 11–13; *he exhorts others to trust in God; to be of good courage; and to expect strength for their hearts,* 14.

V. DAY. EVENING PRAYER

A Psalm of David

A. M. cir. 3426
B. C. cir. 578
A. U. C. cir. 176
Olymp. L.
cir. annum tertium

THE LORD *is* [a]my light and
[b]my salvation; whom shall
I fear? [c]the LORD *is* the strength
of my life; of whom shall I be
afraid?
2 When the wicked, *even* mine enemies and
my foes, [d]came upon me to [e]eat up my flesh,
they stumbled and fell.
3 [f]Though a host should encamp
against me, my heart shall not
fear: though war should rise
against me, in this *will* I *be* confident.
4 [g]One *thing* have I desired of the LORD,
that will I seek after; that I may [h]dwell in
the house of the LORD all the days of my life,
to behold [i]the [k]beauty of the LORD, and to
inquire in his temple.
5 For [l]in the time of trouble he shall hide

[a]Psa. lxxxiv. 11; Isa. lx. 19, 20; Mic. vii. 8——[b]Exod. xv. 2——[c]Psa. lxii. 2, 6; cxviii. 14, 21; Isa. xii. 2 [d]Heb. *approached against me*——[e]Psa. xiv. 4

[f]Psa. iii. 6——[g]Psa. xxvi. 8——[h]Psa. lxv. 4; Luke ii. 37——[i]Or, *the delight*——[k]Psa. xc. 17——[l]Psa. xxxi. 20; lxxxiii. 3; xci. 1; Isa. iv. 6

NOTES ON PSALM XXVII

In the *Hebrew* and *Chaldee* this Psalm has no other title than simply לדוד *ledavid: To* or *For David.* In the *Syriac:* "For David; on account of an infirmity which fell upon him." In the *Vulgate, Septuagint, Arabic,* and *Æthiopic,* it has this title: "A Psalm of David, before he was anointed." The *Anglo-Saxon* omits all the titles. For this title there is no authority in fact. However, it may be just necessary to state that David appears to have received the royal unction three times: 1. In Bethlehem, from the hand of Samuel, in the house of his father Jesse; 1 Sam. xvi. 13. 2. At Hebron, after the death of Saul, by the men of Judah; 2 Sam. ii. 4. 3. By the elders of Israel, at Hebron, after the death of Ishbosheth, when he was acknowledged king over all the tribes; 2 Sam. v. 3. At which of these anointings the Psalm was written, or whether before any of them, we know not; nor is the question to be decided. Some commentators say that it is a Psalm belonging to the *captivity,* and upon that system it may be well interpreted. And lastly, it has been contended that it was written by David after he had been in danger of losing his life by the hand of a gigantic Philistine, and must have perished had he not been succoured by Abishai; see the account 2 Sam. xxi. 17; and was counselled by his subjects not to go out to battle any more, *lest he should extinguish the light of Israel.* To these advisers he is supposed to make the following reply:—

Verse 1. *The Lord* is *my light and my salvation*] This light can never be extinguished by man; the Lord is my salvation, my safeguard, my shield, and my defence; of whom then should I be afraid?

Verse 2. *When the wicked—came upon me*] Near as I appeared to you to be in danger of losing my life, I was safe enough in the hands of the Lord; and those who thought to *have eaten me up, stumbled,* failed of their purpose, and *fell;* the Philistine lost his own life.

Verse 3. *Though a host should encamp against me*] I am so confident of the Almighty's protection, that were I *alone,* and encompassed by a host, I would not fear. I am in the hand of God; and while in that hand, I am safe.

Verse 4. *One* thing *have I desired*] If I am grown too old, and from that circumstance unable to serve my country, I shall then prefer a retirement to the tabernacle, there to serve God the rest of my days. There I shall behold his glory, and there I may *inquire* and get important answers respecting Israel.

But though these words may be thus interpreted, on the above supposition, that David penned the Psalm on the occasion of his escape from the Philistine, and the desire expressed by his subjects that he should go no more out to war; yet it appears that they more naturally belong to the *captivity,* and that this verse especially shows the earnest longing of the captives to return to their own land, that they might enjoy the benefit of Divine worship.

Verse 5. *He shall hide me in his pavilion*] בסכה *besuccoh, in his tabernacle.* I would make his temple my residence; I would dwell with God, and be in continual safety. *Pavilion* comes from *papilio* and παπιλιων, a *butterfly.* It signifies a *tent* made of cloth stretched out on poles, which in form resembles in some measure the insect above named.

In the secret of his tabernacle] Were there no other place, he would put me in the *holy of holies,* so that an enemy would not dare to approach me.

He shall set me upon a rock.] He shall so *strengthen* and *establish* me, that my enemies shall not be able to prevail against me. He shall hide me where they cannot find me, or put me out of the reach of the fiery darts of the wicked. He who lives *nearest to God* suffers least from temptation. "Draw nigh to God, and he will draw nigh to thee: resist the devil, and he will flee from thee."

A. M. cir. 3426
B. C. cir. 578
A. U. C. cir. 176
Olymp. L.
cir. annum
tertium

me in his pavilion: in the secret
of his tabernacle shall he hide
me; he shall [m]set me upon a rock.
6 And now shall [n]mine head
be lifted up above mine enemies round about
me; therefore will I offer in his tabernacle
sacrifices [o]of joy; I will sing, yea, I will sing
praises unto the LORD.

7 Hear, O LORD, *when* I cry
with my voice: have mercy also
upon me, and answer me.
8 [p]*When thou saidst,* [q]Seek
ye my face; my heart said unto thee, Thy
face, LORD, will I seek.
9 [r]Hide not thy face *far* from me; put not
thy servant away in anger: thou hast been [s]my

A. M. cir. 3426
B. C. cir. 578
A. U. C. cir. 176
Olymp. L.
cir. annum
tertium

[m]Psa. xl. 2——[n]Psa. iii. 3——[o]Heb. *of shouting*——[p]Or, *My heart said unto thee, Let my face seek thy face,* &c.

[q]Psa. xxiv. 6; cv. 4——[r]Psa. lxix. 17; cxliii. 7——[s]Psa. xl. 7; lxiii. 7; lxx. 5

Verse 6. *Now shall mine head be lifted up*] We shall most assuredly be redeemed from this captivity, and restored to our own land, and to the worship of our God in his own temple. There shall we offer sacrifices of joy; we will sing praises unto the Lord, and acknowledge that it is by his might and mercy alone that we have been delivered.

Verse 7. *Hear, O Lord,* when *I cry*] This is the utmost that any man of common sense can expect—*to be heard when he cries.* But there are multitudes who suppose God will bless them whether they *cry or not;* and there are others, and not a few, who although they *listlessly pray* and *cry* not, yet imagine God must and will hear them! God will answer them that *pray and cry;* those who do *not* are most likely to be without the blessings which they so much need.

Verse 8. When thou saidst, *Seek ye my face*] How much labour and skill have been employed to make sense of this verse as it stands in our translation! The original words are the following, from which our Version has been forcibly extracted:—

לך אמר לבי בקשו פני את פניך יהוה אבקש *lecha amar libbi bakkeshu panai; eth paneycha, Yehovah, abakkesh;* of which I believe the true rendering to be as follows: "Unto thee, my heart, he hath said, Seek ye my face. Thy face, O Jehovah, I will seek. O my heart, God hath commanded thee to seek his face." Then, *his face I will seek.* Which may be paraphrased thus: *Unto thee,* his Church, God *hath said, Seek ye,* all who compose it, *my face.* To which *I,* his Church, have answered, *Thy face, O Jehovah, I will seek.* On referring to Archbishop *Secker,* I find that he, and indeed Bishop *Horsley,* are of the same mind.

I had formerly proposed another method of reading this difficult verse. Suspecting that some *error* had got into the text, for בקשו פני *bakkeshu panay,* "seek ye my face," I had substituted אבקש פניך *abakkesh paneycha,* "I will seek thy face;" or with the *Vulgate* and *Septuagint,* בקשתי פניך *bakkesti paneycha,* "I have sought thy face," *exquisivit te facies mea,* *Εξεζητησα το προσωπον σου.* And this small alteration seemed to make a good sense: "My heart said unto thee, I have sought thy face, (or, I will seek thy face,) and thy face, O Lord, I will seek." I have not only *done* what it was my duty and interest to do, but I will *continue to do* it. Some have proposed to *mend* the text thus: לך לך אמר לבי *lech lecha, amar libbi,* "Go to, saith my heart," נבקש פני יהוה *nebakkesh peney Yehovah,* "Let us seek the face of Jehovah." This is rather a violent emendation, and is supported by neither MSS. nor *Versions.* The whole verse is wanting in one of Dr. Kennicott's MSS. On the whole I prefer what is first proposed, and which requires no alteration in the text; next, that of the *Vulgate* and *Septuagint.*

The old *Psalter* paraphrases thus: **Til the saide my hert, the my face soght: thy face, lord, I sal seke.** "The gernyng of my hert that spekes til god, and he anely heres: saide **til the my face,** that es my presence soght the and na nother thyng. And fra now I sal seke thy face lastandly, til my dede; and that I fynd my sekyng:" i. e., To thee, said my heart; thee my face sought: thy face, O Lord, I shall seek. "**The gerning of my hert,** that spekes til God, and he anely heres, **til the my face;** that es, my presence soght the and no nother thyng: **and fra now I sal seke thy face** lastandly, til my dede, and that I fynd my sekyng:" i. e., The yearning strong desire of my heart, which speaks to God, and he alone hears; my face is to thee; that is, myself sought thee, and none other thing, and from now I shall seek thee lastingly till my death, and till that I find what I seek.

Verse 9. *Hide not thy face—from me*] As my face is towards thee wheresoever I am, so let thy face be turned towards me. In a Persian MS. poem entitled شاه وگدا *Shah we Gudda,* "The King and the Beggar," I have found a remarkable couplet, most strangely and artificially involved, which expresses exactly the same sentiment:—

روي ما سوي تست از همه رو
سوي ما روي تست از همه سو

One meaning of which is—

OUR *face is towards* THEE in all our ways;
THY *face is towards* US in all our intentions.

Something similar, though not the same sentiment is in *Hafiz,* lib. i., gaz. v., cap. 2:—

با مريدان رو بسوي كعبه چون اريم چون
رو بسوي خانه خمار دارد پير ما

How can we with the disciples *turn our face towards* the kaaba,
When our spiritual instructer *turns his face towards* the wine-cellar?

I shall subjoin a higher authority than either:—

Ὁτι οφθαλμοι Κυριου επι δικαιους,
Και ωτα αυτου εις δεησιν αυτων·
Προσωπον δε Κυριου επι ποιουντας κακα.
1 Pet. iii. 12.

A. M. cir. 3426 B. C. cir. 578 A. U. C. cir. 176 Olymp. L. cir. annum tertium

help; leave me not, neither forsake me, O God of my salvation.
10 [t]When my father and my mother forsake me, then the LORD [u]will take me up.
11 [v]Teach me thy way, O LORD, and lead me in a [w]plain path, because of [x]mine enemies.
12 [y]Deliver me not over unto the will of mine enemies: for [z]false witnesses are risen up against me, and such as [a]breathe out cruelty.
13 *I had fainted,* unless I had believed to see the goodness of the LORD [b]in the land of the living.
14 [c]Wait on the LORD: be of good courage, and he shall strengthen thine heart: wait, I say, on the LORD.

---

[t]Isa. xlix. 15——[u]Heb. *will gather me;* Isa. xl. 11——[v]Psa. xxv. 4; lxxxvi. 11; cxix.——[w]Heb. *a way of plainness;* Psa. xxvi. 12——[x]Heb. *those which observe me;* Psa. v. 8; liv. 5——[y]Psa. xxxv. 25

[z]1 Sam. xxii. 9; 2 Sam. xvi. 7, 8; Psa. xxxv. 11——[a]Acts ix. 1——[b]Psa. lvi. 13; cxvi. 9; cxlii. 5; Jer. xi. 19; Ezek. xxvi. 20——[c]Psa. xxxi. 24; lxii. 1, 5; cxxx. 5; Isa. xxv. 9; Hab. ii. 3

For the *eyes of the Lord* are *upon* the righteous;
And *his ears* to their supplication:
And the *face of the Lord* is *upon* the workers of evil.

Verse 10. *When my father and my mother forsake me*] Or, more literally, "For my father and my mother have forsaken me; but the Lord hath gathered me up." My parents were my protectors *for a time;* but the Lord has been my Protector *always.* There is no time in which I do not fall under his merciful regards.

Verse 11. *Teach me thy way*] Let me know the gracious designs of thy providence towards me, that my heart may submit to thy will.

And lead me in a plain path] In the path of righteousness, because of mine enemies, who watch for my halting.

Verse 12. *Deliver me not over unto the will of mine enemies*] *To their soul* בנפש *benephesh;* their whole soul thirsts for my destruction. Let them not be gratified. They have suborned witnesses against me, but they are false witnesses: unmask their wickedness, and confound their counsels.

Verse 13. I had fainted, *unless I had believed*] The words in italics are supplied by our translators; but, far from being necessary, they injure the sense. Throw out the words *I had fainted,* and leave a *break* after the verse, and the elegant figure of the psalmist will be preserved: "Unless I had believed to see the goodness of the Lord in the land of the living" ——What! what, alas! should have become of me!

Dr. *Hammond* has observed that there is a remarkable elegance in the original, which, by the use of the beautiful figure *aposiopesis,* makes an abrupt breaking off in the midst of a speech. He compares it to the speech of *Neptune* to the winds that had raised the tempest to drown the fleet of Æneas.—*Æneid.* lib. i., ver. 131.

Eurum ad se zephyrumque vocat: dehinc talia fatur;
Tantane vos generis tenuit fiducia vestri?
Jam cœlum terramque, meo sine numine, venti,
Miscere, et tantas audetis tollere moles?
Quos ego—sed motos præstat componere fluctus.

To Eurus and the western blast he cried,
Does your high birth inspire this boundless pride?
Audacious winds! without a power from me,
To raise at will such mountains on the sea?
Thus to confound heaven, earth, the air, and main;
Whom I——but, first, I'll calm the waves again.
PITTS.

Verse 14. *Wait on the Lord*] All ye who are in distress, *wait on the Lord.* Take me for an example. I waited on him, and *he strengthened my heart;* wait ye on him, and he *will strengthen your heart.* You cannot be unsuccessful; fear not. *Wait, I say, on the Lord;* wait for his succour in doing his will. *Age viriliter,* says the *Vulgate;* act like a man, *hope, believe, work,* and *fear not.*

ANALYSIS OF THE TWENTY-SEVENTH PSALM

There are *four* general *parts* in this Psalm. David shows,

I. How free he is from fear in any danger; and he shows also the cause of his confidence, ver. 1, 2, 3.

II. He expresses his love to God's house and his religion, ver. 4, 5, 6.

III. He prays for succour and support, ver. 7, &c.

IV. He exhorts others to dependence on the Lord, ver. 14.

I. It is possible (independently of the reason given in the notes) that some person, friend or foe, might ask David how he felt during the persecutions raised against him by Saul? To whom he may be supposed to return this answer: "I was never disheartened, never in despair; and the reason was, God was my *Light* to guide me, my *Rock* to save me, and my *Strength* to sustain and support me: 'The Lord is my light,' &c." And this he amplifies in the next two verses: 1. By *experience:* he had already found this true: "When the wicked, even mine enemies, came upon me to eat up my flesh, they stumbled and fell." 2. He puts a *case:* "Though a host should encamp against me, my heart shall not fear; though war should rise against me, in this will I be confident."

The arguments for his confidence were, 1. God's *goodness,* ver. 1. 2. His own *experience,* ver. 2. To which he adds, 3. What *God would do for him.*

1. He would hide him in his tabernacle, ver. 5.
2. That though his father and mother should forsake him, God would take him up, ver. 10.
3. That he should see the *goodness* of God in the land of the living, ver. 13.

II. He expresses his great love and affection to the house of God: "One thing I have desired," and in this he was constant. "THAT (emphatically) I will seek after; that I may dwell in the house of the Lord all the days of my life." For *three* ends:—

1. "To behold the beauty of the Lord." To taste how good and gracious he is.

2. "To inquire in his temple." There to search the mind of God.

3. "To offer in his temple sacrifices of joy, and to sing praises to the Lord."

And this was another argument of his security: "For in the time of trouble he will hide me in his pavilion—he shall set me upon a rock, and my head shall be lifted up." And—

III. He prays for succour and support.

1. For *audience*, and an *answer:* "Hear, O Lord, when I cry; have mercy upon me, and answer me."

2. The *ground* of his prayer; his having willingly received the commandment of God: "He hath said, Seek ye my face. Thy face, O Lord, will I seek."

3. The *matter* of his prayer in *general:* "Hide not thy face from me; put not thy servant away in anger." In which he had good hope of success from former experience. "Thou hast been my help;" be to me now as thou hast been: "Leave me not, nor forsake me, O God of my salvation," &c.

4. The *matter* of his prayer in *particular:* "Teach me thy way, O God; lead me in a plain path." That is, teach me what to do that I may please thee, and "lead me in a plain path," that I may escape the snares of my enemies. "Deliver me not over to their will," for they seek my ruin. 1. They are perjured men: "False witnesses have risen up again me." 2. They are mischievously bent: "They breathe out cruelty."

5. And their cruelty and falsehood are so great that "unless I had believed to see the goodness of the Lord in the land of the living," what would have become of me!

IV. He concludes with an *exhortation* that all others would consider his example, and in their greatest extremities be courageous, and put their trust in God as he did: "Wait on the Lord, be of good courage, and he shall strengthen thy heart; wait, I say, on the Lord." Be an expectant; for he that has promised to come will come, and will not tarry. But wait *actively;* be not *idle.* Use the *means* of grace; *read, hear, pray, believe, work.* Acknowledge him in all thy ways, and he will direct thy steps. They that wait upon the Lord shall never be confounded.

PSALM XXVIII

A righteous man in affliction makes supplication to God, and complains of the malice of his enemies, 1–4; *whom he describes as impious, and whose destruction he predicts,* 5. *He blesses God for hearing his prayers, and for filling him with consolation,* 6, 7; *then prays for God's people,* 8, 9.

A Psalm of David

A. M. cir. 3426
B. C. cir. 578
A. U. C. cir. 176
Olymp. L. cir. annum tertium

UNTO thee will I cry, O LORD my rock; [a]be not silent [b]to me: [c]lest, *if* thou be silent to me, I become like them that go down into the pit.

2 Hear the voice of my supplications, when I cry unto thee, [d]when I lift up my hands [e]toward [f]thy holy oracle.

[a]Psa. lxxxiii. 1——[b]Heb. *from me*——[c]Psa. lxxxiv. 4; cxliii. 7——[d]1 Kings vi. 22, 23; viii. 28, 29; Psa. v. 7

[e]Or, *toward the oracle of thy sanctuary*——[f]Psalm cxxxviii. 2

NOTES ON PSALM XXVIII

This Psalm is of the same complexion with the two preceding; and belongs most probably to the times of the captivity, though some have referred it to David in his persecutions. In the *five* first verses the author prays for support against his enemies, who appear to have acted treacherously against him. In the *sixth* and *seventh* he is supposed to have gained the victory, and returns with songs of triumph. The *eighth* is a chorus of the people sung to their conquering *king.* The *ninth* is the prayer of the king for his people.

Verse 1. *O Lord my rock*] צורי *tsuri* not only means *my rock,* but *my fountain,* and the *origin* of all the good I possess.

If *thou be silent*] If thou do not answer in such a way as to leave no doubt that thou hast heard me, I shall be as a dead man. It is a modern refinement in theology which teaches that no man *can know* when God hears and answers his prayers, but by an *induction of particulars,* and by an *inference* from his *promises.* And, on this ground, how can any man fairly presume that he is heard or answered at all? May not his *inductions* be no other than the *common occurrences* of *providence?* And may not *providence* be no more than the *necessary occurrence of events?* And is it not possible, on this skeptic ground, that there is *no God* to hear or answer? True religion knows nothing of these abominations; it teaches its votaries to pray to God, to expect an answer from him, and to look for the Holy Spirit to bear witness with their spirits that they are the sons and daughters of God.

Verse 2. *Toward thy holy oracle.*] דביר קדשך *debir kodshecha; debir* properly means that place in the holy of holies from which God gave oracular answers to the high priest. This is a presumptive proof that there was a *temple* now standing; and the custom of stretching out the hands in prayer *towards the temple,* when the Jews were at a distance from it, is here referred to.

A. M. cir. 3426
B. C. cir. 578
A. U. C. cir. 176
Olymp. L.
cir. annum
tertium

3 [g]Draw me not away with the wicked, and with the workers of iniquity, [h]which speak peace to their neighbours, but mischief *is* in their hearts.

4 [i]Give them according to their deeds, and according to the wickedness of their endeavours: give them after the work of their hands; render to them their desert.

5 Because [k]they regard not the works of the LORD, nor the operation of his hands, he shall destroy them, and not build them up.

6 Blessed *be* the LORD, because he hath heard the voice of my supplications.

7 The LORD *is* [l]my strength and my shield; my heart [m]trusted in him, and I am helped: therefore my heart greatly rejoiceth; and with my song will I praise him.

8 The LORD *is* [n]their strength, and he *is* the [o]saving [p]strength of his anointed.

9 Save thy people, and bless [q]thine inheritance: [r]feed them also, [s]and lift them up for ever.

[g]Psa. xxvi. 9——[h]Psa. xii. 2; lv. 21; lxii. 4; Jer. ix. 8——[i]2 Tim. iv. 14; Rev. xviii. 6——[k]Job xxxiv. 27; Isa. v. 12——[l]Psa. xviii. 2——[m]Psa. xiii. 5; xxii. 4

[n]Or, *his strength*——[o]Heb. *strength of salvations*——[p]Psa. xx. 6——[q]Deut. ix. 29; 1 Kings viii. 51, 53——[r]Or, *rule;* Psa. lxxviii. 71——[s]Ezra i. 4

Verse 3. *Draw me not away*] Let me not be involved in the punishment of the wicked.

Verse 4. *Give them*] Is the same as *thou wilt give them;* a prophetic declaration of what their lot will be.

Verse 5. *They regard not the works of the Lord*] They have no knowledge of the true God, either as to his *nature,* or as to his *works.*

He shall destroy them, and not build them up.] This is a remarkable prophecy, and was literally fulfilled: the Babylonian empire was destroyed by Cyrus, and never built up again; for he founded the Persian empire on its ruins. Even the place where Babylon stood is now no longer known.

Verse 7. *The Lord* is *my strength*] I have the fullest persuasion that he hears, will answer, and will save me.

Verse 8. *The Lord* is *their strength*] Instead of למו *lamo, to them,* eight MSS. of *Kennicott* and *De Rossi* have לעמו *leammo, to his people;* and this reading is confirmed by the *Septuagint, Syriac, Vulgate, Æthiopic, Arabic,* and *Anglo-Saxon.* This makes the passage more precise and intelligible; and of the truth of the reading there can be no reasonable doubt. "The Lord is the strength of his PEOPLE, and the saving strength of his anointed." Both *king* and *people* are protected, upheld, and saved by him.

Verse 9. *Save thy people*] Continue to preserve them from all their enemies; from idolatry, and from sin of every kind.

Bless thine inheritance] They have taken thee for their God; thou hast taken them for thy people.

Feed them] רעה *raah* signifies both to *feed* and to *govern. Feed them,* as a *shepherd* does his *flock; rule them,* as a *father* does his *children.*

Lift them up for ever.] Maintain thy true Church; let no enemy prevail against it. Preserve and magnify them for ever. *Lift them up:* as hell is the bottomless pit in which damned spirits sink down for ever; or, as Chaucer says, *downe all downe;* so heaven is an endless height of glory, in which there is an eternal rising or exaltation. Down, all down; up, all up; for ever and ever.

ANALYSIS OF THE TWENTY-EIGHTH PSALM

There are *three* parts in this Psalm:—

I. A prayer, ver. 1-6.

II. A thanksgiving, ver. 6-9.

III. A prayer for the Church, ver. 9.

I. The first part is a prayer to God; in which he first requests audience, ver. 2: "Hear me." And his prayer is so described, that it sets forth most of the conditions requisite in one that prays:—

1. The *object*—GOD: "Unto thee, O Lord, do I cry."

2. His *faith:* "To thee I cry, who art my rock."

3. His *fervour:* It was an ardent and vehement prayer: "I cry."

4. *Humility;* it was a supplication: "Hear the voice of my supplication."

5. His *gesture:* "I lift up my hands."

6. According to God's ORDER: "Towards thy holy temple."

1. The argument he uses to procure an audience; the danger he was in: "Lest, if thou be silent, I become like them that go down to the pit."

2. Then he expresses what he prays for, which is, that either

1. He might not be corrupted by the fair persuasions of hypocrites:

2. Or that he might not be partaker of their punishments: "Draw me not away with the wicked." Upon whom he sets this mark: "Who speak peace—but mischief is in their hearts."

3. Against whom he uses this imprecation, which is the second part of his prayer: "Give them according to their own deeds," &c.

4. For which he gives this reason: They were enemies to God and to his religion; far from repentance, and any hope of amendment: "They regard not the words of the Lord, nor the operation of his hands; therefore he shall destroy them, and not build them up."

II. Then follows an excellent form of thanksgiving, which he begins with "Blessed be the Lord;" and assigns the reasons, which express the chief parts of thanksgiving.

1. That God heard him: "He hath heard the voice of my supplication."

2. That he would be his Protector: "The Lord is my strength and my shield."

3. For his grace of confidence: "My heart trusted in him."

4. That from him he had relief: "I am helped."

5. The testification and annunciation of this gratitude: "Therefore my heart greatly re-

joiceth; and with my song will I praise him." He remembers the indenture: "I will DELIVER THEE,—thou shalt PRAISE ME." And, therefore, with heart and tongue he gives thanks.

6. And that God might have all the honour, he repeats what he said before: "The Lord is their strength," &c., that is, of all them that were with him.

III. He concludes with a prayer, in which he commends the whole Church to God's care and tuition.

1. "Save thy people," in the midst of these tumults and distractions.

2. "Bless thine inheritance;" that they increase in knowledge, piety, and secular prosperity.

3. "Feed them:" Give them a godly king.

4. "Lift them up for ever:" Make their name famous among the Gentiles; let them increase and multiply till thy Church embraces all nations, and kindreds, and people, and tongues. This hath the Lord promised.

PSALM XXIX

The psalmist calls upon the great and mighty to give thanks unto God, and to worship him in the beauty of holiness, on account of a tempest that had taken place, 1, 2. *He shows the wonders produced by a thunderstorm, which he calls the* voice of God, 3–9. *Speaks of the majesty of God,* 10; *and points out the good he will do to his people,* 11.

A Psalm of David

A. M. cir. 2985 B. C. cir. 1019 Davidis, Regis Israelitarum, cir. annum 37

GIVE [a]unto the LORD, O [b]ye
mighty, give unto the LORD
glory and strength.

2 Give unto the LORD [c]the
glory due unto his name; worship the LORD
[d]in [e]the beauty of holiness.

3 The voice of the LORD *is*
upon the waters: [f]the God of
glory thundereth: the LORD *is*
upon [g]many waters.

4 The voice of the LORD *is* [h]powerful; the
voice of the LORD *is* [i]full of majesty.

5 The voice of the LORD breaketh the ce-

[a]1 Chron. xvi. 28, 29; Psa. xcvi. 7, 8, 9——[b]Heb. *ye sons of the mighty*——[c]Heb. *the honour of his name* [d]Or, *in his glorious sanctuary*

[e]2 Chronicles xx. 21——[f]Job xxxvii. 4, 5 [g]Or, *great waters*——[h]Heb. *in power*——[i]Heb. *in majesty*

NOTES ON PSALM XXIX

In the Hebrew, this is called *A Psalm for David.* The *Vulgate* says, "A Psalm of David, when the tabernacle was completed." The *Septuagint* says: "A Psalm of David, at the going out or exodus of the tabernacle." The *Arabic* states it to be "A prophecy concerning the incarnation; and concerning the ark and the tent." Num. v. 12. The *Syriac,* "A Psalm of David, concerning oblation." The Psalm was probably written to commemorate the abundant rain which fell in the days of David, after the heavens had been shut up for three years; 2 Sam. xxi. 1-10.

Verse 1. *O ye mighty*] בני אלים *beney elim,* "sons of the strong ones," or "sons of rams." The *Chaldee* has, "Ye hosts of angels, sons of God." The *Vulgate* has, "Offer to the Lord, ye sons of God; offer to the Lord the sons of rams;" in this rendering agree the *Septuagint, Æthiopic, Arabic,* and *Anglo-Saxon.* The old Psalter has, **Bringes til Lord ye goddes sonnes; brynges til Lord sonnes of wether:** which it paraphrases thus: that es, yourself, sonnes of apostles, that war leders of goddes folk; qwam ye study to folow.

Glory and strength.] Ascribe all excellence and might to him.

The whole Psalm is employed in describing the effects produced by a thunder-storm which had lately taken place.

Verse 2. *The glory due unto his name*] Rather, *the glory of his name.* His name is *Mercy;* his nature is *love.* Ascribe *mercy, love, power,* and *wisdom* to him. All these are implied in the name *Jehovah.*

In the beauty of holiness.] בהדרת קדש *behadrath kodesh,* "the beautiful garments of holiness." Let the priests and Levites put on their best and cleanest apparel; and let the whole service be conducted in such a way as to be no dishonour to the Divine Majesty. The *Vulgate* and others read, *In the palace of his holiness.* Let all go to the temple, and return thanks to God for their preservation during this dreadful storm. See on ver. 9.

Verse 3. *The voice of the Lord*] THUNDER, so called, Exod. ix. 23, 28, 29; Job xxxvii. 4; Psa. xviii. 13; Isa. xxx. 30. On this subject see the note on Job xxxvii. 4, where there is a particular description of the nature and generation of thunder; and of the *lightning, clap, rain,* and other *phenomena* which accompany it.

Upon many waters.] The clouds, which Moses calls the waters which are above the firmament.

Verse 4. Is *powerful*] There is no agent in universal nature so powerful as the electric fluid. It destroys life, tears castles and towers to pieces, rends the strongest oaks, and cleaves the most solid rocks: universal animate nature is awed and terrified by it. To several of these effects the psalmist here refers; and for the illustration of the whole I must refer to the above notes on Job.

Full of majesty.] No sound in nature is so tremendous and majestic as that of *thunder;* it is the most fit to represent the voice of God.

Verse 5. *Breaketh the cedars*] Very tall trees attract the lightning from the clouds, by which

A. M. cir. 2985 B. C. cir. 1019 Davidis, Regis Israelitarum, cir. annum 37

dars; yea, the LORD breaketh
[k]the cedars of Lebanon.
6 [l]He maketh them also to
skip like a calf; Lebanon and
[m]Sirion like a young unicorn.
7 The voice of the LORD [n]divideth the flames
of fire.
8 The voice of the LORD shaketh the wilderness; the LORD shaketh the wilderness of
[o]Kadesh.
9 The voice of the LORD maketh [p]the hinds [q]to calve, and
discovereth the forests: and in
his temple [r]doth every one speak
of *his* glory.
10 The LORD [s]sitteth upon the flood; yea,
[t]the LORD sitteth King for ever.
11 [u]The LORD will give strength unto his
people; the LORD will bless his people with
peace.

---

[k]Isa. ii. 13——[l]Psa. cxiv. 4——[m]Deut. iii. 9——[n]Heb. *cutteth out*——[o]Num. xiii. 26——[p]Job xxxix. 1, 2, 3——[q]Or, *to be in pain*——[r]Or, *every whit of it uttereth*, &c.——[s]Gen. vi. 17; Job xxxviii. 8, 25——[t]Psa. x. 16——[u]Psa. xxviii. 8

---

they are often torn to pieces. *Woods* and *forests* give dreadful proof of this after a thunder-storm.

Verse 7. *Divideth the flames of fire.*] The forked zigzag lightning is the cause of *thunder;* and in a thunder-storm these lightnings are variously dispersed, smiting houses, towers, trees, men, and cattle, in different places.

Verse 8. *The wilderness of Kadesh.*] This was on the frontiers of Idumea and Paran. There may be a reference to some terrible thunder-storm and earthquake which had occurred in that place.

Verse 9. *Maketh the hinds to calve*] Strikes terror through all the tribes of animals; which sometimes occasions those which are pregnant to cast their young. This, I believe, to be the whole that is meant by the text. I meddle not with the *fables* which have been published on this subject both by *ancients* and *moderns.*

Discovereth the forests] Makes them sometimes evident in the darkest night, by the sudden flash; and often by setting them on fire.

And in his temple] Does this refer to the effect which a dreadful thunder-storm often produces? Multitudes run to places of worship as asylums in order to find safety, and pray to God. See on ver. 2.

Verse 10. *The Lord sitteth upon the flood*] יהוה למבול ישב *Yehovah lammabbul yashab,* "Jehovah sat upon the deluge." It was Jehovah that commanded those waters to be upon the earth. He directed the storm; and is here represented, after all the confusion and tempest, as sitting on the floods, appeasing the fury of the jarring elements; and reducing all things, by his governing influence, to regularity and order.

Sitteth king for ever.] He governs universal nature; whatsoever he wills he does, in the heavens above, in the earth beneath, and in all deep places. Every phenomenon is under his government and control. There is something very like this in Virgil's description of Neptune appeasing the storm raised by Juno for the destruction of the fleet of Æneas. See at the end of this Psalm.

Verse 11. *The Lord will give strength*] Prosperity in our secular affairs; success in our enterprises; and his blessing upon our fields and cattle.

The Lord will bless his people with peace.] Give them victory over their enemies, and cause the nations to be at peace with them; so that they shall enjoy uninterrupted prosperity. The plentiful rain which God has now sent is a foretaste of his future blessings and abundant mercies.

In the note on ver. 10 I have referred to the following description taken from Virgil. Did he borrow some of the chief ideas in it from the 29th Psalm? The reader will observe several coincidences.

Interea magno misceri murmure pontum,
Emissamque hyemem sensit Neptunus, et imis
Stagna refusa vadis: graviter commotus, et alto
Prospiciens, summa placidum caput extulit unda.
Disjectam Æneæ toto videt æquore classem,
Fluctibus oppressos Troas, cœlique ruina.

* * * * *

Eurum ad se zephyrumque vocat: dehinc talia fatur

* * * * *

Sic ait: et dicto citius tumida æquora placat,
Collectasque fugat nubes, solemque reducit.
Cymothoë simul, et Triton adnixus acuto
Detrudunt naves scopulo; levat ipse tridenti;
Et vastas aperit syrtes, et temperat æquor,
Atque rotis summas levibus perlabitur undas.

* * * * *

Sic cunctus pelagi cecidit fragor, æquora postquam
Prospiciens genitor, cæloque invectus aperto,
Flectit equos, curruque volans dat lora secundo.
Æn. lib. i., ver. 124.

"Mean time, imperial Neptune heard the sound
Of raging billows breaking on the ground.
Displeased, and fearing for his watery reign,
He rears his awful head above the main,
Serene in majesty; then rolled his eyes
Around the space of earth, of seas, and skies.
He saw the Trojan fleet dispersed, distressed,
By stormy winds and wintry heaven oppressed.

* * * * *

He summoned Eurus and the Western Blast,
And first an angry glance on both he cast;
Then thus rebuked.

* * * * *

He spoke; and while he spoke, he soothed the sea,
Dispelled the darkness, and restored the day.
Cymothoë, Triton, and the sea-green train
Of beauteous nymphs, and daughters of the main,

Clear from the rocks the vessels with their
hands;
The god himself with ready trident stands,
And opes the deep, and spreads the moving
sands;
Then heaves them off the shoals: where'er he
guides
His finny coursers, and in triumph rides,
The waves unruffle, and the sea subsides.

*   *   *   *   *

So when the father of the flood appears,
And o'er the seas his sovereign trident rears,
Their fury fails: he skims the liquid plains
High on his chariot; and with loosened reins,
Majestic moves along, and awful peace maintains.

DRYDEN.

Our God, Jehovah, sitteth upon the flood: yea, Jehovah sitteth King for ever.

The heathen god is drawn by his *sea-horse*, and *assisted* in his work by *subaltern deities:* Jehovah sits on the flood an everlasting Governor, ruling all things by his *will*, maintaining order, and dispensing strength and peace to his people. The description of the Roman poet is fine; that of the Hebrew poet, majestic and sublime.

ANALYSIS OF THE TWENTY-NINTH PSALM

There are two *parts* in this Psalm:—

I. The *exhortation* itself, ver. 1, 2.

II. The *reasons* on which it is founded. These are drawn,

1. From his *power*, ver. 3, to ver. 11.

2. From the *protection* he affords to his people, ver. 11.

I. The *exhortation*, which is singular. It proceeds from a king, and not from a common man; a prince, a great prince; and reminds princes and great men that there is *One greater than they;* and that, therefore, they should yield unto him his *due honour and worship.*

1. That they *freely* yield and *give* it up: for which he is very earnest, as appears from the urged *repetition, give, give, give.*

2. That in *giving* this, they must understand they are giving him no more than *his due:* "Give him the honour due to his name."

3. *What* they are to give: *glory* and *strength.* 1. They must make his *name to be glorious.* 2. They must attribute their *strength* to him.

4. That they *bow before* and *adore* him.

5. That they *exhibit* this honour in the proper PLACE: "In his temple; and in the beauty of holiness."

II. And that they may be more easily persuaded to give the Lord the honour due to his name, he proposes *two reasons* to be considered:—

First. His *power;* for although *they* be *mighty ones*, his power is infinitely beyond theirs; which is seen in his *works of nature;* but, omitting many others, he makes choice of the *thunder*, and the *effects* it produces.

1. From its *nature:* for howsoever philosophers may assign it to *natural causes*, yet religious men will look higher; and, when they hear those fearful noises in the air, will confess, with the psalmist, that it is *the voice of the Lord*, which he repeats here *seven* times; and this voice has affrighted the stoutest-hearted sinners, and the mightiest of tyrants.

2. From the *place* where this voice is given: "The voice of the Lord is upon the waters; upon many waters."

3. From its *force* and *power.* They are not vain and empty noises, but strike a terror: "The voice of the Lord is powerful; the voice of the Lord is full of majesty."

4. From its *effects;* which he explains by an induction:—

1. Upon the strong TREES, *the cedars of Lebanon:* "The voice of the Lord breaks the cedars," &c.

2. Upon the *firmest* MOUNTAINS, even *Lebanon* and *Sirion;* for sometimes the thunder is accompanied with an *earthquake*, and the mountains *skip like a calf.*

3. Upon the *air;* which is, to common minds, no small wonder; for, as nothing is more contrary to *fire* than *water*, it is next to miraculous how, out of a *watery* cloud, such *flames* of *fire* should be darted. "The voice of the Lord divideth the flames of fire."

4. In the *brute creation;* for it makes them fear and leave their caves, dens, and woods; yea, makes some of them cast their young: "The voice of the Lord shaketh the wilderness," &c.; "it maketh the hinds to calve."

5. In the mighty *rains* which follow upon it; when the cataracts of heaven are opened, and such floods of water follow that a man might fear that the earth was about to be overwhelmed by a *second inundation.* Out of all which he draws this conclusion: "The Lord sitteth upon the flood; the Lord sitteth a King for ever;" therefore, the earth is not destroyed.

Secondly. His *second* reason is drawn from the *works of grace.* 1. When He moves men to acknowledge his voice, and to give him glory in his temple: "In his temple doth every man speak of his honour." 2. By the *security* He gives to his people, even in the time when he utters his voice, and *speaks in thunder;* whereas the *wicked* then tremble and quake: "The Lord will give strength unto his people; the Lord will bless his people with peace," i. e., bodily security, and peace of conscience.

PSALM XXX

The psalmist returns thanks to God for deliverance from great danger, 1–3. *He calls upon the saints to give thanks to God at the remembrance of his holiness, because of his readiness to save,* 4, 5. *He relates how his mind stood affected before this great trial, and how soon an unexpected change took place,* 6, 7; *mentions how, and in what terms, he prayed for mercy,* 8–10; *shows how God heard and delivered him, and the effect it had upon his mind,* 11, 12.

VI. DAY. MORNING PRAYER

A Psalm *and* Song [a]*at* the dedication of the house of David

A. M. cir. 2987 B. C. cir. 1017 Davidis, Regis Israelitarum, cir. annum 39

I WILL extol thee, O LORD;
for thou hast [b]lifted me up,
and hast not made my foes to
[c]rejoice over me.

2 O LORD my God, I cried unto thee, and
thou hast [d]healed me.

3 O LORD, [e]thou hast brought
up my soul from the grave: thou
hast kept me alive, that I should
not [f]go down to the [g]pit.

A. M. cir. 2987 B. C. cir. 1017 Davidis, Regis Israelitarum, cir. annum 39

4 [h]Sing unto the LORD, O ye saints of his,
and give thanks [i]at the remembrance of his
holiness.

5 For [k]his [l]anger *endureth but* a moment;

[a]Deuteronomy xx. 5; 2 Samuel v. 11; vi. 20——[b]Psa. xxviii. 9——[c]Psalm xxv. 2; xxxv. 19, 24——[d]Psalm vi. 2; ciii. 3——[e]Psalm lxxxvi. 13——[f]Psalm xxviii 1——[g]Psa. xl. 2; lv. 23; lxxxviii. 4, 6; cxliii. 7; Prov. i. 12

[h]1 Chron. xvi. 4; Psa. xcvii. 12——[i]Or, *to the memorial*——[k]Psalm ciii. 9; Isaiah xxvi. 20; liv. 7, 8; 2 Corinthians iv. 17——[l]Hebrew, there is but *a moment in his anger*

NOTES ON PSALM XXX

This *Psalm* or *song* is said to have been made or used *at the dedication of the house* of David, or rather the dedication of a house or temple; for the word *David* refers not to הבית *habbayith*, the *house*, but to מזמור *mizmor*, a *Psalm*. But what temple or house could this be? Some say, the *temple* built by *Solomon;* others refer it to the *dedication* of the *second temple* under Zerubbabel; and some think it intended for the dedication of a *third* temple, which is to be built in the days of the Messiah. There are others who confine it to the *dedication of the house which David built* for himself on Mount Sion, after he had taken Jerusalem from the Jebusites; or to the purgation and re-dedication of his own house, that had been defiled by the wicked conduct of his own son Absalom. *Calmet* supposes it to have been made by David on the dedication of the place which he built on the threshing floor of Araunah, after the grievous *plague* which had so nearly desolated the kingdom, 2 Sam. xxiv. 25; 1 Chron. xxi. 26. All the parts of the Psalm agree to this: and they agree to this so well, and to no other hypothesis, that I feel myself justified in modelling the comment on this principle alone.

Verse 1. *I will extol thee—for thou hast lifted me up*] I will lift thee up, for thou hast lifted me up. Thou hast made me blessed, and I will make thee glorious. Thou hast magnified me in thy mercy; and I will show forth thy praise, and speak good of thy name.

I have made some remarks on this Psalm in the Introduction.

In this Psalm we find *seven* different states of mind distinctly marked:—

1. It is implied, in the *first verse*, that David had been in great distress, and nearly overwhelmed by his enemies.

2. He extols God for having lifted him up, and having preserved him from the cruelty of his adversaries, ver. 1-3.

3. He is brought into great prosperity, trusts in what he had received, and forgets to depend wholly on the Lord, ver. 4-6.

4. The Lord hides his face from him, and he is brought into great distress, ver. 7.

5. He feels his loss, and makes earnest prayer and supplication, ver. 8-10.

6. He is restored to the Divine favour, and filled with joy, ver. 11.

7. He purposes to glory in God alone, and to trust in him for ever, ver. 12.

As it is impossible for any man to have passed through *all these states* at the same time; it is supposed that the Psalm, like many others of the same complexion, has been formed out of the *memoranda of a diary.* See this point illustrated in the Introduction.

Thou hast lifted me up] Out of the pit into which I had fallen: the vain curiosity, and want of trust in God, that induced me to number the people. Bishop *Horsley* translates, *Because thou hast depressed me.* I thank God for my humiliation and afflictions, because they have been the means of teaching me lessons of great profit and importance.

Verse 2. *Thou hast healed me.*] Thou hast removed the plague from my people by which they were perishing in *thousands* before my eyes.

Verse 3. *Thou hast brought up my soul from the grave*] I and my people were both about to be cut off; but thou hast spared us in mercy, and given us a most glorious respite.

Verse 4. *Sing unto the Lord, O ye saints of his*] Ye *priests,* who wait upon him in his sanctuary, and whose business it is to offer prayers and sacrifices for the people, magnify him for the mercy he has now showed in staying this most destructive plague.

Give thanks at the remembrance of his holiness.] "Be ye holy," saith the Lord, "for I am holy." He who can give thanks at the *remembrance* of his holiness, is one who *loves holiness;* who *hates sin;* who longs to be saved from it; and takes encouragement at the recollection of God's holiness, as he sees in this the *holy nature* which *he* is to share, and the *perfection* which he is *here* to attain. But most who call themselves Christians hate the doctrine of holiness; never hear it inculcated without pain; and the principal part of their studies, and those of their pastors, is to find out *with how little holiness they can rationally expect to enter into the kingdom of God.* O fatal and soul-destroying delusion! How long will a holy God suffer such abominable doctrines to pollute his Church, and destroy the souls of men?

Verse 5. *For his anger* endureth but *a moment*] There is an elegant abruptness in these words in the Hebrew text. This is the literal translation: "For a moment in his anger. Lives in his favour. In the evening weeping may lodge: but in the morning exultation." So good is God, that he cannot delight in either the depression or ruin of his creatures. When he afflicts, it is for our advantage, that we may be partakers of his holiness, and be not condemned with the world. If he be *angry* with us, it is but for a *moment;* but when we have recourse to him, and seek his face, his *favour*

A. M. cir. 2987
B. C. cir. 1017
Davidis, Regis
Israelitarum,
cir. annum
39

[m]in his favour *is* life: weeping
may endure [n]for a night, but
[o]joy [p]*cometh* in the morning.
6 And [q]in my prosperity I said,
I shall never be moved.
7 LORD, by thy favour thou hast [r]made my
mountain to stand strong: [s]thou didst hide thy
face, *and* I was troubled.
8 I cried to thee, O LORD; and unto the
LORD I made supplication.
9 What profit *is there* in my blood, when I
go down to the pit? [t]Shall the
dust praise thee? shall it declare
thy truth?
10 Hear, O LORD, and have
mercy upon me: LORD, be thou my helper.
11 [u]Thou hast turned for me my mourning
into dancing: thou hast put off my sackcloth,
and girded me with [v]gladness;
12 To the end that [w]*my* glory may sing praise
to thee, and not be silent. O LORD my God,
I will give thanks unto thee for ever.

A. M. cir. 2987
B. C. cir. 1017
Davidis, Regis
Israelitarum,
cir. annum
39

---

[m]Psalm lxiii. 3——[n]Hebrew, *in the evening*——[o]Psa. cxxvi. 5——[p]Hebrew, *singing*——[q]Job xxix. 18——[r]Hebrew, *settled strength for my mountain*——[s]Psalm civ. 29——[t]Psalm vi. 5; lxxxviii. 11; cxv. 17; cxviii. 17; Isaiah xxxviii. 18——[u]2 Samuel vi. 14; Isaiah lxi. 3; Jeremiah xxxi. 4——[v]Psalm iv. 7; xlv. 15; cv. 43; Isaiah xxx. 29——[w]That is, my *tongue*, or my *soul;* see Gen. xlix. 6; Psa. xvi. 9; lvii. 8

---

is soon obtained, and there are *lives* in that favour—the *life* that *now is*, and the *life* that is *to come.* When *weeping* comes, it is only to *lodge* for the *evening;* but *singing* will surely come in the *morning.* This description of God's slowness to anger, and readiness to save, is given by a man long and deeply acquainted with God as his *Judge* and as his *Father.*

Verse 6. *In my prosperity I said, I shall never be moved.*] Peace and prosperity had seduced the heart of David, and led him to suppose that *his mountain*—his dominion, *stood so strong*, that adversity could never affect him. He wished to know the physical and political strength of his kingdom; and, forgetting to depend upon God, he desired Joab to make a *census* of the people; which God punished in the manner related in 2 Sam. xxiv., and which he in this place appears to acknowledge.

Verse 7. *Thou didst hide thy face*] Thou didst show thyself displeased with me for my pride and forgetfulness of thee: and then I found how vainly I had trusted in an arm of flesh.

Verse 8. *I cried to thee, O Lord*] I found no help but *in him* against whom I had sinned. See his confession and prayer, 2 Sam. xxiv. 17.

Made supplication.] Continued to urge my suit; was instant in prayer.

Verse 9. *What profit* is there *in my blood*] My being cut off will not magnify thy mercy. Let not the sword, therefore, come against me. If spared and pardoned, I will declare thy truth; I will tell to all men what a merciful and gracious Lord I have found. *Hear*, therefore, *O Lord;* ver. 10.

Verse 11. *Thou hast turned—my mourning into dancing*] Rather *into piping.* I have not prayed in vain. Though I deserved to be cut off from the land of the living, yet thou hast spared me, and the remnant of my people. Thou hast *taken away my sackcloth*, the emblem of my distress and misery, and *girded me with gladness*, when thou didst say to the destroying angel, when he stood over Jerusalem ready to destroy it: "It is enough, stay now thy hand;" 2 Sam. xxiv. 16.

Verse 12. *To the end that* my *glory may sing*] The word כבוד *cabod*, which we here translate *glory*, is sometimes taken to signify the *liver.* Here it is supposed to mean the *tongue;* why not the heart? But does not David mean, by *his glory*, the *state* of *exaltation* and *honour* to which God had raised him, and in which he had before too much trusted; forgetting that he held it in a state of dependence on God? Now he was disciplined into a better sentiment. My *glory* before had sung praise to myself; *in* it I had rested; *on* it I had presumed; and intoxicated with my success, I sent Joab to number the people. Now my *glory* shall be employed for *another purpose;* it shall give thanks to God, and *never be silent.* I shall *confess* to all the world that all the good, the greatness, the honour, the wealth, prosperity, and excellence I possess, came from God alone; and that I hold them on his mere good pleasure. It is so; therefore, "O Lord my God, I will give thanks unto thee for ever."

The old *Psalter* translates and paraphrases the last verse thus:—**That my joy syng til the, and I be noght stanged: Lord my God withouten ende I sal schryf til the.** The dede and the sorrow of oure syn God turnes in til joy of remission; and scheres oway oure sekk—(drives away our distress) and umgyfs (surrounds) qwen we dye, with gladness. **That oure joy syng til hym**, that has gyfen us that joy; for we be **no more stanged** (stung) with conscience of syn: na drede of dede or of dome; bot **withouten ende** we sal loue (praise) him. Na tunge may telle na herte may thynk the mykelnes of joy that es in louing [praising] of hym in gast, and in sothfastnes, i. e., *spirit* and *truth.*

ANALYSIS OF THE THIRTIETH PSALM

There are *two* parts in this Psalm:—

I. The *giving of thanks* for delivery from a great danger, 1, 2, 3.

II. An *exhortation* to others to follow his example, and thus acknowledge God's merciful dealings with them, ver. 4-12.

I. He begins with thanksgiving: "I will extol thee, O Lord;" and adds the *causes.*

1. "Thou hast lifted me up," as one out of a deep dark pit.

2. "Thou hast not made my foes to triumph over me;" but rather turned their mirth into sadness.

3. "Thou hast healed me;"—both in body and mind.

4. "Thou hast brought up my soul from the grave;" restored me to life, when apparently condemned to death.

5. He earnestly sought these blessings: "O Lord my God, I cried unto thee," and thou didst for me all that I have mentioned.

II. After having given thanks, he calls on the saints to acknowledge and celebrate the goodness of God to him and to others: "Sing unto the Lord," &c. And to induce them to do this, he gives the instance in himself, that God was angry with him, but soon appeased.

1. He was angry, but his anger *endured but a moment;* but *life*, and a continuance of it, are from his favour.

2. And justly angry he was for his sin and carnal confidence: "In my prosperity I said, I shall never be moved."

3. The *effect* of his anger was: "He hid his face, and I was troubled."

This is the example that he sets before the saints, that they be not secure when the world goes well with them; lest they have experience of God's displeasure, as he had.

Next he shows the *means* he used to avert God's wrath; and this he proposes as a pattern for all to follow in like cases.

1. He betook himself to *prayer*. 2. He sets down the *form* he used.

1. He that is ill sends for the physician—so did I. This was the fruit of my chastisement; I cried unto thee, O Lord; and unto the Lord I made supplication.

2. And the *form* he used was this:—I earnestly pleaded with God thus: 1. "What profit is there in my blood when I go down to the pit?" 2. "Shall the dust praise thee? shall it declare thy truth?" 3. Can a dead man praise thee, or canst thou make good thy promises to the dead? 4. And he concluded with, "Hear, O Lord, and have mercy upon me; O Lord, be thou my helper."

3. He shows the effect of his prayer: "Thou hast turned my mourning into dancing, thou hast put off my sackcloth, and girded me with gladness."

4. For what end God did this: "That my glory may sing praise to thee, and not be silent. O Lord my God, I will give thanks to thee for ever."

Now, O ye saints, 1. You see my case; 2. You see what course I took; 3. You see the effect; 4. You see the end why God was so good to me, that I should praise him. To you, who are in my state, I propose my example. Betake yourselves to God in your necessities; and, having obtained deliverance by earnest prayer and faith, remember to return praise to God for his ineffable goodness.

PSALM XXXI

The psalmist, with strong confidence in God, in a time of distress prays earnestly for deliverance, 1–5. *He expresses his abhorrence of evil,* 6; *gratefully mentions former interpositions of God,* 7, 8; *continues to detail the miseries of his case,* 9–18; *points out the privileges of them that fear God,* 19, 20; *shows that God had heard his prayers, notwithstanding he had given himself over for lost,* 21, 22; *calls on the saints to love God, and to have confidence in him, because he preserves the faithful, and plentifully rewards the proud doer,* 23, 24.

To the chief Musician, A Psalm of David

A. M. cir. 2942
B. C. cir. 1062
Sauli, Regis
Israelitarum,
cir. annum
34

IN [a]thee, O LORD, do I put
my trust; let me never be
ashamed: [b]deliver me in thy
righteousness.
2 [c]Bow down thine ear to me; deliver me
speedily: be thou [d]my strong
rock, for a house of defence to
save me.
3 [e]For thou *art* my rock and
my fortress; therefore [f]for thy name's sake
lead me, and guide me.

A. M. cir. 2942
B. C. cir. 1062
Sauli, Regis
Israelitarum,
cir. annum
34

[a]Psa. xxii. 5; xxv. 2; lxxi. 1; Isa. xlix. 23——[b]Psa. cxliii. 1——[c]Psa. lxxi. 2

[d]Heb. *to me for a rock of strength*——[e]Psa. xviii. 1
[f]Psa. xxiii. 3; xxv. 11; cix. 21; cxliii. 11; Jer. xiv. 7

NOTES ON PSALM XXXI

This Psalm contains no notes of *time* or *place*, to help us to ascertain *when, where,* or on *what account* it was written. Nor have we any certain evidence relative to the *author:* it might have been written by *David* during his persecution by Saul. Some think *Jeremiah* to have been the author: the *thirteenth* verse begins exactly with the same words as Jer. xx. 10. There are several other apparent references to passages in the book of Jeremiah, which shall be produced in the notes.

Verse 1. *In thee, O Lord, do I put my trust*] I confide in thee for every good I need: *let me not be confounded* by not receiving the end of my faith, the supply of my wants, and the salvation of my soul.

Verse 2. *Bow down thine ear*] Listen to my complaint. Put thy ear to my lips, that thou mayest hear all that my *feebleness* is capable of uttering. We generally put our ear near to the lips of the sick and dying, that we may hear what they say. To this the text appears to allude.

Strong rock] Rocks, rocky places, or caves in the rocks, were often *strong places* in the land of Judea. To such natural fortifications

A. M. cir. 2942
B. C. cir. 1062
Sauli, Regis
Israelitarum,
cir. annum
34

4 Pull me out of the net that
they have laid privily for me:
for thou *art* my strength.
5 [g]Into thine hand I commit
my spirit: thou hast [h]redeemed me, O LORD
God of truth.
6 I have hated them [i]that regard lying vanities: but I trust in the LORD.
7 I will be glad and rejoice in thy mercy:
for thou hast considered my trouble; thou hast
[k]known my soul in adversities;

8 And hast not [l]shut me up
into the hand of the enemy:
[m]thou hast set my foot in a large
room.
9 Have mercy upon me, O LORD, for I am
in trouble: [n]mine eye is consumed with grief,
yea, my soul and my belly.
10 For my life is spent with grief, and my
years with sighing: my strength faileth because of mine iniquity, and [o]my bones are consumed.

A. M. cir. 2942
B. C. cir. 1062
Sauli, Regis
Israelitarum,
cir. annum
34

[g]Luke xxiii. 46; Acts vii. 59——[h]Exod. xv. 13; Deut. xiii. 5; xxi. 8——[i]Jonah ii. 8——[k]John x. 27

[l]Deut. xxxii. 30; 1 Sam. xvii. 46; xxiv. 18——[m]Psa. iv. 1; xviii. 19——[n]Psa. vi. 7——[o]Psa. xxxii. 3; cii. 3

allusions are repeatedly made by the Hebrew poetic writers.

Verse 4. *Pull me out of the net*] They have hemmed me in on every side, and I cannot escape but by miracle.

Verse 5. *Into thine hand I commit my spirit*] These words, as they stand in the *Vulgate*, were in the highest credit among our ancestors; by whom they were used in all dangers, difficulties, and in the article of death. *In manus tuas, Domine, commendo spiritum meum,* was used by the sick when about to expire, if they were sensible; and if not, the priest said it in their behalf. In *forms of prayer* for sick and dying persons, these words were frequently inserted in Latin, though all the rest of the prayer was English; for it was supposed there was something sovereign in the *language* itself. But let not the abuse of such words hinder their usefulness. For an ejaculation nothing can be better; and when the pious or the tempted with confidence use them, nothing can exceed their effect. "Into thy hands I commend my spirit; for thou hast redeemed me, O Lord God of truth." I give my soul to thee, for it is thine: thou hast redeemed it by thy blood; it is safe nowhere but in thy hand. Thou hast promised to save them that trust in thee; thou art the *God of truth*, and canst not deny thyself. But these words are particularly sanctified, or *set apart* for this purpose, by the use made of them by our blessed Lord just before he expired on the cross. "And when Jesus had cried with a loud voice, he said, Πατερ, εις χειρας σου παρατιθεμαι το πνευμα μου· 'Father, into thy hands I commend my spirit,'" Luke xxiii. 46. The rest of the verse was not *suitable* to the Saviour of the world, and therefore he omits it; but it is suitable to us who have been redeemed by that sacrificial death. St. Stephen uses nearly the same words, and they were the last that he uttered. Acts vii. 59.

Verse 6. *I have hated them*] That is, I have abominated their ways. *Idolaters* are the persons of whom David speaks.

I trust in the Lord.] While *they* trust in *vanities, vain things;* (for *an idol is nothing in the world;*) and in *lying* vanities; (for much is *promised* and nothing *given;*) *I* trust in Jehovah, who is God all-sufficient, and is my Shepherd, and therefore I shall lack no good thing.

Verse 7. *Thou hast known my soul in adversities*] When all forsook me; when none could help me; when I could not save my own life; when my enemies were sure that I could not escape; then I found *thee* to be my Friend and Supporter. When *friend,* so called, finds it convenient not to know his friend in affliction and poverty, then thou didst acknowledge me as thine own, all worthless as I was. Human friendships may fail; but the Friend of sinners never fails. Cicero defines a real friend, *Amicus certus in re incerta cernitur:* "A friend in need is a friend indeed." Reader, such a Friend is the *Lord.*

Verse 8. *Thou hast set my foot in a large room.*] Many hair-breadth escapes David had for his life; at that time especially when, playing before Saul, the furious king took a spear and endeavoured to pierce him through the body, but he escaped and got to the deserts. Here God, who had saved his life, set his *feet in a large room.* The seventh and eighth verses speak of what God had done previously for him.

Verse 9. *Mine eye is consumed*] He now returns, and speaks of his present situation. Grief had brought many tears from his eyes, many agonies into his soul, and many distressful feelings into his whole frame.

My soul and my belly.] The *belly* is often taken for the whole body. But the term *belly* or *bowels*, in such as case as this, may be the most proper; for in distress and misery, the *bowels* being the most tender part, and in fact the very *seat of compassion,* they are often most affected. In Greek the word σπλαγχνον signifies a *bowel,* and σπλαγχνιζομαι signifies *to be moved with compassion;* to feel misery in the bowels at the sight of a person in pain and distress.

Verse 10. *My life is spent with grief*] My life is a life of suffering and distress, and by grief my days are shortened. *Grief* disturbs the functions of life, prevents the due concoction of food, injures the digestive organs, destroys appetite, impairs the nervous system, relaxes the muscles, induces morbid action in the animal economy, and hastens death. These effects are well expressed in the verse itself.

My years with sighing] אנחה *anachah.* This is a mere *natural* expression of grief; the very *sounds* which proceed from a distressed mind; *an-ach-ah!* common, with little variation, to all nations, and nearly the same in all languages. The *och-och-on* of the Irish is precisely the same sound, and the same sense. Thousands of beauties of this kind are to be found in the sacred language.

A. M. cir. 2942
B. C. cir. 1062
Sauli, Regis
Israelitarum,
cir. annum
34

11 [p]I was a reproach among all mine enemies, but [q]especially among my neighbours, and a fear to mine acquaintance: [r]they that did see me without fled from me.

12 [s]I am forgotten as a dead man out of mind: I am like [t]a broken vessel.

13 [u]For I have heard the slander of many: [v]fear *was* on every side: while they [w]took counsel together against me, they devised to take away my life.

14 But I trusted in thee, O LORD: I said, Thou *art* my God.

15 My times *are* in thy hand: deliver me from the hand of mine enemies, and from them that persecute me.

16 [x]Make thy face to shine upon thy servant: save me for thy mercies' sake.

17 [y]Let me not be ashamed, O LORD; for I have called upon thee: let the wicked be ashamed, *and* [z]let [a]them be silent in the grave.

A. M. cir. 2942
B. C. cir. 1062
Sauli, Regis
Israelitarum,
cir. annum
34

18 [b]Let the lying lips be put to silence; which [c]speak [d]grievous things proudly and contemptuously against the righteous.

19 [e]*O* how great *is* thy goodness, which thou hast laid up for them that fear thee; *which* thou hast wrought for them that trust in thee before the sons of men!

20 [f]Thou shalt hide them in the secret of thy presence from the pride of man: [g]thou shalt keep them secretly in a pavilion from the strife of tongues.

21 Blessed *be* the LORD: for he [h]hath showed me his marvellous kindness [i]in a [k]strong city.

---

[p]Psa. xli. 8; Isa. liii. 4——[q]Job xix. 13; Psa. xxxviii. 11; lxxxviii. 8, 18——[r]Psa. lxiv. 8——[s]Psa. lxxxviii. 4, 5 [t]Heb. *a vessel that perisheth*——[u]Jer. xx. 10——[v]Jer. vi. 25; xx. 3; Lam. ii. 22——[w]Matt. xxvii. 1——[x]Num. vi. 25, 26; Psa. iv. 6; lxvii. 1——[y]Psa. xxv. 2

[z]1 Sam. ii. 9; Psa. cxv. 17——[a]Or, *let them be cut off for the grave*——[b]Psa. xii. 3——[c]1 Sam. ii. 3; Psa. xciv. 4; Jude 15——[d]Heb. *a hard thing*——[e]Isa. lxiv. 4; 1 Cor. ii. 9——[f]Psa. xxvii. 5; xxxii. 7——[g]Job v. 21 [h]Psa. xvii. 7——[i]1 Sam. xxiii. 7——[k]Or, *fenced city*

Verse 11. *I was a reproach*] When proscribed at the court of Saul, my *enemies* triumphed, and loaded me with execrations; my *neighbours* considered me as a dangerous man, now deservedly driven from society; my *acquaintance*, who knew me best, were afraid to hold any communication with me; and *they* who *saw* me in *my exile* avoided me as if affected with a contagious disorder.

Verse 12. *I am forgotten as a dead man*] I am considered as a person adjudged to death. *I am like a broken vessel*—like a thing totally useless.

Verse 13. *I have heard the slander of many*] To this and the two foregoing verses the reader may find several parallels; Jer. xviii. 18 to the end of chap. xix., and ten first verses of chap. xx. This has caused several to suppose that Jeremiah was the author of this Psalm.

Verse 14. *But I trusted in thee*] Hitherto thou hast been my Helper, and thou art my God; I have taken thee for my eternal portion.

Verse 15. *My times* are *in thy hand*] The events of my life are under thy control. No danger can happen to me without thy foresight; thou seest what is prepared for or meditated against me; thou canst therefore deliver me from mine enemies.

Verse 16. *Make thy face to shine upon thy servant*] Only let me know that thou art reconciled to and pleased with me, and then, come what will, all must be well.

Save me for thy mercies' sake.] Literally, *Save me in thy mercy.*

Verse 17. *Let the wicked be ashamed*] Those who traduce my character and lay snares for my life; let them be confounded.

Verse 18. *Let the lying lips be put to silence*] As to my enemies, persecutors, and slanderers, abate their pride, assuage their malice, and confound their devices. See Jer. xviii. 18.

Verse 19. O *how great* is *thy goodness*] God's goodness is infinite; there is enough for *all*, enough for *each*, enough for *evermore*. It is laid up where neither devils nor men can reach it, and it is laid up for *them that fear the Lord;* therefore every one who trembles at his word, may expect all he needs from this Fountain that can never be dried up.

Which *thou hast wrought*] Thou hast already prepared it; it is the work of thy own hands; thou hast provided it and proportioned it to the necessities of men, and all who trust in thee shall have it. And for them especially it is prepared *who trust in thee before men*—who boldly confess thee amidst a crooked and perverse generation.

Verse 20. *Thou shalt hide them in the secret of thy presence*] בסתר פניך *besether paneycha*, "With the covering of thy countenance." Their life shall be so hidden with Christ in God, that their enemies shall not be able to find them out. To such a hiding-place Satan himself dare not approach. There *the pride of man* cannot come.

Thou shalt keep them secretly in a pavilion] Thou shalt put them in the innermost part of thy tent. This implies that they shall have much communion and union with God; that they shall be transformed into his likeness, and have his highest approbation.

Verse 21. *In a strong city.*] If this Psalm was written by David, this must refer to his taking refuge with *Achish, king of Gath*, who gave him *Ziklag*, a fortified city, to secure himself and followers in. See 1 Sam. xxvii. 6. This is more likely than that it was *Keilah*, where he only had intimation of the traitorous design of the inhabitants to deliver him up to Saul; so that the place was no refuge to him, howsoever fortified. Perhaps the passage may mean that, under the protection of God, he was as safe as if he had been in a fortified city.

A. M. cir. 2942
B. C. cir. 1062
Sauli, Regis
Israelitarum,
cir. annum
34

22 For [l]I said in my haste,
[m]I am cut off from before thine
eyes: nevertheless thou heardest
the voice of my supplications
when I cried unto thee.
23 [n]O love the LORD, all ye his saints: *for*
the LORD preserveth the faithful,
and plentifully rewardeth the
proud doer.
24 [o]Be of good courage, and
he shall strengthen your heart, all ye that hope
in the LORD.

A. M. cir. 2942
B. C. cir. 1062
Sauli, Regis
Israelitarum,
cir. annum
34

---

[l]1 Sam. xxiii. 26; Psa. cxvi. 11——[m]Isa. xxxviii. 11, 12; Lam. iii. 54; Jonah ii. 4
[n]Psalm xxxiv. 9
[o]Psalm xxvii. 14

Verse 22. *I said in my haste*] Not duly adverting to the promise of God, I was led to conclude that my enemies were so strong, so numerous, and had so many advantages against me, that I must necessarily fall into and by their hands; however, I continued to pray, and thou didst hear the voice of my supplication.

Verse 23. *O love the Lord, all ye his saints*] It is only the *saints* that can love God, as they only are made partakers of the Divine nature. *Holy spirits* can love God, who is the fountain of their holiness; and the *saints* should love him.

Preserveth the faithful] Those who, being filled with the love of God, bring forth the fruits of that love—universal obedience to the will of God; for to such persons his commands are not grievous, their *duty* is their *delight;* while a man is *faithful* to the grace he has received, that is, uses and improves the talents with which God has intrusted him, God's service is perfect freedom.

The proud doer.] The man of the proud heart, haughty and supercilious carriage, and insulting and outrageous conduct. A *proud man* is peculiarly odious in the sight of God; and in the sight of reason how absurd! A sinner, a fallen spirit, an heir of wretchedness and corruption—proud! Proud of what? Of an indwelling devil! Well; such persons shall be *plentifully rewarded.* They shall get their *due*, their *whole due*, and *nothing but their due.*

Verse 24. *Be of good courage, and he shall strengthen your heart*] In 1 Cor. xvi. 13, St. Paul says, "Watch ye, stand fast in the faith; quit you like men; be strong:" *Γρηγορειτε, στηκετε εν τῃ πιστει, ανδριζεσθε, κραταιουσθε.* The latter words he seems to have borrowed from the *Septuagint*, who translate, "Be of good courage, and he shall strengthen your heart," by *Ανδριζεσθε και κραταιουσθω ἡ καρδια ὑμων·* "Act like men, and your hearts shall be strengthened."

They that hope in God, and are endeavouring to walk carefully before him, may take courage at all times, and expect the fulness of the blessing of the Gospel of peace.

ANALYSIS OF THE THIRTY-FIRST PSALM

This Psalm is composed and mixed of divers affections; for David sometimes prays, sometimes gives thanks; now he complains, now he hopes; at one time fears, at another exults. This vicissitude of affection is *six-fold*, and it may very well divide the Psalm.

I. With great confidence he prays to God; ver. 1-6.

II. He exults for mercy and help received; ver. 7, 8.

III. He grievously complains of the misery he was in; ver. 9-14.

IV. He prays again, upon the strength of God's goodness; ver. 15-18.

V. He admires, exults in, and proclaims God's goodness; ver. 19-22.

VI. He exhorts others to love God, and be courageous; ver. 23, 24.

I. In the six first verses he prays to God, and shows his reasons:—

1. That he be never ashamed in his hope: "Let me never be ashamed."

2. That he be delivered, "speedily delivered."

3. That God would be "his rock, and a house of defence, to save him."

4. That God would lead and guide him: "Lead me, and guide me."

5. That God would "pull his feet out of the net which they had laid for him."

The *reasons* on which he founds his prayer and expectations:—

1. His faith and confidence: "In thee, O Lord, I put my trust."

2. The reason of his faith: "Thou art my ROCK and FORTRESS."

3. His deliverance would be to the honour of God: "For thy name's sake."

4. Thou art my strength; exert it in my behalf.

5. I rely upon thee: "Into thy hands I commit my spirit."

6. I expect thee to do for me as thou hast ever done: "Thou hast redeemed me."

7. I rely on thee alone, I seek no vain helps: "I have hated them that regard lying vanities; but I trust in the Lord."

His *petition* and his *reasons* are in effect the same; his confidence in God to be his *Deliverer, Fortress, Rock, Redeemer,* &c.

II. He exults for mercy and help already received, and by the experience of that, doubts the less in this: "I will be glad and rejoice in thy mercy." And his reason follows from his experience: 1. "For thou hast considered my trouble." 2. "Thou hast known my soul in adversity." 3. "Thou hast not shut me up into the hand of the enemy." 4. But "hast set my feet in a large room."

III. He prays, and grievously complains of what he suffered *within* and *without.*

1. He *prays:* "Have mercy upon me, O Lord."

2. Then he *complains,* and his complaint shows the reason of his prayer.

1. *Within*—at home, he was in a distressed state: "I am in trouble; my eye is consumed with grief; my years with sighing; my strength faileth; my bones are consumed."

2. *Without*—I have no comfort either from friends or enemies.

1. "I was a reproach among all my enemies."

2. My *friends* stand afar off: "I was a reproach, especially among my neighbours." "A fear to my acquaintance." "They that did see me without fled from me."

3. He shows the greatness of his grief, and the scorn he endured: "I am forgotten as a

dead man;" "I am as a broken vessel," vile and useless.

4. I am mocked by the people: "I have heard the slander of many."

5. And the consequence was mischievous. 1. "Fear is on every side." 2. While they conspired, or "took counsel against my life." 3. And their counsel was, "to take away my life." What more could my enemies do, or my friends permit?

IV. After his complaint he comforts himself with his chief reason, *the goodness of God.* I have trusted in thee, O Lord, and said, Thou art my God. Let them conspire, take counsel, and devise what they can; yet I know, except thou permit them, they are not able to do it. "My times are in thy hand," not in *theirs.*

He then begins to pray again, and his prayer consists of *three* parts: 1. Deprecation. 2. Supplication. 3. Imprecation.

1. A *deprecation:* "Deliver me from the hands of my enemies," &c.

2. A *supplication:* "Make thy face to shine upon thy servant; save me." "Let me not be ashamed, for I have called upon thee."

3. An *imprecation:* 1. "Let the wicked be ashamed, and be silent in the grave." 2. "Let the lying lips be put to silence, which speak grievous things," &c.

In this imprecation *four arguments* are used to enforce it:—

1. The *quality* of their persons: "They are wicked, impious men."

2. There is *no truth* in them: "They have lying lips." 1. Their *words* are false. 2. Their *actions* are worse: *They speak grievous things,* and that *against the righteous.* 3. But their *intention* is worst of all, for they do it *proudly, contemptuously, disdainfully, despitefully;* all proceeding from a *bad heart.*

V. In the *fifth* part he sets out the *abundant goodness of the Lord* to his people, and exclaims, in holy rapture, "O how great is thy goodness which thou hast laid up for them that fear thee—which thou hast wrought for them that trust in thee before the sons of men!"

This goodness of God is always treasured up, and to be had at all times. But observe: 1. It is *laid up* for none, nor *wrought* for any one, but *them that fear the Lord.* 2. And for those *who put their trust in him,* and acknowledge him, his cause, his people, and his cross, *before the sons of men.* And the acts of his goodness are here specified:—

1. "Thou shalt hide them in the secret of thy presence from the pride of man."

2. "Thou shalt keep them secretly in a pavilion from the strife of tongues." Upon which consideration he breaks out into praise: 1. "Blessed be the Lord, for he hath showed me his marvellous kindness." 2. He *corrects* his error, and former mistake: "I said in my haste, (rashly, imprudently,) I am cut off from before thine eyes; nevertheless thou heardest the voice of my supplication."

VI. The last part is an *exhortation to the saints:* 1. That they *love God.* 2. That they be of *good courage;* for he was the same God still, and would be as good to others as he was to him.

1. That they *love God,* and that for two reasons:—1. Because the "Lord preserveth the faithful." This is his *mercy.* 2. That he "plentifully rewardeth the proud doer." This is his *justice.*

2. That they *be of good courage;* for then "he shall strengthen your heart, all ye that hope in the Lord." They were not to despair, but keep their hearts firmly fixed in the profession of the truth, which would be a seal of their *hope.*

PSALM XXXII

True blessedness consists in remission of sin, and purification of the heart, 1, 2. *What the psalmist felt in seeking these blessings,* 3–5. *How they should be sought,* 6, 7. *The necessity of humility and teachableness,* 8, 9. *The misery of the wicked,* 10. *The blessedness of the righteous,* 11.

VI. DAY. EVENING PRAYER

[a]*A Psalm* of David, Maschil

A. M. cir. 2970
B. C. cir. 1034
Davidis, Regis
Israelitarum,
cir. annum
22

BLESSED *is he whose* [b]trans-
gression *is* forgiven, *whose*
sin *is* covered.
2 Blessed *is* the man unto
whom the LORD [c]imputeth not
iniquity, and [d]in whose spirit
there is no guile.
3 When I kept silence, my
bones waxed old through my roaring all the
day long.

[a]Or, A Psalm *of David giving instruction*——[b]Psa. lxxxv. 2; Rom. iv. 6, 7, 8——[c]2 Cor. v. 19——[d]John i. 47

NOTES ON PSALM XXXII

The *title* of this Psalm is significant, לדוד משכיל *ledavid maskil,* A Psalm *of David, giving instruction, an instructive Psalm;* so called by way of eminence, because it is calculated to give the highest instruction relative to the guilt of sin, and the blessedness of pardon and holiness, or *justification* and *sanctification.* It is supposed to have been composed after David's transgression with Bath-sheba, and subsequently to his obtaining pardon. The *Syriac* entitles it, "A Psalm of David concerning the sin of Adam, who dared and transgressed; and a prophecy concerning Christ, because through him we are to be delivered from hell." The

A. M. cir. 2970
B. C. cir. 1034
Davidis, Regis
Israelitarum,
cir. annum
22

4 For day and night thy [e]hand
was heavy upon me: my moisture is turned into the drought of
summer. Selah.
5 I acknowledge my sin unto thee, and
mine iniquity have I not hid. [f]I said, I will
confess my transgressions unto the LORD; and
thou forgavest the iniquity of my sin. Selah.
6 [g]For this shall every one that is godly
[h]pray unto thee [i]in a time when thou mayest
be found: surely in the floods of
great waters they shall not come
nigh unto him.
7 [k]Thou *art* my hiding place;
thou shalt preserve me from trouble; thou
shalt compass me about with [l]songs of deliverance. Selah.
8 I will instruct thee and teach thee in the
way which thou shalt go: [m]I will guide thee
with mine eye.

A. M. cir. 2970
B. C. cir. 1034
Davidis, Regis
Israelitarum,
cir. annum
22

[e]1 Sam. v. 6, 11; Job xxxiii. 7; Psa. xxxviii. 2——[f]Prov. xxviii. 13; Isa. lxv. 24; Luke xv. 18, 21 &c.; 1 John i. 9——[g]1 Tim. i. 16——[h]Isa. lv. 6; John vii. 34

[i]Heb. *in a time of finding*——[k]Psa. ix. 9; xxvii. 5; xxxi. 20; cxix. 114——[l]Exod. xv. 1; Judg. v. 1; 2 Sam. xxii. 1——[m]Heb. *I will counsel* thee, *mine eye* shall be *upon thee*

Arabic says, "David spoke this Psalm prophetically concerning the redemption." The *Vulgate*, *Septuagint*, and *Æthiopic*, are the same in meaning as the *Hebrew*.

Verse 1. *Blessed* is he whose *transgression* is *forgiven*] In this and the following verse *four* evils are mentioned: 1. *Transgression*, פשע *pesha*. 2. *Sin*, חטאה *chataah*. 3. *Iniquity*, עון *avon*. 4. *Guile*, רמיה *remiyah*. The *first* signifies the *passing over a boundary, doing what is prohibited*. The *second* signifies the *missing of a mark*, not doing what was commanded; but is often taken to express *sinfulness*, or sin in the future, producing transgression in the life. The *third* signifies *what is turned out of its proper course or situation; any* thing *morally distorted* or *perverted. Iniquity*, what is contrary to *equity* or *justice*. The *fourth* signifies *fraud, deceit, guile*, &c. To remove these evils, *three* acts are mentioned: *forgiving, covering*, and not *imputing*. 1. TRANSGRESSION, פשע *pesha*, must be *forgiven*, נשוי *nesui*, borne away, i. e., by a vicarious sacrifice; for *bearing sin*, or *bearing away sin*, always implies this. 2. SIN, חטאה *chataah*, must be *covered*, כסוי *kesui*, hidden from the sight. It is odious and abominable, and must be put out of sight. 3. INIQUITY, עון *avon*, which is *perverse* or *distorted*, must not be imputed, לא יחשב *lo yachshob*, must *not be reckoned to his account*. 4. GUILE, רמיה *remiyah*, must be annihilated from the soul: *In whose spirit there is no* GUILE. The man whose *transgression* is forgiven; whose *sin* is hidden, God having cast it as a millstone into the depths of the sea; whose iniquity and perversion is not reckoned to his account; and whose *guile*, the deceitful and desperately wicked heart, is annihilated, being emptied of sin and filled with righteousness, is necessarily a happy man.

The old *Psalter* translates these two verses thus: **Blissid qwas wikednes es for gyben, and qwas synnes is hyled** (covered.) **Blisful man til qwam Lord retted** (reckoneth) **noght Syn: ne na treson es in his gast** (spirit.) In vain does any man look for or expect happiness while the *power* of sin *remains*, its *guilt unpardoned*, and its *impurity* not *purged away*. To the person who has got such blessings, we may say as the psalmist said, אשרי *ashrey, O the blessedness of that man, whose transgression is forgiven!* &c.

St. Paul quotes this passage, Rom. iv. 6, 7, to illustrate the doctrine of *justification by faith;* where see the notes.

Verse 3. *When I kept silence*] Before I humbled myself, and confessed my sin, my soul was under the deepest horror. "I roared all the day long;" and felt the hand of God heavy upon my soul.

Verse 5. *I acknowledged my sin*] When this confession was made thoroughly and sincerely, and I ceased to *cover* and *extenuate my offence*, then thou didst forgive the iniquity of my sin. I felt the hardness of heart: I felt the deep distress of soul; I felt power to confess and abhor my sin; I felt confidence in the mercy of the Lord; and I felt the forgiveness of the iniquity of my sin.

Selah.] This is all true; I *know* it; I *felt* it; I *feel* it.

Verse 6. *For this shall every one that is godly*] Because thou art merciful; because thou hast shown mercy to all who have truly turned to thee, and believed in thee; every one who fears thee, and hears of this, *shall pray unto thee* in an acceptable time, *when thou mayest be found;* in the time of finding. When the heart is softened and the conscience alarmed, that is a time of finding. God is ever ready; men are not so. Who can pray with a hard heart and a dark mind? While you feel relentings, pray.

Surely in the floods] In violent trials, afflictions, and temptations; when the rains descend, the winds blow, and the floods beat against that godly man who prays and trusts in God; "they shall not come nigh him," so as to weaken his confidence or destroy his soul. His *house* is founded on a *rock*.

Verse 7. *Thou* art *my hiding place*] An allusion, probably, to the *city of refuge:* "Thou shalt preserve me from trouble." The avenger of blood shall not be able to overtake me. And being encompassed with an impregnable wall, I shall feel myself *encompassed with songs of deliverance*—I shall know that I am safe.

Verse 8. *I will instruct thee*] These are probably the Lord's words to David. Seeing thou art now sensible of the mercy thou hast received from me, and art purposing to live to my glory, I will give thee all the assistance requisite. I will become thy *Instructor*, "and will teach thee," in all occurrences, "the way thou shouldst go." I will keep *mine eyes* upon thee, and thou shalt keep thine upon me: as I go, thou must follow me; and I will continually watch for thy good.

A. M. cir. 2970 B. C. cir. 1034 Davidis, Regis Israelitarum, cir. annum 22

9 [n]Be ye not as the horse, *or*
as the mule, *which* have [o]no understanding: whose mouth must
be held in with bit and bridle,
lest they come near unto thee.
10 [p]Many sorrows *shall be* to the wicked:
but [q]he that trusteth in the
LORD, mercy shall compass him
about.
11 [r]Be glad in the LORD, and
rejoice, ye righteous: and shout for joy, all
ye that are upright in heart.

[n]Prov. xxvi. 3; James iii. 3——[o]Job xxxv. 11——[p]Prov. xiii. 21; Rom. ii. 9

[q]Psa. xxxiv. 8; lxxxiv. 12; Prov. xvi. 20; Jer. xvii. 7
[r]Psa. lxiv. 10; lxviii. 3

Verse 9. *Be ye not as the horse* or *as the mule*] They will only act by *force* and *constraint;* be not like *them;* give a *willing service* to your Maker. "They have no understanding;" you have a *rational soul,* made to be guided and influenced by *reason.* The service of your God is a *reasonable service;* act, therefore, as a *rational being.* The horse and the mule are turned with difficulty; they must be constrained with *bit* and *bridle.* Do not *be like them;* do not oblige your Maker to have continual recourse to afflictions, trials, and severe dispensations of providence, to keep you in the way, or to recover you after you have gone out of it.

Verse 10. *Many sorrows* shall be *to the wicked*] Every *wicked* man is a *miserable* man. God has wedded sin and misery as strongly as he has holiness and happiness. God hath joined them together; none can put them asunder.

But he that trusteth in the Lord] Such a person is both safe and happy.

Verse 11. *Be glad—and rejoice*] Let every *righteous soul* rejoice and glory, but let it be *in the Lord.* Man was made for *happiness,* but his happiness must be founded on holiness: and holiness, as it comes from God, must be retained by continual union with him. Probably this verse belongs to the next Psalm, and was originally its first verse.

Analysis of the Thirty-second Psalm

This Psalm is *doctrinal,* and shows the happiness of the man whose sin is pardoned, and who is himself restored to the favour and image of God. It is called *maschil,* or *instruction;* and the reason of this is shown at the *eighth* verse: "I will instruct thee, and teach thee." In it we have instruction, especially on these *three* points, which divide the Psalm:—

I. The happy state of a justified person, ver. 1, 2.

II. The unhappy condition of that man who is not assured that he is justified and reconciled to God, ver. 3, 4. And the way is prescribed how to gain this assurance, ver. 5.

III. A lesson given for obedience after a man is brought into that state, ver. 8, 9.

I. The prophet first instructs us in what *justification* consists:—

I. It is a *free remission,* a *covering of sin;* a *nonimputation of iniquities.* 2. In what state a person must be in order to obtain it. He must be honest, sincere, and upright in heart; deeply penitent, feeling the guilt of sin, and acknowledging its enormity. He must avoid *guile* or deceit; and not excuse, palliate, or extenuate his sin, but confess it.

II. This he proves by his own experience: he hid his sin, he confessed it not; and was, in consequence, miserable.

1. I held my peace I confessed not. I did not ask pardon: "When I kept silence," &c.

2. I was wounded with the sting of a guilty conscience; fears, horrors, troubles of soul, came upon me: "My bones waxed old through my roaring."

3. And then he shows the *way* he took to *regain* happiness; it was a *contrary course* to that above; he concealed his sin no longer. 1. "I acknowledged my sin unto thee, and mine iniquity I have not hidden." 2. "I said, I will confess my transgressions to the Lord."

Of which the effects were various:—

1. Upon *himself.* He recovered his happiness in being justified: "Thou forgavest the iniquity of my sin."

2. On the *whole Church:* "For this shall every one that is godly pray unto thee."

3. *Comfort* in *extremities,* and safety in the greatest danger: "Surely in the floods of great waters," in an inundation of calamities, *they*—the troubles—*shall not come nigh him* who depends upon God's goodness and mercy, and is reconciled to him. And he shows the reason from his own experience. God was his *Protector:* 1. "Thou art my hiding place: thou shalt preserve me from trouble." 2. "Thou shalt compass me about with songs of deliverance."

III. And now David sets down the duty of a justified person; that he is, after his pardon, obedient to God; and that not out of compulsion, but *freely* and *willingly.* In order to this, God condescends to be his *Instructor.*

1. "I will instruct;" give thee general counsel.

2. "I will guide thee with mine eye." A good servant needs no *stripes;* he will observe *nutum,* the *nod,* or *nictum heri,* the *wink of the master.* As my eye is always over you, carefully to instruct; so be you as ready to observe it.

3. Be not like *beasts:* the HORSE, *headlong;* the MULE, *headstrong;* "whose mouths must be held in with bit and bridle," lest they fling, kick, hurt, or kill thee. *Constrained obedience* is for a *beast; free* and *voluntary obedience,* for a *man.*

4. Besides, to quicken your obedience, I will teach you two reasons. 1. From inconvenience and loss: "Many sorrows shall be to the wicked:" their griefs, troubles and punishments, are many and grievous. Be not, therefore, disobedient like the wicked. 2. From the *gain.* Your obedience shall be rewarded, and that amply: "He that trusteth in the Lord, mercy shall compass him round about." It shall be like the *girdle* with which he *is girded.* God will be present with him in his troubles. He shall perceive that he is in favour with God, that his sins are pardoned, and that he is an heir of eternal life.

Upon which he concludes with this exhortation: "Be glad in the Lord, and rejoice, ye righteous; and shout for joy, all ye that are upright in heart." For this rejoicing there is great cause; for this doctrine of free remission of sin can alone quiet a guilty conscience. And this pardon can only be obtained by faith in Christ Jesus.

PSALM XXXIII

The Lord is praised for his works of creation, 1–9; *and for the stability of his own counsels,* 10, 11. *The blessedness of the people who have the knowledge of the true God, his grace, and providence,* 12–15. *The vanity of all earthly dependence,* 16, 17. *The happiness of them that fear God, and trust in his mercy,* 18–22.

REJOICE [a]in the LORD, O ye righteous:
for [b]praise is comely for the upright.
2 Praise the LORD with harp: sing unto him
with the psaltery [c]*and* an instrument of ten
strings.
3 [d]Sing unto him a new song; play skilfully with a loud noise.
4 For the word of the LORD *is* right; and
all his works *are done* in truth.
5 [e]He loveth righteousness and judgment:
[f]the earth is full of the [g]goodness of the
LORD.
6 [h]By the word of the LORD were the heavens made, and [i]all the host of them [k]by the
breath of his mouth.
7 [l]He gathereth the waters of the sea together as a heap: he layeth up the depth in
storehouses.

[a]Psa. xxxii. 11; xcvii. 12——[b]Psa. cxlvii. 1——[c]Psa. xcii. 3; cxliv. 9——[d]Psa. xcvi. 1; xcviii. 1; cxliv. 9; cxlix. 1; Isa. xlii. 10; Rev. v. 9——[e]Psa. xi. 7; xlv. 7

[f]Psa. cxix. 64——[g]Or, *mercy*——[h]Gen. i. 6, 7; Heb. xi. 3; 2 Pet. iii. 5——[i]Gen. ii. 1——[k]Job xxvi. 13 [l]Gen. i. 9; Job xxvi. 10; xxxviii. 8

NOTES ON PSALM XXXIII

This Psalm has no *title* in the Hebrew and it was probably written on no particular occasion, but was intended as a hymn of praise in order to celebrate the power, wisdom, and mercy of God. Creation and providence are its principal subjects; and these lead the psalmist to glance at different parts of the ancient Jewish history. In eight of *Kennicott's* MSS., this Psalm is written as a part of the preceding.

Verse 1. *Rejoice in the Lord*] It is very likely that the *last* verse of the preceding Psalm was formerly the *first* verse of this. As this Psalm has no *title,* the verse was the more easily separated. In the preceding Psalm we have an account of the happiness of the justified man: in this, such are taught how to glorify God, and to praise him for the great things he had done for them.

Praise is comely for the upright.] It is *right* they should give thanks to Him, who is the fountain whence they have received all the good they possess and thankfulness becomes the lips of the upright.

Verse 2. *Praise the Lord with harp*] כנור *kinnor;* probably something like our *harp:* but Calmet thinks it the ancient *testudo,* or lyre with three strings.

The psalter] נבל *nebel.* Our translation seems to make a *third* instrument in this place, by rendering עשור *asor, an instrument of ten strings;* whereas they should both be joined together, for נבל עשור *nebel-asor* signifies the *nebal,* or *nabla,* with ten strings, or holes. Calmet supposes this to have resembled our *harp.* In one of *Kennicott's* MSS., this Psalm begins with the second verse.

Verse 3. *Sing unto him a new song*] Do not wear out the old forms: fresh mercies call for new songs of praise and gratitude.

Play skilfully with a loud noise.] Let *sense* and *sound* accompany each other; let the style of the music be suited to the words. This *skill* is possessed by few singers. They can make a *loud noise,* but they cannot adapt *sound* to *sense.*

Verse 4. *The word of the Lord* is *right*] He is infinitely wise, and can make no mistakes; and all his works are done in truth. All the words, laws, promises, and threatenings of God are perfectly true and just. The dispensations of his providence and mercy are equally so. When he *rewards* or *punishes,* it is according to *truth* and *justice.*

Verse 5. *He loveth righteousness*] What he delights in himself, he loves to see in his followers.

The earth is full of the goodness of the Lord.] To hear its worthless inhabitants complain, one would think that God dispensed *evil,* not *good.* To examine the operation of his hand, every thing is marked with mercy and there is no place where his goodness does not appear. The *overflowing kindness* of God fills the earth. Even the iniquities of men are rarely a bar to his goodness: he causes his sun to rise on the evil and the good, and sends his rain upon the *just* and the *unjust.*

Verse 6. *By the word of the Lord were the heavens made*] This is illustrated in the 9th verse: "He spake, and it was done; he commanded, and it stood fast." This evidently refers to the account of the creation, as it stands in the first chapter of Genesis.

Verse 7. *He gathereth the waters of the sea together*] He separated the *water* from the *earth* and, while the latter was collected into continents, islands, mountains, hills, and valleys, the former was collected into *one place,* and

8 Let all the earth fear the LORD: let all the inhabitants of the world stand in awe of him.

9 For [m]he spake, and it was *done;* he commanded, and it stood fast.

10 [n]The LORD [o]bringeth the counsel of the heathen to naught: he maketh the devices of the people of none effect.

11 [p]The counsel of the LORD standeth for ever, the thoughts of his heart [q]to all generations.

12 [r]Blessed *is* the nation whose God *is* the LORD; *and* the people *whom* he hath [s]chosen for his own inheritance.

13 [t]The LORD looketh from heaven; he beholdeth all the sons of men.

14 From the place of his habitation he looketh upon all the inhabitants of the earth.

15 He fashioneth their hearts alike; he [u]considereth all their works.

16 [v]There is no king saved by the multitude of a host: a mighty man is not delivered by much strength.

17 [w]A horse *is* a vain thing for safety: neither shall he deliver *any* by his great strength.

18 [x]Behold, the eye of the LORD *is* [y]upon them that fear him, upon them that hope in his mercy;

[m]Gen. i. 3; Psa. cxlviii. 5——[n]Isa. viii. 10; xix. 3 [o]Heb. *maketh frustrate*——[p]Job xxiii. 13; Prov. xix. 21; Isaiah xlvi. 10——[q]Hebrew, *to generation and generation*——[r]Psalm lxv. 4; cxliv. 15——[s]Exodus xix. 5; Deuteronomy vii. 6

[t]2 Chron. xvi. 9; Job xxviii. 24; Psa. xi. 4; xiv. 2; Prov. xv. 3——[u]Job xxxiv. 21; Jer. xxxii. 19——[v]Psa. xliv. 6——[w]Psalm xx. 7; cxlvii. 10; Proverbs xxi. 31 [x]Job xxxvi. 7; Psalm xxxiv. 15; 1 Peter iii. 12——[y]Psalm cxlvii. 11

called *seas;* and by his all-controlling power and providence the waters have been retained in their place, so that they have not returned to drown the earth: and he has so adapted the *solar* and *lunar influence* exerted on the waters, that the tides are only raised to certain heights, so that they cannot overflow the shores, nor become dissipated in the atmospheric regions. In this one economy there is a whole circle of science. The quantity of matter in the sun, moon, and in the earth, are all adjusted to each other in this astonishing provision: the *course* of the *moon,* and the *diurnal* and *annual revolutions of the earth,* are all concerned here; and so concerned, that it requires some of the nicest of the Newtonian calculations to ascertain the laws by which the whole is affected.

Verse 8. *Let all the earth fear the Lord*] He who has thus *bound,* can *unloose;* he who has *created,* can *destroy.* He has promised life and prosperity *only* to the *godly;* let the *ungodly* stand in awe of him.

Verse 10. *The counsel of the heathen to naught*] This appears to be similar to what is mentioned in the second *Psalm;* the useless attempts of the Gentiles to prevent the extension of the kingdom of Christ in the earth: and it may refer to similar attempts of ungodly nations or men to prevent the promulgation of the Gospel, and the universal dissemination of truth in the world.

Verse 11. *The counsel of the Lord*] What he has determined shall be done. He determined to make a world, and he made it; to create man, and he created him. He determined that at a certain period God should be manifested in the flesh, and it was so; that he should taste death for every man, and he did so; that his Gospel should be preached in all the world; and behold it has already nearly overrun the whole earth. All his other counsels and thoughts, which refer to the *future,* shall be accomplished in their times.

Verse 12. *Blessed* is *the nation*] O how happy is that nation which has יהוה *Jehovah* for its אלהים *Elohim;* the self-existent and eternal Lord for its covenant God; one who should unite himself to it by connections and ties the most powerful and endearing! The word אלהים *Elohim,* which we translate GOD, refers to that economy in which God is manifested in the flesh.

The people whom *he hath chosen*] The *Jews,* who were *elected* to be his *heritage,* whom he preserved as such for two thousand years, and whom he has *reprobated* because of their unbelief and rebellion, and elected the Gentiles in their place.

Verse 13. *The Lord looketh from heaven*] This and the following verse seem to refer to God's *providence.* He sees all that is done in the earth, and his eye is on all the children of men.

Verse 15. *He fashioneth their hearts alike*] *He forms their hearts in unity;* he has formed them *alike;* they are all the *works of his hands:* and he has formed them with the same powers, faculties, passions, &c.; body and spirit having the same essential properties in every human being.

Verse 16. *There is no king saved by the multitude of a host*] Even in the midst of the most *powerful* and *numerous army,* no *king* is in *safety* unless he have God's protection. A king is but a *man,* and may as easily lose his life as one of his common soldiers.

A mighty man is not delivered by much strength.] There are times in which his might can be of no avail to him: and unless the *mighty,* the *wise,* the *honourable,* &c., have the protection of God, there is no time in which their *might* may not be turned into *weakness,* their *wisdom* into *folly,* and their *dignity* into *disgrace.*

Verse 17. *A horse* is *a vain thing for safety*] Even the horse, with all his fleetness, is no sure means of escape from danger: the *lion* or the *tiger* can overtake him or he may stumble, fall, and destroy his rider.

Verse 18. *Behold, the eye of the Lord*] Though all the above are unavailing, yet here is one thing that can never fail; "the eye of the Lord"—the watchful providence of the Most High, "is upon them that fear him, upon them that hope in his mercy."

19 To deliver their soul from death, and
[z]to keep them alive in famine.
20 [a]Our soul waiteth for the LORD: [b]he
is our help and our shield.
21 For our [c]heart shall rejoice in him, because we have trusted in his holy name.
22 Let thy mercy, O LORD, be upon us,
according as we hope in thee.

[z]Job v. 20; Psa. xxxvii. 19——[a]Psa. lxii. 1, 5; cxxx. 6——[b]Psa. cxv. 9, 10, 11——[c]Psa. xiii. 5; Zech. x. 7; John xvi. 22

Verse 19. *To deliver their soul from death*] To watch over and protect them in all sudden dangers and emergencies, so that they shall not *lose their* LIVES *by any accident.*

And to keep them alive in famine.] Not only prevent *sudden death* by an instantaneous interposition of my power, but keep them from a lingering death, by *extraordinary* supplies granted them in an *extraordinary manner;* because I am all in all, and all everywhere.

Verse 20. *Our soul waiteth*] Our whole life is employed in this blessed work; we *trust* in nothing but him; neither in multitudes of armed men, nor in natural strength, nor in the fleetest animals, nor in any thing human: we trust in Him alone "who is our help and our shield."

Verse 21. *For our heart shall rejoice in him*] Here is the fruit of our confidence: our *souls are always happy,* because we have taken God for our *portion.*

Verse 22. *Let thy mercy, O Lord, be upon us*] We cannot abide in this state unless upheld by thee; and, as we disclaim all *merit,* we seek for a continuance of thy *mercy;* and this we cannot expect but in a continual dependence on thee. "Let thy mercy, O Lord be upon us, according as we hope in thee."

Analysis of the Thirty-third Psalm

This Psalm is *eucharistic:* the contents are—

I. An *exhortation* to *praise* God, ver. 1, 2, 3.

II. The *arguments* he uses to enforce the duty, 4-19.

III. The *confidence* of God's people in his name. Their happiness, and petition, 20-22.

I. In the three first verses he exhorts men to praise God: but whom?

1. The *upright;* those who are not upright, cannot praise God.

2. That it be done with *zeal* and *affection;* with *singing,* with *voice,* and the *instruments* then in use; with some *new song,* composed on the occasion, for some new mercy; and that the whole be *skilfully* expressed.

II. This he urges on several good grounds:—

1. The first *argument,* in general drawn from the *truth,* the *faithfulness,* the *justice,* and *goodness* of God: 1. "For the word of the Lord is right." 2. "All his works are done in truth." 3. "He loveth righteousness and judgment." 4. "The earth is full of his goodness."

2. His *second argument* is drawn from God's power in the creation of all things, and that by his word alone, ver. 6, 7, 9; and upon it introduces, "Let all the earth fear the Lord; let all the inhabitants of the world stand in awe of him."

3. His *third argument* is drawn from God's *providence* in governing the world, which may easily be discerned by those who will diligently consider his ways and proceedings, both to other people and to his Church.

1. He makes void all enterprises undertaken against his will, not only of single men, but of whole nations. "The Lord bringeth the counsel of the heathen to naught; he maketh the devices of the people of none effect."

2. Whereas, on the contrary, what he hath decreed shall be done. "The counsel of the Lord standeth for ever; the thoughts of his heart to all generations." On the consideration of which he breaks out into this *epiphonema,* or joyous reflection: "Blessed is the nation whose God is the Lord! and the people whom he hath chosen for his own inheritance!"

After which he returns to his discourse on God's *providence,* and by a *hypotyposis,* or splendid imagery, amplifies his former argument. For he sets God before us, as some great king on his throne, providing for all the parts of his empire, examining all causes, and doing justice to every one.

1. "The Lord looks from heaven, and beholds all the sons of men."

2. "From the place of his habitation he looks upon all the inhabitants of the earth."

3. And he is not an *idle spectator:* "He sees and considers their hearts and their works."

And he sees in what they *put their confidence;* in their *armies,* their *strength,* their *horse,* but not in *him.* But all in vain; for "there is no king saved by the multitude of a host: a mighty man is not delivered by much strength. A horse is a vain thing for safety." Multitude, strength, &c., without God, are useless.

Hitherto he had given a proof of God's providence towards *all men,* but now he descends to a particular proof of it, by his care over his *Church,* which he wonderfully guides, defends, and protects, in all dangers and assaults: and that notice may be taken of it, he begins with, *Behold!*

1. "Behold, the eye of the Lord," his tenderest care, "is over them that fear him, upon them that hope in his mercy."

2. "To deliver their soul from death, and keep them alive in famine."

III. The three last verses contain the acclamation of God's people, who place all their hope and trust in him; for, being stimulated by the former arguments, they do *three* things:—

1. They profess and express their *faith* and *dependence* on God: "Our soul waiteth on God, he is our help and our shield."

2. They declare the *hope* by which they are upheld, and how *comforted:* "For our heart shall rejoice in him, because we have trusted in his holy name."

3. Upon this hope they commend themselves by prayer to God; "Let thy mercy, O Lord, be upon us, according as we hope in thee."

PSALM XXXIV

David praises God, and exhorts others to do the same, 1–3; *shows how he sought the Lord, and how he was found of him,* 4–6. *All are exhorted to taste and see the goodness of God; with the assurance of support and comfort,* 7–10. *He shows the way to attain happiness and long life,* 11–16; *the privileges of the righteous, and of all who sincerely seek God,* 17–22.

A Psalm of David, when he changed his behaviour before [a]Abimelech; who drove him away, and he departed

A. M. cir. 2942
B. C. cir. 1062
Sauli, Regis
Israelitarum,
cir. annum
34

I WILL [b]bless the LORD at all
times: his praise *shall* continually *be* in my mouth.
2 My soul shall make her
[c]boast in the LORD: [d]the humble shall hear
thereof, and be glad.

3 O [e]magnify the LORD with
me, and let us exalt his name
together.
4 I [f]sought the LORD, and he
heard me, and delivered me from all my
fears.
5 [g]They looked unto him, and were lightened; and their faces were not ashamed.

A. M. cir. 2942
B. C. cir. 1062
Sauli, Regis
Israelitarum,
cir. annum
34

---

[a]Or, *Achish;* 1 Samuel xxi. 13——[b]Ephesians v. 20; 1 Thessalonians v. 18; 2 Thessalonians i. 3; ii. 13
[c]Jer. ix. 24; 1 Cor. i. 31; 2 Cor. x. 17

[d]Psa. cxix. 74; cxlii. 7——[e]Psa. lxix. 30; Luke i. 46
[f]Matt. vii. 7; Luke xi. 9——[g]Or, *They flowed* unto him

NOTES ON PSALM XXXIV

The *title* states that this is "A Psalm of David, when he changed his behaviour before Abimelech; who drove him away, and he departed." The history of this transaction may be found in 1 Sam. xxi.; on which chapter see the notes. But *Abimelech* is not the person there mentioned; it was *Achish,* king of Gath, called here *Abimelech,* because that was a common name of the Philistine kings. Neither MS. nor version reads *Achish* in this place; and all the versions agree in the title as it stands in our version, except the *Syriac,* which states it to be "A Psalm of David, when he went to the house of the Lord, that he might give the first-fruits to the priests."

Of the *occasion* of this Psalm, as stated here, I have given my opinion in the notes on 1 Sam. xxi., to which I have nothing to add. On the whole I prefer the view taken of it by the *Septuagint,* which intimates that "David fell into an epileptic fit; that he frothed at the mouth, fell against the doorposts, and gave such unequivocal evidences of being subject to epileptic fits, and during the time his intellect became so much impaired, that *Achish Abimelech* dismissed him from his court." This saves the character of David; and if it cannot be vindicated in this way, then let it fall under reproach as to this thing; for hypocrisy, deceit, and falsehood, can never be right in the sight of God, whatever men may ingeniously say to excuse them.

This is the *second* of the *acrostic* or *alphabetical Psalms,* each verse beginning with a consecutive letter of the Hebrew alphabet. But in this Psalm some derangement has taken place. The verse which begins with ו *vau,* and which should come in between the *fifth* and *sixth,* is totally wanting; and the *twenty-second* verse is entirely out of the series; it is, however, my opinion that this verse (the *twenty-second*) which now begins with פ *phe,* פודה *podeh, redeemeth,* was originally written ופודה *vepodeh* or with פדה *padah,* as more than a hundred of Dr. *Kennicott's* MSS. read it, thus making ופדה *vepodah, "and* will redeem" and this reads admirably in the above connection. I shall here place the verses at one view, and the reader shall judge for himself:

Ver. 5. "They looked unto him, and were enlightened: and their faces were not ashamed."

Ver. 22. "AND the Lord will redeem the soul of his servants, and none of them that trust in him shall be desolate."

Ver. 6. "This poor man cried, and the Lord heard *him,* and saved him out of all his troubles."

Ver. 7. "The angel of the Lord encampeth round about them that fear him, and delivereth them."

Thus we find the connection complete, with the above emendation.

Verse 1. *I will bless the Lord at all times*] He has laid me under endless obligation to him, and I will praise him while I have a being.

Verse 2. *My soul shall make her boast*] Shall *set itself to praise* the Lord—shall consider this its chief work.

The humble] ענוים *anavim,* the afflicted, such as *David* had been.

Verse 3. *Magnify the Lord with me*] גדלו ליהוה *gaddelu layhovah,* "make greatness to Jehovah;" show his greatness; and let "us exalt his name," let us show how *high* and *glorious* it is.

Verse 4. *I sought the Lord*] This is the *reason* and *cause* of his gratitude. I sought the Lord, and he heard me, and delivered me out of all my fears. This answers to the history; for when David heard what the servants of Achish said concerning him, "he laid up the words in his heart, and was greatly afraid," 1 Sam. xxi. 13. To save him, God caused the epileptic fit to seize him; and, in consequence, he was dismissed by Achish, as one whose defection from his master, and union with the Philistines, could be of no use, and thus David's life and honour were preserved. The reader will see that I proceed on the ground laid down by the *Septuagint.* See before, verse 1.

Verse 5. *They looked unto him*] Instead of הביטו *hibbitu,* they *looked,* several of Dr. *Kennicott's* and *De Rossi's* MSS. have הביטו *habbitu,* with the point *pathach,* "Look ye."

And their faces were not ashamed.] Some

A. M. cir. 2942
B. C. cir. 1062
Sauli, Regis
Israelitarum,
cir. annum
34

6 [h]This poor man cried, and
the LORD heard *him,* and [i]saved
him out of all his troubles.
7 [k]The angel of the LORD [l]en-
campeth round about them that fear him, and
delivereth them.
8 O [m]taste and see that the LORD *is* good:
[n]blessed is the man *that* trusteth in him.
9 [o]O fear the LORD, ye his saints: for *there*
is no want to them that fear him.
10 [p]The young lions do lack, and suffer
hunger: [q]but they that seek the LORD shall
not want any good *thing.*
11 Come, ye children, hearken unto me:
[r]I will teach you the fear of the LORD.

12 [s]What man *is he*
that desireth life, *and* loveth
many days, that he may see
good?
13 Keep thy tongue from evil, and thy lips
from [t]speaking guile.
14 [u]Depart from evil, and do good; [v]seek
peace, and pursue it.
15 [w]The eyes of the LORD *are* upon the
righteous, and his ears *are open* unto their
[x]cry.
16 [y]The face of the LORD *is* against them
that do evil, [z]to cut off the remembrance of
them from the earth.
17 *The righteous* cry, and [a]the LORD hear-

A. M. cir. 2942
B. C. cir. 1062
Sauli, Regis
Israelitarum,
cir. annum
34

[h]Psa. iii. 4——[i]Ver. 17, 19; 2 Sam. xxii. 1——[k]Dan. vi. 22; Heb. i. 14——[l]See Gen. xxxii. 1, 2; 2 Kings vi. 17; Zech. ix. 8——[m]1 Pet. ii. 3——[n]Psa. ii. 12——[o]Psa. xxxi. 23——[p]Job iv. 10, 11——[q]Psa. lxxxiv. 11——[r]Psa. xxxii. 8——[s]1 Pet. iii. 10, 11

[t]1 Pet. ii. 22——[u]Psa. xxxvii. 27; Isa. i. 16, 17——[v]Rom. xii. 18; Heb. xii. 14——[w]Job xxxvi. 7; Psa. xxxiii. 18; 1 Pet. iii. 12——[x]Ver. 6, 17——[y]Lev. xvii. 10; Jer. xliv. 11; Amos ix. 4——[z]Proverbs x. 7——[a]Verse 6, 15, 19; Psa. cxlv. 19, 20

MSS., and the *Complutensian Polyglot,* make this clause the beginning of a new verse and as it begins with a *vau,* ופניהם *upheneyhem,* "*and* their faces," they make it supply the place of the verse which appears to be lost; but see what is said in the introduction before the *first* verse.

Verse 6. *This poor man cried*] זה עני *zeh ani,* "This *afflicted* man," *David.*

Verse 7. *The angel of the Lord encampeth round*] I should rather consider this angel in the light of a *watchman going round his circuit,* and having for the objects of his especial care such as *fear the Lord.*

Verse 8. *O taste and see that the Lord* is *good*] Apply to him by faith and prayer; plead his *promises,* he will fulfil them; and you shall know in consequence, that *the Lord is good.* God has put it in the power of every man to *know* whether the religion of the Bible be true or false. The *promises* relative to enjoyments in this life are the grand tests of Divine revelation. These must be fulfilled to all them who with deep repentance and true faith turn unto the Lord, if the revelation which contains them be of God. Let any man in this spirit approach his Maker, and plead the *promises* that are suited to his case, and he will soon know whether the doctrine be of God. He shall *taste,* and then *see, that the Lord is good,* and that the *man is blessed who trusts in him.* This is what is called *experimental religion;* the living, operative knowledge that a true believer has that he is passed from death unto life; that his sins are forgiven him for Christ's sake, the Spirit himself bearing witness with his spirit that he is a child of God. And, as long as he is faithful, he carries about with him the testimony of the Holy Ghost; and he knows that he is of God, by the Spirit which God has given him.

Verse 9. There is *no want to them that fear him.*] He who truly *fears* God *loves* him; and he who *loves* God *obeys* him, and to him who *fears, loves,* and obeys God, there can be no want of things essential to his happiness, whether spiritual or temporal, for this life or for that which is to come. This verse is wanting in the *Syriac.*

Verse 10. *The young lions do lack*] Instead of כפירים *kephirim,* the young lions, one of *Kennicott's* MSS. has כבירים *cabbirim,* "powerful men." The *Vulgate, Septuagint, Æthiopic, Syriac, Arabic,* and *Anglo-Saxon* have the same reading. *Houbigant* approves of this; and indeed the sense and connection seem to require it. My old *Psalter* reads:—**The Ryche had nede; and thai hungerd: but sekand Lard sal noght be lessed of alle gode.** That es, says the paraphrase, with outen lessyng thai sal have God; that es alle gode; for in God is al gode.

Verse 11. *Come, ye children*] All ye that are of an *humble, teachable* spirit.

I will teach you the fear of the Lord.] I shall introduce the *translation* and *paraphrase* from my old Psalter; and the rather because I believe there is a reference to that very improper and unholy method of teaching youth the system of heathen mythology before they are taught one sound lesson of true divinity, till at last their *minds* are *imbued* with *heathenism,* and the vicious conduct of gods, goddesses, and heroes, here very properly called *tyrants, becomes* the model of their own; and they are as heathenish *without* as they are heathenish *within.*

Trans. **Cummes sones heres me: dred of Lard I sal gou lere.**

Par. **Cummes** with trauth and luf: **sones,** qwam I gette in haly lere: **heres me.** With eres of hert. **I sal lere you,** noght the fabyls of poetes; na the storys of tyrauntz; bot the dred of oure Larde, that wyl bryng you til the felaghschippe of aungels; and thar in is lyfe." I need not paraphrase this paraphrase, as it is plain enough.

Verse 12. *What man* is he that *desireth life*] He who wishes to live long and to live happily, let him act according to the following directions. For a comment upon this and the *four* ensuing verses, see the notes on 1 Peter iii. 10-12.

Verse 17. The righteous *cry*] There is no

A. M. cir. 2942 B. C. cir. 1062 Sauli, Regis Israelitarum, cir. annum 34

eth, and delivereth them out of
all their troubles.
18 [b]The LORD *is* nigh [c]unto
[d]them that are of a broken heart;
and saveth [e]such as be of a contrite spirit.
19 [f]Many *are* the afflictions of the righteous: [g]but the LORD delivereth him out of
them all.
20 He keepeth all his bones:
[h]not one of them is broken.
21 [i]Evil shall slay the wicked:
and they that hate the righteous
[k]shall be desolate.
22 The LORD [l]redeemeth the soul of his
servants: and none of them that trust in him
shall be desolate.

[b]Psa. cxlv. 18——[c]Psa. li. 17; Isa. lvii. 15; lxi. 1; lxvi. 2——[d]Heb. *to the broken of heart*——[e]Heb. *contrite of spirit*——[f]Prov. xxiv. 16; 2 Tim. iii. 11, 12

[g]Ver. 6, 17——[h]John xix. 36——[i]Psa. xciv. 23——[k]Or, *shall be guilty*——[l]2 Sam. iv. 9; 1 Kings i. 29; Psa. lxxi. 23; ciii. 4; Lam. iii. 58

word in the present *Hebrew* text for righteous; but all the *versions* preserve it. I suppose it was lost through its similitude to the word צעקו *tsaaku*, they cry צעקו צדיקים *tsaaku tsaddikim*, the righteous cry.

Verse 18. *A broken heart*] נשברי לב *nishberey leb*, the heart *broken* to *shivers*.

A contrite spirit.] דכאי רוח *dakkeey ruach*, "the beaten-out spirit." In both words the *hammer* is necessarily implied; in breaking to pieces the ore first, and then plating out the metal when it has been separated from the ore. This will call to the reader's remembrance Jer. xxiii. 29: "Is not my word like as a fire, saith the Lord? And like a *hammer* that breaketh the *rock* in pieces?" The *breaking to shivers*, and *beating out*, are metaphorical expressions: so are the *hammer* and the *rock*. What the large *hammer* struck on a rock by a powerful hand would do, so does the word of the Lord when struck on the sinner's heart by the power of the Holy Spirit. The *broken heart*, and the *contrite spirit*, are two essential characteristics of true repentance.

Verse 19. *Many* are *the afflictions of the righteous*] No commander would do justice to a brave and skilful soldier, by refusing him opportunities to put his skill and bravery to proof by combating with the adversary; or by preventing him from taking the *post of danger* when necessity required it. The righteous are God's soldiers. He suffers them to be tried, and sometimes to enter into the hottest of the battle and in their victory the power and influence of the grace of God is shown, as well as their faithfulness.

Delivereth him out of them all.] He may well combat heartily, who knows that if he fight in the Lord, he shall necessarily be the conqueror.

Verse 20. *He keepeth all his bones*] He takes care of his life; and if he have *scars*, they are honourable ones.

Verse 21. *Evil shall slay the wicked*] The very thing in which they delight shall become their bane and their ruin.

They that hate the righteous] All persecutors of God's people shall be followed by the chilling blast of God's displeasure in this world; and if they repent not, shall perish everlastingly.

Verse 22. *The Lord redeemeth*] Both the *life* and *soul* of God's followers are ever in danger, but God is continually redeeming both.

Shall be desolate.] Literally, *shall be guilty*. They shall be preserved from sin, and neither forfeit *life* nor soul. This verse probably should come in after the fifth. See the introduction to this Psalm.

ANALYSIS OF THE THIRTY-FOURTH PSALM

This Psalm is composed with great art, and this must be attended to by those who would analyze it. The scope of it is to praise God, and to instruct in his fear. Its parts are, in general, the following:—

I. He praises God himself, and calls upon others to follow his example, 1-8.

II. He assumes the office of a teacher, and instructs both young and old in the fear of the Lord, 9-22.

1. He praises God, and expresses himself thus:—1. I will bless the Lord. 2. His praise shall be in my mouth. 3. It shall be in my mouth continually. 4. It shall be expressed by a *tongue* affected by the *heart:* "My soul shall make her boast in the Lord." 5. And so long would he continue it till others should be moved to do the like: "The humble shall hear thereof, and be glad."

2. Upon which he calls upon others to join with him: "O magnify the Lord with me, and let us exalt his name together." And to encourage them he proposes his own example: "I sought the Lord," &c. Should it be said this was a singular mercy shown to David which others are not to expect, he in effect replies, No; a mercy it is, but it belongs to all that seek God: "They looked unto him," &c. But should not this satisfy, and should they rejoin, This poor man (David) cried, and the Lord heard him, but David was in the Divine favour; he may be supposed to reply by this general maxim: "The angel of the Lord encampeth round about them that fear him;" and be they who they may, *if they fear God*, this is their privilege.

II. Now he assumes the chair of the teacher; and the lessons are *two:*—

1. That they make a trial of God's goodness: "O taste and see that the Lord is good."

2. That they become his servants: "O fear ye the Lord, for there is no want," &c.

And this he illustrates by a comparison: "The young lions (or, the rich and the powerful) may lack and suffer hunger," but they *that seek the Lord* shall not.

These promises and blessings belong only to them that fear the Lord and lest some should imagine they had this fear, and were entitled to the promise, he shows them what this fear is.

He calls an assembly, and thus addresses them: "Come, ye children, and hearken unto me and I will teach you the fear of the Lord." That fear of the Lord which, if a man be desirous of life, and to see many days, shall satisfy him; and if he be ambitious to see good, the peace of a quiet *soul* and a good conscience shall lodge with him.

1. Let him be sure to take care of his tongue: "keep thy tongue from evil, and thy lips that they speak no guile."

2. Let him act according to justice: "Depart from evil."

3. Let him be charitable, ready to do good works: "Do good."

4. Let him be peaceable: "Seek peace, and pursue it."

These are the characteristics of those who fear the Lord, and seek him; and they shall want no manner of thing that is good.

It may be objected: The righteous are exposed to afflictions, &c., and ungodly men have power and prosperity; to which it may be answered: Afflictions do not make the godly *miserable*, nor does prosperity make the wicked *happy*. 1. As to the righteous, they are always objects of God's merciful regards: "For the eyes of the Lord are upon the righteous, and his ears are open to their prayers." But, 2. "The face of the Lord is against those who do evil," &c.

These points he illustrates:—

1. The righteous cries, and the Lord heareth him, and delivereth him out of all his troubles; either, 1. By taking *them* from *him* or, 2. By taking *him* from *them*.

2. "The Lord is nigh to them that are of a broken heart," &c. Thus he comforts, confirms, and strengthens.

3. Although the afflictions of the righteous are many, yet the Lord delivers him out of them all; makes him patient, constant, cheerful in all, superior to all.

4. "He keeps all his bones." He permits him to suffer no essential hurt.

But as to the ungodly, it is not so with them; the very root of their perdition is their malice, which they show, 1. To God; 2. To good men.

1. "Evil shall slay the wicked."

2. "And they that hate the righteous shall be desolate."

And then David concludes the Psalm with this excellent sentiment; Though God may suffer his servants to come into trouble, yet he delivers them from it. For it belongs to redemption to free one from misery; for no man can be redeemed who is under no hardship. This shall be done, says David. The "Lord redeemeth the souls of his servants, and none of them that trust in him shall be desolate." The Lord redeems from *trouble* and *affliction*, as well as from *sin*. He knows how to deliver the godly *from* temptation; and he knows how to preserve them *in* it. But it is his *servants* that he redeems, not his *enemies*. The *servant* may confidently look to his *master* for support.

PSALM XXXV

The psalmist, in great straits, prays for his personal safety, 1–3; *and for the confusion of his enemies,* 4–8; *expresses his confidence in God,* 9, 10; *mentions his kindness to those who had rewarded him evil for his good,* 11–16; *appeals to God against them,* 17–26; *prays for those who befriended him; and praises God for his goodness,* 27, 28.

VII. DAY. MORNING PRAYER

A Psalm of David

A. M. cir. 2943
B. C. cir. 1061
Sauli, Regis
Israelitarum,
cir. annum
35

PLEAD [a]*my cause,* O LORD, with them that strive with me: [b]fight against them that fight against me.

2 [c]Take hold of shield and buckler, and stand up for mine help.

3 Draw out also the spear, and stop *the way* against them that persecute me: say unto my soul, I *am* thy salvation.

A. M. cir. 2943
B. C. cir. 1061
Sauli, Regis
Israelitarum,
cir. annum
35

4 [d]Let them be confounded and put to shame that seek after my soul: let them be [e]turned back and brought to confusion that devise my hurt.

[a]Psa. xliii. 1; cxix. 154; Lam. iii. 58——[b]Exod. xiv. 25——[c]Isa. xlii. 13

[d]Verse 26; Psalm xl. 14, 15; lxx. 2, 3——[e]Psalm cxxix. 5

NOTES ON PSALM XXXV

There is nothing in the *title* worthy of remark. The Psalm is simply attributed to David, and was most probably of his composing; and refers to the time of his persecution by Saul and his courtiers. The *Syriac* says it was composed when the Idumeans attacked David. The Arabic says it is a prophecy concerning the incarnation, and concerning the things practised against Jeremiah by the *people*. Some think that our Lord's sufferings are particularly pointed out here; and Bishop *Horsley* thinks that verses 11 to 16 apply more literally and exactly to Christ than to any other whomsoever.

Verse 1. *Plead* my cause, *O Lord*] Literally, *Contend, Lord, with them that contend with me.* The word is often used in a *forensic* or *law* sense.

Verse 2. *Take hold of shield and buckler*] Let them be discomfited in battle who are striving to destroy my life. It is by the *shield* and *buckler* of *others*, not any of his *own*, that God overthrows the enemies of his people. This is spoken merely after the manner of men.

Verse 3. *Say unto my soul, I* am *thy salvation.*] Give me an assurance that thou wilt defend both body and soul against my adversaries.

Verse 4. *Let them be confounded*] Let none of their projects or devices against me succeed. Blast all their designs.

The *imprecations* in these verses against enemies are all *legitimate*. They are not against the *souls* or *eternal welfare* of those sinners,

A. M. cir. 2943
B. C. cir. 1061
Sauli, Regis
Israelitarum,
cir. annum
35

5 [f]Let them be as chaff before
the wind: and let the angel of
the LORD chase *them.*
6 Let their way be [g]dark [h]and
slippery: and let the angel of the LORD persecute them.
7 For without cause have they [i]hid for me
their net *in* a pit, *which* without cause they
have digged for my soul.
8 Let [k]destruction come upon him [l]at unawares; and [m]let his net that he hath hid
catch himself: into that very destruction let
him fall.
9 And my soul shall be joyful in the LORD:
[n]it shall rejoice in his salvation.
10 [o]All my bones shall say, LORD, [p]who *is* like
unto thee, which deliverest the poor from him
that is too strong for him, yea,
the poor and the needy from
him that spoileth him?
11 [q]False [r]witnesses did rise
up; [s]they laid to my charge *things* that I
knew not.
12 [t]They rewarded me evil for good *to* the
[u]spoiling of my soul.
13 But as for me, [v]when they were sick, my
clothing *was* sackcloth: I [w]humbled my soul
with fasting; [x]and my prayer returned into
mine own bosom.
14 I [y]behaved myself [z]as though *he had*
been my friend *or* brother: I bowed down
heavily, as one that mourneth *for his*
mother.
15 But in mine [a]adversity they rejoiced,

A. M. cir. 2943
B. C. cir. 1061
Sauli, Regis
Israelitarum,
cir. annum
35

---

[f]Job. xxi. 18; Psa. i. 4; lxxxiii. 13; Isa. xxix. 5; Hos. xiii. 3——[g]Heb. *darkness and slipperiness*——[h]Psa. lxxiii. 18; Jer. xxiii. 12——[i]Psa. ix. 15——[k]1 Thess. v. 3 [l]Heb. which *he knoweth not of*——[m]Psa. vii. 15, 16; lvii. 6; cxli. 9, 10; Prov. v. 22——[n]Psa. xiii. 5——[o]See Psa. li. 8 [p]Exod. xv. 11; Psa. lxxi. 19

[q]Hebrew, *Witnesses of wrong*——[r]Psalm xxvii. 12 [s]Heb. *they asked me*——[t]Psa. xxxviii. 20; cix. 3, 4, 5; Jer. xviii. 20; John x. 32——[u]Heb. *depriving*——[v]Job xxx. 25; Psa. lxix. 10, 11——[w]Or, *afflicted*——[x]Matt. x. 13; Luke x. 6——[y]Heb. *walked*——[z]Heb. *as a friend, as a brother to me*——[a]Heb. *halting;* Psalm xxxviii. 17

---

but against their *schemes* and *plans* for *destroying the life of an innocent man;* and the holiest Christian may offer up such prayers against his adversaries. If a man aim a blow at another with a design to take away his life, and the blow would infallibly be mortal if it took place, and the person about to be slain see that by breaking the arm of his adversary he may prevent his own death, and thus save his enemy from *actual* murder; it is his duty to prevent this double evil by breaking the arm of the blood-thirsty man. It is on this principle that David prays against his adversaries in the first eight verses of this Psalm.

Verse 5. *Let the angel of the Lord chase* them.] By *angel* we may either understand one of those *spirits*, whether good or bad, commonly thus denominated, or *any thing* used by God himself as the instrument of their confusion.

Verse 6. *Let their way be dark*] Let them lose their way, be entangled in morasses and thickets, and be confounded in all their attempts to injure me. All these phrases are *military;* and relate to *ambushes, hidden snares, forced marches* in order to *surprise*, and *stratagems* of different kinds.

Verse 7. *For without cause have they hid for me their net* in *a pit*] The word שחת *shachath*, a *pit*, belongs to the second member of this verse; and the whole should be read thus: For without a cause they have hidden for me their net, without a cause they have digged a *pit* for my life. They have used every degree and species of cunning and deceit to ruin me.

Verse 8. *Let his net that he hath hid*] See the notes on Psa. vii. 15 and 16.

Verse 9. *My soul*] My life, thus saved—

Shall be joyful in the Lord] I am so circumstanced at present as to be in the utmost danger of being destroyed by my foes; if I escape, it must be by the strong arm of the Lord; and to him shall the glory be given.

Verse 10. *All my bones shall say*] My life being preserved, all the members of my body shall magnify thy saving mercy.

Deliverest the poor] This is a general maxim: God is peculiarly mindful of the poor. Where secular advantages are withheld, there is the more need for spiritual help. God considers this, and his kind providence works accordingly.

Verse 11. *False witnesses did rise up*] There is no doubt that several of this kind were found to depose against the life of David; and we know that the wicked Jews employed such against the life of Christ. See Matt. xxvi. 59, 60.

They laid to my charge things *that I knew not.*] They produced the most unfounded charges; things of which I had never before heard.

Verse 12. To *the spoiling of my soul*] *To destroy my life;* so נפש *nephesh* should be translated in a multitude of places, where our translators have used the word *soul.*

Verse 13. *When they were sick*] This might refer to the case of Absalom, who was much beloved of his father, and for whose life and prosperity he no doubt often prayed, wept, and fasted.

My prayer returned into mine own bosom.] Though from the wayward and profligate life they led, they did not profit by my prayers, yet God did not permit me to pray in vain. They were like alms given to the miserable for God's sake, who takes care to return to the merciful man tenfold into his bosom. The *bosom* is not only the place where the Asiatics carry their purses, but also where they carry any thing that is given to them.

Verse 14. *Mourneth* for his *mother.*] כאבל אם *caabel em*, as a mourning mother. How expressive is this word!

Verse 15. *But in mine adversity they rejoiced*] How David was mocked and insulted

A. M. cir. 2943
B. C. cir. 1061
Sauli, Regis
Israelitarum,
cir. annum
35

and gathered themselves together: *yea,* [b]the abjects gathered themselves together against
me, and I knew *it* not; they did
[c]tear *me,* and ceased not:
16 With hypocritical mockers in feasts,
[d]they gnashed upon me with their teeth.
17 LORD, how long wilt thou [e]look on?
rescue my soul from their destructions, [f]my[g]
darling from the lions.
18 [h]I will give thee thanks in the great congregation: I will praise thee among [i]much
people.
19 [k]Let not them that are mine enemies
[l]wrongfully rejoice over me: *neither* [m]let them
wink with the eye [n]that hate me without a cause.
20 For they speak not peace: but they devise deceitful matters against *them that are*
quiet in the land.
21 Yea, they [o]opened their mouth wide
against me, *and* said, [p]Aha, aha, our eye hath
seen *it.*
22 *This* thou hast [q]seen, O
LORD: [r]keep not silence: O
LORD, be not [s]far from me.
23 [t]Stir up thyself, and awake
to my judgment, *even* unto my cause, my God
and my Lord.
24 [u]Judge me, O LORD, my God, [v]according
to thy righteousness; and [w]let them not rejoice over me.
25 [x]Let them not say in their hearts, [y]Ah,
so would we have it: let them not say, [z]We
have swallowed him up.
26 [a]Let them be ashamed and brought to
confusion together that rejoice at mine hurt:
let them be [b]clothed with shame and dishonour that [c]magnify *themselves* against me.
27 [d]Let them shout for joy, and be glad, that
favour [e]my righteous cause: yea, let them [f]say
continually, Let the LORD be magnified, [g]which
hath pleasure in the prosperity of his servant.
28 [h]And my tongue shall speak of thy righteousness *and* of thy praise all the day long.

A. M. cir. 2943
B. C. cir. 1061
Sauli, Regis
Israelitarum,
cir. annum
35

[b]Job xxx. 1, 8, 12——[c]Job xvi. 9——[d]Job xvi. 9; Psa. xxxvii. 12; Lam. ii. 16——[e]Hab. i. 13——[f]Heb. *my only one*——[g]Psa. xxii. 20——[h]Psa. xxii. 25, 31; xl. 9, 10; cxi. 1——[i]Heb. *strong*——[k]Psa. xiii. 4; xxv. 2; xxxviii. 16——[l]Heb. *falsely;* Psa. xxxviii. 19——[m]Job xv. 12; Prov. vi. 13; x. 10——[n]Psa. lxix. 4; cix. 3; cxix. 161; Lam. iii. 52; John xv. 25——[o]Psa. xxii. 13——[p]Psa. xl. 15; liv. 7; lxx. 3——[q]Exod. iii. 7; Acts vii. 34

[r]Psa. xxviii. 1; lxxxiii. 1——[s]Psa. x. 1; xxii. 11, 19; xxxviii. 21; lxxi. 12——[t]Psa. xliv. 23; lxxx. 2——[u]Psa. xxvi. 1——[v]2 Thess. i. 6——[w]Ver. 19——[x]Psa. xxvii. 12; lxx. 3; cxl. 8——[y]Heb. *Ah, ah, our soul*——[z]Lam. ii. 16——[a]Ver. 4; Psa. xl. 14——[b]Psa. cix. 29; cxxxii. 18 [c]Psa. xxxviii. 16——[d]Rom. xii. 15; 1 Cor. xii. 26 [e]Heb. *my righteousness;* Prov. viii. 18——[f]Psa. lxx. 4 [g]Psa. cxlix. 4——[h]Psa. l. 15; li. 14; lxxi. 24

in the case of Absalom's rebellion by Shimei and others, is well known.

The abjects] נכים *nechim,* the *smiters,* probably hired assassins. They were everywhere lying in wait, to take away my life.

Verse 16. *With hypocritical mockers in feasts*] These verses seem to be prophetic of the treatment of Christ. *They did tear me, and I knew it not.* They blindfolded and buffeted him; they placed him in such circumstances as not to be able to discern who insulted him, except by a supernatural knowledge. *With hypocritical mockers in feasts* may also relate prophetically to our Lord's sufferings. Herod clothed him in a purple robe, put a *reed* in his hand for a sceptre, bowed the knee before him, and set him at naught. Here their hypocritical conduct (pretending one thing while they meant another) was manifest, and possibly this occurred at one of Herod's *feasts.*

Verse 17. *My darling*] יחידתי *yechidathi, my only one,* Psa. xxii. 20. *My united one,* or *He that is alone.* Perhaps this may relate to Christ. See the note on Psa. xxii. 20.

Verse 18. *I will give thee thanks in the great congregation*] I hope to be able to attend at the tabernacle with thy followers, and there publicly express my gratitude for the deliverance thou hast given me.

Verse 19. *That are mine enemies*] Saul and his courtiers.

Verse 21. *They opened their mouth wide*] Gaped upon me to express their contempt.

And *said, Aha, aha, our eye hath seen* it.] They said, האח האח *heach, heach,* the last syllable in each word being a protracted strongly guttural sound, marking insult and triumph at the same time. It is the word which we translate *Ah,* ver. 25.

Verse 22. This *thou hast seen*] I have no need to adduce evidences of these wrongs; thou, to whom I appeal, hast seen them. Therefore,

Verse 23. *Stir up thyself, and awake to my judgment*] I have delivered my cause into thy hand, and appeal to thee as my Judge; and by thy decision I am most willing to abide.

Verse 24. *Judge me, O Lord my God*] The manner of his appeal shows the strong confidence he had in his own innocence.

Verse 25. *Swallowed him up.*] בלענוהו *billaanuhu, we have gulped him down.*

Verse 26. *Let them be ashamed*] This may be a prophetic declaration against Saul and his courtiers. They were ashamed, confounded, clothed with shame, and dishonoured. All these took place in Saul's last battle with the Philistines, where he lost his crown and his life, and came to a most dishonourable end.

Verse 27. *Let them shout for joy and be glad*] While my enemies are confounded, let my friends exult in the Lord; and let them all praise him for his marvellous kindness to me.

Verse 28. *And my tongue shall speak*] I, who am chiefly concerned, and who have received most, am under the greatest obligation; and it will require the constant gratitude and obedience of my whole life to discharge the mighty debt I owe.

Analysis of the Thirty-fifth Psalm

This Psalm may be divided into *three* parts:—

I. A prayer for defence against his enemies. In which he prays, 1. For protection, ver. 1, 2, 3, 17, 19, 22, 23, 24, 25. And, 2. Imprecates evil to fall on their counsels and designs.

II. A bitter complaint against the malice of his enemies, which he pours out into the ears of God as motives to plead his cause, ver. 7, 11, 12, 13, 14, 15, 16, 19, 20, 21.

III. An expression of his trust and confidence in God for help and deliverance; his joy in it, ver. 9, 10; his thanks for it, ver. 18, 28; and a motive to others to do the like, ver. 27.

1. In the courts of men and princes innocent persons are often oppressed by false accusations and calumnies, persecuted and overborne by power.

He then, *first*, prays to God to be his Advocate, his Patron, and his Protector: 1. "Plead my cause, O Lord, with them that strive against me." 2. "Fight against them that fight against me," &c. 3. "Say unto my soul, I am thy salvation." Assure me of thy favour.

He *secondly*, begins an imprecation against his enemies: 1. "Let them be confounded and put to shame," ver. 4. 2. "Let them be as chaff before the wind," ver. 5. 3. "Let their way be dark and slippery," ver. 6. 4. "Let destruction come upon him unawares," ver. 8.

And here he inserts some reasons for his *petition* and *imprecation:*—

1. From the *justice* of *his* cause, and *their injustice:* "Without cause they hid for me their net," ver. 7.

2. From his gratitude; that, being delivered, he would be thankful: "And my soul shall be joyful in the Lord," &c., ver. 9, 10.

3. From his enemies' dealings with him, ver. 11-17.

II. He then enters upon his complaint; and lays to their charge,

1. *Perfidiousness,* extreme malice, and perjury: "False witnesses did rise," &c.

2. *Ingratitude.* They rewarded me evil for good. Good he did to them; for, when they were afflicted, he fasted and prayed for them.

3. They were *cruel* to him: "In my adversity they rejoiced."

4. They *mocked* him and made him their cruel sport: "The abjects gathered themselves together against me," &c.

5. And a *conspiracy* in all, ver. 20, 21.

Then he returns again to his petition; and expostulates with God, wondering that he should be so patient with them: "Lord, how long wilt thou look on? Rescue my soul from destruction," &c.

And, to move God the sooner to do it, he repeats his former reason, ver. 9, engaging himself to be thankful: "I will give thee thanks in the great congregation; I will praise thee among much people."

He continues his suit to the end of the Psalm; sometimes *praying,* at others *imprecating.*

1. He deprecates: "Let not my enemies wrongfully rejoice over me, neither let them wink with the eye," &c. And that God may be the readier to hear him, and stay their joy and triumph, he subjoins these reasons: 1. "For they speak not peace." 2. "They devise deceitful matters against them that are quiet in the land." 3. They are impudent, lying people: "Yea, they opened their mouth wide against me," &c. This is a truth; this is not hidden from thee: "This thou hast seen," and from them to thee I turn my eyes; and thus renew my prayer:—

1. "Keep not silence." Do not appear to neglect my cause; nor to let them pass on with impunity.

2. "Stir up thyself, and awake to my judgment," &c. Defend me, and confound them:—

3. "Judge me according to thy righteousness," which suffers not the just to be always oppressed.

4. "Let them not rejoice over me," and, in me, over the truth, and over a just cause.

5. "Let them not say in their hearts, So would we have it," &c.

6. But rather let that befall them which I have prayed for: "Let them be ashamed,—brought to confusion,—and clothed with shame and dishonour, that magnify themselves against me."

III. In the conclusion he expresses his trust and confidence in God; and intimates that if he be heard, then he, and the whole Church, and all good men, will rejoice together.

1. To them he first directs his speech: "Let them shout for joy that favour my righteous cause; yea, let them say continually; Let the Lord be magnified, which hath pleasure in the prosperity of his servant."

2. He then declares what effect this will have upon him in particular: "My tongue shall speak of thy righteousness and of thy praise all the day long."

PSALM XXXVI

The miserable state of the wicked, 1–4. *The excellence of God's mercy in itself, and to his followers,* 5–9. *He prays for the upright,* 10; *for himself, that he may be saved from pride and violence,* 11; *and shows the end of the workers of iniquity,* 12.

To the chief Musician, *A Psalm* of David the servant of the LORD

THE transgression of the wicked saith within my heart, *that* [a]*there is* no fear of God before his eyes.

2 For [b]he flattereth himself in his own eyes, [c]until his iniquity be found to be hateful.

3 The words of his mouth *are* iniquity and [d]deceit: [e]he hath left off to be wise, *and* to do good.

4 [f]He deviseth [g]mischief upon his bed; he setteth himself [h]in a way *that is* not good; he abhorreth not evil.

5 [i]Thy mercy, O LORD, *is* in the heavens; *and* thy faithfulness *reacheth* unto the clouds.

---

[a]Rom. iii. 18——[b]Deut. xxix. 19; Psalm x. 3; xlix. 18 [c]Heb. *to find his iniquity to hate*——[d]Psa. xii. 2

[e]Jer. iv. 22——[f]Prov. iv. 16; Mic. ii. 1——[g]Or, *vanity* [h]Isa. lxv. 2——[i]Psa. lvii. 10; cviii. 4

NOTES ON PSALM XXXVI

The *title* in the Hebrew is, *To the conqueror, to the servant of Jehovah, to David.* The *Syriac* and *Arabic* suppose it to have been composed on occasion of Saul's persecution of David. *Calmet* supposes, on good grounds, that it was written during the Babylonish captivity. It is one of the finest Psalms in the whole collection.

Verse 1. *The transgression of the wicked saith within my heart*] It is difficult to make any sense of this line as it now stands. How can *the transgression of the wicked speak within my heart?* But instead of לבי *libbi*, MY *heart*, four of *Kennicott's* and *De Rossi's* MSS. have לבו *libbo*, HIS *heart*. "The speech of transgression to the wicked is in the midst of his heart." "There is no fear of God before his eyes." It is not by *example* that such a person sins; the *fountain* that sends forth the impure streams is *in his own heart*. There the spirit of transgression lives and reigns; and, as he has no *knowledge* of God, so he has no *fear of God;* therefore, there is no check to his wicked propensities: all come to full effect. Lust is conceived, sin is brought forth vigorously, and transgression is multiplied. The reading above proposed, and which should be adopted, is supported by the *Vulgate, Septuagint, Syriac, Æthiopic, Arabic*, and *Anglo-Saxon*. This latter reads the sentence thus: **Cwæð se unrihtwisa þæt he agylte on him sylfum: nis ege Godes ætforan eagan his**; which I shall give as nearly as possible in the order of the original. "Quoth the unrightwise, that he do guilt in himself: is not fear God's at fore eyes his." That is, The unrighteous man saith in himself that he will sin: God's fear is not before his eyes. The old *Psalter*, in *language* as well as *meaning*, comes very near to the Anglo-Saxon: **The unrightwis saide that he trespas in hym self: the drede of God es noght before his een.** And thus it paraphrases the passage: **The unrpghtwis**, that es the kynde [the whole generation] of wyked men; **saide in hym self**, qwar man sees noght; **that he trespas**, that es, he synne at his wil, als [as if] God roght noght [did not care] qwat he did; and so it es sene, **that the drede of God es noght by fore his een**; for if he dred God, he durst noght so say."

I believe these *versions* give the true sense of the passage. The psalmist here paints the true state of the *Babylonians:* they were *idolaters* of the grossest kind, and worked iniquity with greediness. The account we have in the book of *Daniel* of this people, exhibits them in the worst light; and profane history confirms the account. Bishop *Horsley* thinks that the word פשע *pesha*, which we render *transgression*, signifies the *apostate* or *devil*. *The devil says to the wicked, within his heart, There is no fear;* i. e., no cause of fear: "God is not before his eyes." Placing the colon after *fear* takes away all ambiguity in connection with the reading, HIS *heart*, already contended for. The *principle of transgression, sin in the heart, says*, or suggests to every *sinner, there is no cause for fear:* go on, do not fear, for there is no danger. He obeys this suggestion, goes on, and acts wickedly, as "God is not before his eyes."

Verse 2. *For he flattereth himself*] He is ruled by the suggestion already mentioned; endeavours to persuade himself that he may safely follow the propensities of his own heart, *until his iniquity be found to be hateful.* He sins so boldly, that at last he becomes detestable. Some think the words should be thus understood: "He smootheth over in his own eyes with respect to the finding out of his iniquity, to hate it. That is, he sets such a false gloss in his own eyes upon his worst actions, that he never finds out the blackness of his iniquity; which, were it perceived by him, would be hateful even to himself."—Bishop *Horsley.*

Verse 3. *The words of his mouth* are *iniquity*] In the principle; *and deceit* calculated to pervert others, and lead them astray.

He hath left off to be wise, and *to do good.*] His heart is become foolish, and his actions wicked. He has cut off the connection between himself and all righteousness.

Verse 4. *He deviseth mischief upon his bed*] He seeks the silent and undisturbed watches of the night, in order to fix his plans of wickedness.

He setteth himself] Having laid his *plans*, he fixes his *purpose* to do what is bad; and he does it without any checks of conscience or abhorrence of evil. He is bent only on mischief, and lost to all sense of God and goodness. A finished character of a perfect sinner.

Verse 5. *Thy mercy, O Lord,* is *in the heavens*] That is, thou art abundant, infinite in thy mercy; else such transgressors must be immediately cut off; but thy long-suffering is intended to lead them to repentance.

Thy faithfulness reacheth *unto the clouds*] עד שחקים *ad shechakim*, to the eternal regions; above all visible space. God's *faithfulness* binds him to fulfil the *promises* and *covenants* made by his mercy. Blessings from the *heavens*, from the *clouds*, from the *earth*, are promised by God to his followers; and his *faithfulness* is in all those places, to distribute to his followers the mercies he has promised.

Verse 6. *Thy righteousness* is *like the great mountains.*] כהררי אל *keharerey El, like the mountains of God;* exceeding high mountains; what, in the present language of *geology*, would

6 Thy righteousness *is* like [k]the great mountains; [l]thy judgments *are* a great deep: O
LORD, [m]thou preservest man and beast.
7 [n]How [o]excellent *is* thy loving-kindness,
O God! therefore the children of men
[p]put their trust under the shadow of thy
wings.
8 [q]They shall be [r]abundantly satisfied
with the fatness of thy house; and thou shalt
make them drink of [s]the river [t]of thy
pleasures.
9 [u]For with thee *is* the fountain of life: [v]in
thy light shall we see light.
10 O [w]continue thy loving-kindness [x]unto
them that know thee; and thy righteousness
to the [y]upright in heart.

[k]Heb. *the mountains of God*——[l]Job xi. 8; Psa. lxxvii. 19; Rom. xi. 33——[m]Job vii. 20; Psalm cxlv. 9; 1 Tim. iv. 10——[n]Psalm xxxi. 19——[o]Hebrew, *precious* [p]Ruth ii. 12; Psa. xvii. 8; xci. 4——[q]Psa. lxv. 4

[r]Heb. *watered*——[s]Job xx. 17; Rev. xxii. 1——[t]Psa. xvi. 11——[u]Jer. ii. 13; John iv. 10, 14——[v]1 Pet. ii. 9 [w]Heb. *draw out at length*——[x]Jer. xxii. 16——[y]Psa. vii. 10; xciv. 15; xcvii. 11

be called *primitive mountains*, those that were formed at the beginning; and are not the effects of *earthquakes* or *inundations*, as *secondary* and *alluvial mountains* are supposed to be.

Thy judgments are *a great deep*] תהום רבה *tehom rabbah, the great abyss;* as incomprehensible as the *great chaos*, or first matter of all things which God created in the beginning, and which is mentioned Gen. i. 2, *and darkness was on the face*, תהום *tehom, of the deep*, the vast profound, or what is *below all* conjecturable *profundity*. How astonishing are the thoughts in these two verses! What an idea do they give us of the mercy, truth, righteousness, and judgments of God!

The old *Psalter*, in paraphrasing *mountains of God*, says, **Thi ryghtwisnes**, that es, ryghtwis men, er gastly hilles of God; for thai er hee in contemplacioun, and soner resayves the lyght of Crist. Here is a metaphor taken from the *tops* of *mountains* and *high hills* first catching the *rays of the rising sun.* "Righteous men are spiritual hills of God; for they are *high* in contemplation, and *sooner* receive the *light of Christ.*" It is really a very fine thought; and much beyond the rudeness of the times in which this Psalter was written.

Man and beast.] Doth God take care of cattle? Yes, he appoints the lions their food, and hears the cry of the young ravens; and will he not provide for the poor, especially the poor of his people? He will. So infinitely and intensely good is the nature of God, that it is his delight to make all his creatures happy. He preserves the *man*, and he preserves the *beast;* and it is his providence which supplies the *man*, when his propensities and actions level him with the *beasts* that perish.

Verse 7. *How excellent* is *thy loving-kindness*] He asks the question in the way of admiration; but expects no answer from angels or men. It is indescribably excellent, abundant, and free; and, "therefore, the children of Adam put their trust under the shadow of thy wings." They trust in thy good *providence* for the supply of their *bodies;* they trust in thy *mercy* for the salvation of their *souls*. These, speaking after the *figure*, are the *two wings* of the Divine goodness, under which the children of men take refuge. The allusion may be to the *wings of the cherubim*, above the mercy-seat.

Verse 8. *They shall be abundantly satisfied*] ירוין *yirveyun*, they *shall be saturated*, as a thirsty field is by showers from heaven. *Inebriaduntur*, they shall be inebriated.—*Vulgate.* **That sal be drunken of the plenteuoste of thi house.** —Old *Psalter*. This refers to the joyous expectation they had of being restored to their own land, and to the ordinances of the temple.

Of the river of thy pleasures.] נחל אדניך *nachal adaneycha*, (or עדנך *edencha*, as in four MSS.,) *the river of thy Eden*. They shall be restored to their paradisaical estate; for here is a reference to the *river* that ran through the *garden of Eden, and watered it;* Gen. ii. 10. Or the *temple*, and under it the *Christian Church*, may be compared to this *Eden;* and the *gracious influences of God* to be had in his *ordinances*, to the *streams* by which that *garden* was *watered*, and its fertility promoted.

Verse 9. *For with thee* is *the fountain of life*] This, in Scripture phrase, may signify a *spring of water;* for such was called among the Jews *living water*, to distinguish it from *ponds, tanks*, and *reservoirs*, that were supplied by water either received from the *clouds*, or conducted into them by *pipes* and *streams* from other quarters. But there seems to be a higher allusion in the sacred text. כי עמך מקור חיים *ki immecha mekor chaiyim*, "For with thee is the vein of lives." Does not this allude to the great *aorta*, which, receiving the blood from the heart, distributes it by the arteries to every part of the human body, whence it is conducted back to the heart by means of the *veins*. *As* the *heart*, by means of the great *aorta*, distributes the blood to the remotest parts of the body; so, GOD, by Christ Jesus, conveys the life-giving streams of his providential goodness to all the worlds and beings he has created, and the influences of his grace and mercy to every soul that has sinned. All spiritual and temporal good comes *from* Him, the FATHER, *through* Him, the SON, to every part of the creation of God.

In thy light shall we see light.] No man can illuminate his own soul; all understanding must come from above. Here the metaphor is changed, and God is compared to the *sun* in the firmament of heaven, that gives light to all the *planets* and their *inhabitants*. "God said, Let there be light; and there was light;" by that light the eye of man was enabled to behold the various works of God, and the beauties of creation: so, when God speaks light into the dark heart of man, he not only beholds his own deformity and need of the salvation of God, but he beholds the "light of the glory of God in the face of Jesus Christ;" "God, in Christ, reconciling the world to himself." "In thy light shall we see light." This is literally true, both in a spiritual and philosophical sense.

Verse 10. *O continue thy loving-kindness*]

11 Let not the foot of pride come against me, and let not the hand of the wicked remove me.

12 There are the workers of iniquity fallen: they are cast down, [z]and shall not be able to rise.

[z]Psa. i. 5

Literally, "Draw out thy mercy." The allusion to the *spring* is still kept up.

Unto them that know thee] To them who *acknowledge thee* in the midst of a crooked and perverse generation.

And thy righteousness] That *grace* which *justifies the ungodly*, and *sanctifies the unholy.*

To the upright in heart.] לישרי לב *leyishrey leb, to the straight of heart;* to those who have but *one end* in view, and *one aim* to that *end.* This is true of every genuine *penitent*, and of every true *believer*.

Verse 11. *Let not the foot of pride come against me*] Let me not be trampled under foot by proud and haughty men.

Let not the hand of the wicked remove me.] תנדני *tenideni, shake me*, or *cause me to wander*. Both these verses may have immediate respect to the captives in Babylon. The Jews were, when compared with the Babylonians, *the people that knew God;* for *in Jewry was God known*, Psa. lxxvi. 1; and the psalmist prays against the treatment which the Jews had received from the proud and insolent Babylonians during the *seventy* years of their captivity: "Restore us to our own land; and let not the proud foot or the violent hand ever *remove us from our country* and its *blessings;* the *temple*, and its *ordinances*."

Verse 12. *There are the workers of iniquity fallen*] THERE, in Babylon, are the workers of iniquity fallen, and so *cast down that they shall not be able to rise.* A prophecy of the destruction of the Babylonish empire by Cyrus. That it was destroyed, is an historical fact; that they were never able to recover their liberty, is also a fact; and that Babylon itself is now blotted out of the map of the universe, so that the site of it is no longer known, is confirmed by every traveller who has passed over those regions.

The word שם *sham*, THERE, has been applied by many of the fathers to the *pride* spoken of in the preceding verse. *There*, in or by pride, says *Augustine*, do all sinners perish. *There*, in heaven, have the evil angels fallen through pride, says St. *Jerome*. *There*, in paradise, have our first parents fallen, through pride and disobedience. *There*, in hell, have the proud and disobedient angels been precipitated.—*Eusebius, &c.* THERE, by pride, have the *persecutors* brought God's judgments upon themselves. See *Calmet*. But the first interpretation is the best.

ANALYSIS OF THE THIRTY-SIXTH PSALM

The object of this Psalm is to implore God, out of his goodness, that he would deliver the upright from the pride and malice of the wicked.

I. The psalmist sets down the character of a wicked man, and his fearful state, 1-5.

II. He makes a narrative in commendation of God's mercy, 6-10.

III. He prays for a continuance of God's goodness to his people, petitions against his proud enemy, and exults at his fall, 10-12.

I. The character of a wicked man:—

1. "There is no fear of God before his eyes;" and from this, as an evil root, all the other evils spring: and thus he enters on an induction of particulars.

2. "He flattereth himself in his own eyes." A great sin, in his eyes, is no sin: vice is virtue; falsehood, truth.

3. In this he continues, "until his iniquity be found to be hateful;"—till God, by some heavy judgment, has passed his sentence against it.

4. He is full of hypocrisy and deceit; "the words of his mouth are iniquity and deceit;" he gives goodly words, but evil is in his heart.

5. He has renounced all wisdom and goodness: "He hath left off to be wise, and to do good."

6. He enters deliberately and coolly into evil plans and designs: 1. "He deviseth mischief upon his bed." 2. "He sets himself (of firm purpose) in the way that is not good. 3. "He abhors not evil." He invents wickedness; he labours to perfect it; yea, though it be of the deepest stain, he abhors it not.

II. How comes it that such wicked men are permitted to live? How is it that God can bear patiently with such workers of iniquity? The psalmist answers this question by pointing out God's mercy, from which this long-suffering proceeds; which he considers in a *twofold* point of view: 1. *Absolute* and *general*, extending to all. 2. *Particular*, which is exhibited to the faithful only.

1. *General.* God is good to all; which is seen in his bountifulness, fidelity, justice; and in his preservation of all things: 1. "Thy mercy, O Lord, is in the heavens." Thou preservest them. Thy *faithfulness* reacheth *unto the clouds.* They water the earth, as thou hast promised. 3. "Thy righteousness is like the great mountains." Immovable. 4. "Thy judgments are a great deep." Unsearchable, and past finding out. 5. "Thou, Lord, preservest man and beast." In thee we live, move, and have our being.

2. In *particular*. He is especially careful of his followers. The providence by which he sustains them is, 1. A precious thing: "O, how excellent (quam pretiosa) how precious is thy loving-kindness, O Lord!" The operation of which, in behalf of the faithful, is hope, confidence, and comfort in distress: "Therefore the children of men shall put their trust under the shadow," &c. 2. The effects of this, the plenty of all good things prepared for them: 1. "They shall be abundantly satisfied with the goodness of thy house." 2. "Thou shalt make them drink of the river of thy pleasures." To which he adds the cause: "For with thee is the fountain of life; in thy light we shall see light."

III. He concludes with a *prayer*, 1. For all God's people. 2. For himself.

1. He prays that this excellent and precious mercy may light on all those who serve God sincerely: "O continue thy loving-kindness to them that know thee."

2. He *prays* for himself; that he may be defended from the pride and violence of wicked

men: "Let not the foot of pride come against me; and let not the hand of the wicked remove me."

3. Lastly, he closes all with this *exultation:* "There are the workers of iniquity fallen!" There, when they promised themselves peace and security, and said, Tush! no harm shall happen to us; *there* and *then* are they fallen: "They are cast down, and shall not be able to rise."

PSALM XXXVII

Godly directions for those who are in adversity not to envy the prosperity of the wicked, because it is superficial, and of short duration, 1–22; *to put their confidence in God, and live to his glory, as this is the sure way to be happy in this life, and in that which is to come,* 23–40.

VII. DAY. EVENING PRAYER

A Psalm of David

FRET [a]not thyself because of evil-doers, neither be thou envious against the workers of iniquity.

2 For they shall soon be cut down [b]like the grass, and wither as the green herb.

3 Trust in the LORD, and do good; *so* shalt thou dwell in the land, and [c]verily thou shalt be fed.

---

[a]Ver. 7; Psa. lxxiii. 3; Prov. xxiii. 17; xxiv. 1, 19

[b]Psa. xc. 5, 6——[c]Heb. *in truth* or *stableness*

NOTES ON PSALM XXXVII

In the *title* this Psalm is attributed to *David* by the *Hebrew*, and by most of the *Versions:* but it is more likely it was intended as an instructive and consoling ode for the captives in Babylon, who might feel themselves severely tempted when they saw those idolaters in prosperity; and themselves, who worshipped the true God, in affliction and slavery. They are comforted with the prospect of speedy deliverance; and their return to their own land is predicted in not less than *ten* different places in this Psalm.

This Psalm is one of the *acrostic* or *alphabetical* kind: but it differs from those we have already seen, in having *two* verses under each letter; the first only exhibiting the *alphabetical letter* consecutively. There are a few anomalies in the Psalm. The *hemistich*, which should begin with the letter ע *ain*, has now a ל *lamed* prefixed to the word with which it begins, לעולם *leolam;* and the hemistich which should begin with ת *tau* (ver. 39) has now a ו *vau* prefixed, ותשועת *utheshuath.* It appears also that the letters ד *daleth*, כ *caph*, and ק *koph*, have each lost a hemistich; and ע *ain*, half a one. The manner in which this Psalm is printed in Dr. *Kennicott's* Hebrew Bible gives a full view of all these particulars. To the English reader some slighter differences may appear; but it should be observed, that the verses in our English Bibles are not always divided as those in the Hebrew. In all the Psalms that have a *title*, the *title* forms the *first* verse in the Hebrew; but our translation does not acknowledge any of those titles as a *part* of the Psalm, and very properly leaves them out of the enumeration of the verses.

Verse 1. *Fret not thyself because of evil doers*] It is as foolish as it is wicked to repine or be envious at the prosperity of others. Whether they are godly or ungodly, it is God who is the dispenser of the *bounty* they enjoy; and, most assuredly, he has a right to do what he will with his own. To be envious in such a case, is to arraign the providence of God. And it is no small condescension in the Almighty to reason with such persons as he does in this Psalm.

Verse 2. *For they shall soon be cut down*] They have their portion in this life; and their enjoyment of it cannot be long, for their breath is but a vapour that speedily vanishes away. They fall before death, as the *greensward* does before the *scythe* of the *mower*.

Verse 3. *Dwell in the land*] Do not flee to foreign climes to escape from that providence which, for thy own good, denies thee affluence in thy own country.

And verily thou shalt be fed.] God will provide for thee the *necessaries* of life: its *conveniences* might damp thy intellect in its *inventions*, and lead thee into *idleness;* and its *superfluities* would induce thee to pamper thy *passions* till the concerns of thy *soul* would be absorbed in those of the *flesh* and, after having lived an *animal* life, thou mightest die without God, and perish everlastingly.

The original, ורעה אמונה *ureeh emunah*, might be translated, "and feed by faith." The *Septuagint* has και ποιμανθησῃ επι τῳ πλουτῳ αυτης, *and thou shalt feed upon its riches.* The *Vulgate*, *Æthiopic*, and *Arabic*, are the same. The *Syriac*, *seek faith.* The *Chaldee*, *be strong in the faith.* The *Anglo-Saxon*, ⁊ þu birt feded on welum hir, *and feeded thou shalt be in its welfare.* Old *Psalter*, **and thu sal be fed in ryches of it.** But it is probable that אמונה *emunah* here signifies *security*. *And thou shalt be fed in security.*

Dr. *Delaney* supposed that the Psalm might have been written by David in the behalf of *Mephibosheth*, who, being falsely accused by his servant *Ziba*, had formed the resolution to *leave a land* where he had met with such bad treatment. David, being convinced of his innocence,

4 [d]Delight thyself also in the LORD; and he shall give thee the desires of thine heart.

5 [e]Commit[f] thy way unto the LORD; trust also in him, and he shall bring *it* to pass.

6 [g]And he shall bring forth thy righteousness as the light, and thy judgment as the noonday.

7 [h]Rest[i] in the LORD, [k]and wait patiently for him: [l]fret not thyself because of him who prospereth in his way, because of the man who bringeth wicked devices to pass.

8 Cease from anger, and forsake wrath: [m]fret not thyself in any wise to do evil.

9 [n]For evil doers shall be cut off: but those that wait upon the LORD, they shall [o]inherit the earth.

10 For [p]yet a little while, and the wicked *shall* not *be:* yea, [q]thou shalt diligently consider his place, and it *shall* not *be.*

11 [r]But the meek shall inherit the earth; and shall delight themselves in the abundance of peace.

12 The wicked [s]plotteth against the just, [t]and gnasheth upon him with his teeth.

13 [u]The LORD shall laugh at him: for he seeth that [v]his day is coming.

14 The wicked have drawn out the sword, and have bent their bow, to cast down the poor and needy, *and* to slay [w]such as be of upright conversation.

15 [x]Their sword shall enter into their own heart, and their bows shall be broken.

---

[d]Isa. lviii. 14——[e]Heb. *Roll thy way upon the LORD* [f]Psa. lv. 22; Prov. xvi. 3; Matt. vi. 25; Luke xii. 22; 1 Pet. v. 7——[g]Job xi. 17; Mic. vii. 9——[h]Psa. lxii. 1 [i]Heb. *Be silent to the LORD*——[k]Psa. lxii. 5; Isa. xxx. 15; Jer. xiv. 22; Lam. iii. 25, 26; 1 Thess. i. 10

[l]Ver. 1, 8; Jer. xii. 1——[m]Psa. lxxiii. 3; Eph. iv. 26 [n]Job xxvii. 13, 14——[o]Ver. 11, 22, 29; Isa. lvii. 13 [p]Heb. x. 36, 37——[q]Job vii. 10; xx. 9——[r]Matt. v. 5 [s]Or, *practiseth*——[t]Psa. xxxv. 16——[u]Psa. ii. 4——[v]1 Sam. xxvi. 10——[w]Heb. *the upright of way*——[x]Mic. v. 6

---

entreats him to dwell in the land, with the assurance of *plenty* and *protection.* It is more likely that it is addressed to the *captives in Babylon;* and contains the promise that they shall return to their own land, and again enjoy *peace* and *plenty.*

Verse 4. *Delight thyself also in the Lord*] Expect all thy happiness *from* him, and seek it *in* him.

The desires of thine heart.] משאלות *mishaloth,* the *petitions.* The godly man never indulges a *desire* which he cannot form into a *prayer* to God.

Verse 5. *Commit thy way unto the Lord*] גול על יהוה *gol al Yehovah,* ROLL *thy way upon the Lord:* probably, a metaphor taken from the *camel,* who lies down till his load be *rolled* upon him.

He shall bring it *to pass.*] יעשה *yaaseh,* "He will *work.*" Trust God, and he will work for thee.

Verse 6. *Thy righteousness as the light*] As God said in the beginning, "Let there be light, and there was light;" so he shall say, Let thy innocence appear, and it will appear as suddenly and as evident as the *light* was at the beginning.

Verse 7. *Rest in the Lord*] דום *dom,* "be silent, be *dumb.*" Do not find fault with thy Maker; he does all things well for others, he will do all things well for thee.

And wait patiently for him] והתחולל לו *vehithcholel lo,* and *set thyself* to expect him; and be *determined* to expect, or wait for him. Such is the import of a verb in the *hithpoel* conjugation.

A heathen gives good advice on a similar subject:—

Nil ergo optabunt homines? Si consilium vis,
Permittes ipsis expendere Numinibus, quid
Conveniat nobis, rebusque sit utile nostris.
Nam pro jucundis aptissima quæque dabunt Di.
Carior est illis homo, quam sibi.

JUV. Sat. x. 346.

"What then remains? Are we deprived of will?
Must we not wish, for fear of wishing ill?
Receive my counsel, and securely move;
Intrust thy pastime to the powers above.
Leave them to manage for thee, and to grant
What their unerring wisdom sees thee want.
In goodness, as in greatness, they excel:
Ah, that we loved ourselves but half so well!"

DRYDEN.

Verse 9. *They shall inherit the earth.*] The word ארץ *arets,* throughout this Psalm, should be translated *land,* not *earth;* for it is most probable that it refers to the *land of Judea;* and in this verse there is a promise of their *return* thither.

Verse 10. *For yet a little while, and the wicked* shall *not* be] A prediction of the destruction of Babylon. This empire was now in its splendour; and the captives lived to see it totally overturned by Cyrus, so that even the shadow of its power did not remain.

Thou shalt diligently consider his place] ואיננו *veeynennu, and he is not.* The ruler is killed; the city is taken; and the whole empire is overthrown, in one night! And now even the place where Babylon stood cannot be ascertained.

Verse 11. *But the meek*] ענוים *anavim,* the *afflicted,* the poor Jewish captives.

Shall inherit the earth] ארץ *arets,* the *land* of *Judea,* given by God himself as an *inheritance* to their fathers, and to their posterity for ever. See ver. 9.

Verse 13. *He seeth that his day is coming.*] The utter desolation of your oppressors is at hand. All this may be said of every *wicked man.*

Verse 14. *The wicked have drawn out the sword*] There is an irreconcilable enmity in the souls of sinners against the godly; and there is much evidence that the idolatrous Babylonians *whetted their tongue like a sword, and shot out their arrows, even bitter words,* to malign the poor captives, and to insult them in every possible way.

Verse 15. *Their sword shall enter into their*

16 [y]A little that a righteous man hath *is* better than the riches of many wicked.
17 For [z]the arms of the wicked shall be broken: but the LORD upholdeth the righteous.
18 The LORD [a]knoweth the days of the upright: and their inheritance shall be [b]for ever.
19 They shall not be ashamed in the evil
time: and [c]in the days of famine they shall
be satisfied.
20 But the wicked shall perish, and the enemies of the LORD *shall be* as [d]the fat of lambs:
they shall consume; [e]into smoke shall they
consume away.
21 The wicked borroweth and payeth not
again: but the [f]righteous showeth mercy, and
giveth.
22 [g]For *such as be* blessed of him shall inherit the earth; and *they that be* cursed of
him [h]shall be cut off.
23 [i]The steps of a *good* man are [k]ordered
by the LORD: and he delighteth in his
way.
24 [l]Though he fall, he shall not be utterly
cast down; for the LORD upholdeth *him with*
his hand.
25 I have been young, and *now* am old; yet
have I not seen the righteous forsaken, nor
his seed [m]begging bread.

[y]Prov. xv. 16; xvi. 8; 1 Tim. vi. 6——[z]Job xxxviii. 15; Psa. x. 15; Ezek. xxx. 21, &c.——[a]Psa. i. 6——[b]Isa. lx. 21——[c]Job v. 20; Psa. xxxiii. 19——[d]Heb. *the preciousness of lambs*——[e]Psa. cii. 3

[f]Psa. cxii. 5, 9——[g]Prov. iii. 33——[h]Ver. 9——[i]1 Sam. ii. 9; Prov. xvi. 9——[k]Or, *established*——[l]Psa. xxxiv. 19, 20; xl. 2; xci. 12; Prov. xxiv. 16; Mic. vii. 8; 2 Cor. iv. 9——[m]Job xv. 23; Psa. lix. 15; cix. 10

own heart] All their execrations and maledictions shall fall upon themselves, and their power to do mischief shall be *broken*.

Verse 16. *A little that a righteous man hath*] This is a solid *maxim*. Whatever a good man has, has God's blessing in it; even the *blessings* of the wicked are *cursed*.

Verse 17. *The arms of the wicked*] Their power to do evil. Of this they are often deprived. *Talents* lent and abused shall be resumed, and the misuser called to a severe account by the Lord of the talents.

Verse 18. *The Lord knoweth the days of the upright*] He is acquainted with all his *circumstances, sufferings*, and *ability* to bear them; and he will either *shorten his trials* or *increase his power*. The Lord also *approves* of the man and his concerns; and his *inheritance shall be for ever*. He shall have God for his portion, here and hereafter. This is probably another indirect promise to the captives that they shall be restored to their own land. See ver. 11.

Verse 19. *They shall not be ashamed*] They have expressed strong confidence in the Lord; and he shall so work in their behalf that their enemies shall never be able to say, "Ye have trusted in your God, and yet your enemies have prevailed over you." No; for even *in the days of famine they shall be satisfied*.

Verse 20. *The enemies of the Lord* shall be *as the fat of lambs*] This verse has given the critics some trouble. Several of the Versions read thus: "But the enemies of the Lord, as soon as they are exalted to honour, shall vanish; like smoke they vanish." If we follow the *Hebrew*, it intimates that *they shall consume as the fat of lambs*. That is, as the *fat* is *wholly consumed* in sacrifices by the fire on the altar, so shall they consume away in the fire of God's wrath.

Verse 21. *The wicked borroweth*] Is often reduced to *penury*, and is obliged to become debtor to those whom he before despised.

And payeth not again] May *refuse* to do it, because he is a *wicked man;* or be *unable* to do it, because he is reduced to *beggary*.

But the righteous showeth mercy] Because he has received mercy from God, therefore he shows mercy to men. And even to his enemies *he showeth mercy, and giveth;* his *heart* being disposed to it by the influence of *Divine grace*, and his hand being enabled to do it by the blessing of God's *providence*.

Verse 22. *Shall inherit the earth*] ארץ *arets*, the *land*, as before. See ver. 11.

Shall be cut off.] A *wicked Jew* shall meet with the same fate as a *wicked Babylonian;* and a *wicked Christian* shall fare no better.

Verse 23. *The steps of a* good *man are ordered by the Lord*] There is nothing for *good* in the text. גבר *geber* is the original word, and it properly signifies *a strong man*, a *conqueror* or *hero;* and it appears to be used here to show, that even the *most powerful* must be supported by the Lord, otherwise their strength and courage will be of little avail.

And he delighteth in his way.] When *his steps are ordered by the Lord, he delighteth in his way*, because it is that into which his own good Spirit has directed him. Or, the *man delights in God's way*—in the *law* and *testimonies* of his Maker.

Verse 24. *Though he fall, he shall not be utterly cast down*] The original is short and emphatic כי יפל לא יוטל *ki yippol, lo yutal*, which the *Chaldee* translates, "Though he should fall into sickness, he shall not die;" for which the reason is given, because *the Lord sustains by his hand*. Though he may for a time fall under the power of his adversaries, as the Jews have done under the Babylonish captivity, he shall not be forsaken. The right hand of God shall sustain him in his afflictions and distresses; and at last God will give him a happy issue out of them all. Neither the *text* nor any of the *Versions* intimate that a *falling into sin* is meant; but a falling into *trouble, difficulty, &c.*

Verse 25. *I have been young, and* now *am old*] I believe this to be literally true in all cases. I am now grey-headed myself; I have travelled in different countries, and have had many opportunities of seeing and conversing with religious people in all situations in life; and I have not, to my knowledge, seen one instance to the contrary. I have seen no *righteous man forsaken*, nor any *children* of the righteous *begging their*

26 [n]*He is* [o]ever merciful, and lendeth; and his seed *is* blessed.

27 [p]Depart from evil, and do good; and dwell for evermore.

28 For the LORD [q]loveth judgment, and forsaketh not his saints; they are preserved for ever: [r]but the seed of the wicked shall be cut off.

29 [s]The righteous shall inherit the land, and dwell therein for ever.

30 [t]The mouth of the righteous speaketh wisdom, and his tongue talketh of judgment.

31 [u]The law of his God *is* in his heart; none of his [v]steps shall slide.

32 The wicked [w]watcheth the righteous, and seeketh to slay him.

33 The LORD [x]will not leave him in his hand, nor [y]condemn him when he is judged.

34 [z]Wait on the LORD, and keep his way, and he shall exalt thee to inherit the land: [a]when the wicked are cut off, thou shalt see *it*.

35 [b]I have seen the wicked in great power, and spreading himself like [c]a green bay-tree.

36 Yet he [d]passed away, and, lo, he *was* not:

---

[n]Deut. xv. 8, 10; Psa. cxii. 5, 9——[o]Heb. *all the day* [p]Psa. xxxiv. 14; Isa. i. 16, 17——[q]Psa. xi. 7——[r]Psa. xxi. 10; Prov. ii. 22; Isa. xiv. 20——[s]Prov. ii. 21 [t]Matt. xii. 35——[u]Deut. vi. 6; Psa. xl. 8; cxix. 98; Isa. ii. 7

[v]Or, *goings*——[w]Psalm x. 8——[x]2 Peter ii. 9 [y]Psalm cix. 31——[z]Verse 9; Psalm xxvii. 14; Proverbs xx. 22——[a]Psalm lii. 5, 6; xci. 8——[b]Job v. 3——[c]Or, *a green tree that groweth in his own soil*——[d]Job xx. 5, &c.

---

bread. God puts this honour upon all that fear him; and thus careful is he of *them*, and of their *posterity*.

Verse 26. He is *ever merciful, and lendeth*] כל היום חונן *kol haiyom chonen*, "all the day he is compassionate." He is confirmed in the habit of godliness: he feels for the distresses of men, and is ready to divide and distribute to all that are in necessity.

And his seed is *blessed.*] The preceding words were not spoken casually; *his seed*, his *posterity, is blessed;* therefore they are not abandoned *to beg their bread.*

Verse 27. *Depart from evil, and do good*] Seeing the above is so, *depart from all evil*—avoid all sin; and let not this be sufficient, *do good.* The grace of God ever gives this *twofold power* to all who receive it; strength to *overcome evil*, and strength to *do that which is right.*

Dwell for evermore.] Be for ever an inhabitant of God's house. This may be also a promise of return to their own land, and of permanent residence there. See ver. 9, 11, &c.

Verse 28. *Forsaketh not his saints*] את חסידיו *eth chasidaiv, his merciful* or *compassionate ones;* those who, through love to him and all mankind, are ever ready to give of their substance to the poor.

But the seed of the wicked shall be cut off.] The children who follow the wicked steps of wicked parents shall, like their parents, be cut off. God's *judgments descend to posterity*, as well as his *mercies.*

Verse 29. *The righteous shall inherit the land*] If this be not another promise of return to their own land, from that of their captivity, it must be spiritually understood, and refer to their eternal dwelling with God in glory.

Verse 30. *The mouth of the righteous speaketh wisdom*] Foolish and corrupt conversation cannot come out of their mouth. They are taught of God, and they speak according to the wisdom that is from above.

Verse 31. *The law of his God* is *in his heart*] The Lord promised that a time should come in which he would make a *new covenant* with the house of Israel; he would put his laws in their minds, and in their hearts he would write them. This is fulfilled in the case above.

None of his steps shall slide.] His holy heart always dictates to his *eyes*, his *mouth*, his *hands*, and his *feet.* The precepts which direct his conduct are not only *written in his Bible*, but also *in his heart.*

Verse 32. *The wicked watcheth the righteous, and seeketh to slay him.*] Similar to what is said ver. 8: "The wicked plotteth against the righteous." But it is added, ver. 33: "The Lord will not leave him in his hands;" he will confound his devices, and save his own servants.

Verse 34. *Wait on the Lord, and keep his way*] This is the *true mode of waiting on God* which the Scripture recommends; *keeping God's way*—using all his ordinances, and living in the spirit of obedience. He who *waits* thus is sure to have the farther blessings of which he is in pursuit. קוה *kavah*, to *wait*, implies the *extension of a right line from one point to another.* The first *point* is the human *heart;* the *line* is its *intense desire;* and the *last point* is GOD, *to* whom this *heart* extends this *straight line* of *earnest desire* to be filled with the fulness of the blessing of the Gospel of peace.

And he shall exalt thee to inherit the land] If ye keep his way, and be faithful to him in your exile, he will *exalt you, lift you up* from your present abject state, to inherit the land of your fathers. See before, ver. 9, 11, &c.

When the wicked are cut off, thou shalt see it.] They did see the destruction of the Babylonish king, *Belshazzar*, and his empire; and it was in consequence of that destruction that they were enlarged.

Verse 35. *I have seen the wicked in great power, and spreading himself like a green bay-tree.*] Does not this refer to Nebuchadnezzar, king of Babylon, and to the *vision* he had of the *great tree which was in the midst of the earth, the head of which reached up to heaven?* See Dan. iv. 10, &c.

Verse 36. *Yet he passed away*] Both *Nebuchadnezzar* and his wicked successor, *Belshazzar;* and on the destruction of the latter, when God had *weighed him in the balance, and found him wanting, numbered his days*, and consigned him to death, his *kingdom was delivered to the Medes and Persians;* and thus the Babylonian empire was destroyed.

yea, I sought him, but he could not be
found.
37 Mark the perfect *man,* and behold the
upright: for [e]the end of *that* man *is* peace.
38 [f]But the transgressors shall be destroyed
together: the end of the wicked shall be
cut off.
39 But [g]the salvation of the righteous *is*
of the LORD: *he is* their strength [h]in the time
of trouble.
40 And [i]the LORD shall help them, and deliver them: he shall deliver them from the
wicked, and save them, [k]because they trust
in him.

---

[e]Isa. xxxii. 17; lvii. 2——[f]Psa. i. 4; lii. 5——[g]Psa. iii. 8
[h]Psa. ix. 9

[i]Isa. xxxi. 5——[k]1 Chron. v. 20; Dan. iii. 17, 28; vi. 23

Verse 37. *Mark the perfect man*] Him who is described above. Take notice of him: he is *perfect in his soul,* God having saved him from all sin, and filled him with his own *love* and *image.* And he is *upright* in his *conduct;* and his *end,* die when he may or where he may, is peace, quietness, and assurance for ever.

Almost all the *Versions* translate the *Hebrew* after this manner: *Preserve innocence, and keep equity in view; for the man of peace shall leave a* numerous *posterity.*

Bishop *Horsley* thus translates: "Keep (thy) loyalty, and look well to (thy) integrity; for a posterity is (appointed) for the perfect man." He comes nearer to the original in his *note* on this verse: "Keep innocency, and regard uprightness; for the perfect man hath a posterity:" "but the rebellious shall be destroyed together; the posterity of the wicked shall be cut off," ver. 38.

Dr. *Kennicott's* note is, "אחרית *acharith,* which we render *latter end,* is *posterity,* Psa. cix. 13. The *wicked* and all his race to be destroyed, the *pious man* to have a numerous progeny, see his sons' sons to the *third* and *fourth* generation. See Job viii. 19, xviii, 13-20."

I think the original cannot possibly bear *our translation.* I shall produce it here, with the literal version of *Montanus:*—

pax viro novissimum quia; rectum vide et, integrum custodi
שמר תם וראה ישר כי אחרית לאיש שלום

The nearest translation to this is that of the *Septuagint* and *Vulgate:* Φυλασσε ακακιαν, και ιδε ευθυτητα, ὁτι εστιν εγκαταλειμμα ανθρωπῳ ειρηνικῳ· Custodi innocentiam, et vide æquitatem; quoniam, sunt reliquiæ homini pacifico. "Preserve innocence, and behold equity; seeing there is a posterity to the pacific man." The *Syriac* says, "Observe simplicity, and choose rectitude; seeing there is a good end to the man of peace." The reader may choose. Our common version, in my opinion, cannot be sustained. The 38th verse seems to confirm the translation of the *Septuagint* and the *Vulgate,* which are precisely the same in meaning; therefore I have given one translation for both.

The old *Psalter* deserves a place also: **Kepe unnoyandnes, and se evenhede; for tha relykes er til þ pesful man.**

Verse 39. *The salvation of the righteous* is *of the Lord*] It is the Lord who made them *righteous,* by blotting out their sins, and infusing his Holy Spirit into their hearts; and it is by his grace they are continually sustained, and finally brought to the kingdom of glory: "He is their strength in the time of trouble."

Verse 40. *The Lord—shall deliver them*] For they are always exposed to trials, and liable to fall.

Because they trust in him.] They keep faith, prayer, love, and obedience in continual exercise. They continue to *believe* in, *love,* and *obey God;* and he continues to *save them.*

ANALYSIS OF THE THIRTY-SEVENTH PSALM

What is here delivered may be reduced to these two general heads:—

I. He sets down the duty of a good man, which is to be patient, and put his confidence in God when he sees the wicked prosper and flourish.

II. He gives many reasons to prove the propriety of such conduct.

I. He begins with an interdict, and then descends to give some directions.

1. His interdict is, "Fret not thyself," &c. Be not angry nor envious; to which he adds this reason, that their prosperity is but short: "For they shall be cut down," &c.

2. Then he sets down some directions and rules to prevent *fretting* and *anger.*

1. The first is a perpetual rule for our whole life: "Trust in the Lord." Rely not on human helps, friends, riches, &c.

2. "Be good." Increase not thy state by evil arts or means.

3. "Dwell in the land." Desert not thy station.

4. "And verily thou shalt be fed." Enjoy quietly what thou hast at present.

5. "Delight thyself in the Lord." Be pleased with his way.

6. "Commit thy way unto the Lord." Labour in an honest vocation, and leave the rest to him; for "he will work for thee."

7. "Rest in the Lord." Acquiesce in his will and the dispensations of his providence; wait patiently for him; his time is the best. And then he repeats his interdict: "Fret not thyself."

II. Then he resumes his *former* reason, mentioned ver. 2, and amplifies it by an *antithesis,* viz., that it shall be well with the good, ill with the wicked, ver. 9, 10, 11; and so it falls out for the *most part,* but not always; which is enough for temporal blessings.

1. "Evil doers shall be cut off; but those who wait on the Lord shall inherit the land."

2. "Yet a little while, and the wicked shall not be," &c.

To this he adds a *second* reason, taken from the providence of God:—

1. In protecting the righteous, and confounding their enemies.

2. In blessing the little they have; in which he seems to remove a double objection: the first, about the tyranny of the wicked over the righteous; the second, that they are commonly in want and poverty.

The first temptation, by which many pious souls are troubled, is the power, the cruelty, and the implacable hatred of wicked men: "The wicked plotteth against the just, and gnasheth upon him." To which the psalmist answers, "The Lord shall laugh at him; for he seeth that his day of *punishment* is coming." Yea, "but the wicked have drawn out their sword, and bent their bow," which is beyond plotting and derision, "to cast down the poor, and slay such as are of an upright conversation." To which he answers, Be it so: "Their sword shall enter into their own heart, and their bow shall be broken."

The other temptation is beggary and poverty, than which nothing is more afflictive. The ungodly swim in wealth; but the godly are commonly poor, and therefore exposed to contempt; for poverty reckons up no reputable genealogy. To this he answers: "A little that the righteous hath is better than the riches of many wicked." *Better*, because used better; *better*, because possessed with contentment; *better*, because it has God's blessing upon it. And this he proves by many reasons:—

1. "For the arms of the wicked (their riches) shall be broken; but the Lord upholdeth the righteous."

2. "The Lord knoweth the days (good or bad) of the upright." He loves them, and they are his care; and "their inheritance shall be for ever," firm and stable.

3. "They shall not be ashamed in the evil time," nor destitute, nor forsaken of necessaries; for "in the days of famine they shall be satisfied."

But with rich wicked men it is not so. Though they abound in wealth, yet they shall insensibly consume and perish, "as the fat of lambs," burnt upon the altar, "vanisheth into smoke and passeth away."

4. And yet there is another blessing on the good man's little: he has often over and above, and something to spare to *give*, whereas the wicked is a borrower, with this bad quality, that *he payeth not again*. "But the righteous showeth mercy, and giveth."

Of which he gives this reason: for "such as God blesseth shall possess the earth;" and "they that be cursed of him shall be cut off." They may *have*, but not *enjoy*, the goods of this life.

And thus much the psalmist proved by his own experience: "I have been young, and now am old; yet have I not seen the righteous forsaken, nor his seed begging their bread." His liberality was the cause of it; "He is ever merciful, and lendeth; and his seed is blessed."

A third reason of God's protection is, that God upholds him: "The steps of a good man are ordered of the Lord;" and should he by infirmity fall into error, or get into trouble or affliction, "he shall not be utterly cast down, for the Lord upholdeth him with his hand." He shall have his judgment corrected by God's teaching, and no disease shall be able to remove him till God's work be done *in him*, and *by him*.

In the rest of the Psalm he makes a repetition of all that went before: he repeats his chief rule, his promises, his comforts, and his threatenings.

He begins with this rule, ver. 3: "Depart from evil and do good, and dwell for evermore." In which he exhorts to obedience, and in both parts brings instances of repentance, mortification, and vivification, which he fortifies with a double reason, as before.

1. A promise to the godly: "For the Lord loveth righteousness; he forsaketh not his saints; they are preserved for ever."

2. A threatening to the wicked: "But the seed of the wicked shall be cut off." These two reasons he resumes, amplifies, and illustrates.

First, That of the righteous: "The righteous shall inherit the land," &c.; and that you may know whom he means by the righteous, he sets down his character.

1. He is one whose mouth speaks wisdom. He speaks reverently of God's justice and providence.

2. One *whose mouth talks of judgment;* i. e., of that only which is just and right.

3. "The law of God is in his heart;" not in his tongue alone, or in his brain.

4. "None of his steps shall slide." He keeps on his right way, and will not be seduced. Yet this righteous man has his enemies, ver. 13-15: "For the wicked watcheth the righteous, and seeketh to slay him."

But although he has his enemies, yet has he also his protector: "The Lord will not leave him in his hand," &c.; therefore "wait on the Lord, and keep his way, and he shall exalt thee. When the wicked are cut off, thou shalt see it."

Secondly, For they shall be cut off, as was said before, ver. 28; and this he knew from his own experience: "I have seen the wicked in great power, and flourishing like a green bay-tree; yet I passed by, and lo, he was gone; I sought him, but he could not be found."

And what he observed, others, if attentive and diligent, may observe also, both in respect of the righteous and the wicked. 1. For "mark the perfect man, and behold the upright; for the end of that man is peace." 2. "But the transgressors shall be destroyed together; the end of the wicked shall be cut off."

Should the cause be inquired why God does these things, it is added, that this sums up all the doctrine of the Psalm:—

1. "The salvation of the righteous is of the Lord; he will save them because they trust in him."

2. On the contrary, "the wicked shall be cut off and perish, because they trust not in him."

PSALM XXXVIII

David prays God to have mercy upon him, and gives a most affecting account of his miserable state, 1–10; *complains of his being forsaken by his friends, and cruelly persecuted by his enemies,* 11–16; *confesses his sin; and earnestly implores help,* 17–22.

VIII. DAY. MORNING PRAYER

A Psalm of David, [a]to bring to remembrance

A. M. cir. 2970
B. C. cir. 1034
Davidis, Regis
Israelitarum,
cir. annum
22

O [b]LORD, rebuke me not in thy wrath: neither chasten me in thy hot displeasure.
2 For [c]thine arrows stick fast
in me, and [d]thy hand presseth me sore.
3 *There is* no soundness in my flesh because of thine anger; [e]neither *is there any* [f]rest in my bones because of my sin.
4 For [g]mine iniquities are gone over mine head: as a heavy burden they are too [h]heavy for me.
5 My wounds stink *and* are corrupt because of my foolishness.
6 I am [i]troubled; [k]I am bowed
down greatly; [l]I go mourning all the day long.
7 For my loins are filled with a [m]loathsome *disease:* and *there is* [n]no soundness in my flesh.
8 I am feeble and sore broken: [o]I have roared by reason of the disquietness of my heart.
9 LORD, all my desire *is* before thee; and my groaning is not hid from thee.

[a]Psa. lxx. title——[b]Psa. vi. 1——[c]Job vi. 4——[d]Psa. xxxii. 4——[e]Psalm vi. 2——[f]Hebrew, *peace* or *health* ——[g]Ezra ix. 6; Psa. xl. 12——[h]Matt. xi. 28

[i]Heb. *wried*——[k]Psa. xxxv. 14——[l]Job xxx. 28; Psa. xlii. 9; xliii. 2——[m]Job vii. 5——[n]Ver. 3——[o]Job iii. 24; Psa. xxii. 1; Isa. lix. 11

NOTES ON PSALM XXXVIII

The title in the HEBREW states this to be *A Psalm of David, to bring to remembrance.* The CHALDEE; "A Psalm of David for a good memorial to Israel." The VULGATE, SEPTUAGINT, and ÆTHIOPIC: "A Psalm of David, for a commemoration concerning the Sabbath." The ARABIC: "A Psalm in which mention is made of the Sabbath; besides, it is a thanksgiving and a prophecy." Never was a title more misplaced or less expressive of the contents. There is no mention of the *Sabbath* in it; there is no *thanksgiving* in it, for it is deeply *penitential;* and I do not see that it contains any *prophecy.* The SYRIAC: "A Psalm of David, when they said to the Philistine king, Achish, This is David, who killed Goliath; we will not have him to go with us against Saul. Besides, it is a form of confession for us." It does not appear that, out of all the titles, we can gather the true intent of the Psalm.

Several conjectures have been made relative to the *occasion* on which this Psalm was composed; and the most likely is, that it was in reference to some severe affliction which David had after his illicit commerce with Bath-sheba; but of what nature we are left to conjecture from the *third, fifth,* and *seventh* verses. Whatever it was, he deeply repents for it, asks pardon, and earnestly entreats support from God.

Verse 1. *O Lord, rebuke me not*] He was sensible that he was suffering under the displeasure of God; and he prays that the chastisement may be in *mercy,* and not in *judgment.*

Verse 2. *Thine arrows stick fast in me*] This, no doubt, refers to the *acute pains* which he endured; each appearing to his feeling as if an arrow were shot into his body.

Verse 3. *No soundness in my flesh*] This seems to refer to some *disorder* which so affected the *muscles* as to produce *sores* and *ulcers;* and so affected his *bones* as to leave him no peace nor rest. In short, he was completely and thoroughly diseased; and all this he attributes to his sin, either as being its natural consequence, or as being inflicted by the Lord as a punishment on its account.

Verse 4. *Mine iniquities are gone over mine head*] He represents himself as one sinking in *deep waters,* or as one oppressed by a *burden* to which his strength was unequal.

Verse 5. *My wounds stink* and *are corrupt*] Taking this in connection with the rest of the Psalm, I do not see that we can understand the word in any *figurative* or *metaphorical* way. I believe they refer to *some disease* with which he was at this time afflicted; but whether the *leprosy,* the *small pox,* or some other disorder that had attacked the whole system, and showed its virulence on different parts of the outer surface, cannot be absolutely determined.

Because of my foolishness.] This may either signify *sin* as the cause of his present affliction, or it may import an affliction which was the consequence of that *foolish levity* which prefers the momentary gratification of an irregular passion to health of body and peace of mind.

Verse 6. *I am troubled*] In mind. *I am bowed down*—in body. I am altogether afflicted, and full of distress.

Verse 7. *For my loins are filled with a loathsome* disease] Or rather, a *burning;* נקלה *nikleh,* from קלה *kalah,* to *fry, scorch,* &c., hence נקלה *nikleh, a burning,* or *strongly feverish disease.*

There is *no soundness in my flesh.*] All *without* and all *within* bears evidence that the whole of my solids and fluids are corrupt.

Verse 8. *I am feeble and sore broken*] I am so exhausted with my disease that I feel as if on the brink of the grave, and unfit to appear before God; therefore "have I roared for the disquietness of my heart."

That David describes a *natural disease* here cannot reasonably be doubted; but what that disease was, who shall attempt to say? However, this is evident, that whatever it was, he most deeply deplored the cause of it; and as he worthily lamented it, so he found mercy at the hand of God. It would be easy to show a disease of which what he here enumerates are the very general symptoms; but I forbear, because in this I might attribute to one what, perhaps, in Judea would be more especially descriptive of another.

Verse 9. *Lord, all my desire* is *before thee*] I long for nothing so much as thy favour; and for this my heart is continually going out after

A. M. cir. 2970
B. C. cir. 1034
Davidis, Regis
Israelitarum,
cir. annum
22

10 My heart panteth, my
strength faileth me: as for [p]the
light of mine eyes, it also [q]is
gone from me.

11 [r]My lovers and my friends [s]stand aloof
from my [t]sore; and [u]my kinsmen [v]stand
afar off.

12 They also that seek after my life [w]lay
snares *for me:* and they that seek my hurt
[x]speak mischievous things, and [y]imagine deceits all the day long.

13 But [z]I, as a deaf *man,* heard not; [a]and
I was as a dumb man *that* openeth not his
mouth.

14 Thus I was a man that heareth not,
and in whose mouth *are* no reproofs.

15 For [b]in thee, O LORD, [c]do I hope: thou
wilt [d]hear, O LORD my God.

16 For I said, *Hear me,* [e]lest
otherwise they should rejoice over
me: when my [f]foot slippeth, they
[g]magnify *themselves* against me.

A. M. cir. 2970
B. C. cir. 1034
Davidis, Regis
Israelitarum,
cir. annum
22

17 For I *am* ready [h]to halt, and my sorrow *is* continually before me.

18 For I will [i]declare mine iniquity; I will
be [k]sorry for my sin.

19 But mine enemies [l]*are* lively, *and* they
are strong: and they that [m]hate me wrongfully are multiplied.

20 They also [n]that render evil for good are
mine adversaries; [o]because I follow *the thing*
that good *is.*

21 Forsake me not, O LORD: O my God,
[p]be not far from me.

22 Make haste [q]to help me, O LORD [r]my
salvation.

---

[p]Psa. vi. 7; lxxxviii. 9——[q]Heb. is *not with me* [r]Psa. xxxi. 11——[s]Luke x. 31, 32——[t]Heb. *stroke* [u]Or, *my neighbours*——[v]Luke xxiii. 49——[w]2 Sam. xvii. 1, 2, 3——[x]2 Sam. xvi. 7, 8——[y]Psa. xxxv. 20——[z]See 2 Sam. xvi. 10——[a]Psa. xxxix. 2, 9——[b]Or, *thee do I wait for*——[c]2 Sam. xvi. 12; Psa. xxxix. 7——[d]Or, *answer*

[e]Psalm xiii. 4——[f]Deut. xxxii. 35——[g]Psa. xxxv. 26 [h]Heb. *for halting;* Psa. xxxv. 15——[i]Psa. xxxii. 5; Prov. xxviii. 13——[k]2 Cor. vii. 9, 10——[l]Heb. being *living, are strong*——[m]Psalm xxxv. 19——[n]Psalm xxxv. 12——[o]See 1 John iii. 12; 1 Peter iii. 13——[p]Psalm xxxv. 22——[q]Heb. *for my help*——[r]Psalm xxvii. 1; lxii. 2, 6; Isa. xii. 2

---

thee. Instead of אדני *Adonai, Lord,* several of Dr. *Kennicott's* MSS. have יהוה *Yehovah.*

Verse 10. *My heart panteth*] סחרחר *sech-archar, flutters, palpitates,* through fear and alarm.

My strength faileth] Not being able to take nourishment.

The light of mine eyes—is gone] I can scarcely discern any thing through the general decay of my health and vigour, particularly affecting my sight.

Verse 11. *My lovers*] Those who professed much affection for me; my friends, רעי *reai,* my *companions,* who never before left my company, *stand aloof.*

My kinsmen] קרובי *kerobai,* my *neighbours,* stand afar off. I am deserted by all, and they stand off because of נגעי *nigi,* my *plague.* They considered me as suffering *under a Divine judgment;* and, thinking me an *accursed being,* they avoided me lest they should be infected by my disease.

Verse 12. *They also that seek after my life*] They act towards me as *huntsmen* after their prey; *they lay snares to take away my life.* Perhaps this means only that they *wished* for his death, and would have been glad to have had it in their power to end his days. Others *spoke all manner of evil of him,* and *told falsities* against him *all the day long.*

Verse 13. *But I, as a deaf* man] I was conscious of my guilt; I could not vindicate myself; and I was obliged in silence to bear their insults.

Verse 14. *No reproofs.*] תוכחות *tochachoth, arguments* or *vindications;* a forensic term. I was as a man accused in open court, and I could make no *defence.*

Verse 15. *In thee, O Lord, do I hope*] I have no helper but thee.

Thou wilt hear, O Lord my God.] Thou art eternal in thy compassions, and wilt hear the prayer of a penitent soul. In the printed copies of the Hebrew text we have אדני אלהי *Adonai Elohai, Lord my God;* but, instead of אדני *Adonai,* one hundred and two of *Kennicott's* and *De Rossi's* MSS. read יהוה *Yehovah.* As this word is never pronounced by the Jews, and they consider it dreadfully sacred, in reading, wherever it occurs, they pronounce אדני *Adonai;* and we may well suppose that Jewish scribes, in writing out copies of the sacred Scriptures, would as naturally write *Adonai* for *Yehovah,* as they would in reading supply the *former* for the *latter.*

Verse 16. *When my foot slippeth*] They watched for my halting; and when my foot slipped, they rejoiced that I had fallen into sin!

Verse 17. *For I* am *ready to halt*] Literally, *I am prepared to halt.* So completely infirm is my soul, that it is impossible for me to take one right step in the way of righteousness, unless strengthened by thee.

Verse 18. *I will declare mine iniquity*] I will confess it with the deepest humiliation and self-abasement.

Verse 19. *But mine enemies* are *lively*] Instead of חיים *chaiyim, lively,* I would read חינם *chinam, without cause;* a change made by the half of one letter, a נ *nun* for a י *yod.* See the parallel places, Psa. xxxv. 19; lxxix. 5. See also the Preliminary Dissertation to Dr. *Lowth's* Isaiah, p. 40: "But without cause my enemies have strengthened themselves; and they who wrongfully hate me are multiplied." Here the one member of the verse answers to the other.

Verse 20. *Because I follow* the thing that *good* is.] The translation is as bad as the sentence is awkward. תחת רדופי טוב *tachath rodpi tob, because I follow goodness.* There is a remarkable addition to this verse in the Arabic: "They have rejected me, the beloved one, as an abominable dead carcass; they have pierced my body with nails." I suppose the Arabic translator meant to refer this to Christ.

None of the other Versions have any thing like this addition; only the Æthiopic adds, "They rejected their brethren as an unclean carcass." St. Ambrose says this reading was found in some Greek and Latin copies in his time; and Theodoret has nearly the same reading with the Arabic: Και απερριψαν με τον αγαπητον, ως νεκρον εβδελυγμενον· "And they cast me, the beloved, out, as an abominable dead carcass." Whence this reading came I cannot conjecture.

Verse 21. *Forsake me not, O Lord*] Though all have forsaken me, do not thou.

Be not far from me] Though my friends keep aloof, be thou near to help me.

Verse 22. *Make haste to help me*] I am dying; save, Lord, or I perish. Whoever carefully reads over this Psalm will see what a grievous and bitter thing it is to sin against the Lord, and especially to sin after having known his mercy, and after having escaped from the corruption that is in the world. Reader, be on thy guard; a life of righteousness may be lost by giving way to a moment's temptation, and a fair character sullied for ever! Let him that most assuredly standeth take heed lest he fall.

'Tis but a grain of sweet that one can sow,
To reap a harvest of wide-wasting wo.

Analysis of the Thirty-eighth Psalm

This Psalm may be divided into *two* parts:—

I. A *deprecation;* begun ver. 1, and continued in ver. 21, 22.

II. A *grievous complaint* of sin, disease, misery, God's anger, the ingratitude of his friends, coldness of his acquaintances, and cruelty of his enemies; all which he uses as arguments to induce God to help him; continued from ver. 2 to ver. 20.

I. In the first part he deprecates God's anger, and entreats a mitigation of it; though rebuked, let it not be in wrath; if corrected, let it not be in rigour: "O Lord, rebuke me not in thy wrath," &c.

II. His *complaint*, on which he falls instantly, and amplifies in a variety of ways.

1. From the prime cause, God: "Thine arrows stick fast in me," &c.

2. From the impulsive cause: "His *sin*, his *iniquities*," ver. 4; "His *foolishness*," ver. 5.

3. From the *weight* of his afflictions, which were, in general, "the arrows of God which stuck in him; the hand of God, by which he was pressed;" which were so grievous "that there was no soundness in his flesh—no rest in his bones."

4. By an induction of particulars, where he declares many effects of the disease:—

1. Putrefaction of his flesh: "My wounds stink, and are corrupt."

2. The *uncomfortable posture* of his *body:* "I am troubled, I am bowed down greatly."

3. Torment in his bowels, &c.: "My loins are filled with a loathsome disease."

4. Diseases through the whole system: "There is no soundness in my flesh."

5. Debility and grievous plague: "I am feeble," &c.

6. Anguish that forced him to cry out: "I have roared," &c.

7. His heart was disquieted: "The disquietness of my heart." But that it might appear that he had not lost his hold of his hope and his confidence in God, he directs his speech to him, and says: "Lord, all my desire is before thee, and my groaning is not hidden from thee."

8. He had a palpitation or trembling of heart: "My heart pants."

9. His strength decayed: "My strength fails."

10. A defect of sight: "The sight of my eyes is gone from me."

All these calamities David suffered from within. He was tormented in body and mind; but had he any comfort from without? Not any.

1. None from his friends: "My lovers and my friends stand aloof." 2. As for his enemies, they even then added to his affliction: "They also that seek after my life lay snares for me." In purpose, word, and deed, they sought to undo him.

He next shows his behaviour in these sufferings; he murmured not, but was silent and patient. "I was as a deaf man;—I was as a dumb man." He made no defence.

This he uses as an argument to induce the Lord to mitigate his sufferings; and of his patience he gives the following reasons:—

1. His reliance on God for audience and redress: "For in thee, O Lord, do I hope; thou wilt hear me."

2. For this he petitions; for to God he was not silent, though deaf and dumb to man. For *I said, Hear me!* and the assurance that he should be heard made him patient; for if not heard, his enemies would triumph: "Hear me, lest otherwise they should rejoice over me."

3. He was thus patient when his grief was extreme: "For I am ready to halt, and my sorrow is continually before me." I am under a bitter cross; and I know that if I be thy servant, I must bear my cross; therefore, I take it up, and suffer patiently.

4. This cross I have deserved to bear; it comes on account of mine iniquity, and I will not conceal it: "I will declare mine iniquity; I will be sorry for my sin." I suffer *justly*, and therefore have reason to be patient.

He complains again of his enemies. Though he suffered justly, yet this was no excuse for their cruelty; he complains of their strength, their number, and their hatred. My enemies are *living*, while I am at *death's door;* they are *multiplied* while I am *minished;* they render me *evil* for the *good* I have done *them.*

Then he concludes with a petition to God, in which he begs *three* things:—

1. God's presence: "Forsake me not, O Lord; my God, be not far from me."

2. He begs for help: "Help me, O Lord."

3. And prays that this help may come speedily: "Make haste to help me."

And these three petitions are directed to the Most High, as the God of his salvation: "O Lord, my salvation;" my deliverer from sin, guilt, pain, death, and hell.

In this Psalm, deeply descriptive of the anguish of a penitent soul, most persons, who feel distress on account of sin, may meet with something suitable to their case.

PSALM XXXIX

The psalmist's care and watchfulness over his thoughts, tongue, and actions, 1–3. *He considers the brevity and uncertainty of human life,* 4–7; *prays for deliverance from sin,* 8–11; *and that he may be protected and spared till he is fitted for another world,* 12, 13.

To the chief Musician, *even* to [a]Jeduthun, A Psalm of David

A. M. cir. 2970
B. C. cir. 1034
Davidis, Regis
Israelitarum,
cir. annum
22

I SAID, I will [b]take heed to
my ways, that I sin not with
my tongue: I will keep [c]my[d]
mouth with a bridle, [e]while the
wicked is before me.
2 [f]I was dumb with silence, I held my
peace, *even* from good; and my sorrow was
[g]stirred.
3 My heart was hot within me, while I was
musing [h]the fire burned: *then*
spake I with my tongue.

A. M. cir. 2970
B. C. cir. 1034
Davidis, Regis
Israelitarum,
cir. annum
22

4 LORD, [i]make me to know mine
end, and the measure of my days,
what it *is; that* I may know [k]how frail I *am*.
5 Behold, thou hast made my days *as* a
handbreadth; and [l]mine age *is* as nothing
before thee: [m]verily every man [n]at his best
state *is* altogether vanity. Selah.
6 Surely every man walketh in [o]a [p]vain

[a]1 Chron. xvi. 41; xxv. 1; Psa. lxii., lxxvii. title——[b]1 Kings ii. 4; 2 Kings x. 31——[c]Heb. *a bridle* or *muzzle for my mouth*——[d]Psa. cxli. 3; James iii. 2——[e]Col. iv. 5——[f]Psa. xxxviii. 13——[g]Heb. *troubled*

[h]Jer. xx. 9——[i]Psa. xc. 12; cxix. 84——[k]Or, *what time I have* here——[l]Psa. xc. 4——[m]Ver. 11; Psa. lxii. 9; cxliv. 4——[n]Heb. *settled*——[o]Heb. *an image*——[p]1 Cor. vii. 31; James iv. 14

NOTES ON PSALM XXXIX

The *title* says, *To the chief Musician, Jeduthun himself, A Psalm of David.* It is supposed that this *Jeduthun* is the same with *Ethan*, 1 Chron. vi. 44, compared with 1 Chron. xvi. 41; and is there numbered among the sons of *Merari.* And he is supposed to have been one of the *four masters of music*, or *leaders of bands*, belonging to the temple. And it is thought that David, having composed this Psalm, gave it to *Jeduthun and his company* to sing. But several have supposed that *Jeduthun* himself was the author. It is very likely that this Psalm was written on the same occasion with the preceding. It relates to a grievous malady by which David was afflicted after his transgression with Bath-sheba. See what has been said on the foregoing Psalm.

Verse 1. *I said, I will take heed to my ways*] I must be *cautious* because of my *enemies;* I must be *patient* because of my *afflictions;* I must be *watchful* over my tongue, lest I offend my GOD, or give my *adversaries* any cause to speak evil of me.

Verse 2. *I held my peace,* even *from good*] "I ceased from the words of the law," says the *Chaldee.* I spoke nothing, *either good or bad.* I did not even defend myself.

My sorrow was stirred.] My afflictions increased, and I had an exacerbation of pain. It is a hard thing to be denied the benefit of *complaint* in sufferings, as it has a tendency to relieve the mind, and indeed, in some sort, to call off the attention from the *place* of actual suffering: and yet undue and extravagant *complaining* enervates the mind, so that it becomes a double prey to its sufferings. On both sides there are *extremes:* David seems to have steered clear of them on the right hand and on the left.

Verse 3. *My heart was hot within me*] A natural feeling of repressed grief.

While I was musing] What was at first a simple sensation of *heat* produced a *flame;* the *fire broke out* that had long been *smothered.* It is a metaphor taken from vegetables, which, being heaped together, begin to heat and ferment, if not scattered and exposed to the air; and will soon produce a *flame*, and consume themselves and every thing within their reach.

Verse 4. *Lord, make me to know mine end*] I am weary of life; I wish to know *the measure of my days*, that I may see how long I have to suffer, and *how frail* I am. I wish to know what is *wanting* to make up the number of the days I have to live.

Verse 5. *My days* as *a handbreadth*] My life is but a *span; σπιθαμη του βιου.*

And mine age is *as nothing*] כאין *keein*, as *if it were not before thee.* All *time* is swallowed up in thy *eternity.*

Verily every man at his best state] כל אדם נצב *col adam nitstab*, "every man that *exists*, is vanity." All his projects, plans, schemes, &c., soon come to nothing. His body also moulders with the dust, and shortly passes both from the *sight* and *remembrance* of men.

Verse 6. *Walketh in a vain show*] בצלם *betselem*, in a *shadow.* He is but the *semblance* of being: he *appears* for a while, and then *vanisheth* away. Some of the fathers read, "Although every man walketh in the image of God, yet they are disquieted in vain."

He heapeth up riches, *and knoweth not who shall gather them.*] He *raketh together.* This is a metaphor taken from *agriculture:* the husbandman rakes the corn, &c., together in the field, and yet, so uncertain is life, that he knows not who shall gather them into the granary!

Verse 7. *And now, Lord, what wait I for?*] Have I any object of pursuit in life, but to regain thy *favour* and thine *image.*

Verse 8. *Deliver me from all my transgressions*] I seek the pardon of my sins; I expect it from thy *mercy.* Grant it, "that I be not the reproach of the foolish," (the godless and the profane,) who deride my expectation, and say no such blessings can be had. Let them know, by thy saving me, that there is a God who hear-

A. M. cir. 2970
B. C. cir. 1034
Davidis, Regis
Israelitarum,
cir. annum
22

show; surely they are disquieted
in vain: [q]he heapeth up *riches*,
and knoweth not who shall
gather them.
7 And now, LORD, what wait I for? [r]my
hope *is* in thee.
8 Deliver me from all my transgressions:
make me not [s]the reproach of the foolish.
9 [t]I was dumb, I opened not my mouth;
because [u]thou didst *it*.
10 [v]Remove thy stroke away from me: I
am consumed by the [w]blow of thine hand.

[q]Job xxvii. 17; Eccles. ii. 18, 21, 26; v. 14; Luke xii. 20, 21——[r]Psa. xxxviii. 15——[s]Psa. xliv. 13; lxxix. 4——[t]Lev. x. 3; Job xl. 4, 5; Psa. xxxviii. 13——[u]2 Sam. xvi. 10; Job ii. 10——[v]Job ix. 34; xiii. 21——[w]Heb. *conflict*——[x]Heb. *that which is to be desired in him to melt away*

11 When thou with rebukes
dost correct man for iniquity,
thou makest [x]his beauty [y]to consume away like a moth: [z]surely
every man *is* vanity. Selah.
12 Hear my prayer, O LORD, and give ear
unto my cry; hold not thy peace at my tears:
[a]for I *am* a stranger with thee, *and* a sojourner, [b]as all my fathers *were*.
13 [c]O spare me, that I may recover
strength, before I go hence, and [d]be no
more.

A. M. cir. 2970
B. C. cir. 1034
Davidis, Regis
Israelitarum,
cir. annum
22

[y]Job iv. 19; xiii. 28; Isa. l. 9; Hos. v. 12——[z]Ver. 5——[a]Lev. xxv. 23; 1 Chron. xxix. 15; Psa. cxix. 19; 2 Corinthians v. 6; Hebrews xi. 13; 1 Pet. i. 17; ii. 11——[b]Genesis xlvii. 9——[c]Job x. 20, 21; xiv. 5, 6——[d]Job xiv. 10, 11, 12

eth prayer, and giveth his Holy Spirit to all them that ask him.

Verse 10. *Remove thy stroke away from me*] This seems to be a figure taken from *gladiators*, or persons *contending in single combat*. One is wounded so as to be able to maintain the fight no longer: he therefore *gives in*, and prays his adversary to spare his life. I am conquered; I can hold the contest no longer: thou art too powerful for me. He cries what our ancestors used to term *craven;* the word spoken by him who was conquered in the battle *ordeal*, or *trial by combat*.

Verse 11. *When thou with rebukes dost correct man*] תוכחות *tochachoth* signifies a *vindication of proceedings in a court of law*, a *legal defence*. When God comes to maintain the credit and authority of his law against a sinner, he "causes his beauty to consume away:" a metaphor taken from the case of a culprit, who, by the arguments of counsel, and the unimpeachable evidence of witnesses, has the facts all proved against him, grows pale, looks terrified; his fortitude forsakes him, and he faints in court.

Surely every man is vanity.] He is incapable of resistance; he falls before his Maker; and none can deliver him but his *Sovereign* and *Judge*, against whom he has offended.

Selah.] This is a true saying, an everlasting truth.

Verse 12. *Hear my prayer*] Therefore, O Lord, show that mercy upon me which I so much need, and without which I must perish everlastingly.

I am a stranger with thee] I have not made this earth my home; I have not trusted in any arm but thine. Though I have sinned, I have never denied thee, and never cast thy words behind my back. I knew that *here* I had no continuing city. *Like my fathers*, I looked for a city that has permanent foundations, in a better state of being.

Verse 13. *O spare me*] Take me not from this *state* of *probation* till I have a thorough preparation for a *state of blessedness*. This he terms *recovering his strength*—being restored to the *favour* and *image* of God, from which he had fallen. This should be the daily cry of every human spirit: Restore me to thine image, guide me by thy counsel, and then receive me to thy glory!

Analysis of the Thirty-ninth Psalm

This Psalm was apparently written on the same occasion as the preceding. The psalmist is still suffering as before, yet is silent and patient; but the suffering at last becoming very sharp, he could hold his peace no longer: then he spoke. And we have reason to be thankful that he broke silence, as whoever considers the weighty truths which he spoke must allow.

There are *three* parts in this Psalm:—

I. His own account of his resolution to keep silence, ver. 1, and the consequences of it, ver. 2, 3.

II. His expostulation with God on the shortness, uncertainty, and frailty of life, ver. 4, 5, 6.

III. His petition to have his sin pardoned, ver. 8; to be saved from punishment, ver. 10; and for farther grace and respite, ver. 12, 13.

I. David acquaints us with his resolution: *I said*—I fully purposed to keep silence.

1. "I said, I will take heed to my ways, that I sin not with my tongue."

2. This resolution he kept for a while: "I was dumb; I held my peace even from good," even from making a just defence.

3. But in this I found great difficulty, nay, impossibility.

1. For all the time "my sorrow was stirred." My pain was increased by silence.

2. "My heart was hot." I was strongly incited to utter my mind.

3. "And, while thus musing, the fire burned;" what was within I saw should not be longer concealed: "Then spake I with my tongue."

II. He expostulates with God: and, being greatly oppressed both in body and mind, prays to know how long he is to live; or, rather, how soon he may get rid of his maladies, false friends, and deceitful enemies. Many considerations render his life uncomfortable.

1. It is very brittle and frail: "Make me to know how frail I am."

2. It is very *short:* "Behold, thou hast made my days as a handbreadth."

3. Yea, when carefully considered, it was

even less, of no consideration: "Mine age is as nothing before thee."

4. It was full of vanity: "Verily, every man at his best estate (in his strength, riches, power) is altogether vanity." His labours promise much, perform little.

5. It is unstable and uncertain, as a *shadow*. "Surely, every man walketh in a vain shadow."

6. It is full of trouble and inquietude: "Surely, they are disquieted in vain."

7. Man labours for he knows not whom: "He heapeth up riches, and knoweth not who shall gather them."

Notwithstanding all this, he finds that even here God is a sufficient Portion for them that trust in him. Let others toil for riches; admire dignities, empires, pleasures; let them be proud of these, and complain that their life is too short to enjoy them; I have a stronger hold; I am persuaded that the Lord will have mercy upon me, and be my Support in all the troubles and uncertainties of life: "And now, Lord, what wait I for? My hope is in thee."

III. On this confidence he again begins to pray,—

1. For remission of sin: "Deliver me from all my transgressions."

2. For defence against malicious tongues: "Make me not a reproach to the foolish."

3. For submission under Divine chastisement: "I was dumb, because thou didst it."

4. For a removal of his punishment: "Take away thy plague from me."

1. And he adds the cause;—either remove thy hand, or I must needs perish: "I am even consumed by the blow of thy hand."

2. This he amplifies by the similitude of a moth; and adds a second reason: "When thou with rebukes dost correct man, thou makest his beauty to consume away like the moth," which frets and destroys a garment. And, for confirmation, delivers his former opinion, which is to be considered as an incontrovertible maxim: "Surely, every man is vanity. Selah." Mark that!

3. To which he adds a *third*—the consideration of our present condition in this life. We and all our fathers are but pilgrims in this life: "I am a stranger with thee, and a sojourner, as all my fathers were." Therefore, spare me.

Faith has always to struggle with difficulties. Though he was confident, ver. 7, that God was his hope; yet his calamities, his sickness, his enemies, the brevity, fugacity, and troubles of life, come ever into his memory; and, therefore, he prays again for them. And this rises by a climax or gradation:—

1. He prays for audience: "Hear my prayer, O Lord!"

2. That his *cry*, for such it was, be heard: "Give ear unto my cry."

3. For admission of his tears: "Hold not thy peace at my tears. The reason, as *a stranger*. Thy grace, thy favour.

4. For some relaxation and ease: "O spare me, that I may recover strength;" which he urges with this motive, "before I go hence, and be no more." Restore me to thy favour in *this life*. Hereafter, it will be too late to expect it. Let me not die *unsaved!*

PSALM XL

The benefit of confidence in God, 1–3. *The blessedness of those who trust in God*, 4, 5. *The termination of the Jewish sacrifices in that of Christ*, 6–8. *The psalmist's resolution to publish God's goodness*, 9, 10: *he prays to be delivered from evils*, 11–13; *against his enemies*, 14, 15; *and in behalf of those who are destitute*, 16, 17.

To the chief Musician, A Psalm of David

A. M. cir. 2971
B. C. cir. 1033
Davidis, Regis Israelitarum, cir. annum 23

I [a]WAITED [b]patiently for the LORD; and he inclined unto me, and heard my cry.

2 He brought me up also out of [c]a horrible pit, out of [d]the miry clay, and [e]set my feet upon a rock, *and* [f]established my goings.

3 [g]And he hath put a new song in my mouth,

[a]Heb. *In waiting I waited*——[b]Psa. xxvii. 14; xxxvii. 7
[c]Heb. *a pit of noise*

[d]Psa. lxix. 2, 14——[e]Psa. xxvii. 5——[f]Psa. xxxvii. 23
[g]Psa. xxxiii. 3

NOTES ON PSALM XL

The TITLE, "To the chief Musician," we have already seen, and it contains nothing worthy of particular remark. Concerning the *occasion* and *author* of this Psalm there has been a strange and numerous diversity of opinions. I shall not trouble the reader with sentiments which I believe to be ill founded; as I am satisfied the Psalm was composed by *David*, and about the same time and on the *same occasion* as the two preceding; with this difference, that *here* he magnifies God for having bestowed the mercy which he sought *there*. It is, therefore, a *thanksgiving* for his recovery from the *sore disease* by which he was afflicted in his body, and for his restoration to the Divine favour. The *sixth*, *seventh*, and *eighth* verses contain a remarkable prophecy of the incarnation and sacrificial offering of Jesus Christ. From the *eleventh* to the end contains a new subject, and appears to have belonged to *another Psalm*. It is the same as the *seventieth* Psalm; only it wants the two first verses.

Verse 1. *I waited patiently for the Lord*] The two preceding Psalms are proofs of the

A. M. cir. 2971
B. C. cir. 1033
Davidis, Regis
Israelitarum,
cir. annum
23

even praise unto our God:
[h]many shall see *it*, and fear,
and shall trust in the LORD.
4 [i]Blessed *is* that man that
maketh the LORD his trust, and [k]respecteth
not the proud, nor such as [l]turn aside to
lies.
5 [m]Many, O LORD my God, *are* thy wonderful works *which* thou hast done, [n]and thy
thoughts *which are* to us-ward:
[o]they cannot be reckoned up in
order unto thee: *if* I would declare and speak *of them*, they
are more than can be numbered.
6 [p]Sacrifice and offering thou didst not desire; mine ears hast thou [q]opened: burnt-
offering and sin-offering hast thou not required.

A. M. cir. 2971
B. C. cir. 1033
Davidis, Regis
Israelitarum,
cir. annum
23

[h]Psalm lii. 6——[i]Psalm xxxiv. 8; Jeremiah xvii. 7——[k]Psalm ci. 3, 7——[l]Psalm cxxv. 5——[m]Exod. xi. 15; Job v. 9; ix. 10; Psalm lxxi. 15; xcii. 5; cxxxix. 6, 17——[n]Isaiah lv. 8——[o]Or, *none can order them unto thee*——[p]1 Sam. xv. 22; Psa. xl. 6; l. 8; li. 16; Proverbs xxi. 3; Eccles. v. 1; Isaiah i. 11; lxvi. 3; Hosea vi. 6; Matthew ix. 13; xii. 7; Hebrews x. 5——[q]Hebrew, *digged;* Exodus xxi. 6

patience and *resignation* with which David waited for the mercy of God. The reader is requested to consult the notes on them.

And heard my cry.] The two preceding Psalms show how he *prayed* and *waited; this* shows how he *succeeded*.

Verse 2. *A horrible pit*] Literally, the *sounding pit;* where nothing was heard except the howlings of wild beasts, or the hollow sounds of winds reverberated and broken from the craggy sides and roof.

The miry clay] Where the longer I stayed the deeper I sank, and was utterly unable to save myself. The *Syriac* and *Arabic* translate, "The pit of perdition, and the mud of corruption." These are figurative expressions to point out the dreary, dismal, ruinous state of sin and guilt, and the utter inability of a condemned sinner to save himself either from the guilt of his conscience, or the corruption of his heart.

Set my feet upon a rock] Thou hast changed my state from *guilt* to *pardon;* from *corruption* to *holiness;* in consequence of which *my goings are established*. I have now power over all sin, and can walk steadily in the way that leads to God's kingdom.

Verse 3. *A new song*] Cheerfulness and joy had long been strangers to him. He seemed to live to utter the most doleful complaints, and be a prey to suffering and wretchedness. *Praise* for a sense of God's favour was a *new* song to him. The word is often used to signify *excellence:* I will sing a most *excellent* and *eminent* song.

Many shall see it] I will publish it abroad; *and fear*—to sin against the Lord, knowing by my example what a grievous and bitter thing it is.

And shall trust in the Lord.] Even the worst of sinners shall not despair of mercy, being penitent, when they see that I have found favour in his sight.

Verse 4. *Blessed* is *that man*] The man must be blessed and happy who casts his soul, with all its burden of sin and wretchedness, at the footstool of God's mercy; for he will save all who come to him through the Son of his love.

Verse 5. *Many*—are *thy wonderful works*] The psalmist seems here astonished and confounded at the *counsels*, *loving-kindnesses*, and *marvellous works* of the Lord, not in *nature*, but in *grace;* for it was the mercy of God towards himself that he had now particularly in view.

Verse 6. *Sacrifice and offering*] The apostle, Heb. x. 5, &c., quoting this and the two following verses, says, *When he* (the Messiah) *cometh into the world*—was about to be incarnated, *He saith*—to God the Father, *Sacrifice and offering thou wouldst not*—it was never thy *will* and design that the sacrifices under thy own law should be considered as making atonement for sin; they were only designed to point out my incarnation and consequent sacrificial death: and therefore *a body hast thou prepared me*, by a miraculous conception in the womb of a virgin; according to thy word, *The seed of the woman shall bruise the head of the serpent.*

A body hast thou prepared me.—The quotation of this and the two following verses by the apostle, Heb. x. 5, &c., is taken from the *Septuagint*, with scarcely any variety of reading: but, although the general meaning is the same, they are widely different in verbal expression in the Hebrew. David's words are אזנים כרית לי *oznayim caritha lli*, which we translate, *My ears hast thou opened;* but they might be more properly rendered, *My ears hast thou bored;* that is, Thou hast made me *thy servant for ever*, to dwell in thine own house: for the allusion is evidently to the custom mentioned Exod. xxi. 2, &c.: "If thou buy a Hebrew servant, six years he shall serve, and in the seventh he shall go out free: but if the servant shall positively say, I love my master, &c., I will not go out free; then his master shall bring him to the doorpost, and shall bore his ear through with an awl, and he shall serve him for ever."

But how is it possible that the Septuagint and the apostle should take a meaning so totally different from the sense of the Hebrew? Dr. Kennicott has a very ingenious conjecture here: he supposes that the Septuagint and apostle express the meaning of the words as they stood in the copy from which the Greek translation was made; and that the present Hebrew text is corrupted in the word אזנים *oznayim*, *ears*, which has been written through carelessness for אז גוה *az gevah*, THEN, a BODY. The first syllable, אז *az*, THEN, is the same in both; and the latter, נים, which, joined to אז makes אזנים *oznayim*, might have been easily mistaken for גוה *gevah*, BODY; נ *nun* being very like ג *gimel;* י *yod* like ו *vau;* and ה *he* like final ם *mem;* especially if the line on which the letters were written in the MS. hap-

A. M. cir. 2971
B. C. cir. 1033
Davidis, Regis
Israelitarum,
cir. annum
23

7 Then said I, Lo, I come: in
the volume of the book *it is*
[r]written of me,
8 [s]I delight to do thy will, O
my God: yea, thy law *is* [t]within [u]my heart.
9 [v]I have preached righteousness in the great
congregation: lo, [w]I have not refrained my lips, O LORD, [x]thou knowest.
10 [y]I have not hid thy righteousness within my heart; I have declared thy faithfulness and thy salvation: I have not con-

[r]Luke xxiv. 44——[s]Psalm cxix. 16, 24, 47, 92; John iv. 34; Romans vii. 22——[t]Hebrew, *in the midst of my bowels*——[u]Psalm xxxvii. 31; Jeremiah xxxi. 33; 2 Corinthians iii. 3——[v]Psalm xxii. 22, 25; xxxv. 18——[w]Psalm cxix. 13——[x]Psalm cxxxix. 2
[y]Acts xx. 20, 27

pened to be blacker than ordinary, which has often been a cause of mistake, it might then have been easily taken for the under-stroke of the *mem*, and thus give rise to a corrupt reading; add to this, the root כרה *carah* signifies as well to *prepare*, as to *open*, *bore*, &c. On this supposition the ancient copy translated by the Septuagint, and followed by the apostle, must have read the text thus: אז גוה כרית לי *az gevah charitha lli;* Σωμα δε κατηρτισω μοι· *Then a body thou hast prepared me:* thus the Hebrew text, the version of the Septuagint, and the apostle, will agree in what is known to be an indisputable fact in Christianity; namely, that Christ was *incarnated* for the sin of the world.

The *Æthiopic* has nearly the same reading: the *Arabic* has both, "A body hast thou prepared me, and mine ears thou hast opened." But the *Syriac*, the *Chaldee*, and the *Vulgate*, agree with the present Hebrew text; and none of the MSS. collated by *Kennicott* and *De Rossi* have any various reading on the disputed words.

It is remarkable, that all the offerings and sacrifices which were considered to be of an atoning or cleansing nature, offered under the law, are here enumerated by the psalmist and the apostle, to show that *none* of them, nor *all* of them, could take away sin; and that the grand sacrifice of Christ was that alone which could do it.

Four kinds are here specified, both by the psalmist and the apostle: viz. SACRIFICE, זבח *zebach*, θυσια; OFFERING, מנחה *minchah*, προσφορα; BURNT-OFFERING, עולה *olah*, ὁλοκαυτωμα; SIN-OFFERING, חטאה *chataah*, περι ἁμαρτιας. Of all these we may say, with the apostle, it was impossible that the blood of bulls and goats, &c. should take away sin.

Thou hast had no pleasure.—Thou couldst never be pleased with the victims under the law; thou couldst never consider them as atonements for sin, as they could never satisfy thy justice, nor make thy law honourable.

Verse 7. *In the volume of the book*] במגלת ספר *bimegillath sepher*, "in the *roll* of the book." Anciently, books were written on skins, and rolled up. Among the Romans, these were called *volumina*, from *volvo*, *I roll;* and the Pentateuch in the Jewish synagogues is still written in this way. There are two wooden rollers; on one they roll *on*, on the other they roll *off*, as they proceed in reading. One now lying before me, written on vellum, is *two feet two inches* in *breadth*, and *one hundred and two feet long.* To roll and unroll such a MS. was no easy task; and to be managed must lie flat on a table. This contains the Pentateuch only, and is without *points*, or any other Masoretic distinction. The *book* mentioned here must be the *Pentateuch*, or five books of Moses; for, in David's time no other part of Divine revelation had been committed to writing. This whole book speaks about Christ, and his accomplishing the *will* of God, not only in "the seed of the woman shall bruise the head of the serpent," and "in thy seed shall all the nations of the earth be blessed;" but in all the *sacrifices* and sacrificial rites mentioned in the law.

Verse 8. *To do thy will*] God *willed* not the sacrifices under the law, but he *willed* that a human victim of infinite merit should be offered for the redemption of mankind. That there might be *such a victim*, a *body* was prepared for the eternal Logos, and in that body *he came* to do the *will of God;* that is, to suffer and die for the sins of the world.

1. Hence we see that the sovereign WILL of God is that Jesus should be incarnated; that he should suffer and die; or, in the apostle's words, *taste death for every man;* that all should believe on him, and be saved from their sins; for this is the WILL of God, our *sanctification.*

2. And as the apostle grounds this on the words of the Psalm, we see that it is the WILL of *God* that that system shall end; for as the essence of it is contained in its *sacrifices*, and God says he *will* not have these, and has appointed the *Messiah* to do his will, i. e., to *die for men*, hence it necessarily follows, from the psalmist himself, that the introduction of the Messiah into the world is the abolition of the law; and that his sacrifice is that which shall last for ever.

Verse 9. *I have preached righteousness*] I think it best to refer these words to Christ and his apostles. In consequence of his having become a sacrifice for sin, the Jewish sacrificial system being ended, the middle wall of partition was broken down, and the door of faith, the doctrine of justification by faith, opened to the Gentiles. Hence the Gospel was preached in all the world, and the mercy of God made known to the Gentiles; and thus *righteousness* —justification by faith, was preached *in the great congregation*—to Jews and Gentiles, throughout the Roman empire.

The great congregation, both in this and the following verse, I think, means the Gentiles, contradistinguished from the Jews.

The word *righteousness* means the plan or method of salvation by Jesus Christ—God's method of justifying sinners by faith, without the deeds of the law. See Rom. iii. 25, 26, and the notes there.

Verse 10. *Thy faithfulness*] This means the exact fulfilment of the promises made by the prophets relative to the incarnation of Christ,

A. M. cir. 2971
B. C. cir. 1033
Davidis, Regis
Israelitarum,
cir. annum
23

cealed thy loving-kindness and
thy truth from the great congregation.
11 Withhold not thou thy tender
mercies from me, O LORD: [z]let thy loving-
kindness and thy truth continually preserve me.
12 For innumerable evils have compassed
me about: [a]mine iniquities have taken hold
upon me, so that I am not able to look up;
they are more than the hairs of mine head:
therefore [b]my heart [c]faileth me.
13 [d]Be pleased, O LORD, to deliver me: O
LORD, make haste to help me.

[z]Psalm xliii. 3; lvii. 3; lxi. 7——[a]Psalm xxxviii. 4
[b]Psalm lxxiii. 26——[c]Hebrew, *forsaketh*——[d]Psalm
lxx. 1, &c.——[e]Psalm xxxv. 4, 26; lxx. 2, 3; lxxi. 13

14 [e]Let them be ashamed and
confounded together that seek
after my soul to destroy it; let
them be driven backward and
put to shame that wish me evil.
15 [f]Let them be [g]desolate for a reward of
their shame that say unto me, Aha, aha.
16 [h]Let all those that seek thee rejoice and
be glad in thee: let such as love thy salvation
[i]say continually, The LORD be magnified.
17 [k]But I *am* poor and needy; *yet* [l]the
LORD thinketh upon me: thou *art* my help
and my deliverer; make no tarrying, O my God.

A. M. cir. 2971
B. C. cir. 1033
Davidis, Regis
Israelitarum,
cir. annum
23

[f]Psalm lxx. 3——[g]Psalm lxxiii. 19——[h]Psalm lxx. 4
[i]Psalm xxxv. 27——[k]Psalm lxx. 5——[l]1 Peter
5, 7

and the opening of the door of faith to the *Gentiles.*

Loving-kindness] Shows the gift itself of Jesus Christ, the highest proof that God could give to a lost world of his *mercy, kindness,* and *loving-kindness.*

Verse 11. *Thy tender mercies*] רחמיך *rachameycha,* such propensities and feelings as a mother bears to her child; or animals in general to their young.

Let thy loving-kindness] חסדך *chasdecha,* thy overflowing and superabundant mercy.

And thy truth] What is revealed in thy word: *continually preserve me. Mercy* to help me, *truth* to direct me; and, by the operation of both, I shall be continually preserved from sin and evil.

Verse 12. *Innumerable evils have compassed me about*] This part does not comport with the preceding; and either argues a former experience, or must be considered a part of another Psalm, written at a different time, and on another occasion, and, were we to prefix the two first verses of the *seventieth* Psalm to it we should find it to be a Psalm as complete in itself as that is.

They are more than the hairs of mine head] This could not be said by any person who was exulting in the pardoning mercy of God, as David was at the time he penned the commencement of this Psalm.

Verse 15. *That say unto me, Aha, aha.*] האח האח *heach, heach.* See on Psa. xxxv. 21.

Verse 16. *Let all those that seek thee—be glad*] In making prayer and supplication to thee, let them ever find thee, that they may magnify thee for the blessings they receive.

Love thy salvation] Who earnestly desire to be saved from sin: saved in thy *own way,* and on thy *own terms.*

The Lord be magnified.] Let God be praised continually for the continual blessings he pours down.

Verse 17. *But I* am *poor*] עני *ani,* afflicted, greatly depressed.

And needy] אביון *ebyon,* a *beggar.* One utterly destitute, and seeking help.

The Lord thinketh upon me] The words are very emphatic; אדני *Adonai,* my prop, my support, *thinketh,* יחשב *yachshab,* meditateth, *upon me.* On which he concludes: "Thou art my help and deliverer." Seeing that my miserable state occupies thy *heart,* it will soon *employ* thy *hand.* Thou, who meditatest upon me, wilt deliver me.

Make no tarrying] Seeing thou art *disposed to help,* and I am in such *great necessity,* delay not, but come speedily to my assistance. The old *Psalter* speaks to this effect: "Let us not be so long under distress and misery that we lose our patience, or our love to thee."

ANALYSIS OF THE FORTIETH PSALM

There are *two* main parts in this Psalm:—

I. A *thanksgiving,* ver. 1-11.

II. A *prayer,* from ver. 12 to the end.

Thankfulness consists in the exercise of two virtues, *truth* and *justice.*

1. Truth calls upon us to acknowledge the *benefit,* and *him* from whom we receive it.

2. Justice obliges us to be grateful, and to perform some duties as evidences of our thankful minds; and both these we meet with in the first part.

I. David begins with a profession of thankfulness; shows his *confidence:* "I waited patiently for the Lord;" then shows the success, or what God did for him.

1. "He inclined his ear, and heard my cry."

2. "He brought me out of the horrible pit, and out of the miry clay."

3. "He set my feet upon a rock." Being redeemed from danger, he set me in a safe place.

4. "He established my goings." He confirmed my steps, so that I slipped and slided no more.

5. And he hath moved me to be thankful: "He hath put a new song in my mouth." The deliverance was not common, and therefore the praise should not be common, but expressed by a new and exquisite song.

And in this he supposed his example would be a common document. Many shall see my deliverance and my thanksgiving, and shall fear God, and acknowledge his *grace,* his *providence,* and *protection;* and be led thereby to put their trust in him. And then he produces his *form* of *thanksgiving:*—

First, He pronounces the man blessed who relies on God. 1. "Blessed is the man that maketh the Lord his trust." 2. "And blessed is he who respects not the proud;" men proud of their wealth and power, or such as turn aside to lies.

Secondly, Then by exclamation admires God's *mercies*, and goodness to his people. 1. For their grandeur and multitude: "Many, O Lord my God, are thy works." 2. For their supernatural appearance: "Thy wonderful works." 3. For the incomparable wisdom by which they are ordered: "Many, O Lord, are thy wondrous works; and thy thoughts to us-ward, they cannot be reckoned up," &c.

And having acknowledged his thankfulness, he speaks of the other part, his gratitude; to which, in equity, he thought himself bound, viz., to be obedient to God's voice, which is, indeed, the best sacrifice, and far beyond all those that are offered by the law; as is apparent in *Christ*, to whom these words and the obedience contained in them are principally attributed: by way of accommodation, they belong to every one of his members who means to be thankful for his redemption.

And, first, he tells us that outward worship is of little worth, if sincerity and true piety be wanting: "Sacrifice and offering thou didst not require." Not these absolutely, but as subservient to the true piety, and significative of the obedience of Christ unto death.

2. To this end "mine ears hast thou opened;" bored, made docile, and taken me for thy servant.

3. And I will be thy voluntary and obedient servant: "Then said I, Lo, I come!" I am ready to hear thy commands.

4. He describes his ready obedience:—

1. That he performed it cheerfully: "I delight to do thy will."

2. That he did it heartily: "Thy law is in my heart." The obedience of eyes, hands, and feet may be hypocritical; that which is of the heart cannot. The heart thou requirest, and the heart thou shalt have; and to that purpose "I have put thy law in my heart."

3. He did this for the benefit of others: he published the Gospel. 1. "I have preached righteousness in the great congregation." 2. "I have not refrained my lips; that thou knowest." 3. "I have not hid thy righteousness within my heart." 4. "I have declared thy faithfulness and thy salvation." 5. "I have not concealed thy loving-kindness and truth from the great congregation."

In this verse we have the commendation of the Gospel, that it is *righteousness.* Jesus, who is the sum and substance of it, *justifies* and *sanctifies*. It is God's *truth* and *faithfulness*, for in it his promises are performed. It is our *salvation*, freeing us from sin, death, the curse of the law, and hell-fire. It must, as such, be preached in the great congregation. And to it *obedience* must be yielded; and to this *four things* are necessary:—

1. The help of God's Spirit: "Thou hast opened mine ears."

2. A ready and willing mind: "Then said I, Lo, I come."

3. A ready performance in the work: "I delight to do thy will."

4. That respect be had to God's law: "Thy law is within my heart."

But all that is here spoken must be considered as resting on the sacrificial offering which Christ made; for we must be justified by his blood; and through him alone can we have remission of sins, the help of God's Spirit, or any power to do any kind of good.

II. This second part of the Psalm appears rather to be a part of another, or a Psalm of itself, as it relates to a different subject.

In the *first* part of the following prayer we have the sorrowful sighing of a distressed heart, vented in the most earnest petitions on account of the greatness of its sins, and the evils by which it was surrounded. A fear of being cut off causes the penitent to pray, "Withhold not thou thy mercy from me, O Lord." 1. "For innumerable evils have compassed me," &c. 2. "My iniquities have taken fast hold upon me," &c. 3. "Therefore my heart faileth me." My agony is great, my vital spirit fails; and therefore he prays again, 4. "Be pleased, O Lord, to deliver me! make haste to help me!"

The *second* part of his prayer is for the confusion of his *wicked enemies:* "Let them be ashamed and confounded together, that say, Aha! aha!"

The *third* part of the prayer is for *all good men.* Let all those who seek thee be joyful and glad in thee; let them say, "The Lord be magnified."

In the *close* he prays for *himself;* and to move Divine mercy the sooner,—

1. He puts himself in the number of the poor and afflicted. He boasts not that he is a king, a prophet, a great man; but "I am poor and needy."

2. He shows his hope and confidence: "Yet the Lord thinketh upon me."

3. He casts himself wholly upon God: "Thou art my help and my deliverer."

4. Therefore delay not: "Make no tarrying, O my God!"

PSALM XLI

The blessedness of the man who is merciful to the poor, 1–3. *The psalmist complains of his enemies, and prays for support,* 4–10; *and blesses God for having heard his prayer, and preserved him from his adversaries,* 11, 12. *A fine doxology closes the Psalm,* 13.

VIII. DAY. EVENING PRAYER

To the chief Musician, A Psalm of David

A. M. cir. 2971
B. C. cir. 1033
Davidis, Regis
Israelitarum,
cir. annum
23

BLESSED [a]*is* he that considereth [b]the poor: the LORD
will deliver him [c]in time of
trouble.
2 The LORD will preserve him, and keep him
alive: *and* he shall be blessed upon the earth:
[d]and [e]thou wilt not deliver him unto the will
of his enemies.
3 The LORD will strengthen him upon the
bed of languishing: thou wilt [f]make all his
bed in his sickness.
4 I said, LORD, be merciful
unto me: [g]heal my soul; for I
have sinned against thee.
5 Mine enemies speak evil of
me, When shall he die, and his name perish?
6 And if he come to see *me,* he [h]speaketh
vanity: his heart gathereth iniquity to itself;
when he goeth abroad, he telleth *it.*
7 All that hate me whisper together against
me: against me do they devise [i]my hurt.
8 [k]An evil disease, *say they,* cleaveth fast
unto him: and *now* that he lieth he shall
rise up no more.

A. M. cir. 2971
B. C. cir. 1033
Davidis, Regis
Israelitarum,
cir. annum
23

[a]Proverbs xiv. 21——[b]Or, *the weak* or *sick*——[c]Hebrew, *in the day of evil*——[d]Psalm xxvii. 12——[e]Or, *do not thou deliver*——[f]Heb. *turn*

[g]2 Chron. xxx. 20; Psa. vi. 2; cxlvii. 3——[h]Psa. xii. 2; Prov. xxvi. 24, 25, 26——[i]Heb. *evil to me*——[k]Hebrew, *A thing of Belial*

NOTES ON PSALM XLI

The *title* as before. The *Syriac* says it was "A Psalm of David, when he appointed overseers to take care of the poor." The *Arabic* says, "It is a prophecy concerning the incarnation; and also of the salutation of Judas." It appears to me to have been written on the same occasion as the three former, and to relate to David's malady and cure, and the evil treatment he had from his enemies during his affliction. Our Lord, by accommodation, applies the ninth verse to the treachery of Judas, John xiii. 18; but as to any other direct reference to Christ, or his history, I believe the Psalm has none.

Verse 1. *Blessed is he that considereth*] God is *merciful;* he will have man to *resemble* him: as far as he is *merciful,* feels a *compassionate heart,* and uses a *benevolent hand,* he *resembles* his Maker; and the mercy he shows to others God will show to him. But it is not a *sudden impression* at the sight of a person in distress, which obliges a man to give something for the relief of the sufferer, that constitutes the *merciful character.* It is he *who considers the poor;* who endeavours to find them out; who looks into their circumstances; who is in the habit of doing so; and actually, according to his power and means, *goes about to do good;* that is the merciful man, of whom God speaks with such high approbation, and to whom he promises a rich reward.

Verse 2. *The Lord will preserve him, and keep him alive*] It is worthy of remark, that *benevolent persons,* who *consider* the *poor,* and especially the *sick poor;* who *search cellars, garrets, back lanes,* and *such abodes of misery,* to find them out, (even in the places where contagion keeps its seat,) very seldom fall a prey to their own benevolence. The Lord, in an especial manner, keeps them *alive,* and preserves them; while many, who endeavour to keep far from the contagion, are assailed by it, and fall victims to it. God loves the merciful man.

Verse 3. *The Lord will strengthen him*] Good, benevolent, and merciful as he is, he must also die: but he shall not die as other men; he shall have peculiar consolations, refreshment, and support, while passing *through the valley of the shadow of death.*

Thou wilt make all his bed] הפכת *haphachta,* thou hast *turned up, tossed,* and *shaken* it; and thou wilt do so to *all his bed*—thou wilt not leave one *uneasy place* in it—not one *lump,* or any *unevenness,* to prevent him from sleeping. Thou wilt do every thing, consistently with the accomplishment of the great decree, "Unto dust thou shalt return," to give him ease, refreshment, and rest. We may sum up the privileges of the merciful man: 1. He is generally *blessed,* ver. 1. 2. He will be *delivered in the time of trouble,* ver. 1. 3. He will be *preserved* by a particular providence, ver. 2. 4. He shall be *kept alive* amidst infection and danger, ver. 2. 5. He *shall be blessed on the earth* in his temporal concerns, ver. 2. 6. His *enemies* shall not be able to spoil or destroy him, ver. 2. 7. He shall be *strengthened on a bed of languishing,* to enable him to bear his afflictions, ver. 3. 8. He shall have *ease, comfort,* and *support* in his *last hours,* ver. 3.

Verse 4. *I said, Lord, be merciful unto me*] I need thy mercy especially, because I have sinned against thee, and my sin is a *deadly wound* to my *soul;* therefore *heal* my *soul, for it has sinned against thee.*

Verse 5. *Mine enemies speak evil*] It is often a good man's lot to be evil spoken of; to have his *motives,* and even his most *benevolent acts,* misconstrued.

Verse 6. *And if he come to see* me] This may relate to *Ahithophel;* but it is more likely that it was to some other person who was his secret enemy, who pretended to come and inquire after his health, but with the secret design to see whether death was *despatching his work.*

When *he goeth abroad, he telleth* it.] He makes several observations on my dying state; intimates that I am suffering deep remorse for secret crimes; that God is showing his displeasure against me, and that I am full of sorrow at the approach of death.

Verse 7. *All that hate me whisper together against me*] This is in consequence of the *information* given by the *hypocritical friend,* who came to him with the *lying tongue,* and whose *heart gathereth iniquity to itself,* which, when *he went abroad,* he told to others as ill-minded as himself, and they also drew their wicked inferences.

Verse 8. *An evil disease,* say they, *cleaveth*

A. M. cir. 2971
B. C. cir. 1033
Davidis, Regis
Israelitarum,
cir. annum
23

9 [l]Yea, [m]mine own familiar
friend, in whom I trusted, [n]which
did eat of my bread, hath [o]lifted
up *his* heel against me.

10 But thou, O LORD, be merciful unto
me, and raise me up, that I may requite
them.

11 By this I know that thou favourest me,
because mine enemy doth not
triumph over me.

12 And as for me, thou upholdest me in mine integrity, and
[p]settest me before thy face for ever.

13 [q]Blessed *be* the LORD God of Israel
from everlasting, and to everlasting. Amen,
and Amen.

A. M. cir. 2971
B. C. cir. 1033
Davidis, Regis
Israelitarum,
cir. annum
23

---

[l]2 Sam. xv. 12; Job xix. 19; Psa. lv. 12, 13, 20; Jer. xx. 10 — [m]Heb. *the man of my peace* — [n]Obad. 7; John xiii. 18 — [o]Heb. *magnified* — [p]Job xxxvi. 7; Psa. xxxiv. 15 — [q]Psa. cvi. 48

---

fast unto him] דבר בליעל יצוק בו *debar beliyaal yatsuk bo*, a *thing*, *word*, or *pestilence of Belial, is poured out upon him.* His disease is of no common sort; it is a *diabolical* malady.

He shall rise up no more.] His disease is incurable without a miracle; and he is too much hated of God to have one wrought for him. Some apply this to the death and resurrection of Christ; he *lieth*—he is *dead* and buried; he shall never *rise again* from the dead.

Verse 9. *Mine own familiar friend*] This is either a direct prophecy of the treachery of Judas, or it is a fact in David's distresses which our Lord found so similar to the falsity of his treacherous disciple, that he applies it to him, John xiii. 18. What we translate *mine own familiar friend*, איש שלומי *ish shelomi*, is *the man of my peace.* The man who, with the שלום לך *shalom lecha, peace be to thee!* kissed me; and thus gave the agreed-on signal to my murderers that I was the person whom they should seize, hold fast, and carry away.

Did eat of my bread] Was an *inmate in my house.* Applied by our Lord to Judas, when eating with him out of the same dish. See John xiii. 18, 26. Possibly it may refer to *Ahithophel*, his counsellor, the *man of his peace*, his prime minister; who, we know, was the strength of Absalom's conspiracy.

Verse 10. *Raise me up*] Restore me from this sickness, *that I may requite them.* This has also been applied to our Lord; who, knowing that he *must die*, prays that he *may rise again*, and thus disappoint the malice of his enemies.

Verse 11. *By this I know that thou favorest me*] If thou hadst not been on my side, I had perished by this disease; and then my enemies would have had cause to triumph.

This also has been applied to our Lord; and *Calmet* says it is the greatest proof we have of the divinity of Christ, that he did not permit the malice of the Jews, nor the rage of the devil, to prevail against him. They might persecute, blaspheme, mock, insult, crucify, and slay him; but his *resurrection* confounded them; and by it he gained the victory over sin, death, and hell.

Verse 12. *Thou upholdest me*] I am still enabled to show that my heart was upright before God.

Settest me before thy face for ever.] Thou showest that thou dost *approve* of me: that I stand *in thy presence*, under the smiles of thy approbation.

This also has been applied to our Lord, and considered as pointing out his *mediatorial office* at the right hand of God.

Verse 13. *Blessed* be *the Lord God of Israel*] By all these circumstances and events glory shall redound to the name of God for ever; for the *record* of these things shall never perish, but be published from one generation to another; and it has been so.

From everlasting, and to everlasting.] מהעולם ועד העולם *mehaolam vead haolam; From the hidden time to the hidden time;* from that which had no beginning to that which has no end.

To which he subscribes, *Amen and Amen. Fiat, fiat.—Vulgate.* Γενοιτο, γενοιτο.—*Septuagint.* The *Chaldee* says, "And let the righteous say, Amen, and Amen." ſyȝebletſod dꞃihten ȝod iſꞃahela fꞃam ƿoꞃulde ⁊ on ƿoꞃulde. beohit ſyhitſƿa. "Be blessed, Lord God of Israel, from world, and in world. Be it! So be it!"—*Anglo-Saxon.* To which the Old *Psalter* approaches very nearly: **Blyssed Lord God of Isrel, fra werld, and in werld: Be it done! be it done.** Thus illustrated by the same, **Fra werld in wereld**; that es, fra the bygynnyng of this wereld, in til wereld that lastes ay. **Be it done, be it done.** This dubblying schews that it es at do of al men. In *Latyn*, it es, *fiat, fiat!* in *Ebru*, *Amen Amen* es writyn: tharfore that *Aquila* translated *vere*, vel *fideliter*, that es, *sothfastly* or *trew.*

Thus ends what the Hebrews call the *first book* of Psalms; for the reader will recollect that this book is divided by the Jews into *five* books, the first of which ends with this Psalm.

This *doxology*, Dr. *Kennicott* supposes, may have been added by the collector of this book; and he thinks that the division into *books* is *not arbitrary;* and that the Psalms were collected at different times by different persons. See the *Introduction.* There is certainly a considerable *variety* in the *style* of the several books; in the examination of which the Hebrew critic will not lose his labour.

ANALYSIS OF THE FORTY-FIRST PSALM

In this Psalm David shows how men should, and how commonly they do, carry themselves towards men in affliction and trouble.

I. They should behave compassionately and kindly, which would tend to their own happiness, and cause them to find mercy from God, ver. 1-4.

II. But they commonly behave unkindly, and afflict the afflicted, ver. 4-10.

III. On which unkindness he flies to God, and prays for mercy, ver. 11; shows his hope and confidence in God, ver. 11, 12.

I. He begins with an excellent grave sentence: "Blessed is he who considereth the poor;" that is, any man in trouble and want, &c. This is a happy man. His particular comforts and privileges are *six:*—

1. "The Lord will deliver him in the time of trouble."

2. The Lord will *preserve* him, "that he faint not in his troubles."

3. The Lord will *keep him alive.* Prolong his life and days.

4. "He shall be blessed upon earth:" God shall enrich him, and bless his substance.

5. He shall not be delivered unto the will of his enemies,—never to their full desires, though often into their hands.

6. "The Lord will strengthen him upon a bed of languishing," and make all his bed in his *sickness:* he shall have comfort and assurance of God's favour.

II. He begins the second part with an ejaculation:—

1. "I said, The Lord be merciful unto me!" pardon my sin.

2. "Heal my soul:" extract the sting of sin, and all inward corruption.

3. He prays thus, because he is sensible that he "has sinned against the Lord."

The complaint against himself being ended, he begins to complain of others.

1. Of their hatred and malice: "Mine enemies speak evil of me."

2. Of their cruelty; they longed for his death: "When shall he die, and his name perish?" they would have even his memorial cut off.

3. Their perfidious dealing and dissimulation. They came to visit him: but it was fraudulently to search out his counsels, and to entrap him in his words; and then to detail them abroad: "If he come to see me," &c.

4. Of their plots and conspiracies: "All they that hate me whisper," &c.

5. Their exultation at his misery: "An evil disease, say they, cleaveth unto him," &c.

6. Of the perfidiousness of some particular friend, perhaps Ahithophel: "Yea, mine own familiar friend hath lifted up his heel against me."

III. And then, against all these evils, and in his own defence, he prays: "But thou, O Lord, be merciful unto me, and raise me up." For which he gives these reasons:—

1. That thereby, as a king, he should have power to do justice on traitors: "That I may requite them."

2. By this he should have experience of God's favour: "By this I know thou favourest me," &c.

3. It will be a testimony unto me that thou favourest not only my person, but my cause: "As for me, thou upholdest me in mine integrity, and settest me before thy face for ever."

The Psalm, and with it the *first book* of the Psalms, according to the Jewish division, is closed with a doxology to God: "Blessed be the Lord God of Israel, from everlasting to everlasting. Amen and Amen."

PSALM XLII

The psalmist earnestly longs for the ordinances of the Lord's house, 1–4; *describes his deep distress,* 5–7; *endeavours to take comfort from the consideration that the Lord would appear in his behalf,* 8, 9; *speaks of the insults of his enemies,* 10; *and again takes encouragement,* 11.

To the chief Musician, [a]Maschil, for the sons of Korah

AS the hart [b]panteth after the water brooks, so panteth my soul after thee, O God.

2 [c]My soul thirsteth for God, for [d]the living God: when shall I come and appear before God?

[a]Or, A Psalm *giving instruction of the sons,* &c.; see 1 Chron. vi. 33, 37; xxv. 5

[b]Heb. *brayeth*——[c]Psa. lxiii. 1; lxxxiv. 2; John vii. 37——[d]1 Thess. i. 9

NOTES ON PSALM XLII

The *title, To the chief Musician, giving instruction to the sons of Korah.* This is the first of the Psalms that has this title prefixed, and it is probable that such Psalms were composed by the *descendants of Korah* during the Babylonish captivity, or by some eminent person among those descendants, and that they were used by the Israelites during their long captivity, as means of consolation: and, indeed, most of the Psalms which bear this inscription are of the *consoling* kind and the sentiments appear to belong to that period of the Jewish history, and to none other. The word משכיל *maskil,* from שכל *sakal,* signifies to *make wise,* to *direct wisely,* to *give instruction;* and here is so understood by our translators, who have left this signification in the *margin;* and so the *Versions* in general.

The *Syriac* says, "It is a Psalm which David sung when he was an exile, and desired to return to Jerusalem." The *Arabic* says: "A Psalm for the backsliding Jews."

Verse 1. *As the hart panteth after the water brooks*] The *hart* is not only fond of feeding near some water for the benefit of *drinking,* "but when he is hard hunted, and nearly spent, he will take to some river or brook, in which," says *Tuberville,* "he will keep as long as his breath will suffer him. Understand that when a hart is spent and sore run, his last refuge is to the water; and he will commonly descend down the streame and swimme in the very middest thereof; for he will take as good heede as he can to touch no boughes or twygges that grow upon the sides of the river, for feare lest the hounds should there take sent of him. And sometimes the hart *will lye under the water,* all but *his very nose;* and I have seene divers lye so until the hounds have been upon

3 [e]My tears have been my meat day and
night, while [f]they continually say unto me,
Where *is* thy God?
4 When I remember these *things,* [g]I pour
out my soul in me: for I had gone with the
multitude, [h]I went with them to the house of
God, with the voice of joy and praise, with a
multitude that kept holyday.
5 [i]Why art thou [k]cast down, O my soul?
and *why* art thou disquieted in me? [l]hope thou
in God: for I shall yet [m]praise him [n]*for* the
help of his countenance.
6 O my God, my soul is cast down within
me: therefore will I remember thee from the
land of Jordan, and of the Hermonites, from
[o]the hill Mizar.
7 [p]Deep calleth unto deep at the noise of
thy waterspouts: [q]all thy waves and thy billows are gone over me.
8 Yet the LORD will [r]command his loving-

[e]Psa. lxxx. 5; cii. 9——[f]Ver. 10; Psa. lxxix. 10; cxv. 2 [g]Job xxx. 16; Psa. lxii. 8——[h]Isa. xxx. 29——[i]Ver. 11; Psa. xliii. 5——[k]Heb. *bowed down*——[l]Lam. iii. 24 [m]Or, *give thanks*

[n]Or, *his presence is salvation*——[o]Or, *the little hill;* Psa. cxxxiii. 3——[p]Jer. iv. 20; Ezek. vii. 26——[q]Psa. lxxxviii. 7; Jonah ii. 3——[r]Lev. xxv. 21; Deut. xxviii. 8; Psa. cxxxiii. 3

them, before they would rise; for *they are constrayned to take the water as their last refuge.*"—*Tuberville's* Art of Venerie, chap. xl. Lond. 4to., 1611.

The above extracts will give a fine illustration of this passage. The hart feels himself almost entirely spent; he is nearly hunted down; the dogs are in full pursuit; he is parched with thirst; and in a burning heat pants after the water, and when he comes to the river, plunges in *as his last refuge.* Thus pursued, spent, and nearly ready to give up the ghost, the psalmist *pants for God,* for the *living God!* for him who can give *life,* and save from *death.*

Verse 2. *When shall I come*] When, when shall I have the privilege of appearing in his courts *before God?* In the mouth of a *Christian* these words would import: "*When* shall I see my heavenly country? *When* shall I come to God, the Judge of all, and to Jesus, the Mediator of the new covenant?" He who is a *stranger* and a *pilgrim* here below, and feels a heart full of piety to God, may use these words in this sense; but he who feels himself here at home, whose soul is not spiritual, wishes the earth to be eternal, and himself eternal on it—feels no panting after the *living God.*

Verse 3. *My tears have been my meat day and night*] My longing has been so intense after spiritual blessings, that I have forgotten to take my necessary food; and my sorrow has been so great, that I have had no appetite for any. I feel more for the honour of my God and his truth than for myself, when the idolaters, who have thy people in captivity, insultingly cry, *Where* is *thy God?*

Verse 4. *When I remember these* things] Or, *these things I shall remember.* They often occur to me, and sharpen my distressful feelings. My soul is dissolved, becomes weak as water, when I reflect on what I have had, and on what I have lost. Or, *I pour out my soul to myself* in deep regrets and complaints, when reflecting on these things. I once enjoyed all the ordinances of God, and now I have none. I once had the joyous communion of saints in God's ordinances; but that communion no longer exists, for there are no ordinances to support it. There was a *multitude* to worship God in public; with these *I often went:* but, alas, this is no more; now there are found only a few *solitary individuals* who sigh for the desolations of Zion. *There* we had our holy days, our appointed *feasts,* to commemorate the wonderful works of the Lord; now there are no processions, no festivals, no joyous assemblies; all is desolation in Zion, and all is mourning in our captivity. I have endeavoured to give a general sense to this verse, but there are several difficulties in it; and different commentators and critics have given it a great variety of translations, and as many different meanings. My plan will not permit me to follow them. Much may be seen in Dr. *Horsley's* work on this verse.

Verse 5. *Why art thou cast down, O my soul?*] Bad as the times are, desolate as Jerusalem is, insulting as are our enemies, hopeless as in the sight of man our condition may be, yet there is no room for *despair.* All things are possible to God. We have a promise of restoration; he is as good as he is powerful; hope therefore in him.

I shall yet praise him] For my restoration from this captivity. He is the health of my soul. I shall have the *light and help of his countenance,* his approbation, and a glorious deliverance wrought by his right hand.

Verse 6. *O my God, my soul is cast down*] It is impossible for me to lighten this load; I am full of discouragements, notwithstanding I labour to hope in thee.

Therefore will I remember thee from the land of Jordan] That is, from Judea, this being the chief river of that country.

And of the Hermonites] הרמונים the *Hermons,* used in the *plural* because Hermon has a *double* ridge joining in an angle, and rising in many summits. The river *Jordan,* and the mountains of *Hermon,* were the most striking features of the holy land.

From the hill Mizar.] מהר מצער *mehar mitsar, from the little hill,* as in the *margin. The little hill* probably means *Sion,* which was little in comparison of the Hermons.—Bishop *Horsley.* No such hill as Mizar is known in India.

Verse 7. *Deep calleth unto deep*] One wave of sorrow rolls on me, impelled by another. There is something *dismal* in the sound of the original; תהום אל תהום קורא *tehom el tehom kore;* something like "And hollow howlings hung in air." *Thompson's Ellenore.* Or like *Homer's* well known verse:—

Βη δ' ακεων παρα θινα πολυφλοισβοιο θαλασσης.

kindness in the daytime, and [s]in the night his
song *shall be* with me, *and* my prayer unto
the God of my life.
9 I will say unto God my rock, Why hast
thou forgotten me? [t]why go I mourning because of the oppression of the enemy?
10 *As* with a [u]sword in my bones, mine enemies reproach me; [v]while they say daily unto
me, Where *is* thy God?
11 [w]Why art thou cast down, O my soul?
and why art thou disquieted within me? hope
thou in God: for I shall yet praise him,
who is the health of my countenance, and
my God.

[s]Job xxxv. 10; Psa. xxxii. 7; lxiii. 6; cxlix. 5——[t]Psa. xxxviii. 6; xliii. 2

[u]Or, *killing*——[v]Verse 3; Joel ii. 17; Mic. vii. 10——[w]Ver. 5; Psa. xliii. 5

"He went silently along the shore of the vastly-sounding sea." Il. i., ver. 34.

The rolling up of the waves into a swell, and the break of the top of the swell, and its *dash* upon the shore, are surprisingly represented in the sound of the two last words.

The psalmist seems to represent himself as cast away at sea; and by wave impelling wave, is carried to a rock, around which the surges dash in all directions, forming *hollow* sounds in the creeks and caverns. At last, several waves breaking over him, tear him away from that rock to which he clung, and where he had a little before found a resting-place, and, apparently, an escape from danger. "All thy waves and thy billows are gone over me;" he is then whelmed in the deep, and God alone can save him.

Waterspouts] A large tube formed of clouds by means of the electric fluid, the base being uppermost, and the point of the tube let down perpendicularly from the clouds. This tube has a particular kind of *circular motion* at the point; and being hollow within, attracts vast quantities of water, which it pours down in torrents upon the earth. These spouts are frequent on the coast of Syria; and Dr. *Shaw* has often seen them at *Mount Carmel.* No doubt the psalmist had often seen them also, and the ravages made by them. I have seen vast gullies cut out of the sides of mountains by the fall of *waterspouts*, and have seen many of them in their fullest activity.

Verse 8. *The Lord will command*] Every day the Lord will give an especial commission to his loving-kindness to visit me. During the night I shall sing of his mercy and goodness; and alternately mingle my *singing* with *prayer* for a continuance of his mercy, and for power to make the best use of these visitations.

Verse 9. *I will say unto God my rock*] God, my Fortress and Support.

Why hast thou forgotten me?] This and the following verse is badly pointed in our Bibles: "Why go I mourning as with a sword in my bones because of the oppression of the enemy? Mine enemies reproach me daily, while they say unto me, Where is thy God?" See on ver. 3. Their reproaches are to my soul as cutting and severe as a sword thrust into my body, and separating between my bones; because these reproaches are intended to fall on thee, my God, as if thou hadst not power to save us from the hands of our oppressors.

Verse 11. *Why art thou cast down*] There is no reason why thou shouldst despair. God will appear and release thee and thy brother captives and soon thy sighing and sorrowing shall flee away.

Who is *the health of my countenance*] As a healthy state of the constitution shows itself in the appearance of the face; God will so rejoice thy heart, heal all thy spiritual maladies, that thy face shall testify the happiness that is within thee.

There is a curious gloss on the first verse of this Psalm in my old *Psalter*, which I cannot withhold from the reader. The author translates and paraphrases the verse thus:—

Trans. **Als the Hert yernes til the welles of waters; so my saule yernes til the God.**

Par. This Psalm es al of perfite men, that er brinnand in the flamme of Goddes luf, and passes in til the contemplatyf lif: and tharfore it es sungen in the office of the dede men: for than haf thai, that thai yearned; that es, the syght of God. Far thi, sais he, *als the Hert that has eten the nedder, gretely yernes to com til the welles of waters for to drynk and wax yong ogayne:* so destroyed in me vices and unclennes, my saule desyres with brinnand yernyng, to come til the God.

Ælian, *Appian*, *Aristotle*, *Nicander*, and *Pliny*, all inform us that one cause why the hart thirsts for the waters is, that *they eat serpents*, and that the *poison* of them diffused through their entrails produces a *burning heat* and *fever*, to ease and cure themselves of which they have recourse to *water*. Many of the *fathers* tell the same tale, and from them the paraphrast in the old Psalter has borrowed what is inserted above: "Like as the hart, which has eaten the adder, greatly longs to come to the fountains of water to drink, that he may grow young again." The hart is undoubtedly a *cunning* animal; but it would be as difficult to believe that he *eats serpents* as it would be to believe that he seeks for and eats the *fresh water crab* or *cray fish*, in order to cure and make him grow young again, as *Eusebius*, *Didymus*, *Theodoret*, *Jerome*, *Epiphanius*, *Gregory Nyssen*, and others of the primitive fathers gravely inform us.

Analysis of the Forty-second Psalm

The psalmist, driven from the assemblies of God's people, complains; and as men overwhelmed with troubles are also oppressed with grief, so is he; and as they abruptly express their thoughts, so does he; for sometimes he *expostulates*, sometimes he *complains*, sometimes he *corrects* and *checks* himself for his weakness. One while he opens his *doubts*, and presently again sets forth his *confidence* in God. It is difficult on this account to analyze this Psalm; but it may be reduced to these *four heads:*—

I. The zeal of the psalmist to serve God in God's own house; ver. 1, 2, 4, 6.

II. His complaint and expressions of grief for

his absence, for his affliction, and his enemies' insults on that ground; ver. 3, 4, 7, 10.

III. His expostulation with his soul for its diffidence, ver. 5, 6; and again with God for his desertion, ver. 9.

IV. His faith and confidence in God's promises; ver. 5, 8, 11.

I. 1. He begins with an expression of his grief for his exile from the ordinances of God, and the assemblies of his people. And he sets forth his zeal and longing desire under the expressive similitude of a hard-hunted and thirsty stag: "As the hart panteth," &c.; ver. 1, 2.

2. He shows the state he was in. 1. "My tears have been my meat day and night;" ver. 3. 2. And the cause was the bitter sarcasm of his enemies: "Where is now thy God?" Where is thy Protector? him in whom thou trustest?

II. That which added to his grief was that which gave occasion to this sarcasm, his banishment from the sanctuary.

1. When I remember these things, my absence, their insults, I pour out my heart to myself; *tear* follows *tear*, and one complaint succeeds to another.

2. And much reason I have to grieve when I compare my present with my former condition. Formerly "I went with the multitude to the house of God,—with the voice of joy and praise," &c. I had *gone; now* I *cannot* and *must not go.*

III. Hitherto he had expressed his zeal, his sorrow, and his complaints, with their causes. These put his soul in a sad condition; and thus he expostulates with himself:—

1. Blaming himself for his weakness and diffidence: "Why art thou cast down, O my soul," &c.

2. Then presently fortifies himself in God's promises: "Hope thou in God, for I shall yet praise him," &c.

In all which is described the combat that a good man has when he is in heaviness through manifold temptation, and finds great difficulty to struggle between hope and despair; but at last conquers by faith, and inherits the promises.

3. But his conflict is not yet over; he exclaims again, and still more affectingly, "O my God, my soul is cast down." Of which he assigns two causes:—

1. That though he was ready to remember and serve God, yet he was forced to do it in an improper place. He remembered the pleasant *land of Palestine*, the stately *mountains of Hermon*, and the *little hill of Sion:* but *there* he could not worship; he was in an enemy's country, and in captivity in that country.

2. The greatness and continual succession of his troubles: "Deep calleth unto deep." Calamity on calamity, one trial on the heels of another; so that he might well say, "All thy waves and thy billows are gone over me."

3. And yet he despairs not, he encourages himself in the Lord: "Yet the Lord will command his loving-kindness," &c. 1. "His song shall be with me." 2. "And my prayer unto the God of my life."

IV. On which he grows more confident and courageous, and again expostulates, not now with his *soul*, as before, but with his GOD: "I will say unto God my rock."

1. "Why hast thou forgotten me?"

2. "Why go I mourning because of the oppression of the enemy?"

3. Why am I wounded with grief, "as with a sword in my bones," while they use the sarcasm, "Where is now thy God?"

But in the conclusion, after all his complaints and expostulations, he gains a full assurance of God's favour and protection.

1. Chiding himself for his discontent and diffidence, "Why art thou cast down?"

2. Then he encourages his heart in God's goodness and faithfulness: "Hope thou in God, for I shall yet praise him, who is the health of my countenance, and my God."

The *forty-third* is most probably a part of this Psalm: they should be read and expounded together, as the subject is not complete in either, taken as separate Psalms. See, therefore, on the following.

PSALM XLIII

The psalmist begs God to take his part against his enemies, 1, 2; *to send his light and truth to guide him to the tabernacle,* 3; *promises, if brought thither, to be faithful in the Divine service,* 4; *chides himself for despondency, and takes courage,* 5.

JUDGE [a]me, O God, and [b]plead my cause
against an [c]ungodly nation: O deliver me
[d]from the deceitful and unjust man.

2 For thou *art* the God of [e]my strength:
why dost thou cast me off? [f]why go I mourning because of the oppression of the enemy?

[a]Psalm xxvi. 1; xxxv. 24——[b]Psalm xxxv. 1——[c]Or, *unmerciful*

[d]Heb. *from a man of deceit and iniquity*——[e]Psalm xxviii. 7——[f]Psa. xlii. 9

NOTES ON PSALM XLIII

There is no *title* to this Psalm in the *Hebrew*, nor in the *Chaldee*. The *Syriac* says it was composed "by David when Jonathan told him that Saul intended to slay him." The *Arabic* says of this, as of the preceding, that it is a *prayer for the backsliding Jews.* It is most evidently on the same subject with the *forty-second* Psalm, had the same author or authors, and contains the remaining part of the complaint of the captive Jews in Babylon. It is written as a part of the *forty-second* Psalm in *forty-six* of *Kennicott's* and *De Rossi's* MSS.

Verse 1. *Judge me, O God, and plead my cause*] ריבה ריבי *ribah ribi*, a forensic term, properly enough translated, *plead my cause, be my counsellor and advocate.*

3 [g]O send out thy light and thy truth: let them lead me; let them bring me unto [h]thy holy hill, and to thy tabernacles.

4 Then will I go unto the altar of God, unto God [i]my exceeding joy: yea, upon the harp will I praise thee, O God my God.

5 [k]Why art thou cast down, O my soul? and why art thou disquieted within me? hope in God: for I shall yet praise him, *who is* the health of my countenance, and my God.

[g]Psa. xl. 11; lvii. 3——[h]Psa. iii. 4

[i]Heb. *the gladness of my joy*——[k]Psa. xlii. 5, 11

Ungodly nation] The Babylonians; the impious, perfidious, wicked, and deceitful Babylonians.

The deceitful and unjust man.] Nebuchadnezzar.

Verse 2. *For thou* art *the God of my strength*] The psalmist speaks here, as in other places, in the person of the whole Israelitish people then captive in Babylon. We still acknowledge thee for our God. *Why are we cast off?* Now that we are humbled and penitent, why are we not enlarged? Why are we not saved from this oppression of the Babylonians?

Verse 3. *O send out thy light and thy truth*] We are in *darkness* and *distress*, O send *light* and *prosperity;* we look for the fulfilment of thy *promises;* O send forth thy *truth*. Let thy *light* guide me to thy *holy hill*, to the country of my fathers; let thy *truth* lead me to thy tabernacles, there to worship thee in *spirit* and in *truth*.

Verse 4. *Then will I go unto the altar*] When thy *light*—a *favourable turn in our affairs*, leads us to the land of our fathers, and thy *truth*—the *fulfilment of thy gracious promises*, has placed us again at the door of thy tabernacles, then will we go to *thy altar*, and joyfully offer those sacrifices and offerings which thy law requires, and rejoice in thee with exceeding great joy.

Verse 5. *Why art thou cast down*] Though our deliverance be delayed, God has not forgotten to be gracious. The vision, the prophetic declaration relative to our captivity, was for an appointed time. Though it appear to tarry, we must wait for it. In the end it will come, and will not tarry; why then should we be discouraged? Let us still continue to trust in God, for we *shall yet praise him* for the fullest proofs of his approbation in a great outpouring of his benedictions.

Analysis of the Forty-third Psalm

This Psalm, which is of the same nature with the former, and properly a part or continuation of it, contains *two chief* things:—

I. A *petition*, which is double. 1. One in the *first* verse. 2. The other in the *fourth* verse.

II. A *comfortable apostrophe* to his own soul, ver. 5.

First, He petitions God,—

1. That, being *righteous*, he would be his Judge: "Judge me, O Lord."

2. That, being *merciful*, he would plead his cause: "Plead my cause."

3. That, being *almighty*, he would deliver him: "Deliver me," ver. 1.

For this petition he assigns *two* reasons:—

1. The unmerciful disposition of his enemies. 1. They were a factious, bloody, inhuman people: "Plead my cause against an ungodly nation," גוי לא חסיד *goi lo chasid*, "a people without mercy." 2. They were men of deceit and iniquity: "Deliver me from the deceitful and unjust man," ver. 1.

2. The other reason he draws from the nature of God, and his relation to him: "For thou art the God of my strength." Thou hast promised to defend me. On this he expostulates: 1. "Why hast thou cast me off?" For so, to the eye of sense, it at present appears. 2. "Why go I mourning, because of the oppression of the enemy?" ver. 2.

Secondly, The second part of his petition is, that he may be restored to God's favour, and brought back to his own country, ver. 3.

1. "O send forth thy light and thy truth," the light of thy favour and countenance, and make thy promises true to me: "Let them lead me," ver. 3.

2. "Let them guide me;"—whither? To dignity and honours? No, I ask not those: I ask to be guided to thy holy hill and tabernacles, where I may enjoy the exercises of piety in thy pure worship, ver. 3.

Thirdly, That he might the better move God to hear his petition, he does as good as *vow* that he would be thankful, and make it known how good God had been to him.

1. "Then will I go unto the altar of God, my exceeding joy." The joy and content he would take in this should not be of an ordinary kind.

2. "Yea, upon the harp will I praise thee, O God." His joy should be expressed outwardly by a Psalm, doubtless composed for the occasion; the singing of which should be accompanied by the *harp*, or such instruments of music as were *then* commonly used in the Divine worship.

The petitions being ended, and now confident of audience and favour, he thus addresses his heavy and mournful heart, as in the former Psalm: 1. Chiding himself. 2. Encouraging himself.

1. "Why art thou cast down, O my soul? and why art thou disquieted within me?" Chiding.

2. "Hope in God: for I shall yet praise him, who is the health of my countenance, and my God." Encouraging. See notes and analysis of the preceding Psalm.

PSALM XLIV

***The psalmist recounts the mercies of God; shows to his people how God in ancient times gave them the victory over all their enemies,* 1–8; *points out their present miserable state,* 9–16; *asserts that they have not apostatized, and appeals to God for the truth of his assertion,* 17–22; *and calls upon the Lord for deliverance from their enemies,* 23–26.**

IX. DAY. MORNING PRAYER

To the chief Musician for the sons of Korah, Maschil

WE have heard with our ears, O God, [a]our
fathers have told us, *what* work thou
didst in their days, in the times of old.
2 *How* [b]thou didst drive out the heathen
with thy hand, and plantedst them: *how* thou
didst afflict the people, and cast them out.
3 For [c]they got not the land in possession
by their own sword, neither did their own
arm save them: but thy right hand, and thine
arm, and the light of thy countenance, [d]be-
cause thou hadst a favour unto them.
4 [e]Thou art my King, O God: command
deliverances for Jacob.
5 Through thee [f]will we push down our
enemies: through thy name will we tread
them under that rise up against us.
6 For [g]I will not trust in my bow, neither
shall my sword save me.
7 But thou hast saved us from our enemies,
and [h]hast put them to shame that hated us.
8 [i]In God we boast all the day long, and
praise thy name for ever. Selah.
9 But [k]thou hast cast off, and put us to
shame; and goest not forth with our armies.
10 Thou makest us to [l]turn back from the
enemy: and they which hate us spoil for themselves.
11 [m]Thou hast given us [n]like sheep *appointed* for meat; and hast [o]scattered us
among the heathen.

[a]Exod. xii. 26, 27; Psa. lxxviii. 3——[b]Exod. xv. 17; Deut. vii. 1; Psa. lxxviii. 55; lxxx. 8——[c]Deut. viii. 17; Josh. xxiv. 12——[d]Deut. iv. 37; vii. 7, 8——[e]Psa. lxxiv. 12——[f]Dan. viii. 4——[g]Psa. xxxiii. 16; Hos. i. 7 [h]Psa. xl. 14

[i]Psa. xxxiv. 2; Jer. ix. 24; Rom. ii. 17——[k]Psa. lx. 1, 10; lxxiv. 1; lxxxviii. 14; lxxxix. 38; cviii. 11——[l]Lev. xxvi. 17; Deut. xxviii. 25; Josh. vii. 8, 12——[m]Rom. viii. 36——[n]Heb. *as sheep of meat*——[o]Deut. iv. 27; xxviii. 64; Psa. lx. 1

NOTES ON PSALM XLIV

The *title* here is the same as that in Psa. xlii.; which see. The *Syriac* says it was "A Psalm of the sons of Korah, which the people and Moses sung at Horeb." Such titles are fancies to which no credit should be attached. Like the preceding, it appears to belong to the time of the *captivity*.

Verse 1. *We have heard with our ears*] The psalmist begins with recounting the marvellous interpositions of God in behalf of the Jewish people, that he might the better strengthen his confidence, and form a ground on which to build his expectation of additional help.

Verse 2. *Thou didst drive out the heathen*] The Canaanites were as a bad tree planted in a good soil, and bringing forth bad fruit with great luxuriance. God plucked up this bad tree from the roots, and in its place planted the Hebrews as a good tree, a good vine, and caused them to take root, and fill the land.

Verse 3. *For they got not the land*] Neither by their valour, nor cunning, nor for their merit; yet, they were obliged to fight. But how did they conquer? By the right hand of the Lord, and by his arm; by his strength alone, and the *light of his countenance*—his favour most manifestly shown unto them.

Verse 4. *Thou art my king*] What thou wert to *them*, be to *us*. We believe in thee as they did; we have sinned and are in captivity, but we repent and turn unto thee; command, therefore, deliverances to Jacob, for we are the descendants of him in whose behalf thou hast wrought such wonders.

Verse 5. *Through thee will we push down*] *Through thy* WORD, במימרא *bemeimra*, "Thy substantial Word."—*Chaldee*. If thou be with us, who can be successfully against us? Literally, "We will toss them in the air with our horn;" a metaphor taken from an ox or bull tossing the dogs into the air which attack him.

Through thy name] Jehovah; the infinite, the omnipotent, the eternal Being; whose power none is able to resist.

Verse 6. *I will not trust in my bow*] As he is speaking of what God had already done for his forefathers, these words should be read in the *past* tense: "We have not trusted," &c.

Verse 8. *In God we boast*] We have told the heathen how great and powerful our God is. If thou do not deliver us by thy mighty power, they will not believe our report, but consider that we are held in bondage by the superior strength of their gods.

Verse 9. *But thou hast cast off*] Our enemies have dominion over us.

And goest not forth with our armies.] Were we to attempt to muster our several tribes, and form a *host*, like our fathers when they came out of Egypt, thou wouldst not accompany us as thou didst them: the horses and chariots of the Babylonians would soon overtake and destroy us.

Verse 10. *Thou makest us to turn back*] This thou didst: and our enemies, profiting by the occasion, finding our strength was departed from us, made us an easy prey, captivated our persons, and spoiled us of our property.

Verse 11. *And hast scattered us among the heathen.*] This most evidently alludes to the

12 [p]Thou sellest thy people [q]for nought, and dost not increase *thy wealth* by their price.

13 [r]Thou makest us a reproach to our neighbours, a scorn and a derision to them that are round about us.

14 [s]Thou makest us a byword among the heathen, [t]a shaking of the head among the people.

15 My confusion *is* continually before me, and the shame of my face hath covered me,

16 For the voice of him that reproacheth and blasphemeth; [u]by reason of the enemy and avenger.

17 [v]All this is come upon us; yet have we not forgotten thee, neither have we dealt falsely in thy covenant.

18 Our heart is not turned back, [w]neither have our [x]steps declined from thy way.

19 Though thou hast sore broken us in [y]the place of dragons, and covered us [z]with the shadow of death.

20 If we have forgotten the name of our God, or [a]stretched out our hands to a strange god;

21 [b]Shall not God search this out? for he knoweth the secrets of the heart.

22 [c]Yea, for thy sake are we killed all the day long; we are counted as sheep for the slaughter.

23 [d]Awake, why sleepest thou, O LORD? arise, [e]cast *us* not off for ever.

24 [f]Wherefore hidest thou thy face, *and* forgettest our affliction and our oppression?

---

[p]Isa. lii. 3, 4; Jer. xv. 13——[q]Heb. *without riches* [r]Deut. xxviii. 37; Psa. lxxix. 4; lxxx. 6——[s]Jer. xxiv. 9——[t]2 Kings xix. 21; Job xvi. 4; Psa. xxii. 7——[u]Psa. viii. 2——[v]Dan. ix. 13——[w]Job xxiii. 11; Psalm cxix. 51, 157——[x]Or, *goings*

[y]Isa. xxxiv. 13; xxxv. 7——[z]Psa. xxiii. 4——[a]Job xi. 13; Psa. lxviii. 31——[b]Job xxxi. 14; Psa. cxxxix. 1; Jer. xvii. 10——[c]Rom. viii. 36——[d]Psa. vii. 6; xxxv. 23; lix. 4, 5; lxxviii. 65——[e]Ver. 9——[f]Job xiii. 24; Psa. xiii. 1; lxxxviii. 14

---

captivity. From the successful wars of the kings of Assyria and Chaldea against the kings of Israel and Judah, and the dispersion of the tribes under Tiglath-pileser, Shalmaneser, and Nebuchadnezzar, Jews have been found in every province of the east; there they settled, and there their successors may be found to the present day.

Verse 12. *Thou sellest thy people for nought*] An allusion to the mode of disposing of slaves by their proprietors or sovereigns. Instead of seeking profit, thou hast made us a present to our enemies.

Verse 14. *Thou makest us a byword*] We are evidently abandoned by thee, and are become so very miserable in consequence, that we are a proverb among the people: "See the Hebrews! *see their misery and wretchedness! see how low the wrath of God has brought down an offending people!*" And the worst curse that can be imprecated against a wicked nation is: "*Mayest thou become as wretched as the Jews;*" or as the old *Psalter:* "**Thou has seet us reprobe til our neghburs: scornyng and hethyng til tha that er in our umgang.** That es, gref, tourment that es of our neghburs, and that hethyng es noght sone gave or passand, that we suffer of tha, that er al aboute us. When men sais *so byfal ye, als byfel him.*"

Verse 17. *Yet have we not forgotten thee*] These are bold words; but they must be understood in a qualified sense. We have not *apostatized* from thee; we have not *fallen into idolatry.* And this was strictly true: the charge of idolatry could never be brought against the Jewish nation from the time of the captivity, with sufficient evidence to support it.

Verse 19. *Thou hast sore broken us in the place of dragons*] Thou hast delivered us into the hands of a fierce, cruel, and murderous people. We, as a people, are in a similar state to one who has strayed into a wilderness, where there are no human inhabitants; who hears nothing round about him but the hissing of serpents, the howling of beasts of prey, and the terrible roaring of the lion; and who expects every moment to be devoured.

Verse 20. *If we have forgotten the name of our God*] *That name,* יהוה *Yehovah,* by which the true God was particularly distinguished, and which implied the exclusion of all other objects of adoration.

Or stretched out our hands] Made supplication; offered prayer or adoration to any *strange god*—a god that we had not known, nor had been acknowledged by our fathers. It has already been remarked, that from the time of the Babylonish captivity the Jews never relapsed into idolatry.

It was customary among the ancients, while praying, to *stretch out their hands* towards the *heavens,* or the *image* they were worshipping, as if they expected to *receive* the favour they were asking.

Verse 21. *Shall not God search this out?*] We confidently appeal to the true God, the searcher of hearts, for the truth of this statement.

Verse 22. *For thy sake are we killed all the day long*] Because of our attachment to thee and to thy religion, we are exposed to continual death; and some of us fall a daily sacrifice to the persecuting spirit of our enemies, and we all carry our lives continually in our hands. In the same state were the primitive Christians; and St. Paul applies these words to their case, Rom. viii. 36.

Verse 23. *Awake, why sleepest thou, O Lord?*] That is, Why dost thou appear as one asleep, who is regardless of the safety of his friends. This is a *freedom of speech* which can only be allowed to inspired men; and in their mouths it is always to be *figuratively* understood.

Verse 24. *Wherefore hidest thou thy face*] Show us the cause why thou withdrawest from us the testimony of thy approbation.

25 For [g]our soul is bowed down to the dust: our belly cleaveth unto the earth.

26 Arise [h]for our help, and redeem us for thy mercies' sake.

[g]Psa. cxix. 25

[h]Heb. *a help for us*

Verse 25. *Our soul is bowed down*] Our life is drawing near to the grave. If thou delay to help us, we shall become extinct.

Verse 26. *Arise for our help*] Show forth thy power in delivering us from the hands of our enemies.

Redeem us] Ransom us from our thraldom.

For thy mercies' sake.] למען חסדך *lemaan chasdecha, On account of thy mercy.* That we may have that proper view of thy mercy which we should have, and that we may magnify it as we ought to do, redeem us. The Vulgate has, Redime nos, propter nomen tuum, "Redeem us on account of thy name;" which the old *Psalter* thus paraphrases: "Help us in ryghtwysness, and by us (buy,) that es, delyver us, that we be withouten drede; and al this for thi name Jehsu; noght for oure merite."

Analysis of the Forty-fourth Psalm

In this Psalm are livelily expressed the sufferings, the complaints, the assurances, the petitions which are offered to God by good men, who suffer, together with others, in the common afflictions that God brings on his people.

The parts are *two:*—

I. A *petition* from ver. 24 to the end.

II. The *arguments* by which the petition is quickened, from ver. 1 to 24.

First, He begins with the *arguments,* of which the first is drawn from God's goodness, of which he gives in particular, his benefits and miracles done for their fathers; as if he had said, "This thou didst for them; why art thou so estranged from us?"

I. "We have heard with our ears, O God, and our fathers have told us what works thou didst in their days, and in the times of old." The particulars of which are,—

1. "How thou didst drive out the heathen," namely, the Canaanites.

2. "How thou plantedst them."

3. "How thou didst afflict the people, and cast them out," ver. 2.

II. This we acknowledge to be thy word; expressed thus:—

1. "How thou didst drive out the heathen;" negatively, by remotion of what some might imagine: "They got not the land in possession by their own sword, neither was it their own arm that helped them," ver. 3. "Not unto us, O Lord, not unto us, but unto thy name be the praise."

2. "How thou plantedst them;" positively: "For it was thy right hand and thy arm, and the light of thy countenance." A mere *gratuito:* "because thou hadst a favour unto them;" no other reason can be assigned but that, ver. 3.

3. Upon this consideration, by an apostrophe, he turns his speech to God, and sings a song of triumph, of which the strains are,—

1. An open confession: "Thou art my king, O God."

2. A petition: "Send help unto Jacob," ver. 4.

3. A confident persuasion of future victory; but still with God's help and assistance, ver. 5, 6, 7. 1. "Through thee will we push down our enemies." 2. "Through thee will we tread them under that rise up against us." All through thee; *in thy name, by thy power.*

4. An abrenunciation of his own power or arm: "For I will not trust in my bow, neither shall my sword save me."

5. A reiteration, or a second ascription of the whole victory to God: "But thou hast saved us from our enemies; thou hast put them to shame that hated us," ver. 7.

6. A grateful return of thanks; which is indeed the tribute God expects, and which we are to pay upon our deliverance: "In God we boast all the day long, and praise thy name for ever."

Secondly, The second argument by which he wings his petition is drawn from the condition which, for the present, God's people were in, before he had done wonders for their deliverance; but now he had delivered them to the will of their enemies. This would move a man to think that his good will was changed toward them: "But thou hast cast us off, and put us to shame, and goest not forth with our armies."

Of which the consequences are many and grievous, although we acknowledge that all is from thee, and comes from thy hand and permission.

1. The *first* is: "Thou makest us to turn back from the enemy," ver. 10.

2. The *second,* We become a prey: "They which hate us spoil for themselves," ver. 10.

3. The *third,* We are devoured: "Thou hast given us as sheep appointed for meat;" killed cruelly, and when they please, ver. 11.

4. The *fourth,* We are driven from our country, and made to dwell where they will plant us: "Thou hast scattered us among the heathen;" (inter gentes,) and that is a great discomfort, to live among people *without God in the world.*

5. The *fifth,* We are become slaves, sold and bought as beasts; and that for any price, upon any exchange: "Thou sellest thy people for nought, and dost not increase thy wealth by their price," ver. 12; puts them off as worthless things.

6. The *sixth,* We are made a scorn, a mock; and to whom? To our enemies: but that might be borne; but even to our friends and neighbours: "Thou makest us a reproach to our neighbours, a scorn and derision to them that are round about us."

And this he amplifies,—

1. From the circumstance that they are a proverb of reproach: "Thou makest us a byword among the heathen."

That in scorn any one that would used a scornful gesture toward them: "We are become a shaking of the head among the people."

3. That this insulting is continual: "My confusion is daily before me."

4. It is superlative; shame so great that he had not what to say to it: "The shame of my face hath covered me."

5. It is public; their words and gestures are not concealed; they speak out what they please: "Ashamed I am for the voice of him that reproacheth and blasphemeth; for the enemy and avenger."

Thirdly, And yet he useth a third argument, that the petition may be the more grateful, and more easily granted; drawn from the constancy and perseverance of God's people in the profession of the truth, notwithstanding this heavy loss, persecution, and affliction: "All this is come upon us;"—thus we are oppressed, devoured, banished, sold, derided; *yet* we continue to be thy servants still, we retain our faith, hope, service.

1. *We have not forgotten thee*, not forgotten thou art our God. We acknowledge no idols.

2. *We have not dealt falsely in thy covenant.* We have not juggled in thy service, dealing with any side for our advantage, renouncing our integrity.

3. *Our heart is not turned back.* Our heart is upright, not turned back to the idols our fathers worshipped.

4. *Our steps are not gone out of thy way.* Slip we may, but not revolt; no, not though great calamities are come upon us. 1. *Broken.* 2. *Broken in the place of dragons*, i. e., enemies fierce as dragons. 3. *Though covered with the shadow of death.* Now, that all this is true we call our God to witness, who knoweth the very secrets of the heart, and is able to revenge it: "We have not forgotten the name of our God, or stretched out our hands," &c. "Shall not God search it out? for he knows the very secret of the heart."

Fourthly. But the last argument is more pressing than the other three. It is not for any thing we have done to those that oppress us, that we are thus persecuted by them; it is for thee, it is because we profess thy name, and rise up in defence of thy truth: "Yea, for thy sake are we killed all the day long; for thy sake are we counted as sheep for the slaughter." The sum then is: Since thou hast been a good God to our fathers; since we suffered great things under bitter tyrants; since, notwithstanding all our sufferings, we are constant to thy truth; since these our sufferings are for thee, *for thy sake*, thy truth; therefore *awake, arise, help us*, for upon these grounds he commences his petition.

II. This is the *second* part of the Psalm, which begins at ver. 23, and continues to the end, in which petition there are these degrees:—

1. That God, who to flesh and blood, in the calamities of his Church, seems to sleep, would awake and put an end to their trouble: "Awake, why sleepest thou, O Lord," ver. 23.

2. That he would arise and judge their cause, and not seem to neglect them as abjects: "Arise, cast us not off for ever," ver. 23.

3. That he would show them some favour, and not seem to forget their miseries: "Wherefore hidest thou thy face, and forgettest our affliction and oppression?"

4. *Lastly*, That he would be their helper, and actually deliver them: "Arise for our help, and redeem us for thy mercies' sake."

And that this petition might be the sooner and more readily granted, he briefly repeats the second argument: "For our soul is bowed down to the dust, our belly cleaveth to the earth," ver. 25. Brought we are as low as low may be, even to the dust, to death, to the grave.

PSALM XLV

The contents of this Psalm are generally summed up thus: The majesty and grace of Christ's kingdom; or an epithalamium of Jesus Christ and the Christian Church; the duty of this Church, and its privileges. The Psalm contains a magnificent description of the beauty, ornaments, valour, justice, and truth of the Divine Bridegroom; the beauty, magnificence, and riches of the bride, who was to become mother of a numerous and powerful posterity. The preamble is found in the title and verse 1. *The description and character of the Bridegroom,* 2–9. *The address to the bride by her companions,* 10–15. *A prediction of her numerous and glorious descendants,* 16, 17.

To the chief Musician [a]upon Shoshannim, for the sons of Korah, [b]Maschil, A Song of loves

A. M. cir. 2996 B. C. cir. 1008 Salomonis, Reg. Israelitarum, cir. annum 8

MY heart [c]is inditing a good matter: I speak of the things which I have made touching the king: my tongue *is* the pen of a ready writer.

2 Thou art fairer than the children of men: [d]grace is poured into thy lips: therefore God hath blessed thee for ever.

[a]Psa. lxix., lxxx. title——[b]Or, *of instruction*

[c]Heb. *boileth* or *bubbleth up*——[d]Luke iv. 22

NOTES ON PSALM XLV

The title is nearly the same with that of Psalm lxix. and lxxx. "To the chief musician, *or master of the band of those who played* on the six-stringed instruments, giving instruction, for the sons of Korah; a song of loves, *or amatory ode;* or a song of the beloved maids." The *Vulgate* and *Septuagint* have, *For those who shall be changed*, or brought into another state, which some have interpreted as relating to the *resurrection of the just;* but if I could persuade myself that the title came by Divine inspiration, I would say it more properly belonged to the calling and conversion of the Gentiles, and bringing them over from idolatry to the worship of the true God. By some the word ששנים *shoshannim*, is translated *lilies;* and a world of labour has been spent to prove that these *lilies* mean the saints, Jesus Christ

A. M. cir. 2996
B. C. cir. 1008
Salomonis, Reg.
Israelitarum,
cir. annum
8

3 Gird thy [e]sword upon *thy*
thigh, [f]O *most* mighty, with thy
glory and thy majesty.
4 [g]And in thy majesty [h]ride
prosperously because of truth
and meekness *and* righteousness;
and thy right hand shall teach
thee terrible things.

A. M. cir. 2996
B. C. cir. 1008
Salomonis, Reg.
Israelitarum,
cir. annum
8

[e]Isa. xlix. 2; Heb. iv. 12; Rev. i. 16; xix. 15——[f]Isa. ix. 6——[g]Rev. vi. 2——[h]Heb. *prosper thou, ride thou*

himself, and the Divine light which is a banner to them that fear him. I cannot believe that any such meaning is intended, and, consequently, I cannot attempt to interpret the Psalm after this model. I believe it to be an epithalamium, or nuptial song, which primarily respected Solomon's marriage with the daughter of Pharaoh; and that it probably has a prophetic reference to the conversion of the Gentiles, and the final aggrandisement of the Christian Church.

Verse 1. *My heart is inditing a good matter*] רחש *rachash*, boileth or bubbleth up, as in the margin. It is a metaphor taken from a fountain that sends up its waters from the earth in this way. The Vulgate has *eructavit*, which is most literally translated by the old Psalter: **Mi hert ryfted gude word.** **Bealcetted heopte min.** *My heart belcheth.*—Anglo-Saxon.

I speak of the things which I have made touching the king] אמר אני מעשי למלך, literally, "I dedicate my work unto the king." Or, as the *Psalter*, **I say my werkes til the kyng.** This was the general custom of the Asiatic poets. They repeated their works before princes and honourable men; and especially those parts in which there was either a direct or constructive compliment to the great man. Virgil is reported to have a part of his Æneid before Augustus, who was so pleased with it that he ordered *ten* sestertia to be given him for every line. And the famous Persian poet Ferdusi read a part of his Shah Nameh before Sultan Mahmoud, who promised him *thirty thousand* denars for the poem.

My tongue is *the pen of a ready writer.*] I shall compose and speak as fluently the Divine matter which is now in my heart, as the most expert scribe can write from my recitation. **My tung of maister swiftly wrytand.** "That es, my tung is pen of the Haly Gast; and nout but als his instrument, wham he ledis als he wil. For I speke noght bot that he settis on my tung; als the pen dos noght withouten the writer. **Swyftly wrytand**, for the vertu of goddes inspiracioun is noght for to thynk with mons study, that he schewes til other of the purete of heven; that es some for to com that he wrytes."—Old *Psalter*.

Verse 2. *Thou art fairer than the children of men*] By whom are these words spoken? As this is a regular epithalamium, we are to consider that the bride and bridegroom have compliments paid them by those called the friends of the bridegroom, and the companions or maids of the bride. But it seems that the whole Psalm, except the first verse, was spoken by those who are called in the title ידידת *yedidoth*, the *beloved maids*, or *female companions*, who begin with his perfections, and then describe hers. And afterwards there is a prophetical declaration concerning his issue. We may, therefore, consider that what is spoken here is spoken by companions of the bride, or what are called *yedidoth* in the *title*. It would be unauthenticated to say Solomon was the most beautiful man in the universe; but to the perfections of the Lord Jesus they may be safely applied.

Grace is poured into thy lips] This probably refers to his speech, or the gracious words which he spoke. Solomon was renowned for wisdom, and especially the wisdom of his conversation. The queen of Sheba came from the uttermost parts of the land to hear the wisdom of Solomon; and so far did she find him exceeding all his fame, that she said *one half had not been told her:* but behold, *a greater than Solomon is here. No man ever spoke like this man,* his enemies themselves being judges.

God hath blessed thee for ever.] This, I am afraid, could in no sense be ever spoken of Solomon; but of the man Christ Jesus it is strictly true.

Verse 3. *Gird thy sword upon* thy *thigh, O* most *mighty*] This clause should be translated, *O hero, gird thy sword upon thy thigh!* This, I think, cannot be spoken of Solomon. He was not a warlike prince: he never did any feats of arms. It has been said he would have been a warrior, if he had had enemies; it might have been so: but the words more properly apply to Christ, who is King of kings, and Lord of lords; whose sword with two edges, proceeding from his mouth, cuts all his adversaries to pieces.

With thy glory and thy majesty.] Be as warlike as thou art glorious and majestic. Solomon's court was splendid, and his person was majestic. These words may be well said of him. But the majesty and glory of Christ are above all: he is higher than all the kings of the earth; and has a name above every name; and at it every knee shall bend, and every tongue confess.

Verse 4. *In thy majesty ride prosperously*] These words cannot be spoken of Solomon; they are true only of Christ. His *riding* is the prosperous progress of his Gospel over the earth. He uses no sword but the sword of the Spirit; and what religion, system of truth, pretended or real, ever made such progress as the religion of Christ has done, without one sword being ever drawn to propagate it from the first introduction of Christianity to the present time? His Gospel is TRUTH, proclaiming HUMILITY, ענוה *anvah*, and RIGHTEOUSNESS. This, indeed, is the *sum* of the Gospel; and an *epitome* of its operations in the hearts of men. 1. The Gospel is a revelation of *eternal* TRUTH, in opposition to all *false* systems of religion, and to all *figurative* and *ceremonial representations* of the true religion. It is *truth* concerning GOD, his NATURE, and his WORKS. It is *truth* concerning MAN, his ORIGIN, his INTENTS, his DUTIES, and his END. It is truth in what it says concerning the *natural*, the *moral*, and the *invisible world.* 2. It teaches the doctrine of *meekness* or HUMILITY; opposes *pride* and *vain glory;* strips man of his *assumed merits;* proclaims and enforces the *necessity* of *humiliation* or *repentance* because of sin, *humiliation* under the

A. M. cir. 2996 B. C. cir. 1008 Salomonis, Reg. Israelitarum, cir. annum 8

5 Thine [l]arrows *are* sharp in
the heart of the king's enemies;
whereby the people fall under
thee.
6 [k]Thy throne, O God, *is* for ever and ever:
the sceptre of thy kingdom *is* a right sceptre.
7 [l]Thou lovest righteousness, and hatest
wickedness; therefore [m]God,
[n]thy God, [o]hath anointed thee
with the oil [p]of gladness above
thy fellows.
8 [q]All thy garments *smell* of myrrh, and
aloes, *and* cassia, out of the ivory palaces,
whereby they have made thee glad.

A. M. cir. 2996 B. C. cir. 1008 Salomonis, Reg. Israelitarum, cir. annum 8

[i]Num. xxiv. 8; 2 Sam. xxii. 15; Job vi. 4——[k]Psa. xciii. 2; Heb. i. 8——[l]Psa. xxxiii. 5

[m]Or, *O God*——[n]Isa. lxi. 1——[o]1 Kings i. 39, 40 [p]Psa. xxi. 6——[q]Cant. i. 3

providential hand of God, and *humility* in imitation of the character of the Lord Jesus Christ throughout life. 3. The Gospel teaches RIGHTEOUSNESS: shows the nature of *sin, wrong, injustice, transgression,* &c.; works *righteousness* in the *heart;* and *directs* and *influences* to the *practice* of it in all the *actions of life.* The Gospel leads him who is under its influences to *give to all their due;* to GOD, to his *neighbour,* to *himself.* And it is by the propagation of *truth, humility,* and *righteousness,* that the earth has become so far *blessed,* and the kingdom of Christ become extended among men.

And thy right hand shall teach thee terrible things.] The *Chaldee* is different: "And the Lord will teach thee to perform terrible things by thy right hand." The *Arabic:* "And with admiration shall thy right hand direct thee." The *Septuagint:* "And thy right hand shall lead thee wonderfully." To the same purpose are the *Vulgate, Anglo-Saxon,* and the old *Psalter.* The meaning is, Nothing shall be able to resist thee, and the judgments which thou shalt inflict on thine enemies shall be terrible.

Verse 5. *Thine arrows* are *sharp*] The arrows here may mean the convictions produced in the hearts of men by the preaching of the Gospel. The King is God himself; his enemies are sinners of all sorts. The people, the Jews, thousands of whom were pricked in their hearts under the preaching of *Peter* and others. All *fall* before Christ; those who received the word rose again by repentance and faith; those who did not, fell down—all down!

Verse 6. *Thy throne, O God,* is *for ever*] כסאך אלהים עולם ועד *kisacha Elohim olam vaed.* "O God, thy throne is for ever, and eternal!" The word *Elohim* here is the very *first* term or *name* by which the Supreme God has made himself known to the children of men. See Gen. i. 1; and this very verse the apostle, Heb. i. 8, has applied to Jesus Christ. On this I shall make a very short remark, but it shall be conclusive: If the apostle did not believe Jesus Christ to be the true and eternal God, he has utterly misapplied this Scripture.

The translation in the old Psalter, and the paraphrase will, on this controverted text, be considered of some importance: **Thi settil God in werld of werlde: wande of ryghtyng wande of thi kyngedome.** Here he loues [celebrates] God Crist of dome. **Thi settil** of demyng and of kynges pouste. God es werld of werld for al that he demes es noght chaunged and that byfalles the, for the wande that es ceptre and the governyng of thi kyngdom **es wande of ryghtyng,** that ryghtes croked men this es the wand of goddes evenes that ay es ryght and never croked that reules ryghtwis men and smytes wiked men. The reader will observe a blank space between the word **Crist** and **of dome:** it is the same in the original. A word has been so carefully erased with the *scalpel* in the above place, that not a vestige of a letter is left. From the following words I should suspect it to have been **kynge** or **lard.** *Here he praises God, Christ, king of judgment.* However this may be, it is evident that this ancient commentator understood the word *God* to be applied to Christ. I have given the sentence as it is *pointed* in the original.

Verse 7. *Oil of gladness*] As an evidence that all causes of *mourning, sorrow,* and *death,* were at an end; as in the state of mourning the ancients did not anoint themselves.

I have mentioned above that the author of the Epistle to the Hebrews, chap. i. 8, 9, quotes verses 6, 7, of this Psalm. I shall subjoin the substance of what I have written on these verses in that place:—

"Verse 8. *Thy throne, O God,* is *for ever and ever.*—If this be said of the Son of God, i. e., Jesus Christ, then Jesus Christ must be God; and indeed the design of the apostle is to prove this. The words here quoted are taken from Psa. xlv. 6, 7, which the ancient Chaldee paraphrast, and the most intelligent rabbins, refer to the Messiah. On the third verse of this Psalm, 'Thou art fairer than the children of men,' the *Targum* says: 'Thy beauty, מלכא משיחא *malca Meshicha, O King Messiah,* is greater than the children of men.' *Aben Ezra* says: 'This Psalm speaks of David, or rather of his Son the *Messiah,* for this is his name, Ezek. xxxiv. 24: *And David my servant shall be a prince over them for ever.*' Other rabbins confirm this opinion.

"This verse is very properly considered a proof, and indeed a strong one, of the divinity of Christ; but some late versions of the New Testament have endeavoured to avoid the evidence of this proof by translating the word thus: 'God is thy throne for ever and ever;' and if this version be correct, it is certain that the text can be no proof of the doctrine. Mr. Wakefield vindicates this translation at large in his *History of Opinions;* and ὁ Θεος being the *nominative* case is supposed to be sufficient justification of this version. In answer to this it may be stated that the *nominative* case is often used for the *vocative,* particularly by the Attics, and the whole scope of the place requires it should be so used here; and with due deference to all of a contrary opinion, the original Hebrew cannot be consistently translated any other way; כסאך אלהים עולם ועד *kisacha Elohim olam vaed,* 'Thy throne, O God, is for ever, and to eternity.' It is in both worlds, and extends over all time, and will exist through all endless duration. To this our Lord seems to

A. M. cir. 2996
B. C. cir. 1008
Salomonis, Reg.
Israelitarum,
cir. annum
8

9 [r]Kings' daughters *were*
among thy honourable women:
[s]upon thy right hand did stand
the queen in gold of Ophir.

10 Hearken, O daughter, and
consider, and incline thine ear;
[t]forget also thine own people,
and thy father's house;

A. M. cir. 2996
B. C. cir. 1008
Salomonis, Reg.
Israelitarum,
cir. annum
8

[r]Cant. vi. 8 — [s]See 1 Kings ii. 9 — [t]See Deut. xxi. 13

refer, Matt. xxviii. 18: 'All power is given unto me, both in HEAVEN and EARTH.' My *throne*, i. e., my *dominion*, extends from the creation to the consummation of all things. These I have made, and these I uphold; and from the end of the world, throughout eternity, I shall have the same *glory*—sovereign unlimited power and authority, which I had with the Father before the world began; John xvii. 5. I may add that none of the ancient Versions has understood it in the way contended for by those who deny the Godhead of Christ, either in the Psalm from which it is taken, or in this place where it is quoted. Aquila translates אלהים *Elohim*, by Θεε, *O God*, in the vocative case; and the Arabic adds the sign of the vocative يا *ya*, reading the place thus: كرسي يا الله الي ابد الابد *korsee yallaho ila abadilabada*, the same as in our Version. And even allowing that ὁ Θεος here is to be used as the *nominative* case, it will not make the sense contended for without adding εστι to it, a reading which is not countenanced by any *Version*, nor by any MS. yet discovered. Wiclif, Coverdale, and others, understood it as the nominative, and translated it so; and yet it is evident that this nominative has the power of the vocative: **Forsothe to the sone God thi troone into the world of world: a gerde of equite the gerde of thi reume.** I give this, pointing and all, as it stands in my old MS. Bible. *Wiclif* is nearly the same, but is evidently of a more modern cast: **But to the sone he seith, God thy trone is into the world of world, a gherd of equyte is the gherd of thi rewme.** *Coverdale* translates it thus: 'But unto the sonne he sayeth: God, thi seate endureth for ever and ever: the cepter of thy kyngdome is a right cepter.' *Tindal* and others follow in the same way, all reading it in the *nominative* case, with the force of the *vocative;* for none of them has inserted the word εστι, *is*, because not authorized by the original; a word which the opposers of the Divinity of our Lord are obliged to *beg*, in order to support their interpretation.

"*A sceptre of righteousness.*—The sceptre, which was a sort of staff or instrument of various forms, was the ensign of government, and is here used for government itself. This the ancient Jewish writers understand also of the Messiah.

"Verse 9. *Thou hast loved righteousness.*—This is the characteristic of a just governor; he abhors and suppresses iniquity; he countenances and supports righteousness and truth.

"*Therefore God*, even *thy God.*—The original, δια τουτον εχρισε δε, ὁ Θεος, ὁ Θεος σου, may be thus translated: 'Therefore, O God, thy God hath anointed thee.' The form of speech is nearly the same with that in the preceding verse; but the sense is sufficiently clear if we read: 'Therefore God, thy God, hath anointed thee,' &c.

"*With the oil of gladness.*—We have often had occasion to remark that anciently *kings*, *priests*, and *prophets*, were consecrated to their several offices by anointing, and that this signified the gifts and influences of the Divine Spirit. Christ, ὁ χριστος, signifies *The anointed One*, the same as the Hebrew Messiah; and he is here said to be 'anointed with the oil of gladness above his fellows.' None was ever constituted *prophet*, *priest*, and *king*, but himself: some were kings only, prophets only, and priests only; others were kings and priests, or priests and prophets, or kings and prophets; but none had ever the *three offices* in his own person but Jesus Christ; and none but himself can be a King over the universe, a Prophet to all intelligent beings, and a Priest to the whole human race. Thus he is infinitely exalted *beyond his fellows*—all that had ever borne the regal, prophetic, or sacerdotal offices.

"Some think that the word μετοχους, *fellows*, refers to *believers* who are made partakers of the same Spirit, but cannot have its infinite plenitude. The first sense seems the best. *Gladness* is used to express the *festivities* which took place on the inauguration of kings," &c.

Verse 8. *All thy garments* smell *of myrrh*] The Asiatics are very partial to perfumes; every thing with them is perfumed, and especially their garments. And the *ivory palaces* mentioned are the *wardrobes* inlaid with ivory, in which their numerous changes of raiment were **deposited.** *Myrrh* and *aloes* are well known; *cassia* is probably the bark or wood of the *cinnamon* tree. These with *frankincense*, *galbanum* and other odoriferous drugs, were and are frequently used in the perfumes of the Asiatic nations.

Whereby they have made thee glad.] Referring to the effect of strong perfumes refreshing and exhilarating the spirits.

Verse 9. *Kings' daughters* were *among*] Applied to Solomon, these words have no difficulty. We know he had *seven hundred* wives, *princesses;* and the mention of those here may be intended only to show how highly respected he was among the neighbouring sovereigns, when they cheerfully gave him their daughters to constitute his harem. If we apply it to Solomon's marriage with the daughter of the king of Egypt, it may signify no more than the *princesses* and *ladies* of *honour* who accompanied her to the Israelitish court. Applied to *Christ*, it may signify that the Gospel, though preached particularly to the *poor*, became also the means of salvation to many of the *kings*, *queens*, and *nobles*, of the earth. The *Chaldee* interprets the *queen standing at his right hand*, by the *law;* and the *honourable women*, by the different *regions* and *countries* coming to *receive that law from his right hand.* Perhaps by *kings' daughters* may be meant different regions and countries, which are represented as constituting the *families* of potentates. Whole nations shall be converted to the Christian faith; and the *queen*—the Christian Church, shall be most elegantly adorned with all the graces and good works which at once constitute and adorn the Christian character.

Verse 10. *Hearken, O daughter, and consider*] This is the beginning of the address by the *companions of the bride* to their mistress; after

A. M. cir. 2996
B. C. cir. 1008
Salomonis, Reg. Israelitarum, cir. annum 8

11 So shall the king greatly
desire thy beauty: [u]for he *is* thy
LORD; and worship thou him.
12 And the daughter of Tyre
shall be there with a gift; *even* [v]the
rich among the people shall entreat [w]thy
favour.
13 [x]The king's daughter *is* all glorious
within: her clothing *is* of wrought gold.
14 [y]She shall be brought unto the king in
raiment of needlework: the virgins her companions that follow her shall be
brought unto thee.
15 With gladness and rejoicing
shall they be brought: they shall
enter into the king's palace.
16 Instead of thy fathers shall be thy children, [z]whom thou mayest make princes in
all the earth.
17 [a]I will make thy name to be remembered in all generations: therefore shall the
people praise thee for ever and ever.

A. M. cir. 2996
B. C. cir. 1008
Salomonis, Reg. Israelitarum, cir. annum 8

---

[u]Psa. xcv. 6; Isa. liv. 5——[v]Psa. xxii. 29; lxxii. 10; Isa. xlix. 23; lx. 3——[w]Heb. *thy face*——[x]Rev. xix. 7, 8——[y]Cant. i. 4——[z]1 Pet. ii. 9; Rev. i. 6; v. 10; xx. 6——[a]Mal. i. 11

---

having, in the preceding verses, addressed the bridegroom; or, rather, given a description of his person, qualities, and magnificence. Suppose the daughter of Pharaoh to be intended, the words import: Thou art now become the spouse of the most magnificent monarch in the universe. To thee he must be all in all. *Forget* therefore *thy own people*—the Egyptians, and take the Israelites in their place. *Forget* also *thy father's house;* thou art now united to a new family. *So shall the king*—Solomon, *greatly desire thy beauty*—thou wilt be, in all respects, pleasing to him. And it is right thou shouldst act so; for he is now become *thy lord* —thy supreme governor. *And worship thou him*—submit thyself reverently and affectionately to all his commands.

Taken in reference to *Christ* and the *Gospel*, this is an address to the Gentiles to forsake their idolatrous customs and connexions, to embrace Christ and his Gospel in the spirit of reverence and obedience, with the promise that, if beautified with the graces of his Spirit, Christ will delight in them, and take them for his peculiar people; which has been done.

Verse 12. *The daughter of Tyre* shall be there *with a gift*] The Tyrians shall pay tribute to thy spouse, and assist him in all his grand and magnificent operations.

As, at this time, Tyre was the greatest maritime and commercial city in the world, it may be here taken as representing those places which lay on the coasts of the sea, and carried on much traffic; such as parts of Syria, Egypt, Asia Minor, Greece, Italy, France, the British Isles, &c., which first received the Gospel of Christ and were the instruments of sending it to all the other nations of the earth.

Rich among the people] The most powerful and opulent empires, kingdoms, and states, shall embrace Christianity, and entreat the *favour* of its Author.

Verse 13. *The king's daughter* is *all glorious within*] This, in some sense, may be spoken of Solomon's bride, the daughter of the king of Egypt; and then the expression may refer either to the cultivation of her mind, or the ornaments and splendour of her palace. The Asiatic queens, sultanas, and begums, scarcely ever appear in public. They abide in the harem in the greatest luxury and splendour; and to this, as its literal meaning, the text may possibly refer.

Her clothing is *of wrought gold.*] Of the most costly embroidery: her palace, and her person, are decorated in the very highest state of elegance and magnificence.

Spiritually, the *king's daughter* may mean the *Christian Church* filled with the mind that was in Christ, and adorned with the graces of the Holy Spirit; while the whole of its outward conduct is pure and holy, ornamented with the works of faith and love, and always bringing forth the fruits of the Spirit.

Verse 14. *She shall be brought unto the king*] When an Asiatic princess is brought to her spouse, she is inclosed in a *palakee*, and no part of her person is visible. She is attended by her principal friends and companions, who *follow* the palakee, and the ceremony is accompanied with great *rejoicing;* and thus they *enter into* the *palace of the king.*

This part of this parabolical Psalm may refer to the glories of a future state. The Christian Church shall be brought to the KING eternal in the *great day*, adorned with the graces of the Divine Spirit; and thus shall all the redeemed of the Lord enter *into the king's palace*—into the everlasting joy of their Lord.

Verse 16. *Instead of thy fathers shall be thy children*] This is the *third* part, or prophetic declaration relative to the numerous and powerful issue of this marriage. Instead of the kindred, which thou hast left behind in Egypt, thou shalt have numerous children. This cannot refer either to Solomon, or to the daughter of Pharaoh; for there is no evidence that he ever had a child by Pharaoh's daughter; and it is very certain that Rehoboam, Solomon's successor, was not son to the daughter of Pharaoh; nor did any princes of that line ever occupy a foreign throne; nor by successive generations ever continue the remembrance of Solomon and his Egyptian queen. The *children* mentioned here are generally supposed to mean the *apostles* and their *successors in the Christian ministry;* founding Churches all over the world, by whom the Christian name becomes a memorial through all the earth.

Verse 17. *Therefore shall the people praise thee*] They shall magnify the heavenly Bridegroom, and sing the wonderful displays of his love to the Church, his spouse. And the constant use of this Psalm in the Christian Church is a literal fulfilment of the prophecy.

ANALYSIS OF THE FORTY-FIFTH PSALM

The type of the *Messiah* is *Solomon;* of the *Church*, especially of the *Gentiles* to be espoused, *Pharaoh's daughter.*

There are *three* parts in this Psalm:—

I. A preface, ver. 1, 2.

II. The body of this Psalm contains two commendations,—

1. Of the bridegroom, from ver. 3 to 9.

2. Of the bride, from ver. 10 to 15.

III. The conclusion promissory and laudatory, ver. 16 to 17.

I. In the preface the prophet commends the subject he is to treat of,—

1. Signifying that it is *a good thing; good*, as speaking of the Son of God, who is the *chief good*.

2. And *good* for us; for, on our union with the Church, and Christ's union with that, depends our eternal good.

That the author of this Psalm, and the subject of it, is God: the psalmist was but the pen to write, for he was full of the Holy Ghost. Therefore, his heart was inditing, and his tongue followed the dictate of his heart, and presently became the instrument of a ready writer, viz., of the Holy Spirit: "My tongue is the pen of a ready writer."

Thus, having endeavoured to gain over his auditory, 1. By the commendation of the matter of which he is to treat, viz., that it is *good*. 2. That it tends to a good end, viz., the *honour of the King*, that is, Christ, the King of the Church: he then enters on the main business, which has two particulars.

II. 1. He turns his speech to Christ, the King, and commends him for many eminent and excellent endowments:—

1. His beauty: "Thou art fairer than the children of men."

2. His elocution: "Grace is poured into thy lips."

3. For his valour: "O hero, gird thy sword upon thy thigh."

4. For his prosperity in his kingdom: "In thy majesty ride prosperously."

5. For his just administration of public affairs. "Ride on, because of truth, meekness, and righteousness."

6. For his battles and conquests: "Thy right hand shall teach thee terrible things. Thy arrows are sharp in the hearts of the king's enemies, whereby the people shall fall under thee."

7. For the stability and eternity of his power: "Thy throne, O God, is for ever and ever."

8. For his justice and equity: "The sceptre of thy kingdom is a right sceptre. Thou lovest righteousness, and hatest iniquity."

9. For the fulness of his gifts and graces, beyond all others: "Therefore God—hath anointed thee with the oil of gladness above thy fellows."

10. For the splendour of his apparel and buildings. "All thy garments smell of myrrh, &c., out of the ivory palaces." There is nothing we can call good, great, or excellent; nothing praiseworthy in a prince; that may not be found in this king.

2. From the bridegroom he proceeds to the bride, which here means the universal Church; whom he sets forth:—

1. By her attendants; no mean persons: *kings' daughters* and *honourable women*.

2. By her name, title, and dignity: a *queen*.

3. By her place: she *stood on the right hand*, the place of confidence and respect.

4. By her attire and vesture: *she stood in a vesture of gold of Ophir*.

In the midst of this great *encomium* he breaks off and, by an *apostrophe*, turns his speech to the Church lest she should forget herself in the height of her honour; giving her this good counsel:—

1. "Hearken, O daughter!" mark what Christ saith unto thee.

2. "Consider." Look about, and see what is done for thee.

3. "Incline thine ear." Be obedient.

4. "Forget thine own people, and thy father's house." Leave all for Christ; leave thy old way, old opinions, and old companions.

5. The consequence of which will be, "The king shall greatly desire thy beauty."

6. And there is the utmost reason that thou shouldst hear, and be obedient, and conformable to his will. 1. For, "He is the Lord thy God, and thou shalt worship him." 2. This will promote thy interest: "Tyre shall be there with a gift, and the rich among the people shall entreat thy favour."

This counsel and admonition being ended, he returns again to the encomium of the spouse, and commends her,—

1. For her inward virtues and endearments: "The king's daughter (that is, the Church) is all glorious within."

2. For her externals; whether doctrine, morals, offices, which are, as it were, her clothing: "It is of wrought gold."

3. For her rites and ceremonies,—they are a *needlework* of divers colours, in divers Churches.

4. Her maids of honour, *virgins;* holy and sincere souls. Believers, pure in heart, life, and doctrine, living in every particular Church. These, *her companions, shall follow her:* 1. These shall be brought to thee (the Church) from all nations. 2. They shall be brought with joy and gladness, and enter into the king's palace. Gladly and willingly, shall they enter her courts here below, and afterwards be received to mansions in heaven.

5. For her fruitfulness. She shall have many children, good, and great. For the fathers, patriarchs, prophets, and priests, under the *Old Law;* apostles, evangelists, and their successors, under the *New;* that they may be made princes in all lands. Her officers are not contemptible.

III. The conclusion which is gratulatory. For this honour the Church would,

1. Set up a memorial to the honour of the Bridegroom: "I will make thy name to be remembered in all generations."

2. The praise of the heavenly Bridegroom shall be ever perpetuated: "Therefore, shall the people praise thee for ever and ever."

The Christian Church shall ever proclaim the name of Jesus, as the name alone in which salvation is to be found; and as the eternal Fountain of all blessings.

PSALM XLVI

The confidence of believers in God, 1–3. *The privileges of the Church,* 4, 5; *her enemies, and her helper,* 6, 7. *God's judgments in the earth,* 8, 9. *He will be exalted among the heathen, and throughout the earth,* 10, 11.

To the chief Musician [a]for the sons of Korah, [b]a Song upon [c]Alamoth

A. M. 3485
B. C. 519
A. U. C. 235
Anno Darii
I., Regis
Persarum, 6

GOD *is* our [d]refuge and
strength, [e]a very present
help in trouble.
2 Therefore will not we fear,
though the earth be removed, and though the
mountains be carried into [f]the midst of the sea;
3 [g]*Though* the waters thereof roar *and*
be troubled, *though* the mountains shake
with the swelling thereof.
Selah.
4 *There is* [h]a river, the streams
whereof shall make glad [i]the
city of God, the holy *place* of the tabernacles
of the Most High.
5 God *is* [k]in the midst of her; she shall not
be moved: God shall help her, [l]*and that*
right early.
6 [m]The heathen raged, the kingdoms were

[a]Or, *of*——[b]Psa. xlviii., lxvi——[c]1 Chron. xv. 20
[d]Psa. lxii. 7, 8; xci. 2; cxlii. 5——[e]Deut. iv. 7; Psa. cxlv. 18——[f]Heb. *the heart of the seas*——[g]Psa. xciii. 3, 4; Jer. v. 22; Matt. vii. 25——[h]See Isa. viii. 7——[i]Psa. xlviii. 1, 8; Isa. lx. 14

[k]Deut. xxiii. 14; Isa. xii. 6; Ezek. xliii. 7, 9; Hos. xi. 9; Joel ii. 27; Zeph. iii. 15; Zech. ii. 5, 10, 11; viii. 3
[l]Heb. *when the morning appeareth;* see Exod. xiv. 24, 27; 2 Chronicles xx. 20; Psalm xxx. 5; cxliii. 8——[m]Psa. ii. 1

NOTES ON PSALM XLVI

The *title* in the *Hebrew* is, "To the chief musician for the sons of Korah; an ode upon *Alamoth*, or *concerning the virgins*:" possibly meaning a choir of *singing girls*. Some translate the word *secrets* or *mysteries;* and explain it accordingly. *Calmet* thinks it was composed by the descendants of Korah, on their return from the Babylonian captivity, when they had once more got peaceably settled in Jerusalem; and that the disturbances to which it refers were those which took place in the *Persian empire* after the death of *Cambyses*, when the *Magi* usurped the government. Many other interpretations and conjectures are given of the occasion of this fine ode. *Houbigant* thinks it was made on occasion of an *earthquake*, which he supposes took place on the *night* that all Sennacherib's army was destroyed. Dr. *Kennicott* thinks that *alamoth* means a musical instrument. All I can pretend to say about it is, that it is a very *sublime ode;* contains much consolation for the Church of God; and was given by the inspiration of his Holy Spirit.

Verse 1. *God is our refuge*] It begins abruptly, but nobly; ye may trust in whom and in what ye please: but GOD (ELOHIM) *is our refuge and strength.*

A very present help] A help found to be very powerful and effectual in straits and difficulties. The words are very emphatic: עזרה בצרות נמצא מאד *ezerah betsaroth nimtsa meod*, "He is found an exceeding, or superlative help in difficulties." Such we have found him, and therefore celebrate his praise.

Verse 2. *Therefore will not we fear*] Let what commotions will take place in the earth, we will trust in the all-powerful arm of God. Probably the *earthquake* referred to, here means *political commotions*, such as those mentioned under the title; and by *mountains*, kings or secular states may be intended.

Verse 3. *Though the waters thereof roar*] *Waters*, in prophetic language, signify people; and, generally, people in a state of political commotion, here signified by the term *roar*. And by these strong agitations of the people, the *mountains*—the secular rulers, *shake with the swelling thereof*—tremble, for fear that these popular tumults should terminate in the subversion of the state. This very people had seen all Asia in a state of war. The Persians had overturned Asia Minor, and destroyed the Babylonian empire: they had seen Babylon itself sacked and entered by the Persians; and Cyrus, its conqueror, had behaved to them as a father and deliverer. While their oppressors were destroyed, themselves were preserved, and permitted to return to their own land.

Verse 4. There is *a river, the streams whereof*] The Chaldee understands the *river*, and its *streams* or *divisions*, as pointing out various peoples who should be converted to the faith, and thus make glad the city of God, Jerusalem, by their flowing together to the worship of the true God.

But the *river* may refer to the vast Medo-Persian army and its divisions: those branches which took Babylon; and, instead of ruining and destroying the poor Jews, preserved them alive, and gave them their liberty; and thus the city of God, and the tabernacle of the Most High, were gladdened.

Verse 5. *God* is *in the midst of her*] God will not abandon them that trust in him; he will maintain his own cause; and, if his Church should at any time be attacked, he will help her, *and that right early*—with the utmost speed. As soon as the onset is made, God is there to resist. As by the day-break the shadows and darkness are dissipated; so by the bright rising of Jehovah, the darkness of adversity shall be scattered.

Verse 6. *The heathen raged*] There had been terrible wars on all hands, and mighty states were crushed, when the poor Jews were, by the especial favour of God, kept in peace and safety.

A. M. 3485
B. C. 519
A. U. C. 235
Anno Darii
I., Regis
Persarum, 6

moved: he uttered his voice,
[n]the earth melted.
7 [o]The LORD of hosts *is* with
us; the God of Jacob *is* [p]our
refuge. Selah.
8 [q]Come, behold the works of the LORD,
what desolations he hath made in the earth.
9 [r]He maketh wars to cease unto the end of
the earth; [s]he breaketh the bow,
and cutteth the spear in sunder;
[t]he burneth the chariot in the fire.
10 Be still, and know that I
am God: [u]I will be exalted among the heathen,
I will be exalted in the earth.
11 [v]The LORD of hosts *is* with us; the
God of Jacob *is* our refuge. Selah.

A. M. 3485
B. C. 519
A. U. C. 235
Anno Darii
I., Regis
Persarum, 6

[n]Josh. ii. 9, 24——[o]Ver. 11; Num. xiv. 9; 2 Chron. xiii. 12——[p]Heb. *a high place for us;* Psa. ix. 9——[q]Psa. lxvi. 5——[r]Isa. ii. 4——[s]Psa. lxxvi. 3——[t]Ezek. xxxix. 9——[u]Isa. ii. 11, 17——[v]Ver. 7

Kingdoms were moved while they were preserved.

He uttered his voice] These words seem to refer to thunder, lightning, and earthquake. The expressions, however, may be figurative, and refer to the wars and desolations already mentioned. God gave the command; and one empire was cast down, and another was raised up.

Verse 7. *The Lord of hosts* is *with us*] We, feeble Jews, were but a handful of men; but the *Lord of hosts*—the God of armies, was on our side. Him none could attack with hope of success, and his legions could not be overthrown.

The God of Jacob] The God who appeared to Jacob in his distress, and saved him out of all his troubles, appeared also for us his descendants, and has amply proved to us that he has not forgotten his covenant.

Verse 8. *Come, behold the works of the Lord*] See empires destroyed and regenerated; and in such a way as to show that a supernatural agency has been at work. By the hand of God alone could these great changes be effected.

Verse 9. *He maketh wars to cease*] By the death of Cambyses, and setting Darius, son of Hystaspes, upon the Persian throne, he has tranquillized the whole empire. That same God who for our unfaithfulness has delivered us into the hands of our enemies, and subjected us to a long and grievous captivity and affliction, has now turned our captivity, and raised us up the most powerful friends and protectors in the very place in which we have been enduring so great a fight of afflictions.

He breaketh the bow] He has rendered useless all the implements of war; and so profound and secure is the general tranquillity, that the *bow* may be safely *broken*, the *spear snapped asunder*, and the *chariot burnt in the fire*.

Verse 10. *Be still, and know that I* am *God*] הרפו *harpu, Cease* from your provocations of the Divine justice; cease from murmuring against the dispensations of his providence; cease from your labour for a season, that ye may deeply reflect on the severity and goodness of God—severity to those who are brought down and destroyed; goodness to you who are raised up and exalted:—cease from sin and rebellion against your God; let that disgrace you no more, that we may no more be brought into distress and desolation.

Know that I am *God*] Understand that I am the Fountain of power, wisdom, justice, goodness, and truth.

I will be exalted among the heathen] By the dispensation of punishments, the heathen shall know me to be the God of justice; by the publication of my Gospel among them, they shall know me to be the God of goodness.

I will be exalted in the earth.] I will have my salvation proclaimed in every nation, among every people, and in every tongue.

Verse 11. *The Lord of hosts* is *with us*] Having heard these declarations of God, the people cry out with joy and exultation, The Lord of hosts, the God of armies, is with us; we will not fear what man can do unto us.

The God of Jacob is *our refuge.*] He who saved our fathers will save us, and will never abandon his people in distress.

Selah.] This is a firm, lasting, unshaken, well-tried truth.

ANALYSIS OF THE FORTY-SIXTH PSALM

Two things especially are to be considered in this Psalm:—

I. The confidence the Church has in God, ver. 1-8.

II. The exhortation to consider him as the Lord of hosts, the Punisher of the refractory and disobedient nations, often by means of *war;* and the only Giver of peace and tranquillity, ver. 8-10.

I. He begins with a maxim which is the ground of all the confidence which the people of God can have. God is our *Asylum*, or place of *refuge* to fly to; our *Strength, Stay, Munition*, on which to rely: "A very present help to deliver us in time of trouble."

From which maxim this conclusion is drawn: "therefore will we not fear;" not even in the greatest calamities, nor in the midst of the most numerous adversaries. This he expresses, first, *metaphorically;* next, in *plain terms:*—

1. Though the earth on which the Church is seated be moved or removed.

2. "Though the mountains be carried into the midst of the sea;" that is, the greatest and strongest empires and kingdoms should be ruined and overwhelmed.

3. "Though the waters roar and be troubled." Though multitudes of people threaten, and join their forces to ruin the Church.

4. "Though the mountains (i. e., kingdoms) shake with the swelling thereof." *Waters* mean people, Rev. xvii.

More plainly, for we have the interpretation of these metaphors, ver. 6: "Though the heathen raged, and the kingdoms were moved," yet we were not afraid, nor will we fear. We have a fine illustration of this bold feeling (from a consciousness of rectitude, and consequently Divine protection) from the pen of a heathen poet:—

Justum et tenacem propositi virum
Non civium ardor prava jubentium,
Non vultus instantis tyranni,
Mente quatit solida: Neque Auster,
Dux inquieti turbidus Adriæ,
Nec fulminantis magna Jovis manus.
Si fractus illabatur orbis,
Impavidum ferient ruinæ.
HOR. Car. lib. iii., od. 3.

"The man, in conscious virtue bold,
Who dares his secret purpose hold,
Unshaken hears the crowd's tumultuous cries;
And the impetuous tyrant's angry brow defies.
Let the wild winds that rule the seas,
Tempestuous all their horrors raise;
Let Jove's dread arm with thunders rend the spheres;
Beneath the crush of worlds, undaunted he appears."
FRANCIS.

2. Of this undaunted state of mind he next descends to show the *reasons:*—

1. "There is a river," &c. The *city of God* was *Jerusalem*, the type of the *Church;* and the *holy place* of *the tabernacles* was the *temple.* The little *Shiloh*, that ran softly, watered *Jerusalem;* and the *promises* of the Gospel, that shall always flow in the Church, shall *make glad* the hearts of God's people.

2. "God is in the midst of her," to keep, to defend her; "therefore she shall not be moved," i. e., utterly removed, but "shall remain for ever."

3. "God shall help her and deliver her;" *right early*—in the proper season.

4. "He uttered his voice, and the earth melted." The hearts of the men of the earth, that exalted themselves against his Church, at the least word uttered from his mouth, *melted*—were struck with fear and terror.

5. "The Lord of hosts is with us." And even the armies of our *enemies* are at *his* command, and will fight for us whenever he pleases: "He is the Lord of all hosts."

6. "The God of Jacob is our refuge." He is our *Asylum*, and he will save us, ver. 7, 11.

II. The *second* part contains *two exhortations:*—

1. He calls on all to *behold the works of the Lord;* and he produces *two* instances worthy of observation: 1. JUDGMENT is his work, and he afflicts refractory and sinful nations by WAR: "See what desolations he hath made in the earth!" 2. PEACE is his work: "He maketh war to cease to the end of the earth."

2. Then, in the person of God, he exhorts the enemies of the Church to be quiet; for their endeavours are vain, and their rage is to no purpose: "Be still, and know that I am God."

3. And he concludes with a gracious promise, of being celebrated *among the heathen, and through the whole earth.*

PSALM XLVII

The Gentiles are invited to celebrate the praises of God as the Sovereign of the world, 1, 2. *The Jews exult in his kindness to them*, 3, 4. *All then join to celebrate his Majesty, as reigning over the heathen, and gathering the dispersed Jews and Gentiles together into one Church*, 5–9.

IX. DAY. EVENING PRAYER

To the chief Musician, A Psalm [a]for the sons of Korah

A. M. 3485
B. C. 519
A. U. C. 235
Anno Darii I., Regis Persarum, 6

O [b]CLAP your hands, all ye
people; shout unto God
with the voice of triumph.
2 For the LORD most high *is*
[c]terrible; [d]*he is* a great King
over all the earth.
3 [e]He shall subdue the people
under us, and the nations under
our feet.
4 He shall choose our [f]inheritance for us,

[a]Or, *of*——[b]Isa. lv. 12——[c]Deut. vii. 21; Neh. i. 5; Psa. lxxvi. 12——[d]Mal. i. 14——[e]Psa. xviii. 47——[f]1 Pet. i. 4

NOTES ON PSALM XLVII

The *title*, "A Psalm for the sons of Korah," has nothing remarkable in it. The Psalm was probably written about the same time with the preceding, and relates to the happy state of the Jews when returned to their own land. They renewed their praises and promises of obedience, and celebrate him for the deliverance they had received. See the *introduction* to the preceding Psalm. In a spiritual sense, it appears to relate to the *calling of the Gentiles* to be made partakers of the blessings of the Gospel with the converted Jews.

Verse 1. *O clap your hands, all ye people*] Let both Jews and Gentiles magnify the Lord: the Jews, for being *delivered* from the *Babylonish captivity;* the *Gentiles*, for being called to enter into the glorious liberty of the children of God.

Verse 2. *For the Lord most high* is *terrible*] He has insufferable majesty, and is *a great King*—the mightiest of all emperors, for he is Sovereign over the whole earth.

Verse 3. *He shall subdue the people under us*] He shall do again for us what he had done for our forefathers—give us dominion over our enemies, and establish us in our own land. I would rather read this in the *past tense*, relative to what God did for their fathers in destroying the Canaanites, and giving them the promised land for their possession, and taking the people for his own inheritance. This is also applied to the *conversion of the Gentiles*, who, on the rejection of the Jews, have become his inheritance; and whom he has chosen to

A. M. 3485
B. C. 519
A. U. C. 235
Anno Darii
I., Regis
Persarum, 6

the excellency of Jacob whom he
loved. Selah.
5 [g]God is gone up with a shout,
the LORD with the sound of a
trumpet.
6 Sing praises to God, sing praises: sing
praises unto our King, sing praises.
7 [h]For God *is* the King of all the earth:
[i]sing ye praises [k]with understanding.
8 [l]God reigneth over the heathen: God sitteth upon the throne
of his holiness.
9 [m]The princes of the people
are gathered together, [n]*even* the people of
the God of Abraham: [o]for the shields of
the earth *belong* unto God: he is [p]greatly
exalted.

[g]Psa. lxviii. 24, 25——[h]Zech. xiv. 9——[i]1 Cor. xiv. 15, 16——[k]Or, every one *that hath understanding* [l]1 Chron. xvi. 31; Psa. xciii. 1; xcvi. 10; xcvii. 1; xcix. 1; Rev. xix. 6

[m]Or, *The voluntary of the people are gathered* into *the people of the God of Abraham*——[n]Rom. iv. 11, 12 [o]Psa. lxxxix. 18——[p]Psa. cxii. 9; Isa. ii. 11, 17; xxxiii. 10; Phil. ii. 9

inherit all those spiritual blessings typified by the sacrifices and other significant rites and ceremonies of the Jewish Church.

Verse 5. *God is gone up with a shout*] Primarily, this may refer to the rejoicing and sounding of trumpets, when the ark was lifted up to be carried on the shoulders of the Levites. But it is generally understood as a *prophetic declaration* of the *ascension of our Lord Jesus Christ;* and the *shout* may refer to the exultation of the evangelists and apostles in preaching Christ crucified, buried, risen from the dead, and ascended to heaven, ever to appear in the presence of God for us. This was the *triumph of the apostles;* and the conversion of multitudes of souls by this preaching was the *triumph of the cross of Christ.*

Verse 6. *Sing praises*] זמרו *zammeru:* this word is *four* times repeated in this short verse, and shows at once the *earnestness* and *happiness* of the people. They are the words of *exultation* and *triumph.* Feel your obligation to God; express it in thanksgiving: be thankful, be eternally thankful, to God your King.

Verse 7. *For God* is *the King of all the earth*] He is not *your* King only, but the King of the *universe.* He has no *limited power*, no *confined* dominion.

Sing ye praises with understanding] זמרו משכיל *zammeru maskil, sing an instructive song.* Let *sense* and *sound* go together. Let your *hearts* and *heads* go with your *voices. Understand* what you *sing;* and *feel* what you *understand;* and let the *song* be what will *give instruction in righteousness* to them that hear it. ſyngaþ ƿiſlice, *Sing wisely.*—Anglo-Saxon. Multitudes *sing foolishly.*

Verse 8. *God reigneth over the heathen*] Though this is literally true in God's universal dominion, yet *more* is here meant. God *reigns over the heathen* when, by the preaching of the Gospel, they are brought into the Church of Christ.

God sitteth upon the throne of his holiness.] He is a holy God; he proclaims holiness. His laws are holy, he requires holiness, and his genuine *people* are all holy. The *throne of his holiness* is the *heaven of heavens;* also the *temple* at Jerusalem; and, lastly, the *hearts of the faithful.*

Verse 9. *The princes of the people are gathered together*] נדיבי עמים *nedibey ammim.* The *voluntary people*—the *princely, noble*, or *free-willed people;* those who gladly receive the word of life; those who, like the *Bereans*, were of a *noble* or *liberal disposition;* and, when they heard the Gospel, searched the Scriptures to see whether these things were so. It is a similar word which is used Psa. cx. 3; and I believe both texts speak of the same people—the *Gentiles who gladly come unto his light*, and present themselves a *free-will offering* to the Lord.

The people of the God of Abraham] Who were Abraham's people? Not the *Jews;* the covenant was made with him while yet in *uncircumcision.* Properly speaking, the *Gentiles* are those whom he *represented;* for the covenant was made with him while yet a *Gentile;* and in his seed all the *nations*—the *Gentiles*, of the earth were to be *blessed.* The *people of the God of Abraham* are the *Gentiles*, who, receiving the Gospel, are made partakers of the *faith of Abraham*, and are his *spiritual children.* The God of Abraham has Abraham's spiritual posterity, the believing Gentiles, for his own people.

The shields of the earth belong *unto God.*] The *Septuagint* translate this οἱ κραταιοι, *the strong ones of the earth.* The *Vulgate* reads, Quoniam dii fortes terræ vehementer elevati sunt; "Because the strong gods of the earth are exceedingly exalted." These are supposed to mean *kings* and *rulers of provinces* which were present at the dedication of the temple; (for some suppose the Psalm to have been composed for this solemnity;) and that they are said here to be *greatly exalted*, because they exercised a very high degree of power over their respective districts. The words refer to something by which the inhabitants of the earth are defended; God's providence, guardian angels, &c., &c.

He is greatly exalted.] Great as secular rulers are, God is greater, and is above all; King of kings and Lord of lords; and the hearts of kings and governors are in his hand; and he turns them whithersoever he pleases.

ANALYSIS OF THE FORTY-SEVENTH PSALM

This Psalm, under the figure of the ark being brought into the temple, foretells the ascension of Christ to heaven; who was the true ark of the covenant, and the propitiatory or mercy-seat. It contains a prophecy of Christ's kingdom, and has *two* especial parts:—

First, An invitation to sing praises to Christ.

Secondly, The reasons why we should do it.

1. The ascension of Christ is typified under the ark's ascension, ver. 1: "God is gone up with a shout; the Lord with the sound of a trumpet."

2. On which he invites the people to do now what was then done, "that we clap our hands,

and sing praises." This should be done, 1. Cheerfully: "Clap your hands;" for this is a sign of inward joy, Nah. iii. 19. 2. Universally: "O clap your hands, all ye people." 3. Vocally: "Shout unto God with the voice of triumph." 4. Frequently: "Sing praises—sing praises—sing praises—sing praises," ver. 6, and again "sing praises," ver. 7. It cannot be done too frequently. 5. Knowingly and discreetly: "Sing ye praises with understanding;" know the reason why ye are to praise him.

3. Now these reasons are drawn from his *greatness* and from his *goodness.*

1. He is GREAT. 1. He is the Lord Most High; 2. He is terrible; 3. He is a great King over all the earth. All power, at his ascension, was given unto him in heaven and earth.

2. He is GOOD. 1. In collecting his Church by subduing the nations, not by the *sword*, but by his word and Spirit, by which he would subdue their iniquities, the iniquity of the *Jew* first, and then of the *Gentile;* for the law was to come out of Zion, and the word of the Lord from Jerusalem. To the discipline of that religion both were to submit; and therefore both might well be said "to be subdued to us, and brought under our feet."

2. In honouring and rewarding his Church: "He shall choose out our inheritance for us, the excellency of Jacob whom he loved."

1. His Church was his *choice:* "It is a chosen generation, a peculiar people."

2. His *heritage;* for he will dwell among them, and provide an inheritance for them; blessings on earth and glory in heaven.

3. This is "the excellency of Jacob;" of Jacob after the Spirit; the kingdom, priesthood, and all the promises made unto Jacob and the fathers being theirs.

4. The cause: "His love only—he chose—the excellency of Jacob whom he loved."

3. In the increase and amplification of his Church: "God is *now* the king of all the earth;" not of the *Jews* only, for he "reigns over the heathen" also. He "sits upon a throne of holiness;" rules by his holy word and Spirit. 1. Making them holy who were unholy. 2. They are "a willing people" also. For the princes—the volunteers, among the people, are gathered together; even the people of the God of Abraham—the Gentiles, converted and reconciled to God.

4. In protecting his Church; whether by himself, or by the *princes* he raises up; by his *providence*, or his *angels*, or all together. For the "shields of the earth belong *unto* God." Secular rulers, and ecclesiastical governors, are shields of the Church. But God is the *Head* of it, and the *Chief:* "He is greatly exalted."

PSALM XLVIII

The ornaments and the privileges of the Church, 1–8. *The duty of God's people,* 9–14.

A Song *and* Psalm [a]for the sons of Korah

A. M. 3485 B. C. 519 A. U. C. 235 Anno Darii I., Regis Persarum, 6

GREAT *is* the LORD, and greatly to be praised [b]in the city of our God, *in* the [c]mountain of his holiness.

2 [d]Beautiful for situation, [e]the joy of the whole earth, *is* Mount Zion, [f]*on* the sides of the north, [g]the city of the great King.

[a]Or, *of*——[b]Psa. xlvi. 4; lxxxvii. 3——[c]Isa. ii. 2, 3; Mic. iv. 1; Zech. viii. 3

[d]Psa. l. 2; Jer. iii. 19; Lam. ii. 15; Dan. viii. 9; xi. 16 [e]Ezek. xx. 6——[f]Isa. xiv. 13——[g]Matt. v. 35

NOTES ON PSALM XLVIII

The *title: A Song* and *Psalm for the sons of Korah.* To which the *Vulgate, Septuagint, Æthiopic,* and *Arabic* add, *for the second day of the week;* for which I believe it would be difficult to find a meaning. It is evidently of the same complexion with the two preceding, and refers to the Jews returned from captivity; and perhaps was sung at the dedication of the second temple, in order to return thanks to the Lord for the restoration of their political state, and the reestablishment of their worship.

Verse 1. *Great* is *the Lord*] This verse should be joined to the last verse of the preceding Psalm, as it is a continuation of the same subject; and indeed in some of *Kennicott's* MSS. it is written as a part of the foregoing. *That* concluded with *He is greatly exalted; this* begins with *Great is the Lord, and greatly to be praised;* i. e., He should be praised according to his greatness; no common praise is suited to the nature and dignity of the Supreme God.

In the city of our God] That is, in the *temple;* or in Jerusalem, where the temple was situated.

The mountain of his holiness.] Mount Moriah, on which the temple was built. The ancient city of Jerusalem, which David took from the Jebusites, was on the *south* of Mount Zion, on which the temple was built, though it might be said to be more properly on Mount *Moriah*, which is one of the *hills* of which Mount Zion is composed. The temple therefore was to the *north* of the city, as the psalmist here states, ver. 2: "Beautiful for situation, the joy of the whole earth, is Mount Zion, on the sides of the north, the city of the great King." But some think that it is the *city* that is said to be on the *north*, and *Reland* contends that the temple was on the *south* of the city.

Verse 2. *The joy of the whole earth*] Commentators have been greatly puzzled to show in what sense Zion, or the temple, could be said to be the *joy of the whole earth.* If we take the earth here for the *habitable* globe, there is no sense in which it ever was the joy of the whole earth; but if we take כל הארץ *col haarets,* as

A. M. 3485
B. C. 519
A. U. C. 235
Anno Darii
I., Regis
Persarum, 6

3 God is known in her palaces
for a refuge.
4 For, lo, [h]the kings were assembled, they passed by together.
5 They saw *it, and* so they marvelled; they
were troubled, *and* hasted away.
6 Fear [i]took hold upon them there, [k]*and*
pain, as of a woman in travail.
7 Thou [l]breakest the ships of Tarshish
[m]with an east wind.
8 As we have heard, so have we seen in
[n]the city of the LORD of hosts, in the city of
our God: God will [o]establish it for ever.
Selah.
9 We have thought of [p]thy loving-kindness,
O God, in the midst of thy
temple.
10 According to [q]thy name,
O God, so *is* thy praise unto the
ends of the earth: thy right hand is full of
righteousness.
11 Let Mount Zion rejoice, let the daughters
of Judah be glad, because of thy judgments.
12 Walk about Zion, and go round about
her: tell the towers thereof.
13 [r]Mark ye well her bulwarks, [s]consider
her palaces; that ye may tell *it* to the generation following.
14 For this God *is* [t]our God for ever and
ever: he will [u]be our guide *even* unto death.

[h]2 Samuel x. 6, 14, 16, 18, 19——[i]Exod. xv. 15——[k]Hos. xiii. 13——[l]Ezek. xxvii. 26——[m]Jer. xviii. 17——[n]Ver. 1, 2——[o]Isa. ii. 2; Mic. iv. 1——[p]Psa. xxvi. 3; xl. 10

[q]Deut. xxviii. 58; Joshua vii. 9; Psalm cxiii. 3; Mal. i. 11, 14——[r]Hebrew, *Set your heart to her bulwarks*——[s]Or, *raise up*——[t]Psa. xlviii. 14; lxxvii. 13; xcv. 7——[u]Isa. lviii. 11

signifying the *whole of this land,* (and it has no other meaning,) the assertion is plain and easy to be understood, for the temple was considered the *ornament* and *glory* of the whole *land* of Judea.

Verse 3. *God is known in her palaces for a refuge.*] All those who worship there in spirit and truth, find God for their refuge. But the words may be understood: God is known for the defence of her palaces; and with this view of the subject agree *the three* following verses.

Verse 4. *For, lo, the kings were assembled*] Many of the neighbouring potentates, at different times, envied the prosperity of the Jewish nation, and coveted the riches of the temple; but they had no power against it till the cup of Jewish transgression was full. In vain did they *assemble*—confederate, and invade the land. *Saw it*—reconnoitered the place; *marvelled* at its excellence and strength, for *they were troubled*—struck with fear; *hasted away* for fear of destruction, for *fear took hold on them* as pains seize on a *woman in travail.* Those who came to destroy were glad to make their own escape.

Verse 7. *Thou breakest the ships of Tarshish*] *Calmet* thinks this may refer to the discomfiture of *Cambyses,* who came to destroy the land of Judea. "This is apparently," says he, "the same *tempest* which struck dismay into the land-forces of Cambyses, and wrecked his fleet which was on the coasts of the Mediterranean sea, opposite to his army near the port of *Acco,* or the *Ptolemais;* for Cambyses had his quarters at *Ecbatana,* at the foot of Mount Carmel; and his army was encamped in the valley of Jezreel." *Ships of Tarshish* he conjectures to have been large stout vessels, capable of making the voyage of *Tarsus,* in Cilicia.

Verse 8. *As we have heard, so have we seen*] Our fathers have declared what mighty works thou didst in their time; and we have seen the same. God has often interposed and afforded us a most miraculous defence. So it was when they were invaded by the Assyrians, Syrians, Egyptians, Babylonians, Persians and the Greeks under Alexander.

The city of the Lord of hosts] His *hosts* defended the city, and it was known to be *the city of the great King.*

God will establish it for ever.] This must refer to the true temple, the Christian Church, of which the Jewish Church was a type. The *type* perished, but the *antitype* remained, and will remain till time shall be no more.

Selah.] So be it; and so it will be for evermore.

Verse 9. *We have thought of thy loving-kindness*] We went to thy temple to worship thee; we meditated on thy goodness; we waited for a display of it; and the panic that in the first instance struck *us,* was transferred to our *enemies;* and *fear took hold upon them, they marvelled, were troubled,* and *hasted away.*

Verse 10. *According to thy name*] As far as thou art known, so far art thou praised; and where thou art known, thou *wilt* have praise to the end of the earth. And why? "Thy right hand is full of righteousness." Thou art continually dispensing thy blessings to the children of men.

Verse 11. *Let Mount Zion rejoice*] The temple is restored in majesty, which was threatened with total destruction; it is again repaired.

Let the daughters of Judah be glad] That thou hast turned her captivity, and poured out thy judgments upon her oppressors.

Verse 12. *Walk about Zion*] Consider the beauty and magnificence of the temple, count the towers by which it is fortified.

Verse 13. *Mark ye well her bulwarks*] See the *redoubts* by which she is defended.

Consider her palaces] See her *courts, chambers, altars,* &c., &c.; make an exact register of the whole, that ye may have to tell to your children how Jerusalem was built in troublesome times; how God restored you; and how he put it into the hearts of the heathen to assist to build, beautify, and adorn the temple of our God.

Verse 14. *For this God*] Who did all these wonderful things,—

Is *our God*] He is our portion, and he has taken us for his people.

He will be our guide] Through all the snares and difficulties of life,—

Even *unto death*] He will never leave us;

and we, by his grace, will never abandon him. He is just such a God as we need; infinite in *mercy, goodness*, and *truth*. He is *our Father*, and we are the *sons and daughters* of God Almighty. Even unto and in death, he will be our portion.

Analysis of the Forty-eighth Psalm

Under the type of Jerusalem is set down the happiness of the Church, which is always protected by the Divine favour. There are *three* parts in this Psalm:—

I. The excellences and privileges of the city of God, ver. 1-3.

II. A narration of a miraculous deliverance she obtained, and the terror that fell upon her enemies, ver. 4-8.

III. An exhortation to consider it, and to praise God, ver. 9-14.

I. The psalmist begins with a *maxim:* "Great is the Lord, and greatly to be praised." Great in himself; and greatly to be praised for *all things*, in *all places;* but especially in the *city of our God*, in the *mountain of holiness.*

Then he descends to set forth the excellences and ornaments of the Church.

1. It is "the city of God," built and governed by him, and in it he resides.

2. "It is a holy mountain:" The *religion* in it is holy; the *people*, a holy people.

3. "It is beautiful for situation:" God has put his beauty upon it.

4. "The joy of the whole earth is Mount Zion:" The joy and ornament of all the land of Judea then, and afterwards of the whole world, because the law was to come out of Zion.

5. "It is the city of the great King," i. e., God. He founded, and rules in it.

6. "God is known in her palaces:" In her is the knowledge of God; yea, and by an experimental knowledge, he is found to be an asylum, a *sure refuge.*

II. And it is well that it is so; for Jerusalem, *i. e.*, the Church, has many and great enemies, which (ver. 5) the prophet begins to describe; and desires that notice may be taken of them, for he points them out with "Lo! or Behold!"

1. They are many and powerful. They were "kings," a plurality of them.

2. Confederate kings: "The kings were assembled." United power is the more effectual.

But all the endeavours of those kings, those confederate kings, came to nothing.

1. "They passed by together:" together they came, together they vanished.

2. "They saw—they marvelled:" They saw the strength of this city, and wondered how it could be so strangely delivered out of their hands.

3. On this they were troubled, they trembled, and hasted away. *Fear* took hold upon them; which the prophet illustrates by a double similitude: 1. By a travailing woman; "Fear took hold upon them, and pain, as of a woman in travail." 2. By the fear of mariners at sea, when euroclydon threatens to destroy their ship; their amazement was such "as when thou breakest the ships of Tarshish with an east wind."

III. In this third part of the Psalm there are *two* especial points:—

A grateful acknowledgment of God's protection of his Church: "As we have heard, so have we seen in the city of our God." We have heard that he will protect this city, and we see that he hath done it; and persuaded we are that he will always do it: "God will establish it for ever."

2. And this shall never be forgotten by us: "We have thought of thy loving-kindness in the midst of thy temple."

3. And so thought of it as to praise thee for it: "According to thy name so is thy praise; thy right hand is full of righteousness." All the earth shall know that thou dost help with thy powerful hand thy afflicted and oppressed people. Thou wilt punish their adversaries, "for thy right hand is full of righteousness—and justice."

The second point of this third part is an exhortation to God's people.

1. That they exult and rejoice for what God does for them: "Let Mount Zion rejoice, let the daughters of Judah be glad, because of thy judgments," in defending thy Church, and punishing their enemies.

2. That they take especial notice of his miraculous deliverance of Jerusalem; that, notwithstanding the army was great that lay against it, yet no harm was done: "Walk about Zion, tell the towers thereof; mark well her bulwarks, and her palaces." See whether they be not all standing and entire.

3. And do it for this end: "That you may tell it to the generation following." Leave it on record how miraculously God hath delivered you.

4. For this there are *two* strong reasons: 1. "For this God," who protects and defends us, "is our God for ever." 2. "He will be our guide unto death." He will not leave us when all the world leaves us. In the time in which we need him most, we shall find him most powerfully present to help us. Therefore, exult, rejoice, mark it; and make it known to the generations to come.

PSALM XLIX

All men are invited to attend to lessons of wisdom relative to the insufficiency of earthly good to save or prolong life; to secure the resurrection from the dead, 1–9. Death is inevitable, 10. The vain expectations of rich men, 11–13. Death renders all alike, 14. The psalmist encourages and fortifies himself against envying the apparently prosperous state of the wicked, who are brutish, and die like beasts, 15–20.

To the chief Musician, A Psalm [a]for the sons of Korah

HEAR this, all *ye* people; give ear, all *ye* inhabitants of the world:

2 Both [b]low and high, rich and poor, together.

3 My mouth shall speak of wisdom; and the meditation of my heart *shall be* of understanding.

4 [c]I will incline mine ear to a parable: I will open my dark saying upon the harp.

5 Wherefore should I fear in the days of evil: *when* [d]the iniquity of my heels shall compass me about?

6 They that [e]trust in their wealth, and boast themselves in the multitude of their riches;

7 None *of them* can by any means redeem his brother, nor [f]give to God a ransom for him:

8 (For [g]the redemption of their soul *is* precious, and it ceaseth for ever:)

9 That he should still live for ever, *and* [h]not see corruption.

10 For he seeth *that* [i]wise men die, likewise the fool and the brutish person perish, [k]and leave their wealth to others.

11 Their inward thought *is, that* their

[a]Or, *of*——[b]Psa. lxii. 9——[c]Psa. lxxviii. 2; Matt. xiii. 35——[d]Psa. xxxviii. 4——[e]Job xxxi. 24, 25; Psa. lii. 7; lxii. 10; Mark x. 24; 1 Tim. vi. 17

[f]Matt. xvi. 26——[g]Job xxxvi. 18, 19——[h]Psa. lxxxix. 48——[i]Eccles. ii. 16——[k]Prov. xi. 4; Eccles. ii. 18, 21

NOTES ON PSALM XLIX

The *title, To the chief Musician, A Psalm for the sons of Korah*, has nothing particular in it; and the *Versions* say little about it. One of the descendants of the children of Korah might have been the author of it; but *when* or on *what occasion* it was made, cannot now be discovered. The author aimed to be *obscure*, and has succeeded; for it is very difficult to make out his meaning. It is so much in the style of the Book of Job, that one might believe they had the same author; and that this Psalm might have made originally a part of that book. "It seems," says Dr. *Dodd*, "to be a meditation on the vanity of riches, and the usual haughtiness of those who possess them. As a remedy for this, he sets before them the near prospect of death, *from* which no riches can save, *in* which no riches can avail. The author considers the subject he is treating as a kind of wisdom concealed from the world; a mystery, an occult science with respect to the generality of mankind." Dr. *Kennicott* has given an excellent translation of this Psalm, which is very literal, simple, and elegant; and by it the reader will be convinced that a good translation of a difficult passage is often better than a comment.

Verse 1. *Hear this, all* ye *people*] The four first verses contain the author's exordium or introduction, delivered in a very pompous style, and promising the deepest lessons of wisdom and instruction. But what was *rare* then is *common-place* now.

Verse 4. *I will incline mine ear to a parable*] This was the general method of conveying instruction among the Asiatics. They used much figure and metaphor to induce the reader to study deeply in order to find out the meaning. This had its use; it obliged men to *think* and *reflect* deeply; and thus in some measure taught them the use, government, and management of their *minds*.

My dark saying upon the harp.] Music was sometimes used to soothe the animal spirits, and thus prepare the mind for the prophetic influx.

Verse 5. *The iniquity of my heels*] Perhaps עקבי *akebai*, which we translate *my heels*, should be considered the contracted plural of עקבים *akebim, supplanters.* The verse would then read thus: "Wherefore should I fear in the days of evil, though the iniquity of my supplanters should compass me about." The *Syriac* and *Arabic* have taken a similar view of the passage: "Why should I fear in the evil day, when the iniquity of my enemies compasses me about." And so Dr. *Kennicott* translates it.

Verse 7. *None* of them *can by any means redeem his brother*] Wealth cannot save from death; brother, however rich, cannot save his brother; nor will God accept *riches* as a ransom for the *life* or *soul* of any transgressor. To procure health of body, peace of mind, redemption from death, and eternal glory, riches are sought for and applied in vain.

Verse 8. *For the redemption of their soul* is *precious*] It is of too high a price to be redeemed with corruptible things, such as *silver* or *gold*, and has required the sacrificial death of Christ.

And it ceaseth for ever] This is very obscure, and may apply to the *ransom* which *riches* could produce. That ransom must be for ever unavailable, because of the *value of the soul.* Or this clause should be added to the following verse, and read thus: "And though he cease to be, (וחדל *vechadal,*) during the hidden time, (לעולם *leolam;*) yet he shall live on through eternity, (ויחי עוד לנצח *vichi od lanetsach,*) and not see corruption." This is probably the *dark saying* which it was the design of the author to utter in a parable, and leave it to the ingenuity of posterity to find it out. The verb חדל *chadal* signifies a *cessation of being* or *action*, and עולם *olam* often signifies *hidden time*, that which is not *defined*, and the *end* of which is not *ascertained*, though it is frequently used to express *endless duration.* This translation requires no alteration of the original text, and conveys a precise and consistent meaning.

Verse 10. *For he seeth* that *wise men die*] Though they may be rich, and their wisdom teach them the best method of managing their riches so as to derive all the good from them they can possibly produce, yet *they* die as well as the *fool* and the poor ignorant man; and their wealth is left to others who will be equally disappointed in their expectation from it.

Verse 11. *Their inward thought* is, that *their*

houses *shall continue* for ever, *and* their dwelling places [l]to all generations; they [m]call *their* lands after their own names.

12 Nevertheless [n]man *being* in honour abideth not: he is like the beasts *that* perish.

13 This their way *is* their [o]folly: yet their posterity [p]approve their sayings. Selah.

14 Like sheep they are laid in the grave; death shall feed on them; and [q]the upright shall have dominion over them in the morning; [r]and their [s]beauty shall consume [t]in the grave from their dwelling.

15 But God [u]will redeem my soul [v]from the power of [w]the grave: for he shall receive me. Selah.

16 Be not thou afraid when one is made rich, when the glory of his house is increased;

17 [x]For when he dieth he shall carry nothing away: his glory shall not descend after him.

18 Though [y]while he lived [z]he blessed his soul: and *men* will praise thee, when thou doest well to thyself.

19 [a]He shall [b]go to the generation of his fathers; they shall never see [c]light.

20 [d]Man *that is* in honour, and understandeth not, [e]is like the beasts *that* perish.

---

[l]Heb. *to generation and generation*——[m]Gen. iv. 17 [n]Ver. 20; Psa. xxxix. 5; lxxxii. 7——[o]Luke xii. 20 [p]Heb. *delight in their mouth*——[q]Psa. xlvii. 3; Dan. vii. 22; Mal. iv. 3; Luke xxii. 30; 1 Cor. vi. 2; Rev. ii. 26; xx. 4——[r]Job iv. 21; Psalm xxxix. 11——[s]Or, *strength* [t]Or, *the grave* being *a habitation to every one of them*

[u]Psalm lvi. 13; Hosea xiii. 14——[v]Hebrew, *from the hand of the grave*——[w]Or, *hell*——[x]Job xxvii. 19 [y]Hebrew, *in his life*——[z]Deuteronomy xxix. 19; Luke xii. 19——[a]Hebrew, The soul *shall go*——[b]Gen xv. 15——[c]Job xxxiii. 30; Psalm lvi. 13——[d]Verse 12 [e]Eccles. iii. 19

---

houses shall continue *for ever*] Thus, by interpolation, we have endeavoured to patch up a sense to this clause. Instead of קרבם *kirbam*, their *inward part*, the *Septuagint* appear to have used a copy in which the second and third letters have been transposed קברם *kibram*, *their sepulchres;* for they translate: Και οἱ ταφοι αυτων οικιαι αυτων εις τον αιωνα· "For their graves are their dwellings for ever." So six or seven feet long, and two or three wide, is sufficient to hold the greatest conqueror in the universe! What a small house for the quondam possessor of numerous palaces and potent kingdoms!

They call their *lands after their own names.*] There would have been no evil in this if it had not been done on an infidel principle. They expected no state but the *present;* and if they could not continue themselves, yet they took as much pains as possible to perpetuate their *memorial.*

Verse 12. *Man* being *in honour abideth not*] However rich, wise, or honourable, they must die; and if they die not with a sure hope of eternal life, they die like beasts. See on ver. 20.

Verse 13. *Their posterity approve their sayings.*] Go the same way; adopt their maxims.

Verse 14. *Like sheep they are laid in the grave*] לשאול *lishol, into sheol*, the place of *separate* spirits.

Death shall feed on them מות ירעם *maveth yirem*, "Death shall feed them!" What an astonishing change! All the good things of life were once their portion, and they lived only to eat and drink; and now they *live in sheol*, and *Death himself feeds them!* and with what? Damnation. *Houbigant* reads the verse thus: "Like sheep they shall be laid in the place of the dead; death shall feed on them; their morning shepherds rule over them; and their flesh is to be consumed. Destruction is to them in their folds."

Verse 15. *But God will redeem my soul from the power of the grave*] מיד שאול *miyad sheol*, "from the hand of sheol." That is, by the plainest construction, I shall have a resurrection from the dead, and an entrance into his glory; and death shall have no dominion over me.

Verse 16. *Be not thou afraid when one is made rich*] Do not be envious; do not grieve: it will do you no harm; it will do him no good. All he gets will be left behind; he can carry nothing with him. Even his glory must stay behind; he shall mingle with the common earth.

Verse 18. *He blessed his soul*] He did all he could to procure himself animal gratifications, and he was applauded for it; for it is the custom of the world to praise them who pay most attention to their secular interest; and he who attends most to the concerns of his soul is deemed weak and foolish, and is often persecuted by an ungodly world.

Verse 19. *They shall never see light.*] Rise again they shall; but they shall never see the light of glory, for there is prepared for them the *blackness of darkness* for ever.

Verse 20. *Man* that is *in honour*] The rich and honourable man who has no spiritual understanding, is a *beast* in the sight of God. The spirit of this maxim is, A man who is in a dignified official situation, but destitute of learning and sound sense, is like a beast. The important place which he occupies reflects no honour upon him, but is disgraced by him. Who has not read the fable of the beautifully carved head? It was every thing that it should be, but had no *brains.*

This verse has been often quoted as a proof of the *fall of man;* and from ילין *yalin*, (in ver. 12,) which signifies *to lodge for a night*, it has been inferred that Adam fell on the same day on which he was created, and that he did not spend a single night in the terrestrial paradise. Adam, who was in a state of glory, did not remain in it one night, but became stupid and ignorant as the beasts which perish. But we may rest assured this is no meaning of the text.

Analysis of the Forty-ninth Psalm

The doctrine taught by this Psalm is the following: That rich men be not proud of their wealth, nor poor men dejected nor humbled at their mean estate, since all men are mortal; and it is not the wealth of the one can make them happy, nor the poverty of the others can make them unhappy, there being another life by which the condition of both is to be judged.

The Psalm has *three* parts:—

I. An *exordium* or *preface:* ver. 1-4.

II. The *matter* proposed, debated, and argued, from ver. 5 to 16.

III. The *advice* or *admonition* given, from. ver. 16 to 20.

I. In the *exordium,*—

1. He calls together his auditory: "All people, all nations, low, high, rich, and poor;" because what he speaks concerns all.

2. Then he calls them to be attentive. "Hear, give ear."

3. He labours to make them teachable, by commending the matter of which he treats; they are not frivolous, but weighty and important things: 1. "My mouth shall speak of wisdom," &c. I will speak of what I know, and speak so that others may understand. 2. "I will incline my ear." I will teach you nothing but what I teach myself. 3. It is a *parable* which I am about to deliver, and will require all your attention. 4. That it may be brought to your ear with more delight, I shall accompany it with the *harp:* "I will open my dark saying upon the harp."

II. Having now assembled his congregation; endeavoured to make them attentive, docile, and well-disposed, lest any should suppose that he was envious at the prosperity of the wicked, or had so little trust in God that he lived in terror of his adversaries; he says, "Wherefore should I fear in the days of evil, though the iniquity of my supplanters surrounds me?" He had no reason thus to fear; but the wealthy and ambitious had. And this he demonstrates *two ways:* for he takes away happiness from the *one,* ver. 6-15, and places happiness in the other, ver. 16.

1. They that trust in their wealth, and boast themselves in the multitude of their riches, are not happy, ver. 6. For wealth will not deliver in the evil day.

1. It will save no man's life: "None of them (the rich men) can redeem his brother, nor give to God a ransom for him." God will not be bribed to save any man's life.

2. It will save no man's soul. The ransom required for that is more valuable than any thing the earth can produce.

3. Suppose he was wise, and a long-lived man, yet he must die at last: "For he seeth that wise men die; likewise the fool, and the brutish."

4. Which sufficiently shows the vanity of their riches: 1. They leave them. 2. They leave these great riches. 3. They leave them to others; sometimes to children, but often to strangers, such as they thought never would have entered into their labours.

5. "Their thoughts are vain." For, 1. "Their inward thoughts are that their houses shall continue," &c. 2. To this end, "They call their lands after their own names;" they not only study to be *rich,* but they are *vain-glorious* also.

But their study is, 1. Vanity. 2. Folly.

1. *Vanity:* "Nevertheless, man being in honour, abideth not;" a change there will be, and the most glorious man will be *like the beasts that perish.*

2. *Folly:* "This their way is their foolishness." A great foolery to place their chief good in riches; yet their posterity act in the same way, tread in their steps, and pant after riches and honours.

To correct this propensity, he lays before them certain considerations relative to their future condition:—

1. "Like sheep they are laid in the grave." That is their common condition; like sheep they are fatted for slaughter.

2. "Death shall feed on them." The second death; for, like *Dives,* they *shall be burned in hell;* and the *fire that cannot be extinguished* shall feed upon their souls and bodies.

3. In the morning of the resurrection, the "upright shall have power over them." The *righteous* shall shine like the sun, when *they* shall be Christ's footstool. The *godly* shall be placed on the right hand, and seated on thrones to judge them; when *they* shall be seated on the left, and be condemned.

4. "Their beauty shall consume in the grave." Their riches, power, and glory, shall wax old as doth a garment: "For the figure of this world passeth away." Therefore the *rich* of this world, and the *possessors of great glory, are not happy.* He therefore sets down the *happy man:* the man who trusts in God, and lives to him, he is happy in life, notwithstanding his afflictions, and he shall be happy for ever. Therefore he says, "God will redeem my soul from the power of the grave," &c.

1. He shall redeem me. All good men's souls.

2. Not from the grave, for die we must; but from the *hand,* that is, the dominion and power, of death: "Death shall not reign over them."

3. The reason is, For *he shall receive me*—adopt me into his family, and make me a partaker of the Divine nature.

III. On these considerations, relative to good and bad men, and their different conditions, he admonishes the good that they be not troubled at the prosperity of the wicked: "Be not thou afraid," &c.

1. Not at the great wealth of the rich: "Be not afraid when one is made rich."

2. Not at the glory and honour of the mighty: "Nor when the glory of his house is increased."

And he repeats the former reason: "For when he dieth, he shall carry nothing away; his glory shall not descend after him." Their happiness, such as it was, was only momentary.

This he amplifies: Be it granted that they flattered themselves, and were flattered by others.

1. "Though while he lived he blessed his own soul." "Soul, take thy ease," &c.

2. Though men will praise thee, and sound in thy ears, Well done! "so long as thou doest well to thyself,"—heapest up riches, and followest after honour.

1. A mortal thou art, short-lived as all that went before thee: "He shall go to the generation of his fathers." And,

2. If wicked, be cast into utter darkness: "They shall never see the light."

3. Surely any man, however rich, however great, who understands not thus much, must be a beast; and with this sentiment concludes the Psalm; and it is doubled that it may be remembered: "Man, who is in honour, and understandeth not, is like the beasts that perish." Even while he lives, without this understanding, his life is little more than the life of the beast.

PSALM L

God, the Sovereign Judge, cites before his throne all his people, and the priests and the judges, 1–6; *and reproaches them for their vain confidence in the sacrifices they had offered,* 7–13; *and shows them the worship he requires,* 14, 15; *and then enters into a particular detail of their hypocrisy, injustice, and union with scandalous transgressors; all of whom he threatens with heavy judgments,* 16–22. *The blessedness of him who worships God aright, and walks unblamably,* 23.

X. DAY. MORNING PRAYER

A Psalm of [a]Asaph

THE [b]mighty God, *even* the LORD, hath
spoken, and called the earth from the
rising of the sun unto the going down thereof.
2 Out of Zion, [c]the perfection of beauty,
[d]God hath shined.
3 Our God shall come, and shall not keep
silence: a [e]fire shall devour before him, and
it shall be very tempestuous round about him.
4 [f]He shall call to the heavens from above,
and to the earth, that he may judge his people.
5 Gather [g]my saints together unto me;
[h]those that have made a covenant with me by
sacrifice.
6 And [i]the heavens shall declare his

[a]Or, *for Asaph;* see 1 Chron. xv. 17; xxv. 2; 2 Chron. xxix. 30——[b]Neh. ix. 32; Isa. ix. 6; Jer. xxxii. 18——[c]Psa. xlviii. 2——[d]Deut. xxxiii. 2; Psa. lxxx. 1——[e]Lev. x. 2; Num. xvi. 35; Psa. xcvii. 3; Dan. vii. 10——[f]Deut. iv. 26; xxxi. 28; xxxii. 1; Isa. i. 2; Mic. vi. 1, 2——[g]Deut. xxxiii. 3; Isa. xiii. 3——[h]Exod. xxiv. 7——[i]Psa. xcvii. 6

NOTES ON PSALM L

In the *title* this is said to be *A Psalm of Asaph.* There are *twelve* that go under his name; and most probably he was author of each, for he was of high repute in the days of David, and is mentioned *second* to him as a composer of psalms: *Moreover Hezekiah the king, and the princes, commanded the Levites to sing praise unto the Lord, with the* WORDS *of* DAVID, *and of* ASAPH *the* SEER. His band, sons or companions, were also eminent in the days of David, as we learn from 1 Chron. xxv., &c. *Asaph* himself was one of the *musicians* who *sounded with cymbals of brass,* 1 Chron. xv. 19. And he is mentioned with great respect, Neh. xii. 46: *And in the days of* DAVID *and* ASAPH *of old* there were CHIEF *of the* SINGERS, *and* SONGS *of* PRAISE *and* THANKSGIVING *unto God.* He was certainly a *prophetic* man: he is called a *seer*—one on whom the *Spirit of God rested;* and seems from this, his education, and natural talent, to be well qualified to *compose* hymns or psalms in the honour of God. Persons capable of judging, on a comparison of those Psalms attributed to *Asaph* with those known to be of *David,* have found a remarkable *difference* in the *style.* The style of David is more *polished, flowing, correct,* and *majestic,* than that of Asaph, which is more *stiff* and *obscure.* He has been compared to *Persius* and to *Horace;* he is *keen, full of reprehensions,* and his subjects are generally of the *doleful* kind; which was probably caused by his living in times in which there was great corruption of manners, and much of the displeasure of God either *theatened* or *manifested.* It is not known on what particular *occasion* this Psalm was written; but at most times it was suitable to the state of the Jewish Church.

Verse 1. *The mighty God,* even *the Lord, hath spoken*] Here the *essential names* of God are used: אל אלהים יהוה EL, ELOHIM, YEHOVAH, *hath spoken.* The *six first verses* of this Psalm seem to contain a description of the *great judgment:* to any minor consideration or fact it seems impossible, with any propriety, to restrain them. In this light I shall consider this part of the Psalm, and show,—

First, The preparatives to the coming of the great Judge. *El Elohim Jehovah hath spoken, and called the earth*—all the children of men, *from the rising of the sun unto the going down thereof. Out of Zion, the perfection of beauty,* (מכלל יפי *michlal yophi,* the beauty where all perfection is comprised,) *God hath shined,* ver. 1, 2. 1. He has sent his Spirit to convince men of sin, righteousness, and judgment. 2. He has sent his WORD; has made a revelation of himself; and has declared both his law and his Gospel to mankind: "Out of Zion, the perfection of beauty, God hath shined," ver. 2. For out of Zion the law was to go forth, and the word of the Lord from Jerusalem. Isa. ii. 3.

Secondly, The accompaniments. 1. His approach is proclaimed, ver. 3: "Our God shall come." 2. The trumpet proclaims his approach: "He shall not keep silence." 3. Universal nature shall be shaken, and the earth and its works be burnt up: "A fire shall devour before him, and it shall be very tempestuous round about him," ver. 3.

Thirdly, The witnesses are summoned and collected, and collected from all quarters; some from heaven, and some from earth. 1. Guardian angels. 2. Human associates: "He shall call to the heavens from above, and to the earth, that he may judge his people," ver. 4.

Fourthly, The procedure. As far as it respects the righteous, orders are issued: "Gather my saints," those who are saved from their sins and made holy, "together unto me." And that the word *saints* might not be misunderstood, it is explained by "those that have made a covenant with me by sacrifice;" those who have entered into union with God, through the sacrificial offering of the Lord Jesus Christ. All the rest are passed over in silence. We are told who they are that shall enter into the joy of their Lord, viz., only the *saints,* those who have made a covenant with God by sacrifice. All, therefore, who do not answer this description are excluded from glory.

Fifthly, The final issue: all the angelic host,

righteousness: for [k]God *is* judge himself.
Selah.
7 [l]Hear, O my people, and I will speak; O
Israel, and I will testify against thee: [m]I *am*
God, *even* thy God.
8 [n]I will not reprove thee [o]for thy sacrifices
or thy burnt-offerings, *to have been* continually before me.
9 [p]I will take no bullock out of thy house,
nor he-goats out of thy folds.
10 For every beast of the forest *is* mine, *and*
the cattle upon a thousand hills.
11 I know all the fowls of the mountains: and the wild beasts of the field *are*
[q]mine.
12 If I were hungry, I would not tell thee:
[r]for the world *is* mine, and the fulness thereof.
13 Will I eat the flesh of bulls, or drink the
blood of goats?
14 [s]Offer unto God thanksgiving; and [t]pay
thy vows unto the Most High:
15 And [u]call upon me in the day of trouble:
I will deliver thee, and thou shalt [v]glorify me.
16 But unto the wicked God saith, What

[k]Psa. lxxv. 7——[l]Psa. lxxxi. 8——[m]Exod. xx. 2——[n]Isa. i. 11; Jer. vii. 22——[o]Hos. vi. 6——[p]Mic. vi. 6; Acts xvii. 25——[q]Heb. *with me*——[r]Exod. xix. 5; Deut. x. 14; Job xli. 11; Psa. xxiv. 1; 1 Cor. x. 26, 28

[s]Hos. xiv. 2; Heb. xiii. 15——[t]Deut. xxiii. 21; Job xxii. 27; Psa. lxxvi. 11; Eccles v. 4, 5——[u]Job xxii. 27; Psa. xci. 15; cvii. 6, 13, 19, 28; Zech. xiii. 9——[v]Ver. 23; Psa. xxii. 23

and all the redeemed of the Lord, join in applauding acclamation at the decision of the Supreme Judge. The heavens (for the earth is no more, it is burnt up) shall declare his righteousness, the exact justice of the whole procedure, where justice alone has been done without partiality, and without severity; nor could it be otherwise, *for God is Judge himself.* Thus the assembly is dissolved; the righteous are received into everlasting glory, and the wicked turned into hell, with all those who forget God. Some think that the sentence against the wicked is that which is contained from ver. 16 to ver. 22. See the *analysis* at the end, and particularly on the six first verses, in which a somewhat different view of the subject is taken.

Verse 7. *Hear, O my people*] As they were now amply informed concerning the nature and certainty of the general judgment, and were still in a state of probation, Asaph proceeds to show them the danger to which they were exposed, and the necessity of repentance and amendment, that when that great day should arrive, they might be found among those who had made a covenant with God by sacrifice. And he shows them that the sacrifice with which God would be well pleased was quite different from the bullocks, he-goats, &c., which they were in the habit of offering. In short, he shows here that God has intended to abrogate those sacrifices, as being no longer of any service: for when the people began to trust in them, without looking to the thing signified, it was time to put them away. When the people began to pay Divine honours to the *brazen serpent,* though it was originally an ordinance of God's appointment for the healing of the Israelites, it was ordered to be taken away; called *nehushtan,* a bit of brass; and broken to pieces. The sacrifices under the Jewish law were of God's appointment; but now that the people began to put their trust in them, God despised them.

Verse 8. *I will not reprove thee*] I do not mean to find fault with you for not offering sacrifices; you have offered them, they *have been continually before me:* but you have not offered them in the proper way.

Verse 10. *Every beast of the forest* is *mine*] Can ye suppose that ye are laying me under *obligation* to you, when ye present me with a part of my own property?

Verse 12. *The world* is *mine, and the fulness thereof.*] Ye cannot, therefore, give me any thing that is not my own.

Verse 13. *Will I eat the flesh of bulls*] Can ye be so simple as to suppose that I appointed such sacrifices for my own gratification? All these were significative of a spiritual worship, and of the sacrifice of that Lamb of God which, in the fulness of time, was to take away, in an *atoning manner*, the sin of the world.

Verse 14. *Offer unto God thanksgiving; and pay thy vows unto the Most High*] זבח *zebach,* "sacrifice unto God, אלהים *Elohim,* the תודה *todah, thank-offering,*" which was the same as the *sin-offering,* viz. *a bullock, or a ram, without blemish;* only there were, in addition, "unleavened cakes mingled with oil, and unleavened wafers anointed with oil; and cakes of fine flour mingled with oil and fried," Lev. vii. 12.

And pay thy vows] נדריך *nedareycha,* "thy vow-offering, to the Most High." The *neder* or *vow-offering* was *a male without blemish, taken from among the beeves, the sheep, or the goats.* Compare Lev. xxii. 19 with ver. 22. Now these were offerings, in their spiritual and proper meaning, which God required of the people: and as the sacrificial system was established for an especial end—to show the *sinfulness of sin,* and the *purity of Jehovah,* and to show how sin could be *atoned for, forgiven,* and *removed;* this system was now to end in the thing that it signified,—the grand sacrifice of Christ, which was to make *atonement, feed, nourish,* and *save* the souls of believers unto eternal life; to excite their praise and thanksgiving; *bind* them to God Almighty by the most solemn *vows* to live to him in the spirit of *gratitude* and *obedience* all the days of their life. And, in order that they might be able to hold fast faith and a good conscience, they were to make continual *prayer to God,* who promised to hear and *deliver them, that they might glorify him,* ver. 15.

From the 16th to the 22nd verse Asaph appears to refer to the final rejection of the Jews from having any part in the true *covenant sacrifice.*

Verse 16. *But unto the wicked*] The bloodthirsty priests, proud Pharisees, and ignorant scribes of the Jewish people.

hast thou to do to declare my statutes, or *that*
thou shouldest take my covenant in thy mouth?
17 [w]Seeing thou hatest instruction, and
[x]castest my words behind thee.
18 When thou sawest a thief, then thou
[y]consentedst with him, and [z]hast been [a]par-
taker with adulterers.
19 [b]Thou givest thy mouth to evil, and [c]thy
tongue frameth deceit.
20 Thou sittest *and* speakest against thy
brother; thou slanderest thine own mother's
son.
21 These *things* hast thou done, [d]and I kept
silence; [e]thou thoughtest that I was altogether
such an one as thyself: *but* [f]I will reprove
thee, and set *them* in order before thine
eyes.
22 Now consider this, ye that [g]forget God,
lest I tear *you* in pieces, and *there be* none to
deliver.
23 [h]Whoso offereth praise glorifieth me:
and [i]to him [k]that ordereth *his* conversation *aright* will I show the salvation of
God.

---

[w]Rom. ii. 21, 22——[x]Neh. ix. 26——[y]Rom. i. 32
[z]Heb. *thy portion* was *with adulterers*——[a]1 Tim. v. 22
[b]Heb. *Thou sendest*——[c]Psa. lii. 2——[d]Eccles. viii. 11, 12; Isa. xxvi. 10; lvii. 11——[e]See Rom. ii. 4——[f]Psa. xc. 8
[g]Job viii. 13; Psa. ix. 17; Isa. li. 13——[h]Psa. xxvii. 6; Rom. xii. 1——[i]Gal. vi. 16——[k]Heb. *that disposeth* his *way*

Verse 17. *Seeing thou hatest instruction*] All these rejected the counsel of God against themselves; and refused to receive the instructions of Christ.

Verse 18. *When thou sawest a thief*] Rapine, adulteries, and adulterous *divines*, were common among the Jews in our Lord's time. The Gospels give full proof of this.

Verse 21. *These* things *hast thou done*] My eye has been continually upon you, though my judgments have not been poured out: and because I was *silent*, thou didst suppose *I was such as thyself; but I will reprove thee*, &c. I will visit for these things.

Verse 22. *Now consider this*] Ye have forgotten your God, and sinned against him. He has marked down all your iniquities, and has them *in order* to exhibit against you. Beware, therefore, *lest he tear you to pieces, when there is none to deliver;* for none can deliver you but the *Christ* you reject. And how can ye escape, if ye neglect so great a salvation?

Verse 23. *Whoso offereth praise*] These are the very same words as those in ver. 14, זבח תודה; and should be read the same way independently of the *points*, *zebach todah*, "sacrifice the thank-offering." Jesus is the great *eucharistic sacrifice;* offer him up to God in your faith and prayers. By this sacrifice is God *glorified*, for in him is God *well pleased;* and it was by the *grace* or *good pleasure of God* that he *tasted death for every man.*

Ordereth his *conversation*] שם דרך *sam derech*, DISPOSETH *his way.—Margin. Has his way* THERE, שם דרך *sham derech*, as many MSS. and old editions have it; or *makes that his custom.*

Will I show the salvation of God.] אראנו *arennu*, I will cause him to see בישע *beyesha*, into the salvation of God; into God's method of saving sinners by Christ. He shall witness my saving power even to the uttermost; such a salvation as it became a God to bestow, and as a fallen soul needs to receive; the salvation from all sin, which Christ has purchased by his death. **I sall scheu til him, the hele of God**; that es Jeshu, that he se him in the fairehed of his majeste.—*Old Psalter.*

Analysis of the Fiftieth Psalm

The prophet, by a *prosopopœia*, brings in God prescribing rules for his own worship. The point in debate is: *How God will be honoured in his own Church?* And as none can teach this but God, he brings him in speaking to his people.

The Psalm has *two* general parts:—

I. The *majesty* and *authority* of the person who is to judge this debate, ver. 1-6.

II. The *sentence* which he pronounces, ver. 7-23.

The prophet begins with calling an *assize.* He summons a *court*, presents us with a *judge*, produces *witnesses*, cites those who are to *answer*, and, having seated the Judge on his throne, gives forth his *charge.*

I. *First.* He *presents*, 1. The *Judge*, in authority and majesty: "The mighty God, even the Lord, hath spoken," ver. 1.

2. The *place* to which he comes to hold his court—the *Church:* "Out of Zion, the perfection of beauty; God hath shined." To Zion the *law* was given; and *out of* Zion the law was to come, by which he would judge; and therefore it was rightly said, "Out of Zion the Lord hath shined."

3. His *appearance*, which is *terrible.* It was so when he gave his *law* on Mount *Sinai;* and it will be so when he comes to require it: "Our God shall come, and shall not keep silence; a fire shall devour before him, and it shall be very tempestuous round about him." See 2 Pet. iii. 10; Luke xxi. 25, 26.

Secondly. Those who are *cited* to appear before him—his *saints*—those who had undertaken to worship him as he had appointed: "Gather my saints together; those who have made a covenant with me by sacrifice."

Thirdly. Against these he produces his *witnesses*, whom he collects, 1. From *heaven;* 2. From *earth.* "He shall call the heavens from above, and the earth, that he may judge his people." Including the inhabitants of the whole earth, "from the rising of the sun until the going down thereof." And his *award* shall be universally approved: "The heavens shall declare his righteousness—his just method of procedure; for God himself is Judge."

II. Next follows the *charge* given by God himself the Judge; and, to engage attention, he proclaims: "Hear, O my people, and I will speak," &c.

1. "I am God;" therefore, worship and obedience are due to me from all creatures.

2. "I am thy God; and thou art my people;" therefore, due from thee especially.

3. "I will speak." I will judge and determine this controversy about my worship.

4. "I will testify against thee," and convict thee of what thou hast done amiss.

There is a *twofold worship:* 1. *Ceremonial* and external. 2. *Spiritual* and moral. And I will *speak* and *testify* of both.

It was the *duty* of the people to bring the sacrifice, and perform the ceremonies appointed by the law: but God is not pleased with the outward act merely; nothing pleases him where the heart and affections are wanting.

1. "I will not reprove thee for thy sacrifices." These thou bringest, and these I accept. But in this I reprove thee, because thou thinkest that I must be pleased with the *external service*, howsoever performed; and that thou hast a right to expect pardon and all other blessings.

2. Unless the heart be penitent, and the offerings be made in faith, I will not accept them: "I will take no bullock out of thy house, nor he-goat," &c. And this for *two* reasons:—

1. I do not need them: "Every beast of the forest is mine—the cattle on a thousand hills—the fowls of the mountain—the wild beasts of the field—the world and its fulness."

2. My perfection is such that I could not use them: "Thinkest thou that I will eat the flesh of bulls, or drink the blood of goats?"

The heathen priests taught the people that the gods *fed* on the *odour* of the sacrifices; and they represented them as complaining of being *starved*, when they were withheld!

For these reasons the sacrifices, as you have performed them, do not please me; but I shall acquaint you with those that do please me; *thanksgiving* and *prayer* or *invocation*.

1. *Thankfulness:* "Offer unto God thanksgiving, and pay thy vows," &c.

2. *Invocation:* "Call upon me in the day of trouble."

Which being done, he makes an *indenture* with us:

1. On *his* part, that he will *save us:* "I will deliver thee."

2. On *our* part, that we give him the *glory* of our *salvation:* "Thou shalt glorify me."

3. And yet he makes an *exception* to some men's *prayers* and *praises*, *hypocrites* and *impious men. Praise is not comely in the mouth of a sinner*, and petitions offered by the *profane* shall not be heard.

1. "To the wicked God saith, What hast thou to do to declare my statutes," &c.

2. The reason is: Thou professest to love me, but in works thou deniest me: for thou hatest instruction, and hast cast my words behind thee: how then can I be pleased with thee? I shall now prove this against thee.

1. Thou hast broken the *eighth* commandment: "Thou sawest the thief, and consentedst to him,"—joinedst with him to carry off the spoil; or, when he *stole*, thou didst *receive*.

2. Thou hast broken the *seventh* commandment. "Thou hast been a partaker with the adulterers."

3. And the *ninth:* "Thou givest thy mouth to evil, and thy tongue frameth deceit;—thou sittest and speakest against thy brother, and slanderest thy own mother's son." Thou didst do all this deliberately. Thou didst *sit* and *speak*.

4. Thou hast broken the *first* commandment. Because I did not execute judgment upon thy evil works, "thou thoughtest that I was altogether such a one as thyself;" or, in a word, that there was *no God*, or none worthy of fear and reverence.

This wickedness I will not suffer to go unpunished; for the day will come when "I will reprove thee,—set thy sins in order before thee, and punish the wickedness which thou hast attempted to hide. Yet in *judgment* God remembers *mercy;* he gives warning to the wicked, and threatens that he may spare, and that they may repent and perish not.

1. *Now*, while you have respite, *consider this*, that God is not pleased with outward rites and formalities, and that they who trust in merely having performed them are far from being in a safe state. They do the outward work, and *forget God.* Take heed, lest as a lion he rush out upon you, and *tear you to pieces.*

2. To the pure and spiritual worshippers he makes a gracious promise of *defence*, *help*, and *salvation. He who sacrifices the thank-offering*, with an humble, believing heart, *glorifies me;* and to him who *places his feet in that path*, and THERE determinately abides, going the right way which God's word directs, *I will show the salvation of God*—he shall be saved; and shall know that he worships not God in vain. See the preceding *notes* on this Psalm.

PSALM LI

The psalmist, with a deeply penitent heart, prays for remission of sins, 1–4; *which he confesses, and deeply deplores,* 5–14; *states his willingness to offer sacrifice, but is convinced that God prefers a broken heart to all kinds of oblations,* 15–17; *prays for the restoration of the walls of Jerusalem, and promises that then the Lord's sacrifice shall be properly performed,* 18, 19.

To the chief Musician, A Psalm of David, [a]when Nathan the prophet came unto him, after he had gone in to Bath-sheba

A. M. cir. 2971
B. C. cir. 1033
Davidis, Regis Israelitarum, cir. annum 23

HAVE mercy upon me, O God, according to thy loving-kindness: according unto the multitude of thy tender mercies, [b]blot out my transgressions.

2 [c]Wash me throughly from mine iniquity, and cleanse me from my sin.
3 For [d]I acknowledge my transgressions: and my sin *is* ever before me.
4 [e]Against thee, thee only, have I sinned, and done *this* evil [f]in thy sight: [g]that thou might-

[a]2 Sam. xii. 1; xi. 2, 4——[b]Ver. 9; Isa. xliii. 25; xliv. 22; Col. ii. 14——[c]Hebrews ix. 14; 1 John i. 7, 9; Rev. 1. 5

[d]Psa. xxxii. 5; xxxviii. 18——[e]Gen. xx. 6; xxxix. 9; Lev. v. 19; vi. 2; 2 Sam. xii. 13——[f]Luke xv. 21 [g]Rom. iii. 4

NOTES ON PSALM LI

The *title* is long: "To the chief Musician, A Psalm of David, when Nathan the prophet came unto him, after he had gone in to Bath-sheba." The propriety of this title has been greatly suspected, says Bishop *Horsley:* "That this Psalm was not written on the occasion to which the title refers, is evident from the 4th and 18th verses. The 4th verse ill suits the case of David, who laid a successful plot against Uriah's life, after he had defiled his bed: and the 18th verse refers the Psalm to the time of the captivity, when Jerusalem lay in ruins." Dr. *Kennicott* is of the same mind. He says: "The title is misplaced; that it was written during the *captivity*, and the cessation of the temple worship; the author under great depression of mind, arising from the guilt of some crime, probably some compliance with heathen idolatry, not *murder* nor *adultery;* is *plain* from the 4th verse, "Against THEE ONLY have I sinned."

The crime mentioned in the *title* was not only against God, but against the whole order of civil society; against the life of the noble and valiant captain whose wife Bath-sheba was, and against every thing sacred in friendship and hospitality. It was a congeries of sins against God and society. Were it not for the 4th, 18th, and 19th verses, the rest of the Psalm would accord well enough with the *title*, and the deep penitence it expresses would be suitable enough to David's state. But see on verses 4, 18, 19.

Verse 1. *Have mercy upon me, O God*] Without mercy I am totally, finally ruined and undone.

According to thy loving-kindness] Mark the gradation in the sense of these three words, *Have* MERCY *on me,* חנני *chonneni; thy* LOVING-KINDNESS, חסדך *chasdecha;—thy* TENDER MERCIES, רחמיך *rachameycha,* here used to express the Divine compassion. The propriety of the order in which they are placed deserves particular observation.

The *first*, rendered *have mercy* or *pity*, denotes that kind of affection which is expressed by moaning over an object we love and pity; that natural affection and tenderness which even the brute creation show to their young by the several noises they respectively make over them.

The *second*, rendered *loving-kindness*, denotes a strong proneness, a ready, large, and liberal disposition, to goodness and compassion, powerfully prompting to all instances of *kindness* and bounty; flowing as freely as waters from a perpetual fountain. This denotes a higher degree of goodness than the former.

The *third*, rendered *tender mercies*, denotes what the Greeks called σπλαγχνιζεσθαι, that *most tender pity* which we signify by the moving of the heart and bowels, which argues the highest degree of compassion of which nature is susceptible. See *Chandler*.

Blot out my transgressions] מחה *mecheh, wipe out.* There is a reference here to an *indictment:* the psalmist knows what it contains; he pleads guilty, but begs that the writing may be *defaced;* that a proper fluid may be applied to the parchment, *to discharge the ink*, that no record of it may ever appear against him: and this only the *mercy, loving-kindness,* and *tender compassions* of the Lord can do.

Verse 2. *Wash me throughly*] הרבה כבסני *harbeh cabbeseni,* "Wash me again and again,—cause my washings to be multiplied." My stain is deep; ordinary purgation will not be sufficient.

Verse 3. *For I acknowledge my transgressions*] I know, I feel, I confess that I have sinned.

My sin is *ever before me.*] A true, deep, and unsophisticated mark of a genuine penitent. Wherever he turns his face, he sees his sin, and through it the eye of an angry God.

Verse 4. *Against thee, thee only, have I sinned*] This verse is supposed to show the impropriety of affixing the above *title* to this Psalm. It could not have been composed on account of the matter with Bath-sheba and the murder of Uriah; for, surely, these sins could not be said to have been committed against God ONLY, if we take the words of this verse in their common acceptation. That was a *public* sin, grievous, and against society at large, as well as against the peace, honour, comfort, and *life* of an innocent, brave, and patriotic man. This is readily granted: but see below.

That thou mightest be justified when thou speakest] Perhaps, to save the propriety of the *title*, we might understand the verse thus: David, being *king*, was not liable to be called to account by any of his *subjects;* nor was there any *authority* in the land by which he could be *judged* and *punished.* In this respect, *God* ALONE was *greater than the king;* and to *him* ALONE, as king, he was responsible. *Nam quando rex deliquit,* SOLI DEO *reus est; quia hominem non habet qui ejus facta dijudicet,* says *Cassiodorus.* "For when a king transgresses, he is accountable to GOD ONLY; for there is no person who has authority to take cognizance of his conduct." On this very maxim, which is a maxim in all countries, David might say, *Against thee only have I sinned.* "I cannot be called to the bar of my subjects; but I arraign myself before thy bar. They can neither judge nor condemn me; but thou canst: and such are my crimes that thou wilt be justified in the

A. M. cir. 2971
B. C. cir. 1033
Davidis, Regis
Israelitarum,
cir. annum
23

est be justified when thou speakest, *and* be clear when thou
judgest.
5 [h]Behold, I was shapen in ini-
quity; [i]and in sin did my mother [k]conceive me.
6 Behold, thou desirest truth [l]in the inward
parts; and in the hidden *part* thou shalt make
me to know wisdom.
7 [m]Purge me with hyssop, and I shall be
clean: wash me, and I shall be [n]whiter than
snow.

8 Make me to hear joy
and gladness; *that* the bones
which thou hast broken [o]may
rejoice.
9 [p]Hide thy face from my sins, and [q]blot
out all mine iniquities.
10 [r]Create in me a clean heart, O God;
and renew [s]a right spirit within me.
11 Cast me not away [t]from thy presence; and take not thy [u]Holy Spirit
from me.

[h]Job xiv. 4; Psa. lviii. 3; John. iii. 6; Rom. v. 12; Eph. ii. 3——[i]Job xiv. 4——[k]Heb. *warm me*——[l]Job xxxviii. 36——[m]Lev. xiv. 4, 6, 49; Num. xix. 18; Heb. ix. 19

[n]Isa. i. 18——[o]Matt. v. 4——[p]Jer. xvi. 17——[q]Ver. 1——[r]Acts xv. 9; Eph. ii. 10——[s]Or, *a constant spirit*——[t]Gen. iv. 14; 2 Kings xiii. 23——[u]Rom. viii. 9; Eph. iv. 30

eyes of all men, and cleared of all *severity*, shouldst thou inflict upon me the heaviest punishment." This view of the subject will reconcile the Psalm to the *title*. As to the eighteenth and nineteenth verses, we shall consider them in their own place; and probably find that the objection taken from *them* has not much weight.

Verse 5. *Behold, I was shapen in iniquity*] A genuine penitent will hide nothing of his state; he sees and bewails, not only the *acts* of sin which he has committed, but the *disposition* that led to those acts. He deplores, not only the *transgression*, but the *carnal mind*, which is enmity against God. The light that shines into his soul shows him the very source whence transgression proceeds; he sees his fallen nature, as well as his sinful life; he asks *pardon* for his transgressions, and he asks *washing* and *cleansing* for his inward defilement. Notwithstanding all that *Grotius* and others have said to the contrary, I believe David to speak here of what is commonly called *original sin;* the propensity to evil which every man brings into the world with him, and which is the fruitful source whence all transgression proceeds. The word חוללתי *cholalti*, which we translate *shapen*, means more properly, *I was brought forth from the womb;* and יחמתני *yechemathni* rather signifies *made me warm*, alluding to the whole process of the formation of the *fetus in utero*, the formative heat which is necessary to develope the parts of all embryo animals; to incubate the *ova* in the female, after having been impregnated by the male; and to bring the whole into such a state of maturity and perfection as to render it capable of subsisting and growing up by aliment received from *without*. "As my parts were developed in the womb, the sinful principle diffused itself through the whole, so that body and mind grew up in a state of corruption and moral imperfection."

Verse 6. *Behold, thou desirest truth*] I am the very reverse of what I should be. *Thou desirest truth in the heart;* but in me there is nothing but sin and falsity.

Thou shalt make me to know wisdom.] Thou wilt teach me to restrain every inordinate propensity, and to act according to the dictates of sound wisdom, the rest of my life.

Verse 7. *Purge me with hyssop*] תחטאני *techatteeni*, "thou shalt make a sin-offering for me;" probably alluding to the cleansing of the leper: Lev. xiv. 1, &c. The priest took two clean birds, cedar-wood, scarlet, and hyssop; one of the birds was killed; and the living bird, with the scarlet, cedar, and hyssop, dipped in the blood of the bird that had been killed, and then sprinkled over the person who had been infected. But it is worthy of remark that this ceremony was not performed till the plague of the leprosy had *been healed* in the leper; (Lev. xiv. 3;) and the ceremony above mentioned was for the purpose of *declaring* to the people that the man was healed, that he might be restored to his place in society, having been healed of a disease that the finger of God alone could remove. This David seems to have full in view; hence he requests the *Lord* to *make the sin-offering for him*, and to show to the people that he had accepted him, and cleansed him from his sin.

Verse 8. *Make me to hear joy*] Let me have a full testimony of my reconciliation to thee; that the soul, which is so deeply distressed by a sense of thy displeasure, may be healed by a sense of thy pardoning mercy.

Verse 9. *Hide thy face from my sins*] The sentiment here is nearly the same as that in ver. 3: *His sin was ever before his own face;* and he knew that the eye of God was constantly upon him, and that his purity and justice must be highly incensed on the account. He therefore, with a just horror of his transgressions, begs God to *turn away his face from them*, and to blot them out, so that they may never more be seen. See the note on ver. 1.

Verse 10. *Create in me a clean heart*] *Mending* will not avail; my heart is altogether corrupted; it must be *new made*, made as it was in the beginning. This is exactly the sentiment of St. Paul: *Neither circumcision availeth any thing, nor uncircumcision, but a new creation;* and the salvation given under the Gospel dispensation is called a being *created anew in Christ Jesus.*

A right spirit within me.] רוח נכון *ruach nachon*, a constant, steady, determined spirit; called ver. 12, רוח נדיבה *ruach nedibah*, a *noble spirit*, a *free*, *generous*, *princely* spirit; cheerfully giving up itself to thee; no longer *bound* and *degraded* by the sinfulness of sin.

Verse 11. *Cast me not away from thy presence*] Banish me not from thy house and ordinances.

Take not thy Holy Spirit from me.] I know I

A. M. cir. 2971
B. C. cir. 1033
Davidis, Regis
Israelitarum,
cir. annum
23

12 Restore unto me the joy of
thy salvation; and uphold me
with thy [v]free spirit.
13 *Then* will I teach transgressors thy ways; and sinners shall be converted unto thee.
14 Deliver me from [w]blood-guiltiness, [x]O
God, thou God of my salvation: *and* [y]my
tongue shall sing aloud of thy righteousness.
15 O LORD, open thou my lips; and my
mouth shall show forth thy praise.
16 For [z]thou desirest not sacrifice; [a]else
would I give *it:* thou delightest
not in burnt-offering.
17 [b]The sacrifices of God
are a broken spirit: a broken
and a contrite heart, O God, thou wilt not
despise.
18 Do good in thy good pleasure unto Zion:
build thou the walls of Jerusalem.
19 Then shalt thou be pleased with [c]the sacrifices of righteousness, with burnt-offering
and whole burnt-offering; then shall they
offer bullocks upon thine altar.

A. M. cir. 2971
B. C. cir. 1033
Davidis, Regis
Israelitarum,
cir. annum
23

[v]2 Corinthians iii. 17——[w]Hebrew, *bloods*——[x]2 Samuel xi. 17; xii. 9——[y]Psalm xxxv. 28——[z]Numbers xv. 27, 30; Psalm xl. 6; l. 8; Isaiah i. 11; Jeremiah vii. 22; Hosea vi. 6——[a]Or, *that I should give it*——[b]Psa. xxxiv. 18; Isaiah lvii. 15; lxvi. 2——[c]Psalm iv. 5; Mal. iii. 3

have sufficiently grieved it to justify its departure for ever; in consequence of which I should be consigned to the blackness of darkness,—either to utter despair, or to a hard heart and seared conscience; and so work iniquity with greediness, till I fell into the pit of perdition. While the Spirit stays, painfully convincing of sin, righteousness, and judgment, there is hope of salvation; when it departs, then the hope of redemption is gone. But while there is any *godly sorrow*, any *feeling* of regret for having sinned against God, any *desire* to seek mercy, then the case is not hopeless; for these things prove that the light of the Spirit is not withdrawn.

Verse 12. *Restore unto me the joy of thy salvation*] This is an awful prayer. And why? Because it shows he *once* HAD *the joy of God's salvation; and had* LOST *it by sin!*

Uphold me with thy *free spirit.*] Prop me up; support me with a princely spirit, one that will not stoop to a mean or base act. See on ver. 10.

Verse 13. Then *will I teach transgressors*] I will show myself to be grateful; I will testify of thy loving-kindness; I will call on transgressors to consider the error of their ways; and shall set before them so forcibly thy *justice* and *mercy*, that sinners shall be converted unto thee. With a little change I can adopt the language of Dr. *Delaney* on this place: "Who can confide in his own strength, when he sees David fall? Who can despair of Divine mercy when he sees *him* forgiven? Sad triumph of sin over all that is great or excellent in man! Glorious triumph of grace over all that is shameful and dreadful in sin!"

Verse 14. *Deliver me from blood-guiltiness*] This is one of the expressions that gives most colour to the propriety of the title affixed to this Psalm. Here he may have in view the *death of Uriah*, and consider that *his blood* cries for vengeance against him; and nothing but the mere mercy of God can wipe this blood from his conscience. The prayer here is earnest and energetic: *O God! thou God of my salvation! deliver me!* The *Chaldee* reads, "Deliver me (מדין קטול *middin ketol*) from the judgment of slaughter."

My tongue shall sing aloud] My tongue shall praise thy righteousness. I shall testify to all that thou hast the highest displeasure against sin, and wilt excuse it in no person; and that so merciful art thou, that if a sinner turn to thee with a deeply penitent and broken heart, thou wilt forgive his iniquities. None, from my case, *can* ever *presume;* none, from my case, *need* ever *despair*.

Verse 15. *O Lord, open thou my lips*] My heart is believing unto righteousness; give me thy peace, that my tongue may make confession unto salvation. He could not praise God for pardon till he felt that God had pardoned him; then his lips would be opened, and his tongue would show forth the praise of his Redeemer.

Verse 16. *For thou desirest not sacrifice*] This is the same sentiment which he delivers in Psa. xl. 6, &c., where see the notes. There may be here, however, a farther meaning: Crimes, like mine, are not to be expiated by any sacrifices that the law requires; nor hast thou appointed in the law any sacrifices to atone for deliberate murder and adultery: if thou hadst, I would cheerfully have given them to thee. The matter is before thee as Judge.

Verse 17. *The sacrifices of God* are *a broken spirit*] As my crimes are such as admit of no legal atonement, so thou hast reserved them to be punished by exemplary acts of justice, or to be pardoned by a sovereign act of mercy: but in order to find this mercy, thou requirest that the heart and soul should deeply feel the transgression, and turn to thee with the fullest compunction and remorse. This thou hast enabled me to do. I have the broken spirit, רוח נשברה *ruach nishbarah;* and the broken and contrite heart, לב נשבר ונדכה *leb nishbar venidkeh.* These words are very expressive. שבר *shabar* signifies exactly the same as our word *shiver*, to *break into pieces*, to *reduce into splinters;* and דכה *dakah*, signifies to *beat out thin*,—to *beat out masses of metal, &c., into laminæ* or *thin plates*. The spirit broken all to pieces, and the heart broken all to pieces, stamped and beaten out, are the sacrifices which, in such cases, thou requirest; and these "thou wilt not despise." We may now suppose that God had shone upon his soul, healed his broken spirit, and renewed and removed his broken and distracted heart; and that he had now received the answer to the preceding prayers. And here the Psalm properly ends; as, in the two following verses, there is nothing similar to what we find in the rest of this very nervous and most important composition.

Verse 18. *Do good in thy good pleasure unto Zion*] This and the following verse most evidently refer to the time of the *captivity*, when the *walls of Jerusalem were broken down*, and the *temple service entirely discontinued;* and, consequently, are long posterior to the times of David. Hence it has been concluded that the Psalm was not composed by David, nor in his time and that the *title* must be that of some other Psalm inadvertently affixed to this. The fourth verse has also been considered as decisive against this *title:* but the note on that verse has considerably weakened, if not destroyed, that objection. I have been long of opinion that, whether the *title* be properly or improperly affixed to this Psalm, these *two verses* make no part of it: the subject is totally dissimilar; and there is no rule of analogy by which it can be interpreted as belonging to the *Psalm*, to the *subject*, or to the *person*. I think they originally made a Psalm of themselves, a kind of *ejaculatory prayer* for the *redemption of the captives from Babylon*, the *rebuilding of Jerusalem*, and *the restoration of the temple worship*. And, taken in this light, they are very proper and very expressive.

The cxviith Psalm contains only *two verses;* and is an *ejaculation of praise from the captives who had just then returned from Babylon*. And it is a fact that this Psalm is written as a *part* of the cxvith in no less than *thirty-two* of *Kennicott's* and *De Rossi's* MSS.; and in some early editions. Again, because of its smallness, it has been absorbed by the cxviiith, of which it makes the *commencement*, in *twenty-eight* of *Kennicott's* and *De Rossi's* MSS. In a similar way I suppose the two last verses of this Psalm to have been absorbed by the preceding, which originally made a complete Psalm of themselves; and this absorption was the more easy, because, like the cxviith it has no *title*. I cannot allege a similar evidence relative to these two verses, as ever having made a distinct Psalm; but of the fact I can have no doubt, for the reasons assigned above. And I still think that Psalm is too dignified, too energetic, and too elegant, to have been the composition of any but David. It was not Asaph; it was not any of the sons of Korah; it was not Heman or Jeduthun: the hand and mind of a greater master are here.

Analysis of the Fifty-first Psalm

In general the Psalm contains David's prayer,—

I. For himself, ver. 1-12.

II. Three vows or promises, ver. 13-18.

III. For the Church, ver. 18, 19.

I. David being in deep distress on account of his sins, prays to God for *mercy:* and while he feels that he is unworthy of the name of *king*, or *God's anointed*, of *his son*, or of *his servant*, he uses *no plea of his* own *merit*, but, —1. Of the loving-kindness of God: "According to thy loving-kindness." 2. Of the compassion of God: "According to the multitude of thy tender mercies."

The general petition for mercy being offered, next he offers *three* particular petitions:—

First. He prays for *forgiveness of sins.* The fact was past, but the guilt remained: therefore, he earnestly petitions: "Put away mine iniquities;" my sin is a deep stain: "Wash me throughly from mine iniquities, and cleanse me from my sin," *multiply* washing; my sin is a *deep* defilement.

To this petition he joins *confession of sin;* from which we may learn the conditions requisite in a genuine confession:—

He considers the *nature* of his sin; he feels the *weight* of it, the *burden*, and the *anguish* of it; and *abhors* it.

1. "I know mine iniquity." It is no longer hidden from me.

2. "It is ever before me;" and the sight breaks my heart.

3. He uses different *epithets* for it, in order to aggravate the guilt, and deepen the repentance. 1. It is *transgression*, פשע *pesha*, rebellion. 2. It is *iniquity*, עון *avon*, crooked dealing. 3. It is *sin*, חטאת *chattath*, error and wandering.

Then he begins his earnest *confession:* "I have sinned." And this he aggravates by several circumstances:—

1. Of the *person*. It is "against thee;" a good and gracious God, who of a *shepherd* made me a *king* over thy own people. *Against thee*, the great and terrible God. The people are my *subjects*, and they cannot judge me: it is against *thee* I have sinned, and to *thee* I must give account, and by *thee* be judged and punished.

2. Of the *manner*. It was an *impudent* sin; not committed by *surprise*, but done openly: "In thy sight." Therefore, the threatenings by thy prophet are all right. Whatever punishment thou mayest inflict upon me, both thy justice and mercy will stand clear: "That thou mightest be justified," &c.

3. He shows from what *root* his sin sprang; from his *original corruption:* "Behold, I was shapen in iniquity, and in sin did my mother conceive me." I am all corruption *within*, and defilement *without*. The evil fountain hath sent forth bitter waters.

4. Another aggravation of his sin was, that he was in *principle* devoid of that which God *loves:* "Thou desirest truth in the inward parts."

5. The greatest aggravation of all was, his having sinned against light and knowledge. God had endued him with *wisdom in the hidden part*, by the motions of his own Spirit; but he had permitted his passions to obscure that light, and had quenched the Spirit.

Having made this general confession, he names the *particular sin* that lay heaviest on his conscience: "Deliver me from blood-guiltiness." And then renews his petition for *pardon* under a *type* then in use, and a *metaphor*. The type, *hyssop;* the metaphor, *wash me*.

1. "Purge me with hyssop." With a bunch of hyssop, dipped in the blood of the paschal lamb, the Israelites sprinkled their doors. It was also used in the sprinkling of the *leper*, and in the *sacrifice for sin:* and the *blood* and *sprinkling* were a *type of Christ's blood*, and the pardon and holiness that came through it. Sprinkled with this, David knew he must be clean; "for the blood of Christ cleanseth from all sin;" and it is "the blood of Christ that justifies."

2. *Sanctified* also he wishes to be; and there, he says, *Wash me*. And this is done by the influence of God's Spirit: "I will sprinkle clean water upon you, and you shall be clean," Ezek. xxxvi. 25.

Secondly. David, having ended his *petitions for pardon*, proceeds,—

1. To pray that the *evil effects* which had been produced by his sin might be removed: "Make me to hear joy and gladness," &c.

2. That his *body*, which was in a pining condition, might be restored: "That the bones which thou hast broken may rejoice."

3. A *third* evil effect of his sin was, that God's face, that is, his favour, was turned away from him: he therefore begs,—

(1) "Hide thy face from my sins." Remember them not against me.

(2) "And blot out mine iniquities." I know there is a long and black catalogue in thy book against me; blot it out; blot out the handwriting of ordinances that is against me.

Thirdly. Now follows David's *last* petition; in which he again craves more particularly the grace of *sanctification.* He first prayed for *remission;* next for *reconciliation;* and now for *renovation*, which he asks of God in the *three* following verses: 1. "Create in me a clean heart." 2. "Renew a right spirit within me." 3. "Cast me not away from thy presence." 4. "Take not thy Holy Spirit from me." 5. "Restore unto me the joy of thy salvation." 6. "Uphold me with thy free spirit." In which petitions we are to consider,—

1. The *subject* on which the work is to be done. The *heart,—the spirit.* For as the heart is that part that first lives in nature; so it is the first that lives in grace. The work must begin *within*, else *outward* renovation will be to little purpose.

2. The *work* itself, which is,—

1. A *creation.* Sin had reduced David's heart to *nothing* in respect to heavenly affections and things; and to bring it into a state in which it would answer the *end of its creation*, was to bring *something* out of *nothing;* which, in all cases, is the work of Almighty God: "Create in me, O God," &c.

2. It is a *renovation.* All in David was the *old man*, nothing left of the *new man.* He prays, therefore, to be renewed in the spirit of his mind: "Renew a right spirit within me."

3. *Reconciliation* and *restitution.* Cast me not away—as a dead man; nor take away thy Spirit from me, by which I live: "Cast me not away;—take not thy Holy Spirit from me."

4. A *confirmation* in what was good. *Uphold —confirm me.*

3. WHO was to do this work? Not *himself;* GOD alone. Therefore, he prays: "O God, create;—O Lord, renew;—uphold by thy Spirit."

4. The *quality* of this. A *cleansing*—implied in these remarkable words:—a *right spirit,*—a *holy spirit,*—a *free spirit;* in which some have thought they saw the *mystery of the* HOLY TRINITY.

1. A *right spirit.* He felt that he might easily go *wrong;* a *crooked* and *perverse* spirit had prevailed within him, which had led him out of the *right way* to salvation: "Renew in me a RIGHT spirit."

2. A *holy spirit;* one opposed to the *carnal spirit* that was *enmity* against God, the motions and desires of which were from the flesh, and tended only to its gratification: "Take not thy Holy Spirit from me." It is God's Holy Spirit that makes the spirit of man *holy. Holiness of heart* depends on the indwelling of the *Holy Ghost.*

3. A *free spirit.* A *noble*, a *princely* spirit. Ever since his fall he felt he did nothing good; but by *constraint*, he was in *bondage* to corruption. There was no *dignity* in his mind, sin had *debased* it. "Ennoble me by a birth from above," and by thy *noble Spirit uphold me!*

II. He had now presented his *three petitions*, and now he makes his *vows:* 1. To teach others; 2. To praise God; and, 3. To offer him such a sacrifice as he could accept.

His *first* vow. 1. *Then*, after pardon obtained, "I shall teach;" for a man under guilt is not able to declare *pardon* to others.

2. "I will teach thy way to sinners;" viz.: that to the *stubborn* thou wilt show thyself *froward;* but to the *penitent* thou wilt show *mercy.*

The *effect* of which will be: "Sinners shall be converted unto thee." They who hear of thy *justice* and *mercy*, as manifested in my case, will *fear*, and turn from *sin;* have *faith*, and turn to THEE.

His *second* vow and promise is to *praise God:* "My tongue shall sing aloud of thy righteousness." But to this he was 1. *Unapt;* and must be so till received into *favour.* And, 2. *Unable*, till he received the healthful Spirit of the grace of God. Therefore he prays for a capacity to do both: 1. "Deliver me from blood-guiltiness, O God; then my tongue shall sing." 2. "O Lord, open my lips—and my mouth shall show forth thy praise."

His *third* promise is about a *sacrifice*, not of any *animal*, but of a "broken spirit; a broken and contrite heart," which he knew God would not despise. 1. "Thou desirest no sacrifice, else I would give it thee." No *outward* sacrifice can be of any avail if the *heart* be not offered. 2. Nor will the *heart* be accepted if it be not *sacrificed.* "The broken spirit and contrite heart," this sacrifice he vowed to bring.

III. Having finished his *prayers* and *vows* for himself, he forgets not *Jerusalem.* He petitions for God's Church; and the reason might be, that he was afraid Jerusalem would suffer because of his sins; for *peccant reges, plectuntur Achivi*, "the king sins, the people suffer." This was the case when he sinned against God by numbering the people.

His *method* and his *charity* in this are both instructive.

1. His *method.* 1. To be reconciled to God himself; and then, 2. To pray for others. "The prayers of the righteous avail much."

2. His *charity;* for we are always bound "to remember the afflictions of Joseph, and pray for the peace of Jerusalem." He prays,

1. That God, who out of his good pleasure did choose a Church, would out of his mere good will *do it good*, and preserve it: "Do good, in thy good pleasure, to Zion."

2. That he would have a special favour, even to the *building:* "Build thou the walls of Jerusalem;" for these fall not alone; religion and the service of God fall, when the people permit their churches and chapels to be dilapidated or get out of repair. Of this there are multitudes of proofs.

3. For the consequence of Jerusalem's prosperity would be this, that "religion would flourish with it;" then there would be *sacrifices, burnt-offerings*, and *holocausts:* "Then they shall offer bullocks upon thine altar."

4. And, what is yet *more* and *better*, *we* shall offer, and THOU wilt accept: "Then thou shalt

be pleased with the sacrifices of righteousness." Being reconciled to thee, justified, and sanctified; and righteous in all our conduct; all our sacrifices, springing from thy own grace and love in us, shall find a gracious acceptance. See the note on ver. 18.

PSALM LII

The psalmist points out the malevolence of a powerful enemy, and predicts his destruction, 1–5. *At which destruction the righteous should rejoice,* 6, 7. *The psalmist's confidence in God,* 8, 9.

To the chief Musician, Maschil, *A Psalm* of David, [a]when Doeg the Edomite came and [b]told Saul, and said unto him, David is come to the house of Ahimelech

A. M. cir. 2942 B. C. cir. 1062 Sauli, Regis Israelitarum, cir. annum 34

WHY boastest thou thyself in
mischief, O [c]mighty man?
the goodness of God *endureth*
continually.
2 [d]Thy tongue deviseth mischief; [e]like a
sharp razor, working deceitfully.
3 Thou lovest evil more than good; *and*
[f]lying rather than to speak
righteousness. [g]Selah.
4 Thou lovest all devouring words, [h]O *thou* deceitful
tongue.
5 God shall likewise [i]destroy thee for ever,
he shall take thee away, and pluck thee out
of *thy* dwelling place, and [k]root thee out of
the land of the living. Selah.

A. M. cir. 2942 B. C. cir. 1062 Sauli, Regis Israelitarum, cir. annum 34

---

[a]1 Sam. xxii. 9——[b]Ezek. xxii. 9——[c]1 Sam. xxi. 7 [d]Psa. l. 19——[e]Psa. lvii. 4; lix. 7; lxiv. 3——[f]Jer. ix. 4, 5

[g]Psa. iii. 2, 4, 8; iv. 2, 4; vii. 5; ix. 16, &c.——[h]Or, *and the deceitful tongue*——[i]Heb. *beat thee down*——[k]Prov. ii. 22

NOTES ON PSALM LII

The *title* is, "To the chief Musician, an instructive Psalm of David, when Doeg the Edomite came and informed Saul, and said to him, David is come to the house of Ahimelech." The history to which this alludes is the following: David, having learned that Saul was determined to destroy him, went to take refuge with Achish, king of Gath: in his journey he passed by *Nob*, where the tabernacle then was, and took thence the sword of Goliath; and, being spent with hunger, took some of the shew-bread. *Doeg*, an Edomite, one of the domestics of Saul, being there, went to Saul, and informed him of these transactions. Saul immediately ordered Ahimelech into his presence, upbraided him for being a partisan of David, and ordered Doeg to slay him and all the priests. Doeg did so, and there fell by his hand eighty-five persons. And Saul sent and destroyed *Nob* and all its inhabitants, old and young, with all their property; none escaping but *Abiathar*, the son of Ahimelech, who immediately joined himself to David. The account may be found 1 Sam. xxi. 1-7, xxii. 9-23. All the Versions agree in this title except the *Syriac*, which speaks of it as a Psalm directed against vice in general, with a prediction of the destruction of evil.

Though the Psalm be evidently an invective against some great, wicked, and tyrannical man, yet I think it too mild in its composition for a transaction the most barbarous on record, and the most flagrant vice in the whole character of Saul.

Verse 1. *Why boastest thou thyself*] It is thought that Doeg *boasted* of his loyalty to Saul in making the above discovery; but the information was aggravated by circumstances of falsehood that tended greatly to inflame and irritate the mind of Saul. Exaggeration and lying are common to all informers.

***O mighty man?*] This character scarcely comports with Doeg, who was only *chief of the herdsmen of Saul*, 1 Sam. xxi. 7; but I grant this is not decisive evidence that the Psalm may not have Doeg in view, for the chief *herdsman* may have been a man of credit and authority.**

Verse 2. *Deviseth mischiefs*] Lies and slanders proceeding from the tongue argue the desperate wickedness of the heart.

***Like a sharp razor, working deceitfully.*] Which instead of taking off the beard, cuts and wounds the flesh; or as the operator who, when pretending to trim the beard, cuts the throat.**

Verse 3. *Thou lovest evil*] This was a finished character. Let us note the particulars: 1. He boasted in the power to do evil. 2. His tongue devised, studied, planned, and spoke mischiefs. 3. He was a deceitful worker. 4. He loved evil and not good. 5. He loved lying; his delight was in falsity. 6. Every word that tended to the destruction of others he loved. 7. His tongue was deceitful; he pretended friendship while his heart was full of enmity, ver. 1-4. Now behold the *punishment:*—

Verse 5. *God shall likewise destroy thee*] 1. God shall *set himself* to destroy thee; יתצך *yittotscha*, "he will pull down thy building;" he shall unroof it, dilapidate, and dig up thy foundation. 2. He shall bruise or break thee to pieces for ever; thou shalt have neither strength, consistence, nor support. 3. He will mow thee down, and sweep thee away like dust or chaff, or light hay in a whirlwind, so that thou shalt be scattered to all the winds of heaven. Thou shalt have no residence, no tabernacle: *that* shall be entirely destroyed. Thou shalt be rooted out for ever from the land of the living. The bad fruit which it has borne shall bring God's curse upon the tree; it shall not merely wither, or die, but it shall be plucked up from the roots, intimating that such a sinner shall die a violent death. *Selah.* So it shall be, and so it ought to be.

A. M. cir. 2942
B. C. cir. 1062
Sauli, Regis
Israelitarum,
cir. annum
34

6 [l]The righteous also shall see,
and fear, [m]and shall laugh at
him:
7 Lo, *this is* the man *that* made
not God his strength; but [n]trusted in the
abundance of his riches, *and* strengthened
himself in his [o]wickedness.

8 But I *am* [p]like a green olive-
tree in the house of God: I trust
in the mercy of God for ever
and ever.
9 I will praise thee for ever, because thou
hast done *it:* and I will wait on thy name;
[q]for *it is* good before thy saints.

A. M. cir. 2942
B. C. cir. 1062
Sauli, Regis
Israelitarum,
cir. annum
34

---

[l]Job xxii. 19; Psa. xxxvii. 34; xl. 3; lxiv. 9; Mal. i. 5——[m]Psa. lviii. 10——[n]Psa. xlix. 6——[o]Or, *substance*——[p]Jer. xi. 16; Hos. xiv. 6——[q]Psa. liv. 6

Verse 6. *The righteous also shall see, and fear*] The thing shall be done in the sight of the saints; they shall see God's judgments on the workers of iniquity; and they shall *fear* a God so holy and just, and feel the necessity of being doubly on their guard lest they fall into the same condemnation. But instead of ויראו *veyirau*, "and they shall fear," three of *Kennicott's* and *De Rossi's* MSS., with the *Syriac*, have וישמחו *veyismachu*, "and shall rejoice;" and, from the following words, "and shall laugh at him," this appears to be the true reading, for *laughing* may be either the consequence or accompaniment of *rejoicing*.

Verse 7. *Made not God his strength*] Did not make God his *portion*.

In the abundance of his riches] Literally, in the *multiplication of his riches*. He had got much, he hoped to get more, and expected that his *happiness* would *multiply* as his *riches* multiplied. And this is the case with most rich men.

Strengthened himself in his wickedness.] Loved money instead of God; and thus his depravity, being increased, was *strengthened*.

Crescit amor nummi, quantum ipsa pecunia crescit.

"In proportion to the increase of wealth, so is the love of it."

Where is the religious man, in whose hands money has multiplied, who has not lost the spirit of piety in the same ratio? To prevent this, and the perdition to which it leads, there is no way but opening both hands to the *poor*.

Verse 8. *But I* am *like a green olive-tree in the house of God*] *I shall be in the house of God*, full of spiritual vigour, bringing forth evergreen leaves and annual fruit, as the *olive* does when planted in a proper soil and good situation. It does not mean that there were *olive-trees* planted *in* God's house; but *he* was in God's house, as the olive was in *its* proper place and soil.

I trust in the mercy of God] The *wicked man* trusts in his riches: *I* trust in my God. *He*, like a bad tree, bringing forth poisonous fruit, shall be cursed, and pulled up from the roots; *I*, like a healthy olive in a good soil, shall, under the influence of God's mercy, bring forth fruit to his glory. As the olive is ever green, so shall I flourish in the mercy of God for *ever and ever*.

Verse 9. *I will praise thee for ever*] Because I know that all my good comes from thee; therefore, will I ever praise thee for that good.

I will wait on thy name] I will expect all my blessings from the all-sufficient *Jehovah*, who is *eternal* and *unchangeable*.

It is *good before thy saints.*] It is right that I should expect a continuation of thy blessings by *uniting with thy saints in using thy ordinances*. Thus I shall *wait*.

Analysis of the Fifty-second Psalm

There are *three* parts in this Psalm:—

I. An *invective* against Doeg, and a *prediction* of his fall, ver. 1-5.

II. The *comfort* which God's people should take in this, ver. 6, 7.

III. The *security* and *flourishing* state of those who trust in God, and the psalmist's thanks for it, ver. 8, 9.

I. David begins with an abrupt *apostrophe* to Doeg: "Why boastest thou thyself in mischief, thou mighty man?" And answers that this boasting was but vain; because *the goodness of God* endureth *continually*. This was sufficient to quiet all those who might be afraid of his *boasting*. Having given a *general character* of this man, as having a *delight* in *mischief*, he enters into *particulars;* and especially he considers the bad use he made of his *tongue*.

1. *Thy tongue deviseth mischief, like a razor working deceitfully*. Perhaps there may be here a reference to a case where a man, employed to take off or trim the beard, took that opportunity to cut the throat of his employer. In this manner had Doeg often acted; while pretending by his *tongue* to favour, he used it in a deceitful way to ruin the character of another.

2. "Thou lovest evil more than good:" his wickedness was *habitual;* he *loved* it.

3. "Thou lovest lying more than righteousness:" he was an *enemy* to the *truth*, and by lies and flatteries a destroyer of *good men*.

4. This is expressed more fully in the next verse: "Thou lovest all deceitful words, O thou false tongue!" he was all *tongue;* a *man of words:* and these the most deceitful and injurious.

This is his character; and now David foretells his fall and destruction, which he amplifies by a congeries of words. 1. "God shall likewise destroy thee for ever." 2. "He shall take thee away." 3. "He shall pluck thee out of thy dwelling place." 4. "He shall root thee out of the land of the living." See the notes.

II. Then follows how God's people should be affected by Doeg's fall.

1. "The righteous shall see it and fear:" they shall reverence God more than formerly, as taking vengeance on this singularly wicked man.

2. They shall *laugh at him*, using this bitter sarcasm, "Lo, this is the man that made not God his strength," &c.; he trusted in his *gold* more than in his *God*.

III. But such a fearful end shall not fall on any good man: while the wicked is plucked up from the roots, the righteous shall flourish like a healthy olive-tree.

1. "As for me, I am like the green olive-tree;" ever fruitful and flourishing.

2. I am planted in the house of the Lord; and derive all my nourishment from him, through his ordinances.

3. The olive is perhaps one of the most useful trees in the world. Its *fruit* and its *oil* are of great use to the inhabitants of those countries where the olive is cultivated; and are transported to most parts of the world, where the culture of the olive is unknown.

4. The reason why he shall be like the olive: his faith in God: "I trust in the mercy of God for ever."

Hence, the psalmist's *conclusion* is full of confidence:—

1. "I will praise thee for ever, because thou hast done it."

2. "I will wait on thy name:" I will continue to use those means by which thou communicatest thy grace to the soul.

3. I shall do this because it is my duty, and because it is right in the sight of thy people: "For it is good before thy saints."

PSALM LIII

The sentiments of atheists and deists, who deny Divine Providence; their character: they are corrupt, foolish, abominable, and cruel, 1–4; *God fills them with terror,* 5; *reproaches them for their oppression of the poor,* 5. *The psalmist prays for the restoration of Israel,* 6.

X. DAY. EVENING PRAYER

To the chief Musician upon Mahalath, Maschil, *A Psalm* of David

THE [a]fool hath said in his heart, *There is*
no God. Corrupt are they, and have
done abominable iniquity: [b]*there is* none that
doeth good.

2 God [c]looked down from heaven upon the
children of men, to see if there were *any*
that did understand, that did [d]seek God.

3 Every one of them is gone back: they are
altogether become filthy; *there is* none that
doeth good, no, not one.

4 Have the workers of iniquity [e]no knowledge? who eat up my people *as* they eat
bread: they have not called upon God.

5 [f]There [g]were they in great fear, *where* no
fear was: for God hath [h]scattered the bones
of him that encampeth *against* thee: thou hast
put *them* to shame, because God hath despised
them.

6 [i]O [k]that the salvation of Israel *were*
come out of Zion! When God bringeth back
the captivity of his people, Jacob shall rejoice,
and Israel shall be glad.

[a]Psalm x. 4; xiv. 1, &c.——[b]Romans iii. 10——[c]Psa. xxxiii. 13——[d]2 Chronicles xv. 2; xix. 3——[e]Jeremiah iv. 22——[f]Leviticus xxvi. 17, 36; Proverbs xxviii. 1——[g]Hebrew, *they feared a fear;* Psalm xiv. 5——[h]Ezekiel vi. 5——[i]Psalm xiv. 7——[k]Heb. *who will give salvations, &c.*

NOTES ON PSALM LIII

The *title, To the chief Musician upon Mahalath, an instructive Psalm of David.* The word מחלת *machalath,* some translate the *president;* others, the *master* or *leader of the dance;* others, *hollow instruments;* others, *the chorus.* A *flute pipe,* or *wind instrument* with *holes,* appears to be what is intended. "To the chief player on the flute;" or, "To the master of the band of pipers."

Verse 1. *The fool hath said in his heart*] The whole of this Psalm, except a few inconsiderable differences, is the same as the *fourteenth;* and, therefore, the same *notes* and *analysis* may be applied to it; or, by referring to the *fourteenth,* the reader will find the subject of it amply explained. I shall add a few short notes.

Have done abominable iniquity] Instead of עול *avel, evil* or *iniquity,* eight of *Kennicott's* and *De Rossi's* MSS. have עלילה *alilah, work,* which is nearly the same as in Psa. xiv.

Verse 4. *Have the workers of iniquity*] For פעלי *poaley, workers* seventy-two of *Kennicott's* and *De Rossi's* MSS., with several ancient editions, the *Chaldee,* though not noticed in the Latin translation in the *London Polyglot,* the *Syriac, Vulgate, Septuagint, Æthiopic,* and the *Arabic,* with the *Anglo-Saxon,* add the word כל *col, all,*—ALL *the workers of iniquity;* which is the reading in the parallel place in Psa. xiv. It may be necessary to observe, that the *Chaldee,* in the *Antwerp* and *Paris Polyglots,* and in that of *Justinianus,* has not the word כל *col,* ALL.

Have not called upon God] אלהים *Elohim;* but many MSS. have יהוה *Yehovah,* LORD.

Verse 5. *For God hath scattered the bones of him that encampeth* against *thee: thou hast put them to shame, because God hath despised them.*] The reader will see, on comparing this with the fifth and sixth verses of Psa. xiv., that the words above are mostly *added* here to what is said *there;* and appear to be levelled against the *Babylonians,* who sacked and ruined Jerusalem, and who were now sacked and ruined in their turn. The sixth verse of Psa. xiv., "Ye have shamed the counsel of the poor, because the Lord is his refuge," is added here by more than twenty of *Kennicott's* and *De Rossi's* MSS.

Verse 6. *O that the salvation of Israel were come out of Zion!*] I have already shown that the proper translation is, "Who shall give from Zion salvation to Israel?" The word *salvation* is in the *plural* here, *deliverances:* but many MSS., with the *Septuagint, Vulgate, Arabic,* and *Anglo-Saxon,* have it in the *singular.*

When God bringeth back] *When Jehovah bringeth back,* is the reading of more than twenty of *Kennicott's* and *De Rossi's* MSS., with the *Septuagint, Syriac,* and *Chaldee,* and *Justinianus'* Polyglot Psalter.

For larger notes and an analysis, the reader is requested to refer to Psa. xiv.; and for a comparison of the two Psalms he may consult Dr. *Kennicott's* Hebrew Bible, where, under Psa. xiv., in the lower margin, the variations are exhibited at one view.

PSALM LIV

The psalmist complains that strangers were risen up against him to take away his life, 1–3; *expresses his confidence in God that he will uphold him, and punish his enemies,* 4, 5; *on which he promises to sacrifice to God,* 6; *he speaks of his deliverance,* 7.

To the chief Musician on Neginoth, Maschil, *A Psalm* of David, [a]when the Ziphims came and said to Saul, Doth not David hide himself with us?

A. M. cir. 2943
B. C. cir. 1061
Sauli, Regis
Israelitarum,
cir. annum
35

SAVE me, O God, by thy name, and judge me by thy strength.

2 Hear my prayer, O God; give ear to the words of my mouth.

3 For [b]strangers are risen up against me, and oppressors seek after my soul; they have not set God before them. Selah.

4 Behold, God *is* mine helper: [c]the LORD *is* with them that uphold my soul.

5 He shall reward evil unto [d]mine enemies: cut them off [e]in thy truth.

6 I will freely sacrifice unto thee: I will praise thy name, O LORD; [f]for *it is* good.

7 For he hath delivered me out of all trouble: [g]and mine eye hath seen *his desire* upon mine enemies.

[a]1 Samuel xxiii. 19; xxvi. 1——[b]Psalm lxxxvi. 14——[c]Psalm cxviii. 7——[d]Hebrew, *those that observe me;* Psa. v. 8——[e]Psa. lxxxix. 49——[f]Psa. lii. 9; c. 5; cvi. 1; cvii. 1; cxviii. 1, 29; cxxxv. 3; cxxxvi. 1; cxlv. 9——[g]Psa. lix. 10; xcii. 11

NOTES ON PSALM LIV

The title is, "To the chief Musician upon Neginoth, an instructive Psalm of David, when the Ziphites came to Saul, and said, Doth not David conceal himself among us?"

Ziph was a village in the southern part of Palestine. David having taken refuge in the mountains of that country, the Ziphites went to Saul, and informed him of the fact. Saul, with his army, immediately went thither, and was on one side of a mountain while David was on the other. Just when he was about to fall into the hands of his merciless pursuer, an express came to Saul that the Philistines had invaded Israel, on which he gave up the pursuit, and returned to save his country, and David escaped to En-gedi. See the account in 1 Sam. xxiii. 19-29. It is supposed to have been after this deliverance that he composed this Psalm. *Neginoth,* from נגן *nagan,* to *strike* or *play* on some kind of instrument, probably signifies *stringed instruments,* such as were played on with a *plectrum.*

Verse 1. *Save me, O God, by thy name*] Save me by *thyself* alone; so *name* here may be understood. The *name of God* is often *God himself.* David was now in such imminent danger of being taken and destroyed, that no human means were left for his escape; if God therefore had not interfered, he must have been destroyed. See the *introduction* above.

Verse 2. *Hear my prayer*] In his straits he had recourse to God; for from him alone, for the reasons alleged above. his deliverance must proceed.

Verse 3. *Strangers are risen up against me*] The *Ziphites.*

And oppressors] Saul, his courtiers, and his army.

They have not set God before them.] It is on *no religious account,* nor is it to accomplish any *end,* on which they can ask the *blessing* of God.

Selah.] This is true.

Verse 4. *Behold, God* is *mine helper*] This would naturally occur to him when he saw that Saul was obliged to leave the pursuit, and go to defend his territories, when he was on the very point of seizing him. God, whose providence is ever watchful, had foreseen this danger, and stirred up the Philistines to make this inroad just at the time in which Saul and his army were about to lay hands on David. Well might he then say, "Behold, God is mine helper."

Is *with them that uphold my soul.*] נפשי *naphshi,* my *life.* This may even refer to the *Philistines,* who had at this time made an inroad on Israel. God was even with his own enemies, by making them instruments to save the life of his servant.

Verse 5. *He shall reward evil*] Saul and his courtiers, instead of having God's approbation, shall have his curse.

Cut them off in thy truth.] Thou hast *promised* to save me; these have purposed to destroy me. Thy *truth* is engaged in my defence; they will destroy me if permitted to *live:* to save *thy truth,* and to accomplish its *promises, thou must cut them off.*

Verse 6. *I will freely sacrifice unto thee*] Or, *I will sacrifice nobly unto thee.* Not only with a *willing mind*, but with a *liberal hand* will I bring sacrifice unto thee.

For it is *good*] Thy *name* is *good;* it is descriptive of thy nature; full of goodness and mercy to man. And *it is good* to be employed in such a work: whoever worships thee in sincerity is sure to be a gainer. To him who orders his conversation aright, thou dost show thy salvation.

Verse 7. *For he hath delivered me*] Saul had now decamped; and was returned to save his territories; and David in the meanwhile escaped to En-gedi. God was most evidently the author of this deliverance.

Mine eye hath seen his desire *upon mine enemies.*] It is not likely that this Psalm was written after the *death of Saul;* and therefore David could not say that *he had seen his desire.* But there is nothing in the text for *his desire;* and the words might be translated, *My eye hath seen my enemies*—they have been *so near* that I could plainly discover them. Thus almost all the *Versions* have understood the text. *I have seen them,* and yet they were not permitted to approach me. God has been my Deliverer.

Analysis of the Fifty-fourth Psalm

There are *three parts* in this Psalm:—

I. David's prayer for help and salvation, ver. 1-3.

II. His confidence that he should have help, ver. 4, 5.

III. His *gratitude* and *obedience*, ver. 6, 7.

1. David's petition: 1. "Save me." 2. "Plead my cause." 3. "Hear my prayer." 4. "Give ear to my words." He is much in earnest; and yet does not desire his prayer to be heard unless his *cause be just.* If just, then let *God plead it.*

2. He produces *two* grounds upon which he petitions: 1. God's *name.* 2. God's *strength.* 1. He that calls on the name of the Lord shall be saved; I call: "Save me in thy name!" 2. Thou art a *powerful* God, able to do it: "Save me in thy strength."

The greatness of his danger causes him to urge his prayer.

1. His enemies were *strangers;* from whom no favour could be expected.

2. They were *violent oppressors*—formidable, cruel tyrants, from whom he could expect no mercy.

3. They were such as could be satisfied with nothing less than his blood: "They rise to seek after my life."

4. They had no *fear of God:* "They have not set God before them."

II. Notwithstanding they are all that I have already stated; and, humanly speaking, I have nothing but destruction to expect; yet I will not fear: because, 1. God is *with me.* 2. He is *against them.*

1. "God is my helper:" as he has promised, so he has done, and will do, to me.

2. "God is with them also who uphold my soul. Selah." *Behold this!*

But he opposes them who oppose me; is an enemy to them who are mine enemies.

1. "He shall reward evil" to such: of this being assured, he proceeds to imprecate.

2. Destroy thou them: "Cut them off in thy truth." Thou hast promised that it *shall be well with the righteous;* and that *snares, fire, and brimstone, shall be rained on the wicked.* Let God be true: *Fiat justitia; ruat cœlum, pereat mundus.* They *must be cut off.*

III. For such a mercy David promises not to be unthankful.

1. For this he would offer a *princely sacrifice:* "I will freely sacrifice."

2. He would praise the name of the Lord: "I will praise thy name."

For this he gives *two* reasons:—

1. That which *internally* moved him: "For it is good."

2. That which was *outwardly impulsive;* his *deliverance.* 1. His deliverance was great and effectual: "Thou hast delivered me out of all my trouble." 2. His danger was so *imminent* that, humanly speaking, there was no escape. The enemy was within sight who was bent on his destruction; yet *he* was delivered; and *they* were confounded. On these accounts it was right that he should sing praise, and offer sacrifice. To the grateful God is bountiful.

PSALM LV

David, in great danger and distress from the implacable malice of his enemies, calls on God for mercy, 1–5; *wishes he had the wings of a dove, that he might flee away, and be at rest,* 6–8; *prays against his enemies, and describes their wickedness,* 9–11; *speaks of a false friend, who had been the principal cause of all his distresses,* 12–14; *again prays against his enemies,* 15; *expresses his confidence in God,* 16–18; *gives a farther description of the deceitful friend,* 19–21; *encourages himself in the Lord, and foretells the destruction of his foes,* 22, 23.

To the chief Musician on Neginoth, Maschil, *A Psalm* of David

A. M. cir. 2981
B. C. cir. 1023
Davidis, Regis
Israelitarum,
cir. annum
33

GIVE ear to my prayer, O
God; and hide not thyself
from my supplication.
2 Attend unto me, and hear me:
I [a]mourn in my complaint, and make a noise;
3 Because of the voice of the enemy, because
of the oppression of the wicked: [b]for they cast
iniquity upon me, and in wrath they hate me.
4 [c]My heart is sore pained within me: and
the terrors of death are fallen upon me.
5 Fearfulness and trembling are come upon
me, and horror hath [d]overwhelmed me.
6 And I said, O that I had
wings like a dove! *for then*
would I fly away, and be at
rest.

A. M. cir. 2981
B. C. cir. 1023
Davidis, Regis
Israelitarum,
cir. annum
33

7 Lo, *then* would I wander far off, *and* remain in the wilderness. Selah.
8 I would hasten my escape from the windy
storm *and* tempest.
9 Destroy, O LORD, *and* divide their tongues:
for I have seen [e]violence and strife in the city.
10 Day and night they go about it upon the
walls thereof: mischief also and sorrow *are*
in the midst of it.

[a]Isaiah xxxviii. 14——[b]2 Samuel xvi. 7, 8; xix. 19——[c]Psalm cxvi. 3——[d]Hebrew, *covered me*——[e]Jeremiah vi. 7

NOTES ON PSALM LV

The *title*, "To the chief Musician upon Neginoth, *A Psalm* of David, giving instruction." This is the same as the preceding, which see.

Verse 1. *Give ear to my prayer*] The frequency of such petitions shows the great earnestness of David's soul. If God did not hear and help, he knew he could not succeed elsewhere; therefore he continues to knock at the gate of God's mercy.

Verse 2. *I mourn in my complaint*] בשיחי *besichi*, in my *sighing;* a strong *guttural* sound, expressive of the natural accents of sorrow.

And make a noise] I am in a *tumult*—I am strongly *agitated.*

Verse 3. *They cast iniquity upon me*] To give a colourable pretence to their rebellion, they charge me with horrible crimes; as if they had said: Down with such a wretch; he is not fit to reign. Clamour against the person of the sovereign is always the watch-word of *insurrection*, in reference to *rebellion.*

Verse 4. *The terrors of death are fallen upon me.*] I am in hourly expectation of being massacred.

Verse 5. *Fearfulness*] How natural is this description! He is in *distress;*—he *mourns;*—*makes a noise;*—*sobs* and *sighs;*—his *heart is wounded;*—he expects nothing but *death;*—this produces *fear;*—this produces *tremor*, which terminates in that *deep apprehension* of *approaching* and *inevitable ruin* that *overwhelms* him with *horror.* No man ever described a wounded heart like David.

Verse 6. *O that I had wings like a dove!*] He was so surrounded, so hemmed in on every side by his adversaries, that he could see no way for his escape unless he had wings, and could take flight. The *dove* is a bird of very rapid wing; and some of them passing before his eyes at the time, might have suggested the idea expressed here.

And be at rest.] Get a *habitation.*

Verse 7. *Would I wander far off*] He did escape; and yet his enemies were *so near*, as to *throw stones at him:* but he escaped beyond Jordan. 2 Sam. xvii. 22, 23.

A passage in the *Octavia* of SENECA has been referred to as being parallel to this of David. It is in the answer of *Octavia* to the *Chorus*, Acts v., ver. 914-923.

Quis mea digne deflere potest
Mala? Quæ lacrymis nostris quæstus
Reddet Aedon? cujus pennas
Utinam miseræ mihi fata darent!
Fugerem *luctus ablata meos*
Penna volucri, procul et cœtus
Hominum tristes *sedemque feram.*
Sola in vacuo nemore, et tenui
Ramo pendens, querulo possem
Gutture mœstum fundere murmur.

My woes who enough can bewail?
O what notes can my sorrows express?
Sweet Philomel's self e'en would fail
To respond with her plaintive distress.
O had I her wings I would fly
To where sorrows I ne'er should feel more,
Upborne on her plumes through the sky,
Regions far from mankind would explore.
In a grove where sad silence should reign,
On a spray would I seat me alone;
In shrill lamentations complain,
And in wailings would pour forth my moan.

J. B. CLARKE.

Verse 8. *The windy storm*] From the sweeping wind and tempest—Absalom and his party and the mutinous people in general.

Verse 9. *Destroy, O Lord*] *Swallow them up*—confound them.

Divide their tongues] Let his counsellors give opposite advice. Let them never agree, and let their devices be confounded. And the prayer was heard. Hushai and Ahithophel gave opposite counsel. Absalom followed that of *Hushai;* and *Ahithophel*, knowing that the steps advised by Hushai would bring Absalom's affairs to ruin, went and hanged himself. See 2 Sam. xv., xvi., and xvii.

Violence and strife in the city.] They have been concerting violent measures; and thus are full of contention.

Verse 10. *Day and night they go about*] This and the following verse show the state of Jerusalem at this time. Indeed, they exhibit a fair view of the state of any city in the beginning of an *insurrection.* The leaders are plotting continually; going about to strengthen their party, and to sow new dissensions by misrepresentation, hypocrisy, calumny, and lies.

A. M. cir. 2981
B. C. cir. 1023
Davidis, Regis
Israelitarum,
cir. annum
33

11 Wickedness *is* in the midst
thereof: deceit and guile depart
not from her streets.
12 [f]For *it was* not an enemy
that reproached me; then I could have borne
it: neither *was it* he that hated me *that* did
[g]magnify *himself* against me; then I would
have hid myself from him.
13 But *it was* thou, [h]a man mine equal, [i]my
guide, and mine acquaintance.
14 [k]We took sweet counsel together, *and*
[l]walked unto the house of God in company.
15 Let death seize upon them, *and* let them
[m]go down quick into [n]hell: for wickedness *is*
in their dwellings, *and* among them.
16 As for me, I will call upon
God; and the LORD shall save
me.
17 [o]Evening, and morning,
and at noon, will I pray, and cry
aloud: and he shall hear my voice.
18 He hath delivered my soul in peace from
the battle *that was* against me: for [p]there
were many with me.
19 God shall hear, and afflict them, [q]even
he that abideth of old. Selah. [r]Because
they have no changes, therefore they fear not
God.
20 He hath [s]put forth his hands against such
as [t]be at peace with him: [u]he hath broken his
covenant.
21 [v]*The words* of his mouth were smoother

A. M. cir. 2981
B. C. cir. 1023
Davidis, Regis
Israelitarum,
cir. annum
33

---

[f]Psa. xli. 9——[g]Psa. xxxv. 26; xxxviii. 16——[h]Heb. *a man according to my rank*——[i]2 Sam. xv. 12; xvi. 23; Psa. xli. 9; Jer. ix. 4——[k]Heb. *Who sweetened counsel*——[l]Psa. xlii. 4——[m]Num. xvi. 30——[n]Or, *the grave*——[o]Dan. vi. 10; Luke xviii. 1; Acts iii. 1; x. 3, 9, 30; 1 Thess. v. 17——[p]2 Chron. xxxii. 7, 8——[q]Deut. xxxiii. 27——[r]Or, *with whom* also there be *no changes, yet they fear not God*——[s]Acts xii. 1——[t]Psalm vii. 4——[u]Hebrew, *he hath profaned*——[v]Psalm xxviii. 3; lvii. 4; lxii. 4; lxiv. 3; Prov. v. 3, 4; xii. 18

Verse 12. It was *not an enemy*] It is likely that in all these *three* verses Ahithophel is meant, who, it appears, had been at the bottom of the conspiracy from the beginning; and probably was the first mover of the vain mind of Absalom to do what he did.

Verse 14. *Walked unto the house of God in company.*] Or with haste; for the rabbins teach that we should walk *hastily* TO the temple, but *slowly* FROM it.

Verse 15. *Let death seize upon them*] This is a prediction of the sudden destruction which should fall on the ringleaders in this rebellion. And it was so. *Ahithophel*, seeing his counsel rejected, *hanged* himself. *Absalom* was defeated; and, fleeing away, he was suspended by the hair in a tree, under which his mule had passed; and being found thus by Joab, he was despatched with *three darts;* and the *people* who espoused his interests were almost all cut off. They fell by the sword, or perished in the woods. See 2 Sam. xviii. 8.

Let them go down quick into hell] Let them go down alive into the pit. Let the earth swallow them up! And something of this kind actually took place. Absalom and his army were defeated; *twenty thousand* of the rebels were slain on the field; and *the wood devoured more people that day than the sword devoured*, 2 Sam. xviii. 7, 8. The words might be rendered, "Death shall exact upon them; they shall descend alive into sheol." And death did *exact* his debt upon them, as we have seen above.

Verse 16. *I will call upon God*] He foresaw his deliverance, and the defeat of his enemies, and therefore speaks confidently, "The Lord shall save me;" or, as the *Targum*, "The WORD of the Lord shall redeem me."

Verse 17. *Evening, and morning, and at noon, will I pray*] This was the custom of the pious Hebrews. See Dan. vi. 10. The Hebrews began their day in the *evening*, and hence David mentions the *evening first.* The rabbins say, Men should pray three times each day, because the day changes three times. This was observed in the primitive Church; but the times, in different places, were various. The old *Psalter* gives this a curious turn: "At *even* I sall tel his louing (*praise*) what tim Crist was on the Crosse: and at *morn* I sall schew his louing, what tim he ros fra dede. And sua he sall here my voyce at *mid day*, that is sitand at the right hand of his fader, wheder he stegh (*ascended*) at mid day."

Verse 18. *He hath delivered my soul*] My *life* he has preserved in perfect safety from the sword; *for there were many with me:* "for in many afflictions his WORD was my support."—*Targum.* Or David may refer to the *supernatural assistance* which was afforded him when his enemies were so completely discomfited.

Verse 19. *Because they have no changes*] At first Absalom, Ahithophel, and their party, carried all before them. There seemed to be a very general defection of the people; and as in their first attempts they suffered no *reverses*, therefore they feared not God. Most of those who have few or no afflictions and trials in life, have but little religion. They become sufficient to themselves, and call not upon God.

Verse 20. *He hath put forth his hands*] A farther description of Ahithophel. He betrayed his friends, and he broke his covenant with his king. He had agreed to serve David for his own emolument, and a stipulation was made accordingly; but while receiving the king's pay, he was endeavouring to subvert the kingdom, and destroy the life of his sovereign.

Verse 21. *Were smoother than butter*] He was a complete courtier, and a deep, designing hypocrite besides. His words *were as soft as butter, and as smooth as oil*, while he meditated war; and the fair words which were intended to *deceive*, were intended also to *destroy:* they *were drawn swords.* This is a literal description of the words and conduct of Absalom, as we learn from the inspired historian, 2 Sam.

A. M. cir. 2981
B. C. cir. 1023
Davidis, Regis
Israelitarum,
cir. annum
33

than butter, but war *was* in
his heart: his words were softer
than oil, yet *were* they drawn
swords.
22 [w]Cast thy [x]burden upon the LORD,
and he shall sustain thee: [y]he shall never
suffer the righteous to be
moved.
23 But thou, O God, shalt bring
them down into the pit of destruc-
tion: [z]bloody [a]and deceitful men [b]shall [c]not
live out half their days; but I will trust in thee.

A. M. cir. 2981
B. C. cir. 1023
Davidis, Regis
Israelitarum,
cir. annum
33

[w]Psa. xxxvii. 5; Matt. vi. 25; Luke xii. 22; 1 Pet. v. 7——[x]Or, *gift*——[y]Psa. xxxvii. 24——[z]Psa. v. 6

[a]Heb. *men of bloods and deceit*——[b]Heb. *shall not half their days*——[c]Job xv. 32; Prov. x. 27; Eccles. vii. 17

xv. 2, &c. He was accustomed to wait at the gate; question the persons who came for justice and judgment; throw out broad hints that the king was negligent of the affairs of his kingdom, and had not provided an effective magistracy to administer justice among the people; and added that if he were appointed judge in the land, justice should be done to all. He bowed also to the people, and kissed them; and thus *he stole the hearts of the men of Israel.* See the passages referred to above.

Verse 22. *Cast thy burden upon the Lord*] Whatever cares, afflictions, trials, &c., they may be with which thou art oppressed, lay them upon him.

And he shall sustain thee] He shall bear both thee and thy burden. What a glorious promise to a tempted and afflicted soul! God will carry both *thee* and thy *load.* Then cast *thyself* and *it* upon *him.*

He shall never suffer the righteous to be moved.] While a man is righteous, trusts in and depends upon God, he will never suffer him to be shaken. *While he trusts in God, and works righteousness,* he is as safe as if he were in heaven.

Verse 23. *But thou, O God, shalt bring them down into the pit of destruction*] The *Chaldee* is emphatic: "And thou, O Lord, by thy WORD (במימרך *bemeymerach*) shalt thrust them into the deep gehenna, the bottomless pit, whence they shall never come out; the *pit of destruction,* where all is amazement, horror, anguish, dismay, ruin, endless loss, and endless suffering."

Bloody and deceitful men shall not live out half their days] So we find, if there be an appointed time to man upon earth, beyond which he cannot pass; yet he may so live as to provoke the justice of God to cut him off *before* he arrives at that period; yea, before he has reached *half way* to that limit. According to the decree of God, he might have lived the *other half;* but he has not done it.

But I will trust in thee.] Therefore I shall not be moved, and shall live out all the days of *my* appointed time.

The fathers in general apply the principal passages of this Psalm to our Lord's sufferings, the treason of Judas, and the wickedness of the Jews; but these things do not appear to me fairly deducible from the text. It seems to refer plainly enough to the rebellion of Absalom. "The consternation and distress expressed in verses 4, 5, 6, 7, and 8, describe the king's state of mind when he fled from Jerusalem, and marched up the mount of Olives, weeping. The *iniquity cast upon the psalmist* answers to the complaints artfully laid against the king by his son of a negligent administration of justice: and to the reproach of *cruelty* cast upon him by Shimei, 2 Sam. xv. 2, 4; xvi. 7, 8. The *equal,* the *guide,* and the *familiar friend,* we find in *Ahithophel,* the confidential counsellor, first of David, afterwards of his son Absalom. The *buttery mouth* and *oily words* describe the insidious character of *Absalom,* as it is delineated, 2 Sam. xv. 5-9. Still the believer, accustomed to the double edge of the prophetic style, in reading this Psalm, notwithstanding its agreement with the occurrences of David's life, will be led to think of David's great *descendant,* who endured a bitter agony, and was the victim of a baser treachery, in the same spot where David is supposed to have uttered *these complaints."—Bishop Horsley.*

ANALYSIS OF THE FIFTY-FIFTH PSALM

There are *five* general parts in this *Psalm:*—

I. The psalmist entreats God to hear his prayer, ver. 1, 2.

II. He complains of his trouble, ver. 3-8.

II. He prays against his enemies, and shows the causes, ver. 8-15.

IV. He takes courage upon assurance of God's help, and his enemies' overthrow, ver. 15-21.

V. An epilogue, in which he exhorts all men to rely upon God, ver. 22, 23.

I. He begs audience.

1. "Give ear—hide not thyself—attend—hear me."

2. "My prayer—supplication—that I mourn—complain—make a noise." Affected he was with the sense of what he prayed for, and he was therefore earnest in it.

II. This in general; but next, in particular, he mentions the causes of his complaint, and earnestness to God, that he might be heard both in regard of his enemies, and the condition he was now in. The danger he was in was very great; escape he could not without God's help, for his enemies persecuted him very sore.

1. They slandered and calumniated him, and threatened him: "Because of the voice," &c.

2. They vexed, pressed upon him, and oppressed him: "Because of the oppression of the wicked."

3. They plotted his ruin, devolved, and *cast iniquity upon him*—charged him home.

4. They were implacable, angry, and hated him: "In wrath they hate me."

Then, as to his own person, he was in a sad, heavy, doleful condition.

1. "My heart is sore pained within me." His grief was inward.

2. "The terrors of death are fallen upon me." He saw nothing but death before him.

3. "Fearfulness and trembling are come upon me." Which are the outward effects of fear.

4. "And a horrible dread within hath overwhelmed me." Amazement followed his fear.

And he illustrates this his condition by the counsel he took with his own heart. Upon the deliberation the result was, that he would speedily fly away, fly into the wilderness, as if he might be safer among beasts than such men.

1. "And I said." That was the result upon his debate with himself.

2. "O that I had wings like a dove!" It is a fearful creature of a swift wing. In fear he was, and he would fly as fast and as far as the dove from the eagle.

3. As far, even to some remote land, where I should have rest from these wicked men.

And he amplifies and explains himself again:—

1. That he would fly far away, even to some desolate place out of their reach: "Lo, then would I wander far off, and remain in the wilderness."

2. That he would do it with speed: "I would hasten my escape from the windy storm and tempest." Such turbulent and impetuous creatures his enemies were that threw down all before them, as a wind, storm, and tempest.

III. To his prayer he adds an imprecation:—

1. "Destroy them, O Lord; destroy them in their own counsels."

2. Or else, "divide their tongue." Let them not agree in their counsels.

Of this he gives the reason in the following words: viz., that they were a band of violent, contentious, ungodly, troublesome, crafty, and fraudulent people.

1. Violent they were, and litigious: "I have seen violence and strife in the city."

2. Ungodly, and workers of iniquity they were; and incessant in it: "Day and night they go about it upon the walls thereof: mischief also and sorrow are in the midst of it."

3. Crafty and fraudulent also: "Deceit and guile depart not from her streets." It was then a city, a corporation, a society of evil doers.

And of this he produces an instance, which whether it were some bosom friend of *David* who stole out of the city of *Keilah*, and betrayed his counsels to *Saul;* or else *Ahithophel*, who, being formerly his great favourite and counsellor, fell to *Absalom*, it is uncertain. Whoever it was, such a treacherous person there was, and of him he complains: and well he might; for ουδεν μειζον ἑλκος η φιλος αδικων, "there is not a greater sore than a treacherous friend." This treachery he exaggerates most eloquently by an incrementum and apostrophe, drawing his aggravation from the laws of friendship, which he had broken. Had it been an enemy, he could have borne it; but that it was a friend was intolerable, and also inexcusable. Thus the climax stands:—

1. "For it was not an enemy that reproached me; then I could have borne it."

2. "Neither was it he that hated me that did magnify himself," that is, arise and insult me; "then I would have hid myself from him," never admitted him to my bosom.

But mark this emphatic adversative, for now he turns his speech to the man:—

1. "It was thou," emphatically *thou*, principally and beyond all others. None *but thou.*

2. "A man," according to my own rank, mine equal; my guide or counsellor; my acquaintance, my own familiar friend.

3. "We took sweet counsel together." One to whom I communicated my secrets.

4. "And walked unto the house of God in company." Professors we were of the same religion.

Now all these circumstances much heighten and aggravate the treachery: that thou, my equal, my director, my familiar friend, one whom I made the master of all my secrets, one who was a great professor of the same religion with me, that *thou* shouldst betray me, even break my heart. Συ τεκνον; *Judas—betrayest thou?*

Being thus much wronged and moved, as he had just reason, he begins again with an imprecation, not only on him, but on all who believed him, even upon the whole faction: "Let death seize upon them, and let them go down quick into hell," have *Korah, Dathan*, and *Abiram's* wages. And he adds the reason. They are signally and incorrigibly wicked: "For wickedness is in their dwellings, and among them."

IV. Hitherto hath *David* prayed, complained, imprecated; but now he shows how he recovered courage again, being certain of God's help, and a revenge to be taken on his enemies.

1. "As for me, I will call upon God fervently, and the Lord shall save me."

2. "Evening, and morning, and at noon-day," incessantly, "will I pray and cry aloud; and he shall hear me."

3. And I pray in faith; experience I have of his deliverance; he hath done it, and he will do it again. "He hath redeemed my soul in peace from the battle which was against me." Even in the midst of the battle, I was as safe as in a time of peace; miraculously delivered, as if there had been no danger.

4. "For there were many with me." *Many enemies*, say some; others, *many angels.* Those refer it to the danger; these, to the protection. Many enemies round about me, and then it is a wonder I should be delivered. Many angels press to help me, and then it was no wonder that my life was saved. But as for the ungodly, it was not so with them; for this *verse* is opposed to the former.

1. "God shall hear," viz., me and my prayers, and the wrongs they do me.

2. "And shall afflict them," i. e., my enemies.

3. "Even he that abideth of old. Selah." Mark that, for He is immutable. His power and strength is the same, and his care and love to his people; therefore, he will afflict them.

And, besides, there are those who will provoke him to it,—

1. Because "they have no changes." Obstinate they are, impertinent, and change not their ways. Or else they prosper, they have perpetual success, and meet with no alteration; this makes them secure and proud.

2. "They fear not God." They ask, "Who is the Lord, that we should let Israel go?"

3. They are truce-breakers, violators of oaths, leagues, covenants, articles of war. "He (that is, some chief commander among them) hath put forth his hands, made war, imbrued his hands in blood, against such as are at peace with him." He hath broken and profaned his covenant—his oath.

4. He is a gross hypocrite; his deeds answer not to his words: "The words of his mouth were smoother than butter, but war was in his heart; his words were softer than oil, yet they were drawn swords."

V. In the *epilogue* of the Psalm he exhorts good men to rely upon God: "Cast thy burden (the cares, troubles, &c., with which thou art loaded) on the Lord;" and he fits it to his present purpose, both as it concerns the godly and the ungodly.

1. To the godly he gives this comfort: 1. "He (that is, God) shall sustain thee." He will uphold thee, and give thee strength under the heaviest burdens. "Come unto me, all ye that are heavy laden." 2. "He shall never suffer the righteous to be moved." With the temptation he will also give the issue; pressed they may be, but not oppressed so as finally to be overthrown.

2. To the ungodly. 1. Overthrown they shall be, and utterly destroyed: "Thou, O God, shalt bring them down into the pit of destruction;" the grave—hell. 2. "Bloody and deceitful men shall not live out half their days." They come commonly to some untimely death, as *Absalom* and *Ahithophel*, concerning whom the Psalm was composed.

He concludes with the use he would make of it; as if he had said: Let these bloody and deceitful men repose their confidence in their armies, in their violence, in their crafty and subtle ways; I will take another course: "But I will trust in thee."

PSALM LVI

David prays for support against his enemies, whose wickedness he describes, 1–6; *and foretells their destruction,* 7; *expresses his confidence in God's mercy, expects deliverance, and promises thanksgiving and obedience,* 8–13.

XI. DAY. MORNING PRAYER

To the chief Musician upon Jonath-elem-rechokim, [a]Michtam of David, when the [b]Philistines took him in Gath

A. M. cir. 2942
B. C. cir. 1062
Sauli, Regis
Israelitarum,
cir. annum
34

BE [c]merciful unto me, O God; for man would swallow me up: he fighting daily oppresseth me.

2 [d]Mine enemies would daily
[e]swallow *me* up: for *they be*
many that fight against me, O
thou Most High.

A. M. cir. 2942
B. C. cir. 1062
Sauli, Regis
Israelitarum,
cir. annum
34

3 What time I am afraid, I will trust in thee.

4 [f]In God I will praise his word, in [g]God

[a]Or, *a golden* Psalm *of David;* so Psa. xvi.——[b]1 Sam. xxi. 11——[c]Psa. lvii. 1

[d]Heb. *Mine observers;* Psa. liv. 5——[e]Psa. lvii. 3
[f]Ver. 10, 11——[g]1 Chron. v. 20; Psa. v. 11; vii. 1; ix. 10

NOTES ON PSALM LVI

The *title* of this Psalm is very long: "To the conqueror, concerning the dumb dove in foreign places: golden Psalm of David." The *Vulgate* translates the original thus: "to the end. For the people who were afar off from holy things." "This inscription David placed here for a title when the Philistines took him in Gath;" so the *Septuagint* and *Æthiopic*. The *Chaldee* is profuse: "To praise, for the congregation of Israel, which are compared to the silence of a dove, when they were afar off from their cities; but being returned, they praise the Lord of the world; like David, contrite and upright, when the Philistines kept him in Gath." The *Syriac:* "A thanksgiving of the righteous man, because he was delivered from his enemy, and from the hand of Saul. Also concerning the Jews and Christ." *Bochart* translates, "To the tune of the dove in the remote woods."

If the title be at all authentic, David may mean himself and his companions by it, when he escaped from the hands of the Philistines; particularly from the hands of Achish, king of Gath. אלם *elem* signifies to *compress* or *bind together;* also, a *small band* or *body of men:* and יונת *yonath*, from ינה *yanah*, to *oppress* or *afflict*, is properly applied to the *dove*, because of its being so *defenceless*, and often becoming the *prey* of ravenous birds. It is possible, therefore, that the title may imply no more than—"A prayer to God in behalf of himself and the *oppressed band* that followed him, and shared his misfortunes in *distant places*."

Others will have it to mean a simple direction "To the master of the band, to be sung to the time of a well-known ode, called 'The dumb dove, in distant places.'" There is no end to conjectures, and all the *titles* in the whole book are not worth one hour's labour. Perhaps there is not one of them *authentic*. They may have been *notices* that such a Psalm was to be sung to *such and such a tune;* giving the *catch-words* of some well-known song or ode: a custom that prevails much among us in songs and hymns, and is to be found even among the Asiatics.

Verse 1. *Be merciful unto me*] I am assailed both at home and abroad. I can go nowhere without meeting with enemies: unless thou, who art the Fountain of mercy and the *Most High*, stand up in my behalf, my enemies will most undoubtedly prevail against me. *They fight against me continually*, and I am in the utmost danger of *being swallowed up* by them.

Verse 2. *O thou Most High.*] מרום *marom.* I do not think that this word expresses any attribute of God, or indeed is at all addressed to him. It signifies, literally, *from on high*, or *from a high* or *elevated place:* "For the multitudes fight against me from the high or elevated place;" the place of *authority*—the court and cabinet of Saul.

Most of the *Versions* begin the next verse with this word: "From the light of the day, though I fear, yet will I trust in thee." From the time that *persecution waxes hot against me*, though I often am seized with fear, yet I am enabled to maintain my trust in thee. Dr. *Kennicott* thinks there is a corruption here, and proposes to read: "I look upwards all the day long."

Verse 4. *In God I will praise his word*] באלהים *belohim* may mean here, *through God*,

A. M. cir. 2942 B. C. cir. 1062 Sauli, Regis Israelitarum, cir. annum 34

I have put my trust; [h]I will
not fear what flesh can do unto
me.
5 Every day they wrest my
words: all their thoughts *are* against me
for evil.
6 [i]They gather themselves together, they
hide themselves, they mark my steps, [k]when
they wait for my soul.
7 Shall they escape by iniquity? in *thine*
anger cast down the people, O God.
8 Thou tellest my wanderings: put thou
my tears into thy bottle: [l]*are they* not in thy
book?

9 When I cry *unto thee,* then
shall mine enemies turn back:
this I know; for [m]God *is*
for me.
10 [n]In God will I praise *his* word: in the
LORD will I praise *his* word.
11 In God have I put my trust: I will not
be afraid what man can do unto me.
12 Thy vows *are* upon me, O God: I will
render praises unto thee.
13 For [o]thou hast delivered my soul from
death: *wilt* not *thou deliver* my feet from
falling, that I may walk before God in [p]the
light of the living?

A. M. cir. 2942 B. C. cir. 1062 Sauli, Regis Israelitarum, cir. annum 34

---

[h]Psa. cxviii. 6; Isa. xxxi. 3; Heb. xiii. 6——[i]Psa. lix. 3; cxl. 2——[k]Psa. lxxi. 10

[l]Mal. iii. 16——[m]Rom. viii. 31——[n]Ver. 4——[o]Psa. cxvi. 8——[p]Job xxxiii. 30

---

or *by the help of God, I will praise his word.* And, that he should have cause to do it, he says, "In God I have put my trust," and therefore he says, "I will not fear what flesh can do unto me." Man is but FLESH, *weak* and *perishing;* God is an infinite SPIRIT, *almighty* and *eternal.* He repeats this sentiment in the *tenth* and *eleventh* verses.

Verse 5. *Every day they wrest my words*] They have been spies on my conduct continually; they collected all my sayings, and wrested my words out of their proper sense and meaning, to make them, by *inuendos,* speak treason against Saul. They are full of evil purposes against me.

Verse 6. *They gather themselves together*] They form cabals; have secret meetings and consultations how they may most effectually destroy me, under the pretence of justice and safety to the state.

They hide themselves] They do all secretly.

They mark my steps] They are constantly at my heels.

They wait for my soul.] They lie in wait for my *life.* Our translators have missed the meaning of נפש *nephesh* and ψυχε,—which generally signify the *animal life,* not the immortal spirit, —more than any other words in the Old or New Testament.

Verse 7. *Shall they escape by iniquity?*] Shall such conduct go unpunished? Shall their address, their dexterity in working iniquity, be the means of their escape? No. "In anger, O God, wilt thou cast down the people."

Verse 8. *Thou tellest my wanderings*] Thou seest how often I am obliged to *shift the place* of my *retreat.* I am hunted every where; but thou *numberest* all my *hiding-places,* and seest how often I am in danger of losing my life.

Put thou my tears into thy bottle] Here is an allusion to a very ancient custom, which we know long obtained among the *Greeks* and *Romans,* of putting the tears which were shed for the death of any person into small phials, called *lacrymatories* or *urnæ lacrymales* and offering them on the tomb of the deceased. Some of these were of *glass,* some of *pottery,* and some of *agate, sardonyx,* &c. A small one in my own collection is of *hard baked clay.*

Are they *not in thy book?*] Thou hast taken an exact account of all the tears I have shed in relation to this business; and thou wilt call my enemies to account for *every tear.*

Verse 9. *When I cry* unto thee, *then shall mine enemies turn back*] As soon as they know that I call upon thee, then, knowing that thou wilt hear and save, my enemies will immediately take flight. The cry of faith and prayer to God is more dreadful to our spiritual foes than the war-whoop of the Indian is to his surprised brother savages.

This I know] I have often had experience of the Divine interposition; and I know it will be so now, *for God is with me.* He who has *God* WITH *him* need not fear the face of any adversary.

Verses 10, 11. See on ver. 4, where the same words occur.

Verse 12. *Thy vows* are *upon me*] I have promised in the most solemn manner to be thy servant; to give my whole life to thee; and to offer for my preservation sacrifices of praise and thanksgiving.

Reader, what hast *thou vowed* to God? To renounce the devil and all his works, the pomps and vanities of this wicked world, and all the sinful desires of the flesh; to keep God's holy word and commandment, and to walk before him all the days of thy life. These things hast *thou vowed;* and these *vows* are *upon thee.* Wilt thou *pay* them?

Verse 13. *Thou hast delivered my soul from death*] My *life* from the *grave,* and my *soul* from *endless perdition.*

My feet from falling] Thou hast preserved me from taking any false way, and keepest me steady in my godly course; and so supportest me that I may continue to *walk before thee in the light of the living,* ever avoiding that which is evil, and moving towards that which is good; letting my light shine before men, that they may see my good works, and glorify my Father which is in heaven. *To walk before God* is to please him; the *light of the living* signifies the whole course of human life, with all its *comforts* and *advantages.*

Analysis of the Fifty-sixth Psalm

David, in banishment among the Philistines, and being then in great danger of his life, complains, and professes his confidence in God.

The contents of this Psalm are the following:—

I. David's *prayer*, ver. 1, 7, 8.

II. The *cause;* the fear of his enemies, whom he describes, ver. 1, 2, 5, 6.

III. His *confidence* in God's word, ver. 3, 4, 9, 10, 11.

IV. His *thankfulness*, ver. 4, 10, 12, 13.

I. He begins with a prayer for mercy. Little was he likely to find from man; from his God he expected it; and therefore he prays: "Be merciful unto me, O God."

II. And then presently he subjoins the *cause;* the danger he was in by his bloody and cruel enemies, whom he begins to describe:—

1. From their *insatiable rapacity*. Like a wolf they would *swallow me up*. Enemies at home and abroad would swallow me up.

2. From the *time*. Daily they would do it; without intermission.

3. From their *number:* "Many there be that fight against me."

Of these he gives us a farther description in the fifth and sixth verses:—

1. From their *incessant malice:* "Every day they wrest my words. All their thoughts are against me for evil."

2. From their *secret treachery*, *craft*, and *vigilance:* "They gather themselves together, they hide themselves;" their counsels lying, as it were, in ambush for me. "They mark my steps." Go where I will, they are at my heels.

3. From their *implacable hatred;* nothing could satisfy them but his blood: "They lay wait for my soul."

In the very midst of this complaint, he inserts his courage and confidence.

1. "What time I am afraid, I will trust in thee."

2. "I will not fear." He rises higher: even when he fears, he will not fear. His word, his promise, is passed to me for protection; and I will trust in it: "In God will I praise his word; in God have I put my trust, I will not fear what flesh, (for the proudest, the mightiest enemy I have, is but flesh, *and all flesh is grass,*) I will not then fear what flesh can do unto me."

This *reason* he repeats again, ver. 10, 11.

1. "In God I will praise his word; in the Lord I will praise his word."

2. "In God have I put my trust, I will not fear what man can do to me."

III. And this, his *confidence*, he quickens and animates,—

1. From his assurance that God would punish and bring down his enemies: "Shall they escape for their iniquity?" No, no; "in thine anger thou wilt cast them down."

2. From his *assurance* of God's *tutelage*, and paternal eye over him in all his dangers, griefs, complaints, petitions, and banishment.

Men think God does not meddle with little things: he knew otherwise.

1. "Thou tellest," and hast upon account, "my wanderings;" my flights, exile.

2. "Thou puttest my tears into thy bottle;" preservest them as rich wine.

3. Thou keepest a record for them: "Are they not in thy book?"

4. Thou puttest my enemies to flight: "When I cry unto thee, then I know mine enemies shall be turned back; for God is with me."

IV. And therefore, at last, he concludes with thanks, to which he holds himself bound by *vow*.

1. "Thy vows are upon me:" I owe thee thanks by vow, and I will pay them. "I will render praises unto thee."

2. The *reason* is, "For thou hast delivered my soul from death."

3. Thou wilt deliver me: "Wilt not thou deliver my feet from falling?"

4. The end is, "That I may walk before God in the light of the living." That I may live awhile, and walk as before thy eye; as in thy sight, uprightly, sincerely, and prosperously. That in me men may behold how powerfully thou hast saved both my body and soul.

PSALM LVII

David cries to God for mercy, with the strongest confidence of being heard, 1–3; *he describes his enemies as lions,* 4; *thanks God for his deliverance,* 5; *and purposes to publish the praises of the Lord among his people,* 6–11.

To the chief Musician, [a]Al-taschith, Michtam of David, [b]when he fled from Saul in the cave

A. M. cir. 2943 B. C. cir. 1061 Sauli, Regis Israelitarum, cir. annum 35

BE [c]merciful unto me, O God,
be merciful unto me: for
my soul trusteth in thee: [d]yea,
in the shadow of thy wings will
I make my refuge, [e]until *these* calamities be
overpast.
2 I will cry unto God most high; unto God
[f]that performeth *all things* for me.
3 [g]He shall send from heaven, and save me
[h]*from* the reproach of him that would [i]swal-
low me up. Selah. God [k]shall
send forth his mercy and his
truth.
4 My soul *is* among lions:
and I lie *even among* them that are set on
fire, *even* the sons of men, [l]whose teeth *are*
spears and arrows, and [m]their tongue a sharp
sword.
5 [n]Be thou exalted, O God, above the heavens; *let* thy glory *be* above all the earth.
6 [o]They have prepared a net for my steps;
my soul is bowed down: they have digged a

A. M. cir. 2943 B. C. cir. 1061 Sauli, Regis Israelitarum, cir. annum 35

[a]Or, *Destroy not, A golden* Psalm——[b]1 Sam. xxii. 1; xxiv. 3; Psa. cxlii. title——[c]Psa. lvi. 1——[d]Psa. xvii. 8; lxiii. 7——[e]Isa. xxvi. 20——[f]Psa. cxxxviii. 8 [g]Psa. cxliv. 5, 7

[h]Or, *he reproacheth him that would swallow me up* [i]Psa. lvi. 1——[k]Psa. xl. 11; xliii. 3; lxi. 7——[l]Prov. xxx. 14——[m]Psa. lv. 21; lxiv. 3——[n]Ver. 11; Psa. cviii. 5——[o]Psa. vii. 15, 16; ix. 15

NOTES ON PSALM LVII

The *title* is, *To the chief Musician, Al-taschith,* (destroy not,) *a golden Psalm of David,* (or one to be engraven,) *when he fled from Saul in the cave.* It is very likely that this Psalm was made to commemorate his escape from Saul in the cave of *En-gedi,* where Saul had entered without knowing that David was there, and David cut off the skirt of his garment. And it is not improbable that, when he found that Saul was providentially delivered into his hand, he might have formed the hasty resolution to take away his life, as his companions counselled him to do; and in that moment the Divine monition came, אל תשחת *al tascheth! Destroy not! lift not up thy hand against the Lord's anointed!* Instead, therefore, of taking away his *life,* he contented himself with taking away his *skirt,* to show him that he had been in his power. When, afterwards, he composed the Psalm, he gave it for *title* the words which he received as a Divine warning. See the history, 1 Sam. xxiv. See also my note upon the *fourth* verse of that chapter.

Verse 1. *Be merciful unto me*] To show David's deep earnestness, he repeats this *twice;* he was in great danger, surrounded by implacable enemies, and he knew that God alone could deliver him.

My soul trusteth in thee] I put my *life* into thy hand; and my *immortal spirit* knows no other portion than thyself.

In the shadow of thy wings] A metaphor taken from the brood of a hen taking shelter under her wings when they see a bird of prey; and there they continue to *hide themselves* till their *enemy disappears.* In a *storm,* or *tempest of rain,* the mother covers them with her wings to afford them shelter and defence. This the psalmist has particularly in view, as the following words show: "Until these calamities be overpast."

Verse 2. *I will cry unto God most high*] He is the *Most High;* and therefore far above all my enemies, though the *prince of the power of the air* be at their head.

Unto God, לאל *lael,* unto the *strong God,* one against whom no human or diabolic might can prevail. David felt his own *weakness,* and he knew the *strength* of his adversaries; and therefore he views God under those *attributes* and *characters* which were suited to his state. This is a great *secret* in the Christian life; few pray to God *wisely;* though they may do it *fervently.*

That performeth all things *for me.*] Who *works* for me; גמר *gomer,* he who *completes* for me, and will bring all to a happy issue.

Verse 3. *He shall send from heaven, and save me*] Were there no human agents or earthly means that he could employ, he would send his angels from heaven to rescue me from my enemies. Or, He will give his command from heaven that this may be done on earth.

Selah] I think this word should be at the *end* of the verse.

God shall send forth his mercy and his truth.] Here *mercy* and *truth* are personified. They are the *messengers* that God will send from heaven to save me. His *mercy* ever inclines him to help and save the distressed. This he has *promised* to do; and his *truth* binds him to fulfil the promises or engagements his mercy has made, both to saints and sinners.

Verse 4. *My soul* is *among lions*] בתוך לבאם *bethoch lebaim.* I agree with Dr. *Kennicott* that this should be translated, "My soul dwells in *parched places,*" from לאב *laab,* he thirsted. And thus the *Chaldee* seems to have understood the place, though it be not explicit.

I lie even among *them that are set on fire*] I seem to be among *coals.* It is no ordinary rage and malice by which I am pursued: each of my enemies seems determined to have my life.

Verse 5. *Be thou exalted, O God, above the heavens*] Let the glory of thy mercy and truth be seen in the heavens above, and in the earth beneath. Several of the fathers apply what is said above to the *passion* of our Lord, and what is said here to his *resurrection.*

Verse 6. *They have prepared a net for my steps*] A gin or springe, such as huntsmen put in the places which they know the prey they seek frequents: such, also, as they place in *passages in hedges,* &c., through which the game creeps.

They have digged a pit] Another method of catching game and wild beasts. They dig a pit, cover it over with weak sticks and turf.

A. M. cir. 2943
B. C. cir. 1061
Sauli, Regis
Israelitarum,
cir. annum
35

pit before me, into the midst
whereof they are fallen *themselves.* Selah.
7 [p]My heart is [q]fixed, O
God, my heart is fixed: I will sing and give
praise.
8 Awake up, [r]my glory: awake, psaltery
and harp: I *myself* will awake early.
9 [s]I will praise thee, O LORD,
among the people: I will sing
unto thee among the nations.
10 [t]For thy mercy *is* great
unto the heavens, and thy truth unto the
clouds.
11 [u]Be thou exalted, O God, above the
heavens: *let* thy glory *be* above all the earth.

[p]Psa. cviii. 1, &c.——[q]Or, *prepared*——[r]Psa. xvi. 9; xxx. 12; cviii. 1, 2

[s]Psa. cviii. 3——[t]Psa. xxxvi. 5; lxxi. 19; ciii. 11; cviii. 4——[u]Ver. 5

The beasts, not suspecting danger where none appears, in attempting to walk over it, fall through, and are taken. Saul digged a pit, laid snares for the life of David; and fell into one of them himself, particularly at the cave of *En-gedi;* for he entered into the very pit or cave where David and his men were hidden, and his life lay at the generosity of the very man whose life he was seeking! The rabbins tell a curious and instructive tale concerning this: "God sent a spider to weave her web at the mouth of the cave in which David and his men lay hid. When Saul saw the spider's web over the cave's mouth, he very naturally conjectured that it could neither be the haunt of *men* nor *wild beasts;* and therefore went in with confidence to repose." The *spider* here, a vile and contemptible animal, became the instrument in the hand of God of saving David's life, and of confounding Saul in his policy and malice. This may be a *fable;* but it shows by what apparently insignificant *means* God, the universal ruler, can accomplish the greatest and most beneficent *ends.* Saul continued to dig pits to entrap David; and at last fell a prey to his own obstinacy. We have a proverb to the same effect: *Harm watch, harm catch.* The *Greeks* have one also: Ἡ τε κακη βουλη τῳ βουλευσαντι κακιστη, "An evil advice often becomes most ruinous to the adviser." The *Romans* have one to the same effect:—

Neque enim lex justior ulla est
Quam necis artificem arte perire sua.

"There is no law more just than that which condemns a man to suffer death by the instrument which he has invented to take away the life of others."

Verse 7. *My heart is fixed*] My heart is *prepared* to do and suffer thy will. It is *fixed*—it has made the *firmest purpose* through his strength by which I can do all things.

Verse 8. *Awake up, my glory*] Instead of כבודי *kebodi,* "my glory," one MS., and the *Syriac,* have כנורי *kinnori,* "my harp." Dr. *Kennicott* reads כבורי *kebori,* which he supposes to be some instrument of music; and adds that the instrument used in church-music by the Ethiopians is now called כבר *kaber.* I think the *Syriac* likely to be the true reading: "Awake up, my harp; awake, psaltery and harp: I will awake early." Such *repetitions* are frequent in the Hebrew poets. If we read *my glory,* it may refer either to his *tongue;* or, which is more likely, to his *skill in composition,* and in *playing on different instruments.* The *five* last verses of this Psalm are nearly the same with the *five* first verses of Psa. cviii. The reason of this may be, the *notes* or *memoranda* from the *psalmist's diary* were probably, through mistake, twice copied. The insertion at the beginning of the cviiith Psalm seems to bear no relation to the rest of that ode.

Rabbi Solomon Jarchi tells us that *David had a harp at his bed's head, which played of itself when the north wind blew on it; and then David arose to give praise to God.* This account has been treated as a *ridiculous fable* by grave Christian writers. I would however hesitate, and ask one question: Does not the account itself point out an instrument then well known, similar to the comparatively lately discovered *Æolian harp?* Was not *this* the instrument hung at David's bed's head, which, when the night breeze (which probably blew at a certain time) began to act upon the cords, sent forth those dulcet, those heavenly sounds, for which the Æolian harp is remarkable? "Awake, my harp, at the *due time:* I will not wait for thee *now,* I have the strongest cause for gratitude; I will awake earlier than usual to sing the praises of my God."

Verse 9. *Among the people*] The *Israelites.*

Among the nations.] The *Gentiles* at large. A prophecy either relating to the Gospel times, Christ being considered as the Speaker: or a prediction that these Divine compositions should be sung, both in synagogues and in Christian churches, in all the nations of the earth. And it is so: wherever the name of Christ is known, there is David's known also.

Verse 10. *Thy mercy* is *great unto the heavens*] It is as far above all human description and comprehension as the heavens are above the earth. See the notes on Psa. xxxvi. 5, 6, where nearly the same words occur.

Verse 11. *Be thou exalted, O God, above the heavens*] The same sentiments and words which occur in verse 5. See the note there.

David was not only in a happy state of mind when he wrote this Psalm, but in what is called a state of *triumph.* His confidence in God was unbounded; though encompassed by the most ferocious enemies, and having all things against him except God and his innocence. David will seldom be found in a more blessed state than he here describes. Similar faith in God will bring the same blessings to every true Christian in similar circumstances.

ANALYSIS OF THE FIFTY-SEVENTH PSALM

The contents of this Psalm are,—

I. David's *petition,* ver. 1.

II. The *reasons* which induced him to offer it, ver. 2-6.

III. His *resolution* to give God due praise, ver. 5, 7-11.

I. His *petition* is ardent. The *repetition* shows this: it is for grace and protection: "Be merciful unto me, be merciful unto me, O God!"

II. He adduces his *reasons* to persuade the Lord to be merciful.

First reason. The faith and confidence he had in God: "My soul trusteth in thee; and under the shadow of thy wings," as the chicken does under those of the hen, "shall be my refuge until these calamities be overpast."

Second reason. The sufficiency and efficiency of God: "I will call upon God."

1. He is the *Most High;* then he is sufficient and able to deliver me.

2. He will perform all things for me: therefore he will effect this.

In the following verse he insists on this argument.

"He shall send from heaven." He will do it in a miraculous way, if there be no other way: "He will send from heaven, and save me. He will send forth his mercy and his truth;" he will *perform* his *word*, and *graciously* save me.

The *third reason* of his petition is the extreme danger he was then in by a cruel and merciless enemy.

1. "My soul is among the lions," a ravenous, strong, and bloody creature.

2. "I lie even among those who are set on fire." Their anger and hatred to me are implacable.

3. Even among those whose "teeth are spears and arrows, and their tongue a sharp sword." They wound by calumniating me. A *spear* wounds near; an *arrow*, afar off; a *sword*, at hand: *near* or *far off*, they spare not to disgrace me.

He now brings another *argument*, stronger than all the rest, viz., *God's glory.* It will be to his glory to be merciful, to save, and to deliver; and therefore he prays: "Be thou exalted, O God, above the heavens, and let thy glory," &c. That is, Let not the wicked triumph; but display thy power, and assert thy glory; which, if thou do, thy glory will be conspicuous *above*—in the heavens, and *below*—over all the earth.

He then begins his complaint, describing the practices of his enemies:—

1. "They have prepared a net for my feet." They lay *snares* as fowlers do.

2. Through which "my soul is bowed down." My life is in extreme danger.

3. "They have digged a pit before me;" intending to take me like some wild beast; but, praised be God I foresee the event. "They are fallen into the pit themselves."

III. In confidence of this David gives thanks, which may be considered a *fourth* argument; for there is no such way to procure a new favour as to be *thankful.* Our thanksgiving should consist of *two* especial points: 1. Commemoration; 2. Declaration.

1. He that will be thankful should treasure up in his *heart* and *memory* the kindness that is done to him. This David had done: "My heart is fixed, my heart is fixed."

2. After he remembers it, he should be *affected* by it, and *resolve* on it. So does David. My heart is *ready, prepared, fixed. I will* be thankful. I am *determined.*

3. It is not enough that a man have a thankful heart; he must *declare* it, and make publicly known what God has done for him: "I will sing, and give praise."

4. He should use all means in his power to make it known; *tongue, psaltery, harp,* are all little enough. To these he addresses himself: "Awake, tongue, lute, harp," &c.

5. He must not do it carelessly: "Awake! Awake! Myself will awake."

6. He must take the first opportunity, and not delay it: "I will awake EARLY."

7. He should do it in such a way as most tends to God's glory: "I will praise thee among the people—I will sing of thee among the nations."

That all this may be done, David gives a sufficient reason,—God's *mercy* and *truth.* His infinite *mercy* in *promising,* his *truth* in *performing:* "Thy mercy is great unto the heavens; thy truth unto the clouds."

And then he concludes with a repetition of the *fifth* verse: "Be thou exalted above the heavens, and thy truth unto the clouds." Let all give thee the glory due to thy name.

PSALM LVIII

David reproves wicked counsellors and judges, who pervert justice, and stir up the strong against the weak and innocent, 1–5. *He foretells their destruction, and describes the nature of it,* 6–9. *The righteous, seeing this, will magnify God's justice and providence,* 10, 11.

To the chief Musician, [a]Al-taschith, [b]Michtam of David

A. M. cir. 2943 B. C. cir. 1061 Sauli, Regis Israelitarum, cir. annum 35

DO ye indeed speak righteousness, O congregation? do ye judge uprightly, O ye sons of men?

2 Yea, in heart ye work wickedness; [c]ye weigh the violence of your hands in the earth.

3 [d]The wicked are estranged from the

[a]Or, *Destroy not, A golden* Psalm *of David*——[b]Psa. lvii. title

[c]Psa. xciv. 20; Isaiah x. 1——[d]Psalm li. 5; Isa. xliii. 8

NOTES ON PSALM LVIII

The *title* seems to have no reference to the subject of the Psalm. See the introduction to the preceding. Saul having attempted the life of David, the latter was obliged to flee from the court, and take refuge in the deserts of Judea. Saul, missing him, is supposed by Bishop

A. M. cir. 2943
B. C. cir. 1061
Sauli, Regis
Israelitarum,
cir. annum
35

womb: they go astray [e]as
soon as they be born, speaking
lies.
4 [f]Their poison *is* [g]like the
poison of a serpent: *they are* like [h]the
deaf [i]adder *that* stoppeth her
ear;
5 Which will not hearken to
the voice of charmers, [k]charming
never so wisely.

A. M. cir. 2943
B. C. cir. 1061
Sauli, Regis
Israelitarum,
cir. annum
35

[e]Heb. *from the belly*——[f]Psa. cxl. 3; Eccles. x. 11——[g]Heb. *according to the likeness*——[h]Jer. viii. 17——[i]Or, *asp*——[k]Or, be *the charmer never so cunning*

Patrick to have called a council, when they, to ingratiate themselves with the monarch, adjudged David to be guilty of treason in aspiring to the throne of Israel. This being made known to David was the cause of this Psalm. It is a good lesson to all kings, judges, and civil magistrates; and from it they obtain maxims to regulate their conduct and influence their decisions; and at the same time they may discern the awful account they must give to God, and the dreadful punishment *they* shall incur who prostitute justice to serve sinister ends.

Verse 1. *Do ye indeed speak righteousness*] Or, O cabinet, seeing ye profess to act according to the principles of justice, why do ye not give righteous counsels and just decisions, ye sons of men? Or, it may be an irony: What excellent judges you are! well do ye judge according to law and justice, when ye give decisions not founded on any law, nor supported by any principle of justice! To please your master, ye pervert judgment; and take part against the innocent, in order to retain your places and their emoluments. Saul's counsellors appear to have done so, though in their consciences they must have been satisfied of David's innocence.

Verse 2. *Yea, in heart ye work wickedness*] With their *tongues* they had spoken maliciously, and given evil counsel. In their *hearts* they meditated nothing but wickedness. And though in their *hands* they held the *scales of justice*, yet in their use of them they were *balances of injustice and violence*. This is the *fact* to which the psalmist alludes, and the *figure* which he uses is that of *justice with her scales* or *balances*, which, though it might be the emblem of the court, yet it did not prevail in the *practice* of these magistrates and counsellors.

Verse 3. *The wicked are estranged from the womb*] "This," says Dr. *Kennicott*, "and the next *two* verses, I take to be the answer of Jehovah to the question in the *two* first verses, as the 6th, 7th, and 8th, are the answer of the psalmist, and the remainder contains the decree of Jehovah." He calls these *wicked* men, men who had been always wicked, originally and naturally bad, and brought up in falsehood, flattery, and lying. The part they acted now was quite in character.

Verse 4. *Their poison* is *like the poison of a serpent*] When they bite, they convey poison into the wound, as the serpent does. They not only injure you by outward acts, but by their malevolence they poison your reputation. They do you as much evil as they can, and propagate the worst reports that others may have you in abhorrence, treat you as a bad and dangerous man; and thus, as the poison from the bite of the serpent is conveyed into the whole mass of blood, and circulates with it through all the system, carrying death every where; so their injurious speeches and vile insinuations circulate through society, and poison and blast your reputation in every place. Such is the *slanderer*, and such his influence in society. *From* such no reputation is safe; *with* such no character is sacred; and *against* such there is no defence. God alone can shield the innocent from the envenomed tongue and lying lips of such inward monsters in the shape of men.

Like the deaf adder that *stoppeth her ear*] It is a fact that cannot be disputed with any show of reason, that in ancient times there were persons that charmed, lulled to inactivity, or professed to charm, serpents, so as to prevent them from biting. See Eccles. x. 11; Jer. viii. 17. The prince of Roman poets states the fact, VIRG. Ecl. viii., ver. 71.

Frigidus in prati *cantando* rumpitur anguis.

"In the meadows the cold snake is burst by incantation."

The same author, Æn. vii., ver. 750, gives us the following account of the skill of Umbro, a priest of the Marrubians:—

Quin et *Marrubia* venit de gente sacerdos,
Fronde super galeam, et felici comptus oliva,
Archippi regis missu, fortissimus *Umbro;*
Vipereo generi, et graviter spirantibus *hydris*,
Spargere qui *somnos cantuque* manuque solebat,
Mulcebatque iras, et morsus arte levabat.

"*Umbro*, the brave *Marubian* priest, was there,
Sent by the *Marsian monarch* to the war.
The smiling olive with her verdant boughs
Shades his bright helmet, and adorns his brows.
His *charms* in peace the furious serpent *keep*,
And *lull the envenomed viper's race to sleep:*
His healing hand allayed the raging pain;
And at his touch the poisons fled again."
PITT.

There is a particular sect of the Hindoos who profess to bring serpents into subjection, and deprive them of their poison, by *incantation*. See at the end of this Psalm.

Verse 5. *Which will not hearken to the voice of charmers*] The old Psalter translates and paraphrases these two verses curiously:—

Vulg. Furor illis secundum similitudinem serpentis; sicut aspidis surdæ et obturantis aures suas: Quæ non exaudiet vocem incantantium et venefici incantantis sapienter.

Trans. **Wodnes** (madness) **til thaim aftir the liking of the neddir, as of the snake doumb and stoppand her eres.**

Paraph. Right calles he tham **wod,** (*mad,*) for thai hafe na witte to se whider thai ga: for thai louke thair eghen, and rennys till the are thaire wodness til clumsthed that wil noght be turned as of the snake that festis (*fastens*)

A. M. cir. 2943
B. C. cir. 1061
Sauli, Regis
Israelitarum,
cir. annum
35

6 [l]Break their teeth, O God, in
their mouth: break out the great
teeth of the young lions, O
LORD.
7 [m]Let them melt away as waters *which* run
continually: *when* he bendeth *his bow to shoot*
his arrows, let them be as cut in pieces.
8 As a snail *which* melteth, let *every one of*
them pass away; [n]*like* the untimely birth of
a woman, *that* they may not see the sun.
9 Before your pots can feel the
thorns, he shall take them away
[o]as with a whirlwind, [p]both living, and in *his* wrath.
10 [q]The righteous shall rejoice when he
seeth the vengeance: [r]he shall wash his feet
in the blood of the wicked.
11 [s]So that a man shall say, Verily *there is*
[t]a reward for the righteous: verily he is a
God that [u]judgeth in the earth.

A. M. cir. 2943
B. C. cir. 1061
Sauli, Regis
Israelitarum,
cir. annum
35

---

[l]Job iv. 10; Psa. iii. 7——[m]Josh. vii. 5; Psa. cxii. 10——[n]Job iii. 16; Eccles. vi. 3——[o]Prov. x. 25——[p]Heb. *as living as wrath*

[q]Psa. lii. 6; lxiv. 10; cvii. 42——[r]Psa. lxviii. 23——[s]Psa. xcii. 15——[t]Heb. *fruit of the*, &c.; Isa. iii. 10——[u]Psa. lxvii. 4; xcvi. 13; xcviii. 9

---

the ta ere til the erth, and the tother ere stoppis with hir taile: Sua do thai that thai here not Godis word; thai stope thair eris with luf of erthli thing that thai delite thaim in; and with thair taile, that es with all synnes, that thai will noght amend.

Trans. **The whilk salle noght here the voyce of charmand, and of the venim in akare of charmand wisli.**

Paraph. This snake stopis hir eres that she be noght broth to light; for if she herd it, she come forth sone, he charmes swa wysli in his craft. Swa the wikkid men wil noght here the voyce of Crist and his lufers that are wys charmes; for thi wild (*would*) bring them till light of heven. Wyt ye well (*know*) that he (i. e., *Christ*) lufes noght charmars and venim makers but be (*by*) vices of bestes, he takes lickening of vices of men.

It seems as if there were a species of *snake* or *adder* that is *nearly deaf;* and as their instinct informs them that if they listen to the sounds which charmers use they shall become a prey; therefore they stop their ears to prevent the little hearing they have from being the means of their destruction. To this the *Old Psalter* refers. We have also an account of a species of *snake*, which, if it cast its eye on the charmer, feels itself obliged to come out of its hole; it therefore keeps close, and takes care neither to *see* nor be *seen.* To this also the Old Psalter alludes; and of this *fact*, if it be one, he makes a good use.

Verse 6. *Break their teeth*] He still compares Saul, his captains, and his courtiers, to *lions;* and as a lion's power of doing mischief is greatly lessened if all his teeth be broken, so he prays that God may take away their power and means of pursuing their bloody purpose. But he may probably have the serpents in view, of which he speaks in the preceding verse: *break their teeth—destroy the fangs* of these serpents, in which *their poison* is contained. This will amount to the same meaning as above. Save me from the *adders*—the sly and poisonous slanderers: save me also from the *lions*—the tyrannical and blood-thirsty men.

Verse 7. *Let them melt away as waters*] Let them be minished away like the waters which sometimes run in the desert, but are soon evaporated by the *sun*, or absorbed by the *sand.*

When *he bendeth* his bow] When my adversaries aim their envenomed shafts against me, let their arrows not only fall short of the mark, but he broken to pieces in the flight. Some apply this to GOD. When he bends his bow against them, they shall all be exterminated.

Verse 8. *As a snail* which *melteth*] The *Chaldee* reads the verse thus: "They shall melt away in their sins as water flows off; as the creeping snail that smears its track; as the untimely birth and the blind mole, which do not see the sun."

The original word שבלול *shablul*, a *snail*, is either from שביל *shebil*, a *path*, because it leaves a *shining path* after it by emitting a portion of *slime*, and thus *glaring* the ground; and therefore might be emphatically called the *path-maker;* or from ישב *yashab* to *dwell*, ב *be*, *in*, לול *lul*, a *winding* or *spiral shell*, which is well known to be its house, and which it always *inhabits;* for when it is not coiled up within this shell, it carries it with it wheresoever it goes. See *Bochart.* These figures need no farther explanation.

Verse 9. *Before your pots can feel the thorns*] Ye shall be destroyed with a sudden destruction. From the time that the fire of God's wrath is kindled about you, it will be but as a moment before ye be entirely consumed by it: so very short will be the time, that it may be likened to the heat of the first blaze of dry thorns under a pot, that has not as yet been able to penetrate the metal, and warm what is contained in it.

A whirlwind] Or the suffocating *simoom* that destroys life in an instant, without previous warning: so, without *pining sickness*—while ye are *living*—lively and active, the whirlwind of God's wrath shall sweep you away.

Verse 10. *The righteous shall rejoice when he seeth the vengeance*] He shall have a strong proof of the Divine providence, of God's hatred against sinners, and his continual care of his followers.

He shall wash his feet in the blood of the wicked.] This can only mean that the slaughter would be so great, and at the same time so very nigh to the dwelling of the righteous, that he could not go out without dipping his feet in the blood of the wicked. The *Syriac*, *Vulgate*, *Septuagint*, *Æthiopic*, *Arabic*, and *Anglo-Saxon*, read *hands* instead of *feet.* Every thing that is *vindictive* in the Psalms must be considered as totally alien from the spirit of the Gospel, and not at all, under our dispensation, to be imitated. If the passage above be *really* vindictive, and it certainly will admit of the interpretation given above, it is to be considered as not belonging to that state in which the Son of man is come, not to *destroy* men's lives, but to *save*.

Verse 11. *So that a man shall say*] That is, people, seeing these just judgments of God, shall say, There is a reward (פרי *peri, fruit*) to the righteous man. He has not sown his seed in vain; he has not planted and watered in vain: he has the fruit of his labours, he eats the fruit of his doings. But wo to the wicked, it is ill with him; for the reward of his hands has been given him.

He is a God that judgeth in the earth] There is a God who does not entirely defer judgment till the judgment-day; but executes judgment now, even in this earth; and thus continues to give such a proof of his hatred to sin and love to his followers, that every considerate mind is convinced of it. And hence arise the indisputable maxims: "There is, even *here*, a reward for the righteous;" "There is a God who, even *now*, judgeth in the earth."

I have seen Indian priests who professed to charm, not only serpents, but the most ferocious wild beasts; even the enraged elephant, and the royal tiger! Two priests of *Budhoo*, educated under my own care, repeated the *Sanscrit incantations* to me, and solemnly asserted that they had seen the power of them repeatedly and successfully put to the test. I have mislaid these incantations, else I should insert them as a curiosity; for to *charms* of the same nature the psalmist most undoubtedly alludes.

The term חובר *chober*, which we translate *charmer*, comes from חבר *to join*, or *put together;* i. e., certain unintelligible words or sentences, which formed the *spell*.

I once met with a man who professed to remove diseases by pronouncing an unintelligible jingling jargon of words oddly tacked together. I met with him one morning proceeding to the cure of a horse affected with the *farcin*. With a very grave countenance he stood before the diseased animal, and, taking off his hat, devoutly muttered the following words; which, as a matter of peculiar favour, he afterwards taught me, well knowing that *I* could never use them successfully, *because not taught me by a woman;* "for," said he, "to use them with success, a *man* must be taught them by a *woman*, and a *woman* by a *man*." What the genuine orthography may be I cannot pretend to say, as I am entirely ignorant of the language, if the words belong to any language: but the following words exactly express his sounds:—

Murry fin a liff cree
Murry fin a liss cree
Ard fin deriv dhoo
Murry fin firey fu
Murry fin elph yew.

When he had repeated these words *nine* times, he put on his hat and walked off; but he was to return the next morning, and so on for *nine* mornings successively, always *before he had broken his fast*. The *mother* of the above person, a very old woman, and by many reputed a *witch*, professed to do miracles by pronouncing, or rather *muttering*, certain *words* or *sounds*, and by *measuring* with a cord the diseased parts of the sick person. I saw her practise twice: 1st, on a person afflicted with a violent headache, or rather the effects of a *coup de soleil;* and, 2ndly, on one who had got a dangerous mote or splinter in his eye. In the *first* case she began to measure the head, round the temples, marking the length; then from the vertex, under the chin, and so up to the vertex again, marking that length. Then, by observing the dimensions, passed judgment on the *want of proportion* in the two admeasurements, and said the brain was compressed by the sinking down of the skull. She then began her incantations, *muttering* under her breath a supplication to certain divine and angelic beings, *to come and lift up the bones, that they might no longer compress the brain.* She then repeated her admeasurements, and showed how much was gained towards a restoration of the *proportions* from the *spell* already *muttered.* The spell was again muttered, the *measurements* repeated, and at each time a comparison of the first measurement was made with the succeeding, till at last she said she had the due proportions; that the disease, or rather the *cause* of it, was removed; and that the operations were no longer necessary.

In the case of the *diseased eye*, her manner was different. She took a cup of clean pure water, and washed her mouth well. Having done so, she filled her mouth with the same water, and walked to and fro in the apartment (the patient sitting in the midst of the floor) *muttering* her *spell*, of which nothing could be heard but a *grumbling noise.* She then emptied her mouth into a clean white bason, and showed the motes which had been conveyed out of the patient's eye into the water in her mouth, while engaged in *muttering the incantation!* She proffered to teach me her wonder-working words; but the sounds were so very uncouth, if not barbarous, that I know no combination of letters by which I could convey the pronunciation.

Ridiculous as all this may appear, it shows that this incantation work is conducted in the present day, both in *Asia* and *Europe*, where it is professed, in precisely the same manner in which it was conducted formerly, by pronouncing, or rather *muttering certain words* or *sounds*, to which they attach *supernatural power* and *efficiency.* And from this came the term *spell:* Anglo-Saxon ꞅpell. a *word*, a *charm*, composed of such supposed *powerful words;* and **ƿyꞃcan ꞅpell** *wyrkan spell* signified among our ancestors *to use enchantments.*

Analysis of the Fifty-eighth Psalm

David deprecates the danger that hung over his head from Saul and his council.

The Psalm is divided into *three* parts:—

I. A sharp invective, or reprehension of his enemies, ver. 1.

II. An imprecation, or denunciation of God's judgment on them, ver. 6-9.

III. The benefits that from thence redound to the righteous, ver. 10, 11.

I. 1. David begins with an apostrophe, and figures it with an *erotesis*, which makes his reproof the sharper. 1. "O congregation;" O ye counsel of Saul. 2. "Do you indeed speak righteously?" 3. "Do ye judge uprightly, O ye sons of men?" By which he intimates that indeed they do neither.

2. Which in the next verse he affirms in plain terms, and brings home to their charge: "Yea, in heart you work wickedness; you weigh the violence of your hands in the earth;" heart and hand are bent to do evil, which the words, well considered, do exaggerate. 1. They were iniquities, a plurality of them. 2. It was their work. 3. Their hearty work. 4. Their handy work. 5. Weighed out by their scale of justice. 6. Which, indeed, under the colour of justice, was but violence. 7. And it was in this earth—in *Israel*, where no such thing was to be done.

3. This, their wickedness, he amplifies, both from their origin and progress:—

1. The root of it was very old; brought into the world with them: 1. "The wicked are estranged from the womb:" from God and all goodness. 2. "They go astray:" from their cradle they take the wrong way. 3. "As soon as they be born, speaking lies:" from their birth inclined to falsehood.

2. And in this their falsehood they are malicious and obstinate. 1. *Malicious.* The poison of their tongue is like the poison of a serpent, innate, deadly. 2. *Obstinate.* For they will not be reclaimed by any counsel or admonition: They are like the deaf adder that stoppeth her ear, which refuseth to hear the voice of the charmer, "charm he never so wisely."

II. Their wickedness, malice, and obstinacy, being so great, he now prays against and devotes them to God's judgment. He prays, in general, for their ruin, esteeming them no better than lions. Saul, the *old lion;* and his council, *lions' whelps.*

1. To God he turns his speech; and prays against their means to hurt, whether near or afar off.

2. And thence, against their persons: "O God, break their teeth in their mouth; break out the great teeth of the lions." O Lord, remove their strength; their nearest instruments to hurt, to destroy: "O God, when they purpose to harm us, let it be in vain; when he bends his bow to shoot his arrows, let them be as cut in pieces."

Thus let it fall to their arms: but as for their persons,—

1. "Let them melt away as waters." Great brooks, that run with great force from the mountains, and overrun for a little while the valleys; but run quickly into the channels, and thence to the sea, and are swallowed up.

2. Let them be *as a snail* that melts in her passage, and leaves a slimy track behind, which yet quickly passeth away. So let them be like a snail, which, when its shell is taken off, grows cold and dies.

3. Let them be "like the untimely fruit of a woman, that they may not see the sun."

4. "Before your pots can feel the thorns"—ere they do mischief, "He shall take them away as with a whirlwind, both living and in his wrath."

III. The *benefits* which, from his judgment upon the wicked, shall flow to the righteous.

1. Joyfulness: "The righteous shall rejoice when he seeth the vengeance."

2. Amendment. Being warned thus, "He shall wash his footsteps in their blood." Their slaughter shall be great; and he shall be near it, yet unhurt.

3. Confirmation of their faith, and giving glory to God: "So that a man shall say, Verily, there is a reward for the righteous: doubtless, there is a God that judgeth in the earth."

PSALM LIX

The psalmist prays for deliverance from his enemies, whose desperate wickedness he describes, 1–7; *professes strong confidence in God,* 8–10; *speaks of the destruction of his enemies,* 11–15; *praises God for benefits already received; and determines to trust in him,* 16, 17.

XI. DAY. EVENING PRAYER

To the chief Musician, [a]Al-taschith, [b]Michtam of David; [c]when Saul sent, and they watched the house to kill him

A. M. cir. 3559 B. C. cir. 445 Artaxerxis I., R. Persarum, cir. annum 20

DELIVER [d]me from mine
enemies, O my God: [e]defend me from them that rise up
against me.

2 Deliver me from the workers
of iniquity, and save me from
bloody men.

3 For, lo, they lie in wait for
my soul: [f]the mighty are gathered against
me; [g]not *for* my transgression, nor *for* my
sin, O LORD.

[a]Or, *Destroy not, A golden* Psalm *of David*——[b]Psa. lvii. title——[c]1 Sam. xix. 11

[d]Psa. xviii. 48——[e]Heb. *set me on high*——[f]Psa. lvi. 6 [g]1 Sam. cxiv. 11

NOTES ON PSALM LIX

The *title*, "To the chief Musician, Al-taschith, Michtam of David," has already occurred: and perhaps means no more than that the present Psalm is to be sung as Psa. lvii., the *first* which bears this title. But there is here added the supposed occasion on which David made this

A. M. cir. 3559
B. C. cir. 445
Artaxerxis I.,
R. Persarum,
cir. annum
20

4 They run and prepare themselves without *my* fault: [h]awake
[i]to help me, and behold.
5 Thou therefore, O LORD God
of hosts, the God of Israel, awake to visit all
the heathen: be not merciful to any wicked
transgressors. Selah.
6 [k]They return at evening; they make a
noise like a dog, and go round about the city.
7 Behold, they belch out with their mouth:
[l]swords *are* in their lips: for
[m]who, *say they,* doth hear?
8 But [n]thou, O LORD, shalt
laugh at them: thou shalt have
all the heathen in derision.
9 *Because of* his strength will I wait upon
thee: [o]for God *is* [p]my defence.
10 The God of my mercy shall [q]prevent
me: God shall let me see [r]*my desire* upon
[s]mine enemies.

A. M. cir. 3559
B. C. cir. 445
Artaxerxis I.,
R. Persarum,
cir. annum
20

[h]Psa. xxxv. 23; xliv. 23——[i]Heb. *to meet me*——[k]Ver. 14——[l]Psa. lvii. 4; Prov. xii. 18——[m]Psa. x. 11, 13; lxiv. 5; lxxiii. 11; xciv. 7——[n]1 Sam. xix. 16; Psa. ii. 4

[o]Verse 17; Psalm lxii. 2——[p]Heb. *my high place*——[q]Psa. xxi. 3——[r]Psa. liv. 7; xcii. 11; cxii. 8——[s]Heb. *mine observers;* Psa. lvi. 2

Psalm: it was, "when Saul sent, and they watched the house to kill him." When the reader considers the whole of this Psalm carefully, he will be convinced that the *title* does not correspond to the contents. There is scarcely any thing in it that can apply to the circumstances of Saul's sending his guards by night to keep the avenues to the house of David, that when the morning came they might seize and slay him; and of his being saved through the information given him by his wife Michal, in consequence of which he was let down through a window, and so escaped. See 1 Sam. xix. 10, 11. There is not in the whole Psalm any positive allusion to this history; and there are many things in it which show it to be utterly inconsistent with the facts of that history. The Psalm most evidently agrees to the time of Nehemiah, when he was endeavouring to rebuild the walls of Jerusalem, when the enterprise was first mocked; then opposed by Sanballat the Horonite, Tobiah the Ammonite, and Geshem the Arabian, who watched day and night that they might cause the work to cease; and laid ambuscades for the life of Nehemiah himself. Every part of the Psalm agrees to this: and I am therefore of *Calmet's* opinion, that the Psalm was composed in that time, and probably by *Nehemiah*, or by *Esdras*.

Verse 1. *Deliver me from mine enemies, O my God*] A very proper prayer in the mouth of Nehemiah, when resisted in his attempts to rebuild the walls of Jerusalem by Sanballat, Tobiah, and Geshem, who opposed the work, and endeavoured to take away the life of the person whom God had raised up to restore and rebuild Jerusalem. I conceive the Psalm to have been made on this occasion; and on this hypothesis alone I think it capable of consistent explanation.

Verse 2. *The workers of iniquity*] Principally Sanballat the Horonite, Tobiah the Ammonite, and Geshem the Arabian; who were the chief enemies of the poor returned captives.

Bloody men.] The above, who sought the destruction of the Israelites; and particularly, that of Nehemiah, whom *four* several times they endeavoured to bring into an ambush, that they might take away his life. See Neh. vi. 1-4.

Verse 3. *For, lo, they lie in wait for my soul*] For my *life.* See the passages referred to above.

Verse 4. *They run and prepare themselves*] They leave no stone unturned that they may effect my destruction and prevent the building.

Verse 5. *O Lord God of hosts*] This was a proper view to take of God, when Israel, a *handful* of poor distressed captives were surrounded and oppressed by the heathen chiefs above mentioned, and their several tribes. But Jehovah, *God of hosts*, was the *God of Israel;* and hence Israel had little to fear.

Be not merciful to any wicked transgressors.] Do not favour the cause of these wicked men. They are בגדי און *bogedey aven*, "changers of iniquity:" they go through the whole round of evil; find out and exercise themselves in all the *varieties of transgression.* How exactly does this apply to Nehemiah's foes! They sought, by open attack, wiles, flattery, foul speeches, fair speeches, threats, and ambuscades, to take away his life. Do not show them favour, that they may not succeed in their wicked designs. The prayer here is exactly the same in sentiment with that of Nehemiah, chap. iv. 4, 5. Hear, our God, for we are despised; turn their reproach upon their own heads;—cover not their iniquity, "and let not their sin be blotted out."

Verse 6. *They return at evening*] When the beasts of prey leave their dens, and go prowling about the cities and villages to get offal, and entrap domestic animals, these come about the city to see if they may get an entrance, destroy the work, and those engaged in it.

Verse 7. *They belch out with their mouth*] They use the lowest insult, the basest abuse. They deal in sarcasm, ridicule, slander, and lies.

Verse 8. *Thou, O Lord, shalt laugh at them*] They have mocked us; God will turn them and their schemes into ridicule and contempt: "Thou shalt have all these heathenish nations in derision."

Verse 9. Because of *his strength will I wait upon thee*] With this reading, I can make no sense of the passage. But instead of עזו *uzzo*, his strength," עזי *uzzi*, "*my* strength," is the reading of *fourteen* of *Kennicott's* and *De Rossi's* MSS., of the *Vulgate*, *Septuagint*, *Chaldee*, and, in effect, of the *Æthiopic*, *Syriac*, and *Arabic;* and also of the *Anglo-Saxon. To thee I commit all* MY *strength;* all I have I derive from thee, and all the good I possess I attribute to thee. The old Psalter translates, **My strenght I shall kepe till the, for myn uptaker thou art.** See on ver. 17.

Verse 10. *The God of my mercy shall prevent me*] The mercy of God shall go before me, and thus help me in all my doings.

God shall let me see my desire] The sentence is short. *God will let me see concerning my enemies*, i. e., how he will treat them.

A. M. cir. 3559
B. C. cir. 445
Artaxerxis I., R. Persarum, cir. annum 20

11 [t]Slay them not, lest my
people forget: scatter them by
thy power; and bring them
down, O LORD our shield.

12 [u]*For* the sin of their mouth *and* the
words of their lips let them even be taken in
their pride: and for cursing and lying *which*
they speak.

13 [v]Consume *them* in wrath, consume *them*,
that they *may* not *be*: and [w]let them know
that God ruleth in Jacob unto the ends of the
earth. Selah.

14 And [x]at evening let them
return; *and* let them make a
noise like a dog, and go round
about the city.

15 Let them [y]wander up and down [z]for
meat, [a]and grudge if they be not satisfied.

16 But I will sing of thy power; yea, I
will sing aloud of thy mercy in the morning:
for thou hast been my defence and refuge in
the day of my trouble.

17 Unto thee, [b]O my strength, will I sing: [c]for
God *is* my defence, *and* the God of my mercy.

---

[t]So Genesis iv. 12, 15——[u]Proverbs xii. 13; xviii. 7
[v]Psa. vii. 9——[w]Psa. lxxxiii. 18——[x]Ver. 6——[y]Job xv. 23; Psa. cix. 10

[z]Hebrew, *to eat*——[a]Or, *If they be not satisfied, then they will stay all night*——[b]Psalm xviii. 1——[c]Verses 9, 10

Verse 11. *Slay them not, lest my people forget*] I believe the Chaldee gives the true sense of this verse: "Do not slay them suddenly, lest my people should forget. Drive them from their habitations by thy power, and reduce them to poverty *by the loss* of their property." Preserve them long in a state of chastisement, that Israel may see thou hast undertaken for them: that thy hand is on the wicked for evil, and on them for good. The Canaanites were not suddenly destroyed; they were left to be pricks in the eyes and thorns in the sides of the Israelites. It is in a sense somewhat similar that the words are used here.

Verse 12. For *the sin of their mouth*] This verse has puzzled all the commentators. If we take חטאת *chattath* for *sin-offering* instead of *sin*, we shall get a better sense. Some of Nehemiah's enemies made a profession of the Jewish religion. Tobiah and his son were allied by marriage to the Jews; for Eliashib the priest had married his grandson to the daughter of *Sanballat;* and this produced a connexion with *Tobiah*, the fast friend of Sanballat. Besides, this very priest had given Tobiah one of the *great chambers in the house of the Lord*, where formerly the *meat-offerings*, *the frankincense*, *the vessels*, and *the tithe of the corn* and *wine* and *oil* were kept; Neh. xiii. 4, 5, 7, 8, 9. And there were *children of Tobiah* (probably the same family) who professed to be of the *Levites*, *Nethinim*, or *children of Solomon's servants;* but as they could not show *their father's house and their seed*, whether they were of Israel; these, and others which were children of the priests, were put out of the priesthood, and out of the sacred service, as polluted; as having sprung from intermarriages with heathens. See Ezra ii. 59, 60, 61, 62. Tobiah was expelled from the house of the Lord by Nehemiah, and all his household stuff thrown out of doors: Neh. xiii. 7, 8. And this was doubtless one ground of the enmity of Tobiah to Nehemiah; and in this verse of the Psalm he may allude particularly to his occupancy of the chamber of offerings, which offerings, instead of being given to the Levites, were consumed by Tobiah and his household. This may be fairly gathered from Neh. xiii. 5, 10, 11. Here then we have the *sin of their mouth;* their *eating* the offerings that belonged to the Levites; so that the temple service was deserted, the Levites being obliged to go and till the ground in order to obtain the means of life. And if we take חטאת *chattath* for *sin-offering*, it may refer to *promises* of sacrifice and offering which Tobiah and his family made, but never performed. They ate instead of offering them; and here was the *sin of their mouth*, in connexion with the *words of their lips*, and their *cursing and lying which they spake*, for which the psalmist calls upon the Lord *to consume them, that they may not* be, ver. 13.

Verse 14. *At evening let them return*] He had mentioned before, ver. 6, that these persons came like beasts of prey round the city striving to get in, that they might take possession. Now, being fully assured of God's protection, and that they shall soon be made a public example, he says, *Let them return and make a noise like a dog*, &c., like dogs, jackals, and other famished creatures, who come howling about the city-walls for something to eat, and wander up and down for meat, grumbling because they are not satisfied, ver. 15. Nehemiah had made up all the breaches; and had the city guarded so well day and night, by watches who continually relieved each other, that there was no longer any fear of being taken by surprise: and now they must feel like the hungry beasts who were disappointed of their prey.

Verse 16. *I will sing of thy power*] For it was because thy *hand* was upon me for good, that I have thus succeeded in my enterprises.

Yea, I will sing aloud of thy mercy] I shall publish abroad what thou hast done; and done not for *my worthiness*, nor for the *worthiness* of the *people;* but for thy own *mercy's* sake.

In the day of my trouble.] When I came with small means and feeble help, and had the force and fraud of many enemies to contend with, besides the corruption and unfaithfulness of my own people; *thou* wast then *my defence;* and in all attacks, whether *open* or *covered*, *my* sure *refuge*. I will, therefore, *sing of thy mercy in the morning*—I will *hasten* to acquit myself of a duty I owe to thee for such singular interpositions of mercy and power.

Verse 17. *Unto thee, O my strength*] A similar sentiment to that expressed, ver. 9. But the words are very emphatic: *God is my strength; God is my elevation. My God is my mercy.* I have nothing good but what I have from God. And all springs from his dwelling in me. God, therefore, shall have all the glory, both now and for ever.

As many persons may still think that the inscription to this Psalm is correct, the following analysis may be applied in that way; or considered as containing a general resolution of the Psalm, without referring it to any particular occasion.

Analysis of the Fifty-ninth Psalm

The contents of this Psalm are:—

I. The psalmist's prayer for deliverance, ver. 1, 2, and against his foes, ver. 5.

II. He complains of and expresses his enemies' cruelty and improbity, ver. 3-8.

III. He comforts himself, being confident of his own preservation, ver. 8-10.

1. And of their punishment, for which he prays, ver. 14.

2. And of their vain endeavours, for which he insults over them, ver. 14, 15.

IV. He concludes with thanks, ver. 16, 17.

I. He begins with a petition for deliverance, defence, salvation; and urges it from the qualities of his enemies.

1. "Deliver me, defend me from mine enemies:" 1. "Them that rise up against me." 2. "From the workers of iniquity." 3. "From bloody men." These considerations make him pray, "O my God, deliver," &c.

2. And yet, more particularly, he expresses their cruelty and treachery; to aggravate which he pleads his innocence towards them.

II. 1. Their cruelty: "Lo, they lie in wait for my soul."

2. Their treachery: "The mighty are gathered against me." They run and prepare themselves.

3. 1. They are diligent about it: "They return at evening." 2. *Mad*, and set to do it: "They make a noise like a dog," and threaten boldly. 3. Unwearied and obdurate in their purpose: "They go round about the city." 4. Impudent, and brag what they will do to me: "Behold, they belch out with their mouth." 5. And their words are bloody: "Swords are in their lips."

4. And the cause of this is, that they are proud and atheistical. *Who*, say they, *doth hear?* They think themselves secure, supposing they may contemn God and man; neither regarding what is done or becomes of poor *David*.

5. In the midst of which aggravations he asserts his own innocence: "They gather themselves together, not for my transgression, nor for my sin, O Lord."

Then he renews his petition:—

1. Awake to help me, and behold: "Thou, therefore, the Lord God of hosts, the God of Israel." 1. The Lord God of hosts; therefore, powerful. 2. The God of Israel; therefore, merciful.

2. "Awake to visit all the heathen," *i, e.*, punish the heathen; and the Israelites, in this no better.

3. And be not merciful to any wicked transgressors, *i. e.*, obstinate nations.

III. To this rage and implacable hatred of his enemies he now begins to oppose the comfort he had in God's promises. This I know,—

1. "Thou, O Lord, shalt laugh at them." As it were in sport, destroy them, be their power never so great: "Thou wilt laugh them to scorn."

2. Them and all that are like them: "Thou shalt have all the heathen in derision."

3. I confess that Saul's strength is great; but my Protector is greater: "Because of his strength will I wait upon thee, for God is my defence."

4. This I am assured also, "that the God of my mercy," that hath hitherto showed me mercy, "shall prevent me," come in season to my help. "And God shall let me see my desire upon mine enemies."

And to the 16th verse he expresses what his desires were:—

1. Negatively; he would not have them slain and eradicated; and he gives his reason for it: "Slay them not, lest my people forget;" for a dead man is quickly out of mind, and his punishment also, and few the better for it.

2. Positively; the first degree of which is dispersion, vagrancy, banishment. *Scatter them*, which however severe a judgment, let *the Jews* witness.

2. Humiliation: "Bring them down, O Lord, our shield." Bring them from their power, command, honour, to a low degree, which is no small heart-breaking to a great spirit. *Fuimus Troes*, is never remembered without a groan.

And now he assigns the cause why he would have them scattered, and brought low; that their blasphemies and lies may never be forgotten, but stand as a terror to all liars and blasphemers.

1. "For the sin of their mouth, and the words of their lips, let them even be taken in their pride;" the Jews cried Beelzebub, *nolumus hunc;* and they were taken.

2. "And for cursing and lying which they speak." They cursed themselves: "His blood be upon us;" and upon them, indeed, it was.

3. He goes on in his desires. "Consume them, O Lord," emphatically, "consume them in wrath, that they may not be;" which, at first sight, appears contrary to the first desire, "Slay them not:" but he speaks not of their life as if he would have it consumed; but he desires only a consumption of their power, royalty, command. And so these words are a farther explication of his second desire, "Bring them down." He would have them brought down in their strength, dignity, command, wealth, riches, which made them proud; that they might never be able to oppose God any more, hurt his people, trample upon religion and his Church; but he would have them live.

4. And shows the end why he would have them live, and still remain—that they might know by their calamities and miseries, that "it is God that ruleth in Jacob, and unto the ends of the earth;" that he doth wonderfully govern and preserve his Church that is scattered over all the earth.

5. And now by a bitter *epitrope*, or rather *synchoresis*, he insults over them. In the sixth verse he showed their double diligence to do mischief.

1. "They return at evening." Well, *esto;* be it so; "At evening let them return."

2. "They make a noise like a dog." Well; "let them make a noise like a dog."

3. "And go round about the city." Well; "let them go round about the city."

They know that they shall be in a miserable poor mean condition:—

1. "Let them wander up and down for meat." Let them find no settled habitation, but seek necessary food in a strange nation.

2. "And grudge if they be not satisfied." Let them be always grudging, if they have not con-

tent. If they be not satisfied, they will stay all night; be importunate and unmannerly beggars.

IV. The conclusion is a doxology, and contains David's thanks that *God is his defence*, his refuge, his strength. Of him, therefore, he makes his song.

1. "I will sing of thy power."

2. "I will sing of thy mercy." 1. "Aloud." 2. "In the morning."

3. The reason he gives: "For thou hast been my refuge and defence in the day of my trouble."

Both he repeats again:—

1. "Unto thee, O my strength, will I sing."

2. The reason: "For God is my defence, and the God of my mercy."

And he joins these two attributes, *strength* and *mercy*. Take away *strength* from him, and he cannot, remove *mercy*, and he will not, protect. Both must go together; *power* that he can, *mercy* that he will; otherwise it is in vain that we hope for help from him. David found God to be both, and for both he extols him.

PSALM LX

The psalmist complains of the desolations which had fallen on the land; prays for deliverance, 1–5; *and promises himself victory over Shechem, Succoth, Gilead, Ephraim, Moab, Idumea, and the Philistines, by the special help and assistance of God,* 6–12.

To the chief Musician [a]upon Shushan-eduth, [b]Michtam of David, to teach; [c]when he strove with Aram-naharaim and with Aram-zobah, when Joab returned, and smote of Edom in the valley of salt twelve thousand

A. M. cir. 3464
B. C. cir. 540
Olymp. LX.
cir. annum primum
A. U. C. cir. 214

O GOD, [d]thou hast cast us off,
thou hast [e]scattered us, thou
hast been displeased: O turn
thyself to us again.

2 Thou hast made the earth
to tremble; thou hast broken it:
[f]heal the breaches thereof; for it
shaketh.

3 [g]Thou hast showed thy people hard things:
[h]thou hast made us to drink the wine of
astonishment.

---

[a]Psa. lxxx. *title*——[b]Or, *A golden* Psalm——[c]2 Sam. viii. 3, 13; 1 Chron. xviii. 3, 12——[d]Psa. xliv. 9

[e]Heb. *broken*——[f]2 Chron. vii. 14——[g]Psa. lxxi. 20——[h]Isa. li. 17, 22; Jer. xxv. 15

NOTES ON PSALM LX

The title, "To the chief Musician upon the *hexachord*, or *lily of the testimony*, a golden Psalm of David, for instruction; when he strove with Aram Naharaim, Syria of the two rivers (Mesopotamia) and Aram-Zobah, Syria of the watchmen, (Cœlosyria,) when Joab returned, and smote twelve thousand Edomites in the Valley of Salt." I have only to remark here that there is nothing in the contents of this Psalm that bears any relation to this title. According to the title it should be a *song of victory and triumph;* instead of which the first part of it is a tissue of *complaints* of *disaster* and *defeat*, caused by the Divine desertion. Besides, it was not *Joab* that slew *twelve thousand* men in the *Valley of Salt;* it was *Abishai*, the brother of Joab; and the number *twelve thousand* here is not correct; for there were *eighteen thousand* slain in that battle, as we learn from 1 Chron. xviii. 12. The *valley of salt* or *salt pits* is in Idumea. To reconcile the difference between the numbers, various expedients have been hit on; but still the insuperable objection remains; the *contents* of this Psalm and this *title* are in opposition to each other. That the Psalm deplores a *defeat*, is evident from the three first and two last verses. And the *Targumist* seems to have viewed it in this light, perhaps the proper one, by expressing the title thus: "To give praise for the ancient testimony, (סהדותא *sahadutha*,) of the sons of Jacob and Laban, (see Gen. xxxi. 47,) an exemplar by the hand of David, to give instruction when he gathered together the people, and passed by the *heap of testimony*, (איגר סהדותא *ayegar sahadutha*,) and set the battle in array against Aram, which is by the Euphrates; and against Aram, which is by Izobah. And after this Joab returned and smote the Idumeans in the Valley of Salt; and of the armies of David and Joab there fell *twelve thousand* men." The Psalm, therefore, seems to deplore this disastrous event; for although they had the victory at last, *twelve thousand* of the troops of Israel were justly considered too great a sacrifice for such a conquest, and a proof that God had not afforded them that succour which they had long been in the habit of receiving. The latter part of the Psalm seems to be intended to put God in remembrance of his ancient promise of putting Israel in possession of the whole land by driving out the ancient iniquitous inhabitants. Others consider the Psalm as descriptive of the distracted state of the land after the fatal battle of Gilboa, till David was anointed king of the whole at Hebron.

This is the *last* of the *six Psalms* to which מכתם *michtam* is prefixed; the others are Psa. xvi., lvi., lvii., lviii., and lix. I have said something relative to this word in the introduction to Psa. xvi.; but some *observations* of Mr. Harmer lead me to consider the subject more at large. It is well known that there were *seven* most eminent Arabic *poets* who flourished *before* and at the commencement of the career of *Mohammed:* their names were *Amriolkais*,

A. M. cir. 3464 B. C. cir. 540 Olymp. LX. cir. annum primum A. U. C. cir. 214

4 [l]Thou hast given a banner
to them that feared thee, that it
may be displayed because of the
truth. Selah.

5 [k]That thy beloved may be
delivered; save *with* thy right
hand, and hear me.

6 God hath [l]spoken in his holi-

[l]Psa. xx. 5——[k]Psa. cviii. 6, &c. [l]Psa. lxxxix. 35

Amru, *Hareth*, *Tharafah*, *Zohair*, *Lebeid*, and *Antarah*. These poets produced *each a poem*, which because of its excellence was deemed worthy to be *suspended* on the walls of the *temple of Mecca;* and hence the collection of the seven poems was termed Al Moallakat, *The Suspended;* and Al Modhahebat, *The Gilded* or *Golden*, because they were written in *letters of gold* upon the Egyptian papyrus. The six *michtams* of David might have this title for the same reason; they might have been *written in letters of gold*, or on *gilded vellum*, or the *Egyptian papyrus;* for the word מכתם *michtam* is generally supposed to signify *golden*, and כתם *kethem* is used to signify *gold*, probably *stamped* or *engraven* with *figures* or *letters*. That the *Moallakat* were written in this way, there can be no question; and that the works of men of great eminence in Asiatic countries are still thus written, my own library affords ample evidence. Copies of the following works are written on paper all *powdered with gold, with gold borders, and highly illuminated anwans or titles:* The MISNAVI of *Jelaluddeen Raumy;* The DEEVAN of *Zuheer Faryabi;* The HADIKATUSANI, or *Garden of Praise;* The SUHBET AL ABRAR; The DEEVAN of *Hafiz;* GULISTAN of *Saady;* DEEVAN of *Shahy*, with many more, all works of eminent authors, written in the finest manner, ruled with gold borders, &c.

Copies of the *Koran* are often done in the same manner: one in 12mo., so thickly *powdered over with gold* that the *ground* on which the text is written appears to be almost *totally gilded;* another large *octavo, all powdered with gold*, and *golden flowers* down every margin; another small *octavo*, that might be almost called the *Codex Aureus*, with rich *golden borders* on every page. And, lastly, one in large *folio*, which besides superbly illuminated *anwans*, has *three gold lines in every page;* one at the *top*, one in the *middle*, and one at the *bottom*. To the above may be added a small *folio*, that opens out about *eleven feet*, every page of which is like a plate of solid gold, with the characters engraven on it. It is a *collection of elegant extracts*. Another of the *same kind*, large folio, opens out *sixty-two feet*, on which every page is finished in the same manner, with a vast variety of borders, sprigs, and flowers. And to close the whole, a copy of the *Borda*, supposed to be the most elegant MS. in Europe, entirely covered with *gold flowers* and *lines*, the writing the most perfect I ever saw; so that of this MS. it might be truly said, splendid as it is, *materiam superabit opus*.

As Mr. Harmer has alluded to accounts which he has collected from other writers in order to illustrate the *michtams* of David, I have above produced a number of *evidences* to bear witness to the *fact* that such is and such was the custom in the east, to write the works of the most eminent authors in *letters of gold*, or *on a page highly ornamented with the utmost profusion of golden lines, figures, flowers*, &c. In this way these Psalms might have been written, and from this circumstance they may have derived their name. I may just add, that I think these *titles* were made long after the Psalms were composed.

Verse 1. *O God, thou hast cast us off*] Instead of being our *general* in the battle, thou hast left us to ourselves; and then there was only the *arm of flesh* against the *arm of flesh*, numbers and physical power were left to decide the contest. We have been scattered, our ranks have been broken before the enemy, and thou hast caused the whole land to tremble at our bad success; the people are become divided and seditious. "Thou hast made the land to tremble, even the breaches of it, for it shaketh, it is all in commotion," ver. 2.

Verse 3. *Thou hast made us to drink the wine of astonishment*] We reel as *drunken* men; we are *giddy*, like those who have drank too much wine; but *our giddiness* has been occasioned by the *astonishment* and *dismay* that have taken place in consequence of the prevalence of our enemies, and the unsettled state of the land. It has been remarked that the *three first* verses of this Psalm do not agree with the rest, and it also appears that the *three first* verses of Psa. lxxxv. do not agree with the rest of *that* Psalm. But let them change places, and the three first verses of this be set instead of the three first verses of Psa. lxxxv., and let those be placed here instead of these, and then the whole of each Psalm will be consistent. This was first suggested by Bishop *Hare*, and the supposition seems to be well founded. Some imagine that the whole of the Psalm refers to the distracted state of the land after the death of Saul till the time that David was anointed king over all Israel, at Hebron; others, to the disastrous war with the *Syrians*. See before.

Verse 4. *Thou hast given a banner*] נס *nes*, a *sign*, something that was capable of being fixed on a pole.

That it may be displayed] להתנוסס *lehithnoses, that it may be unfurled*.

Because of the truth.] מפני קשט *mippeney koshet, from the face of truth;* which has been thus paraphrased: If we have displayed the *ensign of Israel*, and gone forth against these our enemies, who have now made such a terrible breach among us, (ver. 1-3,) it was *because of thy truth*—the *promises* of victory which we supposed would attend us at all times.

Mr. *Mudge*, thus: "Thou givest to them that fear thee a signal to be displayed before the truth. That thy favoured ones may be delivered, clothe thy right arm with victory, and answer us. God speaketh in his sanctuary, I will exult; I shall portion out Shechem, and measure the valley of Succoth." The *fourth* verse seems to mean that God had appointed for the consolation of his people a certain *signal* of favour, with which therefore he prays him to answer them. This, accordingly, he does. *God speaketh in his sanctuary*, called דביר *debir* or *oracle* for that very reason. What he desires

A. M. cir. 3464 B. C. cir. 540 Olymp. LX. cir. annum primum A. U. C. cir. 214

ness; I will rejoice, I will
[m]divide [n]Shechem, and mete
out [o]the valley of Succoth.
7 Gilead *is* mine, and Manas-
seh *is* mine; [p]Ephraim also *is* the strength
of mine head; [q]Judah *is* my lawgiver:
8 [r]Moab *is* my washpot; [s]over Edom will
I cast out my shoe: [t]Philistia, [u]triumph thou
because of me.
9 Who will bring me *into* the [v]strong
city? who will lead me into
Edom?
10 *Wilt* not thou, O God, *which*
[w]hadst cast us off? and *thou,* O
God, *which* didst [x]not go out with our armies?
11 Give us help from trouble: for [y]vain *is*
the [z]help of man.
12 Through God [a]we shall do valiantly:
for he *it is that* shall [b]tread down our
enemies.

A. M. cir. 3464 B. C. cir. 540 Olymp. LX. cir. annum primum A. U. C. cir. 214

[m]Josh. i. 6——[n]Gen. xii. 6——[o]Josh. xiii. 27——[p]See Deut. xxxiii. 17——[q]Gen. xlix. 10——[r]2 Sam. viii. 2 [s]Psa. cviii. 9; 2 Sam. viii. 14——[t]2 Sam. viii. 1——[u]Or, *triumph thou over me;* (by an irony;) see Psa. cviii. 10

[v]Heb. *city of strength;* 2 Sam. xi. 1; xii. 26——[w]Ver. 1; Psa. xliv. 9; cviii. 11——[x]Josh. vii. 12——[y]Psa. cxi. 8; cxlvi. 3——[z]Heb. *salvation*——[a]Num. xxiv. 18; 1 Chron. xix. 13——[b]Isa. lxiii. 3

then, as he stands imploring the mercy of God before the oracle, is, that he may see the *usual signal of favour* proceed from it; a *voice*, perhaps joined with some *luminous emanation*, whence the phrase of *the light of God's countenance*. The expression in the *sixth* verse seems to be proverbial, and means, "I shall divide the spoils of my enemies with as much ease as the sons of Jacob portioned out Shechem, and measured out for their tents the valley of Succoth." Mr. *Harmer* gives a very ingenious illustration of the *giving the banner*. "*Albertus Aquensis* informs us that when Jerusalem was taken in 1099 by the crusaders, about *three hundred* Saracens got on the roof of a very high building, and earnestly begged for quarter; but could not be induced by any *promises* of safety to come down, till they had received the *banner of Tancred,* one of the crusade generals, as *a pledge of life.* The event showed the faithlessness of these zealots, they put the whole to the sword. But the Saracens surrendering themselves upon the *delivering of a standard* to them, proves in how strong a light they looked upon the *giving a banner*, since it induced them to trust *it*, when they would not trust *any promises.* Perhaps the *delivery of a banner* was anciently esteemed in like manner an obligation to *protect;* and the psalmist might here consider it in this light when he says, *Thou hast shown thy people hard things;* but *thou hast given a banner to them that fear thee.* Though thou didst for a time give up thy Israel into the hands of their enemies, thou hast now given them an assurance of thy having received them under thy protection. Thus God *gave them a banner* or standard that it might be displayed, or *lifted up;* or rather, *that they may lift up a banner to themselves,* or encourage themselves with the confident persuasion that they are under the protection of God: *because of the truth*—the word of promise, which is an *assurance of protection*—like *the giving me and my people a banner*, the surest of pledges."—*Harmer's* Observations. See at the end of the chapter.

Verse 6. *God hath spoken*] Judah shall not only be re-established in Jerusalem, but shall possess Samaria, where *Shechem is*, and the country beyond Jordan, in which is situated the *valley of Succoth. Dividing* and *meting* out signify *possession.*

Verse 7. *Gilead* is *mine*] This country was also beyond Jordan, and *Manasseh* and *Ephraim* are put for the *tribes* that formed the kingdom of Israel. All these, after the return from the captivity, formed but one people, the Jews and Israelites being united.

The strength of mine head] It shall be the principal support of the new-found kingdom, when all distinctions shall be buried.

Judah is *my lawgiver*] This tribe was chief of all those who returned from the captivity; and *Zerubbabel,* who was their leader, was *chief of that tribe*, and of the *family of David.* As this part of the Psalm appears to relate to the return of the captives from Babylon, and their repossession of their own land, the psalmist may refer, not only to the promises of their restoration, but also to the principal person under whose superintendence they returned.

Verse 8. *Moab* is *my washpot*] The Moabites shall be reduced to the *meanest* slavery.

Over Edom will I cast out my shoe] I will make a complete conquest of Idumea, and subject the Edomites to the meanest offices, as well as the Moabites.

Philistia, triumph thou because of me.] John *Hyrcanus* subdued the Idumeans, and caused them to receive circumcision, and profess the Jewish religion. The words here seem to predict their entire subjugation.

In an essay for a new translation of the Bible, there is what appears to me a correct paraphrase of the *seventh* and *eighth* verses: "Gilead and Manasseh have submitted unto me; Ephraim furnishes me with valiant men, and Judah with men of prudence and wisdom. I will reduce the Moabites to servitude; I will triumph over the Edomites, and make them my slaves; and the Philistines shall add to my triumph."

Verse 9. *Who will bring me* into *the strong city?*] If this part of the Psalm, from the *sixth* to the *twelfth* verse, refer to *the return of the captives from Babylon*, as I think probable; then the *strong city* may mean either *Petra*, the capital of *Idumea; Bozra*, in Arabia, near the mountains of Gilead; *Rabba*, the capital of the Ammonites; or *Tyre*, according to the *Chaldee*, the capital of Phœnicia; or *Jerusalem* itself, which, although dismantled, had long been one of the strongest cities of the east. Or it may imply, Who shall give me the dominion over the countries already mentioned? who will lead me into Edom? who will give me the dominion over that people?

Verse 10. Wilt *not thou, O God*] It is God alone from whom we can expect our enlargement. He who has cast us off, and has abandoned us in battle; it is that very God alone from whom we expect complete enlargement, the repossession of our own land, and the subduction of the surrounding nations; and we expect this, because he has graciously *promised* these mercies.

Verse 11. *Give us help from trouble: for vain* is *the help of man.*] We have done all we can do, and have trusted too much in ourselves; now, Lord, undertake for us.

Verse 12. *Through God we shall do valiantly*] Through thee *alone* shall we do valiantly; thou *alone* canst tread down our enemies; and to thee *alone* we look for conquest.

The author to whom *Harmer* refers in the note on the *fourth* verse, is one of the writers in a work entitled *Gesta dei per Francos*, fol. Hanoviæ, 1611, 2 vols. And the places quoted by *Harmer* may be found in vol. i., p. 282; and as the passage is singular, and a good use has been made of it for the illustration of a difficult passage, I shall lay the words of the original before the reader: "Proxima ab hinc die sabbati clarescente, quidam Sarracenorum spe vitæ in summitatem tecti domus præcelsæ Solomonis ab armis elapsi, circiter trecenti, confugerant. Qui multa prece pro vita flagitantes, in mortis articulo positi, nullius fiducia aut promissione audebant descendere, *quousque vexillum Tankradi in signum protectionis vivendi susceperunt.* Sed minime misellis profuit. Nam plurimis super hoc indignantibus, et Christianis furore commotis, ne unus quidem illorum evasit."

It is very properly added by *Albertus*, that the noble spirit of *Tancred* was filled with indignation at this most horrible breach of faith; and he was about to take a summary revenge on the instigators and perpetrators of this unprincipled butchery, when the *chiefs* interposed, and not only maintained the expediency of the massacre that had already been committed, *but the necessity of putting all the inhabitants to the sword.* On this the savage fiends, called *Christians*, flew to arms, and made a universal slaughter of all that remained of the inhabitants. They drew out the prisoners, chopped off their heads, stabbed all they met with in the streets, and—but I can translate no farther; it is too horrible. I shall give my author's words, who was an ecclesiastic, and wrote down the account from eye-witnesses: "Concilio hoc accepto, (the determination of the *chiefs* to put all to the sword,) tertio die post victoriam egressa est sententia a *majoribus:* et ecce universi arma rapiunt, et miserabili cæde in omne vulgus Gentilium, quod adhuc erat residuum, exsurgunt, alios producentes e vinculis et decollantes: alios per vicos et plateas civitatis inventos trucidantes, quibus antea causa pecuniæ, aut humana pietate pepercerunt. Puellas vero, mulieres, matronas nobiles, et fætas cum puellis tenellis detruncabant, aut lapidibus obruebant, in nullis aliquam considerantes ætatem. E contra, puellæ, mulieres, matronæ, metu momentaneæ mortis angustiatæ et horrore gravissimæ necis concussæ Christianos in jugulum utriusque sexus debacchantes ac sævientes, medios pro liberanda vita amplexabantur, quædam pedibus eorum advolvebantur, de vita et salute sua illos nimium miserando fletu et ejulatu solicitantes. Pueri vero quinquennes aut triennes matrum patrumque crudelem casum intuentes, una miserum clamorem et fletum multiplicabant. Sed frustra hæc pietatis et misericordiæ signa fiebant: nam Christiani sic neci totum laxaverunt animum, ut non lugens masculus aut fæmina, nedum infans unius anni vivens, manum percussoris evaderet. Unde plateæ totius civitatis *Jerusalem* corporibus extinctis virorum et mulierum, lacerisque membris infantium, adeo stratæ et opertæ fuisse referuntur, ut non solum in vicis, soliis et palatiis, sed etiam in locis desertæ solitudinis copia occisorum reperiretur innumerabilis." Gesta Dei Vol. I., p. 283.

This is one specimen of the spirit of the crusaders, and is it any wonder that God did not shine on such villanous measures! No wonder that the Mohammedans have so long hated the name of *Christian*, when they had no other specimen of Christianity than what the conduct of these ferocious brutes exhibited; and these were called *Gesta Dei*, the *transactions* of God!

There are many difficulties in this Psalm; whether they are in general removed by the preceding notes, the reader must judge. The following analysis is constructed on the supposition that the Psalm speaks of the distracted state of the kingdom from the fatal battle of Gilboa, in which Saul fell, to the death of Ish-bosheth, when the whole kingdom was united under David.

Analysis of the Sixtieth Psalm

Before David's time, and in the beginning of his reign, Israel was in a distressed condition; he composed and quieted the whole. Edom only was not vanquished. In this Psalm he gives thanks for his victories, and prays for assistance for the conquest of Edom.

There are *three* general parts in this Psalm:—

I. A commemoration of the former lamentably distracted condition of the Israelites, ver. 1, 2, 3.

II. The condition of it under his reign much better, ver. 4-9.

III. His thankfulness in ascribing all his victories to God, ver. 9-12.

I. In the first he shows that God was angry with Israel. On which he laments the effects of his anger. 2. And then prays for the aversion: 1. "O Lord, thou hast (or hadst) cast us off." 2. "Thou hast scattered us abroad; thou hast been displeased." 3. "Thou hast made the earth to tremble." 4. "Thou hast broken it." 5. "Thou hast showed thy people hard things." 6. "Thou hast given us to drink the wine of astonishment." Every syllable of which *congeries* will appear to be most true when we examine the history of the Israelites before *Saul's* reign, under his government, and upon his death; and the first entrance of *David* upon his reign; his wars with the house of *Saul*, until *Ish-bosheth* was taken out of the way.

All which wars, civil and external, with the calamities that flowed from them, he imputes to God's anger: "Thou hast been displeased," ver. 1.

2. And upon it he prays: "O turn thee to us again." Let us again enjoy thy countenance. 2. "Heal the breaches of the land." Close the wounds made by these contentions: they were not closed; for it adds, "It shaketh."

II. And now the condition of it was much

better; all being brought under one king, and he victorious over his foreign enemies.

1. "Thou hast now given a banner to them that fear thee." All *Israel*—all those that are thy servants, are brought to acknowledge thee, and fight under one standard; in effect, have received me as their sole king, their factions and parties being quieted.

2. "That it may be displayed." Set up, that Israel may know under whom to fight, and whose part to take.

3. "Because of thy truth." Who by this hast made it appear that it was no fiction nor ambition of mine to set up this standard; but a *truth* that I was by *Samuel*, by thy special appointment, anointed to be king; and I am now invested with the crown for the performance of thy truth and promise.

4. And the end is especially, that I should bring deliverance to thy servants: it was that "thy beloved may be delivered." That the godly and good men, and those that fear thee, living hitherto oppressed, and in these distractions kept low, might be delivered.

5. Which, that it may be done, he inserts a short ejaculation for himself and them: "Save with thy right hand, and hear thou me." And now he begins to commemorate the *particulars* that God had done for him, and the several victories he had obtained; also, in what manner he ruled this people. All which he prefaces with this *oracle:*—

"God hath spoken in his holiness." He certainly and *truly* hath promised to save us: "I will be glad and rejoice in it." With much joy and gladness I will enter upon the kingdom, being confirmed by his promise, which I will administer in a different manner; my government shall be *paternal* to the *Israelites*, which are his people; but more severe to the *Moabites*, *Ammonites*, *Edomites*, and *Syrians*, because they are aliens to the commonwealth of *Israel.*

1. "I will divide Shechem, and mete out the valley of Succoth." I will bring under my power those places of Israel; and, as a true lord of them, I will *divide* and *measure out* what portions I shall think fit to the inhabitants.

2. "Gilead also is mine, and Manasseh is mine." The Israelites that followed the house of *Saul* are come into my power, and I will divide and apportion them also. Yet, as being mine, I will deal mildly with them.

3. Of *Ephraim* I shall make reckoning. Ephraim "shall be the strength of my head." As this tribe had more *men* than any other, so they were great *soldiers;* and these he esteemed as his *life-guard.*

4. "Judah is my lawgiver." His chief counsel were of this tribe, in whom, with himself, was the legislative power, according to the prophecy of Jacob: "The sceptre shall not depart from Judah, nor a lawgiver from between his feet, till Shiloh come." And thus, having showed his kingdom, and the administration over the Israelites, he passes to the *strangers* whom he had conquered, over whom he would carry a severe hand, putting them into a slavish subjection, and to base offices.

1. "Moab is my washpot." A servant to hold the bason, and to wash my feet.

2. "Over Edom I will cast my shoe." Trample on their necks.

3. "Philistia, triumph thou because of me:" which is either spoken ironically, as if he would say: "O Philistine, whom I have subdued, go, go triumph because I have conquered thee." Or else, "Triumph thou in the triumph I shall celebrate for my conquest; bear among the rest thy part, though unwillingly. Follow the train with acclamations, and proclaim me thy king."

III. After the enumerations of his victories, and form of government, that no man should take this for a vain boast of his own strength, he thankfully ascribes all the glory to God, both of which he had done, and what he was yet to do. One people he had yet to conquer; and that could not be done except that God, who had hitherto gone out with his armies, would again vouchsafe to lead them; and, therefore, he asks,—

1. "Who will bring me into the strong city? who will lead me into Edom?" No question, had *Joab*, *Abishai*, &c., or any of his worthies, been by, they would have striven who should have performed this service. Every one would have said, "I will be the man."

2. But he prevents them all; and returns this answer to himself, that none but God should do it, and that he was persuaded that he would do it; even that God who was formerly displeased with them, had cast them off, but was now reconciled: "Wilt not thou, O God, lead us into the strong city which hadst cast us off? and thou, O God, bring us into Edom, which didst not go forth with our armies."

3. And to that purpose he prays, "Give us help from trouble." And he adds his reason, that nothing can be well done without God's assistance; for the strength, power, prudence, and skill of man, without God, are to little purpose: "Vain is the help of man."

And he concludes all with this *epiphonema:* "In God we shall do great or valiant acts; for he it is that shall tread down our enemies." In war these two must be joined, and indeed in all actions. HE, *we;* GOD and *man.*

1. "We shall do valiantly," for God helps not remiss, or cowardly, or negligent men.

2. And yet, that being done, the work is *his:* "He shall tread down;" the blow and overthrow are not to be attributed to *us*, but to HIM.

PSALM LXI

The psalmist's prayer for those who were banished from their own land, and from the ordinances of God, 1, 2. *He praises God for his past mercies*, 3; *purposes to devote himself entirely to his service*, 4, 5. *He prays for the king*, 6, 7; *and promises to perform his vow to the Lord daily*, 8.

To the chief Musician upon Neginah, *A Psalm* of David

A. M. cir. 3468 B. C. cir. 536 Olymp. LXI. cir. annum primum A. U. C. cir. 218

HEAR [a]my cry, O God; attend unto my prayer.
2 From the end of the earth will I cry unto thee, when my heart is overwhelmed: lead me to the rock *that* is higher than I.
3 For thou hast been a shelter for me, *and* [b]a strong tower from the enemy.
4 [c]I will abide in thy tabernacle for ever: [d]I will [e]trust in the covert of thy wings. Selah.

A. M. cir. 3468 B. C. cir. 536 Olymp. LXI. cir. annum primum A. U. C. cir. 218

5 For thou, O God, hast heard my vows: thou hast given *me* the heritage of those that fear thy name.
6 [f]Thou [g]wilt prolong the king's life: *and* his years [h]as many generations.
7 He shall abide before God for ever: O prepare mercy [i]and truth, *which* may preserve him.
8 So will I sing praise unto thy name for ever, that I may daily perform my vows.

[a]1 Kings xviii. 37——[b]Prov. xviii. 10——[c]Psa. xxvii. 4——[d]Psa. xvii. 8; lvii. 1; xci. 4——[e]Or, *make my refuge*——[f]Psa. xxi. 4

[g]Heb. *thou shalt add days to the days of the king* [h]Heb. *as generation and generation*——[i]Psa. xl. 11; Prov. xx. 28

NOTES ON PSALM LXI

The *title, To the chief Musician upon Neginath*, נגינת. The verb נגן *nagan* signifies to *strike* or *play on a musical instrument*, especially one of the *stringed* kind; but the נגינות *neginoth*, as it is written in about *thirty* MSS., may signify either the *players* on the *instruments* or the *instruments* themselves. The Psalm appears to have been written about the close of the captivity; and the most judicious interpreters refer it to that period. On this supposition the notes are formed.

Verse 1. *Hear my cry, O God*] In the midst of a long and painful captivity, oppressed with suffering, encompassed with cruel enemies and isolent masters, I address my humble prayer to THEE, *O my God*.

Verse 2. *From the end of the earth*] ארץ *arets* should be here translated *land*, not *earth*, and so it should be in numerous places besides. But here it seems to mean the *country beyond the Euphrates;* as it is thought to do, Psa. lxv. 5, 8, called there also *the ends of the earth* or *land*. It may be remarked that the Jews were always more pious and devoted to God in their afflictions and captivities, than when in their own land, in ease and affluence. But who can bear prosperity? How many hearts filled with heavenly *ardour* in affliction and persecution have grown *cold* under the beams of the sun of prosperity!

Lead me to the rock that *is higher than I*.] Direct me to a place of refuge and safety. It is a metaphorical expression; and *Calmet* interprets it of the liberty granted to the Jews by Cyrus to return to their own land. This was a privilege far *higher* than any thing they could expect. The fathers think Jesus Christ is meant by this *high rock*.

Verse 3. *Thou hast been a shelter for me*] During the whole duration of the captivity God marvellously dealt with the poor Jews; so that, although they were cast down, they were not utterly forsaken.

Verse 4. *I will abide in thy tabernacle*] The greater portion of those Psalms which were composed during and after the captivity, says *Calmet*, had *Levites* and *priests* for their authors. Hence we find the ardent desire so frequently expressed of seeing the *temple;* of *praising God there;* of spending their lives in that place, performing the functions of their sacred office. There I *shall sojourn;*—there I *shall dwell,—be at rest,—be in safety,—be covered with thy wings*, as a bird in its nest is covered with the wings of its mother. These simple comparisons, drawn from rural affairs and ordinary occurrences, are more pleasing and consolatory in the circumstances in question, than allegories derived from subjects the most noble and sublime.

Verse 5. *Hast heard my vows*] Often have I purposed to be wholly thine,—to serve thee alone,—to give up my whole life to thy service: and thou hast heard me, and taken me at my word; and given me that heritage, the privilege of enjoying thee in thy ordinances, which is the lot of them that *fear thy name*. The Psalm seems to have been composed either after the captivity, or at the time that Cyrus published his decree in their favour, as has been remarked before.

Verse 6. *Thou wilt prolong the king's life*] The words are very emphatic, and can refer to no ordinary person. Literally, "Days upon days thou wilt add to the king; and his years shall be like the generations of this world, and the generations of the world to come." This is precisely the paraphrase I had given to this text before I had looked into the *Chaldee Version;* and to which I need add nothing, as I am persuaded no earthly king is intended: and it is Christ, as *Mediator*, that "shall abide before God for ever," ver. 7. Neither to David, nor to any earthly sovereign, can these words be applied.

Verse 7. *He shall abide before God for ever*] Literally, "He shall sit for ever before the faces of God." He shall ever appear in the presence of God for us. And he ever *sits at the right hand of the Majesty on high;* for he undertook this office after having, by his sacrificial offering, made atonement for our sins.

Prepare mercy and truth, which *may preserve him.*] As *Mediator*, his attendants will ever be *mercy* and *truth.* He will dispense the *mercy* of God, and thus fulfil the *truth* of the various promises and predictions which had preceded his incarnation. There is an obscurity in this clause, חסד ואמת מן ינצרהו *chesed veemeth man yintseruhu*, owing to the particle מן *man*, which some translate *who* or *what;* and others, *number thou*, from מנה *manah*, to count. *Houbigant*, and he is followed by Bishop *Lowth*, would read מיהוה *miyehovah*, *Mercy and truth from Jehovah shall preserve him.* The *Anglo-Saxon* has, **mildheortnysse ⁊ soþfæstnysse his, hwilc seceþ?** Mildheartedness, and soothfastness his, who seeketh? which is nearly the rendering of the old Psalter: **Mercy and sothfastnes of him, wha sall seke?** Dr. *Kennicott* says, מן *man* is a *Syriasm;* and should be translated *quæso-utinam*, I beseech thee,—I wish,—O that! On this very ground *Coverdale* appears to have translated, **O let thy lovynge mercy and faithfulnes preserve him!** The sense I have given above I conceive to be the true one.

Verse 8. *So will I sing praise unto thy name for ever*] For the benefits which I have received, and hope to receive endlessly from thee, I will to all perpetuity praise thee.

That I may daily perform my vows.] While I live, I shall יום יום *yom, yom*, "day by day," each day as it succeeds, render to thee my vows—act according to what I have often *purposed*, and as often *promised.* The Chaldee ends remarkably: "Thus I will praise thy name for ever, when I shall perform my vows in the day of the redemption of Israel; and in the day in which the King Messiah shall be anointed, that he may reign."

The *ancient Jews* were full of the expectation of the Messiah; the *Jews of the present day* have given up their *hope.*

Analysis of the Sixty-first Psalm

The author of this Psalm prays and vows perpetual service to God. It is composed of *two* parts:—

I. His prayer, ver. 1, 2, 3.

II. His vow, ver. 4-8.

He begins with a prayer, in which he begs,—

1. Audience: "Hear my cry, O God; attend unto my prayer," ver. 1.

2. The reason to enforce it.

1. He was in banishment, in the farther part of the land of Judah: "From the end of the earth will I cry unto thee."

2. He was in extremity: "When my heart is overwhelmed."

3. For defence: "Lead me to the rock that is higher than I;" that is, To some safe and defenced place to which my enemies may have no access, whither without thy help I cannot ascend.

And he adds a reason to this part of his prayer drawn from his own experience: "For thou hast been a shelter for me, and a strong tower from the enemy."

His faith now presents him as delivered; and, therefore, he *vows*,—

1. "I will abide in thy tabernacle for ever." I will return, and adore thee in thy temple.

2. "I will trust in the covert of thy wings." He alludes to the cherubim, whose wings cover the ark.

And for this he assigns many reasons also:—

1. "For thou, O God, hast heard my vows," i. e., my prayers.

2. "Thou hast given me the heritage of those that fear thy name;" made me king over thy people, and more fully performed to me the promise made to *Abraham*, in the land of Canaan.

3. "Thou wilt prolong the king's life."

4. "And his years," i. e., in his posterity, "as many generations;" of which the beginning of the next verse is the prediction. "He shall abide before God for ever."

And now David, assuring himself of the crown, and that his posterity should inherit it, puts forth an earnest vote for that which should establish it: "O prepare mercy and truth, which may preserve him; i. e., me thy king;" for these two *virtues*, *mercy*, i. e., *clemency*, and *truth*, do commend a king, and make him dear to his subjects; for in the practice of these it is not possible that his government should be harsh, unjust, or tyrannical.

Which if it please God to bestow upon him, then he makes a new vow: "So will I sing praise unto thy name for ever."

Though here this appears to be a new vow, yet he had vowed it before, and engaged to discharge; for in singing praise to God's name, he should but pay what by vow he had often undertaken: "I will sing praise unto thy name for ever, that I may daily perform my vows."

PSALM LXII

David, in imminent danger, flees to God for help and safety, 1, 2; *points out the designs of his adversaries*, 3, 4; *encourages his soul to wait on God*, 5–8; *shows the vanity of trusting in man, and of trusting in riches*, 9, 10; *and concludes with asserting that power and mercy belong to God, and that he will give to every man according to his works*, 11, 12.

XII. DAY. MORNING PRAYER

To the chief Musician, to [a]Jeduthun, A Psalm of David

A. M. cir. 2981 B. C. cir. 1023 Davidis, Regis Israelitarum, cir. annum 33

[b]TRULY [c]my soul [d]waiteth
upon God: from him *com-*
eth my salvation.
2 [e]He only *is* my rock and
my salvation; *he is* my [f]defence; [g]I shall
not be greatly moved.
3 How long will ye imagine mischief against
a man? ye shall be slain all of you: [h]as a
bowing wall *shall ye be, and as* a tottering
fence.
4 They only consult to cast *him* down from
his excellency: they delight in
lies: [i]they bless with their
mouth, but they curse [k]inwardly.
Selah.
5 [l]My soul, wait thou only upon God; for
my expectation *is* from him.
6 He only *is* my rock and my salvation: *he*
is my defence; I shall not be moved.
7 [m]In God *is* my salvation and my glory: the
rock of my strength, *and* my refuge, *is* in God.
8 Trust in him at all times; ye people, [n]pour
out your heart before him: God *is* [o]a refuge
for us. Selah.

A. M. cir. 2981 B. C. cir. 1023 Davidis, Regis Israelitarum, cir. annum 33

[a]1 Chron. xxv. 1, 3——[b]Or, *Only*——[c]Psa. xxxiii. 20——[d]Heb. *is silent;* Psa. lxv. 1——[e]Ver. 6——[f]Heb. *high place;* Psa. lix. 9, 17——[g]Psa. xxxvii. 24——[h]Isa. xxx.13

[i]Psalm xxviii. 3——[k]Hebrew, *in their inward parts*——[l]Ver. 1, 2——[m]Jer. iii. 23——[n]1 Sam. i. 15; Psa. xlii. 4; Lam. ii. 19——[o]Psa. xviii. 2

NOTES ON PSALM LXII

The *title*, "To the chief Musician, to Jeduthun," may mean that the Psalm was sent to him who was the chief or leader of the band of the family of Jeduthun. It appears that *Asaph, Jeduthun*, and *Heman*, were chief singers in the time of David; that they, with their families, presided over different departments of the vocal and instrumental worship in the tabernacle, 1 Chron. xxv. 1, &c.; that they were holy men, full of the Divine Spirit, (a thing very rare among singers and performers in these latter days,) and that *they prophesied with harps, with psalteries, and with cymbals;* that Jeduthun had *six* sons thus employed; that himself prophesied with a harp to give thanks and praise to God, ver. 3; and that the sons of Jeduthun were appointed by *lot* to the different courses. The *eighth* course fell to his son *Jeshaiah*, ver. 15; the *twelfth*, to *Hashabiah*, ver. 19; and the *fourteenth*, to *Mattithiah*, ver. 21.

Will our modern performers on instruments of music in churches and chapels, pretend to the *prophetic influence?* If they do not, and cannot, how dare they quote such passages in vindication of their practice, which can be no better than a dulcet noise without its original meaning, and alien from its primary use? Do they indeed *prophesy* with *harps*, and *psalteries*, and *cymbals?* or with their *play-house aggregate* of fiddles and flutes, bass-viols and bassoons, clarionets and kettle-drums? Away with with such trumpery and pollution from the worship and Church of Christ!

Though it is not very clear from the Psalm itself on what occasion it was composed, yet it is most likely it was during the rebellion of Absalom; and perhaps at the particular time when David was obliged to flee from Jerusalem.

Verse 1. *Truly my soul waiteth upon God*] I do not think that the original will warrant this translation, אך אל אלהים דומיה נפשי *ak el Elohim dumiyah naphshi*, "Surely to God only is my soul dumb." I am subject to God Almighty. He has a right to lay on me what he pleases; and what he lays on me is much less than I deserve: therefore am I *dumb* before God. The *Vulgate*, and almost all the Versions, have understood it in this sense: Nonne Deo subjecta erit anima mea? Shall not my soul be subject to God? In other words, God alone has a right to dispose of my *life* as he pleases.

Verse 2. *I shall not be greatly moved.*] Having God for my *rock*—strong fortified place, for my *salvation*—continual safety, and my *defence*—my elevated tower, which places me out of the reach of my enemies; *I shall not be greatly moved*—I may be *shaken*, but cannot be *cast down*.

Verse 3. *How long will ye imagine mischief*] The original word, תהותתו *tehothethu*, has been translated variously; *rush upon, rage against, stir yourselves up, thrust against:* the root is התת *hathath* or התה *hathah, to rush violently upon, to assault.* It points out the disorderly riotous manner in which this rebellion was conducted.

As a bowing wall—a tottering fence.] Ye are just ready to fall upon others, and destroy them; and in that fall yourselves shall be destroyed: "Ye shall be slain the whole of you."

Verse 4. *To cast* him *down from his excellency*] They are consulting to dethrone me, and use treachery and falsehood in order to bring it about: "They delight in lies."

They bless with their mouth] Probably alluding to Absalom's blandishments of the people. He flattered them in order to get the sovereign rule. Or it may refer to the people of Jerusalem, whose perfidy he saw, while they were full of professions of loyalty, &c.; but he could not trust them, and therefore retired from Jerusalem.

Verse 5. *Wait thou only upon God*] There is none but him in whom thou canst safely trust; and to get his help, resign thyself into his hands; be subject to him, and be silent before him; thou hast what thou hast deserved. See on ver. 1.

Verse 7. *In God* is *my salvation*] על אלהים *al Elohim*, "Upon God is my salvation;" he has taken it *upon himself*. *And my glory*—the preservation of my *state*, and the safety of my *kingdom*.

Verse 8. *Trust in him—ye people*] All ye who are faithful to your king, continue to trust in God. The usurper will soon be cast down, and your rightful sovereign restored to his

A. M. cir. 2981
B. C. cir. 1023
Davidis, Regis
Israelitarum,
cir. annum
33

9 [p]Surely men of low degree
are vanity, *and* men of high degree *are* a lie: to be laid in the
balance, they *are* [q]altogether
lighter than vanity.
10 Trust not in oppression, and become not
vain in robbery: [r]if riches increase, set not
your heart *upon them.*

[p]Psa. xxxix. 5, 11; Isa. xl. 15, 17; Rom. iii. 4——[q]Or, *alike*——[r]Job xxxi. 25; Psa. lii. 7; Luke xii. 15; 1 Tim. vi. 17——[s]Job xxxiii. 14——[t]Rev. xix. 1——[u]Or, *strength*

11 God hath spoken [s]once;
twice have I heard this;
that [t]power [u]*belongeth* unto
God.
12 Also unto thee, O LORD, *belongeth* [v]mercy:
for [w]thou renderest to every man according to
his work.

A. M. cir. 2981
B. C. cir. 1023
Davidis, Regis
Israelitarum,
cir. annum
33

[v]Psa. lxxxvi. 15; ciii. 8; Dan. ix. 9——[w]Job xxxiv. 11; Prov. xxiv. 12; Jer. xxxii. 19; Ezek. vii. 27; xxxiii. 20; Matt. xvi. 27; Rom. ii. 6; 1 Cor. iii. 8; 2 Cor. v. 10; Eph. vi. 8; Col. iii. 25; 1 Pet. i. 17; Rev. xxii. 12

government. Fear not the threatenings of my enemies, for *God will be a refuge for us.*

Verse 9. *Men of low degree* are *vanity*] בני אדם *beney Adam,* which we here translate *men of low degree,* literally, *sons of Adam,* are put in opposition to בני איש *beney ish, men of high degree,* literally, the *sons of substance,* or children of substantial men. *Adam* was the name of the first man when formed out of the *earth; Ish* was his name when united to his wife, and they became one flesh. *Before,* he was the *incomplete* man; *after,* he was the *complete* man; for it seems, in the sight of God, it requires the male and female to make one *complete human being.* אנוש *enosh* is another name given to man; but this concerns him in his low, fallen, wretched estate: it properly signifies *weak, poor, afflicted, wretched man.*

Common men can give no help. They are *vanity,* and it is folly to trust in them; for although they may be *willing,* yet they have no *ability* to help you: "Rich men are a lie." They promise much, but perform nothing; they cause you to *hope,* but mock your *expectation.*

To be laid in the balance] במאזנים לעלות *bemozenayim laaloth, In the balances they ascend:* exactly answerable to our phrase, *they kick the beam.*

They are *altogether* lighter *than vanity.*] Literally, *Both of them united are vanity,* המה מהבל יחד *hemmah mehebel yachad.* Put both together in one scale, and *truth* in the opposite, and both will kick the beam. They weigh nothing, they avail nothing.

Verse 10. *Trust not in oppression*] Do not suppose that my unnatural son and his partisans can succeed.

Become not vain in robbery] If ye have laid your hands on the spoils of my house, do not imagine that these ill-gotten riches will prosper. God will soon scatter them to all the winds of heaven. All oppressors come to an untimely end; and all property acquired by injustice has God's curse on it.

Verse 11. *God hath spoken once*] God has *once* addressed his people in giving the law on Mount Sinai. The *Chaldee* translates the whole passage thus: "God hath spoken one law, and twice have we heard this from the mouth of Moses the great scribe, that strength is before God: and it becomes thee, O God, to show mercy to the righteous; for thou renderest to man according to his works."

Twice have I heard this] Except some of the *ancient* Versions, almost every version, translation, and commentary has missed the sense and meaning of this verse. I shall set down the text: אחת דבר אלהים שתים זו שמעתי *achath dibber Elohim; shetayim zu shamati;* of which the true version is this: *Once hath God spoken; these two things have I heard.* Now what are the *two things* he had heard? 1. כי עז לאלהים *ki oz lelohim,* "That strength is the Lord's;" that is, He is the *Origin* of *power.* 2. ולך אדני חסד *ulecha Adonai, chased;* "and to thee, Lord, is mercy;" that is, He is the *Fountain* of *mercy.* These, then, are the *two* grand truths that the *law,* yea, the whole *revelation* of God, declares through every page. He is the *Almighty;* he is the *most merciful;* and hence the *inference:* The powerful, just, and holy God, the most merciful and compassionate Lord, *will* by and by *judge the world,* and *will render to man according to his works.* How this beautiful meaning should have been unseen by almost every interpreter, is hard to say: these verses contain one of the most instructive truths in the Bible.

ANALYSIS OF THE SIXTY-SECOND PSALM

The intent of this Psalm is to teach men to trust in God; and not to trust in wealth, or strength, nor in the power or promise of men.

It may be divided into the *five* following parts:—

I. David's confidence in God, ver. 1, 2.

II. The mischievous but vain attempts of his enemies, ver. 3, 4.

III. He encourages himself and others in the same confidence, ver. 5-9.

IV. That no trust is to be put in men, nor riches, ver. 9, 10.

V. The grounds of our confidence in God, ver. 11, 12.

I. In the first verses David expresses, or rather labours to express, as appears by his frequent repetition of the same thing in divers words, his trust, hope, and confidence in God:—

1. "Truly, my soul waiteth upon God." I acquiesce in his will.

2. "From him comes my salvation." If I be *safe* in my greatest troubles, it is from him.

3. "He only is my rock, and my salvation; he is my defence so that I shall not greatly be moved." He is to me what a rock or tower of defence is to such as flee to them.

II. And upon this he infers that the mischievous attempts of his bitterest adversaries are but vain; with them he expostulates; them he checks, and over them he insults.

1. "How long will ye imagine mischief against a man?" i. e., *me*. He chides their obstinacy.

2. "Ye shall be slain all of you;" and their ruin he declares by a double similitude; "Ye shall be as a bowing wall;" whence when some stones begin to start out or fall, the rest follow: or *as a tottering fence*, that is easily thrown down.

Next, by the description of their manners, he intimates the cause of their ruin.

1. "They only consult to cast him down from his excellency;" their counsel is to destroy David.

2. "They delight in lies;" invent lies and tales to destroy him.

3. Flatterers and dissemblers are they: "They bless with their mouth but they curse inwardly;" no wonder then, if destined to the slaughter, "if they be as a broken wall," &c.

III. And lest his heart faint and fail through the multitude of temptations, he first encourages himself to be confident still. Secondly, persuades others to do so.

1. He encourages himself, making use of the words of the first and second verses for reasons: "My soul, wait thou only upon God; for my expectation is from him: he only is my rock, and my salvation; he is my defence, I shall not be moved. In God is my salvation, and my glory; the rock of my strength, and my refuge, is in God."

2. He exhorts others to do the like: "Trust in him, ye people," which he amplifies:—

1. By assignation of the time: "Trust in him at all times:" in prosperity, that he be not secure; in adversity, that he be not heartless.

2. And in our saddest occasions he shows what is to be done, that we bring our grievances and complaints before God, and with an honest heart open them: "Pour out your heart (that is, the griefs of your hearts) before him."

3. Adding this reason: "God is a refuge for us."

IV. So are not other things; whether, 1. *Men*. 2. *Wealth*, especially unjustly got.

1. Not men; there is no credit or trust to be put in them of *any degree*. 1. "Surely men of low degree are vanity," 2. "And men of high degree are a lie." The *low* are not *able;* the *high deceive* our hopes.

"Put them into the balance; they are altogether lighter than vanity." Make trial of them, as of things in a scale, and you shall find them so vain and light that they carry no proportion to what is weighty, but ascend as an empty scale.

2. Nor *wealth*, nor *riches;* especially if unjustly heaped together: "Trust not in oppression, and become not vain in robbery: if riches increase, set not your heart upon them."

V. In the *close*, he sets down the grounds of his confidence, taken upon God's word: "God hath spoken; twice have I heard the same;" or, "I have heard these two things:"—

1. "That power belongs to God;" and therefore he is to be trusted.

2. "That mercy belongs to God;" and therefore, also, you may have the utmost confidence in him.

The consequence of both is, "Thou renderest to every one according to his works," bonis vera, malis mala: rely upon him. *Bad* work cannot have *good* wages; *good* work cannot have *bad* wages. "What a man soweth, that shall he also reap." "The righteous shall inherit glory, but shame shall be the promotion of fools." A man may deserve hell by a wicked life; but he cannot merit heaven by a good life because he cannot do good but through the grace of God, and the merit of the work belongs to the grace by which it was wrought. Reader, hear God's sentence on this subject: "The *wages* of sin is death." This is desert. "But the *gift* of God is eternal life." Here is no desert, for it is "by Jesus Christ our Lord." To him be glory for ever. Amen.

PSALM LXIII

David's soul thirsts after God, while absent from the sanctuary, and longs to be restored to the Divine ordinances, 1, 2. *He expresses strong confidence in the Most High, and praises him for his goodness,* 3–8; *shows the misery of those who do not seek God,* 9, 10; *and his own safety as king of the people,* 11.

A Psalm of David, [a]when he was in the wilderness of Judah

A. M. cir. 2943
B. C. cir. 1061
Sauli, Regis
Israelitarum,
cir. annum
35

O GOD, thou *art* my God; early will I seek thee: [b]my soul thirsteth for thee, my flesh longeth for thee in a dry and [c]thirsty land, [d]where no water is;

2 To see [e]thy power and thy glory, so *as* I have seen thee in the sanctuary.

A. M. cir. 2943
B. C. cir. 1061
Sauli, Regis
Israelitarum,
cir. annum
35

[a]1 Sam. xxii. 5; xxiii. 14, 15, 16——[b]Psa. xlii. 2; lxxxiv. 2; cxliii. 6——[c]Heb. *weary*

[d]Heb. *without water*——[e]See 1 Sam. iv. 21; 1 Chron. xvi. 11; Psa. xxvii. 4; lxxviii. 61

NOTES ON PSALM LXIII

The *title* of this Psalm is, *A Psalm of David, when he was in the wilderness of Judea;* but instead of *Judea*, the *Vulgate*, *Septuagint*, *Æthiopic*, *Arabic*, several of the ancient Latin *Psalters*, and several of the *Latin fathers*, read *Idumea*, or *Edom;* still there is no evidence that David had ever taken refuge in the *deserts of Idumea*. The *Hebrew* text is that which should be preferred; and all the MSS. are in its favour. The *Syriac* has, "Of David, when he

A. M. cir. 2943
B. C. cir. 1061
Sauli, Regis Israelitarum, cir. annum 35

3 [f]Because thy loving-kindness
is better than life, my lips shall
praise thee.
4 Thus will I bless thee
[g]while I live: I will lift up my hands in thy name.
5 My soul shall be [h]satisfied as *with* [i]marrow and fatness; and my mouth shall praise
thee with joyful lips:
6 When [k]I remember thee
upon my bed, *and* meditate on
thee in the *night* watches.
7 Because thou hast been my
help, therefore [l]in the shadow of thy wings
will I rejoice.
8 My soul followeth hard after thee: thy
right hand upholdeth me.

A. M. cir. 2943
B. C. cir. 1061
Sauli, Regis Israelitarum, cir. annum 35

[f]Psa. xxx. 5——[g]Psa. civ. 33; cxlvi. 2——[h]Psa. xxxvi. 8
[i]Heb. *fatness*

[k]Psa. xlii. 8; cxix. 55; cxlix. 5——[l]Psa. xvii. 8; xxxvi. 7; lvii. 1; lxi. 4; xci. 4

said to the king of Moab, My father and mother fled to thee from the face of Saul; and I also take refuge with thee." It is most probable that the Psalm was written when David took refuge in the forest of *Hareth*, in the wilderness of Ziph, when he fled from the court of Achish. But Calmet understands it as a prayer by the captives in Babylon.

Verse 1. *O God, thou* art *my God*] He who can say so, and feels what he says, need not fear the face of any adversary. He has God, and all sufficiency in him.

Early will I seek thee] From the dawn of day. *De luce*, from the light, *Vulgate;* as soon as day breaks; and often before this, for his eyes prevented the night-watches; and he longed and watched for God more than they who watched for the morning. The old Psalter says, **God my God, til the fram light I wake**; and paraphrases thus: God of all, thurgh myght; thu is my God, thurgh lufe and devocion; speciali till the I wak. **Fra light**, that is, fra thy tym that the light of thi grace be in me, that excites fra night of sine. And makes me wak till the in delite of luf, and swetnes in saul. Thai **wak** till God, that setes all thar thoght on God, and for getns the werld. Thai **slep** till God, that settis thair hert on ani creatur.—I **wak** till the, and that gars me thirst in saule and body.

What first lays hold of the heart in the morning is likely to occupy the place all the day. First impressions are the most durable, because there is not a multitude of ideas to drive them out, or prevent them from being deeply fixed in the moral feeling.

In a dry and thirsty land] בארץ *beerets*, IN a land: but several MSS. have כארץ *keerets*, AS a dry and thirsty land, &c.

Verse 2. *To see thy power and thy glory—in the sanctuary.*] In his public ordinances God had often showed his *power* in the judgments he executed, in the terror he impressed, and in awakening the sinful; and his glory in delivering the tempted, succouring the distressed, and diffusing peace and pardon through the hearts of his followers. God shows his *power* and *glory* in his *ordinances;* therefore *public worship* should never be neglected. *We must see God*, says the old Psalter, *that he may see us.* In his temple he dispenses his choicest blessings.

Verse 3. *Thy loving-kindness* is *better than life*] This is the language of every regenerate soul. But O how few prefer the approbation of God to the blessings of life, or even to life itself in *any circumstances!* But the psalmist says, *Thy loving-kindness*, חסדך *chasdecha*, thy *effusive mercy, is better* מחיים *mechaiyim, than* LIVES: *it is better than*, or *good beyond*, countless *ages* of *human existence.*

My lips shall praise thee.] Men praise, or *speak well*, of power, glory, honour, riches, worldly prospects and pleasures; but the truly religious *speak well* of GOD, in whom they find infinitely more satisfaction and happiness than worldly men can find in the possession of all *earthly good.*

Verse 4. *I will lift up my hands in thy name.*] I will take God for my portion. I will dedicate myself to him, and will take him to witness that I am upright in what I profess and do. Pious Jews, in every place of their dispersion, in all their prayers, praises, contracts, &c., *stretched out their hands towards Jerusalem,* where the true God had his temple, and where he manifested his presence.

Verse 5. *My soul shall be satisfied*] I shall have, in the true worshipping of thee, as complete a sensation of spiritual sufficiency and happiness, so that no desire shall be left unsatisfied, as any man can have who enjoys health of body, and a fulness of all the necessaries, conveniences, and comforts of life.

Verse 6. *When I remember thee upon my bed*] I will lie down in thy fear and love; that I may sleep soundly under thy protection, and awake with a sense of thy presence and approbation; and when I awake in the *night watches*, or be awakened by them, I will spend the waking moments in meditation upon thee.

Verse 7. *Therefore in the shadow of thy wings*] I will get into the very secret of thy presence, into the holy of holies, to the *mercy-seat*, over which the *cherubs extend their wings.* If the psalmist does not allude to the *overshadowing* of the *mercy-seat* by the *extended wings of the cherubim*, he may have in view, as a metaphor, the young of fowls, seeking shelter, protection, and warmth under the wings of their mothers. See the same metaphor, Psa. lxi. 4. When a bird of prey appears, the chickens will, by natural instinct, run under the wings of their mothers for protection.

The old *Psalter* translates, **And in hiling of thi wenges I sall joy.** The paraphrase is curious. "Thou art my helper, in perels; and I can joy in gode dedes in thi hiling, (covering,) for I am thi bride, (bird,) and if thou hil (cover) me noght, the glede (kite) will rawis me, (carry me away.")

Verse 8. *My soul followeth hard after thee*] דבקה נפשי אחריך *dabekah naphshi achareycha,* "My soul cleaves (or) is glued after thee." This phrase not only shows the *diligence* of the pursuit, and the *nearness* of the attainment,

A. M. cir. 2943
B. C. cir. 1061
Sauli, Regis
Israelitarum,
cir. annum
35

9 But those *that* seek my soul,
to destroy *it,* shall go into the
lower parts of the earth.
10 [m]They [n]shall fall by the
sword: they shall be a portion for foxes.

11 But the king shall rejoice
in God; [o]every one that sweareth by him shall glory: but the
mouth of them that speak lies
shall be stopped.

A. M. cir. 2943
B. C. cir. 1061
Sauli, Regis
Israelitarum,
cir. annum
35

[m]Heb. *They shall make him run out* like water *by the hands of the sword*

[n]Ezek. xxxv. 5——[o]Deut. vi. 13; Isa. xlv. 23; lxv. 16; Zeph. i. 5

but also the *fast hold* he had got of the mercy of his God.

Verse 9. *Lower parts of the earth.*] They are appointed, in the just judgment of God, to destruction; they shall be slain and buried in the earth, and shall be seen no more. Some understand the passage as referring to the punishment of *hell;* which many supposed to be in the *centre of the earth.* So the old *Psalter,*—*Thai sall entir in till lagher pine of hell. Lagher* or *laigher*, lower, undermost.

Verse 10. *They shall fall by the sword*] *They shall be poured out by the hand of the sword,* Heb. That is, their life's blood shall be shed either in war, or by the hand of justice.

They shall be a portion for foxes.] They shall be left *unburied,* and the *jackals* shall feed upon their dead bodies. Or, being all cut off by utter destruction, their *inheritance* shall be left for the *wild beasts.* That which was their *portion* shall shortly be the *portion* of the wild beasts of the forest. If he here refers to the destruction of the *Babylonians*, the prediction has been literally fulfilled. Where ancient Babylon stood, as far as it can be ascertained, is now the *hold of dangerous reptiles and ferocious beasts.* The *jackal*, or *chokal*, is a very ravenous beast, and fond of *human flesh.* It devours dead bodies, steals infants out of the lap of their mothers, devours alive the *sick* who are left by the side of the *Ganges*, and even in the streets of Calcutta has been known to eat persons who were in a state of intoxication. WARD'S *Customs.*

Verse 11. *But the king shall rejoice*] David shall come to the kingdom according to the promise of God. Or, if it refer to the *captivity*, the *blood royal* shall be preserved in and by *Zerubbabel* till the *Messiah* come, who shall be David's spiritual successor in the kingdom for ever.

That sweareth by him] It was customary to swear *by the life of the king.* The *Egyptians* swore *by the life of Pharaoh;* and *Joseph* conforms to this custom, as may be seen in the book of *Genesis*, chap. xlii. 15, 16. See also 1 Sam. i. 26, and xvii. 55, and Judith xi. 7. But here it may refer to GOD. He is THE KING, and *swearing by his name* signifies *binding* themselves by his *authority*, *acknowledging* his *supremacy*, and *devoting* themselves to his *glory* and *service* alone.

The *Chaldee* has: "And the King shall rejoice במימר אלהא *bemeymar Eloha*, in the WORD of God;" or, in the WORD GOD; *Meymar*, WORD, being taken here *substantially*, as in many other places, by the Targumist.

The mouth of them that speak lies] The mouth of those who acknowledge *lying vanities*, that worship *false gods*, shall be *stopped.* All false religions shall be destroyed by the prevalence of the truth. For he, CHRIST, shall *reign* till all his enemies are put under his feet. "Thy kingdom come, and hell's o'erpower: and to thy sceptre all subdue." Amen and Amen.

ANALYSIS OF THE SIXTY-THIRD PSALM

The *contents* are,—

I. David's ardent desire to be in the assembly of the saints, ver. 1. And the *reasons* on which this desire was founded, ver. 2, 3, 4, 5.

II. That though *absent* from God's ordinances, yet he forgot not his Maker, ver. 6, 7, 8.

III. A double *prophecy.* 1. What should befall his enemies, ver. 9, 10. And, 2. What should come to himself, ver. 11.

I. 1. In the *first part* he states his confidence in God, as the foundation of his desires, contemplations, meditations, invocations, and consolations: "O God, thou art my God," ver. 1.

2. Then he expresses his fervent desire and ardent affection. 1. "Early will I seek thee." THEE, not other things. 2. "My soul thirsteth for thee," &c. There is no doubt that he wanted many things in this barren thirsty land; but of this he does not complain, but of his want of God in the sanctuary.

And so he expresses himself in the following verse: He *was about to see the power and glory of God in the sanctuary, as he had formerly done.* He gives the *reason* of this: "Because thy loving-kindness is better than life," ver. 3. To see thy goodness in the use of thy ordinances, I count far beyond all the *blessings of life;* and could I again be admitted there, these effects would follow:—

1. Praise: "My lips shall praise," &c., ver. 4.

2. Invocation and prayer: "I will lift up my hands," &c., ver. 4.

3. The satisfaction he should receive from these: "My mouth shall be satisfied as with marrow and fatness," &c., ver. 5.

II. Though David is now in the wilderness, he does not forget his duty.

1. Even there he remembered God upon his bed; and meditated, &c., ver. 6.

2. "Because thou hast been my help; therefore," &c., ver. 7.

3. "My soul followeth hard after thee," &c., ver. 8. It is evident, therefore, that even here David was not without comfort; for, 1. He meditates, and remembers what God had done for him. 2. He remembers that he had been his help; and therefore he rejoices. 3. He still adheres to him, and *follows hard after him* for help still.

III. And now, being secure of God's protection, he foretells, 1. What would befall his *enemies;* and, 2. What would come to himself.

1. To his *enemies*, ruin: "Those who seek after my soul, they shall go (some) into the lower parts of the earth," the grave or hell.

Others should "fall by the sword," lie unburied, and be devoured by wild beasts.

——————'Ελωρια τευχε κυνεσσιν,
Οιωνοισι τε πασι. Il., I. ver. 4.

"Whose limbs, unburied on the naked shore,
Devouring dogs and hungry vultures tore."
POPE.

2. To *himself*, honour and a crown: "But the king (David) shall rejoice in God." The reason is,—

1. "Every one that swears by him," that is who worships and fears God, an oath being put by *synecdoche* for the whole worship of God. See the notes.

2. "The mouth of them that speak lies," utter blasphemies, curses, and perjuries, or pray and confess to strange gods, "shall be stopped;" they shall be ashamed and confounded, and an end be put to their iniquity by a sudden and violent death. The *mouth of God's people* shall *glory;* but the *mouth of the wicked* shall be *stopped*, and be silent in the dust.

PSALM LXIV

The psalmist prays for preservation from the wicked, 1, 2; *whom he describes*, 3–6; *shows their punishment*, 7, 8; *and the effect that this should have on the godly*, 9, 10.

To the chief Musician, A Psalm of David

A. M. cir. 3436
B. C. cir. 568
A. U. C. cir. 186
Olymp. LIII. cir. annum primum

HEAR my voice, O God, in
my prayer: preserve my
life from fear of the enemy.
2 Hide me from the secret
counsel of the wicked; from the insurrection
of the workers of iniquity:
3 [a]Who whet their tongue like a sword,
[b]*and* bend *their bows to shoot* their arrows,
even bitter words:
4 That they may shoot in secret
at the perfect: suddenly do they
shoot at him, and fear not.
5 [c]They encourage themselves
in an evil [d]matter: they commune [e]of laying
snares privily; [f]they say, Who shall see them?
6 They search out iniquities; [g]they accomplish [h]a diligent search: both the inward
thought of every one *of them*, and the heart
is deep.

A. M. cir. 3436
B. C. cir. 568
A. U. C. cir. 186
Olymp. LIII. cir. annum primum

[a]Psa. xi. 2; lvii. 4——[b]Psa. lviii. 7; Jer. ix. 3——[c]See Prov. i. 11——[d]Or, *speech*——[e]Heb. *to hide snares*

[f]Psa. x. 11; lix. 7——[g]Or, *we are consumed by that which they have throughly searched*——[h]Heb. *a search searched*

NOTES ON PSALM LXIV

The *title, To the chief Musician*, or *conqueror, A Psalm of David*. The *Syriac* says, "composed by David when warned by Gad the prophet, who said, Stay not in Masrob, because Saul seeks thy life." Some think it was composed by David when he was persecuted by Saul; or during the rebellion of Absalom. But *Calmet* thinks it is a complaint of the captives in Babylon.

Verse 1. *Hear my voice*] The psalmist feared for his life, and the lives of his fellow-captives; and he sought help of God. He *prayed*, and he lifted up his *voice;* and thus showed his *earnestness*.

Verse 2. *Hide me from the secret counsel*] They *plotted* his destruction, and then formed *insurrections* in order to accomplish it.

Workers of iniquity] Those who made *sin* their *labour*, their daily employment; it was their *occupation* and *trade*. It is supposed that by this title the Babylonians are intended. See Psa. vi. 3; xiv. 4; xxxvi. 12; liii. 4; lix. 2.

Verse 3. *Who whet their tongue like a sword*] They *devise* the evil they shall speak, and meditate on the most provoking, injurious, and *defamatory words;* as the soldier *whets* his sword that he may thereby the better cut down his enemies.

Their arrows—bitter words] Their defamatory sayings are here represented as deadly as *poisoned arrows;* for to such is the allusion here made.

Verse 4. *That they may shoot in secret*] They *lurk*, that they may take their aim the more surely, and not miss their mark.

Suddenly] When there is no fear apprehended, because none is seen.

Verse 5. *They commune of laying snares*] They lay snares to *entrap* those whom they cannot slay by *open* attack or private *ambush*.

Verse 6. *They search out iniquities; they accomplish a diligent search*] The word חפש *chaphash*, which is used *three* times, as a noun and a verb, in this sentence, signifies *to strip off the clothes*. "They investigate iniquities; they perfectly investigate an investigation." Most energetically translated by the old *Psalter:* **Thai ransaked wickednesses; thai failled ransakand in ransaking.** To *ransack* signifies to search every corner, to examine things part by part, to turn over every leaf, to leave no hole or cranny unexplored. But the word *investigate* fully expresses the meaning of the term, as it comes either from *in*, taken privately, and *vestire*, to *clothe*, *stripping the man bare*, that he may be exposed to all shame, and be the more easily wounded; or from the word *investigo*, which may be derived from *in*, *intensive*, and *vestigium*, the *footstep* or *track* of man or beast. A metaphor from hunting the stag; as the *slot*, or *mark of his foot*, is diligently sought out, in order to find whither he is gone, and whether he is *old* or *young*, for huntsmen can determine the age by the *slot*. *Tuberville*, in his Treatise on *Hunting*, gives rules to form this judgment. To this the next verse seems to refer.

A. M. cir. 3436 B. C. cir. 568 A. U. C. cir. 186 Olymp. LIII. cir. annum primum

7 [i]But God shall shoot at them
with an arrow; suddenly [k]shall
they be wounded.
8 So they shall make [l]their
own tongue to fall upon themselves: [m]all that
see them shall flee away.
9 [n]And all men shall fear, and shall [o]declare
the work of God; for they
shall wisely consider of his
doing.
10 [p]The righteous shall
be glad in the LORD, and shall trust in
him; and all the upright in heart shall
glory.

[i]Psa. vii. 12, 13——[k]Heb. *their wound shall be*——[l]Prov. xii. 13; xviii. 7 [m]Psa. xxxi. 11; lii. 6——[n]Psa. xl. 3——[o]Jer. l. 28; li. 10 [p]Psa. xxxii. 11; lviii. 10; lxviii. 3

Verse 7. *But God shall shoot at them* with *an arrow*] They endeavour to *trace* me out, that they may shoot me; but God will *shoot at them.* This, if the Psalm refer to the times of David, seems to be prophetic of Saul's death. The *archers* pressed upon him, and sorely wounded him with their arrows. 1 Sam. xxxi. 3.

Verse 8. *Their own tongue to fall upon themselves*] All the plottings, counsels, and curses, they have formed against me, shall come upon themselves.

Verse 9. *And all men shall fear*] They endeavoured to *hide* their mischief; but God shall so punish them that all shall *see it,* and shall acknowledge in their chastisement the just judgment of God. The wicked, in consequence, *shall fear,* and,

Verse 10. *The righteous shall be glad*] They shall see that God does not abandon his followers to the malice of bad men. The rod of the wicked may *come into the heritage of the just;* but *there* it shall not *rest. Calmet* thinks that this is a prediction of the destruction of the Chaldeans, in consequence of which the Jewish people became highly respected by all the surrounding nations. But it may be applied more *generally* to the enmity of the wicked against the righteous, and how God counterworks their devices, and vindicates and supports his own followers.

Analysis of the Sixty-fourth Psalm

I. The psalmist, in danger, commends his cause to God, ver. 1, 2.

II. Complains of his enemies, who are described by their inward devices, and outward conduct, ver. 3-6.

III. He foretells their ruin, and the consequences, ver. 7-10.

I. 1. He prays in general: "Hear my voice."

2. Then in special, that his life may be safe: "Hide me from the secret counsel," &c., ver. 2.

He describes his enemies, generally:—

1. They were wicked men.
2. They were workers of iniquity.
3. They worked secret counsels against him.
4. They acted according to their counsels.

II. After this general character, he particularly describes their villany.

1. They were calumniators; no *sword* sharper than their tongue, no *arrow* swifter than their accusations.

They were *diligent* and *active* to wound his credit; and the evil of their conduct was aggravated by *two* circumstances: 1. It was in *secret;* 2. It was against the *innocent* and *upright:* "They whet their sword; and bend their bow, to shoot their arrows," &c.

2. They were *obstinate* and *confirmed* in mischief:—1. "They encourage themselves in an evil thing." 2. "They commune," lay their heads together how to lay snares, &c.

3. They are *impudent* and *atheistical:* "They say, Who shall see them?"

4. They are *indefatigable*—they are carried on with an earnest desire to do mischief; they invent all crafty ways to circumvent the righteous.

5. All this they do *subtly, craftily:* "Both the inward thought and heart of them is deep;" it is not easy to find out their snares.

III. Now he foretells, 1. Their *punishment;* and, 2. The *event.*

1. Their *punishment* was to be hasty, sharp, deadly, and very just. 1. "God shall shoot at them with an arrow; suddenly shall they be wounded." 2. Most just. For they shall "make their own tongues fall upon themselves." By their *tongues* did they *mischief;* by their *tongues* shall they *fall.*

2. The *event* shall be *double:* 1. In *general,* to *all;* 2. In *particular,* to the *righteous.*

1. Universally: "All that see them shall flee away,"—fear, desert, forsake them.

2. All men "shall see and declare the work of the Lord, and consider it as his doing."

The *effect* it shall have on the righteous. They shall acknowledge God's justice; and farther,—

1. They *shall be glad* in the Lord—in the judgments he has shown.

2. They shall *trust in him*—that he will always protect and deliver them.

3. They *shall glory*—make their *boast* in God, and tell to all the wonders which in his justice and his mercy he has wrought for them.

PSALM LXV

God is praised for the fulfilment of his promises, and for his mercy in forgiving sins, 1–3. *He is praised for the wonders that he works in nature, which all mankind must acknowledge,* 4–8; *for the fertilizing showers which he sends upon the earth, and the abundance thereby produced both for men and cattle,* 9–13.

XII. DAY. EVENING PRAYER

To the chief Musician, A Psalm *and* Song of David

A. M. cir. 3484
B. C. cir. 520
A. U. C. cir. 234
Darii I., R. Per.
cir. annum
secundum

PRAISE [a]waiteth for thee, O
God, in Sion: and unto thee
shall the vow be performed.
2 O thou that hearest prayer,
[b]unto thee shall all flesh come.
3 [c]Iniquities [d]prevail against me: *as for*
our transgressions, thou shalt
[e]purge them away.
4 [f]Blessed *is the man whom*
thou [g]choosest, and causest to
approach *unto thee, that* he may dwell in thy
courts: [h]we shall be satisfied with the goodness of thy house, *even* of thy holy temple.
5 *By* terrible things in righteousness wilt

A. M. cir. 3484
B. C. cir. 520
A. U. C. cir. 234
Darii I., R. Per.
cir. annum
secundum

[a]Heb. *is silent;* Psa. lxii. 1——[b]Isa. lxvi. 23——[c]Psa. xxxviii. 4; xl. 12——[d]Hebrew, *Words* or *Matters of iniquities*

[e]Psa. li. 2; lxxix. 9; Isa. vi. 7; Heb. ix. 14; 1 John i. 7, 9——[f]Psa. xxxiii. 12; lxxxiv. 4——[g]Psa. iv. 3——[h]Psa. xxxvi. 8

NOTES ON PSALM LXV

The *title,* "To the chief Musician or conqueror, a Psalm and Song of David." So the *Hebrew;* and, in effect, the *Chaldee, Æthiopic,* and best copies of the *Septuagint.* The *Arabic* has, "A Psalm of David concerning the transmigration of the people."

The *Vulgate* is singular: "A Psalm of David. A hymn of Jeremiah and Ezekiel for the people of the transmigration, when they began to go out," from Babylon, understood. This title is of no authority; it neither accords with the *subject* of the Psalm, nor with the *truth of history. Calmet* has very properly remarked that *Jeremiah* and *Ezekiel* were never found *together*, to compose this Psalm, neither *before, at*, nor *after* the captivity. It should therefore be utterly rejected. In the *Complutensian* edition *Haggai* is added to *Jeremiah* and *Ezekiel*, all with equal propriety.

It is supposed to have been written after a great drought, when God had sent a plentiful rain on the land. I rather think that there was no direct drought or rain in the prophet's view, but a celebration of the praises of God for his giving rain and fruitful seasons, and filling men's mouths with food, and their hearts with gladness. There is a particular providence manifested in the quantity of rain that falls upon the earth, which can neither be too much admired nor praised.

Verse 1. *Praise waiteth for thee*] Praise is *silent* or *dumb* for thee. *Thou* alone art worthy of praise; all other perfections are lost in thine; and he who considers *thee* aright can have no other subject of adoration.

Unto thee shall the vow be performed.] All offerings and sacrifices should be made to thee. All human spirits are under obligation to live to and serve thee. All Jews and Christians, by circumcision and baptism, belong to thee; and they are all bound to *pay the vow* of their respective *covenants* to thee alone; and the spirit of this *vow* is, to love thee with all their powers, and to serve thee with a perfect heart and willing mind, all the days of their life.

Verse 2. *Unto thee shall all flesh come.*] All *human beings* should pray to God; and from him alone the sufficient portion of human spirits is to be derived. It is supposed to be a prediction of the calling of the Gentiles to the faith of the Gospel of Christ. A minister, immensely *corpulent*, began his address to God in the pulpit with these words: "O thou that hearest prayer, unto thee shall all flesh come!" and most unluckily laid a strong *emphasis* on ALL FLESH. The coincidence was ominous; and I need not say, the people were not edified, for the effect was ludicrous. I mention this fact, which fell under my own notice, to warn those who minister in righteousness to avoid expressions which may be capable, from a similar circumstance, of a ludicrous application. I have known many good men who, to their no small grief, have been encumbered with a preternatural load of muscles; an evil to be deprecated and deplored.

Verse 3. *Iniquities prevail against me*] This is no just rendering of the original, דברי עונת גברו מני *dibrey avonoth gaberu menni;* "iniquitous words have prevailed against me," or, "The words of iniquity are strong against me." All kinds of calumnies, lies, and slanders have been propagated, to shake my confidence, and ruin my credit.

Our transgressions, thou shalt purge them away.] Whatsoever offences we have committed against thee, thou wilt pardon; תכפרם *tecapperem,* thou wilt make *atonement* for them, when with hearty repentance and true faith we turn unto thee. This verse has been abused to favour Antinomian licentiousness. The true and correct translation of the former clause will prevent this.

The old Scottish Version of this verse, in their *singing Psalms,* is most execrable:—

"Iniquities, I must confess,
Prevail against me do:
And as for our trans-gres-si-ons,
Them purge away wilt thou."

O David, if thou art capable of hearing such abominable doggerel substituted for the nervous words thou didst compose by the inspiration of the Holy Ghost, what must thou feel, if chagrin can affect the inhabitants of heaven!

Verse 4. *Blessed* is the man whom *thou choosest*] This is spoken in reference to the *priests* who were *chosen of God* to minister at the tabernacle; and who were permitted *to approach, draw nigh,* to the Divine Majesty by the various offerings and sacrifices which they presented.

We shall be satisfied with the goodness of thy house] Though *we* are not priests, and have not the great felicity to minister before thee in holy things; yet *we* can worship at thy temple, feel the outpouring of thy Spirit, and be made happy with the blessings which thou dispensest there to thy true worshippers.

Verse 5. By *terrible things in righteousness*] The *Vulgate* joins this clause to the preceding verse: "Thy holy temple is wonderful in righteousness: thou wilt hear us, O God of our salvation." But the psalmist may refer to those

A. M. cir. 3484
B. C. cir. 520
A. U. C. cir. 234
Darii I., R. Per.
cir. annum
secundum

thou answer us, O God of our
salvation; *who art* the confidence of [i]all the ends of the
earth, and of them that are afar
off *upon* the sea:
6 Which by his strength setteth fast the
mountains; [k]*being* girded with power:
7 [l]Which stilleth the noise of the seas, the
noise of their waves, [m]and the tumult of the
people.
8 They also that dwell in the uttermost
parts are afraid at thy tokens: thou makest
the outgoings of the morning and evening [n]to
rejoice.
9 Thou [o]visitest the earth, and [p]waterest[q]
it: thou greatly enrichest it [r]with
the river of God, *which* is full of
water: thou preparest them corn,
when thou hast so provided for it.

A. M. cir. 3484
B. C. cir. 520
A. U. C. cir. 234
Darii I., R. Per.
cir. annum
secundum

10 Thou waterest the ridges thereof abundantly: [s]thou settlest the furrows thereof:
[t]thou makest it soft with showers: thou
blessest the springing thereof.
11 Thou crownest [u]the year with thy goodness; and thy paths drop fatness.
12 They drop *upon* the pastures of the wilderness: and the little hills [v]rejoice on every side.
13 The pastures are clothed with flocks;
[w]the valleys also are covered over with corn;
they shout for joy, they also sing.

---

[i]Psalm xxii. 27——[k]Psalm xciii. 1——[l]Psa. lxxxix. 9; cvii. 29; Matthew viii. 26——[m]Psalm lxxvi. 10; Isa. xvii. 12, 13——[n]Or, *to sing*——[o]Deut. xi. 12——[p]Or, *after thou hadst made it to desire* rain——[q]Gen. ii. 6; Leviticus xxvi. 4; Deuteronomy xi. 14; 1 Kings xviii. 44, 45; Psalm lxviii. 9, 10; civ. 13; Jeremiah v. 24; Matthew v. 45——[r]Psalm xlvi. 4——[s]Or, *thou causest* rain *to descend* into *the furrows thereof*——[t]Heb. *thou dissolvest it*——[u]Hebrew, *the year of thy goodness*——[v]Heb. *are girded with joy*——[w]Isa. lv. 12

---

wonderful displays of God's providence in the change of seasons, and fertilization of the earth; and, consequently, in the sustenance of all animal beings.

The confidence of all the ends of the earth] Thou art the hope of thy people scattered through different parts of the world, and through the isles of the sea. This passage is also understood of the vocation of the Gentiles.

Verse 6. *Setteth fast the mountains*] It is by thy strength they have been raised, and by thy power they are girded about or preserved. He represents the mountains as being formed and pitched into their proper places by the mighty hand of God; and shows that they are preserved from splitting, falling down, or mouldering away, as it were, by a girdle by which they are surrounded. The image is very fine. They were hooped about by the Divine power.

Verse 7. *Stilleth the noise of the seas*] Thou art Sovereign over all the operation of sea and land. Earthquakes are under thy control: so are the flux and reflux of the sea; and all storms and tempests by which the great deep is agitated. Even the *headstrong multitude* is under thy control; for thou stillest the madness of the people.

Verse 8. *Are afraid at thy tokens*] Thunder and lightning, storms and tempests, eclipses and meteors, tornadoes and earthquakes, are proofs to all who dwell even in the remotest parts of the earth, that there is a Supreme Being who is wonderful and terrible in his acts. By these things an eternal power and Godhead become manifest even to the most barbarous. From this verse to the end of the Psalm there is a series of the finest poetic imagery in the world.

The outgoings of the morning, &c.] The *rising* and *setting* sun, the morning and evening twilight, the invariable succession of day and night, are all ordained by thee, and contribute to the happiness and continuance of man and beast. Or, All that fear thee praise thee in the *morning*, when they go to their work, and in the *evening*, when they return home, for thy great goodness manifested in the continuance of their strength, and the success of their labour.

Verse 9. *Thou visitest the earth*] God is represented as going through the whole globe, and examining the wants of every part, and directing the *clouds* how and where to deposit their fertilizing showers, and the *rivers* where to direct their beneficial courses.

The river of God] Some think the *Jordan* is meant; and the visiting and watering refer to rain after a long drought. But the *clouds* may be thus denominated, which properly are the origin of rivers.

Thou preparest them corn] Or, Thou wilt prepare them corn, because "thou hast provided for it." Thou hast made all necessary provision for the fertilization of the earth. Thou hast endued the ground with a vegetative power. Rains, dews, and the genial heat of the sun enable it to put forth that power in providing grass for cattle, and corn for the service of man.

Verse 10. *Thou waterest the ridges*] In seed-time thou sendest that measure of rain that is necessary, in order to prepare the earth for the plough; and then, when the *ridges* are thrown into *furrows*, thou makest them *soft* with showers, so as to prepare them for the expansion of the seed, and the vegetation and developement of the embryo plant.

Thou blessest the springing thereof.] Literally, *Thou wilt bless its germinations*—its *springing buds*. Thou watchest over the young sprouts; and it is by thy tender, wise, and provident care that the *ear* is formed; and by thy bountiful goodness that *mature grains* fill the *ear;* and that *one* produces *thirty, sixty,* or a *hundred* or a *thousand* fold.

Verse 11. *Thou crownest the year*] A full and *plentiful harvest* is the *crown* of the year; and this springs from the unmerited *goodness* of God. This is the *diadem* of the earth. עטרת *ittarta, Thou encirclest*, as with a *diadem*. A most elegant expression, to show the progress of the sun through the *twelve* signs of the zodiac, producing the seasons, and giving a sufficiency of light and heat alternately to all places on the surface of the globe, by its north and south declination (amounting to 23° 28′ at the solstices) on each side of the equator. A more beautiful image could not have been chosen; and the very appearance of the *space* termed the *zodiac* on a celestial globe, shows with what propriety the idea of a *circle* or *diadem* was conceived by this inimitable poet.

Thy paths drop fatness.] מעגליך *magaleycha*, "thy orbits." The various planets, which all have their revolutions within the zodiacal space, are represented as contributing their part to the general fructification of the year. Or perhaps the solar revolution through the *twelve* signs, dividing the year into *twelve* parts or months, may be here intended; the *rains* of *November* and *February*, the *frosts* and *snows* of *December* and *January*, being as necessary for the fructification of the soil, as the gentle *showers* of *spring*, the warmth of *summer*, and the *heat* and *drought* of *autumn*. The earth's diurnal rotation on its axis, its annual revolution in its orbit, and the moon's course in accompanying the earth, are all *wheels* or *orbits* of God, which drop fatness, or produce fertility in the earth.

Verse 12. *The pastures of the wilderness*] Even the places which are not cultivated have their *sufficiency of moisture*, so as to render them proper places of pasturage for cattle. The terms *wilderness* and *desert*, in the Sacred Writings, mean, in general, places *not inhabited* and *uncultivated*, though abounding with timber, bushes, and herbage.

The little hills rejoice] Literally, *The hills gird themselves with exultation*. The metaphor appears to be taken from the frisking of lambs, bounding of kids, and dancing of shepherds and shepherdesses, in the joy-inspiring summer season.

Verse 13. *The pastures are clothed with flocks*] Cattle are seen in every plain, avenue, and vista, feeding abundantly; and the *valleys* are *clothed*, and wave with the richest *harvests;* and transports of joy are heard every where in the cheerful songs of the peasantry, the singing of the birds, the neighing of the horse, the lowing of the ox, and the bleating of the sheep. Claudian uses the same image:—

Viridis amictus montium.

"The green vesture of the mountains."

Shout for joy, they also sing.] They are not loud and unmeaning sounds, they are both music and harmony in their different notes; all together form one great concert, and the *bounty of God* is the subject which they all celebrate. What an inimitable description! And yet the nervous Hebrew is not half expressed, even by the amended translation and paraphrase above.

Analysis of the Sixty-fifth Psalm

This is wholly a poem of thanksgiving; and teaches us *how*, and for *what*, we are to praise God. 1. For *spiritual;* 2. For *temporal* blessings; and, 3. This *publicly; in Zion*—in his *Church*.

It has *two* general parts:—

I. Praise to God for his blessings to his followers, ver. 1-5.

II. His common benefits to all mankind, ver. 6-13.

I. He sets forth God's grace to his followers, of which he reckons several particulars:—

1. He has established a public ministry among them, and *an atoning sacrifice*.

2. He directs and hears their prayers; and to him by sacrifice, prayer, and praise, may all human beings come.

3. Though evil tongues may prevail against them for a time, yet he will deliver them.

4. The *transgressions* committed against him he will accept an *atonement for*, and *pardon*, ver. 1-4. See the notes.

5. All that truly worship him in his ordinances shall be made partakers of spiritual blessedness: "We shall be satisfied with the goodness of thy house," ver. 4.

6. He works powerfully and terribly, but righteously, in behalf of his followers, against their enemies: "By terrible things in righteousness," ver. 5. 1. He *answers* them when they call. 2. By *terrible* things,—as in *Egypt*, the *wilderness*, &c. 3. And the *motive* to it is, his *justice* or *righteousness*, by which he punishes his enemies, and gives retribution to his people.

All this he concludes with a double *eulogy* of God:

1. Showing what he is *peculiarly* to his people: "O God of our salvation."

2. What he is to ALL; "the confidence of all the ends of the earth," for he sustains all, be they where they may.

II. He descends from his *peculiar providence*, —the care he takes of, and the benefits he bestows on, his *Church*,—to his *general providence*, his ordering and sustaining the *whole world;* which he amplifies:—

1. "By his strength he setteth fast the mountains," &c., which is true literally: but, *tropologically*, it may mean *kingdoms* and *states*.

2. He stilleth the noise of the sea,—and of the waves,—for to them he sets bounds: "And the tumult of the people." He stills devils, tyrants, armies, seditions, &c.

3. He does this so, that even those who are in the *uttermost parts of the sea* are afraid at his tokens. They see from the phenomena of nature how powerful and fearful God is.

4. The *sun*, *moon*, *planets*, and *stars* are under his guidance. *Day* and *night* are ordered by him: "Thou makest the outgoings of the morning and evening to rejoice."

5. The earth and its inhabitants are his peculiar care: "Thou visitest the earth," &c., ver. 9-11.

In all which the prophet shows God's mercy, 1. In the *rain*. 2. In the *rivers*. 3. In the *growing of the corn*. 4. In *providing grass for cattle*. 5. In providing *store* in the *summer* and *autumn*. 6. His *clouds* drop fatness upon the earth, and all nature rejoices. The meaning of all is, Man may plough, sow, dig, manure, prune, watch, fence, &c.; but it is God that gives the increase.

For an account of the *imagery* here employed, see the notes. The Psalm is grand beyond description, and can never be sufficiently admired.

PSALM LXVI

The psalmist exhorts all to praise God for the wonders he has wrought, 1–4; calls on Israel to consider his mighty acts in behalf of their fathers, 5–7; his goodness in their own behalf, 8–12; he resolves to pay his vows to God, and offer his promised sacrifices, 13–15; calls on all to hear what God had done for his soul, 15–20.

To the chief Musician, A Song *or* Psalm

A. M. cir. 3484 B. C. cir. 520 Darii I., R. Persarum, cir. annum secundum

MAKE [a]a joyful noise unto
God, [b]all ye lands:
2 Sing forth the honour of his
name: make his praise glorious.
3 Say unto God, How [c]terrible *art thou in*
thy works! [d]through the greatness of thy
power shall thine enemies [e]submit[f] themselves unto thee.
4 [g]All the earth shall worship thee, and
[h]shall sing unto thee; they shall sing *to* thy
name. Selah.
5 [i]Come and see the works of God: *he is*
terrible *in his* doing toward the children of men.
6 [k]He turned the sea into dry
land: [l]they went through the
flood on foot: there did we rejoice in him.
7 He ruleth by his power for ever; [m]his
eyes behold the nations: let not the rebellious
exalt themselves. Selah.
8 O bless our God, ye people, and make the
voice of his praise to be heard:
9 Which [n]holdeth our soul in life, and [o]suf-
fereth not our feet to be moved.
10 For [p]thou, O God, hast proved
us: [q]thou hast tried us, as silver is
tried.

A. M. cir. 3484 B. C. cir. 520 Darii I., R. Persarum, cir. annum secundum

[a]Psa. c. 1——[b]Heb. *all the earth*——[c]Psa. lxv. 5——[d]Psa. xviii. 44——[e]Or, *yield feigned obedience;* Psa. xviii. 44; lxxxi. 15——[f]Heb. *lie*——[g]Psa. xxii. 27; lxvii. 3; cxvii. 1——[h]Psa. xcvi. 1, 2

[i]Psa. xlvi. 8——[k]Exod. xiv. 21——[l]Josh. iii. 14, 16——[m]Psalm xi. 4——[n]Hebrew, *putteth*——[o]Psalm cxxi. 3——[p]Psalm xvii. 3; Isaiah xlviii. 10——[q]Zech. xiii. 9; 1 Pet. i. 6, 7

NOTES ON PSALM LXVI

There is nothing particular in the *title* of the Psalm. It is not attributed to *David* either by the *Hebrew, Chaldee, Syriac, Septuagint, Vulgate,* or *Æthiopic.* The *Arabic* alone prefixes the name of *David.* The *Vulgate, Septuagint, Æthiopic,* and *Arabic,* call it a *psalm of the resurrection:* but for this there is no authority. By many of the ancients it is supposed to be a celebration of the restoration from the Babylonish captivity. Others think it commemorates the deliverance of Israel from Egypt, their introduction into the Promised Land, and the establishment of the worship of God in Jerusalem.

Verse 1. *Make a joyful noise*] Sing aloud to God, *all ye lands*—all ye people who, from different parts of the Babylonish empire, are now on return to your own land.

Verse 2. *The honour of his name*] Let his glorious and merciful acts be the *subject* of your songs.

Verse 3. *How terrible* art thou] Consider the plagues with which he afflicted Egypt before he brought your fathers from their captivity, which obliged all his enemies to submit.

Thine enemies submit themselves] Literally, *lie unto thee.* This was remarkably the case with *Pharaoh* and the *Egyptians.* They promised again and again to let the people go, when the hand of the Lord was upon them: and they as frequently falsified their word.

Verse 4. *All the earth*] The whole land shall worship *thee.* There shall no more an *idol* be found among the tribes of Israel. This was literally true. After the Babylonish captivity the Israelites never relapsed into idolatry.

Selah.] Remark it: this is a well attested truth.

Verse 5. *Come and see the works of God*] Let every man lay God's wonderful dealings with us to heart; and compare our deliverance from *Babylon* to that of our fathers from *Egypt.*

Verse 6. *He turned the sea into dry land*] This was a plain miracle: no human art or contrivance could do this. Even in the bed of the waters THEY *did rejoice in him.* WE have not less cause to praise and be thankful.

Verse 7. *He ruleth by his power*] His *omnipotence* is employed to support his followers, and cast down his enemies.

His eyes behold the nations] He sees what they purpose, what they intend to do; and what they will do, if he restrain them not.

Let not the rebellious exalt themselves.] They shall not succeed in their designs: they have their own aggrandizement in view, but thou wilt disappoint and cast them down.

Selah.] Mark this. It is true.

Verse 8. *O bless our God*] Who have so much cause as you to sing praises to the Lord? Hear what he has done for you:

Verse 9. *Which holdeth our soul in life*] Literally, "he who placeth our soul בחיים *bachaiyim,* in lives." We are preserved *alive,* have *health* of body, and feel the *life* of God in our hearts.

And suffereth not her feet to be moved.] Keeps us steadfast in his testimonies. We have our *life,* our *liberty,* and our *religion.* O, what hath the Lord wrought for us! "Make, therefore, the voice of his praise to be heard." Let God and man know you are thankful.

Verse 10. *For thou, O God, hast proved us*] This is a metaphor taken from *melting* and *refining metals;* afflictions and trials of various kinds are represented as a *furnace* where *ore* is melted, and a *crucible* where it is *refined.* And this metaphor is used especially to represent cases where there is *doubt* concerning the purity of the metal, the quantity of alloy, or even the nature or kind of metal subjected to the trial. So God is said to *try the Israelites*

A. M. cir. 3484
B. C. cir. 520
Darii I.,
R. Persarum,
cir. annum
secundum

11 [r]Thou broughtest us into
the net; thou laidest affliction
upon our loins.
12 [s]Thou hast caused men to
ride over our heads; [t]we went through fire and
through water: but thou broughtest us out
into a [u]wealthy *place*.
13 [v]I will go into thy house with burnt-
offerings; [w]I will pay thee my vows,
14 Which my lips have [x]uttered, and my
mouth hath spoken, when I was in trouble.
15 I will offer unto thee burnt sacrifices of
[y]fatlings, with the incense of rams; I will
offer bullocks with goats.
Selah.
16 [z]Come *and* hear, all ye that
fear God, and I will declare what
he hath done for my soul.
17 I cried unto him with my mouth, and he
was extolled with my tongue.
18 [a]If I regard iniquity in my heart, the
LORD will not hear *me:*
19 *But* verily God [b]hath heard *me;* he hath
attended to the voice of my prayer.
20 Blessed *be* God, which hath not turned
away my prayer, nor his mercy from me.

[r]Lam. i. 13——[s]Isa. li. 23——[t]Isa. xliii. 2——[u]Heb. *moist*——[v]Psa. c. 4; cxvi. 14, 17, 18, 19——[w]Eccles. v. 4——[x]Heb. *opened*

[y]Heb. *marrow*——[z]Psa. xxxiv. 11——[a]Job xxvii. 9; Prov. xv. 29; xxviii. 9; Isa. i. 15; John ix. 31; James iv. 3——[b]Psa. cxvi. 1, 2

that he *might know what was in them;* and *whether they would keep his testimonies:* and then, according to the issue, his conduct towards them would appear to be founded on reason and justice.

Verse 11. *Thou broughtest us into the net*] This refers well to the case of the Israelites, when, in their departure from Egypt, pursued by the Egyptians, having the Red Sea before them, and no method of escape, Pharaoh said, "The wilderness hath shut them in,—they are entangled;" comparing their state to that of a *wild beast* in a *net*.

Affliction upon our loins.] Perhaps this alludes to that sharp *pain in the back and loins* which is generally felt on the apprehension of *sudden* and *destructive danger*.

Verse 12. *Thou hast caused men to ride over our heads*] Thou hast permitted us to fall under the dominion of our enemies; who have treated us as broken infantry are when the cavalry dashes among their disordered ranks, treading all under the horses' feet.

We went through fire and through water] Through afflictions of the most torturing and *overwhelming* nature. To represent such, the metaphors of *fire* and *water* are often used in Scripture. The old *Psalter* considers these trials as a proof of the uprightness of those who were tried—**We passid thurgh fire and watir:** that is, thurgh wa and wele, as a man that leves noght his waye for hete na for kald, for dry na for wette; **and thou out lede us** fra tribulacyon **intill koling** (cooling) that is, in till endles riste, that we hope to hafe after this travell.

Wealthy place.] *Well watered* place, to wit, the land of *Judea*.

Verse 13. *I will go into thy house with burnt-offerings*] Now that thou hast restored us to our own land, and established us in it, we will establish thy worship, and offer all the various kinds of sacrifices required by thy law.

I will pay thee my vows] We often *vowed*, if thou wouldst deliver us from our bondage, to worship and *serve thee alone:* now thou hast heard our prayers, and hast delivered us; therefore will we fulfil our engagements to thee. The old *Psalter* gives this a pious turn:—**I sall yelde till the my wowes**, that is, the vowes of louying (praising) the; whilk vowes my lipes divisid sayand, that I am noght, and thou arte all: and I hafe nede of the, noght thou of me. This is a right distinction—It is certainly a *good distinction*, and it is strictly true. The all-*sufficient* God needs not his *creatures*.

Verse 14. *When I was in trouble.*] This is generally the time when good resolutions are formed, and vows made; but how often are these forgotten when affliction and calamity are removed!

Verse 15. *I will offer, &c.*] Thou shalt have the best of the herd and of the fold; the lame and the blind shall never be given to thee for sacrifice.

The incense of rams] The fine effluvia arising from the burning of the pure fat.

Verse 16. *Come* and *hear, all ye that fear God*] While in captivity, the psalmist had sought the Lord with frequent prayer for his own personal salvation, and for the deliverance of the people; and God blessed him, heard his prayer, and turned the captivity. Now that he is returned in safety, he is determined to perform his vows to the Lord; and calls on all them that fear their Maker, who have any religious reverence for him, to attend to his account of the Lord's gracious dealings with him. He proposes to tell them his spiritual experience, what he needed, what he earnestly prayed for, and what God has done for him. Thus he intended to teach them by *example*, more powerful always than *precept*, however weighty in itself, and impressively delivered.

Verse 17. *I cried unto him with my mouth*] My prayer was fervent; he heard and answered; and my tongue celebrated his mercies; and he as graciously received my *thanksgiving*, as he compassionately heard my *prayer*.

Verse 18. *If I regard iniquity in my heart*] "If I have seen (ראיתי *raithi*) iniquity in my heart," if I have known it was there, and *encouraged* it; if I *pretended* to be what I *was not;* if I *loved iniquity*, while I *professed to pray* and be *sorry* for *my sin; the Lord,* אדני *Adonai*, my Prop, Stay, and Supporter, would not have heard, and I should have been left without *help* or *support*.

Verse 19. *Verily God hath heard me*] A sure proof that my prayer was upright, and my heart honest, before him.

Verse 20. *Blessed* be *God*] I therefore praise God, who has not turned aside my prayer, and who has not withheld his mercy from me. Thus he told them what God had done for his soul.

ANALYSIS OF THE SIXTY-SIXTH PSALM

There are *five parts* in this Psalm:—

I. An *invitation.*

1. To praise God, ver. 1-4.

2. To consider his works, ver. 5-7.

II. A *repetition* of the *invitation*, ver. 8, for the benefit and deliverance lately received, ver. 9-12.

III. A *protestation* and *vow* for himself, that he would serve the Lord, ver. 13-15.

IV. A *declaration* of *God's goodness* to him, which he invites all to come and hear, ver. 16-19.

V. A *doxology*, with which he concludes, ver. 20.

I. The invitation to praise God affectionately and heartily.

1. "Make a joyful song." 2. "Sing the honour of his name." 3. "Make his praise glorious." 4. "Say unto God," &c. Where he prescribes the *form* in which God shall be praised.

He calls all men to *consider his works*, and the double effect:—1. On God's *enemies.* 2. On his *people.*

1. On his enemies, a *feigned obedience*, ver. 3. See the note.

2. On his people, a *willing service*, ver. 4.

He calls on them again, ver. 5, to consider God's works, specially in delivering his people: 1. At the *Red Sea.* 2. In *passing Jordan* on foot, ver. 6.

He calls them to *behold God's power* and providence. 1. His *power* in ruling. 2. His *providence* in beholding, and, 3. His *justice* in punishing the rebellious, ver. 7.

II. He again invites them to praise God for some *special* mercy, without which they would have been destroyed, ver. 8. 1. He kept them *alive.* 2. *Suffered not their feet* to *slip*, ver. 9. 3. He *tried*, that he might purify, them.

He illustrates this trial by *five* similes taken, —1. From *silver.* 2. From a *net.* 3. From a *burden* laid on the loins. 4. From *bondage and slavery*—men rode over us. 5. From *fire and water;* useful *servants*, but cruel *masters*, ver. 10-12.

But the *issue* of all these trials was good:—they were brought *through* all, and profited by *each.*

III. For this he gives thanks, and purposes to *pay his vows.*

1. He would attend God's worship: "I will go into thy house," ver. 13.

2. He would there present his offerings, ver. 14.

3. These should be of the *best kind*, ver. 15.

IV. He declares God's *goodness*, and *invites all that fear God to hear what he has got to say.* Not of what he was *to offer* to God, but of what God *had done for him.*

1. He cried to God, and he heard him.

2. He took care to *avoid iniquity*, that his prayers might not be cast out: "For God heareth not sinners."

V. He closes the Psalm with a doxology, blessing God that, not through his *merit*, but his own *mercy*, he had heard and answered him. He attributes nothing to himself, but all mercy to his God, ver. 20.

PSALM LXVII

The psalmist prays for the enlargement of God's kingdom, 1, 2; *calls upon all nations to serve him, because he judges and governs righteously*, 3–5; *promises prosperity to the faithful and obedient*, 6, 7.

To the chief Musician on Neginoth, A Psalm *or* Song

A. M. cir. 3484
B. C. cir. 520
Darii I.,
R. Persarum,
cir. annum
secundum

GOD be merciful unto us, and
bless us; *and* [a]cause his
face to shine [b]upon us. Selah.
2 That [c]thy way may be known
upon earth, [d]thy saving health
among all nations.
3 [e]Let the people praise thee,
O God; let all the people praise
thee.

A. M. cir. 3484
B. C. cir. 520
Darii I.,
R. Persarum,
cir. annum
secundum

Num. vi. 25; Psa. iv. 6; xxxi. 16; lxxx. 3, 7, 19; cxix. 135 —— [b]Heb. *with us* —— [c]Acts xviii. 25 —— [d]Luke ii. 30, 31; Tit. ii. 11 —— [e]Psa. lxvi. 4

NOTES ON PSALM LXVII

The *title* here is the same with that of Psalm iv., where see the notes. It is supposed to have been written at the return from the Babylonish captivity, and to foretell the conversion of the Gentiles to the Christian religion. The prayer for their salvation is very energetic.

Verse 1. *God be merciful unto us*] Show the Jewish people thy mercy, bless them in their bodies and souls and give a full evidence of thy approbation. This is nearly the same form of blessing as that used Num. vi. 25, where see the notes.

Verse 2. *That thy way may be known*] That thy will, thy gracious designs towards the children of men, thy way of reconciling them to thyself, of justifying the ungodly, and sanctifying the unholy, may be known to all the nations upon the earth! God's *way* is God's *religion;* what *he walks in* before men; and in which men must *walk* before him. A man's religion

A. M. cir. 3484 B. C. cir. 520 Darii I., R. Persarum, cir. annum secundum

4 O let the nations be glad and
sing for joy: for [f]thou shalt judge
the people righteously, and [g]gov-
ern the nations upon earth. Selah.
5 Let the people praise thee, O God; let
all the people praise thee.
6 [h]*Then* shall the earth
yield her increase; *and* God,
even our own God, shall bless
us.
7 God shall bless us, and [i]all the ends of
the earth shall fear him.

A. M. cir. 3484 B. C. cir. 520 Darii I., R. Persarum, cir. annum secundum

[f]Psa. xcvi. 10, 13; xcviii. 9——[g]Heb. *lead*——[h]Lev. xxvi. 4; Psa. lxxxv. 12; Ezek. xxxiv. 27——[i]Psa. xxii. 27

is his *way* of worshipping God, and going to heaven. The whole Gospel is called *this way*, Acts xix. 9.

Thy saving health] ישועתך *yeshuathecha*, "thy salvation." The great *work* which is performed in God's *way*, in destroying the power, pardoning the guilt, cleansing from the infection, of all sin; and filling the soul with holiness, with the mind that was in Christ. Let *all nations*—the whole Gentile world, know that *way*, and this *salvation!*

Verse 3. *Let the people praise thee*] When this is done, the *people*—the Gentiles, will praise thee; all will give thanks to God for his unspeakable gift.

Verse 4. *Glad and sing for joy*] They shall be made happy in thy salvation. Even their political state shall be greatly meliorated; for God will be acknowledged the supreme Judge; *their laws* shall be founded on *his word;* and the nations of the earth shall be *governed* according to judgment, justice, and equity.

Selah.] This is true. There are innumerable facts to confirm it. All the nations who have received the Gospel of Christ have been benefited *politically*, as well as *spiritually*, by it.

Verse 5. *Let the people praise thee*] Seeing the abundance of the blessings which the Gentiles were to receive, he calls again and again upon them to magnify God for such mercies.

Verse 6. *The earth yield her increase*] As the ground was *cursed* for the sin of man, and the *curse* was to be *removed* by *Jesus Christ*, the fertility of the ground should be influenced by the preaching of the Gospel; for as the people's minds would become enlightened by the truth, they would, in consequence, become capable of making the most *beneficial discoveries* in *arts* and *sciences;* and there should be an especial blessing on the toil of the pious husbandman. Whenever true religion prevails, every thing partakes of its beneficent influence.

Verse 7. *God shall bless us*] He shall ever be *speaking good* to us, and ever showering down good things upon us.

The last clause of the *sixth verse* should be joined to the *seventh*, as it is in several of the *Versions*, and should be in all. Many of the *fathers*, and several *commentators*, have thought that there is a reference to the *Holy Trinity* in the triple repetition of the word God: "God, our God, shall bless us; God shall bless us;" thus paraphrased in the old *Psalter:* "Blis us God the Fader: and our God the sone: and blis us and multipli us God the Hali Gast; that swa drede him God, all the endis of erth; for he wil comme to deme rightwysly that unrightwysly was demed. He that kan drede him, he cesses noght to lufe him."

When or by *whom* this Psalm was written cannot be ascertained. It seems to be simply a prophecy concerning the calling of the Gentiles, the preaching of the apostles, and the diffusion and influence of Christianity in the world. It is a fine piece of devotion; and it would be nearly impossible to read or repeat it with a cold and unaffected heart.

Analysis of the Sixty-seventh Psalm

This Psalm may be divided into *three* parts:—

I. A general *prayer*, ver. 1. And the *reason* of it, ver. 2.

II. A double *vow*, ver. 3, 4. With the *reason.* The vow repeated, ver. 6.

III. The *effects* that were to follow, ver. 6, 7.

1. The first part, a *prayer for mercy:* "God be merciful to us!" for *God's mercy* is the fountain of all our blessings.

2. Then *bless us* through that mercy with *temporal* and *spiritual* good.

3. "Cause his face to shine." Give us a sense of thy *approbation.*

4. Let these blessings be extended *to all men.* For this reason: 1. "That thy way," thy will, word, worship, &c., "may be known upon earth." 2. "Thy saving health," the redemption by Christ, "to all nations."

II. Then shall God be honoured; one will readily flow from the other; for *mercy* brings *knowledge* of God and his goodness; and this knowledge brings *praise.* This verse is emphatic:—

1. In respect of the object; "Thee," not strange gods.

2. All *shall praise*—not *mutter* or *meditate* praise, but make it illustrious.

3. This should be done *frequently*, an example of which we have in this Psalm.

4. It should be done *cheerfully*, with a glad heart; not *words* merely, but *affections* of praise.

For this also he gives a *reason* which is twofold:—

1. His *equity* in judging: "Thou shalt judge the people righteously."

2. His *wisdom* in governing. Thou shalt *lead them*, תנחם *tanchem*, thy government shall be full of *wise teaching:* "Wisdom and knowledge shall be the stability of his times."

III. The *effects* of his blessing, and our praise.

1. "The earth shall yield her increase:" the *people* shall be *multiplied;* the *harvests* shall be *ample*, and the *Church* shall *overflow* with converts.

2. God shall *bless this increase;* for, without this, temporal blessings may become a curse. He doubles this that it may not be forgotten.

3. The last and finest effect is, that God shall be worshipped over all the earth: "All the ends of the earth shall fear him." Amen. The *fear of God* is frequently used to express the whole of his worship.

PSALM LXVIII

The psalmist calls upon God to arise, bless his people, and scatter his enemies, 1–3; *exhorts them to praise him for his greatness, tenderness, compassion, and judgments,* 4–6; *describes the grandeur of his march when he went forth in the redemption of his people,* 7, 8; *how he dispensed his blessings,* 9, 10; *what he will still continue to do in their behalf,* 11–13; *the effects produced by the manifestation of God's majesty,* 14–18; *he is praised for his goodness,* 19, 20; *for his judgments,* 21–23; *he tells in what manner the Divine worship was conducted,* 24–27; *how God is to be honoured,* 28–31; *all are invited to sing his praises, and extol his greatness,* 32–35.

XIII. DAY. MORNING PRAYER

To the chief Musician, A Psalm *or* Song of David

A. M. cir. 2962 B. C. cir. 1042 Dav. Reg. Isr. cir. annum 14

LET [a]God arise, let his enemies be scattered; let them
also that hate him flee [b]before him.
2 [c]As smoke is driven away, *so* drive *them*
away: [d]as wax melteth before the fire, *so* let
the wicked perish in the presence of God.
3 But [e]let the righteous be glad; let them
rejoice before God: yea, let them [f]exceed-
ingly rejoice.

4 [g]Sing unto God, sing praises
to his name: [h]extol him that rideth
upon the heavens [i]by his name
JAH, and rejoice before him.

A. M. cir. 2962 B. C. cir. 1042 Davidis, Regis Israelitarum, cir. annum 14

5 [k]A father of the fatherless, and a judge
of the widows, *is* God in his holy habitation.
6 [l]God setteth the solitary [m]in families:
[n]he bringeth out those which are bound with
chains: but [o]the rebellious dwell in a dry
land.
7 O God, [p]when thou wentest forth before

[a]Numbers x. 35; Isaiah xxxiii. 3——[b]Hebrew, *from his face*——[c]Isaiah ix. 18; Hosea xiii. 3——[d]Psa. xcvii. 5; Micah i. 4——[e]Psalm xxxii. 11; lviii. 10; lxiv. 10——[f]Hebrew, *rejoice with gladness*——[g]Psalm lxvi. 4

[h]Deut. xxxiii. 26; ver. 33——[i]Exod. vi. 3——[k]Psa. x. 14, 18; cxlvi. 9——[l]1 Sam. ii. 5; Psa. cxiii. 9——[m]Heb. *in a house*——[n]Psa. cvii. 10, 14; cxlvi. 7; Acts xii. 6, &c.——[o]Psa. cvii. 34, 40——[p]Exod. xiii. 21; Judg. iv. 14; Hab. iii. 13

NOTES ON PSALM LXVIII

In the *title* of this Psalm there is nothing particular to be remarked. It is probable that this Psalm, or a part of it at least, might have been composed by Moses, to be recited when the Israelites journeyed. See Num. x. 35; and that David, on the same model, constructed this Psalm. It might have been sung also in the ceremony of transporting the ark from Kirjath-jearim, to Jerusalem; or from the house of Obed-edom to the tabernacle erected at Sion.

I know not how to undertake a comment on this Psalm: it is the most difficult in the whole Psalter; and I cannot help adopting the opinion of *Simon De Muis:* In hoc Psalmo tot ferme scopuli, tot labyrinthi, quot versus, quot verba. Non immerito crux ingeniorum, et interpretum opprobrium dici potest. "In this Psalm there are as many precipices and labyrinths as there are verses or words. It may not be improperly termed, the torture of critics, and the reproach of commentators." To attempt any thing *new* on it would be dangerous; and to say what has been so often said would be unsatisfactory. I am truly afraid to fall over one of those *precipices*, or be endlessly entangled and lost in one of these *labyrinths.* There are customs here referred to which I do not fully understand; there are *words* whose meaning I cannot, to my own satisfaction, ascertain; and allusions which are to me inexplicable. Yet of the composition itself I have the highest opinion: it is sublime beyond all comparison; it is constructed with an art truly admirable; it possesses all the dignity of the sacred language; none but David could have composed it; and, at this lapse of time, it would require no small influence of the Spirit that was upon him, to give its true interpretation. I shall subjoin a few notes, chiefly philological; and beg leave to refer the reader to those who have written *profusely* and *laboriously* on this sublime Psalm, particularly *Venema, Calmet, Dr. Chandler*, and the writers in the *Critici Sacri.*

Verse 1. *Let God arise*] This was sung when the Levites took up the ark upon their shoulders; see Num. x. 35, 36, and the notes there.

Verse 4. *Extol him that rideth upon the heavens by his name JAH*] "Extol him who sitteth on the throne of glory, in the ninth heaven; YAH is his name; and rejoice before him."—*Targum.*

בערבות *baaraboth*, which we render *in the high heavens*, is *here* of doubtful signification. As it comes from the root ערב *arab*, to mingle, (hence *ereb* the evening or *twilight*, because it appears to be formed of an *equal mixture of light and darkness;* the *Septuagint* translate it δυσμων, the *west*, or *setting* of the sun; so does the *Vulgate* and others;) probably it may mean the *gloomy desert*, through which God, in the chariot of his glory, led the Israelites. If this interpretation do not please, then let it be referred to the *darkness* in which God is said to dwell, through which the *rays of his power and love*, in the various dispensations of his power and mercy, shine forth for the comfort and instruction of mankind.

By his name Jah] יה *Yah*, probably a contraction of the word יהוה *Yehovah;* at least, so the ancient Versions understood it. It is used but in a few places in the sacred writings. It might be translated *The Self existent.*

Verse 6. *The solitary in families*] יחדים *yechidim*, the *single persons.* Is not the meaning, God is the Author of marriage; and children, the legal fruit of it, are an inheritance from him?

Verse 7. *O God, when thou wentest forth*] This and the following verse most manifestly refer to the passage of the Israelites through the wilderness.

A. M. cir. 2962 B. C. cir. 1042 Davidis, Regis Israelitarum, cir. annum 14

thy people, when thou didst
march through the wilderness;
Selah:
8 [q]The earth shook, the heavens also dropped at the presence of God:
even Sinai itself *was moved* at the presence
of God, the God of Israel.
9 [r]Thou, O God, didst [s]send a plentiful
rain, whereby thou didst [t]confirm thine inheritance, when it was weary.
10 Thy congregation hath dwelt therein:
[u]thou, O God, hast prepared of thy goodness
for the poor.
11 The LORD gave the word: great *was* the
[v]company of those that published *it.*
12 [w]Kings of armies [x]did
flee apace: and she that
tarried at home divided the
spoil.
13 [y]Though ye have lien among the pots,
[z]*yet shall ye be as* the wings of a dove covered
with silver, and her feathers with yellow
gold.
14 [a]When the Almighty scattered kings [b]in
it, it was *white* as snow in Salmon.
15 The hill of God *is as* the hill of Bashan;
a high hill *as* the hill of Bashan.
16 [c]Why leap ye, ye high hills? [d]*this is*
the hill *which* God desireth to dwell in; yea,
the LORD will dwell *in it* for ever.

---

[q]Exod. xix. 16, 18; Judg. v. 4; Isa. lxiv. 1, 3——[r]Deut xi. 11, 12; Ezek. xxxiv. 26——[s]Heb. *shake out*——[t]Heb. *confirm it*——[u]Deut. xxvi. 5, 9; Psa. lxxiv. 19——[v]Heb. *army*——[w]Num. xxxi. 8, 9, 54; Josh. x. 16; xii. 8

[x]Heb. *did flee, did flee*——[y]Psa. lxxxi. 6——[z]Psa. cv. 37——[a]Num. xxi. 3; Josh. x. 10; xii. 1, &c.——[b]Or, *for her, she was*——[c]Psa. cxiv. 4, 6——[d]Deut. xii. 5, 11; 1 Kings ix. 3; Psa. lxxxvii. 1, 2; cxxxii. 13, 14

Verse 9. *Didst send a plentiful rain*] גשם נדבות *geshem nedaboth*, a *shower of liberality.* I believe this to refer to the *manna* by which God refreshed and preserved alive the weary and hungry Israelites.

Verse 10. *Thy congregation hath dwelt therein*] חיתך *chaiyathecha, thy living creature;* τα ζωα, *Septuagint; animalia, Vulgate;* so all the Versions. Does not this refer to the *quails* that were brought to the camp of the Israelites, and *dwelt*, as it were, *round about it?* And was not *this*, with the *manna* and the *refreshing rock*, that *goodness which God had provided for the poor*—the needy Israelites?

Verse 11. *Great* was *the company of those that published* it.] המבשרות צבא רב *hammebasseroth tsaba rab;* "Of the female preachers there was a great host." Such is the literal translation of this passage; the reader may make of it what he pleases. Some think it refers to the *women* who, with music, songs, and dances, celebrated the victories of the Israelites over their enemies. But the publication of *good news*, or of any *joyful event*, belonged to the *women.* It was they who announced it to the people at large; and to this universal custom, which prevails to the *present day*, the psalmist alludes. See this established in the note on Isa. xl. 9.

Verse 12. *Kings of armies did flee*] *Jabin* and the kings of the Canaanites, who united their forces to overwhelm the Israelites.

And she] Deborah the prophetess, a *woman* accustomed to *tarry at home*, and take care of the family; she divided the spoils, and vanquished their kings.

Verse 13. *Though ye have lien among the pots*] The prophet is supposed here to address the tribes of *Reuben* and *Gad*, who remained in their *inheritances*, occupied with *agricultural, maritime*, and *domestic affairs*, when the other tribes were obliged to go against *Jabin*, and the other Canaanitish kings. Ye have been thus occupied, while your brethren sustained a desperate campaign; but while you are inglorious, they obtained the most splendid victory, and dwell under those rich tents which they have taken from the enemy; coverings of the most beautiful colours, adorned with gold and silver. The words בירקרק חרוץ *birakrak charuts, native gold*, so exceedingly and splendidly *yellow* as to approach to *greenness*—from ירק *yarak, to be green;* and the doubling of the last syllable denotes an excess in the denomination—*excessively green—glistering green.* The *Targum* gives us a curious paraphrase of this and the following verse: "If ye, O ye kings, slept among your halls, the congregation of Israel, which is like a dove covered with the clouds of glory, divided the prey of the Egyptians, purified silver, and coffers full of the finest gold. And when it stretched out its hands in prayer over the sea, the Almighty cast down kingdoms; and for its sake cooled hell like snow, and snatched it from the shadow of death." Perhaps the Romanists got some idea of purgatory here. For the sake of the righteous, the flames of hell are extinguished!

Verse 15. *The hill of God* is as *the hill of Bashan*] This and the following verse should be read thus: "Is Mount Bashan the craggy mount, Mount Bashan, the mount of God? Why envy ye, ye craggy mounts? This is the mount of God in which he has desired to dwell." The *Targum* countenances this translation: Mount *Moriah*, the place where our fathers of old worshipped God, is chosen to build on it the house of the sanctuary, and Mount *Sinai* for the giving of the law. Mount *Bashan*, Mount *Tabor*, and *Carmel* are rejected; they are made as Mount *Bashan*."

Verse 16. *Why leap ye, ye high hills?*] "God said, Why leap ye, ye high hills? It is not pleasing to me to give my law upon high and towering hills. Behold, Mount Sinai is low; and the WORD of the Lord has desired to place on it the Divine majesty. Moreover, the Lord dwells for ever in the heaven of heavens."—*Targum.*

The psalmist is speaking particularly of the mountains of Judea, and those of Gilead; the former were occupied by the Canaanites, and the others by Og, king of Bashan, and Sihon, king of the Amorites, whom Moses defeated.

A. M. cir. 2962
B. C. cir. 1042
Davidis, Regis
Israelitarum,
cir. annum
14

17 [e]The chariots of God *are* twenty thousand, [f]*even* thousands of angels: the LORD *is* among them, *as in* Sinai, in the holy *place*.

18 [g]Thou hast ascended on high, [h]thou hast led captivity captive: [i]thou hast received gifts [k]for men; yea, *for* [l]the rebellious also, [m]that the LORD God might dwell *among them*.

19 Blessed *be* the LORD, *who* daily loadeth us *with benefits, even* the God of our salvation. Selah.

20 *He that is* our God *is* the God of salvation; and [n]unto God the LORD *belong* the issues from death.

21 But [o]God shall wound the head of his enemies, [p]*and* the hairy scalp of such a one as goeth on still in his trespasses.

A. M. cir. 2962
B. C. cir. 1042
Davidis, Regis
Israelitarum,
cir. annum
14

22 The LORD said, I will bring [q]again from Bashan, I will bring *my people* again [r]from the depths of the sea:

23 [s]That thy foot may be [t]dipped in the blood of *thine* enemies, [u]*and* the tongue of thy dogs in the same.

24 They have seen thy goings, O God; *even* the goings of my God, my King, in the sanctuary.

25 [v]The singers went before, the players on instruments *followed* after; among *them were* the damsels playing with timbrels.

26 Bless ye God in the congregations, *even*

---

[e]Deut. xxxiii. 2; 2 Kings vi. 16, 17; Dan. vii. 10; Heb. xii. 22; Rev. ix. 16——[f]Or, even *many thousands*——[g]Acts i. 9; Eph. iv. 8——[h]Judg. v. 12——[i]Acts ii. 4, 33——[k]Heb. *in the man*——[l]1 Tim. i. 13——[m]Psa. lxxviii. 60

[n]Deut. xxxii. 39; Prov. iv. 23; Rev. i. 18; xx. 1——[o]Psa. cx. 6; Hab. iii. 13——[p]Psa. lv. 23——[q]Num. xxi. 33——[r]Exod. xiv. 22——[s]Psa. lviii. 10——[t]Or, *red*——[u]1 Kings xxi. 19——[v]1 Chron. xiii. 8; xv. 16; Psa. xlvii. 5

Verse 17. *The chariots of God* are *twenty thousand*] רבתים אלפי שנאן *ribbothayim alpey shinan*, "two myriads of thousands doubled." Does not this mean simply *forty thousand?* A myriad is 10,000; two myriads, 20,000; these doubled, 40,000. Or thus: 10,000+10,000+20,000=40,000. The Targum says, "The chariots of God are two myriads; *two thousand* angels draw them; the majesty of God rests upon them in holiness on Mount Sinai." But what does this mean? We must die to know.

Verse 18. *Thou hast ascended on high*] When the ark had reached the top of Sion, and was deposited in the place assigned for it, the singers joined in the following chorus. This seems to be an allusion to a *military triumph*. The conqueror was placed on a very elevated chariot.

Led captivity captive] The conquered kings and generals were usually tied behind the chariot of the conqueror—bound to it, bound together, and walked after it, to grace the triumph of the victor.

Thou hast received gifts for men] "And *gave* gifts *unto* men;" Eph. iv. 8. At such times the conqueror threw money among the crowd. *Thou hast received gifts among men*, באדם *baadam*, IN MAN, in human nature; and *God manifest in the flesh* dwells among mortals! *Thanks be to God for his unspeakable* GIFT! By establishing his *abode among the rebellious*, the prophet may refer to the conquest of the land of Canaan, and the country beyond Jordan.

Yea, for *the rebellious also*] Even to the rebellious. Those who were his enemies, who traduced his character and operations, and those who fought against him now submit to him, and share his munificence; for it is the property of a hero to be generous.

That the Lord God might dwell among them.] יה אלהים *yah Elohim*, the *self-existing God;* see on ver. 4. The conqueror now coming to fix his abode among the conquered people to organize them under his laws, to govern and dispense justice among them. The whole of this is very properly applied by St. Paul, Eph. iv. 5, to the *resurrection and glory of Christ;* where the reader is requested to consult the *note*.

Verse 19. *Blessed* be *the Lord*, who *daily loadeth us*] With benefits is not in the text. Perhaps it would be better to translate the clause thus: "Blessed be Adonai, our Prop day by day, who supports us." Or, "Blessed be the Lord, who supports us day by day." Or as the *Vulgate, Septuagint*, and *Arabic:* "Blessed be the Lord daily, our God who makes our journey prosperous; even the God of our salvation." The *Syriac*, "Blessed be the Lord daily, who hath chosen our inheritance." The word עמס *amas*, which we translate *to load*, signifies to *lift, bear up, support*, or *to bear a burden for another*. Hence it would not be going far from the ideal meaning to translate: "Blessed be the Lord day by day, who bears our burdens for us." But *loadeth us with benefits* is neither a *translation* nor *meaning*.

Verse 20. *The issues from death.*] The *going out* or *exodus* from *death*—from the land of Egypt and house of bondage. Or the expression may mean, Life and death are in the hand of God. "He can create, and he destroy."

Verse 21. *The hairy scalp*] קדקד שער *kodkod sear*. Does this mean any thing like the Indian *scalping?* Or does it refer to a *crest* on a *helmet* or *headcap?* I suppose the latter.

Verse 22. *From the depths of the sea*] All this seems to speak of the defeat of the Egyptians, and the miraculous passage of the Red Sea.

Verse 23. *That thy foot may be dipped in the blood*] God will make such a slaughter among his enemies, the Amorites, that thou shalt walk over their dead bodies; and beasts of prey shall feed upon them.

Verse 24. *They have seen thy goings*] These kings of the Amorites have seen thy terrible majesty in their discomfiture, and the slaughter of their subjects.

Verse 25. *The singers went before*] This verse appears to be a description of the procession.

Verse 26. *Bless ye God*] This is what they sung.

A. M. cir. 2962
B. C. cir. 1042
Davidis, Regis
Israelitarum,
cir. annum
14

the Lord, [w]from [x]the fountain
of Israel.
27 There *is* [y]little Benjamin
with their ruler, the princes of
Judah [z]*and* their council, the princes of Zebulun, *and* the princes of Naphtali.
28 Thy God hath [a]commanded thy strength: strengthen, O God, that which thou hast wrought for us.
29 Because of thy temple at Jerusalem [b]shall kings bring presents unto thee.
30 Rebuke [c]the company of spearmen, [d]the multitude of the bulls, with the calves of the people, *till every one* [e]submit himself with pieces of silver: [f]scatter thou the people *that* delight in war.
31 [g]Princes shall come out of
Egypt; [h]Ethiopia shall soon
[i]stretch out her hands unto
God.
32 Sing unto God, ye kingdoms of the earth; O sing praises unto the LORD; Selah:
33 To him [k]that rideth upon the heavens of heavens, *which were* of old; lo, [l]he doth [m]send out his voice, *and that* a mighty voice.
34 [n]Ascribe ye strength unto God: his excellency *is* over Israel, and his strength *is* in the [o]clouds.
35 O God, [p]*thou art* terrible out of thy holy places: the God of Israel *is* he that giveth strength and power unto *his* people. Blessed *be* God.

A. M. cir. 2962
B. C. cir. 1042
Davidis, Regis
Israelitarum,
cir. annum
14

[w]Or, ye that are *of the fountain of Israel*——[x]Deut. xxxiii. 28; Isa. xlviii. 1——[y]1 Sam. ix. 21——[z]Or, with *their company*——[a]So Psa. xlii. 8——[b]1 Kings x. 10, 24, 25; 2 Chron. xxxii. 23; Psa. lxxii. 10; lxxvi. 11; Isa. lx. 16, 17——[c]Or, *the beast of the reeds;* Jer. li. 32, 33 [d]Psa. xxii. 12

[e]2 Sam. viii. 2, 6——[f]Or, *he scattereth*——[g]Isa. xix. 19, 21——[h]Psa. lxxii. 9; Isa. xlv. 14; Zeph. iii. 10 Acts viii. 27——[i]Psa. xliv. 20——[k]Psa. xviii. 10. civ. 3; ver. 4——[l]Psa. xxix. 3, &c.——[m]Heb. *give* [n]Psa. xxix. 1——[o]Or, *heavens*——[p]Psa. xlv. 4; lxv. 5; lxvi. 3; lxxvi. 12

Verse 27. *There* is *little Benjamin*] This is a description of another part of the procession.

Verse 28. *Thy God hath commanded*] This and the following verses is what they sung.

Verse 30. *Rebuke the company of spearmen*] חית קנה *chaiyath kaneh, the wild beast of the reed*—the *crocodile* or *hippopotamus*, the emblem of Pharaoh and the Egyptians: thus all the *Versions*. Our translators have mistaken the meaning; but they have put the true sense in the *margin*.

Verse 31. *Ethiopia shall soon stretch out her hands unto God.*] This verse had its literal fulfilment under Solomon, when Egypt formed an alliance with that king by his marriage with Pharaoh's daughter; and when the queen of Sheba came to Jerusalem to hear the wisdom of Solomon. But as this may be a *prophetic declaration* of the spread of Christianity, it was literally fulfilled after the resurrection of our Lord. There were *Egyptians* at Jerusalem on the day of Pentecost, who, St. Hilary tells us, on their return to their own country proclaimed what they had seen, and became in that country the ambassadors of Christ. The *Ethiopian eunuch* was one of the first among the Gentiles who received the Gospel. Thus *princes* or *chief men came out of Egypt*, and *Ethiopia stretched out her hands to God.* The words themselves refer to the sending ambassadors, and making alliances. The Hebrew is very emphatic: כוש תריץ ידיו לאלהים *cush tarits yadaiv lelohim; Cush will cause her hands to run out to God.* She will, with great *alacrity* and delight, surrender her *power* and *influence* unto God. The *Chaldee* paraphrases well: "The sons of Cush will run, that they may spread out their hands in prayer before God."

Verse 32. *Sing unto God*] All the inhabitants of the earth are invited to sing unto God, to acknowledge him as their God, and give him the praise due to his name.

Verse 33. *Rideth upon the heavens*] He who manages the heavens, directing their course and influence, he formed every orb, ascertained its motion, proportioned its solid contents to the orbit in which it was to revolve, and the other bodies which belong to the same system. As an able and skilful rider manages his horse, so does God the sun, moon, planets, and all the hosts of heaven.

He doth send out his voice] At his *word of command* they run, shed, or reflect their light; and without the smallest deviations obey his will.

Mighty voice.] He thunders in the heavens, and men tremble before him.

Verse 34. *His strength* is *in the clouds.*] This refers to the bursting, rattling, and pounding of thunder and lightning; for all nations have observed that this is an irresistible agent; and even the most enlightened have looked on it as an especial manifestation of the power and sovereignty of God.

Verse 35. *O God*, thou art *terrible out of thy holy places*] The sanctuary and heaven. Out of the former he had often shone forth with consuming splendour; see the case of Korah and his company: out of the latter he had often appeared in terrible majesty in storms, thunder, lightning, &c.

He that giveth strength and power unto his *people.*] Therefore that people must be invincible who have this strong and irresistible God for their support.

Blessed be *God.*] He alone is worthy to be worshipped. Without him nothing is wise, nothing holy, nothing strong; and from him, as the inexhaustible Fountain, all good must be derived. His *mercy* over his creatures is equal to his *majesty* in the universe; and as he has all good in his possession, so is he willing to deal it out, to supply the utmost necessities of his creatures. Blessed be God! The *Arabic* adds, *Alleluiah!*

The best *analysis* I find of this Psalm is that by Bishop Nicholson. I shall give it at large, begging the reader to refer particularly to those passages on which the preceding notes are written, as in some of them the analysis gives a different view of the subject. The old Psalter gives the whole Psalm a spiritual and mystical interpretation. And this is commonly the case in the commentaries of the *fathers*.

Analysis of the Sixty-eighth Psalm

There are many conjectures as to the occasion of the composing of this Psalm; but the most probable is, that it was composed by *David* when he brought up the ark of God, which was the type of the Church and symbol of God's presence, to Jerusalem. After the ark was sent home by the Philistines, it rested first in the obscure lodge of *Aminadab;* it then for a time stayed with Obed-edom, nearly sixty years in both places. It was David's care to provide a fit room for it in the head of the tribes, even in his own city; and to express his joy, and honour the solemnity, David led the way, dancing with all his might in a linen ephod; and all the house of *Israel* followed with shouts and instruments of music in a triumphant manner. Now, that the choir might not want to know how to express their joyful affections, the sweet singer of Israel made this anthem, beginning the verse himself, as was commanded at the removal of the ark, Num. x. 35. The Psalm has *six* parts:—

I. The entrance, or exordium, ver. 1-4.

II. The invitation to praise God, ver. 4.

III. The confirmation of it by many arguments, ver. 4-24.

IV. A lively description of triumph, or pomp of the ark's deportation, ver. 24-28.

V. A petition, which has three parts, ver. 28-31.

VI. An exhortation to all nations to praise God, ver. 31 to the end.

I. "Let God arise" is either a prayer or acclamation; a prayer that he would, or an acclamation that he does, show his power and presence. Of which the consequence would be double:—

1. Towards his enemies, destruction; for he prays, "Let his enemies be scattered; let those that hate him fly before him."

He illustrates it by a twofold comparison:—

(1) "As smoke (when it is at the highest) is driven away, so drive them away."

(2) "As wax melteth before the fire, so let the wicked perish in the presence of God."

2. Towards good men, his servants; which is quite contrary to the other: "Let the righteous be glad; let them rejoice before God; yea, let them exceedingly rejoice." Thus it happened; for when the *ark* was taken by the *Philistines*, the glory was departed from *Israel*, and there was nothing but sadness and sorrow: but with the return of the *ark* the glory returned and all was joy and gladness.

II. And so, by an apostrophe, he turns his speech to all good men, and exhorts them to praise God.

1. "Sing unto God." Let it be done with your voice publicly.

2. *Psallite:* "Sing praises to his name," with instruments of music."

3. "Extol him." Show his way, as in a triumph. Thus, when our Saviour rode into Jerusalem they cut down branches, and strewed their garments in the way.

III. And so David enters upon his confirmation, producing his reasons why they should praise God.

1. Drawn from his majesty: "He rideth upon the heavens;" that is, he rules in the heavens.

2. From the essence: "By his name Jah," the contraction of Jehovah, *I am.* He gives essence to all things; therefore, "rejoice before him."

3. From his general providence and goodness towards his Church.

(1) "He is the father of the fatherless." Loves, cares, and provides an inheritance for them.

(2) "A judge of the widows." He cares for his people when deserted, and for whom no man cares, and when exposed to injury. Such is God in his holy habitation; whose presence is represented by this ark.

(3) "God setteth the solitary in families." He makes the barren woman to keep house, and to be the joyful mother of children. As also the barren woman—the Gentile Church that had no husband, to bring forth children to God.

(4) He brings forth those which are bound with chains; as Joseph, Jeremiah, Daniel, Peter, Paul.

4. On the contrary: "But the rebellious dwell in a dry land;" perish with want and hunger.

IV. From his special providence toward his people *Israel*, which he introduces by an elegant apostrophe: "O God, when thou wentest forth before thy people;" thus amplified:—

1. God's going before them, and marching along with them in *Egypt*, in the wilderness. These signs manifested his presence: "The earth shook, the heavens also dropped at the presence of God: even Sinai itself was moved at the presence of God, the God of Israel."

2. God's provision for them after he gave them the possession of the good land. He fed, sustained them there, counted them his inheritance, and gave them rain and fruitful seasons: "Thou, O God, didst send a plentiful rain, whereby thou didst confirm thine inheritance, when it was weary. The congregation hath dwelt therein: thou, O God, hast prepared of thy goodness for the poor."

3. The victories he gave them over their enemies, ver. 12, which he prefaces by imitation of the song of the victory, sung usually by the women and damsels of those times, ver. 11: "The Lord gave the word," that is, either the *word of war, or* else the *song;* and then "Great was the company of those that published it." As Miriam, Deborah, &c. And in these songs they sang, "Kings of armies did flee apace; and she that tarried at home divided the spoil." So great was the prey.

4. The deliverance he sends from troubles, and the joy he gives after them. "Though ye have lien among the pots," that is, cast aside as some useless or broken pot, the offscouring of all things; "yet shall ye be as the wings of a dove

covered with silver, and her feathers with yellow gold;" i. e., shining and glorious. The allusion seems to be taken from some standard, whose portraiture and device was a dove so overlaid. The Babylonian ensign was a dove. But see the note on this passage.

And this he farther declares by another similitude: "When the Almighty scattered kings in it:" or *for her, i. e.*, his Church, *it was white*—glittering, glorious, to be seen afar off; "it was white as snow in Salmon," with which it is generally covered.

5. From God's especial presence among them, which, that he might make it more evident, David enters upon the commendation of the hill of Sion to which the ark was at this time brought, comparing it with other hills, especially with *Bashan*. That is a hill of God; a high, plentiful, and fertile hill. As if he had said, So much I grant. But, "why leap ye, ye high hills?" Why are ye so proud? Why do ye boast your vines, your fruits, your pastures, your cattle? Sion has the pre-eminence of you all in two respects:—

1. For God's continual habitation and common presence is there: "This is the hill which God desireth to dwell in; yea, the Lord will dwell in it for ever."

2. For his defence of it. "The chariots of God are twenty thousand, even thousands of angels:" and these are for the defence of Sion, his Church; "for God is among them as in Sinai, in the holy place;" in glory and majesty, in Sinai, and in Sion.

And yet he goes on to persuade us to praise God, 1. For his strange and wonderful works. 2. For the performance of his promises. Among his great works there was none so glorious as the ascension of our Saviour, of which the ark's ascension to Jerusalem at this time was a type.

First. 1. Before the ark David and the people used this acclamation: "Thou hast ascended on high." Thou, O God, whose presence is shadowed out by the ark, hast ascended from an obscure house to a kingly palace, *Sion*.

2. "Thou hast led captivity captive;" those that led us captives being captives themselves, and now led in *triumph*.

3. "Thou hast received gifts for men;" spoils and gifts from the conquered kings; or who may become homagers unto him, and redeem their peace.

4. "Yea, for the rebellious also:" Formerly so, but now tributaries.

5. "That the Lord God might dwell among them;" might have a certain place to dwell in; and the ark not be carried, as before, from place to place.

This is the literal sense; but the mystical refers to our Saviour's ascension. St. Paul says, Eph. iv. 8:

1. "Thou hast ascended on high:" when the cloud carried him from earth to heaven.

2. "Thou hast led captivity," those who captured us, "captive;" death, the devil, sin, the power of hell, the curse of the law.

3. "He received, and gave gifts to men:" The *apostles*, *evangelists*, *prophets*, *doctors*, and *teachers*, were these gifts—graces, gifts of the Spirit.

4. "Yea, for the rebellious also:" Paul, a persecutor; Austin, a Manichæan.

5. "That the Lord God might dwell among them:" for to that end St. Paul says these gifts were given, "to the work of the ministry, to the edification of the Church, to the building up of the body of Christ." Eph. iv. 12, &c.

The two effects of his ascension then were, one towards his enemies, the other for his friends: "When thou ascendest up on high,"—

1. "Thou leddest captivity captive:" this was the consequence to his enemies.

2. "Thou receivedst, and gavest gifts:" This for his friends. For which he sings, "Blessed be God;" for he comes over both again:—

1. The gifts to his friends: "Blessed be the Lord, who daily loadeth us with benefits, even the God of our salvation." "He that is our God is the God of salvation; and unto God the Lord belong the issues from death." He knows many ways to deliver in death itself, when there is no hope.

2. The conquest of his enemies; for such he counts obstinate impenitent sinners; those he will destroy: "God shall wound the head of his enemies, and the hairy scalp of such a one as goeth on still in his trespasses."

Secondly, His last argument is, God's performance of his promise to save them. When you were in the wilderness; when you fought with *Og*, king of *Bashan;* when at the Red Sea, I delivered you. The Lord saith still to his people:—

1. "I will bring again from Bashan;" from equally great dangers.

2. "I will bring my people again from the depths of the sea:" when there is no hope.

3. And for thy enemies, they shall be destroyed by a great effusion of blood: "That thy foot may be dipped in the blood of thine enemies, and the tongue of thy dogs in the same;" thou shalt waste, and make a great slaughter.

4. And now he descends to set before our eyes the pomp and show which was used in the ascent and bringing back of the *ark*, and the proceeding of it.

1. The people were present to witness it: "They have seen thy goings, O God; even the goings of my God, my King, in the sanctuary."

2. The manner of the pomp: "The singers went before, the players on instruments followed after; among them were the damsels playing with timbrels."

3. In the pomp they were not silent; and that they be not, he exhorts them: "Bless ye God in the congregations, even the Lord, from the fountain of Israel,"—Jacob's posterity.

4. And he gives in the catalogue of the tribes that were present, but these especially,—

1. "There is little Benjamin," Jacob's youngest son, or now the least, wasted with war, "with their ruler," the chief prince of their tribe.

2. "The princes of Judah, and their council."

3. "The princes of Zebulun, and the princes of Naphtali;" the farthest tribes, therefore the nearest.

V. And in the midst of the pomp he makes a prayer which has three vows, before which he prefixes the acknowledgment that all the power and strength of *Israel* was from God: "Thy God hath commanded thy strength." He then prays,—

1. For the confirmation, establishment, and continuance of this strength: "Strengthen, O God, that which thou hast wrought for us;" and let this be evinced "by the kings and tributaries that shall bring gifts. Because of thy temple at Jerusalem shall kings bring presents unto thee."

2. For the conquest and subduing of the enemy, until they become tributaries, and do homage: "Rebuke the company of spearmen, the multitude of the bulls, with the calves of the people;" kings, princes, and their potent subjects; "till every one submit himself with pieces of silver: scatter thou the people that delight in war." See the note.

3. For the increase of Christ's kingdom, of which David was but a type, by the access of the *Gentiles.* "Princes shall come out of Egypt; Ethiopia shall soon stretch out her hands unto God." These, by a *synecdoche,* being put for all nations.

VI. This excellent Psalm draws now towards a conclusion; and it is a resumption of that which he principally intended; that is, that God be blessed, honoured, praised. He first exhorts, then shows the reasons for it.

1. He exhorts all nations to perform this duty: at first, the Jews, but now all universally: "Sing unto God, ye kingdoms of the earth; O sing praises unto the Lord."

2. His reasons to induce them to do it.

The majesty of God testified,—

1. By his works: "To him that rideth upon the heaven of heavens, which were of old."

2. His power, in his thunder, in his word: "He doth send out his voice, and that a mighty voice."

3. His wise protection of and providence over his people: "Ascribe ye strength unto God: his excellency is over Israel, and his strength is in the clouds."

4. His communication of himself to his Church in particular: 1. "O God, thou art terrible out of thy holy places." 2. "The God of Israel is he that giveth strength and power unto his people." 3. "Blessed be God." With this *epiphonema* he concludes.

PSALM LXIX

The psalmist describes his afflicted state, and the wickedness of his adversaries, 1–21; *he declares the miseries that should come upon his enemies,* 22–28; *enlarges on his afflicted state, and expresses his confidence in God,* 29–34; *prophesies the restoration of the Jews to their own land and temple,* 35, 36.

XIII. DAY. EVENING PRAYER

To the chief Musician [a]upon Shoshannim, *A Psalm* of David

SAVE me, O God; for [b]the waters are
come in unto *my* soul.
2 [c]I sink in [d]deep mire, where *there is* no
standing: I am come into [e]deep waters, where
the floods overflow me.
3 [f]I am weary of my crying: my throat is
dried: [g]mine eyes fail while I wait for my God.
4 They that [h]hate me without a cause are
more than the hairs of mine head: they that
would destroy me, *being* mine enemies wrongfully, are mighty: then I restored *that* which
I took not away.

[a]Psa. xlv. title——[b]Ver. 2, 14, 15; Jonah ii. 5——[c]Psa. xl. 2——[d]Heb. *the mire of depth*

[e]Heb. *depth of waters*——[f]Psa. vi. 6——[g]Psa. cxix. 82, 123; Isa. xxxviii. 14——[h]Psa. xxxv. 19; John xv. 25

NOTES ON PSALM LXIX

The *title* is: "To the chief Musician upon Shoshannim, *A Psalm* of David." See this title explained on Psalm xlv.

The Psalm is supposed to have been written *during the captivity,* and to have been the work of some Levite Divinely inspired. It is a very fine composition, equal to most in the Psalter. Several portions of it seem to have a reference to our Lord; to his advent, passion, resurrection, the vocation of the Gentiles, the establishment of the Christian Church, and the reprobation of the Jews. The *ninth* verse is quoted by St. John, chap. ii. 17. The *twenty-first* verse is quoted by St. *Matthew,* chap. xxvii. 34, 48; by St. *Mark,* chap. xv. 23; by St. *John,* chap. xix. 29; and applied to the sufferings of our Lord, in the treatment he received from the Jews. St. *Paul* quotes the *twenty-second* as a prophecy of the wickedness of the Jews, and the punishment they were to receive. He quotes the *twenty-third* verse in the same way. See the marginal references. Those portions which the writers of the New Testament apply to our Lord, we may apply also; of others we should be careful.

Verse 1. *The waters are come in unto* my *soul.*] I am in the deepest distress. The waters have broken their dikes, and are just ready to sweep me away! Save me, Lord! In such circumstances I can have no other help.

In the *first, second, third, fourteenth,* and *fifteenth* verses, the psalmist, speaking in the person of the captives in Babylon, compares their captivity to an *abyss of waters,* breaking all bounds, and ready to swallow them up; to a *deep mire,* in which there was no solid bottom, and no *standing;* and to a *pit,* in which they were about to *be inclosed* for ever. This is strongly figurative, and very expressive.

Verse 3. *I am weary of my crying*] A pathetic description of the state of the poor captives for about *seventy* years.

Verse 4. *Then I restored* that *which I took not away.*] I think, with Calmet, that this is

5 O God, thou knowest my foolishness; and
my [i]sins are not hid from thee.
6 Let not them that wait on thee, O Lord
GOD of hosts, be ashamed for my sake: let
not those that seek thee be confounded for my
sake, O God of Israel.
7 Because for thy sake I have borne reproach; shame hath covered my face.
8 [k]I am become a stranger unto my brethren, and an alien unto my mother's children.
9 [l]For the zeal of thine house hath eaten
me up: [m]and the reproaches of them that reproached thee are fallen upon me.
10 [n]When I wept, *and chastened* my soul
with fasting, that was to my reproach.
11 I made sackcloth also my garment; [o]and
I became a proverb to them.
12 They that sit in the gate speak against
me; and [p]I *was* the song of the [q]drunk-
ards.
13 But as for me, my prayer *is* unto thee,
O LORD, [r]*in* an acceptable time; O God, in
the multitude of thy mercy hear me, in the
truth of thy salvation.
14 Deliver me out of the mire, and let me
not sink: [s]let me be delivered from them that
hate me, and out of [t]the deep waters.
15 Let not the waterflood overflow me, neither let the deep swallow me up, and let not
the pit [u]shut her mouth upon me.
16 Hear me, O LORD; [v]for thy loving-kindness *is* good: [w]turn unto me according to the
multitude of thy tender mercies.
17 And [x]hide not thy face from thy servant;
for I am in trouble: [y]hear me speedily.

[i]Heb. *guiltiness*——[k]Psa. xxxi. 11; Isa. liii. 3; John i. 11; vii. 5——[l]Psa. cxix. 139; John ii. 17——[m]See Psa. lxxxix. 50, 51; Rom. xv. 3——[n]Psa. xxxv. 13, 14——[o]1 Kings ix. 7; Jer. xxiv. 9——[p]Job xxx. 9; Psa. xxxv. 15, 16

[q]Heb. *drinkers of strong drink*——[r]Isa. xlix. 8; lv. 6; 2 Cor. vi. 2——[s]Psa. cxliv. 7——[t]Ver. 1, 2, 15——[u]Num. xvi. 33——[v]Psa. lxiii. 3——[w]Psa. xxv. 16; lxxxvi. 16 [x]Psa. xxvii. 9; cii. 2——[y]Heb. *make haste to hear me*

a sort of *proverbial* expression, like such as these, "Those who suffered the wrong, pay the costs." Delirant reges, plectuntur Achivi. "Kings sin, and the people are punished." "The fathers have eaten sour grapes, and the children's teeth are set on edge." Our fathers have grievously sinned against the Lord, and we their posterity suffer for it. See on verse 12. Some have applied it to our Lord. I restored, by my suffering and death, that image of God and the Divine favour, which I took not away. That is, In my *human nature* I expiated the crime that *human beings* had committed against God. But such applications are very gratuitous.

Verse 5. *Thou knowest my foolishness*] Though we have been brought into captivity in consequence of the crimes of our fathers, yet we have guilt enough of our own to merit a continuation of our miseries. How can such words as are in this verse be attributed to our blessed Lord, however they may be twisted or turned?

Verse 6. *Be ashamed for my sake*] The sins of the Jews were a great stumbling-block in the way of the conversion of the Gentiles. They had been the *peculiar people* of the Lord. "How," say the Gentiles, "can a pure and holy Being love such people?" They were now *punished* for their crimes. "How," say the Gentiles, "can God deal so hardly with those whom he professes to love?" The pious among the captives felt keenly, because this reproach seemed to fall upon their gracious and merciful God.

Verse 7. *For thy sake I have borne reproach*] The Gentiles have said, "Why such an obstinate attachment to the *worship* of a Being who treats you so rigorously, and who interests not himself in your comfort and deliverance?" And in these cutting reproaches some of the ungodly *Jews* took a part: "I am an alien to my mother's children."

Verse 9. *The zeal of thine house hath eaten me up*] The strong desire to promote thy glory has absorbed all others. All the desires of my *body* and *soul* are wrapped up in this. This verse is very properly applied to our Lord, John ii. 17, who *went about doing good;* and gave up his life, not only for the redemption of man, but to "magnify the law, and make it honourable."

Verse 12. *They that sit in the gate*] At the gates were the courts for public justice; *there* were complaints lodged, and causes heard. No doubt many vexatious complaints were made against the poor captives; and false accusations, through which they grievously suffered; so that, literally, they were often "obliged to restore that which they had not taken away." See ver. 4.

The song of the drunkards.] These poor miserable people were exposed to all sorts of indignities. Though the conduct is base, the exultation over a fallen enemy is frequent. How miserable was this lot! Forsaken by friends, scorned by enemies, insulted by inferiors; the scoff of libertines, and the song of drunkards; besides hard travail of body, miserably lodged and fed; with the burning crown of all, a deep load of guilt upon the conscience. To such a life any death was preferable.

Verse 13. *My prayer* is *unto thee, O Lord,* in *an acceptable time*] This seems to refer to the *end of the captivity*, which Jeremiah had said should last *seventy years*, Jer. xxv. 11, 12: "The whole land shall be a desolation, and an astonishment; and these nations shall serve the king of Babylon seventy years. And it shall come to pass, when seventy years are accomplished, that I will punish the king of Babylon," &c. The conclusion of this period was the *accepted time* of which the psalmist speaks. *Now*, they incessantly pray for the fulfilment of the promise made by Jeremiah: and to hear them, would be the *truth* of God's *salvation;* it would show the promise to be *true*, because the *salvation*—the *deliverance*, was granted.

Verse 16. *Thy loving-kindness* is *good*] The

18 Draw nigh unto my soul, *and* redeem it: deliver me because of mine enemies.

19 Thou hast known [z]my reproach, and my shame, and my dishonour: mine adversaries *are* all before thee.

20 Reproach hath broken my heart; and I am full of heaviness: and I [a]looked *for some* [b]to take pity, but *there was* none; and for [c]comforters, but I found none.

21 They gave me also gall for my meat; [d]and in my thirst they gave me vinegar to drink.

22 [e]Let their table become a snare before them: and *that which should have been* for *their* welfare, *let it become* a trap.

23 [f]Let their eyes be darkened, that they see not; and make their loins continually to shake.

24 [g]Pour out thine indignation upon them, and let thy wrathful anger take hold of them.

25 [h]Let [i]their habitation be desolate; *and* [k]let none dwell in their tents.

26 For [l]they persecute [m]*him* whom thou hast smitten; and they talk to the grief of [n]those whom thou hast wounded.

27 [o]Add [p]iniquity unto their iniquity: [q]and let them not come into thy righteousness.

28 Let them [r]be blotted out of the book of the living, [s]and not be written with the righteous.

29 But I *am* poor and sorrowful: let thy salvation, O God, set me up on high.

30 [t]I will praise the name of God with a song, and will magnify him with thanksgiving.

31 [u]*This* also shall please the LORD better than an ox *or* bullock that hath horns and hoofs.

---

[z]Psa. xxii. 6, 7; Isa. liii. 3; Heb. xii. 2——[a]Psa. cxlii. 4; Isa. lxiii. 5——[b]Heb. *to lament* with me——[c]Job xvi. 2——[d]Matt. xxvii. 34, 48; Mark xv. 23; John xix. 29 [e]Rom. xi. 9, 10——[f]Isa. vi. 9, 10; John xii. 39, 40; Rom. xi. 10; 2 Cor. iii. 14——[g]1 Thess. ii. 16——[h]Matt. xxiii. 38; Acts i. 20——[i]Heb. *their palace*——[k]Heb. *let there not be a dweller*——[l]See 2 Chron. xxviii. 9; Zech. i. 15 [m]Isa. liii. 4——[n]Heb. *thy wounded*——[o]Rom. i. 28 [p]Or, *punishment of iniquity*——[q]Isa. xxvi. 10; Rom. ix. 31——[r]Exod. xxxii. 32; Phil. iv. 3; Rev. iii. 5; xiii. 8——[s]Ezek. i. 39; Luke x. 20; Heb. xii. 23——[t]Psa. xxviii. 7——[u]Psa. l.13, 14, 23

---

word חסד *chesed* signifies *exuberance of kindness;* and the word רחמים *rachamim*, which we translate *tender mercies*, signifies such *affection* as *mothers* bear to their *young:* and in God, there is רב *rob*, a *multitude*, of *such tender mercies* towards the children of men!

Verse 18. *Deliver me because of mine enemies.*] Probably they now began to think that the redemption of these captives was not an impossible thing; that it was not far off; and therefore they had great rage, because they found their time was but short.

Verse 19. *Thou hast known my reproach*] This is one of the most forcible appeals to mercy and compassion that was ever made. The language of these two verses is inimitable; and the sentiment cannot be mended. I can devise no comment that would not lessen their effect.

Verse 21. *They gave me also gall for my meat*] Even the *food*, necessary to preserve us in their slavery, was frequently mingled with what rendered it unpleasant and disgusting, though not absolutely unwholesome. And vinegar, sour small wines, was given us for our beverage. This is applied to our Lord, Matt. xxvii. 34, where the reader is requested to consult the notes.

Verse 22. *Let their table become a snare*] The execrations here and in the following verses should be read in the *future* tense, because they are *predictive;* and not in the *imperative mood*, as if they were the offspring of the psalmist's resentment: "Their table SHALL become a snare;—their eyes SHALL be darkened; —thou WILT pour out thine indignation upon them;—thy wrathful anger SHALL take hold of them;—their habitation SHALL be desolate,—and none SHALL dwell in their tents."

The psalmist *prophesies* that the evils which they had inflicted on the Israelites should be visited on themselves; that as they had made them *eat*, *drink*, *labour*, and *suffer*, so God should in his judgment treat them.

Verse 27. *Add iniquity unto their iniquity*] תנה עון על עונם *tenah avon al avonam; give iniquity*, that is, the *reward* of it, *upon* or *for their iniquity*. Or, as the original signifies *perverseness*, treat their *perverseness* with *perverseness:* act, in thy judgments, as *crookedly* towards them as they dealt *crookedly* towards thee. They shall get, in the way of punishment, what they have dealt out in the way of oppression.

Verse 28. *Let them be blotted out*] They *shall* be blotted out from the land of the living. They shall *be cut off from life*, which they have forfeited by their cruelty and oppression. The psalmist is speaking of *retributive* justice; and in this sense all these passages are to be understood.

And not be written with the righteous.] They shall have no title to that *long life* which God has promised to his followers.

Verse 29. *I am poor and sorrowful*] Literally, *I am laid low, and full of pain* or *grief.* Hence the prayer, "Let thy salvation, O God, set me on high!" My oppression has laid me *low;* thy salvation shall make me *high!*

Verse 31. *An ox* or *bullock that hath horns and hoofs.*] Oxen offered in sacrifice had their horns and hoofs *gilded;* and the psalmist might mention these parts of the victim more particularly, because they were more *conspicuous.* Others think that *full-grown* animals are intended, those that had perfect *horns*, in opposition to *calves* or *steers.* I think the first the preferable sense; for the horns, &c., of consecrated animals are thus ornamented in the east to the present day.

32 [v]The [w]humble shall see *this, and* be glad:
and [x]your heart shall live that seek God.
33 For the LORD heareth the poor, and despiseth not [y]his prisoners.
34 [z]Let the heaven and earth praise him, the
seas, [a]and every thing that [b]moveth therein.
35 [c]For God will save Zion, and will build
the cities of Judah: that they may dwell
there, and have it in possession.
36 [d]The seed also of his servants shall inherit it: and they that love his name shall
dwell therein.

[v]Psalm xxxiv. 2——[w]Or, *meek*——[x]Psa. xxii. 26
[y]Eph. iii. 1——[z]Psa. xcvi. 11; cxlviii. 1; Isa. xliv. 23; xlix. 13——[a]Isa. lv. 12——[b]Heb. *creepeth*——[c]Psa. li. 18; Isa. xliv. 26——[d]Psa. cii. 28

Verse 32. *The humble shall see* this, and *be glad*] Those who are *low*, pressed down by misfortune or cruelty, shall see this and take courage; expecting that thou wilt lift *them* up also; and thus the heart of those who seek the Lord shall be *revived.*

Verse 33. *For the Lord heareth the poor*] אביונים *ebyonim, of the beggars.* He perhaps refers here to the case of the captives, many of whom were reduced to the most abject state, so as to be obliged to beg bread from their heathen oppressors.

His prisoners.] The captives, shut up by his judgments in Chaldea, without any civil liberty, like culprits in a prison.

Verse 34. *Let the heaven and earth praise him*] The psalmist has the fullest confidence that God will turn their captivity, and therefore calls upon all creatures to magnify him for his mercy.

Verse 35. *God will save Zion*] This fixes the Psalm to the time of the captivity. There was no *Zion* belonging to the Jews in the time of *Saul,* when those suppose the Psalm to be written who make David the author; for David, after he came to the throne, won the stronghold of Zion from the Jebusites. 2. Sam. v. 7; 1 Chron. xi. 5.

Will build the cities of Judah] This refers to the return from the captivity, when all the destroyed cities should be rebuilt, and the Jews repossess their forfeited heritages. Some apply this to the redemption of the human race; and suppose that *Zion* is the type of the Christian Church into which the Gentiles were to be called. What evangelists and apostles apply to our Lord, we safely may. What others see so clearly in this Psalm relative to Gospel matters, I cannot discern.

Analysis of the Sixty-ninth Psalm

There are *three* parts in this Psalm:—

I. The psalmist's *prayer*, and the *reasons* for it, ver. 1-21.

II. *Declaration* of God's *judgments* against his enemies, ver. 22-28.

III. His *profession of thanks*, ver. 29-36.

I. His *prayer:* "Save me, O God!" And then his reasons.

1. His present condition: "The waters are come in unto my soul."
2. "I sink in deep mire."
3. "I am come into deep waters."
4. "I am weary of my crying."
5. "My throat is dried" with calling on thee.
6. "Mine eyes fail while I wait for my God."

When he considered his enemies, he found reason to cry. They were,

1. *Malicious:* "They hate me without a cause."
2. *Numerous:* "More than the hairs of my head."
3. *Powerful:* "My enemies are mighty," ver. 1-4.

1. He declares his innocence with respect to their accusations, and the oppression he suffered: "I restored that which I took not away."
2. Begs to be heard, lest he should be confounded before his enemies.
3. Shows that he *suffers* for God's *cause.*
4. He was *zealous* for the Divine worship.
5. He was a deep *penitent.*

On which account he was a subject of reproach:—

1. To the *high*—those who sat in the gate.
2. To the *low* and *base:* "I was the song of the drunkards."

He renews his *petition*, and presses on God to hear him:—

1. Because of his being *ready to sink*, ver. 13-15.
2. Because of *God's goodness*, *mercy*, and *truth:* "In the multitude of thy mercies," &c.
3. Because he was *God's servant*, and would not desert his Master.
4. Because of his *enemies*, who would have a sinful triumph if he was not delivered.

And he pleads their *ill usage* as a reason why God should help him.

1. They were *scorners*, and God knew it: "They are all before thee," ver. 19.
2. *Reproach* had almost *broken his heart.*
3. His *friends* had *abandoned him*, ver. 20.
4. His *enemies* were *inhuman:* "They gave me gall," &c., ver. 22.

II. *Prophetic declaration of God's judgments* against them:—

1. Their "table should be a snare to them," ver. 22.
2. They should be given up to judicial *blindness*, ver. 23.
3. They should be *enfeebled in their bodies:* "Make their loins shake," ver. 23.
4. God's "wrath should be poured out upon them," ver. 24.
5. Their *country* should be *wasted*, ver. 25.
6. They should have the *punishment* due to their *iniquity*, ver. 27.
7. They should come to an *untimely* death: "Let them be blotted out," ver. 28.

III. His *profession* of *thanks.* Having spoken of his own condition, that he was *poor* and sorrowful, he now breaks out into praise:—

1. "I will praise the name of God," ver. 30.

2. This will be the most *acceptable sacrifice*, ver. 31.

The *effect* of his *deliverance* would be *double:*—

1. It would "gladden the poor," ver. 32, 33.

2. All "creatures would take an interest in it," ver. 34. All shall praise God.

And for this he gives the following *reasons:*—

1. God's *goodness* to his Church: "He will save Zion."

2. He will *confirm his kingdom* among them: "He will build," &c.

3. They shall have peace and security: "That they may dwell there, and have it in possession," ver. 35.

4. All that *love his name* should have it *perpetually*, ver. 36.

The cruel, the oppressor, the scorner, the irreligious, the hypocrite, shall have nothing of God's approbation here, and shall be excluded from his heavenly kingdom for ever.

PSALM LXX

The psalmist prays for speedy deliverance, 1; *prays against those who sought his life*, 2, 3; *and for the blessedness of those who sought God*, 4; *urges his speedy deliverance*, 5.

To the chief Musician, *A Psalm* of David, [a]to bring to remembrance

A. M. cir. 2981
B. C. cir. 1023
Davidis, Regis
Israelitarum,
cir. annum
33

MAKE *haste*, [b]O God, to deliver me; make haste [c]to
help me, O LORD.
2 [d]Let them be ashamed and
confounded that seek after my soul: let them
be turned backward, and put to confusion,
that desire my hurt.
3 [e]Let them be turned back for a reward of
their shame that say, Aha,
aha.

A. M. cir. 2981
B. C. cir. 1023
Davidis, Regis
Israelitarum,
cir. annum
33

4 Let all those that seek thee
rejoice and be glad in thee: and
let such as love thy salvation say continually,
Let God be magnified.
5 [f]But I *am* poor and needy: [g]make
haste unto me, O God: thou *art* my help
and my deliverer; O LORD, make no tarrying.

[a]Psalm xxxviii. title——[b]Psalm xl. 13, &c.; lxxi. 12——[c]Heb. *to my help*

[d]Psa. xxxv. 4, 26; lxxi. 13——[e]Psa. xl. 15——[f]Psa. xl. 17——[g]Psa. cxli. 1

NOTES ON PSALM LXX

The *title* in the *Hebrew* is, *To the chief Musician*, A Psalm *of David, to bring to remembrance.* There seems little sense in this title. It seems to intimate that the Psalm was written as a memorial that David had been in sore affliction, and that God had delivered him. So the *Vulgate, Septuagint, Æthiopic*, and *Arabic*. It is almost word for word the same with *the five last verses of* Psalm xl., to the notes on which the reader is referred.

Verse 1. *Make haste to help me*] I am in extreme distress, and the most imminent danger. *Haste to help me, or I am lost.*

Verse 2. *Let them be turned backward*] They are coming in a *body* against me. Lord, stop their progress!

Verse 3. *That say, Aha, aha.*] האח האח *heach! heach!* a note of supreme contempt. See on Psa. xl. 15.

Verse 4. *Let God be magnified.*] Let his glory, mercy, and kindness, continually appear in the *increase* of his own work in the souls of his followers!

Verse 5. *But I* am *poor and needy*] עני ואביון *ani veebyon*, I am a poor man, and a beggar—an *afflicted beggar;* a sense of my poverty causes me to beg.

Thou art *my help*] I know thou hast enough, and to spare; and therefore I come to *thee*.

Make no tarrying.] My wants are many, my danger great, my time short. O God, delay not!

ANALYSIS OF THE SEVENTIETH PSALM

The contents of this Psalm are the following:—

I. The prayer of David for himself, that he may be freed from his enemies, ver. 1, repeated ver. 5.

II. For the speedy overthrow of the wicked, ver. 2, 3.

III. For the prosperity of the godly, ver. 4.

IV. The arguments he uses to induce God to answer his prayer.

1. His miserable condition: "I am poor and needy."

2. God's office: "Thou art my Helper and Redeemer."

For a farther analysis, see at the end of the *fortieth* Psalm.

PSALM LXXI

The prophet, in confidence, prays for God's favour, 1–5; *recounts God's kindness to him from youth to old age*, 6–9; *shows what his adversaries plot against him, and prays for their confusion*, 10–13; *promises fidelity, and determines to be a diligent preacher of righteousness even in old age*, 14–19; *takes encouragement in God's mercy, and foresees the confusion of all his adversaries*, 20–24.

XIV. DAY. MORNING PRAYER

A. M. cir. 2981
B. C. cir. 1023
Davidis, Regis
Israelitarum,
cir. annum
33

IN [a]thee, O LORD, do I put my
trust: let me never be put to
confusion.
2 [b]Deliver me in thy righteousness, and cause me to escape: [c]incline
thine ear unto me, and save me.
3 [d]Be [e]thou my strong habitation, whereunto I may continually resort: thou hast given
[f]commandment to save me; for thou *art* my
rock and my fortress.
4 [g]Deliver me, O my God, out of the hand
of the wicked, out of the hand of the unrighteous and cruel man.
5 For thou *art* [h]my hope, O Lord GOD:
thou art my trust from my youth.
6 [i]By thee have I been holden up from the
womb: thou art he that took me out of my
mother's bowels: my praise *shall be* continually of thee.

A. M. cir. 2981
B. C. cir. 1023
Davidis, Regis
Israelitarum,
cir. annum
33

7 [k]I am as a wonder unto
many; but thou *art* my strong
refuge.
8 Let [l]my mouth be filled
with thy praise *and with* thy honour all the day.
9 [m]Cast me not off in the time of old age;
forsake me not when my strength faileth.
10 For mine enemies speak against me; and
they that [n]lay wait for my soul [o]take counsel
together,
11 Saying, God hath forsaken him: persecute
and take him; for *there is* none to deliver *him*.
12 [p]O God, be not far from me: O my God,
[q]make haste for my help.
13 [r]Let them be confounded *and* consumed
that are adversaries to my soul: let them be
covered *with* reproach and dishonour that seek
my hurt.
14 But I will hope continually, and will yet
praise thee more and more.

---

[a]Psalm xxv. 2, 3; xxxi. 1——[b]Psalm xxxi. 1——[c]Psa. xvii. 6——[d]Psalm xxxi. 2, 3——[e]Hebrew, *Be thou to me for a rock of habitation*——[f]Psalm xliv. 4——[g]Psa. cxl. 1, 4——[h]Jer. xvii. 7, 17——[i]Psa. xxii. 9, 10; Isaiah xlvi. 3

[k]Isa. viii. 18; Zech. iii. 8; 1 Cor. iv. 9——[l]Psa. xxxv. 28——[m]Ver. 18——[n]Heb. *watch*, or *observe*——[o]2 Sam. xvii. 1; Matt. xxvii. 1——[p]Psa. xxii. 11, 19; xxxv. 22; xxxviii. 21, 22——[q]Psa. lxx. 1——[r]Ver. 24; Psa. xxxv. 4, 26; xl. 14; lxx. 2

NOTES ON PSALM LXXI

There is no *title* to this Psalm either in the *Hebrew* or *Chaldee;* and the reason is, it was written as a part of the preceding Psalm, as appears by about *twenty-seven* of *Kennicott's* and *De Rossi's* MSS. The *Vulgate*, *Septuagint*, *Æthiopic*, and *Arabic*, have, "A Psalm of David for the sons of Jonadab, and the first of those who were led captives." For the *first*, *second*, and *third* verses, see the notes on their parallels, Psa. xxxi. 1-3.

Verse 3. *Be thou my strong habitation*] Instead of מעון *maon, habitation*, many of *Kennicott's* and *De Rossi's* MSS. read מעוז *maoz, munition* or *defence.* Be thou my rock of defence.

Thou hast given commandment to save me] Thou hast determined my escape, and hast ordered thy angels to guard me. See Psa. xci. 11, 12.

Verse 4. *Out of the hand of the wicked*] Probably his unnatural son *Absalom*, called here רשע *rasha*, the WICKED, because he had violated all laws, human and Divine.

The unrighteous and cruel man.] Probably *Ahithophel* who was the iniquitous counsellor of a wicked and rebellious son.

Verse 5. *My trust from my youth.*] When I was born into the world, thou didst receive me, and thou tookest me under thy especial care. "My praise *shall be* continually of thee." Rather, *I have always made thee my boast.*

Verse 7. *I am as a wonder unto many*] I am כמופת *kemopheth*, "as a portent," or "type:" I am a *typical person;* and many of the things that happen to *me* are to be considered in reference to *him* of whom I am a type. But he may mean, I am a *continual prodigy.* My low estate, my slaying the lion and the bear, conquering the Philistine, escaping the fury of Saul, and being raised to the throne of Israel, are all so many *wonders* of thy providence, and effects of thy power and grace.

Verse 9. *Cast me not off in the time of old age*] The original might be translated and paraphrased thus: "Thou wilt not cast me off till the time of old age; and according to the failure of my flesh, thou wilt not forsake me." My expectation of rest and happiness will not be deferred till the time that I shall be an aged man. Thou wilt not withdraw thy presence from me as my flesh decays, and as my natural strength abates; but, on the contrary, as my outward man decays, my inward man shall be renewed day by day. It was in David's *old age* that the rebellion of Absalom took place.

Verse 10. *Lay wait for my soul*] They seek to destroy my *life.*

Verse 11. *God hath forsaken him*] "God, who has been his special help all through life, and who has guarded him so that no hand could be raised successfully against him, has now cast him off; therefore we shall easily prevail against him. His present adversity shows that God is no longer his friend." Thus *men* judge. "Secular prosperity is a proof of God's favour: adversity is a proof of his displeasure." But this is not God's way, except in especial judgments, &c. He never manifests his pleasure or displeasure by secular good or ill.

Verse 13. *Let them be confounded*] They *shall* be confounded: these are *prophetic* denunciations.

Verse 14. *I will hope continually*] I shall expect deliverance after deliverance, and blessing after blessing; and, in consequence, I will praise thee more and more. As thy blessings abound, so shall my praises.

A. M. cir. 2981 B. C. cir. 1023 Davidis, Regis Israelitarum, cir. annum 33

15 [s]My mouth shall show forth thy righteousness *and* thy salvation all the day; for [t]I know not the numbers *thereof*.

16 I will go in the strength of the Lord God: I will make mention of thy righteousness, *even* of thine only.

17 O God, thou hast taught me from my youth: and hitherto have I declared thy wondrous works.

18 [u]Now also [v]when I am old and grey-headed, O God, forsake me not; until I have showed [w]thy strength unto *this* generation, *and* thy power to every one *that* is to come.

19 [x]Thy righteousness also, O God, *is* very high, who hast done great things: [y]O God, who *is* like unto thee!

20 [z]*Thou,* which hast showed me great and sore troubles, [a]shalt quicken me again, and shalt bring me up again from the depths of the earth.

21 Thou shalt increase my greatness, and comfort me on every side.

22 I will also praise thee [b]with [c]the psaltery, *even* thy truth, O my God: unto thee will I sing with the harp, O thou [d]Holy One of Israel.

23 My lips shall greatly rejoice when I sing unto thee; and [e]my soul, which thou hast redeemed.

24 [f]My tongue also shall talk of thy righteousness all the day long: for [g]they are confounded, for they are brought unto shame, that seek my hurt.

[s]Ver. 8, 24; Psa. xxxv. 28——[t]Psa. xl. 5; cxxxix. 17, 18——[u]Ver. 9——[v]Heb. *unto old age and grey hairs*——[w]Heb. *thine arm*——[x]Psa. lvii. 10——[y]Psa. xxxv. 10; lxxxvi. 8; lxxxix. 6, 8

[z]Psa. lx. 5——[a]Hos. vi. 1, 2——[b]Heb. *with the instrument of psaltery*——[c]Psa. xcii. 1, 2, 3; cl. 3——[d]2 Kings xix. 22; Isa. lx. 9——[e]Psa. ciii. 4——[f]Ver. 8, 15——[g]Ver. 13

Verse 15. *I know not the numbers*] I must be continually in the spirit of gratitude, praise, and obedience; for thy blessings to me are innumerable.

Verse 16. *I will go*] אבוא *abo*, I will enter, i. e., into the tabernacle, in the strength or *mightinesses of Adonai Jehovah*, the supreme God, who is my *Prop, Stay*, and *Support*.

I will make mention of thy righteousness] I will continually record and celebrate the *acts of thy mercy and goodness*. They are without number, (verse 15,) and of these alone will I speak.

Verse 17. *Thou hast taught me from my youth*] I have had thee for my continual instructor: and thou didst begin to teach me thy fear and love from my tenderest infancy. Those are well taught whom God instructs; and when he teaches, there is no delay in learning.

Verse 18. *Old and grey-headed*] In the *ninth* verse he mentioned the circumstance of *old age;* here he *repeats* it, with the addition of *hoary-headedness*, which, humanly speaking, was calculated to make a deeper impression in his favour. Though all these things are well known to God, and he needs not our information, yet he is pleased to say, "Come now, and let us *reason* together." And when his children plead and reason with him, they are acting precisely as he has commanded.

Verse 19. *Thy righteousness*—is *very high*] עד מרום *ad marom*—is up to the exalted place, reaches *up to heaven*. The mercy of God fills all *space* and *place*. It crowns in the heavens what it governed upon earth.

Who hast done great things] גדלות *gedoloth*. Thou hast worked *miracles*, and displayed the *greatest acts of power*.

Who is like unto thee!] מי כמוך *mi camocha*. God is alone,—who can resemble him? He is eternal. He can have none *before*, and there can be none *after;* for in the infinite *unity* of his *trinity* he is that eternal, unlimited, impartible, incomprehensible, and uncompounded ineffable Being, whose *essence* is hidden from all created intelligences, and whose *counsels* cannot be fathomed by any creature that even his own hand can form. WHO IS LIKE UNTO THEE! will excite the wonder, amazement, praise, and adoration of angels and men to all eternity.

Verse 20. Thou, *which hast showed me great and sore troubles*] *Multiplied straits* and difficulties. And thou hast only *showed* them. Hadst thou permitted them to have *fallen upon me* with all their own energy and natural consequences, they would have destroyed me. As it was, I was nearly buried under them.

Shalt quicken me again] Shalt revive me—put new life in me. This has been applied to the passion of our Lord, and his resurrection; for it is added, Thou

Shalt bring me up again from the depths of the earth.] Death shall not prey upon my body; thy Holy One can see no corruption. As applicable to David, it might mean his being almost overwhelmed with afflictions; and his deliverance was like a life from the dead.

Verse 21. *Thou shalt increase my greatness*] Thou wilt restore me to my throne and kingdom; and it shall be done in such a way that all shall see it was the hand of God; and I shall have the more honour on the account.

Comfort me on every side.] I shall have friends in all quarters; and the *tribes* on all sides will support me.

Verse 22. *I will also praise thee with the psaltery*] בכלי נבל *bichli nebel, with the instrument nebel.* Unto thee will I sing with the harp; בכנור *bechinnor*, with the *kinnor*. Both were *stringed instruments*, and the principal used in the Jewish worship; and with which, or any thing like them, in Divine worship, *we*, as *Christians*, have nothing to do.

Verse 23. *My lips shall greatly rejoice—and my soul*] My *lips* shall use words expressive of my *soul's* happiness and gratitude. Thou hast *redeemed* me; and thou shalt have the eternal praise.

Verse 24. *Talk of thy righteousness*] The *righteousness of God* is frequently used in this

Psalm, and in other places, to signify his justice, judgments, faithfulness, truth, mercy, &c. There are few words of more *general* import in the Bible.

They are confounded] The counsel of Ahithophel is *confounded*, and turned to foolishness; and he was so *ashamed* that he went and hanged himself. As to the vain and wicked Absalom, he met with the fate that he had meditated against his father. Though not yet done, David sees all these things as actually accomplished; for he had got a Divine assurance that God would bring them to pass.

Analysis of the Seventy-first Psalm

The *parts* of this Psalm, generally, are these *two:*—

I. A *prayer* that God would help and deliver him, which he urges by many arguments, ver. 1-21.

II. His *vow of thanksgiving*, ver. 22 to the end.

I. 1. His petition in general: "Let me never be put to confusion."

2. He intimates the *cause:* "I put my trust in thee," &c., ver. 2.

To induce the Lord to hear, he uses many *arguments*, drawn,—

1. From his *justice* and *equity:* "Deliver me in thy righteousness."

2. From his *word* and *promise:* "Thou hast given commandment," &c.

3. From his *power:* "Thou art my rock," &c.

4. From his *relation* to him: "My God, my hope."

5. From the *qualities* of his *adversaries:* "They were wicked, unrighteous, and cruel."

6. From his *confidence:* "Thou art my hope."

7. From his *gracious providence:* "By thee have I been holden up," &c.

8. From his *thankful heart:* "My praise shall be continually," &c.

9. He had *none to trust to* but God: "Thou art my refuge."

3. He resumes his *prayer:* "Cast me not off in the time of old age," &c.

He describes his enemies:—

1. They were continual *calumniators:* "Mine enemies speak against me."

2. They *laboured* to take away his *life*.

3. They *studied mischief* against him: "They take counsel together."

4. Their *words* were *cruel:* "God hath forsaken him; persecute," &c.

4. He resumes his prayer, and predicts his enemies' downfall: "O my God, be not far from me; make haste for my help."

He prays against his enemies,—

1. "Let them be confounded," &c.: they shall be confounded.

2. He expresses his hope: "I will hope continually."

3. And his purpose of *gratitude:* "I will praise thee more and more."

4. He pleads from his *past experience* of God's mercy to him.

1. God had "taught him from his youth" both by his word and Spirit.

2. Hitherto he had "declared God's wondrous works."

3. Therefore, "forsake me not now that I am old and grey-headed."

4. I have still *much to do:* "Until I have showed thy strength," &c.

From all these considerations he feels gratitude, and praises God.

1. Thy righteousness is very high. There is nothing like IT.

2. God is wonderful: "There is none like HIM."

Of all this he had full and satisfactory proof.

1. Thou *hast showed me troubles*—"sore troubles."

2. Yet thou *shalt revive me.*

3. Thou "shalt bring me from the depths of the earth."

4. "Thou shalt increase my greatness."

5. "Thou shalt support me on every side."

II. The SECOND *part* contains David's *thanksgiving.*

1. He will praise the *truth* of the "Holy One of Israel:" not only with *nebel* and *kinnor*—instruments of music then used,—

2. But with his *lips* and *soul; heart* and *mouth* going together.

3. With his *tongue;* speaking of God's goodness to *others.*

4. And for this reason, "They are confounded, for they are brought to shame that seek my hurt."

PSALM LXXII

David prays to God for Solomon, 1; *prescribes Solomon's work,* 2; *the effects of his administration,* 3–7; *the extent of his dominion,* 8–11; *his mercy and kindness to the poor, and the perpetuity of his praise,* 12–17. *God is blessed for his power and goodness; and the psalmist prays that the whole earth may be filled with his glory,* 18–20.

A Psalm [a]for [b]Solomon

A. M. 2989
B. C. 1015
Davidis, Regis
Israelitarum,
cir. annum
40

GIVE the king thy judgments,
O God, and thy righteous-
ness unto the king's son.
2 [c]He shall judge thy people
with righteousness, and thy poor with judgment.
3 [d]The mountains shall bring peace to the
people, and the little hills, by righteousness.
4 [e]He shall judge the poor of
the people, he shall save the
children of the needy, and shall
break in pieces the oppressor.
5 They shall fear thee [f]as long as the sun
and moon endure, throughout all generations.
6 [g]He shall come down like rain upon
the mown grass: as showers *that* water the
earth.

A. M. 2989
B. C. 1015
Davidis, Regis
Israelitarum,
cir. annum
40

[a]Or, *of*——[b]Psa. cxxvii. title——[c]Isa. xi. 2, 3, 4; xxxii. 1
[d]Psa. lxxxv. 10; Isa. xxxii. 17; lii. 7

[e]Isa. xi. 4——[f]Ver. 7, 17; Psa. lxxxix. 36, 37——[g]2 Sam. xxiii. 4; Hos. vi. 3

NOTES ON PSALM LXXII

The *title* לשלמה *lishelomoh*, we translate, *A Psalm for Solomon*. The *Chaldee* says, "By the hand of Solomon, spoken prophetically." The *Syriac*, "A Psalm of David, when he had constituted Solomon king." All the other *Versions* attribute it to *Solomon* himself. But in the conclusion of the Psalm it appears to be attributed to *David*. "The prayers of David the son of Jesse are ended." It is most probably a Psalm of David, composed in his last days, when he had set this beloved son on the throne of the kingdom. "Then," says *Calmet*, "transported with joy and gratitude, he addressed this Psalm to God, in which he prays him to pour out his blessings on the young king, and upon the people. He then, wrapped up in a Divine enthusiasm, ascends to a higher subject; and sings the glory of the Messiah, and the magnificence of his reign. Hence it is that we may see in this Psalm a great number of expressions which cannot relate to Solomon, unless in a hyperbolical and figurative sense; but, applied to Christ, they are literally and rigorously exact."

Verse 1. *Give the king thy judgments*] Let Solomon receive *thy law*, as the civil and ecclesiastical code by which he is to govern the kingdom.

And thy righteousness unto the king's son.] *Righteousness* may signify *equity*. Let him not only rule according to the *strict letter of thy law*, that being the *base* on which all his decisions shall be founded; but let him rule also according to *equity*, that *rigorous justice* may never become *oppressive*. Solomon is called here *the king*, because now set upon the Jewish throne; and he is called *the king's son*, to signify his *right* to that throne on which he now sat.

Verse 2. *He shall judge thy people with righteousness*] With justice and mercy mixed, or according to *equity*.

And thy poor with judgment.] Every one according to the *law* which thou hast *appointed;* but with especial tenderness to the *poor* and *afflicted*.

Verse 3. *The mountains shall bring peace*] Perhaps *mountains* and *hills* are here taken in their *figurative* sense, to signify *princes* and *petty governors;* and it is a prediction that all governors of provinces and magistrates should administer equal justice in their several departments and jurisdictions; so that universal *peace* should be preserved, and the people be every where *prosperous;* for שלום *shalom* signifies both peace and prosperity, for without the former the latter never existed.

But what is the meaning of "the little hills by righteousness?" Why, it has no meaning: and it has none, because it is a false division of the verse. The word בצדקה *bitsedakah, in righteousness*, at the end of verse 3, should begin verse 4, and then the sense will be plain. Ver. 3: "The mountains and the hills shall bring prosperity to the people." Ver. 4: "In righteousness he shall judge the poor of the people: he shall save the children of the needy, and shall break in pieces the oppressor."

The *effects*, mentioned in the *fourth* verse, show that King Solomon should act according to the law of his God; and that all officers, magistrates, and governors, should minister equal rights through every part of the land. The *Septuagint* has the true division: *Αναλαβετω τα ορη ειρηνην τῳ λαῳ σου, και οἱ βουνοι· Εν δικαιοσυνῃ κρινει τους πτωχους του λαου, κ. τ. λ.* "The mountains shall bring peace to thy people, and the hills: In righteousness shall he judge the poor of thy people," &c.

Verse 5. *They shall fear thee*] There is no sense in which this can be spoken of *Solomon*, nor indeed of any other man: it belongs to *Jesus Christ*, and to him alone. He is the *Prince of peace*, who shall be *feared* and *reverenced* "through all generations, and as long as the sun and moon endure."

Verse 6. *He shall come down like rain upon the mown grass*] The word גז *gez*, which we translate *mown grass*, more properly means *pastured grass* or *pastured land;* for the *dew* of the night is intended to restore the grass which has been eaten in the course of the day. This very idea the *Chaldee* has seized, and renders the place thus: "He shall descend gently, like rain upon the grass which has been eaten by the locust." But there seems to be a reference to the *thick night dews* which in summer fall on the pasturages, and become the means of restoring the grass consumed in the day-time by the cattle. This is finely expressed by the most accomplished of all poets and agriculturists:—

Et quantum longis carpent armenta diebus,
Exigua tantum gelidus ros nocte reponet.
VIRG. Geor. ii., ver. 201.

"For what the day devours, the nightly dew
Shall to the morn by pearly drops renew."
DRYDEN.

Or to leave *poetry*, which always says *too much* or *too little*, the plain prose is:—

A. M. 2989
B. C. 1015
Davidis, Regis Israelitarum, cir. annum 40

7 In his days shall the righteous flourish; [h]and abundance
of peace [i]so long as the moon
endureth.

8 [k]He shall have dominion also from sea to
sea, and from the river unto the ends of the
earth.

9 [l]They that dwell in the wilderness shall
bow before him; [m]and his enemies shall lick
the dust.

10 [n]The kings of Tarshish and of the isles
shall bring presents: the kings of
Sheba and Seba shall offer gifts.

11 [o]Yea, all kings shall fall
down before him: all nations
shall serve him.

12 For he [p]shall deliver the needy when he
crieth; the poor also, and *him* that hath no
helper.

13 He shall spare the poor and needy, and
shall save the souls of the needy.

14 He shall redeem their soul from deceit

A. M. 2989
B. C. 1015
Davidis, Regis Israelitarum, cir. annum 40

---

[h]Isa. ii. 4; Dan. ii. 44; Luke i. 33——[i]Heb. *till* there be *no moon*——[k]See Exod. xxiii. 31; 1 Kings iv. 21, 24; Psa. ii. 8; lxxx. 11; lxxxix. 25; Zech. ix. 10

[l]Psa. lxxiv. 14——[m]Isa. xlix. 23; Mic. vii. 17——[n]2 Chron. ix. 21; Psa. xlv. 12; lxviii. 29; Isa. xlix. 7; lx. 6, 9 [o]Isa. xlix. 22, 23——[p]Job xxix. 12

"And as much as the flocks crop in the long
days,
So much shall the cold dew restore in one
short night."

As showers that *water the earth.*] The influence of the *doctrine* and *Spirit* of Christ on the soul of man shall be as *grateful*, as *refreshing*, and as *fructifying*, as the nightly dews on the cropped fields, and the *vernal showers* on the cultivated lands. Without his influence all tillage is vain; without him there can neither be seed nor fruit.

Verse 7. *In his days shall the righteous flourish*] There was nothing but peace and prosperity all the days of Solomon: for, "In his days Judah and Israel dwelt safely; every man under his vine and under his fig-tree, from Dan even to Beersheba;" 1 Kings iv. 25.

So long as the moon endureth] עד בלי ירח *ad beli yareach*, "Till there be no more moon."

Verse 8. *He shall have dominion also from sea to sea*] The best comment on this, as it refers to Solomon, may be found in 1 Kings iv. 21, 24: "And Solomon reigned over all kingdoms, from the river unto the land of the Philistines, and unto the border of Egypt; for he had dominion over all on this side the river, from Tiphsah even to Azzah, over all the kings on this side the river; and he had peace on all sides round about him."

Solomon, it appears, reigned over all the provinces from the river *Euphrates* to the land of the *Philistines*, even to the frontiers of *Egypt*. The *Euphrates* was on the *east* of Solomon's dominions; the *Philistines* were *westward*, on the *Mediterranean sea;* and *Egypt* was on the *south*. Solomon had therefore, as tributaries, the kingdoms of *Syria*, *Damascus*, *Moab*, and *Ammon*, which lay between the *Euphrates* and the *Mediterranean*. Thus he appears to have possessed all the land which God covenanted with Abraham to give to his posterity.

Unto the ends of the earth.] Or *land*, must mean the tract of country *along the Mediterranean sea*, which was the *boundary of the land* on that side: but, as the words may refer to Christ, every thing may be taken in its utmost latitude and extent.

Verse 9. *They that dwell in the wilderness*] The ציים *tsiyim*, termed *Ethiopians* by the *Vulgate*, *Septuagint*, *Æthiopic*, and *Arabic*. The *Syriac* terms them *the islands*. But it is likely that those who dwell by the sea-coasts, and support themselves by navigation and fishing, are here intended.

His enemies shall lick the dust.] Shall be so completely subdued, that they shall be reduced to the most abject state of vassalage, till they shall become proselytes to the Jewish faith.

Verse 10. *The kings of Tarshish and of the isles shall bring presents*] Though Solomon did not reign over *Cilicia*, of which *Tarsus* was the capital, yet he might receive *gifts*, not in the sense of *tribute;* for מנחה *minchah*, the word here used, signifies a *gratitude* or *friendly offering*.

The kings of Sheba and Seba] Both countries of Arabia. From the former came the *queen of Sheba*, to hear the wisdom of Solomon. And she brought exceeding great *presents* or *gifts*, but not in the way of *tribute*, for Solomon had no jurisdiction in her country. And certainly many sovereigns, to obtain his *friendship*, sent him various presents of the choicest produce of their respective countries; and no doubt he did with them as with the queen of Sheba, gave them gifts in return. Hence the word אשכר *eshcar* is used, which signifies "a *compensative present*, made on account of benefits received."

Verse 11. *All kings shall fall down before*] They shall reverence him on account of his great wisdom, riches, &c.

All nations shall serve him.] All the surrounding nations. This and the preceding verses are fully explained by 1 Kings x. 23-25: "King Solomon exceeded all the kings of the earth for riches and for wisdom. And all the earth sought unto Solomon to hear his wisdom. And they brought every man his present, vessels of silver, and vessels of gold, and garments, and armour, and spices, horses and mules, a rate year by year." If we take these expressions to mean literally *all the habitable globe*, then they cannot be applied to Solomon; but if we take them as *they are most evidently used by the sacred writer*, then they are literally true. When all the earth shall be brought to receive the Gospel of Christ, then they may be applied to *him*.

Verse 12. *He shall deliver the needy when he crieth*] The poor and the rich shall, in the administration of justice, be equally respected; and the strong shall not be permitted to oppress the weak.

Verse 14. *From deceit and violence*] Be-

A. M. 2989 B. C. 1015 Davidis, Regis Israelitarum, cir. annum 40

and violence: and [q]precious shall
their blood be in his sight.
15 And he shall live, and to
him [r]shall be given of the gold
of Sheba: prayer also shall be made for him
continually; *and* daily shall he be praised.
16 There shall be a handful of corn in the
earth upon the top of the mountains; the fruit
thereof shall shake like Lebanon: [s]and *they*
of the city shall flourish like grass of the earth.
17 [t]His name [u]shall endure for ever: [v]his
name shall be continued as long
as the sun: and [w]*men* shall be
blessed in him: [x]all nations shall
call him blessed.
18 [y]Blessed *be* the LORD God, the God of
Israel, [z]who only doeth wondrous things.
19 And [a]blessed *be* his glorious name for
ever: [b]and let the whole earth be filled *with*
his glory; Amen, and Amen.
20 The prayers of David the son of Jesse
are ended.

[q]Psalm cxvi. 15——[r]Hebrew, one *shall give*——[s]1 Kings iv. 20——[t]Psalm lxxxix. 36——[u]Hebrew, *shall be* [v]Heb. *shall be as a son to continue his father's name for ever*

[w]Gen. xii. 13; xxii. 18——[x]Luke i. 48——[y]1 Chron. xxix. 10; Psa. xli. 13; cvi. 48——[z]Exod. xv. 11; Psa. lxxvii. 14; cxxxvi. 4——[a]Neh. ix. 5——[b]Num. xiv. 21; Zech. xiv. 9

cause they are poor and uneducated, they are liable to be *deceived;* and because they are *helpless*, they are liable to *oppression;* but his equal justice shall duly consider these cases; and no man shall suffer because he is deceived, though the *letter of the law* may be against him.

And precious shall their blood be] If the blood or life of such a person shall have been spilt by the hand of violence, he shall seek it out, and visit it on the murderer, though he were the chief in the land. He shall not be screened, though he were of the blood royal, if he have wilfully taken away the life of a man.

Verse 15. *To him shall be given of the gold of Sheba*] The Arabians shall pay him tribute.

Prayer also shall be made for him continually] In all conquered countries *two* things marked the subjection of the people: 1. Their money was stamped with the name of the conqueror. 2. They were obliged to pray for him in their acts of public worship.

Daily shall he be praised.] He shall not act by the conquered like conquerors in general: he shall treat them with benignity; and shall give them the same laws and privileges as his natural subjects, and therefore "he shall be daily praised." All shall speak well of him.

Verse 16. *There shall be a handful of corn*] The earth shall be exceedingly fruitful. Even a handful of corn sown on the top of a mountain shall grow up strong and vigorous; and it shall be, in reference to *crops* in *other times*, as the *cedars of Lebanon* are to *common trees* or *shrubs:* and as the earth will bring forth in handfuls, so the *people* shall be *multiplied* who are to consume this great produce.

And they *of the city shall flourish like grass of the earth.*] There have been many puzzling criticisms concerning this verse. What I have given I believe to be the *sense.*

Verse 17. *His name shall endure for ever*] Hitherto this has been literally fulfilled. Solomon is celebrated in the *east* and in the *west*, in the *north* and in the *south;* his writings still remain, and are received, both by *Jews* and by *Gentiles*, as a revelation from God; and it is not likely that the name of the author shall ever perish out of the records of the world.

All nations shall call him blessed.] Because of the extraordinary manner in which he was *favoured* by the Most High. I well know that all these things are thought to belong properly to Jesus Christ; and, in reference to him, they are all true, and *ten thousand* times more than these. But I believe they are all properly applicable to Solomon: and it is the business of the commentator to find out the literal sense, and historical fact, and not seek for allegories and mysteries where there is no certain evidence of their presence. Where the sacred writers of the New Testament quote passages from the Old, and apply them to our Lord, we not only *may* but *should* follow them. And I am ready to grant there may be many other passages equally applicable to him with those they have quoted, which are not thus applied. Indeed, HE is the sum and substance of the whole Scripture. HE spoke by his Spirit in the prophets; and *himself* was the subject of their declarations. See our Lord's saying, Luke xxiv. 44.

Verse 18. *Blessed* be *the Lord God*] David foresaw all Solomon's *grandeur;* his *justice, equity*, and the *happiness* of the *subjects* under his government; and his soul has, in consequence, sensations of pleasure and gratitude to God, which even his own wondrous pen cannot describe. But it is worthy of remark, that God did not reveal to him the *apostasy* of this beloved son. He did not foresee that this once holy, happy, wise, and prosperous man would be the means of debasing the Divine worship, and establishing the grossest idolatry in Israel. God hid *this* from his eyes, that his heart might not be grieved, and that he might die in peace. Besides, there was still much *contingency* in the business. God would not predict a thing as *absolutely certain*, which was still poised between a *possibility of being and not being;* the scale of which he had left, as he does all contingencies, to the free-will of his creature to turn.

Who only doeth wondrous things.] God alone works *miracles:* wherever there is a *miracle*, there is God. *No creature* can *invert* or *suspend* the *course* and *laws* of *nature;* this is properly the work of God. Jesus Christ, most incontrovertibly, wrought such miracles; therefore, most demonstrably, Jesus Christ is GOD.

Verse 19. *Let the whole earth be filled* with *his glory*] Let the Gospel—the light, the Spirit, and power of Christ, fill the world.

Amen] So *let* it be.

And Amen.] So it *shall be.* Hallelujah!

Verse 20. *The prayers of David the son of*

Jesse are ended.] This was most probably the *last Psalm* he ever wrote. There may be several in the after part of this book which were written by him; but they were probably composed in a former period of his life, for this was the *end* of the *poetic prayers of David the son of Jesse.* Those that were found afterwards have got out of their proper connexion.

Analysis of the Seventy-second Psalm

David being near his death, makes his prayer for his son Solomon, that he may be a just, peaceable, and great king, and his subjects happy under his government. But this is but the *shell* of the Psalm: the *kernel* is Christ and his kingdom, under whom righteousness, peace, and felicity shall flourish, and *unto whom all nations shall do homage for ever and ever.*

The parts of this Psalm are the following, viz.:—

I. The petition, ver. 1.

II. The general declaration of the qualities of this kingdom, ver. 2, 3, 4.

III. The particular unfolding of these in their effects, ver. 4-18.

IV. The doxology, ver. 18-20.

I. David, being taught by experience how hard a matter it is to govern a kingdom well, prays God to assist his son *Solomon,* to whom, being near death, he was to leave his crown and sceptre.

1. "Give the king thy judgments, O God;" the true knowledge of thy law.

2. "And thy righteousness unto the king's son;" that he may not decline to the right or left hand, but administer by justice, judge for God.

II. For then this will follow:—

1. Justice will flourish in his kingdom: "He shall judge thy people with righteousness, and thy poor with judgment."

2. And peace also, and prosperity: "The mountains," that is, the chief magistrates; "and the little hills,"—the lesser officers, shall bring peace to the people: but "by righteousness," for justice upholds the world.

III. And now he proceeds to unfold himself upon the two former generals: first, *justice;* then, *peace.*

Of justice he assigns two effects:—

1. The defence of good men: "He shall judge the poor of the people; he shall save the children of the needy."

2. The punishment of the wicked: "He shall break in pieces the oppressor."

The consequences of peace are,—

1. Fear, and reverence, and the service of God: "They shall fear thee as long as the sun and moon endure, throughout all generations."

2. Plenty and abundance: "He shall come down like rain upon the mown grass; as showers that water the earth."

3. Prosperity of good men: "In his days shall the righteous flourish; and abundance of peace so long as the moon endureth."

Now he shows the greatness and amplitude of this kingdom, which will not be so true of *Solomon* as of *Christ* and his kingdom.

1. His kingdom will be very large: "He shall have dominion from sea to sea, and from the river unto the ends of the earth."

2. His subjects shall be many. Some willingly, others against their will, shall obey him: "They that dwell in the wilderness shall bow before him. His enemies shall lick the dust,"—crouch at his feet.

3. Homage shall be done to him by Asiatic, European, and Arabian princes. 1. "The kings of Tarshish and of the isles shall bring presents, the kings of Sheba and Seba shall offer gifts." 2. "Yea, all kings shall fall down before him; all nations shall serve him."

He sets down many excellent qualities of this king:

1. He should be ready to do good; a gracious lord to the meanest subject: "For he shall deliver the needy when he crieth; the poor also, and him that hath no helper."

2. He should be far from loading his subjects with exactions: "He shall spare the poor and shall save the souls of the needy."

3. Far from all tyranny: "He shall redeem their soul from deceit and violence."

4. Far from shedding innocent blood: "And precious shall their blood be in his sight."

And as he shall be kind and loving to his subjects, so shall his subjects show great love and affection to him.

1. They shall pray for his life: "He shall live."

2. And they shall offer him presents: "And to him shall be given of the gold of Arabia."

3. They shall pray for him: "Prayer also shall be made for him continually."

4. They shall speak well of him: "Daily shall he be praised."

And that which would induce them to it might be, that besides the equity and justice, love and kindness he showed to all, they find that under him they enjoy great plenty and abundance of all things.

1. For the earth brought forth corn, and the mountains afforded them an ample harvest: "There shall be a handful of corn in the earth, upon the top (the highest part) of the mountains; the fruit thereof shall shake (stand so thick that the ears shall brush one against another) as the trees in Lebanon."

2. The kingdom shall abound in people: "They of the city shall flourish like grass of the earth," which is thick and green. In a word, the king shall be dear to his people; and they shall love his name when living, and honour him when dead, and continue it to all posterities.

1. "His name shall endure for ever: his name shall be continued as long as the sun."

2. "Men shall be blessed in him." God shall bless thee, as he did Solomon.

3. "All nations shall call him blessed." Acknowledge his happiness, and wish a blessing to themselves after Solomon's example.

IV. In the close of the Psalm, as usual, he gives thanks for taking into consideration the happiness that was to accrue to his people under such a king, even when he was laid in the grave. He breaks forth,

1. "Blessed be the Lord God, the God of Israel, who only doeth wondrous things;" for indeed such a king is a wonder, and it is the grace of God must make him such.

2. And again: "Blessed be his glorious name for ever."

3. And that not in Judea alone, but in all the world: "And let the whole world be filled with his glory. Amen, amen."

"The prayers of David the son of Jesse are ended." Of which some, indeed most, judge this was the last prayer David made. See the notes at the end of the Psalm.

With the *seventy-second* Psalm the SECOND BOOK of the Psalter ends, according to the division of the Jewish Masoretes. The THIRD BOOK commences with a series, chiefly composed by other inspired writers.

THE following poetical version of some of the principal passages of the foregoing Psalm was made and kindly given me by my much respected friend, *James Montgomery*, Esq., of Sheffield. I need not tell the intelligent reader that he has seized the spirit, and exhibited some of the principal beauties, of the Hebrew bard; though, to use his own words in his letter to me, his "hand trembled to touch the harp of Zion." I take the liberty here to register a wish, which I have strongly expressed to himself, that he would favour the Church of God with a metrical version of the whole book.

Hail to the Lord's Anointed,
Great David's greater Son!
Hail! In the time appointed,
His reign on earth begun!
He comes to break oppression,
To let the captive free,
To take away transgression,
And reign in equity.

He comes with succour speedy
To those who suffer wrong;
To help the poor and needy,
And bid the weak be strong;
To give them songs for sighing,
Their darkness turn to light,
Whose souls, in misery dying,
Were precious in his sight.

By such shall he be feared
While sun and moon endure,
Beloved, adored, revered,
For he shall judge the poor,
Through changing generations,
With justice, mercy, truth,
While stars maintain their stations,
And moons renew their youth.

He shall come down like showers
Upon the fruitful earth,
And joy, and hope, like flowers,
Spring in his path to birth:
Before him, on the mountains,
Shall Peace, the herald, go,
And righteousness, in fountains,
From hill to valley flow.

Arabia's desert-ranger
To him shall bow the knee;
The Æthiopian stranger
His glory come to see:
With offerings of devotion,
Ships from the isles shall meet
To pour the wealth of ocean
In tribute at his feet.

Kings shall fall down before him,
And gold and incense bring;
All nations shall adore him,
His praise all people sing:
For he shall have dominion
O'er river, sea, and shore,
Far as the eagle's pinion,
Or dove's light wing, can soar.

For him shall prayer unceasing,
And daily vows, ascend;
His kingdom still increasing,—
A kingdom without end;
The mountain-dews shall nourish
A need in weakness sown,
Whose fruit shall spread and flourish
And shake like Lebanon.

O'er every foe victorious,
He on his throne shall rest,
From age to age more glorious,—
All-blessing, and all-blest:
The tide of time shall never
His covenant remove;
His name shall stand for ever,
His name—what is it?—LOVE.

PSALM LXXIII

The psalmist speaks of God's goodness to his people, 1; *shows how much he was stumbled at the prosperity of the wicked, and describes their state,* 2–12; *details the process of the temptation, and the pain he suffered in consequence,* 13–16; *shows how he was delivered, and the dismal reverse of the state of the once prosperous ungodly man, by which his own false views were corrected,* 17–22; *his great confidence in God, and the good consequences of it,* 23–28.

XIV. DAY. EVENING PRAYER

[a]*A Psalm of* [b]Asaph

TRULY [c]God *is* good to Israel, *even* to such as are [d]of a clean heart.

2 But as for me, my feet were almost gone; my steps had well nigh slipped.

3 [e]For I was envious at the foolish, *when* I saw the prosperity of the wicked.

4 For *there are* no bands in their death: but their strength *is* [f]firm.

5 [g]They *are* not [h]in trouble *as other* men; neither are they plagued [i]like *other* men.

6 Therefore pride compasseth them about as a chain; violence covereth them [k]*as* a garment.

7 [l]Their eyes stand out with fatness: [m]they have more than heart could wish.

8 [n]They are corrupt, and [o]speak wickedly *concerning* oppression: they [p]speak loftily.

---

[a]Or, *A Psalm for Asaph*——[b]Psa. l. title——[c]Or, *Yet* [d]Heb. *clean of heart*——[e]Job xxi. 7; Psa. xxxvii. 1; Jer. xii. 1——[f]Heb. *fat*——[g]Job xxi. 6——[h]Heb. *in the trouble of* other *men*——[i]Heb. *with*

[k]So Psa. cix. 18——[l]Job xv. 27; Psa. xvii. 10; cxix. 70; Jer. v. 28——[m]Heb. *they pass the thoughts of the heart* [n]Psa. liii. 1——[o]Hos. vii. 16——[p]2 Pet. ii. 18; Jude 16

NOTES ON PSALM LXXIII

THIS is the commencement of the THIRD BOOK of the *Psalter;* and the Psalm before us has for title, *A Psalm of Asaph;* or, as the *margin* has it, *A Psalm for Asaph.* The title in the Hebrew is מזמור לאסף *mizmor leasaph;* "A Psalm of Asaph:" and it is likely that this *Asaph* was the composer of it; that he lived under the Babylonish captivity; and that he published this Psalm to console the Israelites under bondage, who were greatly tried to find themselves in such outward distress and misery, while a people much more wicked and corrupt than they, were in great prosperity, and held them in bondage.

Verse 1. *Truly God* is *good to Israel*] Captives as they were, they still had many blessings from God; and they had promises of deliverance, which must be fulfilled in due time.

Such as are of a clean heart.] Those who have a clean heart must have inward happiness: and, because they resemble God, they can never be forsaken by him.

Verse 2. *My feet were almost gone*] I had nearly given up my confidence. I was ready to find fault with the dispensations of providence; and thought the Judge of all the earth did not do right.

Verse 3. *I was envious at the foolish*] I saw persons who *worshipped not* the true God, and others who were *abandoned to all vices,* in possession of every temporal comfort, while the godly were in straits, difficulties, and affliction. I began then to doubt whether there was a wise providence; and my mind became *irritated.* It seems to have been a maxim among the ancient heathens, Θεου ονειδος τους κακους ευδαιμονειν, "The prosperity of the wicked is a reproach to the gods." But they had no just conception of a state of future rewards and punishments. Besides, man could not bear prosperity. If men had uninterrupted comforts here, perhaps not one soul would ever seek a preparation for heaven. Human trials and afflictions, the *general warfare of human life,* are the highest proof of a providence as benevolent as it is wise. Were the state of human affairs different from what it is, hell would be more thickly peopled; and there would be fewer inhabitants in glory. There is reason to doubt whether there would be *any religion* upon earth had we nothing but temporal prosperity. Indeed, all the following verses are proofs of it.

Verse 4. *No bands in their death*] Many of the godly have sore conflicts at their death. Their enemy then thrusts sore at them that they may fall; or that their confidence in their God may be shaken. But of this the ungodly know nothing. Satan will not molest *them;* he is sure of his prey; they are entangled, and cannot now break their nets; their consciences are seared, they have no sense of guilt. If they think at all of another world, they presume on that mercy which they never sought, and of which they have no distinct notion. Perhaps, "they die without a sigh or a groan; and thus go off as quiet as a lamb"—to the slaughter.

Verse 6. *Pride compasseth them about as a chain*] Perhaps there is an allusion here to the office which some of them bore. *Chains of gold,* and *golden rings,* were ensigns of magistracy and civil power. As these chains encompassed their necks, or the rings their wrists and fingers, as the signs of the *offices* in virtue of which they acted; so חמס *chamas,* violence, oppressive conduct, encompassed them. They made no other use of their great power, than to oppress the poor and the needy; and to drive things to extremities. The *Chaldee,* instead of *a chain,* represents this as a crown or diadem, which they had formed out of the plunder of the poor and defenceless.

Verse 7. *Their eyes stand out with fatness*] "Their countenance is changed because of fatness."—*Chaldee.* By fatness, or corpulency, the natural lines of the face are *changed,* or rather *obliterated.* The characteristic distinctions are gone; and we see little remaining besides the *human hog.*

They have more than heart could wish.] I doubt this translation. *Whose heart* ever said, *I have enough,* which had not its portion with God? It would be more literal to say, "They surpass the thoughts of their heart." They have *more* than they *expected,* though *not more* than they *wish.*

Verse 8. *They are corrupt*] ימיקו *yamiku,* they *mock, act dissolutely.*

And speak wickedly concerning *oppression*] They vindicate excessive acts of government: they push justice to its rigour. They neither show equity, lenity, nor mercy; they are cruel, and they *vindicate* their proceedings.

9 They set their mouth [q]against the heavens, and their tongue walketh through the earth.

10 Therefore his people return hither: [r]and waters of a full *cup* are wrung out to them.

11 And they say, [s]How doth God know? and is there knowledge in the Most High?

12 Behold, these *are* the ungodly, who [t]prosper in the world; they increase *in* riches.

13 [u]Verily I have cleansed my heart *in* vain, and [v]washed my hands in innocency.

14 For all the day long have I been plagued, and [w]chastened every morning.

15 If I say, I will speak thus; behold I should offend *against* the generation of thy children.

16 [x]When I thought to know this, [y]it *was* too painful for me,

17 Until [z]I went into the sanctuary of God; *then* understood I [a]their end.

---

[q]Rev. xiii. 6——[r]Psa. lxxv. 8——[s]Job xxii. 13; Psa. x. 11; xciv. 7——[t]Ver. 3——[u]Job xxi. 15; xxxiv. 9; xxxv. 3; Mal. iii. 14——[v]Psa. xxvi. 6

[w]Heb. *my chastisement* was——[x]Eccles. viii. 17. [y]Heb. *it* was *labour in mine eyes*——[z]Psa. lxxvii. 13 [a]Psa. xxxvii. 38

Verse 9. *Set their mouth against the heavens*] They blaspheme God, ridicule religion, mock at Providence, and laugh at a future state.

Their tongue walketh through the earth.] They find fault with every thing; they traduce the memory of the just in heaven, and ridicule the saints that are upon earth. They criticise every dispensation of God.

Verse 10. *Therefore his people return hither*] There are very few verses in the Bible that have been more variously translated than this; and, like the man in the fable, they have blown the *hot* to *cool* it, and the *cold* to *warm* it. It has been translated, "Therefore God's people fall off to them; and thence they reap no small advantage." And, "Therefore let his people come before them; and waters in full measure would be wrung out from them." That is, "Should God's people come before them, they would squeeze them to the utmost; they would wring out all the juice in their bodies." The *Chaldee* has, "Therefore, are they turned against the people of the Lord, that they may bruise and beat them with mallets; that they may pour out to them abundance of tears." The *Vulgate*, "Therefore shall my people return here, and days of abundance shall be found by them." The *Septuagint* is the same. The *Æthiopic*, *Arabic*, and *Syriac*, nearly the same. The *Hebrew* text is, לכן ישוב עמו הלם ומי מלא ימצו למו *lachen yashub ammo* (עמי *ammi*) *halom; umey male yimmatsu lamo;* "Therefore shall my people be converted, where they shall find abundance of waters." That is, The people, seeing the iniquity of the Babylonians, and feeling their oppressive hand, shall be converted to me; and I shall bring them to their own land, where they shall find an abundance of all the necessaries of life. I believe this to be the meaning; and thus we find their afflictions were sanctified to them; for they obliged them *to return to God*, and then God caused them to return to their own land. The *Vulgate* translates ומי מלא *umey male*, "abundance of waters," by *et dies pleni*, "and days of plenty;" for it has read ימי *yemey*, *days*, for ומי *umey*, *and waters*. Almost all the *Versions* support this reading; but it is not acknowledged by any MS. The old *Psalter* is here mutilated.

Verse 11. *They say, How doth God know?*] My people are so stumbled with the prosperity of the wicked, that they are ready in their temptation to say, "Surely, God cannot know these things, or he would never dispense his favours thus." Others consider these words as the saying of the *wicked:* "We may oppress these people as we please, and live as we list; God knows nothing about it."

Verse 12. *These* are *the ungodly*] The people still speak. It is the ungodly that prosper, the irreligious and profane.

Verse 13. *I have cleansed my heart* in *vain*] It is no advantage to us to worship the true God, to walk according to the law of righteousness, and keep the ordinances of the Most High.

Verse 14. *For all the day long have I been plagued*] Far from enjoying worldly prosperity, we are not only *poor*, but we are *afflicted* also; and every *succeeding day* brings with it some new trouble.

Verse 15. *If I say, I will speak thus*] I have at last discovered that I have reasoned incorrectly; and that I have the uniform testimony of all thy children against me. From generation to generation they have testified that the Judge of all the earth does right; they have trusted in thee, and were never confounded. They also met with afflictions and sore trials, but thou didst bring them safely through all, didst sustain them in the worst, and sanctifiedst the whole to their eternal good.

Verse 16. *When I thought to know this*] When I reviewed the history of our fathers, I saw that, though thou hadst from time to time hidden thy face because of their sins, yet thou hadst never utterly abandoned them to their adversaries; and it was not reasonable to conclude that thou wouldst do now what thou hadst never done before; and yet the continuance of our captivity, the oppressive hardships which we suffer, and the small prospect there is of release, puzzle me again. These things have been very *painful* to *me*.

Verse 17. *Until I went into the sanctuary*] Until, in the use of thy ordinances, I entered into a deep consideration of thy secret counsels, and considered the future state of the righteous and the wicked; that the unequal distribution of temporal good and evil argued a future judgment; that the present is a state of trial; and that God exercises his followers according to his godly wisdom and tender mercy. Then light sprang up in my mind, and I was assured that all these exercises were for our benefit, and that the prosperity of the wicked here was

18 Surely [b]thou didst set them in slippery places: thou castedst them down into destruction.

19 How are they *brought* into desolation, as in a moment! they are utterly consumed with terrors.

20 [c]As a dream when *one* awaketh; *so,* O LORD, [d]when thou awakest, thou shalt despise their image.

21 Thus my heart was [e]grieved, and I was pricked in my reins.

22 [f]So foolish *was* I, and [g]ignorant: I was *as* a beast [h]before thee.

23 Nevertheless I *am* continually with thee: thou hast holden *me* by my right hand.

24 [i]Thou shalt guide me with thy counsel, and afterward receive me *to* glory.

25 [k]Whom have I in heaven *but thee?* and *there is* none upon earth *that* I desire beside thee.

26 [l]My flesh and my heart faileth: *but* God

[b]Psa. xxxv. 6—[c]Job xx. 8; Psa. xc. 5; Isa. xxix. 7, 8 [d]Psa. lxxviii. 65—[e]Ver. 3—[f]Psa. xcii. 6; Prov. xxx. 2

[g]Heb. *I knew not*—[h]Heb. *with thee*—[i]Psa. xxxii. 8; Isa. lviii. 8—[k]Phil. iii. 8—[l]Psa. lxxxiv. 2; cxix. 81

a prelude to their destruction. And this I saw to be their *end.*

That this Psalm was written during the *captivity,* there is little room to doubt. How then can the psalmist speak of the *sanctuary?* There was none at Babylon; and at Jerusalem it had been long since destroyed? There is no way to solve this difficulty but by considering that מקדשי *mikdeshey* may be taken in the sense of *holy places*—places set apart for prayer and meditation. And that the captives had such places in their captivity, there can be no doubt; and the place that is set apart to meet God in, for prayer, supplication, confession of sin, and meditation, is *holy* unto the Lord; and is, therefore, his *sanctuary,* whether a *house* or the open *field. Calmet* thinks by holy meditations a view of the Divine secrets, to which he refers, ver. 24, is here meant.

Verse 18. *Thou didst set them in slippery places*] Affluence is a slippery path; few have ever walked in it without *falling.* It is possible to be *faithful* in the *unrighteous mammon,* but it is very *difficult.* No man should *desire riches;* for they bring with them so many cares and temptations as to be almost *unmanageable.* Rich men, even when pious, are seldom happy; they do not enjoy the consolations of religion. A good man, possessed of very extensive estates, unblamable in his whole deportment, once said to me: "There must be some strange malignity in riches thus to keep me in continual bondage, and deprive me of the consolations of the Gospel." Perhaps to a person to whom his estates are a snare, the words of our Lord may be *literally* applicable: "Sell what thou hast, and give to the poor; and thou shalt have treasure in heaven: and come, take up thy cross, and follow me." But he went away sorrowful, for he had great possessions! May we not then say with the psalmist, *Surely thou didst set them in slippery places,* &c.?

Verse 19. *Are they* brought *into desolation*] This is often a literal fact. I have known several cases where persons, very rich, have by sudden losses been brought into desolation as in a moment; in consequence of which *they were utterly consumed in terrors.*

Verse 20. *As a dream when* one *awaketh*] So their goods fled away. Their *possession* was a *dream*—their *privation, real.*

Thou shalt despise their image.] While destitute of true religion, whatever appearance they had of greatness, nobility, honour, and happiness; yet in the sight of God they had no more than the *ghost* or *shade* of excellence, which God is said here to *despise.* Who would be rich at such risk and dishonour?

Verse 21. *Thus my heart was grieved*] The different views which I got of this subject quite confounded me; I was equally astonished at their sudden overthrow and my own ignorance. I felt as if I were a *beast* in stupidity. I permitted my mind to be wholly occupied with *sensible things,* like the beasts that perish, and did not look into a future state; nor did I consider, nor submit to, the wise designs of an unerring Providence.

Verse 23. *I am continually with thee*] I now see that myself and my people are under thy guardian care; that we are continually upheld by thee; and while in thy *right hand,* we shall not be utterly cast down.

Verse 24. *Thou shalt guide me with thy counsel*] After we have suffered awhile, receiving directions and consolations from thy good Spirit, by means of thy prophets, who are in the same captivity with ourselves; thou wilt grant us deliverance, restore us to our own land, and crown us with honour and happiness. Any sincere follower of God may use these words in reference to this and the coming world. *Thy counsel*—thy WORD and SPIRIT, shall *guide me* through life; and when I have done and suffered thy righteous will, thou wilt *receive me into thy* eternal *glory.*

Verse 25. *Whom have I in heaven* but thee?] The original is more emphatic: מי לי בשמים ועמך לא חפצתי בארץ *mi li bashshamayim; veimmecha lo chaphatsti baarets.* "Who is there to me in the heavens? And with thee I have desired nothing in the earth." No man can say this who has not taken God for his portion in reference to both worlds.

Verse 26. *My flesh—faileth*] I shall soon die: *and my heart*—even my natural courage, will fail; and no support but what is *supernatural* will then be available. Therefore, he adds,—

God is *the strength of my heart*] Literally, *the rock of my heart.*

And my portion] Allusion is here made to the division of the promised land. I ask no inheritance below; I look for one above. I do not look for this in the possession of any *place;* it is GOD alone that can content the desires and wishes of an immortal spirit. And even this would not satisfy, had I not the prospect of its being *for ever,* לעולם *leolam,* "to eternity!"

is the [m]strength of my heart, and [n]my portion for ever.

27 For, lo, [o]they that are far from thee shall perish: thou hast destroyed all them that [p]go a whoring from thee.

28 But *it is* good for me to [q]draw near to God: I have put my trust in the Lord GOD, that I may [r]declare all thy works.

[m]Heb. *rock*——[n]Psa. xvi. 5; cxix. 57——[o]Psa. cxix. 155

[p]Exod. xxxiv. 15; Num. xv. 39; James iv. 4——[q]Heb. x. 22——[r]Psa. cvii. 22; cxviii. 17

Verse 27. *They that are far from thee shall perish*] The term perish is generally used to signify a *coming to nothing*, being *annihilated;* and by some it is thus applied to the *finally impenitent*, they shall all be *annihilated.* But where is this to be found in the Scriptures? In no part, properly understood. In the new heavens and the new earth none of the wicked shall be found; for therein dwells righteousness—nothing but God and righteous spirits; but at the same time the wicked shall be in their own place. And to suppose that they shall be *annihilated*, is as great a heresy, though scarcely so absurd, as to believe that the pains of damnation are *emendatory*, and that *hell-fire* shall burn out. There is presumptive evidence from Scripture to lead us to the conclusion, that if there be not eternal punishment, glory will not be eternal; as the same terms are used to express the duration of both. No human spirit that is not *united* to God can be saved. *Those who are* FAR FROM THEE *shall perish*—they shall be *lost, undone, ruined;* and that without remedy. Being *separated from God* by sin, they shall never be *rejoined;* the great gulf must be between them and their Maker *eternally.*

All them that go a whoring from thee.] That is, all that worship false gods; all idolaters. This is the only meaning of the word in such a connexion. I have explained this elsewhere.

Verse 28. It is *good for me to draw near*] We have already seen that those who are *far off* shall perish; therefore, it is *ill for them.* Those who *draw near*—who come in the true *spirit of sacrifice*, and with the only available offering, the Lord Jesus, shall be finally saved; therefore, it is *good* for *them.*

I have put my trust in the Lord God] I confide in *Jehovah, my Prop and Stay.* I have taken him for my portion.

That I may declare all thy works.] That I may testify to all how good it is to *draw nigh to God;* and what a *sufficient portion* he is to the soul of man.

The *Vulgate, Septuagint, Æthiopic*, and *Arabic*, add, *in the gates of the daughter of Sion.* These words appear to make a better finish; but they are not acknowledged by any Hebrew MS.

ANALYSIS OF THE SEVENTY-THIRD PSALM

The prophet shows the grief that many good men feel at the prosperity of the wicked, and the distresses of the godly; but at last, consulting the will of God, he finds that the felicity of the wicked ends in wretchedness, and the crosses of the godly are the way to happiness; and, with this consideration, he gains quiet to his troubled mind. Let the question be, Who is the *happy man?* The *godly* or *ungodly?* And then the parts of the Psalm will be as follows:—

I. The arguments produced for the happiness of the wicked, ver. 1-9.

II. The impression these arguments make in carnal minds, ver. 2, 3, 10-14.

III. The rejection of these doubts and impressions, ver. 15-17.

IV. The refutation of the former arguments, ver. 18-20.

V. The psalmist's censure of himself for his precipitate judgment, ver. 21, 22.

VI. His full resolution of the doubt, after the full examination of the reasons on both sides. That true happiness consists in *union with God;* and therefore the wicked, who are *far from him*, however they flourish, are unhappy, ver. 23-28.

But, more particularly, the Psalm is divisible into the following parts:—

I. There is, *first*, an assertion: "Certainly, God is good to Israel, to such as are of a clean heart," ver. 1. But can this comport with their present afflicted state? With this he was greatly harassed, ver. 2. He saw the wicked in prosperity, which he states in several particulars.

II. What carnal minds think of them.

1. They have no conflicts in their death, ver. 4.

2. They are not troubled like other men, ver. 5.

3. They are proud and haughty, ver. 6, and yet are not punished.

4. They are oppressive tyrants: "Violence covereth them."

5. They feed luxuriously, ver. 7.

6. They speak evil against the poor, ver. 8.

7. They even speak against God, and all the dispensations of his providence: "Their tongue walketh through the earth," ver. 9.

8. They assert that he takes no cognizance of their ways, ver. 10, 11.

III. The evil conclusion formed from these premises refuted.

1. It is the ungodly that prosper in the earth, ver. 12.

2. If so, then of what avail are my religious observances and sufferings, &c.? ver. 13, 14.

He resolves the question,—

1. From *the testimony of* ALL *the godly*, ver. 15.

2. He tried to solve it by *reason*, but did not succeed, ver. 16.

3. He *consults with God*, and the whole is made plain, ver. 17.

From him he learns,—

1. That the happiness of the wicked is *unstable*, ver. 18.

2. They stand on a *precipice*, and are *cast down*, ver. 19.

3. Their desolation comes *suddenly* and *unexpectedly*, ver. 19.

4. Their ruin is *fearful:* "They are consumed with terrors."

5. Thus it is demonstrated that their happiness was vain, empty, as unsubstantial as a *dream*, ver. 20.

IV. He now acknowledges that he had formed

an erroneous judgment. 1. That he gave way to *animosity*. 2. That he acted rather like a *beast* than a *man*, in looking only to the present life, ver. 21, 22. He now receives instruction and encouragement.

1. The godly are not neglected: "They are continually with God," ver. 23.

2. They are tenderly *led* as by *the hand* of a loving father, ver. 23.

3. They are directed by the *word* and *Spirit* of God, ver. 24.

4. They are often *crowned* with signal marks of God's esteem, even in this life, ver. 24.

V. His resolution to live to God, as he sees that such alone are happy.

1. He expects nothing in *heaven* but God: "Whom have I in heaven," &c.

2. He will seek no other portion on *earth:* "There is none on earth," ver. 25.

3. I will cleave to him in life and death: "When my flesh and my heart fail."

4. My confidence in him shall be unshaken, ver. 26.

VI. He draws two conclusions from what he had learned:—

1. They that are far from God *perish*.

2. They that *draw nigh* to him are saved, ver. 27.

Therefore, I will so trust in God that I shall be able to declare his works, ver. 28.

PSALM LXXIV

The psalmist complains of the desolations of the sanctuary, and pleads with God, 1–3; *shows the insolence and wickedness of their enemies,* 4–8; *prays to God to act for them as he had done for their fathers, whom, by his miraculous power, he had saved,* 9–17; *begs God to arise, and vindicate his own honour against his enemies, and the enemies of his people,* 18–23.

[a]Maschil of Asaph

O GOD, why hast thou [b]cast *us* off for
ever? *why* doth thine anger [c]smoke
against [d]the sheep of thy pasture?
2 Remember thy congregation, [e]*which* thou
hast purchased of old; the [f]rod [g]of thine
inheritance, *which* thou hast redeemed; this
Mount Zion, wherein thou hast dwelt.
3 Lift up thy feet unto the perpetual desolations; *even* all *that* the enemy hath done
wickedly in the sanctuary.
4 [h]Thine enemies roar in the midst of thy
congregations; [i]they set up their ensigns *for*
signs.
5 *A man* was famous according as he had
lifted up axes upon the thick trees.
6 But now they break down [k]the carved
work thereof at once with axcs and hammers.
7 [l]They [m]have cast fire into thy sanctuary,
they have defiled [n]*by casting down* the dwelling-place of thy name to the ground.

[a]Or, A Psalm *for Asaph to give instruction*——[b]Psa. xliv. 9, 23; lx. 1, 10; lxxvii. 7; Jer. xxxi. 37; xxxiii. 24——[c]Deut. xxix. 20——[d]Psa. xcv. 7; c. 3——[e]Exod. xv. 16; Deut. ix. 29

[f]Or, *tribe*——[g]Deut. xxxii. 9; Jer. x. 16——[h]Lam. ii. 7——[i]Dan. vi. 27——[k]1 Kings vi. 18, 29, 32, 35——[l]2 Kings xxv. 9——[m]Heb. *They have sent thy sanctuary into the fire*——[n]Psa. lxxxix. 39

NOTES ON PSALM LXXIV

The *title* is, *Maschil of Asaph*, or, "A Psalm of Asaph, to give instruction." That this Psalm was written at a time when the *temple* was ruined, *Jerusalem* burnt, and the prophets scattered or destroyed, is evident. But it is not so clear whether the desolations here refer to the days of *Nebuchadnezzar*, or to the desolation that took place under the *Romans* about the *seventieth* year of the Christian era. *Calmet* inclines to the former opinion; and supposes the Psalm to be a lamentation over the *temple* destroyed by Nebuchadnezzar.

Verse 1. *O God, why hast thou cast* us *off for ever?*] Hast thou determined that we shall never more be thy people? Are we never to see an end to our calamities?

Verse 2. *Remember thy congregation,* which *thou hast purchased of old*] We are the descendants of that people whom thou didst take unto thyself; the children of Abraham, Isaac, and Jacob. Wilt thou never more be reconciled to us?

Verse 3. *Lift up thy feet*] Arise, and return to us; our desolations still continue. Thy sanctuary is profaned by thine and our enemies.

Verse 4. *Thine enemies roar*] Thy people, who were formerly a distinct and separate people, and who would not even touch a Gentile, are now obliged to mingle with the most profane. Their boisterous mirth, their cruel mockings, their insulting commands, are heard every where in all our assemblies.

They set up their ensigns for *signs.*] שמו אותתם אתות *samu othotham othoth*, they set up their standards in the place of ours. All the ensigns and trophies were those of our enemies; our own were no longer to be seen.

The *fifth, sixth*, and *seventh* verses give a correct historical account of the ravages committed by the Babylonians, as we may see from 2 Kings xxv. 4, 7, 8, 9, and Jer. lii. 7, 18, 19: "And the city was broken up, and all the men fled by night by the way of the gate. They took Zedekiah, and slew his sons before his eyes; and put out his eyes, and bound him with fetters of brass, and carried him to Babylon. And on the *second* day of the *fifth* month of the *nineteenth* year of Nebuchadnezzar, Nebuzaradan, the captain of the guard, came unto Jerusalem; and he burnt the house of the Lord, and the king's house, and every great man's house; and all the houses of Jerusalem burnt he with fire. And they broke down the walls of Jerusalem round about. And the pillars of brass and the bases, and the brazen sea, they broke in pieces, and carried the brass to Babylon.

8 [o]They said in their hearts, Let us [p]destroy them together: they have burned up all the synagogues of God in the land.

9 We see not our signs: [q]*there is* no more any prophet: neither *is there* among us any that knoweth how long.

10 O God, how long shall the adversary reproach? shall the enemy blaspheme thy name for ever?

11 [r]Why withdrawest thou thy hand, even thy right hand? pluck *it* out of thy bosom.

12 For [s]God *is* my King of old, working salvation in the midst of the earth.

13 [t]Thou didst [u]divide the sea by thy strength: [v]thou brakest the heads of the [w]dragons in the waters.

14 Thou brakest the heads of leviathan in

[o]Psa. lxxxiii. 4——[p]Heb. *break*——[q]1 Sam. iii. 1; Amos viii. 11; 1 Mac. iv. 46——[r]Lam. ii. 3

[s]Psa. xliv. 4——[t]Exod. xiv. 21——[u]Heb. *break* [v]Isa. li. 9, 10; Ezek. xxix. 3; xxxii. 2——[w]Or, *whales*

And the pots, shovels, snuffers and spoons, and the fire pans and bowls, and such things as were of gold and silver, they took away." Thus they broke down, and carried away, and destroyed this beautiful house; and in the true barbarian spirit, neither sanctity, beauty, symmetry, nor elegance of workmanship, was any thing in their eyes. What *hammers* and *axes* could ruin, was ruined; Jerusalem was totally destroyed, and its walls laid level with the ground. Well might the psalmist sigh over such a desolation.

Verse 8. *Let us destroy them*] Their object was totally to annihilate the political existence of the Jewish people.

They have burned up all the synagogues of God in the land.] It is supposed that there were no *synagogues* in the land till after the Babylonish captivity. How then could the Chaldeans burn up any in Judea? The word מועדי *moadey*, which we translate *synagogues*, may be taken in a more general sense, and mean *any places* where *religious assemblies* were held: and that such places and assemblies did exist long *before* the Babylonish captivity, is pretty evident from different parts of Scripture. It appears that Elisha kept such at his house on the *sabbaths* and *new moons*. See 2 Kings iv. 23. And perhaps to such St. James may refer, Acts xv. 23, a species of *synagogues*, where *the law was read of old, in every city of the land.* And it appears that such religious meetings were held at the house of the Prophet *Ezekiel*, chap. xxxiii. 31. And perhaps every prophet's house was such. This is the only place in the *Old Testament* where we have the word *synagogue.* Indeed, wherever there was a *place* in which God met with *patriarch* or *prophet*, and any memorial of it was *preserved*, there was a מועד *moed*, or place of religious meeting; and all such places the Chaldeans would destroy, pursuant to their design to extinguish the Jewish religion, and blot out all its memorials from the earth. And this was certainly the most likely means to effect their purpose. How soon would Christianity be destroyed in England if all the churches, chapels, and places of worship were destroyed, and only the poor of the people left in the land; who, from their circumstances, could not build a place for the worship of God! After such desolation, what a miracle was the restoration of the Jews!

Verse 9. *We see not our signs*] "They have taken away all our trophies, and have left us no memorial that God has been among us. Even thou thyself hast left us destitute of all those *supernatural evidences* that have so often convinced us that thou wert among us of a truth." But we may say that they were not totally destitute even of these. The preservation of Daniel in the lion's den, and of the three Hebrews in the fiery furnace; the metamorphosis of Nebuchadnezzar; the handwriting that appeared to Belshazzar; were all so many prodigies and evidences that God had not left them without proofs of his *being* and his *regard.*

There is *no more any prophet*] There was not one among them in that place that could tell them *how long* that captivity was yet to endure. But there were prophets in the captivity. *Daniel* was one; but his prophecies were confined to one place. *Ezekiel* was another, but he was among those captives who were by the river *Chebar*. They had not, as usual, prophets who went *to* and *fro* through the land, preaching repentance and remission of sins.

Verse 11. *Why withdrawest thou thy hand*] It has been remarked, that as the outward habit of the easterns had no sleeves, the hands and arms were frequently covered with the folds of the robe; and in order to do any thing, the hand must be disentangled and drawn out. The literal version of the *Hebrew* is: "To what time wilt thou draw back thy hand; yea, thy right hand, from within thy bosom?" *Consume;* that is, manifest thy power, and *destroy* thy adversaries. I have, in the *introduction* to the book of Psalms, spoken of the old metrical version by *Sternhold* and *Hopkins*, and have stated that it was formed from the original text. A proof of this may be seen by the learned reader in this and the preceding verse; where, though their version is harsh, and some of their expressions quaint almost to ridicule, yet they have hit the true meaning which our prose translators have missed:—

Ver. 10. When wilt thou once, Lord, end this shame,
And cease thine en'mies strong?
Shall they always blaspheme thy name,
And rail on thee so long?

Ver. 11. Why dost thou draw thy hand aback,
And hide it in thy lap?
O pluck it out, and be not slack
To give thy foes a rap!

Verse 12. *For God* is *my King of old*] We have always acknowledged thee as our sovereign; and thou hast reigned as a king in the midst of our land, dispensing salvation and deliverance from the *centre* to every part of the *circumference.*

Verse 13. *Thou didst divide the sea*] When our fathers came from Egypt.

Thou brakest the heads of the dragons in the

pieces, *and* gavest him [x]*to be* meat [y]to the
people inhabiting the wilderness.
15 [z]Thou didst cleave the fountain and the
flood: [a]thou driedst up [b]mighty rivers.
16 The day *is* thine, the night also *is*
thine: [c]thou hast prepared the light and
the sun.
17 Thou hast [d]set all the borders of the earth:
[e]thou hast [f]made summer and winter.
18 [g]Remember this, *that* the enemy hath
reproached, O LORD, and *that* [h]the foolish
people have blasphemed thy name.
19 O deliver not the soul [i]of thy turtle-
dove unto the multitude *of the wicked:* [k]forget not the congregation of thy poor for ever.
20 [l]Have respect unto the covenant: for
the dark places of the earth are full of the
habitations of cruelty.
21 O let not the oppressed return ashamed:
let the poor and needy praise thy name.
22 Arise, O God, plead thine own cause:
[m]remember how the foolish man reproacheth
thee daily.
23 Forget not the voice of thine enemies:
the tumult of those that rise up against thee
[n]increaseth continually.

[x]Num. xiv. 9——[y]Psa. lxxii. 9——[z]Exod. xvii. 5, 6; Num. xx. 11; Psa. cv. 41; Isa. xlviii. 21——[a]Josh. iii. 13, &c.——[b]Heb. *rivers of strength*——[c]Gen. i. 14, &c. [d]Acts xvii. 26——[e]Gen. viii. 22

[f]Heb. *made them*——[g]Ver. 22; Rev. xvi. 19——[h]Psa. xxxix. 8——[i]Cant. ii. 14——[k]Psa. lxviii. 10——[l]Gen. xvii. 7, 8; Lev. xxvi. 44, 45; Psa. cvi. 45; Jer. xxxiii. 21 [m]Ver. 18; Psa. lxxxix. 51——[n]Heb. *ascendeth;* Jonah i. 2

waters.] Pharaoh, his captains, and all his hosts were drowned in the Red Sea, when attempting to pursue them.

Verse 14. *The heads of leviathan*] Leviathan might be intended here as a personification of the *Egyptian government;* and its *heads*, Pharaoh and his chief captains.

To the people inhabiting the wilderness.] Probably meaning the *birds and beasts of prey.* These were the people of the wilderness, which fed on the dead bodies of the Egyptians, which the tides had cast ashore. The *Vulgate, Septuagint, Æthiopic*, and *Arabic* read, "Thou hast given him for meat to the Ethiopians," or Abyssinians.

Verse 15. *Thou didst cleave the fountain*] Thou didst cleave the *rock* in the wilderness, of which all the congregation drank.

Thou driedst up mighty rivers.] Does not this refer to the cutting off the waters of the Jordan, so that the people passed over dry-shod?

Verse 16. *The day* is *thine, the night also* is *thine*] Thou art the Author of light, and of the sun, which is the means of dispensing it.

Verse 17. *Thou hast set all the borders of the earth*] Thou alone art the Author of all its grand *geographical* divisions.

Thou hast made summer and winter.] Thou hast appointed that peculiarity in the poise and rotation of the earth, by which the *seasons* are produced.

Verse 18. *Remember this*] The heathen not only deny these things, but give the honour of them to their false gods, and thus blaspheme thy name.

Verse 19. *Deliver not the soul of thy turtle-dove*] Thy people Israel are helpless, defenceless, miserable, and afflicted: O deliver them no longer into the power of their brutal adversaries.

Verse 20. *Have respect unto the covenant*] הבט לברית *habbet labberith.* Pay attention to the *covenant sacrifice;* to that offered by Abraham, Gen. xv. 9, &c., when the contracting parties, God and Abram, passed through between the separated parts of the covenant sacrifice. An indisputable type of Jesus Christ; and of God and man meeting in his sacrificed humanity.

The dark places of the earth] The caves, dens, woods, &c., of the *land* are full of robbers, cut-throats, and murderers, who are continually destroying thy people, so that the holy seed seems as if it would be entirely cut off and the *covenant* promise thus be rendered void.

The words may either apply to *Chaldea* or *Judea.* Judea was at this time little else than a den of robbers, its own natural inhabitants being removed. Chaldea was infested with hordes of banditti also.

Verse 21. *Let not the oppressed return ashamed*] Do not permit thy people to be so diminished, that when, according to thy promise, they are restored to their own land, they may appear to be but a handful of men.

Verse 22. *Plead thine own cause*] Thy honour is concerned, as well as our safety and salvation. *The fool*—the idolater, *reproacheth thee daily*—he boasts of the superiority of his idols, by whose power, he asserts, we are brought under their domination.

Verse 23. *Forget not the voice*] While we pray to thee for our own salvation, we call upon thee to vindicate thy injured honour: and let all the nations see that thou lovest thy followers, and hatest those who are thy enemies. Let not man prevail against thee or thine.

ANALYSIS OF THE SEVENTY-FOURTH PSALM

This Psalm divides itself into *two* parts:—

I. The Psalmist's complaint, ver. 1-10.

II. His prayer, ver. 10-23.

Both the complaint and petition are summarily comprised in the *three* first verses; and afterwards amplified throughout the Psalm.

I. He expostulates with God about their calamity.

1. From the author of it: "Thou, O God."

2. From the extremity of it: "Cast us not off."

3. From the duration of it: "For ever."

4. From the cause: "Thy anger smokes against us."

5. From the object of it: "The sheep of thy pasture."

To his complaint he subjoins his *petition;* in which every word has the strength of an argument.

1. "Remember thy congregation:" Thy chosen people.

2. "Whom thou hast purchased:" By a mighty hand from Pharaoh.

3. "Of old:" Thy people ever since thy covenant with Abraham.

4. "The rod of thine inheritance;" dwelling in that land which thou didst *measure* out to them.

5. "Whom thou hast redeemed:" From the Canaanites, &c.

6. "This Mount Zion, wherein thou hast dwelt:" Where we gave thee the worship which belonged to the true God; and thou wert pleased with our sacrifices and services. *Remember* this people, and all these engagements; and "cast us not off for ever."

7. "Lift up thy feet:" Consider thy *own dishonour;* they are *thy enemies* as well as *ours.* See what they have done against thee, thy *temple*, thy *ordinances.* Look at their *blasphemies*, and avenge the quarrel of thy *covenant*, ver. 3-11.

Consider what thou hast done for our forefathers.

1. Thou hast been long *our King* and Deliverer. See the proofs, ver. 12-15.

2. Thy general *providence* respects all men. Thou hast given them *light;* the *sun* and *moon*, the *vicissitude of seasons*, &c., ver. 16, 17.

II. The psalmist's *prayer:*—

1. That God would *remember* the *reproaches* of his *enemies*, ver. 18.

2. That he would *deliver the souls* of his *children*, ver. 19.

3. That he would not forget "the congregation of the poor," ver. 19.

4. That he *would remember his covenant* with Abram, to make them an innumerable people, and a blessing to all mankind, ver. 20.

5. That, when they did return, they might not be a diminished people; for their enemies were determined to destroy them, ver. 21.

6. That they might be led from all considerations to *praise his name*, ver. 21.

At the conclusion he urges his petition:—

1. "Arise,—plead thine own cause."

2. "Remember the foolish."

3. "Forget not thine enemies."

4. They make a *tumult*, and their partisans *daily increase*, ver. 22, 23.

PSALM LXXV

The psalmist praises God for present mercies, 1; *the Lord answers, and promises to judge the people righteously,* 2, 3; *rebukes the proud and haughty,* 4, 5; *shows that all authority comes from himself,* 4–7; *that he will punish the wicked,* 8; *the psalmist resolves to praise God,* 9; *and the Most High promises to cast down the wicked, and raise up the righteous,* 9, 10.

XV. DAY. MORNING PRAYER

To the chief Musician, [a]Al-taschith, [b]A Psalm *or* Song [c]of Asaph

UNTO thee, O God, do we give thanks,
unto thee do we give thanks: for *that*
thy name is near thy wondrous works declare.
2 [d]When I shall receive the congregation I
will judge uprightly.
3 The earth and all the inhabitants thereof
are dissolved: I bear up the pillars of it. Selah.
4 I said unto the fools, Deal not fool-

[a]Or, *Destroy not*——[b]Psa. lvii. title

[c]Or, *for Asaph*——[d]Or, *When I shall take a set time*

NOTES ON PSALM LXXV

The *title* is, *"To the chief Musician*, or conqueror, *Al-taschith*, destroy not, *A Psalm* or *Song of Asaph."* See this title Al-taschith explained Psa. lvii. The *Chaldee* supposes that this Psalm was composed at the time of the pestilence, when David prayed the Lord *not to destroy the people.* Some of the Jews suppose that *Al-taschith* is the beginning of a Psalm, to the air of which this Psalm was to be set and sung. The Psalm seems to have been composed during the captivity; and appears to be a continuation of the subject in the preceding.

Verse 1. *Unto thee, O God, do we give thanks*] Thou canst not forget thy people. The numerous manifestations of thy providence and mercy show that thou art not far off, but near: this

Thy wondrous works declare.] These words would make a proper conclusion to the preceding Psalm, which seems to end very abruptly. The *second* verse is the commencement of the Divine answer to the prayer of *Asaph.*

Verse 2. *When I shall receive the congregation*] When the proper time is come that the congregation, my people of Israel, should be brought out of captivity, and received back into favour, I shall not only enlarge them, but punish their enemies. They shall be cut off and cast out, and become a more miserable people than those whom they now insult. I will destroy them as a nation, so that they shall never more be numbered among the empires of the earth.

Verse 3. *The earth and all the inhabitants thereof are dissolved*] They all depend on me; and whenever I withdraw the power by which they exist and live, they are immediately dissolved.

I bear up the pillars of it.] By the word of my power all things are upheld; and without me nothing can subsist. Those who consider this Psalm to have been written by David before he was anointed king over ALL *Israel*, understand the words thus: "All is at present in a state of confusion; violence and injustice reign: but when 'I shall receive the *whole* congregation,' when all the tribes shall acknowledge me as *king*, I will reorganize the whole constitution. It is true that the *land* and *all its inhabitants are dissolved*—unsettled and unconnected by the bands of civil interest. The whole system is disorganized: 'I bear up the pillars of it;' the expectation of the *chief people* is placed upon *me;* and it is the hope they have of my coming speedily to the throne of all Israel that prevents them from breaking out into actual rebellion."

Verse 4. *I said unto the fools*] I have given

ishly: and to the wicked, [e]Lift not up the
horn:

5 Lift not up your horn on high: speak *not*
with a stiff neck.

6 For promotion *cometh* neither from the
east, nor from the west, nor from the [f]south.

7 But [g]God *is* the Judge: [h]he putteth down
one, and setteth up another.

8 For [i]in the hand of the LORD *there is* a
cup, and the wine is red; it is [k]full of mixture: and he poureth out of the same: [l]but
the dregs thereof, all the wicked of the earth
shall wring *them* out, *and* drink *them*.

9 But I will declare for ever; I will sing
praises to the God of Jacob.

10 [m]All the horns of the wicked also will I
cut off; *but* [n]the horns of the righteous shall
be exalted.

[e]Zechariah i. 21——[f]Hebrew, *desert*——[g]Psalm l. 6; lviii. 11——[h]1 Samuel ii. 7; Daniel ii. 21——[i]Job xxi. 20; Psa. lx. 3; Jeremiah xxv. 15; Revelation xiv. 10; xvi. 19——[k]Proverbs xxiii. 30——[l]Psalm lxxiii. 10——[m]Psalm ci. 8; Jeremiah xlviii. 25——[n]Psalm lxxxix. 17; cxlviii. 14

the idolatrous Chaldeans sufficient warning to abandon their idols, and worship the true God; but they would not. I have also charged the wicked, to whom for a season I have delivered you because of your transgressions, not to *lift up their horn*—not to use their *power* to oppress and destroy. They have, notwithstanding, abused their power in the persecutions with which they have afflicted you. For all these things they shall shortly be brought to an awful account. On the term *horn*, see the note on Luke i. 69.

Verse 5. *Speak* not with *a stiff neck*.] Mr. *Bruce* has observed that the Abyssinian kings have a *horn* on their *diadem;* and that the keeping it erect, or in a projecting form, makes them appear as if they had a *stiff neck;* and refers to this passage for the antiquity of the usage, and the *appearance* also.

Verse 6. *For promotion* cometh *neither from the east, &c.*] As if the Lord had said, speaking to the Babylonians, None of all the surrounding powers shall be able to help you; none shall pluck you out of my hand. I am the *Judge:* I will pull you down, and set my afflicted people up, ver. 7.

Calmet has observed that the Babylonians had Media, Armenia, and Mesopotamia on the EAST; and thence came Darius the Mede: that it had Arabia, Phœnicia, and Egypt on the WEST; thence came Cyrus, who overthrew the empire of the Chaldeans. And by the *mountains of the desert,* מדבר הרים *midbar harim,* which we translate SOUTH, Persia, may be meant; which government was established on the ruins of the Babylonish empire. No help came from any of those powers to the sinful Babylonians; they were obliged to drink the *cup of the red wine* of God's judgment, even to the very *dregs.* They were to receive no *other* punishment; this one was to *annihilate* them as a people for ever.

Verse 8. *It is full of mixture*] Alluding to that mingled potion of stupifying drugs given to criminals to drink previously to their execution. See a parallel passage to this, Jer. xxv. 15-26.

Verse 9. *I will sing praises to the God of Jacob.*] These are the words of the psalmist, who magnifies the Lord for the promise of deliverance from their enemies.

Verse 10. *All the horns of the wicked*] All their *power* and *influence,* will I cut off; and will exalt and extend the *power* of the righteous. The psalmist is said to *do these things,* because he is as the *mouth* of God to *denounce* them. All was punctually fulfilled: the *wicked*—the Babylonians, were all cut off; the *righteous*—the Jews, called so from the holy covenant, *which required righteousness,* were delivered and *exalted.*

ANALYSIS OF THE SEVENTY-FIFTH PSALM

Bishop *Nicholson* supposes that *David* was the author of this Psalm; and that he composed it on his inauguration or entrance upon the kingdom; and by it he gives us an example of a good king.

There are *three* chief parts in this Psalm:—

I. A doxology, ver. 1; repeated, ver. 9.

II. His profession how to perform the regal office, ver. 2, 3, 10.

III. His rebuke of foolish men for mistakes occasioned,—

1. Partly by their *pride* when they rise to great places, ver. 4, 5.

2. That they do not consider whence their preferment comes, ver. 6, 7.

3. That they judge not rightly of afflictions, ver. 8.

I. The doxology or thanksgiving.

1. He *doubles* it to show that it should be *frequently* done: "Unto thee do we give thanks; unto thee," &c.

2. His reason for it: "For that thy name is near,"—thy help is always at hand. "The Lord is nigh to all that call upon him."

3. Of which he had experience in his exaltation to the kingdom, which he calls God's "wondrous works."

II. How the office of a good king is to be discharged.

1. I will judge uprightly.

2. To rectify disorders. They had need of a just and upright king. 1. The land and its inhabitants were disorganized. 2. He was the only stay and support of the state: "I bear up the pillars."

III. His rebuke of bad men.

1. They were *fools,* and dealt unjustly.

2. *Wicked,* and vaunted their wealth and power.

3. They used their *power* to oppress.

4. They were *obstinate* in their oppression of the poor. He refers to their false judgments.

1. They supposed that their authority and influence came by their own *merit;* and for them they were accountable to none.

2. They did not consider that *God* was the author of power, &c.

3. Their third mistake was, they imputed afflictions to a wrong cause, and did not consider that they came from God.

To show this, the Psalmist uses an elegant comparison, comparing God to the master of a feast, who invites and entertains all kinds of men at his table; who has a cup of mixed wine in his hand, by which he represents the *miseries* of this life. To all God reaches this cup; and *every one drinks* of it, some more, some less.

1. "In the hand of the Lord there is a cup." He apportions the afflictions of men.

2. "The wine is red." The high-coloured feculent wine, i. e., *afflictions.*

3. "It is full of mixture;" not all *sour*, nor *sweet*, nor *bitter.* The strength of it is tempered by God to the circumstances of his creatures.

4. "He poureth out of the same." He gives to all, some even to his own children. ALL *must drink of this cup.*

5. But the *lees* or *dregs* of it "all the wicked of the earth shall wring out." Those who are incorrigible have afflictions without benefit; they wring the dregs out. On them God's judgments fall without mitigation.

He concludes the Psalm with—

1. A repetition of his thanks: "I will declare for ever; I will sing praises to the God of Jacob."

2. A protestation of his duty: 1. "I will cut off the horns of the wicked." 2. "I will exalt the horns of the righteous." Those who exalt themselves shall be abased: those who humble themselves shall be exalted.

Tu regere imperio populos, Romane, memento,
(Hæ tibi erunt artes) pacisque imponere morem;
Parcere subjectis, et debellare superbos.
VIRG. Æn. lib. vi., ver. 851.

"But, Rome, 'tis thine alone, with awful sway,
To rule mankind, and make the world obey,
Disposing peace and war thy own majestic
way:
To tame the proud, the fettered slave to free:
These are imperial arts, and worthy thee."
DRYDEN.

These lines of the Roman poet contain precisely the same sentiment that is expressed in the *tenth* verse of the Psalm. And thus God acts in the government of the world, dealing with nations as they have dealt with others: so the conquerors are conquered; the oppressed, raised to honour and dominion.

PSALM LXXVI

The true God known in Judah, Israel, Salem, and Zion, 1, 2. *A description of his defeat of the enemies of his people,* 3–6. *How God is to be worshipped,* 7–9. *He should be considered as the chief Ruler: all the potentates of the earth are subject to him,* 10–12.

To the chief Musician on Neginoth, A Psalm *or* Song [a]of Asaph

A. M. cir. 3294 B. C. cir. 710 Ezechiæ, Regis Judææ, cir. annum 17

IN [b]Judah *is* God known:
his name *is* great in Israel.
2 In Salem also is his tabernacle, and his dwelling place
in Zion.
3 [c]There brake he the arrows of the bow, the shield,
and the sword, and the battle.
Selah.
4 Thou *art* more glorious *and* excellent
[d]than the mountains of prey.

A. M. cir. 3294 B. C. cir. 710 Ezechiæ, Regis Judææ, cir. annum 17

[a]Or, *for Asaph*——[b]Psa. xlviii. 1, &c.——[c]Psa. xlvi. 9; Ezek. xxxix. 9——[d]Ezek. xxxviii. 12, 13; xxxix. 4

NOTES ON PSALM LXXVI

The *title*, "To the chief Musician on Neginoth, a Psalm *or* Song of Asaph." See the titles to Psalms iv. and vi. The *Vulgate, Septuagint,* and others have, "A Psalm for the Assyrians;" and it is supposed to be a thanksgiving for the defeat of the Assyrians. The Syriac says it is a thanksgiving for the taking of Rabbah, belonging to the children of Ammon. It is considered by some of the best commentators to have been composed after the defeat of Sennacherib. That it was composed after the death of David, and after the two kingdoms of Israel and Judah were separated, is evident from the first verse. If *Asaph* was its author, it could not be the *Asaph* that flourished in the days of David but some other gifted and Divinely inspired man of the same name, by whom several others of the Psalms appear to have been composed during the captivity.

Verse 1. *In Judah* is *God known*] The true God revealed himself to the *Jews.* The *Israelites*, after the separation of the tribes, had the same knowledge, but they greatly corrupted the Divine worship; though still God was *great*, even in Israel.

Verse 2. *In Salem also is his tabernacle*] *Salem* was the ancient name of *Jebus*, afterward called *Jerusalem.* Here was the *tabernacle* set up; but afterwards, when the *temple* was built on *Mount Zion*, there was his *habitation.* The Psalm was evidently composed after the building of Solomon's temple.

Verse 3. *There brake he the arrows of the bow*] רשפי *rishphey*, the *fiery arrows.* Arrows, round the heads of which inflammable matter was rolled, and then ignited, were used by the ancients, and shot into towns to set them on fire; and were discharged among the towers and wooden works of besiegers. The Romans called them *phalaricæ;* and we find them mentioned by Virgil, Æn. lib. ix., ver. 705:—

Sed magnum stridens contorta phalarica venit,
Fulminis acta modo.

On this passage *Servius* describes the *phalarica* as a dart or spear with a spherical leaden head to which fire was attached. Thrown by a strong hand, it killed those whom it hit, and set fire to buildings, &c. It was called *phalarica* from the towers called *phalæ* from which it was generally projected. In allusion to these St. Paul speaks of the *fiery darts of the devil,* Eph. vi.

A. M. cir. 3294
B. C. cir. 710
Ezechiæ, Regis
Judææ,
cir. annum
17

5 [e]The stout-hearted are spoiled, [f]they have slept their sleep: and none of the men of might have found their hands.

6 [g]At thy rebuke, O God of Jacob, both the chariot and horse are cast into a dead sleep.

7 Thou, *even* thou, *art* to be feared: and [h]who may stand in thy sight when once thou art angry?

8 [i]Thou didst cause judgment to be heard from heaven; [k]the earth feared, and was still,

A. M. cir. 3294
B. C. cir. 710
Ezechiæ, Regis
Judææ,
cir. annum
17

9 When God [l]arose to judgment, to save all the meek of the earth. Selah.

10 [m]Surely the wrath of man shall praise thee: the remainder of wrath shalt thou restrain.

---

[e]Isa. xlvi. 12——[f]Psa. xiii. 3; Jer. li. 39——[g]Exod. xv. 1, 21; Ezek. xxxix. 20; Nah. ii. 13; Zech. xii. 4 [h]Nah. i. 6

[i]Ezek. xxxviii. 20——[k]2 Chron. xx. 29, 30——[l]Psa. ix. 7, 8, 9; lxxii. 4——[m]See Exod. ix. 16; xviii. 11; Psa. lxv. 7

16, to the note on which the reader is requested to refer.

The shield and the sword] If this refers to the destruction of Sennacherib's army, it may be truly said that God rendered useless all their warlike instruments, his angel having destroyed 185,000 of them in one night.

Verse 4. *Than the mountains of prey.*] This is an address to Mount *Zion*. Thou art more illustrious and excellent than all the mountains of prey, i. e., where wild beasts wander, and prey on those that are more helpless than themselves. Zion was the place where GOD *dwelt;* the other mountains were the *abode* of *wild beasts*.

Verse 5. *The stout-hearted are spoiled*] The boasting blasphemers, such as Rab-shakeh, and his master Sennacherib, the king of Assyria.

They have slept their sleep] They were asleep in their tent when the destroying angel, the suffocating wind, destroyed the whole; they over whom it passed never more awoke.

None of the men of might] Is not this a strong irony? Where are your mighty men? their boasted armour, &c.?

Verse 6. *At thy rebuke*] It was not by any human means that this immense army was overthrown; it was by the power of God alone. Not only *infantry* was destroyed, but the *cavalry* also.

The chariot and horse] That is, the chariot horses, as well as the men, were

Cast into a dead sleep.] Were all suffocated in the same night. On the destruction of this mighty host, the reader is requested to refer to the notes on 2 Kings xix.

Verse 7. *Thou,* even *thou,* art to be *feared*] The Hebrew is simple, but very emphatic: אתה נורא אתה *attah nora attah,* "Thou art terrible; thou art." The repetition of the *pronoun* deepens the sense.

When once thou art angry?] Literally, *From the time thou art angry.* In the moment thy wrath is kindled, in that moment judgment is executed. How awful is this consideration! If *one hundred and eighty-five thousand* men were in one moment destroyed by the wrath of God, canst *thou,* thou poor, miserable, feeble sinner, resist his will, and turn aside his thunder!

Verse 8. *Thou didst cause judgment to be heard*] When God declared by his prophet that the enemy should not prevail, but on the contrary be destroyed, *the earth*—the *land,* and by *metonymy* the *inhabitants* of the land, were struck with astonishment and terror, so as not to be able to move. The great boaster Sennacherib, who carried terror, dismay, and desolation every where, was now struck with dumb amazement; and the angel of the Almighty, in a moment, stopped the breath of those hosts in which he confided.

Verse 9. *The meek of the earth.*] The *humbled* or *oppressed people of the land.* The poor *Jews,* now utterly helpless, and calling upon the Lord for succour.

Verse 10. *Surely the wrath of man shall praise thee*] The rage of Sennacherib shall only serve to manifest thy glory. The stronger he is, and the more he threatens, and the weaker thy people, the more shall thy majesty and mercy appear in his destruction and their support.

The remainder of wrath shalt thou restrain.] The Hebrew gives rather a different sense: "Thou shalt gird thyself with the remainder of wrath." Even after thou hast sent this signal destruction upon Sennacherib and his army, thou wilt continue to pursue the *remnant* of the persecutors of thy people; their wrath shall be the cause of the excitement of thy justice to destroy them. As a man *girds* himself with his girdle, that he may the better perform his work, so thou wilt gird thyself *with wrath,* that thou mayest destroy thy enemies. A good maxim has been taken from this verse: "God often so *counterworks* the evil designs of men against his cause and followers, that it turns out to their advantage and his glory; nor does he permit them to go to the extent of what they have *purposed,* and of what they are *able* to perform. He *suffers* them to do *some mischief,* but not *all* they *would* or *can* do." But how different is the reading of the *Vulgate! Quoniam cogitatio hominis confitebitur tibi: et reliquiæ cogitationis diem festum agent tibi:* "The thought of man shall praise thee; and the remains of thought shall celebrate a feast day to thee." The *Septuagint* and the *Æthiopic* have understood the text in the same way. Some translate thus: "Certainly, the ferocity of the man (Sennacherib) shall praise thee: and thou shalt gird thyself with the spoils of the furious." The spoils of this great army shall be a booty for thy people. Probably this is the true notion of the place. The old *Psalter* renders it thus: **For thoght of man sal schrife** (confess) **to the, and levyngs** (remains) **of thoght a feste day till the sal wirk.** The paraphrase is curious, of which this is the substance: "When man forsakes perfitly his synne, and sithen (afterwards) rightwisness werks; it is a feste day; whenne the conscience is clered, and makes feste with the swetnes of goddes

A. M. cir. 3294
B. C. cir. 710
Ezechiæ, Regis
Judææ,
cir. annum
17

11 [n]Vow, and pay unto the LORD your God: [o]let all that be round about him bring presents [p]unto him that ought to be feared.

12 He shall cut off the spirit of princes: [q]*he is* terrible to the kings of the earth.

[n]Eccles. v. 4, 5, 6——[o]2 Chron. xxxii. 22, 23; Psa. lxviii. 29; lxxxix. 7——[p]Heb. *to fear*——[q]Psa. lxviii. 35

lufe, restand fra besynes of any creatur in erth: Than is God at hame with his spouse dwelland."

Verse 11. *Vow, and pay unto the Lord*] *Bind* yourselves to him, and forget not your *obligations.*

Let all that be round about him] All the neighbouring nations, who shall see God's judgments against his enemies, should

Bring presents unto him] Give him that homage which is due unto him.

That ought to be feared.] למורא *lammora,* "to the terrible One;" lest they be consumed as the Assyrians have been.

Verse 12. *He shall cut off the spirit of princes*] Even in the midst of their conquests, he can fill them with terror and dismay, or cut them off in their career of victory.

He is *terrible to the kings of the earth.*] "He is the only Ruler of princes;" to him they must account. And a terrible account most of them will have to give to the great God; especially those who, instigated by the desire of dominion, have, in the lust of conquest which it generates, laid countries waste by fire and sword, making widows and orphans without number, and extending the empire of desolation and death.

Thus *all* are under his dominion, and are accountable to him. Even those whom *man* cannot bring to justice, God will; and to judge *them* is one grand use of a *final judgment-day.*

ANALYSIS OF THE SEVENTY-SIXTH PSALM

In this Psalm there are *three* parts:—

I. The prerogative of Judah and Israel, ver. 1, 2.

II. A narration of God's majesty in the Church, ver. 3-11.

III. An exhortation to worship and serve God.

I. The prerogatives of the Jews above all other nations.

1. God was *known* among them: "In Judah is God known."

2. His *name* was *great* in *Israel.* Illustrious for his manifold deliverances.

3. At *Salem* was his tabernacle,—his *seat of worship,* his peculiar presence.

4. His dwelling in *Zion,*—his constant habitation.

II. A narration of God's power and majesty.

He was *glorious* among good men; *more glorious than the mountains of prey*—kingdoms acquired by violence, murder, and robbery.

And this *glory* was manifest in the following particulars:—

1. They who came to *spoil* were *spoiled,* ver. 5.

2. They were *slain:* "They have slept their sleep," ver. 5.

3. They could make no head against their destroyer, though they were both *numerous* and *strong:* "None of the men of might have found their hands," ver. 5.

The cause of their consternation:—

1. The *rebuke* of God, ver. 6.

2. He was *terrible:* "None could stand in his sight," ver. 7.

3. He was *determinate:* "Judgment was heard from heaven," ver. 8. Sennacherib and his host were destroyed.

The *effects* produced by this were,

1. Praise from the wicked: "They shall acknowledge this as the hand of God." ver. 10.

2. Victory; though they rally, and return again to the battle, they shall be routed: "The remainder of wrath shalt thou restrain," ver. 10. See the notes.

III. He exhorts all to praise him:—1. "Vow, and pay." 2. "Fear and submit to him," ver. 11.

This exhortation he founds on the following REASONS:—

1. "He shall cut off the spirit of princes;" take away from tyrants their prudence and courage.

2. "He is terrible to the kings of the earth." They also shall know that he is God.

PSALM LXXVII

The psalmist's ardent prayer to God in the time of distress, 1–4. *The means he used to excite his confidence,* 5–12. *God's wonderful works in behalf of his people,* 13–20.

To the chief Musician, [a]to Jeduthun, A Psalm [b]of Asaph

I [c]CRIED unto God with my voice, *even* unto God with my voice; and he gave ear unto me.

2 [d]In the day of my trouble I [e]sought the LORD: [f]my sore ran in the night, and ceased not: my soul refused to be comforted.

[a]Psa. xxxix., lxii., title——[b]Or, *for Asaph*——[c]Psa. iii. 4

[d]Psa. l. 15——[e]Isa. xxvi. 9, 16——[f]Heb. *my hand*

NOTES ON PSALM LXXVII

The *title,* "To the chief Musician, (or conqueror,) to Jeduthun, A Psalm of Asaph." On this title we may observe that both *Asaph* and *Jeduthun* were celebrated singers in the time of David, and no doubt were masters or leaders of bands which long after their times were called by their names. Hence Psalms composed during and after the captivity have these names prefixed to them. But there is reason to believe also, that there was a person of the name

3 I remembered God, and was troubled: I complained, and [g]my spirit was overwhelmed. Selah.

4 Thou holdest mine eyes waking: I am so troubled that I cannot speak.

5 [h]I have considered the days of old, the years of ancient times.

6 I call to remembrance [i]my song in the night: [k]I commune with mine own heart: and my spirit made diligent search.

7 [l]Will the LORD cast off for ever? and will he [m]be favourable no more?

8 Is his mercy clean gone for ever? doth [n]*his* promise fail [o]for evermore?

9 Hath God [p]forgotten to be gracious? hath he in anger shut up his tender mercies? Selah.

10 And I said, This *is* [q]my infirmity: *but I will remember* the years of the right hand of the Most High.

---

[g]Psa. cxlii. 3; cxliii. 4——[h]Deut. xxxii. 7; Psa. cxliii. 5; Isa. li. 9——[i]Psa. xlii. 8——[k]Psa. iv. 4——[l]Psa. lxxiv. 1

[m]Psalm lxxxv. 1——[n]Romans ix. 6——[o]Hebrew, *to generation and generation*——[p]Isaiah xlix. 15——[q]Psa. xiii. 22

---

of *Asaph* in the captivity at Babylon. The author must be considered as speaking in the persons of the captive Israelites. It may however be adapted to the case of any individual in spiritual distress through strong temptation, or from a sense of the Divine displeasure in consequence of backsliding.

Verse 1. *I cried unto God*] The *repetition* here marks the earnestness of the psalmist's soul; and the word *voice* shows that the Psalm was not the issue of private *meditation*, but of deep mental trouble, which forced him to *speak* his griefs *aloud*.

Verse 2. *My sore ran in the night, and ceased not*] This is a most unaccountable translation; the literal meaning of ידי נגרה *yadi niggerah*, which we translate *my sore ran*, is, *my hand was stretched out*, i. e., in prayer. He continued during the whole night with his voice and hands lifted up to God, *and ceased not*, even in the midst of great discouragements.

Verse 3. *My spirit was overwhelmed.*] As the verb is in the *hithpael* conjugation, the word must mean *my spirit was overpowered in itself*. It purposed to involve itself in this calamity. I felt exquisitely for my poor suffering countrymen.

"The generous mind is not confined at home;
It spreads itself abroad through all the public,
And feels for every member of the land."

Verse 4. *Thou holdest mine eyes waking*] Literally, *thou keepest the watches of mine eyes*—my grief is so great that I cannot sleep.

I am so troubled that I cannot speak.] This shows an *increase* of sorrow and anguish. At *first* he felt his misery, and *called aloud*. He receives more light, sees and feels his deep wretchedness, and then his words are swallowed by excessive distress. His woes are too big for utterance. "Small troubles are loquacious; the great are dumb." Curæ leves loquuntur; ingentes stupent.

Verse 5. *I have considered the days of old*] חשבתי *chishshabti, I have counted up;* I have reckoned up the various dispensations of thy mercy in behalf of the distressed, marked down in the history of our fathers.

Verse 6. *I call to remembrance my song in the night*] I do not think that נגינתי *neginathi* means *my song.* We know that נגינת *neginath* signifies some *stringed* musical instrument that was struck with a *plectrum;* but here it possibly might be applied to the *Psalm* that was played on it. But it appears to me rather that the psalmist here speaks of the circumstances of composing the short ode contained in the *seventh, eighth,* and *ninth verses;* which it is probable he sung to his harp as a kind of dirge, if indeed he had a harp in that distressful captivity.

My spirit made diligent search.] The verb חפש *chaphas* signifies such an investigation as a man makes who is obliged to *strip himself* in order to do it; or, *to lift up coverings*, to search fold by fold, or in our phrase, *to leave no stone unturned.* The Vulgate translates: "Et scopebam spiritum meum." As *scopebam* is no pure Latin word, it may probably be taken from the Greek *σκοπεω scopeo*, "to look about, to consider attentively." It is however used by no author but St. Jerome; and by him only here and in Isa. xiv. 23: *And I will sweep it with the besom of destruction;* scopabo eam in scopa terens. Hence we see that he has formed a verb from a noun *scopæ*, a *sweeping brush* or *besom;* and this sense my old Psalter follows in this place, translating the passage thus: **And I sweped my gast;** which is thus paraphrased: "And swa I sweped my gaste, (I swept my soul,) that is, I purged it of all fylth."

Verse 7. *Will the Lord cast off for ever?*] Will there be no end to this captivity? Has he not said, "Turn, ye backsliders; for I am married unto you; I will heal your backsliding, and love you freely." *Will he* then *be favourable no more?* Thus the psalmist pleads and reasons with his Maker.

Verse 8. *For evermore?*] לדר ודר *ledor vador*, "to generation and generation." From race to race. Shall no mercy be shown even to the remotest generation of the children of the offenders?

Verse 9. *Hath God—in anger shut up his tender mercies?*] The *tender mercies* of God are the *source* whence all his kindness to the children of men flows. The metaphor here is taken from a *spring*, the mouth of which is closed, so that its waters can no longer run in the same channel; but, being confined, break out, and take some other course. Wilt thou take thy mercy from the Israelites, and give it to some other people? This he most certainly did. He took it from the *Jews*, and gave it to the *Gentiles*.

Verse 10. *And I said, This* is *my infirmity*] The Hebrew is very obscure, and has been differently translated: ואמר חלותי היא שנות ימין עליון *vaomar challothi hi shenoth yemin elyon;* "And I said, Is this my weakness? Years the right

11 [r]I will remember the works of the LORD:
surely I will remember thy wonders of old.
12 I will meditate also of all thy work, and
talk of thy doings.
13 [s]Thy way, O God, *is* in the sanctuary:
[t]who *is so* great a God as *our* God?
14 Thou *art* the God that doest wonders:
thou hast declared thy strength among the
people.
15 [u]Thou hast with *thine* arm redeemed thy
people, the sons of Jacob and Joseph. Selah.
16 [v]The waters saw thee, O God, the waters
saw thee; they were afraid: the depths also
were troubled.
17 [w]The clouds poured out water: the skies
sent out a sound: [x]thine arrows also went
abroad.
18 The voice of thy thunder *was* in the
heaven: [y]the lightnings lightened the world:
[z]the earth trembled and shook.
19 [a]Thy way *is* in the sea, and thy path in the
great waters, [b]and thy footsteps are not known.
20 [c]Thou leddest thy people like a flock by
the hand of Moses and Aaron.

---

[r]Psa. cxliii. 5——[s]Psa. lxxiii. 17——[t]Exod. xv. 11 [u]Exod. vi. 6; Deut. ix. 29——[v]Exod. xiv. 21; Josh. iii. 15, 16; Psa. cxiv. 3; Hab. iii. 8, &c.——[w]Heb. *The clouds were poured forth with water*

[x]2 Sam. xxii. 15; Hab. iii. 11——[y]Psa. xcvii. 4 [z]2 Sam. xxii. 8——[a]Hab. iii. 15——[b]Exod. xiv. 28 [c]Exod. xiii. 21; xiv. 19; Psa. lxxviii. 52; lxxx. 1; Isa. lxiii. 11, 12; Hos. xii. 13

---

hand of the Most High." If חלותי *challothi* comes from חלה *chalah*, and signifies to *pray*, as *De Dieu* has thought, then his translation may be proper: Precari hoc meum est; mutare dextram Altissimi. "To pray, this my business; to change the right hand of the Most High." I can do nothing else than pray; God is the Ruler of events. Mr. *N. M. Berlin* translates, "Dolere meum hoc *est;* mutare *est* dextra Altissimi." *To grieve is my portion; to change* (my condition) *belongs to the right hand of the Most High.* Here שנות *shenoth*, which we translate *years*, is derived from שנה *shanah*, to *change.* This latter appears to me the better translation; the sum of the meaning is, "I am in deep distress; the Most High alone can change my condition." The old Psalter, following the *Vulgate,*—Et dixi, Nunc cœpi: hæc mutatio dexteræ Excelsi,—translates: **And I said, Now I began this chaunchyng of ryght hand of hihegh** (highest) Alswa say, God sal noght kast al man kynde fra his sigt with outen ende: for nowe I began to understand the syker; (the truth;) that man sal be brogt to endles; and thar fore, now I said, that this chaunchyng fra wreth to mercy, is thrugh Ihu Criste that chaunges me fra ill to gude, fra noy to gladnes.

Once more, *Coverdale*, who is followed by Matthews and Becke, takes the passage by storm: "At last I came to this poynte, that I thought; O why art thou so foolish? The right hande of the Most Hyest can chaunge all."

Verse 11. *I will remember the works of the Lord*] I endeavour to recollect what thou hast done in behalf of our fathers in past times; in no case hast thou cast them off, when, with humbled hearts, they sought thy mercy.

Verse 13. *Thy way*—is *in the sanctuary*] See Psa. lxxiii. 17. I must go to the sanctuary now to get *comfort*, as I went before to get *instruction.* What a mercy to have the privilege of drawing near to God in his ordinances! How many doubts have been solved, fears dissipated, hearts comforted, darknesses dispelled, and snares broken, while waiting on God in the means of grace!

Some understand the words, *Thy way is in holiness*—all thy dispensations, words, and works are holy, just and true. And as is thy majesty, so is thy mercy! O, who is so great a God as our God?

Verse 14. *Thou—doest wonders*] Every act of God, whether in nature or grace, in creation or providence, is wondrous; surpasses all *power* but his own; and can be comprehended only by his own *wisdom.* To the *general observer*, his *strength* is most apparent; to the *investigator of nature*, his *wisdom;* and to the genuine *Christian*, his *mercy* and *love.*

Verse 15. *The sons of Jacob and Joseph.*] "The sons which Jacob begat and Joseph nourished." says the *Chaldee.* The Israelites are properly called the sons of Joseph as well as of Jacob, seeing *Ephraim* and *Manasseh*, his sons, were taken into the number of the tribes. All the latter part of this Psalm refers to the deliverance of the Israelites from Egypt; and the psalmist uses this as an argument to excite the expectation of the captives. As God delivered *our fathers* from *Egypt*, so we may expect him to deliver *us* from *Chaldea.* It required his *arm* to do the former, and that arm is not shortened that it cannot save.

Verse 16. *The waters saw thee*] What a fine image! He represents God approaching the Red Sea; and the waters, seeing him, took fright, and ran off before him, dividing to the right and left to let him pass. I have not found any thing more majestic than this.

The depths also were troubled.] Every thing appears here to have *life* and *perception.* The *waters* see the Almighty, do not wait his coming, but in terror flee away! The deeps, uncovered, are astonished at the circumstance; and as they cannot fly, they are filled with trouble and dismay. Under the hand of such a poet, *inanimate nature* springs into *life;* all *thinks, speaks, acts;* all is in motion, and the dismay is general.

Verse 17. *The clouds poured out water*] It appears from this that there was a violent *tempest* at the time of the passage of the Red Sea. There was a violent storm of *thunder, lightning,* and *rain.* These *three* things are distinctly marked here. 1. "The skies sent out a sound:" the THUNDER. 2. "Thine arrows went abroad:" the LIGHTNING. 3. "The clouds poured out water:" the RAIN. In the next verse we have, 4. An EARTHQUAKE: "The earth trembled and shook," ver. 18.

Verse 19. *Thy way* is *in the sea*] Thou didst walk through the sea, thy path was through a multitude of waters.

Thy footsteps are not known.] It was evident from the *effects* that God was there: but his *track* could not be discovered; still he is the Infinite Spirit, without parts, limits, or passions. No object of sense.

Verse 20. *Thou leddest thy people like a flock*] This may refer to the *pillar of cloud and fire.* It went before them, and they followed it. So, in the eastern countries, the shepherd does not *drive*, but *leads*, his flock. He goes *before* them to find them pasture, and they regularly *follow* him.

By the hand of Moses and Aaron.] They were God's agents; and acted, in *civil* and *sacred* things, just as directed by the Most High.

Analysis of the Seventy-seventh Psalm

In this Psalm the prophet shows the bitter agony which a troubled spirit undergoes from a sense of God's displeasure; and the comfort which it afterwards receives through faith in his promises.

There are *two* parts in this Psalm:—

I. The psalmist sets forth the strife between the flesh and the spirit; and how the flesh tempts the spirit to despair, and calls in question the goodness of God, ver. 1-10.

II. Next, he shows the victory of the spirit over the flesh; being raised, encouraged, and confirmed by the nature, promises, and works of God, ver. 11-20.

This is an excellent Psalm, and of great use in spiritual desertion.

I. The *strife.* The prophet betakes himself to God. 1. He prays. 2. Prays often. 3. Prays earnestly. 4. And with a troubled soul. The Psalm is, therefore, not the expression of a *despairing* soul, but of one that has a great conflict with temptation.

Though he complains, yet he despairs not.

I. His complaint is bitter, and he sets down how he was exercised.

1. He found no intermission; day and night he was in distress. His voice was continually lifted up, and his hands constantly stretched out to God in prayer. When no man saw him, he prayed. His complaint was in *secret*, and far from *hypocrisy*, which always loves to have *witnesses.*

2. He refused to be comforted, ver. 2.

3. Even the "remembrance of God troubled him," ver. 3.

4. His *soul* was *overwhelmed*, ver. 3.

5. He became at last *speechless* through grief, ver. 4.

6. All *sleep* departed from him, ver. 4.

II. He shows that his grief was aggravated by a consideration of the happiness he once enjoyed, but had lost.

1. He had considered the days of old, ver. 5.

2. He could rejoice in and praise God, ver. 6.

3. But now, on diligent search, all good is gone, ver. 6.

4. His debate between hope and despair, which leads him to break out in the following interrogations: 1. Will the Lord cast off for ever? 2. Will he be favourable no more? 3. Is his mercy clean gone? 4. Doth his promise fail? 5. Hath God forgotten to be gracious? 6. Hath he in anger shut up his tender mercies? ver. 7-9.

II. How he is restored.

1. He begins with a correction of himself: "I said, This is my infirmity," ver. 10.

2. Takes encouragement from a remembrance,—

(1) Of God's *ways:* "I will remember—the right hand of the Most High," ver. 10.

(2) Of his works: "I will remember thy wonders of old," ver. 11.

3. On these he will *meditate* and *discourse*, ver. 12.

(1) He then addresses his speech to God; who he understands is to be sought in his *sanctuary*, ver. 13.

(2) And who is "infinitely great and good," ver. 13.

(3) Who has declared his strength among the people, ver. 14.

(4) And particularly to the descendants of Jacob, ver. 15.

III. He amplifies the story of their deliverance from Egypt by several instances of God's power.

1. In the Red Sea: "The waters saw thee," ver. 16.

2. In the heavens: "The clouds poured out water, ver. 17.

3. In the earth: "The earth trembled and shook," ver. 18.

IV. The final cause of all was that he might lead his people out of their bondage, and destroy their enemies, ver. 19, 20.

PSALM LXXVIII

An enumeration of the principal effects of the goodness of God to his people, 1–16; *of their rebellions and punishment,* 17–33; *their feigned repentance,* 34–37; *God's compassion towards them,* 38, 39; *their backsliding, and forgetfulness of his mercy,* 40–42; *the plagues which he brought upon the Egyptians,* 43–51; *the deliverance of his own people, and their repeated ingratitude and disobedience,* 52–58; *their punishment,* 59–64; *God's wrath against their adversaries,* 65, 66; *his rejection of the tribes of Israel and his choice of the tribe of Judah, and of David to be king over his people,* 67–72.

XV. DAY. EVENING PRAYER

[a]Maschil [b]of Asaph

A. M. cir. 3074
B. C. cir. 930
Assæ, Regis
Judææ,
cir. annum
26

GIVE [c]ear, O my people, *to*
my law: incline your ears
to the words of my mouth.
2 [d]I will open my mouth in a
parable: I will utter dark sayings of old:
3 [e]Which we have heard and known, and
our fathers have told us.
4 [f]We will not hide *them* from their children,
[g]showing to the generation to come the praises
of the LORD, and his strength, and his wonderful works that he hath done.
5 For [h]he established a testimony in Jacob,
and appointed a law in Israel, which he commanded our fathers, that [i]they should make
them known to their children:
6 [k]That the generation to come might know
them, even the children *which*
should be born; *who* should arise
and declare *them* to their children:

A. M. cir. 3074
B. C. cir. 930
Assæ, Regis
Judææ,
cir. annum
26

7 That they might set their hope in God,
and not forget the works of God, but keep his
commandments:
8 And [l]might not be as their fathers, [m]a
stubborn and rebellious generation; a generation [n]*that* [o]set not their heart aright, and
whose spirit was not steadfast with God.
9 The children of Ephraim, *being* armed,
and [p]carrying bows, turned back in the day
of battle.
10 [q]They kept not the covenant of God, and
refused to walk in his law;
11 And [r]forgat his works, and his wonders
that he had showed them.

---

[a]Psa. lxxiv. title——[b]Or, A Psalm *for Asaph to give instruction*——[c]Isa. li. 4——[d]Psa. xlix. 4; Matt. xiii. 35 [e]Psa. xliv. 1——[f]Deut. iv. 9; vi. 7; Joel i. 3——[g]Exod. xii. 26, 27; xiii. 8, 14; Josh. iv. 6, 7——[h]Psa. cxlvii. 19 [i]Deut. iv. 9; vi. 7; xi. 19

[k]Psa. cii. 18——[l]2 Kings xvii. 14; Ezek. xx. 18 [m]Exod. xxxii. 9; xxxiii. 3; xxxiv. 9; Deut. ix. 6, 13; xxxi. 27; Psa. lxviii. 6——[n]Heb. that *prepared not their heart* [o]Ver. 37; 2 Chron. xx. 33——[p]Heb. *throwing forth* [q]2 Kings xvii. 15——[r]Psa. cvi. 13

NOTES ON PSALM LXXVIII

The *title, Maschil of Asaph;* or, according to the *margin,* A Psalm *for Asaph to give instruction;* contains nothing particular. The *Arabic* has, "A sermon from Asaph to the people." The Psalm was probably not written by David, but *after* the separation of the *ten* tribes of Israel, and *after* the days of Rehoboam, and *before* the Babylonish captivity, for the *temple* was still standing, ver. 69. *Calmet* supposes that it was written in the days of *Asa,* who had gained, by the aid of the Syrians, a great victory over the Israelites; and brought back to the pure worship of God many out of the tribes of *Ephraim, Manasseh,* and *Simeon.* See 2 Chron. xv. and xvi.

Verse 1. *Give ear, O my people*] This is the *exordium* of this very pathetic and instructive discourse.

Verse 2. *In a parable*] Or, I will give you *instruction* by numerous *examples;* see Psa. xlix. 1-4, which bears a great similarity to this; and see the notes there. The term *parable,* in its various acceptations, has already been sufficiently explained; but משל *mashal* may here mean *example,* as opposed to תורה *torah, law* or *precept,* ver. 1.

Verse 3. *Which we have heard and known*] We have heard the *law,* and known the *facts.*

Verse 4. *We will not hide* them] In those ancient times there was very *little reading,* because *books* were exceedingly scarce; *tradition* was therefore the only, or nearly the only, means of preserving the memory of past events. They were handed down from father to son by *parables* or *pithy sayings,* and by *chronological poems.* This very Psalm is of this kind, and must have been very useful to the Israelites, as giving instructions concerning their ancient history, and recounting the wonderful deeds of the Almighty in their behalf.

Verse 5. *A testimony in Jacob*] This may signify the various *ordinances, rites,* and *ceremonies* prescribed by the law; and the word *law* may mean the *moral* law, or system of religious *instruction,* teaching them their duty to God, to their neighbour, and to themselves. These were commanded to the *fathers*—the *patriarchs* and *primitive Hebrews,* that they should make them known to their children, who should make them known to the generation that was to come, whose children should also be instructed that they might declare them to their children; to the end that their hope might be in God, that they might not forget his works, and might keep his commandments: that they might not be as their fathers, but have their heart right and their spirit steadfast with God, ver. 6-8. *Five* generations appear to be mentioned above: 1. Fathers; 2. Their children; 3. The generation to come; 4. And their children; 5. And their children. They were never to lose sight of their history throughout all their generations. Some think the *testimony* here may mean the *tabernacle.*

Verse 9. *The children of Ephraim—turned back*] This refers to some defeat of the Ephraimites; and some think to that by the *men of Gath,* mentioned 1 Chron. vii. 21. R. D. *Kimchi* says this defeat of the Ephraimites was in the desert; and although the story be not mentioned in the law, yet it is written in the Books of the Chronicles, where we read, on the occasion of "Zabad the Ephraimite, and Shuthelah, &c., whom the men of Gath, who were born in the land, slew; and Ephraim their father mourned many days, and his brethren came to comfort him," 1 Chron. vii. 20-22: but to what defeat of the Ephraimites this refers is not certainly known; probably the *Israelites* after the division of the two kingdoms are intended.

Verse 10. *They kept not the covenant of God*] They abandoned his worship, both *moral* and *ritual.* They acted like the Ephraimites in

A. M. cir. 3074 B. C. cir. 930 Assæ, Regis Judææ, cir. annum 26

12 [s]Marvellous things did he in the sight of their fathers, in the land of Egypt, [t]*in* the field of Zoan.

13 [u]He divided the sea, and caused them to pass through; and [v]he made the waters to stand as a heap.

14 [w]In the daytime also he led them with a cloud, and all the night with a light of fire.

15 [x]He clave the rocks in the wilderness, and gave *them* drink as *out of* the great depths.

16 He brought [y]streams also out of the rock, and caused waters to run down like rivers.

17 And they sinned yet more against him by [z]provoking the Most High in the wilderness.

18 And [a]they tempted God in their heart by asking meat for their lust.

19 [b]Yea, they spake against God; they said, Can God [c]furnish a table in the wilderness?

20 [d]Behold, he smote the rock, that the waters gushed out, and the streams overflowed; can he give bread also? can he provide flesh for his people?

21 Therefore the LORD heard *this*, and [e]was wroth: so a fire was kindled against Jacob, and anger also came up against Israel;

A. M. cir. 3074 B. C. cir. 930 Assæ, Regis Judææ, cir. annum 26

22 Because they [f]believed not in God, and trusted not in his salvation:

23 Though he had commanded the clouds from above, [g]and opened the doors of heaven,

24 [h]And had rained down manna upon them to eat, and had given them of the corn of heaven.

25 [i]Man did eat angels' food: he sent them meat to the full.

26 [k]He caused an east wind [l]to blow in the heaven: and by his power he brought in the south wind.

27 He rained flesh also upon them as dust, and [m]feathered fowls like as the sand of the sea:

28 And he let *it* fall in the midst of their camp, round about their habitations.

29 [n]So they did eat, and were well filled: for he gave them their own desire;

30 They were not estranged from their lust. But [o]while their meat *was* yet in their mouths,

[s]Exod. vii., viii., ix., x., xi., xii.——[t]Gen. xxxii. 3; Num. xiii. 22; ver. 43; Isa. xix. 11, 13; Ezek. xxx. 14——[u]Exod. xiv. 21——[v]Exod. xv. 8; Psa. xxxiii. 7——[w]Exod. xiii. 21; xiv. 24; Psa. cv. 39——[x]Exod. xvii. 6; Num. xx. 11; Psa. cv. 41; 1 Cor. x. 4——[y]Deut. ix. 21; Psa. cv. 41——[z]Deut. ix. 22; Psa. xcv. 8; Heb. iii. 16——[a]Exod. xvi. 2——[b]Num. xi. 4

[c]Hebrew, *order*——[d]Exod. xvii. 6; Num. xx. 11——[e]Num. xi. 1, 10——[f]Heb. iii. 18; Jude 5——[g]Gen. vii. 11; Mal. iii. 10——[h]Exod. xvi. 4, 14; Psa. cv. 40; John vi. 31; 1 Cor. x. 3——[i]Or, *Every one did eat the bread of the mighty;* Psa. ciii. 20——[k]Num. xi. 31——[l]Heb. *to go*——[m]Hebrew, *fowl of wing*——[n]Numbers xi. 20——[o]Numbers xi. 33

the above case, who threw down their bows and arrows, and ran away.

Verse 12. *The field of Zoan.*] "In campo Taneos," *Vulgate. Tanis* was the capital of Pharaoh, where Moses wrought so many miracles. It was situated in the *Delta*, on one of the most easterly branches of the *Nile*. It was afterwards called *Thanis;* and from *it* the district was called the *Thanitic Canton*. See *Calmet*. Dr. *Shaw* thinks *Zoan* was intended to signify *Egypt* in general.

Verse 13. *He divided the sea, and caused them to pass through*] The reader is requested to consult the notes on the parallel passages marked in the margin on this verse and verses 14, 15, 16, 17, &c., where all these miracles are largely explained.

Verse 18. *By asking meat for their lust.*] לנפשם *lenaphsham*, "for their souls," i. e., *for their lives;* for they said in their hearts that the *light bread*, the *manna*, was not sufficient to sustain their natural force, and preserve their lives. It seems, however, from the expression, that they were wholly *carnal;* that they had no *spirituality* of mind: they were *earthly, animal*, and *devilish*.

Verse 22. *They believed not in God*] After all the miracles they had seen. they were not convinced that there was a Supreme Being! and, consequently, they did *not trust in his salvation*—did not expect the *glorious rest* which he had promised them. Their descendants in the present day are precisely in this state. Multitudes of them disbelieve the Divine origin of their *law*, and have given up all hopes of a *Messiah*.

Verse 24. *The corn of heaven.*] The *manna*. It fell about their camp in the form of seeds; and as it appeared to come down from the clouds, it was not improperly termed *heavenly corn*, or *heavenly grain*, דגן שמים *degan shamayim*. The word *shamayim* is frequently taken to express the *atmosphere*.

Verse 25. *Man did eat angels' food*] לחם אבירים אכל איש *lechem abbirim achal ish*, "Man did eat the bread of the mighty ones;" or, *each person ate*, &c. They ate such bread as could only be expected at the tables of the *rich* and *great;* the best, the most delicate food. How little did this gross people know of the sublime excellence of that which they called *light bread*, and which they said their *soul loathed;* Num. xxi. 5! It was a type of Jesus Christ, for so says St. Paul: "They all ate the same spiritual meat, and drank the same spiritual drink," &c., 1 Cor. x. 3, 4. And our Lord calls himself "the bread that came down from heaven, that giveth life unto the world," John vi. 31-35: but a Jew sees nothing but with the eyes of *flesh*. It is true their doctors or rabbins are full of allegories, mysteries, and conceits; but they are, in general, such as would disgrace

A. M. cir. 3074
B. C. cir. 930
Assæ, Regis
Judææ,
cir. annum
26

31 The wrath of God came
upon them, and slew the fattest
of them, and [p]smote down the
[q]chosen *men* of Israel.
32 For all this [r]they sinned still, and [s]be-
lieved not for his wondrous works.
33 [t]Therefore their days did he consume in
vanity, and their years in trouble.
34 [u]When he slew them, then they sought
him: and they returned and inquired early
after God.
35 And they remembered that [v]God *was*
their rock, and the high God [w]their Redeemer.
36 Nevertheless they did [x]flat-
ter him with their mouth, and
they lied unto him with their
tongues.
37 For [y]their heart was not right with him,
neither were they steadfast in his covenant.
38 [z]But he, *being* full of compassion, forgave *their* iniquity, and destroyed *them* not:
yea, many a time [a]turned he his anger away,
and [b]did not stir up all his wrath.
39 For [c]he remembered [d]that they *were*
but flesh; [e]a wind that passeth away, and
cometh not again.

---

[p]Heb. *made to bow*——[q]Or, *young men*——[r]Num. xiv., xvi., xvii.——[s]Ver. 22——[t]Num. xiv. 29, 35; xxvi. 64, 65——[u]See Hos. v. 15——[v]Deut. xxxii. 4, 15, 31 [w]Exod. xv. 13; Deut. vii. 8; Isa. xli. 14; xliv. 6; lxiii. 9

[x]Ezek. xxxiii. 31——[y]Ver. 8——[z]Num. xiv. 18 20——[a]Isa. xlviii. 9——[b]2 Kings xxi. 29——[c]Psa. ciii. 14, 16——[d]Gen. vi. 3; John iii. 6——[e]Job vii. 7, 16; James iv. 14

---

the *Cabinet des Fees*, and would not be tolerated in the *nursery*. O, how thick a veil hangs over their *gross* and *hardened hearts*.

Verse 26. *He caused an east wind to blow*] See the note on Num. xi. 31.

Verse 32. *For all this they sinned still*] How astonishing is this! They were neither *drawn* by *mercies*, nor *awed* by *judgments!* But we shall cease to wonder at this, if we have a thorough acquaintance with our own hearts.

Verse 33. *Their days did he consume in vanity*] By causing them to wander forty years in the wilderness, *vainly expecting* an end to their labour, and the enjoyment of the promised rest, which, by their rebellions, they had forfeited.

Verse 34. *When he slew them*] While his judgments were upon them, then they began to humble themselves, and deprecate his wrath. When they saw some fall, the rest began to tremble.

Verse 35. *That God* was *their rock*] They recollected in their affliction that Jehovah was their *Creator*, and their *Father;* the *Rock*, the *Source*, not only of their *being*, but of all their *blessings;* or, that he was their sole *Protector*.

And the high God their Redeemer.] ואל עליון גאלם *veel elyon goalam*, "And the strong God, the Most High, their kinsman." That one who possessed the *right of redemption;* the *nearest akin* to him who had *forfeited* his *inheritance;* so the word originally means, and hence it is often used for a *redeemer*. The Hebrew word גאל *goel* answers to the Greek *σωτηρ*, a *saviour;* and is given to the *Lord Jesus Christ*, the *strong God*, the *Most High*, the *Redeemer of a lost world*. After this verse there is the following Masoretic note: חצי הספר *chatsi hassepher*, "The middle of the book." And thus the reader has arrived at the *middle of the Psalter*, a book for excellence unparalleled.

Verse 36. *Nevertheless they did flatter him with their mouth*] What idea could such people have of God, whom they supposed they could thus deceive? They promised well, they called him their God, and their fathers' God; and told him how good, and kind, and merciful he had been to them. Thus, *their mouth flattered him*. And they said that, whatever the Lord their God commanded them to *do*, they would perform.

And they lied unto him.] I think the *Vulgate* gives the true sense of the Hebrew: Dilexerunt eum in ore suo; et lingua sua mentiti sunt ei,—"They loved him with their mouth; and they lied unto him with their tongue." "That is," says the old *Psalter*, "thai sayde thai lufed God, bot thai lighed, als thair dedes schewes; for thai do noght als thai hight; for when God ceses to make men rad; than cese thai to do wele."

Verse 37. *Their heart was not right*] When the *heart* is *wrong*, the *life* is *wrong;* and because their heart was not right with God, therefore they were not faithful in his covenant.

Verse 38. *But he*, being *full of compassion*] Feeling for them as a *father* for his children.

Forgave their *iniquity*] יכפר *yechapper*, made an *atonement* for their iniquity.

And did not stir up all his wrath.] Though they often grieved his Spirit, and rebelled against him, yet he seldom punished them; and when he did chastise them, it was as a tender and merciful Father. *He did not stir up all his wrath*—the punishment was much less than the iniquity deserved.

Verse 39. *He remembered that they* were but *flesh*] Weak mortals. He took their feeble perishing state always into *consideration*, and knew how much they needed the whole of their state of *probation;* and therefore he bore with them to the uttermost. How merciful is God!

A wind that passeth away, and cometh not again.] I believe this to be a bad translation, and may be productive of error; as if when a man dies his being were ended, and death were an eternal sleep. The original is, רוח הולך ולא ישוב *ruach holech velo yashub:* and the translation *should* be, "The spirit goeth away, and it doth not return." The present life is the state of probation; when therefore the *flesh*—the *body*, fails, the *spirit* goeth away into the eternal world, and returneth not hither again. Now God, being full of compassion, spared them, that their salvation might be accomplished before they went into that state where there is no *change;* where the pure are pure still, and the defiled are defiled still. All the *Versions* are right; but the polyglot translator of the *Syriac*, ܪܘܚܐ *rocho*, has falsely put

A. M. cir. 3074
B. C. cir. 930
Assæ, Regis
Judææ,
cir. annum
26

40 How oft did they [f]provoke[g]
him in the wilderness, *and* grieve
him in the desert!
41 Yea, [h]they turned back and
tempted God, and [i]limited the Holy One
of Israel.
42 They remembered not his hand, *nor* the
day when he delivered them [k]from the enemy.
43 How [l]he had [m]wrought his signs in
Egypt, and his wonders in the field of Zoan:
44 [n]And had turned their rivers into blood;
and their floods, that they could not drink.
45 [o]He sent divers sorts of flies among them,
which devoured them; and [p]frogs, which destroyed them.
46 [q]He gave also their increase unto the
caterpillar, and their labour unto
the locust.

A. M. cir. 3074
B. C. cir. 930
Assæ, Regis
Judææ,
cir. annum
26

47 [r]He [s]destroyed their vines
with hail, and their sycamore-
trees with [t]frost.
48 [u]He [v]gave up their cattle also to the
hail, and their flocks to [w]hot thunderbolts.
49 He cast upon them the fierceness of his
anger, wrath, and indignation, and trouble, by
sending evil angels *among them*.
50 [x]He made a way to his anger; he spared
not their soul from death, but gave [y]their life
over to the pestilence;
51 [z]And smote all the first-born in Egypt;
the chief of *their* strength in [a]the tabernacles
of Ham:

---

[f]Or, *rebel against him*——[g]Ver. 17; Psa. xcv. 9, 10; Isaiah vii. 13; lxiii. 10; Eph. iv. 30; Heb. iii. 16, 17——[h]Num. xiv. 22; Deut. vi. 16——[i]Ver. 20——[k]Or, *from affliction*——[l]Ver. 12; Psa. cv. 27, &c.——[m]Heb. *set*——[n]Exod. vii. 20; Psa. cv. 29——[o]Exod. viii. 24; Psa. cv. 31——[p]Exod. viii. 6; Psa. cv. 30

[q]Exod. x. 13, 15; Psa. cv. 34, 35——[r]Exod. ix. 23, 25; Psa. cv. 33——[s]Heb. *killed*——[t]Or, *great hail stones*——[u]Exod. ix. 23, 24, 25; Psa. cv. 32——[v]Heb. *He shut up*——[w]Or, *lightnings*——[x]Heb. *He weighed a path*——[y]Or, *their beasts to the murrain;* Exod. ix. 3, 6——[z]Exod. xii. 29; Psa. cv. 36; cxxxvi. 10——[a]Psa. cvi. 22

---

ventus, wind, instead of *spiritus*, soul or spirit. The *Arabic* takes away all ambiguity:

خرج لم يعد بعد ✡ ذكرانهم لحم وروح اذا

"He remembered that they were flesh; and a spirit which, when it departs, does not again return." The human being is composed of flesh and spirit, or body and soul; these are easily separated, and, when separated, the body turns to dust, and the spirit returns no more to animate it in a state of probation. *Homer* has a saying very like that of the psalmist:—

Ανδρος δε ψυχη παλιν ελθειν ουτε ληιστη,
Ουθ' ἑλετη, επει αρ κεν αμειψεται ἑρκος οδοντων.

Il. ix., ver., 408.

"But the soul of man returns no more; nor can it be acquired nor caught after it has passed over the barrier of the teeth."

Pope has scarcely given the passage its genuine meaning:—

"But from our lips the vital spirit fled,
Returns no more to wake the silent dead."

And the *Ossian-like* version of *Macpherson* is but little better: "But the life of man returns no more; nor acquired nor regained is the soul which once *takes its flight on the wind*." What has the *wind* to do with the ἑρκος οδοντων of the Greek poet?

Several similar sayings may be found among the Greek poets; but they all suppose the *materiality* of the soul.

Verse 41. *Limited the Holy One of Israel.*] The *Chaldee* translates, "And the Holy One of Israel they signed with a sign." The Hebrew word התוו *hithvu* is supposed to come from the root תוה *tavah*, which signifies to *mark;* and hence the letter ת *tau*, which in the ancient Hebrew character had the form of a cross X, had its name probably because it was used as a *mark*. Mr. *Bate* observes that in *hithpael* it signifies to *challenge* or *accuse;* as one who gives his *mark* or *pledge* upon a trial, and causes his adversary to do the same. Here it most obviously means an insult offered to God.

Verse 44. *Turned their rivers into blood*] See on Exod. vii. 20.

Verse 45. *He sent—flies—and frogs*] See on Exod. viii. 6, 24.

Verse 46. *The caterpillar, and—the locust.*] See on Exod. x. 13.

Verse 47. *He destroyed their vines with hail*] Though the *vine* was never plentiful in Egypt, yet they have some; and the wine made in that country is among the most delicious. The *leaf* of the vine is often used by the Egyptians of the present day for wrapping up their mincemeat, which they lay leaf upon leaf, season it after their fashion, and so cook it, making it a most exquisite sort of food, according to Mr. *Maillet*.

And their sycamore-trees] This tree was very useful to the ancient Egyptians, as all their *coffins* are made of this wood; and to the modern, as their barques are made of it. Besides, it produces a kind of *fig*, on which the common people in general live; and Mr. *Norden* observes that "they think themselves well regaled when they have a piece of bread, a couple of sycamore figs, and a pitcher of water from the Nile." The loss therefore of their *vines* and *sycamore-trees* must have been very distressing to the Egyptians.

Verse 48. *He gave up their cattle*] See on Exod. ix. 23.

Verse 49. *By sending evil angels*] This is the first mention we have of *evil angels*. There is no mention of them in the account we have of the plagues of Egypt in the Book of Exodus, and what they were we cannot tell: but by what the psalmist says here of their operations, they were the sorest plague that God had sent; they were marks of the *fierceness of his anger, wrath, indignation, and trouble*. Some think the *destroying angel* that slew all the first-born

A. M. cir. 3074 B. C. cir. 930 Assæ, Regis Judææ, cir. annum 26

52 But [b]made his own people
to go forth like sheep, and guided
them in the wilderness like a
flock.

53 And he [c]led them on safely, so that they
feared not: but the sea [d]overwhelmed [e]their
enemies.

54 And he brought them to the border of
his [f]sanctuary, *even to* this mountain, [g]*which*
his right hand had purchased.

55 [h]He cast out the heathen also before
them, and [i]divided them an inheritance by
line, and made the tribes of Israel to dwell in
their tents.

56 [k]Yet they tempted and provoked the
most high God, and kept not his testimonies:

57 But [l]turned back, and dealt
unfaithfully like their fathers:
they were turned aside [m]like a
deceitful bow.

A. M. cir. 3074 B. C. cir. 930 Assæ, Regis Judææ, cir. annum 26

58 [n]For they provoked him to anger with
their [o]high places, and moved him to jealousy
with their graven images.

59 When God heard *this,* he was wroth,
and greatly abhorred Israel:

60 [p]So that he forsook the tabernacle of
Shiloh, the tent *which* he placed among men;

61 [q]And delivered his strength into captivity, and his glory into the enemy's hand.

62 [r]He gave his people over also unto the
sword; and was wroth with his inheritance.

63 The fire consumed their young men; and

[b]Psa. lxxvii. 20——[c]Exod. xiv. 19, 20——[d]Exod. xiv. 27, 28; xv. 10——[e]Heb. *covered*——[f]Exod. xv. 17 ——[g]Psa. xliv. 3——[h]Psa. xliv. 2——[i]Josh. xiii. 7; xix. 51; Psa. cxxxvi. 21, 22——[k]Judg. ii. 11, 12——[l]Ver. 41; Ezek. xx. 27, 28

[m]Hosea vii. 16——[n]Deut. xxxii. 16, 21; Judg. ii. 12, 20; Ezek. xx. 28——[o]Deut. xii. 2, 4; 1 Kings xi. 7; xii. 31——[p]1 Samuel iv. 11; Jeremiah vii. 12, 14; xxvi. 6, 9——[q]Judges xviii. 30——[r]1 Samuel xiv. 10

is what is here intended; but this is distinctly mentioned in ver. 51. An *angel* or *messenger* may be either *animate* or *inanimate; a disembodied spirit* or *human being;* any *thing* or *being* that is an instrument *sent of God* for the punishment or support of mankind.

Verse 54. *The border of his sanctuary*] קדשו *kodsho,* "of his holy place," that is, the *land of Canaan,* called afterwards *the mountain* which *his right hand had purchased;* because it was a *mountainous country,* widely differing from Egypt, which was a long, continued, and almost perfect *level.*

Verse 57. *They were turned aside like a deceitful bow.*] The eastern bow, which when at rest is in the form of a ⌒, must be *recurved,* or *turned the contrary way,* in order to be what is called *bent* and *strung.* If a person who is unskilful or weak attempt to *recurve* and string one of these bows, if he take not great heed it will spring back and regain its quiescent position, and perhaps break his arm. And sometimes I have known it, when bent, to *start aside,* and regain its quiescent position, to my no small danger, and in one or two cases to my injury. This image is frequently used in the sacred writings; but no person has understood it, not being acquainted with the eastern *bow* ⌒, which must be *recurved,* or bent the contrary way, ⏜⏝ in order to be proper for use. If not well made, they will fly back in discharging the arrow. It is said of the *bow* of Jonathan, *it turned not back,* 2 Sam. i. 22, לא נשוג אחור *lo nasog achor,* "did not twist itself backward." It was a good bow, one on which he could depend. Hosea, chap. vii. 16, compares the unfaithful Israelites to a *deceitful bow;* one that, when bent, would suddenly start aside and recover its former position. We may find the same passage in Jer. ix. 3. And this is precisely the kind of bow mentioned by *Homer,* Odyss. xxi., which none of Penelope's suitors could bend, called καμπυλα τοξα and αγκυλα τοξα, the *crooked bow* in the state of rest; but τοξον παλιντονον, the *recurved bow* when prepared for use. And of this trial of *strength* and *skill* in the bending of the bow of Ulysses, none of the critics and commentators have been able to make any thing, because they knew not the instrument in question. On the τοξου θησις of *Homer,* I have written a dissertation elsewhere. The image is very correct; these Israelites, when brought out of their natural bent, soon recoiled, and relapsed into their former state.

Verse 60. *He forsook the tabernacle of Shiloh*] The Lord, offended with the people, and principally with the *priests,* who had profaned his holy worship, gave up his ark into the hands of the Philistines. And so true it is that he *forsook the tabernacle of Shiloh,* that he never returned to it again. See 1 Sam. vi. 1; 2 Sam. vi.; 1 Kings viii. 1; where the several removals of the ark are spoken of, and which explain the remaining part of this Psalm. Because God suffered the Philistines to take the ark, it is said, ver. 61: "He delivered his strength into captivity, and his glory into the enemy's hand;" and ver. 67, that "he refused the tabernacle of Joseph, and chose not the tribe of Ephraim;" for *Shiloh* was in the tribe of *Ephraim* the son of Joseph; and God did not suffer his ark to return thither, but to go to *Kirjath-jearim,* which was in the tribe of *Benjamin;* from thence to the house of *Obed-edom:* and so to *Zion* in the tribe of *Judah,* as it follows, ver. 68.

The *tabernacle* which Moses had constructed in the wilderness remained at Shiloh, even after the *ark* was taken by the Philistines, and afterwards sent to Kirjath-jearim. From Shiloh it was transported to *Nob;* afterwards to Gibeon, apparently under the reign of Saul; and it was there at the commencement of Solomon's reign, for this prince went thither to offer sacrifices, 1 Kings iii. 4. From the time in which the temple was built, we know not what became of the tabernacle of Moses: it was probably laid up in some of the chambers of the temple. See *Calmet.*

Verse 63. *Their maidens were not given to*

A. M. cir. 3074 B. C. cir. 930 Assæ, Regis Judææ, cir. annum 26

[s]their maidens were not [t]given
to marriage.
64 [u]Their priests fell by the
sword; and [v]their widows made
no lamentation.
65 Then the LORD [w]awaked as one out of
sleep, *and* [x]like a mighty man that shouteth
by reason of wine.
66 And [y]he smote his enemies in the
hinder part: he put them to a perpetual
reproach.
67 Moreover he refused the tabernacle of
Joseph, and chose not the tribe of Ephraim:
68 But chose the tribe of Judah,
the Mount Zion [z]which he loved.
69 And he [a]built his sanctuary
like high *palaces,* like the earth
which he hath [b]established for ever.
70 [c]He chose David also his servant, and
took him from the sheepfolds:
71 [d]From following the [e]ewes great with
young he brought him [f]to feed Jacob his
people, and Israel his inheritance.
72 So he fed them according to the [g]inte-
grity of his heart; and guided them by the
skilfulness of his hands.

[s]Jer. vii. 34; xvi. 9; xxv. 10——[t]Heb. *praised*——[u]1 Sam. iv. 11; xxii. 18——[v]Job xxvii. 15; Ezek. xxiv. 23——[w]Psa. xliv. 23——[x]Isa. xlii. 13——[y]1 Sam. v. 6, 12; vi. 4——[z]Psa. lxxxvii. 2

[a]1 Kings vi——[b]Heb. *founded*——[c]1 Sam. xvi. 11, 12; 2 Sam. vii. 8——[d]Heb. *from after*——[e]Gen. xxxiii. 13; Isa. xl. 11——[f]2 Sam. v. 2; 1 Chron. xi. 2——[g]1 Kings ix. 4

marriage.] הוללו *hullalu,* were not celebrated with marriage songs. It is considered a calamity in the east if a maiden arrives at the age of *twelve years* without being *sought* or *given in marriage.*

Verse 64. *Their priests fell by the sword*] Hophni and Phinehas, who were slain in that unfortunate battle against the Philistines in which the ark of the Lord was taken, 1 Sam. iv. 11.

A Chaldee *Targum* on this passage says, "In the time in which the ark of the Lord was taken by the Philistines, Hophni and Phinehas, the two priests, fell by the sword at Shiloh; and when the news was brought, their wives made no lamentation, for they both died the same day."

Verse 65. *Then the Lord awaked*] He seemed as if he had totally disregarded what was done to his people, and the reproach that seemed to fall on himself and his worship by the capture of the ark.

Like a mighty man] כגבור *kegibbor, like a hero that shouteth by reason of wine.* One who, going forth to meet his enemy, having taken a sufficiency of wine to refresh himself, and become a proper stimulus to his animal spirits, *shouts*—gives the *war-signal* for the *onset;* impatient to meet the foe, and sure of victory. The idea is not taken from the case of a *drunken man.* A person in such a state would be very unfit to meet his enemy, and could have little prospect of conquest.

Verse 66. *He smote his enemies in the hinder part*] This refers to the *hemorrhoids* with which he afflicted the Philistines. See the note on 1 Sam. v. 6-10.

Verse 67. *He refused the tabernacle of Joseph*] See the note on ver. 60.

Verse 69. *He built his sanctuary like high* palaces] כמו רמים *kemo ramim,* which several of the *Versions* understand of the *monoceros* or *rhinoceros.* The temple of God at Jerusalem was the *only one* in the land, and stood as *prominent* on Mount Zion as the horn of the unicorn or rhinoceros does upon his snout. And there *he established* his ark, to go no more out as long as the temple should last. Before this time it was frequently in a migratory state, not only in the wilderness, but afterwards in the promised land. See the notes on ver. 60.

Verse 70. *He chose David*] See the account, 1 Sam. xvi. 11, &c.

Verse 71. *From following the ewes*] Instances of this kind are not unfrequent in the ancient Greek and Roman history. *Crœsus* said that *Gyges,* who was the first of his race, was a *slave,* and rose to *sovereignty,* succeeding his predecessor, *of whose sheep he had been the pastor.*

Verse 72. *So he fed them*] Here David is mentioned as *having terminated his reign.* He *had* fed the people, *according to the integrity of his heart,* for that was ever disposed to do the will of God in the administration of the kingdom: and his *hand* being *skilful* in war, he always led them out to victory against their enemies.

ANALYSIS OF THE SEVENTY-EIGHTH PSALM

The psalmist, considering that it is God's command that his works be not forgotten, but that the father should deliver his former doings to posterity, that they might be to them both *comfort* and *instruction, deter them from sin, and persuade them to fear God,* gives in this Psalm a long catalogue of God's dealings with his people, even from their coming out of Egypt to the conclusion of the reign of David.

There are *three* principal parts in this Psalm:—

I. A *preface,* in which the psalmist exhorts men to learn and declare the way of God, ver. 1-9.

II. A *continued narrative* of God's administration among the people, and their *stubbornness, disobedience,* and *contumacy;* together with the *punishments* which God inflicted upon them, ver. 9-67.

III. His *mercy,* manifested in the midst of judgment; that he did not cut them off, but, after the rejection of Ephraim, (Israel,) made choice of Judah, Zion, and David.

I. In the PREFACE or *exordium* he labours to gain attention: "Give ear, O my people," ver. 1.

1. Shows that he is about to deliver doctrines and precepts from heaven. It is God's law, and

it should be heard: 1. For its excellence, ver. 2. 2. For its certainty, ver. 3.

2. He shows the *end*, which is another argument for attention. 1. It must not be hidden from their children, that God might be praised, ver. 4. 2. And his power magnified; and 3. His people edified, ver. 5.

Then follow the *duties* of their *children*, which are *three:* 1. That they might *know* God, his law, his works, ver. 6. 2. That they might *trust* in him, ver. 7. 3. That they might be *obedient*, ver. 8.

II. The NARRATION. Their fathers were stubborn and rebellious, of which he gives several examples:—

1. In *Ephraim:* "They turned back in the day of battle," ver. 9.

2. They kept not the *covenant* of God, ver. 10.

3. They *forgat his works* in Egypt, ver. 11.

The psalmist extends this narrative, and shows, 1. God's goodness; 2. Israel's obstinacy; 3. Their punishment.

I. His *goodness* in bringing them out of Egypt in such a marvellous way, ver. 12. 1. He divided the Red Sea, ver. 13. 2. He made the waters to stand on a heap, ver. 13.

1. His *care* in guiding them: 1. In the daytime by a *cloud*, ver. 14. 2. In the night by *fire*, ver. 14.

2. His *love* in providing for them. 1. He clave the rock that they might have water, ver. 15. 2. He caused these waters to follow them as rivers, ver. 16. 3. And thus they had an abundant supply, ver. 16.

II. *Israel's* obstinacy. 1. They sinned. 2. More and more. 3. Provoked the Holy One of Israel, ver. 17, 18.

They were *incredulous.*

1. They *tempted* God by desiring *other supplies* than his providence had designed. He gave them *manna;* they would have *flesh.*

2. They questioned his *power*, ver. 19.

3. They were foolishly *impatient*, and must have immediately whatever they thought proper, else they murmured. They said, 1. He smote the rock, and the *water* gushed out. 2. But can he give *bread* also? ver. 20.

III. Their *punishment.* 1. The Lord was wroth, ver. 21. 2. A *fire was kindled.* 3. Because they *believed him not*, nor trusted in his salvation, ver. 22.

He provided *manna* for them; an especial blessing, on various considerations.

1. It came from heaven, ver. 23.

2. It came abundantly. He "rained it down," ver. 24.

3. It was *most excellent:* "Man did eat angels' food," ver. 25.

Weary of this, they desired *flesh.* In this also God heard them. 1. He brought *quails.* 2. In abundance. 3. Brought them to and about the *camp*, so that they had no labour to find them, ver. 25, 26, 28. 4. They were all *gratified* with them, ver. 29.

See God's *justice* in their punishment, and the cause of it. 1. They were "not estranged from their lust," ver. 30. 2. His *wrath* came upon them. 3. It came *suddenly.* 4. It *slew* them. 5. Even the *chief* of them, ver. 31.

See their *sin* notwithstanding. 1. For all this, they sinned yet more. 2. They were incredulous, ver. 32. 3. He caused them to consume their days in vanity. 4. And their years (forty long years) in trouble, ver. 33.

They began apparently to relent. 1. They sought him. 2. They returned. 3. They sought after God. 4. They remembered that he was their Rock. 5. And the Most High their Redeemer, ver. 34, 35.

But in this, their *apparent* amendment, they were guilty—1. Of *hypocrisy*, ver. 36. 2. Of *insincerity*, ver. 37. 3. Of *instability:* "They were not steadfast in his covenant," ver. 37.

On a review of this, the prophet extols the *goodness* of God that bore with such a people.

1. He opened to them the *fountain of mercy:* "He being full of compassion."

2. He displayed an *act* of this mercy: "He forgave their iniquity."

3. Though he punished *in a measure*, yet he restrained his vindictive justice, and destroyed them not, ver. 38.

His motives for this tenderness: 1. He remembered that they were but *flesh.* 2. That, their *probation* once ended, their state was fixed for ever, ver. 39. See the note.

He proceeds with the story of their *rebellions.* 1. They provoked him often in the wilderness. 2. They grieved him in the desert, ver. 40. 3. They *returned to sin*, tempted him. 4. Insulted him. 5. And forgat all his past mercies, ver. 41-43. More particularly, 1. They remembered not his hand, ver. 42. 2. Nor his signs in Egypt, ver. 44.

The wonders which he wrought in Egypt. *Five* of the plagues mentioned:—

First plague. He turned their *rivers into blood*, ver. 44.

Fourth plague. He sent *divers flies*, ver. 45.

Second plague. The *frogs* destroyed them, ver. 45.

Eighth plague. The *locusts*, ver. 46.

Seventh plague. Their *vines*, &c. were destroyed, ver. 47.

1. He cast upon them the fierceness of his wrath. 2. Sent evil angels among them. 3. And made a *path for his anger*, ver. 49.

The *first plague.* He gave their life to the pestilence, ver. 50.

The *last* plague. He slew their first-born, ver. 51.

He now gives a recital of God's mercy in the following particulars:

1. He brought his people through the Red Sea, ver. 52.

2. He guided them as a flock.

3. He kept them in safety, ver. 53.

4. He did not suffer them still to wander, but brought them,—1. To the border of his sanctuary. 2. Even to Mount Zion. 3. Cast out the heathen before them. 4. And divided them an inheritance by lot, ver. 54, 55.

Yet still, 1. "They tempted and provoked him." 2. "Kept not his testimonies." 3.

"Turned aside" from his worship. 4. Were *unfaithful*. 5. And *idolatrous*, ver. 55-58.

For this,—1. God's wrath grows more hot against the people. 2. He greatly abhorred Israel. 3. Forsook the tabernacle. 4. Delivered up the ark. 5. Gave the people to the sword. 6. Gave up the priests to death. 7. And brought upon them general desolation, ver. 59-64.

Once more, God—1. Remembers them in mercy. 2. Fixes his *tabernacle* among them. 3. Chooses *David* to be their king. 4. During the whole of whose days they had prosperity in all things, ver. 65-72.

Behold here the goodness and severity of God. Reader, learn wisdom by what those have suffered.

PSALM LXXIX

The psalmist complains of the cruelty of his enemies and the desolations of Jerusalem, and prays against them, 1–7. *He prays for the pardon and restoration of his people, and promises gratitude and obedience,* 8–13.

XVI. DAY. MORNING PRAYER

A Psalm of [a]Asaph

O GOD, the heathen are come into [b]thine
inheritance; [c]thy holy temple have they
defiled; [d]they have laid Jerusalem on heaps.
2 [e]The dead bodies of thy servants have
they given *to be* meat unto the fowls of the
heaven, the flesh of thy saints unto the beasts
of the earth.
3 Their blood have they shed like water
round about Jerusalem; [f]and *there was* none
to bury *them*.
4 [g]We are become a reproach to our neighbours, a scorn and derision to them that are
round about us.
5 [h]How long, LORD? wilt thou be angry for
ever? shall thy [i]jealousy burn like fire?
6 [k]Pour out thy wrath upon the heathen
that [l]have not known thee, and upon the
kingdoms that have [m]not called upon thy
name.
7 For they have devoured Jacob, and laid
waste his dwelling-place.
8 [n]O remember not against us [o]former iniquities: let thy tender mercies speedily prevent us: for we are [p]brought very low.

[a]Or, *for Asaph*——[b]Exod. xv. 17; Psa. lxxiv. 2——[c]Psa. lxxiv. 7; 1 Mac. i. 31, 39——[d]2 Kings xxv. 9, 10; 2 Chron. xxxvi. 19; Mic. iii. 12——[e]Jer. vii. 33; xvi. 4; xxxiv. 20; 1 Mac. vii. 17——[f]Psa. cxli. 7; Jer. xiv. 16; xvi. 4; Rev. xi. 9——[g]Psa. xliv. 13; lxxx. 6

[h]Psa. lxxiv. 1, 9, 10; lxxxv. 5; lxxxix. 46——[i]Zeph. i. 18; iii. 8——[k]Jer. x. 25; Rev. xvi. 1——[l]Isa. xlv. 4, 5; 2 Thess. i. 8——[m]Psa. liii. 4——[n]Isa. lxiv. 9——[o]Or, *the iniquities of them that were before us*——[p]Deut. xxviii. 43; Psa. cxlii. 6

NOTES ON PSALM LXXIX

The *title*, *A Psalm of Asaph*, must be understood as either applying to a person of the name of *Asaph* who lived under the captivity; or else to the *family of Asaph;* or to a *band* of *singers* still bearing the name of that *Asaph* who flourished in the days of *David;* for most undoubtedly the Psalm was composed during the Babylonish captivity, when the city of Jerusalem lay in heaps, the temple was defiled, and the people were in a state of captivity. *David* could not be its author. Some think it was composed by *Jeremiah;* and it is certain that the *sixth* and *seventh* verses are exactly the same with Jer. x. 25: "Pour out thy fury upon the heathen that know thee not, and upon the families that call not on thy name: for they have eaten up Jacob, and devoured him, and consumed him; and have made his habitation desolate."

Verse 1. *The heathen are come into thine inheritance*] Thou didst cast them *out*, and take thy people *in;* they have cast *us* out, and now taken possession of the land that belongs to *thee*. They have defiled the temple, and reduced Jerusalem to a heap of ruins; and made a general slaughter of thy people.

Verse 2. *The dead bodies of thy servants*] It appears that in the destruction of Jerusalem the Chaldeans did not bury the bodies of the slain, but left them to be devoured by birds and beasts of prey. This was the grossest inhumanity.

Verse 3. There was *none to bury* them.] The Chaldeans would not; and the Jews who were not slain were carried into captivity.

Verse 4. *We are become a reproach to our neighbours*] The Idumeans, Philistines, Phœnicians, Ammonites, and Moabites, all gloried in the subjugation of this people; and their insults to them were mixed with blasphemies against God.

Verse 5. *How long, Lord?*] Wilt thou continue thine anger against us; and suffer us to be insulted, and thyself blasphemed?

Verse 6. *Pour out thy wrath*] Bad as we are, we are yet less wicked than they. We, it is true, have been unfaithful; but they never knew thy name, and are totally abandoned to idolatry.

Verse 7. *Laid waste his dwelling-place.*] The *Chaldee* understands this of the *temple*. This, by way of eminence, was Jacob's *place*. I have already remarked that these two verses are almost similar to Jer. x. 25, which has led many to believe that *Jeremiah* was the author of this Psalm.

Verse 8. *Remember not against us former*

9 [q]Help us, O God of our salvation, for
the glory of thy name: and deliver us, and
purge away our sins, [r]for thy name's
sake.
10 [s]Wherefore should the heathen say,
Where *is* their God? let him be known
among the heathen in our sight *by* the [t]reveng-
ing of the blood of thy servants *which is* shed.
11 Let [u]the sighing of the prisoner come
before thee; according to the greatness of [v]thy
power [w]preserve thou those that are appointed to die;
12 And render unto our neighbours [x]seven-
fold into their bosom [y]their reproach,
wherewith they have reproached thee, O
LORD.
13 So [z]we thy people and sheep of thy
pasture will give thee thanks for ever:
[a]we will show forth thy praise [b]to all generations.

[q]2 Chron. xiv. 11——[r]Jer. xiv. 7, 21——[s]Psa. xlii. 10; cxv. 2——[t]Heb. *vengeance*——[u]Psa. cii. 20——[v]Heb. *thine arm*——[w]Heb. *reserve the children of death*

[x]Gen. iv. 15; Isa. lxv. 6, 7; Jer. xxxii. 18; Luke vi. 38——[y]Psa. lxxiv. 18, 22; xcv. 7——[z]Psa. lxxiv.1; c. 3 [a]Isa. xliii. 21——[b]Heb. *to generation and generation*

iniquities] Visit us not for the sins of our forefathers.

Speedily prevent us] Let them *go before us*, and turn us out of the path of destruction; for there is no help for us but in *thee*.

We are brought very low.] Literally, "We are greatly thinned." Few of us remain.

Verse 9. *Purge away our sins*] כפר *capper*, be *propitiated*, or *receive an atonement* (על חטאתינו *al chattotheynu*) *on account of our sins*.

Verse 10. *Where is their God?*] Show *where* thou art by rising up for our redemption, and the infliction of deserved punishment upon our enemies.

Verse 11. *The sighing of the prisoner*] The poor captive Israelites in Babylon, who sigh and cry because of their bondage.

Those that are appointed to die] בני תמותה *beney themuthah*, "sons of death." Either those who were condemned to death because of their crimes, or condemned to be destroyed by their oppressors. Both these senses apply to the Israelites: they were sons of death, i. e., worthy of death because of their sins against God; they were condemned to death or utter destruction, by their Babylonish enemies.

Verse 12. *Sevenfold into their bosom*] That is, Let them get in this world what they deserve for the cruelties they have inflicted on us. Let them suffer in captivity, who now have us in bondage. Probably this is a *prediction*.

Verse 13. *We thy people*] Whom thou hast chosen from among all the people of the earth.

And sheep of thy pasture] Of whom thou thyself art the *Shepherd*. Let us not be destroyed by those who are thy enemies; and we, in all our generations, will give thanks unto thee for ever.

Analysis of the Seventy-ninth Psalm

This Psalm contains the *four* following parts:—

I. A complaint for the desolation of Jerusalem, ver. 1-5.

II. A deprecation of God's anger, ver. 5.

III. A twofold petition:—

1. Against the enemies of God's people, ver. 6, 7, 10-12.

2. For the people, ver. 8, 9.

IV. A doxology, ver. 13.

I. The complaint is bitter, and is amplified by a *climax*,—

1. "The heathen are come into thine inheritance," ver. 1.

2. "The holy temple they have defiled," ver. 1.

3. "They have laid Jerusalem in heaps," ver. 2.

4. They have exercised cruelty towards the dead.

5. "They have shed blood like water," ver. 3.

6. They have not even buried those whom they slaughtered.

7. "We are become a reproach, a scorn, and a derision," ver. 4.

II. Next comes the cause of their calamity.

1. God's anger was kindled because of their sins, ver. 5.

2. This anger he deprecates, ver. 5.

III. The twofold prayer,—

1. Against the enemy: 1. Pour out thy wrath on *them*, not on *us*, ver. 6; 2. He adds the reason: "They have devoured Jacob." ver. 7.

2. The second part of the prayer is in behalf of the people: 1. "Remember not against us former offences," ver. 8. 2. "Let thy mercy prevent us." The reasons: "We are brought very low." 3. His prayer is directed for help to the God of salvation. 4. For deliverance and pardon of sin, ver. 9.

His arguments to prevail with God:—

1. The blasphemy of the heathen, ver. 10.

2. The misery of the people, ver. 11. And another prayer against the enemy, ver. 12.

IV. The doxology.

1. We, who are thy people, will be thankful.

2. We will leave a record of thy mercy to all generations, ver. 13.

PSALM LXXX

A prayer for the captives, 1–3. *A description of their miseries*, 4–7. *Israel compared to a vineyard*, 8–14. *Its desolate state, and a prayer for its restoration*, 15–19.

To the chief Musician [a]upon Shoshannim-Eduth, A Psalm [b]of Asaph

GIVE ear, O Shepherd of Israel, thou that leadest Joseph [c]like a flock; [d]thou that dwellest *between* the cherubims, [e]shine forth.

2 [f]Before Ephraim and Benjamin and Manasseh stir up thy strength, and [g]come *and* save us.

3 [h]Turn us again, O God, [i]and cause thy face to shine; and we shall be saved.

4 O LORD God of hosts, how long [k]wilt thou be angry against the prayer of thy people?

5 [l]Thou feedest them with the bread of tears; and givest them tears to drink in great measure.

6 [m]Thou makest us a strife unto our neighbours: and our enemies laugh among themselves.

7 [n]Turn us again, O God of hosts, and cause thy face to shine; and we shall be saved.

8 Thou hast brought [o]a vine out of Egypt; [p]thou hast cast out the heathen, and planted it.

9 Thou [q]preparedst *room* before it, and didst cause it to take deep root, and it filled the land.

[a]Psa. xlv., lxix. title——[b]Or, *for Asaph*——[c]Psa. lxxvii. 20——[d]Exod. xxv. 20, 22; 1 Sam. iv. 4; 2 Sam. vi. 2; Psa. xcix. 1——[e]Deut. xxxiii. 2; Psa. l. 2; xciv. 1 [f]Num. ii. 18–23——[g]Heb. *come for salvation to us* [h]Ver. 7, 19; Lam. v. 21

[i]Num. vi. 25; Psa. iv. 6; lxvii. 1——[k]Heb. *will thou smoke;* Psa. lxxiv. 1——[l]Psa. xlii. 3; cii. 9; Isa. xxx. 20 [m]Psa. xliv. 13; lxxix. 4——[n]Ver. 3, 19——[o]Isa. v. 1, 7; Jer. ii. 21; Ezek. xv. 6; xvii. 6; xix. 10——[p]Psa. xliv. 2; lxxviii. 55——[q]Exod. xxiii. 28; Josh. xxiv. 12

NOTES ON PSALM LXXX

The *title:* see Psa. xlv., lx., and lxix., where every thing material is explained. This Psalm seems to have been written on the same occasion with the former. One ancient MS. in the public library in Cambridge writes the *eightieth* and the *seventy-ninth* all as one Psalm; the subject-matter is precisely the same—was made on the same occasion, and probably by the same author.

Verse 1. *O Shepherd of Israel*] The subject continued from the last verse of the preceding Psalm.

Leadest Joseph] *Israel* and *Joseph* mean here the whole of the Jewish tribes; all were at this time in captivity; all had been the people of the Lord; all, no doubt, made supplication unto him now that his chastening hand was upon them; and for all the psalmist makes supplication.

That dwellest between *the cherubims*] It was between the cherubim, over the *cover* of the ark, called the *propitiatory* or *mercy-seat*, that the glory of the Lord, or symbol of the Divine Presence, appeared. It is on this account that the Lord is so often said *to dwell between the cherubim.* Of these symbolical beings there is a long and painful account, or system of conjectures, in *Parkhurst's* Hebrew Lexicon, of about twenty quarto pages, under the word כרב *carab.*

Shine forth.] Restore thy worship; and give us such evidences of thy presence *now*, as our fathers had under the first tabernacle, and afterwards in the temple built by Solomon.

Verse 2. *Before Ephraim and Benjamin and Manasseh*] It is supposed that these three tribes represent the whole, Benjamin being incorporated with Judah, Manasseh comprehending the country beyond Jordan, and Ephraim all the rest.—*Dodd.*

Verse 3. *Turn us again*] השיבנו *hashibenu, convert* or *restore us.* There are *four* parts in this Psalm, *three* of which end with the above words; see the *third, seventh,* and *nineteenth* verses; and *one* with words similar, ver. 14.

Verse 5. *Thou feedest them with the bread of tears*] They have no peace, no comfort, nothing but continual sorrow.

In great measure.] שליש *shalish, threefold.* Some think it was a certain *measure* used by the Chaldeans, the real capacity of which is not known. Others think it signifies *abundance* or *abundantly.*

Verse 6. *Thou makest us a strife*] The neighbouring districts have a controversy about us; we are a subject of contention to them. A people so wonderfully preserved, and so wonderfully punished, is a mystery to them. They see in us both the *goodness* and *severity* of God. Or, all the neighbouring nations join together to malign and execrate us. We are hated by all; derided and cursed by all.

Verse 8. *Thou hast brought a vine out of Egypt*] This is a most elegant metaphor, and every where well supported. The same similitude is used by Isaiah, chap. v. 1, &c.; by Jeremiah, chap. ii. 21; by Ezekiel, chap. xvii. 5, 6; by Hosea, chap. x. 1; by Joel, chap. i. 7; by Moses, Deut. xxxii. 32, 33; and often by our Lord himself, Matt. xx. 1, &c.; xxi. 33, &c.; Mark xii. 1, &c. And this was the ordinary figure to represent the Jewish Church. We may remark several analogies here:—

1. This vine was brought out of Egypt that it might be planted in a better and more favourable soil. The Israelites were brought out of their Egyptian bondage that they might be established in the land of Canaan, where they might grow and flourish, and worship the true God.

2. When the husbandman has marked out a proper place for his vineyard, he hews down and roots up all other trees; gathers out the stones, brambles, &c., that might choke the young vines, and prevent them from being fruitful. So God cast out the *heathen nations* from the land of Canaan, that his pure worship might be established, and that there might not remain there any incitements to idolatry.

Verse 9. *Thou preparedst—before it*] 3. When the ground is properly cleared, then it is well digged and manured, and the vines are placed in the ground at proper distances, &c. So when God had cast out the heathen, he caused the land to be divided by lot to the different tribes, and then to the several families of which these tribes were composed.

And didst cause it to take deep root] 4. By sheltering, propping up, and loosening the

10 The hills were covered with the shadow of it, and the boughs thereof *were like* [r]the goodly cedars.

11 She sent out her boughs unto the sea, and her branches [s]unto the river.

12 Why hast thou *then* [t]broken down her hedges, so that all they which pass by the way do pluck her?

13 The boar out of the wood doth waste it, and the wild beast of the field doth devour it.

14 Return, we beseech thee, O God of hosts: [u]look down from heaven, and behold, and visit this vine;

15 And the vineyard which thy right hand hath planted, and the branch *that* thou madest [v]strong for thyself.

16 *It is* burned with fire, *it is* cut down: [w]they perish at the rebuke of thy countenance.

17 [x]Let thy hand be upon the man of thy right hand, upon the son of man *whom* thou madest strong for thyself.

18 So will not we go back from thee: quicken us, and we will call upon thy name.

19 [y]Turn us again, O LORD God of hosts, cause thy face to shine; and we shall be saved.

[r]Heb. *the cedars of God*——[s]Psa. lxxii. 8——[t]Psa. lxxxix. 40, 41; Isa. v. 5; Nah. ii. 2——[u]Isa. lxiii. 15

[v]Isa. xlix. 5——[w]Psa. xxxix. 11; lxxvi. 7——[x]Psa. lxxxix. 21——[y]Ver. 3, 7

ground about the tender plants, they are caused to take a deep and firm rooting in the ground. Thus did God, by especial manifestations of his kind providence, support and protect the Israelites in Canaan; and by various religious ordinances, and civil institutions, he established them in the land; and, by the ministry of priests and prophets, did every thing necessary to make them *morally fruitful.*

It filled the land.] 5. To multiply vines, the gardener cuts off a shoot from the old tree, leaving a joint or knob both at top and bottom; then plants it in proper soil; the lower knob furnishes the *roots*, and the upper the *shoot*, which should be carefully trained as it grows, in order to form another vine. By these means one tree will soon form a complete vineyard, and multiply itself to any given quantity. Thus God so carefully, tenderly, and abundantly blessed the Israelites, that they increased and multiplied; and, in process of time, filled the whole land of Canaan. Vines are propagated, not only by *cuttings*, but by *layers, seed, grafting*, and *inoculation.*

Verse 10. *The hills were covered*] 6. The vine, carefully cultivated in a suitable soil, may be spread to any extent. In the land of Judea it formed shades under which the people not only sheltered and refreshed themselves in times of sultry heats; but it is said they even ate, drank, and dwelt under the shelter of their vines. See 1 Kings iv. 25; Mic. iv. 4; 1 Mac. xiv. 12. God so blessed the Jews, particularly in the days of David and Solomon, that all the neighbouring nations were subdued—the Syrians, Idumeans, Philistines, Moabites, and Ammonites.

Verse 11. *She sent out her boughs unto the sea, and her branches unto the river.*] The Israelitish empire extended from the River *Euphrates* on the east to the *Mediterranean Sea* on the west, and from the same Euphrates on the north of the promised land to its farthest extent on the south; Syria bounding the north, and Arabia and Egypt the south. And this was according to the promises which God had made to the fathers, Exod. xxiii. 31; Deut. xi. 24.

Verse 12. *Why hast thou broken down*] 7. When a vineyard is planted, it is properly *fenced* to preserve it from being trodden down, or otherwise injured by beasts; and to protect the fruit from being taken by the unprincipled passenger. So God protected Jerusalem and his temple by his own almighty arm; and none of their enemies could molest them as long as they had that protection. As it was *now spoiled*, it was a proof that that protection had been withdrawn; therefore the psalmist addresses the Lord with, "Why hast thou broken down her hedges?" Had God continued his protection, Jerusalem would not have been destroyed.

Verse 13. *The boar out of the wood*] Nebuchadnezzar, king of Babylon, who was a fierce and cruel sovereign. The allusion is plain. The wild *hogs* and *buffaloes* make sad havoc in the *fields* of the *Hindoos*, and in their *orchards:* to keep them out, men are placed at night on covered stages in the fields.

Verse 14. *Return—O God of hosts*] Thou hast *abandoned* us, and therefore our enemies have us in captivity. *Come back* to us, and we shall again be restored.

Behold, and visit this vine] Consider the state of thy own people, thy own worship, thy own temple. Look down! Let thine eye affect thy heart.

Verse 15. *The vineyard which thy right hand hath planted*] Thy holy and pure worship, which thy Almighty power had established in this city.

And the branch—thou madest strong for thyself.] The original is ועל בן *veal ben*, "and upon the SON whom thou hast strengthened for thyself." Many have thought that the *Lord Jesus* is meant. And so the *Chaldee* understood it, as it translates the passage thus: ועל מלכא משיחא *veal* MALCA MESHICHA, "And upon the King Messiah, whom thou hast strengthened for thyself." The Syriac, Vulgate, Septuagint, Æthiopic, and Arabic, have, "the Son of man," as in the *seventeenth* verse. *Eighteen* of *Kennicott's* and *De Rossi's* MSS. have בן אדם *ben Adam*, "Son of man;" and as the *Versions* have all the same reading, it was probably that of the original copies. As *Christ* seems here to be intended, this is the *first place* in the Old Testament where the title *Son of man* is applied to him. The old Psalter understands this of *setting Christ at the right hand of God.*

Verse 17. *The man of thy right hand*] The

only person who can be said to be at the right hand of God as intercessor, is JESUS the MESSIAH. Let him become our Deliverer: appoint him for this purpose, and let his strength be manifested in our weakness! By whom are the Jews to be restored, if indeed they ever be restored to their own land, but by JESUS CHRIST? By HIM alone can they find mercy; through HIM *alone* can they ever be reconciled to God.

Verse 18. *So will not we go back from thee*] We shall no more become *idolaters:* and it is allowed on all hands that the Jews were never guilty of idolatry after their return from the Babylonish captivity.

Quicken us] Make us *alive*, for we are nearly as good as *dead.*

We will call upon thy name.] We will invoke thee. Thou shalt be for ever the object of our adoration, and the centre of all our hopes.

Verse 19. *Turn us again*] Redeem us from this captivity.

O Lord God of hosts] Thou who hast all power in heaven and earth, the innumerable *hosts* of both worlds being at thy command.

Cause thy face to shine] Let us know that thou art *reconciled* to us. Let us once more enjoy thy *approbation.* Smile upon thy poor rebels, weary of their sins, and prostrate at thy feet, imploring mercy.

And we shall be saved.] From the power and oppression of the Chaldeans, from the guilt and condemnation of our sins, and from thy wrath and everlasting displeasure. Thus, O God, *save* us!

ANALYSIS OF THE EIGHTIETH PSALM

The parts of this Psalm are the following:—

I. A prayer, ver. 1-3.

II. A complaint by way of expostulation, ver. 4-7.

III. In the *twelve* last verses, to move God's mercy, he, 1. Shows God's love to Israel under the allegory of a vine, ver. 8-12. 2. Deplores the waste made upon it, ver. 12, 13. 3. Prays for its restoration, ver. 13-18.

IV. He makes a vow of perpetual service, ver. 19.

I. The *first* part, his *petition*, ver. 1. 1. For audience, ver. 2. 2. For assistance, ver. 3. 3. For grace to amend, ver. 3.

The arguments he uses to induce the Lord to hear. 1. He was formerly their Shepherd. 2. He sat between the cherubim, on the *mercy-seat.* 3. He has only to *shine forth*, and show himself; and they shall be saved.

II. The *second* part, his complaint. He complains, 1. That God was angry with them. 2. That the people were in the most distressed circumstances, ver. 5. 3. Of what they suffered from their neighbours, ver. 6.

On which he redoubles his prayer. 1. Turn us. 2. Cause thy face to shine. And, 3. Then we shall be saved, ver. 7.

III. The *third* part: what God *had done* for his people. 1. He brought the vine out of Egypt, ver. 8. 2. He cast out the heathen, ver. 8. 3. He planted it. 4. He prepared the soil for it. 5. He caused it to take deep root. 6. And it filled the land, from the *river* Euphrates to the Mediterranean Sea, ver. 9-11.

He deplores the *waste* made upon it. 1. The fence was broken down. 2. It was spoiled by those who passed by, and by the wild beasts.

Then he prays, 1. Look down from heaven. 2. Visit this vine. 3. It is cut down. 4. It is burnt with fire. 5. Let thy power in its behalf be shown by the Man of thy right hand. See the notes.

Some think *Zerubbabel* is meant; others think the *Jewish nation* is thus called *the son of man*, and the *man of God's right hand.*

IV. The *last* part of the Psalm: gratitude and obedience are promised. 1. We will backslide no more, ver. 18. 2. We are nearly dead; quicken us, and we will live to thee. 3. We will invoke thy name. We will serve thee alone, and never more bow down to any strange god, ver. 18.

All these things considered, he thinks he has good ground for his prayer; and therefore confidently *repeats* what he had twice before said: "Turn us again, O Lord God of hosts, cause thy face to shine," &c.

PSALM LXXXI

An exhortation to the people to praise God for his benefits, 1–7; *and to attend to what he had prescribed*, 8–10; *their disobedience lamented*, 11; *the miseries brought on themselves by their transgressions*, 12–16.

To the chief Musician [a]upon Gittith, *A Psalm* [b]of Asaph

SING aloud unto God our strength: make
a joyful noise unto the God of Jacob.

2 Take a psalm, and bring hither the timbrel, the pleasant harp with the psaltery.

3 Blow up the trumpet in the new moon

[a]Psa. viii. title

[b]Or, *for Asaph*

NOTES ON PSALM LXXXI

The *title* is the same as to Psalm viii, which see. There are various opinions concerning the *occasion* and *time* of this Psalm: but it is pretty generally agreed that it was either written *for* or used *at* the celebration of the Feast of Trumpets, (see on Lev. xxiii. 24,) which was held on the first day of the month *Tisri*, which was the beginning of the Jewish year; and on that day it is still used in the Jewish worship. According to Jewish tradition, credited by many learned Christians, the world was created in *Tisri*, which answers to our *September.* The

in the time appointed, on our solemn feast day.

4 For [c]this *was* a statute for Israel, *and* a law of the God of Jacob.

5 This he ordained in Joseph *for* a testimony, when he went out [d]through the land of Egypt: [e]*where* I heard a language *that* I understood not.

6 [f]I removed his shoulder from the burden: his hands [g]were delivered from [h]the pots.

7 [i]Thou calledst in trouble, and I delivered thee; [k]I answered thee in the secret place of thunder: I [l]proved thee at the waters of [m]Meribah. Selah.

8 [n]Hear, O my people, and I will testify unto thee: O Israel, if thou wilt hearken unto me;

9 [o]There shall no [p]strange god be in thee; neither shalt thou worship any strange god.

10 [q]I *am* the LORD thy God, which brought thee out of the land of Egypt: [r]open thy mouth wide, and I will fill it.

11 But my people would not hearken to my voice; and Israel would [s]none of me.

[c]Lev. xxiii. 24; Num. x. 10——[d]Or, *against*——[e]Psa. cxiv. 1——[f]Isa. ix. 4; x. 27——[g]Heb. *passed away* [h]Exodus i. 14——[i]Exodus ii. 23; xiv. 10; Psa. l. 15 [k]Exod. xix. 19——[l]Exod. xvii. 6, 7; Num. xx. 13

[m]Or, *strife*——[n]Psalm l. 7——[o]Exodus xx. 3, 5 [p]Deut. xxxii. 12; Isa. xliii. 12——[q]Exod. xx. 2——[r]Psa. xxxvii. 3, 4; John xv. 7; Eph. iii. 20——[s]Exod. xxxii. 1; Deut. xxxii. 15, 18

Psalm may have been used in celebrating the Feast of Trumpets on the first day of Tisri, the Feast of Tabernacles on the *fifteenth* of the same month, the *creation* of the world, the Feasts of the New Moons, and the deliverance of the Israelites from Egypt; to all which circumstances it appears to refer.

Verse 1. *Sing aloud unto God our strength*] There is much *meaning* here: as God is our *strength*, let that strength be devoted to his service; therefore, sing *aloud!* This is principally addressed to the *priests* and *Levites*.

Verse 2. *Take a psalm*] זמרה *zimrah*. I rather think that this was the name of a *musical instrument*.

Bring hither the timbrel] תף *toph;* some kind of *drum* or *tom tom*.

The pleasant harp] כנור *kinnor*. Probably a *sistrum*, or something like it. A STRINGED instrument.

With the psaltery.] נבל *nebel*, the *nabla*. The *cithara, Septuagint*.

Verse 3. *Blow up the trumpet*] שופר *shophar*, a species of *horn*. Certainly a *wind* instrument, as the two last were *stringed* instruments. Perhaps some chanted a *psalm* in *recitativo*, while all these *instruments* were used as *accompaniments*. In a *representative* system of religion, such as the Jewish, there must have been much *outside* work, all emblematical of better things: no proof that such things should be continued under the Gospel dispensation, where outsides have disappeared, shadows flown away, and the *substance* alone is presented to the *hearts* of mankind. He must be ill off for proofs in favour of instrumental music in the Church of Christ, who has recourse to practices under the Jewish ritual.

The feast of the *new moon* was always proclaimed by sound of trumpet. Of the ceremonies on this occasion I have given a full account in my *Discourse on the Eucharist*. For want of astronomical knowledge, the poor Jews were put to sad shifts to know the real time of the new moon. They generally sent persons to the top of some hill or mountain about the time which, according to their supputations, the new moon should appear. The first who saw it was to give immediate notice to the Sanhedrin; they closely examined the reporter as to his credibility, and whether his information agreed with their calculations. If all was found satisfactory, the president proclaimed the new moon by shouting out מקדש *mikkodesh! "It is consecrated."* This word was repeated *twice* aloud by the people; and was then proclaimed every where by *blowing of horns*, or what is called the sound of *trumpets*. Among the Hindoos some feasts are announced by the sound of the *conch* or *sacred shell*.

Verse 4. *This was a statute for Israel*] See the statute, Num. x. 10, and Lev. xxiii. 24.

Verse 5. *I heard a language I understood not.*] This passage is difficult. *Who* heard? And *what* was heard? All the *Versions*, except the *Chaldee*, read the pronoun in the *third* person, instead of the *first*. "*He* heard a language that *he* understood not." And to the Versions *Kennicott* reforms the text, שפת לא ידעה ישמע *sephath lo yadah yisma;* "a language which *he* did not understand *he* heard." But what was that *language?* Some say the *Egyptian;* others, who take *Joseph* to signify the *children of Israel* in general, say it was the declaration of God by Moses, that Jehovah was the true God, that he would deliver their *shoulder from their burdens, and their hands from the pots*—the moulds and furnaces in which they formed and baked their brick.

Verse 7. *Thou calledst in trouble*] They had *cried* by reason of their burdens, and the cruelty of their task-masters; and God heard that cry, and delivered them. See Exod. iii. 7, &c.

In the secret place of thunder] On Mount Sinai; where God was *heard*, but not *seen*. They heard a *voice*, but they saw no *shape*.

At the waters of Meribah.] See this transaction, Exod. xvii. 1, &c.

Verse 8. *Hear, O my people*] These are nearly the same words with those spoken at the giving of the law, Exod. xx. 2.

Verse 10. *Open thy mouth wide*] Let thy desires be ever so extensive, I will gratify them if thou wilt be faithful to me. Thou shalt lack no manner of thing that is good.

Verse 11. *Israel would none of me.*] לא אבה לי *lo abah li*, They willed me not, they would not have me for their God.

12 [t]So I gave them up [u]unto their own hearts' lust: *and* they walked in their own counsels.

13 [v]O that my people had hearkened unto me, *and* Israel had walked in my ways;

14 I should soon have subdued their enemies, and turned my hand against their adversaries.

15 [w]The haters of the LORD should have [x]submitted [y]themselves unto him: but their time should have endured for ever.

16 He should [z]have fed them also [a]with the finest of the wheat: and with honey [b]out of the rock should I have satisfied thee.

[t]Acts vii. 42; xiv. 16; Rom. i. 24, 28——[u]Or, *to the hardness of their hearts*, or *imaginations*——[v]Deut. v. 29; x. 12, 13; xxxii. 29; Isa. xlviii. 18——[w]Psa. xviii. 45; Rom. i. 30

[x]Or, *yielded feigned obedience;* Psa. xviii. 44; lxvi. 3——[y]Hebrew, *lied*——[z]Deuteronomy xxxii. 13, 14; Psalm cxlvii. 14——[a]Hebrew, *with the fat of wheat* [b]Job xxix. 6

Verse 12. *Unto their own hearts' lust*] To the *obstinate wickedness* of their heart.

In their own counsels.] God withdrew his restraining grace, which they had abused; and then they fulfilled the inventions of their wicked hearts.

Verse 13. *O that my people had hearkened unto me,—Israel had walked in my ways*] Nothing can be more plaintive than the original; *sense* and *sound* are surprisingly united. I scruple not to say to him who understands the Hebrew, however learned, he has never found in any poet, Greek or Latin, a finer example of deep-seated grief, unable to express itself in appropriate words without frequent interruptions of sighs and sobs, terminated with a mournful cry.

לו עמי שמע לי
ישראל בדרכי יהלכו

Lo ammi shomea li
Yishrael bidrachi yehallechu!

He who can give the proper guttural pronunciation to the letter ע *ain;* and gives the ו *vau*, and the י *yod*, their full Asiatic sound, not pinching them to death by a compressed and worthless European enunciation; will at once be convinced of the propriety of this remark.

Verse 14. *I should soon have subdued*] If God's promise appeared to fail in behalf of his people, it was because they rejected his counsel, and walked in their own. While they were faithful, they prospered; and not one jot or tittle of God's word failed to them.

Verse 15. *Their time should have endured for ever.*] That is, Their *prosperity* should have known no end.

Verse 16. *With the finest of the wheat*] מחלב חטה *mecheleb chittah;* literally, *with the fat of wheat*, as in the *margin*.

Honey out of the rock] **And he fed thaim of the grese of whete: And of the hony stane he thaim filled.** Old *Psalter*. Thus paraphrased: "He fed thaim with the body of Criste and gastely understandyng; and of hony that ran of the stane, that is, of the wisedome that is swete to the hert." Several of the fathers understand this place of Christ.

ANALYSIS OF THE EIGHTY-FIRST PSALM

The contents of this Psalm are the following:—

I. The psalmist exhorts them to celebrate God's name in their festivals, ver. 1-4.

II. The reasons why they should do this: God's benefits conferred on Israel, ver. 5-10.

III. Israel's ingratitude, and its consequences, ver. 11, 12.

IV. God's love and call to amendment, with the reasons for obedience, ver. 13-16.

I. He exhorts them to rejoice: but this must be, 1. *In God*, ver. 1. 2. At his *festivals*, ver. 2, 3.

II. The reasons. 1. It was God's command, ver. 4. 2. It was an ancient ordinance, ver. 5. 3. Their deliverance from base servitude, ver. 6. 4. When in deep affliction, ver. 7. 5. In a miraculous manner, ver. 7. 6. His mercy shown at the waters of Meribah, ver. 7. 7. His giving them his law, ver. 8, 9.

He then inculcates obedience, for which he gives *three* reasons: 1. "I am the Lord thy God," ver. 10. 2. Who *redeemed* thee from bondage, ver. 10. 3. He will make thee *truly happy:* "Open thy mouth wide, and I will fill it," ver. 10.

III. Israel's ingratitude, and its consequences. 1. God gave them up; left them to themselves, ver. 12. 2. They walked in their own counsels, ver. 12. And came to ruin.

IV. God's love and call, &c.

He calls them to repentance, ver. 13. The fruits of which would be *three* great benefits. 1. The subjugation of their enemies, ver. 14. 2. A long uninterrupted prosperity. 3. An abundance of all temporal and spiritual blessings, ver. 15, 16.

Under the emblems of the *finest wheat*, and the *purest honey* from the hives of bees in the rocks, where they abounded in Judea, he shows them that his followers should have so much of earthly and spiritual blessings, that they should be *satisfied*, and say, It is enough. But, alas! Israel would not be obedient; and, therefore, Israel is under the curse.

PSALM LXXXII

A warning to corrupt judges, 1, 2; *an exhortation to them to dispense justice without respect of persons,* 3–5; *they are threatened with the judgments of the Lord,* 6–8.

XVI. DAY. EVENING PRAYER

A Psalm [a]of Asaph

A. M. cir. 3092 B. C. cir. 912 Josaphati, Regis Judææ, cir. annum 3

GOD [b]standeth in the congregation of the mighty; he
judgeth among [c]the gods.
2 How long will ye judge unjust-
ly, and [d]accept the persons of the wicked? Selah.
3 [e]Defend the poor and fatherless: [f]do
justice to the afflicted and needy.
4 [g]Deliver the poor and needy: rid *them*
out of the hand of the wicked.
5 They [h]know not, neither will
they understand; they walk
on in darkness: [i]all the foundations of the earth are [k]out of
course.
6 [l]I have said, Ye *are* gods; and all of
you *are* children of the Most High.
7 But [m]ye shall die like men, and fall like
one of the princes.
8 [n]Arise, O God, judge the earth: [o]for thou
shalt inherit all nations.

A. M. cir. 3092 B. C. cir. 912 Josaphati, Regis Judææ, cir. annum 3

---

[a]Or, *for Asaph*——[b]2 Chron. xix. 6; Eccles. v. 8——[c]Exod. xxi. 6; xxii. 28——[d]Deut. i. 17; 2 Chron. xix. 7; Prov. xviii. 5——[e]Heb. *Judge*——[f]Jer. xxii. 3——[g]Job xxix. 12; Prov. xxiv. 11

[h]Mic. iii. 1——[i]Psa. xi. 3; lxxv. 3——[k]Heb. *moved*——[l]Exod. xxii. 9, 28; ver. 1; John x. 34——[m]Job xxi. 32; Psa. xlix. 12; Ezek. xxxi. 14——[n]Mic. vii. 2, 7——[o]Psa. ii. 8; Rev. xi. 15

NOTES ON PSALM LXXXII

This Psalm, which, in the *title*, is attributed to *Asaph*, was probably composed in the time when *Jehoshaphat* reformed the courts of justice throughout his states; see 2 Chron. xix. 6, 7, where he uses nearly the same words as in the beginning of this Psalm.

Verse 1. *God standeth in the congregation of the mighty*] The Hebrew should be translated, "God standeth in the assembly of God." God is among his people; and he presides especially in those courts of justice which himself has established. The *Court of King's Bench* is properly the place where the *king presides*, and where he is supposed to be always present. But the kings of England seldom make their appearance there. King James I. sometimes attended: at such times it might be said, "The *king* is in the *king's* court." I believe the case above to be similar. Judges! beware what you do! God is in his court, and in the midst (of the assembly) God will judge. See *Parkhurst* under אלה.

Verse 2. *Accept the persons of the wicked?*] "Lift up their faces," encourage them in their oppressions.

Selah.] "Mark this:" ye *do* it, and sorely shall ye *suffer* for it.

Verse 3. *Defend the poor*] You are their natural *protectors* under God. They are *oppressed: punish* their *oppressors*, however rich or powerful: and *deliver them.*

Verse 5. *They know not*] The judges are not acquainted with the law of God, on which all their decisions should be founded.

Neither will they understand] They are ignorant, and do not wish to be instructed. They will not learn; they cannot teach. Happy England! How different from Judea, even in the days of Jehoshaphat! All thy judges are learned, righteous, and impartial. Never did greater men in their profession dignify any land or country.—(1822.)

All the foundations of the earth] "All the civil institutions of the land totter." Justice is at the *head* of all the institutions in a well regulated state: when that gets poisoned or perverted, every evil, political and domestic, must prevail; even *religion* itself ceases to have any influence.

Verse 6. *Ye* are *gods*] Or, with the prefix of כ *ke*, the particle of *similitude*, כאלהים *keelohim*, "like God." Ye are my *representatives*, and are clothed with my power and authority to dispense judgment and justice, therefore *all of them* are said to be *children of the Most High.*

Verse 7. *But ye shall die like men*] כאדם *keadam*, "ye shall die like *Adam*," who fell from his high perfection and dignity as ye have done. Your high office cannot secure you an immortality.

And fall like one of the princes.] *Justice* shall pursue you, and *judgment* shall overtake you; and you shall be executed like public *state criminals.* You shall not, in the course of nature, fall into the grave; but your life shall be brought to an end by a *legal sentence*, or a *particular judgment* of God.

Verse 8. *Arise, O God, judge the earth*] Justice is perverted in the land: take the sceptre, and rule thyself.

For thou shalt inherit all nations.] Does not this last verse contain a prophecy of our Lord, the calling of the Gentiles, and the prevalence of Christianity over the earth? Thus several of the *fathers* have understood the passage. It is only by the universal spread of Christianity over the world, that the reign of righteousness and justice is to be established: and of whom can it be said that *he shall inherit all nations*, but of *Jesus Christ?*

Analysis of the Eighty-second Psalm

There are *three* parts in this Psalm:—

I. The prophet's proclamation, ver. 1.

II. God's controversy with the judges of the land, ver. 2-7.

III. The prophet's prayer that God would rise and judge, ver. 8.

I. God's presence proclaimed in court. At an assize the judge sits in the midst of the justices: "God standeth in the congregation," &c., ver. 1.

II. 1. He *reproves* them, ver. 2. 1. For their unjust judgment: "Ye judge unjustly." 2. For their obstinate continuance in it: "How long will ye," &c. Ye have not done it once, but often. 3. For their partiality: "they accepted persons," ver. 2.

2. He *exhorts* them to do their duty. 1. "Defend the poor and fatherless." Do right to

every man. 2. "Deliver the poor and needy," ver. 3.

3. He acquaints them with the events that shall follow where justice is not done: all is out of order; and the judges are the cause of it.

1. Through ignorance: "They know not the law," ver. 5.

2. Through obstinacy: "They will not learn it," ver. 5.

3. Through their determination to walk in their own way, ver. 5: "They walk on in darkness."

4. They shall in consequence be brought, 1. To an untimely death: "Ye shall die like men." 2. To a shameful death: "Ye shall fall like one of the princes," ye shall have a mighty fall, ver. 7.

III. The prophet's prayer. Since judgment and justice have failed in the land, he says, 1. "Arise, O Lord!" He does not say, Arise, O people, and put down those unjust judges. No; their function is from God, and God alone is to *reform*, or *strip*, or *punish* them. 2. "Judge the earth." Take the state of all people into thy consideration: there is much injustice in the earth. 3. For this petition he gives a reason: "For thou shalt inherit all nations," ver. 8. Publish thy own laws, appoint thy own officers, and let them in thy name dispense righteousness and true holiness throughout the world.

PSALM LXXXIII

The psalmist calls upon God for immediate help against a multitude of confederate enemies who had risen up against Judah, 1–5. *He mentions them by name,* 6–8; *shows how they were to be punished,* 9–17; *and that this was to be done for the glory of God,* 18.

A Song *or* Psalm [a]of Asaph

A. M. vir. 3108 B. C. cir. 896 Josaphati, Regis Judææ, cir. annum 19

KEEP [b]not thou silence, O
God: hold not thy peace,
and be not still, O God.
2 For, lo, [c]thine enemies make
a tumult: and they that [d]hate thee have lifted
up the head.
3 They have taken crafty counsel against thy
people, and consulted [e]against
thy hidden ones.
4 They have said, Come, and
[f]let us cut them off from *being*
a nation; that the name of Israel may be no
more in remembrance.
5 For they have consulted together with one
[g]consent: they are confederate against thee:

A. M. cir. 3108 B. C. cir. 896 Josaphati, Regis Judææ, cir. annum 19

[a]Or, *for Asaph*——[b]Psa. xxviii. 1; xxxv. 22; cix. 1——[c]Psa. ii. 1; Acts iv. 25——[d]Psa. lxxi. 15

[e]Psa. xxvii. 5; xxxi. 20——[f]See Esth. iii. 6, 9; Jer. xi. 19; xxxi. 36——[g]Heb. *heart*

NOTES ON PSALM LXXXIII

The title, *A Song* or *Psalm of Asaph*, contains nothing particular. Among a multitude of conjectures relative to the *time* and *occasion* of this Psalm, that which refers it to the confederacy against *Jehoshaphat*, king of Judah, mentioned 2 Chron. xx., is the most likely. The following reasons make it probable: 1. The children of *Ammon*, that is, the *Ammonites* and *Moabites*, were the principal movers in the war. 2. The *Idumeans* came to their assistance, 2 Chron. xx. 22; with certain *Ammonites* or *Meonians*, referred to here in ver. 8, and in 2 Chron. xx. 1. 3. There were also in this confederacy many *strangers* of *Syria*, and from beyond the sea, most likely the Dead Sea, which seems to indicate the *Assyrians*, *Hagaranes*, and *Ishmaelites*, designed expressly here, ver. 7, 8. 4. In that transaction there was a prophet of the race of *Asaph*, named *Jahaziel*, who foretold to *Jehoshaphat* their total overthrow, 2 Chron. xx. 14, &c., and probably this *Jahaziel* is the same with *Asaph*, the author of this Psalm. In the course of the notes we shall see other circumstances relative to the war of the *Moabites* and *Ammonites* against *Jehoshaphat*, which illustrates several particulars in this Psalm. See *Calmet*.

Verse 1. *Keep not thou silence*] A strong appeal to God just as the confederacy was discovered. Do not be inactive; do not be neuter. Thy honour and our existence are both at stake.

Verse 2. *Thine enemies make a tumult*] They are not merely the enemies of *thy people*, but they are the enemies of *thyself*, thy worship, ordinances, and laws: "They make a tumult," they *throng* together.

They—have lifted up the head.] They have made an irruption into the land of Judea, and encamped at *En-gedi*, by the Dead Sea, 2 Chron. xx. 1, 2.

Verse 3. *Consulted against thy hidden ones.*] צפוניך *tsephuneycha*, *Thy hidden things; places; persons.* "The hidden things in thy treasures."—CHALDEE. "Thy holy ones."—SYRIAC. "Thy saints."—VULGATE and SEPTUAGINT; and so the *Æthiopic* and *Arabic*. The *people of Israel* are probably meant. Or perhaps the *temple*, the *ark*, and the *treasures of the temple*, are intended.

Verse 4. *Let us cut them off*] Let us exterminate the whole race, that there may not be a record of them on the face of the earth. And their scheme was well laid: *eight* or *ten* different nations united themselves in a firm bond to do this; and they had kept their purpose so secret that the king of Judah does not appear to have heard of it till his territories were actually invaded, and the different bodies of this coalition had assembled at En-gedi. Never was Judah before in greater danger.

Verse 5. *They have consulted together with one consent*] With a united heart, לב יחדו *leb yachdav*. Their heart and soul are in the work.

They are confederate against thee] "They

A. M. cir. 3108 B. C. cir. 896 Josaphati, Regis Judææ, cir. annum 19

6 [h]The tabernacles of Edom,
and the Ishmaelites; of Moab,
and the Hagarenes;
7 Gebal, and Ammon, and
Amalek; the Philistines with the inhabitants
of Tyre;
8 Assur also is joined with them: [i]they
have holpen the children of Lot. Selah.
9 Do unto them as *unto* the [k]Midianites; as
to [l]Sisera, as *to* Jabin, at the brook of Kison:
10 *Which* perished at En-dor:
[m]they became *as* dung for the
earth.
11 Make their nobles like
[n]Oreb, and like Zeeb: yea, all their princes
as [o]Zebah, and as Zalmunna:
12 Who said, Let us take to ourselves the
houses of God in possession.
13 [p]O my God, make them like a wheel; [q]as
the stubble before the wind.

A. M. cir. 3108 B. C. cir. 896 Josaphati, Regis Judææ, cir. annum 19

[h]See 2 Chron. xx. 1, 10, 11——[i]Heb. *they have been an arm to the children of Lot*——[k]Numbers xxxi. 7; Judg. vii. 22

[l]Judg. iv. 15, 24; v. 21——[m]2 Kings ix. 37; Zeph. i. 17——[n]Judg. vii. 25——[o]Judg. vii. 12, 21——[p]Isa. xvii. 13, 14——[q]Psa. xxxv. 5

have made a covenant," ברית יכריתו *berith yachrithu*, "they have cut the covenant sacrifice." They have slain an animal, divided him in twain, and passed between the pieces of the victim; and have thus bound themselves to accomplish their purpose.

Verse 6. *The tabernacles of Edom*] The *tents* of these different people are seen in the grand encampment. *Tents* are probably mentioned because it was the custom of some of these people, particularly the *Ishmaelites*, to live a migratory or wandering life; having no fixed habitation, but always abiding in tents. Their posterity remain to the present day, and act and live in the same manner.

Hagarenes] These people dwelt on the east of *Gilead;* and were nearly destroyed in the days of Saul, being totally expelled from their country, 1 Chron. v. 10, but afterwards recovered some strength and consequence; but *where* they dwelt after their expulsion by the Israelites is not known.

Verse 7. *Gebal*] The *Giblites*, who were probably the persons here designed, were a tribe of the ancient inhabitants of the land of Canaan, and are mentioned as unconquered at the death of Joshua, chap. xiii. 5. They are called *stone-squarers* or *Giblites*, 1 Kings v. 18, and were of considerable assistance to Hiram, king of Tyre, in preparing timber and stones for the building of the temple. They appear to have been eminent in the days of Ezekiel, who terms them the "ancients of Gebal, and the wise men thereof," who were ship-builders, chap. xxvii. 3. What is now called *Gibyle*, a place on the Mediterranean Sea, between Tripoli and Sidon, is supposed to be the remains of the city of the *Giblites*.

Ammon and *Moab* were the descendants of the children of *Lot*. Their bad origin is sufficiently known. See Gen. xix. 30, &c. Calmet supposes that *Ammon* is put here for *Men* or *Maon*, the *Meonians*, a people who lived in the neighbourhood of the Amalekites and Idumeans. See the notes on 2 Chron. xx. 1; xxvi. 7.

Amalek] The Amalekites are well known as the ancient and inveterate enemies of the Israelites. They were neighbours to the Idumeans.

The Philistines] These were tributaries to Jehoshaphat, 2 Chron. xvii. 11; but it seems they took advantage of the present times, to join in the great confederacy against him.

The inhabitants of Tyre] These probably joined the confederacy in hopes of making conquests, and extending their territory on the *main land*.

Verse 8. *Assur also is joined*] The *Ammonites* might have got those auxiliaries from beyond the Euphrates, against Jehosphaphat, as formerly they were brought against David. See 2 Sam. x. 16.

They have holpen the children of Lot.] The Ammonites, who appear to have been the chief instigators in this war.

Verse 9. *Do unto them as* unto *the Midianites*] Who were utterly defeated by *Gideon*, Judg. vii. 21, 22.

As to *Sisera*] Captain of the army of *Jabin*, king of Canaan, who was totally defeated by *Deborah* and *Barak*, near Mount *Tabor*, by the river *Kishon;* and himself, after having fled from the battle, slain by *Jael*, the wife of *Heber*, the Kenite. See Judg. iv. 15, &c.

Verse 10. *Perished at En-dor*] This refers to the defeat of the *Midianites* by *Gideon*, who were encamped in the valley of *Jezreel*, at the foot of Mount *Gilboa*, and near to *Tabor*, Judg. vi. 33, vii. 1, and consequently in the environs of *En-dor*. There *Gideon* attacked and defeated them; and, in various places during their flight, they were destroyed, and left to rot upon the earth. Judg. vii. 22-25.

Verse 11. *Make their nobles like Oreb, and like Zeeb*] They were two of the chiefs, or generals, of the Midianites; and were slain in the pursuit of the Midianites, by the men of Ephraim; and their heads brought to *Gideon* on the other side of Jordan. Judg. vii. 24, 25.

Yea, all their princes as Zebah, and as Zalmunna] These were kings of *Midian*, who were encamped at *Karkor* with *fifteen thousand* men, whom Gideon attacked there, and defeated, and took the kings prisoners; and finding that they had killed his own brothers slew them both. See Judg. viii 10-21. Of the Midianites there fell at this time *one hundred and twenty thousand* men.

Verse 12. *Let us take to ourselves the houses of God in possession.*] Nearly the words spoken by the confederates when they came to attack Jehoshaphat. *They come* (says the king in address to God) *to cast us out of thy possession, which thou hast given us to inherit.* See 2 Chron. xx. 11.

Verse 13. *O my God, make them like a wheel*] Alluding to the manner of threshing corn in the east. A *large broad wheel* was rolled over the grain on a threshing-floor, which was generally in the open air; and the grain being thrown up by a shovel against the wind the chaff was thus separated from it, in the place where it was threshed.

A. M. cir. 3108 B. C. cir. 896 Josaphati, Regis Judææ, cir. annum 19

14 As the fire burneth a wood,
and as the flame [r]setteth the
mountains on fire;
15 So persecute them [s]with thy
tempest, and make them afraid with thy storm.
16 [t]Fill their faces with shame; that they
may seek thy name, O LORD.
17 Let them be confounded
and troubled for ever; yea, let
them be put to shame, and
perish:
18 [u]That *men* may know that thou, whose
[v]name alone *is* JEHOVAH, *art* [w]the Most
High over all the earth.

A. M. cir. 3108 B. C. cir. 896 Josaphati, Regis Judææ, cir. annum 19

[r]Deut. xxxii. 22——[s]Job ix. 17——[t]Psa. xxxv. 4, 26 [u]Psa. lix. 13——[v]Exod. vi. 3——[w]Psa. xcii. 8

Verse 14. *The flame setteth the mountains on fire*] This may refer to the burning of the straw and chaff, after the grain was threshed and winnowed. And as their threshing-floors were situated often on the *hills* or *mountains*, to take the advantage of the wind, the *setting the mountains on fire* may refer to the burning of the *chaff*, &c., in those places. Let them be like *stubble* driven away by the *wind*, and burnt by the *fire*.

Verse 15. *So persecute them*] In this and the two following verses we find several awful execrations; and all this seems to be done in reference to that ancient custom, "pouring execrations on an enemy previously to battle." Of this I have already given specimens in this work; and the reader is particularly requested to refer to the case of Balaam being hired by the king of Moab to curse Israel previously to his intended attack: see the note on Num. xxii. 6, where the subject is treated at large.

This custom prevailed much among the *Romans*, and the ancient *Druids* of *Britain*. In all cases the *priests* were employed to utter the execrations, as they were supposed to have the greatest influence with the gods, in whose name the curses were uttered.

Verse 16. *That they may seek thy name*] Let them be confounded in all their attempts on Israel; and see, so manifestly, that thou hast done it, that they may invoke thy name, and be converted to thee.

Verse 17. *Let them—perish*] That is, in their present attempts. Some have objected to the execrations in this Psalm, without due consideration. None of these execrations refer either to their *souls* or to their *eternal state;* but merely to their *discomfiture in their present attempts.* Suppose the continental powers should join together to subjugate Britain, and destroy the Protestant religion; is there a Christian in the land that would not be justified in meeting them with the same or similar execrations? On the knees of my soul would I offer every one of them to God against such invaders. Selah.—A. C.

Verse 18. *That* men *may know*] That they may acknowledge, and be converted to thee. Here is no *malice;* all is *self-defence.*

Analysis of the Eighty-third Psalm

This Psalm divides itself into *four* parts:—

I. A short ejaculation, ver. 1.

II. A complaint against God's enemies, which is the reason of this prayer, ver. 2-10.

III. A fearful imprecation against them, ver. 12-17.

IV. The charitable ends proposed, ver. 18.

I. The *ejaculation* or prayer: "Keep not thou silence—be not still." Thy enemies are *loud* in their threatenings, and *active* in their endeavours, to destroy thy *people* and *thy worship:* "Hold not thy peace!"

II. He complains—These are enemies, 1. To thy people, ver. 2. 2. To God himself, ver. 5. Then he describes them, ver. 6-8.

1. They were banditti—spoilers: They "make a tumult," ver. 2.

2. Proud and arrogant: "They have lifted up the head," ver. 2.

3. They were subtle and crafty: "They have taken crafty counsel," ver. 3.

4. They carried their cunning counsel into acts of aggression: "Come, and let us cut them off," &c., ver. 4.

5. They were conspirators,—1. Against God. 2. Against his people. All the world against God and his Church! Not an uncommon case.

6. He gives us a *catalogue* of these conspirators, ver. 6-8: *Edom*, &c.

III. *He prays to God against them.* In which there are *four* particulars: 1. Their fall and ruin. 2. Their persecution. 3. Their terror. 4. Their disgrace.

These he illustrates by *five* similitudes: 1. Of a *wheel* that, running on, crushes all under it successively. 2. Of *stubble* or *chaff*, easily driven away by the *wind*, ver. 13. 3. Of a *wood* or *forest* in a state of general *conflagration*, ver. 14. 4. Of a *flame* that even consumes the *mountains*, ver. 14.

Their fall and ruin he wished to be—

1. *Speedy* and *perpetual:* "Do unto them as unto the Midianites," &c., ver. 9-13.

2. *Sudden* and *violent:* "As fire," ver. 13.

3. *Terrible* and *shameful:* "Fill their faces with shame," ver. 15, 16.

There are here *three* particulars of their punishment: 1. *Flight.* 2. *Terror.* 3. *Shame* and *ignominy.*

IV. The charitable ends proposed. These were *two:*—

1. That they might *seek after God*, be converted to him, ver. 16.

2. That they might *know him to be Jehovah*, the only true God, that they might be saved from all idolatry, ver. 18.

The spirit of this prayer is, 1. If they will not *seek* thee, and be converted, let them be *confounded* in their attempts against thy people. 2. If they will not *acknowledge* thee, let them be utterly *routed and overthrown:* "Let them be put to shame, and perish!"

PSALM LXXXIV

The psalmist longs for communion with God in the sanctuary, 1–3. *The blessedness of those who enjoy God's ordinances,* 4–7. *With confidence in God, he prays for restoration to his house and worship,* 8–12.

To the chief Musician [a]upon Gittith, A Psalm [b]for the sons of Korah

HOW [c]amiable *are* thy tabernacles, O
LORD of hosts!
2 [d]My soul longeth, yea, even fainteth for
the courts of the LORD: my heart and my
flesh crieth out for the living God.
3 Yea, the sparrow hath found a house, and
the swallow a nest for herself, where she may
lay her young, *even* thine altars, O LORD of
hosts, my King and my God.
4 [e]Blessed *are* they that dwell in thy house;
they will be still praising thee. Selah.
5 Blessed *is* the man whose strength *is* in
thee; in whose heart *are* the ways *of them:*
6 *Who* passing through the valley [f]of[g] Baca
make it a well; the rain also [h]filleth the
pools.

[a]Psa. viii. title——[b]Or, *of*——[c]Psa. xxvii. 4——[d]Psa. xlii. 1, 2; lxiii. 1; lxxiii. 26; cxix. 20——[e]Psa. lxv. 4

[f]Or, *of mulberry trees make him a well, &c.*——[g]2 Sam. v. 22, 23——[h]Heb. *covereth*

NOTES ON PSALM LXXXIV

The *title* here is the same as that of Psalm lxxxi., only that was for *Asaph*, this *for the sons of Korah.* This person was one of the chief rebels against Moses and Aaron; there were *three*, *Korah*, *Dathan*, and *Abiram*, who made an insurrection; and the earth opened, and swallowed them and their partisans up, Num. xvi. The children of Dathan and Abiram perished with their fathers; but by a particular dispensation of Providence, the children of *Korah* were *spared.* See Num. xxvi. 11, and the *note* there. The family of *Korah* was continued in Israel; and it appears from 1 Chron. xxvi. 1-19 that they were still employed about the temple, and were *porters* or *keepers of the doors.* They were also *singers* in the temple; see 2 Chron. xx. 19. This Psalm might have been sent to them to be sung, or one of themselves might have been its author.

Verse 1. *How amiable* are *thy tabernacles*] In this *plural* noun he appears to include all the *places* in or near the temple where acts of Divine worship were performed. The holy of holies, the holy place, the altar of incense, the altar of burnt-offering, &c., &c.; all called here God's *tabernacles* or *dwelling-places;* for wherever God was worshipped, there he was supposed to dwell.

Verse 2. *My soul longeth*] It is a Levite that speaks, who ardently longs to regain his place in the temple, and his part in the sacred services.

My heart and my flesh] All the desires of my *soul* and *body;* every *appetite* and *wish*, both *animal* and *spiritual*, long for thy service.

Verse 3. *Yea, the sparrow hath found a house*] It is very unlikely that sparrows and swallows, or birds of any kind, should be permitted to build their nests, and hatch their young, in or about altars which were kept in a state of the *greatest purity;* and where *perpetual fires* were kept up for the purpose of sacrifice, burning incense, &c. Without altering the text, if the clause be read in a parenthesis, the absurdity will be avoided, and the sense be good. "My heart crieth out for the living God, (even the sparrow hath found a house, and the swallow דרור *deror*, the *ring-dove*, a nest for herself, where she may lay her young,) for thine altars, O Lord of hosts!" Or, read the parenthesis last: "My heart crieth out for the living God; for thine altars, O Lord of hosts, my King and my God. Even the sparrow hath found out a house, and the swallow (ring-dove) a nest for herself, where she may lay her young;" but I have no place, either of rest or worship, understood. The *Chaldee* translates thus: "Even the pigeon hath found a house, and the turtle-dove hath a nest, because their young may be offered lawfully upon thine altars, O Lord of hosts, my King and my God." Or, as a *comparison* seems to be here intended, the following may best express the meaning: "Even as the sparrow finds out (seeks) a house, and the swallow her nest in which she may hatch her young; so I, thine altars, O Lord of hosts, my King and my God."

Verse 4. *Blessed* are *they that dwell in thy house*] They who have such a constant habitation in thy temple as the sparrow or the swallow has in the house wherein it has built its nest.

They will be still praising thee.] They will find it good to draw nigh unto God, as he always pours out his Spirit on his sincere worshippers.

Verse 5. *The man whose strength* is *in thee*]

"Who life and strength from thee derives;
And by thee moves and in thee lives."

In whose heart are *the ways* of them] This is no sense. The original, however, is obscure: מסלות בלבבם *mesilloth bilebabam*, "the high ways are in their hearts;" that is, the roads winding to thy temple. Perhaps there is a reference here to the *high roads* leading to the *cities of refuge.* We wish to escape from the hands and dominion of these murderers, and the roads that lead to Jerusalem and the temple we think on with delight; our hearts are with them, we long to be travelling on them.

Verse 6. *Passing through the valley of Baca make it a well*] Instead of בכא *bacha*, a *mulberry-tree, seven* MSS. have בכה *becheh, mourning.* I believe *Baca* to be the same here as *Bochim*, Judg. ii. 1-5, called *The Valley of Weeping.* Though they pass through this barren and desert place, they would not fear evil, knowing that thou wouldst supply all their wants; and even in the sandy desert cause them to find pools of water, in consequence of

7 They go [i]from [k]strength to strength, *every one of them* in Zion [l]appeareth before God.

8 O LORD God of hosts, hear my prayer: give ear, O God of Jacob. Selah.

9 [m]Behold, O God our shield, and look upon the face of thine anointed.

10 For a day in thy courts *is* better than a thousand. [n]I had rather be a doorkeeper in the house of my God, than to dwell in the tents of wickedness.

11 For the LORD God *is* a [o]sun and [p]shield: the LORD will give grace and glory: [q]no good *thing* will he withhold from them that walk uprightly.

12 O LORD of hosts, [r]blessed *is* the man that trusteth in thee.

---

[i]Or, *from company to company*——[k]Prov. iv. 18; 2 Cor. iii. 18——[l]Deut. xvi. 16; Zech. xiv. 16——[m]Gen. xv. 1; ver. 11

[n]Heb. *I would choose rather to sit at the threshold* [o]Isa. lx. 19——[p]Gen. xv. 1; ver. 9; Psa. cxv. 9, 10, 11; cxix. 114; Prov. ii. 7——[q]Psa. xxxiv. 9, 10——[r]Psa. ii. 12

---

which they shall advance with renewed strength, and shall meet with the God of Israel in Zion.

The rain also filleth the pools.] The *Hebrew* may be translated differently, and has been differently understood by all the *Versions*. גם ברכות יעטה מורה *gam berachoth yaateh moreh;* "Yea, the instructor is covered or clothed with blessings." While the followers of God are passing through the *wilderness* of this world, God *opens* for them *fountains* in the *wilderness, and springs in the dry places.* They *drink* of the *well-spring of salvation;* they are not destitute of their *pastors.* God takes care to give his followers *teachers* after his own heart, that shall feed them with knowledge; and while they are watering the people they are watered themselves; for God *loads them with his benefits,* and the people *cover* them with their *blessings.*

Verse 7. *They go from strength to strength*] They proceed from one degree of grace to another, gaining Divine virtue through all the steps of their probation.

Every one of them *in Zion appeareth before God.*] This is a paraphrase, and a bad one, but no translation. They shall proceed from strength to strength, יראה אל אלהים בציון *yeraeh el Elohim betsiyon,* "The God of gods shall be seen in Zion." God shall appear in their behalf, as often as they shall seek him; in consequence of which they shall increase in spiritual strength.

Some think there is a reference here to *companies* of people going up to Jerusalem from different parts of the land, blending together as they go on, so that the crowd is continually increasing. This meaning our translators have put in the *margin.*

Verse 8. *Hear my prayer*] Let us be restored to thy sanctuary, and to thy worship.

Verse 9. *Behold, O God, our shield*] We have no Protector but thee. Thou seest the deadly blows that are aimed at us; cover our souls; protect our lives!

Look upon the face of thine anointed.] Consider the supplications sent up by him whom thou hast appointed to be Mediator between thee and man—thy *Christ.* But some apply this to *David,* to *Zerubbabel,* to the *people of Israel;* and each has his reasons.

Verse 10. *A day in thy courts* is *better than a thousand.*] Not only better than *one thousand* in captivity, as the *Chaldee* states, but any where else. For in God's courts we meet with God the King, and are sure to have what petitions we offer unto him through his Christ.

I had rather be a doorkeeper] O what a strong desire does this express for the ordinances of God! Who *now* prefers the worship of God to genteel, gay, honourable, and noble company, to mirthful feasts, public entertainments, the stage, the oratorio, or the ball! Reader, wouldst thou rather be in thy *closet,* wrestling in prayer, or reading the Scriptures on thy knees, than be at any of the above places? How often hast thou sacrificed thy *amusement,* and *carnal delight,* and *pleasures,* for the benefit of a pious heart-searching sermon? Let conscience speak, and it will tell thee.

Verse 11. *For the Lord God* is *a sun and shield*] To *illuminate, invigorate,* and *warm;* to *protect* and *defend* all such as prefer him and his worship to every thing the earth can produce.

It is remarkable that not one of the *Versions* understand the שמש *shemesh,* as signifying *sun,* as we do. They generally concur in the following translation: "For the Lord loveth mercy and truth, and he will give grace and glory." The *Chaldee* says, "The Lord is as a high wall and a strong shield; grace and glory will the Lord give, and will not deprive those of blessedness who walk in perfection." Critics in general take the word as signifying a *defence* or a *guard.* Instead of שמש *shemesh, sun, Houbigant* reads שמר *shemer,* a *keeper* or *guardian,* and says that to represent God as the *sun* is without example in the sacred writings. But is not Mal. iv. 2, a parallel passage to this place? "Unto you that fear my name shall the *Sun of righteousness arise with healing in his wings.*" No MS. countenances the alteration of *Houbigant.*

The Lord will give grace] To pardon, purify, and save the soul from sin: and then he will *give glory* to the *sanctified* in his eternal kingdom; and even *here* he withholds no good thing from them that walk uprightly. Well, therefore, might the psalmist say, verse 12, "O Lord of hosts, blessed is the man that trusteth in thee."

ANALYSIS OF THE EIGHTY-FOURTH PSALM

This Psalm may be divided into the following parts:—

I. The psalmist, absent from the public worship of God, shows his love to the house of God, and his desire to be present in it, ver. 1-3.

II. The happiness of those who continue in that assembly, ver. 4-7.

III. He prays for restoration to it, and sets down the causes, ver. 8-11.

IV. The blessedness of the man who trusts in God, ver. 12.

I. 1. He begins with the pathetical exclamation, "How amiable are thy tabernacles!" A mode of expression which intimates *there is none equal to them.*

2. He expresses his ardent affection to the house of God:—1. "My soul longeth," &c. 2. "My heart and flesh cry out," &c.

3. He laments his absence from God's house. The *sparrows* and *swallows* have their respective houses, where they may be present, build, hatch their young, &c., but he could have no access to God's house. And this he expresses in an affecting appeal to God to move his pity:—1. "O Lord of hosts!" I acknowledge thee as my *Leader.* 2. "My King." I acknowledge myself as thy *subject.* 3. "My God." Whom I serve, and have taken for my portion.

II. The happiness of those who have liberty to worship God in his temple.

1. "Blessed are they." They enjoy thy ordinances, and have blessings in all.

2. "Who dwell:" Who continue in union with God, ever prizing his ordinances.

3. "They will be still praising thee:" As being continually happy in thy presence.

"Blessed is the man whose strength is in thee:" Who knows his own weakness, and depends upon thee for his continual support.

This is the happiness of those who are near God's house: but there is a happiness for those also whose hearts are there, though their bodies are detained at a distance from it.

1. Blessed are they in whose hearts are the ways of them, ver. 5.

2. Even when they are passing through desert and inhospitable countries, ver. 6.

3. "They go from strength to strength:" 1. They get from one place of protection to another. 2. They increase in the Divine light and life. 3. They get many companions on the way.

III. His prayer. 1. He begs to be heard. 2. He remembers God, who succoured *Jacob* in weakness and distress. 3. He considers himself as the *anointed* of God, and under his especial care, ver. 8. He wishes to be employed, even in the meanest offices, in the house of God, which he illustrates by an opposition of *time, place,* and *persons.*

1. *Time. One day* in thy courts is better than a *thousand out of it.*

2. *Place. God's house,* to the *tents* of wickedness.

3. *Persons.* A doorkeeper, a Korahite at the temple, rather than an emperor in his palace.

For this he gives *five* reasons:—

1. "The Lord is a sun:" He dispels darkness, comforts, warms, gives life.

2. He is a *shield:* The Defender and Protector of his followers.

3. He *gives grace,* to prepare for heaven.

4. *Glory,* to crown that grace.

5. He is all-sufficient. "He will withhold no good thing."

But sinners and hypocrites need not expect these blessings; they are for them that walk uprightly.

1. They must *walk*—go on, be constant, abide in the way.

2. They must be *upright*—truly sincere and obedient.

IV. The blessedness of the man who trusts in God. "O Lord of hosts, blessed is the man that trusts in thee!" This acclamation may be intended to answer an objection: "If those be blessed who dwell in thy temple, then those must be wretched who are exiled from it." No, says the psalmist; though there be many advantages enjoyed by those who can attend the ordinances of God, and some may attend them without profit; yet he who trusts in God can never be confounded. Faith in God will always be crowned; and, when absent through necessity, every place is a temple.

"Though fate command me to the farthest verge
Of the green earth——————
Yet God is ever present, ever felt,
In the wide waste as in the city full;
And where he vital breathes, there must be joy.

PSALM LXXXV

Thanksgiving to God for restoration to the Divine favour, 1–3; *prayer for farther mercies,* 4–7; *the psalmist waits for a gracious answer in full confidence of receiving it,* 8. *He receives the assurance of the greatest blessings, and exults in the prospect,* 9–13.

To the chief Musician, A Psalm [a]for [b]the sons of Korah

A. M. cir. 3468 B. C. cir. 536 Cyri, R. Persarum, cir. annum primum

LORD, thou hast been [c]favourable unto thy land: thou hast [d]brought back the captivity of Jacob.

2 [e]Thou hast forgiven the iniquity of thy people, thou hast covered all their sin. Selah.

A. M. cir. 3468 B. C. cir. 536 Cyri, R. Persarum, cir. annum primum

3 Thou hast taken away all thy wrath:

[a]Psa. xlii. title——[b]Or, *of*——[c]Or, *well pleased;* Psa. lxxvii. 7

[d]Ezra i. 11; ii. 1; Psa. xiv. 7; Jer. xxx. 18; xxxi. 23; Ezek. xxxix. 25; Joel iii. 1——[e]Psa. xxxii. 1

NOTES ON PSALM LXXXV

The *title* of this Psalm we have seen before, Psa. xlii. As to the *time,* it seems to have been written during, or even after, the return from the Babylonish captivity. In the *three* first verses the psalmist acknowledges the goodness of God in bringing the people back to their own land; he next prays to God to restore them to their ancient prosperity. In the spirit of prophecy, he waits on God, and hears him promise to do it; and then exults in the prospect of so great a good. The whole Psalm seems also to have a reference to the redemption of the world by Jesus Christ.

Verse 1. *Lord, thou hast been favourable*] Literally, *Thou hast been well pleased with thy land.*

A. M. cir. 3468 B. C. cir. 536 Cyri, R. Persarum, cir. annum primum

[f]thou hast turned *thyself* from
the fierceness of thine anger.
4 [g]Turn us, O God of our
salvation, and cause thine anger
toward us to cease.
5 [h]Wilt thou be angry with us for ever?
wilt thou draw out thine anger to all generations?
6 Wilt thou not [i]revive us again: that thy
people may rejoice in thee?
7 Show us thy mercy, O LORD,
and grant us thy salvation.
8 [k]I will hear what God the
LORD will speak: for [l]he will
speak peace unto his people, and to his saints:
but let them not [m]turn again to folly.
9 Surely [n]his salvation *is* nigh them that
fear him; [o]that glory may dwell in our land.
10 Mercy and truth are met together; [p]righteousness and peace have kissed *each other.*

[f]Or, *thou hast turned thine anger from waxing hot;* Deut. xiii. 17——[g]Psa. lxxx. 7——[h]Psa. lxxiv. 1; lxxix 5; lxxx. 4——[i]Hab. iii. 2——[k]Hab. ii. 1

[l]Zech. ix. 10——[m]2 Pet. ii. 20, 21——[n]Isa. xlvi. 13 [o]Zech. ii. 5; John i. 14——[p]Psa. lxxii. 3; Isa. xxxii. 17; Luke ii. 14

Thou hast brought back the captivity] This seems to fix the *time* of the Psalm to be after the return of the Jews from Babylon.

Verse 2. *Thou hast forgiven the iniquity*] נשאת עון *nasatha avon, Thou hast borne,* or *carried away, the iniquity.* An allusion to the ceremony of the *scapegoat.*

Thou hast covered all their sin.] As thou hast freely *forgiven* it, its offensiveness and abominable nature no longer *appear.* The whole is put *out of sight;* and, as we are restored from our captivity, the *consequences* no longer *appear.*

Selah.] This is true. Our return to our own land is the full proof.

Verse 3. *Thou hast taken away*] אספת *asaphta,* "Thou hast *gathered up* all thy wrath." This carries on the *metaphor* in the *second* verse: "Thou hast *collected* all thy wrath, and *carried it away* with all our iniquities."

Verse 4. *Turn us, O God of our salvation*] Thou hast turned our captivity; now convert our souls. And they find a *reason* for their prayer in an attribute of their God; *the God of their salvation.* And as his work was to *save,* they beg that *his anger towards them might cease.* The Israelites were not restored from their captivity *all at once.* A few returned with *Zerubbabel;* some more with *Ezra* and *Nehemiah;* but a great number still remained in *Babylonia, Media, Assyria, Egypt,* and other *parts.* The request of the psalmist is, to have a complete restoration of all the Israelites from all places of their dispersion.

Verse 5. *Wilt thou draw out thine anger*] We have already suffered much and long; our fathers have suffered, and we have succeeded to their distresses. Draw not out thy anger against us from generation to generation.

Verse 6. *Wilt thou not revive us*] We have long had the sentence of death in ourselves; and have feared an utter extinction. Shall not our nation yet live before thee? Shall we not become once more numerous, pious, and powerful; that

Thy people may rejoice in thee?] As the Source of all our mercies; and give thee the glory due to thy name?

Verse 7. *Show us thy mercy*] Blot out all our sins.

And grant us thy salvation.] Give us such a complete deliverance as is worthy of thy *majesty* and *mercy* to bestow!

Verse 8. *I will hear what God the Lord will speak*] The psalmist goes as a prophet to consult the Lord; and, having made his request, waits an answer from the spirit of prophecy. He is satisfied that the answer will be gracious; and having received it he relates it to the people.

He will speak peace] He will give *prosperity* to *the people* in general; and to *his saints*—his followers, in particular.

But let them not turn again to folly.] Let them not abuse the mercy of their God, by sinning any more against him.

Verse 9. *Surely his salvation* is *nigh*] To him who *fears* God, and trembles at his word, his salvation is nigh at hand.

That glory may dwell in our land.] That thy worship may be restored, the temple rebuilt, and the Divine shechinah, or symbol of the presence of God, resume its place. The pure and undefiled religion of God preached, professed, and experienced in a nation, is the *glory* of that land. The Prophet *Haggai* had said that *the glory of the latter house*—the temple built after their return from Babylon, *should be greater than the glory of the former,* viz., of that built by Solomon: but, as a building, it was far inferior to the former; yet it had a *superior* glory in being visited by Jesus Christ. This was the glory that excelled.

Verse 10. *Mercy and truth are met together*] It would be more simple to translate the original,—

חסד ואמת נפגשו
צדק ושלום נשקו

Chesed veemeth niphgashu;
Tsedek veshalom nashaku,—

"Mercy and truth have met on the way;
Righteousness and peace have embraced."

This is a remarkable text, and much has been said on it: but there is a beauty in it which, I think, has not been noticed.

Mercy and *peace* are on one side; *truth* and *righteousness* on the other. *Truth* requires *righteousness; mercy* calls for *peace.*

They meet together on the way; one going to make inquisition for sin, the other to plead for reconciliation. Having met, their differences on certain considerations, not here particularly mentioned, are adjusted; and their mutual claims are blended together in one common interest; on which *peace* and *righteousness* immediately embrace. Thus, *righteousness* is given to *truth,* and *peace* is given to *mercy.*

Now, *Where* did these meet? In Christ Jesus. *When* were they reconciled? When he poured out his life on Calvary.

A. M. cir. 3468
B. C. cir. 536
Cyri,
R. Persarum,
cir. annum
primum

11 [q]Truth shall spring out
of the earth; and righteousness shall look down from
heaven.
12 [r]Yea, the LORD shall give *that which is*
good; and [s]our land shall yield
her increase.
13 [t]Righteousness shall go before him; and shall set *us* in the
way of his steps.

[q]Isa. xlv. 8——[r]Psa. lxxxiv. 11; James i. 17 [s]Psa. lxvii. 6——[t]Psa. lxxxix. 14

Verse 11. *Truth shall spring out of the earth*] In consequence of this wonderful *reconciliation*, the truth of God shall prevail among men. The *seeds* of it shall be so plentifully sown by the preaching of Christ and his apostles that true religion shall be diffused over the world.

And righteousness shall look down from heaven.] And be delighted with the reformation of the sons of Adam; and shall be so satisfied with the glorious work which is carried forward, that,

Verse 12. *The Lord shall give—good*] הטוב *hattob*, THE GOOD *thing*—what is the supreme good, the *summum bonum*, for which man has searched in vain through all his generations. Those who are reconciled to him through the Son of his love shall enjoy the *favour* of their God; to have which is the supreme happiness of man.

Our land shall yield her increase.] There shall be neither *dearth* nor *barrenness;* for *truth*, that *springs out of the earth*, shall yield an abundant harvest, in the conversion of all nations to the faith of our Lord Jesus Christ.

Verse 13. *Righteousness shall go before him*] Perhaps this verse may receive its best solution from Rom. iii. 25: "Whom God hath set for a propitiation through faith in his blood, to declare his RIGHTEOUSNESS for the remission of sins that are past." This term the apostle uses to point out *God's method of justifying* or *saving mankind.* And this, in the preaching of the pure Gospel, is ever *going before* to point out the Lord Jesus, and the redemption that is in his blood. And thus going before him, the sinner, who feels his need of salvation, is *Set—in the way of his steps;* as Bartimeus sat by the way-side begging, by which way Jesus walked; and when he came where he was, heard his prayer, and restored him his sight. Or, *righteousness*—the pure and holy law of God, must be proclaimed as broken by sinners, and calling aloud for vengeance, before they can see and feel their need of Christ crucified. By the preaching of the law they are prepared to receive the grace of the Gospel.

ANALYSIS OF THE EIGHTY-FIFTH PSALM

Mystically, this Psalm may be considered as treating of the redemption of the world by Jesus Christ. It has the *three* following parts:—

I. An acknowledgment of God's former mercies, ver. 1-3.

II. A petition on that ground that he would repeat them, ver. 4-7.

III. A profession of obedience, and an advice to continue in it, ver. 8. That men may be partakers of the promises, both *spiritual*, ver. 9, 10, 11; and *temporal*, ver. 12, which shall be fulfilled to those who keep in the ways of God, ver. 13.

I. In the *three* first verses, the psalmist commemorates God's mercies to his people; of which his *good will* or *favour* is the Fountain. These mercies are, 1. *Temporal:* "Thou hast been favourable unto thy land," &c., ver. 1. 2. *Spiritual:* 1. "Thou hast forgiven the iniquities of thy people:" Justification. 2. "Thou hast taken away all thy wrath:" Reconciliation.

II. Upon this he founds a prayer: "Turn us, O God."

1. Thou hast turned away the captivity. Restore and convert us.

2. Thou hast brought us back. Revive our hearts, that they may rejoice in thee.

3. Thou hast been reconciled to our *fathers*. Be reconciled to *us*.

4. Thou hast forgiven the iniquity of thy people. Save us.

III. He promises obedience: "I will hear what God will speak;" and I shall hear nothing from him but what is for his own glory, and his people's good.

1. "He will speak peace:" He will turn all their sufferings to their advantage.

2. But they must hear, and be steady. They must "not turn again to folly;" let them remember this.

3. To such his promise is sure: "His salvation is nigh them."

4. And it comes, that "glory may dwell in our land;" that it may be crowned with peace and plenty.

In this prosperity of theirs, there shall be a combination of *mercy*, *truth*, *justice*, and *peace*.

1. "Justice and peace shall embrace;" for there is such a league between these two, that where *peace* is made without *justice*, it cannot long continue: and *mercy* and *truth* must; for it is inconsistent with mercy to be in concord with falsehood.

2. "Truth shall spring out of the earth." Men shall observe it in all their transactions, contracts, and promises.

3. "Righteousness shall look down from heaven." God will smile on this state of things, and pour out upon them the continual dew of his blessing.

4. In a word, 1. They shall enjoy all *spiritual* blessings; for the "Lord shall give that which is good." 2. And all *temporal;* "for the land shall yield her increase."

For these mercies he sets down our duty:—

1. "Righteousness shall go before him." All his saints shall walk before him in righteousness and true holiness.

"And this righteousness shall set them in the

way of his steps." It shall teach them to walk constantly and steadily in the way of his commandments all the days of their life.

By many of the ancients and moderns the whole of this Psalm has been applied to Christ, and his salvation. See the preceding notes.

PSALM LXXXVI

The psalmist prays to God for support, from a conviction that he is merciful, good, ready to forgive, and that there is none like him, 1–8; *all nations shall bow before him because of his wondrous works,* 9, 10; *he prays to be instructed, and promises to praise God for his great mercy,* 11–13; *describes his enemies, and appeals to God,* 14–16; *begs a token for God, that his enemies may be confounded,* 17.

XVII. DAY. MORNING PRAYER

[a]A Prayer of David

BOW down thine ear, O LORD, hear me:
for I *am* poor and needy.

2 Preserve my soul; for I *am* [b]holy: O thou
my God, save thy servant [c]that trusteth in thee.

3 [d]Be merciful unto me, O LORD: for I
cry unto thee [e]daily.

4 Rejoice the soul of thy servant: [f]for unto
thee, O LORD, do I lift up my soul.

5 [g]For thou, LORD, *art* good, and ready to
forgive; and plenteous in mercy unto all them
that call upon thee.

6 Give ear, O LORD, unto my prayer;
and attend to the voice of my supplications.

7 [h]In the day of my trouble I will call upon
thee: for thou wilt answer me.

8 [i]Among the gods *there is* none like unto
thee, O LORD; [k]neither *are there any works*
like unto thy works.

9 [l]All nations whom thou hast made shall
come and worship before thee, O LORD; and
shall glorify thy name.

10 For thou *art* great, and [m]doest wondrous
things: [n]thou *art* God alone.

[a]Or, *A Prayer,* being a Psalm *of David*——[b]Or, *one whom thou favourest*——[c]Isa. xxvi. 3——[d]Psa. lvi. 1; lvii. 1——[e]Or, *all the day*——[f]Psa. xxv. 1; cxliii. 8 [g]Ver. 15; Psa. cxxx. 7; cxlv. 9; Joel ii. 13——[h]Psa. l 15

[i]Exodus xv. 11; Psalm lxxxix. 6——[k]Deut. iii. 24 [l]Psa. xxii. 31; cii. 18; Isa. xliii. 7; Rev. xv. 4——[m]Exod. xv. 11; Psa. lxxii. 18; lxxvii. 15——[n]Deut. vi. 3; xxxii. 39; Isa. xxxvii. 16; xliv. 6; Mark xii. 29; 1 Cor. viii. 4; Eph. iv. 6

NOTES ON PSALM LXXXVI

The *title* attributes this Psalm to *David;* and in this all the *Versions* agree: but in its structure it is the same with those attributed to the *sons of Korah;* and was probably made during the captivity. It is a very suitable prayer for a person labouring under affliction from persecution or calumny.

Verse 1. *Bow down thine ear*] Spoken after the manner of men: I am so *low,* and so *weak,* that, unless thou *stoop to me,* my voice cannot reach thee.

Poor and needy.] I am afflicted, and destitute of the necessaries of life.

Verse 2. *Preserve my soul*] Keep it as in a strong place.

For I am *holy*] כי חסיד אני *ki chasid ani,* for I am merciful. The spirit of this prayer is,

"The mercy I to others show,
That mercy show to me!"

Save thy servant] I have long taken thee as my *Master* and *Lord;* I receive the word from thy mouth, and *obey* thee.

Verse 3. *Be merciful unto me*] I have no *merit;* I plead none, but trust in thee alone.

I cry unto thee daily.] My state deeply affects me; and I incessantly cry for thy salvation.

Verse 4. *Rejoice the soul of thy servant*] I want spiritual blessings; I want such consolations as thou dost impart to them that love thee; I present that soul to thee which I wish thee to console.

Verse 5. *For thou, Lord,* art *good*] I found my expectations of help on thy own goodness, through which thou art always ready to forgive. And I found it also on thy well-known character, to which all thy followers bear testimony, viz., that "thou art plenteous in mercy unto all them that call upon thee."

Verse 6. *Give ear, O Lord*] Attend to *me.* Millions call upon thee for help and mercy; but who has more need than myself? That the psalmist was deeply in earnest, his conduct shows. 1. He *prayed.* 2. His prayer was vehement; he lifted up his *voice.* 3. He continued in prayer; he abounded in *supplications.*

Verse 7. *Thou wilt answer me.*] Because thou art good, merciful, and ready to forgive; and I call upon thee fervently, and seek thee in thy own way.

Verse 8. *Among the gods* there is *none like unto thee, O Lord*] None that trusted in an idol ever had help in time of need; none that prayed to any of them ever had an answer to his petitions. *Thou* savest; *they* cannot; thou *upholdest;* they must be *upheld* by their foolish worshippers. *Thou art my Director,* אדני *Adonai;* but they cannot *direct* nor *teach;* they have mouths, but they speak not.

Verse 9. *All nations*] Thy word shall be proclaimed among all the Gentiles: they shall receive thy testimony, and worship thee as the only true and living God.

Verse 10. *For thou* art *great*] Almighty, infinite, eternal.

And doest wondrous things] ועשה נפלאות *veoseh niphlaoth;* thou art the *Worker of mir-*

11 [o]Teach me thy way, O LORD; I will walk
in thy truth: unite my heart to fear thy
name.
12 I will praise thee, O LORD my God,
with all my heart: and I will glorify thy name
for evermore.
13 For great *is* thy mercy toward me: and
thou hast [p]delivered my soul from the lowest
[q]hell.
14 O God, [r]the proud are risen against me,
and the assemblies of [s]violent *men* have sought
after my soul; and have not set thee before
them.
15 [t]But thou, O LORD, *art* a God full of
compassion, and gracious, long suffering, and
plenteous in mercy and truth.
16 O [u]turn unto me, and have mercy upon
me; give thy strength unto thy servant, and
save [v]the son of thine handmaid.
17 Show me a token for good; that they
which hate me may see *it,* and be ashamed:
because thou, LORD, hast holpen me, [w]and
comforted me.

---

[o]Psa. xxv. 4; xxvii. 11; cxix. 33; cxliii. 8——[p]Psa. lvi. 13; cxvi. 8——[q]Or, *grave*——[r]Psa. liv. 3——[s]Heb. *terrible*——[t]Exod. xxxiv. 6; Num. xiv. 18; Neh. ix. 17; ver. 5; Psa. ciii. 8; cxi. 4; cxxx. 4, 7; cxlv. 8; Joel ii. 13——[u]Psa. xxv. 16; lxix. 16——[v]Psa. cxvi. 16; Luke i. 38, 48 [w]Isa. xlix. 13; li. 12; Matt. v. 4

---

acles. This thou hast done in numerous instances, and thereby showed thy infinite power and wisdom.

This appears to be a prophecy of the calling of the Gentiles to the faith of Christ, and the evidence to be given to his Divine mission by the *miracles* which he should work.

Thou art God alone.] Συ ει ὁ Θεος μονος ὁ μεγας.—*Sept. Thou art the only,* THE GREAT *God.* In this the *Æthiopic* and *Arabic* agree.

Verse 11. *Teach me thy way*] Instruct me in the steps I should take; for without thy teaching I must go astray.

Unite my heart] יחד לבבי *yached lebabi, join* all the purposes, resolutions, and affections of my heart *together,* to fear and to glorify thy name. This is a most important prayer. A *divided* heart is a great curse; *scattered* affections are a miserable plague. When the *heart* is not at *unity* with itself, the work of religion cannot go on. *Indecision* of *mind* and *division* of *affections* mar any work. The *heart* must be *one,* that the *work* may be *one.* If this be wanting, all is wrong. This is a prayer which becomes the mouth of every Christian.

Verse 12. *I will praise thee—with all my heart*] When my *heart* is *united* to fear thy name, then shall I praise thee with my *whole heart.*

Verse 13. *Thou hast delivered my soul from the lowest hell.*] This must mean more than the *grave;* a *hell below hell*—a place of perdition for the soul, as the grave is a place of corruption for the *body.*

Verse 14. *The assemblies of violent* men] עדת עריצים *adath aritsim,* the *congregation of the terrible ones.* Men of violent passions, violent counsels, and violent acts; and, because they have power, *terrible* to all.

Have not set thee before them.] Who sins that sets God before his eyes? Who does not sin that has no consciousness of the Divine presence?

Verse 15. *But thou, O Lord*] What a wonderful character of God is given in this verse! אדני *Adonai,* the Director, Judge, and Support;—but instead of אדני *Adonai, thirty-four* of Kennicott's MSS. have יהוה *Yehovah,* the self-existent and eternal Being;—אל *El,* the strong God; רחום *rachum,* tenderly compassionate; חנון *channun,* the Dispenser of grace or favour; ארך אפים *erech appayim,* suffering long, not easily provoked; רב חסד *rab chesed,* abundant in blessings; and אמת *emeth,* faithful and true. Such is the God who has made himself more particularly known to us in Christ. The scanty language of our ancestors was not adequate to a full rendering of the original words: **⁊ ðu driht god gemildsiend ⁊ mildheort, geþyldig, ⁊ mucel mildheortnysse ⁊ soþfæst.** "**And** thu driht God gemildsiend, and mildheort, gethyldig and mucel mildheortnysse and sothfæst.—And thou, Lord God, art mild, and mildhearted, patient, and of much mildheartedness, and soothfast,"—steady in truth.

In the old *Psalter* the language is but little improved: **And thou Lorde God mercier, and mercyful, sufferand, and of mykel mercy, and sothefast.**

The word **mercier** is interpreted, *doand dede of mercy.*

Verse 16. *O turn unto me*] He represents himself as following after God; but he cannot overtake him; and then he prays that he would *turn* and meet him through pity; or give him *strength* that he might be able to hold on his race.

Give thy strength unto thy servant] The *Vulgate* renders, Da imperium tuum puero tuo, "Give thy empire to thy child." The old *Psalter:* **Gyf empyre to thi barne, and make safe the son of thi hand mayden.** *Thi barne*—thy tender child. **cnapan** or **cnafan þinum,** Anglo-Saxon; *thy knave;* signifying either a *serving man* or a *male child.* As many *servants* were found to be purloiners of their masters' property, hence the word **cnapan,** and **cnafan,** and *knave,* became the title of an unprincipled servant. The term *fur,* which signifies a *thief* in Latin, for the same reason became the appellative of a *dishonest servant.*

Quid domini facient, audent cum talia FURES?

When servants (*thieves*) do such things, what may not be expected from the masters?
VIRG. Ecl. iii. 16.

So PLAUTUS, speaking of a *servant,* Aulul. ii. 46, says: Homo es trium literarum, "Thou art a man of *three* letters," i. e., FUR, a *thief.* The word *knave* is still in use, but is always taken in a bad sense. The *paraphrase* in the old *Psalter* states the *handmaid* to be the *kirk,* and the *son* of this *handmaid* to be a *true believer.*

Verse 17. *Show me a token for good*] עשה

עמי אות *aseh immi oth*, "*Make* with me a sign." Fix the honourable mark of thy name upon me, that I may be known to be thy servant. There seems to be an allusion here to the *marking of a slave*, to ascertain whose property he was. The *Anglo-Saxon*, **do mid me tacn on gode**, "do with me a token in good." Old *Psalter:* **Do with me signe in gude.** From **tacn** *tacn* we have our word *token*, which signifies a *sign*, *mark*, or *remembrancer* of something beyond itself; a *pledge* that something, then specified, shall be *done* or *given*. Give me, from the influence of thy Spirit in my heart, a *pledge* that the blessings which I now ask shall be given in due time. But he wished for such a sign as his enemies might see; that they might know God to be his helper, and be confounded when they sought his destruction.

Analysis of the Eighty-sixth Psalm

This Psalm is a continued prayer, and may be divided into *four* parts:—

I. The *first* part is a petition for safety, drawn from *his own person*, ver. 1-4.

II. The *second*, a quickening of the same petition, drawn from the *person* and *nature* of *God*, ver. 5-13.

III. The *third*, taken from the *quality* of his *adversaries*, ver. 14.

IV. The *fourth*, a conjunction of all these *three;* the *first*, ver. 15; the *second*, ver. 16; the *third*, ver. 17.

I. The reasons of his petition, drawn from *himself*.

1. "Bow down thine ear." Reason: "I am poor and needy," ver. 1.

2. "Preserve my soul." Reason: "I am holy," or merciful, ver. 2.

3. "Save thy servant." Reason: "He puts his trust in thee," ver. 3.

4. "Be merciful unto me." Reason: "I cry unto thee daily," ver. 4.

5. "Rejoice the soul of thy servant." Reason: "For unto thee do I lift up my soul," ver. 4.

II. A quickening of the petition, drawn from the *nature of God*.

1. "For thou, Lord, art good," &c., ver. 5, 6.

2. "I will call upon thee: for thou wilt answer me," ver. 7.

3. "There is none like unto thee," ver. 8.

4. "Nor any works like unto thy works," ver. 8. This shall be amply proved: for

5. "All nations," now worshipping idols, "shall be converted to thee," ver. 9.

6. "Because thou art great, and doest wondrous things," ver. 10.

On this reason, that there is none like God,—

1. He begs to be governed by his word and Spirit, ver. 11.

2. Promises to praise him for his great mercy, ver. 12, 13.

III. He presses another argument taken from his *enemies*.

1. They were *proud:* "The proud are risen against me."

2. They were *powerful:* "The assemblies of violent men."

3. They were *ungodly:* "They did not set thee before them," ver. 14.

IV. He amplifies his former argument.

1. From the *nature of God:* "Thou art full of compassion," &c., ver. 15.

2. From his *own condition:* "Turn unto me, and have mercy upon me," ver. 16.

3. From the *quality of his adversaries:* "Show me a token—that they which hate me may be ashamed," ver. 17.

PSALM LXXXVII

The nature and glorious privileges of Zion and Jerusalem, 1–3. *No other city to be compared to this*, 4. *The privilege of being born in it*, 5, 6. *Its praises celebrated*, 7.

A Psalm *or* Song [a]for the sons of Korah

A. M. cir. 3468 B. C. cir. 536 Cyri, R. Persarum, cir. annum primum

HIS foundation *is* [b]in the holy
mountains.
2 [c]The LORD loveth the gates
of Zion more than all the dwellings of Jacob.

3 [d]Glorious things are spoken
of thee, O city of God. Selah.
4 I will make mention [e]of Rahab and Babylon to them that
know me: behold Philistia, and Tyre, with
Ethiopia; this *man* was born there.

A. M. cir. 3468 B. C. cir. 536 Cyri, R. Persarum, cir. annum primum

[a]Or, *of*——[b]Psa. xlviii. 1——[c]Psa. lxxviii. 67, 68

[d]See Isa. lx.——[e]Psa. lxxxix. 10; Isa. li. 9

NOTES ON PSALM LXXXVII

The *title, A Psalm* or *Song for the sons of Korah*, gives us no light into the *author* or *meaning* of this Psalm. It begins and ends so abruptly that many have thought it to be only a *fragment* of a larger Psalm. This opinion is very likely. Those who suppose it to have been made when Jerusalem was rebuilt and fortified, imagine it to have been an exclamation of the author on beholding its beauty, and contemplating its privileges. If this opinion be allowed, it will account for the apparent abruptness in the beginning and end. As to its general design it seems to have been written in praise of Jerusalem; and those who are for *mystic* meanings, think that it refers to the Christian Church; and, on this supposition it is interpreted by several writers, both ancient and modern. To pretend to have found out the true meaning would be very absurd. I have done the best I could to give its *literal* sense.

Verse 1. *His foundation* is *in the holy mountains.*] Jerusalem was founded on the mountains or hills of *Zion* and *Moriah*. The after increase of the population obliged the inhabitants to inclose all the contiguous hills; but *Zion* and *Moriah* were the principal. We know that ancient Rome was built on *seven hills.*

Verse 2. *The Lord loveth the gates of Zion*

A. M. cir. 3468
B. C. cir. 536
Cyri,
R. Persarum,
cir. annum
primum

5 And of Zion it shall be said,
This and that man was born in
her; and the Highest himself
shall establish her.
6 [f]The LORD shall count, when he [g]writeth
up the people, *that* this *man* was
born there. Selah.
7 As well the singers as the
players on instruments *shall be*
there: all my springs *are* in thee.

A. M. cir. 3468
B. C. cir. 536
Cyri,
R. Persarum,
cir. annum
primum

---

[f]Psa. xxii. 30

[g]Ezek. xiii. 9

---

more than all the dwellings of Jacob.] That is, he preferred Zion for his habitation, to be the place of his temple and sanctuary, before any other place in the promised land. Mystically, the Lord prefers the Christian Church to the Jewish: the latter was only a type of the former; and had no glory by reason of the glory that excelleth. To this position no exception can be made.

Verse 3. *Glorious things are spoken of thee*] Or, there are glorious words or doctrines in thee. Does this refer to the glorious doctrines of the Christian Church? These are glorious sayings indeed.

Verse 4. *I will make mention of Rahab*] The meaning seems to be, *Rahab*, i. e., *Egypt*, *Babylon*, *Tyre*, *Philistia*, and *Ethiopia* are not so honourable as *Jerusalem*. To be born in any of them is no privilege when compared with being a native of Jerusalem: their cities are but heads of villages; Jerusalem alone is a CITY. I have met with a very similar sentiment in a Persian work, of which I know not the author:

چه مصر و چه شام و چه بر و بحر
همه رستاي اند و شيرازي شهر

Tche Mesr, o tche Sham, o tche Birr o Buhr.
Hemè rustaee and, we Sheerazee Shuhr.

What celebrity can *Egypt* or *Syria*, or any thing on *earth* or on the *sea*, pretend to?
"When compared to *Sheeraz*, those are but *villages*, but this alone is a CITY."

The meaning seems to be the same in both the *Hebrew* and *Persian* poet.

Verse 5. *This and that man was born in her*] It will be an honour to any person to have been born in Zion. But how great is the honour to be *born from above*, and be a citizen of the Jerusalem that is from above! To be children of God, by faith in Christ Jesus! The *Targum* has, "David the king, and Solomon his son, were brought up here."

The Highest himself shall establish her.] The Christian Church is built on the foundation of the prophets and apostles; Jesus Christ himself being the Cornerstone.

Verse 6. *The Lord shall count, when he writeth up the people*] בכתוב עמים *bichthob ammim*, in the register of the people. When he takes account of those who dwell in Jerusalem, he will particularly note those who were born in Zion.

This has an easy spiritual meaning. When God takes an account of all *professing Christians*, he will set apart those for inhabitants of the New Jerusalem who were born in Zion, who were born again, received a new nature, and were fitted for heaven.

Verse 7. *As well the singers, &c.*] Perhaps, this may mean no more than, The burden of the songs of all the singers and choristers shall be, "All my fountains (ancestors and posterity) are in thee;" and consequently, entitled to all thy privileges and immunities. Instead of שרים *sharim*, "singers," many MSS. and early printed editions have, *sarim*, "princes." Some for מעיני *mayenai*, "my fountains," would read with several of the *Versions*, מעוני *meoney*, "habitations;" but no MS. yet discovered supports this reading.

It would be a very natural cause of exultation, when considering the great privileges of this royal city, to know that all his friends, family, and children, were citizens of this city, were entered in God's register, and were entitled to his protection and favour. Applied to the Christian Church, the privileges are still higher: born of God, enrolled among the living in Jerusalem, having their hearts purified by faith, and being washed and made clean through the blood of the covenant, and sealed by the Holy Spirit of promise, such have a right to the inheritance among the saints in light. I need not add that *springs*, *wells*, *fountains*, and *cisterns*, and *waters* are used metaphorically in the sacred writings for children, posterity, fruitful women, people, &c.; see among others Prov. v. 15, 16; Psa. lxviii. 26; Isa. xlviii. 1; and Rev. xvii. 15. The old *Psalter* understands the whole as relating to Gospel times; and interprets it accordingly. Bishop Horne takes it in the same sense. The whole Psalm is obscure and difficult. I will venture a literal version of the whole, with a few explanatory interpolations, instead of notes, in order to cast a little more light upon it.

1. A Psalm *to be sung* by the posterity of Korah. A *prophetic* song.

2. "Jehovah loves his foundation, the city built by him on holy mountains. He loves the gates of Zion more than all the habitations of Jacob."

3. "Honourable things are declared of thee, O city of God. Selah."

4. "I will number Egypt and Babylon among my worshippers; behold Philistia and Tyre! They shall be born in the same place." They shall be considered as born in the city of God.

5. "But of Zion it shall be said, This one, and that one," persons of different nations, "was born in it, and the Most High shall establish it."

6. "Jehovah shall reckon in the registers of the people, This one was born there."

7. "The people shall sing, as in leading up a choir, All my fountains," the springs of my happiness, "are in thee."

I have nearly followed here the version of Mr. *N. M. Berlin*, who wonders that there should be any doubt concerning this translation of the last verse, when *Symmachus* and *Aquila*, who must have well known the sense of the Masoretic text, have translated: Και ᾳδοντης ως χοροι πασαι πηγαι εν σοι· "And they shall sing, as in leading up a dance, *All my fountains are in thee."* The translation cannot be far from the meaning.

ANALYSIS OF THE EIGHTY-SEVENTH PSALM

This Psalm contains marks of the beauty and perfection of the Church.

1. Its *foundation.* The author is GOD, it is *his foundation;* not laid in the *sand,* but upon the *mountains;* not common, but *holy mountains,* ver. 1.

2. The *Lord loveth his Church*—this assembly, beyond all others: "The Lord loveth," &c., ver. 2.

3. All the prophets have spoken *glorious things* concerning it, and have considered it as the "city of God," ver. 3.

4. One of the *glorious things* spoken of it was the *conversion* of the *Gentiles* to it. So here *Egyptians, Babylonians, Tyrians, Ethiopians,* &c., are to be gathered into it by regeneration. They shall all be brought to *know* the true God; and shall be classed in the multitude of those *who know him,* i. e., who offer him a pure and holy worship, ver. 4.

5. By having the word of God in this true Church, they shall be converted to God; so that it may be said, "This and that man were born to God in it," ver. 5.

6. All other cities shall decay and perish; but the Church of God, the city of the Great King, shall be *established for ever,* the gates of hell shall never prevail against it, ver. 5.

7. The converted Gentiles shall have equal privileges with the converted Jews; and in the Christian Church they shall all *be enrolled* without difference or precedence, ver. 6.

8. They shall *enjoy a perpetual solemnity.* They shall ever have cause to *sing* and *rejoice,* ver. 7.

9. The highest privilege is that in God's Church he opens the *fountains of living water;* in his ordinances God dispenses every blessing; every sincere and upright soul rejoices in opportunities to wait on God in his ordinances. Such a one can sing, "All my springs are in thee." All other *fountains* are *muddy;* this alone is as *clear as crystal.* Worldly springs yield no pure delight; all there are mixed and turbulent: all here are refreshing, satisfying, delightful.

PSALM LXXXVIII

The earnest prayer of a person in deep distress, abandoned by his friends and neighbours, and apparently forsaken of God, 1–18.

A Song *or* Psalm [a]for the sons of Korah, to the chief Musician upon Mahalath [b]Leannoth, [c]Maschil of [d]Heman the Ezrahite

O LORD [e]God of my salvation, I have [f]cried day *and* night before thee:

2 Let my prayer come before thee: incline thine ear unto my cry;

3 For my soul is full of troubles; and my life [g]draweth nigh unto the grave.

[a]Or, *of*——[b]That is, *To humble*——[c]Or, A Psalm *of Heman the Ezrahite, giving instruction*

[d]1 Kings iv. 31; 1 Chron. ii. 6——[e]Psa. xxvii. 9; li. 14——[f]Luke xviii. 7——[g]Psa. cvii. 18

NOTES ON PSALM LXXXVIII

Perhaps the *title* of this Psalm, which is difficult enough, might be thus translated: "A Poem to be sung to the conqueror, by the sons of Korah, responsively, in behalf of a distressed person; to give instruction to Heman the Ezrahite." *Kennicott* says this Psalm has *three* titles, but the last only belongs to it; and supposes it to be the prayer of a person shut up in a separate house, because of the leprosy, who seems to have been in the last stages of that distemper; this disease, under the Mosaic dispensation, being supposed to come from the immediate stroke of God. *Calmet* supposes it to refer to the captivity; the Israelitish nation being represented here under the figure of a person greatly afflicted through the whole course of his life. By some *Heman* is supposed to have been the author; but who he was is not easy to be determined. *Heman* and *Ethan,* whose names are separately prefixed to this and the following Psalm, are mentioned as the grandsons of Judah by his daughter-in-law Tamar, 1 Chron. ii. 6, for they were the sons of Zerah, his immediate son by the above. "And Tamar, his daughter-in-law, bare him Pharez and Zerah," ver. 4. "And the sons of Zerah, Zimri, and Ethan, and Heman, and Calcol, and Dara, (or Darda,") ver. 6. If these were the same persons mentioned 1 Kings iv. 31, they were *eminent in wisdom;* for it is there said that Solomon's wisdom "excelled the wisdom of all the children of the east country, and all the wisdom of Egypt. For he was wiser than all men; than Ethan the Ezrahite, and Heman, and Chalcol, and Darda, the sons of Mahol," ver. 30, 31. Probably *Zerah* was also called *Mahol.* If the Psalms in question were written by these men, they are the *oldest* poetical compositions extant; and the *most ancient part of Divine revelation,* as these persons lived at least *one hundred and seventy* years before Moses. This may be true of the *seventy-eighth* Psalm; but certainly not of the following, as it speaks of transactions that took place long afterwards, at least as late as the days of *David,* who is particularly mentioned in it. Were we sure of Heman as the author, there would be no difficulty in applying the whole of the Psalm to the state of the Hebrews in Egypt, persecuted and oppressed by Pharaoh. But to seek or labour to reconcile matters contained in the *titles* to the Psalms, is treating them with too much respect, as many of them are wrongly placed, and none of them Divinely inspired.

Verse 1. *O Lord God of my salvation*] This is only the *continuation of prayers and supplications* already often sent up to the throne of grace.

Verse 2. *Let my prayer come before thee*]

4 [h]I am counted with them that go down
into the pit: [i]I am as a man *that hath* no
strength:
5 Free among the dead, like the slain that
lie in the grave, whom thou rememberest no
more: and they are [k]cut off [l]from thy hand.
6 Thou hast laid me in the lowest pit, in
darkness, in the deeps.

---

[h]Psa. xxviii. 1——[i]Psa. xxxi. 12

[k]Isa. liii. 8——[l]Or, *by thy hand*

It is weak and helpless, though fervent and sincere: take all hinderances out of its way, and let it have a free passage to thy throne. One of the finest thoughts in the Iliad of *Homer* concerns *prayer;* I shall transcribe a principal part of this incomparable passage—incomparable when we consider its origin:—

Και γαρ τε Λιται εισι Διος κουραι μεγαλοιο,
Χωλαι τε, ῥυσσαι τε, παραβλωπες τ' οφθαλμω·
Αἱ ῥα τε και μετοπισθ' Ατης αλεγουσι κιουσαι·
'Η δ' Ατη σθεναρη τε και αρτιπος· οὑνεκα πασας
Πολλον ὑπεκπροθεει, φθανει δε τε πασαν επ' αιαν,
Βλαπτουσ' ανθρωπους· αἱ δ' εξακεονται οπισσω·
'Ος μεν τ' αιδεσεται κουρας Διος, ασσον ιουσας,
Τονδε μεγ' ωνησαν, και τ' εκλυον ευξαμενοιο.
'Ος δε κ' ανηνηται, και τε στερεως αποειπῃ,
Λισσονται δ' αρα ταιγε Δια Κρονιωνα κιουσαι,
Τῳ Ατην ἁμ' ἑπεσθαι, ἱνα βλαφθεις αποτισῃ.
Αλλ', Αχιλευ, πορε και συ Διος κουρῃσιν ἑπεσθαι
Τιμην, ἡτ' αλλων περ επιγναμπτει φρενας εσθλων.
Iliad., ix. 498-510.

Prayers are Jove's daughters; wrinkled, lame, slant-eyed,
Which, though far distant, yet with constant pace
Follow *offence.* Offence, robust of limb,
And treading firm the ground, outstrips them all,
And over all the earth, before them runs
Hurtful to man: *they,* following, heal the hurt.
Received respectfully when they approach,
They yield us aid, and listen when we pray.
But if we slight, and with obdurate heart
Resist them, to Saturnian Jove they cry.
Against, us supplicating, that *offence*
May cleave to us for vengeance of the wrong.
Thou, therefore, O Achilles! honour yield
To *Jove's own daughters,* vanquished as the brave
Have ofttimes been, by honour paid to thee.
COWPER.

On this allegory the translator makes the following remarks: "*Wrinkled,* because the countenance of a man, driven to prayer by a consciousness of guilt, is sorrowful and dejected. *Lame,* because it is a remedy to which men recur late, and with reluctance. *Slant-eyed,* either because in that state of humiliation they fear to lift up their eyes to heaven, or are employed in taking a retrospect of their past misconduct. The whole allegory, considering *when* and *where* it was composed, forms a very striking passage."

Prayer to God for mercy must have the qualifications marked above. *Prayer comes from God.* He *desires* to save us: this desire is impressed on our hearts by his Spirit, and *reflected* back to himself. Thus says the allegory, "Prayers are the daughters of Jupiter." But they are *lame,* as *reflected light* is much *less intense* and *vivid* than *light direct.* The desire of the heart is afraid to go into the presence of God, because the man knows, *feels,* that he has sinned against goodness and mercy. They are *wrinkled*—dried up and withered, with incessant longing: even the *tears* that refresh the soul are dried up and exhausted. They are *slant-eyed;* look aside through shame and confusion; dare not look God in the face. But *transgression* is strong, bold, impudent, and destructive: it treads with a *firm step* over the earth, bringing down curses on mankind. *Prayer and repentance follow,* but generally at a *distance.* The heart, being hardened by the deceitfulness of sin, does not *speedily* relent. They, however, *follow:* and when, with humility and contrition, they approach the throne of grace, they are *respectfully received.* God acknowledges them *as his offspring,* and *heals* the *wounds* made by *transgression.* If the heart remain *obdurate,* and the man *will not humble himself* before his God, then his *transgression cleaves to him,* and the heartless, lifeless prayers which he may offer in that state, presuming on God's mercy, will turn against him; and to such a one the sacrificial death and mediation of Christ are in vain. And this will be the case especially with the person who, having received an offence from another, *refuses to forgive.* This latter circumstance is that to which the poet particularly refers. See the whole passage, with its context.

Verse 4. *I am counted with them, &c.*] I am as good as dead; nearly destitute of life and hope.

Verse 5. *Free among the dead*] במתים חפשי *bammethim chophshi,* I rather think, means *stripped among the dead.* Both the *fourth* and *fifth* verses seem to allude to a *field of battle:* the *slain* and the *wounded,* are found scattered over the plain; the *spoilers* come among them, and strip, not only the *dead,* but those also who appear to be *mortally wounded,* and cannot recover, and are so feeble as not to be able to *resist.* Hence the psalmist says, "I am counted with them that go down into the pit; I am as a man that hath no strength," ver. 4. And I am stripped among the dead, like the mortally wounded (חללים *chalalim*) that lie in the grave. "Free among the dead," *inter mortuos liber,* has been applied by the fathers to our Lord's voluntary death: all others were *obliged* to die; he alone *gave up his life,* and could take it again, John x. 18. He went into the grave, and came out when he *chose.* The dead are *bound* in the grave; *he was free,* and not obliged to continue in that state as *they* were.

They are cut off from thy hand.] An allusion to the roll in which the general has the names of all that compose his army under their respective officers. And when one is killed, he is erased from this register, and *remembered no more,* as belonging to the army; but his name is entered among those who are dead, in a separate book. This latter is termed the *black book,* or the *book of death;* the other is called the *book of life,* or the *book* where the *living*

7 Thy wrath lieth hard upon me, and [m]thou hast afflicted *me* with all thy waves. Selah.

8 [n]Thou hast put away mine acquaintance far from me; thou hast made me an abomination unto them: *I am* shut up, and I cannot come forth.

9 [o]Mine eye mourneth by reason of affliction: LORD, I have called daily upon thee, [p]I have stretched out my hands unto thee.

10 [q]Wilt thou show wonders to the dead? shall the dead arise *and* praise thee? Selah.

11 Shall thy loving-kindness be declared in the grave? *or* thy faithfulness in destruction?

12 [r]Shall thy wonders be known in the dark? [s]and thy righteousness in the land of forgetfulness?

13 But unto thee have I cried, O LORD; and [t]in the morning shall my prayer prevent thee.

14 LORD, why castest thou off my soul? *why* hidest thou thy face from me?

15 I *am* afflicted and ready to die from *my* youth up: *while* [u]I suffer thy terrors I am distracted.

16 Thy fierce wrath goeth over me; thy terrors have cut me off.

17 They came round about me [v]daily like water; they compassed me about together.

18 [w]Lover and friend hast thou put far from me, *and* mine acquaintance into darkness.

[m]Psa. xlii. 7——[n]Job xix. 13; Psa. xxxi. 11; cxlii. 4——[o]Psa. xxxviii. 10——[p]Job xi. 13; Psa. cxliii. 6——[q]Psa. vi. 5; xxx. 9; cxv. 17; cxviii. 17; Isa. xxxviii. 18

[r]Job x. 21; Psa. cxliii. 3——[s]Psa. xxxi. 12——[t]Psa. v. 3——[u]Job vi. 4——[v]Or, *all the day*——[w]Psalm xxxi. 11; xxxviii. 11

are enrolled. From this circumstance, expressed in different parts of the sacred writings, the doctrine of unconditional reprobation and election has been derived. How wonderful!

Verse 7. *Thou hast afflicted* me *with all thy waves.*] The figures in this verse seem to be taken from a tempest at sea. The storm is fierce, and the waves cover the ship.

Verse 8. *Thou hast made me an abomination*] This verse has been supposed to express the *state of a leper*, who, because of the infectious nature of his disease, is *separated* from his *family*—is *abominable* to all, and at last *shut up* in a *separate house*, whence he does not *come out* to mingle with society.

Verse 10. *Wilt thou show wonders to the dead?*] מתים *methim, dead men.*

Shall the dead] רפאים *rephaim*, "the manes or departed spirits."

Arise and *praise thee?*] Any more in this life? The *interrogations* in this and the two following verses imply the strongest *negations.*

Verse 11. Or *thy faithfulness in destruction?*] *Faithfulness* in God refers as well to his *fulfilling his threatenings* as to his *keeping his promises.* The wicked are threatened with such *punishments* as their crimes have deserved; but *annihilation* is no *punishment.* God therefore does not intend to *annihilate* the wicked; their *destruction* cannot declare the *faithfulness of God.*

Verse 12. *The land of forgetfulness?*] The place of *separate spirits*, or the *invisible world.* The heathens had some notion of this state. They feigned a river in the invisible world, called *Lethe*, Ληθη, which signifies *oblivion*, and that those who drank of it remembered no more any thing relative to their former state.

——————Animæ, quibus altera fato
Corpora debentur, *lethæi* ad *fluminis undam*
Securos latices et *longa oblivia potant.*
VIRG. Æn. vi. 713.

To all those souls who round the river wait
New mortal bodies are decreed by fate;
To yon *dark stream* the gliding ghosts repair,
And quaff *deep draughts* of *long oblivion* there.

Verse 13. *Shall my prayer prevent thee.*] It shall get *before* thee; I will not wait till the accustomed time to offer my morning sacrifice, I shall call on thee long before others come to offer their devotions.

Verse 14. *Why castest thou off my soul?*] Instead of *my soul*, several of the ancient *Versions* have *my prayer.* Why dost thou refuse to *hear* me, and thus abandon me to *death?*

Verse 15. *From* my *youth up.*] I have always been a child of sorrow, afflicted in my body, and distressed in my mind. There are still found in the Church of God persons in similar circumstances; persons who are continually mourning for themselves and for the desolations of Zion. A disposition of this kind is sure to produce an unhealthy body; and indeed a weak constitution may often produce an enfeebled mind; but where the *terrors of the Lord* prevail, there is neither health of *body* nor peace of *mind.*

Verse 16. *Thy fierce wrath goeth over me.*] It is a mighty flood by which I am overwhelmed.

Verse 17. *They came round about me daily like water*] Besides his spiritual conflicts, he had many enemies to grapple with. The waves of God's displeasure broke over him, and his enemies came around him like water, increasing more and more, rising higher and higher, till he was at last on the point of being submerged in the flood.

Verse 18. *Lover and friend*] I have no comfort, and neither *friend* nor *neighbour* to sympathize with me.

Mine acquaintance into darkness.] All have forsaken me; or מידעי מחשך *meyuddai machsach*, "Darkness is my companion." Perhaps he may refer to the *death* of his acquaintances; all were gone; there was none left to console him! That man has a dismal lot who has outlived all his old friends and acquaintances; well may such complain. In the removal of their friends they see little else than the triumphs of death. *Khosroo*, an eminent Persian poet, handles this painful subject with great delicacy and beauty in the following lines:—

رفتم سوي خطيره بكريستيم بزار
از هجره دوستان كه اسير فنا شدند
گفتم ايشان كجا شدند و خطر
داد از صدا جواب ايشان كجا

Ruftem sauee khuteereh bekerestem bezar
Az Hijereh Doostan ke aseer fana shudend:
Guftem *Eeshah Kuja shudend?* ve Khatyr
Dad az sada jouab *Eeshan Kuja!*

"Weeping, I passed the place where lay my friends
Captured by death; in accents wild I cried,
Where are they? And stern Fate, by Echo's voice,
Returned in solemn sound the sad *Where are they?*"
J. B. C.

ANALYSIS OF THE EIGHTY-EIGHTH PSALM

There are *four* parts in this Psalm:—

I. A petition, ver. 1, 2.

II. The cause of this petition, his misery, which he describes, ver. 3-9.

III. The effects produced by this miserable condition: 1. A special prayer, ver. 10-12; 2. An expostulation with God for deliverance, ver. 10-12.

IV. A grievous complaint, ver. 14-18.

The psalmist offers his petition; but before he begins, he lays down four arguments why it should be admitted,—

1. His confidence and reliance on God: "O Lord God of my salvation."

2. His earnestness to prevail: "I have cried."

3. His assiduity: "Day and night."

4. His sincerity: "I have cried before thee."

And then he tenders his request for audience: "Let my prayer come before thee, incline thine ear unto my cry."

II. And then next he sets forth the pitiful condition he was in, that hereby he might move God to take compassion, which he amplifies several ways:—

1. From the weight and variety of his troubles; many they were, and pressed him to death. "For my soul is full of troubles, and my life draweth nigh to the grave."

2. From the danger of death in which he was. Which is illustrated by three degrees:—

1. That he was *moribundus, dying*, no hope of life in him even by the estimate of all men: "I am counted with them that go down to the pit; I am as a man that hath no strength."

2. That he was *plane mortuus, nearly dead;* but as a dead man, "free among the dead;" freed from all the business of this life; as far separate from them as a dead man.

3. Yea, dead and buried: "Like the slain that lie in the grave; whom thou rememberedst no more;" i. e., to care for in this life; and "they are cut off from thy hand," i. e., thy providence, thy custody, as touching matter of this life.

And yet he farther amplifies his sad condition by two similitudes:—

1. Of a man in some deep dark dungeon: "Thou hast laid me in the lowest pit, in darkness, in the deeps;" as was Jeremiah, chap. xxxvii.

2. Of a man in a wreck at sea, that is compassed with the waves, to which he compares God's anger: "Thy wrath lieth hard upon me, and thou hast afflicted me with all thy waves." One wave impels another. The recurrence of his troubles was perpetual; one no sooner gone but another succeeded.

And, to add to this his sorrow, his friends, whose visits in extremity used to alleviate the grief of a troubled soul, even these proved perfidious, and came not to him; he had no comfort with them; which was also God's doing, and thus augmented his grief.

The *auxesis* or *augmentation* is here very elegant:

1. "Thou hast put away mine acquaintance from me." THOU.

2. "Thou hast made me an abomination to them." No less; *an abomination.*

3. "I am shut up, I cannot come forth." As a man in prison, I cannot come at them, and they will not come to me.

III. The effect of which grievous affliction was threefold: 1. An internal grief and wasting of the body; 2. An ardent affection in God; and, 3. An expostulation with God.

1. "My eye mourns by reason of affliction." An evidence that I am troubled and grieved to the heart, that my eye droops and fails; for when the animal and vital spirits suffer a decay, the eye will quickly, by her dimness, deadness, and dulness, discover it.

2. It produced an ardent affection, a continuance and assiduity in prayer, which is here made evident by the adjuncts.

1. His *voice:* "I have called daily upon thee." It was, 1. A cry; 2. It was continual.

2. By the extension of his hands: "I have stretched out my hands to thee." Men used to do so when they expected help; when they looked to receive; whence we sometimes say, Lend me thy hand.

3. The third effect was, an expostulation with God, in which he presseth to spare his life from the inconvenience that might thereby happen, viz., that he should be disabled to praise God, and celebrate his name, as he was bound and desired to do, among the living: an argument used before, Psa. vi. 3. This argument, though it savours too much of human frailty, yet he thought by it to move God, who above all things is jealous of his own glory, which by his death he imagines will suffer loss; and therefore he asks,—

1. "Wilt thou show wonders among the dead?" That is, thy desire is to set forth thy honour, which cannot be done if I go to the grave, except by some miracle I should be raised from thence.

2. "Shall the dead arise again and praise thee?" It is the living that shall show forth thy praise, thy power, and goodness; thy fidelity in keeping thy promises to the sons of men. The dead, as dead, cannot do this; and they return not from the grave, except by miracle.

3. "Shall thy lovingkindness be declared in the grave, or thy faithfulness in destruction? shall thy wonders be known in the dark, or thy righteousness in the land of forgetfulness?" Such is the grave, a place of oblivion; for *Abraham* is ignorant of us. The goodness and faithfulness of God, which he makes known to us in this life, are not known nor can be declared by the dead: the living see them; they have experience of them; and therefore he desires that his life may be spared to that end, lest if he die now that faculty should be taken from him; he

should no longer be able to resound the praise of God, which is the end for which men ought to desire life.

IV. He returns to his complaint; and again repeats what he had said before, and almost in the same words, and gives *three* instances:—

1. In his prayer: "But unto thee have I cried, O Lord; and in the morning shall my prayer prevent thee." He prayed earnestly, early, not drowsily; for he did prevent God: he prayed, and would continue in prayer; and yet all in vain.

2. For God seems to be inexorable, of which he complains: "Lord, why castest thou off my soul? why hidest thou thy face from me?" Even the best of God's servants have sometimes been brought to that strait, that they have not had a clear sense of God's favour, but conceived themselves neglected and deserted by him, and discountenanced.

His *second* instance is, his present affliction, mentioned before, ver. 4, 5, 6, 7: "I am afflicted and ready to die," which he here exaggerates:—

1. From the time and continuance of it; for he had borne it "even from his youth up."

2. From the cause. It did not proceed from any outward or human cause; that might have been borne and helped: but it was an affliction sent from God: "Thy terrors have I suffered;" it came from a sense of God's wrath.

3. From an uncomfortable effect. It wrought in his soul amazement, unrest, a perpetual trouble and astonishment: "Thy terrors have I suffered with a troubled mind: "I am distracted with them."

He amplifies this wrath by the former similes, ver. 7; waves and water.

1. "Thy fierce wrath goes over me;" as waves over a man's head at sea. "Thy terrors have cut me off;" as a weaver's thrum.

2. "They came round about me like water; daily like water."

3. "They compassed me about together," as if they conspired my ruin: "all thy waves," ver. 7.

His *third* instance, which is the same, ver. 8. The perfidiousness and desertion of friends: a loving friend is some comfort in distress; but this he found not: "Lover and friend hast thou put far from me, and mine acquaintance into darkness." They appear no more to me to give me any counsel, help, or comfort, than if they were hidden in perpetual darkness. His case, therefore, was most deplorable.

PSALM LXXXIX

The psalmist shows God's great mercy to the house of David, and the promises which he had given to it of support and perpetuity, 1–37; *complains that, notwithstanding these promises, the kingdom of Judah is overthrown, and the royal family nearly ruined,* 38–45; *and earnestly prays for their restoration,* 46–52.

XVII. DAY. EVENING PRAYER

[a]Maschil of [b]Ethan the Ezrahite

[c]I WILL sing of the mercies of the LORD for ever: with my mouth will I make known thy faithfulness [d]to all generations.

2 For I have said, Mercy shall be built up for ever: [e]thy faithfulness shalt thou establish in the very heavens.

3 [f]I have made a covenant with my chosen, I have [g]sworn unto David my servant,

[a]Or, A Psalm *for Ethan the Ezrahite, to give instruction* [b]1 Kings iv. 31; 1 Chron. ii. 6——[c]Psa. ci. 1

[d]Heb. *to generation and generation;* so ver. 4——[e]Psa. cxix. 89——[f]1 Kings viii. 16——[g]2 Sam. vii. 11, &c.

NOTES ON PSALM LXXXIX

It is most probable that this Psalm was composed during the captivity. Of *Ethan* and *Heman* we have already seen something in the introduction to the preceding Psalm; see also the parallel places in the margin. The *title* should probably be translated,—*To give instruction to Ethan the Ezrahite.* The *Chaldee* has, "A good instruction, delivered by Abraham, who came from the east country." The *Septuagint* and *Æthiopic* have *Ethan the Israelite;* the *Arabic* has *Nathan the Israelite.*

The Psalm divides itself into *two* grand parts; the first extends from ver. 1 to 37, in which the psalmist shows God's mercy to the house of David, and the promises which he has given to it of support and perpetuity. The *second* part begins with ver. 38, and ends with the Psalm; and in it the author complains that, notwithstanding these promises, the kingdom of Judah is overthrown and the royal family ruined; and he entreats the Lord to remember his covenant made with that family, and restore them from their captivity.

Verse 1. *I will sing of the mercies of the Lord*] I will celebrate the mercy of God to the house of Jacob; the mercy that has been shown to our fathers from time *immemorial.*

To all generations] What I say concerning thy mercy and goodness, being inspired by thy Spirit, is not only *true,* but shall be *preserved* by the Divine providence for ever.

Verse 2. *Mercy shall be built up for ever*] God's *goodness* is the *foundation* on which his *mercy rests;* and from that source, and on that foundation, acts of mercy shall flow and be built up for ever and ever.

Thy faithfulness shalt thou establish] What thou hast promised to do to the children of men on earth, thou dost register in heaven; and thy promise shall never fail.

Verse 3. *I have made a covenant with my chosen*] I have made a covenant with Abraham, Isaac, and Jacob; and renewed it with Moses and Joshua in reference to the Israelites

4 [h]Thy seed will I establish for ever,
and build up thy throne [i]to all generations.
Selah.
5 And [k]the heavens shall praise thy wonders,
O LORD: thy faithfulness also in the congregation of the saints.
6 [l]For who in the heaven can be compared
unto the LORD? *who* among the sons of the
mighty can be likened unto the LORD?
7 [m]God is greatly to be feared in the assembly of the saints, and to be had in reverence
of all *them that are* about him.
8 O LORD God of hosts, who *is* a strong
LORD [n]like unto thee? or to thy faithfulness
round about thee?
9 [o]Thou rulest the raging of the sea: when
the waves thereof arise, thou stillest them.
10 [p]Thou hast broken [q]Rahab in pieces, as
one that is slain; thou hast scattered thine
enemies [r]with thy strong arm.

[h]Ver. 29, 36——[i]See ver. 1——[k]Psa. xix. 1——[l]Psa. xl. 5; lxxi. 19; lxxxvi. 8; cxiii. 5——[m]Psa. lxxvi. 7, 11 [n]Exod. xv. 11; 1 Sam. ii. 2; Psa. xxxv. 10; lxxi. 19

[o]Psa. lxv. 7; xciii. 3, 4; cvii. 29——[p]Exod. xiv. 26, 27, 28; Psa. lxxxvii. 4; Isa. xxx. 7; li. 9——[q]Or, *Egypt* [r]Heb. *with the arm of thy strength*

in general: but I have made one with David in especial relation to himself and posterity, of whom, according to the flesh, the Christ is to come. And this is the covenant with David:—

Verse 4. *Thy seed will I establish for ever, and build up thy throne to all generations.*] And this covenant had most incontestably Jesus Christ in view. This is the *seed*, or posterity, that should sit on the throne, and reign for ever and ever. David and his family are long since become extinct; none of his race has sat on the Jewish throne for more than *two thousand* years: but the Christ has reigned invariably since that time, and will reign till all his enemies are put under his feet; and to this the psalmist says *Selah.* It will be so; it is so; and it cannot be otherwise; for the Lord hath *sworn* that he shall have an *everlasting kingdom*, as he has an *everlasting priesthood.*

Verse 5. *The heavens shall praise thy wonders*] The works that shall be wrought by this descendant of David shall be so plainly miraculous as shall prove their origin to be Divine: and both saints and angels shall join to celebrate his praises.

Thy faithfulness also] All thy promises shall be fulfilled; and particularly and supereminently those which respect the *congregation of the saints*—the assemblies of Christian believers.

Verse 6. *For who in the heaven*] שחק *shachak* signifies the ethereal regions, all visible or unbounded space; the universe. Who is like Jesus? Even in his *human nature* none of *the sons of the mighty* can be compared with him. He atones for the sin of the world, and saves to the uttermost all who come unto God through him.

This may also be considered a reproof to idolaters. Is there any among the heavenly hosts like to God? Even the most glorious of them were made by his hands. Can the stars, or the more distant planets, or the moon, or the sun, be likened unto God most high?

Who *among the sons of the mighty*] Instead of אלים *elim, mighty ones,* four of *Kennicott's* and *De Rossi's* MSS. have איל *eil, strength:*— sons of strength, strong persons. Several of the *Versions* seem to have read אלהים *Elohim,* GOD, instead of אלים *elim,* strong ones. So my old Psalter, following the *Vulgate:*—**For wha in the clowdes sal be evened to Lorde; like sal be to God in sons of God!** which it paraphrases thus: "Emang al haly men nane may be evened to Ihu Crist: and nane may be like to hym in God's sons: for he is God's son be kynde, and thai thrugh grace."

Verse 7. *God is greatly to be feared*] In all religious assemblies the deepest reverence for God should rest upon the people. Where this does not prevail, there is no true worship. While some come with a proper Scriptural boldness to the throne of grace, there are others who come into the presence of God with a reprehensible, if not sinful, boldness.

Verse 8. *O Lord God of hosts*] Thou who hast all armies at thy command, and canst serve thyself by every part of thy creation, whether animate or inanimate.

Who is a strong Lord] See ver. 6.

Thy faithfulness round about thee?] Or, more properly, *thy faithfulness is round about thee.* Thou still keepest thy promises *in view.* God's *truth* leads him to fulfil his promises: they stand round his throne as the faithful servants of an eastern monarch stand round their master, waiting for the moment of their dismission to perform his will.

Verse 9. *Thou rulest the raging of the sea*] Whoever has seen the sea in a storm, when its waves run what is called *mountain high,* must acknowledge that nothing but omnipotent power could rule its raging.

When the waves thereof arise, thou stillest them.] Thou governest both its *flux* and *reflux.* Thou art the Author of *storms* and *calms.* There may be a reference here to the passage of the Red Sea, and the strong wind that agitated its waves at that time; as the next verse seems to indicate.

Verse 10. *Thou hast broken Rahab*] Thou hast destroyed the power of *Egypt,* having overthrown the king and its people when they endeavoured to prevent thy people from regaining their liberty.

As one that is slain] The whole clause in the original is, אתה דכאת כחלל רהב *attah dikkitha kechalal Rahab,* "Thou, like a hero, hast broken down Egypt." Dr. *Kennicott* has largely proved that חלל *chalal,* which we render *wounded, slain,* &c., means a *soldier, warrior, hero;* and it is certain that this sense agrees better with it than the other in a great number of places. Mr. *Berlin* translates, Tu contrivisti ut cadaver Ægyptum; "Thou hast bruised down Egypt like a dead carcass." The whole strength of Egypt could avail nothing against thee. Thou didst trample them down as easily as if they had all been dead carcasses.

11 [s]The heavens *are* thine, the earth also
is thine: *as for* the world and the fulness
thereof, thou hast founded them.
12 [t]The north and the south thou hast
created them: [u]Tabor and [v]Hermon shall
rejoice in thy name.
13 Thou hast [w]a mighty arm: strong is thy
hand, *and* high is thy right hand.
14 [x]Justice and judgment *are* the [y]habitation
of thy throne: [z]mercy and truth shall go
before thy face.
15 Blessed *is* the people that know the
[a]joyful sound: they shall walk, O LORD, in
the [b]light of thy countenance.
16 In thy name shall they rejoice all the day:
and in thy righteousness shall they be exalted.
17 For thou *art* the glory of their strength:
[c]and in thy favour our horn shall be exalted.
18 For [d]the LORD *is* our defence; and the
Holy One of Israel *is* our King.
19 Then thou spakest in vision to thy Holy
One, and saidst, I have laid help upon *one
that is* mighty; I have exalted *one* [e]chosen
out of the people.

---

[s]Gen. i. 1; 1 Chron. xxix. 11; Psa. xxiv. 1, 2; l. 12 —— [t]Job xxvi. 7 —— [u]Josh. xix. 12, 22; Judg. iv. 6, 12, 14; viii. 18; 1 Sam. x. 3; 1 Chron. vi. 17; Jer. xlvi. 18; Hos. v. 1 —— [v]Josh. xii. 1 —— [w]Hebrew, *an arm with might* —— [x]Psalm xcvii. 2 —— [y]Or, *establishment* —— [z]Psa. lxxxv. 13 —— [a]Num. x. 10; xxiii. 21; Psa. xcviii. 6 —— [b]Psa. iv. 6; xliv. 3 —— [c]Ver. 24; Psa. lxxv. 10; xcii. 10; cxxxii. 17 —— [d]Or, *our shield* is *of the LORD, and our king* is *of the Holy One of Israel;* Psa. xlvii. 9 —— [e]Ver. 3; 1 Kings xi. 34

Verse 11. *The heavens* **are** *thine*] **Thou art the Governor of all things, and the Disposer of all events.**

The world] **The terraqueous globe.**

And the fulness] **All the generations of men.** *Thou hast founded them*—**thou hast** *made* **them, and dost** *sustain* **them.**

After this verse, the *Editio Princeps* **of the Hebrew Bible, printed at Soncini, 1488, adds:—**

לך יום אף לך לילה

lailah lecha aph yom lecha

אתה הכינות מאור ושמש

vashamesh maor hachinotha attah

To thee is the day; also to thee is the night:
Thou hast prepared the light and the sun.

But these same words are found in Psa. lxxiv. 16.

Verse 12. *The north and the south*] **It is generally supposed that by these** *four* **terms all the four quarters of the globe are intended.** *Tabor,* **a mountain of Galilee, was on the** *west* **of Mount** *Hermon,* **which was beyond Jordan, to the** *east* **of the source of that river.**

Verse 14. *Justice and judgment* **are** *the habitation of thy throne*] **The throne—the government, of God, is founded in** *righteousness* **and** *judgment.* **He knows what is right; he sees what is right; he does what is right; and his** *judgments* **are ever according to righteousness. His decisions are all** *oracles;* **no one of them is ever reversed.**

Mercy and truth shall go before thy face.] **These shall be the** *heralds* **that shall announce the coming of the Judge. His** *truth* **binds him to fulfil all his declarations; and his** *mercy* **shall be shown to all those who have fled for refuge to the hope that is set before them in the Gospel. See the notes on Psa. lxxxv. 10, 11.**

Verse 15. *Blessed* **is** *the people*] **"O the blessednesses of that people (אשרי העם** *ashrey haam***) that know the joyful sound;" that are spared to hear the sound of the trumpet on the morning of the** *jubilee,* **which proclaims deliverance to the captives, and the restoration of all their forfeited estates. "They shall walk vigorously (יהלכון** *yehallechun***) in the light of thy countenance" (באור פניך** *beor paneycha***)—the full persuasion of the approbation of God their** *Father, Redeemer,* **and** *Sanctifier.*

Verse 16. *In thy name shall they rejoice*] **Or, "greatly exult," יגילון** *yegilun;* **"all that day," היום** *haiyom,* **the jubilee, referred to above.**

And in thy righteousness] **In the declaration of thy righteousness for the remission of sins that are past, Rom. iii. 25, 26.**

Shall they be exalted.] **They shall be justified freely from all things, be purified from all unrighteousness, grow in grace, and in the knowledge of Jesus Christ here below, and at last be exalted to his right hand to reign with him for ever. The jubilee was a type of the Gospel, and under that type the psalmist here speaks of the glorious advent of the Lord Jesus, and the great happiness of believers in him. Let it be observed that the letters in the above Hebrew words called** *paragogic,* **as ן** *nun* **in יהלכון** *yehallechuN,* **and יגילון** *yegiluN,* **always increase and deepen the meaning of the words to which they are attached.**

Verse 17. *For thou* **art** *the glory of their strength*] **They are strong in faith, and give glory to thee, because they know that their strength cometh from the Lord of hosts.**

And in thy favour our horn shall be exalted.] **Instead of תרום** *tarum,* **"shall be exalted," תרים** *tarim,* **"thou shalt exalt," is the reading of several MSS.: but תרום** *tarum,* **"shall be exalted," is supported by** *forty-four* **of** *Kennicott's* **MSS., and** *sixty* **of** *De Rossi's,* **as well as by several ancient editions, with the** *Septuagint, Syriac, Vulgate,* **and** *Arabic* **Versions. In the enjoyment of the Divine favour they shall grow more** *wise,* **more** *holy,* **more** *powerful,* **and, consequently, more** *happy.*

Verse 19. *Then thou spakest in vision to thy holy one*] **Instead of חסידך** *chasidecha,* **"thy holy one," חסידיך** *chasideycha,* **"thy holy ones," is the reading of** *sixty-three* **of** *Kennicott's* **and** *seventy-one* **of** *De Rossi's* **MSS., and a great number of** *editions* **besides.**

If we take it in the *singular,* **it most probably means** *Samuel,* **and refers to the** *revelation* **God gave to him relative to his appointment of** *David* **to be king in the stead of Saul. If we take it in the** *plural,* **it may mean not only** *Samuel,* **but also** *Nathan* **and** *Gad.*

20 [f]I have found David my servant; with
my holy oil have I anointed him:
21 [g]With whom my hand shall be established: mine arm also shall strengthen
him.
22 [h]The enemy shall not exact upon him;
nor the son of wickedness afflict him.
23 [i]And I will beat down his foes before
his face, and plague them that hate him.
24 But [k]my faithfulness and my mercy *shall*
be with him: and [l]in my name shall his horn
be exalted.
25 [m]I will set his hand also in the sea, and
his right hand in the rivers.
26 He shall cry unto me, Thou *art* [n]my
father, my God, and [o]the rock of my salvation.
27 Also I will make him [p]*my* first-born,
[q]higher than the kings of the earth.
28 [r]My mercy will I keep for him for evermore, and [s]my covenant shall stand fast with
him.
29 [t]His seed also will I make *to endure* for
ever, [u]and his throne [v]as the days of heaven.
30 [w]If his children [x]forsake my law, and
walk not in my judgments;
31 If they [y]break my statutes, and keep not
my commandments;
32 Then [z]will I visit their transgression
with the rod, and their iniquity with stripes.

---

[f]1 Sam. xvi. 1, 12——[g]Psa. lxxx. 17——[h]2 Sam. vii. 10——[i]2 Sam. vii. 9——[k]Psa. lxi. 7——[l]Ver. 17——[m]Psa. lxxii. 8; lxxx. 11——[n]2 Sam. vii. 14; 1 Chron. xxii. 10——[o]2 Sam. xxii. 47——[p]Psa. ii. 7; Col. i. 15, 18

[q]Num. xxiv. 7——[r]Isa. lv. 3——[s]Ver. 34——[t]Ver. 4, 36——[u]Ver. 4; Isa. ix. 7; Jer. xxxiii. 17——[v]Deut. xi. 21——[w]2 Sam. vii. 14——[x]Psa. cxix. 53; Jer. ix. 13——[y]Heb. *profane my statutes*——[z]2 Sam. vii. 14; 1 Kings xi. 31

For what God revealed to *Samuel* relative to David, see 2 Sam. vii. 5, &c.; 1 Chron. xi. 2, 3; and for what he said to *Nathan* on the same subject, see 1 Chron. xvii. 3, 7-15. All the *Versions* have the word in the *plural.*

Verse 20. *I have found David my servant*] This is the sum of what God had said in prophetic *visions* to his *saints* or holy persons, *Samuel, Nathan,* and *Gad;* see the parallel places in the *margin.* Here the psalmist begins to reason with God relative to David, his posterity, and the perpetuity of his kingdom; which promises appear now to have utterly failed, as the throne had been overturned, and all the people carried into captivity. But all these things may have reference to *Christ* and his kingdom; for we are assured that David was a type of the Messiah.

Verse 22. *The enemy shall not exact upon him*] None of his enemies shall be able to prevail against him. It is worthy of remark that David was never overthrown; he finally conquered every foe that rose up against him. Saul's persecution, Absalom's revolt, Sheba's conspiracy, and the struggle made by the partisans of the house of Saul after his death, only tended to call forth David's skill, courage, and prowess, and to seat him more firmly on his throne. The Philistines, the Ammonites, the Syrians, &c., united all their forces to crush him, but in vain: "God beat down all his foes before his face," and variously *plagued* those who opposed him, ver. 23.

Verse 25. *I will set his hand also in the sea*] This was literally fulfilled in David. *Hand* signifies power or authority; he set his hand on the sea in *conquering* the Philistines, and extending his empire along the coast of the Mediterranean Sea, from Tyre to Pelusium. All the coasts of the Red Sea, the Persian Gulf, and the Arabic Ocean, might be said to have been under his *government,* for they all paid tribute to *him* or his son Solomon.

His right hand in the rivers] First, the Euphrates: he subjected all Syria, and even a part of Mesopotamia; 2 Sam. viii. 3; 1 Chron. xviii. 3. He also took Damascus, and consequently had his *hand* or authority over the river Chrysorrhoes, or Baraddi; and in his conquest of all Syria his hand must have been on the *Orontes* and other rivers in that region. But if this be considered as referring to the typical David, we see that *He* was never conquered; he never lost a battle; the hosts of hell pursued him in vain. Satan was discomfited, and all his enemies bruised under his feet. Even over *death* he triumphed; and as to his dominion, it has spread and is spreading over all the isles of the sea, and the continents of the world.

Verse 27. *I will make him* my *first-born*] I will deal with him as a father by his *first-born son,* to whom a double portion of possessions and honours belong. *First-born* is not always to be understood *literally* in Scripture. It often signifies simply a *well-beloved,* or *best-beloved son;* one preferred to all the rest, and distinguished by some eminent prerogative. Thus God calls Israel *his son,* his *first-born,* Exod. iv. 22. See also Ecclus. xxxvi. 12. And even Ephraim is called God's *first-born,* Jer. xxxi. 9. In the same sense it is sometimes applied even to *Jesus Christ himself,* to signify his super-eminent dignity; not the *eternal Sonship* of his *Divine nature,* as inveterate prejudice and superficial thinking have supposed.

Verse 29. *His seed also will I make* to endure *for ever*] This can apply only to the spiritual David. The posterity of David are long since extinct, or so blended with the remaining Jews as to be utterly indiscernible; but Jesus ever liveth, and his seed (*Christians*) are spread, and are spreading over all nations; and *his* throne is eternal. As to his *manhood,* he is of the house and lineage of David; the government is upon his shoulders, and of its increase there shall be no end, upon the throne of David and on his kingdom to order it and to establish it with judgment and justice, from henceforth even for ever. Isa. ix. 7.

Verse 30. *If his children forsake my law*] See the notes on 2 Sam. vii. 13, where this

33 [a]Nevertheless my lovingkindness [b]will I not utterly take from him, nor suffer my faithfulness [c]to fail.

34 My covenant will I not break, nor alter the thing that is gone out of my lips.

35 Once have I sworn [d]by my holiness [e]that I will not lie unto David.

36 [f]His seed shall endure for ever, and his throne [g]as the sun before me.

37 It shall be established for ever as the moon, and *as* a faithful witness in heaven. Selah.

38 But thou hast [h]cast off and [i]abhorred, thou hast been wroth with thine anointed.

39 Thou hast made void the covenant of thy servant; [k]thou hast profaned his crown *by casting it* to the ground.

40 [l]Thou hast broken down all his hedges; thou hast brought his strong holds to ruin.

41 All that pass by the way spoil him: he is [m]a reproach to his neighbours.

42 Thou hast set up the right hand of his adversaries; thou hast made all his enemies to rejoice.

43 Thou hast also turned the edge of his sword, and hast not made him to stand in the battle.

44 Thou hast made his [n]glory to cease, and [o]cast his throne down to the ground.

45 The days of his youth hast thou shortened: thou hast covered him with shame. Selah.

[a]2 Sam. vii. 13——[b]Heb. *I will not make void from him*——[c]Heb. *to lie*——[d]Amos iv. 2——[e]Heb. *If I lie*——[f]2 Sam. vii. 16; Luke i. 33; John xii. 34; ver. 4, 29——[g]Psa. lxxii. 5, 17; Jer. xxxiii. 20

[h]1 Chron. xxviii. 9; Psa. xliv. 9; lx. 1, 10——[i]Deut. xxxii. 19; Psa. lxxviii. 59——[k]Psa. lxxiv. 7; Lam. v. 16——[l]Psa. lxxx. 12——[m]Psa. xliv. 13; lxxix. 4——[n]Heb. *brightness*——[o]Verse 39

and some of the following verses are explained.

Verse 34. *My covenant will I not break*] My determination to establish a spiritual kingdom, the head of which shall be Jesus, the son of David, shall never fail. My prophets have declared this, and I will not alter the thing that is gone out of my mouth.

Verse 35. *Once have I sworn*] I have made one determination on this head, and have bound myself by my holiness; it is impossible that I should change, and there needs no second oath, the one already made is of endless obligation.

Verse 36. *His throne as the sun*] Splendid and glorious! dispensing light, heat, life, and salvation to all mankind.

Verse 37. *As the moon, and* as *a faithful witness in heaven.*] That is, as long as the sun and moon shall endure, as long as *time* shall last, his kingdom shall last among men. The moon appears to be termed *a faithful witness* here, because by her particularly *time* is measured. Her *decrease* and *increase* are especially observed by every nation, and by these time is generally estimated, especially among the eastern nations. *So many moons is a man old; so many moons since such an event happened;* and even their years are reckoned by *lunations.* This is the case with the Mohammedans to the present day. Or the *rainbow* may be intended; that sign which God has established in the cloud; that faithful witness of his that the earth shall no more be destroyed by water. As long therefore as the *sun,* the *moon,* and the *rainbow* appear in the heavens, so long shall the spiritual David reign, and his seed prosper and increase.

Selah.] It is confirmed; it shall not fail.

Verse 38. *But thou hast cast off*] Hitherto the psalmist has spoken of the *covenant of God with David* and his family, which led them to expect all manner of prosperity, and a perpetuity of the Jewish throne; now he shows what appears to him a failure of the promise, and what he calls in the next verse the *making void the covenant of his servant.* God cannot lie to David; how is it then that his *crown is profaned,* that it is cast *down to the ground;* the land being possessed by strangers, and the twelve tribes in the most disgraceful and oppressive captivity?

Verse 40. *Thou hast broken down all his hedges*] Thou hast permitted the land to be stripped of all defence; there is not even one strong place in the hands of thy people.

Verse 41. *All that pass by the way spoil him.*] The land is in the condition of a vineyard, the hedge of which is broken down, so that they who pass by may pull the grapes, and dismantle or tear down the vines. The *Chaldeans* and the *Assyrians* began the ravage; the *Samaritans* on the one hand, and the *Idumeans* on the other, have completed it.

Verse 42. *Thou hast set up the right hand of his adversaries*] Thou hast given them that *strength* which thou didst formerly give to thy own people; therefore *these* are depressed, *those* exalted.

Verse 43. *Thou hast also turned the edge of his sword.*] The arms and military prowess of thy people are no longer of any use to them; THOU art *against* them, and therefore they are fallen. In what a perilous and hopeless situation must that soldier be who, while defending his life against his mortal foe, has his sword *broken,* or its *edge turned;* or, in modern warfare, whose *gun misses fire!* The *Gauls,* when invaded by the Romans, had no method of *hardening iron;* at every blow their swords *bended,* so that they were obliged, before they could strike again, to put them under their foot or over their knee, to straighten them; and in most cases, before this could be done, their better armed foe had taken away their life! The edge of their sword was turned, so that they could not stand in battle; and hence the *Gauls* were conquered by the Romans.

Verse 44. *Thou hast made his glory to cease*] The kingly dignity is destroyed, and there is neither *king* nor *throne* remaining.

Verse 45. *The days of his youth hast thou shortened*] Our kings have not reigned half

46 [p]How long, LORD? wilt thou hide thyself for ever? [q]shall thy wrath burn like fire?

47 [r]Remember how short my time is: wherefore hast thou made all men in vain?

48 [s]What man *is he that* liveth, and shall not [t]see death? shall he deliver his soul from the hand of the grave? Selah.

49 LORD, where *are* thy former lovingkindnesses, *which* thou [u]swarest unto David [v]in thy truth?

50 Remember, LORD, the reproach of thy servants; [w]*how* I do bear in my bosom *the reproach of* all the mighty people;

51 [x]Wherewith thine enemies have reproached, O LORD; wherewith they have reproached the footsteps of thine anointed.

52 [y]Blessed *be* the LORD for evermore. Amen, and Amen.

[p]Psa. lxxix. 5——[q]Psa. lxxviii. 63——[r]Job vii. 7; x. 9; xiv. 1; Psa. xxxix. 5; cxix. 84——[s]Psa. xlix. 9

[t]Heb. xi. 5——[u]2 Sam. vii. 15; Isa. lv. 3——[v]Psa. liv. 5 [w]Psa. lxix. 9, 19——[x]Psa. lxxiv. 22——[y]Psa. xli. 13

their days, nor lived out half their lives. The *four* last kings of Judea reigned but a short time, and either died by the sword or in captivity.

Jehoahaz reigned only *three months*, and was led captive to Egypt, where he *died*. *Jehoiakim* reigned only *eleven years*, and was tributary to the Chaldeans, who *put him to death*, and cast his body into the common sewer. *Jehoiachin* reigned *three months* and *ten days*, and was led *captive* to Babylon, where he continued in prison to the time of Evilmerodach, who, though he loosed him from prison, never invested him with any power. *Zedekiah*, the last of all, had reigned only *eleven years* when he was taken, *his eyes put out*, was *loaded with chains*, and thus carried to Babylon. Most of these kings died a violent and *premature* death. Thus the *days of their youth*—of their power, dignity, and life, *were shortened*, and they themselves *covered with shame*. *Selah;* so it most incontestably is.

Verse 46. *How long, Lord?*] The promise cannot utterly fail. When then, O Lord, wilt thou restore the kingdom to Israel?

Verse 47. *How short my time is*] If thou deliver not speedily, none of the present generations shall see thy salvation. Are all the remnants of our tribes created in vain? shall they never see happiness?

Verse 48. *What man* is he that *liveth*] All men are mortal, and death is uncertain and no man, by wisdom, might, or riches, can deliver his life from the *hand*—the power, of death and the grave.

Verse 49. *Lord, where* are *thy former lovingkindnesses*] Wilt thou not deal with *us* as thou didst with our *fathers?* Didst thou not swear unto David that thou wouldst distinguish *him* as thou didst *them?*

Verse 50. *I do bear in my bosom*] Our enemies, knowing our confidence, having often heard our boast in thee, and now seeing our low and hopeless estate, mock us for our confidence, and blaspheme *thee*. This wounds my soul; I cannot bear to hear thy name blasphemed among the heathen. *All these mighty people* blaspheme the God of Jacob.

Verse 51. *They have reproached the footsteps of thine anointed.*] They search into the whole history of thy people; they trace it up to the earliest times; and they find we have been disobedient and rebellious; and on this account we suffer much, alas, *deserved* reproach. The *Chaldee* gives this clause a singular turn: "Thy enemies have reproached the slowness of the footsteps of the feet of thy Messiah, O Lord. We have trusted in him as our great Deliverer, and have been daily in expectation of his coming: but there is no deliverer, and our enemies mock our confidence." This expectation seems *now* wholly abandoned by the Jews: they have rejected the *true Messiah*, and the ground of their expectation of *another* is now cut off. When will they turn unto the Lord? When shall the veil be taken away from their hearts?

> "Bend by thy grace, O *bend* or *break*
> The *iron sinew* in their neck!"

Verse 52. *Blessed* be *the Lord for evermore.*] Let him treat us as he will, his name deserves eternal praises: our affliction, though great, is less than we have deserved.

This verse concludes the THIRD BOOK of the PSALTER; and, I think, has been added by a later hand, in order to make this *distinction*, as every *Masoretic* Bible has something of this kind at the end of each book. The verse is wanting in one of *Kennicott's* and one of *De Rossi's* MSS.; in *another* it is written without points, to show that it does not belong to the text, and in *three* others it is written *separately* from the text. It is found, however, in all the ancient *Versions*. The *Chaldee* finishes thus: "Blessed be the name of the Lord in this world. Amen and Amen. Blessed be the name of the Lord in the world to come. Amen and Amen." And the reader will find no difficulty to subscribe his Amen, so be it.

ANALYSIS OF THE EIGHTY-NINTH PSALM

In this Psalm the stability and perpetuity of Christ's kingdom, of which the kingdom of David was but a type, are excellently described and foretold.

The *parts* of this Psalm are these:—

I. The *argument* and *sum* of the whole; the loving-kindness and the truth of God, ver. 1, 2.

II. The *particular instance* of God's goodness and truth in making a covenant with David, ver. 3, 4.

III. A *doxology* in which God is praised for his wonders, faithfulness, power, providence, justice, judgment, mercy, and truth, ver. 3-15

IV. The *happy state* of God's people, ver. 15-19.

V. A *special example* of God's goodness towards his Church, *exemplified* in David, but *verified* in Christ, ver. 20-28.

VI. How David's *posterity should be dealt with*, on their disobedience, ver. 29-38.

VII. An *expostulation* on the contrary events, where the psalmist deplores the ruined state of the Jewish kingdom, ver. 38-47.

VIII. A *petition* for mercy and restoration, ver. 48-51.

IX. The *conclusion*, in which the psalmist blesseth God for the hope he has in his favour, in all states, ver. 52.

I. The *argument* or *sum* of the Psalm set down in the *first verse*, and amplified by the reason in the *second*.

1. "I will sing." I will set this forth in a song; because, 1. It is the fittest way to express joy for any thing. 2. It will be best inculcated in this way. 3. It will be more easily remembered; and, 4. More easily delivered to others, in order to be remembered. Many ancient histories had not been preserved at all, had they not been delivered in *poetry*.

2. "Of thy mercies." Plurally, for they are many; and a song of this kind should be of *all*.

3. "For ever." Intentionally, not in himself, not actually; for as a wicked man, could he live always, would sin always; so a good man, could he live here for ever, would sing for ever of the mercies of the Lord.

4. "With my mouth will I make known," &c. While I live I will make them known, and when I am dead they shall be known by the record which I leave behind. His reason for it is, because God's mercy is everlasting; it is therefore proper to be the subject of everlasting song.

1. "For I have said." This is an indubitable truth.

2. "Mercy shall be built up for ever." It is not exhausted in one age, but, as a house built on a strong foundation, it shall be firm, and last from age to age.

3. "Thy faithfulness shalt thou establish." As is thy *mercy*, so is thy faithfulness, perpetual as the heavens.

II. For the proof of God's goodness and truth he produces the instance of the covenant made with David, where he brings in God speaking:—

1. "I have made a covenant with my chosen." I have made this covenant through my mere mercy, not on account of their merits. I have chosen David, not because he *deserved* it, but because he is fit for it.

2. "I have sworn." In compassion to the weakness of men, I have condescended to bind myself by an oath; and the covenant and the oath are extant. 2 Sam. vii. 11.

3. The tenor of the covenant is, "Thy seed will I establish for ever, and build up thy throne to all generations." *Thy seed*—this is true of Christ only, who was of the seed of David, and of whose kingdom there shall be no end. The words are not to be understood of David's earthly kingdom, but of Christ's spiritual kingdom, for that alone will be established for ever.

III. A Doxology. What the psalmist undertook in the *first* part he now performs, and thus he begins: "The heavens shall praise." By these some understand the Church, and the preachers in the Church; others, the *angels:* both are true. God's *followers* and his *angels* praise him; and the subject of their praise is:—

1. God's *wondrous works*, and his *truth*. 2. The manner in which he showed his works and his truth, in promising the Messiah, and in so faithfully keeping that promise.

And now he sings praise to his majesty, setting forth his power in *three* respects:—

1. By way of comparison; there is nothing in heaven or earth equal to it, ver. 6-8.

2. By his agency in governing the world: as, for example, the *sea*, Thou stillest the raging of it, &c.

3. The creation of all things; the world and its fulness.

The other part of the praise, sung both by the prophets and the angels, is taken from his attributes, summed up in ver. 14: "Justice and judgment are the habitation of thy throne; mercy and truth shall go before thy face."

He represents God as a great King sitting in his throne; the *basis* of which is, 1. *Justice* and *Judgment*. 2. The *attendants* are *mercy* and *truth*.

1. Justice, which defends his subjects, and does every one right.

2. Judgment, which restrains rebels, and keeps off injuries.

3. Mercy, which shows compassion, pardons, supports the weak.

4. Truth, that performs whatsoever he promiseth.

IV. And in regard that God is powerful, just, merciful, faithful, he takes an occasion to set out the happy condition of God's people, who live under this King.

"Blessed are the people that know the joyful sound:" that is, do know that God is present with them, and his kingly Majesty is at hand to protect them. The phrase is taken from *Moses*. For the law was given by sound of trumpet. The calling of the feasts was by sound of trumpet: at that sound they removed; at that sound they assembled. *Balaam* said, "The sound of a king is among them." Happy, then, are the people that know the joyful sound. God presents their King speaking, ruling, defending, pardoning them. Or it may refer to the year of jubilee, (see the notes.) That they are happy, the effects do evince; which are:—

1. "They shall walk in the light of thy countenance," i. e., though beset with troubles, yet they shall walk confidently, being assured of God's favour.

2. "In thy name shall they rejoice all the day long." Their joy is firm.

3. "In thy righteousness shall they be exalted." They shall get a name, strength. In their union and communion with God they shall be happy.

Confident, yea, joyful and strong they are in all temptations; which yet they have not from themselves. All is from God. For "thou art the glory of their strength, and in thy favour our horn shall be exalted. For the Lord is our defence, the Holy One of Israel is our King."

V. The doxology being now ended, and the happiness of God's people expressed and proved, the prophet now enlarges himself upon the covenant formerly mentioned, ver. 4, 5, exemplified in *David*, but truly verified in *Christ*. Which he continues to verse 30.

1. "Then," i. e., when *David* was chosen to be king, and invested with the regal robe.

2. "Thou spakest in vision to thy Holy One." To *Samuel* for his anointing; and saidst,

3. "I have laid help upon one that is mighty; I have exalted one chosen out of the people." That is, *David* in type, but *Christ* in the antitype. So explained, "I have found *David* my servant; with my holy oil have I anointed him."

To which there follow the promises made to him:—

1. For his establishment and confirmation in the throne: "With whom my hand shall be established; mine arm also shall strengthen him."

2. For protection against his enemies: "The enemy shall not exact upon him, nor the son of wickedness afflict him."

3. A conquest over his enemies: "And will beat down his foes before his face, and plague them that hate him."

4. And that there be no doubt of the performance of these ample promises, nor yet those that follow, the prophet interposes the cause, viz., the faithfulness and mercy of God. In mercy he said it, and it should so come to pass: "But my faithfulness and mercy shall be with him." And now he goes on:—

5. "His horn shall be exalted." His power shall be greatly increased.

And this his exaltation appears:—

1. In the dilatation of his empire: "I will set his hand also in the sea, and his right hand in the rivers," i. e., from the sea to *Euphrates*, 2 Sam. viii.

2. In the honour done him, to call God Father, his God, his Rock: "He shall call to me, Thou art my Father, my God, and the Rock of my salvation."

3. Then that God asserts and fixes this prerogative upon him, acknowledging him to be his Son; his first-born Son: "Also I will make him my first-born, higher than the kings of the earth."

4. In the perpetuity of his kingdom, which is rightly attributed to God's mercy; as ver. 25: "My mercy will I keep for him for evermore, and my covenant shall stand fast with him."

5. In the promise made to his seed: "His seed also will I make to endure for ever, and his throne as the days of heaven."

VI. And next the prophet puts a case, and answers it: But what, if *David's* seed transgress God's covenant, break his laws, violate his statutes, become rebels and disobedient; will God then *keep covenant with them? shall his seed endure for ever? and his throne as the days of heaven?* To this doubt God answers, from ver. 30 to 38; showing us how David's seed, if they transgress, shall be dealt with.

1. "If his children forsake my law;" that is, my whole doctrine of worship, religion, faith, &c.

2. "And walk not in my judgments;" i. e., in those laws which set out rewards and punishments.

3. "If they break my statutes." Those statutes I have set down for my service, the rites, ceremonies, new moons, Sabbaths, sacrifices, circumcision, passover, &c.

4. "And keep not my commandments;" that is, the decalogue and moral law. In a word, if they become vicious in their morals, and profane, and rebels in my worship and religion.

This then shall happen unto them,—escape they shall not, but shall soundly smart for it. They shall feel,—1. *The rod;* and, 2. *The scourge.* Then,

1. "I will visit (that is, punish) their transgression with the rod."

2. "And their iniquity with stripes." Which was often done by the *Babylonians, Antiochus*, &c. And yet in judgment I will remember mercy. I will remember my covenant, my promise, my word, my oath, and will make that good. I will not totally cast off David's seed; which I mean not after the flesh, for that is long since cast off, but after the Spirit. *Christ*, which was of the seed of *David*, and those which are his seed, viz., the Church, shall enjoy the benefit of my covenant and oath for ever: "Nevertheless, my loving-kindness will I not utterly take from him, nor suffer my faithfulness to fail. My covenant will I not break, nor alter the thing gone out of my lips."

And that there be no doubt of this, he brings in God repeating his oath and covenant.

1. His oath: "Once have I sworn by my holiness;" that is, by myself, who am holy.

2. His covenant: "That I will not lie unto David; for his seed shall endure for ever, and his throne as the sun before me. It shall be established for ever as the moon, and as a faithful witness in heaven." As the sun and moon are not liable to any ruinous mutations, no more is this covenant: they must endure to the end of the world; and so must this covenant. They are faithful witnesses in heaven; and so we are to seek for the performance of this covenant in heaven; not in the earth, the covenant being about a heavenly kingdom, not an earthly; it being evident that the kingdom of *David* on earth has failed many ages since: but that of *Christ* shall never fail.

VII. Now that *David's* kingdom did fail, or at least was brought to a low ebb, is the complaint in the following words, which flesh and blood considering, gave a wrong judgment upon it, as if God did nothing less than perform his oath and covenant. This is what the prophet lays to God's charge: "But thou hast cut off and abhorred, thou hast been wroth with thine anointed." Both king and people are cast aside, than which nothing seems more contrary to thy covenant.

Thou hast made void the covenant of thy servant, of which there are many lamentable consequences:—

1. "His crown is cast to the ground." The glory of his kingdom trampled upon.

2. "His hedges broken down." His strongholds brought to ruin.

3. "All that pass by the way spoil him." He is exposed to all rapine and plunder.

4. "He is a reproach to his neighbour." Exposed to all contumely and disgrace.

5. "Thou hast set up the right hand of his enemies, and made all his adversaries to rejoice." Thou seemest to take part with the enemy against him, and makest him to exult and rejoice in oppressing him.

6. "Thou hast also turned the edge of his sword, (blunted his sword that was wont to slay,) and hast not made him to stand in the battle," but to fly and turn his back.

7. "Thou hast made his glory (the glory, dignity, authority of his kingdom) to cease, and cast his crown to the ground."

8. "The days of his youth hast thou shortened;" cut him off in the prime and strength of his years. "Thou hast covered him with shame;" made his opulent, glorious kingdom ignominious; which was true in divers of *David's* posterity, especially *Jehoiakim*.

These were the sad complaints which the prophet pours out; but he quickly recovers and recalls his thoughts; and that he may move God to help, he falls to prayer, which is very pathetic.

VIII. He considers the nature of God as kind, loving, merciful, slow to anger; and asks,—

1. "How long, Lord? wilt thou hide thyself for ever?" Hide thy favour?

2. "Shall thy wrath burn like fire?" An element that hath no mercy.

He then uses other arguments, pathetically expressed, to move God to pity:—

1. Drawn from the brevity of man's life: "Remember how short my time is."

2. From the end for which man was created; not in vain, but to be an object of God's goodness and favour.

3. From the weakness and disability of man. His life is short; and can he lengthen it? "What man is he that liveth, and shall not see death?" Yea, though he live long, yet he is a mortal creature: "Shall he deliver his soul from the grave?"

4. From the covenant, of which he puts God in mind: "Lord, where are thy former lovingkindnesses, which thou swarest to David in thy truth?"

5. From the ignominy, scorns, sarcasms, by enemies cast upon them, which he desires God to look upon. 1. "Remember, Lord, the reproach of thy servant." 2. "And how I do bear in my bosom." Not spoken afar off, but in my hearing, and to my face, as if poured and emptied into my bosom; the *rebukes* not of this or that man, but of *many people.*

6. And lastly, that these reproaches, in effect, fall upon God. For they who reproach God's servants are his enemies: "Remember the reproaches"—1. "Wherewith thine enemies have reproached, O Lord." 2. "Wherewith they have reproached the footsteps of thine anointed," i. e., either whatsoever he says or does; or else by *footsteps* is to be understood the latter end of *David's* kingdom, which was indeed subject to reproach. 3. But the *Chaldee* paraphrast by *footsteps* understands the coming of the Messiah in the flesh; which, because it was long promised and men saw not performed, many derided, mocked, and reproached, as vain.

IX. The close of this long Psalm is a *benediction*, by which the prophet, after his combat with flesh and blood about the performance of the covenant, composes his troubled soul, and acquiesces in God; blessing him for whatever falls out, breaking forth into:—

1. "Blessed be the Lord for evermore:" Blessed be his name, who does and orders all things for the best of his people, although in the midst of calamities and troubles he seems to desert them.

2. And that we may know that he did this from his heart, he seals it with a double Amen. "Amen, Amen." So I wish it; so be it.

PSALM XC

The eternity of God, 1, 2; *the frailty of the state of man,* 3–9; *the general limits of human life,* 10; *the danger of displeasing God,* 11; *the necessity of considering the shortness of life, and of regaining the favour of the Almighty,* 12; *earnest prayer for the restoration of Israel,* 13–17.

XVIII. DAY. MORNING PRAYER

[a]A Prayer [b]of Moses the man of God

LORD, [c]thou hast been our dwelling-place
[d]in all generations.

2 [e]Before the mountains were brought forth,
or ever thou hadst formed the earth and the
world, even from everlasting to everlasting,
thou *art* God.

[a]Or, *A Prayer* being a Psalm *of Moses*——[b]Deut. xxxiii. 1——[c]Deut. xxxiii. 27; Ezek. xi. 16

[d]Hebrew, *in generation and generation*——[e]Proverbs viii. 25, 26

NOTES ON PSALM XC

The *title* of this Psalm is, *A Prayer of Moses the man of God.* The *Chaldee* has, "A prayer which Moses the prophet of the Lord prayed when the people of Israel had sinned in the wilderness." All the *Versions* ascribe it to Moses; but that it could not be of Moses the *lawgiver* is evident from this consideration, that the age of man was not then *seventy* or *eighty years,* which is here stated to be its almost universal limit, for Joshua lived *one hundred and ten* years, and Moses himself *one hundred and twenty;* Miriam his sister, *one hundred and thirty;* Aaron his brother, *one hundred and twenty-three;* Caleb, *four-score and five* years; and their contemporaries lived in the same proportion. See the note on ver. 4. Therefore the Psalm cannot at all refer to such *ancient* times. If the *title* be at all authentic, it must refer to some *other person* of that name; and indeed איש אלהים *ish Elohim,* a man of God, a divinely inspired man, agrees to the times of the prophets, who were thus denominated. The Psalm was doubtless composed during or after the captivity; and most probably on their return, when they were engaged in rebuilding the temple; and this, as Dr. *Kennicott* conjectures, may be *the work of their hands,* which they pray God to *bless* and *prosper.*

Verse 1. *Lord, thou hast been our dwelling-place*] מעון *maon;* but instead of this several MSS. have מעוז *maoz,* "place of defence," or "refuge," which is the reading of the *Vulgate, Septuagint, Arabic,* and *Anglo-Saxon.* Ever since thy covenant with Abraham thou hast been the Resting-place, Refuge, and Defence of thy people Israel. Thy mercy has been lengthened out from generation to generation.

Verse 2. *Before the mountains were brought forth*] The mountains and hills *appear* to have been everlasting; but as they were *brought forth* out of the womb of eternity, there was a *time* when *they were not:* but THOU hast been *ab æternitate a parte ante, ad æternitatem a parte post;* from the eternity that is past, be-

3 Thou turnest man to destruction; and sayest, [f]Return, ye children of men.

4 [g]For a thousand years in thy sight *are but* as yesterday [h]when it is past, and *as* a watch in the night.

5 Thou carriest them away as with a flood; [i]they are *as* a sleep; in the morning [k]*they are* like grass *which* [l]groweth up.

6 [m]In the morning it flourisheth, and groweth up; in the evening it is cut down, and withereth.

7 For we are consumed by thine anger, and by thy wrath are we troubled.

8 [n]Thou hast set our iniquities before thee, our [o]secret *sins* in the light of thy countenance.

9 For all our days are [p]passed away in thy wrath: we spend our years [q]as a tale *that is told.*

10 [r]The days of our years *are* threescore years and ten; and if by reason of strength *they be* fourscore years, yet *is* their strength

---

[f]Genesis iii. 19; Eccles. xii. 7——[g]Ecclus. xviii. 10; 2 Peter iii. 8——[h]Or, *when he hath passed* them——[i]Psa. lxxiii. 20——[k]Psalm ciii. 15; Isaiah xl. 6——[l]Or, *is changed*——[m]Psalm xcii. 7; Job xiv. 2——[n]Psalm l. 21; Jeremiah xvi. 17——[o]Psalm xix. 12——[p]Heb. *turned away*——[q]Hebrew, Or, *as a meditation*——[r]Hebrew, As for *the days of our years, in them* are *seventy years*

---

fore time began; to the eternity that is after, when time shall have an end. This is the highest description of the *eternity* of God to which human language can reach.

Verse 3. *Thou turnest man to destruction*] Literally, Thou shalt turn dying man, אנוש *enosh*, to the small dust, דכא *dacca* but thou wilt say, Return, ye children of Adam. This appears to be a clear and strong promise of the *resurrection* of the human body, after it has long slept, mingled with the *dust of the earth.*

Verse 4. *For a thousand years in thy sight*] As if he had said, Though the resurrection of the body may be a *thousand* (or any indefinite number of) years distant; yet, when these are past, they are *but as yesterday*, or a single *watch of the night.* They pass through the mind in a moment, and appear no longer in their duration than the time required by the mind to reflect them by thought. But, short as they appear to the eye of the mind, they are *nothing* when compared with the *eternity* of God! The author probably has in view also that economy of Divine justice and providence by which the life of man has been shortened from *one thousand years* to *threescore years and ten*, or *fourscore.*

Verse 5. *Thou carriest them away as with a flood*] Life is compared to a *stream*, ever *gliding away;* but sometimes it is as a *mighty torrent*, when by reason of *plague, famine*, or *war*, thousands are swept away daily. In particular cases it is a *rapid stream*, when the *young* are suddenly carried off by consumptions, fevers, &c.; this is the *flower that flourisheth* in the *morning*, and in the *evening* is *cut down* and *withered.* The whole of life is like a *sleep* or as a *dream.* The eternal world is *real;* all *here* is either *shadowy* or *representative.* On the whole, *life* is represented as a *stream; youth*, as *morning; decline of life*, or *old age*, as *evening; death*, as *sleep;* and the *resurrection* as the *return of the flowers* in *spring.* All these images appear in these curious and striking verses, 3, 4, 5, and 6.

Verse 7. *We are consumed by thine anger*] *Death* had not entered into the world, if men had not fallen from God.

By thy wrath are we troubled] Pain, disease, and sickness are so many proofs of our defection from original rectitude. The *anger* and *wrath* of God are moved against all *sinners.* Even in protracted life we *consume away*, and only seem to live in order to die.

"Our wasting lives grow shorter still,
As days and months increase;
And every beating pulse we tell
Leaves but the number less."

Verse 8. *Thou hast set our iniquities before thee*] Every one of our transgressions is *set before thee;* noted and minuted down in thy awful register!

Our secret sins] Those committed in darkness and privacy are easily discovered by thee, being shown by the splendours of thy face shining upon them. Thus we light a candle, and bring it into a dark place to discover its contents. O, what can be hidden from the all-seeing eye of God? Darkness is no darkness to him; wherever he comes there is a profusion of light—for God is light!

Verse 9. *We spend our years as a tale*] The *Vulgate* has: Anni nostri sicut aranea meditabuntur; "Our years pass away like those of the spider." Our *plans* and *operations* are like the *spider's web;* life is as *frail*, and the *thread* of it as *brittle*, as one of those that constitute the well-wrought and curious, but *fragile*, habitation of that insect. All the *Versions* have the word *spider;* but it neither appears in the *Hebrew*, nor in any of its MSS. which have been collated.

My old *Psalter* has a curious paraphrase here: "Als the iran (spider) makes vayne webe for to take flese (flies) with gile, swa our yeres ere ockupide in ydel and swikel castes about erthly thynges; and passes with outen frute of gude werks, and waste in ydel thynkyns." This is *too true* a picture of most lives.

But the *Hebrew* is different from all the *Versions.* "We consume our years (כמו הגה *kemo hegeh*) like a groan." We live a dying, whining, complaining life, and at last a *groan* is its termination! How amazingly expressive!

Verse 10. *Threescore years and ten*] See the note on the *title* of this Psalm. This Psalm could not have been written by *Moses*, because the *term* of human life was much more *extended* when he flourished than *eighty* years at the most. Even in *David's* time many lived *one hundred* years, and the author of *Ecclesiasticus*, who lived after the captivity, fixed this term at *one hundred* years at the most (chap. xviii. 9;)

labour and sorrow; for it is soon cut off, and we fly away.
11 Who knoweth the power of thine anger? even according to thy fear, *so is* thy wrath.
12 [s]So teach *us* to number our days, that we may [t]apply *our* hearts unto [u]wisdom.
13 Return, O LORD, how long? and let it [v]repent thee concerning thy servants.
14 O satisfy us early with thy mercy; [w]that we may rejoice and be glad all our days.
15 Make us glad according to the days *wherein* thou hast afflicted us, *and* the years *wherein* we have seen evil.
16 [x]Let thy work appear unto thy servants, and thy glory unto their children.
17 [y]And let the beauty of the LORD our God be upon us: and [z]establish thou the work of our hands upon us; yea, the work of our hands establish thou it.

[s]Psa. xxxix. 4——[t]Heb. *cause to come*——[u]Job xxviii. 28; Psa. cxi. 10; Prov. ix. 10

[v]Deut. xxxii. 36; Psa. cxxxv. 14——[w]Psa. lxxxv. 6; cxlix 2——[x]Heb. iii. 2——[y]Psa. xxvii. 4——[z]Isa. xxvi. 12

but this was merely a general average, for even in our country we have many who exceed *a hundred years.*

Yet is their strength labour and *sorrow*] This refers to the infirmities of old age, which, to those well advanced in life, produce *labour* and *sorrow.*

It is soon cut off] *It*—the *body*, is soon cut off.

And we fly away.] The *immortal spirit* wings its way into the eternal world.

Verse 11. *Who knoweth the power of thine anger?*] The afflictions of *this life* are not to be compared to the *miseries* which await them who live and die without being reconciled to God, and saved from their sins.

Verse 12. *So teach* us *to number our days*] Let us deeply consider our own frailty, and the shortness and uncertainty of life, that we may live for eternity, acquaint ourselves with thee, and be at peace; that we may die in thy favour, and live and reign with thee eternally.

Verse 13. *Return, O Lord, how long?*] Wilt thou continue angry with us for ever?

Let it repent thee] הנחם *hinnachem, be comforted*, rejoice over them to do them good. Be glorified rather in our salvation than in our destruction.

Verse 14. *O satisfy us early*] Let us have thy mercy soon, (literally, *in the morning.*) Let it now shine upon us, and it shall seem as the morning of our days, and we shall exult in thee all the days of our life.

Verse 15. *Make us glad according to the days*] Let thy people have as many years of *prosperity* as they have had of *adversity.* We have now suffered *seventy* years of a most distressful captivity.

Verse 16. *Let thy work appear unto thy servants*] That thou art working for us we know; but O, let thy work *appear!* Let us *now see*, in our deliverance, that thy thoughts towards us were mercy and love.

And thy glory] Thy pure worship be established among our *children* for ever.

Verse 17. *And let the beauty of the Lord*] Let us have thy *presence, blessing*, and *approbation*, as our fathers had.

Establish thou the work of our hands] This is supposed, we have already seen, to relate to their *rebuilding the temple*, which the surrounding heathens and Samaritans wished to hinder. We have begun, do not let them demolish our work; let the top-stone be brought on with shouting, *Grace, grace* unto it.

Yea, the work of our hands] This repetition is wanting in *three* of *Kennicott's* MSS., in the *Targum*, in the *Septuagint*, and in the *Æthiopic.* If the repetition be genuine, it may be considered as marking great earnestness; and this earnestness was to get the temple of God rebuilt, and his pure worship restored. The pious Jews had this more at heart than their own restoration; it was their highest grief that the temple was destroyed and God's ordinances suspended; that his enemies insulted them, and blasphemed the worthy name by which they were called. Every truly pious man feels more for God's glory than his own temporal felicity, and rejoices more in the prosperity of God's work than in the increase of his own worldly goods.

A FEW INSTANCES OF MODERN LONGEVITY

In the year 1790 I knew a woman in the city of Bristol, Mrs. *Somerhill*, then in the 106th year of her age. She read the smallest print without spectacles, and never had used any helps to decayed sight. When she could not go any longer to a place of worship, through the weakness of her limbs, she was accustomed to read over the whole service of the Church for each day of the year as it occurred, with all the *Lessons, Psalms*, &c. She had been from its commencement a member of the Methodist Society; heard Mr. *John Wesley* the first sermon he preached when he visited Bristol in 1739; and was so struck with his clear manner of preaching the doctrine of *justification through faith*, that, for the benefit of hearing *one more sermon* from this apostolic man, she followed him *on foot* to Portsmouth, a journey of *one hundred and twenty-five* miles! On my last visit to her in the above year, I was admitted by a *very old decrepit woman*, then a widow of *seventy-five* years of age, and the *youngest daughter* of Mrs. Somerhill. I found the aged woman's faculties strong and vigorous, and her eyesight unimpaired, though she was then confined to her bed, and was hard of hearing. She died rejoicing in God, the following year.

Agnes Shuner is another instance. She lived at Camberwell in Surrey; her husband, *Richard Shuner*, died in 1407, whom she survived *ninety-two* years. She died in 1499, aged *one hundred and nineteen* years.

The *Countess of Desmond* in Ireland. On the ruin of the house of Desmond, she was obliged at the age of *one hundred and forty* to travel from Bristol to London, to solicit relief from the court, being then reduced to *poverty.* She renewed her teeth *two* or *three* times, and died in 1612, aged *one hundred and forty-five* years.

Thomas Parr, of Winnington, in Shropshire, far outlived the term as set down in the Psalm. At the age of *eighty-eight* he married his first wife, by whom he had *two* children. At the age of *one hundred and two* he fell in love with *Catharine Milton*, by whom he had an illegitimate child, and for which he did penance in the Church! At the age of *one hundred and twenty*, he married a widow woman; and when he was *one hundred and thirty* could perform any operation of husbandry. He died at the age of *one hundred and fifty-two*, A. D. 1635. He had seen *ten* kings and queens of England.

Thomas Damme, of Leighton, near Minshul in Cheshire, lived *one hundred and fifty-four* years, and died A. D. 1648.

Henry Jenkins, of Ellerton upon Swale, in Yorkshire, was sent, when a boy of about *twelve* years of age, with a *cart load of arrows* to Northallerton, to be employed in the battle of *Flodden Field*, which was fought September 9, 1513. He was a *fisherman;* and often *swam* in the rivers when he was more than *one hundred* years of age! He died A. D. 1670, being then *one hundred and sixty-nine* years of age!

I shall add one foreigner, *Peter Toston*, a peasant of Temiswar, in Hungary. The remarkable longevity of this man exceeds the age of *Isaac five* years; of *Abraham, ten;* falls short of *Terah's*, Abraham's father, *twenty;* and exceeds that of *Nahor*, Abraham's grandfather, *thirty-seven* years. He died A. D. 1724, at the extraordinary age of *one hundred and eighty-five!*

Analysis of the Ninetieth Psalm

There are four parts in this Psalm:—

I. An ingenuous acknowledgment of God's protection of the people, ver. 1, 2.

II. A lively narration of the mortality of man, the fragility and brevity of his life, together with the misery of it, ver. 2-7.

III. The causes: man's rebellion and God's anger for it, ver. 7-12.

IV. A petition, which is double: 1. That God would instruct man to know his fragility. 2. That he would return, and restore him to his favour, ver. 12-17.

I. In the beginning the psalmist freely acknowledges what God had always been unto his people. What he is in himself, and his own nature.

1. To his people he had always been a refuge, as it were, a dwelling-place: though they had been pilgrims and sojourners in a strange land for many years, yet he had been, nay dwelt, among them; and no doubt he alludes to the tabernacle of God that was pitched among them as an evidence of his presence and protection: "Lord, thou hast been our dwelling-place (a secure place to rest in) in all generations," Deut. xxxiii. 1-6.

2. But in himself he was from everlasting: other creatures had a beginning, and their creation and ornaments from him. He, the Eternal Being, "Before the mountains were brought forth, or ever thou hadst formed the earth, and the world, even from everlasting to everlasting thou art God." Not like man, then, whose mutability, fragility, mortality, brevity, he next describes.

II. "Thou turnest man to destruction." Though framed according to thy own image, yet he is but an earthen vessel; to that pass thou bringest him, till he be broken to pieces, broken as a potter's vessel. To him thou sayest, "Return, ye children of men, (of Adam,) return; for dust thou art, and to dust shalt thou return." The mortality of man may not be then attributed to diseases, chance, fortune, &c., but to God's decree, pronounced on man upon his disobedience. First, then, let the sons of *Adam* remember that they are mortal; next, that their life is but very short. Suppose a man should live the longest life, and somewhat longer than the oldest patriarch, a thousand years; yet, let it be compared with eternity, it is as nothing: "A thousand years in thy sight are but as yesterday, when it is past;" but as a day which is short, as a day which is past and forgotten; which the *prophet* farther illustrates by elegant similitudes.

1. "And as a watch in the night." A time of three hours' continuance, which is but the eighth part of a natural day, and so far less than he said before. The flower of our youth, our constant age, and our old age, may well be the three hours of this watch; and wise they are that observe their stations in either of them.

2. "Thou carriest them away as with a flood." As a sudden inundation of waters our life passeth; we swell and fall. Or, As all waters come from the sea, and return thither; so from the earth we came, and thither return. Or, We are as water spilt on the earth, which cannot be gathered up again.

3. "They are as a sleep," or rather a dream; all our happiness a dream of felicity. In our dreams many pleasant, many fearful things are presented; we pass half our time in sleep; drowsily, it is certain, for our life is σκιας οναρ, *the shadow of a dream.*—Pindar.

4. Or we are like grass: "In the morning they are like grass that groweth up: in the morning it flourisheth and groweth up, in the evening it is cut down and withereth." The herb hath its morning and evening, and its mid-day, and so hath our life; *naturally* it fades, or *violently* it is cut off.

III. After he had spoken of and explained our mortality, the brevity, the misery of our life, he next descends to examine the causes of it, which are two. 1. God's anger; and that which brought it upon us, our own iniquities.

1. God's anger: "We consume away by thine anger; and by thy wrath are we troubled." The cause, then, of death and disease is not the decay of the radical moisture, or defect of natural heat; but that which brought these defects upon us, *God's wrath* because of *sin*.

2. Our own sin: For this anger of God was not raised without a just cause; he is a just Judge, and proceeds not to punishment, but upon due examination and trial; and to that end he takes an account, not only of our open sins, but even of our secret faults, such as are not known to ourselves, or such as we labour to conceal from others.

1. "Thou hast set our iniquities before thee."

2. "And our secret sins in the light of thy countenance." No hypocrisy, no contempt, can escape thine eye: all to thee is revealed, and clear as the light.

3. And then he repeats the effect, together with the cause: "Therefore all our days (viz., the *forty* years in the wilderness and the *seventy* in captivity) are passed away in thy wrath." 2. "We spend our days as a tale that is told;" *et fabula fies*, the tale ended, it vanisheth, and is thought of no more.

4. And as for our age, it is of no great

length: "The days of our years are threescore years and ten." To that time some men may be said to live, because the faculties of their souls are tolerably vigorous, and their bodies proportionately able to execute the offices of life.

But allow that it so happen, which happens not to many, "that by reason of strength," some excellent natural constitution, "a man arrive to fourscore years," yet our life is encumbered with these *three* inconveniences, labour, sorsow, and brevity.

1. It is laborious, even labour itself. One is desirous to be rich, another wise; this man potent, another prudent, or at least to seem so; and this will not be without labour: "All is affliction of spirit."

2. Sorrow; for our life is only the shadow of real life.

3. Short; for it is soon cut off, and we flee away: *Avolat umbra.* 1. God's anger for sin is not laid to heart; and of this the *prophet* in the next verse sadly complains: "Who knows the power of thy anger?" Thine anger is great for sin; the power of it fearful and terrible. Thou canst and wilt cast sinners into hell-fire; but who regards it? Thy threats to men seem to be old wives' fables. 2. "Even according to thy fear, so is thy wrath;" but be it that this stupidity possess men, yet this is certain, that thy wrath is great; and it shall be executed according to thy fear, in such proportion as men have stood in fear of thee. They that have in a reverential fear stood in awe of thee shall escape it; they that have contemned and slighted thy wrath shall feel it to the uttermost.

IV. Upon all the former considerations the psalmist converts his words to a prayer, in which he implores God's mercy, that he would turn, 1. The stupidity of men into wisdom. 2. Our calamity into felicity. 3. His wrath into compassion. And, 4. Our sorrow into joy. For the first he begins thus:—

1. "So teach us to number our days," to cast up the labour, the sorrow, the brevity, the fugacity; thy anger, our sin, that caused it.

2. "That we may apply our hearts unto wisdom;" be no more stupid and secure, but wise; wise, to avoid thy anger, wise to set a true estimate on this life, and wise in time to provide for another.

3. "So teach us;" for God must teach it, or it will not be learned: this wisdom comes from above.

Secondly, he deprecates God's anger: "Return, O Lord, how long? and let it repent thee concerning thy servants."

Thirdly, he begs restoration to God's favour; and what will follow upon it, peace of conscience.

1. "O satisfy us with thy mercy." We hunger for it as men do for meat.

2. Early let it be done, quickly, before our sorrows grow too high, and overwhelm us.

3. With thy mercy; not with wealth, delights, &c.

4. And with a perpetual joy of heart: "That we may be glad and rejoice all our days."

5. And let our joy bear proportion to our sorrows: "Make us glad according to the days wherein thou hast afflicted us, and the years wherein we have seen evil."

6. This is the work he calls God's work; for as to punish is his strange work, Isa. xxviii., so to have pity and mercy is his own proper work; and this he desires that it should be made manifest: "Let thy work appear unto thy servants, and thy glory unto their children."

Fourthly, he begs for success in all their work and labours.

1. "Let the beauty of the Lord our God be upon us;" for no action of ours is beautiful, except the beauty of God be stamped upon it; done by his direction, his rule, his word, and to his glory.

2. And therefore he prays, and repeats this prayer: "Establish thou the work of our hands upon us; yea, the work of our hands establish thou it." There must be *opus*, our work; for God blesseth not the idle. 2. And *opus manuum*, a laborious work. 3. God's direction, his word the rule. 4. A good end in it, for that is his beauty upon it. 5. So it will be established, confirmed, ratified. 6. And, lastly, know that there is no blessing to be expected without prayer; and therefore he prays, "Let the beauty of the Lord our God be upon us." See the notes on this Psalm.

PSALM XCI

The safety of the godly man, and his confidence, 1, 2. *How he is defended and preserved,* 3–10. *The angels of God are his servants,* 11, 12; *and he shall tread on the necks of his adversaries,* 13. *What God says of, and promises to, such a person,* 14–16.

HE [a]that dwelleth in the secret place of the Most High shall [b]abide [c]under the shadow of the Almighty.

2 [d]I will say of the LORD, *He is* my refuge and my fortress: my God; in him will I trust.

[a]Psa. xxvii. 5; xxxi. 20; xxxii. 7——[b]Heb. *lodge*

[c]Psa. xvii. 8——[d]Psa. cxlii. 5

NOTES ON PSALM XCI

This Psalm has no *title* in the Hebrew; nor can it be determined on what occasion or by whom it was composed. It is most likely by the author of the preceding; and is written as a *part* of it, by *fifteen* of *Kennicott's* and *De Rossi's* MSS., commencing before the *repetition* of the four last words of the *ninetieth.* It is allowed to be one of the finest Psalms in the whole collection. Of it *Simon de Muis* has said: "It is one of the most excellent works of this kind which has ever appeared. It is impossible to imagine any thing more solid, more

3 Surely [e]he shall deliver thee from the
snare of the fowler, *and* from the noisome
pestilence.
4 [f]He shall cover thee with his feathers, and
under his wings shalt thou trust: his truth
shall be thy shield and buckler.
5 [g]Thou shalt not be afraid for the terror
by night; *nor* for the arrow *that* flieth by
day;
6 *Nor* for the pestilence *that* walketh in
darkness; *nor* for the destruction *that* wasteth at noonday.

---

[e]Psa. cxxiv. 7——[f]Psa. xvii. 8; lvii. 1; lxi. 4——[g]Job v. 19, &c.; Psa. cxii. 7; cxxi. 6; Prov. iii. 23, 24; Isa. xliii. 2

---

beautiful, more profound, or more ornamented. Could the Latin or any modern languages express thoroughly all the beauties and elegancies as well of the *words* as of the *sentences*, it would not be difficult to persuade the reader that we have no poem, either in *Greek* or *Latin*, comparable to this Hebrew ode."

Verse 1. *He that dwelleth in the secret place*] The *Targum* intimates that this is a *dialogue* between *David*, *Solomon*, and *Jehovah*. Suppose we admit this,—then

DAVID asserts: "He who dwelleth in the secret place of the Most High shall abide under the shadow of the Almighty," ver. 1.

SOLOMON answers: "I will say of the Lord, He is my refuge and my fortress; my God, in him will I trust," ver. 2.

DAVID replies, and tells him what blessings he shall receive from God if he abide faithful, ver. 3-13.

Then the SUPREME BEING is introduced, and confirms all that *David* had spoken concerning *Solomon*, ver. 14-16: and thus this sacred and instructive dialogue ends.

In the secret place of the Most High] Spoken probably in reference to the *Holy of holies*. He who enters legitimately there shall be covered with the cloud of God's glory—the protection of the all-sufficient God. This was the privilege of the *high priest* only, under the law: but under the new covenant all believers in Christ *have boldness to enter into the holiest by the blood of Jesus;* and those who thus enter are safe from every evil.

Verse 2. *I will say of the Lord*] This is my experience: "He is my fortress, and in him will I continually trust."

Verse 3. *Surely he shall deliver thee*] If thou wilt act thus, then the God in whom thou trustest will deliver thee from the snare of the fowler, from all the devices of Satan, and from all dangerous maladies. As the original word, דבר *dabar*, signifies a *word spoken*, and *deber*, the same *letters*, signifies *pestilence;* so some translate one way, and some another: he shall deliver thee from the evil and *slanderous word;* he shall deliver thee from the *noisome pestilence*—all blasting and injurious *winds*, *effluvia*, &c.

Verse 4. *He shall cover thee with his feathers*] He shall act towards thee as the hen does to her brood,—take thee under his wings when birds of prey appear, and also shelter thee from chilling blasts. This is a frequent metaphor in the sacred writings; see the parallel texts in the *margin*, and the notes on them. The *Septuagint* has Εν τοις μεταφρενοις αυτου επισκιασει σοι· *He will overshadow thee between his shoulders;* alluding to the custom of parents carrying their weak or sick children on their backs, and having them covered even there with a mantle. Thus the Lord is represented carrying the Israelites in the wilderness. See Deut. xxxii. 11, 12, where the metaphor is taken from the *eagle*.

His truth shall be thy *shield and buckler*] His revelation; his Bible. That truth contains promises for all times and circumstances; and these will be invariably fulfilled to him that trusts in the Lord. The fulfilment of a promise relative to defence and support is to the soul what the best shield is to the body.

Verse 5. *The terror by night*] Night is a time of terrors, because it is a time of treasons, plunder, robbery, and murder. The godly man lies down in peace, and sleeps quietly, for he trusts his body, soul, and substance, in the hand of God; and he knows that he who keepeth Israel neither slumbers nor sleeps. It may also mean all *spiritual foes,—the rulers of the darkness of this world*. I have heard the following petition in an evening family prayer: "Blessed Lord, take us into thy protection this night; and preserve us from disease, from sudden death, from the violence of fire, from the edge of the sword, from the designs of wicked men, and from the influence of malicious spirits!"

Nor *for the arrow*] The *Chaldee* translates this verse, "Thou shalt not fear the demons that walk by night; nor the arrow of the angel of death which is shot in the day time." Thou needest not to fear a sudden and unprovided-for death.

Verse 6. Nor *for the pestilence* that *walketh in darkness;* nor *for the destruction* that *wasteth at noonday*.] The rabbins supposed that the empire of death was under two demons, one of which ruled by *day*, the other by *night*. The *Vulgate* and *Septuagint* have—the *noonday devil*. The ancients thought that there were some demons who had the power to injure particularly at *noonday*. To this *Theocritus* refers, Id. i. ver. 15:—

> Ου θεμις, ω ποιμαν, το μεσαμβρινον, ου θεμις αμμιν
> Συρισδεν· τον Πανα δεδοικαμες· η γαρ απ' αγρας
> Τανικα κεκμακως αμπαυεται, εντι γε πικρος,
> Και οἱ αει δριμεια χολα ποτι ῥινι καθηται.

"It is not lawful, it is not lawful, O shepherd, to play on the flute at *noonday:* we fear Pan, who at that hour goes to sleep in order to rest himself after the fatigues of the chase; *then he is dangerous*, and his wrath easily kindled."

Lucan, in the horrible account he gives us of a grove sacred to some barbarous power, worshipped with the most horrid rites, refers to the same superstition:—

> Lucus erat longo nunquam violatus ab ævo,
> Non illum cultu populi propiore frequentant,
> Sed cessere deis: *medio* cum *Phœbus in axe est*,
> Aut *cœlum nox atra tenet*, pavet ipse sacerdos
> Accessus, dominumque timet deprendere luci.
> LUCAN. lib. iii., ver. 399.

7 A thousand shall fall at thy side, and ten
thousand at thy right hand; *but* it shall not
come nigh thee.
8 Only [h]with thine eyes shalt thou behold
and see the reward of the wicked.
9 Because thou hast made the LORD *which*
is [i]my refuge, *even* the Most High, [k]thy
habitation;
10 [l]There shall no evil befall thee, neither
shall any plague come nigh thy dwelling.
11 [m]For he shall give his angels charge
over thee, to keep thee in all thy
ways.
12 They shall bear thee up in *their*
hands, [n]lest thou dash thy foot against a
stone.
13 Thou shalt tread upon the lion and
[o]adder: the young lion and the dragon shalt
thou trample under feet.
14 Because he hath set his love upon me,

[h]Psa. xxxvii. 34; Mal. i. 5——[i]Ver. 2——[k]Psa. lxxi. 3; xc. 1——[l]Prov. xii. 21——[m]Psa. xxxiv. 7; lxxi. 3; Matt. iv. 6; Luke iv. 10, 11; Heb. i. 14——[n]Job v. 23; Psa. xxxvii. 24——[o]Or, *asp*

"Not far away, for ages past, had stood
An old inviolated sacred wood:—
The pious worshippers approach not near,
But shun their gods, and kneel with distant fear:
The *priest* himself, when, or the *day* or *night*
Rolling have reached their full *meridian* height,
Refrains the gloomy paths with wary feet,
Dreading the *demon* of the grove *to meet;*
Who, terrible to sight, at *that fixed hour*
Still treads the round about this dreary bower." ROWE.

It has been stated among the heathens that the gods should be worshipped *at all times*, but the *demons* should be worshipped at *mid-day:* probably because these demons, having been employed during the *night*, required *rest at noonday;* and that was the most proper time to appease them. See *Calmet* on this place. Both the *Vulgate* and *Septuagint* seem to have reference to this superstition.

The *Syriac* understands the passage of a *pestilential wind*, that *blows at noonday. Aquila* translates, *of the bite of the noonday demon.*

Verse 7. *A thousand shall fall at thy side*] *Calmet* thinks this place should be translated thus: "A thousand enemies may fall upon thee on one side, and ten thousand may fall upon thee on thy right hand: but they shall not come nigh thee to take away thy life." It is a promise of perfect protection, and the utmost safety.

Verse 8. *The reward of the wicked.*] Thou shalt not only be safe thyself, but thou shalt see all thy enemies discomfited and cast down.

Verse 9. *Because thou hast made the Lord*] Seeing thou hast taken Jehovah, the Most High, for thy portion and thy refuge, *no evil shall come nigh thy dwelling;* thou shalt be safe in thy soul, body, household, and property, ver. 10. Every pious man may expect such protection from his *God* and *Father.*

Verse 11. *He shall give his angels charge over thee*] Evil spirits may attempt to injure thee; but they shall not be able. The *angels of God* shall have an especial charge to accompany, defend, and preserve thee; and against their power, the influence of evil spirits cannot prevail. These will, when necessary, turn thy steps out of the way of danger; ward it off when it comes in thy ordinary path; suggest to thy mind prudent counsels, profitable designs, and pious purposes; and thus minister to thee as a child of God, and an heir of salvation.

To keep thee in all thy ways.] The path of duty is the way of safety. Thou canst not reasonably expect protection if thou walk not in the way of obedience. *Thy ways* are the paths of duty, which God's word and providence have marked out for thee. The *way of sin* is not *thy way*—thy *duty*, thy *interest.* Keep in *thy own ways*, not in those of *sin*, *Satan*, the *world*, and the *flesh;* and God will take care of thee.

Verse 12. *They shall bear thee up in* their *hands*] Take the same care of thee as a *nurse* does of a weak and tender child; lead thee,—teach thee to walk,—lift thee up out of the way of danger, "lest thou shouldst dash thy foot against a stone," receive any kind of injury, or be prevented from pursuing thy path with safety and comfort.

Let us remember that it is GOD, whose these angels are; HE gives them charge—from HIM they receive their commission,—to HIM they are responsible for their charge. From God thou art to expect them; and for their help he alone is to receive the praise. It is expressly said, *He shall give his angels charge;* to show that they are not to be *prayed to* nor *praised;* but GOD *alone*, whose *servants* they are. See the note on Matt. iv. 6.

Verse 13. *Thou shalt tread upon the lion and adder*] Even the king of the forest shall not be able to injure thee; should one of these attack thee, the angels whom God sends will give thee an easy victory over him. And even the *asp*, (פתן *pethen,*) one of the most venomous of serpents, shall not be able to injure thee.

The asp is a very small serpent, and peculiar to Egypt and Libya. Its poison kills without the possibility of a remedy. Those who are bitten by it die in about from three to eight hours; and it is said they die by sleep, without any kind of *pain.* Lord *Bacon* says the asp is less painful than all the other instruments of death. He supposes it to have an affinity to *opium*, but to be less disagreeable in its operation. It was probably on this account that *Cleopatra*, queen of Egypt, chose to die by the asp, as she was determined to prevent the designs of *Augustus*, who intended to have carried her captive to Rome to grace his *triumph.*

The dragon shalt thou trample] The תנין *tannin*, which we translate *dragon*, means often any large aquatic animal; and perhaps here the *crocodile* or *alligator.*

Verse 14. *Because he hath set his love upon me*] Here the *Most High* is introduced as confirming the word of his servant. He has fixed his *love*—his heart and soul, on me.

therefore will I deliver him: I will set him on high, because he hath [p]known my name.

15 [q]He shall call upon me, and I will answer him: [r]I *will be* with him in trouble; I will deliver him and [s]honour him.

16 With [t]long life will I satisfy him, and show him my salvation.

[p]Psa. ix. 10——[q]Psa. l. 15——[r]Isa. xliii. 2

[s]1 Sam. ii. 30——[t]Heb. *length of days;* Prov. iii. 2

Therefore will I deliver him] I will save him in all troubles, temptations, and evils of every kind.

I will set him on high] I will place him *out of the reach* of all his enemies. I will *honour* and *ennoble* him, *because he hath known my name*—because he has loved, honoured, and served me, and rendered me that worship which is my due. He has *known* me to be the God of infinite mercy and love.

Verse 15. *He shall call upon me*] He must *continue to pray;* all his blessings *must come in this way;* when he *calls*, I will *answer* him—I will give him whatever is best for him.

I will be *with him in trouble*] Literally, *I am with him.* עמו אנכי *immo anochi;* as soon as the trouble comes, *I am there.*

I will deliver him] For his good I may permit him to be exercised for a time, but *delivered* he shall be.

And honour him] אכבדהו *acabbedehu*, "I will glorify him." I will *load* him with *honour;* that honour that comes from God. I will even show to men how highly I prize such.

Verse 16. *With long life*] Literally, *With length of days will I fill him up.* He shall neither live a useless life, nor die before his time. He shall live happy and die happy.

And show him my salvation.] ואראהו בישועתי *vearehu bishuathi*, "I will make him see (or contemplate) in my salvation." He shall discover infinite lengths, breadths, depths, and heights, in my salvation. He shall feel boundless desires, and shall discover that I have provided boundless gratifications for them. He shall dwell in my glory, and throughout eternity increase in his resemblance to and enjoyment of me. Thus shall it be done to the man whom the Lord delighteth to honour; and he delights to honour that man who *places his love on him.* In a word, he shall have *a long life* in this world, and an *eternity of blessedness* in the world to come.

Analysis of the Ninety-first Psalm

The full intent and purpose of this Psalm is to encourage and exhort the godly in all extremities, pressures, troubles, temptations, afflictions, assaults, inward or outward; in a word, in all dangers to put their trust and confidence in God, and to rely upon his protection.

There are *two* parts in this Psalm:—

I. A general proposition, in which is given an assurance of help and protection to every godly man, ver. 1: "He that dwelleth," &c.

II. The proof of this by three witnesses:—

1. Of the just man, in whose person the *psalmist* speaks, ver. 2: "I will say of the Lord," &c.

2. Of the prophet, ver. 3: "Surely he shall deliver thee from the snare," &c.; which he amplifies by an enumeration of the dangers, God's assistance, and the angels' protection, ver. 3-14.

3. Of God himself, whom he brings in speaking to the same purpose, ver. 14-16.

I. The first part or verse is a universal proposition, in which is contained a comfortable and excellent promise made by the Holy Ghost of security, viz., that God's help shall never be wanting to those who truly put their hope and trust in him: "He that dwelleth in the secret place of the Most High shall abide (or lodge) under the shadow of the Almighty."

1. *He,*—be he who he will, rich or poor, king or people; God is no respecter of persons.

2. "That dwells." For that he must be sure to do, constantly, daily, firmly, rest and acquiesce in God, to persevere in the faith of his promise, and carry that about him, else he cannot be assured by this promise.

3. "In the secret place." For his aid and defence is not as some strong-hold or castle which is visible; it is a secret and invisible fortress, known only to a faithful soul. In that he may repose his hope, as a means and secondary defence; but he dwells, relies, rests in that help of God which is secret, and is not seen except by the eye of faith.

4. "Of the Most High." And upon this he relies, because he is the *Most High. Above* he is, and sees all; nothing is hid from him. And again, *above* he is, sits in the highest throne, and rules all. All things are under his feet; he can therefore deliver his people from all troubles and dangers. Yea, he will do it for this faithful man; he that relies and trusts in him shall never be frustrated of his hope; protected he shall be; he shall be safe. 1. "He dwells, therefore he shall abide." He shall lodge quietly—securely. 2. "He dwells in the secret place, therefore he shall abide under the shadow." In the cool, the favour, the cover from the heat. 3. "He dwelleth in the secret place of the Most High, therefore he shall abide under the shadow of the Almighty;" i. e., of the all-powerful God, of the God of heaven; of that God whose name is Shaddai, All-sufficient; by which name he made his promise to Abraham, Gen. xvii. 1.

II. This proposition being most certainly true, in the next place the psalmist explains it. And that no man may doubt of it, descends to prove it by three witnesses: first, of a just man; secondly, of the prophet; thirdly, of God himself.

He brings in the just man thus speaking in his own person: "I will say unto the Lord, He is my refuge, my fortress, my God; in him will I trust." Is it so? "Shall he that dwells in the secret of the Most High, abide under the shadow of the Almighty?" Therefore I will say, in the person of all just men, to the Lord, that hath no superior, that hath no peer; to that Lord to whose command all things are subject, and who can be commanded by none; I will say to him,—

1. "Thou art my refuge." If pursued, I will flee to thee as a sanctuary.

2. "Thou art my fortress." If set upon, I will betake myself to thee as a strong tower.

3. "Thou art my God." If assaulted by men or devils, thou, the Most High; thou, Almighty,

art a God able to defend me, and therefore "I will hope in thee;" I will dwell, trust, rely upon thee and this thy promise, in every temptation and danger.

Next, to assert the truth of this, he brings in the attestation of the prophet; for, being moved by the Holy Ghost, he saith as much, "Surely he shall deliver thee;" and then falls upon the particulars, from which the godly man shall be delivered, set down in many metaphors.

1. "He shall deliver thee from the snare of the fowler;" the deceits of evil men or devils.

2. "From the noisome pestilence," all danger to which we are incident, by plague, war, or famine.

Again, when thou art little in thine own eyes,—

1. "He shall cover thee," as the hen does her young, "with his feathers; and under his wings shalt thou trust," secured from the rain, the storm, the heat of the sun, and the birds of prey.

2. When thou art grown up, and able to encounter an enemy in the field, he shall help thee to a shield and buckler, and that shall be his truth, his veracity, thy faith in it; and which is yet more,—

Thou shalt not be afraid,—

1. "For the terror by night;" any hidden secret temptation, danger, treachery, detraction, conspiracy.

2. "Nor for the arrow that flies by day;" any open persecution, calamity, fraud, assault, invasion.

3. "Nor for the pestilence that walks in darkness;" the machinations of wicked men hatched in the dark.

4. "Nor for the destruction that wasteth at noon-day;" the bold threats and decrees of tyrants and persecutors.

Moller observes rightly that the promises of deliverance here made do not belong to one or other kind of evil, but to all kinds of calamities, open or secret, and so may be applicable to any; some of which steal upon us, as in the night secretly; others overwhelm as in the day, openly. But the promise is general, as Bellarmine well observes; whether the danger come by day or night, those who trust in God are armed with his shield of truth against it. "For if God be for us, who can be against us?" Rom. viii.

The prophet goes on, and confirms the godly in their security by the dissimilarity or unlike condition of wicked men. When thou shalt be safe, they shall fall.

1. "A thousand shall fall at thy side, on thy left hand," overcome by adversity.

2. "Ten thousand on thy right hand," flattered into sin by prosperity. "But neither the fear by night, nor the arrow by day, shall come nigh thee."

3. And, which is another cause of comfort and pleasure: "Only with thine eyes shalt thou behold, and see the reward of the wicked;" which sometimes falls out in this life, as the *Israelites* saw the Egyptians dead upon the sea-shore; *Moses* and *Aaron* saw *Dathan* and *Abiram* swallowed up quick, &c. But it shall be amply fulfilled at the last judgment, Matt. xxv. Of which security, comfort, content, the *prophet* in the next verse gives the reason; the danger shall not come nigh thee; when they fall thou shalt see it, and consider it with content. "Because thou hast made the Lord, which is my refuge, even the Most High, thy habitation;" thou trustest in him as I do; and therefore shalt have the like protection, deliverance, comfort, that I by his promise have. Farther, "there shall no evil befall thee, neither shall any plague come nigh thy dwelling." But the just man may say, I am secure that no evil shall befall me; I desire to know how I may be kept so, that I fall not among thieves. This *objection* the *prophet prevents*, saying, in effect, Fear not, "for he shall give his angels charge over thee, to keep thee in all thy ways; they shall bear thee up in their hands, lest thou dash thy foot against a stone."

In which verses consider,—

1. That the good man is protected by angels; many angels have a care of one poor man.

2. That they are commanded by God to do it; for are not they ministering spirits sent by God to that end? Heb. i. 14.

3. That it is a particular administration, a charge given to the poorest, the meanest saint.

4. That they are to keep, to look to, defend thee, and what is thine; thou hast an invisible guard.

5. But then mark the limitation and restriction; it is in "all thy ways," in the walk of thy vocation to which God hath called thee; either walk in them, or the angels have no charge to keep thee.

6. Lastly, "In all thy ways;" not in *one* but *all;* for the ways of men are many, and in *all* he needs the custody of angels: 1. The law is a way, and the way of the law is manifold. 2. Our works and operations are manifold; which are our way too. 3. Our life is a way, and there be many parts and conditions of our life, various ages, manifold states; and in all these ways we need a guardian, for we may slip in every law, in every operation, in every age, in every state of life.

Which that it be not done, God hath given his angels charge over us: to keep us only; nay, which is more,—

1. "They shall bear thee," as kind mothers and nurses do their children.

2. "They shall bear thee in their hands;" the will, understanding, wisdom, and power are, as it were, the angels' hand; with all these they will bear us.

3. "That thou dash not thy foot;" that is, thy affections, which carry the soul to good or bad.

4. "Against a stone;" which are all difficulties and obstacles.

And, which is yet more, under their custody we shall tread under foot Satan, and all his accomplices; him, a roaring lion, an old serpent, a fierce dragon, and all his associates, tyrants, persecutors, and hypocrites; for such is the promise; "Thou shalt tread upon the lion and adder; the young lion and dragon shalt thou trample under feet."

5. "In the mouth of two or three witnesses shall every word stand, saith God;" and here we find the law strictly observed: it was to be proved, that all who truly trust in God were to be protected by God; of which one witness was the *just man*, ver. 2; another, the testimony of the Spirit by the *prophet*, from verse 3 to this verse; to which a third, we have here even God himself; for in these three last verses the *prophet* brings Him, God himself, testifying this great and comfortable truth with his own mouth:—

1. "Because he hath set his love upon me," pleased me, loved me, adhered to me, hoped in me, trusted to me with a filial love and adherence.

2. "Because he hath known my name," acknowledged my power, wisdom, goodness; these are the causes and conditions presupposed in the protected.

3. "He shall call upon me." Invocation is necessary also. "Therefore I will deliver him, I will answer him, I will be with him in trouble, I will honour him. I will glorify him, or set him on high;" and the second, "I will deliver him; with long life will I satisfy him, and show him my salvation."

1. "I will deliver him," by the shield, by my angels, by other ways, directly or indirectly, yet so that it be remembered that I do it; for these shall not deliver without me.

2. "I will answer him;" answer his desires, answer his prayers, so they be *cries*.

3. "I will be with him in trouble;" join myself close to him, go into prison with him as it were, suffer with him, and think myself pursued when he is persecuted, give him comfort even then; they sung in prison; he neither delivers the martyrs from death, nor does he forsake them.

4. "I will honour him:" for the names of those who suffered for his sake are honourable; "precious in the sight of the Lord is the death of his saints."

These promises may belong to this life; those that follow to the other.

1. "I will deliver him." For the just by death are freed from the present and all future miseries: "Blessed are the dead, for they rest from their labours."

2. "I will glorify him." As if it were not enough to deliver him; such a thing in this life may fall out, as it happened to Joseph, Job, David, Daniel; but the true glory no question must be, "when the righteous shall shine like the sun, be set upon their thrones, and judge the twelve tribes of Israel."

3. "With long life will I satisfy him," i. e., with eternal felicity, with a continuance in bliss, which shall be eternal; for without eternity even length of days cannot satisfy; as appears by old men, who yet have complained of a short life.

4. And that the *prophet* speaks of this eternal felicity is more than probable, because he adds, "I will show him my salvation;" I will show him Jesus, my salvation; that is, I will bring to pass, that when through his whole life I have given him sufficient evidences of my fatherly affection, I will at last translate him to a place where he shall no longer live by faith, but shall see, and experimentally feel, what he hath believed.

PSALM XCII

The psalmist shows the duty and advantage of praising God, 1–3; *speaks of the grandeur of God's works*, 4–6; *the fall of the wicked*, 7–9; *the happiness of the righteous*, 10–14; *and all this founded on the perfections of God.*

A Psalm *or* Song for the Sabbath day

IT *is a* [a]good *thing* to give thanks unto the
LORD, and to sing praises unto thy name,
O Most High:
2 To [b]show forth thy loving-kindness in
the morning, and thy faithfulness [c]every
night.
3 [d]Upon an instrument of ten strings, and

[a]Psa. cxlvii. 1——[b]Psa. lxxxix. 1——[c]Heb. *in the nights*——[d]2 Chron. xxiii. 5; Psa. xxxiii. 2

NOTES ON PSALM XCII

The *title*, *A Psalm* or *Song for the Sabbath*, gives no information concerning the *time*, *occasion*, or *author*. The *Chaldee*, has "Praise, and a song which the first man spoke concerning the Sabbath:" but this is an idle conceit; and, though entertained by some *rabbins*, has been followed by none of the *Versions*. *Calmet* supposes the Psalm to have been composed by some of the Levites during or near the close of the Babylonish captivity, acknowledging the mercy of God, and foreseeing the desolation of their enemies, and their own return to Jerusalem, and their temple service.

Verse 1. It is a *good* thing *to give thanks*] This Psalm begins very *abruptly*. *Good to confess unto the Lord.* He *had been* acknowledging God's goodness, and praising him for his mercy; and now he breaks out and tells how good he felt this employment to be.

Verse 2. *To show forth thy loving-kindness*] חסדך *chasdecha*, thy abundant mercy, *in the morning*—that has preserved me throughout the night, and brought me to the beginning of a new day: *and thy faithfulness in the night*, that has so amply fulfilled the promise of preservation during the course of the day. This verse contains a general plan for morning and evening prayer.

Verse 3. *Upon an instrument of ten strings*] Eusebius, in his comment on this Psalm, says: Ψαλτηριον δε δεκαχορδον, ἡ του Ἁγιου Πνευματος δια των αισθητηριων πεντε μεν του σωματος, ισαριθμων δε της ψυχης δυναμεων, επιτελουμενη λατρεια· "The *Psaltery of ten strings* is the worship of the Holy Spirit, performed by means of the *five* senses of the body, and by the *five* powers of the soul." And, to confirm this interpretation, he quotes the apostle, 1 Cor. xiv. 15: "I will pray with the spirit, and with the understanding also; I will sing with the spirit, and with the understanding also." "As the mind has its influence by which it moves the body, so the spirit has its own influence by which it moves the soul." Whatever may be thought of this gloss, one thing is pretty evident from it, that *instrumental music* was not in use in the Church of Christ in the time of Eusebius, which was near

upon the psaltery; [e]upon the harp with [f]a
solemn sound.
4 For thou, LORD, hast made me glad
through thy work: I will triumph in the works
of thy hands.
5 [g]O LORD, how great are thy works! *and*
[h]thy thoughts are very deep.
6 [i]A brutish man knoweth not; neither doth
a fool understand this.
7 When [k]the wicked spring as the grass, and
when all the workers of iniquity do flourish;
it is that they shall be destroyed for ever:

8 [l]But thou, LORD, *art most* high for ever
more.
9 For, lo, thine enemies, O LORD, for, lo,
thine enemies shall perish; all the workers of
iniquity shall [m]be scattered.
10 But [n]my horn shalt thou exalt like *the*
horn of an unicorn: I shall be [o]anointed with
fresh oil.
11 [p]Mine eye also shall see *my desire* on
mine enemies, *and* mine ears shall hear *my*
desire of the wicked that rise up against me.
12 The [q]righteous shall flourish like the

[e]Or, *upon the solemn sound with the harp*——[f]Heb. *Higgaion;* Psa. ix. 16——[g]Psa. xl. 5; cxxxix. 17——[h]Isa. xxviii. 29; Rom. xi. 33, 34——[i]Psa. lxxiii. 22; xciv. 8——[k]Job xii. 6; xxi. 7; Psa. xxxvii. 1, 2, 35, 38; Jer. xii. 1, 2; Mal. iii. 15——[l]Psa. lvi. 2; lxxxiii. 18——[m]Psa. lxviii. 1; lxxxix. 10——[n]Psa. lxxxix. 17, 24——[o]Psa. xxiii. 5——[p]Psa. liv. 7; lix. 10; cxii. 8——[q]Psa. lii. 8; Isa. lxv. 22; Hos. xiv. 5, 6

the middle of the *fourth* century. Had any such thing then existed in the Christian Church, he would have doubtless alluded to or spiritualized it; or, as he quoted the words of the apostle above, would have shown that *carnal usages* were substituted for *spiritual exercises.* I believe the whole verse should be translated thus: *Upon the asur, upon the nebel, upon the higgayon, with the kinnor.* Thus it stands in the Hebrew.

Verse 4. *For thou, Lord, hast made me glad through thy work*] I am delighted with thy conduct towards me; with the work of thy *providence*, the works of thy *grace*, and thy works of *creation.*

Verse 5. *How great are thy works!*] They are multitudinous, stupendous, and splendid: *and thy thoughts*—thy designs and counsels, *from* which, *by* which, and *in reference* to which, they have been formed; *are very deep*—so profound as not to be fathomed by the comprehension of man.

Verse 6. *A brutish man knoweth not*] איש בער *ish baar*, the human hog—the stupid bear—the *boor;* the man who is all flesh; in whom *spirit* or *intellect* neither seems to work nor exist. The *brutish man*, who never attempts to see God in his works.

Neither doth a fool understand this.] כסיל *kesil*, the fool, is different from בער *baar*, the brutish man; the latter *has mind*, but it is buried in flesh; the former has *no mind*, and his stupidity is unavoidable.

Verse 7. *When the wicked spring as the grass*] This is a lesson which is frequently inculcated in the sacred writings. The favour of God towards man is not to be known by outward prosperity; nor is his disapprobation to be known by the adverse circumstances in which any person may be found. When, however, we see the wicked flourish, we may take for granted that their *abuse* of God's mercies will cause him to cut them off as cumberers of the ground; and, dying in their sins, *they are destroyed for ever.*

Verse 8. *High for evermore.*] *They* are brought down and destroyed; but the Lord is exalted eternally, both for his judgments and his mercies.

Verse 10. *Like* the horn of *a unicorn.*] ראים *reeym*, perhaps here, the *oryx* or *buffalo.* But the *rhinoceros* seems to be the real *monoceros* of the Scriptures.

I shall be anointed with fresh oil.] Perhaps the allusion is here not to any *sacramental* anointing, but to such anointings as were frequent among the Asiatics, especially after bathing, for the purpose of health and activity.

Verse 11. *Mine eye also shall see,*—and *mine ears shall hear*] Even in my own times my enemies shall be destroyed; and of this destruction I shall either be an *eye-witness* or have authentic *information.*

Verse 12. *The righteous shall flourish like the palm-tree*] Very different from the wicked, ver. 7, who are likened to *grass.* These shall have a *short duration;* but those shall have a long and useful life. They are compared also to the *cedar of Lebanon*, an incorruptible wood, and extremely long-lived. Mr. *Maundrell*, who visited those trees in 1697, describes them thus: "These noble trees grow among the snow, near the highest part of Lebanon. Some are very old, and of prodigious bulk. I measured one of the largest, and found it *twelve* yards *six* inches in girt, and yet sound; and *thirty-seven* yards in the spread of its boughs. At about *five* or *six* yards from the ground, it was divided into *five* limbs, each of which was equal to a large tree." Some of these trees are supposed to have lived upwards of *one thousand* years! The figure of the *palm-tree* gives us the idea of *grandeur* and *usefulness.* The *fruit* of the palm-tree makes a great part of the *diet* of the people of *Arabia*, part of *Persia*, and *Upper Egypt.* The *stones* are ground down for the camels; the *leaves* are made into *baskets;* the *hard boughs*, or rather *strong leaves*, some being *six* or *eight* feet in length, make *fences;* the *juice* makes *arrack;* the *threads* of the web-like integument between the leaves make *ropes*, and the rigging of small vessels; and the *wood* serves for slighter buildings and fire-wood. In short, the *palm* or *date tree*, and the *olive*, are two of the most excellent and useful productions of the forest or the field.

The *cedar* gives us the idea of *majesty, stability, durableness*, and *incorruptibility.* To these *two* trees, for the most obvious reasons, are the righteous compared. *William Lithgow*, who travelled through the *holy land* about A. D. 1600, describes the cedars of Mount *Leba-*

palm-tree: he shall grow like a cedar in Lebanon.

13 Those that be planted in the house of the LORD shall flourish [r]in the courts of our God.

14 They shall still bring forth fruit in old age; they shall be fat and [s]flourishing;

15 To show that the LORD *is* upright: [t]*he is* my rock, and [u]*there is* no unrighteousness in him.

[r]Psa. c. 4; cxxxv. 2——[s]Heb. *green*——[t]Deut. xxxii. 4——[u]Rom. ix. 14

non as "being in number twenty-four, growing after the manner of oaks, but a great deal taller, straighter, and thicker, and the branches growing so straight, and interlocking, as though they were kept by art: and yet from the root to the top they bear no boughs, but grow straight and upwards like to a palm-tree. Their circle-spread tops do kiss or embrace the lower clouds, making their grandeur overlook the highest bodies of all other aspiring trees. The nature of this tree is, that it is always green, yielding an odoriferous smell, and an excellent kind of fruit, like unto apples, but of a sweeter taste, and more wholesome. The roots of some of these cedars are almost destroyed by the shepherds, who have made fires thereat, and holes where they sleep; yet nevertheless they flourish green above, in the tops and branches." —Lithgow's 17 years' Travels, 4to., London, 1640.

Verse 13. *Those that be planted in the house of the Lord*] I believe the *Chaldee* has the true meaning here: "His children shall be planted in the house of the sanctuary of the Lord, and shall flourish in the courts of our God." As these trees flourish in their respective soils and climates, so shall the *righteous* in the ordinances of God. I do not think there is any allusion to either *palm-trees* or *cedars*, planted near the tabernacle or temple.

Verse 14. *They shall still bring forth fruit in old age*] They shall continue to grow in grace, and be fruitful to the end of their lives. It is a rare case to find a man in old age full of faith, love, and spiritual activity.

Verse 15. *To show that the Lord is upright*] Such persons show how faithful God is to his promises, how true to his word, how kind to them who trust in him. He is the *Rock*, the *Fountain*, whence all good comes.

There is *no unrighteousness in him.*] He does nothing *evil*, nothing *unwise*, nothing *unkind*. He is both *just* and *merciful.*

Analysis of the Ninety-second Psalm

I. A general proposition, ver. 1: "It is good to give thanks to the Lord," &c.; which is explained ver. 2, 3, and applied ver. 4.

II. A particular narration of such works, in which the goodness and faithfulness of God do especially consist, viz., the creation and government of the world, ver. 4, 5. And of the last he gives two instances:—

1. One in wicked men; of their stupidity, ver. 6. Then of their sudden extirpation, ver. 7, 8, 9.

2. Another in the godly, whose prosperity is great, ver. 10-14, and security certain, ver. 15.

I. He begins with a maxim: 1. "It is good," i. e., just, profitable, pleasant, and commendable, "to give thanks to the Lord." 2. "And to sing praises (with heart and tongue) to thy glorious name, O thou Most High."

And both parts he explains. 1. That we give thanks at all times, morning and evening, in prosperity and in adversity; and in our praises especially to remember his loving-kindness and faithfulness. These must be the matter of our thanksgiving: "It is good to show forth thy loving-kindness in the morning, and thy faithfulness every night," ver. 2; and by all manner of means, ver. 3.

And thus the maxim being proposed and explained, he applies it to himself, and shows his own practice, and the reason of it: "For thou, Lord, hast made me glad through thy work; I will triumph in the works of thy hands," ver. 4.

1. "Thou hast made me glad." He was first delighted and affected with God's work.

2. And then he exults and triumphs in it. The heart must be first truly affected with the work of God before a man shall take any true content or delight in it.

II. He had made mention of the works of God; and now he farther opens what they are: First, The creation of the universe; Secondly, His especial providence in ordering the things of this world, particularly about man.

1. First, he begins with the work of creation, upon which he enters, not with less than an admiration: "O Lord, how great are thy works! and thy thoughts are very deep." As if he said, I cannot be satisfied in the contemplation of them. There is such a depth in them, that I cannot attain to it, nor comprehend it.

2. And he ends it, not without an indignation, that the wise men of the world, who yet in his judgment, for their disregard of it, are but fools, should not consider it. In the creature they look after nothing but profit and pleasure, in which regard they are but fools. *For this brutish man knows not* how great are his works; *this fool understands not* how deep are his cogitations.

And that he may illustrate their folly the more, from the work of creation he comes to God's work of governance of the world; and shows, that as they who would be and are reputed wise, are mistaken in the one, so also they are mistaken in the other; for they think the ungodly, and such as flourish in power and wealth, happy, and that the righteous men, sometimes oppressed, are unhappy: and upon these two instances, he insists to the end of the Psalm. First, he instances the ungodly: *When the wicked spring up*—rise on a sudden, (for such a time there is,) *as the grass*, that grows insensibly and in a night; *and when all the workers of iniquity do flourish*—become very conspicuous, exalted in power and pride, and abound in wealth; who would not now take them for happy men? No, saith our prophet, it is not so.

1. This their felicity is the greatest infelicity: It is, "that they may perish," be destroyed.

2. "That they may perish for ever." Remember the rich man in the Gospel.

3. And this their destruction is from God, that sits on the throne, and is immutable in his decrees and ways. They flourish and are exalted; but it is but for a moment: "But thou,

Lord, art most high for evermore." And thou wilt execute thy decree upon them.

4. Which the prophet fully opens in the next verse, which the *epizeuxis* makes more emphatical: "For, lo, thine enemies, O Lord, for, lo, thine enemies shall perish; and all the workers of iniquity shall be scattered."

1. Behold, they were green, they *flourished:* but the change shall be sudden.

2. They were *enemies, thy enemies, workers of iniquity;* therefore cursed with a curse.

3. "They shall perish, they shall be scattered;" they rose, they flourished as grass, and they shall be scattered as dry grass, which the wind blows from the face of the earth.

His second instance is the godly, whose happy condition he demonstrates, 1. In *hypothesi,* or in himself, ver. 10, 11; and, 2. In *thesi;* in all others that be true members of the mystical Church of Christ, ver. 12-15.

He instanceth in himself, that his condition is not like the ungodly. He shot not up as the fading grass, but his strength and power should be as a unicorn.

1. "But my horn shalt thou exalt as the horn of a unicorn;" that is, my power, and glory, and felicity shall still mount higher.

2. "And I shall be anointed with fresh oil." Anointed to be king over *Israel,* by *Samuel,* with a horn of oil;—by God, with the gracious oil of his Spirit.

3. And that which adds to my flourishing estate: "My eye shall see my desire upon my enemies, and my ears shall hear my desire of the wicked that rise up against me;" which David lived to see and hear in the ruin of *Saul* and his house.

And that which the prophet said of himself he now transfers to all just and righteous men, whom he compares to the *palm* and *cedar.*

1. "The righteous shall flourish like a palm-tree." So a good Christian; the greater weight he carries, the more he flourishes.

2. "He shall grow like a cedar in Lebanon." Cedar-wood is not consumed by worms or time; nor the Church by antiquity nor persecution. The gates of hell shall not prevail against it, nor any true member of it.

Of which the reason is, because these *palms* and *cedars*—these righteous men, are planted, set by faith, watered by the word and sacraments, rooted by charity in the Church, which is the house of the Lord; and therefore they *shall flourish*—be green and vigorous, *in the courts of our God.*

Nay, which is yet more, they shall be full of sap and laden with fruit.

1. "They shall bring forth fruit in their old age." It shall be contrary to them, as with other trees. Those grow fruitless, and bear not when they grow old; these are then most laden with the fruits of grace.

2. "They shall be fat and flourishing." Other trees, when old, are hard and dry; these then are fat in juice, and flourish in good works.

3. And the reason of this vigour, of the continuance of this radical and vital moisture to old age, is, that they bring forth fruit, which is specified in the last verse: "That they might show forth God's faithfulness, praise him for that," as it is in the second verse. 1. "That they might show that the Lord is upright,"—just and righteous in himself. 2. "That he is a Rock,"—a sure, stable foundation to trust to. 3. "And that there is no unrighteousness in him,"—no injustice; though for a time he suffer the wicked to flourish, and the just to be under the cross. For in his good time he will show his justice in rewarding the just, and punishing the unjust.

PSALM XCIII

The universal government of God, 1, 2; *the opposition to that government,* 3, 4; *the truth of God's testimonies,* 5.

XVIII. DAY. EVENING PRAYER

A. M. cir. 3468 B. C. cir. 536 Cyri, R. Persarum, cir. annum primum

THE [a]LORD reigneth, [b]he is
clothed with majesty; the
LORD is clothed with strength,
[c]*wherewith* he hath girded himself: [d]the world also is established, that it cannot be moved.
2 [e]Thy throne *is* established[f] of old: thou *art* from everlasting.

[a]Psa. xcvi. 10; xcvii. 1; xcix. 1; Isa. lii. 7; Rev. xix. 6 [b]Psa. civ. 1——[c]Psa. lxv. 6

[d]Psa. xcvi. 10——[e]Psa. xlv. 6; Prov. viii. 22, &c. [f]Heb. *from them*

NOTES ON PSALM XCIII

This Psalm has no *title* either in the Hebrew or Chaldee. The *Vulgate, Septuagint, Æthiopic,* and *Arabic,* state it to be "A song of praise of David for the day preceding the Sabbath, when the earth was founded;" but in such a title there is no information on which any man can rely. This Psalm is written as a part of the preceding in *twelve* of *Kennicott's* and *De Rossi's* MSS. It was probably written at the close of the captivity by the *Levites,* descendants of Moses.

Verse 1. *The Lord reigneth*] He continues to govern every thing he has created; and he is every way qualified to govern all things, for *he is clothed with majesty and with strength*—dominion is his, and he has supreme power to

A. M. cir. 3468 B. C. cir. 536 Cyri, R. Persarum, cir. annum primum

3 The floods have lifted up,
O LORD, the floods have lifted
up their voice; the floods lift
up their waves.
4 [g]The LORD on high *is* mightier than the
noise of many waters, *yea, than*
the mighty waves of the sea.
5 Thy testimonies are very
sure: holiness becometh thine
house, O LORD, [h]for ever.

[g]Psa. lxv. 7; lxxxix. 9

[h]Heb. *to length of days*

exercise it; and *he has so established the world* that nothing can be driven out of order; all is ruled by him. *Nature* is his agent: or rather, nature is the sum of the laws of his government; the operations carried on by the Divine energy, and the effects resulting from those operations.

He hath girded himself] The *girding with strength* refers to the *girding* in order to *strengthen the loins, arms, knees*, &c. When a Hindoo is about to set off on a journey, to lift a burden, or to do something that requires exertion, he *binds firmly* his loose upper garment round his loins.—WARD.

Verse 2. *Thy throne is established of old*] There never was a time in which God did not reign, in which he was not a supreme and absolute Monarch; for he is from *everlasting*. There never was a time in which he was not; there never can be a period in which he shall cease to exist.

Verse 3. *The floods have lifted up*] Multitudes of people have confederated against thy people; and troop succeeds troop as the waves of the sea succeed each other.

Verse 4. *The Lord—*is *mightier than the noise of many waters*] Greater in strength than all the *peoples* and *nations* that can rise up against him.

Mighty waves of the sea.] Even the most powerful empires can prevail nothing against him; therefore those who trust in him have nothing to fear.

Verse 5. *Thy testimonies are very sure*] Thou wilt as surely fulfil thy word as thou wilt keep possession of thy throne.

Holiness becometh thine house] Thy *nature* is holy, all thy *works* are holy, and thy *word* is holy; therefore, thy *house*—thy *Church*, should be holy. The *building* itself should be *sanctified*—should be so *consecrated* to thy worship alone, that it shall never be employed in any other service. The *ministers* of this Church should be holy, the *members* holy, the *ordinances* holy; its *faith*, its *discipline*, and its *practice* holy. And this at all times, and in all circumstances; for holiness becometh thine house—for ever," לארך ימים *le-orech yamim*, for length of days. During the whole lapse of time; till the sun and moon shall be no more. The old *Psalter* says the house of God is *man's saule;* and of this house holiness is נאוה *naavah*, "the *ornament;*" it produces that meek and quiet spirit which is in the sight of God of great price. No decoration of person nor simplicity of dress can supply the place of this heavenly clothing.

ANALYSIS OF THE NINETY-THIRD PSALM

In this Psalm it is the purpose of the prophet to comfort the Church, oppressed by tyrants and persecutors; and yet she shall not utterly fail. The gates of hell shall not prevail against her; because Christ sits in his Church as *King*. The sum of it is,—

I. The magnificence and power of Christ our eternal King, ver. 1, 2.

II. That he defends his Church in the day of a storm, ver. 3, 4.

III. That his laws are holy, and his Church also, ver. 5.

I. The prophet in the first verse describes our King:

First. From his office:—

1. "He reigns." He is the great and chief Monarch; he is no idle spectator of things below; but wisely, and justly, and powerfully administers all things.

2. He is a glorious King: "He is clothed with majesty."

3. He is a potent King: "The Lord is clothed with strength."

4. He is a warlike King: "He hath girded himself," buckled his sword upon his armour; for offence towards his enemies, for defence of his kingdom.

Secondly. From his kingdom:—

1. It is universal: "The world."

2. It is fixed, firm, and stable: "The world is also established, and cannot be moved."

3. It is an everlasting kingdom: "From everlasting to everlasting; thy throne is established of old: thou art from everlasting."

II. But in this his kingdom there are those who raise tumults, commotions, and rebellions. These he compares to swelling waters and foaming waves.

1. "The floods," that is, tyrants, persecutors, &c., "have lifted up, O Lord, the floods have lifted up their voice; the floods lift up their waves." The Church dwells in the sea; and the waves of tyranny, ambition, and malice, beat furiously upon it.

2. Well, be it so; yet "the Lord on high is mightier than the noise of many waters; yea, than the mighty waves of the sea." He wonderfully and strangely hath showed his might in getting himself the victory over all persecutors, and propagating and enlarging his kingdom over all the earth in despite of his enemies.

III. 1. And as his kingdom is immovable, so are the laws by which it is governed fixed and unalterable also: "Thy testimonies are very sure." The Gospel is an eternal Gospel; the doctrine thereof is holy and inviolable; by which God hath declared his good will to man, and what he requires of all his loving subjects; which is, that they be a holy people. For,

2. "Holiness becomes thy house for ever." The temple, the priests, the people, must be a holy nation; for ever correspondent to the holiness of his law and testimonies: "Be ye holy, for I am holy." "Holiness becomes thy house, O Lord, for ever."

PSALM XCIV

An appeal to God against oppressors, 1–7. *Expostulations with the workers of iniquity,* 8–11. *God's merciful dealings with his followers,* 12–15; *and their confidence in him,* 16–19. *The punishment of the wicked foretold,* 20–23.

O LORD [a]God, [b]to whom vengeance belongeth; O God, to whom vengeance belongeth, [c]show thyself.
2 [d]Lift up thyself, thou [e]Judge of the earth:
render a reward to the proud.
3 LORD, [f]how long shall the wicked, how
long shall the wicked triumph?
4 *How long* shall they [g]utter *and* speak
hard things? *and* all [h]the workers of iniquity
boast themselves?
5 They break in pieces thy people, O LORD,
and afflict thine heritage.
6 They slay the widow and the stranger, and
murder the fatherless.
7 [i]Yet they say, The LORD shall not see,
neither shall the God of Jacob regard *it.*
8 [k]Understand, ye brutish among the people: and *ye* fools, when will ye be wise?
9 [l]He that planted the ear, shall he not
hear? he that formed the eye, shall he not
see?
10 He that chastiseth the heathen, shall not
he correct? he that [m]teacheth man knowledge,
shall not he know?

[a]Heb. *God of revenges*——[b]Deut. xxxii. 35; Nah. i. 2——[c]Hebrew, *shine forth;* Psa. lxxx. 1——[d]Psa. vii. 6——[e]Gen. xviii. 25——[f]Job xx. 5——[g]Psalm xxxi. 18; Jude 15

[h]Job xxxi. 3; xxxiv. 8, 22; Prov. x. 29; Luke xiii. 27——[i]Psalm x. 11, 13; lix. 7——[k]Psalm lxxiii. 22; xcii. 6——[l]Exod. iv. 11; Prov. xx. 12——[m]Job xxxv. 11; Isa. xxviii. 26; 1 Cor. ii. 13; 1 John ii. 27

NOTES ON PSALM XCIV

This Psalm has no *title* either in the *Hebrew* or *Chaldee.* The *Vulgate, Septuagint, Æthiopic,* and *Arabic,* have "A Psalm of David, for the fourth day of the week;" but this gives us no information on which we can rely. In *three* of *Kennicott's* MSS. it is written as a *part* of the preceding. It is probably a prayer of the captives in Babylon for deliverance; and was written by the descendants of Moses, to whom some of the preceding Psalms have been attributed. It contains a description of an iniquitous and oppressive government, such as that under which the Israelites lived in Babylon.

Verse 1. *O Lord God, to whom vengeance belongeth*] God is the author of *retributive justice,* as well as of *mercy.* This retributive justice is what we often term *vengeance,* but perhaps improperly; for vengeance with us signifies an excitement of *angry passions,* in order to *gratify* a *vindictive spirit,* which supposes itself to have received some real injury; whereas what is here referred to is that simple act of justice which gives to all their due.

Verse 2. *Lift up thyself*] Exert thy power.

Render a reward to the proud.] To the Babylonians, who oppress and insult us.

Verse 3. *How long shall the wicked triumph?*] The wicked are often in prosperity; and this only shows us of how little worth riches are in the sight of God, when he bestows them on the most contemptible of mortals. But their time and prosperity have their *bounds.*

Verse 4. *They utter* and *speak*] יביאו *yabbiu,* their hearts *get full* of pride and insolence; and then, from the abundance of such vile hearts, the mouth *speaks;* and the speech is of *hard things, threatenings* which they are determined to execute, *boastings* of their power, authority, &c.

Verse 5. *They break in pieces thy people*] This was true of the Babylonians. Nebuchadnezzar slew many; carried the rest into captivity; ruined Jerusalem; overturned the temple; sacked, pillaged, and destroyed all the country.

Verse 6. *They slay the widow*] Nebuchadnezzar carried on his wars with great cruelty. He carried fire and sword every where; spared neither *age, sex,* nor *condition.* The *widow,* the *orphan,* and the *stranger,* persons in the most desolate condition of life, were not distinguished from others by his ruthless sword.

Verse 7. *The Lord shall not see*] This was either the language of *infidelity* or *insult.* Indeed, what could the Babylonians know of the true God? They might consider him as the God of a *district* or *province,* who knew nothing and did nothing out of his own territories.

Verse 8. *Understand, ye brutish*] These are the same expressions as in Psa. xcii. 6, on which see the note.

Verse 9. *He that planted the ear, shall he not hear?*] This is allowed to be an unanswerable mode of argumentation. Whatever is found of excellence in the *creature,* must be derived from the *Creator,* and exist in him in the plenitude of infinite excellence. God, says St. *Jerome,* is all *eye,* because he sees all; he is all *hand,* because he does all things; he is all *foot,* for he is every where present. The psalmist does not say, He that planted the ear, *hath he not an ear?* He that formed the eye, *hath he not eyes?* No; but, Shall he not *hear?* Shall he not *see?* And why does he say so? To prevent the error of humanizing God, of attributing members or corporeal parts to the infinite Spirit. See *Calmet.*

Verse 10. *He that chastiseth the heathen, shall not he correct?*] YOU, who are heathens, and heathens of the most abandoned kind.

He that teacheth man knowledge] We here supply *shall not he know?* But this is not acknowledged by the *original,* nor by any of the *Versions.* Indeed it is not necessary; for either the words contain a simple proposition, "It is

11 [n]The LORD knoweth the thoughts of man, that they *are* vanity.

12 [o]Blessed *is* the man whom thou chastenest, O LORD, and teachest him out of thy law;

13 That thou mayest give him rest from the days of adversity, until the pit be digged for the wicked.

14 [p]For the LORD will not cast off his people, neither will he forsake his inheritance.

15 But judgment shall return unto righteousness: and all the upright in heart [q]shall follow it.

16 Who will rise up for me against the evildoers? *or* who will stand up for me against the workers of iniquity?

17 [r]Unless the LORD *had been* my help, my soul had [s]almost dwelt in silence.

18 When I said, [t]My foot slippeth; thy mercy, O LORD, held me up.

19 In the multitude of my thoughts within me thy comforts delight my soul.

20 Shall [u]the throne of iniquity have fellowship with thee, which [v]frameth mischief by a law?

21 [w]They gather themselves together against

---

[n]1 Cor. iii. 20——[o]Job v. 17; Prov. iii. 11; 1 Cor. xi. 32; Hebrews xii. 5, &c.——[p]1 Samuel xii. 22; Romans xi. 1, 2

[q]Heb. shall be *after it*——[r]Psa. cxxiv. 1, 2——[s]Or, *quickly*——[t]Psa. xxxviii. 16——[u]Amos vi. 3——[v]Psa. lviii. 2; Isa. x. 1——[w]Matt. xxvii. 1

---

he who teacheth man knowledge," or this clause should be read in connexion with ver. 11: "Jehovah, who teacheth man knowledge, knoweth the devices of man, that they are vanity." As he teaches *knowledge* to man, must he not *know* all the reasonings and devices of the human heart?

Verse 12. *Blessed* is *the man whom thou chastenest*] תיסרנו *teyasserennu*, whom thou *instructest; and teachest him out of thy law. Two* points here are worthy of our most serious regard: 1. God gives *knowledge* to man: gives him *understanding* and *reason.* 2. He gives him a *revelation* of himself; he places before that *reason* and *understanding* his *Divine law.* This is God's system of teaching; and the human intellect is his gift, which enables man to understand this teaching. We perhaps may add a *third* thing here; that as by sin the understanding is darkened, he gives the Holy Spirit to dispel this darkness from the intellect, in order that his word may be properly apprehended and understood. But he gives no *new faculty;* he removes the impediments from the old, and invigorates it by his Divine energy.

Verse 13. *That thou mayest give him rest*] He whom God instructs is made wise unto salvation; and he who is thus taught has rest in his soul, and peace and confidence in adversity.

Verse 14. *The Lord will not cast off his people*] Though they are now suffering under a grievous and oppressive captivity, yet the Lord hath not utterly cast them off. They are his inheritance, and he will again restore them to their own land.

Verse 15. *But judgment shall return unto righteousness*] If we read יושב *yosheb, shall sit*, for ישוב *yashub, shall return*, which is only placing the ו *vau* before the ש *shin* instead of after it, we have the following sense: *Until the just one shall sit in judgment, and after him all the upright in heart.* Cyrus has the epithet צדק *tsedek*, the *just one*, in different places in the Prophet Isaiah. See Isa. xli. 2, 10; xlv. 8; li. 5. It was Cyrus who gave liberty to the Jews; who appeared as their deliverer and conductor to their own land, and they are all represented as *following* in his *train.*

Verse 16. *Who will rise up for me*] Who is he that shall be the deliverer of thy people? Who will come to our assistance against these wicked Babylonians?

Verse 17. *Unless the Lord* had been *my help*] Had not God in a strange manner supported us while under his chastising hand, we had been utterly cut off.

My soul had almost dwelt in silence.] The *Vulgate* has *in inferno*, in *hell* or the *infernal world;* the *Septuagint*, τῳ ᾀδῃ, *in the invisible world.*

Verse 18. *When I said, My foot slippeth*] When I found myself so weak and my enemy so strong, that I got *first* off my guard, and then off my *centre* of *gravity*, and my fall appeared inevitable,—

Thy mercy, O Lord, held me up.] יסעדני *yisadeni, propped me.* It is a metaphor taken from any thing *falling*, that is *propped, shored up*, or *buttressed.* How often does the *mercy* of God thus prevent the ruin of weak believers, and of those who have been unfaithful!

Verse 19. *In the multitude of my thoughts*] Of my griefs, (*dolorum*, Vulgate;) my sorrows, (οδυνων, Septuagint.) According to the multitude of my trials and distresses, have been the consolations which thou hast afforded me. Or, While I have been deeply *meditating* on thy wondrous grace and mercy, Divine light has broken in upon my soul, and I have been filled with delight.

Verse 20. *Shall the throne of iniquity*] No wicked king, judge, or magistrate shall ever stand in thy presence. No countenance shall such have from thy grace or providence.

Which frameth mischief] Devise, plan, and execute, as if they acted by a positive law, and were strictly enjoined to do what they so much delighted in.

Verse 21. *They gather themselves together*] In every thing that is *evil*, they are in *unity.* The devil, his angels, and his children, all join and draw together when they have for their object the destruction of the works of the Lord. But this was particularly the case with respect to the poor Jews among the Babylonians: they were objects of their continual hatred, and they laboured for their destruction.

This and the following verses have been applied to our Lord, and the treatment he met with both from his own countrymen and from the soul of the righteous, and [x]condemn the innocent blood.

22 But the LORD is [y]my defence; and my God *is* the rock of my refuge.

23 And [z]he shall bring upon them their own iniquity, and shall cut them off in their own wickedness; *yea,* the LORD our God shall cut them off.

[x]Exod. xxiii. 7; Prov. xvii. 15——[y]Psa. lix. 9; lxii. 2, 6——[z]Psa. vii. 16; Prov. ii. 22; v. 22

the Romans. They pretended to "judge him according to the law, and framed mischief against him;" they "assembled together against the life of the righteous one," and "condemned innocent blood;" but God evidently interposed, and "brought upon them their own iniquity," according to their horrible imprecation: "His blood be upon us and upon our children!" God "cut them off in their own iniquity." All this had, in reference to him, a most literal fulfilment.

Verse 22. *The rock of my refuge.*] Alluding to those natural fortifications among rocks, which are frequent in the land of Judea.

Verse 23. *Shall cut them off*] This is *repeated,* to show that the destruction of the Babylonians was fixed and indubitable: and in reference to the Jews, the persecutors and murderers of our Lord and his apostles, it was not less so. *Babylon* is totally destroyed; not even a *vestige* of it remains. The *Jews* are no longer a nation; they are scattered throughout the world, and have no certain place of abode. They do not possess even one *village* on the face of the earth.

The last verse is thus translated and paraphrased in the old Psalter:—

Trans. **And he sal yelde to thaim thair wickednes, and in thair malice he sall skater thaim: skater thaim sal Lorde oure God.**

Par. Alswa say efter thair il entent, that thai wil do gude men harme; he sall yelde thaim pyne, and in thair malice thai sal be sundred fra the hali courte of hevene, and skatred emang the wiked fendes of hell.

For different views of several parts of this Psalm, see the *Analysis.*

ANALYSIS OF THE NINETY-FOURTH PSALM

In this Psalm the parts are,—

I. A petition for vengeance upon the wicked, ver. 1, 2.

II. A pitiful complaint, with the causes of it, which were two:—

1. The delay of God's judgments on them, ver. 3, 4.

2. Their insolence, oppression of the poor, and blasphemy against God, ver. 4-7.

III. A sharp reprehension of their blasphemy and atheism, and the refutation of it.

IV. A consolation to all good men, that God will punish the wicked and defend the righteous, ver. 12-23. Which is confirmed,—

1. From God's faithfulness, who hath promised, and will perform it, ver. 14.

2. From David's own experience, ver. 16-20.

3. From God's hatred of injustice, tyranny, and oppression, ver. 20, 21. 1. Which will cause him to be a rock and defence to his people, ver. 22. 2. A severe revenger to the oppressors, ver. 23.

1. He begins with a petition that God would take vengeance of the oppressors of his people: "O Lord God, to whom vengeance belongs, to whom vengeance belongs;" as if he had said, Thou art the most powerful Lord, a God of justice and power, and hast vengeance in thine own hand. Therefore now—

1. "Show thyself." Appear, shine forth evidently, and apparently show thy justice, ver. 1.

2. "Lift up thyself, thou Judge of the earth." Do thy office of judicature; ascend thy throne and tribunal, as judges use to do when they give judgment.

3. "Render a reward unto the proud." For the proud humble themselves not unto thee; they repent not.

II. And now the prophet begins to complain that, by the delay of God's judgment, wicked men were hardened in their impiety, and gloried in their villany.

1. "How long? how long?" This thy forbearance seems tedious; especially since the wicked grow worse and worse by it, and insult over us the more.

2. "For they triumph in their strength." They glory in their prosperity, and in their wickedness.

3. "They utter and speak hard things." Boldly, rashly, proudly, they threaten ruin to thy Church.

4. "They are workers of iniquity, and they boast themselves." It is not sufficient for them to do ill, but they boast of it.

Now to what end do they make use of all these? The consequence is lamentable—the event sad. The effects are lamentable, for in their fury and injustice—

1. "They break in pieces thy people, O Lord." The people dedicated to thee.

2. "They afflict thine heritage." The people that thou hast chosen for thy possession.

3. "They slay the widow," destitute of the comfort of a husband;—1. "And the stranger." A man far from his friends and country. 2. "And murder the fatherless." All which thou hast taken into thy protection, and commanded that they be not wronged. Exod. xxii.; Deut. xxiv. Yet such is their fury, that they spare neither sex, nor age, nor any condition of men.

"Yet they say, The Lord shall not see, neither shall the God of Jacob regard it." This is their impiety; this is their blasphemy; this is the true cause of all their injustice, tyranny, cruelty, and oppression.

III. Now our prophet sets himself seriously to reprehend and confute this. By an *apostrophe* he turns to them, and calls them fools; and proves by a manifest argument that they are fools; demonstrating, from the cause to the effect, that God is neither deaf nor blind, as they presumed and conceived: and urgeth them emphatically,—

1. "Understand, ye brutish among the people. O ye fools, when will ye be wise?" What! will ye be brutish always? will ye never have common sense in your heads?

2. "He planted the ear," caused you to hear; "and shall he not then hear?"

3. *He formed the eye* with all the tunicles, and put into it the faculty of vision by which you see; "and shall he not see?" To say the

contrary, is as if you should affirm that the fountain that sends forth the stream had no water in it; or the sun that enlightens the world had no light; or the fire that warms, no heat. Are these affirmations fit for wise men? Neither is it, that the God of Jacob doth not hear nor see.

4. "He chastiseth the heathen," as *Sodom, Gomorrah,* &c.; or he chastises them by the checks of their own conscience; "and shall not he then correct you," who go under the name of his people, and yet so impiously blaspheme?

5. "He that teacheth man knowledge"—hath endued him with a reasonable soul, and made him capable of all arts and sciences; is he stupid? is he without understanding? "Shall not he know?" He looks into your hearts, and knows your thoughts and counsels, and findeth them all vain: "The Lord knows the thoughts of man, that they are but vanity." With which he concludes his reprehension.

IV. And so from them he comes to the good man, and shows his happiness, whom he labours to comfort in his extremities, pronouncing him *blessed:* "Blessed is the man." And his blessedness lies in three things:—

1. In his sufferings; because when he is punished, he is but chastised, and his chastisements are from the Lord: "Blessed is the man whom thou chastenest."

2. In his teaching; for when he is chastised, he is but taught obedience to the law of God, taught *out of thy law.*

3. In consideration of the end; that he feel not, but bear more moderately, the injuries of the wicked; for the end why God chastiseth and teacheth thee out of his law is: *That he may give thee rest*—a quiet and even soul, *from the days of adversity;* and that thou shouldst expect with patience, *till the pit be digged up for the ungodly.* Such a day there is, and the day will come. Hell is as ready to receive the sinner, as a grave digged up for a dead body. Expect, therefore, their punishment and thy deliverance with a quiet mind. For which he gives *three* reasons:—

The *first* reason is, that though God for a time seem to be angry, and suffer his people to be afflicted, yet he will not utterly neglect and forsake them:—

1. "For the Lord will not cast off his people, neither will he forsake his inheritance."

2. A day of judgment and execution of justice shall come, "when judgment shall return unto righteousness."

A *second* confirmation of the comfort he gave to the Church in affliction is drawn from his own experience, ver. 16-20.

1. Object. Yea, but this time of judgment may be long; in the meanwhile it is necessary to have some helper and help against the persecutions and injuries of cruel men. Who will arise for me, and labour to protect me in so great a concourse of devils or mischievous men? "Who will stand up for me, and defend me against the workers of iniquity?"

Resp. Even he that then stood up for me. No man, but God alone. He did it; and "unless the Lord had been my help, my soul had almost dwelt in silence;" I had been laid in the grave among the dead, saith David, ver. 17.

2. *If I said,* and complained to him, that I was in any danger, *my foot slips*—I was tempted and ready to fall, *thy mercy, O Lord, held me up;* in mercy he lent me his hand, and sustained me.

3. "In the multitude of my thoughts within me thy comforts delight my soul:"—

(1) The *thoughts within me* were sorrows of heart, and many they were, occasioned from within, from without; *a multitude of them.*

(2) "Thy comforts delight my soul." As were the troubles in the flesh, so were comforts in my soul.

His *third* reason, to comfort the Church in affliction, is drawn from the nature of God, to whom all iniquity is hateful.

1. "Shall the throne of iniquity have fellowship with thee?" Thou art a just God, and wilt thou have any thing to do, any society, with those that sit upon thrones and seats of justice, and execute injustice?

2. "Which frame mischief by a law," i. e., frame wicked laws; or, under the colour of law and justice, oppress the innocent. With those who do injustice by the sword of justice, God will have no fellowship.

3. And yet there is a third pretence of wicked men to colour their proceedings against innocent men. The first was their *throne,* the second was the *law,* and the third is their *council,* and consultations in them. These they call to that end. They meet by troops as thieves; they assemble, they convene in synods; "they gather themselves together," and that to a most wicked end:—

1. "Against the soul of the righteous." Θηρευσαι, To hunt.—*Septuagint.*

2. "To condemn the innocent blood." Their laws are *Draco's* laws. Now what shall the poor innocent do in such a case? How shall he be comforted? Help he must not expect from man; from man it cannot come; it must come from heaven; and therefore let him say with *David,* Though my enemies rage as they list, and exercise all cruelties towards me, under a pretence of zeal, piety, and legal justice; yet

1. "The Lord is my defence," so that their treachery and plots shall not hurt me.

2. "My God is the rock of my refuge," on whom my hope shall safely rely.

3. "I am fully assured, for I have his word and his promise engaged for it."

1. "That he shall bring upon them their own iniquity;" that is, that the iniquity of the wicked man shall return upon his own head.

2. "And shall cut them off in their own wickedness;" not so much for their sin as for the malice of it.

3. Which for assurance of it he repeats, and explains who it is that shall do it: "Yea, the Lord our God shall cut them off;" the Lord, whose providence they derided; "our God," the God of Jacob, whom they contemned, ver. 7, he "shall cut them off;" they shall have no part with his people.

PSALM XCV

An invitation to praise *God*, 1, 2. *The reason on which this is founded, the majesty and dominion of God*, 3–5. *An invitation to* pray *to God*, 6. *And the reasons on which that is founded*, 7. *Exhortation not to act as their fathers had done, who rebelled against God, and were cast out of his favour*, 8–11.

XIX. DAY. MORNING PRAYER

O COME, let us sing unto the LORD: [a]let
us make a joyful noise to [b]the rock of our
salvation.

2 Let us [c]come before his presence with
thanksgiving, and make a joyful noise unto
him with psalms.

3 For [d]the Lord *is* a great God, and a great
King above all gods.

4 [e]In his hand *are* the deep places of
the earth; [f]the strength of the hills *is* his
also.

5 [g]The [h]sea is *his*, and he made it: and his
hands formed the dry *land*.

6 O come, let us worship and bow down:
let [i]us kneel before the LORD our Maker.

7 For he *is* our God; and [k]we *are* the
people of his pasture, and the sheep of

[a]Psa. c. 1——[b]Deut. xxxii. 15; 2 Sam. xxii. 47
[c]Heb. *prevent his face*——[d]Psa. xcvi. 4; xcvii. 9; cxxxv. 5
[e]Heb. *in whose*

[f]Or, *the heights of the hills* are *his*——[g]Heb. *Whose the sea is*——[h]Gen. i. 9, 10——[i]1 Cor. vi. 20——[k]Psa. lxxix. 13; lxxx. 1; c. 3

NOTES ON PSALM XCV

This Psalm is also without a *title*, both in the *Hebrew* and *Chaldee:* but is attributed to *David* by the *Vulgate*, *Septuagint*, *Æthiopic*, *Arabic*, and *Syriac;* and by the *author* of the Epistle to the Hebrews, chap. iv. 3-7. *Calmet* and other eminent critics believe that it was composed during the time of the *captivity*, and that the apostle only followed the *common opinion* in quoting it as the production of *David*, because in general the Psalter was attributed to him.

The Psalm is a solemn invitation to the people, when assembled for public worship, to praise God from a sense of his great goodness; and to be attentive to the instructions they were about to receive from the reading and expounding of the law; and or these accounts it has been long used in the Christian Church, at the commencement of public service, to prepare the people's minds to worship God in spirit and in truth.

Houbigant, and other learned divines, consider this Psalm as composed of *three* parts. 1, The part of the *people*, ver. 1 to the middle of ver. 7. 2. The part of the *priest* or *prophet*, from the middle of ver. 7 to the end of ver. 8. 3. The part of *Jehovah*, ver. 9-11. It is written as a part of the preceding Psalm by *nine* of *Kennicott's* and *De Rossi's* MSS.; but certainly it must have been originally an ode by itself, as the subject is widely different from that in the foregoing.

Verse 1. *O come, let us sing*] Let us *praise* God, not only with the most joyful accents which can be uttered by the *voice;* but let us also praise him with *hearts* tuned to gratitude, from a full sense of the manifold benefits we have already received.

The rock of our salvation.] The strong *Fortress* in which we have always found *safety*, and the *Source* whence we have always derived *help* for our souls. In both these senses the word *rock*, as applied to God, is used in the Scriptures.

Verse 2. *Let us come before his presence*] פניו *panaiv*, his faces, with thanksgiving, בתודה *bethodah*, with *confession*, or *with the confession-offering*. *Praise* him for what he has already done, and *confess* your unworthiness of any of his blessings. The *confession-offering*, the great *atoning sacrifice*, can alone render your *acknowledgment of sin* and *thanksgiving* acceptable to a *holy* and *just* God.

Verse 3. *For the Lord* is *a great God*] Or, "A great God is Jehovah, and a great King above all gods;" or, "God is a great King over all." The Supreme Being has *three* names here: אל EL, יהוה JEHOVAH, אלהים ELOHIM, and we should apply none of them to *false gods*. The *first* implies his *strength;* the *second* his *being* and *essence;* the *third*, his *covenant relation* to mankind. In public worship these are the views we should entertain of the Divine Being.

Verse 4. *In his hand* are *the deep places of the earth*] The greatest deeps are *fathomed by him.*

The strength of the hills is *his also.*] And to him the *greatest heights* are *accessible*.

Verse 5. *The sea* is *his*] The sea and the dry land are equally his, for he has formed them both, and they are his property. He governs and disposes of them as he sees good. He is the absolute Master of universal nature. Therefore there is no other object of worship nor of confidence.

Verse 6. *O come, let us worship*] *Three* distinct words are used here to express *three different acts of adoration:* 1. *Let us worship*, נשתחוה *nishtachaveh*, let us *prostrate* ourselves; the highest act of adoration by which the *supremacy* of God is acknowledged. 2. *Let us bow down*, נכרעה *nichraah*, let us *crouch* or *cower down, bending the legs under*, as a dog in the presence of his master, which solicitously waits to receive his commands. 3. *Let us kneel*, נברכה *nibrachah, let us put our knees to the ground*, and thus put ourselves in the *posture* of those who *supplicate*. And let us consider that all this should be done in the *presence* of HIM who is *Jehovah our Creator*.

Verse 7. *For he* is *our God*] Here is the reason for this service. He has condescended to enter into a *covenant* with us, and he has taken us for his own; therefore—

We are the people of his pasture] Or, rather,

his hand. [l]To-day if ye will hear his
voice,
8 Harden not your heart, [m]as in the [n]pro-
vocation, *and* as *in* the day of temptation in
the wilderness:
9 When [o]your fathers tempted me, proved
me, and [p]saw my work.
10 [q]Forty years long was I grieved with *this*
generation, and said, It *is* a people that do err
in their heart, and they have not known my
ways:
11 Unto whom [r]I sware in my wrath
[s]that they should not enter into my
rest.

[l]Heb. iii. 7, 15; iv. 7——[m]Exod. xvii. 2, 7; Num. xiv. 22, &c.; xx. 13; Deut. vi. 16——[n]Heb. *contention* [o]Psa. lxxviii. 18, 40, 56; 1 Cor. x. 9

[p]Num. xiv. 22——[q]Heb. iii. 10, 17——[r]Num. xiv. 23, 28, 30; Heb. iii. 11, 18; iv. 3, 5——[s]Heb. *if they enter into my rest*

as the *Chaldee*, *Syriac*, *Vulgate*, and *Æthiopic* read, "We are his people, and the sheep of the pasture of his hand." We are his own; he feeds and governs us, and his powerful *hand* protects us.

To-day if ye will hear his voice] *To-day*—you have no time to lose; *to-morrow* may be too late. God calls to-day; to-morrow he may be silent. This should commence the eighth verse, as it begins what is supposed to be the part of the *priest* or *prophet* who now exhorts the people; as if he had said: Seeing you are in so good a spirit, do not forget your own resolutions, and harden not your hearts, "as your fathers did in Meribah and Massah, in the wilderness;" the *same fact* and the *same names* as are mentioned Exod. xvii. 7; when the people murmured at *Rephidim*, because they had no water; hence it was called *Meribah*, contention or provocation, and *Massah*, temptation.

Verse 9. *When your fathers tempted me*] *Tried* me, by their insolence, unbelief, and blasphemy. They *proved* me—they had full proof of my power to save and to destroy. There *they saw my works*—they saw that nothing was too hard for God.

Verse 10. *Forty years long*] They did nothing but murmur, disbelieve, and rebel, from the time they began their journey at the *Red Sea* till they passed over Jordan, a period of *forty* years. During all this time God was *grieved* by *that generation;* yet he seldom showed forth that *judgment* which they most righteously had deserved.

It is a people that do err in their heart] Or, according to the *Chaldee*, These are *a people whose idols are in their hearts.* At any rate they had not God there.

They have not known my ways] The verb ידע *yada*, *to know*, is used here, as in many other parts of Scripture, to express *approbation.* They knew God's ways well enough; but they did not *like* them; and would not walk in them. "These wretched men," says the old Psalter, "were gifnen to the lufe of this lyfe: knewe noght my ways of mekenes, and charite: for thi in my wreth I sware to thaim; that es, I sett stabely that if thai sall entre in till my rest;" that is, they shall not enter into my rest.

This ungrateful people did not approve of God's ways—they did not enter into his designs—they did not conform to his commands—they paid no attention to his miracles—and did not acknowledge the benefits which they received from his hands; therefore God determined that they should not enter into the *rest* which he had promised to them on condition that, if they were obedient, they should inherit the promised land. So none of those who came out of Egypt, except *Joshua* and *Caleb*, entered into Canaan; all the rest died in the wilderness, wherein, because of their disobedience, God caused them to wander *forty* years.

It is well known that the land of Canaan was a type of heaven, where, after all his toils, the good and faithful servant is to enter into the joy of his Lord. And as those Israelites in the wilderness were not permitted to enter into the land of Canaan because of their unbelief, their distrust of God's providence, and consequent disobedience, St. Paul hence takes occasion to exhort the Jews, Heb. iv. 2-11, to accept readily the terms offered to them by the Gospel. He shows that the words of the present Psalm are applicable to the state of Christianity; and intimates to them that, if they persisted in obstinate refusal of those gracious offers, *they* likewise would fall according to the same example of unbelief.—*Dodd.*

Analysis of the Ninety-fifth Psalm

This Psalm contains *two* parts:—

I. An exhortation to praise God, to adore, worship, kneel, ver. 1, 2, 6.

II. Reasons to persuade to it.

1. God's mercies, ver. 3, 4, 5, 7.

2. His judgments in punishing his own people *Israel* for neglect of this duty.

I. The psalmist begins this *Psalm* with an earnest invitation, including himself; saying,—

1. "O come, let us;" come along with me. Though a king, he thought not himself exempted.

2. And the assembly being come together, he acquaints them what they came for:—

1. "To sing to the Lord." 1. Heartily, joyfully: "Let us make a joyful noise;" make a *jubilee* of it. 2. Openly, and with a loud voice: "Let us make a joyful noise with Psalms." 3. Reverently, as being in his eye, "his presence." 4. Gratefully: "Let us come before his presence with thanksgiving."

2. "To worship, to bow down, to kneel," ver. 6. Adoration, humble adoration; outward worship—that of the body, as well as inward—that of the soul, is his due; and that for these reasons:—

II. 1. Because he is "the Rock of our salvation;" whether temporal or spiritual. So long as we rely on him as a Rock, we are safe from the tyranny of men, from the wrath of God, from the power of the devil, death, and hell.

2. Because he is "a great God, and a great King above all gods," Jehovah, a God whose name is *I am*, an incommunicable name to any other; for his essence is from himself, and immutable; all others derivative and mutable; and the *great* Jehovah, great in power, majesty, and glory; for he "is above all gods."

3. The whole orb of the earth is under his

power and dominion: "In his hands are all the corners of the earth; the strength of the hills is his also." The globe in all its extensions is subject to him.

4. And no wonder, for he is the Creator of both, which is another argument: "The sea is his, and he made it; and his hands formed the dry land."

5. "He is our Maker," the Creator and Lord of men also.

6. *Our Lord God* in particular, for he hath called us to be his inheritance: "For we are the people of his pasture, and the sheep of his hand."

In which duty, if we fail, he proposeth what is to be expected by the example of the *Israelites.*

I. God gave them a day, and he gives it to you; it is the *hodie*, to-day, of your life.

2. In this day he speaks, he utters his voice: outwardly he speaks by his word; inwardly, by his Spirit.

3. This you are bound to hear, to obey.

4. And it is your own fault if you hear it not, for you may hear it if you will; to that purpose he hath given you a day: "To-day if you will hear his voice."

5. Suppose you hear it not; the cause is, the hardness of your hearts: and take heed of it; "harden not your hearts."

For then it will be with you as it was with the Israelites.

1. "As in the day of temptation in the wilderness," at *Meribah* and *Massah.*

2. "When your fathers," the Israelites that then lived, "tempted me and proved me." They asked whether God was among them or not? They questioned my power, whether I was able to give them bread and water, and flesh?

3. And they found that I was able to do it: "They saw my works;" for I brought them water out of the rock, and gave them bread from heaven, and flesh also.

Their stubbornness was of long continuance, and often repeated, for it lasted *forty* years: "Forty years was I grieved with this generation;" which drew God to pass this censure and verdict upon them:—

1. His censure was, that they were an obstinate perverse people, "a people that do always err in their hearts;" that were led by their own desires, which caused them to err; the way of God they would not go in; they knew it not, that is, they liked it not.

2. This verdict upon them: "Unto whom I sware in my wrath, that they should not enter into my rest;" i, e., literally, into the land of *Canaan* that I promised them. The oath is extant, Num. xiv: "As I live, saith the Lord, your carcasses shall fall in the wilderness;" and in the wilderness they did fall, every one, except *Caleb* and *Joshua*, a fearful example against stubbornness and disobedience. Let him that readeth understand.

PSALM XCVI

All the inhabitants of the earth are invited to praise the Lord, 1–3. *His supreme majesty,* 3–6. *The tribes of Israel are invited to glorify him,* 7–9; *and to proclaim him among the heathen,* 10. *The heavens and the earth are commanded to rejoice in him,* 11–13.

A. M. 3489
B. C. 515
A. U. C. 239
Darii I.,
R. Persarum,
anno sexto

O [a]SING unto the LORD a new song: sing unto the LORD, all the earth.

2 Sing unto the LORD, bless his name; show forth his salvation from day to day.

3 Declare his glory among the heathen, his wonders among all people.

A. M. 3489
B. C. 515
A. U. C. 239
Darii I.,
R. Persarum,
anno sexto

[a]1 Chron. xvi. 23–33; Psa. xxxiii. 3

NOTES ON PSALM XCVI

This Psalm has no *title*, either in the *Hebrew* or *Chaldee*. The *Syriac:* "Of David. A prophecy of the advent of Christ, and the calling of the Gentiles to believe in him." The *Vulgate, Septuagint, Æthiopic,* and *Arabic* have, "A Song of David, when the House was built after the Captivity." We have seen in 1 Chron. xvi. 23-33 a Psalm nearly like this, composed by David, on bringing the ark to Sion, from the house of Obed-edom. See the notes on the above place. But the Psalm, as it stands in the *Chronicles*, has *thirty* verses; and this is only a section of it, from the *twenty-third* to the *thirty-third*. It is very likely that this part was taken from the Psalm above mentioned, to be used at the dedication of the *second temple.* The *one hundred and fifth* Psalm is almost the same as that in Chronicles, but much more extensive. Where they are in the *main* the same, there are differences for which it is not easy to account.

Verse 1. *Sing unto the Lord a new song*] A song of peculiar excellence, for in this sense the term *new* is repeatedly taken in the Scriptures. He has done extraordinary things for us, and we should *excel* in praise and thanksgiving.

Verse 2. *Show forth his salvation from day to day.*] The original is very emphatic, בשרו מיום ליום ישועתו *basseru miyom leyom yeshuatho*, "Preach the Gospel of his salvation from day to day." To the same effect the Septuagint, Ευαγγελιζεσθε ἡμεραν εξ ἡμερας το σωτηριον αυτου, "Evangelize his salvation from day to day."

Verse 3. *Declare his glory among the heathen.*] The heathen do not know the true God: as his being and attributes are at the foundation of all religion, these are the first subjects of instruction for the Gentile world. *Declare,* ספרו *sapperu, detail, number out* his *glory,* כבודו *kebodo*, his *splendour* and *excellence.*

His wonders among all people.] Declare also to the *Jews* his wonders, נפלאותיו *niphleothaiv, his miracles.* Dwell on the works which he

A. M. 3489
B. C. 515
A. U. C. 239
Darii I.,
R. Persarum,
anno sexto

4 For [b]the LORD *is* great, and
[c]greatly to be praised: [d]he *is* to
be feared above all gods.
5 For [e]all the gods of the nations *are* idols: [f]but the LORD made the
heavens.
6 Honour and majesty *are* before him:
strength and [g]beauty *are* in his sanctuary.
7 [h]Give unto the LORD, O ye kindreds of
the people, give unto the LORD glory and
strength.
8 Give unto the LORD the glory [i]*due unto*
his name: bring an offering, and come into
his courts.
9 O worship the LORD [k]in [l]the beauty of
holiness: fear before him, all
the earth.
10 Say among the heathen *that*
[m]the LORD reigneth: the world
also shall be established that it shall not be
moved: [n]he shall judge the people righteously.
11 [o]Let the heavens rejoice, and let the
earth be glad; [p]let the sea roar, and the fulness thereof.
12 Let the field be joyful, and all that *is* therein: then shall all the trees of the wood rejoice
13 Before the LORD: for he cometh, for he
cometh to judge the earth: [q]he shall judge
the world with righteousness, and the people
with his truth.

A. M. 3489
B. C. 515
A. U. C. 239
Darii I.,
R. Persarum,
anno sexto

[b]Psa. cxlv. 3——[c]Psa. xviii. 3——[d]Psa. xcv. 3 [e]See Jer. x. 11, 12——[f]Psa. cxv. 15; Isa. xlii. 5——[g]Psa. xxix. 2——[h]Psa. xxix. 1, 2——[i]Heb. *of his name* [k]Psa. xxix. 2; cx. 3

[l]Or, *in the glorious sanctuary*——[m]Psa. xciii. 1; xcvii. 1; Rev. xi. 15; xix. 6——[n]Ver. 13; Psa. lxvii. 4; xcviii. 9 [o]Psa. lxix. 34——[p]Psa. xcviii. 7, &c.——[q]Psa. lxvii. 4; Rev. xix. 11

shall perform in Judea. The miracles which Christ wrought among the Jews were full proof that he was not only the *Messiah*, but the *mighty power of God*.

Verse 4. *He* is *to be feared above all gods.*] I think the two clauses of this verse should be read thus:—

Jehovah is great, and greatly to be praised.
Elohim is to be feared above all.

I doubt whether the word אלהים *Elohim* is ever, by fair construction, applied to false gods or idols. The *contracted* form in the following verse appears to have this meaning.

Verse 5. *All the gods of the nations* are *idols*] אלהי *elohey.* All those reputed or worshipped as gods among the heathens are אלילים *elilim, vanities, emptinesses, things of nought.* Instead of being *Elohim*, they are *elilim;* they are not only not GOD, but they are *nothing.*" "Jehovah made the heavens." He who is the Creator is alone worthy of adoration.

Verse 6. *Honour and majesty* are *before him*] Does this refer to the cloud of his glory that preceded the ark in their journeying through the wilderness? The words *strength* and *beauty*, and *glory and strength*, ver. 7, are those by which the ark is described, Psa. lxxviii. 61.

Verse 7. *Ye kindreds of the people*] Ye families, all the *tribes* of Israel in your respective *divisions.*

8. *Come into his courts.*] Probably referring to the *second temple.* The reference must be either to the *tabernacle* or *temple.*

Verse 9. *Worship the Lord in the beauty of holiness*] I think בהדרת קדש *behadrath kodesh*, signifies *holy ornaments*, such as the high priest wore in his ministrations. These were given him for *glory* and *beauty;* and the psalmist calls on him to put on his sacerdotal garments, to bring his offering, מנחה *minchah*, and come into the courts of the Lord, and perform his functions, and make intercession for the people.

Verse 10. *Say among the heathen* that *the Lord reigneth*] *Justin Martyr*, in his dialogue with *Trypho* the Jew, quotes this passage thus: Ειπατε εν τοις εθνεσι, ὁ Κυριος εβασιλευσε απο του ξυλου, "Say among the nations, the Lord ruleth *by the wood*," meaning the *cross;* and accuses the Jews of having blotted this word out of their Bibles, because of the evidence it gave of the truth of Christianity. It appears that this reading did exist anciently in the *Septuagint*, or at least in some ancient copies of that work, for the reading has been quoted by *Tertullian*, *Lactantius*, *Arnobius*, *Augustine*, *Cassiodorus*, *Pope Leo*, *Gregory of Tours*, and others. The reading is still extant in the ancient *Roman* Psalter, *Dominus regnavit a ligno*, and in some others. In an ancient MS. copy of the Psalter before me, while the text exhibits the commonly received reading, the margin has the following gloss: *Regnavit a ligno crucis*, "The Lord reigns by the wood of the cross." My old *Scotico-Latin* Psalter has not *a ligno* in the text, but seems to refer to it in the paraphrase: **For Criste regned efter the dede on the crosse.** It is necessary, however, to add, that no such words exist in any copy of the Hebrew text now extant, nor in any MS. yet collated, nor in any of the ancient Versions. Neither *Eusebius* nor *Jerome* even refer to it, who wrote comments on the Psalms; nor is it mentioned by any *Greek* writer except *Justin Martyr*.

The world also shall be established] The word תבל *tebel* signifies the *habitable globe*, and may be a metonymy here, the container put for the contained. And many think that by it the *Church* is intended; as the *Lord*, who is announced to the heathen as reigning, is understood to be Jesus Christ; and *his judging among the people*, his establishing the holy Gospel among them, and governing the nations by its laws.

Verse 11. *Let the heavens rejoice*] The publication of the Gospel is here represented as a universal blessing; the *heavens*, the *earth*, the *sea*, and its *inhabitants*, the *field*, the *grass*, and the *trees* of the *wood*, are all called to rejoice at this glorious event. This verse is well and harmoniously translated in the old Psalter:—

Fayne be hevenes,—and the erth glad;
Styrde be the see,—and the fulnes of it;
Joy sal feldes,—and al that ere in thaim.

And the paraphrase is at least curious:—

Hevens, haly men. **Erthe,** meke men that receyves lare (learning.) **Feldes,** that is even men, mylde and softe: they shall joy in Criste. **And all that is in thaim,** that es, strengh, wyttes & skill."

I shall give the remaining part of this ancient paraphrase, which is an echo of the opinion of most of the Latin fathers.

Verse 12. **Thou sal glad al the trese of woddes.—Thou,** that is in another lyfe. **Trese of woddes.**—Synful men that were fyrst withouten frut, and sithen taken into God's temple.

Verse 13. **For he coms, he coms. He coms,** fyrste to be man.—Sythen **he comes** to deme the erth.

He sal deme in evenes the erth:—and folk in his sothfastnes. Nothing is evener, or sothfaster, than that he geder with hym perfyte men; to deme and to deperte to the rig hande (thaim) that did mercy:—pase to the lefte hande (thaim) that did it nogt.

The psalmist here in the true spirit of poetry, gives life and intelligence to universal nature, producing them all as exulting in the reign of the Messiah, and the happiness which should take place in the earth when the Gospel should be universally preached. These predictions seem to be on the eve of complete fulfilment. Lord, hasten the time! For a fuller explanation see the following analysis.

Analysis of the Ninety-sixth Psalm

Although this Psalm was composed by David at the bringing back of the ark, yet most ancient and modern Christian expositors acknowledge it a prophecy of Christ's kingdom, to be enlarged by the accession of all the Gentiles, and finally, his coming to judgment.

There are *two* parts in this Psalm:—

I. A general exhortation to both Jews and Gentiles to praise God, ver. 1-3.

II. A prophecy of Christ's kingdom, described by its greatness, ver. 4, 5; the honours and glory, ver. 6; of the majesty of the King, ver. 7, 8.

1. The amplitude of this kingdom, ver. 10.
2. His judicature in it, ver. 11-13.

I. 1. The invitation to praise God for the benefits conferred on the whole earth by Christ, ver. 1-3. 1. That the praise be full, he thrice repeats, "O sing, sing, sing;" to the honour of the Trinity, says *Bellarmine*, obscurely intimated in the Old, but plainly to be preached in the New, Testament. 2. "Show forth." Give praise by thanks and singing. 3. "Declare." Carry good news—the Gospel of glad tidings.

2. The song to be sung must be new: "Sing unto the Lord a new song." New, for a new benefit; new, to be sung by new people; new, as being on a most excellent subject.

3. It was to be sung "by the whole earth." By new men, and all the world over; for God was not now to be known in *Judea* only, but by all nations.

4. It must be continually sung, from day to day, without cessation; for as one day succeeds another, so should there be a continual succession in his praise.

Afterwards he expresses the benefits for which the whole earth is to praise him, which is for the redemption of the world by his Son.

1. He shows forth his salvation, which he has conferred on mankind by Christ.

2. "Declare his glory among the heathen, his wonders among all people." Salvation was a glorious work, full of wonders. And this was to be evangelized, as before to the *Jews* by the *prophets*, so now to *all people* by the *apostles*.

II. And that this exhortation might appear more reasonable, he presents God as a king, and sets down the greatness, amplitude, and equity of his kingdom.

1. "Sing to the Lord all the earth, for he is Lord of the whole earth." 1. "The Lord is great." Great in power, wisdom, goodness, mercy, dominion, riches; great in every way of greatness. 2. "He is greatly to be praised," or worthy of all praise, for his innumerable benefits. He bestows them, spiritually and temporally, in his creation, redemption, and preservation of the world. What is praiseworthy in any king may be found superlatively in him.

2. "He is to be feared above all gods;" for he can cast body and soul into hell. They, though called gods, can do neither good nor hurt; the devils, who set them up, believe that he is above them, and they tremble. Sing to him then, for the supremacy is his; he is above all gods. If there be other gods, show their works; produce the heavens they have made, or the earth they have framed. It is our God alone who "made the heavens, and all things that are in them;" fear him, and not them.

The prophet elegantly derides the heathenish gods, and the heathen for fearing them.

1. For the multitude of them, for they were many; which is contrary to the nature of God, who must be but one, for there can be but one Supreme.

2. For their division: one of the *Ammonites; another* of the *Moabites;* one of the *Philistines;* many of the *Assyrians, Egyptians, Greeks, Romans:* their gods were according to the number of their cities; three hundred Jupiters, thirty thousand deities.

3. They were *elilim, Dii minores. Moloch* had the rule of the *sun; Astarte*, of the *moon; Ceres*, of *corn; Pluto*, of *hell; Neptune*, of the *sea*, &c. Their power was not universal, as the power of God ought to be.

4. Lastly, in the opposition, which plainly shows the difference between God and idols. They are but the work of men's hands. Our God is a creator; he made the heavens, and all that is contained in and under them. He then is terrible, and to be feared; not those diminutive, vain, unprofitable gods of the nations.

And so, having removed out of his way all the gods of the nations, he returns to our God and King. Having said "he was great, greatly to be feared, and praised above all gods," he now sets forth his majesty to the eye of the subject and stranger: *Honour, majesty, strength, beauty;* so says our prophet: "Honour and majesty are before him, strength and beauty are in his sanctuary." God is invisible; but his honour and majesty, strength and beauty, may be easily observed in his ordering, governing, and preserving the whole world and his Church; both which may be justly called his sanctuary, and the last *his holy place*.

He has proved God to be a universal King, and now he endeavours to persuade his subjects, all kindreds of people, to return to their king his tribute, his honour and worship, which he comprehends in these words: *Give—bring* an *offering—worship—fear—proclaim him to be King.*

1. "Give unto the Lord;" and again, "Give unto the Lord glory and strength." Give freely to him, and alone attribute to him the glory of your being and well-being, that he made and redeemed you, and that by the strength of his right hand he has plucked you out of the hands of your enemies. This was the glorious work of his mercy and power.

2. "Give unto the Lord the honour due to his name." It is a debt; and a debt, in equity, must be paid. The honour due to his name is to acknowledge him to be holy, just, true, powerful: "The Lord, the faithful God,"—"good, merciful, long-suffering," &c. Defraud not his name of the least honour.

3. "Bring an offering, and come into his courts." *Appear not before the Lord empty,* as the *Jews* were commanded; to which the prophet alludes. "They had their sacrifices, and we also have our spiritual sacrifices, acceptable to God through Jesus Christ," to bring; 1 Peter ii. 5. These are the sacrifices of a contrite heart. Bring these when you enter into his courts, and into his house of prayer.

4. "O worship the Lord in the beauty of holiness." They who enter into the presence of a king presently fall on their knees in token of submission and homage; in the presence of your King do the same. *Adore*, and remember to do it in the beauty of holiness; referred to the material temple, it is by relation a *holy place*, and should not be profaned; a beautiful place, and should not be defaced, but kept beautiful. If referred to the spiritual temple, the temple of the Holy Ghost is to be beautiful with holiness; a holy life, holy virtues, beautiful garments, righteousness and true holiness.

5. "Fear before him, all the earth." Join fear to your worship, for a man may be bold in the presence of his king. "Serve the Lord with fear, and rejoice with reverence." There is a fear which arises out of an apprehension of greatness and excellency in the person, together with our dependence on and our submission to him, which in body and mind makes us step back, and keep at a distance. This kind of fear produces reverence and adoration, and this the prophet here means.

6. "Say among the heathen, the Lord reigns;" or, as some say: "The Lord reigns among the heathen." Be heralds; and proclaim, with the sound of the trumpet, *God reigns, God is King.*

The prophet begins to set forth the amplitude of Christ's kingdom:—

1. Before, it was confined to Judea, but is now enlarged: "All nations are become his subjects; he reigns among the heathen."

2. Its stability: "The world shall be established, that it shall not be moved." The laws of this kingdom are not to be altered, as were the laws of Moses, but fixed and established for ever. The Gospel is an eternal Gospel, a standing law.

3. The equity to be observed in it: "He shall judge the people righteously," for he shall give to those who observe his laws, rewards; to those who despise them, break them, and say, "We will not have this man to reign over us," condign punishment.

4. The prophet, having described the King, and the state of his kingdom, exults in spirit, as if he had seen him coming to sit upon the throne. He calls, not the *Gentiles* only, whom it did very nearly concern, but all creatures, to rejoice in him; *heaven, earth, sea, trees, fields*, &c. Although there are who by *heaven* understand *angels; by the earth, men;* by the *sea, troublesome spirits;* by *trees* and *fields*, the *Gentiles* who were to believe; yet this need not be thought strange, because such *prosopopœias* are frequent in Scripture. The meaning is, that as the salvation was universal, so he would have the joy to be universal: "Let the heavens rejoice, and let the earth be glad; let the sea roar, and the fulness thereof. Let the field be joyful, and all that is therein: then shall the trees of the wood rejoice before the Lord."

He incites all creatures to rejoice for Christ's coming, both for the first and for the second: for the first, in which he consecrated all things; for the second, in which he will free all things from corruption, Rom. viii. 19-22.

1. "For he cometh, for he cometh to judge the earth."—Which first part of the verse the fathers refer to his first coming, when he was incarnate, and came to redeem the world by his death: and was to the end to judge, that is to rule and govern, the world by his word, ordinances, and Spirit.

2. And again: "He shall come to judge the world with righteousness, and the people with his truth:" which coming, though terrible to the wicked, will be joyful and comfortable to the righteous. For, says our Lord, "Lift up your heads, for your redemption draweth near;" and to comfort them, and terrify the wicked, he tells them he will judge with equity, that is, in justice and in truth, according to his word and promise. He will accept no man's person, but render to every man according to his works.

PSALM XCVII

The reign of Jehovah, its nature and blessedness, 1, 2. *He is fearful to the wicked*, 3–6. *Idolaters shall be destroyed*, 7. *The blessedness of the righteous*, 8–12.

A. M. 3489
B. C. 515
A. U. C. 239
Darii I.,
R. Persarum,
anno sexto

THE [a]LORD reigneth; let the earth rejoice; let the [b]multitude of [c]isles be glad *thereof*.

2 [d]Clouds and darkness *are* round about him: [e]righteousness and judgment *are* the [f]habitation of his throne.

[a]Psa. xcvi. 10——[b]Heb. *many* or *great isles*——[c]Isa. lx. 9

[d]1 Kings viii. 12; Psa. xviii. 11——[e]Psa. lxxxix. 14
[f]Or, *establishment*

NOTES ON PSALM XCVII

This Psalm has no *title* either in the *Hebrew* or *Chaldee; and in fourteen* of *Kennicott's* and *De Rossi's* MSS. it is written as a part of the preceding. In the *Vulgate* it is thus entitled, *Psalmus David, quando terra ejus restituta est.* "A Psalm of David when his land was restored;" the meaning of which I suppose to be, after he had obtained possession of the kingdom of Israel and Judah, and became king over all the tribes; or perhaps, after he had gained possession of all those countries which were originally granted to the Israelites in the Divine promise. See 1 Chron. xviii. 1, 2. The *Septuagint* is nearly to the same purpose, *ὁτι ἡ γη αυτου καθισταται*, "when his land was established:" so the *Æthiopic* and *Arabic*. The *Syriac* has, "A Psalm of David, in which he predicts the advent of Christ, (i. e., in the flesh,) and through it his last appearing, (i. e., to judgment.") The author of the Epistle to the Hebrews, chap. i. 6, quotes a part of the *seventh* verse of this Psalm, and applies it to Christ. Who the author was is uncertain: it is much in the spirit of David's finest compositions; and yet many learned men suppose it was written to celebrate the Lord's power and goodness in the restoration of the Jews from the *Babylonish captivity.*

Verse 1. *The Lord reigneth*] Here is a simple proposition, which is a self-evident axiom, and requires no proof: JEHOVAH is *infinite* and *eternal;* is possessed of *unlimited power* and *unerring wisdom;* as he is the *Maker*, so he must be the *Governor*, of all things. His authority is absolute, and his government therefore universal. In all places, on all occasions, and in all times, Jehovah reigns.

But this supreme King is not only called יהוה YEHOVAH, which signifies his infinite and eternal being, unlimited power, and unerring wisdom; and, as Creator, his *universal government;* but he is also אדני ADONAI, the *Director* and *Judge*. He *directs* human actions by his *word, Spirit*, and *Providence.* Hence are his *laws* and *revelation* in general; for the governed should know their governor, and should be acquainted with his laws, and the reasons on which *obedience* is founded. As *Adonai* or *Director*, he shows them the difference between good and evil; and their duty to their God, their neighbours, and themselves: and he finally becomes the *Judge* of their actions. But as his law is holy, and his commandment holy, just, and good, and man is in a fallen, sinful state; hence he *reveals* himself as אלהים ELOHIM, *God*, entering into a *gracious covenant* with mankind, to enlighten his darkness, and help his infirmities; that he may see what is *just*, and be *able* to do it. But as this will not cancel the sins *already committed*, hence the necessity of a Saviour, an atonement; and hence the incarnation, passion, death, and resurrection of our Lord Jesus. This is the *provision* made by the great God for the more effectual administration of his kingdom upon earth. *Jehovah, Adonai, Elohim* reigneth; *et his animadversis*, and these points considered, it is no wonder that the psalmist should add,

Let the earth rejoice; let the multitude of isles be glad] The *earth*, the *terraqueous globe;* especially, here, the *vast continents*, over every part of which God's dominion extends. But it is not confined to *them;* it takes in the *islands* of the sea; all the *multitude* of those islands, even to the smallest inhabited rock; which are as much the objects of his care, the number of their inhabitants considered, as the vastest continents on which are founded the mightiest empires. All this government springs from his *holiness, righteousness*, and *benignity;* and is exercised in what we call *providence*, from *pro*, for, before, and *video*, to see, which word is well defined and applied by CICERO: *Providentia est, per quam futurum aliquid videtur, antequam factum sit.* "Providence is that by which any thing future is seen before it takes place." *De Invent.* c. 53. And, in reference to a *Divine* providence, he took up the general opinion, viz., *Esse deos, et eorum providentia mundum administrari. De Divinat.* c. 51, *ad finem.* "There are gods; and by their providence the affairs of the world are administered."

This providence is not only *general*, taking in the *earth* and its *inhabitants, en masse;* giving and establishing *laws* by which all things shall be governed; but it is also *particular;* it takes in the multitudes of the *isles*, as well as the vast *continents;* the different *species* as well as the *genera;* the *individual*, as well as the *family.* As every *whole* is composed of its *parts*, without the smallest of which it could not be a whole; so all *generals* are composed of *particulars.* And by the *particular* providence of God, the *general* providence is formed; he takes care of each *individual;* and, consequently, he takes care of the *whole.* Therefore, on the *particular* providence of God, the *general* providence is built; and the *general* providence could not exist without the *particular*, any more than a *whole* could subsist independently of its *parts.* It is by this particular providence that God governs *the multitude of the isles*, notices the *fall of a sparrow, bottles the tears* of the mourner, and *numbers the hairs* of his followers. Now, as God is an infinitely *wise* and *good* Being, and governs the world in *wisdom* and *goodness*, the *earth* may well *rejoice*, and *the multitude of the isles be glad.*

Verse 2. *Clouds and darkness* are *round about him*] It is granted that this is a subject which cannot be comprehended. And why? Because God is *infinite;* he acts from his own *counsels*, which are *infinite;* in reference to *ends* which are also *infinite:* therefore, the *reasons* of his government cannot be comprehended by the feeble, limited powers of man. There must be *clouds and darkness*—an impenetrable obscurity, round about him; and we can no more

A. M. 3489
B. C. 515
A. U. C. 239
Darii I.,
R. Persarum,
anno sexto

3 [g]A fire goeth before him,
and burneth up his enemies
round about.
4 [h]His lightnings enlightened
the world: the earth saw, and trembled.
5 [i]The hills melted like wax at the presence
of the LORD, at the presence of
the LORD of the whole earth.
6 [k]The heavens declare his
righteousness, and all the people
see his glory.
7 [l]Confounded be all they that serve graven

A. M. 3489
B. C. 515
A. U. C. 239
Darii I.,
R. Persarum,
anno sexto

[g]Psa. xviii. 8; l. 3, Dan. vii. 10; Hab. iii. 5——[h]Exod. xix. 18; Psa. lxxvii. 18; civ. 32

[i]Judg. v. 5; Mic. i. 4; Nah. i. 5——[k]Psa. xix. 1; l. 6
[l]Exod. xx. 4; Lev. xxvi. 1; Deut. v. 8; xxvii. 15

comprehend him in what is called *æternitas a parte ante*—the eternity that passed before *time* commenced, than we can in the *æternitas a parte post*—the eternity that is to come, when time shall be no more. Yet such a Being cannot but *see* all things *clearly*, and *do* all things *well;* therefore the psalmist properly asserts,—

Righteousness and judgment are *the habitation of his throne.*] *Righteousness,* צדק *tsedek,* the principle that acts according to *justice* and *equity;* that gives to all their *due,* and ever holds in all things an *even balance. And judgment,* משפט *mishpat,* the principle that *discerns, orders, directs,* and *determines* every thing according to truth and justice: these form *the habitation of his throne;* that is, his government and management of the world are according to these; and though we cannot see the *springs,* the *secret counsels,* and the *times,* which this *omniscient* and *almighty* FATHER must ever have in his own power, yet we may rest assured that all his administration is wise, just, holy, good, and kind. For, although his counsels be inscrutable, and the dispensations of his providence be sometimes apparently unequal, yet righteousness and judgment are the habitation of his throne.

In this most sublime description the psalmist, by the *figure* termed *prosopopœia,* or personification, gives *vitality* and *thought* to all the subjects he employs; here, the very *throne* of God is *animated; righteousness* and *judgment* are two *intellectual beings* who support it. The *fire,* the *lightnings,* the *earth,* the *heavens* themselves, are all intellectual beings, which either accompany, go before him, or proclaim his majesty.

Verse 3. *A fire goeth before him*] Literally, this and the following verse may refer to the electric fluid, or to manifestations of the Divine displeasure, in which, by means of *ethereal fire,* God consumed his enemies. But *fire* is generally represented as an accompaniment of the appearances of the Supreme Being. He appeared on *Mount Sinai* in the midst of *fire, thunder,* and *lightnings,* Exod. xix. 16-18. Daniel, chap. vii. 9, 10, represents the Sovereign Judge as being on a throne which was a *fiery flame,* and the *wheels* of his chariot like *burning fire;* and a *fiery stream* issuing from it, and coming forth from before him. St. *Paul* tells us (2 Thess. i. 8) that the Lord Jesus shall be revealed from heaven with his mighty angels, in *flaming fire;* and St. *Peter,* (2 Epist. iii. 7, 10, 11,) that when the Lord shall come to judgment the heavens and the earth shall be destroyed by *fire,* the heavens shall pass away with a *great noise,* the *elements melt with fervent heat,* and the *earth* and its works be *burnt up.* Here then, will appear,—

"Our God in grandeur, and our world on fire."

Burneth up his enemies round about.] The fire is his pioneer which destroys all the hinderances in his way, and makes him a plain passage.

Verse 4. *His lightnings enlightened the world*] Though this be no more than a majestic description of the coming of the Lord, to confound his enemies and succour his followers, yet *some spiritualize* the passage, and say, the *lightnings* signify the *apostles,* who *enlightened* the world by their heavenly doctrine.

The earth saw, and trembled.] The earth is represented as a sentient being. It saw the terrible majesty of God; and trembled through terror, fearing it should be destroyed on account of the wickedness of its inhabitants.

Verse 5. *The hills melted like wax*] The fire of God seized on and liquefied them, so that they no longer opposed his march; and the mountains before him became a plain.

The Lord of the whole earth.] אדון כל הארץ *adon col haarets,* the Director, Stay, and Support of the whole earth. The universal Governor, whose jurisdiction is not confined to any one place; but who, having created all, governs all that he has made.

Verse 6. *The heavens declare his righteousness*] They also, in this poetic description, become *intelligent* beings, and proclaim the majesty and the mercy of the Most High. Metaphorically, they may be said to declare his glory. Their magnitude, number, revolutions, order, influence, and harmony, proclaim the wondrous skill, matchless wisdom, and unlimited power of the Sovereign of the universe. See the notes on Psalm xix.

And all the people see his glory.] Whatsoever God has made proclaims his eternal power and Godhead; and who, from a contemplation of the work of his hands, can be ignorant of his being and providence?

Verse 7. *Confounded be all they*] Rather, *They shall be confounded that boast themselves in idols.* There is a remarkable play on the *letters* here, המתהללים *hammithhalelim,* who move like madmen; referring to the violent gestures practised in idolatrous rites.

Of idols] באלילים *baelilim,* in vanities, emptinesses; who "make much ado about nothing," and take a *mad* and *painful* pleasure in *ridiculous* and *unprofitable* ceremonies of religion.

Worship him] WHO? JESUS: so says the apostle, Heb. i. 6. Who will dare to dispute his authority?

All ye *gods.*] Οἱ αγγελοι αυτου, *his angels: so* the *Septuagint* and the *apostle:* "Let all the angels of God worship him:" and the words are most certainly applied to the Saviour of the world by the author of the Epistle to the Hebrews; see the note there. The *Chaldee* says: "All nations who worship idols shall adore him."

A. M. 3489 B. C. 515 A. U. C. 239 Darii I., R. Persarum, anno sexto

images, that boast themselves of
idols: [m]worship him, all *ye* gods.
8 Zion heard, and was glad;
and the daughters of Judah rejoiced because of thy judgments, O LORD.
9 For thou, LORD, *art* [n]high above all the
earth: [o]thou art exalted far above all gods.
10 Ye that love the LORD, [p]hate evil: [q]he
preserveth the souls of his saints;
[r]he delivereth them out of the
hand of the wicked.
11 [s]Light is sown for the righteous, and gladness for the upright in heart.
12 [t]Rejoice in the LORD, ye righteous;
[u]and give thanks [v]at the remembrance of his
holiness.

[m]Heb. i. 6——[n]Psa. lxxxiii. 18——[o]Exod. xviii. 11; Psa. xcv. 4; xcvi. 5——[p]Psa. xxxiv. 14; xxxvii. 27; ci. 3; Amos v. 15; Rom. xii. 9——[q]Psa. xxxi. 23; xxxvii. 28; cxlv. 20; Prov. ii. 8

[r]Psalm xxxvii. 39, 40; Daniel iii. 28; vi. 22, 27——[s]Job xxii. 28; Psalm cxii. 4; Proverbs iv. 18——[t]Psalm xxxiii. 1——[u]Psalm xxx. 4——[v]Or, *to the memorial*

Verse 8. *Zion heard, and was glad*] All the land of *Israel*, long desolated, heard of the judgments which God had shown among the enemies of his people.

And the daughters of Judah] All the villages of the land—*Zion* as the mother, and all the *villages* in the country as her *daughters*, rejoice in the deliverance of God's people.

Verse 9. *For thou, Lord,* art *high*] Thou art infinitely exalted above *men* and *angels*.

Verse 10. *Ye that love the Lord, hate evil*] Because it is inconsistent with his love to you, as well as your love to him.

He preserveth the souls of his saints] The *saints,* חסידיו *chasidaiv, his merciful people:* their *souls*—lives, are precious in his sight. He *preserves* them; keeps them from every evil, and every enemy.

Out of the hand of the wicked.] From his *power* and influence.

Verse 11. *Light is sown for the righteous*] The Divine light in the soul of man is a seed which takes root, and springs up and increases *thirty, sixty,* and *a hundred* fold. *Gladness* is also a seed: it is *sown,* and, if carefully improved and cultivated, will also multiply itself into *thousands.* Every grace of God is a *seed,* which he intends should produce a *thousand* fold in the hearts of genuine believers. We do not so much require *more* grace from God, as the *cultivation* of what we have received. God will not give more, unless we improve what we have got. Remember *the parable of the talents.* Let the *light* and *gladness* be faithfully cultivated, and they will multiply themselves till the whole body shall be full of light, and the whole soul full of happiness. But it is the *righteous* only for whom the *light* is sown; and the *upright in heart* alone for whom the *gladness* is sown.

The words may also signify that, however *distressed* or *persecuted* the *righteous* and the *upright* may be, it shall not be always so. As surely as the *grain* that is sown in the earth shall vegetate, and bring forth its proper fruit in its season, so surely shall *light*—prosperity, and *gladness*—comfort and peace, be communicated to them. They also will *spring up* in due time.

Verse 12. *Rejoice in the Lord, ye righteous*] It is your privilege to be *happy.* Exult in him through whom ye have received the atonement. *Rejoice;* but let it be *in the Lord.* All other joy is the *mirth of fools,* which is as the *crackling of thorns under a pot*—it is a luminous blaze for a moment, and leaves nothing but smoke and ashes behind.

At the remembrance of his holiness.] But why should you give thanks at the remembrance that God is holy? Because he has said, *Be ye holy; for I am holy:* and in *holiness* alone true *happiness* is to be found. *As he, therefore, who hath called you is holy; so be ye holy in all manner of conversation.* False Christians hate the doctrine of Christian holiness; they are willing to be holy in another, but not holy in themselves. There is too much cross-bearing and self-denial in the doctrine of holiness for them. A perfect heart they neither expect nor wish.

The analysis considers the whole Psalm as relating to Jesus Christ and the last judgment: so it was understood by several of the ancient fathers. The reader may take it in either sense.

ANALYSIS OF THE NINETY-SEVENTH PSALM

There are *three* parts in this Psalm, if we interpret it as referring to our blessed Lord:—

I. A *prophetical* description of his power and glory, especially at the *day of judgment,* ver. 1-6.

II. A manifest difference between the states of idolaters and the people of God, ver. 7-9.

III. An exhortation to love God and hate evil; and the reason on which it is founded: a two-fold gracious reward, ver. 10-12.

I. The psalmist begins with a solemn acclamation: "The Lord reigneth." He is the supreme King; and he will use his kingly power both now and in the day of judgment. 1. For the good of his subjects. 2. For the confusion of his enemies.

1. For "clouds and darkness are round about him," as when he gave the law on Mount Sinai. 2. "Righteousness and judgment are the habitation of his throne;" and therefore a just sentence shall come forth *against* his *enemies,* and in *behalf* of his *friends,* ver. 2-5. 3. His appearance shall be very glorious; for the "heavens shall declare it, and all people shall see it," ver. 6.

II. The difference between the state of idolaters and the people of God.

1. *Confusion* and a *curse* shall fall upon the *former:* "They shall be confounded," &c., ver. 7.

2. He exhorts all in power, men—*magistrates,* &c., and all who excel in strength—*angels,* to worship him: "Worship him, all ye gods," ver. 7. All confidence should be reposed in him.

3. God's people rejoice when they find that it is their own Lord who is coming to judgment:

"Zion heard, and was glad; the daughters of Judah rejoiced," ver. 8.

4. And they rejoiced chiefly in knowing that their God "was high above all the earth, and exalted far above all gods," ver. 9.

III. The *expostulation*, which gives us the *character* by which God's people may be known. He exhorts them to *love God, and to hate evil.* Hence we see that the true followers of God, 1. Love him; 2. Hate evil, as the infallible consequence of loving him, ver. 10.

He shows them the gracious reward which God promises.

1. "He preserveth the souls of his saints." Often their *lives*, in an especial manner, are *preserved* by him; but always their *souls*. The accuser of the brethren shall not hurt them.

2. "He delivereth them out of the hands of the wicked." Sometimes out of their hand, that they fall not into it; and sometimes out of their hand, when they are in it. This is their *first* reward, ver. 10.

A *second* reward is in the next verse: that in their miseries they shall be filled with spiritual happiness, when perhaps they little expect it: "Light is sown for the righteous, and gladness for the upright in heart," ver. 11.

1. By *light* we may understand a peculiar manifestation of God's favour; comfort, peace, and joy; or deliverance from their spiritual and temporal oppressors.

2. This is *sown* as a seed. For the light of comfort, of peace of conscience, and joy in the Holy Spirit, though it may be clouded in times of heaviness, through manifold temptations, yet it will spring forth again, like the corn, which, after it is sown, lies hidden for some time, under the clods of the earth; yet all that time it is *vegetating* and coming forth to public view. And deliverance from their enemies, though slow, will come; though the rod of the wicked *come* into the lot of the just, it shall not *rest* there.

3. From these premises the psalmist draws this conclusion: Since God is preparing those blessings for you that fear and love him, then, 1. "Rejoice in the Lord;" glory in him as the Fountain of your blessedness. 2. "Give thanks at the remembrance of his holiness." Remember the good he has done you, the grace he has bestowed on you, and the holiness you may yet receive from him; and rejoice in the encouragement, and give thanks. Rejoice that ye may be *holy*, for in that your *happiness* consists.

PSALM XCVIII

God is celebrated for his wondrous works, 1, 2; *for the exact fulfilment of his gracious promises,* 3. *The manner in which he is to be praised,* 4–6. *Inanimate creation called to bear a part in this concert,* 7, 8. *The justice of his judgments,* 9.

XIX. DAY. EVENING PRAYER

A Psalm

A. M. 3489
B. C. 515
A. U. C. 239
Darii I.,
R. Persarum,
anno sexto

O [a]SING unto the LORD a new song, for [b]he hath done marvellous things: [c]his right hand, and his holy arm hath gotten him the victory.

2 [d]The LORD hath made known his salvation: [e]his righteousness hath he [f]openly showed in the sight of the heathen.

3 He hath [g]remembered his mercy and his truth toward the house of Israel: [h]all the ends of the earth have seen the salvation of our God.

4 [i]Make a joyful noise unto the LORD, all

A. M. 3489
B. C. 515
A. U. C. 239
Darii I.,
R. Persarum,
anno sexto

[a]Psa. xxxiii. 3; xcvi. 1; Isa. xlii. 10——[b]Exod. xv. 11; Psa. lxxvii. 16; lxxxvi. 10; cv. 5; cxxxvi. 4; cxxxix. 14——[c]Exod. xv. 6; Isa. lix. 16; lxiii. 5——[d]Isa. lii. 10; Luke ii. 30, 31

[e]Isaiah lxii. 2; Romans iii. 25, 26——[f]Or, *revealed*——[g]Luke i. 54, 55, 72——[h]Isa. xlix. 6; lii. 10; Luke ii. 30, 31; iii. 6; Acts xiii. 47; xxviii. 28——[i]Psalm xcv. 1; c. 1

NOTES ON PSALM XCVIII

In the *Hebrew* this is simply termed מזמור *mizmor*, a Psalm. In the *Chaldee, A prophetic Psalm.* In the *Vulgate, Septuagint, Æthiopic, A Psalm of David.* In the *Syriac* it is attributed to *David*, and stated to be composed concerning the "Restoration of the Israelites from Egypt; but is to be understood spiritually of the advent of the Messiah, and the vocation of the Gentiles to the Christian faith."

The Psalm in its subject is very like the *ninety-sixth*. It was probably written to celebrate the deliverance from the Babylonish captivity; but is to be understood prophetically of the redemption of the world by Jesus Christ.

Verse 1. *A new song*] A song of *excellence*. Give him the *highest* praise. See on Psa. xcvi. 1.

Hath done marvellous things] נפלאות *niphlaoth*, "miracles;" the same word as in Psa. xcvi. 3, where we translate it *wonders.*

His holy arm] His Almighty power,—

Hath gotten him the victory.] הושיעה לו *hoshiah llo*, "hath made salvation to himself."

Verse 2. *Made known his salvation*] He has delivered his people in such a way as to show that it was supernatural, and that their confidence in the unseen God was not in vain.

Verse 3. *He hath remembered his mercy*] His gracious promises to their forefathers.

A. M. 3489 B. C. 515 A. U. C. 239 Darii I., R. Persarum, anno sexto

the earth: make a loud noise,
and rejoice, and sing praise.
5 Sing unto the LORD with the
harp; with the harp, and the
voice of a psalm.
6 [k]With trumpets, and sound of cornet,
make a joyful noise before the LORD the
King.
7 [l]Let the sea roar, and the
fulness thereof; the world, and
they that dwell therein.
8 Let the floods [m]clap *their*
hands: let the hills be joyful together.
9 Before the LORD; [n]for he cometh to
judge the earth: with righteousness shall he
judge the world, and the people with equity.

[k]Numbers x. 10; 1 Chronicles xv. 28; 2 Chronicles xxix. 27

[l]Psalm xcvi. 11, &c.——[m]Isaiah lv. 12——[n]Psalm xcvi. 10, 13

And his truth] Faithfully accomplishing what he had promised. All this was fulfilled under the Gospel.

Verse 5. *With—the voice of a Psalm.*] I think זמרה *zimrah*, which we translate *Psalm*, means either a *musical instrument*, or a *species of ode* modulated by different voices.

Verse 6. *With trumpets*] חצצרות *chatsotseroth*. Some kind of tubular instruments, of the form and management of which we know nothing.

And sound of cornet] שופר *shophar*, the word commonly used for what we call *trumpet*.

Verse 7. *Let the sea roar*] These are either fine poetic images; or, if we take them as referring to the promulgation of the Gospel, by the *sea* all maritime countries and commercial nations may be intended.

Verse 8. *Let the floods clap* their *hands*] נהרות *neharoth*, properly *the rivers*—possibly meaning immense *continents*, where only *large rivers* are found; thus including *inland* people, as well as *maritime nations*, and those on the sea-coasts generally; as in those early times little more than the *coasts* of the sea were known. The Gospel shall be preached in the most secluded nations of the world.

Let the hills be joyful] All the inhabitants of *rocky* and *mountainous* countries.

Verse 9. *For he cometh to judge the earth*] He comes to make known his salvation, and show his merciful designs to all the children of men.

With righteousness shall he judge the world] His word shall not be confined; all shall know him, from the least to the greatest: he shall show that he is loving to every man, and hateth nothing that he hath made. See the notes on Psa. xcvi. There is a very great similarity between this Psalm and the Song or *Magnificat* of the Blessed Virgin. I shall note some of the parallels, chiefly from Bishop Nicholson.

This Psalm is an evident prophecy of Christ's coming to save the world; and what is here *foretold* by David is, in the Blessed *Virgin's* song, chanted forth as being *accomplished.* David is the *Voice*, and Mary is the *Echo*.

1. DAVID. "O sing unto the Lord a new song." (The *Voice.*)
   MARY. "My soul doth magnify the Lord." (The *Echo.*)
2. DAVID. "He hath done marvellous things." (The *Voice.*)
   MARY. "He that is mighty hath done great things." (The *Echo.*)
3. DAVID. "With his own right hand and holy arm hath he gotten himself the victory." (The *Voice.*)
   MARY. "He hath showed strength with his arm and scattered the proud in the imagination of their hearts." (The *Echo.*)
4. DAVID. "The Lord hath made known his salvation; his righteousness hath he openly showed," &c. (The *Voice.*)
   MARY. "His mercy is on them that fear him, from generation to generation." (The *Echo.*)
5. DAVID. "He hath remembered his mercy and his truth toward the house of Israel." (The *Voice.*)
   MARY. "He hath holpen his servant Israel, in remembrance of his mercy." (The *Echo.*)

These parallels are very striking; and it seems as if Mary had this Psalm in her eye when she composed her song of triumph. And this is a farther argument that the whole Psalm, whether it record the deliverance of Israel from Egypt, or the Jews from the Babylonish captivity, is yet to be ultimately understood of the redemption of the world by Jesus Christ, and the proclamation of his Gospel through all the nations of the earth: and taken in this view, no language can be too strong, nor poetic imagery too high, to point out the unsearchable riches of Christ.

ANALYSIS OF THE NINETY-EIGHTH PSALM

This Psalm has the *two* following parts:—

I. An *exhortation* to sing to the Lord, and the *reasons* of it, ver. 1-3.

II. A *new invitation* to praise him, and that it be *universal*, ver. 4-9.

I. He calls upon them to praise God: 1. *Sing*—a *song* or hymn, to *the Lord*—and to none other. *A new song*—a song of excellency.

For this exhortation and command he gives the reasons. His work was a work of power and holiness.

1. "He hath done marvellous things." He has opened his greatness and goodness in the work of redemption. What *marvels* has not Christ done? 1. He was conceived by the Holy Ghost. 2. Born of a virgin. 3. Healed all manner of diseases. 4. Fed thousands with a few loaves and fishes. 5. Raised the dead. 6. And what was more *marvellous*, died himself. 7. Rose again by his own power. 8. Ascended to heaven. 9. Sent down the Holy Ghost. 10. And made his apostles and their testimony the instruments of enlightening, and ultimately converting, the world.

2. "His right hand and his holy arm hath got him the victory." 1. It was all *his own work*, whatever were the *instruments;* for without his energy they could do nothing. 2. It was his *holy arm*—no *bloody sword*, but a *holy hand*, to do a *holy work*. 3. "He got himself the victory" over *sin*, *Satan*, *death*, and *hell*.

3. This salvation was *made known:*—1. By *himself* to the *Jews*. 2. By his *apostles* to *all nations*.

4. This salvation has been *applied*. 1. He hath showed his *righteousness*—his method of *justifying sinners* through his own blood, and *sanctifying* them by his own Spirit. 2. This he hath *openly* showed, plainly revealing the whole in his Gospel. 3. He has done this in the *sight of the heathen*, calling them to be partakers of the same salvation promised to Abraham and to his posterity, both *Jews* and *Gentiles*.

5. That which moved him to do this; his *mercy*, and *truth:* 1. "He hath remembered his mercy." This mercy was to the *house of Israel*, and through them to the *Gentiles;* for the Gentiles were the *first* in the promise and covenant. There was no *Jew* when the covenant was made with Abraham: it was made with him while he was yet in uncircumcision; consequently the *Gentiles*, the *whole human race*, were originally included in that covenant. The descendants of Jacob were made depositaries of it for a season; but they, not having benefited by it, were rejected, and the salvation of Christ was given to the Gentiles, for whom it was originally intended, and who have kept the faith, and are daily profiting by it. 2. It is called *mercy;* for it was the merest mercy that said: "The seed of the woman shall bruise the serpent's head." 3. He *remembered* this; it was never out of the Divine mind; "Jesus was the Lamb slain from the foundation of the world." 4. As this mercy was intended for every human soul; so it is here *prophectically* said: "All the ends of the earth have seen the salvation of our God." This Gospel has been preached, is now in the course of being preached, and shortly will be preached to every people under heaven.

II. A new invitation to praise God; and to do this in every possible way.

1. "Make a joyful noise." Jump for joy, because of this most glorious news.

2. As *all* are interested in it, so let *all* do it: "All the earth."

3. In all possible ways. With *harp*, *psaltery*, *trumpet*, *cornet;* with *vocal*, *chordal*, and *pneumatic* music. But it is the *joyful* music, the *heart* music, which the Lord seeks.

4. "Before the Lord." In his immediate presence. Let all be sincere, pure, and holy. Remember the eye of the Lord is upon you: do not draw near with your *lips*, *pipes*, or *stringed* instruments, while your *hearts* are far from him.

5. And to make the music full, as if the inanimate creation had *ears* and *hands* to give an *applause* at the relation, and *feet* to *dance* because of it, he says: "Let the sea roar, the floods clap their hands, and the hills be joyful together."

And for all this he gives a reason, with which he concludes: "For he cometh to judge the earth;" which may be referred to his *first* and *second* coming.

1. If to the *first*, then the sense is—Let all creatures rejoice because he comes to *judge*, that is, to enlighten, order, and govern the world. For this purpose he was incarnated, suffered, died, and rose again for the redemption of mankind; and has sent his holy *Gospel* to enlighten the world, and his *Spirit* to apply its truths to the hearts of men.

2. If we consider this as referring to his *last coming*, then let all men rejoice, as he comes to destroy evil, to root out incorrigible sinners, and to make a new heaven and a new earth.

3. All this shall be done with that rectitude of judgment, that there shall be nothing crooked, oblique, or savouring of iniquity in it: "For he shall judge the world, and the people with equity."

PSALM XCIX

The empire of God in the world and the Church, 1, 2. *He ought to be praised*, 3. *Justice and judgment are his chief glory*, 4. *He should be worshipped as among the saints of old, whom he graciously answered and saved*, 5–8. *Exalt him because he is holy*, 9.

A. M. cir. 3489
B. C. cir. 515
A. U. C. 239
Darii I.,
R. Persarum,
anno sexto

THE [a]LORD reigneth; let the people tremble: [b]he sitteth *between* the cherubims; let the earth [c]be moved.

2 The LORD *is* great in Zion; and he *is* [d]high above all the people.

3 Let them praise [e]thy great

A. M. 3489
B. C. 515
A. U. C. 239
Darii I.,
R. Persarum,
anno sexto

[a]Psalm xciii. 1——[b]Exodus xxv. 22; Psalm xviii. 10; lxxx. 1——[c]Heb. *stagger*——[d]Psa. xcvii. 9——[e]Deut. xxviii. 58; Rev. xv. 4

NOTES ON PSALM XCIX

The *Hebrew* and *Chaldee* have no *title;* all the *versions* but the *Chaldee* attribute it to *David*. The *Syriac* says it concerns "the slaughter of the Midianites which Moses and the children of Israel had taken captive; and is a prophecy concerning the glory of the kingdom of Christ." But the mention of *Samuel* shows that it cannot be referred to the time of *Moses*. *Calmet* thinks that it was sung at the dedication of the city, or of the second temple, after the return from the Babylonish captivity. Eight of *Kennicott's* and *De Rossi's* MSS. join it to the preceding psalm.

Verse 1. *The Lord reigneth*] See the note on Psa. xcvii. 1.

Let the people tremble] He will establish his kingdom in spite of his enemies; let those who oppose him tremble for the consequences.

He sitteth between *the cherubims*] This is in reference to the *ark*, at each end of which was a

A. M. 3489
B. C. 515
A. U. C. 239
Darii I.,
R. Persarum,
anno sexto

and terrible name; *for* it *is*
holy.
4 [f]The king's strength also
loveth judgment; thou dost establish equity, thou executest judgment and
righteousness in Jacob.
5 [g]Exalt ye the LORD our God, and worship at [h]his footstool; *for* [i]he [k]*is* holy.
6 [l]Moses and Aaron among his priests, and
Samuel among them that call upon his name;
they [m]called upon the LORD, and
he answered them.
7 [n]He spake unto them in the
cloudy pillar: they kept his testimonies, and the ordinance *that* he gave them.
8 Thou answeredst them, O LORD our God:
[o]thou wast a God that forgavest them, though
[p]thou tookest vengeance of their inventions.
9 [q]Exalt the LORD our God, and worship at
his holy hill; for the LORD our God *is* [r]holy.

[f]Job xxxvi. 5, 6, 7——[g]Verse 9——[h]1 Chronicles xxviii. 2; Psalm cxxxii. 7——[i]Or, *it is holy*——[k]Leviticus xix. 2——[l]Exodus xvii. 4; 1 Samuel vii. 9; Jeremiah xv. 1——[m]Exodus xiv. 15; xv. 25; 1 Samuel vii. 9; xii. 18——[n]Exodus xxxiii. 9

[o]Num. xiv. 20; Jer. xlvi. 28; Zeph. iii. 7——[p]See Exod. xxxii. 2, &c.; Num. xx. 12, 24; Deut. ix. 20 [q]Ver. 5; Exod. xv. 2; Psa. xxxiv. 3; cxviii. 28——[r]Lev. xxi. 8; 1 Sam. ii. 2; Psa. xxii. 3; cxlv. 17; Isa. vi. 3; John xvii. 11

cherub of glory; and the *shechinah*, or symbol of the Divine Presence, appeared on the lid of the ark, called also the *mercy-seat*, between the cherubim. *Sitting between the cherubim* implies God's *graciousness* and *mercy*. While then, in his reign, he was terrible to sinners, he is on the *throne of grace* to all who fear, love, and obey him. Though this *symbol* were not in the *second* *temple*, yet the Divine Being might very well be thus denominated, because it had become one of his titles, he having thus appeared under the *tabernacle* and *first temple*.

Verse 2. *The Lord* is *great in Zion*] It is among his own worshippers that he has manifested his *power* and *glory* in an especial manner. *There* he is known, and *there* he is worthily magnified.

Verse 3. *Let them praise thy great and terrible name*] Let them confess thee to be great and terrible: let them tremble before thee.

For *it* is *holy*.] קדוש הוא *kadosh hu*. As this not only ends this verse but the *fifth* also, and in effect the *ninth*, it seems to be a species of *chorus* which was sung in a very solemn manner at the conclusion of each of these parts. His *holiness*—the immaculate purity of his nature, was the reason why he should be exalted, praised, and worshipped.

Verse 4. *The king's strength*] If this Psalm were written by David, he must mean by it that he was God's *vicegerent* or *deputy*, and that, even as king, God was *his strength*, and the *pattern* according to which equity, judgment, and righteousness should be executed in Jacob.

Verse 5. *Worship at his footstool*] Probably meaning the *ark* on which the Divine glory was manifested. Sometimes the *earth* is called God's *footstool*, Matt. v. 35, Isa. lxvi. 1; sometimes *Jerusalem;* sometimes the *temple*, Lam. ii. 1; sometimes the *tabernacle*, Psa. xxxii. 7; and sometimes the *ark*, 1 Chron. xxviii. 2. The Israelites, when they worshipped, turned their faces toward the *ark*, because that was the place where was the symbol of the Divine Presence.

For *he* is *holy*.] The burden chanted by the *chorus*.

Verse 6. *Moses and Aaron*] As Moses and Aaron among the priests, and as Samuel among the prophets, worshipped God in humility, gratitude, and the spirit of obedience, and received the strongest tokens of the Divine favour; so worship ye the Lord, that he may bless, support, and save you. Moses was properly the priest of the Hebrews before Aaron and his family were appointed to that office.

Verse 7. *He spake unto them in the cloudy pillar*] That is, he directed all their operations, marchings, and encampments by this cloudy pillar. See Exod. xxxiii. 9.

They kept his testimonies] Do ye the same, and God will be *your* portion as he was *theirs*.

Verse 8. *Thou—forgavest them*] When the people had sinned, and wrath was about to descend on them, Moses and Aaron interceded for them, and they were not destroyed.

Tookest vengeance of their inventions.] God spared them, but showed his displeasure at their misdoings. He chastised, but did not consume them. This is amply proved in the history of this people.

Verse 9. *Worship at his holy hill*] Worship him *publicly* in the *temple*.

For the Lord our God is *holy*.] The words of the *chorus;* as in the *third* and *fifth* verses.

Analysis of the Ninety-ninth Psalm

There are *two* parts in this Psalm:—

I. A description of the kingdom of God.

1. From the *majesty* and *terror* of it against his enemies, ver. 1-3.

2. From its *equity* in the execution of *judgment* and *justice*, ver. 4.

3. From his *patience* and *clemency* in giving audience to his servants, ver. 6-8.

II. A demand of praise and honour of all that acknowledge him for their King, begun at the *third* verse, repeated at the *fifth*, and continued in the *last*. The Psalm contains a prophecy of the kingdom of Christ, and its glory.

I. 1. The terror, power, and majesty of this kingdom: "The Lord reigneth." 1. He bids defiance to his enemies: "Let the people tremble." 2. "He sitteth between the cherubim." He is always present with his people; they need not fear, though *the earth be moved*. 3. "He is great in Zion." More potent and higher than all people. 4. "His name is great and terrible." His *enemies* have every thing to *fear*, while his *friends* have every thing to *hope*.

2. The psalmist describes this kingdom, from its *justice* and *equity*. 1. "He loveth judgment." This is one of his perfections. 2. "He establishes equity." Gives just and equal laws to all. 3. "He executes judgment in Jacob." None of his followers shall live without law; they are obedient children, living according to his will. 4. And therefore he requires them to *exalt and*

adore him. 5. They are to *worship at his footstool*—all their approaches are to be made in the *deepest reverence*, with the *truest self-abasement*. 6. "For he is holy;" and he requires all his followers to be holy also.

3. He describes it from the *mercy* and *clemency* of the ruler. 1. He showed his mercy and *kindness* to *Moses*, *Aaron*, and *Samuel*, as intercessors for the people. "They called upon God," for themselves and for the people; "and he answered them." 1. See the intercession of Moses, Exod. xxxii. 31; 2. Of *Aaron*, Num. xvi. 46-48. 3. Of *Samuel*, 1 Sam. vii. 5, 9, 10. 4. He spake to *Moses*, Exod. xxxiii. 8, 9, 11; and to *Aaron*, Num. xii. 5-8.

And now he adds the *reason* why he heard them:—

1. "They kept his testimonies." Those precepts that were common to all others.

2. "And the ordinances that he gave them." As public persons who were to rule in Church and state.

And that it was a great mercy that the Lord heard them, the prophet acknowledges by this *apostrophe*—

1. "Thou answeredst them, O Lord our God." Which the history shows.

2. "Thou forgavest them;" that is, the *people* for whom they prayed: for in Hebrew the *relative* is often put without an *antecedent*.

3. "Thou tookest vengeance of their inventions." The *golden calf* was broken to pieces, Exod. xxxii.; and the *false gods* were put away 1 Sam. vii. The people were not consumed, though their sin was in a certain manner visited upon them. See Num. xiv. 23, 30, and xx. 12.

II. The psalmist concludes with a *demand of praise* to this kind God.

1. "Exalt the Lord." Show that he is high, holy, just, good, and kind.

2. "Worship at his holy hill." Attend his public worship, and show a godly example in this way to all others. He who is indifferent about the *public worship* of God is generally not less so in *private devotion*.

3. The reason for all this is: "The Lord our God is holy." He requires this worship because it is a chief *means* by which he communicates *his holiness* to his followers. Without this holiness there is no happiness here, and without it none shall ever see God. Get *holiness*, that you may get happiness *here*, and heaven *hereafter*.

PSALM C

All nations are exhorted to praise the Lord, 1, 2; *to acknowledge him to be the Sovereign God and their Creator, and that they are his people and the flock of his pasture*, 3; *to worship him publicly, and be grateful for his mercies*, 4. *The reasons on which this is founded; his own goodness, his everlasting mercy, and his ever-during truth*, 5.

[a]A Psalm of [b]Praise

A. M. 3489 B. C. 515 A. U. C. 239 Darii I., R. Persarum, anno sexto

MAKE [c]a joyful noise unto the LORD, [d]all ye
lands.
2 Serve the LORD with gladness: come before his presence
with singing.
3 Know ye that the LORD he *is*
God: [e]*it is* he *that* hath made
us, [f]and not we ourselves; [g]*we are* his peo-

[a]Psa. cxlv. title——[b]Or, *thanksgiving*——[c]Psa. xcv. 1; xcviii. 4——[d]Heb. *all the earth*

[e]Psa. cxix. 73; cxxxix. 13, &c.; cxlix. 2; Eph. ii. 10
[f]Or, *and his we are*——[g]Psa. xcv. 7; Ezek. xxxiv. 30, 31

NOTES ON PSALM C

This Psalm is entitled in the Hebrew מזמור לתודה *mizmor lethodah*, not "A Psalm of Praise," as we have it, but "A Psalm for the confession, or *for the confession-offering*," very properly translated by the Chaldee: שבחא על קורבן תודתא *shibcha al kurban todetha*, "Praise for the sacrifice (or *offering*) of confession." The *Vulgate*, *Septuagint*, and *Æthiopic* have followed this sense. The Arabic attributes it to *David*. The Syriac has the following prefixed: "Without a name. Concerning Joshua the son of Nun, when he had ended the war with the Ammonites: but in the new covenant it relates to the conversion of the Gentiles to the faith." It is likely that it was composed after the captivity, as a form of thanksgiving to God for that great deliverance, as well as an inducement to the people to consecrate themselves to him, and to be exact in the performance of the acts of public worship.

Verse 1. *Make a joyful noise*] הריעו *hariu*, *exult, triumph, leap for joy*.

All ye lands.] Not only Jews, but Gentiles, for the Lord bestows his benefits on all with a liberal hand.

Verse 2. *Serve the Lord with gladness*] It is your privilege and duty to be happy in your religious worship. The religion of the true God is intended to remove human misery, and to make mankind happy. He whom the religion of Christ has not made happy does not understand that religion, or does not make a proper use of it.

Verse 3. *Know ye that the Lord he* is *God*] Acknowledge in every possible way, both in public and private, that Jehovah, the uncreated, self-existent, and eternal Being, is *Elohim*, the God who is in covenant with man, to instruct, redeem, love, and make him finally happy.

It is *he* that *hath made us*] He is our *Creator* and has consequently the only right in and over us.

And not we ourselves] ולא אנחנו *velo anachnu*. I can never think that this is the true reading, though found in the present Hebrew text, in the *Vulgate*, *Septuagint*, *Æthiopic*, and *Syriac*. Was there ever a people on earth, however grossly heathenish, that did believe, or could believe, that *they had made themselves*?

A. M. 3489
B. C. 515
A. U. C. 239
Darii I.,
R. Persarum,
anno sexto

ple, and the sheep of his
pasture.
4 [h]Enter into his gates
with thanksgiving, *and* into
his courts with praise: be thankful unto
him, *and* bless his name.
5 For the LORD *is* good;
[i]his mercy *is* everlasting; and
his truth *endureth* [k]to all generations.

[h]Psa. lxvi. 13; cxvi. 17, 18, 19——[i]Psa. cxxxvi. 1, &c.——[k]Heb. *to generation and generation;* Psa. lxxxix. 1

In *twenty-six* of *Kennicott's* and *De Rossi's* MSS. we have ולו אנחנו *velo anachnu*, "and HIS we are;" לו *lo*, the pronoun, being put for לא *lo*, the *negative* particle. This is the reading of the *Targum*, or Chaldee paraphrase, ודיליה אנחנא *vedileyh anachna*, "and his we are," and is the reading of the text in the Complutensian Polyglot, of both the Psalters which were printed in 1477, and is the *keri*, or marginal reading in most Masoretic Bibles. Every person must see, from the nature of the subject that it is the genuine reading. The position is founded on the maxim that what a man invents, constructs out of his own materials, without assistance in genius, materials or execution from any other person, is HIS OWN; and to it, its use, and produce, he has the only right. *God made us;* therefore *we are* HIS: we are his people, and should acknowledge him for our God; we are the sheep of his pasture, and should devote the lives to him constantly which he continually supports.

Verse 4. *Enter into his gates with thanksgiving*] Publicly worship God; and when ye come to the house of prayer, be thankful that you have such a privilege; and when you *enter his courts*, praise him for the permission. The word בתודה *bethodah*, which we render *with thanksgiving*, is properly *with the confession-offering* or *sacrifice*. See on the *title*.

Bless his name.] Bless *Jehovah*, that he is your *Elohim;* see ver. 3. In our liturgic service we say, "Speak good of his name;" we cannot do otherwise; we have nothing *but good* to speak of our God.

Verse 5. *For the Lord* is *good*] GOODNESS, the perfect, eternal opposition to all *badness* and *evil*, is essential to God. *Mercy* and *compassion* are modifications of his *goodness;* and as his *nature* is *eternal*, so his *mercy*, springing from his *goodness*, must be *everlasting*. And as TRUTH is an essential characteristic of an infinitely intelligent and perfect nature; therefore *God's truth* must endure *from generation to generation*. Whatsoever he has *promised* must be fulfilled, through all the successive generations of men, as long as sun and moon shall last.

As this is a very important Psalm, and has long made a part of our *public worship*, I shall lay it before the reader in the oldest vernacular Versions I have hitherto met with,—the *Anglo-Saxon* and the *Anglo-Scottish*, with a literal interlineary translation of the former.

The Anglo-Saxon Hundredth Psalm

Rhyme ye the Lord all earth, serve the Lord in
1. **Idrymeð drihtne, eall eorðe, ðeowiað drihtne on**
bliss;
blisse;
Infare in sight his in blithness;
2. **Infarað on gesyhðe hys on bliðnysse;**

Wit ye, for that Lord he is God, he did us
3. **Witaðge forðonðe drihten he is God, he dyde us,**
& not self we;
⁊ na selfe we;
Folk his & sheep leeseway his; fare into gates his in
4. **Folc his ⁊ sceap læswe his, infarað gatu his on**
confession, into courts is in hymns, confess
andetnysse. on cafertunas, his on ymnum andettað
him.
him;
Praise name his, for that winsom is; Lord thro'
5. **Heriað naman his forðande winsom is; driht on**
eternity mildheartedness his, & unto on kindred & kindred
ecnysse mildheortnyssa his ⁊ oð on cynrine ⁊ cynrine
sothfastnes his
soðfæstnys his.

The reader will see that, in order to make this translation as literal as possible, I have preserved some old English words which we had from the Anglo-Saxon, and which have nearly become obsolete: e. g., *Infare*, "to go in;" *blithness*, "joy, exultation;" *wit ye*, "know ye;" *did*, the preterite of *to do*, "made, created," the literal translation of the Hebrew, עשה *asah, he made; leeseway*, "pasturage on a common;" *winsom*, "cheerful, merry;" *mildheartedness*, "tenderness of heart, compassion;" *sothfastness*, "steady to the sooth or truth, fast to truth."

I might have noticed some various readings in Anglo-Saxon MSS.; e. g., ver. 1. for **Idrymeð** *idrymeth*, "rhyme ye;" **winsumiað** *winsumiath*, "be winsom, be joyful." And ver. 5, for **winsum** *winsom*, "cheerful;" **swete,** *swete*, "sweet."

Anglo-Scottish Version of the Hundredth Psalm

1. **Joyes to God al the erth; serves to Lord in gladnes.**
2. **Enters in his sight with joying.**
3. **Wittes for Lorde he is God; he made us and nogt we;**
4. **Folke of hym, and schepe of his pasture; enters the gates of him in schrift; hys Halles in ympnys; schryves to hym.**
5. **Loues his name, for soft is Lorde; withouten end in his mercy; and in generation and generation the sothfastnes of hym.**

Thus our forefathers *said* and *sung* in heart and mouth and with their tongues made confession to salvation. There are but few words here which require explanation: Ver. 3, *Wittes*, "wot ye, know ye." Ver. 4, *Schrift*, "confession;" *schryves*, "confess ye." Ver. 5, *Loues*, "praise ye, laud ye." *Sothfastness*, as above, steadfastness in the truth.

ANALYSIS OF THE HUNDREDTH PSALM

There are *two* parts in this Psalm:—

I. An *exhortation* to praise God, and the manner in which it is to be done, ver. 1-4.

II. The *reasons* on which this is founded, ver. 3-5.

I. In his exhortation to praise God it is required,—

1. That the praise be *universal:* "All ye lands."

2. That it be *hearty:* "Make a joyful noise." Let the soul be cheerful in the work.

3. That it be not *partial* nor restrained: "Make a joyful noise—serve—be glad—sing—be thankful—give praise—bless his name." The various expressions show the completeness of this blessed word.

4. That it be sincere—done in *his presence.*

5. That it be an *intelligent* service: "Know ye."

6. That it be *frequent* and *public:* "Enter his gates—go into his courts."

7. That *gratitude* shall be a part of it: "With thanksgiving."

II. The *reasons* on which this is grounded; they are,—

1. Drawn from the *nature* of God: "Know ye that Jehovah is Elohim," the true God; therefore, alone worthy to be worshipped.

2. Drawn from the *benefits* bestowed on us: 1. "He has made us"—capable of knowing him, and being eternally happy with him. 2. He has called upon us by his *grace* to be "his people, and the sheep of his pasture." He both *governs* and *feeds* us.

And that we may be the more cheerful in this work he puts us in mind of the Divine *attributes* engaged in our redemption, *goodness, mercy,* and *truth.*

1. "He is good." This is his very *nature.*

2. "He is merciful." This *flows* from his *goodness.*

3. "He is true;" keeping covenant for ever with them that fear him; and *fulfilling* all his *promises* to the believing and obedient.

And that we may have the more confidence,

1. "His mercy is everlasting." It *continues* through all the changes and chances of this life to them who trust in him; and extends through all the generations of men.

2. His truth is like his mercy, it is pledged to fulfil his promises. "God is not man that he should lie;" he has promised, and will save to the uttermost all who come to him through Christ Jesus: "Be therefore thankful to him, and speak good of his name."

PSALM CI

The subject proposed, mercy and judgment, 1. *The psalmist's resolution in respect to his private conduct,* 2. *He will put away evil, inward and outward,* 3. *No evil person shall stand in his presence,* 4; *nor any slanderer of his neighbour,* 4, 5. *He will encourage the faithful and upright,* 6; *but the deceitful, the liars, and the profligate, he will cast out of the city of God,* 7, 8.

A Psalm of David

A. M. cir. 2949 B. C. cir. 1055 Ante I. Ol. 279 Ante Urbem Conditam 302

I [a]WILL sing of mercy and
judgment: unto thee, O
LORD, will I sing.
2 I will [b]behave myself wisely
in a perfect way. O when wilt
thou come unto me? I will
[c]walk within my house with a
perfect heart.
3 I will set no [d]wicked thing before mine

[a]Psa. lxxxix. 1——[b]1 Sam. xviii. 14

[c]1 Kings ix. 4; xi. 4——[d]Heb. *thing of Belial*

NOTES ON PSALM CI

The *Hebrew* and all the *Versions* attribute this Psalm to *David.* It shows us the resolutions he formed when he came to the throne; and it is a perfect model according to which a wise prince should regulate his conduct and his government.

Verse 1. *I will sing of mercy and judgment*] David might say, Adverse and prosperous providences have been of the utmost use to my soul; therefore, I will thank God for *both.* Or, as he was probably now called to the government of *all the tribes,* he might make a resolution that he would show חסד *chesed,* incessant benevolence, to the upright; and משפט *mishpat,* the execution of judgment, to the wicked; and would make the conduct of God the model of his own.

Verse 2. *I will behave myself wisely*] God's law prescribes a perfect way of life; in this perfect way I have professed to walk, and I must act *wisely* in order to walk in it.

When wilt thou come unto me?] I can neither walk in this way, nor grow *wise* unto salvation, unless *thou come unto me* by thy grace and Spirit; for without thee I can do nothing.

I will walk within my house] It is easier for most men to walk with a perfect heart in the *Church,* or even in the *world,* than in their *own families.* How many are as meek as lambs among *others,* when at *home* they are *wasps* or *tigers!* The man who, in the midst of family provocations, maintains a Christian character, *being meek, gentle,* and *long-suffering* to his *wife,* his *children,* and his *servants,* has got a *perfect heart,* and adorns the doctrine of God his Saviour in all things.

The original is very emphatic: אתהלך *ethhallech,* "I will set myself to walk," I will make it a determined point thus to walk. I will bear and forbear with children, servants, &c., not speaking rashly, nor giving way to bad tempers. Through various motives a man will behave with propriety and decorum among others; but none of these motives operate in his own house, where he feels himself *master,* and consequently under no restraint.

A. M. cir. 2949 B. C. cir. 1055 Ante I. Ol. 279 Ante Urbem Conditam 302

eyes: [e]I hate the work of them [f]that turn aside; *it* shall not cleave to me.

4 A froward heart shall depart from me: I will not [g]know a wicked *person.*

5 Whoso privily slandereth his neighbour, him will I cut off: [h]him that hath a high look and a proud heart will not I suffer.

6 Mine eyes *shall be* upon the faithful of the land, that they may dwell with me: he that walketh [i]in a perfect way, he shall serve me.

7 He that worketh deceit shall not dwell within my house: he that telleth lies [k]shall not tarry in my sight.

8 I will [l]early destroy all the wicked of the land; that I may cut off all wicked doers [m]from the city of the LORD.

[e]Psa. xcvii. 10——[f]Josh. xxiii. 6; 1 Sam. xii. 20, 21; Psa. xl. 4; cxxv. 5——[g]Matt. vii. 23; 2 Tim. ii. 19 [h]Psa. xviii. 27; Prov. vi. 17

[i]Or, *perfect in the way;* Psalm cxix. 1——[k]Hebrew, *shall not be established*——[l]Psa. lxxv. 10; Jer. xxi. 12 [m]Psalm xlviii. 2, 8

Verse 3. *I will set no wicked thing before mine eyes*] I will undertake no unjust wars; will enter into no sinful alliances; will not oppress my subjects by excessive taxation, to support extravagance in my court. I will not look favourably on *things* or *words of Belial.* What is *good for nothing* or evil in its operation, what is wicked in its principle, and what would lead me away from righteousness and truth, I will never set before my eyes.

Them that turn aside] I shall particularly abominate the conduct of those who apostatize from the true religion, and those who deny its Divine authority, and who live without having their conduct governed by its influence, such shall never be put in a place of political trust or confidence by me.

Verse 4. *A froward heart*] Rash and headstrong men shall not be employed by me.

I will not know a wicked person.] I will give no countenance to sinners of any kind; and whatever is *evil* shall be an object of my abhorrence.

Verse 5. *Whoso privily slandereth his neighbour*] All flatterers and time-servers, and those who by insinuations and false accusations endeavour to supplant the upright, that they may obtain their offices for themselves or their dependants, will I consider as enemies to the state, I will abominate, and expel them from my court.

The Chaldee gives a remarkable meaning to the Hebrew, מלשני בסתר רעהו *melasheni bassether reehu,* which we translate, *Whoso privily slandereth his neighbour,* and which it renders thus, דמשתעי לישן תליתי על חבריה *demishtaey lishan telitai al chabreyah:* "He who speaks with the *triple tongue* against his neighbour." That is, the tongue by which he slays *three* persons, viz., 1. The *man* whom he slanders; 2. *Him* to whom he *communicates* the slander; and, 3. *Himself,* the slanderer. Every slanderer has his *triple tongue,* and by every slander inflicts those *three* deadly wounds. Such a person deserves to be *cut off.* On this subject St. Jerome speaks nearly in the same way: Ille qui detrahit, et se, et illum qui audit, demergit; "He who slanders ruins both himself and him who hears him;" he might have added, *and him who is slandered,* for this is often the case; the *innocent* are ruined by detraction.

A high look and a proud heart] One who is seeking preferment; who sticks at nothing to gain it; and one who behaves himself haughtily and insolently in his office.

Will not I suffer.] לא אוכל *lo uchal,* I cannot away with. These persons especially will I drive from my presence, and from all state employments.

Verse 6. *Mine eyes*] My approbation.

Upon the faithful] The humble, upright followers of God.

That they may dwell with me] Be my confidants and privy counsellors. No irreligious or wicked man, whatever his abilities may be, shall be countenanced or supported by me. I will purify my court from the base, the irreligious, the avaricious, the venal, the profligate, and the wicked.

He that walketh in a perfect way] He that is truly religious.

He shall serve me.] Shall be my prime minister, and the chief officer in my army, and over my finances.

Verse 7. *He that worketh deceit—that telleth lies*] I will expel from my court all sycophants and flatterers. *Tiberius* encouraged flatterers; *Titus burned* some, *banished* several others, and *sold* many for *slaves.*

Verse 8. *I will early destroy*] I will take the first opportunity of destroying all the wicked of the land. I will purify my court, purge Jerusalem, and cleanse the whole land of every abomination and abominable person; so that the city of my God, where *holiness* alone should dwell, shall indeed become *the Holy City;* that the *state* may be made *prosperous,* and the *people* happy. Such an administration must have been a good one, where such pious caution was used in choosing all the officers of the state.

Analysis of the Hundred and First Psalm

There are *two* parts of this Psalm:—

I. The *sum,* with the dedication of it, ver. 1.

II. The full explanation of *mercy* and *judgment,* and how practised:—

1. Towards *himself,* ver. 2-5.
2. Towards *ungodly* men, ver. 4, 5, 7, 8.
3. Towards all *good* men, ver. 6.

I. The sum of the Psalm, *mercy* and *judgment,* the two great virtues of a king.

1. *Mercy* in countenancing, giving audience, judging, and rewarding the good.

2. *Judgment* in discountenancing, being a terror to and punishing the evil doers.

II. He begins with his *own* reformation and that of his *house,* that he may set a godly example to his *kingdom.*

1. "I will behave myself wisely:" most act *foolishly;* I shall be guided by Divine wisdom.

2. "I am in a perfect way:" I have professed to believe in the God of Israel, and I must walk suitably to this profession.

3. "When wilt thou come unto me?" I am sincere in my resolves; but without thee I can do nothing. Stand by me, and I will walk uprightly.

In his house he resolves, "I will walk within my house with a perfect heart."

1. "I will walk:" it shall be my constant employment.

2. "I will walk in my house:" I will see that my *family* fear God.

3. "I will walk with a perfect heart:" I shall do nothing for *show;* all shall be sincere and pious.

In order to walk in this perfect way, he promises,—

1. "I will set no wicked thing before my eyes:" evil desires enter more frequently into the soul by the *eye* than by any of the other senses.

2. "I hate the work of them that turn aside:" he that would leave sin must hate and abhor it: he that *leaves God* is an object of abhorrence.

3. "It shall not cleave to me:" it will cleave to him who cleaves to it. He who does not *hate* it, will *cleave* to it.

He shows what he will be towards the *ungodly.*

1. "A froward heart shall depart from me:" the headstrong, stubborn, and refractory.

2. "I will not know the wicked:" I shall not only not approve of such, but I will cultivate no acquaintance with them.

These wicked persons he particularizes. They are,

1. *Slanderers:* "Him that slandereth his neighbour I will cut off."

2. *The ambitious:* "Him that hath a high look," who wants influence and honour.

3. The *proud:* the haughty, who thinks all born to be his vassals.

How he will treat the *godly.*

1. "His eye shall be upon the faithful." Of them he will take especial care; he shall dwell with me.

2. The truly religious, "he that walks in a perfect way," shall be employed by himself. "He shall serve me."

He farther states what he will do in reference to the *ungodly.*

1. No fraudulent person shall dwell in his house: "He that worketh deceit," &c.

2. *Liars shall be banished out of his sight.*

In this work he tells us how he would proceed.

1. "I will early destroy." I will make *despatch,* that the *land* be not polluted.

2. The *end,* in reference to the Church: "I will cut off the wicked from the city of the Lord." The city, the seat of government, the place of God's *altars,* must be kept pure. There must be a thorough, a radical reform. No corruption or abuse, either in things *political, domestic,* or *religious,* shall be tolerated. All must be holy, as he who has called us is holy. This was a reformation according to God's word; not according to the caprice of the multitude.

PSALM CII

The complaint and miserable state of the poor captives, 1–11; *the expectation of deliverance,* 12–14; *the conversion of the heathen,* 15–18; *the termination of the captivity,* 19–22; *the great frailty of man,* 23, 24; *the unchangeableness of God,* 25–27; *the permanence of the Church,* 28.

XX. DAY. MORNING PRAYER

A Prayer [a]of the afflicted, [b]when he is overwhelmed, and poureth out his complaint before the LORD

HEAR my prayer, O LORD, and let my cry
[c]come unto thee.

2 [d]Hide not thy face from me in the day *when*
I am in trouble; [e]incline thine ear unto me:
in the day *when* I call answer me speedily.

3 [f]For my days are consumed [g]like smoke,
and [h]my bones are burned as a hearth.

4 My heart is smitten, and [i]withered like
grass; so that I forget to eat my bread.

[a]Or, *for*——[b]Psa. lxi. 2; cxlii. 2——[c]Exod. ii. 23; 1 Sam. ix. 16; Psa. xviii. 6——[d]Psa. xxvii. 9; lxix. 17 [e]Psa. lxxi. 2; lxxxviii. 2

[f]Psa. cxix. 83; James iv. 14——[g]Or, (as some read,) *into smoke*——[h]Job xxx. 30; Psa. xxxi. 10; Lam. i. 13 [i]Psa. xxxvii. 2; ver. 11

NOTES ON PSALM CII

The *Hebrew,* and nearly all the *Versions,* give the following *title* to this Psalm: *A prayer of the afflicted, when he is overwhelmed, and pours out his sighing before the Lord.* There seems to be little doubt that this is the prayer of the captives in Babylon, when, towards the end of the captivity, they were almost worn out with oppression, cruelty, and distress. The Psalm has been attributed to *Daniel,* to *Jeremiah,* to *Nehemiah,* or to some of the other *prophets* who flourished during the time of the captivity. The author of the Epistle to the Hebrews has applied the *twenty-fifth, twenty-sixth,* and *twenty-seventh* verses to our Lord, and the perpetuity of his kingdom.

Verse 1. *Hear my prayer*] The chief parts of the Psalm answer well to the title: it is the *language of the deepest distress,* and well directed to *Him* from whom alone help can come.

Verse 3. *My days are consumed like smoke*] He represents himself (for the psalmist speaks in the name of the people) under the notion of a *pile of combustible matter,* placed upon a *fire,* which soon consumes it; part flying away in *smoke,* and the residue lying on the hearth in the form of *charred coal* and *ashes.* The *Chaldeans* were the *fire,* and the *captive Jews* the *fuel,* thus converted into *smoke* and *ashes.*

Verse 4. *My heart is smitten, and withered like grass*] The metaphor here is taken from

5 By reason of the voice of my groaning
[k]my bones cleave to my [l]skin.
6 [m]I am like [n]a pelican of the wilderness:
I am like an owl of the desert.
7 I [o]watch, and am as a sparrow [p]alone
upon the house-top.
8 Mine enemies reproach me all the day;
and they that are [q]mad against me are [r]sworn
against me.
9 For I have eaten ashes like bread, and
[s]mingled my drink with weeping,
10 Because of thine indignation and thy
wrath: for [t]thou hast lifted me up, and cast
me down.
11 [u]My days *are* like a shadow that
declineth; and [v]I am withered like
grass.
12 But [w]thou, O LORD, shalt endure for
ever; and [x]thy remembrance unto all generations.
13 Thou shalt arise, *and* [y]have mercy upon
Zion: for the time to favour her, yea, the
[z]set time is come.
14 For thy servants take pleasure in [a]her
stones, and favour the dust thereof.
15 So the heathen shall [b]fear the name of
the LORD, and all the kings of the earth thy
glory.
16 When the LORD shall build up Zion,
[c]he shall appear in his glory.

---

[k]Job xix. 20; Lam. iv. 8——[l]Or, *flesh*——[m]Job xxx. 29——[n]Isaiah xxxiv. 11; Zephaniah ii. 14——[o]Psa. lxxvii. 4——[p]Psalm xxxviii. 11——[q]Acts xxvi. 11 [r]Acts xxiii. 12——[s]Psalm xlii. 3; lxxx. 5——[t]Psalm xxx. 7——[u]Job xiv. 2; Psalm cix. 23; cxliv. 4; Eccles. vi. 12——[v]Verse 4; Isaiah xl. 6, 7, 8; James i. 10 [w]Verse 26; Psalm ix. 7; Lamentations v. 19——[x]Psalm cxxxv. 13——[y]Isaiah lx. 10; Zechariah i. 12——[z]Isaiah xl. 2——[a]Psalm lxxix. 1——[b]1 Kings viii. 43; Psalm cxxxviii. 4; Isa. lx. 3——[c]Isa. lx. 1, 2

---

grass cut down in the meadow. It is first *smitten* with the *scythe*, and then *withered* by the *sun*. Thus the Jews were smitten with the judgments of God; and they are now withered under the fire of the *Chaldeans*.

Verse 6. *I am like a pelican of the wilderness*] It may be the *pelican* or the *bittern*. The original, קאת *kaath*, is mentioned Lev. xi. 18, and is there described. See the note.

Owl of the desert.] כום *cos*, some species of *owl;* probably the night raven. See the notes referred to above.

Verse 7. *As a sparrow alone*] צפור *tsippor*, seems to be often used for any small bird, such as the *swallow*, *sparrow*, or the like. *Bochart* supposes the *screech owl* is intended.

Verse 8. *They that are mad against me are sworn against me.*] The Chaldeans are determined to destroy us; and they have bound themselves *by oath* to do it. See a similar case related Acts xxiii. 12-14, where a number of Jews had bound themselves by an *oath* neither to eat nor drink till they had slain Paul.

Verse 9. *I have eaten ashes like bread*] Fearful of what they might do, we all humbled ourselves before thee, and sought thy protection; well knowing that, unless we were supernaturally assisted, we must all have perished; our enemies having sworn our destruction.

Verse 10. *For thou hast lifted me up, and cast me down.*] Thou hast lifted me on high, that thou mightest dash me down with the *greater force*. We were *exalted* in thy *favour* beyond any people, and now thou hast made us the *lowest* and most *abject* of the children of men.

Verse 11. *My days* are *like a shadow that declineth*] Or rather, *My days decline like the shadow*. I have passed my *meridian*, and the sun of my prosperity is about to set for ever. There may be here an allusion to the declination of the sun towards the south, which, by shortening their days, would greatly lengthen their nights. Similar to the exclamation of a contemporary prophet, Jer. viii. 20: "The harvest is past, the summer is ended, and we are not saved." There is now scarcely any human hope of our deliverance.

Verse 12. *But thou, O Lord, shalt endure for ever*] Our life is a shadow; we can scarcely be called *beings* when compared with thee, for thou art *eternal*. Have mercy upon us, *creatures of a day*, and thy kindness shall be a *memorial* in all our *generations*.

Verse 13. *Thou shalt arise*, and *have mercy upon Zion*] While he is humbled at the footstool of mercy, and earnestly praying for mercy, an answer of peace is given; he is assured, not only that they *shall be delivered*, but that the time of deliverance is *at hand*. The *set time*—the *seventy* years predicted by Jeremiah, was ended; and God gave him to see that he was ever mindful of his promises.

Verse 14. *Thy servants take pleasure in her stones*] Though Jerusalem was at this time in a heap of ruins, yet even her rubbish was sacred in the eyes of the pious; for this had been *the city of the great King*.

Verse 15. *So the heathen shall fear the name of the Lord*] It is granted that after the edict of Cyrus to restore and rebuild Jerusalem, which was about *four hundred and ninety* years before Christ, the name of the true God was more generally known among the heathen; and the translating the Sacred Writings into Greek, by the command of Ptolemy Philadelphus, king of Egypt, about *two hundred and eighty-five* years before the Christian era, spread a measure of the light of God in the Gentile world which they had not before seen. Add to this, the disperson of the Jews into different parts of the Roman empire, after Judea became a Roman province, which took place about *sixty* years before the advent of our Lord; and we may consider these as so many preparatory steps to the conversion of the heathen by the Gospel of our Lord Jesus Christ. And to this last general illumination of the Gentile world the psalmist must allude here, when he speaks of "the heathen fearing God's name, and all the kings of the earth his glory."

Verse 16. *When the Lord shall build up Zion*]

17 [d]He will regard the prayer of the destitute, and not despise their prayer.

18 This shall be [e]written for the generation to come: and [f]the people which shall be created shall praise the LORD.

19 For he hath [g]looked down from the height of his sanctuary; from heaven did the LORD behold the earth;

20 [h]To hear the groaning of the prisoner; to loose [i]those that are appointed to death;

21 To [k]declare the name of the LORD in Zion, and his praise in Jerusalem;

22 When the people are gathered together, and the kingdoms, to serve the LORD.

23 He [l]weakened my strength in the way; he [m]shortened my days.

24 [n]I said, O My God, take me not away in the midst of my days: [o]thy years *are* throughout all generations.

25 [p]Of old hast thou laid the foundation of the earth: and the heavens *are* the work of thy hands.

26 [q]They shall perish, but [r]thou shalt [s]endure: yea, all of them shall wax old like a garment; as a vesture shalt thou change them, and they shall be changed:

27 But [t]thou *art* the same, and thy years shall have no end.

28 [u]The children of thy servants shall continue, and their seed shall be established before thee.

[d]Neh. i. 6, 11; ii. 8——[e]Rom. xv. 4; 1 Cor. x. 11 [f]Psa. xxii. 31; Isa. xliii. 21——[g]Deut. xxvi. 15; Psa. xiv. 2; xxxiii. 13, 14——[h]Psa. lxxix. 11——[i]Heb. *the children of death*——[k]Psa. xxii. 22——[l]Heb. *afflicted* [m]Job xxi. 21

[n]Isa. xxxviii. 10——[o]Psa. xc. 2; Hab. i. 12——[p]Gen. i. 1; ii. 1; Heb. i. 10——[q]Isa. xxxiv. 4; li. 6; lxv. 17; lxvi. 22; Rom. viii. 20; 2 Pet. iii. 7, 10, 11, 12——[r]Ver. 12——[s]Heb. *stand*——[t]Mal. iii. 6; Heb. xiii. 8; James i. 17——[u]Psa. lxix. 36

It is such a difficult thing, so wholly improbable, so far out of the reach of human power, that when God does it, he must manifest his power and glory in a most extraordinary manner.

Verse 17. *The prayer of the destitute*] הערער *haarar* of him who is laid in utter ruin, who is entirely wasted.

Verse 18. *The people which shall be created*] "The Gentiles, who shall be brought to the knowledge of salvation by Christ," as the *Syriac* states in its inscription to this Psalm: how often the conversion of the soul to God is represented as a *new creation*, no reader of the New Testament need be told. See Eph. ii. 10, iv. 24; 2 Cor. v. 17; Gal vi. 15. Even the publication of the Gospel, and its influence among men, is represented under the notion of "creating a new heaven and a new earth," Isa. lxv. 17, 18.

Verse 19. *For he hath looked down*] This, with the three following verses, seems to me to contain a glorious prophecy of the incarnation of Christ, and the gathering in of the Jews and the Gentiles to him. *The Lord looks down from heaven*, and sees the whole earth groaning and travailing in pain; his eye affects his heart, and he purposes their salvation.

Verse 20. *To hear the groaning*] By sin, all the inhabitants of the earth are *miserable.* They have broken the Divine laws, are under the arrest of judgment, and all cast into *prison.* They have been tried, *found guilty*, and *appointed to die;* they *groan* under their chains, are alarmed at the prospect of death, and implore mercy.

Verse 21. *To declare the name of the Lord*] To publish that Messenger of the Covenant in whom the name of the Lord is, that Messiah in whom the fulness of the Godhead dwelt; and to commence at *Jerusalem*, that the first offers of mercy might be made to the Jews, from whom the word of reconciliation was to go out to all the ends of the earth.

Verse 22. *When the people are gathered together*] When all the *Gentiles* are enlightened, and the kings of the earth brought to pay homage to the King of kings.

Verse 23. *He weakened my strength in the way*] We are brought so low in our captivity by oppression, by every species of hard usage, and by death, that there is now no hope of our restoration by any efforts of our own.

Verse 24. *I said, O my God*] This and the following verses seem to be the *form of prayer* which the captives used previously to their deliverance.

Thy years are *throughout all generations.*] This was a frequent argument used to induce God to hear prayer. We are *frail* and *perishing;* thou art *everlasting:* deliver us, and we will glorify thee.

Verse 25. *Of old hast thou laid the foundation*] None taught of God ever imagined the world to have been *eternal. Of old,* לפנים *lephanim*, before there were any *faces* or *appearances*, thou didst lay the foundations of the earth. It was created by thee; it did not grow by *accretion* or *aggregation* from a *pre-existent nucleus.* There was *nothing;* and thou didst produce *being—substance* or *matter.* Out of that created matter thou didst make the *earth* and the *heavens.*

Verse 26. *They shall perish*] Nothing can be eternal *a parte ante*, or *a parte post*, but thyself. Even that which thou hast created, because not necessarily *eternal*, must be perishable; necessary *duration* belongs to God only; and it is by his will and energy alone that universal nature is preserved in existence, and preserved from running into speedy disorder, decay, and ruin.

Yea, all of them shall wax old] Every thing must *deteriorate*, unless *preserved* by thy *renewing* and *invigorating energy.* Even the *heavens* and the *earth* are subject to this law; for that which is not, from the infinite perfection of its own nature, ETERNAL, must be perishable; therefore the heavens and the earth must necessarily come to an end. They contain the *seeds* of their own dissolution. It is true that in sublunary things, the *vicissitudes of seasons* is a sort of check to the principle of dissolution; but it only partially corrects this tendency. Even the productions of the earth *wear out* or *deteriorate*. Plant the same seed or grain for several years consecutively, and it degenerates so as at last not to be worth the labour of tillage, however expensively the soil may be manured in which it is planted. I may instance in *wheat* and in the *potatoe*, the two grand supporters of life in European countries. All other seeds and plants, as far as they have fallen under my observation, are subject to the same law.

Verse 27. *But thou* art *the same*] ואתה הוא *veattah* HU, *but thou art* HE, that is, *The* ETERNAL; and, consequently, he who only has *immortality*.

Thy years shall have no end.] לא יתמו *lo yittammu*, "they shall not be completed." Every thing has its revolution—its conception, growth, perfection, decay, dissolution, and death, or corruption. It may be said that *regeneration* restores all these substances; and so it does in a measure, but not without *deterioration*. The *breed of animals*, as well as *vegetables*, *wears out;* but God's eternal round has *no completion*. I repeat it,—what is *necessarily eternal* is unchangeable and imperishable; all created beings are perishable and mutable, because not eternal. God alone is eternal; therefore God alone is imperishable and immutable.

Verse 28. *The children of thy servants shall continue*] Thy *Church* shall be permanent, because founded *on thee;* it shall live throughout all the revolutions of time. And as thy followers are made *partakers of the Divine nature*, they shall live in *union with God* in the other world, deriving *eternal duration* from the *inexhaustible Fountain* of *being*. Nothing can be permanent but by God's supporting and renewing influence.

Analysis of the One Hundred and Second Psalm

There are *two* general parts in this Psalm:—

I. A description of the calamities of the Church, under the person of an afflicted man, ver. 1-11.

II. The consolation afforded in these calamities, and the ground of it, ver. 12-28.

I. The description, &c., is formed into a *prayer* proposed in the *two first verses:*—

1. "Hear my prayer."

2. "Hide not thy face."

In this prayer he complains, and shows his wretched state by various metaphors or figures.

1. A consumption of strength: "My days are consumed."

2. From continual *weeping:* "My bones cleave to my skin."

3. From his *solitude:* "Like a pelican in the wilderness."

4. From his continual *watching:* "I watch, and am like a sparrow," &c.

5. From the *reproach* of his enemies. "Mine enemies reproach me."

6. From his *sadness:* "I have eaten ashes like bread."

All these increased, from a *sense of God's displeasure.*

1. "Because of thine indignation."

2. Because of his *sufferings:* "Thou hast lifted me up, and hast cast me down."

3. And the *effect* produced: "My days are as a shadow."

II. He comforts himself in the promises of God:—

1. "I am withered like grass: but thou shalt endure for ever."

2. I shall soon be forgotten; "but thy remembrance is unto all generations."

3. Thou seemest to take no heed: but "thou wilt arise."

He was the more confident,—

1. Because the *set time* to favour Zion was come.

2. This he saw more clearly from the *concern* with which God had filled the hearts of the people: "Thy servants take pleasure in her stones."

3. He consoled himself in the prospect of the *conversion of the heathen* themselves: "So the heathen shall fear thy name."

4. For this he gives a particular reason: Because "the Lord shall build up Zion."

5. And he will do this, because of the *prayers of the people:* "He will regard the prayer," &c.

This should be done in such a *manner*, that,—

1. *Record* should be made of it: "This shall be written."

2. And it should be a blessing to those that were unborn: "The people which shall be created shall praise the Lord."

And for this he assigns the *proper reasons.*

1. "The Lord looked down from heaven."

2. "He heard the groans of the prisoners."

These mercies call for *gratitude* and *obedience:*—

1. They should "declare the name of the Lord."

2. And this will take place "when the people are gathered together," &c.

The psalmist fears that he shall *not live* to see this deliverance:—

1. "For he weakened my strength in the way,—he shortened my days."

2. Yet he earnestly desires to see it: "Take me not away."

To strengthen this petition, he pleads God's *unchangeableness;* and he proves God to be *eternal*, because he is *immutable.*

1. Not so the *earth*, for it had a *beginning:* "Of old thou hast laid," &c.

2. Not so the *heavens;* for they are "the work of thy hands."

3. Neither shall they continue: "They shall perish," &c.

But God is *always the same.* Every thing that is *mutable* acquires by its change some *property, quality, form* or *accident*, which *it had not before:* but God, being an infinite Spirit, and infinitely perfect, can suffer no loss, can have no addition. For as he *wants nothing*, nothing can be *added* to him; as he *inhabits eternity*, nothing can be *taken from him.* In him, therefore, there is no possibility of *change;* and, consequently, none of *decay* or *perishing.*

From these considerations the psalmist draws this comfortable conclusion:—

1. His Church and servants shall continue also: "The children of thy servants,"—the apostles, with the patriarchs, shall dwell in thy kingdom—in the new Jerusalem.

2. "And their seed;" as many as are begotten by the Gospel, if they remain in the faith that works by love, "shall be established,"—persevere, remain, continue *before thee*—live in thy presence for ever. As thou art eternal, so thou wilt unite them to thyself and make *them* eternally happy.

PSALM CIII

God is praised for his benefits to his people, 1, 2; *he forgives their iniquities, and heals their diseases,* 3; *redeems their lives, crowns them with loving-kindness,* 4; *satisfies them with good things, renews their youth,* 5; *he helps the oppressed, makes his ways known, is merciful and gracious, and keeps not his anger for ever,* 6–9; *his forbearance, and pardoning mercy,* 10–12; *he is a tender and considerate Father,* 13, 14; *the frail state of man,* 15, 16; *God's everlasting mercy, and universal dominion,* 17–19; *all his angels, his hosts, and his works, are invited to praise him,* 20–22.

A. M. cir. 3468
B. C. cir. 536
Cyri,
R. Persarum,
cir. annum
primum

A Psalm of David

BLESS [a]the LORD, O my
soul: and all that is within
me, *bless* his holy name.
2 Bless the LORD, O my soul,
and forget not all his benefits:
3 [b]Who forgiveth all thine iniquities;
who [c]healeth all thy dis-
eases;
4 Who [d]redeemeth thy life
from destruction; [e]who crowneth
thee with loving-kindness and tender mercies;
5 Who satisfieth thy mouth with good *things;*
so that [f]thy youth is renewed like the eagle's.

[a]Ver. 22; Psa. civ. 1; cxlvi. 1——[b]Psa. cxxx. 8; Isa. xxxiii. 24; Matt. ix. 2, 6; Mark ii. 5, 10, 11; Luke vii. 47

[c]Exod. xv. 26; Psa. cxlvii. 3; Jer. xvii. 14——[d]Psa. xxxiv. 22; lvi. 13——[e]Psa. v. 12——[f]Isa. xl. 31

NOTES ON PSALM CIII

The *inscription* in the *Hebrew*, and in all the *Versions*, gives this Psalm to *David;* and yet many of the ancients believed it to refer to the times of the captivity, or rather to its *conclusion*, in which the redeemed Jews give thanks to God for their restoration. It is a Psalm of inimitable sweetness and excellence; contains the most affectionate sentiments of gratitude to God for his mercies; and the most consoling motives to continue to trust in God, and be obedient to him.

Verse 1. *Bless the Lord*] He calls on his soul, and all its faculties and powers, to magnify God for his mercies. Under such a weight of obligation the *lips* can do little; the soul and all its powers must be engaged.

Verse 2. *Forget not all his benefits*] Call them into recollection; particularize the chief of them; and here record them for an everlasting memorial.

Verse 3. *Who forgiveth*] The benefits are the following, 1. Forgiveness of sin. 2. Restoration of health: "Who healeth all thy diseases."

Verse 4. *Who redeemeth*] 3. Preservation from destruction. הגואל *haggoel*, properly, *redemption of life by the kinsman;* possibly looking forward, in the spirit of prophecy, to him who became partaker of our flesh and blood, that he might have the right to redeem our souls from death by dying in our stead. 4. Changing and ennobling his state; weaving a crown for him out of *loving-kindness* and *tender mercies.*

Verse 5. *Who satisfieth thy mouth*] 5. For continual communications of spiritual and temporal good; so that the vigour of his mind was constantly supported and increased.

Thy youth is renewed like the eagle's.] There is such a vast variety of the eagle, or genus *Falco*, that it is not easy to determine which is meant here. The Hebrew נשר *neser* is a general name for such as were known in the land of Judea; which were probably such as belong to the genus *Aquila*, comprehending *forty-one* species and *seven* varieties.

There are as many *legends* of the *eagle* among the ancient writers, as there are of some saints in the calendar; and all *equally true.* Even among *modern divines, Bible Dictionary* men, and such like, the most ridiculous tales concerning this bird continue to be propagated; and no small portion of them have been crowded into comments on this very verse. One specimen my *old Psalter* affords, which, for its curiosity, I shall lay before the reader:—

Trans. **Newed sal be als of aeren thi youthed.**

Par. The arne when he is greved with grete elde, his neb waxis so gretely, that he may nogt open his mouth and take mete: bot then he smytes his neb to the stane, and has away the solgh, and than he gaes til mete, and be commes yong a gayne. Swa Criste duse a way fra us oure elde of syn and mortalite, that settes us to ete oure brede in hevene, and newes us in hym.

The plain English of all this is:—

"When the arne [*eagle*, from the Anglo-Saxon **earn**, a word which Dr. Jamieson has not entered in his dictionary] is oppressed with old age, his bill grows so much that he cannot open his mouth in order to take meat. He then smites his bill against a stone, and breaks off the slough—the excrescence that prevented him from eating; and then he goes to his ordinary food, and becomes young again. So Christ takes away from us our old age of sin and death, and gives us to eat that bread which comes down

A. M. cir. 3468
B. C. cir. 536
Cyri,
R. Persarum,
cir. annum
primum

6 [g]The LORD executeth righteousness and judgment for all
that are oppressed.
7 [h]He made known his ways
unto Moses, his acts unto the children of
Israel.
8 [i]The LORD is merciful and gracious, slow
to anger, and [k]plenteous in mercy.
9 [l]He will not always chide: neither will he
keep *his anger* for ever.
10 [m]He hath not dealt with us after our sins;
nor rewarded us according to
our iniquities.
11 [n]For [o]as the heaven is
high above the earth, *so* great is
his mercy toward them that fear him.
12 As far as the east is from the west *so* far
hath he [p]removed our transgressions from us.
13 [q]Like as a father pitieth *his* children, *so*
the LORD pitieth them that fear him.
14 For he knoweth our frame; [r]he remembereth that we *are* dust.

A. M. cir. 3468
B. C. cir. 536
Cyri,
R. Persarum,
cir. annum
primum

[g]Psalm cxlvi. 7——[h]Psalm cxlvii. 19——[i]Exod. xxxiv. 6, 7; Numbers xiv. 18; Deuteronomy v. 10; Nehemiah ix. 17; Psalm lxxxvi. 15; Jeremiah xxxii. 18 [k]Hebrew, *great of mercy*——[l]Psalm xxx. 5; Isaiah lvii. 16; Jeremiah iii. 5; Micah vii. 18——[m]Ezra ix. 13 [n]Psalm lvii. 10; Ephesians iii. 18——[o]Hebrew, *according to the height of the heaven*——[p]Isaiah xliii. 25; Mic. vii. 18——[q]Mal. iii. 17——[r]Psa. lxxviii. 39

from heaven: and thus gives us a new life in himself."

I believe the meaning of the psalmist is much more simple: he refers to the *moulting* of birds, which, in most, takes place annually, in which they cast their old feathers and get a new plumage. To express this, he might as well have chosen any bird, as this is common to all the feathered race; but he chose the *king of the birds*, because of his bulk, his strength, and vivacity.

The *long life* of the eagle might have induced the psalmist to give it the preference. An eagle was nine years in the possession of *Owen Holland*, Esq., of Conway, in Wales, and had lived *thirty-two* years in the possession of the gentleman who made it a present to him: but of its previous age, for it came from Ireland, we are not informed. *Keysler* relates that an eagle died at Vienna, after a confinement of *one hundred and four* years!

The *eagle* can subsist a long time without food. That first mentioned above, through the neglect of a servant, was *twenty-one* days without food, and yet survived this long fast.

The meaning and moral of the psalmist are not difficult of comprehension. The Israelites, when redeemed from their captivity, should be so blessed by their God that they should reacquire their political strength and vigour; and should be so quickened by the Divine Spirit, that old things should be passed away, and all things become new.

Verse 6. *The Lord executeth*] This shall be done because the Lord will avenge his elect who have cried unto him day and night for his deliverance: "He is slow to anger;" but he will punish. "He is plenteous in mercy," and he will save. The persevering sinner shall be destroyed; the humble penitent shall be saved.

Verse 7. *He made known his ways unto Moses*] From the earliest part of our history he has been our protector and defence. His wonderful *acts* in behalf of the *children of Israel* are so many *proofs* of his *mercy*, power, and goodness; and so many *reasons* why *we* should now trust in him.

Verse 8. *The Lord is merciful*] See the note on Psa. lxxxvi. 15.

Verse 9. *He will not always chide*] He will not contend with us continually. He has often reproved, often punished us; but his mercy ever rejoiced over judgment.

Verse 10. *He has not dealt with us after our sins*] He has never apportioned our *punishment to* our *sins*, nor has he regulated the exercise of his *mercy* by our *merits*.

Verse 11. *For as the heaven is high above the earth*] Great and provoking as our crimes may have been, yet his mercies have, in their magnitude and number, surpassed these, as far as the heavens are elevated beyond the earth.

Verse 12. *As far as the east is from the west*] As the east and the west can never meet in one point, but be for ever at the same distance from each other, so our sins and their decreed punishment are removed to an eternal distance by his mercy.

Verse 13. *Like as a father pitieth his children*] This is a very emphatic verse, and may be thus translated: "As the tender compassions of a father towards his children; so the tender compassions of Jehovah towards them that fear him." Nothing can place the tenderness and concern of God for his creatures in a stronger light than this. What yearnings of bowels does a *father* feel toward the *disobedient child*, who, sensible of his ingratitude and disobedience, falls at his parent's feet, covered with confusion and melted into tears, with, "Father, I have sinned against heaven, and before thee, and am not worthy to be called thy son!" The same in *kind*, but infinitely more exquisite, does God feel when the penitent falls at his feet, and implores his mercy through Christ crucified.

Verse 14. *For he knoweth our frame*] יצרנו *yitsrenu*, "our formation;" the *manner* in which we are constructed, and the *materials* of which we are made. He knows we cannot contend with him, and if he uses his power against us, we must be crushed to destruction. In all his conduct towards us he considers the frailty of our nature, the untowardness of our circumstances, the strength and subtlety of temptation, and the sure party (till the heart is renewed) that the tempter has within us. Though all these things are against us, yet it must ever be said, whatever use we make of it, "the grace of God is sufficient for us." But alas! who makes use of that sufficient grace? Here, then, is cause for condemnation. But, O amazing mercy! if any man sin, we have an advocate with the Father, Jesus Christ the righteous. And like as a father pitieth his children, so the Lord pitieth them that fear him; for he knoweth our frame, he remembereth that we are but

A. M. cir. 3468
B. C. cir. 536
Cyri,
R. Persarum,
cir. annum
primum

15 *As for* man, [s]his days *are*
as grass: [t]as a flower of the
field, so he flourisheth.
16 For the wind passeth over
it, and [u]it is gone; and [v]the place thereof
shall know it no more.

17 But the mercy of the LORD *is* from everlasting to everlasting upon them that fear him,
and his righteousness unto [w]children's children;

18 [x]To such as keep his covenant, and to
those that remember his commandments to do
them.

19 The LORD hath prepared
his [y]throne in the heavens;
and [z]his kingdom ruleth over
all.

A. M. cir. 3468
B. C. cir. 536
Cyri,
R. Persarum,
cir. annum
primum

20 [a]Bless the LORD, ye his angels, [b]that
excel in strength, that [c]do his commandments,
hearkening unto the voice of his word.

21 Bless ye the LORD, all *ye* [d]his hosts;
[e]*ye* ministers of his, that do his pleasure.

22 [f]Bless the LORD, all his works in all
places of his dominion: [g]bless the LORD, O
my soul.

---

[s]Psa. xc. 5, 6; 1 Pet. i. 24——[t]Job xiv. 1, 2; James i. 10, 11——[u]Hebrew, *it is not*——[v]Job vii. 10; xx. 9——[w]Exod. xx. 6——[x]Deut. vii. 9——[y]Psa. xi. 4——[z]Psa. xlvii. 2; Dan. iv. 25, 34, 35

[a]Psa. cxlviii. 2——[b]Heb. *mighty in strength*; see Psa. lxxviii. 25——[c]Matt. vi. 10; Heb. i. 14——[d]Gen. xxxii. 2; Josh. v. 14; Psa. lxviii. 17——[e]Dan. vii. 9, 10; Heb. i. 14——[f]Psa. cxlv. 10——[g]Ver. 1

---

dust. The man who can say, in the face of these Scriptures, *Let us sin that grace may abound*, is a brute and demon, who has neither lot nor part in this thing.

Verse 15. *His days are as grass*] See the note on Psa. xc. 5.

Verse 16. *The wind passeth over it*] Referring perhaps to some blasting pestilential wind.

Verse 17. *The mercy of the Lord is from everlasting to everlasting*] חסד *chesed* signifies more particularly the *exuberant goodness of God*. This is an attribute of his nature, and must be from everlasting to everlasting; and hence, his righteousness (צדקת *tsidketh*)—his merciful *mode of justifying the ungodly*, is extended from one generation to another.

Unto children's children.] It is still in force, and the doctrine of reconciliation through Christ shall continue to be preached till the conclusion of time.

Verse 18. *To such as keep his convenant*] The spirit of which was, *I will be your* GOD; WE *will be thy* PEOPLE. From the covenant came the *commandments*, and their obligation *to remember and do them;* and on such *keepers* of the covenant, and *doers* of the commandments, God promises to pour out his mercy through all generations.

Verse 19. *The Lord hath prepared his throne in the heavens*] There he is Sovereign; but his dominion extends equally over all the earth; for his *kingdom*—regal government, influence, and sway, *ruleth over all.*

Verse 20. *Bless the Lord, ye his angels*] Every person who has a sense of God's goodness to his soul feels his own powers inadequate to the praise which he ought to offer; and therefore naturally calls upon the holiest of men, and the supreme angels, to assist him in this work.

That excel in strength] Some take גברי כח *gibborey coach* the *mighty in strength*, for another class of the hierarchy,—*they that do his commandments, hearkening to his words;* and consider them to be that order of beings who are particularly employed in operations among and for the children of men; probably such as are called *powers* in the New Testament.

Verse 21. *All ye his hosts;* ye *ministers of his*] We know almost nothing of the economy of the heavenly host; and, therefore, cannot tell what is the difference between *angels, mighty powers, hosts*, and *ministers* who do his pleasure. All owe their being and all its blessings to God; all depend upon his bounty; and without him they can do nothing; therefore, all should praise him.

Verse 22. *Bless the Lord, all his works*] Let every thing he has done be so considered as to show forth his praise.

Bless the Lord, O my soul.] Let *me* never forget my obligation to his mercy; for with tender mercies and loving-kindness has he crowned me. I will therefore be thankful unto him, and speak good of his name.

ANALYSIS OF THE ONE HUNDRED AND THIRD PSALM

There are *three* parts in this Psalm:—

I. The *exordium*, in which the psalmist invites his own soul to praise the Lord, ver. 1, 2.

II. The *narration*, being a declaration of God's benefits conferred on him and others, and the causes of those benefits, ver. 3-19.

III. The *conclusion*, in which he calls on all creatures to assist him in praising the Lord, ver. 20-22.

I. The *exordium*,—

1. Bless God. Think on the benefit, and praise the Benefactor.

2. Let the *soul* join in this. Let it be done heartily; *lip-labour* is little worth.

3. "All that is within me." Every faculty,—understanding, will, memory, judgment, affections, desires, &c.

4. "Bless Jehovah," who gave thee thy being, and all thy blessings.

5. "Forget not his benefits." Most forget their obligations both to God and man; but *ingratitude*, which is the source of *forgetfulness*, is abominable.

6. "All his benefits." Thou hast already forgotten many; forget no more. The word גמולי *gemuley*, signifies, literally, *retributions* or *recompenses*, as the *Vulgate* has well expressed it. And of what kind are these *recompenses?* Invariably *good* for *evil;* nor hast thou ever offered him one accent of praise that he has not compensated with a *blessing* of *infinite value.*

II. The *narration.* A declaration of benefits. 1. To *himself.* 2. To the *Church.* These were,—1. *Spiritual;* 2. *Temporal* benefits.

First spiritual benefit—*justification:* "He forgiveth all thine iniquities."

Second spiritual benefit—*regeneration* or *sanctification:* "Healeth all thy diseases."

Third spiritual benefit—*redemption* from the first and second death, in consequence of being thus justified and sanctified.

Fourth spiritual benefit—*glorification* anticipated: "Who crowneth thee with loving-kindness and tender mercy." The *crown* comes from the *loving-kindness* and *tender mercy* of God; not from any *merit* in man.

The *temporal* benefits are,—

1. Abundance of the necessaries of life: "Who satisfieth thy mouth with good things."

2. Health and long life: "Thy youth is renewed like the eagle's." See the note on this passage.

The benefits to the whole *Church are,*—

1. *Defence* and *deliverance:* "The Lord executes judgment."

2. *Manifestation* of *his will:* "He made known his ways," &c.

All these spring from the *four attributes* mentioned below,—

1. "He is merciful," רחום *rachum,* bearing a paternal affection to his intelligent creatures, especially to those who fear him.

2. "Gracious," חנון *channun,* the Giver of grace and favour; for he who has a fatherly heart will *give.*

3. "Slow to anger," ארך אפים *erech appayim, long in nostrils,* not hasty; not *apt to be angry.*

4. "Plenteous in mercy," רב חסד *rab chesed, multiplying kindness.* Gives abundantly from his own *bounty,* not according to our *merit.*

The effects of all these are,—

1. Because he is *merciful:* "He will not always chide."

2. Because he is *gracious:* "He deals not with us after our sin."

3. Because he is *slow to anger:* "He will not keep his anger forever."

4. Because he is *plenteous in mercies:* His mercies surpass our sins as much as heaven surpasses the earth.

5. Because he is *like a father:* He "pities his children;" considers their frame, and makes all the allowance that *justice* mingled with *mercy* can make.

6. And as he is *righteous*—true, and faithful in performing his covenant, his mercy is everlasting to those that fear him.

But let it be remembered who they are that have a right to expect such blessings:—

1. "Those who fear him."

2. "Those who keep his covenant."

3. "Those who remember his commandments, and do them."

That he is *able* to do all that he has promised, the psalmist marks his *dominion:*—

1. It is not circumscribed: "His throne is in heaven."

2. It takes in all *places* and all *nations.* For "his kingdom ruleth over all;" he is King of kings, and Lord of lords.

III. The *conclusion.* For these benefits he invites all creatures to praise the Lord.

1. The *angels,* whom he describes,—1. From their *excellence:* "Ye that excel in strength." 2. From their *obedience:* "Ye that do his commandments." 3. From their *readiness and cheerfulness* in it: "Ye that hearken to the voice of his words,"—who are ever ready, at the slightest intimation, to perform his will.

2. All the *hosts* or *armies* of God,—archangels, principalities, dominions, powers, thrones, &c.

3. He invites all the creatures of God to praise him, whether *animate* or *inanimate:* "All creatures, in all places of his dominion." This extends throughout immensity. For this there is the strongest reason—he *made* all—*rules* over all—"is in all places" *with* all—*preserves* all—*moves* all.

4. To show that he who calls upon others will not be backward himself to praise God; as he began, so he concludes, with "Bless the Lord, O my soul!" Thus he had the high praises of God continually in his mouth.

And thus finishes this most excellent and inimitable Psalm. The *old Psalter* concludes thus: "Blysses to Lorde al his werks in ilk stede of his Lordschip: blisse my saule to Lorde. When men well lyfes, al thair werks blysses God. Fra blyssyng we cum forth to blyssyngs, gawe agayne, and tharein dwell we."

The more we praise God, the more occasion we shall see to praise him, and the more spiritually minded we shall become. *Praise* proceeds from *gratitude;* gratitude from a sense of *obligation;* and both *praise* and *gratitude* will be in *proportion* to the *weight* of that obligation; and the *weight* will be in proportion to the *sense* we have of God's *great goodness* and our own *unworthiness.* As the reader's heart may be in a heavenly frame, I shall help him to express his feelings by the following *inimitable verses,* which express the substance of the preceding Psalm:—

From all that dwell below the skies
Let the Creator's praise arise!
Let the Redeemer's grace be sung
In every land, by every tongue!

Eternal are thy mercies, Lord!
Eternal truth attends thy word!
Thy praise shall sound from shore to shore,
Till sun shall rise and set no more.

Praise God, from whom all blessings flow!
Praise Him, all creatures here below!
Praise Him above, ye heavenly host!
Praise Father, Son, and Holy Ghost!
Amen and Amen.

PSALM CIV

The majesty and power of God manifested in the creation of the heavens and the atmosphere, 1–3; *of the earth and sea,* 4–9; *of the springs, fountains, and rivers,* 10–13; *of vegetables and trees,* 14–18; *of the sun and moon,* 19; *of day and night, and their uses,* 20–23; *of the riches of the earth,* 24; *of the sea, its inhabitants, and its uses,* 25, 26; *of God's general providence in providing food for all kinds of animals,* 27–31; *of earthquakes and volcanoes,* 32. *God is praised for his majesty, and the instruction which his works afford,* 33, 34. *Sinners shall be destroyed,* 35.

XX. DAY. EVENING PRAYER

A. M. cir. 3468 B. C. cir. 536 Cyri, R. Persarum, cir. annum primum

BLESS [a]the LORD, O my soul. O LORD my God, thou art very great; [b]thou art clothed with honour and majesty.

2 [c]Who coverest *thyself* with light as *with* a garment: [d]who stretchest out the heavens like a curtain:

3 [e]Who layeth the beams of his chambers

[a]Psa. ciii. 1; ver. 35——[b]Psa. xciii. 1

[c]Dan. vii. 9——[d]Isa. xl. 22; xlv. 12——[e]Amos ix. 6

NOTES ON PSALM CIV

This Psalm has no title either in the Hebrew or Chaldee; but it is attributed to David by the Vulgate, Septuagint, Æthiopic, Arabic, and Syriac. It has the following title in the Septuagint, as it stands in the Complutensian Polyglot: *Ψαλμος τῳ Δαυιδ ὑπερ της του κοσμου συστασεως·* "A Psalm of David concerning the formation of the world." The Syriac says it is "A Psalm of David when he went with the priests to adore the Lord before the ark." It seems a continuation of the preceding Psalm; and it is written as a part of it in *nine* of Kennicott's and De Rossi's MSS. It is properly a poem on the works of God in the creation and government of the world; and some have considered it a sort of epitome of the history of the creation, as given in the book of Genesis.

Verse 1. *O Lord my God, thou art very great*] The works of God, which are the subject of this Psalm, particularly show the grandeur and majesty of God. The strongest proofs of the being of God, for common understandings, are derived from the works of creation, their magnitude, variety, number, economy, and use. And a proper consideration of those works presents a greater number of the attributes of the Divine nature than we can learn from any other source. Revelation alone is superior.

Verse 2. *Who coverest* thyself *with light*] Light, insufferable splendour, is the robe of the Divine Majesty. *Light* and *fire* are generally the accompaniments of the Supreme Being, when he manifests his presence to his creatures. He appeared thus to *Abraham* when he made a covenant with him, Gen. xv. 17; and to *Moses* when he appointed him to bring the people out of Egypt, Exod. iii. 2; and when he gave him his law on Sinai, Exod. xix. 18. Moses calls *God a consuming fire*, Deut. iv. 24. When *Christ* was transfigured on the mount, his face shone like the sun, and his garment was white as the light, Matt. xvii. 2. And when the Lord manifests himself to the prophets, he is always surrounded with *fire*, and the most brilliant *light.*

Bishop *Lowth* has some fine remarks on the *imagery* and *metaphors* of this Psalm. The *exordium,* says he, is peculiarly magnificent, wherein the majesty of God is described, so far as we can investigate and comprehend it, from the admirable construction of nature; in which passage, as it was for the most part necessary to use translatitious images, the sacred poet has principally applied those which would be esteemed by the Hebrews the most elevated, and worthy such an argument; for they all, as it seems to me, are taken from the *tabernacle.* We will give these passages verbally, with a short illustration:—

הוד והדר לבשת *hod vehadar labashta.*

"Thou hast put on honour and majesty."

The original, לבשת, is frequently used when speaking of the *clothing* or *dress* of the *priests.*

Verse 2. עטה אור כשלמה *oteh or cassalmah.*

"Covering thyself with light as with a garment."

A manifest symbol of the Divine Presence; the light conspicuous in the holiest is pointed out under the same idea; and from this single example a simile is educed to express the ineffable glory of God generally and universally.

נוטה שמים כיריעה *noteh shamayim kayeriah.*

"Stretching out the heavens like a curtain."

The word יריעה, rendered here *curtain*, is that which denotes the *curtains* or *uncovering* of the whole *tabernacle.* This may also be an allusion to those curtains or awnings, stretched over an area, under which companies sit at weddings, feasts, religious festivals, curiously *painted under*, to give them the appearance of the visible heavens in the night-season.

Verse 3. המקרה במים עליותיו *hamekareh bammayim aliyothaiv.*

"Laying the beams of his chambers in the waters."

The sacred writer expresses the wonderful nature of the *air* aptly, and regularly constructed, from various and flux elements, into one continued and stable series, by a metaphor drawn from the singular formation of the *tabernacle*, which, consisting of many and different parts, and easily reparable when there was need, was kept together by a perpetual juncture and contignation of them all together. The poet goes on:—

השם עבים רכובו *hassem abim rechubo,*
המהלך על כנפי רוח *hamehallech al canphey ruach.*

"Making the clouds his chariot,
Walking upon the wings of the wind."

He had first expressed an image of the Divine Majesty, such as it resided in the holy of holies, discernible by a certain investiture of the most splendid light; he now denotes the same from

A. M. cir. 3468
B. C. cir. 536
Cyri,
R. Persarum,
cir. annum
primum

in the waters: [f]who maketh the
clouds his chariot: [g]who walketh upon the wings of the
wind:
4 [h]Who maketh his angels spirits; [i]his
ministers a flaming fire:
5 [k]*Who* [l]laid the foundations of the earth,
that it should not be removed for ever.
6 [m]Thou coveredst it with the deep as *with*
a garment: the waters stood
above the mountains.
7 [n]At thy rebuke they fled;
at the voice of thy thunder they
hasted away.
8 [o]They [p]go up by the mountains; they go
down by the valleys unto [q]the place which
thou hast founded for them.
9 [r]Thou hast set a bound that they may

A. M. cir. 3468
B. C. cir. 536
Cyri,
R. Persarum,
cir. annum
primum

---

[f]Isa. xix. 1——[g]Psa. xviii. 10——[h]Heb. i. 7——[i]2 Kings ii. 11; vi. 17——[k]Heb. *He hath founded the earth upon her bases*——[l]Job xxvi. 7; xxxviii. 4, 6; Psa. xxiv. 2; cxxxvi. 6; Eccles. i. 4

[m]Genesis vii. 19——[n]Genesis viii. 1——[o]Or, *The mountains ascend, the valleys descend*——[p]Genesis viii. 5——[q]Job xxxviii. 10, 11——[r]Job xxvi. 10; Psalm xxxiii. 7; Jer. v. 22

---

that light of itself which the Divine Majesty exhibited, when it moved together with the ark, sitting on a circumambient cloud, and carried on high through the air. That seat of the Divine Presence is even called by the sacred historians, as its proper name, המרכבה *hammercabah*, THE CHARIOT.

Verse 4. עשה מלאכיו רחות *oseh malachaiv ruchoth*,
משרתיו אש להט *mesharethaiv esh lohet.*

The elements are described as prompt and expedite to perform the Divine commands, like angels or ministers serving in the tabernacle; the Hebrew word משרתיו *mesharethaiv* being a word most common in the sacred ministrations.

Verse 5. יסד ארץ על מכוניה *yasad erets al mechoneyha*,
בל תמוט עולם ועד *bal tammot olam vaed.*

"Laying the earth upon its foundations,
That it should not be shaken for evermore."

This image Bishop Lowth thinks evidently taken from the *tabernacle*, which was so laid upon its foundations that nothing could move it, and the dispensation to which it was attached, till the end purposed by the secret counsel of God was accomplished: and thus the *earth* is established, till the end of its creation shall be fully answered; and then it and its works shall be burnt up. On the above ground, the stability of the sanctuary and the stability of the earth are sometimes mentioned in the same words.

Verse 6. *Thou coveredst it with the deep*] This seems to be spoken in allusion to the creation of the earth, when it was without form and void, and darkness was upon the face of the deep, and the waters invested the whole, till God separated the dry land from them; thus forming the seas and the terraqueous globe. The poet Ovid has nearly the same idea:—

Densior his tellus, elementaque grandia traxit,
Et pressa est gravitate sua; circumfluus humor
Ultima possedit, solidumque coercuit orbem.
Met. lib. i., ver. 29.

Earth sinks beneath, and draws a numerous throng
Of ponderous, thick, unwieldy seeds along:
About her coasts unruly waters roar;
And, rising on a ridge, insult the shore.
DRYDEN.

Verse 7. *At thy rebuke they fled*] When God separated the *waters which were above the firmament* from those *below*, and caused the *dry land to appear.* He commanded the separation to take place; and the waters, as if instinct with life, hastened to obey.

At the voice of thy thunder] It is very likely God employed the *electric fluid* as an agent in this separation.

Verse 8. *They go up by the mountains; they go down by the valleys*] Taking the words as they stand here, *springs* seem to be what are intended. But it is difficult to conceive how the water could ascend, through the fissures of mountains, to their tops, and then come down their sides so as to form rivulets to water the valleys. Most probably all the springs in mountains and hills are formed from waters which fall on their tops in the form of rain, or from clouds that, passing over them, are arrested, and precipitate their contents, which, sinking down, are stopped by some solid strata, till, forcing their way at some aperture at their sides, they form springs and fountains. Possibly, however, *vapours* and *exhalations* are understood; these by *evaporation* ascend to the tops of mountains, where they are condensed and precipitated. Thus the vapours ascend, and then come down to the valleys, forming fountains and rivulets in those places which the providence of God has allotted them; that is, continuous valleys, with such a degree of *inclination* as determines their waters to run in that direction till they reach another river, or fall into the ocean.

Some have thought there is a reference to the *breaking up of the fountains of the great deep*, at the time of the flood; while the protrusion of the waters would raise the circumambient crust, so as to form mountains, the other parts, falling in to fill up the vacuum occasioned by the waters which were thrown up from the central abyss, would constitute *valleys.*

Ovid seems to paraphrase this verse:—

Jussit et extendi campos, subsidere valles,
Fronde tegi sylvas, lapidosos surgere montes.
Met. lib. i., ver. 43.

"He shades the woods, the valleys he restrains
With rocky mountains, and extends the plains."
DRYDEN.

Verse 9. *Thou hast set a bound that they may not pass*] And what is this *bound?* The *flux*

A. M. cir. 3468
B. C. cir. 536
Cyri,
R. Persarum,
cir. annum
primum

not pass over; [s]that they turn
not again to cover the earth.
10 [t]He sendeth the springs
into the valleys, *which* [u]run
among the hills.
11 They give drink to every beast of the
field: the wild asses [v]quench their thirst.
12 By them shall the fowls of the heaven
have their habitation, *which* [w]sing among the
branches.
13 [x]He watereth the hills from his chambers: [y]the earth is satisfied with
[z]the fruit of thy works.
14 [a]He causeth the grass to
grow for the cattle, and herb for
the service of man: that he may bring forth
[b]food out of the earth;
15 And [c]wine *that* maketh glad the heart of
man, *and* [d]oil to make *his* face to shine, and
bread *which* strengtheneth man's heart.
16 The trees of the LORD are full of *sap;*
the cedars of Lebanon, [e]which he hath planted;

A. M. cir. 3468
B. C. cir. 536
Cyri,
R. Persarum,
cir. annum
primum

---

[s]Genesis ix. 11, 15——[t]Heb. *Who sendeth*——[u]Heb. *walk*——[v]Hebrew, *break*——[w]Hebrew, *give a voice*——[x]Psalm cxlvii. 8——[y]Psalm lxv. 9, 10——[z]Jeremiah x. 13; xiv. 22——[a]Genesis i. 29, 30; iii. 18; ix. 3; Psalm cxlvii. 8——[b]Psalm cxxxvi. 25; cxlvii. 9; Job xxviii. 5——[c]Judges ix. 13; Psalm xxiii. 5; Proverbs xxxi. 6, 7——[d]Hebrew, *to make* his *face shine with oil,* or *more than oil*——[e]Num. xxiv. 6

---

and *reflux* of the sea, occasioned by the solar and lunar *attraction*, the *rotation* of the earth on its own axis, and the *gravitation* of the waters to the centre of the earth. And what is the *cause* of all these? The will and energy of God. Thus the sea is prevented from drowning the earth equally where there are *flat shores* as where the sea seems hemmed in by huge mounds of land and mountains. The *above*, not *these*, are the *bounds which it cannot pass, so that they cannot turn again to cover the earth.*

Verse 10. *He sendeth the springs into the valleys*] *Evaporation* is guided and regulated by Divine Providence. The sun has a certain power to raise a certain portion of vapours from a given space. God has apportioned the *aqueous* to the *terrene surface*, and the solar attraction to both. There is just as much *aqueous surface* as affords a sufficiency of vapours to be raised by the solar attraction to water the *earthy surface*. Experiments have been instituted which prove that it requires a given space of aqueous surface to provide vapours for a given space of terrene surface; and the proportion appears ordinarily to be *seventeen of water* to *three of earth;* and this is the proportion that the aqueous bears to the terrene surface of the globe. See Ray's three Physico-theological Discourses.

Verse 11. *The wild asses quench their thirst.*] The פרא *pere*, *onager* or *wild ass*, differs in nothing from the *tame ass*, only it has not a broken spirit, and is consequently more lively and active. It is so very swift that no horse except the Arab barb can overtake it. It is a gregarious animal, and they go in troops to feed and to drink. It is very timid, or rather jealous of its liberty, and therefore retires deep into the desert; yet even there the providence of God regards it; springs are provided, and it has the instinct to find them out.

Verse 12. *By them shall the fowls of the heaven have their habitation*] All fowls love verdure, and have their residence where they can find wood and water.

Verse 13. *From his chambers*] The *clouds*, as in ver. 3.

The earth is satisfied] The inhabitants of it.

Verse 14. *He causeth the grass to grow for the cattle*] Doth God care for oxen? Yes, and there is not a beast of the field that does not share his merciful regards.

And herb for the service of man] Plants, esculent herbs, and nutritive grain in general; and thus *he brings forth food* (לחם *lechem, bread*) *out of the earth.* In the germination and growth of a grain of wheat there is a profusion of miracles. God takes care of man, and of all those animals which are so necessary to the convenience and comfort of man.

Verse 15. *And wine*] *Wine*, in moderate quantity, has a wondrous tendency to revive and invigorate the human being. *Ardent spirits* exhilarate, but they *exhaust* the strength; and every dose leaves man the worse. Unadulterated wine, on the contrary, *exhilarates* and *invigorates:* it makes him cheerful, and provides for the continuance of that cheerfulness by *strengthening* the *muscles*, and *bracing* the *nerves*. This is its *use*. Those who continue drinking till wine inflames them, *abuse* this mercy of God.

Oil to make his *face to shine*] That is, to anoint the body; and particularly those parts most exposed to the sun and weather. This is of high importance in all arid lands and sultry climates. By it the pores are kept open, and perspiration maintained.

Bread which *strengtheneth man's heart.*] In hunger not only the *strength* is prostrated, but the *natural courage* is also abated. *Hunger* has no enterprise, emulation, nor courage. But when, in such circumstances, a little bread is received into the stomach, even before concoction can have time to prepare it for nutriment, the *strength* is restored, and the *spirits* revived. This is a surprising effect; and it has not yet been satisfactorily accounted for.

Three of the choicest and most important articles of life are here mentioned: WINE, for the support of the vital and intellectual spirits; BREAD, for the support of the nervous and muscular system; and OIL, as a seasoner of food, and for those *unctions* so necessary for the maintenance of health. Where *wine, oil,* and *bread* can be had in sufficient quantities, there *animal food*, ardent spirits, and all high-seasoned aliments, may be well dispensed with. Heavy taxes on these necessaries of life are taxes on *life*, itself; and infallibly lead to adulteration of the articles themselves; especially *wine* and *oil*, which, in countries where they are highly taxed, are no longer to be found pure.

Verse 16. *The trees of the Lord are full* of sap] ישבעו *yisbeu*, "are saturated."

A. M. cir. 3468
B. C. cir. 536
Cyri,
R. Persarum,
cir. annum
primum

17 Where the birds make their
nests: *as for* the stork, the fir-
trees *are* her house.
18 The high hills *are* a refuge
for the wild goats; *and* the rocks for [f]the
conies.
19 [g]He appointed the moon for seasons: the
sun [h]knoweth his going down.
20 [i]Thou makest darkness, and it is night;
wherein [k]all the beasts of the forests do creep
forth.
21 [l]The young lions roar after their prey,
and seek their meat from God.

22 The sun ariseth, they
gather themselves together, and
lay them down in their dens.
23 Man goeth forth unto [m]his
work and to his labour until the evening.
24 [n]O LORD, how manifold are thy works!
in wisdom hast thou made them all: the earth
is full of thy riches.
25 *So is* this great and wide sea, wherein
are things creeping innumerable, both small
and great beasts.
26 There go the ships: *there is* that [o]levia-
than, *whom* thou hast [p]made to play therein.

A. M. cir. 3468
B. C. cir. 536
Cyri,
R. Persarum,
cir. annum
primum

[f]Prov. xxx. 26——[g]Gen. i. 14——[h]Job xxxviii. 12
[i]Isa. xlv. 7——[k]Heb. *all the beasts thereof do trample on the forest*——[l]Job xxxviii. 39; Joel i. 20——[m]Gen. iii. 19
[n]Prov. iii. 19——[o]Job xli. 1——[p]Heb. *formed*

The cedars of Lebanon] God's providence not only extends to *men* and *cattle*, but also to the *trees* of the field and forest. Many of these are not only sustained, but *planted* by his providence. Who ever planted the seeds of the cedars of Lebanon, or of the thousands of woods and forests on the globe? God himself sowed those seeds, and they have sprung up and flourished without the care of man.

Verse 17. *Where the birds make their nests*] צפרים *tsipporim* signifies *swallows*, *sparrows*, and *small birds* in general; here opposed to the חסידה *chasidah* or *stork*. Perhaps the *heron* may be understood, which is said to be the first of all birds to build her nest, and she builds it on the very highest trees. The general meaning is, that God has provided shelter and support for the greatest and smallest birds; they are all objects of his providential regard.

Verse 18. *The high hills* are *a refuge*] The barren tops of the highest hills, and the craggy abrupt precipices of the most stupendous rocks, are not without their uses: they afford protection, refuge, and food, for creatures whose dispositions and habits are suited to such places; and thus no part of the creation is useless. The creatures who are their inhabitants are necessary *links* in the great *chain* of animated beings, and show the wisdom and providence of God.

For a description of the *coney*, see Lev. xi. 5. The יעל *yael*, translated here the *wild goat*, is no doubt a creature of the *stag* or *deer* kind; the *ibex*, *chamois*, *antelope*, &c.

Verse 19. *He appointed the moon for seasons*] The heathens thought that the *sun* and *moon* were gods, and worshipped them as such. The psalmist shows, 1. That they are creatures dependent on God for their being and continuance; and, 2. That they were made for the use of man. See what has been said on these luminaries in the notes on Gen. i.

Verse 20. *Thou makest darkness*] It is not the design of God that there should be either constant *darkness* or constant *light*. That man may *labour*, he gives him, by means of the *sun*, the *light of the day;* and that he may *rest* from his labour, and get his strength recruited, he gives him *night*, and comparative *darkness*. And as it would not be convenient for man and the wild beasts of the forest to collect their food *at the same time*, he has given the *night* to them as the proper time to procure their prey, and the *day* to rest in. When MAN *labours*, THEY *rest; when* MAN *rests*, THEY *labour*.

Verse 21. *The young lions roar after their prey*] It is said of the lion, that his *roaring* is so terrible as to astonish and quite unnerve the beast which he pursues; so that, though fleeter than himself, it falls down and becomes an easy prey.

Verse 22. *The sun ariseth*] The dawn of day is the warning for *man* to arise and betake himself to his work; and is the warning to *them* to retire to their dens.

Verse 24. *O Lord, how manifold are thy works*] In this verse there are *three* propositions: 1. The works of the Lord are multitudinous and varied. 2. They are so constructed as to show the most consummate wisdom in their *design*, and in the *end* for which they are formed. 3. They are all God's *property*, and should be used only in reference to the end for which they were created. All *abuse* and *waste* of God's creatures are spoil and robbery on the property of the Creator. On this verse Mr. *Ray* has published an excellent work, entitled, "The Wisdom of God in the Creation," which the reader will do well, not only to consult, but carefully to read over and study.

Verse 25. *This great and wide sea*] The original is very emphatic: זה הים גדול ורחב ידים *zeh haiyam gadol urechab yadayim*, "This very sea, great and extensive of hands." Its waters, like *arms*, encompassing all the terrene parts of the globe. I suppose the psalmist was within sight of the Mediterranean when he wrote these words.

Verse 26. *There go the ships*] By means of navigation countries the most remote are connected, and all the inhabitants of the earth become known to each other. He appears at this time to have seen the ships under sail.

That leviathan] This may mean the *whale*, or any of the large marine animals. The *Septuagint* and *Vulgate* call it *dragon*. Sometimes the *crocodile* is intended by the original word.

To play therein.] Dreadful and tempestuous as the sea may appear, and uncontrollable in its billows and surges, it is only the field of *sport*, the *play-ground*, the *bowling-green* to those huge marine monsters.

A. M. cir. 3468 B. C. cir. 536 Cyri, R. Persarum, cir. annum primum

27 [q]These wait all upon thee; that thou mayest give *them* their meat in due season.

28 *That* thou givest them they gather: thou openest thine hand, they are filled with good.

29 Thou hidest thy face, they are troubled: [r]thou takest away their breath, they die, and return to their dust.

30 [s]Thou sendest forth thy spirit, they are created: and thou renewest the face of the earth.

31 The glory of the LORD [t]shall endure for ever: the LORD [u]shall rejoice in his works.

32 He looketh on the earth, and it [v]trembleth: [w]he toucheth the hills, and they smoke.

33 [x]I will sing unto the LORD as long as I live: I will sing praise to my God while I have my being.

34 My meditation of him shall be sweet: I will be glad in the LORD.

35 Let [y]the sinners be consumed out of the earth, and let the wicked be no more. [z]Bless thou the LORD, O my soul. Praise ye the LORD.

---

[q]Psa. cxxxvi. 25; cxlv. 15; cxlvii. 9——[r]Job xxxiv. 14, 15; Psa. cxlvi. 4; Eccles. xii. 7——[s]Isa. xxxii. 15; Ezek. xxxvii. 9

[t]Heb. *shall be*——[u]Gen. i. 31——[v]Hab. iii. 10——[w]Psa. cxliv. 5——[x]Psa. lxiii. 4; cxlvi. 2——[y]Psa. xxxvii. 38; Prov. ii. 22——[z]Ver. 1

Verse 27. *These wait all upon thee*] The innumerable *fry* of the smaller aquatic animals, as well as *whales, dolphins, porpoises*, and *sharks*, all have their meat from God. He has in his gracious providence furnished that sort of food which is suitable to all. And this provision is *various;* not only for *every kind* of fish does God provide food, but a *different kind* of aliment for each in its different *periods* of *growth*. Here are displayed the goodness and infinitely varied providence of God: "He giveth them their meat in due season."

Verse 28. That *thou givest them they gather*] All creatures are formed with such and such digestive organs, and the food proper for them is provided. Infinitely varied as are living creatures in their habits and internal economy, so are the aliments which God has caused the *air*, the *earth*, and the *waters* to produce.

Thou openest thine hand] An allusion to the act of scattering grain among fowls.

Verse 29. *Thou hidest thy face*] If thou bring dearth or famine on the *land*, contagion in the *air*, or any destruction on the provision made by the *waters*, then beasts, fowl, and fish die, and are dissolved.

Verse 30. *Thou sendest forth thy spirit, they are created*] יבראון *yibbareun*, "They are created again."

And thou renewest the face of the earth.] Do not these words plainly imply a *resurrection* of the bodies which have died, been dissolved, or turned to dust? And is not the brute creation principally intended here? Is it not on this account it is said, ver. 31, "the glory of the Lord shall endure for ever, (לעולם *leolam*,)" to be manifest in those *times* which are *secret*, when *Jehovah* himself *shall rejoice in his works;* when the brute creation shall be delivered from the bondage of its corruption? See the notes on Rom. viii. 19-23.

Verse 32. *He looketh on the earth*] Even the look of God terrifies all created nature!

He toucheth the hills] So easy is it for God to burn up the earth and the works thereof, that even his *touch* kindles the mountains into flames! See *Etna, Vesuvius, Stromboli*, &c.; these are *ignited* by the touch of God. How majestic are these figures!

The renewal of the earth, and re-creation of deceased animals, shall take place when he shall shake terribly the heavens and the earth; when they shall be wrapped together as a scroll, and the earth and its works be dissolved, that is, after the general *convulsion* and *conflagration* of the world.

Verse 33. *I will sing unto the Lord*] The psalmist exulting in the glorious prospect of the renovation of all things, breaks out in triumphant anticipation of the great event, and says, I will sing unto the Lord בחיי *bechaiyai*, with my *lives*, the life that I *now* have, and the *life* that I *shall have* hereafter.

I will sing praise to my God] בעודי *beodi*, "in my eternity;" my going on, my endless progression. What astonishing ideas! But then, how shall this great work be brought about? and how shall the new earth be inhabited with righteous spirits only? The answer is,

Verse 35. *Let the sinners be consumed out of the earth, and let the wicked be no more.*] Or, He shall consume the wicked and ungodly, till no more of them be found. Then the wicked shall be turned into hell, with all the nations that forget God. No wonder, with these prospects before his eyes, he cries out, "Bless Jehovah, O my soul! Hallelujah!" And *ye* that hear of these things, *bless the Lord* also.

ANALYSIS OF THE HUNDRED AND FOURTH PSALM

The scope of this Psalm is the same with that of the former, i. e., to excite them to praise God in consideration of his benefits; but yet on a different ground. In the former, for the benefits of grace conferred upon his Church; in this, for the gifts of nature bestowed in general upon all. Those flow immediately from his mercy; these, from his power, wisdom, and goodness, and depend upon his providence, and are manifest in the creation, governance, and preservation of all things. The creature then is the subject of this Psalm, relative to which we have a long but very methodical narration.

I. The exhortation proposed briefly, ver. 1.

II. The exhortation urged by the inspection of the fabric, the beauty, order, and government of the world, ver. 1-33.

III. The duty practised by himself, ver. 33, 34.

IV. An imprecation on them that neglect the duty, ver. 35.

I. He begins with a double apostrophe:—

1. To his own soul, to praise God: "Bless the Lord, O my soul;" which was the conclusion of the former Psalm.

2. To his God: "O Lord my God," whom he describes to be great and glorious. That he may set forth his majesty and glory, borrowing his figure from the person of some great king, presenting himself very glorious to his people in his robes, in his pavilion, with a glittering canopy extended over his throne; sometimes in his chariot, drawn by the swiftest horses, with his nobles, ministers, and servants, waiting on his pleasure.

In this way he describes the majesty of God in the works of the first and second day, for by that order he proceeds in setting forth God's works, that in which they were made.

1. His robe is the light, the work of the first day, which is the purest, the most illustrious and cheerful of all God's creatures. With this "he is clothed as with a garment," for he is light, John i. 1; and he dwells in that inaccessible light that no man hath seen, nor can see, 1 Tim. vi. 16.

2. His pavilion stretched round about him is the heavens, the work of the second day. These are as the hangings and curtains of his chamber of presence, by his fiat and power stretched out as we now see them: "He stretched out the heavens as a curtain."

3. His palace built in a most miraculous manner. The beams are laid, not as usual on a solid body, but upon that which is most fluent: "He lays the beams of his chambers in the waters." In Gen. i. 7 we read of the "waters above the firmament," which were a part of the second day's work; and of these the prophet surely speaks.

4. His chariot, the clouds: "Who makes the clouds his chariot." Upon these he rides in a most wonderful manner, in all places he pleases; which are now in this place, and then instantly removed to another.

5. The horses that draw it, the *winds*, *alipedes*, as the poets feigned the horses who drew the chariot of the sun. The psalmist intends to show that by the power of God they are brought upon the face of heaven, and removed at his pleasure.

6. His attendants, angels: "He maketh his angels spirits, his ministers a flaming fire." No creature of greater quickness and agility than a *spirit*, no element more active than *fire*. These blessed spirits he sends forth as he pleases, to defend his servants; and as a flame of fire to consume and burn up his enemies: in which appears his might and majesty.

II. Next, the prophet descends from the heavens, and out of the air, and speaks of the work of the third day; and begins with the earth, that element which is best known to us, in which he shows the power and wisdom of God many ways.

1. In the foundation of it upon its centre. Strange it is that so great and heavy a body should remain in the midst of it and not sink; this the prophet attributes to the power and providence of God: "Who laid the foundations of the earth that it should not be removed for ever."

2. Another part of his providence about the *earth* was, that the water, being the lighter element, covered the earth, and thus rendered it useless. God, either by taking some parts of the upper superficies out of the earth in some places, made it more hollow, and putting them in others, made it convex; or in other words, by raising some and depressing others, made room for the sea; this was the work of God's word, and the prophet speaks of this in the three following verses.

1. He shows in what condition the *earth* was in the first creation; it was covered, and under water: "Thou coveredst it with the deep as with a garment; the waters stood above the mountains."

2. He shows that the earth became uncovered by the voice, power, and fiat of God: "Let the waters be gathered together into one place, and let the dry land appear." This the psalmist here calls the rebuke of God, the voice of thunder; for God no sooner spake than it was done: "At thy rebuke they fled, at the voice of thy thunder they were afraid."

3. And so there became a new world. The mountains and valleys take the lower place; the mists and vapours *go up by the mountains.*

4. There they inclose them: "Thou hast set a bound," &c. Yet not violently kept there, but restrained by an ordinary law of nature, it being natural for water to descend to the lower places.

III. He next speaks of the rivers and springs, and shows God's wonderful providence over them:—

1. "He sendeth the springs," the streams of water, from the hills "into the valleys."

2. "The end of this infinitely declares God's providence; it is for the sustenance of beasts and fowls, or they must perish for thirst: "The springs and rivers give drink to every beast of the field, the wild asses," &c.

IV. But the springs and rivers cannot water all parts of the earth; therefore, his wisdom devised the rain and the clouds.

"He watereth the hills from his chambers." The effect of which is,—

1. In general, the satisfaction of the earth, which, being thirsty, gapes for rain: "The earth is satisfied with the fruit of thy works."

2. In particular, the effects and consequences of the dews. 1. Grass for the cattle: "He causeth the grass to grow for the cattle." 2. Herbs for meat and medicine: "And herbs for the service of man." 3. All kinds of food: "And that he may bring forth food." 4. "And wine that makes glad the heart of man," lawfully used. 5. "And oil to make his face to shine." Oil supplies and strengthens the nerves, and keeps the flesh smooth, fresh, and youthful. 6. "And bread which strengtheneth man's heart;"

for it is always the chief and necessary part of the service.

V. Neither hath the God of providence forgotten to provide us trees for shade, building, and fuel, as well as to yield us fruit.

1. "The trees of the Lord also." His trees, because he first made them, and now causes them to grow. "They are full of sap," which is another effect of the rain.

2. "Where the birds make their nests."

3. Other creatures are not forgotten; not the goats nor the conies: "For the high hills," &c.

The psalmist next mentions the work of the fourth day; the creation of the two great luminaries, the sun and the moon.

1. "God appointed the moon for certain seasons."

2. "And the sun knoweth his going down."

And in this division of time, the providence of God is admirable: "Thou makest darkness, and it is night."

1. For the good of the beasts, even the wildest, that they be sustained. 1. The night comes, and the beasts of the forest creep forth: "The young lions," &c. 2. Again, the day appears: "The sun ariseth, and they appear not," &c.

2. For the good of man: "Man goeth forth to his labour." Labour he must all day, and then take rest: "Labour till the evening."

Upon the consideration of all which the prophet exclaims: "O God, how manifold are thy works! in wisdom hast thou made them all: the earth is full of thy riches."

1. "How manifold are thy works." How great, how excellent, how worthy of praise! such that I cannot express them.

2. "In wisdom hast thou made them all." Nothing is done by chance or rashness, but with great reason; neither too much nor too little.

3. "All the earth is full of thy riches." No place, no part of it, but thy works proclaim that thou art a bountiful and most wise Creator; an open handed and liberal bestower of riches.

The prophet has hitherto set forth God's wisdom in his works; in the heavens, air, the earth; and now he descends into the sea.

1. In the amplitude of it: It is the *great and wide sea.*

2. In the abundance of the fish, the work of the fifth day: "Wherein are things creeping innumerable."

3. In the useful art of navigation, which God taught by Noah's ark: "There go the ships."

4. In the whale: "There is that leviathan."

And the conservation of the creature now follows, from verse 27 to 30; where their dependence is shown upon the providence of God, both for their meat, life, and continuation of their *species.*

1. "These all wait upon thee;" they expect till thou givest.

2. "That thou mayest give them their meat." Meat fit for every season of the year, and when they want it.

3. "That thou givest them they gather." That, and no more nor less: and his power and blessing must co-operate with the second causes.

4. This he farther explains: "Thou openest thine hand, and they are filled with good."

Farther, life and death are in thy power. Death, and the forerunner of it; trouble.

1. "Thou hidest thy face;" seemest displeased, and withdrawest help and assistance; "and they are troubled."

2. "Thou takest away their breath; they die."

And life also.

1. "Thou sendest forth thy spirit," a vital spirit, by restoring new individuals to every species.

2. And by this "thou renewest the face of the earth;" which, if not done, the whole would fail in an age.

Now, after this long catalogue of the creatures, and God's power, wisdom, and goodness made most manifest in the creation, governance, and sustentation of them, he descends, ver. 32.

1. "Let the glory of the Lord," his glory, for his wisdom, and goodness and power, "endure for ever." Hallowed be his name!

2. "The Lord shall rejoice in his works." Let man be so careful to use them well, that by the abuse he grieve not God, and cause him to repent that he made them.

3. Which if it happen, it would be remembered that he is a God, and able to punish the ungrateful person: "For if he looketh on the earth with a threatening brow, it trembleth."

He makes then an open profession of his own practice.

1. "I will sing unto the Lord as long as I live," &c.

2. And this he would do with delight: "My meditation of him shall be sweet," &c.

3. And he concludes with an imprecation against unthankful and negligent persons, who regard not the works of God, and will not see his glory, power, wisdom, and goodness, in his creating, governing, and sustaining this universe; and therefore very little praise him. Against these he prays that they may be confounded or converted.

"But, O my soul," be not thou like to them,—"bless the Lord. Hallelujah."

PSALM CV

An exhortation to praise God for his wondrous works, 1–5; *his goodness to Abraham, Isaac, and Jacob,* 6–16; *to Joseph in Egypt,* 17–22; *to Israel in Egypt,* 23–25; *to Moses in the same land,* 26; *the plagues sent on the Egyptians,* 27–36; *the deliverance of the Israelites out of Egypt,* 37, 38; *how he supported them in the wilderness,* 39–43; *and brought them into Canaan,* 44, 45.

XXI. DAY. MORNING PRAYER

A. M. cir. 3468
B. C. cir. 536
Cyri,
R. Persarum,
cir. annum
primum

O [a]GIVE thanks unto the
LORD; call upon his name:
[b]make known his deeds among
the people.

2 Sing unto him, sing psalms unto him:
[c]talk ye of all his wondrous works.

3 Glory ye in his holy name: let the heart
of them rejoice that seek the LORD.

4 Seek the LORD, and his strength: [d]seek
his face evermore.

5 [e]Remember his marvellous works that he
hath done; his wonders, and the judgments
of his mouth;

6 O ye seed of Abraham his servant, ye
children of Jacob his chosen.

7 He *is* the LORD our God: [f]his judgments
are in all the earth.

8 He has [g]remembered his covenant for ever,
the word *which* he commanded
to a thousand generations.

A. M. cir. 3468
B. C. cir. 536
Cyri,
R. Persarum,
cir. annum
primum

9 [h]Which *covenant* he made
with Abraham, and his oath
unto Isaac;

10 And confirmed the same unto Jacob for
a law, *and* to Israel *for* an everlasting covenant:

11 Saying, [i]Unto thee will I give the land
of Canaan, [k]the lot of your inheritance:

12 [l]When there were *but* a few men in number; yea, very few, [m]and strangers in it.

13 When they went from one nation to another, from *one* kingdom to another people;

14 [n]He suffered no man to do them wrong:
yea, [o]he reproved kings for their sakes;

15 *Saying,* Touch not mine anointed, and
do my prophets no harm.

16 Moreover [p]he called for a famine upon

[a]1 Chron. xvi. 8–22; Isa. xii. 4——[b]Psa. cxlv, 4. 5, 11——[c]Psa. lxxvii. 12; cxix. 27——[d]Psa. xxvii. 8——[e]Psa. lxxvii. 11——[f]Isa. xxvi. 9——[g]Luke i. 72——[h]Gen. xvii. 2; xxii. 16, &c.; xxvi. 3; xxviii. 13; xxxv. 11; Luke i. 73; Heb. vi. 17——[i]Gen. xiii. 15; xv. 18——[k]Heb. *the cord*——[l]Gen. xxxiv. 30; Deut. vii. 7; xxvi. 5——[m]Heb. xi. 9——[n]Gen. xxxv. 5——[o]Gen. xii. 17; xx. 3, 7——[p]Gen. xli. 54

NOTES ON PSALM CV

We find several verses of this Psalm in 1 Chron. xvi., from which it is evident that David was the author of the principal part of it: but it was probably enlarged and sung at the restoration of the people from the Babylonish captivity. The *hallelujah* which terminates the preceding Psalm, is made the *title* of this by the *Vulgate, Septuagint, Æthiopic,* and *Arabic:* but it has no title either in the *Hebrew* or *Chaldee.* The Syriac considers it a paraphrase on the words, "Fear not, Jacob, to go down into Egypt; and teach us spiritually not to fear when we are obliged to contend with devils; for God is our shield, and will fight for us." The Psalm is a history of God's dealings with Abraham and his posterity, till their settlement in the promised land.

Verse 1. *O give thanks*] He had been meditating on God's gracious dealings with their fathers; and he calls upon himself and all others to magnify God for his mercies.

Verse 2. *Talk ye of all his wondrous works.*] נפלאתיו *niphleothaiv,* "of his miracles." Who have so many of these to boast of as Christians! Christianity is a tissue of miracles; and every part of the work of grace on the soul is a miracle. Genuine Christian converts may talk of miracles from morning to night; and they *should talk of them,* and recommend to others their miracle-working God and Saviour.

Verse 3. *Glory ye in his holy name*] Show the name Jesus: exult in it—praise it. His name was called *Jesus;* because he came to save his people from their sins.

Let the heart of them rejoice] That is, the heart of those *shall* rejoice who seek the Lord: therefore it is added,—

Verse 4. *Seek the Lord*] Worship the one only Supreme Being, as the only and all-sufficient good for the soul of man.

And his strength] Man is *weak;* and needs connexion with the *strong* God that he may be enabled to avoid evil and do good.

Seek his face] Reconciliation to him. Live not without a sense of his favour.

Evermore.] Let this be thy chief business. In and above all thy seeking, seek this.

Verse 5. *Remember his marvellous works*] Keep up communion with thy Maker, that thou mayest neither forget him nor his works.

The judgments of his mouth] Whatsoever he has spoken concerning good or evil. His commands, promises, threatenings; and particularly what he has foretold, and what he has done.

Verse 6. *O ye seed of Abraham*] Ye Jews especially, who have been the peculiar objects of the Divine favour.

Verse 7. *He is the Lord our God*] He is *Jehovah,* the self-existent and eternal God. He is *our God,* he is our portion; has taken us for his people, and makes us happy in his love.

The following abstract of the history of the Israelites presents but few difficulties. See the notes on Psalm lxxviii.

Verse 12. But *a few men*] When all appearances were against them, and nothing but the arm of God could have brought them through their difficulties, and given them a settlement in the promised land.

Verse 13. *When they went from one nation to another*] From several circumstances in the history of the travels of the ancient Hebrews, we find that the wilderness through which they then passed was well peopled.

Verse 15. *Touch not mine anointed*] It is supposed that the *patriarchs* are here intended; but the whole people of Israel may be meant. They were a kingdom of *priests* and *kings*

A. M. cir. 3468
B. C. cir. 536
Cyri,
R. Persarum,
cir. annum
primum

the land: he brake the whole
[q]staff of bread.
17 [r]He sent a man before
them, *even* Joseph, *who* [s]was
sold for a servant:
18 [t]Whose feet they hurt with fetters: [u]he
was laid in iron:
19 Until the time that his word came: [v]the
word of the LORD tried him.
20 [w]The king sent and loosed him; *even* the
ruler of the people, and let him go free.
21 [x]He made him lord of his house, and
ruler of all his [y]substance:
22 To bind his princes at his pleasure; and
teach his senators wisdom.
23 [z]Israel also came into Egypt; and Jacob
sojourned [a]in the land of Ham.
24 And [b]he increased his people greatly;
and made them stronger than their enemies.
25 [c]He turned their heart to hate his people, to deal subtilly with his servants.
26 [d]He sent Moses his servant; *and* Aaron
[e]whom he had chosen.
27 [f]They showed [g]his signs among them,
[h]and wonders in the land of Ham.
28 [i]He sent darkness, and made it dark;
and [k]they rebelled not against his word.

29 [l]He turned their waters into
blood, and slew their fish.
30 [m]Their land brought forth
frogs in abundance, in the
chambers of their kings.

A. M. cir. 3468
B. C. cir. 536
Cyri,
R. Persarum,
cir. annum
primum

31 [n]He spake, and there came divers sorts
of flies, *and* lice in all their coasts.
32 [o]He [p]gave them hail for rain, *and* flaming fire in their land.
33 [q]He smote their vines also and their fig-
trees; and brake the trees of their coasts.
34 [r]He spake, and the locusts came, and
caterpillars, and that without number,
35 And did eat up all the herbs in their
land, and devoured the fruit of their ground.
36 [s]He smote also all the first-born in their
land, [t]the chief of all their strength.
37 [u]He brought them forth also with silver
and gold: and *there was* not one feeble *person* among their tribes.
38 [v]Egypt was glad when they departed:
for the fear of them fell upon them.
39 [w]He spread a cloud for a covering; and
fire to give light in the night.
40 [x]*The people* asked, and he brought quails
and [y]satisfied them with the bread of heaven.
41 [z]He opened the rock, and the waters

[q]Lev. xxvi. 26; Isa. iii. 1; Ezek. iv. 16——[r]Gen. xlv. 5; l. 20——[s]Gen. xxxvii. 28, 36——[t]Gen. xxxix. 20; xl. 15——[u]Heb. *his soul came into iron*——[v]Gen. xli. 25——[w]Gen. xli. 14——[x]Gen. xli. 40——[y]Heb. *possession*——[z]Gen. xlvi. 6——[a]Psa. lxxviii. 51; cvi. 22——[b]Exod. i. 7——[c]Exod. i. 8, &c.——[d]Exod. iii. 10; iv. 12, 14——[e]Num. xvi. 5; xvii. 5——[f]Exod. vii., viii., ix., x., xi., xii.; Psa. lxxviii. 43, &c.——[g]Heb. *words of his signs*——[h]Psa. cvi. 22——[i]Exod. x. 22——[k]Psa. xcix. 7

[l]Exod. vii. 20; Psa. lxxviii. 44——[m]Exod. viii. 6; Psa. lxxviii. 45——[n]Exod. viii. 17, 24; Psa. lxxviii. 45——[o]Exod. ix. 23, 25; Psa. lxxviii. 48——[p]Heb. *He gave their rain hail*——[q]Psa. lxxviii. 47——[r]Exod. x. 4, 13, 14; Psa. lxxviii. 46——[s]Exod. xii. 29; Psa. lxxviii. 51——[t]Gen. xlix. 3——[u]Exod. xii. 35——[v]Exod. xii. 33——[w]Exod. xiii. 21; Neh. ix. 12——[x]Exod. xvi. 12, &c.; Psa. lxxviii. 18, 27——[y]Psa. lxxviii. 24, 25——[z]Exod. xvii. 6; Num. xx. 11; Psa. lxxviii. 15, 16; 1 Cor. x. 4

unto God; and *prophets*, *priests*, and *kings* were always *anointed*.

Verse 19. *Until the time that his word came*] This appears to refer to the completion of Joseph's interpretation of the dreams of the chief butler and baker.

The word of the Lord tried him.] This seems to refer to the interpretation of Pharaoh's dreams, called אמרת יהוה *imrath Yehovah*, "the oracle of the Lord," because sent by him to Pharaoh. See Gen. xli. 25, and *Kennicott in loco*.

Verse 25. *He turned their heart*] "Their heart was turned." So the *Syriac* and *Arabic*. After befriending the Hebrews on Joseph's account, to whom they were so deeply indebted, finding them to multiply greatly in the land, and at last to become more powerful than the Egyptians themselves, they turned their attention to the adoption of measures, in order to prevent the Hebrews from possessing themselves of the government of the whole land; they curtailed them of their privileges, and endeavoured to depress them by all possible means, and by a variety of legal enactments. This appears to be the sole meaning of the phrase, "He turned their heart;" or, "their heart was turned."

Verse 27. *They showed his signs*] Here is a reference to the *plagues* with which God afflicted the Egyptians. See the places in the margin, and the notes on them.

Verse 28. *They rebelled not against his word.*] Instead of ולא מרו *velo maru*, "they rebelled," some think that a ש *shin* has been lost from before the word, and that it should be read ולא שמרו *velo shamru*, "they did not observe *or* keep his word." Or the words may be spoken of *Moses* and *Aaron;* they received the commandment of God, and they did not rebel against it. They believed what he had spoken, and acted according to his orders. It could not be spoken of the *Egyptians;* for they rebelled against his words through the whole course of the transactions.

Verse 33. *He smote their vines also, and their fig trees*] This is not mentioned in Exodus; but we have had it before, Psalm lxxviii. 47.

Verse 41. *He opened the rock, and the waters gushed out*] See the note on Exod. xvii. 6, to

A. M. cir. 3468
B. C. cir. 536
Cyri,
R. Persarum,
cir. annum
primum

gushed out; they ran in the dry places *like* a river.
42 For he remembered [a]his holy promise, *and* Abraham his servant.
43 And he brought forth his people with joy, *and* his chosen with [b]gladness:
44 [c]And gave them the lands of the heathen: and they inherited the labour of the people;
45 [d]That they might observe his statutes, and keep his laws. [e]Praise ye the LORD.

A. M. cir. 3468
B. C. cir. 536
Cyri,
R. Persarum,
cir. annum
primum

[a]Genesis xv. 14——[b]Hebrew, *singing*——[c]Deuteronomy vi. 10, 11; Joshua xiii. 7, &c.; Psalm lxxviii. 55——[d]Deuteronomy iv. 1, 40; vi. 21-25——[e]Hebrew, *Hallelujah*

which I can now add, that a piece of this rock, broken off by the hand of my nephew, E. S. A. Clarke, in the course of the present year [1822,] now lies before me. It is fine *granite;* and so well distinguished as a granite, that the *feldt-spar*, the *mica*, and the *quartz*, of which granite is composed, appear very distinctly. It is worthy of remark, that, as *granite* is supposed, in the most accredited *systems of geology*, to be the very *basis* of the *earth*, the *original rock*, and all other substances to be superimpositions upon it, and as the decompositions of the *feldt-spar* produce pure vegetable earth, this rock should be used for this purpose, and should be an emblem of Jesus Christ, the Creator and Redeemer of the human race; and that it should signify him who is the *basis of all things;* who upholds all by the word of his power; without whom nothing is *stable*, nothing *fruitful;* from whom alone the *water of life* proceeds; and in whose name only is salvation. *And that rock* (in the wilderness) *was Christ!* and it is the only *remaining emblem* of him in creation.

Verse 45. *That they might observe his statutes*] That they might be properly *instructed*, and properly *disciplined*. This is the end proposed by Divine revelation: men are to be made wise unto salvation, and then to be brought under the yoke of obedience. He who is not conformed to God's word shall not enter into Christ's kingdom.

ANALYSIS OF THE HUNDRED AND FIFTH PSALM

The *title* of this Psalm is *Hallelujah*, as are also the two following; and the first fifteen verses of it were sung at the bringing up of the ark by *David*, 1 Chron. xvi.

The scope of it is the same with the two former Psalms, "that we praise God;" but yet with this difference: in the hundred and third, that he be magnified "for his benefits of redemption;" in the hundred and fourth, "for the manifestation of his power and providence in creating, governing, and sustaining the world;" but in this, "for the gracious covenant he made with Abraham, and, in him, with his whole Church."

I. An exhortation to praise God, ver. 1-7.

II. An enumeration of the favours God bestowed to persuade to it, from ver. 7 to the end.

I. He that loves his prince truly desires also that others should magnify and honour him. This was David's case; he was a true lover of his God, and set a true estimate upon him. He honoured and praised God himself, and desired that others should do the same outwardly and inwardly, with heart and tongue: he thought all too little, and therefore, he repeats the duty often, and shows how it is to be done.

1. By giving of thanks: "O give thanks unto the Lord."

2. By invocation: "Call upon his name."

3. By communication: "Make known his deeds among the people."

4. By voices, psalms, and hymns: "Sing unto him; sing psalms unto him."

5. By frequent colloquies of his works: "Talk ye of all his wondrous works."

6. By boasting of him: "Glory ye in his holy name." Profess that you are happy men, that God's holy name was ever made known to you. "He that glories, let him glory in the Lord;" 2 Cor. xi.

He invites all outwardly to exhibit praise; and now he advises that it be done inwardly also, with exultation and gladness of heart.

1. "Let the heart of them rejoice." The Holy Spirit does not sing but out of a joyous heart.

2. "Let them seek the Lord." For, indeed, they only who seek him rejoice heartily: they can acquiesce in God, in his promises of grace, pardon, and acceptance; which is so necessary to every one who will make his approaches to the throne of grace, and have his praise rendered acceptable, that the prophet seriously urges the duty:—

(1) "Seek the Lord." Cast all impiety and wickedness away: seek him.

(2) "Seek his strength." Which at that time was the ark, it being the symbol of his presence Seek him in his Church.

(3) "Seek his face evermore." His favour, and grace, and reconciliation; seek them in his word and sacraments, &c.

(4) "Evermore seek him." Now and then is too little; it must be our constant work.

Having thus spoken of the heart, he comes to the memory: "Remember, forget not." And the things to be remembered are, 1. *His marvellous works.* 2. *His wonders.* 3. *His judgments;* which three are the substance of this whole Psalm, and are explained according to their heads. They ought to be particularly remembered by the Israelites, the posterity of Abraham, and the sons of Jacob.

"Remember his marvellous works," &c. "O ye seed of Abraham, his servant; ye children of Jacob, his chosen." Remember that he made *Abraham* and chose *Jacob* to be his servants, gave you laws, and showed you with what rites he would be worshipped. Forget them not.

II. But at the *seventh* verse the prophet begins his narration; and tells the *Israelites*, and in them us, what marvellous works God had done for his people, all which he presses as arguments to his people that they should praise, honour, worship, and obey him. There is much reason for it.

1. "He is the Lord our God." The same argument prefaces the commandments: "I am the Lord thy God."

2. "His judgments are in all the earth." He is a mighty Monarch, and has all nature under his empire.

And if neither of these move, yet there is another, drawn from his many and infinite favours: "On you Israelites," and all mankind as well; for on the fall of man his covenant was, *That the seed of the woman should bruise the serpent's head;* and this he forgot not: "He hath remembered his covenant," &c.

1. "Which covenant he made with Abraham," and confirmed it by sacrifice, Gen. xv. 13.

2. "His oath unto Isaac," Gen. xxvi. 3, 4.

3. "And confirmed the same unto Jacob for a law," &c.; Gen. xxviii. 13, 14, 15.

4. The form of the covenant recited: "Saying, Unto thee will I give," &c.; for it was divided to the tribes by lots.

Which covenant God made with their fathers and them, not out of any merit that could be in them; Deut. viii. 4, 5, 6; Josh. xxiv. 2.

1. "When there were but a few men," and humble; "yea, very few."

2. And they "strangers" in the land. For the patriarchs only sojourned in *Canaan.*

3. Yea, "when they went from one nation to another," &c.

Now when they were in this condition, *very few, strangers, sojourners,* and *pilgrims,* God protected and defended them.

1. "He suffered no man to do them wrong," &c.; no, not the greatest, for "he reproved even kings for their sakes."

2. For he gave the command: "Touch not mine anointed,"—*Abraham, Isaac,* and *Jacob,* who were anointed with the Holy Ghost, though not with material oil; "and do my prophets no harm," i. e., the same men, for they were prophets. *Abraham* foresaw the bondage of his seed in *Egypt; Isaac* foretold what should befall *Esau's* posterity, Gen. xxvii.; and *Jacob,* by a prophetical spirit, gave his blessings, Gen. xlix. Of *Abraham* it is expressly said, "He is a prophet, and he shall pray for thee," Gen. xx. 7.

Two of these mercies, the covenant and protection, are already named; and now he goes on and insists upon the third, verses 16-23, for which there was infinite matter of praise for the wonderful wisdom of God, that brought out of the greatest evils the chiefest good, by preserving their lives in *Egypt* in the midst of famine, Gen. xxxvii.

1. "Moreover he called for a famine upon the land." It came not by chance.

2. "He brake the whole staff of bread," the upholder of our lives; and this he brake when he ordered that there should be no ploughing, sowing, nor harvest, Gen. xlv.

3. By this famine the patriarchs were to suffer; yet God provided for their subsistence: "He sent a man, (a wise man,) before them,"—Joseph.

4. This Joseph was sold by the envy and cruelty of his brethren.

And now he comes, 1. To his base usage. 2. His advancement.

1. By the false accusation of *Potiphar's* wife, who turned her base love into hatred: "His feet were hurt with fetters of iron."

2. "He was laid in iron;" or, as some read, "the iron entered into his soul." Grief that he should lie under foul aspersions.

There he lay: "Until the time that his word came." So long then he lay in prison, and no longer.

1. "Until the time that his word came:" his word—God's word for his deliverance. Or, as others: "Joseph's word to the butler."

2. "The word of the Lord tried him." God tried his patience: or the interpretation of the dreams proved that by the Lord he spake.

And now follows his honour and advancement:—

1. *Pharaoh,* by his *butler,* hearing of *Joseph's* wisdom: "He sent," &c.

2. "Even the ruler of the people let him go free." A work fit for a king.

And his advancement follows:—

1. "He made him lord of his house."

2. "A ruler of all his substance." A viceroy, a grand vizier.

The king's end in it; not only in the famine to provide bread for their bodies, but for the good of their souls.

1. To punish the rebellious: "To bind his princes at his pleasure."

2. To instruct his counsellors in wisdom, arts, sciences, religion. It is supposed that all the learning in which the Egyptians excelled was first taught them by *Joseph.*

The fourth benefit follows of God towards his people, ver. 22-37, which was their nourishment, increase in Egypt, their oppression, and deliverance.

1. He begins with Jacob's descent thither: 1. "Israel also, Joseph's father, went down into Egypt," Gen. xlvi. 2. "And Jacob with all his family," &c.

2. He proceeds with their strange increase there; for it is wonderful that in so short a time they should grow into such a multitude, Exod. i. 7. At their going out they were six hundred thousand, besides children, Exod. xii. 37: "And he increased his people greatly, and made them stronger than their enemies," Exod. i. 9.

This was the occasion of their afflictions, bondage, and sufferings; for,—

1. "He turned the Egyptians' hearts to hate his people." He suffered them to be turned: "For there arose another king," &c.

2. "And to deal subtilly with his people. Come on, say they," &c.

"To set over them taskmasters," &c.; Exod. i. 11. But when they saw "that the more they afflicted them, the more they multiplied," ver. 12, then they ordered "that all the male children should be strangled by the midwives," ver. 16. And when even this would not do, then *Pharaoh* charged "that every son that was born," &c., ver. 22. Thus subtilly they dealt; but it did not hinder their multiplication. There is no counsel against God.

Now God, seeing their affliction, and hearing their groans, sent them a deliverer.

1. "He sent Moses his servant, and Aaron whom he had chosen."

2. "They showed his signs among them." 1. To the Israelites; 2. "And wonders in the land of Ham."

The catalogue follows:—

1. "He sent darkness," &c.

2. "He turned their waters into blood," &c.

3. "The land brought forth frogs," &c.

4. "He spake, and there came divers sorts of flies," &c.

5. "He gave them hail for rain," &c.
6. "He smote the vines also, and the fig-trees," &c.
7. "He spake, and the locusts came," &c.
8. "He smote also the first-born of their land," &c.

These were the wonders that God wrought in Egypt by the hand of *Moses* and *Aaron* for the deliverance of his people, which the psalmist briefly records that they might remember—be thankful, and praise him.

The fifth benefit that the psalmist records is, that God brought not out his people beggars, but enriched them with the spoils of Egypt.

1. "He brought them forth with silver and gold." For they were sent by God to ask jewels: and when the Jews pretend by their example to rob more honest men than themselves, when they can show an immediate commission from God to do it, I am content that they borrow, and never restore; rob and spoil whom they please. Till this be shown, they are thieves and sacrilegious persons.

2. Farther, they left the *Egyptians* afflicted with some strange disease, of which their first-born had died; yet they were healthy: "There was not one, no, not one feeble person, among them."

The terror of them was so great, and the fear of death so instant, that, regarding not their jewels, they urged them to be gone—they thrust them out; which the prophet expresses: "Egypt was glad when they departed."

The sixth benefit follows after their departure, which was "the pillar of cloud by day, and of fire by night. He spread a cloud for a covering," &c.; which most interpret as if the cloud kept off the heat of the sun; and therefore the prophet says: "He spread it for a covering."

The seventh benefit was *quails* and *manna*:—

1. "The people asked, and he brought quails." Those given Exod. xvi.

2. "And satisfied them with the bread of heaven"—*manna*, because it was made of the sweet dew descending from the air, and therefore called heavenly bread; the earth having nothing to do with its production.

The eighth benefit was the water out of the rock; "for they travelled through a dry wilderness."

1. "He opened the rock." He did not turn the rock into water, but opened a passage for the fountain he had made.

2. *For the waters gushed out* upon the passage being made for them.

3. "And they ran in dry places."

Now here he inserts the reason both of the former and latter benefits, which was his covenant and promise to Abraham: "For he remembered his holy promise," &c.

The ninth benefit was, he brought them not only out of Egypt; but that too in such a manner that they had reason to exult and triumph, Exod. xv.: "And he brought forth his people with joy," &c.

And to make the number of his benefits complete, he adds a tenth, which was the exact fulfilling of his promise, his introduction of them into *Canaan*, ejection of the inhabitants, and the donation of their inheritances to his people, which they afterwards possessed.

"He gave them the lands of the heathen," &c. The houses they built not, the vines they planted not, the lands they tilled not, fell to them.

For which benefits God requires no more than their obedience: this he requires as his due and tribute. He bestowed so many benefits on them for one end only: "That they might observe his statutes, and keep his laws." Hallelujah! "Let *your* light so shine before men, that they may glorify your Father who is in heaven."

PSALM CVI

God is praised for his manifold mercies, 1–3. *The prophet prays for himself*, 4, 5. *A recapitulation of the history of the Hebrew people: of God's mercies toward them, and their rebellions*, 6–39. *The judgments and afflictions which their transgressions brought upon them*, 40–42. *God's mercy to them notwithstanding their transgressions*, 43–46. *He prays for their restoration*, 47, 48.

XXI. DAY. EVENING PRAYER

PRAISE [a]ye the LORD. [b]O [c]give thanks unto the LORD; for *he is* good: for his mercy *endureth* for ever.

2 [d]Who can utter the mighty acts of the LORD? *who* can show forth all his praise?

3 Blessed *are* they that keep judgment, *and* he that [e]doeth righteousness at [f]all times.

[a]Heb. *Hallelujah*——[b]1 Chron. xvi. 34——[c]Psa. cvii. 1; cxviii. 1; cxxxvi. 1

[d]Psa. xl. 5——[e]Psa. xv. 2——[f]Acts xxiv. 16; Gal. vi. 9

NOTES ON PSALM CVI

As a part of the preceding Psalm is found in 1 Chron. xvi., so the first and two last verses of *this* are found in the same place, (ver. 34-36,) and yet it is supposed by eminent commentators to be a prayer of the captives in Babylon, who acknowledge the mercies of God, confess their own sins, and those of their forefathers, and implore the Lord to gather them from among the heathen, and restore them to their own country. In none of the *Versions* except the *Syriac* has it any title, except HALLELUJAH, *Praise ye the Lord*, the word with which the original commences. The *Syriac* gives us a sort of table of its contents; or rather shows us the subjects to which it may be *applied*, and the uses we should make of it. After stating that it has *no* title, it says, "It calls upon men to observe the Divine precepts, and teaches us that the

4 [g]Remember me, O LORD, with the favour
that thou bearest unto thy people: O visit me
with thy salvation;
5 That I may see the good of thy chosen,
that I may rejoice in the gladness of thy nation, that I may glory with thine inheritance.
6 [h]We have sinned with our fathers, we have
committed iniquity, we have done wickedly.
7 Our fathers understood not thy wonders in
Egypt; they remembered not the multitude of
thy mercies; [i]but provoked *him* at the sea,
even at the Red Sea.
8 Nevertheless he saved them [k]for his name's
sake, [l]that he might make his mighty power
to be known.
9 [m]He rebuked the Red Sea also, and it was

[g]Psa. cxix. 132——[h]Lev. xxvi. 40; 1 Kings viii. 47; Dan. ix. 5——[i]Exod. xiv. 11, 12

[k]Ezek. xx. 14——[l]Exod. ix. 16——[m]Exod. xiv. 21; Psa. xviii. 15; Nah. i. 4

more the Jews transgressed, the more we should fear. That we should not talk together in the Church, nor ever contend with our brethren on any account; and especially when we assist in the celebration of the Divine mysteries and in prayer: and that when we sin we should repent." All this is very good: but it would be difficult to find these subjects in the Psalm, or any thing on which they could be rationally founded. But it shows us that the Scriptures were very easily *accommodated* to particular uses, not originally intended: and hence arose much of the practice of *spiritualizing* and *allegorizing;* which, to say the least of it, has been of no use to the Church of Christ.

Verse 1. *Praise ye the Lord*] This, which is a sort of *title*, is wanting in several MSS., and in the Syriac Version.

O give thanks unto the Lord; for he is good] Ye who live by his bounty should praise his mercy. God is the good Being, and of all kinds of good he is the Author and Dispenser. That the term *God* among our Anglo-Saxon ancestors, expressed both the Supreme Being and *good* or *goodness*, is evident from the Anglo-Saxon version of this clause: **andettað drihtne forðon god, forðon on worulda mildheortnyssa.** "Confess Lord for that God, (or good,) for that on world mildheartness his." Which the old Psalter thus translates and paraphrases:—

Trans. **Schrifes to Lorde for he is gude; for in worlde the mercy of him.**

Par. Schryfes synes, and louyngs to God. for he is gude of kynde, that nane do bot aske his mercy; for it lastes to the worlds ende in wriches whame it comfortes and delyvers: and the blysfulhede that is gyfen thrugh mercy is endles. That is:—

Confess your sins, and give praise to God, for he is good in his nature to all that ask his mercy; for it lasts to the world's end in comforting and delivering the wretched: and the blessedness that is given through mercy is endless.

Verse 2. *Who can utter the mighty acts of the Lord?*] His acts are all acts of *might;* and particularly those in behalf of his followers.

Verse 3. *Blessed* are *they that keep judgment*, and *he that doeth righteousness at all times.*] How near do the *Anglo-Saxon*, the ancient *Scottish Version*, and the *present translation*, approach to each other!

Anglo-Saxon. **Eadig þaðe healdað dom, ⁊ doþ rihtwisnysse on ælcere tide.** "Blessed they that holdeth doom, and doth righteousness in ilkere tide."

Anglo-Scottish. Blisful tha that kepes dome, and duse rightwisnes in ilk tyme.

Those are truly blessed, or happy, whose hearts are devoted to God, and who live in the habit of obedience. Those, the general tenor of whose life is not conformed to the will of God, have no true happiness.

Verse 4. *Remember me*] This and the following clauses are read in the plural by several MSS.: *Remember* US—*that* WE *may rejoice,*—*that* WE *may glory*, &c.: and thus *all the Versions* except the *Chaldee;* and this is more agreeable to the context.

Verse 5. *That I may see the good of thy chosen*] That I may *enjoy* the good, for so the word *see* is understood among the Hebrews. "Blessed are the pure in heart, for they shall *see* God,"—they shall *enjoy* him, possess his favour, and be made like unto him.

Verse 6. *We have sinned*] Here the confession begins; what preceded was only the *introduction* to what follows: *Our forefathers sinned*, and suffered; we, like them, have sinned, and do suffer.

Verse 7. *Our fathers understood not*] They did not regard the operation of God's hands; and therefore they understood neither his designs nor their own interest.

At the sea, even *at the Red Sea.*] Some of the rabbins suppose that the repetition of the words point out *two* faults of the Israelites at the Red Sea. 1. They murmured against Moses for bringing them out of Egypt, when they saw the sea before them, and Pharaoh behind them. 2. When the waters were divided, they were afraid to enter in, lest they sould stick in the mud which appeared at the bottom. The word seems to be added by way of explanation, and perhaps may refer to the above: *they provoked* על ים *al yam*, "AT the sea;" בים סוף *beyam suph*, "IN the sea *Suph*," or *Red Sea*. They provoked him *at* it and *in* it.

Verse 8. *He saved them for his name's sake*] למען שמו *lemaan shemo*, "on account of his name;" to manifest his own power, goodness, and perfections. There was nothing which he could draw from them as a reason why he should save them; therefore he drew the reason from himself. There is a singular gloss in the old *Psalter* on this verse: "Whan thai cam oute of Egypt to the rede Se, whare thai were closed on a syde with a hylle that na man mygt passe: on another side was the rede See: behynde tham was men of Egypt foluand; and for this thai began to gruch, forgetand Gods mygt: bot than he safed tham, depertand the Se in twelfe, to ilk kynde of Isrel a passage." It seems as if this author thought there were *twelve* passages made through the Red Sea, that each tribe should have a passage to itself.

Verse 9. *He rebuked the Red Sea*] In the

dried up: so [n]he led them through the depths, as through the wilderness.

10 And he [o]saved them from the hand of him that hated *them,* and redeemed them from the hand of the enemy.

11 [p]And the waters covered their enemies: there was not one of them left.

12 [q]Then believed they his words; they sang his praise.

13 [r]They [s]soon forgat his works; they waited not for his counsel:

14 [t]But [u]lusted exceedingly in the wilderness, and tempted God in the desert.

15 [v]And he gave them their request; but [w]sent leanness into their soul.

16 [x]They envied Moses also in the camp, *and* Aaron the saint of the LORD.

17 [y]The earth opened and swallowed up Dathan, and covered the company of Abiram.

18 [z]And a fire was kindled in their company; the flame burned up the wicked.

19 [a]They made a calf in Horeb and worshipped the molten image.

20 Thus [b]they changed their glory into the similitude of an ox that eateth grass.

21 They [c]forgat God their Saviour, which had done great things in Egypt;

22 Wondrous works in [d]the land of Ham, *and* terrible things by the Red Sea.

23 [e]Therefore he said that he would destroy them, had not Moses his chosen [f]stood before him in the breach, to turn away his wrath, lest he should destroy *them.*

24 Yea, they despised [g]the [h]pleasant land, they [i]believed not his word:

25 [k]But murmured in their tents, *and* hearkened not unto the voice of the LORD.

26 [l]Therefore he [m]lifted up his hand against them, to overthrow them in the wilderness:

27 [n]To [o]overthrow their seed also among the nations, and to scatter them in the lands.

28 [p]They joined themselves also unto Baal-peor, and ate the sacrifices of the dead.

29 Thus they provoked *him* to anger with their inventions: and the plague brake in upon them.

30 [q]Then stood up Phinehas, and executed judgment: and *so* the plague was stayed.

31 And that was counted unto him [r]for righteousness unto all generations for evermore.

32 [s]They angered *him* also at the waters of strife, [t]so that it went ill with Moses for their sakes:

[n]Isa. lxiii. 11, 12, 13, 14——[o]Exod. xiv. 30——[p]Exod. xiv. 27, 28; xv. 5——[q]Exod. xiv. 31; xv. 1——[r]Exod. xv. 24; xvi. 2; xvii. 2; Psa. lxxviii. 11——[s]Heb. *They made haste, they forgat*——[t]Num. xi. 4, 33; Psa. lxxviii. 18; 1 Cor. x. 6——[u]Heb. *lusted a lust*——[v]Num. xi. 31; Psa. lxxviii. 29——[w]Isa. x. 16——[x]Num. xvi. 1, &c. [y]Num. xvi. 31, 32; Deut. xi. 6——[z]Num. xvi. 35, 46 [a]Exod. xxxii. 4——[b]Jer. ii. 11; Rom. i. 23——[c]Psa. lxxviii. 11, 12——[d]Psa. lxxviii. 51; cv. 23, 27——[e]Exod. xxxii. 10, 11, 32; Deut. ix. 19, 25; x. 10; Ezek. xx. 13

[f]Ezek. xiii. 5; xxii. 30——[g]Deut. viii. 7; Jer. iii. 19. Ezek. xx. 6——[h]Heb. *a land of desire*——[i]Heb. iii. 18 [k]Num. xiv. 2, 27——[l]Num. xiv. 28, &c.; Psa. xcv. 11; Ezek. xx. 15; Heb. iii. 11, 18——[m]Exod. vi. 8; Deut. xxxii. 40——[n]Heb. *To make them fall*——[o]Lev. xxvi. 33; Psa. xliv. 11; Ezek. xx. 23——[p]Num. xxv. 2, 3; xxxi. 16; Deut. iv. 3; xxxii. 17; Hos. ix. 10; Wisd. xiv. 15; Rev. ii. 14——[q]Num. xxv. 7, 8——[r]Num. xxv. 11, 12, 13 [s]Num. xx. 3, 13; Psa. lxxxi. 7——[t]Num. xx. 12; Deut. i. 37; iii. 26

descriptions of the psalmist *every thing has life.* The *sea* is an *animated being,* behaves itself proudly, is rebuked, and retires in confusion.

Verse 10. *The hand of him that hated* them] Pharaoh.

Verse 12. *Then believed they*] Just while the miracle was before their eyes.

Verse 13. *They soon forgat his works*] Three days afterwards, at the waters of Marah, Exod. xv. 24.

They waited not for his counsel] They were impatient, and would not wait till God should in his own way fulfil his own designs.

Verse 15. *Sent leanness*] They despised the manna, and called it *light,* that is, *innutritive, bread.* God gave *flesh* as they desired, but gave no blessing with it; and in consequence they did not fatten, but grew *lean* upon it. Their souls also suffered want.

Verse 16. *They envied Moses*] A reference to the case of *Korah* and his company.

Aaron the saint.] The *anointed,* the *high priest* of the Lord.

Verse 20. *Thus they changed their glory*] That is, their God, who was their glory; and they worshipped an ox in his stead. See the use St Paul makes of this, Rom. i. 23; see also the note there. The incorruptible God was thus served by all the heathen world.

Verse 22. *Wondrous works in the land of Ham*] The plagues inflicted on the *Egyptians.* Egypt is called the *Land of Ham* or *Cham,* because it was peopled by *Misraim* the son of *Cham.*

Verse 23. *Moses his chosen*] Or elect; (Vulgate, *electus ejus; Septuagint,* ὁ εκλεκτος αυτου;) the person that he had *appointed* for this work. It would be very difficult to show that this word in any part of the Old Testament refers to the *eternal state* of any man, much less to the doctrine of *unconditional election* and *reprobation.*

Verse 28. *They joined themselves also unto Baalpeor*] The *Vulgate, Septuagint,* and others, have *Belphegor;* the *Syriac* and *Arabic,* the *idol Phegor,* or *Phaaur;* the ע *ain* in the word being pronounced as *gh.*

Ate the sacrifices of the dead] מתים *methim,*

33 [u]Because they provoked his spirit, so that he spake unadvisedly with his lips.

34 [v]They did not destroy the nations [w]concerning whom the LORD commanded them:

35 [x]But were mingled among the heathen, and learned their works.

36 And [y]they served their idols: [z]which were a snare unto them.

37 Yea, [a]they sacrificed their sons and their daughters unto [b]devils.

38 And shed innocent blood, *even* the blood of their sons and of their daughters, whom they sacrificed unto the idols of Canaan: and [c]the land was polluted with blood.

39 Thus were they [d]defiled with their own works, and [e]went a whoring with their own inventions.

40 Therefore [f]was the wrath of the LORD kindled against his people, insomuch that he abhorred [g]his own inheritance.

41 And [h]he gave them into the hand of the heathen; and they that hated them ruled over them.

42 Their enemies also oppressed them, and they were brought into subjection under their hand.

43 [i]Many times did he deliver them; but they provoked *him* with their counsel, and were [k]brought low for their iniquity.

44 Nevertheless he regarded their affliction, when [l]he heard their cry:

45 [m]And he remembered for them his covenant, and [n]repented [o]according to the multitude of his mercies.

46 [p]He made them also to be pitied of all those that carried them captives.

47 [q]Save us, O LORD our God, and gather

---

[u]Numbers xx. 10——[v]Judges i. 21, 27, 28, 29, &c. [w]Deuteronomy vii. 2, 16; Judges ii. 2——[x]Judges ii. 2; iii. 5, 6; Isa. ii. 6; 1 Cor. v. 6——[y]Judges ii. 12, 13, 17, 19; iii. 6, 7——[z]Exodus xxiii. 33; Deuteronomy vii. 16; Judges ii. 3, 14, 15——[a]2 Kings xvi. 3; Isaiah lvii. 5; Ezekiel xvi. 20; xx. 26——[b]Leviticus xvii. 7; Deut. xxxii. 17; 2 Chron. xi. 15; 1 Cor. x. 20——[c]Num. xxxv. 33——[d]Ezek. xx. 18, 30, 31

[e]Lev. xvii. 7; Num. xv. 39; Ezek. xx. 30——[f]Judg. ii. 14, &c.; Psalm lxxviii. 59, 62——[g]Deut. ix. 29 [h]Judg. ii. 14; Neh. ix. 27, &c.——[i]Judg. ii. 16; Neh. ix. 27, &c.——[k]Or, *impoverished*, or *weakened*——[l]Judg. iii. 9; iv. 3; vi. 7; x. 10; Neh. ix. 27, &c.——[m]Lev. xxvi. 41, 42——[n]Judg. ii. 18——[o]Psa. li. 1; lxix. 16; Isa. lxiii. 7; Lam. iii. 32——[p]Ezra ix. 9; Jer. xlii. 12——[q]1 Chron. xvi. 35, 36

---

of *dead men.* Most of the heathen idols were *men*, who had been deified after their death; many of whom had been execrated during their life.

Verse 33. *They provoked his spirit*] המרו *himru*, from מרה *marah, to rebel:* they brought it into a rebellious state; he was soured and irritated, and was off his guard.

So that he spake unadvisedly with his lips.] For this *sentence* we have only these *two words* in the Hebrew, ויבטא בשפתיו *vayebatte bisephathaiv, he stuttered* or *stammered with his lips*, indicating that he was transported with anger. See the notes on Num. xx. 10-12.

Verse 36. *They served their idols*] עצביהם *atsabbeyhem*, their *labours* or *griefs*—idols, so called because of the *pains* taken in *forming* them, the *labor* in *worshipping* them, and the *grief* occasioned by the *Divine judgments* against the people for their idolatry.

Verse 37. *They sacrificed their sons and their daughters unto devils.*] See the places referred to in the margin. That *causing their sons and their daughters to pass through the fire to Moloch* did not always mean they *burnt them to death* in the flames, is very probable. But all the heathen had *human sacrifices;* of this their history is full. *Unto devils,* לשדים *lashshedim*, to *demons. Devil* is never in Scripture used in the *plural;* there is but ONE *devil*, though there are MANY *demons.*

Verse 39. *And went a whoring.*] By *fornication, whoredom,* and *idolatry*, the Scripture often expresses *idolatry and idolatrous acts.* I have given the reason of this in other places. Besides being false to the true God, to whom they are represented as *betrothed* and *married*, (and their acts of idolatry were breaches of this solemn engagement,) the worship of idols was frequently accompanied with various acts of *impurity.*

The translation in the *Anglo-Saxon* is very remarkable: ⁊ hi fyrenligeredon, *and they fornicated.* In *Anglo-Saxon*, fyren signifies to *fire, to ignite;* fyrenan, to *commit adultery.* So fyrenhicgend is a *prostitute*, a *whore;* and fyren ligenian is to *go a whoring*, to *fornicate;* probably from fyr, or fyren, to *fire*, and ligan, to *lie*, or liccera, *a glutton;*—one *who lies with fire*, who is *ignited* by it, who is *greedily intent* upon the act by which he is *inflamed.* And do not the words themselves show that in former times whoredom was punished, as it is now, by a disease which produces the *sensation of burning* in the unhappy prostitutes, whether male or female? And to this meaning the following seems particularly to be *applicable.*

Verse 40. *Therefore was the wrath of the Lord kindled*] God *kindled a fire* in his judgments for those who by their flagitious conduct had *inflamed* themselves with their idols, and the *impure rites* with which they were worshipped.

Verse 43. *Many times did he deliver them*] See the Book of *Judges;* it is a history of the rebellions and deliverances of the Israelites.

Verse 46. *He made them also to be pitied*] This was particularly true as to the Babylonish captivity; for *Cyrus* gave them their liberty; *Darius* favoured them, and granted them several privileges; and *Artaxerxes* sent back Nehemiah, and helped him to rebuild Jerusalem and the temple. See the Books of Ezra and Nehemiah; and see *Calmet.*

Verse 47. *Save us, O Lord—and gather us*]

us from among the heathen, to give thanks unto thy holy name, *and* to triumph in thy praise.

48 [r]Blessed *be* the LORD God of Israel from everlasting to everlasting: and let all the people say, Amen. [s]Praise ye the LORD.

---

[r]Psa. xli. 13

[s]Heb. *Hallelujah*

These words, says *Calmet*, are found in the hymn that was sung at the ceremony of bringing the ark to Jerusalem, 1 Chron. xvi.; but it is supposed they were added by Ezra or some other prophet: here they are in their natural place. The author of the Psalm begs the Lord to gather the Israelites who were dispersed through different countries; for at the dedication of the second temple, under Nehemiah, (where it is probable this Psalm, with the cvth and the cviith, was sung,) there were very few Jews who had as yet returned from their captivity.

Verse 48. *Blessed* be *the Lord God of Israel*] Here both *gratitude* and *confidence* are expressed; *gratitude* for what God had already wrought, and *confidence* that he would finish the great work of their restoration.

From everlasting to everlasting] מן האולם ועד העולם *min haolam vead haolam*, "from the hidden term to the hidden term," from the beginning of time to the end of time, from eternity and on to eternity. **Fram ƿorulde ⁊ oð ƿorulde,** *Anglo-Saxon.* **Fra worlde and into worlde,** *old Psalter;* which it paraphrases thus: Fra with outen beginning, & withouten endyng.

And let all the people say, Amen.] Let the people join in the prayer and in the thanksgiving, that God may hear and answer. *Anglo-Saxon:* **⁊ cƿeðe eall folc, beo hit beo hit;** "And, quoth all folk, be it, be it." *Hallelujah*—Praise ye Jehovah! Let his name be eternally magnified! Amen.

This is the end of the *fourth book* of the Psalms.

ANALYSIS OF THE ONE HUNDRED AND SIXTH PSALM

The intention of the prophet in this Psalm is to express God's long-suffering in bearing with rebellious sinners, and yet in pardoning them upon the confession of their sins, and turning to him; both which he exemplifies by a long narration of Israel's rebellions, repentance, and turning to God, and God's dealing with them, which gave him just occasion to praise God, and to pray for his Church and people.

I. An exhortation to praise God, with the reasons in general, ver. 1; and who are fit to perform this duty, ver. 2, 3.

II. A petition and prayer directed to God in his own person for the whole Church, and the end of it, ver. 4, 5.

III. A confession of sin, particularly of the Israelites', together with God's patience with them, and their repentance, ver. 646.

IV. His prayer that God would collect his Church out of all nations, that they might meet and praise him, ver. 47, 48.

I. "Praise ye the Lord, O give thanks unto the Lord." To this the prophet invites, for two reasons:—

1. "Because he is good." He is beforehand with us, and prevents men with many benefits.

2. "Because his mercy endures for ever." It is everlasting, and far exceeds our sins and miseries; for after men have offended him, and deserve no mercy, yet he receives the penitent offenders. But who is sufficient for these things? Who is fit to praise him, and set forth his mercies? "Who can utter the mighty acts of the Lord?" That is, the infinite benefits exhibited to his people. Or, Who can show forth all his praise in preserving, pardoning, and propagating his Church?

They alone are happy men "who keep judgment, and do righteousness at all times."

1. They are happy in prosperity and adversity, they dwell in the house of God, under his protection.

2. "They keep his judgments." Follow in their lives the strict rules of the Divine law, by which they judge all their actions, and so keep faith and a good conscience.

3. "They do righteousness at all times." They approve that which is right, true, and just; condemn, hate, and punish what is unjust: such are fit to praise God with their tongues, because they praise him in their lives.

II. After the prophet had invited men to praise God, and showed who were fit to do it, he begins his petition, which he proposes in his own person for the whole Church.

1. "Remember me." Me; but not me alone, rather thy whole Church. By what we suffer, thou hast seemed to forget thy covenant and promise; but now call it to mind again.

2. Which I expect, not for any desert of mine, but merely from thy good will: "Remember me with the favour," &c.

3. "O visit me;" but not in wrath, for such a visitation there is; but in mercy and grace.

4. "With thy salvation." Save me at this time from my sins, and from my present calamities.

And to this end I desire thy favour, thy salvation.

1. "That I may see the good of thy chosen." Be a partaker of and in their happiness.

2. "That I may rejoice in the gladness of thy nation." Partake of it.

3. "That I may glory with thine inheritance." Glorify thee with them.

But observe here the three eminent titles given to God's Church:—

1. They are a "chosen" people; which is a glorious and gracious title, and intimates favour.

2. They are his "nation," his peculiar people.

3. They are his "inheritance."

III. In the following part of the Psalm, from ver. 7 to 46, he makes use of a new argument to move God to mercy. He represents not the present condition the people of God are in, not their captivity, miseries, and afflictions, but ingenuously confesses how they had offended God, and how justly they suffered.

1. "We have sinned with our fathers." Trodden in their steps, and filled up the measure of their sins.

2. "We have committed iniquity." Not only from infirmity, but choice.

3. "We have done wickedly." The intent and purpose in it was evil. And by these three steps he exaggerates the sin; the *act*, the *frequency*, the *intent;* as every true confessionist to God ought never to extenuate, but to aggravate the offence against himself.

And because he had mentioned their fathers at large, now he instances their rebellions: "Our fathers understood not thy wonders in Egypt;" that is, they laid them not to heart.

1. "They remembered not the multitude of thy mercies," &c. When they saw Pharaoh's army on one side, and the sea on the other, they grew heartless, diffident, and murmured.

2. This was their sin at that time; but God was then merciful to them: "Nevertheless he saved them."

For which he assigns two reasons:—

1. "For his name's sake." To advance his glory and honour.

2. "That he might make his mighty power to be known." Pharaoh and the Egyptians might have taken notice of it by the plagues he had already brought upon them.

In the following verses, by a distribution, he shows the manner of their deliverance.

1. By God's rebuke, and drying up of the sea: "He rebuked the Red Sea also," &c.

2. By the unheard-of way: "He led them through the depths as through the wilderness;" there was no more water there to offend them than in the sands of Arabia.

3. By the consequence of it: "And he saved them by the hand of him," &c.

4. "And the waters covered their enemies," &c.

The effect was, for the present,

1. It extorted from them a confession that God was true in his promises: "Then believed they his words."

2. It excited them to praise him: "They sang his praise," Exod. xv. But these very men who were forced to confess his power and sing his praises for the overthrow of Pharaoh in the Red Sea, were scarcely departed from those banks, when they, for want of a little bread and water, grew as impatient and distrustful as they were before.

1. They made haste to forget: "They soon forgot;" which aggravates their sin.

2. They forgot his omnipotence, his providence.

3. "They waited not for his council." With patience they expected not the end, why God in his wisdom suffered them now to wait, which was, to prove their faith, hope, and love.

4. And what they did at this time they did also at others: "For they lusted exceedingly in the wilderness."

Now God yielded to these desires of the people: "He gave them bread, flesh, and water."

1. And he gave them their request, Exod. xvi. 12.

2. "But he sent leanness into their souls." Which certainly has reference to the quails in Num. xi. 20 and 33, where the people ate, and died of plague.

Another rebellion the prophet now touches, which was, when they rose up against the king and the priest.

1. "They envied also Moses in the camp;" objecting that he had usurped a power over them, and taken it upon his own head.

2. "And Aaron, the saint of the Lord." He whom God had chosen, anointed, and sanctified to the priest's office.

The punishment follows, Num. xvi.

1. "The earth opened, and swallowed up Dathan, and covered the congregation of Abiram."

2. "And a fire was kindled in their company; the flame burned up the wicked." That is, the *two hundred and fifty* men that presumed to offer incense; and presently after the *fourteen thousand seven hundred* that murmured, and objected to *Moses* and *Aaron* that they had killed the people of the Lord.

Still the prophet goes on in his story of Israel's stubbornness and rebellion; and comes to their grand sin, their idolatry in erecting the golden calf, Exod. xxxii.

1. "They made a calf in Horeb," &c., contrary to God's command.

2. "Thus they changed their glory." That is, the true God, who was indeed their glory, "into the similitude of an ox," a brute beast, "that eateth grass," a base creature, which much aggravates their sin.

3. But the *prophet* aggravates their stupidity and folly: "They forgat God," &c.

In the following verse are expressed God's just anger and mercy,—

1. His anger against their sins: "Therefore he saith," &c. Pronounced his will to destroy them.

2. His mercy, in that he spared them at the intercession of Moses: "Had not Moses his chosen stood before him in the breach." The breach and division which this sin had made between God and his people, like that in the wall of a besieged town, in which some valiant captain stands, and opposes himself against the assault of the enemy; so did Moses.

For his object was the same, it was "to turn away his wrath lest he should destroy;" and the end was answered—it was turned away.

Farther yet, he calls to mind a new rebellion, which fell out upon the report of the spies sent to search the land, Num. xiii. 26, &c., and xiv.

1. "They despised the pleasant land," and wished to return into Egypt, Num. xiv. 1-5.

2. "They believed not his word;" for they said, "Hath the Lord brought us," &c.

3. "But murmured in their tents, and hearkened not," &c., Num. xiv. "Therefore he lifted up his hand against them," &c. As their sin, so their punishment, is extant; Num. xiv. 29: "Your carcasses shall fall in the wilderness; ye shall not come into the land."

This punishment fell upon the murmurers themselves; but if their children should be guilty of the like rebellion, they should not escape, for they too should be *overthrown;* which is fully brought to pass.

The prophet joins to that of the golden calf another piece of idolatry in the wilderness, to which there was joined fornication also, by the counsel of *Balaam* and the policy of Balak. This caused them to eat and sacrifice to their god, Num. xxv., which the prophet next insists upon,—

1. "They joined themselves to Baal-peor," because the idol was set up upon that mountain.

2. "And ate the offerings of the dead." They left the sacrifice of the living God, and ate those meats which were offered to dead idols.

Upon which there followed God's wrath and their own punishment:—

1. God was angry: "For they provoked him to wrath."

"And the plague brake in upon them" like mighty waters, or as an army into a city at a breach; for there died of it *twenty-four thousand*, Num. xxv. 9.

In the former idolatry God's anger was averted by the intercession of *Moses;* in this, by the execution of judgment by *Phinehas;* for—

1. "There stood up Phinehas;" moved, no question, with a zeal for God's honour.

2. "And he executed judgment upon Zimri and Cozbi;" for which (let men conceive as they please—I see nothing to the contrary) he had his commission from Moses, or rather God; Num. xxv. 4, 5.

3. The event was, the plague was stayed; the execution of offenders pacifies the anger of God.

Which zeal of his was well rewarded: "This was accounted to him for righteousness," &c. This act was an act of righteousness, and an ample reward he had for it; for God established the dignity of the high priesthood in *Phinehas* and his posterity, as long as the Jewish commonwealth continued.

The prophet comes to another remarkable sin of the Jews, Num. xx., where the people chid Moses for want of water:—

1. "They angered him also at the waters of strife," when they contradicted *Moses*.

2. "So that it went ill with Moses for their sakes;" for, being disturbed with choler, "he spake unadvisedly with his lips,"—"Hear now, ye rebels," &c.; and he smote the rock. By their murmuring they so provoked his spirit to bitterness, that he who at other times was cheerful, and ready to obey God's commands, now acted with reluctance.

Hitherto the prophet has set down several rebellions of the Jews during their abode in the wilderness; and now he shows how they behaved themselves after they came into the land of *Canaan*. Better, a man would think, they should be after God had fulfilled his word to them; but an Ethiopian cannot change his skin, nor they their manners; disobedient, stubborn, and rebellious they remained.

1. God had expressly commanded that the nations of *Canaan* should be destroyed, Deut. vii. 1, 2, 3: "But they did not destroy the nations," &c.

2. "But they mingled among the heathen:" in leagues and marriages, Judg. ii. and iii.

3. "And learned their works:" many superstitious and evil customs.

But, beyond all, they learned to be idolaters; forsook God for the devil.

1. "They served their idols, which was a snare unto them," for that they became their slaves, Judg. ii., &c.

2. "Yea, they sacrificed their sons," &c., to Moloch.

3. With inhuman sin, they "shed innocent blood;" the blood of innocent children, &c.

The consequences of which are double. First, A double pollution. Secondly, A heavy punishment.

1. A pollution of the land: "The land was defiled with blood."

2. A pollution of their own souls: "Thus were they defiled with their own works."

The judgment, or punishment, now follows; and a signification whence it proceeded; it came not by chance, but by God's order and anger.

1. "Therefore was the wrath of the Lord kindled," &c. For their idolatry, murder, whoredom; so that he was not only angry, but his anger was kindled to a flame.

2. Insomuch "that he abhorred his own inheritance."

And the punishment he inflicted on them was very just,—

1. "He gave them into the hand," that is, the power, "of the heathen." God had given the heathen into their hands to destroy them; which, because they did not, but learned their works, therefore God gave them into the hands of the heathen.

2. He made them their lords; and hard masters they were, as plainly appears from the Book of Judges, and 1 Samuel.

And *little* they; for the prophet in the next verse adds,

1. "Their enemies oppressed them:" tyrants, oppressors they were. Read the Book of Judges, &c.

2. "They were brought into subjection," &c., under the Philistines, Moabites, Ammonites, &c.

In which condition God did not forget them, for "many times did he deliver them;" not once only, but often, as by *Gideon*, *Jephthah*, *Deborah*, *Samson*, and others. But, O the ingratitde of a sinful nation! instead of serving God, "they provoked him with their counsel," that is, by following the dictates of their own hearts.

And so were very justly brought into the same case they were before; for "they were brought low for their iniquity."

And now the prophet adds, which indeed he infers through the whole Psalm, the wonderful and immutable good will of God to them. Though he forgave and delivered them upon their repentance, and they in a short time provoked him again; yet he received them to grace, even after their relapses. And the causes that moved him to this were external and internal.

The cause that outwardly and occasionally moved him to it was their affliction and cry: "He regarded their affliction," &c.

But the cause that inwardly swayed him was his word passed to them, and his mercy.

1. His word and his promise were passed to "Abraham, to be their God;" and he would not break it. "And he remembered for them his covenant."

2. His tender affection that he bare them; this caused him to repent, and grieve that they should be in misery. "He repented," &c.

3. And the effect which all these causes had was beneficial to them even in their bondage and captivity; for even their very enemies' hearts were often turned to do them good, as is evident in *Jeremiah*, *David*, *Daniel*, *Ezra*, *Zerubbabel*, *Mordecai*, and indeed the whole nation under the *Babylonian*, *Philistian*, *Egyptian*, and *Persian* kings, which the prophet sets down, ver. 46: "He made them also to be pitied of all those that carried them captives." According to the saying of the wise man: "When a man's ways please God, he will make his very enemies to be at peace with him," Prov. xvi. 7.

4. And this sense makes the way plainer to what follows, the petition and the doxology; for if God showed himself merciful in the time of his anger, and made it apparent even to the

very view of their enemies, encouragement they might have,—

1. To pray: "Save us, O Lord our God, and gather us from among the heathen," &c.

2. Then to give thanks: 1. "Blessed be the Lord God of Israel from everlasting to everlasting. 2. And for it let the people do their duty; that is, the solemn and necessary forms: "Let all the people say, Amen. Hallelujah."

PSALM CVII

A thanksgiving of the people for deliverance from difficulties and dangers; their state compared to a journey through a frightful wilderness, 1–9; *to confinement in a dreary dungeon*, 10–16; *to a dangerous malady*, 17–22; *to a tempest at sea*, 23–32. *The psalmist calls on men to praise God for the merciful dispensations of his providence, in giving rain and fruitful seasons, after affliction by drought and famine*, 33–38; *for supporting the poor in affliction, and bringing down the oppressors*, 39–41. *The use which the righteous should make of these providences*, 42; *and the advantage to be derived from a due consideration of God's merciful providence*, 43.

XXII. DAY. MORNING PRAYER

O [a]GIVE thanks unto the LORD, for [b]*he is* good: for his mercy *endureth* for ever.

2 Let the redeemed of the LORD say *so*, [c]whom he hath redeemed from the hand of the enemy;

[a]Psa. cvi. 1; cxviii. 1; cxxxvi. 1

[b]Psa. cxix. 68; Matt. xix. 17——[c]Psa. cvi. 10

NOTES ON PSALM CVII

This Psalm has no title, either in the Hebrew, or any of the Versions; the word "Hallelujah," which is prefixed to some of the latter, is no title, but was most probably borrowed from the conclusion of the preceding Psalm. The author is unknown; but it was probably like Psalms cv. and cvi., made and sung at the dedication of the second temple. The three Psalms seem to be on the same subject. In them the author has comprised the marvellous acts of the Lord towards his people; the transgressions of this people against God; the captivities and miseries they endured in consequence; and finally God's merciful kindness to them in their restoration from captivity, and re-establishment in their own land.

This Psalm seems to have been sung in parts: the 8th, 15th, 21st, and 31st verses, with the 6th, 13th, 19th, and 28th, forming what may be called the burden of the song. In singing of which the whole chorus joined.

We may easily perceive that the Psalm must have been sung in alternate parts, having a double burden, or *intercalary* verse often recurring, and another immediately following, giving a reason for the former. See the 8th and 9th, the 15th and 16th, the 21st and 22nd, the 31st and 32nd, and the 42nd and 43rd, which may be reckoned under the same denomination.

Dr. Lowth, in his 29th prelection, has made some excellent remarks on this Psalm. "It is observable," says he, "that after each of the intercalary verses one is added, expressive of deliverance or praise. I would farther observe, that if the Psalm be supposed to be made with a view to the *alternate* response of one side of the choir to the other, then it may be considered as if it were written exactly after the method of the ancient *pastorals*, where, be the subject of their verse what it will, each swain endeavours to excel the other; and one may perceive their thoughts and expressions gradually to *arise* upon each other; and hence a manifest beauty may be discovered in this Divine pastoral. We will suppose, then, that the author composed it for the use of his brethren the Jews, when, in the joy of their hearts, they were assembled after their return from captivity. At such a time, what theme could be so proper for the subject of his poem, as the manifest goodness of Almighty God? The first performers, therefore, invite the whole nation to praise God for this; a great instance of it being their late return from captivity. At ver. 10, the other side take the subject, and rightly observe that the return of their great men, who were actually in chains, was a more remarkable instance of God's mercy to them, than the return of the people in general, who were only dispersed, we may suppose, up and down the open country. Then the first performers beautifully compare this unexpected deliverance to that which God sometimes vouchsafes to the languishing dying man, when he recalls, as it were, the sentence of death, and restores him to his former vigour. The others again compare it, with still greater strength and expression, to God's delivering the affrighted *mariner* from all the dreadful horrors of the ungovernable and arbitrary ocean. But the *first*, still resolved to outdo the rest, recur to that series of wonderful works which God had vouchsafed to their nation, ver. 32, and of which they had so lately such a convincing proof. Wherefore at last, as in a common chorus, they all conclude with exhorting each other to a serious consideration of these things, and to make a proper return to Almighty God for them.

"No doubt the composition of this Psalm is admirable throughout; and the descriptive part of it adds at least its share of beauty to the whole; but what is most to be admired is its *conciseness*, and withal the expressiveness of the diction, which strikes the imagination with inimitable elegance. The *weary* and *bewildered traveller*, the miserable *captive* in the hideous dungeon, the sick and dying man, the *seaman foundering* in a storm, are described in so affecting a manner, that they far exceed any thing of the kind, though never so much laboured." I

3 And [d]gathered them out of the lands, from the east, and from the west, from the north, and [e]from the south.

4 They [f]wandered in [g]the wilderness in a solitary way; they found no city to dwell in.

5 Hungry and thirsty, their soul fainted in them.

6 [h]Then they cried unto the LORD in their trouble, *and* he delivered them out of their distresses.

7 And he led them forth by the [i]right way, that they might go to a city of habitation.

8 [k]O that *men* would praise the LORD *for* his goodness, and *for* his wonderful works to the children of men!

9 For [l]he satisfieth the longing soul, and filleth the hungry soul with goodness.

10 Such as [m]sit in darkness and in the shadow of death, *being* [n]bound in affliction and iron;

11 Because they [o]rebelled against the words of God, and contemned [p]the counsel of the Most High:

12 Therefore he brought down their heart with labour; they fell down, and *there was* [q]none to help.

---

[d]Psa. cvi. 47; Isa. xliii. 5, 6; Jer. xxix. 14; xxxi. 8, 10; Ezek. xxxix. 27, 28——[e]Heb. *from the sea*——[f]Ver. 40 [g]Deut. xxxii. 10——[h]Ver. 13, 19, 28; Psa. l. 15; Hos. v. 15——[i]Ezra viii. 21

[k]Ver. 15, 21, 31——[l]Psa. xxxiv. 10; Luke i. 53 [m]Luke i. 79——[n]Job xxxvi. 8——[o]Lam. iii. 42——[p]Psa. lxxiii. 24; cxix. 24; Luke vii. 30; Acts xx. 27——[q]Psa. xxii. 11; Isa. lxiii. 5

---

may add that had such an *Idyl* appeared in *Theocritus* or *Virgil*, or had it been found as a scene in any of the *Greek tragedians*, even in *Æschylus* himself, it would have been praised up to the heavens, and probably been produced as their master-piece.

Verse 1. *O give thanks*] Here is a duty prescribed; and the reasons of it are immediately laid down. 1. He is *good*. This is his nature. 2. *His mercy* endureth *for ever*. This is the *stream* that flows from the *fountain* of his goodness.

Verse 2. *Let the redeemed of the Lord say so*] For they have had the fullest proof of this goodness, in being saved by the continuing stream of his mercy.

Verse 3. *And gathered them out of the lands*] Though many Jews returned into Jerusalem from various parts of the world, under the reigns of *Darius Hystaspes*, *Artaxerxes*, and *Alexander the Great;* yet this prophecy has its completion only under the Gospel, when all the ends of the earth hear the salvation of God.

Verse 4. *They wandered in the wilderness*] Here begins the FIRST *comparison:* the Israelites in captivity are compared to *a traveller in a dreary, uninhabited, and barren desert*, spent with hunger and thirst, as well as by the fatigues of the journey, ver. 5.

Verse 6. *Then they cried unto the Lord*] When the Israelites began to pray heartily, and the eyes of all the tribes were as the eyes of one man turned unto the Lord, then he delivered them out of their distresses.

Verse 7. *That they might go to a city of habitation.*] God stirred up the heart of *Cyrus* to give them liberty to return to their own land: and *Zerubbabel*, *Ezra*, and *Nehemiah*, at different times, brought many of them back to Judea.

Verse 8. *O that* men *would praise the Lord*] This is what is called the *intercalary verse*, or *burden* of each *part* of this *responsive song:* see the *introduction*. God should be praised because he is *good*. We naturally speak highly of those who are eminent. God is infinitely excellent, and should be celebrated for his *perfections*. But *he does wonders for the children of men;* and, therefore, men should *praise the Lord*. And he is the more to be praised, because these wonders, נפלאות *niphlaoth*, miracles of mercy and grace, are done for the *undeserving*. They are done לבני אדם *libney Adam*, for the children of *Adam*, the corrupt descendants of a rebel father.

Verse 9. *For he satisfieth the longing soul*] This is the reason which the psalmist gives for the *duty* of thankfulness which he prescribes. *The longing soul,* נפש שוקקה *nephesh shokekah, the soul that pushes forward in eager desire* after salvation.

Verse 10. *Such as sit in darkness*] Here begins the SECOND *similitude*, which he uses to illustrate the state of the captives in Babylon, viz., that of *a prisoner in a dreary dungeon.* 1. *They sit in* or *inhabit darkness*. They have no light, no peace, no prosperity. 2. "In the shadow of death." The place where death reigns, over which he has projected his shadow; those against whom the sentence of death has been pronounced. 3. They are *bound* in this darkness, have no liberty to revisit the light, and cannot escape from their executioners. 4. They are *afflicted*, not only by want and privation in general, but they are tortured in the prison, עני *oni*, afflicted, humbled, distressed. 5. Their fetters are such as they cannot break; they are *iron*. The reason of their being in this wretched state is given.

Verse 11. *Because they rebelled against the words of God*] 1. God showed them their duty and their interest, and commanded them to obey his word; but they cast off all subjection to his authority, acted as if they were independent of heaven and earth, and broke out into open rebellion against him. 2. He *counselled* and exhorted them to return to him: but they contemned his advice, and turned his counsel into ridicule. 3. As lenient means were ineffectual, he visited them in judgment: hence it is added,

Verse 12. *He brought down their heart with labour*] He delivered them into the hands of their enemies. and, as they would not be under subjection to GOD, he delivered them into slavery to wicked men: "So they fell down, and there was none to help;" God had forsaken them because they had forsaken him.

13 [r]Then they cried unto the LORD in their
trouble, *and* he saved them out of their distresses.
14 [s]He brought them out of darkness, and
the shadow of death, and brake their bands in
sunder.
15 [t]O that *men* would praise the LORD *for*
his goodness, and *for* his wonderful works to
the children of men!
16 For he hath [u]broken the gates of brass,
and cut the bars of iron in sunder.
17 Fools [v]because of their transgression,
and because of their iniquities, are afflicted.
18 [w]Their soul abhorreth all manner of
meat; and they [x]draw near unto the gates of
death.
19 [y]Then they cry unto the LORD in their
trouble, *and* he saveth them out of their distresses.
20 [z]He sent his word, and [a]healed them,
and [b]delivered *them* from their destructions.
21 [c]O that *men* would praise the LORD *for*
his goodness, and *for* his wonderful works
to the children of men!
22 And [d]let them sacrifice the sacrifices of
thanksgiving, and [e]declare his works with
[f]rejoicing.
23 They that go down to the sea in ships,
that do business in great waters;
24 These see the works of the LORD, and
his wonders in the deep.
25 For he commandeth, and [g]raiseth [h]the
stormy wind, which lifteth up the waves
thereof.
26 They mount up to the heaven, they go
down again to the depths: [i]their soul is
melted because of trouble.
27 They reel to and fro, and stagger like

[r]Ver. 6, 19, 28——[s]Psa. lxviii. 6; cxlvi. 7; Acts xii. 7, &c.; xvi. 26, &c.——[t]Ver. 8, 21, 31——[u]Isa. xlv. 2——[v]Lam. iii. 39——[w]Job xxxiii. 20——[x]Job xxxiii. 22; Psa. ix. 13; lxxxviii. 3——[y]Ver. 6, 13, 28——[z]2 Kings xx. 4, 5; Psa. cxlvii. 15, 18; Matt. viii. 8

[a]Psa. xxx. 2; ciii. 3——[b]Job xxxiii. 28, 30; Psa. xxx. 3; xlix. 15; lvi. 13; ciii. 4——[c]Ver. 8, 15, 31——[d]Lev. vii. 12; Psa. l. 14; cxvi. 17; Heb. xiii. 15——[e]Psa. ix. 11; lxxiii. 28; cxviii. 17——[f]Heb. *singing*——[g]Heb. *maketh to stand*——[h]Jonah i. 4——[i]Psa. xxii. 14; cxix. 28; Nah. ii. 10

Verse 13. *Then they cried unto the Lord in their trouble*] This was the salutary effect which their afflictions produced: they began to cry to God for mercy and help; and God mercifully heard their prayer, and reversed their state; for,

Verse 14. *He brought them out of darkness*] 1. Gave them again peace and prosperity. 2. Repealed the *sentence of death*. 3. "Unbound the poor prisoners." 4. Broke their iron bonds in sunder.

Verse 15. *O that* men, *&c.*] This is the *intercalary verse*, or *burden*, of the *second* part, as it was of the *first*. See verse 8.

Verse 16. *For he hath broken*] This is the *reason* given for thanks to God for his deliverance of the captives. It was not a simple deliverance; it was done so as to manifest the *irresistible* power of God. He tore the prison in pieces, and cut the bars of iron asunder.

Verse 17. *Fools because of their transgression*] This is the THIRD *comparison;* the captivity being compared to *a person in a dangerous malady*. Our Version does not express this clause well: *Fools* מדרך פשעם *midderech pisham, because of the way of their transgressions, are afflicted*. Most human maladies are the fruits of sin; *misery* and *sin* are married together in bonds that can never be broken.

Verse 18. *Their soul abhorreth all manner of meat*] A natural description of a sick man: appetite is gone, and all desire for food fails; nutriment is no longer necessary, for death has seized upon the whole frame. See a similar image, Job xxxiii. 20.

Verse 10. *Then they cry*] The effect produced by affliction as before.

Verse 20. *He sent his word, and healed them*] He spoke: "Be thou clean, be thou whole;" and immediately the disease departed; and thus they were *delivered from the destructions* that awaited them.

Verse 21. *O that* men, *&c.*] The *intercalary* verse, or *burden*, as before.

Verse 22. *And let them sacrifice*] For their *healing* they should bring a *sacrifice;* and they should offer the *life* of the innocent animal unto God, as he has spared their *lives;* and let them thus *confess* that God has spared *them* when they deserved to die; and let them *declare* also "his works with rejoicing;" for who will not rejoice when he is delivered from *death?*

Verse 23. *They that go down to the sea in ships*] This is the FOURTH *comparison*. Their captivity was as dangerous and alarming as a dreadful tempest at sea to a weather-beaten mariner.

Verse 24. *These see the works of the Lord*] Splendid, Divinely impressive, and glorious in *fine weather*.

His wonders in the deep.] Awfully terrible in a *tempest*.

Verse 25. *For he commandeth*] And what less than the command of God can raise up such winds as seem to heave old Ocean from his bed?

Verse 26. *They mount up to the heaven*] This is a most natural and striking description of the state of a ship at sea in a storm: when the *sea* appears to *run mountains high*, and the vessel seems for a moment to stand on the sharp ridge of one most stupendous, with a valley of *a frightful depth* between it and a similar mountain, which appears to be flying in the midst of heaven, that it may submerge the hapless bark, when she descends into the valley of death below. This is a sight the most terrific that can be imagined: nor can any man conceive or form an adequate idea of it, who has not himself been at sea in such a storm.

Their soul is melted because of trouble.] This

a drunken man, and [k]are at their wit's end.

28 [l]Then they cry unto the LORD in their trouble, and he bringeth them out of their distresses.

29 [m]He maketh the storm a calm, so that the waves thereof are still.

30 Then are they glad because they be quiet; so he bringeth them unto their desired haven.

31 [n]O that *men* would praise the LORD *for* his goodness, and *for* his wonderful works to the children of men!

32 Let them exalt him also [o]in the congre-

[k]Hebrew, *all their wisdom is swallowed up*——[l]Verse 6, 13, 19

[m]Psa. lxxxix. 9; Matt. viii. 26——[n]Ver. 8, 15, 21 [o]Psa. xxii. 22, 25; cxi. 1

is not less expressive than it is *descriptive.* The action of raising the vessel to the clouds, and precipitating her into the abyss, seems to dissolve the very soul: the whole mind seems to melt away, so that neither feeling, reflection, nor impression remains, nothing but the apprehension of inevitable destruction! When the ship is buffeted between conflicting waves, which threaten either to tear her asunder or crush her together; when she *reels to and fro, and staggers like a drunken man,* not being able to hold any certain course; when *sails* and *masts* are an incumbrance, and the *helm* of no use; when all *hope of safety* is taken away; and when the experienced *captain*, the skilful *pilot*, and the hardy *sailors*, cry out, with a voice more terrible than the cry of fire at midnight, *We are* ALL *lost! we are all* LOST! then, indeed, are they *at their wit's end;* or, as the inimitable original expresses it, וכל חכמתם תתבלע *vechol chochmatham tithballa,* "and all their skill is swallowed up,"—seems to be gulped down by the frightful abyss into which the ship is about to be precipitated. Then, indeed, can the hand of God alone "bring them out of their distresses." Then, a cry to the Almighty (and in such circumstances it is few that can lift up such a cry) is the only means that can be used to save the perishing wreck! Reader, dost thou ask why I paint thus, and from whose authority I describe? I answer: Not from any books describing storms, tempests, and shipwrecks; not from the relations of shipwrecked marines; not from viewing from the shore a tempest at sea, and seeing a vessel beat to pieces, and all its crew, one excepted, perish. Descriptions of this kind I have read, with the shipwrecked mariner I have conversed, the last scene mentioned above I have witnessed: but none of these could give the fearful impressions, the tremendous and soul-melting apprehensions, described above. "*Where* then have you had them?" I answer, From the great deep. I have been at sea in the storm, and in the circumstances I describe; and, having *cried to the Lord in my trouble,* I am spared to describe the storm, and recount the tale of his mercy. None but either a man inspired by God, who, in describing, will show things *as they are*, or one who has been actually in these circumstances, can tell you with what propriety the psalmist speaks, or utter the thousandth part of the dangers and fearful apprehensions of those concerned in a tempest at sea, where all the winds of heaven seem collected to urge an already crazy vessel among the most tremendous rocks upon a lee shore! God save the reader from such circumstances!

When, in the visitation of the winds,
He takes the ruffian billows by the top,
Curling their monstrous heads, and hanging them,
With deafening clamours, on the slippery clouds,
That with the hurly death itself awakes!

HENRY IV.

A storm at sea—*the lifting the vessel to the clouds*—her *sinking into the vast marine valleys*—the *melting of the soul*—and *being at their wit's end*, are well touched by several of the ancient poets. See particularly Virgil's description of the storm that dispersed the fleet of Æneas, who was himself not unacquainted with the dangers of the sea:—

Tollimur in cœlum curvato gurgite, et idem
Subducta ad manes imos descendimus unda.

ÆN. iii., 364.

Now on a towering arch of waves we rise,
Heaved on the bounding billows to the skies.
Then, as the roaring surge retreating fell,
We shoot down headlong to the gates of hell.

PITT.

Rector in incerto est, nec quid fugiatve, petatve,
Invenit: ambiguis ars stupet ipsa malis.

"The pilot himself is in doubt what danger to shun; or whither to steer for safety he knows not: his skill is nonplussed by the choice of the difficulties before him."

See more in the analysis.

Verse 29. *He maketh the storm a calm*] He causes the storm to stand *dumb*, and *hushes* the waves. See the original, where *sense* and *sound* emphatically meet:—

יקם סערה לדממה ויחשו גליהם

galleyhem vaiyecheshu lidemamah secrah yakem

He shall cause the whirlwind to stand *dumb*, and he shall *hush* their billows.

Verse 30. *Then are they glad because they be quiet*] The turbulence of the sea being hushed, and the waves still, they rejoice to see an end to the tempest; and thus, having fine weather, a smooth sea, and fair wind, they are speedily brought to the *desired haven.*

Verse 31. *O that men*] The *intercalary* verse, or *burden*, as before. See ver. 8.

Verse 32. *Let them exalt him also in the congregation*] Their deliverance from such imminent danger, and in a way which clearly showed the Divine interposition, demands, not only gratitude of heart and the song of praise at the end of the storm, but when they come to *shore* that they *publicly* acknowledge it in the congregation of God's people. I have been often pleased, when in sea-port towns, to see and hear notes sent to the minister from pious sailors, returning thanks to the Almighty for preservation from shipwreck, and, in general, from the gation of the people, and praise him in the assembly of the elders.

33 He [p]turneth rivers into a wilderness, and
the watersprings into dry ground;

34 A [q]fruitful land into [r]barrenness, for the
wickedness of them that dwell therein.

35 [s]He turneth the wilderness into a standing water, and dry ground into watersprings.

36 And there he maketh the hungry to
dwell, that they may prepare a city for habitation;

37 And sow the fields, and plant vineyards,
which may yield fruits of increase.

38 [t]He blesseth them also, so that they [u]are
multiplied greatly; and suffereth not their cattle to decrease.

39 Again, they are [v]minished and brought
low through oppression, affliction, and sorrow.

40 [w]He poureth contempt upon princes, and
causeth them to wander in the [x]wilderness, *where there is* no way.

41 [y]Yet setteth he the poor on high, [z]from
affliction, and [a]maketh *him* families like a flock.

42 [b]The righteous shall see *it,* and rejoice:
and all [c]iniquity shall stop her mouth.

43 [d]Whoso *is* wise, and will observe these
things, even they shall understand the lovingkindness of the LORD.

---

[p]1 Kings xvii. 1, 7——[q]Gen. xiii. 10; xiv. 3; xix. 25 [r]Heb. *saltness*——[s]Psa. cxiv. 8; Isa. xli. 18——[t]Gen. xii. 2; xvii. 16, 20——[u]Exod. i. 7——[v]2 Kings x. 32 [w]Job xii. 21, 24——[x]Or, *void place*

[y]1 Sam. ii. 8; Psa. cxiii. 7, 8——[z]Or, *after*——[a]Psa. lxxviii. 52——[b]Job xxii. 19; Psa. lii. 6; lviii. 10——[c]Job v. 16; Psa. lxiii. 11; Prov. x. 11; Rom. iii. 19——[d]Psa. lxiv. 9; Jer. ix. 12; Hos. xiv. 9

---

dangers of the sea; and for bringing them back in safety to their own port. Thus "they exalt the Lord in the congregation, and praise him in the assembly of the elders." And is it not something of this kind that the psalmist requires?

Verse 33. *He turneth rivers into a wilderness*] After having, as above, illustrated the state of the Jews in their captivity, and the deliverance which God wrought for them, he now turns to the general conduct of God in reference to the poor and needy; and his gracious interpositions in their behalf, the providential supply of their wants, and his opposition to their oppressors. *On account of the wickedness of men*, he sometimes changes a *fruitful land into a desert.* See the general state of Egypt in the present time: once a fertile land; now an arid, sandy wilderness. Again, by his blessing on honest industry, he has changed deserts into highly fertile ground. And, as for the wickedness of their inhabitants, many lands are cursed and rendered barren; so, when a people acknowledge him in all their ways, he blesses their toil, gives them rain and fruitful seasons, and fills their hearts with joy and gladness.

Verse 26. *And there he maketh the hungry to dwell*] All this seems to apply admirably to the first colonists of any place. They flee from a land of want, an *ingrata terra* that did not repay their toil, and they seek the wilderness where the land wants only cultivation to make it produce all the necessaries of life. He, by his providence, so guides their steps as to lead them to *rivers* which they can navigate, and from which they can procure plenty of fish, and shows them *wells* or *springs* which they have not digged. The *hungry dwell there;* and jointly agree, for convenience and defence, *to build them a city for habitation.* They sow the fields which they have cleared; and plant vineyards, and orchards which yield them increasing fruits, ver. 37, and he multiplies their cattle greatly, and does not suffer them to decrease, ver. 38. What a fine picture is this of the first peopling and planting of *America*, and of the multiplication and extension of that people; of the Divine blessing on their industry, and the general and astonishing prosperity of their country! May they never again know what is spoken in the following verse:

Verse 39. *Again, they are minished*] Sometimes by war, or pestilence, or famine. How minished and brought low was the country already spoken of, by the long and destructive war which began in 1775, and was not ended till 1783! And what desolations, minishings, and ruin have been brought on the fertile empires of Europe by the war which commenced in 1792, and did not end till 1814! And how many millions of lives have been sacrificed in it, and souls sent unprepared into the eternal world! When God makes inquisition for blood, on whose heads will he find the blood of these slaughtered millions? Alas! O, alas!

Verse 40. *He poureth contempt upon princes*] How many have lately been raised from *nothing*, and set upon thrones! And how many have been cast down from thrones, and reduced to nothing! And where are now those mighty troublers of the earth? On both sides they are in general gone to give an account of themselves to God. And what an account!

Where there is *no way.*] Who can consider the fate of the late emperor of the French, *Napoleon*, without seeing the *hand of God* in his downfall! All the powers of Europe were leagued against him in vain; they were as stubble to his bow. "HE *came*, HE *saw*, and HE *conquered*" almost every where, till God, by a *Russian* FROST, destroyed his tens of thousands of veteran troops. And afterwards his armies of *raw conscripts* would have overmatched the world had not a particular providence intervened at *Waterloo*, when all the *skill* and *valour* of his opponents had been nearly reduced to nothing. How terrible art thou, O Lord, in thy judgments! Thou art fearful in praises, doing wonders.

The dreary rock of St. Helena, where there was no way, saw a period to the mighty conqueror, who had *strode* over all the countries of Europe!

Verse 41. *Yet setteth he the poor on high*] This probably refers to the case of the *Israelites* and their restoration from captivity. But these are incidents which frequently occur, and mark the superintendence of a *benign Providence*, and the hand of a just *God;* and are applicable to a multitude of cases.

Verse 42. *The righteous shall see it*] The wicked are as inconsiderate as they are obstinate and headstrong.

And rejoice] To have such ample proofs that God ruleth in the earth, and that none that trust in him shall be desolate.

All iniquity shall stop her mouth.] God's judgments and mercies are so evident, and so distinctly marked, that atheism, infidelity, and irreligion are confounded, and the cause of error and falsehood has become hopeless. It was only the *mouth* that could do any thing; and that only by *lies, calumnies,* and *blasphemies:* but God *closes this mouth,* pours *contempt* upon the *head* and *judgment* upon the *heart.* This may also be applied to the case of the *Israelites* and the *Babylonians.* The former, when they turned to God, became *righteous; the* latter were a personification of *all iniquity.*

Verse 43. *Whoso* is *wise*] That is, He that is wise, he that fears God, and regards the operation of his hand *will observe*—lay up and keep, *these things.* He will hide them in his heart, that he sin not against Jehovah. He will encourage himself in the Lord, because he finds that he is a *never-failing spring of goodness* to the righteous.

They shall understand the loving-kindness of the Lord] חסדי יהוה *chasdey Yehovah,* the *exuberant goodness of Jehovah.* This is his peculiar and most prominent characteristic among men; for "judgment is his strange work." What a wonderful discourse on Divine Providence, and God's management of the world, does this inimitable Psalm contain! The *ignorant* cannot read it without profit; and by the study of it, the *wise man* will become yet wiser.

Analysis of the One Hundred and Seventh Psalm

The title of this Psalm is *Hallelujah,* because it sets forth the praises of God for delivering such as are oppressed from four common miseries; after each of which is expressed those intercalary verses: "O that men would praise the Lord," &c.; " They cried unto the Lord in their trouble." It also praises God for his providence in its effects.

I. A preface in which he exhorts all to praise God, especially the redeemed, ver. 1, 2.

II. A declaration of his goodness in particular.

I. To the travellers and strangers, famished, ver. 3-9.

2. To the prisoners and captives, ver. 10-16.

3. To the sick, ver. 16-23.

4. To the mariners, ver. 23-32.

III. A praise of God's power and providence. which is evidently seen in the changes and varieties in the world, of which he gives many instances, that prove him to be the sole Disposer and Governor of the universe, ver. 33-42.

IV. The conclusion, which sets forth the use we are to make of it, ver. 42, 43.

I. 1. This Psalm, like the former, begins: "That we celebrate and set forth God's praise," and for the same reasons. "O give thanks unto the Lord;" 1. "For he is good;" 2. And merciful: "For his mercy endureth for ever."

2. And those whom he invites to perform this duty are all who are sensible that they have received any mercy or goodness from him in either soul or body, whom he calls the redeemed of the Lord; that men may know, when they are freed from any evil, that it is not by chance or their wisdom: God's hand is in it; he is the First Cause; the rest are only his instruments.

1. "Let the redeemed of the Lord say," i. e., that he is good and merciful.

2. "They say so whom he hath redeemed," &c. If the Holy Ghost means, when he speaks of our redemption by Christ, *the enemy,* the devil, or some tyrant, tribulation, &c.; then a corporeal and temporal redemption is meant. The next verse seems to refer to their banishment.

3. "And gathered them out of the lands," &c. Which is yet as true of our spiritual redemption. Matt. viii. 11; John x. 16; and xi. 52.

II. Most expositors begin the *second* part at the second verse, but some at the fourth; but it is not material. In those two there was mention made of God's goodness in their deliverance, in their collection from all lands. But the following is a declaration of what they suffered during their absence from their country. And this is the misery which the prophet first instances in this place, then shows the course the travellers took, and lastly acquaints us with the manner of their deliverance. Their misery was—

1. "That they wandered." No small discomfort for an ingenious native to go from place to place as a vagrant. God's people were for a time pilgrims; "few and evil were their days."

2. The place adds to their misery. Travellers are not confined always to solitary places, they occasionally have company; but these "wandered in the wilderness in a solitary place," &c. Literally it was fulfilled in the *Israelites,* while they travelled through the wilderness.

3. "Hungry and thirsty." Men may wander and be solitary; and yet have a sufficient supply of food; but God's people sometimes fast, as *Elijah, David,* &c.

4. And the famine was so great "that their soul," that is, their life, "was ready to faint." This is the *incrementum* that the prophet uses to aggravate the misery of the travellers, and the several steps by which it rises.

The prophet shows the course which these travellers and hungry souls took for ease and help; and that it did not fail them, nor any one else who has tried it.

1. "Then in their trouble." God let them be brought into trouble to bring them back to himself.

2. "They cried." In their petition they were very earnest; it was no cold prayer, which froze on the way before it got to heaven; but fervent. *A cry.*

3. "And they cried." Not to any false god, but *unto the Lord.*

The success was answerable to their desire.

1. In general, "He delivered them out of their distresses."

2. But in particular, the deliverance was every way fit.

1. "They wandered in the wilderness," &c., ver. 4. "But he led them forth, that they might go to a city of habitation."

2. "They were hungry, and thirsty," &c. But "he filled the hungry soul," &c.

And upon this he concludes his exhortation to praise God, which he is so earnest for them to do, that he inserts the exhortation between each mention of the mercies.

1. The Lord delivered: "The Lord led them forth." Praise him then.

2. Of his mere mercy, not of desert. "For he is good."

3. And the effects of his goodness were seen in his works; let his praise then be as public as his works: "O that men," &c.

The *second* corporeal misery to which men are subject is captivity and imprisonment; he then shows the course the captives took, and God's mercy in their deliverance.

1. Captives; they were taken by the enemy, put in dungeons and prisons, where they were debarred the comfort of the sun: "For they sat in darkness," &c., and in fear of death.

2. Besides, in this place "they were fast bound with affliction," &c., because of their rebellion against the Lord: "The iron entered into their soul." "He brought them low;" but they sought help of the Lord.

"They cried unto the Lord in their trouble." "And found the same favour as the travellers did. "And he saved them out of their distresses."

The manner was suitable to their distress.

1. "For they sat in darkness," &c. "But he brought them out," &c.

2. "They were bound in affliction and iron," &c. The prison was not so strong but he was stronger, and delivered them from captivity. Now the psalmist interposes his thanksgiving: "O that men," &c.

The *third* misery is some great sickness or pining away of the body under some grievous disease, such as when stung by fiery serpents, as the Israelites. 1. He describes the danger under which they languished. 2. Shows the method they took for their recovery.

1. The appellation he fastens on the diseased persons, *fools;* not but that, generally speaking, they were wise enough; but in that they sinned with a high hand against God, "they are fools."

2. Now such *fools* God often smites with an incurable disease: "Fools, because of their transgression," &c. Not but that all sickness is from sin; but this that the prophet speaks of was their general apostasy, rebellion, and contempt of God's will and commandment.

The effect was lamentable and double.

1. "Their soul abhorred all manner of meat." Meat, with which the life of man is sustained, became loathsome to them, the disease was so grievous.

2. And deadly too; no art of the physician could cure them. "For they drew near to the gates of death," that is, the grave, where Death exercises his power, as the judges of Israel did in the gates.

But these, being but dead men in the eye of man, took the same course as they did before.

1. "They cried unto the Lord in their trouble."

2. And by God's blessing they recovered; God was alone their Physician.

3. This was the manner of their cure. "He saved them out of their distress."

1. "He sent his word, and healed them." He said the word only, and they were made whole. Or if any medicine were made use of, it was his word which made it medicinal, as in the case of the bunch of figs, and therefore the prophet uses an apt word to put them in mind. "He sent his word," as a great prince sends forth his ambassadors to do his commands. Most probably the centurion had this in his mind when he said, "Say the word only, and my servant shall be whole."

2. "And he delivered them from their destructions," which are opposed to their previous danger. "They drew nigh," &c.

3. But he exhorts the saved to be thankful: "O that men," &c.

And he adds,

1. "Let them sacrifice their sacrifices."

2. But with these conditions and limitations: 1. That it be with a thankful heart, for an outward sacrifice is nothing. 2. That with the sacrifice there go an annunciation; that men *declare* and *publish* that the cure came from God. 3. That it be done with rejoicing; that we have an experience of God's presence, favour, and mercy, for which the heart ought to rejoice more than for the cure of the body.

The *fourth* misery arises from the danger at sea.

1. He describes.

2. Shows the course they take in a storm.

3. And the event following upon their prayers.

Upon which he calls upon them, as upon the three before, to praise God.

1. "They that go down to the sea in ships." For the sea is lower than the earth.

2. "That do business in great waters." As merchants, mariners, &c.

3. "These men see the works of the Lord," &c. Others hear of them by relation, but these see them: they see the great whales, innumerable kinds of fish, and monsters; islands dispersed and safe in the waves; whirlpools, quicksands, rocks; and have experience of the virtue of the loadstone. They discover many stars we know not; and they behold the vast workings of the sea, which fill the most valiant with fear.

4. "For he commandeth," &c.

Now he describes the tempest:—

1. From the cause. God speaks the word.

2. By it "he raiseth the stormy wind."

3. Which, inspired by his word, "lifts up the waves thereof."

—Fluctus ad sidera tollit.

"The waves arise to heaven."

4. "They" (that is, the passengers) "mount up to heaven," &c.

Hi summo in fluctu pendent, his unda dehiscens.

"They hung upon the wave; the sea yawns under them; and the bottom seems to be laid bare between the surges."

5. "Their soul is melted because of trouble." Their spirit fails.

Extemplo Æneæ solvuntur frigora membra.

"The limbs of the hero himself dissolve with terror."

6. "They reel to and fro." Tossed this way and that way.

Tres Eurus ab alto in brevia, et syrtes urget.

"They are dashed against the shoals and quicksands."

7. "They stagger and totter," &c. An apt simile.

Cui dubii stantque labantque pedes.

"They cannot keep their feet."

8. "And are at their wit's end." Omnis sapientia eorum absorbetur.—"Their judgment roves; their art fails; their skill is at an end."

Et meminisse viæ media Palinurus in unda.

"Even the pilot loses his way in the troubled deep."

Hitherto the prophet has poetically described the tempest and storm; and now he gives an account of the course they took to save their lives. "Then they cried unto the Lord," &c. An old proverb says: Qui nescit orare, discat navigare. "He who knows not how to pray, let him learn to be a sailor."

And the consequence of their praying was:

"And he brings them out," &c. In this manner:—

1. " He makes the storm a calm."

———Dicto citius tumida æquora placat.

"By his word the swelling sea becomes calm."

2. "So that the waves thereof are still." Et cunctus pelagi cecidit fragor. "And the noise of it is hushed to silence."

3. "Then they are glad," &c., no more reeling to and fro; whence arises their joy.

——Læto testantur gaudia plausu.

"The clapping of hands expresses their joy."

4. And to increase it: "So he brings them to their desired haven."

———Magno telluris amore,
Egressi optata nautæ potiuntur arena,
Et sale tabentes artus in littore ponunt.

"The weather-beaten marines having reached the shore, in an ecstacy of joy kiss the sand, and lay themselves down upon the beach."

And now, in the last place, he calls upon them to pay their tribute of thankful duty for the miracle done them in their preservation: "O that men would praise the Lord," &c.

And probably in their danger they might have made a vow, which is frequently done in such cases. Read the Life of *Nazianzen.* This vow the prophet would have them pay openly.

1. "Let them exalt him also in the congregation," &c.

2. And that not only before the promiscuous multitude; but " let them praise him in the assembly of the elders," &c. Sua tabula sacer votiva paries indicat, uvida suspendisse potenti vestimenta maris Deo. "Let them here suspend their votive tablet; and hang their wet clothes against a wall, as a grateful offering to him who rules the seas."

III. The prophet had exalted God's mercies in freeing men from these four miseries and calamities; these travellers through the wilderness, captivity, sickness, shipwreck; and now he manifests his power, providence, and wisdom, in the vicissitudes we meet with below. In the earth we see strange mutations; in kingdoms, wonderful revolutions; yet we must go higher, and not rest short of the hand which governs all.

The prophet first instances the earth's changes.

1. "He turns rivers into a wilderness," &c. The fertility of any land arises from its rivers, as is apparent in Egypt from the overflowing of the *Nile.* And when Elisha would free the soil from barrenness, he first healed the waters. The drying up of rivers produces famine, and when the channels are directed from their courses, the fruitful land becomes a wilderness.

2. And the cause of this is: "The iniquity of them that dwell therein."

On the contrary, God illustrates his mercy by sometimes changing the wilderness into a fruitful and abundant place.

1. "He turneth the wilderness into a standing water," &c. They shall be fruitful for man's sake.

2. "For there he makes the hungry to dwell." God puts it into men's minds to plant colonies in some newly found and good land, where the hungry find plenty and are satisfied.

3. And to build houses: "That they may prepare a city," &c.

Pars aptare locum tecto, pars ducere muros.

"Some dig out the foundations, others raise the walls."

4. The endeavours of the colonists are: 1. "To sow fields." 2. "To plant vineyards." Which was the first trade in the world.

5. And God's blessing on those endeavours: "God blessed them also." 1. In children: "So that they multiplied greatly." 2. In cattle: "And suffered not their cattle to decrease."

But there is nothing in this world perpetual and stable: even those whom God had sometimes blessed and enriched continued not at one stay.

1. These are "minished, and brought low."

2. These are "worn out by oppression," &c. By some public calamity, war, famine, invasion, &c.

Even monarchs are subject to changes.

1. "He pours contempt upon princes." It is a heavy judgment for princes, civil or ecclesiastical, to become contemptible; for then the reins of discipline are let loose, confusion follows, and all things grow worse. And this *for the iniquity of those,* &c.

2. "He causeth them to wander in the wilderness," &c., which clause is subject to a double interpretation.

Either that he suffers princes to err in their counsels, lives, and example; or they enact unjust laws, favour wicked men, or oppress the good. But in the following verse there is some comfort.

"Yet setteth he the poor man on high," &c. Delivers him from all affliction.

"And maketh him families like a flock." Becomes his shepherd, and governs him by his special providence.

IV. He concludes the Psalm with an *epiphonema,* in which he persuades good men to consider the former promises, and lay them to heart; to observe the whole course of God's providence, that they impute not the changes of the world to chance or fortune, but bless God for all his dispensations.

1. "The righteous shall see it," &c. Consider, meditate upon it.

2. "And rejoice." When they are assured that God is their Guardian, and that all he lays upon them is for their real good.

"And all iniquity shall stop her mouth." By the observation of the event, at last evil doers shall not have cause to laugh and blaspheme, but to confess that all is justly and wisely done by God.

And this consideration is that of the wise man who looks afar off.

1. "Who is wise," &c., so as to mark these changes in the world properly.

2. "And they shall understand the loving-kindness of the Lord." It shall be seen by them how ineffable is his mercy towards those who truly fear him, and call upon his name: but our life is hid with Christ in God.

PSALM CVIII

The psalmist encourages himself to praise the Lord for mercies he had received, 1–5. *He prays for the Divine succour,* 6; *and encourages the people to expect their restoration, and the enjoyment of all their former privileges and possessions,* 7–13.

XXII. DAY. EVENING PRAYER

A Song *or* Psalm of David

O [a]GOD, my heart is fixed; I will sing and give praise, even with my glory.

2 [b]Awake, psaltery and harp: I *myself* will awake early.

3 I will praise thee, O LORD, among the people: and I will sing praises unto thee among the nations.

4 For thy mercy *is* great above the heavens: and thy truth *reacheth* unto the [c]clouds.

5 [d]Be thou exalted, O God, above the heavens: and thy glory above all the earth;

6 [e]That thy beloved may be delivered: save *with* thy right hand, and answer me.

7 God hath spoken in his holiness; I will rejoice, I will divide Shechem, and mete out the valley of Succoth.

8 Gilead *is* mine; Manasseh *is* mine; Ephraim also *is* the strength of mine head; [f]Judah *is* my lawgiver;

9 Moab *is* my washpot; over Edom will I cast out my shoe; over Philistia will I triumph.

10 [g]Who will bring me into the strong city? who will lead me into Edom?

11 *Wilt* not *thou,* O God, *who* hast cast us off? and wilt not thou, O God, go forth with our hosts?

12 Give us help from trouble: for vain *is* the help of man.

13 [h]Through God we shall do valiantly: for he *it is that* shall tread down our enemies.

[a]Psa. lvii. 7——[b]Psa. lvii. 8–11——[c]Or, *skies*——[d]Psa. lvii. 5, 11

[e]Psa. lx. 5, &c.——[f]Gen. xlix. 10——[g]Psa. lx. 9 [h]Psa. lx. 12

NOTES ON PSALM CVIII

This Psalm is compounded of *two Psalms* which we have had already under review. The 1st, 2nd, 3rd, 4th, and 5th verses, are the same with the 7th, 8th, 9th, 10th, and 11th verses of Psalm lvii. And the 6th, 7th, 8th, 9th, 10th, 11th, 12th, and 13th, are the same with the 5th, 6th, 7th, 8th, 9th, 10th, 11th, and 12th of Psalm lx. The *variations* are few, and of little moment, and the explanation may be seen in the notes on the preceding Psalms, which need not be repeated here. That the Psalms referred to were made by *David,* and were applicable to the *then* state of his affairs, has been the opinion of many; and it is probable that the captives in Babylon composed *this* out of two above, and applied it to the state of their affairs. Their captivity being now ended, or nearly at an end, they look and pray for their restoration to their own land, as amply as it was possessed in the most prosperous days of *David.* The *Syriac* considers it as a prophecy of the vocation of the Gentiles. The *Hebrew* and all the *Versions* attribute it to *David.*

Verse 1. *Even with my glory.*] My greatest glory shall be in publishing thy praise. Some make the *glory* here to mean the LORD himself; some, the ARK of the *covenant;* some, the SOUL of the *psalmist;* others, his TONGUE; some, the GIFT OF PROPHECY; and some, the psalmist's SPIRIT OR VEIN of *poetry.* See the notes on Psalm lvii. 8.

Verse 3. *Among the people*] The *Jews.*

Among the nations.] The *Gentiles.* Wherever this Psalm is sung or read, either among *Jews* or *Gentiles, David* may be said to sing praise to God.

Verse 7. *God hath spoken in his holiness*] בקדשו *bekodsho;* some think this means *in his Holy One,* referring to the *Prophet Jeremiah,* who predicted the captivity, its duration of *seventy* years, and the deliverance from it.

Verse 10. *The strong city*] The possession of the *metropolis* is a sure proof of the subjugation of the country.

Verse 13. *Through God we shall do valiantly*] From him we derive our courage, from him our strength, and by him our success.

[For the ANALYSIS, see the Psalms from which our is composed.]

PSALM CIX

The psalmist speaks against his inveterate enemies, 1–5. *He prays against them, and denounces God's judgments,* 6–15. *The reason on which this is grounded,* 16–20. *He prays for his own safety and salvation, using many arguments to induce God to have mercy upon him.*

To the chief Musician, A Psalm of David

A. M. cir. 2981 B. C. cir. 1023 Davidis, Regis Israelitarum, cir. annum 33

HOLD [a]not thy peace, O God of my praise;

2 For the mouth of the wicked and the [b]mouth of the deceitful [c]are opened against me: they have spoken against me with a lying tongue.

3 They compassed me about also with words of hatred; and fought against me [d]without a cause.

4 For my love they are my adversaries: but I *give myself unto* prayer.

5 And [e]they have rewarded me evil for good, and hatred for my love.

6 Set thou a wicked man over him: and

[a]Psa. lxxxiii. 1——[b]Heb. *mouth of deceit*——[c]Heb. *have opened* themselves

[d]Psa. xxxv. 7; lxix. 4; John xv. 25——[e]Psa. xxxv. 7, 12 xxxviii. 20

NOTES ON PSALMS CIX

The *title* of this Psalm, *To the chief Musician, A Psalm of David,* has already often occurred, and on it the *Versions* offer nothing new. The *Syriac* says it is "a Psalm of David, when the people, without his knowledge, made *Absalom* king; on which account he was slain: but to us (Christians) he details the passion of Christ." That it contains a prophecy against *Judas* and the enemies of our Lord, is evident from Acts i. 20. Probably, in its primary meaning, (for such a meaning it certainly has,) it may refer to *Ahithophel.* The execrations in it should be rendered in the *future* tense, as they are mere prophetic denunciations of God's displeasure against sinners. Taken in this light, it cannot be a stumbling-block to any person. God has a right to denounce those judgments which he will inflict on the workers of iniquity. But perhaps the whole may be the execrations of *David's* enemies against himself. See on ver. 20. *Ahithophel,* who gave evil counsel against *David,* and being frustrated hanged himself, was no mean prototype of *Judas* the traitor; it was probably on this account that *St. Peter,* Acts i. 20, applied it to the case of *Judas,* as a prophetic declaration concerning him, or at least a subject that might be accommodated to his case.

Verse 1. *Hold not thy peace*] Be not silent; arise and defend my cause.

Verse 2. *The mouth of the wicked and—the deceitful are opened against me*] Many persons are continually uttering calumnies against me. Thou knowest my heart and its innocence; vindicate my uprightness against these calumniators.

Verse 4. *For my love they are my adversaries*] In their behalf I have performed many acts of kindness, and they are my adversaries notwithstanding; this shows principles the most vicious, and hearts the most corrupt. Many of the fathers and commentators have understood the principal part of the things spoken here as referring to our Lord, and the treatment he received from the Jews; and whatever the original intention was, they may safely be applied to this case, as the 2nd, 3rd, 4th, and 5th verses are as highly illustrative of the conduct of the Jewish rulers towards our Lord as the following verses are of the conduct of Judas; but allowing these passages to be prophetic, it is the *Jewish state* rather than an *individual,* against which these awful denunciations are made, as it seems to be represented here under the person and character of an extremely hardened and wicked man; unless we consider the curses to be those of *David's* enemies. See the note on verse 20.

But I give myself unto *prayer*] ואני תפלה *vaani thephillah;* "And I prayer." The *Chaldee:* ואנא אצלי *vaana atsalley,* "but I pray." This gives a good sense, which is followed by the *Vulgate, Septuagint, Æthiopic, Arabic,* and *Anglo-Saxon.* The *Syriac,* "I will pray for them." This, not so correctly; as dreadful *imprecations,* not *prayers,* follow. But probably the whole ought to be interpreted according to the mode laid down, verse 20. The translation and paraphrase in the old Psalter are very simple:—

Trans. **For that thyng that thai sulde hafe lufed me, thai bakbited me; bot I prayed.**

Par. That is, thai sulde haf lufed me for I was godson, and thai bakbited me sayande, in Belzebub he castes oute fendes; bot I prayed for thaim.

Verse 6. *Let Satan stand at his right hand.*] *As the word* שטן *satan* means an *adversary* simply, though sometimes it is used to express the evil spirit *Satan,* I think it best to preserve here its grammatical meaning: "Let an *adversary* stand at his right hand:" i. e., Let him be *opposed* and *thwarted* in all his purposes.

All the *Versions* have *devil,* or some equivocal word. The ARABIC has ابليس *eblees.* the chief

A. M. cir. 2981 B. C. cir. 1023 Davidis, Regis Israelitarum, cir. annum 33

let [f]Satan [g]stand at his right
hand.
7 When he shall be judged, let
him [h]be condemned: and [i]let his
prayer become sin.
8 Let his days be few; *and* [k]let another
take his [l]office.
9 [m]Let his children be fatherless, and his
wife a widow.
10 Let his children be continually vagabonds, and beg: let
them seek *their bread* also out
of their desolate places.
11 [n]Let the extortioner catch all that he
hath; and let the strangers spoil his labour.
12 Let there be none to extend mercy unto
him: neither let there be any to favour his
fatherless children.

A. M. cir. 2981 B. C. cir. 1023 Davidis, Regis Israelitarum, cir. annum 33

---

[f]Zech. iii. 1——[g]Or, *an adversary*——[h]Heb. *go out guilty*, or *wicked*——[i]Prov. xxviii. 9

[k]Ac s 1. 20——[l]Or, *charge*——[m]Exod. xxii. 24——[n]Job v. 5; xviii. 9

---

of the apostate spirits; but the name is probably corrupted from the GREEK διαβολος *diabolos;* from which the LATIN *diabolus*, the ITALIAN *diavolo*, the SPANISH *diablo*, the FRENCH *diable*, *the* IRISH or CELTIC *diabal*, the DUTCH *duivel*, the GERMAN *teufel*, *the* ANGLO-SAXON *deofal*, and the ENGLISH *devil*, are all derived. The original, διαβολος, comes from δια βαλλειν, to *shoot* or *pierce through*.

Verse 7. *Let him be condemned*] יצא רשע *yetse rasha*. "Let him come out a wicked man;" that is let his wickedness be made manifest.

Let his prayer become sin.] Thus paraphrased by Calmet: "Let him be accused, convicted, and condemned, and let the *defence* which he brings for his justification only serve to deepen his guilt, and hasten his condemnation." I once more apprise the reader, that if these are not the words of *David's* enemies against himself, (see on verse 20,) they are *prophetic denunciations* against a rebellious and apostate person or people, hardened in crime, and refusing to return to God.

Verse 8. *Let another take his office.*] The original is פקדתו *pekuddatho*, which the margin translates *charge*, and which literally means *superintendance, oversight, inspection* from actual *visitations*. The translation in our common Version is too technical. *His bishopric*, following the *Septuagint*, επισκοπην, and *Vulgate*, *episcopatum*, and has given cause to some light people to be *witty*, who have said, "The first bishop we read of was bishop Judas." But it would be easy to convict this witticism of blasphemy, as the word is used in many parts of the sacred writings, from Genesis downward, to signify offices and officers, appointed either by God immediately, or in the course of his providence, for the accomplishment of the most important purposes. It is applied to the patriarch *Joseph*, Gen. xxxix. 4, ויפקדהו *vaiyaphkidehu*, *he made him bishop*, alias *overseer;* therefore it might be as *wisely* said, and much more correctly, "The first bishop we read of was bishop Joseph;" and many such bishops there were of God's making long before Judas was born. After all, Judas was no *traitor* when he was appointed to what is called his *bishopric*, *office*, or *charge* in the apostolate. Such witticisms as these amount to no argument, and serve no cause that is worthy of defence.

Our common Version, however, was not the first to use the word: it stands in the *Anglo-Saxon* ⁊ biscophad his, onfo oðer, "and his episcopacy let take other." The old Psalter is nearly the same; I shall give the whole verse: **Fa be made his days, and his bysshopryk another take.** "For Mathai was sett in stede of Judas; and his days was *fa* that hynged himself."

Verse 9. *Let his children be fatherless, &c.*] It is said that Judas was a married man, against whom this verse, as well as the preceding is supposed to be spoken; and that it was to support them that he stole from the bag in which the property of the apostles was put, and of which he was the treasurer.

Verse 10. *Let his children—beg*] The father having lost his *office*, the children must necessarily be destitute; and this is the hardest lot to which any can become subject, after having been born to the expectation of an ample fortune.

Verse 11. *Let the strangers spoil his labour.*] Many of these execrations were literally fulfilled in the case of the miserable Jews, after the death of our Lord. They were not only expelled from their own country, after the destruction of Jerusalem, but they were prohibited from returning; and so taxed by the Roman government, that they were reduced to the lowest degree of poverty. *Domitian* expelled them from Rome; and they were obliged to take up their habitation without the gate Capena, in a wood contiguous to the city, for which they were obliged to pay a rent, and where the whole of their property was only a *basket and a little hay.* See JUVENAL, Sat. ver. 11:—

Substitit ad veteres arcus, madidamque Capenam:
Hic ubi nocturnæ Numa constituebat amicæ,
Nunc sacri fontis nemus, et delubra locantur
Judæis: quorum cophinus, fœnumque supellex:
Omnis enim populo mercedem pendere jussa est
Arbor, et ejectis mendicat silva Camœnis.

He stopped a little at the conduit gate,
Where Numa modelled once the Roman state;
In nightly councils with his nymph retired:
Though now the sacred shades and founts are hired
By banished Jews, who their whole wealth can lay
In a small basket, on a wisp of hay.
Yet such our avarice is, that every tree
Pays for his head; nor sleep itself is free;
Nor place nor persons now are sacred held,
From their own grove the Muses are expelled.
DRYDEN.

The same poet refers again to this wretched state of the Jews, Sat. vi., ver. 541; and shows to what vile extremities they were reduced in order to get a morsel of bread:—

A. M. cir. 2981
B. C. cir. 1023
Davidis, Regis
Israelitarum,
cir. annum
33

13 [o]Let his posterity be cut off; *and* in the generation following let their [p]name be blotted out.

14 [q]Let the inquity of his fathers be remembered with the LORD; and let not the sin of his mother [r]be blotted out.

15 Let them be before the LORD continually, that he may [s]cut off the memory of them from the earth.

16 Because that he remembered not to show mercy, but persecuted the poor and needy man, that he might even slay the [t]broken in heart.

17 [u]As he loved cursing, so let it come unto him: as he delighted not in blessing, so let it be far from him.

A. M. cir. 2981
B. C. cir. 1023
Davidis, Regis
Israelitarum,
cir. annum
33

18 As he clothed himself with cursing like as with his garment, so let it [v]come [w]into his bowels like water, and like oil into his bones.

19 Let it be unto him as the garment *which* covereth him, and for a girdle wherewith he is girded continually.

20 *Let* this *be* the reward of mine adversaries from the LORD, and of them that speak evil against my soul.

21 But do thou for me, O GOD the Lord,

[o]Job xviii. 19; Psalm xxxvii. 28——[p]Prov. x. 7——[q]Exod. xx. 5——[r]Neh. iv. 5; Jer. xviii. 23——[s]Job xviii. 17; Psa. xxxiv. 16——[t]Psa. xxxiv. 18——[u]Prov. xiv. 14; Ezek. xxxv. 6——[v]Num. v. 22——[w]Heb. *within him*

Cum dedit ille locum, cophino fœnoque relicto,
Arcanam Judæa tremens mendicat in aurem,
Interpres legum Solymarum, et magna sacerdos
Arboris, ac summi fida internuncia cœli.
Implet et illa manum, sed parcius, ære minuto.
Qualia cunque voles Judæi somnia vendunt.

Here a *Jewess* is represented as coming from the wood mentioned above, to gain a few *oboli* by fortune-telling; and, trembling lest she should be discovered, she leaves her *basket* and *hay*, and whispers lowly in the ear of some female, from whom she hopes employment in her line. She is here called by the poet the *interpretess of the laws of Solymae*, or Jerusalem, and the *priestess of a tree*, because obliged, with the rest of her nation, to lodge in a *wood;* so that she and her countrymen might be said *to seek their bread out of desolate places, the stranger having spoiled their labour.* Perhaps the whole of the Psalm relates to their infidelities, rebellions, and the miseries inflicted on them from the crucifixion of our Lord till the present time. I should prefer this sense, if what is said on ver. 20 be not considered a better mode of interpretation.

Verse 13. *Let his posterity be cut off*] It is a fact that the *distinction* among the Jewish tribes in entirely lost. Not a Jew in the world knows from what tribe he is sprung; and as to the royal family, it remains nowhere but in the person of Jesus the Messiah. He *alone* is the Lion of the tribe of Judah. Except as it exists in him, *the name is blotted out.*

Verse 16. *Persecuted the poor and needy man*] In the case of Jesus Christ all the dictates of justice and mercy were destroyed, and they persecuted this poor man unto death. They acted from a diabolical malice. On common principles, their opposition to Christ cannot be accounted for.

Verse 17. *As he loved cursing, so let it come unto him*] The Jews said, when crucifying our Lord, *His blood be upon us and our children!* Never was an imprecation more dreadfully fulfilled.

Verse 18. *Let it come into his bowels like water*] Houbigant thinks this is an allusion to the *waters of jealousy;* and he is probably right,—the bitter waters that produce the curse. See Num. v. 18.

Verse 19. *And for a girdle*] Let the curse *cleave* to him throughout life: as the girdle binds all the clothes to the body, let the curse of God bind all mischiefs and maladies to his body and soul.

The *Hindoos, Budhists*, and others often wear a *gold* or *silver chain* about their waist. One of those chains, once the ornament of a *Moudeliar* in the island of Ceylon, lies now before me: it is silver, and curiously wrought.

Verse 20. Let *this* be *the reward of mine adversaries from the Lord, and of them that speak evil against my soul.*] Following the mode of interpretation already adopted, this may mean: All these maledictions shall be fulfilled on my enemies; they shall have them for their reward. So all the opposition made by the Jews against our Lord, and the obloquies and execrations wherewith they have loaded him and his religion, have fallen upon themselves; and they are awful examples of the wrath of God abiding on *them* that believe not.

But is not this verse a *key to* all that preceded it? The original, fairly interpreted, will lead us to a somewhat different meaning: זאת פעלת שטני מאת יהוה והדברים רע על נפשי *zoth peullath soteney meeth Yehovah, vehaddoberim ra al naphshi.* "This is the work of my adversaries before the Lord, and of those who speak evil against my soul," or *life.* That is, all that is said from the *sixth* to the *twentieth* verse consists of the evil words and imprecations of my enemies against my soul, laboring to set the Lord, by imprecations, against me, that their curses may take effect. This, which is a reasonable interpretation, frees the whole Psalm from *every difficulty.* Surely, the curses contained in it are more like those which proceed from the mouth of the wicked, than from one inspired by the Spirit of the living God. Taking the words in this sense, which I am persuaded is the best, and which the *original* will well bear and several of the *Versions* countenance, then our translation may stand just as it is; only let the reader remember that at the *sixth* verse David begins to tell *how his enemies cursed* HIM, *while he prayed for* THEM.

Verse 21. *But do thou for me*] While they

A. M. cir. 2981
B. C. cir. 1023
Davidis, Regis
Israelitarum,
cir. annum
33

for thy name's sake: because
thy mercy *is* good, deliver thou
me,
22 For I *am* poor and needy,
and my heart is wounded within me.
23 I am gone [x]like the shadow when it
declineth: I am tossed up and down as the
locust.
24 My [y]knees are weak through fasting;
and my flesh faileth of fatness.
25 I became also [z]a reproach unto them:
when they looked upon me [a]they shaked their
heads.
26 Help me, O LORD my God: O save me
according to thy mercy:
27 [b]That they may know that
this *is* thy hand; *that* thou,
LORD, hast done it.
28 [c]Let them curse, but bless
thou: when they arise, let them be ashamed;
but let [d]thy servant rejoice.
29 [e]Let mine adversaries be clothed with
shame, and let them cover themselves with
their own confusion, as with a mantle.
30 I will greatly praise the LORD with my
mouth; yea, [f]I will praise him among the
multitude.
31 For [g]he shall stand at the right hand of
the poor, to save *him* [h]from those that condemn his soul.

[x]Psa. cii. 11; cxliv. 4——[y]Heb. xii. 12——[z]Psa. xxii. 6, 7——[a]Matt. xxvii. 39——[b]Job xxxvii. 7——[c]2 Sam. xvi. 11, 12——[d]Isa. lxv. 14

[e]Psa. xxxv. 26; cxxxii. 18——[f]Psa. xxxv. 18; cxi. 1——[g]Psa. xvi. 8; lxxiii. 23; cx. 5; cxxi. 5——[h]Heb. *from the judges of his soul*

use horrible imprecations against me, and load me with their curses, *act thou for me*, and *deliver me* from their maledictions. While they *curse*, do thou *bless*. This verse is a farther proof of the correctness of the interpretation given above.

Verse 22. *I* am *poor and needy*] I am *afflicted* and *impoverished;* and *my heart is wounded*—my very *life* is sinking through distress.

Verse 23. *I am gone like the shadow*] "I have walked like the declining shadow,"—I have passed my meridian of health and life; and as the sun is going below the horizon, so am I about to go under the earth.

I am tossed up and down as the locust.] When swarms of locusts take wing, and infest the countries in the east, if the wind happen to blow *briskly*, the swarms are agitated and driven upon each other, so as to appear to be heaved to and fro, or tossed up and down. Dr. *Shaw*, who has seen this, says it gives a lively idea of the comparisons of the psalmist.

Verse 24. *My knees are weak through fasting*] That *hunger* is as soon felt in *weakening the knees*, as in producing an *uneasy sensation in the stomach*, is known by all who have ever felt it. Writers in all countries have referred to this effect of hunger. Thus *Tryphioderus*, Il. Excid. ver. 155:—

Τειρομενου βαρυθειεν ατερπεϊ γουνατα λιμῳ.

"Their knees might fail, by hunger's force subdued;
And sink, unable to sustain their load."
MERRICK.

So PLAUTUS, Curcul, act. ii., scen. 3:—

Tenebræ oboriuntur, genua inedia succidunt.

"My eyes grow dim; my knees are weak with hunger."

And LUCRETIUS, lib. iv. ver. 950:—

Brachia, palpebræque cadunt, poplitesque procumbunt.

"The arms, the eyelids fall; the knees give way."

Both the *knees* and the *sight* are particularly affected by hunger.

Verse 25. When *they looked upon me they shaked their heads.*] Thus was David treated by *Shimei*, 2 Sam. xvi. 5, 6, and our blessed Lord by the *Jews*, Matt. xxvii. 39.

Verse 27. *That they may know that this is thy hand*] Let thy help be so manifest in my behalf, that they may see it is thy hand, and that thou hast undertaken for me. Or, if the words refer to the passion of our Lord, Let them see that I suffer not on my own account; "for the transgression of my people am I smitten."

Verse 28. *Let them curse, but bless thou*] See on ver. 20: Of the mode of interpretation recommended there, this verse gives additional proof.

Verse 29. *Let them cover themselves*] He here retorts their own curse, ver. 18.

Verse 30. *I will greatly praise the Lord*] I have the fullest prospect of deliverance, and a plenary vindication of my innocence.

Verse 31. *He shall stand at the right hand of the poor*] Even if Satan himself be the accuser, God will vindicate the innocence of his servant. Pilate and the Jews condemned our Lord to death as a malefactor; God showed his immaculate innocence by his resurrection from the dead.

The whole of this Psalm is understood by many as referring solely to *Christ*, the traitor *Judas*, and the *wicked Jews*. This is the view taken of it in the analysis.

ANALYSIS OF THE HUNDRED AND NINTH PSALM

The later expositors expound this Psalm of *Doeg Ahithophel*, and other persecutors of *David;* and so it may be understood in the type; but the ancient fathers apply it to *Judas*, and the Jews who put Christ to death; which opinion, being more probable, and because Peter (Acts i. 20) applies a passage out of ver. 8 to *Judas*, I shall expound the Psalm as of Christ, whom David personated, and of *Judas*, and the malicious *Jews*, as understood in the persons of his wicked and slanderous enemies.

The Psalm has four parts:—

I. A short ejaculation, ver. 1, and the reasons expressed in a complaint of the fraud and malice of his enemies, ver. 6.

II. A bitter imprecation against their fury, ver. 6-21.

III. A supplication presented to God for himself, and the reasons, ver. 21-30.

IV. A profession of thanks.

I. He begins with an ejaculation: "Hold not thy peace, O God of my praise."

1. Either actively, that is, "O God, whom I praise," even in the greatest calamities.

2. Or passively; "Who art my praise:" The Witness and Advocate of my innocency when I am condemned by malicious tongues; which sense appears best for this place.

"Hold not thy peace." *Tacere*, to be silent, in Scripture, when referred to God, is to connive, to rest, to appear not to regard; and, on the contrary, *loqui*, to speak, to do something for revenge or deliverance; it is what David here asks, that, when the malice of his enemies arrived at its height, God should not suffer them, but show his displeasure.

Then by way of complaint, he describes their malicious nature, which he aggravates by an elegant gradation. "For the mouth of the wicked:" and they were, 1. Impious. 2. Deceitful. 3. Liars.

1. "For the mouth of the wicked:" *Caiaphas*, *Judas*, the *priests*, *Jews*, &c.

2. "And the mouth of the deceitful," &c. *They sought to entrap him in his words.*

3. "They have spoken against me," &c. "He casteth out devils through Beelzebub," &c.

And yet the mischief rises higher, even to hatred and malice.

1. "They compassed me about," &c. Manifesting in plain words the malice they carried in their hearts. "This man is not of God," &c.

2. "They hated me without a cause:" Wantonly, idly. They were not only evil, deceitful, and malicious; but very ungrateful. "He went about doing good;" and "How often would I have gathered you," &c.; and for this love they returned hatred.

1. "For my love, they are my adversaries:" But, nevertheless,

2. "I give myself to prayer:" "Father, forgive them; they know not," &c. Which base ingratitude of theirs he opens in fuller words. "They have rewarded me evil." And Theognis truly says,

Ἡ χαρις αλλαξαι την φυσιν ου δυναται.

No kindness can invert an evil nature:

A Jew will ever be a Jew.

II. The prophet, having complained of the malice, spiteful usage, and ingratitude of his nation, their crafty dealing with him, and their lies against him, proceeds to pray against them, and that in most bitter and fearful imprecations. Enemies he foresaw they would be to the flourishing state of Christ's Church, and that nothing had power to restrain or amend them; and therefore he curses them with a curse the most bitter that ever fell from the lips of man. In particular *Judas*, who was guide to them who took Jesus, is pointed out; but, as Augustine observes, he represented the person of the whole synagogue; therefore, it is involved necessarily. But some understanding these curses as uttered by the Jews against *David*. See the note on ver. 20.

1. "Set thou a wicked man over him," &c.: A fearful imprecation. Subject him to the will of some impious and wicked man, to whose lust and violence he may be no better than a slave. Others understand by *a wicked man* a false teacher, who may seduce him by false doctrines.

2. "Let Satan stand at his right hand:" Have full power over him. Let him stand; which signifies a perpetual endeavour to urge him forward till he effect his intended mischief. And so it was with *Judas* and the *Jews;* Satan was their guide, and they followed him.

The second is, "When he shall be judged, let him be condemned;"—find no mercy, no favour, at the judge's hands; thus, when *Judas*, accused and condemned by his own conscience, went to the high priest, who had bribed him, he would not acquit him; and *Judas*, in despair and grief for his sin, "went out and hanged himself."

The third, "Let his prayer become sin:" He turned his ear from hearing God, why then should God hear him? No prayer is acceptable to God but through Christ, and that out of a sincere heart; any other prayers become sin.

The fourth is the shortening of their life and honour.

1. "Let his days be few:" Length of days is promised only to the obedient, and is a blessing: but the prayer is that this man's life be a short one, and so Judas's was.

2. "And let another take his office:" Which must be applied to *Judas*, since St. Peter (Acts i. 20) so interprets it; and it is at this day as true of the Jews, for they have no high priest. Another, after the order of *Melchizedek*, has succeeded Aaron's priesthood.

The fifth is—

1. "Let his children be fatherless," &c.: Which follows on the former curse.

2. "Let his children be continually vagabonds, and beg:" And such the Jews are to this day; and beggars they were for a long time after the overthrow of Jerusalem.

The sixth execration is upon his goods.

1. "Let the extortioner catch all that he hath:" Probably the publicans.

2. "And let the strangers spoil his labour:" Which was verified by the soldiers of *Titus*, who ripped up the bellies of the captive *Jews* to see if they had swallowed gold.

But the prophet again returns to his children.

1. "Let there be none to extend mercy unto him," &c.: To beg, or to want, is a misery; but there is some comfort in it when beggars meet with some to relieve it. But the prophet says, Let there be none to pity him, or his. *Judas* found none to pity him.

2. Men, because they must die themselves, desire, if possible, to be immortal in their issue. *Bellarmine* observes that *Judas* had no issue; for that *Matthias*, who came in his place, did not derive his office from him. Though a posterity of the *Jews* remained after the flesh, yet, in the next generation, their ecclesiastical and civil polity was at an end; and since their dispersion they are without king, without priest, without sacrifice, without altar, without ephod, and without teraphim, as foretold by *Hosea*.

3. "Let the iniquity of his fathers be remembered," &c.: This imprecation answers God's threat: "I will visit the iniquity of the fathers upon the children." And this curse has come upon the Jews to the uttermost; they are self-

devoted: "Let his blood be upon us, and upon our children." The guilt of his blood is yet upon them; the iniquity of their fathers is yet remembered; and the sin of their mother, the synagogue, is not yet done away.

He repeats again the sin of their fathers, and the sin of the synagogue; this verse being but the exposition of the former.

1. "Let them be before the Lord continually:" The sin their father and mother committed, never let it be forgotten by God.

2. "That he may cut off the memory," &c.: Except it be in contempt.

The prophet having now finished his execrations, acquaints us with the causes of them.

1. Their want of pity to them in distress: "Have ye no regard, all ye that pass by?" Lam. i. 12. It is but just then "that they find judgment without mercy, that would show no mercy."

2. So far from that, "that he persecuted the poor and needy man," &c., which is the second cause; the inhumanity of *Judas* and the Jews against Christ, who is here called—1. *Poor*, because, "when he was rich, for our sakes he became poor, that we through his poverty might be rich;" 2 Cor. ix. 2. *The needy man:* "For the foxes have holes," &c.; Luke ix. 58. 3. *The broken in heart.* For he was in agony, and his soul was troubled, when he sweated great drops of blood; when he cried, "My God, my God!" not with compunction or contrition for any fault he had committed, but from a sense of pain, and his solicitude for the salvation of mankind.

In this verse there is noted the extreme cruelty and inhumanity of the *Jews;* for whoever persecutes a man for his life is inclined to it either from some real or supposed injury, or else through envy: but Christ was humble and lowly in heart; he went about doing good, and yet they persecuted him.

But, thirdly, he complains: "He loved cursing;" therefore, it is but reason that he should have what he loved: "As he clothed himself with cursing—so let it come," &c. No man can love a curse or hate a blessing, if it be proposed to the will under the form of a curse or blessing: but a man is said to love a curse when he follows a wicked course, and avoids the blessing of a good life. This *Judas* and the *Jews* did: *Judas*, by loving money more than his Master; the Jews, by—"Let his blood," &c.

Neque enim lex justior ulla est, &c.

It is just that a man should suffer for his own wicked inventions. But the prophet adds, Let it sit close to him as a garment; let it be converted into his substance: let him carry it perpetually, &c.

1. "As he clothed himself with cursing," &c. As in clothes he delights in.

2. "So let it come as waters," &c. As the stomach concocts and turns every thing into the very flesh of the animal; so let his curse be converted into his nature and manners.

3. "Let it come as oil into his bones," &c. Oil will pierce the bones; water will not.

This curse must be of great efficacy; he must always carry it.

1. "Let it be unto him," &c. Stick close as a garment.

2. "And for a girdle," &c. Compass him round about.

For a garment some read *pallium;* a cloak that a man puts off at home, and calls for when he goes abroad: thus let God set an outward mark upon him; let him be known as a cast-away.

If *Doeg* were the type of *Judas*, as most agree, in this Psalm, then by the girdle might be understood *cingulum militare*, the military girdle, which, while they were of that profession, they cast not off: and he, *Doeg*, being a military man, the curse was to cleave to him, and compass him as his girdle.

The prophet concludes this part of the Psalm with an exclamation, as being persuaded his curses were not in vain.

"Let this be the reward of mine adversaries," &c., who say that I am a deceiver, and deny me to be the Saviour of the world.

III. The prophet now turns from curses to prayer: and in the person of Christ, directs it to God for protection and deliverance both of himself and the whole Church.

1. "But do thou for me," &c. He asks help against his persecutors on these three grounds: 1. Because his Lord was *Jehovah*, the fountain of all being and power. 2. Because it would be for his honour: "Do it for thy name's sake." Thy faithfulness and goodness to the Church, and justice in executing vengeance on her enemies. 3. Do it, *because thy mercy is good*—easily inclined to succour the miserable.

2. "Deliver me," may have reference to Christ's prayer, "Father, save me from this hour," &c.

1. "Deliver me," for I am destitute of all human help.

2. "Deliver me," for my heart is wounded within me.

And to these he adds many other reasons; and uses two similes, the one drawn from the shadow of the evening, the other from the *locust.*

1. "I am gone like a shadow:" &c. Which passes away in a moment silently: so was Christ led away as a prisoner, without any murmur: "He was led as a lamb," &c.; Isa. liii. Thus the apostles and martyrs died patiently.

2. "I am tossed up and down as the locust." From one tribunal to another, as the locust carried from place to place, Exod. x. 12, 19.

Secondly, he reasons from his bodily debility.

1. "My knees are weak through fasting." The little sustenance Christ took before his passion, and his watching in prayer all night.

2. "And my flesh faileth of fatness," through the excess of his fatigue, and the anguish of his Spirit: thus he could not bear his cross.

3. A third reason why God should pity and deliver is drawn from the opprobrious usage and the scorn they put upon him, than which there is nothing more painful to an ingenuous and noble nature: "I am become also a reproach unto them," &c. The *four* Gospels are an ample comment upon this verse.

The second part of his prayer is for a speedy resurrection: "Help me, O Lord my God: O save me," &c. And he supports his petition with a strong reason, drawn from the final cause: "Save me, that they may know," &c. That all men, the Jews especially, may be convinced by my rising again, in despite of the watch and the seal, that it was not their malice and power that brought me to this ignominious death, but that my passion, suffering, and death proceeded from thy hand: "By his resurrection he was declared," Rom. i. 4. And in the close of his prayer he sings a triumph over his enemies, the *devil*, *Judas*, the *Jews*, those bitter enemies to him and his Church.

1. "Let them curse." Speak evil of me and my followers.

2. "But bless thou." Bless all nations that have faith in me.

3. "When they arise." For, 1. Arise they will, and endeavour by every means to destroy my kingdom; 2. But "let them be ashamed." Confounded that their wishes are frustrated.

4. "But let thy servant (which condition Christ took upon himself) rejoice;" because thy name is thereby glorified.

And he continues his exercrations by way of explanation. "Let mine adversaries," &c, be confounded at the last day, for their ingratitude and malice, before angels and men.

IV. He closes all with thanks, which he opposes to the confusion of the wicked.

1. "I will greatly praise the Lord." With affection and a great jubilee.

2. "I will praise him among the multitude." Before all the world.

For which he assigns this reason,—

1. "He shall stand at the right hand of the poor." That is, such as are *poor in spirit*, who ask and find mercy from God: to such I will be as a shield and buckler.

2. "I will stand at the right hand of the poor, to save him," &c. From the devil and all his instruments. Christ is the all-covering shield of his Church: "He hath blotted out the handwriting of ordinances," &c. So that, cum a mundo damnamur, a Christo ab solvemur. "When we are condemned by the world, we are absolved by Christ."

PSALM CX

The Messiah sits in his kingdom at the right hand of God, his enemies being subdued under him, 1, 2. *The nature and extent of his government*, 3. *His everlasting priesthood*, 4. *His execution of justice and judgment*, 5, 6. *The reason on which all this is founded, his passion and exaltation*, 7.

XXIII. DAY. MORNING PRAYER

A Psalm of David

A. M. cir. 2989
B. C. cir. 1015
Davidis, Regis Israelitarum, cir. annum 40

THE [a]LORD said unto my Lord, Sit thou at my right hand, until I make thine enemies thy footstool.

2 The LORD shall send the rod of thy strength out of Zion: rule thou in the midst of thine enemies.

3 [b]Thy people *shall be* willing in the day of thy power, [c]in the beauties of holiness [d]from

[a]Matt. xxii. 44; Mark xii. 36; Luke xx. 42; Acts ii. 34; 1 Cor. xv. 25; Heb. i. 13; 1 Pet. iii. 22; see Psa. xlv. 6, 7

[b]Judg. v. 2——[c]Psa. xcvi. 9——[d]Or, *more than the womb of the morning; thou shalt have*, &c.

NOTES ON PSALM CX

The *Hebrew*, and all the *Versions*, except the *Arabic*, attribute this Psalm to *David:* nor can this be doubted, as it is thus attributed in the New Testament; see the places in the margin. We have in it the celebration of some great potentate's accession to the crown; but the subject is so grand, the expressions so noble, and the object raised so far above what can be called *human*, that no history has ever mentioned a prince to whom a literal application of this Psalm can be made. To Jesus Christ alone, to his everlasting priesthood and government, as King of kings and Lord of lords, can it be applied.

The *Jews*, aware of the advantage which the Christian religion must derive from this Psalm, have laboured hard and in vain to give it a contrary sense. Some have attributed it to *Eliezer*, the servant or steward of Abraham; and state that he composed it on the occasion of his master's victory over the *four* kings at the valley of *Shaveh*, Gen. xiv. Others say it was done by *David*, in commemoration of his victory over the Philistines. Others make *Solomon* the author. Some refer it to *Hezekiah*, and others to *Zerubbabel*, &c.: but the bare reading of the Psalm will show the vanity of these pretensions. A King is described here who is *David's* Lord, and sits at the right hand of God; a conqueror, reigning at Jerusalem, King from all eternity—having an everlasting priesthood, Judge of all nations, triumphing over all potentates, indefatigable in all his operations, and successful in all his enterprises. Where has there ever appeared a prince in whom all these characters met? There never was one, nor is it possible that there ever can be one such, the Person excepted to whom the Psalm is applied by the authority of the Holy Spirit himself. That the Jews who lived in the time of our Lord believed this Psalm to have been written by David, and that it spoke of the Messiah alone, is evident from this, that when our Lord quoted it, and drew arguments from it in favour of his mission, Matt. xxii. 42, they did not attempt to gainsay it. St. *Peter*, Acts ii. 34, and St. *Paul*, 1 Cor. xv. 25; Heb. i. 13, v. 6, 10, vii. 17, x. 12, 13, apply it to show that Jesus is the Messiah. Nor was there any attempt to contradict them; not even an intimation that they had misapplied it, or mistaken its meaning. Many of the later Jews also have granted that it applied to the *Messiah*, though they dispute its application to Jesus of Nazareth. All the critics and commentators whom I have consulted apply it to our Lord; nor does it appear to me to be capable of interpretation on any other ground. Before I proceed to take a general view of it, I shall set down the chief of the *various readings* found in the MSS. on this Psalm.

Verse 1. *Said unto my Lord.* Instead of לאדני

A. M. cir. 2989 B. C. cir. 1015 Davidis, Regis Israelitarum, cir. annum 40

the womb of the morning: thou
hast the dew of thy youth.
4 The LORD hath sworn, and
[e]will not repent, [f]Thou *art* a
priest for ever after the order of Melchizedek.
5 The LORD [g]at thy right hand shall strike
through kings [h]in the day of his wrath.
6 He shall judge among the
heathen, he shall fill *the places*
with the dead bodies; [i]he shall
wound the heads over [k]many
countries.
7 [l]He shall drink of the brook in the way:
[m]therefore shall he lift up the head.

A. M. cir. 2989 B. C. cir. 1015 Davidis, Regis Israelitarum, cir. annum 40

[e]Num. xxiii. 19——[f]Heb. v. 6; vi. 20; vii. 17, 21; see Zech. vi. 13——[g]Psa. xvi. 8——[h]Psa. ii. 5, 12; Rom. ii. 5; Rev. xi. 18——[i]Psa. lxviii. 21; Hab. iii. 13——[k]Or, *great*——[l]Judg. vii. 5, 6——[m]Isa. liii. 12

ladoni, "my Lord," one MS. seems to have read ליהוה *layhovah*, "Jehovah said unto Jehovah, 'Sit thou on my right hand,'" &c. See *De Rossi.*

Thy footstool. הדם לרגליך *hadom leragleycha*, "the footstool to thy feet." But *eight* MSS. drop the prefix ל *le;* and read the word in the *genitive* case, with the *Septuagint*, *Vulgate*, and *Arabic.* Many also read the word in the *singular* number.

Ver. 3. Instead of בהדרי קדש *behadrey kodesh*, "in the beauties of holiness," בהררי קדש *beharerey kodesh*, "in the mountains of holiness," is the reading of *thirty-four* of *Kennicott's* MSS., and *fifty-three* of those of *De Rossi*, and also of several printed editions.

Instead of ילדתך *yaldutheca*, "of thy youth," ילדתיך *yaladticha*, "I have begotten thee," is the reading, as to the *consonants*, of *sixty-two* of *Kennicott's* and *twenty-three* of *De Rossi's* MSS., and of some ancient editions, with the *Septuagint*, *Arabic*, and *Anglo-Saxon.*

Ver. 4. *After the order*, על דברתי *al dibrathi*, דברתו *dibratho*, "HIS order," is the reading of *twelve* of *Kennicott's* and *De Rossi's* MSS.

Ver. 5. *The Lord*, אדני *adonai:* but יהוה *Yehovah* is the reading of a great number of the MSS. in the above collections.

Ver. 6. Instead of בגוים *baggoyim*, "among the heathens" or *nations*, גוים *goyim*, "he shall judge the *heathen*," is the reading of one ancient MS.

Instead of ראש *rosh*, "the head," ראשי *rashey*, "the heads," is the reading of one MS., with the *Chaldee*, *Septuagint*, *Vulgate*, and *Anglo-Saxon.*

Ver. 7. For ירים *yarim*, "he shall lift up," ירום *yarom*, "shall be lifted up," is the reading of *six* MSS. and the *Syriac.*

Instead of ראש *rosh*, "THE head," ראשו *rosho*, "HIS head," is the reading of *two* MSS. and the *Syriac.*

A few add הללו יה *halelu Yah*, "Praise ye Jehovah;" but this was probably taken from the beginning of the following Psalm.

The learned *Venema* has taken great pains to expound this Psalm: he considers it a Divine oracle, partly relating to David's Lord, and partly to David himself.

1. David's Lord is here inducted to the highest honour, regal and sacerdotal, with the promise of a most flourishing kingdom, founded in Zion, but extending *every where*, till every enemy should be subdued.

2. David is here promised God's protection; that his enemies shall never prevail against him; but he must go through many sufferings in order to reach a state of glory.

3. The time in which this oracle or prophecy was delivered was probably a little after the time when David had brought home the ark, and before he had his wars with the neighbouring idolatrous nations. The kingdom was *confirmed* in his hand; but it was not yet *extended* over the neighbouring nations.

Verse 1. *The Lord said unto my Lord*] *Jehovah* said unto my *Adoni.* That David's Lord is the Messiah, is confirmed by our Lord himself and by the apostles Peter and Paul, as we have already seen.

Sit thou at my right hand] This implies the possession of the utmost confidence, power, and preeminence.

Until I make thine enemies] Jesus shall reign till all his enemies are subdued under him. Jesus Christ, as GOD, ever dwelt in the fulness of the Godhead; but it was as *God-man* that, after his resurrection, he was raised to the *right hand of the Majesty on high*, ever to appear in the presence of God for us.

Verse 2. *The rod of thy strength*] *The Gospel*—the *doctrine of Christ crucified;* which is the powerful sceptre of the Lord that bought us; is *quick and powerful*, *sharper than any two-edged sword;* and is the power of God to salvation to all them that believe.

The kingdom of our Lord was to be founded in Zion; and thence, by gradual conquests, to be extended over the whole earth. It was in Zion the preaching of the Gospel first began; and it is by the Gospel that Christ *rules*, even *in the midst of his enemies;* for the Gospel extends a moralizing influence over multitudes who do not receive it to their salvation.

Verse 3. *Thy people* shall be *willing in the day of thy power*] This verse has been wofully perverted. It has been supposed to point out the irresistible operation of the grace of God on the souls of the elect, thereby making them willing to receive Christ as their Saviour. Now, whether this doctrine be true or false, it is not in this text, nor can it receive the smallest countenance from it. There has been much spoken against the doctrine of what is called *free will* by persons who seem not to have understood the term. *Will* is a free principle. *Free will* is as absurd as *bound will;* it is not *will* if it be *not free;* and if it be *bound* it is no *will. Volition* is essential to the being of the soul, and to all rational and intellectual beings. This is the most essential discrimination between *matter* and *spirit.* MATTER can have no *choice;* SPIRIT has. Ratiocination is essential to intellect; and from these *volition* is inseparable. God uniformly treats *man* as a *free agent;* and on this principle the whole of Divine revelation is constructed, as is also the doctrine of future rewards and punishments. If man be *forced* to believe, *he* believes not at all; it is the *forcing power* that believes, not the *machine* forced.

If he be forced to *obey*, it is the forcing power that *obeys;* and he, as a machine, shows only the effect of this irresistible force. If man be incapable of *willing good*, and *nilling evil*, he is incapable of being *saved* as a rational being; and if he acts only under an *overwhelming compulsion*, he is as incapable of being damned. In short, this doctrine reduces him either to a *punctum stans*, which by the *vis inertiæ* is incapable of being moved but as acted upon by foreign influence; or, as an intellectual being, to nonentity. "But if the text supports the doctrine laid upon it, vain are all these reasonings." *Granted.* Let us examine the text. The Hebrew words are the following: עמך נדבת ביום חילך *ammecha nedaboth beyom cheylecha*, which literally translated are, *Thy princely people*, or *free people, in the day of thy power;* and are thus paraphrased by the *Chaldee:* "Thy people, O house of Israel, who willingly labour in the law, thou shalt be helped by them in the day that thou goest to battle."

The *Syriac* has: "This praiseworthy people in the day of thy power."

The *Vulgate:* "With thee is the principle or origin (principium) in the day of thy power." And this is referred, by its interpreters, to the Godhead of Christ; and they illustrate it by John i. 1: *In principio erat Verbum*, "In the beginning was the Word."

The *Septuagint* is the same; and they use the word as St. John has it in the Greek text: Μετα σου ἡ αρχη εν ἡμερᾳ της δυναμεως σου· "With thee is the Arche, or principle, in the day of thy power."

The *Æthiopic* is the same; and the *Arabic* nearly so, but rather more express: "The government, رياسة *riasat*, exists with thee in the day of thy power."

The *Anglo-Saxon*, **mid ðe fruma on dæge mægnas þines.** "With thee the principle in day of thy greatness."

The old *Psalter*, **With the begynnyngs in day of thi vertu.** Which it thus paraphrases: "I, the fader begynnyng with the, begynnyng I and thou, an begynnyng of al thyng in day of thi vertu."

Coverdale thus: "In the day of thy power shal my people offre the free-will offeringes with a holy worship." So *Tindal*, *Cardmarden*, *Beck*, and the *Liturgic Version.*

The *Bible* printed by *Barker*, the king's printer, 4to. Lond. 1615, renders the whole verse thus: "Thy people *shall come* willingly at the time *of assembling* thine army in the holy beauty; the youth of thy womb *shall be* as the morning dew."

By the authors of the *Universal History*, vol. iii., p. 223, the whole passage is thus explained: "The Lord shall send the rod, or sceptre, of thy power out of Sion," i. e., out of the tribe of Judah: compare Gen. xlix. 20, and Psa. lxxviii. 68. "Rule thou over thy free-will people;" for none but such are fit to be Christ's subjects: see Matt. xi. 29. "In the midst of thine enemies," Jews and heathens; or, in a spiritual sense, the world, the flesh, and the devil. "In the day of thy power," i. e., when all power shall be given him, both in heaven and earth; Matt. xxviii. 18. "In the beauties of holiness," which is the peculiar characteristic of Christ's reign, and of his religion.

None of the *ancient Versions*, nor of our *modern translations*, give any sense to the words that countenances the doctrine above referred to; it merely expresses the character of the people who shall constitute the kingdom of Christ. נדב *nadab* signifies to be *free, liberal, willing, noble;* and especially *liberality in bringing offerings to the Lord*, Exod. xxv. 2; xxxv. 21, 29. And נדיב *nadib* signifies a *nobleman*, a *prince*, Job xxi. 8; and also *liberality.* נדבה *nedabah* signifies a *free-will offering*—an offering made by superabundant gratitude; one *not commanded:* see Exod. xxxvi. 3; Lev. vii. 16, and elsewhere. Now the עם נדבות *am nedaboth* is the people of liberality—the princely, noble, and generous people; Christ's real subjects; his own children, who form his Church, and are the salt of the world; the bountiful people, who live only to get good from God that they may do good to man. Is there, has there ever been, any religion under heaven that has produced the *liberality*, the *kindness*, the *charity*, that characterize *Christianity?* Well may the followers of Christ be termed the *am nedaboth*—the cheerfully beneficent people. They *hear* his call, come *freely*, stay *willingly*, act *nobly*, live *purely*, and obey *cheerfully.*

The *day of Christ's* power is the time of the Gospel, the reign of the Holy Spirit in the souls of his people. *Whenever* and *wherever* the Gospel is preached in sincerity and purity, *then* and *there* is the day or time of Christ's power. It is the time of his exaltation. The days of his *flesh* were the days of his *weakness;* the time of his *exaltation* is the day of his *power.*

In the beauties of holiness] בהדרי קדש *behadrey kodesh*, "In the splendid garments of holiness." An allusion to the beautiful garments of the high priest. Whatever is intended or expressed by superb garments, they possess, in holiness of heart and life, indicative of their Divine birth, noble dispositions, courage, &c. Their garb is such as becomes the children of so great a King. Or, They shall appear on *the mountains of holiness*, bringing glad tidings to Zion.

From the womb of the morning] As the *dew* flows from the womb of the morning, so shall all the godly from thee. They are *the dew of thy youth;* they are the *offspring* of thy own *nativity.* As the human nature of our Lord was begotten by the creative energy of God in the womb of the Virgin; so the followers of God are born, not of blood, nor of the will of the flesh, but by the Divine Spirit.

Youth may be put here, not only for *young men*, but for *soldiers;*—so the *Trojana juventus* "the Trojan troops," or *soldiers*, in Virgil, Æn. i. ver. 467;—and for persons, courageous, heroic, strong, active, and vigorous. Such were the apostles, and first preachers of the Gospel; and, indeed, all genuine Christians. They may be fully compared to *dew*, for the following reasons:—

1. Like dew, they had their origin from heaven.
2. Like dew, they fructified the earth.
3. Like dew, they were innumerable.
4. Like dew, they were diffused over the earth.
5. Like dew, they came from the morning; the *dawn*, the *beginning* of the *Gospel day* of salvation.

1. As the morning arises in the East, and the *sun*, which produces it, proceeds to the West; so was the coming of the Son of man, and of his disciples and apostles.

2. They began in the East—Asia Proper and

Asia Minor; and shone unto the WEST—Europe, America, &c. Scarcely any part of the world has been hidden from the bright and enlivening power of the Sun of Righteousness; and *now* this glorious sun is walking in the greatness of its strength.

Saw ye not the cloud arise,
Little as a human hand?
Now it spreads along the skies,
Hangs o'er all the thirsty land.
Lo, the promise of a *shower*
Drops already from above;
But the Lord will shortly pour
All the spirit of his love.

The heavenly dew is dropping every where from the womb of the morning; and all the ends of the earth are about to see the salvation of God.

Verse 4. *The Lord hath sworn*] Has most firmly purposed, and will most certainly perform it, feeling himself bound by his *purpose*, as an *honest man* would by his *oath*.

And will not repent] Will never change this purpose; it is perfectly without condition, and without contingency. Nothing is left here to the will of man or angel. Christ shall be incarnated, and the Gospel of his salvation shall be preached over the whole earth. This is an *irresistible decree* of that God who loves mankind.

Thou art *a priest for ever*] The word כהן *cohen* signifies, not only a *priest*, but also a *prince;* as, in the patriarchal times, most heads of families had and exercised both *political* and *sacerdotal authority* over all their descendants. Every priest had a *threefold* office: 1. He was an *instructor* of the family or tribe over which he presided. 2. He *offered sacrifices* for the sins of the people, to reconcile them to God, and give them access to his presence. 3. He was their *mediator*, and interceded for them. So is Christ, the grand, the universal *Instructor*, by his word and Spirit; the *Lamb of God*, who, by his *sacrificial offering* of himself, takes away the sin of the world, and still continues to exhibit himself before the throne in his sacrificial character; and also the great *Mediator* between God and man: and in these characters he is a PRIEST *for ever*. He will instruct, apply the sacrificial offering, and intercede for man, till time shall be no more.

After the order of Melchizedek.] For the elucidation of this point, the reader is requested to refer to the notes on Gen. xiv. 18, 19, and to the *observations* at the end of that chapter, where the subject, relative to the *person*, *name*, and *office* of this ancient king, is fully discussed; and it will be necessary to read that note, &c., as if appended to this place.

Melchizedek was *king of Salem*, that is, *king of Jerusalem;* for *Salem* was its ancient name: but שלם *salem* signifies *peace*, and צדק *tsedek*, *righteousness*. Christ is styled the *Prince of peace;* and he is the *king* that rules in the empire of righteousness; and all *peace* and *righteousness* proceed from him, Heb. vii. 2.

He is *priest after the order of Melchizedek*—after his *pattern;* in the same kind or manner of way in which this ancient king was priest.

Calmet properly observes that there were *three orders* of priesthood. 1. That of *royalty*. All ancient kings being, in virture of their office, *priests* also. This seems to have been considered as the *natural right* of royalty, as it obtained in almost every nation of the earth, from the beginning of the world down to the end of the Roman empire. 2. That of the *first-born.* This right appertained naturally to Reuben, as the first-born in the family of Jacob. 3. That of the *Levites*, instituted by God himself, and taken from *Reuben*, because of his transgression. The Levitical *priesthood* ended with the *Jewish polity;* and that also of the *first-born*, which had been absorbed in it. This *order*, therefore, was not perpetual; it was intended to last only for a time. But that of *royalty* is perpetual, though not now in general use, because founded in what is called *natural right.* It is, therefore, according to this most ancient order, that Christ is a Priest for ever. The kings of England as *heads of the Church*, appointing all bishops, continue to assume, in a certain way, this original right.

Melchizedek is said to be "without father, without mother, without beginning of days, or end of life." We have no account of his *parents;* nothing of his *birth;* nothing of his *death.* Christ, as to his Divine nature, is without father or mother, and without beginning of days; nor can he have any end. Other priests could not continue by reason of death; but he is the Eternal, he cannot die, and therefore can have no successor: *"He is a priest* FOR EVER." Therefore, as Melchizedek was a priest and a king, and had no successor, so shall Christ be: of the increase and government of his kingdom there shall be no end.

Melchizedek was *priest of the Most High God;* and consequently not of *one people* or *nation*, but of the *universe. Aaron* was priest of *one people*, and for a *time* only; JESUS is priest of *all mankind*, and *for ever.* He tasted death for every man; he is the King eternal; he has the keys of hell and of death. As God is the King and Governor of all human beings, Christ, being the *priest of the Most High God*, must also be the *priest for* and *over* all whom this most high God made and governs; and therefore he is the priest, the atoning sacrifice, of the *whole human race.* In this the main similitude consists between the *order of Melchizedek* and *that of Christ.*

Verse 5. *The Lord at thy right hand*] Here *Venema* thinks the Psalm speaks of *David.* As Jesus is at the right hand of God, so he will be at thy hand, giving thee all the support and comfort requisite.

Shall strike through kings] As he did in the case of Abraham, Gen. xiv. 1-16, (for to this there seems to be an allusion,) where he smote *four kings*, and *filled the pits* with the *dead bodies* of their troops. That the allusion is to the above transaction seems the most probable; because in the same chapter, where the *defeat of the four kings* is mentioned, we have the account of *Melchizedek coming to meet Abraham*, and receiving the *tenth of the spoils.*

Verse 6. *He shall judge among the heathen*] David shall greatly extend his dominion, and rule over the *Idumeans, Moabites, Philistines*, &c.

He shall fill—with the dead bodies] He shall fill pits—make heaps of slain; there shall be an immense slaughter among his enemies.

He shall wound the heads] He shall so bring down the power of all the neighbouring kings, as to cause them to acknowledge him as their lord, and pay him tribute.

Verse 7. *He shall drink of the brook in the way*] He shall have sore travail, and but little ease and refreshment: but he shall still go *on* from conquering to conquer.

Therefore shall he lift up the head.] Or *his head.* He shall succeed in all his enterprises, and at last be peaceably settled in his ample dominions.

But these verses, as well as the former, may be applied to our Lord. The fifth verse may be an address to Jehovah: *Adonai at thy right hand,* O Jehovah, *shall smite kings*—bring down all powers hostile to his empire, *in the day of his wrath*—when, after having borne long, he arises and shakes terribly the rulers of the earth.

Ver. 6. *He shall judge,* give laws, *among the heathen*—send his Gospel to the whole *Gentile world. He shall fill* the field of battle with the dead bodies of the slain, who had resisted his empire, and would not have him to reign over them.

He shall wound the heads over many countries.—This must be spoken against some *person* possessing a very extensive sway. Perhaps Antichrist is meant; he who has so *many countries* under his *spiritual domination.* Christ shall destroy every person, and every thing, which opposes the universal spread of his own empire. He will be a *King,* as well as a *Priest* for ever.

Ver. 7. *He shall drink of the brook*—he shall suffer sorely, and even *die* in the struggle: but in that death his enemies shall all perish; and *he shall lift up the head*—he shall rise again from the dead, possessing all power in heaven and earth, *ascend* to the throne of glory, and reign till time shall be no more. He must suffer and die, in order to have the *triumphs* already mentioned.

While all have acknowledged that this Psalm is of the utmost importance, and that it speaks of Christ's *priesthood* and *victories,* it is amazing how various the interpretations are which are given of different passages. I have endeavoured to give the general sense in the preceding notes, and to explain all the particular expressions that have been thought most *difficult:* and by giving the *various readings* from the MSS., have left it to the learned reader to make farther improvements.

It has, however, long appeared to me that there is a *key* by which all the difficulties in the Psalm may be unlocked. As this has not been suggested by any other, as far as I know, I shall without apology lay it before the reader:—

The hundred and tenth Psalm is a WAR SONG, and every phrase and term in it is MILITARY.

1. In the *first* place may be considered here the *proclamation* of the *Divine purpose* relative to the *sacerdotal, prophetic,* and *regal offices* of the LORD JESUS CHRIST: *"Jehovah said unto my Lord,* SIT THOU ON MY RIGHT HAND."

2. A grievous *battle,* and consequent *victory* over the enemy, foretold: I WILL MAKE THINE ENEMIES THE FOOTSTOOL TO THY FEET, ver. 1.

3. The *ensign* displayed: "THE LORD SHALL SEND FORTH THE ROD OF THY STRENGTH;" the *pole* on which the banner shall be *displayed,* at the *head* of his *strength*—his numerous and *powerful forces.*

4. The *inscription, device,* or *motto* on this *ensign:* "RULE THOU IN THE MIDST OF THINE ENEMIES," ver. 2.

5. The *muster of the troops.* A host of bold, spirited *volunteers;* not *mercenaries,* neither *kidnapped* nor *impressed;* but עם נדבות *am nedaboth,* a volunteer people; high-born, loyal subjects; veteran soldiers; every man *bringing gifts* to his General and King.

6. The *regimentals* or *uniform* in which they shall appear: "THE BEAUTIES OF HOLINESS;" הדרי קדש *hadrey kodesh, the splendid garments of holiness.* The apparel showing the *richness* of the *King,* and the *worth* and *order* of the *soldiers;* every man being determined to do his duty, and feeling assured of conquest. The Lacedæmonian soldiers were clothed in *scarlet;* and never went to battle without *crowns* and *garlands* upon their heads, being always sure of victory. *Potter's* Ant., vol. ii., p. 55.

7. The *number* of the troops: THEY SHALL BE AS THE DROPS OF DEW AT BREAK OF DAY:—*innumerable;* and this shall be in consequence ילדתך *yalduthecha,* of *thy nativity*—the *manifestation of Jesus.* THOU shalt be born unto *men;* THEY shall be born of *thy Spirit,* ver. 3.

8. The *title* of the *commander:* "THOU ART A PRIEST," כהן *cohen* a *Priest* and a *Prince.* So was *Agamemnon* in *Homer,* and *Æneas* in *Virgil.* Both were *princes;* both were *priests* and both were *heroes.*

9. The *perpetuity* of this office: "FOR EVER;" לעולם *leolam,* for *futurity*—for *all time*—till the earth and the heavens are no more.

10. The *resolution* of *setting* up such a *Priest* and *King,* and *levying* such an *army:* ACCORDING TO THE ORDER OF MELCHIZEDEK. The *Commander, muster,* and *establishment* of the *corps* shall be according to the *plan* of that *ancient king* and *priest;* or, translating the words literally, על דברתי מלכי צדק *al dabarti malki tsedek,* all shall be executed as *I have spoken to my righteous king;* I have sworn, and will not change my purpose. All my purposes shall be fulfilled. This *speaking* may refer to the *purpose,* ver. 1, confirmed by an *oath,* ver. 4.

11. *Victory* gained: ADONAI AT THY RIGHT HAND HATH TRANSFIXED (מחץ *machats*) KINGS IN THE DAY OF HIS WRATH, i. e., of *battle* and *victory.* Jesus, the Almighty King and Conqueror, fights and gains his battles, while *sitting* at the *right hand* of the *Majesty on high,* ver. 5.

12. *Judgment* instituted and executed: "HE SHALL JUDGE AMONG THE HEATHEN," בגים *baggoyim, among the nations.* He shall bring forth, judge, and condemn his enemies; and he shall *fill pits with the bodies* of executed criminals, ver. 6.

13. *False religion,* supporting itself by the *secular arm,* under the name of *true religion,* shall be destroyed. מחץ ראש על ארץ רבה *machats rosh al erets rabbah;* "He smites the head that is over an extensive land" or country. The *priesthood* that is not according to the *order of Melchizedek* shall be destroyed; and all *government* that is not according to him who is the eternal King and Priest, shall be brought down and annihilated. Who is this great HEAD? this *usurping power?* this *antichristian authority?* Let the Italian archbishop answer, ver. 6.

14. *Refreshment* and *rest,* the fruits of the victories which have been gained: "HE SHALL DRINK OF THE BROOK IN THE WAY; THEREFORE, SHALL HE LIFT UP THE HEAD." He and his victorious army, having defeated and pursued his enemies, and being spent with fatigue and thirst, are refreshed by drinking from a rivulet providentially met with in the way. But the rout being now complete and final,

15. The emperor is proclaimed and *triumphs:*

God lifts up the HEAD,—ראש *rosh*, the CHIEF, the CAPTAIN; as the word often means. Jesus, the *Captain of our salvation*, has a complete *triumph;* eternal peace and tranquillity are established. The *Messiah* is all in all—the last enemy, *Death*, is destroyed. Jesus, having overcome, has sat down with the Father upon his throne; and his *soldiers*, having also overcome through the blood of the Lamb, seated with him on the same throne, are for ever with the Lord. They *see him as he is;* and eternally contemplate and enjoy his glory:—

"Far from a world of grief and sin,
With God eternally shut in."

Hallelujah! The Lord God Omnipotent reigneth! Amen, Amen.

ANALYSIS OF THE ONE HUNDRED AND TENTH PSALM

This Psalm is short in appearance, but deep and copious in mysteries. The subject, without doubt, is *Christ;* since both *St. Peter* (Acts ii. 34) and *St. Paul* (Heb. i. 13) expound it of Christ; and in Matt. xxii. 44 Christ applies it to himself.

In this Psalm Christ is described as a Priest and a King.

I. Christ's kingdom, in the three first verses.

II. His priesthood, from the fourth to the seventh.

I. In reference to his kingdom the prophet acquaints us, 1. With his person; 2. With his power, and the acquisition of it; 3. The continuance of it; 4. The execution of it—First, Over his enemies; Secondly, Over his own people, which is the sum of the three first verses.

1. The person who was to reign was David's Lord; his son according to the flesh, but his Lord as equal to God; Phil. ii. 6, 7. As made flesh, and born of a virgin, the son of David; but as *Immanuel*, the Lord of David, which the Jews not understanding could not reply to Christ's question, Matt. xxii. 45.

2. As to his power, the Author of it was God: "The Lord said to my Lord," &c. Decreed it from everlasting. And again, "The Seed of the woman," &c.

3. And of his kingdom. He took possession, when the Lord said unto him, "Sit thou on my right hand." Christ, as the Son of God, was ever at God's right hand, equal to him in might and majesty; but, as man, was exalted to honour, not before his glorious ascension, Acts ii. 34; Ephes. i. 20; Phil. ii. 9.

4. For the continuance of it. It is to be UNTIL, which notes, not a portion of time, but a perpetuity. "Sit TILL *I* make," &c. Sit at God's right hand, that is, in power and glory, till he shall say to all the wicked, "Depart from me," Matt. xxv., but not so as to be then dethroned. But when once all his enemies shall be made his footstool, then he shall visibly rule, "sitting at his Father's right hand for evermore;" go on to reign, neither desist to propagate and enlarge thy kingdom, till all men bow the knee to thy name, till all opponents be overthrown.

The beginning of this kingdom was in Zion: "The Lord shall send," &c.

1. The rod of his power was his sceptre; that is, "His word, the Gospel, the wisdom of God," 1 Thess. ii. 13; "The sword of the Spirit," Ephes. vi. 17; "The mighty power of God," &c., Rom. i. 16.

2. And this was to be sent out of *Zion*, Isa. xxiii. "It behoved Christ to suffer," &c., Luke xxiv. 46. The sound of the apostle's words went into all lands; but Zion must first hear, Acts xiii. 46.

And now the prophet comes to the execution of his power: "Rule thou in the midst," &c. Converting all such as believe his Gospel, and confounding those who will not have him to reign over them. Now these enemies are the most in number; for the Church however greatly increased, is still surrounded by Turks, Jews, &c. *Rule* thou; be thou Ruler; go on, and set up thy standard universally; for believers are easily dealt with; they love thy government.

1. "For thy people shall be willing." Not forced by compulsion; "they shall flow together as water," Isa. ii.

2. But not before thy grace has brought down their hearts: "In the day of thy power," that is, in the days of thy solemn assemblies, when the Gospel light shall be sent forth, and the apostles and messengers go abroad to preach thy truth.

3. The third quality of this good people is, "that they be holy." For some read the words thus: "They shall offer freewill-offerings with a holy worship." Our last translators point it, "Thy people shall be willing in the day of thy power." Here they pause, and read on thus: "In the beauty of holiness from the womb of the morning." The *Vulgate, In splendoribus sanctorum*, "In the splendour of the saints," and stops there; but let the reading be as it will, all expositors are agreed that holiness must be the ornament of Christ's Church:—

4. Which sanctity these good people have not from themselves, but by the influence of the Holy Spirit, for "they shall worship in the beauty," &c. This is a very difficult place, and the rendering of it is so various, so perplexed by the several modes of pointing it, that the difficulty is increased. But see the notes. The fathers expound this passage of Christ himself, and the later divines, of his people, which is most probable. By their *youth* they understand their regeneration; by the *dews*, the graces bestowed on them; which come immediately from God. The prophet phrases it, "From the womb of the morning." As if the Holy Ghost had said, "The preaching of thy word shall bring forth a great and good people, plentiful as the drops of the morning dew. As the secret and refreshing dews come from heaven to refresh the earth, so thy power, regenerating the hearts of men by the secret operation of thy Holy Spirit, shall produce an immortal seed, children begotten to God. 'Thou hast the dew,' the grace of God, to beautify thy youth, and to make them holy by the direct influence of thy Spirit, to produce entire regeneration."

II. The prophet, having foretold Christ's kingdom, now predicts his priesthood, under which his prophetical office may be implied. That Messiah was to be a priest at his coming, God sware:—

1. "The Lord sware." His word of assurance was given with his oath. In the priesthood of Christ lies the main weight of our redemption; therefore God swears that he shall be a priest to offer himself, and to intercede for us, without which he had in vain been our Prophet and our King.

2. "And will not repent." This is also added for our greater assurance. God is sometimes represented as repenting, as in the case of *Nineveh;* but now that he was to save the world by this Priest, his Son, he takes an oath to do it, and he will not repent. His sentence for judgment is ever conditional; but his decree for mercy is absolute. "He will not repent," &c.

The matter of the oath follows: "Thou art a priest for ever, after the order of Melchizedek."

1. *Thou* is emphatical: *Thou—David's* Lord, art a Priest, and none such a Priest as *thou.*

2. *Art;* for this priest was the *I am;* therefore, justly said, *Thou art.*

3. *A Priest;* whose office the apostle describes, Heb. v. 1.

4. *For ever*—Not as Aaron and his successors, who were priests, &c., Heb. vii. 23, 24.

5. *After the order*—The right, the law, the custom, the rites. See the notes.

6. *Of Melchizedek.*—Which is opposed to the order of *Aaron.* He was not then to be a priest after the order of *Aaron* but by a former and higher order.

The difference lies in this:—

1. In the constitution of him to the priesthood. He was made with an oath; and so were not any of Aaron's order, Heb. vii. 20, 21.

2. In the succession. In Aaron's priesthood, the high priest, being mortal, died, and another succeeded; but this priest, as *Melchizedek,* "had neither beginning of days nor end of life," Heb. vii.

3. *Melchizedek* was priest and king: so was Christ. *Aaron* was only a priest.

4. "Aaron and his sons offered up oxen," &c., Lev. xvi. 6. "But Christ, being holy," &c., offered no sacrifice for *himself,* but for *our* sins, Isa. liii. 9.

5. "Aaron was a local priest; but Christ an universal priest," John iv. 22.

6. "Aaron was anointed with material oil; Christ, with the Holy Ghost," Luke iv. 18, 21.

7. "Aaron's priesthood was temporary; Christ's for ever."

A priest is to be,—

1. A person taken from among men, but select, fit for the office; thus was Christ a perfect man.

2. A priest must be ordained by God: "For no man," &c. "So Christ glorified not himself to be made a high priest." "Thou art my Son," &c.

3. The high priest was ordained of men in things pertaining to God, to be their advocate, mediator, interpreter, and reconciler, in all those things in which men make their addresses to God, or God is to signify his will to them; and so was Christ, for he is the Advocate, the Mediator for his people; he reconciles them to God, he interprets his will to us by preaching his Gospel to the poor.

4. The high priest was ordained that he might offer gifts and sacrifices for sin. Their sacrifices were the blood of bulls, &c.; but Christ was most infinitely precious, even *his own blood,* Eph. v. 2; Heb. ix. 26, x. 10-12.

5. The high priest must have compassion on the ignorant, and those who are out of the way; such was Christ: "For we have not," &c., Heb. iv. 15.

6. Lastly, the high priest was compassed with infirmities; and so was Christ: "In all things it became him," &c. "He took our infirmities," &c.

It remains now to show,—

1. How he is "a priest for ever?"

2. How a priest "after the order of Melchizedek?"

He is "a priest for ever," in respect to his person, office, and effect.

1. In respect of his person and office. For he succeeded no priest, his vocation being immediate. Neither is any to succeed him in this priesthood; "for he lives for ever," and therefore needs not, as the priests under the old law, any successor to continue his priesthood.

2. A priest he is for ever in respect of the effect: because by that sacrifice which he once offered on the cross he purchased the inestimable effects of redemption and eternal salvation, in which sense the priesthood is eternal.

"That Christ is a priest for ever" is evident; but it remains to be shown how he is *a priest after the order*—the rite, the manner, the word, and power given and prescribed to *Melchizedek.*

1. This *Melchizedek* was king of *Salem,* and priest of the most high God, Gen. xiv.; so was Christ a King of *Jerusalem* above, God's own city, and a priest, "offering himself a sacrifice for sin."

2. *Melchizedek* is by interpretation *king of righteousness;* so is Christ *the Lord our righteousness,* Jer. xxiii. 6; 1 Cor. i. 30.

3. *Melchizedek is king of Salem,* i. e., peace; so Christ is the Prince of peace, Isa. ix. 6.

4. "Melchizedek was without father or mother;" so was this our priest, as revealed by God to us, "without beginning of days or end of life," as touching his Godhead.

5. "Melchizedek blessed Abraham;" so Christ us "in turning every one of us away from his iniquities."

6. "Melchizedek brought forth bread and wine to refresh Abraham's army;" so Christ instituted the sacrament, set forth in bread and wine, to refresh the hungry and thirsty souls of his genuine followers.

After the prophet had said "that the Messiah shall be a priest," &c., he intimates in this verse that, notwithstanding all opposition that shall be made against him, yet his priesthood should be eternal; for,

1. "The Lord is on thy right hand." Giving thee power in defence of his Church.

2. "And this thy Lord shall strike through kings," &c. The greatest of thy enemies.

3. "In the day of his wrath." For such a day there is, and it will come, when the proudest tyrant shall not escape.

In the following verse Christ is described as a valiant conqueror.

1. "He shall rule and judge." Not only the Jews, but all people.

2. "He shall fill the places," &c. Make such a slaughter among his enemies, as enraged soldiers do in the storming of a city, when they fill the trenches with the dead bodies.

"He shall wound the heads," &c. Even kings and monarchs, those in the greatest power and authority.

The prophet, through the whole of the Psalm, had spoken of Christ's exaltation: that he was set at God's right hand; by oath was made a priest; and that, in defence of his kingdom and priesthood, he would subdue, conquer, and break to pieces his enemies. In this last verse he tells us by what means he came to this honour: his cross was the way to the crown; his passion and humiliation, to his exaltation: "He," saith David, "shall drink of the brook by the way; therefore, shall he lift up his head;" as if he had said, with the apostle: "He humbled himself, and became obedient to death," &c.

1. "He shall drink." To drink, is to be afflicted, Jer. xlix. 12.

2. "He shall drink of the brook," נחל *nachal*, of the torrent; and that is more than of the cup, for a cup contains but a certain portion of sorrows, but a torrent, a whole flood of miseries. In a cup, that which is drunk may be clear and clean; but in a torrent, a man can expect nothing but muddy and troubled water. Thus the prophet intimates here that the drink offered him should be much and troubled. And in his passion he descended into the depth of the torrent, and drank deep of it.

3. "In the way." On his journey that preceded his resurrection and ascension.

But *claritas humilitatis præmium*, "glory is the reward of humility." Because he thus humbled himself and willingly underwent his death and passion, for the glory of his Father, and the salvation of man; therefore shall God "lift up his head." He shall ascend into heaven; sit on his right hand, and be constituted the Judge of quick and dead. He shall rise from the dead and have all power committed to him in heaven and earth.

PSALM CXI

The psalmist praises the Lord, and extols his works as great, honourable, glorious, and magnificent, 1–4; *his providence and kindness to his followers,* 5–8; *the redemption he has granted to his people,* 9. *The fear of the Lord is the beginning of wisdom,* 10.

A. M. cir. 3469
B. C. cir. 535
Cyri,
R. Persarum,
cir. annum
secundum

PRAISE [a]ye the LORD. [b]I
will praise the LORD with
my whole heart, in the assembly of the upright, and *in*
the congregation.

2 [c]The works of the LORD *are*
great, [d]sought out of all them
that have pleasure therein.
3 His work *is* [e]honourable and
glorious; and his righteousness endureth for
ever.

A. M. cir. 3469
B. C. cir. 535
Cyri,
R. Persarum,
cir. annum
secundum

[a]Heb. *Hallelujah*——[b]Psa. xxxv. 18; lxxxix. 5; cvii. 32; cix. 30; cxlix. 1

[c]Job xxxviii., xxxix., xl., xli.; Psa. xcii. 5; cxxxix. 14; Rev. xv. 3——[d]Psa. cxliii. 5——[e]Psa. cxlv. 4, 5, 10

NOTES ON PSALM CXI

This is one of the *alphabetical* or *acrostic* Psalms: but it is rather different from those we have already seen, as the first *eight* verses contain each *two members;* and each member commences with a consecutive letter of the Hebrew alphabet. But the two last verses are composed of *three members* each, characterized the same way, making *twenty-two members* or hemistichs in the whole, to each of which a consecutive letter of the alphabet is prefixed. But this division is not proper: it should follow the arrangement in the Hebrew poetry, where every hemistich stands by itself, and each contains a complete sense. The Psalm has no *title* in the Hebrew, unless the word *Hallelujah* be considered as such; and the thanksgivings which it contains were probably composed for the benefit of the Jews after their return from captivity.

Verse 1. *I will praise the Lord with* my *whole heart*] If we profess to "sing to the praise and glory of God," the *heart*, and the *whole heart*, without division and distraction, must be employed in the work.

In the assembly] בסוד *besod*, in the *secret assembly*—the *private religious meetings* for the *communion of saints. And in the congregation,* עדה *edah*, the *general assembly—the public congregation.* There were such meetings as the former ever since God had a Church on the earth; and to convey general information, there must be *public assemblies.*

Verse 2. *The works of the Lord* are *great*] גדלים *gedolim, vast* in *magnitude; as* רבים *rabbim* signifies their *multitude* and *variety.*

A. M. cir. 3469
B. C. cir. 535
Cyri,
R. Persarum,
cir. annum
secundum

4 He hath made his wonderful works to be remembered: [f]the LORD *is* gracious and full of compassion.

5 He hath given [g]meat [h]unto them that fear him: he will ever be mindful of his covenant.

6 He hath showed his people the power of his works, that he may give them the heritage of the heathen.

7 The works of his hands *are* [i]verity and judgment; [k]all his commandments *are* sure.

8 [l]They [m]stand fast for ever and ever, *and are* [n]done in truth and uprightness.

A. M. cir. 3469
B. C. cir. 535
Cyri,
R. Persarum,
cir. annum
secundum

9 [o]He sent redemption unto his people: he hath commanded his covenant for ever: [p]holy and reverend *is* his name.

10 [q]The fear of the LORD *is* the beginning of wisdom: [r]a good understanding have all they that [s]do *his commandments:* his praise endureth for ever.

---

[f]Psa. lxxxvi. 5; ciii. 8——[g]Heb. *prey*——[h]Matt. vi. 26, 33——[i]Rev. xv. 3——[k]Psa. xix. 7——[l]Isa. xl. 8; Matt. v. 18——[m]Heb. are *established*——[n]Psa. xix. 9; Rev. xv. 3

[o]Matt. i. 21; Luke i. 68——[p]Luke i. 49——[q]Deut. iv. 6; Job xxviii. 28; Prov. i. 7; ix. 10; Eccles. xii. 13; Ecclus. i. 16——[r]Or, *good success;* Prov. iii. 4——[s]Heb. *that do them*

Sought out] Investigated, carefully examined.

Of all them that have pleasure therein.] By all that delight in them: by every genuine philosopher; every lover of nature; he who traces out the great First Cause by means of his works. And the man that does so will be astonished at the perfections of the Creator, and admire all the operations of his hands.

Verse 3. *His work* is *honourable, &c.*] He has done nothing in *nature* or *grace* that does not redound to his own honour and glory; and because all is done in *righteousness*, it *endureth for ever.*

Verse 4. *He hath made his wonderful works*] He who seeks them out will never *forget* them; and every thing of God's framing is done in such a way, as to strike the imagination, interest the senses, and charm and edify the intellect. But the psalmist may here intend principally the works of God in behalf of the Jewish people; and particularly in their deliverance from the Babylonish captivity, which this Psalm is supposed to celebrate.

Verse 5. *He hath given meat*] טרף *tereph*, PREY. This may allude to the *quails* in the wilderness. The word signifies what is taken in *hunting*—wild beasts, venison, or *fowls* of any kind; particularly such as were proper for food. It also signifies *spoil* taken from enemies. And he may also refer to the wondrous manner in which they were fed and supported during their captivity; and by his support he proved that he was mindful of his covenant. He had promised such blessings; he was faithful to his promises.

Verse 6. *The power of his works*] They have seen that these things did not arrive in the common course of nature; it was not by might nor by power, but by the Spirit of the Lord of hosts they were done. And it required a display of the power of God to give them the heritage of the heathen.

Verse 7. *Verity and judgment*] His works are *verity* or *truth*, because they were wrought for the fulfilment of the promises he made to their fathers. And they were *just;* for their punishment was in consequence of their infidelities: and the punishment of the Babylonians was only in consequence of their gross iniquities; and in both respects he had proved his work to be according to justice and judgment.

Verse 8. *They stand fast for ever*] סמוכים *semuchim*, they are *propped up, buttressed, for ever.* They can never fail; for God's power supports his works, and his providence preserves the record of what he has done.

Verse 9. *He sent redemption*] He sent Moses to redeem them out of Egypt; various *judges* to deliver them out of the hands of their oppressors; Ezra, Nehemiah, and Zerubbabel, to deliver them from Babylon; and the Lord Jesus to redeem a whole lost world from sin, misery, and death.

Holy and reverend is *his name.*] The word *reverend* comes to us from the Latins, *reverendus*, and is compounded of *re*, intensive, and *vereor*, to be *feared;* and *most* or *right* reverend, *reverendissimus*, signifies *to be greatly feared.* These terms are now only titles of ecclesiastical respect, especially in the *Protestant* ministry; but there was a time in which these were no empty titles. Such was the power of the clergy, that, when they walked not in the fear of the Lord, they caused the *people to fear*, and *they themselves* were to *be feared;* but, when the *secular power* was added to the *spiritual*, they were then truly *reverendi* and *reverendissimi, to be feared* and *greatly to be feared.* But *reverend* is not applied to God in this way; nor does the word נורא *nora* bear this signification; it rather means *terrible: Holy and terrible*, or *holy and tremendous, is his name.* This title belongs not to *man;* nor does any minister, in assuming the title *reverend*, assume *this.* Indeed, the word *reverend*, as now used, gives us a very imperfect conception of the original term. *Holy and tremendous is God's name.* He is glorious in holiness, fearful in praises, doing wonders, both in the way of judgment and in the way of mercy.

Verse 10. *The fear of the Lord* is *the beginning of wisdom*] The original stands thus: ראשית חכמה יראת יהוה *reshith chokmah, yirath Yehovah, The beginning of wisdom* is *the fear of Jehovah. Wisdom* itself begins with this *fear;* true *wisdom* has this for its commencement. It is the first ingredient in it, and is an essential part of it. In vain does any man pretend to be *wise* who does *not fear the Lord;* and he who fears the Lord departs from evil: he who lives in sin neither fears God, nor is wise.

A good understanding have all they that do his commandments] These last words we add as necessary to make up the sense; but there is no need of this expedient, as the words of the original literally read thus: "The beginning of wisdom is the fear of Jehovah; good discernment to the doers." That is, They who act according to the dictates of wisdom, the commencement of which is the fear of Jehovah, have a sound understanding, discern their duty and their interest, and live to secure their own peace, their neighbour's good, and God's glory.

Analysis of the Hundred and Eleventh Psalm

It is supposed that this hymn was set by the author to be sung at the passover; and that it might be the more readily learned and remembered, the colons are in number as many as, and arranged in the order of, the letters of the Hebrew alphabet. It is an exhortation to praise God for his wonderful benefits bestowed on the world at large, and especially on Israel and the Church.

There are *three* parts in this Psalm:—

I. A resolution of the psalmist to praise God; the manner in which he would do so; and the company with whom he would do it, ver. 1.

II. An expression of the reasons which moved him to praise God, viz., his admirable benefits, special and general, ver. 2-9.

III. An inference from the premises by way of sentiment in which he commends the fear of God, ver. 10.

I. The title of this Psalm is, "Hallelujah, praise ye the Lord;" and he adds,—

1. "I will praise the Lord." And shows how it should be done.

2. Not hypocritically; not with the lips only, but "with the heart."

3. "With the whole heart."

4. Not only secretly, but also "in the assembly of the upright," &c. 1. Both in the assembly, where these good and upright men are. 2. And also in a mixed multitude, and secretly among good men.

II. And, having made a pious confession of his readiness to practise the duty, he next sets down the ground and matter of his praise.

First. His works of *power*, in the creation and conservation of the world, or the favours shown to the Church: "And these works of the Lord are great." 1. *Great*, not only for variety and beauty, but also in base creatures his wisdom is admirable, and to be admired. 2. *Great;* for it was great to take to himself a people out of another people, to make a covenant with them, and to reveal his promises, and give them a law, to settle among them a policy for Church and state. 3. Fools and impious men, indeed, but little consider these works; they think not of their Author: but in the eyes of all wise men "they are sought out," &c.

Secondly. His works of wisdom, in governing the creatures he has created, and in guiding and collecting his Church. 1. It is *honourable;* and much more so its Author. 2. And *glorious;* far above the works of princes. 3. And *righteous:* "He is a righteous God, and his righteousness endureth for ever." For he never departs from the exact rule of justice.

Which record must be kept:—

"He hath made his wonderful works," &c. As in the Jewish hosts.

Thirdly. His works of *mercy.* They proceed from mere mercy: "For the Lord is gracious," &c. 1. "Gracious," in doing these works. 2. "Full of compassion," as a father towards his children.

Of these the prophet gives several instances:—

1. "He hath given meat," &c. He nourished his people for forty years in the wilderness, giving them meat from heaven.

2. "He will ever be mindful," &c. Notwithstanding their provocations.

3. "He hath showed his people," &c. As in the turning of *Jordan* backwards, overthrowing *Jericho*, staying the sun and moon, &c.

4. "That he might give them," &c. By the expulsion of the Canaanites: "The works of the Lord are great," &c.

He now uses an acclamation: "The works of his hands are,"—

1. *Verity.* Making good his promise to *Abraham.*

2. *Judgment.* Executed on idolaters and profane persons.

And shows unto all the world that,—

1. "All his commandments are sure." That his laws, especially his moral laws, are of everlasting obligation on all.

2. That these commands "stand fast for ever;" for they are established in truth, equity, justice, and reason.

The prophet next speaks of a mercy far exceeding all the rest, the work of human redemption by Christ. This may be thus expounded, and better than in reference to the redemption of Israel out of Egypt.

1. "He sent redemption," &c. A Redeemer so long promised.

2. "He hath commanded his covenant," &c. Which is still extant.

III. The prophet, having enumerated many of God's works of power, wisdom, and mercy, concludes the Psalm with three acclamations.

"Holy and reverend," &c. Either in his service, or whenever he is signified.

1. *Holy*—unpolluted by hypocrisy. The command is, "Be ye holy, for I am holy."

2. *Reverend*—not rashly or negligently performed. Or, as some read it, *terrible;* and it is a fearful thing to fall into the hands of the living God.

The second acclamation follows upon the preceding:—

1. This fear "is the beginning of wisdom." For these men begin to be wise; "to eschew evil, and do good."

2. This fear, if it be right, will be practical: "For a good understanding," &c.

The third acclamation is, "His praise endureth for ever." Which some refer to God, others to man; but both are true. For the praise must continue for ever: "His power, mercy," &c.

If referred to man then the sense will be,—

1. "His praise." For "they that dwell in thy house," &c.; Psa. lxxxiv. 4.

2. Or "His praise." The commendation of a good man "will be had in everlasting remembrance," Psa. cxii. 6. "The name of the wicked shall rot," &c.; Prov. x. 7. "Well done, thou good and faithful servant," &c.; Matt. xxv. 21. His praise is in this world lasting, but in the world to come everlasting.

PSALM CXII

***The blessedness of the man that fears the Lord, both as it regards himself and his family,* 1–3; *his conduct to his family, his neighbours, and the poor,* 4–9; *the envy of the wicked at his prosperity,* 10.**

A. M. cir. 3469
B. C. cir. 535
Cyri,
R. Persarum,
cir. annum
secundum

PRAISE [a]ye the LORD. [b]Blessed *is* the man *that* feareth the LORD, *that* [c]delighteth greatly in his commandments.

2 [d]His seed shall be mighty upon earth: the generation of the upright shall be blessed.

3 [e]Wealth and riches *shall be* in his house: and his righteousness endureth for ever.

4 [f]Unto the upright there ariseth light in the darkness: *he is* gracious, and full of compassion, and righteous.

5 [g]A good man showeth favour, and lendeth: he will guide his affairs [h]with [i]discretion.

6 Surely [k]he shall not be moved for ever: [l]the righteous shall be in everlasting remembrance.

A. M. cir. 3469
B. C. cir. 535
Cyri,
R. Persarum,
cir. annum
secundum

7 [m]He shall not be afraid of evil tidings: his [n]heart is fixed, [o]trusting in the LORD.

8 His heart *is* established, [p]he shall not be afraid until he [q]see *his desire* upon his enemies.

9 [r]He hath dispersed, he hath given to the poor, [s]his righteousness endureth for ever; his [t]horn shall be exalted with honour.

10 [u]The wicked shall see *it,* and be grieved; [v]he shall gnash with his teeth, and [w]melt away: [x]the desire of the wicked shall perish.

---

[a]Heb. *Hallelujah*——[b]Psa. cxxviii. 1——[c]Psa. cxix. 16, 35, 47, 70, 143——[d]Psa. xxv. 13; xxxvii. 26; cii. 28
[e]Matt. vi. 33——[f]Job xi. 17; Psa. xcvii. 11——[g]Psa. xxxvii. 26; Luke vi. 35——[h]Eph. v. 15; Col. iv. 5
[i]Heb. *judgment*——[k]Psa. xv. 5——[l]Prov. x. 7

[m]Prov. i. 33——[n]Psa. lvii. 7——[o]Psa. lxiv. 10
[p]Prov. iii. 33——[q]Psa. lix. 10; cxviii. 7——[r]2 Cor. ix. 9
[s]Deut. xxiv. 13; ver. 3——[t]Psa. lxxv. 10——[u]See Luke xiii. 28——[v]Psalm xxxvii. 12——[w]Psalm lviii. 7, 8
[x]Prov. x. 28; xi. 7

NOTES ON PSALM CXII

This is another of the acrostic or alphabetical Psalms, under the title *Hallelujah.* It is formed exactly as the preceding in the division of its verses. It has *ten* verses in the whole: the first eight contain each two hemistichs, beginning with a consecutive letter of the alphabet; the *ninth* and *tenth* verses, three each, making twenty-two in the whole. It is understood to have been written after the captivity, and probably by Zechariah and Haggai: to them it is ascribed by the Vulgate.

Verse 1. *Blessed* is *the man* that *feareth the Lord*] This seems to be the continuation of the preceding Psalm: *there* it was asserted that the *beginning of wisdom was the fear of the Lord;* and *here* the blessedness of the man who *thus fears* is stated.

That *delighteth greatly*] It is not enough to *fear God*, we must also *love him: fear* will deter us from *evil; love* will lead us to *obedience.* And the more a man fears and loves God, the more obedient will he be; till at last he *will delight greatly in the commandments* of his Maker.

Verse 2. *His seed shall be mighty*] זרעו *zaro,* his *posterity.* So the word should always be understood in this connection.

Verse 3. *Wealth and riches* shall be *in his house*] This is often the case: a godly man must save both *time* and *money.* Before he was converted he lost much time, and squandered his money. All this he now saves, and therefore wealth and riches must be in his house; and if he do not distribute to the necessities of the poor, they will continue to accumulate till they be his curse; or God will, by his providence, sweep them away. Both צדקה *tsedakah* and *δικαιοσυνη* are often used to signify, not only *justice* and *righteousness,* but also *beneficence* and *almsgiving;* and this is most probably the meaning here. See ver. 9.

Verse 4. *There ariseth light in the darkness*] The upright are always happy; and when tribulations come, God lifts up the light of his countenance upon him, and causes all occurences to work together for his good.

He is *gracious, and full of compassion, and righteous.*] He enjoys the *favour* of God; that *grace* makes him *compassionate;* and in the general tenor of his conduct he is righteous. From these principles he *shows favour* (ver. 5) to him that *needs* it; that is, to the real poor he *gives* of his substance; and others he obliges by *lending,* they not being utterly in want, but standing in need only of a little *present help.* But he takes heed to *whom* he *gives* and to *whom* he *lends;* that in the first case his bounty may be well applied, and in the second he may not oblige the person who only seeks, under the notion of a *loan,* to appropriate the money *borrowed.* To prevent evils of this kind he acts prudently, and *guides his affairs with discretion,* ver. 5.

Verse 7. *He shall not be afraid of evil tidings*] He knows that God governs the world, therefore he fears not for futurity. And as to the *calumnies* of men, he fears *them* not, because *his heart is fixed*—determined to walk in the path of duty, whatever persecutions he may suffer, for *he trusts in the Lord.*

Verse 8. *His heart* is *established*] סמוך לבו *samuch libbo,* "his heart is propped up;" he is *buttressed up* by the strength of his Maker.

Verse 9. *He hath dispersed*] He has scattered abroad his munificence; he has given particularly to the *poor;* his *righteousness*—his almsgiving, his charity, *remaineth for ever.* See on ver. 3.

His horn] His power and authority *shall be exalted with honour.* He shall rise to influence only through his own worth, and not by extortion or flattery.

Verse 10. *The wicked shall see* it] רשע *rasha,* the *wicked one.* Some think *Satan* is meant. It is distinguished from רשעים *reshaim, wicked men,* in the conclusion of the verse.

Shall gnash with his teeth] Through spite and ill will.

And melt away] Through envy and hopeless expectation of similar good; for *his desire* in reference to *himself,* and in reference to him who is the object of his *envy, shall perish*—shall come to nothing.

Analysis of the Hundred and Twelfth Psalm

The psalmist, having put it down for an infallible maxim, in the close of the former Psalm, "that the fear of the Lord is the beginning of wisdom," in this sets down the felicity of that man who fears God, in several particulars.

There are two parts in this Psalm:—

I. A general proposition, that he is blessed.

II. An enumeration of particulars in which that blessedness consists, from ver. 2 to the end.

I. To the first part he prefixes a hallelujah, "praise the Lord," which is the intent and scope of the Psalm; that he be praised for those rewards of piety he bestows on such as fear him.

He delivers this one general proposition to persuade them to piety: "Blessed is the man," &c., that believes, honours, and serves him.

For fear a man should mistake, supposing he fears the Lord when he really does not, he adds these three restrictions to his proposition:—

1. "Keep his commandments." An obedient fear.

2. "He delights in them," &c. Is pleased with their equity, and loves them.

3. "He delights greatly," &c. It must be a thankful and ready fear, performed with alacrity and earnestness, done with all the heart.

II. In the rest of the Psalm he insists on what this blessedness consists in:—

1. That the righteous shall have temporal goods, and that they shall be blessings.

2. That though they shall enjoy them, they are not exempted from crosses, 2 Tim. iii. 12.

3. That God distributes these temporal blessings not equally, but most profitably for him.

This being premised, he enumerates the blessings here promised:—

1. "His seed shall be mighty," &c. Which was verified in Abraham and his posterity: "I will show mercy to thousands," &c.

2. "Wealth and riches," &c. That is, abundance of all things *shall be in his house,* and remain in it for his just dealing; and contentment preserves his well obtained goods to his posterity.

3. "Unto the upright there ariseth light," &c. The light of counsel and consolation, in the midst of doubts, tribulations, and afflictions, which the prophet ascribes to God's mercy and goodness.

4. He hath bowels of compassion, of which he shows two effects: 1. "A good man showeth favour," &c. Easily forgives an injury. 2. Imagines he is not born for himself, but to do good to others.

5. "He will guide his affairs with discretion." Discern between truth and falsehood; be no accepter of persons, but in all things just and upright.

6. He is patient and constant. Troubles and dangers may increase; but in the midst of all he looks to heaven, and remains firm in his principles.

7. "The righteous shall be had," &c. His name is written in the book of life, and it is precious in the Church, such as those of the martyrs; while the wicked are detested, such as Judas, Cain, Pilate. At the last day the one shall have "Come, ye blessed;" the other, "Go, ye cursed."

8. "He shall not be afraid of evil tidings." Scandals may arise; but he remembers "the servant is not above his lord," therefore he bears all patiently, and for these reasons: 1. "Because his heart is fixed," &c. He has a sure rock; God will clear his innocency. 2. "His heart is established," &c. He knows God will take care of him.

9. The ninth felicity to the righteous is, God has given him a charitable heart. 1. "He hath dispersed," acts liberally, that others as well as himself may reap. 2. He does it freely, without looking for any thing again: "He gives." 3. "He hath given to the poor." To those who need his kindness.

For this liberality he is a great gainer in two respects:—

1. "The good work he hath done," &c. His charity and piety are increased by it.

2. "His horn," &c. His power, honour, dignity, and glory.

His last felicity is,

1. "The wicked shall see it," and be grieved at his felicity.

2. "He shall gnash his teeth" as a mad dog, and seek his ruin.

3. But shall not be able to harm him: "The desire of the wicked shall perish." He that fears God is a happy man; he that fears him not, most unhappy. Reader, in what state art thou? Happy or unhappy?

PSALM CXIII

An exhortation to bless God for his own excellencies, 1–6; *and for his great mercy to the poor and necessitous*, 7–9.

A. M. cir. 3469
B. C. cir. 535
Cyri,
R. Persarum,
cir. annum
secundum

PRAISE [a]ye the LORD.
[b]Praise, O ye servants of
the LORD, praise the name of
the LORD.
2 [c]Blessed be the name of the LORD from
this time forth and for evermore.
3 [d]From the rising of the sun unto the going
down of the same the LORD's name is to be
praised.
4 The LORD *is* [e]high above all nations, *and*
[f]his glory above the heavens.
5 [g]Who *is* like unto the LORD our
God, who [h]dwelleth on
high.
6 [i]Who humbleth *himself* to
behold *the things that are* in
heaven, and in the earth!
7 [k]He raiseth up the poor out of the dust,
and lifteth the needy out of the dunghill;
8 That he may [l]set *him* with princes, *even*
with the princes of his people.
9 [m]He maketh the barren woman [n]to keep
house, *and to be* a joyful mother of children.
Praise ye the LORD.

A. M. cir. 3469
B. C. cir. 535
Cyri,
R. Persarum,
cir. annum
secundum

[a]Heb. *Hallelujah*——[b]Psa. cxxxv. 1——[c]Dan. ii. 20——[d]Isa. lix. 19; Mal. i. 11——[e]Psa. xcvii. 9; xcix. 2——[f]Psa. viii. 1——[g]Psa. lxxxix. 6——[h]Heb. *exalteth himself to dwell*

[i]Psa. xi. 4; cxxxviii. 6; Isa. lvii. 15——[k]1 Sam. ii. 8; Psa. cvii. 41——[l]Job xxxvi. 7——[m]1 Sam. ii. 5; Psa. lxviii. 6; Isa. liv. 1; Gal. iv. 27——[n]Heb. *to dwell in a house*

NOTES ON PSALM CXIII

Psalms cxiii., cxiv., cxv., cxvi., cxvii., and cxviii., form the great *Hallel*, and were sung by the Jews on their most solemn festivals, and particularly at the *passover*. To these reference is made by the *evangelists*, Matt. xxvi. 30, and Mark xiv. 26, there called the *hymn* which Jesus and his disciples sung at the passover, for the whole of the Psalms were considered as one grand hymn or thanksgiving. It was probably composed after the return from the captivity. It has no title but *Hallelujah* in the *Hebrew* and ancient *Versions*.

Verse 1. *Praise, O ye servants*] Probably an address to the Levites. The Anglo-Saxon has **heriað cnapan drihꞇ**, *praise the Lord, ye knaves*. Knapa or knave signified among our ancestors a *servant;* sometimes a *male, a young man.*

Verse 3. *From the rising of the sun*] From morning to evening be always employed in the work. Or it may be a call on *all mankind* to praise God for his innumerable mercies to the *human race.* Praise him from *one end of the world unto the other.* And therefore the psalmist adds,

Verse 4. *The Lord* is *high above all nations*] He governs all, he provides for all; therefore let all give him praise.

Verse 5. *Who* is *like unto the Lord*] Those who are highly exalted are generally unapproachable; they are proud and overbearing; or so surrounded with *magnificence* and *flatterers*, that to them the poor have no access; but *God, though infinitely* exalted, *humbleth himself to behold* even *heaven* itself, and much more does he *humble himself* when he condescends to behold *earth* and her inhabitants; (ver. 6.) But so does he love his creatures that he rejoices over even the meanest of them to do them good.

Verse 7. *He raiseth up the poor*] The poorest man, in the meanest and most abject circumstances, is an object of his merciful regards. He may here allude to the wretched state of the captives in Babylon, whom God raised up out of that dust and dunghill. Others apply it to the resurrection of the dead.

Verse 8. *With the princes*] נדיבים *nedebim* very properly translated by the Anglo-Saxon **ealdormannum,** the aldermen, the most respectable of his people.

Verse 9. *He maketh the barren woman to keep house*] This is a figure to point out the *desolate, decreasing state* of the captives in Babylon, and the happy change which took place on their return to their own land. These are nearly the words of Hannah, 1 Sam. ii. 5.

ANALYSIS OF THE HUNDRED AND THIRTEENTH PSALM

The scope of this Psalm is the same with those that went before, that is, to excite men to praise God.

This Psalm contains three parts:—

I. An exhortation to God's servants to praise him.

II. A form set down how and where to praise him, ver. 2, 3.

III. The reasons to persuade us to it. 1. By his infinite power, ver. 4, 5. 2. His providence, as displayed in heaven and earth, ver. 6.

I. The prophet exhorts men "to praise the Lord;" and,

1. He doubles and trebles his exhortation, that it be not coldly but zealously done, or else to show that he alone is worthy of praise.

2. "Praise the Lord, O ye servants," &c.: They are to praise him, for he is their Lord; praise him likewise with a pure heart.

II. The manner of praising him. Say,

1. "Blessed be the name of the Lord." Job i.

2. "From this time forth," &c.: In prosperity or adversity, in this life or the future.

3. "From the rising of the sun," &c.: In all places, even over all the world.

III: And now follow the reasons to persuade men to praise God.

1. Because of his majesty, infinite power, and glory, which extend not to earth alone, but heaven also: "The Lord is high above," &c.

2. Because of his providence, benignity, and bounty, which being united with so much majesty, appear the more admirable. "Who is like the Lord," &c. None in heaven or on earth are to be compared to him. "Yet he

humbleth himself," &c. He is present with the highest angels, and with the poorest of his creatures, to help them.

In "humbling himself to behold the things on earth" he gives two instances: 1. In states and kingdoms. 2. In private families.

1. In states: "He raiseth up the poor," &c.: Let then no man say, that God does not regard them that are of low estate; he raiseth up the poor, to the end "that he may set him with the princes," &c.

2. In private families: "He maketh the barren woman," &c. "Children are a heritage of the Lord." Some expositors refer the meaning of this last verse to the Church of the *Gentiles:* "Rejoice, O barren," &c. Isa. liv. 1.

PSALM CXIV

Miracles wrought at the exodus of the Israelites from Egypt, at the Red Sea, and at Jordan, 1–6; *and at the rock of Horeb,* 7, 8.

XXIII. DAY. EVENING PRAYER

A. M. cir. 3469
B. C. cir. 535
Cyri,
R. Persarum,
cir. annum
secundum

WHEN [a]Israel went out of
Egypt, the house of Jacob
[b]from a people of strange language;
2 [c]Judah was his sanctuary, *and* Israel his
dominion.
3 [d]The sea saw *it*, and fled: [e]Jordan was
driven back.
4 [f]The mountains skipped like rams, *and*
the little hills like lambs.
5 [g]What *ailed* thee, O thou
sea, that thou fleddest? thou
Jordan, *that* thou wast driven
back?
6 Ye mountains, *that* ye skipped like rams;
and ye little hills, like lambs?
7 Tremble, thou earth, at the presence
of the LORD, at the presence of the God of
Jacob;
8 [h]Which turned the rock *into* a standing
water, the flint into a fountain of waters.

A. M. cir. 3469
B. C. cir. 535
Cyri,
R. Persarum,
cir. annum
secundum

---

[a]Exodus xiii. 3——[b]Psalm lxxxi. 5——[c]Exodus vi. 7; xix. 6; xxv. 8; xxix. 45, 46; Deuteronomy xxvii. 9 [d]Exodus xiv. 21; Psalm lxxvii. 16

[e]Joshua iii. 13, 16——[f]Psalm xxix. 6; lxviii. 16 [g]Hab. iii. 8 [h]Exodus xvii. 6; Numbers xx. 11; Psalm cvii. 35

NOTES ON PSALM CXIV

This Psalm has no *title*. The word *Hallelujah* is prefixed in all the Versions except the *Chaldee* and *Syriac*. It seems like a fragment, or a part of another Psalm. In many MSS. it is only the *beginning* of the following; both making but one Psalm in all the Versions, except the *Chaldee*. It is elegantly and energetically composed; but begins and ends very abruptly, if we separate it from the following. As to the *author* of this Psalm, there have been various opinions; some have given the honour of it to *Shadrach, Meshech,* and *Abed-nego;* others to *Esther;* and others, to *Mordecai.*

Verse 1. *A people of strange language*] This may mean no more than a *barbarous* people; a people whom they did not know, and who did not worship their God. But it is a fact that the language of the Egyptians in the time of Joseph was so different from that of the Hebrews that they could not understand each other. See Psa. lxxxi. 5; Gen. xlii. 23.

The *Chaldee* has here מעמי ברבראי *meammey barbarey*, which gives reason to believe that the word is *Chaldee*, or more properly *Phœnician*. See this word fully explained in the note on Acts xxviii. 2. My old *Psalter* understood the word as referring to the *religious* state of the Egyptians: **In gangyng of Isrel oute of Egipt, of the house of Jacob fra hethen folke.**

Verse 2. *Judah was his sanctuary*] He set up his true worship among the Jews, and took them for his peculiar people.

And *Israel his dominion.*] These words are a proof, were there none other, that this Psalm was composed *after* the days of David, and *after* the division of the tribes, for then the distinction of *Israel* and *Judah* took place.

Verse 3. *The sea saw* it, *and fled*] Mr. Addison has properly observed (see Spect. No. 461) that the author of this Psalm designedly works for effect, in pointing out the miraculous driving back the Red Sea and the river Jordan, and the commotion of the hills and mountains, without mentioning any *agent*. At last, when the reader sees the sea rapidly retiring from the shore, Jordan retreating to its source, and the mountains and hills running away like a flock of affrighted sheep, that the passage of the Israelites might be every where uninterrupted; then the *cause* of all is suddenly introduced, and the *presence of God* in his grandeur solves every difficulty.

Verse 5. *What* ailed *thee, O thou sea*] The original is very abrupt; and the *prosopopœia*, or personification very fine and expressive:—

What to thee, O sea, that thou fleddest away!
O Jordan, that thou didst roll back!
Ye mountains, that ye leaped like rams!
And ye hills, like the young of the fold!

After these very sublime interrogations, God appears; and the psalmist proceeds as if answering his own questions:—

At the appearance of the Lord, O earth, thou
didst tremble;
At the appearance of the strong God of Jacob.
Converting the rock into a pool of waters;
The granite into water springs.

I know the present Hebrew text reads חולי *chuli*, "tremble thou," in the *imperative;* but almost all the *Versions* understood the word in *past* tense, and read as if the psalmist was answering his own questions, as stated in the translation above. "Tremble thou, O earth." As if he had said, Thou mayest well tremble, O earth, at the presence of the Lord, at the presence of the God of Jacob.

Verse 8. *The flint*] I have translated חלמיש *challamish*, GRANITE; for such is the rock of Horeb, a piece of which now lies before me.

This short and apparently imperfect Psalm, for elegance and sublimity, yields to few in the whole book.

It is so well translated in the old *Psalter*, that I think I shall gratify the reader by laying it before him.

Ver. 1. **In gangyng of Isrel oute of Egipt,**
Of the house of Jacob fra hethen folke.
Ver. 2. **Made is Jude his halawyng**
Isrel might of hym.
Ver. 3. **The se sawe and fled,**
Jurdan turned is agayne;
Ver. 4. **Hawes gladed als wethers,**
And hilles als lambes of schepe.
Ver. 5. **What is to the se, that thou fled?**
And thou Jordane that thou ert turned agayne?
Ver. 6. **Hawes gladded als wethers?**
And hils als lambs of schepe.
Ver. 7. **Fra the face of Lorde styrde is the erth,**
Fra the face of God of Jacob;
Ver. 8. **That turnes the stane in stank of waters,**
And roche in wels of waters.

And, as a still more ancient specimen of our language, I shall insert the Anglo-Saxon, with a literal reading, line for line, as near to the Saxon as possible, merely to show the affinity of the languages.

Ver. 1. **On uꞇᵹanᵹe Iꞅꞃael oꝼ Eᵹẏpꞇan;**
huꞅ Iacob oꝼ ꝼolce ælðeoꝺiᵹum.
Ver. 2. **ᵹeƿoꞃꝺen iꞅ Iuꝺea halᵹune hiꞅ,**
Iꞅꞃael anꝺƿealꝺ hiꞅ.
Ver. 3. **Sæ ᵹeꞅeah ⁊ ꝼleah**
Ioꞃꝺan ᵹeciꞃꞃeꝺ iꞅ unꝺeꞃbæc.
Ver. 4. **Munꞇaꞅ hi ꝼæᵹnoꝺon ꞅƿa ꞃammaꞅ**
⁊ beoꞃᵹaꞅ ꞅƿa ꞅƿa lamb ꞅceap.
Ver. 5. **Hƿæꞇ iꞅ ðe ꞅæ ꝥ þu ꝼluᵹe**
⁊ þu ea, ꝼoꞃðon ᵹecyꞃꞃeꝺ iꞅ unꝺeꞃbæc?
Ver. 6. **Munꞇaꞅ ᵹeꝼæᵹnoꝺon ꞅƿa ꞅƿa ꞃammaꞅ**
⁊ hylla ꞅƿa ꞅƿa lambꞃa ꞅceapa.
Ver. 7. **ꝼꞃam anꞅine ꝺꞃihꞇneꞅ aꞅꞇyꞃoꝺ iꞅ eoꞃðe**
ꝼꞃam anꞅine ᵹoꝺeꞅ Iacob
Ver. 8. **Seðe ᵹecyꞃꝺe ꞅꞇan on meꞃe ƿæꞇeꞃa**
⁊ cluꝺaꞅ on ƿyllan ƿæꞇeꞃa.

Ver. 1. On outgang Israel of Egypt,
House Jacob of folk foreigners;
Ver. 2. Made is Jacob holyness his;
Israel andweald (government) his.
Ver. 3. Sea saw, and flew!
Jordan turned underback!
Ver. 4. Mounts they fain (rejoiced) so (as) rams,
And burghs (hillocks) so (as) lamb-sheep.
Ver. 5. What is the sea, that thou flew?
And thou river for that thou turned is underback?
Ver. 6. Mounts ye fained (rejoiced) so so rams;
And hills so so lambs-sheep.
Ver. 7. From sight Lord's stirred is earth;
From sight God of Jacob.
Ver. 8. Who turned stone in mere waters;
And cliffs in wells waters.

I have retained some words above in nearly their Saxon form, because they still exist in our old writers; or, with little variation, in those of the present day:—

Ver. 2. *Andweald*, government. Hence *weal* and *wealth*, *commonweal* or *wealth;* the general government, that which produces the *welfare* of the country.

Ver. 4. *Fægnodon*, fained—desired fervently, felt delight in expectation.

Ver 4. *Burgh*, a hill—a mound or heap of earth, such as was raised up over the dead. Hence a *barrow;* and hence the word *bury*, to inhume the dead.

Ver. 8. *Mere*, or meer, a large pool of water, a lake, a *lough*, still in use in the north of England. Gentlemen's ponds, or large sheets of water so called; and hence *Winander-mere*, a large lake in Westmoreland. Mere also signifies *limit* or *boundary;* hence the *Mersey*, the river which divides Lancashire from Cheshire, and serves as a *boundary* to both counties. The *mere* that spreads itself out to the *sea*.

Instead of *cludas*, which signifies *rocks*, one MS. has **clyꝼ** *clyf*, which signifies *a craggy mountain* or *broken rock*.

The reader will see from this specimen how much of our ancient language still remains in the present; and perhaps also how much, in his opinion, we have amplified and improved our mother tongue.

Analysis of the Hundred and Fourteenth Psalm

David in this Psalm chants forth the wonderful works and miracles that God wrought, when he brought forth Israel out of Egypt.

This Psalm has *two* parts:—

I. A narration of Israel's deliverance, amplified by the state they were in, ver. 1; the state to which they were brought, ver. 2; the miracles then done, ver. 3; and the law given, ver. 4.

II. A *prosopopœia* set down by way of dialogue: 1. The prophet asks the sea and *Jordan* why they fled, ver. 5, 6. 2. To which the answer is, that "the earth trembled," &c., ver. 7, 8.

I. In the narration, Israel's condition is set down by way of comparison, in order that their deliverance might make the deeper impression. We must recollect that *Jacob* and *Judah* in this place signify the whole nation of the Israelites that descended out of Jacob's loins; but of the house of *Jacob* there is made particular mention, because with him they came into *Egypt;* and of *Judah*, because from him they were called *Jews*. This being premised. 1. We are presented with the condition of the Jews *before* their deliverance; before they were formed into a state or Church; they were among "a people of a strange language."

2. The condition of the Jews *after* their deliverance: "When Israel went out of Egypt," &c., then "Judah was his sanctuary," &c. 1. "His sanctuary:" A people sanctified and adopted by him, consecrated to his worship as holy temples and sanctuaries, and having a holy priest to govern them in points of piety. 2. "His dominion:" In which he reigned as King by his laws and Spirit, and appointed godly magistrates to rule them in matters of policy; for the government was a theocracy, till they cast it off by choosing a king.

The prophet explains the manner of their

deliverance, which was by miracles and signs; and gives us these instances:—

1. "The sea saw it, and fled," as the people advanced to it. "At the presence of the Lord it turned back all night," Exod. xiv. In a poetical strain he attributes this to the sense of the sea. "The sea saw," &c.

2. "Jordan was driven back," &c. Forty years after, when they were entering the promised land, then Jordan suffered a long reflux, Josh. iv.

3. At *Sinai*, when the law was given, then the mountains and hills quaked: "The mountains skipped like rams," &c.

II. This Psalm abounds with poetical imagery; and having related the wonderful deliverances wrought for God's people, the psalmist expostulates with the sea and mountains, and interrogates them as to what so strangely altered their course. "What ailed thee, O thou sea, &c.?—Ye mountains that ye skipped like rams," &c.

To which, in the person of the earth speaking to herself, the prophet answers; thus making both a *prosopopœia* and an *apostrophe*.

1. "Tremble, thou earth, at the presence of the Lord," &c. As if it had been said, Would you know the reason why we fly? The cause is, the Lord has appeared and showed his force and power, and laid his commands upon us; and therefore, not abiding his presence, the mountains are moved, &c.

2. Of his power this miracle is sufficient for an instance: "Which turned the rock into a standing water, the flint into a fountain of waters." Causing not only waters to flow from thence, but turning the very substance of a flint, which is apter to yield fire than water, into that fluid element, Num. xx. [See the note on ver. 8.]

PSALM CXV

God alone is to be glorified, 1–3. *The vanity of idols*, 4–8. *Israel, the house of Aaron, and all that fear God, are exhorted to trust in the Lord*, 9–11. *The Lord's goodness to his people, and his gracious promises*, 12–16. *As the dead cannot praise him, the living should*, 17, 18.

A. M. cir. 3469
B. C. cir. 535
Cyri,
R. Persarum,
cir. annum
secundum

NOT [a]unto us, O LORD, not
unto us, but unto thy name
give glory, for thy mercy, *and*
for thy truth's sake.

2 Wherefore should the heathen say, [b]Where
is now their God?

3 [c]But our God *is* in the heavens: he hath done whatsoever
he hath pleased.

4 [d]Their idols *are* silver and
gold, the work of men's hands.

5 They have mouths, but they speak not:

[a]See Isa. xlviii. 11; Ezek. xxxvi. 32——[b]Psa. xlii. 3, 10; lxxix. 10; Joel ii. 17

[c]1 Chron. xvi. 26; Psa. cxxxv. 6; Dan. iv. 35——[d]Deut. iv. 28; Psa. cxxxv. 15, 16, 17; Jer. x. 3, &c.

NOTES ON PSALM CXV

This Psalm is written as a part of the preceding by *eighteen* of *Kennicott's* and *fifty-three* of *De Rossi's* MSS.; by some ancient editions the *Septuagint*, the *Syriac*, the *Vulgate*, the *Æthiopic*, the *Arabic*, and the *Anglo-Saxon*. The old *Anglo-Scottish* Psalter reads it consecutively with the foregoing. Who the author of both was, we know not, nor on what occasion it was written. It seems to be an *epinikion* or triumphal song, in which the victory gained is entirely ascribed to Jehovah.

Verse 1. *Not unto us, O Lord*] We take no merit to ourselves; as thine is the kingdom, and the power in that kingdom, so is thy glory.

For *thy mercy*, and *for thy truth's sake*.] Thy mercy gave thy promise, thy truth fulfilled it.

Verse 2. *Wherefore should the heathen say*] This appears to refer to a time in which the Israelites had suffered some sad reverses, so as to be brought very low, and to be marked by the heathen.

Verse 3. *He hath done whatsover he hath pleased.*] There was too much cause for his abandoning us to our enemies; yet he still lives and rules in heaven and in earth.

Verse 4. *Their idols* are *silver*, &c.] They are metal, stone, and wood. They are generally made in the form of man, but can neither see, hear, smell, feel, walk, nor speak. How brutish to trust in such! And next to these, in stupidity and inanity, must they be who form them, with the expectation of deriving any good from them. So obviously vain was the whole system of idolatry, that the more serious heathens ridiculed it, and it was a butt for the jests of their freethinkers and buffoons. How keen are those words of Juvenal!—

————————Audis,
Jupiter, hæc? nec labra moves, cum mittere vocem.
Debueras, vel marmoreus vel aheneus? aut cur
In carbone tuo charta pia thura soluta
Ponimus, et sectum vituli jecur, albaque porci
Omenta? ut video, nullum discrimen habendum est
Effigies inter vestras, statuamque Bathylli.
SAT. xiii., ver. 113.

"Dost thou hear, O Jupiter, these things? nor move thy lips when thou oughtest to speak out, whether thou art of marble or of bronze? Or, why do we put the sacred incense on thy altar from the opened paper, and the extracted liver of a calf, and the white caul of a hog? As far as I can discern there is no difference between thy statue and that of Bathyllus."

This irony will appear the keener, when it is known that Bathyllus was a fiddler and player, whose image by the order of Polycrates, was erected in the temple of Juno at Samos. See

A. M. cir. 3469
B. C. cir. 535
Cyri,
R. Persarum,
cir. annum
secundum

eyes have they, but they see
not:
6 They have ears, but they
hear not: noses have they, but
they smell not:
7 They have hands, but they handle not:
feet have they, but they walk not: neither
speak they through their throat.
8 [e]They that make them are like unto them;
so is every one that trusteth in them.
9 [f]O Israel, trust thou in the LORD: [g]he
is their help and their shield.
10 O house of Aaron, trust in the LORD: he
is their help and their shield.
11 Ye that fear the LORD, trust in the LORD:
he *is* their help and their shield.
12 The LORD hath been mindful of us: he
will bless *us;* he will bless the
house of Israel; he will bless
the house of Aaron.
13 [h]He will bless them that
fear the LORD, *both* small [i]and great.
14 The LORD shall increase you more and
more, you and your children.
15 Ye *are* [k]blessed of the LORD [l]which
made heaven and earth.
16 The heaven, *even* the heavens, *are* the
LORD'S: but the earth hath he given to the
children of men.
17 [m]The dead praise not the LORD, neither
any that go down into silence.
18 [n]But we will bless the LORD from this
time forth and for evermore. Praise the
LORD.

[e]Psa. cxxxv. 18; Isa. xliv. 9, 10, 11; Jonah ii. 8; Hab. ii. 18, 19——[f]See Psa. cxviii. 2, 3, 4; cxxxv. 19, 20 [g]Psa. xxxiii. 20; Prov. xxx. 5

[h]Psa. cxxviii. 1, 4——[i]Heb. *with*——[k]Gen. xiv. 19 [l]Gen. i. 1; Psa. xcvi. 5——[m]Psa. vi. 5; lxxxviii. 10, 11, 12; Isa. xxxviii. 18——[n]Psa. cxiii. 2; Dan. ii. 20

Isa. xli. 1. &c.; xlvi. 7; Jer. x. 4, 5, &c.; and Psa. cxxxv. 15, 16.

Verse 9. *O Israel*] The body of the Jewish people.

Verse 10. *O house of Aaron*] All the different classes of the priesthood.

Verse 11. *Ye that fear the Lord*] All real penitents, and sincere believers, *trust in the Lord*, in the almighty, omniscient, and infinitely good Jehovah.

He is their help and shield] He is the succour, support, guardian, and defence of all who put their confidence in him.

Verse 12. *The Lord hath been mindful*] He has never yet wholly abandoned us to our enemies.

He will bless the house of Israel] He will bless the people as a nation; he will bless the priesthood and Levites; he will bless all of them who fear him, great and small, in whatsoever station or circumstances found. There is a great deal of emphasis in this verse: several words are redoubled to make the subject the more affecting. I give a literal translation:—

Ver. 12: "The Lord has been mindful of us; he will bless the house of Israel; he will bless the house of Aaron. Ver. 13: He will bless them that fear Jehovah, the small with the great. Ver. 14: Jehovah will add upon you, upon you and upon all your children. Ver. 15: Blessed are ye of the Lord, the Maker of heaven and earth. Ver. 16: The heavens of heavens are the Lord's: but the earth he hath given to the sons of Adam."

Jehovah is absolute Master of the universe. He has made the heavens of heavens, and also the earth; and this he gives to the children of Adam. When he exiled him from *paradise*, he turned him out into the *earth*, and gave it to him and his sons for ever, that they might dress, till, and eat of its produce all their days.

Verse 17. *The dead praise not the Lord*] המתים *hammethim*, those dead men who worshipped as gods dumb idols, dying in their sins, worship not Jehovah; nor can any of those who *go down into silence* praise thee: earth is the place in which to praise the Lord for his mercies, and get a preparation for his glory.

Verse 18. *But we will bless the Lord*] Our fathers, who received so much from thy bounty, are *dead;* their *tongues* are *silent* in the *grave;* we are in their place, and wish to magnify thy name, for thou hast dealt bountifully with us. But grant us those farther blessings before we die which we so much need; and we will praise thee as *living* monuments of thy mercy, and the praise we begin *now* shall continue for ever and ever.

The *Targum*, for "neither any that go down into silence," has "nor any that descend into the house of earthly sepulture," that is, the *tomb*. The Anglo-Saxon: **⁊ na ealle þaðe nyðerastigað on helle,** *neither all they that go down into hell.* **Nogh the dede sal loue the Lorde, ne al that lyghtes in hell.** Old Psalter. The word *hell* among our ancestors meant originally the *covered*, or *hidden obscure* place, from helan, to *cover* or *conceal:* it now expresses only the *place* of *endless torment.*

ANALYSIS OF THE HUNDRED AND FIFTEENTH PSALM

The prophet, being zealous of God's honour, which the heathens were solicitous to give to their idols, earnestly beseeches God to manifest that power which belongs to him alone, and which he will not give to another.

This Psalm, has *four* parts:—

I. His petition for God's honour, ver. 1; which belongs to no idol, ver. 3-9.

II. An exhortation to praise God, and hope in him, ver. 10-12.

III. The benefit that will arise from it; a blessing, ver. 12-16.

IV. A profession, that for the blessing they will bless God, ver. 17, 18.

1. Some join this Psalm to the former, conceiving that the prophet, having expressed the

goodness of God in the deliverance of his people from *Egypt*, would not have any of the glory attributed to *Moses* or *Aaron*, but wholly to God. Therefore he begins:—

1. "Not unto us," &c. Or any leader among us.

2. "But unto thy name," &c. We seek it not; take it wholly to thyself.

And this, for these reasons, he desires might always be shown to his people.

1. "Give glory to thy name," &c. For the manifestation of his mercy.

2. "Do it for thy truth's sake." As a promise-keeping God.

3. "Wherefore should the heathen say," &c. Give them not occasion to blaspheme, as if thou hadst forsaken thy people. Should the heathen ask, we can answer: "As for our God, he is in the heavens, which his miracles testify. He can deliver or afflict his people as he pleases."

But where are their gods?

1. "Their idols are silver and gold." The mere productions of the earth.

2. "The work of men's hands." Works, and not makers of works.

3. They are of no use or power, though formed like men: "For they have mouths," &c. "They have hands, but they handle not," &c. They have not the power of articulating sounds; they are lower than even the beasts that perish.

The prophet, having thus described the idols, now notices their makers.

1. "They that make them," &c. Quite senseless people.

2. "So is every one that puts his trust," &c. Christ says, "Having eyes," &c. Mark viii.

II. The prophet, having passed this sarcasm upon the idols and idolaters, leaves them, and exhorts the *Israelites*.

1. "O Israel, trust thou," &c. You are God's servants; and to encourage them he adds, "He is their help," &c. The protector of the whole nation.

2. "O house of Levi," &c. You are the leaders and guides in religion; and therefore, you ought especially to trust in him who is the shield of your tribe.

3. "Ye that fear the Lord," &c. In whatever nation you live; for all who fear him, and do righteously, are accepted of him.

III. That this exhortation might be the deeper rooted, he puts them in mind that God "hath been mindful of us," by his special providence.

1. "He will bless the house of Israel" as a nation.

2. "He will bless the house of Aaron" as the priesthood.

3. "He will bless them that fear the Lord," &c., without distinction.

The prophet, taking his example from God, pours his blessing upon them also, and upon their children.

1. "The Lord shall increase you," &c.

2. "Ye are the blessed of the Lord," &c. Though the world speak evil of you.

3. "The Lord which made heaven and earth." Which words are added that they may be assured that their blessings are real, and come forth from his hand directly and alone.

4. They come from one able to bless; for, 1. *The heaven*, even *the heavens*, &c. In them he especially shows his presence, majesty, and glory; but sends his dews and rain upon the earth. 2. As for the earth, *he hath given it*, &c., that by his blessing upon their labours they might have food and raiment; therefore praise him.

IV. For this is the true end of their being: which he illustrates by an antithesis.

1. "For the dead praise not the Lord," &c. These temporal blessings are not felt by the dead—they need them not: but the living should render continual thanks for them to God their author.

2. But we that are upon earth enjoy his protection and temporal care of us; and besides we have his far richer spiritual blessings; therefore, "we will bless the Lord," &c., by ourselves while we live, and aim by our instructions and prayers that our posterity may do the same when we are gone down into silence.

3. However, ye that are alive this day, "praise ye the Lord."

PSALM CXVI

The psalmist praises God for his deliverance from thraldom, which he compares to death and the grave, 1–9. *The exercises through which he had passed*, 10, 11. *His gratitude for these mercies, and resolution to live to God's glory*, 12–19.

XXIV. DAY. MORNING PRAYER

A. M. cir. 3489
B. C. cir. 515
Darii I.,
R. Persarum,
cir. annum
sextum

I [a]LOVE the LORD, because
he hath heard my voice *and*
my supplications.
2 Because he hath inclined
his ear unto me, therefore will I
call upon *him* [b]as long as I live.
3 [c]The sorrows of death compassed me, and the pains of hell
[d]gat hold upon me: I found trouble and sorrow.

A. M. cir. 3489
B. C. cir. 515
Darii I.,
R. Persarum,
cir. annum
sextum

[a]Psa. xviii. 1——[b]Heb. *in my days*

[c]Psa. xviii. 4, 5, 6——[d]Heb. *found me*

NOTES ON PSALM CXVI

This Psalm is also without a *title*, and its *author* is unknown. It appears to have been written after the captivity, and to be a thanksgiving to God for that glorious event. The psalmist compares this captivity to *death* and the *grave;* and shows the happy return to the promised land, called here *The land of the living*. The people recollect the vows of God

A. M. cir. 3489
B. C. cir. 515
Darii I.,
R. Persarum,
cir. annum
sextum

4 Then called I upon the
name of the LORD; O LORD,
I beseech thee, deliver my
soul.
5 [e]Gracious *is* the LORD, and [f]righteous;
yea, our God *is* merciful.
6 The LORD preserveth the simple: I was
brought low, and he helped me.
7 Return unto thy [g]rest, O my
soul: for [h]the LORD hath dealt
bountifully with thee.
8 [i]For thou hast delivered my
soul from death, mine eyes from tears, *and*
my feet from falling.
9 I will walk before the LORD [k]in the land
of the living.

A. M. cir. 3489
B. C. cir. 515
Darii I.,
R. Persarum,
cir. annum
sextum

[e]Psa. ciii. 8——[f]Ezra ix. 15; Neh. ix. 8; Psa. cxix. 137; cxlv. 17——[g]Jer. vi. 16; Matt. xi. 29——[h]Psa. xiii. 6; cxix. 17——[i]Psa. lvi. 13——[k]Psa. xxvii. 13

which were upon them, and purpose to fulfil them. They exult at being enabled to worship God in the temple at Jerusalem.

The *Syriac*, which abounds in conjectural prefaces, supposes this Psalm to have been written on the occasion of Saul coming to the mouth of the cave in which David lay hidden; but spiritually taken, it relates to the bringing of a new people, the Gentiles, to the Christian faith. In a few MSS. this Psalm is joined to the preceding. Many think it relates wholly to the passion, death, and triumph of Christ. Most of the fathers were of this opinion.

Verse 1. *I love the Lord because he hath heard*] How vain and foolish is the *talk*, "To love God for his benefits to us is mercenary, and cannot be pure love!" Whether pure or impure, there is no other love that can flow from the heart of the creature to its Creator. *We love him*, said the holiest of Christ's disciples, *because he first loved us;* and the increase of our love and filial obedience is in proportion to the increased sense we have of our obligation to him. We love him for the benefits bestowed on us. *Love begets love.*

Verse 2. *Because he hath inclined his ear*] The psalmist represents himself to be so sick and weak, that he could scarcely speak. The Lord, in condescension to this weakness, is here considered as *bowing down his ear to the mouth of the feeble suppliant*, that he may receive every word of his prayer.

Therefore will I call upon him] I have had such blessed success in my application to him, that I purpose to invoke him as long as I shall live. He th. t prays much will be emboldened to pray more, because none can supplicate the throne of grace in vain.

Verse 3. *The sorrows of death*] חבלי מות *chebley maveth*, the *cables* or *cords of death;* alluding to their bonds and fetters during their captivity; or to the cords by which a criminal is bound, who is about to be led out to execution; or to the bandages in which the dead were enveloped, when head, arms, body, and limbs were all *laced down* together.

The pains of hell] מצרי שאול *metsarey sheol*, the *straitnesses of the grave.* So little expectation was there of life, that he speaks as if he were condemned, executed, and *closed* up in the tomb. Or, he may refer here to the *small niches* in cemeteries, where the coffins of the dead were placed.

Because this Psalm has been used in the thanksgiving of women after safe delivery, it has been supposed that the pain suffered in the act of parturition was equal for the time to the torments of the damned. But this supposition is shockingly absurd; the utmost power of human nature could not, for a moment, endure the wrath of God, the deathless worm, and the unquenchable fire. The body must die, be decomposed, and be built up on indestructible principles, before this punishment can be borne.

Verse 5. *Gracious* is *the Lord*] In his own nature.

And righteous] In all his dealings with men.

Our God is *merciful.*] Of tender compassion to all penitents.

Verse 6. *The Lord preserveth the simple*] פתאים *pethaim*, which all the Versions render *little ones.* Those who are meek and lowly of heart, who feel the spirit of little children, these he preserves, as he does little children; and he mentions this circumstance, because the Lord has a peculiar regard for these *young ones*, and gives his angels charge concerning them. Were it otherwise, children are exposed to so many dangers and deaths, that most of them would fall victims to accidents in their infancy.

Verse 7. *Return unto thy rest, O my soul*] God is the *centre* to which all immortal spirits tend, and in connexion with which alone they can find *rest.* Every thing *separated* from its *centre* is in a state of *violence;* and, if intelligent, cannot be happy. All human souls, while separated from God by sin, are in a state of violence, agitation, and misery. From God all spirits come; to him all must return, in order to be finally happy. This is true in the general case; though, probably, the *rest* spoken of here means the *promised land*, into which they were now *returning.*

A proof of the late origin of this Psalm is exhibited in this verse, in the words למנוחיכי *limenuchaichi*, "to thy rest," and עליכי *alaichi*, "to thee," which are both *Chaldaisms.*

Verse 8. *Thou hast delivered my soul from death*] Thou hast rescued my *life* from the *destruction* to which it was exposed.

Mine eyes from tears] Thou hast turned my *sorrow* into *joy.*

My feet from falling.] Thou hast taken me out of the land of *snares* and *pitfalls*, and brought me into a *plain path.* How very near does our ancient mother tongue come to this:—**Forðon he nerode sawle mine of deaðe, eagan mine of tearum, fet mine of slide.** *For thou he nerode sawle mine of deathe, eagan mine of tearum; fet mine of slide.* And this language is but a little improved in the old Psalter:—

For he toke my saule fra dede; my eghen fra teres; my fete fra slippyng.

Verse 9. *I will walk before the Lord*] אתהלך *ethhallech*, I will *set myself to walk.* I am *determined to walk;* my *eyes* are now bright-

A. M. cir. 3489
B. C. cir. 515
Darii I.,
R. Persarum,
cir. annum
sextum

10 [l]I believed, therefore have
I spoken: I was greatly afflicted:
11 [m]I said in my haste, [n]All
men *are* liars.
12 What shall I render unto the LORD *for*
all his benefits toward me?
13 I will take the cup of salvation, and
call upon the name of the
LORD.
14 [o]I will pay my vows unto
the LORD now in the presence
of all his people.
15 [p]Precious in the sight of the LORD *is*
the death of his saints.

A. M. cir. 3489
B. C. cir. 515
Darii I.,
R. Persarum,
cir. annum
sextum

---

[l]2 Cor. iv. 13——[m]Psa. xxxi. 22——[n]Rom. iii. 4

[o]Ver. 18; Psa. xxii. 25; Jonah ii. 9——[p]Psa. lxxii. 14

---

ened, so that I can *see;* my feet are *strengthened*, so that I can *walk;* and my *soul* is *alive*, so that I can *walk* with the *living*.

The *Vulgate*, the *Septuagint*, the *Æthiopic*, the *Arabic*, and the *Anglo-Saxon* end this Psalm here, which is numbered the cxivth; and begin with the *tenth* verse another Psalm, which they number cxvth; but this division is not acknowledged by the *Hebrew*, *Chaldee*, and *Syriac*.

Verse 10. *I believed, therefere have I spoken*] Distressed and afflicted as I was, I ever believed thy promises to be true; but I had great struggles to maintain my confidence; for my afflictions were great, oppressive, and of long standing.

It is scarcely worth observing that the letters called *heemantic* by the Hebrew grammarians, and which are used in forming the *derivatives* from the *roots*, are taken from the *first* word in this verse, האמנתי *heemanti*, "I have believed;" as the *prefixes* in that language are found in the technical words משה וכלב *Mosheh vecaleb*, "Moses and Caleb;" and the *formatives* of the *future* are found in the word איתן *eythan*, "strength."

Verse 11. *I said in my haste*] This is variously translated: *I said in my flight*, CHALDEE. In my *excess*, or ecstasy, VULGATE. In my *ecstasy*, εκστασει, SEPTUAGINT. فى تحيرى *fi tahayury*, in my *giddiness*, ARABIC. In my *fear* or *tremor*, SYRIAC. **Ic cpæð on utᵹanᵹe minum,** *I quoth in outgoing mine*, when I was *beside* myself, ANGLO-SAXON. **In myn oute passyng,** *old Psalter*. When passion got the better of my reason, when I looked not at God, but at my afflictions, and the impossibility of human relief.

All men are *liars.*] כל האדם כזב *col haadam cozeb*, "the whole of man is a lie." Falsity is diffused through his nature; deception proceeds from his tongue; his actions are often counterfeit. He is imposed on by others, and imposes in his turn; and on none is there any dependence till God converts their heart.

"O what a thing were man, if his *attires*
Should *alter* with his *mind*,
And, like a *dolphin's skin*,
His *clothes* combine with his desires!
Surely if each one saw another's heart,
There would be no commerce;
All would disperse,
And live apart." HERBERT.

To the same purpose I shall give the following Italian proverb:—

Con arte e con inganno,
Si vive mezzo l'anno.
Con inganno e con arte
Si vive l' altro parti.

"Men live half the year by deceit and by art;
By art and deceit men live the other part."

Who gives this bad character of mankind? MAN.

Verse 12. *What shall I render*] מה אשיב *mah ashib*, "What shall I return?"

For his benefits] תגמולוהי *tagmulohi*, "His retributions," the returns he had made to my prayers and faith.

Verse 13. *I will take the cup of salvation*] Literally, *The cup of salvation*, or *deliverance*, *will I lift up*. Alluding to the action in taking the *cup of blessing* among the Jews, which, when the person or master of the family *lifted up*, he said these words, "Blessed be the Lord, the Maker of the world, who has created the fruit of the vine!"

But it may probably allude to the libation-offering, Num. xxviii. 7; for the *three* last verses seem to intimate that the psalmist was now at the temple, offering the meat-offering, drink-offering, and sacrifices to the Lord. *Cup* is often used by the Hebrews to denote *plenty* or *abundance.* So, *the cup of trembling*, an abundance of *misery; the cup of salvation*, an abundance of *happiness.*

And call upon the name of the Lord.] I will *invoke* his name, that I may get more of the same blessings; for the only *return* that God requires is, that we ask for *more.* Who is like GOD? One reason why we should never more come to a fellow-mortal for a favour is, we have received so many already. A strong reason why we should claim the utmost salvation of God is, because we are already *so much in debt* to his mercy. Now this is the only way we have of discharging our debts to God; and yet, strange to tell, every such attempt to discharge the debt only serves to *increase* it! Yet, notwithstanding, the debtor and creditor are represented as both *pleased*, both *profited*, and both *happy* in each other! Reader, pray to him, invoke his name; receive the cup—accept the *abundance of salvation* which he has provided thee, that thou mayest love and serve him with a perfect heart.

Verse 14. *I will pay my vows unto the Lord now in the presence of all his people.*] He was probably now bringing his offering to the temple. These words are repeated, ver. 18.

Verse 15. *Precious in the sight of the Lord*] Many have understood this verse as meaning, "the saints are too precious in the Lord's sight, lightly to give them over to death:" and this, *Calmet* contends, is the true sense of the text. Though they have many enemies, their lives are precious in his sight, and their foes shall not prevail against them.

A. M. cir. 3489
B. C. cir. 515
Darii I.,
R. Persarum,
cir. annum
sextum

16 O LORD, truly [q]I *am* thy
servant; I *am* thy servant, *and*
[r]the son of thine handmaid:
thou hast loosed my bonds.

17 I will offer to thee [s]the sacrifice of thanksgiving, and will call upon the name of the LORD.

18 [t]I will pay my vows unto
the LORD now in the presence of
all his people,

19 In the [u]courts of the LORD's
house, in the midst of thee, O Jerusalem.
Praise ye the LORD.

[q]Psalm cxix. 125; cxliii. 12——[r]Psalm lxxxvi. 16——[s]Lev. vii. 12; Psa. l. 14; cvii. 22——[t]Ver. 14——[u]Psa. xcvi. 8; c. 4; cxxxv. 2

Verse 16. *I* am *thy servant*] Thou hast preserved me alive. I live *with, for*, and *to* THEE. I am thy *willing domestic, the son of thine handmaid*—like one born in thy house of a woman already thy property. I am a *servant*, son of *thy servant*, made free by thy kindness; but, refusing *to go out*, I have had my *ear bored to thy door-post*, and am to continue by *free choice* in thy house for ever. He alludes here to the case of the servant who, in the year of jubilee being entitled to his liberty, refused to leave his master's house; and suffered his ear to be bored to the door-post, as a proof that by his own consent he agreed to continue in his master's house for ever.

Verse 17. *I will offer to thee*] As it is most probable that this Psalm celebrates the *deliverance from Babylon*, it is no wonder that we find the psalmist so intent on performing the *rites* of his religion in the temple at Jerusalem, which had been burnt with fire, and was now reviving out of its ruins, the temple service having been wholly interrupted for nearly fourscore years.

Verse 19. *In the midst of thee, O Jerusalem.*] He speaks as if present in the city, offering his vowed *sacrifices* in the temple to the Lord.

Most of this Psalm has been applied to *our Lord* and his *Church;* and in this way it has been considered as *prophetic;* and, taken thus, it is innocently accommodated, and is very edifying. This is the interpretation given of the whole by the *old Psalter*.

ANALYSIS OF THE HUNDRED AND SIXTEENTH PSALM

This Psalm is gratulatory; for it shows how great straits the psalmist was brought into, from which God delivered him.

This Psalm has *three* parts:—

I. The psalmist makes profession of his love, and shows the reasons of it: God's goodness in hearing and delivering him from his low and sad condition, ver. 1-9.

II. He professes his duty and faith, ver. 9-11.

III. He promises to be thankful, and in what manner, ver. 12-19.

I. He begins with the expression of his content and love: "I love the Lord." And he gives these reasons:—

1. "Because he hath heard," &c. This is reason enough why I should love him.

2. "Because he hath inclined," &c. An evidence that he was heard. Upon which experience that he was heard he adds: "Therefore will I call," &c.

Another reason which moved him to love God was, that he heard him in the extremity of his deep distress; for,—

1. "The sorrows of death," &c. Death is the king of fear.

2. "The pains of hell," &c. He feared the anger of God for his sins.

3. "I found trouble and sorrow." The psalmist was sensible of his condition: though others might suppose him compassed with prosperity, yet he knew himself distressed.

But he prayed to the Lord.

1. "Then." In these troubles and pangs.

2. "I called upon," &c. Invocation to God was his sole refuge.

3. "O Lord, I beseech thee," &c. He sets down the very words of his prayer.

And then, that he might show that he prayed to God in faith and hope, he points out the attributes of God for the encouragement of others.

1. "God is gracious." It is he who inspires prayer and repentance, remits sin, and pardons those who fly in faith to him for mercy.

2. "And righteous and just." He will perform what he has promised.

3. "Yea, our God is merciful." He mingles mercy with his justice; he corrects with a father's hand, and loves to forgive rather than to punish. Of which David gives an instance in himself: "I was brought low, and he helped me." And all others may find the same who come in the way that I did to him for pardon.

Another reason he gives for loving God was, the tranquillity of soul he found after this storm was over: "Therefore, return unto thy rest, O my soul." Hitherto thou hast been tossed up and down on the waves of sorrow, finding no port or haven: now faith has opened to thee a harbour where thou mayest be safe: "For the Lord hath dealt," &c.: but of his infinite mercy he has given thee joy for sadness.

He attributes to him the whole of his work.

1. "Thou hast delivered," &c. Turned my heaviness into joy, by removing all fear of death.

2. "Thou hast delivered my eyes," &c. Made me joyful.

3. "Thou hast delivered my feet," &c. When my infirmity is great, the devil takes advantage of me that I might fall; but now thou hast settled my feet—made me able to resist him. And this God does for all who call upon him, and trust in him.

II. The psalmist, having expressed his sorrows and God's goodness, now professes his dutiful attachment, 1. By his obedience; 2. By a faithful confession of his errors, and future confidence.

1. "I will walk before the Lord," &c. Be careful to please God, by walking not after the flesh, but after the Spirit.

He professes his faith, on which he will evermore rely.

1. "I believed, and therefore," &c. Which confidence came from faith.

2. "I was greatly afflicted," &c.; but I became

docile and humble to the Spirit of God. When David was tossed between hope and despair, he found those sorrows were not easily quieted; for "I said in my haste," &c.

Which clause is differently understood by commentators.

1. Some suppose it to be an amplification of his former grief. I was so amazed, and overwhelmed with sorrow, that if any one reminded me of God's promises, "I said in my haste, All men are liars." I will not believe God; he hath no care for me.

2. Others again refer this clause to the preceding: They talk of happiness and felicity, but none is to be found in the land of the living.

3. Some again refer it to *Absalom*, who deceived *David* by his vow at *Hebron;* or to *Ahithophel*, who revolted from him.

4. Again, others suppose that he taxed even *Samuel* himself that he spoke not by God's Spirit, when he anointed him king over Israel; because, during Saul's persecution, there appeared so little hope of it. But the first sense is the most cogent.

III. Henceforth, to the end of the Psalm, David declares his gratitude: "What shall I render to the Lord," &c. As if he had said, I acknowledge the benefits God has bestowed upon me; but in what way can I best evince my gratitude?

1. "I will take the cup of salvation." Here interpreters vary as to what is to be understood by the *cup of salvation.* 1. Some refer it to the ucharistical sacrifices of the old law, in which, when a man offered a sacrifice to God for some deliverance, he made a feast to the people, as did David, 1 Chron. i., ii., iii. 2. The fathers understood it of the cup of patience and affliction, which is often in Scripture called a cup, Matt. xx. 22. 3. But here it seems to signify plenty, abundance, &c. See the note.

2. "I will pay my vows," &c. It was usual in God's service to make vows, or to confess his name in an open assembly. God cares for all his people, however circumstanced; for *precious in the sight of the Lord* is *the death of his saints.* The servants of God trouble themselves in vain when they distrust him; for in life he is with them, and in death he will not forsake them.

The psalmist does not become proud upon God's favours; but in all humility, though a king, he exclaims,—

1. "O Lord, truly I *am* thy servant," &c.

2. And yet no slave, but a willing servant: "Thou hast loosed my bonds,"—taken from my neck the bonds of fear: thou hast made me thy servant through love.

3. And therefore will I do what thy servants ought to do.

Showing his earnestness he repeats again, "I will offer to thee the sacrifice of thanksgiving, and will call upon the name of the Lord. I will pay my vows unto the Lord now in the presence of all his people, in the courts of the Lord's house, in the midst of thee, O Jerusalem. Praise ye the Lord." *Within* the Church, and at all times, he would praise and do him worship. What is not done according to God's word and Spirit is of little service. He who neglects *public worship* is not very likely to keep up private devotion, either in his *family* or in his *closet.* "I will pay my vows in the midst of thee, O Jerusalem."

PSALM CXVII

The psalmist calls upon the nations of the world to praise the Lord for his mercy and kindness, and for the fulfilment of his promises, 1, 2.

A. M. cir. 3489 B. C. cir. 515 Darii I., R. Persarum, cir. annum sextum

O [a]PRAISE the LORD, all ye nations: praise him, all ye people.

2 For his merciful kindness is great toward us: and the [b]truth of the LORD *endureth* for ever. Praise ye the LORD.

A. M. cir. 3489 B. C. cir. 515 Darii I., R. Persarum, cir. annum sextum

[a]Rom. xv. 11 — [b]Psa. c. 5

NOTES ON PSALM CXVII

This is the shortest Psalm in the whole collection; it is written as a part of the preceding in thirty-two of *Kennicott's* and *De Rossi's* MSS., and is found thus printed in some ancient editions. The whole Psalm is omitted in one of *Kennicott's* and in two of *De Rossi's* MSS. It celebrates the redemption from the Babylonish captivity, the grand type of the redemption of the world by our Lord Jesus.

The *Syriac* says: "It was spoken concerning Ananias and his followers when they came out of the furnace; but it also foretells the vocation of the Gentiles by the preaching of the Gospel." In this way St. Paul applies it, Rom. xv. 11.

Verse 1. *O praise the Lord, all ye nations*] Let all the *Gentiles* praise him, for he provides for their eternal salvation.

Praise him, all ye people.] All ye *Jews*, praise him; for ye have long been his peculiar people. And while he sends his Son to be *a light to the Gentiles*, he sends him also to be *the glory of his people Israel.*

Verse 2. *For his merciful kindness is great*] גבר *gabar*, is *strong:* it is not only *great* in *bulk* or *number*, but it is *powerful;* it *prevails* over *sin*, *Satan*, *death*, and *hell.*

And the truth of the Lord endureth *for ever.*] Whatsoever he has *promised*, that he will most infallibly *fulfil.* He has promised to *send his Son into the world*, and thus he *has done.* He his promised that he should *die for transgressors*, and this he *did.* He has promised to *receive all who come unto him* through Christ

Jesus, and this he invariably *does*. He has promised that his *Gospel shall be preached in every nation*, and this he *is doing;* the truth of the Lord remaineth for ever. Therefore, *Praise ye the Lord!*

Analysis of the Hundred and Seventeenth Psalm

This Psalm contains a *doxology* to God for his *mercy* and *truth;* and it is *prophetical*, having reference to the calling of the Gentiles; Rom. xv. 11.

It contains two parts:—

I. An *exhortation* to praise God.

II. The *reason* for it.

I. 1. He speaks to the *Gentiles:* "Praise the Lord, all ye nations." Praise him for the *promise* of salvation; and then, when fulfilled, praise him for the *enjoyment* of this salvation,—for the *remission* of sins, and gift *of the Holy Ghost*.

2. He speaks to the converted *Jews*, whom he notes under the name of *people*, as they are called Psa. ii. 1; Acts iv. 25. As they and the *Gentiles* are intended to make *one Church*, so they should join in the praise of him *of whom the whole family in heaven and earth is named.*

II. The *reason* given:—

1. Because *his mercy is great*. It is strong; *confirmed* toward us, in sending his Son to save both Jews and Gentiles from their sins.

2. Because the truth of his promises is *fulfilled*. The promised Messiah *is come*, and *has performed* all that was prophesied of him.

3. Because this truth is *forever*. His *promises* and their *fulfilment* belong to *all generations*. There will never be another Messiah; Jesus is the true one: he tasted death for every man; he forgives iniquity, transgression, and sin; and his blood cleanses from all unrighteousness. Now, for all this, "Praise ye the Lord!"

[*N. B.* Proclaiming the eternal mercy of God in Christ is more likely to persuade sinners to return to their Maker than all the fire of hell.]

PSALM CXVIII

A general exhortation to praise God for his mercy, 1–4. *The* psalmist, *by his own experience, encourages the people to trust in God, and shows them the advantage of it*, 5–9; *then describes his enemies, and shows how God enabled him to destroy them*, 10–13. *The* people *rejoice on the account*, 15, 16. *He speaks again of the help he received from the Lord; and desires admission into the temple, that he may enter and praise the Lord*, 17–19. *The gate is opened*, 20. *He offers praise*, 21. *The* priests, &c., *acknowledge the hand of the Lord in the deliverance wrought*, 22–24. *The psalmist prays for prosperity*, 25. *The priest performs his office, blesses the people, and* all *join in praise*, 26, 27. *The* psalmist *expresses his confidence*, 28. *The* general doxology, *or chorus*, 29.

O [a]GIVE thanks unto the LORD; for *he is* good: because his mercy *endureth* for ever.

2 [b]Let Israel now say, that his mercy *endureth* for ever.

[a]1 Chron. xvi. 8, 24; Psa. cvi. 1; cvii. 1; cxxxvi. 1

[b]See Psa. cxv. 9, &c.

NOTES ON PSALM CXVIII

Most probably David was the author of this Psalm, though many think it was written after the captivity. It partakes of David's spirit, and every where shows the hand of a *master*. The *style* is grand and noble; the *subject*, majestic.

Dr. *Kennicott*, who joins this and the *hundred and seventeenth* Psalm together, considers the whole as a *dialogue*, and divides it accordingly. The whole of the *hundred and seventeenth* he gives to the *psalmist* as *part* the *first*, with the first four verses of the *hundred and eighteenth.* The *second part*, which is from the *fifth* verse to the *twenty-first* inclusive, he gives to the *Messiah*. The *third part*, from the *twenty-second* verse to the *twenty-seventh*, he gives to the *chorus*. And the *fourth part*, the *twenty-eighth* and *twenty-ninth* verses, he gives to the *psalmist*. Of the whole he has given an improved version.

Bishop *Horsley* is still different. He considers the *hundred and seventeenth* Psalm as only the exordium of this. The whole poem, he states, is a triumphant processional song. The scene passes at the front gate of the temple. A *conqueror* with his train appears before it; he demands admittance to return thanks for his deliverance and final success, in an expedition of great difficulty and danger. The *conqueror* and his *train* sing the *hundred and seventeenth* Psalm, and the first four verses of the *hundred and eighteenth*, as they advance to the gate of the temple, in this manner.—The *hundred and seventeenth* Psalm, *Chorus of the whole procession.* The *first* verse of the *hundred and eighteenth Psalm*, A *single voice*. The *second*, Another *single voice.* The *third*, A third *single voice*. The *fourth*, *Chorus of the whole procession.* Arrived at the temple gate, the *conqueror alone* sings the *fifth*, *sixth*, and *seventh* verses. The *eighth* and *ninth* are sung by his *train* in *chorus*. The *conqueror*, again *alone*, sings the *tenth*, *eleventh*, *twelfth*, *thirteenth*, and *fourteenth* verses. His *train*, in *chorus*, sing the *fifteenth* and *sixteenth*. The *conqueror alone* sings the *seventeenth*, *eighteenth*, and *nineteenth* verses. The *twentieth* is sung by the *priests* and *Levites* within, in *chorus*. The *twenty-fifth* by the *conqueror alone* within the gates. The *twenty-sixth*, by the *priests* and *Levites* in *chorus*. The *twenty-seventh*, by the

3 Let the house of Aaron now say, that his mercy *endureth* for ever.

4 Let them now that fear the LORD say, that his mercy *endureth* for ever.

5 [c]I called upon the LORD [d]in distress: the LORD answered me, *and* [e]*set me* in a large place.

6 [f]The LORD *is* [g]on my side; I will not fear: what can man do unto me?

7 [h]The LORD taketh my part with them that help me: therefore shall [i]I see *my desire* upon them that hate me.

8 [k]*It is* better to trust in the LORD than to put confidence in man.

9 [l]*It is* better to trust in the LORD than to put confidence in princes.

10 All nations compassed me about: but in the name of the LORD will I [m]destroy them.

11 They [n]compassed me about; yea, they compassed me about: but in the name of the LORD I will destroy them.

12 They compassed me about [o]like bees; they are quenched [p]as the fire of thorns: for in the name of the LORD I will [q]destroy them.

---

[c]Psa. cxx. 1——[d]Heb. *out of distress*——[e]Psa. xviii. 19——[f]Psa. xxvii. 1; lvi. 4, 11; cxlvi. 5; Isa. li. 12; Heb. xiii. 6——[g]Heb. *for me*——[h]Psa. liv. 4——[i]Psa. lix. 10

[k]Psa. xl. 4; lxii. 8, 9; Jer. xvii. 5, 7——[l]Psa. cxlvi. 3——[m]Heb. *cut them off*——[n]Psa. lxxxviii. 17——[o]Deut. i. 44——[p]Eccles. vii. 6; Nah. i. 10——[q]Heb. *cut down*

---

conqueror's train in *chorus.* The *twenty-eighth,* by the *conqueror alone.* The *twenty-ninth,* by the *united chorus* of *priests* and *Levites,* and the *conqueror's train,* all within the gates. "Now," the learned bishop adds, "the *Jewish temple* was a type of *heaven;* the *priests* within represent the *angelic host* attending round the throne of God in heaven; the *Conqueror* is *Messiah;* and his *train,* the *redeemed.*" On this distribution the bishop has given a new version. The simple distribution into parts, which I have given in the *contents,* is, in my opinion, the best. Ingenious as Dr. *Kennicott* and Bishop *Horsley* are, they seem to me too *mechanical.* This is the last of those Psalms which form the great *hallel,* which the Jews sung at the end of the *passover.*

Verse 2. *Let Israel now say*] Seeing the hand of the Lord so visibly, and the deliverance gained, that *God's mercy endureth for ever.*

Verse 3. *The house of Aaron*] The priesthood is still preserved, and the temple worship restored.

Verse 4. *That fear the Lord*] All sincere penitents and genuine believers. See the notes on Psa. cxv. 9-11.

Verse 5. *I called upon the Lord*] I am a standing proof and living witness of God's mercy. Take encouragement from me.

Verse 7. *The Lord taketh my part with them that help me*] Literally, *The Lord is to me among my helpers. Therefore shall I see* my desire *upon them that hate me.* Literally, *And I shall look among them that hate me.* As God is on my side, I fear not to look the whole of them in the face. I shall see them defeated.

Verse 8. *Better to trust in the Lord*] Man is feeble, ignorant, fickle, and capricious; it is better to trust in Jehovah than in such.

Verse 9. *In princes.*] Men of high estate are generally *proud, vain-glorious, self-confident,* and *rash:* it is better to trust in God than in them. Often they *cannot* deliver, and often they *will not* when they *can.* However, in the concerns of our *salvation,* and in matters which belong to *Providence,* they can do nothing.

Verse 10. *All nations compassed me about*] This is by some supposed to relate to David, at the commencement of his reign, when all the neighbouring Philistine nations endeavoured to prevent him from establishing himself in the kingdom. Others suppose it may refer to the Samaritans, Idumeans, *Ammonites,* and others, who endeavoured to prevent the Jews from rebuilding their city and their temple after their return from captivity in Babylon.

But in the name of the Lord will I destroy them.] Dr. *Kennicott* renders אמילם *amilam,* "I shall *disappoint them;*" Bishop *Horsley,* "I cut them to pieces;" Mr. *N. Berlin, repuli eas,* "I have *repelled* them." "I will *cut them off;*" *Chaldee. Ultus sum in eos,* "I am *avenged* on them;" *Vulgate.* So the *Septuagint.*

Verse 12. *They compassed me about like bees; they are quenched as the fire of thorns*] I shall refer to Dr. *Delaney's* note on this passage. The reader has here in miniature two of the finest images in Homer; which, if his curiosity demands to be gratified, he will find illustrated and enlarged, Iliad ii., ver. 86.

——————— Επεσσευοντο δε λαοι.
Ηΰτε εθνεα εισι μελισσαων αδιναων,
Πετρης εκ γλαφυρης αιει νεον ερχομεναων,
Βοτρυδον δε πετονται επ' ανθεσιν ειαρινοισιν,
Αἱ μεν τ' ενθα ἁλις πεποτηαται, αἱ δε τε ενθα·
Ὡς των εθνεα πολλα νεων απο και κλισιαων
Ηϊονος προπαροιθε βαθειης εστιχοωντο
Ιλαδον εις αγορην.

——————— The following host,
Poured forth by thousands, darkens all the coast.
As from some rocky cleft the shepherd sees,
Clustering in heaps on heaps, the driving bees,
Rolling and blackening, swarms succeeding swarms,
With deeper murmurs and more hoarse alarms:
Dusky they spread a close embodied crowd,
And o'er the vale descends the living cloud;
So from the tents and ships a lengthening train
Spreads all the beach, and wide o'ershades the plain;
Along the region runs a deafening sound;
Beneath their footsteps groans the trembling ground.
POPE.

The other image, *the fire consuming the thorns,* we find in the same book, ver. 455:—

Ηΰτε πυρ αϊδηλον επιφλεγει ασπετον ὑλην,
Ουρεος εν κορυφης· ἑκαθεν δε τε φαινεται αυγη·
Ὡς των ερχομενων, απο χαλκου θεσπεσιοιο
Αιγλη παμφανοωσα δι' αιθερος ουρανον ἱκεν.

13 Thou hast thrust sore at me that I might fall: but the LORD helped me.

14 [r]The LORD *is* my strength and song, and is become my salvation.

15 The voice of rejoicing and salvation *is* in the tabernacles of the righteous: the right hand of the LORD doeth valiantly.

16 [s]The right hand of the LORD is exalted: the right hand of the LORD doeth valiantly.

17 [t]I shall not die, but live, and [u]declare the works of the LORD.

18 The LORD hath [v]chastened me sore: but he hath not given me over unto death.

19 [w]Open to me the gates of righteousness: I will go in to them, *and* I will praise the LORD:

20 [x]This gate of the LORD, [y]into which the righteous shall enter.

21 I will praise thee: for thou hast [z]heard me, and [a]art become my salvation.

22 [b]The stone *which* the builders refused is become the head *stone* of the corner.

23 [c]This is the LORD'S doing: it *is* marvellous in our eyes.

24 This *is* the day *which* the LORD hath made; we will rejoice and be glad in it.

25 Save now, I beseech thee, O LORD: O LORD, I beseech thee, send now prosperity.

26 [d]Blessed *be* he that cometh in the name of the LORD: we have blessed you out of the house of the LORD.

27 God *is* the LORD, which hath showed us [e]light: bind the sacrifice with cords, *even* unto the horns of the altar.

28 Thou *art* my God, and I will praise thee: [f]*thou art* my God, I will exalt thee.

29 [g]O give thanks unto the LORD, for *he is* good: for his mercy *endureth* for ever.

[r]Exod. xv. 2; Isa. xii. 2——[s]Exod. xv. 6——[t]Psa. vi. 5; Hab. i. 12——[u]Psa. lxxiii. 28——[v]2 Cor. vi. 9 [w]Isa. xxvi. 2——[x]Psa. xxiv. 7——[y]Isa. xxxv. 8; Rev. xxi. 27; xxii. 14, 15——[z]Psa. cxvi. 1——[a]Ver. 14 [b]Matt. xxi. 42; Mark xii. 10; Luke xx. 17; Acts iv. 11; Ephesians ii. 20; 1 Peter ii. 4, 7——[c]Hebrew, *This is from the LORD*——[d]Matthew xxi. 9; xxiii. 39; Mark xi. 9; Luke xix. 38; see Zechariah iv. 7——[e]Esther viii. 16; 1 Peter ii. 9——[f]Exodus xv. 2; Isaiah xxv. 1 [g]Ver. 1

As on some mountain, through the lofty grove,
The crackling flames ascend and blaze above;
The fires expanding, as the winds arise,
Shoot their long beams, and kindle half the skies;
So, from the polished arms, and brazen shields,
A gleamy splendour flashed along the fields.
POPE.

The arms resembling a gleaming *fire* is common both to the psalmist and Homer; but the idea of that fire being *quenched* when the army was *conquered*, is peculiar to the psalmist.

Verse 13. *Thou hast thrust sore at me*] In pushing thou hast pushed me that I might fall.

But the Lord helped me.] Though he possessed skill, courage, and strength, yet these could not have prevailed had not God been his *helper;* and to him he gives the glory of the victory.

Verse 15. *The voice of rejoicing*] *Formerly* there was nothing but wailings; but *now* there is universal joy because of the *salvation*—the deliverance, which God has wrought for us.

Verse 16. *The right hand of the Lord is exalted*] Jehovah *lifted up* his right hand, and with it performed prodigies of power.

Verse 17. *I shall not die*] I was nigh unto death; but I am preserved,—preserved to publish the wondrous works of the Lord.

Verse 19. *Open to me the gates*] Throw open the doors of the temple, that I may enter and perform my vows unto the Lord.

Verse 20. *This gate of the Lord*] Supposed to be the answer of the Levites to the request of the king.

Verse 21. *I will praise thee*] He is now got within the gates, and breaks out into thanksgivings for the mercies he had received. *He is become my salvation*—he himself hath saved me from all mine enemies.

Verses 22, 23. *The stone* which *the builders refused*] See a full elucidation of these two verses in the notes on Matt. xxi. 42.

Verse 24. *This* is *the day* which *the Lord hath made*] As the Lord hath called me to triumph, this is the day which he hath appointed for that purpose. This is a *gracious opportunity;* I will improve it to his glory.

Verse 25. *Save now, I beseech thee*] These words were sung by the Jews on the feast of tabernacles, when carrying green branches in their hands; and from the הושיעה נא *hoshiah nna*, we have the word *hosanna.* This was sung by the Jewish children when Christ made his public entry into Jerusalem. See Matt. xxi. 9, and see the note there, in which the word and the circumstance are both explained.

Verse 26. *We have blessed you*] The answer of the Levities to the king.

Verse 27. *God is the Lord*] Rather אל יהוה *El Yehovah*, the strong God Jehovah.

Which hath showed us light] ויאר לנו *vaiyaer lanu*, "And he will illuminate us." Perhaps at this time a Divine splendour shone upon the whole procession; a proof of God's approbation.

Bind the sacrifice with cords] The *Chaldee* paraphrases this verse thus: "Samuel the prophet said, Bind the little one with chains for a solemn sacrifice, until ye have sacrificed him and sprinkled his blood on the horns of the altar." It is supposed that the words refer to the feast of tabernacles, and חג *chag* here means the *festival victim.* Several translate the original "keep the festival with thick boughs of the horns of the altar." In this sense the *Vulgate* and *Septuagint* understood the passage. David in this entry into the temple was a type of our blessed Lord, who made a similar entry, as related Matt. xxi. 8-10.

Verse 29. *O give thanks unto the Lord*] This is the general doxology or chorus. All join in thanksgiving, and they *end* as they began: "His mercy endureth for ever." It began at the creation of man; it will continue till the earth is burnt up.

Analysis of the Hundred and Eighteenth Psalm

The parts of this Psalm are the following:—

I. An exhortation to praise God for his mercy, ver. 1-5.

II. A persuasion to trust in God, and that from the psalmist's own example, who called upon God, and was delivered from trouble, ver. 5-14.

III. The exultation of the Church for it, ver. 15-18.

IV. A solemn thanksgiving kept for it, and in what manner it was celebrated, ver. 19-27.

V. A short doxology.

1. The psalmist invites all to praise God: "O give thanks," &c., and adds his reasons:—

1. "For he is good." How briefly and powerfully spoken! He is absolutely good.

2. "He is good, and ever good." To us he is a merciful God, which flows from his goodness; his mercy created, redeemed, protects, and will crown. us. Thus his mercy extends especially to his people; therefore,—

1. "Let Israel now say," &c. The whole nation.

2. "Let the house of Aaron," &c. That whole consecrated tribe.

3. "Let them now that fear the Lord," &c. Proselytes, &c.

II. And thus, having given a general recommendation of his mercy, he descends to instance in what it consists; that is, God's great deliverance of him.

1. "I was in distress,' &c. A frequent case with God's people, as well as with David.

2. "I called upon the lord," &c. I fled to him, not trusting in myself, and found mercy.

3. "The Lord answered me, and set me in a large place." This was the issue.

Upon which experience the psalmist exults, and attributes it to God's mercy.

1. "The Lord is my helper," &c. The Lord is for me, therefore I shall not suffer.

2. "The Lord takes my part," &c. I shall be in safety, while my enemies will be cast down, and the Church freed.

From which he deduces a third inference:—

1. "It is better to trust in the Lord," &c. He is both able and willing to help.

2. "It is better to trust in the Lord than to put confidence in princes." *David* found this in the case of *Achish*, king of *Gath*.

In a song of triumph he acquaints us in what dangers he was, and from which God delivered him. It is good then to trust in the Lord.

1. "All nations compassed me about," &c., but to no purpose.

2. "They compassed me about; yea, they compassed me about," &c.

3. "They compassed me about like bees," &c. Angry, and armed with stings; but my trust is alone in the Lord. In his name, and by his help, "I will destroy them."

He told us of a multitude of enemies; and for the overthrow of these he sang his triumph.

1. "Thou hast thrust sore at me," &c. I was in great danger; there was little hope of escape.

2. "But the Lord helped me." No help was in myself, but the Lord.

In the next verse he fully acknowledges the Lord as his strength.

1. "My strength." By which I resist my enemies.

2. "My salvation." To deliver me from my enemies.

3. "My song." Him whom I joyfully sing after my deliverance.

III. And that this song might be fuller, he calls for the whole choir to sing with him. His delivery concerned the whole Church, and therefore it must be sung by the whole Church; and so it was kept as a jubilee, a day of thanksgiving.

1. "The voice of rejoicing," &c. They congratulate their own safety in mine.

2. "The right hand of the Lord," &c. This anthem the whole choir sang.

Now this anthem was no sooner ended by the choir, than the psalmist took his harp again; and, exulting over his enemies, sings, "I shall not die," &c. Not be heart-broken, but "declare the works of the Lord."

And among his works this is one:—

1. "The Lord hath chastened me sore," &c. Within have I struggled hard with sin; without have I been assaulted with bitter enemies.

2. "But he hath not given me over," &c. I acknowledge in this his fatherly affection.

IV. It is supposed that this Psalm was composed by *David*, in order that it might be sung when the people and the priests were assembled before the Lord, for the purpose of thanksgiving; we may, with *Junius*, form it into a dialogue.

1. David speaks of the *priests* and *Levites* who had the care of the tabernacle: "Open to me the gates," &c., that is, the Lord's house; "for I will go in to them," &c.

2. To this the priests reply, "This is the gate," &c. The sole gate of justice that leads to him.

David replies, showing in brief his reason: "I will praise thee," &c.; and to the *twenty-eighth* verse, he shows how God had settled him in his kingdom, making him "the head of the corner;" which words, though they refer to David, there is no doubt of their having reference also to Christ, of whom *David* was a type; and of Christ then I shall rather interpret them.

"The stone which the builders refused," &c.

1. The Church is sometimes in Scripture called a building; the saints are the living stones, and Christ is "the chief Corner-stone."

2. But the *Jews*, the priests, to whom belonged the office of building the Church, refused this stone: "We will not have this man," &c.

3. But "he is become the head of the corner." And whoever is not connected with him cannot be saved. 1. "This was the Lord's doing," &c.

That Christ became our salvation. 2. "And it is marvellous in our eyes." And so it ever must be, that Christ should die, the just for the unjust, to bring us to God.

In commemoration of so great a work, a day should be set apart.

1. "This is the day," &c. Which without doubt was the day of the resurrection; the Lord making it a high and holy day.

2. "We will be glad and rejoice," &c. Adam's fall was a doleful day. On the day of Christ's resurrection we will be glad.

3. In the midst of our rejoicing we will pray, and sound forth Hosanna to the Son of David. This was done by the people on the entering of Christ into *Jerusalem*. It was the opinion of the Jews that this form of acclamation would be used before the *Messiah*.

The whole prophecy of Christ's coming, riding into Jerusalem in triumph, rejection, passion, &c., being thus explained, the prophet puts this into the mouths of the priests:—

"We have blessed you." All true happiness is under this King.

2. "Out of the house of the Lord," &c. From out of the Church.

3. "God is the Lord," &c. Revealed unto us his Son as the Light of the world.

4. "Bind the sacrifice with cords," &c. Be thankful to him, and meet in the Church to celebrate your thanksgivings.

V. The prophet concludes with a doxology.

1. "Thou art my God," I have taken thee for my portion.

2. "And I will praise thee;" which he doubles: "Thou art my God, and I will exalt thee." Which repetition shows his ardent desire of evincing his gratitude.

And thus the psalmist concludes with the same exhortation with which he began the Psalm.

"O give thanks unto the Lord, for he is good; for his mercy endureth for ever." And let him that readeth, and him that heareth, say, Amen!

THIS is an uncommonly fine Psalm, and among the many noble ones it is one of the most noble. Its beauties are so many and so prominent that every reader, whose mind is at all influenced by spiritual things, must see, feel, and admire them.

The 22nd verse, "The stone which the builders rejected is become the head stone of the corner," must have been a *proverbial* expression; but what gave birth to it I cannot find; but, like all other proverbs, it doubtless had its origin from some *fact*. One thing is evident from the Jewish doctors. The most enlightened of them understand this as a prophecy of the *Messiah;* and it was this general opinion, as well as the knowledge that the Spirit of prophecy thus intended it, that caused our Lord to apply it to himself, Matt. xxi. 42; nor did any of them attempt to dispute the propriety of the application.

PSALM CXIX

The various excellencies and important uses of the law or revelation of God.

XXIV. DAY. EVENING PRAYER

א ALEPH

BLESSED *are* the [a]undefiled in the way, [b]who walk in the law of the LORD.

2 Blessed *are* they that keep his testimonies, *and that* seek him with the whole heart.

3 [c]They also do no iniquity: they walk in his ways.

[a]Or, *perfect* or *sincere*——[b]Psa. cxxviii. 4

[c]1 John iii. 9; v. 18

NOTES ON PSALM CXIX

This is another of the *alphabetical* or *acrostic* Psalms. It is divided into *twenty-two* parts, answering to the *number* of letters in the *Hebrew alphabet.* Every *part* is divided into *eight verses;* and each verse begins with that letter of the alphabet which forms the *title* of the part, *e. g.:* The *eight* first verses have א *aleph* prefixed, the second *eight* ב *beth,* each of the *eight* verses beginning with *that* letter; and so of the rest. All *connexion,* as might be naturally expected, is sacrificed to this artificial and methodical arrangement.

It is not easy to give any general *Analysis* of this Psalm; it is enough to say that it treats in general on the privileges and happiness of those who observe the law of the Lord. That law is exhibited by various names and epithets tending to show its various excellences. Earnest prayers are offered to God for wisdom to understand it, and for grace to observe it faithfully. These particulars may be collected from the *whole* composition, and appear less or more in *every part.*

The words which express that *revelation* which God had then given to men, or some *particular characteristic* of it, are generally reckoned to be the *ten* following: 1. *Testimonies;* 2. *Commandments;* 3. *Precepts;* 4. *Word;* 5. *Law;* 6. *Ways;* 7. *Truth;* 8. *Judgments;* 9. *Righteousness;* 10. *Statutes.* To these some add the following: 1. *Faithfulness;* 2. *Judgment;* 3. *Name;* but these are not used in the sense of the other *ten* words. I believe it is almost universally asserted that in *every verse* of this Psalm one or other of those *ten* words is used, except in ver. 122; but on a closer inspection we shall find that none of them is used in the above sense in the 84th, 90th, 121st, 122nd, and 132nd. See the notes on these verses.

To save myself unnecessary repetition, and the reader time and trouble, I shall here, once for all, explain the above words, which the reader will do well to keep in remembrance.

1. The LAW, תורה TORAH, from ירה *yarah,* to

4 Thou hast commanded *us* to [d]keep thy precepts diligently.

5 O that my ways were directed to [e]keep thy statutes!

[d]Exod. xv. 26; Isa. xxviii. 10, 13——[e]Lev. xviii. 5, 26; xix. 19; xx. 8, 22; Deut. iv. 20; vi. 2; xxvi. 17; xxviii. 45; xxx. 10

direct, guide, teach, make straight, or *even, point forward;* because it *guides, directs*, and *instructs* in the way of righteousness; makes our path *straight*, shows what is *even* and *right*, and points us *onward* to peace, truth, and happiness. It is even our *school-master* to bring us to Christ, that we may be justified through faith; and by it is the knowledge of sin.

II. STATUTES, חקים CHUKKIM, *from* חק *chak*, to *mark, trace out, describe*, and *ordain;* because they *mark out* our way, describe the line of conduct we are to pursue, and *order* or *ordain* what we are to observe.

III. PRECEPTS, פקודים PIKKUDIM, *from* פקד *pakad*, to *take notice* or *care* of a thing, to *attend*, have *respect to*, to *appoint*, to *visit;* because they take *notice* of our way, have *respect* to the whole of our life and conversation, *superintend, overlook*, and *visit* us in all the concerns and duties of life.

IV. COMMANDMENTS, מצות MITSVOTH, from צוה *tasvah* to *command, order, ordain;* because they show us what we should do, and what we should leave undone, and exact our obedience.

V. TESTIMONIES, עדות EDOTH, from עד *ad*, denoting *beyond, farther, all along*, to *bear witness*, or *testimony*. The rites and ceremonies of the law; because they point out matters *beyond* themselves, being *types* and *representations* of the good things that were to come.

VI. JUDGMENTS, משפטים MISHPATIM, from שפט *shaphat*, to *judge, determine, regulate, order*, and *discern*, because they *judge* concerning our words and works; show the *rules* by which they should be *regulated;* and cause us to *discern* what is *right* and *wrong*, and *decide* accordingly.

VII. TRUTH, אמונה EMUNAH, from אמן *aman*, to *make steady, constant*, to *settle, trust, believe*. The *law* that is established, steady, confirmed, and ordered in all things, and sure; which should be *believed* on the authority of God, and *trusted* to as an infallible *testimony* from Him who cannot *lie* nor deceive.

VIII. WORD, דבר *dabar*, from the same root, to *discourse, utter one's sentiments, speak consecutively* and *intelligibly;* in which it appears to differ from מלל *malal*, to *utter articulate sounds*. Any prophecy or immediate communication from heaven, as well as the whole body of Divine revelation, is emphatically called דבר יהוה *debar Yehovah, the word of Jehovah*. On the same ground we call the whole *Old and New Testament* THE WORD OF THE LORD, as we term the volume in which they are contained THE BIBLE—THE BOOK. In his revelation God speaks to man; shows him, in a clear, concise, intelligible, and rational way, his interest, his duty, his privileges; and, in a word, the reasonable service that he requires of him.

IX. WAY, דרך DERECH, from the same root, to *proceed, go on, walk, tread*. The *way* in which God goes in order to instruct and save man; the *way* in which man must tread in order to be safe, holy, and happy. *God's manner of acting or proceeding* in providence and grace; and the *way* that man should take in order to answer the end of his creation and redemption.

X. RIGHTEOUSNESS, צדקה TSEDAKAH, from צדק *tsadak*, to *do justice*, to *give full weight*. That which teaches a man to give to all their *due;* to give GOD his *due*, MAN his *due*, and HIMSELF his *due;* for every man has duties to *God*, his *neighbor*, and *himself*, to perform. This word is applied to God's *judgments, testimonies*, and *commandments;* they are all *righteous*, give to all their *due*, and require what is due from every one.

The *three* words, which some *add* here, are, 1. FAITHFULNESS, אמונה EMUNAH: but see this under No. VII.; nor does it appear in ver. 90, where it occurs, to be used as a characteristic of God's *law*, but rather his exact fulfilment of his *promises* to man.

The *second* is JUDGMENT, משפט *mishpat*. See this under No. VI.: it occurs in ver. 84 and 121: "When wilt thou execute judgment," &c.; but is not used in those places as one of the *ten words*.

The *third* is NAME, שם *shem*, see ver. 132: but this is no characteristic of God's law; it refers here simply to himself. *Those that love thy* NAME is the same as *those that love* THEE. Bishop *Nicholson* inserts *promises* among the *ten* words: but this occurs no where in the Psalm.

We might, and with much more propriety, add a *fourth*, אמרה IMRAH, from אמר *amar*, to *branch out, spread*, or *diffuse itself*, as the *branches of a tree;* and which is often used for a *word spoken, a speech*. This often occurs in the Psalm: and we regularly translate it *word*, and put no difference or distinction between it and דבר *dabar*, No. VIII.: but it is not exactly the *same;* דבר *dabar* may apply more properly to *history, relation, description*, and such like; while, אמרתך *imrathecha, thy word*, may mean an *immediate oracle*, delivered solemnly from God to his prophet for the instruction of men. But the two words appear often indifferently used; and it would not be easy to ascertain the different shades of meaning between these two roots.

Having thus far introduced the Psalm to the reader's attention, I should probably speak at large of the *elegance* of its composition, and the *importance* and *utility* of its matter. Like all other portions of Divine revelation, it is elegant, important, and useful; and while I admire the fecundity of the psalmist's genius, the unabating flow of his poetic vein, his numerous synonyms, and his *copia verborum*, by which he is enabled to expand, diversify, and illustrate the same idea; presenting it to his reader in all possible points of view, so as to render it pleasing, instructive, and impressive; I cannot rob the rest of the book of its just praise by setting this, as many have done, above all the pieces it contains. It is by far the largest, the most artificial, and most diversified; yet, in proportion to its length, it contains the fewest ideas of any Psalm in the Book.

6 [f]Then shall I not be ashamed, when I have respect unto all thy commandments.

7 [g]I will praise thee with uprightness of heart, when I shall have learned [h]thy righteous judgments.

8 I will keep thy statutes: O forsake me not utterly.

[f]Job xxii. 26; 1 John ii. 28——[g]Ver. 171

[h]Heb. *judgments of thy righteousness*

Several of the ancients, particularly the *Greek fathers*, have considered it as an abridgement of David's life; in which he expresses all the states through which he had passed; the trials, persecutions, succours, and encouragements he had received. The *Latin fathers* perceive in it all the morality of the Gospel, and rules for a man's conduct in every situation of life. Cassiodorus asserts that it contains the sentiments of the prophets, apostles, martyrs, and all the saints. In the introduction to the Book of Psalms I have conjectured that many of them were composed from notes taken at different times, and in widely different circumstances; hence the different states described in the same Psalm, which could not have been at one and the same time the experience of the same person. It is most likely that this Psalm was composed in this way; and this, as well as its *acrostical* arrangement, will account for its general want of connexion.

Though the most judicious interpreters assign it to the times of the Babylonish captivity; yet there are so many things in it descriptive of David's state, experience, and affairs, that I am led to think it might have come from his pen; or if composed at or under the captivity, was formed out of his notes and *memoranda*.

I shall now make short remarks on the principal subjects in each part; and, at the end of each, endeavour by the *Analysis* to show the *connexion* which the *eight* verses of each have among themselves, and the use which the reader should make of them. In all the *Versions* except the *Chaldee* this Psalm is numbered cxviii.

LETTER א ALEPH.—*First Division*

Verse 1. *Blessed* are *the undefiled in the way*] אשרי תמימי דרך *ashrey temimey darech*, "O the blessedness of the perfect ones in the way." This Psalm begins something like the *first*, where see the notes. By the *perfect*, which is the proper meaning of the original word, we are to undertsand those who sincerely believe what God has spoken, religiously observe all the rules and ceremonies of his religion, and have their lives and hearts regulated by the spirit of love, fear, and obedience. This is farther stated in the *second* verse.

Verse 3. *They also do no iniquity*] They avoid all idolatry, injustice, and wrong; and they walk in God's ways, not in those ways to which an evil heart might entice them, nor those in which the thoughtless and the profligate tread.

Verse 4. *Thy precepts diligently.*] מאד *meod*, "superlatively, to the uttermost." God has never given a commandment, the observance of which he knew to be *impossible*. And to whatsoever he has commanded he requires *obedience;* and *his grace is sufficient for us.* We must not trifle with God.

Verse 5. *O that my ways were directed*] "I wish that my way may be *confirmed* to *keep thy statutes.*" Without thee I can do nothing; my soul is *unstable* and *fickle;* and it will continue *weak* and *uncertain* till thou *strengthen* and establish it.

Verse 6. *Then shall I not be ashamed*] Every act of transgression in the wicked man tends to *harden his heart;* and render it *callous.* If a man who fears God is so unhappy as to fall into sin, his conscience reproaches him, and he is *ashamed* before God and man. This is a full proof that God's Spirit has not utterly departed from him, and that he may repent, believe and be *healed.*

Unto all thy commandments.] God requires *universal obedience*, and all things are possible to him whom Christ strengthens; and all things are possible to him that believes. *Allow* that *any* of God's commandments *may* be transgressed, and we shall soon have the whole decalogue set aside.

Verse 8. *O forsake me not utterly.*] עד מאד *ad meod*, "to utter dereliction;" never leave me to my own strength, nor to my own heart!

ANALYSIS OF LETTER ALEPH.—*First Division*

I. In this first *octonary* the prophet commends to us the law of God, and persuades us to practise it by two arguments: 1. Happiness, ver. 1, 2. 2. The excellence of the Lawgiver, ver. 4.

II. He shows his affection to this law, desiring grace to keep it, ver. 5.

On which he knew there would follow two effects:

1. Peace of conscience: "He should not be ashamed," &c.

2. Thankfulness to God for his teaching, ver. 7.

"Blessed are they who are undefiled in the way," &c.

"Blessed are they who keep his testimonies," &c.

"They also do no iniquity," &c.

I. The *first argument* used by the prophet to persuade men to obedience is *blessedness.* He that would be happy must be obedient; and his obedience, if true, may be thus discerned:—

1. "He must be undefiled in the way." Keep himself from sin.

2. "He must walk in the law of the Lord," &c. Which is the *rule* of our faith, life, and worship.

3. "He must keep his testimonies." Search them out in God's word.

4. "He must seek him with a whole heart." With sincerity search his law to the utmost, both what it *bids*, and what it *forbids*, in order to know the mind of the Lawgiver.

5. "They also do no iniquity." They work no iniquity with 1. Purpose of heart; 2. Delight; 3. With perseverance; 4. Nor at all, when the heart is fully sanctified unto God; Christ dwelling in it by faith.

6. *They walk in his way*, which the wicked

ב BETH

9 Wherewithal shall a young man cleanse his way? by taking heed *thereto* according to thy word.

10 With my whole heart have I [i]sought thee: O let me not [k]wander from thy commandments.

11 [l]Thy word have I hid in mine heart, that I might not sin against thee.

12 Blessed *art* thou, O LORD: [m]teach me thy statutes.

13 With my lips have I [n]declared all the judgments of thy mouth.

[i]2 Chron. xv. 15——[k]Ver. 21, 118——[l]Psa. xxxvii. 31; Luke ii. 19, 51——[m]Ver. 26, 33, 64, 68, 108, 124, 135; Psa. xxv. 4——[n]Psa. xxxiv. 11

do not: but the righteous have taken it for their path through life; and should they at any time swerve from it, they come back by repentance and confession to God.

The prophet's *second argument* to persuade to obedience is the authority of the Lawgiver. All disobedience proceeds either from contempt of God's laws, or rebellion against them: but David brings to our mind the authority of the Lawgiver, from a consideration of *who* he is who commands our obedience as his servants: "Thou hast commanded that we keep," &c.

1. *Thou*, who knowest when we err, and wilt punish us.

2. *Hast commanded*—absolutely enjoined.

3. *That we keep*, &c.—they cannot be dispensed with.

4. *Diligently*, &c. Not negligently or lazily, or Satan will take advantage of us.

II. The blessedness promised to the keepers of God's law moved the prophet to send forth this ardent prayer, "O that my ways," &c.

1. *David* was a great king, and yet desires to be obedient.

2. He answers God's *command* by a *prayer*, to be enabled to perform it by his grace.

3. "O that my ways," &c. My counsels, actions, &c., were conformable to the straitness and regularity of thy law.

4. He knew he could not be too closely united to God, and therefore he prays to be directed.

Which prayer he knew God would hear; and that the effect would be quietness of soul, and boldness at a throne of grace.

1. "Then shall I not be confounded," &c. If his heart were right with God, he should not fly from him, as did *Adam:* that was the effect of disobedience.

2. If God *directed his ways* to the keeping of his commandments, he should find no amazement in his conscience, but holy boldness.

And this effect will produce another fruit, a thankful heart.

1. "I will praise thee." Give thee thanks for they grace and assistance.

2. "With uprightness of heart." Not with his tongue only, but with an honest and upright heart.

3. But this could not be done till God had taught him: "I will praise thee when I shall have learned," &c. Not to know them only with my *understanding*, but to make them the *rule of my life*, which cannot be but by the *influence* of the *Spirit of* GOD.

And what follows upon this will be a firm purpose of heart to be obedient to God's laws.

1. "I will keep thy statutes." So am I fully resolved and decreed with myself. And it is a great help to godliness to *resolve to live a godly life;* for how shall that be *performed* which is not purposed.

2. And yet this purpose or conclusion he makes in *God's strength;* and therefore constantly prays: "O forsake me not utterly." Without thy aid I can do nothing: but if at any time in thy just judgment thou desert me, that I may know and feel my own weakness, and learn the better to fly to thee, let it not be an utter desertion. Forsake me not, neither too much nor too long.

LETTER ב BETH—*Second Division*

Verse 9. *A young man cleanse his way*] ארח *orach*, which we translate *way* here, signifies a *track*, a *rut*, such as is made by the wheel of a cart or chariot. A *young sinner* has no *broad beaten* path; he has his *private ways* of offence, his *secret pollutions:* and how shall he *be cleansed* from these? how can he be saved from what will destroy mind, body, and soul? Let him hear what follows; the description is from God.

1. He is to *consider* that his way is *impure;* and how abominable this must make him appear in the sight of God.

2. He must examine it *according to God's word*, and carefully hear what God has said concerning *him* and *it*.

3. He must *take heed* to it, לשמר *lishmor*, to *keep guard*, and *preserve his way*—his general course of life, from all defilement.

Verse 10. *With my whole heart have I sought thee*] 4. He must *seek God;* make *earnest prayer* and *supplication* to him for Divine *light*, for a *tender conscience*, and for *strength* to walk uprightly. 5. His *whole heart;* all his affections must be engaged here, or he cannot succeed. If he keep any affection for the idol or abomination; if his *heart* do not give it before the Lord, he may make many prayers, but God will answer none of them. 6. He must *take care to keep in the path of duty*, of abstinence and self-denial; not permitting either his *eye*, his *hand*, or his *heart* to *wander* from the *commandments* of his Maker.

Verse 11. *Thy word have I hid in my heart*] 7. He must *treasure* up those portions of *God's word* in his mind and heart which speak against uncleanness of every kind; and that recommend purity, chastity, and holiness. The word of Christ should dwell *richly* in him. If God's word be only in his *Bible*, and not also in his *heart*, he may soon and easily be surprised into his *besetting* sin.

Verse 12. *Blessed* art *thou*] 8. He must *acknowledge the mercy of God*, in so far preserving him from all the *consequences* of his sin. 9. He should beg of him to become his *teacher*, that his heart and conscience might be *instructed* in the *spirituality* of his statutes.

Verse 13. *With my lips have I declared*] **10.**

14 I have rejoiced in the way of thy testimonies, as *much as* in all riches.

15 I will [o]meditate in thy precepts, and have respect unto thy ways.

16 I will [p]delight myself in thy statutes: I will not forget thy word.

ג GIMEL

17 [q]Deal bountifully with thy servant, *that* I may live, and keep thy word.

18 [r]Open thou mine eyes, that I may behold wondrous things out of thy law.

19 [s]I *am* a stranger in the earth: hide not thy commandments from me.

20 [t]My soul breaketh for the longing *that it hath* unto thy judgments at all times.

21 Thou hast rebuked the proud *that are* cursed, which do [u]err from thy commandments.

---

[o]Psalm i. 2; verse 23, 48, 78——[p]Psalm i. 2; verse 35, 47, 70, 77——[q]Psalm cxvi. 7——[r]Hebrew, *reveal* [s]Genesis xlvii. 9; 1 Chronicles xxix. 15; Psalm xxxix. 12; 2 Corinthians v. 6; Hebrew xi. 13——[t]Psalm cxlii. 1, 2; lxiii. 1; lxxxiv. 2; verse 40, 131——[u]Ver. 10, 110, 118

He should *declare* to his own heart, and to all his *companions in iniquity*, God's *judgments* against himself and them; that if his *long-suffering mercy* have not made a proper impression on their hearts, they may tremble at his approaching *judgments.*

Verse 14. *I have rejoiced*] 11. He must consider it his *chief happiness* to be found in the *path of obedience*, giving his whole heart and strength to God; and when enabled to do it, he should rejoice more in it than if he had gained thousands of gold and silver. O how great is the treasure of a tender and approving conscience!

Verse 15. *I will meditate*] 12. He should encourage self-examination and reflection; and meditate frequently on God's words, works, and ways; and especially on his gracious dealings towards him. 13. He should *keep his eye* upon *God's steps;* setting the example of his Saviour before his eyes, going *where* he would *go*, and *nowhere* else; *doing* what he would *do*, and *nothing* else; keeping the *company* that he would *keep*, and *none* else; and doing every thing in reference to the *final judgment.*

Verse 16. *I will delight myself*] The word is very emphatical: אשתעשע *eshtaasha, I will skip about and jump for joy.* 14. He must exult in God's word as his treasure, live in the spirit of obedience as his work, and ever glory in God, who has called him to such a *state* of salvation. 15. He must never forget what God has *done for him, done in him,* and promised *farther to do;* and he must not *forget* the *promises* he had made, and the *vows* of the Lord that are upon him. Any young man who attends to these *fifteen* particulars will get his impure way cleansed; victory over his sin; and, if he abide faithful to the Lord that bought him, an eternal heaven at last among them that are *sanctified.*

Analysis of Letter Beth.—*Second Division*

In the first part the psalmist, having commended God's law, from its Author—God, and its end—happiness, shows us in the *second* part the efficacy and utility of it to a *holy life*, without which there can be no *happiness.* And in order to show this effect, he chooses the most unlikely *subject.*

I. A *young man*, in whom the law of the members is most strong; he wants experience; he is headstrong, and generally under the government, not of reason nor religion, but of his own passions.

II. The psalmist shows that, to cleanse the way of such, he must "take heed to them," watch over them, and "remember his Creator in the days of his youth."

As a man must become *holy* in order to be *happy*, he shows how this holiness is to be attained, and adduces his own experience.

1. Seek God with thy "whole heart." Be truly sensible of your wants.

2. Keep and remember what God says: "Thy words have I hidden," &c.

3. Reduce all this to practice: "That I might not sin against thee."

4. Bless God for what he has given: "Blessed art thou," &c.

5. Ask more: "Teach me thy statutes."

6. Be ready to communicate his knowledge to others: "With my lips have I declared."

7. Let it have a due effect on thy own heart: "I have rejoiced," &c.

8. Meditate frequently upon them: "I will meditate," &c.

9. Deeply reflect on them: "I will have respect," &c. As food undigested will not nourish the body, so the word of God not considered with deep meditation and reflection will not feed the soul.

10. Having pursued the above course, he should continue in it, and then his happiness would be secured: "I will not forget thy word. I will (in consequence) delight myself in thy statutes."

Letter ג Gimel.—*Third Division*

Verse 17. *Deal bountifully*] גמל *gemol, reward* thy servant. Let him have the return of his faith and prayers, that the Divine *life* may be preserved in his soul! Then he will keep thy word. From גמל *gamal*, to reward, &c., comes the name of ג *gimel*, the *third* letter in the Hebrew alphabet, which is prefixed to every verse in this *part*, and commences it with its own name. This is a stroke of the psalmist's *art* and *ingenuity.*

Verse 18. *Open thou mine eyes*] גל עיני *gal eynai, reveal my eyes,* illuminate my understanding, take away the veil that is on my heart, and then shall I see wonders in thy law. The Holy Scriptures are plain enough; but the heart of man is *darkened* by sin. The *Bible* does not so much need a *comment*, as the *soul* does the *light of the Holy Spirit.* Were it not for the darkness of the human intellect, the things relative to salvation would be easily apprehended.

22 [v]Remove from me reproach and contempt; for I have kept thy testimonies.

23 Princes also did sit *and* speak against me: *but* thy servant did [w]meditate in thy statutes.

24 [x]Thy testimonies also *are* my delight *and* [y]my counsellors.

ד DALETH

25 [z]My soul cleaveth unto the dust: [a]quicken thou me according to thy word.

26 I have declared my ways, and thou heardest me: [b]teach me thy statutes.

27 Make me to understand the way of thy precepts: so [c]shall I talk of thy wondrous works.

28 [d]My soul [e]melteth for heaviness; strengthen thou me according unto thy word.

29 Remove from me the way of lying: and grant me thy law graciously.

30 I have chosen the way of truth: thy judgments have I laid *before me.*

---

[v]Psa. xxxix. 8——[w]Ver. 15——[x]Ver. 77, 92——[y]Heb. *men of counsel*——[z]Psa. xliv. 25——[a]Ver. 40; Psa. cxliii. 11——[b]Ver. 12; Psa. xxv. 4; xxvii. 11; lxxxvi. 11 [c]Psa. cxlv. 5, 6——[d]Psa. cvii. 26——[e]Heb. *dropped*

Verse 19. *I am a stranger in the earth*] In the *land.* Being obliged to wander about from place to place, I am like a *stranger* even in my *own country.* If it refer to the *captives* in *Babylon,* it may mean that they felt themselves there as in a state of *exile;* for, although they had been *seventy* years in it, they still felt it as a *strange* land, because they considered Palestine their *home.*

Verse 20. *My soul breaketh*] We have a similar expression: *It broke my heart, That is heart-breaking, She died of a broken heart.* It expresses excessive longing, grievous disappointment, hopeless love, accumulated sorrow. By this we may see the *hungering* and *thirsting* which the psalmist had after righteousness, often mingled with much *despondency.*

Verse 21. *Thou hast rebuked the proud*] This was done often in the case of David; and was true also in reference to the Babylonians, who held the Israelites in subjection, and whose kings were among the proudest of human beings. Instead of זדים *zedim,* the *proud,* some MSS. read זרים *zarim, strangers,* and one reads גוים *goyim,* the *heathen;* and so the *Syriac.*

Verse 22. *Remove from me reproach and contempt*] Of these the captives in Babylon had a more than ordinary load.

Verse 23. *Princes also did sit*] It is very likely that the *nobles* of Babylon did often, by wicked misrepresentations, render the minds of the kings of the empire evil affected towards the Jews.

Verse 24. *Thy testimonies also* are—*my counsellors.*] אנשי עצתי *anshey atsathi,* "the men of my counsel." I sit with them; and I consider every testimony thou hast given as a particular counsellor; one whose advice I especially need.

The Analysis will farther explain the particular uses of this part.

Analysis of Letter Gimel.—*Third Division*

In this division the psalmist—

I. Reckons up the *impediments* he may meet with in endeavouring to keep God's law.

II. Prays God to remove them.

First impediment. A *dead soul* and a *dull heart;* and therefore he prays for grace that he may *live* and keep *God's word.*

Second impediment. Blindness of understanding: "Open my eyes, that I may see wonders in thy law." The wonderful equity, wisdom, and profit of it.

Third impediment. His *wayfaring* and *uncertain situation:* I am a "stranger upon the earth;" therefore, "hide not thy commandments from me." Should I be frequently destitute of thy ordinances, leave me not without thy Spirit's teaching.

Fourth impediment. His *infirmity* and *imperfection:* "My soul breaks," &c. I wish to be at *all times,* what I am *sometimes,* full of desire, fervour, zeal, prayer, and faith. Then shall I be what I should be, when my heart is *steady* in seeking thy salvation.

Fifth impediment. Pride of heart. This he saw in *others,* and was afraid that it might take place in himself; and he knew if it did, he should *wander from the commandment,* and come under a *curse.*

Sixth impediment. The *reproach* and *contempt* he met with in consequence of his endeavours to live a godly life. Against this he prays as a grievous temptation: "Remove from me reproach and contempt."

Seventh impediment. The *rulers of the people plotted against his life;* they even met in council about it: "Princes did also sit and speak against me." It is difficult to bear reproach even for Christ's sake; though it should be a matter of glorying: but he must be strong in the faith, who can stand against *keen raillery,* and *state persecution.*

But what effect had all this upon the psalmist?

1. He cleaved to God's *testimonies,* and conscientiously *observed* them.

2. He made them his *counsellors*—drew all his wisdom from them; and he was amply rewarded, for they became *his delight.* Every man profits who is faithful to his God.

Letter ד Daleth.—*Fourth Division*

Verse 25. *My soul cleaveth unto the dust*] It would be best to translate נפשי *naphshi, my life;* and then *cleaving to the dust* may imply an apprehension of *approaching death;* and this agrees best with the petition.

Quicken thou me] חיני *chaiyeni,* "make me alive." Keep me from going down into the dust.

Verse 26. *I have declared my ways*] ספרתי *sipparti,* "I have numbered my ways;" I have searched them out; I have investigated them. And that he had earnestly *prayed* for pardon of what was wrong in them, is evident; for he adds, "Thou heardest me."

Verse 28. *My soul melteth*] דלף *dalaph* sig-

31 I have stuck unto thy testimonies: O
LORD, put me not to shame.

32 I will run the way of thy commandments,
when thou shalt [f]enlarge my heart.

XXV. DAY. MORNING PRAYER

ה HE

33 [g]Teach me, O LORD, the way of thy
statutes; and I shall keep it [h]*unto* the end.

34 [i]Give me understanding, and I shall keep
thy law; yea, I shall observe it with *my* whole
heart.

35 Make me to go in the path of thy commandments; for therein do I [k]delight.

36 Incline my heart unto thy testimonies,
and not to [l]covetousness.

37 [m]Turn [n]away mine eyes from [o]beholding
vanity; *and* [p]quicken thou me in thy way.

---

[f]1 Kings iv. 29; Isa. lx. 5; 2 Cor. vi. 11——[g]Ver. 12——[h]Ver. 112; Matt. x. 22; Rev. ii. 26——[i]Ver. 73; Prov. ii. 6; James i. 5——[k]Ver. 16

[l]Ezek. xxxiii. 31; Mark vii. 21, 22; Luke xii. 15; 1 Tim. vi. 10; Heb. xiii. 5——[m]Isa. xxxiii. 15——[n]Heb. *make to pass*——[o]Prov. xxiii. 5——[p]Ver. 40

---

nifies *to distil*, to *drop* as *tears from the eye.* As my distresses cause the *tears* to *distil* from my eyes, so the overwhelming load of my afflictions causes my life to *ebb* and *leak* out.

Verse 29. *The way of lying*] The propensity to *falsity* and *prevarication;* whatsoever is contrary to *truth. Remove me* from its solicitations, and *remove* it from *me.* "Grant me thy law graciously;" give it to me as a rule of moral conduct; but give it to me graciously through the *Gospel;* and then it will not be the letter that killeth, but will be sanctified to me, so as to become to me holy, just, and GOOD.

Verse 30. *I have chosen the way of truth*] And that I may continue in it, "remove from me the way of lying." See above.

Verse 31. *I have stuck*] דבקתי *dabakti*, I have *cleaved* to, been *glued* to, them: the same word as in ver. 25. My *soul cleaves* as much to *thy testimonies*, as my *life* has *cleaved* to the *dust.*

O Lord, put me not to shame.] Let my sins and follies be blotted out by thy mercy; and so *hide* and *cover* them that they shall never appear, either in *this* or the *coming world,* to my *shame* and *confusion!* How many need to be importunate with God in this prayer!

Verse 32. *I will run*] The particle כי, which we translate *when,* should be translated *because: Because thou shalt enlarge,* or dilate, *my heart;* make plain my path by cleansing me from my impurity, and taking the hinderances out of my way. I *will* then *run* without dread of stumbling, and every day make sensible progress.

ANALYSIS OF LETTER DALETH.—*Fourth Division*

The psalmist—

I. Sets down the state of an *imperfect* man.

II. *Confesses* it.

III. *Asks grace and mercy.*

IV. *Professes* what in consequence he would do.

I. 1. "My soul cleaveth unto the dust:" His affections cleaved to things below, instead of being set on things above.

2. "Quicken thou me:" Give me a life *according to thy law.* By cleaving to the earth, he was earthly; by cleaving to the flesh, he was carnal; but by living according to the spiritual law, he was to become one spirit with God.

II. He *confesses* his imperfections.

1. "I have declared my ways." I acknowledge all my wanderings, sins, follies, and unfaithfulness; I have hidden nothing from thee.

2. Thou didst *hear me;* forgavest me out of thy mere mercy.

3. Do the like now: "Teach me thy statutes." These two things should be sought together: *mercy* to pardon, and *grace* to assist and renew.

III. He proceeds in this *prayer.*

1. "Make me to understand:" Where the *mind* is *darkened,* the *heart* cannot be *well ordered.*

2. He that asks *good things* from God should ask them for a *good end:* "Make me to understand; so shall I talk," &c.

3. He would show *God's wondrous works:* I shall talk of thy wondrous *law,*—thy wondrous *Gospel,*—thy wondrous *mercy* in saving sinners,—the wondrous *means* thou usest, &c.

IV. He returns to his confession, and states what he *purposes to do.*

1. "My soul melts:" I am full of trouble and distress.

2. "Strengthen thou me:" Give me the grace thou hast promised.

3. "Remove from me the way of lying:" Give me power to avoid all sin.

4. "Grant me thy law graciously:" Print the matter of it in my heart, and abolish my corruption.

5. He *chooses the truth.*

6. He *adheres* to it.

7. He will *continue* in it.

8. Yea, and with *greater diligence* than ever. To make up for lost time, he will now *run:* and, while running, keep in God's way. Some run, but they run *out* of it.

LETTER ה HE.—*Fifth Division*

Verse 33. *Teach me, O Lord, the way of thy statutes*] To understand the spiritual reference of all the statutes, &c., under the law, required a teaching which could only come from God.

I shall keep it unto *the end.*] Here is a *good thing* asked for a good *end.* He wishes for heavenly teaching; not to make a parade of it, but to enable him to discern his duty, that he might act accordingly.

Verse 34. *With* my *whole heart.*] I will not trifle with my God, I will not divide my affections with the world; God shall have all.

Verse 36. *Not to covetousness.*] Let me have no inordinate love for gain of any kind, nor for any thing that may grieve thy Spirit, or induce me to seek my happiness here *below.*

Verse 37. *From beholding vanity*] An idol,

38 [q]Stablish thy word unto thy servant, who *is devoted* to thy fear.

39 Turn away my reproach, which I fear: for thy judgments *are* good.

40 Behold, I have [r]longed after thy precepts: [s]quicken me in thy righteousness.

ו VAU

41 [t]Let thy mercies come also unto me, O LORD, *even* thy salvation, according to thy word.

42 [u]So shall I have wherewith to answer him that reproacheth me: for I trust in thy word.

43 And take not the word of truth utterly out of my mouth; for I have hoped in thy judgments.

44 So shall I keep thy law continually for ever and ever.

45 And I will walk [v]at liberty: for I seek thy precepts.

[q]2 Sam. vii. 25——[r]Ver. 20——[s]Ver. 25, 37, 88, 107, 149, 156, 159——[t]Psa. cvi. 4; ver. 77

[u]Or, *So shall I answer him that reproacheth me in a thing* ——[v]Heb. *at large*

worldly pleasure, beauty, finery; any thing that is vain, empty, or transitory. Let me not *behold* it; let me not *dwell upon* it. Let me remember *Achan:* he *saw,*—he *coveted,*—he *took,*—he *hid* his theft, and was *slain* for his sin.

Verse 38. *Stablish thy word*] Fulfil the promises thou hast made to me.

Verse 39. *Turn away my reproach, which I fear*] This may be understood of the reproach which a man may meet with in consequence of living a godly life, for such a life was never *fashionable* in any *time* or *country.* But I have found the following note on the passage: "I have done a *secret evil;* my soul is sorry for it: if it become *public,* it will be a heavy reproach to me. O God, turn it away, and let it never meet the eye of man!"—*Anon.*

Verse 40. *Behold, I have longed*] Thou searchest the heart; thou knowest that I have long desired thy salvation; thou seest that this desire still remains. Behold it! it is thy work; and through thy mercy I breathe after thy mercy.

Quicken me] I am *dying;* O give me the spirit of life in Christ Jesus!

ANALYSIS OF LETTER HE.—*Fifth Division*

In this part, which is wholly *precatory,* the psalmist prays,—

I. That God would *illuminate* his mind.

II. That he would *remove all those hinderances* which might prevent him from doing his duty.

I. 1. The first petition is for illumination: "Teach me;" point me out *what* I am to *learn,* and *how* I am to learn it.

2. The second is, "Give me understanding." Let me *comprehend,* that I may *profit* by this teaching.

3. The *end* for which he asks,—that he "may keep the law."

He specifies the manner: 1. He will be no *temporizer;* he will keep it "to the end." 2. He will be no *hypocrite;* he will keep it "with his whole heart."

1. He prays for *power:* "Make me to go." Without thy Spirit's help I can do nothing: I do not know the way without thy *teaching;* I cannot walk in it without thy *help.*

2. He wishes to go in *the path;* the way in which all God's followers have walked.

3. It is a *path,* not a public road; a path where no *beast* goes, and *men* seldom.

4. He gives a *reason* why his petition should be granted: "Therein do I delight."

II. He prays to have all impediments removed.

1. "Incline my heart." Bind it down to a willing obedience.

2. "Not to covetousness." Keep me from the *love* of *money,* the *world,* the *creature.*

3. He prays against the *desire of the eye:* "Turn away mine eyes." Let the eye of my body be turned away *from* vanity; the eye of my mind turned away *to* thee.

4. Let me find the benefit of this turning: "Stablish thy word,"—make good thy word; give me grace to stand.

5. For which he gives this reason: "I am thy servant, and am devoted to thy fear."

6. He is afraid of the consequences if he be not faithful: "Turn away my reproach." Let it not be said, at the day of judgment, "I was hungry, and you gave me no meat," &c.

7. He knows if God condemns it must be justly: "For thy judgments are good." *Man* may *condemn* where *thou approvest; he* may *approve* where *thou condemnest. Thy judgments* alone *are good.*

8. He concludes, desiring the Lord to look on the state of his heart: "Behold!" 1. Is not my heart right before thee? 2. If so, *quicken me; make me alive,* and *keep me alive!* Without the *latter,* the *former* will answer no end.

LETTER ו VAU.—*Sixth Division*

Verse 41. *Let thy mercies come*] Let me speedily see the accomplishment of all my prayers! Let me have *thy salvation*—such a deliverance as it becomes thy greatness and goodness to impart. Let it be *according to thy word*—thy exceeding great and precious promises.

Verse 42. *So shall I have wherewith to answer*] Many say, "My hope in thy mercy is vain;" but when thou fulfillest thy promises to me, then shall I answer to the confusion of their infidelity.

Verse 43. *Take not the word of truth*] Grant that the assurances which thy prophets have given to the people of approaching deliverance may not fall to the ground; let it appear that *they* have spoken *thy mind,* and that *thou* hast fulfilled *their word.*

Verse 45. *I will walk at liberty*] When freed from the present bondage, we shall rejoice in obedience to thy testimonies; we shall *delight* to keep all thy ordinances.

46 [w]I will speak of thy testimonies also before kings, and will not be ashamed.

47 And I will [x]delight myself in thy commandments, which I have loved.

48 My hands also will I lift up unto thy commandments, which I have loved; and I will [y]meditate in thy statutes.

ז ZAIN

49 Remember the word unto thy servant, upon which thou hast caused me to [z]hope.

50 This *is* my [a]comfort in my affliction: for thy word hath quickened me.

51 The proud have had me greatly [b]in derision: *yet* have I not [c]declined from thy law.

52 I remembered thy judgments of old, O LORD; and have comforted myself.

53 [d]Horror hath taken hold upon me, because of the wicked that forsake thy law.

54 Thy statutes have been my songs in the house of my pilgrimage.

[w]Psa. cxxxviii. 1; Matt. x. 18, 19; Acts xxvi. 1, 2 [x]Ver. 16——[y]Ver. 15——[z]Ver. 74, 81, 147

[a]Rom. xv. 4——[b]Jer. xx. 7——[c]Job xxiii. 11; Psa. xliv. 18; ver. 157——[d]Ezra ix. 3

Verse 46. *I will speak—before kings*] Dr. *Delaney* supposes that this is spoken in reference to *Achish, king of Gath*, whom David had instructed in the Jewish religion; but we have already seen that it is most likely that the Psalm was compiled under the Babylonish captivity. But the words may with more propriety be referred to the case of *Daniel*, and other bold and faithful Israelites, who spoke courageously before *Nebuchadnezzar*, *Belshazzar*, and *Darius*. See the books of *Daniel*, *Ezra*, and *Nehemiah*.

Verse 47. *Thy commandments, which I have loved.*] O shame to Christians who feel so little affection to the *Gospel of Christ*, when we see such cordial, conscientious, and inviolate attachment in a Jew to the laws and ordinances of Moses, that did not afford a thousandth part of the privileges!

Verse 48. *My hands also will I lift up*] I will present every victim and sacrifice which the law requires. I will make prayer and supplication before thee, lifting up holy hands without wrath and doubting.

ANALYSIS OF LETTER VAU.—*Sixth Division*

The psalmist prays for *mercy*, and promises to show his *thankfulness two ways:*—

I. By a bold confession of God's law.

II. By holy obedience to it.

The whole section consists of two petitions and six promises.

I. i. *First petition.* "Let thy mercies come also unto me—even thy salvation." He joins these two, *mercy* and *salvation*, as *cause* and *effect;* for God's *mercy* can alone bring *salvation.*

This being granted, he vows to be thankful and courageous.

1. He vows to confess God's law, and answer any adversary who may say, "It is vain for him to hope in the Lord," by showing that God has fulfilled his word.

2. That he *will put his trust in God;* because he is omnipotent and merciful.

ii. The *second petition* is, "Take not the word of truth utterly out of my mouth." For which he gives a reason: "I have hoped in thy judgments."

1. "Take not thy word," in which I boast and glory before my adversaries.

2. "Take not the word out of my mouth," so that I dare not speak nor openly profess it.

3. "Take it not away utterly." If for my unfaithfulness thou shouldst shut my mouth for a time, restore thy favour to me, that I may again make confession unto salvation.

4. For which he gives this reason: "I have hoped," &c. I trust in thy fidelity and justice, that thou wilt accomplish, in *promises* and *threatenings*, whatsoever thou hast engaged to perform.

II. Now he shows his *thankfulness* by determining to make confession of God's mercy in a holy life; serving God.

1. With a *free heart:* "I will walk at liberty;" sin shall have no dominion over me.

2. *With a loosened tongue:* "I will speak of thy testimonies also before kings." It is a difficult thing to speak to great men concerning their salvation; it requires great boldness, and equal *humility. Rudeness*, under the guise of *zeal*, spoils every good.

3. With *hearty affection:* "I will delight myself." He who can *delight* in his *duty* has made considerable progress in *piety.*

4. With *corresponding practice:* "My hands will I lift up." My life shall declare that I have not received the grace of God in vain.

5. With a *considerate mind:* "I will meditate in thy statutes." My understanding shall frequently examine them, approve of them, and turn them over to a heart full of fervent affection.

6. This was a work to which he *was accustomed:* "I have loved thy commandments and statutes." Love feels no loads, and habit is a second nature.

LETTER ז ZAIN.—*Seventh Division*

Verse 49. *Remember the word*] Thou hast *promised* to redeem us from our captivity; on that *word* we have built our *hope. Remember* that thou hast thus promised, and *see* that we thus *hope.*

Verse 50. *This* is *my comfort*] While enduring our harsh captivity, we anticipated our enlargement; and thy *word of promise* was the *means* of keeping our souls *alive.*

Verse 51. *The proud have had me*] We have been treated, not only with oppressive *cruelty*, but also with *contempt*, because we still professed to *trust in thee*, the living God, who because of our transgressions hadst been greatly displeased with us; *yet we have not declined from thy law.*

Verse 52. *I remembered thy judgments of*

55 [e]I have remembered thy name, O LORD, in the night, and have kept thy law.
56 This I had, because I kept thy precepts.

ח CHETH

57 [f]*Thou art* my portion, O LORD: I have said that I would keep thy words.
58 I entreated thy [g]favour with *my* whole heart: be merciful unto me [h]according to thy word.
59 I [i]thought on my ways, and turned my feet unto thy testimonies.
60 I made haste, and delayed not to keep thy commandments.

---

[e]Psa. lxiii. 6——[f]Psa. xvi. 5; Jer. x. 16; Lam. iii. 24——[g]Heb. *face;* Job xi. 19——[h]Ver. 41——[i]Luke xv. 17, 18

---

old] The word *judgments* is here taken for *providential dealing;* and indeed *kind treatment;* that which God showed to the Hebrews in bearing with and blessing them. And it was the recollection of *these judgments* that caused him to *comfort* himself.

Verse 53. *Horror hath taken hold upon me*] The word זלעפה *zilaphah,* which we render *horror,* is thought to signify the pestilential burning wind called by the Arabs *simoom.* Here it strongly marks the idea that the psalmist had of the destructive nature of *sin;* it is pestilential; it is corrupting, mortal.

Verse 54. *Thy statutes have been my songs*] During our captivity all our consolation was derived from singing thy praises, and chanting among our fellow-captives portions of thy law, and the precepts it contains.

Verse 55. *I have remembered thy name*] Thou art *Jehovah;* and as *our God* thou hast made thyself known unto us. In the deepest *night* of our affliction this has consoled me.

Verse 56. *This I had, because I kept thy precepts.*] Though thou didst leave us under the power of our enemies, yet thou hast not left us without the consolations of thy Spirit.

ANALYSIS OF LETTER ZAIN.—*Seventh Division*

In this part the psalmist—

I. Prays.

II. Shows his trust in God, notwithstanding his discouragements.

III. Commends the word of God, by showing what blessed effects it had produced in him.

I. 1. He prays: "Remember;" accomplish and perfect thy promise. God's promises are made to prayer and faith; if men do not exert these, God will not fulfil the others.

2. "Made to thy servant:" The promises are made to the *obedient.* It is in vain to desire God to remember *his promises* made to *us,* if we make no conscience to perform *our promises* made to *him.*

3. "Wherein thou hast caused me to put my trust:" This is a forcible argument to induce God to fulfil his promises. They are thy promises; thou hast made them to us; and thou hast caused us to hope, because made by thee, that they shall be fulfilled.

II. He shows that the hope he had in God made him steady, even in afflictions.

1. "This is my comfort in affliction:" That is, God's word and promise.

2. "Thy word hath quickened me;" brought me *life, strength,* and *courage.*

3. He mentions his afflictions. 1. The proud have had me in derision. 2. Yet I have not declined from thy law. 3. For in my afflictions I remembered thy judgments; his casting down the proud and exalting the humble. And, 4. From these considerations he derived comfort.

III. His knowledge of God's purity and judgments caused him to commiserate the state of the wicked.

1. "Horror hath taken hold upon me:" For those who trampled under foot God's word, and persecuted the righteous, he grieved; not because of the evil they did him, but of the evil they did themselves. He describes those men.

2. They forsook God's laws. Probably *apostate* Israelites.

3. He was not without consolation, though much afflicted and harassed. He took delight in God's law, and made his *songs* of it.

4. And this was a source of joy to him both day and night.

5. He concludes with this acclamation: "This I had;" I had this spirit, this power, this comfort, "because I kept thy precepts." While I suffered *for* God, I was enabled to rejoice *in* God. As I made him my portion, so he has been my praise.

LETTER ח CHETH.—*Eighth Division*

Verse 57. Thou art *my portion, O Lord*] From the *fifty-seventh* to the *sixtieth* verse may be seen the *progress* of the work of grace on the human heart, from the first dawn of heavenly light till the soul is filled with the fulness of God. But as I consider this Psalm as *notes* selected from *diaries* of past experience, formed at different times; and that the author has been obliged, for the support of his *acrostic* plan, to interchange circumstances, putting that sometimes *behind* which in the order of grace comes *before;* because, to put it in its right place, the *letters* would not accord with the *alphabetical arrangement;* I shall therefore follow what I conceive to be its *order* in the *connexion of grace,* and not in the *order* in which the words are here laid down.

Verse 59. FIRST.—*I thought on my ways*] חשבתי *chashabti,* I deeply pondered them; I turned them upside down; I viewed my conduct on all sides. The word, as used here, is a metaphor taken from *embroidering,* where the *figure* must appear the *same* on the *one side* as it does on the *other;* therefore, the cloth must be turned on each side every time the needle is set in, to see that the stitch be fairly set. Thus narrowly and scrupulously did the psalmist examine his conduct; and the result was, a deep conviction that he had departed from the way of God and truth.

SECONDLY.—*And turned my feet unto thy testimonies.*] Having made the above discovery, and finding himself under the displeas-

61 The [k]bands of the wicked have robbed me: *but* I have not forgotten thy law.

62 [l]At midnight I will rise to give thanks unto thee, because of thy righteous judgments.

63 I *am* a companion of all *them* that fear thee, and of them that keep thy precepts.

64 [m]The earth, O LORD, is full of thy mercy: [n]teach me thy statutes.

---

[k]Or, *companies*——[l]Acts xvi. 25

[m]Psa. xxxiii. 5——[n]Ver. 12, 26

---

ure of God, he abandoned every evil way, took God's word for his directory, and set out fairly in the way of life and salvation.

Verse 60. THIRDLY.—*I made haste, and delayed not*] He did this with the utmost *speed;* and did not trifle with his convictions, nor seek to drown the voice of conscience.

The original word, which we translate *delayed not*, is amazingly emphatical. ולא התמהמהתי *velo hithmahmahti*, I did not stand *what-what-whating;* or, as we used to express the same sentiment, *shilly-shallying* with myself: I was *determined*, and so set out. The *Hebrew* word, as well as the *English*, strongly marks indecision of mind, positive action being suspended, because the mind is so unfixed as not to be able to make a choice.

Verse 58. FOURTHLY.—Being determined in his heart, he tells us, *I entreated thy favour with* my *whole heart.* He found he had sinned; that he needed *mercy;* that he had no time to lose; that he must be importunate; and therefore he sought that mercy *with all his soul.*

FIFTHLY.—Feeling that he *deserved* nothing but wrath, that he had no *right* to any good, he cries for *mercy* in the way that God had promised to convey it: "Be merciful unto me!" And to this he is encouraged only by the *promise* of God; and therefore prays, "Be merciful unto me ACCORDING to thy WORD."

Verse 57. SIXTHLY.—To keep himself firm in his present resolutions, he binds himself unto the Lord. "I have said that I would keep thy words." Thy vows are upon me, and I must not add to my guilt by breaking them.

SEVENTHLY.—He did not seek in vain; God reveals himself in the fulness of blessedness to him, so that he is enabled to exclaim, *Thou art my portion, O Lord!* My whole soul trusts in thee; my spirit rests supremely satisfied with thee. I have no other inheritance, nor do I desire any. Here then is the *way* to *seek*, the *way* to *find*, and the *way* to be *happy.* Other effects of this conversion may be seen below.

Verse 61. *The bands of the wicked have robbed me*] חבלי *chebley*, the *cables*, *cords*, or *snares* of the wicked. They have *hunted* us like wild beasts; many they have taken for prey, and many they have destroyed.

Verse 62. *At midnight I will rise*] We are so overpowered with a sense of thy goodness, that in season and out of season we will return thee thanks.

Verse 63. *I* am *a companion*] This was the natural consequence of his own conversion; he abandoned the workers of iniquity, and associated with them that feared the Lord.

Verse 64. *The earth is full of thy mercy*] What an astonishing operation has the grace of God! In the midst of want, poverty, affliction, and bondage, it makes those who possess it happy! When Christ dwells in the heart by faith, we have nothing but *goodness* around us. Others may complain; but to us even the earth appears full of the mercy of the Lord.

ANALYSIS OF LETTER CHETH.—*Eighth Division*

In this part we have—

I. The assertion of the psalmist, that *God* was his *portion;* and his resolution upon it to keep God's law.

II. His *prayer* for grace to enable him to do it.

III. His *profession* of *duty* and a *holy life.*

IV. His *concluding* acclamation and *prayer.*

I. "Thou art my portion:" Let others choose as they please, *thou* art sufficient for *me;* I ask no more.

1. And on this I resolve to be thy *obedient servant:* "I have said, that I would keep thy words."

2. But thou knowest I am unable without thy grace to do this; therefore I must entreat thy favour: "Be merciful unto me." There are three helps to a godly life, all which we meet here, viz.:—

1. *Determination.* This makes a man *begin* well: "I have said."

2. *Supplication.* This makes a man *continue* well: "I entreated."

3. *Consideration.* This makes a man, when he *errs, come back* to the way again.

II. He was ready to co-operate with grace: "I have thought on my ways." If we be not workers with God, vain are our prayers. *Two things* are required of us: 1. *Aversion* from evil. 2. *Conversion* to good. Both must meet together.

1. Aversion from evil: "I thought on my ways." But he did not rest here.

2. Conversion to good: "I turned my feet unto thy testimonies."

III. And his sincerity is shown many ways:—

1. By his *readiness* and *zeal:* "I made haste, and delayed not."

2. By his *courage* and *constancy.* Though he was *plundered*, for his adherence to God, *by the bands of the wicked*, yet he *did not forget God's law.*

3. By his *fervour* about it. He was always employed in the work; and would rather take something from his natural rest, than not gratify his hunger and thirst after righteousness: "At midnight I will rise to give thanks."

4. By *selecting his company.* "He who walks with the lame will learn to limp:" therefore, avoiding the society of the wicked, he seeks the company of them *that fear the Lord* and *keep his precepts.*

IV. He concludes with an *acclamation* and *prayer.*

1. "The earth, O Lord, is full of thy mercy." There is not a creature that is not a partaker of thy goodness; let *me* have my portion in it.

2. "Teach me thy statutes." That is, continue to instruct me. I need constant teaching, line upon line, and precept upon precept. Teach thou, and I will learn; and as I learn from thy teaching, I will practise by thy grace.

ט TETH

65 Thou hast dealt well with thy servant, O LORD, according unto thy word.

66 Teach me good judgment and knowledge: for I have believed thy commandments.

67 [o]Before I was afflicted I went astray: but now have I kept thy word.

68 Thou *art* [p]good, and doest good; [q]teach me thy statutes.

69 The proud have [r]forged a lie against me: *but* I will keep thy precepts with *my* whole heart.

70 [s]Their heart is as fat as grease; *but* I [t]delight in thy law.

71 [u]*It is* good for me that I have been afflicted; that I might learn thy statutes.

72 [v]The law of thy mouth *is* better unto me than thousands of gold and silver.

---

[o]Ver. 71; Jer. xxxi. 18, 19; Heb. xii. 11——[p]Psa. cvi. 1; cvii. 1; Matt. xix. 17——[q]Ver. 12, 26——[r]Job xiii. 4; Psa. cix. 2

[s]Psa. xvii. 10; Isa. vi. 10; Acts xxviii. 27——[t]Ver. 35
[u]Ver. 67; Heb. xii. 10, 11——[v]Ver. 127; Psa. xix. 10; Prov. viii. 10, 11, 19

LETTER ט TETH.—*Ninth Division*

Verse 65. *Thou hast dealt well with thy servant*] Whatsoever thy word has promised, thou hast fulfilled. Every *servant* of God can testify that God has done him nothing but *good*, and therefore he can speak *good* of his name.

Verse 66. *Teach me good judgment and knowledge*] טוב טעם ודעת למדני *tob taam vedaath lammedeni. Teach me* (to have) *a good taste and discernment.* Let me see and know the importance of Divine things, and give me a *relish* for them.

Verse 67. *Before I was afflicted I went astray*] Many have been humbled under affliction, and taught to know themselves and humble themselves before God, that probably without this could never have been saved; after this, they have been serious and faithful. *Affliction* sanctified is a great blessing; unsanctified, it is an additional curse.

Verse 68. *Thou* art *good*] And because thou art good, *thou doest good;* and because thou delightest to do good, *teach me thy statutes.*

Verse 69. *The proud have forged a lie*] The poor captives in Babylon had their conduct and motives continually misrepresented, and themselves belied and calumniated.

Verse 70. *Their heart is as fat as grease*] They are egregiously stupid, they have fed themselves without fear; they are become *flesh —brutalized,* and given over to vile affections, and have no kind of *spiritual relish:* but *I delight in thy law*—I have, through thy goodness, a *spiritual feeling* and a spiritual appetite.

Verse 71. It is *good for me that I have been afflicted*] See on ver. 67.

Verse 72. *The law of thy mouth* is *better*] Who can say this? Who *prefers* the law of his God, the Christ that bought him, and the heaven to which he hopes to go, when he can live no longer upon earth, *to thousands of gold and silver?* Yea, how many are there who, like Judas, *sell their Saviour* even for *thirty* pieces of silver? Hear this, ye lovers of the world and of money!

As the letter ט *teth* begins but few words, not forty, in the Hebrew language, there is less *variety* under this division than under any of the preceding.

ANALYSIS OF LETTER TETH.—*Ninth Division*

The psalmist, having been afflicted, shows,—

I. How graciously God dealt with him, in bringing him profitably through it.

II. Prays for a right judgment and knowledge.

III. Expresses his love to God's law, and the value he set upon it.

I. The psalmist gives thanks for mercy granted in affliction.

1. "Thou hast dealt graciously with thy servant." Graciously in afflicting him, and graciously in relieving him.

2. And this thou hast done "according to thy word." Thou hast fulfilled thy *promise.*

II. He prays to be taught of God:—

1. "Teach me good judgment." Many judge badly; for they think that affliction is a sign of God's displeasure. Let me have that *good judgment* that receives it as a fatherly correction from thee.

2. He asks for *science* and *knowledge.* A spiritual perception, and taste for heavenly things.

3. For this he gives his reason: "I have believed thy commandments." If we believe not God, we cannot profit by his word.

4. There is something remarkable in the *manner* of asking: 1. A good or *sound judgment.* 2. *Knowledge;* for without a *sound judgment, knowledge* is of no use.

III. He acknowledges that God's *chastisements* had done him *good.*

1. "Before I was afflicted." Prosperity is often the mother or error.

2. "Now I have kept thy word." Schola crucis, schola lucis, "The school of the cross is the school of light."

3. He acknowledges that the *good God* had done him *good.* To have a right notion of God is a great blessing.

IV. Much of the psalmist's *affliction* proceeded from *wicked men.* These he describes:—

1. They were *proud.* Pride is the mother of *rebellion,* both against *God* and *man.*

2. They were *liars.* Evil speaking and calumny are the first weapons of persecutors.

3. They *forged* these lies; they invented them. There was none *ready* to their hand, so they framed some to serve their purpose.

4. The psalmist opposes them with *humility* and *truth:* "I will keep thy precepts."

5. He shows more particularly their *moral character:* "Their heart was as fat as grease;" they were *stupid, brutish, hoggish.* Their *god* was their *belly.* 1. Because they abounded in *wealth,* they were *proud.* 2. Because they *pampered* themselves, they were *stupid,* and incapable of *moral feeling.* The *fat* is the least *sensible* part of the animal system.

XXV. DAY. EVENING PRAYER

י YOD

73 [w]Thy hands have made me and fashioned me: [x]give me understanding, that I may learn thy commandments.

74 [y]They that fear thee will be glad when they see me; because [z]I have hoped in thy word.

75 I know, O LORD, that thy judgments *are* [a]right, and [b]*that* thou in faithfulness hast afflicted me.

76 Let, I pray thee, thy merciful kindness be [c]for my comfort, according to thy word unto thy servant.

77 [d]Let thy tender mercies come unto me, that I may live: for [e]thy law *is* my delight.

78 Let the proud [f]be ashamed; [g]for they dealt perversely with me without a cause: *but* I will [h]meditate in thy precepts.

79 Let those that fear thee turn unto me, and those that have known thy testimonies.

80 Let my heart be sound in thy statutes; that I be not ashamed.

[w]Job x. 8; Psa. c. 3; cxxxviii. 8; cxxxix. 14——[x]Ver. 34, 144——[y]Psa. xxxiv. 2——[z]Ver. 49, 147——[a]Heb. *righteousness*

[b]Heb. xii. 10——[c]Heb. *to comfort me*——[d]Verse 41 [e]Verse 24, 47, 174——[f]Psalm xxv. 3——[g]Verse 86 [h]Verse 23

V. He shows the *condition* of the godly.

1. They see God's hand in their afflictions.
2. They learn his statutes.
3. They prefer his word to all earthly treasures; and,
4. They persevere in this heavenly disposition, because they continue to depend on God.

LETTER י YOD.—*Tenth Division*

Verse 73. *Thy hands have made me*] Thou hast formed the *mass* out of which I was made; and *fashioned me*—thou hast given me that particular *form* that distinguishes me from all thy other creatures.

Give me understanding] As thou hast raised me above the beasts that perish in my *form* and *mode of life, teach me* that I may live for a higher and nobler end, in loving, serving, and enjoying thee for ever. Show me that I was made for *heaven*, not for *earth*.

Verse 74. *They that fear thee*] They who are truly religious *will be glad*—will rejoice, at this farther proof of the saving power of God.

Verse 75. *I know—that thy judgments are right*] All the dispensations of thy providence are laid in *wisdom*, and executed in *mercy:* let me see that it is through this wisdom and mercy that I have been afflicted.

Verse 76. *Thy merciful kindness*] Let me derive my comfort and happiness from a diffusion of thy love and mercy, חסדך *chasdecha*, thy exuberant goodness, through my soul.

Verse 77. *Let thy tender mercies*] רחמיך *rachameycha, thy fatherly and affectionate feelings.*

Verse 78. *Let the proud be ashamed*] To reduce a *proud man* to *shame*, is to humble him indeed. Let them be *confounded. Without cause*—without any colourable pretext, have they persecuted me.

Verse 79. *Let those that fear thee*] The truly pious.

Turn unto me] Seeing thy work upon me, they shall acknowledge me as a *brand plucked from the burning.*

Verse 80. *Let my heart be sound in thy statutes*] Let it be *perfect*—all given up to thee, and all possessed by thee.

ANALYSIS OF LETTER YOD.—*Tenth Division*

I. In the first place the psalmist prays for understanding, *comfort*, and *mercy;* and uses this argument, I am thy creature: "Thy hands have fashioned me."

II. He prays for *understanding:* Give me *heavenly light* and *influence.*

III. He prays for this that he may *learn God's commandments.* This was his *end.*

1. He endeavours to persuade God to this by the *benefit* that others would receive from seeing his *conversion:* "They that fear thee will be glad," &c.

2. He acknowledges that, if he was at any time *deserted*, it was because he was unfaithful, and that it was in very faithfulness that God had corrected him; therefore God's judgments were right.

3. He prays that God's *merciful kindness* may be extended to him. But this prayer he would not presume to have offered, had he not been authorized and encouraged by God's word: "According to thy word." When God gives a *promise*, he *binds* himself to *fulfil* it.

4. He desires to be treated as a *child* in the *heavenly family;* and therefore prays for God's *fatherly mercies*—his *bowels of compassion.*

5. And he prays for them for this *end*, "that he may live." And here also he adds a reason why he should be heard: "Thy law is my delight."

6. He puts up another petition for his enemies, if they will take timely warning: "Let the proud be ashamed;" let them see their unprincipled conduct and *blush* that they have been persecuting and calumniating innocent people.

7. He next expresses his own resolution: "I will meditate on thy statutes." Howsoever they deal with me, I will cleave unto my God.

8. He prays that he may be acknowledged by the *godly:* "Let them that fear thee turn unto me." God's Church is a communion of saints, and to them has God so distributed his graces that one stands in need of another. Where one *doubts*, the light of another may *solve his difficulty.* One *grieves;* another may *comfort* him. One is *tempted;* another may uphold and re store him. This company the psalmist would have joined to him for these ends.

9. He prays that he may be *sound in the faith*, for without this he could not be *steady* in his *obedience.* Though an *orthodox creed* does not constitute true religion, yet it is the basis of it, and it is a great blessing to have it; and *sound-*

כ CAPH

81 [i]My soul fainteth for thy salvation: *but* [k]I hope in thy word.

82 [l]Mine eyes fail for thy word, saying, When wilt thou comfort me?

83 For [m]I am become like a bottle in the smoke; *yet* do I not forget thy statutes.

84 [n]How many *are* the days of thy servant? [o]when wilt thou execute judgment on them that persecute me?

85 [p]The proud have digged pits for me, which *are* not after thy law.

86 All thy commandments *are* [q]faithful: [r]they persecute me [s]wrongfully; help thou me.

87 They had almost consumed me upon earth; but I forsook not thy precepts.

88 [t]Quicken me after thy loving-kindness; so shall I keep the testimony of thy mouth.

---

[i]Psalm lxxiii. 26; lxxxiv. 2——[k]Ver. 74, 114——[l]Ver. 123; Psalm lxix. 3——[m]Job xxx. 30——[n]Psalm xxxix. 4——[o]Revelation vi. 10

[p]Psalm xxxv. 7; Proverbs xvi. 27——[q]Hebrew, *faithfulness*——[r]Ver. 78——[s]Psalm xxxv. 19; xxxviii. 19——[t]Ver. 40

---

ness of mind is a strong help to the retention of a sound creed.

Finally, he shows the *end* for which he desires this blessing, that "he may not be ashamed." That he may continue sincere and upright, have dominion over all sin, give no place to secret iniquities, and that he may never be put to the blush before God or man. Reader, beg of God to enable *thee* to lay these things profitably to heart.

LETTER כ CAPH.—*Eleventh Division*

Verse 81. *My soul fainteth for thy salvation*] I have longed so incessantly after *thy salvation*—the complete purification and restoration of my soul, that my very spirits are exhausted.

"My heartstrings groan with deep complaint;
My soul lies panting, Lord, for thee;
And every limb and every joint
Stretches for perfect purity."

Verse 82. *Mine eyes fail*] With *looking up* for the fulfilment of thy promise, as my heart fails in longing after thy presence.

Verse 83. *Like a bottle in the smoke*] In the eastern countries their *bottles* are made of *skins;* one of these hung in the smoke must soon be *parched* and *shrivelled up*. This represents the exhausted state of his body and mind by long bodily affliction and mental distress.

Verse 84. *How many* are *the days of thy servants*] Dost thou not know that I have few to live, and they are full of trouble?

When wilt thou execute judgment on them that persecute me?] Shall not the pride of the Chaldeans be brought down, the arm of their strength broken, and thy people delivered? In this verse there is none of the *ten* words used in reference to God's law.

Verse 85. *The proud have digged pits*] The *Vulgate*, *Septuagint*, *Æthiopic*, and *Arabic*, translate this verse thus: "They have recited to me unholy fables, which are not according to thy law." They wish us to receive their *system of idolatry*, and the *tales* concerning their *gods;* but these *are not according to thy law*. The *Anglo-Saxon* is the same: **ƿi cyðon me þa unꞃiꞇƿiꞅa ꞅpellunᵹa ac na ꞅƿa ꞅƿa æ þin**; *They quothed me the unrightwise spells; but no so so law thine.*

Verse 87. *They had almost consumed me*] Had it not been for thy mercy, we had all been destroyed under this oppressive captivity.

Verse 88. *Quicken me*] Make and keep me *alive*.

So shall I keep] Without the spiritual *life* there is no *obedience;* we must therefore rise from the *dead*, and be *quickened* by the Spirit of Christ.

ANALYSIS OF LETTER CAPH.—*Eleventh Division*

I. In this section the psalmist laments his being grieved with some inward anguish.

II. Complains of his enemies.

III. Expresses his hope and constancy; and,

IV. Prays to God for comfort and grace.

I. 1. He begins with a sad complaint: "My soul fainteth." As the body will fail if it want natural food, so will the soul if it get not the bread of life.

2. His eyes also failed with *looking up*. The blessing was long delayed.

3. Yet *he hoped in God's word*. He knew that it would not fail.

4. He made complaint: "When wilt thou comfort me?"

5. His state was most deplorable; his body *dried* and *shrivelled up* through long *fasting* and *affliction*, so that it resembled a leathern bottle hung up in the smoke.

6. Yet still he continued faithful: "I do not forget thy statutes."

II. He complains against his enemies.

1. How long he should be obliged to suffer them.

2. He inquires "when the Lord will execute judgments."

He describes these enemies from their *qualities:*—

1. They were *proud*. They would not bow down to nor acknowledge God.

2. They were *treacherous*. They *digged pits for him*—used every kind of means in order to destroy him; cruel, treacherous, and cowardly.

3. They were *impious*. In heart and conduct they were not "according to God's law."

4. They acted without a *shadow of justice; wrongfully* against *law and justice*.

III. He prays for *succour:* "Help thou me." Here are three things of especial note: 1. O THOU, who art infinite. 2. *Help;* for thou hast all power in heaven and in earth. 3. *Me*, who cannot stand against my enemies; but "I trust in thee."

IV. 1. He closes with a frequent petition: "Quicken thou me—make me alive." All true religion consists in the LIFE *of God* in the SOUL *of man*.

ל LAMED

89 [u]For ever, O LORD, thy word is settled in heaven.

90 Thy faithfulness *is* [v]unto all generations: thou hast established the earth, and it [w]abideth.

91 They continue this day according to [x]thine ordinances: for all *are* thy servants.

92 Unless [y]thy law *had been* my delights, I should then have perished in mine affliction.

93 I will never forget thy precepts: for with them thou hast quickened me.

94 I *am* thine, save me; for I have sought thy precepts.

95 The wicked have waited for me to destroy me: *but* I will consider thy testimonies.

96 [z]I have seen an end of all perfection: *but* thy commandment *is* exceeding broad.

---

[u]Psa. lxxxix. 2; Matt. xxiv. 34, 35; 1 Pet. i. 25——[v]Hebrew, *to generation and generation;* Psa. lxxxix. 1

[w]Hebrew, *standeth*——[x]Jer. xxxiii. 25——[y]Ver. 24
[z]Matt. v. 18; xxiv. 35

---

2. The *manner* in which he wishes to be quickened: "After thy loving-kindness." He wishes not to be raised from the *death of sin* by *God's thunder*, but by the *loving voice* of a *tender Father*.

3. The *effect* it should have upon him: "So shall I keep the testimony of thy mouth." Whatever thou *speakest* I will *hear, receive, love,* and *obey*.

LETTER ל LAMED.—*Twelfth Division*

Verse 89. *For ever, O Lord, thy word is settled in heaven.*] Thy purposes are all settled above, and they shall all be fulfilled below.

Verse 90. *Thy faithfulness*] That which binds thee to accomplish the promise made. And this shall be, not for an age merely, but from generation to generation; for thy promises refer to the whole duration of time.

Thou hast established the earth] Thou hast given it its appointed place in the system, and there it abideth.

Verse 91. *They continue this day*] This verse should be thus read: *All are thy servants; therefore, they continue this day according to thy ordinances.* "All the celestial bodies are governed by thy power. Thou hast given an ordinance or appointment to each, and each fulfils thy will in the place thou hast assigned it."

Verse 92. *Unless thy law* had been *my delights*] Had we not had the consolations of religion, we should long ago have died of a broken heart.

Verse 93. *I will never forget thy precepts*] How can I? It is by them I *live*.

Verse 94. *I* am *thine, save me*] He who can say this need fear no evil. In all trials, temptations, dangers, afflictions, persecutions, I am thine. Thy enemies wish to destroy me! Lord, look to thy servant; thy servant looks to thee. O how sovereign is such a word against all the evils of life! *I am* THINE! therefore *save thine* OWN!

Verse 96. *I have seen an end of all perfection*] Literally, "Of all consummations I have seen the end:" as if one should say, Every thing of human origin has its limits and end, howsoever extensive, noble, and excellent. All arts and sciences, languages, inventions, have their respective principles, have their limits and ends; as they came from man and relate to man, they shall end with man: but thy law, thy revelation, which is a picture of thy own mind, an external manifestation of thy own perfections, conceived in thy infinite ideas, in reference to eternal objects, is exceeding broad; transcends the limits of creation; and extends illimitably into eternity! This has been explained as if it meant: All the real or pretended perfection that men can arrive at in this life is nothing when compared with what the law of God requires. This saying is *false* in itself, and is no *meaning* of the text. Whatever God requires of man he can, by his grace, work in man.

ANALYSIS OF LETTER LAMED.—*Twelfth Division*

This section contains an *encomium* of the WORD of GOD; of its perfection and immutability; and of the *comfort* the psalmist received from it.

I. In the *three* first verses the psalmist shows that God's word is *immutable*, by an instance in the *creatures*.

1. In the HEAVENS. They *continue* to *this day* as he made them in the beginning.

2. In the EARTH. As it was *established* in the beginning, so it *abideth*.

3. So also of the other heavenly bodies. *They* also *abide* as they were created; and answer still, most exactly, the ends for which they were made.

4. The *reason* of which is, "All are God's servants," made to *obey* his will: and from obedience they never swerve.

II. He shows the *excellence* of this word by a *rare effect* it had on himself: "Unless thy law had been my delight, I should have perished." No such comfort in trouble as God's word and promise. This he remembers with gratitude.

1. "I will never forget thy precepts." Only those forget them who reap no good from them.

2. This word had *quickened* him, i. e., God speaking and working by that word.

3. He will therefore be the *Lord's servant* for ever: "I am thine."

4. He knows he cannot continue so, but by *Divine help:* "Save me!"

5. He shows his love to God's word: "He seeks his precepts," that he may obey them.

III. He needed the help of God, because he had *inveterate enemies*. These he describes:

1. By their *diligence:* "The wicked have waited for me."

2. By their *cruelty:* "They waited to destroy me."

3. His *defence* against them. I will consider אתבנן *ethbonen*, I will set myself to consider. I will use all proper means to enable me to understand them.

מ MEM

97 O how love I thy law! [a]it *is* my meditation all the day.

98 Thou through thy commandments hast made me [b]wiser than mine enemies: for [c]they *are* ever with me.

99 I have more understanding than all my teachers: [d]for thy testimonies *are* my meditation.

100 [e]I understand more than the ancients because I keep thy precepts.

101 I have [f]refrained my feet from every evil way, that I might keep thy word.

102 I have not departed from thy judgments: for thou hast taught me.

103 [g]How sweet are thy words unto my [h]taste! *yea, sweeter* than honey to my mouth!

104 Through thy precepts I get understanding: therefore [i]I hate every false way.

---

[a]Psa. i. 2——[b]Deut. iv. 6, 8——[c]Heb. *it is ever with me* [d]2 Tim. iii. 15——[e]Job xxxii. 7, 8, 9

[f]Prov. i. 15——[g]Psa. xix. 10; Prov. viii. 11——[h]Heb. *palate*——[i]Ver. 128

IV. Having shown the perfection of God's word,—

1. In *establishing* and *upholding* the *frame of the world.*

2. In bringing comfort to the soul. In the close,

3. He compares it to all other things which we esteem as *excellent* and *perfect,—riches, honours, crowns, sceptres, kingdoms,* &c., over which the word of God has still the pre-eminence; they perish, but it endures for ever: "I have seen an end of all perfection." Jonah's *gourd* was smitten by a *worm;* the *golden head* had *feet* of *clay;* the most *beautiful form* shall dissolve into *dust; Babylon,* the wonder of the world, has *perished* from the face of the earth; the fairest day is succeeded by *midnight;* and so of other things: "but the commandment is exceeding broad:" all the principles of justice are contained in it; no just notion of God without it; all the rules of a holy life, and all the promises of life eternal, are found in it. It is the word of God, and it endureth for ever. When the heavens and the earth are no more, this word shall stand up and flourish.

LETTER מ MEM.—*Thirteenth Division*

Verse 97. *O how love I thy law*] This is one of the strongest marks of a gracious and pious heart, cast in the mould of obedience. Such love the precepts of Christ: in his commandments they delight; and this delight is shown by their making them frequent subjects of their *meditation.*

Verse 98. *Wiser than mine enemies*] Some have thought that this Psalm was composed by *Daniel,* and that he speaks of himself in these verses. Being instructed by God, he was found to have more *knowledge* than any of the Chaldeans, magicians, soothsayers, &c., &c.; and his wisdom soon appeared to the whole nation vastly superior to theirs.

Verse 99. *I have more understanding than all my teachers*] As he had entered into the spiritual nature of the law of God, and saw into the exceeding breadth of the commandment, he soon became wiser than any of the *priests* or even *prophets* who instructed him.

Verse 100. *I understand more than the ancients*] God had revealed to him more of that *hidden wisdom* which was in his law than he had done to any of his predecessors. And this was most literally true of *David,* who spoke more fully about *Christ* than any who had gone before him; or, indeed, followed after him. His compositions are, I had almost said, a *sublime Gospel.*

Verse 101. *I have refrained my feet*] By avoiding all sin, the spirit of wisdom still continues to rest upon me.

Verse 103. Sweeter *than honey to my mouth!*] What deep communion must this man have had with his Maker! These expressions show a soul filled with God. O Christians, how vastly *superior* are our privileges! and alas! how vastly *inferior* in general, are our consolations, our communion with God, and our heavenly-mindedness!

Verse 104. *Through thy precepts I get understanding*] Spiritual knowledge increases while we tread in the path of *obedience.* Obedience is the grand means of *growth* and *instruction.* Obedience trades with the talent of grace, and thus grace becomes multiplied.

ANALYSIS OF LETTER MEM.—*Thirteenth Division*

In this division we see,—

I. The affection of the psalmist to the law of God.

II. The great benefits he derived from it.

I. 1. "O how I love thy law." God alone knows how great that love is which I feel.

2. As true love always seeks opportunities of conversing with the beloved object, the psalmist shows his in *meditation* on God's law by day and night.

He gives us several *encomiums* on God's word:—

1. The *wisdom* he derived from it. It made him *wiser than his enemies.* It taught him how to conduct himself towards them, so as to disappoint many of their plans, and always insure his own peace.

2. It made him *wiser than his teachers.* Many, even of the *Jewish teachers,* took upon them to *teach* that to others which they had *never learned* themselves. He must have been wiser than these. Many in the present day take upon themselves the character of *ministers of Jesus Christ,* who have never felt his Gospel to be the power of God to their salvation. A simple woman, who is converted to God, and feels the *witness of his Spirit* that she is his child, has *a thousand* times more true wisdom than such persons, though they may have learned many languages and many sciences.

3. It made him *wiser than the ancients*—than any of the *Jewish elders,* who had not made that word the subject of their deep study and meditation.

A *second encomium.* God's word *gives power*

XXVI. DAY. MORNING PRAYER

נ NUN

105 [k]Thy word *is* a [l]lamp unto my feet,
and a light unto my path.
106 [m]I have sworn, and I will perform
it, that I will keep thy righteous judgments.
107 I am afflicted very much: [n]quicken me,
O LORD, according unto thy word.
108 Accept, I beseech thee, [o]the freewill-
offerings of my mouth, O LORD, [p]and teach
me thy judgments.
109 [q]My soul *is* continually in my hand: yet
do I not forget thy law.
110 [r]The wicked have laid a snare for me:
yet I [s]erred not from thy precepts.
111 [t]Thy testimonies have I taken as a
heritage for ever: for [u]they *are* the rejoicing
of my heart.
112 I have inclined mine heart [v]to perform thy statutes alway, [w]*even unto* the end.

[k]Proverbs vi. 23——[l]Or, *candle*——[m]Neh. x. 29
[n]Ver. 88——[o]Hos. xiv. 2; Heb. xiii. 15——[p]Ver. 12, 26
[q]Job xiii. 14

[r]Psalm cxl. 5; cxli. 9——[s]Verse 10, 21——[t]Deuteronomy xxxiii. 4——[u]Verse 77, 92, 174——[v]Hebrew, *to do*——[w]Ver. 33

over sin: "I have refrained:" and the psalmist was no *speculatist;* he was in every respect a *practical* man.

A *third encomium* is, the more a man resists evil forbidden by that law, and practices righteousness commanded by it, the stronger he grows. The psalmist *refrained from every evil way,* that he might *keep God's word.*

Lest any one should think that he pretends to have acquired all these excellencies by his own *study* and *industry,* he asserts that he had nothing but what he had received: "I have not departed," &c.; "for THOU hast taught me."

A *fourth encomium* is, that God's law gives indescribable *happiness* to them who love and obey it: "How sweet are thy words," &c.

II. In the last verse he proves all that he said by the blessed effects of God's word upon himself.

1. He got *understanding* by it. He became learned, wise, and prudent.

2. He was enabled to *hate every false way*—false religion, lying vanities, empty pleasures; and every thing that did not tend to and prepare for an eternity of blessedness.

LETTER נ NUN.—*Fourteenth Division*

Verse 105. *Thy word* is *a lamp*] This is illustrated thus by *Solomon,* Prov. vi. 23: "The *commandment* is a *lamp;* and the *law* is *light;* and *reproofs of instruction* are the *way* of *life.*" God's word is a *candle* which may be held in the hand to give us light in every *dark place* and *chamber;* and it is a *general light* shining upon all *his works,* and upon all *our ways.*

Verse 106. *I have sworn*] Perhaps this means no more than that he had renewed his *covenant* with God; he had *bound* himself to love and serve him only.

Verse 107. *I am afflicted very much*] עד מאד *ad meod,* "to extremity, excessively." We are in the most oppressive captivity.

Quicken me] Deliver us from our bondage.

Verse 108. *The freewill-offerings of my mouth*] נדבות פי *nidboth pi,* the *voluntary offerings which I have promised.* Or, As we are in *captivity,* and cannot sacrifice to thee, but *would* if we *could;* accept the *praises* of our *mouth,* and the *purposes* of our *hearts,* instead of the sacrifices and offerings which we *would* bring to thy altar, but *cannot.*

Verse 109. *My soul* is *continually in my hand*] נפשי *naphshi, my life;* that is, it is in *constant danger* every hour I am on the confines of death. The expression signifies to be in *continual danger.* So *Xenarchus* in Athenæus, lib. xiii., c. 4: Εν τη χειρι την ψυχην εχοντα, "having the life in the hand;" which signifies continual danger and jeopardy. There is something like this in the speech of *Achilles* to *Ulysses,* HOM. Il. ix., ver. 322:—

Αιει εμην ψυχην παραβαλλομενος πολεμιζειν·

"Always presenting my life to the dangers of the fight."

My soul is in thy hand, is the reading of the *Syriac, Septuagint, Æthiopic,* and *Arabic;* but this is a *conjectural* and *useless* emendation.

Verse 110. *The wicked have laid a snare*] Thus their lives were continually exposed to danger.

Verse 111. *As a heritage*] In ver. 57 he says, God *is my portion,* חלקי *chelki.* In this he says, *Thy testimonies have I taken as a heritage,* נחל *nachal.* To these he was *heir;* he had *inherited* them from his fathers, and he was determined to leave them to his *family* for ever. If a man can leave nothing to his child but a *Bible,* in that he bequeaths him the greatest treasure in the universe.

Verse 112. *I have inclined mine heart*] I used the power God gave me, and turned to his testimonies with all mine heart. When we *work with God,* we can *do all things.*

ANALYSIS OF LETTER NUN.—*Fourteenth Division*

In this division the psalmist points out farther excellencies of God's word, in the use of it. 1. God's word was a *lamp to his feet* to guide him through every dark place. 2. It was a *light to his path,* ever showing him generally the way in which he should walk.

1. He therefore resolves to keep it, and binds himself to fulfil his resolution. As the lamp was going before, and the light was shining, it was necessary that he should walk while the light shone. He therefore, 1. Binds himself by an *oath* or vow: "I have sworn." 2. He will be *faithful* to his oath: "I will perform it." 3. Not merely to admire, but to *keep* God's word. 4. Not its *promises* merely, but its *righteous judgments.*

2. And this he will do in all circumstances, even in *extreme affliction.* Then he requests *two* things from the Lord. 1. That he would "accept the freewill-offerings of his mouth."

ס SAMECH

113 I hate *vain* thoughts: but thy law do I love.

114 [x]Thou *art* my hiding place and my shield: [y]I hope in thy word.

115 [z]Depart from me, ye evil doers: for I will keep the commandments of my God.

116 Uphold me according unto thy word, that I may live: and let me not [a]be ashamed of my hope.

117 Hold thou me up, and I shall be safe: and I will have respect unto thy statutes continually.

118 Thou hast trodden down all them that [b]err from thy statutes: for their deceit *is* falsehood.

119 Thou [c]puttest away all the wicked of the earth [d]*like* dross: therefore I love thy testimonies.

120 [e]My flesh trembleth for fear of thee; and I am afraid of thy judgments.

---

[x]Psa. xxxii. 7; xci. 1——[y]Ver. 81——[z]Psa. vi. 8; cxxxix. 19; Matt. vii. 23——[a]Psa. xxv. 2; Rom. v. 5; ix. 33; x. 11——[b]Ver. 21——[c]Heb. *causest to cease*——[d]Ezek. xxii. 18——[e]Hab. iii. 16

All his praises, thanksgivings, and vows. 2. That he would "teach him his judgments," that he might perform what he had vowed.

3. He shows the difficulties he was in: 1. "My soul is continually in my hand." I am in continual danger. He had got the *sword of the Spirit*, and his life depended on the use he made of it: if the soldier, whose life depends on his *drawn sword*, does not use it well, his enemy kills him. 2. Hence he says, "I do not forget thy law." I am making a proper use of my sword. 3. And that I have need of it is evident, for "the wicked have laid a snare for me." 4. This did not intimidate him: he did not leave the *path of duty* for fear of a *snare* being in that path: "I erred not from thy precepts." I did not *go about* to seek a *safer* way.

4. He keeps his resolution, and vows still. 1. He preferred God's testimonies even to the land of Canaan, to riches and crowns: "I have taken them for my heritage." 2. He delighted in them: "They are the rejoicing of my heart."

5. In this work he was determined to *continue:* 1. "I have inclined my heart." The counsel of the soul is like a balance; and the mind, which hath the commanding power over the affections, inclines the balance to that which it judges best. 2. It was to *perform it*, that he thus *inclined his heart*. 3. And this, not for a *time*, or on some *particular occasion*, but *always*, and unto *the end*. Then the *end of life* would be the *beginning of glory*.

LETTER ס SAMECH.—*Fifteenth Division*

Verse 113. *I hate* vain *thoughts*] I have hated סעפים *seaphim*, "tumultuous, violent men." I abominate all *mobs* and *insurrections*, and troublers of the public peace.

Verse 114. *My hiding place*] My asylum.

And my shield] There is a time in which I may be called to *suffer in secret;* then thou *hidest me*. There may be a time in which thou callest me to *fight;* then thou art my *Shield* and *Protector*.

Verse 115. *Depart from me*] *Odi profanum vulgus, etarceo*, I abominate the profane, and will have no communion with them. I drive them away from my presence.

Verse 116. *Uphold me*] סמכני *sammecheni*, prop me up; give me thyself to *lean upon*.

Verse 117. *Hold thou me up*] I shall grow weary and faint in the way, if not strengthened and *supported* by thee.

And I shall be safe] No soul can be *safe*, unless upheld by thee.

Verse 118. *Thou hast trodden down*] All thy enemies will be finally trodden down under thy feet.

Their deceit is *falsehood*.] Their elevation is a *lie*. The wicked often become *rich* and *great*, and affect to be *happy*, but it is all *false;* they have neither a *clean* nor *approving conscience*. Nor can they have *thy* approbation; and, consequently, no true *blessedness*.

Verse 119. *Thou puttest away all the wicked of the earth* like *dross*] There is no *true metal* in them: when they are tried by the *refining fire*, they are burnt up; they fly off in fumes, and come to no amount. There is probably an allusion here to the *scum* or *scoriæ* at the *surface of melting metals*, which is swept off previously to casting the metal into the mould.

Therefore I love thy testimonies.] Thy *testimonies* will stand; and thy *people* will stand; because thou who didst give the one, and who upholdest the other, art *pure, immovable*, and *eternal*.

Verse 120. *My flesh trembleth for fear of thee*] I know thou art a just and holy God: I know thou requirest truth in the inner parts. I know that thou art a Spirit, and that they who worship thee must worship thee in spirit and in truth; and I am often *alarmed* lest I *fall short*. It is only an assurance of my interest in thy mercy that can save me from *distressing fears and harassing doubts*. It is our privilege to know we are in God's favour; and it is not less so to maintain a continual filial fear of offending him. A true conception of God's justice and mercy begets reverence.

ANALYSIS OF LETTER SAMECH.—*Fifteenth Division*

In this section the psalmist—

I. Declares his hatred to wickedness, and his detestation of wicked men.

II. Expresses his love to God's law.

III. Prays for grace to sustain him in the observance of it.

IV. Foretells the destruction of the wicked.

I. "I hate vain thoughts;" not only *evil* itself, but the *thought* that leads to it.

II. 1. "Thy law do I love:" I strive to keep every *affection* exercised on its *proper object*.

2. This is my privilege: for thou art, 1. "My hiding-place," that public evils may not reach me; and 2. "My shield," to ward off the fiery darts of the wicked one.

3. To God, therefore, and his word, he would adhere in all extremities; and would have no communion with the wicked. 1. These he would *drive away* as the pests of piety: "Depart from

ע AIN

121 I have done judgment and justice: leave me not to mine oppressors.

122 Be [f]surety for thy servant for good: let not the proud oppress me.

123 [g]Mine eyes fail for thy salvation, and for the word of thy righteousness.

124 Deal with thy servant according unto thy mercy, and [h]teach me thy statutes.

125 [i]I *am* thy servant; give me understanding, that I may know thy testimonies.

126 *It is* time for *thee,* LORD, to work: *for* they have made void thy law.

127 [k]Therefore I love thy commandments above gold; yea, above fine gold.

128 Therefore I esteem all *thy* precepts *concerning* all *things to be* right; *and* I [l]hate every false way.

[f]Heb. vii. 22——[g]Ver. 81, 82——[h]Ver. 12——[i]Psa. cxvi. 16

[k]Verse 72; Psalm xix. 10; Proverbs viii. 11
[l]Verse 104

me." 2. Because he would *"keep* the commandments of God," while the others were bent on *breaking* them.

III. He prays for the grace of God to sustain him.

1. "Uphold me:" if thou do not, I *fall.*

2. "Hold thou me up:" for I am *falling.* One part of this prayer is against the *occurrence* of evil; the other, against evil as *actually taking place.*

IV. He foretells the destruction of wicked men.

1. "Thou hast trodden down:" they who *tread thy commandments* under *their feet* shall be *trodden down* under *thy feet.* The *first* treading shall bring on the *second.*

2. They *deceive* themselves in supposing thou wilt not resent this. This is a *deception,* and a dangerous one too, for it is against the most positive declarations of thy *truth,* therefore it is *falsehood.*

3. This is most certain, for "thou puttest away all the wicked of the earth like dross;" they are utterly vile, and of no account in thy sight.

4. "Therefore I love thy testimonies." And for this, among others reasons, that I may avoid their *judgments.*

5. Foreseeing the *judgments* to fall on the wicked, it was necessary that he should be filled with a salutary *fear.* 1. "My flesh trembleth." Happy is he who by other men's harms learns to be wise. 2. We should work out our salvation with fear and trembling. God is *holy* and *just* as well as *merciful;* therefore we should fear before him. 3. Because he saw those judgments coming on the wicked, he desired to be *established in God's holy fear.* In all cases the old proverb is true: "Too much familiarity breeds contempt."

LETTER ע AIN.—*Sixteenth Division*

Verse 121. *I have done judgment and justice*] I have given the best *decision* possible on every case that came before me; and I have endeavoured to *render* to all their *due.*

Verse 122. *Be surety for thy servant*] ערב *arob,* give a pledge or token that thou wilt help me in times of necessity. Or, *Be bail for thy servant.* What a word is this! Pledge thyself for me, that thou wilt produce me *safely* at the judgment of the great day. Then sustain and keep me blameless till the coming of Christ. Neither of these two verses has any of the *ten words* in reference to God's *law* or *attributes.* The *judgment* and the *justice* refer to the psalmist's own conduct in ver. 121. The *hundred and twenty-second* has no word of the kind.

Verse 123. *Mine eyes fail*] See on ver. 82.

Verse 125. *I* am *thy servant*] See on ver. 94.

Verse 126. It is *time for* thee, *Lord, to work*] The *time* is fulfilled in which thou hast promised deliverance to thy people. *They*—the Babylonians,

Have made void thy law.] They have filled up the measure of their iniquities.

Verse 127. *Therefore I love thy commandments*] I see thou wilt do all things well. I will trust in thee.

Above gold] מזהב *mizzahab,* more than *resplendent gold;* gold without any stain or rust.

Yea, above fine gold.] ומפז *umippaz, above solid gold;* gold separated from the dross, perfectly *refined.*

Verse 128. *All* thy *precepts* concerning *all* things to be *right*] There are too many *supplied* words here to leave the text unsuspected. All the ancient versions, except the *Chaldee,* seem to have omitted the second כל *col,* ALL, and read the text thus: "Therefore I have walked straight in all thy precepts." I go straight on in all thy precepts, hating every false way. I neither turn to the right hand nor to the left; the *false ways* are *crooked; thy way* is *straight.* I am going to heaven, and that way lies *straight before me.* To walk in the way of *falsity* I cannot, because I *hate* it; and I hate such ways because God hates them.

ANALYSIS OF LETTER AIN.—*Sixteenth Division*

In this part the psalmist,

I. Makes a profession of his integrity.

II. Prays for protection against his enemies.

III. Resolves to walk in the right way.

I. He makes a profession of his integrity:—

1. "I have done judgment and justice."

2. Though he had done so, yet he was not free from calumny and oppression. He commends, therefore, his righteous cause to God: "Leave me not to mine oppressors."

3. "Be surety for thy servant:" give me an assurance that thou wilt stand by me.

4. "Let not the proud oppress me." For miserable are the destitute when they fall into such hands.

II. He shows us how he had prayed against his enemies, and for God's salvation.

"Mine eyes fail." My faith is almost gone, and the eye of my mind become dim.

2. It was the *salvation* of God he had in view: "For thy salvation."

3. The ground on which he prayed was *the word of God's righteousness.*

פ PE

129 Thy testimonies *are* wonderful: therefore doth my soul keep them.

130 The entrance of thy words giveth light; [m]it giveth understanding unto the simple.

131 I opened my mouth, and panted: for I [n]longed for thy commandments.

132 [o]Look thou upon me, and be merciful unto me, [p]as [q]thou usest to do unto those that love thy name.

133 [r]Order my steps in thy word: and [s]let not any iniquity have dominion over me.

134 [t]Deliver me from the oppression of man: so will I keep thy precepts.

135 [u]Make thy face to shine upon thy servant; and [v]teach me thy statutes.

136 [w]Rivers of waters run down mine eyes, because they keep not thy law.

[m]Psa. xix. 7; Prov. i. 4——[n]Ver. 20——[o]Psa. cvi. 4 [p]2 Thess. i. 6, 7——[q]Heb. *according to the custom toward those, &c.*

[r]Psa. xvii. 5——[s]Psa. xix. 13; Rom. vi. 12——[t]Luke i. 74——[u]Psa. iv. 6——[v]Ver. 12, 26——[w]Jer. ix. 1; xiv. 17; see Ezek. ix. 4

He proceeds in his prayer; and begs God to deal with him as a needy *servant*, and also an *ignorant scholar*.

1. "Deal with thy servant." I am ready to do thy will; but treat me in thy *mercy*.

2. "Teach me thy statutes." I wish to learn what thy will is; and when I know it, faithfully to do it.

He urges the same request, with nearly the same reasons for it: "I am thy servant." I am no *stranger* to thee. I have frequently come to thee to get grace to enable me to serve thee. I am one of thy domestics, a member of thy Church.

He comes now with his complaint.

1. "It is time for thee to work." Thy *enemies* are *strong*, and thy *people weak*.

2. "They have made void thy law." They have entirely trampled it under foot.

III. The zeal of the psalmist increased as the love of many waxed cold.

1. "Therefore," because they despise thy word, ordinances, and people.

2. "I love thy commandments." As they hate, so I love. When we love God's commandments, it is a sign that we have not received the grace of God in vain.

3. To show the greatness of his love, he says, I love thy commandments "above gold; yea, above fine gold." My love is greater to thy *law*, than that of the miser is to his bags.

4. He received all God's precepts to be right; and he takes not some, but the whole of them.

5. Whatever gain *idolatry* and *time-serving* might hold out to him, he abominated it, because he *hated every false way*. His love of God, his law, and holiness, was greater than his love of life.

LETTER פ PE.—*Seventeenth Division*

Verse 129. *Thy testimonies* are *wonderful*] There is a height, length, depth, and breadth in thy word and testimonies that are truly astonishing; and on this account my soul loves them, and I deeply study them. The more I study, the more light and salvation I obtain.

Verse 130. *The entrance of thy words giveth light*] פתח *pethach*, the *opening* of it: when I open my Bible to read, light springs up in my mind. Every sermon, every prayer, every act of faith, is an *opening* by which light is let into the seeking soul.

Verse 131. *I opened my mouth, and panted*] A metaphor taken from an animal exhausted in the chase. He runs, open-mouthed, to take in the cooling air; the heart beating high, and the muscular force nearly expended through fatigue. The psalmist sought for salvation, as he would run from a ferocious beast for his life. Nothing can show his earnestness in a stronger point of view.

Verse 132. *As thou usest to do*] Treat me as thy mercy has induced thee to treat others in my circumstances. Deal with me as thou dealest with thy *friends*.

Verse 133. *Order my steps*] הכן *hachen*, make them *firm;* let me not walk with a halting or unsteady step.

Have dominion over me.] בי *bi*, IN *me*. Let me have no governor but God; let the throne of my heart be filled by him, and none other.

Verse 135. *Make thy face to shine*] Give me a sense of thy approbation. Let me know, by the testimony of thy Spirit in my conscience, that thou art reconciled to me. The godly in all ages derived their happiness from a consciousness of the Divine favour. The witness of God's spirit in the souls of believers was an essential principle in religion from the foundation of the world.

Verse 136. *Rivers of waters run down mine eyes*] How much had this blessed man the honour of God and the salvation of souls at heart! O for more of that spirit which mourns for the transgressions of the land! But we are not properly convinced of the exceeding sinfulness of sin.

ANALYSIS OF LETTER PE.—*Seventeenth Division*

In this division the psalmist—

I. Praises God's word.

II. Shows his affection to it.

III. Prays for grace to keep it.

IV. Mourns for those who do not.

1. The eulogy he gives to God's word here is from a *new quality* not mentioned before. "Thy testimonies are wonderful;" wondrous mysteries are contained in the Divine oracles.

1. The *ceremonial* law is wonderful, because the mystery of our redemption by the blood of Christ is pointed out in it.

2. The *prophecies* are wonderful, as predicting things, humanly speaking, so uncertain, and at such great distance of time, with so much accuracy.

3. The *decalogue* is wonderful, as containing in a very few words all the principles of justice and charity.

4. Were we to go to the *New Testament*, here wonders rise on wonders! All is astonishing; but the psalmist could not have had this in view.

צ TSADDI

137 [x]Righteous *art* thou, O LORD, and upright *are* thy judgments.

138 [y]Thy testimonies *that* thou hast commanded *are* [z]righteous and very [a]faithful.

139 [b]My zeal hath [c]consumed me, because mine enemies have forgotten thy words.

140 [d]Thy word *is* very [e]pure: therefore thy servant loveth it.

141 I *am* small and despised: *yet* do not I forget thy precepts.

142 Thy righteousness *is* an everlasting righteousness, and thy law *is* [f]the truth.

143 Trouble and anguish have [g]taken hold on me: *yet* thy commandments *are* [h]my delights.

144 The righteousness of thy testimonies *is* everlasting: [i]give me understanding, and I shall live.

[x]Ezra ix. 15; Neh. ix. 33; Jer. xii. 1; Dan. ix. 7 [y]Psa. xix. 7, 8, 9——[z]Heb. *righteousness*——[a]Heb. *faithfulness*——[b]Psa. lxix. 9; John ii. 17——[c]Heb. *cut me off*

[d]Psa. xii. 6; xviii. 30; xix. 8; Prov. xxx. 5——[e]Heb. *tried* or *refined*——[f]Ver. 151; Psa. xix. 9; John xvii. 17——[g]Heb. *found me*——[h]Verse 77——[i]Verse 34, 73, 169

The second eulogy is, that God's law is *the dispenser of light.*

1. The entrance of it, the first chapter of Genesis; what light does that pour on the mind of man! What knowledge of the most important things, which we should never have known without it!

2. *It gives light to the simple*—to those who are not *double;* who have but *one end* in view, and one *aim* to that end.

3. Of those *simple ones* or *babes* our Lord speaks, Matt. xi. 25, and St. Paul, 1 Cor. i. 25, 26, &c.

II. The psalmist shows that he was one of those *simple* ones.

1. "He opened his mouth" by prayer, and sought the spirit of light and piety.

2. He *panted* after it as men do that want breath, and are longing to get fresh air.

3. And this he did because "he longed for God's commandments;" had a vehement desire to know and keep them.

III. He now betakes himself to prayer, and acquaints us with the petitions he had offered.

1. He said, "Look upon me." Consider thy poor, dependent, helpless creature.

2. "Have mercy upon me." Look, not with the indignation which I deserve, but with the mercy which thou knowest I need.

3. "As thou usest to do." Act by me as thou dost by them that love thee.

4. "Order my steps." Give me grace to be obedient. Many look for *mercy to pardon their sin*, but do not look for *grace* to enable them to be *obedient.*

5. "Let not any iniquity have dominion over me." Let me be saved from all my spiritual captivity.

6. "Deliver me from the oppression of men." Let neither wicked men nor wicked spirits rule over me.

7. "Make thy face to shine upon me!" Let me have thy light, thy peace, and thy *approbation.*

8. "And teach me thy statutes." Keep me at thy feet, under continual instruction.

IV. He concludes by telling how he grieved for the wickedness of others and the dishonour of God. If we grieve not for others, their sin may become ours. See Ezek. ix. 8; 1 Cor. v. 2.

LETTER צ TSADDI.—*Eighteenth Division*

Verse 137. *Righteous* art *thou*] Thou art infinitely holy in thy nature; and therefore thou art *upright in thy judgments*—all thy dispensations to men.

Verse 138. *Thy testimonies*] Every thing that proceeds from thee partakes of the perfections of thy nature.

Verse 139. *My zeal hath consumed me*] My earnest desire to promote thy glory, and the pain I feel at seeing transgressions multiplied, have worn down both my flesh and spirits.

Verse 140. *Thy word* is *very pure*] צרופה *tseruphah*, it is *purification.* It is not a *purified thing*, but a *thing* that *purifies.* "Now ye are *clean*," said Christ, "by the *word* I have spoken unto you." God's word is a *fire* to *purify* as well as a *hammer* to *break.*

Verse 141. *I* am *small and despised*] And on these accounts have every thing to *fear.* Being *small*, I cannot *resist;* being *despised*, I am in *danger;* but even all this does not induce me to start aside, or through the fear of man to be unfaithful to thee.

Verse 142. *Thy righteousness* is *an everlasting righteousness*] The word צדק *tsedek* is a word of very extensive meaning in the Bible. It signifies, not only God's inherent righteousness and perfection of nature, but also his method of treating others; his plan of redemption; *his method of saving others.* And the word δικαιοσυνη, which answers to it, in the *Septuagint* and in the *New Testament*, is used with the same latitude of meaning, and in the same sense; particularly in that remarkable passage, Rom. iii. 25, 26, where see the notes. Thy merciful method of dealing with sinners and justifying the ungodly will last as long as the earth lasts; and thy *law* that witnesses this, in all its pages, is *the truth.*

Verse 143. *Trouble and anguish*] I am exercised with various trials from men and devils.

Have taken hold on me] But still I cleave to my God, and am *delighted* with his law.

Verse 144. *The righteousness of thy testimonies* is *everlasting*] Thy *moral law* was not made for *one people*, or for one *particular time;* it is as imperishable as thy *nature*, and of *endless obligation.* It is that law by which all the children of Adam shall be judged.

Give me understanding] To know and practise it.

And I shall live.] Shall glorify thee, and live eternally; not for the *merit* of having done it, but because thou didst fulfil the work of the law in my heart, having saved me from condemnation by it.

XXVI. DAY. EVENING PRAYER

ק KOPH

145 I cried with *my* whole heart; hear me, O LORD: I will keep thy statutes.

146 I cried unto thee; save me, [k]and I shall keep thy testimonies.

147 [l]I prevented the dawning of the morning, and cried: [m]I hoped in thy word.

148 [n]Mine eyes prevent the *night* watches, that I might meditate in thy word.

149 Hear my voice according unto thy loving-kindness: O LORD, [o]quicken me according to thy judgment.

150 They draw nigh that follow after mischief: they are far from thy law.

151 Thou *art* [p]near, O LORD; [q]and all thy commandments *are* truth.

152 Concerning thy testimonies, I have known of old that thou hast founded them [r]for ever.

---

[k]Or, *that I may keep*——[l]Psa. v. 3; lxxxviii. 13; cxxx. 6 [m]Ver. 74——[n]Psa. lxiii. 1, 6

[o]Ver. 40, 154——[p]Psa. cxlv. 18——[q]Ver. 86, 143, 172 [r]Luke xxi. 33

ANALYSIS OF LETTER TSADDI.—*Eighteenth Division*

In this division the psalmist—

I. Commends the law of God, from its Author, its equity, its purity, and its perpetuity.

II. A consideration of which led him to love and delight in it, though opposed by many enemies.

I. 1. "Righteous art thou." Thou *alterest* not with *times*, thou *changest* not with *persons*, thou art *ever the same.*

2. Thy *judgments*, in giving rewards and dispensing punishments, are upright.

3. Thy *testimonies*, that declare this, are *righteous* and *faithful.*

He consequently felt an ardent *zeal* for God's glory.

1. This "zeal consumed him," and he expresses the cause.

2. Men "forgot God's words." He pined away for grief on this account. He turns to another *character* of God's law.

"Thy word is very pure."

1. It is *pure* in itself, and the *purifier* of the heart.

2. On this account he *loved* it; and we know that "love is the fulfilling of the law."

A *third* effect was a careful remembrance of it, though tried by his enemies.

1. "I am small." Of no weight nor authority; have no secular power.

2. "Despised." Have no credit nor respect.

3. "Yet do I not forget thy precepts." Nothing can move me while upheld by thee; and thou wilt uphold me while I cleave unto thee.

A *fourth* commendation of God's law is its *immutability.*

1. It is immutable, and can never be dispensed with. It is a *righteousness* that is everlasting.

2. It is *the truth:* 1. It has priority of all laws; 2. Contains no falsehood.

3. Its promises and threatenings shall all be punctually fulfilled.

II. He *loved* and *delighted* in it, notwithstanding he had *trouble* and *anguish.*

1. *Trouble* and *anguish.* The righteous are often under the cross.

2. Yet "thy commandments are my delights." While faithful to thee, all my afflictions are sanctified to me, so that I can *rejoice* while I suffer.

He speaks again about the *immutability* of God's word.

1. "The righteousness of thy testimonies," Thy word is like thyself, for it comes from thee.

2. "Give me understanding." I always stand in need of *teaching.*

3. "And I shall live." All is *death* without thee. Live in *me*, that I may live *by* thee.

LETTER ק KOPH.—*Nineteenth Division*

Verse 145. *I cried with* my *whole heart*] The whole soul of the psalmist was engaged in this good work. He whose *whole heart* cries to God will never rise from the throne of grace without a blessing.

Verse 147. *I prevented the dawning*] קדמתי *kiddamti*, "I went before the dawn or twilight."

Verse 148. *Mine eyes prevent*] קדמו *kiddemu*, "go before the watches." Before the watchman proclaims the hour, I am awake, meditating on thy words. The Jews divided the night into three watches, which began at what we call six o'clock in the evening, and consisted each of four hours. The Romans taught them afterwards to divide it into four watches of three hours each; and to divide the day and night into twelve hours each; wherein different guards of soldiers were appointed to watch. At the proclaiming of each watch the psalmist appears to have risen and performed some act of devotion. For a remarkable custom of our Saxon ancestors, see the note on ver. 164.

Verse 150. *They draw nigh*] They are just at hand who seek to destroy me.

They are far from thy law.] They are *near* to all *evil*, but *far* from *thee.*

Verse 151. *Thou* art *near*] As they are *near* to destroy, so art thou *near* to *save.* When the enemy comes in as a flood, the Spirit of the Lord lifts up a standard against him.

Verse 152. *Concerning thy testimonies, I have known of old*] קדם ידעתי *kedem yedati*, "Long ago I have known concerning thy testimonies. Thou hast designed that thy testimonies should bear reference to, and evidence of, those glorious things which thou hast provided for the salvation of men; and that this should be an everlasting testimony. They continue, and Christ is come.

ANALYSIS OF LETTER KOPH.—*Nineteenth Division*

I. The psalmist is earnest in his prayers for deliverance.

II. He shows the *end* for which he desires it.

ר RESH

153 [s]Consider mine affliction, and deliver me: for I do not forget thy law.

154 [t]Plead my cause, and deliver me: [u]quicken me according to thy word.

155 [v]Salvation *is* far from the wicked: for they seek not thy statutes.

156 [w]Great *are* thy tender mercies, O LORD: [x]quicken me according to thy judgments.

157 Many *are* my persecutors and mine enemies; *yet* do I not [y]decline from thy testimonies.

158 I beheld the transgressors, and [z]was grieved; because they kept not thy word.

159 Consider how I love thy precepts: [a]quicken me, O LORD, according to thy lovingkindness.

160 [b]Thy word *is* true *from* the beginning: and every one of thy righteous judgments *endureth* for ever.

---

[s]Psa. ix. 13; Lam. v. 1——[t]1 Sam. xxiv. 15; Psa. xxxv. 1; Mic. vii. 9——[u]Ver. 40——[v]Job v. 4——[w]Or, *Many*——[x]Ver. 149

[y]Psa. xliv. 18; ver. 51——[z]Ver. 136; Ezek. ix. 4
[a]Ver. 25, 37, 40, 88, 107, 149, 154, 156; Psa. cxliii. 11
[b]Heb. *The beginning of thy word is true*

III. The *necessity* of its being speedy, as his enemies were at hand.

I. 1. His prayer was *earnest;* it was a *cry,* rather than a *petition.*

2. It was *sincere:* "I cried with my whole heart." There was no hypocrisy in it.

3. It was *in season:* "I prevented the dawning of the morning."

4. It was *out of season:* "Mine eyes prevent the night-watches."

What he prayed for,—

1. *Audience:* "Hear me, O Lord."
2. *Deliverance:* "Save me."
3. *Increase of grace:* "Quicken me."

II. The *end* for which he prayed.

1. That he might *keep God's statutes.*

2. That he might keep *his testimonies.* See the explanation of these words at the beginning of this Psalm.

3. That he might *meditate* on God's word.

4. That he might *increase* in the *life* of God.

The *arguments* he uses:—

1. His *faith* and *hope.* I cried, because I *waited* and *hoped* in thy word.

2. *God's mercy.* According to thy lovingkindness.

3. The *danger* he was in from his *pursuing enemies.*—1. *They draw nigh.* 2. They are *mischievously* bent. 3. They are most *impious* men. *Far from the law of God;* they despised and hated it.

III. Near as they may be to *destroy,* thou art nearer to *save.*

1. "Thou art near:" They cannot come where thou art not.

2. "All thy commandments are truth:" And thou hast commanded us to *trust in thee;* and therefore we shall not fear evil. Thou wilt *support* thy *servants,* and *destroy* thine *enemies.*

He concludes with an *acclamation:*—

1. "Concerning thy testimonies:" Thy *will,* which thou hast testified in thy word.

2. "I have known of old:" Ever since I looked into them, began to study and practice them.

3. "That thou hast founded them for ever:" They are of eternal truth, immutable and indispensable. And this is the anchor of our souls, that we may not be carried away by trials and temptations. Not one tittle of God's truth has ever failed any of his sincere followers. No one promise of his that has been sought by faith in Christ has ever been unfulfilled. Blessed be God!

LETTER ר RESH.—*Twentieth Division*

Verse 153. *Consider mine affliction*] *See mine affliction* or *humiliation:* but the *eye of the Lord affects his heart;* and therefore he never *sees* the distresses of his followers without *considering* their situation, and *affording* them help.

Verse 154. *Plead my cause*] ריבה ריבי *ribah ribi.* "Be my Advocate in my suit." Contend for us against the Babylonians, and bring us out of our bondage.

According to thy word.] Spoken by thy prophets for our comfort and encouragement.

Verse 155. *Salvation* is *far from the wicked*] There is no hope of their conversion.

For they seek not thy statutes.] And they who *do not seek, shall not find.*

Verse 156. *Great* are *thy tender mercies*] They are רבים *rabbim, multitudes.* They extend to *all* the *wretchednesses* of *all men.*

Verse 158. *I beheld the transgressors, and was grieved*] Literally, *I was affected with anguish.*

Verse 160. *Thy word* is *true* from *the beginning*] ראש *rosh,* the *head* or *beginning* of thy word, is *true.* Does he refer to the *first word* in the Book of *Genesis,* בראשית *bereshith,* "in the beginning?" The learned reader knows that ראש *rash,* or *raash,* is the *root* in that word. Every word thou hast spoken from the first in *Bereshith* (Genesis) to the end of the law and prophets, and all thou wilt yet speak, as flowing from the *fountain of truth,* must be true; and all shall have in due time, their fulfilment. And all these, thy words endure *for ever.* They are *true,* and *ever will be true.*

ANALYSIS OF LETTER RESH.—*Twentieth Division*

I. 1. The psalmist begins with a petition: "Consider my affliction."

2. Begs that God would help him: "Deliver me."

3. The reason for both: "I do not forget thy law."

4. He begs God to be his Advocate: 1. "Plead my cause." At the bar of men a just cause often miscarries for want of an able advocate, and is borne down by an unjust judge. Be *thou* my Advocate, and I shall not fail. 2. "Quicken me:" Revive my hopes, give *new life* to my soul.

II. He believes he shall be heard, because—

1. "Salvation is far from the wicked:" But he does not *forget God's law.*

ש SCHIN

161 [c]Princes have persecuted me without a cause: but my heart standeth in awe of thy word.

162 I rejoice at thy word, as one that findeth great spoil.

163 I hate and abhor lying: *but* thy law do I love.

164 Seven times a day do I praise thee, because of thy righteous judgments.

---

[c]1 Sam. xxiv. 11, 14; xxvi. 18; ver. 23

---

2. "They seek not God's statutes:" But he *meditates* in God's law *day* and *night*.

III. If he ever miscarries, or comes short, he flees to God for mercy.

1. On God's mercies he bestows two epithets: 1. They are *great* or *many*, and they *endure for ever*. 2. They are *tender;* they are *misericordiæ*, q. d., *miseria cordis*, feelings which occasion *pain* and *distress* to the *heart*. רחמים *rachamim*, such as *affect* and flow from the *tender yearnings of the bowels*. The word signifies what a *mother* feels for the *infant* that lay in her *womb*, and hangs on her *breast*.

2. He prays to be *quickened*. Let me not *die*, but *live*.

IV. He complains of his adversaries:—

1. They are *many:* Many *devils*, many *men;* many *visible*, more *invisible*.

2. Yet he continued steadfast: "I do not decline," &c.

3. They were "transgressors:" Not simple *sinners*, but *workers of iniquity*.

4. He was greatly distressed on their account: "I beheld them, and was grieved."

V. He brings this as a proof of his attachment to God.

1. "Consider how I love:" No man dare say to God, "Look upon *me*," but he who is persuaded that when God looks upon him *he will like him*. This was a sure proof of the psalmist's sincerity.

2. He loves not merely the *blessings* he receives from God, but he loves God's *law;* and none will love this, who does not delight in *obedience*. And how few are there of this character, even in the Church of God!

3. And because he loves he prays to be *quickened*. The soul only which is spiritually *alive*, can *obey*.

VI. He concludes with a commendation of God's word.

1. "Thy word is true," in its *principle* and in all its details, from Adam to Moses; from Moses to Christ; from Christ to the present time; and from the present time to the end of the world.

2. For it "endures for ever:" All other things wear out or decay; lose their *testimony*, and become *obsolete*. But God will ever bear testimony to his own *word*, and continue to support its veracity by fulfilling it to all successive generations.

LETTER ש SCHIN.—*Twenty-first Division*

Verse 161. *Princes have persecuted me*] This may refer to what was done by *prime ministers*, and the rulers of provinces, to sour the king against the *unfortunate Jews*, in order still to detain them in bondage. In reference to *David*, the plotting against him in Saul's court, and the dangers he ran in consequence of the jealousies of the Philistine lords while he sojourned among them, are well known.

My heart standeth in awe] They had probably offers made them of enlargement or melioration of condition, providing they submitted to some idolatrous conditions; but they knew they had to do with a jealous God; their hearts *stood in awe*, and they were thereby kept from sin.

Verse 162. *As one that findeth great spoil.*] שלל רב *shalal rab*. This appears to refer to such *spoil* as is acquired by *stripping the dead* in a field of battle, taking the rich garments of the slain chiefs; or it may refer to *plunder* in general. As God *opened his eyes* he *beheld wonders in his law;* and each discovery of this kind was like finding a prize.

Verse 163. *I—abhor lying*] Perhaps they might have made the confessions which the Chaldeans required, and by mental reservation have kept an inward firm adherence to their creed; but this, in the sight of the God of truth, must have been *lying;* and at such a sacrifice they would not purchase their enlargement, even from their captivity.

Verse 164. *Seven times a day do I praise thee*] We have often seen that *seven* was a number expressing *perfection*, *completion*, &c., among the Hebrews; and that it is often used to signify *many*, or an *indefinite number*, see Prov. xxiv. 16; Lev. xxvi. 28. And here it may mean no more than that his soul was filled with the spirit of gratitude and praise, and that he very frequently expressed his joyous and grateful feelings in this way. But *Rabbi Solomon* says this is to be understood literally, for they praised God *twice* in the morning before reading the decalogue, and *once* after; *twice* in the evening before the same reading, and *twice* after; making in the whole *seven* times. The Roman Church has prescribed a similar service.

In a manuscript Saxon Homily, Domin. 3, in Quadrag, A. D. 971, I find the following singular directions:—

eallum Cristenum mannum es beboden ꝥ hi ealne heora licheman seofon siðum gebletsion mid Cristes rode tacne

1. **ærest on arne morgen.**
2. **oþre siðe on undern tid.**
3. **ðriddan siðe on midne dæg.**
4. **feorðan siðe on non tid.**
5. **fiftan siðe on æfen.**
6. **sýxtan siðe on niht ær he reste.**
7. **seoðan siðe on uhtan huru he hine gode be.**

Every Christian man is commanded that he always his body seven times bless with the sign of Christ's cross.

1. First, at day-break.
2. Second time at undern tide, (nine o'clock in the morning.)
3. The third time at midday.
4. The fourth time at noon-tide. (3 o'clock P. M.)
5. The fifth time in the evening.

165 [d]Great peace have they which love thy law: and [e]nothing shall offend them.

166 [f]LORD, I have hoped for thy salvation, and done thy commandments.

167 My soul hath kept thy testimonies; and I love them exceedingly.

168 I have kept thy precepts and thy testimonies: [g]for all my ways *are* before thee.

ת TAU

169 Let my cry come near before thee, O LORD: [h]give me understanding according to thy word.

170 Let my supplication come before thee: deliver me according to thy word.

171 [i]My lips shall utter praise, when thou hast taught me thy statutes.

172 My tongue shall speak of thy word: for all thy commandments *are* righteousness.

173 Let thine hand help me; for [k]I have chosen thy precepts.

174 [l]I have longed for thy salvation, O LORD; and [m]thy law *is* my delight.

175 Let my soul live, and it shall praise thee; and let thy judgments help me.

176 [n]I have gone astray like a lost sheep: seek thy servant; for I do not [o]forget thy commandments.

---

[d]Prov. iii. 2; Isa. xxxii. 17——[e]Heb. *they shall have no stumbling block*——[f]Gen. xlix. 18; ver. 174 [g]Prov. v. 21——[h]Ver. 144——[i]Ver. 7

[k]Josh. xxiv. 22; Prov. i. 29; Luke x. 42——[l]Ver. 166 [m]Ver. 16, 24, 47, 77, 111——[n]Isa. liii. 6; Luke xv. 4, &c.; 1 Pet. ii. 25——[o]Ver. 16, 83, 93, 109, 141, 153

---

6. The sixth time at night ere he go to rest.
7. The seventh time at midnight. A good man would do so if he awoke.

It seems that the *sign of the cross* was thought sufficient, even without prayer.

Verse 165. *Great peace have they*] They have peace in their conscience, and joy in the Holy Spirit; and

Nothing shall offend] Stumble, or put them out of the way.

Verse 166. *Lord, I have hoped*] Thou hast *promised deliverance*, and I have *expected* it on the *ground* of that *promise.*

Verse 167. *My soul hath kept*] I have not attended to the *latter* merely, but my spirit has entered into the spirit and design of thy testimonies.

Verse 168. *For all my ways* are *before thee.*] Thou knowest that I do not lie; thy eye has been upon my heart and my conduct, and thou knowest that I have endeavoured to walk before thee with a perfect heart.

ANALYSIS OF LETTER SCHIN.—*Twenty-first Division*

In this section the psalmist shows,—

I. His love to God; and

II. The ardour and perfection of that love.

I. The *first* sign of his love was, that it stood in the midst of persecution.

1. "Princes have persecuted."
2. But "without a cause," though they pretended many.
3. "But my heart standeth in awe." My love and confidence have due respect to thy infinite justice and immaculate purity.

The *second sign* of his love is the *joy* and *delight* he took in *God's law;* it was greater than a conqueror could feel at the fortunate issue of a battle, and the spoils of the vanquished, howsover rich or immense.

The *third sign* was his *hatred to all inquity:* "I hate and abhor lying."

The *fourth sign* was his fervour and earnestness in devotion: "Seven times," &c.

The *fifth sign* was the satisfaction he took in the *welfare of others.*

1. "Great peace have they which love thy law."
2. "Nothing shall offend them." They go on their way rejoicing; and they that love God *rejoice with them that do rejoice.*

II. He shows the *perfection* of his love,—

1. By his *hope* and *confidence:* "Lord, I have hoped," &c.
2. By his *obedience:* "And done thy commandments."
3. By *keeping God's testimonies* with all *his soul.*

And this he repeats.

1. "I have kept thy precepts and thy testimonies."
2. I have *done* this through the *purest motives*, as thou knowest: "For all my ways are before thee." Whatever he did he did in God's sight; for he well knew that the eye of the Lord was constantly upon him.

For other particulars see the preceding notes.

LETTER ת TAU.—*Twenty-second Division*

Verse 169. *Let my cry come near before thee*] This is really a fine image; it is of frequent occurrence, and is little heeded. Here the psalmist's cry for deliverance is *personified;* made an intelligent being, and sent up to the throne of grace to negotiate in his behalf. He pursues this *prosopopœia* in the next verse, and sends his *supplication* in the same way. I have already had occasion to refer to a similar figure in *Homer*, where prayers are represented as the *daughters of Jupiter.* See on Psa. lxxxviii. 2.

Verse 171. *My lips shall utter praise*] תהלה *tehillah*, a song of praise.

Verse 172. *My tongue shall speak of thy word*] There is a curious *distinction* here. In the preceding verse he says, "My lips shall utter;" here no reference is made to *articulate sounds*, except as affixed to musical notes. In *this verse* he says, "My tongue shall speak;" here *articulate* and *intelligible* words are intended. He first utters sounds connected with words expressive of his grateful feelings; in the second he speaks words, principally those which God himself had spoken, containing promises of support, purposes relative to the redemption of his people, and denunciations against their enemies.

Verse 173. *Let thine hand help me*] Exert thy *power* in my defence.

Verse 175. *Let my soul live*] Let my *life* be *preserved,* and my *soul quickened!*

Verse 176. *I have gone astray like a lost sheep*] A sheep, when it has once lost the flock, strays in such a manner as to render the prospect of its own return utterly hopeless. I have seen them bleating when they have lost the flock, and when answered by the others, instead of turning to the *sound,* have gone on in the same direction in which they were straying, their bleatings answered by the rest of the flock, till they were out of hearing! This fact shows the propriety of the next clause.

Seek thy servant] I shall never find *thee;* come to the wilderness, take *me* up, and carry me to the flock. See the notes on the parable of *the lost sheep,* Luke xv. 4, &c. The psalmist began with "Blessed are the undefiled in the way, who walk in the law of the Lord;" and he concludes with "I have gone astray like a lost sheep; seek thy servant." And thus, conscious of the blessedness of those who are in the way or righteousness, he desires to be brought into it, that he may walk in newness of life. Ver. 1: "It is a good way, and they are blessed that walk in it." Verse the *last,* "Bring me into this way, that I may be blessed." And thus the Psalm, in sentiment, returns into itself; and the *latter* verse is so connected with the *former,* as to make the whole a perfect *circle,* like the serpent biting its own tail.

There is one extraordinary perfection in this Psalm: *begin* where you will, you seem to be at the commencement of the piece; *end* where you will, you seem to close with a complete *sense.* And yet it is not like the Book of *Proverbs,* a tissue of detached sentences; it is a *whole* composed of many *parts,* and all apparently as necessary to the perfection of the Psalm, as the different *alphabetical letters* under which it is arranged are to the formation of a complete alphabet. Though there be a continual recurrence of the *same words,* which would of itself prevent it from having a pleasing effect upon the ear, yet these words are so connected with a vast *variety* of others, which show their force and meaning in still new and impressive points of light, that *attention* is still excited, and *devotion* kept alive, during the whole reading. It is constructed with admirable art, and every where breathes the justest and highest encomiums on the revelation of God; shows the glories of the God who gave it, the necessities and dependence of his intelligent creatures, the bounty of the Creator, and the praise and obedience which are his due. It is elegant throughout; it is full of beauties, and I have endeavoured in the preceding notes to mark some of them; but the number might have been greatly multiplied. To no Psalm can its own words be better applied, ver. 18: "Open thou mine eyes, that I may behold wondrous things out of thy law."

ANALYSIS OF LETTER TAU.—*Twenty-second Division*

In this last section the psalmist seems to sum up all his preceding exercises.

I. He prays.

II. Gives thanks.

III. Confesses his errors.

IV. Craves mercy; and,

V. Promises obedience.

I. In the first two verses he *prays for his prayers,* begging God to accept them.

1. "Let my cry come near before thee!"

2. "Let my supplication come before thee!" This repetition shows his earnestness, fervency, importunity, and perseverance. See Luke xi. 1, &c.

That for which he prays is, 1. *Understanding;* 2. *Deliverance.*

1. "Give me understanding." I want more light.

2. Give me this "according to thy word." In the measure which thou hast promised.

3. And give it to me for this *end,* that I may know thy law, be obedient to its precepts, and finally, by thy mercy, obtain everlasting life.

4. "Deliver me according to thy word." I want *salvation,* and that *measure* of it which thy word promises.

II. He gives thanks.

1. "My lips shall utter praise." I will celebrate thy praises with songs.

2. "My tongue shall speak." I shall set forth thy wondrous deeds.

3. Shall show that all thy commandments are righteousness; just, holy, impartial.

4. But these things I cannot do till "thou hast taught me thy statutes."

III. He proceeds to other parts of prayer:—

1. "Let thy hand help me." My own *strength* will avail little.

2. "I have chosen thy statutes:" and without thy help I cannot obey them.

3. "I have longed for thy salvation." Thou knowest my heart is right with thee.

4. "And thy law is my delight." A man naturally *longs* for that which he delights to possess.

Here he notes *three* things:—

1. I have "chosen thy precepts."

2. I have "longed for thy salvation."

3. "Delighted in thy law;" therefore "let thy hand be with me."

He prays for,—

1. *Life:* "Let my soul live."

2. "And it shall praise thee." When the soul is dead to God, there is neither *gratitude* nor *obedience.*

3. "Let thy judgments help me." Cause the *merciful dispensations of thy providence* ever to work in my behalf. In this sense the word *judgments* is frequently taken in this Psalm.

IV. He confesses his errors.

1. "I have gone astray," departed from thee, my Shepherd.

2. "And like a lost sheep too." See the note.

3. My errors, however, have not been *wilful* and *obstinate.* I did not sufficiently watch and pray, and my *sheep-like simplicity* was practised upon by my arch enemy.

4. The consequence, however, has been, I am *lost*—far from thy fold. But thou didst come to seek and save that which was lost.

5. Therefore, O Lord, *seek me.* I am in the *wilderness;* leave the *ninety and nine* that do not need thee as I do, and seek me; for, by thy grace, I seek thee.

V. I look for thee in the spirit of *obedience.*

1. Seek thy *servant.* I am ready to do thy will, though I erred from thy ways.

2. "I do not forget thy commandments," though I have often come short of my duty.

These words may be very suitable to a person who has *backslidden*, and who is returning to God with a penitent and believing heart.

1. Though he had *fallen*, the light of God continued to shine into his conscience.

2. He had not *forgotten God's way*, nor lost sight of his own state. The word of the Lord, applied by his Spirit, 1. When he was slumbering, *awakened* him. 2. When he was dead, *quickened* him. 3. When he was in danger, *preserved* him. 4. When he was wounded, *cured* him. 5. When he was assailed by his foes, *armed* and *defended* him. 6. And by this word he was *nourished* and *supported*. It was ever well with the psalmist, and it is ever well with all the followers of God, when *they do not forget God's word.*

It may be just necessary to note here, that if this Psalm be considered as belonging to the *times of the Babylonish captivity*, which it most probably does, the psalmist, though speaking in *his own person*, is ever to be considered as speaking *in the persons of all the captives in Babylon.*

PSALM CXX

The psalmist, in great distress, calls on the Lord for deliverance from calumny and defamation, 1, 2; *shows the punishment that awaits his persecutor,* 3, 4; *deplores the necessity of his residence with the ungodly,* 5–7.

XXVII. DAY. MORNING PRAYER

A Song of Degrees

IN [a]my distress I cried unto the LORD, and he heard me.

2 Deliver my soul, O LORD, from lying lips, *and* from a deceitful tongue.

3 [b]What shall be given unto thee? or what shall be [c]done unto thee, thou false tongue?

[a]Psa. cxviii. 5; Jonah iv. 2——[b]Or, *What shall the deceitful tongue give unto thee?* or, *What shall it profit thee?*——[c]Heb. *added*

NOTES ON PSALM CXX

This Psalm, and all the rest that follow it, to the end of Psalm cxxxiv., *fifteen* in number, are called Psalms of Degrees; for thus the Hebrew title המעלות *hammaaloth* is generally translated, as coming from the root עלה *alah*, to *ascend* or *mount upwards.* Hence מעלות *maaloth, steps* or *stairs for ascending*, 1 Kings x. 19, 20; 2 Kings ix. 13. But as the word may be applied to *elevation* in general, hence some have thought that it may here signify the *elevation of voice;* "these Psalms being sung with the *highest elevations of voice and music.*" Others have thought the word expresses rather the *matter* of these Psalms, as being of peculiar *excellence:* and hence *Junius* and *Tremellius* prefix to each *Canticum excellentissimum*, "A most excellent ode."

R. D. Kimchi says, "There were *fifteen steps* by which the priests ascended into the temple, on each of which they sang one of these *fifteen* Psalms." This opinion I find referred to in the Apocryphal Gospel of *the birth of Mary:* "Her parents brought her to the temple, and set her upon one of the steps. Now there are *fifteen steps* about the temple, by which they go up to it, according to the *fifteen Psalms of Degrees.*" But the existence of such *steps* and *practices* cannot be proved.

Aben Ezra supposes that the word means some kind of *tune* sung to these Psalms. It is more likely, if the *title* be really *ancient*, that it was affixed to them on account of their being sung on the *return from the Babylonish captivity*, as the people were *going up* to Jerusalem; for though some of them are attributed to *David*, yet it is very probable that they were all made long after his time, and probably during the captivity, or about the end of it. The author of these *fifteen* Psalms is not known; and most probably they were not the work of one person. They have been attributed to *David*, to *Solomon*, to *Ezra*, to *Haggai*, to *Zechariah*, and to *Malachi*, without any positive evidence. They are, however, excellent in their kind, and written with much elegance; containing strong and nervous sentiments of the most exalted piety, expressed with great felicity of language in a few words.

Verse 1. *In my distress*] Through the causes afterwards mentioned.

I cried unto the Lord] Made strong supplication for help.

And he heard me.] Answered my prayer by comforting my soul.

It appears to be a prayer of the *captives* in Babylon for complete liberty; or perhaps he recites the prayer the Israelites had made previously to their restoration.

Verse 2. *Lying lips*, and *from a deceitful tongue.*] From a people without faith, without truth, without religion; who sought by lies and calumnies to destroy them.

Verse 3. *What shall be given unto thee?*] Thou art worthy of the heaviest punishments.

Verse 4. *Sharp arrows*] The *Chaldee* has, "The strong, sharp arrows are like lightning from above, with coals of *juniper* kindled in hell beneath." On the *juniper*, see the note on Job xxx. 4, where this passage is explained. *Fiery arrows, or arrows wrapped about with inflamed combustibles*, were formerly used in sieges to set the places on fire. See my notes on Eph. vi. 16.

4 [d]Sharp arrows of the mighty, with coals of juniper.

5 Wo is me that I sojourn in [e]Mesech, [f]*that* I dwell in the tents of Kedar!

6 My soul hath long dwelt with him that hateth peace.

7 I *am* [g]*for* peace: but when I speak, they *are* for war.

[d]Or, It is as *the sharp arrows of the mighty* man *with coals of juniper*——[e]Gen. x. 2; Ezek. xxvii. 13——[f]Gen. xxv. 13; 1 Sam. xxv. 1; Jer. xlix. 28, 29——[g]Or, a man *of peace*

Verse 5. *That I sojourn in Mesech*] The *Chaldee* has it, "Wo is me that I am a stranger with the Asiatics, (אוסאי *useey,*) and that I dwell in the tents of the Arabs." *Calmet*, who understands the Psalm as speaking of the state of the captives in *Babylon* and its *provinces*, says, "Meshec was apparently the father of the Mosquians, who dwelt in the mountains that separate Iberia from Armenia, and both from Colchis. These provinces were subjugated by Nebuchadnezzar; and it is evident from 2 Kings xvii. 23, 24, xviii. 11, xix. 12, 13, that many of the Jews were held in captivity in those countries. As to *Kedar*, it extended into *Arabia Petræa*, and towards the Euphrates; and is the country afterwards known as the country of the *Saracens*."

Verse 6. *My soul hath long dwelt with him that hateth peace.*] A restless, barbarous, warlike, and marauding people.

Verse 7. *I am for peace*] We love to be quiet and peaceable; but they are continually engaged in excursions of rapine and plunder. It is evident that the psalmist refers to a people like the *Scenitæ* or *wandering Arabs*, who live constantly in *tents*, and subsist by robbery; plundering and carrying away all that they can seize. The poor captives wished them to cultivate the arts of peace, and live quietly; but they would hear of nothing but their old manner of life.

Analysis of the Hundred and Twentieth Psalm

The psalmist in distress—

I. Flees to God by prayer.

II. Sets forth the miseries of a foul and deceitful tongue.

III. Complains of his banishment.

I. 1. He is in distress, and *cries* to the Lord; the surest and best way.

2. He tells us of the *success* of his prayer: "God heard him."

3. Of the matter of it: "Lord, I beseech thee deliver my soul!" 1. "From lying lips." Detractions, calumnies, and defamations. 2. From "a deceitful tongue," which, under the colour of friendship, covers deceit. A *detractor* does his mischief *openly*, a *flatterer* secretly; so that when *a deceitful tongue* is joined with *lying lips*, the mischief is intolerable.

II. He sets forth the evil that shall fall on such deceivers and slanderers.

1. *Arrows*—which wound afar off, suddenly and invisibly.

2. *Sharp arrows, well-headed* and *keen*, that can pierce deeply.

3. "Sharp arrows of the mighty," shot by a *strong hand*, and so much the more dangerous.

4. "With coals—inflamed arrows," such as set all things on *fire*.

5. "With coals of juniper," which of all coals are the *hottest*, and *keep fire the longest*.

III. The psalmist complains of his *banishment*.

1. He laments his situation on account of the wickedness of the people among whom he sojourned.

2. They were barbarous and inhuman, enemies to piety and civility.

3. His state was the more intolerable, as it had been of *long duration:* "My soul hath long dwelt," &c.

His *disposition* was quite contrary to theirs.

1. "I am for peace." I wish to live in peace, and cultivate it.

2. But when I *speak of peace*, they are *for war;* They are fierce and inhuman. It was said of the Macedonians in Philip's time, Illis pacem esse bellum et bellum pacem. "To them peace was war, and war was peace." Such were the people of the provinces, among whom many of the Israelites were in captivity.

PSALM CXXI

The resolution of a godly man, 1, 2. *The safety and prosperity of such, as they and theirs shall be under the continual protection of God*, 3–8.

A Song of Degrees

I [a]WILL lift up mine eyes unto the hills, from whence cometh my help.

2 [b]My help *cometh* from the Lord, which made heaven and earth.

3 [c]He will not suffer thy foot to be

[a]Or, *Shall I lift up mine eyes to the hills? whence should my help come?* see Jer. iii. 23——[b]Psa. cxxiv. 8——[c]1 Sam. ii. 9; Prov. iii. 23, 26

NOTES ON PSALM CXXI

This appears to be a prayer of the Jews in their captivity, who are solicitous for their restoration. It is in the form of a *dialogue*.

Ver. 1, 2. The person who worships God speaks the *two* first verses, "I will lift up mine eyes—my help cometh,"—ver. 1, 2.

Ver. 3. The ministering priest answers him, "He will not suffer thy foot to be moved." "He that keepeth thee will not slumber," ver. 3.

To which the worshipper answers, that he

moved: [d]he that keepeth thee will not slumber.

4 Behold, he that keepeth Israel shall neither slumber nor sleep.

5 The LORD *is* thy keeper: the LORD *is* [e]thy shade [f]upon thy right hand.

6 [g]The sun shall not smite thee by day, nor the moon by night.

7 The LORD shall preserve thee from all evil: he shall [h]preserve thy soul.

8 The LORD shall [i]preserve thy going out and thy coming in from this time forth, and even for evermore.

---

[d]Psa. cxxvii. 1; Isa. xxvii. 3——[e]Isa. xxv. 4——[f]Psa. xvi. 8; cix. 31——[g]Psa. xci. 5; Isa. xlix. 10; Rev. vii. 16——[h]Psa. xli. 2; xcvii. 10; cxlv. 20——[i]Deut. xxviii. 6; Prov. ii. 8; iii. 6

---

knows that "he who keepeth Israel shall neither slumber nor sleep," ver. 4; but he seems to express a *doubt* whether *he* shall be an object of the Divine attention.

Ver. 5, &c. The priest resumes; and, to the conclusion of the Psalm, gives him the most positive assurances of God's favour and protection.

Verse 1. *Unto the hills*] Jerusalem was built upon a mountain; and Judea was a mountainous country; and the Jews, in their several dispersions, *turned towards* Jerusalem when they offered up their prayers to God.

Verse 2. *My help* cometh *from the Lord*] There is no help for me but in my God; and I expect it from no other quarter.

Verse 3. *He will not suffer thy foot to be moved*] The foundation, God's infinite power and goodness, on which thou standest, cannot be moved; and whilst thou standest on this basis, thy foot cannot be moved.

Verse 4. *He that keepeth Israel*] The Divine Being represents himself as a *watchman*, who takes care of the city and its inhabitants during the night-watches; and who is never overtaken with slumbering or sleepiness. There is a thought in the *Antigone* of *Sophocles*, that seems the counterpart of this of the psalmist.

Ταν σαν, Ζευ, δυναμιν τις ανδρων
Ὑπερβασιᾳ κατασχοι,
Ταν ουθ' ὑπνος αἱ—
ρει ποθ' ὁ παντογηρως,
Ακαματοι τε θεων
Μηνες;

Antig. ver. 613, Edit. *Johnson.*

Shall men below control great Jove above,
Whose eyes by all-subduing sleep
Are never closed, as feeble mortals' are;
But still their watchful vigil keep
Through the long circle of th' eternal year?

FRANKLIN.

Verse 6. *The sun shall not smite thee by day*] Thus expressed by the *Chaldee:* "The morning spectres shall not smite thee by day, during the government of the sun; nor the nocturnal spectres by night, during the government of the moon." I believe the psalmist simply means, they shall not be injured by *heat* nor *cold;* by a *sun-stroke* by day, nor a *frost-bite* by night.

Verse 7. *The Lord shall preserve thee from all evil*] Spiritual and corporeal, *natural* and *moral.*

He shall preserve thy soul.] Take care of thy *life*, and take care of thy soul.

Verse 8. *Thy going out and thy coming in*] Night and day—in all thy business and undertakings; and this through the whole course of thy life: *for evermore.*

ANALYSIS OF THE HUNDRED AND TWENTY-FIRST PSALM

The scope of this Psalm is to show that God alone is the refuge of the distressed.

I. While some are looking for earthly comfort and support, "I will lift up mine eyes unto the hills," &c.

II. Faith sees God, the only helper; and says, "My help is the Lord."

And the *first reason* for this is given: God's omnipotence and sufficiency. "The Lord that made heaven and earth," and is consequently the author and dispenser of all spiritual and temporal blessings.

And the *second reason* is, his *grace* and *goodness;* "he will not suffer thy foot to be moved."

A *third reason* is, his watchful care: "He that keepeth thee will not slumber."

III. The *end* which God proposes in his watching,—to *keep them.*

1. He is the "Keeper of Israel." He guards his Church; he is as a wall of fire about it.

2. He is a *shade.* This certainly refers to that kind of *umbraculum*, or *parasol*, which was in very ancient use in the eastern countries. The sense of the passage is, Neither the day of prosperity nor the night of adversity shall hurt thee; nor the heat of persecution, nor the coldness of friends or relatives: all these shall work for thy good.

3. "He shall preserve thee from all evil;"—and,

4. Especially from every thing that might hurt thy *soul:* "He shall preserve thy soul."

The psalmist concludes with this encouraging assurance.

1. "The Lord shall preserve thy going out." We are always beginning or ending some action, going abroad or returning home; and we need the protecting care of God in all.

2. "From this time forth." Now that thou hast put thy whole trust and confidence in God, he will be thy continual portion and defence in all places, in all times, in all actions; in life, in prosperity, in adversity, in death, in time, and in eternity.

PSALM CXXII

The satisfaction of a gracious soul in the use of God's ordinances, 1, 2. *Description of the internal government of Jerusalem,* 3–5. *Prayers for its peace and prosperity,* 6–9.

A Song of Degrees of David

A. M. cir. 3468
B. C. cir. 536
Cyri,
R. Persarum,
cir. annum
primum

I WAS glad when they said unto me, [a]Let us go into the house of the LORD.

2 Our feet shall stand within thy gates, O Jerusalem.

3 Jerusalem is builded as a city that is [b]compact together.

4 [c]Whither the tribes go up, the tribes of the LORD, unto [d]the testimony of Israel, to give thanks unto the name of the LORD.

5 [e]For there [f]are set thrones of judgment, the thrones of the house of David.

A. M. cir. 3468
B. C. cir. 536
Cyri,
R. Persarum,
cir. annum
primum

6 [g]Pray for the peace of Jerusalem: they shall prosper that love thee.

7 Peace be within thy walls, *and* prosperity within thy palaces.

8 For my brethren and companions' sakes, I will now say, Peace *be* within thee.

9 Because of the house of the LORD our God I will [h]seek thy good.

---

[a]Isa. ii. 3; Zech. viii. 21——[b]See 2 Sam. v. 9——[c]Exod. xxiii. 17; Deut. xvi. 16——[d]Exod. xvi. 34

[e]Deut. xvii. 8; 2 Chron. xix. 8——[f]Heb. *do sit*——[g]Psa. li. 18——[h]Neh. ii. 10

NOTES ON PSALM CXXII

In the preceding Psalms we find the poor captives crying to God for deliverance; here they are returning thanks that they find they are permitted to return to their own land and to the ordinances of their God.

Verse 1. *I was glad when they said*] When Cyrus published an edict for their return, the very first object of their thanksgiving was the kindness of God in permitting them to return to his ordinances.

Verse 2. *Our feet shall stand*] For *seventy* years we have been exiled from our own land; our *heart* was in Jerusalem, but our *feet* were in Chaldea. Now God has turned our captivity, and our *feet* shall shortly stand *within the gates of Jerusalem.* What a transition from misery to happiness! and what a subject for rejoicing!

Verse 3. *Jerusalem—compact together.*] It is now well rebuilt, every part contributing to the strength of the whole. It is also a state of great political and spiritual union. It is the *centre* of union to all the tribes, for each tribe has an equal interest in that God who is worshipped there.

Verse 4. *The testimony of Israel*] There is the *ark*, where the presence of God is manifested; there is the holy of holies; and there all the tribes assembled to worship Jehovah. He no doubt alludes to the assembling of the tribes *annually* at each of the *three* grand national festivals.

Verse 5. *There are set thrones of judgment*] There were the *public courts*, and thither the people went to obtain justice; and while the *thrones of the house of David* were there, they had justice.

Verse 6. *Pray for the peace of Jerusalem*] שלום *shalom* signifies both *peace* and *prosperity.* Let her *unanimity* never be *disturbed;* let her *prosperity* ever be on the *increase!*

They shall prosper that love thee.] In the peace and prosperity of the city, they shall find their peace and their prosperity; and even on this ground they should *love* the city, and labour to promote its best interests. There is a remarkable *alliteration* in this verse, the letter ש *shin* frequently recurring.

שאלו שלום ירושלם ישליו אהביך

*Sh*aalu *sh*elom yeru*sh*alam yi*sh*layu ohabeycha.

"Ask ye the prosperity of Jerusalem; they shall be quiet that love thee."

There are remarkable specimens of similar *alliteration* to be found in *all poets*, ancient and modern. This formed the chief feature of our *ancient poetry.* Thus in *Peter the ploughman:*—

"In a *s*omers *s*eysoun whan *s*ete was the *s*onne
I *s*choop me in a *s*hrowde as I a *s*heep were."

And the same manner often appears, even in Milton himself. See the *Il Penseroso:*—

"Oft, on a plat of rising ground,
I hear the *far-off curfew* sound
Over some wide-watered *sh*ore,
*S*winging *s*low with *s*ullen roar."

Verse 7. *Peace be within thy walls*] This is the *form of prayer* that they are to use: "May *prosperity* ever reside within thy walls, on all the people that dwell there; and tranquillity within thy palaces or high places, among the *rulers* and *governors* of the people."

Verse 8. *For my brethren and companions' sakes*] Because this city is the abode of my kinsfolk and countrymen, I will wish it prosperity. I will promote its peace and tranquillity by all means in my power. I will affectionately say, *May peace be within thee!*

Verse 9. *Because of the house of the Lord our God*] Particularly will I wish thee well, because thou art the *seat of religion*, the place where our merciful God has condescended to dwell.

To the captives in Babylon the Prophet *Jeremiah* had given this charge, chap. xxix. 7: "And seek שלום *shalom*, the *prosperity* of the city, whither I have caused you to be carried captives, and pray unto the Lord for it; for in the *prosperity* thereof ye shall have *prosperity*."

Was this a *duty* for the *captives? Yes.* And is it the duty of every man for his *own country?* God, nature, common sense, and self-interest say, YES! And what must we think of the wretches who not only do not thus pray, but labour to destroy the public peace, to subvert the government of their country, to raise seditions, and to destroy all its civil and religious institutions? *Think* of them! Why, that *hemp* would be *disgraced* by hanging them.

There is a fine picture given us here of the state of Jerusalem after the restoration of the Jews. The *walls* were finished, the *city* rebuilt, beautiful, strong, and regular; the temple and its worship were restored, the *courts of justice* were re-established, the *constituted authorities* in *Church* and *state* were doing their duty; and God was pouring out his blessing upon all. Who could see this without praying, May God increase thy peace, and establish thy prosperity for ever!

ANALYSIS OF THE HUNDRED AND TWENTY-SECOND PSALM

The psalmist, in the person of the people,—

I. Expresses his joy that he might join with the Church in God's service, ver. 1, 2.

II. Commends the Church, under the name of Jerusalem, for her unity, ver. 3; religious worship, ver. 4; civil and ecclesiastical policy, ver. 5.

III. Exhorts all to pray for its peace and prosperity, ver. 6; and puts the form of prayer into their mouths, ver. 7.

IV. Shows his own readiness to do this, and offers up his supplications, ver. 8, 9.

I. The psalmist congratulates himself and the people on the restoration of God's worship:—

1. He expresses his own joy: "I was glad."

2. To hear of the unanimity of the people mutually exhorting each other to it: "When they said unto me."

3. "Let us go into the house of the Lord." Let us *all* go, hear his word, give him thanks, and make prayers and supplications to him.

II. He commends Jerusalem *three* ways:—

1. For its *unity:* it was compact together; it was united in itself; and united, both in *politics* and *religion*, in its *inhabitants.*

2. For its being the *place of God's worship:* 1. For "thither the tribes go up" thrice in the year, as was ordained, Exod. xxiii. 14, to celebrate their deliverance from Egypt, in keeping the *passover.* 2. The giving of the law, in the feast of *pentecost.* 3. Their preservation in the wilderness, in the feast of *tabernacles.*

These tribes are "the tribes of the Lord." A very honourable title,

"Unto the testimony of Israel." To the ark of the covenant, the pledge of the covenant between God and the people.

The *end* for which they went up: "To give thanks unto the name of the Lord."

3. He commends Jerusalem for its civil and ecclesiastical policy: 1. "For there are set thrones of judgment." The tribunals and courts of justice are there. 2. "The thrones of the house of David." The court and throne of a legitimate sovereign.

III. He exhorts the tribes to *pray for* a continuance of its present happy state.

1. "Pray for the peace," &c. It is our duty to pray for the *prosperity* of the *nation* and of the *Church of God.*

2. "They shall prosper that love thee." Those who love both are *blessed*, those who do not are *cursed.*

3. And that we may know the prayer that God will hear, he puts one in our mouth, "Peace be within thy walls, and prosperity within thy palaces." It is well to join *peace* and *prosperity* together. *Peace* without *prosperity* is but a secure possession of *misery;* and *prosperity* without *peace* is but a dubious and uncertain *felicity.*

1. "Peace be within thy walls." Not only thy *fortifications, civil and religious institutions*, but also among all thy *officers, soldiers*, and *inhabitants*, for they constitute the strength and safety of the kingdom.

2. "And prosperity within thy palaces." In the king's house, his family, his ministers; if there be dissensions there, ruin will soon follow.

IV. The psalmist shows his own readiness to do this.

1. "I will now say, Peace be within thee." So should all the ministers of religion pray.

2. "I will seek thy good." So should the king and every officer of state resolve. All should be united in so good a work. They should not seek *their own good*, but the *good*, not the *goods*, of *the people.*

For this the psalmist gives *these* reasons:—

1. "For my brethren and companions' sakes." We are not only subjects of one king, citizens of the same city, but we have all one God and Father.

2. "Because of the house of the Lord." For the maintenance of true religion. If *religion* fail, the *kingdom* will fail; prosperity will be at an end; the nation will be divided, distracted, destroyed. Religion, the true religion in a country, is the *consolation* of the *good*, and the *bridle* that holds in the jaws of the *wicked.* Let us all pray for the prosperity of pure and undefiled religion, and the prosperity of the state!

PSALM CXXIII

The prayer and faith of the godly, 1, 2. *They desire to be delivered from contempt*, 3, 4.

A Song of Degrees

UNTO thee [a]lift I up mine eyes, O thou [b]that dwellest in the heavens.

2 Behold, as the eyes of servants *look* unto the hand of their masters, *and* as the eyes of a maiden unto the hand of her mistress; so our eyes *wait* upon the LORD our God, until that he have mercy upon us.

3 Have mercy upon us, O LORD, have mercy upon us: for we are exceedingly filled with contempt.

4 Our soul is exceedingly filled with the scorning of those that are at ease, *and* with the contempt of the proud.

[a]Psa. cxxi. 1; cxli. 8

[b]Psa. ii. 4; xi. 4; cxv. 3

NOTES ON PSALM CXXIII

This Psalm is probably a complaint of the captives in Babylon relative to the contempt and cruel usage they received. The author is uncertain.

Verse 1. *Unto thee lift I up mine eyes*] We have no hope but in thee; our eyes look upward; we have expectation from thy *mercy* alone.

Verse 2. *As the eyes of servants*] We now wait for thy commands, feeling the utmost readiness to obey them when made known to us. The words may be understood as the language of dependence also. As slaves expect their *support* from their masters and mistresses; so do we ours from thee, O Lord! Or, As servants look to their masters and mistresses, to *see how they do their work*, that they may do it in the same way; so do we, O Lord, that we may learn of thee, and do thy work in thy own Spirit, and after thy own method. Some think that there is a reference here to the *chastisement of slaves* by their masters, who, during the time they are receiving it, keep their eyes fixed on the hand that is inflicting punishment upon them, professing deep sorrow, and entreating for mercy. And this sense seems to be countenanced by the following words:—

Verse 3. *Have mercy upon us, O Lord*] Chastise us no more; we will no more revolt against thee.

We are exceedingly filled with contempt.] We not only suffer grievously from our captivity, but are treated in the most contemptuous manner by our masters.

Verse 4. *Those that are at ease*] The Babylonians, who, having subdued all the people of the neighbouring nations, lived *at ease*, had none to contend with them, and now became luxurious, *indolent*, and *insolent:* they were contemptuous and proud.

ANALYSIS OF THE HUNDRED AND TWENTY-THIRD PSALM

The oppressed followers of God make application to him for mercy. In this application they express *three* things:—

I. Their confidence in God.

II. Prayer for mercy.

III. An account of their oppressors.

I. Their trust in God.

1. "Unto thee lift I up mine eyes." We trust in thee *alone*.

2. "O thou that dwellest in the heavens." Infinitely raised above us; but affected with our miserable condition, and always ready to help us.

This he shows by a double similitude:—

1. "As the eyes of servants," i. e., *men-servants*, "look unto the hand of their masters."

2. "As the eyes of a maiden unto the hand of her mistress:" both might be beaten; and here both beg to be saved from farther stripes.

3. "So our eyes," &c. God's children are always looking up to him.

4. "Until that he have mercy;" abate his stripes, and take off his hand.

II. Their prayer for mercy.

1. Before they *lifted their eyes* to God, but now they *cry* for mercy.

For this *crying*, they give the following reasons:—

1. "We are exceedingly filled with contempt." To *suffer contempt* is *much;* to be *filled* with it is *more;* and to be *exceedingly filled* with it is *worst* of all.

2. We are *scorned:* they join *words* and *actions* to show how much they despise us.

III. They give the *character* of those by whom they suffer.

1. They are *at ease*—loaded with wealth, and sunk in indolence.

2. They are *proud*—puffed up with a sense of their own importance; and this leads them to despise others. Proud men are for the most part empty, shallow-pated men: and contempt and scorn from such wounds deeply; especially if they rise, as they often do, from the *dunghill.* The sick *lion* in the fable found it extremely galling to be kicked by the *foot* of an *ass.*

PSALM CXXIV

A thanksgiving of the godly for extraordinary deliverances, 1–6. *The great danger they were in*, 7. *Their confidence in God*, 8.

A Song of Degrees of David

A. M. cir. 3494 B. C. cir. 510 Assueri, R. Persarum, cir. annum duodecimum

IF *it had not been* the LORD
who was on our side, [a]now
may Israel say;
2 If *it had not been* the LORD who
was on our side, when men rose up against us:
3 Then they had [b]swallowed us up quick,
when their wrath was kindled against us:
4 Then the waters had overwhelmed us, the
stream had gone over our soul:
5 Then the proud waters had
gone over our soul.
6 Blessed *be* the LORD, who
hath not given us *as* a prey to
their teeth.
7 Our soul is escaped [c]as a bird out of the
snare of the fowlers: the snare is broken, and
we are escaped.
8 [d]Our help *is* in the name of the LORD,
[e]who made heaven and earth.

A. M. cir. 3494 B. C. cir. 510 Assueri, R. Persarum, cir. annum duodecimum

[a]Psalm cxxix. 1——[b]Psalm lvi. 1, 2; lvii. 3; Proverbs i. 12

[c]Psa. xci. 3; Prov. vi. 5——[d]Psa. cxxi. 2——[e]Gen. i. 1; Psa. cxxxiv. 3

NOTES ON PSALM CXXIV

In our present Hebrew copies this Psalm is attributed to *David*, לדוד *ledavid;* but this inscription is wanting in *three* of *Kennicott's* and *De Rossi's* MSS., as also in the *Septuagint*, *Syriac*, *Vulgate*, *Æthiopic*, and *Arabic;* and in most of the ancient *fathers*, Greek and Latin, who found no other inscription in their copies of the text than *A Psalm of degrees.* It was composed long after David's days; and appears to be either a thanksgiving for their deliverance from the Babylonish captivity, or for a remarkable deliverance from some potent and insidious enemy after their return to Judea. Or, what appears to be more likely, it is a thanksgiving of the Jews for their escape from the general massacre intended by Haman, prime minister of Ahasuerus, king of Persia. See the whole Book of *Esther*.

Verse 1. *If* it had not been *the Lord*] If God had not, in a very especial manner, supported and defended us, we had all been swallowed up alive, and destroyed by a sudden destruction, so that not one would have been left. This might refer to the plot against the whole nation of the Jews by Haman, in the days of Mordecai and Esther; when by his treacherous schemes the Jews, wheresoever dispersed in the provinces of Babylon, were all to have been put to death in one day. This may here be represented under the figure of an earthquake, when a chasm is formed, and a whole city and its inhabitants are in a moment swallowed up alive.

Verse 5. *Then the proud waters*] The proud *Haman* had nearly brought the flood of desolation over our lives.

Verse 7. *Our soul is escaped as a bird out of the snare*] This is a fine image; and at once shows the *weakness* of the Jews, and the *cunning* of their adversaries. Haman had laid the snare completely for them; humanly speaking there was no prospect of their escape: but the *Lord was on their side;* and the providence that induced Ahasuerus to call for the book of the records of the kingdom to be read to him, as well indeed as the once very improbable advancement of Esther to the throne of Persia, was the means used by the Lord for the preservation of the whole Jewish people from extermination. God thus *broke the snare*, and the *bird escaped;* while the poacher was caught in his own trap, and executed. See the Book of Esther, which is probably the best comment on this Psalm.

Verse 8. *Our help* is *in the name of the Lord*] בשום מימרא דיי *beshum meymra deyai*, Chaldee, "In the name of the WORD of the LORD." So in the second verse, "Unless the WORD of the LORD had been our Helper:" *the substantial* WORD; not a *word spoken*, or a *prophecy* delivered, but the person who was afterwards termed Ὁ Λογος του Θεου, *the* WORD OF GOD. This deliverance of the Jews appears to me the most natural interpretation of this Psalm: and probably *Mordecai* was the author.

ANALYSIS OF THE HUNDRED AND TWENTY-FOURTH PSALM

The people of God, newly escaped from some great danger, acknowledge it, and celebrate God as their Deliverer.

I. The psalmist begins abruptly, as is usual in pathetical expressions.

1. "If it had not been the Lord:" and so deeply was he affected with a sense of God's goodness, and the narrowness of the escape, that he repeats it: "Unless the Lord," &c. Nothing else could have saved us.

2. "Now may Israel say;" the whole body of the Jewish people may well acknowledge this.

3. "When men rose up:" when they were all leagued against us as one man to destroy us; and, humanly speaking, our escape was impossible.

II. This danger and escape the psalmist illustrates by *two metaphors:*—

1. The *first* is taken from *beasts* of prey: "They had swallowed us up quick." They would have rushed upon us, torn us in pieces, and swallowed us down, while life was quivering in our limbs.

This they would have done in their *fury.* The plot was laid with great *circumspection* and *caution;* but it would have been executed with a *resistless fury.*

2. The *second* similitude is taken from *waters* which had broken through dikes, and at once submerged the whole country: "The stream had gone over our soul;" the *proud waters,* resistless now the dikes were broken, would have *gone over our soul*—destroyed our life.

III. He next acknowledges the *deliverance.*

1. "We are not given a prey to their teeth."

2. It is the blessed God who has preserved us: "Blessed be God," &c.

As this deliverance was *beyond expectation,* he illustrates it by *another metaphor,* a *bird* taken in, but escaping from, a *snare.*

1. We were in "the snare of the fowler."

2. But "our soul is escaped."

3. And the fowler disappointed of his prey. The disappointment of Haman was, in all its circumstances, one of the most mortifying that ever occurred to man.

IV. He concludes with a grateful acclamation.

1. "Our help is in the name of the Lord." In open assaults, and in *insidious attacks,* we have no helper but God; and from him our deliverance must come.

2. This help is sufficient; for he made the *heaven* and *earth;* has both under his government; and can employ both in the support, or for the *deliverance,* of his followers.

Or, take the following as a plainer analysis:—

I. 1. The *subtlety* of the adversaries of the Church in laying snares to entrap it, as fowlers do birds, ver. 7.

2. Their *cruelty* in seeking to tear it to pieces, as some ravenous beasts of prey do; or, as mighty inundations that overthrow all in their way, ver. 3-6.

II. The cause of this subtlety and cruelty: wrath and displeasure, ver. 3.

III. The delivery of the Church from both, by the power and goodness of God, ver. 1, 2, 6, 7.

IV. The duty performed for this deliverance; praises to God, ver. 6.

PSALM CXXV

The safety of those who trust in God, 1, 2. *God's protecting providence in behalf of his followers,* 3. *A prayer for the godly,* 4. *The evil lot of the wicked,* 5.

A Song of Degrees

A. M. cir. 3559 B. C. cir. 445 Artaxerxis I., R. Persarum, cir. annum vigesimum

1 THEY that trust in the LORD *shall be* as Mount Zion, *which* cannot be removed, *but* abideth for ever.

2 *As* the mountains *are* round about Jerusalem, so the LORD *is* round about his people from henceforth even for ever.

3 For [a]the rod of [b]the wicked shall not rest upon the lot of the righteous; lest the righteous put forth their hands unto iniquity.

4 Do good, O LORD, unto *those that be* good

[a]Prov. xxii. 8; Isa. xiv. 5

[b]Heb. *wickedness*

NOTES ON PSALM CXXV

This Psalm is without a *title:* it belongs most probably to the times after the captivity; and has been applied, with apparent propriety, to the opposition which *Sanballat* the Horonite, *Geshem* the Arabian, and *Tobiah* the Ammonite, gave to the Jews while employed in rebuilding the walls of Jerusalem, and restoring the temple.

Verse 1. *They that trust in the Lord*] Every faithful Jew who confides in Jehovah shall stand, in those *open* and *secret attacks* of the enemies of God and truth, as *unshaken* as *Mount Zion;* and shall not be moved by the power of any adversary.

Verse 2. As *the mountains* are *round about Jerusalem*] Jerusalem, according to *Sandys,* was situated on a rocky mountain every way to be ascended, except a little on the north, with steep ascents and deep valleys, naturally fortified. It is surrounded with other *mountains,* at no great distance, as if placed in the midst of an amphitheatre; for on the *east* is Mount *Olivet,* separated from the city by the *valley of Jehoshaphat,* which also encompasses a part of the *north;* on the *south,* the mountain of *Offiner* interposed with the *valley of Gehinnom;* and on the *west* it was formerly fenced with the *valley of Gihon,* and the *mountains* adjoining. The situation was such as to be easily rendered impregnable.

The Lord is *round about his people*] He is *above, beneath, around* them; and *while they keep within it,* their fortress is impregnable, and they can suffer no evil.

Verse 3. *For the rod of the wicked shall not rest upon the lot of the righteous*] Rod, here, may be taken for *persecution,* or for *rule;* and then it may be thus interpreted: "The wicked shall not be permitted to *persecute always,* nor to have a *permanent rule.*" In our *liturgic version* this clause is thus rendered: "The rod of the ungodly cometh not into the lot of the righteous." "This," said one of our forefathers, "is neither *truth* nor *scripture. First,* it is not *truth;* for the rod of the wicked *doth come* into the inheritance of the righteous, and that *often.*

A. M. cir. 3559
B. C. cir. 445
Artaxerxis I.,
R. Persarum,
cir. annum
vigesimum

and to *them that are* upright in
their hearts.
5 As for such as turn aside
unto their [c]crooked ways, the
LORD shall lead them forth
with the workers of iniquity:
but [d]peace *shall be* upon
Israel.

[c]Prov. ii. 15

[d]Psa. cxxviii. 6; Gal. vi. 16

Secondly, it is not *scripture;* for the text saith, 'The rod of the wicked shall not rest there.' It may *come*, and stay for a time; but it shall not be permitted to abide."

This is only *one*, and not the *worst*, of the many sad blemishes which deform the Version in our national Prayer-book. In short, the Version of the Psalms in that book is wholly unworthy of regard; and should be thrown aside, and that in the *authorized Version* in the Bible substituted for it. The people of God are misled by it; and they are confounded with the *great* and *glaring differences* they find between it and what they find in their Bibles, where they have a version of a much better character, delivered to them by the authority of *Church* and *state*. Why do not our present excellent and learned prelates lay this to heart, and take away this sore stumbling-block out of the way of the people? I have referred to this subject in the *introduction to the Book of Psalms*.

Lest the righteous put forth] Were the wicked to *bear rule* in the Lord's vineyard, religion would soon become extinct; for the great mass of the people would conform to their rulers. Fear not your enemies, while ye fear God. Neither *Sanballat*, nor *Tobiah*, nor *Geshem*, nor any of God's foes, shall be able to set up their *rod*, their *power* and *authority*, here. While you are faithful, the Lord will laugh them to scorn.

Verse 4. *Do good, O Lord, unto* those that be *good*] Let the upright ever find thee his sure defence! Increase the *goodness* which thou hast already bestowed upon them; and let all who are *upright in heart* find thee to be their stay and their support!

Verse 5. *As for such as turn aside*] Who are not *faithful;* who *give way to sin;* who *backslide*, and walk in a *crooked way*, widely different from the *straight way* of the *upright*, ישרים *yesharim*, the *straight* in heart; they shall be *led forth* to punishment *with the* common *workers of iniquity*. Thus thy Church will be purified, and thy *peace* rest *upon* thy true *Israel*. Let him that readeth understand.

ANALYSIS OF THE HUNDRED AND TWENTY-FIFTH PSALM

It is the purpose of the psalmist to comfort the people of God,—

I. By an assurance of their perpetuity, both from God's presence and protection, ver. 1, 2.

II. That though he may permit them to be harassed by the wicked, yet he will not leave them under their rod, ver. 3.

III. He prays for the good; and,

IV. Sets down the portion of the wicked, ver. 4, 5.

I. A general promise of the perpetuity of the Church; that is, of them "that trust in God."

1. "They that trust in the Lord:" "The congregation of God's faithful people, who have the pure word of God preached, and the sacraments duly administered," Acts xix.

2. "Shall be as Mount Zion," secure and immovable; immovable, because a *mountain*,—a *holy* mountain,—and particularly *dear* to God.

3. "Which abideth for ever:" So surely as *Mount Zion* shall never be *removed*, so surely shall the *Church of God* be *preserved*. Is it not strange that wicked and idolatrous powers have not joined together, dug down this mount, and carried it into the sea, that they might nullify a promise in which the people of God exult! Till ye can carry Mount Zion into the Mediterranean Sea, the Church of Christ shall grow and prevail. Hear this, ye murderous Mohammedans!

4. "As the mountains are round about Jerusalem,"—to fortify it.

5. "So the Lord is round about his people"—to preserve them.

6. "From henceforth, even for ever:" Through both *time* and *eternity*.

II. 1. But the Church is often persecuted and harassed. Granted; for the "rod," the power and scourge, "of the wicked, may come into the heritage of the righteous."

2. But then may it not finally prevail? No: for though it *come*, it shall not *rest*.

3. And why? Because it might finally destroy the Church, pervert the good, and cause them to join issue with the ungodly. Therefore, "they shall not be tempted above that they are able."

III. Therefore the psalmist prays,—

1. "Do good to the good:" Give them *patience*, and keep them *faithful*.

2. And "to the upright in heart:" Let not the *weak* and the *sincere* be overcome by their enemies:

IV. He sets down the *lot of the ungodly:*—

1. "They turn aside."

2. They get into *crooked paths;* they get into the *spirit of the world*, and are *warped* into its *crooked* and *winding* ways.

3. They shall be condemned, and *then led forth to* punishment. The backslider in heart shall be filled with his own ways; he shall have *writhing* in pain, for *crooked walking* in sin.

4. But while this is their portion, "peace," prosperity, and blessedness, "shall be upon Israel."

PSALM CXXVI

The joy of the Israelites on their return from captivity, and the effect their deliverance had upon the heathen, 1–3. *The prayer which they had offered up*, 4. *The inference they draw from the whole*, 5, 6.

XXVII. DAY. EVENING PRAYER

A Song of Degrees

A. M. cir. 3468 B. C. cir. 536 Cyri, R. Persarum, cir. annum primum

WHEN the LORD [a]turned
again the captivity of Zion,
[b]we were like them that dream.
2 Then [c]was our mouth filled
with laughter, and our tongue
with singing: then said they
among the heathen, The LORD
[d]hath done great things for them.
3 The LORD hath done great things for us;
whereof we are glad.

[a]Heb. *returned the returning of Zion;* Psa. liii. 6; lxxxv. 1; Hos. vi. 11; Joel iii. 1 [b]Acts xii. 9——[c]Job viii. 21——[d]Heb. *hath magnified to do with them*

NOTES ON PSALM CXXVI

This Psalm is not of David, has no title in the Hebrew or any of the Versions, and certainly belongs to the close of the captivity. It might have been composed by *Haggai* and *Zechariah*, as the *Syriac* supposes; or by *Ezra*, according to others. It is beautiful, and highly descriptive of the circumstances which it represents.

Verse 1. *When the Lord turned again the captivity*] When Cyrus published his decree in favour of the Jews, giving them liberty to return to their own land, and rebuild their city and temple.

We were like them that dream.] The news was so unexpected that we doubted for a time the truth of it. We believed it was too good news to be true, and thought ourselves in a dream or illusion. When the Romans had vanquished Philip, king of Macedon, they restored liberty to the Grecian cities by proclamation. It was done at the time of the Isthmian games, and by the crier, who went into the circus to proclaim them; none but the Roman general T. Quintius knowing what was to be done. Multitudes from all Greece were there assembled; and the tidings produced nearly the same effect upon them, according to Livy, that the publication of the decree of Cyrus did on the Jews, according to what is here related by the psalmist. I shall give the substance of this account from the Roman historian. When the Romans had sat down to behold the games, the herald with his trumpet went into the arena, according to custom, to proclaim the several games. Silence being obtained, he solemnly pronounced the following words:—

SENATUS ROMANUS ET T. QUINCIUS IMPERATOR, PHILIPPO REGE MACEDONIBUSQUE DEVICTIS; LIBEROS, IMMUNES, SUIS LEGIBUS ESSE JUBET CORINTHIOS, PHOCENSES, LOCRENSESQUE OMNES, ET INSULAM EUBŒAM, ET MAGNETAS, THESSALOS, PERRHÆBOS, ACHÆOS, PHTHIOTAS.

"The Roman Senate, and T. Quintius the general, having vanquished king Philip and the Macedonians, do ordain that the Corinthians, Phocensians, all the Locrensians, the island of Eubœa, the Magnesians, Thessalians, Perrhæbians, Acheans, and Phthiotians, shall be free, be delivered from all taxes, and live according to their own laws."

The effect that this produced on the astonished Grecians who were present, is related by this able historian in a very natural and affecting manner; and some parts of it *nearly in the words of the psalmist.*

Audita voce præconis, majus gaudium fuit, quam quod universum homines caperent. Vix satis se credere se quisque audisse: alii alios intueri mirabundi velut *somnii vanam speciem: guod ad guemque pertineret, suarum aurium fidei minimum credentes, proximos interrogabant.* Revocatur præco, cum unusquisque non audire, sed videre libertatis suæ nuncium averit, iterum pronunciaret eadem. Tum ab certo jam gaudio tantus cum clamore plausus est ortus, totiesque repetitus, ut facile appareret, nihil omnium bonorum multitudini gratius quam LIBERTATEM esse.

T. LIV. *Hist.*, lib xxxiii., c. 32.

This proclamation of the herald being heard, there was such joy, that the people in general could not comprehend it. Scarcely could any person believe what he had heard. They gazed on each other, wondering as if it had been *some illusion, similar to a dream;* and although all were interested in what was spoken, none could trust his own ears, but inquired each from him who stood next to him what it was that was proclaimed. The herald was again called, as each expressed the strongest desire not only to hear, but see the messenger of his own liberty: the herald, therefore, repeated the proclamation. When by this repetition the glad tidings were confirmed, there arose such a shout, accompanied with repeated clapping of hands, as plainly showed that *of all good things none is so dear to the multitude* as LIBERTY.

O that God may raise up some other deliverer to save *these same cities* with their *inhabitants*, from a worse yoke than ever was imposed upon them by the king of Macedon; and from a servitude which has now lasted three hundred years longer than the *captivity* of the Israelites in the empire of Babylon!

Constantinople was taken by the *Turks* in 1453; and since that time till the present, (October, 1822,) three hundred and sixty-nine years have elapsed. Why do the *Christian* powers of Europe stand by, and see the ark of their God in captivity; the holy name by which they are called despised and execrated; the vilest indignities offered to those who are called Christians, by barbarians the most cruel, ferocious, and abominable that ever disgraced the name of man? Great God, vindicate the cause of the distressed Greeks as *summarily*, as *effectually*, as *permanently*, as thou once didst that of thy oppressed people the Jews! Let the *crescent* never more *fill* its *horns* with a *victory*, nor with the spoils of any who are called by the sacred name of JESUS: but let it *wane* back into total darkness; and know no

A. M. cir. 3468 B. C. cir. 536 Cyri, R. Persarum, cir. annum primum

4 Turn again our captivity, O
LORD, as the streams in the
south.
5 [e]They that sow in tears shall
reap in [f]joy.
6 He that goeth forth and weepeth, bearing [g]precious seed, shall
doubtless come again with rejoicing, bringing his sheaves *with*
him.

A. M. cir. 3468 B. C. cir. 536 Cyri, R. Persarum, cir. annum primum

[e]See Jer. xxxi. 9, &c. — [f]Or, *singing*——[g]Or, *seed basket*

change for the better, till illuminated by the *orient splendour* of the *Sun of righteousness!* Amen! Amen!

How signally has this prayer been thus far answered! Three great Christian powers, the *British*, the *French*, and the *Russian*, have taken up the cause of the oppressed Greeks. The Turkish fleet has been attacked in the Bay of Navarino by the combined fleets of the above powers in October, 1827, under the command of the British Admiral, Sir Edward Codrington, and totally annihilated. After which, the Mohammedan troops were driven out of Greece and the Morea; so that the whole of Greece is cleared of its oppressors, and is now under its own government, protected by the above powers.—March, 1829.

Verse 2. *Then was our mouth filled with laughter*] The same effect as was produced on the poor liberated Grecians mentioned above.

Then said they among the heathen] The liberty now granted was brought about in so extraordinary a way, that the very *heathens* saw that the hand of the great Jehovah must have been in it.

Verse 3. *The Lord hath done great things for us*] We acknowledge the hand of our God. *Deus nobis hæc otia fecit*, "God alone has given us this enlargement."

We are glad.] This is a mere burst of ecstatic joy. O how happy are we!

Verse 4. *Turn again our captivity*] This is either a recital of the prayer they had used *before* their deliverance; or it is a prayer for those who *still remained* in the provinces beyond the Euphrates. The Jewish captives did not all return at *once;* they came back at different times, and under different leaders, Ezra, Nehemiah, Zerubbabel, &c.

As the streams in the south.] Probably the *Nile* is meant. It is now pretty well known that the Nile has its origin in the kingdom of *Damot;* and runs from *south* to *north* through different countries, till, passing through Egypt, it empties itself into the Mediterranean Sea. It it possible, however, that they might have had in view some *rapid rivers* that either rose in the south, or had a *southern* direction; and they desired that their return might be as rapid and as *abundant* as the waters of those rivers. But we know that the Nile proceeds from the south, divides itself into several *streams* as it passes through Egypt, and falls by *seven mouths* into the Mediterranean.

Verse 5. *They that sow in tears shall reap in joy.*] This is either a *maxim* which they gather from their own history, or it is a *fact* which they are now witnessing. We see the benefit of humbling ourselves under the mighty hand of God; we have now a sweet return for our bitter tears. Or, We *have* sown in tears; now we reap in joy. We are restored after a long and afflicting captivity to our own country, to peace, and to happiness.

Verse 6. *He that goeth forth and weepeth, bearing precious seed*] The metaphor seems to be this: A poor farmer has had a very bad harvest: a very scanty portion of grain and food has been gathered from the earth. The *seed time* is now come, and is very unpromising. Out of the famine a little seed has been saved to be sown, in hopes of another crop; but the badness of the present season almost precludes the entertainment of hope. But he must sow, or else despair and perish. He carries his all, his *precious seed*, with him in his *seed basket;* and with a sorrowful heart commits it to the furrow, watering it in effect with his tears, and earnestly imploring the blessing of God upon it. God hears; the season becomes mild; he beholds successively the *blade*, the *ear*, and the *full corn* in the ear. The appointed weeks of harvest come, and the grain is very productive. He fills his arms, his carriages with the sheaves and shocks; and returns to his large expecting family in triumph, praising God for the wonders he has wrought. So shall it be with this handful of *returning Israelites.* They also are to be *sown*--scattered all over the land; the blessing of God shall be upon them, and their faith and numbers shall be abundantly increased. The return here referred to, *Isaiah* describes in very natural language: "And they shall bring all your brethren for an offering to the Lord out of all nations, upon horses, and in chariots, and in litters, upon mules, and upon swift beasts, to my holy mountain Jerusalem, saith the Lord, as the children of Israel bring an offering in a clean vessel into the house of the Lord," chap. lxvi., ver. 20.

ANALYSIS OF THE HUNDRED AND TWENTY-SIXTH PSALM

The parts of this Psalm are *three:*—

I. An expression of joy for their strange deliverance from captivity.

II. A prayer for the return of the remaining part.

III. A moral collected by the psalmist from it.

1. The psalmist celebrates their return, and amplifies it *three* ways:—

1. From the cause, *Jehovah.* Cyrus gave a commission for it; but it was the Lord who disposed his heart so to do: "When the Lord turned," &c.

2. From the *manner* of it. It was strange and wonderful; they could scarcely believe it.

3. From the *joy* at it, inward and external. 1. Their "mouths were filled with laughter." 2. Their "tongue with singing." A thankful tongue expressed the feelings of a thankful heart.

That God did this for them he proves by two evidences:—

1. The *heathen:* "Then said they among the heathen." They saw that they were permitted to return by virtue of a royal edict; that the

very king who gave the commission was named by a prophet; that they had rich gifts given them, the vessels of gold and silver restored, &c. Who could do all these things but GOD?

2. The *Jews.* It is true, said the Jews, what you acknowledge. 1. "The Lord hath done great things for us." Beyond our merit, beyond our hope. 2. "Whereof we are glad," for we are freed from a galling yoke.

II. But there were some Jews left behind, for whom they pray.

1. "Turn their captivity also." Put it in their hearts to join their brethren. Several, no doubt, stayed behind, because they *had married strange wives,* &c.

2. "Turn it as the streams in the south." Or, as some read it, *streams of water on a parched land.* Judea has been lying waste; we need many hands to cultivate it. When all join together in this work the land will become *fruitful,* like the parched ground when powerful rivulets are sent through it in all directions.

III. The benefit of this will be great; for although it may cost us much *hard labour* and *distress* in the beginning, yet the maxim will hold good—"They who sow in tears shall reap in joy." Which the psalmist amplifies in the next verse.

1. "He that goeth forth and weepeth." The poor husbandman, for the reasons given above and in the notes, *bearing precious seed*—seed bought with a high price, which augments his grief, being so poor.

2. "He shall doubtless come again"—in harvest *with joy,* having a plentiful crop; for every grain sown at least one full-fed ear of corn, with at the lowest *thirty-fold.* Some maxims are to be gathered from the whole: Penitential sorrow shall be followed by the joy of pardoning mercy; he that bears the cross shall wear the crown; and, trials and difficulties shall be followed by peace and prosperity.

PSALM CXXVII

The necessity of God's blessing on every undertaking, without which no prosperity can be expected, 1, 2. *Children are a heritage from the Lord,* 3, 4. *A fruitful wife is a blessing to her husband,* 5.

A Song of Degrees [a]for Solomon

A. M. cir. 3559
B. C. cir. 445
Artaxerxis I.,
R. Persarum,
cir. annum
vigesimum

EXCEPT the LORD build the
house, they labour in vain
[b]that build it: except [c]the LORD
keep the city, the watchman
waketh *but* in vain.

2 *It is* vain for you to rise
up early, to sit up late, to [d]eat
the bread of sorrows: *for* so
he giveth his beloved sleep.

A. M. cir. 3559
B. C. cir. 445
Artaxerxis I.,
R. Persarum,
cir. annum
vigesimum

3 Lo, [e]children *are* a heritage of the LORD:
and [f]the fruit of the womb *is his* reward.

[a]Or, *of Solomon;* Psa. lxxii. title——[b]Heb. that are *builders of it in it*——[c]Psa. cxxi. 3, 4, 5

[d]Gen. iii. 17, 19——[e]Gen. xxxiii. 5; xlviii. 4; Josh. xxiv. 3, 4——[f]Deut. xxviii. 4

NOTES ON PSALM CXXVII

The *Hebrew, Chaldee,* and *Vulgate* attribute this Psalm to Solomon. The *Syriac* says it is "A Psalm of David concerning Solomon; and that it was spoken also concerning Haggai and Zechariah, who forwarded the building of the temple." The *Septuagint, Æthiopic, Arabic,* and *Anglo-Saxon* have no title, but simply "A Psalm of Degrees." It was most likely composed for the building of the second temple, under Nehemiah, and by some prophet of that time.

Verse 1. *Except the Lord build the house*] To build a house is taken in *three* different senses in the sacred writings. 1. To build the temple of the Lord, which was called הבית *habbeith, the house,* by way of eminence. 2. To build any ordinary house, or place of dwelling. 3. To have a numerous offspring. In this sense it is supposed to be spoken concerning the Egyptian midwives; that because they feared the Lord, therefore he built them houses. See the note on Exod. i. 21. But, however, the above passage may be interpreted, it is a fact that בן *ben, a son,* and בת *bath, a daughter,* and בית *beith, a house,* come from the same root בנה *banah, to build;* because sons and daughters build up a household, or constitute a *family,* as much and as really as stones and timber constitute a *building.* Now it is true that unless the good hand of God be upon us we cannot prosperously build a place of worship for his name. Unless we have his blessing, a dwelling-house cannot be comfortably erected. And if his blessing be not on our children, the house (the family) may be built up, but instead of its being the house of God, it will be the synagogue of Satan. All marriages that are not under God's blessing will be a private and public curse. This we see every day.

Except the Lord keep the city] When the returned Jews began to restore the walls of Jerusalem, and rebuild the city, Sanballat, Tobiah, and others formed plots to prevent it. Nehemiah, being informed of this, set up proper watches and guards. The enemy, finding this, gathered themselves together, and determined to fall upon them at once, and cut them all off. Nehemiah, having gained intelligence of this also, armed his people, and placed them behind the wall. Sanballat and his company, finding that the Jews were prepared for resistance, abandoned their project; and Nehemiah, to prevent surprises of this kind, kept one-half of the people always under arms, while the other half was employed in the work. To this the psalmist alludes; and in effect says, Though you should watch constantly, guard every place, and keep on your armour ready to repel every attack, yet remember the success of all depends upon the presence and blessing of God. While, therefore, ye are not slothful in business, be fervent in spirit, serving the Lord; for there is no success either in spiritual or secular undertakings but in consequence of the benediction of the Almighty.

Verse 2. It is *vain for you to rise up early*]

A. M. cir. 3559
B. C. cir. 445
Artaxerxis I.,
R. Persarum,
cir. annum
vigesimum

4 As arrows *are* in the hand
of a mighty man; so *are* children of the youth.
5 Happy *is* the man that [g]hath
his quiver full of them: [h]they
shall not be ashamed, but they
[i]shall speak with the enemies in
the gate.

A. M. cir. 3559
B. C. cir. 445
Artaxerxis I.,
R. Persarum,
cir. annum
vigesimum

[g]Heb. *hath filled his quiver with them*——[h]See Job v. 4; Prov. xxvii. 11

[i]Or, *shall subdue*, as Psalm xviii. 47; or, *destroy*

There seems to be here an allusion to the daily and nightly watches which Nehemiah instituted. The people are worn out with constant labour and watching; he therefore divided them in such a manner, that they who had worked in the day should rest by night, and that they who worked by night should rest in the day; and thus *his beloved*, a title of the Jews, *the beloved of God*, got sleep, due refreshment, and rest. As for Nehemiah and his servants, they never put off their clothes day or night but for washing.

Verse 3. *Lo, children* are *a heritage of the Lord*] That is, To many God gives children in place of temporal good. To many others he gives houses, lands, and thousands of gold and silver, and with them the womb that beareth not; and these are their inheritance. The poor man has from God a number of children, without lands or money; these are his inheritance; and God shows himself their father, feeding and supporting them by a chain of miraculous providences. Where is the *poor man* who would give up his *six children*, with the prospect of having *more*, for the *thousands* or *millions* of him who is the *centre* of his *own existence*, and has neither *root* nor *branch* but his forlorn solitary self upon the face of the earth? Let the fruitful family, however poor, lay this to heart: "Children are a heritage of the Lord; and the fruit of the womb is his reward." And he who gave them will feed them; for it is a fact, and the *maxim* formed on it has never failed, "Wherever God sends mouths, he sends meat." "Murmur not," said an Arab to his friend, "because thy family is large; know that it is for *their sakes* that God feeds *thee*."

Verse 4. *As arrows* are *in the hand of a mighty man*] Each child will, in the process of time, be a *defence* and *support* to the family, as arrows in the quiver of a skilful and strong archer; the more he has, the more enemies he may slay, and consequently the more redoubted shall he be.

Children of the youth.] The children of *young people* are always more strong and vigorous, more healthy, and generally longer lived than those of *elderly*, or comparatively *elderly persons. Youth* is the time for marriage; I do not mean *infancy* or a comparative *childhood*, in which several fools join in marriage who are scarcely fit to leave the *nursery* or *school.* Such couples generally disagree; they cannot bear the *boyish* and *girlish* petulancies and caprices of each other; their own growth is hindered, and their offspring, (if any,) have never much better than an *embryo* existence. On the other hand *age* produces only a *dwarfish* or *rickety* offspring, that seldom live to procreate; and when they do, it is only to perpetuate deformity and disease. It would be easy to assign reasons for all this; but the interpretation of Scripture will seldom admit of *physiological details.* It is enough that God has said, *Children of the youth* are strong and active, *like arrows in the hands of the mighty.*

Verse 5. *Happy* is *the man that hath his quiver full of them*] This is generally supposed to mean *his house full of children*, as his *quiver* if full of *arrows;* but I submit whether it be not more congenial to the metaphors in the text to consider it as applying to the *wife:* "Happy is the man who has a breeding or fruitful wife;" this is the *gravida sagittis pharetra* "the quiver pregnant with arrows." But it may be thought the metaphor is not natural. I think otherwise: and I know it to be in the *Jewish style*, and the style of the times of the captivity, when this Psalm was written, and we find the *pudendum muliebre*, or human *matrix*, thus denominated, Ecclus, xxvi. 12: *Κατεναντι παντος πασσαλου καθησεται, και εναντι βελους ανοιξει φαρετραν.* The reader may consult the place in the *Apocrypha*, where he will find the verse well enough translated.

With the enemies in the gate.] "When he shall contend with his adversaries in the gate of the house of judgment."—*Targum.* The reference is either to *courts of justice*, which were held at the *gates* of *cities*, or to *robbers* who endeavour to force their way into a *house* to spoil the inhabitants of their goods. In the *first case* a man falsely accused, who has a numerous family, has as many witnesses in his behalf as he has children. And in the *second case* he is not afraid of *marauders*, because his house is well defended by his active and vigorous sons. It is, I believe, to this last that the psalmist refers.

This Psalm may be entitled, "The Soliloquy of the happy Householder:—The poor man with a large loving family, and in annual expectation of an increase, because his wife, under the Divine blessing, is fruitful." All are blessed of the Lord, and his hand is invariably upon them for good.

Analysis of the Hundred and Twenty-seventh Psalm

The Jews were at this time very busy in rebuilding their temple, and the houses and walls of their city; and the prophet teaches them that, without the assistance of God, nothing will be blessed or preserved, and that their children are his especial blessing also. This the prophet shows by these words repeated, *nisi, nisi, frustra, frustra*, and proves it by an induction.

I. In civil affairs, whether in house or city.

1. "Except the Lord build the house," &c. God must be the chief builder in the family; his blessing and help must be prayed for, for the nourishment of wife, children, servants, cattle, &c.

2. "Except the Lord keep the city," &c. And so it is in kingdoms and commonwealths. The *Jews* had now a trowel in one hand, and a sword in the other, for fear of their enemies: but the prophet tells them that the Lord must be their

protector and keeper, else their watch, magistrates, judges, &c., would be of little value.

And this he illustrates by an elegant *hypothesis* of an industrious man who strives to be rich, but looks not to God.

1. "He riseth early." He is up with the rising of the sun.

2. "He sits up late." Takes little rest.

3. "He eats the bread of sorrow." Defrauds himself of necessary food. His mind is full of anxiety and fear: but all this without God's blessing is vain: "It is vain for you to rise up early," &c. On the contrary, he who loves and fears God has God's blessing: "For so he gives his beloved sleep," in the place of fear and distraction.

II. The prophet then sets down the blessing a man possesses in his children. In reference to their birth,

1. "Lo, children are a heritage," &c. They are alone the Lord's gift.

2. As regarding their education: being brought up in the fear of the Lord, they become generous spirits: "As arrows are in the hand of a mighty man," &c. enabled to do great actions, and to defend themselves and others.

And the benefit will redound to the father in his old age.

1. "Happy is the man that hath," &c. Of such good children.

2. "He shall not be ashamed," &c. He shall be able to defend himself, and keep out all injuries, being fortified by his children. And if it so happen that he has a cause pending in the gate, to be tried before the judges, he shall have the patronage of his children, and not suffer in his plea for want of advocates: his sons shall stand up in a just cause for him.

PSALM CXXVIII

The blessedness of the man that fears the Lord, 1. *He is blessed in his labour,* 2; *in his wife and children,* 3, 4; *in the ordinances of God,* 5; *and in a long life and numerous posterity,* 6.

A Song of Degrees

A. M. cir. 3559
B. C. cir. 445
Artaxerxis I.,
R. Persarum,
cir. annum
vigesimum

BLESSED [a]*is* every one that
feareth the LORD; that
walketh in his ways.
2 [b]For thou shalt eat the labour
of thine hands: happy *shalt* thou *be,* and *it*
shall be well with thee.
3 Thy wife *shall be* [c]as a fruitful vine by the
sides of thine house: thy children [d]like
olive plants round about thy
table.
4 Behold, that thus shall the man
be blessed that feareth the LORD.
5 [e]The LORD shall bless thee out of Zion:
and thou shalt see the good of Jerusalem all
the days of thy life.
6 Yea, thou shalt [f]see thy children's children, *and* [g]peace upon Israel.

[a]Psa. cxii. 1; cxv. 13; cxix. 1——[b]Isa. iii. 10——[c]Ezek. xix. 10——[d]Psa. lii. 8; cxliv. 12——[e]Psa. cxxxiv. 3——[f]Gen. l. 23; Job xlii. 16——[g]Psa. cxxv. 5

NOTES ON PSALM CXXVIII

This Psalm has no *title,* either in the *Hebrew* or any of the *Versions;* though the *Syriac* supposes it to have been spoken of *Zerubbabel,* prince of Judah, who was earnestly engaged in building the temple of the Lord. It seems to be a continuation of the preceding Psalm, or rather the *second* part of it. The man who is stated to have a numerous offspring, in the *preceding Psalm,* is here represented as *sitting at table* with his large family. A person in the mean while coming in, sees his happy state, speaks of his comforts, and predicts to him and his all possible future good. And why? Because the man and his family "fear God, and walk in his ways."

Verse 2. *Thou shalt eat the labour of thine hands*] Thou shalt not be exempted from *labour.* Thou shalt *work:* But God will *bless* and *prosper* that work, and thou and thy family shall eat of it. Ye shall all live on the produce of your own labour, and the hand of violence shall not be permitted to deprive you of it. Thus,

Happy shalt *thou* be, *and* it shall be *well with thee.*] Thou shalt have prosperity.

Verse 3. *Thy wife* shall be *as a fruitful vine*] Thy *children,* in every corner and apartment of thy house, shall be the evidences of the fruitfulness of thy wife, as *bunches of grapes* on every *bough* of the vine are the proofs of its being in a healthy thriving state. Being *about the house sides,* or *apartments,* is spoken of the *wife,* not the *vine;* being *around the table* is spoken of the *children,* not of the *olive-plants.* It does not appear that there were any *vines* planted *against the walls* of the houses in Jerusalem, nor any *olive-trees* in *pots* or *tubs* in the inside of their houses; as may be found in different parts of Europe.

Verse 4. *Thus shall the man be blessed that feareth the Lord.*] A *great price* for a small consideration. Fear God, and thou shalt have as much domestic good as may be useful to thee.

Verse 5. *The Lord shall bless thee out of Zion*] In all thy approaches to him in his house by prayer, by sacrifice, and by offering, thou shalt have his especial blessing. Thou shalt thrive every *where,* and in all *things.*

And thou shalt see the good of Jerusalem] Thou shalt see the cause of God flourish in thy lifetime, and his Church in great prosperity.

Verse 6. *Yea, thou shalt see thy children's children*] Thou shall not die till thou have seen thy family all settled in the world, and those of them who may be *married* blessed with children.

And *peace upon Israel.*] This is the same conclusion as in Psa. cxxv.; and should be translated, *Peace be upon Israel!* May God favour his own cause, and bless all his people!

ANALYSIS OF THE HUNDRED AND TWENTY-EIGHTH PSALM

In this Psalm the prophet persuades men to fear God upon the several rewards that attend upon piety.

It is divided into *three* parts.

I. He describes the pious man, and pronounces him blessed, ver. 1.

II. He proposes the particulars of his blessing, ver. 2-6.

III. He gives his acclamation to it, ver. 4.

I. He describes the man who is to expect the blessing. Two qualities he must have:—

1. He must "fear the Lord." Fear, and not decline from him.

2. He must "walk in his ways." This is the true character of his fear.

3. This man shall be "blessed." Whether rich or poor, high or low; all such shall experience the blessing of the Lord.

II. And the blessedness consists in three particulars.

1. He shall enjoy those goods he has honestly obtained with his hands: "For thou shalt eat the labour of thine hands:" his happiness consists not in having much, but in enjoying what he has.

2. "Happy shalt thou be," &c. Able to help others, and leave to thy children.

3. Happy he shall be in his marriage, if his choice be prudent, and in the Lord: 1. "His wife shall be," &c. *Fetifera, non sterilis.* 2. Upon the walls of thy house. Staying at home, and caring for the things of the house, while her husband is taking care abroad.

4. Happy in his children: 1. "Thy children like olive-plants." Fresh, green, spreading, fruitful, and pledges of peace: not like sharp and prickly thorns. 2. "Round about thy table." Sit, eat, and converse with thee.

III. The acclamation follows these temporal blessings: "Thus shall the man be blessed," &c. In his goods, wife, and children.

But there is a blessing far beyond these, the sum of which is,—

1. God's blessing: "The Lord shall bless thee," &c. By a federal, a Church blessing.

2. "Thou shalt see the good of Jerusalem," &c. The prosperity of the Church.

3. "Yea, thou shalt see thy children's children."

Et natos natorum, et qui nascuntur ab illis.

"Thy children's children, and those born of *them.*"

4. "And peace upon Israel." A flourishing commonwealth and kingdom: for by peace is understood all prosperity.

PSALM CXXIX

The Jews give an account of the afflictions which they have passed through, 1–3. *And thank God for their deliverance,* 4. *The judgments that shall fall on the workers of iniquity,* 5–8.

A Song of Degrees

MANY [a]a time have they afflicted me from [b]my youth, [c]may Israel now say:

2 Many a time have they afflicted me from my youth: yet they have not prevailed against me.

3 The plowers plowed upon my back: they made long their furrows.

4 The LORD *is* righteous: he hath cut asunder the cords of the wicked.

5 Let them all be confounded and turned back that hate Zion.

---

[a]Or, *Much*——[b]See Ezek. xxiii. 3; Hos. ii. 15; xi. 1——[c]Psa. cxxiv. 1

NOTES ON PSALM CXXIX

This Psalm was written *after* the captivity; and contains a reference to the many tribulations which the Jews passed through from their *youth*, i. e., the earliest part of their history, their bondage in Egypt. It has no *title* in any of the *Versions*, nor in the *Hebrew text*, except the general one of *A Psalm of Degrees.* The *author* is uncertain.

Verse 1. *Many a time have they afflicted me*] The Israelites had been generally in affliction or captivity from the earliest part of their history, here called *their youth.* So Hos. ii. 15: "She shall sing as in the *days of her youth*, when she came up out of *the land of Egypt.*" See Jer. ii. 2, and Ezek. xvi. 4, &c.

Verse 2. *Yet they have not prevailed*] They endeavoured to annihilate us as a people; but God still preserves us as his own nation.

Verse 3. *The plowers plowed upon my back*] It is possible that this mode of expression may signify that the people, during their captivity, were cruelly used by *scourging*, &c.; or it may be a sort of proverbial mode of expression for *the most cruel usage.* There really appears here to be a reference to a *yoke*, as if they had actually been *yoked to the plough*, or to *some kind of carriages*, and been obliged to draw like *beasts of burden.* In this way St. Jerome understood the passage; and this has the more likelihood, as in the next verse God is represented as *cutting them off* from these draughts.

Verse 4. *The Lord—hath cut asunder the cords of the wicked.*] The words have been applied to the sufferings of Christ; but I know not on what authority. No such scourging could take place in his case, as would justify the expression,—

"The ploughers made long furrows there,
Till all his body was one wound."

It is not likely that he received more than *thirty-nine* stripes. The last line is an unwarranted assertion.

Verse 5. *Let them all be confounded*] They shall be confounded. They who *hate Zion*, the Church of God, hate God himself; and all such must be dealt with as *enemies*, and be utterly *confounded.*

6 Let them be as [d]the grass *upon* the housetops, which withereth afore it groweth up:

7 Wherewith the mower filleth not his hand; nor he that bindeth sheaves his bosom.

8 Neither do they which go by say, [e]The blessing of the LORD *be* upon you: we bless you in the name of the LORD.

[d]Psa. xxxvii. 2

[e]Ruth ii. 4; Psa. cxviii. 26

Verse 6. *As the grass* upon *the housetops*] As in the east the roofs of the houses were *flat*, seeds of various kinds falling upon them would naturally vegetate, though in an imperfect way; and, because of the want of proper nourishment, would necessarily *dry* and *wither* away. If *grass*, the *mower* cannot make *hay* of it; if *corn*, the *reaper* cannot make a *sheaf* of it. Let the Babylonians be like such herbage—good for nothing, and come to nothing.

Withereth afore it groweth up] Before שלק *shalak*, it is *unsheathed;* i. e., before it *ears*, or comes to *seed*.

Verse 8. *Neither do they which go by say*] There is a reference here to the *salutations* which were *given* and *returned* by the reapers in the time of the *harvest*. We find that it was customary, when the master came to them into the field, to say unto the reapers, *The Lord be with you!* and for them to answer, *The Lord bless thee!* Ruth ii. 4. Let their land become desolate, so that no harvest shall ever more appear in it. No interchange of benedictions between owners and reapers. This has literally taken place: Babylon is utterly destroyed; no harvests grow near the place where it stood.

Analysis of the Hundred and Twenty-ninth Psalm

The intent of the prophet in composing this Psalm is to comfort the Church in affliction, and to stir her up to glorify God for his providence over her, always for her good, and bringing her enemies to confusion, and a sudden ruin.

It is divided into *three* parts:—

I. The indefatigable malice of the enemies of the Church, ver. 1, 3.

II. That their malice is vain. God saves them, ver. 2, 4.

III. God puts into the mouth of his people what they may say to their enemies, even when their malice is at the highest.

I. "Many a time have they afflicted me," &c. In which observe,—

1. That afflictions do attend those who will live righteously in Christ Jesus.

2. These afflictions are many: "Many a time," &c.

3. That they begin with the Church: "From my youth." Prophets, martyrs, &c.

4. This affliction was a heavy affliction: "The plowers plowed upon my back," &c. They dealt unmercifully with me, as a husbandman does with his ground.

II. But all their malice is to no purpose.

1. "Yet they have not prevailed against me." To extinguish the Church.

2. The reason is, "The Lord is righteous." And therefore he protects all those who are under his tuition, and punishes their adversaries.

3. "The Lord is righteous," &c. Cut asunder the ropes and chains with which they made their furrows: "He hath delivered Israel," &c.

III. In the following verses, to the end, the prophet, by way of prediction, declares the vengeance God would bring upon his enemies, which has *three* degrees:—

1. "Let them all be confounded," &c. Fail in their hopes against us.

2. "Let them be as the grass," &c. That they quickly perish. Grass on the housetops is good for nothing: "Which withereth afore it groweth up," &c. Never is mowed, nor raked together.

3. "Neither do they which go by say, The blessing of the Lord," &c. No man says so much as, God speed him! as is usual to say to workmen in harvest: but even this the enemies of the Church, and of God's work, say not, for they wish it not.

PSALM CXXX

The prayer of a penitent to God, with confession of sin, 1–3. *Confidence in God's mercy, and waiting upon him,* 4, 6. *Israel is encouraged to hope in the Lord, because of his willingness to save,* 7, 8.

A Song of Degrees

OUT [a]of the depths have I cried unto thee, O LORD.

2 LORD, hear my voice: let thine ears be attentive to the voice of my supplications.

3 [b]If thou, LORD, shouldest mark iniquities, O LORD, who shall stand?

[a]Lam. iii. 55; Jonah ii. 2

[b]Psa. cxliii. 2; Rom. iii. 20, 23, 24

NOTES ON PSALM CXXX

This Psalm has no title nor author's name, either in the Hebrew, or in any of the Versions; though the Syriac says it was spoken of Nehemiah the priest. It was most probably composed during the captivity; and contains the complaint of the afflicted Jews, with their hopes of the remission of those sins which were the cause of their sufferings, and their restoration from captivity to their own land. This is one of those called *penitential Psalms*.

Verse 1. *Out of the depths*] The captives in Babylon represent their condition like those

4 But *there is* [c]forgiveness with thee, that
[d]thou mayest be feared.
5 [e]I wait for the LORD, my soul doth wait,
and [f]in his word do I hope.
6 [g]My soul *waiteth* for the LORD more than
they that watch for the morning: [h]*I say,*
more than they that watch for the morning.
7 [i]Let Israel hope in the LORD: for [k]with
the LORD *there is* mercy, and with him *is* plenteous redemption.
8 And [l]he shall redeem Israel from all his
iniquities.

[c]Exod. xxxiv. 7——[d]1 Kings viii. 40; Psa. ii. 11; Jer. xxxiii. 8, 9——[e]Psa. xxvii. 14; xxxiii. 20; xl. 1; Isa. viii. 17; xxvi. 8; xxx. 18——[f]Psa. cxix. 81

[g]Psa. lxiii. 6; cxix. 147——[h]Or, *which watch unto the morning*——[i]Psa. cxxxi. 1——[k]Psa. lxxxvi. 5, 15; Isa. lv. 7——[l]Psa. ciii. 3, 4; Matt. i. 21

who are in a prison—an abyss or deep ditch, ready to be swallowed up.

Verse 2. *Lord, hear my voice*] They could have no helper but God, and to him they earnestly seek for relief.

Verse 3. *If thou—shouldest mark iniquities*] If thou shouldst set down every deviation in thought, word, and deed from thy holy law; and if thou shouldst call us into judgment for all our infidelities, both of heart and life; O Lord, who could stand? Who could stand such a trial, and who could stand acquitted in the judgment? This is a most solemn saying; and if we had not the doctrine that is in the next verse, who could be saved?

Verse 4. *But* there is *forgiveness with thee*] Thou canst forgive; mercy belongs to thee, as well as judgment. The doctrine here is the doctrine of St. John: "If any man sin, we have an Advocate with the Father, Jesus Christ the righteous; and he is the propitiation for our sins; and not for ours only, but also for *the sins* of the whole world." "Hear, O heavens, and give ear, O earth; for the Lord hath spoken!" Jesus has died for our sins; therefore God *can be just, and yet the justifier of him who believeth in Jesus.*

Verse 5. *I wait for the Lord*] The word קוה *kavah*, which we translate *to wait*, properly signifies the *extension of a cord from one point to another.* This is a fine metaphor: *God* is one point, the *human heart* is the other; and the *extended cord* between both is the *earnest believing desire* of *the soul.* This *desire, strongly extended* from the *heart* to *God,* in every mean of grace, and when there is none, is the *active, energetic waiting* which God requires, and which will be successful.

Verse 6. More than *they that watch for the morning.*] I believe the original should be read differently from what it is here. The *Chaldee* has, "More than they who observe the morning watches, that they may offer the morning oblation." This gives a good sense, and is, perhaps, the true meaning. Most of the Versions have, "From the morning to the night watches." Or the passage may be rendered, "My soul waiteth for the Lord from the morning watches to the morning watches." That is, "I wait both day and night."

Verse 7. *Let Israel hope in the Lord*] This, to hope for salvation, is their *duty* and their *interest.* But what *reason* is there for this *hope?* A twofold reason:—

1. *With the Lord* there is *mercy*] החסד *hachesed,* THAT *mercy, the fund, the essence* of mercy.

2. *And with him* is *plenteous redemption.*] והרבה עמו פדות *veharabbah immo peduth;* and *that abundant redemption,* that to which there is none like, the *Fountain* of *redemption, the Lamb of God which taketh away the sin of the world.* The article ה, both in הרבה *harabbah* and החסד *hachesed,* is very emphatic.

Verse 8. *He shall redeem Israel*] Και αυτος λυτρωσει, "He will make a ransom for Israel," He will *provide a great price* for Israel, and by it will *take away all his iniquities.* I would not restrict this to Israel in Babylon. Every *believer* may take it to himself. God perfectly justifies and perfectly sanctifies all that come unto him through the Son of his love.

ANALYSIS OF THE HUNDRED AND THIRTIETH PSALM

In this Psalm the Spirit of God proposes to us the case of a person oppressed with the wrath of God against sin, yet flying to him for comfort, remission, and purification.

I. Acknowledging his miserable condition, he prays to be heard, ver. 12.

II. He desires remission of sin, ver. 3, 4.

III. He expresses his hope and confidence, ver. 5, 6.

IV. He exhorts God's people to trust in him, ver. 7, 8.

I. The psalmist likens himself to a man in the bottom of a pit:—

1. "Out of the depths have I cried," &c. A true penitent cries out of the depth of his misery, and from the depth of a heart sensible of it.

2. "Lord, hear my voice." Although I be so low, thou canst hear me.

3. "Let thine ears be attentive," &c. Or I cry in vain.

II. But there was a reason why God should not hear. He was a grievous sinner; but all men are the same; therefore,

1. "If thou, Lord, shouldest mark iniquity." And I have nothing of my own but it to bring before thee, yet execute not thy just anger on account of my transgressions; for,

2. "There is mercy with thee," &c. True repentance requires two things, the recognition of our own misery and the persuasion of God's mercy. Both are needful; for if we know not the former, we shall not seek mercy; and if we despair of mercy, we shall never find it.

3. "That thou mayest be feared." Not with a servile but a filial fear, which involves prayer, faith, hope, love, adoration, giving of thanks, &c. This fear leads to God's throne as a merciful and pardoning God.

III. The method of God's servants in their addresses to heaven is, that they believe, hope, pray, and expect. Thus did the psalmist.

1. "I expect the Lord." In faith.

2. "My soul doth wait." His expectation was active and real, and proceeded from fervency of heart.

3. His expectation was not presumptive, but grounded upon God's word and promise: "In his word is my hope."

4. "My soul waiteth for the Lord." Which he illustrates by the similitude of a watchman who longs for the morning.

5. "I wait for the Lord more than they," &c. It was now night with him, darkness and misery were upon his soul; the morning he expected was the remission of his sins, which must come from God's mercy. For this he eagerly waited.

IV. He proposes his own example to God's people:—

1. "Let Israel hope in the Lord," like me, and cry from the depths.

2. "For with the Lord there is mercy." This is the reason and encouragement for the hope. Mercy flows from him.

3. "And with him is redemption." Which we need, being all sold under sin; and this redemption was purchased for us by the death of his Son.

4. And this redemption is *plentiful;* for by it he has redeemed the whole world, 1 John i. 2.

5. And this is to take effect upon Israel: "For he shall redeem Israel," &c. It is not, as the Jews expected, a temporal redemption, but a spiritual, as the angel told Joseph: "His name shall be called Jesus; for he shall save his people from their sins."

PSALM CXXXI

The psalmist professes his humility, and the peaceableness of his disposition and conduct, 1, 2. *Exhorts Israel to hope in God,* 3.

A Song of Degrees of David

LORD, my heart is not haughty, nor mine eyes lofty: [a]neither do I [b]exercise myself in great matters, or in things too [c]high for me.

2 Surely I have behaved and quieted [d]myself, [e]as a child that is weaned of his mother: my soul *is* even as a weaned child.

3 [f]Let Israel hope in the LORD [g]from henceforth and for ever.

[a]Rom. xii. 16——[b]Heb. *walk*——[c]Heb. *wonderful;* Job xlii. 3; Psa. cxxxix. 6

[d]Heb. *my soul*——[e]Matt. xviii. 3; 1 Cor. xiv. 20——[f]Psa. cxxx. 7——[g]Heb. *from now*

NOTES ON PSALM CXXXI

Some think that David composed this Psalm as a vindication of himself, when accused by Saul's courtiers that he affected the crown, and was laying schemes and plots to possess himself of it. Others think the Psalm was made during the captivity, and that it contains a fair account of the manner in which the captives behaved themselves, under the domination of their oppressors.

Verse 1. *Lord, my heart is not haughty*] The principle of *pride* has no place in my heart; and consequently the *high, lofty,* and *supercilious look* does not appear in my eyes. I neither *look up,* with desire to obtain, to the *state* of others, nor *look down* with contempt to the meanness or poverty of those below me. And the whole of my conduct proves this; for *I have not exercised myself*—walked, *in high matters,* nor associated myself with the higher ranks of the community, nor in *great matters,* נפלאות *niphlaoth, wonderful* or sublime things; *too high for me,* ממני *mimmeni, alien from me,* and that do not belong to a person in my sphere and situation in life.

Verse 2. *I have behaved and quieted myself, as a child*] On the contrary, I have been under the rod of others, and when chastised have not complained; and my *silence* under my affliction was the fullest proof that I neither *murmured* nor *repined,* but received all as coming from the hands of a just God.

My soul is even as a weaned child.] I felt I must forego many conveniences and comforts which I once enjoyed; and these I gave up without repining or demurring.

Verse 3. *Let Israel hope in the Lord*] Act all as I have done; trust in him who is the God of justice and compassion; and, after you have suffered awhile, he will make bare his arm and deliver you. Short as it is, this is a most instructive Psalm. He who acts as the psalmist did, is never likely to come to mischief, or do any to others.

ANALYSIS OF THE HUNDRED AND THIRTY-FIRST PSALM

I. The psalmist, having been accused of proud and haughty conduct, protests his innocence, states his humble thoughts of himself, and the general meekness of his deportment.

II. That his confidence was in God; in him he trusted, and therefore was far from ambition.

III. And by his own example calls on Israel to trust in God as he did.

I. He protests his humility.

1. There was no *pride* in his heart; and he calls God to witness it: "Lord, my heart is not haughty."

2. There was no *arrogance* in his carriage: "Nor mine eyes lofty."

3. Nor in his undertakings: "Neither do I exercise myself in great matters." He kept himself within his own bounds and vocation, and meddled not with state affairs.

II. What preserved him from *pride* was *humility.* He brought down his desires, and wants, and views to his circumstances.

1. "Surely I have behaved and quieted myself." Have I not given every evidence of my mild and peaceable behaviour? and I certainly never permitted a high thought to rise within me.

2. I acted as the *child weaned* from his mother. When once deprived of my comforts, and brought into captivity, I submitted to the will of God, and brought down my mind to my circumstances.

III. He proposes his own example of humility and peaceableness for all Israel to follow.

1. "Let Israel hope." Never despair of God's mercy, nor of his gracious providence. The *storm* will be succeeded by *fair* and *fine weather.*

2. "Let Israel hope in the Lord." Never content yourselves with merely supposing that in the course of things these afflictions will wear out. No; look to God, and depend on him, that *he* may bring them to a happy conclusion.

Remember that he is *Jehovah.*

1. Wise to plan.
2. Good to purpose.
3. Strong to execute, and will withhold no good thing from them that walk uprightly.
4. Trust *from henceforth.* If you have not begun before, begin now.
5. And do not be weary; trust *for ever.* Your case can never be out of the reach of God's power and mercy.

PSALM CXXXII

The psalmist prays that God would remember his promises to David, 1. *His purpose to bring the ark of the Lord into a place of rest,* 2–5. *Where it was found, and the prayer in removing it,* 6–9. *The promises made to David and his posterity,* 10–12. *God's choice of Zion for a habitation, and his promises to the people,* 13–17. *All their enemies shall be confounded,* 18.

XXVIII. DAY. MORNING PRAYER

A Song of Degrees

A. M. cir. 3489 B. C. cir. 515 Darii I., R. Persarum, cir. annum sextum

LORD, remember David, *and* all his afflictions:

2 How he sware unto the LORD
[a]*and* vowed unto [b]the mighty
God of Jacob;
3 Surely I will not come into the tabernacle
of my house, nor go up into my bed;
4 I will [c]not give sleep to mine eyes, *or*
slumber to mine eyelids,
5 Until I [d]find out a place
for the LORD, [e]a habitation for
the mighty *God* of Jacob.
6 Lo, we heard of it [f]at
Ephratah: [g]we found it [h]in the fields of the
wood.
7 We will go into his tabernacles: [i]we will
worship at his footstool.
8 [k]Arise, O LORD, into thy rest; thou, and
[l]the ark of thy strength.
9 Let thy priests [m]be clothed with righteous-

A. M. cir. 3489 B. C. cir. 515 Darii I., R. Persarum, cir. annum sextum

[a]Psalm lxv. 1——[b]Gen. xlix. 24——[c]Prov. vi. 4 [d]Acts vii. 46——[e]Heb. *habitations*——[f]1 Sam. xvii. 12 [g]1 Sam. vii. 1

[h]1 Chron. xiii. 5——[i]Psa. v. 7; xcix. 5——[k]Num. x. 35; 2 Chron. vi. 41, 42——[l]Psa. lxxviii. 61——[m]Job xxix. 14; ver. 16; Isa. lxi. 10

NOTES ON PSALM CXXXII

Some attribute this Psalm to *David*, but without sufficient ground; others, to *Solomon*, with more likelihood; and others, to some inspired author at the conclusion of the captivity, which is, perhaps, the most probable. It refers to the building of the second temple, and placing the ark of the covenant in it.

Verse 1. *Lord, remember David*] Consider the promises thou hast made to this thy eminent servant, that had respect, not only to *him* and to his *family*, but to all the *Israelitish people.*

Verse 2. *How he sware unto the Lord*] It is only in this place that we are informed of David's vow to the Lord, relative to the building of the temple; but we find he had fully purposed the thing.

Verse 3. *Surely I will not come*] This must refer to the *situation* of the temple; or, as we would express it, he would not pass another day till he had found out the *ground* on which to build the temple, and projected the *plan*, and devised *ways* and *means* to execute it. And we find that he would have acted in all things according to his oath and vow, had God permitted him. But even after the Lord told him that Solomon, not he, should build the house, he still continued to show his good will by collecting treasure and materials for the building, all the rest of his life.

Verse 5. *The mighty* God *of Jacob.*] עביר יעקב *abir yaacob*, the *Mighty One of Jacob.* We have this epithet of God for the first time, Gen. xlix. 24. Hence, perhaps, the *abirim* of the heathen, the stout ones, the *strong beings.*

Verse 6. *Lo, we have heard of it at Ephratah*] This may be considered as a continuation of David's vow; as if he had said: As I had determined to build a temple for the ark, and heard that it was at *Ephratah*, I went and found it in the *fields of Jaar*, יער;—not the wood, but Kirjath Jaar or Jearim, where the ark was then

A. M. cir. 3489
B. C. cir. 515
Darii I.,
R. Persarum,
cir. annum
sextum

ness; and let thy saints shout
for joy.
10 For thy servant David's
sake turn not away the face of
thine anointed.
11 [n]The LORD hath sworn *in* truth unto
David; he will not turn from it; [o]Of the
fruit of [p]thy body will I set upon thy
throne.
12 If thy children will keep my covenant
and my testimonies that I shall teach them,
their children shall also sit upon thy throne
for evermore.
13 [q]For the LORD hath chosen Zion; he
hath desired *it* for his habitation.
14 [r]This *is* my rest for ever:
here will I dwell; for I have
desired it.
15 [s]I [t]will abundantly bless her provision:
I will satisfy her poor with bread.
16 [u]I will also clothe her priests with salvation: [v]and her saints shall shout aloud for joy.
17 [w]There will I make the horn of David to
bud: [x]I have ordained a [y]lamp for mine
anointed.
18 His enemies will I [z]clothe with shame:
but upon himself shall his crown flourish.

A. M. cir. 3489
B. C. cir. 515
Darii I.,
R. Persarum,
cir. annum
sextum

[n]Psa. lxxxix. 3, 4, 33, &c.; cx. 4——[o]2 Sam. vii. 12; 1 Kings viii. 25; 2 Chron. vi. 16; Luke i. 69; Acts ii. 30——[p]Heb. *thy belly*——[q]Psa. xlviii. 1, 2——[r]Psa. lxviii. 16——[s]Psa. cxlvii. 14

[t]Or, *surely*——[u]2 Chron. vi. 41; ver. 9; Psa. cxlix. 4——[v]Hos. xi. 12——[w]Ezek. xxix. 21; Luke i. 69——[x]See 1 Kings xi. 36; xv. 4; 2 Chron. xxi. 7——[y]Or, *candle*——[z]Psa. xxxv. 26; cix. 29

lodged;—and having found it, he entered the tabernacle, ver. 7; and then, adoring that God whose presence was in it, he invited him to arise and come to the place which he had prepared for him.

Verse 8. *Arise, O Lord, into thy rest; thou and the ark of thy strength.*] Using the same expressions which Solomon used when he dedicated the temple, 2 Chron. vi. 41, 42. There are several difficulties in these passages. *Ephratah* may mean the *tribe of Ephraim;* and then we may understand the place thus: "I have learned that the ark had been in the tribe of Ephraim, and I have seen it at Kirjath-jearim, or *Field of the woods;* but this is not a proper place for it, for the Lord hath chosen Jerusalem." It is true that the ark did remain in that tribe from the days of Joshua to Samuel, during *three hundred and twenty-eight* years; and thence it was brought to Kirjath-jearim, where it continued *seventy* years, till the commencement of the reign of David over *all* Israel.

But if we take verses 6, 7, and 8, *not* as the continuation of David's vow, but as the *words of the captives in Babylon,* the explanation will be more plain and easy: "We have heard, O Lord, from our fathers, that thy tabernacle was formerly a long time at Shiloh, in the tribe of Ephraim. And our history informs us that it has been also at Kirjath-jearim, the fields of the wood; and afterwards it was brought to Jerusalem, and there established: but Jerusalem is now ruined, the temple destroyed, and thy people in captivity. Arise, O Lord, and re-establish thy dwelling-place in thy holy city!" See *Calmet* and others on this place.

Verse 9. *Let thy priests be clothed with righteousness*] Let them be as remarkable for *inward holiness* as they are for the splendour of their *holy vestments.*

Verse 10. *The face of thine anointed.*] David. Remember thy promises to him, that he may be restored to thee and to thy worship.

Verse 11. *The Lord hath sworn*] As David sware to the Lord, so the Lord swears to David, that he will establish his throne, and place his posterity on it: and that he had respect to David's Antitype, we learn from St. Peter, Acts ii. 30, where see the note. This verse with the following refers to the spiritual David, and the Christian Church.

Verse 12. *If thy children will keep my covenant*] This was conditional with respect to the posterity of David. They have been driven from the throne, because they did not keep the Lord's covenant; but the true David is on the throne, and his posterity forms the genuine Israelites.

Verse 13. *The Lord hath chosen Zion*] Therefore neither *Shiloh* nor *Kirjath-jearim* is the place of his rest.

Verse 14. *This* is *my rest for ever*] Here the Christian Church is most indubitably meant. This is *God's place* for ever. After this there never will be another *dispensation;* Christianity closes and completes all communications from heaven to earth. God has nothing greater to give to mankind on this side heaven; nor does man need any thing better; nor is his nature capable of any thing more excellent.

Verse 15. *I will abundantly bless her provision*] There shall be an abundant provision of salvation made for mankind in the Christian Church. Our Lord's *multiplication of the loaves* was a *type* and *proof* of it.

Verse 16. *I will also clothe her priests*] All Christian ministers, *with salvation;* this shall appear in all their conduct. *Salvation—redemption from all sin* through the blood of the Lamb, shall be their great and universal message.

Verse 17. *There will I make the horn of David to bud*] *There,* in the *Christian Church,* the power and authority of the spiritual David shall appear.

I have ordained a lamp] I have taken care to secure a *posterity,* to which the promises shall be expressly fulfilled.

Verse 18. *His enemies will I clothe with shame*] Every opponent of the Christian cause shall be confounded.

But upon himself shall his crown flourish.] There shall be no end of the government of Christ's kingdom. From verse 11 to the end, the spiritual David and his posterity are the subjects of which the Psalm treats.

Analysis of the Hundred and Thirty-second Psalm

This Psalm is divided into *three* parts:—

I. A petition, before which is David's care and vow to settle the ark, and with what reverence they would settle it in the temple; and he sets down the solemn prayer then used, ver. 1-10.

II. An explication of the promises made unto David for the continuance of his kingdom in his posterity, ver. 11, 12, and God's love to his Church, ver. 13.

III. A prophecy, spoken in the person of God, for the stability of Christ's Church; and the blessings upon the people, the priests, and the house of David, from ver. 14 to the end.

I. In all prayer a man must reflect upon God's promise; otherwise he cannot pray in faith.

1. "Lord, remember David:" Thy promises made to him. First he prays for the king; then for the ecclesiastics, ver. 8, 9; then for the people, ver. 8.

2. "And all his afflictions:" Many he had before he was king; and one of the greatest was the settling of the ark.

Now this his ardent and sincere desire appears by his oath. And now,—

1. "How he sware unto the Lord," &c.

2. The substance of which was, "Surely I will not come," &c.

Now this is hyperbolical; for we must not conceive that he went not into his house or bed till he found out a place to build God's house. But see the note.

1. "I will not come into—my house:" So as to forget to build God's house.

2. "Nor go up into my bed:" Or let any thing make me forget the work.

3. "I will not give sleep," &c.: But make provision for building the temple.

And here the prophet inserts two verses by way of gratitude.

First, he exults for the news of the ark: "Lo, we heard of it at Ephratah," &c.

By *Ephratah* some understand the land of *Ephraim*, in which the ark remained at Shiloh. Being afterwards sent home, it was found in the field of Joshua; thence conveyed to the house of *Amminadab*, who dwelt in *Kirjath-jearim*, that signifies a *woody city*. Hence, David might well say, "And found it in the fields of the wood," &c.

And the place for the ark being found, he calls on Israel, saying,

1. "We will go into his tabernacles." Now the ark is rested in Mount Zion.

2. "And we will worship," &c. Not make rash approaches to the ark, but come with reverence, and bow in his presence.

The ark being brought into the temple, he uses this solemn form:—

1. "Arise, O Lord," &c. He prays and invites him to dwell in his temple.

2. "Into thy rest." To pass no more from place to place.

3. "Thou, and the ark of thy strength." Show thy power and strength, as thou didst at *Jordan*, &c.

Before the ark in the temple he prays,—

1. "Let thy priests be clothed," &c. Inwardly, in heart and soul.

2. "Let thy saints shout," &c. With a cheerful voice, for the ark rests.

3. "For thy servant David's sake," &c. 1. David is not here to be taken absolutely for his person only, as having the covenants and promises made to him, but for the promise' sake. 2. "Turn not away," &c. Suffer me not to depart from thy presence unheard.

II. The prophet now proceeds to count up the promises made to *David*, which God confirmed by oath, in which we are to observe, 1. The manner of the promise: "The Lord hath sworn in truth," &c. It was merciful to promise; but more so to bind himself by oath. 2. The matter of his oath expressed ver. 11-14.

1. For the seed of David, as respects Christ, is categorical and absolute: "Of the fruit of thy body," &c. Which word St. *Peter* refers to Christ, Acts ii. 30. According to the flesh he was David's seed; for by the *mother's* side Christ was to be David's seed, not by the father's.

2. For the seed of David, as it relates to his posterity, the oath is hypothetical and conditional: "If thy children will keep," &c.

As the external kingdom was by this oath annexed to one family, so the external worship was assigned by it to one place.

1. "For the Lord hath chosen Zion," &c.

2. "This is my rest for ever." Zion was the seat of the sanctuary till the coming of the Messiah. But Zion was but a type of Christ's Church, which he hath chosen to be his rest for ever.

III. The prophet represents God as promising good things to his Church.

1. Such abundance of temporal things that the poor shall not want: "I will abundantly bless her provision," &c.

2. That her "priests shall be clothed with salvation," &c.

3. "There will I make the horn of David to flourish," &c. That is, the kingdom of the Messiah.

4. The fourth benefit God promises is the confusion of their enemies, and the eternal authority in this kingdom: "His enemies will I clothe with shame, but upon himself shall his crown flourish."

PSALM CXXXIII

The comfort and benefit of the communion of saints, 1–3.

A Song of Degrees of David

A. M. cir. 3489
B. C. cir. 515
Darii I.,
R. Persarum,
cir. annum
sextum

BEHOLD, how good and how pleasant *it is* for [a]brethren to dwell [b]together in unity!

2 *It is* like [c]the precious ointment upon the head, that ran down upon the beard, *even* Aaron's beard: that went down to the skirts of his garments;

3 As the dew of [d]Hermon, *and as the dew* that descended upon the mountains of Zion: for [e]there the LORD commanded the blessing, *even* life for evermore.

[a]Gen. xiii. 8; Heb. xiii. 1——[b]Heb. *even together* [c]Exod. xxx. 25, 30

[d]Deut. iv. 48——[e]Lev. xxv. 21; Deut. xxviii. 8; Psa. xlii. 8

NOTES ON PSALM CXXXIII

There are different opinions concerning this Psalm; the most probable is, that it represents the priests and Levites returned from captivity, and united in the service of God in the sanctuary. This, the preceding, and the following, appear to make one subject. In the *one hundred and thirty-second*, the Lord is entreated to enter his temple, and pour out his benediction; in the *one hundred and thirty-third*, the beautiful order and harmony of the temple service is pointed out; and in the *one hundred and thirty-fourth*, all are exhorted to diligence and watchfulness in the performance of their duty. It is attributed to David by the Hebrew, the Syriac, and the Vulgate; but no name is prefixed in the Septuagint, Æthiopic, Arabic, and Anglo-Saxon.

Verse 1. *Behold, how good and how pleasant*] Unity is, according to this scripture, a *good* thing and a *pleasant;* and especially among *brethren*—members of the same family, of the same Christian community, and of the same nation. And why not among the great family of mankind? On the other hand, *disunion* is bad and hateful. The former is from heaven; the latter, from hell.

Verse 2. *Like the precious ointment*] The composition of this holy anointing oil may be seen, Exod. xxx. 23; *sweet cinnamon, sweet calamus, cassia lignea*, and *olive oil.* The odour of this must have been very agreeable, and serves here as a metaphor to point out the exquisite excellence of brotherly love.

Ran down upon the beard] The oil was poured upon the head of Aaron so profusely as to run down upon his garments. It is customary in the east to pour out the oil on the head so profusely as to reach every limb.

Verse 3. *As the dew of Hermon*, and as the dew *that descended upon the mountains of Zion*] This was not Mount Zion, ציון *tsiyon*, in Jerusalem, but *Sion*, שיאן which is a part of Hermon, see Deut. iv. 48: "Mount Sion, which is Hermon." On this mountain the dew is very copious. Mr. Maundrell says that "with this dew, even in dry weather, their tents were as wet as if it had rained the whole night." This seems to show the strength of the comparison.

For there] Where this *unity* is.

The Lord commanded the blessing] That is, an *everlasting life.* There he pours out his blessings, and gives a long and happy life.

For other particulars, see the commentators *passim*, and the following *analysis.*

ANALYSIS OF THE HUNDRED AND THIRTY-THIRD PSALM

In this Psalm the blessings of peace and unity are recommended and described, whether in the Church, family, or kingdom.

I. *It is*, says the prophet, *a good and pleasant thing*, &c., ver. 1.

II. He declares both by similitudes.

1. The pleasantness, by the *ointment* with which the high priest was anointed.

2. The goodness, by the *dew* which fell upon the mountains.

3. But in plainer terms, by the *blessing of God* upon the head of the peaceful.

1. The prophet begins with an encomium of peace, unity, and concord.

1. "Behold." Take notice of it in its effects.

2. "How good and pleasant," &c. He admires, but cannot express it.

3. The *encomium* itself is expressed by two epithets: 1. *It is good*, and brings much profit. 2. *It is pleasant*, and brings much content with it.

4. The concord itself is thus expressed: *Brethren*, either in a Church, family, or kingdom, should be of one soul, and intent on the common good.

II. The pleasantness is compared to "the precious ointment upon the head."

1. All benefit from this concord; princes, nobles, and people. *The head, beard*, and *skirts.*

2. It sends forth a sweet and reviving savour.

3. It is as balsam poured into wounds.

The profit he compares to the dews: "As the dew of Hermon," &c., gently descending, and fructifying and enriching the ground.

And this he sets down without any metaphor: "For there the Lord commanded the blessing," &c.; which approbation he manifests by the abundance he pours where concord and unity are found.

1. He commands his blessing. Makes all creatures useful to them.

2. His blessing is prosperity, good success. To bless is to benefit.

3. This he calls life; for with troubles, griefs, &c., a man's life is no life. A quiet life those shall have who live in peace, without dissensions respecting religion or in matters connected with the state.

PSALM CXXXIV

An exhortation to praise God in his sanctuary, 1–3.

A. M. cir. 3489
B. C. cir. 515
Darii I.,
R. Persarum,
cir. annum
sextum

A Song of Degrees

BEHOLD, bless ye the LORD,
[a]all *ye* servants of the LORD,
[b]which by night stand in the
house of the LORD.

2 [c]Lift up your hands [d]*in* the
sanctuary, and bless the LORD.
3 [e]The LORD that made heaven
and earth [f]bless thee out of
Zion.

A. M. cir. 3489
B. C. cir. 515
Darii I.,
R. Persarum,
cir. annum
sextum

---

[a]Psa. cxxxv. 1, 2——[b]1 Chron. ix. 33——[c]1 Tim. ii. 8

[d]Or, in *holiness*——[e]Psa. cxxiv. 8——[f]Psa. cxxviii 5; cxxxv. 21

NOTES ON PSALM CXXXIV

This is the last of the fifteen Psalms called *Psalms of degrees.* Who was the author is uncertain; it is attributed to *David* only by the *Syriac;* it is intimately connected with the two preceding Psalms, and is an exhortation to the priests and Levites who kept nightly watch in the temple, to the assiduous in praising the Lord. It seems to consist of *two* parts: 1. An exhortation, probably from the high priest, to those priests and Levites who kept watch in the temple by night, to spend their time profitably, and duly celebrate the praises of God, ver. 1, 2. The *second* part, which is contained in the third verse, is the prayer of the priests and Levites for the *high priest,* who seems now to be going to his rest.

Verse 1. *Behold, bless ye the Lord*] I believe הנה *hinneh* should be taken here in the sense of *take heed!* Be upon your guard; you serve a jealous God; provoke him not.

Which by night stand] Who minister during the night.

Verse 2. *Lift up your hands* in *the sanctuary*] קדש *kodesh,* "*in* holiness:" or, as the SYRIAC, ܠܩܘܕܫܐ *lekoudishe,* "to holiness;" *in sancta,* VULGATE; and εις τα ἁγια, SEPTUAGINT; "in holy things;" or, as the ÆTHIOPIC, "in the house of the sanctuary." The expression seems very similar to that of St. Paul, 1 Tim. ii. 8: "Lifting up holy hands, without wrath and doubting."

Bless the Lord.] That is, speak good of his name: tell the wonders he has wrought, and show that his name is exalted.

Verse 3. *The Lord that made heaven and earth*] Who governs and possesses all things; and who can give you every spiritual and earthly blessing.

Bless thee out of Zion.] As if they had said, "We will attend to your orders; go in peace, and may God shower down his blessings upon you!" The blessing pronounced by the priests was the following: "The Lord bless thee and keep thee! The Lord make his face shine upon thee, and he gracious unto thee! The Lord lift up his countenance upon thee, and give thee peace!" Num. vi. 24-26.

ANALYSIS OF THE HUNDRED AND THIRTY-FOURTH PSALM

In this Psalm the prophet—

I. Exhorts the Levites and ministers of religion to attend the appointed hours of prayer.

II. Then the ministers bless the people.

1. 1. "Behold, bless ye the Lord."

2. Yet principally, "all ye servants of the Lord:" Choose out of the people to this service.

3. "Which by night stand in the house of the Lord," &c.: In the temple ye ought not to be sleepy, or forget your duty.

4. Therefore, "lift up your hands," &c., before the ark of the covenant which was the symbol of his presence.

5. "Bless the Lord," &c.

II. The other part of your office is to bless the people; let not that be forgotten, but say,—

1. "The Lord bless thee:" Let them know from whom the blessing comes.

2. "Out of Zion:" So long as they remain in the unity of the Church; there was none to be expected out of *Zion.*

3. "The Lord that made:" &c. He that hath power to bless hath given, and must give, his blessing to all creatures, without which they will not be blessed to thee; therefore, bless him.

PSALM CXXXV

An exhortation to praise God for his goodness and greatness, 1–5; *for his wonders in nature,* 6, 7; *his wonders done in Egypt,* 8, 9; *in the wilderness,* 10–12; *for his goodness to his people,* 13, 14. *The vanity of idols,* 15–18. *Israel, with its priests and Levites, exhorted to praise the Lord,* 19–21.

A. M. cir. 3489
B. C. cir. 515
Darii I.,
R. Persarum,
cir. annum
sextum

PRAISE ye the LORD. Praise ye the name of the LORD; [a]praise *him,* O ye servants of the LORD.

2 [b]Ye that stand in the house of the LORD, in [c]the courts of the house of our God,

3 Praise the LORD; for [d]the LORD *is* good: sing praises unto his name; [e]for *it is* pleasant.

4 For [f]the LORD hath chosen Jacob unto himself, *and* Israel for his peculiar treasure.

5 For I know that [g]the LORD *is* great, and *that* our LORD *is* above all gods.

6 [h]Whatsoever the LORD pleased, *that* did he in heaven, and in earth, in the seas, and all deep places.

7 [i]He causeth the vapours to ascend from the ends of the earth; [k]he maketh lightnings for the rain; he bringeth the wind out of his [l]treasuries.

8 [m]Who smote the first-born of Egypt, [n]both of man and beast.

A. M. cir. 3489
B. C. cir. 515
Darii I.,
R. Persarum,
cir. annum
sextum

9 [o]*Who* sent tokens and wonders into the midst of thee, O Egypt, [p]upon Pharaoh, and upon all his servants.

10 [q]Who smote great nations, and slew mighty kings;

11 Sihon king of the Amorites, and Og king of Bashan, and [r]all the kingdoms of Canaan:

12 [s]And gave their land *for* a heritage, a heritage unto Israel his people.

13 [t]Thy name, O LORD, *endureth* for ever; *and* thy memorial, O LORD, [u]throughout all generations.

14 [v]For the LORD will judge his people, and he will repent himself concerning his servants.

15 [w]The idols of the heathen *are* silver

---

[a]Psa. cxiii. 1; cxxxiv. 1——[b]Luke ii. 37——[c]Psa. xcii. 13; xcvi. 8; cxvi. 19——[d]Psa. cxix. 68——[e]Psa. cxlvii. 1——[f]Exod. xix. 5; Deut. vii. 6, 7; x. 15——[g]Psa. xcv. 3; xcvii. 9——[h]Psa. cxv. 3——[i]Jer. x. 13; li. 16——[k]Job xxviii. 25, 26; xxxviii. 24, &c.; Zech. x. 1——[l]Job xxxviii. 22——[m]Exod. xii. 12, 29; Psa. lxxviii. 51; cxxxvi. 10

[n]Heb. *from man unto beast*——[o]Exod. vii., viii., ix., x., xiv.——[p]Psa. cxxxvi. 15——[q]Num. xxi. 24, 25, 26, 34, 35; Psa. cxxxvi. 17, &c.——[r]Josh. xii. 7——[s]Psa. lxxviii. 55; cxxxvi. 21, 22——[t]Exod. iii. 15; Psa. cii. 12——[u]Heb. *to generation and generation*——[v]Deut. xxxii. 36——[w]Psa. cxv. 4, 5, 6, 7, 8

NOTES ON PSALM CXXXV

This Psalm is intimately connected with the preceding. It is an exhortation addressed to the *priests* and *Levites,* and to all *Israel,* to publish the praises of the Lord. The conclusion of this Psalm is nearly the same with Psalm cxv.; and what is said about *idols,* and the effects of the power of God, seems to be taken from it and the tenth chapter of Jeremiah; and from these and other circumstances it appears the Psalm was written *after the captivity;* and might, as *Calmet* conjectures, have been used at the dedication of the second temple.

Verse 1. *Praise ye the Lord*] This may be considered as the *title,* for it has none other.

Praise ye the name of the Lord] Perhaps the original הללו את שם יהוה *halelu eth shem Yehovah,* should be translated, *Praise ye the name Jehovah;* that is, Praise God in his infinite essence of being, holiness, goodness, and truth.

Verse 2. *Ye that stand*] Priests and Levites. For which he gives several reasons.

Verse 3. *The Lord* is *good*] Here is the *first reason* why he should be praised; and a *second* is subjoined:—

For it is *pleasant.*] It is becoming to acknowledge this infinite Being, and our dependence on him; and it is truly comfortable to an upright mind to be thus employed.

Verse 4. *For the Lord hath chosen Jacob*] This is a *third* reason. He has taken the Israelites for his peculiar people, סגלתו *segullatho,* his peculiar treasure; and now has brought them home to himself from their captivity and wanderings.

Verse 5. *The Lord* is *great*] Unlimited in his power: *another* reason.

Is *above all gods.*] Every class of *being,* whether idolized or not; because he is the Fountain of existence. This is a *fifth* reason.

Verse 6. *Whatsoever the Lord pleased*] All that he has done is *right,* and therefore it is *pleasing* in his sight. He is the author of all existence. Angels, men, spirits, the heavens, the earth, and all their contents, were made by him, and are under his control.

Verse 7. *He causeth the vapours to ascend*] Dr. Shaw thinks that the account here refers to the *autumnal* rains in the *east.* Of them he speaks as follows: "Seldom a night passes without much *lightning* in the north-west quarter, but not attended with *thunder;* and when this *lightning* appears in the west or south-west points, it is a sure sign of the approaching *rain,* which is often followed by *thunder.* A squall of wind and clouds of dust are the sure forerunners of the first rain." This account induces Mr. *Harmer* to believe that the word נשאים *nesiim,* should be translated *clouds,* not *vapours.* It shows that God—

Maketh lightnings for the rain] The squalls of wind bring on these *refreshing showers,* and are therefore *precious things* of the *treasuries of God;* and when he *thunders,* it is the *noise of waters in the heavens.* See Jer. x. 13, which contains almost the same words as those in this verse: "When he uttereth his voice, there is a multitude of waters in the heavens; and he causeth the vapours to ascend from the ends of the earth; he maketh lightnings with rain, and bringeth forth the wind out of his treasuries."

Verse 8. *Who smote the first-born of Egypt*] See the parallel passages.

Verse 14. *The Lord will judge his people*] He will do them justice against their enemies.

Verse 15. *The idols of the heathen*] This

A. M. cir. 3489
B. C. cir. 515
Darii I.,
R. Persarum,
cir. annum
sextum

and gold, the work of men's
hands.
16 They have mouths, but
they speak not; eyes have they,
but they see not;
17 They have ears, but they hear
not; neither is there *any* breath in their
mouths.
18 They that make them are like unto them:
so is every one that trusteth in
them.
19 [x]Bless the LORD, O house
of Israel: bless the LORD, O
house of Aaron:
20 Bless the LORD, O house of Levi: ye
that fear the LORD, bless the LORD.
21 Blessed be the LORD [y]out of Zion, which
dwelleth at Jerusalem, [z]Praise ye the LORD.

A. M. cir. 3489
B. C. cir. 515
Darii I.,
R. Persarum,
cir. annum
sextum

[x]Psa. cxv. 9, &c.——[y]Psa. cxxxiv. 3

[z]Judg. v. 2; 1 Chron. xvi. 4; xxiii. 30; xxv. 3

verse and the following, to the end of the 18th, are almost word for word the same as verses 4-8 of Psalm cxv., where see the notes.

Verse 17. To this verse one of Kennicott's MSS. adds the 6th and 7th verses of Psalm cxv.

Verse 19. *Bless the Lord, O house, &c.*] See similar verses, Psa. cxv. 9-13, and the notes there.

Verse 21. *Blessed be the Lord out of Zion*] Who has once more restored our temple and city, and now condescends to *dwell* with us *in Jerusalem.*

ANALYSIS OF THE HUNDRED AND THIRTY-FIFTH PSALM

In this Psalm the prophet invites the servants of God, and especially his ministers, to praise God, ver. 1, 2, from arguments drawn,

I. From his goodness, particularly in choosing Israel, ver. 3, 4.

II. From the greatness and power showed in his works, ver. 5-8.

III. From his justice showed to the enemies of Israel, ver. 1-13.

IV. From his loving-kindness extended and promised still to his servants, ver. 13, 14.

V. Having derided the vanity of idols, ver. 15-19, he returns to his exhortation calling upon them to bless God, ver. 19-21.

I. He calls upon the ministers of religion especially to attend the recitation of Divine praises:—

1. "Praise ye the Lord," &c.
2. "Ye that stand."

And now, repeating his words again, he produces his reason of inducement:—

1. Because the Lord is worthy of praise: "For he is good," &c. Not comparatively, but absolutely good.

2. "Sing praises unto his name," &c. Because it is no painful duty, but pleasant.

3. Praise him for his love to Israel; for this you owe him gratitude: "For the Lord hath chosen Jacob," &c. 2. "And Israel for his peculiar treasure."

II. The next argument he uses is drawn from his greatness.

1. From his empire and universal dominion in heaven and earth: "Whatsoever the Lord pleased," &c. Nothing is impossible to him: but he does all from his free will, not from any necessity.

2. "He doth all things," &c. In all places; heaven, earth, seas, and hell.

And these last words the prophet amplifies,—

1. In the earth. Causing the vapours to ascend from the ends of the earth, from all parts, which are endued with several qualities.

2. In the air. "He maketh lightning for rain."

3. In the water. "For he bringeth the winds out of his treasuries." Nothing is more obscure than the generation of the winds.

III. The fourth argument the prophet uses to persuade men to praise God, is from the vengeance he executes on the enemies of his people.

1. Upon the Egyptians. "Who smote the first-born of Egypt," &c.

2. "Who sent tokens and wonders," &c. "And he smote great nations," &c.

IV. To the commemoration of the justice God exercised upon their *enemies*, the prophet exhorts them to extol God.

1. "Thy name, O Lord," &c.
2. "And thy memorial," &c.

And the reason is drawn from his mercy.

1. "For the Lord will judge his people." Judge their cause, and deliver them.

2. "And he will repent himself," &c. If they repent, and turn to him.

The prophet, having proved that God is great in himself, now proves that he is above all gods, which are but vanity.

1. From their composition: "Silver and gold."

2. From their makers: "The work of men's hands."

3. From their impotency: "They have mouths," &c.

4. From the nature of their worshippers: "They that make them," &c.

Lastly, he invites all true worshippers of God to praise him, because they are lively images of the living God, from whom all their faculties have proceeded. To this he invites—

1. All *Israel:* "Bless the Lord, O house of Israel."

2. The priests: "Bless the Lord, O house of Aaron."

3. The Levites: "Bless the Lord, O house of Levi."

4. Lastly, all the laity: "Ye that fear the Lord bless the Lord."

To which he adds his own note, concluding—

1. "Blessed be the Lord out of Zion." Where he shows his presence by the ark.

2. "Which dwelleth at Jerusalem." Who, though in essence he is every where, yet more especially manifests his presence in his Church by his indwelling Spirit.

Therefore, let all the people bless the Lord for his great mercy: but let the citizens of *Zion* and *Jerusalem* never cease to praise him.

PSALM CXXXVI

An exhortation to give thanks to God for various mercies granted to all men, 1–9; *particularly to the Israelites in Egypt,* 10–12; *at the Red Sea,* 13–15; *in the wilderness,* 16–20; *and in the promised land,* 21, 22; *for the redemption of the captives from Babylon,* 23, 24; *and for his providential mercies to all,* 25, 26.

XXVIII. DAY. EVENING PRAYER

A. M. cir. 3489 B. C. cir. 515 Darii I., R. Persarum, cir. annum sextum

O [a]GIVE thanks unto the
LORD; for *he is* good: [b]for
his mercy *endureth* for ever.
2 O give thanks unto [c]the God
of gods: for his mercy *endureth* for ever.
3 O give thanks to the LORD of lords: for
his mercy *endureth* for ever.
4 To him [d]who alone doeth great wonders:
for his mercy *endureth* for ever.
5 [e]To him that by wisdom made the heavens: for his mercy *endureth* for ever.
6 [f]To him that stretched out the earth
above the waters: for his mercy *endureth*
for ever.
7 [g]To him that made great lights: for his
mercy *endureth* for ever:

[a]Psa. cvi. 1; cvii. 1; cxviii. 1——[b]1 Chron. xvi. 34, 41; 2 Chron. xx. 21——[c]Deut. x. 17——[d]Psa. lxxii. 18——[e]Gen. i. 1; Prov. iii. 19; Jer. li. 15——[f]Gen. i. 9; Psa. xxiv. 2; Jer. x. 12——[g]Gen. i. 14——[h]Gen. i. 16

8 [h]The sun [i]to rule by day:
for his mercy *endureth* for ever:
9 The moon and stars to rule
by night: for his mercy *endureth*
for ever.
10 [k]To him that smote Egypt in their first-
born: for his mercy *endureth* for ever:
11 [l]And brought out Israel from among
them: for his mercy *endureth* for ever:
12 [m]With a strong hand, and with a stretched-
out arm: for his mercy *endureth* for ever.
13 [n]To him which divided the Red Sea into
parts: for his mercy *endureth* for ever:
14 And made Israel to pass through the
midst of it: for his mercy *endureth* for ever:
15 [o]But [p]overthrew Pharaoh and his host in
the Red Sea: for his mercy *endureth* for ever.

A. M. cir. 3489 B. C. cir. 515 Darii I., R. Persarum, cir. annum sextum

[i]Heb. *for the rulings by day*——[k]Exod. xii. 29; Psa. cxxxv. 8——[l]Exod. xii. 51; xiii. 3, 17——[m]Exod. vi. 6——[n]Exod. xiv. 21, 22; Psa. lxxviii. 13——[o]Exod. xiv. 27; Psa. cxxxv. 9——[p]Heb. *shaked off*

NOTES ON PSALM CXXXVI

This Psalm is little else than a repetition of the preceding, with the burden, כי לעולם חסדו *ki leolam chasdo,* "because his mercy endureth for ever," at the end of every verse. See below. It seems to have been a *responsive song:* the first part of the verse sung by the *Levites,* the burden by the *people.* It has no title in the Hebrew, nor in any of the Versions. It was doubtless written after the captivity. The *author* is unknown.

Verse 1. *O give thanks unto the Lord: for he is good*] This sentiment often occurs: the *goodness* of the Divine nature, both as a *ground* of *confidence* and of *thanksgiving.*

For his mercy endureth *for ever*] These words, which are the *burden* of every verse, כי לעולם חסדו *ki leolam chasdo,* might be translated: "For his tender mercy is to the coming age:" meaning, probably, if the Psalm be *prophetic,* that peculiar display of his compassion, the redemption of the world by the Lord Jesus. These very words were prescribed by *David* as an acknowledgment, to be used continually in the Divine worship, see 1 Chron. xvi. 41: also by *Solomon,* 2 Chron. vii. 3. 6, and observed by *Jehoshaphat,* 2 Chron, xx. 21; all acknowledging that, however rich in mercy God was to them, the most extensive displays of his goodness were reserved for *the age to come;* see 1 Pet. i. 10-12: "Of which salvation the prophets have inquired, and searched diligently, who prophesied of the grace that should come unto you,—unto whom it was revealed, that not unto themselves, but unto us, they did minister the things which are now reported unto you by them that preached the Gospel unto you by the power of the Holy Ghost sent down from heaven," &c.

Verse 2. *The God of gods*] לארני הארנים *ladonai haadonim.* As *adonai* signifies *director,* &c., it may apply here, not to *idols,* for God is not their god; but to the priests and spiritual rulers; as *Lord* of *lords* may apply to *kings* and *magistrates,* &c. He is God and ruler over all the rulers of the earth, whether in things *sacred* or *civil.*

Verse 4. *Who alone doeth great wonders*] MIRACLES. No power but that which is *almighty* can work miracles, נפלאות *niphlaoth,* the *inversion,* or *suspension,* or *destruction* of the laws of nature.

Verse 5. *By wisdom made the heavens*] In the contrivance of the celestial bodies, in their relations, connexions, influences on each other, revolutions, &c., the wisdom of God particularly appears.

Verse 6. *Stretched out the earth above the waters*] Or, *upon the waters.* This seems to refer to a *central abyss of waters,* the existence of which has not been yet disproved.

Verse 7. *Great lights*] See the notes on the parallel passages in *Genesis,* &c.

Verse 10. *Smote Egypt in their first-born*] This was one of the heaviest of strokes: a great part of the rising generation was cut off; few but old persons and children left remaining.

Verse 13. *Divided the Red Sea into parts*] Some of the Jews have imagined that God made

A. M. cir. 3489
B. C. cir. 515
Darii I.,
R. Persarum,
cir. annum
sextum

16 [q]To him which led his people through the wilderness: for
his mercy *endureth* for ever.
17 [r]To him which smote
great kings: for his mercy *endureth* for
ever:
18 [s]And slew famous kings: for his mercy
endureth for ever:
19 [t]Sihon, king of the Amorites: for his
mercy *endureth* for ever:
20 [u]And Og the king of Bashan: for his
mercy *endureth* for ever:
21 [v]And gave their land for a heritage:
for his mercy *endureth* for
ever:
22 *Even* a heritage unto Israel
his servant: for his mercy *endureth* for ever.
23 Who [w]remembered us in our low estate:
for his mercy *endureth* for ever:
24 And hath redeemed us from our enemies:
for his mercy *endureth* for ever.
25 [x]Who giveth food to all flesh: for his
mercy *endureth* for ever.
26 O give thanks unto the God of heaven:
for his mercy *endureth* for ever.

A. M. cir. 3489
B. C. cir. 515
Darii I.,
R. Persarum,
cir. annum
sextum

[q]Exod. xiii. 18; xv. 22; Deut. viii. 15——[r]Psa. cxxxv. 10, 11——[s]Deut. xxix. 7——[t]Num. xxi. 21——[u]Num. xxi. 33

[v]Josh. xii. 1, &c.; Psa. cxxxv. 12——[w]Gen. viii. 1; Deut. xxxii. 36; Psa. cxiii. 7——[x]Psa. civ. 27; cxlv. 15; cxlvii. 9

twelve paths through the Red Sea, that each tribe might have a distinct passage. Many of the *fathers* were of the same opinion; but is this very likely?

Verse 16. *Which led his people through the wilderness*] It was an astonishing miracle of God to support so many hundreds of thousands of people in a wilderness totally deprived of all necessaries for the life of man, and that for the space of *forty* years.

Verse 23. *Who remembered us in our low estate*] He has done much for our *forefathers;* and he has done much for us, in delivering us, when we had no helper, from our long captivity in Babylon.

Verse 25. *Giveth food to all flesh*] By whose *universal providence* every intellectual and animal being is supported and preserved. The appointing every *living thing* food, and that sort of food which is suited to its nature, (and the nature and habits of animals are endlessly diversified,) is an overwhelming proof of the wondrous providence, wisdom, and goodness of God.

The Vulgate, Arabic, and Anglo-Saxon, add a twenty-seventh verse, by repeating here ver. 3 very unnecessarily.

Analysis of the Hundred and Thirty-sixth Psalm

This Psalm has the same argument with the preceding. It is divided into *three* parts:—

I. A general exhortation to praise God for his goodness and majesty, ver. 1, 2, 3.

II. A declaration of that goodness and majesty in their effects, ver. 4-10.

III. A conclusion fit for the exordium, ver. 26.

1. Of his creation, ver. 4-10.
2. Of his providence in preserving the Church, and punishing her enemies, ver. 10-25.
3. That his providence extends to all his creatures, ver. 25.

I. In the *three* first verses the prophet invites us to praise God for his mercy and goodness. And in these *three* verses expositors find the Trinity:—

1. *Jehovah.* God the Father, who is the Fountain of being.
2. *God the Son.* Who is God of gods, and over all.
3. *The Holy Ghost.* Who is Lord of lords.

The psalmist's reasons for calling upon us thus to praise him are, "for he is good: for his mercy endureth for ever."

The prophet now begins to praise God for his wonderful works, and which he alone was able to do.

1. "Who hath done wonderful things." Such as the work of creation.
2. "For his mercy endureth for ever." In sustaining and preserving all things.

"To him give thanks" for the wisdom manifested in the heavens; for, contemplate them as we may, they appear full of beauty, order, and splendour.

Praise him for the formation of the earth, as the mansion of man.

Give thanks "to him that stretched out," &c. Naturally this could not be, because the earth is heavier than water: but God hath made furrows for the waters to flow into, that man and beast might live on the earth.

"For his mercy endureth for ever." In this there was a threefold mercy:—

1. In reference to the *earth.* To make it something of nothing.
2. As respects the *water.* To prepare for it a settled place.
3. In regard to *man.* To whom he gave the earth uncovered from water, and yet plentifully supplied with rivers and fruits.

The third instance is the two great luminaries and the stars, in the three following verses. These do astonishingly adorn the heaven, and profit the earth. The sun and moon illuminate the earth, and comfort us. Perhaps the prophet instances these because they are alike blessings bestowed upon and shared by all the world.

II. From the wonderful works of the creation the prophet descends to those of his providence, in the preservation of the Church; and instances it in the redemption of his people *Israel* from the land of *Egypt,* &c., dwelling at large upon it, ver. 10-22.

In these verses the prophet records how God performed to *Israel* all the offices of a good Captain, Guide, Leader, and even Father; for he fed them with bread from heaven, gave them water out of the rock, caused that their clothes wore not out, cured their sick, defended them from their enemies, &c.

All this God did for them before they entered *Canaan.* And then the prophet reminds them how they rebelled against God, and he humbled them by bringing the *Philistines* and the *Babylonian* kings against them, who conquered and subjected them: but when they cried to him, he turned their captivity; for "he remembered us when we were in our low estate," &c.; "and hath redeemed us from our enemies," &c.

Lastly, that his goodness is not only extended over his people, but his *creatures;* to all *flesh,* which word signifies every thing that hath life.

III. He concludes as he began, "O give thanks unto the God of heaven," &c. The prophet calls him the *God of heaven,* because he alone made the heavens, and has his throne there, having the whole world under him; and by his wisdom and providence he preserves, moderates, and governs all things.

PSALM CXXXVII

The desolate and afflicted state of the captives in Babylon, 1, 2. *How they were insulted by their enemies,* 3, 4. *Their attachment to their country,* 5, 6. *Judgments denounced against their enemies,* 7–9.

BY the rivers of Babylon, there we sat down, yea, we wept, when we remembered Zion.

2 We hanged our harps upon the willows in the midst thereof.

3 For there they that carried us away captive required of us [a]a song; and they that [b]wasted[c] us *required of us* mirth, *saying,* Sing us *one* of the songs of Zion.

4 How shall we sing the LORD's song in a [d]strange land?

5 If I forget thee, O Jerusalem, let my right hand forget *her cunning.*

6 If I do not remember thee, let my [e]tongue

[a]Heb. *the words of a song*——[b]Heb. *laid us on heaps*

[c]Psa. lxxix. 1——[d]Heb. *land of a stranger*——[e]Ezek. iii. 26

NOTES ON PSALM CXXXVII

The *Vulgate, Septuagint, Æthiopic,* and *Arabic,* say, ridiculously enough, a *Psalm of David for Jeremiah.* Anachronisms with those who wrote the *titles* to the Psalms were matters of no importance. *Jeremiah* never was at Babylon; and therefore could have no part in a Psalm that was sung on the banks of its rivers by the Israelitish captives. Neither the *Hebrew* nor *Chaldee* has any *title;* the *Syriac* attributes it to *David.* Some think it was sung when they returned from Babylon; others, while they were there. It is a matter of little importance. It was evidently composed *during* or at the *close* of the *captivity.*

Verse 1. *By the rivers of Babylon*] These might have been the *Tigris* and *Euphrates,* or their *branches,* or *streams* that flowed into them. In their captivity and dispersion, it was customary for the Jews to hold their religious meetings on the banks of rivers. Mention is made of this Acts xvi. 13, where we find the Jews of Philippi resorting to *a river side, where prayer was wont to be made.* And sometimes they built their synagogues here, when they were expelled from the cities.

Verse 2. *We hanged our harps upon the willows*] The ערבים *arabim* or *willows* were very plentiful in Babylon. The great quantity of them that were on the banks of the *Euphrates* caused Isaiah, chap. xv. 7, to call it *the brook* or *river of willows.* This is a most affecting picture. Perhaps resting themselves after toil, and wishing to spend their time religiously, they took their harps, and were about to sing one of the songs of Zion; but, reflecting on their own country, they became so filled with distress, that they unstrung their harps with one consent, and hung them on the willow bushes, and gave a general loose to their grief. Some of the Babylonians, who probably attended such meetings for the sake of the music, being present at the time here specified, desired them to *sing one of Zion's songs:* this is affectingly told.

Verse 3. *They that carried us away captive required of us a song*] This was as *unreasonable* as it was *insulting.* How could they who had reduced us to slavery, and dragged us in chains from our own beautiful land and privileges, expect us to sing a sacred ode to please them, who were enemies both to us and to our God? And how could those *who wasted us* expect *mirth* from people in captivity, deprived of all their possessions, and in the most abject state of poverty and oppression?

Verse 4. *How shall we sing the Lord's song*] איך נשיר *eich! nashir; O, we sing!* Who does not hear the *deep sigh* in the strongly guttural sound of the original איך *eich!* wrung, as it were, from the bottom of the heart? *Can* WE, in this state of *slavery,*—WE, *exiles,* from our *country,*—WE, *stripped* of all our *property,*—WE, reduced to *contempt* by our *strong enemy,*—WE, *deprived* of our *religious privileges,*—WE, *insulted* by our *oppressors,*—WE, in the land of *heathens,*—WE *sing,* or be *mirthful* in these *circumstances?* No: God does not expect it; man should not wish it; and it is base in our enemies to require it.

Verse 5. *If I forget thee, O Jerusalem*] Such conduct would be, in effect, a renunciation of our land; a tacit acknowledgment that we were reconciled to our bondage; a concession that we were pleased with our captivity, and could profane holy ordinances by using them as means of *sport* or *pastime* to the heathen. No: *Jerusalem!* we remember thee and thy Divine ordinances; and especially thy *King* and our

cleave to the roof of my mouth; if I prefer
not Jerusalem above [f]my chief joy.
7 Remember, O LORD, [g]the children of
Edom in the day of Jerusalem; who said,
[h]Rase *it,* rase *it, even* to the foundation thereof.

8 O daughter of Babylon, [i]who art to be
[k]destroyed; happy *shall he be,* [l]that[m] rewardeth thee as thou hast served us.
9 Happy *shall he be,* that taketh and [n]dash-
eth thy little ones against [o]the stones.

---

[f]Heb. *the head of my joy*——[g]Jer. xlix. 7, &c.; Lam. iv. 22; Ezek. xxv. 12; Obad. 10, &c.; 1 Esd. iv. 45 [h]Heb. *Make bare*——[i]Isa. xiii. 1, 6, &c.; xlvii. 1; Jer. xxv. 12; l. 2

[k]Hebrew, *wasted*——[l]Hebrew, *that recompenseth unto thee thy deed which thou didst to us*——[m]Jeremiah l. 15, 29; Rev. xviii. 6——[n]Isaiah xiii. 16——[o]Hebrew, *the rock*

God, whose indignation we must bear, because we have sinned against him.

Let my right hand forget] Let me forget the use of my right hand. Let me forget that which is dearest and most profitable to me; and let me lose my skill in the management of my harp, if I ever prostitute it to please the ungodly multitude or the enemies of my Creator!

Verse 6. *Let my tongue cleave*] Let me lose my *voice*, and all its powers of *melody;* my *tongue*, and all its *faculty* of *speech;* my *ear*, and its *discernment* of *sounds;* if I do not prefer my *country*, my *people*, and the *ordinances of my God*, beyond all these, and whatever may constitute the *chiefest joy* I can possess in aught else beside. This is truly *patriotic*, truly noble and dignified. Such sentiments can only be found in the hearts and mouths of those slaves whom the grace of God has made *free*.

Verse 7. *Remember—the children of Edom*] It appears from Jer. xii. 6; xxv. 14; Lam. iv. 21, 22; Ezek. xxv. 12; Obad. 11-14; that the *Idumeans* joined the army of Nebuchadnezzar against their brethren the Jews; and that they were main instruments in rasing the walls of Jerusalem even to the ground.

Verse 8. *O daughter of Babylon, who art to be destroyed*] Or, *O thou daughter of Babylon the destroyer*, or, *who art to be ruined*. In being reduced under the empire of the Persians, Babylon was already greatly humbled and brought low from what it was in the days of Nebuchadnezzar; but it was afterwards so totally ruined that not a vestige of it remains. After its capture by Cyrus, A. M. 3468, it could never be considered a capital city; but it appeared to follow the fortunes of its various conquerors till it was, as a city, finally destroyed.

Rewardeth thee as thou hast served us.] This was Cyrus, who was chosen of God to do this work, and is therefore called *happy*, as being God's agent in its destruction. Greater desolations were afterwards brought upon it by *Darius Hystaspes*, who took this city after it had revolted, and slaughtered the inhabitants, men and women, in a barbarous manner. Herod. lib. iii.

Verse 9. *Happy—that taketh and dasheth thy little ones*] That is, So oppressive hast thou been to all under thy domination, as to become universally hated and detested; so that those who may have the last hand in thy destruction, and the total extermination of thy inhabitants, shall be reputed *happy*—shall be *celebrated* and *extolled* as those who have rid the world of a curse so grievous. These prophetic declarations contain no excitement to any person or persons to commit acts of cruelty and barbarity; but are simply *declarative* of what would take place in the order of the retributive providence and justice of God, and the general opinion that should in consequence be expressed on the subject; therefore *praying for the destruction of our enemies* is totally out of the question. It should not be omitted that the Chaldee considers this Psalm a *dialogue*, which it thus divides:—The *three* first verses are supposed to have been spoken by the *psalmist*, *By the rivers*, &c. The Levites answer from the porch of the temple, in ver. 4, *How shall we sing*, &c. The voice of the *Holy Spirit* responds in ver. 5, 6, *If I forget thee*, &c. *Michael, the prince of Jerusalem*, answers in ver. 7, *Remember, O Lord*, &c. *Gabriel, the prince of Zion*, then addresses *the destroyer of the Babylonish nation*, in ver. 8, 9, *Happy shall be he that rewardeth thee*, &c. To slay all when a city was sacked, both male and female, old and young, was a common practice in ancient times. Homer describes this in words almost similar to those of the psalmist:—

> Ὑίας τ' ολλυμενους, ἑλκυσθεισας τε θυγατρας,
> Και θαλαμους κεραϊζομενους, και νηπια τεκνα
> Βαλλομενα προτι γαιῃ εν αινῃ δηϊοτητι,
> Ἑλκομενας τε νυους ολοῃς ὑπο χερσιν Αχαιων.
>
> Il. lib. xxii., ver. 62.

> My heroes slain, my bridal bed o'erturned;
> My daughters ravished, and my city burned:
> My bleeding infants dashed against the floor;
> These I have yet to see; perhaps yet more.
>
> POPE.

These excesses were common in all barbarous nations, and are only prophetically declared here. He shall be reputed *happy*, *prosperous*, and *highly commendable*, who shall destroy Babylon.

ANALYSIS OF THE HUNDRED AND THIRTY-SEVENTH PSALM

When this Psalm was composed, the *Jews* were in captivity in *Babylon*, far from their own country, the temple, and the public exercises of religion; and the scoff and scorn of their enemies; and they contrast what they were with what they are. This Psalm has *two* parts:—

I. The complaint of *Israel*. Because of the insults of the *Babylonians*, they deplore their sad condition, long for the temple, and their return to *Jerusalem*, ver. 1-7.

II. An imprecation or prayer for vengeance, on their persecutors, ver. 7-9.

I. Their complaint arises from their captivity, and it is aggravated.—

1. From the place, *Babylon:* "By the rivers of Babylon." A place far from their country; who were aliens from the covenant made by God with *Abraham*, scorners of their religion, had laid waste their city and forced them to base and servile labour.

2. From the continuance of their captivity

and misery: "There we sat down," &c. Took up the seats allotted to us, and that for *seventy* years.

3. From the effects it produced: "Yea, we wept," &c.

4. From the cause which drew these tears. The remembrance of what they had enjoyed, (now lost,) the services of religion: "We wept when we remembered Zion," &c.

5. From the intenseness of their grief, which was so great that they could not even tune their harps: "We hung our harps," &c.

That which increased their grief was the joy their enemies manifested at it.

1. THERE, in a strange land, the place of our captivity.

2. "THEY that carried us away captive."

3. "They required of us a song." They required of us mirth, saying,

4. O thou *Jew* or captive, come now, "sing us one of the songs of Zion."

To this sarcasm the captive Jews return a double answer.

"How shall we sing the Lord's song in a strange land?" You are aliens, and this is a strange land; we cannot sing God's service there, which is destined to his honour, to you, or in this place without offending our God.

They reply by a protestation of their hope and constancy in religion, and accurse themselves if they do not continue in it.

1. "If I forget thee," &c. Forget the worship and feasts I kept there.

2. "If I do not remember thee," &c. If I do not prefer and make mention of Jerusalem, then "let my tongue cleave," &c. Let me no more have the use of that excellent organ of God's glory. It would be unworthy of my religion, and a dishonour to my God to sing the songs of Zion thus circumstanced, and to scoffers and aliens.

II. This seems to be the sense of the first part of the Psalm. The second part has reference to the imprecations poured out against *Edom* and *Babylon*, both persecutors of God's people. The Babylonians carried them away captive, and the *Edomites* persecuted their brethren with the sword, Amos i. 12.

1. Against Edom.

(1) "Remember, O Lord, the children of Edom," &c. How they carried themselves towards thy people on that day when thy anger smote against them, and the Babylonians carried us away.

(2) *Remember* how they added to our affliction, saying, "Rase it," &c.

2. Against *Babylon*. To her he turns his speech by an apostrophe; but at the same time foretells her ruin: "O daughter of Babylon," &c. Thou seemest to thyself to be most happy; but thy ruin approaches. Shortly after, the *Medes*, led by *Cyrus*, destroyed them.

(1) "Happy shall he be that rewardeth," &c. [See the notes.]

(2) "Happy shall he be that taketh and dasheth thy little ones," &c. [See the notes.]

PSALM CXXXVIII

The psalmist praises the Lord for his mercies to himself, 1–3. *He foretells that the kings of the earth shall worship him*, 4, 5. *God's condescension to the humble*, 6. *The psalmist's confidence*, 7, 8.

A Psalm of David

A. M. cir. 2956 B. C. cir. 1048 Davidis, Regis Israelitarum, cir. annum decimum

I WILL praise thee with my whole heart: [a]before the gods will I sing praise unto thee.
2 [b]I will worship [c]toward thy holy temple, and praise thy name for thy loving-kindness and for thy truth: for thou hast [d]magnified thy word above all thy name.

A. M. cir. 2956 B. C. cir. 1048 Davidis, Regis Israelitarum, cir. annum decimum

[a]Psa. cxix. 46——[b]Psa. xxviii. 2 [c]1 Kings viii. 29, 30; Psa. v. 7——[d]Isa. xlii. 21

NOTES ON PSALM CXXXVIII

The *Hebrew* and all the *Versions* attribute this Psalm to *David*, and it is supposed to have been made by him when, delivered from all his enemies, he was firmly seated on the throne of Israel. As the *Septuagint* and *Arabic* prefix also the names of *Haggai* and *Zechariah*, it is probable that it was used by the Jews as a *form of thanksgiving* for their deliverance from all their enemies, and their ultimate settlement in their own land, after Ahasuerus, supposed by Calmet to be *Darius Hystaspes*, had married *Esther*, before which time they were not peaceably *settled* in their own country.

Verse 1. *I will praise thee with my whole heart*] I have received the highest favours from thee, and my whole soul should acknowledge my obligation to thy mercy. The Versions and several MSS. add יהוה *Yehovah*, "I will praise thee, O LORD," &c.

Before the gods will I sing] נגד אלהים *neged Elohim*, "in the presence of Elohim;" most probably meaning before the ark, where were the sacred symbols of the Supreme Being. The *Chaldee* has, *before the judges*. The *Vulgate*, *before the angels*. So the *Septuagint*, *Æthiopic*, *Arabic*, and *Anglo-Saxon*. The Syriac, *Before kings will I sing unto thee.* This place has been alleged by the Roman Catholics as a proof that the holy angels, who are present in the assemblies of God's people, take their prayers and praises, and present them before God. There is nothing like this in the *text;* for supposing, which is not granted, that the word *elohim* here signifies *angels*, the praises are not *presented to them*, nor are *they requested to present them before God;* it is simply said, *Before elohim will I sing praise unto* THEE. Nor could there be need of any intermediate agents, when it was well known that God himself was present in the sanctuary,

A. M. cir. 2956
B. C. cir. 1048
Davidis, Regis
Israelitarum,
cir. annum
decimum

3 In the day when I cried
thou answeredst me, *and*
strengthenedst me *with* strength
in my soul.
4 [e]All the kings of the earth shall praise
thee, O LORD, when they hear the words of
thy mouth.
5 Yea, they shall sing in the ways of the
LORD: for great *is* the glory of the LORD.
6 [f]Though the LORD *be* high, yet [g]hath he
respect unto the lowly: but the
proud he knoweth afar off.
7 [h]Though I walk in the midst
of trouble, thou wilt revive me:
thou shalt stretch forth thine hand against
the wrath of mine enemies, and thy right
hand shall save me.
8 [i]The LORD will perfect *that which* concerneth me: thy mercy, O LORD, *endureth* for ever:
[k]forsake not the works of thine own hands.

A. M. cir. 2956
B. C. cir. 1048
Davidis, Regis
Israelitarum,
cir. annum
decimum

[e]Psalm cii. 15, 22——[f]Psalm cxiii. 5, 6; Isa. lvii. 15 [g]Prov. iii. 34; James iv. 6; 1 Pet. v. 5

[h]Psa. xxiii. 3, 4——[i]Psa. lvii. 2; Phil. i. 6——[k]See Job x. 3, 8; xiv. 15

sitting between the cherubim. Therefore this opinion is wholly without support from this place.

Verse 2. *For thy loving-kindness*] Thy *tender mercy* shown to me; and for the fulfilment of thy *truth*—the promises thou hast made.

Thou hast magnified thy word above all thy name.] All the *Versions* read this sentence thus: "For thou hast magnified above all the name of thy holiness," or, "thy holy name." Thou hast proved that thou hast all *power* in heaven and in earth, and that thou art *true* in all thy words. And by giving the word of *prophecy*, and fulfilling those words, thou hast *magnified thy holy name above all things*—thou hast proved thyself to be *ineffably great*. The original is the following: כי הגדלת על כל שמך אמרתך *ki higdalta al col shimcha, imrathecha*, which I think might be thus translated: "For thou hast magnified thy name and thy word over all," or, "on every occasion." *Kennicott* reads, "He preferred *faithfulness to his promise* to the attribute of his *power*." I believe my own translation to be nearest the truth. There may be some corruption in this clause.

Verse 3. With *strength in my soul.*] Thou hast endued my soul with many graces, blessings, and heavenly qualities.

Verse 4. *All the kings of the earth*] Of the land: all the neighbouring nations, seeing what is done for us, and looking in vain to find that any human agency was employed in the work, will immediately see that it was *thy hand;* and consequently, by *confessing* that it was *thou*, will give praise to thy name.

Verse 5. *They shall sing in the ways of the Lord*] They shall admire thy *conduct*, and the *wondrous workings* of thy providence; if they should not even unite with thy people.

Verse 6. *Though the Lord* be *high*] Infinitely *great* as God is, he regards even the lowest and most inconsiderable part of his creation; but the *humble* and *afflicted* man attracts his notice particularly.

But the proud he knoweth afar off.] He beholds them at a distance, and has them in utter derision.

Verse 7. *Though I walk in the midst of trouble*] I have had such experience of thy mercy, that let me fall into whatsoever trouble I may, yet I will trust in thee. Thou wilt *quicken* me, though I were *ready to die;* and thou wilt deliver me from the *wrath of my enemies.*

Verse 8. *The Lord will perfect*] Whatever is farther necessary to be done, he will do it.

Forsake not the works of thine own hands.] My body—my soul; thy work *begun in my soul;* thy work in *behalf of Israel;* thy work in the evangelization of the world; thy work in the salvation of mankind. Thou wilt not forsake these.

ANALYSIS OF THE HUNDRED AND THIRTY-EIGHTH PSALM

I. In the three first verses of this Psalm David promises a grateful heart, and to sing the praises of God, because he had heard his cries, and sent him comfort and deliverance.

II. In the three next he shows what future kings would do, when the works and truth of God should be made known to them.

III. In the two last verses he professes his confidence in God; shows what he hopes for from him; and, in assurance that God will perfect his works, prays him not to desert or forsake him.

I. The prophet shows his thankfulness, which he illustrates and amplifies.

1. "I will praise thee with my whole heart." Sincerely, cordially.

2. "Before the gods," &c. Publicly, before potentates, whether angels or kings.

3. "I will worship toward," &c. It is true God ruleth as King in his palace: there will I bow; it is the symbol of his presence.

4. "And praise thy name," &c. From a feeling sense of thy goodness. 1. "For thy loving-kindness," &c. In calling me to the kingdom from the sheepfold. 2. "And for thy truth." In performing thy promise. By which,

5. "Thou hast magnified," &c. This clause is differently read. "Thou hast magnified thy name in thy word; *by* performing thy word above all things." Or, "Thou hast magnified thy name and thy word above all things." See the notes.

6. "In the day when I cried," &c. Finite creatures as we are, we must sometimes faint in our temptations and afflictions, if not strengthened by God.

II. The prophet, having set down what God had in mercy done for him in calling him *from following the ewes*, &c., and *making him king*, and performing *his promises to him;* seeing all this, the prophet judges it impossible but that the neighbouring and future kings should acknowledge the miracle and praise God. This appears the literal sense: but it may have reference to the conversion of kings in future ages to the faith.

1. "All the kings of the earth," &c. Or the future kings of Israel.

2. "Yea, they shall sing in the ways," &c. His mercy, truth, clemency, &c.: "For great is the glory of the Lord." Righteous and glorious in all his works, of which this is one. "Though the Lord be high," &c. Of which David was an instance. "But the proud," &c., he removes far from him. Saul and others are examples of this.

III. Because *God who is high*, &c. And David, being conscious of his own humility of mind, confidently expects help from God.

1. "Though I walk," &c. Exposed on all sides to trouble.

2. "Thou wilt revive me." Preserve me safe and untouched.

3. "Thou shalt stretch forth thy hand," &c. Restrain the power of my enemies.

4. "And thy right hand," &c. Thy power; thy *Christ*, who, in Isa. liii. is called *the arm of the Lord.*

The last verse depends on the former. Because the prophet knew that many troubles and afflictions remained yet to be undergone; therefore he was confident that the same God would still deliver and make his work perfect.

1. "The Lord will perfect," &c. Not for my merits, but his mercy.

2. Of which he gives the reason: "Thy mercy, O Lord," &c. It does not exist only for a moment, but it is eternal.

3. And he concludes with a prayer for God to perfect his work: "Forsake not the work," &c. Thou who hast begun this work, increase and perfect it; because it is thy work alone, not mine. If we desire that God should perfect any work in us, we must be sure that it is his work, and look to him continually.

PSALM CXXXIX

A fine account of the omniscience of God, 1–6; *of his omnipresence*, 7–12; *of his power and providence*, 13–16. *The excellence of his purposes*, 17, 18. *His opposition to the wicked*, 19, 20; *with whom the godly can have no fellowship*, 21, 22.

XXIX. DAY. MORNING PRAYER

To the chief Musician, A Psalm of David

O LORD, [a]thou hast searched me, and
known *me*.

2 [b]Thou knowest my downsitting and mine
uprising, thou [c]understandest my thought
afar off.

3 [d]Thou [e]compassest my path and my

[a]Psa. xvii. 3; Jer. xii. 3——[b]2 Kings xix. 27——[c]Matt. ix. 4; John ii. 24, 25——[d]Job xxxi. 4——[e]Or, *winnowest*

NOTES ON PSALM CXXXIX

The *title* of this Psalm in the *Hebrew* is, *To the chief Musician*, or, *To the Conqueror, A Psalm of David.* The *Versions* in general follow the Hebrew. And yet, notwithstanding these testimonies, there appears internal evidence that the Psalm was not written by *David*, but *during* or *after the time of the captivity*, as there are several *Chaldaisms* in it. See verses 2, 3, 7, 9, 19, 20, collated with Dan. ii. 29, 30; iv. 16; vii. 28; some of these shall be noticed in their proper places.

As to the *author*, he is unknown; for it does not appear to have been the work of *David.* The composition is worthy of him, but the language appears to be *lower* than his time.

Concerning the *occasion*, there are many conjectures which I need not repeat, because I believe them unfounded. It is most probable that it was written on *no particular occasion*, but is a moral lesson on the wisdom, presence, providence, and justice of God, without any reference to any circumstance in the *life of David*, or in the *history of the Jews.*

The Psalm is very sublime; the sentiments are grand, the style in general highly elevated, and the images various and impressive. The first part especially, that contains so fine a description of the wisdom and knowledge of God, is inimitable.

Bishop *Horsley's* account of this Psalm is as follows:—

"In the first twelve verses of this Psalm the author celebrates God's perfect knowledge of man's thoughts and actions; and the reason of this wonderful knowledge, *viz.*, that God is the Maker of man. Hence the psalmist proceeds, in the four following verses, 13, 14, 15, 16, to magnify God as ordaining and superintending the formation of his body in the womb. In the 17th and 18th he acknowledges God's providential care of him in every moment of his life; and in the remainder of the Psalm implores God's aid against impious and cruel enemies, professing his own attachment to God's service, that is, to the true religion, and appealing to the Searcher of hearts himself for the truth of his professions.

The composition, for the purity and justness of *religious sentiment*, and for the force and beauty of the images, is certainly in the very first and best style. And yet the frequent *Chaldaisms* of the diction argue *no very high antiquity.*

Verse 1. *O Lord, thou hast searched me*] חקרתני *chakartani;* thou hast *investigated* me; *thou hast thoroughly acquainted thyself* with my whole soul and conduct.

Verse 2. *My downsitting and mine uprising*] Even these inconsiderable and casual things are under thy continual notice. I cannot so much as *take a seat*, or *leave it*, without being marked by thee.

Thou understandest my thought] לרעי *lerei*, "my cogitation." This word is *Chaldee*, see Dan. ii. 29, 30.

Afar off.] While the figment is forming that shall produce them.

Verse 3. *Thou compassest my path*] זרית

lying down, and art acquainted *with* all my
ways.
4 For *there is* not a word in my tongue, *but,*
lo, O LORD, [f]thou knowest it altogether.
5 Thou hast beset me behind and before,
and laid thine hand upon me.
6 [g]*Such* knowledge *is* too wonderful for me;
it is high, I cannot *attain* unto it.
7 [h]Whither shall I go from thy Spirit? or
whither shall I flee from thy presence?
8 [i]If I ascend up into heaven, thou *art* there:
[k]if I make my bed in hell, behold thou *art there.*
9 *If* I take the wings of the morning, *and*
dwell in the uttermost parts of the sea;
10 Even there shall thy hand lead me, and
thy right hand shall hold me.
11 If I say, Surely the darkness shall cover
me; even the night shall be light about me.
12 Yea, [l]the darkness [m]hideth not from thee;
but the night shineth as the day: [n]the darkness and the light *are* both alike *to thee.*
13 For thou hast possessed my reins: thou
hast covered me in my mother's womb.
14 I will praise thee; for I am fearfully *and*

---

[f]Heb. iv. 13——[g]Job xlii. 3; Psa. xl. 5; cxxxi. 1 [h]Jer. xxiii. 24; Jonah i. 3——[i]Amos ix. 2, 3, 4——[k]Job xxvi. 6; Prov. xv. 11

[l]Job xxvi. 6; xxxiv. 22; Dan. ii. 22; Heb. iv. 13 [m]Heb. *darkeneth not*——[n]Hebrew, *as is the darkness so is the light*

---

zeritha thou dost winnow, ventilate, or *sift* my path; and my lying down, רבעי *ribi*, my *lair*, my *bed*.

And art acquainted] *Thou treasurest up*. This is the import of סכן *sachan*. Thou hast the *whole number* of my ways, and the steps I took in them.

Verse 4. There is *not a word in my tongue*] Although (כי *ki*) *there be not a word in my tongue, behold, O Jehovah, thou knowest the whole of it*, that is, thou knowest all my *words before* they are *uttered*, as thou knowest all my *thoughts* while as yet they are *unformed*.

Verse 5. *Thou hast beset me behind and before*] אחור וקדם צרתני *achor vekodam tsartani*, "The hereafter and the past, thou hast formed me." I think Bishop Horsley's emendation here is just, uniting the two verses together. "Behold thou, O Jehovah, knowest the whole, the hereafter and the past. Thou hast formed me, and laid thy hand upon me."

Verse 6. Such *knowledge* is *too wonderful*] I think, with *Kennicott*, that פלאיה דעת *pelaiah daath* should be read פלאי הדעת *peli haddaath*, "THIS knowledge," ממני *mimmenni*, "is beyond or above me." This change is made by taking the ה *he* from the end of פלאיה *pelaiah*, which is really *no word*, and joining it with דעת *daath;* which, by giving it an *article*, makes it demonstrative, הדעת *haddaath*, "THIS knowledge." *This kind of knowledge*, God's knowledge, that takes in all things, and their reasons, essences, tendencies, and issues, is far beyond me.

Verse 7. *Whither shall I go from thy Spirit?*] Surely רוח *ruach* in this sense must be taken *personally*, it certainly cannot mean either *breath* or *wind;* to render it so would make the passage ridiculous.

From thy presence?] מפניך *mippaneycha*, "from thy faces." Why do we meet with this word so frequently in the *plural* number, when applied to God? And why have we his *Spirit*, and his *appearances* or *faces*, *both* here? A *Trinitarian* would at once say, "The plurality of persons in the Godhead is intended;" and who can *prove* that he is mistaken?

Verse 8. *If I ascend*] Thou art in *heaven*, in thy glory; in *hell*, in thy vindictive justice; and in all *parts of earth, water, space, place*, or *vacuity*, by thy *omnipresence*. Wherever I am, there art thou; and where I cannot be, thou art there. Thou fillest the heavens and the earth.

Verse 11. *Surely the darkness shall cover me*] Should I suppose that this would serve to screen me, immediately this *darkness* is turned into *light*.

Verse 12. *Yea, the darkness hideth not from thee*] Darkness and light, ignorance and knowledge, are things that stand in relation to us; God sees equally in *darkness* as in *light;* and *knows* as perfectly, however man is enveloped in *ignorance*, as if all were *intellectual brightness*. What is to us *hidden* by *darkness*, or *unknown* through *ignorance*, is perfectly *seen* and *known* by God; because he is all sight, all hearing, all feeling, all soul, all spirit—*all* in ALL, and infinite in himself. He lends to every thing; receives nothing from any thing. Though his *essence* be *unimpartible*, yet his *influence* is *diffusible* through time and through eternity. Thus God makes himself known, seen, heard, felt; yet, in the infinity of his essence, neither angel, nor spirit, nor man can see him; nor can any creature comprehend him, or form any idea of the *mode* of his existence. And yet vain man would be wise, and ascertain his foreknowledge, eternal purposes, infinite decrees, with all operations of infinite love and infinite hatred, and their *objects specifically* and *nominally*, from all eternity, as if himself had possessed a being and powers co-extensive with the Deity! O ye wise fools! Jehovah, the fountain of eternal perfection and love, is as unlike your *creeds*, as he is unlike *yourselves*, forgers of doctrines to prove that the source of infinite benevolence is a *streamlet of capricious love* to thousands, while he is an overflowing, eternal, and irresistible *tide* of *hatred* to millions of millions both of angels and men! The antiproof of such doctrines is this: he bears with such blasphemies, and does not consume their abettors. "But nobody holds these doctrines." Then I have written against *nobody;* and have only to add the prayer, May no such doctrines ever disgrace the page of history; or farther dishonour, as they have done, the annals of the Church!

Verse 13. *Thou hast possessed my reins*] As the Hebrews believed that the *reins* were the first part of the human fetus that is formed, it may here mean, thou hast laid the foundation of my being.

Verse 14. *I am fearfully* and *wonderfully*

wonderfully made; marvellous *are* thy works;
and *that* my soul knoweth [o]right well.
15 [p]My[q] substance was not hid from thee,
when I was made in secret, *and* curiously
wrought in the lowest parts of the earth.
16 Thine eyes did see my substance, yet
being unperfect; and in thy book [r]all *my*
members were written, [s]*which* in continuance
were fashioned, when *as yet there was* none
of them.
17 [t]How precious also are thy thoughts
unto me, O God! how great is the sum of
them.
18 *If* I should count them, they are more in
number than the sand: when I awake, I am
still with thee.

[o]Heb. *greatly*——[p]Job x. 8, 9; Eccles. xi. 5——[q]Or, *strength* or *body*

[r]Heb. *all of them*——[s]Or, what *days they should be fashioned*——[t]Psa. xl. 5

made] The texture of the human body is the most complicated and curious that can be conceived. It is, indeed, *wonderfully made;* and it is withal so exquisitely *nice* and *delicate*, that the slightest accident may impair or destroy in a moment some of those parts essentially necessary to the continuance of life; therefore, we are *fearfully made.* And God has done so to show us our *frailty*, that we should walk with *death*, keeping *life* in view; and feel the necessity of *depending* on the all-wise and continual superintending care and providence of God.

Verse 15. *My substance was not hid from thee*] עצמי *atsmi*, my *bones* or *skeleton.*

Curiously wrought] רקמתי *rukkamti*, embroidered, *made of needle-work.* These two words, says Bishop Horsley, describe the two principal parts of which the human body is composed; the *bony skeleton*, the *foundation* of the whole; and the *external covering* of muscular flesh, tendons, veins, arteries, nerves, and skin; a curious *web of fibres.* On this passage Bishop *Lowth* has some excellent observations: "In that most perfect hymn, where the immensity of the omnipresent Deity, and the admirable wisdom of the Divine Artificer in framing the human body, are celebrated, the poet uses a remarkable metaphor, drawn from the nicest tapestry work:—

When I was formed in secret;
When I was wrought, as with a needle, in
the lowest parts of the earth.

"He who remarks this, (but the man who consults *Versions* only will hardly remark it,) and at the same time reflects upon the wonderful composition of the human body, the various implication of veins, arteries, fibres, membranes, and the 'inexplicable texture' of the whole frame; will immediately understand the beauty and elegance of this most apt translation. But he will not attain the whole force and dignity, unless he also considers that the most artful embroidery with the needle was dedicated by the Hebrews to the *service of the sanctuary;* and that the proper and singular use of their work was, by the immediate prescript of the Divine law, applied in a certain part of the *high priest's dress*, and in the *curtains* of the *tabernacle*, Exod. xxviii. 39; xxvi. 36; xxvii. 16; and compare Ezek. xvi. 10; xiii. 18. So that the psalmist may well be supposed to have compared the wisdom of the Divine Artificer particularly with that specimen of human art, whose dignity was through religion the highest, and whose elegance (Exod. xxxv. 30-35) was so exquisite, that the sacred writer seems to attribute it to a Divine inspiration."

In the lowest parts of the earth.] The womb of the mother, thus expressed by way of delicacy.

Verse 16. *Thine eyes did see my substance*] גלמי *golmi*, my *embryo state*—my yet indistinct mass, when all was *wrapped up* together, before it was gradually unfolded into the lineaments of man. "Some think," says Dr. Dodd, "that the allusion to *embroidery* is still carried on. As the embroiderer has still his work, pattern, or *carton*, before him, to which he always recurs; so, by a method as exact, were all my members *in continuance fashioned*, i. e., from the rude embryo or mass they daily received some degree of figuration; as from the rude skeins of variously coloured silk or worsted, under the artificer's hands, there at length arises an unexpected beauty, and an accurate harmony of colours and proportions."

And in thy book all my members *were written*] "All those members lay open before God's eyes; they were discerned by him as clearly as if the *plan* of them had been *drawn in a book*, even to the least figuration of the body of the child in the womb."

Verse 17. *How precious also are thy thoughts*] רעיך *reeycha*, thy *cogitations;* a *Chaldaism*, as before.

How great is the sum of them!] מה עצמו ראשיהם *mah atsemu rasheyhem; How strongly rational are the heads or principal subjects of them!* But the word may apply to the *bones*, עצמות *atsamoth*, the structure and uses of which are most curious and important.

Verse 18. If *I should count them*] I should be glad to enumerate so many interesting particulars: but they are beyond calculation.

When I awake] Thou art my Governor and Protector night and day.

I am still with thee.] All my steps in life are ordered by thee: I cannot go out of thy presence; I am ever under the influence of thy Spirit.

The subject, from the 14th verse to the 16th inclusive, might have been much more particularly illustrated, but we are taught, by the peculiar delicacy of expression in the Sacred Writings, to avoid, as in this case, the entering too minutely into *anatomical details.* I would, however, make an additional observation on the subject in the 15th and 16th verses. I have already remarked the elegant allusion to *embroidery*, in the word רקמתי *rukkamti*, in the astonishing texture of the human body; all of which is said to be done *in secret*, בסתר *bassether*, in the *secret place*, viz., *the womb of the mother*, which, in the conclusion of the verse, is by a delicate choice of expression termed *the lower parts of the earth.*

19 Surely thou wilt [u]slay the wicked, O God:
[v]depart from me, therefore, ye bloody men.
20 For they [w]speak against thee wickedly,
and thine enemies take *thy name* in vain.
21 [x]Do not I hate them, O LORD, that hate
thee? and am not I grieved with those that
rise up against thee?

22 I hate them with perfect hatred: I count
them mine enemies.
23 [y]Search me, O God, and know my heart:
try me, and know my thoughts:
24 And see if *there be any* [z]wicked
way in me, and [a]lead me in the way everlasting.

[u]Isa. xi. 4——[v]Psa. cxix. 115——[w]Jude 15——[x]2 Chron. xix. 2; Psa. cxix. 151

[y]Job xxxi. 6; Psa. xxvi. 2——[z]Heb. *way of pain* or *grief*
[a]Psa. v. 8; cxliii. 10

The *embryo* state, גלם *golem*, has a more forcible meaning than our word *substance* amounts to. גלם *galam* signifies *to roll* or *wrap up together;* and expresses the state of the fetus before the constituent members were developed. The best system of modern philosophy allows that *in semine masculino* all the members of the future animal are contained; and that these become slowly developed or *unfolded*, in the case of *fowls*, by *incubation;* and in the case of the more perfect *animals*, by gestation in the maternal matrix. It is no wonder that, in considering these, the psalmist should cry out, *How precious*, or *extraordinary, are thy thoughts! how great is the sum*—heads or outlines, *of them!* The *particulars* are, indeed, beyond comprehension; even the *heads*—the *general* contents, of thy works; while I endeavour to form any tolerable notion of them, *prevail over me*—they confound my *understanding*, and are vastly too multitudinous for my *comprehension*.

Verse 19. *Surely thou wilt slay the wicked*] The remaining part of this Psalm has no visible connexion with the preceding. I rather think it a *fragment*, or a part of some other Psalm.

Ye bloody men.] אנשי דמים *anshey damim*, *men of blood*, men *guilty of death*.

Verse 20. *Thine enemies take* thy name *in vain.*] Bishop *Horsley* translates the whole verse thus:—

"They have deserted me who are disobedient to thee;
"They who are sworn to a rash purpose—thy refractory adversaries."

The *original* is obscure: but I cannot see these things in it. Some translate the Hebrew thus: "Those who oppose thee iniquitously seize unjustly upon thy cities;" and so almost all the *Versions*. The words, thus translated, may apply to *Sanballat, Tobiah*, and the other enemies of the returned Jews, who endeavoured to drive them from the land, that they might possess the cities of Judea.

Verse 21. *Do not I hate them*] I hold their conduct in abomination.

Verse 22. *With perfect hatred*] Their *conduct*, their *motives*, their *opposition* to *thee*, their *perfidy* and *idolatrous purposes*, I perfectly abhor. With them I have neither part, interest, nor affection.

Verse 23. *Search me, O God*] *Investigate* my conduct, *examine* my *heart*, put me to *the test*, and *examine* my *thoughts*.

Verse 24. *If* there be any *wicked way*] דרך עצב *derech otseb: a way of idolatry*, or of *error*. Any thing false in *religious principle;* any thing contrary to *piety* to thyself, and love and benevolence to man. And he needed to offer such prayer as this, while filled with indignation against the *ways* of the *workers of iniquities;* for he who hates, *utterly hates*, the practices of any man, is not far from hating the *man himself*. It is very difficult

"To hate the sin with all the heart,
And yet the sinner love."

Lead me in the way everlasting.] בדרך עולם *bederech olam, in the old way*—the way in which our *fathers* walked, who worshipped thee, the infinitely pure Spirit, in *spirit* and in *truth*. Lead me, guide me, as thou didst them. We have ארח עולם *orach olam*, the *old path*, Job xxii. 15. "The two words דרך *derech* and ארח *orach*, differ," says Bishop *Horsley*, "in their figurative senses: *derech* is the *right way*, in which a man *ought* to go; *orach* is the way, *right* or *wrong*, in which a man *actually goes by habit*." The way that is right in a man's own eyes is seldom the way to God.

ANALYSIS OF THE HUNDRED AND THIRTY-NINTH PSALM

David, having had aspersions laid upon him, calls upon God in this Psalm to witness his innocency. Now, that this his appeal be not thought unreasonable, he presents God in his two especial attributes, omniscience and omnipresence; then he shows he loved goodness, and hated wickedness.

This Psalm is divided into four parts:—

I. A description of God's omniscience, ver. 1-7.

II. A description of his omnipresence, ver. 7-18.

III. David's hatred to evil and evil men, ver. 19-23.

IV. A protestation of his own innocency, which he offers to the trial of God, ver. 23, 24.

I. He begins with God's omniscience: "O Lord, thou hast searched me," &c. Examined me with scrutiny.

He searches and knows our actions.

1. "Thou knowest," &c. When and for what reasons I ever act.

2. "Thou understandest my thoughts," &c. Thou knowest my counsels and thoughts.

3. "Thou compassest my path," &c. The end I aim at.

4. "There is not a word," &c. Every word and thought thou knowest.

And for this he gives this reason: God is our Maker: "Thou hast beset me," &c. These *two* arguments prove that God knows all things.

1. God knows all the past and future: "Beset behind and before."

2. He governs man: "Thou God madest man,"

&c. The prophet concludes this Divine attribute, omniscience, with an acclamation: "Such knowledge," &c. It is beyond my reach and capacity.

II. From God's omnipresence the prophet argues that man cannot hide any thing from God, for he is every where present.

1. "Where shall I go," &c. That I may be hid from thy knowledge.

2. "Or whither shall I flee," &c. From thy face and eye.

There is no place that is not before thee.

1. "If I ascend up to heaven," &c.

2. "If I make my bed in hell," &c.

3. "If I take the wings of the morning," &c.

And among many instances that might be brought forward to prove God's omniscience and omnipresence, we may simply instance the formation of a child in the womb.

1. "Thou hast possessed my reins," &c. Thou hast undertaken wholly to frame, and cherish me when formed.

2. "Thou hast covered me," &c. Clothed me with flesh, skin, bones, &c.

Then the prophet breaks out in admiration of God's works.

1. "I will praise thee," &c.

2. "I am fearfully," &c. His works are enough to strike all men with reverential fear.

3. "Marvellous are thy works."

Then he proceeds with the formation of the infant embryo.

1. "My substance," &c. My strength, my essence. "Is not hid," &c.

2. "When I was made in secret," &c. In the secret cell of my mother's womb.

3. "And curiously wrought," &c. The word in the Hebrew signifies to interweave coloured threads. Man is a curious piece, and the variety of his faculties shows him such. [See the notes.]

4. "In the lowest parts of the earth," &c. In the womb, where it is as secret if God wrought it in *the lowest part of the earth.*

5. "Thine eyes did see my substance," &c. When in embryo, and without any distinct parts.

6. "And in thy book," &c. The idea of them was with thee, as the picture in the eye of the painter.

7. Which *in continuance*, &c.

The prophet closes this part with an exclamation.

1. "How precious also are thy thoughts," &c. In this and other respects.

2. "O how great is the sum of them." They are infinite.

3. And for this cause: "When I awake," &c., thy wisdom and providence are ever before my mind, and my admiration is full of them.

The prophet, having ended his discourse on the omniscience and omnipresence of God, justifies himself at God's tribunal.

1. "Surely thou wilt slay the wicked," &c. I dare not then associate with them.

2. "Depart, therefore, from me," &c. Keep at a distance.

3. "For they speak against thee wickedly," &c. Blaspheme my God.

So far from giving them the right hand of fellowship, he asks,—

1. "Do not I hate them, O Lord," &c. I hate them as sinners, but feel for and pity them as men.

2. Then he returns this answer to himself, "Yea, I hate them," &c. I count them my enemies, for they are thine.

IV. Lastly, it would appear that his heart was sincere and pure, or he would not abide such a trial.

1. "Search me, O God:" In the beginning of the Psalm he showed what God did; now he entreats him to do it.

2. "Try me," &c. Examine my heart and my ways.

3. "And see if there be any wicked way," &c. Presumptuous sins.

4. "And lead me in the way everlasting." This was the end proposed by his trial; that, if God saw any wickedness in him that might seduce him, he would withdraw him from it; and lead him to think, and devise, and do those things which would bring him to life eternal.

PSALM CXL

The psalmist prays against his enemies, 1–6; *returns thanks for help*, 7; *describes his enemies, and prays farther against them*, 8–11. *His confidence in God*, 12, 13.

To the chief Musician, A Psalm of David

A. M. cir. 2943 B. C. cir. 1061 Sauli, Regis Israelitarum, cir. annum 35

DELIVER me, O LORD, from
the evil man: [a]preserve me
from the [b]violent man;
2 Which imagine mischiefs in
their heart; [c]continually are
they gathered together *for* war.
3 They have sharpened their
tongues like a serpent; [d]adders'
poison *is* under their lips. Selah.

[a]Ver. 4——[b]Heb. *man of violence*

[c]Psa. lvi. 6——[d]Psa. lviii. 4; Rom. iii. 13

NOTES ON PSALM CXL

The *Hebrew*, and all the *Versions*, attribute this Psalm to *David;* and it is supposed to contain his complaint when persecuted by Saul. The *Syriac* determines it to the time when Saul endeavoured to transfix David with his spear.

Verse 1. *From the evil man*] Saul, who was full of envy, jealousy, and cruelty against David, to whom both himself and his kingdom were under the highest obligations, endeavoured by every means to destroy him.

Verse 2. *They gathered together*] He and his courtiers form plots and cabals against my life.

Verse 3. *They have sharpened their tongues*] They employ their time in forging lies and

A. M. cir. 2943
B. C. cir. 1061
Sauli, Regis
Israelitarum,
cir. annum
35

4 [e]Keep me, O LORD, from
the hands of the wicked; [f]pre-
serve me from the violent man;
who have purposed to overthrow
my goings.

5 [g]The proud have hid a snare for me, and
cords; they have spread a net by the way-
side; they have set gins for me. Selah.

6 I said unto the LORD, Thou *art* my God:
hear the voice of my supplication, O LORD.

7 O God the LORD, the strength of my
salvation, thou hast covered my head in the
day of battle.

8 Grant not, O LORD, the desires of the
wicked: further not his wicked device; [h]*lest*[i]
they exalt themselves. Selah.

9 *As for* the head of those that
compass me about, [k]let the
mischief of their own lips cover
them.

10 [l]Let burning coals fall upon them; let
them be cast into the fire; into deep pits,
that they rise not up again.

11 Let not [m]an [n]evil speaker be established
in the earth: evil shall hunt the violent man
to overthrow *him*.

12 I know that the LORD will [o]maintain the
cause of the afflicted, *and* the right of the
poor.

13 Surely the righteous shall give thanks
unto thy name; the [p]upright shall dwell
in thy presence.

[e]Psa. lxxi. 4——[f]Ver. 1——[g]Psa. xxxv. 7; lvii. 6; cxix. 110; cxli. 9; Jer. xviii. 22——[h]Or, *let them* not *be exalted*——[i]Deut. xxxii. 27——[k]Psa. vii. 16; xciv. 23; Prov. xii. 13; xviii. 7——[l]Psa. xi. 6

[m]Heb. *a man of tongue*——[n]Or, *an evil speaker, a wicked man of violence, be established in the earth; let him be hunted to* his *overthrow*——[o]1 Kings viii. 45; Psa. ix. 4——[p]Job i. 1; Psa. lxviii. 10; Prov. ii. 21; xi. 20; xiv. 11

calumnies against me; and those of the most virulent nature.

Verse 4. *Preserve me from the violent man*] Saul again; who was as headstrong and violent in all his measures, as he was cruel, and inflexibly bent on the destruction of David.

Verse 5. *Have hid a snare for me*] They hunted David as they would a dangerous wild beast: one while striving to *pierce* him with the spear; another to *entangle* him in their snares, so as to take and sacrifice him before the people, on pretence of his being an *enemy to the state.*

Selah] This is the truth.

Verse 7. *Thou hast covered my head*] Not only when I fought with the proud blaspheming Philistine; but in the various attempts made against my life by my sworn enemies.

Verse 8. *Further not his wicked device*] He knew his enemies still desired his death, and were plotting to accomplish it; and here he prays that God may disappoint and confound them. The *Chaldee* understands this of *Doeg.*

Verse 10. *Let burning coals*] The *Chaldee* considers this as spoken against *Ahithophel,* who was head of a conspiracy against David; and translates this verse thus: "Let coals from heaven fall upon them, precipitate them into the fire of hell, and into miry pits, from which they shall not have a resurrection to eternal life." This is a proof that the Jews did believe in a resurrection of the body, and an eternal life for that body, in the case of the righteous.

Verse 11. *Let not an evil speaker be established*] איש לשון *ish lashon,* "a man of tongue." There is much force in the rendering of this clause in the *Chaldee* גבר דמשתעי לישן תליתי *gebar demishtai lishan telithai,* "The man of detraction, or *inflammation,* with the *three-forked tongue.*" He whose tongue is *set on fire from hell;* the tale-bearer, slanderer, and dealer in scandal: *with the three-forked tongue;* wounding *three* at once: his *neighbour* whom he slanders; the *person* who receives the slander; and *himself* who deals in it. What a just description of a character which God, angels, and good men must detest! Let not such a one be established in the land; let him be unmasked; let no person trust him; and let all join together to hoot him out of society. "He shall be hunted by the angel of death, and thrust into hell."—CHALDEE.

Verse 12. *The cause of the afflicted*] Every person who is *persecuted* for righteousness' sake has God for his *peculiar help* and *refuge;* and the *persecutor* has the same God for his *especial enemy.*

Verse 13. *The righteous shall give thanks*] For thou wilt support and deliver him.

The upright shall dwell in thy presence.] Shall be admitted to the most intimate intercourse with God.

The *persecuted* have ever been dear to God Almighty; and the *martyrs* were, in an especial manner, his delight; and in proportion as he loved *those,* so must he hate and detest *these.*

ANALYSIS OF THE HUNDRED AND FORTIETH PSALM

David, being persecuted by Saul, *Doeg,* and the men of *Ziph,* prays to God against their evil tongues. But the fathers apply it more largely to the Church, in its persecution by wicked men and devils.

The Psalm is divided into *four* parts:—

I. A petition to be delivered from his enemies, whom he describes, ver. 1-6.

II. A protestation of his confidence in God, ver. 6, 7.

III. A prayer against them, ver. 8-11.

IV. A manifestation of his hope, that God will maintain his just cause, ver. 12, 13.

I. He first summarily proposes his petition.

1. "Deliver me, O Lord," &c. From Saul, *Doeg,* or the devil.

2. "Preserve me," &c. From his violence and malice, and their effects. 1. Evil counsels, and wicked stratagems: "Which imagine mischief," &c. 2. From their evil words, which were consonant with their thoughts.

"They have sharpened their tongues," &c. With calumnies and frauds.

"Like a serpent," &c. Their bitter words are as the poison of the *viper* and *adder*, or the *asp*, which, without pain, extinguishes life.

He repeats his petition: "Keep me, O Lord," &c.

To move God, he shows their intentions.

1. "They have purposed," &c.: To make me walk slowly, or not at all, in the ways of God; to turn me back.

2. The method they took to attain their purpose: "The proud have laid a snare," &c.: as hunters do for birds and beasts. So the devil shows the bait, but hides the hook: under pleasure he hides the bitterness of its reward and consequences.

II. He implores aid from God against the evil and danger.

1. "I said unto the Lord," &c. I do not cast away my confidence.

2. "Hear the voice," &c.

Better to show the ground of his constancy, he declares,—

1. What esteem he had for his God: "Thou art the strength," &c. My fortification against all my enemies.

2. What he had formerly done for him: "Thou hast covered my head," &c.

III. The other part of his petition consists in praying against their plots.

1. "Grant not, O Lord," &c. Let them not have their wishes.

2. "Further not his wicked device," &c. Give them no prosperity in them.

3. "Lest they exalt themselves," &c. Triumph in my being conquered by them.

After praying against them, predicts their punishment: "As for the head of those that compass me about," &c.

1. "Let the mischief of their own lips," &c.

2. Deal severely with them: "Let burning coals," &c. Let them suffer extreme punishment: "Let them be cast into the fire," &c.

3. "Let not an evil speaker," &c.—a liar, flatterer, &c., "be established in the earth."

4. "Evil shall hunt," &c. Give no rest, but pursue the wicked man to his utter ruin; all those who persecute the Church, who write their laws in her blood.

IV. To the infliction of punishment on the wicked, he subjoins, by an antithesis, the promise of God for the defence of the righteous, and so concludes.

1. "I know," &c. Am certainly persuaded by my own experience, and the example of my forefathers, whom thou hast delivered in their trials and temptations.

2. "That the Lord will maintain," &c. He may defer his help and deliverance; but he will not take it from them.

And this he confirms and amplifies from the final cause, which is double.

1. That they praise him: "Surely the righteous shall give thanks," &c. Being delivered, they attribute the honour, not to themselves, or their innocency or merit, but give the glory of his grace and love to God alone.

2. That they remain before him in his Church militant and triumphant. That they may "dwell in thy presence," &c. Walk before his face here, dwell in his favour, and enjoy the beatific vision hereafter.

PSALM CXLI

The psalmist prays that his devotions may be accepted, 1, 2. *That he may be enabled so to watch that he do not offend with his tongue; and that he may be preserved from wickedness*, 3, 4. *His willingness to receive reproof*, 5. *He complains of disasters*, 6, 7. *His trust in God, and prayer against his enemies*, 8–10.

A Psalm of David

A. M. cir. 2943
B. C. cir. 1061
Sauli, Regis
Israelitarum,
cir. annum
35

LORD, I cry unto thee: [a]make
haste unto me; give ear unto my voice, when I cry unto thee.
2 Let [b]my prayer be [c]set
forth before thee [d]*as* incense;
and [e]the lifting up of my hands
as [f]the evening sacrifice.
3 Set a watch, O LORD, before
my mouth; keep the door of my lips.

A. M. cir. 2943
B. C. cir. 1061
Sauli, Regis
Israelitarum,
cir. annum
35

[a]Psa. lxx. 5——[b]Rev. v. 8; viii. 3, 4——[c]Heb. *directed*——[d]Rev. viii. 3——[e]Psa. cxxxiv. 2; 1 Tim. ii. 8——[f]Exod. xxix. 39

NOTES ON PSALM CXLI

This Psalm is generally attributed to *David*, and considered to have been composed during his persecution by Saul. Some suppose that he made it at the time that he formed the resolution to go to *Achish, king of Gath;* see 1 Sam. xxvi. It is generally thought to be an *evening prayer*, and has long been used as such in the service of the Greek Church. It is in several places very obscure.

Verse 1. *Lord, I cry unto thee*] Many of David's Psalms begin with *complaints;* but they are not those of *habitual plaint* and *peevishness.* He was in frequent troubles and difficulties, and he always sought help in God. He ever appears *in earnest;* at no time is there any evidence that the devotion of David was *formal.* He *prayed, meditated, supplicated, groaned, cried*, and even *roared*, as he tells us, for the disquietude of his soul. He had speedy answers; for he had much *faith*, and was always in *earnest.*

Verse 2. As *incense*] Incense was offered every morning and evening before the Lord, on the golden altar, before the veil of the sanctuary. Exod. xxix. 39, and Num. xxviii. 4.

As *the evening sacrifice.*] This was a burnt-offering, accompanied with flour and salt. But it does not appear that David refers to any

A. M. cir. 2943
B. C. cir. 1061
Sauli, Regis
Israelitarum,
cir. annum
35

4 Incline not my heart to *any*
evil thing, to practise wicked
works with men that work iniquity: [g]and let me not eat of
their dainties.
5 [h]Let [i]the righteous smite me; *it shall be*
a kindness: and let him reprove me; *it shall*
be an excellent oil, *which* shall not break my
head: for yet my prayer also *shall be* in their
calamities.
6 When their judges are overthrown in stony
places, they shall hear my words; for they
are sweet.
7 Our bones are scattered [k]at
the grave's mouth, as when one
cutteth and cleaveth *wood* upon
the earth.
8 But [l]mine eyes *are* unto thee, O GOD
the Lord: in thee is my trust; [m]leave not
my soul destitute.
9 Keep me from [n]the snares *which* they
have laid for me, and the gins of the workers
of iniquity.
10 [o]Let the wicked fall into their own nets,
whilst that I withal [p]escape.

[g]Prov. xxiii. 6——[h]Prov. ix. 8; xix. 25; xxiii. 12; Gal. vi. 1——[i]Or, *Let the righteous smite me kindly, and reprove me; let not* their *precious oil break my head*, &c.

[k]2 Cor. i. 9——[l]2 Chron. xx. 12; Psa. xxv. 15; cxxiii. 1, 2——[m]Heb. *make not my soul bare*——[n]Psa. cxix. 110; cxl. 5; cxlii. 3——[o]Psa. xxxv. 8——[p]Heb. *pass over*

sacrifice, for he uses not זבח *zebach*, which is almost universally used for a *slaughtered animal;* but מנחה *minchah*, which is generally taken for a *gratitude-offering* or *unbloody* sacrifice. The literal translation of the passage is, "Let my prayer be established for incense before thy faces; and the lifting up of my hands for the evening oblation." The psalmist appears to have been at this time at a distance from the sanctuary, and therefore could not perform the Divine worship in the way prescribed by the law. What could he do? Why, as he could not worship according to the *letter* of the law, he will worship God according to the *spirit;* then *prayer* is accepted in the place of *incense;* and the *lifting up of his hands, in gratitude and self-dedication* to God, is accepted in the place of the *evening minchah* or *oblation.* Who can deplore the necessity that obliged the psalmist to worship God in this way?

Verse 3. *Set a watch, O Lord, before my mouth*] While there are so many spies on my actions and words, I have need to be doubly guarded, that my enemies may have no advantage against me. Some think the prayer is against *impatience;* but if he were now going to Gath, it is more natural to suppose that he was praying to be preserved from *dishonouring the truth*, and from making *sinful concessions* in a heathen land; and at a court where, from his circumstances, it was natural to suppose he might be *tempted to apostasy* by the heathen party. The following verse seems to support this opinion.

Verse 4. *Let me eat not of their dainties.*] This may refer either to eating things *forbidden by the law;* or to the partaking in *banquets* or *feasts in honour of idols.*

Verse 5. *Let the righteous smite me*] This verse is extremely difficult in the original. The following translation, in which the *Syriac, Vulgate, Septuagint, Æthiopic*, and *Arabic* nearly agree, appears to me to be the best: "Let the righteous chastise me in mercy, and instruct me: but let not the oil of the wicked anoint my head. It shall not adorn (יני *yani*, from נוה *navah*) my head; for still my prayer shall be against their wicked works."

The oil of the wicked may here mean his *smooth flattering speeches;* and the psalmist intimates that he would rather suffer the *cutting* reproof of the righteous than the *oily talk* of the flatterer. If this were the case, how few are there now-a-days of his mind! On referring to Bishop *Horsley*, I find his translation is something similar to my own:—

Let the just one smite me, let the pious remove me.
Let not the ointment of the impious anoint my head.
But still I will intrude in their calamities.

Verse 6. *When their judges are overthrown in stony places*] בידי סלע *biyedey sela*, "In the hands of the rock." Does this *rock* signify a *strong* or *fortified place;* and its *hands* the *garrison* which have occupied it, by whom these judges were overthrown? If we knew the occasion on which this Psalm was made, we might be the better able to understand the *allusions* in the text.

They shall hear my words; for they are sweet.] Some think there is here an allusion to David's generous treatment of Saul in the cave of En-gedi, and afterwards at the hill of Hachilah, in this verse, which might be translated: "Their judges have been dismissed in the rocky places; and have heard my words, that they were sweet." Or perhaps there may be a reference to the *death of Saul* and his *sons*, and the very disastrous defeat of the Israelites at *Gilboa.* If so, the *seventh* verse will lose its chief difficulty, *Our bones are scattered at the grave's mouth;* but if we take them as referring to the *slaughter of the priests at Nob*, then, instead of translating לפי שאול *lephi sheol, at the grave's mouth*, we may translate *at the command of Saul;* and then the verse will point out the *manner* in which those servants of the Lord were massacred; *Doeg cut them in pieces; hewed them down* as one cleaveth wood. Some understand all this of the *cruel usage* of the captives in Babylon. I could add other conjectures, and contend for my own; but they are all too vague to form a just ground for decided opinion.

Verse 8. *But mine eyes* are *unto thee*] In all times, in all places, on all occasions, I will cleave unto the Lord, and put my whole confidence in him.

Verse 10. *Let the wicked fall into their own*

nets] This is generally the case; those who lay snares for others fall into them themselves. *Harm watch, harm catch*, says the old adage. How many cases have occurred where the spring guns that have been set for thieves have shot some of the family! I have known some dismal cases of this kind, where some of the most amiable lives have been sacrificed to this accursed machine.

Whilst—I withal escape.] They alone are guilty; they alone spread the nets and gins; I am innocent, and God will cause me to escape.

Analysis of the Hundred and Forty-first Psalm

The contents and sum of the Psalm are the following:—

I. His prayer, ver. 1, 2.

II. That God would restrain his tongue, and compose his mind, that through anger or impatience he offend not, ver. 3, 4.

III. He prays that if he must be reproved, it be by the just, not the unjust man, ver. 5; whose judgment he declares, ver. 5, 6, and will not have any society with him.

IV. He shows the malice of the wicked to good men, ver. 6, 7.

V. He puts his trust in God, and prays to be delivered from snares, ver. 8-10.

I. 1. "Lord, I cry unto thee," &c. Speedily hear my prayer, which is fervently and affectionately addressed to thee.

2. "Let my prayer be set forth before thee," &c. Which was offered with the sacrifice. Why does David pray that his prayer might be accepted as the evening rather than the morning sacrifice? Perhaps the evening sacrifice might be more noble, as a figure of Christ's sacrifice on the cross, which was in the evening.

II. His second petition is, that God would restrain his tongue, that he might know when to speak and when to be silent. The metaphor is taken from the watch and gate of a city, which, to be safely kept, no one must be suffered to go in or out that ought not. The gate will not be sufficient without the watch; for it will be always shut, or ever open.

His third petition is for his heart, because it is deceitful above all things. Man is weak without the grace of God.

1. "Incline not my heart," &c. Suffer it not to be bent, or set on any evil thing.

2. "Incline not my heart to practices," &c. To do iniquity, being invited by their example.

3. "Let me not eat," &c. Partake with them in their feasts, doctrines, feigned sanctity, power, riches, or dignities.

III. His fourth petition is, that if reproved, it may be in the kindness of friendship, not revenge or bitterness.

1. "Let the righteous smite me," &c. Smite with a reproof.

2. "It shall be a kindness," &c. I shall account it an act of charity, and I will love him for it.

3. "And let him reprove me," &c. An excellent oil, to heal my wounds of sin.

IV. His next petition he prefaces thus: "Let my prayer," &c. "When their judges are overthrown," &c., refers to the judicature: the chief seats, authorities, &c., are swallowed up, as men are by the sea; as the ship is dashed against the rock, and broken to pieces.

And this sense the following verse will justify: "Our bones are scattered," &c. They beset me and my company so closely, that we despair of life; and our bones must be scattered here and there in the wilderness, except thou, O Lord, succour us.

V. Therefore he presents his last petition, which has two parts. 1. "But mine eyes are unto thee," &c. 2. "Leave not my soul destitute."

1. For his own safety: "Leave not my soul," &c. Let me not fall into their hands.

2. Which prayer is grounded on his confidence in God: "Mine eyes are unto thee," &c. I depend on and look to thee alone for deliverance.

3. "Keep me from the snares," &c. From their frauds and ambushes.

Lastly, he imprecates confusion on the heads of his enemies.

1. "Let the wicked fall," &c.

2. "Whilst that I withal escape." Pass by or through them unhurt.

PSALM CXLII

The psalmist, in great distress and difficulty, calls upon God, 1–7.

XXIX. DAY. EVENING PRAYER

[a]Maschil [b]of David; A Prayer [c]when he was in the cave

I [d]CRIED unto the LORD with my voice; with my voice unto the LORD did I make my supplication.

2 [e]I poured out my complaint before him; I showed before him my trouble.

3 [f]When my spirit was overwhelmed within me, then thou knewest my path. [g]In the way wherein I walked have they privily laid a snare for me.

[a]Psa. lvii. title——[b]Or, A Psalm *of David, giving instruction*——[c]1 Sam. xxii. 1; xxiv. 3

[d]1 Sam. vii. 8; Psa. cvii. 19——[e]Psa. cii. title; Isa. xxvi. 16——[f]Psa. cxliii. 4——[g]Psa. cxl. 5

NOTES ON PSALM CXLII

The title says, "An Instruction of David," or a Psalm of David giving instruction; "A Prayer when he was in the cave."

David was *twice* in great peril in *caves*. 1. At the cave of *Adullam*, when he fled from Achish, king of Gath, 1 Sam. xxii. 2. When he was in the cave of *En-gedi*, where he had taken refuge from the pursuit of Saul; and the latter, without knowing that David was in it, had gone into it on some necessary occasion,

4 [h]I [i]looked on *my* right hand, and beheld, but [k]*there was* no man that would know me: refuge [l]failed me; [m]no man cared for my soul.

5 I cried unto thee, O LORD: I said, [n]Thou *art* my refuge *and* [o]my portion [p]in the land of the living.

6 Attend unto my cry; for I am [q]brought very low: deliver me from my persecutors; for they are stronger than I.

7 Bring my soul out of prison, that I may praise thy name: [r]the righteous shall compass me about; [s]for thou shalt deal bountifully with me.

---

[h]Psa. lxix. 20——[i]Or, *Look on the right hand, and see* [k]Psa. xxxi. 11; lxxxviii. 8, 18——[l]Heb. *perished from me* [m]Heb. *no man sought after my soul*

[n]Psa. xlvi. 1; xci. 2——[o]Psa. xvi. 5; lxxiii. 26; cxix. 57; Lam. iii. 24——[p]Psa. xxvii. 13——[q]Psa. cxvi. 6 [r]Psa. xxxiv. 2——[s]Psa. xiii. 6; cxix. 17

---

1 Sam. xxiv. If the inscription can be depended on, the *cave of En-gedi* is the most likely of the two, for the scene laid here. But were there doubts concerning the legitimacy of the title, I should refer the Psalm to the state of the captives in Babylon, to which a great part of the Psalms refer. Bishop *Horsley* calls it "A Prayer of the Messiah taken and deserted." It may be so: but where is the *evidence*, except in the conjectural system of *Origen*.

Verse 1. *I cried unto the Lord*] See on the *first* verse of the preceding Psalm.

Verse 3. *Then thou knewest my path.*] When Saul and his army were about the cave in which I was hidden, *thou knewest my path*—that I had then no way of escape but by *miracle:* but thou didst not permit them to *know* that I was wholly in their power.

Verse 4. There was *no man that would know me*] This has been applied to the time in which our Lord was deserted by his disciples. As to the case of David in the cave of En-gedi, he had no refuge: for what were the handful of men that were with him to Saul and his army?

Verse 5. *Thou* art *my refuge*] Even in these most disastrous circumstances, I will put my trust in thee.

Verse 6. *I am brought very low*] Never was I so near total ruin before.

Deliver me from my persecutors] They are now in full possession of the only means of my escape.

They are stronger than I.] What am I and my men against this well-appointed armed multitude, with their king at their head.

Verse 7. *Bring my soul out of prison*] Bring נפשי *naphshi*, my *life*, out of this *cave* in which it is now *imprisoned;* Saul and his men being in possession of the entrance.

The righteous shall compass me about] יכתרו *yachtiru*, they *shall crown me;* perhaps meaning that the pious Jews, on the death of Saul, would cheerfully join together to make him king, being convinced that God, by his *bountiful dealings with him*, intended that it should be so. The *old Psalter*, which is imperfect from the *twenty-first* verse of Psalm cxix. to the end of Psalm cxli., concludes this Psalm thus: "Lede my saule oute of corrupcion of my body; that corrupcion is bodely pyne, in whilk my saule is anguyst; after that in Godes house, sal al be louyng (praising) of the."

ANALYSIS OF THE HUNDRED AND FORTY-SECOND PSALM

The substance of this Psalm is the earnest prayer of the psalmist that he might be delivered from the danger he was in.

The parts are,

I. An exordium; in which he

1. Shows what he did in his trouble; took himself to prayer, ver. 1, 2.

2. Then his consternation and anxiety of mind, which arose from the malice and craft of his enemies, and want of help from his friends, ver. 3, 4.

II. His address and petition to God, ver. 5-7.

1. The two first verses show the psalmist's intention. "I cried unto the Lord," &c. 2. "I poured out my supplication," &c.

This he amplifies,—

1. From his vehemence: "I cried, I supplicated."

2. From the object: "Unto the Lord." I invoked him, and no other.

3. From the instrument: "With my voice."

4. From his humility in prayer. It was a *supplication.*

5. From his free and full confession: "I poured out," &c.

6. From his sincerity and confidence in God.

The reason was:—

1. This I did "when my spirit was overwhelmed," &c. There being no sufficiency in me, I betook myself to the all-sufficient God.

2. "For thou knowest my path," &c. My actions and intentions.

The craft and subtlety of his enemies, especially *Saul.*

1. "In the way wherein I walked," &c. My vocation.

2. "Have they privily laid," &c. Saul gave him his daughter *Michal* to be a snare to him; and a dowry he must have of a hundred foreskins of the Philistines, that David might fall by their hands.

His destitution in the time of trouble.

1. "I looked on my right hand," &c. But no friend was near: "There was no man," &c. The miserable have few friends.

2. "Refuge failed me," &c. I had no place of safety.

3. "No man cared," &c. Regarded my life, or cared if I perished.

II. The psalmist, having no human help, calls upon God.

1. "Thou art my refuge," &c. My hiding-place.

2. "Thou art my portion," &c. While I live in this world.

Then he sends up his prayer, fortified by a double argument.

1. From the lamentable condition he was brought into: "I was brought low," &c.

2. From the malice and power of his enemies: "Deliver me," &c.

Again he renews his prayer, and presses it from the final cause: "Bring my soul," &c.

Upon which follow two effects:—

1. His gratitude: "That I may praise thy name."

2. That of others: "The righteous shall compass me," &c. Come unto me.

3. The reason for this: "For thou shalt deal bountifully with me." Bestow favours upon me, having delivered me from my former miseries; which men seeing, who are commonly the friends of prosperity, will magnify and resort to me.

PSALM CXLIII

The psalmist prays for mercy, and deprecates judgment, 1, 2. *His persecutions,* 3. *His earnest prayer for deliverance,* 4–9. *Prays for God's quickening Spirit,* 10, 11. *And for the total discomfiture of his adversaries,* 12.

A Psalm of David

A. M. cir. 2981 B. C. cir. 1023 Davidis, Regis Israelitarum, cir. annum 33

HEAR my prayer, O LORD, give ear to my supplications: [a]in thy faithfulness answer me, *and* in thy righteousness.

2 And [b]enter not into judgment with thy servant: for [c]in thy sight shall no man living be justified.

3 For the enemy hath persecuted my soul; he hath smitten my life down to the ground; he hath made me to dwell in darkness as those that have been long dead.

4 [d]Therefore is my spirit overwhelmed within me; my heart within me is desolate.

A. M. cir. 2981 B. C. cir. 1023 Davidis, Regis Israelitarum, cir. annum 33

5 [e]I remember the days of old; I meditate on all thy works; I muse on the work of thy hands.

6 [f]I stretch forth my hands unto thee: [g]my soul *thirsteth* after thee, as a thirsty land. Selah.

7 Hear me speedily, O LORD: my spirit faileth: hide not thy face from me, [h]lest [i]I be like unto them that go down into the pit.

8 Cause me to hear thy loving-kindness [k]in the morning; for in thee do I trust: [l]cause me to know the way wherein I should walk; for [m]I lift up my soul unto thee.

---

[a]Psa. xxxi. 1——[b]Job xiv. 3——[c]Exod. xxxiv. 7; Job iv. 17; ix. 2; xv. 14; xxv. 4; Psa. cxxx. 3; Eccles. vii. 20; Rom. iii. 20; Gal. ii. 16——[d]Psa. lxxvii. 3; cxlii. 3

[e]Psa. lxxvii. 5, 10, 11——[f]Psa. lxxxviii. 9——[g]Psa. lxiii. 1——[h]Psa. xxviii. 1——[i]Or, *for I am become like,* &c.; Psa. lxxxviii. 4——[k]See Psa. xlvi. 5——[l]Psa. v. 8 [m]Psa. xxv. 1

NOTES ON PSALM CXLIII

The *Hebrew* and all the *Versions* attribute this Psalm to *David;* and the *Vulgate, Septuagint, Æthiopic* and *Arabic* state that it was composed on the rebellion of his son Absalom: nor is there any thing in the Psalm that positively disagrees with this inscription. This is the last of the seven Psalms styled *penitential.*

Verse 1. *In thy faithfulness answer me*] Thou hast promised to support me in my difficulties, and, though my children should forsake me, never to withdraw thy loving-kindness from me. See the present unnatural rebellion of my son. Lord, undertake for me!

Verse 2. *Enter not into judgment*] אל תבוא *al tabo.* Do not come into court, either as a *Witness* against me, or as a *Judge,* else I am ruined; for thou hast seen all my ways that they are evil, and thy justice requires thee to punish me. Nor can any soul that has ever lived be justified in the sight of thy justice and righteousness. Had I my desert from thee, I should have worse than even my unnatural son intends me. O what a relief is *Jesus crucified* to a soul in such circumstances!

Verse 3. *He hath made me to dwell in darkness*] Literally, *in dark places.* This may be understood of David's taking refuge in *caves* and *dens* of the earth, to escape from his persecuting son; yea, even to take refuge in the *tombs,* or *repositories* of the dead.

Verse 4. *Therefore is my spirit*] I am deeply depressed in spirit, and greatly afflicted in body.

My heart within me is desolate.] It has no companion of its sorrows, no sympathetic friend. I am utterly destitute of comfort.

Verse 5. *I remember the days of old*] Thou hast often helped me, often delivered me. I will therefore trust in thee, for thy mercy is not clean gone from me.

Verse 6. *I stretch forth my hands*] This is a natural action. All in distress, or under the influence of *eager desire,* naturally extend their hands and arms, as if to catch at help and obtain succour.

As a thirsty land.] Parched and burned by the sun, longs for rain, so does my thirsty soul for the living God.

Verse 7. *Hear me speedily*] מהר *maher, make haste* to answer me. A few hours, and my state may be irretrievable. In a short time my unnatural son may put an end to my life.

Verse 8. *Cause me to hear thy loving-kindness in the morning*] This petition was probably offered in the *night-season.* David had despatched his messengers in all directions; and prays to God that he might by the morning get some good news.

Cause me to know the way wherein I should walk] Absalom and his partisans are in possession of all the country. I know not in what direction to go, that I may not fall in with

A. M. cir. 2981
B. C. cir. 1023
Davidis, Regis
Israelitarum,
cir. annum
33

9 Deliver me, O LORD, from
mine enemies: I [n]flee unto thee
to hide me.
10 [o]Teach me to do thy
will; for thou *art* my God: [p]thy Spirit
is good; lead me into [q]the land of uprightness.

11 [r]Quicken me, O LORD,
for thy name's sake: for thy
righteousness' sake bring my
soul out of trouble.
12 And of thy mercy [s]cut off mine enemies,
and destroy all them that afflict my soul: for
[t]I *am* thy servant.

A. M. cir. 2981
B. C. cir. 1023
Davidis, Regis
Israelitarum,
cir. annum
33

---

[n]Heb. *hide me with thee*——[o]Psa. xxv. 4, 5; cxxxix. 24——[p]Neh. ix. 20

[q]Isa. xxvi. 10——[r]Psa. cxix. 25, 37, 40, &c.——[s]Psa. liv. 5——[t]Psa. cxvi. 16

---

them: point out by thy especial providence the path I should take.

Verse 9. *I flee unto thee to hide me.*] That I may not be *found* by my enemies, who seek my life to destroy it.

Verse 10. *Teach me to do thy will*] רצונך *retsonecha*, thy *pleasure.* To be found doing the will of God is the only safe state for man.

Thy Spirit is *good*] The Author of every *good desire* and *holy purpose.*

Lead me] *Let it lead me* by its continued inspirations and counsels.

Into the land of uprightness.] "Into a right land," CHALDEE. Into the place where I shall be safe. The old Psalter has, **Thi goste gude sal lede me into rygt lande.**

Verse 11. *Quicken me*] I am as a dead man, and my hopes are almost dead within me.

Verse 12. *And of thy mercy*] To *me* and the *kingdom.*

Cut off mine enemies] Who, if they succeed, will destroy the very *form of godliness.* The steps he has already taken show that even *morality* shall have no countenance, if Absalom reign.

I am thy servant.] Whoever is disloyal to me, I will love and serve thee.

For a full explanation of this Psalm, as applied to penitents, see the analysis.

ANALYSIS OF THE HUNDRED AND FORTY-THIRD PSALM

David, being driven from *Jerusalem* by his son *Absalom,* wisely calls to mind his sin, as being the cause of it.

This Psalm has four parts:—

I. A prayer for remission of sin, grounded on God's promise, ver. 1; not on his own worthiness, ver. 2.

II. A narration of the sad state of his affairs, ver. 3, 4.

III. The comfort he received in his sad condition, and whence, ver. 5, 6.

IV. His petition, containing many particulars and reasons, ver. 7 to the end.

I. He prays for audience: "Hear my prayer, O Lord," &c. He does not plainly express the matter he prayed for; but it may be gathered from the context that it was for remission of sin.

1. "In thy faithfulness," &c. Thou art a faithful God, and hast promised to pardon the penitent. I am a penitent; have mercy on me.

2. "And in thy righteousness," &c. Which here signifies mercy, loving-kindness.

This sense appears more plainly from the next verse.

1. "And enter not into judgment," &c. Call me not to a strict account at the bar of thy justice. This he deprecates; so that *Justitia* in the former verse could not be taken for that justice.

2. "For in thy sight," &c. Not I, nor any other man: pardon me, then, for the sake of thy mercy and promise, not my merits.

II. And now he enters upon the narration of his sad condition.

1. "For the enemy hath persecuted," &c. My son Absalom seeks my life: but it was Satan who enticed me to adultery and homicide.

2. "He hath smitten," &c. Humbled me; made me a lover of earth, vile in thy sight.

3. "He hath made me to dwell," &c. After Satan had entangled me with earthly pleasures, I was in spiritual darkness, and saw not the way of life, any more than those who have been long dead.

The effect this darkness produced was fear and consternation.

1. "Therefore is my spirit," &c. I suffered a kind of swoon in my soul; I was ready to faint when I considered thy holiness and my impurity.

2. "My heart within me," &c. Far from comfort in heavy trouble.

III. In this sadness of heart and mind,—

1. "I remember the days of old," &c. Thy past kindness to me and to others.

2. "I meditate," &c. I did not slightly run them over, but pondered on them.

And I derived great profit from my meditation; for,

1. "I stretch forth my hands," &c. I began earnestly to pray to thee.

2. "My soul thirsteth," &c. After thy righteousness, as the dry land wanting water. For as the earth without rain has no consistence, but is pulverized; so the soul not moistened with the grace of God falls on the right and left hand into temptation, and brings forth no fruit to God's glory.

IV. The sad case in which David was, upon a sense of God's indignation, makes him seek out a remedy.

1. "Hear me speedily," &c. And his reason for this is the sad condition in which he was till God was pacified for his sin.

2. "Hide not thy face," &c. Thy presence, thy favour.

His next petition resembles the former in substance.

1. "Cause me to hear," &c. Thy pardoning mercy out of thy word; it is thy Spirit which must work with it to save me.

2. "In the morning," &c. Betimes, speedily, quickly, &c.

3. His reason: "For in thee do I trust," &c. I did not let go my hold even in my extremity; but still hoped against hope.

His third petition is—

1. "Cause me to know," &c. The psalmist,

being truly penitent, fears to relapse into his pardoned sin, and prays to God for grace and direction.

2. His reason: "For I lift up my soul," &c. My purpose, to serve thee.

His fourth petition is—

1. "Deliver me, O Lord," &c. From the devil and all his temptations.

2. His reason: "I flee unto thee," &c. From them.

His fifth petition resembles his third.

1. "Teach me to do thy will," &c. Both by an active and passive obedience may I know thy will perfectly; in adversity, to submit to it; in prosperity, to do it without pride or presumption.

2. His reason: "For thou art my God." Who hast promised me thy help; and from whom all my good proceeds, being and well-being.

His sixth petition: "Thy Spirit is good." Not mine. Let then thy good Spirit instruct and lead me in the right way.

His seventh petition is—

1. "Quicken me, O Lord," &c. Restore life; justify me fully.

2. "For thy name's sake." Not my merits, but thy mercy, and the glory that will accrue to thy name in pardoning a penitent soul.

3. He goes on: "For thy righteousness' sake," &c. Freedom he desires; but still at the hands of God's infinite mercy.

His last petition is for the destruction of Satan's kingdom.

1. "Of thy mercy cut off mine enemies," &c.

2. His reason: "For I am thy servant," &c. A follower; one under thy patronage and protection; one of thy family honoured with the dignity of being thy servant, and well contented and pleased to perform my duty and service.

PSALM CXLIV

The psalmist praises God for his goodness, 1, 2. *Exclamations relative to the vanity of human life,* 3, 4. *He prays against his enemies,* 5–8; *and extols God's mercy for the temporal blessings enjoyed by his people,* 9–15.

XXX. DAY. MORNING PRAYER

A Psalm of David

A. M. cir. 2981 B. C. cir. 1023 Davidis, Regis Israelitarum, cir. annum 33

BLESSED *be* the LORD [a]my
strength, [b]which teacheth
my hands [c]to war, *and* my
fingers to fight:
2 [d]My [e]goodness, and my fortress; my
high tower, and my deliverer; my shield, and
he in whom I trust; who subdueth my people under me.
3 [f]LORD, what *is* man, that
thou takest knowledge of him!
or the son of man, that thou makest account
of him!
4 [g]Man is like to vanity: [h]his days *are*
as a shadow that passeth away.

---

[a]Heb. *my rock;* Psa. xviii. 2, 31——[b]2 Sam. xxii. 35; Psa. xviii. 34——[c]Heb. *to the war,* &c.——[d]2 Sam. xxii. 2, 3, 40, 48

[e]Or, *My mercy*——[f]Job vii. 17; Psa. viii. 4; Heb. ii. 6——[g]Job iv. 19; xiv. 2; Psa. xxxix. 5; lxii. 9——[h]Psa. cii. 11

NOTES ON PSALM CXLIV

The *Hebrew*, and all the *Versions*, attribute this Psalm to *David*. The *Vulgate, Septuagint, Æthiopic*, and *Arabic*, term it, *A Psalm of David against Goliath*. The *Syriac* says, "A Psalm of David when he slew Asaph, the brother of Goliath." *Calmet* thinks, and with much probability, that it was composed by David after the death of Absalom, and the restoration of the kingdom to peace and tranquillity. From a collation of this with Psa. xviii., of which it appears to be an *abridgment*, preserving the same ideas, and the same forms of expression, there can be no doubt of both having proceeded from the same pen, and that David was the author. There is scarcely an expression here of peculiar importance that is not found in the prototype; and for *explanation* I must refer generally to the above Psalm.

Verse 1. *Teacheth my hands to war*] To use *sword, battle-axe*, or *spear*.

And *my fingers to fight*] To use the *bow and arrows*, and the *sling*.

Verse 2. *Who subdueth my people*] Who has once more reduced the nation to a state of loyal obedience. This may refer to the peace after the rebellion of Absalom.

Verse 3. *Lord, what* is *man*] See the notes on Psa. viii. 4, 5. *What is Adam, that thou approvest of him?* Can he do any thing worthy of thy notice? Or *the son of feeble perishing man, that thou shouldest hold him in repute?* What care, love, and attention, dost thou lavish upon him!

Verse 4. *Man is like to vanity*] אדם להבל דמה *Adam lahebel damah*, literally, *Adam is like to Abel*, exposed to the same miseries, accidents, and murderers; for in millions of cases the hands of brothers are lifted up to shed the blood of brothers. What are wars but fratricide in the great human family?

His days are *as a shadow*] The life of *Abel* was promissory of much blessedness; but it afforded merely the *shadow* of *happiness*. He was pure and holy, beloved of his parents, and beloved of God; but, becoming the object of his brother's envy, his life became a sacrifice to his piety.

A. M. cir. 2981
B. C. cir. 1023
Davidis, Regis
Israelitarum,
cir. annum
33

5 [i]Bow thy heavens, O LORD, and come down: [k]touch the mountains, and they shall smoke.

6 [l]Cast forth lightning, and scatter them: shoot out thine arrows, and destroy them.

7 [m]Send thine [n]hand from above; [o]rid me, and deliver me out of great waters, from the hand of [p]strange children;

8 Whose mouth [q]speaketh vanity, and their right hand *is* a right hand of falsehood.

9 I will [r]sing a new song unto thee, O God: upon a psaltery *and* an instrument of ten strings will I sing praises unto thee.

10 [s]*It is he* that giveth [t]salvation unto kings: who delivereth David his servant from the hurtful sword.

11 [u]Rid me, and deliver me from the hand of strange children, whose mouth speaketh vanity, and their right hand *is* a right hand of falsehood:

A. M. cir. 2981
B. C. cir. 1023
Davidis, Regis
Israelitarum,
cir. annum
33

12 That our sons *may be* [v]as plants grown up in their youth; *that* our daughters *may be* as corner stones, [w]polished *after* the similitude of a palace:

13 *That* our garners *may be* full, affording [x]all manner of store: *that* our sheep may bring forth thousands and ten thousands in our streets:

14 *That* our oxen *may be* [y]strong to labour; *that there be* no breaking in, nor going out; that *there be* no complaining in our streets.

15 [z]Happy *is that* people, that is in such a case: *yea,* happy *is that* people, whose God *is* the LORD.

---

[i]Psa. xviii. 9; Isa. lxiv. 1——[k]Psa. civ. 32——[l]Psa. xviii. 13, 14——[m]Psa. xviii. 16——[n]Heb. *hands* [o]Ver. 11; Psa. lxix. 1, 2, 14——[p]Psa. liv. 3; Mal. ii. 11 [q]Psa. xii. 2——[r]Psa. xxxiii. 2, 3; xl. 3

[s]Psa. xviii. 50——[t]Or, *victory*——[u]Ver. 7, 8——[v]Psa. cxxviii. 3——[w]Heb. *cut*——[x]Heb. *from kind to kind* [y]Heb. *able to bear burdens,* or *loaden* with flesh——[z]Deut. xxxiii. 29; Psa. xxxiii. 12; lxv. 4; cxlvi. 5

Verse 5. *Bow thy heavens*] See the note on Psa. xviii. 9.

Verse 6 *Cast forth lightning*] See the note, ib. ver. 13, 14.

Verse 7. *Deliver me out of great waters*] See the note, ib. ver. 16.

Verse 9. *I will sing a new song*] A song of peculiar excellence. I will pour forth all my *gratitude,* and all my *skill,* on its composition. See on Psa. xxxiii. 2, 3.

Verse 10. He *that giveth salvation unto kings*] *Monarchy,* in the principle, is from God: it is that *form of government* which, in the course of the Divine providence, has principally prevailed; and that which, on the whole, has been most beneficial to mankind. God, therefore, has it under his peculiar protection. It is by him that kings reign; and by his special providence they are protected.

Verse 12. *That our sons* may be *as plants*] God had promised to his people, being faithful, THREE *descriptions* of BLESSINGS, Deut. xxviii. 4. 1. The *fruit of the body*—sons and daughters. 2. The *fruits of the ground*—grass and corn in sufficient plenty. 3. *Fruit of the cattle*—"the increase of kine, and flocks of sheep." These are the blessings to which the psalmist refers here, as those in which he might at present exult and triumph: blessings *actually enjoyed* by his people at large; proofs of his mild and paternal government, and of the especial blessing of the Almighty. The people who *were in such a state,* and revolted, had no excuse: they were doubly guilty, as ungrateful both to *God* and *man.*

Verse 13. That *our garners, &c.*] *Our garners are full.* These are not *prayers* put up by David *for such blessings:* but *assertions,* that such blessings were actually in possession. All these expressions should be understood in the *present tense.*

Ten thousands in our streets.] בחצתינו *bechutsotheynu* should be translated in our *pens* or *sheep-walks;* for *sheep bringing forth* in the *streets* of cities or towns is absurd.

Verse 14. *Our oxen* may be *strong to labour*] We have not only an abundance of cattle; but they are of the most strong and vigorous breed.

No breaking in] So well ordered is the *police* of the kingdom, that there are no depredations, no robbers, house-breakers, or marauding parties, in the land; no sudden incursions of neighbouring tribes or banditti breaking into fields or houses, carrying away property, and taking with them the people to sell them into captivity: there is no such *breaking in,* and no such *going out,* in the nation. My *enemies* are either become *friends,* and are united with me in political interests; or are, *through fear,* obliged to *stand aloof.*

Verse 15. *Happy* is that *people*] "O how happy are the people!" Such were his people; and they had not only all this secular happiness, but they had *Jehovah for their God;* and in him had a ceaseless fountain of strength, protection, earthly blessings, and eternal mercies! A people in such a case to rebel, must have the curse of God and man.

ANALYSIS OF THE HUNDRED AND FORTY-FOURTH PSALM

This Psalm is divided into *three* parts:—

I. A thanksgiving, ver. 1-5.

II. A petition, ver. 5-11.

III. A discussion on happiness, and in what it consists, ver. 12, to the end.

I. The prophet gives thanks, and praises God.

1. "Blessed be the Lord:" &c. Who has taught me in a general way the art of war, in a particular way the use of the sling; giving me skill, &c.

2. "He is my strength," &c. The strength I have is from him.

3. "My goodness," &c. Benignity or mercy.

4. "My fortress," &c. To him I fly as to a stronghold.

5. "And my Deliverer." Therefore will I trust in him.

From the consideration of so many benefits, the psalmist exclaims, "Lord what is man," &c.

To which question he replies,—

1. "Man is like to vanity." If God be not his fulness and strength.

2. "His days," &c. God is always the same; but man changes every moment.

II. He prays for God's assistance: "Bow thy heavens," &c. "Cast forth lightning," &c. If men will not acknowledge thy mercy, let them see thy judgments. This first part of his petition against his enemies being ended, he prays,—

1. "Rid me, and deliver me:" &c. From dangers of men.

2. "From the hand of strange children:" &c. Moabites, Philistines, &c.

Upon whom he sets these two characters.

1. "Whose mouth speaketh vanity:" &c. Lies, insincere words.

2. "At their right hand:" &c. They use their power to oppress and deceive.

Then the psalmist exclaims, as in a short hymn—

1. "I will sing a new song," &c. And this I will do because "thou hast given victory," &c. "Thou hast delivered David," &c., from Saul, Absalom, &c.

2. And then he repeats, and concludes his petition as before: "Rid me," &c.

III. His petition being ended, he discourses on the nature of happiness, which is of two kinds, temporal and spiritual. The addition of temporal blessings is pleasant, and promised to the obedient: but godliness is the only safety in this, and especially in the life to come: "For godliness," &c. God created temporal *goods* not merely for the wicked; they are often the rewards of piety. The psalmist therefore prays,—

1. "That our sons," &c. They are the pillars of a house; let them be flourishing.

2. "That our daughters," &c. Stones that join the building, beautiful as well as useful.

3. "That our garners may be full," &c. That we may have abundance.

4. "That our sheep," &c. Our flocks' increase.

5. "That our oxen," &c. May be healthy and strong.

6. "That there be no breaking," &c. No plundering among us.

7. "That there be no complaining," &c. No want of bread, or any cause of tumult. David prays that, during his reign, the people may be happy, and enjoy the fruits of peace.

Then he concludes the Psalm with this acclamation:—

1. "Happy is that people," &c. Those he has described.

2. "Yea, happy," &c. That have the true God for their God; who know God to be their Father, and that he takes care of them, providing for their temporal necessities, and supplying all their spirtual wants. Others understand these words, not as prayers, but as a description of the state *David* and his people were then in. See the notes.

PSALM CXLV

God is praised for his unsearchable greatness, 1, 2; *for his majesty and terrible acts*, 3, 6; *for his goodness and tender mercies to all*, 7–9; *for his power and kingdom*, 10–13; *for his kindness to the distressed*, 14; *for his providence*, 15–17. *He hears and answers prayer*, 18–20. *All should praise him*, 21.

David's [a]*Psalm* of praise

I WILL extol thee, my God, O King; and I will bless thy name for ever and ever.

2 Every day will I bless thee; and I will praise thy name for ever and ever.

3 [b]Great *is* the LORD, and greatly to be

[a]Psa. c. title

[b]Psa. xcvi. 4; cxlvii. 5

NOTES ON PSALM CXLV.

This Psalm is attributed to *David* by the *Hebrew* and all the *Versions.* It is the last of the *acrostic* Psalms; and should contain twenty-two verses, as answering to the twenty-two letters of the Hebrew alphabet; but the verse between the thirteenth and fourteenth, beginning with the letter נ *nun*, is lost out of the present Hebrew copies; but a translation of it is found in the *Syriac, Septuagint, Vulgate, Æthiopic, Arabic,* and *Anglo-Saxon.* See below. It is an incomparable Psalm of praise; and the rabbins have it in such high estimation, that they assert, if a man with sincerity of heart repeat it three times a-day, he shall infallibly enjoy the blessings of the world to come. It does not appear on what particular occasion it was composed; or, indeed, whether there was any occasion but gratitude to God for his ineffable favours to mankind.

Verse 1. *I will extol thee*] I will raise thee on high, I will lift thee up.

I will bless thy name] לעולם ועד *leolam vaed, for ever and onward,* in this and the coming world. This sort of expressions, which are

praised; [c]and [d]his greatness *is* unsearchable.
4 [e]One generation shall praise thy works to another, and shall declare thy mighty acts.
5 I will speak of the glorious honour of thy majesty and of thy wondrous [f]works.
6 And *men* shall speak of the might of thy terrible acts: and I will [g]declare thy greatness.
7 They shall abundantly utter the memory of thy great goodness, and shall sing of thy righteousness.
8 [h]The LORD *is* gracious, and full of compassion; slow to anger, and [i]of great mercy.
9 [k]The LORD *is* good to all: and his tender mercies *are* over all his works.
10 [l]All thy works shall praise thee, O LORD; and thy saints shall bless thee.
11 They shall speak of the glory of thy kingdom, and talk of thy power;
12 To make known to the sons of men his mighty acts, and the glorious majesty of his kingdom.
13 [m]Thy kingdom *is* [n]an everlasting king-

[c]Hebrew, *and of his greatness* there is *no search*——[d]Job v. 9; ix. 10; Romans xi. 33——[e]Isaiah xxxviii. 19——[f]Hebrew *things* or *words*——[g]Hebrew *declare it*——[h]Exodus xxxiv. 6, 7; Numbers xiv. 18; Psalm lxxxvi. 5, 15; ciii. 8——[i]Hebrew, *great in mercy*——[k]Psalm c. 5; Nahum i. 7——[l]Psalm xix. 1——[m]Psalm cxlvi. 10; 1 Timothy i. 17——[n]Hebrew, *a kingdom of all ages*

very difficult to be translated, are on the whole well expressed by those words, in a hymn of Mr. Addison:—

Through all eternity to thee
A joyful song I'll raise;
But O, eternity's too short
To utter all thy praise!

This contains a strong *hyperbole;* but allowable in such cases.

Verse 3. *His greatness* is *unsearchable.*] Literally, *To his mightinesses there is no investigation.* All in God is *unlimited* and *eternal.*

Verse 4. *One generation*] Thy *creating* and *redeeming* acts are recorded in thy *word;* but thy *wondrous providential dealings* with mankind must be handed down by tradition, from generation to generation; for they are in continual occurrence, and consequently innumerable.

Verse 8. *The Lord* is *gracious*] His holy nature is ever *disposed* to show favour.

Full of compassion] Wherever he sees misery, his eye affects his heart.

Slow to anger] When there is even the *greatest provocation.*

Of great mercy.] Great in his *abundant mercy.* These *four* things give us a wonderful display of the goodness of the Divine nature.

Verse 9. *The Lord* is *good to all*] There is not a soul out of hell that is not continually under his *most merciful regards;* so far is he from *willing* or *decreeing before their creation* the damnation of any man.

His tender mercies] His *bowels of compassion* are over all his works; he feels for his intelligent offspring, as the most *affectionate mother* does for the child of her own bosom. And through this matchless mercy, these bowels of compassion, his son Jesus tasted death for every man. How far is all that is here spoken of the nature of God opposed to the Molochian doctrine of the eternal decree of reprobation!

"His grace for every soul is free:
For *his, who forged the dire decree;*
For every reprobate and me."

Verse 10. *All thy works shall praise thee*] Whom? The God *who is good to all.*

Thy saints] חסידיך *chasideycha,* thy *compassionate ones;* those who are partakers of thy *great mercy,* ver. 8. These shall *bless thee,* because they know, they *feel,* that thou willest the salvation of all. The dark, the gloomy, the hard-hearted, the narrow-minded bigots, who never have had thy love shed abroad in their hearts, can unfeelingly deal in the damnation of their fellows.

Verse 12. *To make known*] They delight to recommend their God and Father to others.

Verse 13. *Thy dominion* endureth] There is neither age nor people in and over which God does not manifest his *benignly ruling* power. As the above verse begins with the letter מ *mem,* the next in the order of the alphabet should begin with נ *nun:* but that verse is totally wanting. To say it never was in, is false, because the alphabet is not complete without it; and it is an unanswerable argument to prove the careless manner in which the Jews have preserved the Divine records. Though the *Syriac, Septuagint, Vulgate, Æthiopic, Arabic,* and *Anglo-Saxon,* have a verse, not in the Hebrew text, that answers to the נ *nun,* which is found in no printed copy of the Hebrew Bible; yet one MS., now in Trinity College, Dublin, has it thus, I suppose by correction, in the bottom of the page:—

נאמן יהוה בכל דבריו וחסיד בכל מעשיו:

Neeman Yehovah bechol debaraiv; vechasid bechol maasaiv.

"The Lord is faithful in all his words; and merciful in all his works."

Πιστος Κυριος εν τοις λογοις αυτου· και όσιος εν πασι τοις εργοις αυτου.—SEPTUAGINT.

Fidelis Dominus in omnibus verbis suis: et sanctus in omnibus operibus suis.—VULGATE.

These two Versions, the *Septuagint* and *Vulgate,* are the same with the Hebrew given above. The *Anglo-Saxon* is the same:—

ᵹetrywe driht on eallum wordum heora; ⁊ halig on eallum weorcum his. "True Lord in all words his; and holy in all works his."

The *Latin* text in my old Psalter is the same with the present printed Vulgate: "Fidelis Dominus in omnibus verbis suis; et sanctus in omnibus operibus suis." Thus translated in the same MSS.: **Lorde true in all his words; and holy in al his workes.**

dom, and thy dominion *endureth* throughout all generations.

14 The LORD upholdeth all that fall, and [o]raiseth up all *those that be* bowed down.

15 [p]The eyes of all [q]wait upon thee; and [r]thou givest them their meat in due season.

16 Thou openest thine hand, [s]and satisfiest the desire of every living thing.

17 The LORD *is* righteous in all his ways, and [t]holy in all his works.

18 [u]The LORD *is* nigh unto all them that call upon him, to all that call upon him [v]in truth.

19 He will fulfil the desire of them that fear him: he also will hear their cry, and will save them.

20 [w]The LORD preserveth all them that love him: but all the wicked will he destroy.

21 My mouth shall speak the praise of the LORD: and let all flesh bless his holy name for ever and ever.

[o]Psa. cxlvi. 8——[p]Psa. civ. 27——[q]Or, *look unto thee* [r]Psa. cxxxvi. 25——[s]Psa. civ. 21; cxlvii. 9

[t]Or, *merciful* or *bountiful*——[u]Deut. iv. 7——[v]John iv. 24——[w]Psa. xxxi. 23; xcvii. 10

It is remarkable that the whole verse is wanting in the *Vulgate*, as published in the *Complutensian* Polyglot, as also the *Antwerp* and *Paris* Polyglots, which were taken from it. It is wanting also in the Polyglot Psalter of *Porus*, because he did not find it in the Hebrew text.

Verse 14. *The Lord upholdeth all that fall*] נפלים *nophelim*, the *falling*, or those who are not able to keep their feet; the weak. He *shores* them up; he is their *prop*. No man falls through his own weakness *merely;* if he rely on God, the strongest foe cannot shake him.

Verse 15. *The eyes of all wait upon thee*] What a fine figure! The *young* of all animals look up to *their parents for food.* God is here represented as the *universal Father*, providing food for every living creature.

In due season] The kind of food that is suited to every animal, and to all the *stages of life* in *each animal.* This is a wonderful mystery. It is a fact that all are thus provided for; but *how* is it done? All expect it from God, and not one is dsappointed! For,

Verse 16. *Thou openest thine hand*] What a hand is this that holds in it all the food that meets the desires and necessities of the universe of creatures! A very large volume might be written upon this: The proper kinds of food for the various classes of animals.

Verse 17. *The Lord* is *righteous*] It was the similarity of *this* to the omitted verse, which should have been the *fourteenth*, that caused *it* to be omitted.

Verse 18. *The Lord* is *nigh*] Whoever calls upon God in truth, with a sincere and upright heart, one that *truly desires* his salvation, to that person *God is nigh.* The following verse shows he is not only *near* to praying people, but 1. He will *hear their cry.* 2. *Fulfil their desires.* 3. *Save them.* Reader, lift up thy soul in prayer to this merciful God.

Verse 20. *The Lord preserveth*] He is the keeper of all them that love him.

But all the wicked will be destroy.] They call not upon him; they fight against him, and he will confound and destroy them. There is something curious in the שומר *shomer*, the keeper or guardian of the pious; he is שמיר *shamid*, the destroyer of the wicked. The first word implies he is continually keeping them; the second, that he *causes* the others to be *destroyed.*

Verse 21. *Let all flesh bless his holy name*] He is good to all, wants to save all, actually feeds and preserves all. And as near as שמר *shamar* is to שמד *shamad*, so near is he a *Saviour* to those who stand on the brink of *destruction*, if they will look to him.

For the application of all this Psalm to the Church of Christ, see the *analysis*.

ANALYSIS OF THE HUNDRED AND FORTY-FIFTH PSALM

This hymn is most excellent, both as it regards matter and style. The matter is praise to God; the style, the Hebrew alphabet, the better to assist our memories in recording God's praise.

This Psalm contains,—

I. A proem, or protestation to praise God, ver. 1, 2.

II. A celebration of Divine praises through the whole Psalm, from these arguments:—

I. From the greatness of God, ver. 3.

II. From his wonderful works, ver. 4, which he distinguishes under the following heads:—

1. They are glorious and beautiful, majestic and wonderful, ver. 5.
2. Marvellous, and full of terror, ver. 6.
3. Amiable, and full of goodness, ver. 7-9.

But all wonderful.

III. From his kingdom, and government of it, and in it, ver. 10-21.

IV. A conclusion, ver. 21, in which he performs his protestation of praising God.

I. In the two first verses the psalmist acquaints us what he will do with the whole.

1. "I will extol, I will bless, I will praise."
2. "Thee, my God, my King." I am thy servant, though an earthly king.
3. "Every day," &c. No day shall pass without my praising thee.
4. "For ever and ever." I shall now begin, and a succession of men will continue to hymn and praise thee till the consummation of all things.

II. The first thing he praises God for is his essence. *Great.*

I. "Great is the Lord, and greatly to be praised." Of course this follows:—

"And his greatness is unsearchable." Past our weak capacity to comprehend; higher than the heavens, deeper than hell, having no end. Or if *great* here refer to him as King, then in respect to the extension of his empire over every living creature, he is *great;* he rules over the hearts of the children of men, over their thoughts and affections, and nothing is hidden from his sight.

II. From the essence of God the psalmist passes to his works and effects, which yet set forth his praise: "One generation shall praise," &c. Each age is an eyewitness of thy mighty acts and mercy. From a general consideration of these works he then particularizes:—

1. "For the heavens declare," &c. The sun, moon, and stars, in their splendour, magnitude, and perpetual motion, show forth God's honour and majesty.

2. A second kind of works are the terrible acts of his justice, such as the deluge, the fire of Sodom, Pharaoh's overthrow in the Red Sea, the earth opening to swallow up *Korah*, *Dathan*, and *Abiram*.

Then there follow his acts of love and mercy, spoken of at large.

1. "Thy great works shall abundantly utter," &c. Thy bounty shall make all generations eloquent in thy praise, *and shall sing of thy righteousness*, in exhibiting thy promised blessings, in bestowing temporal benefits; but above all, in the gifts of thy grace:—In the incarnation, passion, resurrection, ascension, the coming of the Holy Ghost, calling of the Gentiles, justification, sanctification, and eternal life; for all these, and each of them, men shall abundantly utter thy righteousness.

2. "The Lord is gracious," &c.

3. "The Lord is good to all," &c.

4. "His tender mercies are over," &c. Even to the most wicked, God gives time and opportunity for repentance, before he cuts them off.

III. The prophet having sung of God's great works in glory, terror, and mercy, now adds, "All thy works shall praise thee, O Lord." And now he begins a new matter, the erection of his peculiar kingdom in his Church: "A peculiar people," &c. His saints. These will continue to mark thy wonders, and sing to thy glory: these, *thy saints, shall bless thee* for all and in all thy acts. "They shall speak of the glory of thy kingdom," &c. "To make known to the sons of men," &c. "Thy kingdom is an everlasting kingdom," &c. Now the power and glory of Christ's kingdom differ in a fourfold manner from that of the sons of men.

1. The kings on earth require obedience from their subjects; they exact subsidies, tributes, taxes, &c.

2. Earthly kings glory in their power, and rejoice in their dignity; but their crown is full of thorns, anxiety, care, &c.

3. Earthly kings reign but for a time, Christ for ever. 1. "They shall speak of the glory," &c. Excelling all others. 2. "To make known," &c. Thy acts far beyond theirs. 3. "Thy kingdom is an everlasting kingdom," &c. Not so theirs.

The prophet having described Christ's kingdom, begins to extol the qualities and virtues of a good king, which agrees with Christ.

I. His *veracity*.

II. His *probity:* "The Lord is faithful," &c.

III. This is another quality of a good king, so to govern his subjects that they fall not, or to raise them if fallen. Christ sustains and upholds his people, or restores them if they fall from him and return by repentance to him; this was exemplified in *David*, *Peter*, the *prodigal*, &c. "The eyes of all," &c. "Thou openest thine hand," &c.

IV. Liberality and bounty are excellent qualities in a king who cares for his subjects, and may properly be applied to Christ, who provides for his Church in all things. And—

1. "The eyes of all wait upon thee." In expectation.

2. "And thou givest," &c. It is a gift, not a debt.

3. "Their meat." Every thing fit for them.

4. "In due season." When fit and necessary.

5. "Thou openest thine hand." Givest bountifully.

6. "And satisfiest," &c. The covetous always want; content is from God.

7. "The desire of every living thing," &c. "The Lord is righteous," &c.

V. This is another virtue of a good king, and refers to Christ. "The Lord is nigh unto all them," &c.

VI. This is the sixth quality of a good king, to show himself ready of access to all who implore his aid.

1. *Faith*. For he that prays without it will not be answered.

2. *Hope and confidence*. He prays not seriously who hopes not to be heard.

3. *Love*. No man prays who hates God.

4. *Desire*. Nor that desires not to obtain.

5. *Attention and intention*, without which prayer is idle. "The Lord will fulfil," &c.

VII. The seventh quality of a good king is to grant petitions.

1. "He will fulfil," &c. But with limitation: "So they fear him."

2. "He also will hear their cry." When it is earnest and sincere.

3. "And will save them:" "The Lord preserveth all them," &c.

VIII. The eighth quality of a good king is to spare the humble and destroy the proud. *Parcere subjectis, et debellare superbos.*—VIRGIL. Which Christ will do; he preserves his martyrs in patience, and then receives them into glory.

IV. The conclusion is an acclamation, and answers to the beginning of the Psalm.

1. "My mouth shall speak," &c. This will I do while I live.

2. "And let all flesh," &c. And let all follow his example in giving due praise to this bountiful God.

PSALM CXLVI

The psalmist, full of gratitude, purposes to praise God for ever, 1, 2; *and exhorts not to trust in man, not even the most powerful; for which he gives his reasons,* 3, 4. *The great advantage of trusting in God,* 5. *The mercies which they who trust in God may expect,* 6–9. *The Divine government is everlasting,* 10.

PRAISE [a]ye the LORD. [b]Praise the LORD,
O my soul.
2 [c]While I live will I praise the LORD: I
will sing praises unto my God while I have
any being.
3 [d]Put not your trust in princes, *nor* in
the son of man, in whom *there is* no [e]help.
4 [f]His breath goeth forth, he returneth to
his earth; in that very day [g]his thoughts
perish.
5 [h]Happy *is he* that *hath* the God of Jacob
for his help, whose hope *is* in the LORD his
God:
6 [i]Which made heaven, and earth, the sea,
and all that therein *is:* which keepeth truth
for ever:
7 [k]Which executeth judgment for the oppressed: [l]which giveth food to the hungry.
[m]The LORD looseth the prisoners:
8 [n]The LORD openeth *the eyes of* the blind:
[o]the LORD raiseth them that are bowed down:
the LORD loveth the righteous:

[a]Hebrew, *Hallelujah*——[b]Psalm ciii. 1——[c]Psalm civ. 33——[d]Psalm cxviii. 8, 9; Isaiah ii. 22——[e]Or, *salvation*——[f]Psalm civ. 29; Ecclesiastes xii. 7; Isaiah ii. 22——[g]See 1 Corinthians ii. 6——[h]Psalm cxliv. 15; Jeremiah xvii. 7——[i]Genesis i. 1; Revelation xiv. 7 [k]Psalm ciii. 6——[l]Psalm cvii. 9——[m]Psalm lxviii. 6; cvii. 10, 14——[n]Matthew ix. 30; John ix. 7–32 [o]Psalm cxlv. 14; cxlvii. 6; Luke xiii. 13

NOTES ON PSALM CXLVI

This is the first of the Psalms called *Hallelujah* Psalms, of which there are *five*, and which conclude the book. No author's name is prefixed to this, either in the *Hebrew* or *Chaldee.* But the *Syriac, Vulgate, Septuagint, Æthiopic,* and *Arabic*, attribute it to *Haggai* and *Zechariah.* It was probably written after the captivity, and may refer to the time when Cyrus, prejudiced by the enemies of the Jews, withdrew his order for the rebuilding of the walls of Jerusalem, to which revocation of the royal edict the *third* verse may refer: *Put not your trust in princes*, &c.

Verse 2. *While I live will I praise*] The true feeling of a heart overpowered with a sense of God's goodness.

While I have any being.] בעודי *beodi*, in my continuance, in my progression, my eternal existence. This is very expressive.

Verse 3. *Put not your trust in princes*] This may refer, as has been stated above, to Cyrus, who had revoked his edict for the rebuilding of Jerusalem. Perhaps they had begun to suppose that they were about to owe their deliverance to the Persian king. God permitted this change in the disposition of the king, to teach them the *vanity of confidence in men,* and the necessity of *trusting in himself.*

Verse 4. *His breath goeth forth*] His existence depends merely, under God, on the *air* he breathes. When he ceases to *respire* he ceases to *live;* his body from that moment begins to claim its affinity to the earth; and all his thoughts, purposes, and projects, whether good or evil, come to nought and *perish.* He, then, who has no other dependence, must necessarily be *miserable.*

Verse 5. *Happy* is he *that* hath *the God of Jacob for his help*] While he that trusts in man is *miserable,* he that trusts in God is *happy. In the son of man,* בן אדם *ben Adam, there is no help,* תשועה *teshuah,* no *saving principle.* Every *son of Adam* naturally comes into the world without this, and must continue so till the *Lord open the eyes of the blind,* ver. 8; but a measure of light is given from that true Light *which lighteth every man that cometh into the world.* This son of Adam returns to his earth, לאדמתו *leadmatho,* to *the ground,* from which he was taken; this refers directly to Gen. ii. 7; iii. 19. But he that has the God for his help who helped *Jacob* in his distress, and was with him, and sustained him in and through all adversities, can never be destitute; for this God *changes not;* he lives for ever, and his projects cannot perish. He has *purposed* that Israel shall be delivered from this captivity. *Cyrus may change,* but *God will not; trust therefore in* HIM. He has all power; he *made heaven and earth;* he has them under his government and at his disposal; and should *earth* itself fail, *heaven* endures. And he keeps his *truth for ever;* and therefore his promises must be fulfilled to them that trust in him. *Fear not.*

Verse 7. *Which executeth judgment for the oppressed*] For those who suffer by *violence* or *calumny.* This may refer to the Israelites, who suffered much by *oppression* from the *Babylonians,* and by *calumny* from the *Samaritans,* &c., who had prejudiced the king of Persia against them.

Giving food to the hungry.] No doubt he fed the poor captives by many displays of his peculiar providence.

The Lord looseth the prisoners] And as he has sustained you so long *under* your captivity, so will he bring you *out* of it.

Verse 8. *Openeth* the eyes of *the blind*] He brings us out of our prison-house, from the *shadow of death,* and *opens our eyes* that we may behold the *free light* of the day. And it is the Lord only that can open the eyes of any son of Adam, and give him to see his wretchedness, and where help and salvation may be found.

Raiseth them that are bowed down] Through a sense of their guilt and sinfulness.

9 [p]The LORD preserveth the strangers; he relieveth the fatherless and widow: [q]but the way of the wicked he turneth upside down.

10 [r]The LORD shall reign for ever, *even* thy God, O Zion, unto all generations. Praise ye the LORD.

[p]Deut. x. 8; Psa. lxviii. 5——[q]Psa. cxlvii. 6

[r]Exod. xv. 18; Psa. x. 16; cxlv. 13; Rev. xi. 15

The Lord loveth the righteous] These he makes partakers of a *Divine nature;* and he loves those who bear his own image.

Verse 9. *Preserveth the strangers*] He has *preserved you strangers* in a strange land, where you have been in captivity for *seventy* years; and though in an *enemy's country*, he has provided for the *widows* and *orphans* as amply as if he had been in the promised land.

The way of the wicked he turneth upside down.] He *subverts, turns aside.* They shall not do all the wickedness they wish; they shall not do all that is in their power. In their career he will either *stop* them, turn them *aside*, or *overturn* them.

Verse 10. *The Lord shall reign for ever*] Therefore he can never fail; and he is *thy God, O Zion.* Hitherto he has helped *you* and your *fathers;* and has extended that help from *generation to generation.* Therefore trust in him and bless the Lord.

ANALYSIS OF THE HUNDRED AND FORTY-SIXTH PSALM

The subject of this Psalm is the same with the former.

It is divided into *four* parts:—

I. An exhortation to praise God, ver. 1. Which the psalmist resolves to do, ver. 2.

II. A dehortation from confidence in man, ver. 3, 4.

III. He pronounces them happy who trust in God, ver. 5.

IV. And to persuade to this he uses every reason, ver. 6, to the end.

I. He begins with a dialogism.

1. "He speaks to all: "Praise ye the Lord."

2. Then by an apostrophe he truns to himself: "Praise the Lord, O my soul."

3. And his soul answers: "While I live," &c. While I am, while I shall be.

II. But the prophet, for fear men should trust too much in the great, and not rely wholly upon God, exhorts them: "Put not your trust in princes," &c.

He gives his reasons for the warning:—

1. Because of their impotency: "There is no help in them," &c.

2. Because of their mortality: "Their breath goeth forth," &c.

III. If a man will be happy, the prophet shows him that he must rely upon God alone; for,

1. "Happy is he that hath," &c. Him in whom *Jacob* trusted.

2. "And whose hope," &c. Not in short-lived man.

And this he confirms by many reasons:—

I. From his omnipotence: "He is God the Creator," &c.

II. From his veracity: "Who keeps truth for ever," &c. His word is passed for our protection, and he can and will keep it.

III. From his justice: "He executeth judgment," &c.

IV. From his mercy.

1. "He giveth food," &c. Relieves men in their necessities.

2. "The Lord looseth the prisoner." Another act of grace, again.

3. "The Lord openeth the eyes," &c. Whether spiritually or corporeally.

4. "The Lord raiseth them that are bowed down," &c. By sin or misery.

V. From his love: "The Lord loveth," &c. Of which the effects are:—

1. "The Lord preserveth," &c.

2. "He delivereth the fatherless," &c.

3. But the ungodly find a far different effect: "But the way of the wicked," &c. He makes their glory to perish utterly.

PSALM CXLVII

The psalmist praises God for his goodness to Jerusalem, 1–3; *shows his great mercy to them that trust in him,* 4–6; *he extols him for his mercies, and providential kindness,* 7–11; *for his defence of Jerusalem,* 12–15; *for his wonders in the seasons,* 16–18; *and his word unto Jacob,* 19, 20.

XXX. DAY. EVENING PRAYER

A. M. cir. 3485
B. C. cir. 519
Darii I.,
R. Persarum,
cir. annum
secundum

PRAISE ye the LORD: for [a]*it is* good to sing praises unto our God; [b]for *it is* pleasant; *and* [c]praise is comely.

2 The LORD doth [d]build up Jerusalem: [e]he gathereth together the outcasts of Israel.

3 [f]He healeth the broken in heart, and bindeth up their [g]wounds.

[a]Psa. xcii. 1——[b]Psa. cxxxv. 3——[c]Psa. xxxiii. 1——[d]Psa. cii. 16——[e]Deut. xxx. 3

[f]Psa. li. 17; Isa. lvii. 15; lxi. 1; Luke iv. 18——[g]Hebrew, *griefs*

NOTES ON PSALM CXLVII

This Psalm, which is without *title* in the *Hebrew, Chaldee,* and *Vulgate,* is attributed by the other *Versions* to *Haggai* and *Zechariah.* It was probably penned after the captivity, when the Jews were busily employed in *rebuilding Jerusalem*, as may be gathered from the *second* and *thirteenth* verses. It may be necessary to remark that all the Versions, except the *Chal-*

A. M. cir. 3485 B. C. cir. 519 Darii I., R. Persarum, cir. annum secundum

4 [h]He telleth the number of
the stars; he calleth them all by
their names.
5 [i]Great *is* our LORD, and of
[k]great power: [l]his [m]understanding *is* infinite.
6 [n]The LORD lifteth up the meek: he casteth the wicked down to the ground.
7 Sing unto the LORD with thanksgiving:
sing praise upon the harp unto our God:
8 [o]Who covereth the heaven with clouds,
who prepareth rain for the earth, who maketh
grass to grow upon the mountains.
9 [p]He giveth to the beast his food, *and* [q]to
the young ravens which cry.
10 [r]He delighteth not in the strength of the
horse: he taketh not pleasure in
the legs of a man.
11 The LORD taketh pleasure
in them that fear him, in those
that hope in his mercy.
12 Praise the LORD, O Jerusalem; praise
thy God, O Zion.
13 For he hath strengthened the bars of thy
gates; he hath blessed thy children within thee.
14 [s]He [t]maketh peace *in* thy borders, *and*
[u]filleth thee with the [v]finest of the wheat.
15 [w]He sendeth forth his commandment
upon earth: his word runneth very swiftly.
16 [x]He giveth snow like wool: he scattereth the hoar frost like ashes.

[h]See Gen. xv. 5; Isa. xl. 26——[i]1 Chron. xvi. 25; Psa. xlviii. 1; xcvi. 4; cxlv. 3——[k]Nah. i. 3——[l]Heb. *of his understanding* there is *no number*——[m]Isa. xl. 28 [n]Psa. cxlvi. 8, 9——[o]Job xxxviii. 26, 27; Psa. civ. 13, 14 [p]Job xxxviii. 41; Psa. civ. 27, 28; cxxxvi. 25; cxlv. 15

[q]Job xxxviii. 41; Matt. vi. 26——[r]Psa. xxxiii. 16, 17, 18; Hos. i. 7——[s]Heb. *Who maketh thy border peace* [t]Isa. lx. 17, 18——[u]Psa. cxxxii. 15——[v]Heb. *fat of wheat;* Deut. xxxii. 14; Psa. lxxxi. 16——[w]Psa. cvii. 20; Job xxxvii. 12——[x]Job xxxvii. 6

dee, divide this Psalm at the end of the *eleventh* verse, and begin a new Psalm at the *twelfth.* By this division the numbers of the Psalms agree in the Versions with the *Hebrew;* the former having been, till now, *one behind.*

Verse 1. *Praise is comely.*] It is decent, befitting, and proper that every intelligent creature should acknowledge the Supreme Being: and as he does nothing *but good* to the children of men, so they should *speak good of his name.*

Verse 2. *The Lord doth build up*] The psalmist appears to see the *walls* rising under his eye, because the *outcasts of Israel*, those who had been in *captivity*, are now *gathered together* to do the work.

Verse 3. *He healeth the broken in heart*] שבורי, *the shivered* in heart. From the root שבר *shabar*, to *break in pieces*, we have our word *shiver*, to break into *splinters*, into *shivers.* The heart broken in pieces by a sense of God's displeasure.

Verse 4. *He telleth the number of the stars*] He whose knowledge is so exact as to tell every star in heaven, can be under no difficulty to find out and collect all the scattered exiles of Israel.

Verse 5. *His understanding* is *infinite.*] To *his intelligence there is no number:* though he *numbers* the *stars*, his *understanding* is without *number.* It is infinite; therefore, he *can know*, as he *can do*, all things.

Verse 6. *The Lord lifteth up the meek*] The humbled, the afflicted.

Verse 7. *Sing unto the Lord*] ענו *enu*, sing a responsive song, sing in parts, answer one another.

Verse 8. *Who covereth the heaven with clouds*] Collects the vapours together, in order to cause it to rain upon the earth. Even the direction of the winds, the collection of the clouds, and the descent of the rain, are under the especial management of God. These things form a part of his *providential management of the world.*

Maketh grass to grow upon the mountains.] After this clause the *Vulgate*, the *Septuagint*, *Æthiopic*, *Arabic*, and *Anglo-Saxon*, add, *and herb for the service of man.* It appears that a *hemistich*, or *half-line*, has been lost from the *Hebrew* text; which, according to the above *Versions*, must have stood thus: ועשב לעבדת האדם *veeseb laabodath haadam*, as in Psa. civ. 14: "And herbage for the service of mankind."

Verse 10. *He delighteth not*] The *horse*, among all animals, is most delighted in by man for *beauty*, *strength*, and *fleetness.* And a *man's legs*, if well proportioned, are more admired than even the finest features of his face. Though God has made *these*, yet they are not his peculiar delight.

Verse 11. *The Lord taketh pleasure in them that fear him*] That are truly religious.

In those that hope is his mercy.] Who are just beginning to seek the salvation of their souls. Even the *cry of the penitent* is pleasing in the ear of the Lord. With this verse the *hundred and forty-sixth* Psalm ends in all the *Versions*, except the *Chaldee.* And the *hundred and forty-seventh* commences with the 12th verse. I believe these to be two distinct Psalms. The subjects of them are not exactly the same, though something similar; and they plainly refer to different periods.

Verse 13. *He hath strengthened the bars of thy gates*] He has enabled thee to complete the *walls of Jerusalem.* From the former part of the Psalm it appears the *walls were then in progress;* from this part, they appear to be *completed*, and provisions to be brought into the city, to support its inhabitants. The *gates* were set up and well secured by *bars*, so that the grain, &c., was in safety.

Verse 14. *He maketh peace*] They were now no longer troubled with the Samaritans, Moabites, &c.

Verse 15. *He sendeth forth his commandment*] His substantial word. It is here personified, מימרא *meymra*, Chaldee; and appears to be a very active agent running every where, and performing the purposes of his will.

Verse 16. *He giveth snow like wool*] Falling

A. M. cir. 3485
B. C. cir. 519
Darii I.,
R. Persarum,
cir. annum
secundum

17 He casteth forth his ice like
morsels: who can stand before
his cold?
18 [y]He sendeth out his word,
and melteth them: he causeth his wind to
blow, *and* the waters flow.
19 [z]He showeth [a]his word
unto Jacob, [b]his statutes and his
judgments unto Israel.
20 [c]He hath not dealt so with
any nation: and *as for his* judgments, they
have not known them. Praise ye the LORD.

[y]Ver. 15; see Job xxxvii. 10——[z]Deut. xxxiii. 2, 3, 4; Psa. lxxvi. 1; lxxviii. 5; ciii. 7

[a]Heb. *his words*——[b]Mal. iv. 4——[c]See Deut. iv. 32, 33, 34; Rom. iii. 1, 2

down in large flakes; and in this state nothing in nature has a nearer resemblance to fine white *wool.*

Scattereth the hoar frost like ashes.] Spreading it over the whole face of nature.

Verse 17. *He casteth forth his ice*] קרחו *korcho,* (probably *hailstones,*) like crumbs.

Who can stand before his cold?] At particular times the cold in the *east* is so very intense as to kill man and beast. *Jacobus de Vitriaco,* one of the writers in the *Gesta Dei per Francos,* says, that in an expedition in which he was engaged against Mount Tabor, on the 24th of December, the cold was so intense that many of the poor people, and the beasts of burden, died by it. And *Albertus Aquensis,* another of these writers, speaking of the cold in Judea, says, that *thirty* of the people who attended Baldwin I. in the mountainous districts near the Dead Sea, were killed by it; and that in that expedition they had to contend with horrible hail and ice, with unheard-of *snow and rain.* From this we find that the winters are often very severe in Judea; and in such cases as the above, we may well call out, "Who can stand against his cold!"

Verse 18. *He sendeth out his word*] He gives a command: the *south wind* blows; the *thaw* takes place; and the *ice* and *snow* being liquefied, the *waters flow,* where before they were bound up by the ice.

Verse 19. *He showeth his word unto Jacob*] To no nation of the world beside had God given a revelation of his will.

Verse 20. *And* as for his *judgments*] The wondrous ordinances of his law, no nation had known them; and consequently, did not know the glorious things in futurity to which they referred.

Analysis of the Hundred and Forty-seventh Psalm

The parts of this Psalm are *two:*—

I. An exhortation to praise God, ver. 1, which is repeated, ver. 7 and 12.

II. The arguments to persuade to it: God's bounty, wisdom, power, providence, justice, and mercy; dwelt on through the whole Psalm.

I. The exhortation is briefly proposed, "Praise the Lord." Which the prophet, as the chanter of the choir, begins; and then more fully repeats, "Sing unto the Lord," &c. And again, "Praise the Lord, O Jerusalem," &c., ver. 12; where the *Arabic, Greek,* and *Latin* translators begin a new Psalm: but in the *Hebrew* they are conjoined, and form but one hymn.

The prophet, having ended his exhortation, adds his reasons for it.

1. It is pleasant and becoming.

2. His bounty in building *Jerusalem,* and bringing back the dispersed, ver. 2. In comforting the distressed, ver. 3. For his wisdom, ver. 4. For his power, ver. 5. For his mercy and justice, ver. 6.

His first arguments are drawn from the thing itself.

I. Good: "For it is good," &c.

For many reasons this may be called *good.*

1. For it is God's command, and must not be neglected.

2. It elevates the heart from earth to heaven.

3. Good again, because we are bound to it by obligations.

II. "To praise God is pleasant."

1. Because it proceeds from love.

2. Because it is pleasant to perform our duty, and the end of our creation.

3. Because God is pleased with it: "He that offereth me praise, glorifieth me," &c.

4. Because God is pleased with the virtues of faith, hope, charity, humility, devotion, &c., of which praise is the effect.

III. "It is comely." There is no sin greater than that of ingratitude.

These are the first arguments the prophet uses, and they are drawn from the nature of the thing itself: they may apply to all ages of the Church.

He dwells upon the deliverance of *Israel* from captivity.

1. "The Lord doth build up" his Church, the seat of his sanctuary. He hath restored our policy and religion.

2. "He gathereth together," &c. The banished and scattered ones; the Gentiles.

3. "He healeth the broken in heart," &c. Oppressed by captivity or sin.

4. "And bindeth up," &c. Like a good surgeon.

The second argument is drawn from his *wisdom.*

1. "He telleth the number of the stars," &c. A thing to man impossible.

2. "He calleth them," &c. They are his army, and he knows them.

By the stars in this place some understand God's saints.

1. The stars are infinite in number. So are the saints.

2. Among them are planets. Saints have their circuits; and always revolve round him, the Sun of righteousness.

3. The stars shine clearest in the night. The saints in persecution.

4. One star differeth from another in glory. Some saints excel others in piety.

5. The stars are above. The saints' conversation is in heaven.

6. The stars are obscured by clouds. The Church is sometimes obscured by affliction and persecution.

His third argument is drawn from God's *power:* "Great is the Lord," &c.

His fourth argument is drawn from God's *justice* and *mercy.*

1. His mercy: "The Lord lifteth up the meek," &c. Sustains and exalts them.

2. His justice: "He casteth the wicked down," &c. They shall not always triumph.

But, before the prophet proceeds farther, he repeats:—

1. "Sing unto the Lord with thanksgiving." Do it in words.

2. "Sing praises upon the harp," &c. Do it in works.

Then he proceeds to argue from God's *providence.*

1. "Who covereth the heaven," &c. Not to obscure, but fructify the earth.

2. "Who maketh grass to grow," &c. By his blessing on the most barren places.

3. "He giveth to the beast," &c. They gather it from his supplies.

4. "And to the young ravens," &c. No bird suffers its young so soon to provide for themselves; but God hears and sends them food. *Christ* himself uses this argument to encourage us to rely on God's providence, Matt. vi.

Should the distrustful *Jew* argue, Alas, we have no strength, ammunition, horse, or armour, the prophet replies:—

1. "He delighteth not," &c. When used as a warlike creature.

2. "He taketh not pleasure," &c. In the nimbleness of man, when used for warlike preparations.

But he delights in his servants.

1. "The Lord taketh pleasure," &c. In those who obey and love him.

2. "In those that hope," &c. Have faith and confidence in him.

3. He again repeats his proposition, and calls upon the Church to perform it: "Praise the Lord, O Jerusalem," &c. "Thy God, O Zion." Should others be negligent, be not ye.

He then adds four reasons why *Zion* should praise him: 1. Security and defence. 2. Benediction. 3. Peace. 4. Substance.

1. Security: "For he hath strengthened," &c.

2. Benediction: "He hath blessed," &c. His officers with wisdom, &c.

3. Peace: "He maketh peace." *The vision of peace* is the literal interpretation of the word *Jerusalem.*

4. Provision: "Filleth thee with the finest of the wheat," &c.

That *God* has done this for Jerusalem, is evident from his general providence over the world. And this argument the prophet uses: "He sendeth forth his commandment upon earth," &c. For,

1. "He giveth snow like wool." Beautiful in appearance, and in order to preserve vegetables from the nipping but necessary frost, when long continued.

2. "He scattereth the hoar frost," &c. Thickening the air with it like ashes; freezing all the vapours that float in it.

3. "He casteth forth his ice," &c. Fragments of ice.

4. "Who can stand before his cold?" Endure it unprovided.

But having described all these powerful agents, the prophet next shows how easily they are governed by his *word.*

1. "He sendeth out his word, and melteth them."

2. "He causeth his wind to blow," &c. And the ice and snow return to water. All these are his, and on him we must depend for safety and comfort.

By these God teaches alike nations to acknowledge him.

But there are particular acts which refer to his people; for,

1. "He showeth his word," &c. By *Moses* and the prophets.

2. "He hath not dealt so," &c. None at that time, but since to his Church.

3. "As for his judgments," &c. His evangelical precepts. He is sending forth his word; the nations could not find out his precepts otherwise: therefore for this *praise ye the Lord.*

PSALM CXLVIII

The psalmist calls on all the creation to praise the Lord. The angels and visible heavens, 1–6; *the earth and the sea,* 7; *the meteors,* 8; *mountains, hills, and trees,* 9; *beasts, reptiles, and fowls,* 10; *kings, princes, and mighty men,* 11; *men, women, and children,* 12, 13; *and especially all the people of Israel,* 14.

A. M. cir. 3485 B. C. cir. 519 Darii I., R. Persarum, cir. annum secundum

PRAISE [a]ye the LORD. Praise
ye the LORD from the heavens: praise him in the heights.
2 [b]Praise ye him, all his angels: praise ye him, all his hosts.
3 Praise ye him, sun and moon: praise him, all ye stars of light.

[a]Heb. *Hallelujah* [b]Psa. ciii. 20, 21

NOTES ON PSALM CXLVIII

This Psalm has no title: but by the *Syriac* it is attributed to *Haggai* and *Zechariah;* and the *Septuagint* and the *Æthiopic* follow it. As a hymn of praise, this is the most sublime in the whole book.

Verse 1. *Praise ye the Lord from the heavens*] The *Chaldee* translates, "Praise the Lord, ye holy creatures from the heavens. Praise him, ye armies of supreme angels. Praise him, all ye angels who minister before him." מן השמים *min hashshamayim* signifies whatever belongs to the heavens, all their inhabitants; as מן הארץ *min haarets,* ver. 7, signifies all that belongs to the earth, all its inhabitants and productions.

Verse 3. *Praise ye him, sun and moon*] The meaning of this address and all others to *inanimate nature,* is this: Every work of God's hand partakes so much of his perfections, that

A. M. cir. 3485
B. C. cir. 519
Darii I.,
R. Persarum,
cir. annum
secundum

4 Praise him, [c]ye heavens of
heavens, and [d]ye waters that *be*
above the heavens.
5 Let them praise the name of
the LORD: for [e]he commanded, and they were
created.
6 [f]He hath also established them for ever and
ever: he hath made a decree which shall not
pass.
7 Praise the LORD from the earth, [g]ye dragons, and all deeps:
8 Fire, and hail; snow, and
vapour; stormy wind [h]fulfilling
his word:
9 [i]Mountains, and all hills;
fruitful trees, and all cedars:
10 Beasts, and all cattle; creeping things,
and [k]flying [l]fowl:
11 Kings of the earth, and all people; princes, and all judges of the earth:
12 Both young men, and maidens; old men,
and children:

[c]1 Kings viii. 27; 2 Cor. xii. 2——[d]Gen. i. 7——[e]Gen. i. 1, 6, 7; Psa. xxxiii. 6, 9——[f]Psa. lxxxix. 37; cxix. 90, 91; Jer. xxxi. 35, 36; xxxiii. 25——[g]Isa. xliii. 20

[h]Psa. cxlvii. 15–18——[i]Isa. xliv. 23; xlix. 13; lv. 12——[k]Heb. *birds of wing*——[l]Gen. i. 26; ii. 19; vii. 23; viii. 17; ix. 2, 20; Deut. iv. 17; Ezek. xxxix. 17; Dan. vii. 6

it requires only to be studied and known, in order to show forth the manifold *wisdom*, *power*, and *goodness* of the Creator.

Sars of light] The brightest and most luminous stars: probably the planets may be especially intended.

Verse 4. *Heavens of heavens*] Heavens exceeding heavens. Systems of systems extending as far beyond the solar system, as it does beyond the lowest deeps. The endless systematic concatenation of worlds.

Ye waters that be *above the heavens.*] This refers to Gen. i. 7, where see the notes. Clouds, vapours, air, exhalations, rain, snow, and meteors of every kind.

Verse 5. *He commanded, and they were created.*] He spake the word expressive of the idea in his infinite mind; and they sprang into being according to that idea.

Verse 6. *He hath also stablished them*] He has determined their respective *revolutions*, and the *times* in which they are performed, so exactly to show his all-comprehensive wisdom and skill, that they have never passed the line marked out by his *decree*, nor intercepted each other in the vortex of space, through revolutions continued for nearly 6000 years.

Verse 7. *Praise the Lord from the earth*] As, in the first address, he calls upon the heavens, and all that *belong to them;* so here, in this second part, he calls upon the earth, and all *that belong to it.*

Ye dragons] תנינים *tanninim*, whales, porpoises, sharks, and sea-monsters of all kinds.

And all deeps] Whatsoever is contained in the sea, whirlpools, eddies, ground tides, with the astonishing flux and reflux of the ocean.

Every thing, in its *place* and *nature*, shows forth the perfections of its Creator.

Verse 8. *Fire, and hail; snow, and vapours*] All kinds of meteors, water, and fire, in all their forms and combinations. And *air*, whether in the gentle *breeze*, the *gale*, the *whirlwind*, the *tempest*, or the *tornado;* each accomplishing an especial purpose, and fulfilling a particular *will* of the Most High.

Verse 9. *Mountains, and all hills*] Whether *primitive, secondary*, or *alluvial;* of *ancient* or *recent formation*, with all their *contents*, quarries, mines, and minerals. But what a profusion of wisdom and skill is lavished on these! To instance only in the different metals, earths, and minerals; especially the precious stones.

Fruitful trees] עץ פרי *ets peri, fruit trees* of all kinds.

And all cedars] Every kind of *forest tree.* The formation of the *fruits*, their infinitely varied *hues* and savours, proclaim the unsearchable wisdom and goodness of God: not less so, the *growth, structure*, and *various qualities* and *uses* of the *forest trees.*

Verse 10. *Beasts*] החיה *hachaiyah, wild beasts* of every kind.

All cattle] בהמה *behemah*, all *domestic animals;* those used for the service of the *house*, and those for *agricultural* purposes.

Creeping things] All the class of *reptiles*, from the *boa constrictor*, that can combat, kill, and swallow whole the *royal tiger*, to the *cobra de manille*, a poisonous reptile as small as a *fine needle;* with those still smaller animals that are found in water, and require the power of the microscope to bring them to view. In the production, preservation, habits, and properties of all these, there is a profusion of wisdom and economy that would require ages to exhibit.

Flying fowl] The structure of fowls is astonishing; and the exact *mathematical manner* in which *flying fowls swim* the air, and steer their course wheresoever they will; the feathers, and their *construction*, with the *muscles* which give them motion; strike the observer of nature with *astonishment* and *delight.*

Verse 11. *Kings of the earth*] As being representatives of the Most High; and *all people*—the nations governed by them. *Princes*, as governors of provinces, and *all judges* executing those laws that bind man to man, and regulate and preserve civil society; *praise God*, from whom ye have derived your *power* and *influence:* for *by him kings reign.* And let the *people* magnify God for *civil* and *social institutions*, and for the *laws* by which, under him, their *lives* and *properties* are preserved.

Verse 12. *Both young men, and maidens*] Who are in the bloom of youth, and in the height of health and vigour; know that God is your Father; and let the morning and energy of your days be devoted to *him.*

Old men, and children] Very appropriately united here, as the *beginning* and *conclusion* of *life* present nearly the same passions, appetites, caprices, and infirmities: yet in both the beneficence, all-sustaining power, and goodness of God are seen.

A. M. cir. 3485
B. C. cir. 519
Darii I.,
R. Persarum,
cir. annum
secundum

13 Let them praise the name of the LORD: for [m]his name alone is [n]excellent; [o]his glory *is* above the earth and heaven.

14 [p]He also exalteth the horn of his people, [q]the praise of all his saints; *even* of the children of Israel, [r]a people near unto him. Praise ye the LORD.

[m]Psa. viii. 1; Isa. xii. 4——[n]Heb. *exalted*——[o]Psa. cxiii. 4——[p]Psa. lxxv. 10——[q]Psa. cxlix. 9——[r]Eph. ii. 17

Verse 13. *Let them*] All already specified, *praise the name of Jehovah*, because he excels all beings: and *his glory*, as seen in creating, preserving, and governing all things, is על *al*, *upon* or *over*, the *earth* and *heaven*. All *space* and *place*, as well as the *beings* found in them, show forth the manifold wisdom and goodness of God.

Verse 14. *He also exalteth the horn*] Raises to power and authority *his people*.

The praise] Jehovah is the subject of the praise of all his *saints*.

A people near unto him.] The only people who know him, and make their approaches unto him with the *sacrifices* and *offerings* which he has himself prescribed. Praise ye the Lord!

O what a hymn of praise is here! It is a *universal chorus!* All created nature have a share, and all perform their respective parts.

All *intelligent beings* are especially called to praise him who made them in his love, and sustains them by his beneficence. *Man* particularly, in all the stages of his being—*infancy*, *youth*, *manhood*, and *old age:* all human beings have their peculiar interest in the great Father of the spirits of all flesh.

He loves *man*, wheresoever found, of whatsoever colour, in whatever circumstances, and in all the stages of his pilgrimage from his *cradle* to his *grave*.

Let the *lisp* of the *infant*, the *shout* of the *adult*, and the *sigh* of the *aged*, ascend to the universal parent, as a gratitude-offering. He guards those who *hang upon the breast;* controls and directs the *headstrong* and *giddy*, and sustains *old age* in its infirmities; and sanctifies to it the sufferings that bring on the termination of life.

Reader, this is thy God! How great, how good, how merciful, how compassionate! Breathe thy soul up to him; breathe it into him; and let it be preserved in his bosom till mortality be swallowed up of life, and all that is imperfect be done away.

Jesus is thy sacrificial offering; Jesus is thy Mediator. He has taken thy humanity, and placed it on the throne! He creates all things new; and faith in his blood will bring thee to his glory! Amen! hallelujah!

The beautiful morning hymn of Adam and Eve, (Paradise Lost, book v., line 153, &c.,)—

"These are thy glorious works, Parent of good;
Almighty, thine this universal frame," &c.—

has been universally admired. How many have spoken loud in its praises; who have never attempted to express their feelings in a stanza of the *hundred and forty-eighth* Psalm! But to the rapturous adorers of Milton's poetry what is the song of David, or this grand music of the spheres! Know this, O forgetful man, that *Milton's* morning hymn is a *paraphrase of this Psalm*, and is indebted to it for every excellency it possesses. It is little else than the psalmist speaking in English instead of Hebrew verse.

ANALYSIS OF THE HUNDRED AND FORTY-EIGHTH PSALM

The psalmist calls upon the whole creation to be instrumental in praising God. By which he shows,—

I. His ardent desire that God be praised. As if creatures, endowed with reason, were too few, therefore he calls on inanimate things to join and be heralds of his wondrous works.

II. His intention; what he would and could have done.

III. That what could be done should be done.

IV. That all really do praise him in their kind and manner.

This Psalm is disposed into excellent distribution.

1. He calls upon celestial creatures in general; 2. In particular. 1. On angels: "Praise ye the Lord from the heavens," &c. Ye of celestial order. 2. "Praise him in the heights," &c. The heavens above. 3. "Praise him, all his hosts," &c. Which in St. Luke are called *the heavenly host*.

2. "Praise ye him, sun, moon, and stars." Though not with the voice, yet by your beauty, motion, light, efficacy, &c.

He mentions the whole body of the heavenly orbs.

1. "Praise him, ye heavens of heavens," &c. The highest state of bliss.

2. "And ye waters," &c. All the orbs above the air, in Scripture called *heavens;* and the *waters* that are above the firmament.

And in the two next verses he gives the reason.

1. "He commanded," &c. They are his creatures, therefore,—

2. "He hath established them," &c. They are incorruptible.

From the heavens he now descends to the earth, air, water, &c.: "Praise the Lord from the earth," &c. All ye elementary substances.

1. "Ye dragons." Whales, great fishes.
2. "All deeps." All kinds of waters.
3. "Fire and hail," &c. Meteors, &c.
4. "Mountains and hills," &c.
5. "Fruitful trees," &c. Trees fit to build with and fruit-trees.
6. "Beasts and all cattle." Both wild and tame.
7. "Creeping things," &c. Worms and serpents.
8. "And all flying fowls."

And, lastly, he cites all mankind to praise God.

1. "The highest kings," &c. They who command, and they who obey.

2. "Princes, and all judges," &c. All inferior magistrates.

3. "Both young men and maidens." Both sexes.

4. "Old men and children,"—all ages: "Let them praise the name of the Lord."

And for this reason:—

1. "For his name is excellent alone." No name is so sublime and worthy.

2. "His glory is above the earth and heaven." All good comes from him.

The prophet concludes this Psalm with God's goodness to the Church, which furnishes him with another reason:—

1. He also "exalts the horn," &c. The power and glory of his people.

2. "He is the praise," &c. The Guide of *Israel.*

3. "Even of the children of Israel," &c. A people consecrated to God. All which is to be understood not merely of *Israel* according to the flesh, but God's spiritual Church. Now those who are true *Israelites*, and those especially, he excites to sing,—

"Hallelujah! Praise ye the Lord!"

PSALM CXLIX

All the congregation are invited to praise God for his mercies, 1–3. *Their great privileges,* 4, 5. *Their victories,* 6–9.

PRAISE [a]ye the LORD. [b]Sing unto the
LORD a new song, *and* his praise in the
congregation of saints.
2 Let Israel rejoice in [c]him that made him:
let the children of Zion be joyful in their
[d]King.
3 [e]Let them praise his name [f]in the dance:
let them sing praises unto him with the
timbrel and harp.
4 For [g]the LORD taketh pleasure in his
people: [h]he will beautify the meek with salvation.
5 Let the saints be joyful in glory: let them
[i]sing aloud upon their beds.

[a]Heb. *Hallelujah*——[b]Psa. xxxiii. 3; Isa. xlii. 10——[c]See Job xxxv. 10; Psa. c. 3; Isa. liv. 5——[d]Zech. ix. 9; Matt. xxi. 5——[e]Psa. lxxxi. 2; cl. 4——[f]Or, *with the pipe*——[g]Psa. xxxv. 27——[h]Psa. cxxxii. 16——[i]Job xxxv. 10

NOTES ON PSALM CXLIX

This seems to be an *epinikion*, or *song of triumph*, after some glorious victory; probably in the time of the *Maccabees.* It has been also understood as predicting the success of the Gospel in the nations of the earth. According to the *Syriac*, it concerns the *new temple*, by which the *Christian Church* is meant. It has no *title* in the Hebrew, nor in any of the *Versions*, and no *author's* name.

Verse 1. *Sing unto the Lord a new song*] That is, as we have often had occasion to remark, an *excellent song*, the best we can possibly pronounce. So the word חדש *chadash* is often understood; and so the word *novus*, "new," was often used among the Latin writers:—

Pollio amat nostram, quamvis sit rustica, musam.
Pollio et ipse facit NOVA CARMINA.
VIRG. Ecl. iii., ver. 84.

Pollio loves my lines, although rude:
Pollio himself makes *excellent* odes.

Tamely and inexpressively translated by Dryden:—

"Pollio my rural verse vouchsafes to read.
My Pollio writes himself."

O what a falling off is here!

Servius, in his comment on *nova*, says, *magna, miranda. Nova* means *great, admirable.*

So on *novum nectar*, Ecl. v., ver. 71, he says, id est, *magna dulcedo;* "nectar of EXCELLENT flavour."

Congregation of saints.] The *Israelites*, who were, by *profession* and *by injunction*, a *holy people.*

Verse 2. *In him that made him*] Let them remember in their exultations to give all glory to the *Lord;* for he is the Author of their *being* and their *blessings.* And let them know that he is their *King* also; that they should submit to his *authority*, and be guided and regulated in their hearts and conduct by his *laws.*

Verse 3. *Let them praise his name in the dance*] במחול *bemachol, with the pipe*, or some kind of *wind music*, classed here with תף *toph*, the *tabor* or *drum*, and כנור *kinnor*, the *harp.* "מחול *machol*," says *Parkhurst*, "*some fistular wind-instrument of music, with holes*, as *a flute, pipe*, or *fife*, from חל *chal, to make a hole or opening.*" I know no place in the Bible where מחול *machol* and מחלת *machalath* mean *dance* of any kind; they constantly signify some kind of *pipe.*

Verse 4. *The Lord taketh pleasure in his people*] The pleasure or good will of God is in his people: he loves them ardently, and will load them with his benefits, while they are *humble* and *thankful;* for,

He will beautify] יפאר *yephaer*, he will make *fair, the meek*, ענוים *anavim*, the *lowly*, the *humble with salvation*, בישועה *bishuah;* which St. Jerome thus translates, *Et exaltabit mansuetos in Jesu*, "And he will exalt the meek in Jesus." Whether this rendering be correct or not, there is no other way by which the *humble soul* can be exalted, but by JESUS, as the redeeming Saviour.

Verse 5. *Let the saints be joyful in glory*]

6 *Let* the high *praises* of God *be* [k]in their mouth, and [l]a two-edged sword in their hand;

7 To execute vengeance upon the heathen, *and* punishments upon the people;

8 To bind their kings with chains, and their nobles with fetters of iron;

9 [m]To execute upon them the judgment written: [n]this honour have all his saints. Praise ye the LORD.

[k]Heb. *in their throat*——[l]Heb. iv. 12; Rev. i. 16

[m]Deut. vii. 1, 2——[n]Psa. cxlviii. 14

Let them be gloriously joyful: seeing themselves so *honoured* and so *successful*, let them be joyful. God has put *glory* or *honour* upon them; let them give him the thanks due to his name.

Sing aloud upon their beds.] While they are reclining on their *couches*. At their festal banquets, let them shout the praises of the Lord. In imitation of this we often have at our public entertainments the following words sung, taken from the *Vulgate* of Psalm cxv. 1: NON NOBIS DOMINE NON NOBIS; sed NOMINI TUO da GLORIAM! super MISERICORDIA TUA et VERITATE TUA. "Not unto us, O Lord, not unto us, but unto thy name give glory, for thy mercy and for thy truth's sake." Let them mingle their feasting with Divine songs. This reclining on couches, while they take their food, is still practised in Asiatic countries.

Verse 6. Let *the high* praises *of God*] Let them sing songs the most sublime, with the loudest noise consistent with *harmony*.

And a two-edged sword in their hand] Perhaps there is an allusion here to the manner in which the Jews were obliged to labour in rebuilding the walls of Jerusalem: "Every one with one of his hands wrought in the work, and with the other hand held a weapon," Neh. iv. 17.

The *two-edged sword*, in Hebrew, is פיפיות *pipiyoth*, "mouth mouths."

Verse 7. *To execute vengeance upon the heathen*] This may refer simply to their purpose of defending themselves to the uttermost, should their enemies attack them while building their wall: and they had every reason to believe that God would be with them; and that, if their enemies did attack them, they should be able to inflict the severest punishment upon them.

Punishments upon the people] The unfaithful and treacherous *Jews;* for we find that some, even of their *nobles*, had joined with *Sanballat* and *Tobiah;* (see Neh. vi. 17-19:) and it appears also that many of them had formed alliances with those heathens, which were contrary to the law; see Neh. xiii. 15-29.

Verse 8. *To bind their kings with chains, and their nobles with fetters of iron*] That is, if these kings, governors of provinces, and chiefs among the people, had attacked them, God would have enabled them to defeat them, take their generals prisoners, and lead them in triumph to Jerusalem. It is certain also that in the times of the *Maccabees* the Jews had many signal victories over the *Samaritans, Philistines*, and *Moabites;* and over *Antiochus*, king of *Syria*. See the Books of the *Maccabees*. To these the psalmist may here refer in a *hyperbolical* way, not unusual in poetry and in songs of triumph.

Verse 9. *To execute upon them the judgment written*] In Deut. vii. 1, &c., God promises his people complete victory over all their enemies, and over the heathen. God repeatedly promises such victories to his faithful people; and this is, properly speaking, the *judgment written*, i. e., foretold.

This honour have all his saints.] They shall all be supported, defended, and saved by the Lord. Israel had this honour, and such victories over their enemies, while they continued faithful to their God. When they relapsed into iniquity, their enemies prevailed against them; they were defeated, their city taken, their temple burnt to the ground, more than a million of themselves slaughtered, and the rest led into captivity; and, scattered through the world, they continue without king, or temple, or true worship, to the present day.

"But do not these last verses contain a *promise* that all the nations of the earth shall be brought under the dominion of the *Church of Christ;* that all *heathen* and *ungodly kings* shall be put down, and *pious men* put in their places?" I do not think so. I believe God never intended that his Church should have the civil government of the world. His *Church*, like its *Founder* and *Head*, will never be a *ruler and divider among men*. The men who, under pretence of *superior sanctity*, affect this, are not of God; the truth of God is not in them; they are puffed up with pride, and fall into the condemnation of the devil. *Wo unto the inhabitants of the earth*, when the *Church* takes the *civil government* of the world into its hand! Were it possible that God should trust *religious people* with civil government, *anarchy* would soon ensue; for every professed believer in Christ would consider himself on a par with any other and every other believer, the *right to rule* and the *necessity to obey* would be immediately lost, and every man would do what was right in his own eyes; for, where the grace of God makes *all equal*, who can presume to say, I have Divine authority to govern my fellow? The Church of Rome has claimed this right; and the pope, in consequence, became a secular prince; but the nations of the world have seen the vanity and iniquity of the claim, and refused allegiance. Those whom it did govern, with force and with cruelty did it rule them; and the odious yoke is now universally cast off. Certain *enthusiasts* and *hypocrites*, not of that Church, have also attempted to set up a *fifth monarchy*, a *civil government* by the SAINTS! and diabolic saints they were. To such pretenders God gives neither countenance nor support. The secular and spiritual government God will ever keep distinct; and the Church shall have no power but that of *doing good;* and this only in proportion to its holiness, heavenly-mindedness, and piety to God. That the verses above may be understood in a *spiritual sense*, as applicable to the influence of the *word of God preached*, may be seen in the following analysis.

Analysis of the Hundred and Forty-ninth Psalm

In this Psalm the saints of God are excited to give due thanks.

I. For the grace and favour received from God, ver. 1-5.

II. For the glory and privileges they shall receive, ver. 5-9.

I. "Let Israel rejoice," &c. The saints. Which he amplifies:

1. The saints: "For praise is not comely in the mouth of sinners."

2. The quality of the song: "A new song." By renewed men.

From the place in which it must be done. The public congregation.

4. From the manner. With alacrity.

5. From the object. God, their Creator and King: "Let Israel rejoice," &c.

And this part he concludes with a strong reason:

1. "For the Lord taketh pleasure," &c. He loves those who most resemble him in holiness and purity.

2. "He will beautify the meek," &c. The people who trust him he will save.

II. And now he describes their future glory.

1. "Let the saints," &c. None others will he beautify.

2. "Let them rejoice," &c. The mansions prepared for them in heaven. There they rest from labour, but not from praise.

Their work is twofold: Present and future.

1. Present: "The high praises," &c. The highest that can be thought of.

2. For the future: "Let a two-edged sword," &c. When Christ shall come to judgment, the saints at the last shall be judges.

Then the exercise of this judiciary power shall be,

1. "To execute vengeance," &c. To judge them to punishment.

2. "To bind their kings with chains," &c. The phrase is metaphorical. "Bind him hand and foot," &c.; Matt. xxii. Christ's iron sceptre shall bruise the head of his enemies.

3. "To execute upon them the judgment written," &c. Against evil-doers.

He concludes with an acclamation. This *glory* of sitting with Christ and judging the world, is the glory of all saints. *Hallelujah.*

PSALM CL

A general exhortation to praise God, 1, 2. *With the trumpet, psaltery, and harp,* 3. *With the timbrel and dance, stringed instruments and organs,* 4. *With the cymbals,* 5. *All living creatures are called upon to join in the exercise.*

PRAISE [a]ye the Lord. Praise God in his
sanctuary: praise him in the firmament
of his power.

2 [b]Praise him for his mighty acts: praise
him according to his excellent [c]greatness.

3 Praise him with the sound of the [d]trum-

[a]Heb. *Hallelujah*——[b]Psa. cxlv. 5, 6

[c]Deut. iii. 24——[d]Or, *cornet;* Psa. xcviii. 6

NOTES ON PSALM CL.

This Psalm is without title and author in the *Hebrew*, and in all the ancient versions. It is properly the full chorus of all *voices* and *instruments* in the temple, at the conclusion of the grand *Hallelujah*, to which the five concluding Psalms belong.

Verse 1. *Praise God in his sanctuary*] In many places we have the compound word הללו־יה *halelu-yah,* praise ye Jehovah; but this is the first place in which we find הללו־אל *halelu-el,* praise God, or the strong God. Praise him who is Jehovah, the infinite and self-existent Being; and praise him who is God, *El* or *Elohim,* the great God in covenant with mankind, to bless and save them unto eternal life.

In his sanctuary—in the temple; in whatever place is dedicated to his service. Or, *in his holiness*—through his own holy influence in your hearts.

The firmament of his power.] Through the whole expanse, to the utmost limits of his power. As רקיע *rakia* is the firmament of vast expanse that surrounds the globe, and probably that in which all the celestial bodies of the solar system are included, it may have that meaning here. Praise him whose power and goodness extend through all worlds; and let the inhabitants of all those worlds share in the grand chorus, that it may be universal.

Verse 2. *For his mighty acts*] Whether manifested in creation, government, mercy or justice.

His excellent greatness.] כרב גדלו *kerob gudlo,* according to the multitude of his magnitude, or of his majesty. **Æfter mænigfealdnysse mucelnysse his;** After the manyfoldness of his mickleness.—Anglo-Saxon. After the mykelnes of his greathede.—Old Psalter. Let the praise be such as is becoming so great, so holy, and so glorious a Being.

Verse 3. *The sound of the trumpet*] שופר *sophar,* from its noble, cheering, and majestic sound; for the original has this ideal meaning.

With the psaltery] נבל *nebel;* the nabla, a hollow stringed instrument; perhaps like the *guitar,* or the old *symphony.*

And harp.] כנור *kinnor,* another *stringed* instrument, played on with the *hands* or *fingers.*

pet: [e]praise him with the psaltery and
harp.
4 Praise him [f]with the timbrel and [g]dance:
praise him with [h]stringed instruments and
organs.

5 Praise him upon the loud [i]cymbals:
praise him upon the high-sounding cymbals.
6 Let every thing that hath breath praise
the LORD. Praise ye the LORD.

[e]Psa. lxxxi. 2; cxlix. 3——[f]Exod. xv. 20——[g]Or, *pipe;* Psa. cxlix. 3

[h]Psa. xxxiii. 2; xcii. 3; cxliv. 9; Isa. xxxviii. 20——[i]1 Chron. xv. 16, 19, 28; xvi. 5; xxv. 1, 6

Verse 4. *Praise him with the timbrel*] תף *toph, drum, tabret,* or *tomtom,* or *tympanum* of the ancients; a skin stretched over a broad hoop; perhaps something like the *tambarine.* Anglo-Saxon; glig-beam, the *glad pipe. Taburne;* Old Psalter.

And dance] מחול *machol,* the *pipe.* The *croude* or *crowthe:* Old Psalter; a species of *violin.* It never means *dance;* see the note on Psa. cxlix. 3. *Crwth* signifies a *fiddle* in Welsh.

Stringed instruments] מנים *minnim.* This literally signifies *strings put in order;* perhaps a *triangular kind of hollow instrument* on which the strings were regularly placed, growing *shorter* and *shorter* till they came to a *point.* This would give a variety of sounds, from a deep bass to a high treble. In an ancient MS. Psalter before me, David is represented in two places, playing on such an instrument. It may be the sambuck, or psaltery, or some such instrument.

Organs.] עוגב *ugab.* Very likely the *syrinx* or *mouth organ; Pan's pipe;* both of the ancients and moderns. The *fistula, septem, disparibus nodis conjuncta,* made of seven pieces of cane or thick *straw,* of unequal lengths, applied to the lips, each blown into, according to the *note* intended to be expressed. This instrument is often met with in the ancient *bucolic* or *pastoral* writers.

Verse 5. *Loud cymbals*] צלצלים *tseltselim.* Two hollow plates of brass, which, being struck together, produced a sharp clanging sound. This instrument is still in use. What the *high-sounding cymbals* meant I know not; unless those of a *larger make,* struck above the head, and consequently emitting a louder sound.

Verse 6. *Let every thing that hath breath*] Either to make a vocal noise, or a sound by blowing into *pipes, fifes, flutes, trumpets,* &c. Let all join together, and put forth all your *strength* and all your *skill* in sounding the praises of Jehovah; and then let a *universal burst* with HALLELUJAH! close the grand ceremony. It is evident that this Psalm has no other meaning than merely the summoning up all the *voices,* and all the *instruments,* to complete the service in FULL CHORUS.

Of such peculiar importance did the *Book of Psalms* appear to our blessed Lord and his apostles, that they have quoted nearly fifty of them several times in the New Testament. There is scarcely a state in human life that is not distinctly marked in them; together with all the variety of experience which is found, not merely among *pious Jews,* but among *Christians,* the most deeply acquainted with the things of Christ.

The minister of God's word, who wishes to preach *experimentally,* should have frequent recourse to this sacred book; and by considering the various parts that refer to Jesus Christ and the Christian Church, he will be able to build up the people of God on their most holy faith; himself will grow in grace, and in the knowledge of God; and he will ever have an abundance of the most profitable *matter* for the edification of the Church of Christ.

ANALYSIS OF THE HUNDRED AND FIFTIETH PSALM

This Psalm is the same with the former. In the *hundred and forty-eighth,* all creatures are invited to praise God; in the *hundred and forty-ninth,* men especially, and those who are in the Church; but in this, that they praise him with all kinds of instruments.

I. An invitation to praise God, which word he repeats thirteen times, according to the thirteen attributes of God, as the rabbins reckon them.

II. That this be done with all sorts of instruments, intimating that it is to be performed with all the care, zeal, and ardency of affection.

I. Throughout the Psalm he calls on men to praise God.

1. "Praise God in his sanctuary." Or in your hearts, which are the temples of the Holy Ghost.

2. "Praise him in the firmament," &c. His magnificence when he sits on his throne. Some understand the Church by it, in which his saints shine as stars in the firmament.

3. "Praise him for his mighty acts," &c. The works of his power.

4. "Praise him according," &c. Whereby he excels all things; he being absolutely great, they only comparatively so.

II. The prophet desires that no way be omitted by which we may show our zeal and ardency in praising him.

1. "Praise him with the sound of the trumpet," &c. An instrument used in their solemn feasts.

2. "Praise him with the psaltery," &c. And with these they sing, so that there is also music with the voice.

3. "Praise him with the timbrel," &c. In the choir with many voices.

4. "Praise him with stringed instruments," &c. Lutes, viols, organs, &c.

5. "Praise him upon the high-sounding cymbals," &c. An instrument which yields a loud sound, as bells among us.

His conclusion is of universal reference, "Let every thing," &c.

1. "Every thing that hath breath," &c. That hath faculty or power to do it.

2. "Every thing that hath life," &c. Whether spiritual, as angels; or animal, as man and beasts. Or, metaphorically, such as, though inanimate, may be said to praise God, because they obey his order and intention. Thus, all things praise God, because all things that have

life or being derive it immediately from himself.

MASORETIC NOTES ON THE BOOK OF PSALMS

Number of verses, *two thousand five hundred and twenty-seven. Middle* verse. Psa. lxxviii. 36. *Sections, nineteen.*

At the end of the *Syriac* we have this colophon:—

"The hundred and fifty Psalms are completed. There are *five* books, *fifteen* Psalms of *degrees*, and *sixty* of *praises*. The number of *verses* is *four thousand eight hundred and thirty-two*. There are some who have added *twelve* others; but we do not need them. And may God be praised for ever!"

At the end of the *Arabic* is the following:—

The end of the *five books* of Psalms. The *first* book ends with the *fortieth* Psalm; the *second*, with the *seventieth* Psalm; the *third*, with the *eightieth* Psalm; the *fourth*, with the *hundred and fifteenth;* and the *fifth*, with the *last* Psalm, i. e., the *hundred and fiftieth.*

PSALM CLI

Besides these *hundred and fifty* Psalms, there is *one* additional in the *Syriac, Septuagint, Æthiopic,* and *Arabic,* of which it will be necessary to say something, and to give a translation.

1. The Psalm is not found in the *Hebrew*, nor in the *Chaldee*, nor in the *Vulgate*.

2. It is found, as stated, above, in the *Syriac, Septuagint, Æthiopic,* and *Arabic;* but not in the *Anglo-Saxon*, though *Dom. Calmet* has stated the contrary. But I have not heard of it in any MS. of that version; nor is it in Spelman's printed copy.

3. It is mentioned by *Apollinaris, Athanasius, Euthymius, Vigilius, Tapsensis,* and *St. Chrysostom.*

4. It has never been received either by the *Greek* or *Latin* Church; nor has it ever been considered as *canonical*.

5. It is certainly *very ancient*, stands in the *Codex Alexandrinus*, and has been printed in the *Paris* and *London Polyglots*.

6. Though the *Greek* is considered the most authentic copy of this Psalm, yet there are some things in the *Syriac* and *Arabic* necessary to make a full sense. The *Arabic* alone states the *manner* of Goliath's death.

The *title* is, "A Psalm in the handwriting of David, beyond the number of the Psalms, composed by David, when he fought in single combat with Goliath." I shall make it as complete as I can from the different versions.

I WAS the least among my brethren; and the youngest in my father's house; and I kept also my father's sheep.

2 My hands made the organ; and my fingers joined the psaltery.

3 And who told it to my LORD? [*Arab.:* And who is he who taught me?] The LORD himself, he is my Master, and the Hearer of all that call upon him.

4 He sent his angel, and took me away from my father's sheep; and anointed me with the oil of his anointing. [Others, *the oil of his mercy.*]

5 My brethren were taller and more beautiful than I; nevertheless the LORD delighted not in them.

6 I went out to meet the Philistine, and he cursed me by his idols.

7 [*Arab.:* In the strength of the LORD I cast three stones at him. *I smote* him in the forehead, and felled him to the earth.]

8 And I drew out his own sword from its sheath, and cut off his head, and took away the reproach from the children of Israel.

NOTES ON PSALM CLI.

If we were sure this was David's composition, we should not be willing to see it *out of the number of the Psalms*, or standing among the *apocryphal* writings. As a matter of *curiosity* I insert it; as, if a forgery, it is very ancient; and I leave it to the intelligent reader to add his own *notes*, and form his own *analysis*.

The subscription to the Syriac says some add *twelve* more. The *Codex Alexandrinus* has fourteen more. They are the following:—

1. The Song of Moses and the children of Israel, Exod. xv. 1, &c.
2. Ditto, from Deut. xxii. 1, &c.
3. The Song of Hannah, 1 Sam. ii. 1, &c.
4. The prayer of Isaiah, Isa. xxvi. 2, &c.
5. The prayer of Jonah, Jonah, ii. 3, &c.
6. The prayer of Habakkuk, Hab. iii. 2, &c.
7. The prayer of Hezekiah, Isa. xxxviii. 10, &c.
8. The prayer of Manasseh, see the *Apocrypha*.
9. The prayer of Azarias, or of the Three Children.—*Apocrypha.*
10. The Hymn of our Fathers, see the *Benedicite omnia opera* in the *Liturgy*.
11. The *Magnificat*, or Song of the Blessed Virgin, Luke i. 46, &c.
12. The *Nunc dimittis*, or Song of Simeon, Luke ii. 29, &c.
13. The prayer of Zacharias, Luke i. 68, &c.
14. The Ὕμνος ἑωθινος, or, Morning Hymn as used in the service of the *Greek Church*.

My old Psalter seems to have copied such authority as the *Codex Alexandrinus*, for it has added several similar pieces, after the *hundred and fiftieth* Psalm, where we read, *Explicit Psalmos, incipit canticum Ysaie.*

1. The Hymn of Isaiah, Isa. xii. 1, &c.
2. The Prayer of Hezekiah, Isa. xxxviii. 10-20, inclusive.
3. The Prayer of Hannah, 1 Sam. ii. 1, &c.
4. The Song of Moses at the Red Sea, Exod. xv. 1-19.
5. The Prayer of Habakkuk.
6. The Song of Moses, Deut. xxii. 1-43.
7. The *Magnificat*, or Song of the Blessed Virgin, Luke i. 46-55.
8. The ten commandments.
9. There are several curious maxims, &c., which follow the commandments, such as *Seven werkes of Mercy; Seven gastely werkes of Mercy; Seven Virtues; The keeping of the five senses; Fourteen points of trouthe.* Another head, which is torn off. Lastly, *some godly advices* in poetry, which terminate the book.

I suppose these hymns were added on the same principle that the general assembly of the Kirk of Scotland added, by an act of 1479 and 1750, a number of verses and portions of the sacred writings, among which are several of the above, to their authorized version of the Psalms of David in metre, to be sung in all kirks and families.

SKETCH
OF THE
LIFE AND CHARACTER OF DAVID

WHEN the historical books of the Old Testament were under consideration, I formed the resolution to say but little on those parts where the history of David is concerned, till I should come to the end of the Psalms, where, if I did not give a general history of his life, I might at least draw his character. But so many facts in David's history were found to require illustration, I was obliged often to anticipate my design, and enter into discussions which I had hoped to be able to produce with good effect at the end of his writings. I must therefore refer back to several particulars in the Books of Samuel, Kings, and Chronicles, that concern the history of this most extraordinary man; and the objections produced against his spirit and conduct by persons not friendly to Divine revelation.

Where I have found David to blame, I have not palliated his conduct; and though it is with me a maxim to lean to the most favourable side when examining the characters of men, yet I hope I have nowhere served the cause of *Antinomianism*, which I abominate, nor endeavoured to render any thing, morally evil, venial, because it was found in the conduct of a religious man or a prophet. Vice must never be countenanced, though individuals, on the whole highly respectable, suffer by its disclosure, which disclosure should take place only when the interests of religion and truth absolutely require it.

David, Doud, or *Daoud,* דוד, the son of Jesse, of an obscure family in the tribe of Judah, and of the inconsiderable village of Bethlehem, in the same tribe, was born, according to the best accounts, A. M. 2919, B. C. 1085. He was the youngest of eight sons, and was keeper of his father's sheep. David was descended from *Jacob* by his son *Judah,* in that line which united both the *regal* and *sacerdotal* functions; and in his own person were conjoined the *regal* and *prophetic* offices. It is supposed he was anointed by Samuel, about A. M. 2934, when he was but about *fifteen* years of age; and that he slew Goliath in A. M. 2942, when he was in the *twenty-third* or *twenty-fourth* year of his age. He became king of Judah after the death of Saul, A. M. 2949; and king of all Israel, A. M. 2956, when he was about *thirty-seven* years of age, and died A. M. 2989, B. C. 1015, when he was about *seventy-one* years old.

He is often mentioned by the *Asiatic* writers, and by *Mohammed,* in the *Koran,* in these words, "Daoud slew Geealout; (Goliath;) and God gave him a kingdom and wisdom, and taught him whatsoever he wished to know."

Hussain Vaez, one of the commentators on the Koran, observes on the above passage: "That Goliath was of such an enormous size that his armour, which was of *iron,* weighed *one thousand* pounds; and that his helmet alone weighed *three hundred;* nevertheless David slung a stone with such force as to break through the helmet, pierce the skull, and beat out the Philistine's brains.

"God gave him the gift of prophecy, and the Book *Ziboor;* (Psalms;) and taught him to make hair and sackcloth, which was the work of the prophets; and instructed him in the language of birds, which, with the stones of the field, were obedient to him, and iron was softened by his hands. During the *forty* days which he spent in bewailing his sins, plants grew where he watered the ground with his tears."

The Mohammedans all allow that the *Ziboor,* or Book of Psalms, was given to David by *immediate inspiration,* and that it contains 150 sourats or chapters. His skill in music is also proverbial among the Mohammedans. Hence some verses in the *Anvari Soheely,* which are to this effect: "You decide the greatest difficulties with as much ease as *Daoud* touched the chords of his lyre when he chanted his Psalms."

If we could persuade the Mohammedans that the *Book of Psalms* which we now possess was the real work of David, something would be gained towards their conversion. But they say the Jews have corrupted it, as the Christians have the *Angeel*, (Gospel,) and the book which they produce as the Psalms of David consists of extracts only from the Psalms, with a variety of other matters which have no relation either to David or his work.

In the sacred writings David is presented to our view—1. As a shepherd; 2. A musician; 3. A skilful military leader; 4. A hero; 5. A king; 6. An ecclesiastical reformer; 7. A prophet; 8. A type of Christ; 9. A poet; and 10. A truly pious man.

1. David stands before the world in his history and writings as a private person destitute of ambition, apparently in a low, if not mean, situation in life, contributing to the support of a numerous family, of which he formed a part, by keeping the sheep of his father in the wilderness or champaign country in the vicinity of Bethlehem. In those times, and in such a rocky and mountainous country as Judea, this situation required a person of considerable *address*, *skill*, *courage*, and *muscular strength*. The flock must not only be led out and in to find the proper pasture, but their maladies must be skilfully treated, and they defended against the attacks of wild beasts, than which none could be more formidable for rapacity and strength than the *lion* and the *bear*. These were among the savage inhabitants of the country of Judea, and were the destroyers of the flocks, and the terror of the shepherds. The land was also infested with *banditti*, or lawless solitary rovers, who sought by depredations among the flocks to live at the expense of others. The office therefore of a *shepherd* was neither *mean* nor *unimportant*, as a principal part of the property of the Jews consisted in their flocks.

From the ancient history of all civilized nations we learn that the persons thought qualified for it were such as had a liberal education, good natural parts, and were highly trustworthy and courageous. These most evidently were all combined in the character of David. That his *education* was good, his language and skill in music prove; and that his *mind* was highly cultivated, the depth, sublimity, and purity of his compositions demonstrate; and that his *courage* and *personal strength* must have been great, his slaying the lion and bear that had attacked the flock under his protection, are the clearest proofs.

2. His *skill in music* was so great as to be proverbial. In this curious art he excelled all his contemporaries, so as alone to acquire the character of the *sweet singer of Israel*. His success in quieting the turbulent and maniacal spirit of Saul by his performances on the lyre stand strongly marked in his history; and the effects produced were equal to any mentioned in the now fabulous histories of Greece or Rome. The wondrous harp of Orpheus, by which beasts and birds were enraptured, and the very stones and trees moved in harmony together, so as to compose of themselves the celebrated city of Thebes, we may well leave out of the question, as the fable is too gross to be credited, unless we take the exposition of an ancient author, *Philodemus*, some fragments of whose works have been recovered from the ruins of Herculaneum, from which we learn that the fable of the building of Thebes by the melody of his lyre arose from the fact that he was a musician who attended the builders, played to them during their labour, by whose contributions he earned a competent support, and caused them to go so lightly through their work, that he was hyperbolically said to have built the walls of the city by the power of his music. Nothing can be more natural than this explanation, nor could any thing serve better for the foundation of the fable. Indeed it has been conjectured by one of David's biographers, Dr. Delaney, that the history of David was the origin of that of Orpheus. The coincidence of the times, and the other circumstances alleged by this entertaining writer, have not served to persuade me of the truth of his hypothesis. We can amply support the credit of the Hebrew musician without impairing the credibility of the history and identity of the person of the ancient Greek lyrist.

It is not likely, however, that David was a performer on one kind of instrument only. There were many kinds of musical instruments in his time that were all used in the ordinances of religion, and apparently employed in those parts of it where the compositions of David were used. *Calmet* and others have properly divided these instruments into three classes. 1. STRINGED *instruments*. 2. WIND *instruments*. And 3. Such as were played on by a PLECTRUM.

I. STRINGED *instruments*. 1. The *nabla*, or psaltery. 2. The *kinnor*. 3. The *cythera* or *azur*, an instrument of ten chords. 4. The *symphony*. 5. The *Sambuck*. 6. The *minnim*.

II. WIND *instruments*. 1. The *chatsotserah*. 2. The *shophar*, or trumpet. 3. The *keren, or* horn. 4. The *ugab*, a species of organ. 5. The *mashrokitha*, or syrinx. 6. The *machalath*, a species of pipe or fife. 7. The *chalil*, or flute.

III. Instruments which required a PLECTRUM. 1. The *toph*, a drum, tomtom, or tambarine. 2. The *tseltselim*, or sistrum. 3. The *shalishim*, or triangle. 4. The *metsiltayim*, a species of bell.

As all these instruments were used in the service of God, and most of them are mentioned in the Psalms, it is very likely that such a consummate musician and poet played on the whole.

3. That David was a *skilful military leader*, requires little proof. When for the safety of his own life he was obliged to leave the court of Saul, and become an exile in the wilds of a country so much indebted to his courage and valour, he was under the necessity of associating to himself men of desperate fortunes and of no character. These, to the amount of *four hundred*, he so disciplined and managed, as to soften their lawless disposition, and repress their propensity to plunder and rapine, so that they never went on any expedition that was not under his direction, and made no inroads but what tended to strengthen the hands of his countrymen, and weaken those of their enemies. Neither by day nor night, so complete was his authority over them, were they permitted to take even a lamb or a kid from the flock of any man, though they had frequent opportunities of doing so in countries so thinly inhabited, and where the flocks were numerous. On the contrary they were *protectors* of the different herds which were fed in those parts of the wilderness where they were obliged to sojourn. To have succeeded in disciplining such a description of men is highly to the credit of his address and skill, especially when we consider that they were composed of such as had run away from the claims of their *creditors;* from the authority of their *masters;* who

were *distressed* in their circumstances, and *discontented* with the government, or their situation in life, 1 Sam. xxii. 2. I question much whether any of the heroes of the last or present century, from *Peter* and *Frederick* the Great down to Napoleon Bonaparte, destitute of all subsidiary authority, and without any *other officer* to assist them in the command, could have disciplined *four hundred* such men, brought them under perfect obedience, and prevented them from indulging their restless and marauding spirit with so many temptations before their eyes, while prey was so easy to be acquired, and their general privations rendered such supplies necessary.

4. As a *hero*, David appears very conspicuous, if we take this word in its general acceptation, *a man eminent for bravery.* And here his proffering to fight with Goliath, the famous Philistine champion who had defied and terrified all the hosts of Israel, is at once a proof of his *bravery* and *patriotism.* In very remote times, and down to a late period, military etiquette permitted feuds and civil broils to be settled by single combat. In the presence of the hostile armies, previously to the shock of general battle, a man either stepped out from the ranks, or by a *herald* bid defiance to any person in the hostile army, and stipulated certain conditions of combat, in order to spare the effusion of blood; to the exact fulfilment of which he pledged himself and his party. This was done very circumstantially in the case before us. When the Israelities and the Philistines had drawn up their forces in battle array at Ephes-dammim, a champion of Gath called *Goliath*, of gigantic stature and strength, came out of the camp of the Philistines, and stood and cried unto the armies of Israel: "Why are ye come out to set your battle in array? Choose you a man for you, and let him come down to me. If he be able to fight with me, and to kill me, then will we be your servants; but if I prevail against him, and kill him, then shall ye be our servants, and serve us." And concluded with defying the armies of Israel. Saul, though he was a man of great personal courage, and the whole Israelitish army, were greatly dismayed at this challenge; and the more particularly so, because no man dared to take it up, notwithstanding the king had offered "to enrich the accepter with great gifts, give him his daughter in marriage, and make his father's house free in Israel;" 1 Sam. xvii. 1, &c. David had come to the camp with provisions for his brothers who were in Saul's army; (for it appears that the Israelitish militia bore their own expenses when their services were requisite for the safety of their country;) and hearing the defiance of the Philistine, proposed to take up the challenge; and having obtained Saul's consent, went forth, fought and slew the Philistine in the manner related in the chapter quoted above.

On numerous occasions he signalized himself in the same way; his natural courage, heightened by his constant dependence on God, never forsook him, and was always invincible. He was the life of his kingdom, and the soul of his army; knew well how to distinguish and employ eminent abilities, had the ablest generals, and the address to form a multitude of heroes like himself.

He had a company of champions, or as they are generally termed *worthies* or *mighty men*, to the number of thirty-seven. The account given of these (2 Sam. xxiii.) would almost render credible the legend of King Arthur and the Knights of the Round Table; and it is probable that the first idea of that ancient romance was taken from the genuine history of David and his thirty-seven champions.

5. How David would have acquitted himself as a *lawgiver* we cannot tell; for God had taken care to leave nothing of this kind to the wisdom, folly, or caprice of any man. The laws were all made and the constitution framed by Jehovah himself; and no legitimate king of the Jews was permitted to enact any new laws, or abrogate or change the old. The faithful and constitutional king was he who ruled according to the laws already established, as well in religious as in civil matters; for although the Jewish theocracy was somewhat changed by the election of Saul, yet the monarch was considered only as the *vicegerent* of the Almighty; and David, taking care to abide by the laws as they then were, and governing his subjects accordingly, was said to be *after God's own heart*, or *a man after God's own heart:* and this is the sense in which this phrase is to be understood. And as David took great care that no innovation should be made in the *constitution*, that the law of God should be the law of the empire, and ruled according to that law, therefore he was most properly said to be *a man after God's own heart*, to fulfil all his counsels; and by this faithful attachment to the laws he was contradistinguished from Saul, who in several respects changed that law, and made not a few attempts to alter it in some of its most essential principles. On these grounds God rejected *him* and chose David.

But as a *civil magistrate* David's conduct was unimpeachable: his court was regulated according to the maxims of the Divine law; and the universal prosperity of his kingdom is a decisive proof that judgment and justice were faithfully administered in it. The *strong* did not oppress the *weak*, nor the *rich* the *poor;* and, although the empire was seldom at rest from war during his reign, yet it was so conducted that his subjects were neither *oppressed* nor *impoverished.* Many of his Psalms bear testimony to these matters, as they contain appeals to God relative to the sincerity of his heart, the uprightness of his conduct, and his impartiality in administering justice among the people. To David the cry of the distressed was never uttered in vain; and the curse of the widow and fatherless was never pronounced against him for a neglect of justice, or partiality in administering it according to the laws.

6. David, I think, may be fitly ranked among *ecclesiastical reformers;* for, although the *grand body* of the Jewish religion was so firmly fixed, that it could not be changed, yet there were *several circumstances* in the *form* of Divine worship that appear to have been left to the pious discretion of the Jewish prophets, priests, and kings, to improve as time and circumstances might require. That God might be constantly worshipped, that the Jewish ritual might be carefully observed, and all the Divinely appointed ecclesiastical persons have their proper share of the public service, David divided the *thirty-eight thousand Levites* into courses, assigning to each course its particular service, 1 Chron. xxiii. He did the same by the *priests*, *porters*, *singers*, &c.; and appointed *twelve captains* to serve each a month, and

have the rule and inspection of the different courses and orders, to see that the worship of God was properly conducted. The *twenty-third, twenty-fourth, twenty-fifth, twenty-sixth,* and *twenty-seventh* chapters of the *first* book of Chronicles, give a very detailed and circumstantial account of the improvements which David made in the *form* and *execution* of the different parts of public worship. Almost every pious king of Judah had matters of this kind to regulate and settle: but it appears that David's plan was so perfect, that it became a standard; and when any decay took place in the form of public worship, the chief aim of the succeeding kings was, to reduce every thing to the form in which David had left it. This is a full proof of the perfection of his plan.

7. That David was favoured with the *gift* of *prophecy,* is, I think, universally allowed. And although there have been prophets *pro tempore,* who were not remarkable for piety, yet there never was one on whom the prophetic Spirit *rested,* that was not truly pious. All such had deep communion with God: their souls were upright, and their bodies became temples of the Holy Ghost. This was most assuredly the case with David: the prophetic Spirit overshadowed and rested upon him; in general he held deep communion with God; and even in his Psalms, we can scarcely say *when* he does not prophesy. Some learned and very pious men consider the whole Psalter as a tissue of prophecies concerning Christ and his kingdom; and in this way our Lord and his apostles quote many of them. Could we really ascertain which were David's, perhaps we might find them all of this description; though the subjects to which they apply might not be so clearly distinct: but there were so many written *before, at, under,* and *after,* the Babylonish captivity, that are become so mixed with those of David, that it is difficult, and in some cases impossible, to ascertain them. Where he evidently prophesies of Christ and his Church, I have particularly remarked it in the notes. I have not gone so far as some learned and pious commentators have gone, in applying the Psalms to Christ and his Church, because I was not satisfied that they have such reference. Even those which are of David's composition, and have reference to Christ, are so mixed up with his own state, that it is often impossible to say when the Psalmist prophesies of the *Root of Jesse,* and when he simply refers to his own circumstances: and, on the whole, I am only sure of those which are thus quoted by our Lord and his apostles.

8. That David was a *type* of Christ is proved by the Scriptures themselves, see Jer. xxx. 9: "They shall serve the Lord their God, and DAVID their king, whom I will raise up unto them;" Ezek. xxxiv. 23: "And I will set up one shepherd over them, and he shall feed them, even my servant DAVID; he shall feed them, and he shall be their shepherd." Ver. 24: "And I the Lord will be their God, and my servant DAVID a prince among them." See also Ezek. xxxvii. 24; and compare this with Jer. xxiii. 4, 5; John x. 11; Heb. xiii. 24; 1 Pet. ii. 25; and v. 4; Hosea, chap. iii. ver. 5, speaks in the same way: "Afterward shall the children of Israel return, and seek the Lord their God, and DAVID their king; and shall fear the Lord and his goodness in the latter days." That none of these scriptures speak of *David, son of Jesse,* is evident from this, that Hosea lived three hundred years *after* David, Jeremiah four hundred and seventy-three, and Ezekiel four hundred and ninety-three.

But in what was David a *type of Christ?* Principally, I think, in the *name* דויד *David,* which signifies *the beloved one,* that one more loved than any other; and this is what is expressed from heaven by God himself, when he says, *This is my Son,* 'Ο Αγαπητος, εν ᾡ ευδοκησα, THE BELOVED ONE, *in whom I have delighted.* This is the *genuine David;* the *man after my own heart.* He was his *type* also, in being a *royal prophet*—one in whom the Holy Spirit dwelt, and one who was a truly *spiritual king;* a character that seldom occurs in the history of the world.

Were we to consult those who have *laboured* on the *types,* we might find all the following resemblances *stated;* and, in their way, wondrously *proved!* David was a type of Christ, 1. In his originally mean appearance. 2. In his mean education. 3. In his unction. 4. In his eminent qualifications. 5. In his various persecutions. 6. In his enemies. 7. In his distresses. 8. In his deliverance. 9. "In his victories and conquests. And, 10. In his taking to wife the adulterous woman, and thereby bringing guilt upon himself." See *Parkhurst.* All the first *nine* particulars might be *controverted,* as not having any thing in them exclusively typical; and the *tenth* is horrible, if not blasphemous. No analogies, no metaphorical meanings can support this abominable position. I have already given my opinion: to elucidate the particulars above, I shall never attempt.

9. But the highest merit of David, and that which seems to have been almost exclusively *his own,* was his *poetic genius.* As a Divine poet, even God himself had created none greater, either *before* or *since.* In this science and gift he is therefore the *chef-d'œuvre* of the Almighty. *Moses* wrote some fine verses; *Solomon* two fine poems, an *ode* and an *elegy.* The prophets, particularly *Isaiah,* in several *chapters* of his prophecy; *Jeremiah,* in his book of *Lamentations;* and some of the *minor prophets,* in a few *select verses,* have given us specimens of a profound poetical genius; but we have no *whole* like that of David. The *sublimity,* the *depth,* the *excursive fancy,* the *discursive power,* the *vast compass* of *thought,* the knowledge of *heaven* and *earth,* of *God* and *nature,* the work of the Spirit, the endlessly varied temptations of Satan, the knowledge of the human heart, the travail of the soul, the full comprehension of the *prosopopœia* or *personification* of the whole of *inanimate nature,* of every *virtue,* and of every *vice,* the immense grasp of thought embodying and arranging, and afterwards clothing in suitable language, the vast assemblage of ideas furnished by the natural and spiritual world; in a word, the spirit of poetry, the true *genie createur,* the του ποιητου ποιησις, *framework of the framer, the poetry of the poet,* not the *fiction* of the *inventive* genius; but the production of truth, hidden before in the bosom of God and nature, and exhibited in the most pleasing colours, with the most impressive pathos and irresistible harmonic diction: these qualities, these supramundane excellences, are found in no other poet that ever graced the annals of the world; they exist in their perfection only in David king of Israel. What is peculiarly remarkable in David is, he has succeeded to the very high-

est degree in every species of poetic composition that has for its *object* the glory of God and the welfare of man; and there is not one poet who has succeeded him, that has not failed when he attempted to sing of God, the punishment and rewards of the future world, and the unsearchable riches of Christ.

The *hymns* which he produced have been the general song of the universal Church; and men of all nations find in these compositions a language at once suitable to their feelings, and expressive of their highest joys and deepest sorrows, as well as of all the endlessly varied wishes and desires of their hearts. Hail, thou sweet singer of Israel! thy voice is still heard in all the assemblies of the saints.

In my notes on different places of the Psalter I have taken the opportunity of pointing out some of the beauties of these incomparable productions. But I must here state that the true excellence of this work will never be fully known, till it be translated according to its *rythmical* order, or *hemistich plan*, in which the harmony of its versification will be felt, and the whole be much more easily apprehended and practically understood. Had we a second *Lowth* to take up *David*, as the *first* did *Isaiah*, the Church of God would have the utmost reason to rejoice; and each devout penitent and believer would be enabled to sing more with the *spirit* and the *understanding*, than they can possibly do in taking up the best translation of the Psalms, whether *metrical* or *prosaic*, now extant.

We have no less than *four* versions, *two in prose* and *two in verse*, given by public authority to the good people of this land. Of the former there is one in the public service of the Church, compiled out of various translations; and one by King James's translators, in the authorized version of the Bible: the latter indescribably the better of this class. The *two metrical* versions are by *Sternhold*, *Hopkins*, and *others*, and by *Brady* and *Tate*. The former is the most just and literal: but none of them worthy of the subject. All these have already passed under review.

10. That there should have been any doubt entertained as to the *piety of David* appears very strange: most certainly, no man ever gave more unequivocal proofs of piety and devotedness to God than he gave. It was utterly impossible that any man could have written such Psalms as David has, whose soul was not deeply imbued with the Spirit of holiness; and this appears, not only in his *writings*, but in his *general conduct*. That in some cases he grievously departed from God, who would attempt to deny? His adultery with Bathsheba, and the consequent murder of the brave Uriah, were crimes of a very deep dye. I can say no more on these, than I have said already in my notes on 2 Sam. xi., and in the observations at the end of that chapter; and to these I beg to refer the reader. His pretended *cruelty* to the *Ammonites* has been adduced as a proof of a *hard* and *wicked heart*. See the notes on 2 Sam. xii. 31, where this charge is shown to be *unfounded*. Whatever obliquities have been charged against him, from *facts* recorded in his history, have already been amply considered where the facts are mentioned. But all these, make the worst of them we can, are but *insulated facts;* they never existed in *habit*, they made no part of his *general character;* and his *repentance* on the account of that which was his great blot, was the deepest and most exemplary we have on record. If a man have fallen into sin, and made the speediest return to God by confession and repentance, he proves that that transgression *is no part of his character*. He does not *repeat* it; he loathes and abhors it. It requires *malice* against God's book to say this crime was a part of David's *character*. Adultery and murder were no part of the character of David; he fell *once* into the first, and endeavoured to cover it by the death of an innocent man; but who can prove that he ever *repeated* either? While it is granted that a man of God *should* never sin against his Maker, it must also be granted that, in a state of *probation*, a holy man *may* sin; that such *may* be renewed unto repentance, and sin against their God no more, are also possible cases. And it is not less possible that a holy man of God may fall into sin, continue in it, repeat it and re-repeat it, and rise no more. Of this dreadful possibility the Scripture gives ample proof. There are but few in the Church of God that have kept their garments unspotted from the world, and retained their first love: but it *should have been otherwise;* and had they watched unto prayer, they would not have fallen. I only contend for the *possibility*, not for the *necessity*, of the case. And I contend that, in the case of David, a life so long, so holy, so useful, and, except in these instances, so truly exemplary, entitles him to the character of *a holy man of God;* and, allowing but a little for the dispensation under which he lived, *one of the holiest, if not* THE *holiest*, that ever wore a crown, or wielded a sceptre. For the supposition that on his death-bed he retracted the promise of life to Shimei, see the notes on 1 Kings ii. 9, where he is amply vindicated.

On the whole, I can cheerfully sum up all in the words of Dr. *Delaney:* "David was a *true believer*, a *zealous adorer* of God, *teacher* of his *law* and *worship*, and *inspirer* of his *praise*. A glorious *example*, a *perpetual* and *inexhaustible fountain* of true piety. A consummate and unequalled *hero*, a skilful and fortunate *captain*, a steady *patriot*, a wise *ruler*, a faithful, generous, and magnanimous *friend;* and, what is yet rarer, a no less generous and magnanimous *enemy*. A true *penitent*, a *Divine musician*, a sublime *poet*, an inspired *prophet*. By birth a *peasant*, by merit a *prince*. In youth a *hero*, in manhood a *monarch*, and in age a *saint*."

The matters of Bathsheba and Uriah are almost his only *blot*. There he sinned deeply; and no man ever suffered more in his body, soul, and domestic affairs, than he did in consequence. His penitence was as deep and extraordinary as his crime; and nothing could surpass both, *but* that eternal mercy that took away the guilt, assuaged the sorrow, and restored this most humbled transgressor to character, holiness, happiness, and heaven. Reader, let the God of David be exalted for ever!

***Corrected for the Press*, March 15*th*, 1829.—A. C.**

INTRODUCTION

TO THE

PROVERBS OF SOLOMON,

THE SON OF DAVID, KING OF ISRAEL

THERE has scarcely been any dispute concerning either the *author* or *Divine authority* of this book, either in the *Jewish* or *Christian* Church: all allow that it was written by Solomon; and the general belief is, that he wrote the book by Divine *inspiration.*

It has, indeed, been supposed that Solomon *collected* the major part of these proverbs from those who had preceded him, whether *Hebrews* or *heathens;* but the latter opinion has been controverted, as derogating from the *authority* of the book. But this supposition has very little weight; for, whatever of *truth* is found *in* or *among* men, came originally from God; and if he employed an inspired man to collect those *rays of light*, and *embody* them for the use of his Church, he had a right so to do, and to claim his *own* wheresoever found, and, by giving it a *new authentication*, to render it more useful in reference to the end for which it was originally communicated. God is the *Father of lights*, and from him came all true wisdom, not only in its discursive teachings, but in all its detached maxims for the government and regulation of life. I think it very likely that Solomon did not *compose* them all; but he collected every thing of this kind within his reach, and what was according to the Spirit of truth, by which he was inspired, he condensed in this book; and as the Divine Spirit gave it, so the providence of God has preserved it, for the use of his Church.

That true Light, which lightens every man that cometh into the world, first taught men to acknowledge himself as the Fountain and Giver of all good; and then by *short maxims*, conveyed in terse, energetic words, taught them to regulate their conduct in life, in respect to the dispensations of his providence, and in reference to each other in domestic, social, and civil life; and this was done by such *proverbs* as we find collected in this book. The different changes that take place in society; the new relations which in process of time men would bear to each other; the invention of arts and sciences; and the *experience* of those who had particularly considered the ways of the Lord, and marked the operations of his hands; would give rise to many maxims, differing from the original stock only in their application to those *new relations* and *varying circumstances.*

The *heathen* who had any connection with the first worshippers of the Almighty would observe the maxims by which *they* regulated the affairs of life, and would naturally borrow from them; and hence those *original teachings* became diffused throughout the world; and we find there is not an ancient nation on earth that is without its *code of proverbs* or proverbial maxims. The ancient SANSCRIT is full of them; and they abound in the *Persian* and *Arabic* languages, and in all the *dialects* formed from these, in all the countries of the East. The HEETOPADESA of Vishnoo Sarma, the *Anvari Soheili*, the *Bahar Danush*, *Kalila we Dumna*, and all the other *forms* of that *original* work; the fables of *Lockman*, *Æsop*, *Phædrus*, *Avienus*, &c., are collections of proverbs, illustrated by their application to the most important purposes of domestic, social, and civil life.

Those nations with which we are best acquainted have their collections of proverbs; and perhaps those with which we are unacquainted have theirs also. Messrs. *Visdelou* and *Galand* formed a collection of *Asiatic* proverbs, and published it in their supplement to the *Bibliotheque Orientale* of *D'Herbelot*. This is a collection of very great worth, curiosity, and importance. Mr. J. *Ray*, F. R. S., formed a collection of this kind, particularly of such as are or have been in use in Great Britain: this is as curious as it is entertaining and useful.

The term PROVERB, *proverbium*, compounded of *pro*, for, and *verbum*, a word, speech, or saying, leads us to an original meaning of the thing itself. It was an *allegorical* saying, where "more was meant than met the eye"—a *short saying* that stood for a *whole discourse*, the words of which are metaphorical; e. g., this of the rabbins: "I have given thee my lamp: give me thy lamp. If thou keep my lamp, I will keep thy lamp; but if thou quench my lamp, I will quench thy lamp." Here the word *lamp* is a metaphor: 1. For *Divine revelation*. 2. For the *human soul*. I have given thee my *word* and *Spirit;* give me thy *soul* and *heart*. If thou *observe* my *word*, and *follow* the dictates of my *Spirit*, I will *regulate* thy *heart*, and *keep* thy *soul* from every evil; but if thou *disobey* my *word*, and *quench* my *Spirit*, I will withdraw my Spirit, leave thee to the *hardness* and *darkness* of thy own heart, and send thee at last into outer *darkness*. Such as this is properly the *proverb;* the *word* which stands *for a discourse*.

But the Hebrew משלים *meshalim*, from משל *mashal*, to *rule* or *govern*, signifies a set or collection of *weighty*, *wise*, and therefore *authoritative*, *sayings*, whereby a man's whole conduct, civil and religious, is to be governed; sayings containing rules for the government of life. Or, as the Divine author himself expresses it in the beginning of the first chapter, the design is to lead men "to know wisdom and instruction, to perceive the words of understanding; to receive the instruction of wisdom, justice, and judgment, and equity; to give subtilty to the simple, and to the young man knowledge and discretion," ver. 2, 3. This was the design of *proverbs;* and perhaps it would be impossible to find out a better definition of the design and object of those of Solomon, than is contained in the two preceding verses. See my Dissertation on Parabolical Writing, at the end of the notes on Matt. xiii.

Of the *three thousand proverbs* which Solomon spoke, we have only those contained in this book and in *Ecclesiastes;* and of the *one thousand and five songs* which he made, only the *Canticles* have been preserved: or, in other words, of all his numerous works in *divinity*, *philosophy*, *morality*, and *natural history*, only the *three* above mentioned, bearing his name, have been admitted into the sacred canon. His *natural history* of *trees* and *plants*, of *beasts*, *fowls*, and *fishes*, (for on all these he wrote,) is totally lost. *Curiosity*, which never says, *It is enough*, would give up the three we have for those on the *animal* and *vegetable kingdom*, which are lost. What God judged of importance to the eternal interests of mankind, is preserved; and perhaps we know the vegetable and animal kingdoms now as well through *Linnæus* and *Buffon*, and their *followers*, as we should have known them, had Solomon's books on natural history come down to our time. Others would investigate *nature*, and to them those researches were left. Solomon spoke by inspiration; and therefore to him *Divine doctrines* were communicated, that he might teach them to man. *Every man in his order*.

The book of *Proverbs* has been divided into *five* parts:

I. A *master* is represented as instructing his *scholar*, giving him admonitions, directions, cautions, and excitements to the study of wisdom, chap. i. to ix.

II. This part is supposed to contain the Proverbs of Solomon, *properly so called;* delivered in distinct, independent, general sentences. From chap. ix. to xxii. 17.

III. In this part the tutor again addresses himself to his pupil, and gives him fresh admonitions to the study of wisdom; which is followed by a set of instructions, delivered *imperatively* to the pupil, who is supposed all the while to be standing before him. From chap. xxii. 17 to chap. xxv.

IV. This part is distinguished by being a *selection* of Solomon's Proverbs, made by the *men of Hezekiah*, conjectured to be Isaiah, Hosea, and Micah, who all flourished under that reign. This part, like the *second*, is composed of distinct, unconnected sentences, and extends from chap. xxv. to xxx.

V. The *fifth* part contains a set of wise expostulations and instructions, which *Agur*, the son of *Jakeh*, delivered to his pupils, *Ithiel* and *Ucal*, chap. xxx. And the thirty-first chapter contains the instructions which a *mother*, who is not named, gave to *Lemuel* her son, being earnestly desirous to guard him against vice, to establish him in the principles of justice, and to have him married to a wife of the best qualities. These two last chapters may be considered a kind of *Appendix* to the book of Proverbs: see Dr. *Taylor;* but others suppose that the thirty-first chapter contains *Bathsheba's* words to *Solomon*, and his commendation of his mother.

There are many *repetitions* and some *transpositions* in the book of Proverbs, from which it is very probable that they were not all made at the same time; that they are the work of different authors, and have been collected by various hands: but still the sum total is delivered to us by Divine inspiration; and whoever might have been the original authors of *distinct parts*, the Divine Spirit has made them all its own by handing them to us in this form. Some attribute the collection, i. e., the formation of this collection, to *Isaiah;* others, to *Hilkiah*, and *Shebna* the scribe; and others, to *Ezra*.

That Solomon could have borrowed little from his predecessors is evident from this consideration, that all uninspired ethic writers, who are famous in history, lived *after his times.* Solomon began to reign A. M. 2989, which was 239 years before the *first Olympiad;* 479 before *Cyrus*, in whose time flourished the *seven wise men of Greece;* 679 before *Alexander the Great*, under whose reign flourished *Socrates*, *Plato*, and *Aristotle;* and 1011 before the *birth of Christ*. Therefore to the *Gentiles* he could be but little, if at all, indebted.

It is impossible for any description of persons to read the book of Proverbs without profit. *Kings* and *courtiers*, as well as those engaged in *trade*, *commerce*, *agriculture*, and the *humblest walks* of life, may here read lessons of instruction for the regulation of their conduct in their respective circumstances. *Fathers*, *mothers*, *wives*, *husbands*, *sons*, *daughters*, *masters*, and *servants*, may here also learn their respective duties; and the most excellent rules are laid down, not only in reference to *morality*, but to *civil policy* and *economy*. Many *motives* are employed by the wise man to accomplish the end at which he aims; motives derived from *honour*, *interest*, *love*, *fear*, *natural affection*, and *piety* towards God. The principal object he has in view is, to inspire a deep reverence for God, fear of his judgments and an ardent love for wisdom and virtue. He exhibits injustice, impiety, profligacy, idleness, imprudence, drunkenness, and almost every vice, in such livelycolours as to render every man ashamed of them who has any true respect for his interest, honour, character, or health. And as there is nothing so directly calculated to ruin young men, as *bad company*, *debauch*, and *irregular connections*, he labours to fortify his disciples with the most convincing reasons against all these vices, and especially against *indolence*, *dissipation*, and the company of *lewd women*.

Maxims to regulate life in all the conditions already mentioned, and to prevent the evils already described, are laid down so copiously, clearly, impressively, and in such *variety*, that every man who wishes to be instructed may take what he chooses, and, among multitudes, those which he likes best.

Besides the original *Hebrew*, the book of Proverbs exists in the following ancient versions: the *Chaldee*, *Septuagint*, *Syriac*, *Vulgate*, and *Arabic*. But the Septuagint takes greater liberty with the sacred text than any of the rest: it often *transposes*, *changes*, and *adds;* and all these to a very considerable extent. This is the version which is quoted in the *New Testament*. Several of these *additions*, as well as the most important *changes*, the reader will find noticed in the following notes; but to mark them all would require a translation of almost the whole *Greek text*. How our *forefathers* understood several passages will be seen by quotations from an ancient MS. in my possession, which begins with this book, and extends to the conclusion of the New Testament. It is well written upon strong vellum, in very large folio, and highly illuminated in the beginning of each book, and first letter of each chapter. The language is more antiquated than in the translation commonly attributed to Wiclif. It was once the property of *Thomas à Woodstock*, youngest son of Edward III., and brother of John of Gaunt and the Black Prince. I have often quoted this MS. in my notes on the New Testament.

A. CLARKE.

THE
PROVERBS

Year from the Creation, 3004.—Year before the birth of Christ, 996.—Year before the vulgar era of Christ's nativity, 1000.—Year since the Deluge, according to Archbishop Usher and the English Bible, 1348.—Year from the destruction of Troy, 185.—Year before the first Olympiad, 224.—Year before the building of Rome, 247.

CHAPTER I

The design of the proverbs, 1–6. An exhortation to fear God, and believe his word, because of the benefit to be derived from it, 7–9; to avoid the company of wicked men, who involve themselves in wretchedness and ruin, 10–19. Wisdom, personified, cries in the streets, and complains of the contempt with which she is treated, 20–23. The dreadful punishment that awaits all those who refuse her counsels, 24–33.

A. M. cir. 3004
B. C. cir. 1000
Ante I. Olymp. cir. 224
Ante U. C. cir. 247

THE [a]proverbs of Solomon
the son of David, king of
Israel;
2 To know wisdom and in-
struction; to perceive the words of understanding;
3 To [b]receive the instruction
of wisdom, justice, and judgment, and [c]equity;
4 To give subtilty to the
[d]simple, to the young man knowledge and
[e]discretion.

[a]1 Kings iv. 32; ch. x. 1; xxv. 1; Eccles. xii. 9——[b]Ch. ii. 1, 9——[c]Heb. *equities*——[d]Ch. ix. 4——[e]Or, *advisement*

NOTES ON CHAP. I

Verse 1. *The proverbs of Solomon*] For the meaning of the word *proverb*, see the *introduction;* and the *dissertation upon parabolical writing* at the end of the notes on Matt. xiii. Solomon is the first of the sacred writers whose name stands at the head of his works.

Verse 2. *To know wisdom*] That is, this is the design of parabolical writing in *general;* and the *particular* aim of the present work.

This and the two following verses contain the interpretation of the term *parable*, and the author's design in the whole book. The first verse is the *title*, and the next three verses are an explanation of the nature and design of this very important tract.

Wisdom] חכמה *chochmah* may mean here, and in every other part of this book, not only that Divine science by which we are enabled to *discover the best end*, and *pursue it by the most proper means;* but also the whole of that *heavenly teaching* that shows us both ourselves and God, directs us into all truth, and forms the whole of *true religion.*

And instruction] מוסר *musar*, the *teaching* that discovers all its parts; to *understand*, to *comprehend* the words or doctrines which should be comprehended, in order that we may become wise to salvation.

Verse 3. *To receive the instruction*] השכל *haskel*, the deliberately *weighing* of the points contained in the *teaching*, so as to find out their *importance.*

Equity] משרים *mesharim*, *rectitude.* The pupil is to receive *wisdom and instruction, the words of wisdom and understanding, justice and judgment*, so perfectly as to excel in all. *Wisdom* itself, personified, is his teacher; and when God's wisdom teaches, there is no delay in learning.

Verse 4. *To give subtilty to the simple*] The word *simple*, from *simplex*, compounded of *sine*, without, and *plica*, a fold, properly signifies *plain* and *honest*, one that has no *by-ends* in view, who is *what he appears to be;* and is opposed to *complex*, from *complico*, to *fold together*, to make *one rope* or *cord* out of *many strands;* but because *honesty and plaindealing* are so rare in the world, and none but the *truly religious man* will practise them, farther than the *fear of the law* obliges him, hence *simple* has sunk into a state of progressive deterioration. At first, it signified, as above, *without fold, unmixed, uncompounded:* this was its *radical* meaning. Then, as applied to *men*, it signified *innocent, harmless, without disguise;* but, as such persons were rather an *unfashionable* sort of people, it sunk in its meaning to *homely, homespun, mean, ordinary.* And, as worldly men, who were seeking their portion in this life, and had little to do with religion, supposed that *wisdom, wit*, and *under-*

A. M. cir. 3004 B. C. cir. 1000 Ante I. Olymp. cir. 224 Ante U. C. cir. 247

5 [f]A wise *man* will hear, and
will increase learning; and a
man of understanding shall attain unto wise counsels:

6 To understand a proverb, and [g]the interpretation; the words of the wise, and their [h]dark sayings.

7 [i]The fear of the LORD *is*
[k]the beginning of knowledge:
but fools despise wisdom and instruction.

8 [l]My son, hear the instruction of thy father, and forsake not the law of thy mother.

[f]1 Chron. xxvi. 14; chap. ix. 9; chap. xi. 30; xiii. 14, 20; xv. 2——[g]Or, *an eloquent speech*——[h]Psa. lxxviii. 2

[i]Job xxviii. 28; Psa. cxi. 10; chap. ix. 10; Eccles. xii. 13 [k]Or, *the principal part*——[l]Chap. iv. 1; vi. 20

standing, were given to men that they might make the best of them in reference to the *things of this life*, the word sunk still lower in its meaning, and signified *silly, foolish;* and there, to the dishonour of our language and morals, it stands! I have taken those acceptations which I have marked in Italics out of the *first dictionary* that came to hand—*Martin's;* but if I had gone to *Johnson*, I might have added to SILLY, *not wise, not cunning. Simplicity*, that meant at first, as MARTIN defines it, *openness, plaindealing, downright honesty*, is now degraded to *weakness, silliness, foolishness.* And these terms will continue thus degraded, till *downright honesty* and *plaindealing* get again into vogue. There are two Hebrew words generally supposed to come from the *same root*, which in our common version are rendered *the simple,* פתאים *pethaim*, and פתים or פתיים *pethayim;* the former comes from פתא *patha*, to be *rash, hasty;* the latter, from פתה *pathah, to draw aside, seduce, entice.* It is the first of these words which is used here, and may be applied to *youth;* the *inconsiderate*, the *unwary*, who, for want of knowledge and experience, act *precipitately.* Hence the *Vulgate* renders it *parvulis*, little ones, young children, or *little children*, as my old MS.; or *very babes*, as *Coverdale.* The *Septuagint* renders it ακακοις, those that are *without evil;* and the *versions* in general understand it of those who are *young, giddy*, and *inexperienced.*

To the young man] נער *naar* is frequently used to signify such as are in the *state of adolescence, grown up boys*, very well translated in my old MS. **yunge fulwaxen;** what we would now call the *grown up lads.* These, as being giddy and inexperienced, stand in especial need of lessons *of wisdom and discretion.* The Hebrew for *discretion*, מזמה *mezimmah*, is taken both in a *good* and *bad* sense, as זם *zam*, its root, signifies to *devise* or *imagine;* for the *device* may be either *mischief*, or the *contrivance* of some *good purpose.*

Verse 5. *A wise* man *will hear*] I shall not only give such instructions as may be suitable to the youthful and inexperienced, but also to those who have much knowledge and understanding. So said St. Paul: *We speak wisdom among them that are perfect.* This and the following verse are connected in the old MS. and in *Coverdale:* "By hearyinge the wyse man shall come by more wysdome; and by experience he shall be more apte to understonde a parable and the interpretation thereof; the wordes of the wyse and the darke speaches of the same."

Verse 6. *Dark sayings.*] חידת *chidoth*, enigmas or riddles, in which the Asiatics abounded. I believe *parables*, such as those delivered by our Lord, nearly express the meaning of the original.

Verse 7. *The fear of the Lord*] In the preceding verses Solomon shows the *advantage* of acting according to the dictates of wisdom; in the following verses he shows the *danger* of acting contrary to them. *The fear of the Lord* signifies that *religious reverence* which every intelligent being owes to his Creator; and is often used to express the *whole of religion*, as we have frequently had occasion to remark in different places. But *what* is *religion?* The love of God, and the love of man; the *former* producing *all obedience* to the *Divine will;* the *latter*, every *act of benevolence* to one's fellows. The love of God shed abroad in the heart by the Holy Spirit produces the deepest religious reverence, genuine piety, and cheerful obedience. To love one's neighbour as himself is the second great commandment; and as *love* worketh no ill to one's neighbour, *therefore it is said* to be *the fulfilling of the law.* Without *love*, there is no *obedience;* without *reverence*, there is neither *caution, consistent conduct*, nor *perseverance* in righteousness.

This fear or religious reverence is said to be *the beginning of knowledge;* ראשית *reshith*, the *principle*, the *first moving influence*, begotten in a tender conscience by the Spirit of God. No man can ever become *truly wise*, who does not begin with God, the fountain of knowledge; and he whose mind is influenced by the fear and love of God will learn more in a month than others will in a year.

Fools despise] אוילים *evilim*, evil men. Men of bad hearts, bad heads, and bad ways.

Verse 8. *My son, hear*] *Father* was the title of *preceptor*, and *son*, that of *disciple* or *scholar*, among the Jews. But here the reference appears to be to the *children of a family;* the *father* and the *mother* have the principal charge, in the first instance, of their children's instruction. It is supposed that these parents have, themselves, the fear of the Lord, and that they are capable of giving the best counsel to their children, and that they set before them a strict example of all godly living. In vain do parents give *good advice* if their own conduct be not consistent. The *father* occasionally gives *instruction;* but he is not always in the *family*, many of those occupations which are necessary for the family support being carried on abroad. The *mother*—she is constantly *within doors*, and to her the regulation of the family belongs; therefore she has and gives *laws.* The wise man says in effect to every child, "Be obedient to thy mother within, and carefully attend to the instructions of thy father, that thou mayest the better see the *reasons* of obedience; and learn from him how thou art to get thy bread honestly in the world."

A. M. cir. 3004
B. C. cir. 1000
Ante I. Olymp. cir. 224
Ante U. C. cir. 247

9 For [m]they *shall be* [n]an ornament of grace unto thy head, and
chains about thy neck.
10 My son, if sinners entice
thee, [o]consent thou not.
11 If they say, Come with us, let us [p]lay
wait for blood, let us lurk privily for the innocent without cause:
12 Let us swallow them up alive as the
grave; and whole, [q]as those that go down
into the pit:
13 We shall find all precious substance, we
shall fill our houses with spoil:
14 Cast in thy lot among us; let us all have
one purse:
15 My son, [r]walk not thou in the way with
them; [s]refrain thy foot from
their path:
16 [t]For their feet run to evil,
and make haste to shed blood.
17 Surely in vain the net is spread [u]in the
sight of any bird.
18 And they lay wait for their *own* blood;
they lurk privily for their *own* lives.
19 [v]So *are* the ways of every one that is
greedy of gain; *which* taketh away the life
of the owners thereof.
20 [w]Wisdom [x]crieth without; she uttereth
her voice in the streets:
21 She crieth in the chief place of concourse,
in the openings of the gates: in the city
she uttereth her words, *saying,*

---

[m]Chap. iii. 22——[n]Hebrew, *an adding*——[o]Genesis xxxix. 7, &c.; Psalm i. 1; Ephesians v. 11——[p]Jeremiah v. 26——[q]Psalm xxviii. 1; cxliii. 7——[r]Psalm i. 1; chap. iv. 14——[s]Psalm cxix. 101——[t]Isaiah lix. 7; Romans iii. 15——[u]Hebrew, *in the eyes of every thing that hath a wing*——[v]Chap. xv. 27; 1 Timothy vi. 10——[w]Hebrew, *Wisdoms,* that is, *excellent wisdom*——[x]Chap. i. 8, &c.; ix. 3; John vii. 37

Verse 9. *An ornament of grace unto thy head, and chains*] That is, filial respect and obedience will be as ornamental to thee as *crowns, diadems,* and golden chains and pearls are to others.

Political dignity has been distinguished in many nations by a *chain of gold about the neck.* Solomon seems here to intimate, if we follow the metaphor, that the surest way of coming to distinguished eminence, in civil matters, is to act according to the principles of *true wisdom,* proceeding from the *fear of God.*

Verse 10. *If sinners entice thee, consent thou not.*] אל תבא *al tobe,* WILL—*not.* They can do thee no harm unless thy will join in with them. God's eternal purpose with respect to man is, that his *will* shall be *free;* or, rather, that the *will,* which is *essentially* FREE, shall never be forced nor be forceable by any power. Not even the devil himself can lead a man into sin till he *consents.* Were it not so, how could God judge the world?

Verse 11. *If they say, Come with us*] From all accounts, this is precisely the way in which the workers of iniquity form their partisans, and constitute their marauding societies to the present day.

Let us lay wait for blood] Let us rob and murder.

Let us lurk privily] Let us lie in ambush for our prey.

Verse 12. *Let us swallow them up alive*] Give them as hasty a death as if the earth were suddenly to swallow them up. This seems to refer to the destruction of a whole village. Let us destroy man, woman, and child; and then we may seize on and carry away the whole of their property, and the booty will be great.

Verse 14. *Cast in thy lot*] Be a *frater conjuratus,* a sworn brother, and thou shalt have an equal share of all the spoil.

Common sense must teach us that the words here used are such as must be spoken when a gang of cutthroats, pickpockets, &c., are associated together.

Verse 16. *For their feet run to evil*] The whole of this verse is wanting in the *Septuagint,* and in the *Arabic.*

Verse 17. *Surely in vain the net is spread in the sight of any bird.*] This is a *proverb* of which the wise man here makes a particular use; and the meaning does not seem as difficult as some imagine. The wicked are represented as *lurking privily* for the innocent. It is in this way alone that they can hope to destroy them and take their substance; for if their designs were *known,* proper precautions would be taken against them; for it would be *vain to spread the net in the sight of those birds* which men wish to ensnare. Attend therefore to my counsels, and they shall never be able to ensnare *thee.*

Verse 18. *They lay wait for their* own *blood*] I believe it is the *innocent* who are spoken of here, for whose *blood* and *lives* these *lay wait* and *lurk privily;* certainly not *their own,* by any mode of construction.

Verse 19. Which *taketh away the life*] A *covetous* man is in effect, and in the sight of God, a murderer; he wishes to get all the *gain* that can accrue to any or all who are in the same business that he follows—no matter to him how many families starve in consequence. This is the very case with him who sets up shop after shop in different parts of the same town or neighbourhood, in which he carries on the same business, and endeavours to *undersell* others in the same trade, that he may get all into his own hand.

Verse 20. *Wisdom crieth*] Here wisdom is again *personified,* as it is frequently, throughout this book; where nothing is meant but the *teachings* given to man, either by *Divine revelation* or the voice of the Holy Spirit in the heart. And this voice of *wisdom* is opposed to the *seducing language* of the wicked mentioned above. This voice is everywhere heard, in public, in private, in the streets, and in the house. Common sense, universal experience, and the law of justice written on the heart, as

A. M. cir. 3004
B. C. cir. 1000
Ante I. Olymp. cir. 224
Ante U. C. cir. 247

22 How long, ye simple ones, will ye love simplicity? and the scorners delight in their scorning, and fools hate knowledge?

23 Turn you at my reproof: behold, [y]I will pour out my spirit unto you, I will make known my words unto you.

24 [z]Because I have called, and ye refused; I have stretched out my hand, and no man regarded;

25 But ye [a]have set at naught all my counsel, and would none of my reproof:

26 [b]I also will laugh at your calamity; I will mock when your fear cometh;

27 When [c]your fear cometh as desolation, and your destruction cometh as a whirlwind, when distress and anguish cometh upon you.

28 [d]Then shall they call upon me, but I will not answer; they shall seek me early, but they shall not find me:

A. M. cir. 3004
B. C. cir. 1000
Ante I. Olymp. cir. 224
Ante U. C. cir. 247

29 For that they [e]hated knowledge, and did not [f]choose the fear of the LORD:

30 [g]They would none of my counsel: they despised all my reproof.

31 Therefore [h]shall they eat of the fruit of their own way, and be filled with their own devices.

32 For the [i]turning away of the simple shall slay them, and the prosperity of fools shall destroy them.

33 But [k]whoso hearkeneth unto me shall dwell safely, and [l]shall be quiet from fear of evil.

---

[y]Joel ii. 28——[z]Isa. lxv. 12; lxvi. 4; Jer. vii. 13; Zech. vii. 11——[a]Psa. cvii. 11; ver. 30; Luke vii. 30——[b]Psa. ii. 4——[c]Ch. x. 24——[d]Job xxvii. 9; xxxv. 12; Isa. i. 15; Jer. xi. 11; xiv. 12; Ezek. viii. 18; Mic. iii. 4; Zech. vii. 13; James iv. 3——[e]Job xxi. 14; ver. 22——[f]Psa. cxix. 173——[g]Ver. 25; Psa. lxxxi. 11——[h]Job iv. 8; ch. xiv. 14; xxii. 8; Isa. iii. 11; Jer. vi. 19——[i]Or, *ease of the simple*——[k]Psa. xxv. 12, 13——[l]Psa. cxii. 7

---

well as the law of God, testify against rapine and wrong of every kind.

Verse 22. *Ye simple ones*] פתים *pethayim*, ye who have been *seduced* and *deceived*. See on ver. 4.

Verse 23. *Turn you at my reproof*] לתוכחתי *lethochachti*, at my *convincing mode* of *arguing;* attend to my *demonstrations*. This is properly the meaning of the original word.

I will pour out my spirit unto you] "I wil expresse my mynde unto you;" COVERDALE. **Loo I shall bryngen forth to you my Spirit**; *Old MS. Bible*. If you will hear, ye shall have ample instruction.

Verse 24. *Because I have called*] These and the following words appear to be spoken of the persons who are described, ver. 11-19, who have refused to return from their evil ways till arrested by the hand of justice; and here the wise man points out their deplorable state.

They are now about to suffer according to the demands of the law, for their depredations. They now wish they had been guided by wisdom, and had chosen the fear of the Lord; but it is too late: die they must, for their crimes are proved against them, and *justice* knows nothing of *mercy*.

This, or something like this, must be the wise man's meaning; nor can any thing spoken here be considered as applying or applicable to the *eternal* state of the persons in question, much less to the case of any man convinced of sin, who is crying to God for mercy. Such persons as the above, condemned to die, may call upon justice for pardon, and they may do this *early, earnestly;* but they will call in vain. But no poor penitent sinner on this side of eternity can call upon God early, or seek him through Christ Jesus earnestly for the pardon of his sins, without being heard. Life is the time of probation, and while it lasts the vilest of the vile is within the reach of mercy. It is only in *eternity* that the state is irreversibly fixed, and where that which was guilty must be guilty still. But let none harden his heart because of this longsuffering of God; for if he die in his sin, where God is he shall never come. And when once shut up in the unquenchable fire, he will not pray for mercy, as he shall clearly see and feel that the hope of his redemption is entirely cut off.

Verse 27. *Your destruction cometh as a whirlwind*] כסופה *kesuphah*, as the all-prostrating blast. *Sense* and *sound* are here well expressed. *Suphah* here is the gust of wind.

Verse 29. *They hated knowledge*] This argues the deepest degree of intellectual and moral depravity.

Verse 32. *For the turning away of the simple*] This difficult place seems to refer to such a case as we term *turning king's evidence;* where an accomplice saves his own life by impeaching the rest of his gang. This is called his *turning* or *repentance*, משובה *meshubah;* and he was the most likely to turn, because he was of the פתים *pethayim, seduced* or *deceived* persons. And this evidence was given against them when they were in their prosperity, שלוה *shalvah*, their *security*, enjoying the fruits of their depredations; and being thus in a state of fancied *security*, they were the more easily taken and brought to justice.

Verse 33. *But whoso hearkeneth unto me shall dwell safely*] The man who hears the *voice of wisdom* in preference to the *enticements* of the *wicked*. He shall dwell in *safety*, ישכן בטח *yishcan betach*, he shall *inhabit safety* itself; he shall be completely safe and secure; and *shall be quiet from the fear of evil*, having a full consciousness of his own innocence and God's protection. *Coverdale* translates, "And have ynough without eney feare of evell." What the just man has he got honestly; and he has the blessing of God upon it. It is the reverse with the thief, the knave, the cheat, and the extortioner: Male parta pejus dilabuntur; "Ill gotten, worse spent."

CHAPTER II

The teacher promises his pupil the highest advantages, if he will follow the dictates of wisdom, 1–9. *He shall be happy in its enjoyment,* 10, 11; *shall be saved from wicked men,* 12–15; *and from the snares of bad women,* 16–19; *be a companion of the good and upright; and be in safety in the land, when the wicked shall be rooted out of it,* 20–22.

A. M. cir. 3004 B. C. cir. 1000 Ante I. Olymp. cir. 224 Ante U. C. cir. 247

MY son, if thou wilt receive
my words, and [a]hide my
commandments with thee;
2 So that thou incline thine
ear unto wisdom, *and* apply thine heart to
understanding;
3 Yea, if thou criest after knowledge, *and*
[b]liftest up thy voice for understanding;
4 [c]If thou seekest her as silver, and searchest for her as *for* hid treasures;
5 Then shalt thou understand the fear of
the LORD, and find the knowledge of God.
6 [d]For the LORD giveth wisdom: out of his
mouth *cometh* knowledge and understanding.
7 He layeth up sound wisdom for the righteous: [e]*he is* a buckler to them
that walk uprightly.
8 He keepeth the paths of judgment, and [f]preserveth the way
of his saints.
9 Then shalt thou understand righteousness,
and judgment, and equity; *yea,* every good path.
10 When wisdom entereth into thine heart,
and knowledge is pleasant unto thy soul;
11 Discretion shall preserve thee, [g]under-
standing shall keep thee:
12 To deliver thee from the way of the evil
man, from the man that speaketh froward
things;
13 Who leave the paths of uprightness, to

A. M. cir. 3004 B. C. cir. 1000 Ante I. Olymp. cir. 224 Ante U. C. cir. 247

[a]Ch. iv. 21; vii. 1——[b]Heb. *givest thy voice*——[c]Ch. iii. 14; Matt. xiii. 43——[d]1 Kings iii. 9, 12; James i. 5

[e]Psa. lxxxiv. 11; chap. xxx. 5——[f]1 Sam. ii. 9; Psa. lxvi. 9——[g]Chap. vi. 22

NOTES ON CHAP. II.

Verse 1. *My son*] Here the *tutor* still continues to instruct his *disciple.*

Hide my commandments with thee] Treasure them up in thy *heart,* and then act from them through the medium of thy *affections.* He who has the rule of his *duty* only in his *Bible* and in his *head,* is not likely to be a steady, consistent character; his heart is not engaged, and his obedience, in any case, can be only *forced,* or done from a *sense of duty:* it is not the obedience of a *loving, dutiful child,* to an *affectionate father.* But he who has the word of God in his *heart,* works *from his heart;* his heart goes with him in all things, and he delights to do the will of his heavenly Father, because *his law is in his heart.* See chap. iii. 3.

Verse 4. *If thou seekest her as silver*] How do men seek money? What will they not do to get rich? Reader, seek the salvation of thy soul as earnestly as the covetous man seeks wealth; and be ashamed of thyself, if thou be less in earnest after the *true riches* than he is after *perishing wealth.*

Hid treasures] The original word signifies property of any kind *concealed* in the earth, in caves or such like; and may also mean *treasures,* such as the *precious metals* or *precious stones,* which are presumptively known to exist in such and such *mines.* And how are these sought? Learn from the following circumstance: In the Brazils *slaves* are employed to scrape up the soil from the bed of the Rio Janeiro, and wash it carefully, in order to find particles of *gold* and *diamonds;* and it is a law of the state, that he who finds a diamond of so many carats shall have his *freedom.* This causes the greatest ardour and diligence in searching, washing out the soil, picking, &c., in order to find such diamonds, and the greatest anxiety for success; so precious is *liberty* to the human heart. This method of searching for gold and precious stones is alluded to in chap. iii. 13-15. In this way Solomon wishes men to seek for wisdom, knowledge, and understanding; and he who succeeds finds the *liberty* of the children of God, and is saved from the *slavery* of *sin* and the *empire of death.*

Verse 7. *He layeth up sound wisdom*] תושיה *tushiyah.* We have met with this word in Job; see chap. v. 12; vi. 13; xi. 6; xii. 16. See especially the note on Job xi. 6, where the different acceptations of the word are given. *Coverdale* translates, "He preserveth the welfare of the righteous." It is difficult to find, in any language, a term proper to express the original meaning of the word; its seems to mean generally the *essence* or *substance* of a thing, THE thing itself—that which is *chief* of its *kind. He layeth up* WHAT IS ESSENTIAL *for the righteous.*

Verse 9. *Then shalt thou understand*] He who is taught of God understands the whole law of *justice, mercy, righteousness,* and *truth;* God has written this on his heart. He who understands these things by *books* only is never likely to practise or profit by them.

Verse 11. *Discretion shall preserve thee*] מזמה *mezimmah.* See on chap. i. 4. Here the word is taken in a good sense, a *good device.* The man *invents purposes* of good; and all his *schemes, plans,* and *devices,* have for their object God's glory and the good of man: he deviseth liberal things, and by liberal things he shall stand. *Coverdale* translates, "Then shall COUNSEL preserve thee." A very good translation, much better than the present.

Verse 12. *The man that speaketh froward*

A. M. cir. 3004
B. C. cir. 1000
Ante I. Olymp. cir. 224
Ante U. C. cir. 247

[h]walk in the ways of darkness;
14 Who [i]rejoice to do evil,
and [k]delight in the frowardness
of the wicked;
15 [l]Whose ways *are* crooked, and *they* froward in their paths:
16 To deliver thee from [m]the strange woman,
[n]*even* from the stranger *which* flattereth with
her words;
17 [o]Which forsaketh the guide of her
youth, and forgetteth the covenant of her
God.
18 For [p]her house inclineth
unto death, and her paths unto
the dead.
19 None that go unto her re-
turn again, neither take they hold of the paths
of life.
20 That thou mayest walk in the way of good
men, and keep the paths of the righteous.
21 [q]For the upright shall dwell in the land,
and the perfect shall remain in it.
22 [r]But the wicked shall be cut off from
the earth, and the transgressors shall be [s]rooted
out of it.

[h]John iii. 19, 20——[i]Ch. x. 23; Jer. xi. 15——[k]Rom. i. 32——[l]Psa. cxxv. 5——[m]Chap. v. 20——[n]Chap. v. 3; vi. 24; vii. 5

[o]See Mal. ii. 14, 15——[p]Chap. vii. 27——[q]Psa. xxxvii. 29——[r]Job xviii. 17; Psa. xxxvii. 28; civ. 35
[s]Or, *plucked up*

things.] תהפכות *tahpuchoth*, things of *subversion;* from תפך *taphach*, to *turn* or *change* the *course of a thing.* Men who wish to *subvert* the *state* of things, whether *civil* or *religious;* who are seditious themselves, and wish to make others so. These speak much of *liberty* and *oppression*, deal greatly in *broad assertions*, and endeavour especially to corrupt the minds of *youth.*

Verse 16. *The stranger* which *flattereth with her words*] החליקה *hechelikah*, she that *smooths* with her words. The original intimates the *glib, oily* speeches of a *prostitute.* The English *lick* is supposed to be derived from the original word.

Verse 17. *Which forsaketh the guide of her youth*] Leaves her father's house and instructions, and abandons herself to the public.

The covenant of her God.] Renounces the *true religion*, and mixes with *idolaters;* for among them prostitution was enormous. Or by the *covenant* may be meant the *matrimonial contract*, which is a *covenant made in the presence of God between the contracting parties*, in which they bind themselves to be faithful to each other.

Verse 18. *For her house inclineth unto death*] It is generally in *by* and *secret places* that such women establish themselves. They go out of the *high road* to get a residence; and every step that is taken towards their house is a step towards *death.* The path of sin is the path of ruin: the path of duty is the way of safety. For *her paths* incline *unto the dead*, רפאים *rephaim*, the *inhabitants of the invisible world.* The woman who abandons herself to prostitution soon *contracts*, and generally *communicates, that disease*, which, above all others, signs the speediest and most effectual *passport* to the *invisible world.* Therefore it is said,

Verse 19. *None that go unto her return again*] There are very few instances of prostitutes ever returning to the paths of sobriety and truth; perhaps *not one* of such as become prostitutes *through a natural propensity to debauchery.* Among those who have been *deceived, debauched*, and *abandoned*, many have been reclaimed; and to such alone *penitentiaries* may be useful; to the others they may only be incentives to farther sinning. *Rakes* and *debauchees* are sometimes converted: but most of them *never lay hold on the path of life;* they have had their *health* destroyed, and never *recover* it. The original, חיים *chaiyim*, means *lives;* not only the *health* of the *body* is destroyed, but the *soul* is *ruined.* Thus the unhappy man may be said to be *doubly* slain.

Verse 20. *That thou mayest walk*] Therefore thou shalt walk.

Verse 22. *Transgressors*] בוגדים *bogedim.* The *garment men*, the *hypocrites;* those who *act borrowed characters*, who go under a *cloak; dissemblers.* All such shall be *rooted out of the land;* they shall not be blessed with *posterity.* In general it is so: and were it not so, one evil offspring succeeding another, *adding* their *own* to their *predecessors'* vices, the earth would become so exceedingly corrupt that a *second flood*, or a *fire*, would be necessary to purge it.

CHAPTER III

An exhortation to obedience, 1–4; *trust in God's providence,* 5, 6; *to humility,* 7, 8; *to charity,* 9, 10; *to submission to God's chastenings,* 11, 12. *The profitableness of wisdom in all the concerns of life,* 13–26. *No act of duty should be deferred beyond the time in which it should be done,* 27, 28. *Brotherly love and forbearance should be exercised,* 29, 30. *We should not envy the wicked,* 31, 32. *The curse of God is in the house of the wicked; but the humble and wise shall prosper,* 33–35.

A. M. cir. 3004
B. C. cir. 1000
Ante I. Olymp. cir. 224
Ante U. C. cir. 247

MY son, forget not my law;
[a]but let thine heart keep
my commandments:
2 For length of days, and
[b]long life, and [c]peace, shall they add to thee.
3 Let not mercy and truth forsake thee:
[d]bind them about thy neck; [e]write them upon
the table of thine heart:
4 [f]So shalt thou find favour and [g]good understanding in the sight of God and man.

[a]Deut. viii. 1; xxx. 16, 20——[b]Heb. *years of life*——[c]Psa. cxix. 165——[d]Exod. xiii. 9; Deut. vi. 8; chap. vi. 21; vii. 3——[e]Jer. xvii. 1; 2 Cor. iii. 3——[f]Psa. cxi. 10; see 1 Sam. ii. 26; Luke ii. 52; Acts ii. 47; Rom. xiv. 18

5 [h]Trust in the LORD with
all thine heart; [i]and lean not
unto thine own understanding.
6 [k]In all thy ways acknowledge him, and
he shall [l]direct thy paths.
7 [m]Be not wise in thine own eyes: [n]fear the
LORD, and depart from evil.
8 It shall be [o]health to thy navel, and
[p]marrow [q]to thy bones.

A. M. cir. 3004
B. C. cir. 1000
Ante I. Olymp. cir. 224
Ante U. C. cir. 247

[g]Or, *good success*——[h]Psa. xxxvii. 3, 5——[i]Jer. ix. 23——[k]1 Chron. xxviii. 9——[l]Jer. x. 23——[m]Rom. xii. 16——[n]Job i. 1; chap. xvi. 6——[o]Heb. *medicine*——[p]Heb. *watering* or *moistening*——[q]Job xxi. 24

NOTES ON CHAP. III

Verse 1. *My son*] The preceptor continues to deliver his lessons.

Forget not my law]. *Remember* what thou hast *heard*, and *practise* what thou dost *remember;* and let all obedience be *from the heart:* "Let thy heart keep my commandments.

Verse 2. *For length of days*] THREE eminent *blessings* are promised here: 1. ארך ימים *orech yamim*, long days; 2. שנות חיים *shenoth chaiyim*, years of lives; 3. שלום *shalom*, prosperity; i. e. health, long life, and abundance.

Verse 3. *Let not mercy and truth forsake thee*] Let these be thy constant *companions* through life.

Bind them about thy neck] Keep them constantly *in view. Write them upon the table of thine heart*—let them be thy *moving principles; feel* them as well as *see* them.

Verse 4. *So shalt thou find favour*] Thou shalt be acceptable to God, and thou shalt enjoy a sense of his approbation.

And good understanding] Men shall *weigh* thy character and conduct; and by this *appreciate* thy motives, and give thee credit for sincerity and uprightness. Though religion is frequently persecuted, and religious people suffer at first where they are not fully *known;* yet a truly religious and benevolent character will in general be prized wherever it is well known. The envy of men is a proof of the excellence of that which they envy.

Verse 5. *Trust in the Lord with all thine heart*] This is a most important precept: 1. God is the *Fountain* of all good. 2. He has made his intelligent creatures *dependent* upon himself. 3. He requires them to be *conscious* of that dependence. 4. He has *promised* to communicate what they need. 5. He commands them to *believe* his promise, and look for its fulfilment. 6. And to do this without doubt, fear, or distrust; "with their whole heart."

Lean not unto thine own understanding] אל תשען *al tishshaen*, do not *prop* thyself. It is on GOD, not on *thyself*, that thou art commanded to *depend*. He who trusts in his own heart is a fool.

Verse 6. *In all thy ways acknowledge him*] Begin, continue, and end every work, purpose, and device, with God. Earnestly pray for his *direction* at the *commencement;* look for his continual *support* in the *progress;* and so begin and continue that all may terminate in his glory: and then it will certainly be to thy good; for we never *honour God*, without *serving ourselves*. This passage is well rendered in my old MS. Bible:—**Habe trost in the Lord of all thin herte and ne lene thou to thi prudence: in alle thi weys think hym, and he shal right rulen thi goynges; ne be thou wiis anentis thiself.** *Self-sufficiency* and *self-dependence* have been the ruin of mankind ever since the fall of Adam. The grand sin of the human race is their continual endeavour to *live independently of God*, i. e., to be *without God in the world. True religion* consists in considering God the fountain of all good, and expecting all good from him.

Verse 8. *It shall be health to thy navel*] We need not puzzle ourselves to find out what we may suppose to be a more *delicate* meaning for the original word שר *shor* than *navel;* for I am satisfied a more proper cannot be found. It is well known that it is by the *umbilical cord* that the *fetus* receives its nourishment all the time it is in the womb of the mother. It receives nothing by the *mouth*, nor by any other means: by *this* alone all nourishment is received, and the circulation of the blood kept up. When, therefore, the wise man says, that "trusting in the Lord with the whole heart, and acknowledging him in all a man's ways, &c., shall be health to the navel, and marrow to the bones;" he in effect says, that this is as essential to the life of God in the soul of man, and to the continual growth in grace, as the *umbilical cord* is to the *life* and *growth of the fetus* in the womb. Without the *latter*, no human being could ever exist or be born; without the *former*, no *true religion* can ever be found. *Trust* or *faith* in God is as necessary to derive grace from him to nourish the soul, and cause it to grow up unto eternal life, as the *navel string* or *umbilical cord* is to the human being in the first stage of its existence. I need not push this illustration farther: the good sense of the reader will supply what *he knows*. I might add much on the subject.

And marrow to thy bones.] This metaphor is not less proper than the preceding. All the larger *bones* of the body have either a large *cavity*, or they are *spongious*, and full of little cells: in both the one and the other the *oleaginous* substance, called *marrow*, is contained in proper vesicles, like the fat. In the larger *bones* the *fine oil*, by the gentle heat of the

A. M. cir. 3004 B. C. cir. 1000 Ante I. Olymp. cir. 224 Ante U. C. cir. 247

9 [r]Honour the LORD with thy
substance, and with the first-
fruits of all thine increase:
10 [s]So shall thy barns be filled
with plenty, and thy presses shall burst out
with new wine.
11 [t]My son, despise not the chastening of the
LORD: neither be weary of his correction:
12 For whom the LORD loveth he correcteth;
[u]even as a father the son *in whom* he delighteth.
13 [v]Happy *is* the man
that findeth wisdom, and [w]the
man *that* getteth understanding.
14 [x]For the merchandise of it *is* better than
the merchandise of silver, and the gain thereof
than fine gold.
15 She *is* more precious than rubies: and
[y]all the things thou canst desire are not to be
compared unto her.

[r]Exod. xxii. 29; xxiii. 19; xxxiv. 26; Deut. xxvi. 2, &c.; Mal. iii. 10, &c.; Luke xiv. 13——[s]Deut. xxviii. 8——[t]Job v. 17; Psa. xciv. 12; Heb. xii. 5, 6; Rev. iii. 19

[u]Deut. viii. 5——[v]Ch. viii. 34, 35——[w]Heb. *the man that draweth out understanding*——[x]Job xxviii. 13, &c.; Psa. xix. 10; ch. ii. 4; viii. 11, 19; xvi. 16——[y]Matt. xiii. 44

body, is exhaled through the pores of its small vesicles, and enters some narrow passages which lead to certain fine canals excavated in the substance of the bone, that the marrow may supply the *fibres of the bones*, and render them less liable to break. *Blood-vessels* also penetrate the *bones* to supply this *marrow* and this *blood;* and consequently the *marrow* is supplied in the infant by means of the *umbilical cord.* From the *marrow* diffused, as mentioned above, through the *bones*, they derive their *solidity* and *strength.* A simple experiment will cast considerable light on the use of the *marrow* to the *bones:*—Calcine a *bone*, so as to destroy all the *marrow* from the cells, you will find it exceedingly *brittle.* Immerse the same bone in *oil* so that the cells may be all replenished, which will be done in a few minutes; and the bone reacquires a considerable measure of its *solidity* and *strength;* and would acquire the *whole*, if the *marrow* could be *extracted* without otherwise injuring the texture of the *bone.* After the calcination, the bone may be reduced to powder by the hand; after the *impregnation with the oil*, it becomes *hard, compact*, and *strong.* What the marrow is to the *support* and *strength* of the *bones*, and the *bones* to the *support* and *strength* of the *body;* that, *faith* in God, is to the *support, strength, energy*, and *salvation* of the *soul.* Behold, then, the force and elegance of the wise man's metaphor. Some have rendered the last clause, *a lotion for the bones.* What is this? How are the *bones washed?* What a pitiful destruction of a most beautiful metaphor!

Verse 9. *Honour the Lord with thy substance*] The מנחה MINCHAH or gratitude-offering to God, commanded under the *law*, is of endless obligation. It would be well to give a portion of the *produce* of *every article* by which we get our support to *God*, or to the *poor*, the representatives of Christ. This might be done either in *kind*, or by the *worth* in *money.* Whatever God sends us in the way of secular prosperity, there is a *portion of it* always for the poor, and for God's cause. When that *portion* is thus disposed of, the rest is *sanctified;* when it is *withheld*, God's curse is upon the whole. Give to the *poor*, and God will give to *thee.*

Verse 11. *Despise not the chastening of the Lord*] The word מוסר *musar* signifies *correction, discipline*, and *instruction. Teaching* is essentially necessary to show the man the *way* in which he is to go; *discipline* is necessary to render that *teaching effectual;* and, often, *correction* is requisite in order to bring the mind into *submission*, without which it cannot acquire *knowledge.* Do not therefore reject this procedure of God; humble thyself under his mighty hand, and open thy eyes to thy own interest; and then thou wilt learn *specially* and *effectually.* It is of no use to *rebel;* if thou do, thou *kickest against the pricks*, and every act of rebellion against him is a *wound* to thine own *soul.* God will either *end* thee or *mend* thee; wilt thou then *kick* on?

Verse 12. *Whom the Lord loveth*] To encourage thee to bear correction, know that it is a proof of God's love to thee; and thereby he shows that he treats thee as a father does his son, even that one to whom he bears the fondest affection.

The last clause the *Septuagint* translate μαστιγοι δε παντα υἱον ὁν παραδεχεται, "and chasteneth every son whom he receiveth;" and the *apostle*, Heb. xii. 6, quotes this *literatim.* Both clauses certainly amount to the same sense. *Every son whom he receiveth*, and *the son in whom he delighteth*, have very little difference of meaning.

Verse 13. *Happy* is *the man* that *findeth wisdom*] This refers to the advice given in chap. ii. 4; where see the note.

Verse 14. *For the merchandise*] סחר *sachar*, the *traffic*, the *trade* that is carried on by *going through countries* and *provinces* with such articles as they could carry on the backs of camels, &c.; from סחר *sachar*, to *go about, traverse.* **Chaffarynge;** Old MS. Bible.

And the gain thereof] תבואתה *tebuathah*, its *produce;* what is gained by the articles after all expenses are paid. The *slaves*, as we have already seen, got their *liberty* if they were so lucky as to find a diamond of so many carats' weight; he who *finds wisdom*—the *knowledge* and *salvation of God*—gets a greater prize; for he obtains the *liberty of the Gospel*, is adopted into the *family of God*, and made an *heir* according to the hope of an eternal life.

Verse 15. *She* is *more precious than rubies*] מפנינים *mippeninim.* The word principally means *pearls*, but may be taken for *precious stones* in general. The root is פנה *panah*, he *looked, beheld;* and as it gives the idea of the eye always being turned towards the observer, Mr. Parkhurst thinks that it means the *load-*

A. M. cir. 3004 B. C. cir. 1000 Ante I. Olymp. cir. 224 Ante U. C. cir. 247

16 [z]Length of days *is* in her
right hand; *and* in her left hand
riches and honour.
17 [a]Her ways *are* ways of
pleasantness, and all her paths *are* peace.
18 She *is* [b]a tree of life to them that lay
hold upon her: and happy *is every one* that
retaineth her.
19 [c]The LORD by wisdom hath founded the
earth; by understanding hath he [d]established
the heavens.
20 [e]By his knowledge the
depths are broken up, and [f]the
clouds drop down the dew.
21 My son, let not them de-
part from thine eyes: keep sound wisdom
and discretion:
22 So shall they be life unto thy soul, and
[g]grace to thy neck.
23 [h]Then shalt thou walk in thy way safely,
and thy foot shall not stumble.
24 [i]When thou liest down, thou shalt not

A. M. cir. 3004 B. C. cir. 1000 Ante I. Olymp. cir. 224 Ante U. C. cir. 247

---

[z]Chap. viii. 18; 1 Tim. iv. 8——[a]Matt. xi. 29, 30 [b]Gen. ii. 9; iii. 22——[c]Psa. civ. 24; cxxxvi. 5; chap. viii. 27; Jer. x. 12; li. 15

[d]Or, *prepared*——[e]Gen. i. 9——[f]Deut. xxxiii. 28; Job xxxvi. 28——[g]Chap. i. 9——[h]Psa. xxxvii. 24; xci. 11, 12; chap. x. 9——[i]Lev. xxvi. 6; Psa. iii. 5; iv. 8

---

stone; see the note on Job xxviii. 18, where this subject is considered at large. If the oriental *ruby*, or any other precious stone, be intended here, the word may refer to their being *cut* and *polished*, so that they present different *faces*, and reflect the light to you in whatever direction you may look at them.

All the things thou canst desire] Superior to every thing that can be an object of desire here below. But who believes this?

Verse 16. *Length of days* is *in her right hand*] A wicked man shortens his days by *excesses;* a righteous man prolongs his by *temperance.*

In her left hand riches and honour.] That is, her hands are full of the choicest benefits. There is nothing to be understood here by the *right hand* in preference to the *left.*

Verse 17. *Her ways* are *ways of pleasantness*] These blessings of true religion require little comment. They are well expressed by the poet in the following elegant verses:—

"*Wisdom Divine!* Who tells the price
Of Wisdom's costly merchandise?
Wisdom to silver we prefer,
And *gold* is *dross* compared to her.
Her hands are fill'd with length of days,
True riches, and *immortal praise;*—
Riches of Christ, on all bestow'd,
And honour that descends from God.

To purest joys she all invites,
Chaste, holy, spiritual *delights;*
Her ways are ways of pleasantness,
And *all her* flowery *paths are peace.*
Happy the man that finds the grace,
The blessing of God's chosen race;
The *wisdom coming from above,*
The *faith* that sweetly *works by love!*"

WESLEY.

Verse 18. *She* is *a tree of life*] עץ חיים *ets chaiyim*, "the tree of lives," alluding most manifestly to the tree so called which God in the beginning planted in the garden of Paradise, by eating the fruit of which all the wastes of nature might have been continually repaired, so as to prevent death for ever. This is an opinion which appears probable enough. The blessings which wisdom—true religion—gives to men, preserve them *in* life, comfort them *through* life, cause them to triumph in *death*, and ensure them a glorious *immortality.*

Verse 19. *The Lord by wisdom hath founded the earth*] Here wisdom is taken in its proper acceptation, for that infinite knowledge and skill which God has manifested in the creation and composition of the earth, and in the structure and economy of the heavens. He has established the *order* as well as the *essence* of all things; so that though they *vary* in their *positions*, &c., yet they never *change* either their *places*, or their *properties. Composition* and *analysis* are not *essential changes;* the original *particles*, their *forms* and *properties*, remain the same.

Verse 20. *By his knowledge the depths are broken up*] He determined in his wisdom how to *break up* the *fountains of the great deep*, so as to *bring a flood of waters upon the earth;* and by his knowledge those fissures in the earth through which *springs* of water arise have been appointed and determined; and it is by his skill and influence that *vapours* are exhaled, suspended in the *atmosphere*, and afterwards precipitated on the earth in *rain, dews*, &c. Thus the wisest of men attributes those effects which we suppose to spring from *natural causes* to the Supreme Being himself.

Verse 21. *Let not them depart from thine eyes*] Never forget that God, who is the author of nature, directs and governs it in all things; for it is no self-determining agent.

Keep sound wisdom and discretion] תושיה ומזמה *tushiyah umezimmah.* We have met with both these words before. *Tushiyah* is the *essence* or *substance* of a thing; *mezimmah* is the *resolution* or *purpose* formed in reference to something good or excellent. To acknowledge God as the author of all good, is the *tushiyah*, the *essence*, of a godly man's creed; to *resolve* to *act according* to the directions of his wisdom, is the *mezimmah*, the *religious purpose*, that will bring good to ourselves and glory to God. These bring *life to the soul*, and are *ornamental* to the man who acts in this way, ver. 22.

Verse 24. *When thou liest down*] In these verses (23-26) the wise man describes the confidence, security, and safety, which proceed from a consciousness of innocence. Most people are afraid of *sleep*, lest they should never awake, because they feel they are not prepared to appear before God. They are neither innocent nor pardoned. True believers know that God is their keeper night and day; they have

A. M. cir. 3004
B. C. cir. 1000
Ante I. Olymp. cir. 224
Ante U. C. cir. 247

be afraid: yea, thou shalt lie
down, and thy sleep shall be
sweet.
25 [k]Be not afraid of sudden
fear, neither of the desolation of the wicked
when it cometh.
26 For the LORD shall be thy confidence, and
shall keep thy foot from being taken.
27 [l]Withhold not good from [m]them to whom
it is due, when it is in the power of thine hand
to do *it*.
28 [n]Say not unto thy neighbour, Go, and
come again, and to-morrow I will give; when
thou hast it by thee.
29 [o]Devise not evil against thy neighbour,
seeing he dwelleth securely by thee.
30 [p]Strive not with a man
without cause, if he have done
thee no harm.
31 [q]Envy thou not [r]the oppressor, and choose none of his ways.
32 For the froward *is* abomination to the
LORD: [s]but his secret *is* with the righteous.
33 [t]The curse of the LORD *is* in the house
of the wicked: but [u]he blesseth the habitation
of the just.
34 [v]Surely he scorneth the scorners: but
he giveth grace unto the lowly.
35 The wise shall inherit glory: but shame
[w]shall be the promotion of fools.

[k]Psa. xci. 5; cxii. 7——[l]Rom. xiii. 7; Gal. vi. 10——[m]Heb. *the owners thereof*——[n]Lev. xix. 13; Deut. xxiv. 15——[o]Or, *Practise no evil*——[p]Rom. xii. 48——[q]Psa. xxxvii. 1; lxxiii. 3; chap. xxiv. 1——[r]Heb. *a man of violence*——[s]Psa. xxv. 14——[t]Lev. xxvi. 14, &c.; Psa. xxxvii. 22; Zech. v. 4; Mal. ii. 2——[u]Psalm i. 6——[v]James iv. 6; 1 Pet. v. 5——[w]Hebrew, *exalteth the fools*

strong confidence in him that he will be their director, and not suffer them to take any *false step* in life, ver. 23. They go to rest in perfect confidence that God will watch over them; hence their *sleep*, being undisturbed with foreboding and evil dreams, is *sweet* and refreshing, ver. 24. They are not apprehensive of any *sudden destruction*, because they know that all things are under the control of God; and they are satisfied that if *sudden destruction* should fall upon their wicked neighbour, yet God knows well how to preserve *them*, ver. 25. And all this naturally flows from the Lord being their confidence, ver. 26.

Verse 27. *Withhold not good from them to whom it is due*] מבעליו *mibbealaiv, from the lords of it.* But who are they? The *poor. And what art thou, O rich man?* Why, thou art a *steward*, to whom God has given substance that thou mayest divide with the poor. They are the right owners of every farthing thou hast to spare from thy own support, and that of thy family; and God has given the surplus for their sakes. Dost thou, by hoarding up this treasure, deprive the *right owners* of their property? If this were a *civil case*, the law would take thee by the throat, and lay thee up in prison; but it is a case in which GOD alone judges. And what will he do to thee? Hear! "He shall have judgment without mercy, who hath showed no mercy;" James ii. 13. *Read, feel, tremble, and act justly.*

Verse 28. *Say not unto thy neighbour*] Do not refuse a kindness when it is in thy power to perform it. If thou have the means *by thee*, and thy neighbour's necessities be pressing, do not put him off till the *morrow*. Death may take either him or thee before that time.

Verse 30. *Strive not with a man*] Do not be of a litigious, quarrelsome spirit. Be not under the influence of too nice a sense of honour. If thou must appeal to judicial authority to bring him that wrongs thee to reason, avoid all enmity, and do nothing in a spirit of revenge. But, if he *have done thee no harm*, why contend with him? May not others in the same way contend with and injure *thee?*

Verse 31. *Envy thou not the oppressor*] O how bewitching is *power!* Every man desires it; and yet all hate *tyrants*. But query, if all had *power*, would not the major part be *tyrants?*

Verse 32. *But his secret*] סודו *sodo, his secret assembly;* godly people meet there, and God dwells there.

Verse 33. *The curse of the Lord*] No godly people meet in such a house; nor is God ever an *inmate* there.

But he blesseth the habitation of the just.] He considers it as his *own temple*. There he is worshipped in spirit and in truth; and hence God makes it his *dwelling-place*.

Verse 34. *Surely he scorneth the scorners; but he giveth grace unto the lowly.*] The *Septuagint* has Κυριος ὑπερηφανοις αντιτασσεται, ταπεινοις δε διδωσι χαριν. *The Lord resisteth the proud; but giveth grace to the humble.* These words are quoted by St. *Peter*, 1st Epist. v. 5, and by St. *James*, chap. iv. 6, just as they stand in the *Septuagint*, with the change of ὁ Θεος, *God*, for Κυριος, *the Lord*.

Verse 35. *The wise*] The person who follows the dictates of wisdom, as mentioned above, *shall inherit glory;* because, being one of the *heavenly family*, a *child of God*, he has thereby heaven for his *inheritance; but fools*, such as those mentioned chap. i. and ii., shall have *ignominy* for their *exaltation*. Many such fools as Solomon speaks of are exalted to the *gibbet* and *gallows*. The way to prevent this and the like evils, is to attend to the voice of wisdom.

CHAPTER IV

The preceptor calls his pupils, and tells them how himself was educated, 1–4; *specifies the teachings he received,* 5–19; *and exhorts his pupil to persevere in well-doing, and to avoid evil,* 20–27.

A. M. cir. 3004 B. C. cir. 1000 Ante I. Olymp. cir. 224 Ante U. C. cir. 247

HEAR, [a]ye children, the instruction of a father, and
attend to know understanding.
2 For I give you good doctrine,
forsake ye not my law.
3 For I was my father's son, [b]tender and
only *beloved* in the sight of my mother.
4 [c]He taught me also, and said unto me,
Let thine heart retain my words: [d]keep my
commandments, and live.
5 [e]Get wisdom, get understanding: forget *it* not; neither decline from the words of my
mouth.
6 Forsake her not, and she shall preserve
thee: [f]love her, and she shall keep thee.
7 [g]Wisdom *is* the principal thing; *therefore*
get wisdom: and with all thy getting get understanding.
8 [h]Exalt her, and she shall promote thee:

A. M. cir. 3004 B. C. cir. 1000 Ante I. Olymp. cir. 224 Ante U. C. cir. 247

---

[a]Psalm xxxiv. 11; chap. i. 8——[b]1 Chron. xxix. 1——[c]1 Chron. xxix. 9; Eph. vi. 4——[d]Chap. vii. 2

[e]Chap. ii. 2, 3——[f]2 Thess. ii. 10——[g]Matt. xiii. 44; Luke x. 42——[h]1 Sam. ii. 30

NOTES ON CHAP. IV

Verse 1. *Hear, ye children*] Come, my pupils, and hear how a father instructed his child. Such as *I* received from *my father* I give to you; and they were the teachings of a wise and affectionate parent to his only son, a peculiar object of his regards, and also those of a *fond mother.*

He introduces the subject thus, to show that the teaching he received, and which he was about to give them, was the most excellent of its kind. By this he ensured their attention, and made his way to their heart. Teaching by *precept* is good; teaching by *example* is better; but teaching *both by precept and example* is best of all.

Verse 4. *He taught me also, and said*] Open thy heart to receive my instructions—receive them with affection; when heard, retain and practise them; and thou shalt live—the great purpose of thy being brought into the world shall be accomplished in thee.

Verse 5. *Get wisdom*] True religion is essential to thy happiness; never *forget* its teachings, nor go *aside* from the path it prescribes.

Verse 6. *Forsake her not*] Wisdom personified is here represented as a *guardian* and *companion,* who, if not forsaken, will continue faithful; if loved, will continue a protector.

Verse 7. *Wisdom* is *the principal thing*] ראשית חכמה *reshith chochmah,* "wisdom is the principle." It is the *punctum saliens* in all religion to know the true God, and *what* he requires of man, and *for what* he has made man; and to this must be added, under the Christian dispensation, *to know Jesus Christ whom he hath sent,* and for *what end* HE was *sent,* the *necessity* of his being *sent,* and the *nature* of that *salvation* which he has *bought by his own blood.*

Get wisdom] Consider this as thy *chief gain;* that in reference to which all *thy* wisdom, knowledge, and endeavours should be directed.

And with all thy getting] Let this be thy *chief property.* While thou art passing through things temporal, do not lose those things which are eternal; and, while *diligent in business,* be *fervent in spirit, serving the Lord.*

Get understanding.] Do not be contented with the lessons of wisdom merely; do not be satisfied with having a sound religious creed; *devils* believe and tremble; but see that thou properly *comprehend* all that thou hast learnt; and see that thou rightly apply all that thou hast been taught.

Wisdom prescribes the best end, and the means best calculated for its attainment. *Understanding* directs to the ways, times, places, and opportunities of practising the lessons of wisdom. *Wisdom* points out the *thing requisite; understanding* sees to the *accomplishment* and *attainment. Wisdom sees;* but *understanding feels.* One *discovers,* the other *possesses.*

Coverdale translates this whole verse in a very remarkable manner: "The chefe poynte of wyssdome is, that thou be wyllynge to opteyne wyssdome; and before all thy goodes to get the understandynge." This is *paraphrase,* not *translation.* In this version *paraphrase* abounds.

The translation in my old MS. Bible is very simple: **Begynnynge of wisdam, welle thou wisdam: in al thi wisdam, and in al thi possioun, purchas prudence.** He is already wise who seeks wisdom; and he is wise who knows its value, seeks to possess it. The whole of this verse is wanting in the *Arabic,* and in the best copies of the *Septuagint.*

Instead of קנה חכמה *keneh chochmah, get wisdom,* the *Complutensian* Polyglot has קנה בינה *keneh binah, get understanding;* so that in it the verse stands, "Wisdom is the principle, get understanding; and in all thy getting, get understanding." This is not an error either of the *scribe,* or of the *press,* for it is supported by *seven* of the MSS. of *Kennicott* and *De Rossi.*

The *Complutensian, Antwerp,* and *Paris* Polyglots have the *seventh* verse in the *Greek* text; but the two latter, in general, copy the former.

Verse 8. *She shall bring thee to honour*] There is nothing, a strict life of piety and benevolence excepted, that has such a direct tendency to *reflect honour* upon a man, as the careful *cultivation of his mind.* One of *Bacon's* aphorisms was, *Knowledge is power;* and it is truly astonishing to see what *influence* true learning has. Nothing is so universally respected, provided the learned man be a *consis-*

A. M. cir. 3004 B. C. cir. 1000 Ante I. Olymp. cir. 224 Ante U. C. cir. 247

she shall bring thee to honour,
when thou dost embrace her.
9 She shall give to thine head
[i]an ornament of grace: [k]a
crown of glory shall she deliver to thee.
10 Hear, O my son, and receive my sayings;
[l]and the years of thy life shall be many.
11 I have taught thee in the way of wisdom;
I have led thee in right paths.
12 When thou goest, [m]thy steps shall not
be straitened; [n]and when thou runnest, thou
shalt not stumble.
13 Take fast hold of instruction; let *her* not
go: keep her; for she *is* thy
life.
14 [o]Enter not into the path of
the wicked, and go not in the
way of evil *men.*
15 Avoid it, pass not by it, turn from it, and
pass away.
16 [p]For they sleep not, except they have
done mischief; and their sleep is taken away,
unless they cause *some* to fall.
17 For they eat the bread of wickedness, and
drink the wine of violence.
18 [q]But the path of the just [r]*is* as the

[i]Chap. i. 9; iii. 22——[k]Or, *she shall compass thee with a crown of glory*——[l]Chapter iii. 2——[m]Psalm xviii. 36——[n]Psalm xci. 11, 12——[o]Psalm i. 1; chapter i. 10, 15——[p]Psalm xxxvi. 4; Isaiah lvii. 20——[q]Matthew v. 14, 45; Philippians ii. 15——[r]2 Samuel xxiii. 4

tent moral character, and be not proud and overbearing; which is a disgrace to genuine literature.

Verse 9. *A crown of glory*] A tiara, diadem, or crown, shall not be more honourable to the princely wearer, than sound wisdom—true religion—coupled with deep learning, shall be to the Christian and the scholar.

Verse 10. *The years of thy life shall be many.*] Vice and intemperance impair the health and shorten the days of the wicked; while true religion, sobriety, and temperance, prolong them. The principal part of our diseases springs from "indolence, intemperance, and disorderly passions." Religion excites to *industry*, promotes *sober habits*, and destroys *evil passions*, and *harmonizes* the soul; and thus, by preventing many diseases, necessarily prolongs life.

Verse 12. *Thy steps shall not be straitened*] True wisdom will teach thee to keep out of embarrassments. A man under the influence of true religion *ponders* his paths, and carefully *poises occurring circumstances;* and as the fear of God will ever lead him to act an upright and honest part, so his way in business and life is both *clear* and *large.* He has no *by-ends* to serve; he *speculates* not; he uses neither *trick* nor *cunning* to effect any purpose. Such a man can never be embarrassed. *His steps are not straitened;* he sees his way always plain; and when a favourable tide of Providence shows him the necessity of increased *exertion*, he *runs*, and is in no danger of *stumbling.*

Verse 13. *Take fast hold*] החזק *hachazek, seize it strongly*, and keep the hold; and do this as *for life.* Learn all thou canst, retain what thou hast learnt, and keep the reason continually in view—*it is for thy life.*

Verse 14. *Enter not into the path of the wicked*] Never *associate* with those whose life is irregular and sinful; never *accompany* them in any of their acts of transgression.

Verse 15. *Avoid it*] Let it be the serious purpose of thy soul to shun every appearance of evil.

Pass not by it] Never, for the sake of worldly gain, or through complaisance to others, *approach the way* that thou wouldst not wish to be found in when God calls thee into the eternal world.

Turn from it] If, through *unwatchfulness* or *unfaithfulness*, thou at any time get *near* or *into the way* of sin, *turn from it* with the utmost speed, and humble thyself before thy Maker.

And pass away.] Speed from it, run for thy life, and get to the utmost distance; eternally diverging so as never to come near it whilst thou hast a being.

Verse 16. *Except they have done mischief*] The *night* is their time for spoil and depredation. And they must gain some *booty*, before they *go to rest.* This I believe to be the meaning of the passage. I grant, also, that there may be some of so malevolent a disposition, that they cannot be easy unless they can injure others, and are put to excessive pain when they perceive any man in *prosperity*, or receiving a kindness. The address in *Virgil*, to an ill-natured shepherd is well known:—

Et cum vidisti puero donata, dolebas:
Et si non aliqua nocuisses, mortuus esses.
Eclog. iii. 14.

"When thou sawest the gifts given to the lad, thou wast distressed; and hadst thou not found some means of doing him a mischief, thou hadst died."

Verse 17. *For they eat the bread of wickedness*] By *privately* stealing.

And drink the wine of violence.] By *highway robbery.*

Verse 18. *But the path of the just*] The path of the wicked is gloomy, dark, and dangerous; that of the righteous is open, luminous, and instructive. This verse contains a fine metaphor; it refers to the *sun* rising above the horizon, and the increasing twilight, till his beams shine full upon the earth. The original, הולך ואור עד נכון היום *holech vaor ad nechon haiyom*, may be translated, "going and illuminating unto the prepared day." This seems plainly to refer to the progress of the rising *sun* while below the horizon; and the gradual increase of the light occasioned by the reflection of his rays by means of the *atmosphere*, till at last he is completely elevated above the horizon, and then the *prepared day* has fully taken place, the sun having risen *at the determined time.* So, the truly wise man is but in his twilight here below; but he is in a state

A. M. cir. 3004 B. C. cir. 1000 Ante I. Olymp. cir. 224 Ante U. C. cir. 247

shining light, that shineth more
and more unto the perfect day.
19 [s]The way of the wicked *is*
as darkness: they know not at
what they stumble.
20 My son, attend to my words; incline
thine ear unto my sayings.
21 [t]Let them not depart from thine
eyes; [u]keep them in the midst of thine
heart.
22 For they *are* life unto those that find
them, and [v]health [w]to all their flesh.
23 Keep thy heart [x]with all
diligence; for out of it *are* the
issues of life.
24 Put away from thee [y]a froward mouth, and perverse lips put far from
thee.
25 Let thine eyes look right on, and let thine
eyelids look straight before thee.
26 Ponder the path of thy feet, and [z]let all
thy ways be established.
27 [a]Turn not to the right hand nor to the
left: [b]remove thy foot from evil.

---

[s]1 Sam. ii. 9; Job xviii. 5, 6; Isa. lix. 9, 10; Jer. xxiii. 12; John xii. 35——[t]Chap. iii. 3, 21——[u]Chap. ii. 1 [v]Chap. iii. 8; xii. 18; [w]Heb. *medicine*——[x]Heb. *above all keeping*

[y]Heb. *frowardness of mouth, and perverseness of lips* [z]Or, *all thy ways shall be ordered aright*——[a]Deuteronomy v. 32; xxviii. 14; Josh. i. 7——[b]Isaiah i. 16; Rom. xii. 9

---

of glorious *preparation* for the realms of everlasting light; till at last, emerging from darkness and the shadows of death, he is ushered into the full blaze of endless felicity. Yet previously to his enjoyment of this glory, which is prepared for him, he is *going*—walking in the commandments of his God blameless; and *illuminating*—reflecting the light of the salvation which he has received on all those who form the circle of his acquaintance.

Verse 21. *Keep them in the midst of thine heart.*] Let them be wrapped up in the very *centre of thy affections;* that they may give spring and energy to every desire, word, and wish.

Verse 23. *Keep thy heart with all diligence*] "Above all keeping," guard thy heart. He who knows any thing of himself, knows how apt his affections are to go astray.

For out of it are *the issues of life.*] תוצאות חיים *totseoth chaiyim,* "the goings out of lives." Is not this a plain allusion to the *arteries* which carry the blood from the heart through the whole body, and to the utmost extremities? As long as the heart is capable of receiving and propelling the blood, so long *life* is continued. Now as the heart is the fountain whence all the streams of life proceed, care must be taken that the fountain be not stopped up nor injured. A double watch for its safety must be kept up. So in spiritual things: the heart is the seat of the Lord of life and glory; and the streams of spiritual life proceed from him to all the powers and faculties of the soul. Watch with all diligence, that this fountain be not sealed up, nor these streams of life be cut off. Therefore "put away from thee a froward mouth and perverse lips—and let thy eyes look straight on." Or, in other words, look *inward*—look *onward*—look *upward.*

I know that the *twenty-third* verse is understood as principally referring to the evils which proceed from the heart, and which must be guarded against; and the good purposes that must be formed in it, from which *life* takes its colouring. The former should be opposed; the latter should be encouraged and strengthened. If the heart be pure and holy, all its purposes will be just and good. If it be impure and defiled, nothing will proceed from it but abomination. But though all this be true, I have preferred following what I believe to be the *metaphor* in the text.

Verse 24. *A froward mouth*] Beware of hastiness, anger, and rash speeches.

And perverse lips] Do not delight in nor acquire the *habit* of *contradicting* and *gainsaying;* and beware of *calumniating* and *backbiting* your neighbour.

Verse 26. *Ponder the path of thy feet*] *Weigh* well the part thou shouldst act in life. See that thou contract no bad *habits.*

Verse 27. *Turn not to the right hand nor to the left*] Avoid all crooked ways. Be an upright, downright, and straight-forward man. Avoid *tricks, wiles,* and *deceptions* of this kind.

To this the *Septuagint* and *Vulgate* add the following verse: *Αυτος δε ορθας ποιησει τας τροχιας σου, τας δε πορειας σου εν ειρηνη προαξει.* Ipse autem rectos faciet cursus tuos; itinera autem tua in pace producet. "For himself will make thy paths straight and thy journeyings will he conduct in prosperity." The *Arabic* has also a clause to the same effect. But nothing like this is found in the *Hebrew, Chaldee,* or *Syriac;* nor in the *Vulgate,* as printed in the *Complutensian* Polyglot; nor in that of *Antwerp* or of *Paris;* but it is in the Greek text of those editions, in the *editio princeps* of the Vulgate, in *five* of my own MSS., and in the old MS. Bible. *De Lyra* rejects the clause as a *gloss* that stands on no authority. If an *addition,* it is certainly *very ancient;* and the promise it contains is true, whether the clause be authentic or not.

CHAPTER V

Farther exhortations to acquire wisdom, 1, 2. *The character of a loose woman, and the ruinous consequences of attachment to such,* 3–14. *Exhortations to chastity and moderation,* 15–21. *The miserable end of the wicked,* 22, 23.

A. M. cir. 3004
B. C. cir. 1000
Ante I. Olymp. cir. 224
Ante U. C. cir. 247

MY son, attend unto my wisdom, *and* bow thine ear to
my understanding:
2 That thou mayest regard
discretion, and *that* thy lips may [a]keep knowledge.
3 [b]For the lips of a strange woman drop *as*
a honey-comb, and her [c]mouth *is* [d]smoother
than oil:
4 But her end is [e]bitter as wormwood, [f]sharp
as a two-edged sword.
5 [g]Her feet go down to death; her steps take
hold on hell.
6 Lest thou shouldest ponder the path of life,
her ways are moveable, *that* thou canst not
know *them*.
7 Hear me now therefore, O ye children,
and depart not from the words
of my mouth.
8 Remove thy way far from
her, and come not nigh the door
of her house:
9 Lest thou give thine honour unto others,
and thy years unto the cruel:
10 Lest strangers be filled with [h]thy wealth;
and thy labours *be* in the house of a stranger;
11 And thou mourn at the last, when thy
flesh and thy body are consumed,
12 And say, How have I [i]hated instruction,
and my heart [k]despised reproof;
13 And have not obeyed the voice of my
teachers, nor inclined mine ear to them that
instructed me!
14 I was almost in all evil in the midst

[a]Mal. ii. 7——[b]Chap. ii. 16; vi. 24——[c]Heb. *palate* [d]Psa. lv. 21——[e]Eccles. vii. 26——[f]Heb. iv. 12

[g]Chap. vii. 27——[h]Heb. *thy strength*——[i]Chap. i. 29 [k]Chap. i. 25; xii. 1

NOTES ON CHAP. V

Verse 1. *Attend unto my wisdom*] Take the following lessons from my *own experience*.

Verse 3. *The lips of a strange woman*] One that is not *thy own*, whether Jewess or heathen.

Drop as *a honey-comb*] She uses the most deceitful, flattering, and alluring speeches: as the droppings of the honey out of the comb are the sweetest of all.

Verse 4. *Bitter as wormwood*] כלענה *Kelaanah*, like the *detestable* herb *wormwood*, or something analogous to it: something as excessive in its *bitterness*, as *honey* is in its *sweetness*.

Verse 5. *Her feet go down to death*] She first, like a serpent, infuses her *poison*, by which the whole *constitution* of her paramour is infected, which soon or late brings on *death*.

Her steps take hold on hell.] First, the *death of the body;* and then the damnation of the soul. These are the *tendencies* of connections with such women.

Verse 6. *Lest thou shouldest ponder*] To prevent thee from reflecting on thy present conduct, and its consequences, *her ways are moveable*—she continually varies her allurements.

Thou canst not know them.] It is impossible to conceive all her tricks and wiles: to learn these in all their varieties, is a part of the *science* first taught in that infernal trade.

Verse 7. *Hear me—O ye children*] בנים *banim*, sons, *young men* in general: for these are the most likely to be deceived and led astray.

Verse 8. *Come not nigh the door of her house*] Where there are generally such exhibitions as have a natural tendency to excite impure thoughts, and irregular passions.

Verse 9. *Lest thou give thine honour*] The *character* of a *debauchee* is universally detested: by this, even those of *noble blood* lose their *honour* and *respect*.

Thy years unto the cruel] Though all the blandishments of love dwell on the tongue, and the excess of fondness appear in the whole demeanour of the *harlot* and the *prostitute;* yet *cruelty* has its throne in their hearts; and they will *rob* and *murder* (when it appears to answer their ends) those who give their *strength*, their *wealth*, and their *years* to them. The unfaithful *wife* has often murdered her own husband for the sake of her paramour, and has given *him* over to justice in order to save herself. Murders have often taken place in brothels, as well as robberies; for the vice of *prostitution* is one of the parents of *cruelty*.

Verse 11. *When thy flesh and thy body are consumed*] The word שאר *shear*, which we render body, signifies properly the *remains*, *residue*, or *remnant* of a thing: and is applied here to denote the *breathing carcass*, *putrid* with the *concomitant disease* of debauchery: a public reproach which the justice of God entails on this species of iniquity. The *mourning* here spoken of is of the most excessive kind: the word נחם *naham* is often applied to the *growling of a lion*, and the *hoarse incessant murmuring* of the sea. In the line of my duty, I have been often called to attend the deathbed of such persons, where *groans* and *shrieks* were incessant through the *jaculating* pains in their bones and flesh. Whoever has witnessed a closing scene like this will at once perceive with what force and propriety the wise man speaks. And *How have I hated instruction*, and *despised the voice of my teachers!* is the unavailing cry in that terrific time. Reader, whosoever thou art, lay these things to heart. Do not *enter* into their sin: once *entered*, thy *return* is nearly hopeless.

Verse 14. *I was almost in all evil*] This vice, like a whirlpool, sweeps all others into its vortex.

In the midst of the congregation and assembly.] **In the mydel of the Curche and of the Synagoge.**—Old MS. Bible. Such persons, however sacred the place, carry about with *them eyes full of adultery, which cannot cease from sin.*

A. M. cir. 3004 B. C. cir. 1000 Ante I. Olymp. cir. 224 Ante U. C. cir. 247

of the congregation and assembly.
15 Drink waters out of thine
own cistern, and running waters
out of thine own well.
16 Let thy fountains be dispersed abroad,
and rivers of waters in the streets.
17 Let them be only thine own, and not
strangers' with thee.
18 Let thy fountain be blessed: and rejoice
with [l]the wife of thy youth.
19 [m]*Let her be as* the loving hind and pleasant roe; let her breasts [n]satisfy thee at all
times; and [o]be thou ravished al-
ways with her love.
20 And why wilt thou, my son,
be ravished with [p]a strange woman, and embrace the bosom of a stranger?
21 [q]For the ways of man *are* before the
eyes of the LORD, and he pondereth all his
goings.
22 [r]His own iniquities shall take the wicked
himself, and he shall be holden with the cords
of his [s]sins.
23 [t]He shall die without instruction; and
in the greatness of his folly he shall go astray.

[l]Mal. ii. 14——[m]See Cant. ii. 9; iv. 5; vii. 3——[n]Heb. *water thee*——[o]Heb. *err thou always in her love*——[p]Ch. ii. 16; vii. 5——[q]2 Chron. xvi. 9; Job xxxi. 4; xxxiv. 21; chap. xv. 3; Jer. xvi. 17; xxxii. 19; Hos. vii. 2; Heb. iv. 13——[r]Psa. ix. 15——[s]Heb. *sin*——[t]Job iv. 21; xxxvi. 12

Verse 15. *Drink waters out of thine own cistern*] Be satisfied with thy own wife; and let the wife see that she reverence her husband; and not tempt him by inattention or unkindness to seek elsewhere what he has a right to expect, but cannot find, at *home.*

Verse 16. *Let thy fountains be dispersed abroad*] Let thy children lawfully begotten be numerous.

Verse 17. *Let them be only thine own*] The off-spring of a legitimate connection; a *bastard brood,* however numerous, is no credit to any man.

Verse 18. *Let thy fountain be blessed*] יהי מקורך ברוך *yehi mekorecha baruch. Sit vena tua benedicta.* Thy *vein;* that which carries off streams from the fountain of *animal life,* in order to *disperse them abroad,* and *through the streets.* How *delicate* and correct is the *allusion* here! But anatomical allusions must not be pressed into detail in a commentary on Scripture.

Verse 19. *The loving hind and pleasant roe*] By אילת *aiyeleth,* the *deer;* by יעלה *yaalah,* the *ibex* or mountain *goat,* may be meant.

Let her breasts satisfy thee] As the infant is satisfied with the breasts of its mother; so shouldst thou be with the wife of thy youth.

Verse 21. *For the ways of a man*] Whether they are public or private, God sees all the steps thou takest in life.

Verse 22. *He shall be holden with the cords of his sins.*] Most people who follow unlawful pleasures, think *they can give them up whenever they please;* but sin *repeated* becomes *customary;* custom soon engenders *habit;* and habit in the end assumes the form of *necessity;* the man becomes *bound with his own cords,* and so is *led captive by the devil at his will.*

Verse 23. *He shall die without instruction*] This is *most likely,* and it is a *general* case; but even *these* may repent and live.

CHAPTER VI

Exhortations against becoming surety for others, 1–5; *against idleness, from the example of the ant,* 6–11; *description of a worthless person,* 12–15; *seven things hateful to God,* 16–19; *the benefits of instruction,* 20–23; *farther exhortations against bad women, and especially against adultery,* 24–33; *what may be expected from jealousy,* 34, 35.

A. M. cir. 3004 B. C. cir. 1000 Ante I. Olymp. cir. 224 Ante U. C. cir. 247

MY son, [a]if thou be surety for
thy friend, *if* thou hast
stricken thy hand with a stranger,
2 Thou art snared with the
words of thy mouth, thou art taken
with the words of thy mouth.
3 Do this now, my son, and
deliver thyself when thou art

[a]Chap. xi. 15; xvii. 18; xx. 16; xxii. 26; xxvii. 13

NOTES ON CHAP. VI

Verse 1. *If thou be surety for thy friend*] לרעך *lereacha,* for thy *neighbour;* i. e., any person. If thou pledge thyself in behalf of another, thou takest the burden off him, and placest it on thine own shoulders; and when he knows he has got one to stand between him and the demands of law and justice, he will feel little responsibility; his spirit of exertion will become crippled, and listlessness as to the event will be the consequence. His own character will suffer little; his property nothing, for his friend bears all the burden: and perhaps the very person for whom he bore this burden treats him with neglect; and, lest the

A. M. cir. 3004
B. C. cir. 1000
Ante I. Olymp. cir. 224
Ante U. C. cir. 247

come into the hand of thy
friend; go, humble thyself, [b]and
make sure thy friend.
4 [c]Give not sleep to thine
eyes, nor slumber to thine eyelids.
5 Deliver thyself as a roe from the hand *of*
the hunter, and as a bird from the hand of the
fowler.
6 [d]Go to the ant, thou sluggard; consider
her ways, and be wise:
7 Which having no guide, overseer, or ruler,
8 Provideth her meat in the summer, *and*
gathereth her food in the harvest.
9 [e]How long wilt thou sleep,
O sluggard? when wilt thou
arise out of thy sleep?
10 *Yet* a little sleep, a little
slumber, a little folding of the hands to sleep:
11 [f]So shall thy poverty come as one that
travelleth, and thy want as an armed man.
12 A naughty person, a wicked man, walketh
with a froward mouth.
13 [g]He winketh with his eyes, he speaketh
with his feet, he teacheth with his fingers;
14 Frowardness *is* in his heart; [h]he deviseth
mischief continually; [i]he [k]soweth discord.

A. M. cir. 3004
B. C. cir. 1000
Ante I. Olymp. cir. 224
Ante U. C. cir. 247

[b]Or, *so shalt thou prevail with thy friend*——[c]Psa. cxxxii. 4——[d]Job xii. 7——[e]Chap. xxiv. 33, 34

[f]Ch. x. 4; xiii. 4; xx. 4——[g]Job xv. 12; Psa. xxxv. 19; ch. x. 10——[h]Mic. ii. 1——[i]Ver. 19——[k]Heb. *casteth forth*

restoration of the pledge should be required, will avoid both the sight and presence of his friend. *Give* what thou canst; but, except in extreme cases, be *surety* for no man. *Striking* or *shaking hands* when the *mouth had once made the promise,* was considered as the *ratification* of the engagement; and thus the man became *ensnared with the words of his mouth.*

Verse 3. *Do this—deliver thyself*] Continue to press him for whom thou art become surety, to pay his creditor; give him no rest till he do it, else thou mayest fully expect to be left to pay the debt.

Verse 5. *Deliver thyself as a roe*] צבי *tsebi,* the antelope. If thou art got into the snare, get out if thou possibly canst; make every *struggle* and *exertion,* as the antelope taken in the net, and the bird taken in the snare would, in order to get free from thy captivity.

Verse 6. *Go to the ant, thou sluggard*] נמלה *nemalah,* the *ant,* is a remarkable creature for *foresight, industry,* and *economy.* At the proper seasons they collect their food—not in the *summer* to lay up for the *winter;* for they sleep during the winter, and eat not; and therefore such hoards would be to them useless; but when the food necessary for them is most plentiful, then they collect it for their consumption in the proper seasons. No insect is more *laborious,* not even the *bee* itself; and none is more *fondly attached* to or more *careful* of its young, than the ant. When the young are in their *aurelia* state, in which they appear like a small *grain* of *rice,* they will bring them out of their nests, and lay them near their holes, for the benefit of the sun; and on the approach of *rain,* carefully remove them, and deposit them in the nest, the hole or entrance to which they will cover with a piece of thin stone or tile, to prevent the wet from getting in. It is a fact that they do not lay up any meat for winter; nor does Solomon, either here or in chap. xxx. 25, assert it. He simply says that they provide their food in summer, and gather it in harvest; these are the most proper times for a stock to be laid in for their consumption; not in *winter;* for no such thing appears in any of their nests, nor do they need it, as they *sleep* during that season; but for autumn, during which they wake and work. Spring, summer, and autumn, they are incessant in their labour; and their conduct affords a bright example to men.

Verse 10. Yet *a little sleep, a little slumber*] This, if not the *language,* is the *feeling* of the sluggard. The *ant* gathers its food in summer and in harvest, and sleeps in winter when it has no work to do. If the sluggard would work in the day, and sleep at night, it would be all proper. The ant yields him a lesson of reproach.

Verse 11. *So shall thy poverty come as one that travelleth*] That is, with slow, but surely approaching steps.

Thy want as an armed man.] That is, with irresistible fury; and thou art not prepared to oppose it. The *Vulgate, Septuagint,* and *Arabic* add the following clause to this verse:—"But if thou wilt be diligent, thy harvest shall be as a fountain; and poverty shall flee far away from thee."

It is also thus in the Old MS. Bible: **If forsothe unslow thou shul ben; shul comen as a welle thi rip; and nede fer shal fleen fro thee.**

Verse 12. *A naughty person*] אדם בליעל *adam beliyal,* "Adam good for nothing." When he lost his innocence. **A man apostata;** Old MS. Bible.

A wicked man] איש און *ish aven.* He soon became a general transgressor after having departed from his God. All his posterity, unless restored by Divine grace, are men of Belial, and sinners by trade; and most of them, in one form or other, answer the character here given. They yield their members instruments of unrighteousness unto sin.

Verse 13. *He winketh with his eyes, he speaketh with his feet, he teacheth with his fingers*] These things seem to be spoken of debauchees; and the following quotation from Ovid, Amor. lib. i., El. iv., ver. 15, shows the whole process of the villany spoken of by Solomon:

Cum premit ille torum, vultu comes ipsa modesto
Ibis, ut accumbas: clam mihi *tange pedem.*
Me specta, *nutusque* meos, *vultum que loquacem*
Excipe *furtivas,* et refer ipsa, *notas.*
Verba superciliis sine voce loquentia dicam
Verba leges *digitis, verba notata mero.*
Cum tibi succurrit Veneris lascivia nostræ,
Purpureas tenero *pollice tange genas,* &c., &c.

A. M. cir. 3004
B. C. cir. 1000
Ante I. Olymp. cir. 224
Ante U. C. cir. 247

15 Therefore shall his calamity
come suddenly; suddenly shall
he [l]be broken [m]without remedy.
16 These six *things* doth the LORD hate:
yea, seven *are* an abomination [n]unto him.
17 [o]A [p]proud look, [q]a lying tongue, and
[r]hands that shed innocent blood,
18 [s]A heart that deviseth wicked imaginations, [t]feet that be swift in running to mischief,
19 [u]A false witness *that* speaketh lies, and
he [v]that soweth discord among brethren.
20 [w]My son, keep thy father's commandment, and forsake not the law of thy mother:
21 [x]Bind them continually upon thine
heart, *and* tie them about thy
neck.
22 [y]When thou goest, it shall
lead thee; when thou sleepest,
[z]it shall keep thee; and *when* thou awakest,
it shall talk with thee.
23 [a]For the commandment *is* a [b]lamp; and
the law *is* light; and reproofs of instruction
are the way of life:
24 [c]To keep thee from the evil woman, from
the flattering [d]of the tongue of a strange
woman.
25 [e]Lust not after her beauty in thine heart;
neither let her take thee with her eye-lids.
26 For [f]by means of a whorish woman *a*
man is brought to a piece of bread: [g]and [h]the

[l]Jer. xix. 11——[m]2 Chron. xxxvi. 16——[n]Heb. *of his soul*——[o]Psa. xviii. 27; ci. 5——[p]Heb. *Haughty eyes*——[q]Psa. cxx. 2, 3——[r]Isa. i. 15——[s]Gen. vi. 5——[t]Isa. lix. 7; Rom. iii. 15——[u]Psa. xxvii. 12; chap. xix. 5, 9——[v]Ver. 14——[w]Chap. i. 8; Eph. vi. 1

[x]Chap. iii. 3; vii. 3——[y]Chap. iii. 23, 24——[z]Chap. ii. 11——[a]Psa. xix. 8; cxix. 105——[b]Or, *candle*——[c]Chap. ii. 16; v. 3; vii. 5——[d]Or, *of the strange tongue*——[e]Matt. v. 28——[f]Chap. xxix. 3——[g]Gen. xxxix. 14——[h]Heb. *the woman of a man*, or *a man's wife*

The whole *elegy* is in the same strain: it is translated in *Garth's* Ovid, but cannot be introduced here.

Verse 14. *He deviseth mischief*] He plots schemes and plans to bring it to pass.

He soweth discord.] Between men and their wives, by seducing the latter from their fidelity. See the preceding quotation.

Verse 15. *Suddenly shall he be broken*] Probably alluding to some punishment of the adulterer, such as being *stoned to death.* A multitude shall join together, and so overwhelm him with stones, that he shall have his flesh and bones broken to pieces; and there shall be *no remedy*—none to deliver or pity him.

Verse 16. *These six—doth the Lord hate*] 1. *A proud look*—exalted eyes; those who will not condescend to look on the rest of mankind. 2. *A lying tongue*—he who neither loves nor tells *truth.* 3. *Hands that shed innocent blood*, whether by murder or by battery. 4. *A heart that deviseth wicked imaginations*—the heart that *fabricates* such, lays the foundation, builds upon it, and completes the superstructure of *iniquity.* 5. *Feet that be swift in running to mischief*—he who works iniquity with greediness. 6. *A false witness that speaketh lies*—one who, even on his oath before a court of justice, tells any thing but the truth.

Seven are *an abomination unto him*] נפשו *naphsho*, "to his soul." The seventh is, *he that soweth discord among brethren*—he who troubles the peace of a family, of a village, of the state; all who, by lies and misrepresentations, strive to make men's minds evil-affected towards their brethren.

Verse 20. *Keep thy father's commandment*] See on Chap. i. 8.

Verse 21. *Bind them continually upon thine heart*] See on chap. iii. 3. And see a similar command, to which this is an allusion, Deut. vi. 6-8.

Verse 22. *When thou goest, it shall lead thee*] Here the *law* is *personified;* and is represented as a nurse, teacher, and guardian, by night and day. An upright man never *goes* but as directed by God's word, and led by God's Spirit.

When thou sleepest] He commends his body and soul to the protection of his Maker when he lies down and sleeps in peace. And when he awakes in the morning, the promises and mercies of God are the first things that present themselves to his recollection.

Verse 23. *For the commandment* is *a lamp*] It illuminates our path. It shows us how *we should walk* and *praise God.*

And the law is *light*] A *general light*, showing the *nature* and *will* of GOD, and the *interest* and *duty* of MAN.

And reproofs of instruction] Or, that instruction which reproves us for our sins and errors leads us into the way of life.

Verse 24. *To keep thee from the evil woman*] Solomon had suffered sorely from this quarter; and hence his repeated cautions and warnings to others. The *strange woman* always means one that is not a man's own; and sometimes it may also imply a *foreign harlot*, one who is also a *stranger* to the God of Israel.

Verse 25. *Neither let her take thee with her eye-lids.*] It is a very general custom in the East to *paint the eye-lids.* I have many Asiatic drawings in which this is expressed. They have a method of *polishing the eyes* with a preparation of *antimony*, so that they appear with an indescribable lustre; or, as one who mentions the fact from observation, "Their eyes appear to be swimming in bliss."

Verse 26. *By means of a whorish woman*] In following lewd women, a man is soon reduced to poverty and disease. The *Septuagint* gives this a strange turn: Τιμη γαρ πορνης, ὁση και ἑνος αρτου. "For the price or hire of a whore is about one loaf." So *many* were they in the land, that they hired themselves out for a *bare subsistence.* The *Vulgate*, *Syriac*, and *Arabic*, give the same sense. The old MS. Bible has it thus: **The price forsothe of a strumpet is**

A. M. cir. 3004
B. C. cir. 1000
Ante I. Olymp. cir. 224
Ante U. C. cir. 247

adulteress will [i]hunt for the precious life.

27 Can a man take fire in his bosom, and his clothes not be burned?

28 Can one go upon hot coals, and his feet not be burned?

29 So he that goeth in to his neighbour's wife; whosoever toucheth her shall not be innocent.

30 *Men* do not despise a thief, if he steal to satisfy his soul when he is hungry;

31 But *if* he be found, [k]he shall restore sevenfold; he shall give all the substance of his house.

32 *But* whoso committeth adultery with a woman [l]lacketh [m]understanding: he *that* doeth it destroyeth his own soul.

33 A wound and dishonour shall he get; and his reproach shall not be wiped away.

34 For jealousy *is* the rage of a man: therefore he will not spare in the day of vengeance.

35 [n]He will not regard any ransom; neither will he rest content, though thou givest many gifts.

[i]Ezek. xiii. 18——[k]Exod. xxii. 1, 4——[l]Chap. vii. 7

[m]Heb. *heart*——[n]Heb. *He will not accept the face of any ransom*

unneth oon lof: the woman forsothe taketh the precious liif of a man. The sense of which is, and probably the sense of the *Hebrew* too, While the man hires the whore for a *single loaf* of bread; the woman thus hired taketh his *precious life.* She extracts his energy, and poisons his constitution. In the first clause אשה זונה *ishshah zonah* is plainly a *prostitute*; but should we render אשת *esheth,* in the second clause, an *adulteress?* I think not. The versions in general join אשת איש *esheth ish,* together, which, thus connected, signify no more than *the wife of a man;* and out of this we have made *adulteress,* and *Coverdale* a *married woman.* I do not think that the Old MS. Bible gives a good sense; and it requires a good deal of paraphrase to extract the common meaning from the text. Though the following verses seem to countenance the common interpretation, yet they may contain a complete sense of themselves; but, taken in either way, the sense is good, though the construction is a little violent.

Verse 27. *Can a man take fire*] These were proverbial expressions, the meaning of which was plain to every capacity.

Verse 29. *So he that goeth in to his neighbour's wife*] As sure as he who takes *fire into his bosom,* or who *walks* upon *live coals,* is burnt thereby; so sure he that seduces his neighbour's wife *shall be guilty.* That is, he shall be punished.

Verse 30. *Men do not despise a thief, if he steal*] Every man pities the poor culprit who was perishing for lack of food, and stole to *satisfy his hunger;* yet no law *clears* him: he is bound to make restitution; in some cases *double,* in others *quadruple* and *quintuple;* and if he have not property enough to make restitution, to be sold for a *bondman;* Exod xxii. 1-4; Lev. xxv. 39.

Verse 32. But *whoso committeth adultery*] The case understood is that of a *married man:* he has a wife; and therefore is not in the circumstances of the *poor thief,* who stole to *appease his hunger, having nothing to eat.* In this alone the *opposition* between the two cases is found: the *thief had no food,* and he stole some; the married man had a *wife,* and yet went in to *the wife of his neighbour.*

Destroyeth his own soul.] Sins against *his life;* for, under the law of Moses, adultery was punished with *death;* Lev. xx. 10; Deut. xxii. 22.

Verse 33. *A wound and dishonour shall he get*] Among the *Romans,* when a man was caught in the fact, the injured husband took the law into his own hand; and a large *radish* was thrust up into the anus of the transgressor, which not only overwhelmed him with infamy and disgrace, but generally caused his death.

Verse 34. *Jealousy* is *the rage of a man: therefore he will not spare*] He will not, when he has detected the adulterer in the fact, wait for the slow progress of the law: it is then to him the *day of vengeance;* and in general, he avenges himself on the spot, as we see above.

Verse 35. *He will not regard any ransom*] This is an injury that admits of *no compensation.* No *gifts* can satisfy a man for the injury his honour has sustained; and to take a *bribe* or a *ransom,* would be setting up *chastity* at a price.

CHAPTER VII

A farther exhortation to acquire wisdom, in order to be preserved from impure connections, 1–5. The character of a harlot, and her conduct towards a youth who fell into her snare, 6–23. Solemn exhortations to avoid this evil, 24–27.

A. M. cir. 3004
B. C. cir. 1000
Ante I. Olymp. cir. 224
Ante U. C. cir. 247

MY son, keep my words, and
[a]lay up my commandments
with thee.
2 [b]Keep my commandments,
and live; [c]and my law as the apple of thine
eye.
3 [d]Bind them upon thy fingers, write them
upon the table of thine heart.
4 Say unto wisdom, Thou *art* my sister; and
call understanding *thy* kinswoman:
5 [e]That they may keep thee from the strange
woman, from the stranger *which* flattereth
with her words.
6 For at the window of my house I looked
through my casement,
7 And beheld among the simple ones, I discerned among [f]the youths, a young man [g]void
of understanding,

[a]Chap. ii. 1——[b]Lev. xviii. 5; chap. iv. 4; Isa. lv. 3——[c]Deut. xxxii. 10——[d]Deut. vi. 8; xi. 18; chap. iii. 3; vi. 21——[e]Chap. ii. 16; v. 3; vi. 24——[f]Heb. *the sons*——[g]Chap. vi. 32; ix. 4, 16

A. M. cir. 3004
B. C. cir. 1000
Ante I. Olymp. cir. 224
Ante U. C. cir. 247

8 Passing through the street
near the corner; and he went the
way to her house.
9 [h]In the twilight, [i]in the
evening, in the black and dark night:
10 And, behold, there met him a woman *with*
the attire of a harlot, and subtle of heart.
11 ([k]She *is* loud and stubborn; [l]her feet
abide not in her house:
12 Now *is she* without, now in the streets,
and lieth in wait at every corner.)
13 So she caught him, and kissed him, *and*
[m]with an impudent face said unto him,
14 [n]*I have* peace-offerings with me; this day
have I payed my vows.
15 Therefore came I forth to meet thee,
diligently to seek thy face, and I have found
thee.

[h]Job xxiv. 15——[i]Heb. *in the evening of the day*——[k]Chap. ix. 13——[l]1 Tim. v. 13; Titus ii. 5——[m]Hebrew, *she strengthened her face, and said*——[n]Hebrew, *Peace-offerings* are *upon me*

NOTES ON CHAP. VII

Verse 1. *My son, keep my words*] See chap. ii. 1.

Verse 2. *As the apple of thine eye.*] As the pupil of the eye, which is of such essential necessity to sight, and so easily injured.

Verse 3. *Bind them upon thy fingers*] See on chap. iii. 3.

Verse 4. *Thou* art *my sister*] Thou art my dearest friend, and I will treat thee as such.

Verse 5. *The strange woman*] The *prostitute*, the *adulteress*.

Verse 6. *I looked through my casement*] The *casement* is a small aperture in a large window, or a window opening on hinges. Here it means the *lattice*, for they had no *glass windows* in the East. And the *latticed* windows produced a *double* advantage: 1. Making the apartments sufficiently private; and 2. Admitting fresh air to keep them cool.

Verse 7. *Among the simple ones*] The inexperienced, inconsiderate young men.

A young man void of understanding] חסר לב *chasar leb*, "destitute of a heart." He had not wisdom to discern the evil intended; nor courage to resist the flatteries of the seducer.

Verse 8. *He went the way to her house.*] She appears to have had a corner house sufficiently remarkable; and a way from the main street to it.

Verse 9. *In the twilight, in the evening*] Some time after sun-setting; before it was *quite dark*.

In the black and dark night] When there were neither *lamps* nor *moon-shine*.

Verse 10. *A woman* with *the attire of a harlot*] It appears that sitting in some open place, and covering the face, or having a veil of a peculiar kind on, was the evidence of a harlot; Gen. xxxviii. 14, 15-19. No doubt, in Solomon's time, they had other distinctions. In all other countries, and in all times, *the show of their countenance did testify against them; they declared their sin as Sodom; they hid it not.* However, this does not seem to have been a mere prostitute; for she was, according to her own declaration, a *married woman*, and kept house, ver. 19, if her assertions relative to this were not falsehoods, and calculated the better to render him secure, and prevent the suspicion of endangering himself by cohabiting with a common woman; which I am rather inclined to think was the case, for she was *subtle of heart.*

Verse 11. *She* is *loud and stubborn*] המיה *homiyah*, she is never *at rest*, always *agitated;* busily employed to gain her end, and this is *to go* into the *path of error:* סררת *sorereth*, "turning aside;" preferring any way to the right way. And, therefore, it is added, *her feet abide not in her house;* she gads abroad; and this disposition probably first led her to this vice.

Verse 12. *Now* is she *without*] She is continually exposing herself, and showing by her gait and gestures *what* she *is*, and *what* she *wants*. These two verses are a *parenthesis*, intended to show the character of the woman.

Verse 13. *So she caught him*] Laid *fast hold* on him, and *kissed him*, to show that she was affectionately attached to him.

And with an impudent face] העזה פניה *heezzah paneyha*, "she strengthened her countenance," assumed the most confident look she could; endeavoured to appear friendly and sincere.

Verse 14. I have *peace-offerings with me*] More literally, "the sacrifices of the peace-offerings are with me." *Peace-offerings* שלמים *shelamim*, were offerings the spiritual design of which was to make peace between God and man, to make up the *breach* between them which sin had occasioned; see the notes on Lev. vii., where every kind of sacrifice offered under the law is explained. When the *blood* of

A. M. cir. 3004
B. C. cir. 1000
Ante I. Olymp. cir. 224
Ante U. C. cir. 247

16 I have decked my bed with
coverings of tapestry, with carved
works, with [o]fine linen of Egypt.
17 I have perfumed my bed
with myrrh, aloes, and cinnamon.
18 Come, let us take our fill of love until
the morning: let us solace ourselves with
loves.
19 For the good man *is* not at home, he is
gone a long journey:
20 He hath taken a bag of money [p]with him,
and will come home at [q]the day appointed.
21 With [r]her much fair speech she caused
him to yield, [s]with the flattering of her lips
she forced him.
22 He goeth after her [t]straight-
way, as an ox goeth to the
slaughter, or as a fool to the correction of the stocks:
23 Till a dart strike through his liver; [u]as
a bird hasteth to the snare, and knoweth not
that it *is* for his life.
24 Hearken unto me now, therefore, O ye
children, and attend to the words of my mouth.
25 Let not thine heart decline to her ways,
go not astray in her paths.
26 For she hath cast down many wounded:
yea, [v]many strong *men* have been slain by her.
27 [w]Her house *is* the way to hell, going
down to the chambers of death.

A. M. cir. 3004
B. C. cir. 1000
Ante I. Olymp. cir. 224
Ante U. C. cir. 247

[o]Isa. xix. 9——[p]Heb. *in his hand*——[q]Or, *the new moon* [r]Chap. v. 3——[s]Psa. xii. 2

[t]Heb. *suddenly*——[u]Eccles. ix. 12——[v]Neh. xiii. 26 [w]Chap. ii. 18; v. 5; ix. 13

these was poured out at the altar, and the *fat* burnt there, the *breast* and *right shoulder* were the priest's portion; but the rest of the carcass belonged to the sacrificer, who might carry it home, and make a feast to his friends. See Lev. iii. 1-11. Much light is cast on this place by the *fact* that the gods in many parts of the East are actually worshipped in *brothels,* and fragments of the *offerings* are divided among the wretches who fall into the snare of the prostitutes.—WARD'S *Customs.*

Have I payed my vows] She seems to insinuate that she had *made a vow for the health and safety of this young man;* and having done so, and prepared the sacrificial banquet, came actually out to seek him, that he might partake of it with her, ver. 15. But, as she intended to proceed farther than mere *friendship,* she was obliged to avail herself of the *night season,* and the *absence of her husband.*

Verse 16. *I have decked my bed*] ערשי *arsi,* "my couch or sofa;" distinguished from משכבי *mishcabi,* "my bed," ver. 17, *the place to sleep on,* as the other was *the place to recline on* at *meals.* The *tapestry,* מרבדים *marbaddim,* mentioned here seems to refer to the covering of the *sofa;* exquisitely *woven* and *figured* cloth. חטבות אטון *chatuboth etun,* the *Targum* translates *painted carpets,* such as were manufactured in *Egypt;* some kind of *embroidered* or *embossed stuff* is apparently meant.

Verse 17. *I have perfumed my bed with myrrh*] מר *mor,* "aloes," אהלים *ahalim,* and "cinnamon," קנמון *kinnamon.* We have taken our names from the original words; but probably the *ahalim* may not mean *aloes,* which is no *perfume;* but *sandal wood,* which is very much used in the East. She had used every means to excite the passions she wished to bring into action.

Verse 18. *Come, let us take our fill of love*] נרוה דדים *nirveh dodim,* "Let us revel in the breasts;" and then it is added, "Let us solace ourselves with loves," נתעלסה באהבים *nithallesah boohabim;* "let us gratify each other with loves, with the utmost delights." This does not half express the original; but I forbear. The speech shows the *brazen face* of this woman, well translated by the *Vulgate,* "Veni, inebriemur uberibus; et fruamur cupidinis amplexibus." And the *Septuagint* has expressed the spirit of it: Ελθε, και απολαυσωμεν φιλιας—δευρο, και εγκυλισθωμεν ερωτι. "Veni, et fruamur amicitia —Veni, et colluctemur cupidine." Though varied in the words, all the *versions* have expressed the same thing. In the old MS. Bible, the speech of this woman is as follows:—**I have arrayed with cordis my litil bed, and spred with peyntid tapetis of Egipt: I have springid my ligginge place with mirre and aloes and canelcum, and be we inwardly drunken with Tetis, and use we the coveytied clippingis to the tyme that the dai wax light.** The original itself is too gross to be literally translated; but quite in character as coming from the mouth of an abandoned woman.

Verse 19. *For the good man*] Literally, "For the man is not in his house."

Verse 20. *He hath taken*] Literally, "The money bag he hath taken in his hand." He is gone a journey of itinerant merchandising. This seems to be what is intended.

And *will come home at the day appointed.*] ליום הכסא *leyom hakkase,* the *time fixed* for a return from such a journey. The *Vulgate* says, "at the full moon." The *Targum,* "the day of the assembly." In other words, He will return by the *approaching festival.*

Verse 21. *With her much fair speech*] With her blandishments and lascivious talk, she overcame all his scruples, and constrained him to yield.

Verse 22. *As an ox goeth to the slaughter*] The original of this and the following verse has been variously translated. Dr. *Grey* corrects and translates thus: "He goeth after her straightway, as an ox goeth to the SLAUGHTER; as a DOG to the CHAIN; and as a DEER till the DART strike through his liver; as a BIRD hasteneth to the SNARE, and knoweth not that it is for its life." Very slight alterations in the Hebrew text produce these differences; but it is not necessary to pursue them; all serve to mark the stupidity and folly of the man who is led away by enticing women or who lives a life of intemperance.

Verse 24. *Hearken unto me now, therefore, O*

ye children] Ye that are young and inexperienced, seriously consider the example set before your eyes, and take warning at another's expense.

Verse 26. *For she hath cast down many wounded: yea, many strong* men *have been slain by her.*] That is, such like women have been the ruin of many. חללים *chalalim*, which we render *wounded*, also signifies *soldiers* or men of war; and עצמים *atsumim*, which we render *strong men*, may be translated *heroes*. Many of those who have distinguished themselves in the field and in the cabinet have been overcome and destroyed by their mistresses. History is full of such examples.

Verse 27. *Her house* is *the way to hell*] שאול *sheol*, the *pit*, the *grave*, the *place of the dead*, the *eternal* and *infernal world*. And they who, through such, fall into the *grave*, descend lower, into *the chambers of death;* the place where pleasure is at an end, and *illusion* mocks no more.

CHAPTER VIII

The fame and excellence of wisdom, and its manner of teaching, 1–4; *the matter of its exhortations,* 5–12; *its influence among men,* 13–21; *its antiquity,* 22–31; *the blessedness of attending to its counsels,* 32–35; *the misery of those who do not,* 36.

A. M. cir. 3004 B. C. cir. 1000 Ante I. Olymp. cir. 224 Ante U. C. cir. 247

DOTH not [a]wisdom cry? and
[b]understanding put forth
her voice?
2 She standeth in the top of high
places, by the way in the places of the paths.
3 She crieth at the gates, at the entry of the
city, at the coming in at the
doors.
4 Unto you, O men, I call; and
my voice *is* to the sons of man.
5 O ye simple, understand wisdom: and ye
fools, be ye of an understanding heart.

[a]Chap. i. 20; ix. 3 — [b]Psa. cxix. 130; cxlvii. 5

NOTES ON CHAP. VIII.

Verse 1. *Doth not wisdom cry?*] Here wisdom is again *personified;* but the *prosopopœia* is carried on to a greater length than before, and with much more variety. It is represented in this chapter in a *twofold* point of view: 1. Wisdom, the *power of judging rightly*, implying *the knowledge of Divine and human things.* 2. As an *attribute* of God, particularly displayed in the various and astonishing works of *creation.* Nor has it *any other meaning* in this whole chapter, whatever some of the fathers may have dreamed, who find allegorical meanings every where. The wise man seems as if suddenly awakened from the distressful contemplation which he had before him,—of the ruin of young persons in both worlds by means of debauchery,—by the voice of wisdom, who has *lifted up her voice* in the most public places, where was the *greatest concourse* of the people, to warn the yet unsnared, that they might avoid the way of seduction and sin; and cause those who love her to *inherit substance*, and to have their *treasuries filled* with durable riches.

Verse 2. *In the places of the paths.*] בית נתיבת נצבה *beith nethiboth nitstsabah*, "The constituted house of the paths." Does not this mean the house of public worship? the tabernacle or temple, which stands a centre to the surrounding villages, the paths from all the parts leading to and terminating at it? In such a place, where the holy word of God is read or preached, there in a particular manner does wisdom *cry*, and *understanding lift up her voice.* There are the warnings, the precepts, and the promises of eternal truth; there the *bread of God* is broken to his children, and thither they that *will* may come and take the *water* of *life* freely.

Verse 3. *She crieth at the gates*] This might be well applied to the preaching of Jesus Christ and his apostles, and their faithful successors in the Christian ministry. He went to the *temple*, and proclaimed the righteousness of the Most High: he did the same in the *synagogues*, on the *mountains*, by the *sea-side*, in the *villages*, in the *streets* of the *cities*, and in *private houses.* His disciples followed his track: in the *same way*, and in the *same spirit*, they proclaimed the unsearchable riches of Christ. God's *wisdom* in the hearts of his true ministers directs them to go and to seek sinners. There are, it is true, temples, synagogues, churches, chapels, &c.; but hundreds of thousands never frequent them, and therefore do not hear the voice of truth: *wisdom*, therefore, *must go to them*, if she wishes them to receive her instructions. Hence the zealous ministers of Christ go still to the *highways* and *hedges*, to the *mountains* and *plains*, to the *ships* and the *cottages*, to persuade sinners to turn from the error of their ways, and accept that redemption which was procured by the sacrificial offering of Jesus Christ.

Verse 4. *Unto you, O men*] אישים *ishim*, men of *wealth* and *power*, *will I call;* and not to you alone, for my voice is אל בני אדם *al beney Adam*, "to all the descendants of Adam;" to the whole human race. As Jesus Christ tasted death for every man, so the Gospel proclaims salvation to all: *to* YOU—to every individual, my voice is addressed. *Thou* hast sinned; and *thou* must perish, if not saved by grace.

Verse 5. *O ye simple*] פתאים *pethaim*, ye that are *deceived*, and with flattering words and fair speeches deluded and *drawn away.*

Ye fools] כסילים *kesilim*, ye stupid, stiff-necked, senseless people. That *preaching* is never likely to do much good, that is not *pointed;* specifying and describing vices, and charging them home on the consciences of

A. M. cir. 3004 B. C. cir. 1000 Ante I. Olymp. cir. 224 Ante U. C. cir. 247

6 Hear; for I will speak of [c]ex-
cellent things; and the opening
of my lips *shall be* right things.
7 For my mouth shall speak
truth; and wickedness *is* [d]an abomination to
my lips.
8 All the words of my mouth *are* in righteousness; *there is* nothing [e]froward or perverse in them.
9 [f]They *are* all plain to him that understandeth, and right to them that find knowledge.
10 Receive my instruction, and not silver;
and knowledge rather than choice
gold.
11 [g]For wisdom *is* better than
rubies; and all the things that
may be desired are not to be compared to it.
12 I wisdom dwell with [h]prudence, and find
out knowledge of witty inventions.
13 [i]The fear of the LORD *is* to hate evil:
[k]pride, and arrogancy, and the evil way, and
[l]the froward mouth, do I hate.
14 Counsel *is* mine, and sound wisdom: I
am understanding; [m]I have strength.

A. M. cir. 3004 B. C. cir. 1000 Ante I. Olymp. cir. 224 Ante U. C. cir. 247

[c]Ch. xxii. 20——[d]Heb. *the abomination of my lips* [e]Heb. *wreathed*——[f]Ch. xiv. 6——[g]Job xxviii. 15, &c.; Psa. xix. 10; cxix. 127; ch. iii. 14, 15; iv. 5, 7; xvi. 16

[h]Or, *subtilty*——[i]Chapter xvi. 6——[k]Chapter vi. 17 [l]Chapter iv. 24——[m]Eccles. vii. 19; Psa. xviii. 1; xix. 14; xxii. 19; xxxi. 4

transgressors. Where this is *not done*, the congregation is unconcerned; no man supposes he has any thing to do in the business, especially if the preacher takes care to tell them, "These were the crimes of Jews, Romans, Greeks, of the people at Corinth, Philippi, Thessalonica, Laodicea, and of heathens in general; but I hope better things of you, who have been born in a Christian land, and baptized in the Christian faith." Thus he arms their *consciences* in double brass against the good effects of his own teaching.

Verse 6. *Hear; for I will speak of excellent things*] נגידים *negidim*, things which are pre-eminent, and manifestly superior to all others. The teaching is not *trifling*, though addressed to *triflers*.

The opening of my lips shall be *right things.*] מישרים *meysharim*, things which are calculated to correct your false notions, and set straight your crooked ways. Hence she declares,

Verse 7. *My mouth shall speak truth*] TRUTH, without *falsity*, or any mixture of *error*, shall be the whole matter of my discourse.

Verse 8. *All the words*—are *in righteousness*] בצדק *betsedek*, in justice and equity, testifying what man *owes* to his God, to his neighbour, and to himself; giving to each his *due*. This is the true import of צדק *tsadak*.

There is *nothing froward*] נפתל *niphtal*, tortuous, involved, or difficult.

Or perverse] עקש *ikkesh*, distorted, leading to obstinacy. On the contrary,

Verse 9. *They* are *all plain*] נכחים *nechochim*, straight forward, over against every man, level to every capacity. This is true of all that concerns the salvation of the soul.

To them that find knowledge.] When a man gets the *knowledge* of *himself*, then he sees all the *threatenings* of God to be *right*. When he obtains the knowledge of GOD in *Christ*, then he finds that all the *promises* of God are *right* —yea and amen.

Verse 10. *Receive my instruction, and not silver*] A Hebrew idiom; *receive my instruction* in preference to silver.

Verse 11. *Wisdom* is *better than rubies*] See on chap. iii. 15.

Verse 12. *I wisdom dwell with prudence*] Prudence is defined, *wisdom applied to practice;* so wherever true wisdom is, it will lead to action, and its activity will be always in reference to the *accomplishment of the best ends by the use of the most appropriate means.* Hence comes what is here called *knowledge of witty inventions*, דעת מזמות אמצא *daath mezimmoth emtsa*, "I have found out knowledge and contrivance." The farther wisdom proceeds in man, the more *practical* knowledge it gains; and finding out the nature and properties of things, and the general course of providence, it can *contrive* by new combinations to produce new results.

Verse 13. *The fear of the Lord* is *to hate evil*] As it is impossible to hate *evil* without loving *good;* and as hatred to *evil* will lead a man to abandon the *evil way;* and *love to goodness* will lead him to do what is *right* in the sight of God, under the influence of that Spirit which has given the *hatred to evil*, and inspired the *love of goodness:* hence this implies the sum and substance of *true religion*, which is here termed *the fear of the Lord.*

Verse 14. *Counsel* is *mine*] *Direction* how to act in all circumstances and on all occasions must come from *wisdom:* the *foolish* man can give no *counsel*, cannot show another how he is to act in the various changes and chances of life. The wise man alone can give this counsel; and he can give it only as continually receiving instruction from God: for this Divine wisdom can say, תושיה TUSHIYAH, *substance, reality, essence,* all belong to me: I am the *Fountain* whence all are derived. Man may be wise, and good, and prudent, and ingenious; but these he derives from me, and they are *dependently* in him. But in *me* all these are *independently* and *essentially* inherent.

And sound wisdom] See above. This is a totally false translation: תושיה *tushiyah* means essence, substance, reality; the source and substance of good. How ridiculous the support derived by certain authors from this translation in behalf of their system! See the writers on and quoters of Prov. viii.

I have strength.] Speaking still of wisdom, as communicating rays of its light to man, it enables him to bring every thing to his aid; to construct machines by which *one man* can do the work of *hundreds*. From it comes all *mathematical learning*, all *mechanical knowledge;* from it originally came the *inclined plane*, the *wedge*, the *screw*, the *pulley*, in all its *multiplications;* and the *lever*, in all its

A. M. cir. 3004 B. C. cir. 1000 Ante I. Olymp. cir. 224 Ante U. C. cir. 247

15 [n]By me kings reign, and princes decree justice.
16 By me princes rule, and nobles, *even* all the judges of the earth.
17 [o]I love them that love me; and [p]those that seek me early shall find me.
18 [q]Riches and honour *are* with me; *yea,* durable riches and righteousness.
19 My fruit *is* better than gold; yea, than fine gold; and my revenue than choice silver.
20 I [s]lead in the way of righteousness, in the midst of the paths of judgment:
21 That I may cause those that love me to inherit substance: and I will fill their treasures.
22 [t]The LORD possessed me in the beginning of his way, before his works of old.
23 [u]I was set up from everlasting, from

[n]Dan. ii. 21; Rom. xiii. 1——[o]1 Sam. ii. 30; Psa. xci. 14; John xiv. 21——[p]James i. 5——[q]Ch. iii. 16; Matt. vi. 33——[r]Chap. iii. 14; ver. 10——[s]Or, *walk*——[t]Chap. iii. 19; Ecclus. xxiv. 9; John i. 1——[u]Psa. ii. 6

combinations and *varieties*, came from this wisdom. And as all these can produce prodigies of *power*, far surpassing all kinds of *animal energy*, and all the effects of the utmost efforts of muscular force; hence the maxim of Lord Bacon, "Knowledge is power," built on the maxim of the *tushiyah* itself; לי גבורה *li geburah*, MINE IS STRENGTH.

Verse 15. *By me kings reign*] Every wise and prudent king is such through the influence of Divine wisdom. And just laws and their righteous administration come from this source. In this and the following verse *five degrees* of *civil power* and *authority* are mentioned. 1. מלכים *melachim*, KINGS. 2. רזנים *rozenim*, CONSULS. 3. שרים *sarim*, PRINCES, CHIEFS of the people. 4. נדיבים *nedibim*, NOBLES. And 5. שפטים *shophetim*, JUDGES or CIVIL MAGISTRATES. All orders of government are from God. Instead of שפטי ארץ *shophetey arets*, "judges of the earth," שפטי צדק *shophetey tsedek*, "righteous judges," or "judges of righteousness," is the reading of *one hundred and sixty-two* of Kennicott's and De Rossi's MSS., both in the text and in the margin, and of several ancient editions. And this is the reading of the *Vulgate*, the *Chaldee*, and the *Syriac;* and should undoubtedly supersede the other.

Verse 17. *I love them that love me*] Wisdom shows itself; teaches man the knowledge of himself; shows him also the will of God concerning him; manifests the snares and dangers of life, the allurements and unsatisfactory nature of all sensual and sinful pleasures, the blessedness of true religion, and the solid happiness which an upright soul derives from the peace and approbation of its Maker. If, then, the heart embraces this wisdom, follows this Divine teaching, and gives itself to God, his love will be shed abroad in it by the influence of the Holy Spirit. Thus we love God because he hath first loved us; and the more we love him, the more we shall feel of his love, which will enable us to love him yet *more and more;* and thus we may go on increasing to eternity. Blessed be God!

And those that seek me early shall find me.] Not merely *betimes in the morning*, though he who does so shall find it greatly to his advantage; (see on Psa. iv.;) but early *in life*—in *youth*, and as near as possible to the first dawn of *reason*. To the *young* this gracious promise is particularly made: if *they* seek, they *shall find*. Others, who are old, may seek and find; but *never to such advantage* as they would have done, had they sought *early*. Youth is the *time* of *advantage* in every respect: it is the time of *learning*, the time of *discipline;* the time of *improvement*, the time of *acquiring useful, solid*, and *gracious habits*. As the *first-fruits* always belong to God, it is *God's time;* the time in which he is peculiarly gracious; and in which, to sincere youthful seekers, he pours out his benefits with great profusion. "They that seek me early shall find me."

Hear, ye *young*, and ye *little ones!* God offers himself now to *you*, with all his treasures of grace and glory. Thank him for his ineffable mercy, and embrace it without delay.

Verse 18. *Riches and honour* are *with me*] Often the wise, prudent, and discreet man arrives literally to *riches* and *honour;* but this is not *always* the case. But there are *other riches* of which he *never fails;* and these seem to be what Solomon has particularly in view, *durable riches and righteousness;* the treasure deposited by God in earthen vessels.

Verse 20. *I lead in the way of righteousness*] Nothing but the teaching that comes from God by his *word* and *Spirit* can do this.

Verse 22. *The Lord possessed me in the beginning of his way*] Wisdom is not *acquired* by the Divine Being; *man*, and even *angels, learn it* by *slow* and *progressive* degrees; but in God it is as eternally inherent as any other essential attribute of his nature. The *Targum* makes this wisdom a *creature*, by thus translating the passage: אלהא בראני בריש בריתיה *Elaha barani bereish biriteiah*, "God created me in the beginning of his creatures." The *Syriac* is the same. This is as absurd and heretical as some modern glosses on the same passage.

Verse 23. *I was set up from everlasting*] נסכתי *nissachti*, "I was diffused or poured out," from נסך *nasach*, "to diffuse, pour abroad, as a spirit or disposition," Isa. xxix. 10. See *Parkhurst*. Or from סך *sach*, "to cover, overspread, smear over, as with *oil;*" to be *anointed* king. Hence some have translated it, *principatum habui*, I had the principality, or was a ruler, governor, and director, from eternity. All the schemes, plans, and circumstances, relative to creation, government, providence, and to all being, *material, animal*, and *intellectual*, were conceived in the Divine mind, by the Divine wisdom, from eternity, *or ever the earth was.* There was no *fortuitous creation*, no *jumbling concourse of original atoms*, that entered into the composition of *created beings;* all was the

A. M. cir. 3004
B. C. cir. 1000
Ante I. Olymp. cir. 224
Ante U. C. cir. 247

the beginning, or ever the earth
was.
24 When *there were* no depths,
I was brought forth; when *there*
were no fountains abounding with water.
25 [v]Before the mountains were settled, before the hills was I brought forth:
26 While as yet he had not made the earth,
nor the [w]fields, nor [x]the highest part of the
dust of the world.
27 When he prepared the heavens, I *was*
there: when he set [y]a compass upon the face
of the depth:

A. M. cir. 3004
B. C. cir. 1000
Ante I. Olymp. cir. 224
Ante U. C. cir. 247

28 When he established the
clouds above: when he strengthened the fountains of the deep:
29 [z]When he gave to the sea
his decree, that the waters should not pass his
commandment: when [a]he appointed the foundations of the earth:
30 [b]Then I was by him, *as* one brought up
with him: [c]and I was daily *his* delight, rejoicing always before him:
31 Rejoicing in the habitable part of his
earth; and [d]my delights *were* with the sons
of men.

---

[v]Job xv. 7, 8——[w]Or, *open places*——[x]Or, *the chief part* [y]Or, *a circle*——[z]Gen. iv. 9, 10; Job xxxviii. 10, 11; Psa. xxxiii. 7; civ. 9; Jer. v. 22——[a]Job xxxviii. 4——[b]John i. 1, 2, 18——[c]Matt. iii. 17; Col. i. 13——[d]Psa. xvi. 3

---

effect of the *plans* before conceived, laid down, and at last acted upon by God's eternal wisdom.

Verse 24. *When* there were *no depths*] תהמות *tehomoth*, before the original chaotic mass was formed. See Gen. i. 2.

I was brought forth] חוללתי *cholalti*, "I was produced as by labouring throes." Mr. *Parkhurst* thinks that the heathen poets derived their idea of *Minerva's* (wisdom's) being born of Jupiter's brain, from some such high poetic personification as that in the text.

Verse 26. *The highest part of the dust of the world*] ראש עפרות תבל *rosh aphroth tebel*, "the first particle of matter." The *prima materia*, the primitive atom. All these verses (3-29) are a periphrasis for *I existed before creation;* consequently before *time* was. I dwelt in God as a principle which might be communicated in its influences to intellectual beings when formed.

Verse 27. *When he prepared the heavens, I* was *there*] For there is no part of the creation of God in which wisdom, skill, contrivance, are more manifest, than in the construction of the visible heavens.

When he set a compass upon the face of the depth] Does not this refer to the establishment of the *law of gravitation?* by which all the particles of matter, tending to a *common centre*, would produce in all bodies the *orbicular* form, which we see them have; so that even the *waters* are not only retained within their boundaries, but are subjected to the *circular form*, in their great aggregate of seas, as other parts of matter are. This is called here *making a compass*, בחקו חוג *bechukko chug*, sweeping a circle; and even this on *the face of the deep*, to bring the chaotic mass into *form*, regularity, and order.

Verse 28. *The clouds above*] שחקים *shechakim*, "the ethereal regions," taking in the whole of the atmosphere, with all its meteors, clouds, vapours, &c.

Verse 29. *When he gave to the sea his decree*] When he assigned its limits, adjusted its saltness, and proportioned the *extent of the surface* to the quantity of *vapours* to be raised from it, for the irrigation of the terrene *surface*.

The foundations of the earth] Those irreversible laws by which all its motions are governed; its annual and diurnal rotation, and particularly its *centrifugal* and *centripetal forces;* by the former of which it has its *annual motion* round the sun like all other planets; and by the *latter* all its particles are prevented from *flying off*, notwithstanding the great *velocity* of its motion round its own axis, which causes *one thousand and forty-two* miles of its equator to pass under any given point in the heavens in the course of a single *hour!* These are, properly speaking, *the foundations of the earth;* the *principles* on which it is constructed, and the *laws* by which it is governed.

Verse 30. *Then I was with him,* as *one brought up*] אמון *amon*, a *nursling*, a *darling* child. Wisdom continues its parable, says *Calmet;* and represents itself as a new-born child which is ever near its parent, and takes pleasure to see him act, and to sport in his presence. This is poetical and highly figurative; and they who think they find the deity of Jesus Christ in these metaphors should be very cautious how they apply such terms as these; so that while they are endeavouring to defend the truth, they *may do nothing against the truth*, in which most of them unhappily fail.

Rejoicing always before him] All the images in this verse are borrowed from the state and circumstances of a *darling*, affectionate, playful child; as any one will be convinced who examines the *Hebrew text.*

Verse 31. *Rejoicing in the habitable part of his earth*] There God displays especially his wisdom in ordering and directing *human beings*, and in providing for their wants. The *wisdom* of God is in an especial manner manifested in his *providence.*

My delights were *with the sons of men.*] This Divine wisdom, as it delighted in the creation of man, so it continues to delight in his *instruction.* Hence it is represented as offering its lessons of instruction continually, and using every means and opportunity to call men from folly and vice to sound knowledge, holiness, and happiness. It is to man that God especially gives *wisdom;* and he has it in the form of *reason* beyond all other creatures; therefore it is said, "My delights are with the sons of men;" to them I open my choicest treasures. They alone are capable of *sapience, intelligence*, and *discursive reason.*

A. M. cir. 3004
B. C. cir. 1000
Ante I. Olymp. cir. 224
Ante U. C. cir. 247

32 Now therefore hearken unto me, O ye children: for [e]blessed *are they that* keep my ways.

33 Hear instruction, and be wise, and refuse it not.

34 [f]Blessed *is* the man that heareth me, watching daily at my gates, waiting at the posts of my doors.

35 For whoso findeth me findeth life, and shall [g]obtain [h]favour of the LORD.

36 But he that sinneth against me [i]wrongeth his own soul: all they that hate me love death.

[e]Psa. cxix. 1, 2; cxxviii. 1, 2; Luke xi. 28——[f]Chap. iii. 13, 18——[g]Heb. *bring forth*——[h]Ch. xii. 2——[i]Ch. xx. 2

Verse 32. *Now therefore*] Since I delight so much in conveying instruction; since I have the happiness of the *children of Adam* so much at heart, *hearken unto me;* and this is for your own interest, for *blessed* are they who *keep my ways.*

Verse 34. *Watching daily at my gates*] Wisdom is represented as having a *school* for the instruction of men; and seems to point out some of the most *forward* of her *scholars* coming, through their intense desire to learn, even *before the gates were opened,* and waiting there for admission, that they might hear *every word* that was uttered, and not lose one accent of the heavenly teaching. *Blessed are such.*

Verse 35. *Whoso findeth me*] The wisdom that comes from God, teaching to avoid evil and cleave to that which is good; *findeth life*—gets that knowledge which qualifies him to answer the *purposes* for which he was *made;* for he is *quickened with* Christ, and made a partaker of the Divine life. *Christ dwells in his heart by faith;* he *lives a new life,* for Christ *liveth* in him; the law of the *spirit of life* in Christ Jesus makes him free from the *law* of *sin* and *death. And shall obtain favour of the Lord.* The more he walks after the Divine counsel, the more he obtains of the Divine image; and the more he resembles his Maker, the more he partakes of the Divine favour.

Verse 36. *Wrongeth his own soul*] It is not *Satan,* it is not *sin,* properly speaking, that hurts him; it is *himself.* If he received the teaching of God, *sin would have no dominion over him;* if he *resisted the devil,* the devil would *flee from him.*

Love death.] They do it in *effect,* if not in *fact;* for as they love sin, that leads to *death,* so they may be justly said to love *death,* the wages of sin. He that works in this case, works for wages; and he must love the *wages,* seeing he *labours* so hard in the *work.*

I HAVE gone through this fine chapter, and given the best exposition of it in my power. I have also, as well as others, *weighed every word,* and closely examined their *radical* import, their connection among themselves, and the connection of the subject of the chapter with what has gone before, and with what follows after; and I cannot come, conscientiously, to *any other* interpretation than that which I have given. I am thoroughly satisfied that it speaks not one word either about the *Divine* or *human nature of Christ,* much less of any *eternal filiation* of his *Divinity.* And I am fully persuaded, had there not been a preconceived creed, no soul of man, by fair criticism, would have ever found out that fond opinion of the eternal sonship of the Divine nature, which so many commentators persuade us they find here. That it has been thus applied in *early ages,* as well as in *modern times,* I am sufficiently aware; and that many other portions of the Divine records have been appealed to, in order to support a particular opinion, and many that were false in themselves, must be known to those who are acquainted with the *fathers.* But many quote *them* who know nothing of them. As to the fathers in general, they were not all agreed on this subject, some supposing *Christ,* others the *Holy Spirit,* was meant in this chapter. But of these we may safely state, that there is not a *truth* in the most orthodox creed, that cannot be proved by their authority, nor a *heresy* that has disgraced the Romish Church, that may not challenge them as its abettors. In points of *doctrine,* their authority is, *with me,* nothing. The WORD of GOD alone contains my creed. On a number of points I can go to the Greek and Latin fathers of the Church, to know what *they believed,* and what the *people of their respective communions* believed; but after all this I must return to *God's word,* to know what he would have ME to believe. No part of a *Protestant creed* stands on the decision of *fathers* and *councils.* By appealing to the Bible alone, as the only rule for the faith and practice of Christians, they confounded and defeated their papistical adversaries, who could not prove their doctrines but by *fathers* and *councils.* Hence their peculiar doctrines stand in their ultimate proof upon THESE; and *those* of Protestantism on the BIBLE. Some late writers upon this subject, whose names I spare, have presumed much on *what they have said on this subject;* but before any man, who seeks for sober truth, will receive any of their *conclusions,* he will naturally look whether their *premises* be sound, or whether from *sound principles* they have drawn *legitimate conclusions.* They say this chapter is a sufficient foundation to build their doctrine on. I say it is no foundation at all; that it never has been proved, and never can be proved, that it speaks at all of the doctrine in question. It has nothing to do with it. On this conviction of mine, their proofs drawn from this chapter must go with *me* for *nothing.* I have been even shocked with reading over some things that have been *lately written* on the subject. I have said in my heart, They have taken away my ETERNAL LORD, and I know not where they have laid him. I cannot believe their doctrine; I never did; I hope I never shall. I believe in the holy Trinity; in three persons in the Godhead, of which none is before or after another. I believe JEHOVAH, JESUS, the HOLY GHOST to be one infinite, eternal GODHEAD, subsisting ineffably in *three persons.* I believe Jesus the Christ to be, as to his *Divine nature,* as *unoriginated* and *eternal* as JEHOVAH himself; and with the *Holy*

Ghost to be one infinite Godhead, *neither* person being *created*, *begotten*, nor *proceeding*, more than another: as to its *essence*, but *one* TRINITY, in an infinite, eternal and inseparable UNITY. And this TRIUNE GOD is the object of my faith, my adoration, and my confidence. But I believe not in an eternal sonship or generation of the Divine nature of Jesus Christ. *Here* I have long stood, *here* I now stand, and *here* I trust to stand in the hour of death, in the day of judgment, and to all eternity. Taking the Scriptures in general, I find a *plurality* in the Divine nature; taking the grand *part* mentioned, Matt. iii. 16, 17, I find that *plurality* restrained to a *trinity*, in the most unequivocal and evident manner: Jesus, who was baptized in Jordan; the HOLY GHOST, who descended upon him who was baptized; and the FATHER, manifested by the VOICE from heaven that said, "This is my beloved Son, in whom I am well pleased." And how that person called JESUS the CHRIST, in whom dwelt all the fulness of the Godhead bodily, could be called the *Son of God*, I have shown in my note on Luke i. 35.

Some writers, in their defence of the doctrine above, which I venture to say *I do not believe*, have made reflections, in real or pretended pity, on the belief of their Trinitarian brethren, which have very little to do with candour: viz., "How the supporters of this hypothesis can avoid either the error of Tritheism on the one hand, or Sabellianism on the other, is difficult to conceive." Now, the supporters of the doctrine of the underived and unbegotten eternity of Christ's Divine nature might as well say of them: How the supporters of the eternal sonship of Christ can avoid the error of Arianism on the one hand, and Arianism on the other, it is difficult to conceive. But I would not say so; for though I know Arians who hold that doctrine, and express their belief nearly in the same words; yet I know many most conscientious Trinitarians who hold the doctrine of the eternal sonship, and yet believe in the proper deity, or eternal godhead, of Jesus Christ. After all, as a very wise and excellent man lately said: "While we have every reason to be satisfied of the soundness of each other's faith, we must allow each to explain his own sentiments in his own *words:* here, in the *words* used in explanation, a little latitude may be safely allowed." To this correct sentiment I only add:—

> Scimus; et hanc veniam petimusque damusque vicissim.—HORACE.

"I grant it; and the license give and take."

I have passed the *waters of strife*, and do not wish to recross them: the wrath of man worketh not the righteousness of God. I will have nothing to do with ill-tempered, abusive men; I wish them more light and better manners.

And while I am on this subject, let me add one thing, which I am sure will not please all the generation of his people; and it is this: that Jesus Christ, having taken upon him human nature, which was afterwards crucified, and expired upon the cross, did by those acts make a full, perfect, and sufficient offering, sacrifice, and atonement for the sin of the whole world. That he died, paid down the *redemption price*, for *every soul of man*, that *was ever born* into the world, and *shall ever be born* into it. That all who lay hold on the hope set before them shall be saved; (and all *may* thus lay hold;) and none shall perish but those who would not come to Christ that they might have life. And that men perish, not because they were not redeemed, but because they would not accept of the redemption.

To conclude on this subject, it will be necessary to refer the reader to the remarkable *opposition* that subsists between *this* and the *preceding chapter*. *There*, the *prostitute* is represented as *going out into the streets* to seek her prey; and the *alluring words* of *carnal wisdom* to excite the animal appetite to sinful gratification, which she uses: *here*, heavenly *wisdom* is represented as *going out* into the *streets*, to the *high places*, the *gates of the city*, to counteract her designs, and lead back the simple to God and truth.

These *personifications* were frequent among the Jews. In the Book of *Ecclesiasticus* we find a similar personification, and expressed in almost *similar terms;* and surely none will suppose that the writer of that Apocryphal book had either the Christian doctrine of the *Trinity*, or the *sonship of Christ* in view.

I will give a few passages:—

"WISDOM shall *glory* in the *midst of her people;* in the *congregation* of the Most High shall *she open her mouth*, and triumph before his power. I *came out of the mouth of the Most High*, and covered the earth as a cloud. I *dwelt in the high places;* I alone *compassed the circuit of the heaven*, and walked in the *bottom of the deep*, in the waves of the sea, and in all the earth. *He created me from the beginning, before the world;* and I shall never fail. I am the mother of fair love, and fear, and knowledge, and holy hope. I therefore, *being eternal*, am given to all my children which are named of him. *Come unto me*, and fill *yourselves with my fruits*. I also came out as a brook from a river, and a conduit into a garden," &c., &c., Eccl. xxiv. 1, &c. This kind of personification of wisdom we have had in the preceding chapters; and in the following chapter we shall find the figure still kept up.

CHAPTER IX

Wisdom builds her house, makes her provision for a great feast, calls her guests, and exhorts them to partake of her entertainment, 1–6. *Different admonitions relative to the acquisition of wisdom*, 7–12. *The character and conduct of a bad woman*, 13–18.

A. M. cir. 3004
B. C. cir. 1000
Ante I. Olymp. cir. 224
Ante U. C. cir. 247

WISDOM hath [a]builded her
house, she hath hewn out
her seven pillars:
2 [b]She hath killed [c]her beasts;
[d]she hath mingled her wine, she hath also
furnished her table.
3 She hath [e]sent forth her maidens: [f]she
crieth [g]upon the highest places
of the city.
4 [h]Whoso *is* simple, let him
turn in hither: *as for* him that
wanteth understanding, she saith to him,
5 [i]Come, eat of my bread, and drink of the
wine *which* I have mingled.

[a]Matthew xvi. 18; Ephesians ii. 20, 21, 22; 1 Pet. ii. 5——[b]Matthew xxii. 3, &c.——[c]Hebrew, *her killing*——[d]Verse 5; chapter xxiii. 30——[e]Romans x. 15

[f]Chapter viii. 1, 2——[g]Verse 14——[h]Verse 16; chapter vi. 32; Matthew xi. 25——[i]Verse 2; Cant. v. 1; Isa. lv. 1; John vi. 27

NOTES ON CHAP. IX.

The same Wisdom speaks here who spoke in the preceding chapter. *There* she represented herself as manifest in all the *works of God* in the natural world; all being constructed according to counsels proceeding from an infinite understanding. *Here*, she represents herself as the great *potentate*, who was to rule all that she had constructed; and having an immense *family* to provide for, had made an abundant *provision*, and calls all to partake of it. This, says *Calmet*, is the continuation of the parable begun in the preceding chapter, where wisdom is represented as a venerable lady, whose real beauties and solid promises are opposed to the false allurements of PLEASURE, who was represented in the seventh chapter under the idea of a debauched and impudent woman. *This one*, to draw young people into her snares, describes the *perfumes*, the *bed*, and the *festival* which she has prepared. WISDOM acts in the same way: but, instead of the debauchery, the false pleasures, and the criminal connections which *pleasure* had promised, offers her guests a strong, well-built, magnificent palace, chaste and solid pleasures, salutary instructions, and a life crowned with blessedness. This is the sum and the substance of the parable; but as in the preceding part, so in this, men have produced strange creatures of their own brain, by way of explanation. One specimen of this mode of interpretation may suffice.

The *house* built by wisdom is the holy *humanity of Jesus Christ;* the *seven pillars* are the *seven sacraments*, or the *seven gifts of the Holy Ghost*, or the *whole of the apostles, preachers, and ministers of the Church;* the *slain beasts* are the *sacrifice of Christ's body* upon the cross; and the *bread* and *mingled wine* are the *bread* and *wine* in the *sacrament of the Lord's Supper!*—FATHERS and DOCTORS.

If we have recourse to any other particulars than those given above in the summary of the chapter, let us follow the first part of the parable, where wisdom is represented as laying the plan of the creation; and then perhaps we may say with safety, that wisdom, having *produced* the grand *ichnograph* or *ground plot* of the whole, with all the requisite *elevations* and *specifications* of *materials*, comes to show us, in this part, that the whole has been *constructed on this plan;* and specifies the *end* for which this august building has been raised.

Verse 1. *Wisdom hath builded her house*] The eternal counsel of God has framed the *universe.*

She hath hewn out her seven pillars] Every thing has been so constructed as to exhibit a scene of grandeur, stability, and durableness.

Verse 2. *She hath killed her beasts*] God has made the most ample provision for the innumerable tribes of animal and intellectual beings, which people the whole vortex of created nature.

Verse 3. *She hath sent forth her maidens*] The wisdom of God has made use of the *most proper means* to communicate Divine knowledge to the inhabitants of the earth; as a good and gracious Creator wills to teach them *whence* they *came*, *how* they are *supported*, *whither* they are *going*, and for what *end* they were formed. It is a custom to the present day, in Asiatic countries, to send their invitations to guests by a company of *females*, preceded by eunuchs: they go to the doors of the invited, and deliver their message.

Verse 4. *Whoso* is *simple*] Let the young, heedless, and giddy attend to my teaching.

Him that wanteth understanding] Literally, *he that wanteth a heart;* who is without *courage*, is *feeble* and *fickle*, and *easily drawn* aside from the holy commandment.

Verse 5. *Come, eat of my bread*] Not only receive my instructions, but *act* according to my directions.

Drink of the wine—I have mingled.] Enter into my counsels; be not contented with *superficial knowledge* on any subject, where any thing *deeper* may be attained. Go by the *streams* to the *fountain head.* Look into the *principles* on which they were formed; investigate their *nature*, examine their *properties*, acquaint thyself with their *relations, connections, influences*, and various *uses.* See the *skill, power*, and *goodness* of God in their creation. And when thou hast learned all within thy reach, know that thou knowest but little of the manifold wisdom of God. Let what thou hast learned humble thee, by showing thee how very little thou dost know. Thou hast drunk of the *provided wine;* but that *wine* was mingled with *water*, for God will hide pride from man. He dwells only on the surface of religious and philosophical learning, who does not perceive and feel that he is yet but a *child* in knowledge; that he *see through a glass darkly;* that he *perceives men like trees walking;* and that there are lengths, breadths, depths, and heights, in the works and ways of God, which it will require an eternity to fathom. Here below the pure wine is mingled with water: but this is God's work. Yet there is enough; do not therefore be contented with a little. To this subject the words of the poet may be well applied:—

A *little learning* is a dangerous thing;
Drink deep, or taste not the Pierian spring:
For *scanty draughts intoxicate* the brain,
But *drinking largely sobers* us again.

POPE

A. M. cir. 3004
B. C. cir. 1000
Ante I. Olymp. cir. 224
Ante U. C. cir. 247

6 Forsake the foolish, and live; and go in the way of understanding.

7 He that reproveth a scorner getteth to himself shame: and he that rebuketh a wicked *man getteth* himself a blot.

8 [k]Reprove not a scorner, lest he hate thee: [l]rebuke a wise man, and he will love thee.

9 Give *instruction* to a wise *man,* and he will be yet wiser: teach a just *man,* [m]and he will increase in learning.

10 [n]The fear of the LORD *is* the beginning of wisdom: and the knowledge of the Holy *is* understanding.

11 [o]For by me thy days shall be multiplied, and the years of thy life shall be increased.

A. M. cir. 3004
B. C. cir. 1000
Ante I. Olymp. cir. 224
Ante U. C. cir. 247

12 [p]If thou be wise, thou shalt be wise for thyself: but *if* thou scornest, thou alone shalt bear *it.*

13 [q]A foolish woman *is* clamorous: *she is* simple, and knoweth nothing.

14 For she sitteth at the door of her house, on a seat [r]in the high places of the city,

15 To call passengers who go right on their ways:

16 [s]Whoso *is* simple, let him turn in hither: and *as for* him that wanteth

[k]Matt. vii. 6——[l]Psa. cxli. 5——[m]Matt. xiii. 12——[n]Job xxviii. 28; Psa. cxi. 10; chap. i. 7

[o]Chap. iii. 2, 16; x. 27——[p]Job xxxv. 6, 7; chap. xvi. 26——[q]Chap. vii. 11——[r]Ver. 3——[s]Ver. 4

Among the ancient *Jews, Greek,* and *Romans,* wine was rarely drank without being mingled with water; and among ancient writers we find several ordinances for this. Some direct *three parts* of water to *one of wine;* some *five* parts; and *Pliny* mentions some wines that required *twenty* waters: but the most common proportions appear to have been *three parts of water* to *two of wine.* But probably the יין מסך *yayin masach,* mingled wine, was wine mingled, *not* with *water,* to make it *weaker;* but with *spices* and other ingredients to make it *stronger.* The ingredients were *honey, myrrh, mandragora, opium,* and such like, which gave it not only an *intoxicating* but *stupifying* quality also. Perhaps the *mixed wine* here may mean *wine* of the *strongest* and *best quality,* that which was good to cheer and refresh the heart of man.

If we consider the *mixed wine* as meaning this *strong wine,* then the import of the metaphor will be, a thorough investigation of the works of God will invigorate the soul, strengthen all the mental powers, enlarge their capacity, and enable the mind to take the most exalted views of the *wonders of God's skill* manifested in the *operations of his hand.*

Verse 6. *Forsake the foolish*] For the companion of fools must be a fool.

And live] Answer the *end* for which thou wert *born.*

Verse 7. *He that reproveth a scorner*] לץ *lets,* the person who *mocks* at sacred things; the *libertine,* the *infidel;* who turns the most serious things into ridicule, and, by his *wit,* often succeeds in rendering the person who reproves him ridiculous. Wisdom seems here to intimate that it is vain to attempt by reproof to amend such: and yet we must not suffer sin upon our neighbour; at all hazards, we must deliver our own soul. But no reproof should be given to any, but in the *spirit of love* and deep concern; and when they contradict and blaspheme, leave them to God.

Verse 9. *Give* instruction *to a wise* man] Literally *give to the wise, and he will be wise.* Whatever you give to such, they reap profit from it. They are like the bee, they extract honey from every flower.

Verse 10. *The fear of the Lord*] See on chap. i. 7. The knowledge of the holy; קדשים *kedoshim,* of the holy ones: *Sanctorum,* of the saints.—*Vulgate.* Βουλη ἁγιων, the counsel of the holy persons.

Verse 11. *For by me thy days shall be multiplied*] Vice shortens human life, by a necessity of consequence: and by the same, righteousness lengthens it. There is a long addition here in the *Septuagint, Syriac,* and *Vulgate:* "He who trusts in falsity feeds on the winds; and is like him who chases the fowls of heaven. He forsakes the way of his own vineyard, and errs from the paths of his own inheritance. He enters also into lonely and desert places, and into a land abandoned to thirst; and his hands collect that which yieldeth no fruit."

Verse 12. *If thou be wise*] It is thy own interest to be religious. Though thy example may be very useful to thy neighbours and friends, yet the chief benefit is to *thyself.* But if thou *scorn*—refuse to receive—the doctrines of wisdom, and die in thy sins, *thou alone* shalt suffer the vengeance of an offended God.

Verse 13. *A foolish woman* is *clamorous*] Vain, empty women, are those that make *most noise.* And she that is *full* of clamour, has generally *little* or no *sense.* We have had this character already, see chap. vii. 11. The translation of the *Septuagint* is very remarkable: Γυνη αφρων και θρασεια, ενδεης ψωμου γινεται, "A lewd and foolish woman shall be in need of a morsel of bread."

Verse 14. *For she sitteth at the door of her house*] Her conduct here marks at once her *folly, impudence,* and *poverty.* See above on chap. vii. 6, &c., where the reader will find a similar character.

Verse 16. *Whoso* is *simple, let him turn in hither*] FOLLY or PLEASURE here personified, uses the very same expressions as employed by *Wisdom,* ver. 4. Wisdom says, "Let the simple turn in to me." No, says Folly, "Let the simple turn in to me." If he turn in to *Wisdom,* his folly shall be taken away, and he shall become wise; if he turn in to *Folly,* his darkness will be thickened, and his folly will remain.

Wisdom sets up her school to instruct the ignorant:

Folly sets her school up next door, to defeat the designs of Wisdom.

A. M. cir. 3004
B. C. cir. 1000
Ante I. Olymp. cir. 224
Ante U. C. cir. 247

understanding, she saith to
him,
17 [t]Stolen waters are sweet, and
bread [u]*eaten* in secret is pleasant.
18 But he knoweth not that
[v]the dead *are* there; *and that*
her guests *are* in the depths of
hell.

A. M. cir. 3004
B. C. cir. 1000
Ante I. Olymp. cir. 224
Ante U. C. cir. 247

[t]Chap. xx. 17——[u]Heb. *of secrecies*

[v]Chap. ii. 18; vii. 27

Thus the saying of the satirist appears to be verified:—

"Wherever God erects a *house* of *prayer*,
The devil surely builds a *chapel* there.
And it is found upon examination,
The *latter* has the *larger congregation*."
De Foe.

Verse 17. *Stolen waters are sweet*] I suppose this to be a proverbial mode of expression, importing that *illicit pleasures are sweeter than those which are legal*. The meaning is easy to be discerned; and the conduct of multitudes shows that they are ruled by this adage. On it are built all the *adulterous intercourses* in the land.

Verse 18. *But he knoweth not that the dead are there*] See on chap. ii. 18. He does not know that it was in this way the first apostates from God and truth walked. רפאים *rephaim; γιγαντες*, the GIANTS.—*Septuagint*. The *sons of men*, the *earth-born*, to distinguish them from the *sons of God*, those who were *born from above*. See the notes on Gen. vi. 1, &c.

Her guests are *in the depths of hell*.] Those who have been drawn out of the way of understanding by *profligacy* have in general lost their *lives*, if not their *souls*, by their folly. The *Septuagint*, *Syriac*, and *Arabic* make a long addition to this verse: "But draw thou back, that thou mayest not die in this place; neither fix thy eyes upon her; so shalt thou pass by those strange waters. But abstain thou from strange waters, and drink not of another's fountain, that thou mayest live a long time, and that years may be added to thy life." Of this *addition* there is nothing in the *Hebrew*, the *Chaldee*, or the *Vulgate*, as now printed: but in the *editio princeps* are the following words:—Qui enim applicabitur illi descendet ad inferos; nam qui abscesserit ab ea salvabitur. These words were in the copy *from which* my old MS. Bible has been made, as the following version proves: **Who forsoth schal ben joyned to hir, schal falle doun in to hell: for whi he that goth awai fro hir, schal be saved.** Three of my own MSS. have the same reading.

CHAPTER X

It is impossible to give summaries *of such chapters as these, where almost* every verse *contains a* separate subject. *Our common version not being able to exhibit the contents as usual, simply says, "From this chapter to the five and twentieth are sundry observations upon moral virtues, and their opposite vices." In general the wise man states in this chapter the difference between the wise and the foolish, the righteous and the wicked, the diligent and the idle. He speaks also of love and hatred, of the good and the evil tongue, or of the slanderer and the peace-maker.*

A. M. cir. 3004
B. C. cir. 1000
Ante I. Olymp. cir. 224
Ante U. C. cir. 247

THE proverbs of Solomon.
[a]A wise son maketh a glad
father: but a foolish son *is* the
heaviness of his mother.
2 [b]Treasures of wicked-
ness profit nothing: [c]but
righteousness delivereth from
death.

A. M. cir. 3004
B. C. cir. 1000
Ante I. Olymp. 224
Ante U. C. cir. 247

[a]Ch. xxv. 20; xvii. 21, 25; xix. 13; xxix. 3, 15——[b]Psa. xlix. 6, &c.; ch. xi. 4; Luke xii. 19, 20——[c]Dan. iv. 27

NOTES ON CHAP. X.

Verse 1. *The proverbs of Solomon*] Some ancient MSS. of the *Vulgate* have *Proverbiorum liber secundus*, "The second book of the Proverbs." The preceding *nine* chapters can only be considered as an *introduction*, if indeed they may be said to make even a *part*, of the proverbs of Solomon, which appear to commence only at the tenth *chapter*.

A wise son maketh a glad father] The parallels in this and several of the succeeding chapters are those which *Bishop Lowth* calls the *antithetic;* when two lines correspond with each other by an opposition of *terms* and *sentiments;* when the second is contrasted with the first; sometimes in *expression*, sometimes in *sense* only. Accordingly the degrees of antithesis are various; from an exact contraposition of *word to word*, through a whole sentence, down to a general *disparity*, with something of a *contrariety* in the two propositions, as:—

A wise son rejoiceth in his father.
But a foolish son is the grief of his mother.

Where *every word* has its *opposite;* for the terms *father* and *mother* are, as the logicians say, relatively opposite.

Verse 2. *Treasures of wickedness*] Property gained by wicked means.

Delivered from death] Treasures gained by

A. M. cir. 3004
B. C. cir. 1000
Ante I. Olymp. cir. 224
Ante U. C. cir. 247

3 [d]The LORD will not suffer the soul of the righteous to famish: but he casteth away [e]the substance of the wicked.

4 [f]He becometh poor that dealeth *with* a slack hand: but [g]the hand of the diligent maketh rich.

5 He that gathereth in summer *is* a wise son: *but* he that sleepeth in harvest *is* [h]a son that causeth shame.

6 Blessings *are* upon the head of the just: but [i]violence covereth the mouth of the wicked.

7 [k]The memory of the just *is* blessed: but the name of the wicked shall rot.

8 The wise in heart will receive commandments: [l]but [m]a prating fool [n]shall fall.

9 [o]He that walketh uprightly walketh surely: but he that perverteth his ways shall be known.

10 [p]He that winketh with the eye causeth sorrow: [q]but a prating fool [r]shall fall.

11 [s]The mouth of a righteous *man is* a well of life: but [t]violence covereth the mouth of the wicked.

12 Hatred stirreth up strifes: but [u]love covereth all sins.

13 In the lips of him that hath understanding wisdom is found: but [v]a rod is for the back of him that is void of [w]understanding.

14 Wise *men* lay up knowledge: but [x]the mouth of the foolish *is* near destruction.

---

[d]Psa. x. 14; xxxiv. 9, 10; xxxvii. 25——[e]Or, *the wicked for* their *wickedness*——[f]Ch. xii. 24; xix. 15 [g]Ch. xiii. 4; xxi. 5——[h]Ch. xii. 4; xvii. 2; xix. 26——[i]Ver. 11; Esth. vii. 8——[k]Psa. ix. 5, 6; cxii. 6; Eccles. viii. 10 [l]Ver. 10——[m]Heb. *a fool of lips*——[n]Or, *shall be beaten*

[o]Psa. xxiii. 4; ch. xxviii. 18; Isa. xxxiii. 15, 16——[p]Ch. vi. 13——[q]Ver. 8——[r]Or, *shall be beaten*——[s]Psa. xxxvii. 30; ch. xiii. 14; xviii. 4——[t]Psa. cvii. 42; ver. 6 [u]Ch. xvii. 9; 1 Cor. xiii. 4; 1 Pet. iv. 8——[v]Ch. xxvi. 3 [w]Heb. *heart*——[x]Ch. xviii. 7; xxi. 23

---

robbery often bring their possessors to an untimely death; but those gained by righteous dealing bring with them no such consequences.

Verse 3. *But he casteth away the substance of the wicked.*] But instead of רשעים *reshaim*, *the wicked*, בוגדים *bogedim*, *hypocrites*, or *perfidious* persons, is the reading of *twelve* or *fourteen* of *Kennicott's* and *De Rossi's* MSS., and some *editions;* but it is not acknowledged by any of the ancient versions.

The righteous have God for their feeder; and because of his infinite bounty, they can never famish for want of the bread of life. On the contrary, the wicked are often, in the course of his providence, deprived of the property of which they make a bad use.

Verse 4. *He becometh poor*] God has ordered, in the course of his providence, that he who will not *work* shall not *eat*. And he always blesses the work of the *industrious* man.

Verse 5. *He that gathereth in summer*] All the work of the field should be done in the *season suitable to it*. If *summer* and *harvest* be neglected, in vain does a man expect the fruits of *autumn*.

Verse 6. *Violence covereth the mouth of the wicked.*] As *blessings shall be on the head of the just*, so the *violence of the wicked shall cover their face* with shame and confusion. Their own violent dealings shall be visited upon them. **The mouth forsoth of unpitous men wickidnesse coverith.**—*Old MS. Bible.* "The forehead of the ungodly is past shame, and presumptuous."—*Coverdale.*

Verse 7. *The memory of the just* is *blessed*] Or, *is a blessing.*

But the name of the wicked shall rot.] This is another antithesis; but there are only two antithetic terms, for *memory* and *name* are synonymous.—*Lowth.* The very name of the wicked is as offensive as putrid carrion.

Verse 8. *A prating fool shall fall.*] This clause is repeated in the *tenth* verse. The *wise man will receive the commandment: but the shallow blabbing fool shall be cast down.* See verse 10.

Verse 9. *He that walketh uprightly*] The upright man is always *safe;* he has not *two characters* to support; he goes straight forward, and is never afraid of *detection*, because he has never been influenced by *hypocrisy* or *deceit.*

Verse 10. *He that winketh with the eye*] Instead of the latter clause, on which see ver. 8, the *Septuagint* has, ὁ δε ελεγχων μετα παρρησιας ειρηνοποιει· "but he that reproveth with freedom, maketh peace." This is also the reading of the *Syriac* and *Arabic*. A faithful open reproving of sin is more likely to promote the peace of society than the passing it by slightly, or taking no notice of it; for if the wicked turn to God at the reproof, the law of *peace* will soon be established in his heart, and the law of kindness will flow from his tongue.

Verse 11. *The mouth of a righteous* man is *a well of life*] מקור חיים *mekor chaiyim*, is the *vein of lives;* an allusion to the *great aorta*, which conveys the blood from the heart to every part of the body. The latter clause of this verse is the same with that of verse 6.

Verse 12. *Hatred stirreth up strifes*] It seeks for occasions to provoke enmity. It delights in broils. On the contrary, love conciliates; removes aggravations; puts the best construction on every thing; and pours *water*, not *oil*, upon the *flame*.

Verse 13. *A rod* is *for the back of him*] He that *can learn*, and *will not learn*, should be *made to learn*. The rod is a most powerful instrument of knowledge. Judiciously applied, there is a lesson of profound wisdom in every *twig*.

Verse 14. *Wise* men *lay up knowledge*] They keep secret every thing that has a tendency to disturb domestic or public peace; but the foolish man blabs all out, and produces much mischief. Think much, speak little, and always think before you speak. This will promote your own peace and that of your neighbour.

A. M. cir. 3004
B. C. cir. 1000
Ante I. Olymp. cir. 224
Ante U. C. cir. 247

15 [y]The rich man's wealth *is*
his strong city: the destruction
of the poor *is* their poverty.
16 The labour of the righteous
tendeth to life: the fruit of the wicked to sin.
17 He *is in* the way of life that keepeth instruction: but he that refuseth reproof [z]erreth.
18 He that hideth hatred *with* lying lips, and
[a]he that uttereth a slander, *is* a fool.
19 [b]In the multitude of words there wanteth
not sin: but [c]he that refraineth his lips *is* wise.
20 The tongue of the just *is as* choice silver: the heart of the wicked *is* little worth.
21 The lips of the righteous feed many: but
fools die for want [d]of wisdom.
22 [e]The blessing of the LORD, it maketh
rich, and he addeth no sorrow
with it.
23 [f]*It is* as sport to a fool to
do mischief: but a man of understanding hath wisdom.
24 [g]The fear of the wicked, it shall come
upon him: but [h]the desire of the righteous
shall be granted.
25 As the whirlwind passeth, [i]so *is* the wicked no *more:* but [k]the righteous *is* an everlasting foundation.
26 As vinegar to the teeth, and as smoke to
the eyes, so *is* the sluggard to them that send
him.
27 [l]The fear of the LORD [m]prolongeth days:
but [n]the years of the wicked shall be shortened.

A. M. cir. 3004
B. C. cir. 1000
Ante I. Olymp. cir. 224
Ante U. C. cir. 247

[y]Job xxxi. 24; Psa. lii. 7; ch. xviii. 11; 1 Tim. vi. 17——[z]Or, *causeth to err*——[a]Psa. xv. 3——[b]Eccles. v. 3——[c]James iii. 2——[d]Heb. *of heart*——[e]Gen. xxiv. 35; xxvi. 12; Psalm xxxvii. 22——[f]Chap. xiv. 9; xv. 21

[g]Job xv. 21——[h]Psa. cxlv. 19; Matt. v. 6; 1 John v. 14, 15——[i]Psa. xxxvii. 9, 10——[k]Ver. 30; Psa. xv. 5; Matt. vii. 24, 25; xvi. 18——[l]Chap. ix. 11——[m]Heb. *addeth*——[n]Job xv. 32, 33; xxii. 16; Psa. lv. 23; Eccles. vii. 17

Verse 15. *The rich man's wealth* is *his strong city*] Behold a mystery in providence; there is not a *rich man* on earth but becomes such by means of the *poor!* Property comes from the *labour* of the *poor*, and *the king himself is served of the field.* How unjust, diabolically so, is it to *despise* or *oppress* those by whose labour all property is acquired!

The destruction of the poor is *their poverty.*] A man in abject poverty never arises out of this pit. They have no nucleus about which property may aggregate. The poet spoke well:—

Haud facile emergunt, quorum virtutibus obstat
Res angusta domi.

'They rarely emerge from poverty, whose exertions are cramped by want at home."

Verse 16. *The labour of the righteous*] The good man labours that he may be able to *support life;* this is his *first* object: and then to have *something to divide with the poor;* this is his *next* object.

The fruit of the wicked to sin.] This man lives to eat and drink, and his property he spends in riot and excess. God's blessings are cursed to him.

Verse 17. *He* is in *the way of life*] The truly religious man accumulates knowledge that he may the better know how to live to God, and do most good among men.

Verse 18. *He that hideth*] This is a common case. How many, when full of resentment, and deadly hatred, meditating revenge and cruelty, and sometimes even murder, have pretended that they *thought nothing of the injury they had sustained;* had *passed by the insult,* &c.! Thus *lying lips* covered the malevolence of a wicked heart.

Verse 19. *In the multitude of words*] It is impossible to speak much, and yet speak nothing but truth; and injure no man's character in the mean while.

Verse 20. *The heart of the wicked* is *little worth*] כמעט *kimat,* is like little or nothing; or is *like dross,* while the tongue of the just is like *silver.* A sinner's heart is worth nothing, and is good for nothing; and yet because it is his most *hidden part,* he vaunts of its *honesty, goodness,* &c.! Yes, yes; it is very honest and good, only the devil is in it! that is all.

Verse 22. *The blessing of the Lord, it maketh rich*] Whatever we receive in the way of providence, has God's blessing in it, and will do us good. Cares, troubles, and difficulties come with all property not acquired in this way; but God's blessing gives simple enjoyment, and levies no tax upon the comfort.

Verse 23. It is *a sport to a fool to do mischief*] What a millstone weight of iniquity hangs about the necks of most of the *jesters, facetious* and *witty* people! "How many lies do they tell in jest, to go to the devil in earnest!"

Verse 24. *The fear of the wicked*] The wicked is full of fears and alarms; and all that he has dreaded and more than he has dreaded, shall come upon him. The righteous is always *desiring* more of the salvation of God, and God will exceed even his utmost desires.

Verse 25. *As the whirlwind passeth*] As tornadoes that sweep every thing away before them; so shall the wrath of God sweep away the wicked; it shall leave him neither branch nor root. But the righteous, being built on the *eternal foundation,* יסוד עולם *yesod olam,* shall never be shaken.

Verse 26. *As vinegar to the teeth*] The *acid* softening and dissolving the *alkali* of the bone, so as to impair their texture, and render them incapable of *masticating;* and as *smoke* affects the eyes, irritating their tender vessels, so as to give pain and prevent distinct vision; so the sluggard, the lounging, thriftless messenger, who never returns in time with the desired answer.

A. M. cir. 3004
B. C. cir. 1000
Ante I. Olymp. cir. 224
Ante U. C. cir. 247

28 The hope of the righteous
shall be gladness: but the [o]ex-
pectation of the wicked shall
perish.
29 The way of the LORD *is* strength to
the upright: but [p]destruction *shall be* to the
workers of iniquity.
30 [q]The righteous shall never be removed:
but the wicked shall not inhabit
the earth.
31 [r]The mouth of the just
bringeth forth wisdom: but the
froward tongue shall be cut out.
32 The lips of the righteous know what is
acceptable: but the mouth of the wicked
speaketh [s]frowardness.

A. M. cir. 3004
B. C. cir. 1000
Ante I. Olymp. cir. 224
Ante U. C. cir. 247

[o]Job viii. 13; xi. 20; Psa. cxii. 10; chap. xi. 7——[p]Psa. i. 6; xxxvii. 20

[q]Psa. xxxvii. 22, 29; cxxv. 1; ver. 25——[r]Psa. xxxvii. 30
[s]Heb. *frowardness*

Verse 28. *The expectation of the wicked shall perish.*] A wicked man is always imposing on himself by the *hope of God's mercy* and *final happiness;* and he continues *hoping,* till he dies without receiving that *mercy* which alone would entitle him to that *glory.*

Verse 29. *The way of the Lord* is *strength*] In the path of *obedience* the upright man ever finds his *strength renewed;* the more he *labours* the *stronger* he grows. The same sentiment as that in Isa. xl. 31.

Verse 30. *The righteous shall never be removed*] Because he is built on the *eternal foundation.* See on ver. 25.

Verse 31. *The froward tongue shall be cut out.*] This probably alludes to the punishment of *cutting out the tongue* for *blasphemy, treasonable speeches, profane swearing,* or such like. **The tunge of schrewis schal perishen.**—Old MS. Bible. Were the tongue of every *shrew* or *scold* to be extracted, we should soon have much less *noise* in the world.

Verse 32. *The lips of the righteous know what is acceptable*] And what they believe to be most pleasing and most profitable, that they speak; but the wicked man knows as well what is *perverse,* and that he speaketh forth. As the love of God is not in his heart; so the law of kindness is not on his lips.

CHAPTER XI

A parallel of the advantages of the righteous and wise, opposed to the miseries of the wicked and the foolish. True and false riches.

A. M. cir. 3004
B. C. cir. 1000
Ante I. Olymp. cir. 224
Ante U. C. cir. 247

A [a]FALSE [b]balance *is* abomination to the LORD: but
[c]a just weight *is* his delight.
2 [d]*When* pride cometh, then
cometh shame: but with the lowly *is* wisdom.
3 [e]The integrity of the upright shall guide
them: but the perverseness of transgressors
shall destroy them.
4 [f]Riches profit not in the day of wrath:
but [g]righteousness delivereth
from death.
5 The righteousness of the perfect shall [h]direct his way: but
the wicked shall fall by his own wickedness.
6 The righteousness of the upright shall deliver them: but [i]transgressors shall be taken
in *their own* naughtiness.
7 [k]When a wicked man dieth, *his* expecta-

A. M. cir. 3004
B. C. cir. 1000
Ante I. Olymp. cir. 224
Ante U. C. cir. 247

[a]Lev. xix. 35, 36; Deut. xxv. 13–16; ch. xvi. 11; xx. 10, 23——[b]Heb. *balances of deceit*——[c]Heb. *a perfect stone*
[d]Chap. xv. 33; xvi. 18; xviii. 12; Dan. iv. 30, 31

[e]Chap. xiii. 6——[f]Chap. x. 2; Ezek. vii. 19; Zeph. i. 18; Ecclus. v. 8——[g]Gen. vii. 1——[h]Heb. *rectify*
[i]Chap. v. 22; Eccles. x. 8——[k]Chap. x. 28

NOTES ON CHAP. XI

Verse 1. *A false balance* is *abomination*] This refers to the balance itself deceitfully constructed, so that it is sooner turned at one end than at the other. This is occasioned by *one end* of the *beam* being *longer* than the other.

But a just weight] אבן שלמה *eben shelemah,* the *perfect stone,* probably because weights were first made of stone; see the law, Deut. xxv. 13-35.

Verse 2. When *pride cometh*] The proud man thinks much more of himself than any other can do; and, expecting to be treated according to his own supposed worth, which treatment he seldom meets with, he is repeatedly mortified, ashamed, confounded, and rendered indignant.

With the lowly] צנועים *tsenuim,* ταπεινων, the *humble,* the *modest,* as opposed to the *proud,* referred to in the first clause. The humble man looks for nothing but justice; has the meanest opinion of himself; expects nothing in the way of commendation or praise; and can never be disappointed but in receiving praise, which he neither expects nor desires.

Verse 4. *Riches profit not in the day of wrath*] Among men they can do all things; but they cannot purchase the remission of sins, nor turn aside the wrath of God when that is poured out upon the opulent transgressor.

Verse 7. *When a wicked man dieth*] HOPE is a great blessing to man in his present state of trial and suffering; because it leads him to expect a favourable termination of his ills. But *hope* was not made for the *wicked;* and yet

A. M. cir. 3004, B. C. cir. 1000, Ante I. Olymp. cir. 224, Ante U. C. cir. 247

tion shall perish: and the hope
of unjust *men* perisheth.
8 [l]The righteous is delivered
out of trouble, and the wicked
cometh in his stead.
9 A [m]hypocrite with *his* mouth destroyeth
his neighbour: but through knowledge shall
the just be delivered.
10 [n]When it goeth well with the righteous,
the city rejoiceth: and when the wicked perish, *there is* shouting.
11 [o]By the blessing of the upright the city
is exalted: but it is overthrown by the mouth
of the wicked.
12 [p]He that is void of wisdom despiseth
his neighbour: but a man of understanding
holdeth his peace.
13 [q]A [r]talebearer revealeth
secrets: but he that is of a faithful spirit concealeth the matter.
14 [s]Where no counsel *is*, the
people fall: but in the multitude of counsellors
there is safety.
15 [t]He that is surety for a stranger [u]shall
smart *for it:* and he that hateth [v]suretiship
is sure.
16 [w]A gracious woman retaineth honour:
and strong *men* retain riches.
17 [x]The merciful man doeth good to his
own soul: but *he that is* cruel troubleth his
own flesh.
18 The wicked worketh a deceitful work:
but [y]to him that soweth righteousness *shall be*
a sure reward.

---

[l]Chap. xxi. 18——[m]Job viii. 13——[n]Esth. viii. 15; chap. xxviii. 12, 28——[o]Chap. xxix. 8——[p]Heb. *destitute of heart*——[q]Lev. xix. 16; chap. xx. 19——[r]Heb. *He that walketh*, being *a talebearer*

[s]1 Kings xii. 1, &c.; chap. xv. 22; xxiv. 6——[t]Chap. vi. 1——[u]Heb. *shall be sore broken*——[v]Heb. *those that strike* hands——[w]Chap. xxxi. 30——[x]Matt. v. 7; xxv. 34, &c.——[y]Hos. x. 12; Gal. vi. 8, 9; James iii. 18

---

they are the very persons that most abound in it! They hope to be saved, and get at last to the kingdom of God; though they have their face towards perdition, and refuse to turn. But their hope goes no farther than the *grave*. There the wicked man's expectation is cut off, and his hope perishes. But to the *saint*, the *penitent*, and the *cross-bearers* in general, what a treasure is *hope!* What a balm through life!

Verse 8. *The wicked cometh in his stead.*] Often God makes this distinction; in public calamities and in sudden accidents he rescues the righteous, and leaves the wicked, who has filled up the measure of his iniquities, to be seized by the hand of death. *Justice*, then, does its own work; for *mercy* has been rejected.

Verse 9. *A hypocrite with* his *mouth*] חנף *chaneph* might be better translated *infidel* than *hypocrite*. The latter is one that pretends to religion; that uses it for *secular purposes*. The former is one who *disbelieves* Divine revelation, and accordingly is *polluted*, and lives in *pollution*. This is properly the force of the original word. Such persons deal in calumny and lies, and often thus destroy the character of their neighbour. Besides, they are very zealous in propagating their own infidel notions; and thus, by this means, destroy their neighbour; but the experimental knowledge which the *just* have of God and his salvation prevents them from being ensnared.

Verse 10. *When it goeth well*] An upright, pious, sensible man is a great blessing to the neighbourhood where he resides, by his example, his advice, and his prayers. The considerate prize him on these accounts, and rejoice in his prosperity. But when the *wicked perish*, who has been a general curse by the contagion of his example and conversation, there is not only no regret expressed for his decease, but a *general joy* because God has removed him.

Verse 12. *He that is void of wisdom*] A foolish man is generally abundant in his censures; he dwells on the *defects* of his neighbour, and is sure to bring them into the most prominent view. But a *man of understanding*—a prudent, sensible man, hides those defects wherever he can, and puts the most charitable construction on those which he cannot conceal.

Verse 13. *A talebearer*] הולך רכיל *holech rachil*, the walking busybody, the trader in scandal.

Revealeth secrets] Whatever was confided to him he is sure to publish abroad. The word means a *hawker*, or *travelling chapman*. Such are always great newsmongers; and will tell even their *own secrets*, rather than have nothing to say.

Verse 15. *He that is surety for a stranger shall smart* for it] He shall find evil upon evil in it. See on chap. vi. 1.

Verse 16. *A gracious woman retaineth honor*] Instead of this clause, the *Septuagint* have, Γυνη ευχαριστος εγειρει ανδρι δοξαν, "A gracious woman raiseth up honour to the man;" Θρονος δε ατιμιας γυνη μισουσα δικαια, "But she that hateth righteous things is a throne of dishonour." A good wife is an honour to her husband; and a bad wife is her husband's reproach: if this be so, how careful should a man be whom he marries!

Verse 17. *The merciful man doeth good to his own soul*] Every gracious disposition is increased while a man is exercised in showing mercy. No man can show an act of disinterested mercy without benefiting his own soul, by improving his moral feeling.

But he that is *cruel troubleth his own flesh.*] We seldom see a peevish, fretful, vindictive man either in good health, or good plight of body. I have often heard it observed of such, "He frets his flesh off his bones."

Verse 18. *Worketh a deceitful work*] An *unstable* work; nothing is durable that he does, except his crimes.

A. M. cir. 3004
B. C. cir. 1000
Ante I. Olymp. cir. 224
Ante U. C. cir. 247

19 As righteousness *tendeth* to
life: so he that pursueth evil
pursueth it to his own death.
20 They that are of a froward
heart *are* abomination to the LORD: but
such as are upright in *their* way *are* his delight.
21 [z]*Though* hand *join* in hand, the wicked
shall not be unpunished: but [a]the seed of the
righteous shall be delivered.
22 *As* a jewel of gold in a swine's snout, *so*
is a fair woman which [b]is without discretion.
23 The desire of the righteous *is* only good:
but the expectation of the wicked [c]*is*
wrath.
24 There is that [d]scattereth, and yet increaseth: and *there is* that withholdeth more
than is meet, but *it tendeth* to poverty.
25 [e]The [f]liberal soul shall be made fat:
[g]and he that watereth shall be
watered also himself.
26 [h]He that withholdeth corn,
the people shall curse him: but
[i]blessing *shall be* upon the head of him that
selleth *it*.
27 He that diligently seeketh good procureth
favour: [k]but he that seeketh mischief, it shall
come unto him.
28 [l]He that trusteth in his riches shall fall:
but [m]the righteous shall flourish as a branch.
29 He that troubleth his own house [n]shall
inherit the wind: and the fool *shall be* servant to the wise of heart.
30 The fruit of the righteous *is* a tree of
life; and [o]he that [p]winneth souls *is* wise.
31 [q]Behold the righteous shall be recompensed in the earth: much more the wicked
and the sinner.

[z]Chap. xvi. 5——[a]Psa. cxii. 2——[b]Heb. *departeth from*——[c]Rom. ii. 8, 9——[d]Psa. cxii. 9——[e]2 Cor. ix. 6, 7, 8, 9, 10——[f]Or, *The soul of blessing*——[g]Matt. v. 7 [h]Amos viii. 5, 6——[i]Job xxix. 13——[k]Esth. vii. 10; Psa. vii. 15, 16; ix. 15, 16; x. 2; lvii. 6

[l]Job xxxi. 24; Psa. lii. 7; Mark x. 24; Luke xii. 21; 1 Tim. vi. 17——[m]Psa. i. 3; lii. 8; xcii. 12, &c.; Jer. xvii. 8——[n]Eccles. v. 16——[o]Dan. xii. 3; 1 Cor. ix. 19, &c.; James v. 20——[p]Heb. *taketh*——[q]Jer. xxv. 29; 1 Pet. iv. 17, 18

Verse 19. *Righteousness* tendeth *to life*] True godliness promotes health, and is the best means of lengthening out life; but wicked men live not out half their days.

Verse 21. Though *hand* join *in hand*] Let them confederate as they please, to support each other, justice will take care that they escape not punishment. The Hindoos sometimes ratify an engagement by one person *laying his right hand on the hand of another*.—WARD.

Verse 22. *A jewel of gold in a swine's snout*] That is, beauty in a woman destitute of good breeding and modest carriage, is as becoming as a gold ring on the snout of a swine. *Coverdale* translates thus: "A fayre woman without discrete maners, is like a ringe of golde in a swyne's snoute." In Asiatic countries the *nose jewel* is very common: to this the text alludes.

Verse 24. *There is that scattereth, and yet increaseth*] The bountiful man, who gives to the poor, never turning away his face from any one in distress, the Lord blesses his property, and the bread is multiplied in his hand. To the same purpose the following verse.

Verse 25. *The liberal soul shall be made fat*] He who gives to the distressed, in the true spirit of charity, shall get a hundred fold from God's mercy. How wonderful is the Lord! He gives the *property*, gives the *heart* to use it aright, and *recompenses* the man for the deed, though all the fruit was found from himself!

He that watereth] A man who distributes in the right spirit gets more good himself than the poor man does who receives the bounty. Thus *it is more blessed to give than to receive.*

Verse 26. *He that withholdeth corn*] Who refuses to sell because he hopes for a dearth, and then he can make his own price.

The people shall curse him] Yes, and God shall curse him also; and if he do not return and repent, he will get God's curse, and the curse of the poor, which will be a *canker* in his *money* during *time*, and in his *soul* throughout *eternity*.

Verse 29. *Shall inherit the wind*] He who dissipates his property by riotous living, shall be as unsatisfied as he who attempts to feed upon *air*.

Verse 30. *The fruit of the righteous is a tree of life*] עץ חיים *ets chaiyim*, "the tree of lives." It is like that tree which grew in the paradise of God; increasing the bodily and mental vigour of those who ate of it.

He that winneth souls is wise.] Wisdom seeks to reclaim the wanderers; and he who is influenced by wisdom will do the same.

Verse 31. *Behold, the righteous shall be recompensed in the earth, &c.*] The *Septuagint*, *Syriac*, and *Arabic* read this verse as follows: "And if the righteous scarcely be saved, where shall the ungodly and the sinner appear?" And this St. Peter quotes *literatim*, 1st Epist. iv. 18, where see the note.

CHAPTER XII

Of the benefit of instruction, and the cultivation of piety. The virtuous woman. The different lot of the just and unjust. The humane man. The industrious man. The fool and the wise man. The uncharitable. The excellence of the righteous. The slothful is in want. Righteousness leads to life, &c.

A. M. cir. 3004
B. C. cir. 1000
Ante I. Olymp. cir. 224
Ante U. C. cir. 247

WHOSO loveth instruction
loveth knowledge: but he
that hateth reproof *is* brutish.
2 [a]A good *man* obtaineth favour of the LORD: but a man of wicked devices will he condemn.
3 A man shall not be established by wickedness: but the [b]root of the righteous shall
not be moved.
4 [c]A virtuous woman *is* a crown to her
husband: but she that maketh ashamed *is* [d]as
rottenness in his bones.
5 The thoughts of the righteous *are* right:

[a]Chapter viii. 35——[b]Chapter x. 25——[c]Chapter xxxi. 23; 1 Corinthians xi. 7——[d]Chapter xiv. 30
[e]Chapter i. 11, 18——[f]Chapter xiv. 3

but the counsels of the wicked
are deceit.
6 [e]The words of the wicked
are to lie in wait for blood:
[f]but the mouth of the upright shall deliver
them.
7 [g]The wicked are overthrown, and *are*
not: but the house of the righteous shall
stand.
8 A man shall be commended according to
his wisdom: [h]but he that is [i]of a perverse
heart shall be despised.
9 [k]*He that is* despised, and hath a servant,

A. M. cir. 3004
B. C. cir. 1000
Ante I. Olymp. cir. 224
Ante U. C. cir. 247

[g]Psalm xxxvii. 36, 37; chapter xi. 21; Matthew vii. 24, 25, 26, 27——[h]1 Samuel xxv. 17——[i]Hebrew *perverse of heart*——[k]Chapter xiii. 7

NOTES ON CHAP. XII

Verse 1. *Whoso loveth instruction*] מוסר *musar*, discipline or correction, *loves knowledge;* for correction is the way to knowledge.

But he that hateth reproof is *brutish.*] בער *baar*, he is a bear; and expects no more benefit from correction than the *ox* does from the *goad.*

Verse 2. *A good* man *obtaineth favour*] First, it is God who makes him *good;* for every child of Adam is *bad* till the grace of God changes his heart. Secondly, while he walks in the path of obedience he increases in *goodness*, and consequently in the *favour of the Lord.*

Verse 3. *A man shall not be established by wickedness*] Evil is always variable: it has no *fixed principle*, except the *root* that is in the human heart; and even that is ever assuming *new forms.* Nothing is *permanent* but *goodness;* and that is *unchangeable*, because it comes from GOD. The *produce* of goodness is *permanent*, because it has God's *blessing* in it: the *fruit* of *wickedness*, or the *property* procured by wickedness, is *transitory*, because it has God's curse in it. The righteous has his *root* in God; and therefore *he shall not be moved.*

Verse 4. *A virtuous woman* is *a crown to her husband*] אשת חיל *esheth chayil*, a *strong woman.* Our word *virtue* (*virtus*) is derived from *vir*, a *man;* and as *man* is the *noblest* of God's creatures, virtue expresses what is becoming to man; what is *noble, courageous*, and *dignified:* and as *vir*, a man, comes from *vis*, power or *strength;* so it implies what is *strong* and *vigorous* in principle: and as in uncivilized life *strength* and *courage* were considered the very highest, because apparently the most necessary, of all *virtues;* hence the term itself might have become the denomination of all *excellent moral qualities;* and is now applied to whatever constitutes the *system of morality* and *moral duties.* In some parts of the world, however, where *arts* and *sciences* have made little progress, *strength* is one of the first qualifications of a *wife*, where the labours of the field are appointed to them. It is not an uncommon sight in different parts of Africa, to see the wives (*queens*) of the kings and chiefs going out in the morning to the plantations, with their mattock in their hand, and their youngest child on their back; and when arrived at the ground, lay the young *prince* or *princess* upon the earth, which when weary of lying on one side, will roll itself on the other, and thus continue during the course of the day, without uttering a single whimper, except at the intervals in which its mother gives it suck; she being employed all the while in such *labour* as we in Europe generally assign to our *horses.* In these cases, the *strong wife* is the highest acquisition; and is *a crown to her husband*, though he be *king* of *Bonny* or *Calabar.* It is certain that in ancient times the *women* in Judea did some of the severest work in the fields, such as *drawing water* from the wells, and watering the flocks, &c. On this account, I think, the words may be taken literally; and especially when we add another consideration, that a woman healthy, and of good *muscular powers*, is the most likely to produce and properly rear up a *healthy offspring;* and children of this kind are a *crown* to their parents.

Is *as rottenness in his bones.*] Does not this refer to a woman irregular in her manners, who by her *incontinence* not only maketh her husband *ashamed*, but contracts and communicates such diseases as bring *rottenness into the bones?* I think so. And I think this was the view taken of the text by *Coverdale*, who translates thus: "A stedfast woman is a crowne unto her hussbonde: but she that behaveth herself unhonestly is a corruption in his bones."

Verse 7. *The wicked are overthrown*] Seldom does God give such a long life or numerous offspring.

But the house of the righteous shall stand.] God blesses their progeny, and their families continue long in the earth; whereas the wicked seldom have many generations in a direct line. This is God's mercy, that the entail of iniquity may be in some sort cut off, so that the same vices may not be strengthened by successive generations. For generally the *bad root* produces not only a *bad plant*, but one *worse than itself.*

Verse 9. He that is *despised, and hath a servant*] I believe the *Vulgate* gives the true *sense* of this verse: Melior est pauper, et sufficiens sibi; quam gloriosus, et indigens pane.

A. M. cir. 3004 B. C. cir. 1000 Ante I. Olymp. cir. 224 Ante U. C. cir. 247

is better than he that honoureth
himself, and lacketh bread.
10 [l]A righteous *man* regardeth the life of his beast: but
the [m]tender mercies of the wicked *are*
cruel.
11 [n]He that tilleth his land shall be satisfied with bread: but he that followeth vain
persons [o]*is* void of understanding.
12 The wicked desireth [p]the net of evil
men: but the root of the righteous yieldeth
fruit.
13 [q]The [r]wicked is snared by the transgression of *his* lips: [s]but the just shall come
out of trouble.
14 [t]A man shall be satisfied
with good by the fruit of *his*
mouth: [u]and the recompense of a
man's hands shall be rendered
unto him.
15 [v]The way of the fool *is* right in his own
eyes: but he that hearkeneth unto counsel *is*
wise.
16 [w]A fool's wrath is [x]presently known:
but a prudent *man* covereth shame.
17 [y]*He that* speaketh truth showeth forth
righteousness: but a false witness deceit.
18 [z]There is that speaketh like the piercings of a sword: but the tongue of the wise
is health.

[l]Deut. xxv. 4——[m]Or, *bowels*——[n]Gen. iii. 19 [o]Chap. vi. 32——[p]Or, *the fortress*——[q]Heb. *The snare of the wicked is in the transgression of lips*——[r]Chap. xviii. 7——[s]2 Pet. ii. 9

[t]Chap. xiii. 2; xviii. 20——[u]Isa. iii. 10, 11——[v]Chap. iii. 7; Luke xviii. 11——[w]Chap. xxix. 11——[x]Heb. *in that day*——[y]Chapter xiv. 5——[z]Psa. lviii. 4; lix. 7; lxiv. 3

"Better is the poor man who provides for himself, than the proud who is destitute of bread." The versions in general agree in this sense. This needs no comment. There are some who, through *pride of birth*, &c., would rather starve, than put their hands to menial labour. Though they may be *lords*, how much to be preferred is the *simple peasant*, who supports himself and family by the drudgery of life!

Verse 10. *A righteous* man *regardeth the life of his beast*] One principal characteristic of a *holy man* is *mercy:* cruelty is unknown to him; and his benevolence extends to the meanest of the brute creation. Pity rules the heart of a pious man; he can do nothing that is *cruel.* He considers what is best for the comfort, ease, health, and life of the *beast* that serves him; and he knows that God himself *careth for oxen:* and one of the ten commandments provides *a seventh part of time* to be allotted for the *rest of labouring beasts* as well as for *man.*

I once in my travels met with the *Hebrew* of this clause on the *sign board* of a public inn: יודע צדיק נפש בהמתו *yodea tsaddik nephesh behemto.* "A righteous man considereth the life of his beast;" which, being very appropriate, reminded me that I should feed my horse.

The tender mercies of the wicked are *cruel.*] אחזרי *achzari*, are *violent, without mercy, ruthless.* The wicked, influenced by Satan, can show no other disposition than what is in their master. If they *appear* at any time *merciful*, it is a *cloak* which they use to cover purposes of cruelty. To accomplish its end, iniquity will assume any garb, speak mercifully, extol benevolence, sometimes even *give to the poor!* But, timeo Danaos, et dona ferentes. The *cry of fire at midnight*, provided it be in another's dwelling, is more congenial to their souls than the *cry of mercy.* Look at the *human fiends*, "out-heroding Herod," in *horse races, bruising matches*, and *cock fights*, and in wars for the extension of territory, and the purposes of ambition. The *hell* is yet undescribed, that is suited to such monsters in cruelty.

Verse 11. *He that tilleth his land*] God's blessing will be in the labour of the honest agriculturist.

But he that followeth vain persons] He who, while he should be cultivating his ground, preparing for a future crop, or reaping his harvest, associates with *fowlers, coursers of hares, hunters of foxes*, or those engaged in any champaign amusements, is void of understanding; and I have known several such come to beggary.

To this verse the *Septuagint* add the following clause: Ὁς εστιν ἡδυς εν οινων διατριβαις, εν τοις ἑαυτου οχυρωμασι καταλειψει ατιμιαν. "He who is a boon companion in banquets, shall leave dishonour in his own fortresses." This has been copied by the *Vulgate* and the *Arabic.* That is, The man who frequents the ale-house enriches *that*, while he *impoverishes* his own *habitation.*

Verse 12. *The wicked desireth the net of evil* men] They applaud their ways, and are careful to imitate them in their wiles.

Verse 13. *The wicked is snared by the transgression of* his *lips*] A man who deals in *lies* and *false oaths* will sooner or later be found out to his own ruin. There is another proverb as true as this: *A liar had need of a good memory;* for as the *truth* is not in *him*, he *says* and *unsays*, and often *contradicts himself.*

Verse 16. *A fool's wrath is presently known*] We have a proverb very like this, and it will serve for illustration:—

A fool's bolt is soon shot.

A weak-minded man has no *self-government;* he is easily angered, and generally speaks whatever comes first to his mind.

Verse 18. *There is that speaketh*] Instead of בוטה *boteh, blabbing out, blustering*, several MSS. have בוטח *boteach*, TRUSTING: and instead of כמדקרות *kemadkeroth*, AS *the piercings*, seven MSS., with the *Complutensian Polyglot*, have במדקרות *bemadkeroth*, IN *the piercings.* "There is that *trusteth in* the piercings of a sword: but the tongue of the wise is health." But I suppose the *former* to be the true reading.

A. M. cir. 3004
B. C. cir. 1000
Ante I. Olymp. cir. 224
Ante U. C. cir. 247

19 The lip of truth shall be
established for ever: [a]but a
lying tongue *is* but for a moment.
20 Deceit *is* in the heart of them that
imagine evil: but to the counsellors of peace
is joy.
21 There shall no evil happen to the just:
but the wicked shall be filled with mischief.
22 [b]Lying lips *are* abomination to the
LORD: but they that deal truly *are* his delight.
23 [c]A prudent man concealeth knowledge:
but the heart of fools proclaimeth foolishness.

[a]Psa. lii. 5; chap. xix. 9——[b]Chap. vi. 17; xi. 20; Rev. xxii. 15——[c]Chap. xiii. 16; xv. 2

A. M. cir. 3004
B. C. cir. 1000
Ante I. Olymp. cir. 224
Ante U. C. cir. 247

24 [d]The hand of the diligent
shall bear rule: but the [e]sloth-
ful shall be under tribute.
25 [f]Heaviness in the heart of
man maketh it stoop: but [g]a good word
maketh it glad.
26 The righteous *is* more [h]excellent than
his neighbour: but the way of the wicked seduceth them.
27 The slothful *man* roasteth not that which
he took in hunting: but the substance of a
diligent man *is* precious.
28 In the way of righteousness *is* life; and
in the pathway *thereof there is* no death.

[d]Chap. x. 4——[e]Or, *deceitful*——[f]Chap. xv. 43——[g]Isa l. 4——[h]Or, *abundant*

Verse 19. *A lying tongue* is *but for a moment.*] *Truth* stands for ever; because its *foundation* is indestructible: but *falsehood* may soon be detected; and, though it gain credit for a while, it had that credit because it was supposed to be *truth.*

Verse 21. *There shall no evil happen to the just*] No, for all things work together for good to them that love God. Whatever occurs to a righteous man God turns to his advantage. But, on the other hand, the *wicked are filled with mischief:* they are hurt, grieved, and wounded, by every occurrence; and nothing turns to their profit.

Verse 23. *A prudent man concealeth knowledge*] "If a fool hold his peace he may pass for a wise man." I have known men of some learning, so intent on immediately informing a company how well cultivated their minds were, that they have passed either for *insignificant pedants* or *stupid asses.*

Verse 24. *The hand of the diligent shall bear rule*] And why? because by his *own industry* he is *independent;* and every such person is respected wherever found.

Verse 25. *Heaviness in the heart of a man maketh it stoop*] Sorrow of heart, hopeless love, or a sense of God's displeasure—these prostrate the *man,* and he becomes a *child* before them.

But a good word maketh it glad.] A single good or favourable word will remove despondency; and that word, "Son, be of good cheer, thy sins are forgiven thee," will instantly remove despair.

Verse 26. *The righteous* is *more excellent than his neighbour*] That is, if the neighbour be a wicked man. The spirit of the proverb lies here: The POOR *righteous man* is *more excellent* than his *sinful neighbour,* though *affluent* and *noble.* The *Syriac* has it, "The righteous deviseth good to his neighbour." A late commentator has translated it, "The righteous explore their pastures." How מרעהו can be translated THEIR *pastures* I know not; but none of the *versions* understood it in this way. The *Vulgate* is rather singular: Qui negligit damnum propter amicum, justus est. "He who neglects or sustains a loss for the sake of his friend, is a just man." The *Septuagint* is insufferable: "The well-instructed righteous man shall be his own friend." One would hope these translators meant *not exclusively;* he should love his neighbour as himself.

Verse 27. *The slothful* man *roasteth not that which he took in hunting*] Because he is a *slothful* man, he does not hunt for prey; therefore gets *none,* and cannot *roast,* that he may *eat.* There is some obscurity in the *original,* on which the *versions* cast little light. *Coverdale* translates the whole verse thus: "A discreatfull man schal fynde no vauntage: but he that is content with what he hath, is more worth than golde." My old MS. Bible: **The gylful man schal not fynd wynnynge: and the substance of a man schal ben the pris of gold.**

By translating רמיה *remiyah* the *deceitful,* instead of the *slothful man,* which appears to be the genuine meaning of the word, we may obtain a good sense, as the *Vulgate* has done: "The deceitful man shall not find gain; but the substance of a (just) man shall be the price of gold." But our common version, allowing רמיה *remiyah* to be translated *fraudulent,* which is its proper meaning, gives the best sense: "The fraudulent man roasteth not that which he took in hunting," the justice of God snatching from his mouth what he had acquired *unrighteously.*

But the substance of a diligent man] One who by honest industry acquires all his property—*is precious,* because it has the blessing of God in it.

Verse 28. *In the way of righteousness* is *life*] חיים *chaiyim, lives; life* temporal, and *life* eternal.

And in *the pathway* thereof there is *no death.*] Not only do the *general precepts* and *promises* of God lead *to life eternal,* and promote *life temporal;* but every *duty,* every *act of faith, patience of hope,* and *labour of love,* though requiring much *self-abasement, self-denial,* and often an *extension* of *corporal strength,* all *lead to life.* For in every case, in every particular, "the path of duty is the way of safety." The latter clause is only a repetition of the *sense* of the former.

CHAPTER XIII

Various moral sentences; the wise child; continence of speech; of the poor rich man and the rich poor man; ill-gotten wealth; delay of what is hoped for; the bad consequences of refusing instruction; providing for one's children; the necessity of correcting them, &c.

A. M. cir. 3004
B. C. cir. 1000
Ante I. Olymp. cir. 224
Ante U. C. cir. 247

A WISE son *heareth* his father's instruction: [a]but a
scorner heareth not rebuke.
2 [b]A man shall eat good by
the fruit of *his* mouth: but the soul of the
transgressors *shall eat* violence.
3 [c]He that keepeth his mouth keepeth his
life: *but* he that openeth wide his lips shall
have destruction.
4 [d]The soul of the sluggard desireth, and
hath nothing: but the soul of the diligent shall
be made fat.
5 A righteous *man* hateth lying: but a
wicked *man* is loathsome, and
cometh to shame.
6 [e]Righteousness keepeth *him*
that is upright in the way: but
wickedness overthroweth [f]the sinner.
7 [g]There is that maketh himself rich, yet
hath nothing: *there is* that maketh himself
poor, yet *hath* great riches.
8 The ransom of a man's life *are* his riches:
but the poor heareth not rebuke.
9 The light of the righteous rejoiceth: [h]but
the [i]lamp of the wicked shall be put out.
10 Only by pride cometh contention: but

A. M. cir. 3004
B. C. cir. 1000
Ante I. Olymp. cir. 224
Ante U. C. cir. 247

[a]1 Sam. ii. 25——[b]Chap. xii. 14——[c]Psa. xxxix. 1; chap. xxi. 23; James iii. 2——[d]Chap. x. 4

[e]Chap. xi. 3, 5, 6——[f]Heb. *sin*——[g]Chap. xii. 9——[h]Job xviii. 5, 6; xxi. 17; ch. xxiv. 20——[i]Or, *candle*

NOTES ON CHAP. XIII

Verse 1. *A wise son* heareth *his father's instruction*] The child that has had a proper *nurturing*, will profit by his father's counsels; but the child that is permitted to fulfil *its own will* and *have its own way*, will jest at the reproofs of its parents.

Verse 3. *He that keepeth his mouth keepeth his life*] How often have the foolish, headstrong, and wicked, forfeited their lives by the *treasonable* or *blasphemous* words they have spoken! The *government of the tongue* is a *rare* but useful talent.

But *he that openeth wide his lips*] He that puts no bounds to his loquacity, speaks on every subject, and gives his judgment and opinion on every matter. It has often been remarked that God has given us *two* EYES, that we may SEE *much; two* EARS, that we may HEAR *much;* but has given us but ONE *tongue*, and that fenced in with teeth, to indicate that though we *hear* and *see much*, we should *speak* but *little*.

Verse 4. *The soul of the sluggard desireth, and* hath *nothing*] We often hear many religious people expressing a *desire to have more of the Divine life*, and yet never get *forward* in it. How is this? The reason is, they *desire*, but do not *stir themselves up* to lay hold upon the Lord. They are always learning, but never able to come to the knowledge of the truth. They *seek* to enter in at the strait gate, but are not able, because they do not *strive*.

Verse 7. *There is that maketh himself rich*] That labours hard to acquire money, *yet hath nothing;* his excessive *covetousness* not being satisfied with what he possesses, nor permitting him to enjoy *with comfort* what he has acquired. The fable of *the dog in the manger* will illustrate this.

There is *that maketh himself poor, yet* hath *great riches.*] "As poor," said St. Paul, "yet making many rich; as having nothing, yet possessing all things." The former is the *rich poor* man; the latter is the *poor rich* man.

As the words are here in the *hithpael* conjugation, which implies *reflex action*, or the *action performed on one's self*, and often signifies *feigning* or *pretending* to be what one *is not*, or *not* to be what one *is;* the words may be understood of persons who *feign* or *pretend* to be either *richer* or *poorer* than they *really are*, to accomplish some particular purpose. "There is that *feigneth himself* to be *rich*, yet hath *nothing;* there is that *feigneth himself* to be *poor*, yet hath *great riches*." Both these characters frequently occur in life.

Verse 8. *The ransom of a man's life*] Those who have riches have often much trouble with them; as they had much trouble to *get* them, so they have much trouble to *keep* them. In despotic countries, a rich man is often accused of some capital crime, and to save his life, though he may be quite innocent, is obliged to give up his riches; but the *poor*, in such countries, are put to no trouble.

Verse 9. *The light of the righteous rejoiceth*] They shall have that measure of prosperity which shall be best for them; but the wicked, howsoever prosperous for a time, shall be brought into desolation. *Light* and *lamp* in both cases may signify *posterity*. The righteous shall have a joyous posterity; but that of the wicked shall be cut off. So 1 Kings xi. 36: "And unto his son will I give one tribe, that David my servant may have a *light* (נר *ner*, a *lamp*) always before me." xv. 4: "Nevertheless for David's sake did the Lord give them a *lamp*, to set up his *son* after him." See also Psa. cxxxii. 17, and several other places.

Verse 10. *By pride cometh contention*] Perhaps there is not a *quarrel* among *individuals* in private life, nor a *war* among nations, that does not proceed from *pride* and *ambition*. Neither *man* nor *nation* will be content to be *less* than another; and to acquire the wished-for *superiority* all is thrown into general confusion, both in public and private life. It was to destroy this *spirit of pride*, that Jesus was manifested in the *extreme of humility* and *humiliation* among men. The salvation of Christ is a *deliverance* from *pride*, and a being clothed

A. M. cir. 3004 B. C. cir. 1000 Ante I. Olymp. cir. 224 Ante U. C. cir. 247

with the well advised *is* wisdom.

11 [k]Wealth *gotten* by vanity shall be diminished: but he that gathereth [l]by labour shall increase.

12 Hope deferred maketh the heart sick: but [m]*when* the desire cometh, *it is* a tree of life.

13 Whoso [n]despiseth the word shall be destroyed: but he that feareth the commandment [o]shall be rewarded.

14 [p]the law of the wise *is* a fountain of life, to depart from [q]the snares of death.

15 Good understanding giveth favour: but the way of transgressors *is* hard.

16 [r]Every prudent *man* dealeth with knowledge: but a fool [s]layeth open *his* folly.

17 A wicked messenger falleth into mischief but [t]a [u]faithful ambassador *is* health.

A. M. cir. 3004 B. C. cir. 1000 Ante I. Olymp. cir. 224 Ante U. C. cir. 247

18 Poverty and shame *shall be to* him that refuseth instruction: but [v]he that regardeth reproof shall be honoured.

19 [w]The desire accomplished is sweet to the soul: but *it is* abomination to fools to depart from evil.

20 He that walketh with wise *men* shall be wise: but a companion of fools [x]shall be destroyed.

21 [y]Evil pursueth sinners: but to the righteous good shall be repayed.

22 A good *man* leaveth an inheritance to his children's children: and [z]the wealth of the sinner *is* laid up for the just.

[k]Chap. x. 2; xx. 21——[l]Heb. *with the hand*——[m]Ver. 19——[n]2 Chron. xxxvi. 16——[o]Or, *shall be in peace* [p]Chap. x. 11; xiv. 27; xvi. 22——[q]2 Sam. xxii. 6 [r]Chap. xii. 23; xv. 2——[s]Heb. *spreadeth*

[t]Chap. xxv. 23——[u]Heb. *an ambassador of faithfulness*——[v]Chap. xv. 5, 31——[w]Ver. 12——[x]Heb. *shal be broken*——[y]Psa. xxxii. 10——[z]Job xxvii. 16, 17; chap. xxviii. 8; Eccles. ii. 26

with *humility.* As far as we are *humble*, so far we are *saved.*

Verse 11. *Wealth* gotten *by vanity*] Wealth that is not the result of *honest industry* and *hard labour* is seldom permanent. All fortunes acquired by speculation, lucky hits, and ministering to the pride or luxury of others, &c., soon become dissipated. They are not gotten in the way of Providence, and have not God's blessing, and therefore are not permanent.

Verse 12. *Hope deferred maketh the heart sick*] When once a *good* is discovered, *want* of it felt, *strong desire* for the possession excited, and the promise of attainment made on grounds unsuspected, so that the *reality* of the *thing* and the *certainity* of the *promise* are manifest, *hope* posts forward to *realize the blessing. Delay* in the gratification pains the mind; the increase of the delay prostrates and sickens the heart; and if *delay sickens the heart*, ultimate *disappointment kills* it. *But* when the thing desired, hoped for, and expected comes, it is a tree of life, עץ חיים *ets chaiyim*, "the tree of lives;" it comforts and invigorates both body and soul. To the tree of lives, in the midst of the gardens of paradise, how frequent are the allusions in the writings of Solomon, and in other parts of the Holy Scriptures! What deep, and perhaps yet unknown, mysteries were in this tree!

Verse 13. *Whoso despiseth the word*] The revelation which God has in his mercy given to man—*shall be destroyed;* for there is no other way of salvation but that which it points out.

But he that feareth the commandment] That respects it so as to obey it, walking as this revelation directs—*shall be rewarded;* shall find it to be his highest interest, and shall be in *peace* or *safety*, as the Hebrew word ישלם may be translated.

Verse 14. *The law of the wise* is *a fountain of life*] Perhaps it would be better to translate, "The law is to the wise man a fountain of life." It is the same to him as the "vein of lives," מקור חיים *mekor chaiyim*, the great *aorta* which transmits the blood from the heart to every part of the body. There seems to be here an allusion to the *garden of paradise*, to the *tree of lives*, to the *tempter*, to the baleful *issue* of that temptation, and to the *death* entailed on man by his *unwisely* breaking the *law* of his God.

Verse 15. *The way of transgressors* is *hard.*] Never was a truer saying; most sinners have *more pain* and *difficulty* to get their souls damned, than the righteous have, with all their cross-bearings, to get to the kingdom of heaven.

Verse 17. *A wicked messenger*] The *Septuagint:* Βασιλευς θρασευς, *a bold king;* instead of מלאך *malach*, *a messenger*, they had read מלך *melech*, a *king:* but they are singular in this rendering; none of the other versions have it so. He that betrays the counsels of his government, or the interests of his country, will sooner or later fall into mischief; but he that faithfully and loyally fulfils his mission, shall produce *honour* and *safety* to the commonwealth.

Verse 19. *The desire accomplished*] See on ver. 12.

Verse 20. *He that walketh with wise* men *shall be wise*] To *walk* with a person implies *love* and *attachment;* and it is impossible not *to imitate those we love.* So we say, "Show me his company, and I'll tell you the man." Let me know the company he keeps, and I shall easily guess his moral character.

Verse 22. *A good* man *leaveth an inheritance*] He files many a *prayer* in heaven in their behalf, and his good *example* and *advices* are remembered and quoted from generation to generation. Besides, whatever property he left was *honestly* acquired, and *well-gotten goods are permanent.* The general experience of men shows this to be a common case; and that *property ill-gotten seldom reaches to the third generation.* This even the *heathens* observed. Hence:

De male quæsitis non gaudet tertius hæres.

A. M. cir. 3004 B. C. cir. 1000 Ante I. Olymp. cir. 224 Ante U. C. cir. 247

23 [a]Much food *is in* the tillage
of the poor: but there is *that is*
destroyed for want of judgment.
24 [b]He that spareth his rod hateth his son:
but he that loveth him chasten-
eth him betimes.
25 [c]The righteous eateth to
the satisfying of his soul: but
the belly of the wicked shall want.

[a]Chap. xii. 11——[b]Chap. xix. 18; xxii. 15; xxiii. 13; xxix. 15, 17——[c]Psa. xxxiv. 10; xxxvii. 3

"The third generation shall not possess the goods that have been unjustly acquired."

Verse 23. That is *destroyed for want of judgment.*] O, how much of the *poverty* of the *poor* arises from their own want of management! They have little or no economy, and no foresight. When they get any thing, they speedily spend it; and a *feast* and a *famine* make the chief *varieties* of their life.

Verse 24. *He that spareth his rod hateth his son*] That is, if he *hated* him, he could not do him a greater disservice than not to correct him when his *obstinacy* or *disobedience* requires it. We have met with this subject already, and it is a favourite with Solomon. See the places referred to in the margin.

The Rev. Mr. Holden makes some sensible observations on this passage: "By the neglect of early correction the desires (passions) obtain ascendancy; the temper becomes irascible, peevish, querulous. Pride is nourished, humility destroyed, and by the habit of indulgence the mind is incapacitated to bear with firmness and equanimity the cares and sorrows, the checks and disappointments, which *flesh is heir to.*"

Verse 25. *To the satisfying of his soul*] His desires are all moderate; he is contented with his circumstances, and is pleased with the lot which God is pleased to send. The wicked, though he use all *shifts* and *expedients* to acquire earthly good, not sticking even at *rapine* and *wrong*, is frequently in real want, and always dissatisfied with his portion. *A contented mind is a continual feast.* At such feasts he eats not.

CHAPTER XIV

Various moral sentiments. The antithesis between wisdom and folly, and the different effects of each.

A. M. cir. 3004 B. C. cir. 1000 Ante I. Olymp. cir. 224 Ante U. C. cir. 247

EVERY [a]wise woman [b]build-
eth her house: but the foolish plucketh it down with her
hands.
2 He that walketh in his uprightness feareth
the LORD: [c]but *he that is* perverse in his
ways despiseth him.
3 In the mouth of the foolish *is* a rod of
pride: [d]but the lips of the wise
shall preserve them.
4 Where no oxen *are* the crib
is clean: but much increase *is*
by the strength of the ox.
5 [e]A faithful witness will not lie: but a false
witness will utter lies.
6 A scorner seeketh wisdom, and *findeth it*

[a]Chap. xxiv. 3——[b]Ruth iv. 11——[c]Job xii. 4 [d]Chap. xii. 6 [e]Exod. xx. 16; xxiii. 1; chap. vi. 19; xii. 17; ver. 25

NOTES ON CHAP. XIV

Verse 1. *Every wise woman buildeth her house*] By her prudent and industrious management she *increases property* in the family, *furniture* in the *house*, and *food* and *raiment* for her household. This is the true *building of a house.* The *thriftless* wife acts differently, and the opposite is the result. Household *furniture*, far from being *increased*, is *dilapidated;* and her *household* are *ill-fed*, *ill-clothed*, and *worse educated.*

Verse 3. *The mouth of the foolish* is *a rod of pride*] The reproofs of such a person are *ill-judged* and *ill-timed*, and generally are conveyed in *such language* as renders them not only ineffectual, but displeasing, and even *irritating.*

Verse 4. *But much increase* is *by the strength of the ox.*] The *ox* is the most profitable of all the *beasts* used in *husbandry.* Except merely for *speed*, he is almost in every respect superior to the horse. 1. He is *longer lived.* 2. Scarcely liable to any *diseases.* 3. He is *steady*, and always *pulls fair* in his gears. 4. He *lives*, *fattens*, and *maintains* his strength on what *a horse will not eat*, and therefore is supported on one third the cost. 5. His *manure* is more profitable. And, 6, When he is worn out in his labour his *flesh* is good for the nourishment of man, his *horns* of great utility, and his *hide* almost invaluable. It might be added, he is *little or no expense* in *shoeing*, and his *gears* are much more *simple*, and much less *expensive*, than those of the *horse.* In all large farms *oxen* are greatly to be preferred to *horses.* Have but patience with this most patient animal, and you will soon find that *there is much increase by the strength* and labour *of the ox.*

Verse 6. *A scorner seeketh wisdom*] I believe the *scorner* means, in this book, the man

A. M. cir. 3004
B. C. cir. 1000
Ante I. Olymp. cir. 224
Ante U. C. cir. 247

not; but [f]knowledge is easy
unto him that understandeth.
7 Go from the presence of a
foolish man, when thou per-
ceivest not *in him* the lips of knowledge.
8 The wisdom of the prudent *is* to understand his way: but the folly of fools *is* deceit.
9 [g]Fools make a mock at sin; but among
the righteous *there is* favour.
10 The heart knoweth [h]his own bitterness;
and a stranger doth not intermeddle with his
joy.
11 [i]The house of the wicked shall be overthrown: but the tabernacle of
the upright shall flourish.
12 [k]There is a way which
seemeth right unto a man,
but the [l]end thereof *are* the ways of
death.
13 Even in laughter the heart is sorrowful;
and [m]the end of that mirth *is* heaviness.
14 The backslider in heart shall be [n]filled
with his own ways; and a good man *shall be*
satisfied from himself.
15 The simple believeth every word: but
the prudent *man* looketh well to his going.

A. M. cir. 3004
B. C. cir. 1000
Ante I. Olymp. cir. 224
Ante U. C. cir. 247

[f]Chap. viii. 9; xvii. 24——[g]Chap. x. 23——[h]Heb. *the bitterness of his soul*

[i]Job viii. 15——[k]Chap. xvi. 25——[l]Rom. vi. 21
[m]Chap. v. 4; Eccles. ii. 2——[n]Chap. i. 31; xii. 14

that *despises* the *counsel of God;* the *infidel.* Such may *seek wisdom;* but he never can find it, because he does not seek it *where* it is to be found; neither in the *teaching of God's Spirit,* nor in the *revelation* of his *will.*

Verse 7. *When thou perceivest not—the lips of knowledge.*] Instead of דעת *daath, knowledge,* several MSS. *have* שקר *sheker, a lie.* How this reading came I cannot conjecture. The meaning of the adage is plain: Never associate with a vain, empty fellow, when thou perceivest he can neither *convey* nor *receive* instruction.

Verse 8. Is *to understand his way*] Instead of הבין *habin,* to *understand,* הכין *hachin,* to DIRECT his way, is found in one MS. It makes a very good sense.

Verse 9. *Fools make a mock at sin*] And only *fools* would do so. But he that makes a *sport* of *sinning,* will find it *no sport* to suffer the vengeance of an eternal fire. Some learned men by their criticisms have brought this verse into embarrassments, out of which they were not able to extricate it. I believe we shall not come much nearer the sense than our present version does.

Verse 10. *The heart knoweth his own bitterness*] מרת נפשו *morrath naphsho,* "The bitterness of its soul." Under spiritual sorrow, the *heart* feels, the *soul* feels; all the *animal* nature feels and suffers. But when the peace of God is spoken to the troubled soul, the joy is indescribable; the *whole man* partakes of it. And a stranger to these religious feelings, to the travail of the soul, and to the witness of the Spirit, does not *intermeddle* with them; he does not understand them: indeed they may be even foolishness to him, because they are spiritually discerned.

Verse 12. *There is a way which seemeth right unto a man*] This may be his *easily besetting sin,* the *sin of his constitution,* the *sin of his trade.* Or it may be *his own false views of religion:* he may have an *imperfect repentance,* a *false faith,* a *very false creed;* and he may persuade himself that he is in the direct way to heaven. Many of the papists, when they were burning the saints of God in the flames at Smithfield, thought they were doing God service! And in the late Irish massacre, the more of the Protestants they *piked to death, shot,* or *burnt,* the more they believed they deserved of God's favour and their Church's gratitude. But cruelty and murder are the *short road,* the *near way,* to eternal perdition.

Verse 13. *Even in laughter the heart is sorrowful*] Many a time is a *smile* forced upon the *face,* when the heart is in *deep distress.* And it is a hard task to put on the *face of mirth,* when a man has a *heavy heart.*

Verse 14. *The backslider in heart shall be filled with his own ways*] 1. Who is the *backslider?* סוג *sug.* 1. The man who once walked in the ways of religion, but has *withdrawn* from them. 2. The man who once *fought manfully* against the world, the devil, and the flesh; but has *retreated* from the battle, or joined the enemy. 3. The man who once belonged to the congregation of the saints, but is now *removed* from them, and is set down in the synagogue of Satan.

2. But who is *the backslider in* HEART? 1. Not he who was *surprised* and *overcome* by the power of temptation, and the weakness of his own heart. 2. But he who drinks down iniquity with greediness. 3. Who gives cheerful way to the bent of his own nature, and now delights in fulfilling the lusts of the flesh and of the mind. 4. Who loves sin as before he loved godliness.

3. What are *his own ways?* Folly, sin, disappointment, and death; with the apprehension of the wrath of God, and the sharp twingings of a guilty conscience.

4. What is implied in being *filled with his own ways?* Having his soul *saturated* with folly, sin, and disappointment. At last ending here below in death, and then commencing an eternal existence where the *fire is not quenched,* and under the influence of that *worm that never dieth.* Alas, alas! who may abide when God doeth this?

And a good man shall be satisfied *from himself.*] 1. Who is the good man? (איש טוב *ish tob.*) 1. The man whose heart is right with God, whose *tongue* corresponds to his heart, and whose *actions* correspond to both. 2. The man who is every thing that the *sinner* and *backslider* are not.

2. *He shall be* satisfied *from himself*—he shall have the testimony of his own conscience, that in simplicity and godly sincerity, not with

A. M. cir. 3004 B. C. cir. 1000 Ante I. Olymp. cir. 224 Ante U. C. cir. 247

16 °A wise *man* feareth, and
departeth from evil: but the fool
rageth, and is confident.
17 *He that is* soon angry dealeth
foolishly: and a man of wicked devices is hated.
18 The simple inherit folly: but the prudent
are crowned with knowledge.
19 The evil bow before the good; and the
wicked at the gates of the righteous.
20 [p]The poor is hated even of his own neighbour: but [q]the rich *hath* many friends.
21 He that despiseth his neighbour sinneth:
[r]but he that hath mercy on the poor, happy
is he.
22 Do they not err that devise evil? but
mercy and truth *shall be* to them
that devise good.
23 In all labour there is profit:
but the talk of the lips *tendeth*
only to penury.
24 The crown of the wise *is* their riches:
but the foolishness of fools *is* folly.
25 [s]A true *witness* delivereth souls: but a
deceitful *witness* speaketh lies.
26 In the fear of the LORD *is* strong confidence; and his children shall have a place of
refuge.
27 [t]The fear of the LORD *is* a fountain of
life, to depart from the snares of death.
28 In the multitude of people *is* the king's

A. M. cir. 3004 B. C. cir. 1000 Ante I. Olymp. cir. 224 Ante U. C. cir. 247

---

[o]Chap. xxii. 3——[p]Chap. xix. 7——[q]Heb. *many are the lovers of the rich*——[r]Psa. xli. 1; cxii. 9——[s]Ver. 5——[t]Chap. xiii. 14

---

fleshly wisdom, but by the grace of God, he has his conversation among men.

3. He shall have God's Spirit to testify with his spirit that he is a child of God. He hath the witness in himself that he is born from above. The Spirit of God in his conscience, and the testimony of God in his Bible, show him that he belongs to the heavenly family. It is not from creeds or confessions of faith that he derives his satisfaction: he gets it from heaven, and it is sealed upon his heart.

Verse 16. *A wise* man *feareth*] He can never *trust in himself*, though he be *satisfied from himself*. He knows that *his sufficiency* is of GOD; and he has that *fear* that causes him to *depart from evil*, which is a guardian to the *love* he feels. Love renders him cautious; the other makes him confident. His *caution* leads him *from sin;* his *confidence* leads him *to God.*

Verse 17. *He that is soon angry*] קצר אפים *ketsar appayim*, "short of nostrils:" because, when a man is angry, his *nose is contracted*, and drawn up towards his eyes.

Dealeth foolishly] He has no time for reflection; *he* is *hurried* on by his passions, *speaks* like a *fool*, and *acts* like a *madman*.

Verse 19. *The evil bow before the good*] They are almost *constrained* to show them *respect;* and the *wicked*, who have wasted their substance with riotous living, *bow before the gates of the righteous*—of benevolent men—begging a morsel of bread.

Verse 20. *But the rich* hath *many friends.*] Many who *speak* to him the *language* of *friendship;* but if they profess *friendship* because he is *rich*, there is not *one real friend* among them. There is a fine saying of Cicero on this subject: Ut hirundines festivo tempore præsto sunt, frigore pulsæ recedunt: ita falsi amici sereno tempore præsto sunt: simul atque fortunæ hiemem viderint, evolant omnes.—Lib. iv., ad Herenn. "They are like *swallows*, who fly off during the winter, and quit our cold climates; and do not return till the warm season: but as soon as the winter sets in, they are all off again." So Horace:—

Donec eris felix, multos numerabis amicos:
Nullus ad amissas ibit amicus opes.

"As long as thou art prosperous, thou shalt have many friends: but who of them will regard thee when thou hast lost thy wealth?"

Verse 21. *He that despiseth his neighbor sinneth*] To despise a man because he has some natural blemish is *unjust, cruel,* and *wicked.* He is not the *author* of his *own imperfections;* they did not occur through his *fault* or *folly;* and if he *could,* he *would not retain them.* It is, therefore, *unjust* and wicked to despise him for what is not his *fault*, but his *misfortune.*

But he that hath mercy on the poor] Who reproaches no man for his *poverty* or *scanty intellect*, but divides his bread with the hungry—*happy is he;* the blessing of God, and of them that were ready to perish, shall come upon *him.*

Verse 23. *In all labour there is profit*] If a man work at his trade, he gains by it; if he cultivate the earth, it will yield an increase; and in *proportion* as he *labours*, so will be his *frofit:* but he who *talks* much *labours* little. And a man *words* is seldom a man of *deeds. Less talk and more work*, is one of our own ancient advices.

Verse 24. But *the foolishness of fools* is *folly.*] The *Targum* reads, *The honour of fools is folly.* The fool, from his foolishness, produces acts of folly. This appears to be the meaning.

Verse 26. *In the fear of the Lord* is *strong confidence*] From this, and from genuine Christian experience, we find that the *fear* of *God* is highly consistent with the *strongest confidence* in his mercy and goodness.

Verse 27. *The fear of the Lord* is *a fountain of life*] מקור חיים *mekor chaiyim*, the *vein of lives.* Another allusion to the great *aorta* which carries the blood from the heart to all the extremities of the body. Of this phrase, and the *tree of lives*, Solomon is particularly fond. See on chap. iv. 23; x. 12.

Verse 28. *In the multitude of people*] It is the interest of every state to promote *marriage* by every means that is just and prudent; and to discourage, disgrace, and debase *celibacy;* to render *bachelors* incapable, after a given age, of all public employments: and to banish *nun-*

A. M. cir. 3004 B. C. cir. 1000 Ante I. Olymp. cir. 224 Ante U. C. cir. 247

honour: but in the want of people *is* the destruction of the prince.
29 [u]*He that is* slow to wrath *is* of great understanding: but *he that is* [v]hasty of spirit exalteth folly.
30 A sound heart *is* the life of the flesh: but [w]envy [x]the rottenness of the bones.
31 [y]He that oppresseth the poor reproacheth [z]his Maker: but he that honoureth him hath mercy on the poor.
32 The wicked is driven away in his wickedness: but [a]the righteous hath hope in his death.
33 Wisdom resteth in the heart of him that hath understanding; but [b]*that which is* in the midst of fools is made known.
34 Righteousness exalteth a nation: but sin *is* a reproach [c]to any people.
35 [d]The king's favour *is* toward a wise servant: but his wrath is *against* him that causeth shame.

A. M. cir. 3004 B. C. cir. 1000 Ante I. Olymp. cir. 224 Ante U. C. cir. 247

[u]Chap. xvi. 32; James i. 19——[v]Heb. *short of spirit* [w]Psa. cxii. 10——[x]Chap. xii. 4——[y]Chap. xvii. 5; Matt. xxv. 40, 45——[z]See Job xxxi. 15, 16; chap. xxii. 2

[a]Job xiii. 15; xix. 26; Psa. xxiii. 4; xxxvii. 37; 2 Cor. i. 9; v. 8; 2 Tim. iv. 18——[b]Chap. xii. 16; xxix. 11 [c]Heb. *to nations*——[d]Matt. xxiv. 45, 47

neries and *monasteries* from all parts of their dominions;—they have ever, from their invention, contributed more to vice than virtue; and are positively point blank against the law of God.

Verse 29. That is *hasty of spirit*] קצר רוח *ketsar ruach*, "the short of spirit;" one that is easily irritated; and, being in a passion, he is agitated so as to be literally *short of breath*. Here put in opposition to ארך אפים *erech appayim, long of nostrils;* see on ver. 17; and of the same import with St. Paul's μακροθυμια, longsuffering, longmindedness. See on Eph. iv. 2.

Verse 30. *A sound heart* is *the life of the flesh*] A healthy state of the *blood*, and a proper *circulation* of that stream of life, is the grand cause, in the hand of God, of *health* and *longevity*. If the heart be diseased, *life* cannot be long continued.

Verse 31. *He that oppresseth the poor reproacheth his Maker*] Because the *poor*, or comparatively *poor*, are, in the order of God, *a part of the inhabitants of the earth;* and every man who loves God will *show mercy to the poor*, for with this God is peculiarly delighted. *The poor have we ever with us*, for the excitement and exercise of those benevolent, compassionate, and merciful feelings, without which men had been but little better than brutes.

Verse 32. *The wicked is driven away in his wickedness*] He does not *leave life cheerfully*. Poor soul! Thou hast no *hope* in the other world, and thou leavest the present with the utmost *regret!* Thou wilt not *go* off; but God will *drive* thee.

But the righteous hath hope in his death.] He rejoiceth to depart and be with Christ: to him death is gain; he is not reluctant to *go*—he *flies* at the call of God.

Verse 34. *But sin* is *a reproach to any people.*] I am satisfied this is not the sense of the original, וחסד לאמים חטאת *vechesed leummim chattath;* which would be better rendered, *And mercy is a sin-offering for the people.* The *Vulgate* has, *Miseros autem facit populos peccatum*, "sin makes the people wretched." Ελασσονουσι δε φυλας ἁμαρτιαι; "But sins lessen the tribes."—*Septuagint.* So also the *Syriac* and *Arabic.* The plain meaning of the original seems to be, *A national disposition to mercy* appears in the sight of God as a *continual sin-offering.* Not that it atones for the sin of the people; but, *as* a sin-offering is pleasing in the sight of the God of mercy, so is a merciful disposition in a nation. This view of the verse is consistent with the purest doctrines of free grace. And what is the true sense of the words, we should take at all hazards and consequences: we shall never trench upon a *sound creed* by a *literal interpretation* of God's words. No nation has more of this *spirit* than the British nation. It is true, we have too many *sanguinary laws;* but the *spirit* of the people is widely different.

If any one will contend for the *common version*, he has my consent; and I readily agree in the saying, *Sin is the reproach of any people.* It is the *curse* and *scandal* of man. Though I think what I have given is the true meaning of the text.

Verse 35. *The king's favour* is *toward a wise servant*] The king should have an intelligent man for his *minister;* a man of deep sense, sound judgment, and of a *feeling, merciful disposition.* He who has not the *former* will plunge the nation into *difficulties;* and he who has not the *latter* will embark her in *disastrous wars.* Most wars are occasioned by *bad ministers, men of blood*, who cannot be happy but in endeavouring to unchain the spirit of discord. Let every humane heart pray, *Lord, scatter thou the people who delight in war! Amen—so be it. Selah!*

CHAPTER XV

The soft answer. Useful correction. Stability of the righteous. The contented mind. The slothful man. The fool. The covetous. The impious. The wicked opposed to the righteous; to the diligent; and to the man who fears the Lord.

A. M. cir. 3004
B. C. cir. 1000
Ante I. Olymp. cir. 224
Ante U. C. cir. 247

A [a]SOFT answer turneth
away wrath: but [b]grievous
words stir up anger.
2 The tongue of the wise useth
knowledge aright: [c]but the mouth of fools
[d]poureth out foolishness.
3 [e]The eyes of the LORD *are* in every place,
beholding the evil and the good.
4 [f]A wholesome tongue *is* a tree of life:
but perverseness therein *is* a breach in the
spirit.
5 [g]A fool despiseth his father's instruction: [h]but he that regardeth reproof is prudent.
6 In the house of the righteous *is* much treasure: but in the revenues of the wicked is
trouble.
7 The lips of the wise disperse knowledge:
but the heart of the foolish *doeth* not so.
8 [i]The sacrifice of the wicked *is* an abomination unto the LORD: but the prayer of the
upright *is* his delight.
9 The way of the wicked *is* an abomination unto the LORD: but he loveth him
that [k]followeth after righteousness.
10 [l]Correction *is* [m]grievous
unto him that forsaketh the way;
and [n]he that hateth reproof shall die.
11 [o]Hell and destruction *are* before the
LORD; how much more then [p]the hearts of
the children of men?
12 [q]A scorner loveth not one that reproveth
him; neither will he go unto the wise.
13 [r]A merry heart maketh a cheerful countenance: but [s]by sorrow of the heart the
spirit is broken.
14 The heart of him that hath understanding seeketh knowledge: but the mouth of
fools feedeth on foolishness.
15 All the days of the afflicted *are* evil:
[t]but he that is of a merry heart *hath* a continual feast.
16 [u]Better *is* little with the fear of the
LORD, than great treasure and trouble therewith.
17 [v]Better *is* a dinner of herbs where love
is, than a stalled ox and hatred therewith.

A. M. cir. 3004
B. C. cir. 1000
Ante I. Olymp. cir. 224
Ante U. C. cir. 247

[a]Judg. viii. 1, 2, 3; chap. xxv. 15——[b]1 Sam. xxv. 10, &c.——1 Kings xii. 13, 14, 16——[c]Ver. 28; chap. xii. 23; xiii. 16——[d]Heb. *belcheth* or *bubbleth*——[e]Job xxxiv. 21; chap. v. 21; Jer. xvi. 17; xxxii. 19; Heb. iv. 14——[f]Heb. *The healing of the tongue*——[g]Chap. x. 1——[h]Ch. xiii. 18; ver. 31, 32——[i]Chap. xxi. 27; xxviii. 9; Isa. i. 11; lxi. 8; lxvi. 3; Jer. vi. 20; vii. 22; Amos v. 22——[k]Ch. xxi. 21; 1 Tim. vi. 11——[l]Or, *Instruction*——[m]1 Kings xxii. 8——[n]Chap. v. 12; x. 17——[o]Job xxvi. 6; Psa. cxxxix. 8——[p]2 Chron. vi. 30; Psa. vii. 9; xliv. 21; John ii. 24, 25; xxi. 17; Acts i. 24——[q]Amos v. 10; 2 Tim. iv. 3——[r]Chap. xvii. 22——[s]Chap. xii. 25——[t]Chap. xvii. 22——[u]Psa. xxxvii. 16; Chap. xvi. 8; 1 Tim. vi. 6——[v]Chap. xvii. 1

NOTES ON CHAP. XV

Verse 1. *A soft answer*] Gentleness will often disarm the most furious, where positive derangement has not taken place; one angry word will always beget another, for the disposition of one spirit always begets its own likeness in another: thus kindness produces kindness, and rage produces rage. Universal experience confirms this proverb.

Verse 2. *Useth knowledge aright*] This is very difficult to know:—*when* to *speak*, and *when* to be *silent; what* to *speak*, and *what* to leave *unspoken;* the *manner* that is best and most suitable to the *occasion*, the *subject*, the *circumstances*, and the *persons.* All these are difficulties, often even to the wisest men. Even *wise counsel* may be *foolishly* given.

Verse 3. *The eyes of the Lord* are *in every place*] He not only sees all things, by his omnipresence, but his *providence* is everywhere. And if the consideration that *his eye is in every place*, have a tendency to *appal* those whose *hearts are not right before him*, and who seek for *privacy*, that they may *commit iniquity;* yet the other consideration, that his *providence* is *everywhere*, has a great tendency to encourage the upright, and all who may be in *perilous* or *distressing* circumstances.

Verse 4. *A wholesome tongue* is *a tree of life*] Here again is an allusion to the paradisiacal tree, עץ חיים *ets chaiyim*, "the tree of lives."

Verse 8. *The sacrifice of the wicked* is *an abomination*] Even the most *sedulous attendance* on the *ordinances* of God, and *performance* of the *ceremonies of religion*, is an abomination to the Lord, if the *heart* be not right with him, and the observance do not flow from a principle of pure devotion. No *religious acts* will do in place of *holiness to the Lord.*

The prayer of the upright is *his delight.*] What a *motive* to be *upright;* and what a motive to the upright to *pray!* But who is the *upright?* The man who is *weary of sin*, and *sincerely desires* the salvation of God; as well as he who has already received a measure of that salvation. Hence it is said in the next verse, "He loveth him that followeth after righteousness."

Verse 11. *Hell and destruction*] שאול ואבדון *sheol vaabaddon. Hades*, the invisible world, the place of separate spirits till the resurrection: and *Abaddon*, the place of *torment;* are ever under the eye and control of the Lord.

Verse 13. *By sorrow of the heart the spirit is broken.*] Every kind of *sorrow worketh death*, but that which is the offspring of true repentance. This alone is healthful to the soul. The indulgence of a disposition to *sighing* tends to destroy life. Every *deep sigh* throws off a portion of the vital *energy.*

Verse 16. *Better* is *little with the fear of the Lord*] Because where the fear of God is, there are *moderation* and *contentment* of spirit.

Verse 17. *Better* is *a dinner of herbs*] Great

A. M. cir. 3004
B. C. cir. 1000
Ante I. Olymp. cir. 224
Ante U. C. cir. 247

18 [w]A wrathful man stirreth
up strife: but *he that is* slow to
anger appeaseth strife.
19 [x]The way of the slothful
man is as a hedge of thorns: but the way of
the righteous [y]*is* made plain.
20 [z]A wise son maketh a glad father: but
a foolish man despiseth his mother.
21 [a]Folly *is* joy to *him that is* [b]destitute of
wisdom: [c]but a man of understanding walketh uprightly.
22 [d]Without counsel purposes are disappointed: but in the multitude of counsellors
they are established.
23 A man hath joy by the answer of his
mouth: and [e]a word *spoken* [f]in due season,
how good *is it!*
24 [g]The way of life *is* above to the wise,
that he may depart from hell beneath.
25 [h]The LORD will destroy the house of the
proud: but [i]he will establish the border of the
widow.
26 [k]The thoughts of the wicked *are* an abomination to the
LORD: [l]but *the words* of the
pure *are* [m]pleasant words.
27 [n]He that is greedy of gain troubleth his
own house: but he that hateth gifts shall
live.
28 The heart of the righteous [o]studieth to
answer: but the mouth of the wicked poureth
out evil things.
29 [p]The LORD *is* far from the wicked: but
[q]he heareth the prayer of the righteous.
30 The light of the eyes rejoiceth the
heart: *and* a good report maketh the bones
fat.
31 [r]The ear that heareth the reproof of life
abideth among the wise.
32 He that refuseth [s]instruction despiseth
his own soul: but he that [t]heareth reproof
[u]getteth understanding.
33 [v]The fear of the LORD *is* the instruction
of wisdom; and [w]before honour *is* humility.

[w]Chap. xxvi. 21; xxix. 22——[x]Chap. xxii. 5——[y]Heb. is *raised up as a causey*——[z]Chap. x. 1; xxix. 3——[a]Ch. x. 23——[b]Heb. *void of heart*——[c]Eph. v. 15——[d]Chap. xi. 14; xx. 18——[e]Chap. xxv. 11——[f]Heb. *in his season* [g]Phil. iii. 20; Col. iii. 1, 2——[h]Chap. xii. 7; xiv. 11 [i]Psa. lxviii. 5, 6; cxlvi. 9

[k]Chap. vi. 16, 18——[l]Psa. xxxvii. 30——[m]Heb. *words of pleasantness*——[n]Chap. xi. 19; Isa. v. 8; Jer. xvii. 11——[o]1 Pet. iii. 15——[p]Psa. x. 1; xxxiv. 16 [q]Psa. cxlv. 18, 19——[r]Ver. 5——[s]Or, *correction*——[t]Or, *obeyeth*——[u]Heb. *possesseth a heart*——[v]Chap. i. 7 [w]Chap. xviii. 12

numbers of *indigent Hindoos* subsist wholly on *herbs*, fried in oil, and mixed with their rice.

Verse 19. *The way of the slothful* man is *as a hedge of thorns*] Because he is *slothful*, he imagines *ten thousand* difficulties in the way which cannot be surmounted; but they are all the creatures of his own *imagination*, and that imagination is formed by his *sloth*.

Verse 22. *But in the multitude of counsellors*] See note on chap. xi. 14. But רב יועצים *rob yoatsim* might be translated, chief or master of the council, the prime minister.

Verse 24. *The way of life* is *above to the wise*] There is a *treble* antithesis here: 1. The way of the *wise*, and that of the *fool*. 2. The one is *above*, the other *below*. 3. The one is of *life*, the other is of *death*.

Verse 25. *The house of the proud*] Families of this description are seldom continued long. The Lord hates *pride;* and those that will not be *humble* he will *destroy*.

Verse 27. *He that is greedy of gain*] He who *will* be rich; *troubleth his own house*—he is a torment to himself and his family by his avariciousness and penury, and a curse to those with whom he deals.

But he that hateth gifts] Whatever is *given to pervert judgment*.

Verse 28. *The heart of the righteous studieth to answer*] His tongue never runs before his wit; he never speaks rashly, and never unadvisedly; because he *studies*—ponders, his thoughts and his words.

Verse 29. *The Lord* is *far from the wicked*] He is neither near to *hear*, nor near to *help*.

Verse 30. *The light of the eyes rejoiceth the heart*] Nature and art are continually placing before our view a multitude of the most resplendent images, each of which is calculated to give pleasure. The man who has a *correct judgment*, and an *accurate eye*, may not only *amuse*, but *instruct* himself endlessly, by the beauties of nature and art.

Verse 31. *The ear that heareth the reproof*] That receives it gratefully and obeys it. "Advice is for them that will take it;" so says one of our own old proverbs; and the meaning here is nearly the same.

Verse 32. *Despiseth his own soul*] That is, *constructively;* for if the instruction lead to the *preservation* of *life* and *soul*, he that neglects or despises it throws all as much in the way of danger as if he actually hated himself.

Verse 33. *The fear of the Lord*] See note on chap. i. 7. Much is spoken concerning this *fear;* 1. It is the *beginning of wisdom*. 2. It is also the *beginning of knowledge*. And, 3. It is the *instruction of wisdom*. Wisdom derives its most important lessons from the fear of God. He who fears God much, is well taught.

And before honour is *humility*.] That is, few persons ever arrive at *honour* who are not *humble;* and those who from low life have risen to places of trust and confidence, have been remarkable for humility. We may rest assured that the *providence* of God will never elevate a proud man; such God beholds *afar off*. He may get into places of trust and profit, but God will *oust* him, and the people will curse him, and curse his memory. So will it ever be with bad ministers and advisers of the crown.

CHAPTER XVI

Man prepares, but God governs. God has made all things for himself; he hates pride. The judgments of God. The administration of kings; their justice, anger, and clemency. God has made all in weight, measure, and due proportion. Necessity produces industry. The patient man. The lot is under the direction of the Lord.

A. M. cir. 3004
B. C. cir. 1000
Ante I. Olymp. cir. 224
Ante U. C. cir. 247

THE [a]preparations [b]of the
heart in man, [c]and the answer of the tongue, *is* from the
LORD.
2 [d]All the ways of a man *are* clean in his
own eyes: but [e]the LORD weigheth the spirits.

3 [f]Commit [g]thy works unto
the LORD, and thy thoughts shall
be established.
4 [h]The LORD hath made all
things for himself: [i]yea, even the wicked for
the day of evil.

A. M. cir. 3004
B. C. cir. 1000
Ante I. Olymp. cir. 224
Ante U. C. cir. 247

[a]Ver. 9; chap. xix. 21; xx. 24; Jer. x. 23——[b]Or, *dispostings*——[c]Matt. x. 19, 20——[d]Chap. xxi. 2——[e]1 Sam. xvi. 7

[f]Psa. xxxvii. 5; lv. 22; Matt. vi. 25; Luke xii. 22; Phil. iv. 6; 1 Pet. v. 7——[g]Heb. *Roll*——[h]Isa. xliii. 7; Rom. xi. 36——[i]Job xxi. 30; Rom. ix. 22

NOTES ON CHAP. XVI

Verse 1. *The preparations of the heart in man*] The Hebrew is לאדם מערכי לב *leadam maarchey leb*, which is, literally, "To man are the dispositions of the heart; but from the Lord is the answer of the tongue." Man proposes his wishes; but God answers as he thinks proper. The former is the free offspring of the heart of man; the latter, the free volition of God. Man may *think* as he pleases, and *ask* as he lists; but God will *give*, or *not give*, as he thinks proper. This I believe to be the *meaning* of this shamefully tortured passage, so often vexed by critics, their doubts, and indecisions. God help them! for they seldom have the faculty of making any subject *plainer!* The text does not say that the "preparations," rather *dispositions* or *arrangements*, מערכי *maarchey*, "of the heart," as well as "the answer of the tongue, *is* from the Lord;" though it is generally understood so; but it states that the *dispositions* or *schemes* of the heart (are) man's; but the answer of the tongue (is) the Lord's. And so the principal *versions* have understood it.

Hominis est animam preparare; et Domini gubernare linguam.—VULGATE. "It is the part of man to prepare his soul: it is the prerogative of the Lord to govern the tongue." מן בר נש תרעיתא דלבא ומן יי ממללא דלישנא *min bar nash taritha delibba; umin yeya mamlala delishana.*—CHALDEE. "From the son of man is the counsel of the heart; and from the Lord is the word of the tongue." The SYRIAC is the same. Καρδια ανδρος λογιζεσθω δικαια, ινα ὑπο του Θεου διορθωθῃ τα διαβηματα αυτῃ.—SEPTUAGINT. "The heart of man deviseth righteous things, that its goings may be directed by God."

The ARABIC takes great latitude: "All the works of an humble man are clean before the Lord; and the wicked shall perish in an evil day." **Of a man is to maken redy the inwitt: and of the Lorde to goberne the tunge.**—Old MS. Bible.

"A man maye well purpose a thinge in his harte: but the answere of the tonge cometh of the Lorde."—COVERDALE.

MATTHEW'S Bible, 1549, and BECKE'S Bible of the same date, and CARDMARDEN'S of 1566, follow *Coverdale*. The Bible printed by *R. Barker*, at Cambridge, 4to., 1615, commonly called the *Breeches Bible*, reads the text thus:—"The preparations of the hart *are* in man; but the answere of the tongue *is* of the Lord." So that it appears that our *first*, and all our *ancient versions*, understood the text in the same way; and this, independently of critical torture, is the genuine meaning of the *Hebrew text*. That very valuable version published in *Italian*, at Geneva, fol. 1562, translates thus: Le dispositioni del cuore sono de l'huomo; ma la risposta del la lingua è dal Signore. "The dispositions of the heart are of man; but the answer of the tongue is from the Lord."

The *modern European versions*, as far as I have seen, are the same. And when the word *dispositions, arrangements, schemes*, is understood to be the proper meaning of the *Hebrew term*, as shown above, the sense is *perfectly sound;* for there may be a *thousand schemes* and *arrangements* made in the heart of man, which he may earnestly wish God to bring to full effect, that are neither for *his good* nor *God's glory;* and therefore it is his interest that God has the *answer* in his own power. At the same time, there is no intimation here that *man can prepare his own heart to wait upon, or pray unto the Lord;* or that from the *human heart* any thing *good* can come, *without Divine influence;* but simply that he may have many *schemes* and *projects* which he may beg God to accomplish, that are not of *God*, but from *himself*. Hence our own proverb: "Man proposes, but God disposes." I have entered the more particularly into the consideration of this text, because some are very strenuous in the support of our vicious reading, from a supposition that the other defends the *heterodox* opinion of *man's sufficiency* to think any thing *as of himself*. But while they deserve due credit for their orthodox caution, they will see that no such imputation can fairly lie against the plain grammatical translation of the Hebrew text.

Verse 3. *Commit thy works unto the Lord*] See that what thou doest is commanded; and then begin, continue, and end all in his name. *And thy thoughts shall be established*—these schemes or arrangements, though formed in the heart, are agreeable to the Divine will, and therefore shall be established. His *thoughts*—his meditations—are right; and he begins and ends his work in the Lord; and therefore all issues well.

Verse 4. *The Lord hath made all* things *for*

A. M. cir. 3004 B. C. cir. 1000 Ante I. Olymp. cir. 224 Ante U. C. cir. 247

5 [k]Every one *that is* proud in heart *is* an abomination to the LORD: [l]*though* hand *join* in hand, he shall not be [m]unpunished.

6 [n]By mercy and truth iniquity is purged: and [o]by the fear of the LORD *men* depart from evil.

7 When a man's ways please the LORD, he maketh even his enemies to be at peace with him.

8 [p]Better *is* a little with righteousness, than great revenues without right.

9 [q]A man's heart deviseth his way: [r]but the LORD directeth his steps.

10 [s]A divine sentence *is* in the lips of the

[k]Chap. vi. 17; viii. 13——[l]Chap. xi. 21——[m]Heb. *held innocent*——[n]Dan. iv. 27; Tob. xii. 9; Luke xi. 41——[o]Chap. xiv. 16

[p]Psa. xxxvii. 16; Chap. xv. 16——[q]Ver. 1; chap. xix. 21——[r]Psa. xxxvii. 23; Prov. xx. 23; Jer. x. 24——[s]Heb. *Divination*

himself] He has so framed and executed every part of his creation, that it manifests his wisdom, power, goodness, and truth.

Even the wicked for the day of evil.] וגם רשע ליום רעה *vegam rasha leyom raah.* The whole verse is translated by the *Chaldee* thus: "All the works of the LORD are for those who obey him; and the wicked is reserved for the evil day."

As רעה *raah* literally signifies to *feed*, it has been conjectured that the clause might be read, *yea, even the wicked he feeds by the day*, or *daily.*

If we take the words as they stand in our present version, they mean no more than what is expressed by the *Chaldee* and *Syriac:* and as far as we can learn from their present *confused state*, by the *Septuagint* and *Arabic*, that "the wicked are reserved for the day of punishment." *Coverdale* has given, as he generally does, a good sense: "The Lorde doth all thinges for his owne sake; yea, and when he kepeth the ungodly for the daye of wrath." He does not *make* the *wicked* or *ungodly man;* but when *man has made himself such*, even *then* God bears with him. But if he repent not, when the measure of his iniquity is filled up, he shall fall under the wrath of God his Maker.

Verse 5. Though *hand* join *in hand, he shall not be unpunished.*] The day of wrath shall come on the wicked, whatever means he may take to avoid it. See chap. xi. 21.

Verse 6. *By mercy and truth iniquity is purged*] This may be misunderstood, as if a man, by *showing mercy* and *acting according to truth*, could atone for his own iniquity. The *Hebrew* text is not ambiguous: בחסד ואמת יכפר עון *bechesed veemeth yechapper avon;* "By mercy and truth he shall atone for iniquity." *He*—God, *by* his *mercy*, in sending his son Jesus into the world,—"shall make an atonement for iniquity" according to his *truth*—the word which he declared by his holy prophets since the world began. Or, if we retain the present version, and follow the *points* in יכפר *yecuppar*, reading "iniquity is purged" or "atoned for," the sense is unexceptionable, as we refer the *mercy* and the *truth* to GOD. But what an awful comment is that of *Don Calmet*, in which he expresses, not only his *own opinion*, but the *staple doctrine* of his own *Church*, the Romish! The reader shall have his own words: "'L'iniquité se rachete par la misericorde et la verité.' On expie ses pechèz par des œuvres de *misericorde* envers le prochein; par la clemence, par la douceur, par compassion, par les aumônes: et par la *verité*—par la fidelité, la bonne foi, la droiture, l'equité dans le commerce. Voyez Prov. iii. 3, xiv. 22, xx. 28." "'Iniquity is redeemed by mercy and truth.' We expiate our sins by works of *mercy* towards our neighbour; by clemency, by kindness, by compassion, and by alms: and by *truth—by* fidelity, by trustworthiness, by uprightness, by equity in commerce." If this be so, why was Jesus incarnated? Why his agony and bloody sweat, his cross and passion, his death and burial, his resurrection and ascension? Was it only to *supply* a sufficient portion of *merit* for those who had *neglected to make a fund for themselves?* Is the guilt of sin so small in the sight of Divine justice, that a man can atone for it by *manifesting good dispositions towards his neighbours*, by *giving some alms*, and not doing those things for which he might be *hanged?* Why then did God make such a mighty matter of the redemption of the world? Why send his Son at all? An *angel* would have been *more* than sufficient; yea, even a *sinner*, who had been converted by his own compassion, alms-deeds, &c., would have been sufficient. And is not this the very doctrine of this most awfully fallen and corrupt Church? Has she not provided a *fund of merit* in her *saints*, of what was more than requisite for *themselves*, that it might be *given*, or *sold out*, to those who had not enough of their own? Now such is the doctrine of the Romish Church—grossly absurd, and destructively iniquitous! And because men cannot believe this, cannot believe these monstrosities, that Church will burn them to ashes. Ruthless Church! degenerated, fallen, corrupt, and corrupting! once a *praise*, now a *curse*, in the earth. Thank the blessed God, whose blood alone can expiate sin, that he has a Church upon the earth; and that the *Romish* is not the *Catholic* Church; and that it has not that political power by which it would subdue all things to itself.

Verse 7. *When a man's ways please the Lord*] God is the guardian and defence of all that fear and love him; and it is truly astonishing to see how wondrously God works in their behalf, raising them up friends, and turning their enemies into friends.

Verse 9. *A man's heart deviseth his way*] This is precisely the same sentiment as that contained in the first verse, on the true meaning of which so much has been already said.

Verse 10. *A divine sentence*] קסם *kesem*, "divination," as the margin has it. Is the meaning as follows? Though *divination* were applied to a righteous king's lips, to induce him

A. M. cir. 3004
B. C. cir. 1000
Ante I. Olymp. cir. 224
Ante U. C. cir. 247

king: his mouth transgresseth not in judgment.

11 A [t]just weight and balance *are* the LORD'S: [u]all the weights of the bag *are* his work.

12 *It is* an abomination to kings to commit wickedness: for [v]the throne is established by righteousness.

13 [w]Righteous lips *are* the delight of kings; and they love him that speaketh right.

14 [x]The wrath of a king *is as* messengers of death: but a wise man will pacify it.

15 In the light of the king's countenance *is* life; and [y]his favour *is* [z]as a cloud of the latter rain.

16 [a]How much better *is it* to get wisdom than gold? and to get understanding rather to be chosen than silver?

17 The highway of the upright *is* to depart from evil: he that keepeth his way preserveth his soul.

18 [b]Pride goeth before destruction, and a haughty spirit before a fall.

A. M. cir. 3004
B. C. cir. 1000
Ante I. Olymp. cir. 224
Ante U. C. cir. 247

19 Better *it is to be* of an humble spirit with the lowly, than to divide the spoil with the proud.

20 [c]He that handleth a matter wisely shall find good: and whoso [d]trusteth in the LORD, happy *is* he.

21 The wise in heart shall be called prudent: and the sweetness of the lips increaseth learning.

22 [e]Understanding *is* a well-spring of life unto him that hath it: but the instruction of fools *is* folly.

23 [f]The heart of the wise [g]teacheth his mouth, and addeth learning to his lips.

24 Pleasant words *are as* a honey-comb, sweet to the soul, and health to the bones.

25 [h]There is a way that seemeth right unto a man; but the end thereof *are* the ways of death.

26 [i]He [k]that laboureth, laboureth for himself; for his mouth [l]craveth it of him.

27 [m]An ungodly man diggeth up evil: and

---

[t]Lev. xix. 36; chap. xi. 1——[u]Heb. *all the stones* [v]Chap. xxv. 5; xxix. 14——[w]Chap. xiv. 35; xxii. 11 [x]Chap. xix. 12; xx. 2——[y]Chap. xix. 12——[z]Job xxix. 23; Zech. x. 1——[a]Chap. viii. 11, 19——[b]Chap. xi. 2; xvii. 19; xviii. 12——[c]Or, *He that understandeth a matter*

[d]Psa. ii. 12; xxxiv. 8; cxxv. 1; Isa. xxx. 18; Jer. xvii. 7 [e]Chap. xiii. 14; xiv. 27——[f]Psa. xxxvii. 30; Matt. xii. 34 [g]Heb. *maketh wise*——[h]Chap. xiv. 12——[i]See chap. ix. 12; Eccles. vi. 7——[k]Heb. *The soul of him that laboureth* [l]Heb. *boweth unto him*——[m]Heb. *A man of Belial*

---

to punish the innocent and spare the guilty, yet *would not his lips transgress in judgment;* so firmly attached is he to God, and so much is he under the Divine *care* and *influence.* Whatever judgment such a one pronounces, it may be considered as a decision from God.

Verse 11. *All the weights of the bag* are *his*] Alluding, probably, to the *standard weights* laid up in a bag in the *sanctuary,* and to which all weights in common use in the land were to be referred, in order to ascertain whether they were just: but some think the allusion is to the *weights* carried about by merchants in their *girdles,* by which they weigh the money, silver and gold, that they take in exchange for their merchandise. As the *Chinese* take no *coin* but *gold* and *silver* by weight, they carry about with them a sort of small *steelyard,* by which they weigh those metals taken in exchange.

Verse 12. It is *an abomination to kings, &c.*] In all these verses the wise man refers to *monarchical government rightly administered.* And the proverbs on this subject are all plain.

Verse 16. *How much better—to get wisdom than gold?*] Who believes this, though spoken by the wisest of men, under Divine inspiration?

Verse 17. *The highway of the upright*] The upright man is ever departing from evil; this is his *common road:* and by keeping *on* in this way, *his soul is preserved.*

Verse 18. *Pride goeth before destruction*] Here *pride* is personified: it walks along, and has destruction in its train.

And a haughty spirit before a fall.] Another personification. A *haughty spirit* marches on, and *ruin* comes after.

In this verse we find the following *Masoretic* note in most Hebrew Bibles. חצי הספר *chatsi hassepher:* "the *middle* of the book." This verse is the *middle verse;* and the first *clause* makes the middle of the *words* of the book of Proverbs.

Verse 22. *Understanding* is *a well-spring of life*] מקור חיים *mekor chaiyim;* another allusion to the *artery* that carries the blood from the heart to distribute it to all the extremities of the body.

Verse 23. *The heart of the wise teacheth his mouth*] He has a wise heart; he speaks as it dictates; and therefore his speeches are all speeches of wisdom.

Verse 24. *Pleasant words* are as *a honey-comb*] The honey of which is *sweeter* than that which has been expressed from it, and has a much *finer flavour* before it has come in contact with the atmospheric air.

Verse 25. *There is a way that seemeth right*] This whole verse is precisely the same as that chap. xiv. 12.

Verse 26. *He that laboureth*] No thanks to a man for his labour and industry; if he do not *work* he must *starve.*

Verse 27. *An ungodly man diggeth up evil*] How will the following suit?

Effodiuntur opes irritamenta malorum

"*Wealth, the incitement to all evil, is digged up* out the earth."

A. M. cir. 3004
B. C. cir. 1000
Ante I. Olymp. cir. 224
Ante U. C. cir. 247

in his lips *there is* as a burning
fire.
28 [n]And froward man [o]soweth
strife: and [p]a whisperer separateth chief friends.
29 A violent man [q]enticeth his neighbour,
and leadeth him in the way *that is* not good.
30 He shutteth his eyes to devise froward
things: moving his lips he bringeth evil to pass.
31 [r]The hoary head *is* a crown
of glory, *if* it be found in the way
of righteousness.
32 [s]*He that is* slow to anger
is better than the mighty; and he that
ruleth his spirit, than he that taketh a
city.
33 The lot is cast into the lap: but the
whole disposing thereof *is* of the LORD.

[n]Chap. vi. 14, 19; xv. 18; xxvi. 21; xxix. 22.——[o]Heb. *sendeth forth*——[p]Chap. xvii. 9——[q]Chap. i. 10, &c.——[r]Chap. xx. 29——[s]Chap. xix. 11

A wicked man labours as much to bring about an evil purpose, as the *quarryman* does to dig up stones.

In his lips—a burning fire.] His words are as *inflammable*, in producing *strife* and *contention* among his neighbours, as *fire* is in igniting dry stubble.

Verse 30. *He shutteth his eyes to devise, &c.*] He *meditates deeply* upon ways and means to commit sin. He shuts his eyes that he may shut out all other ideas, that his whole soul may be in this.

Verse 31. *The hoary head is a crown of glory*] The latter part of the verse is very well added, for many a *sinner* has a *hoary head.*

Verse 32. *He that ruleth his spirit, than he that taketh a city.*] It is much easier to subdue an enemy *without* than one *within.* There have been many kings who had conquered nations, and yet were slaves to their own passions. Alexander, who conquered the world, was a slave to *intemperate anger*, and in a fit of it slew *Clytus*, the best and most intimate of all his friends, and one whom he loved beyond all others.

The spirit of this maxim is so self-evident, that most nations have formed similar proverbs. The classical reader will remember the following in HOR., Odar. lib. ii., Od. 2:—

Latius regnes, avidum domando
Spiritum, quam si Libyam remotis
Gadibus jungas, et uterque Pœnus
Serviat uni.

"By virtue's precepts to control
The furious passions of the soul,
Is over wider realms to reign,
Unenvied monarch, than if Spain
You could to distant Libya join,
And both the Carthages were thine."

FRANCIS.

And the following from OVID is not less striking:

—— Fortior est qui se, quam qui fortissima vincit
Mœnia, nec virtus altius ire potest.

"He is more of a hero who has conquered himself, than he who has taken the best fortified city."

Beyond this self-conquest the highest courage can not extend; nor did their philosophy teach any thing more sublime.

Verse 33. *The lot is cast into the lap*] On the *lot*, see the note on Num. xxvi. 55. How far it may be proper *now* to put difficult matters to the lot, after earnest prayer and supplication, I cannot say. *Formerly*, it was both lawful and efficient; for after it was solemnly cast, the decision was taken as coming immediately from the Lord. It is still practised, and its use is allowed even by writers on civil law. But those who need most to have recourse to the lot are those who have not *piety* to *pray* nor *faith* to trust to God for a positive decision. The lot should never be resorted to in indifferent matters; they should be those of the greatest importance, in which it appears impossible for human prudence or foresight to determine. In such cases the lot is *an appeal to God*, and he disposes of it according to his goodness, mercy, and truth. The result, therefore, cannot be *fortuitous.*

CHAPTER XVII

Contentment. The wise servant. The Lord tries the heart. Children a crown to their parents. We should hide our neighbour's faults. The poor should not be despised. Litigations and quarrels to be avoided. Wealth is useless to a fool. The good friend. A fool may pass for a wise man when he holds his peace.

A. M. cir. 3004
B. C. cir. 1000
Ante I. Olymp. cir. 224
Ante U. C. cir. 247

BETTER *is* a [a]dry morsel,
and quietness therewith,
than a house full of [b]sacrifices
with strife.
2 A wise servant shall have
rule over [c]a son that causeth
shame, and shall have part of the
inheritance among the brethren.

[a]Chap. xv. 17——[b]Or, *good cheer*——[c]Chap. x. 5; xix. 26

NOTES ON CHAP. XVII

Verse 1. *Better* is *a dry morsel*] Peace and contentment, and especially *domestic peace*, are beyond all other blessings.

A house full of sacrifices] A Hindoo priest, who officiates at a festival, sometimes receives so many *offerings* that *his house is filled with them*, so that many of them are damaged before they can be used.—*Ward.*

A. M. cir. 3004
B. C. cir. 1000
Ante I. Olymp. cir. 224
Ante U. C. cir. 247

3 [d]The fining pot *is* for silver, and the furnace for gold: but the LORD trieth the hearts.

4 A wicked doer giveth heed to false lips; *and* a liar giveth ear to a naughty tongue.

5 [e]Whoso mocketh the poor reproacheth his Maker: *and* [f]he that is glad at calamities shall not be [g]unpunished.

6 Children's children *are* the crown of old men; and the glory of children *are* their fathers.

7 [i]Excellent speech becometh not a fool: much less do [k]lying lips a prince.

8 [l]A gift *is as* [m]a precious stone in the eyes of him that hath it: whithersoever it turneth, it prospereth.

9 [n]He that covereth a transgression [o]seeketh love: but [p]he that repeateth a matter separateth *very* friends.

10 [q]A reproof entereth more into a wise man, than a hundred stripes into a fool.

A. M. cir. 3004
B. C. cir. 1000
Ante I. Olymp. cir. 224
Ante U. C. cir. 247

11 An evil *man* seeketh only rebellion: therefore a cruel messenger shall be sent against him.

12 Let [r]a bear robbed of her whelps meet a man, rather than a fool in his folly.

13 Whoso [s]rewardeth evil for good, evil shall not depart from his house.

14 The beginning of strife *is as* when one letteth out water: therefore [t]leave off contention, before it be meddled with.

15 [u]He that justifieth the wicked, and he that condemneth the just, even they both *are* abomination to the LORD.

16 Wherefore *is there* a price in the hand of a fool to get wisdom, [v]seeing *he hath* no heart *to it?*

17 [w]A friend loveth at all times, and a brother is born for adversity.

18 [x]A man void of [y]understanding striketh

[d]Psa. xxvi. 2; chap. xxvii. 21; Jer. xvii. 10; Mal. iii. 3——[e]Chap. xiv. 31——[f]Job xxxi. 29; Obad. 12——[g]Heb. *held innocent*——[h]Psa. cxxvii. 3; cxxviii. 3——[i]Heb. *a lip of excellency*——[k]Heb. *a lip of lying*——[l]Chap. xviii. 16; xix. 6——[m]Heb. *a stone of grace*——[n]Chap. x. 12——[o]Or, *procureth*——[p]Chap. xvi. 28——[q]Or, *A reproof aweth more a wise man than to strike a fool a hundred times*——[r]Hos. xiii. 8——[s]Psa. cix. 4, 5; Jer. xviii. 20; see Rom. xii. 17; 1 Thess. v. 15; 1 Pet. iii, 9——[t]Chap. xx. 3; 1 Thess. iv. 11——[u]Exod. xxiii. 7. chap. xxiv. 24; Isa. v. 23——[v]Ch. xxi. 25, 26——[w]Ruth i. 16; ch. xviii. 24——[x]Ch. vi. 1; xi. 15——[y]Heb; *heart*

Verse 3. *The fining pot* is *for silver*] When *silver* is *mixed*, or suspected to be mixed, with *base metal*, it must be subjected to such a test as the *cupel* to purify it. And gold also must be purified by the action of the *fire*. So God tries hearts. He sends afflictions which penetrate the soul, and give a man to see his state, so that he may apply to the *spirit of judgment* and *the spirit of burning*, to destroy what cannot stand the fire, to separate and burn up all the dross.

Verse 4. *A wicked doer giveth heed*] An evil heart is disposed and ever ready to receive evil; and liars delight in lies.

Verse 5. *He that is glad at calamity*] He who is pleased to hear of the misfortune of another will, in the course of God's just government, have his own multiplied.

Verse 7. *Excellent speech becometh not a fool*] This proverb is suitable to those who affect, in public speaking, fine language, which neither comports with their ordinary conversation, nor with their education. Often *fine words* are injudiciously brought in, and are as unbecoming and irrelevant as a cart wheel among clockwork.

Verse 8. *A gift* is as *a precious stone*] It both enriches and ornaments. In the latter clause there is an evident allusion to *cut stones*. Whithersoever you *turn them*, they *reflect the light*, are *brilliant* and *beautiful*.

Verse 10. *A reproof entereth more*] Though the *rod*, judiciously applied, is a *great instrument of knowledge*, yet it is of no use where incurable dulness or want of intellect, prevails. Besides, there are *generous dispositions* on which *counsel* will work more than stripes.

Verse 12. *Let a bear robbed of her whelps*] At which times such animals are peculiarly fierce. See the note on 2 Sam. xvii. 8.

Verse 13. *Whoso rewardeth evil for good*] Here is a most awful warning. As many persons are guilty of the sin of *ingratitude*, and of paying *kindness* with *unkindness*, and *good* with *evil*, it is no wonder we find so much *wretchedness* among men; for God's word cannot fail; evil shall not depart from the houses and families of such persons.

Verse 14. *The beginning of strife* is as *when one letteth out water*] As soon as the smallest breach is made in the dike or dam, the water begins to *press* from all parts *towards the breach;* the resistance becomes too great to be successfully opposed, so that dikes and all are speedily swept away. Such is the beginning of contentions, quarrels, lawsuits, &c.

Leave off contention, before it be meddled with.] As you see what an altercation must lead to, therefore do not begin it. Before it be *mingled together*, התגלע *hithgalla*, before the spirits of the contending parties come into conflict—are joined together in battle, and begin to deal out mutual reflections and reproaches. When you see that the dispute is likely to take this turn, leave it off immediately.

Verse 17. *A friend loveth at all times*] Equally in *adversity* as in *prosperity*. And a *brother*, according to the ties and interests of consanguinity, is *born* to support and comfort a *brother* in *distress*.

Verse 18. *Striketh hands*] *Striking* each

A. M. cir. 3004 B. C. cir. 1000 Ante I. Olymp. cir. 224 Ante U. C. cir. 247

hands, *and* becometh surety in
the presence of his friend.
19 He loveth transgression that
loveth strife: *and* [z]he that exalteth his gate seeketh destruction.
20 [a]He that hath a froward heart findeth no
good: and he that hath [b]a perverse tongue
falleth into mischief.
21 [c]He that begetteth a fool *doeth it* to his
sorrow: and the father of a fool hath no joy.
22 [d]A merry heart doeth good [e]*like* a
medicine: [f]but a broken spirit drieth the
bones.
23 A wicked *man* taketh a gift out of the
bosom [g]to pervert the ways of judgment.

[z]Ch. xvi. 18——[a]Heb. *the froward of heart*——[b]James iii. 8——[c]Ch. x. 1; xix. 13; ver. 25——[d]Chap. xv. 13, 15; xii. 25——[e]Or, *to a medicine*——[f]Psa. xxii. 15

24 [h]Wisdom *is* before him
that hath understanding: but the
eyes of a fool *are* in the ends
of the earth.
25 [i]A foolish son *is* a grief to his father
and a bitterness to her that bare him.
26 [k]Also to punish the just *is* not good, *nor*
to strike princes for equity.
27 [l]He that hath knowledge spareth his
words: *and* a man of understanding is of [m]an
excellent spirit.
28 [n]Even a fool, when he holdeth his
peace, is counted wise: *and* he that shutteth
his lips *is esteemed* a man of understanding.

[g]Exod. xxiii. 8——[h]Ch. xiv. 6; Eccles. ii. 14; viii. 1 [i]Ch. x. 1; xv. 20; xix. 13; ver. 21——[k]Ver. 15; ch. xviii. 5 [l]James i. 19——[m]Or, *a cool spirit*——[n]Job xiii. 5

other's hands, or *shaking hands*, was anciently the *form* in concluding a contract. See notes on chap. vi. 1.

Verse 19. *He that exalteth his gate*] In different parts of Palestine they are obliged to have the doors of their courts and houses *very low*, not more than *three* feet high, to prevent the Arabs, who scarcely ever leave the backs of their horses, from *riding into the courts and houses*, and spoiling their goods. He, then, who, through pride and ostentation, made a *high gate*, exposed himself to *destruction;* and is said here to *seek it*, because he must know that this would be a necessary consequence of *exalting his gate*. But although the above is a fact, yet possibly *gate* is here taken for the *mouth;* and the *exalting of the gate* may mean proud boasting and arrogant speaking, such as has a tendency to kindle and maintain strife. And this interpretation seems to agree better with the scope of the context than the above.

Verse 22. *A merry heart doeth good* like *a medicine*] Instead of נהה *gehah*, a *medicine*, it appears that the *Chaldee* and *Syriac* had read in their copies גוה *gevah*, the body, as they translate in this way. This makes the apposition here more complete: "A merry heart doeth good to the *body;* but a broken spirit drieth the *bones*." Nothing has such a direct tendency to ruin health and waste out life as grief, anxiety, fretfulness, bad tempers, &c. All these work *death*.

Verse 23. *A gift out of the bosom*] Out of his *purse;* as in their *bosoms*, above their girdles, the Asiatics carry their *purses*. I have often observed this.

Verse 24. Are *in the ends of the earth.*] Wisdom is within the *sight* and *reach* of every man: but he whose *desires* are scattered abroad, who is always aiming at impossible things, or is of an unsteady disposition, is not likely to find it.

Verse 26. Nor *to strike princes for equity.*] To fall out with the ruler of the people, and to take off his head under pretence of his not being a *just* or *equitable governor*, is *unjust*. To kill a king on the ground of justice is a most dreadful omen to any land. Where was it ever done, that it promoted the *public prosperity?* No experiment of this kind has ever yet succeeded, howsoever worthless the king might be.

Verse 28. *Even a fool*] He is counted wise *as to that particular*. He may know that he cannot speak well, and he has sense enough to keep from speaking. He is, as to that particular, a wise fool.

A man may be *golden-mouthed* and *silver-tongued* in eloquence; but to know *when* and *where* to *speak* and to be *silent*, is better than *diamonds*. But who that thinks he can speak well can refrain from speaking? His tongue has no rest.

CHAPTER XVIII

The man who separates himself and seeks wisdom. The fool and the wicked man. Deep wisdom. Contention of fools. The talebearer and the slothful. The name of the Lord. Pride and presumption because of riches. Hastiness of spirit. The wounded spirit. The influence of gifts. The lot. The offended brother. The influence of the tongue. A wife a good from God. The true friend.

A. M. cir. 3004 B. C. cir. 1000 Ante I. Olymp. cir. 224 Ante U. C. cir. 247

THROUGH [a]desire a man,
having separated himself,
seeketh *and* intermeddleth with
all wisdom.
2 A fool hath no delight in understanding,
but that his heart may discover itself.
3 When the wicked cometh, *then* cometh
also contempt, and with ignominy reproach.
4 [b]The words of a man's mouth *are as*
deep waters, *and* [c]the well-spring of wisdom
as a flowing brook.
5 [d]*It is* not good to accept
the person of the wicked, to
overthrow the righteous in judgment.
6 A fool's lips enter into contention, and his
mouth calleth for strokes.
7 [e]A fool's mouth *is* his destruction, and his
lips *are* the snare of his soul.
8 [f]The words of a [g]tale-bearer *are* [h]as
wounds, and they go down into the [i]inner-
most parts of the belly.

A. M. cir. 3004 B. C. cir. 1000 Ante I. Olymp. cir. 224 Ante U. C. cir. 247

---

[a]Or, *He that separateth himself, seeketh according to* his *desire,* and *intermeddleth in every business;* see Jude 19 —— [b]Chapter x. 11; xx. 5 —— [c]Psalm lxxviii. 2 —— [d]Leviticus xix. 15; Deuteronomy i. 17; xvi. 19; chapter xxiv. 23; xxviii. 21 —— [e]Chapter x. 14; xii. 13; xiii. 3; Ecclesiastes x. 12 —— [f]Chapter xii. 18; xxvi. 22 —— [g]Or, *whisperer* —— [h]Or, *like as when men are wounded* —— [i]Heb. *chambers*

NOTES ON CHAP. XVIII

Verse 1. *Through desire a man, having separated himself*] The original is difficult and obscure. The *Vulgate, Septuagint,* and *Arabic,* read as follows: "He who wishes to break with his friend, *and* seeks occasions or pretences, shall at all times be worthy of blame."

My old MS. Bible translates, **Occasioun seeketh that wil go awei fro a freend: at al tyme he schal ben wariable.**

Coverdale thus: "Who so hath pleasure to sowe discorde, piketh a quarrel in every thinge."

Bible by *Barker,* 1615: "Fro the desire *thereof* he will separate himself to seeke it, and occupie himself in all wisdome." Which has in the *margin* the following note: "He that loveth wisdom will separate himself from all impediments, and give himself wholly to seek it."

The Hebrew: לתאוה יבקש נפרד בכל תושיה יתגלע *lethaavah yebakkesh niphrad, bechol tushiyah yithgalla.* The nearest translation to the words is perhaps the following: "He who is separated shall seek the desired thing, (i. e., the object of his desire,) and shall intermeddle (mingle himself) with all realities or all essential knowledge." He finds that he can make little progress in the *investigation* of *Divine* and *natural* things, if he have much to do with *secular* or *trifling matters:* he therefore *separates himself* as well from *unprofitable pursuits* as from *frivolous company,* and then *enters into the spirit* of his pursuit; is not satisfied with *superficial* observances, but examines the *substance* and *essence,* as far as possible, of those things which have been the objects of his *desire.* This appears to me the best meaning: the reader may judge for himself.

Verse 2. *But that his heart may discover itself.*] It is a fact that most vain and foolish people are never satisfied in company, but in showing their own *nonsense* and *emptiness.* But this verse may be understood as confirming the view already given of the preceding, and may be translated thus: "But a fool doth not delight in understanding, though it should even manifest itself:" so I understand כי אם בהתגלות *ki im behithgalloth.* The *separated person* seeks understanding in every hidden thing, and feels his toil well repaid when he finds it, even after the most painful and expensive search: the other regards it not, though its *secret springs* should be *laid open to him* without toil or expense.

Verse 3. *When the wicked cometh, &c.*] would it not be better to read this verse thus? "When the wicked cometh contempt cometh; and with ignominy *cometh* reproach." A wicked man is despised even by the wicked. He who falls under ignominy falls under *reproach.*

Verse 4. *The words of a man's mouth*] That is, the wise sayings of a wise man are like *deep waters;* howsoever much you pump or draw off, you do not appear to lessen them.

The well-spring of wisdom] Where there is a *sound understanding,* and a deep, well-informed mind, its wisdom and its counsels are an incessant stream, מקור חכמה *mekor chochmah,* "the vein of wisdom," ever throwing out its healthy streams: but מקור חיים *mekor chaiyim,* "the vein of LIVES," is the reading of *eight* of *Kennicott's* and *De Rossi's* MSS., and is countenanced by the *Septuagint,* πηγη ζωης, "the fountain of life." And so the Arabic, عين حياة This is the more likely to be the *true reading,* because the *figure* of the heart propelling the blood through the great aorta, to send it to all parts of the animal system, is a favourite with *Solomon,* as it was with his father, *David.* See the note on Psa. xxxvi. 9; Prov. x. 11, &c.

Verse 5. *To accept the person of the wicked*] We must not, in judicial cases, pay any attention to a man's *riches, influence, friends, offices,* &c., but judge the case according to its own merits. But when the *wicked* rich man opposes and oppresses the poor *righteous,* then all those things should be utterly forgotten.

Verse 8. *The words of a tale-bearer*] דברי נרגן *dibrey nirgan,* "the words of the whisperer," the *busy-body,* the *busy, meddling croaker. Verba bilinguis,* "the words of the double-tongued."—*Vulgate.* **The wordes of the twisel tunge.**—Old MS. Bible. "The words of a slanderer."—*Coverdale.*

The words of a deceiver, the fair-spoken, deeply-malicious man, though they appear *soft* and *gracious,* are wounds deeply injurious.

The original word is כמתלהמים *kemithlahamim;* they *are as soft* or *simple,* or *undesigning.* But *Schultens* gives another meaning. He observes that لهم *lahamah* in *Arabic* signifies to "swallow down quickly or greedily." Such words are like dainties, eagerly swal-

A. M. cir. 3004
B. C. cir. 1000
Ante I. Olymp. cir. 224
Ante U. C. cir. 247

9 He also that is slothful in
his work is [k]brother to him that
is a great waster.
10 [l]The name of the LORD
is a strong tower: the righteous runneth into
it, and [m]is safe.
11 [n]The rich man's wealth is his strong
city, and as a high wall in his own conceit.
12 [o]Before destruction the heart of man is
haughty, and before honour *is* humility.
13 He that [p]answereth a matter [q]before he
heareth *it,* it *is* folly and shame unto him.
14 The spirit of a man will sustain his infirmity; but a wounded spirit who can bear?
15 The heart of the prudent
getteth knowledge; and the ear
of the wise seeketh knowledge.
16 [r]A man's gift maketh room
for him, and bringeth him before great men.
17 *He that is* first in his own cause *seemeth*
just; but his neighbour cometh and searcheth
him.
18 The lot causeth contentions to cease, and
parteth between the mighty.
19 A brother offended *is harder to be won*
than a strong city: and *their* contentions *are*
like the bars of a castle.
20 [s]A man's belly shall be satisfied with the

[k]Chap. xxviii. 24——[l]2 Sam. xxii. 3, 51; Psa. xviii. 2; xxvii. 1; lxi. 3, 4; xci. 2; cxliv. 2——[m]Heb. *is set aloft*
[n]Chap. x. 15——[o]Chap. xi. 2; xv. 33; xvi. 18

[p]Heb. *returneth a word*——[q]John vii. 51——[r]Gen. xxxii. 20; 1 Samuel xxv. 27; chap. xvii. 8; xxi. 14
[s]Chap. xii. 14; xiii. 2

lowed, because inviting to the taste; like gingerbread, apparently *gilded* over, though with *Dutch leaf*, which is a preparation of *copper;* or *sweetmeats* powdered over with *red candied seeds*, which are thus formed by *red lead;* both deeply ruinous to the tender bowels of the poor little innocents, but, because of their *sweetness* and *inviting colour, greedily swallowed down.* This makes a good reading, and agrees with the latter clause of the verse, "they go down into the innermost parts of the belly."

Verse 9. *He also that is slothful*] A *slothful* man neglects his *work*, and the *materials* go to ruin: the *waster*, he destroys the *materials.* They are both destroyers.

Verse 10. *The name of the Lord* is *a strong tower*] The *name of the Lord* may be taken for the *Lord himself;* he is a *strong tower*, a *refuge*, and *place of complete safety*, to all that trust in him. What a strong fortress is to the besieged, the like is God to his persecuted, tempted, afflicted followers.

Verse 11. *The rich man's wealth*] See chap. x. 15.

Verse 12. *Before destruction*] See on chap. xi. 2; and xvi. 18.

Verse 13. *He that answereth a matter*] This is a common case; before a man can tell out his story, another will begin *his.* Before a man has made his *response*, the other wishes to confute *piecemeal*, though he has had his own speech already. This is foolishness to them. They are ill-bred. There are many also that *give judgment* before they hear the whole of the cause, and express an *opinion* before they hear the state of the case. How absurd, stupid, and foolish!

Verse 14. *The spirit of a man will sustain*] A man sustains the ills of his body, and the trials of life, by the strength and energy of his mind. But if the *mind* be *wounded*, if this be *cast down*, if slow-consuming care and grief have shot the dagger into the soul, what can then sustain the man? Nothing but the unseen God. Therefore, let the afflicted *pray.* A man's *own spirit* has, in general, sufficient fortitude to bear up under the *unavoidable* trials of life; but when the *conscience* is wounded by sin, and the soul is dying by iniquity, *who can lift him up?* God alone; for salvation is of the Lord.

Verse 16. *A man's gift maketh room for him*] It is, and ever has been, a base and degrading practice in Asiatic countries, to bring a gift or present to the great man into whose presence you come. Without this there is no audience, no favour, no *justice.* This arose from the circumstance that men must not approach the *altar of God* without an *offering.* Potentates, wishing to be considered as *petty gods*, demanded a similar homage:—

Munera, crede mihi, capiunt hominesque deosque;
Placatur donis Jupiter ipse suis. OVID.

"Believe me, gifts prevail much with both gods and men: even Jupiter himself is pleased with his own offerings."

Verse 17. He that is *first in his own cause*] Any man may, in the first instance, make out a fair tale, because he has the choice of circumstances and arguments. But when the neighbour cometh and searcheth him, he examines all, dissects all, swears and cross-questions every witness, and brings out truth and fact.

Verse 18. *The lot causeth contentions to cease*] See note on chap. xvi. 33.

Verse 19. *A brother offended* is harder to be won *than a strong city*] Almost all the *versions* agree in the following reading: "A brother assisted by a brother, is like a fortified city; and their decisions are like the bars of a city." *Coverdale* is both plain and terse: "The unitie of brethren is stronger then a castell, and they that holde together are like the barre of a palace." The fable of the dying father, his sons, and the bundle of faggots, illustrates this proverb. Unity among brethren makes them invincible; small things grow great by concord. If we take the words according to the *common version*, we see them express what, alas! we know to be too generally true: that when brothers fall out, it is with extreme difficulty that they can be reconciled. And fraternal enmities are generally strong and inveterate.

Verse 20. *With the fruit of his mouth*] Our own words frequently shape our good or evil fortune in life.

A. M. cir. 3004 B. C. cir. 1000 Ante I. Olymp. cir. 224 Ante U. C. cir. 247

fruit of his mouth; *and* with the
increase of his lips shall he be
filled.
21 [t]Death and life *are* in the
power of the tongue: and they that love it
shall eat the fruit thereof.
22 [u]*Whoso* findeth a wife findeth a good
thing, and obtaineth favour of
the LORD.
23 The poor useth entreaties;
but the rich answereth [v]roughly.
24 A man *that hath* friends must show himself friendly: [w]and there is a friend *that*
sticketh closer than a brother.

A. M. cir. 3004 B. C. cir. 1000 Ante I. Olymp. cir. 224 Ante U. C. cir. 247

---

[t]Matt. xii. 37——[u]Chap. xix. 14; xxxi. 10

[v]James ii. 3——[w]Chap. xvii. 17

Verse 21. *Death and life* are *in the power of the tongue*] This may apply to all men. Many have lost their lives by their tongue, and some have saved their lives by it: but it applies most forcibly to *public pleaders;* on many of their tongues hangs *life* or *death.*

Verse 22. Whoso *findeth a wife findeth a good* thing] *Marriage,* with all its troubles and embarrassments, is a blessing from God; and there are *few cases* where a *wife of any sort* is not better than none, because celibacy is an evil; for God himself hath said, "It is not good for man to be alone." None of the versions, except the *Chaldee,* are pleased with the naked simplicity of the Hebrew text, hence they all add *good:* "He that findeth a GOOD wife findeth a good thing;" and most people, who have not deeply considered the subject, think the assertion, without this qualification, is absurd. Some copies of the *Targum,* and apparently one of *Kennicott's* MSS., have the addition טובה *tobah, good;* but this would be an authority too slender to justify changing the Hebrew text; yet *Houbigant, Kennicott,* and other able critics argue for it. The *Septuagint* is not satisfied without an addition: "But he who puts away a good wife, puts away a good thing: and he that retains an adulteress, is a fool and wicked." In this addition the *Vulgate, Syriac,* and *Arabic,* agree with the *Septuagint.* The *Hebrew* text as it stands, teaches a *general doctrine* by a *simple* but general *proposition:* "He that findeth a wife findeth a good thing." So St. Paul: "Marriage is honourable in all." Had the world been left, in this respect, to the unbridled propensities of man, in what a horrible state would society have been—if indeed society could have existed, or civilization have taken place—if *marriage* had not obtained among men! As to *good wives* and *bad wives,* they are relatively so, in general; and most of them that have been *bad* afterwards, have been *good* at first; and we well know the best things may deteriorate, and the world generally allows that where there are matrimonial contentions, there are *faults on both sides.*

Verse 24. *A man* that hath *friends must show himself friendly*] Love begets love; and love requires love as its recompense. If a man do not maintain a friendly carriage, he cannot expect to retain his friends. Friendship is a good plant; but it requires cultivation to make it grow.

There is a kind of factitious friendship in the world, that, to show one's self *friendly* in it, is very expensive, and in every way utterly unprofitable: it is maintained by expensive *parties. feasts,* &c., where the table groans with dainties, and where the *conversation* is either *jejune* and *insipid,* or *calumnious;* backbiting, talebearing, and scandal, being the general topics of the different squads in company.

There is a friend that *sticketh closer than a brother.*] In many cases the genuine friend has shown more attachment, and rendered greater benefits, than the natural brother. Some apply this to *God;* others to *Christ;* but the text has no such meaning.

But critics and commentators are not agreed on the translation of this verse. The original is condensed and obscure. איש רעים להתרועע *ish reim lehithroea,* or *lehithroeang,* as some would read, who translate: *A man of friends may ring again;* i. e., he may boast and mightily exult: but there is a friend, אהב *oheb,* a *lover,* that sticketh closer, דבק *dabek,* is *glued* or *cemented,* מאח *meach, beyond,* or more than, a brother. The former will continue during *prosperity,* but the latter continues *closely united* to his friend, even in the most disastrous circumstances.

Hence that maxim of *Cicero,* so often repeated, and so well known:—

Amicus certus in re incerta cernitur.

"In doubtful times the genuine friend is known."

A late commentator has translated the verse thus:—

The man that hath many friends is ready to be ruined:
But there is a friend that sticketh closer than a brother. HOLDEN.

"A frende that delyteth in love, doth a man more frendship, and sticketh faster unto him, than a brother."—*Coverdale.*

"A man that hath friends *ought to* show himself friendly, for a friend is nearer than a brother."—BARKER'S *Bible,* 1615.

"A man amyable to felowschip, more a freend schal ben thanne a brother."—Old MS. Bible. The two last verses in this chapter, and the two first of the next, are wanting in the Septuagint and Arabic.

These are the principal varieties; out of them the reader may choose. I have already given my opinion.

CHAPTER XIX

The worth of a poor upright man. Riches preserve friends. False witnesses. False friends. A king's wrath. The foolish son. The prudent wife. Slothfulness. Pity for the poor. The fear of the Lord. The spendthrift son. Obedience to parents.

A. M. cir. 3004 B. C. cir. 1000 Ante I. Olymp. cir. 224 Ante U. C. cir. 247

BETTER [a]*is* the poor that
walketh in his integrity,
than *he that is* perverse in his
lips, and is a fool.
2 Also, *that* the soul *be* without knowledge,
it is not good; and he that hasteth with *his*
feet sinneth.
3 [b]The foolishness of man perverteth his
way; [c]and his heart fretteth against the
LORD.
4 [d]Wealth maketh many friends: but the
poor is separated from his neighbour.
5 [e]A false witness shall not be [f]unpun-
ished, and *he that* speaketh lies shall not
escape.
6 [g]Many will entreat the favour of the
prince: and [h]every man *is* a friend to [i]him
that giveth gifts.
7 [k]All the brethren of the poor do hate him:
how much more do his friends
go [l]far from him? he pursueth
them with words, *yet* they *are*
wanting *to him.*
8 He that getteth [m]wisdom loveth his own
soul: he that keepeth understanding [n]shall
find good.
9 [o]A false witness shall not be unpunished,
and *he that* speaketh lies shall perish.
10 Delight is not seemly for a fool; much
less [p]for a servant to have rule over princes.
11 [q]The [r]discretion of a man deferreth his
anger; [s]and *it is* his glory to pass over a
transgression.
12 [t]The king's wrath *is* as the roaring of a
lion: but his favour *is* [u]as dew upon the grass.
13 [v]A foolish son *is* the calamity of his father: [w]and the contentions of a wife *are* a
continual dropping.

---

[a]Chap. xxviii. 6——[b]Chap. xiv. 24; xv. 2, 14——[c]Psa. xxxvii. 7——[d]Chap. xiv. 20——[e]Ver. 9; Exod. xxiii. 1; Deut. xix. 16, 19; chap. vi. 19; xxi. 28——[f]Heb. *held innocent*——[g]Chap. xxix. 26——[h]Chap. xvii. 8; xviii. 16; xxi. 14——[i]Heb. *a man of gifts*——[k]Chap. xiv. 20

[l]Psa. xxxviii. 11——[m]Heb. *a heart*——[n]Ch. xvi. 20——[o]Ver. 5——[p]Ch. xxx. 22; Eccles. x. 6, 7——[q]Ch. xiv. 29; James i. 19——[r]Or, *prudence*——[s]Ch. xv i. 32——[t]Ch. xvi. 14, 15; xx. 2; xxviii. 15——[u]Hos. xiv. 5——[v]Ch. x. 1; xv. 20; xvii. 21, 25——[w]Ch. xxi. 9, 19; xxvii. 15

NOTES ON CHAP. XIX

Verse 1. *Better* is *the poor*] The upright poor man is always to be preferred to the rich or *self-sufficient* fool.

Verse 2. *Also,* that *the soul* be *without knowledge,* it is *not good*] Would it not be plainer, as it is more *literal,* to say, "Also, to be without knowledge, is not good for the soul?" The soul was made for God; and to be without his *knowledge,* to be *unacquainted with him,* is not only *not good,* but the *greatest evil* the soul can suffer, for it involves all other evils. The *Chaldee* and *Syriac* have: "He who knows not his own soul, it is not good to him." "Where no discretion is, there the soul is not well."—*Coverdale.*

And he that hasteth with his *feet sinneth.*] And this will be the case with him who is not Divinely instructed. A *child* does nothing *cautiously,* because it is uninstructed; a *savage* is also *rash* and *precipitate,* till *experience* instructs him. A man who has not the knowledge of God is incautious, rash, headstrong, and precipitate: and hence he *sinneth*—he is continually *missing the mark,* and wounding his own soul.

Verse 3. *The foolishness of man*] Most men complain of cross providences, because they get into straits and difficulties through the *perverseness of their ways;* and thus *they fret against God;* whereas, in every instance, they are the causes of their own calamities. O how inconsistent is man!

Verse 4. *The poor is separated from his neighbour.*] Because he has the "disease of all-shunned poverty."

Verse 7. *Do hate him*] They *shun* him as they do the person they *hate.* They neither *hate* him *positively,* nor *love* him: they *disregard* him; they will have nothing to do with him. שנא *sana* signifies not only to hate, but to show a less degree of love to one than another. So Jacob loved Rachel, but hated Leah—showed her less affection than he did to Rachel.

Verse 10. *Delight is not seemly for a fool*] תענוג *taanug,* splendid or luxurious living, rank, equipage, &c. These sit ill on a *fool,* though he be by birth a *lord.*

For a servant to have rule over princes.] I pity the king who delivers himself into the hands of his own ministers. Such a one loses his character, and cannot be respected by his subjects, or rather *their* subjects. But it is still worse when a person of mean extraction is raised to the throne, or to any *place of power;* he is generally cruel and tyrannical.

Verse 11. It is *his glory to pass over a transgression.*] "No," says what is termed a *man of honour;* "he must meet me as a gentleman; I must have his blood, let God say what he will." O poor, dastardly coward! thou canst not bear the reproach of poor, flimsy, paltry fellows who ridicule thee, because thou hast refused to commit murder. Such laws should be put down by law; and the man that *gives a challenge* should be hanged, because he *intends* to commit *murder.*

Verse 12. *The king's wrath* is *as the roaring of a lion*] There is nothing more dreadful than the roaring of this tyrant of the forest. At the sound of it all other animals tremble, flee away, and hide themselves. The *king* who is above law, and rules without law, and whose will is his own law, is like the *lion.* This is strongly descriptive of the character of *Asiatic* sovereigns.

Verse 13. *The contentions of a wife* are *a continual dropping.*] The man who has got such a wife is like a tenant who has got a *cottage* with

A. M. cir. 3004
B. C. cir. 1000
Ante I. Olymp. cir. 224
Ante U. C. cir. 247

14 [x]House and riches *are* the
inheritance of fathers: and [y]a
prudent wife *is* from the LORD.
15 [z]Slothfulness casteth into a
deep sleep; and an idle soul shall [a]suffer hunger.

16 [b]He that keepeth the commandment
keepeth his own soul: *but* he that despiseth
his ways shall die.

17 [c]He that hath pity upon the poor lendeth unto the LORD; and [d]that which he hath
given will he pay him again.

18 [e]Chasten thy son while there is hope,
and let not thy soul spare [f]for his crying.

19 A man of great wrath shall suffer punishment: for if thou deliver *him,* yet thou must
[g]do it again.

20 Hear counsel, and receive instruction,
that thou mayest be wise [h]in the latter end.

21 [i]*There are* many devices in a man's
heart; nevertheless the counsel of the LORD,
that shall stand.

22 The desire of a man *is* his kindness;
and a poor man *is* better than a
liar.

A. M. cir. 3004
B. C. cir. 1000
Ante I. Olymp. cir. 224
Ante U. C. cir. 247

23 [k]The fear of the LORD
tendeth to life: and *he that hath*
it shall abide satisfied; he shall not be visited
with evil.

24 [l]A slothful *man* hideth his hand in *his*
bosom, and will not so much as bring it to his
mouth again.

25 [m]Smite a scorner, and the simple [n]will
[o]beware; and [p]reprove one that hath understanding, *and* he will understand knowledge.

26 He that wasteth *his* father, *and* chaseth
away *his* mother, *is* [q]a son that causeth shame,
and bringeth reproach.

27 Cease, my son, to hear the instruction *that*
causeth to err from the words of knowledge.

28 [r]An ungodly witness scorneth judgment:
and [s]the mouth of the wicked devoureth
iniquity.

29 Judgments are prepared for scorners,
[t]and stripes for the back of fools.

---

[x]2 Cor. xii. 14——[y]Chap. xviii. 22——[z]Ch. vi. 9——[a]Ch. x. 4; xx. 13; xxiii. 21——[b]Luke x. 28; xi. 28——[c]Chap. xxviii. 27; Eccles. xi. 1; Matt. x. 42; xxv. 40; 2 Cor. ix. 6, 7, 8; Heb. vi. 10——[d]Or, *his deed*——[e]Ch. xiii. 24; xxiii. 13; xxix. 17——[f]Or, *to his destruction,* or *to cause him to die*——[g]Heb. *add*——[h]Psa. xxxvii. 37

[i]Job xxiii. 13; Psa. xxxiii. 10, 11; ch. xvi. 1, 3; Isa. xiv. 26, 27; xlvi. 10; Acts v. 39; Heb. vi. 17——[k]1 Tim. iv. 8——[l]Ch. xv. 19; xxvi. 13, 15——[m]Ch. xxi. 11——[n]Heb. *will be cunning*——[o]Deut. xiii. 11——[p]Ch. ix. 8——[q]Chap. xvii. 2——[r]Heb. *A witness of Belial*——[s]Job xv. 16; xx. 12, 13; xxxiv. 7——[t]Chap. x. 13; xxvi. 3

---

a *bad roof,* through every part of which the rain either *drops* or *pours.* He can neither *sit, stand, work,* nor *sleep,* without being exposed to these *droppings.* God help the man who is in such a case, with *house* or *wife!*

Verse 14. *A prudent wife* is *from the Lord.*] One who has a good understanding, אשה משכלת *ishshah mascaleth;* who avoids complaining, though she may often have cause for it.

Verse 15. *Into a deep sleep*] תרדמה *tardemah,* the same into which Adam was thrown, before Eve was taken from his side. Sloth renders a man utterly unconscious of all his interests. Though he has frequently felt hunger, yet he is regardless that his continual slothfulness must necessarily plunge him into more sufferings.

Verse 17. *Lendeth unto the Lord*] O what a word is this! God makes himself debtor for every thing that is given to the *poor!* Who would not *advance much* upon such *credit? God will pay it again.* And in no case has he ever forfeited his word.

Verse 18. *Let not thy soul spare for his crying.*] This is a hard precept for a *parent.* Nothing affects the heart of a parent so much as a child's *cries* and *tears.* But it is better that the *child* may be caused to *cry,* when the correction may be healthful to his soul, than that the parent should *cry* afterwards, when the child is grown to *man's* estate, and his evil habits are *sealed for life.*

Verse 19. *A man of great wrath*] He who is of an *irritable, fiery* disposition, will necessarily get himself into many broils; and he that is *surety* for him once is likely to be called on again and again for the same friendly office.

Verse 21. There are *many devices, &c.*] The same sentiment as in chap. xvi. 1, where see the note.

Verse 24. *A slothful* man *hideth his hand in* his *bosom*] Is too lazy to feed himself. If he dip his hand *once* in the dish, he is too lazy to put it in a *second* time. It is a strange case that a man, through his excessive slothfulness, would rather starve than put himself to the trouble to eat.

Verse 26. *He that wasteth* his *father*] Destroys his substance by riotous or extravagant living, so as to embitter his latter end by poverty and affliction; and adds to this wickedness the *expulsion of his aged* widowed *mother* from the paternal house; *is a son of shame*—a most shameful man; and *a son of reproach*—one whose conduct cannot be sufficiently execrated. **Who tormentith the fader, and fleeth the modir, schenful schal ben, and unblisful.**—Old MS. Bible. The common reading of the *Vulgate* is, *et fugat matrem, and expels his mother;* but the *Old Bible* was taken from a copy that had *fugit matrem, shuns* his *mother, flees* away from her, *leaves her* to affliction and penury. It is prostitution of the term to call such, *man.*

Verse 27. *Cease, my son*] Hear nothing that would lead thee away from God and his truth.

Verse 29. *Stripes for the back of fools.*] *Profane* and *wicked* men expose themselves to the punishments denounced against such by just laws. Avoid, therefore, both their company and their end.

CHAPTER XX

Against wine and strong drink. We should avoid contentions. The sluggard. The righteous man. Weights and measures. Tale-bearers. The wicked son. The wise king. The glory of young men. The beauty of old men. The benefit of correction.

A. M. cir. 3004
B. C. cir. 1000
Ante I. Olymp. cir. 224
Ante U. C. cir. 247

WINE [a]*is* a mocker, strong
drink *is* raging: and whosoever *is* deceived thereby is not
wise.
2 [b]The fear of a king *is* as the roaring of a
lion: *whoso* provoketh him to anger [c]sinneth
against his own soul.
3 [d]*It is* an honour for a man to cease from
strife: but every fool will be meddling.
4 [e]The sluggard will not plough by reason
of the [f]cold; [g]*therefore* shall he beg in harvest and *have* nothing.
5 [h]Counsel in the heart of man *is like* deep
water: but a man of understanding will draw
it out.
6 [i]Most men will proclaim every one his
own [k]goodness; but [l]a faithful
man who can find?

A. M. cir. 3004
B. C. cir. 1000
Ante I. Olymp. cir. 224
Ante U. C. cir. 247

7 [m]The just *man* walketh in
his integrity: [n]his children *are*
blessed after him.
8 [o]A king that sitteth in the throne of
judgment scattereth away all evil with his
eyes.
9 [p]Who can say, I have made my heart
clean, I am pure from my sin?
10 [q]Divers [r]weights, *and* [s]divers measures,
both of them *are* alike abomination to the
LORD.
11 Even a child is [t]known by his doings,
whether his work *be* pure, and whether *it be*
right.

[a]Gen. ix. 21; chap. xxiii. 29, 30; Isa. xxviii. 7; Hos. iv. 11; [b]Chap. xvi. 14; xix. 12——[c]Chap. viii. 36——[d]Ch. xvii. 14——[e]Chap. x. 4; xix. 24——[f]Or, *winter*——[g]Ch. xix. 15——[h]Chap. xviii. 4——[i]Chap. xxv. 14; Matt. vi. 2; Luke xviii. 11——[k]Or, *bounty*——[l]1 Sam. xxii. 14; Psa. xii. 10; chap. xxviii. 20; Luke xviii. 8

[m]2 Cor. i. 12——[n]Psa. xxxvii. 26; cxii. 2——[o]Ver. 26——[p]1 Kings viii. 46; 2 Chron. vi. 36; Job xiv. 4; Psa. li. 5; Eccles. vii. 20; 1 Cor. iv. 4; 1 John i. 3——[q]Deut. xxv. 13, &c.; ver. 23; chap. xi. 1; xvi. 11; Mic. vi. 10, 11——[r]Heb. *A stone and a stone*——[s]Heb. *an ephah and an ephah*——[t]Matt. vii. 16

NOTES ON CHAP. XX

Verse 1. *Wine is a mocker*] It *deceives* by its *fragrance*, *intoxicates* by its *strength*, and renders the intoxicated *ridiculous*.

Strong drink] שכר *shechar*, any strong fermented liquor, whether of the *vine*, *date*, or *palm* species.

Verse 2. *The fear of a king*] Almost the same with chap. xix. 12, which see.

Verse 3. It is *an honour for a man*] The same sentiment as chap. xix. 11.

Verse 4. *The sluggard will not plough*] For other parts of this character, see the preceding chapter. It is seldom that there is a *season* of very cold weather in Palestine; very cold *days* sometimes occur, with wind, rain, and sleet. They begin their ploughing in the latter end of *September*, and sow their early wheat by the middle of *October*. And this is often the case in England itself. The meaning of the proverb is: the slothful man, under the pretence of unfavourable weather, neglects cultivating his land till the proper time is elapsed.

Verse 5. *Counsel in the heart of man*] Men of the deepest and most comprehensive minds are rarely apt, unsolicited, to join in any discourse, in which they might appear even to the greatest advantage; but a *man of understanding* will *elicit* this, by questions framed for the purpose, and thus *pump* up the salubrious waters from the deep and capacious well. The metaphor is fine and expressive.

Verse 6. *Most men will proclaim*] **Many men merciful ben clepid: a feithful man forsoth, who schal finde?**—Old MS. Bible.

Verse 8. *A king that sitteth in the throne of judgment*] Kings should see to the administration of the *laws*, as well as of the *state transactions*, of their kingdom. In the British constitution there is a *court* for the *king*, called the *King's Bench*, where he *should* sit, and where he is always *supposed* to be sitting. The *eyes*—the *presence*, of the monarch in such a place, *scatter evil*—he sees into the case himself, and gives right judgment, for he can have no *self-interest*. Corrupt judges, and falsifying counsellors, cannot stand before him; and the *villain* is too deeply struck with the *majesty* and state of the monarch, to *face out* iniquity before him.

Verse 9. *Who can say, I have made my heart clean*] No man. But thousands can testify that the blood of Jesus Christ has cleansed them from all unrighteousness. And he is *pure from his sin*, who is justified freely through the redemption that is in Jesus.

Verse 10. *Divers weights and divers measures*] **A peise and a peise**;—Old MS. Bible: from the French *pois*, weight. Hebrew: "A stone and a stone; an ephah and an ephah." One the *standard*, the other *below* it; one to *buy* with, the other to *sell* by.

Verse 11. *Even a child is known by his doings*] That is, in general terms, the *effect* shows the nature of the cause. "A childe is known by his conversation," says *Coverdale*. A child is easily detected when he has done evil; he immediately begins to excuse and vindicate himself, and profess his innocence, almost before accusation takes place. Some think the words should be understood, *every child will dissemble;* this amounts nearly to the meaning given above. But probably the principal thing

A. M. cir. 3004 B. C. cir. 1000 Ante I. Olymp. cir. 224 Ante U. C. cir. 247

12 [u]The hearing ear, and the
seeing eye, the LORD hath made
even both of them.
13 [v]Love not sleep, lest thou
come to poverty; open thine eyes, *and* thou
shalt be satisfied with bread.
14 *It is* naught, *it is* naught, saith the
buyer: but when he is gone his way, then he
boasteth.
15 There is gold, and a multitude of rubies:
but [w]the lips of knowledge *are* a precious
jewel.
16 [x]Take his garment that is surety *for* a
stranger: and take a pledge of
him for a strange woman.
17 [y]Bread [z]of deceit *is* sweet
to a man; but afterwards his
mouth shall be filled with gravel.
18 [a]*Every* purpose is established by counsel: [b]and with good advice make war.
19 [c]He that goeth about *as* a tale-bearer
revealeth secrets: therefore meddle not with
him [d]that [e]flattereth with his lips.
20 [f]Whoso curseth his father or his mother,
[g]his [h]lamp shall be put out in obscure darkness.

A. M. cir. 3004 B. C. cir. 1000 Ante I. Olymp. cir. 224 Ante U. C. cir. 247

---

[u]Exod. iv. 11; Psa. xciv. 9——[v]Chapter vi. 9; xii. 11; xix. 15; Rom. xii. 11——[w]Job xxviii. 12, 16, 17, 18, 19; chapter iii. 15; viii. 11——[x]Chapter xxii. 26, 27; xxxii. 13——[y]Chapter ix. 17——[z]Hebrew, *Bread of lying*, or *falsehood*——[a]Chapter xv. 22; xxiv. 6——[b]Luke xiv. 31——[c]Chapter xi. 13——[d]Rom. xvi. 18——[e]Or, *enticeth*——[f]Exod. xxi. 17; Lev. xx. 9; Matt. xv. 4——[g]Job xviii. 5, 6; chapter xxiv. 20——[h]Or, *candle*

---

intended by the wise man is, that we may easily learn from the *child* what the *man* will be. In general, they give indications of those *trades* and *callings* for which they are adapted by nature. And, on the whole, we cannot go by a surer guide in preparing our children for future life, than by observing their early propensities. The future *engineer* is seen in the little *handicraftsman* of two years old. Many children are crossed in these early propensities to a particular calling, to *their* great prejudice, and the loss of their parents, as they seldom settle at, or succeed in, the business to which they are tied, and to which nature has given them no tendency. These infantine predilections to particular callings, we should consider as indications of Divine Providence, and its calling of them to that work for which they are peculiarly fitted.

Verse 12. *The hearing ear and the seeing eye*] Every *good* we possess comes from God; and we should neither use our *eyes*, nor our *ears*, nor *any thing* we possess, but in strict subserviency to his will.

Verse 13. *Love not sleep, lest thou come to poverty*] Sleep, indescribable in its nature, is an indescribable *blessing;* but how often is it turned into a *curse!* It is like *food;* a certain measure of it restores and invigorates exhausted nature; more than *that* oppresses and destroys life. A lover of sleep is a paltry, insignificant character.

Verse 14. It is *naught*, it is *naught, saith the buyer*] How apt are men to decry the goods they wish to purchase, in order that they may get them at a *cheaper rate;* and, when they have made their bargain and carried it *off*, *boast* to others at how much *less* than its *value* they have obtained it! Are such honest men? Is such knavery actionable? Can such be punished only in *another* world? St. Augustine tells us a pleasant story on this subject: A certain mountebank published, in the full theatre, that at the next entertainment he would *show to every man* present *what was in his heart.* The time came, and the concourse was immense; all waited, with deathlike silence, to hear what he would say to each. He stood up, and in a single sentence redeemed his pledge:—

VILI vultis EMERE, et CARO VENDERE.

"You all wish to BUY CHEAP, and SELL DEAR."

He was applauded; for every one felt it to be a description of his own heart, and was satisfied that all others were similar. "In quo dicto levissimi scenici omnes tamen conscientias invenerunt suas."—DE TRINITATE, lib. xiii., c. 3; OPER. vol. vii., col. 930.

Verse 15. *There is gold*] *Gold* is valuable, *silver* is valuable, and so are *jewels;* but the *teachings* of *sound knowledge* are more valuable than all.

Verse 16. *Take his garment that is surety* for *a stranger*] I suppose the meaning to be, If a stranger or unknown person become surety in a case, greater caution should be used, and such security taken from this *stranger* as would prevent him from running away from his engagements.

Verse 17. *Bread of deceit* is *sweet*] Property acquired by *falsehood, speculation*, &c., without labour, is pleasant to the unprincipled, slothful man; but there is a *curse* in it, and the issue will prove it.

Verse 18. *With good advice make war.*] Perhaps there is not a precept in this whole book so little regarded as this. Most of the *wars* that are undertaken are wars of injustice, ambition, aggrandizement, and caprice, which can have had no previous *good counsel.* A minister, who is perhaps neither a *good* nor a *great* man, counsels his king to make war; the *cabinet* must be brought into it, and a *sufficient number* out of the states of the kingdom gained over to support it. By and by, what was begun through *caprice* must be maintained through *necessity.* Places must be created, and offices must be filled with needy dependents, whose interest it may be to *protract the war*, till they get enough to pay their debts, and secure independence for life. And for these most important ends the blood of the country is spilled, and the treasures of the people exhausted! I have met with a fact precisely of this kind under the reign of Louis XIV.

Verse 20. *Whoso curseth his father*] Such persons were put to death under the law; see

A. M. cir. 3004 B. C. cir. 1000 Ante I. Olymp. cir. 224 Ante U. C. cir. 247

21 [i]An inheritance *may be* gotten hastily at the beginning;
[k]but the end thereof shall not
be blessed.
22 [l]Say not thou, I will recompense evil;
but [m]wait on the LORD, and he shall save
thee.
23 [n]Divers weights *are* an abomination unto
the LORD; and [o]a false balance *is* not good.
24 [p]Man's goings *are* of the LORD; how
can a man then understand his own way?
25 *It is* a snare to the man *who* devoureth
that which is holy, and [q]after vows to make
inquiry.
26 [r]A wise king scattereth the
wicked, and bringeth the wheel
over them.
27 [s]The spirit of man *is* the
[t]candle of the LORD, searching all the inward
parts of the belly.
28 [u]Mercy and truth preserve the king:
and his throne is upholden by mercy.
29 The glory of young men *is* their strength:
and [v]the beauty of old men *is* the gray
head.
30 The blueness of a wound [w]cleanseth
away evil: so *do* stripes the inward parts of
the belly.

A. M. cir. 3004 B. C. cir. 1000 Ante I. Olymp. cir. 224 Ante U. C. cir. 247

---

[i]Chap. xxviii. 20——[k]Hab. ii. 6——[l]Deut. xxxii. 35; chap. xvii. 13; xxiv. 29; Rom. xii. 17, 19; 1 Thess. v. 15; 1 Peter iii. 9——[m]2 Sam. xvi.12——[n]Verse 10——[o]Heb. *balances of deceit*

[p]Psa. xxxvii. 23; chap. xvi. 9; Jer. x. 23——[q]Eccles. v. 4, 5——[r]Psa. ci. 5, &c.; ver. 8——[s]1 Cor. ii. 11 [t]Or, *lamp*——[u]Psa. ci. 1; chap. xxix. 14——[v]Ch. xvi. 31 [w]Heb. is *a purging medicine against evil*

Exod. xxi. 17; Lev. xx. 9; and here it is said, Their *lamp shall be put out*—they shall have no *posterity;* God shall cut them off both *root* and *branch.*

Verse 21. *An inheritance—gotten hastily*] Gotten by *speculation;* by *lucky hits;* not in the fair *progressive* way of *traffic,* in which money has its *natural increase.* All such inheritances are short-lived; God's blessing is not in them, because they are not the produce of *industry;* and they lead to *idleness, pride, fraud,* and *knavery.* A speculation in trade is a public nuisance and curse. How many honest men have been ruined by such!

Verse 22. *I will recompense evil*] Wait on the Lord; judgment is his, and his judgments are sure. In the mean time pray for the conversion of your enemy.

Verse 24. *Man's goings* are *of the Lord*] He, by his providence, governs all the great concerns of the world. Man often traverses these operations; but he does it to his own damage. An old writer quaintly says: "They who will carve for themselves shall cut their fingers."

Verse 25. Who *devoureth* that which is *holy*] It is a sin to take that which belongs to *God,* his *worship,* or his *work,* and devote it to one's own use.

And after vows to make inquiry.] That is, if a man be *inwardly* making a *rash vow,* the fitness or unfitness, the necessity, expediency, and propriety of the thing should be first carefully considered. But how foolish to make the vow first, and afterwards to inquire whether it was right in the sight of God to do it! This equally condemns all rash and inconsiderate conduct. My old MS. Bible translates, **Falling is of men often to bowen to seyntis, and after, the bouw is agen drawen.** Is it possible that *Wiclif* could have translated this verse thus? as it strongly countenances *vows to* and *invocations of saints.*

Verse 26. *Bringeth the wheel over them.*] He threshes them in his anger, as the *wheel does the grain on the threshing-floor.* Every one knows that grain was separated from its husks, in Palestine, by the feet of the oxen trampling among the sheaves, or bringing a rough-shod wheel over them. Asiatic kings often threshed their people, to bring out their property; but this is not what is intended here.

Verse 27. *The spirit of man* is *the candle of the Lord*] God has given to every man a *mind,* which *he so enlightens by his own Spirit,* that the man knows how to distinguish good from evil; and *conscience,* which springs from this, searches the inmost recesses of the soul.

Verse 28. *Mercy and truth preserve the king*] These are the brightest jewels in the royal crown; and those kings who are most governed by them have the stablest government.

Verse 29. *The glory of young men* is *their strength*] Scarcely any young man affects to be wise, learned, &c.; but all delight to *show their strength* and to be *reputed strong. Agility,* one evidence of strength, they particularly *affect;* and hence their various trials of strength and fleetness in public exercises.

And the beauty of old men is *the gray head.*] They no longer affect *strength* and *agility,* but they affect *wisdom, experience, prudent counsels,* &c., and are fond of being *reputed wise,* and of having respect paid to their *understanding* and *experience.*

Verse 30. *The blueness of a wound*] חברות *chabburoth,* from חבר *chabar,* to *unite,* to *join together.* Does it not refer to the cicatrice of a wound when, in its healing, the two lips are brought *together?* By this union the wound is *healed;* and by the previous discharge the lacerated ends of fibres and blood-vessels are purged away. So *stripes,* though they hurt for the time, become the means of *correcting* and *discharging* the *moral evil* of the inmost soul, the vice of the *heart,* the *easily-besetting sin.*

In this chapter, verses *fourteen* to *nineteen,* inclusive, are wanting in the *Septuagint* and *Arabic;* and the *tenth, eleventh, twelfth,* and *thirteenth,* come in after the *twenty-second.* It is difficult to account for these variations, unless they were occasioned by the change of leaves in MSS.

CHAPTER XXI

The king's heart is in the hand of God. We should practise mercy and justice. The lying tongue. The quarrelsome woman. The punishment of the wicked. The uncharitable. The private gift. The happiness of the righteous. The wicked a ransom for the righteous. The treasures of the wise. He who guards his tongue. Desire of the sluggard. The false witness. Salvation is of the Lord.

A. M. cir. 3004
B. C. cir. 1000
Ante I. Olymp. cir. 224
Ante U. C. cir. 247

THE king's heart *is* in the
hand of the LORD, *as* the
rivers of water: he turneth it
whithersoever he will.
2 [a]Every way of a man *is* right in his own
eyes: [b]but the LORD pondereth the hearts.
3 [c]To do justice and judgment *is* more acceptable to the LORD than sacrifice.
4 [d]A [e]high look, and a proud heart, *and*
[f]the ploughing of the wicked, *is* sin.
5 [g]The thoughts of the diligent *tend* only to
plenteousness; but of every one *that is* hasty
only to want.
6 [h]The getting of treasures by a lying
tongue *is* a vanity tossed to and
fro of them that seek death.
7 The robbery of the wicked
shall [i]destroy them; because
they refuse to do judgment.
8 The way of man *is* froward and strange:
but *as for* the pure, his work *is* right.
9 [k]*It is* better to dwell in a corner of the
housetop, than with [l]a brawling woman in [m]a
wide house.
10 [n]The soul of the wicked desireth evil:
his neighbour [o]findeth no favour in his eyes.
11 [p]When the scorner is punished, the simple is made wise: and when the wise is

A. M. cir. 3004
B. C. cir. 1000
Ante I. Olymp. cir. 224
Ante U. C. cir. 247

---

[a]Chap. xvi. 2——[b]Ch. xxiv. 12; Luke xvi. 15——[c]1 Sam. xv. 22; Psa. l. 8; chap. xv. 8; Isa. i. 11, &c.; Hos. vi. 6; Mic. vi. 7, 8——[d]Chap. vi. 17——[e]Heb. *Haughtiness of eyes*——[f]Or, *the light of the wicked*——[g]Chap. x. 4; xiii. 4

[h]Ch. x. 2; xiii. 11; xx. 21; 2 Pet. ii. 3——[i]Heb. *saw them*, or *dwell with them*——[k]Ver. 19; ch. xix. 13; xxv. 24; xxvii. 15——[l]Heb. *a woman of contentions*——[m]Heb. *a house of society*——[n]James iv. 5——[o]Heb. *is not favoured*——[p]Chap. xix. 25

NOTES ON CHAP. XXI

Verse 1. *The king's heart* is *in the hand of the Lord*] The Lord is the only ruler of princes. He alone can govern and direct their counsels. But there is an allusion here to the Eastern method *of watering their lands*. Several canals are dug from one stream; and by opening a particular sluice, the husbandman can direct a stream to whatever part he please: so the king's heart, wherever it turns; i. e., to whomsoever he is disposed to show favour. As the land is enriched with the streams employed in irrigation; so is the favourite of the king, by the royal bounty: and God can induce the king to give that bounty to whomsoever he will. See *Harmer*.

Verse 2. *The Lord pondereth the hearts.*] Every man feels strongly attached to his own opinions, modes of acting, &c.; and though he will not easily give up any thing to the judgment of a neighbour, whom he will naturally consider at least as fallible as himself, yet he should consider that the unerring eye of God is upon him; and he should endeavour to see that what he does is acceptable in the eye of his Maker and Judge.

Verse 3. *To do justice and judgment*] The words of Samuel to Saul. See note on 1 Sam. xv. 23.

Verse 4. *A high look*] The evidence of pride, self-conceit, and vanity. *A proud heart*, from which the *high look*, &c., come.

And *the ploughing*] נר *ner*, *lucerna*, the *lamp*, the prosperity and posterity of the wicked; *is sin*—it is evil in the *seed*, and evil in the *root*, evil in the *branch*, and evil in the *fruit*. They are full of sin themselves, and what they do is sinful.

Verse 6. *Of them that seek death*] Instead of מבקשי *mebakshey*, "them that seek," several MSS., some ancient editions, with *Symmachus*, the *Septuagint*, *Vulgate*, and *Arabic*, have מקשי *mokeshey*, the *snares*. He who gets treasures by a lying tongue, pursues vanity into the snares of death. Our common translation may be as good. But he who, by the snares of his *tongue*, endeavours to *buy* and *sell* to the *best advantage*, is *pursuing what* is *empty in itself;* and he is *ensnared* by *death*, while he is attempting to *ensnare* others.

Verse 7. *The robbery of the wicked*] The wicked shall be *terrified* and *ruined* by the means they use to aggrandize themselves. And as they refuse to do judgment, they shall have judgment without mercy.

Verse 9. *In a corner of the housetop*] A shed raised on the *flat roof:*—*a wide house;* בית חבר *beith chaber*, "a house of fellowship;" what we should call a *lodging-house*, or a *house occupied by several families*. This was usual in the *East*, as well as in the *West*. Some think a *house of festivity* is meant: hence my old MS. Bible has, **the hous and feste.**

Verse 11. *When the scorner is punished*] When those who mock at religion, blaspheme against its Author, and endeavour to poison society, and disturb the peace of the community by their false doctrine, meet with that degree of punishment which their crimes, as far as they affect the public peace, deserve; then *the simple*, who were either led away, or in danger of being led away, by their pernicious doctrines, *are made wise*. And when those thus *made wise* are *instructed* in the important truths which have been decried by those unprincipled men, then they receive knowledge; and one

A. M. cir. 3004 B. C. cir. 1000 Ante I. Olymp. cir. 224 Ante U. C. cir. 247

instructed, he receiveth knowledge.
12 The righteous *man* wisely
considereth the house of the
wicked: *but God* overthroweth the wicked
for *their* wickedness.
13 [q]Whoso stoppeth his ears at the cry of
the poor, he also shall cry himself, but shall
not be heard.
14 [r]A gift in secret pacifieth anger: and a
reward in the bosom strong wrath.
15 *It is* joy to the just to do judgment: [s]but
destruction *shall be* to the workers of iniquity.
16 The man that wandereth out of the way
of understanding shall remain in the congregation of the dead.
17 He that loveth [t]pleasure *shall be* a poor
man: he that loveth wine and oil shall not be
rich.
18 [u]The wicked *shall be* a ransom for the
righteous, and the transgressor for the upright.
19 [v]*It is* better to dwell [w]in the wilderness,
than with a contentious and an
angry woman.

A. M. cir. 3004 B. C. cir. 1000 Ante I. Olymp. cir. 224 Ante U. C. cir. 247

20 [x]*There is* treasure to be
desired and oil in the dwelling
of the wise; but a foolish man spendeth it up.
21 [y]He that followeth after righteousness
and mercy findeth life, righteousness, and
honour.
22 [z]A wise *man* scaleth the city of the
mighty, and casteth down the strength of the
confidence thereof.
23 [a]Whoso keepeth his mouth and his
tongue keepeth his soul from troubles.
24 Proud *and* haughty scorner *is* his name,
who dealeth [b]in proud wrath.
25 [c]The desire of the slothful killeth him;
for his hands refuse to labour.
26 He coveteth greedily all the day long:
but the [d]righteous giveth and spareth not.
27 [e]The sacrifice of the wicked *is* abomination: how much more, *when* he bringeth
[f]it with a wicked mind?

[q]Matt. vii. 2; xviii. 30, &c.; James ii. 13——[r]Ch. xvii. 8, 23; xviii. 16——[s]Ch. x. 29——[t]Or, *sport*——[u]Ch. xi. 8; Isa. xliii. 3, 4——[v]Ver. 9——[w]Heb. *in the land of the desert*——[x]Psa. cxii. 3; Matt. xxv. 3, 4——[y]Ch. xv. 9; Matt. v. 6

[z]Eccles. ix. 14, &c.——[a]Chap. xii. 13; xiii. 3; xviii. 21; James iii. 2——[b]Heb. *in the wrath of pride*——[c]Chap. xiii. 4——[d]Psa. xxxvii. 26; cxii. 9——[e]Psa. l. 9; chap. xv. 8; Isa. lxvi. 3; Jeremiah vi. 20; Amos v. 22——[f]Heb. *in wickedness*

such public example is made a blessing to thousands. But only *blasphemy* against *God* and the *Bible* should be thus punished. Private opinion the state should not meddle with.

Verse 12. *The righteous* man *wisely considereth*] This verse is understood as implying the *pious concern* of a righteous man, for a wicked family, whom he endeavours by his *instructions* to bring into the way of knowledge and peace.

Verse 13. *Whoso stoppeth his ears*] See the conduct of *the priest* and *Levite* to the man who *fell among thieves;* and let every man learn from this, that he who shuts his ear against the cry of the poor, shall have the ear of God shut against his cry. The words are quite plain; there is no difficulty here.

Verse 16. *The man* once enlightened, *that wandereth out of the way of understanding*, in which he *had* walked, *shall remain*—have a permanent residence—*in the congregation of the dead;* רפאים *rephaim, the lost;* either separate spirits in general, or rather the *assembly of separate spirits*, which had fallen from primitive rectitude; and shall not be restored to the Divine favour; particularly those sinners who were destroyed by the deluge. This passage intimates that those called *rephaim* are in a state of conscious existence. It is difficult to assign the true meaning of the word in several places where it occurs: but it seems to mean the state of separate spirits, i. e., of those separated from their bodies, and awaiting the judgment of the great day: but the *congregation* may also include the *fallen angels*. My old MS. Bible translates, **The man that errith fro the wei of doctrine, in the felowschip of geantis schal wonnen.**

Verse 17. *He that loveth pleasure*] That follows gaming, fowling, hunting, coursing, &c., when he should be attending to the culture of the fields, *shall be a poor man;* and, I may safely add, shall be so deservedly poor, as to have none to pity him.

Verse 18. *The wicked* shall be *a ransom for the righteous*] God often in his judgments cuts off the *wicked*, in order to prevent them from destroying the *righteous*. And in general, we find that the wicked fall into the traps and pits they have digged for the righteous.

Verse 22. *A wise* man *scaleth the city of the mighty*] Wisdom is in many respects preferable to strength, even in the case of defence. See what skill does in the fortification and reduction of strong places.

Verse 25. *The desire of the slothful killeth him*] He desires to eat, drink, and be clothed: but as he does *not labour*, hence he dies with this desire in his heart, envying those who possess plenty through their labour and industry. Hence he is said to *covet greedily all the day long*, ver. 26, while the *righteous*, who has been *laborious* and diligent, has enough to *eat*, and some to *spare*.

Verse 27. When *he bringeth it with a wicked mind?*] If such a person even bring the *sacrifices* and *offerings* which God *requires*, they are an abomination to him, because the man is *wicked;* and if such offerings be *imperfect* in themselves, or of goods *ill-gotten*, or offered by *constraint of custom*, &c., they are doubly abominable.

A. M. cir. 3004
B. C. cir. 1000
Ante I. Olymp. cir. 224
Ante U. C. cir. 247

28 [g]A [h]false witness shall
perish: but the man that heareth
speaketh constantly.
29 A wicked man hardeneth
his face: but *as for* the upright, he [i]directeth
his way.
30 [k]*There is* no wisdom nor understanding
nor counsel against
the LORD.
31 [l]The horse *is* prepared
against the day of battle: but [m]safety[n] *is* of
the LORD.

[g]Chap. xix. 5, 9——[h]Heb. *A witness of lies*——[i]Or, *considereth*——[k]Isa. viii. 9, 10; Jer. ix. 23; Acts v. 39——[l]Psalm xx. 7; xxxiii. 17; Isa. xxxi. 1——[m]Psalm iii. 8——[n]Or, *victory*

Verse 29. *He directeth his way*] Instead of יכין *yachin*, he *directeth*, upwards of *fifty* of *Kennicott's* and *De Rossi's* MSS., several ancient *editions*, with some of the *versions*, read יבין *yabin, he understands;* and because he *understands* his way, he is able to *direct* himself in walking in it.

Verse 31. *The horse* is *prepared against the day of battle*] *Horses* were not used among the Jews before the time of *Solomon*. There was a Divine command against them, Deut. xvii. 16; but Solomon transgressed it; see 1 Kings x. 29. But he here allows that a horse is a vain thing for safety; and that however strong and well appointed *cavalry* may be, still *safety, escape,* and *victory,* are of the Lord. Among the ancient Asiatics, the *horse* was used *only for war; oxen* laboured in the *plough* and *cart;* the *ass* and the *camel* carried *backloads;* and *mules* and *asses* served for *riding*. We often give the credit of a victory to *man*, when they who consider the circumstances see that it came from *God*.

CHAPTER XXII

A good reputation. The rich and the poor. The idle. Good habits formed in infancy. Injustice and its effects. The providence of God. The lewd woman. The necessity of timely correction. Exhortation to wisdom. Rob not the poor. Be not the companion of the froward. Avoid suretyship. Be honest. The industrious shall be favoured.

A. M. cir. 3004
B. C. cir. 1000
Ante I. Olymp. cir. 224
Anti U. C. cir. 247

A [a]*GOOD* name *is* rather to
be chosen than great riches,
and [b]loving favour rather than
silver and gold.
2 [c]The rich and poor meet together:
[d]the LORD *is* the Maker
of them all.
3 [e]A prudent *man* forseeth

[a]Eccles. vii. 1——[b]Or, *favour is better than,* &c.——[c]Ch. xxix. 13; 1 Cor. xii. 21——[d]Job xxxi. 15; chapter xiv. 31——[e]Chapter xiv. 16; xxvii. 12

NOTES ON CHAP. XXII

Verse 1. *A* good *name*] שם *shem*, a *name*, put for reputation, credit, fame. Used nearly in the same way that we use it: "He has got a name;" "his name stands high;" for "He is a man of credit and reputation." טבא *toba*, καλον, حمود *hamood*, and *bonum*, are added by the *Chaldee, Septuagint, Arabic,* and *Vulgate*, all signifying *good* or *excellent*.

Is *rather to be chosen than great riches*] Because character will support a man in many circumstances; and there are many *rich* men that have *no name:* but the *word* of the man of character will go farther than all their riches.

Verse 2. *The rich and poor meet together*] עשיר *ashir*, the *opulent*, whether in money, land, or property; רש *rash*, the man that is destitute of these, and lives by his labour, whether a handicraftsman, or one that tills the ground. In the order of God, the rich and the poor live together, and are mutually helpful to each other. Without the *poor*, the *rich* could not be supplied with the articles which they consume; for the poor include all the labouring classes of society: and without the *rich*, the *poor* could get no *vent* for the *produce* of their *labour*, nor, in many cases, *labour* itself. The *poor* have more *time* to labour than the mere necessaries of life require; their *extra* time is employed in providing a multitude of things which are called the *superfluities* of life, and which the *rich* especially consume. *All* the *poor man's time* is thus employed; and he is *paid* for his *extra labour* by the rich. The *rich* should not despise the *poor*, without whom he can neither have his *comforts*, nor *maintain* his *state*. The poor should not *envy* the *rich*, without whom he could neither get employment, nor the *necessaries of life*.

The Lord is *the Maker of them all.*] Both the *states* are in the order of God's *providence*, and both are *equally* important in his sight. Merely considered as *men*, God loves the *simple artificer* or *labourer* as much as he does the *king;* though the *office* of the latter, because of its entering into the plan of his government of the world, is of infinitely greatly consequence than the *trade* of the *poor artificer*. Neither should *despise* the *other;* neither should *envy* the *other*. Both are useful; both important; both absolutely necessary *to each other's welfare* and *support;* and both are accountable to God for the *manner* in which they acquit themselves in those *duties of life* which God has respectively assigned them. The *abject poor*—those who are destitute of *health* and the *means of life*—God in effect lays at the *rich man's door*, that by his *superfluities* they may be supported. How wise is that ordinance which has made the *rich* and the *poor!* Pity it were not better understood!

Verse 3. *A prudent* man *foreseeth the evil*] God in mercy has denied man the knowledge of

A. M. cir. 3004
B. C. cir. 1000
Ante I. Olymp. cir. 224
Ante U. C. cir. 247

the evil, and hideth himself: but
the simple pass on, and are
punished.
4 [f]By [g]humility *and* the fear
of the LORD *are* riches, honour, and life.
5 [h]Thorns *and* snares *are* in the way of the
froward: [i]he that doth keep his soul shall be
far from them.
6 [k]Train [l]up a child [m]in the way he should
go: and when he is old, he will not depart
from it.
7 [n]The rich ruleth over the poor, and the

[f]Psa. cxii. 3; Matt. vi. 33——[g]Or, *The reward of humility, &c.*——[h]Ch. xv. 19——[i]1 John v. 18——[k]Eph. vi. 4; 2 Tim. iii. 15——[l]Or, *Catechise*——[m]Heb. *in his way*——[n]James ii. 6——[o]Heb. *to the man that lendeth*

A. M. cir. 3004
B. C. cir. 1000
Ante I. Olymp. cir. 224
Ante U. C. cir. 247

borrower *is* servant [o]to the
lender.
8 [p]He that soweth iniquity shall
reap vanity: [q]and the rod of his
anger shall fail.
9 [r]He [s]that hath a bountiful eye shall be
blessed; for he giveth of his bread to the poor.
10 [t]Cast out the scorner, and contention shall
go out; yea, strife and reproach shall cease.
11 [u]He that loveth pureness of heart, [v]*for*
the grace of his lips the king *shall be* his friend.
12 The eyes of the LORD preserve know-

[p]Job iv. 8; Hos. x. 13——[q]Or, *and with the rod of his anger he shall be consumed*——[r]2 Cor. ix. 6——[s]Heb. *Good of eye*——[t]Gen. xxi. 9, 10; Psa. ci. 5——[u]Psa. ci. 6; chap. xvi. 13——[v]Or, and hath *grace in his lips*

futurity; but in its place he has given him *hope* and *prudence.* By *hope* he is continually expecting and anticipating *good;* by *prudence* he derives and employs *means* to secure it. His *experience* shows him that there are many *natural evils* in a current state, the course of which he can neither stem nor divert: *prudence* shows him beforehand the means he may use to step out of their way, and *hide* himself. The *simple*—the inexperienced, headstrong, giddy, and foolish—rush on in the *career of hope,* without *prudence* to regulate, chastise, and guide it; thus they commit many faults, make many miscarriages, and suffer often in consequence; and the commission of crimes leads to punishment.

Verse 5. *Thorns* and *snares*] Various difficulties, trials, and sufferings.

Verse 6. *Train up a child in the way he should go*] The Hebrew of this clause is curious: חנך לנער על פי דרכו *chanoch lannaar al pi darco,* "Initiate the child at the opening (the mouth) of his path." When he comes to the *opening of the way of life,* being able to walk alone, and to choose; stop at this entrance, and begin a series of instructions, how he is to conduct himself in every *step* he takes. Show him the *duties,* the *dangers,* and the *blessings* of the path; give him directions *how* to *perform* the *duties,* how to *escape* the *dangers,* and how to *secure* the *blessings,* which all lie before him. Fix these on his mind by *daily inculcation,* till their *impression* is become *indelible;* then lead him to *practice* by slow and almost imperceptible degrees, till each *indelible impression* becomes a *strongly radicated habit.* Beg incessantly the blessing of God on all this teaching and discipline; and then you have obeyed the injunction of the wisest of men. Nor is there any likelihood that such *impressions* shall ever be effaced, or that such *habits* shall ever be destroyed.

חנך *chanac,* which we translate *train up* or *initiate,* signifies also *dedicate;* and is often used for the *consecrating* any thing, house, or person, to the service of God. *Dedicate,* therefore, in the first instance, your *child* to *God;* and *nurse, teach,* and *discipline* him as God's child, whom he has intrusted to your care. These things observed, and illustrated by your own conduct, the child (you have God's word for it) will never depart from the path of life. *Coverdale* translates the passage thus: "Yf thou teachest a childe what waye he shoulde go, he shall not leave it when he is olde." *Coverdale's* Bible, for generally giving the *true sense* of a passage, and in *elegant language* for the time, has no equal in any of the translations which have followed since. HORACE'S maxim is nearly like that of Solomon:—

Fingit equum tenera docilem cervice magister
Ire viam, quam monstrat eques; venaticus, ex quo
Tempore cervinam pellem latravit in aula,
Militat in sylvis catulus. Nunc adbibe puro
Pectore verba, puer; nunc te melioribus offer.
Quo semel est imbuta recens, servabit odorem
Testa diu. HOR. Ep. lib. i., ep. 2, ver. 64.

"The docile *colt* is form'd with *gentle skill*
To *move obedient* to his *rider's will.*
In the *loud hall* the *hound* is taught to bay
The *buckskin trail'd,* then challenges his prey
Through the *wild woods.* Thus, in your *hour of youth*
From *pure instruction quaff the words of truth:*
The *odours* of the wine that *first* shall stain
The *virgin vessel,* it shall *long retain.*"
FRANCIS.

Verse 7. *The rich ruleth over the poor*] So it is in the order of God, and may be a blessing to *both.*

Verse 8. *He that soweth iniquity*] The *crop* must be according to the *seed.* If a man sow *thistle seed,* is it likely he shall reap *wheat?* If he sow to the *flesh,* shall he not of the flesh reap *destruction?*

Verse 9. *A bountiful eye*] One that disposes him to help all that he sees to be in want; the *bountiful eye* means the *bountiful heart;* for the *heart* looks through the *eye.* The *merciful heart,* even when the *hand* has little or nothing to give, shall be blessed of the Lord.

Verse 11. *He that loveth pureness of heart*] Who aims to be what God would have him to be —*the King* of kings *shall be his Friend.* There is no class of men that value *uprightness* more than *kings;* as none stand so much in need of it in their *servants.*

Verse 12. *The eyes of the Lord*—(the Divine

A. M. cir. 3004
B. C. cir. 1000
Ante I. Olymp. cir. 224
Ante U. C. cir. 247

ledge, and he overthroweth [w]the
words of the transgressor.
13 [x]The slothful *man* saith,
There is a lion without, I shall
be slain in the streets.
14 [y]The mouth of strange women *is* a deep
pit: [z]he that is abhorred of the LORD shall
fall therein.
15 Foolishness *is* bound in the heart of a
child: *but* [a]the rod of correction shall drive
it far from him.

[w]Or, *the matters*——[x]Chap. xxvi. 13——[y]Chap. ii. 16; v. 3; vii. 5; xxiii. 27

16 He that oppresseth the poor
to increase his *riches, and* he that
giveth to the rich, *shall* surely
come to want.

A. M. cir. 3004
B. C. cir. 1000
Ante I. Olymp. cir. 224
Ante U. C. cir. 247

17 Bow down thine ear, and hear the words
of the wise, and apply thine heart unto my
knowledge.
18 For *it is* a pleasant thing if thou keep
them [b]within thee; they shall withal be fitted
in thy lips.
19 That thy trust may be in the LORD, I

[z]Eccles. vii. 26——[a]Ch. xiii. 24; xix. 18; xxiii. 13, 14; xxix. 15, 17——[b]Heb. *in thy belly*

providence) *preserve knowledge.*] This providence has been wonderfully manifested in *preserving the sacred oracles*, and in *preserving many ancient authors*, which have been of great use to the *civil interests of man.*

Verse 13. *The slothful* man *saith*, There is *a lion without*] But *why* does he say so? Because he is a *slothful* man. Remove his slothfulness, and these imaginary difficulties and dangers will be no more. He will not *go abroad* to *work* in the fields, because he thinks there is a *lion* in the *way;* he will not *go out* into the *town* for employment, as he fears to be *assassinated* in the *streets!* From both these circumstances he seeks total cessation from *activity.*

Verse 14. *The mouth of strange women* is *a deep pit*] In chap. xxiii. 27, he says, A *whore* is a DEEP DITCH, and a *strange woman is a* NARROW PIT. The allusions in these *three* places are too plain to be misunderstood. Virgil's hell has been adduced in illustration:—

——————*Sate sanguine Divum,*
Tros Anchisiade, facilis decensus Averni;
Noctes atque dies patet atri janua Ditis:
Sed revocare gradum, superasque *evadere ad auras*,
HOC OPUS; hic LABOR *est.* Pauci *quos æquus amavit*
Jupiter, aut ardens evexit ad æthera virtus,
Dis geniti potuere.
VIRG. *Æn.* lib. vi., ver. 125.

"O glorious prince of brave Anchises' line!
Great godlike hero! sprung from seed divine,
Smooth lies the road to Pluto's gloomy shade;
And *hell's black gates* for ever *stand display'd:*
But 'tis a long unconquerable pain,
To climb to these *ethereal realms* again.
The choice-selected few, whom favouring Jove,
Or their own virtue, rais'd to heaven above,
From these *dark realms emerged again to day;*
The *mighty sons of gods*, and only *they.*
PITT.

Verse 16. *He that oppresseth the poor*] He who, in order to obtain the favour of the *rich* and *great*, either *robs* or *cheats* the *poor*, to make those men *presents;* or gives *in presents* to them, for the sake of *honour* and *reputation*, what he should have given to the *poor*, *shall surely* come to *want.*

Verse 17. *Bow down thine ear*] From this to the end of ver. 21 are contained, not *proverbs*, but *directions* how to *profit* by that which *wisdom* has already delivered; the *nature* of the *instruction*, and the *end* for which it was given.

I shall give a paraphrase of this very important passage:—

I. Solomon addresses his pupils on the use of his past teachings. See on ver. 6.

1. The *wise* man speaks; and all his *words*, not merely his *sentiments*, are to be carefully heard.

2. He speaks *knowledge*—gives *doctrines* true in themselves, and confirmed by *observation* and *experience.*

3. These are to be *heard* with *humility* and deep *attention:* "Bow down thine ear."

4. They must not only be *heard*, but *meditated* and *pondered:* "Apply thine heart to my knowledge."

Verse 18. *For* it is *a pleasant thing if thou keep them within thee*]

II. The pleasure and profit which may be derived from an attentive hearing.

1. They should be *laid up in the heart*—stored, treasured up *within thee.*

2. This will yield high *satisfaction* and *happiness* to the soul: "For *it is* a pleasant thing if thou keep them within thee."

3. The man who thus attends to the teachings of wisdom shall gain an *experimental* knowledge of them, so as to be able to speak of them *suitably, pertinently* and *persuasively:* "They shall withal be fitted in thy lips."

Verse 19. *That thy trust may be in the Lord, I have made known, &c.*]

III. The END for which the wise man gives these instructions:—

1. "That thy trust may be in the Lord." That thou mayest acknowledge HIM as the *Fountain* of all good; and refer every thing to *him.*

2. That this end may be *accomplished*, the instructions are *specific* and *particular:* "I have made known to thee, even to thee."

3. And this has not only been done in times past, "I have made known:" but even in the *present*, "I have made known this day!"

IV. An *appeal* is made to the person himself relative to the *matter* and *importance* of the teaching.

1. "Have I not written to thee excellent things;" שלשים *shalishim*, literally *threefold, thrice*, in *three different ways;* which some think refers to his three books:—1. *Canticles.* 2. *Koheleth*, or Ecclesiastes. And 3. *Proverbs.*

A. M. cir. 3004 B. C. cir. 1000 Ante I. Olymp. cir. 224 Ante U. C. cir. 247

have made known to thee this
day, [c]even to thee.
20 Have not I written to thee
[d]excellent things in counsels and
knowledge,
21 [e]That I might make thee know the certainty of the words of truth: [f]that thou mightest answer the words of truth [g]to them that send unto thee?
22 [h]Rob not the poor, because he *is* poor:
[i]neither oppress the afflicted in the gate:
23 [k]For the LORD will plead
their cause, and spoil the soul of
those that spoiled them.
24 Make no friendship with
an angry man; and with a furious man thou shalt not go:
25 Lest thou learn his ways, and get a snare to thy soul.
26 [l]Be not thou *one* of them that strike hands, *or* of them that are sureties for debts.
27 If thou hast nothing to pay, why should

[c]Or, trust *thou also*——[d]Chapter viii. 6——[e]Luke i. 3, 4——[f]1 Pet. iii. 15——[g]Or, *to those that send thee* [h]Exod. xxiii. 6; Job xxxi. 16, 21; Isa. x. 2; xvii. 14

[i]Zech. vii. 10; Mal. iii. 5——[k]1 Sam. xxiv. 12; xxv. 39; Psa. xii. 5; xxxv. 1, 10; lxviii. 5; cxl. 12; ch. xxiii. 11; Jer. li. 36——[l]Chap. vi. 1; xi. 15

Others, understanding it of the voice of Divine wisdom, suppose the *three* grand divisions of the sacred oracles are intended; viz., 1. The *Law;* 2. The *Prophets;* and 3. The *Hagiographa.* And others interpret it of the *three* grand intellectual sciences:—1. *Morality,* or *Ethics.* 2. *Natural Philosophy,* or *Physics.* 3. *Theology,* or the science of *Divine things* as reported in the Scriptures. But Solomon's books of *Natural Philosophy* are lost.

And lastly, some of the *rabbins* and some Christians find in these *shalishim* the *three senses* of Scripture: 1. *Literal;* 2. *Figurative;* and 3. *Allegorical.*

After all, as we know the term *thrice* was used as the term *seven,* a *certain* number for an *uncertain,* (see Amos i. 11; 2 Cor. xii. 8,) it *may* mean no more here than, *I have written to thee often.* But perhaps it is safer to apply it to the *Scriptures,* and the excellent *doctrines* they contain: for שלשים *shalishim* signifies also *excellent, princely things;* things which become a *king* to *speak.* Indeed, it would not be difficult to prove that there is not one important *art* or *science* which is not alluded to in the Holy Scriptures, and used to illustrate and inculcate heavenly truths.

2. These *excellent, princely,* or *threefold teachings,* consist of two grand parts: 1. COUNSELS, מעצות *moetsoth, from* יעץ *yaats,* to give *advice, counsel,* or *information.* These (1) show thee what thou shouldst *know;* and (2) *advise* thee what thou shouldst do. 2. KNOWLEDGE, דעת *daath,* from ידע *yada,* to *perceive,* or *feel* by means of the senses and *internal perception;* viz., what should be *felt, experienced, known to be true by mental perception,* and by their *influence* on the *heart* and *affections.*

V. All this is done to give the pupil the *fullest satisfaction,* and most plenary *evidence* concerning the *truths* of God.

Verse 21. *That I might make thee know the certainty of the words of truth*]

1. These are words or doctrines of *truth:* 1. They are true in themselves. 2. Come from the God of truth. 3. Are truly *fulfilled* to all that believe.

2. These words of truth are *certain,* קשט *koshet,* they are not of dubious or difficult interpretation; they *point directly* to the great end for which God gave them; they *promise,* and they are *fulfilled.* He who pleads them by faith, receives their *accomplishment* in the spirit and power of Divine love. The Scriptures, as far as they concern the salvation of the soul, are to be *experimentally* understood; and, by this experimental knowledge, every believer has the *witness in himself,* and knows the *certainty* of the words of truth.

VI. What we know ourselves to be true, and of infinite importance to the welfare of men in general, we should carefully proclaim and witness, that they also may believe.

That thou mightest answer the words of truth] 1. When the doctrine of salvation is preached, there will be many *inquirers.* What is this doctrine? Have any persons received these blessings—the remission of sins, witness of the Holy Spirit, purification of the heart, &c., &c.? *Who* are they? What are the collateral arguments that prove these things, and show us that you have not misapprehended the meaning of these Scriptures? 2. Inquiries of this kind should meet with the *speediest* and most distinct *answers;* and the doctrines of *truth* should be *supported* and *illustrated* with the *words of truth.* "That thou mightest answer the words of truth to them that send unto thee."

Verse 22. *Neither oppress the afflicted in the gate*] In judgment let the poor have a fair hearing; and let him not be borne down because he is *poor.* The reader has often seen that courts of justice were held at the *gates* of cities in the East.

Verse 23. *For the Lord will plead their cause*] Wo therefore to them that oppress them, for they will have *God,* not the *poor,* to deal with.

Verse 24. *Make no friendship with an angry man*] *Spirit* has a wonderful and unaccountable influence upon *spirit.* From those with whom we associate we acquire habits, and learn *their ways,* imbibe their *spirit,* show their *tempers,* and walk in their *steps.* We cannot be too choice of our *company,* for we may soon *learn ways* that will *be a snare to our soul.*

Verse 26. *That strike hands*] See on the parallel texts in the margin.

Verse 27. *If thou hast nothing to pay*] Should any man give security for more than he is *worth?* If he does, is it not a fraud on the very face of the transaction?

Why should he take away thy bed from under

A. M. cir. 3004 B. C. cir. 1000 Ante I. Olymp. cir. 224 Ante U. C. cir. 247

he [m]take away thy bed from
under thee?
28 [n]Remove not the ancient [o]land-
mark, which thy fathers have set.

29 Seest thou a man diligent in
his business? he shall stand before kings; he shall not stand
before [p]mean *men*.

A. M. cir. 3004 B. C. cir. 1000 Ante I. Olymp. cir. 224 Ante U. C. cir. 247

[m]Chap. xx. 16——[n]Deut. xix. 14; xxvii. 17; chap. xxiii. 10——[o]Or, *bound*——[p]Heb. *obscure men*

thee?] The *creditor* will not pursue the *debtor* whom he knows to be worth nothing; but he will sue the *bail* or *bondsman*. And why shouldst thou put thyself in such circumstances as to expose thyself to the loss even of thy bed?

Verse 28. *Remove not the ancient landmark*] Do not take the advantage, in ploughing or breaking up a field contiguous to that of thy neighbour, to set the dividing stones *farther* into his *field* that thou mayest *enlarge thy own*. Take not what is not *thy own* in any case. Let all ancient *divisions*, and the *usages* connected with them, be held sacred. Bring in no new *dogmas*, nor *rites*, nor *ceremonies*, into *religion*, or the worship of God, that are not clearly laid down in the *sacred writings*. "Stand in the way; and see, and ask for the old paths, which is the good way, and walk therein; and ye shall find rest for your souls;" Jer. vi. 16. But if any *Church* have lost sight of the *genuine doctrines* of the Gospel, calling them back to these is not *removing the ancient landmarks*, as some have falsely asserted. God gave a law against removing the ancient landmarks, by which the inheritances of tribes and families were distinguished. See Deut. xix. 14, from which these words of Solomon appear to be taken.

Even among the *heathens* the *landmark* was sacred; so sacred that they made a *deity* of it. *Terminus* signifies the *stone* or *post* that served as a *landmark*. And *Terminus* was reputed a *god*, and had offerings made to him. Hence Ovid:—

Tu quoque sacrorum, Termine, finis eras.
Fast. lib. i., ver. 50.

Nox ubi transierit, solito celebratur honore,
Separat indicio qui Deus arva suo.
Termine, sive lapis, sive es defossus in agro
Stipes, ab antiquis sic quoque Numen habes.
Te duo diversa domini pro parte coronant;
Binaque serta tibi, binaque liba ferunt.——
Conveniunt, celebrantque dapes vicinia simplex;
Et cantant laudes, Termine sancte, tuas.
Tu populos, urbesque, et regna ingentia finis:
Omnis erit, sine te, litigiosus ager.
Fast. lib. ii., ver. 639.

Here we find the owners of both fields bringing each his *garland* and *libation* to the honour of this god. They sung its *praises*, put on its top a *chaplet of flowers*, *poured out* the *libation* before it; and the inhabitants of the *country* held a *festival* in its honour. It was, in short, celebrated as the *preserver* of the *bounds* and territorial rights of tribes, cities, and whole kingdoms; and without its testimony and evidence, every field would have been a subject of litigation.

Verse 29. *He shall not stand before mean men.*] חשכים *chashukkim*, *dark* or *obscure persons;* men of no repute. **Na he schal ben before un-noble men.**—Old MS. Bible. "Not amonge the symple people."—*Coverdale*.

The general meaning of the proverb is, "Every diligent, active man, shall be at once independent and respectable."

CHAPTER XXIII

Sobriety in eating and drinking, especially at the tables of the great. Have no fellowship with the covetous. Remove not the ancient landmark. Children should receive due correction. Avoid the company of wine-bibbers. Obedience to parents. Avoid lewd connections. The effect of an unfeeling conscience.

A. M. cir. 3004 B. C. cir. 1000 Ante I. Olymp. cir. 224 Ante U. C. cir. 247

WHEN thou sittest to eat
with a ruler, consider diligently what *is* before thee:
2 And put a knife to thy throat,
if thou *be* a man given to appetite.

3 Be not desirous of his
dainties: for they *are* deceitful
meat.
4 [a]Labour not to be rich:
[b]cease from thine own wisdom.

A. M. cir. 3004 B. C. cir. 1000 Ante I. Olymp. cir. 224 Ante U. C. cir. 247

[a]Chap. xxviii. 20; 1 Tim. vi. 9, 10 [b]Chap. iii. 5; Rom. xii. 16

NOTES ON CHAP. XXIII

Verse 1. *When thou sittest to eat with a ruler*] When invited to the table of thy betters, eat *moderately*. Do not appear as if half starved at home. Eat not of *delicacies* to which thou art not accustomed; they are *deceitful meat;* they please, but they do not profit. They are pleasant to the *sight*, the *taste*, and the *smell;* but they are injurious to *health*. These are prudential cautions; and should be carefully observed by all who would avoid the conduct of a *clown*, and desire to pass for a *well-bred* man.

Verse 2. *Put a knife to thy throat*] Repress thy appetite, and do not be incontinent of speech. Eat, drink, and converse, under a *check*.

Verse 4. *Labour not to be rich*] Let not this be thy object. Labour to provide things *honest*

A. M. cir. 3004
B. C. cir. 1000
Ante I. Olymp. cir. 224
Ante U. C. cir. 247

5 [c]Wilt thou set thine eyes
upon that which is not? for
riches certainly make themselves
wings; they fly away as an
eagle toward heaven.
6 [d]Eat thou not the bread of *him that hath*
[e]an evil eye, neither desire thou his dainty
meats:
7 For as he thinketh in his heart, so *is* he:
Eat and drink, [f]saith he to thee; but his heart
is not with thee.
8 The morsel *which* thou hast eaten shalt
thou vomit up, and lose thy sweet words.
9 [g]Speak not in the ears of a fool: for he
will despise the wisdom of thy words.
10 [h]Remove not the old [i]landmark; and
enter not into the fields of the fatherless:
11 [k]For their redeemer *is* mighty: he shall
plead their cause with thee.
12 Apply thine heart unto instruction, and
thine ears to the words of knowledge.

[c]Heb. *Wilt thou cause thine eyes to fly upon*——[d]Psa. cxli. 4——[e]Deut. xv. 9——[f]Psa. xii. 2——[g]Chap. ix. 8; Matt. vii. 6——[h]Deut. xix. 14; xxvii. 17; chapter xxii. 28——[i]Or, *bound*——[k]Job xxxi. 21; chap. xxii. 23
[l]Chap. xiii. 24; xix. 18; xxii. 15; xxix. 15, 17——[m]1 Cor. v. 5

A. M. cir. 3004
B. C. cir. 1000
Ante I. Olymp. cir. 224
Ante U. C. cir. 247

13 [l]Withhold not correction
from the child: for *if* thou beatest
him with the rod, he shall not die.
14 Thou shalt beat him with
the rod, and [m]shalt deliver his soul from hell.
15 My son, [n]if thine heart be wise, my
heart shall rejoice, [o]even mine.
16 Yea, my reins shall rejoice, when thy lips
speak right things.
17 [p]Let not thine heart envy sinners: but
[q]*be thou* in the fear of the LORD all the day
long.
18 [r]For surely there is an [s]end; and thine
expectation shall not be cut off.
19 Hear thou, my son, and be wise, and
[t]guide thine heart in the way.
20 [u]Be not among winebibbers: among
riotous eaters [v]of flesh:
21 For the drunkard and the glutton shall
come to poverty: and [w]drowsiness shall clothe
a man with rags.

[n]Ver. 24, 25; chap. xxix. 3——[o]Or, *even I* will rejoice——[p]Psa. xxxvii. 1; lxxiii. 3; chap. iii. 31; xxiv. 1
[q]Chap. xxviii. 14——[r]Psa. xxxvii. 37; chap. xxiv. 14; Luke xvi. 25——[s]Or, *reward*——[t]Chap. iv. 23——[u]Isa. v. 22; Matt. xxiv. 49; Luke xxi. 34; Rom. xiii. 13; Eph. v. 18——[v]Heb. *of their flesh*——[w]Chap. xix. 15

in the sight of God and all men; and if thou get wealth, do not forget the *poor*, else God's curse will be a canker even in thy *gold*.

Cease from thine own wisdom.] בינתך *binathecha*, thy own *understanding* or *prudence*. The world says, "Get rich *if* thou canst, and *how* thou canst." Rem, si possis, recte; si non, quocunque modo rem; "Get a fortune *honestly* if thou canst; but if not, get one at all events." This is the devil's counsel, and well it is followed; but Solomon says, and God says, "Cease from thine own counsel." Thou hast an immortal soul, and shalt shortly appear before God. Lay up treasure for heaven, and be rich towards God.

Verse 6. *Of* him that hath *an evil eye*] Never eat with a covetous or stingy man; if he entertains you at his own expense, he grudges every morsel you put in your mouth. This is well marked by the wise man in the next verse: "Eat and drink, saith he: but his heart is not with thee."

Verse 8. *The morsel* which *thou hast eaten*] On reflection thou wilt even blame thyself for having accepted his invitation.

Verse 10. *Remove not the old landmark*] See the preceding chapter, ver. 28.

Enter not into the fields of the fatherless] Take nothing that belongs to an orphan. The heaviest curse of God will fall upon them that do so.

Verse 11. *For their redeemer* is *mighty*] גאלם *goalam*, their *kinsman*. The word means the person who has a right, being next in blood, to *redeem a field* or *estate*, alienated from the family; to avenge *the blood* of a murdered relative, by slaying the murderer; and to take *to wife* a brother's widow, who had died childless, in order to preserve the family. The *strength* here mentioned refers to the *justness* of his claim, the *extent* of his *influence*, and the powerful *abettors* of such a cause. But in reference to the orphans here mentioned, they having no *kinsman*, God takes up, vindicates, and avenges their cause.

Verse 14. *Thou shalt beat him with the rod*] A proper correction of children was a favourite point of discipline with Solomon. We have already seen how forcibly he speaks on this subject. See the notes on the places referred to in the margin.

Verse 18. *Surely there is an end*] יש אחרית *yesh acharith*, there is *another* life; "and thy expectation" of the enjoyment of a blessed immortality "shall not be cut off." The Old MS. Bible reads thus: **For thou schalt hab hop in the last; and thin abiding schal not ben taken awei.** "For the ende is not yet come; and thy pacient abydinge shal not be in vayne."—COVERDALE.

Verse 20. *Be not among winebibbers*] There is much of this chapter spent in giving directions concerning *eating*, *drinking*, and *entertainments* in general. First, the pupil is directed relative to the manner in which he is to conduct himself in his visits to the tables of the *rich* and *great*. 2. Relative to the *covetous*, and his intercourse with them. And 3. To *public entertainments*, where there were generally riot and debauch. The reasons, says *Calmet*, which induced the wise man to give these directions were, 1. The useless expense. 2. The loss of time. 3. The danger from bad company. And 4. The danger of contracting irregular

A. M. cir. 3004
B. C. cir. 1000
Ante I. Olymp. cir. 224
Ante U. C. cir. 247

22 [x]Hearken unto thy father
that begat thee, and despise not
thy mother when she is old.
23 [y]Buy the truth, and sell
it not; *also* wisdom, and instruction, and understanding.
24 [z]The father of the righteous shall greatly
rejoice: and he that begetteth a wise *child*
shall have joy of him.
25 Thy father and thy mother shall be glad,
and she that bare thee shall rejoice.
26 My son, give me thine heart, and let thine
eyes observe my ways.
27 [a]For a whore is a deep ditch; and a
strange woman *is* a narrow pit.
28 [b]She also lieth in wait [c]as *for* a prey,
and increaseth the transgressors among men.
29 [d]Who hath wo? who hath sorrow? who
hath contentions? who hath babbling? who
hath wounds without cause? who
[e]hath redness of eyes?
30 [f]They that tarry long at
the wine; they that go to seek
[g]mixed wine.
31 Look not thou upon the wine when it is
red, when it giveth his colour in the cup, *when*
it moveth itself aright.
32 At the last it biteth like a serpent, and
stingeth like [h]an adder.
33 Thine eyes shall behold strange women,
and thine heart shall utter perverse things.
34 Yea, thou shalt be as he that lieth down
[i]in the midst of the sea, or as he that lieth
upon the top of a mast.
35 [k]They have stricken me, *shalt thou say,*
and I was not sick; they have beaten me, *and*
[l]I [m]felt *it* not: [n]when shall I awake? I will
seek it yet again.

[x]Chapter i. 8; xxx. 17; Eph. vi. 1, 2——[y]Chapter iv. 5, 7; Matt. xiii. 44——[z]Chapter x. 1; xv. 20; ver. 15
[a]Chapter xxii. 14——[b]Chap. vii. 12; Eccles. vii. 26
[c]Or, *as a robber*——[d]Isa. v. 11, 22——[e]Gen. xlix. 12

[f]Chap. xx. 1; Eph. v. 18——[g]Psa. lxxv. 8; chapter ix. 2——[h]Or, *a cockatrice*——[i]Heb. *in the heart of the sea*
[k]Jer. v. 3; chapter xxvii. 22——[l]Heb. *I knew it not*
[m]Eph. iv. 19——[n]See Deut. xxix. 19; Isa. lvi. 12

habits, and of being induced to lead a voluptuous and effeminate life.

Verse 22. *Despise not thy mother when she is old.*] A very necessary caution, as *very old women* are generally helpless, useless, and burdensome: yet these circumstances do not at all lessen the child's *duty.* And this *duty* is strengthened by the Divine command here given.

Verse 23. *Buy the truth*] Acquire the *knowledge of God* at all events; and in order to do this, too much pains, industry, and labour, cannot be expended.

And sell it *not*] When once acquired, let no consideration deprive thee of it. Cleave to and guard it, even at the risk of thy life. *Coverdale* translates: "Labour for to get the treuth; sell not awaye wissdome."

Verse 26. *My son, give me thine heart*] This is the speech of God to every *human soul;* give thy *affections* to *God,* so as to love him with all thy heart, soul, mind, and strength.

And let thine eyes observe my ways.] Be obedient to me in all things. *My son,* thou believest that I AM, and that I AM the *Fountain of all good. Give me thy heart;* it is I alone who can make thee happy. *Observe my ways*—follow me; do what is right in my sight. This exhortation contains *three* words: BELIEVE, LOVE, OBEY! This is the *sum* of God's counsels to every child of man.

Verse 27. *For a whore is a deep ditch*] See on chap. xxii. 14.

Verse 28. *Increaseth the transgressors among men.*] More iniquity springs from this one source of evil, than from any other cause in the whole system of sin. *Women* and *strong drink* cause many millions to *transgress.*

Verse 29. *Who hath wo?*] I believe Solomon refers here to the natural effects of drunkenness. And perhaps אוי *oi,* which we translate *wo,* and אבוי *aboi,* which we translate *sorrow,* are mere natural sounds or vociferations that take place among drunken men, either from illness, or the *nauseating* effects of too much liquor. As to *contentions* among such; *babblings* on a variety of subjects, which they neither understand nor are fit to discuss; *wounds,* got by falling out about nothing; and *red eyes,* bloodshotten with excess of drink, or *black* and *blue eyes* with fighting;—these are such common and general effects of these *compotations,* as naturally to follow from them. So that they who *tarry long at wine,* and use *mixed wine* to make it more inebriating, (see chap. ix. 2,) are the very persons who are most distinguished by the circumstances enumerated above. I need scarcely add, that by *wine* and *mixed wine* all inebriating liquors are to be understood.

Verse 31. *Look not thou upon the wine*] Let neither the *colour,* the *odour,* the *sparkling,* &c., of the wine, when poured out, induce thee to drink of it. However *good* and *pure* it may be, it will to thee be a snare, because thou art addicted to it, and hast no self-command.

Verse 33. *Thine eyes shall behold strange women*] Evil concupiscence is inseparable from drunkenness. Mr. *Herbert* shows these effects well:—

He that is *drunken* may his *mother* kill,
Big with his sister: he hath lost the reins;
Is outlawed by himself. *All kinds of ill*
Did, with his liquor, slide into his veins.
The drunkard forfeits *man;* and doth divest
All worldly right, save what he hath by *beast.*
HERBERT'S *Poems.—The Church Porch.*

Verse 34. *Lieth down in the midst of the sea*] He is utterly regardless of life; which is expressed very forcibly by one in a state of intoxication ascending the *shrouds,* clasping the mast-head, and there *falling asleep;* whence, in a few moments, he must either fall down upon the deck and be dashed to pieces, or fall into the sea and be drowned. Reader, if thou be a man given to this appetite, put a knife to thy throat.

Verse 35. *They have stricken me*] Though beat and abused, full of pain, and exhibiting a frightful figure; yet so drunk was he, as to be insensible who had struck him: still, after all this abuse and disgrace, he purposes to embrace the next opportunity of repeating his excesses! SIN makes a man *contemptible* in life, *miserable* in death, and *wretched* to all eternity. Is it not strange, then, that men should LOVE it?

CHAPTER XXIV

Do not be envious. Of the house wisely built. Counsel necessary in war. Save life when thou canst. Of honey and the honey-comb. Of the just that falleth seven times. We should not rejoice at the misfortune of others. Ruin of the wicked. Fear God and the king. Prepare thy work. The field of the sluggard, and the vineyard of the foolish, described.

A. M. cir. 3004
B. C. cir. 1000
Ante I. Olymp. cir. 224
Ante U. C. cir. 247

BE not thou [a]envious against
evil men, [b]neither desire to
be with them.
2 [c]For their heart studieth destruction, and their lips talk of mischief.
3 Through wisdom is a house builded; and
by understanding it is established:
4 And by knowledge shall the chambers be
filled with all precious and pleasant riches.
5 [d]A wise man *is* [e]strong; yea, a man of
knowledge [f]increaseth strength.
6 [g]For by wise counsel thou shalt make thy
war: and in multitude of counsellors *there is*
safety.
7 [h]Wisdom *is* too high for
a fool: he openeth not his mouth
in the gate.
8 He that [i]deviseth to do evil
shall be called a mischievous person.
9 The thought of foolishness *is* sin: and the
scorner *is* an abomination to men.
10 *If* thou faint in the day of adversity, thy
strength *is* [k]small.
11 [l]If thou forbear to deliver *them that are*
drawn unto death, and *those that are* ready to
be slain;
12 If thou sayest, Behold, we knew it not:
doth not [m]he that pondereth the heart consi-

A. M. cir. 3004
B. C. cir. 1000
Ante I. Olymp. cir. 224
Ante U. C. cir. 247

[a]Psa. xxxvii. 1, &c.; lxxiii. 3; ch. iii. 31; xxiii. 17; ver. 19——[b]Ch. i. 15——[c]Psa. x. 7——[d]Ch. xxi. 22; Eccles. ix. 16——[e]Heb. is *in strength*——[f]Heb. *strengtheneth might*

[g]Chap. xi. 15; xiii. 22; xx. 18; Luke xiv. 31——[h]Psa. x. 5; chap. xiv. 6——[i]Rom. i. 30——[k]Heb. *narrow*
[l]Psa. lxxxii. 4; Isa. lviii. 6, 7; 1 John iii. 16——[m]Chap. xxi. 2

NOTES ON CHAP. XXIV

Verse 3. *Through wisdom is a house builded*] That is, a family; household affairs. See the notes on chap. ix. 1, &c.

Verse 5. *A wise man* is *strong.* His wisdom enables him to construct a great variety of machines, by which, under his own influence, he can do the labour of a hundred or even a thousand men. But in all cases *wisdom* gives *power* and *influence;* and he who *is wise to salvation* can overcome even Satan himself. The *Septuagint* has: "The wise is better than the strong; and the man who has prudence, than a stout husbandman."

Verse 6. *By wise counsel thou shalt make thy war*] See note on chap. xx. 18.

Verse 7. *A fool—openeth not his mouth in the gate.*] Is not put into public offices of trust and responsibility.

Verse 9. *The thought of foolishness* is *sin*] זמת אולת חטאת *zimmath ivveleth chattath.* "The device of folly is transgression;" or, "an evil purpose is sinful;" or, perhaps more literally, "the device of the foolish is sin." It has been variously understood by the *versions.*

"The cunning of the fool is sin."—*Targum.*

"The imprudent man (or fool, αφρων) shall die in sins."—*Septuagint.*

So the *Arabic.*

The thinkynge of the fool is synne.—Old MS. Bible.

Fool is here taken for a *wicked* man, who is not only evil in his *actions*, but every thought of his heart is evil, and that continually. A simple thought *about* foolishness, or about *sin* itself, is not sinful; it is the *purpose* or *device*, the *harbouring* evil thoughts, and *devising how to sin*, that is criminal.

Verse 10. If *thou faint*] If thou give way to discouragement and despair *in the day of adversity*—time of trial or temptation.

Thy strength is *small.*] צר כחכה *tsar cochachah*, thy *strength* is *contracted.* So the old MS. Bible excellently: **Gif sliden thou dispeire, in the dai of angwys, schal be made litil thy strengthe.** In times of trial we should endeavour to be doubly courageous; when a man loses his courage, his strength avails him nothing.

Verse 11. *If thou forbear to deliver*] If thou seest the innocent taken by the hand of lawless power or superstitious zeal, and they are about to be put to death, thou shouldst rise up in their behalf, boldly plead for them, testify to their innocence when thou knowest it; and thus thou wilt not be *guilty of blood;* which thou

A. M. cir. 3004 B. C. cir. 1000 Ante I. Olymp. cir. 224 Ante U. C. cir. 247

der *it?* and he that keepeth thy
soul, doth *not* he know *it?* and
shall *not* he render to *every* man
[n]according to his works?
13 My son, [o]eat thou honey, because *it is*
good; and the honey-comb, *which is* sweet [p]to
thy taste.
14 [q]So *shall* the knowledge of wisdom *be*
unto thy soul: when thou hast found *it,* [r]then
there shall be a reward, and thy
expectation shall not be cut off.
15 [s]Lay not wait, O wicked
man, against the dwelling of the
righteous; spoil not his resting place.
16 [t]For a just *man* falleth seven times, and
riseth up again: [u]but the wicked shall fall into
mischief.
17 [v]Rejoice not when thine enemy falleth,

[n]Job xxxiv. 11; Psa. lxii. 12; Jer. xxxii. 19; Rom. ii. 6; Rev. ii. 23; xxii. 12——[o]Cant. v. 1——[p]Heb. *upon thy palate*——[q]Psa. xix. 10; cxix. 103——[r]Chap. xxiii. 18 [s]Psa. x. 9, 10

[t]Job v. 19; Psa. xxxiv. 19; xxxvii. 24; Mic. vii. 8 [u]Esth. vii. 10; Amos v. 2; viii. 14; Rev. xviii. 21——[v]Job xxxi. 27; Psa. xxxv. 15, 19; chapter xvii. 5; Obadiah 12

wouldst be, if, through any pretence, thou shouldst neglect to save the life of a man unjustly condemned.

Verse 13. *And the honey-comb*] I have often had occasion to remark how much finer the flavour of honey is in the honey-comb than it is after it has been *expressed* from it, and exposed to the action of the air. But it has been asserted that the *honey-comb* is *never eaten;* it must be by those who have no acquaintance with the *apiary.* I have seen the *comb* with its contained honey eaten frequently, and of it I have repeatedly partaken. And that our Lord ate it, is evident from Luke xxiv. 42. Nor can any man who has not eaten it in this way feel the full force of the allusions to the *honey-comb* and its *sweetness* in several parts of the sacred writings. See 1 Sam. xiv. 27; Psa. xix. 10; Prov. v. 3; xvi. 24; xxvii. 7; Cant. iv. 11; v. 1; and the place before us.

Verse 14. *So* shall *the knowledge of wisdom* be *unto thy soul*] True religion, experimental godliness, shall be to thy soul as the honey-comb is to thy mouth.

Then there shall be a reward, and thy expectation shall not be cut off.] This is precisely the same with that in the preceding chapter, ver. 18, where see the note. The word אחרית *acharith,* we translate in the former place *an end,* and here we translate it a *reward;* but there is no place I believe in the sacred writings in which it has any such acceptation; nor can such a meaning be deduced from the root אחר *achar,* which always refers to *behind, after, extremity, latter part, time,* &c., but never carries the idea of *recompense, compensation,* or such like; nor has one of the *versions* understood it so. There is *another state* or *life,* and *thy expectation* of happiness in a *future world shall not be cut off.* In this sense the *versions* all understood it. I will take them as they lie before me.

"Which (wisdom) when thou shalt have found, thou shalt have hope in thy *last days;* and thy hope shall not perish."—*Vulgate.*

"And if thou find it, thou shalt have a *good death;* and hope shall not forsake thee."—*Septuagint.*

"Which, if thou have found, thy *latter days* shall be better than the former; and thy hope shall not be consumed."—*Chaldee.*

"There shall be *an end,* and thy hope shall not be cut off."—*Syriac.*

"For, if thou shalt find her, (wisdom,) *thy death shall be glorious,* and thy hope will not fail thee."—*Arabic.*

Whiche whan thou fyndist thou schalt han in the last thingis, hope: and thin hope schal not perischen.—Old MS. Bible.

"*And there* is GOOD HOPE; yee that hope shal not be in vayne."—*Coverdale.*

This rendering is indefinite, which is not the usual custom of the translator.

Verse 15. *The dwelling of the righteous*] צדיק *tsaddik,* the man who is walking unblameably in all the testimonies of God; who is rendering to every man his due.

Verse 16. *For a just* man] צדיק *tsaddik,* the *righteous,* the same person mentioned above.

Falleth seven times] Gets *very often* into distresses through his *resting place* being *spoiled* by the *wicked man,* the robber, the spoiler of the desert, *lying in wait* for this purpose, ver. 15.

And riseth up again] Though God permit the hand of *violence* sometimes to spoil his *tent, temptations* to assail his *mind,* and *afflictions* to press down his *body,* he constantly emerges; and every time he passes through the furnace, he comes out *brighter* and more refined.

But the wicked shall fall into mischief.] And there they shall *lie;* having no strong arm to uphold them. Yet,

Verse 17. *Rejoice not when thine enemy falleth,* (into this mischief,) *and let not thine heart be glad when he stumbleth*] When he meets with any thing that injures him; for God will not have thee to avenge thyself, or *feel any disposition* contrary to love; for if thou do, the Lord will *be angry,* and may *turn away his wrath from him,* and pour it out on *thee.*

This I believe to be the true sense of these verses: but we must return to the *sixteenth,* as that has been most sinfully misrepresented.

For a just man *falleth seven times.*—That is, say many, "the most righteous man in the world sins seven times a day on an average." Solomon does not say so:—1. There is not a word about *sin* in the text. 2. The word *day* is not in the Hebrew text, nor in any of the *versions.* 3. The word יפול *yippol,* from נפל *naphal,* to *fall,* is never applied to *sin.* 4. When set in opposition to the words *riseth up,* it merely applies to affliction or calamity. See Mic. vii. 8; Amos viii. 4; Jer. xxv. 27; and Psa. xxxiv. 19, 20. "The righteous falls into trouble." See above.

Mr. *Holden* has a very judicious note on this passage: "Injure not a righteous man; for, though he frequently falls into distress, yet, by the superintending care of Providence, 'he

A. M. cir. 3004
B. C. cir. 1000
Ante I. Olymp. cir. 224
Ante U. C. cir. 247

and let not thine heart be glad
when he stumbleth:
18 Lest the LORD see *it,* and
[w]it displease him, and he turn
away his wrath from him.
19 [x]Fret [y]not thyself because of evil *men,*
neither be thou envious at the wicked;
20 For [z]there shall be no reward to the
evil *man;* [a]the [b]candle of the wicked shall
be put out.
21 My son, [c]fear thou the LORD and the
king: *and* meddle not with [d]them that are
given to change:
22 For their calamity shall rise suddenly;
and who knoweth the ruin of them both?
23 These *things* also *belong* to the wise.
[e]*It is* not good to have respect of persons in
judgment.
24 [f]He that saith unto the wicked, Thou
art righteous; him shall the
people curse, nations shall abhor
him:
25 But to them that rebuke
him shall be delight, and [g]a good blessing
shall come upon them.
26 *Every man* shall kiss *his* lips [h]that giveth
a right answer.
27 [i]Prepare thy work without, and make it
fit for thyself in the field; and afterwards
build thine house.
28 [k]Be not a witness against thy neighbour
without cause; and deceive *not* with thy lips.
29 [l]Say not, I will do so to him as he hath
done to me: I will render to the man according to his work.
30 I went by the field of the slothful, and
by the vineyard of the man void of understanding;

A. M. cir. 3004
B. C. cir. 1000
Ante I. Olymp. cir. 224
Ante U. C. cir. 247

[w]Heb. *it be evil in his eyes*——[x]Psa. xxxvii. 1; lxvii. 3; chap. xxiii. 17; ver. 1——[y]Or, *Keep not company with the wicked*——[z]Psa. xi. 6——[a]Job xviii. 5, 6; xxi. 17; chap. xiii. 9; xx. 20——[b]Or, *lamp*——[c]Romans xiii. 7; 1 Peter ii. 27——[d]Heb. *changers*

[e]Lev. xix. 15; Deut. xi. 7; xvi. 19; chap. xviii. 5; xxviii. 21; John vii. 24——[f]Chap. xvii. 15; Isa. v. 23 [g]Heb. *a blessing of good*——[h]Heb. *that answereth right words*——[i]1 Kings v. 17, 18; Luke xiv. 28——[k]Eph. iv. 25——[l]Chap. xx. 22; Matt. v. 39, 44; Rom. xii. 17, 19

riseth up again,' is delivered from his distress, while the wicked are overwhelmed with their misfortunes. That this is the meaning is plain from the preceding and following verses: yet some expound it by the just man often relapsing into sin, and recovering from it; nay, it has even been adduced to prove the doctrine of the final perseverance of the elect. But נפל is never used for falling into sin, but into distress and affliction—as chap. xi. 5, 14; xiii. 17; xvii. 20; xxvi. 27; xxviii. 10, 14, 18."

Verse 18. *And he turn away his wrath from him.*] Wrath is here taken for the effect of wrath, punishment; and the meaning must be as paraphrased above—lest he take the punishment from *him,* and inflict it upon *thee.* And in this way *Coverdale* understood it: "Lest the Lorde be angry, and turn his wrath from him unto thee." Or we may understand it thus: Lest the Lord inflict on thee a *similar punishment;* for if thou get into his *spirit,* rejoicing in the calamities of another, thou deservest punishment.

Verse 20. *For there shall be no reward to the evil* man] אחרית *acharith.* There shall not be the *future state* of *blessedness* to the wicked. See the note on ver. 14. *His candle shall be put out;* his *prosperity* shall finally cease, or he shall have no *posterity.* Some have thought that this text intimates the *annihilation* of sinners; but it refers not to *being,* but to the *state* or *condition* of that being. The wicked shall *be;* but they shall not *be* HAPPY.

Verse 21. *My son, fear thou the Lord and the king*] Pay to each the homage due: to the LORD, Divine honour and adoration; to the *king,* civil respect, civil honour, and political obedience.

Meddle not with them that are given to change] עם שונים אל תתערב *im shonim al titharab:* "And with the changelings mingle not thyself." The *innovators;* those who are always for making experiments on modes of government, forms of religion, &c. The most dangerous spirit that can infect the human mind.

Verse 22. *The ruin of them both?*] *Of* them who do not *fear* the LORD; and of *them* that do not *reverence* the KING.

Verse 23. *These* things *also* belong *to the wise.*] גם אלה לחכמים *gam elleh lachachamim,* "These also to wise." This appears to be a *new section;* and perhaps, what follows belongs to *another collection.* Probably fragments of sayings collected by wise men from the Proverbs of Solomon.

It is *not good to have respect*] Judgment and justice should never be perverted.

Verse 26. *Kiss* his *lips*] Shall treat him with affection and respect.

Verse 27. *Prepare thy work without*] Do nothing without a *plan.* In *winter* prepare seed, implements, tackle, geers, &c., for *seed-time and harvest.*

Verse 28. *Be not a witness*] Do not be forward to offer thyself to bear testimony against a neighbour, in a matter which may prejudice him, where the essential claims of justice do not require such interference; and especially do not do this in a spirit of *revenge,* because he has injured thee before.

Verse 30. *I went by the field of the slothful*] This is a most instructive *parable;* is exemplified every day in a variety of forms; and is powerfully descriptive of the *state* of many a *backslider* and *trifler* in religion. *Calmet* has an excellent note on this passage. I shall give the substance of it.

A. M. cir. 3004 B. C. cir. 1000 Ante I. Olymp. cir. 224 Ante U. C. cir. 247

31 And, lo, [m]it was all grown over
with thorns, *and* nettles had covered the face thereof, and the stone
wall thereof was broken down.
32 Then I saw, *and* [n]considered *it* well: I
looked upon *it, and* received instruction.
33 [o]*Yet* a little sleep, a little
slumber, a little folding of the
hands to sleep:
34 So shall thy poverty come
as one that travelleth; and thy want as [p]an
armed man.

[m]Gen. iii. 18——[n]Heb. *set my heart* [o]Chap. vi. 9, &c.——[p]Heb. *a man of shield*

Solomon often recommends diligence and economy to his disciples. In those primitive times when agriculture was honourable, no man was respected who neglected to cultivate his grounds, who sunk into poverty, contracted debt, or engaged in ruinous securities. With great propriety, a principal part of *wisdom* was considered by them as consisting in the *knowledge* of properly *conducting one's domestic affairs*, and duly cultivating the inheritances derived from their ancestors. Moses had made a law to prevent the rich from utterly depressing the poor, by obliging them to return their *farms* to them on the *Sabbatic year*, and to remit all debts at the *year of jubilee*.

In the civil state of the Hebrews, we never see those enormous and suddenly raised fortunes, which never subsist but in the ruin of numberless families. One of the principal solicitudes of this legislator was to produce, as far as possible in a monarchical state, an equality of property and condition. The ancient *Romans* held agriculture in the same estimation, and highly respected those who had applied themselves to it with success. When they spoke in praise of a man, they considered themselves as giving no mean commendation when they called him a *good husbandman*, an *excellent labourer*. From such men they formed their most valiant generals and intrepid soldiers. CATO *De Re Rustica*, cap. 1. The property which is acquired by these means is most innocent, most solid, and exposes its possessor less to envy than property acquired in any other way. See CICERO *De Officiis*, lib. 1. In Britain the *merchant* is all in all; and yet the waves of the sea are not more uncertain, nor more tumultuous, than the property acquired in this way, or than the agitated life of the speculative merchant.

But let us look more particularly into this very instructive parable:—

I. The owner is described. 1. He was איש עצל *ish atsel*, the loitering, sluggish, slothful man. 2. He was אדם חסר לב *adam chasar leb*, a man that wanted heart; destitute of courage, alacrity, and decision of mind.

II. His circumstances. This man had, 1st, שדה *sadeh*, a sowed field, arable ground. This was the character of his estate. It was *meadow* and *corn* land. 2. He had כרם *kerem*, a *vineyard*, what we would call perhaps *garden* and *orchard*, where he might employ his skill to great advantage in raising various kinds of fruits and culinary herbs for the support of his family.

III. The state of this heritage: 1. "It was grown over with thorns." It had been long neglected, so that even *brambles* were permitted to grow in the fields: 2. "Nettles had covered the face thereof." It was not *weeded*, and all kinds of rubbish had been suffered to multiply: 3. "The stone wall was broken down." This belonged to the *vineyard: it* was neither *pruned* nor *digged;* and the *fence*, for want of timely repairs, had all fallen into ruins, ver. 31.

IV. The *effect* all this had on the attentive observer. 1. *I saw it*, אחזה אנכי *echezeh anochi*, I fixed my attention on it. I found it was no mere report. It is a fact. I myself was an eyewitness of it. 2. *I considered it well*, אשית לבי *ashith libbi*, I put my heart on it. All my feelings were interested. 3. *I looked upon it*, ראיתי *raithi*, I took an *intellectual* view of it. And 4. Thus *I received instruction*, לקחתי מוסר *lakachti musar*, I received a very important lesson from it: but the owner paid no attention to it. He alone was uninstructed; for he "slumbered, slept, and kept his hands in his bosom." Ver. 33. "Hugged himself in his sloth and carelessness."

V. The consequences of this conduct. 1. *Poverty* described as coming like a *traveller*, making sure steps every hour coming nearer and nearer to the door. 2. *Want*, מחסר *machsor*, total destitution; want of all the *necessaries, conveniences*, and *comforts* of life; and this is described as coming *like an armed man* כאיש מגן *keish magen*, as a man with a shield, who comes to destroy this unprofitable servant: or it may refer to a man coming with what we call an execution into the house, armed with the law, to take even his *bed* from the *slumberer*.

From this literal solution any minister of God may make a profitable discourse.

CHAPTER XXV

A new series of Solomon's proverbs. God's glory in mysteries. Observations concerning kings. Avoid contentions. Opportune speech. The faithful ambassador. Delicacies to be sparingly used. Avoid familiarity. Amusements not grateful to a distressed mind. Do good to your enemies. The misery of dwelling with a scold. The necessity of moderation and self-government.

A. M. cir. 3304
B. C. cir. 700
Ol. vigesimæ
cir. annum
primum
A. U. C. cir. 54

THESE [a]*are* also proverbs of
Solomon, which the men of
Hezekiah king of Judah copied
out.
2 [b]*It is* the glory of God to conceal a thing:
but the honour of kings *is* [c]to search out a
matter.
3 The heaven for height, and the earth for
depth, and the heart of kings *is* [d]unsearch-
able.
4 [e]Take away the dross from the silver,
and there shall come forth a
vessel for the finer.
5 [f]Take away the wicked *from*
before the king, and [g]his throne
shall be established in righteousness.
6 [h]Put not forth thyself in the presence of
the king, and stand not in the place of great
men:
7 [i]For better *it is* that it be said unto thee,
Come up hither; than that thou shouldest be
put lower in the presence of the prince whom
thine eyes have seen.

[a]1 Kings iv. 32——[b]Deut. xxix. 29; Rom. xi. 33——[c]Job xxix. 16——[d]Heb. there is *no searching*

[e]2 Tim. ii. 21——[f]Ch. xx. 8——[g]Ch. xvi. 12; xxix. 14——[h]Heb. *Set not out thy glory*——[i]Luke xiv. 8, 9, 10

NOTES ON CHAP. XXV

Verse 1. *These* are *also proverbs of Solomon*] In my old MS. Bible, this verse concludes the preceding chapter. It seems that the remaining part of this book contains proverbs which had been collected by the order of King Hezekiah, and were added to the preceding book as a sort of supplement, having been collected from traditionary sayings of Solomon. And as the men of Hezekiah may mean *Isaiah, Shebna*, and other *inspired* men, who lived in that time, we may consider them as of equal authority with the rest, else such men could not have united them to the sacred book. The chronological notes in the margin of this and the five following chapters denote the time when the proverbs contained in them were collected together in the reign of Hezekiah, about *two hundred and seventy years* after the death of Solomon.

Verse 2. It is *the glory of God to conceal a thing*] This has been understood as referring to the revelation of God's will in his word, where there are many things concealed in *parables, allegories, metaphors, similitudes*, &c. And it is becoming the majesty of God so to publish his will, that it must be *seriously studied* to be understood, in order that the truth may be more prized when it is discovered. And if it be God's glory thus partially to conceal his purposes, it is the glory of a king to search and examine this word, that he may understand how by Him kings reign and princes decree judgment. *Prophecies* are partially concealed; and we cannot fully know their meaning till their accomplishment; and then the *glory of God's wisdom* and *providence* will be more particularly evident, when we see the event correspond so particularly and exactly with the *prediction.* I know not, however, that there are not matters in the Book of God that will not be fully opened till mortality is swallowed up of life. For *here* we see through a glass darkly; but *there*, face to face: *here* we know in part; but *there* we shall know as we also are known.

On this subject I cannot withhold an extract of a letter sent to myself, by a *royal* and *learned* personage.*

"As far as I have presumed to dive into and occupy myself with the sacred volumes, I feel satisfied of their Divine origin and truth. And I am satisfied, likewise, that they contain more matter than any one, and myself in particular, can ever aspire fully to understand. This belief, however, ought in nowise to slacken our diligence, or damp our ardour, in attempting a constant pursuit after the attainment of knowledge and truth; as we may flatter ourselves, although unable to reach the *gate*, we are still approaching nearer to its portals, which of itself is a great blessing." This sentiment will be approved by every pious and enlightened mind.

Verse 3. *The heaven for height*] The simple meaning of this is, the *reasons of state*, in reference to many acts of the *executive government*, can no more be fathomed by the *common people*, than the *height of the heavens* and the *depth of the earth.*

Verse 4. *Take away the dross from the silver*] You cannot have a *pure* silver vessel till you have purified the silver; and no nation can have a king a public blessing till the *wicked*—all bad counsellors, wicked and interested ministers, and sycophants—are banished from the court and cabinet. When the *wise* and *good* only are the king's ministers and advisers, then the throne will be established in righteousness, and his administration be a universal blessing.

Verse 7. *Come up hither*] Our Lord refers to this, see Luke xiv. 8, and the notes there. Be humble; affect not high things; let those who are desperate climb dangerous precipices; keep thyself quiet, and thou shalt live at ease, and in peace. Hear the speech of a wise *heathen* on this subject:—

Quid fuit, ut tutas agitaret Dædalus alas;
Icarus immensas nomine signet aquas?
Nempe quod hic alte, dimissus ille volabat.
Nam pennas ambo nonne habuere suas?
Crede mihi; bene qui latuit, bene vixit; et infra
Fortunam debet quisque manere suam.
Vive sine invidia; mollesque inglorius annos
Exige: amicitias et tibi junge pares.
OVID, *Trist.* lib. iii., El. 4, ver. 21.

"Why was it that *Dœdalus* winged his way safely, while *Icarus* his son fell, and gave name to the Icarian sea? Was it not because the son flew aloft, and the father skimmed the ground? For both were furnished with the same kind of wings. Take my word for it, that he who lives privately lives safely; and every one should live within his own income. Envy no man; pray for a quiet life,

*His Royal Highness, the Duke of Sussex.

A. M. cir. 3304
B. C. cir. 700
Ol. vigesimæ
cir. annum
primum
A. U. C. cir. 54

8 [k]Go not forth hastily to strive,
lest *thou know not* what to do in
the end thereof, when thy neighbour hath put thee to shame.
9 [l]Debate thy cause with thy neighbour *himself;* and [m]discover not thy secret to another:
10 Lest he that heareth *it* put thee to
shame, and thine infamy turn not away.
11 [n]A word [o]fitly spoken *is like* apples of
gold in pictures of silver.
12 *As* an ear-ring of gold, and an ornament
of fine gold, *so is* a wise reprover upon an obedient ear.
13 [p]As the cold of snow in
the time of harvest, *so is* a
faithful messenger to them that send him:
for he refresheth the soul of his masters.
14 [q]Whoso boasteth himself [r]of a false
gift *is like* [s]clouds and wind without rain.
15 [t]By long forebearing is a prince persuaded, and a soft tongue breaketh the bone.

A. M. cir. 3304
B. C. cir. 700
Ol. vigesimæ
cir. annum
primum
A. U. C. cir. 54

[k]Chap. xvii. 14; Matt. v. 25——[l]Matt. v. 25; xviii. 15——[m]Or, *discover not the secret of another*——[n]Chap. xv. 23; Isa. l. 4——[o]Heb. *spoken upon his wheels*

[p]Chap. xiii. 17——[q]Chap. xx. 6——[r]Heb. *in a gift of falsehood*——[s]Jude 12——[t]Gen. xxxii. 4, &c.; 1 Sam. xxv. 24, &c.; chap. xv. 1; xvi. 14

though it should not be dignified. Seek a friend, and associate with thy equals."

Verse 8. *Go not forth hastily to strive*] לרב *lerib*, to enter into a *lawsuit*. Keep from this *pit of the bottomless deep*, unless urged by the direst necessity.

Verse 9. *Debate thy cause with thy neighbour*] Take the advice of friends. Let both sides attend to their counsels; but do not tell the *secret* of thy business to any. After squandering your money away upon lawyers, both *they* and the *judge* will at last leave it to be settled by *twelve* of your fellow citizens! O the folly of going to law! O the blindness of men, and the rapacity of unprincipled lawyers!

On this subject I cannot but give the following extract from Sir *John Hawkins's* Life of Dr. Johnson, which he quotes from Mr. *Selwin*, of London: "A man who deliberates about going to law should have, 1. A good cause; 2. A good purse; 3. A good skilful attorney; 4. Good evidence; 5. Good able counsel; 6. A good upright judge; 7. A good intelligent jury; and with all these on his side, if he have not, 8. *Good luck*, it is odds but he miscarries in his suit." O the glorious uncertainty of the law!

Verse 11. *A word fitly spoken*] על אפניו *al ophannaiv, upon its wheels.* An observation, caution, reproof, or advice, that *comes in naturally, runs* smoothly along, is not *forced* nor *dragged* in, that appears to be without *design*, to rise out of the conversation, and though particularly relative to *one point*, will appear to the company to suit all.

Is like *apples of gold in pictures of silver.*] Is like the refreshing *orange* or beautiful *citron*, served up in *open work* or *filigree baskets*, made of *silver.* The Asiatics excel in *filigree silver work.* I have seen much of it, and it is exquisitely beautiful. The silver wire by which it is done they form into the appearance of numerous *flowers;* and though these wires are *soldered* everywhere at their junctions with each other, yet this is done with such *delicacy* and *skill* as to be scarcely perceptible. I have seen *animals* formed on this *filigree* work, with all *their limbs*, and every *joint* in its *natural play. Fruit-baskets* are made also in this way, and are exquisitely fine. The wise man seems to have this kind of work particularly in view; and the contrast of the *golden yellow fruit* in the exquisitely wrought *silver basket*, which may be all termed *picture work*, has a fine and pleasing effect upon the *eye*, as the contained *fruit* has upon the *palate* at an entertainment in a sultry climate. So the word spoken judiciously and opportunely is as much in its place, as the *golden apples* in the *silver baskets.*

Verse 12. As *an ear-ring of gold*] I believe נזם *nezem* to mean the *nose-ring* with its *pendants;* the left nostril is pierced, and a ring put through it, as in the ear. This is very common in almost every part of the East, among women of condition. This is a farther illustration of the above metaphor.

Verse 13. *As the cold of snow*] That *snow* was frequent in *Judea*, is well known; and that in the East they have *snow-houses*—places dug under ground, where they lay up snow for *summer* use—is also a fact. By means of the mass of snow desposited in them the icy temperature is kept up, so that the snow is easily preserved. The *common method of cooling their wine*, which is as *easy* as it is *effectual*, is by dipping a cloth in *water*, wrapping it round the *bottle*, and then hanging the bottle in the *heat of the sun.* The strong *evaporation* carries off the *caloric* from the wine, and the repetition of the wet cloth in the same exposure, makes the wine almost as cold as *ice.*

How agreeable this must be in a burning climate, may be easily conceived. Perhaps it is this to which the wise man refers; for it is a fact that they could have no *snow in harvest*, unless such as had been *preserved* as mentioned above; but this could be only in a *few places*, and within the reach of a *very few persons.* But cooling their liquors by the *simple mode of evaporation* already explained, was within the reach even of the *labourers in the harvest field.* I think the text favours this supposition; for כצנת שלג *ketsinnath sheleg*, need not be referred to *snow itself* procuring cold, but to a *coldness like that of snow*, procured by *evaporation.* If this interpretation be allowed, all difficulty will be removed.

Verse 14. *A false gift*] מתת שקר *mattath shaker, a lying gift*, one *promised*, but never *bestowed.* "Whoso maketh greate boastes, and giveth nothing;" Coverdale. So the Vulgate: "Vir gloriosus, et promissa non complens;" "A bragging man, who does not fulfil his promises," is like *clouds* which appear to be laden with vapour, and like the *wind* which, though it blow from a rainy quarter, brings no moistness with it. So the vain boaster; he is big with promise, but performs nothing.

Verse 15. *A soft tongue breaketh the bone.*]

A. M. cir. 3304 B. C. cir. 700 Ol. vigesimæ cir. annum primum A. U. C. cir. 54

16 [u]Hast thou found honey? eat so much as is sufficient for thee, lest thou be filled therewith, and vomit it.

17 [v]Withdraw thy foot from thy neighbour's house; lest he be [w]weary of thee, and *so* hate thee.

18 [x]A man that beareth false witness against his neighbour *is* a maul, and a sword, and a sharp arrow.

19 Confidence in an unfaithful man in time of trouble *is like* a broken tooth, and a foot out of joint.

20 *As* he that taketh away a garment in cold weather, *and as* vinegar upon nitre, so *is* he that [y]singeth songs to a heavy heart.

21 [z]If thine enemy be hungry, give him bread to eat; and if he be thirsty, give him water to drink:

22 For thou shalt heap coals of fire upon his head, [a]and the LORD shall reward thee.

23 [b]The [c]north wind driveth away rain: so *doth* an angry countenance [d]a backbiting tongue.

24 [e]*It is* better to dwell in the corner of the house-top, than with a brawling woman, and in a wide house.

25 *As* cold waters to a thirsty soul, so *is* good news from a far country.

26 A righteous man falling down before the wicked *is as* a troubled fountain, and a corrupt spring.

27 [f]*It is* not good to eat much honey: so *for men* [g]to search their own glory *is not* glory.

28 [h]He that *hath* no rule over his own spirit *is like* a city *that is* broken down, *and* without walls.

---

[u]Ver. 27——[v]Or, *Let thy foot be seldom in thy neighbour's house*——[w]Heb. *full of thee*——[x]Psa. lvii. 4; cxx. 3, 4; chap. xii. 18——[y]Dan. vi. 18; Rom. xii. 15——[z]Exod. xxiii. 4, 5; Matt. v. 44; Rom. xii. 20——[a]2 Sam. xvi. 12

[b]Job xxxvii. 22——[c]Or, *The north wind bringeth forth rain; so doth a backbiting tongue an angry countenance* [d]Psa. ci. 5——[e]Chap. xix. 13; xxi. 9, 19——[f]Verse 16 [g]Chap. xxvii. 2——[h]Chap. xvi. 32

This is similar to another proverb on the same subject: "A soft answer turneth away wrath." An *angry* word does nothing but *mischief*.

Verse 16. *Hast thou found honey?*] Make a moderate use of all thy enjoyments. "Let thy moderation be known unto all, and appear in all things."

Verse 17. *Withdraw thy foot*] Another proverb will illustrate this: "Too much familiarity breeds contempt."

Verse 20. As *vinegar upon nitre*] The original word נתר *nather* is what is known among chemists as the *natron* of the ancients and of the Scriptures, and *carbonate of soda*. It is found native in *Syria* and *India*, and occurs as an *efflorescence on the soil*. In *Tripoli* it is found in *crystalline incrustations* of from one third to half an inch thick. It is found also in solution in the water of some lakes in *Egypt* and *Hungary*. The borders of these lakes are covered with crystalline masses, of a grayish white or light brown colour; and in some specimens the *natron* is nearly *pure carbonate of soda*, and the *carbonate* is easily discovered by *effervescing* with an *acid*. It appears to have its Hebrew name from נתר *nathar*, to *dissolve* or *loosen:* because a solution of it in water is *abstersive*, taking out *spots*, &c. It is used in the East for the purposes of *washing*. If *vinegar* be poured on it, Dr. Shaw says a *strong fermentation* immediately takes place, which illustrates what Solomon says here: "The singing of songs to a heavy heart is like vinegar upon natron:" that is, "there is no *affinity* between them; and opposition, colluctation, and strife, are occasioned by any attempt to unite them."

And poureth vyneger upon chalke.—COVERDALE. This also will occasion an *effervescence*. See Jer. ii. 22.

Verse 21. *If thine enemy be hungry*] See this and the next verse explained, Rom. xii. 20.

Verse 22. *Thou shalt heap coals of fire upon his head*] Not to *consume*, but to melt him into kindness; a metaphor taken from smelting metallic ores:—

So artists melt the sullen ore of lead,
By *heaping coals of fire upon its head:*
In the *kind warmth* the metal learns to *glow*,
And *pure from dross* the *silver* runs *below*.
S. WESLEY.

Verse 23. *The north wind driveth away rain*] The *margin* has, "The north wind bringeth forth rain." It is said that the "north wind brings forth rain at Jerusalem, because it brings with it the vapours arising from the sea that lies north of it." The marginal is the *true reading;* and is supported by the *Chaldee*, *Syriac*, and *Septuagint;* but the *Arabic* reads *south wind*.

A backbiting tongue] A *hidden tongue*.

Verse 24. It is *better to dwell in a corner*] See the note on chap. xxi. 9.

Verse 27. It is *not good to eat much honey*] *Coverdale* translates the whole passage thus: "Like as it is not good to eat to muche hony; even so, he that wyll search out hye thinges, it shal be to hevy for him." **As he that etith myche honye, and it is not to him goode; so, that is a sercher of mageste, schal ben oppressid of glorie**—Old MS. Bible. He that searches too much into *mysteries*, is likely to be confounded by them. I really think this is the *meaning* of the place; and shall not puzzle either myself or my reader with the discordant explanations which have been brought forward with the hope of illustrating this passage.

CHAPTER XXVI

Honour is not seemly in a fool. The correction and treatment suitable to such. Of the slothful man. Of him who interferes with matters which do not concern him. Contentions to be avoided. Of the dissembler and the lying tongue.

A. M. cir. 3304
B. C. cir. 700
Ol. vigesimæ cir. annum primum
A. U. C. cir. 54

AS snow in summer, [a]and as
rain in harvest; so honour is
not seemly for a fool.
2 As the bird by wandering,
as the swallow by flying, so [b]the curse causeless shall not come.
3 [c]A whip for the horse, a bridle for the
ass, and a rod for the fool's back.
4 Answer not a fool according to his folly,
lest thou also be like unto him.
5 [d]Answer a fool according to
his folly, lest he be wise in [e]his
own conceit.
6 He that sendeth a message
by the hand of a fool cutteth off the feet,
and drinketh [f]damage.
7 The legs of the lame [g]are not equal: so
is a parable in the mouth of fools.
8 [h]As he that bindeth a stone in a sling, so
is he that giveth honour to a fool.

A. M. cir. 3304
B. C. cir. 700
Ol. vigesimæ cir. annum primum
A. U. C. cir. 54

[a]1 Samuel xii. 17——[b]Numbers xxiii. 8; Deuteronomy xxiii. 5——[c]Psalm xxxii. 9; chapter x. 13 [d]Matthew xvi. 1–4; xxi. 24–27

[e]Hebrew, *his own eyes*——[f]Or, *violence*——[g]Hebrew, *are lifted up*——[h]Or, *As he that putteth a precious stone in a heap of stones*

NOTES ON CHAP. XXVI

Verse 1. *As snow in summer*] None of these is *suitable* to the *time;* and at this unsuitable time, both are *unwelcome: so a fool* to be *in honour* is *unbecoming.*

Verse 2. *As the bird*] צפור *tsippor* is taken often for the *sparrow;* but means generally any small bird. As the *sparrow* flies about the house, and the *swallow* emigrates to strange countries; so an undeserved malediction may flutter about the neighbourhood for a season: but in a short time it will disappear as the bird of passage; and never take effect on the innocent person against whom it was pronounced.

Verse 3. *A whip for the horse*] Correction is as suitable to a fool, as a *whip* is for a horse, or a *bridle* for an ass.

Verse 4. *Answer not a fool*] On this and the following verse Bishop *Warburton*, who has written well on many things, and very indifferently on the doctrine of grace, has written with force and perspicuity: "Had this advice been given simply, and without circumstance, *to answer* the fool, and *not to answer* him, one who had reverence for the text would satisfy himself in supposing that the different directions referred to the *doing* a thing *in* and *out of season;* 1. The reasons given why a *fool should not be answered according to his folly*, is, "lest he (the answerer) should be like unto him." 2. The reason given why *the fool should be answered according to his folly*, is, "lest he (the fool) should be wise in his own conceit."

"1. The cause assigned for *forbidding to answer*, therefore, plainly insinuates that the defender of religion should not imitate the insulter of it in his modes of disputation, which may be comprised in sophistry, buffoonery, and scurrility.

"2. The cause assigned for directing *to answer*, as plainly intimates that the sage should address himself to confute the *fool* upon his own false principles, by showing that they lead to conclusions very wide from, very opposite to, those impieties he would deduce from them. If any thing can allay the *fool's vanity*, and prevent his being *wise in his own conceit*, it must be the dishonour of having his own principles turned against himself, and shown to be destructive of his own conclusions."—*Treatise on Grace. Preface.*

Verse 6. *Cutteth off the feet*] Sending by such a person is utterly useless. My old MS. Bible translates well: **Halt in feet and drinking wickidnesse that sendith wordis bi a foole messager.** Nothing but *lameness* in *himself* can vindicate his sending it by such hands; and, after all, the expedient will be worse than the total omission, for he is likely to *drink wickedness*, i. e., the mischief occasioned by the fool's misconduct. *Coverdale* nearly hits the sense as usual: "He is lame of his fete, yee dronken is he in vanite, that committeth eny thinge to a foole."

Verse 8. *As he that bindeth a stone in a sling, so is he that giveth honour to a fool.*] It is entirely thrown away. This, however, is a difficult proverb; and the *versions* give but little light on the subject. The Hebrew may be translated, "As a piece of precious stone among a heap of stones, so is he that giveth honour to a fool." See the *margin*, and *Parkhurst:* but on this interpretation the meaning would rather be, "It is as useless to throw a jewel among a heap of stones to increase its bulk, as to give honour to a fool."

As he that sendith a stoon into a hepe of monee; so he that gebeth to an unwiisman wirschip.—Old MS. Bible.

"He that setteth a foole in hye dignite, that is even as yf a man dyd caste a precious stone upon the galous."—*Coverdale.* This translator refers to the custom of throwing a stone to the *heap* under which a *criminal lay buried.* The *Vulgate* gives some countenance to this translation: "He who gives honour to a fool is like one who throws a stone to Mercury's heap." *Mercury* was considered the deity who *presided over the highways;* and stones were erected in different places to guide the traveller. Hence those lines of Dr. *Young:*—

"Death stands like Mercuries in every way;
And kindly points us to our journey's end."

A. M. cir. 3304
B. C. cir. 700
Ol. vigesimæ cir. annum primum
A. U. C. cir. 54

9 *As* a thorn goeth up into hand of a drunkard; so *is* a parable in the mouth of fools.

10 [i]The great *God* that formed all *things* both rewardeth the fool, and rewardeth transgressors.

11 [k]As a dog returneth to his vomit; [l]*so* a fool [m]returneth to his folly.

12 [n]Seest thou a man wise in his own conceit? *there is* more hope of a fool than of him.

13 [o]The slothful *man* saith, *There is* a lion in the way; a lion *is* in the streets.

14 *As* the door turneth upon his hinges, so *doth* the slothful upon his bed.

15 [p]The slothful hideth his hand in *his* bosom; [q]it grieveth him to bring it again to his mouth.

16 The sluggard *is* wiser in his own conceit than seven men that can render a reason.

17 He that passeth by, *and* [r]meddleth with strife *belonging* not to him, *is like* one that taketh a dog by the ears.

18 As a mad *man* who casteth [s]firebrands, arrows, and death;

19 So *is* the man *that* deceiveth his neighbour, and saith, [t]Am not I in sport?

A. M. cir. 3304
B. C. cir. 700
Ol. vigesimæ cir. annum primum
A. U. C. cir. 54

20 [u]Where no wood is, *there* the fire goeth out: so [v]where *there is* no [w]tale-bearer, the strife [x]ceaseth.

21 [y]*As* coals *are* to burning coals, and wood to fire; so *is* a contentious man to kindle strife.

22 [z]The words of a tale-bearer *are* as wounds, and they go down into the [a]innermost part of the belly.

23 Burning lips and a wicked heart *are like* a potsherd covered with silver dross.

24 He that hateth [b]dissembleth with his lips, and layeth up deceit within him:

25 [c]When he [d]speaketh fair, believe him not: for *there are* seven abominations in his heart.

26 [e]*Whose* hatred is covered by deceit, his wickedness shall be showed before the *whole* congregation.

27 [f]Whoso diggeth a pit shall fall therein: and he that rolleth a stone, it will return upon him.

28 A lying tongue hateth *those that are* afflicted by it; and a flattering mouth worketh ruin.

---

[i]Or, *A great* man *grieveth all, and he hireth the fool, he hireth also transgressors*——[k]2 Peter ii. 22——[l]Exod. viii. 15——[m]Heb. *iterateth his folly*——[n]Chap. xxix. 20; Luke xviii. 11; Rom. xii. 16; Rev. iii. 17——[o]Chap. xxii. 13——[p]Chap. xix. 24——[q]Or, *he is weary*——[r]Or, *is enraged*——[s]Heb. *flames*, or, *sparks*——[t]Eph. v. 4

[u]Heb. *without wood*——[v]Chap. xxii. 10——[w]Or, *whisperer*——[x]Heb. *is silent*——[y]Chap. xv. 18; xxix. 22 [z]Chap. xviii. 8——[a]Heb. *chambers*——[b]Or, *is known* [c]Psa. xxviii. 3; Jer. ix. 8——[d]Heb. *maketh his voice gracious*——[e]Or, *Hatred is covered in secret*——[f]Psa. vii. 15, 16; ix. 15; x. 2; lvii. 6; ch. xxviii. 10; Eccles. x. 8

Verse 10. *The great* God *that formed all* things] See the *margin*, where this verse is very differently translated. I shall add that of *Coverdale:* "A man of experience discerneth all thinges well: but whoso hyreth a foole, hyreth soch one as wyl take no hede." The רב *rab* may mean either the great God, or a great man: hence the two renderings, in the *text* and in the *margin*.

Verse 11. *As a dog returneth to his vomit*] See note on 2 Pet. ii. 22.

Verse 13. *The slothful* man *saith*] See the note on chap. xxii. 13.

Verse 16. *Than seven men that can render a reason.*] *Seven* here only means *perfection*, *abundance*, or *multitude*. He is wiser in his own eyes than a *multitude* of the wisest men. "Than seven men that sytt and teach."—*Coverdale;* i. e., than seven *doctors* of the *law*, or *heads* of the schools of the *prophets*, who always *sat* while they *taught*.

Verse 17. *He that passeth by*] This proverb stands true *ninety-nine* times out of a *hundred*, where people meddle with *domestic broils*, or differences between *men* and their *wives*.

Verse 19. *Am not I in sport?*] How many hearts have been made sad, and how many reputations have been slain, by this kind of *sport!* "I designed no harm by what I said;" "It was only in jest," &c. *Sportive* as such persons may think their conduct to be, it is as ruinous as that of the *madman* who shoots *arrows*, throws *firebrands*, and projects in all directions *instruments of death*, so that some are wounded, some burnt, and some slain.

Verse 20. *Where no wood is*, there *the fire goeth out*] The tale-*receiver* and the tale-*bearer* are the agents of discord. If none received the slander in the *first* instance, it could not be propagated. Hence our proverb, "The receiver is as bad as the thief." And our *laws* treat them equally; for the *receiver* of stolen goods, knowing them to be stolen, is *hanged*, as well as *he* who *stole them*.

Verse 22. *The words of a tale-bearer*] The same with chap. xviii. 8, where see the note.

Verse 23. *Burning lips and a wicked heart*] Splendid, shining, smooth lips; that is, lips which make great professions of friendship are like a *vessel plated* over with *base metal* to make it resemble *silver;* but it is only a *vile pot*, and even the *outside* is not *pure*.

Verse 25. *When he speaketh fair*] For there are such hypocrites and false friends in the world.

Believe him not] Let all his professions go for nothing.

For there are *seven abominations in his heart.*] That is, he is *full of abominations.*

Verse 27. *Whoso diggeth a pit*] See note on Psa. vii. 15. There is a *Latin* proverb like this: *Malum consilium consultori pessimum,* "A bad counsel, but worst to the giver." *Harm watch; harm catch.*

Verse 28. *A lying tongue hateth* those that are *afflicted by it*] He that injures another hates him in proportion to the injury he has done him; and, strange to tell, in proportion to the *innocence* of the oppressed. The debtor cannot bear the sight of his creditor; nor the knave, of him whom he has injured.

CHAPTER XXVII

To-morrow is uncertain. Self-praise forbidden. Anger and envy. Reproof from a friend. Want makes us feel the value of a supply. A good neighbour. Beware of suretyship. Suspicious praise. The quarrelsome woman. One friend helps another. Man insatiable. The incorrigible fool. Domestic cares. The profit of flocks for food and raiment.

A. M. cir. 3304
B. C. cir. 700
Ol. vigesimæ
cir. annum
primum
A. U. C. cir. 54

BOAST [a]not thyself of [b]to-
morrow; for thou knowest
not what a day may bring forth.
2 [c]Let another man praise
thee, and not thine own mouth; a stranger,
and not thine own lips.
3 A stone *is* [d]heavy, and the sand weighty;
but a fool's wrath *is* heavier than them both.
4 [e]Wrath *is* cruel, and anger *is* outrageous;
but [f]who is *able* to stand before [g]envy?
5 [h]Open rebuke *is* better than secret love.

6 [i]Faithful *are* the wounds of
a friend; but the kisses of an
enemy *are* [k]deceitful.
7 The full soul [l]loatheth a
honey-comb; but [m]to the hungry soul every
bitter thing is sweet.
8 As a bird that wandereth from her nest, so
is a man that wandereth from his place.
9 Ointment and perfume rejoice the heart:
so *doth* the sweetness of a man's friend [n]by
hearty counsel.

A. M. cir. 3304
B. C. cir. 700
Ol. vigesimæ
cir. annum
primum
A. U. C. cir. 54

[a]Luke xii. 19, 20; James iv. 13, &c.——[b]Heb. *to-morrow day*——[c]Chap. xxv. 27——[d]Heb. *heaviness* [e]Heb. *Wrath* is *cruelty, and anger an overflowing*——[f]1 John iii. 12

[g]Or, *jealousy;* chap. vi. 34——[h]Chap. xxviii. 23; Gal. ii. 14——[i]Psa. cxli. 5——[k]Or, *earnest,* or *frequent* [l]Heb. *treadeth under foot*——[m]Job vi. 7——[n]Heb. *from the counsel of the soul*

NOTES ON CHAP. XXVII

Verse 1. *Boast not thyself of to-morrow*] See note on James iv. 13, &c. Do not depend on any future moment for spiritual good which at present thou needest, and God is willing to give, and without which, should death surprise thee, thou must be eternally lost; such as repentance, faith in Christ, the pardon of sin, the witness of the Holy Spirit, and complete renovation of soul. Be incessant in thy application to God for these blessings.

My old MS. Bible translates thus: **Ne glorie thou into the morewenning.** Here we see the derivation of our word *morning;* **morewenning**, from *more*, and *wen* or *won*, to *dwell*, i. e., a *continuance* of time to *live* or *dwell* in your present habitation. Every man wishes to live longer, and therefore wishes for *to-morrow;* and when to-morrow comes, then to-morrow, and so on.

Verse 2. *Let another man praise thee, and not thine own mouth*] We have a similar proverb, which illustrates this: "Self-praise is no commendation."

Verse 4. *Who* is *able to stand before envy?*] The rabbins have a curious story on this subject, and it has been formed by the moderns into a fable. There were two persons, one *covetous* and the other *envious*, to whom a certain person promised to grant whatever they should ask; but *double* to him who should ask *last*. The *covetous* man would not ask *first*, because he wished to get the *double* portion; and the *envious* man would not make the first request because he could not bear the thoughts of thus benefiting his neighbour. However, at last he requested that *one* of his eyes should be taken out, in order that his neighbour might lose both.

Verse 5. *Open rebuke* is *better than secret love.*] *Plutarch* gives an account of a man who, aiming a blow at his enemy's life, cut open an imposthume, which by a salutary discharge saved his life, that was sinking under a disease for which a remedy could not be found. *Partial friendship* covers faults; envy, malice, and revenge, will exhibit, heighten, and even multiply them. The former conceals us from ourselves; the latter shows us the worst part of our character. Thus we are taught the necessity of amendment and correction. In this sense *open rebuke is better than secret love.* Yet it is a *rough medicine*, and none can *desire* it. But the genuine open-hearted friend may be intended, who tells *you* your faults *freely*, but conceals them from all *others;* hence the *sixth* verse: "Faithful are the wounds of a friend."

Verse 8. *As a bird that wandereth from her nest*] Leaving her own brood, places of retreat, and feeding-ground behind, and going into strange countries, where she is exposed to every kind of danger. So is the man who leaves his family connections and country, and goes into strange parts to find employment, better his circumstances, make a fortune, &c. I have seen multitudes of such *wanderers from their place* come to great misery and wretchedness. God's general advice is, "Do good, and dwell in the land; and verily thou shalt be fed."

Verse 9. *Ointment and perfume*] Anointing

A. M. cir. 3304
B. C. cir. 700
Ol. vigesimæ
cir. annum
primum
A. U. C. cir. 54

10 Thine own friend, and thy
father's friend, forsake not; neither go into thy brother's house
in the day of thy calamity: *for*
[o]better *is* a neighbour *that is* near, than a
brother far off.
11 [p]My son, be wise, and make my heart
glad, [q]that I may answer him that reproacheth
me.
12 [r]A prudent *man* foreseeth the evil, *and*
hideth himself; *but* the simple pass on, *and*
are punished.
13 [s]Take his garment that is surety for a
stranger, and take a pledge of him for a
strange woman.
14 He that blesseth his friend with a
loud voice, rising early in the morning, it
shall be counted a curse to
him.
15 [t]A continual dropping in
a very rainy day and a contentious woman are alike.
16 Whosoever hideth her hideth the wind,
and the ointment of his right hand, *which* be-
wrayeth *itself*.
17 Iron sharpeneth iron; so a man sharpeneth the countenance of his friend.
18 [u]Whoso keepeth the fig tree shall eat
the fruit thereof: so he that waiteth on his
master shall be honoured.
19 As in water face *answereth* to face; so
the heart of man to man.
20 [v]Hell and destruction are [w]never full, so
[x]the eyes of man are never satisfied.

[o]Chap. xvii. 17; xviii. 24; see chap. xix. 7——[p]Chap. x. 1; xxiii. 15, 24——[q]Psa. cxxvii. 5——[r]Chap. xxii. 3——[s]See Exodus xxii. 26; chap. xx. 16——[t]Chap. xix. 13——[u]1 Corinthians ix. 7, 13——[v]Chap. xxx. 16; Habakkuk ii. 5——[w]Hebrew, *not*——[x]Ecclesiastes i. 8; vi. 7

the head and various parts of the body with aromatic oil is frequent in the East, and fumigating the beards of the guests at the conclusion of an entertainment is almost universal; as is also sprinkling rose-water, and water highly ordoriferous. Two of the curious vessels which are used for this purpose are now before me; they hold some quarts each, and are beautifully inlaid with silver in the form of sprigs, leaves, &c.

Verse 10. *Thine own friend*] A well and long tried friend is invaluable. Him that has been a friend to thy *family* never *forget*, and never *neglect*. And, in the time of adversity, rather apply to such a one, than go to thy nearest relative, who keeps himself at a distance.

Verse 12. *A prudent* man *foreseeth the evil*] The very same as chap. xxii. 3.

Verse 13. *Take his garment*] The same as chap. xx. 16.

Verse 14. *He that blesseth his friend*] He who makes loud and public protestations of acknowledgments to his friend for favours received, subjects his *sincerity* to suspicion; and remember the Italian proverb elsewhere quoted:—"He who praises you more than he was wont to do, has either deceived you, or is about to do it." Extravagant public professions are little to be regarded.

Verse 15. *A continual dropping*] See chap. xix. 13.

Verse 16. *Whosoever hideth her hideth the wind*] You may as well attempt to repress the blowing of the wind, as the tongue of a scold; and to conceal this unfortunate propensity of a wife is as impossible as to hush the storm, and prevent its sound from being heard.

The ointment of his right hand] You can no more conceal such a woman's conduct, than you can the smell of the aromatic oil with which your hand has been anointed. The Hebrew is very obscure, and is variously translated. *Coverdale* thus: "He that refrayneth her, refrayneth the wynde; and holdith oyle fast in his honde." That is, he attempts to do what is impossible to be done.

Verse 17. *Iron sharpeneth iron*] As *hard iron*, viz., *steel*, will bring a knife to a better edge when it is properly *whetted against* it: so one friend may be the means of *exciting* another to *reflect*, dive deeply into, and illustrate a subject, without which *whetting* or *excitement*, this had never taken place. Had *Horace* seen this proverb in the *Septuagint* translation when he wrote to the *Pisos?*

Ergo fungar vice cotis, acutum
Reddere quæ ferrum valet, exors ipsa secandi.
HOR. ARS. POET., ver. 304.

"But let me sharpen others, as the hone
Gives edge to razors, though itself have none."
FRANCIS.

Verse 19. *As in water face* answereth *to face*] All men's hearts are pretty nearly alike; water is not more like to water, than one heart is to another. Or, as a man sees his face perfectly reflected by the water, when looking into it; so the wise and penetrating man sees generally what is in the heart of another by considering the general tenor of his words and actions.

"Surely, if each man saw another's heart
There would be no commerce;
All would disperse,
And live apart."
HERBERT.

Verse 20. *Hell and destruction are never full*] How hideous must the soul of a covetous man be, when God compares it to *hell and perdition!*

The eyes of man are never satisfied.] As the *grave* can never be filled up with *bodies*, nor *perdition* with *souls;* so the restless desire, the lust of power, riches, and splendour, is never satisfied. Out of this ever unsatisfied desire spring all the changing fashions, the varied amusements, and the endless modes of getting money, prevalent in every age, and in every country.

A. M. cir. 3304
B. C. cir. 700
Ol. vigesimæ
cir. annum
primum
A. U. C. cir. 54

21 [y]*As* the fining pot for silver,
and the furnace for gold; so *is*
a man to his praise.
22 [z]Though thou shouldest
bray a fool in a mortar among wheat with a
pestle, *yet* will not his foolishness depart from
him.
23 Be thou diligent to know the state of
thy flocks, *and* [a]look well to thy herds.
24 For [b]riches *are* not for ever: and doth
the crown *endure* [c]to every
generation?
25 [d]The hay appeareth, and
the tender grass showeth itself,
and herbs of the mountains are gathered.
26 The lambs *are* for thy clothing, and the
goats *are* the price of the field.
27 And *thou shalt have* goats' milk enough
for thy food, for the food of thy household,
and *for* the [e]maintenance for thy maidens.

[y]Ch. xvii. 3——[z]Isa. i. 5; Jer. v. 3; ch. xxiii. 35——[a]Heb. *set thy heart*——[b]Heb. *strength*——[c]Heb. *to generation and generation;* Psa. xxxiii. 11; xlv. 17; xlix. 11; lxxii. 5; lxxxv. 5; lxxxix. 1——[d]Psa. civ. 14——[e]Heb. *life*

Verse 21. As *the fining pot for silver*] As silver and gold are tried by the art of the refiner, so is a man's heart by the praise he receives. If he *feel* it not, he *deserves* it; if he be *puffed up* by it, he is *worthless.*

Verse 22. *Though thou shouldest bray a fool*] Leaving all other conjectures, of which commentators are full, I would propose, that this is a metaphor taken from *pounding metallic ores* in very large mortars, such as are still common in the East, in order that, when subjected to the action of the fire, the metal may be the more easily separated from the ore. However you may try, by *precept* or *example*, or both, to instruct a stupid man, your labour is lost; his foolishness cannot be separated from him. You may purge metals of all their dross; but you cannot purge the fool of his folly.

Verse 23. *The state of thy flocks*] The directions to the end of the chapter refer chiefly to *pastoral* and *agricultural* affairs. Do not trust thy flocks to the shepherd merely; number them thyself; look into their condition; see how they are tended; and when, and with what, and in what proportion, they are fed.

Verse 24. *For riches* are *not for ever*] All other kinds of property are very transitory. Money and the highest civil honours are but for a short season. Flocks and herds, properly attended to, may be multiplied and continued from generation to generation. The *crown* itself is not naturally so permanent.

Verse 25. *The hay appeareth*] Take care that this be timeously *mown*, carefully dried, and safely ricked or housed. And when the *tender grass* and the proper herbs *appear* in *the mountains* in the spring, then send forth the *lambs*, the young of the flock, that they may get suitable pasturage, without too much impoverishing the *home fields;* for by the sale of the *lambs* and *goats*, the *price of the field* is paid—all the landlord's demands are discharged. Either a certain number of lambs, goats, and other cattle, was given to the landlord; or so much money as so many lambs, &c., were then worth.

Verse 26. *The lambs* are *for thy clothing*] So many *fleeces* are given in some places as *rent* to the landlord.

Verse 27. *Goats' milk enough for thy food*] ללחמך *lelachmecha*, "to thy bread;" for they ate the *bread* and *supped the milk* to assist mastication, and help deglutition. And it seems that *bread*, with *goats' milk*, was the general article of food for the *master* and his *family;* and for the *servant maids* who assisted in the household work, and performed the operations required in the *dairy.*

The reader who wishes to see these maxims detailed and illustrated at large, may consult the writers *De Re Rustica*, where he will find much curious information.

CHAPTER XXVIII

The timidity of the wicked. Quick succession in the government of a country is a punishment to the land. Of the poor who oppress the poor. The upright poor man is preferable to the wicked rich man. The unprofitable conduct of the usurer. The prosperity of the righteous a cause of rejoicing. He is blessed who fears always. A wicked ruler a curse. The murderer generally execrated. The faithful man. The corrupt judge. The foolishness of trusting in one's own heart. The charitable man. When the wicked are elevated, it is a public evil.

A. M. cir. 3304
B. C. cir. 700
Ol. vigesimæ
cir. annum
primum
A. U. C. cir. 54

THE [a]wicked flee when no
man pursueth: but the
righteous are bold as a lion.
2 For the transgression of a
land many *are* the princes thereof: but [b]by a man of understanding *and* knowledge the state
thereof shall be prolonged.

[a]Lev. xxvi. 17, 36; Psa. liii. 5——[b]Or, *by men of understanding* and *wisdom shall they likewise be prolonged*

NOTES ON CHAP. XXVIII

Verse 1. *The wicked flee*] Every wicked man, however *bold* he may *appear*, is full of dreary apprehensions relative to both worlds. But the righteous has true courage, being conscious of his own innocence, and the approbation of his God. **The unpitious fleeth.**—Old MS.

A. M. cir. 3304
B. C. cir. 700
Ol. vigesimæ cir. annum primum
A. U. C. cir. 54

3 [c]A poor man that oppresseth
the poor *is like* a sweeping rain
[d]which leaveth no food.
4 [e]They that forsake the law
praise the wicked: [f]but such as keep the law
contend with them.
5 [g]Evil men understand not judgment: but
[h]they that seek the LORD understand all
things.
6 [i]Better *is* the poor that walketh in his
uprightness, than *he that is* perverse *in his*
ways, though he *be* rich.
7 [k]Whoso keepeth the law *is* a wise son:
but he that [l]is a companion of riotous *men*
shameth his father.
8 [m]He that by usury and [n]unjust gain increaseth his substance, he shall
gather it for him that will pity
the poor.
9 [o]He that turneth away his
ear from hearing the law, [p]even his prayer
shall be abomination.
10 [q]Whoso causeth the righteous to go
astray in an evil way, he shall fall himself into
his own pit: [r]but the upright shall have good
things in possession.
11 The rich man *is* wise [s]in his own conceit: but the poor that hath understanding
searcheth him out.
12 [t]When righteous *men* do rejoice, *there is*
great glory: but when the wicked rise, a man
is [u]hidden.

A. M. cir. 3304
B. C. cir. 700
Ol. vigesimæ cir. annum primum
A. U. C. cir. 54

[c]Matt. xviii. 28——[d]Heb. *without food*——[e]Psa. x. 3; xlix. 18; Rom. i. 32——[f]1 Kings xviii. 18, 21; Matt. iii. 7; xiv. 4; Eph. v. 11——[g]Psa. xcii. 6——[h]John vii. 17; 1 Cor. ii. 15; 1 John ii. 20, 27——[i]Chap. xix. 1; ver. 18——[k]Chap. xxix. 3——[l]Or, *feedeth gluttons*

[m]Job xxvii. 16, 17; chapter xiii. 22; Eccles. ii. 26——[n]Heb. *by increase*——[o]Zech. vii. 11——[p]Psa. lxvi. 18; cix. 7; chap. xv. 8——[q]Chap. xxvi. 27——[r]Matt. vi. 33——[s]Heb. *in his eyes*——[t]Ver. 28; chap. xi. 10; xxix. 2; Eccles x. 6——[u]Or, *sought for*

Bible. This word is often used for *impious, wicked, ungodly;* hence it appears that our word *pity* anciently meant *piety* or *godliness.*

Verse 2. *Many are the princes*] *Nations,* as nations, cannot be judged in a future world; therefore, God judges them *here.* And where the *people* are very *wicked,* and the *constitution* very *bad,* the *succession of princes is frequent*—they are generally taken off by an untimely death. Where the people know that the constitution is in their favour, they seldom disturb the prince, as they consider him the guardian of their privileges.

But by a man of understanding] Whether he be a *king,* or the king's *prime minister,* the prosperity of the state is advanced by his counsels.

Verse 3. *A poor man that oppresseth the poor*] Our Lord illustrates this proverb most beautifully, by the parable of the *two debtors,* Matt. xviii. 23. One owed *ten thousand talents,* was insolvent, begged for time, was forgiven. A fellow servant owed this one *a hundred pence:* he was insolvent; but prayed his fellow servant to give him a little time, and he would pay it all. He would not, took him by the throat, and cast him into prison till he should pay that debt. Here the *poor* oppressed the *poor;* and what was the consequence? The oppressing poor was delivered to the tormentors; and the forgiven debt charged to his amount, because *he showed no mercy.* The *comparatively poor* are often shockingly uncharitable and unfeeling towards the *real poor.*

Like *a sweeping rain*] These are frequent in the East; and sometimes carry flocks, crops, and houses, away with them.

Verse 4. *They that forsake the law*] He that transgresses says, in fact, that it is *right to transgress;* and thus other wicked persons are *encouraged.*

Verse 5. *They that seek the Lord understand all* things.] They are wise unto salvation; they "have the unction from the Holy One, and they know all things," 1 John ii. 20, every thing that is essentially needful for them to know, in reference to both worlds.

Verse 8. *He that by usury—increaseth his substance*] By taking unlawful interest for his money; *lending* to a man in great distress money, for the use of which he requires an *exorbitant sum.* O that the names of all those unfeeling, hard-hearted, consummate villains in the nation, who thus take advantage of their neighbour's necessities to enrich themselves. were published at every market cross; and then the delinquents all sent to their brother savages in New Zealand. It would be a happy riddance to the country.

Verse 9. *He that turneth away his ear from hearing the law*] Many suppose, if they *do not know their duty, they shall not be accountable for their transgressions;* and therefore avoid every thing that is calculated to enlighten them. They will not read the Bible, lest they should know the will of God; and they will not attend Divine ordinances for the same reason. But this pretence will avail them nothing; as he that *might have known* his *master's will,* but would not, shall be treated as he shall be who *did know* it, and disobeyed it. Even the *prayers* of such a person as this are reputed *sin* before God.

Verse 10. *Whoso causeth the righteous to go astray*] He who strives to pervert one really converted to God, in order that he may pour contempt on religion, shall fall into that hell to which he has endeavoured to lead the other.

Verse 12. *When righteous* men *do rejoice*] When true religion is no longer persecuted. and the word of God duly esteemed, *there is great glory;* for the word of the Lord has then free course, runs, and is glorified: but *when the wicked rise*—when they are *elevated* to places of trust, and put at the head of civil affairs, then the righteous man is obliged to hide himself; the word of the Lord becomes scarce, and there is no open vision. The *first* was the case in this country, in the days of EDWARD VI.; the *second* in the days of his suc-

A. M. cir. 3304
B. C. cir. 700
Ol. vigesimæ cir. annum primum
A. U. C. cir. 54

13 [v]He that covereth his sins shall not prosper: but whoso confesseth and forsaketh *them* shall have mercy.

14 Happy *is* the man [w]that feareth alway: [x]but he that hardeneth his heart shall fall into mischief.

15 [y]*As* a roaring lion, and a ranging bear; [z]*so is* a wicked ruler over the poor people.

16 The prince that wanteth understanding *is* also a great oppressor: *but* he that hateth covetousness shall prolong *his* days.

17 [a]A man that doeth violence to the blood of *any* person shall flee to the pit; let no man stay him.

18 [b]Whoso walketh uprightly shall be saved: but [c]*he that is* perverse *in his* ways shall fall at once.

19 [d]He that tilleth his land shall have plenty of bread: but he that followeth after vain *persons* shall have poverty enough.

20 A faithful man shall abound with blessings: [e]but he that maketh haste to be rich shall not be [f]innocent.

21 [g]To have respect of persons *is* not good; for, [h]for a piece of bread *that* man will transgress.

A. M. cir. 3304
B. C. cir. 700
Ol. vigesimæ cir. annum primum
A. U. C. cir. 54

22 [i]He [k]that hasteth to be rich *hath* an evil eye, and considereth not that poverty shall come upon him.

23 [l]He that rebuketh a man afterwards shall find more favour than he that flattereth with the tongue.

24 Whoso robbeth his father or his mother, and saith, *It is* no transgression; the same [m]*is* the companion of [n]a destroyer.

25 [o]He that is of a proud heart stirreth up strife: [p]but he that putteth his trust in the LORD shall be made fat.

26 He that trusteth in his own heart is a fool: but whoso walketh wisely, he shall be delivered.

27 [q]He that giveth unto the poor shall not lack: but he that hideth his eyes shall have many a curse.

28 [r]When the wicked rise, [s]men hide themselves: but when they perish, the righteous increase.

---

[v]Psa. xxxii. 3, 5; 1 John i. 8, 9, 10——[w]Psa. xvi. 8; chap. xxiii. 17——[x]Rom. ii. 5; xi. 20——[y]1 Pet. v. 8——[z]Exod. i. 14, 16, 22; Matt. ii. 16——[a]Genesis ix. 6; Exod. xxi. 14——[b]Chap. xix. 9, 25——[c]Ver. 6——[d]Chap. xii. 11——[e]Chap. xiii. 11; xx. 21; xxiii. 4; ver. 22; 1 Tim. vi. 9——[f]Or, *unpunished*

[g]Chap. xviii. 5; xxiv. 23——[h]Ezek. xiii. 19——[i]Or, *he that hath an evil eye hasteth to be rich*——[k]Ver. 20——[l]Chap. xxvii. 5, 6——[m]Chap. xviii. 9——[n]Heb. *a man destroying*——[o]Chap. xiii. 10——[p]1 Tim. vi. 6——[q]Deut. xv. 7, &c.; chap. xix. 17; xxii. 9——[r]Ver. 12; chap. xxix. 2——[s]Job xxiv. 4

---

cessor, MARY I. Popery, cruelty, and knavery, under her, nearly destroyed the Church and the State in these islands.

Verse 13. *He that covereth his sins*] Here is a general *direction* relative to *conversion.* 1. If the sinner do not *acknowledge* his sins; if he *cover* and *excuse* them, and refuse to come to the light of God's word and Spirit, lest his deeds should be reproved, he *shall find no salvation.* God will never admit a *sinful, unhumbled* soul, into his kingdom. 2. But if he confess his sin, with a penitent and broken heart, and, by *forsaking* every evil way, give this proof that he feels his own sore, and the plague of his heart, then he shall *have mercy.* Here is a doctrine of vital importance to the salvation of the soul, which the weakest may understand.

Verse 14. *Happy* is *the man that feareth alway*] That ever carries about with him that reverential and filial fear of God, which will lead him to avoid sin, and labour to do that which is lawful and right in the sight of God his Saviour.

Verse 16. *The prince that wanteth understanding*] A weak prince will generally have wicked ministers, for his weakness prevents him from making a proper choice; and he is apt to prefer them who flatter him, and minister most to his pleasures. The quantum of the king's intellect may be always appreciated by the mildness or oppressiveness of his government. He who plunges his people into expensive wars, to support which they are burdened with taxes, is a prince without understanding. He does not know his own interest, and does not regard that of his people. But these things, though general truths, apply more particularly to those despotic governments which prevail in Asiatic countries.

Verse 17. *That doeth violence to the blood*] He who either *slays* the innocent, or procures his destruction, may flee to *hide* himself: but let none give him protection. The law demands his life, because he is a *murderer;* and let none deprive justice of its claim. Murder is the most horrid crime in the sight of God and man; it scarcely ever goes unpunished, and is universally execrated.

Verse 18. *Shall fall at once*] Shall fall *without resource, altogether.*

Verse 19. *He that tilleth his land*] See chap. xii. 11.

Verse 20. *He that maketh haste to be rich*] See chap. xiii. 11; xx. 21.

Verse 24. *Whoso robbeth his father*] The father's property is as much his own, in reference to the child, as that of the merest *stranger.* He who robs his parents is worse than a common robber; to the act of dishonesty and rapine he adds ingratitude, cruelty, and disobedience. Such a person is *the companion of a destroyer;* he may be considered as a murderer.

Verse 25. *Shall be made fat.*] Shall be prosperous.

Verse 26. *He that trusteth in his own heart is a fool*] For his heart, which is deceitful and desperately wicked, will infallibly deceive him.

Verse 27. *He that giveth unto the poor*] See the notes on the passages referred to in the *margin.*

CHAPTER XXIX

We must not despise correction. The prudent king. The flatterer. The just judge. Contend not with a fool. The prince who opens his ears to reports. The poor and the deceitful. The pious king. The insolent servant. The humiliation of the proud. Of the partner of a thief. The fear of man. The Lord the righteous Judge.

A. M. cir. 3304
B. C. cir. 700
Ol. vigesimæ cir. annum primum
A. U. C. cir. 54

[a]HE, [b]that being often reproved hardeneth *his* neck,
shall suddenly be destroyed, and
that without remedy.

2 [c]When the righteous are [d]in authority, the
people rejoice: but when the wicked beareth
rule, [e]the people mourn.

3 [f]Whoso loveth wisdom rejoiceth his father: [g]but he that keepeth company with harlots spendeth *his* substance.

4 The king by judgment establisheth the
land: but [h]he that receiveth gifts overthroweth it.

5 A man that flattereth his neighbour
spreadeth a net for his feet.

6 In the transgression of an evil man *there
is* a snare: but the righteous doth sing and
rejoice.

7 [i]The righteous considereth
the cause of the poor: *but*
the wicked regardeth not to
know *it.*

A. M. cir. 3304
B. C. cir. 700
Ol. vigesimæ cir. annum primum
A. U. C. cir. 54

8 [k]Scornful men [l]bring a city into a snare:
but wise *men* [m]turn away wrath.

9 *If* a wise man contendeth with a foolish
man, [n]whether he rage or laugh, *there is* no
rest.

10 [o]The [p]bloodthirsty hate the upright: but
the just seek his soul.

11 A [q]fool uttereth all his mind: but a wise
man keepeth it in till afterwards.

12 If a ruler hearken to lies, all his servants
are wicked.

13 The poor and [r]the deceitful man [s]meet
together: [t]the LORD lighteneth both their
eyes.

---

[a]Heb. *A man of reproofs*——[b]1 Sam. ii. 25; 2 Chron. xxxvi. 16; ch. i. 24-27——[c]Esth. viii. 15; ch. xi. 10; xxviii. 12, 28——[d]Or, *increased*——[e]Esth. iii. 15——[f]Ch. x. 1; xv. 20; xxvii. 11——[g]Ch. v. 9, 10; vi. 26; xxviii. 7; Luke xv. 13, 30——[h]Heb. *a man of oblations*

[i]Job xxix. 16; xxxi. 13; Psa. xli. 1——[k]Ch. xi. 11——[l]Or, *set a city on fire*——[m]Ezek. xxii. 30——[n]Matt. xi. 17——[o]Heb. *Men of blood*——[p]Gen. iv. 5, 8; 1 John iii. 12——[q]Judg. xvi. 17; chap. xii. 16; xiv. 33——[r]Or, *the usurer*——[s]Ch. xxii. 2——[t]Matt. v. 45

NOTES ON CHAP. XXIX

Verse 1. *Hardeneth* his *neck*] Becomes *stubborn* and *obstinate.*

Verse 3. *But he that keepeth company*] רעה יאבד *roeh,* he that *feedeth harlots, yeabed, shall utterly destroy* his substance. Has there ever been a single case to the *contrary?*

Verse 4. *He that receiveth gifts*] This was notoriously the case in this kingdom, before the passing of the *Magna Charta,* or *great charter of liberties.* Hence that article in it, Nulli vendemus justitiam; "We will not sell justice to any." I have met with cases in our ancient records where, in order to get his *right,* a man was obliged almost to ruin himself in *presents to the king, queen, and their favourites,* to get the case decided in his favour.

Verse 5. *Spreadeth a net for his feet.*] Beware of a flatterer; he does not flatter merely to please you, but to *deceive you* and *profit himself.*

Verse 9. *Whether he rage or laugh*] *Coverdale* translates, "Yf a wyse man go to lawe with a foole, whether he deale with him frendly or roughly he geteth no rest."

Verse 11. *A fool uttereth all his mind*] A man should be careful to keep his *own secret,* and never tell his whole mind upon any subject, while there are other opinions yet to be delivered; else, if he speak *again,* he must go over his old ground; and as he brings out nothing *new,* he injures his former *argument.*

Verse 12. *If a ruler hearken to lies*] Wherever the system of *espionage* is permitted to prevail, there the system of *falsity* is established; for he who is capable of being a *spy* and informer, is not only capable of telling and swearing lies, but also of cutting his king's or even his *father's* throat. I have seen cases, where the *same spy* received pay from both parties, and deceived both.

Verse 13. *The poor and the deceitful man*] It is difficult to fix the meaning of תככים *techachim,* which we here render the *deceitful man.* The TARGUM has, "The *poor* and the *man* of LITTLE WEALTH." The SEPTUAGINT, "The *usurer* and the DEBTOR." The VULGATE, "The *poor* and CREDITOR." COVERDALE, "The *poor* and the LENDER." OTHERS, "The *poor* and the RICH;" "The *poor* and the OPPRESSORS." I suppose the meaning may be the same as in chap. xxii. 2: "The rich and the poor meet

A. M. cir. 3304
B. C. cir. 700
Ol. vigesimæ
cir. annum
primum
A. U. C. cir. 54

14 [u]The king that [v]faithfully
judgeth the poor, his throne shall
be established for ever.
15 [w]The rod and reproof give
wisdom: but [x]a child left *to himself* bringeth
his mother to shame.
16 When the wicked are multiplied, transgression increaseth: [y]but the righteous shall
see their fall.
17 [z]Correct thy son, and he shall give thee
rest; yea, he shall give delight unto thy soul.
18 [a]Where *there is* no vision, the people
[b]perish: but [c]he that keepeth the law, happy
is he.
19 A servant will not be corrected by words:
for though he understand he will not answer.
20 Seest thou a man *that is* hasty [d]in his
words? [e]*there is* more hope of a fool than
of him.
21 He that delicately bringeth
up his servant from a child shall
have him become *his* son at the
length.

A. M. cir. 3304
B. C. cir. 700
Ol. vigesimæ
cir. annum
primum
A. U. C. cir. 54

22 [f]An angry man stirreth up strife, and a
furious man aboundeth in transgression.
23 [g]A man's pride shall bring him low:
but honour shall uphold the humble in spirit.
24 Whoso is partner with a thief hateth his
own soul: [h]he heareth cursing, and bewray-
eth *it* not.
25 [i]The fear of man bringeth a snare: but
whoso putteth his trust in the LORD [k]shall be
safe.
26 [l]Many seek [m]the ruler's favour: but
every man's judgment *cometh* from the LORD.
27 An unjust man *is* an abomination to the
just; and *he that is* upright in the way *is*
abomination to the wicked.

[u]Chap. xx. 28; xxv. 5——[v]Psa. lxxii. 2, 4, 13, 14——[w]Ver. 17——[x]Chap. x. 1; xvii. 21, 25——[y]Psa. xxxvii. 36; lviii. 10; xci. 8; xcii. 11——[z]Chap. xiii. 24; xix. 18; xxii. 15; xxiii. 13, 14; ver. 15——[a]1 Sam. iii. 1; Amos viii. 11, 12——[b]Or, *is made naked*——[c]John xiii. 17; James i. 25——[d]Or, *in his matters*——[e]Chap. xxvi. 12

[f]Chap. xv. 18; xxvi. 21——[g]Job xxii. 29; chap. xv. 33; xviii. 12; Isa. lxvi. 2; Dan. iv. 30, 31, &c.; Matt. xxiii. 12; Luke xiv. 11; xviii. 14; Acts xii. 23; James iv. 6, 10; 1 Pet. v. 5——[h]Lev. v. 1——[i]Gen. xii. 12; xx. 2, 11——[k]Heb. *shall be set on high*——[l]See Psalm xx. 9; chapter xix. 6——[m]Heb. *the face of a ruler*

together; the Lord is the Maker of them all." Where see the note.

Verse 16. *When the wicked are multiplied*] That, in the *multiplication of the wicked transgression is increased*, requires no proof; but an important doctrine attaches to this. On this account wicked nations and wicked families are cut off and rooted out. Were it not so, righteousness would in process of time be banished from the earth. This will account for many of the numerous instances in which whole families fail.

Verse 18. *Where* there is *no vision*] My old MS. Bible, following the *Vulgate*, translates: **Whan prophecye schal failen, the peple schal ben to scatered.** Where Divine revelation, and the faithful preaching of the sacred testimonies, are neither reverenced nor attended, the ruin of that land is at no great distance.

But he that keepeth the law, happy is *he.*] Go how it may with others, *he* shall be safe. So our Lord: "Blessed are they who hear the word of God, and keep it."

Verse 21. *He that delicately bringeth up his servant*] Such persons are generally forgetful of their obligations, assume the rights and privileges of children, and are seldom good for any thing.

Verse 22. *An angry man stirreth up strife*] His spirit begets its *like* wherever he goes.

And a furious man aboundeth in transgression.] His furious spirit is always carrying him into *extremes*, and each of these is a *transgression.*

Verse 23. *A man's pride shall bring him low*] A proud man is universally despised, and such are often exposed to great mortifications.

Verse 24. *Hateth his own soul*] נפשו *naphsho*, his *life*, as the outraged law may at any time seize on and put him to *death.*

He heareth cursing] אלה *alah*, the *execration* or *adjuration*, (for all culprits were *charged, as before God*, to *tell the truth*,) ולא יגד *velo yaggid, but* HE *will not tell* IT. He has no fear of God, nor reverence for an oath, because his heart is hardened through the deceitfulness of sin.

Verse 25. *The fear of man bringeth a snare*] How often has this led weak men, though *sincere* in their general character, to deny their God, and abjure his people! See the case of *Peter;* and learn from this, O reader, that where the mighty have been slain, *thou* wilt fall, unless thou call on the Strong for *strength*, and for *courage* to use it. Be not ashamed of JESUS, nor of his *people*, nor of his *cross.* Glory in this, that thou knowest *him*, art joined to *them*, and art counted worthy to bear *it.*

Verse 26. *Many seek the ruler's favour*] To be screened from the punishment determined by the law; but should *he* grant the favour sought, and pardon the criminal, this takes not away his guilt in the sight of God, from whom all just judgment proceeds.

Verse 27. *And* he that is *upright in the way*] "But as for those that be in the right waye, the wicked hate them."—COVERDALE.

To this verse the VULGATE adds the following: *Verbum custodiens filius extra perditionem erit;* "The son that keeps the word shall not fall into perdition." This is not in *all copies* of the Vulgate: but it was in that from which my old MS. Bible was made, where it is thus translated: **The sone keping the worde schal ben out of perdicyon.** I believe *verbum* here is intended for the Divine *word;* the revelation from God.

CHAPTER XXX

Agur's confession of faith, 1–6. *His prayer,* 7–9. *Of wicked generations,* 10–14. *Things that are never satisfied,* 15, 16. *Of him who despises his parents,* 17. *Three wonderful things,* 18–20. *Three things that disquiet the land,* 21–23. *Four little but very intelligent animals,* 24–28. *Four things that go well,* 29–31. *A man should cease from doing foolishly, and from strife,* 32, 33.

A. M. cir. 3304 B. C. cir. 700 Ol. vigesimæ cir. annum primum A. U. C. cir. 54

THE words of Agur the son
of Jakeh, *even* [a]the prophecy: the man spake unto
Ithiel, even unto Ithiel and Ucal,
2 [b]Surely I *am* more brutish than *any* man,
and have not the understanding of a man.
3 I neither learned wisdom,
nor [c]have the knowledge of the
holy.
4 [d]Who hath ascended up into
heaven, or descended? [e]who hath gathered
the wind in his fists? who hath bound the

[a]Chap. xxxi. 1——[b]Psa. lxxiii. 22——[c]Heb. *know*——[d]John iii. 13

[e]Job xxxviii. 4, &c.; Psa. civ. 3, &c.; Isa. xl. 12, &c.

NOTES ON CHAP. XXX

Verse 1. *The words of Agur the son of Jakeh*] The words *Agur, Jakeh, Ithiel,* and *Ucal,* have been considered by some as *proper names:* by others, as *descriptive characters.* With some, *Agur* is *Solomon;* and *Jakeh, David;* and *Ithiel* and *Ucal* are epithets of *Christ.*

The *Vulgate* translates, *Verba congregantis filii vomentis: visio, quam locutus est vir, cum quo est Deus, et qui Deo secum morante confortatus, ait.* "The words of the collector, the son of the vomiter: the vision of the man who has God with him, and who is fortified by God dwelling with him, saith."

COVERDALE makes the following words a *title* to the chapter:

"The wordes of Agur the sonne of Jake.

"The prophecie of a true faithfull man, whom God hath helped; whom God hath comforted and nourished."

The whole might be thus translated, keeping near to the *letter:—*

"The words of the epistle of the obedient son." Or,

"The words of the collector, the son of Jakeh. The parable which הגבר *haggeber,* the strong man, the hero, spake unto him who is God with me; to him who is God with me, even the strong God."

The visioun that a man spake with whiche is God, and that God with him, wonyng confortid.—Old MS. Bible.

From this introduction, from the names here used, and from the style of the book, it appears evident that Solomon was not the author of this chapter; and that it was designed to be distinguished from his work by this very preface, which specifically distinguishes it from the preceding work. Nor can the words in verses 2, 3, 8, and 9, be at all applied to Solomon: they suit no part of Solomon's *life,* nor of his *circumstances.* We must, therefore, consider it an *appendix* or *supplement* to the preceding collection; something in the manner of that part which the *men of Hezekiah, king of Judah, had collected.* As to *mysteries* here, many have been found by them who sought for nothing else; but they are all, in my view of the subject, hazarded and precarious. I believe *Agur, Jakeh, Ithiel,* and *Ucal,* to be the *names of persons* who did exist, but of whom we know nothing but what is here mentioned. *Agur* seems to have been a public *teacher,* and *Ithiel* and *Ucal* to have been his *scholars;* and what he delivers to them was done by *prophecy.* It was what the prophets generally term משא *massa,* an ORACLE, something immediately delivered by the *Holy Spirit* for the benefit of man.

Verse 2. *Surely I* am *more brutish*] These words can in no sense, nor by any mode of speech, be true of Solomon: for while he was the *wisest of men,* he could not have said that he *was more brutish than* any *man, and had not the understanding of a man.* It is saying nothing to the purpose, to say he was so *independently of the Divine teaching.* Had he put this in, even by innuendo, it might be legitimate: but he does not; nor is it by fair implication to be understood. Solomon is not supposed to have written the Proverbs *after he fell from God.* Then indeed he might have said he *had been more brutish than any man.* But Agur might have used these words with strict propriety, for aught we know; for it is very probable that he was a *rustic,* without education, and without any human help, as was the prophet Amos; and that all that he knew now was by the *inspiration* of the Almighty, independently of which he was *rustic* and *uneducated.*

Verse 3. *I neither learned wisdom*] I have never been a scholar in any of those schools of the *wise men,* nor *have the knowledge of the holy,* קדשים *kedoshim,* of the *saints* or *holy persons.*

The *Septuagint* give this a different turn: Θεος δεδιδαχε με σοφιαν, και γνωσιν ἁγιων εγνωκα; "God hath taught me wisdom, and the knowledge of the saints I have known."

This may refer to the *patriarchs, prophets,* or *holy men,* that lived before the days of Solomon. That is, the translators might have had these in view.

Verse 4. *Who hath ascended up into heaven, or descended?*] *Calmet* paraphrases this passage thus: "*Who hath* descended, &c. In order to show the truth of what he was about to say, he observes: *I have not the science of the saints;* for how could I have acquired it? Who is he who could attain to that? *Who has ascended to heaven* to learn that science; and *who has descended* in order to publish it? Is the science of salvation one of those things that can be *apprehended* only by *study?* Is it not a pure gift of the goodness of God? Moses, after having shown to the people the will of

A. M. cir. 3304 B. C. cir. 700 Ol. vigesimæ cir. annum primum A. U. C. cir. 54

waters in a garment? who hath
established all the ends of the
earth? what *is* his name, and
what *is* his son's name, if thou
canst tell?
5 [f]Every word of God *is* [g]pure: [h]he *is* a
shield unto them that put their trust in him.

6 [i]Add thou not unto his
words, lest he reprove thee, and
thou be found a liar.
7 Two *things* have I required
of thee; [k]deny me *them* not before I
die:
8 Remove far from me vanity and lies:

A. M. cir. 3304 B. C. cir. 700 Ol. vigesimæ cir. annum primum A. U. C. cir. 54

[f]Psalm xii. 6; xviii. 30; xix. 8; cxix. 140——[g]Heb. *purified*——[h]Psa. xviii. 30; lxxxiv. 11; cxv. 9, 10, 11

[i]Deut. iv. 2; xii. 32; Rev. xxii. 18, 19——[k]Heb. *withhold not from me*

God, said to them: 'This commandment which I command thee this day is not hidden from thee; neither is it far off. It is not in heaven, that thou shouldest say, Who shall go up for us to heaven, and bring it unto us, that we may hear it, and do it?' Deut. xxx. 11, 12. The person whose words we are here examining speaks a knowledge more sublime than that contained in the simple laws of the Lord, common to all the people of Israel. He speaks of the sublime science of the designs of God, of his ways, and of his secrets; and in this sense he affirms he has no knowledge."

Who hath gathered the wind in his fists?] It is as difficult for a mortal man to acquire this Divine science by his own reason and strength, as to collect the winds in his fists. And who can command the spirit of prophecy, so that he can have it whensoever he pleases?

What is *his name?*] Show me the nature of this Supreme Being. Point out his eternity, omniscience, omnipresence, omnipotence; comprehend and describe him, if thou canst.

What is *his son's name*] Some copies of the *Septuagint* have η τι ονομα τοις τικνοιο αυτου; "Or the name of his sons;" meaning, I suppose, the *holy angels*, called his *saints* or *holy ones*, ver. 3.

The *Arabic* has, *What is his name?* وما اسم والده *and what is the name of his father?* him who *begat him*. But the *Chaldee*, the *Syriac*, and the *Vulgate*, read as the *Hebrew*.

Many are of opinion that Agur refers here to the *first* and *second persons* of the *ever-blessed* Trinity. It *may* be so; but who would venture to rest the proof of that most glorious doctrine upon such a *text*, to say nothing of the *obscure author?* The doctrine is true, sublimely true; but many doctrines have suffered in controversy, by improper texts being urged in their favour. Every lover of God and truth should be very choice in his *selections*, when he comes forward in behalf of the *more mysterious doctrines* of the Bible. Quote nothing that is not clear: advance nothing that does not *tell.* When we are obliged to spend a world of critical labour, in order to establish the *sense* of a text which we intend to allege in favour of the doctrine we wish to support, we may rest assured that we *are going the wrong way to work.* Those who indiscriminately amass every text of Scripture *they think* bears upon the subject they defend, give their adversaries great advantage against them. I see many a sacred doctrine suffering through the bad judgment of its friends every day. The Godhead of Christ, salvation by faith, the great atoning sacrifice, and other essential doctrines of this class, are all suffering in this way. My heart says, with deep concern,

Non tali auxilio, nec defensoribus istis,
Tempus eget.

When truth is assailed by all kinds of weapons, handled by the most *powerful foes*, injudicious defenders may be ranked among its enemies. To such we may innocently say, "Keep your cabins; you do assist the storm."

Verse 5. *Every word of God* is *pure*] כל אמרת אלוה צרופה *col imrath eloah tseruphah*, "Every oracle of God is purified." A metaphor taken from the *purifying of metals.* Every thing that God has pronounced, every inspiration which the prophets have received, is pure, without mixture of error, without dross. Whatever trials it may be exposed to, it is always like *gold:* it *bears the fire*, and comes out with the same *lustre*, the same *purity*, and the same *weight.*

He is *a shield unto them*] And *this* oracle among the rest. "He is the defence of *all* them that put their trust in him." לכל *lechol, to all*, is added here by *nineteen* of *Kennicott's* and *De Rossi's* MSS.; for instead of לחסים *lachosim, to the trusters*, they read לכל החוסים *lechol hachosim*, "to EVERY ONE of them that trust." Where the *preposition* and *adjective* are not only added, but the *noun* is written *more full*, and more *emphatic:* but a translation cannot well express it without *paraphrase.*

Verse 6. *Add not thou unto his words*] You can no more increase their *value* by any *addition*, than you can that of *gold* by adding any *other metal to it.* Take care that you *do not* any thing that this word *forbids*, nor leave *undone* any thing that it *commands:* for this is *adding* and *diminishing* in Scripture phrase.

Lest he reprove thee] Lest he try *thy word by fire*, as his has been tried; and it appear that, far from *abiding* the test, the *fire* shows thine to be *reprobate silver;* and so thou be found a *falsifier of God's word*, and a *liar.*

How amply has this been fulfilled in the case of the *Romish Church!* It has *added* all the *gross stuff* in the *Apocrypha*, besides innumerable *legends* and *traditions*, to the word of God! They have been tried by the *refiner's fire.* And this Church has been *reproved*, and *found to be a liar*, in attempting to filiate on the most holy God *spurious writings* discreditable to his nature.

Verse 7. *Two* things *have I required of thee*] These *two petitions* are mentioned in the next verse; and he wishes to have them answered *before he should die.* That is, he wishes the answer *now*, that he may live the rest of his life in the *state* he describes.

Verse 8. *Remove far from me vanity and lies.*] 1. שוא *shav*, all *false shows*, all *false*

A. M. cir. 3304 give me neither poverty nor
B. C. cir. 700 riches; [l]feed me with food
Ol. vigesimæ cir. annum primum [m]convenient for me.
A. U. C. cir. 54 9 [n]Lest I be full, and [o]deny
thee, and say, Who *is* the LORD? or lest I be
poor and steal, and take the name of my God
in vain.

10 [p]Accuse not a servant unto his master,
lest he curse thee, and thou be found guilty.

11 *There is* a generation *that* curseth their
father, and doth not bless their mother.

12 *There is* a generation [q]*that are* pure in
their own eyes, and *yet* is not washed from
their filthiness.

13 *There is* a generation, O A. M. cir. 3304 B. C. cir. 700
how [r]lofty are their eyes! and Ol. vigesimæ
their eyelids are lifted up. cir. annum primum
14 [s]*There is* a generation, A. U. C. cir. 54
whose teeth *are as* swords, and their jaw
teeth *as* knives, [t]to devour the poor from off
the earth, and the needy from *among* men.

15 The horseleech hath two daughters,
crying, Give, give. There are three *things*
that are never satisfied, *yea,* four *things* say
not, [u]*It is* enough:

16 [v]The grave; and the barren womb; the
earth *that* is not filled with water; and the
fire, *that* saith not, *It is* enough.

---

[l]Matt. vi. 11——[m]Heb. *of my allowance*——[n]Deut. viii. 12, 14, 17; xxxi. 20; xxxii. 15; Neh. ix. 25, 26; Job xxxi. 24, 25, 28; Hos. xiii. 6——[o]Heb. *belie* thee [p]Heb. *Hurt not with thy tongue*——[q]Luke xviii. 11

[r]Psa. cxxxi. 1; chap. vi. 17——[s]Job xxix. 17; Psa. lii. 2; lvii. 4; chap. xii. 18——[t]Psa. xiv. 4; Amos viii. 4——[u]Hebrew, *Wealth*——[v]Chap. xxvii. 20; Hab. ii. 5

---

appearances of happiness, every *vain expectation.* Let me not set my heart on any thing that is not *solid, true, durable,* and *eternal.* 2. *Lies,* דבר כזב *debar cazab,* all *words of deception, empty pretensions, false promises, uncertain dependences,* and *words that* FAIL; *promises* which, when they become *due,* are like *bad bills;* they are *dishonoured* because they are found to be *forged,* or the *drawer insolvent.*

From the import of the original, I am satisfied that *Agur* prays against *idolatry, false religion,* and *false worship* of every kind. שוא *shav* is used for an *idol,* a *false god.* Jer. xviii. 15: "My people have forsaken me; they have burnt incense to VANITY;" לשוא *lashshav,* "to an IDOL." Psa. xxxi. 6: "I have hated them that regard lying VANITIES;" הבלי שוא *habley shave,* "vain IDOLS." See also Hos. xii. 11; Jonah ii. 8. And כזב *cazab,* a thing that *fails* or *deceives,* may well apply to the *vain pretensions, false promises,* and *deceptive religious rites* of *idolatry.* So Jer. xv. 18: "Wilt thou be unto me as a liar," כמו אכזב *kemo achzob,* like the false, failing *promises* of the *false gods;* "and as waters that fail;" לא נאמנו *lo neemanu,* that are not *faithful;* not like the *true God,* whose *promises never fail.* According to this view of the subject, *Agur* prays, 1. That he may be preserved from idolatry. 2. That he may put no confidence in any words but those *pure words* of God that never *fail them that trust in him.*

Give me neither poverty nor riches] Here are *three* requests: 1. *Give me not poverty.* The *reason* is added: *Lest,* being *poor, I shall* get into a covetous spirit, and, impelled by *want,* distrust my Maker, and take my neighbour's property; and, in order to excuse, hide, or vindicate my conduct, *I take the name of my God in vain;* תפשתי *taphasti,* "I catch at the name of God." Or, by swearing falsely, endeavour to make myself pass for innocent. **Forswere the name of my God.**—Old MS. Bible. *Coverdale,* "deny or apostatize from him."

2. *Give me not riches.* For which petition he gives a *reason* also: *Lest I be full,* and addict myself to luxurious living, pamper the flesh and starve the soul, and so *deny thee,* the Fountain of goodness; and, if called on to resort to first principles, I say, *Who is Jehovah?* Why should I acknowledge, why should I serve him? And thus cast aside all religion, and all moral obligation.

3. The *third* request is, *Feed me with food convenient for me,* הטריפני לחם חקי *hatripheni lechem chukki;* the meaning of which is, "give me as prey my statute allowance of bread," i. e., my *daily bread,* a sufficient portion for each day. There is an allusion made to *hunting:* "Direct so by thy good providence, that I may each day find sufficient portion to subsist on, as a hunter in the forest prays that he may have good speed." It is the province of a *preacher* to show the importance and utility of such a *prayer,* and *dilate* the *circumstances,* and *expand* the *reasons,* after the *commentator* has shown the *literal sense.*

Verse 10. *Accuse not a servant*] Do not bring a *false* accusation against a *servant,* lest *thou be found guilty* of the falsehood, and he *curse thee* for having traduced his character, and in his turn traduce thine. In general, do not meddle with other people's servants.

Verse 11. There is *a generation*] There are *such persons* in the world. In this and the three following verses the wise man points out *four grand evils* that prevailed in his time.

The *first,* Those who not only did not *honour,* but who *evil-treated,* their *parents.*

Verse 12. The *second,* Those who were *self-righteous,* supposing themselves *pure,* and were *not so.*

Verse 13. The *third,* Those who were *full of vanity, pride,* and *insolence.*

Verse 14. The *fourth,* The *greedy, cruel,* and *oppressive,* and, especially, *oppressive to the poor.*

Verse 15. *The horseleech hath two daughters,* crying, *Give, give.*] "This horseleech," says *Calmet,* "is COVETOUSNESS, and her two daughters are *Avarice* and *Ambition.* They never say, It is enough; they are never satisfied; they are never contented."

Many explanations have been given of this verse; but as all the *versions* agree in render-

A. M. cir. 3304
B. C. cir. 700
Ol. vigesimæ
cir. annum
primum
A. U. C. cir. 54

17 [w]The eye *that* mocketh at
his father, and despiseth to obey
his mother, the ravens of [x]the
valley shall pick it out, and the
young eagles shall eat it.
18 There be three *things which* are too wonderful for me, yea, four which I know not:
19 The way of an eagle in the
air; the way of a serpent upon
a rock; the way of a ship in
the [y]midst of the sea; and the
way of a man with a maid.
20 Such *is* the way of an adulterous
woman; she eateth, and wipeth her mouth,

A. M. cir. 3304
B. C. cir. 700
Ol. vigesimæ
cir. annum
primum
A. U. C. cir. 54

[w]Gen. ix. 22; Lev. xx. 9; chap. xx. 20; xxiii. 22

[x]Or, *the brook*——[y]Heb. *heart*

ing עלורה *alukah* the *horseleech* or *blood-sucker*, the general meaning collected has been, "There are persons so excessively covetous and greedy, that they will scarcely let any live but themselves; and when they lay hold of any thing by which they may profit, they never let go their hold till they have extracted the last portion of good from it." *Horace* has well expressed this disposition, and by the *same emblem*, applied to a *poor poet*, who seizes on and extracts all he can from an *author of repute*, and obliges all to hear him read his wretched verses.

Quem vero arripuit, tenet, occiditque legendo,
Non missura cutem, nisi plena cruoris,
HIRUDO. DE ARTE POET., ver. 475.

"But if he seize you, then the torture dread;
He fastens on you till he reads you dead;
And like a LEECH, voracious of his food,
Quits not his cruel hold till gorged with blood."
FRANCIS.

The word אלוקה *alukah*, which we here translate *horseleech*, is read in no other part of the Bible. May it not, like *Agur*, *Jakeh*, *Ithiel*, and *Ucal*, be a *proper name*, belonging to some well-known *woman* of *his acquaintance*, and well known to *the public*, who had *two daughters* notorious for their *covetousness* and *lechery?* And at first view the following verse may be thought to confirm this supposition: "There are three things that are never satisfied, yea, four things say not, It is enough." the *grave*, the *barren womb*, the *earth*, the *fire*. What an astonishing similarity there is between this and the following *institute*, taken from the *Code of Hindoo Laws*, chap. xx., sec. i., p. 203.

"A *woman* is never satisfied with the copulation of man, no more than a *fire* is satisfied with burning *fuel;* or the *main ocean* is with receiving the *rivers;* or *death*, with the dying of *men* and *animals*." You can no more satisfy these two daughters of Alukah than you can the grave, &c.

Some of the rabbins have thought that *alukah* signifies *destiny*, or the *necessity of dying*, which they say has *two daughters*, *Eden* and *Gehenna*, paradise and hell. The former has never enough of *righteous souls;* the latter, of the *wicked*. Similar to them is the opinion of *Bochart*, who thinks *alukah* means *destiny*, and the *two daughters*, the *grave* and *hell;* into the *first* of which the *body* descends after death, and into the *second*, the *soul*.

The *Septuagint* gives it a curious turn, by connecting the *fifteenth* with the *sixteenth* verse: Τη Βδελλη θυγατερες ησαν αγαπησει αγαπωμεναι, και αἱ τρεις αὑται ουκ ενεπιμπλασαν αυτην, και ἡ τεταρτη ουκ ηρκεσθη ειπειν· Ἱκανον; "The horseleech had three well-beloved daughters; and these three were not able to satisfy her desire: and the fourth was not satisfied, so as to say, It is enough."

After all, I think my own conjecture the most probable. *Alukah* is a proper name, and the two daughters were of the description I have mentioned.

Verse 17. *The eye* that *mocketh at* his *father*] This seems to be spoken against those who *curse their father*, and *do not bless their mother*, ver. 11.

The ravens of the valley] Those which frequent the places where dead carcasses and offal are most likely to be found. The *raven*, the *crow*, the *rook*, the *daw*, the *carrion crow*, and the Cornish *chough*, appear to be all of the same genus. Some of them live on *pulse* and *insects;* others, the *raven* in particular, live on *carrion*.

The young eagles shall eat it.] The mother eagle shall scoop out such an eye, and carry it to the nest to feed her young. Many of the *disobedient to parents* have come to an *untimely end*, and, in the *field of battle*, where many a profligate has fallen, and upon *gibbets*, have actually become the prey of ravenous birds.

Verse 19. *The way of an eagle*] I borrow, with thanks, the very sensible note of the Rev. Mr. Holden on this passage.

"The particle כן *ken* plainly shows that verses 19 and 20 are to be taken in connection; consequently, it is a comparison between the *way of an adulterous woman*, and the *way of the things* here described.

"The *adulterous woman* goes about in search of her deluded victim, like as the *eagle* takes its flight into the air to spy out its prey. She uses every species of blandishment and insinuation to allure and beguile, as the *serpent* employs its windings and sinuous motions to pass along the *rocks;* she pursues a course surrounded with danger, as *a ship in the midst of the sea* is continually exposed to the fury of the tempest, and the hazard of shipwreck; and she tries every means, and exercises all her sagacity, to prevent the discovery of her illicit enjoyments, as a man attempts to conceal his clandestine intercourse *with a maid*. Such is the conduct of a lewd woman, marked by specious dissimulation and traitorous blandishment; *she eateth and wipeth her mouth*—she indulges her adulterous lust, yet artfully endeavours to conceal it, and with unblushing countenance asserts her innocence, exclaiming, *I have done no wickedness*."

CHAUCER's *January* and *May* is an excellent comment on such *wiles* and *protestations*.

The way of a man with a maid.] בעלמה *bealmah with* or *in a maid;* but one of *De Rossi's* MSS. has בעלמיו *bealmaiv*, *in his*

A. M. cir. 3304 B. C. cir. 700 Ol. vigesimæ cir. annum primum A. U. C. cir. 54

and saith, I have done no wickedness.
21 For three *things* the earth
is disquieted, and for four
which it cannot bear.
22 [z]For a servant when he reigneth; and a
fool when he is filled with meat;
23 For an odious *woman* when she is married; and a handmaid that is heir to her mistress.
24 There be four *things which are* little
upon the earth, but they *are* [a]exceeding wise:

[z]Chap. xix. 10; Eccles. x. 7——[a]Heb. *wise, made wise*

A. M. cir. 3304 B. C. cir. 700 Ol. vigesimæ cir. annum primum A. U. C. cir. 54

25 [b]The ants *are* a people
not strong; yet they prepare
their meat in the summer;
26 [c]The conies *are but* a
feeble folk, yet make they their houses in the
rocks;
27 The locusts have no king, yet go they
forth all of them [d]by bands;
28 The spider taketh hold with her hands,
and is in kings' palaces.
29 There be three *things* which go well, yea,
four are comely in going:

[b]Chap. vi. 6, &c.——[c]Psa. civ. 18——[d]Heb. *gathered together*

youth; and with this the SEPTUAGINT, εν νεοτητι, the VULGATE, *in adolescentia*, the SYRIAC and the ARABIC agree; and so also my own MS. Bible:—**The weie of a man in his waxing youthe.** Dr. *Kennicott*, in a *sermon preached at Oxford*, 1765, p. 46, has defended the reading of the *versions*, corroborating it by two MSS., one in the *Harleian*, and the other in the *Bodleian* library, besides that mentioned by *De Rossi*. See *De Rossi's* Var. Lect. Certainly the *way of a man in his youth* contains too many intricacies for human wisdom to explore. He only who searches the heart knows fully its various corrupt principles, and their productions. The common reading may refer to the formation of a child in the womb. But some have understood it of the *immaculate conception*. See my note on Matt. i. 23, where the subject is largely considered.

If we take the *four things* which Agur says were *too wonderful for him*, in their *obvious sense*, there is little difficulty in them. 1. The passage which a bird makes *through the air;* 2. That which is made by a *serpent on a rock;* and, 3. That *made by a ship through the sea*, are such as cannot be ascertained: for who can possibly show the *track* in which either of them has passed? And as to the *fourth*, if it refer to the *suspected incontinence* of one *reputed a virgin*, the *signs* are so *equivocal*, as to be absolutely unascertainable. The existence of the *hymen* has been denied by the ablest anatomists; and the signs of *continence* or *incontinence*, except in the most recent cases, are such as neither *man* nor *woman* can swear to, even to the present day; and they were certainly not less difficult to *Agur* and his *contemporaries*. I shall carry this matter no farther.

Verse 21. *For three* things *the earth is disquieted, and for four* which *it cannot bear*] This is another enigma. *Four* things *insupportable to men*. 1. A *slave, when he becomes ruler*. 2. An *overfed fool*. 3. An *ill-tempered woman, when mistress of a family*. And, 4. A *servant maid, when the rule of the house is committed* to her.

1. A *slave*, when he comes to *bear rule*, is an unprincipled *tyrant*. It has been often observed both in *America* and in the *West Indies*, when it was judged necessary to arm some of the most confidential slaves, that no regiments were used *so cruelly* in the *drill*, &c., as those *black regiments* that had *black officers*.

2. *The overfed fool*. The intellectually *weak man*, who has every thing *at his command*, has generally *manners* which none can bear; and, if a *favourite* with his *master*, he is insupportable to all others.

3. An *ill-tempered woman*, when she gets embarrassed with domestic cares, is beyond bearing.

4. A *servant maid*, when, either through the *death* of the mistress, or the sin of the husband, she is in fact exalted to be head over the family, is so insolent and impudent, as to be hateful to every one, and execrated by all.

Verse 24. *There be four* things] Of which it is said, they are *very little* but *very wise*. 1. The *ants*. 2. The *rabbits*. 3. The *locusts*. 4. The *spider*.

1. The *ants* show their wisdom by *preparing their meat in the summer;* seeking for it and storing it when it may be had; not for *winter consumption*, for they *sleep* all that time; but for *autumn* and *spring*. See the note on chap. vi. 6. The *ants* are a *people;* they have their *houses, towns, cities, public roads*, &c. I have seen several of these, both of the *brown* and large *black ant*.

2. The *rabbits* act curiously enough in the construction of their *burrows;* but the word שפן *shaphan* probably does not here mean the *animal* we call *coney* or *rabbit*. It is most likely that this is what Dr. *Shaw* calls the *Daman-Israel;* a creature very like a rabbit, but never burrowing in the ground, but dwelling in clefts and holes of *rocks*.

3. The *locusts*. These surprising animals we have already met with and described. Though they have no *leader*, yet they go forth by *troops*, some miles in circumference, when they *take wing*.

4. The *spider*. This is a singularly curious animal, both in the manner of *constructing her house*, her *nets*, and *taking* her *prey*. But the habits, &c., of these and such like must be sought in works on *natural history*.

Verse 29. *There be three* things *which go well*] Here is another set of *emblems; four* things which *walk beautifully* and *with majesty*. 1. The *lion*. 2. The *greyhound*. 3. The *he-goat*. And, 4. A *king*.

1. Nothing can be more majestic than the *walk of the lion*. It is deliberate, equal, firm, and in every respect becoming the king of the forest.

2. The *greyhound*. זרזיר מתנים *zarzir moth-*

A. M. cir. 3304
B. C. cir. 700
Ol. vigesimæ
cir. annum
primum
A. U. C. cir. 54

30 A lion, *which is* strongest
among beasts, and turneth not
away for any;
31 A [e]greyhound; [f]a he-
goat also; and a king, against whom *there is*
no rising up.
32 If thou hast done foolishly in lifting up
thyself, or if thou hast thought
evil, [g]*lay* thine hand upon thy
mouth.
33 Surely the churning of milk
bringeth forth butter, and the wringing of the
nose bringeth forth blood: so the forcing of
wrath bringeth forth strife.

[e]Or, *horse*——[f]Heb. *girt in the loins*

[g]Job xxi. 5; xl. 4; Eccles. viii. 3; Mic. vii. 16

nayim, the *girt in the loins;* but what this beast is we do not distinctly know. It is *most likely* that this was the *greyhound*, which in the *East* are remarkably fine, and very *fleet.* Scarcely any thing can be conceived to *go* with greater fleetness, in full chase, than a greyhound with its prey in view: it seems to *swim* over the earth.

3. The *goat*, תיש *tayish.* This is generally allowed to be the *he-goat;* and how he walks, and what *state* he assumes, in the presence of his part of the flock, every one knows, who has at all noticed this animal. The *ram* also, which some suppose to be intended, is both fierce and majestic at the head of the sheep.

4. *And a king, against whom* there is *no rising* up. That is, a king whose court, counsels, and troops, are so firmly united to him, as to render all hopes of successful conspiracy against him utterly vain. He walks boldly and majestically about, being safe in the affections of his people. But the *Hebrew* is singular; it makes but *two words;* and these are they, ומלך אלקום *umelech Alkum*, "and King Alkum." It is a doubt whether this may not be a *proper name*, as *Agur* abounds in them; see *Ithiel, Ucal*, and probably *Alukah*, ver. 15. But it is said, "We know nothing of a king named Alkum." True; nor do we know any thing of *Agur, Ithiel, Ucal*, to say nothing of *Alukah.* And this might have been some remarkable *chieftain*, who carried his victories wherever he went, and was remarkably fortunate. If, however, we separate the word into אל *al*, "not," and קום *kum*, "he arose," we may make the interpretation above given.

Verse 32. *If thou hast done foolishly*] And who has not, at one time or other of his life?

Lay *thine hand upon thy mouth.*] Like the *leper;* and cry to God, *Unclean! unclean!* and *keep silence* to all besides. God will blot out thy offence, and neither the world nor the Church ever know it, for he is merciful; and *man* is rarely able to pass by a sin committed by his fellows, especially if it be one to which himself is by nature not liable or inclined.

Verse 33. *And the wringing*] **Who hugeli snytith drawith out blood.**—Old MS. Bible. This is well expressed in homely phrase. The *Septuagint* have, "draw the milk, and you may have butter; if you press the nostrils you may bring out blood; and if you draw out your discourse to a great length, you may have strife and contention." Avoid, therefore, all strong *excitements* and irritations. *Coverdale's* translation of this verse is very simple: "Whoso chyrneth mylck maketh butter; he that rubbeth his nose, maketh it blede; and he that causeth wrath, bryngeth forth strife."

CHAPTER XXXI

The words and prophecy of King Lemuel, and what his mother taught him, 1, 2. *Debauchery and much wine to be avoided,* 3–7. *How kings should administer justice,* 8, 9. *The praise of a virtuous woman and good housewife, in her economy, prudence, watchfulness, and assiduity in labour,* 10–29. *Frailty of beauty,* 30, 31.

THE words of King Lemuel, [a]the prophecy
that his mother taught him.
2 What, my son? and what, [b]the son of my
womb? and what, the son of my vows?

[a]Chap. xxx. 1

[b]Isa. xlix. 15

NOTES ON CHAP. XXXI

Verse 1. *The words of King Lemuel*] דברי למואל מלך *dibrey lemuel melech*, "The words to Muel the king." So the *Syriac;* and so I think it should be read, the ל *lamed* being the article or *preposition.*

But who is *Muel* or *Lemuel? Solomon*, according to general opinion; and the *mother* here mentioned, *Bath-sheba.* I cannot receive these sayings; for 1. Whoever this was, he appears to have been the *first-born* of his mother: called here emphatically בר בטני *bar bitni*, the *son of my womb;* which is not likely to be true of Solomon, as his mother had been the wife of Uriah, and possibly had borne that rough and faithful soldier some children. 2. It is intimated here that this son had come by a *lawful marriage: hence* בר נדרי *bar nedarai*, the *son of my vow*, her *matrimonial covenant;* for so it is most natural to understand the words. But is there any proper sense in which we can say that this was correct in reference to *David, Bath-sheba*, and *Solomon?* For although the son born in adultery died, it is by

3 [c]Give not thy strength unto women, nor thy ways [d]to that which destroyeth kings.

4 [e]*It is* not for kings, O Lemuel, *it is* not for kings to drink wine; nor for princes strong drink:

5 [f]Lest they drink, and forget the law, and [g]pervert the judgment [h]of any of the afflicted.

6 [i]Give strong drink unto him that is ready to perish, and wine unto those that be [k]of heavy hearts.

7 Let him drink, and forget his poverty, and remember his misery no more.

8 [l]Open thy mouth for the dumb [m]in the cause of all [n]such as are appointed to destruction.

9 Open thy mouth, [o]judge righteously, and [p]plead the cause of the poor and needy.

10 [q]Who can find a virtuous woman? for her price *is* far above rubies.

11 The heart of her husband doth safely trust in her, so that he shall have no need of spoil.

12 She will do him good and not evil all the days of her life.

---

[c]Chap. v. 9——[d]Deut. xvii. 17; Neh. xiii. 26; chap. vii. 26; Hos. iv. 11——[e]Eccles. x. 17——[f]Hos. iv. 11——[g]Heb. *alter*——[h]Heb. *of all the sons of affliction*——[i]Psa. civ. 15——[k]Heb. *bitter of soul;* 1 Sam. i. 10

[l]See Job xxix. 15, 16——[m]1 Samuel xix. 4; Esth. iv. 16——[n]Heb. *the sons of destruction*——[o]Lev. xix. 15; Deut. i. 16——[p]Job xxix. 12; Isa. i. 17; Jer. xxii. 16——[q]Chap. xii. 4; xviii. 22; xix. 14

---

no means likely that Bath-sheba made any particular *vows* relative to *Solomon;* for of her piety, so much vaunted of by some writers, we yet want the proofs.

But, however this may be, there is no evidence whatever that *Muel* or *Lemuel* means *Solomon;* the chapter seems to be much later than his time, and the several *Chaldaisms* which occur in the very opening of it are no mean proof of this. If *Agur* was not the author of it, it may be considered as another *supplement* to the book of Proverbs. Most certainly Solomon did not write it.

The prophecy that his mother taught him.] משא *massa* may here signify the *oracle;* the subject that came by *Divine inspiration;* see on chap. xxx. 1. From this and some other circumstances it is probable that *both* these *chapters* were written by the *same author. Houbigant* thinks that *Massa* here is the name of a *place;* and, therefore, translates, "The words of Lemuel, king of Massa, with which his mother instructed him."

Verse 2. *What, my son?*] The Chaldee בר *bar* is used twice in this verse, instead of the Hebrew בן *ben*, SON. This verse is very elliptical; and commentators, according to their different tastes, have inserted *words*, indeed some of them a whole *sentence*, to make up the sense. Perhaps *Coverdale* has hit the sense as nearly as any other: "These are the wordes of Kynge Lemuel; and the lesson that his mother taughte him. My sonne, thou son of my body, O my deare beloved sonne!"

The son of my vows?] A child born after vows made for offsprings is called the *child* of a person's *vows*.

Verse 3. *Give not thy strength*] Do not waste thy substance on *women*. In such intercourse the *strength* of *body, soul* and *substance* is destroyed. Such connections are those *which destroy kings*, מלכין *melachin*, the *Chaldee* termination instead of the *Hebrew*.

Verse 4. It is *not for kings—to drink wine*] An intemperate man is ill fit to hold the reins of government.

Verse 5. *Lest they drink, and forget the law*] When they should be administering justice, they are found incapable of it; or, if they go into the judgment-seat, may pervert justice.

Verse 6. *Give strong drink unto him that is ready to perish*] We have already seen, that inebriating drinks were mercifully given to condemned criminals, to render them less sensible of the torture they endured in dying. This is what was offered to our Lord; but he refused it. See note on Psa. civ. 15.

Verse 8. *Open thy mouth for the dumb*] For such accused persons as have no counsellors, and cannot plead for themselves.

Are appointed to destruction.] בני חלוף *beney chaloph*, variously translated, *children of passage*—indigent travellers; *children of desolation*—those who have no possessions, or *orphans*. I believe it either signifies those who are strangers, and are *travelling from place to place*, or those who are *ready to perish* in consequence of want or oppression.

Verse 10. *Who can find a virtuous woman?*] This and the following verses are *acrostic*, each beginning with a consecutive letter of the *Hebrew alphabet:* ver. 10, א *aleph;* ver. 11, ב *beth;* ver. 12, ג *gimel;* and so on to the end of the chapter, the last verse of which has the letter ת *tau*. From this to the end of the chapter we have the *character* of a woman of *genuine worth* laid down; *first, in general*, ver. 10, 11, and 12; *secondly*, in its particular or component parts, ver. 13-29; and, *thirdly*, the summing up of the character, ver. 30, 31.

I. Her *general character*.

1. She is a *virtuous woman*—a woman of power and strength. אשת חיל *esheth chayil*, a strong or virtuous wife, full of mental energy.

2. She is *invaluable;* her *price is far above rubies*—no quantity of precious stones can be equal to *her* worth.

Verse 11. *The heart of her husband*]

3. She is an *unspotted* wife. *The heart of her husband doth safely trust in her*—he knows she will take care that a proper provision is made for his household, and will not *waste* any thing. He *has no need for spoil*—he is not obliged to go out on predatory excursions, to provide for his family, at the expense of the neighbouring tribes.

Verse 12. *She will do him good*]

4. She has her husband's happiness in view constantly. She recompenses all his *kindness* to her in *beneficent acts*. For *kind words* she returns *kind deeds*. Her *good* is *unmixed;* she will *do him good*, and *not evil*. 2. *Her good* is

13 She seeketh wool, and flax, and [r]worketh
willingly with her hands.
14 She is like the merchant's ships; she
bringeth her food from afar.
15 [s]She riseth also while it is yet night, and
[t]giveth meat to her household, and a portion
to her maidens.
16 She considereth a field and [u]buyeth it:
with the fruit of her hands she planteth a
vineyard.
17 She girdeth her loins with strength, and
strengtheneth her arms.
18 [v]She perceiveth that her merchandise *is*
good: her candle goeth not out by night.
19 She layeth her hands to the spindle, and
her hands hold the distaff.

---

[r]Eccles. ix. 10; 2 Thess. iii. 10, 12——[s]Rom. xii. 11 [t]Luke xii. 42——[u]Heb. *taketh*——[v]Heb. *She tasteth*

---

not *capricious;* it is *constant* and *permanent,* while she and her husband live. *His heart safely trusts in her,* for *she will do him good all the days of her life.* This is her general character.

Verse 13. *She seeketh wool, and flax, and worketh willingly, &c.*]

II. This is the *second* part of her character, giving the *particulars* of which it is composed.

1. She did not buy *ready woven cloth:* she procured the *raw material,* if *wool,* most probably from her own *flocks;* if *flax,* most probably from her own *fields.*

2. Here she manufactured; for she *worketh willingly with her hands.* And all her labour is a *cheerful service;* her *will,* her *heart,* is in it.

It needs no arguments to prove that women, even of the highest ranks, among the Greeks, Romans, and Israelites, worked with their hands at every kind of occupation necessary for the support of the family. This kind of employment was not peculiar to the *virtuous woman* in the text.

Verse 14. *She is like the merchants' ships*]

3. She acts like merchants. If she buy any thing for her household, she sells sufficient of her *own manufactures* to pay for it; if she *imports,* she *exports:* and she sends articles of her own manufacturing or produce to distant countries; she traffics with the neighbouring tribes.

Verse 15. *She riseth also while it is yet night*]

4. She is an economist of *time;* and when the *nights* are *long,* and the *days short,* her family not only spend a part of the *evening* after sunset in domestic labour, but they all arise *before daylight,* and prepare the *day's food,* that they may not have their labour interrupted. To those who are going to the *fields,* and to the *flocks,* she gives the food necessary for the day: טרף *teref, prey,* a term taken from *hunting,* the object of which was, the supplying their natural wants: hence applied to *daily food.* See notes on chap. xxx. 8. And to the women who are to be employed within she gives חק *chok,* the *task*—the *kind* of work they are to do, the *materials* out of which they are to form it, and the *quantity* she expects from each. Thus all the servants are settled: their food, work, and tasks appointed. Every thing is done *orderly.*

Verse 16. *She considereth a field and buyeth it*]

5. She provides for the growing wants of her family. More land will shortly be needed, for the family is growing up; and having *seen a field* contiguous to her own, which was on sale, she estimates its worth, and purchases it a good bargain; and she pays for it by the *fruit of her own industry.*

6. She does not restrict herself to the bare *necessaries* of life; she is able to procure some of its *comforts.* She plants a *vineyard,* that she may have wine for a *beverage,* for *medicine,* and for *sacrifice.* This also is procured of her own labour. Whatever *goes out* brings its worth *in;* and *barter,* not *buying,* is her chief mode of traffic.

Verse 17. *She girdeth her loins with strength*]

7. She takes care of her own health and strength, not only by means of useful labour, but by healthy exercise. She avoids what might enervate her body, or soften her mind—she is ever active, and *girt* ready for every necessary exercise. Her *loins* are *firm,* and her *arms strong.*

Verse 18. *She perceiveth that her merchandise is good*]

8. She takes care to manufacture the *best articles* of the kind, and to lay on a *reasonable price* that she may secure a *ready sale.* Her *goods* are in high repute, and she knows she can *sell* as much as she can *make.* And she finds that while she pleases her customers, she *increases her own profits.*

9. She is *watchful* and careful. Her *candle*—her *lamp,* burns all night, which is of great advantage in case of sudden alarms; and in the times and places where there were so many *banditti,* this was a very necessary family regulation. Perhaps some works were carried on *during the night,* those employed *sleeping in the daytime.* Thus labour never stood still; whilst some slept, others worked. This was no unusual thing in *ancient times;* and it prevails *now;* but alas! little children are often thus employed to help to support their indigent parents, and to fill the coffers of their unfeeling taskmasters.

Verse 19. *She layeth her hands to the spindle*]

10. She gives an example of *skill* and *industry* to her household. She takes the *distaff,* that on which the *wool* or *flax* was *rolled;* and the *spindle,* that by *twisting* of which she *twisted the thread* with the *right hand,* while she held the *distaff* in the *guard* of the left arm, and drew *down the thread* with the fingers of the left hand. Allowing that *spindle* and *distaff* are proper translations of כישור *kishor,* and פלך *pelech,* this was their *use,* and the *way* in which they were used. The *spindle* and *distaff* are the most *ancient* of all the instruments used for *spinning,* or making *thread.* The *spinning-wheel* superseded them in these countries; but still they were in considerable use till *spinning machinery* superseded both them and the *spinning-wheels* in general.

20 [w]She [x]stretcheth out her hand to the poor;
yea, she reacheth forth her hands to the needy.
21 She is not afraid of the snow for her
household: for all her household *are* clothed
with [y]scarlet.
22 She maketh herself coverings of tapestry;
her clothing *is* silk and purple.
23 [z]Her husband is known in the gates,
when he sitteth among the elders of the
land.
24 She maketh fine linen, and selleth *it*;
and delivereth girdles unto the merchant.
25 Strength and honour *are* her clothing;
and she shall rejoice in time to come.

---

[w]Heb. *She spreadeth*——[x]Eph. iv. 28; Heb. xiii. 16 [y]Or, *double garments*——[z]Chap. xii. 4

Verse 20. *She stretcheth out her hand to the poor*]

11. She is truly charitable. She knows that in *every portion* of a man's *gain* God requires a *lot for the poor;* and if this is not given, God's blessing is not in the rest. And she is not contented to give common alms. While with *one hand* (יד *yad*) she relieves the *general poor*, with *both hands* (ידיה *yadeyha*) she gives *to the needy*, לעני *leaney*, to the *afflicted poor*.

Verse 21. *She is not afraid of the snow*]

12. She is not anxious relative to the health and comfort of her family in the winter season, having provided *clothes sufficient* for each in the cold weather, in addition to those which they wore in the warm season.

For all her household are *clothed with scarlet.*] Not *scarlet*, for the *colour* can avail nothing in keeping off the cold; nor would it be a proper colour for the bogs and dirt of winter. But שנים *shanim*, from שנה *shanah*, to *iterate*, to *double*, signifies not only *scarlet*, so called from being twice or doubly dyed, but also *double garments*, not only the *ordinary coat* but the *surtout* or *great-coat* also, or a *cloak* to cover all. But most probably *double garments*, or *twofold* to what they were accustomed to wear, are here intended. If the *general clothing* be intended, *scarlet* cannot be the meaning, nor did our translators entirely rely on it; and therefore put *double garments*, the true meaning, in the *margin*, from which it cannot be too speedily transferred to the *text*. The *Vulgate* has "duplicibus." And my old MS. very properly, **Alle forsoth hir hoomli men, ben clothid with double.** And *Coverdale*, with equal propriety, "For all hir householde folkes are duble clothed." But if her *husband* and *children* alone are referred to, *scarlet*, which is the general meaning of the term, may be proper enough; as even in *these countries* of ours, *scarlet*, as being a *lively bright* colour, is used in the *winter* dresses.

Verse 22. *She maketh herself coverings of tapestry*]

13. She is not regardless either of her own person, or of the decent, proper appearance of her presses and wardrobe. She has coverings or carpeting for her *guests to sit upon;* she has also tapestry, מרבדים *marbaddim*, either tapestry, carpeting, or quilted work for her *beds;* and her own *clothing* is שש *shesh*, fine flax, or linen cloth, and *purple;* probably for a cloak or mantle. The *fine linen* or *cotton cloth* of Egypt is probably intended. I have often seen it wrapping the bodies of mummies; it is something like our coarse calico. The *purple* was supposed to have been dyed by a precious liquor obtained from the *pinna magna*, a large shellfish, of the *muscle* kind, found on the coast of the Mediterranean Sea. I have seen some of them nearly *two feet* in length. But it is a doubt whether any such liquor was ever obtained from this or any other fish; and the story itself is invented merely to *hide the secret*, the proper method of *dying purple;* which was kept so well that it certainly died with the ancients.

Verse 23. *Her husband is known in the gates*]

14. She is a loving wife, and feels for the *respectability* and *honour* of her husband. He is an *elder* among his people, and he sits as a *magistrate* in the *gate*. He is respected not only on account of the *neatness* and *cleanliness* of his *person* and *dress;* but because he is the husband of a woman who is justly held in universal esteem. And her complete management of household affairs gives him full leisure to devote himself to the civil interests of the community.

Verse 24. *She maketh fine linen, and selleth* it]

15. She is *here* remarkable for carrying on a traffic of *splendid* and *ornamental dresses*, or *habits*, as she is, ver. 13, for "a coarser manufacture." The סדין *sidon* is supposed to come from سدن in Arabic; and to signify a kind of *loose inner garment*, *shirt*, *chemise*, or *fine muslin covering*. Some of these are so exceedingly fine, like the *abrooam*, that when spread on the grass, they are scarcely discernible. Some such garments as these are still worn by *ladies* in *India* and in *China*, and are so *thin* and *transparent*, that every part of the body may be seen through them. I have many representations of persons clothed in this way before me both of the *Chinese*, the *Hindoo*, and the *Malabar ladies*. Probably this eminent Jewish matron had such articles manufactured in her own house. She dealt also in *girdles*. These are still a very general and very expensive article of dress. I have seen them made of *silk*, and highly ornamented with *gold* and *silver thread*, worked into *flowers* and various *curious devices*. The *loose Eastern robe* is confined by these; and the word may also take in the *shawl* of the *turban*, which is often *superb* and *costly*. It is properly the *girdle* for the *head*. As these were generally woven, the consumption was great; and an able artist must have had a good trade.

The *Arabic* gives a remarkable translation of this verse: "She maketh towels, (or tablecloths,) and sells them to the inhabitants of Basra, (a city in Mesopotamia,) and fine linens, and sells them to the Canaanites." My old MS. Bible has, **Sandel sche made and sold, and a litil girdil sche toke to Chanane.** Perhaps לכנעני *lakkenaani, for the merchant*, may stand here for לכנענים *lakkenaanim*, the *Canaanites*.

Verse 25. *Strength and honour* are *her clothing*]

26 She openeth her mouth with wisdom; and in her tongue *is* the law of [a]kindness.

27 She looketh well to the ways of her household, and eateth not the bread of idleness.

28 Her children arise up, and call her blessed; her husband *also*, and he praiseth her.

29 Many daughters [b]have done virtuously, but thou excellest them all.

30 Favour *is* deceitful, and [c]beauty *is* vain: *but* a woman *that* feareth the LORD, she shall be praised.

31 Give her of the fruit of her hands; and let her own works praise her in the gates.

[a]1 Tim. iii. 4——[b]Or, *have gotten riches*

[c]Isa. xxviii. 1, 4

16. All the articles manufactured by herself or under her care have a double perfection: 1. They are *strong*. 2. They are *elegant; Strength and honour are her clothing;* and on account of this *she shall rejoice in time to come;* she shall never have occasion to blush for any thing she has *made*, for any thing she or hers have *worn*, or for any thing she has *sold*. Besides, she has so conducted herself that she has reason to expect that the hand of the Lord shall be still with her, and shall keep her from evil that it may not grieve her.

Verse 26. *She openeth her mouth with wisdom*]

17. He comes now to the *moral management* of her family. 1. She is *wise* and *intelligent;* she has not neglected the cultivation of her *mind*. 2. She is amiable in her carriage, full of good nature, well tempered, and conciliating in her manners and address.

In her tongue is *the law of kindness.*] This is the most distinguishing excellence of this woman. There are very few of those who are called managing women who are not *lords* over their *husbands*, *tyrants* over their *servants*, and *insolent* among their *neighbours*. But this woman, with all her eminence and excellence, was of a *meek* and *quiet spirit*. Blessed woman!

Verse 27. *She looketh well to the ways of her household*]

18. She is a *moral* manager: she takes care that all shall behave themselves well; that none of them shall keep bad company or contract vicious habits. A religious industry, or an industrious religion, is the law of her house. She can instruct them in religion, as well as she can teach them in their labour. In her house, diligence in business, and fervency of spirit, serving the Lord, go hand in hand.

And eateth not the bread of idleness.]

19. She knows that *idleness* leads to *vice;* and therefore every one has *his work*, and every one has his *proper food*. That they may *work well, they are fed well;* and every one, at least, earns the bread that he eats—*eateth not the bread of idleness.*

Verse 28. *Her children arise up, and call her blessed*]

20. She considers a *good education* next to *Divine influence;* and she knows also that if she train up a child in the way he should go, when he is old he will not depart from it. 1. Her children are *well bred;* they *rise up* and pay *due respect*. 2. They are *taught the fear of the Lord*, and obedience to his testimonies; therefore they *call her blessed*. So they are of a decent, orderly, respectable, religious behaviour. 3. Her husband is so satisfied with her conduct towards *himself*, his *household*, his *business*, and their *children*, that he *praiseth her*. He shows himself sensible of her excellence, and encourages her, in her work, by the *commendations* he bestows.

Verse 29. *Many daughters have done virtuously*] This is undoubtedly the speech of the husband, giving testimony to the excellence of his wife: "Her husband also, and he praiseth her, *saying*, 'many daughters,' *women*, 'have done virtuously,' with due propriety as wives, mistresses, and mothers; 'but THOU,' my incomparable wife, 'excellest them all;' ואת עלית על כלנה *veath alith al cullanah*, but THOU hast ascended above the whole of them—thou hast carried every duty, every virtue, and every qualification and excellency, to a *higher perfection*, than any of whom we have ever read or heard." And let the reader seriously consider the above particulars, as specified under the different heads and subdivisions; and he will be probably of the same mind. But high as the character of this Jewish matron stands in the preceding description, I can say that I have met at least *her equal*, in a *daughter* of the Rev. Dr. *Samuel Annesly*, the *wife* of *Samuel Wesley*, sen., rector of Epworth in Lincolnshire, and *mother* of the late extraordinary brothers, *John* and *Charles Wesley*. I am constrained to add this testimony, after having traced her from her *birth* to her *death*, through all the relations that a woman can bear upon earth. Her Christianity gave to her virtues and excellences a heightening, which the Jewish matron could not possess. Besides, she was a woman of great *learning* and information, and of a depth of mind, and reach of thought, seldom to be found among the daughters of Eve, and not often among the sons of Adam.

Verse 30. *Favour* is *deceitful, and beauty* is *vain, &c.*]

III. Here is the *summing up* of the character. 1. *Favour*, חן *chen*, *grace* of manner may be *deceitful*, many a *fair appearance* of this kind is *put on*, *assumed* for certain secular or more unworthy purposes; it is learned by *painful drilling* in *polished seminaries*, and, being the effect of mere *physical discipline*, it continues while the *restraint* lasts; but it is שקר *sheker*, a *lie*, a *mere semblance*, an *outward varnish*. It is not the *effect* of *internal moral regulation;* it is an *outside*, at which the *inside* murmurs; and which, because not *ingenuous*, is a *burden to itself*.

2. *Beauty*, היפי *haiyophi*, elegance of shape, symmetry of features, dignity of mien, and beauty of countenance, are all הבל *hebel*, *vanity; sickness* impairs them, *suffering* deranges them, and *death* destroys them.

3. "But a woman that feareth the Lord," that possesses *true religion*, has that *grace* that *harmonizes the soul*, that *purifies* and *refines* all the *tempers* and *passions*, and that ornament

of beauty, a *meek and quiet mind*, which in the sight of God *is of great price*—

She shall be praised.] This is the lasting grace, the unfading beauty.

Verse 31. *Give her of the fruit of her hands*] This may be a *prayer*. May she long enjoy the fruit of her labours! May she see her children's children, and peace upon Israel!

And let her own works praise her in the gates.] Let what she has done be spoken of for a memorial of her; let her bright example be held forth in the most *public places*. Let it be set before the eyes of every *female*, particularly of every *wife*, and especially of every *mother;* and let them learn from this exemplar, what men have a right to expect in their *wives*, the *mistresses* of *their families*, and the *mothers* of *their children*. Amen.

MASORETIC NOTES ON THIS BOOK

Number of verses in the book of Proverbs, 915.

Middle verse, chap. xvi. 18.

Sections, 8.

The Syriac reckons 1863 verses.

The Arabic concludes thus:—"The discipline of Solomon written out by the friends of Hezekiah, king of Judah, the interpretation or translation of which is extremely difficult, (but) is now completed by the assistance and influence of the Son of God."

IN the *introduction* to the book of Proverbs, among the several *collections* of a similar nature which are mentioned there, I have referred to M. Galand's *Maximes des Orientaux.* From this work, as contained in the supplement to the *Bibliotheque Orientale*, I have translated the following *selection*. They will serve to show the curious reader how many sayings similar to those of Solomon still abound in the East.

ASIATIC PROVERBS

I fear God; and beside him I fear none, but that man who fears him not.

He who knows not his Maker cannot know himself.

Godliness is the greatest wisdom, and impiety the greatest of follies.

The fear of God is the greatest safeguard.

To sin once is too much; but a thousand acts of devotion towards God are not sufficient to honour him.

If a man foresaw his end, and his exit from life, he would abhor his actions, and their deceitfulness.

Life is a sort of sleep, from which many awake not but in death.

The life of man is a path that leads to death.

The orphan is not the person who has lost his father; but he who has neither wisdom, nor a good education.

Want of good sense is worse than all the degrees of poverty.

Nothing so effectually hides what we are as *silence*.

He who has least wisdom has most vanity.

There is no greatness of soul in avenging one's self.

The heart of the fool is in his mouth, and the tongue of the wise man is in his heart.

He who runs with a slack rein, guided only by *hope*, encounters the last moment of his life, and falls.

Envy has no rest.

When you have once received a benefit, render yourself not unworthy of it, by a want of gratitude.

The desire of revenge is a constant hinderance to a happy and contented life.

When you have got an advantage over your enemy, pardon him, in returning God thanks for that advantage.

When you are in prosperity, you need seek no other revenge against him who envies you than the mortification he has from it.

How advantageous must wisdom be to its possessor, seeing it is of so great value as not to be purchased by money!

Nothing obtains pardon more speedily than repentance.

There is no disease so dangerous as the want of common sense.

Of all vices, vanity and a love of contention are the most difficult to be corrected.

Visiting your neighbour is no crime; but your visits should not be so often repeated, as to induce him to say, *It is enough.*

If a prince would worship God in truth, he must remain in his limits, be true to his treaties, be content with what he has, and suffer patiently the privation of what he has not.

Nothing so much resembles flowers planted on a dunghill, as the good which is done to an ignorant or worthless man.

In whatsoever company or society you be, engage not in those matters which concern the *whole;* for if you succeed, the whole company will attribute the success to itself; and if you succeed not, each person will lay the blame on *you.*

When the soul is ready to depart, what avails it whether a man die on a throne or in the dust?

Take and give with equity.

We need not be surprised when those who ask or seek for improper things, fall into misfortunes which they did not expect.

Riches dwell no longer in the hand of a liberal man, than patience in the heart of a lover, or water in a sieve.

As soon as a person takes pleasure in hearing slander, he is to be ranked in the number of slanderers.

That which a man suffers for this world, fills his heart with darkness; but that which he suffers for the other, fills it with light.

The greatest repose which a man can enjoy, is that which he feels in *desiring nothing.*

One seldom finds that which he seeks, when he searches for it with *impatience*.

Do not reproach a man for the sin which he has committed, when God has forgiven him.

He who pushes a jest farther than good breeding requires, shall never fail to be hated or despised.

He who is worthy of being called *a man*, is unshaken in adversity, humble in prosperity, active and bold in danger; and, if he be not learned, has at least a love for learning.

The man who is governed by his passions is in a worse state than the most miserable slave.

Men often give themselves much trouble to succeed in an affair from which they derive only vexation in the end.

He is a free man who desires nothing; and he is a slave who expects that which he wishes.

The advice of a wise man is to be considered as a *prediction*.

Be sincere, though your sincerity should cost you your life.

Live not on credit, and you shall live in liberty.

A wise man practises the three following things: he abandons the world before it abandons him; he builds his sepulchre before the time of entering it; and he does all with a design to please God, before entering into his presence.

He who lords it over those who are below him, shall one day find a master who will lord it over him.

Sin not, if you would have less vexation in the hour of death.

He who takes not counsel beforehand, will surely fail in accomplishing his projects.

Covetousness leads to poverty; but he is truly rich who desires nothing.

He who relates the faults of others to you, designs to relate yours to them.

Watch your friends; except those of whom you are certain; but know, that none can be a *true* friend but he who has the fear of God.

The most perfect pleasures in this world are always mingled with some bitterness.

He who considers consequences with too much attention, is ordinarily a man of no courage.

The world is the hell of the good, and the heaven of the wicked; i. e., it is all the evil that the former shall meet with, and all the good that the latter shall enjoy.

By doing good to those who have evil intentions against you, you thereby shut their mouth.

He who knows well what he is capable of, has seldom bad success.

He who has too good an opinion of himself, drives all others away from him.

He who loves jesting and raillery, brings himself into many troubles.

Partial knowledge is better than total ignorance; if you cannot get what you wish, get what you can.

He who has lost shame may bury his heart.

The poor should get learning in order to become rich; and the rich should acquire it for their ornament.

A man should accommodate himself to the weakness of his inferiors, in order to derive from them the services he requires.

An avaricious man runs straight into poverty. He leads a life of poverty here below; but he must give the account of a *rich man* in the day of judgment.

The greatest advantage that a man can procure for his children, is to have them well educated.

Do good to him who does you evil, and by this means you will gain the victory over him.

Men, because of *speech*, have the advantage over brutes; but beasts are preferable to men whose language is indecent.

If you can do good *to-day*, defer it not till *to-morrow.*

The excellence of many discourses consists in their brevity.

Two things are inseparable from lying; many promises and many excuses.

Deceivers, liars, and all persons who lead an irregular life, are intoxicated by the prosperity which smiles upon them in all things; but that intoxication is the just recompense of their evil actions.

He lives in true repose who bridles his passions.

It is in vain to expect these five things from the following persons: A present from a poor man; service from a lazy man; succour from an enemy; counsel from an envious man; and true love from a prude.

It is unbecoming the character of a wise man to commit the fault for which he reproves others.

A passionate man is capable of nothing; how unfit then is such a person for a governor!

A rich man who is not liberal, resembles a tree without fruit.

You cannot keep your own secret; what cause then have you to complain, if another to whom you have declared it should reveal it?

It is the same with the administration of the affairs of kings as with sea voyages; you may lose, gain, amass treasures, and lose your life.

He who submits to a voluntary poverty neither possesses, nor is possessed by, any thing.

A wicked man should be considered as dead while he is alive; but a good man lives even in the tomb.

No man should undertake any thing till he has thoroughly examined it.

He who possesses any art or science, is at least equal to a great lord.

Honours, employments, and dignities cannot recompense a man for the pains he has taken to acquire them.

On many occasions a good book supplies the place of an agreeable companion.

That day in which a man neither does some good action, nor acquires some useful knowledge, should not be (if possible) numbered in the days of his life.

He who is of a surly and unyielding disposition, never fails to excite troubles even among relatives and friends.

A great monarch should fix a *good reputation* as an object to which he should continually bend his pursuits; because, of all the grandeurs and eminences of this world, this is the only thing that shall survive him.

Leave not till to-morrow what you can perform to-day.

To have pity on one's enemy, when he is in distress, is the mark of a great soul.

He who does good shall not lose his reward. A good action never perishes, neither before God nor before men.

Covetousness proceeds *ad infinitum;* therefore, determine the bounds of your desires, and the objects of your pursuits. He who does not act thus shall never become either rich or happy.

A monarch who considers his own interest should ever abide in his kingdom, and consider himself as a *rose* in the midst of a garden, which continually reposes on *thorns.*

Never despise a man because his employment is mean, or his clothing bad. The *bee* is an insect which is not very pleasing to the sight, yet its hive affords abundance of honey.

The people enjoy *repose* when governed by princes who take none. The monarch who watches causes his people to repose in safety.

Confer your opinion with that of another, for truth is more easily discovered by two than one.

Do not rejoice at the death of your enemy; *your* life is not eternal.

Be always employed, that ye become not slothful; and refer to God all that you acquire by labour, otherwise you shall live in a continual and condemnable idleness.

It is extremely difficult to render him wise who knows nothing; because his ignorance causes him to believe that he knows more than he who attempts to instruct him.

One coat, one house, and one day's food, is enough for you; and should you die at noonday, you will have one half too much.

A covetous man is an enemy to all the poor; and is cursed both in this and the coming world.

Interested friends resemble dogs in public places, who love the bones better than those who throw them.

In order to live well, a man should die to all his passions and every thing that depends on them.

A thousand years of delight do not deserve the risk of our lives for a single moment.

You shall only receive in proportion to what you give.

The service of kings may be compared to a vast sea, where many merchants traffic, some of whom acquire great riches, and others are shipwrecked.

Fear the man who fears you.

Do nothing without design.

Humble yourself in asking, that you may be raised up in obtaining what you request.

A wicked woman in the house of a good man is a hell to him in this world.

It cannot be said of a miser that he possesses his riches, however attached he may be to them.

The thought of evil frequently derives its origin from idleness.

Kings and subjects are equally unhappy, where persons of merit are despised, and where ignorant men occupy the chief places of trust.

Answer those who ask questions of you in such a manner as not to offend them.

The most proper method of punishing an envious person is, to load him with benefits.

Prudence suffers between *impossibility* and *irresolution.*

When you speak, let it be in such a manner as not to require an explanation.

The most precious acquisition is that of a friend.

Never trust to appearance. Behold the *drum:* notwithstanding all its noise, it is *empty* within.

Keep not an evil conscience: but be diffident, to the end that you be never surprised nor deceived.

Nothing remains with punishment or reward.

A wise man by his speeches does things which a hundred armies conjoined could not execute.

Do not speak till you have thought on what you intend to say.

Those who believe they may gain by seditions and commotions never fail to excite them.

The best friends we have in this world are the spies of our actions, who publish our faults.

Hope for nothing from this world, and your soul will enjoy rest.

He who applies himself to acquire knowledge, puts himself in the capacity of possessing all good things.

He who does not succeed in the business in which he is employed, because he is incapable of it, deserves to be excused; for it is to be believed that he has done all he could to accomplish his end.

Every kind of employment requires a particular sort of genius.

Riches increase in proportion as you give to the poor.

The greatest reputation is frequently an embarrassment.

Do not despise a poor man because he is such: the lion is not less noble because he is chained.

A young man who has the wisdom of an old man is considered as an old man among those who are wise.

A righteous prince is the image and shadow of God upon earth.

As soon as virtue begins to discover itself, vice begins its insolent insults.

Can it be said that a man has wisely considered what he has done, when the end corresponds not with what he proposed?

To the end that what you desire may be advantageous to you, never desire any thing but that which is proper for you.

Those who will not forgive an offence are the most accursed of all men.

Though it be pretended that no man can shun his destiny, yet it is well to do nothing without precaution.

It is a double present when given with a cheerful countenance.

Nobility is nothing unless supported by good actions.

Evil speaking and calumny never quit their hold till they have destroyed the innocent on whom they have once seized.

Consider your estate, and leave playing and jesting to children.

Soft words may appease an angry man; bitter words never will.

Would you throw fire on a house in flames to extinguish them?

Continue to speak the truth, though you know it to be hateful.

It is a blessing to a house to have a number of guests at table.

Five things are useless when they are not accompanied each with another thing: advice without effect; riches without economy; science without good manners; almsgiving to improper objects, or without a pure intention; and life without health.

If you wish your enemy never to know your secret, never divulge it to your friend.

Art thou a man in honour? Wouldst thou live without inquietude or remorse? Then do actions worthy of thy character.

When subjects are ill treated by subaltern officers, and cannot make remonstrances to the prince, because the too great authority of ministers of state deprives them of the means; their lot is like to that of a man who, half dead with thirst, approaches the river Nile to drink; but perceiving a *crocodile,* is obliged to perish for lack of water, or submit to be devoured.

It is better to perish with hunger, than to deprive the poor of their bread.

If you be reproved for your faults, do not be angry with him who does it: but turn your anger against the things for which he has reproved you.

Poisonous food is preferable to bad discourse.

Do not discover the faults of others, if you be unwilling to have your own known.

Wage war against yourself, and you will thereby acquire true peace of soul.

One resembles those the company of whom he most frequents.

The best expended riches are those which are given for God's sake.

If you have a dispute with any person, take heed that you say not of him all the evil which you know; otherwise you will leave no room for accommodation.

Your conversation is the index of your intellect, and your actions show the bottom of your heart.

It is more difficult to manage riches well, than to acquire them.

The grandeur of kings is evidenced in the administration of justice.

Honour your parents, and your children will honour you.

Cultivate no friendship with him who loves your enemy.

If you have a friend who takes offence at trifles, break entirely with him, for he is not to be trusted.

The happiness of life is only to be found, when the conscience is pure and clean.

Measure every man with his own measure; i. e., "Do not expect or require from him more than is in him."

Can any man boast who considers what he is come from?

In whatever corner of the world you are, you will have something to suffer.

It will be more profitable for thee to adorn thy inside than thy outside.

The Words of LOCKMAN *to his* SON

My son, I wish thee to observe these *six* maxims which comprehend all the morality of the ancients and moderns.

1. Have no attachment to the world, but in proportion to the short duration of thy life.
2. Serve God with all that fervour which the need thou hast of him demands.
3. Labour for the other life that awaits thee, and consider the time it must endure.
4. Strive to escape that fire, out of which those who are once cast in can never escape.
5. If thou hast temerity enough to sin, measure beforehand the strength thou shalt require to endure the fire of hell, and the chastisements of God.
6. When thou wishest to transgress, seek for a place where God cannot see thee.

The Words of ALI *to his* SONS

My sons, never despise any person: consider your superior as your father, your equal as your brother, and your inferior as your son.

Words addressed by a Mohammedan to the MESSIAH

The heart of the afflicted draws all its consolation from thy words.

The soul receives life and vigour at the bare mention of thy name.

If ever the human spirit be rendered capable of contemplating the mysteries of the Divinity, it is thou alone who givest it the light by which it understands, and the attractions by which it is penetrated.

INTRODUCTION
TO THE
BOOK OF ECCLESIASTES

THE book, entitled *Koheleth*, or *Ecclesiastes*, has ever been received, both by the Jewish and Christian Church, as written under the *inspiration* of the Almighty; and was held to be properly a part of the sacred canon. But while this has been almost universally granted, there has been but little unanimity among learned men and critics as to its *author*. To *Solomon* it has been most generally attributed, both in ancient and modern times.

Grotius, however, conjectured that it was written a long time after Solomon; and he says, at the close of his notes on it, that it was revised in the days of *Zerubbabel* by some learned man, who in the twelfth verse of the last chapter addresses his son *Abihud:* "And farther, by these, my son, be admonished." But such a conjecture appears to have little foundation. This great man was more successful in his criticism on the *language* of the book; showing that there are many words in it which do not savour of the purity of the Hebrew tongue; and are found in the times of the *captivity* and *afterwards*, and such as appear principally in the books of *Ezra* and *Daniel*.

Calovius has on the other hand, not with so much success as he imagined, argued against *Grotius* for the *purity* of the language.

Mr. G. Zirkel of Wurtzburgh published an examination of this book in 1792, in which he endeavours to prove:—

1. That the *style* of Ecclesiastes is that of the *later Hebrew writers*, as appears by the *Chaldaisms*, *Syriasms*, and *Hellenisms* that occur in it.

2. That it may have been written between the years 380 and 130 before Jesus Christ, if not later.

The *Jena* reviewers seem to have thought it to be a *translation* from the *Greek*, and to have been written by a *Jew* of *Alexandria*, while the famous *library* was founding by *Ptolemy Philadelphus* king of Egypt, about the year 240 before Christ. And that it is to this circumstance that chap. xii. 12 alludes, "Of making many books there is no end;" which could not have entered into the head of a Palestine Jew; and such a person might speak with propriety of an *Israel in Jerusalem*, chap. i. 12, being acquainted with an *Israel in Alexandria*.

The Jews in general, and St. *Jerome*, hold the book to be the composition of *Solomon*, and the fruit of his repentance when restored from his idolatry, into which he had fallen through means of the strange or *heathenish women* whom he had taken for *wives* and *concubines*.

Others, of no mean note, who consider Solomon as the author, believe that he wrote it *before* his fall; there being no evidence that he wrote it afterwards; nor, indeed, that he ever recovered from his fall. Besides, it was in his *old age* that his wives turned away his heart from God; and the book bears too many evidences of mental *energy* to allow the supposition that in his *declining age*, after so deep a fall from God, he was *capable* of writing such a treatise. This opinion goes far towards destroying the *Divine inspiration* of the book; for if he did recover and repent, there is no evidence that God gave him back that *Divine inspiration* which he before possessed; for we hear of the Lord appearing to him *twice before his fall*, but of a *third* appearance there is no intimation. And lastly, Of the restoration of Solomon to the favour of God there is no proof in the sacred history; for in the *very place* where we are told that "in his old age his wives turned away his heart from the Lord," we are told of his *death*, without the slightest intimation of his *repentance*. See my character of Solomon at the end of 1 Kings xi.

Nothing, however, of this uncertainty can affect either the character, importance, or utility of the book in question. It is a production of singular worth; and the finest monument we have of the wisdom of the ancients, except the *book of Job*.

But the chief difficulty attending this book is the *principle* on which it should be interpreted. Some have supposed it to be a *dialogue* between a *true believer* and an *infidel*, which makes it to the unwary reader appear abounding with contradiction, and, in some instances, false doctrine; and that the parts must be attributed to their respective speakers, before interpretation can be successfully attempted. I am not convinced that the book has any such structure; though in some places the *opinions* and *sayings* of *infidels* may be quoted; e. g., chap. vii. 16, and in some of the following chapters.

In the year 1763, M. *Desvœux*, a learned foreigner then resident in England, and who was in the British service, wrote and published a *Philosophical and Poetical Essay* on this book, in which he endeavours to prove, that the design of the author was to *demonstrate the immortality of the soul;* and that it is on this principle alone that the book can be understood and explained.

As a late commentator on the Bible has adopted this plan, and interwoven the major part of this dissertation with his notes on the book, I shall introduce the whole of M. *Desvœux's analysis of its contents*, the *propositions*, *arguments*, *proofs*, *illustrations*, *corollaries*, &c., on the ground of which he attempts its illustration:—

The whole of the discourse (he says) may be reduced to the three following *propositions*, each of which is attended with its *apparatus* of *proofs* and *especial observations*.

PROPOSITION I

No labour of man in this world can render him contented, or give him true satisfaction of soul.

PROPOSITION II

Earthly goods and possessions are so far from making us happy, that they may be even viewed as real obstacles to our ease, quiet, and tranquillity of mind.

PROPOSITION III

Men know not what is or is not truly advantageous to them; because they are either ignorant or unmindful of that which must come to pass after their death.

The *three propositions*, with their *proofs* and *illustrations*, are contained in the following analysis:—

PROPOSITION I

Chap.	Ver.	
I.	2, 3.	No labour of man, &c.
	4–11.	First proof.—The course of nature.
	12, &c.	Second proof.—Men's occupations.
	16–18.	First head.—Wisdom or philosophy.
II.	1, 2.	Second head.—Pleasure.
	3–10.	Both jointly.
	11.	General conclusion of the second proof.
		A review of the second proof with special conclusions, relating to every particular therein mentioned, viz.,
	12–17.	I. Wisdom.
	18–23.	II. Riches.
	24–26.	III. Pleasure.
III.	1, &c.	Third proof.—Inconstancy of men's wills.
	9.	Conclusion of the third proof.
		A review of the second and third proofs, considered jointly, with special observations and corollaries.
	10, 11.	First observation.—God is inculpable.
III.	12, 15.	Second observation.—God is the author of whatever befalls us in this world.
	16, 17.	First corollary.—God shall redress all grievances.
	18–21.	Second corollary.—God must be exalted, and man humbled.
	22.	Third corollary.—God allows men to enjoy the present life.
IV.	1.	Fourth proof.—Men's neglect of proper opportunities, evidenced in several instances, viz.,
	1–3.	I. Oppression.
	4.	II. Envy.
	5, 6.	III. Idleness.
	7–12.	IV. Avarice.
V.	13–19.	V. Misapplication of esteem and regard.
		N. B. 1–9 is a digression containing several admonitions, in order to prevent any misconstruction of the foregoing remarks.
	10–12.	IV. Expensive living.

PROPOSITION II.—Chap. v. 13

Chap.	Ver.	
v.	14–17.	First proof. Instability of riches.
vi.	18. 2.	Second proof. Insufficiency of riches to make men happy.
	3–6.	Corollary. The fate of an *abortive* is, on the whole, preferable to that of him who lives without enjoying life.
vi.	7–9.	Third proof. Men's insatiableness.
	10, 11.	General *conclusion* from the *first* and *second propositions*.

PROPOSITION III.—Chap. vi. 12

Chap.	Ver.	
vii.	1, &c.	First proof. Wrong estimation of things.
		A *digression*, intended, like that ver. 1–9, to prevent any misconstruction of the preceding observations; and containing several *advices*, together with a strong commendation of him who gives them, in order to enforce the observation of the *rules* he lays down.
	9–12.	First advice. Do not blame Providence.
	13.	Second advice. Do not judge of Providence.
	14, 15.	Third advice. Submit to Providence.
	16–20.	Fourth advice. Avoid excesses.
	21, 22.	Fifth advice. Do not heed idle reports.
	23–25.	Commendation of the foregoing advices from the author's application of every thing; and especially,
vii.	26–29.	i. Wickedness and ignorance.
viii.	1–8.	ii. Wisdom.
		Second proof. Anticipated judgments.
	9–14.	i. That sin shall go unpunished, because it is so in this world.
ix.	15–6.	ii. That life is preferable to death.
	7–9.	First corollary. Earthly enjoyments are not criminal.
	10.	Second corollary. We must make a proper use of our faculties.
	11–15.	Third proof. Judgments that are seemingly right, but entirely false.
	16, &c.	Fourth proof. Little regard paid to wisdom.
	16.	i. Past services are forgotten.
		ii. The least fault is noticed.
x.	5–19.	iii. Favour gets what is due to merit.
	20.	A caution to prevent the abuse of the preceding remarks.

PRACTICAL INFERENCES

Chap.	Ver.	
xi.	1–4.	i. From the *first* PROPOSITION,—We must give to earthly goods that stability of which they are capable.
	5, 6.	ii. From the *first* and *second* PROPOSITIONS,—We must, in all our conduct, conform to the design of Providence, and leave the success to God.
xii.	7, 8.	iii. From the *three* PROPOSITIONS, but especially from the *third*, we must seek for happiness beyond the grave.
	9–12.	Commendation of the work, from several considerations.
	13, 14.	CONCLUSION of the whole.

This is the whole of M. *Desvœux's Analysis;* and I place it here, that the reader who approves of the *plan* may keep it in view while he is passing through the book. For my own part, I doubt whether the author made any such technical arrangement.

The three propositions which M. Desvœux lays down, and which are so essential to the interpretation he gives of the book, would have been expressly propounded by the inspired writer had he intended such; but they appear nowhere in it, and M. D. is obliged to *assume* or gather them from the general scope of the work. However, on his plan, he has certainly made a number of judicious observations on different passages, though his translations are *generally* too bold, and *seldom* well supported by the original text.

In 1768 was published "Choheleth, or the Royal Preacher, a Poetical Paraphrase of the Book of Ecclesiastes. Most humbly inscribed to the King." 4to. There is no name to this work. The late Rev. John Wesley gives the following account of the work and its author in his *Journals:*—

"Monday, Feb. 8, 1768. I met with a surprising poem, entitled, Choheleth, or the Preacher: it is a paraphrase in tolerable verse on the book of Ecclesiastes. I really think the author of it (a Turkey merchant) understands both the difficult expressions, and the connection of the whole, better than any other either ancient or modern writer whom I have seen. He was at Lisbon during the great earthquake, just then sitting in his night-gown and slippers. Before he could dress himself, part of the house he was in fell, and blocked him up. By this means his life was saved; for all who had run out were dashed to pieces by the falling houses."

Mr. W. seems to have known the author well, but did not like to tell his name. About the year 1789 that eminent man recommended the work to me, and told me several particulars relative to it, which have escaped my memory. I procured the book the first opportunity, and read it with great satisfaction; and from it derived no small portion of information. Having now examined it anew, I can most cordially subscribe to Mr. Wesley's opinion. I really believe that the author understood both the difficult expressions, and the connection of the whole, better than any other writer, whether ancient or modern, at least known to me. Had it comported with my plan, I should have thought a reprint of his work, with the *text*, which he does not insert, and a few philological notes, would have been quite sufficient to have given my readers a safe and general view of the whole work and its design; though I can by no means adopt the author's hypothesis, that the book was written by Solomon *after* he was restored from his grievous apostacy. This is an assumption that never was proved and never can be.

From the *preface* to this work I have selected some general observations, which I consider to be important, and subjoin to this introduction; and what I borrow from the *work* itself I mark with a C, not knowing the author's name. Of the *authenticity* of the book of *Ecclesiastes* I have no doubt; but I must say, the *language* and *style* puzzle me not a little. *Chaldaisms* and *Syriasms* are certainly frequent in it, and not a few *Chaldee words* and terminations; and the style is such as may be seen in those writers who lived at or after the captivity. If these can be reconciled with the age of Solomon, I have no objection; but the attempts that have been made to deny this, and overthrow the evidence, are in my view often trifling, and generally ineffectual. That Solomon, son of David, might have been the *author* of the whole *matter* of this, and a *subsequent writer* put it in his own language, is a possible case; and were this to be allowed, it would solve all difficulties. Let us place the supposition thus: Solomon said all these things, and they are highly worthy of his wisdom; and a Divine writer, *after his time*, who does not mention his name, gives us a faithful version of the whole in his own language.

On other subjects relative to this book, the author of Choheleth shall speak for me.

"I. Not to perplex our readers with the various expositions of the word *Choheleth*, the title of the book in the original, (for in truth we can find none better or more significant than that commonly received, viz., *Ecclesiastes, or the Preacher*,) let us now come to the book itself. Nothing can be more interesting than the subject it treats of, to wit, *the chief or sovereign good* which man, as a rational and accountable being, should here propose to himself. Every human creature, it is certain, naturally aims at happiness; but though all apply themselves with equal ardour to this desirable end, yet such is the violence of passion, and want of reflection in the generality of mankind, that the means they use for obtaining it, instead of conducting them to the safe and direct road, only serve to mislead and bewilder them in dark and intricate labyrinths, where it is impossible to find what they seek for. Now as it was absolutely necessary to convince such men of the vanity of their pursuits, in order to induce them to turn back in the right way, Solomon shows, in the first place, what is *not* happiness, and then what really *is*. Like a skilful physician, he searches deeply into the latent cause of the malady, and then prescribes a radical cure.

"II. In the former disquisition he enumerates all those particulars which mankind are most apt to fix their hearts upon, and shows, from his own dear-bought experience, and the transient and unsatisfactory nature of the things themselves, that no such thing as solid felicity is to be found in any of them. What he asserts on this head carries with it the greater weight, as no man upon earth was ever better qualified to speak decisively on such a subject, considering the opportunities he had of enjoying to the utmost all that this world affords. After having thus cleared away the obstacles to happiness, he enters on the main point, which is to direct us how and where it may be found. This he affirms, at the conclusion of the book, where he recapitulates the sum and substance of the sermon, as some not improperly have styled it, consists in a religious and virtuous life, with which, as he frequently intimates, a man in the lowest circumstances may be happy, and without which one in the highest must be miserable. As the whole book tends to this single point, so, in discussing thereof, many excellent observations are interpersed relating to the various duties of life, from the highest to the lowest station; the advantages resulting even from poverty, the genuine use of riches, and extreme folly of abusing them; the unequal dispensations of Divine Providence; the immortality of the human soul; and great day of final retribution. All these noble and important subjects are treated of in such a style and manner as nothing among the ancients can parallel.

"We have here given the genuine character of this inestimable piece; yet such has been the ignorance, inattention, or depravity of some persons, that it would be hard to find an instance of any thing written on so serious and interesting a subject, which has been so grossly misrepresented. How often has a handle been taken from certain passages, ill understood, and worse applied, to patronise libertinism, by such as pretend to judge of the whole from a single sentence, independent of the rest, without paying the least regard to the general scope or design! According to which rule the most pious discourse that ever was written may be perverted to atheism. Some fanatics have fallen into the contrary extreme; for, on reading that all here below was vanity, they have been so wrong-headed, as to condemn every thing as evil in itself. This world, according to them, cannot be too bitterly inveighed against; and man has nothing else to do with it, but to spend his days in sighing and mourning. But it is evident that nothing could be farther from the preacher's intention: for notwithstanding he speaks so feelingly of the instability and unsatisfactory nature of all sublunary things, and the vanity of human cares, schemes, and contrivances; yet, lest any one should mistake his meaning, he advises every man, at the same time, to reap the fruit of his honest labours, and take the comfort of what he possesses with a sober freedom and cheerful spirit. Not to harass and disturb his mind with anxious cares and restless solicitudes about future events; but to pass the short space which Heaven has allotted him here, as pleasantly as his station will admit, with a quiet conscience. He does not condemn the things themselves, such as science, prudence, mirth, riches, honours, &c.; but only their abuse, that is, the useless studies, unreasonable pursuits, and immoderate desires, of those who pervert God's blessings to their own destruction.

"On this head Solomon gives his sentiments, not only as a divine and philosopher, but like one thoroughly acquainted with the foibles of the human heart. It was not his design to drive people out of the world, or to make them live wretchedly in it; but only that they should think and act like rational creatures; or, in other words, be induced to consult their own happiness.

"There is nothing in the whole body of pagan philosophy so elevated and magnificent, as what some have written on the important subject of this poem: but we find their opinions so various and contradictory, and the most plausible so blended with errors, even those of the *divine Plato* not excepted, that their sublimest sentiments on the *sovereign good* or *ultimate happiness* of man, when compared with those of the royal preacher, not only appear cold and languid, but always leave the mind unsatisfied and restless. We are lost in a pompous flow of words; and dazzled, but not illuminated. One sect, by confining happiness to sensual pleasures, so greatly slackened the cord as to render it wholly useless: another, by their too austere and rigid maxims, stretched it so tight that it snapped asunder; though the experience of all ages has evinced that these latter imposed both on themselves and the world, when they taught that virtue, however afflicted here, was its own reward, and sufficient of itself to render a man completely happy. Even in the brazen bull of *Perillus*, truth will cry out from the rack against such fallacious teachers, and prove them liars. The extravagant figments, therefore, of the *stoical apathy*, no less than those of the *voluptuous epicurean*, both equally vanish at the splendour of the Divine truth delivered by Solomon.

He alone decides the great question in such a manner that the soul is instantly convinced; it need seek no farther.

"III. To prevent all misapprehensions, which a slight and cursory reading of this book is apt to raise in many persons, it will be requisite to observe two cautions: First, that Solomon, who tells us that he applied his heart not only to the search of wisdom and knowledge, but also of folly and madness, frequently speaks, not according to his own sentiments, though he proposes the thing in a naked and simple manner, designedly making use of such terms as might set the picture in a fuller and clearer light, so that we often meet with certain expressions which, unless we search into their true design, seem to have a quite different force and meaning from what the author really intended. We must therefore take particular care to distinguish the doubts and objections of others from Solomon's answers; the want of attending to which has made this book much more obscure than otherwise it would appear. Secondly, we should not judge of the entire discourse from some parts of it; since many things are pertinently said, according to the present subject, which, in themselves, and strictly taken, are far from true. In order to come at the genuine sense, we should form our opinion from the different circumstances of the matter treated of, comparing the antecedent with the consequent passages, and always considering the preacher's real scope and design. By carefully attending to these two cautions, this book will be seen in a very different light from what it now appears in to the generality of readers.

"IV. This book, besides the figurative and proverbial expressions to be found in no other part of the Scripture, is undoubtedly metrical; and, consequently, the grammatization, in many places, not a little perplexed, from the frequent ellipses, abbreviations, transposition of words, and other poetical licenses, allowed in all languages; to say nothing of the carelessness or ignorance of transcribers, as appears from the variety of readings. Yet, notwithstanding we are so little acquainted with the nature of the Hebrew metre, and the propriety of certain phrases which, at this vast distance of time, in a language that has been dead upwards of two thousand years, must unavoidably occasion the same difficulties and obscurities as occur in works of far less antiquity, and in languages more generally studied and better understood; notwithstanding this, I say, a diligent and attentive observer will always find enough to recompense his trouble; and, if he has any taste, cannot avoid being struck with the exquisite beauty and regularity of the plan.

"V. The most judicious commentators have remarked on this book, that we have here a conspicuous example of that form of disputing, which was so justly admired in the soundest of the pagan philosophers; particularly in Socrates, who, whilst others were taken up with abstruse speculations about the nature of things, and investigating the number, motions, distance, and magnitude of the stars, brought down philosophy from the upper regions, and fixed its abode on earth; that is, by teaching such precepts as served for the regulation of life and manners, by far the most useful of all sciences, as being most conducive to the welfare of society, and the general benefit of mankind. Of this we have a noble specimen in the memoirs of that ancient moralist, collected by Xenophon. It is, I think, beyond all contradiction, that no one ever made deeper researches into nature, or had made so great a progress in every branch of science, both speculative and experimental. But what, after all, was the result of his inquiries? A thorough conviction of the inutility of such studies, and how little they conduce towards the obtaining that peace and tranquillity of mind wherein true happiness consists. He applied himself, therefore, to that study which might produce a real and lasting advantage, namely, to render men wise to some purpose; that is, truly virtuous. The manner of his treating this important subject bears some resemblance to that of the celebrated Greek moralist. He does not give us a long roll of dry formal precepts, with which the mind is soon tired; but, to confirm the truth of every thing he says, appeals, not only to his own experience, but to the general sense of unbiassed reason. At the same time he sets before us, in the liveliest colours, the sad effects of vice and folly; and makes use of every incentive to engage the heart to be enamoured with virtue, and pursue its own interest. Whatever he intends to inculcate is first barely proposed, and then more accurately explained and illustrated, though by gentle and almost imperceptible transitions; with this peculiarity, that there is always much more implied than expressed; insomuch that the reader, from a slight hint given him, is left to draw such inferences as his own reflection must naturally suggest. Every thing, in short, is drawn, in this admirable composition, with equal simplicity and elegance; and hath as distinguished a superiority to whatever the best pagan philosophers have given us on the same subject, as the borrowed light of the moon is surpassed by that of the sun in his full meridian lustre; or, to use a still stronger comparison, as Solomon's knowledge of the one true God excelled the idle notion of their fictitious deities."

Some have supposed that the book of Ecclesiastes is a poem. That some poetic lines may be found in it, there is no doubt; but it has nothing in common with poetic books, nor does it exist in the hemistich form in any printed edition or MS. yet discovered. It is plain prose, and is not susceptible of that form in which the Hebrew poetic books appear.

The author already quoted thinks that the book of *Ecclesiastes* is *metrical*. I cannot see this: but it has what is essential to poetry, a truly dignified style; there are no mean, creeping words in it, whether pure Hebrew, or borrowed from any of its dialects. They are all well chosen, nervous, and highly expressive. They are, in short, such as become the subject, and are worthy of that inspiration by which the author was guided.

ECCLESIASTES;

OR,

THE PREACHER

Year from the Creation, according to Archbishop Usher, 3027.—Year from the Flood of Noah, according to the common Hebrew text, 1371.—Year before the birth of Christ, 973.—Year before the vulgar era of Christ's nativity, 977.—N. B. The time when this book was written is very uncertain: the above chronology is agreeable to that contained in the present authorized version.

CHAPTER I

The prophet shows that all human courses are vain, 1–4. *The creatures are continually changing,* 5–8. *There is nothing new under the sun,* 9–11. *Who the prophet was, his estate and his studies,* 12–18.

A. M. cir. 3027
B. C. cir. 977
Ante I. Olymp. cir. 201
Ante U. C. cir. 224

THE words [a]of the Preacher,
the son of David, king of
Jerusalem.
2 [b]Vanity of vanities, saith
the Preacher, vanity of vanities; [c]all *is*
vanity.
3 [d]What profit hath a man of
all his labour which he taketh
under the sun?
4 *One* generation passeth
away, and *another* generation cometh: [e]but
the earth abideth for ever.

[a]Ver. 2, 12; chap. vii. 27; xii. 8, 9, 10——[b]Psa. xxxix. 5, 6; lxii. 9; cxliv. 4; chap. ii. 1, 15, 19, 21, 23; iii. 19; iv. 8, 16; v. 10; vi. 2, 4, 9, 11; vii. 6, 15; viii. 10, 14; ix. 9; xi. 10; xii. 8; Isa. xxx. 28; xl. 17, 23; xli. 29; xliv. 9; lvii. 13; lviii. 9; lix. 4——[c]Rom. viii. 20——[d]Chap. ii. 22; iii. 9——[e]Psa. civ. 5; cxix. 90

NOTES ON CHAP. I

Verse 1. *The words of the Preacher*] Literally, "The words of Choheleth, son of David, king of Jerusalem." But the *Targum* explains it thus: "The words of the prophecy, which Choheleth prophesied; the same is Solomon, son of David the king, who was in Jerusalem. For when Solomon, king of Israel, saw by the spirit of prophecy that the kingdom of Rehoboam his son was about to be divided with Jeroboam, the son of Nebat; and the house of the sanctuary was about to be destroyed, and the people of Israel sent into captivity; he said in his word—*Vanity of vanities* is all that I have laboured, and David my father; they are *altogether vanity.*"

The word קהלת *Koheleth* is a feminine noun, from the root קהל *kahal,* to collect, gather together, assemble; and means, *she who assembles* or *collects a congregation;* translated by the *Septuagint,* Εκκλησιαστης, a *public speaker, a speaker in an assembly;* and hence translated by us *a preacher.* In my old MS. Bible it is explained thus: **a talker to the peple; or togyder cleping.**

Verse 2. *Vanity of vanities*] As the words are an exclamation, it would be better to translate, *O vanity of vanities!* Emptiness of emptinesses. True, substantial good is not to be found in any thing liable to *change* and *corruption.*

The author referred to in the introduction begins his paraphrase thus:—

"O vain deluding world! whose largest gifts
Thine emptiness betray, like painted clouds,
Or watery bubbles: as the vapour flies,
Dispersed by lightest blast, so fleet thy joys,
And leave no trace behind. This serious truth
The royal preacher loud proclaims, convinced
By sad experience; with a sigh repeats
The mournful theme, that nothing here below
Can solid comfort yield: 'tis all a scene.
Of vanity, beyond the power of words
To express, or thought conceive. Let every man
Survey himself, then ask, what fruit remains
Of all his fond pursuits? What has he gain'd,
By toiling thus for more than nature's wants
Require? Why thus with endlness projects rack'd
His heated brain, and to the labouring mind,
Repose denied? Why such expense of time,
That steals away so fast, and ne'er looks back?
Could man his wish obtain, how short the space
For his enjoyment! No less transient here
The time of his duration, than the things

A. M. cir. 3027 B. C. cir. 977 Ante I. Olymp. cir. 201 Ante U. C. cir. 224

5 [f]The sun also ariseth, and
the sun goeth down, and [g]hasteth
to his place where he arose.
6 [h]The wind goeth toward the
south, and turneth about unto the north; it
whirleth about continually, and the wind returneth again according to his circuits.
7 [i]All the rivers run into the sea; yet the
sea *is* not full; unto the place from whence
the rivers come, thither they [k]return again.
8 All things *are* full of labour; man cannot utter *it:* [l]the eye is not
satisfied with seeing, nor the ear
filled with hearing.
9 [m]The thing that hath been,
it *is that* which shall be; and that which is
done *is* that which shall be done: and *there
is* no new *thing* under the sun.
10 Is there *any* thing whereof it may be
said, See, this *is* new? it hath been already
of old time, which was before us.
11 *There is* no remembrance of former

[f]Psa. xix. 5, 6——[g]Heb. *panteth*——[h]John iii. 8——[i]Job xxxviii. 10; Psa. civ. 8, 9——[k]Heb. *return to go*——[l]Proverbs xxvii. 20——[m]Chapter iii. 15

Thus anxiously pursued. For, as the mind,
In search of bliss, fix'd on no solid point,
For ever fluctuates; so our little frames,
In which we glory, haste to their decline,
Nor permanence can find. The human race
Drop like autumnal leaves, by spring revived:
One generation from the stage of life
Withdraws, another comes, and thus makes room
For that which follows. Mightiest realms decay,
Sink by degrees; and lo! new form'd estates
Rise from their ruins. Even the earth itself,
Sole object of our hopes and fears,
Shall have its period, though to man unknown."

Verse 3. *What profit hath a man*] What is the sum of the real good he has gained by all his toils in life? They, in themselves, have neither made him *contented* nor *happy.*

Verse 4. One *generation passeth away*] Men succeed each other in unceasing generations: but the earth is still the same; it undergoes no change that leads to melioration, or greater perfection. And it will continue the same לעולם *leolam,* during the whole course of time; till the end of all things arrives.

Verses 5 and 6. These verses are confused by being falsely divided. The first clause of the *sixth* should be joined to the *fifth* verse.

"The sun also ariseth, and the sun goeth down, and hasteth to his place where he ariseth; going to the south, and circulating to the north."

Verse 6. "The wind is continually whirling about, and the wind returneth upon its whirlings."

It is plain, from the clause which I have restored to the *fifth* verse, that the author refers to the approximations of the sun to the *northern* and *southern tropics,* viz., of *Cancer* and *Capricorn.*

All the *versions* agree in applying the first clause of the *sixth* verse to the *sun,* and not to the *wind.* Our *version* alone has mistaken the meaning. My old MS. Bible is quite correct:

The sunne riisith up, and goth doun, and to his place turnith agein; and there agein riising, goth about bi the south, and then agein to the north.

The author points out two things here: 1. *Day* and *night,* marked by the appearance of the sun above the horizon; proceeding *apparently* from *east to west;* where he sinks under the horizon, and appears to be lost during the night. 2. His *annual course* through the twelve signs of the zodiac, when, from the equinoctial, he proceeds southward to the tropic of Capricorn; and thence turneth about towards the north, till he reaches the tropic of Cancer; and so on.

Verse 7. *All the rivers run into the sea; yet the sea* is *not full*] The reason is, nothing goes into it either by the *rivers* or by *rain,* that does not come from it: and *to the place whence the rivers come,* whether from the *sea* originally by evaporation, or immediately by *rain,* thither they return again; for the water exhaled from the sea by evaporation is collected in the *clouds,* and in rain, &c., falls upon the tops of the mountains; and, filtered through their fissures, produce *streams,* several of which *uniting,* make *rivers,* which flow into the sea. The water is again *evaporated by the sun;* the vapours collected are precipitated; and, being filtered through the earth, become *streams,* &c., as before.

Verse 8. *All things* are *full of labour*] It is impossible to calculate how much anxiety, pain, labour, and fatigue are necessary in order to carry on the *common operations of life.* But an *endless desire* of *gain,* and an *endless curiosity* to *witness* a variety of results, cause men to labour on. The *eye* sees much; but wishes to see more. The *ear* hears of many things; but is curious to have the actual knowledge of them. So *desire* and *curiosity* carry men, under the Divine providence, through all the labours and pains of life.

Verse 9. *The thing that hath been*] Every thing in the whole economy of nature has its *revolutions;* summer and winter, heat and cold, rain and drought, seedtime and autumn, with the whole system of *corruption* and *generation,* alternately succeed each other, so that *whatever has been* shall *be again.* There is really, physically, and philosophically, nothing absolutely new under the sun, in the course of sublunary things. The same is the case in all the revolutions of the heavens.

Verse 10. *Is there* any *thing, &c.*] The original is beautiful. "Is there any thing which will say, See this! it is new?" Men may say this of their discoveries, &c.; but universal nature says, It is not new. *It has been,* and it *will be.*

Verse 11. There is *no remembrance*] I believe the general meaning to be this: Multitudes of *ancient transactions* have been lost,

A. M. cir. 3027 B. C. cir. 977 Ante I. Olymp. cir. 201 Ante U. C. cir. 224

things; neither shall there be
any remembrance of *things* that
are to come with *those* that shall
come after.

12 [n]I the Preacher was king over Israel in
Jerusalem.

13 And I gave my heart to seek and search
out by wisdom concerning all *things* that are
done under heaven: [o]this sore travail hath
God given to the sons of man [p]to be exercised
therewith.

14 I have seen all the works that are done
under the sun; and, behold, all *is* vanity and
vexation of spirit.

15 [q]*That which is* crooked cannot be made
straight: and [r]that which is
wanting cannot be numbered.

16 I communed with mine
own heart, saying, Lo, I am
come to great estate, and have gotten [s]more
wisdom than all *they* that have been before me in Jerusalem: Yea, my heart [t]had
great experience of wisdom and knowledge.

17 [u]And I gave my heart to know wisdom,
and to know madness and folly: I perceived
that this also is vexation of spirit.

18 For [v]in much wisdom *is* much grief:
and he that increaseth knowledge increaseth
sorrow.

[n]Verse 1——[o]Genesis iii. 19; chapter iii. 10——[p]Or, *to afflict them*——[q]Chapter vii. 13——[r]Hebrew, *defect*——[s]1 Kings iii. 12, 13; iv. 30; x. 7, 23; chapter ii. 9——[t]Hebrew, *had seen much*——[u]Chapter ii. 3, 12; vii. 23, 25; 1 Thessalonians v. 21——[v]Chapter xii. 12

because they were not *recorded;* and of many that have been recorded, the *records* are *lost.* And this will be the case with many others which are yet to occur. How many persons, not much acquainted with books, have supposed that certain things were their own discoveries, which have been *written* or *printed* even long before they were born! *Dutens*, in his *Origin of the Discoveries attributed to the Moderns*, has made a very clear case.

Verse 12. *I the Preacher was king*] This is a strange verse, and does not admit of an easy solution. It is literally, "I, Choheleth, have been king over Israel, in Jerusalem." This book, as we have already seen, has been conjectured by some to have been written about the time that *Ptolemy Philadelphus* formed his great library at Alexandria, about *two hundred and eighty-five* years before our Lord; and from the multitude of Jews that dwelt there, and resorted to that city for the sake of commerce, it was said there was an *Israel in Alexandria.* See the *introduction.*

It has also been conjectured from this, that if the book were written by *Solomon*, it was intended to be a *posthumous publication.* "I that *was* king, still continue to preach and instruct you." Those who suppose the book to have been written *after Solomon's fall*, think that he speaks thus through *humility.* "I was once worthy of the name of king: but I fell into all evil; and, though recovered, I am no longer worthy of the name." I am afraid this is not *solid.*

Verse 13. *And I gave my heart to seek and search*] While Solomon was faithful to his God, he diligently cultivated his mind. His giving himself to the study of natural history, philosophy, poetry, &c., are sufficient proofs of it. He had not intuitive knowledge from God; but he had a *capacity* to obtain every kind of knowledge useful to man.

This sore travail] This is the way in which knowledge is to be acquired; and in order to investigate the operations of nature, the most *laborious discussions* and *perplexing experiments* must be instituted, and conducted to their proper results. It is God's determination that knowledge shall be acquired in no other way.

Verse 14. *Behold, all* is *vanity*] After all these discussions and experiments, when even the results have been the most successful, I have found only *rational satisfaction;* but not that *supreme good* by which alone the soul can be made happy.

O curas hominum! O quantum est in rebus inane!

"How anxious are our cares, and yet how vain
The bent of our desires!"

PERS. *Sat.* i., v. 1.

Verse 15. That which is *crooked cannot be made straight*] There are many apparent irregularities and anomalies in nature for which we cannot account; and there are many *defects* that cannot be *supplied.* This is the impression from a *general view* of nature; but the more we study and investigate its operations, the more we shall be convinced that all is a *consecutive* and well-ordered whole; and that in the *chain of nature* not one *link* is broken, deficient, or lost.

Verse 16. *I communed with mine own heart*] Literally, "I spoke, I, with my heart, saying." When successful in my researches, but not happy in my soul, though easy in my circumstances, I entered into my own heart, and there inquired the *cause* of my discontent. He found that, though—1. He had gotten wisdom beyond all men; 2. Wealth and honours more than any other; 3. Practical wisdom more than all his predecessors; 4. Had tried *pleasure* and animal gratification, even to their extremes; yet after all this he had nothing but *vexation of spirit. None* of these *four* things, nor the *whole* of them *conjoined*, could afford him such a *happiness* as satisfies the soul. Why was all this? Because the soul was made for God, and in the possession of him alone can it find happiness.

Verse 17. *To know madness and folly*] הוללות ושכלות *holloth vesichluth.* Παραβολας και επιστημην, "Parables and science."—*Septuagint.* So the *Syriac;* nearly so the *Arabic.*

"What were error and foolishness."—*Coverdale.* Perhaps *gayety* and *sobriety* may be the better meaning for these two difficult words. I can scarcely think they are taken in that *bad sense* in which our translation exhibits them. "I tried pleasure in all its forms; and sobriety and self-abnegation to their utmost extent." Choheleth paraphrases, "Even fools and madmen taught me rules."

Verse 18. *For in much wisdom* is *much grief*] The more we know of *ourselves* the less satisfied shall we be with our own hearts; and the more we know of *mankind* the less willing shall we be to trust them, and the less shall we admire them.

He that increaseth knowledge increaseth sorrow.] And why so? Because, independently of God, the principal objects of knowledge are natural and moral evils.

The *Targum* gives a curious paraphrase here: "The man who multiplies wisdom, when he sins and is not converted to repentance, multiplies the indignation of God against himself; and the man who adds science, and yet dies in his childhood, adds grief of heart to his relatives." A man in science; a foolish child in conduct. How pained must they be who had the expense of his education! But there are many men-children of this sort in every age and country.

CHAPTER II

The vanity of human courses in the works of pleasure, planting, building, equipage, amassing wealth, &c., 1–11. *Wisdom preferable to folly,* 12–14; *yet little difference between the wise and the foolish in the events of life,* 15–17. *The vanity of amassing wealth for heirs, when whether they will be foolish or wise cannot be ascertained,* 18–21. *There is much sorrow in the labour of man,* 22, 23. *We should enjoy what the providence of God gives,* 25, 26.

A. M. cir. 3027
B. C. cir. 977
Ante I. Olymp. cir. 201
Ante U. C. cir. 224

[a]I SAID in mine heart, Go to
now, I will prove thee
with mirth, therefore enjoy pleasure: and, behold, [b]this also *is*
vanity.
2 [c]I said of laughter, *It is* mad: and of
mirth, What doeth it?
3 [d]I sought in mine heart [e]to give myself
unto wine, (yet acquainting mine heart with
wisdom,) and to lay hold on folly, till I might
see what *was* that good for the
sons of men, which they should
do under the heaven [f]all the
days of their life.
4 I made me great works; I builded me
houses; I planted me vineyards:
5 I made me gardens and orchards, and I
planted trees in them of all *kind of* fruits:
6 I made me pools of water, to water therewith the wood that bringeth forth trees:

A. M. cir. 3027
B. C. cir. 977
Ante I. Olymp. cir. 201
Ante U. C. cir. 224

---

[a]Luke xii. 19——[b]Isa. l. 11——[c]Prov. xiv. 13; chap. vii. 6——[d]Chap. i. 17

[e]Heb. *to draw my flesh with wine*——[f]Heb. *the number of the days of their life*

NOTES ON CHAP. II

Verse 1. *I will prove thee with mirth*] This is well expressed by the author so often referred to. Having tried speculative knowledge in vain, passion and appetite whisper,—

"From the rugged thorny road
Of wisdom, which so ill repays thy toil,
Turn back, and enter pleasure's flowery paths.
Go, take thy fill of joy; to passion give
The reins; nor let one serious thought restrain
What youth and affluence prompt."

Verse 2. *I said of laughter,* It is *mad*] Literally, "To laughter I said, O mad one! and to mirth, What is this one doing?"

Solomon does not speak here of a sober enjoyment of the things of this world, but of *intemperate pleasure,* whose two attendants, *laughter* and *mirth* are introduced by a beautiful *prosopopœia* as two persons; and the contemptuous manner wherewith he treats them has something remarkably striking. He tells the *former* to her face that *she is mad;* but as to the *latter,* he thinks her so much beneath his notice, that he only points at her, and instantly turns his back.

Verse 3. *To give myself unto wine,* (*yet acquainting* [נהג *noheg,* "guiding"] *mine heart with wisdom,*)] I did not run into *extremes,* as when I gave up myself to *mirth* and *pleasure. There,* I threw off all restraint; *here,* I took the middle course, to see whether a *moderate* enjoyment of the things of the world might not produce that happiness which I supposed man was created to enjoy here below.

Verse 4. *I builded me houses*] Palace after palace; the house of the forest of Lebanon, 1 Kings vii. 1, &c.; a house for the queen; the temple, &c., 2 Chron. viii. 1, &c.; 1 Kings ix. 10, &c., besides many other buildings of various kinds.

Verse 5. *I made me gardens and orchards*] פרדסים *pardesim,* "paradises." I doubt much whether this be an original *Hebrew* word. فردوس *ferdoos,* is found in the *Persian* and *Arabic;* and signifies a *pleasant garden,* a *vineyard.* Hence our word *paradise,* a place *full of delights.* How well Solomon was qualified to form *gardens, orchards, vineyards, conservatories,* &c., may be at once conceived when we recollect his knowledge of *natural history;* and that he wrote treatises on vegetables and their properties, from the *cedar* to the *hyssop.*

Verse 6. *Pools of water*] *Tanks* and *reservoirs.*

A. M. cir. 3027
B. C. cir. 977
Ante I. Olymp. cir. 201
Ante U. C. cir. 224

7 I got *me* servants and maidens, and had [g]servants born in my house; also I had great possessions of great and small cattle above all that were in Jerusalem before me:

8 [h]I gathered me also silver and gold, and the peculiar treasure of kings and of the provinces: I gat me men singers and women singers, and the delights of the sons of men, *as* [i]musical instruments, and that of all sorts.

9 So [k]I was great, and increased more than all that were before me in Jerusalem: also my wisdom remained with me.

10 And whatsoever mine eyes desired I kept not from them, I withheld not my heart from any joy; for my heart rejoiced in all my labour: and [l]this was my portion of all my labour.

A. M. cir. 3027
B. C. cir. 977
Ante I. Olymp. cir. 201
Ante U. C. cir. 224

11 Then I looked on all the works that my hands had wrought, and on the labour that I had laboured to do: and, behold, all *was* [m]vanity and vexation of spirit, and *there was* no profit under the sun.

12 And I turned myself to behold wisdom, [n]and madness, and folly: for what *can* the man *do* that cometh after the king? [o]*even* that which hath been already done.

13 Then I saw [p]that wisdom excelleth folly, as far as light excelleth darkness.

---

[g]Heb. *sons of my house*——[h]1 Kings ix. 28; x. 10, 14, 21, &c.——[i]Heb. *musical instrument and instruments*
[k]Ch. i. 16——[l]Ch. iii. 22; v. 18; ix. 9——[m]Ch. i. 3, 14

[n]Ch. i. 17; vii. 25——[o]Or, *in those things which have been already done*——[p]Heb. *that there is an excellency in wisdom more than in folly*, &c.

To water therewith the wood] Aqueducts to lead the water from the tanks to different parts.

Verse 7. *Servants and maidens*] For my works, fields, folds, and various domestic labours.

Servants born in my house] Besides those hired from without, he had *married couples* in the precincts of his grounds, palaces, &c., who, when their children grew up, got them employment with themselves.

Great and small cattle] *Oxen, neat, horses, asses, mules, camels*, and such like; with *sheep* and *goats*. And multitudes of most of these he needed, when we are told that his household consumed daily *ten stall-fed oxen, with twenty from the pasture, with a hundred sheep;* besides *harts, roebucks, fallow deer, fatted fowls*, and other kinds of provision. Probably, such another court for splendour and expense was not in the universe.

Verse 8. *The peculiar treasure of kings and of the provinces*] 1. The *taxes* levied off his subjects. 2. The *tribute* given by the neighbouring potentates. Both these make the "peculiar treasure of kings;" *taxes* and *tribute*.

Men singers and women singers] This includes all *instrumental* and *vocal* performers. These may be called the *delights* of the sons of men.

Musical instruments, and that of all sorts.] For these *seven* words, there are only *two* in the original, שדה ושדות *shiddah veshiddoth*. These words are acknowledged on all hands to be utterly unknown, if not utterly inexplicable. Some render them *male* and *female captives;* others, *cups* and *flagons;* others, *cooks* and *confectioners;* others, *a species of musical compositions* derived from a celebrated Phœnician woman named *Sido*, to whom Sanchoniatho attributes the invention of *music*. Others, with more probability, *wives* and *concubines;* of the *former* of whom Solomon had *seven hundred*, and of the *latter, three hundred;* and if these be not spoken of here, they are not mentioned at all; whereas music, and every thing connected with that, was referred to before. The author of *Choheleth* paraphrases thus:—

"To complete
This scene of earthly bliss, how large a span
Of that which most delights the sons of men
Fell to my portion! What a lovely train
Of blooming beauties, by *connubial* ties,
By *purchase*, or the *gifts* of neighbouring kings,
Or *spoils of war*, made mine."

If, after all this, I may add one *conjecture*, it shall be this; שדה *sadeh*, in Hebrew, is a *field*, and occurs in various parts of the Bible. שדות *sadoth* is *fields*, 1 Sam. xxii. 7, the *points* in such a case are of no consideration. May not Solomon be speaking here of *farms upon farms*, or *estates upon estates*, which he had added by purchase to the *common regal portion?* We know that a king of Israel (Ahab) once desired to have a vineyard (Naboth's) which he could not obtain: now, Solomon having spoken before of *gardens, orchards, and vineyards*, why may he not here speak of *supernumerary estates?* Perhaps every man who critically examines the place will be dissatisfied, and have a *conjecture* of his own.

Verse 10. *I withheld not my heart from any joy*] He had every means of gratification; he could desire nothing that was not within his reach; and whatever he wished, he took care to possess.

Verse 11. *And, behold, all* was *vanity*] Emptiness and insufficiency in itself.

And vexation of spirit] Because it promised the good I wished for, but did not, could not, perform the promise; and left my soul discontented and chagrined.

Verse 12. *For what* can *the man* do *that cometh after the king?*] I have examined every thing proposed by *science*, by *maddening pleasure*, and by more refined and regulated *mirth*. I seized on the whole, and used them to the uttermost; and so far, that none ever shall be able to exceed me; as none can, in the course of things, ever have such *power* and *means* of *gratification*.

Verse 13. *Then I saw that wisdom excelleth folly*] Though in none of these pursuits I found the *supreme good*. the happiness my soul longed

A. M. cir. 3027
B. C. cir. 977
Ante I. Olymp. cir. 201
Ante U. C. cir. 224

14 [q]The wise man's eyes *are*
in his head; but the fool walketh
in darkness: and I myself perceiveth also that [r]one event happeneth to them all.
15 Then said I in my heart, As it happeneth
to the fool, so it [s]happeneth even to me; and
why was I then more wise? Then I said
in my heart, that this also *is* vanity.
16 For *there is* no remembrance of the wise
more than of the fool for ever; seeing that
which now *is* in the days to come shall all be
forgotten. And how dieth the [t]wise *man?*
as the fool.
17 Therefore I hated life; because the work
that is wrought under the sun *is* grievous
unto me: for all *is* vanity and vexation of
spirit.

A. M. cir. 3027
B. C. cir. 977
Ante I. Olymp. cir. 201
Ante U. C. cir. 224

18 Yea, I hated all my labour
which I had [u]taken under the
sun: because [v]I should leave it unto the man that shall be after me.
19 And who knoweth whether he shall be a
wise *man* or a fool? yet shall he have rule
over all my labour wherein I have laboured,
and wherein I have showed himself wise under
the sun. This *is* also vanity.
20 Therefore I went about to cause my
heart to despair of all the labour which I took
under the sun.
21 For there is a man whose labour *is* in
wisdom, and in knowledge, and in equity; yet
to a man that hath not laboured therein shall
he [w]leave it *for* his portion. This also *is*
vanity and a great evil.
22 [x]For what hath man of all his labour,

[q]Proverbs xvii. 24; chapter viii. 1——[r]Psalm xlix. 10; chapter ix. 2, 3, 11——[s]Hebrew, *happeneth to me, even to me*——[t]Job v. 13; Psalm xciv. 8; chapter ii. 15; vi. 8; vii. 16; Isa. xliv. 25——[u]Hebrew, *laboured*——[v]Psalm xlix. 10——[w]Hebrew, *give*——[x]Chapter i. 3; iii. 9

after; yet I could easily perceive that wisdom *excelled* the *others*, as far as *light excels darkness*. And he immediately subjoins the reasons.

Verse 14. *The wise man's eyes, &c.*] Well expressed by *Choheleth*:—

"The wise are circumspect, maturely weigh
The consequence of what they undertake,
Good ends propose, and fittest means apply
To accomplish their designs."

But the fool walketh in darkness]

"But fools, deprived
Of reason's guidance, or in darkness grope,
Or, unreflecting like a frantic man,
Who on the brink of some steep precipice
Attempts to run a race with heedless steps,
Rush to their own perdition."

One event happeneth to them all.]

"Though wide the difference, what has human pride
To boast? Even I myself too plainly saw,
That *one event to both alike befalls;*
To various accidents of life exposed,
Without distinction: nor can *wisdom* screen
From *dangers*, *disappointments*, *grief*, and *pain*."

Verse 15. *As it happeneth to the fool*] Literally, "According as the event is to the fool, it happens to me, even me." There is a peculiar beauty and emphasis in the repetition of *me*. Having pointed out the advantages that wisdom has over folly, he takes this opportunity of reminding us of the danger of trusting too much to it, by showing that it is equally subject to the common accidents of life; and, therefore, incapable of making us completely happy. Having given his sentiments on this point in *general* terms, he proceeds to those *particular* instances wherein human prudence chiefly exerts itself; and shows how egregiously it is mistaken in every one of them.—C.

Verse 16. There is *no remembrance*] The wise and the fool are equally subject to death; and, in most instances, they are equally forgotten. *Time* sweeps away all remembrances, except the very *few* out of *millions* which are preserved for a while in the *page of history*.

Verse 17. *Therefore I hated life*] את החיים *et hachaiyim, the lives*, both of the *wise*, the *madman*, and the *fool*. Also all the *stages* of life, the *child*, the *man*, and the *sage*. There was nothing in it worth *pursuing*, no *period* worth *re-living*, and no *hope* that if this were possible I could again be more successful.

Verse 18. *I hated all my labour*] Because, 1. It has not answered the end for which it was instituted. 2. I can enjoy the fruits of it but a short time. 3. I must leave it to others, and know not whether a *wise man*, a *knave*, or a *fool* will possess it.

Verse 19. *A wise* man *or a fool?*] Alas! Solomon, the *wisest* of all men, made the *worst use* of his wisdom, had *three hundred wives* and *seven hundred concubines*, and yet left but *one son* behind him, to possess his *estates* and his *throne*, and that one was the silliest of fools!

Verse 20. *I went about to cause my heart to despair*] What makes all worse, there is no remedy. It is impossible in the present state of things to prevent these evils.

Verse 21. *For there is a man*] Does he not allude to himself? As if he had said, "I have laboured to cultivate my mind in wisdom and in science, in knowledge of men and things, and have endeavoured to establish *equity* and dispense justice. And now I find I *shall leave* all the fruits of my labour to *a man that hath not laboured therein*, and consequently cannot prize what I have wrought." Does he not refer to his son *Rehoboam?*

Verse 22. *For what hath man of all his labour*] *Labour* of *body*, *disappointment* of

A. M. cir. 3027
B. C. cir. 977
Ante I. Olymp. cir. 201
Ante U. C. cir. 224

and of the vexation of his heart, wherein he hath laboured under the sun?

23 For all his days *are* [y]sorrows, and his travail grief; yea, his heart taketh not rest in the night. This is also vanity.

24 [z]*There is* nothing better for a man *than* that he should eat and drink, and *that* he [a]should make his soul enjoy good in his labour. This also I saw, that it *was* from the hand of God.

25 For who can eat, or who else can hasten *hereunto,* more than I?

26 For *God* giveth to a man that *is* good [b]in his sight, wisdom, and knowledge, and joy: but to the sinner he giveth travail, to gather and to heap up, that [c]he may give to *him that is* good before God. This also *is* vanity and vexation of spirit.

[y]Job v. 7; xiv. 1——[z]Chap. iii. 12, 13, 22; v. 18; viii. 15 [a]Or, *delight his senses*

[b]Heb. *before him;* Gen. vii. 1; Luke i. 6——[c]Job xxvii. 16, 17; Prov. xxviii. 8

hope, and *vexation* of *heart,* have been all my portion.

Verse 23. *His days* are *sorrows*] What a picture of human life where the heart is not filled with the peace and love of God! All his *days* are *sorrows;* all his *labours griefs;* all his *nights restless;* for he has no portion but merely what *earth* can give; and that is embittered by the labour of *acquisition,* and the disappointment in the using.

This is also vanity.] Emptiness of good and substantial misery.

Verse 24. There is *nothing better for a man*] The sense of this passage is well expressed in the following lines:—

"For these disorders wouldst thou find a cure,
Such cure as human frailty would admit?
Drive from thee anxious cares; let reason curb
Thy passions; and with cheerful heart enjoy
That little which the world affords; for here,
Though vain the hopes of perfect happiness,
Yet still the road of life, rugged at best,
Is not without its comforts.———
Wouldst thou their sweetness taste, look up to heaven,
And praise the all-bounteous Donor, who bestows
The power to use aright."

Verse 25. *For who can eat—more than I?*] But instead of חוץ ממני *chuts mimmenni, more than I;* חוץ ממנו *chuts mimmennu, without* HIM, is the reading of *eight* of *Kennicott's* and *De Rossi's* MSS., as also of the *Septuagint, Syriac,* and *Arabic.*

"For who maye eat, drynke, or bring enythinge to pass without him?"—COVERDALE.

I believe this to be the true reading. No one can have a true relish of the comforts of life without the Divine blessing. This reading connects all the sentences: "This also I saw, that it was from the hand of God;—for who can eat, and who can relish without HIM? For God giveth to man that is good." It is through his liberality that we have any thing to eat or drink; and it is only through his blessing that we can derive good from the use of what we possess.

Verse 26. *Giveth—wisdom, and knowledge, and joy*] 1. God gives *wisdom*—the knowledge of himself, light to direct in the way of salvation. 2. *Knowledge*—understanding to discern the operation of his hand; *experimental acquaintance* with himself, in the dispensing of his *grace* and the *gifts of his Spirit.* 3. *Joy;* a hundred days of ease for one day of pain; *one thousand* enjoyments for one privation; and to them that believe, *peace of conscience,* and JOY *in the Holy Ghost.*

But to the sinner he giveth travail] He has a life of labour, disappointment, and distress; for because he is an enemy to God, he travails in pain all his days; and, as the wise man says elsewhere, *the wealth of the wicked is laid up for the just.* So he loseth *earthly good,* because he would not take a *heavenly portion* with it.

CHAPTER III

Every thing has its time and season, 1–8. *Men are exercised with labour,* 9, 10. *Every thing is beautiful in its season,* 11. *Men should enjoy thankfully the gifts of God,* 12, 13. *What God does is for ever,* 14. *There is nothing new,* 15. *The corruption of judgment; but the judgments of God are right,* 16, 17. *Man is brutish, and men and brutes die in like manner,* 18–21. *Man may enjoy the fruit of his own labours,* 22.

A. M. cir. 3027
B. C. cir. 977
Ante I. Olymp. cir. 201
Ante U. C. cir. 224

TO every *thing there is* a season, and a [a]time to every
purpose under the heaven.
2 A time [b]to be born, and a
[c]time to die; a time to plant, and a time to
pluck up *that which is* planted;
3 A time to kill, and a time to heal; a time
to break down, and a time to build up;
4 A time to weep, and a time to laugh; a
time to mourn, and a time to dance;
5 A time to cast away stones,
and a time to gather stones together; a time to embrace, and [d]a
time [e]to refrain from embracing;
6 A time to [f]get, and a time to lose; a time
to keep, and a time to cast away;
7 A time to rend, and a time to sew; [g]a
time to keep silence, and a time to speak;
8 A time to love, and a time to [h]hate; a
time of war, and a time of peace.

[a]Ver. 17; chap. viii. 6——[b]Heb. *to bear*——[c]Hebrews ix. 27——[d]Joel ii. 16; 1 Cor. vii. 5——[e]Heb. *to be far from*——[f]Or, *seek*——[g]Amos v. 13——[h]Luke xiv. 26

NOTES ON CHAP. III

Verse 1. *To every* thing there is *a season, and a time to every purpose*] *Two* general remarks may be made on the first *eight* verses of this chapter. 1. God by his providence governs the world, and has determined particular *things* and operations to particular *times*. In those times such things may be done with propriety and success; but if we neglect the appointed seasons, we sin against this providence, and become the authors of our own distresses. 2. God has given to man that portion of duration called TIME; the space in which all the operations of nature, of animals, and intellectual beings, are carried on; but while nature is steady in its course, and animals faithful to their instincts, man devotes it to a great variety of purposes; but very frequently to that for which God never made *time*, *space*, or *opportunity*. And all we can say, when an evil deed is done, is, there was a *time* in which it was done, though God never made *it* for that purpose.

To say any farther on this subject is needless, as the words themselves give in general their own meaning. The Jews, it is true, see in these *times* and *seasons* all the events of their own nation, from the birth of Abraham to the present times; and as to *fathers* and their followers, they see all the events and states of the Christian Church in them!

It is worthy of remark, that in all this list there are but *two* things which may be said to be done generally by the disposal of God, and in which men can have but little influence: the *time of birth*, and the *time of death*. But all the others are left to the option of man, though God continues to overrule them by his providence. The following paraphrase will explain all that is necessary to be generally understood:—

Verse 2. *A time to be born, and a time to die—plant*]

"As in its *mother's womb* the *embryo* lies
A *space determined;* to full growth arrived,
From its dark prison *bursts*, and *sees the light;*
So is the period fix'd when man shall drop
Into the *grave*.—A *time there is to plant*,
And *sow;* another time to *pluck* and *reap*.
Even *nations* have their destined *rise* and *fall:*
Awhile they thrive; and for destruction ripe,
When grown, are rooted up like *wither'd plants*."

Verse 3. *A time to kill,—heal,—break down,—build up.*

"The healing art, when out of season used,
Pernicious proves, and serves to hasten death.
But timely med'cines drooping nature raise,
And health restore.—*Now, Justice* wields her *sword*
With wholesome rigour, nor the offender spares:
But *Mercy* now is more expedient found.
On *crazy fabrics* ill-timed cost bestow'd
No purpose answers, when discretion bids
To *pull them down*, and wait a season fit
To *build anew*."

Verse 4. *A time to weep,—laugh,—mourn,—dance*]

——————— "When private *griefs* affect
The heart, *our tears with decent sorrow flow;*
Nor less becoming, when the *public mourns*,
To vent the *deepest sighs*. But all around
When things a *smiling aspect* bear, our souls
May *well exult;* 'tis then a time for *joy*."

Verse 5. *A time to cast away stones,—to gather stones,—to embrace,—to refrain*]

"One while *domestic cares abortive* prove,
And then *successful*. Nature now invites
Connubial pleasures: but, when *languid* grown,
No less *rejects*."

Verse 6. *A time to get,—to lose,—to keep,—to cast away*]

——————— "*Commerce* produces wealth,
Whilst *time of gaining* lasts; from every point
Blow prosperous gales. Now heaven begins to lower,
And all our hopes are blasted. Prudence bids,
One while, our *treasure to reserve*, and then
With liberal hand to *scatter wide*. How oft
In raging storms, the owner *wisely casts*
Into the deep his precious merchandise,
To save the foundering bark!

Verse 7. *A time to rend,—sew,—keep silence,—speak*]

——————— "Intestine broils
And factions *rend a state:* at length the *breach*
Is *heal'd*, and rest ensues. Wisdom *restrains*
The *tongue*, when *words* are vain: but *now*,
'Tis *time to speak*, and silence would be criminal."

Verse 8. *A time to love,—hate,—of war,—of peace.*]

"*Love* turns to *hatred;* interest or caprice
Dissolves the firmest knot by *friendship* tied.
O'er *rival nations*, with *revenge* inflamed,
Or *lust of power*, fell *Discord* shakes awhile
Her *baleful torch:* now smiling *Peace* returns.

A. M. cir. 3027 B. C. cir. 977 Ante I. Olymp. cir. 201 Ante U. C. cir. 224

9 [i]What profit hath he that
worketh in that wherein he laboureth?
10 [k]I have seen the travail
which God hath given to the sons of men to
be exercised in it.
11 He hath made every *thing* beautiful in
his time: also he hath set the world in their
heart, so that [l]no man can find out the work
that God maketh from the beginning to the
end.

12 [m]I know that *there is* no
good in them, but for *a man* to rejoice, and to do good in his life.
13 And also [n]that every man
should eat and drink, and enjoy the good of
all his labour, it *is* the gift of God.
14 I know that whatsoever God doeth, it
shall be for ever: [o]nothing can be put to it,
nor any thing taken from it: and God doeth
it, that *men* should fear before him.
15 [p]That which hath been is now; and

A. M. cir. 3027 B. C. cir. 977 Ante I. Olymp. cir. 201 Ante U. C. cir. 224

[i]Chap. i. 3——[k]Chap. i. 13——[l]Psa. cxlv. 3; Isa. xl. 13; chap. viii. 17; Rom. xi. 33

[m]Verse 22——[n]Chap. ii. 24——[o]James i. 17——[p]Chap. i. 9

The above paraphrase on the verses cited contains a general view of the *principal occurrences of time*, in reference to the human being, from his cradle to his grave, through all the operations of life.

Verse 9. *What profit hath he*] What real good, what solid pleasure, is derived from all the labours of man? *Necessity* drives him to the principal part of his *cares* and *toils;* he *labours* that he may *eat* and *drink;* and he *eats* and *drinks* that he may be preserved *alive*, and kept from *sickness* and *pain*. Love of *money*, the basest of all passions, and *restless ambition*, drive men to many labours and expedients, which perplex and often destroy them. He, then, who lives without God, travails in pain all his days.

Verse 10. *I have seen the travail*] Man is a sinner; and, because he is such, he suffers.

Verse 11. *Beautiful in his time*] God's works are well done; there are order, harmony, and beauty in them all. Even the *caterpillar* is a finished beauty in all the *changes* through which it passes, when its structure is properly examined, and the *end* kept in view in which each change is to issue. Nothing of this kind can be said of the works of man. The most finished works of art are bungling jobs, when compared with the meanest operation of nature.

He hath set the world in their heart] העולם *haolam*, that *hidden time*—the *period beyond* the present,—ETERNITY. The proper translation of this clause is the following: "Also that eternity hath he placed in their heart, without which man could not find out the work which God hath made from the commencement to the end." God has deeply rooted the idea of *eternity* in every human heart; and every considerate man sees, that all the operations of God refer to that endless duration. See ver. 14. And it is only in eternity that man will be able to discover what God has designed by the various works he has formed.

Verse 12. *I know that* there is *no good in them, but, &c.*] Since God has so disposed the affairs of this world, that the great events of providence cannot be accelerated or retarded by human cares and anxieties, submit to God; make a proper use of what he has given: do thyself *no harm*, and endeavour as much as possible to do others *good*.

Enjoy, and bless thyself; let others share
The transient blessing: 'tis the gift of God.

Verse 14. *I know that whatsoever God doeth, it shall be for ever*] לעולם *leolam*, for *eternity;* in reference to that grand consummation of men and things intimated in ver. 11. God has produced no being that he intends ultimately to destroy. He made every thing in reference to eternity; and, however matter may be changed and refined, animal and intellectual beings shall not be deprived of their *existence*. The brute creation shall be restored, and all human spirits shall live for ever; the *pure* in a state of supreme and endless blessedness, the *impure* in a state of indestructible misery.

Nothing can be put to it] No new order of beings, whether animate or inanimate, can be produced. God *will not* create more; man *cannot* add.

Nor any thing taken from it] Nothing can be *annihilated;* no power but that which can *create* can *destroy*. And whatever he has done, he intended to be a means of impressing a just sense of his being, providence, mercy, and judgments, upon the souls of men. A proper consideration of God's works has a tendency to make man a *religious creature;* that is, to impress his mind with a sense of the *existence* of the *Supreme Being*, and the *reverence* that is due to him. In this sense *the fear of God* is frequently taken in Scripture. The Hebrew of this clause is strongly emphatic: והאלהים עשה שייראו מלפניו *vehaelohim asah sheiyireu millephanaiv;* "And the gods he hath done, that they might fear from before his faces." Even the doctrine of the eternal *Trinity* in *Unity* may be collected from numberless appearances in *nature*. A consideration of the herb *trefoil* is said to have been the means of fully convincing the learned Erasmus of the truth of the assertion, *These Three are One:* and yet *three distinct*. He saw the *same root*, the *same fibres*, the same *pulpy substance*, the *same membraneous covering*, the *same colour*, the *same taste*, the *same smell*, in *every part;* and yet the *three leaves* distinct: but *each* and *all* a *continuation* of the *stem*, and proceeding from the *same root*. Such a fact as this may at least illustrate the doctrine. An intelligent shepherd, whom he met upon the mountains, is said to have exhibited the herb, and the illustration while discoursing on certain difficulties in the Christian faith. When a child, I heard a learned man relate this fact.

Verse 15. *That which hath been is now*] God

A. M. cir. 3027 B. C. cir. 977 Ante I. Olymp. cir. 201 Ante U. C. cir. 224

that which is to be hath already
been; and God requireth [q]that
which is past.

16 And moreover [r]I saw under
the sun the place of judgment, *that* wickedness *was* there; and the place of righteousness, *that* iniquity *was* there.

17 I said in mine heart, [s]God shall judge the righteous and the wicked: for *there is* [t]a time there for every purpose and for every work.

18 I said in mine heart concerning the estate of the sons of men, [u]that God might manifest them, and that they might see that they themselves are beasts.

19 [v]For that which befalleth the sons of
men befalleth beasts; even one
thing befalleth them: as the one
dieth, so dieth the other; yea,
they have all one breath; so that
a man hath no pre-eminence above a beast: for all *is* vanity.

20 All go unto one place; [w]all are of the dust, and all turn to dust again.

21 [x]Who knoweth the spirit [y]of man that [z]goeth upward, and the spirit of the beast that goeth downward to the earth?

22 [a]Wherefore I perceive that *there is* nothing better, than that a man should rejoice in his own works; for [b]that *is* his portion: [c]for who shall bring him to see what shall be after him?

[q]Hebrew, *that which is driven away*——[r]Chapter v. 8——[s]Romans ii. 6, 7, 8; 2 Cor. v. 10; 2 Thess. i. 6, 7——[t]Ver. 1——[u]Or, *that they might clear God, and see,* &c.——[v]Psalm xlix. 12, 20; lxxiii. 22; chapter ii. 16——[w]Genesis iii. 19——[x]Chapter xii. 7——[y]Hebrew, *of the sons of man*——[z]Hebrew, *is ascending*——[a]Chapter ii. 24; v. 18; xi. 9——[b]Chapter ii. 10——[c]Chapter vi. 12; viii. 7; x. 14

governs the world *now,* as he *has governed* it from the beginning; and the revolutions and operations of nature are the *same now,* that they have been from *the beginning.* What we see *now,* is the *same* as has *been seen* by those before us.

And God requireth that which is past] i. e., That it may return again in its proper order. The heavens themselves, taking in their great revolutions, show the same phenomena. Even comets are supposed to have their revolutions, though some of them are hundreds of years in going round their orbits.

But in the *economy of grace,* does not *God require that which is past?* Whatever blessing or influence God gives to the soul of man, he intends shall remain and increase; and it will, if man be faithful. Reader, canst thou produce all the secret inspirations of his Spirit, all the drawings of his love, his pardoning mercy, his sanctifying grace, the heavenly-mindedness produced in thee, thy holy zeal, thy spirit of prayer, thy tender conscience, the witness of the Spirit, which thou didst once receive and enjoy? WHERE *are they? God requireth that which is past.*

Verse 16. *The place of judgment,* that *wickedness* was *there*] The abuse of power, and the perversion of judgment, have been justly complained of in every age of the world. The following paraphrase is good:—

"But what enjoyment can our labours yield,
When e'en the *remedy* prescribed by heaven
To cure disorders proves our deadliest bane?
When God's vicegerents, destined to protect
The weak from insolence of power, to guard
Their lives and fortunes, impious robbers turn?
And, or by force or fraud, deprive of both?—
To what asylum shall the injured fly
From her tribunal, where perverted law
Acquits the guilty, the innocent condemns?"
C.

Verse 17. *For* there is *a time there for every purpose*] Man has *his time* here below, and God shall have *his time* above. At his throne the judged shall be rejudged, and iniquity for ever close her mouth.

Verse 18. *That they might see that they themselves are beasts.*] The author of *Choheleth* has given a correct view of this difficult verse, by a proper translation: "I said in my heart, reflecting on the state of the sons of men, O that God would enlighten them, and make them see that even they themselves are like beasts." These words are to be referred to those in authority who abused their power; particularly to the corrupt magistrates mentioned above.

Verse 19. *For that which befalleth the sons of men befalleth beasts*] From the present comparison of *great men* to *beasts,* the author takes occasion to enforce the subject by mentioning the state of mankind in general, with respect to the *mortality* of their *bodies;* and then, by an easy transition, touches in the next verse on the point which is of such infinite consequence to religion.

As the one dieth, so dieth the other] Animal life is the same both in the *man* and in the *beast.*

They have all one breath] They respire in the same way; and when they cease to respire, animal life becomes extinct.

Befalleth beasts—This is wanting in six of *Kennicott's* and *De Rossi's* MSS.

Verse 20. *All go unto one place*]

"Man was born
To die, nor aught exceeds in this respect
The vilest brute. Both transient, frail, and vain,
Draw the same breath; alike grow old, decay,
And then expire: both to one grave descend;
There blended lie, to native dust return'd."—C.

Verse 21. *Who knoweth the spirit of man*] I think the meaning of this important verse is well taken by the above able writer:—

The nobler part of *man,* 'tis true, survives
The frail corporeal frame: but who regards

The difference? Those who live like beasts,
as such
Would die, and be no more, if their own fate
Depended on themselves. Who once reflects,
Amidst his revels, that the *human soul*,
Of origin celestial, *mounts aloft*,
While that of *brutes* to earth shall *downward go?*"

The word רוח *ruach*, which is used in this and the *nineteenth* verse, has two significations, *breath* and *spirit*. It signifies *spirit*, or an *incorporeal* substance, as distinguished from *flesh*, or a *corporeal* one, 1 Kings xxii. 21, 22, and Isa. xxxi. 3. And it signifies the *spirit* or *soul of man*, Psa. xxxi. 6, Isa. lvii. 16, and in this book, chap. xii. 7, and in many other places. In this book it is used also to signify the *breath*, *spirit*, or *soul* of a beast. While it was said in ver. 19, *they have all one breath*, i. e., the *man* and the *beast* live the same kind of animal life; in this verse, a proper distinction is made between the רוח *ruach*, or *soul* of man, and the רוח *ruach*, or *soul* of the beast: the one *goeth upwards*, the other *goeth downwards*. The literal translation of these important words is this: "Who considereth the (רוח *ruach*) immortal spirit of the sons of Adam, which ascendeth? it is from above; (היא למעלה *hi lemalah;*) and the spirit or breath of the cattle which descendeth? it is downwards unto the earth," i. e., it tends to the earth only. This place gives no countenance to the materiality of the soul; and yet it is the strongest hold to which the cold and fruitless materialist can resort.

Solomon most evidently makes an *essential difference* between the human soul and that of brutes. Both have *souls*, but of different natures: the soul of man was made for *God*, and to *God* it shall return: *God is its portion;* and when a holy soul leaves the body, it goes to *paradise*. The soul of the beast was made to *derive its happiness* from this *lower world*. Brutes shall have a resurrection, and have an endless enjoyment in a *new earth*. The *body* of *man* shall arise, and join his *soul* that is already above; and both enjoy final blessedness in the fruition of God. That Solomon did not believe they had the *same kind of spirit*, and the same *final lot*, as some materialists and infidels say, is evident from chap. xii. 7: "The spirit shall return unto God who gave it."

Verse 22. *A man should rejoice in his own works*] Do not turn God's blessings into sin by perverseness and complaining; make the best of life. God will sweeten its bitters to you, if you be faithful. Remember this is the *state to prepare for glory;* and the evils of life may be so sanctified to you as to work for your good. Though even wretched *without*, you may be happy *within;* for God can make all grace to abound towards you. You may be happy if you please; cry to God, who never rejects the prayer of the humble, and gives his Holy Spirit to all them that ask him.

CHAPTER IV

The vanity of life is increased by oppression, 1–3; by envy, 4; by idleness, 5. The misery of a solitary life, and the advantages of society, 6–12. A poor and wise child; better than an old and foolish king, 13. The uncertainty of popular favour, 14–16.

A. M. cir. 3027 B. C. cir. 977 Ante I. Olymp. cir. 201 Ante U. C. cir. 224

SO I returned, and considered
all the [a]oppressions that are
done under the sun: and behold,
the tears of *such as were* oppressed, and they had no comforter; and on
the [b]side of their oppressors *there was* power;
but they had no comforter.
2 [c]Wherefore I praised the dead which are
already dead more than the living which are
yet alive.
3 [d]Yea, better *is he* than both
they, which hath not yet been,
who hath not seen the evil work
that is done under the sun.
4 Again, I considered all travail, and [e]every
right work, that [f]for this a man is envied of
his neighbour. This *is* also vanity and vexation of spirit.
5 The fool [g]foldeth his hands together, and
eateth his own flesh.

A. M. cir. 3027 B. C. cir. 977 Ante I. Olymp. cir. 201 Ante U. C. cir. 224

[a]Chap. iii. 16; v. 8——[b]Heb. *hand*——[c]Job iii. 17, &c. [d]Job iii. 11, 16, 21; chap. vi. 3——[e]Heb. *all the rightness of work*——[f]Heb. *this is the envy of a man from his neighbour*——[g]Prov. vi. 10; xxiv. 33

NOTES ON CHAP. IV

Verse 1. *Considered all the oppressions*] עשקים *ashukim* signifies any kind of *injury* which a man can receive in his *person*, his *property*, or his *good fame*.

On the side of their oppressors there was *power*] And, therefore, neither protection nor comfort for the oppressed.

Verse 2. *Wherefore I praised the dead*] I considered those happy who had escaped from the pilgrimage of life to the place where the wicked cease from troubling, and where the weary are at rest.

Verse 3. *Which hath not yet been*] Better never to have been born into the world, than to have *seen* and *suffered* so many miseries.

Verse 4. *For this a man is envied*] It is not by injustice and wrong only that men suffer, but through *envy* also. For if a man act uprightly and properly in the world, he soon becomes the object of his neighbour's envy and calumny too. Therefore the encouragement to do good, to act an upright part, is very little. This constitutes a part of the *vain* and *empty* system of human life.

Verse 5. *The fool foldeth his hands*] After all, without *labour* and *industry* no man can

A. M. cir. 3027
B. C. cir. 977
Ante I. Olymp. cir. 201
Ante U. C. cir. 224

6 [h]Better *is* a handful *with* quietness, than both the hands full *with* travail, and vexation of spirit.

7 Then I returned, and I saw vanity under the sun.

8 There is one *alone,* and *there is* not a second; yea, he hath neither child nor brother: yet *is there* no end of all his labour; neither is his [i]eye satisfied with riches; [k]neither *saith he,* For whom do I labour, and bereave my soul of good? This *is* also vanity, yea, it *is* a sore travail.

9 Two *are* better than one; because they have a good reward for their labour.

10 For if they fall, the one will lift up his fellow: but wo to him *that is* alone when he falleth; for *he hath* not another to help him up.

11 Again, if two lie together, then they have heat: but how can one be warm *alone?*

A. M. cir. 3027
B. C. cir. 977
Ante I. Olymp. cir. 201
Ante U. C. cir. 224

12 And if one prevail against him, two shall withstand him; and a threefold cord is not quickly broken.

13 Better *is* a poor and a wise child, than an old and foolish king, [l]who will no more be admonished.

14 For out of prison he cometh to reign; whereas also *he that is* born in his kingdom becometh poor.

15 I considered all the living which walk under the sun, with the [m]second child that shall stand up in his stead.

16 *There is* no end of all the people, *even* of all that have been before them: they also that come after shall not rejoice in him. Surely this also *is* [n]vanity and vexation of spirit.

---

[h]Prov. xv. 16, 17; xvi. 18——[i]Prov. xxvii. 20; 1 John ii. 16——[k]Psa. xxxix. 6

[l]Heb. *who knoweth not to be admonished*——[m]1 Kings xi. 43——[n]Chap. i. 2, 14

---

get any comfort in life; and he who gives way to idleness is the veriest of fools.

Verse 6. *Better* is *a handful* with *quietness*] These may be the words of the *slothful* man, and spoken in vindication of his idleness; as if he had said, "Every man who labours and amasses property is the object of *envy*, and is marked by the oppressor as a subject for spoil; better, therefore, to act as I do; gain little, and have little, and enjoy my handful with quietness." Or the words may contain Solomon's *reflection* on the subject.

Verse 8. *There is one* alone, *and* there is *not a second*] Here *covetousness* and *avarice* are characterized. The man who is the centre of his own existence; has neither wife, child, nor legal heir; and yet is as intent on getting money as if he had the largest family to provide for; nor does he only labour with intense application, but he even refuses himself the comforts of life out of his own gains! This is not only *vanity*, the excess of foolishness, but it is also *sore travail.*

Verse 9. *Two* are *better than one*] Married life is infinitely to be preferred to this kind of life, for the very reasons alleged below, and which require no explanation.

Verse 13. *Better* is *a poor and a wise child*] The *Targum* applies this to *Abraham*. "Abraham was a *poor child* of only *three* years of age; but he had the spirit of prophecy, and he refused to worship the idols which the *old foolish king*—Nimrod—had set up; therefore Nimrod cast him into a furnace of fire. But the Lord worked a miracle and delivered him. Yet here was no knowledge in Nimrod, and he would not be *admonished*." The *Targum* proceeds:

Verse 14. *For out of prison he cometh to reign*] "Then Abraham left the country of the idolaters, where he had been *imprisoned*, and came and *reigned* over the land of Canaan; and Nimrod became *poor* in this world." This is the *fact* to which the ancient rabbins supposed Solomon to allude.

Verse 15. *With the second child that shall stand up*] The *Targum* applies this to the case of *Jeroboam* and *Rehoboam*. History affords many instances of mean persons raised to sovereign authority, and of kings being reduced to the meanest offices, and to a morsel of bread. Agrippa himself ascended the throne of Israel after having been long in prison. See Josephus, Ant. lib. xviii. c. 8. This the heathens attributed to *fortune*.

Si fortuna volet, fies de rhetore consul;
Si volet hæc eadem, fies de consule rhetor.
Juv. Sat. vii., ver. 197.

Though I have given what the Jews suppose to be the allusion in these verses, yet the reader may doubt whether the reference be correct. There is a case implied, whether from *fact* or *assumption* I cannot say; but it seems to be this:

A king who had abused the authority vested in him by oppressing the people, had a son whose prudent conduct promised much comfort to the nation, when he should come to the throne. The father, seeing the popular wish, and becoming jealous of his son, *shut him up in prison*. In the interim the old king either *dies* or is *deposed*, and the son is brought *out of prison*, and *placed on the throne*. Then (ver. 15, 16) multitudes of the people flock to him, and begin to *walk under the sun;* i. e., the prosperous state to which the nation is raised by its redemption from the former tyranny. However, the wise man insinuates that this *sunshine* will not last long. The young king, feeling the reins in his own hands, and being surrounded by those whose interest it was to *flatter* in order to obtain and continue in *court favour*, he also becomes corrupted so that those who come after shall have no cause of rejoicing in him. This appears to be the case; and similar cases have frequently occurred, not only in *Asiatic*, but also in *European* history, I have, in another place, referred to the case of *Rushn Achter*, who was brought *out of prison*, and set upon the *throne of Hindoostan*. This is expressed in the following elegant Persian couplet, where his fortune is represented as similar to that of the patriarch *Joseph:*—

روشن اختر بود اکنون ماه شد
یوسف از زندن بر آمد شاه شد

"The *bright star* is now become a *moon:*
Joseph is taken out of *prison*, and become a *king*."

Rushn Achter signifies a *bright* or *splendid star*.

Verse 16. There is *no end of all the people*] This is supposed to refer to the multitudes of people who hail the advent and accession of a new sovereign; for, as *Suetonius* remarks, *A plerisque adorari solem orientem*, "Most people adore the rising sun." But when the new king becomes old, very few regard him; and perhaps he lives long enough to be as much despised by the very persons who before were ready to worship him. This is also a miserable vanity. Thus the blooming heir—

"Shall feel the sad reverse: honoured awhile;
Then, like his sire, contemn'd, abhorr'd, forgot."
C.

CHAPTER V

The reverence to be observed in attending Divine worship, 1–3. *We should be faithful to our engagements*, 4–7. *The oppression of the innocent*, 8. *The king dependent on the produce of the soil*, 9. *Against covetousness*, 10, 11. *The peace of the honest labourer*, 12. *The evil effect of riches*, 13, 14. *Man cannot carry his property to the grave*, 15–17. *We should thankfully enjoy the blessings of God*, 18–20.

A. M. cir. 3027
B. C. cir. 977
Ante I. Olymp. cir. 201
Ante U. C. cir. 224

KEEP [a]thy foot when thou
goest to the house of God,
and be more ready to hear
[b]than to give the sacrifice of
fools: for they consider not that they do evil.
2 Be not rash with thy mouth, and let not
thine heart be hasty to utter *any* [c]thing before God; for God *is* in heaven, and thou
upon earth: therefore let thy words [d]be few.
3 For a dream cometh through the multitude of business; and [e]a fool's
voice *is known* by multitude of
words.
4 [f]When thou vowest a vow
unto God, defer not to pay it; for *he hath*
no pleasure in fools: [g]pay that which thou
hast vowed.
5 [h]Better *is it* that thou shouldest not vow,
than that thou shouldest vow and not pay.
6 Suffer not thy mouth to cause thy flesh

A. M. cir. 3027
B. C. cir. 977
Ante I. Olymp. cir. 201
Ante U. C. cir. 224

[a]See Exod. iii. 5; Isa. i. 12, &c.——[b]1 Sam. xv. 22; Psalm l. 8; Prov. xv. 8; xxi. 27; Hos. vi. 6——[c]Or, *word* [d]Prov. x. 19; Matt. vi. 7

[e]Prov. x. 19——[f]Num. xxx. 2; Deut. xxiii. 21, 22, 23; Psa. l. 14; lxxvi. 11——[g]Psa. lxvi. 13, 14——[h]Prov. xx. 25; Acts v. 4

NOTES ON CHAP. V

Verse 1. *Keep thy foot*] This verse the *Hebrew* and all the *versions* join to the preceding chapter.

Solomon, having before intimated, though very briefly, that the only cure against human vanity is a due sense of religion, now enters more largely on this important subject, and gives some excellent directions with regard to the right performance of Divine service, the nature of vocal and mental prayer, the danger of rash vows, &c.—C.

The whole verse might be more literally translated thus:—

"Guard thy steps as thou art going to the house of God; and approach to hearken, and not to give the sacrifice of fools, for none of them have knowledge about doing evil." "They offer gifts for their sins, and do not turn from their evil works; for they know not (they distinguish not) between good and evil." See the *Chaldee*.

Verse 2. *Be not rash with thy mouth*] Do not hasten with thy mouth; weigh thy words, feel deeply, think much, speak little.

"When ye approach his altar, on your lips
Set strictest guard; and let your thoughts be pure,
Fervent, and recollected. Thus prepared,
Send up the silent breathings of your souls,
Submissive to his will."
C.

Verse 3. *For a dream cometh*] That is, as *dreams* are generally the effect of the business in which we have been engaged during the day; so a *multitude of words* evidence the feeble workings of the foolish heart.

Verse 4. *When thou vowest a vow*] When in distress and difficulty, men are apt to promise much to God if he will relieve them; but generally forget the vow when the distress or trouble is gone by.

Verse 5. *Better* is it *that thou shouldest not vow, &c.*] We are under *constant obligations* to live to God; no *vow* can make it more so. Yet, there may be cases in which we should bind ourselves to take up some particular cross, to perform some particular duty, to forego some particular attachment that does not tend to bring our souls nearer to God. Then, if fully determined, and strong in faith relative to the point, *bind* and *hold fast;* but if not fully, rationally, and conscientiously determined, "do not suffer thy mouth to cause thy soul to sin."

Verse 6. *Neither say thou before the angel, that it* was *an error*] Nor think of saying "before the cruel angel, who shall exercise author-

A. M. cir. 3027
B. C. cir. 977
Ante I. Olymp. cir. 201
Ante U. C. cir. 224

to sin; [i]neither say thou before
the angel, that it *was* an error:
wherefore should God be angry
at thy voice, and destroy the
work of thine hands?
7 For in the multitude of dreams and many
words *there are* also *divers* vanities: but [k]fear
thou God.
8 If thou [l]seest the oppression of the poor,
and violent perverting of judgment and justice
in a province, marvel not [m]at the matter: for
[n]*he that is* higher than the highest regardeth;
and *there be* higher than they.
9 Moreover the profit of the earth is for all;
the king *himself* is served by the field.
10 He that loveth silver shall not be satisfied with silver; nor he that loveth abundance
with increase: this *is* also
vanity.
11 When goods increase, they
are increased that eat them: and
what good is there to the owners thereof
saving the beholding *of them* with their eyes?
12 The sleep of a labouring man *is* sweet,
whether he eat little or much: but the abundance of the rich will not suffer him to sleep.
13 [o]There is a sore evil *which* I have seen
under the sun, *namely,* riches kept for the
owners thereof to their hurt.
14 But those riches perish by evil travail:
and he begetteth a son, and *there is* nothing in
his hand.
15 [p]As he came forth of his mother's womb,
naked shall he return to go as he came, and

A. M. cir. 3027
B. C. cir. 977
Ante I. Olymp. cir. 201
Ante U. C. cir. 224

[i]1 Cor. xi. 10——[k]Chap. xii. 13——[l]Chap. iii. 16 [m]Heb. *at the will* or *purpose*
[n]Psa. xii. 5; lviii. 11; lxxxii. 1——[o]Chap. vi. 1——[p]Job i. 21; Psa. xlix. 17; 1 Tim. vi. 7

ity over thee in the judgment of the great day, that thou didst it through ignorance."—*Chaldee.* I believe by the *angel* nothing else is intended than the *priest,* whose business it was to take cognizance of *vows* and *offerings.* See Lev. v. 4, 5. In Mal. ii. 7, the priest is called the "angel of the Lord of hosts."

Verse 7. *In—dreams*—are—divers *vanities; but fear thou God.*] If, by the disturbed state of thy mind during the day, or by Satanic influence, thou dream of evil, do not give way to any unreasonable fears, or gloomy forebodings, of any coming mischief:—FEAR GOD. Fear neither the *dream* nor its *interpretation;* God, will take care of and protect thee. Most certainly, he that fears God need fear nothing else. Well may an upright soul say to *Satan* himself, I fear God; and because I fear *him,* I do not fear *thee.*

Verse 8. *If thou seest the oppression of the poor*] For this was a frequent case under all governments; and especially in the *provinces* or *colonies* which being far from the *seat* of government, were generally oppressed by the sovereign's deputies.

Marvel not at the matter] החפץ *hachephets,* the *will,* i. e., of God; which permits such evils to take place; for all things shall work together for good to them that love him.

"Marvel not,
Ye righteous, if his dispensations here
Unequal seem. What, though disorders reign?
He still presides, and with unerring hand
Directs the vast machine. His wisdom can
From discord harmony produce; and make
Even vice itself subservient to his ends."

Verse 9. *The profit of the earth is for all*] The earth, if properly cultivated, is capable of producing food for every living creature; and without cultivation none has a right to expect bread.

The king himself *is served by the field.*] Without the field he cannot have supplies for his own house; and, unless *agriculture* flourish, the necessary expenses of the state cannot be defrayed. Thus, God joins the *head* and *feet* together; for while the peasant is protected by the king as executor of the laws, the king himself is dependent on the peasant; as the wealth of the nation is the fruit of the labourer's toil.

Verse 10. *He that loveth silver shall not be satisfied with silver*] The more he gets, the more he would get; for the saying is true:—

Crescit amor nummi, quantum ipsa pecunia crescit.

"The love of money increases, in proportion as money itself increases."

Verse 11. *When goods increase*] An increase of property always brings an increase of expense, by a multitude of servants; and the owner really possesses no more, and probably *enjoys* much less, than he did, when every day provided its own bread, and could lay up no store for the next. But if he have more *enjoyment,* his cares are multiplied; and he has no kind of profit. "This also is vanity."

Verse 12. *The sleep of a labouring man* is *sweet*] His labour is healthy exercise. He is without possessions, and without cares; his sleep, being undisturbed, is sound and refreshing.

Verse 13. *Riches kept for the owners thereof to their hurt.*] This may be the case through various causes: 1. He may make an improper use of them, and lose his health by them. 2. He may join in an unfortunate partnership and lose all. 3. His riches may excite the desire of the *robber;* and he may spoil him of his goods, and even take away his life. 4. Or, he may leave them to his son, who turns profligate, spends the *whole,* and ruins both his body and soul. I have seen this again and again.

Verse 14. *And he begetteth a son, and* there is *nothing in his hand.*] He has been stripped of his property by unfortunate trade or by plunderers; and he has nothing to leave to his children.

Verse 15. *As he came forth*] However it

A. M. cir. 3027
B. C. cir. 977
Ante I. Olymp. cir. 201
Ante U. C. cir. 224

shall take nothing of his labour,
which he may carry away in his
hand.
16 And this also *is* a sore evil,
that in all points as he came, so shall he go:
and [q]what profit hath he [r]that hath laboured
for the wind?
17 All his days also [s]he eateth in darkness,
and *he hath* much sorrow and wrath with his
sickness.
18 Behold *that* which I have seen: [t]*it* [u]*is*
good and comely *for one* to eat and to drink,
and to enjoy the good of all his
labour that he taketh under the
sun [v]all the days of his life,
which God giveth him: [w]for it *is*
his portion.
19 [x]Every man also to whom God hath given
riches and wealth, and hath given him power
to eat thereof, and to take his portion, and to
rejoice in his labour; this *is* the gift of God.
20 [y]For he shall not much remember the
days of his life; because God answereth *him*
in the joy of his heart.

[q]Chap. i. 3——[r]Prov. xi. 29——[s]Psa. cxxvii. 2
[t]Chap. ii. 24; iii. 12, 13, 22; ix. 7; xi. 9; 1 Tim. vi. 17
[u]Heb. there is *a good which is comely*, &c.
[v]Heb. *the number of the days*——[w]Chap. ii. 10; iii. 22
[x]Chap. ii. 24; iii. 13; vi. 2——[y]Or, *Though* he give *not much*, yet *he remembereth*, &c.

may be, he himself shall carry nothing with him into the eternal world. If he die worth millions, those millions are dead to him for ever; so he has had no real profit from all his labours, cares, anxieties, and vast property!

Verse 17. *All his days also he eateth in darkness*] Even his enjoyments are embittered by *uncertainty.* He fears for his goods; the possibility of being deprived of them fills his heart with anguish. But instead of יאכל *yochel,* "he shall eat," ילך *yelech,* "he shall walk," is the reading of several MSS. *He walks* in darkness—he has no evidence of salvation. There is no ray of light from God to penetrate the gloom; and all beyond life is darkness impenetrable!

And wrath with his sickness.] His *last hours* are *awful;* for,

"Counting on long years of pleasure here,
He's quite unfurnish'd for the world to come."
BLAIR.

He is full of anguish at the *thought* of death; but the *fear* of it is horrible. But if he have a sense of *God's wrath* in his guilty conscience, what horror can be compared with his horror!

Verse 18. *Behold* that *which I have seen*] This is the result of my observations and experience. God gives every man, in the course of his providence, the necessaries of life; and it is his will that he should thankfully use them.

For it is *his portion.*] What is requisite for him in the lower world; without them his life cannot subsist; and earthly blessings are as truly the *portion* of his *body* and *animal life,* as the *salvation of God* is the portion of his soul.

Verse 20. *For he shall not much remember*] The person who acts in this way, extracts all the good requisite from life. He passes through things temporal so as not to lose those that are eternal:—

"Calm and serene, the road of life to him,
Or long or short, rugged or smooth, with thorns
O'erspread, or gay with flowers, is but a *road.*
Such fare as offers grateful he accepts,
And smiling to his *native home* proceeds."
C.

CHAPTER VI

The vanity of riches without use, 1, 2. *Of children and of old age without riches and enjoyment,* 3–7. *Man does not know what is good for himself,* 8–12.

A. M. cir. 3027
B. C. cir. 977
Ante I. Olymp. cir. 201
Ante U. C. cir. 224

THERE [a]is an evil which I
have seen under the sun,
and it *is* common among men;
2 A man to whom God hath
given riches, wealth, and honour, [b]so that he
wanteth nothing for his soul of
all that he desireth, [c]yet God
giveth him not power to eat
thereof, but a stranger eateth it:
this *is* vanity, and it *is* an evil disease.

[a]Chap. v. 13——[b]Job xxi. 10, &c.; Psa. xvii. 14; lxxiii. 7——[c]Luke xii. 20

NOTES ON CHAP. VI

Verse 2. *A man to whom God hath given riches*] A man may possess much earthly goods, and yet enjoy nothing of them. Possession and fruition are not necessarily joined together; and this is also among the *vanities* of life. It is worthy of remark, that it belongs to God as much to give the power to enjoy as it does to give the earthly blessings. A wise heathen saw this:—

Di tibi divitias dederant, artemque fruendi.
HOR. Ep. lib. i., ep. 4, ver. 7.

"The gods had given thee riches, and the art to enjoy them."

A. M. cir. 3027
B. C. cir. 977
Ante I. Olymp. cir. 201
Ante U. C. cir. 224

3 If a man beget a hundred *children,* and live many years, so that the days of his years be many, and his soul be not filled with good, and [d]also *that* he have no burial; I say, *that* [e]an untimely birth *is* better than he.

4 For he cometh in with vanity, and departeth in darkness, and his name shall be covered with darkness.

5 Moreover he hath not seen the sun, nor known *any thing:* this hath more rest than the other.

6 Yea, though he live a thousand years twice *told,* yet hath he seen no good: do not all go to one place?

7 [f]All the labour of man *is* for his mouth, and yet the [g]appetite is not filled.

A. M. cir. 3027
B. C. cir. 977
Ante I. Olymp. cir. 201
Ante U. C. cir. 224

8 For what hath the wise more than the fool? what hath the poor, that knoweth to walk before the living?

9 Better *is* the sight of the eyes [h]than the wandering of the desire: this *is* also vanity and vexation of spirit.

10 That which hath been is named already, and it is known that it *is* man: [i]neither may he contend with him that is mightier than he.

11 Seeing there be many things that increase vanity, what *is* man the better?

12 For who knoweth what *is* good for man in *this* life, [k]all the days of his vain life which he spendeth as [l]a shadow? for [m]who can tell a man what shall be after him under the sun?

---

[d]2 Kings ix. 35; Isaiah xiv. 19, 20; Jeremiah xxii. 19 [e]Job iii. 16; Psa. lviii. 8; chapter iv. 3——[f]Proverbs xvi. 26——[g]Hebrew, *soul*——[h]Hebrew, *than the walking of the soul*

[i]Job ix. 32; Isa. xlv. 9; Jer. xlix. 19——[k]Heb. *the number of the days of the life of his vanity*——[l]Psa. cii. 11; cix. 23; cxliv. 4; James iv. 14——[m]Psa. xxxix. 6; chap. viii. 7

Verse 3. *If a man beget a hundred* children] If he have the most numerous family and the largest possessions, and is so much attached to his riches that he grudges himself a monument; an *abortion* in the eye of reason is to be preferred to such a man; *himself* is contemptible, and his *life* worthless. The abortion *comes in with vanity*—baulks expectation, *departs in darkness*—never opened its eyes upon the light, and *its name is covered with darkness*—it has no place in the family register, or in the chronicles of Israel. This, that hath neither *seen the sun, nor known any thing* is preferable to the *miser* who has his coffers and granaries well furnished, should he have *lived a thousand years,* and had *a hundred children.* He *has seen*—possessed, no good; *and he and the abortion go to one place,* equally unknown, and wholly forgotten.

Verse 7. *All the labour of man*] This is the grand primary object of all human labour; merely to provide for the support of life by procuring things *necessary.* And life only exists for the sake of the soul; because man puts these things in place of *spiritual* good, the *appetite*—the intense desire after the *supreme good*—is not *satisfied.* When man learns to provide as distinctly for his *soul* as he does for his *body,* then he will begin to be happy, and may soon attain his end.

Verse 8. *For what hath the wise more than the fool?*] They must both labour for the same end. Both depend upon the labour of themselves or others for the necessaries of life. Both must eat and drink in order to live; and the rich man can no more eat two meals at a time, than he can comfortably wear two changes of raiment. The necessaries of life are the same to both, and their *condition* in life is nearly similar; liable to the same diseases, dissolution, and death.

Verse 9. *Better* is *the sight of the eyes than the wandering of the desire*] This is translated by the *Vulgate,* as a sort of adage: Melius est videre quod cupias, quam desiderare quod nescias; "It is better to see what one desires than to covet what one knows not." It is better to enjoy the present than to feed one's self with vain desires of the *future.* What we translate *the wandering of desire,* מהלך נפש *mehaloch nephesh,* is the *travelling of the soul.* What is this? Does it simply mean *desire?* Or is there any reference here to the state of *separate spirits?* It however shows the soul to be in a *restless state,* and consequently to be *unhappy.* If Christ dwell in the heart by faith, the soul is then at *rest,* and this is properly the *rest of the people of God.*

Verse 10. *That which hath been is named already*] The *Hebrew* of this verse might be translated, "Who is he who is? His name has been already called. And it is known that he is Adam; and that he cannot contend in judgment with him who is stronger than he."

"What is more excellent than man; yet can he not, in the lawe, get the victory of him that is mightier than he."—COVERDALE.

ADAM is his name; and it at once points out, 1. His *dignity;* he was made in the image of God. 2. His *fall;* he sinned against his Maker, and was cast out of Paradise. And 3. His *recovery* by *Christ;* the *second man* (*Adam*) *was the Lord from heaven,* and a *quickening Spirit.*

Verse 12. *For who knoweth what* is *good for man in* this *life*] Those things which we deem *good* are often *evil.* And those which we think *evil* are often *good.* So ignorant are we, that we run the greatest hazard in making a *choice.* It is better to leave ourselves and our concerns in the hands of the Lord, than to keep them in our own.

For who can tell a man what shall be after him] Futurity is with God. While he lives, man wishes to know what is before him. When he is about to die, he wishes to know what will be after him. All this is vanity; God, because he is merciful, will reveal neither.

CHAPTER VII

The value of a good name, 1. Advantages of sorrow and correction, 2–5. The emptiness of a fool's joy, 6. Of oppression, 7. The end better than the beginning, 8. Against hastiness of spirit, 9. Comparison of former and present times, 10. Excellence of wisdom, 11, 12. Of the dispensations of Providence, 13–15. Against extremes, 16–18. The strength of wisdom, 19. Man is ever liable to sin and mistake, 20. We should guard our words, 21, 22. Difficulty of obtaining wisdom, 23–25. A bad woman dangerous, 26. There are few who are really upright, 27–29.

A. M. cir. 3027
B. C. cir. 977
Ante I. Olymp. cir. 201
Ante U. C. cir. 224

A [a]GOOD name *is* better than
[b]precious ointment; and the
day of death than the day of
one's birth.
2 *It is* better to go to the house of mourning, than to go to the house of feasting: for
that *is* the end of all men; and the living will
lay *it* to his heart.
3 [c]Sorrow *is* better than laughter: [d]for by
the sadness of the countenance the heart is
made better.
4 The heart of the wise *is* in the house of
mourning; but the heart of fools
is in the house of mirth.
5 [e]*It is* better to hear the
rebuke of the wise, than for a
man to hear the song of fools.
6 [f]For as the [g]crackling of thorns under a
pot, so *is* the laughter of the fool: this also *is*
vanity.
7 Surely oppression maketh a wise man
mad; [h]and a gift destroyeth the heart.
8 Better *is* the end of a thing than the beginning thereof: *and* [i]the patient in spirit *is*

A. M. cir. 3027
B. C. cir. 977
Ante I. Olymp. cir. 201
Ante U. C. cir. 224

---

[a]Proverbs xv. 30; xxii. 1——[b]Matthew xxvi. 7; Mark xiv. 3; Luke vii. 37——[c]Or, *Anger*——[d]2 Corinthians vii. 10——[e]See Psalm cxli. 5; Proverbs xiii. 18; xv. 31, 32——[f]Psalm cxviii. 12; chapter ii. 2——[g]Hebrew, *sound*——[h]Exodus xxiii. 8; Deuteronomy xvi. 19——[i]Proverbs xiv. 29

NOTES ON CHAP. VII

Verse 1. *A good name*] Unsatisfactory as all sublunary things are, yet still there are some which are of great consequence, and among them a good name. The place is well paraphrased in the following verses:

"A *spotless name,*
By virtuous deeds acquired, is sweeter far
Than fragant balms, whose odours round diffused
Regale the invited guests. Well may such men
Rejoice at death's approach, and bless the hours
That end their toilsome pilgrimage; assured
That till the race of life is finish'd none
Can be completely blest."

Verse 2. It is *better to go to the house of mourning*] *Birthdays* were generally kept with great festivity, and to these the wise man most probably refers; but according to his maxim, the miseries of life were so many and so oppressive that the day of a man's *death* was to be preferred to the *day of his birth.* But, independently of the allusion, it is much more profitable to visit the house of mourning for the dead than the house of festivity. In the *former* we find occasion for serious and deeply edifying thoughts and reflections; from the *latter* we seldom return with one profitable thought or one solid impression.

Verse 3. *Sorrow* is *better than laughter*] The reason is immediately given; for *by the sorrow of the countenance—the grief* of heart that shows itself in the countenance—

The heart is made better.] In such cases, most men try themselves at the tribunal of their own consciences, and resolve on amendment of life.

Verse 4. *The heart of the wise* is *in the house of mourning*] A wise man loves those occasions from which he can derive spiritual advantage; and therefore prefers *visiting the sick,* and *sympathizing* with those who have *suffered privations* by death. But the *fool*—the gay, thoughtless, and giddy—prefers places and times of diversion and amusement. Here he is prevented from seriously considering either himself or his latter end. The grand fault and misfortune of youth.

Verse 6. *For as the crackling of thorns*] They make a great noise, a great blaze; and are extinguished in a few moments. Such, indeed, comparatively, are the joys of life: they are noisy, flashy, and transitory.

Verse 7. *Oppression maketh a wise man mad*] This has been translated with good show of reason, "Surely oppression shall give lustre to a wise man: but a gift corrupteth the heart." The chief difference here is in the word יהולל *yeholel,* which, from the root הלל *halal,* signifies to *glister, irradiate,* as well as to *move briskly,* to *be mad, furious,* in *a rage;* and certainly the former meaning suits this place best. We cannot think that the wise man—he that is truly religious, (for this is its meaning in the language of Solomon,) can be made *mad* by any kind of oppression; but as he trusts in God, so in patience he possesses his soul.

Verse 8. *Better* is *the end*] We can then judge of the whole, and especially if the matter relate to the conduct of Divine Providence. At the beginning we are often apt to make very rash conjectures, and often suppose that such and such things are against us; and that every thing is going wrong. Dr. *Byrom* gives good advice on such a subject:—

"With patient mind thy course of duty run:
God nothing does, nor suffers to be done,
But thou wouldst do thyself, couldst thou but see
The *end* of all events, as well as HE."

I may add, in the words of our paraphrast,—

A. M. cir. 3027 B. C. cir. 977 Ante I. Olymp. cir. 201 Ante U. C. cir. 224

better than the [k]proud in
spirit.

9 [l]Be not hasty in thy spirit
to be angry: for anger resteth in
the bosom of fools.

10 Say not thou, What is *the cause* that the
former days were better than these? for thou
dost not inquire [m]wisely concerning this.

11 Wisdom [n]*is* good with an inheritance:
and *by it there is* profit [o]to them that see
the sun.

12 For wisdom *is* a [p]defence, *and* money
is a defence: but the excellency of knowledge
is, that wisdom giveth life to
them that have it.

13 Consider the work of God:
for [q]who can make *that* straight,
which he hath made crooked?

14 [r]In the day of prosperity be joyful, but
in the day of adversity consider: God also
hath [s]set the one over against the other, to
the end that man should find nothing after
him.

15 All *things* have I seen in the days of
my vanity: [t]there is a just *man* that perisheth in his righteousness, and there is a wicked

[k]Prov. xxi. 4; xxviii. 25——[l]Prov. xiv. 17; xvi. 32; James i. 19——[m]Heb. *out of wisdom*——[n]Or, *as good as an inheritance; yea, better too*

[o]Chap. xi. 7——[p]Heb. *shadow*——[q]See Job xii. 14; chap. i. 15; Isa. xiv. 27——[r]Chap. iii. 4; Deut. xxviii. 47 [s]Heb. *made*——[t]Chap. viii. 14

"Wait the result, nor ask with frantic rage
Why God permits such things. His ways, though now
Involved in clouds and darkness, will appear
All right, when from thine eyes the mist is clear'd.
Till then, to learn submission to his will
More wisdom shows, than vainly thus to attempt
Exploring what thou canst not comprehend,
And God for wisest ends thinks fit to hide."

C.

Verse 9. *Anger resteth in the bosom of fools.*] A wise man, off his guard, may feel it for a moment: but in him it cannot *rest:* it is a *fire* which he immediately casts out of his breast. But the *fool*—the man who is under the dominion of his own tempers, harbours and fosters it, till it takes the form of malice, and then excites him to seek full revenge on those whom he deems enemies. Hence that class of *dangerous* and *empty fools* called *duellists.*

Verse 10. *The former days were better than these?*] This is a *common saying;* and it is as *foolish* as it is common. There is no weight nor truth in it; but men use it to excuse their crimes, and the folly of their conduct. "In former times, say they, men might be more religious, use more self-denial, be more exemplary." This is *all false.* In former days men were wicked as they are now, and religion was unfashionable: God also is the same *now* as he was *then;* as just, as merciful, as ready to help: and there is no depravity in the age that will excuse your crimes, your follies, and your carelessness.

Among the oriental proverbs I find the following:

"Many say, *This is a corrupt age.* This mode of speaking is not just; it is not the age that is corrupt, but the men of the age."

Verse 11. *Wisdom* is *good with an inheritance*] In this chapter Solomon introduces many observations which appear to be made by objectors against his doctrine; and as he was satisfied of their futility, he proposes them in their own full strength, and then combats and destroys them. It is quite necessary to attend to this; else we shall take the *objector's words* for *those* of *Solomon;* and think, as some have done, that the wise man contradicts and refutes himself. Observations, reflections, and objections of friends and adversaries are frequently introduced in the works of ancient authors, without mentioning them as such. This is frequent, more particularly in *ethic* writers; and we have many specimens in *Horace;* and without this distinction, it would be impossible to make sense of some of his writings. Here, an *objector*, who had listened to the wise man declaiming in favour of wisdom, suddenly interrupts him, and says in effect, "I grant the truth of what you have said. Wisdom is very good in its place; but what is it without property? A man who has a good inheritance may be profited by wisdom, because it will show him how to manage it to the best advantage."

Verse 12. *Wisdom* is *a defence*] To whom Solomon answers: All true *wisdom* is most undoubtedly a great advantage to men in all circumstances; and *money* is also of great use: but it cannot be compared to wisdom. *Knowledge* of Divine and human things is a great blessing. *Money* is the means of supporting our animal life: but *wisdom*—the religion of the true God—gives *life* to *them that have it. Money* cannot procure the favour of God, nor give *life* to the soul.

Verse 13. *Consider the work of God*] Such is the nature of his providence, that it puts money into the hands of few: but wisdom is within the reach of all. The first is not necessary to happiness; therefore, it is not offered to men; the latter is; and therefore God, in his goodness, offers it to the whole human race. The former can rarely be acquired, for God puts it out of the reach of most men, and you cannot *make that straight which he has made crooked;* the latter may be easily attained by every person who carefully and seriously seeks it from God.

Verse 14. *In the day of prosperity be joyful*] When ye receive these temporal gifts from God, enjoy them, and be thankful to the Giver: but remember, this sunshine will not *always* last. God has balanced *prosperity* and *adversity* against each other; and were it not so, how many would put the former in the place of God himself!

Verse 15. *There is a just* man *that perisheth*] This is another objection; as if he had said, "I also have had considerable experience; and I have not discovered any marked approbation of the conduct of the righteous, or disapprobation of that of the wicked. On the

A. M. cir. 3027
B. C. cir. 977
Ante I. Olymp. cir. 201
Ante U. C. cir. 224

man that prolongeth *his life* in
his wickedness.
16 [u]Be not righteous overmuch: neither make thyself over-
wise: why shouldest thou [w]destroy thyself?
17 Be not overmuch wicked, neither be
thou foolish: [x]why shouldest thou die [y]be-
fore thy time?
18 *It is* good that thou shouldest take hold
of this; yea, also from this withdraw not thine
hand: for he that feareth God shall come forth
of them all.
19 [z]Wisdom strengtheneth the wise more
than ten mighty *men* which are in the city.
20 [a]For *there is* not a just man
upon earth, that doeth good, and
sinneth not.
21 Also [b]take no heed unto
all words that are spoken; lest thou hear thy
servant curse thee:
22 For oftentimes also thine own heart
knoweth that thou thyself likewise hast cursed
others.
23 All this have I proved by wisdom;
[c]I said, I will be wise; but it *was* far
from me.
24 [d]That which is far off, and [e]exceeding
deep, who can find it out?

[u]Prov. xxv. 16——[v]Ecclus. iii. 21, 22; Rom. xii. 3——[w]Heb. *be desolate*——[x]Job xv. 32; Psa. lv. 23; Prov. x. 27——[y]Heb. *not in thy time*——[z]Prov. xxi. 22; xxiv. 5; chap. ix. 16, 18

[a]1 Kings viii. 46; 2 Chron. vi. 36; Prov. xx. 9; Rom. iii. 23; 1 John i. 8——[b]Heb. *give not thine heart*——[c]Rom. i. 22——[d]Job xxviii. 12, 20; 1 Tim. vi. 16——[e]Rom. xi. 33

contrary, I have seen a righteous man perish, while employed in the work of righteousness; and a wicked man prosperous, and even exalted, while living wickedly. The former is indeed a victim to his righteousness, while the life and prosperity of the latter were preserved: hence I conclude, it is not prudent, whatever good there may be in religion, and whatever excellence in wisdom, that men should be overmuch righteous, or over-wise: for why should they by austerity and hard study destroy themselves?" So far the objector.

Verse 16. *Why shouldest thou destroy thyself?*] תשומם *tishshomem*, make thyself *desolate*, so that thou shalt be obliged to stand *alone;* neither make thyself over-wise, תתחכם *tithchaccam*, do not pretend to abundance of wisdom. Why shouldest thou be so singular? In other words, and in modern language, "There is no need of all this watching, fasting, praying, self-denial, &c., you carry things to *extremes*. Why should you wish to be reputed singular and precise?" To this the man of God answers:

Verse 17. *Be not overmuch wicked, neither be thou foolish: why shouldest thou die before thy time?*] אל תרשע הרבה *al tirsha harbeh*. Do not multiply wickedness; do not add direct opposition to godliness to the rest of your crimes. Why should you provoke God to destroy you before your time? Perdition will come soon enough. If you will not turn from your sins, and avoid it finally, yet keep out of it as long as you can.

It cannot be supposed, except by those who are totally unacquainted with the nature of true religion, that a man may have *too much holiness, too much of the life of God* in his soul! And yet a learned doctor, in three sermons on this text, has endeavoured to show, out-doing Solomon's infidel, "the *sin, folly,* and *danger* of being righteous overmuch." O rare darkness!

Verse 18. It is *good that thou shouldest take hold of this*] Do not let such an observation slip: *take hold of this; do not forget that.* Get what you can in an honest way; but do not forget to get true religion; for he that fears God will be saved from all evil.

Verse 19. *Wisdom strengtheneth the wise*] One wise, thoroughly learned, and scientific man, may be of more use in fortifying and defending a city, than ten *princes.* Witness the case of *Syracuse*, when attacked by the Romans both by sea and land. *Archimedes*, by his engines, burnt and dashed their fleet to pieces, and destroyed all that came near the walls. And had not the city been betrayed, and he killed, all their force and skill could not have taken it.

Verse 20. There is *not a just man upon earth, that doeth good, and sinneth not.*] לא יחטא *lo yechta*, that *may not sin*. There is not a man upon earth, however just he may be, and habituated to do good, but is *peccable*—liable to commit sin; and therefore should continually watch and pray, and depend upon the Lord. But the text does not say, the *just man does commit sin*, but simply that he *may sin;* and so our translators have rendered it in 1 Sam. ii. 25, twice in 1 Kings viii. 31, 46, and 2 Chron. vi. 36; and the reader is requested to consult the note on 1 Kings viii. 46, where the proper construction of this word may be found, and the doctrine in question is fully considered.

Verse 21. *Also take no heed unto all words that are spoken*] This is good advice, and much for every man's peace through life.

Thy servant curse thee] מקללך *mekallelecha*, make light of thee, speak evil of thee.

Verse 22. *Thou thyself—hast cursed others.*] קללת *kalalta*, thou hast spoken evil; hast vilified others. O, who is free from evil speaking; from uncharitable speaking; from detailing their neighbour's faults, from whispering, talebearing, and backbiting? Do not wonder if God, in his justice, permit *thee* to be calumniated, seeing thou hast so frequently calumniated others. See my discourse on Psa. xv. 1-5.

Verse 23. *All this have I proved by wisdom*] These rules I have laid down for my own conduct, and sought after more wisdom; but have fallen far short of what I wished to be.

Verse 24. *That which is far off*] Though the wisdom that is essential to our salvation may be soon learned, through the teaching of

A. M. cir. 3027 B. C. cir. 977 Ante I Olymp. cir. 201 Ante U. C. cir. 224

25 [f]I [g]applied mine heart to
know, and to search, and to
seek out wisdom, and the reason *of things,* and to know the
wickedness of folly, even of foolishness *and*
madness.

26 [h]And I find more bitter than death the
woman, whose heart *is* snares and nets, *and*
her hands as bands: [i]whoso pleaseth God
shall escape from her; but the sinner shall be
taken by her.

27 Behold, this have I found,
saith [k]the Preacher, [l]*counting*
one by one, to find out the
account:

28 Which yet my soul seeketh, but I find
not: [m]one man among a thousand have I
found; but a woman among all those have I
not found.

29 Lo, this only have I found, [n]that God
hath made man upright; but [o]they have
sought out many [p]inventions.

[f]Heb. *I and my heart compassed*——[g]Chap. i. 17; ii. 12 [h]Prov. v. 3, 4; xxii. 14——[i]Heb. he that is *good before God*——[k]Chap. i. 1, 2

[l]Or, weighing *one thing after another, to find out the reason*——[m]Job xxxiii. 23; Psa. xii. 1——[n]Gen. i. 27 [o]Gen. iii. 6, 7——[p]Psa. xcix. 8; cvi. 29, 39; Prov. viii. 12

the Spirit of wisdom, yet in wisdom itself there are *extents* and *depths* which none can reach or fathom.

Verse 25. *I applied mine heart*] I cast about, סבותי *sabbothi*, I made a circuit; I circumscribed the ground I was to traverse; and all within my circle I was determined to *know*, and to *investigate*, and to *seek out wisdom*, and the *reason of things*. Has man *reason* and *understanding?* If so, then this is his work. God as much calls him to use these powers in this way, as to believe on the Lord Jesus that he may be saved; and he that does not, according to the means in his power, is a slothful servant, from whom God may justly take away the misemployed or not used talent, and punish him for his neglect. Every doctrine of God is a subject both for reason and faith to work on.

To know the wickedness of folly, even of foolishness and *madness.*]

"And my own heart, with scrutiny severe,
By far the harder task survey'd; intent
To trace that wisdom which from heaven descends,
Fountain of living waters, and to explore
The source of human folly, whose foul streams
Intoxicate and kill."—C.

Verse 26. *And I find more bitter than death the woman*] After all his investigation of the *wickedness of folly*, and the *foolishness of madness*, he found nothing equally dangerous and ruinous with the *blandishments of cunning women.* When once the affections are entangled, escape without ruin is almost impossible.

Whoso pleaseth God] The man who walks with God, and he alone, shall escape this sore evil: and even he that fears God, if he get with an artful woman, may be soon robbed of his strength, and become like other men. A bad or artful woman is represented as a *company of hunters*, with *nets*, *gins*, &c., to catch their prey.

Verse 27. Counting *one by one*] I have gone over every particular. I have compared one thing with another; man with woman, his wisdom with her wiles; his strength with her blandishments; his influence with her ascendancy; his powers of reason with her arts and cunning; and in a *thousand* men, I have found *one* thoroughly upright *man;* but among *one thousand* women I have not found *one such.* This is a lamentable account of the *state of morals* in Judea, in the days of the wise King Solomon. Thank God! it would not be difficult to get a *tithe* of *both* in the same number in the present day.

The *Targum* gives this a curious turn:—"There is another thing which my soul has sought, but could not find: a man perfect and innocent, and without corruption, from the days of Adam until *Abraham* the just was born; who was found faithful and upright among the thousand kings who came together to construct the tower of Babel: but a *woman* like to *Sarah* among the wives of all those kings I have not found."

Verse 29. *Lo, this only have I found, that God hath made man upright*] Whatever evil may be now found among men and women, it is not of God; for God made them all upright. This is a singular verse, and has been most variously translated: עשה האלהים את האדם ישר והמה בקשו חשבנות רבים *asah hælohim eth haadam yashar vehemhah bikkeshu chishbonoth rabbim.*

"Elohim has made mankind upright, and they have sought many computations."

"He hath meddled with endless questions."—VULGATE.

"Many reasonings."—SEPTUAGINT, SYRIAC, and ARABIC.

"They seek dyverse sotylties."—COVERDALE.

And he himself mengide with questions without eend.—Old MS. Bible.

The *Targum* considers the text as speaking of *Adam* and *Eve.*

"This have I found out, that the Lord made the first man upright before him, and innocent: but the serpent and Eve seduced him to eat of the fruit of the tree, which gave the power to those who ate of it to discern between good and evil; and was the cause that death came upon him, and all the inhabitants of the earth; and they sought that they might find out *many stratagems* to bring this evil upon all the inhabitants of the world."

I doubt much whether the word חשבנות *chishbonoth* should be taken in a *bad* sense. It may signify the whole of human *devices, imaginations, inventions, artifice,* with all their products; arts, sciences, schemes, plans, and all that they have found out for the destruction or melioration of life. God has given man wondrous faculties; and of them he has made strange uses, and sovereign abuses: and they have been, in consequence, at one time his help, and at another his bane. This is the fair way of understanding this question.

CHAPTER VIII

A man's wisdom makes his face shine, 1. *Kings are to be greatly respected,* 2–4. *Of him who keeps the commandment; of the misery of man; of the certainty of death,* 5–8. *Of him that rules another to his own hurt,* 9. *The end of the wicked,* 10. *God's longsuffering,* 11, 12. *It shall be ill with wicked men,* 13. *Strange events in the course of Providence,* 14, 15. *God's works cannot be found out,* 16, 17.

A. M. cir. 3027
B. C. cir. 977
Ante I. Olymp. cir. 201
Ante U. C. cir. 224

WHO *is* as the wise *man?* and who knoweth the interpretation of a thing? [a]a man's
wisdom maketh his face to shine,
and [b]the [c]boldness of his face shall be
changed.
2 I *counsel thee* to keep the king's commandment, [d]and *that* in regard of the oath of
God.
3 [e]Be not hasty to go out of his sight:
stand not in an evil thing; for
he doeth whatsoever pleaseth
him.
4 Where the word of a king
is, there is power: and [f]who may say unto
him, What doest thou?
5 Whoso keepeth the commandment [g]shall
feel no evil thing: and a wise man's heart
discerneth both time and judgment.
6 Because [h]to every purpose there is time

A. M. cir. 3027
B. C. cir. 977
Ante I. Olymp. cir. 201
Ante U. C. cir. 224

[a]Prov. iv. 8, 9; xvii. 24; see Acts vi. 15——[b]Heb. *the strength*——[c]Deut. xxviii. 50——[d]1 Chron. xxix. 24; Ezek. xvii. 18; Rom. xiii. 5——[e]Chap. x. 4——[f]Job xxxiv. 18——[g]Heb. *shall know*——[h]Chap. iii. 1

NOTES ON CHAP. VIII

Verse 1. *Who knoweth the interpretation*] פשר *pesher*, a pure *Chaldee* word, found nowhere else in the Bible but in the *Chaldee* parts of *Daniel.* "A man's wisdom maketh his face to shine." Every state of the heart shines through the countenance; but there is such an evidence of the contented, happy, pure, benevolent state of the soul in the *face* of a truly pious man, that it must be observed, and cannot be mistaken. In the Hebrew the former clause of this verse ends the preceding chapter. Who has ever been deceived in the appearance of the face that belonged to a savage heart? Those who represent, by painting. or otherwise, a *wise man,* with a *gravely sour face,* striking awe and forbidding approach, have either mistaken the man, or are unacquainted with some essential principles of their art.

The boldness of his face shall be changed.] Instead of ישנא *yeshunne,* which signifies *shall be hated,* many of *Kennicott's* and *De Rossi's* MSS. have ישנה *yeshunneh,* shall be *changed* or *doubled.* Hence the verse might be read, "The wisdom of a man shall illuminate his face; and the strength of his countenance shall be doubled." He shall speak with full confidence and conviction on a subject which he perfectly understands, and all will feel the weight of his observations.

Verse 2. *To keep the king's commandment*] This sentence would be better translated, *I keep the mouth of the king;* I take good heed not to meddle with state secrets; and if I know, to hide them. Or, I am obedient to the commands of the laws; I feel myself bound by whatever the king has decreed.

In regard of the oath of God.] You have sworn obedience to him; keep your oath, for the engagement was made in the *presence of God.* It appears that the Jewish princes and chiefs took an oath of fidelity to their kings. This appears to have been done to *David,* 2 Sam. v. 1-3; to *Joash,* 2 Kings xi. 17; and to *Solomon,* 1 Chron. xxix. 24.

Verse 3. *Be not hasty*] I consider the first *five* verses here as directions to *courtiers,* and the more immediate servants of kings.

Be steadily faithful to your sovereign. *Do not stand in an evil thing.* If you have done wrong, do not endeavour to vindicate yourself before him; it is of no use; his power is *absolute,* and *he will do what* he *pleases.* He will take his *own view* of the subject, and he will *retain* it. The language of a despotic sovereign was ever this, Sic volo sic jubeo, stat pro ratione voluntas; "I will this. I command that. No hesitation! My will is law!" Therefore it is added here, *Where the word of a king* is, there is *power*—influence, authority, *and* the sword. And *who may say unto him,* whether he acts right or wrong, *What doest thou?* ver. 4. No wonder in such governments there are so many *revolutions;* but they are *revolutions* without *amendment,* as it is one *tyrant* rising up to destroy *another,* who, when seated in authority, acts in the way of his predecessor; till another, like himself, do to him as he has done to the former. In our country, after a long trial, we find that a *mixed monarchy* is the safest, best, and most useful form of government: we have had, it is true, unprincipled ministers, who wished to turn our *limited* into an *absolute monarchy;* and they were always ready to state that *an absolute monarchy was best.* Granted; provided the monarch be as *wise,* as *holy,* and as *powerful* as GOD!

Verse 5. *Both time and judgment.*] It is a matter of great importance to be able to discern WHEN and HOW both to *speak* and *act;* but when *time* and *manner* are both determined, the *matter* comes next. WHAT shall *I speak?* WHAT shall *I do? When, how,* and *what,* answer to *time, manner,* and *matter.* To discern all these, and act suitably, is a *lesson* for a *philosopher,* and a *study* for a *Christian.*

Verse 6. *To every purpose there is time*] חפץ *chaphets,* every *volition,* every thing that *depends on the will of man.* He has generally the *opportunity* to do whatever he purposes; and as his purposes are frequently evil, his

A. M. cir. 3027
B. C. cir. 977
Ante I. Olymp. cir. 201
Ante U. C. cir. 224

and judgment, therefore the
misery of man *is* great upon him.
7 [i]For he knoweth not that
which shall be: for who can tell
him [k]when it shall be?
8 [l]*There is* no man that hath power [m]over
the spirit to retain the spirit; neither *hath he*
power in the day of death: and *there is* no
[n]discharge in *that* war; neither shall wickedness deliver those that are given to it.
9 All this have I seen, and applied my heart
unto every work that is done under the sun:
there is a time wherein one man ruleth over
another to his own hurt.
10 And so I saw the wicked buried, who
had come and gone from the place of the holy,
and they were forgotten in the city where they
had so done: this *is* also vanity.
11 [o]Because sentence against an evil work
is not executed speedily, therefore the heart of the sons of
men is fully set in them to do evil.
12 [p]Through a sinner do evil
a hundred times, and his *days* be prolonged,
yet surely I know that [q]it shall be well with
them that fear God, which fear before him:
13 But it shall not be well with the wicked,
neither shall he prolong *his* days, *which are* as
a shadow; because he feareth not before God.
14 There is a vanity which is done upon
the earth; that there be just *men,* unto whom
it [r]happeneth according to the work of the
wicked; again, there be wicked *men,* to whom
it happeneth according to the work of the
righteous: I said that this also *is* vanity.
15 [s]Then I commended mirth, because a man
hath no better thing under the sun, than to
eat, and to drink, and to be merry; for that

A. M. cir. 3027
B. C. cir. 977
Ante I. Olymp. cir. 201
Ante U. C. cir. 224

---

[i]Proverbs xxiv. 22; chapter vi. 12; ix. 12; x. 14——[k]Or, *how it shall be*——[l]Psa. xlix. 6, 7——[m]Job xiv. 5——[n]Or, *casting off* weapons——[o]Psalm x. 6; l. 21; Isaiah xxvi. 10——[p]Isaiah lxv. 20; Romans ii. 5——[q]Psalm xxxvii. 11, 18, 19; Proverbs i. 32, 33; Isaiah iii. 10, 11; Matthew xxv. 34, 41——[r]Psalm lxxiii. 14; chapter ii. 14; vii. 15; ix. 1, 2——[s]Chapter ii. 24; iii. 12, 22; v. 18; ix. 7

---

acts are so too: and in consequence his misery is great.

Verse 8. There is *no man that hath power over the spirit to retain the spirit*] The *Chaldee* has, "There is no man who can rule over the spirit of the breath, so as to prevent the animal life from leaving the body of man." Others translate to this sense: "No man hath power over the *wind* to restrain the wind; and none has power over *death* to restrain him; and when a man engages as a *soldier*, he cannot be discharged from the war till it is ended; and by wickedness no man shall be delivered from any evil." Taking it in this way, these are maxims which contain self-evident truths. Others suppose the verse to refer to the *king* who *tyrannizes* over and oppresses his people. He shall also account to God for his actions; he shall die, and he cannot prevent it; and when he is judged, his wickedness cannot deliver him.

Verse 9. *One man ruleth over another to his own hurt.*] This may be spoken of rulers generally, who, instead of *feeding, fleece the flock;* tyrants and oppressors, who come to an untimely end by their mismanagement of the offices of the state. All these things relate to *Asiatic* despots, and have ever been more applicable to *them* than to any other sovereigns in the world. They were despotic; they still are so.

Verse 10. *Who had come and gone from the place of the holy*] The place of the holy is the sacred office which they held, *anointed* either as *kings* or *priests* to God; and, not having fulfilled the holy office in a holy way, have been carried to their *graves* without *lamentation*, and lie among the dead without remembrance.

Verse 11. *Because sentence*] פתגם *pithgam*, a *Divine decree* or *declaration.* This is no *Hebrew*, but a mere *Chaldee* word, and occurs only in the *later books* of the Bible—*Esther, Ezra* and *Daniel*, and nowhere else but in this place. Because God does not immediately punish every delinquency, men think he disregards evil acts; and therefore they are emboldened to sin on. So this longsuffering of God, which *leadeth to repentance*, is abused so as to *lead to farther crimes!* When men sin against the remedy of their salvation, how can they escape perdition?

Verse 12. *Though a sinner do evil a hundred times*] If God bear so long with a transgressor, waiting in his longsuffering for him to repent and turn to him, surely he will be peculiarly kind to them that *fear him*, and endeavour to walk uprightly before him.

Verse 13. *But it shall not be well with the wicked*] Let not the long-spared sinner presume that, because sentence is not speedily executed on his evil works, and he is suffered to go on to his *hundredth transgression*, God has forgotten to punish. No; *he feareth not before God;* and therefore he shall not ultimately escape.

Verse 14. *There be just* men] See on chap. vii. ver. 16.

Verse 15. *Then I commended mirth*] These are some more of the cavils of the infidel objector: "Since *virtue* is frequently under oppression, and *vice* triumphs in health, and rolls in wealth, I see plainly that we should not trouble ourselves about future things; and therefore should be governed by the maxim Ede, bibe, lude. *Post mortem nulla voluptas.*"

Eat, drink, and *play,*
While here you may;
For soon as death
Has stopp'd your breath,
Ye ne'er shall see a cheerful day.

A. M. cir. 3027 B. C. cir. 977 Ante I. Olymp. cir. 201 Ante U. C. cir. 224

shall abide with him of his labour
the days of his life, which God
giveth him under the sun.
16 When I applied mine heart
to know wisdom, and to see the business that is
done upon the earth: (for also *there is that* neither day nor night seeth sleep with his eyes:)
17 Then I beheld all the work
of God, that [t]a man cannot find
out the work that is done under
the sun: because though a man
labour to seek *it* out, yet he shall not find
it; yea, farther; though a wise *man* think to
know *it,* [u]yet shall he not be able to find *it.*

[t]Job v. 9; chap. iii. 11; Rom. xi. 33

[u]Psa. lxxiii. 16

Verse 16. *When I applied mine heart to know wisdom*] This is the reply of the wise man: "I have also considered these seeming contradictions. God governs the world; but we cannot see the reasons of his conduct, nor know why he does this, omits that, or permits a third thing. We may *study night* and *day*, and deprive ourselves of *rest* and *sleep*, but we shall never fathom the depths that are in the Divine government; but all is right and just. *This* is the state of *probation;* and in it neither can the wicked be punished, nor the righteous rewarded. But eternity is at hand; and then shall every man receive according to his works. He that spends his life in the *eat, drink*, and *play*, will find in that day that he has lost the *time* in *which* he could have prepared for *eternity.*

Verse 17. *Then I beheld all the work of God, that a man cannot find out the work that is done under the sun*] I saw it to be of such a nature—1, That *a man cannot find it out.* 2. That if he *labour to find it out*, he shall not succeed. 3. That though he be *wise*—the *most instructed* among men, and *think* to find it out, he shall find *he is not able.* It is beyond the wisdom and power of man. How vain then are all your *cavils* about Providence. You do not understand it; you cannot comprehend it. Fear God!

CHAPTER IX

No man knows, by any present sign, what is before him, 1. *All things happen alike to all,* 2, 3. *Comparison of the state of the dead and the living,* 4–6. *Enjoy God's mercies, and live to his glory,* 7–10. *The race is not to the swift, nor the battle to the strong,* 11. *Man is ignorant of futurity,* 12, 13. *The account of the little city, and the poor wise man,* 14–18.

A. M. cir. 3027 B. C. cir. 977 Ante I. Olymp. cir. 201 Ante U. C. cir. 224

FOR all this [a]I considered in
my heart even to declare all
this, [b]that the righteous, and the
wise, and their works, *are* in the
hand of God: no man knoweth either love or
hatred *by* all *that is* before them.
2 [c]All *things come* alike to all: *there is*
one event to the righteous, and to the wicked;
to the good and to the clean, and to the unclean; to him that sacrificeth,
and to him that sacrificeth not:
as *is* the good, so *is* the sinner;
and he that sweareth, as *he* that
feareth an oath.
3 This *is* an evil among all *things* that are
done under the sun, that *there is* one event unto
all: yea, also the heart of the sons of men is
full of evil, and madness *is* in their heart while

[a]Heb. *I gave or set to my heart*——[b]Chap. viii. 14

[c]Job xxi. 7, &c.; Psa. lxxiii. 3, 12, 13; Mal. iii. 15

NOTES ON CHAP. IX

Verse 1. *The righteous, and the wise, and their works*, are *in the hand of God*] This is a continuation of the preceding subject; and here the wise man draws a conclusion from what he had seen, and from the well-known character of God, that the *righteous*, the *wise*, and *their conduct*, were all in *the hand of God*, protected by his power, and safe in his approbation: but we cannot judge from the occurrences which take place in life who are the objects of God's love or displeasure.

Verse 2. *All* things come *alike to all*] This is very generally true; but God often makes a difference; and his faithful followers witness many interventions of Divine Providence in their behalf. But there are general blessings, and general natural evils, that equally affect the just and the unjust. But in this all is right; the *evils* that are in *nature* are the effects of the FALL of man; and God will not suspend *general laws*, or *alter* them, to favour *individual* cases. Nor does he design that his approbation or disapprobation shall be shown by any of these occurrences. Every holy man has a testimony of God's approbation in his own heart; and this makes him truly happy, let outward things be as they may. And, in general, what the wicked suffer is the fruit of their own doings. But the general state of nature as to what are called *natural evils*, is just as it ought to be. There is *evil* enough to show that *man has fallen* from God, and *good* enough to show that God deals with him in *mercy.* I cannot see that there is any rational cause for me to stumble at the dispensations of Divine Providence on these accounts.

Verse 3. *The heart of the sons of men is full*

A. M. cir. 3027
B. C. cir. 977
Ante I. Olymp. cir. 201
Ante U. C. cir. 224

they live, and after that *they go*
to the dead.
4 For to him that is joined to
all the living there is hope: for
a living dog is better than a dead lion.
5 For the living know that they shall die:
but [d]the dead know not any thing, neither
have they any more a reward; for [e]the memory of them is forgotten.
6 Also their love and their hatred, and their
envy, is now perished; neither have they any
more a portion for ever in any *thing* that is
done under the sun.

A. M. cir. 3027
B. C. cir. 977
Ante I. Olymp. cir. 201
Ante U. C. cir. 224

7 Go thy way, [f]eat thy bread
with joy, and drink thy wine with
a merry heart; for God now
accepteth thy works.
8 Let thy garments be always white; and
let thy head lack no ointment.
9 [g]Live joyfully with the wife whom thou
lovest all the days of the life of thy vanity,
which he hath given thee under the sun, all the
days of thy vanity: [h]for that *is* thy portion
in *this* life, and in thy labour which thou
takest under the sun.
10 Whatsoever thy hand findeth to do, do

[d]Job xiv. 21; Isa. lxiii. 16——[e]Job vii. 8, 9, 10; Isa. xxvi. 14——[f]Chap. viii. 15

[g]Hebrews, *See* or *enjoy life*——[h]Chap. ii. 10, 24; iii. 13, 22; v. 18

of evil] No wonder then that the curse of God should be frequent in the earth.

Verse 4. *For to him that is joined to all the living there is hope*] While a man lives he hopes to *amend*, and he hopes to have a *better lot;* and thus life is spent, hoping to *grow better*, and hoping to *get more.* The *Vulgate* has, "There is none that shall live always, nor has any hope of such a thing." Perhaps the best translation is the following: "What, therefore, is to be chosen? In him that is living there is hope." Then choose that eternal life which thou hopest to possess.

A living dog is better than a dead lion.] I suppose this was a proverb. The smallest measure of *animal* existence is better than the largest of *dead matter.* The poorest living peasant is infinitely above Alexander the Great.

Verse 5. *The living know that they shall die*] This is so self-evident that none can doubt it; and therefore all that have this conviction should prepare for death and eternal blessedness.

But the dead know not any thing] Cut off from *life*, they know nothing of *what passes under the sun.* Their day of *probation* is ended, and therefore they can have no farther *reward* in living a holy life; nor can they be liable to any *farther punishment* for crimes in a state of probation, that being ended.

Verse 6. *Also their love, and their hatred*] It is evident that he speaks here of the ignorance, want of power, &c., of the *dead*, in reference only to *this life.* And though they have no more a *portion* under the sun, yet he does not intimate that they have none anywhere else. A man threatens to conquer kingdoms, &c. He dies; what are his *threats?*

Verse 7. *Go thy way, eat thy bread with joy*] Do not vex and perplex yourselves with the dispensations and mysteries of Providence; enjoy the blessings which God has given you, and live to his glory; and then *God will accept your works.*

Verse 8. *Let thy garments be always white*] The Jews wore white garments on festal occasions, as emblems of joy and innocence. Be always pure, and always happy. The inhabitants of India are all dressed in clean *white cotton*, and to this is the allusion in the text.

The *Targum* says: "At all times let thy garments be washed and pure from the stain of sin. Acquire a good name, which is likened to the oil of anointing, that blessings may be called down up thy head, and goodness not forsake thee."

Verse 9. *Live joyfully with the wife whom thou lovest*] Marry prudently, keep faithfully attached to the wife thou hast chosen, and rejoice in the labour of thy hands.

Some understand this as the words of the libertine objector: "Live joyfully with the woman whom thou lovest best." But this does not comport so well with the scope of the place.

Verse 10. *Whatsoever thy hand findeth to do*] Examine here the WHAT, the HOW, and the WHY.

I. *What* is necessary to be done in this life, in reference to another? 1. Turn from sin. 2. Repent. 3. Frequent the ordinances of God, and associate with the upright. 4. Read the Scriptures. 5. Pray for pardon. 6. Believe on the Lord Jesus, that thou mayest obtain it. 7. Look for the gift of the Holy Spirit. 8. Bring forth in their seasons the fruits of it—(1) Repentance; (2) Faith; and (3) The Holy Spirit. 9. Live to get good. 10. And to do good. 11. And refer every purpose and act to the eternal world.

II. *How* should these be done? *With thy might.* 1. Be fully convinced of the necessity of these things. 2. Be determined to act according to this conviction. 3. Then act with all thy strength; put forth all thy power in avoiding evil, repenting of sin, &c., &c.

III. *Why* should this be done? 1. Because thou art a dying man. 2. Thou art going into the grave. 3. When thou leavest this life, thy state of probation, with all its advantages, is eternally ended. 4. If thou die in sin, where God is thou shalt never come. For, 1. There is no *work* by which thou mayest profit; 2. No *device* by which thou mayest escape punishment; 3. No *knowledge* of any means of help; and, 4. No *wisdom*—restoration of the soul to the favour and image of God, *in that grave whither thou goest.* Therefore, work while it is called *to-day.*

My old MS. Bible translates this nervously: **Whateuer thinge may thin hond don, besily wirch: for nouther werc, ne resoun, ne wisdom, ne keennyng schuln be a nentis hell, whither thou gost.** Properly speaking, every sinner is *going to hell,* and the wisdom of God calls upon him to turn and live.

A. M. cir. 3027 B. C. cir. 977 Ante I. Olymp. cir. 201 Ante U. C. cir. 224

it with thy might; for *there is*
no work, nor device, nor knowledge, nor wisdom, in the grave,
whither thou goest.
11 I returned, [i]and saw under the sun, that
the race *is* not to the swift, nor the battle to
the strong, neither yet bread to the wise, nor
yet riches to men of understanding, nor yet
favour to men of skill; but time and chance
happeneth to them all.
12 For [k]man also knoweth not his time: as
the fishes that are taken in an
evil net, and as the birds that are
caught in the snare; so *are* the
sons of men [l]snared in an evil
time, when it falleth suddenly upon them.
13 This wisdom have I seen also under the
sun, and it *seemed* great unto me:
14 [m]*There was* a little city, and few men
within it; and there came a great king against
it, and besieged it, and built great bulwarks
against it:

A. M. cir. 3027 B. C. cir. 977 Ante I. Olymp. cir. 201 Ante U. C. cir. 224

[i]Amos ii. 14, 15; Jeremiah ix. 23——[k]Chapter viii. 7

[l]Prov. xxix. 6; Luke xii. 20, 39; xvii. 26, &c.; 1 Thess. v. 3——[m]See 2 Sam. xx. 16–22

Verse 11. *The race* is *not to the swift*] It is not by swiftness, nor by strength and valour, that races are gained and battles won. God causes the *lame* often to take the *prey*, the prize; and so works that the *weak* overthrow the *strong;* therefore, no man should confide in himself. All things are under the government, and at the disposal of God.

But time and chance] עת *eth*, time or opportunity, and פגע *pega*, incident or occurrence,—

Happeneth to them all.] Every man has what may be called *time* and *space* to act in, and *opportunity* to do a particular work. But in this TIME and OPPORTUNITY there is INCIDENT, what *may fall in;* and OCCURRENCE, what may *meet* and frustrate an attempt. These things should be wisely weighed, and seriously balanced; for those *four things* belong to every human *action*. While you have TIME, seek an OPPORTUNITY to do what is right; but calculate on *hinderances* and *oppositions*, because *time* and *opportunity* have their INCIDENT and OCCURRENCE. *Coverdale* translates this verse well: "I sawe that in runnynge, it helpeth not to be swift; in batayll, it helpeth not to be stronge; to fedynge, it helpeth not to be wyse; to riches, it helpeth not to be sutyll; to be had in favoure, it helpeth not to be connynge; but that all lyeth in time and fortune."

Verse 12. *As the birds that are caught*] Man acts so heedlessly, notwithstanding all his wisdom, and all his warnings, that he is often taken, as a *fish* is, by the baited hook; and the *bird* by the baited snare. And thus, *an evil time*, like the snare, gin, trap, hook, falleth suddenly upon them; and they are taken in a moment, and have no means of escaping. How frequently do we see these comparisons illustrated!

Verse 14. There was *a little city, and few men within it*] Here is another proof of the vanity of sublunary things; the *ingratitude of men*, and the *little compensation* that *genuine merit* receives. The little history mentioned here may have either been a *fact*, or intended as an instructive fable. A *little city*, with *few to defend* it, being besieged by a *great king* and a powerful army, was delivered by the *cunning and address of a poor wise man;* and afterwards his *townsmen* forgot *their obligation to him.*

Those who *spiritualize* this passage, making the *little city* the CHURCH, the *few men* the APOSTLES, the *great king* the DEVIL, and the *poor wise man* JESUS CHRIST, abuse the text.

But the *Targum* is not less whimsical: "The *little city* is the human body; *few men in it*, few *good affections* to work righteousness; *the great king*, evil concupiscence, which, like a strong and powerful king, enters into the body to oppress it, and besieges the heart so as to cause it to err; *built great bulwarks against it*—evil concupiscence builds his throne in it wheresoever he wills, and causes it to decline from the ways that are right before God; that it may be taken in the greatest nets of hell, that he may burn it seven times, because of its sins. But there is *found in it a poor wise man*—a good, wise, and holy affection, which prevails over the evil principle, and snatches the body from the judgment of hell, by the strength of its wisdom. Yet, after this deliverance, the man did not remember what the good principle had done for him; but said in his heart, I am innocent," &c.

What a wonderful text has this been in the hands of many a modern *Targumist;* and with what force have the *Keachonians* preached Christ *crucified* from it!

Such a passage as this receives a fine illustration from the case of *Archimedes* saving the city of *Syracuse* from all the Roman forces besieging it by sea and land. He destroyed their ships by his *burning-glasses*, lifted up their galleys out of the water by his machines, dashing some to pieces, and sinking others. One man's wisdom here prevailed for a long time against the most powerful exertions of a mighty nation. In this case, wisdom far exceeded strength. But was not Syracuse taken, notwithstanding the exertions of this poor wise man? No. But it was *betrayed* by the baseness of *Mericus*, a Spaniard, one of the *Syracusan* generals. He delivered the whole district he commanded into the hands of *Marcellus*, the Roman consul, *Archimedes* having defeated every attempt made by the Romans, either by sea or land: yet he commanded no company of men, made no sorties, but confounded and destroyed them by his machines. This happened about 208 years before Christ, and nearly about the time in which those who do not consider Solomon as the author suppose this book to have been written. This wise man was *not remembered;* he was slain by a Roman soldier, while deeply engaged in demonstrating a new problem, in order to his farther operations against the enemies of his country. See *Plutarch*, and the historians of this *Syracusan* war.

When *Alexander* the Great was about to destroy the city *Lampsacus*, his old master *Anaxi-*

A. M. cir. 3027
B. C. cir. 977
Ante I. Olymp. cir. 201
Ante U. C. cir. 224

15 Now there was found in it
a poor wise man, and he by his
wisdom delivered the city; yet
no man remembered that same
poor man.
16 [n]Then said I, Wisdom *is* better than
strength: nevertheless [o]the poor man's wisdom *is* despised, and his words
are not heard.
17 The words of wise *men*
are heard in quiet, more than the
cry of him that ruleth among fools.
18 [p]Wisdom *is* better than weapons of war:
but [q]one sinner destroyeth much good.

A. M. cir. 3027
B. C. cir. 977
Ante I. Olymp. cir. 201
Ante U. C. cir. 224

[n]Prov xxi. 22; xxiv. 5; chap. vii. 19; ver. 18 —— [o]Mark vi. 2, 3 —— [p]Ver. 16 —— [q]Josh. vii. 1, 11, 12

menes came out to meet him. Alexander, suspecting his design, that he would intercede for the city, being determined to destroy it, swore that he would *not* grant him any thing he should ask. Then said Anaximenes, "I desire that you *will destroy* this city." Alexander respected his oath, and the city was spared. Thus, says *Valerius Maximus*, the narrator, (lib. vii. c. iii., No. 4. Extern.,) by this sudden turn of sagacity, this ancient and noble city was preserved from the destruction by which it was threatened. "Hæc velocitas sagacitatis oppidum vetusta nobilitate inclytum exitio, cui destinatum erat, subtraxit."

A stratagem of *Jaddua*, the *high priest*, was the means of preserving *Jerusalem* from being destroyed by *Alexander*, who, incensed because they had assisted the inhabitants of Gaza when he besieged it, as soon as he had reduced it, marched against Jerusalem, with the determination to raze it to the ground; but Jaddua and his priests in their sacerdotal robes, meeting him on the way, he was so struck with their appearance that he not only prostrated himself before the high priest, and spared the city, but also granted it some remarkable privileges. But the case of *Archimedes* and *Syracuse* is the most striking and appropriate in all its parts. That of Anaximenes and Lampsacus is also highly illustrative of the maxim of the wise man: "Wisdom is better than strength."

Verse 16. *The poor man's wisdom* is *despised, and his words are not heard.*] I cannot help pursuing this illustration a little farther. The soldier who found Archimedes busily employed in drawing figures upon the sand, put to him some impertinent question, withal rudely obtruding himself on his operations. To whom this wonderful mathematician replied, "Stand off, soldier, and do not spoil my diagram;" on which the bloody savage struck him dead!

Verse 17. *The words of wise* men are *heard in quiet*] In the tumult of war the words of *Archimedes* were not heard; and his *life* was lost.

Verse 18. *Wisdom* is *better than weapons of war*] So proved in the case of *Archimedes*.

But one sinner] Such as the Roman butcher above mentioned.

Destroyeth much good] Such as were the life and skill of the Syracusan mathematician. One sinner has often injured the work of God; one stumbling-block has sometimes destroyed a revival of religion. Sin acts like a ferment; whatever comes in contact with it, it assimilates to itself.

CHAPTER X

Observations on wisdom and folly, 1–3. *Concerning right conduct towards rulers*, 4. *Merit depressed, and worthlessness exalted*, 5–7. *Of him who digs a pit and removes a landmark*, 8, 9. *The use of wisdom and experience*, 10. *Of the babbler and the fool*, 11–15. *The infant king*, 16. *The well-regulated court*, 17. *Of slothfulness*, 18. *Of feasting*, 19. *Speak not evil of the king*, 20.

A. M. cir. 3027
B. C. cir. 977
Ante I. Olymp. cir. 201
Ante U. C. cir. 224

DEAD [a]flies cause the ointment of the apothecary to
send forth a stinking savour: *so*
doth a little folly him that is in
reputation for wisdom *and* honour.
2 A wise man's heart *is* at his
right hand; but a fool's heart at
his left.
3 Yea also, when he that is a
fool walketh by the way, [b]his wisdom faileth

A. M. cir. 3027
B. C. cir. 977
Ante I. Olymp. cir. 201
Ante U. C. cir. 224

[a]Heb. *Flies of death* —— [b]Heb. *his heart*

NOTES ON CHAP. X

Verse 1. *Dead flies*] Any putrefaction spoils perfume; and so a foolish act ruins the character of him who has the reputation of being wise and good. Alas! alas! in an unguarded moment how many have tarnished the reputation which they were many years in acquiring! Hence, no man can be said to be safe, till he is taken to the paradise of God.

Verse 2. *A wise man's heart* is *at his right hand*] As the *right hand* is ordinarily the best exercised, strongest, and most ready, and the *left* the contrary, they show, 1. The command which the wise man has over his own mind, feelings, passions, &c., and the prudence with which he acts. And, 2. The want of prudence and management in the fool, who has no restraint on his passions, and no rule or guard upon his tongue. The *right hand* and the *left* are used in Scripture to express *good* and *evil*. The wise man is always employed in doing *good;* the fool, in nonsense or evil.

Verse 3. *When—a fool walketh by the way*]

A. M. cir. 3027
B. C. cir. 977
Ante I. Olymp. cir. 201
Ante U. C. cir. 224

him, [c]and he saith to every one
that he *is* a fool.
4 If the spirit of the ruler rise
up against thee, [d]leave not thy
place; for [e]yielding pacifieth great offences.
5 There is an evil *which* I have seen under
the sun, as an error *which* proceedeth [f]from
the ruler:
6 [g]Folly is set [h]in great dignity, and the
rich sit in low place.
7 I have seen servants [i]upon horses, and
princes walking as servants upon the earth.
8 [k]He that diggeth a pit shall fall into it;
and whoso breaketh a hedge, a
serpent shall bite him.
9 Whoso removeth stones shall
be hurt therewith; *and* he that
cleaveth wood shall be endangered thereby.
10 If the iron be blunt, and he do not whet
the edge, then must he put to more strength:
but wisdom *is* profitable to direct.
11 Surely the serpent will bite [l]without enchantment; and a [m]babbler is no better.
12 [n]The words of a wise man's mouth *are*
[o]gracious; but [p]the lips of a fool will swallow
up himself.

---

[c]Prov. xiii. 16; xviii. 2——[d]Chap. viii. 3——[e]1 Sam. xxv. 24, &c.; Prov. xxv. 15——[f]Heb. *from before*. [g]Esth. iii. 1——[h]Heb. *in great heights*——[i]Prov. xix. 10; xxx. 22

[k]Psa. vii. 15; Prov. xxvi. 27——[l]Psa. lviii. 4, 5; Jer. viii. 17——[m]Heb. *the master of the tongue*——[n]Prov. x. 32; xii. 13——[o]Heb. *grace*——[p]Proverbs x. 14; xviii. 7

In every act of life, and in every company he frequents, the irreligious man shows what he is. Vanity, nonsense, and wickedness are his themes: so that in effect *he saith to every one* that *he* is *a fool*.

Verse 4. *If the spirit of the ruler rise up against thee*] If the king get incensed against thee.

Leave not thy place] Humble thyself before him, that is *thy place* and duty; for yielding to him, and not standing stoutly in thy defence, pacifieth *great offences:* and then, when his anger is appeased, he will hear any thing in thy justification, if thou have any thing to offer. This is good advice to a *child* in reference to his *parents*, and to an *inferior* of any kind in reference to his *superiors*.

Several of the fathers understood this differently, *If the spirit of the ruler*—the influence of Satan—*hath risen up against* and prevailed over thee, to bring thee into some sin; *leave not thy place*—do not despair of God's mercy; humble thyself before him, and seek pardon through the Son of his love, and this will be מרפא *marpe*, a *remedy* or *cure* even for חטאים גדולים *chataim gedolim*, great errors or sins. All this is true in itself, whether found in this text or not.

Verse 5. *An error* which *proceedeth from the ruler*] What this error in the ruler is, the two following verses point out: it is simply this—an injudicious distribution of offices, and raising people to places of trust and confidence, who are destitute of *merit*, are neither of *name* nor *family* to excite public confidence, and are without *property;* so that they have no *stake in the country*, and their only solicitude must naturally be to enrich themselves, and provide for their poor relatives. This is frequent in the governments of the world; and *favouritism* has often brought prosperous nations to the brink of ruin. *Folly* was set in *dignity;* the man of property, sense, and name, in a *low place. Servants*—menial men, *rode upon horses*—carried every thing with a high and proud hand; and *princes*,—the nobles of the people, were obliged *to walk by their sides*, and often from the state of things to become in effect *their servants*. This was often the case in this country, during the reign of *Thomas à Becket*, and *Cardinal Woolsey*. These insolent men lorded it over the whole nation; and the people and their gentry were raised or depressed according as their pride and caprice willed. And, through this kind of errors, not only a few sovereigns have had most uncomfortable and troublesome reigns, but some have even lost their lives.

Verse 8. *Whoso breaketh a hedge, a serpent shall bite him.*] While spoiling his neighbour's property, he himself may come to greater mischief: while pulling out the sticks, he may be bit by a serpent, who has his nest there. Some have supposed that נחש *nachash* here means a *thorn;* perhaps from the similarity of its *prick* to the serpent's *sting*. He who forces his way through a hedge will be pricked by the thorns.

Verse 9. *Whoso removeth stones*] This verse teaches care and caution. Whoever *pulls down* an old building is likely to be hurt by the stones; and in *cleaving wood* many accidents occur for want of sufficient caution.

Verse 10. *If the iron be blunt*] If the axe have lost its edge, and the owner do not sharpen it, he must apply the more strength to make it cut: but the *wisdom that is profitable to direct* will teach him, that he should *whet* his *axe*, and *spare* his *strength*. Thus, without wisdom and understanding we cannot go profitably through the meanest concerns in life.

Verse 11. *The serpent will bite without enchantment*] בלא לחש *belo lachash*, without *hissing*. As a snake may bite before it hiss, so also will the babbler, talkative person, or calumniator. Without directly speaking evil, he insinuates, by innuendoes, things injurious to the reputation of his neighbour. **Gif the eddir bite in silence, nothing lasse than he hath that pribily backbiteth.**—Old MS. Bible. "A babbler of his tongue is no better than a serpent that styngeth without hyssynge."—COVERDALE. The *moral* of this saying is simply this: A calumniator is as dangerous as a poisonous serpent; and from the envenomed tongue of slander and detraction no man is safe. The comparing the serpent, נחש *nachash*, to a *babbler*, has something singular in it. I have already supposed that the creature mentioned, Gen. iii. 1, was of the genus *simia*. This has been ridiculed, but not *disproved*.

Verse 12. *The words of a wise man's mouth*]

A. M. cir. 3027
B. C. cir. 977
Ante I. Olymp. cir. 201
Ante U. C. cir. 224

13 The beginning of the words
of his mouth *is* foolishness: and
the end of [q]his talk *is* mischievous madness.
14 [r]A fool also [s]is full of words: a man
cannot tell what shall be; and [t]what shall be
after him, who can tell him?
15 The labor of the foolish wearieth every
one of them, because he knoweth not how to
go to the city.
16 [u]Wo to thee, O land, when thy king *is*
a child, and thy princes eat in the morning!
17 Blessed *art* thou, O land, when thy king
is the son of nobles, and [v]thy princes eat in
due season, for strength, and not
for drunkenness!
18 By much slothfulness the
building decayeth; and through
idleness of the hands the house droppeth
through.
19 A feast is made for laughter, and [w]wine
[x]maketh merry: but money answereth all
things.
20 [y]Curse not the king, no, not in thy
[z]thought; and curse not the rich in thy bed-
chamber: for a bird of the air shall carry the
voice, and that which hath wings shall tell the
matter.

A. M. cir. 3027
B. C. cir. 977
Ante I. Olymp. cir. 201
Ante U. C. cir. 224

[q]Heb. *his mouth*——[r]Prov. xv. 2——[s]Heb. *multiplieth words*——[t]Chap. iii. 22; vi. 12; viii. 7——[u]Isa. iii. 4, 5, 12; v. 11——[v]Prov. xxxi. 4

[w]Psalm civ. 15——[x]Heb. *maketh glad the life*——[y]Exodus xxii. 28; Acts xxiii. 5——[z]Or, *conscience*, figure like, Luke xix. 40

Every thing that proceeds from him is decent and orderly; creditable to himself, and acceptable to those who hear him. But the *lips of the fool*, which speak every thing at random, and have no understanding to guide them, are not only not pleasant to others, but often destructive to himself.

Verse 14. *A man cannot tell what shall be*] A foolish babbling man will talk on every subject, though he can say as little on the *past*, as he can on the *future*.

Verse 15. *He knoweth not how to go to the city.*] I suppose this to be a proverb: "He knows nothing; he does not know his way to the next village." He may labour; but for want of *judgment* he wearies himself to no purpose.

Verse 16. *Wo to thee, O land, when thy king* is *a child*] *Minorities* are, in general, very prejudicial to a state. Regents either disagree, and foment civil wars; or oppress the people. Various discordant interests are raised up in a state during a minority; and the young king, having been under the tutelage of interested men, acts *partially* and *injuriously* to the interests of the people when he comes to the throne; and this produces popular discontent, and a troubled reign.

Thy princes eat in the morning!] They do nothing in order; turn night into day, and day into night; sleep when they should wake, and wake when they should sleep; attending more to chamberings and banquetings, than to the concerns of the state.

Verse 17. *When thy king* is *the son of nobles*] Υἱος ἐλευθερων, the son of freemen; persons well acquainted with the principles of civil liberty, and who rule according to them.—*Septuagint.* Such a one as comes to the throne in a legitimate way, from an ancient regal family, whose right to the throne is incontestable. It requires such a long time to establish a regal right, that the state is in continual danger from *pretenders* and *usurpers*, where the king is not the son of nobles.

And thy princes eat in due season] All persons in places of trust for the public weal, from the king to the lowest public functionary, should know, that the public are exceedingly scandalized at repeated accounts of entertainments, where irregularity prevails, much money is expended, and no good done. These things are drawn into precedent, and quoted to countenance debauch in the inferior classes. The natural division of the day for necessary *repasts* is, Breakfast, *eight*, or *half after;* Dinner, *one*, or *half after;* Supper, *eight*, or *half after*. And these, or even *earliers* hours were formerly observed in these countries. Then we had scarcely any such thing as *gout*, and no *nervous disorders*.

In ancient nations the custom was to eat but *once;* and then about mid-day.

Verse 18. *By much slothfulness*] This is remarkably the case in some countries. Houses are not repaired till they almost fall about the ears of the inhabitants. We have an adage that applies to all such cases: "A stitch in time saves nine."

Verse 19. *A feast is made for laughter*] The object of it is to produce merriment, to banish care and concern of every kind. But who are they who make and frequent such places? Epicures and drunkards generally; such as those of whom *Horace* speaks:

Nos numerus sumus, et fruges consumere nati.
Epist. lib. i., ep. 2, ver. 27.

"Those whose names stand as indications of *men*, the *useless many;* and who appear to be born only to consume the produce of the soil."

But money answereth all] This saying has prevailed everywhere.

Scilicet uxorem *cum* dote, fidemque, *et* amicos,
Et genus, *et* formam regina pecunia *donat;*
Ac bene nummatum *decorat* Suadela, Venusque.
Hor. Ep. lib. i., ep. 6, ver. 36.

"For *gold*, the *sovereign* queen of *all below*,
Friends, honour, birth, and *beauty*, can bestow.
The goddess of *persuasion* forms her train;
And *Venus* decks the *well-bemonied* swain."
Francis.

Verse 20. *Curse not the king*] Do not permit thyself even to think evil of the king; lest thy tongue at some time give vent to thy thoughts, and so thou be chargeable with treason.

For a bird of the air shall carry the voice] Does he refer here to such fowls as the *carrier pigeon*, which were often used to carry letters under their wings to a great distance, and bring back answers? The *Targum* turns it curiously: "Do not speak evil of the king in thy conscience, nor in the secret of thy heart, nor in the most hidden place in thy house, curse not a wise man; for *Raziel* calls daily from heaven upon Mount Horeb, and his voice goes through the whole world; and *Elijah*, the great priest, goes, flying through the air like a winged eagle, and publishes the words which are spoken in secret by all the inhabitants of the earth."

Civil government is so peculiarly of God, that he will have it supported for the benefit of mankind; and those who attempt to disturb it are generally *marked* by his *strong disapprobation*. And though there have been multitudes of treasons hatched in the deepest secrecy; yet, through the providence of God, they have been discovered in the most singular manner. This shows God's care for government.

CHAPTER XI

Give alms to all, 1–4. *The works of God unknown to man*, 5. *Diligence necessary*, 6. *Prosperity frequently succeeded by adversity*, 7, 8. *There will be a day of judgment*, 9, 10.

A. M. cir. 3027
B. C. cir. 977
Ante I. Olymp. cir. 201
Ante U. C. cir. 224

CAST thy bread [a]upon [b]the
waters: [c]for thou shalt find
it after many days.
2 [d]Give a portion [e]to seven,
and also to eight; [f]for thou knowest not what
evil shall be upon the earth.
3 If the clouds be full of rain, they empty
themselves upon the earth: and if the tree fall
toward the south, or toward the
north, in the place where the tree
falleth, there it shall be.
4 He that observeth the wind
shall not sow; and he that regardeth the
clouds shall not reap.
5 As [g]thou knowest not what *is* the way
of the spirit, [h]*nor* how the bones *do grow* in

A. M. cir. 3027
B. C. cir. 977
Ante I. Olymp. cir. 201
Ante U. C. cir. 224

[a]See Isa. xxxii. 20——[b]Heb. *upon the face of the waters*——[c]Deut. xv. 10; Prov. xix. 17; Matt. x. 42; 2 Chron. ix. 8; Gal. vi. 9, 10; Heb. vi. 10

[d]Psa. cxii. 9; Luke vi. 30; 1 Tim. vi. 18, 19——[e]Mic. v. 5——[f]Eph. v. 16——[g]John iii. 8——[h]Psalm cxxxix. 14, 15

NOTES ON CHAP. XI

Verse 1. *Cast thy bread upon the waters*] An allusion to the *sowing of rice;* which was sown upon muddy ground, or ground covered with water, and trodden in by the feet of cattle: it thus took root, and grew, and was *found after many days* in a plentiful harvest. Give alms to the poor, and it will be as seed sown in good ground. God will cause thee *afterwards* to receive it with abundant increase. The *Targum* understands it of giving bread to poor sailors. The *Vulgate* and my *old Bible* have the same idea. **Send thi brede upon men passing waters.**

Verse 2. *Give a portion to seven*] Never cease giving while thou seest a person in distress, and hast wherewithal to relieve him.

Thou knowest not what evil] Such may be the change of times, that thou mayest yet stand in need of similar help thyself. *Do as thou wouldst be done by.*

Verse 3. *If the clouds be full of rain.*] Act as the clouds; when they are full they pour out their water indifferently on the *field* and on the *desert*. By giving charity indiscriminately, it may be that thou wilt often give it to the *unworthy;* but thou shouldst ever consider that he is an object of thy charity, who *appears* to be in real want; and better relieve or give to a *hundred* worthless persons, than pass by one who is in real distress.

Where the tree falleth, there it shall be.] Death is at no great distance; thou hast but a short time to do good. Acquire a heavenly *disposition* while here; for there will be no *change after this life.* If thou die in the love of God, and in the love of man, in that state wilt thou be found in the day of judgment. If a tree about to fall lean to the *north*, to the north it will fall; if to the *south*, it will fall to that *quarter*. In whatever *disposition* or *state of soul* thou diest, in that thou *wilt be found* in the *eternal world*. Death *refines nothing, purifies nothing, kills no sin, helps to no glory.* Let thy continual *bent* and *inclination* be to God, to holiness, to charity, to mercy, and to heaven: then, fall when thou mayest, thou wilt fall well.

Verse 4. *He that observeth the wind shall not sow*] The man that is too scrupulous is never likely to succeed in any thing. If a man neither plough nor sow till the weather is entirely to his mind, the season will in all probability pass before he will have done any thing: so, if thou be too nice in endeavouring to find out who are the *impostors* among those who *profess to be in want*, the real object may perish, whom otherwise thou mightest have relieved, and whose life might have been thereby saved. Those very punctilious and scrupulous people, who will *sift every thing* to the bottom in *every case*, and, before they will act, must be *fully satisfied* on all points, seldom do any good, and are themselves generally good for nothing. While they are *observing the clouds* and *the rain*, others have joined hands with God, and made a poor man live.

Verse 5. *As thou knowest not—the way of the spirit*] *Why* God should have permitted such an such persons to fall into want, and *how* they came into all their distresses, thou canst not tell, no more than thou canst how *their soul* is united to their body, how it came to *inform* that body, or how the *child* was formed in *the womb of its mother*. Nor canst thou discern the *end* which God has in view in these things. *He maketh all*, every thing is open to him; and take heed lest, while pretending motives of scrupulosity and prudence, in not relieving the distresses of those thou pre-

A. M. cir. 3027
B. C. cir. 977
Ante I. Olymp. cir. 201
Ante U. C. cir. 224

the womb of her that is with child: even so thou knowest not the works of God who maketh all.

6 In the morning sow thy seed, and in the evening withhold not thine hand: for thou knowest not whether [l]shall prosper, either this or that, or whether they both *shall be* alike good.

7 Truly the light *is* sweet, and a pleasant *thing it is* for the eyes [k]to behold the sun:

8 But if a man live many years, *and* rejoice in them all; yet let him remember the days of darkness: for they shall be many. All that cometh *is* vanity.

A. M. cir. 3027
B. C. cir. 977
Ante I. Olymp. cir. 201
Ante U. C. cir. 224

9 Rejoice, O young man, in thy youth; and let thy heart cheer thee in the days of thy youth, [l]and walk in the ways of thine heart, and in the sight of thine eyes: but know thou, that for all these *things* [m]God will bring thee into judgment.

10 Therefore remove [n]sorrow from thy heart and [o]put away evil from thy flesh: [p]for childhood and youth *are* vanity.

[i]Heb. *shall be right*——[k]Chap. vii. 11——[l]Num. xv. 39 [m]Chap. xii. 14; Rom. ii. 6–11

[n]Or, *anger*——[o]2 Cor. vii. 1; 2 Tim. ii. 22——[p]Psalm xxxix. 5

tendest to suspect to be *unworthy*, he does not *see* that a *love of money* is the *motive* of thy conduct, and a *want of the bowels of mercy* the *cause* why thou drivest this *suspected* beggar from thy door.

Verse 6. *In the morning sow thy seed*] Be ready at *all times* to show mercy; begin in the *morning*, continue till the *evening*. Thou knowest not the most worthy object; it is enough that God knoweth; and if thy motive be *good*, he will applaud and reward thee; not according to the *worthiness* or *unworthiness* of the *object* of thy charity, but according to the *motive* which induced thee to relieve him.

Verse 7. *Truly the light* is *sweet*] Life is dear to every man as the *light of the sun* is to the *eye*. A man would give all that he has for his life; and it is particularly dear to him when he is in ease and affluence: but let each remember that,

Verse 8. *If a man live many years*] And even have *prosperity* through the whole; yet the *days of darkness*—times of affliction, weakness, and perhaps *old age, will be many.* If he die not a *violent* death, which no man can wish, he will die a *lingering death;* and this is ordinarily attended with many *pains*, and many *sorrows;* therefore let him prepare to meet his God; and to carry this thought through life, that all must terminate in death. The writer of *Ecclesiasticus*, chap. vii. 36, has a good saying, similar to this: "Whatsoever thou takest in hand, remember *thy* END; and thou shalt never do amiss;" ουκ ἁμαρτησεις, *thou wilt not sin.*

Verse 9. *Rejoice, O young man, in thy youth*] *Youth* is devoid of cares; and, consequently, of many perplexities and distresses. Were it not so, we should have no *old men;* nay, perhaps not *one* even of *middle age*. It is in the order of a most gracious God, that the *young* should *rejoice* in their *youth;* but they should make such a moderate use of all their enjoyments, that they may not be confounded in the day of judgment. But, O young man, if thou wilt follow the propensities of thy *own heart*, the noisy mirth of the *fool*, and the dissipation of the *profligate—go on;* take thy full swing; but take this with thee, that "for all these things, God will judge thee;" and if the righteous are scarcely saved, where shall the *ungodly* and the *sinner* appear?

Verse 10. *Therefore remove sorrow*] כעס *caas, anger;* every kind of violent passion, all filthiness of *the flesh* and spirit. "Childhood and youth are vanity;" they pass away and come to nothing. Eternity alone is permanent; live for eternity.

CHAPTER XII

Youth should remember their Creator, 1. *A description of old age and its infirmities, with the causes of death and dissolution*, 2–9. *How the Preacher taught the people knowledge*, 9–11. *General directions, and conclusion of the work*, 12–14.

A. M. cir. 3027
B. C. cir. 977
Ante I. Olymp. cir. 201
Ante U. C. cir. 224

REMEMBER [a]now thy Creator in the days of thy youth, while the evil days come not, nor the years draw nigh, [b]when thou shalt say, I have no pleasure in them.

A. M. cir. 3027
B. C. cir. 977
Ante I. Olymp. cir. 201
Ante U. C. cir. 224

2 While the sun, or the light, or the moon, or the stars, be not

[a]Prov. xxii. 6; Lam. iii. 27

[b]See 2 Sam. xix. 35

NOTES ON CHAP. XII

Verse 1. *Remember thy Creator*] בוראיך *Boreeycha*, thy CREATORS. The word is most certainly in the *plural* number in all our common Hebrew Bibles; but it is in the *singular* number, בורך *Borecha*, in *one hundred and seventy-six* of Dr. *Kennicott's* MSS., and *ninety-six* of *De Rossi's;* in many *ancient editions;* and in all the ancient *versions.* There is no dependence on the *plural* form in most of the modern editions; though there are some edi-

A. M. cir. 3027 B. C. cir. 977 Ante I. Olymp. cir. 201 Ante U. C. cir. 224

darkened, nor the clouds return
after the rain;
3 In the day when the keepers
of the house shall tremble, and the
strong men shall bow themselves,
and [e]the grinders cease because
they are few, and those that look
out of the windows be darkened,

[e]Or, *the grinders fail, because they* grind *little*

tions of great worth which exhibit the word in this form, and among them the *Complutensian*, *Antwerp*, *Paris*, and *London* polyglots.

The evidence, therefore, that this text is supposed to give to the doctrine of the *ever blessed Trinity*, is but precarious, and on it little stress can be laid; and no man who loves truth would wish to support it by dubious witnesses. Injudicious men, by laying stress on texts dubious in themselves, and which may be interpreted a different way, greatly injure the true faith. Though such in their hearts may be friends to the orthodox faith, they are in fact its *worst friends*, and their assistance is such as helps their *adversaries*.

But what does the text say? It addresses the *youth* of both *sexes* throughout the creation; and says in effect:—

I. You are not your own, you have no right to yourselves. God made you; he is your *Creator:* he made you that you might be happy; but you can be happy only *in him*. And as he *created* you, so he *preserves* you; he *feeds, clothes, upholds* you. He has *made* you capable of *knowing*, *loving*, and *serving* him in this world, and of *enjoying* him in his own glory for ever. And when you had *undone yourselves* by *sin*, he sent his Son to *redeem* you by his blood; and he sends his *Spirit* to *enlighten, convince*, and *draw you* away from childishness, from vain and trifling, as well as from sinful, pursuits.

II. *Remember* him; consider that he is your *Creator*, your *loving* and affectionate *Father*. In youth *memory is* strong and tenacious; but, through the *perversion of the heart* by *sin*, young people can *remember any thing* better than GOD. If you get a kindness from a friend, you can *remember* that, and *feel gratitude* for it; and the *person* is therefore *endeared* to you. Have any ever given you such *benefits* as your *Creator?* Your *body* and *soul* came from him; he gave you your *eyes, ears, tongue, hands, feet*, &c. What blessings are these! how *excellent!* how *useful!* how *necessary!* and will you *forget* HIM?

III. *Remember him in thy* YOUTH, in order that you may have a *long* and *blessed life*, that you may be saved from the corruption and misery into which young people in general run; and the evils they entail upon themselves by giving way to the sinful propensities of their own hearts. As in youth all the powers are more active and vigorous, so they are capable of superior enjoyments. *Faith, hope*, and *love*, will be in their best *tenor*, their greatest *vigour*, and in their *least encumbered state*. And it will be *easier* for you to *believe, hope, pray, love, obey*, and *bear your cross*, than it can be in old age and decrepitude.

IV. *Remember him* NOW, in *this part* of your *youth*—you have no certainty of life; *now* is yours, to-morrow may not be. You *are* young; but you may *never* be old. *Now* he waits to be gracious; *to-morrow* may be too late. God *now* calls; his *Spirit* now strives; his *ministers* now exhort. You have now *health;* sin has not now *so much dominion over you* as it will have, increasing by every future moment, if you do not give up your hearts to your Maker.

V. There is another consideration which should weigh with you: should you live to *old age*, it is a very disadvantageous time to begin to serve the Lord in. *Infirmities* press down both body and mind, and the oppressed nature has enough to do to bear its own infirmities; and as there is *little time*, so there is generally *less inclination*, to call upon the Lord. *Evil habits* are strengthened by long continuance; and every desire and appetite in the soul is a strong hold for Satan. There is little time for repentance, little for faith, *none* for obedience. The *evil days* are *come*, and the *years* in which you will feelingly be obliged to say, Alas! "we have no pleasure in them;" and, what is worse, the heart is hardened through the *deceitfulness of sin*.

Verse 2. *While the sun, or the light, or the moon, or the stars, be not darkened*] i. e., in the SPRING, prime, and prosperity of life.

Nor the clouds return] The infirmities of old age of which WINTER is a proper emblem, as *spring* is of *youth*, in the former clause of this verse.

Verse 3. *In the day when the keepers of the house*] The BODY of *man* is here compared to a HOUSE:—mark the metaphors and their propriety.

1. *The keepers shall tremble*—the *hands* become paralytic, as is constantly the case, less or more, in old age.

2. *The strong men shall bow*] The *legs* become feeble, and unable to support the weight of the body.

3. *The grinders cease because they are few*] The *teeth* decayed and mostly lost; the *few* that remain being incapable of properly masticating hard substances or animal food. And so they *cease;* for soft or pulpy substances, which are requisite then, require little or no mastication; and these aliments become their ordinary food.

4. *Those that look out of the windows*] The *optic nerves*, which receive impressions, through the medium of the different *humours* of the eye, from surrounding objects—they *are darkened;* the humours becoming *thick, flat*, and *turbid*, they are no longer capable of transmitting those images in that clear, distinct manner, as formerly. There may be an allusion here to the *pupil* of the eye. Look into it, and you will see *your own image* in extreme minature *looking out* upon you; and hence it has its name *pupillus*, a *little child*, from *pupus*, a *baby*, a *doll;* because the image in the eye resembles such. The *optic nerve* being seated at the *bottom of the eye*, has the images of surrounding objects painted upon it; *it looks out through the different humors.* The different membranes and humours which compose the eye, and serve for vision, are, the *tunica con-*

A. M. cir. 3027 B. C. cir. 977 Ante I. Olymp. cir. 201 Ante U. C. cir. 224

4 And the [d]doors shall be shut
in the streets, when the sound of
the grinding is low, and he shall
rise up at the voice of the bird,
and all [e]the daughters of music shall be
brought low;
5 Also *when* they shall be afraid of *that*
which is high, and fears *shall be*
in the way, and the almond tree
shall flourish, and the grasshopper shall be a burden, and
desire shall fail: because man goeth to [f]his
long home, and [g]the mourners go about the
streets:

A. M. cir. 3027 B. C. cir. 977 Ante I. Olymp. cir. 201 Ante U. C. cir. 224

[d]Psa. cxli. 3——[e]2 Sam. xix. 35

[f]Job xvii. 13——[g]Jer. ix. 17

junctiva, the *tunica sclerotica*, the *cornea*, the *iris*, the *pupil*, the *choroides*, and the *retina*. The *iris* is perforated to admit the rays of light, and is called the *pupil;* the *retina* is a diffusion of the *optic nerve* in the bottom of the eye, on which the images are painted or impressed that give us the *sensation* we term *sight* or *vision*. All these *membranes, humours*, and *nerves*, are more or less *impaired*, thickened, or rendered *opaque*, by *old age;* expressed by the metaphor, "Those that look out of the windows are darkened."

Verse 4. *And the doors shall be shut in the streets*]

5. The *doors*—the *lips*, which are the *doors* by which the *mouth* is *closed*.

6. *Be shut in the streets*] The *cavities* of the *cheeks* and *jaws*, through which the food may be said to *travel* before it is fitted by *mastication* or chewing to go down the *œsophagus* into the stomach. The *doors* or *lips* are *shut* to hinder the food in chewing from dropping out; as the *teeth*, which prevented that before, are now lost.

7. *The sound of the grinding is low*] Little noise is now made in eating, because the *teeth* are either lost, or become so infirm as not to suffer their being pressed close together; and the mouth being kept shut to hinder the food from dropping out, the *sound* in eating is scarcely heard. The *teeth* are divided into *three* kinds:—1. The *dentes incisores*, or *cutting teeth*, in the front of the jaw. 2. The *dentes canini*, or *dog teeth*, those in the sides of the jaws, for *gnawing*, or *tearing* and *separating* hard or *tough substances*. And, 3. *Dentes molares*, or *grinding teeth*, the posterior or *double teeth*, in both jaws, generally termed the *grinders;* because their office is to *grind down* the substances that have been *cut* by the *fore teeth, separated* into their parts or fibres by the *dog teeth*, and thus prepare it for digestion in the stomach.

8. *He shall rise up at the voice of the bird*] His sleep is not *sound* as it used to be; he *slumbers* rather than *sleeps;* and the *crowing of the cock* awakes him. And so much difficulty does he find to *respire* while in bed, that he is glad of the dawn to rise up and get some relief. The chirping of the sparrow is sufficient to awake him.

9. *All the daughters of music shall be brought low*] The VOICE, that wonderful *instrument*, almost endless in the *strength* and *variety* of its *tones*, becomes *feeble* and *squeaking*, and merriment and pleasure are no more. The tones *emitted* are all of the *querulous* or *mournful* kind.

Verse 5. When *they shall be afraid* of that which is *high*]

10. Being so *feeble*, they are afraid to trust themselves to *ascend steps, stairs*, &c., without help. And when they *look upwards*, their heads turn giddy, and they are ready to fall.

11. *Fears* shall be *in the way*] They dare not walk *out*, lest they should meet some danger, which they have not *strength* to repel, nor *agility* to *escape*. A second childishness has taken place—apprehensions, fears, terrors, and weakness.

12. *The almond tree shall flourish*] ינאץ *yenaets*, not *flourish*, but *fall off*. The *hair* begins to change, first *gray*, then *white;* it having no longer that supply of nutritive juices which it once had, this *animal vegetable withers* and *falls off*. The *almond tree*, having *white flowers*, is a fit emblem of a *hoary head;* or as *Hasselquist* says, who observed the tree in full flower in Judea, "like an old man with his *white locks*."

13. *The grasshopper shall be a burden*] Even such an inconsiderable thing as a *locust*, or a very small *insect*, shall be deemed burdensome, their strength is so exceedingly diminished. In cases of the *gout*, especially in *old men*, the *shadow* of a person passing by puts them to acute pain! How much less can they bear the smallest pressure! But probably the words refer to the man himself, who, bent at the loins, and his arms hanging down, exhibits some caricature of the animal in question. The poor grasshopper has become a burden to himself. Another interpretation has been given of the *grasshopper;* but I pass it by as impertinent and contemptible; such commentators appear as if they wished to render the text ridiculous.

14. *Desire shall fail*] Both *relish* and *appetite* for food, even the most *delicate*, that to which they were formerly so much *attached*, now *fails*. The *teeth* are no longer able to *masticate* the food, or have all *dropped out;* the stomach no longer able to digest any thing; and, as the body is no longer capable of receiving nourishment, *appetite* and *relish* necessarily fail.

15. *Because man goeth to his long home*] אל בית עולמו *el beith olamo*, "to the house of his age;" the place destined to receive him, when the *whole race* or *course* of life shall be *finished;* for עולם *olam* takes in the *whole course* or *duration of a thing;* if applied to a *dispensation*, such as the LAW, it takes in its whole *duration;* to the *life* of man, it takes in the *whole life;* to *time*, it includes its whole compass; to *eternity*, it expresses its infinite duration. So *old age* terminates the *olam*, the complete duration of human life; and when life is no longer desired, and nutrition ceases, the *olam* of man is terminated. My old MS. Bible translates it, **The hous of his everlastingness.**

16. He is just departing into the invisible world; and this is known by the *mourners going abount the streets*, the *long hollow groans* and *throat rattlings* which proceed from him;

A. M. cir. 3027
B. C. cir. 977
Ante I. Olymp. cir. 201
Ante U. C. cir. 224

6 Or ever the silver cord be
loosed, or the golden bowl be
broken, or the pitcher be broken
at the fountain, or the wheel
broken at the cistern.

7 [h]Then shall the dust return to the earth
as it was: [i]and the spirit shall return unto
God [k]who gave it.

8 [l]Vanity of vanities, saith the
Preacher, all *is* vanity.

9 And [m]moreover, because the
Preacher was wise, he still taught
the people knowledge; yea, he gave good
heed, and sought out, *and* [n]set in order many
proverbs.

10 The Preacher sought to find out [o]ac-

A. M. cir. 3027
B. C. cir. 977
Ante I. Olymp. cir. 201
Ante U. C. cir. 224

[h]Gen. iii. 19; Job xxxiv. 15; Psa. xc. 3——[i]Chap. iii. 21——[k]Num. xvi. 22; xxvii. 16; Job xxxiv. 14; Isa. lvii. 16; Zech. xii. 1

[l]Psa. lxii. 9; chap. i. 2——[m]Or, *the more wise the Preacher was*, &c.——[n]1 Kings iv. 32——[o]Hebrew, *words of delight*

the sure prognostications of the extreme *debility* and *speedy cessation* of those essential animal functions next mentioned.

Verse 6. *Or ever the silver cord be loosed*] We have already *had* all the *external* evidences of *old age*, with all its attendant infirmities; next follow what takes place *in* the body, in order to produce what is called *death*, or the separation of body and soul.

1. *The silver cord.*—The *medulla oblongata* or *spinal marrow*, from which all the nerves proceed, as itself does from the *brain*. This is termed a *cord*, from its *exact similitude* to one; and a *silver cord*, from its *colour*, as it strikingly exhibits the *silver gray;* and from its *preciousness.* This is said to be *loosed;* as the *nervous system* became a little before, and at the article of death, wholly debilitated. The last *loosing* being the *fall of the under jaw*, the invariable and never-failing evidence of *immediate death;* a few struggles more, and the soul is dismissed from its clay tenement.

2. *The golden bowl be broken*] The *brain* contained in the *cranium*, or skull, and enveloped with the membranes called the *dura* and *pia mater;* here called a *bowl*, from its resemblance to such a vessel, the *container* being put for the *contained;* and *golden* because of its *colour*, and because of its exceeding *preciousness*, as has been noticed in the former case. *Broken*—be rendered *unfit to perform its functions*, neither supplying nor distributing any *nervous energy.*

3. *Or the pitcher be broken at the fountain*] The *vena cava*, which brings back the blood to the *right ventricle* of the heart, here called the *fountain*, המבוע *hammabbua*, the *spring* whence the water *gushes up;* properly applied here to the heart, which by its *systole* and *diastole* (*contraction* and *expansion*) sends out, and afterwards receives back, the blood; for all the blood flows from, and returns back to, the heart.

4. *The wheel broken at the cistern*] The *great aorta*, which receives the blood from the *cistern*, the *left ventricle* of the heart, and distributes it to the different parts of the system. These may be said, as in the case of the *brain* above, to be *broken*, i. e., rendered useless; when, through the *loosening of the silver cord*, the total relaxation of the *nervous system*, the *heart* becomes incapable of *dilatation* and *contraction*, so that the blood, on its return to the *right ventricle* of the heart, is not *received*, nor that already contained in the *ventricles* propelled into the great *aorta*. The *wheel* is used in allusion to the Asiatic *wheels*, by which they raise water from their wells and tanks, and deep cisterns, for domestic purposes, or to irrigate the grounds. Thus, then, the blood becomes stagnate; the lungs cease to respire; the blood is no longer *oxidized;* all motion, voluntary and involuntary, ceases; the body, the house of the immortal spirit, is no longer tenantable, and the soul takes its flight into the eternal world. The man D—I—E—S! This is expressed in the following verse:—

Verse 7. *Then shall the dust return to the earth as it was: and the spirit shall return unto God*]

5. Putrefaction and solution take place; the whole mass becomes decomposed, and in process of time is reduced to dust, from which it was originally made; while the spirit, הרוח *haruach*, that spirit, which God at first breathed into the nostrils of man, when he in consequence became a LIVING SOUL, an intelligent, rational, discoursing animal, returns to God who gave it. Here the wise man makes a most evident distinction between the body and the soul: they are not the same; they are not both matter. The body, which is matter, returns to dust, its original; but the spirit, which is *immaterial*, returns to God. It is impossible that two natures can be more distinct, or more emphatically distinguished. The author of this book was not a materialist.

Thus ends this affecting, yet elegant and finished, picture of OLD AGE and DEATH. See a description of old age similar, but much inferior, to this, in the Agamemnon of Æschylus, v. 76-82.

It has been often remarked that the *circulation of the blood*, which has been deemed a modern discovery by our countryman Dr. *Harvey*, in 1616, was known to Solomon, or whoever was the author of this book: the *fountains*, *cisterns*, *pitcher*, and *wheel*, giving sufficient countenance to the conclusion.

Verse 8. This affecting and minute description of *old age* and *death* is concluded by the author with the same exclamation by which he began this book: *O vanity of vanities*, saith Koheleth, *all is vanity.* Now that man, the masterpiece of God's creation, the delegated sovereign of this lower world, is *turned to dust*, what is there *stable* or worthy of contemplation besides? ALL—ALL is VANITY!

Verse 9. *Because the Preacher was wise, he still taught the people knowledge*] And in order to do this he took *good heed*—considered what would be most useful. *He set in order*—collected and arranged, many parables, probably alluding to the book over which we have already passed.

Verse 10. *He sought to find out acceptable words*] דברי חפץ *dibrey chephets*, words of desire, words of will; the best, the most suitable words; those which the people could best

A. M. cir. 3027 B. C. cir. 977 Ante I. Olymp. cir. 201 Ante U. C. cir. 224

ceptable words: *and that which*
was written *was* upright, *even*
words of truth.
11 The words of the wise *are*
as goads, and as nails fastened *by* the masters
of assemblies, *which* are given from one
shepherd.
12 And farther, by these, my son, be admonished: of making many books *there is* no
end; and [p]much [q]study *is* a
weariness of the flesh.
13 [r]Let us hear the conclusion
of the whole matter: [s]Fear God,
and keep his commandments: for this *is* the
whole *duty* of man.
14 For [t]God shall bring every work into
judgment, with every secret thing, whether *it*
be good, or whether *it be* evil.

[p]Chap. i. 18——[q]Or, *reading*——[r]Or, *The end of the matter, even all that hath been heard,* is——[s]Deut. vi. 2; x. 12

[t]Chap. xi. 9; Matt. xii. 36; Acts xvii. 30, 31; Rom. ii. 16 xiv. 10, 12; 1 Cor. iv. 5; 2 Cor. v. 10

understand. But these words were not such as might merely please the people; they were *words of truth;* such as came from God, and might lead them to him.

Verse 11. *The words of the wise*] Doctrines of faith, illustrated by suitable language, are *as nails fastened* by the *masters of assemblies,* בעלי אספות *baaley asuphoth,* the *masters of collections,* those who had made the best collections of this kind, the *matter* of which was of the most excellent nature; every saying sinking as deeply into the mind, by the *force* of the *truth* contained in it, as a *nail* well *pointed* does into a *board,* when *impelled by the hammer's force.* These *masters of collections* have been supposed to be public persons appointed by the *prince* himself, the *sole shepherd,* to see that nothing was put into the people's hands but what would be profitable for them to read; and that, when any wise man gave public instructions, a good *scribe* sat by to take down the words; and then the master examined what he *had written,* to see that it was *upright,* and that the words were *doctrines of truth.* These were something like our *licensers of the press;* but the existence of such is little more than conjecture.

After all, *masters of assemblies* may mean *public teachers;* that *which was written,* the oracles of God, out of which they instructed the people; the *one Shepherd,* God Almighty, from whom they received their authority and unction to preach the truth; and by the energy of whose *Spirit* the heavenly teaching was fastened in their hearts, as a *well-driven nail* in a *sound piece of wood.*

Verse 12. *And farther, by these, my son, be admonished*] Hear such teachers, and receive their admonitions; and do not receive the grace of God in vain.

Of making many books there is *no end*] Two thousand years have elapsed since this was written; and since that time some millions of treatises have been added, on all kinds of subjects, to those which have gone before. The press is still groaning under and teeming with books, books innumerable; and no one subject is yet *exhausted,* notwithstanding all that has been written on it. And we who live in these *latter times* are no nearer an end, in the investigation of nature and its *properties;* of God, his attributes, his providence, his justice, and his mercy; of man, his animal life, his mode of nutrition and existence, and his soul and its powers; of Jesus, and the redemption by him; of eternity, and what it implies as exhibiting to us the pains of the cursed, and the glories of the blessed. Of several of these we know no more than they who have lived *five thousand* years before us; nor do we know any thing *certainly* by the *endless books* that have been published, except what bears the seal of the God of heaven, as published in that word which was declared by his Spirit.

And much study is *a weariness of the flesh.*] O how true is this! Let the trembling knees, the palsied hands, the darkened eyes, the aching heart, and the puzzled mind of every real student declare! And should none more worthy of the name of student be within reach to consult, the writer of this work is a proof in point.

Verse 13. After all, the sum of the great business of human life is comprised in this short sentence, on which some millions of books have been already written!

FEAR GOD, AND KEEP HIS COMMANDMENTS

1. Know that he is, and that he is a rewarder of them that diligently seek him. 2. Reverence him; pay him adoration. 3. Love him, that you may be happy.

Keep his commandments] They are contained in two words: 1. "Thou shalt love the Lord thy God with all thy heart;" 2. "And thy neighbour as thyself." Blessed be God, much reading and much study are not necessary to accomplish this, which is called כל האדם *col haadam,* the whole of Adam; the whole that God required of the *first man* and of *all his posterity.* But the *Gospel* of Jesus Christ must be understood to comprehend the full force of this short saying.

The word *duty,* added here by our translators, *spoils,* if not perverts, the sense.

The whole passage is rendered with great simplicity by *Coverdale:*—

"The same preacher was not wyse alone: but taught the people knowledge also. He gave good hede, sought out the grounde, and set forth many parables. His diligence was to fynde out acceptable wordes, right scripture, and the wordes of trueth. For the wordes of the wyse are like prickes and nales that go thorow, wherewith men are kepte together: for they are geven of one Shepherd onely. Therefore be warre (my sonne) that above these thou make thee not many and innumerable bookes, nor take dyverse doctrynes in hande, to weery thy body withall.

"Let us heare the conclucion of all thinges: Feare God, and kepe his comaundementes, for that toucheth all men; for God shall judge all workes and secrete thinges, whether they be good or evell."

I shall give the same from my old MS. Bible:—

And wan Ecclesiastes was most wiis he taght the peple, and told out what he had don, and enserchinge maade many parablis. He soght profitable wordis, and wrote most rigt sermons, and ful of trewth. The wordis of wismen as prickis and as nailis into herte pigt: that bi the counseyle of maisteris ben geven of oon scheperd. More thann thes sone myn, ne seche thou; of making many bokes is noon eend, and oft bethinking is tormenting of the flesche. Eend of spekinge alle togydir heere mee. Drede God, and his hestis kepe; that is eche man. Alle thingis that ben maad he schal bringen into dome, for eche erid thinge, whithir good or evyl it be.

Verse 14. *For God shall bring every work into judgment*] This is the *reason* why we should "fear God and keep his commandments." 1. Because there will be a *day of judgment.* 2. Every soul of man shall stand at that bar. 3. God, the infinitely wise, the heart-searching God, will be judge. 4. He will bring to light every *secret thing*—all that has been done since the creation, by all men; whether *forgotten* or *registered;* whether *done in secret* or *in public.* 5. All the works of the *godly,* as well as all the works of the *wicked,* shall be judged in that day; the *good* which the *godly* strove to *conceal,* as well as the *evil* which the *wicked* endeavoured to *hide.* This, then, will be the *conclusion* of the whole mortal story. And although in this world *all is vanity;* yet *there,* "vanities will be vain no more." Every thing, whether *good* or *evil,* will have its own proper, stable, eternal *result.* O God! prepare the reader to give up his accounts with joy in that day! Amen.

Masoretic Notes

Number of verses, 222.
Middle verse, chap. vi. 10.
Sections, 4.

The Arabic subjoins this colophon:—"Praise be to God for ever and ever!"

"By the assistance of the Most High God this book of Ecclesiastes, which is vanity of vanities, written by Solomon the son of David, who reigned over the children of Israel, is completed."

The Syriac has, "The end of the book of Koheleth."

There are others, but they are of no importance.

INTRODUCTION

TO THE

CANTICLES, OR SONG OF SOLOMON

THE book before us is called in the Hebrew שיר השירים Shir Hashshirim, "The Song of Songs;" or, "An Ode of the Odes:" which might be understood, "An Ode *taken* or selected *from others* of a similar kind;" or, "An Ode the *most excellent* of all others;" this being an idiom common to the Hebrew language: e. g., the *God of gods* is the supreme God; the *Lord of lords*, the supreme Lord; the *King of kings*, the supreme King; the *heaven of heavens*, the supreme or highest heaven. It may therefore be designed to express "a song of the *utmost perfection; one of the best that existed, or had ever been penned.*" Perhaps the title may have a reference to the other poetical compositions of Solomon, which were no less than *one thousand and five;* and this was considered the *most excellent* of the whole, and the *only one* that remains, unless we suppose Solomon, with some of the Jews, to be the author of Psalms lxxii. and cxxvii.: but this cannot be proved.

There have been some doubts concerning the author of this book. Some of the rabbins supposed it to be the work of the prophet Isaiah; but this sentiment never gained much credit. Most have, without hesitation, attributed it to Solomon, whose name it bears; and if the book of Ecclesiastes be his, this will follow in course, as the *style* is exactly the same, allowing for the difference of the subject. Both books seem to have been written about the same *time*, and to have had the same *author*.

This book, if written by Solomon, could not have been written in his *old age*, as some have supposed the book of Ecclesiastes to have been; which sentiment is, I think, sufficiently disproved; for we find that long before Solomon's old age he had *three hundred* wives, and *seven hundred* concubines; but at the time this Song was written, Solomon had only *sixty* wives and *eighty* concubines. And the Song most certainly celebrates a *marriage;* whether between *Solomon* and the *daughter of Pharaoh*, or between him and some *Jewish princess*, has not been fully agreed on among critics and commentators. It is most likely to have been *a juvenile* or *comparatively juvenile* production; and indeed the high and glowing colouring, and the strength of the images, are full proofs of this. Though *Anacreon* made amatory odes when he was *bald-headed*, yet neither he nor *any one else*, humanly speaking, could have made such odes as the Canticles when stricken in years.

But to what denomination of writing do the Canticles belong? Are they mere *Odes*, or *Idyls*, or *Pastorals;* or are they an *Epithalamium?* Let us define these terms, and examine the Song of Solomon by them. 1. The Ode is generally understood to be a species of poetry containing sublime and important matter, always *sung*, or accompanied by the *harp*, or some proper *musical instrument*. 2. The Idyl implies a *short poem*, containing some *adventure*. 3. The Pastoral contains what belongs to *shepherds*, and their *occupations*. 4. The Epithalamium is the congratulatory song, sung to a new married pair, wishing them abundant blessings, a numerous and happy offspring, &c. Strictly speaking, the book of Canticles falls under neither of these descriptions: it is rather a composition *sui generis*, and seems to partake more of the nature of what we call a mask, than any thing else; an entertainment for the guests who attended the marriage ceremony, with a *dramatic cast* throughout the whole, though the *persons* who speak and act are not formally introduced. There are so many touches in the form and manner of this Song like those in the *Comus* of Milton, that it leads me to doubt whether the *English poet* has not taken the idea of his *mask* from the *Jewish.*

As to the *persons,* chiefly concerned, it is generally believed that *Solomon* and *Pharaoh's daughter* are the *bridegroom* and *bride;* with their proper *attendants,* viz., companions of the bridegroom, and companions of the bride, with certain *mutes,* who only appear, or are mentioned by others, without taking any particular part in the transactions.

But it is much more easy to be satisfied on the *species* of composition to which this book belongs, than on the *meaning* of the book itself. Is it to be understood in the *obvious manner* in which it presents itself? And are Solomon and his bride, their friends and companions, to be considered as mere *dramatis personæ?* Or are they *typical* or *representative* persons? Does this *marriage* represent a *celestial union?* Do the *speeches* of each contain Divine doctrines? Are the *metaphors,* taken from *earthly* things, to be understood of *spiritual* matters? In a word, does *Solomon* here represent *Jesus Christ?* Is the *daughter of Pharaoh* the *Christian Church;* or, according to some Roman Catholics, the Virgin Mary? Are *watchmen, vineyard-keepers, shepherds,* &c., the *ministers* of the *Gospel? Wine* and *various fruits,* the *influences* and *graces* of the Divine Spirit? &c., &c. How multitudinous and *positive* are the *affirmative* answers to these questions! And yet, though the many agree in the general principle, how various their expositions of the different parts of the piece! And where, all this time, is the *proof* that the *principle* is not misunderstood? As to *conjectures,* they are as *uncertain* as they are endless; and what one pious or learned man may *think* to be the meaning, is no proof to any other that he should make up his mind in the *same way.*

Let us for a moment consider the different opinions held on this book, without entering into the discussion of their propriety or impropriety. They are the following:—

I. It is a plain *epithalamium* on the marriage of Solomon with the *daughter of Pharaoh,* king of Egypt; and is to be understood in no other way.

II. It is an *allegory* relative to the conduct of God towards the Hebrews, in bringing them out of Egypt, through the wilderness to the Promised Land.

III. It is intended to represent the *incarnation* of Jesus Christ, or his marriage with human nature, in reference to its redemption.

IV. It represents Christ's love to the Church or elected souls, and their love to him.

V. It is an *allegorical poem* on the glories of *Jesus Christ* and the *Virgin Mary.*

VI. It is a collection of sacred idyls; the spiritual meaning of which is not agreed on.

Now each of these opinions has its powerful supporters, and each of these has reasons to offer for the support of the opinion which is espoused; and nothing but a direct revelation from God can show us which of these opinions is the correct one, or whether any of them are correct.

The *antiquity* of an opinion, if that be not founded on a *revelation from God,* is no evidence of its truth; for there are many ungodly opinions which are more than a *thousand* years old. And as to *great men* and *great names,* we find them enrolled and arranged on each side of all controversies. It may be asked, What do Christ and his apostles say of it?

1. If Jesus Christ or any of his apostles had referred to it as an *allegory,* and told us the *subject* which it pointed out, the matter would have been *plain:* we should then have had *data,* and had only to proceed in the way of *elucidation.* But we find nothing of this in the New Testament.

2. If they had referred to it as an *allegory,* without intimating the *meaning,* then we should be justified in searching everywhere for that meaning; and *conjecture* itself would have been legal, till we had arrived at some *self-testifying issue.*

3. If they had referred to it at all, in connection with *spiritual* subjects, then we should

have at once seen that it was to be *spiritually understood;* and, comparing spiritual things with spiritual, we must have humbly sought for its spiritual interpretation.

4. Had the *Supreme Being* been introduced, or referred to in any of his *essential attributes,* or by any of the names which he has been pleased to assume in his revelations to men, we should have then seen that the writer was a *spiritual man,* and wrote probably in reference to a *spiritual end;* and, that we should pass by or through his *letter,* in order to get to the *spirit* concealed under it. But none of these things appear in this book: the *name of God* is not found in it; nor is it *quoted* in the *New Testament.* As to certain *references* which its allegorical expositors suppose are made to it, either in the *Gospels, Epistles,* or *Apocalypse,* they are not *express,* and do not, by any thing *in* or *connected with* them, appear *unequivocally* to point out this book. And after all that has been said, I am fully of opinion it is not once referred to in the New Testament. But this is no proof of its not being *canonical,* as there are other books, on which there is no doubt, that are in the same predicament. But still, if it refer so distinctly to Christ and his Church, as some suppose, it certainly would not have been passed over by both evangelists and apostles without pointed and especial notice; and particularly if it points out the *love of Christ to his Church,* and the whole *economy* of God's working in reference to the salvation of the souls of men.

From all this it will appear to the intelligent reader, that the *spiritual meaning* of this book cannot easily be made out: 1. Because we do not know that it is an *allegory.* 2. If one, the *principles* on which such allegory is to be explained do nowhere appear.

Whom then are we to follow in the interpretation of this very singular book? The *Targumist,* who applies it to God and the *Hebrews,* in their journeyings from Egypt to the promised land? *Origen,* who made it a Christian allegory? *Apponius,* who spiritualized it? *Gregory the Great,* who in the main copied them? The *good man,* who in 1717, at Paris, so illustrated it as "to induce men to devote themselves to Jesus Christ and the Virgin Mary?" Mr. *Durham,* Mr. *Robotham,* Mr. *Ainsworth,* Mr. *Romaine,* and Dr. *Gill,* who endeavoured to prove that it concerns *Christ* and *the elect?* Or Mr. *Harmer* and others who acknowledge it to be an inimitable composition, and to be understood only of Solomon and Pharaoh's daughter? Or, finally, Dr. *Mason Good,* who considers it a collection of sacred idyls, the spiritual interpretation of which is not agreed on?

I had for a long time hesitated whether I should say any thing on this book; not because I did not think I understood its chief design and general meaning, for of this I really have no doubt, but because I did not understand it as a *spiritual allegory,* representing the *loves of Christ and his Church.* I must own I see no indubitable ground for this opinion. And is it of no moment whether the *doctrines* drawn from it, by those who allegorize and spiritualize it, be indubitably founded on it or not? The doctrines may be true in themselves, (which is indeed more than can be said of those of most of its interpreters,) but is it not a very *solemn,* and indeed *awful* thing to say, *This* is the *voice* of *Christ* to his *Church, This* is the *voice* of the *Church* to *Christ,* &c., &c., when there is *no proof* from God, nor from any other portion of his word, that these things are so?

It is much better, therefore, if explained or illustrated at all, to take it in its *literal* meaning, and explain it in its *general* sense. I say *general* sense, because there are many passages in it which should not be explained, if taken literally, the references being too delicate; and Eastern phraseology on such subjects is too vivid for European imaginations. Let any sensible and pious medical man read over this book, and, if at all acquainted with Asiatic phraseology, say whether it would be proper, even in medical language, to explain all the descriptions and allusions in this poem.

After what I have said on the difficulty of interpreting this book in a *spiritual* way, it would not be fair to withhold from the reader the general *arguments* on which the *theory* of its allegorical meaning is founded. The principal part of the commentators on this book, especially those who have made it their *separate* study, have in general taken it for granted that their mode of interpretation is incontrovertible; and have proceeded to spiritualize every *figure* and every *verse* as if they had a Divine warrant for all they have said. Their conduct is dangerous; and the result of their well-intentioned labours has been of very little service to the cause of *Christianity* in general, or to the interests of true *morality* in particular. By their mode of interpretation an undignified, not to say mean and carnal, language has been propagated among many well-meaning religious people, that has associated itself too much with *selfish* and *animal affections*, and created feelings that accorded little with the dignified spirituality of the religion of the Lord Jesus. I speak not from report; I speak from observation and experience, and observation not hastily made. The conviction on my mind and the conclusion to which I have conscientiously arrived, are the result of frequent examination, careful reading, and close thinking, at intervals, for nearly *fifty* years; and however I may be *blamed* by some, and *pitied* by others, I must say, and I say it as fearlessly as I do conscientiously, that in this inimitably fine elegant Hebrew ode I see nothing of *Christ* and *his Church*, and nothing that appears to have been *intended* to be *thus* understood; and nothing, if applied in this way, that, *per se*, can promote the interests of vital godliness, or cause the simple and sincere not to "know Christ after the flesh." Here I conscientiously stand. May God help me!

The most rational view of the subject that I have seen is that taken by Mr. *Harmer*, who has indeed detailed and strengthened the arguments of his predecessors who have declared for the *spiritual* meaning. In his "Outlines of a Comment upon Solomon's Song," he supposes that the Song refers to *Solomon's marriage with the daughter of Pharaoh;* and that he had a *Jewish queen*, who is frequently referred to in the work; and that, unless this be allowed, there are several important passages in the book that cannot be understood; and indeed it is on this principle that he finds his chief ground for a *spiritual* and *allegorical* interpretation.

"Whatever was the intention of God," says he, "in bringing about this marriage, and in causing it to be celebrated in such an *extraordinary* manner, *by songs that were directed to be placed among the sacred writings*, it is certain there never was *any resemblance more striking* between the circumstances and transactions of any of the remarkable personages of the Old Testament and those of Messiah, than the *likeness* we may observe between *Solomon marrying a Gentile princess*, and making her *equal in honour and privileges* with his former *Jewish queen*, and in her being *frequently mentioned* afterwards in history, while the other is passed over in *total silence*, and the *conduct of the Messiah towards the Gentile and Jewish Churches*.

"The two remarkable things in the conduct of the Messiah towards the two Churches are the making the Gentiles *fellow heirs* of the same body and partakers of the promises, *without and difference;* and the *giving up to neglect* the Jewish Church, while that of the Gentiles has long flourished in great honour, and been the subject of many a history. St. Paul takes notice of both these circumstances with particular solemnity; of the first, in the *third* chapter of *Ephesians*, and elsewhere; of the other, in the *eleventh* chapter of *Romans*. They are points, then, that deserve great attention.

"They are both called *mysteries*, (Rom. xi. 25, Eph. iii. 3,) that is, things that had been concealed aforetime; but it by no means follows that there were no shadowy representations of these events in the preceding ages, only that they were not *clearly and expressly revealed.*

"*Kingdoms* and *cities* are frequently spoken of in holy writ as *women*. *Sacred* as well as secular bodies of men are represented under that image. *The universal Church* is spoken of under the notion of a *bride*, and the *Messiah* as her *husband*, Eph. v. The two Churches of Jews and Gentiles, or the Church under the Mosaic dispensation and the Church freed from those ceremonies, are represented as *two women*—the one formerly treated as the *principal wife;* and the second, as having been for a long time neglected, but afterwards producing a much more numerous issue than the first—by the prophet Isaiah in his *fifty-*

fourth chapter, according to the explanation St. Paul has given of that passage in Gal. iv. *Particular* Churches are mentioned after the same manner. So, concerning the Church at Corinth, St. Paul says, "I have espoused you to one husband, *that I may present you* as a chaste virgin to Christ;" 2 Cor. xi. 2.

"Since then it is common for the Scriptures to represent the Church of God under the notion of a *woman*, and the Messiah under that of a *husband;* since the two bodies of men —that which worshipped God according to the *Mosaic* rites, and that which observed them *not*—are compared to *two women;* and since the circumstances of these two Churches are such as I have given an account of from St. Paul, it must be acknowledged that there is a lively resemblance between Solomon's espousing the Egyptian princess and the Messiah's admitting the Gentiles to equal privileges with the Jews, whether it was or was not *designed* by God as an emblem and type of it: celebrated by his prophets for this cause, in holy songs; and those songs preserved with care to this day among writings of the *most sacred* kind on that account."

This is the whole of Mr. *Harmer's* argument; see his *Outlines*, pages 74–77. And *what* is proved by it? Nothing, in reference to this book. We know that the *Jewish people*, not the *Church* exclusively, are represented under the notion of a *woman afflicted*, and a *wife unfaithful*, *divorced*, and *forsaken*, &c.; and that the *Corinthians* were represented under the notion of a *chaste virgin espoused to Christ.* And we know that all this was done to show, that as the *marriage union* was the *closest*, *strictest*, and *most sacred* among men, the union of the soul to God, and its connection with him, might be most fitly represented by that union, and unfaithfulness to him by infidelity in the other case. But what has this to do with the *Canticles? Where is the intimation* that *Solomon* represents *Christ; Pharaoh's daughter*, the *Church* of the *Gentiles;* and the *Jewish queen*, the *Church* of the *Israelites?* Nowhere. Why then *assume* the thing that should be *proved;* and then build doctrines on it, and draw inferences from it, as if the *assumption* had been *demonstrated?*

Were this mode of interpretation to be applied to the Scriptures in general, (and why not, if legitimate here?) in what a state would religion soon be! Who could see any thing certain, determinate, and fixed in the meaning of the Divine oracles, when *fancy* and *imagination* must be the standard interpreters? God has *not* left his word to man's will in this way.

Every attempt, however well-intentioned, to revive this thriftless, not to say dangerous, *Origenian* method of seducing the Scriptures to particular creeds and purposes, should be regarded with jealousy; and nothing received as the *doctrine* of the Lord but what may be derived from those *plain words* of the Most High which lie most on a level with the capacities of mankind. Allegory, metaphor, and figures in general, where the design is clearly indicated, which is the case with all those employed by the sacred writers, may come in to *illustrate* and more forcibly to *apply* Divine truth; but to extort celestial meanings from *a whole book*, where no such *indication* is given, is most certainly not the way to arrive at the knowledge of the true God, and of Jesus Christ whom he has sent.

As the Jewish marriages were celebrated for *seven days,* it has been often observed that this Song divides itself into *seven periods*, and describes the *transactions* of each.

I. The FIRST *chapter* represents the *bridegroom* and *bride* as a *shepherd* and *shepherdess.* The bride asks her spouse where he takes his flock at noon, to preserve them from the excessive heat, lest she, in seeking him, should go astray into some strange pastures. After this day, the *first night* succeeds, which is pointed out chap. ii. 4, 5, 6. The bridegroom rises early in the morning, leaves the bride asleep, and goes hastily to the fields to his necessary occupations, ver. 7.

II. The SECOND *night* is pointed out chap. ii. 8, 9, &c. The bridegroom comes to the window of his spouse. She opens it, and he enters; and on the morrow, he returns to the fields to his flocks, ver. 17.

III. The THIRD *night*, the bridegroom having delayed his coming, the bride, being uneasy, arises from her bed, and goes out and inquires of the guards of the city, whether they had seen her beloved. She had not gone far from them till she met with him; she conducts him to her apartment, chap. iii. 1–4. Very early in the morning, he retires to the country, leaving the bride asleep, ver. 5. Afterwards she arises, and goes also to the fields, ver. 6.

The FOURTH *chapter* is an eulogium on the bride's beauty; and seems to be a conversation between the parties in the country. She invites the bridegroom to visit her, chap. v. 1. He leaves his friends, with whom he was feasting, and comes to the door of his spouse, ver. 2. She hesitating to let him in, he withdraws and goes to his garden. The bride follows; but, not knowing whither he had retired, asks the guards of the city, by whom she is maltreated; thence goes to the daughters of Jerusalem, and inquires of them, ver. 3, &c. At last she meets with him, chap. vi. 1, &c., and having spent some time with him, returns.

IV. Chap. vi. 9, points out the FOURTH *night* of the marriage.

V. The FIFTH *night* is pointed out chap. vii. 1, &c. The bridegroom gives his bride nearly the same praise and commendations which he had received from her in the preceding chapters; and early in the morning they go out together to the fields, ver. 11–13.

VI. The SIXTH *night* they pass at a village in the country, at the house of a person who is termed the bride's *mother*, chap. vii. 13, viii. 1–3. She invites her spouse thither, and promises to regale him with excellent fruits and choice wine; and early in the morning the bridegroom arises, leaves the bride asleep as formerly, and retires to the country, chap. viii. 4.

VII. The SEVENTH *night* is passed in the gardens. From chap. viii. 5, we have a series of dialogues between the bride and bridegroom. In the morning the bridegroom, having perceived that they were overheard, begs the bride to permit him to retire. She assents, ver. 13, 14, and exhorts him "to make haste, and be like a roe or a young hart on the mountains of spices."

This is the division, which is in the main most followed, especially by the best critics. But, besides this, several others have been proposed; and the reader, who wishes to enter more particularly into the subject, may consult Bishop *Bossuet*, *Calmet*, and Bishop *Lowth*. For my own part I doubt the propriety of this technical arrangement, and do not think that any thing of the kind was intended by the author. The division is not *obvious;* and therefore, in my apprehension, not *natural*. Of Dr. *Good's* division I shall speak below.

The *dramatis personæ* have been marked by some of the ancient interpreters, and the different portions of the whole Song appointed to several persons who are specified; and this division served for the *basis* of a *commentary*. The most regular division of this kind with which I have met is in a MS. of my own; the Bible which I have often quoted in my *comment*.

This, attributed by some to Wiclif, and by others to an older translator, I have carefully transcribed, with all the distinction of *parts* and *speeches*. The translation is very simple; and in many cases is much more faithful to the meaning of the *Hebrew* text, though in the main taken from the *Vulgate*, than our own version. It is a great curiosity, and certainly was never before printed; and is a fine specimen of our mother tongue as spoken in these countries in M.CCCLX., which may be about the date of this translation. On the common mode of interpretation I venture to assert that my readers will understand this Song ten times better from this translation and its *rubricks*, than they have ever done from all the forms in which it has been presented to them, to the present time. For this addition, I anticipate the thanks of every intelligent reader. The indications of the speakers, printed here in black letter, are all *rubrick*, in the beautiful original. I have added a short glossary on some of the more difficult or obsolete words, which will assist the less experienced reader, under whose notice such remote specimens of his own tongue seldom fall.

Between *twenty* and *thirty* years ago I received from India a *part* of the *Gitagovinda*, or

Songs of *Jayadeva.* This poet, the finest lyric poet of India, flourished before the Christian era; and the poem above, which makes the tenth book of the *Bhagavet,* was written professedly to celebrate the *loves* of *Chrishna* and *Radha,* or *the reciprocal attraction between the Divine goodness* and *the human soul.* The author leaves us in no doubt concerning the *design* of this little *pastoral drama;* for in the conclusion he thus speaks: "Whatever is delightful in the modes of music, *whatever is* DIVINE *in* MEDITATIONS on VISHNU, whatever is exquisite in the sweet art of love, whatever is graceful in the fine strains of poetry; all that, let the happy and wise learn from the Songs of Jayadeva, whose soul is united with the foot of *Narayan.*" *Vishnu* and *Narayan* are epithets of *Chrishna,* or the supreme incarnated god of the Hindoos. I found the general phraseology of this work, and its imagery as well as its *subject,* to correspond so much with those of the *Canticles,* that in the short notes which I wrote on this book in 1798, I proposed the illustration of many of its passages from the *Gitagovinda;* and was pleased to find, several years after, that my view of the subject had been confirmed by that encyclopædia of learning and science, Dr. *Mason Good,* who in his translation of the *Song of Songs,* with *critical notes,* published 1803, 8vo., has illustrated many passages from the *Gitagovinda.*

After having made a selection from this ancient poet for the illustration of the *Canticles,* I changed in some measure my purpose, and determined to give the whole work, and leave it to my readers to apply those passages which they might think best calculated to throw light upon a book which professedly has the *wisest of men* for its *author,* and according to the opinion of many, the most *important doctrines* of the Christian religion for its *subject.* I have not followed the *metrical version* which I received from India, but rather the *prose translation* of Sir William Jones; dividing it into *parts* and *verses,* after the model of the metrical version above mentioned; and adding verbal interpretations of the principal proper names and difficult terms which are contained in the work.

Having been long convinced that the *Chaldee Targum* is at once the oldest and most valuable *comment* upon this book, I have also added this. And here I might say that I have not only followed my own judgment, but that also of a very learned divine, Dr. *John Gill,* who, having preached *one hundred and twenty-two* sermons on the Song of Solomon, to the Baptist congregation at *Horsleydown,* near London, embodied them all in what he calls "*An Exposition*" of this book; to which he added a *translation of the Targum,* with short *explanatory notes,* folio, 1728. This was, however, suppressed in all the later editions of this exposition; but why, I cannot tell. This piece I give to my readers, and for the same reasons alleged by this very learned and excellent man himself:—

"At the end of this exposition I have given," says he, "a version of the *Targum* or *Chaldee paraphrase* upon the whole book, with some notes thereon, induced hereunto by the following reasons:

"*First,* to gratify the curiosity of some who, observing frequent mention and use made of it in my exposition, might be desirous of perusing the whole.

"*Secondly,* for the profitableness thereof. Our learned countryman, Mr. *Broughton,* says, this paraphrase is worth our study both for delight and profit. It expounds several passages of Scripture, and some in the *New Testament,* which I have directed to in my notes upon it; and I am persuaded that the writings of the Jews, the ancient Jews especially, would give us much light into the phraseology and sense of abundance of texts in the New Testament."

It is certain that this paraphrase does very often direct us, or at least confirm us, as to the *persons speaking* in this Song, to know which is of very great use in the explication of it. I shall add another reason: I believe the book of Canticles refers more to the *Jewish* than to the *Christian Church,* and I think the *Targumist* has made a more rational use of it than any of his successors.

I have thus places within the reach of all my readers THREE *especial helps* towards a good understanding of this book: 1. The ancient English translation, with its curious *dramatis personæ*. 2. The *Gitagovinda*, a most curious poem of the spiritual and allegorical kind. 3. The *Chaldee Targum*, the oldest comment on this Song. And I add my prayer, May God guide the reader into all truth, through Christ Jesus! Amen.

On this part of the subject it would be almost criminal not to mention, still more particularly, Dr. *Mason Good's translation* and *notes* on the *Song of Songs*. He has done much to elucidate its phraseology, and his notes are a treasury of critical learning. He considers the book to be a collection of *Sacred Idyls*, *twelve* in number; and his division is as follows:

IDYL I

Royal Bride,	Chap. I.	Verses 2, 3, 4.
Attendant Virgins,	——	Part of the fourth verse, beginning, "We will exult."
Royal Bride,	——	Verses 5, 6, 7.
Attendant Virgins,	——	—— 8.

IDYL II

King Solomon,	Chap. I.	Verses 9, 10, 11.
Royal Bride,	——	—— 12, 13, 14.
King Solomon.	——	—— 15.
Royal Bride,	——	—— 16, 17. Chap. II. Ver. 1.
King Solomon,	—— II.	2.
Royal Bride,		—— 3, 4, 5, 6, 7.

IDYL III

Royal Bride,	Chap. II.	Verses 8, 9, 10, 11, 12, 13, 14, 15, 16, 17.

IDYL IV

Royal Bride,	Chap. III.	Verses 1, 2, 3, 4, 5.

IDYL V

Scene, a Chiosk or Pavilion

Attendant Virgins,	Chap. III.	Verse 6.
Other Virgins,	——	—— 7, 8, 9, 10.
Royal Bride,		—— 11.
King Solomon,	—— IV.	—— 1, 2, 3, 4, 5, 6, 7.

IDYL VI

King Solomon,	Chap. IV.	Verses 8, 9, 10, 11, 12, 13, 14, 15.
Royal Bride,	——	—— 16.
King Solomon,	—— V.	—— 1.
Royal Bride,	——	Part of the first verse, beginning, "Eat, O my friends."

IDYL VII

Royal Bride,	Chap. V.	Verses 2, 3, 4, 5, 6, 7, 8.
Virgins,		9.
Royal Bride,	——	—— 10, 11, 12, 13, 14, 15, 16.
Virgins,	—— VI.	—— 1.
Royal Bride,	——	—— 2, 3.
King Solomon,	——	—— 4, 5, 6, 7, 8, 9, 10.

IDYL VIII

Royal Bride,	Chap. VI.	Verses 11, 12.
Virgins,		—— 13.
Royal Bride,	——	Part of the thirteenth verse, beginning, "What do you expect?"
Virgins,	——	Latter part of the thirteenth verse, beginning "Fortitude."

IDYL IX

Virgins,	Chap. VII.	Verses 1, 2, 3, 4, 5.
King Solomon,	——	—— 6, 7, 8, 9.

IDYL X

Royal Bride,	Chap. VII.	Verses 10, 11, 12, 13.
	—— VIII.	—— 1, 2, 3, 4

IDYL XI

Virgins,	Chap. VIII.	Verse 5.
King Solomon,	——	Part of the fifth verse, beginning, "I excited thee."
Royal Bride,		Verse 6.
King Solomon,		—— 7.

IDYL XII

Royal Bride,	Chap. VIII.	Verse 8.
King Solomon,	——	—— 9.
Royal Bride,	——	—— 10, 11, 12.
King Solomon,	——	—— 13.
Royal Bride,	——	—— 14.

There have been various opinions on this division; and many will still think that much remains yet to be done. Dr. *Good* considers it a *spiritual allegory;* but he does not attempt a spiritual application of any part of it. This perhaps is no mean proof of his good sense and judgment. I have acted in the same way, though not so convinced of its spirituality as Dr. *Good* appears to be. If I took it up in this way, I should explain it *according to my own creed*, as others have done according to *theirs;* and could I lay it down as a maxim, that it is to be spiritually interpreted in reference to the Christian Revelation, I might soon show my reader that it points out the infinite love of God to every human soul, in the incarnation of Christ; the means he uses to bring all mankind to an acquaintance with himself; the redemption of true believers from all unrighteousness, through the inspiration of God's Holy Spirit; their consequent holy life, and godly conversation; the calling of the Gentiles; the restoration of the Jews; and the final judgment! And my comment on this plan would have just as *solid a foundation* as those of my predecessors, from *Origen* to the present day.

To conclude: I advise all young ministers to avoid preaching on Solomon's Song. If they take a text out of it, to proclaim salvation to lost sinners, they must borrow their doctrines from other portions of Scripture, where all is *plain* and *pointed.* And why then leave such, and go out of their way to find allegorical meanings, taking a whole book by storm, and leaving the word of God to serve tables?

It is curious to see the manner in which many preachers and commentators attempt to expound this book. They first assume that the book refers to Christ and his Church; his union with human nature; his adoption of the Gentiles; and his everlasting love to elect souls, gathered out of both people; then take the words bride, bridegroom, spouse, love, watchmen, shepherds, tents, door, lock, &c., &c., and, finding some words either *similar* or *parallel,* in other parts of the sacred writings, which have *there* an allegorical meaning, contend that those *here* are to be similarly understood; and what is spoken of *those* apply to *these;* and thus, in fact, are explaining other passages of Scripture in their own way, while professing to explain the *Canticles!* What eminent talents, precious time, great pains, and industry, have been wasted in this way! One eminent scholar preaches to his congregation *one hundred and twenty-two* sermons upon the Song of Solomon, while all this time the evangelists and apostles have been comparatively forgotten; except only as they are referred to in illustration of the particular creed which such writers and preachers found on this book. How can they account to God for so much time spent on a tract which requires all their ingenuity and skill to make edifying, even on their own plan; a text of which they are not permitted to allege, in controversy, to prove the truth of any disputed doctrine? This, however, is not the fault of any particular *class* of ministers *exclusively;* several of all classes, though of some more than of others, have been found, less or more, labouring at this thriftless craft. Some, having preached on it during the whole of their ministry, have carried it, in a certain way, beyond the grave. An aged minister once told me, in a very solemn manner, that as God had been exceedingly merciful to him in saving his soul, and putting him into the ministry, thus accounting him faithful, he hoped that, when called to the Church above, if any *funeral sermon* were preached for him, it should be from Canticles, chap. i. 8: "Go thy way forth by the footsteps of the flock, and feed thy kids beside the shepherds' tents." That he could have applied these words to his own state, and the use which should be made of his life and death, I have no doubt; but who, from this text, would have chosen to pronounce the funeral oration?

I repeat it, and I wish to be heard by young ministers in particular, take the plainest texts when you attempt to convince men of sin, and build up believers on their most holy faith; and thus show rather your love for their souls than your dexterity in finding out spiritual meanings for obscure passages, on the true signification of which few, either among the learned or pious, are agreed.

I now, according to my promise, lay before my readers a transcript from my own MS. Bible, which is most probably the first translation of this *Song* that was ever made into the English language. I have *added,* for the sake of reference, the *figures* for the present division into verses, in the *margin:* these are not in the MS. The *dramatis personæ,* here in *black* letter, are in *red* in the MS. The *orthography* is scrupulously followed.

THE BOOK OF CANTICLES

[*Carefully transcribed from a MS. of the fourteenth century in the Editor's possession*]

Here begynnyth the Boke that is clepid Songis of Songis, of the Bridulis of Crist and of the Chirche.

CAP. I

The Chirche of the commyng of Crist, spekith seyinge,

2. Kysse he me with the cosse of his mouth.

The voice of the Fadir.

For better ben thi tetis thann wyn, smelling with best oynmentis.

The voice of the Chirche.

3. Oyle held oute thi name: there fore the yunge waxinge wymmen loviden thee ful myche.

The voice of the Chirche to Crist.

4. Drawe me after thee: we schul rennen in the smell of thin oynmentis.

The Chirche seyth of Crist.

Brogte me in the king into his celers. We schul ful out joyen and gladen in thee, myndful of thi tetis upon wyn, rigtmen loven thee.

The Chirche, of hir tribulacyouns.

5. O zee dogtris of Jerusalem, blac I am but
schappli, as the tabernaculis of cedar, as
6. the skynnes of Salomon. Willith not beholden that I be broun; for discolord me hath the sunne. The sones of my modir fogten agein me: thei setiden me keper in vynes: my vyne gerde I kepte not.

The voice of the Chirche to Crist.

7. Schewe thou to me whom lovith my soule, where thou gevest leswe, where thou lygge in myd day: lest to gou vagraunt I begynne aftir the flockis of thi felawes.

The voice of Crist to the Chirche.

8. Gif thou knowest not thee, O thou fair most among wymmen; go oute, and go awei after the steppis of thi flockis and feed thi goot beside the tabernaculis of schepperdis.
9. To my ryding in charis of Pharao, I licned
10. thee, O my leef! Fair ben thy cheekis as
11. of a turture; thi necke as brochis. Golden ribanes we schul maken to thee maad furrede with sylvir.

The voice of the Chirche, of Crist.

12. Whan the king was in his lying place, my
13. maad encense gave his smell. A bundlet of mirre my lemman is to me: between my
14. tetis he schal dwellen. The cluster of cypre tree my lemman to me: in the vynes of Engaddy.

The voice of Crist to the Chirche.

15. Loo thou art fair my leef, loo thou fair: thin eegen of culveris.

The voice of the Chirche to Crist.

16. Loo thou art fair my lemman, and seemli; oure bed is schynynge. The trees of oure hous as cedre; oure couplis cypresse.

CAP. II

The voice of Crist, of him and of the Chirche.

1, 2. I the floure of the feeld, and the lilie of al valeys, as a lilie among thornes, so my leef among dogtris.

The voice of the Chirche, of Crist.

3. As an apple tree among the trees of wodis; so my lemman among sones. Undir the schadewe of him whom I hadde desirede, I satte: and his fruyte sweet to my throote.
4. The king ladde me into his wyne celere, he
5. ordeynede in me charite. Undir leye gee me with floures, settith me about applis; for I languych for love.

The voice of the Chirche, of Crist.

6. The left hond of him undir myn heued; and his rigt hond schal clippen me.

The voice of Crist, of the Chirche.

7. I adjure gou, gee dogtris of Jerusalem, by the capretis and the hertis of feeldis, ne rere gee, ne makith my leef to waken, to the time that sche wille.

The voice of the Chirche, of Crist.

8. The voice of my lemman: Loo, this commith lepinge in mounteynes, and over
9. lepinge hilles. Liic is my lemman to an capret and to an hert, calf of hertis. Loo, he stant behinden our wall beholding by the wyndowis a fer loking thurg the latises.
10. Loo my lemman spekith to me: Riis go thou my leef, my culver my schappli and

11. cum. Now forsothe wynter passide, wedir
12. geed fro, and is gon awei. Floures ap-
peereden in our lond—tyme of cutting is
cummen; the voice of the turtur is herd in
13. oure londe. The fige tree brogt forth his
first figs: The vynes flouryng geven their
smell.

The voice of Crist to the Chirche.

14. Riis, go my leef, my schaply and cum thou
my culver, in the hoolis of the stoon wal.
Schewe thou to me thi face, and soun thi
voice in my eris; thi voice forsoth is sweet,
and thi face seemli.

The voice of Crist to the Chirche agein herytikis.

15. Take gee to us litil foxis that destruyen
vynes: for oure vyne flourede.

The voice of the Chirche, of Crist.

16. My loved to me, and I to him, that is fed
among lilies, to the tyme that the day
17. springe, and schadewis ben bowed in. Turne
agein; liic be thou O my lemman to a
capret, and to the hert, calf of hertis, upon
the mounteynes of Bether.

CAP. III

The voice of the Chirche gedred togyder of Gentilis.

1. In my litil bed by nigtis, I sougt whom
lovede my soule: I sogte him, and I founde
2. not. I schal riisen and gon aboute the
cytee, by tounes and streetis: I schal
sechen whom loveth my soule. I sogt him
3. and found not. There founden me the
wacheris that kepen the cytee.

The Chirche seith of Crist, to the Apostlis.

Wheyther whom loveth my soule, gee
4. seegen? A litil whan I hadde passid hem,
I foond whom lovith my soule; I heeld him
and I schal not leven to the tyme that I
bringe him into the hous of my moder:
and into the bed of hir that gat me.

The voice of Crist, of the Chirche.

5. I adjure gou ge dogtris of Jerusalim, by
capretis and hertis of feeldis, ne reire gee,
ne make gee my leef to waken to the tyme
that sche wille.

The Synagoge, of the Chirche.

6. What is sche this that stiegeth up by
desert, as a litil gerde of smoke of the
swote spyces of mirre and of cense, and of
al pymentarie poudre?

The voice of the Chirche, of Crist.

7. Loo the litil bed of Salomon; sixti stronge
men compassen, of the most strong men of
8. Israel; the whiche alle ben holdinge
swerdis; and to bataile best tagt. Of eche
oon the swerd upon his hip, for the nigt
dredis.

Of Crist, and of the Chirche chosen of Gentilis.

9. A chaier King Salomon maad to him of the
10. trees of Liban. His pileers, he maade
sylveren; the lenying place, golden; the
steiging up, purpure; the myddis he en-
ournede with charite, for the dogteris of
Jerusalem.

The voice of the Chirche, of Crist.

11. Goth out and seeth gee dogtris of Syon,
Kyng Salomon, in the dyademe in the
whiche crowned him his modir, in the dai
of spousing of him; and in the dai of glad-
neese of his herte.

CAP. IV

The voice of Crist to the Chirche.

1. How fair art thou my leef, hou fair ert
thou! Thyn eegen of culveris, with out it
that with ine forth is hid. Thin heris as
the flockis of Got, that steigiden up fro the
the hill of Galaad.
2. Thi teeth as the flockis of clippid scheep
that steigeden up fro the wasching place.
Alle with double lombis in the wombe; and
3. bareyn is not there among hem. Als a
furred sylken fylet, thi lippis, and thy fair
speche swote. Als the brekyng of a powmgarnet, so thy cheekis; without it, that
4. withine forth litt hid. Als the tour of David thi neck that is bild out with pynaclis.
A thousand scheeldis hangen of it al the
5. armour of strong men. Thi two tetis as
two yunge capretis twynglingis of the
6. capret, that ben fed in lilies: to the tyme
that the day brethe out, and the schadewis
ben in bowid. I schal gou to the mount of
7. mirre, and to the hill of cens. Al fair thou
art my leef, and wemm is not in thee.
8. Cumm thou fro Libane my spouse, cumm
fro Liban; cum thou schalt ben crowned
fro the heued of Amana; fro the frount of
Sannir, and of Ermon: fro the couchis
9. liouns, and the hill of Paradise. Thou hast
woundid myn herte myn suster, my spouse,
thou hast woundide myn herte in oon of
thin eegen: and in oon here of thi neck.
10. Hou fair ben thi tetis my suster, my spouse,
fairer ben thi tetis than wyne: and the
smell of thin oynmentis, over alle spices.
11. A dropping honycomb thy lippis, spouse:
honey and mylc undir thi tunge; and the
smell of thi clothing is, as the smell of
12. cens. A closid garden my suster, spouse; a
13. closid gardyn, a welle selid. Thin out send-
ingis is paradis of paumgarnetis: with thi
14. fruytis of applis. Of cypre tree with narde;
and narde with safrun, and fystula and
canel, with alle the trees of Liban, mirre
and aloes, with alle the first oynmentis.
15. The welle of gardynes, the pit of lyvyng
wateris that flowen with burre fro Liban,
Riis North, and cum South, blow thurg my
gardyn, and thei schul flowen swote spyces
of it.

CAP. V

The Chirche seith of Crist.

1. Cum my leef into his gardyn; and ete he
the fruyt of his applis.

Crist seith to the Chirche.

Cum into my gardyn, my sister, my spouse;
I have gadered my mirre with my swote
spices; I ette myn hony comb with myn
hony. I dranke my wyne with my mylc.

Crist to the Apostolis seith.

Etith gee freendis and drinkith: and gee
most derworth beth inwardli maad
2. drunken. I sleep and myn herte wakith.

The voice of the Chirche, of Crist.

The voice of my Lemman knockyng, open
thou to me my sustir, my leef, my culver,
my unwemmynd, for my heud is ful of
dewe, and my temple heris of the droopis
3. of nigtis. I spoylide me my coote; hou
schal I be clothid it? I waschide my feet,
4. hou schal I befoulen hem? my lemman
putte his hond bi the hool; my wombe
inwardly trembled at the touching of him.
5. I rose that I scholde opennen to my lemman. My hondis droppiden mirre; and my
6. fingris ful of best proved mirre. The lacche
of my dore, I opened to my lemman; and
he hadde bowid asyde and passide. My
soule is moltyn as my lemman spac. I
sogte and founde not him. I clepid and he
7. answered not to me. There founden me
keperis that gon about the cytee. Thei
smyten me, and woundiden me; takin my
8. mantill the keperis of the wallis. I adjure
gou ye dogtris of Jerusalem, gif gee schul
fynden my lemman, that gee telle to him,
for I languisch for love.

The voice of freendis seith to the Chirche.

9. Whiche is thy lemman of the loved, O thou
most fair of wymmen? Whiche is thy lemman of the loved? Forsoth thou hast ad-
jured us.

The voice of the Chirche of Crist seith to the freendis.

10. My lemman whiit and roodi chosen of thou-
11. sandis. His heued, best gold; his her as
bunchis of palmys, thick leved blac as a
12. crowe. His eegen as culveris upon litil
ryvers. Of wateris that ben waschid with
mylk; and sitte by the most full flowing of
13. wateris. The cheekis of litil flouris of
14. swote spices plaunted of pimentaries. His
lippis dropping the first myrre; the hondis
of him able to turnen about, golden and
full of jacynctis. His wombe is yvren
15. depertid by saphiris. His lippis marbil
pileeris, that ben foundid upon golden feet.
His fairness as of Lyban, and chosen as of
16. cedre. The throot of him most swote; and
he al desirable. Siche is my loved, and this
is my lemman, gee dogtris of Jerusalem.

CAP. VI

The voice of holi soulis of the Chirche.

1. Whider grede awei thi lemman? O thou
most fair of wymmen? Whither bowiden
doun thi leef, and we schul sechen him
with thee?

The voice of the Chirche, of Crist.

2. My leef went doun into his gardyne to the
floore of swote spices: that there he fed in
3. the gardynes, and lilies he gadired. I to
my leef, and my self, and my leef to me,
that is fed among lilies.

The voice of Crist to the Chirche.

4. Fair thou art my leef; swote and fair as
Jerusalem; ferful as the scheltrun of tentis
5. ordeyned. Turne awei thin eegen fro me;
for thei maden me to fleen awei. Thin
heris as the flockis of sche got, that apeer-
6. eden fro Galaad. Thi teeth as a floc of
scheep that steigeden up fro the wasching place; al with double fruyt of wombe
7. and bareyn there is not in hem. As the
rynde of powmgarnet; so thi cheekis with-
8. out thin hid thingis. Sixty ben queenes,
and eigty ben secundane wiives; and of
yunge waxe wymmen there is no noumbre.
9. Oon is my culver, my perfite: oon is to hir
modir, chosen of hir modir, chosen of hir
that gat hir. There seegen hir the dogtris
of Syon, and most blisful preisiden hir: the
queenes and secundarie wiives preisiden
10. hir. What is sche this that goth forth as
the morewtide, riising fair as the mone,
chosen as the sunne; ferful as of tentis
scheltrun ordeyned.

The voice of the Chirche, of the Synagoge.

11. I wente doun into my gardyne that I
schulde seen the applis of valeys; and beholden gif the vynes hadden flouride, and
12. the poumgarnetis hadden burriouned, I
wiste not, my soule distourbid me, for the
foure horsid cartis of Amynadab.

The voice of the Chirche to the faith of the Natyvyte.

13. Turne agein, turne agein Sunamytis; turne
agein, turne agein that we beholden thee.

The voice of Crist to the Chirche, of the Synagoge.

What schalt thou seen in the Sunamyte,
but queeris of tentis?

CAP. VII

The voice of Crist to the Chirche.

1. Hou fair ben thi goingis in schoon, thou
dogtir of the prince? the jointures of thin
hippis as broochis that ben forgid with
2. hond of the craftisman. Thin navel a turned
cuppe, never needing drinkis. Thi wombe
as an hepe of whete, of whete sett abouten
3. with lilies. Thy two tetis as two yunge
4. capretis, gemelwis of the sche capret. Thi
necke as an yvren tour; thin eegen as the
cysternys in Esebon; that ben in the gate
of the dogtir of the multitude. Thi noose
as the tour of Liban that beholdith ageins
5. damask. Thyn heued as Carmele, thin
heris of thin heued as the purpure of the
6. kyng joined to watir pipis. Hou faire thou
art, and hou seemli thou most derworthe
7. in delicis? Thi stature is lickened to a
palme tree; and thi tetis to clusteris.

Crist, of the holi crosse seith.

8. I seide I schal steigen into a palme tree;
and I schal taken the fruytis of it.

The voice of Crist to the Chirche.

And thi tetis schul ben as the clusteris of a
vyne, and the smel of thi mouth as the
smel of applis; and thi throot as best wyne.

The Chirche seith of Crist.

9. Worthi to my leef to drinken: to the lippis,
10. and to the teeth of him to chewen. I to my
leef and to me the turnynge of him.

The voice of the Chirche to Crist.

11. Cum my leef, go we out into the feeld,
12. dwelle we togydir in townes: erli riise we
to the vyne: see we gif the vyne flouride;
gif the floures, fruytis bringen forth; gif
13. the poumgarnetis flouren? The mandrag-
gis yeven their smel in oure yeatis. Alle
appls newe and olde my leef, I kepte to
thee.

CAP. VIII

The voice of Patriarkis, of Crist.

1. Who to me gevith thee my brother, souking
the tetis of my modir, that I fynde thee
aloon without forth and kysse thee, and
2. now, me, no man dispises. I schal taken
thee and leiden into the hous of my modir,
and into the bed place of hir that gat me.
There thou shalt tecken me, and I schal
geven to thee drinken of spycid wyne, and
3. of the must of my poumgarnetis. The left
hond of him undir my heued, and the rigt
hond of him schal clippen me.

The voice of Crist, of the Chirche.

4. I adjure you, gee dogtris of Jerusalem, ne
rere gee, ne makith to wake my leef, to the
tyme that sche will.

The voice of the Synagoge, of the Chirche.

5. What is sche this that steigith up fro
desert, flowing delices, fast clevyng upon
hir leef?

The voice of Crist to the Synagoge, of the holi Crosse.

Undir an apple tree I rered thee; there
schent is thi modir: there defoulid is sche
6. that gat thee. Putte me as a brooche upon
thi herte; putte me as a brooche upon thin
arme; for strong as deth, love: hard as
helle, gelousnesse: the lampis of it, the
7. lampis of fiir: and of flammes. Many
wateris schal not mown quenchen oute
charitee: ne floodis schal not throwen it
doun. Gif a man gif al the substaunce of
his hous for love, as nogt he dispisith it.

The voice of Crist, to the lynage of holi Chirche.

8. Our sustir a litil child; and tetis sche hath
not. What schal we done to oure sustir, in
the day whann sche is to be spoken to?
9. Gif a wal she is bilden we upon it sylveren
pynnaclis. Gif a dore sche is, joyn we it
with cedre tables.

The voice of the Chirche, answeeringe.

10. I, a wal; and my tetis as a tour; sythen I
am maad be fore thee as pese receyvynge.

The Synagoge, of the Chirche seith.

11. Vyne sche was to pesyble, in hir that hath
peplis; sche toke it to the keperis: a man
takith awei for the fruyte of it, a thousand
sylveren platis.

Crist to the Chirche seith.

12. My vyne before me is; a thousand thi
pesiblis; and two hundrith to hem that
13. kepen the fruytis of it. The whiche dwellest in gardynes freendis herkenen thee:
make me to heeren thi voice.

The voice of the Chirche to Crist.

14. Flee thou my leef, be thou lickened to a
capret, and to an hert, calf of hertis, upon
the mounteynes of swote spices.

Explicit Canticum

The above is taken, literatim, from an ancient MS. once the property of *Thomas à Woodstock*, youngest son of *Edward III.*, and brother to *Edward* the *Black Prince*.

Millbrook, *Feb.* 1, 1823.

EXPLANATION OF THE MOST DIFFICULT WORDS IN THE PRECEDING ANCIENT VERSION OF SOLOMON'S SONG

CHAP. I

Ver.	Word	Meaning
2	Cosse	kisses.
6	Fogten	fought.
7	Leswe	leisure or rest.
8	Goot	plural of *goat*.
9	Charis	chairs or chariots.
10	Leef	*love*, fem. as *lemman*, mas.
—	Turture	turtle dove.
11	Furrede	bordered.
13	Lemman	lover. See Leef.

CHAP. II

Ver.	Word	Meaning
4	Throote	throat.
5	Gee	ye.
6	Heued	head.
—	Clippen	embrace.
7	Capretis	young goats, kids.
—	Rere	rear or raise.

CHAP. III

Ver.	Word	Meaning
3	Sogt	sought, searched for.
4	Seegen	saw.
6	Stiegeth	ascendeth.
—	Gerde	rod or staff.
—	Swote	sweet.
—	Cense	incense.
—	Pymentarie	odoriferous.
8	Tagt	taught.
10	Enournede	strewed.

CHAP. IV

Ver.	Word	Meaning
1	Eegen	eyes.
2	Clipped	shorne.
3	Swote	sweet.
6	Inbowid	declined.
—	Cens	incense.
7	Wemm	defect, wart, mole.
8	Couchis	lairs or dens.
15	Burre	a rippling noise like waters.

CHAP. V

Ver.	Word	Meaning
1	Derworth	most beloved.
2	Culver	dove.
6	Moltyn	melted.
13	Pimentaries	perfumers, confectioners.
14	Yvren	ivory.

CHAP. VI

Ver.	Word	Meaning
4	Scheltrun	covering.
8	Secundane wiives	secondary wives, concubines.
9	Secundarie	*idem.*
10	Morewtide	to-morrow.
11	Burrouned	put forth buds.
13	Queeris	choirs.

CHAP. VII

Ver.	Word	Meaning
3	Gemelwis	twins.
4	Yate	gate.
5	Heris	hairs.
—	Purpure	purple.
8	Tetis	teats, breasts.
12	Gif	if.
13	Yeven	give.

CHAP. VIII

Ver.	Word	Meaning
2	Must	new wine.
3	Clippen	embrace.
5	Clevyng	holding on, leaning.
—	Schent	corrupted.
6	Gelousnesse	jealousy.
9	Pynnaclis	turrets, towers.
11	Pesyble	the peaceful man, i. e., Solomon.
13	Pesiblis	*idem.*

N. B.—There are many other words which, though they appear difficult, a little labour will make out as they differ more in the *spelling* than in the *sense*.

THE
SONG OF SOLOMON

Year from the Creation of the World, according to Archbishop Usher, 2990.—Year from the Flood of Noah, according to the common Hebrew text, 1334.—Year before the birth of Christ, 1010.—Year before the vulgar era of Christ's nativity, 1014.

CHAPTER I

The bride's love to her spouse, 1–5. *She confesses her unworthiness; desires to be directed to the flock,* 6, 7; *and she is directed to the shepherds' tents,* 8. *The bridegroom describes his bride, and shows how he will provide for her, and how comfortably they are accommodated,* 9–17.

A. M. cir. 2990
B. C. cir. 1014
Ante I. Olymp. cir. 238
Ante U. C. cir. 261

THE [a]song of songs, which
is Solomon's.
2 Let him kiss me with the
kisses of his mouth: [b]for [c]thy
love *is* better than wine.
3 Because of the savour of thy good [d]oint-
ments, thy name *is as* ointment poured forth,
therefore do the virgins love thee.

A. M. cir. 2990
B. C. cir. 1014
Ante I. Olymp. cir. 238
Ante U. C. cir. 261

4 Draw me, [e]we will run after
thee: the king [f]hath brought me
into his chambers: we will be
glad and rejoice in thee, we will
remember thy love more than wine: [g]the upright love thee.
5 I *am* black, but comely, O ye daughters of Jerusalem, as the tents of Ke-

[a]1 Kings iv. 32——[b]Chap. iv. 10——[c]Heb. *thy loves* [d]Hos. xi. 4; John vi. 44

[e]Phil. iii. 12, 13, 14——[f]Psa. xlv. 14, 15; John xiv. 2; Eph. ii. 6——[g]Or, *they love thee uprightly*

NOTES ON CHAP. I

Verse 1. *The song of songs*] A song of peculiar excellence. See the *Introduction*. The rabbins consider this superior to all songs. TEN *songs*, says the *Targum*, have been sung; but this excels them all. 1. The *first* was sung by *Adam* when his sin was pardoned. 2. The *second* was sung by Moses and the *Israelites* at the *Red Sea*. 3. The *third* was sung by the *Israelites* when they drank of the *rock* in the wilderness. 4. The *fourth* was sung by *Moses* when summoned to *depart* from this *world*. 5. The *fifth* was sung by *Joshua* when the *sun* and *moon stood still*. 6. The *sixth* was sung by *Deborah and Barak* after the defeat of *Sisera*. 7. The *seventh* was sung by *Hannah* when the Lord promised her a *son*. 8. The *eighth* was sung by *David* for all the *mercies* given him by God. 9. The *ninth* is the present, sung in the spirit of prophecy by *Solomon*. 10. The *tenth* is that which shall be sung by the *children of Israel* when restored from their *captivities*. See the *Targum*.

Verse 2. *Let him kiss me,* &c.] She speaks of the bridegroom in the *third* person, to testify her own *modesty*, and to show him the greater *respect*.

Thy love is *better than wine.*] The *versions* in general translate דדיך *dodeyca*, thy *breasts;* and they are said to represent, spiritually, the *Old* and *New Testaments*.

Verse 3. *Thy name* is as *ointment poured forth*] Ointments and perfumes were, and still are, in great request among the Asiatics. They occur constantly in their entertainments. Thy *name* is as refreshing to my heart, as the best perfumes diffused through a chamber are to the senses of the guests.

Therefore do the virgins love thee.] She means *herself;* but uses this *periphrasis* through modesty.

Verse 4. *Draw me*] Let me have the full assurance of thy affection.

We will run after thee] Speaking in the plural through modesty, while still *herself* is meant.

The king hath brought me] My spouse is a *potentate*, a mighty *king*, no ordinary person.

Into his chambers] He has favoured me with his utmost confidence.

The upright love thee.] The most perfect and accomplished find thee worthy of their highest esteem.

Verse 5. *I am black, but comely*] This is literally true of many of the Asiatic women; though *black* or *brown*, they are exquisitely beautiful. Many of the Egyptian women are still fine; but their *complexion* is much inferior to that of the Palestine females. Though black or swarthy in my complexion, yet am I *comely* —well proportioned in every part.

As the tents of Kedar] I am *tawny*, like the

A. M. cir. 2990
B. C. cir. 1014
Ante I. Olymp. cir. 238
Ante U. C. cir. 261

dar, as the curtains of Solomon.
6 Look not upon me, because
I *am* black, because the sun hath
looked upon me: my mother's children were
angry with me; they made me keeper of the
vineyards; *but* mine own vineyard have I
not kept.
7 Tell me, O thou whom my soul loveth,
where thou feedest, where thou makest *thy*
flock to rest at noon: for why should I be as
[h]one that turneth aside by the
flocks of thy companions?
8 If thou know not, [i]O thou
fairest among women, go thy
way forth by the footsteps of the flock,
and feed thy kids beside the shepherds'
tents.
9 I have compared thee, [k]O my love, [l]to
a company of horses in Pharaoh's chariots.
10 [m]Thy cheeks are comely with rows *of*
jewels, thy neck with chains *of gold.*

A. M. cir. 2990
B. C. cir. 1014
Ante I. Olymp. cir. 238
Ante U. C. cir. 261

[h]Or, *as one that is veiled*——[i]Chap. v. 9; vi. 1——[k]Chap. ii, 2, 10, 13; iv. 1, 7; v. 2; vi. 4; John xv. 14, 15——[l]2 Chronicles i. 16, 17——[m]Ezekiel xvi. 11, 12, 13

tents of the *Arabians*, and like the pavilions of Solomon, probably covered by a kind of *tanned cloth.* The *daughters of Jerusalem* are said to represent the *synagogue;* the *bride*, the *Church of Christ.* It is easy to find spiritual meanings: every *creed* will furnish them.

Verse 6. *Because the sun hath looked upon me*] The bride gives here certain reasons why she was *dark complexioned.* "The sun hath looked upon me." I am sunburnt, tanned by the sun; being obliged, perhaps, through some domestic jealously or uneasiness, to keep much without: "My mother's children were angry; they made me keeper of the vineyards." Here the *brown complexion* of the Egyptians is attributed to the influence of the *sun* or *climate.*

My mother's children were angry with me] Acted *severely.* The bringing of a *foreigner* to the throne would no doubt excite jealousy among the Jewish females; who, from their own superior complexion, national and religious advantages, might well suppose that Solomon should not have gone to *Egypt* for a wife and queen, while *Judea* could have furnished him with every kind of superior excellence.

Verse 7. *Tell me—where thou feedest*] This is spoken as if the parties were shepherds, or employed in the pastoral life. But how this would apply either to *Solomon*, or the *princes of Egypt*, is not easy to ascertain. Probably in the marriage festival there was something like our *masks*, in which persons of quality assumed rural characters and their employments. See that fine one composed by *Milton*, called Comus.

To rest at noon] In hot countries the shepherds and their flocks are obliged to retire to shelter during the burning heats of the noonday sun. This is common in all countries, in the summer heats, where *shelter* can be had.

One that turneth aside] As a *wanderer;* one who, not knowing where to find her companions, wanders fruitlessly in seeking them. It was customary for shepherds to *drive their flocks together* for the purpose of *conversing, playing on the pipe*, or having *trials of skill* in *poetry* or *music.* So Virgil:—

Forte sub arguta consederat ilice Daphnis
Compulerantque greges Corydon et Thyrsis in unum:
Thyrsis oves, Corydon distentas lacte capellas;
Ambo florentes ætatibus, Arcades ambo,
Et cantare pares, et respondere parati.
Ecl. vii. v. 1.

"Beneath a holm repair'd two jolly swains:
Their sheep and goats together grazed the plains;
Both young Arcadians, both alike inspired
To sing and answer as the song required."
Dryden.

This does not express the *sense* of the original: from the different pastures in which they had been accustomed to feed their flocks, *they drove their sheep and goats together* for the purpose mentioned in the pastoral; and, in course, returned to their respective pasturages, when their business was over.

Verse 8. *If thou know not*] This appears to be the reply of the *virgins.* They know not exactly; and therefore direct the bride to the *shepherds*, who would give information.

Verse 9. *I have compared thee—to a company of horses*] This may be translated, more literally, "I have compared thee לססתי *lesusathi*, to *my mare*, in the chariots or courses of Pharaoh;" and so the *versions* understood it. *Mares*, in preference to *horses*, were used both for riding and for chariots in the East. They are much *swifter*, endure more *hardship*, and will go longer *without food*, than either the *stallion* or the *gelding.* There is perhaps no brute creature in the world so beautiful as a fine well-bred horse or mare; and the finest woman in the universe, *Helen*, has been compared to a *horse in a Thessalian chariot*, by *Theocritus.* Idyl. xviii. ver. 28:—

Ὡδε και ἁ χρυσεα Ἑλενα διαφαινετ' εν ἡμιν,
Πιειρη, μεγαλη, ἁτ' ανεδραμεν ογμος αρουρᾳ,
Η καπῳ κυπαρισσος, η ἁρματι Θεσσαλος ἱππος.

"The golden Helen, tall and graceful, appears as distinguished among us as the furrow in the field, the cypress in the garden, or the *Thessalian horse in the chariot.*"

This passage amply justifies the Hebrew bard, in the simile before us. See Jer. vi. 2.

Verse 10. *Thy cheeks are comely*] *D'Arvieux* has remarked that "the Arabian ladies wear a great many *pearls* about their *necks* and *caps.* They have *gold chains* about their *necks* which hang down upon their *bosoms* with strings of coloured gauze; the gauze itself *bordered* with *zechins* and other pieces of *gold coin*, which hang upon their *foreheads* and both *cheeks.*

A. M. cir. 2990
B. C. cir. 1014
Ante I. Olymp. cir. 238
Ante U. C. cir. 261

11 We will make thee borders
of gold with studs of silver.
12 While the king *sitteth* at
his table, my spikenard sendeth
forth the smell thereof.
13 A bundle of myrrh *is* my well-beloved
unto me; he shall lie all night betwixt my
breasts.
14 My beloved *is* unto me *as* a cluster of
[n]camphire in the vineyards of
En-gedi.
15 [o]Behold, thou *art* fair, [p]my
love; behold, thou *art* fair; thou
hast dove's eyes.
16 Behold, thou *art* fair, my beloved, yea,
pleasant: also our bed *is* green.
17 The beams of our house *are* cedar, *and*
our [q]rafters of fir.

[n]Or, *cypress;* chap. iv. 13——[o]Chap. iv. 1; v. 12

[p]Or, *my companion*——[q]Or, *galleries*

The ordinary women wear *small silver coins*, with which they cover their *forehead-piece* like *fish scales*, as this is one of the principal ornaments of their faces." I have seen their *essence bottles* ornamented with festoons of *aspers*, and small pieces of silver *pearls*, *beads*, &c. One of these is now before me.

Verse 11. *Borders of gold*] I have observed several of the *handkerchiefs*, shawls, and head attire of the Eastern women, curiously and expensively worked in the *borders* with *gold* and *silver*, and variously coloured silk, which has a splendid effect.

Verse 12. *While the king* sitteth *at his table*] במסבו *bimsibbo*, in his *circle*, probably meaning the circle of his friends at the marriage festivals, or a *round table*.

Verse 13. *He shall lie all night betwixt my breasts.*] Mr. *Harmer* contends that it is the *bundle of myrrh* which the bride says shall *lie all night betwixt her breasts*, to which she compares the bridegroom, his name being as pleasing and refreshing to her mind, as the myrrh or *stacte* was to her senses, by its continual fragrance.

Verse 14. *A cluster of camphire*] Mr. *Hasselquist* supposes this to mean a *bunch of the Cyprus grape;* but this is supposed to mean a *shrub* so called, not any production of the isle of *Cypress;* the best kinds of which were found at *En-gedi*. This place belonged to the tribe of Judah.

Perhaps the poet alludes to the dark colour of the *hair*, which by the Greeks was not unfrequently compared to the *bunches of grapes;* by no means an unfit similitude for thick black clustering curls. The following lines represent the same idea:—

وفرع يزين اصتن اسود فاحم
اثيث كقن اللنخلة اطتعثكل

"The dark black locks that ornament her neck
Hang thick and clustering like the branchy palm."

Verse 15. *Thou* hast *doves' eyes*] The large and beautiful dove of Syria is supposed to be here referred to, the eyes of which are remarkably fine.

Verse 16. *Also our bed* is *green.*] ערש *eres*, from its use in several places of the Hebrew Bible, generally signifies a *mattress;* and here probably a *green bank* is meant, on which they sat down, being now on a walk in the country. Or it may mean a *bower* in a *garden*, or the nuptial bed.

Verse 17. *The beams of our house* are *cedar*] Perhaps it was under a *cedar tree*, whose vast limbs were interwoven with the ברות *beroth*, a tree of the *cypress* kind, where they now sat. And this natural bower recommended itself to the poet's attention by its strength, loftiness, and its affording them a *shady cover* and *cool retreat*. How natural to break out into the praise of a *bower*, by whose *branches* and *foliage* we are shielded from the intense heat of the sun! Even the *shelter of a great rock in a weary land* is celebrated by the pen of the first of *prophets* and greatest of *poets*, Isa. xxxii. 2.

With this chapter the *first* day of the marriage ceremonies is supposed to end.

CHAPTER II

A description of the bridegroom, and his love to the bride, 1–9. *A fine description of spring,* 10–13. *The mutual love of both,* 14–17.

A. M. cir. 2990
B. C. cir. 1014
Ante I. Olymp. cir. 238
Ante U. C. cir. 261

I AM the rose of Sharon, *and*
the lily of the valleys.
2 As the lily among thorns, so
is my love among the daughters.
3 As the apple tree among
the trees of the wood, so *is* my
beloved among the sons. [a]I
sat down under his shadow with

[a]Heb. *I delighted and sat down, &c.*

NOTES ON CHAP. II

Verse 1. *I* am *the rose of Sharon*] *Sharon* was a very fruitful place, where David's cattle were fed, 1 Chron. xxvii. 29. It is mentioned as a place of excellence, Isa. xxxv. 2, and as a place of flocks, Isa. lxv. 10. Perhaps it would be better, with almost all the *versions*, to translate, "I am the rose of the field." The bridegroom had just before called her *fair;* she with a becoming modesty, represents her beauty as nothing extraordinary, and compares herself to a *common flower of the field*. This, in the warmth of his affection, he denies, insisting that

A. M. cir. 2990 B. C. cir. 1014 Ante I. Olymp. cir. 238 Ante U. C. cir. 261

great delight, [b]and his fruit *was*
sweet to my [c]taste.
4 He brought me to the [d]banqueting house, and his banner
over me *was* love.
5 Stay me with flagons, [e]comfort me with
apples: for I *am* sick of love.
6 [f]His left hand *is* under my head, and his
right hand doth embrace me.
7 [g]I [h]charge you, O ye daughters of Jerusalem, by the roes, and by the hinds of the
field, that ye stir not up, nor awake *my* love,
till he please.

8 The voice of my beloved!
behold, he cometh leaping upon
the mountains, skipping upon
the hills.
9 [i]My beloved is like a roe, or a young
hart: behold, he standeth behind our wall, he
looketh forth at the windows, [k]showing himself through the lattice.
10 My beloved spake, and said unto me,
[l]Rise up, my love, my fair one, and come
away.
11 For, lo, the winter is past, the rain is
over *and* gone;

[b]Rev. xxii. 1, 2——[c]Heb. *palate*——[d]Heb. *house of wine*——[e]Heb. *straw me with apples*——[f]Chap. viii. 3

[g]Heb. *I adjure you*——[h]Chap. iii. 5; viii. 4——[i]Ver. 17——[k]Heb. *flourishing*——[l]Ver. 13

she as much surpasses all other maidens as the flower of the *lily* does the *bramble*, ver. 2.

Verse 3. *As the apple tree*] The bride returns the compliment, and says, *As the apple* or *citron tree is among the trees of the wood*, so is the bridegroom among all other men.

I sat down under his shadow] I am become his spouse, and my union with him makes me indescribably happy.

Verse 4. *He brought me to the banqueting house*] Literally, *the house of wine*. The ancients preserved their wine, not in barrels or dark cellars under ground, as we do, but in large *pitchers*, ranged against the wall in some upper apartment in the house, the place where they kept their most precious effects. We have a proof of this in HOMER:—

Ως φαν· ὁ δ' ὑψοροφον θαλαμον κατεβησατο πατρος
Ευρυν, ὁθι νητος χρυσος και χαλκος εκειτο,
Εσθης τ' εν χηλοισιν, ἁλις τ' ευωδες ελαιον.
Εν δε πιθοι οινοιο παλαιου ἡδυποτοιο
Εστασαν, ακρητον θειον ποτον εντος εχοντες,
'Εξειης ποτε τοιχον αρηροτες· ειποτ' Οδυσσευς
Οικαδε νοστησειε, και αλγεα πολλα μογησας.
Κληϊσται δ' επεσαν σανιδες πυκινως αραρυιαι,
Δικλιδες· εν δε γυνη ταμιη νυκτας τε και ημαρ
Εσχ', κ. τ. λ. Od. lib. ii., ver. 337.

Meantime the lofty rooms the prince surveys,
Where lay the *treasures* of th' Ithacian race.
Here, ruddy *brass* and *gold* refulgent blazed;
There, polished *chests embroider'd vestures* graced.
Here, *pots of oil* breathed forth a rich perfume;
There, *jars of wine* in rows adorn'd the dome.
(Pure flavorous wine, by gods in bounty given,
And worthy to exalt the feasts of heaven.)
Untouch'd they stood, till, his long labours o'er,
The great *Ulysses* reach'd his native shore.
A double strength of bars secured the gates;
Fast by the door wise *Euryclea* waits, &c.

POPE.

Verse 5. *Stay me with flagons*] I believe the original words mean some kind of *cordials* with which we are unacquainted. The *versions* in general understand some kind of *ointment* or *perfumes* by the first term. I suppose the good man was perfectly sincere who took this for his *text*, and, after having repeated, *Stay me with flagons, comfort me with apples, for I am sick of love* sat down, perfectly overwhelmed with his own feelings, and was not able to proceed! But while we admit such a person's sincerity, who can help questioning his judgment?

Verse 7. *I charge you—by the roes*] This was probably some rustic mode of adjuration. The verses themselves require little comment.

With this verse the *first night* of the *first day* is supposed to end.

Verse 8. *Behold, he cometh leaping*] This appears to be highly characteristic of the gambols of the shepherds, and points out the ecstasy with which those who were enamoured ran to their mates. It is supposed that the *second day's eclogue* begins at this verse. The author of what was then called *A New Translation of Solomon's Song*, observes, 1. The bride relates how the bridegroom, attended by his companions, had come under her window, and called upon her to come forth and enjoy the beauties of the spring, ver. 9, 10, 11, &c. 2. She then returns to her narration, chap. iii. 1. The bridegroom did not come according to her wishes. Night came on; she did not find him in her bed; she went out to seek him; found him, and brought him to her mother's pavilion, ver. 4; and then, as before, conjures the virgins not to disturb his repose, ver. 5.

Verse 9. *He standeth behind our wall*] This may refer to the *wall* by which the house was *surrounded*, the space between which and the house constituted the *court*. He was seen first *behind the wall*, and then in the *court;* and lastly came to the *window* of his bride's chamber.

Verse 11. *The winter is past*] Mr. *Harmer* has made some good collections on this part, from Drs. *Shaw* and *Russel*, which I shall transcribe. One part of the winter is distinguished from the rest of it by the people of the East, on account of the *severity of the cold*. At *Aleppo* it lasts about forty days, and is called by the natives *maurbanie*. I would propose it to the consideration of the learned, whether the word here used, and translated *winter*, may not be understood to mean what the *Aleppines* express by the term *maurbanie*. It occurs nowhere else in the Old Testament; and another word is used for the *rainy* part of the year in general. If this thought be admitted, it will greatly illustrate the words of the bridegroom: *Lo, the winter is past; the rain is over, and gone*. For then the last clause will not be explanatory of the first, and signify that the

A. M. cir. 2990
B. C. cir. 1014
Ante I. Olymp. cir. 238
Ante U. C. cir. 261

12 The flowers appear on the
earth; the time of the singing
of birds is come, and the voice
of the turtle is heard in our land;
13 The fig tree putteth forth her green figs,
and the vines *with* the tender grape give a
good smell. [m]Arise, my love, my fair one,
and come away.
14 O my dove, *that art* in the clefts of the
rock, in the secret *places* of the stairs, let me
see thy countenance, [n]let me hear thy voice;
for sweet *is* thy voice, and thy
countenance *is* comely.
15 Take us [o]the foxes, the
little foxes, that spoil the vines:
for our vines *have* tender grapes.
16 [p]My beloved *is* mine, and I *am* his: he
feedeth among the lilies.
17 [q]Until the day break, and the shadows
flee away, turn, my beloved, and be thou [r]like
a roe or a young hart upon the mountains [s]of
Bether.

A. M. cir. 2990
B. C. cir. 1014
Ante I. Olymp. cir. 238
Ante U. C. cir. 261

[m]Ver. 10——[n]Chap. viii. 13——[o]Psa. lxxx. 13; Ezek. xiii. 4; Luke xiii. 32

[p]Chap. vi. 3; vii. 10——[q]Chap. iv. 6——[r]Ver. 9; chap. viii. 14——[s]Or, *of division*

moist part of the year was entirely past; with which, Dr. *Russel* assures us, all pleasantness withdraws at *Aleppo;* but the words will import: "The *maurbanie* is past and over; the weather is become agreeably warm; the rain too is just ceased, and consequently hath left us the prospect of several days of serenity and undisturbed pleasantness."

The weather of Judea was in this respect, I presume, like that at *Algiers;* where, after two or three days of rain, there is usually, according to Dr. *Shaw*, "a week, a fortnight, or more, of fair and good weather. Of such a sort of cessation of rain alone, the bridegroom, methinks, is here to be understood; not of the absolute termination of the rainy season, and the *summer droughts* being come on. And if so, what can the time that is *past* mean but the *maurbanie?* Indeed, Dr. *Russel*, in giving us an account of the excursions of the English merchants at *Aleppo*, has undesignedly furnished us with a good comment on this and the two following verses. These gentlemen, it seems, dine abroad under a tent, in spring and autumn on Saturdays, and often on Wednesdays. They do the same during the good weather in winter; but they live at the gardens in April, and part of May. In the heat of the summer they dine at the gardens, as once or twice a week they dine under a tent in autumn and spring." The cold weather is not supposed by Solomon to have been long over, since it is distinctly mentioned; and the *Aleppines* make these incursions very early; the *narcissus* flowers during the whole of the *maurbanie;* the *hyacinths* and *violets* at least before it is quite over. The appearing of flowers, then, doth not mean the appearing of the first and earliest flowers, but must rather be understood of the earth's being covered with them; which at *Aleppo* is not till after the middle of *February*, a *small crane's bill* appearing on the banks of the river there about the middle of *February*, quickly after which comes a profusion of flowers. The *nightingales*, too, which are there in abundance, not only afford much pleasure by their songs in the gardens, but are also kept tame in the houses, and *let out* at a small rate to divert such as choose it in the city; so that no entertainments are made in the *spring* without a concert of these birds. No wonder, then, that *Solomon* makes the bridegroom speak of the singing of birds; and it teaches us what these birds are, which are expressly distinguished from turtle doves.

Verse 13. *The fig tree putteth forth her green figs*] The fig tree in Judea bears *double* crops; the first of which is ripe in *spring*. But the tree, as I have elsewhere observed, bears figs all the year through, in the climes congenial to it. That is, the fig tree has always *ripe* or *unripe* fruit on it. I never saw a healthy tree naked. But in the beginning of spring they grow fast, and become turgid.

The vines with *the tender grape*] The versions understand this of the *flowers* of the vine. These were formerly put into the new wine (2 lbs. to every cask) to give it a fine flavour.

Verse 14. *My dove—in the clefts of the rock*] He compares his bride hiding herself in her secret chambers and closets to a *dove* in the clefts of the rock.

Verse 15. *Take us the foxes*] That these were ruinous to vines all authors allow. They love the vine, and they are eaten in autumn in some countries, according to *Galen*, when they are very fat with eating the grapes. They abounded in Judea; and did most damage when the clusters were young and tender. It is likely that these are the words of the *bridegroom* to his *companions*, just as he was entering the apartment of his spouse. "Take care of the vineyard: set the traps for the foxes, which are spoiling the vines; and destroy their *young* as far as possible."

Verse 16. *My beloved* is *mine*] The words of the *bride* on his entering: "I am thy own; thou art wholly mine."

He feedeth among the lilies.] The odour with which he is surrounded is as fine as if he passed the night among the sweetest scented flowers.

Verse 17. *Until the day break*] Literally, *until the day breathe;* until the first dawn, which is usually accompanied with the most refreshing *breezes*.

The shadows flee away] Referring to the *evening* or *setting of the sun*, at which all *shadows* vanish.

The mountains of Bether.] Translated also *mountains of division*, supposed to mean the mountains of *Beth-horon*.

There was a place called *Bithron*, 2 Sam. ii. 29, on the other side of Jordan; and as the name signifies PARTITION, it might have had its name from the circumstance of its being divided or separated from Judea by the river Jordan.

With this chapter the *second night* is supposed to end.

CHAPTER III

The bride mentions the absence of her spouse, her search after him, and her ultimate success, 1–5. *A description of the bridegroom, his bed, chariot, &c.,* 6–11.

A. M. cir. 2990
B. C. cir. 1014
Ante I. Olymp. cir. 238
Ante U. C. cir. 261

BY [a]night on my bed I sought
him whom my soul loveth:
I sought him, but I found him
not.
2 I will rise now, and go about the city in
the streets, and in the broad ways I will seek
him whom my soul loveth: I sought him, but
I found him not.
3 [b]The watchmen that go about the city
found me: *to whom I said,* Saw ye him whom
my soul loveth?
4 *It was* but a little that I passed from them,
but I found him whom my soul loveth: I
held him, and would not let him go, until I
had brought him into my mother's house, and
into the chamber of her that conceived me.
5 [c]I charge you, O ye daughters of Jerusalem,
by the roes, and by the hinds of the
field, that ye stir not up, nor awake *my* love,
till he please.
6 [d]Who *is* this that cometh out of the wilderness like pillars of smoke,
perfumed with myrrh and frankincense,
with all powders of the
merchant?

A. M. cir. 2990
B. C. cir. 1014
Ante I. Olymp. cir. 238
Ante U. C. cir. 261

7 Behold his bed, which *is* Solomon's;
threescore valiant men *are* about it, of the
valiant of Israel.
8 They all hold swords, *being* expert in
war: every man *hath* his sword upon his thigh
because of fear in the night.
9 King Solomon made himself [e]a chariot of
the wood of Lebanon.
10 He made the pillars thereof *of* silver, the
bottom thereof *of* gold, the covering of it *of*
purple, the midst thereof being paved *with*
love, for the daughters of Jerusalem.
11 Go forth, O ye daughters of Zion, and
behold King Solomon with the crown wherewith
his mother crowned him in the day of
his espousals, and in the day of the gladness
of his heart.

---

[a]Isa. xxvi. 9——[b]Chap. v. 7——[c]Chap. ii. 7; viii. 4——[d]Chap. viii. 5——[e]Or, *a bed*

NOTES ON CHAP. III

Verse 1. *By night on my bed I sought him*] It appears that the bridegroom only saw the bride *by night:* that on the night referred to here he did not come as usual. The bride, troubled on the account, rose and sought him; inquired of the city guards, and continued to seek till at last she found him, and brought him to her apartment, ver. 2-4.

Verse 4. *Into my mother's house*] The *women* in the East have all *separate apartments,* into which no person ever attempts to enter except the *husband.* We find *Isaac* bringing *Rebecca* into his *mother's tent,* when he made her his wife, Gen. xxiv. 67. What is here related appears to refer to the third night of the nuptials.

Verse 5. *I charge you*] The same adjuration as before, chap. ii. 7.

Verse 6. *Who* is *this that cometh out of the wilderness*] Going to Egypt was called *descending* or *going down,* coming from it was termed *coming up.* The bride, having risen, goes after her spouse to the country, and the clouds of incense arising from her *palanquin* seemed like *pillars of smoke;* and the appearance was altogether so splendid as to attract the admiration of her own women, who converse about her splendour, excellence, &c., and then take occasion to describe Solomon's nuptial bed and chariot. Some think that it is the *bridegroom* who is spoken of here.

With this verse the *third night* is supposed to end.

Verse 7. *Threescore valiant men*] These were the *guards* about the pavilion of the bridegroom, who were placed there *because of fear in the night.* The *security* and *state* of the prince required such a guard as this, and the passage is to be *literally* understood.

Verse 8. *They all hold swords*] They are swordsmen. Every man has a sword, and is well instructed how to use it.

Verse 9. *Of the wood of Lebanon.*] Of the *cedar* that grew on that mount. It is very likely that a *nuptial bed,* not a *chariot,* is intended by the original word אפריון *appiryon. Montanus* properly translates it *sponsarum thalamum,* a nuptial bed. It may, however, mean a *palanquin.*

Verse 10. *The pillars*—of *silver*] The *bedposts* were made of silver, or *cased* with wrought silver plates, like the king's chairs brought from Hanover, now, in one of the staterooms in *Windsor Castle.*

The bottom thereof of *gold*] This may refer to *cords* made of *gold thread,* or to the *mattress,* which was made of cloth ornamented with gold.

The covering—of *purple*] Most probably the *canopy.*

The midst—*paved* with *love*] The *counterpane,* a superb piece of *embroidery,* wrought by some of the noble maids of Jerusalem, and, as a proof of their affection, respect, and love, presented to the bride and bridegroom, on their nuptial day. This is most likely to be the sense of the passage, though some suppose it to refer to the whole court.

A Turkish couch is made of wooden *lattices* painted and gilded; the inside is painted with baskets of flowers and nosegays, intermixed with *little mottoes* according to the fancy of the artist. Solomon's couch may have been of the same kind, and decorated in the same way; and the *paving with love* may refer to the amatory verses worked either on the counterpane, hangings, or embroidered carpet. And as this was done by the *daughters of Jerusalem*, they might have expressed the most striking parts of such a *chaste history of love* as Halaly's *Leely* and *Mejnoon* on the different parts. I see that Dr. *Good* is of this opinion. It is sufficiently probable.

Verse 11. *Go forth, O ye daughters of Zion*] This is the exhortation of the *companions* of the *bride* to the *females* of the *city* to examine the superb appearance of the bridegroom, and especially the *nuptial crown*, which appears to have been made by *Bathsheba*, who it is supposed might have lived till the time of Solomon's marriage with the daughter of Pharaoh. It is conjectured that the *prophet* refers to a *nuptial crown*, Isa. lxi. 10. But a *crown*, both on the *bride* and *bridegroom*, was common among most people on such occasions. The nuptial crown among the Greeks and Romans was only a chaplet or wreath of flowers.

In the day of the gladness of his heart.] The day in which all his wishes were crowned, by being united to that female whom beyond all others he loved.

Here the *third day* is supposed to end.

CHAPTER IV

The bridegroom's description of his bride, her person, her accomplishments, her chastity, and her general excellence, 1–16.

A. M. cir. 2990
B. C. cir. 1014
Ante I. Olymp. cir. 238
Ante U. C. cir. 261

BEHOLD, [a]thou *art* fair, my
love; behold, thou *art* fair;
thou *hast* doves' eyes within
thy locks: thy hair *is* as a
[b]flock of goats, [c]that appear from Mount
Gilead.

2 [d]Thy teeth *are* like a flock *of sheep that*
are even shorn, which came up from the
washing; whereof every one
bear twins, and none *is* barren
among them.

3 Thy lips *are* like a thread of
scarlet, and thy speech *is* comely: [e]thy temples
are like a piece of a pomegranate within thy
locks.

4 [f]Thy neck *is* like the tower of David

[a]Chap. i. 15; v. 12——[b]Chap. vi. 5——[c]Or, *that eat of*, &c.——[d]Chap. vi. 6——[e]Chap. vi. 7——[f]Chap. vii. 4

NOTES ON CHAP. IV

Verse 1. *Thou* hast *doves' eyes within thy locks*] Perhaps this refers rather to a sort of veil worn by many of the Eastern women, but especially in Egypt. It is a species of black cloth made of the hair of some animal, probably the black goat; is suspended from the head by silken cords, one of which comes from the crown of the head, down the forehead, to the upper part of the nose, just under the eyes, at which place the veil begins; for the forehead and the eyes are uncovered, except the cord above mentioned, which is ornamented with gold, silver, and precious stones, according to the circumstances of the wearer. This partial veil not only covers all the face, the eyes and forehead excepted, but the neck also, and hangs loosely down over the bosom. One of them, lately brought from Egypt, now lies before me. But the clause, *within thy locks*, מבעד לצמתך *mibbaad letsammathech*, is not well translated, either by ourselves or by the *versions*. *Jerome's* translation is an indication of the meaning: *Absque eo quod intrinsecus latet; without that*, or independently of that, *which lies hidden within*. The *Septuagint*, *Syriac*, and *Arabic* have, *besides thy silence*. *Calmet* contends that none of these gives the *true meaning*, and that *the word* צמת *tsemath* has not the meaning of *hair* or *locks* wherever it occurs, and has quite a different meaning in Isa. xlvii. 2. St. Jerome on this place expresses himself thus: *Nolentibus qui interpretati sunt transferre nomen quod in Sancta Scriptura sonat* turpitudinem.—Ergo צמתך *tsammathech*, *quod* Aquila *posuit*, verenda mulieris *appellantur cujus etymologia apud eos sonat* sitiens tuus. Calmet translates: *Vous êtes toute belle, mon amie; vous êtes toute belle: vos yeux sont des yeux de colombe; sans ce que la pudeur et la modestie tiennent caché.* I leave the translation of these to the learned reader. See another description under ver. 7.

As a flock of goats] Because it was *black* and sleek, as the hair of the goats of Arabia and Palestine is known to be; which, with its fine undulation, is supposed to bear some resemblance to the *curls* or *plaits* of a woman's tresses. The mountains of *Gilead* were beyond Jordan, on the frontiers of *Arabia Deserta*.

Verse 2. *Thy teeth* are *like a flock*] This comparison appears to be founded on the *evenness*, *neatness*, and *whiteness* of the *newly shorn* and newly *washed* sheep.

Verse 3. *Thy lips* are *like a thread of scarlet*] Both *lips* and *cheeks* were *ruddy; sicut fragmen mali punici.*—VULGATE. *Like the section of a pomegranate*, that side cut off on which is the *finest blush*. This is a good and apt *metaphor*. But the inside may be referred to, as it is finely streaked with red and white melting into each other. She had beautiful *hair*, beautiful *eyes*, beautiful *cheeks* and *lips*, and a most pleasing and dulcet *voice*.

Within thy locks.] See on ver. 1, and on ver. 7.

Verse 4. *Thy neck* is *like the tower of David*] It is certain that *bucklers* were frequently hung about towers, both for their ornaments, and to have them at hand when their use was required; see Ezek. xxvii. 10. But the allusion here may be to those *pillars* which are often seen in armouries on which weapons of

A. M. cir. 2990 B. C. cir. 1014 Ante I. Olymp. cir. 238 Ante U. C. cir. 261

builded [g]for an armoury, whereon there hang a thousand bucklers, all shields of mighty men.
5 [h]Thy two breasts *are* like
two young roes that are twins, which feed
among the lilies.
6 [i]Until the day [k]break, and the shadows
flee away, I will get me to the
mountain of myrrh, and to the
hill of frankincense.
7 [l]Thou *art* all fair, my love;
there is no spot in thee.
8 Come with me from Lebanon, *my* spouse,
with me from Lebanon: look from the top of

[g]Neh. iii. 19——[h]See Prov. v. 19; chap. vii. 3

[i]Chap. ii. 17——[k]Heb. *breathe*——[l]Eph. v. 27

various kinds are hung, formed into a great variety of shapes and very splendid. Whoever has seen the *armoury* in the *tower* of London, or such like places, has most probably seen something very similar to that of which the poet speaks.

Verse 5. *Thy two breasts* are *like two young roes*] I have met with many attempts to support this *similitude*, or rather to show that there is a *similitude;* but I judge them unworthy of citation. The poet speaks the *language of nature;* and in a case of this kind, where the impassioned lover attempts to describe the different perfections of his bride, language often fails him, and his comparisons and similitudes are often without strict correctness. In love songs we have heard ladies' *necks* compared to that of the *swan*, not only for its *whiteness*, but also for its *length!* The description here shows more of *nature* than of *art*, which I consider a high recommendation.

Feed among the lilies.] It may be the *nipples* especially, which the poet compares to the *two young roes;* and the *lilies* may refer to the *whiteness* of the *breasts* themselves.

Verse 6. *Until the day break*] Until the morning *breeze.* See chap. ii. 17.

The shadows flee away] Till the *sun sets.*

Mountain of myrrh] Probably the same as the mountains of *Bether*, chap. ii. 17. Mountains where the trees grew from which *myrrh* and *incense* were extracted.

Verse 7. *Thou* art *all fair*—there is *no spot in thee.*] "My beloved, every part of thee is beautiful; thou hast not a single defect."

The description given of the beauties of *Daphne*, by Ovid, Metam. lib. i. ver. 497, has some similarity to the above verses:—

Spectat inornatos collo *pendere* capillos.
Et, quid si comantur? ait. Videt igne micantes
Sideribus similes oculos; *videt* oscula, *quæ non*
Est vidisse satis. Laudat digitosque, manusque,
Brachiaque, *et* nudos *media plus parte* lacertos.
Si qua latent *meliora putat.*

Her well-turn'd *neck* he view'd, (her neck was bare,)
And on her shoulders her *dishevell'd hair.*
O, were it comb'd, said he, with what a grace
Would every *waving curl* become her face!
He view'd her *eyes*, like heavenly lamps that shone,
He view'd her *lips*, too sweet to view alone;
Her taper fingers, and her panting *breast.*
He praises all he sees; and, for the rest,
Believes the *beauties yet unseen* the best.
Dryden.

Jayadeva describes the beauty of Radha in nearly the same imagery: "Thy *lips*, O thou most beautiful among women, are a *bandhujiva* flower; the lustre of the *madhuca* beams upon thy *cheek;* thine *eye* outshines the blue *lotos;* thy nose is a bud of the *tila;* the *cunda* blossom yields to thy *teeth.* Surely thou descendedst from heaven, O slender damsel! attended by a company of youthful goddesses; and all their beauties are collected in thee." See these poems, and the short notes at the end.

The same poet has a parallel thought to that in ver. 5, "Thy two breasts," &c. The companions of *Radha* thus address her: "Ask those *two round hillocks* which receive pure dew drops from the garland playing on thy neck, and the *buds* on *whose tops* start aloft with the thought of thy beloved."

Verse 8. My *spouse.*] The כלה *callah*, which we translate *spouse*, seems to have a peculiar meaning. Mr. Harmer thinks the *Jewish princess* is intended by it; and this seems to receive confirmation from the bridegroom calling her *sister*, ver. 9, that is, one of the same stock and country; and thus different from the Egyptian bride.

Mr. Harmer's opinion is very probable, that two *queens* are mentioned in this song: one Pharaoh's daughter, the other a Jewess. See his *outlines.* But I contend for no system relative to this song.

Look from the top of Amana, &c.] Solomon, says *Calmet*, by an admirable poetic fiction, represents his beloved as a mountain nymph, wholly occupied in hunting the lion and the leopard on the mountains of Lebanon, Amana, Shenir, and Hermon. As a bold and undisciplined virgin, who is unwilling to leave her wild and rural retreats, he invites her to come from those hills; and promises to deck her with a crown and to make her his bride. Thus the poets represent their goddess *Diana*, and even *Venus* herself:—

Per juga, per sylvas, dumosaque saxa vagatur
Nuda genu, vestem ritu succincta Dianæ;
Hortaturque canes; tutæque animalia prædæ,
Aut pronos lepores, aut celsum in cornua cervum,
Aut agitat damas: at fortibus abstinet apris.
Met. lib. x., ver. 535.

Now buskin'd like the virgin huntress goes
Through woods, and pathless wilds, and mountain snows.
With her own tuneful voice she joys to cheer
The panting hounds that chase the flying deer.
She runs the labyrinth of the fearful hares,
But fearless beasts and dangerous prey forbears.

Mount *Libanus* separates Phœnicia from Syria. *Amanus* is between Syria and Silicia. *Shenir* and *Hermon* are beyond Jordan, to the south of Damascus and Mount Libanus, and northward of the mountains of Gilead. Hermon and Shenir are but different parts of the same chain of mountains which separates *Trachonitis*,

A. M. cir. 2990
B. C. cir. 1014
Ante I. Olymp. cir. 238
Ante U. C. cir. 261

Amana, from the top of Shenir [m]and Hermon, from the lion's dens, from the mountains of the leopards.

9 Thou hast [n]ravished my heart, my sister, *my* spouse; thou hast ravished my heart with one of thine eyes, with one chain of thy neck.

10 How fair is thy love, my sister, *my* spouse! [o]how much better is thy love than wine! and the smell of thine ointments than all spices!

11 Thy lips, O *my* spouse, drop *as* the honey-comb: [p]honey and milk *are* under thy tongue; and the smell of thy garments *is* [q]like the smell of Lebanon.

12 A garden [r]enclosed *is* my sister, *my* spouse; a spring shut up, a fountain sealed.

13 Thy plants *are* an orchard of pomegranates, with pleasant fruits; [s]camphire, with spikenard.

14 Spikenard and saffron; calamus and cinnamon, with all trees of frankincense; myrrh and aloes, with all the chief spices:

15 A fountain of gardens, a well of [t]living waters, and streams from Lebanon.

16 Awake, O north wind; and come, thou south; blow up my garden, *that* the spices thereof may flow out. [u]Let my beloved come into his garden, and eat his pleasant fruits.

---

[m]Deut. iii. 9——[n]Or, *taken away my heart*——[o]Ch. i. 2——[p]Prov. xxiv. 13, 14; chap. v. 1——[q]Gen. xxvii. 27; Hos. xiv. 6, 7——[r]Heb. *barred*——[s]Or, *cypress;* ch. i. 14——[t]John iv. 10; vii. 38——[u]Ch. v. 1

---

or the country of *Manasses*, from Arabia Deserta. For these places, see 2 Kings v. 12, and Deut. iii. 9, where they are probably meant.

Verse 9. *Thou hast ravished my heart*] לבבתני *libbabtini*, "Thou hast hearted me," i. e., taken away my heart; as we say, "He has barked the tree," i. e., he has stripped it of its bark; "He has fleeced the flock," i. e., deprived them of their wool.

With one of thine eyes] באחד מעיניך *beachad meeynayich.* This has been thought a harsh expression, and various emendations have been sought. The *Masoretes* have put באחת *beachath*, "at once," in the margin; and this is confirmed by *twenty* of *Kennicott's* MSS.; but *De Rossi* does not notice it. It is scarcely necessary; the sense to me is clear and good without it. "Even one of thine eyes, or one glance of thine eyes, has been sufficient to deprive me of all power; it has completely overcome me;" for *glance* may be understood, and such forms of speech are common in all languages, when speaking on such subjects. If even taken *literally*, the sense is good; for the poet may refer to a *side glance*, shot in *passing by* or *turning away*, where only *one eye* could be seen. I think this a better sense than that which is obtained from the Masoretic emendation.

With one chain of thy neck] Probably referring to the play of the *cervical muscles*, rather than to *necklaces*, or *ringlets of hair.*

Verse 10. *How much better is thy love*] דדיך *dodayich; Hebrew.* Μαστοι σου; *Septuagint. Ubera tua; Vulgate.* "Thy breasts." And so all the *versions*, except the *Chaldee.*

Smell of thine ointments] Perfumes.

Verse 11. *Thy lips—drop* as *the honey-comb*] Thy words are as delicious to my heart as the first droppings of the honey-comb are to the palate.

Honey and milk are *under thy tongue*] Eloquence and persuasive speech were compared among the ancients to *honey* and *milk.*

Thus Homer, Iliad, lib. i., ver. 247:—

Τοισι δε Νεστωρ
Ηδυεπης ανορουσε, λιγυς Πυλιων αγορητης,
Του και απο γλωσσης μελιτος γλυκιων ῥεεν αυδη.

Experienced Nestor, in *persuasion* skill'd,
Words sweet as honey from his lips distill'd.

But the figure is common to all writers and languages. A similar expression will be seen in the *Gitagovinda.*

Verse 12. *A garden enclosed—a spring shut up, a fountain sealed.*] Different expressions to point out the *fidelity* of the bride, or of the Jewish queen. See the *outlines.* She is *unsullied*, a chaste, pure *virgin.* None has ever *entered* into this *garden;* none has yet *tasted* of this *spring;* the *seal* of this *fountain* has never been *broken.* Among the Athenians, the interior part of the house, called the women's apartment, was not only locked but sealed; so Aristophan., Thesmoph. ver. 422:—

Ειτα δια τουτον ταις γυναικωνιτισιν
Σφραγιδας εμβαλλουσιν ηδη και μοχλους.

And on this account, to the women's apartment
They place seals as well as bolts.

And *seal*, as applicable to chaste conduct, is a phrase well known to the Greeks. Æschylus, in the Agamemnon, praises a woman, σημαντηριον ουδεν διαφθειρασαν, who had not violated her seal of conjugal faith. But Nonnus, lib. ii., uses the form of speech exactly as Solomon does with reference to a pure virgin; he says, Αψαυστον ἑης σφρηγιδα κορειης; "She had preserved *the seal of her virginity untouched.*" All this is plain; but how many will make *metaphors* out of *metaphors!*

Verse 13. *Thy plants* are *an orchard of pomegranates*] This seems to refer to the *fecundity* of the bride or Jewish queen; to the former it would be a *prediction;* to the latter, a *statement* of *what had already taken place.* The word פרדס *pardes*, which we translate an *orchard*, is the same which has given birth to our *paradise*, a *garden of pleasure.* The other expressions, in this and the following verse, seem to refer wholly to matters of a connubial nature.

Verse 15. *A fountain of gardens*] Perhaps גנים *gannim*, "gardens," was originally חיים *chaiyim*, "lives," a *living fountain*, a *continual spring.* See *Houbigant.* But this is expressed afterwards; though there would be nothing improper in saying, "a living fountain, a well of living waters, and streams from Mount Lebanon." A fountain of gardens may mean one so abundant as to be sufficient to supply many gardens, to water many plots of ground, an exuberant fountain. This is the allusion; the reference is plain enough.

Verse 16. *Awake, O north wind; and come, thou south*] It is granted that the *south wind* in Palestine, in the summer, is *extremely hot and troublesome;* therefore, another interpretation of this passage has been proposed by Mr. *Harmer;* who thinks בואי *boi*, which we render *come*, signifies *enter into thy repositories;* and, therefore, supposes the true interpretation of the words to be as follows: "Arise, thou north wind, (and retire, thou south,) blow upon my garden; let the spices thereof flow forth, that my beloved may come into his garden, invited by the coolness and fragrancy of the air, and may eat his pleasant fruits; for, if the *south wind* blow, the *excessive heat* will forbid his taking the air, and oblige him to shut close the doors and windows of his apartments." Others think that he wishes the *winds* from *all directions* to carry throughout the land the *fume* of his spices, virtue, and perfections.

Let my beloved come into his garden] This is the invitation of the *bride:* and if we look not for far-fetched meanings, the sense is sufficiently evident. But commentators on this song sometimes take a *literal* sense where the *metaphor* is evident; at other times they build an *allegory* upon a *metaphor*. The *Gitagovinda* has an elegant passage similar to this. See the place, Part VII., beginning with *Enter, sweet Radha.*

The whole of this chapter is considered to be unconnected with any particular time of the marriage ceremonies.

CHAPTER V

The bridegroom calls on his spouse to admit him, 1–3. *She hesitates; but arising finds him gone, seeks him, and is treated unworthily by the city watch,* 4–7. *Inquires of the daughters of Jerusalem, who question her concerning her beloved,* 8, 9. *This gives her occasion to enter into a fine description of his person and accomplishments,* 10–16.

A. M. cir. 2990 B. C. cir. 1014 Ante I. Olymp. cir. 238 Ante U. C. cir. 261

I [a]AM come into my garden,
my sister, *my* spouse: I have
gathered my myrrh with my
spice; [b]I have eaten my honey-
comb with my honey; I have drunk my wine
with my milk: eat, O [c]friends; drink, [d]yea,
drink abundantly, O beloved.
2 I sleep, but my heart waketh: *it is* the
voice of my beloved [e]that knock-
eth, *saying,* Open to me, my
sister, my love, my dove, my undefiled: for my head is filled with
dew, *and* my locks with the drops of the night.
3 I have put off my coat; how shall I put
it on? I have washed my feet; how shall I
defile them?

[a]Chap. iv. 16——[b]Chap. iv. 11——[c]Luke xv. 7, 10; John iii. 29; xv. 14——[d]Or, *and be drunken* with *loves*——[e]Rev. iii. 20

NOTES ON CHAP. V

Verse 1. *I am come into my garden*] באתי *bathi*, I came, or have come; this should be translated in the *past* tense, as the other *preterite* verbs in this clause. I think the latter clause of the preceding verse should come in here: "Let my beloved come into his garden, and eat his pleasant fruits. I have come into my garden, my sister, callah, or spouse; I have gathered my myrrh," &c. I have taken thee for my spouse, and am perfectly satisfied that thou art pure and immaculate.

Eat, O friends—drink abundantly] These are generally supposed to be the words of the *bridegroom*, after he returned from the *nuptial chamber*, and exhibited those *signs* of his wife's *purity* which the customs of those times required. This being a cause of universal joy, the entertainment is served up; and he invites his companions, and the friends of both parties, to eat and drink abundantly, as there was such a universal cause of rejoicing. Others think that these are the words of the bride to her spouse: but the original will not bear this meaning; the verbs are all plural.

Verse 2. *I sleep, but my heart waketh*] This is a *new part;* and some suppose that the *fifth* day's solemnity begins here. *Though I sleep, yet so* impressed is *my heart* with the excellences of my beloved, that my imagination presents him to me in the most pleasing *dreams* throughout the night. I doubt whether the whole, from this verse to the end of the *seventh*, be not a *dream:* several parts of it bear this resemblance; and I confess there are some parts of it, such as her hesitating to rise, his sudden disappearance, &c., which would be of easier solution on this supposition. Or part of the transactions mentioned might be the *effects of the dream* she had, as rising up suddenly, and going out into the street, meeting with the watchmen, &c., before she was well awake. And her being in so much *disorder* and *dishabille* might have induced them to treat her as a *suspicious person*, or one of questionable *character*. But it is most likely the whole was a *dream*.

For my head is filled with dew.] She supposed he had come in the night, and was standing without, *wet*, and exposed to the inclemency of the weather.

Verse 3. *I have put off my coat*] The bride must have been in a *dream*, or in much *disorder*

A. M. cir. 2990
B. C. cir. 1014
Ante I. Olymp. cir. 238
Ante U. C. cir. 261

4 My beloved put in his hand
by the hole *of the door,* and my
bowels were moved [f]for him.
5 I rose up to open to my beloved; and my hands dropped *with* myrrh,
and my fingers *with* [g]sweet-smelling myrrh,
upon the handles of the lock.
6 I opened to my beloved; but my beloved
had withdrawn himself, *and* was gone: my
soul failed when he spake: [h]I sought him,
but I could not find him; I called him, but he
gave me no answer.
7 [i]The watchmen that went about the city
found me, they smote me, they wounded me;
the keepers of the walls took away my veil
from me.
8 I charge you, O daughters of Jerusalem,
if ye find my beloved, [k]that ye
tell him, that I *am* sick of love.

A. M. cir. 2990
B. C. cir. 1014
Ante I. Olymp. cir. 238
Ante U. C. cir. 261

9 What *is* thy beloved more
than *another* beloved, [l]O thou
fairest among women? what *is* thy beloved
more than *another* beloved, that thou dost
so charge us?
10 My beloved *is* white *and* ruddy, [m]the
chiefest among ten thousand.
11 His head *is as* the most fine gold, his
locks *are* [n]bushy, *and* black as a raven.
12 [o]His eyes *are* as *the eyes* of doves by the
rivers of waters, washed with milk, *and* [p]fitly
set.
13 His cheeks *are* as a bed of spices, *as*
[q]sweet flowers: his lips *like* lilies, dropping
sweet-smelling myrrh.

[f]Or, (as some read,) *in me*——[g]Heb. *passing* or *running about*——[h]1 Sam. x. 21; chap. iii. 1; Luke ii. 44, 45
[i]Chap. iii. 3——[k]Heb. *what*——[l]Chap. i. 8——[m]Heb. *a standard-bearer*

[n]Or, *curled*——[o]Chap. i. 15; iv. 1——[p]Heb. *sitting in fulness,* that is, *fitly placed, and set as a precious stone in the foil of a ring*——[q]Or, *towers of perfumes*

of mind to have made the frivolous excuses here mentioned. The words relate to the case of a person who had gone to take rest on his bed. As they wore nothing but sandals, they were obliged to wash their feet previously to their lying down. I have washed my feet, taken off my clothes, and am gone to bed: I cannot therefore be disturbed. A Hindoo always washes his feet before he goes to bed. If called from his bed, he often makes this excuse, *I shall daub my feet;* and the excuse is reasonable, as the floors are of earth; and they do not wear shoes in the house.—WARD.

Verse 4. *My beloved put in his hand*] If it were a *real scene,* which is mentioned in this and the two following verses, it must refer, from the well-known use of the *metaphors,* to matrimonial endearments. Or, it may refer to his *attempts to open the door,* when she hesitated to arise, on the grounds mentioned ver. 3. But this also bears every evidence of a *dream.*

Verse 5. *My hands dropped* with *myrrh*] It was a custom among the Romans, as *Brissonius, Isidore,* and others relate, to conduct the bride to the house of the bridegroom with lighted torches; and those who brought her *anointed the door-posts with fragant oils,* whence the name *uxor,* or as it was formerly written *unxor,* for a *wife* or *married* woman, because of the *anointing* which took place on the occasion; for sometimes the bride herself *anointed* the *door-posts,* and sometimes those who brought her; probably both at the same time. The same custom might have existed among the Jews. See *Vossius' Etymologicon.*

Verse 7. *Took away my veil*] They tore it off rudely, to discover who she was. See on ver. 2. To tear the veil signifies, in Eastern phrase, to deflower or dishonour a woman.

Verse 8. *I* am *sick of love.*] "I am exceedingly concerned for his absence; and am distressed on account of my thoughtless carriage towards him." The latter clause may be well translated, "What should ye tell him?" Why, "that I am sick of love." This ends the transactions of the *third day* and *night.*

Verse 9. *What* is *thy beloved more than another beloved*] This question gives the bride an opportunity to break out into a highly wrought description of the beauty and perfections of her spouse.

Verse 10. *My beloved* is *white and ruddy*] *Red* and *white,* properly mixed, are essential to a *fine complexion;* and this is what is intimated: he has the *finest complexion among ten thousand persons;* not one in that number is equal to *him.* Literally, "He bears the standard among ten thousand men;" or "He is one before whom a standard is borne," i. e., he is *captain* or *chief* of the whole.

Verse 11. *His head* is as *the most fine gold*] He has the most beautiful head, fine and majestic. Gold is here used to express *excellence.*

His locks are *bushy*] *Crisped* or *curled.* This may refer to his mustachios.

Black as a raven.] His hair is black and glossy.

Verse 12. *His eyes* are *as* the eyes *of doves*] See on chap. iv. ver. 1.

Washed with milk] The *white* of the eye, *exceedingly white.* By the use of *stibium,* in the East, the eye is rendered very *beautiful;* and receives such *a lustre* from the use of this article, that, to borrow the expression of a late traveller, "their eyes appear to be swimming in bliss." I believe this expression to be the meaning of the text.

Fitly set.] Or, as the *margin,* very properly, *sitting in fulness;* not sunk, not contracted.

Verse 13. *His cheeks* are *as a bed of spices*] Possibly meaning a *bed in the garden,* where odoriferous herbs grew. But it has been supposed to refer to his *beard,* which in a *young well-made man* is exceedingly beautiful. I have seen young Turks, who had taken much care of their beards, mustachios, &c., look majestic. Scarcely any thing serves to set off the human face to greater advantage than the *beard,* when

A. M. cir. 2990 B. C. cir. 1014 Ante I. Olymp. cir. 238 Ante U. C. cir. 261

14 His hands *are as* gold rings
set with the beryl: his belly *is as*
bright ivory overlaid *with* sapphires.
15 His legs *are as* pillars of marble, set
upon sockets of fine gold: his countenance *is*
as Lebanon, excellent as the
cedars.
16 [r]His mouth *is* most sweet:
yea, he *is* altogether [s]lovely.
This *is* my beloved, and this *is* my friend, O
daughters of Jerusalem.

[r]Heb. *His palate*

[s]2 Sam. i. 23

kept in proper order. Females admire it in their *suitors* and *husbands.* I have known cases, where they not only *despised* but *execrated* Europeans, whose faces were close shaved. The men perfume their beards often; and this may be what is intended by *spices* and *sweet-smelling myrrh.*

His lips like *lilies*] The שושנים *shoshannim* may mean any flower of the *lily* kind, such as the *rubens lilium,* mentioned by *Pliny,* or something of the *tulip* kind. There are tints in such flowers that bear a very near resemblance to a fine *ruby lip.*

Verse 14. *His hands—gold rings set with the beryl*] This really seems to refer to *gold rings* set with precious stones on the fingers, and perhaps to circlets or bracelets about the wrists. Some suppose it to refer to the roundness and exquisite symmetry of the hand and fingers. תרשיש *tarshish,* which we translate *beryl,* a gem of a sea-green tint, had better be translated *chrysolite,* which is of a *gold* colour.

His belly—bright ivory overlaid with *sapphires.*] This must refer to some *garment* set with *precious stones* which went round his waist, and was peculiarly remarkable. If we take it *literally,* the sense is plain enough. His belly was beautifully white, and the blue veins appearing under the skin resembled the sapphire stone. But one can hardly think that this was intended.

Verse 15. *His legs* are as *pillars of marble*] Exquisitely turned and well-shaped; the *sockets of gold* may refer to his *slippers.* On these a profusion of gold and ornaments are still lavished in Asiatic countries.

His countenance is *as Lebanon*] As Lebanon exalts its head beyond all the other mountains near Jerusalem, so my beloved is tall and majestic, and surpasses in stature and majesty all other men. He is also as *straight* and as *firm* as the *cedars.*

Verse 16. *His mouth* is *most sweet*] His eloquence is great, and his voice is charming. Every word he speaks is sweetness, mildness, and benevolence itself. Then, her powers of description failing, and metaphor exhausted, she cries out, "The whole of him is loveliness. This is my beloved, and this is my companion, O ye daughters of Jerusalem."

CHAPTER VI

The companions of the bride inquire after the bridegroom, 1–3. *A description of the bride,* 4–13.

A. M. cir. 2990 B. C. cir. 1014 Ante I. Olymp. cir. 238 Ante U. C. cir. 261

WHITHER is thy beloved
gone, [a]O thou fairest among
women? whither is thy beloved
turned aside? that we may seek
him with thee.
2 My beloved has gone down into his garden,
to the beds of spices, to feed in
the gardens, and to gather lilies.
3 [b]I *am* my beloved's, and my
beloved *is* mine: he feedeth
among the lilies.
4 Thou *art* beautiful, O my love, as Tirzah,

[a]Chap. i. 8

[b]Chap. ii. 16; vii. 10

NOTES ON CHAP. VI

Verse 1. *Whither is thy beloved gone*] These words are supposed to be addressed to the *bride* by her own *companions,* and are joined to the preceding chapter by the *Hebrew* and all the *versions.*

Verse 2. *My beloved is gone down into his garden*] The answer of the *bride* to her *companions.*

Verse 4. *Beautiful—as Tirzah*] This is supposed to be the address of Solomon to the bride. Tirzah was a city in the tribe of Ephraim, (Josh. xii. 24,) and the capital of that district. It appears to have been *beautiful* in *itself,* and *beautifully situated,* for *Jeroboam* made it his residence before *Samaria* was built; and it seems to have been the ordinary residence of the kings of *Israel,* 1 Kings xiv. 17; xv. 53. Its *name* signifies *beautiful* or *delightful.*

Comely as Jerusalem] This was called *the perfection of beauty,* Psa. xlviii. 2, 3; l. 2. And thus the poet compares the bride's beauty to the *two finest places* in the land of Palestine, and the *capitals* of the *two kingdoms* of *Israel* and *Judah.*

Terrible as an army *with banners.*] This has been supposed to carry an allusion to the *caravans* in the East, and the manner in which they are conducted in their travels by night. The caravans are divided into *companies,* called *cottors,* according to *Thevenet;* and each company is distinguished by the *form* of the *brazier* in which they carry their *lights.* After night, these braziers are placed on the ends of long poles, and carried by a person who walks at the head of the company. Some have *ten* or *twelve* lights, and are of different forms; some *triangular,* or like an N; some like an M, by which each pilgrim readily knows

A. M. cir. 2990
B. C. cir. 1014
Ante I. Olymp. cir. 238
Ante U. C. cir. 261

comely as Jerusalem, [c]terrible
as *an army* with banners.
5 Turn away thine eyes from
me, for [d]they have overcome me:
thy hair *is* [e]as a flock of goats that appear
from Gilead.
6 [f]Thy teeth *are* as a flock of sheep which
go up from the washing, whereof every one
beareth twins, and *there is* not one barren
among them.
7 [g]As a piece of a pomegranate *are* thy
temples within thy locks.
8 There are threescore queens, and fourscore concubines, and virgins without number.
9 My dove, my undefiled is *but* one; she *is*
the *only* one of her mother, she *is* the choice
one of her that bare her. The daughters saw
her, and blessed her; *yea,* the
queens and the concubines, and
they praised her.
10 Who *is* she *that* looketh
forth as the morning, fair as the moon, clear
as the sun, [h]*and* terrible as *an army* with
banners?
11 I went down into the garden of nuts to
see the fruits of the valley, *and* [i]to see
whether the vine flourished, *and* the pomegranates budded.
12 [k]Or ever I was aware, my soul [l]made
me *like* the chariots of Amminadib.
13 Return, return, O Shulamite; return, return, that we may look upon thee. What
will ye see in the Shulamite? As it were the
company [m]of two armies.

A. M. cir. 2990
B. C. cir. 1014
Ante I. Olymp. cir. 238
Ante U. C. cir. 261

[c]Ver. 10——[d]Or, *they have puffed me up*——[e]Ch. iv. 1——[f]Ch. iv. 2——[g]Ch. iv. 3——[h]Ver. 4——[i]Ch. vii. 12

[k]Heb. *I knew not*——[l]Or, *set me on the chariots of my willing people*——[m]Or, *of Mahanaim;* Gen. xxxii. 2

his own company, both by *night* and *day.* A whole caravan, composed of many thousands of *hadgees* or *pilgrims,* divided into various *cottors* or companies, each having its own distinguishing brazier or *light,* must necessarily produce a very *splendid,* if not a *terrible,* appearance.

Verse 5. *Turn away thine eyes*] As the sight of so many fires after night was extremely *dazzling,* and the *eye* could not *bear* the sight, so the *look* of the bride was such as pierced the heart, and quite overwhelmed the person who met it. Hence the bridegroom naturally cries out, "Turn away thine eyes from me, for they have overcome me."

Thy hair is as a flock of goats] See on chap. iv. 1.

Verse 6. *Thy teeth*] See on chap. iv. 2.

Verse 7. *As a piece of a pomegranate*] See on chap. iv. 3.

Verse 8. *There are threescore queens*] Though there be *sixty queens,* and *eighty concubines,* or *secondary wives,* and *virgins innumerable,* in my *harem,* yet thou, *my dove, my undefiled, art* אחת *achath,* ONE, the ONLY ONE, she in whom I delight beyond all.

Verse 9. *The daughters saw her, and blessed her*] Not only the *Jewish women in general* spoke well of her on her arrival, but the *queens* and *concubines praised her* as the most accomplished of her sex.

With this verse the *fourth night* of the marriage week is supposed to end.

Verse 10. *Looketh forth as the morning*] The bride is as lovely as the *dawn* of day, the *Aurora,* or perhaps the *morning star,* VENUS. She is even more resplendent, she is as *beautiful as the* MOON. She even surpasses *her,* for she is as *clear* and *bright* as the SUN; and *dangerous* withal to look on, for she is as formidable as the vast collection of lights that burn by night at the head of every company in a numerous caravan. See the note on ver. 4. The comparison of a fine woman to the splendour of an unclouded *full moon* is continually recurring in the writings of the Asiatic poets.

Verse 11. *I went down into the garden of nuts*] I believe this and the following verse refer at least to the preparations for a farther consummation of the marriage, or examination of the advancement of the bride's pregnancy. But many circumstances of this kind are so interwoven, and often *anticipated* and also *postponed,* that it is exceedingly difficult to arrange the whole so as to ascertain the several parts, and who are the actors and speakers. But other writers find no difficulty here, because they have their system; and that explains all things.

It is probably not the *hazel* but the *almond nut,* that is referred to here.

Verse 12. *The chariots of Amminadib.*] Probably for their great speed these chariots became proverbial. The passage marks a strong agitation of mind, and something like what we term palpitation of the heart. As I am not aware of any *spiritual* meaning here, I must be excused from commenting on that which is *literal. Amminadib* signifies *my noble* or *princely people;* but it may here be a proper name, and Amminadib might be celebrated for his skill and rapidity in driving, as Jehu was.

Verse 13. *Return, O Shulamite*] This appears to be addressed to the bride, as now the confirmed, acknowledged *wife* of *Solomon; for* שולמית *shulammith,* appears to be a *feminine* formed from שלמה *shelomoh,* or שלמון *shelomon,* as we form *Charlotte* from *Charles; Henrietta,* from *Henry; Janette,* from *John,* &c.

The company of two armies.] Or the *musicians of the camps.* She is as terrible as hosts of armed men, on the ground of what is said on verses 4, 5. The two armies may refer to the *choirs* of the bride's *virgins,* and the bridegroom's *companions;* but the similitude is not very perceptible. The *Targum* explains it of "the camps of Israel and Judah:" as if the bridegroom should say, "My beloved possesses all the perfections both of the Israelitish and Jewish women." But how little satisfaction do the best *conjectures* afford!

With this chapter the *fifth night* is supposed to end.

CHAPTER VII

A farther description of the bride, 1–9. *Her invitation to the bridegroom*, 10–13.

A. M. cir. 2990
B. C. cir. 1014
Ante I. Olymp. cir. 238
Ante U. C. cir. 261

HOW beautiful are thy feet
with shoes, [a]O prince's
daughter? the joints of thy
thighs *are* like jewels, the work
of the hands of a cunning workman.
2 Thy navel *is like* a round goblet, *which*
wanteth not [b]liquor: thy belly *is like* a heap
of wheat set about with lilies.
3 [c]Thy two breasts *are* like two young
roes *that are* twins.
4 [d]Thy neck *is* as a tower of ivory; thine
eyes *like* the fish-pools in Heshbon, by the
gate of Bath-rabbim: thy nose *is* as the tower
of Lebanon, which looketh toward Damascus.
5 Thine head upon thee *is* like
[e]Carmel, and the hair of thine
head like purple: the king *is*
[f]held in the galleries.
6 How fair and how pleasant art thou, O
love, for delights!
7 This thy stature is like to a palm tree,
and thy breasts to clusters *of grapes.*
8 I said, I will go up to the palm tree, I
will take hold of the boughs thereof: now
also thy breasts shall be as clusters of the
vine, and the smell of thy nose like apples;
9 And the roof of thy mouth like the best
wine for my beloved, that goeth *down* [g]sweetly,

A. M. cir. 2990
B. C. cir. 1014
Ante I. Olymp. cir. 238
Ante U. C. cir. 261

[a]Psa. xlv. 13——[b]Heb. *mixture*——[c]Chap. iv. 5——[d]Chap. iv. 4——[e]Or, *crimson*——[f]Heb. *bound*——[g]Heb. *straightly*

NOTES ON CHAP. VII

Verse 1. *How beautiful are thy feet with shoes*] "How graceful is thy walking." In the *sixth* chapter the bridegroom praises the *Shulamite*, as we might express it, *from head to foot.* Here he begins a new description, taking her from *foot to head.*

The *shoes, sandals,* or *slippers* of the Eastern ladies are most beautifully formed, and richly embroidered. The *majestic walk* of a beautiful woman in such shoes is peculiarly grand. And to show that such a walk is intended, he calls her a *prince's daughter.*

The joints of thy thighs] Must refer to the ornaments on the beautiful *drawers*, which are in general use among ladies of quality in most parts of the East.

Verse 2. *Thy navel* is like *a round goblet*] This may also refer to some ornamental dress about the *loins.* These suppositions are rendered very probable from hundreds of the best finished and highly decorated drawings of Asiatic *ladies* in my own collection, where every thing appears in the drawings, as in nature.

A heap of wheat set about with lilies.] This is another instance of the same kind. The richly embroidered dresses in the above drawings may amply illustrate this also. Ainsworth supposes the metaphor is taken from a pregnant woman; the child in the womb being nourished by means of the *umbilical cord* or *navel string,* till it is brought into the world. After which it is fed by means of the mother's *breasts*, which are immediately mentioned. Possibly the whole may allude to the bride's *pregnancy.*

Verse 3. *Thy two breasts*] Where the hair and breasts are fine, they are the highest ornaments of the person of a female.

Verse 4. *Thy neck—as a tower of ivory*] High, white, and ornamented with jewellery, *as the tower of David* was with *bucklers.* See on chap. iv. 4.

The fish-pools in Heshbon] Clear, bright, and serene. These must have been very beautiful to have been introduced here in comparison. These two fountains appear to have been situated at the *gate* that led from *Heshbon* to *Rabba,* or *Rabboth Ammon.* There is a propriety in this metaphor, because *fountains* are considered to be the *eyes* of the *earth.*

Thy nose—as the tower of Lebanon] There was doubtless a propriety in this similitude also, which cannot now be discerned. If we are to understand the similitude as taken from the *projecting* form of the *nose,* even here I see nothing striking in the metaphor; for surely the tower of Lebanon did not *project* from the *mountain* as the human *nose* does from the *face.* It is better to acknowledge that there was undoubtedly some fit resemblances; but in what *circumstance* we know not. But some commentators are always extolling the correctness of the imagery in those very difficult places, where no soul sees the similitude but themselves.

Verse 5. *Thine head—like Carmel*] Rising majestically upon thy neck, and above thy shoulders, as Mount Carmel does in its district. Carmel was the name of the mountain where Elijah had his contest with the prophets of Baal. See 1 Kings xviii. 19, &c.

The hair of thine head like purple] Ornamented with *ribbons* and *jewellery* of this *tint.*

The king is *held in the galleries.*] Or is detained in the antechamber. His heart is captivated by thy person and conduct. Some understand the ringlets of the bride's hair.

Verse 6. *How fair and how pleasant*] Thou art every way beautiful, and in every respect calculated to inspire pleasure and delight.

Verse 7. *Like to a palm tree*] Which is remarkably *straight, taper,* and *elegant.*

And thy breasts to clusters of grapes.] *Dates* are the fruit of the palm tree; they grow in clusters; and it is these, not *grapes,* which are intended.

Verse 8. *I will go up to the palm tree*] I will take hold on the boughs of this tree, and climb up by them, in order to gather the clusters of dates at the top. The *rubric* here in the old MS. interprets this of the *cross of Christ.*

Verse 9. *The roof of thy mouth like the best*

A. M. cir. 2990 B. C. cir. 1014 Ante I. Olymp. cir. 238 A. U. C. cir. 261

causing the lips [h]of those that
are asleep to speak.
10 [i]I *am* my beloved's, and
[k]his desire *is* toward me.
11 Come, my beloved, let us go forth into
the field; let us lodge in the villages.
12 Let us get up early to the vineyards;
let us [l]see if the vine flourish, *whether*
the tender grape [m]appear *and*
the pomegranates bud forth:
there will I give thee my
loves.
13 The [n]mandrakes give a smell, and at our
gates [o]*are* all manner of pleasant *fruits,* new
and old, *which* I have laid up for thee, O my
beloved.

A. M. cir. 2990 B. C. cir. 1014 Ante I. Olymp. cir. 238 A. U. C. cir. 261

[h]Or, *of the ancient*——[i]Chap. ii. 16; vi. 3——[k]Psa. xlv. 11

[l]Chap. vi. 11——[m]Heb. *open*——[n]Gen. xxx. 14
[o]Matt. xiii. 52

wine] The *voice* or *conversation* of the spouse is most probably what is meant.

Causing the lips of those that are asleep to speak.] As *good wine* has a tendency to cause the most backward to *speak fluently* when taken in moderation; so a sight of thee, and hearing the charms of thy conversation, is sufficient to excite the most taciturn to speak, and even to become eloquent in thy praises.

Verse 10. *I* am *my beloved's, and his desire* is *toward me.*] It is worthy of remark that the word which we translate *his desire* is the very same used Gen. iii. 16: *Thy desire*, thy ruling appetite, תשוקתך *teshukathech, shall be to thy husband, and he shall rule over thee.* This was a part of the woman's curse. Now here it seems to be *reversed;* for the bride says, *I am my beloved's*, and *his desire* or *ruling appetite* and *affection,* תשוקתו *teshukatho,* is עלי *ali,* UPON ME. The old MS. translates this with considerable force:—**I to my leef, and to me the turnynge of him.**

Verse 11. *Let us go forth into the field*] It has been conjectured that the bridegroom arose early every morning, and left the bride's apartment, and withdrew to the country; often leaving her asleep, and commanding her companions not to disturb her till she should awake of herself. Here the bride wishes to accompany her spouse to the country, and spend a night at his country house.

Verse 12. *Let us get up early to the vineyards*] When in the country, we shall have the better opportunity to contemplate the progress of the spring vegetation; and there she promises to be peculiarly affectionate to him.

Verse 13. *The mandrakes give a smell*] See the note on Gen. xxx. 14, where the *mandrake* is particularly described; from which this passage will receive considerable light. The reader is *requested* to consult it.

All manner of pleasant fruits] Fruits *new* and *old; flowers* and *herbs* of every kind which the season could yield. The literal sense, allowing for the concealing metaphors, is, I believe, of a widely different nature from what is generally given. But this must be left to the reader's sagacity and prudence.

CHAPTER VIII

The love of the bride to her spouse, and the nature of that love, 1–7. *The younger sister,* 8–10. *Solomon's vineyard,* 11, 12. *The confidence of the bride and bridegroom in each other,* 13, 14.

A. M. cir. 2990 B. C. cir. 1014 Ante I. Olymp. cir. 238 A. U. C. cir. 261

O THAT thou *wert* as my brother, that sucked the breasts
of my mother! *when* I should
find thee without, I would kiss
thee; yea, [a]I should not be despised.
2 I would lead thee, *and* bring thee into
my mother's house, *who* would instruct me:
I would cause thee to drink of [b]spiced wine
of the juice of my pomegranate.
3 [c]His left hand *should be*
under my head, and his right
hand should embrace me.
4 [d]I charge you, O daughters of Jerusalem, [e]that ye stir not up, nor awake *my* love,
until he please.

A. M. cir. 2990 B. C. cir. 1014 Ante I. Olymp. cir. 238 A. U. C. cir. 261

[a]Heb. *they should not despise me*——[b]Prov. ix. 2
[c]Chap. ii. 6

[d]Chap. ii. 7; iii. 5——[e]Heb. *why should ye stir up,* or *why,* &c.

NOTES ON CHAP. VIII

Verse 1. *O that thou* wert *as my brother*] The bride, fearing that her fondness for her spouse might be construed into too great a familiarity, wishes that he were *her little brother;* and then she might treat him in the most affectionate manner, and kiss him even in the *streets* without suspicion, and without giving offence to any one.

Verse 2. *Would—bring thee into my mother's house,* who *would instruct me*] She would teach me how to conduct myself towards thee, as she would how to nurse a young child.

To drink of spiced wine] Wine rendered peculiarly strong and invigorating. The bride and bridegroom on the wedding day both drank out of the same cup, to show that they were to *enjoy* and equally *bear* together the *comforts* and *adversities* of life.

Verse 3. *His left hand*] See on chap. ii. 6. With the *fourth* verse the SIXTH *night* of the marriage week is supposed to end.

A. M. cir. 2990
B. C. cir. 1014
Ante I. Olymp. cir. 238
A. U. C. cir. 261

5 [f]Who *is* this that cometh
up from the wilderness, leaning
upon her beloved? I raised thee
up under the apple tree: there
thy mother brought thee forth; there she
brought thee forth *that* bare thee.
6 [g]Set me as a seal upon thine heart, as a
seal upon thine arm: for love *is* strong as
death; jealousy *is* [h]cruel as the grave: the
coals thereof *are* coals of fire, *which hath* a
most vehement flame.
7 Many waters cannot quench love, neither
can the floods drown it: [i]if a
man would give all the substance
of his house for love, it would
utterly be contemned.
8 [k]We have a little sister, and she hath no
breasts: what shall we do for our sister in the
day when she shall be spoken for?
9 If she *be* a wall, we will build upon
her a palace of silver: and if she *be* a
door, we will enclose her with boards of
cedar.
10 I *am* a wall, and my breasts like tow-

[f]Ch. iii. 6——[g]Isa. xlix. 16; Jer. xxii. 24; Hag. ii. 23——[h]Heb. *hard*——[i]Prov. vi. 35——[k]Ezek. xxiii. 33

Verse 5. *That cometh up from the wilderness*] Perhaps the words of the *daughters of Jerusalem*, who, seeing the bride returning from the country, leaning on the arm of her beloved, are filled with admiration at her excellent carriage and beauty.

I raised thee up under the apple tree] The original of this clause is obscure, and has given birth to various translations. The following is nearly literal: "Under the apple tree I excited thee (to espouse me:) there, thy mother contracted thee;—there, she that brought thee forth contracted thee (to me.) Or it may be understood of the following circumstance: The bridegroom found her once asleep under an apple tree, and awoke her; and this happened to be the very place where her mother, taken in untimely labour, had brought her into the world." And here the bridegroom, in his fondness and familiarity, recalls these little adventures to her memory.

The *Vulgate* gives this an abominable meaning.

Sub arbore malo suscitavi te: ibi corrupta est mater tua; ibi violata est genetrix tua; "I raised thee up under the apple tree: it was there that thy mother was corrupted; it was there that she who brought thee forth was violated." Spiritually, all this is applied to Eve losing her purity by sin; and Jesus as the promised seed *raising her up* by the promise of mercy, through the blood of his cross. But the *text* says nothing of this.

Verse 6. *Set me as a seal upon thine heart*] It was customary in the Levant and other places to make impressions of *various kinds* upon the *arms*, the *breast*, and other parts. I have seen these often: some slight punctures are made, and the place rubbed over with a sort of blue powder that, getting between the *cuticle* and *cutis*, is never discharged; it continues in all its distinctness throughout life. The figures of *young women* are frequently thus impressed on the *arms* and on the *breasts*. If the bride alludes to any thing of this kind, which is very probable, the interpretation is easy. Let me be thus depicted upon thine *arm*, which being constantly before thy eyes, thou wilt never forget me; and let me be thus depicted upon thy *breast*, the emblem of the share I have in thy *heart* and affections. Do this as a proof of the love I bear to thee, which is such as nothing but death can destroy; and do it to prevent any *jealousy* I might feel, which is as *cruel as the grave*, and as deadly as *fiery arrows* or poisoned darts shot into the body.

A most vehement flame.] שלהבתיה *shalhebethyah*, "the flame of God;" for the word is divided שלהבת יה *shalhebeth Yah*, "the flame of Jehovah," by *one hundred and sixteen* of Dr. *Kennicott's* MSS., and by *one hundred and fourteen* of those of *De Rossi*. It may mean the *lightning;* or, as our text understands it, a most *vehement* or *intense fire.*

Verse 7. *Many waters*] Neither common nor uncommon *adversities*, even of the most *ruinous* nature, can destroy love when it is *pure;* and *pure love* is such that nothing can *procure* it. If it be not excited naturally, no money can purchase it, no property can procure it, no arts can persuade it. How vain is the thought of *old rich men* hoping to procure the affections of *young women* by loading them with *presents* and *wealth!* No woman can command her affections; they are not in her power. Where they do not rise spontaneously, they can never exist. "If a man would give all the substance of his house for love, it would be utterly contemned." Let the *old*, as well as the *gay* and the *giddy*, think of this.

Verse 8. *We have a little sister*] This young girl belonged most probably to the *bride.*

She hath no breasts] She is not yet marriageable.

What shall we do for our sister] How shall we secure her comfort and welfare?

In the day when she shall be spoken for?] When any person shall demand her in marriage.

Verse 9. *If she* be *a wall*] All these expressions, says *Calmet*, show that it was necessary to provide a husband for this young sister. For a *woman* without a *husband* is like a *wall* without *towers*, and without defence; is like a *gate* or *door* without *bar* or *lock;* and like a *city* without *walls*. They must therefore provide for their sister a *rich, powerful*, and *illustrious* man; qualities here figured by *towers* or *palaces* of *silver*, and *doors* of *cedar*. As it is customary to build *towers* upon a *wall*, and to put *bolts* and *bars* upon a *door* in order to secure it, so the expressions may point out the *defence, protection*, and *guardianship* which they imagined this young woman to require.

Verse 10. *I am a wall, and my breasts like towers*] I am become marriageable, and I stood in need of the *defence* I have now in my beloved; and as soon as I was so, and became

A. M. cir. 2990 B. C. cir. 1014 Ante I. Olymp. cir. 238 A. U. C. cir. 261

ers: then was I in his eyes as
one that found [l]favour.
11 Solomon had a vineyard at
Baal-hamon; [m]he let out the vine-
yard unto keepers; every one for the fruit thereof was to bring a thousand *pieces* of silver.
12 My vineyard, which *is* mine, *is* before
me: thou, O Solomon, *must have* a thousand,
and those that keep the fruit
thereof two hundred.
13 Thou that dwellest in the
gardens, the companions hearken
to thy voice: [n]cause me to hear *it*.
14 [o]Make [p]haste, my beloved, and [q]be
thou like to a roe or to a young hart upon the
mountains of spices.

[l]Heb. *peace*——[m]Matt. xxi. 33——[n]Chap. ii. 14

[o]See Rev. xxii. 17, 20——[p]Heb. *Flee away*——[q]Ch. ii. 17

pleasing in the eyes of my beloved, I was given to him in marriage, and have ever since *found favour in his sight.* As soon then as my sister is in my state, let a proper match be sought out for *her.* These expressions show the solicitude which the bride felt for her sister, and in her favour she wishes to interest her spouse.

Verse 11. *Solomon had a vineyard*] *Calmet* translates and paraphrases the *Hebrew* of these two verses thus: "Ver. 11. *Solomon has a vineyard at Baal-hamon: he has let it out to keepers, each of whom for the fruit of it was to bring a thousand pieces of silver.* Ver. 12. *As for me, my vineyard is before me;* that is, it is my own; I am its proprietor. *Keep thyself, O Solomon, thy thousand pieces of silver, and let those who dress* (thy vineyard) *have two hundred for their trouble.* I neither envy thee thy vineyard, nor them their profits. I am satisfied with my own. My beloved is my vineyard—my heritage; I would not change him for all the riches of the universe."

Some suppose that there is a reference here to some property which Pharaoh had given to Solomon with his daughter. See *Harmer's Outlines*, where this subject is considered at large.

Verse 13. *Thou that dwellest in the gardens*] This is supposed to refer to the bridegroom asking permission of his spouse early in the morning to retire, as was his usual custom. He intimates the *companions* were waiting to *hear*, and he wished to *hear it* in the way of *permission* to depart.

Verse 14. *Make haste, my beloved*] These appear to be the words of the bride giving permission, but entreating him to speed his *return.* What these *mountains of spices* were, we cannot particularly tell; but they must have been thus named from their producing the *trees* on which the *spices* grew. They might have been the same as the *mountains of Bether*, chap. ii. 17, or the *mountains of myrrh*, chap. iv. 6; where see the notes.

Here ends the *seventh night* of the marriage week.

Thus ends this most singular book; the oldest *pastoral* in the world, if it may be ranked among this species of writing. To whatever species of composition it belongs, it is, beyond all controversy, the *finest*, the most *sublime* for *imagery* and *colouring*, that ever came from the pen of man.

In the preceding notes I have carefully avoided all attempts to *spiritualize* this song. My reasons I have already given in the *introduction;* and in the course of writing these short notes I have seen no cause to alter my opinion. Any man may *allegorize* it; that is an easy matter; for when he once considers it to be an *allegory*, his own *creed* will furnish him with enough to *say*, *write*, or *preach*, upon the *spiritual* meanings of every part, which will be an exhibition of his own *confession of faith!* But when he has finished his work, the question will recur, By what authority do you give it *these meanings?* And till the day of judgment none shall be able to say, "I have the authority of God for my exposition."

MASORETIC NOTES

Number of verses in Canticles, 117. Middle verse chap. iv. 14.

THE

TARGUM,[(a)] OR CHALDEE PARAPHRASE

ON THE

SONG OF SONGS

CHAPTER I

Verse 1. *The song of songs, &c.*] The songs and hymns which Solomon the prophet, king of Israel, delivered by the (*b*) spirit of prophecy, before Jehovah, the Lord of the whole world. Ten songs are sung in this world; but this is the most excellent of them all. The *first* song Adam sang, at the time when his sins were forgiven him; and when the Sabbath day came, he put a covering upon his lips, and sang (*c*) a psalm *or* song for the Sabbath day. The *second* song sang Moses with the children of Israel, at the time when the Lord of the world divided the Red Sea for them; *then* they all of them opened their mouths, and sang as one song, as it is written, (*d*) "Then sang Moses and the children of Israel." The *third* song the children of Israel sang at the time that the well of water was given to them, as it is written, (*e*) "Then sang Israel." The *fourth* song Moses the prophet sang, when his time was come to (*f*) depart out of the world, and in which he reproved the people of the house of Israel, as it is written, (*g*) "Give ear, O heavens, and I will speak." The *fifth* song Joshua the son of Nun sang, when he fought in *Gibeon*, and the sun and moon stood still for him (*h*) *thirty* and *six* hours: when they ceased from singing, he himself opened his mouth, and sang this song, as it is written, (*i*) "Then sang Joshua before the Lord." The *sixth* song Barak and Deborah sang, in the day that the Lord delivered Sisera and his army into the hands of the children of Israel, as it is written, (*k*) "Then sang Deborah and Barak, the son of Abinoam." The *seventh* song Hannah sang, at the time when a son was given her by the Lord, as it is written, (*l*) "And Hannah prayed by the spirit of prophecy, and said." The *eighth* song David the king of Israel sang, on the account of all the wonders which the Lord did for him. He opened his mouth, and sang this song, as it is written, (*m*) "And David sang by the spirit of prophecy before the Lord." The *ninth* song Solomon the king of Israel sang by the Holy Spirit before Jehovah, the Lord of the whole world. And the *tenth* song the children of the captivity shall sing at the time when they shall come out of captivity; as it is written and explained by Isaiah the prophet, (*n*) This song shall be unto you for joy in the night, that the feast of the passover is kept holy, and gladness of heart; as *when* the people go to appear before the Lord, three times in the year, with *all*

(*a*) The word תרגום signifies an exposition, or interpretation, or a translation of one language into another; and here of the Hebrew text into the Chaldee language, with an explanation. The first use of these translations was after the return of the Jews from Babylon, where they had almost lost the Hebrew language; and, therefore, were necessary for the understanding the law and the prophets. The translation of the five books of Moses was done by Onkelos, and that of the prophets by Jonathan Ben Uzziel, the former of whom lived a little after Christ, and the latter a little before him: but the translation of the Hagiographa, among which is this book of Canticles, is generally thought to be done by R. Joseph Cæcus. The paraphrase on this book could not have been written till after the finishing of the Talmud, seeing express mention is made of it there.

(*b*) Which is the Holy Spirit, as it is afterwards explained. What the Targum says of this book is the mind of Jewish writers in general. *Vide* Mishna, Tract. Yadaim, c. 3, s. 5. Shirhashirim Rabba, in ver. 1. Midrash Koheleth, in ver. 1. Zohar, in Exod. fol. 59, 3. Jarchi and Aben Ezra, in Præfat. in Cant. Kimchi in 1 Reg. 11, 41.

(*c*) Psa. xcii., which Psalm many Jewish writers think was made by the first man Adam; so Targum in Psa. xcii. Zohar in Gen. fol. 43, 2. Vajikra Rabba, Parash. 10. But in Shemoth Rabba, Parash. 23, it is said that Adam never composed any song: and that the song which Moses and the children of Israel sang at the Red Sea, was the first that ever was sung in the world; and, indeed, it is the first that is mentioned in Scripture.

(*d*) Exod. xv. 1.

(*e*) Num. xxi. 17.

(*f*) A phrase expressive of death. See Phil. i. 23.

(*g*) Deut. xxxii. 1.

(*h*) In Josh. x. 13, it is said, that "the sun stood still in the midst of heaven, and hasted not to go down כיום תמים, "about a whole day," or *a complete day*, which, if we understand of an artificial day, was but twelve hours; and if of a natural day, twenty-four hours. Kimchi, on Josh. x. 13, says that this miracle was wrought in the summer solstice, and on the longest day in the year, which in the land of Canaan consists but of fourteen hours; whereas the Targum here says, the sun stood still thirty-six hours, which makes three artificial days, or one natural day and a half. *Vide* Ecclus. xlvi. 5.

(*i*) So the Targum on Josh. x. 12.]

(*k*) Judg. v. 1.

(*l*) So the Targum on 1 Sam. ii. 1.

(*m*) So the Targum on 2 Sam. xxii. 1.

(*n*) Much to the same purpose is the Targum on Isa. xxx. 29.

kinds of music, and sound of the pipe, when they go up to the mountain of the Lord, to worship before the Lord, the mighty one of Israel.

Verse 2. *Let him kiss me, &c.*] Solomon the prophet said, "Blessed be the name of the Lord," who hath given us the law by the hands of Moses, (*o*) the great scribe, written upon two tables of stone, and the six parts of the (*p*) *Mishna* and *Talmud* (*q*) to study *in;* and he was speaking to us face to face, as a man kisseth his friend, because of the greatness of the love with which he loved us more than (*r*) the *seventy* nations.

Verse 3. *Because of the savour, &c.*] At the report of thy wonders and of thy power, which thou wroughtest for thy people the house of Israel. All the nations trembled who heard of the fame of thy greatness, and of thy favours; and thy holy name was heard in all the earth, which is more excellent than the anointing oil that was poured upon the heads of the kings and priests; and, therefore, the righteous love to walk in thy good way, that they may possess (*s*) this world, and the world to come.

Verse 4. *Draw me, &c.*] When the people of the house of Israel came out of Egypt, the *shechinah* of the Lord of the world went before them (*t*) in a pillar of cloud by day, and in a pillar of fire by night. The righteous of that generation said, Lord of all the world, draw us after thee, and we will run in thy good way; and bring us to the foot of Mount Sinai, and give us the law out of thy treasure house, the firmament; and we will rejoice and be glad, in the (*u*) *twenty-two* letters with which it is written; and we will remember them, and love thy deity; and will withdraw ourselves from the idols of the nations; and all the righteous which do what is right before thee shall fear thee, and love thy commandments.

Verse 5. *I am black, &c.*] When the house of Israel made the calf, their faces became black, like the sons of Cush, (*v*) which dwell in the tents of Kedar: but when they returned by repentance, and were forgiven, the brightness of the glory of their faces was increased, like the angels', because they made curtains for the tabernacle; therefore the *shechinah* of the Lord dwelt among them: and Moses, their master, went up into the (*w*) firmament, and made peace between them and their King.

Verse 6. *Look not upon me, &c.*] The congregation of Israel said before the nations, Do not despise me, because I am blacker than you, for I have done according to your works, and have (*x*) worshipped the sun and moon; for false prophets have been the cause that the fierce anger of the Lord hath come down upon me; and they taught me to worship your idols, and to walk in your laws: but the Lord of the world, who is my God, I have not served, nor walked in his commandments, nor have I kept his statutes and his law.

Verse 7. *Tell me, O thou, &c.*] When the time of Moses the prophet was come, to (*y*) depart out of the world, he said before the Lord, It is revealed unto me that this people will sin, and go into captivity; now show me how they shall be governed and dwell among the nations, whose decrees are grievous as the heat, and as the scorchings of the sun at noon, in the (*z*) summer solstice; and wherefore it is that they shall wander among the flocks of the sons of Esau and Ishmael, who join to thee their idols, for companions.

Verse 8. *If thou know not, &c.*] The holy blessed God said to Moses the prophet, It is their desire to smite the captivity of the congregation of Israel, which is like to a fair damsel: but my soul loveth her, *therefore* let her walk in the ways of the righteous, and let her order her prayer according to the direction of her governors, and let her lead her posterity, and teach her children, which are like to the kids of the goats, to go to the synagogue, and the school; and by that righteousness they shall be governed in the captivity, until the time that I send the King Messiah, and he shall lead them quietly to their habitations; *yea, he shall bring them to* the house of the sanctuary, which David and Solomon, the shepherds of Israel, built for them.

Verse 9. *To a company of horses, &c.*] When Israel went out of Egypt, Pharaoh and his host pursued after them with chariots and horsemen, and their way was shut up on the four sides of them; on the right hand and on the left were wildernesses full of fiery serpents, and behind them was wicked Pharaoh and his army, and before them was the Red Sea. What did the holy blessed God do? He was manifested in the power of his might upon the Red Sea, and dried the sea up; but the mud he did not dry up. The wicked and the mixed multi-

(*o*) So Ezra is called a "scribe of the law of the God of heaven," Ezra vii. 11, 12.

(*p*) The Mishna, which consists of six parts, is a collection of the traditions of the Jews, or their oral law, compiled by R. Judah, about the year of Christ 150.

(*q*) Or the Gemara, as it is read in Targum Triplex, printed with the Pentateuch. Of this Gemara, or Talmud, there are two sorts; the one is called the Jerusalem Talmud, which R. Jochanan collected together, about the year of Christ 230; the other is called the Babylonian Talmud, which was begun by R. Ase, in the year 367, who was succeeded in it by Maremar, in the year 427, and at last was finished by Avina, in the year 500. The former was written for the use of the Jerusalem Jews; the latter, for those in Babylon and other parts, and is most esteemed. It contains the disputations and decisions of the Jewish doctors upon the Mishna. *Vide* Buxtorf, Biblioth. Rab. p. 425.

(*r*) It is a generally received opinion among the Jews that seventy angels descended and confounded the language at Babel, from which time the earth was divided into seventy different nations, speaking seventy different languages. *Vide* Targum Jon. in Gen. xi. 7, 9.

(*s*) A like phrase see in Eph. i. 21; Matt. xii. 32.

(*t*) *Vide* Exod. xiii. 21, 22.

(*u*) The number of Hebrew letters in the alphabet. R. Isaac, in Shirhashirim Rabba in loc., gives the same sense of the words, which he collects from the word בך *bach, in thee,* ב *beth* standing numerically for two, and ך *caph,* for twenty.

(*v*) The Ethiopians. Shirhashirim Rabba in loc. explains the words by Amos ix. 7: "Are ye not as the children of the Ethiopians unto me," &c.

(*w*) It is a received opinion among the Jews that Moses went up into the firmament of heaven; though the Scriptures only signify that he went up into Mount Sinai, and was in the midst of the cloud with God there. So the Targum on ver. 11, 12, 14; and on Psa. lxviii. 18.

(*x*) So it is explained in Shirhashirim Rabba in loc. See Deut. xvii. 3; Job xxxi. 26, 27; 2 Kings xxiii. 5, 11; Ezek. viii. 16.

(*y*) See note on ver. 1.

(*z*) The Jews, as here and elsewhere, call it תקופת תמוז, *tekuphath Tammuz,* "the revolution of Tammuz." The sun is so called Ezek. viii. 14, which was worshipped under this name; it answers in part to our June, when the sun enters into the tropic of Cancer, and is what is meant by this revolution, Maimon. Hilch. Kiddush Hachodesh, c. 9, s. 2. *Vide* Targum, Jon. in Gen. viii. 22.

tude, and the strangers which were among them, said, The waters of the sea he is able to dry up; but the mud he is not able to dry up. In that very hour the fierce anger of the Lord *came* upon them; and he sought to drown them in the waters of the sea, as Pharaoh and his army, his chariots, and his horsemen, and his horses, were drowned; had it not been for Moses, the prophet, who spread his hands in prayer before the Lord, and turned away the anger of the Lord from them. Then he and the righteous of that generation opened their mouths, and sang a song, and passed through the Red Sea on dry land, because of the righteousness of Abraham, Isaac, and Jacob, the beloved of the Lord.

Verse 10. *Thy cheeks are comely, &c.*] When they went out into the wilderness, the Lord said to Moses, How fair is this people; that the words of the law should be given unto them; and they shall be as bridles in their jaws, that they may not depart out of the good way, as a horse turneth not aside that has a bridle in his jaw; and how fair is their neck to bear (*a*) the yoke of my commandments; and it shall be upon them as a yoke upon the neck of a bullock, which plougheth in the field, and feeds both itself and its master!

Verse 11. *We will make thee borders of gold, &c.*] Then was it said to Moses, Go up into the firmament, and I will give thee the two tables of stone, hewed out of the (*b*) sapphire of the throne of my glory, shining as the best gold, disposed in rows, written with my finger, in which are engraven the (*c*) ten words, purer than silver that is purified seven times seven, which is the number of the things explained in them, (*d*) forty-nine ways; and they shall be given by thine hand unto the people of the house of Israel.

Verse 12. *While the king sitteth, &c.*] Whilst Moses their master was in the firmament, to receive the two tables of stone, and the law, and the commandments, the wicked of that generation, and the mixed multitude that was among them, rose up and made a golden calf, and caused their works to stink; and there went out an evil report of them in the world, for before this time a fragrant odour of them was diffused in the world: but afterwards they stank like (*e*) nard, whose smell is very bad; and the plague of leprosy came down upon their flesh.

Verse 13. *A bundle of myrrh, &c.*] At that time the Lord said unto Moses, Go down, for the people have corrupted themselves; desist from *speaking to* me, and I will destroy them. Then Moses returned and asked mercy of the Lord; and the Lord remembered for them the (*f*) binding of Isaac, whom his father bound on (*g*) Mount Moriah, upon the altar; and the Lord turned from his fierce anger, and caused his shechinah to dwell among them as before.

Verse 14. *A cluster of camphire, &c.*] Lo, then went Moses down with the two tables of stone in his hands; and because of the sins of Israel his hands grew heavy, and they fell and were broken. Then went Moses, and ground (*h*) the calf to powder, and scattered the dust of it upon the river, and made the children of Israel drink *it*, and slew all that deserved to die, and went up a second time into the firmament, and prayed before the Lord, and made atonement for the children of Israel; then was he commanded to make a tabernacle and an ark. Immediately Moses hastened, and made the tabernacle, and all its furniture, and the ark; and he put in the ark the two other tables, and appointed the sons of Aaron the priests to offer the offerings upon the altar, and to pour the wine upon the offerings: but from whence had they wine to pour? For in the wilderness they had no proper place for sowing, neither had they fig trees, nor vines, nor pomegranates; but they went to the vineyards of En-gedi, and took clusters of grapes from thence, and pressed wine out of them, and poured it upon the altar, the fourth part of a hin to one lamb.

Verse 15. *Behold, thou art fair, &c.*] When the children of Israel performed the will of their King, he (*i*) himself praised them, in the (*k*) family of the holy angels, and said, How fair are thy works, my daughter, my beloved, O congregation of Israel, in the time that thou doest my will, and studiest in the words of my law; and how well ordered are thy works and thy affairs, as young doves that are fit to be offered up upon the altar!

Verse 16. *Behold, thou art fair, &c.*] The congregation of Israel answered before the Lord of the world, and thus she said, How fair is the shechinah of thy holiness, when thou dwellest among us, and receivest our prayers with acceptance, and when thou dwellest in our beloved bed, and our children are multiplied in the world, and we increase and multiply like a tree that is planted by a fountain of water, whose leaf is fair, and whose fruit is plenteous!

Verse 17. *The beams of our house, &c.*] Solo-

(*a*) It is very common in Jewish writings to compare the law to a yoke; so Targum, in Lam. iii. 27. Mishna, Tract. Berac. c. 2, s. 2. Pirk. Aboth. c. 3, s. 5. Midrash Echa Rabbati, fol. 56, 3. Bereshith Rabba, Parash. 98. Bemidbar Rabba, Parash. 13. See Matt. xi. 29, and Acts xv. 10.

(*b*) So Targ. Jon. in Exod. xxxi. 18. Zohar in Exod. fol. 35, 1. Jarchi in Exod. xxxiv. 1. See Exod. xxiv. 10, and Ezek. i. 26.

(*c*) The decalogue or ten commandments.

(*d*) In Psa. xii. 6, the place here referred to, the "words of the Lord" are said to be "as silver purified seven times;" where by שבעתים *shibathayim* some of the Jewish rabbins, agreeably to the Targum here, understand *seven times seven*, which makes forty-nine; and so many ways they say the law is capable of being interpreted, and that he is a wise man who is acquainted with them. Midrash Agada in Jarchi, in Psa. xii. 6. Midrash Kohelet, in c. 8, v. 1. Vajikra Rabba, Parash. 26, and Yade Mose, in ib. Bemidbar Rabba, Parash. 19.

(*e*) In Buxtorf's Bible it is read כגידא *kegida*, "like wormwood," which, indeed, well agrees with what is said of it; though Matthiolus says of *nard*, that when it has lost its sweet smell it stinks exceedingly. His words are these: Plerumque accidit dum per Indicum et Arabicum mare in Alexandriam defertur, et unde Venetias, ut ascito sibi maris humore (id namque facile sit quod nardus sit siccissima) vel situm contrahat, vel supputrescat: unde postea amissa suaveolentia, graviter oleat.—Matthiolus in Dioscor. l. 1, c. 6.

(*f*) The Jews suppose the binding of Isaac to be very meritorious, and that by virtue of it their sins are expiated and many blessings procured for them; and therefore in the beginning of the year they pray to God, that *in mercy to Israel* he would remember the binding of Isaac. Seder Tephillot, fol. 282, 1, 2. Edit. Basil. 1578. See Targum and Jarchi on Mic. vii. 20. Shirhashirim Rabba in c. 1, 14. Jarchi in Exod. xxxii. 13. Shemoth Rabba, Parash. 44.

(*g*) The Jews say, that in this same place Adam, Cain, Abel, and Noah built altars, and sacrificed. Maimon. Hilch. Beth. Habbechira, c. 2, s. 2. Targum Jon. in Gen. viii. 20, and xxii. 9. Here Solomon afterwards built the temple, 2 Chron. iii. 1.

(*h*) Exod. xxxii. 20.

(*i*) Ch. במימריה *bemeymreyh*, "by his word."

(*k*) The Latin word *familia* is here used by the paraphrast; compare with this Eph. iii. 15, Luke xii. 8.

mon the prophet said, How beautiful is the house of the sanctuary of the Lord, which is built by my hands of wood of (*l*) Gulmish: but far more beautiful will be the house of the sanctuary, which shall be built (*m*) in the days of the King Messiah, whose beams will be of the cedars of the garden of Eden, and whose rafters will be of brutine, fir, and box.

(*l*) A kind of cedar, see Eliæ Levitæ Methurgeman in voce. Targum Jon. in Num. xix. 6, and Ketoreth Hassammim, in ib.

(*m*) The Jews expect a third temple to be built in the days of the Messiah. See R. Abendan. not. in Miclol Yophi, and Abarbinel in Hagg. ii. 9. R. Isaac Chizuk Emun. par. 1, c. 34. Bemidbar Rabba, Parash. 14.

CHAPTER II

Verse 1. *I am the rose of Sharon, &c.*] The congregation of Israel said, When the Lord of the world causes his (*a*) shechinah to dwell in the midst of me, I am like the green daffodil of the garden of Eden, and my works are fair as the rose which is in the plain of the garden of Eden.

Verse 2. *As the lily among thorns, &c.*] But when I turn aside out of the way that is right before me, and he removes the shechinah of his holiness from me, I am like to a rose which flourishes among thorns, by which its leaves are pricked through and torn: even so am I pricked through and torn with wicked edicts, in the captivity among the (*b*) kings of the nations.

Verse 3. *As the apple tree among the trees, &c.*] As the pomecitron tree is beautiful, and to be praised among the unfruitful trees, and all the world knows it; so the Lord of the world was praised among the angels, when he was revealed on Mount Sinai, and gave the law unto his people; in that very hour I desired to sit under the shadow of his shechinah, and the words of his law were (*c*) fixed upon the roof of my mouth, and the reward of his commands is reserved for me in the world to come.

Verse 4. *He brought me, &c.*] The congregation of Israel said, The Lord brought me to the school which is in (*d*) Sinai, to learn the law from the mouth of Moses the great scribe; and the banner of his commandments I took upon me in love, and said, All that the Lord commandeth I will do, and will obey.

Verse 5. *Stay me with flagons, &c.*] But when I heard his voice, which spake out of the midst of the flame of fire, I trembled, and went backwards because of fear. Then I drew near to Moses and Aaron, and said unto them, Receive ye the voice of the words of the Lord, out of the midst of the fire, and bring me to the school, and sustain me with the words of the law on which the world is founded, and put veils upon my neck; *for* the interpretation of the holy words, which are sweet to my palate, are as the apples of the garden of Eden, and I will study in them: perhaps I may be healed by them, for I am sick of love.

Verse 6. *His left hand is under my head, &c.*] When the people of the house of Israel were travelling in the wilderness, they had (*e*) four clouds of glory at the four winds of the world round about them, that the (*f*) evil eye might not rule over them. There was one above them, that the heat and sun, as also the rain and hail, might not have power over them; and one below them, which carried them as a nurse carrieth her sucking child in her bosom; and another ran before them, at the distance of three days journey, (*g*) to level the mountains, and to elevate the plains; and it slew all the fiery serpents and scorpions which were in the wilderness; and it spied out a convenient place for them to lodge in, that they might study in the doctrine of the law, which was given them by the right hand of the Lord.

Verse 7. *I charge you, O ye daughters, &c.*] After that it was commanded Moses, by *the spirit of* prophecy from the Lord, to send spies to spy the land, and when they returned from spying it, they brought an evil report upon the land of Israel, wherefore they tarried forty years in the wilderness. Moses opened his mouth, and thus he said, I adjure you, O congregation of Israel, by the Lord of hosts, and by the fortresses of the land of Israel, that ye presume not to go up to the land of Canaan until it is the will of the Lord; lest the whole generation of warlike men perish from the camp, even as your brethren, the children of Ephraim, (*h*) who went out thirty years from

(*a*) The word shechinah comes from שכן *shachan*, which signifies *to dwell*, and Elias Levita, in his Methurgeman, says that their wise men called the Holy Spirit so, because it dwelt upon the prophets; though perhaps, he says, there may be another sense of it among the Cabalistic doctors, of which he declares himself ignorant. It seems to intend the glorious majesty and presence of God with his Church and people, and is the same with St. John's *σκηνη του Θεου*, *tabernacle* or *habitation of God*, which is said to be with men, Rev. xxi. 3; and may very well be applied to the Messiah, Jesus, who was made flesh, *και εσκηνωσεν*, *and dwelt* among us, John i. 14.

(*b*) In Buxtorf's Bible it is read פלכי *pilkey*, "the provinces of the nations."

(*c*) In Buxtorf's Bible it is read בסימן "*were sweet* to my palate, or taste."

(*d*) The same sense is given of those words in Shirhashirim Rabba in loc., and in Bemidbar Rabba, Parash. 2.

(*e*) The Jews are divided about the number of those clouds which they say attended the Israelites in their travels. R. Josiah says there were *five* of them, four at the four winds, and one went before them. R. Hoshea thinks there were *seven*, four at the four winds, one above, one below, and another that went before them; Bemidbar Rabba, Parash. 1.

(*f*) That is, envy or malice.

(*g*) The same is ascribed to this cloud in Bemidbar Rabba, *ubi supra*, and in Jarchi in Cant. iii. 6.

(*h*) The same story is reported in Targum Jon. in Exod. xiii. 7, where it is said that the number of the slain in this expedition was two hundred thousand mighty men, and that these are the dry bones Ezekiel saw in the valley, which upon his prophesying lived, and became an exceeding great army, Ezek. xxxvii. Something of this story is also hinted at in Shirhashirim Rabba, and Aben Ezra in loc. *Vide* 1 Chron. vii. 21, 22, and Kimchi, in *ibid*.

Egypt, before the time came, and they fell into the hand of the Philistines, which dwell in Gath, and they slew them: but tarry ye unto the end of forty years, and your children shall go up and inherit it.

Verse 8. *The voice of my beloved, &c.*] Solomon the king said, When the people of the house of Israel dwelt in Egypt, their cry went up to the highest heavens. Lo! then was the glory of the Lord revealed to Moses on Mount Horeb; and he sent him into Egypt to deliver them, and to bring them out of the oppression of the tyranny of Egypt; and he leaped over the appointed season through the righteousness of their fathers, who are like to mountains; and he skipped over the time of a hundred and ninety years' (*i*) servitude, through the righteousness of their mothers, who are like to hills.

Verse 9. *My beloved is like a roe, &c.*] The congregation of Israel said, When the glory of the Lord was revealed in Egypt, in the night of the passover, and slew all the first-born, he rode upon a swift cloud, and ran like a roe or a young hart, and protected the houses in which we were, and stood behind our wall, and looked out of the windows, and beheld through the lattices, and saw the blood of the sacrifice of the passover, and the blood of circumcision which was fixed upon our gates; and he hastened from the highest heavens, and saw his people, who eat of the sacrifice of the feast which was roasted with fire, with (*k*) Tamca and Ulshin, and unleavened bread; and he spared us, and did not give power to the destroying angel to destroy us.

Verse 10. *My beloved spake, and said unto me, &c.*] And in the morning my beloved answered, and said unto me, Arise, O congregation of Israel, my love, who *wast so* of old, and *who art* fair in *good* works; go, get thee out from the bondage of the Egyptians.

Verse 11. *For lo, the winter is past, &c.*] For behold, the time of bondage, which is like to winter, is ceased; and the years (*l*) which I spake of to Abraham between the pieces are at an end; and the tyranny of the Egyptians, which is like to a violent rain, is over and gone; neither shall ye see them any more for ever.

Verse 12. *The flowers appear on the earth, &c.*] And Moses and Aaron, (*m*) who are like to branches of palm trees, appeared to do wonders in the land of Egypt; and the time of cutting the first-fruits is come, and the voice of the Holy Spirit of redemption, which I spake of to Abraham your father. Now ye hear what I said unto him; yea, the people whom ye shall serve I will judge, and after that ye shall come forth with great substance; and now it is my pleasure to do what I sware to him by my word.

Verse 13. *The fig tree putteth forth, &c.*] The congregation of Israel, which is like to the first-fruits of figs, opened her mouth, and sang a song at the Red Sea; yea, the babes and sucklings praised the Lord of the world with their tongues. Immediately the Lord of the world said unto them, Arise, O congregation of Israel, my love, and my fair one, and go from hence into the land which I have sworn unto thy fathers.

Verse 14. *O my dove, that art in the clefts of the rock, &c.*] And when wicked Pharaoh (*n*) pursued after the children of Israel, the congregation of Israel was like to a dove that is shut up in the clefts of the rock, when the serpent afflicts within, and the hawk oppresses without; even so the congregation of Israel was shut up on the four sides of the world, for before them was the sea, and behind them enmity (*o*) pursued; and on the two sides of them were the wildernesses, which were full of fiery serpents, which bite and kill the sons of men with their poison. And immediately she opened her mouth in prayer before the Lord, and Bath Kol (*p*) went out from the highest heavens, and thus it said, O thou congregation of Israel, who art like to a clean dove, and which is hid in the closure of the clefts of the rock, and in the secret places of the stairs, show me thy countenance, and thy works, which are right; cause me to hear thy voice, for thy voice is sweet in prayer in the house of the little sanctuary, and thy countenance is fair in good works.

(*i*) The Jews unanimously agree, that from the time of Jacob's going down into Egypt to the coming up of the Israelites from thence were just two hundred and ten years; Targum Jon. in Exod. xii. 40. Shirhashirim Rabba, in c. 2, ver. 11, 17. Shemoth Rabba, Parash. 13. Jarchi in Gen. xv. 13, and in Exod. xii. 40; which some of them collect from the word רדו *redu*, "get you down," used by Jacob, Gen. xlii. 2, when he ordered his sons to go down to Egypt, and buy corn, the letters of which word numerically make up 210. Bemidbar Rabba, Parash. 13. Jarchi in Gen. xlii. 2. R. Abendana not. in Miclol Yophi in Exod. xii. 40; to which two hundred and ten years if we add the one hundred and ninety, which the Targumist here says were skipped over in order to hasten the deliverance of the Israelites from their bondage, there will be just the four hundred years God spake of to Abraham, Gen. xv. 13, and mentioned by Stephen, Acts vii. 6, in which his seed should be a stranger, serve, be afflicted and evil entreated; which four hundred years may be reckoned after this manner: From the birth of Isaac to the birth of Jacob sixty years, Gen. xxv. 26; from thence to the coming of Jacob into Egypt one hundred and thirty years, Gen. xlvii. 9; and from thence to the coming of the children of Israel out of Egypt two hundred and ten years; which completes the number. And if we begin the date from Abraham's going out from Ur of the Chaldees, and allow five years for his dwelling in Haran, as the Jews do, see Aben Ezra in Exod. xii. 40; from whose departure from thence to the birth of Isaac were twenty-five years, Gen. xii. 4, and xxi. 5; which thirty years, being added to the above-said four hundred, make up the number given by Moses, Exod. xii. 40, and by the apostle Paul, Gal. iii. 17.

(*k*) The names of the bitter herbs with which the paschal lamb was eaten, Exod. xii. 8. The same are mentioned in Targum Jon. in Exod. xii. 8; and in some of their writings three other herbs are mentioned, the names of which are Chazareth, Charcabina, and Meror, by which they intend horehound, endive, wild lettuce, cichory, and such like herbs; for they themselves do not seem very well to understand them. See Misna Tract. Pesach. c. 2, s. 6. Jarchi ib., and Maimon. Tract. Chametz. Umetza, c. 7, s. 13.

(*l*) So it is explained in Shirhashirim Rabba, and by Jarchi in loc.

(*m*) So Shirhashirim Rabba, and Jarchi in loc.

(*n*) After the same manner Shirhashirim Rabba, and Jarchi in loc. Shemoth Rabba, Parash. 21.

(*o*) That is, the enemy; compare with this Rom. viii. 7.

(*p*) Frequent mention is made of this in the writings of the Jews. It was a voice from heaven which revealed secrets, foretold future events, decided controversies, and directed in difficult matters; it was used in the second temple in the room of prophecy, which the Jews say then ceased, Talmud Sota, fol. 48, col. 2, and Sanhedrin, fol. 2, col. 4. R. Saadiah Gaon in Dan. ix. 24. Shirhashirim Rabba in c. 8, 9. It is thought by R. Levi Ben. Gerson, in 2 Sam. i., s. 27, to be a more excellent and complete kind of divination; and indeed I am inclined to think that most of those voices which go under this name were the mere illusions of Satan, designed to deceive the people, and lessen the credit of those voices which were heard from heaven in the times of Christ. See Matt. iii. 17, and xvii. 5; John xii. 28.

Verse 15. *Take us the foxes, &c.*] After that they had passed through the sea, they murmured for water; then came wicked Amalek against them, who hated them on the account of the birthright and blessing which Jacob our father took away from Esau; and he came to make war with Israel, for they had made void the words of the law; and wicked Amalek (*q*) stole from under the wings of the clouds of glory *several* persons from the tribe of Dan, and slew them, because the idol of Micah was in their hand. In that very hour the house of Israel, which is like to a vineyard, was condemned to be destroyed, except the righteous of that generation, who were like to the best spice.

Verse 16. *My beloved is mine, &c.*] In that very hour they returned by repentance: then stood Moses the prophet, and prayed before the Lord; and Joshua his minister girded himself, and went out from under the (*r*) wings of the clouds of the glory of the Lord, and with him mighty men that *were* righteous, who in their works are like to the rose; and they made war with Amalek, and they broke Amalek and his people with the anathema of the Lord, and with slaughter, and with breach, and with the edge of the sword.

Verse 17. *Until the day break, &c.*] But in a very few days the children of Israel made the golden calf, and the clouds of glory which covered them removed; and they were left open, and were spoiled of the apparatus of their armour, on which was engraven the Great Name, (*s*) that is explained by seventy names. And the Lord sought to destroy them out of the world; but that he remembered before him the oath which he sware to Abraham, to Isaac, and to Jacob, who were swift in their service, as a roe or a young hart, and the offering which Abraham offered up, *even* Isaac, his own son, on Mount Moriah, and where, before then, he had offered his offering, and divided them equally.

(*q*) In Targ. Jon. in Exod. xvii. 8, where the same story is mentioned, it is said that those men of the tribe of Dan whom Amalek took and slew, were such whom the cloud did not receive and protect because of their idolatry.

(*r*) So Targum Jon. and Jarchi in Exod. xvii. 9, and Shemoth Rabba Parash. 26.

(*s*) This is the name Jehovah, which the Jews think it unlawful to pronounce; and therefore explain it by other names, usually by Adonai or Elohim. Here it is said to be explained by seventy names, sometimes by seventy-two; of which see Galatinus de Arcanis Cath. ver. 1, 2, c. 17, and Schindler, Lex. Pentaglot., p. 1492.

CHAPTER III

Verse 1. *By night on my bed, &c.*] And when the people of the house of Israel saw that the clouds of glory were removed from them, and the holy crown (*a*) that was given to them at Sinai was taken from them, and they were left dark as the night; then they sought the holy crown, which was removed from them, but they found it not.

Verse 2. *I will rise now, &c.*] The children of Israel said one to another, Let us arise, and go and surround the tabernacle of the congregation, which Moses fixed without the camp; and let us seek instruction from the Lord, and the holy shechinah, which is removed from us. And they went about the cities, and in the streets, and in the broad places; but they found it not.

Verse 3. *The watchmen that go about the city, &c.*] The congregation of Israel said, (*b*) Moses and Aaron, and the Levites which keep the charge of the word of the tabernacle of the congregation, who go round about it, found me, and I inquired of them concerning the shechinah of the glory of the Lord, which was removed from me. Moses, the great scribe of Israel, answered, and thus he said: I will go up to the highest heavens, and I will pray before the Lord; perhaps atonement may be made for your transgressions, so that he may cause his shechinah to dwell among you as before.

Verse 4. *It was but a little that I passed, &c.*] It was but a very little time, and the Lord turned from the fierceness of his anger, and commanded Moses the prophet to make the tabernacle of the congregation, and the ark, and caused his shechinah to dwell in it; and the people of the house of Israel offered their offerings, and studied in the words of the law in the chamber (*c*) of the school of Moses their master, and in the chamber of Joshua, the son of Nun, his minister.

Verse 5. *I charge you, &c.*] When the seven nations (*d*) heard that the children of Israel were about to possess their land, they arose as one *man*, and cut down the trees, and stopped up the fountains of water, and destroyed their cities, and fled. The holy blessed God said to Moses the prophet, I have sworn to their fathers, that I will bring their children to inherit a land flowing with milk and honey; but how shall I bring them to a land that is desolate and empty? Now, therefore, I will cause them to stay forty years in the wilderness, and my law shall be mixed with them, and after that those wicked nations shall build what they have destroyed. And then said Moses to the children of Israel, I charge you, O congregation of Israel, by the Lord of hosts, and by the fortresses of the land of Israel, that ye presume not to go up to the land of Canaan until the forty years are ended. When it shall be the good pleasure of the Lord to deliver the inhabitants of the land into your hands, then

(*a*) The same is mentioned in the Targums of Jon. and Jerus. in Exod. xxxii. 25. By this holy crown seems to be meant the shechinah or presence of God, and so it is explained in Shirhashirim Rabba in chap. iv. 12; or else the law, which is very frequently called so, Bemidbar Rabba, Parash. 4. Midrash Kohelet in c. 7, 1. Pirk. Aboth. c. 4, s. 13.

(*b*) These are also supposed to be intended by the watchmen in Shirhashirim Rabba, and by Jarchi and R. Aben Ezra in loc.

(*c*) It was a common practice with the Jewish doctors to teach, dispute, and converse about religion in chambers or upper rooms. See Mishná Tract. Shabbath. c. 1, s. 4.

(*d*) The Hittites, the Girgashites, the Amorites, the Canaanites, the Perizzites, the Hivites, and the Jebusites, Deut. vii. 1.

shall ye pass over Jordan, and the land shall be subdued before you.

Verse 6. *Who is this that cometh out of the wilderness, &c.*] When the Israelites came up out of the wilderness, and passed over Jordan with Joshua the son of Nun, the people of the land said, Who is this choice nation which comes up out of the wilderness, perfumed with the sweet incense, and supported through the righteousness of Abraham, who worshipped and prayed before the Lord on Mount Moriah, and is anointed with the anointing oil, through the righteousness of Isaac, who was bound in that place of the sanctuary which is called the mountain of frankincense; for whom wonders are also wrought through the holiness of Jacob, who wrestled with him until the morning ascended, and prevailed over him, and was delivered, he and the twelve tribes?

Verse 7. *Behold his bed, which is Solomon's, &c.*] When Solomon, the king of Israel, built the house of the sanctuary of the Lord in Jerusalem, the Lord said by his word, How beautiful is the house of this sanctuary, which is built for me by the hands of King Solomon, the son of David! and how beautiful are the priests, when they spread their hands, and stand upon their desks, and bless the people of the house of Israel by the sixty letters (*e*) which were delivered to Moses their master, and with that blessing which surrounds them like a high and strong wall, and by which all the mighty men of Israel prevail and prosper!

Verse 8. *They all hold swords, &c.*] And the priests and the Levites, and all the tribes of Israel, all of them take hold of the words of the law, which are like to a (*f*) sword, in which they employ themselves as men that are expert in war; and every one of them has the (*g*) seal of circumcision sealed upon their flesh, even as it was sealed upon the flesh of Abraham; and by it they prevail as a man that has his sword girt upon his thigh, wherefore they are not afraid of noxious spirits (*h*) and apparitions, which walk in the night.

Verse 9. *King Solomon made himself a chariot, &c.*] King Solomon built for himself (*i*) a holy temple of the trees of (*k*) Zangebila, fir trees, and cedars, which came from Lebanon, and covered it with pure gold.

Verse 10. *He made the pillars thereof, &c.*] And after that he had finished it, he put in the midst of it the ark of the testimony, which is the pillar of the world; and in it the two tables of stone, which Moses placed there in Horeb, which are more precious than silver purified, and more beautiful than the best gold; and he spread and covered over it (*l*) the veil of blue and purple, and between the cherubims which are over the mercy-seat the shechinah of the Lord abode, whose name dwelleth in Jerusalem, above all the cities of the land of Israel.

Verse 11. *Go forth, O ye daughters of Zion, &c.*] When King Solomon came to make the dedication of the house of the sanctuary, a crier went forth in strength; and thus he said, Go forth and see, ye inhabitants of the provinces of the land of Israel, and ye people of Zion, the crown and diadem wherewith the people of the house of Israel crowned King Solomon in the (*m*) day of the dedication of the house of the sanctuary, when he rejoiced with the joy of the feast of tabernacles; for king Solomon kept at that time the feast of tabernacles (*n*) fourteen days.

(*e*) The same is mentioned in Shirhashirim Rabba in loc., and in Bemidbar Rabba, Parash. 11. There being just this number of letters in the forms of blessings with which the priests were to bless the people of Israel, in Num. vi. 24, 25, 26.

(*f*) The law is likewise compared to a sword, in Bereshith Rabba, Parash. 21. See Eph. vi. 17. Heb. iv. 12.

(*g*) The apostle Paul calls circumcision *σημειον περιτομης, σφραγιδα της δικαιοσυνης της πιστεως*, "the sign of circumcision, a seal of the righteousness of faith," Rom. iv. 11.

(*h*) So this "fear in the night" is interpreted by some of the rabbins in Shirhashirim Rabba in loc., and in Bemidbar Rabba, Parash. 11. Though others of them in the said places explain it of the fear of hell, which is like to the night; as they do also in Gemara Rab. Tract. Sanhedrin, c. 1, fol. 7, col. 1.

(*i*) By this chariot R. Aben Ezra also understands the house of the Lord; and in Shirhashirim Rabba, and by Jarchi in loc., it is interpreted of the tabernacle, as it is by some of the Jews, in Bemidbar Rabba, Parash. 12, though others think the ark is intended; and others in the same place would have the world meant, which way they explain it in Zohar in Gen. fol. 2, 1. The word אפריון very properly signifies "the marriage bed," so called from פרה which signifies "to fructify," or "to be fruitful." Hence לבנות אפריון is a very usual phrase with the rabbins to express the celebration of marriage. *Vide* Buxtorf, epist. Heb. lib. 2, ep. 7.

(*k*) Elias Levita, in his Methurgeman on this word, says that this is cinnabar. He seems to mean a kind of red wood, which dyers use; but observes, that some say it is the spice we call ginger. So David de Pomis renders it in his Lex. Heb. fol. 54, 4; and indeed it is joined with pepper in Maimon. Tract. Shebitat Asur, c. 2, s. 6. Biath. Hamikdash, c. 7, s. 13, and Beracoth, c. 8, s. 7. It is most likely to be a kind of cedar.

(*l*) *Vide* Bemidbar Rabba, Parash. 12, Shirhashirim Rabba, and Jarchi in loc.

(*m*) Most of the Jewish writers refer this to the time of the giving of the law on Mount Sinai, and the setting up of the tabernacle by Moses; so Jarchi and Shirhashirim Rabba in loc. Shemoth Rabba, Parash. 52. Vajikra Rabba, Parash. 20, Bemidbar Rabba, Parash. 2 and 12. Præfat. Echa Rabbati. fol. 21, 2.

(*n*) In 1 Kings viii. 65, it is said that "Solomon held a feast seven days and seven days, even fourteen days;" the reason of which distinction is because the first seven days were kept for the dedication of the altar, and the other for the feast of tabernacles; see 2 Chron. vii. 8, 9: whereas our Targumist would have the feast of tabernacles kept the whole fourteen days, contrary to the command in Lev. xxiii. 34. *Vide* R. Levi Ben Gerson, and R. David Kimchi in 1 Reg. viii. 65.

CHAPTER IV

Verse 1. *Behold, thou art fair, &c.*] And in that day King Solomon offered up a (*a*) thousand burnt-offerings upon the altar, and his offerings were graciously accepted by the Lord.

(*a*) In 1 Kings viii. 63, the sacrifice of peace-offerings which Solomon offered was two and twenty thousand oxen, and a hundred and twenty thousand sheep: but the number of burnt-offerings is not mentioned.

Bath Kol (*b*) went forth from heaven; and thus it said, How fair art thou, O congregation of Israel, and how fair are the princes of the congregation and the wise men, (*c*) who sit in the sanhedrin, who enlighten (*d*) the world; the people of the house of Israel, and are like to young doves; yea, even the rest of the children of thy congregation; and the people of the earth are righteous, as the sons of Jacob, (*e*) who gathered stones, and made a heap *thereof* on the mount of Gilead!

Verse 2. *Thy teeth are like, &c.*] How fair are the priests and Levites, who offer up thine offerings, and eat the holy flesh, and the tithes, and the offering of fruits; and are pure from all oppression and rapine, even as clean as Jacob's flocks of sheep when they were shorn, and came up from the brook (*f*) Jabok, among whom there was no oppression or rapine, and they are all of them like to one another, and always bear twins; neither is any barren, or that miscarrieth among them.

Verse 3. *Thy lips are like a thread, &c.*] And the lips of the high priest inquire in prayer, on the day of atonement, before the Lord; and his words turn the transgressions of Israel, which are like to a thread of scarlet, and make them white (*g*) as pure wool; and the king, who is their head, is full of the commandments, as a pomegranate; besides the (*h*) Amarcalin and (*i*) Archonin, who are next the king, who are righteous; neither is there any iniquity in them.

Verse 4. *Thy neck is like the tower, &c.*] And the head of the school, who is thy master, is powerful in righteousness, and mighty in good works, as David king of Israel, by the word of whose mouth the world is restored, who in the doctrine of the law employs himself; *in which* the people of the house of Israel placing their confidence, overcome in war, as if they held in their hands all kinds of warlike instruments of mighty men.

Verse 5. *Thy two breasts, &c.*] Thy two Redeemers which shall redeem thee; (*k*) Messiah the son of David, and Messiah the son of Ephraim, are like to Moses and Aaron, the sons of Jochebed, who may be compared to young roes that are twins; who by their righteousness fed the people of the house of Israel forty years in the wilderness with manna, and with fatted fowls, and water of (*l*) the well of Miriam.

Verse 6. *Until the day break, &c.*] And all the time that the house of Israel held fast in their hands the religion of their righteous fathers, they drove away those noxious spirits that walk in the night-time, or in the morning, or at noonday; because that the shechinah of the glory of the Lord dwelt in the house of the sanctuary, which was built on Mount Moriah; for all the noxious and destroying spirits fled at the smell of the sweet incense.

Verse 7. *Thou art all fair, &c.*] And when thy people, the house of Israel do the will of the Lord of the world, he praises them in the highest heavens; and thus he saith, Thou art all fair, O congregation of Israel, and there is no (*m*) spot in thee.

Verse 8. *Come with me from Lebanon, &c.*] The Lord said by his word, Dwell with me, O congregation of Israel, who art like to a modest (*n*) damsel, and go up with me to the house of the sanctuary, where the heads of the people, which dwell by the river of (*o*) Amana, and the inhabitants that reside on the top of Mount (*p*) Talga, and the people which are in Hermon, shall bring gifts unto thee, and they that inhabit the strong fortified cities, which are as powerful as lions, shall pay tribute to thee; *yea*, an offering *shall be brought* from the cities of the mountains, which are mightier than the leopards.

Verse 9. *Thou hast ravished my heart, &c.*] Fixed upon the (*q*) table of my heart is thy love, O my sister, the congregation of Israel, who art like to a modest damsel; fixed upon the

(*b*) See note on chap. ii. 14.

(*c*) So the words are explained in Shirhashirim Rabba, in loc.

(*d*) So Christ calls his disciples the "light of the world," Matt. v. 14.

(*e*) This refers to the account that is given of what passed between Jacob and Laban, in Gen. xxxi. 46, 47. See Jarchi in loc.

(*f*) This is the ford Jacob passed over with his wives and children, when he went out to meet his brother Esau, Gen. xxxii. 22. Mention is made of it in several other places of Scripture: Deut. ii. 37, and iii. 16; Josh. xii. 2.

(*g*) The Jews say, that when the scape-goat was sent into the wilderness, a scarlet thread was tied to the temple door, which, as soon as the goat was arrived in the wilderness, turned white; which was not only a token to them of its arrival there, but was also an indication of their sins being forgiven; as it is said, "Though your sins be as scarlet, they shall be as white as snow," Isa. i. 18. See Mishna, Tract. Yoma, c. 6, s. 8, and Ez Chayim, *ibid.* This scarlet thread, they say, ceased turning white forty years before the destruction of the temple, which was about the time Jesus Christ, who was typified by the scape-goat, made atonement for sin; Talmud Yoma, fol. 39, col. 2. This tradition the Targumist seems to have in view here.

(*h*) These officers were of the tribe of Levi, Bemidbar Rabba, Parash. 3. Their number was never less than seven; their work was to take the care and charge of the keys of the court; and one might not open the door unless all seven were present, Mishna, Tract. Shekalim, c. 5, s. 2. Maimon. Hilch. Cele Hamikdash, c. 4, s. 17. Jarchi in 2 Reg. xii. 9; though Kimchi, in 2 Reg. xii. 9, and xxii. 4, thinks that they were treasurers, who had the charge of the public money. The etymology given of this word is very different. Baal Aruch says this officer was so called because he was מר על הכל *mar al haccol*, "lord over all:" the same is given in Vajikra Rabba, Parash. 5, where Shebna the treasurer, Isa. xxii. 15, is said to be one of those officers. Elias Levita, in his Methurgeman, says he was so called because אומר כל *omar col*, "he said" or "prescribed" all things.

(*i*) This is from the Greek word Αρχων, and signifies princes, rulers, or governors.

(*k*) The Jews, observing different characters given of the Messiah, which they think irreconcilable in one person, have feigned two Messiahs; the one they call Messiah, the son of David, who shall be a potent, prosperous, and victorious prince; the other, Messiah the son of Ephraim, or Joseph, as he is sometimes called, who shall be exposed to many hardships and sufferings, and at last die in the war of Gog and Magog. Of these two Messiahs, see Talmud, Succah, fol. 52, col. 1. Zohar in Num. fol. 68, 3; 82, 2; 99, 4; and 101, 2. Jarchi in Isa. xxiv. 18. Kimchi, Jarchi, and Aben Ezra in Zech. xii. 10.

(*l*) It is an opinion which obtains among the Jews, that on account of the merits of Moses the manna was given; and on the account of those of Aaron, the clouds of glory; and for the sake of Miriam, the well of water, which they say they enjoyed all the forty years they were in the wilderness. Shirhashirim Rabba in loc. Bemidbar Rabba, Parash. 1 and 13. Targum Jon. and Jarchi in Num. xx. 2.

(*m*) Or plague.

(*n*) Here the Greek word νυμφη is used, as it is also in verses 9, 10, 11, 12, and chap. v. 1.

(*o*) This was one of the rivers of Damascus; see 2 Kings v. 12, where it is read Abana: but both the Masora and Targum read it Amana; and Kimchi thinks it was called by both names.

(*p*) Or "the mountain of snow." Elias Levita, in his Methurgeman, says that Mount Shenir was called so: perhaps Mount Salmon may be meant, which had snow continually upon it; see Psa. lxviii. 14, and R. Aben Ezra, *ibid.*

(*q*) Compare with this 2 Cor. iii. 3.

table of my heart is the love of the least of thy children, who is righteous as one of the great men of the sanhedrin, as one of the kings (*r*) of the house of Judah, on whose neck the crown of the kingdom is put.

Verse 10. *How fair is thy love, &c.*] How fair is thy love to me, my sister, the congregation of Israel, who art like to a modest damsel! How excellent is thy love to me, more than the (*s*) seventy nations; and the good (*t*) report of thy righteous ones is more excellent than all spices!

Verse 11. *Thy lips, O my spouse, &c.*] And when the priests pray in the holy court, their lips drop *as* the honey-comb; and so does thy tongue, O thou modest damsel, when thou deliverest songs and hymns, sweet as milk and honey; and the smell of the (*u*) priests' garments *is* as the smell of Lebanon.

Verse 12. *A garden enclosed, &c.*] Thy women, which are married to modest men, are as a modest damsel, and as the garden of Eden, into which no man hath power to enter except the righteous, whose souls are by angels (*v*) carried into it; and thy virgins are hid and concealed (*w*) in private chambers, and are sealed up because *they are* as a fountain of living water, which comes forth from under the tree, and is parted to the four heads (*x*) of the rivers: but if it is sealed with the great and holy name, it goes forth and flows, and overflows all the world.

Verse 13. *Thy plants are an orchard, &c.*] And thy young men are full of thy commands, as pomegranates, and love their wives, and beget children as righteous as themselves; and their smell, therefore, is as the excellent spices of the garden of Eden, even camphires with nards.

Verse 14. *Spikenard with saffron, &c.*] Nard, and saffron, and calamus, and cinnamon, with all trees of frankincense, pure myrrh, and lign aloes, with all kinds of spices.

Verse 15. *A fountain of gardens, &c.*] And the waters of Siloah (*y*) go softly, with the rest of the waters which flow from Lebanon, to water the land of Israel, for the sake of those who study in the words of the law, which are like to a well of living water; and on the account of the righteousness (*z*) of pouring of water, which they pour upon the altar in the house of the sanctuary, that is built in Jerusalem, which is called (*a*) Lebanon.

Verse 16. *Awake, O north wind, &c.*] And at the north side (*b*) was a table, and upon it (*c*) twelve loaves of shew-bread, and at the south side (*d*) was the lamp to give light; and upon the altar the priests offered up the offerings, and caused the sweet incense to ascend from thence. The congregation of Israel said, Let the merciful God come into the house of the sanctuary, and graciously accept the offerings of his people.

(*r*) Many of the kings of the house of Judah were holy and good men; so Aben Ezra in loc.

(*s*) See note in chap. i. 2.

(*t*) So Jarchi in loc.

(*u*) *Vide* Jarchi in loc.

(*v*) It was an ancient opinion of the Jews, that the ministry of angels was used in carrying the souls of saints to heaven. Thus in Debarim Rabba, Parash. 11, several angels are ordered by God to bring the soul of Moses to him. Agreeably to this notion, it is said in Luke xvi. 22, that "the beggar died, and was carried by the angels into Abraham's bosom.

(*w*) It was very usual with the Eastern people to keep their virgins, especially those of note and esteem, very recluse, and not admit them to public or common conversation; but oblige them to abide much within doors. Hence they are called in the Hebrew language עלמות, from the word עלם, which signifies to hide or cover, because they were not exposed to public view; wherefore the author of the second book of Maccabees calls them *κατακλειστους παρθενους*, "virgins that were shut up;" i. e., in the houses of their parents, in private chambers, as the Targumist here says. See 2 Macc. iii. 19.

(*x*) Regard seems to be had to the river which went out of Eden, mentioned in Gen. ii. 10, and was parted into four heads or rivers, the names of which were Pison, Gihon, Hiddekel, and Euphrates. The Cabalists suppose a great many mysteries to be contained therein; see Zohar in Gen. fol. 85, 2; in Exod. fol. 34, 3; 37, 2, and in Lev. fol. 24, 3, where the name of this river is said to be Jobel, according to Jer. xvii. 8; and so it is in Vajikra Rabba, Parash. 22, and in Bemidbar Rabba, Parash. 21.

(*y*) See Isa. viii. 6, and Aben Ezra upon it, who expounds the text in Isaiah by this in Canticles. Jarchi, in Isa. viii. 6 says the name of this fountain was Gihon. In the New Testament it is called Siloam, John ix. 7, 11; it was a fountain near Jerusalem, Neh. iii. 15.

(*z*) The paraphrast refers here to a ceremony used at the feast of tabernacles, when the people fetched water from Siloam, and brought it to the priest, who poured it upon the altar with the wine of the daily sacrifice; this they say Moses received from God at Mount Sinai, though it is not written. This ceremony of drawing and pouring water at those times was attended with all the demonstrations of joy imaginable, as shouting, leaping, dancing, singing, blowing of trumpets, throwing of citrons, illumination of houses, &c.; insomuch that they say, that those who never saw the rejoicing of drawing water never saw rejoicing in their lives, Mishna, Tract. Succa, c. 4, s. 9, 10, and c. 5, s. 1, 2, 3, 4, 5; Jarchi and Ez Chayim, *ibid.;* Maimon., Tract. Tamidin, c. 10, s. 6, 7, 8; Cele Hamikdash, c. 7, s. 8, and c. 8, s. 6. They fancied the Holy Ghost was much delighted with this vain joy of theirs; nay, that in drawing water they drew him, i. e., procured his descent upon them, and abode with them as a spirit of prophecy, which they say Jonah obtained at this time and in this way; and, therefore, whilst they were performing this ceremony, frequently used those words in Isa. xii. 3: "With joy shall ye draw water out of the wells of salvation;" which they understand of the Holy Ghost, Bereshith Rabba, Parash. 70. Midrash Ruth, fol. 32, 2. Jarchi and Ez Chayim in Mishna, *ubi supra.* To this ceremony Christ is thought to allude, "when in the last day, the great day of this feast of tabernacles, he stood and cried, saying, If any man thirst, let him come unto me and drink: he that believeth on me, as the Scripture hath said, out of his belly shall flow rivers of living water: but this spake he of the Spirit," &c. John vii. 37, 38, 39. *Vide* Tremell., *ibid.*

(*a*) So the temple is called in Zech. xi. 1: "Open thy doors, O Lebanon, that the fire may devour thy cedars," according to the mind of several Jewish interpreters, who, out of Talmud Yoma, fol. 39, 2, relate, that forty years before the destruction of the temple the doors thereof opened of themselves; at which Jochanan Ben Zaccai being affrighted, said, O temple, temple, now know I that thy destruction is at hand; for so prophesied Zechariah, the son of Iddo, of thee, Open thy doors, &c. *Vide* R. Abendam. Not. in Miclol Yophi; Jarchi and Kimchi in Zech. xi. 1.

(*b*) That is, of the sanctuary; see Exod. xl. 22, 23.

(*c*) Lev. xxiv. 5, 6.

(*d*) Exod. xl. 24, 25.

CHAPTER V

Verse 1. *I am come into my garden, &c.*] The holy blessed God said unto his people, the house of Israel, I am come into the house of my sanctuary, which thou hast built for me, O my sister, the congregation of Israel, who *art* like to a modest damsel: I have caused my shechinah to dwell with thee, (*a*) I have received thy sweet incense, which thou hast made on my account; I have sent fire from heaven, and it hath devoured the burnt-offerings, and the holy drink-offerings; the libation of the red and white wine is graciously received by me, which the priests pour out upon mine altar. Now, *therefore*, come, ye priests that love my commandments, and eat what is left of the offerings, and delight yourselves with those good things which are prepared for you.

Verse 2. *I sleep, but my heart waketh, &c.*] After all these words the people of the house of Israel sinned, and he delivered them into the hand of Nebuchadnezzar, king of Babylon, who carried them into captivity; and they were in captivity like a man asleep, that cannot be awaked out of his sleep; wherefore the Holy Ghost warned them by the prophets, and awaked them out of the sleep of their hearts. *Then* answered the Lord of the whole world, and thus he said, Return by repentance, open thy mouth, rejoice and show forth my praise, my sister, my love, O congregation of Israel, who *art* like to a dove for the perfection of thy works; for the hair of my head is filled with thy tears, as a man the hair of whose head is wet with the dew of heaven; and my Nazaritical locks are filled with the drops of thine eyes, as a man whose Nazaritical locks are full of the drops of rain which descend in the night.

Verse 3. *I have put off my coat, &c.*] The congregation of Israel answered in the presence of the prophets, Behold, now have I removed from me the (*b*) yoke of his commandments, and have served the idols of the nations; wherefore, how can I have the face to return to him again? The Lord of the world answered them by the prophets, *saying*, And behold, now I also have removed my shechinah from thee; and how shall I return again, seeing thou hast done evil works? for I have washed my feet from thine uncleanness, and how shall I defile them in the midst of thee with thy evil works?

Verse 4. *My beloved put in his hand, &c.*] When it appeared manifest before the Lord that the people of the house of Israel would not repent and turn unto him, he stretched forth (*c*) his mighty arm against the tribes of Reuben and Gad, and the half tribe of Manasseh; on the other side of Jordan; and he delivered them into the hand of Sennacherib, the king of Assyria, who carried them into captivity, (*d*) to Lachlach, and Chabor, *and to the* rivers of Gozan, and cities of Media; and he took out of their hands the molten calf which Jeroboam, the wicked, set in Lesham-Dan, which was called (*e*) Pamias, in the days of Pekah, the son of Remaliah; and when I heard *it*, my bowels were moved towards them.

Verse 5. *I rose up to open to my beloved, &c.*] And when the mighty stroke of the Lord lay heavy upon me, I repented of my works; and the priests offered up offerings, and burnt the sweet incense: but it was not graciously received, for the Lord of the world shut the (*f*) doors of repentance to my face.

Verse 6. *I opened to my beloved, &c.*] The congregation of Israel said, I was willing to seek instruction from the Lord: but he removed his shechinah from me, and my soul desired the voice of his words. I sought the shechinah of his glory: but I found *it* not. I prayed before him: but he covered the heavens with (*g*) clouds, and did not receive my prayer.

Verse 7. *The watchmen that went about the city, &c.*] The (*h*) Chaldeans, which kept the ways, and besieged the city of Jerusalem all around, joined themselves to me. Some they slew with the sword, and others they carried into captivity. They took the crown royal off the neck of Zedekiah king of Judah, and carried him away to Ribla, (*i*) where the people of Babylon, who besieged the city and kept the walls, put out his eyes.

Verse 8. *I charge you, O daughters of Jerusalem, &c.*] The congregation of Israel said, I charge you, O ye prophets, by the decree of the word of the Lord, that, if your love manifests himself unto you, you tell him that I, who love him, am sick of love.

Verse 9. *What is thy beloved, &c.*] The prophets answered and said, unto the house of Israel, (*k*) Who is this God thou art seeking to worship, O congregation of Israel, *who art* fairer than all the nations? Who is this thou art desirous to fear, that thou dost so charge us?

Verse 10. *My beloved is white and ruddy,*

(*a*) These words are similarly paraphrased in Shirhashirim Rabba, and by Jarchi in loc., and in Bemidbar Rabba, Parash. 13.

(*b*) See note on chap. i. 10.

(*c*) Chald. The stroke of his might.

(*d*) See 2 Kings xvii. 6, and xviii. 11; 1 Chron. v. 26.

(*e*) Leshem being taken by the tribe of Dan, Josh. xix. 47, they call it Dan, after the name of their father; and it seems it was also called Pamias. Both Baal Aruch, and David de Pomis, say that פמיאס *Pamias* was a cave at the head of the river Jordan: and it is asserted by several of the rabbins, that Jordan took its rise from hence, who therefore say that the river was so called, שיורד מדן *sheiyored middan*, "because it descended from Dan," i. e., from Leshem, Dan, or Pamias, Talmud Baba Bathra, fol. 74, col. 2; and Bechoroth. fol. 55, col. 1; Jarchi in Deut. xxxiii. 22; Kimchi in Jos. xix. 47. This in Bereshith Rabba, Parash. 63, is called פניאס *Panias*, as it is also by Josephus, and no doubt is the same which Pliny, in Nat. Hist. 1. 5, c. 18, calls Paneas, who also makes mention in c. 15 of a fountain of the same name, from whence he says the river Jordan sprung. The same is observed by Solinus, in his Polyhistor. c. 48, who calls it by the name of Peneas. Eusebius, in his Eccl. Hist. 1. 7, c. 17, says that the Phœnicians called Cæsarea Philippi Paneas, and speaks of a mountain called Paneius, from whence the river Jordan has its original.

(*f*) In Shirhashirim Rabba, in chap. 5, 2, mention is made of פתח של תשובה "the gate of repentance," which the Lord desired the Israelites to open to him. Agreeably to this phrase, it is observed, in Acts xiv. 27, that "God had opened unto the Gentiles θυραν πιστεως, the door of faith."

(*g*) See Lam. iii. 44.

(*h*) Jarchi by these watchmen understands Nebuchadnezzar and his army. R. Aben Ezra, the kings of Greece. Shirhashirim Rabba, the tribe of Levi.

(*i*) See Jer. iii. 7, 9, 11.

(*k*) *Vide* Jarchi, and Shirhashirim Rabba in loc.

&c.] Wherefore the congregation of Israel began to speak in the praise of the Lord of the world, and thus she said, That God I desire to serve, who in the day is covered with a garment (*l*) white as snow, (*m*) and the brightness of the glory of the Lord, whose face shines as fire, because of the greatness of wisdom and knowledge, for he is making new things every day, and will manifest them to his people in the (*n*) great day, and his banner is over ten thousand times ten thousand angels, who minister before him.

Verse 11. *His head is as the most fine gold, &c.*] His law, (*o*) which is more desirable than the best gold, and the interpretation of the words *thereof*, in which are senses, (*p*) heaps *upon* heaps, and the commandments to them that keep them *are* white as snow; but to those that do not keep them *are* black as the wings of a raven.

Verse 12. *His eyes are as the eyes of doves, &c.*] His eyes look continually (*q*) upon Jerusalem, to do good unto it, and to bless it, from the beginning of the year unto the end of the year, as doves which stand and look upon the water-courses, because of the righteousness of those who sit in the sanhedrin, who study in the law, and give light to a cause, that it may be smooth as milk; and they sit in the house of the school, and (*r*) wait in judgment until they have finished either for absolution or condemnation.

Verse 13. *His cheeks are as a bed of spices, &c.*] The (*s*) two tables of stone which he gave unto his people are written in (*t*) ten lines, like to the rows of a spice garden, producing acute meanings and senses, even as a garden produces spices; and the lips of his wise men which study in the law, drop senses on every side, and the speech of their mouths is as the choice myrrh.

Verse 14. *His hands are as gold rings, &c.*] The twelve tribes of Jacob his servants are included in the plate of the holy crown of gold, and are engraven upon the twelve (*u*) precious stones with the three fathers of the world, Abraham, Isaac, and Jacob. Reuben is engraven on achmad, Simeon is engraven upon akik, Levi is engraven on barkan and affran, Judah is engraven on cachale, Issachar is engraven on ismorad, Zebulun is engraven on gihar, Dan is engraven on birla, Naphtali is engraven on esphor, Gad is engraven on tabeag, Asher is engraven on frozag, Joseph is engraven on meribag, Benjamin is engraven on apantor: these are like to the twelve celestial signs, shining as lamps, polished in their works like ivory, and bright as sapphires.

Verse 15. *His legs are as pillars of marble, &c.*] And the righteous they *are* the pillars of the world, set upon sockets of the best gold; these *are* (*x*) the words of the law, in which they study, and reprove the people of the house of Israel, that they may do his will who is filled with compassion to them, as an old man; and makes the transgressions of the house of Israel

---

(*l*) So the Ancient of days is represented in Dan. vii. 9.

(*m*) In some exemplars these following words are inserted:—"And studies in the twenty-four books of the law, and in the words of prophecy, and in the Holy Writings, and in the night-time employs himself in the six parts of the Mishna," which Buxtorf has omitted in his Bible, though he makes mention of them in his Recensio operis Talmud, p. 232; and indeed they greatly lessen the glory of the Divine Being, though they are designed to extol and magnify the Mishna or oral law.

(*n*) That is, the day of judgment, which in Jude, ver. 6, is called *κρισις μεγαλης ἡμερας*, "the judgment of the great day," when not only the hidden things of darkness and the counsels of the hearts will be made manifest, 1 Cor. iv. 5, but the judgments of God also, Rev. xv. 4.

(*o*) The same way the words are explained in Shirhashirim Rabba, and by Jarchi in loc., and in Vajikra Rabba, Parash. 19. By this head R. Aben Ezra understands the throne of glory.

(*p*) That is, a variety or great multitude of them; for the Jews suppose the law may be interpreted various ways, and that there is not the least thing in it but what contains a great many mysteries. See notes on chap. i. 11.

(*q*) *Vide* Shirhashirim Rabba in loc.

(*r*) That is, they proceed in trying causes slowly and gradually, and not rashly and precipitately, being willing to search thoroughly into them, that they may do justice and pass a right sentence; this is one of the three things the men of the great congregation advised to in Pirke Aboth, c. 1, s. 1, where they say הוו מתונין בדין *havu mittonin bedin*, "Be slow in judgment, settle many disciples, and make a hedge for the law."

(*s*) So Jarchi by "his cheeks" understands the words of Mount Sinai.

(*t*) Every commandment was written in a distinct line by itself, five on one table and five on the other.

(*u*) In the same order are the names of the twelve tribes as engraven on so many precious stones, mentioned in Targum Jerus. in Exod. xxviii. 17, 18, 19, 20; in Shemoth Rabba, Parash. 38; and in Bemidbar Rabba, Parash. 2. Though different names are given of the precious stones, the names of them in the Rabboth are the same with those in Exod. xxviii. In the Targum Jer. are Chaldee names, and in this paraphrase they are different from them. Reuben's stone was the Sardius, Heb. odem, Onk. samkan, Jon. semuktha, Jerus. samkatha. It is so called by all those names from the redness of its colour; here it is called achmad, perhaps from חמד *chamad*, because it is very desirable. Simeon's stone was the topaz, Heb. pitdah, Onk. yarkan, Jon. and Jerus. yarketha, because of its green colour; here it is called akik: but what gem is intended by it is not certain. Levi's stone was the carbuncle, Heb. barketh, Jon. and Jerus, barketha, and here barkan, and so in Onk.; and is so called because of its bright and glistering light. Judah's stone was the emerald, Heb. nophec, Onk. ismaragdin, Jon. ismorad: both seem to mean the smaragd. Jerus. cadcedana, or the chalcedony; here it is called cachale; it is thought to be the smaragd. See Eliæ Levitæ Methurgeman, Buxtorf and Schindler *in voce*. Issachar's stone was the sapphire, Heb. saphir, Onk. shabzez, Jon. sapphirinon, Jerus. sampuryana: all intend the sapphire; here it is called ismorad, or the smaragd. Zebulon's stone was the diamond, Heb. yahalom, Onk. sabhalon; it bears those names from the hardness of it. Jon. cadcodin or chalcedony, Jerus. ein egla, the calves eye; here it is called gihar, which some think to be the jasper. See Buxtorf *in voce*. Dan's stone was the ligure, Heb. leshem, Onk. kankire, Jon. kankirinum, Jerus. zuzin; here it is called birla, which seems to be the beryl. Naphtali's stone was the agate, Heb. shebo, Onk. yarkia, Jon. arkin, Jerus. birzalin; and here it is called espor, which may be thought to be the sapphire. Gad's stone was the amethyst, Heb. achlamah, Onk. and Jon. ein egla, the calves eye, Jerus. smaragdin, the smaragd; and here it is called yabeag: but what is meant by it I know not. Asher's stone was the beryl, Heb. tarshish. Onk. Jon. and Jerus. crum yamma; here it is called frozag. Elias in his Methurgeman says, that a topaz, in the German language, is called frozam. Joseph's stone was the onyx, Heb. shoham, Onk. burla, Jon. berlevath; both seem to intend the beryl, Jerus. bdolcha or bdellium; here it is called meribag, which some take to be the onyx. See Buxtorf *in voce*. Benjamin's stone was the jasper, Heb. jashpeh, Jerus. margalita, a pearl, Onk. pantere, Jon. apanturin; and here apantor, which Elias in his Methurgeman says is so called because it comes from Pontus; but rather because some sorts of jaspers are variegated and spotted like panthers. In the same order were the names of the twelve tribes engraven both upon the stones in the breastplate, and on the two onyx stones upon the shoulders of the ephod, according to Maimon, Tract. Cele Hamikdash. c. 9, s. 1, 7, 9.

(*x*) So these sockets of fine gold are explained in Shirhashirim Rabba, and by Jarchi in loc., in Vajikra Rabba, Parash. 25, and in Bemidbar Rabba, Parash. 10.

as white as snow, and is ready to make victory and war among the nations who have transgressed his word, as a man who is strong and robust as the cedars.

Verse 16. *His mouth is most sweet, &c.*] The words of his mouth are sweet as honey, and all his commandments are more desirable to his wise men than gold and silver; this is the praise of God, who is my beloved, and this is the power of the mighty of the Lord, who is dear to me, O ye prophets who prophesy in Jerusalem.

CHAPTER VI

Verse 1. *Whither is thy beloved gone, &c.*] The prophets (*a*) replied, when they heard the praise of the Lord, from the mouth of the congregation of Israel, and thus they said, For what offence is the shechinah of the Lord removed from thee, O thou *who* art fairer in thy works than all the nations? and which way did thy beloved turn himself when he removed from thy sanctuary? The congregation of Israel said, Because of the sins, transgressions, and rebellion which were found in me. The prophets said, But now return by repentance, and let us arise, both thou and we, and we will pray before him, and seek mercy with thee.

Verse 2. *My beloved is gone down into his garden, &c.*] And the Lord of the world graciously received their prayer, and came down to the sanhedrin of the wise men at Babylon, and gave refreshment unto his people, and brought them out of their captivity by the hands of Cyrus, and Ezra, and Nehemiah, and Zerubbabel the son of Shealtiel, and the elders of Judah; and they built the house of the sanctuary, and appointed priests over the offerings, and Levites over the charge of the holy commandment; and he sent fire from heaven and graciously received the offerings, and the sweet incense; and as a man supplies his own beloved son with dainties, so did he deliciously feed them; and as a man that gathereth roses out of the plains, so did he gather them out of Babylon.

Verse 3. *I am my beloved's, &c.*] And when I served the Lord of the world, who is my beloved, my beloved caused the holy shechinah to dwell with me, and he fed me with dainties.

Verse 4. *Thou are beautiful, O my love, &c.*] The Lord said by his word, How fair art thou, my love, when thou art willing to perform my pleasure! beautiful is the sanctuary which thou hast built for me instead of the former sanctuary, which Solomon, king in Jerusalem, built for me, and thy dread was upon all the people in the day that thy four (*b*) standards marched in the wilderness.

Verse 5. *Turn away thine eyes from me, &c.*] Set thy doctors, the wise men of the great congregation, in a circle over against me, for these (*c*) made me *their* king in the captivity, and fixed the school, for the teaching of my law, and the rest of thy nobles, and the people of the earth justified me by the word of their mouth, as the sons of Jacob, who gathered stones and made a heap (*d*) upon the mount of Gilead.

Verse 6. *Thy teeth are as a flock of sheep, &c.*] And the priests and Levites, who eat thine offerings, and the holy tithes, and the oblation of fruits, are pure from all oppression and rapine, for they are as clean as Jacob's flocks of sheep, when they came up from the brook (*e*) Jabok, for there is no oppression or rapine in them: but they are all of them like one another, and they always bear twins, neither is there any that miscarrieth or is barren among them.

Verse 7. *As a piece of pomegranate, &c.*] And the kingdom of the house of the Hasmonæans (*f*) are all of them full of the commandments, even as a pomegranate; besides Matthias the high priest, and his sons, who are more righteous than them all, who very eagerly established the commandments and the words of the law.

Verse 8. *There are threescore queens, &c.*] At that time the Grecians arose and gathered sixty kings of the children of (*g*) Esau, clothed with coats of mail, riding upon horses, being horsemen, and eighty dukes of the children of Ishmael, riding upon elephants, besides the rest of the nations and languages, of which

---

(*a*) The persons here interrogating are said to be "the nations of the world," in Shirhashirim Rabba, and by Jarchi in loc.

(*b*) Which were those of Judah, Reuben, Ephraim, and Dan. See Num. ii., and Bemidbar Rabba, Parash. 2.

(*c*) So the word הרהיבני is paraphrased in Shirhashirim Rabba in loc.

(*d*) See note on chap. iv. 1.

(*e*) See note on chap. iv. 2.

(*f*) Schindler, in his Lex. Pentaglot. fol. 680, says that Mattathias and his posterity were so called from השמון *Hasmon*, one of their ancestors, though I think there is no evidence of any of their ancestors being of that name. The Jewish writers pretty generally agree that they were so called from the word השמנים *Hashmannim*, which signifies *princes* or *great persons*, and is so used in Psa. lxviii. 32; for they had both the high priesthood and the princely government in their hands. So R. Aben Ezra, R. David Kimchi, and R. Sol. Ben Melec, in Psa. lxviii. 32. David de Pomis, Lex. Heb. fol. 42, 1, and so likewise Scaliger de Emend. Temp. lib. 5, pp. 436, 437; who observes that Mattathias was never so called, nor was he a high priest, though the Targumist here calls him so, but a common priest of the course of Jehoiarib, and of the town of Moddin; (see 1 Mac. ii. 1;) and that this family began to be called by the name of the Hasmonæans, from the times of Simon Hyrcanus, who was both high priest and prince of the Jewish nation, which kind of government continued in that family unto the times of Herod the Great, who destroyed both it and them; and this well agrees with what the paraphrast here says, who manifestly distinguishes the kingdom of the house of the Hasmonæans from Mattathias and his sons, i. e., Judas Maccabæus and Jonathan. Of these Hasmonæans, Jarchi and Aben Ezra explain the 10th and 12th verses of this chapter.

(*g*) *Vide* Aben Ezra and Jarchi in loc., and Bemidbar Rabba, Parash. 14, where those sixty queens and eighty concubines are interpreted of the sons of Noah, Abraham, Ham, Ishmael, and Esau.

there is no number; and they appointed King Alexander to be the general over them, and they came to make war against Jerusalem.

Verse 9. *My dove, my undefiled, is but one, &c.*] And at that time the congregation of Israel, which is like to an unblemished dove, was serving her Lord with a single heart, and was united to the law, and studied in the words of the law with a perfect heart, and her righteousness was as pure as in the day when she came out of Egypt. Lo, the sons of the Hasmonæans, and Matthias, and all the people of Israel, went forth and made war with them, and the Lord delivered them into their hands; which, when the inhabitants of the provinces saw, they blessed them, and the kingdoms of the earth, and the governors, and they praised them.

Verse 10. *Who is she that looketh forth as the morning, &c.*] The nations said, How splendid are the works of this people as the morning; fair are their young men as the moon, and their righteousness as clear as the sun; and their dread was upon all the inhabitants of the earth, as in the time their (*h*) four standards marched in the wilderness!

Verse 11. *I went down into the garden of nuts, &c.*] The Lord of the world said, concerning the second (*i*) temple, which was built (*k*) by the hands of Cyrus, I will cause my shechinah to dwell *there*, to behold the good works of my people, and see whether the wise men, who are like to a vine, multiply and increase, and *whether* their branches are full of good works, as the pomegranates.

Verse 12. *Or ever I was aware, &c.*] And when it appeared manifest before the Lord that they were righteous, and studied in the law, the Lord said by his word, I will not humble them any more, yea, I will not consume them: but will consult with myself to do them good, and to set them, even their excellent ones, in the chariots of (*l*) kings, because of the worthiness of the righteous of that generation, who are like in their works to Abraham their father.

Verse 13. *Return, return, O Shulamite, &c.*] Return unto me, O congregation of Israel, return unto Jerusalem; return unto the house of the doctrine of the law; return to receive the prophecy from the prophets, who have prophesied in the name of the word of the Lord; for what is your goodness, ye lying prophets, to make the people of Jerusalem go astray by your prophecies? for ye speak perverse things against the word of the Lord, to profane the camp of Israel and Judah.

(*h*) See note on ver. 4.

(*i*) So Jarchi interprets this "garden of nuts;" though some of the rabbins in Shirhashirim Rabba think the world is meant; and by the vine, the schools and synagogues; and by the pomegranates, the students in the law.

(*k*) It is said to be built by Cyrus, because he gave the Jews liberty and encouragement to build it; see Ezra i. 2, 3, 4.

(*l*) In Shirhashirim Rabba in loc. these words are referred to the deliverance of the Israelites out of Egypt, and their exaltation over the nations in the land of Canaan; to the raising of David to the throne of Israel, after he had been persecuted by Saul; and to the advancement of Mordecai to great dignity in Babylon, after his mourning in sackcloth and ashes; all which are represented as severally surprising to them.

CHAPTER VII

Verse 1. *How beautiful are thy feet with shoes, &c.*] Solomon said, by the spirit of prophecy from the Lord, How beautiful are the feet of the Israelites, when they come up to appear before the Lord (*a*) three times a year, in sandals of badger *skin*, and offer up their vows and free-will offerings; and their sons which come out of their loins are fair as the gems which were fixed upon the holy (*b*) crown that Bezaleel the artificer made for Aaron the priest.

Verse 2. *Thy navel is like a round goblet, &c.*] And the head of thy school, by whose righteousness all the world is nourished, even as the fetus receives its nourishment through its navel, in its mother's bowels; who shines in the law as the orb of the moon, when he comes to pronounce pure or unclean, to justify or condemn; neither do the words of the law ever fail from his mouth, even as the waters of the great river, which proceeds from Eden, never (*c*) fail; and the seventy wise men are round about him, as a round (*d*) floor, whose treasures are full of the holy tithes, and vows, and free-will offerings which Ezra the priest, and Zerubbabel, and Joshua, and Nehemiah, and

(*a*) That is, at the feast of the passover, at the feast of weeks or pentecost, and at the feast of tabernacles; see Exod. xxiii. 14, 15, 16, 17; 2 Chron. viii. 13. So the words are explained in Shirhashirim Rabba, and by Jarchi in loc.

(*b*) So the plate of gold was called, on which was inscribed "holiness to the Lord," which was fixed to the fore-front of the mitre on Aaron's forehead; see Exod. xxviii. 36, and xxxix. 30. This plate was two fingers broad, and reached from ear to ear; "holiness to the Lord" was written upon it in great letters, standing out, and that either in one line or in two lines; if in two lines, "holiness" was written below, and "to the Lord" above; Maimon. Hilch. Cele Hamikdash, c. 9, s. 1, 2; Ceseph Mishna in *ibid.*, and Jarchi in Exod. xxviii. 36.

(*c*) The same is said of them in Zohar in Exodus, fol. 34, 3, and xxxviii. 2: see Gen. ii. 10, and note on chapter iv. 12.

(*d*) The great sanhedrin consists of seventy persons, besides the nasi or prince, at whose right hand sat Ab Beth Din, or *the father of the house of judgment:* before them sat the two scribes, and the rest of the sanhedrin took their places according to their age or dignity, and sat in a semicircular form, or, as they express it, כחצי גורן עגולה *cachatsi goren agullah*, "as the half of a round corn floor," to which they compare this assembly. So that both the prince and father of the court could see them all, Mishna Tract. Sanhedrin, c. 4, s. 3. Jarchi and Ez Chayim, *ibid.* Maimon. Hilch. Sanhedrin, c. 1, s. 3, and Ceseph Mishna, *ibid.* Shemoth Rabba, Parash. 5. Vajikra Rabba, Parash. 11. R. Aben Ezra in loc. Midrash Echa Rabba Præfat. fol. 38, 4. Midrash Kohelet in chap. i. 11.

Mordecai Bilshan, men of the great (*e*) congregation who are like to roses, decreed for them, because they had strength to study in the law day and night.

Verse 3. *Thy two breasts are like two young roes, &c.*] Thy (*f*) two Redeemers which shall redeem thee, Messiah, the son of David, and Messiah, the son of Ephraim, are like to Moses and Aaron, the sons of Jochebed, who may be compared to two young roes that are twins.

Verse 4. *Thy neck is as a tower of ivory, &c.*] And (*g*) the father of the house of judgment, who determines thy causes, is mighty over thy people to bind them, and to bring him forth who is condemned in judgment, *even* to bring *him* forth, as Solomon the king, who made a tower of ivory, and subjected the people of the house of Israel, and returned them to the Lord of the world. Thy scribes are full of wisdom, as pools of water; and they know how to number the computations of the (*h*) intercalations; and they intercalate the years, and fix the beginning of the months and the beginning of the years at the gate of the house of the great sanhedrin, and the chief of the house of Judah is like to David the king, who built the fortress of Zion, which is called the tower of Lebanon, on which, whoever stands, may number (*i*) all the towers that *are* in Damascus.

Verse 5. *Thine head upon thee is like Carmel, &c.*] The king who is set over thee, a righteous head, *is* as (*k*) Elijah the prophet, who was jealous with a jealousy for the Lord of heaven, and slew the false prophets in the mount of Carmel, and reduced the people of the house of Israel to the fear of the Lord God; and the poor of the people, which go with a bowed-down head because they are poor, shall be clothed in purple, as Daniel was clothed in the city of Babylon, and Mordecai in Shushan, because of the righteousness of Abraham, who long before consulted the Lord of the world; and because of Isaac, whom his father bound in order to offer him up; and because of the holiness of Jacob, who pilled the rods in the gutters.

Verse 6. *How fair and how pleasant art thou, &c.*] King Solomon said, How beautiful art thou, O congregation of Israel, when thou bearest upon thee the yoke of my kingdom, when I correct thee with chastisements for thy transgressions, and thou bearest them in love, and they appear in thy sight as delicious dainties.

Verse 7. *This thy stature is like to a palm tree, &c.*] And when thy priests (*l*) spread their hands in prayer, and bless their brethren, the house of Israel, their four hands are separated like the branches of the palm tree, and their stature is as the date; and thy congregations stand face to face over against the priests, and their faces are bowed to the earth like a cluster of grapes.

Verse 8. *I said, I will go up to the palm tree, &c.*] The Lord said by his word, I will go and try Daniel, and see whether he is able to stand in one temptation as Abraham his father, who is like to a palm tree branch, stood in (*m*) ten temptations; yea, I will also try Hananiah, Mishael, and Azariah, whether they are able to stand in their temptations; for the sake of whose righteousness I will redeem the people of the house of Israel, who are like to clusters of grapes; and the fame of Daniel, Hananiah, Mishael, and Azariah, shall be heard in all the earth; and their smell shall be excellent, like the smell of the apples of the garden of Eden.

Verse 9. *And the roof of thy mouth is like the best wine, &c.*] Daniel and his companions said, We will surely take upon us the decree of the word of the Lord, as Abraham our father, who may be compared to old wine, took it upon him; and we will walk in the way which is right before him, even as Elijah and Elisha the prophets walked, through whose righteousness the dead, which are like to a man asleep, were raised; and as Ezekiel, the son of Buzi, by the prophecy of whose mouth those who were asleep

---

(*e*) This was the sanhedrin or great council, collected by Ezra the scribe, after the return of the Jews from the Babylonish captivity, of which he was president. This assembly consisted of one hundred and twenty persons, of which these here mentioned were the chief. There are others reckoned with them by some, as the three prophets, Haggai, Zechariah, and Malachi, with Daniel, Hananiah, Mishael, Azariah, Seraiah, Relaiah, Mispar, Bigvai, Rehum, and Baanah: the last of this venerable body of men, they say, was Simeon the Just; who, about forty years after the building of the second temple, met Alexander the Great coming against Jerusalem, and appeased him. These men were called אנשי כנסת הגדולה *anshey keneseth haggedolah*, "the men of the great congregation," because they restored the law to its pristine glory, and purged the Jewish Church from those corruptions which had crept into it during the captivity in Babylon. They are said to have received the oral law from the prophets, who had received it from the elders, and they from Joshua, and Joshua from Moses, and to have transmitted it down to posterity, Pirke Aboth, c. 1, s. 1, 2, and Jarchi, *ibid.* Maimon. Præfat. in lib. Yad. *Vide* Buxtorfii Tiberiad. in c. 10.

(*f*) See note on chap. iv. 5.

(*g*) See note on ver. 2.

(*h*) The Jewish year consisted of twelve lunar months, and sometimes they intercalated a thirteenth month, which they called Veadar, or the second Adar, which was always done by the direction and at the pleasure of the sanhedrin; as also the fixing of the beginning of the months, by the phasis or first appearance of the moon, Maimon. Hilch. Kiddush Hachodesh, c. 1, s. 1, 2, 3, 4, 5, 6; c. 4, s. 1, 9, 10, 11, 13, and c. 5, s. 1, 2, 3, 4. The men of the tribe of Issachar were famous for their knowledge in these things, Bereshith Rabba, Parash. 72, Bemidbar Rabba, Parash. 13. Midrash Esth. Parash. 4, and Kimchi in 1 Chron. xii. 32.

(*i*) Jarchi relates out of the Midrash, that from the house of the forest of Lebanon, which Solomon built, a man might number all the houses which were in Damascus.

(*k*) So these words are paraphrased in Shirhashirim Rabba in loc., and in Vajikra Rabba, Parash. 31.

(*l*) When the priests blessed the people, they stretched out their hands and lifted them above their heads, with their fingers spread out; only the high priest never lifted up his above the plate of gold upon the mitre; and though, at the time of blessing, the priests and people stood face to face, right over against each other, yet the priests never looked upon the people, but kept their eyes upon the ground, as in the time of prayer; nor might the people look in the faces of the priests, lest their minds should be disturbed thereby; which ceremony the Targumist here refers to, Maimon. Hilch. Tephila, c. 14, s. 3, 7, 9. Bemidbar Rabba, Parash. 11. Targum Jon. in Num. vi. 23.

(*m*) The same is said in Targum Jerus. in Gen. xxii. 1. Bereshith Rabba, Parash. 56. Bemidbar Rabba, Parash. 15. Pirke Aboth, c. 5, s. 3, and Jarchi, *ibid.;* where he, out of Pirke Eliezer, has given us an account of them in this following order, viz., 1st. Nimrod sought to kill him, and he was hid in a field thirteen years. 2. He cast him into Ur of the Chaldees, or into a furnace of fire. 3. He banished him from the land of his nativity. 4. The Lord brought a famine in his days. 5. Sarah was taken into the house of Pharaoh. 6. The kings came and carried Lot his brother's son away captive. 7. It was shown him between the pieces, that four kingdoms should rule over his children. 8. He was commanded to circumcise himself and his children. 9. To put away Ishmael and his mother. And 10. To slay his son Isaac.

were awaked, even the dead which were in the valley of (*n*) Dura.

Verse 10. *I am my beloved's, &c.*] Jerusalem (*o*) said, All the time that I was walking in the way of the Lord of the world, he caused his shechinah to dwell with me, and his desire was towards me: but when I turned aside out of his paths, he removed his shechinah from me, and carried me away among the nations; and they ruled over me as a man rules over his wife.

Verse 11. *Come, my beloved, let us go forth into the field, &c.*] When the people of the house of Israel sinned, the Lord carried them into captivity, into the land of Seir, the fields of Edom. The congregation of Israel said, I beseech thee, O Lord of the whole world, receive my prayer, which I have prayed before thee, in the cities of the captivity and in the provinces of the people.

Verse 12. *Let us get up early to the vineyards, &c.*] The children of Israel said one to another, Let us get up early in the morning, and let us go to the synagogue and to the school, and let us search in the book of the law, and see whether (*p*) the time of the redemption of the people of the house of Israel, who are like to a vine, is come, that they may be redeemed out of their captivity; and let us inquire of the wise men, whether the righteousness of the righteous, who are full of the commandments as pomegranates, is made manifest before the Lord; whether the time is come to go up to Jerusalem, there to give praise to the God of heaven, and to offer up the burnt-offerings, and the holy drink-offerings.

Verse 13. *The mandrakes give a smell, &c.*] And when it is the pleasure of the Lord to redeem his people out of captivity, it shall be said to the King Messiah, Now is the end of the captivity completed, and the righteousness of the righteous is become sweet as the smell of balsam, and the wise men fix *their* habitations by the gates of the school; they study in the (*q*) words of the scribes, and in the words of the law. Arise now, take the kingdom which I have reserved for thee.

(*n*) In this valley Nebuchadnezzar set up his golden image. Dan. iii. 1. And here the Jews say the children of Ephraim were slain, who went out of Egypt before the time; as also the Israelites, whom the Chaldeans slew when they carried them captive; and that this is the valley Ezekiel was brought into by the Spirit of the Lord, Ezek. xxxvii. 1; and these the dry bones he prophesied over, which lived and stood upon their feet an exceeding great army, Targum Jon. in Exod. xiii. 17. R. Saadiah Gaon in Dan. iii. 1. Jarchi in Ezek. xxxvii. 1.

(*o*) That is, the inhabitants of Jerusalem, or the Shulamite the Church, as in chap. vi. 13. The Church is frequently called so in the Old Testament, and likewise in the New, see Gal. iv. 26; Heb. xii. 22; Rev. xxi. 2, 10.

(*p*) The Jews vainly expect the time of redemption by the Messiah to be future, when it is past many hundred years ago, as they might easily learn from the book of the law and the prophets; particularly from Jacob's prophecy in Gen. xlix. 10, from Haggai's in chap. ii. 6, 7, 8, and from Daniel's weeks in chap. ix. 24, 25, 26. See this fully proved in a book called "The prophecies of the Old Testament respecting the Messiah considered," &c. Chap. iii.

(*q*) The words of the scribes are mentioned before the words of the law, and are, indeed, by the Jews, preferred unto them. They say the words of the beloved, i. e., the wise men, are better than the wine of the law; so they paraphrase the words in Cant. i. 2: they assert that the law cannot be understood without the words of the scribes; that the oral law is the foundation of the written law, and not the written law the foundation of the oral law; and that he that transgresses the words of the wise men as much deserves death, as though he had been guilty of idolatry, murder, or adultery, or profanes the Sabbath; nay, that if these say their right hand is their left, and their left hand is their right, they are obliged to hearken to them, Shirhashirim Rabba, in c. 1, 2. Bemidbar Rabba, Parash. 14. Matteh Dan. Dialog. 3, fol. 31, 3. Jarchi in Deut. xvii. 11. *Vide* Buxtorf, Recensio Operis Talmud. pp. 222, 223, &c.

CHAPTER VIII

Verse 1. *O that thou wert as my brother, &c.*] And when the King Messiah (*a*) shall be revealed unto the congregation of Israel, the children of Israel shall say unto him, Be thou with us for a brother, and let us go up to Jerusalem, and let us suck with thee the senses of the law, as a sucking child sucketh the breasts of its mother; for all the time that I was wandering without my own land, whenever I remembered the name of the great God, and laid down my life for the sake of his Deity, even the nations of the earth did not despise me.

Verse 2. *I would lead thee, and bring thee, &c.*] I will lead thee, O King Messiah, and bring thee to the house of my sanctuary; and thou shalt teach me to fear the Lord, and to walk in his paths; and there will we keep (*b*) the feast of leviathan, and drink old wine, which has been reserved in its grapes ever since

(*a*) The Jews very seldom speak of the birth or nativity of the Messiah as future, but only of a revelation or discovery of him to them, which they expect; for they are under self convictions that he was born long since. Some of them say he was born on the day the house of the sanctuary was destroyed, but is hid because of their sins and transgressions, and that either in the sea, or the walks of the garden of Eden; and some say that he sits among the lepers at the gates of Rome, from whence they expect he will come unto them, R. Aben Ezra, in Cant. vii. 5. Targum in Mic. iv. 8. Talmud Sanhedrin, fol. 98, col. 2. Targum Jerus. in Exod. xii. 42.

(*b*) The Jews expect a very sumptuous feast to be made for the righteous in the days of the Messiah, which will consist of all sorts of flesh, fish, and fowl, of plenty of generous wine, and of a variety of the most delicious fruit; some particulars of which they have thought fit to give, and are as follow: 1. They say an exceeding large ox shall be served up, which they take to be the behemoth in Job xl., of which they say many things monstrous and incredible; as that it lies upon a thousand hills, and feeds upon them all, and drinks up all the waters which are gathered together in a year's time, in the river Jordan, at one draught, Vajikra Rabba, Parash. 22. Bemidbar Rabba, Parash. 21. Targum in Psa. l. 10. Jarchi in *ibid.*, and in Job xl. 20. 2. The next dish is the leviathan and his mate, which they say are "the great whales" mentioned in Gen. i. 21. The male, they say, God castrated, and the female he slew, and salted it against this feast, Talmud Baba Bathra, fol. 74. Targum Jon., Jarchi, and Baal Hatturim in Gen. i. 21. Vajikra Rabba, Parash. 13. Targum Sect. in Esth. iii. 7. Aben Ezra in Dan. xii. 2. 3. They speak of an exceeding large fowl, which they call Ziz, that the day the world was created, and of the pomegranates, the fruits which are prepared for the righteous in the garden of Eden.

Verse 3. *His left hand should be under my head, &c.*] The congregation of Israel said, I am chosen above all people, because I have bound the tephillin (*c*) upon my left hand, and upon my head, and have fixed the mezuzah (*d*) on the right side of my door, in the third part thereof, over against my chamber, so that the noxious spirits have no power to destroy me.

Verse 4. *I charge you, O daughters of Jerusalem, &c.*] The King Messiah shall say, I adjure you, O my people, the house of Israel, wherefore do ye stir up yourselves against the people of the earth to go out of captivity? and why do ye rebel against the army of Gog and (*e*) Magog? tarry a little while until the people which come up to make war against Jerusalem are destroyed; and after that the Lord of the world will remember unto you the mercies of the righteous, and then it will be his good pleasure to redeem you.

Verse 5. *Who is this that cometh up from the wilderness, &c.*] Solomon the prophet said, When the dead shall live, the Mount of *Olives* shall be (*f*) cleaved asunder, and all the dead of Israel shall come out from under it; yea, even the righteous, which die in captivity, shall pass through subterraneous (*g*) caverns, and come out from under the Mount of *Olives:* but the wicked which die and are buried in the land of Israel shall be cast away, (*h*) as a man casts a stone with a sling; then all the inhabitants of the earth shall say, What is the righteousness of this people, which ascend out of the earth, even ten thousand times ten thousand, as in the day they came up out of the wilderness to the land of Israel, and are deliciously fed by the mercies of the Lord, as in the day when they were hid (*i*) under Mount Sinai to receive the law; and in that very hour Zion, which is the (*k*) mother of Israel, shall bring forth her sons, and Jerusalem receive the children of the captivity.

Verse 6. *Set me as a seal upon thine heart, &c.*] The children of Israel said in that day unto their Lord, We pray thee, set us as the signature of a ring upon thine heart, as the signature of a ring upon thine arm, that we may not be carried captive any more; for strong as death is the love of thy Deity, and mighty as hell is the envy which the people bear unto us; and the hatred which they have reserved

---

shall be one part of this entertainment, of which they say many things incredible; as particularly, that when its feet are upon the earth its head reaches the heavens; and when it stretches out its wings, they cover the body of the sun, Baba Bathra, fol. 73, col. 2. Targum amd Kimchi in Psa. l. 10. Vajikra Rabba, Parash. 22. 4. After all this shall be served up a variety of the most pleasant and delightful fruits, which are in the garden of Eden, which the Targumist here speaks of. And lastly, the wine which will then be used will be generous old wine, which, as it is said here and elsewhere, was kept in the grape from the creation of the world, Zohar in Gen. fol. 81, 4. Targum Jon. in Gen. xxvii. 25, and Targum in Eccles. ix. 7. Something of this gross notion seems to have obtained among the Jews in the times of Christ; see Luke xiv. 15. *Vide* Buxtorf Synagog. Jud. c. 50.

(*c*) These were four sections of the law, written on parchments, folded up in the skin of a clean beast, and tied to the head and hand. The four sections were these following, viz.: The first was Exod. xiii. 2–11. The second was Exod. xiii. 11–17. The third was Deut. vi. 4–10. The fourth was Deut. xi. 13–22. Those that were for the head were written and rolled up separately, and put in four distinct places in one skin, which was fastened with strings to the crown of the head towards the face, about the place where the hair ends, and where an infant's brain is tender: and they take care to place them in the middle, that so they may be between the eyes. Those that were for the hand were written in four columns, on one parchment, which, being rolled up, was fastened to the inside of the left arm, where it is fleshy, between the shoulder and the elbow, that so it might be over against the heart. These they call tephillin, from the root פלל *phalal*, "to pray," because they use them in the time of prayer, and look upon them as useful to put them in mind of that duty; in Matt. xxiii. 5, they are called *φυλακτηρια*, *phylacteries*, because they think they *keep* men in the fear of God, are preservatives from sin, nay, from evil spirits, and against diseases of the body; they imagine there is a great deal of holiness in them, and value themselves much upon the use of them, Targum Jon. Jarchi and Baal Hatturim in Exod. xiii. 9, 10, and Deut. vi. 8. Maimon. Hilch. Tephilin, c. 1, s. 1; c. 2, s. 1; c. 3. 1, 2, 3, 4, 5, 6; and c. 4. 1, 2, 25. Matteh Dan. Dialog. 2, fol. 9, 4, and 10, 1. *Vide* Buxtorf Synagog. Jud. c. 9, and Leo Modena's History of the Rites, &c., of the Present Jews, par. 1, c. 11.

(*d*) These were two passages in the law, the one was Deut. vi. 4–10, the other was Deut. xi. 13–22, which were written on a piece of parchment in one column, which, being rolled up and put into a pipe of reed or wood, was fastened to the right side of the door-post: this they imagine was useful to put them in mind of the Divine Being, to preserve them from sin, and from evil spirits, Targum Jon. in Deut. vi. 9. Maimon. Hilch. Tephilin, c. 5, s. 1, 6, and 6, 13. *Vide* Buxtorf Synagog. Jud. c. 31.

(*e*) Magog was one of the sons of Japhet, Gen. x. 2, from whom very probably the people called by those two names sprung, who seem to be the Scythians or Tartars; for Josephus, Antiq. Jud. l. 1, c. 7, calls the Scythians Magogæ; and Hierapolis in Cœlesyria, Pliny (Nat. Hist. l. 5, c. 23) says, was called by the Syrians Magog: and Marcus Paulus Venetus, l. 1, c. 64, says that "the countries of Gog and Magog are in Tartary, which they call Jug (perhaps rather Gog) and Mungug." *Vide* Schindler, Lex. Pent. fol. 288. Mention is made of these in Ezek. xxxviii. and xxxix., Rev. xx. 8, 9; with which last text may be compared what the Targumist here says. The Jewish rabbins, in their writings, very frequently speak of the war of Gog and Magog, which they expect in the days of the Messiah. See Mr. Mede's works, book 1, disc. 48, p. 374, and book 3, pp. 713, 751.

(*f*) See Zech. xiv. 4.

(*g*) The Jews are of opinion, that those of their nation who die and are buried in other lands, at the resurrection of the dead shall not rise where they died and were buried; but shall be rolled through the caverns of the earth, into the land of Canaan, and there rise. This they call גלגול המתים *gilgul hammethim*, "the rolling of the dead," or גלגול המחילות *gilgul hammechiloth*, "the rolling through the caverns," which they represent as very painful and afflicting; and say that this was the reason that Jacob desired he might not be buried in Egypt, and is now one reason why the Jews are so desirous of returning to their own land: nay, at this time the more wealthy and religious among them go thither on this very account, especially when advanced in years, that they may die, and be buried there, and so escape this painful rolling under the earth, Bereshith Rabba, Parash. 96. Midrash Hannealam in Zohar in Gen. fol. 68, 4. Jarchi in Gen. xlvii. 29. Kimchi in Ezek. xxxvii. 12. *Vide* Buxtorf Synagog. Jud. c. 3, and Lex. Talmud, fol. 439.

(*h*) Though the resurrection of the dead is one of the thirteen articles of the Jewish creed, yet many of them are of opinion that it is peculiar to the righteous, and that the wicked shall have no share therein; but that their bodies perish with their souls at death, and shall never rise more, R. David Kimchi, in Psa. i. 5, and in Isa. xxvi. 19. R. Saadiah Gaon, in Dan. xii. 2. *Vide* Pocock. Not. Misc. c. 6, p. 180, &c.

(*i*) The Targumist here refers to a fabulous notion of the Jews, that when the people of Israel came to Mount Sinai to receive the law, the Lord plucked up the mountain, and removed it into the air, and set the people under it, where he gave the law unto them; this they collect from Exod. xix. 17, and Deut. iv. 11. And this, they say, is *the apple tree* under which the Church is here said to be *raised up*, Targum Jon. Jarchi and Baal Hatturim in Exod. xix. 17. Jarchi and Shirhashirim Rabba in loc.

(*k*) So Jerusalem is said to be "the mother of us all," in Gal. iv. 26.

for us is like to the coals of the fire of hell, (*l*) which the Lord created on the second (*m*) day of the creation of the world, to (*n*) burn therein those who commit idolatry.

Verse 7. *Many waters cannot quench love, &c.*] The Lord of the world said unto his people, the house of Israel, If all people (*o*) which are like to the waters of the sea, which are many, were gathered together, they could not extinguish my love unto thee; and if all the kings of the earth, which are like to the waters of a river that runs fiercely, they could not remove thee out of the world: but if a man will give all the substance of his house to obtain wisdom in the captivity, I will return unto him (*p*) double in the world to come; and all the spoils (*q*) which they shall take from the armies of Gog shall be his.

Verse 8. *We have a little sister, &c.*] At that time the angels of heaven shall say to one another, We have one nation in the earth, and her righteousness is very little, and the kings and governors do not bring her forth to make war with the armies of Gog. What shall we do for our sister, in the day when the nations shall speak of going up against her to war?

Verse 9. *If she be a wall, &c.*] Michael (*r*) the prince of Israel shall say, If she is fixed as a wall among the people, and gives silver to procure the (*s*) unity of the name of the Lord of the world, I and you, together with their scribes, will surround her as borders of silver, that the people may have no power to rule over her, even as a worm hath no power to rule over silver; and though she (*t*) is poor in the commandments, we will seek mercies for her from the Lord; and the righteousness of the law shall be remembered to her, in which infants study, being written upon (*u*) the table of the heart, and is placed over against the nations as a cedar.

Verse 10. *I am a wall, &c.*] The congregation of Israel answered and said, I am strong in the words of the law as a wall, and my sons are mighty as a tower; and at that time the congregation of Israel found mercy in the eyes of her Lord, and all the inhabitants of the earth asked of her welfare.

Verse 11. *Solomon had a vineyard at Baal-hamon, &c.*] One nation came up in the lot of the Lord of the world, (*v*) with whom is peace, which is like to a vineyard; (*w*) he placed it in Jerusalem, and delivered it into the hands of the kings of the house of David, who kept it as a vinedresser keeps his vineyard; after that Solomon king of Israel died, it was left in the hands of his son Rehoboam; Jeroboam, the son of Nebat, came and divided the kingdom with him, and took out of his hands ten tribes, according to the word of Ahijah of Shiloh, who was a great man.

Verse 12. *My vineyard, which is mine, &c.*] When Solomon, the king of Israel, heard the prophecy of Ahijah of Shiloh, he sought to (*x*) kill him; but Ahijah fled from Solomon, and went into Egypt. And at that time King Solomon was informed by prophecy that he should rule over the ten tribes all his days: but after his death Jeroboam, the son of Nebat, should rule over them; and the two tribes, Judah and Benjamin, Rehoboam, the son of Solomon, should reign over.

Verse 13. *Thou that dwellest in the gardens,*

(*l*) גהנם *gehinnom*, "the valley of Hinnom," where the idolaters caused their children to pass through the fire to Molech, and burned them, 2 Chron. xxviii. 3, and xxxiii. 6; Jer. vii. 31, and xxxii. 35. R. David Kimchi, in Psa. xxvii. 13, says that Gehinnom was a very contemptible place near Jerusalem, where all manner of filthiness and dead carcasses were cast; and that a continual fire was kept there to burn them: hence the word is used very frequently by the Jewish rabbins, to signify the place where the wicked are punished after death; and so the word γεεννα, is used in the New Testament; see Matt. v. 22, and x. 28, and elsewhere.

(*m*) The same is asserted in Talmud Pesach. fol. 54, 1. Bereshith Rabba, Parash. 4, and 11 and 21. Shemoth Rabba, Parash. 15. Zohar in Deut. fol. 120, 1. Jarchi in Isa. xxx. 33; and yet at other times they reckon hell among the seven things which were created before the world was, Talmud Pesach, fol. 54, 1, and Nedarim. fol. 39, 2. Zohar in Lev. fol. 14, 4. Targum Jon. in Gen. iii. 24. See Matt. xxv. 41.

(*n*) The punishment of the wicked in hell is very frequently expressed by Jewish writers, by their burning in fire and brimstone, Bereshith Rabba, Parash. 6 and 51. Zohar in Gen. fol. 71, 3. Raya Mehimna, *ibid.* in Lev. fol. 7, 2. Targum Jon. and Jerus. in Gen. iii. 24. Targum Jerus. in Gen. xv. 12. Targum in Eccles. viii. 10, and x. 11. Targum in Isa. xxxiii. 14. R. David Kimchi in Isa. xxx. 33. Thus idolaters, with others, are said to "have their part in the lake which burneth with fire and brimstone," Rev. xxi. 8.

(*o*) So the words are explained in Shemoth Rabba, Parash. 49. Bemidbar Rabba, Parash. 2. Zohar in Num. fol. 105, 3. Raya Mehimna, *ibid.* in Gen. fol. 51, 3. Shirhashirim Rabba, Jarchi and Aben Ezra in loc.

(*p*) See Mark x. 30; Luke xviii. 30.

(*q*) See Ezek. xxxix. 9, 10.

(*r*) See Dan. x. 13, 21, and xii. 1. The Jews suppose that every nation or kingdom has an angel set over it, to be its president, protector, and defender; and that Michael was he that presided over Israel.

(*s*) That is, the knowledge of the unity of God. The doctrine of the unity of the Divine Being is the second article of the Jewish creed, where they say that "God is one, and that there is no unity in any respect like his;" this they very much magnify and extol. Hence they often have those words in their mouths, "Hear, O Israel, the Lord our God is one Lord," Deut. vi. 4; which, they think, is entirely inconsistent with a trinity of persons. Hence, says Maimonides, (Hilch. Yesod Hattorah, c. 1, s. 4,) "This God is one, not two, or more than two; but one. For there is no unity like his in any of the individuals which are found in the world; neither is he one in species, which comprehends more individuals, nor one in body, which is divided into parts and extremes, but he is so one, that there is no other unity like it in the world." All which is not so much opposed to the polytheism of the heathens, as to the plurality of persons in the trinity, and the incarnation of Christ. But though modern Jews have exploded the doctrine of the trinity, as inconsistent with that of the unity of the Divine Being, yet their more ancient writers do very manifestly speak of it as the great mystery of faith, Zohar edit. Sultzbac. in Gen. fol. 1, col. 3; in Exod. fol. 18, 3, 4, fol. 58, 1, and fol. 66, 2, 3; in Lev. fol. 27, 2, and in Num. fol. 67, 3. Jetzira. edit. Rittangel. fol. 1, 4, 6, 38, 64. *Vide* Josep. de Voisin. Disp. Theolog. de S. Trinitate, Allix's judgment of the Jewish Church, against the Unitarians, c. 9, 10, 11.

(*t*) In Raya Mehimna in Zohar in Exod. fol. 38, 3, it is said that "no man is poor but he that is so in the law and in the commandments;" and that "the riches of a man lies in them;" and in Vajikra Rabba, Parash. 34, where those words in Prov. xxii. 2, "The rich and poor meet together," are mentioned, it is said, "The rich is he that is rich in the law, and the poor is he that is poor in the law;" see also Zohar in Num. fol. 91, 3; with all which compare 1 Tim. vi. 18.

(*u*) See note on chap. iv. 9.

(*v*) In Shirhashirim Rabba in loc. it is explained in the same way; R. Aben Ezra, by Solomon in the next verse, understands the King Messiah; though it is interpreted of Solomon, king of Israel, by the Targum and Jarchi in loc., by Maimon. Yesod Hattorah, c. 6, s. 12, and in Zohar in Exod. fol. 91, 3.

(*w*) So it is explained of the people of Israel, under the government of Solomon in Shirhashirim Rabba, and by Jarchi and Aben Ezra in loc.

(*x*) This is a very great mistake of the Targumist; for it was Jeroboam, and not Ahijah, who fled into Egypt, whom Solomon sought to kill; see 1 Kings xi. 40.

&c.] Solomon said at the end of his prophecy, The Lord of the world shall say to the congregation of Israel in the end of days, O thou congregation of Israel, which *art* like to a garden highly esteemed of among the nations, and sits in the school with the companions of the sanhedrin, and the rest of the people which hearken to the voice of the chief of the school, and learn from his mouth his words, cause me to hear the law, the voice of thy words, when thou sittest to justify and condemn, and I will consent to whatever thou dost.

Verse 14. *Make haste, my beloved, &c.*] In that very hour the elders of the congregation of Israel shall say, Flee, O my beloved, the Lord of the world, from this defiled earth, and cause thy shechinah to dwell in the highest heavens, and in the time of straits, when we pray before thee, be thou like a roe, which, when it sleeps, (*y*) has one eye shut and the other eye open; or as a young hart, which, when it flees, looks behind it; so do thou look upon us, and consider our sorrow and our affliction, from the highest heavens, until the time *comes* that thou wilt take pleasure in us, and redeem us, and bring us to the mountain of Jerusalem, where the priests shall offer up before thee the sweet incense.

(*y*) The same is mentioned in Shirhashirim Rabba in loc.

THE GITAGOVINDA;

OR THE

SONGS OF JAYADEVA

A mystical poem, supposed to have a near resemblance to the BOOK OF CANTICLES, many passages of which it illustrates.

PART I

THE firmament is obscured by clouds, the woodlands are black with *Tamala* (1) trees.
That youth who roves in the forest must be fearful in the gloom of night.
Go, my daughter; bring the wanderer home to my rustic mansion.
Such was the command of NANDA, (2) the fortunate herdsman; and hence arose the loves of RADHA (3) and MADHAVA, (4) who sported on the bank of *Yamuna,* (5) or hastened eagerly to the secret bower.
If thy soul be delighted with the remembrance of HERI, (6) or sensible to the raptures of love, listen to the voice of JAYADEVA, whose notes are both sweet and brilliant.
O thou who reclinest on the bosom of CAMALA, (7) whose ears flame with gems, and whose locks are embellished with sylvan flowers;
Thou from whom the day-star derived his effulgence, who showedst the venom-breathing CALIYA, (8) who beamedst like a sun on the tribe of YADU, (9) that flourished like a lotos;
Thou, who sittest on the plumage of GARURA, (10) who, by subduing demons, gavest exquisite joy to the assembly of immortals;
Thou, for whom the daughter of JANACA (11) was decked in gay apparel, by whom DUSHANA (12) was overthrown;
Thou, whose eye sparkles like the water-lily, who calledst three worlds into existence;
Thou, by whom the rocks of *Mandar* (13) were easily supported; who sippest nectar from the radiant lips of PEDMA, (14) as the fluttering *Chacora* (15) drinks the moonbeams;

Be victorious, O HERI, *lord of conquest!*

RADHA sought him long in vain, and her thoughts were confounded by the fever of desire.
She was roving in the vernal season, among the twining *Vasantis,* (16) covered with soft blossoms, when a damsel thus addressed her with youthful hilarity:
"The gale that has wantoned round the beautiful clove plant breathes from the hill of MAYLAYA; (17)
The circling arbours resound with the notes of the *Cocila,* (18) and the murmurs of honey-making swarms
Now the hearts of damsels, whose lovers are travelling at a distance, are pierced with anguish;
While the blossoms of *Bacul* (19) are conspicuous among the flowrets covered with bees.
The *Tamala,* with leaves dark and fragrant, claims a tribute from the musk, which it vanquishes;
And the clustering flowers of the *Cinsuca* (20) resembling the nails of *Cama,* (21) with which he rends the hearts of the young.
The full-blown *Cesara* (22) gleams like the sceptre of the world's monarch, love;
And the pointed thyrsus of the *Cetaci* (23) resembles the darts by which lovers are wounded.
See the bunches of *Patali* (24) flowers filled with bees, like the quiver of *Smara* (25) full of shafts,
While the tender blossom of the *Caruna* (26) smiles to see the whole world laying shame aside.
The far-scented *Madhavi* (27) beautifies the trees, round which it twines;
And the fresh *Malica* (28) seduces with rich perfume even the hearts of hermits;
While the *Amra* (29) tree with blooming tresses is embraced by the gay creeper *Atimucta,* (30)
And the blue streams of *Yamuna* wind round the groves of *Vrindavan.* (31)
In this charming season, which gives pain to separated lovers,
Young HERI sports and dances with a company of damsels.
A breeze, like the breath of love, from the fragrant flowers of the *Cetaci,* kindles every heart.

Whilst it perfumes the woods with the prolific dust, which it shakes from the *Mallica* (32) with half opened buds;

And the *Cocila* bursts into song, when he sees the blossoms glistening on the lovely *Rasala*." (33)

The jealous RADHA gave no answer;

And, soon after, her officious friend, perceiving the foe of MURA (34) in the forest, eager for the rapturous embraces of the herdman's daughters, with whom he was dancing,

Thus again addressed his forgotten mistress:

"With a garland of wild flowers, descending even to the yellow mantle that girds his azure limbs,

Distinguished by smiling cheeks, and by ear-rings that sparkle as he plays,

HERI exults in the assemblage of amorous damsels.

One of them presses him with her swelling breast, while she warbles with exquisite melody.

Another, affected by a glance from his eye, stands meditating on the lotos of his face.

A third, on pretence of whispering a secret in his ear, approaches his temples, and kisses them with ardour.

One seizes his mantle, and draws him towards her, pointing to the bower on the banks of *Yamuna*, where elegant *Vanjulas* (35) interweave their branches.

He applauds another who dances in the sportive circle, whilst her bracelets ring, as she beats time with her palms.

Now he caresses one, and kisses another, smiling on a third with complacency;

And now he chases her, whose beauty has most allured him.

Thus the wanton HERI frolics, in the season of sweets, among the maids of *Vraja*, (36)

Who rush to his embraces, as if he were pleasure itself assuming a human form;

And one of them, under a pretext of hymning his divine perfections, whispers in his ear.

'Thy lips, my beloved, are nectar.' "

PART II

RADHA remains in the forest: but, resenting the promiscuous passion of HERI, and his neglect of her beauty, which he once thought superior,

She retires to a bower of twining plants, the summit of which resounds with the humming of swarms engaged in their sweet labours;

And there, fallen languid on the ground, she thus addresses her female companion:

"Though he take recreation in my absence, and smile on all around him,

Yet my soul remembers him, whose beguiling reed modulates an air sweetened by the nectar of his quivering lip,

While his ear sparkles with gems, and his eye darts amorous glances;

Him, whose looks are decked with the plumes of peacocks resplendent with many-coloured moons,

And whose mantle gleams like a dark blue cloud illumined with rainbows;

Him, whose graceful smile gives new lustre to his lips, brilliant and soft as a dewy leaf, sweet and ruddy as the blossom of *Bandhujiva*, (37)

While they tremble with eagerness to kiss the daughters of the herdsmen;

Him, who disperses the gloom with beams from the jewels which decorate his bosom, his wrists, and his ankles;

On whose forehead shines a circlet of sandal wood, which makes even the moon contemptible, when it moves through irradiated clouds;

Him, whose ear-rings are formed of entire gems in the shape of the fish *Macara* (38) on the banners of love.

Even the yellow-robed god, whose attendants are the chief of deities, of holy men, and of demons;

Him who reclines under a gay *Cadumba* (39) tree, who formerly delighted me while he gracefully waved in the dance,

And all his soul sparked in his eye.

My weak mind thus enumerates his qualities; and, though offended, strives to banish offence.

What else can do it? It cannot part with its affection for CRISHNA, whose love is excited by other damsels and who sports in the absence of RADHA.

Bring, O my sweet friend, that vanquisher of the demon *Cesi* (40) to sport with me, who am repairing to a secret bower,

Who look timidly on all sides, who meditate with amorous fancy on his divine transfiguration.

Bring him, whose discourse was once composed of the gentlest words, to converse with me, who am bashful on his first approach,

And express my thoughts with a smile sweet as honey.

Bring him, who formerly slept on my bosom, to recline with me on a green bed of leaves just gathered, while his lips shed dew, and my arms enfold him.

Bring him, who has attained the perfection of skill in love's art, whose hand used to press these firm and delicate spheres, to play with me,
Whose voice rivals that of the *Cocila,* and whose tresses are bound with waving blossoms.
Bring him, who formerly drew me by the locks to his embrace, to repose with me whose feet tinkle, as they move, with rings of gold and of gems,
Whose loosened zone sounds, as it falls; and whose limbs are slender and flexible as the creeping plant.
That god, whose cheeks are beautified by the nectar of his smiles,
Whose pipe drops in his ecstasy from his hand, I saw in the grove encircled by the damsels of *Vraja,* who gazed on him askance from the corners of their eyes.
I saw him in the grove with happier damsels, yet the sight of him delighted me.
Soft is the gale which breathes over yon clear pool, and expands the clustering blossoms of the voluble *Asoca;* (41)
Soft, yet grievous to me in the absence of the foe of MADHU.
Delightful are the flowers of *Amra* trees on the mountain top, while the murmuring bees pursue their voluptuous toil;
Delightful, yet afflicting to me, O friend, in the absence of the youthful *Cesava.*"

PART III

Meantime, the destroyer of CANSA, (42) having brought to his remembrance the amiable RADHA, forsook the beautiful damsels of *Vraja.*
He sought her in all parts of the forest; his whole wound from love's arrow bled again;
He repented of his levity; and, seated in a bower near the bank of *Yamuna,* the blue daughter of the sun
Thus poured forth his lamentation:
"She is departed; she saw me, no doubt, surrounded by the wanton shepherdesses;
Yet, conscious of my fault, I durst not intercept her flight.
Wo is me! she feels a sense of injured honour, and is departed in wrath.
How will she conduct herself? How will she express her pain in so long a separation?
What is wealth to me? What are numerous attendants?
What are the pleasures of the world? What joy can I receive from a heavenly abode?
I seem to behold her face with eyebrows contracting themselves through a just resentment;
It resembles a fresh lotos, over which two black bees are fluttering.
I seem, so present is she to my imagination, even now to caress her with eagerness.
Why then do I seek her in this forest? why do I lament her without cause?
O slender damsel, I know that anger has torn thy soft bosom;
But whither thou art retired, that I know not.
How can I invite thee to return?
Thou art seen by me, indeed, in a vision; thou seemest to move before me.
Ah! why dost thou not rush, as before, to my embrace?
Do but forgive me: never again will I commit a similar offence.
Grant me but a sight of thee, O lovely *Radhica;* for my passion torments me.
I am not the terrible *Mahesa*: (43) a garland of water-lilies with subtle filaments decks my shoulders, not serpents, with twisted folds.
The blue petals of the lotos glitter on my neck; not the azure gleam of poison.
Powdered sandal-wood is sprinkled on my limbs; not pale ashes.
O god of love, mistake me not for *Mahadeva.* (44)
Wound me not again; approach me not in anger;
I love already but too passionately; yet I have lost my beloved.
Hold not in thy hand that shaft barbed with an *Amra* flower.
Brace not thy bow, O conqueror of the world. Is it valour to slay one who faints?
My heart is already pierced by arrows from *Radha's* eyes, black and keen as those of an antelope;
Yet my eyes are not gratified with her presence.
Her eyes are full of shafts; her eyebrows are bows; and the tips of her ears are silken strings.
Thus armed by *Ananga,* (45) the god of desire, she marches, herself a goddess to ensure his triumph over the vanquished universe.
I meditate on her delightful embrace, on the ravishing glances darted from her eye,
On the fragrant lotos of her mouth, on her nectar-dropping speech,
On her lips, ruddy as the berries of the *Bimba* (46) plant;
Yet even my fixed meditation on such an assemblage of charms increases instead of alleviating the misery of separation."

PART IV

The damsel, commissioned by RADHA, found the disconsolate god under an arbour of spreading *Vaniras* by the side of *Yamuna;* where, presenting herself gracefully before him, she thus described the affliction of his beloved:

"She despises essence of sandal-wood, and even by moonlight sits brooding over her gloomy sorrow;

She declares the gale of *Malaya* to be venom; and the sandal-trees, through which it has breathed, to have been the haunt of serpents.

Thus, O MADHAVA is she afflicted in thy absence with the pain which love's dart has occasioned: her soul is fixed on thee.

Fresh arrows of desire are continually assailing her, and she forms a net of lotos leaves as armour for her heart, which thou alone shouldst fortify.

She makes her own bed of the arrows darted by the flowery-shafted god: but when she hoped for thy embrace, she had formed for thee a couch of soft blossoms.

Her face is like a water-lily, veiled in the dew of tears; and her eyes appear like moons eclipsed, which let fall their gathered nectar through pain caused by the tooth of the furious dragon.

She draws thy image with musk in the character of the deity with five shafts, having subdued the *Macar*, or horned shark, and holding an arrow tipped with an *Amra* flower; thus she draws thy picture, and worships it.

At the close of every sentence, O MADHAVA, she exclaims, At thy feet am I fallen, and in thy absence even the moon, though it be a vase full of nectar, inflames my limbs.

Then by the power of imagination she figures thee standing before her; thee, who art not easily attained;

She sighs, she smiles, she mourns, she weeps, she moves from side to side, she laments and rejoices by turns.

Her abode is a forest; the circle of her female companions is a net;

Her sighs are flames of fire kindled in a thicket; herself (alas! through thy absence) is become a timid roe; and love is the tiger who springs on her like YAMA, the genius of death.

So emaciated is her beautiful body, that even the light garland which waves over her bosom she thinks a load.

Such, O bright-haired god, is RADHA when thou art absent.

If powder of sandal-wood finely levigated be moistened and applied to her bosom, she starts, and mistakes it for poison.

Her sighs form a breeze long extended, and burn her like the flame which reduced CANDARPA (47) to ashes.

She throws around her eyes, like blue water-lilies with broken stalks, dropping lucid streams.

Even her bed of tender leaves appears in her sight like a kindled fire.

The palm of her hand supports her aching temple, motionless as the crescent rising at eve.

HERI, HERI, thus in silence she meditates on thy name, as if her wish were gratified, and she were dying through thy absence.

She rends her locks; she pants; she laments inarticulately;

She trembles; she pines; she muses; she moves from place to place; she closes her eyes;

She falls; she rises again; she faints: in such a fever of love she may live, O celestial physician, if thou administer the remedy;

But shouldst thou be unkind, her malady will be desperate.

Thus, O divine healer, by the nectar of thy love must RADHA be restored to health; and if thou refuse it, thy heart must be harder than the thunder-stone.

Long has her soul pined, and long has she been heated with sandal-wood, moonlight, and water-lilies, with which others are cooled;

Yet she patiently and in secret meditates on thee, who alone canst relieve her.

Shouldst thou be inconstant, how can she, wasted as she is to a shadow, support life a single moment?

How can she, who lately could not endure thy absence even an instant, forbear sighing now, when she looks with half-closed eyes on the *Rasala* with blooming branches, which remind her of the vernal season, when she first beheld thee with rapture?"

"Here have I chosen my abode: go quickly to RADHA; sooth her with my message, and conduct her hither."

So spoke the foe of MADHU (48) to the anxious damsel, who hastened back, and thus addressed her companion:

"Whilst a sweet breeze from the hills of *Malaya* comes wafting on his plumes the young god of desire,

While many a flower points his extended petals to pierce the bosoms of separated lovers,

The deity crowned with sylvan blossoms laments, O friend, in thy absence.

Even the dewy rays of the moon burn him; and as the shaft of love is descending, he mourns inarticulately with increasing distraction.

When the bees murmur softly, he covers his ears;

Misery sits fixed in his heart, and every returning night adds anguish to anguish.

He quits his radiant palace for the wild forest, where he sinks on a bed of cold clay, and frequently mutters thy name.

In yon bower, to which the pilgrims of love are used to repair, he meditates on thy form, repeating in silence some enchanting word which once dropped from thy lips, and thirsting for the nectar which they alone can supply.

Delay not, O loveliest of women; follow the lord of thy heart: behold, he seeks the appointed shade, bright with the ornaments of love, and confident of the promised bliss.

Having bound his locks with forest flowers, he hastens to yon arbour, where a soft gale breathes over the banks of *Yamuna;*

There, again pronouncing thy name, he modulates his divine reed.

Oh! with what rapture doth he gaze on the golden dust, which the breeze shakes from expanded blossoms:

The breeze which has kissed thy cheek!

With a mind languid as a drooping wing, feeble as a trembling leaf, he doubtfully expects thy approach, and timidly looks on the path which thou must tread.

Leave behind thee, O friend, the ring which tinkles on the delicate ankle, when thou sportest in the dance;

Hastily cast over thee thy azure mantle, and run to the gloomy bower.

The reward of thy speed, O thou who sparklest like lightning, will be to shine on the blue bosom of MURARI, (49)

Which resembles a vernal cloud, decked with a string of pearls like a flock of white water-birds fluttering in the air.

Disappoint not, O thou lotos-eyed, the vanquisher of MADHU; accomplish his desire.

But go quickly: it is night; and the night also will quickly depart.

Again and again he sighs; he looks around; he re-enters the arbour; he can scarce articulate thy sweet name;

He again smooths his flowery couch; he looks wild; he becomes frantic; thy beloved will perish through desire.

The bright-beamed god sinks in the west, and thy pain of separation may also be removed;

The blackness of the night is increased, and the passionate imagination of GOVINDA (50) has acquired additional gloom.

My address to thee has equalled in length and in sweetness the song of the *Cocila;* delay will make thee miserable, O my beautiful friend.

Seize the moment of delight in the place of assignation with the son of DEVACI, (51) who descended from heaven to remove the burdens of the universe.

He is a blue gem on the forehead of the three worlds, and longs to sip honey like the bee from the fragrant lotos of thy cheek."

But the solicitous maid, perceiving that RADHA was unable, through debility, to move from her arbour of flowery creepers, returned to GOVINDA, who was himself disordered with love, and thus described her situation:

"She mourns, O sovereign of the world, in her verdant bower;

She looks eagerly on all sides in hope of thy approach; then, gaining strength from the delightful idea of the proposed meeting, she advances a few steps, and falls languid on the ground.

When she rises, she weaves bracelets of fresh leaves; she dresses herself like her beloved, and looking at herself in sport, exclaims, 'Behold the vanquisher of MADHU!'

Then she repeats again and again the name of HERI, and catching at a dark blue cloud, strives to embrace it, saying, 'It is my beloved who approaches.'

Thus, while thou art dilatory, she lies expecting thee: she mourns; she weeps; she puts on her gayest ornaments to receive her lord;

She compresses her deep sighs within her bosom; and then, meditating on thee, O cruel, she is drowned in a sea of rapturous imaginations.

If a leaf but quiver, she supposes thee arrived; she spreads her couch; she forms in her mind a hundred modes of delight;

Yet, if thou go not to her bower, she must die this night through excessive anguish."

PART V

By this time the moon spread a net of beams over the groves of *Vrindavan,*

And looked like a drop of liquid sandal on the face of the sky, which smiled like a beautiful damsel;

While its orb with many spots betrayed, as it were, a consciousness of guilt, in having often attended amorous maids to the loss of their family honour.

The moon, with a black fawn couched on its disk, advanced in its nightly course.

But MADHAVA had not advanced to the bower of RADHA, who thus bewailed his delay with notes of varied lamentations:

"The appointed moment is come; but HERI, alas! comes not to the grove.

Must the season of my unblemished youth pass thus idly away?

Oh! what refuge can I seek, deluded as I am by the guile of my female adviser?

The god with five arrows has wounded my heart; and I am deserted by him, for whose sake I have sought at night the darkest recess of the forest.

Since my best beloved friends have deceived me, it is my wish to die;

Since my senses are disordered, and my bosom is on fire—why stay I longer in this world?

The coolness of this vernal night gives me pain, instead of refreshment.

Some happier damsel enjoys my beloved; whilst I, alas! am looking at the gems of my bracelets, which are blackened by the flames of my passion.

My neck, more delicate than the tenderest blossom, is hurt by the garland that encircles it:

Flowers are, indeed, the arrows of love, and he plays with them cruelly.

I make this wood my dwelling: I regard not the roughness of the *Vetas trees;*

But the destroyer of MADHU holds me not in his remembrance!

Why comes he not to the bower of the blooming *Vanjulas*, assigned for meeting?

Some ardent rival, no doubt, keeps him locked in her embrace.

Or have his companions detained him with mirthful recreations?

Else why roams he not through the cool shades?

Perhaps, through weakness, the heart-sick lover is unable to advance even a step!"

So saying, she raised her eyes; and, seeing her damsel return silent and mournful, unaccompanied by MADHAVA, she was alarmed even to frenzy;

And, as if she actually beheld him in the arms of a rival, she thus described the vision which overpowered her intellect:

"Yes, in habiliments becoming the war of love, and with tresses waving like flowery banners,

A damsel, more alluring than RADHA, enjoys the conqueror of MADHU.

Her form is transfigured by the touch of her divine lover; her garland quivers over her swelling bosom;

Her face like the moon is graced with clouds of dark hair, and trembles while she quaffs the nectareous dew of his lip;

Her bright ear-rings dance over her cheeks, which they irradiate; and the small bells on her girdle tinkle as she moves.

Bashful at first, she smiles at length on her embracer, and expresses her joy with inarticulate murmurs;

While she floats on the waves of desire, and closes her eyes dazzled with the blaze of approaching CAMA:

And now this heroine in love's warfare falls, exhausted and vanquished by the resistless MURARI.

But alas! in my bosom prevails the flame of jealousy, and yon moon, which dispels the sorrow of others, increases mine.

See again, where the foe of MURA sports in yon grove, on the bank of the *Yamuna*.

See how he kisses the lip of my rival, and imprints on her forehead an ornament of pure musk, black as the young antelope on the lunar orb!

Now, like the husband of RETI, (52) he fixes white blossoms on her dark locks, where they gleam like flashes of lightning among the curled clouds.

On her breasts, like two firmaments, he places a string of gems like a radiant constellation.

He binds on her arms, graceful as the stalks of the water-lily, and adorned with hands glowing like the petals of its flower, a bracelet of sapphires, which resembles a cluster of bees.

Ah! see how he ties round her waist a rich girdle illumined with golden bells,

Which seem to laugh as they tinkle, at the inferior brightness of the leafy garlands, which lovers hang on their bowers to propitiate the god of desire.

He places her soft foot, as he reclines by her side, on his ardent bosom, and stains it with the ruddy hue of *Yavaca*.

Say, my friend, why pass I my nights in this tangled forest without joy, and without hope,

While the faithless brother of HALADHERA clasps my rival in his arms?

Yet why, my companion, shouldst thou mourn, though my perfidious youth has disappointed me?

What offence is it of thine, if he sport with a crowd of damsels happier than I?

Mark, how my soul, attracted by his irresistible charms, bursts from its mortal frame, and rushes to mix with its beloved.

She, whom the god enjoys, crowned with sylvan flowers,

Sits carelessly on a bed of leaves with him, whose wanton eyes resemble blue water-lilies agitated by the breeze.

She feels no flame from the gales of *Malaya* with him, whose words are sweeter than the water of life.

She derides the shafts of soul-born CAMA with him, whose lips are like a red lotos in full bloom.

She is cooled by the moon's dewy beams, while she reclines with him, whose hands and feet glow like vernal flowers.

No female companion deludes her, while she sports with him, whose vesture blazes like tried gold.

She faints not through excess of passion, while she caresses that youth who surpasses in beauty the inhabitants of all worlds.

O gale, scented with sandal, who breathest love from the regions of the south, be propitious but for a moment:

When thou hast brought my beloved before my eyes, thou mayest freely waft away my soul.

Love, with eyes like blue water-lilies, again assails me, and triumphs;

And, while the perfidy of my beloved rends my heart, my female friend is my foe;

The cool breeze scorches me like a flame, and the nectar-dropping moon is my poison.

Bring disease and death, O gale of *Malaya!* Seize my spirit, O god with five arrows!

I ask not mercy from thee: no more will I dwell in the cottage of my father.

Receive me in thy azure waves, O sister of YAMA, (53) that the ardour of my heart may be allayed."

PART VI

Pierced by the arrows of love, she passed the night in the agonies of despair, and at early dawn thus rebuked her lover, whom she saw lying prostrate before her, and imploring her forgiveness:

"Alas! alas! go, MADHAVA, depart, O CESAVA, (54) speak not the language of guile;

Follow her, O lotos-eyed god, follow her, who dispels thy care.

Look at his eye half opened, red with continual waking through the pleasurable night, yet smiling still with affection for my rival!

Thy teeth, O cerulean youth, are azure as thy complexion, from the kisses which thou hast imprinted on the beautiful eyes of thy darling, graced with dark blue powder;

And thy limbs, marked with punctures in love's warfare, exhibit a letter of conquest written on polished sapphires with liquid gold.

That broad bosom, stained by the bright lotos of her foot, displays a vesture of ruddy leaves over the tree of thy heart, which trembles within it.

The pressure of her lip on thine, wounds me to the soul.

Ah! how canst thou assert that we are one, since our sensations differ thus widely?

Thy soul, O dark-limbed god, shows its blackness externally.

How couldst thou deceive a girl who relied on thee; a girl who burned in the fever of love?

Thou rovest in the woods, and females are thy prey:—what wonder?

Even thy childish heart was malignant; and thou gavest death to the nurse, who would have given thee milk.

Since thy tenderness for me, of which these forests used to talk, has now vanished;

And since thy breast, reddened by the feet of my rival, glows as if thy ardent passion for her were bursting from it,

The sight of thee, O deceiver, makes my (ah! must I say it?) blush at my own affection."

Having thus inveighed against her beloved, she sat overwhelmed in grief, and silently meditated on his charms; when her damsel softly addressed her:

"He is gone: the light air has wafted him away. What pleasure, now my beloved, remains in thy mansion?

Continue not, resentful woman, thy indignation against the beautiful MADHAVA.

Why shouldst thou render vain those round, smooth vases, ample and ripe as the sweet fruit of yon *Tala* tree?

How often and how recently have I said, Forsake not the blooming HERI?

Why sittest thou so mournful? Why weepest thou with distraction, when the damsels are laughing around thee?

Thou hast formed a couch of soft lotos leaves: let thy darling charm thy sight, while he reposes on it.

Afflict not thy soul with extreme anguish: but attend to my words, which conceal no guile.

Suffer CESAVA to approach; let him speak with exquisite sweetness, and dissipate all thy sorrows.

If thou art harsh to him, who is amiable; if thou art proudly silent, when he deprecates thy wrath with lowly prostrations;

If thou showest aversion to him, who loves thee passionately; if, when he bends before thee, thy face be turned contemptuously away;

By the same rule of contrariety the dust of sandal-wood, which thou hast sprinkled, may become poison;

The moon, with cool beams, a scorching sun; the fresh dew, a consuming flame; and the sports of love be changed into agony."

Madhava was not absent long; he returned to his beloved; whose cheeks were healed by the sultry gale of her sighs.

Her anger was diminished, not wholly abated; but she secretly rejoiced at his return, while the shades of night also were approaching.

She looked abashed at her damsel, while he, with faltering accents, implored her forgiveness.

"Speak but one mild word, and the rays of thy sparkling teeth will dispel the gloom of my fears.

My trembling lips, like thirsty *Chacorus*, long to drink the moonbeams of thy cheek.

O my darling, who art naturally so tender-hearted, abandon thy causeless indignation.

At this moment the flame of desire consumes my heart. Oh! grant me a draught of honey from the lotos of thy mouth.

Or if thou beest inexorable, grant me death from the arrows of thy keen eyes.

Make thy arms my chains; and punish me according to thy pleasure.

Thou art my life; thou art my ornament; thou art a pearl in the ocean of my mortal birth:

Oh! be favourable now, and my heart shall externally be grateful.

Thine eyes, which nature formed like blue water-lilies, art become, through thy resentment, like petals of the crimson lotos.

Oh! tinge with their effulgence these my dark limbs, that they may glow like the shafts of love tipped with flowers.

Place on my head that foot like a fresh leaf: and shade me from the sun of my passion, whose beams I am unable to bear.

Spread a string of gems on those two soft globes; let the golden bells of thy zone tinkle, and proclaim the mild edict of love.

Say, O damsel, with delicate speech, shall I dye red with the juice of *Alactaca* those beautiful feet, which make the full blown land-lotos blush with shame?

Abandon thy doubts of my heart, now indeed fluttering through fear of thy displeasure, but hereafter to be fixed wholly on thee;

A heart, which has no room in it for another: none else can enter it, but love, the bodyless god.

Let him wing his arrows; let him wound me mortally; decline not, O cruel, the pleasure of seeing me expire.

Thy face is bright as the moon, though its beams drop the venom of maddening desire;

Let thy nectareous lip be the charmer, who alone has power to lull the serpent, or supply an antidote for his poison.

Thy silence afflicts me: Oh! speak with the voice of music, and let thy sweet accents allay my ardour.

Abandon thy wrath: but abandon not a lover, who surpasses in beauty the sons of men, and who kneels before thee, O thou most beautiful among women.

Thy lips are a *Bandhujiva* flower; the lustre of the *Madhuca* (55) beams on thy cheek;

Thine eye outshines the blue lotos; thy nose is a bud of the *Tila;* (56) the *Cunda* (57) blossom yields to thy teeth;

Thus the flowery-shafted god borrows from thee the points of his darts, and subdues the universe.

Surely thou descendest from heaven, O slender damsel, attended by a company of youthful goddesses; and all their beauties are collected in thee."

PART VII

He spake; and seeing her appeased by his homage, flew to his bower, clad in a gay mantle.

The night now veiled all visible objects; and the damsel thus exhorted *Radha*, while she decked her with beaming ornaments:

"Follow, gentle Radhica, follow the son of Madhu;

His disclosure was elegantly composed of sweet phrases; he prostrated himself at thy feet, and he now hastens to his delightful couch by yon grove of branching *Vanjalas*.

Bind round thy ankle rings beaming with gems; and advance with mincing steps, like the pearl-fed *Marala*.

Drink with ravished ears the soft accents of Heri; and feast on love, while the warbling *Cocilas* obeys the mild ordinance of the flower-darting god.

Abandon delay: see the whole assembly of slender plants, pointing to the bower with fingers of young leaves agitated by the gale, make signals for thy departure.

Ask those two round hillocks, which receive pure dew-drops from the garland playing on thy neck, and the buds whose tops start aloft with the thought of thy darling;

Ask, and they will tell, that thy soul is intent on the warfare of love:

Advance, fervid warrior, advance with alacrity, while the sound of thy tinkling waist-bells shall represent martial music.

Lead with thee some favoured maid; grasp her hand with thine, whose fingers are long and smooth as love's arrows.

March; and with the noise of thy bracelets proclaim thy approach to the youth, who will own himself thy slave.

'She will come; she will exult in beholding me; she will pour accents of delight;

She will enfold me with eager arms; she will melt with affection.'

Such are his thoughts at this moment; and, thus thinking, he looks through the long avenue;

He trembles; he rejoices; he burns; he moves from place to place; he faints, when he sees thee not coming, and falls in his gloomy bower.

The night now dresses in habiliments fit for secrecy the many damsels, who hasten to their places of assignation;

She sets off with blackness their beautiful eyes; fixes dark *Tamala* leaves behind their ears;

Decks their locks with the deep azure of water-lilies, and sprinkles musk on their panting bosoms.

The nocturnal sky, black as the touchstone, tries the gold of their affections,

And is marked with rich lines from the flashes of their beauty, in which they surpass the brightest *Cashmirians*."

RADHA, thus incited, tripped through the forest: but shame overpowered her, when, by the light of innumerable gems on the arms, the neck, and the feet of her beloved,

She saw him at the door of his flowery mansion; then her damsel again addressed her with ardent exultation:

"Enter, sweet RADHA, the bower of HERI; seek delight, O thou whose bosom laughs with the foretaste of happiness.

Enter, sweet RADHA, the bower graced with a bed of *Asoca* leaves; seek delight, O thou whose garland leaps with joy on thy breast.

Enter, sweet RADHA, the bower illumined with gay blossoms; seek delight, O thou whose limbs far excel them in softness.

Enter, O RADHA, the bower made cool and fragrant by gales from the woods of *Malaya;* seek delight, O thou whose amorous lays are softer than breezes.

Enter, O RADHA, the bower spread with leaves of twining creepers; seek delight, O thou whose arms have been long inflexible.

Enter, O RADHA, the bower which resounds with the murmur of honey-making bees; seek delight, O thou whose embrace yields more exquisite sweetness.

Enter, O RADHA, the bower attuned by the melodious band of *Cocilas;* seek delight, O thou whose lips, which outshine the grains of the pomegranate, are embellished, when thou speakest, by the brightness of thy teeth.

Long has he borne thee in his mind; and now, in an agony of desire, he pants to taste nectar from thy lip.

Deign to restore thy slave, who will bend before the lotos of thy foot, and press it to his irradiated bosom.

A slave, who acknowledges himself bought by thee for a single glance from thy eye, and a toss of thy disdainful eyebrow."

She ended; and RADHA with timid joy, darting her eyes on GOVINDA, while she musically sounded the rings of her ankles, and the bells of her zone, entered the mystic bower of her only beloved.

There she beheld her MADHAVA, who delighted in her alone;

Who so long had sighed for her embrace; and whose countenance then gleamed with excessive rapture.

His heart was agitated by her sight, as the waves of the deep are affected by the lunar orb.

His azure breast glittered with pearls of unblemished lustre, like the full bed of the cerulean *Yamuna*, interspersed with curls of white foam.

From his graceful waste flowed a pale yellow robe, which resembled the golden dust of the water-lily scattered over its blue petals.

His passion was inflamed by the glances of her eyes, which played like a pair of water-birds with blue plumage, that sport near a full-blown lotos on a pool in the season of dew.

Bright ear-rings, like two suns, displayed in full expansion the flowers of his cheeks and lips, which glistened with the liquid radiance of smiles.

His looks, interwoven with blossoms, were like a cloud variegated with moonbeams;

And on his forehead shone a circle of odorous oil, extracted from the sandal of *Malaya*, like the moon just appearing on the dusky horizon;

While his whole body seemed in a flame from the blaze of unnumbered gems.

Tears of transport gushed in a stream from the full eyes of RADHA, and their watery glances gleamed on her best beloved.

Even shame, which before had taken its abode in their dark pupils, was itself ashamed, and departed, when the fawn-eyed RADHA gazed on the brightened face of CRISHNA.

While she passed by the soft edge of his couch, and the bevy of his attendant nymphs, pretending to strike the gnats from their cheeks in order to conceal their smiles, warily retired from the bower.

PART VIII

GOVINDA, seeing his beloved cheerful and serene, her lips sparking with smiles, and her eyes speaking desire, thus eagerly addressed her; while she carelessly reclined on the leafy bed strewn with soft blossoms.

Set the lotos of thy foot on this azure bosom; and let this couch be victorious over all who rebel against love.

Give short rapture, sweet RADHA, to NARAYAN, (58) thy adorer.

I do thee homage; I press with my blooming palms thy feet, weary with so long a walk.

O that I were the golden ring that plays round thy ankle!

Speak but one gentle word; bid nectar drop from the bright moon of thy mouth.

Since the pain of absence is removed, let me thus remove the thin vest that enviously hides thy charms.

Blest should I be, if those raised globes were fixed on my bosom, and the ardour of my passion allayed.

Oh suffer me to quaff the liquid bliss of those lips;

Restore with their water of life thy slave, who has long been lifeless, whom the fire of separation has consumed.

Long have these ears been afflicted in thy absence by the notes of the *Cocila*.

Relieve them with the sound of thy tinkling waist-bells, which yield music, almost equal to the music of thy voice.

Why are those eyes half closed? Are they ashamed of seeing a youth to whom thy careless resentment gave anguish?

Oh, let affliction cease, and let ecstasy drown the remembrance of sorrow.

PART IX

In the morning she rose disarrayed, and her eyes betrayed a night without slumber; when the yellow-robed god, who gazed on her with transport, thus meditated on her charms in his heavenly mind:

Though her locks be diffused at random; though the lustre of her lips be faded; though her garland and zone be fallen from their enchanting stations;

And though she hide their places with her hands, looking towards me with bashful silence, yet even thus disarrayed, she fills me with ecstatic delight.

But RADHA, preparing to array herself, before the company of nymphs could see her confusion, spake thus with exultation to her obsequious lover:

Place, O son of YADU, with fingers cooler than sandal-wood, place a circlet of musk on this breast, which resembles a vase of consecrated water, crowned with fresh leaves, and fixed near a vernal bower, to propitiate the god of love.

Place, my darling, the glossy powder, which would make the blackest bee envious, on this eye, whose glances are keener than arrows darted by the husband of RETI.

Fix, O accomplished youth, the two gems, which form part of love's chain, in those ears, whence the antelopes of thine eyes may run downwards, and sport at pleasure.

Place now a fresh circle of musk, black as the lunar spots, on the moon of my forehead; and mix gay flowers on my tresses with a peacock's feathers, in graceful order, that they may wave like the banners of CAMA.

Now replace, O tender-hearted, the loose ornaments of my vesture; and refix the golden bells of my girdle on their destined station, which resembles those hills where the god with five shafts, who destroyed SAMBARA, (59) keeps his elephant ready for battle.

While she spake the heart of YADAVA triumphed; and obeying her sportful behests, he placed musky spots on her bosom and forehead, dyed her temples with radiant hues, embellished her eyes with additional blackness, decked her braided hair and her neck with fresh garlands, and tied on her wrists the loosened bracelets, on her ankles the beamy rings, and round her waist the zone of bells, that sounded with ravishing melody.

Whatever is delightful in the modes of music, whatever is divine in meditations on VISHNU, (60) whatever is exquisite in the sweet art of love, whatever is graceful in the fine strains of poetry, all that let the happy and wise learn from the songs of JAYADEVA, (61) whose soul is united with the foot of NARAYAN.

THE GITAGOVINDA

May that Heri be your support, who expanded himself into an infinity of bright forms, when, eager to gaze with myriads of eyes, on the daughter of the ocean, he displayed his great character of the all-pervading deity, by the multiplied reflections of his divine person in the numberless gems on the many heads of the king of serpents, whom he chose for his couch;

That Heri, who removing his lucid veil from the bosom of Pedma, and fixing his eyes on the delicious buds that grew on it, diverted her attention by declaring that, when she had chosen him as her bridegroom near the sea of milk, the disappointed husband of Pervati (62) drank in despair the venom, which dyed his neck azure!

I have now placed before my readers this extraordinary poem, which I believe will be considered by every adequate judge to be equal, if not superior, to every thing of the kind that has been produced, either by the ancients or moderns. The poem is confessedly *mystical*, relating to the pure and affectionate intercourse between the Deity and human souls; and is capable of a very extended comment, to illustrate its phraseology, and explain its almost numberless allusions to the mythological system of the Hindoos.

But the chief design of its introduction here is to illustrate the phraseology of the Song of Songs. The most superficial reader cannot but be struck with the similarity of the language of the metaphors and imagery. There are few turns of thought in the *Song of Songs* that may not find a parallel in the *Gitagovinda;* and even the strongly impassioned language of *Solomon* may be everywhere supported by that of *Jayadeva,* and *vice versa.* Could it be proved that the love between Christ and the Church were really the subject of the *Canticles*, the *Gitagovinda* might be applied with the utmost success to illustrate and explain all its *imagery*, and all its allusions: but we have no key to unlock its reference; no *data* to which we can confidently refer; and though it be generally allowed to be a *mystic song*, yet all interpreters follow their own creed in its explanation; and it is only on the general subject that any two of them agree. As I am not satisfied that the common method used in its interpretation is either correct or genuine, I have simply avoided the rocks on which others have been wrecked, but have constructed no chart according to which a more prosperous voyage might be projected.

The late learned and pious Mr. *Romaine* seems to have thought that a competent knowledge of the original language might lead to its proper illustration; and is indignant at those who have attempted its explanation without this necessary qualification. Of his knowledge of the sacred language no man doubts. I, also, have brought some acquaintance with the original to bear on the subject; but, though perhaps as well acquainted with the meaning of the words as Mr. Romaine himself, I have not been able to discover his system in the poem; and I dare not by *conjecture* put a meaning on any thing that professes to be a revelation from God. I respect many of its interpreters for their piety and learning, but I cannot follow their steps; they have not proved to me that Solomon's Song refers to the love of Christ and his Church. Let this by my apology with the candid reader for not entering into a more extended comment on this extraordinary book.

ADAM CLARKE.

London, May 1, 1823.

To ascertain some of the *latter* parts of this poem, I have been obliged to trust to my own judgment; as Sir William Jones, from whom I have borrowed these, had not marked any division; and I have had the *original* of the four first parts only.

As to the *old version* of the Canticles which I have introduced, the reader will be pleased to observe, it is that which was used by our forefathers before and after the reformation: one word of which I would not presume to alter or change. It is sacred both by age and use.

NOTES ON THE GITAGOVINDA

(1) TAMALA TREE.—A dark-leaved tree, common in Mat'hura and other parts, but not found in Bengal.—The laurel.
(2) *Nanda.*—The foster father of Crishna.
(3) *Radha.*—One of the principal and favourite mistresses of Crishna.
(4) *Madhava.*—One of the names of Crishna, implying the possession of Ma or Lachmi, his heavenly consort.
(5) *Yamuna.*—Vulgarly called Jumna, the river which flows by Dehlee, Mat'hura, and Ayra.
(6) *Heri.*—A name of Crishna; importing the remover of sin and suffering.
(7) *Camala.*—A name of Lachmi, derived from the lotos.
(8) *Caliya.*—A huge snake, who from the Jumna infested the neighbourhood of Gocul till destroyed by Crishna.
(9) *Yadu.*—The name of a tribe, derived from Yadu, a celebrated Raja, famed to have been descended from the moon.
(10) *Garura.*—Not the vulture known by this name in Bengal; but a fabled bird, answering in some respects to the eagle of Jupiter, and described to be the bearer of Vishnu, the heavenly Crishna.
(11) *Janaca.*—A Raja of Tirhoot, whose daughter Suta was offered in marriage to whoever could draw a bow of immense size; and won by Crishna, in his incarnation of Ramehundra.
(12) *Dushana.*—A demon giant, slain by Crishna in the form of Rama.
(13) *Mandar.*—A mountain of immense size, with which Crishna is said to have churned the ocean in his second incarnation.
(14) *Pedma.*—A name of Lachmi, of the same meaning with Camala.
(15) *Chacora.*—A poetical bird, described like the partridge, but imagined to be enamoured of the moon, and to feed on her beams.
(16) *Vasanti.*—A vernal creeper, bearing a yellow and white flower.
(17) *Maylaya.*—A mountain in the Dekkan, on which sandal trees grow in abundance.
(18) *Cocila.*—An admired singing bird with green plumage, with red beak and feet, common in Mat'hura, and said to sing only in the spring season. The same name is given to a blackbird in Bengal, called the Rocil, which only sings in the night.
(19) *Bacul.*—A beautiful tree, commonly called orbicular, well known in Bengal, by the names of Moulseree and Boulseree.
(20) *Cinsuca.*—A broad-leaved tree, called also the Teisoo, bearing red flowers, shaped like nails.
(21) *Cama.*—The Hindoo god of love.
(22) *Cesara.*—A beautiful flower, with yellow and white petals, better known by the name of Nageisur.
(23) *Cetaci.*—The female Ceyora, a thorny shrub, whose flowers yield a fine perfume.
(24) *Patali.*—A large hollow flower, of which one species is red, the other white.
(25) *Smara.*—A name of the god of love, signifying *ideal.*
(26) *Caruna.*—A delicate creeper, with small red flowers, called in Persian Ishk-peiched, or love-tangler.
(27) *Madhavi.*—A creeper bearing small white flowers.
(28) *Malica.*—A species of jasmine.
(29) *Amra.*—The mango tree; with its flowers the god *Cama* tips his arrows.
(30) *Atimucta.*—A fragrant creeper, which runs to a great extent, called also Midmalut. It bears a flower of yellowish white, sometimes called also Madhavi.
(31) *Vrindavan.*—An extensive forest of Vraja.
(32) *Mallica.*—A species of jasmine, white and odoriferous.
(33) *Rasala.*—An epithet of the mango, implying replete with sweet juice.
(34) *Mura.*—A demon and giant slain by Crishna.
(35) *Vanjula.*—A large tree, called also Varvon, producing white flowers.
(36) *Vraja.*—A country about 170 miles in circumference, between Dehlee and Agra, including the city of Mat'hura, and intersected by the Jumna.
(37) *Bandhujiva.*—A red flower, named likewise Doperheca.
(38) *Macara.*—A horned fish, supposed to be the hammer shark.
(39) *Cadumba.*—A flower tree, vulgarly called Cuddum, very common in Bengal, and much esteemed by the Hindoos.

(40) *Cesi.*—A monster slain by *Vishnu.*
(41) *Asoca.*—A tall tree, somewhat resembling the beech, consecrated to Mahadeva.
(42) *Cansa.*—The maternal uncle of Crishna, destroyed by him for his iniquities.
(43) *Mahesa.*—Literally, mighty lord, an epithet of the god Shiva.
(44) *Mahadeva.*—The great deity; also an attribute of Shiva.
(45) *Ananga.*—A title of the god of love, implying incorporeal.
(46) *Bimba.*—A common plant, called also Cundooree, producing red berries which are eaten by the natives.
(47) *Candarpa.*—A name of *Cama,* the god of love, who having wounded *Siva* with one of his flowery arrows, was by him in revenge reduced to ashes.
(48) *Madhu.*—A giant destroyed by *Crishna.*
(49) *Murari.*—A name of *Crishna.*
(50) *Govinda.*—A name of *Crishna.*
(51) *Devaci.*—The mother of *Crishna.*
(52) *Reti.*—The wife of *Cama,* god of love.
(53) *Yama.*—The genius of Death.
(54) *Cesava.*—A name given to *Crishna,* on account of the fineness of his hair.
(55) *Madhuca.—Bossia.*
(56) *Tila.*—A grain called Sesamum.
(57) *Cunda.*—The jasmine.
(58) *Narayan.*—A name of *Crishna.*
(59) *Sambara.*—A tyrant destroyed by Cama.
(60) *Vishnu.*—A name of *Crishna.*
(61) *Jayadeva.*—A celebrated *Hindoo* poet, the author of the preceding poem.
(62) *Pervati.*—The consort of *Siva.*

THE HOLY BIBLE

CONTAINING THE

OLD AND NEW TESTAMENTS

THE TEXT CAREFULLY PRINTED FROM THE MOST CORRECT COPIES OF THE PRESENT AUTHORIZED TRANSLATION, INCLUDING THE MARGINAL READINGS AND PARALLEL TEXTS

WITH

A COMMENTARY AND CRITICAL NOTES

DESIGNED AS A HELP TO A BETTER UNDERSTANDING OF THE SACRED WRITINGS

BY ADAM CLARKE, LL.D., F.S.A., &c.

A NEW EDITION, WITH THE AUTHOR'S FINAL CORRECTIONS

For whatsoever things were written aforetime were written for our learning, that we through patience and comfort of the Scriptures might have hope.—Rom. xv. 4.

THE OLD TESTAMENT

VOLUME IV.—ISAIAH TO MALACHI

ABINGDON
NASHVILLE

Printed in the United States of America

INTRODUCTION

TO THE

BOOK OF THE PROPHET ISAIAH

On the term *prophet*, and on the nature and several kinds of prophecy, I have already discoursed in different parts of this work. See the notes on Gen. xv. 1, xx. 7, and the preface to the four Gospels, and Acts of the Apostles. A few things only require to be recapitulated. נבא *naba* signifies not only to *foretell future events*, but also to *pray* and *supplicate;* and נביא *nabi*, the *prophet*, was by office not only a *declarer of events still future*, but the general *preacher* of the day; and as he frequently foresaw the approach of disastrous times, such was the wickedness of the people, he employed his time in counselling sinners to turn from the error of their ways, and in making strong prayer and supplication to God to avert the threatened judgments: for such predictions, however apparently *positive* in their *terms*, were generally *conditional;* strange as this may appear to some who, through their general ignorance of every thing but the peculiarities of their own creed, suppose that every occurrence is impelled by an *irresistible necessity*.

To his own conduct, in reference to such matters, God has been pleased to give us a *key* (see Jer. xviii.) which opens all difficulties, and furnishes us with a general comment on his own providence. God is absolute master of his own ways; and as he has made man a *free agent*, whatever concerns him in reference to futurity, on which God is pleased to express his mind in the way of *prophecy*, there is a *condition* generally implied or expressed. As this is but seldom attended to by partial interpreters, who wish by their doctrine of *fatalism* to bind even God himself, many contradictory sentiments are put in the mouths of his prophets.

In ancient times those who were afterwards called PROPHETS were termed SEERS; 1 Sam. ix. 9. הראה *haroeh*, the *seeing person;* he who *perceives mentally* what the design of God is. Sometimes called also חזה *chozeh*, the man who has *visions*, or supernatural *revelations;* 1 Kings xxii. 17; 2 Kings xvii. 13. Both these terms are translated *seer* in our common Version. They were sometimes called *men of God*, and *messengers* or *angels of God*. In their case it was ever understood that all God's prophets had an extraordinary commission and had their message given them by immediate inspiration.

In this the heathen copied after the people of God. They also had their *prophets* and *seers;* and hence their *augurs* and *auguries*, their *haruspices*, and *priestesses*, and their *oracles;* all pretending to be divinely inspired, and to declare nothing but the *truth;* for what was *truth* and *fact* among the *former*, was *affected* and *pretended* among the *latter*.

Many *prophets* and *seers* are mentioned in the sacred writings; but, *fragments* and *insulated prophecies* excepted, we have the works of only SIXTEEN; *four* of whom are termed the *former* or *larger* prophets, and *twelve*, the *latter* or *minor* prophets. They have these epithets, not from *priority of time*, or from *minor importance*, but merely from the places they occupy in the present arrangement of the books in the Bible. and from the relative *size* of their productions.

The Jews reckon *forty-eight prophets*, and *seven prophetesses;* and *Epiphanius*, in a fragment preserved by *Cotelerius*, reckons not fewer than *seventy-three prophets*, and *ten prophetesses;* but in both collections there are many which have no Scriptural pretensions to such a distinguished rank.

INTRODUCTION TO THE BOOK OF ISAIAH

The *succession* of prophets in the Jewish Church is well worthy of note, because it not only manifests the merciful regards of God towards that people, but also the uninterrupted succession of the *prophetic influence*, at least from Moses to Malachi, if not before; for this gift was not withheld under the *patriarchal* dispensation; indeed we might boldly ask any man to show when the time was in which God left himself without a witness of this kind.

To show this succession, I shall endeavour to give the different prophets in order of time.

1. The first man, ADAM, has an undoubted right to stand at the *head of the prophets*, as he does at the head of the *human race*. His declaration concerning marriage, "For this cause shall a man leave his father and mother, and cleave to his wife," is so truly *prophetic*, that no doubt can be formed on the subject. There was then nothing in *nature* or *experience* to justify such an assertion; and he could have it only by Divine inspiration. The millions of instances which have since occurred, and the numerous laws which have been founded on this principle among all the nations of the earth, show with what precision the declaration was conceived, and with what truth it was published to the world. Add to this, his correct *knowledge of the nature of the different animals*, so that he could impose on them names expressive of their respective natures or *propensities;* which proves that he must have acted under a Divine inspiration; for known only to God are all his works from the beginning.

2. ENOCH, the seventh from Adam, is expressly called a *prophet;* and St. Jude, ver. 14, 15, has preserved a fragment of one of his prophecies, relative to the corruption of the antediluvian world, and the approaching judgments of God.

3. NOAH was a *prophet* and *preacher of righteousness*, and predicted the general deluge, and the time of respite which God in his mercy had granted to the offenders of that age.

4. ABRAHAM is expressly called a *prophet* also, Gen. xx. 7; and it appears from Psa. cv. 15, that he partook of the Divine anointing.

5. ISAAC, Gen. xxvii. 27, predicted the future greatness of his son Jacob, and of the race that was to spring from him.

6. JACOB was so especially favoured with the prophetic gift, that he distinctly foretold what should happen to each of his sons. See Gen. xlix.

7. JOSEPH was favoured with several prophetic visions, and had the gift of interpreting dreams which portended *future occurrences;* (see Gen. xxvii., xl., xli.;) and *foretold* the redemption of the Israelites from Egypt; Gen. l. 25. Thus far the prophetic influence extended through the patriarchal dispensation for about *two thousand three hundred and seventy* years from the creation.

With the Jewish dispensation the prophetic gift revived; and,

8. MOSES became one of the most eminent prophets that had ever appeared. He not only enjoyed the continual prophetic afflatus, but had such visions of and intercourse with God as no other person either before or since was favoured with; and by which he was highly qualified to perform the arduous work which God had given him to do, and to frame that *Code of Laws* which had no equal before the promulgation of the *Gospel*. See Deut. xxiv. 10. He predicted expressly the coming of the Messiah. See Deut. xviii. 18.

9. AARON, the brother of Moses, his prime minister and God's high priest, was also a partaker of his Divine influence, and declared the will of God to Pharaoh and the Israelites, not merely from information received from Moses, but also by immediate communication from God. See Exod. iv. 15.

10. MIRIAM, the sister of Moses and Aaron, is expressly called a prophetess, Exod. xv. 20; Num. xii. 2.

11. JOSHUA, who succeeded Moses, was a partaker of the same grace. He was appointed by Moses under the especial direction of God; Num. xxvii. 18–23; Deut. xxxiv. 9; and has always been reckoned among the Jews as one of the prophets. See Ecclus. xlvi. 1–6.

Though I cannot place them in the same rank, yet it is necessary to state that, by the

Jews, several of the *judges* are classed among the prophets; such as *Othniel, Ehud, Samson,* and *Barak.*

12. Deborah, the coadjutor of Barak, is called a *prophetess,* Judg. iv. 4. During her time, and down to the days of Eli the high priest, prophecy had been very scarce, there having been very few on whom the Spirit of the Lord had rested; for "the word of the Lord was scarce in those days, and there was no open vision;" 1 Sam. iii. 1.

13. Hannah, the wife of Elkanah, is supposed to have partaken of the spirit of prophecy; and to have foretold, at least indirectly, the advent of the Messiah, and the glory that should be revealed under the Gospel. See her Song, 1 Sam. ii. 1–10. And what renders this more likely is, that it is on the *model,* and with many of the *expressions,* of this song, that the blessed Virgin composed her *Magnificat,* Luke i. 46–55.

14. Samuel, her son, was one of the most eminent of the Jewish prophets, and was the last, and indeed the *greatest,* of the *judges* of Israel. In his time the prophetic influence seems to have rested upon *many;* so that we find even *whole schools* or *colleges* of *prophets* which were under his direction. See 1 Sam. x. 5, 10, xix. 20, and elsewhere.

15. David united in himself the character of *prophet* and king, in the most eminent manner; and from his reign down to the *captivity* the succession was not only *not interrupted,* but these extraordinary messengers of God became very *numerous.*

16. Gad flourished under his reign, and was emphatically called David's *Seer,* 2 Sam. xxiv. 11; 1 Chron. xxi. 9, 19, 20; and it appears that he had written a Book of Prophecies, which is now lost, 1 Chron. xxix. 29.

17. Nathan lived also under the same reign, 2 Sam. vii. 2; and, in conjunction with *Gad,* composed a book of the acts of David, 1 Chron. xxix. 29.

18. To Solomon also, son of David, the prophetic gift has been attributed. This might be implied in the extraordinary wisdom with which God had endowed him, 1 Kings iii. 5–9; 2 Chron. i. 7, vii. 12; and in his writings several prophetic declarations may be found, even independently of the *supposed* reference to *Christ and his Church* in the *Canticles.*

19. Iddo is termed a *Seer,* 2 Chron. xii. 15, xiii. 22; and was one of Solomon's biographers.

20. Shemaiah lived under *Rehoboam;* he is called *a man of God,* and to him the word of prophecy came relative to Judah and Benjamin, 1 Kings xii. 22–24. Some think this was the same person who was sent to *Jeroboam* relative to his idolatry; see 1 Kings xiii. 1, &c.

21. Ahijah, the Shilonite, prophesied to Jeroboam, 1 Kings xi. 29–39.

22. Hanani the *Seer* prophesied under *Azariah* and Asa, 2 Chron. xvi. 7.

23. Jehu, son of Hanani, prophesied under Jehoshaphat, 1 Kings xvi. 1, 7; 2 Chron. xvi. 7, xix. 2, and xx. 34.

24. Azariah, the son of *Oded,* prophesied under *Asa,* 2 Chron. xv. 1.

25. Elijah prophesied under the reign of *Ahab* and *Jezebel.*

26. Elisha succeeded Elijah under the same reigns. And these eminent men had many disciples on whom the spirit of prophecy rested. *They,* and their *masters,* Elijah and Elisha, prophesied in the kingdoms both of Israel and Judah. Their histories make a prominent part of the first and second Books of Kings; and are well known.

27. Micaiah, the son of Imlah, prophesied under the same reign, 1 Kings xxi. 9.

28. Hosea prophesied under *Jeroboam* the second, king of Israel, and under the reign of *Uzziah,* king of Judah.

29. Isaiah was contemporary with Hosea, but probably began to prophesy a little later than he did.

30. Amos prophesied about the same time.

31. Jonah, son of Amittai, is supposed to have been contemporary with the above.

32. Eliezer, the son of Dodavah, prophesied against *Jehoshaphat* and *Ahaziah,* 2 Chron. xx. 37.

33. Jahaziel, son of Zechariah, prophesied against Judah and Israel under the same reign, 2 Chron. xx. 14.

34. Micah prophesied against Samaria and Jerusalem, in the reigns of *Jotham, Ahaz,* and *Hezekiah.*

35. Oded, father of Azariah, prophesied against *Asa,* 2 Chron. xv. 8.

36. Nahum prophesied under *Hezekiah.*

37. Joel, under *Josiah.*

38. Jeremiah, about the same time.

39. Zephaniah, under the same reign. See their prophecies.

40. Huldah, the prophetess, was contemporary with the above.

41. Igdaliah, called *a man of God,* and probably a prophet, was contemporary with Jeremiah, Jer. xxxv. 4.

42. Habakkuk lived about the end of the reign of *Josiah,* or the beginning of that of *Jehoiakim.*

43. Ezekiel lived under the captivity; and prophesied in Mesopotamia, about the time that Jeremiah prophesied in Jerusalem.

44. Obadiah lived in Judea, after the capture of Jerusalem and before the desolation of Idumea by Nebuchadnezzar.

45. Daniel prophesied in Babylon during the captivity.

46. Haggai prophesied during and after the captivity.

47. Urijah, the son of Shemaiah, prophesied under *Jehoiakim.* See Jer. xxvi. 20, 21.

48. Zechariah, son of Barachiah, flourished in the second year of *Darius,* after the captivity.

49. Malachi lived under *Nehemiah,* and some time after Haggai and Zechariah.

Here is a succession of divinely inspired men, by whom God at sundry times and in divers manners spake unto the fathers, from the beginning of the world down to the restoration from the Babylonish captivity, a period of *three thousand six hundred* years. From the time of Malachi, who was the last of the prophets, till the advent of Christ, a period of nearly *four hundred* years elapsed without vision or prophecy: but during the whole of that interval the Jews had the *law* and *the prophetical writings,* to which, till the time of Christ, there was no necessity to add any thing; for God had with the writings of the last mentioned prophet completed the *canon of the Old Testament,* nothing being farther necessary, till he should, in the fulness of time, superadd the Gospel; and this having taken place, vision and prophecy are now for ever sealed up, and the temple of God is established among all genuine believers in Christ Jesus.

It is not easy to ascertain the *order* in which the *sixteen prophets,* whose writings are preserved, have succeeded to each other. There are *chronological notes* prefixed to several of their prophecies, which assist to settle generally the times of the whole. Several were contemporary, as the reader has already seen in the preceding list. The major and minor prophets may be thus arranged:—

1. Jonah, under the reign of Jeroboam the second.
2. Hosea, under Uzziah, Jotham, Ahaz, &c.
3. Joel, contemporary with Hosea.
4. Amos, under Uzziah and Jeroboam the second.
5. Isaiah, under Uzziah, Jotham, Ahaz, and Hezekiah.
6. Micah, contemporary with Isaiah.
7. Nahum, under the reign of Hezekiah.
8. Habakkuk, under the reign of Manasseh or Josiah.
9. Zephaniah, under Josiah.
10. Jeremiah, from Josiah to Zedekiah.
11. Daniel, under the captivity, after Zedekiah.

12. EZEKIEL, at the same time.
13. OBADIAH, during the captivity.
14. HAGGAI began to prophecy in the second year of Darius.
15. ZECHARIAH, about the same time. See Zech. i. 1, vii. 1.
16. MALACHI, under Nehemiah. The last of all the prophets.

The works of these prophets constitute the principal and most important part of what is called THE BIBLE or *Old Testament.*

ON the *style of the prophets* much has been said by several learned men; particularly *Calmet, Lowth,* Bishop *Newton, Vitringa, Michaelis,* and *Houbigant.* Their chief observations, and especially those most within the reach of the common people, have been selected and abridged with great care and industry by the *Rev. Dr. John Smith,* of Cambleton, in his little Tract entitled "A Summary View and Explanation of the Writings of the Prophets," to which it forms *preliminary observations,* drawn up at the desire of the Scottish Society for propagating Christian Knowledge, in a small 8vo. 1804. From this work I thankfully borrow what concerns the present subject; taking occasion at the same time to recommend the whole to all Christian ministers, to private persons, and to all families who wish to read the prophets to their edification.

"The writings of the prophets, the most sublime and beautiful in the world, lose much of that usefulness and effect which they are so well calculated to produce on the souls of men, from their not being more generally understood. Many prophecies are somewhat dark, till events explain them. They are, besides, delivered in such lofty and figurative terms, and with such frequent allusions to the customs and manners of times and places the most remote, that ordinary readers cannot, without some help, be supposed capable of understanding them. It must therefore be of use to make the language of prophecy as intelligible as may be, by explaining those images and figures of speech in which it most frequently abounds; and this may be done generally, even when the prophecies themselves are obscure.

"Some prophecies seem as if it were not intended that they should be clearly understood before they are fulfilled. As they relate to different periods, they may have been intended for exciting the attention of mankind from time to time both to providence and to Scripture and to furnish every age with new evidence of Divine revelation; by which means they serve the same purpose to the last ages of the world that miracles did to the first. Whereas, if they had been in every respect clear and obvious from the beginning, this wise purpose had been in a great measure defeated. Curiosity, industry, and attention would at once be at an end, or, by being too easily gratified, would be little exercised.

"Besides, a great degree of obscurity is necessary to some prophecies before they can be fulfilled; and if not fulfilled, the consequence would not be so beneficial to mankind. Thus many of the ancient prophecies concerning the destruction of Jerusalem had a manifest relation to the remoter destruction by the Romans, as well as to the nearer one by the Chaldeans. Had the Jews perceived this, which was not indeed clear enough till the event explained it, they would probably have wished to have remained for ever in their captivity at Babylon, rather than expose themselves or their offspring a second time to a destruction so dreadful as that which they had already experienced.

"With respect to our times, by far the greatest number of prophecies relate to events which are now past; and therefore a sufficient acquaintance with history, and with the language and style of prophecy, is all that is requisite to understand them. Some prophecies, however, relate to events still future; and these too may be understood in general, although some particular circumstances connected with them may remain obscure till they are fulfilled. If prophecies were not capable of being understood in general, we should not find the Jews so often blamed in this respect for their ignorance and want of discernment. That they did actually understand many of them when they chose to search the Scriptures we know. Daniel understood, from the prophecies of Jeremiah, the time at which the captivity in Babylon was to be at an end; and the scribes knew from Micah, and told Herod, where the Messiah was to be born. A very little attention might have enabled them in the same manner to understand others, as they probably did; such as the seventy weeks of Daniel; the destruction of the Babylonian empire, and of the other three that were to succeed; and also of the ruin of the people and places around them, Moab, Ammon, Tyre, Sidon, Philistia, Egypt, and Idumea. Perhaps, indeed, a few enigmatical circumstances might have been annexed, which could not be understood till they were accomplished; but the general tenor of the prophecies they could be at no loss to understand. With regard to prophecies still future, we are in a similar situation. It is understood in general, that the Jews will be gathered from their dispersions, restored to their own land, and converted to Christianity; that the fulness of the Gentiles will likewise come in; that Antichrist, Gog and Magog, and all the enemies of the Church will be destroyed; after which the Gospel will remarkably flourish, and be more than ever glorified. But several circumstances connected with those general events must probably remain in the dark till their accomplishment shall clearly explain them.

"But this degree of obscurity which sometimes attends prophecy does not always proceed from the circumstances or subject; it frequently proceeds from the highly poetical and figurative style, in which prophecy is for the most part conveyed, and of which it will be proper to give some account. To speak of all the rhetorical figures with which the prophets adorn their style would lead us into a field too wide, and would be more the province of the rhetorician than of the commentator. It will be sufficient for our purpose at present to attend to the most common of them, consisting of *allegory*, *parable*, and *metaphor*, and then to consider the *sources* from which the prophets most frequently borrow their images in those figures, and the sense which they wish to convey by them.

"By *allegory*, the first of the figures mentioned, is meant that mode of speech in which the writer or speaker means to convey a different idea from what the words in their obvious and primary signification bear. Thus, 'Break up your fallow ground, and sow not among thorns,' (Jer. iv. 3,) is to be understood, not of *tillage*, but of *repentance*. And these words, 'Thy rowers have brought thee into great waters, the east wind hath broken thee in the midst of the seas,' Ezek. xxvii. 26, allude not to the fate of a *ship*, but of a *city*.

"To this figure the *parable*, in which the prophets frequently speak, is nearly allied. It consists in the application of some feigned narrative to some real truth, which might have been less striking or more disagreeable if expressed in plain terms. Such is the following one of Isaiah, v. 1, 2: 'My well-beloved hath a vineyard in a very fruitful hill. And he fenced it, and gathered out the stones thereof, and planted it with the choicest vine, and built a tower in the midst of it, and also made a wine-press therein; and he looked that it should bring forth grapes, and it brought forth wild grapes.' The seventh verse tells us that this *vineyard* was the *house of Israel*, which had so ill requited the favour which God had shown it. On this subject see the dissertation at the end of the notes on Matt. xiii.

"There is, besides, another kind of allegory not uncommon with the prophets, called *mystical allegory* or *double prophecy*. Thus it is said of Eliakim, Isa. xxii. 22: 'And the key of the house of David will I lay upon his shoulder; and he shall open, and none shall shut; and he shall shut, and none shall open.' In the first and obvious sense, the words relate to Eliakim; but in the secondary or mystical sense, to the Messiah. Instances of the same kind are frequent in those prophecies that relate to David, Zerubbabel, Cyrus, and other types of Christ. In the first sense the words relate to the type; in the second, to the antitype. The use of this allegory, however, is not so frequent as that of the former. It is generally confined to things most nearly connected with the Jewish religion; with Israel, Sion, Jerusalem, and its kings and rulers; or such as were most opposite to these, Assyria, Babylon, Egypt, Idumea, and the like. In the former kind of allegory the primitive meaning is dropped, and the figurative only is retained; in this, both the one and the other are preserved, and this is what constitutes the difference.

"But of all the figures used by the prophets the most frequent is the *metaphor*, by which words are transferred from their primitive and plain to a secondary meaning. This figure, common in all poetry and in all languages, is of indispensable necessity in Scripture, which, having occasion to speak of Divine and spiritual matters, could do it only by terms borrowed from sensible and material objects. Hence it is that the sentiments, actions, and corporeal parts, not only of man, but also of inferior creatures, are ascribed to God himself; it being otherwise impossible for us to form any conceptions of his pure essence and incommunicable attributes. But though the prophets, partly from necessity and partly from choice, are thus profuse in the use of metaphors, they do not appear, like other writers, to have the liberty of using them as fancy directed. The same set of images, however diversified in the manner of applying them, is always used, both in allegory and metaphor, to denote the same subjects, to which they are in a manner appropriated. This peculiar characteristic of the Hebrew poetry might perhaps be owing to some rules taught in the prophetic schools, which did not allow the same latitude in this respect as other poetry. Whatever it may be owing to, the uniform manner in which the prophets apply these images tends greatly to illustrate the prophetic style; and therefore it will be proper now to consider the *sources* from which those images are most frequently derived, and the *subjects* and *ideas* which they severally denote. These sources may be classed under four heads; *natural, artificial, religious,* and *historical.*

"I. The first and most copious, as well as the most pleasing source of images in the prophetic writings, as in all other poetry, is *nature;* and the principal images drawn from nature, together with their application, are the following:—

"The *sun, moon,* and *stars,* the highest objects in the natural world, figuratively represent *kings, queens,* and *princes* or *rulers;* the highest in the world politic. 'The moon shall be confounded, and the sun ashamed;' Isa. xxiv. 23. 'I will cover the heavens, and make the stars thereof dark: I will cover the sun with a cloud, and the moon shall not give her light;' Ezek. xxxii. 7.

"*Light* and *darkness* are used figuratively for *joy* and *sorrow,* prosperity and adversity. 'We wait for *light,* but behold *obscurity;* for *brightness,* but we walk in *darkness;*' chap. lix. 9. An uncommon degree of light denotes an uncommon degree of joy and prosperity, and *vice versa.* 'The light of the *moon* shall be as the light of the *sun,* and the light of the sun shall be *sevenfold;*' chap. xxx. 26. The same metaphors are likewise used to denote *knowledge* and *ignorance.* 'If they speak not according to this word, it is because there is no *light* in them;' chap. viii. 20. 'The people that walked in darkness have seen a great *light;*' chap. ix. 2.

"*Dew, moderate rains, gentle streams,* and *running waters* denote the *blessings of the Gospel.* 'Thy *dew* is as the dew of herbs;' chap. xxvi. 19. 'He shall come unto us as the rain;' Hosea vi. 3. 'I will *water* it every moment;' chap. xxvii. 3. 'I will pour *water* on him that is thirsty;' chap. xliv. 3.

"*Immoderate rains* on the other hand, *hail, floods, deep waters, torrents,* and *inundations,* denote *judgments* and *destruction.* 'I will rain upon him an *overflowing rain,* and *great hailstones,*' Ezek. xxxviii. 22. 'Waters rise up out of the north, and shall overflow the land,' Jer. xlvii. 2.

"*Fire* also, and the *east wind,* parching and hurtful, frequently denote the same. 'They shall cast thy choice cedars into the *fire,*' Jer. xxii. 7. 'He stayeth his *rough wind* in the day of the *east wind,*' Isa. xxvii. 8.

"*Wind* in general is often taken in the same sense. 'The *wind* shall eat up all thy pastures,' Jer. xxii. 22. Sometimes it is put for any thing *empty* or *fallacious,* as well as hurtful. 'The prophets shall become *wind,*' Jer. v. 13. 'They have sown the *wind,* and they shall reap the *whirlwind,*' Hos. viii. 7.

"*Lebanon* and *Carmel;* the one remarkable for its *height* and stately *cedars,* was the image of *majesty, strength,* or anything very *great* or *noble.* 'He shall cut down the thickets of the *forest* with iron, and *Lebanon* shall fall by a mighty one,' Isa. x. 34. 'The Assyrian was a *cedar* in Lebanon,' Ezek. xxxi. 3. The other mountain (*Carmel*) being fruitful, and abounding in vines and olives, denoted *beauty* and *fertility.* 'The glory of Lebanon shall be given it, the excellency of *Carmel,*' Isa. xxxv. 2. The vine alone is a frequent image of the Jewish Church. 'I had planted thee a noble *vine,*' Jer. ii. 21.

"*Rams* and *bullocks of Bashan, lions, eagles, sea-monsters,* or any *animals of prey,* are figures frequently used for cruel and oppressive *tyrants* and *conquerors.* 'Hear this word, ye *kine* of *Bashan,* which oppress the poor,' Amos iv. 1. 'The *lion* is come up from his thicket,' Jer. iv. 7. 'A great *eagle* came unto Lebanon, and took the *highest branch* of the cedar,' Ezek. xvii. 3. 'Thou art as a *whale* in the seas,' Ezek. xxxii. 2. 'The *unicorns* shall come down, and their land shall be soaked with blood,' Isa. xxxiv. 7.

"II. The ordinary *occupations* and *customs* of life, with the few *arts* practised at the time, were another source from which the prophets derived many of their figures, particularly,

"From *husbandry* in all its parts, and from its *implements.* 'Sow to yourselves in righteousness, reap in mercy: break up your fallow ground,' Hos. x. 12. 'Put in the *sickle,* for the harvest is ripe,' Joel iii. 13. 'I am pressed under you, as a *wain* under a load of sheaves,' Amos ii. 13. *Threshing* was performed in various ways, (mentioned Isa. xxviii. 24, &c.,) which furnish a variety of images denoting punishment. 'Arise and thresh, O daughter of Zion; for I will make thine *horn* iron, and thy *hoofs* brass,' &c., Micah iv. 13. The operation was performed on rising grounds, where the *chaff* was driven away by the wind, while the *grain* remained; a fit emblem of the *fate of the wicked,* and of the *salvation of the just.* 'Behold, I will make thee a new *threshing-instrument* having teeth; thou shalt thresh the mountains, and beat them small, and thou shalt make the hills as *chaff*. Thou shalt *fan* them, and the wind shall carry them away, and the *whirlwind* shall scatter them,' Isa. xli. 15, 16.

"The *vintage* and *winepress* also furnish many images, obvious enough in their application. 'The *press* is full, the *fats* overflow, for their wickedness is great,' Joel iii. 13. 'I have trod the *winepress* alone. I will tread down the people in mine anger,' Isa. lxiii. 3, &c. As the *vintage* was gathered with *shouting* and *rejoicing,* the ceasing of the vintage-shouting is frequently one of the figures that denote *misery* and *desolation.* 'None shall *tread* with *shouting;* their *shouting* shall be no *shouting,*' Jer. xlviii. 33.

"From the occupation of *tending cattle* we have many images. 'Wo unto the *pastors* that destroy and scatter the *sheep* of my pasture,' Jer. xxiii. 1. The people are the *flock; teachers* and *rulers* the *pastors.* 'Israel is a *scattered sheep,* the lions have driven him away.' 'As a *shepherd* taketh out of the mouth of the lion two legs, or a piece of an ear,' &c., Amos iii. 12. Some of the images derived from *husbandry, tending cattle,* &c., may perhaps appear mean to us; though not to the Jews, whose manner of life was simple and plain, and whose greatest men (such as Moses, David, Gideon, &c.) were often *husbandmen* and *shepherds.* Accordingly, the Messiah himself is frequently described under the character of a *shepherd.* [See *Fleury's* Manners of the Israelites.]

"It was customary in deep mournings to *shave* the *head* and *beard,* to retire to the *house-tops,* which in those countries were flat, and furnished with little chambers adapted to the purposes of devotion or of sequestered grief; also to sing dirges at funerals, and to accompany them with a mournful sort of music; and from these and the like circumstances images are frequently borrowed by the prophets to denote the *greatest danger,* and the *deepest distress.* 'Mine heart shall sound for Moab like pipes.' 'Every head shall be *bald,* and every *beard clipt*—there shall be lamentation on all the *house-tops* of Moab,' Jer. xlviii. 36–38; Isa. xv. 2, 3.

"The mode of *burying in the Jewish sepulchres,* or 'sides of the pit,' and their *Hades,* or state of the dead, supplied many images of the same kind. See observations on Isa. xiv., and Ezek. xxvi. 20.

"According to the barbarous custom of those times, conquerors *drove their captives before them* almost *naked,* and exposed to the intolerable heat of the sun, and the inclemencies of the weather. They afterwards employed them frequently in *grinding at the handmill,* (watermills not being then invented;) hence *nakedness,* and *grinding at the mill,* and *sitting on the ground* (the posture in which they wrought) express captivity. 'Descend and sit in the dust, O virgin daughter of Babylon; take the *millstones*—thy *nakedness* shall be uncovered,' Isa. xlvii. 1–3.

"The *marriage relation* supplied metaphors to express the relation or covenant between God and his people. On the other hand *adultery, infidelity* to the *marriage bed,* &c., denoted any breach of covenant with God, particularly the *love and worship of idols.* 'Turn, O backsliding children, saith the Lord, for I am married unto you,' Jer. iii. 14. 'There were two women, the daughters of one mother, and they committed whoredoms—with their idols have they committed adultery,' &c., Ezek. xxiii. 2–37.

"The *debility* and *stupefaction* caused by *intoxicating liquors* suggested very apt images to express the terrible effects of the Divine judgments on those who are the unhappy objects of them. 'Thou shalt be filled with drunkenness, with the cup of thy sister Samaria,' Ezek. xxiii. 33.

"From the method of *refining metals in the furnace* images are often borrowed to denote the *judgments* inflicted by God on his people, with a view to cleanse them from their sins, as metal from its dross. 'Israel is dross in the midst of the furnace,' Ezek. xxii. 18. 'He shall sit as a refiner and purifier of silver,' Mal. iii. 3.

"Among the other few arts from which the Hebrew poets derive some of their images, are those of the *fuller* and *potter,* Mal. iii. 2, &c.; Jer. xviii. 1, &c.; of which the application is obvious. No less so is that of images derived from *fishing, fowling,* and the *implements* belonging to them; the *hook, net, pit, snare,* &c., which generally denote *captivity* or *destruction.* 'I will send for many fishers, and they shall fish them; and for many hunters, and they shall hunt them; for their iniquity is not hid from mine eyes,' Jer. xvi. 16, 17. 'I will put hooks to thy jaws,' Ezek. xxix. 4. 'Fear, and the pit, and the snare, are upon thee, O inhabitant of the earth,' Isa. xxiv. 17.

"A few images are derived from *building,* as when the Messiah is denoted by a *foundation* and *corner-stone,* Isa. xxviii. 16. The next verse describes the *rectitude* of *judgment* by metaphors borrowed from the *line* and *plummet;* and by *building with precious stones* is denoted a very high degree of *prosperity,* whether applied to church or state, Isa. liv. 11, 12.

"III. Religion, and things connected with it, furnished many images to the sacred poets.

"From the *temple* and its pompous service, from the *tabernacle, shechinah, mercy-seat*, &c., are derived a variety of images, chiefly serving to denote the glory of the Christian Church, the excellency of its worship, God's favour towards it, and his constant presence with it; the prophets speaking to the Jews in terms accommodated to their own ideas. 'And the Lord will create upon every dwelling-place of Mount Zion, and upon her assemblies, a cloud and smoke by day, and the shining of a flaming fire by night; for upon all the glory shall be a covering,' Isa. iv. 5. 'Then will I sprinkle clean water upon you, and ye shall be clean,' Ezek. xxxvi. 25.

"The *ceremonial law*, and especially its distinctions between things *clean* and *unclean*, furnished a number of images, all obvious in their application. 'Wash ye, make you clean, put away the evil of your doings,' Isa. i. 16. 'Their way was before me as the uncleanness of a removed woman,' Ezek. xxxvi. 17.

"The *killing of sacrifices* and *feasting upon them*, serve as metaphors for *slaughter*. 'The Lord hath a sacrifice in Bozrah,' Isa. xxxiv. 6; Ezek. xxxix. 17.

"The *pontifical robes*, which were very splendid, suggested several images expressive of the *glory* of both the Jewish and Christian Church. 'I clothed thee with broidered work,' &c., Ezek. xvi. 10. 'He clothed me with the garments of salvation,' Isa. lxi. 10. The prophets wore a *rough upper garment;* false prophets wore the like, in imitation of true ones; and to this there are frequent allusions. 'Neither shall they wear a rough garment to deceive,' Zech. xiii. 4.

"From the *pots,* and other *vessels* and *utensils* of the temple, are likewise borrowed a few metaphors obvious enough without explanation: 'Every pot in Jerusalem and in Judah shall be holiness,' Zech. xiv. 21.

"The prophets have likewise many images that allude to the *idolatrous rites* of the neighbouring nations, to their *groves* and *high places,* Isa. xxvii. 9, and to the worship paid to their idols, *Baal, Molech, Chemosh, Gad, Meni, Ashtaroth, Tammuz,* &c., Ezek. viii. 10–14.

"IV. Many of the metaphors and images used by the prophets are likewise borrowed from *history,* especially sacred.

"From the *fall of angels:* 'How art thou fallen from heaven, O Lucifer, son of the morning;' Isa. xiv. 12. 'Thou art the anointed cherub,—thou wast upon the holy mountain of God;' Ezek. xxviii. 14. And from *the fall of man:* 'Thou hast been in Eden, the garden of God;' ver. 13.

"From *chaos:* 'I beheld the earth, and, lo! it was without form, and void; and the heavens, and they had no light;' Jer. iv. 23. 'He shall stretch over it the line of devastation, and the plummet of emptiness;' Isa. xxxiv. 11.

"From the *deluge:* 'The windows from on high are open, and the foundations of the earth do shake;' Isa. xxiv. 18.

"From the *destruction of Sodom and Gomorrah:* 'And the streams thereof shall be turned into pitch, and the dust thereof into brimstone, and the land thereof shall become burning pitch;' Isa. xxxiv. 9. Also from the destruction of the Hivites and Amorites, &c., Isa. xvii. 9.

"The *exodus* and *deliverance from Egypt,* is frequently used to shadow forth other great deliverances: 'Thus saith the Lord, who maketh a way in the sea, and a path in the mighty waters,' &c.; Isa. xi. 15, 16; xliii. 16–19; li. 9, 10, &c.

"From the *descent on Sinai:* 'Behold, the Lord cometh forth out of his place, and will come down and tread on the high places of the earth; and the mountains shall be molten under him;' Micah i. 3, 4.

"From the *resurrection,* the *end of the world,* and the *last judgment,* are derived many images, of which the application is natural and obvious: 'Thy dead men shall live, with my dead body shall they arise,—awake and sing, ye that dwell in the dust,' &c.; Isa. xxvi. 19. 'And all the host of heaven shall be dissolved, and the heavens shall be rolled together as a scroll; and all their host shall fall down as a leaf falleth from the vine, and as a falling fig from the fig-tree;' Isa. xxxiv. 4.

"The foregoing account of the images which most frequently occur in the writings of the prophets may be of considerable use in studying their style; but as a thorough knowledge of this must be allowed to be of the highest importance, a few *general remarks* are farther added, although some part of them may appear to be superseded by what has been already observed.

"1. Although the prophets use words so frequently in a figurative or metaphorical meaning; yet we ought not, without necessity, to depart from the primitive and original sense of language; and such a necessity there is, when the plain and original sense is less proper, less suitable to the subject and context, or contrary to other scriptures.

"2. By images borrowed from the world natural the prophets frequently understand something analogous in the world politic. Thus, the *sun, moon, stars*, and *heavenly bodies* denote *kings, queens, rulers*, and *persons* in *great power;* their *increase of splendour* denotes *increase of prosperity;* their *darkening, setting*, or *falling* denotes a *reverse of fortune*, or the entire ceasing of that power or kingdom to which they refer. *Great earthquakes*, and the *shaking of heaven and earth*, denote the *commotion* and *overthrow of kingdoms;* and the *beginning* or *end of the world*, their *rise* or *ruin*.

"3. The *cedars of Lebanon, oaks of Bashan, fir-trees*, and other *stately* trees of the forest, denote *kings, princes, potentates*, and *persons of the highest rank; briers* and *thorns*, the *common people*, or those of the meanest order.

"4. *High mountains* and *lofty hills*, in like manner, denote *kingdoms, republics, states*, and *cities; towers* and *fortresses* signify *defenders* and *protectors; ships of Tarshish*, merchants or commercial people; and the *daughter* of any capital or mother city, the *lesser cities* or *suburbs* around it. *Cities never conquered* are farther styled *virgins*.

"5. The prophets likewise describe *kings* and *kingdoms* by their *ensigns;* as *Cyrus* and the *Romans* by an *eagle*, the *king of Macedon* by a *goat*, and the *king of Persia* by a *ram;* these being the figures on their respective standards, or in the ornaments of their architecture.

"6. The prophets in like manner borrow some of their images from *ancient hieroglyphics*, which they take in their usual acceptation: thus, a *star* was the emblem of a *god* or *hero;* a *horn*, the emblem of *great power* or *strength;* and a *rod*, the emblem of *royalty;* and they signify the same in the prophets.

"7. The same prophecies have frequently a *double meaning;* and refer to different events, the one *near*, the other *remote;* the one *temporal*, the other *spiritual*, or perhaps *eternal*. The prophets having thus several events in their eye, their expressions may be partly applicable to one, and partly to another; and it is not always easy to mark the transitions. Thus, the prophecies relating to the *first* and *second restoration* of the *Jews*, and *first* and *second coming of our Lord*, are often interwoven together; like our Saviour's own prediction (Matt. xxiv.) concerning the *destruction of Jerusalem* and the *end of the world*. What has not been fulfilled in the first, we must apply to the second; and what has been already fulfilled may often be considered as typical of what still remains to be accomplished.

"8. Almost all the prophecies of the *Old Testament*, whatever view they may have to nearer events, are ultimately to be referred to the *New*, where only we are to look for their full completion. Thus *Babylon*, under the *Old Testament*, was a type of *mystical Babylon* under the *New;* and the *king of Syria*, (Antiochus Epiphanes,) a type of *Antichrist;* the *temporal enemies* of the *Jews*, types and figures of the *spiritual enemies* of *Christians*. We must not, however, expect to find always a mystical meaning in prophecy; and when the near and most obvious meaning is plain, and gives a good sense, we need not depart from it, nor be over-curious to look beyond it.

"9. In prophecies, as in parables, we are chiefly to consider the *scope* and *design*, without attempting too minute an explication of all the poetical images and figures which the sacred writers use to adorn their style.

"10. Prophecies of a general nature are applicable *by accommodation* to individuals; most of the things that are spoken of the Church in general being no less applicable to its individual members.

"11. Prophecies of a particular nature, on the other hand, admit, and often require, to be extended. Thus, Edom, Moab, or any of the enemies of God's people, is often put for the whole; what is said of one being generally applicable to the rest.

"12. In like manner, what is said to or of any of God's people, on any particular occasion, is of general application and use; all that stand in the same relation to God having an interest in the same promises.

"13. A *cup of intoxicating liquor* is frequently used to denote the *indignation of God;* and the effects of such a cup, the effects of his displeasure.

"14. As the *covenant of God* with his people is represented under the figure of *marriage;* so their *breach of that covenant*, especially their idolatry, is represented by *whoredom, adultery*, and *infidelity to the marriage bed;* on which the prophets sometimes enlarge, to excite detestation of the crime. The epithet *strange* does likewise, almost always, relate to something connected with *idolatry*.

"15. Persons or nations are frequently said in Scripture to be related to those whom they resemble in their life and conduct. In the same manner, men are denoted by *animals* whose qualities they resemble. A definite number, such as *three, four, seven, ten,* &c., is sometimes used by the prophets for an *indefinite*, and commonly denotes a *great many.*

"16. In the reckoning of time, a *day* is used by the prophets to denote a *year;* and things *still future*, to denote their certainty, are spoken of as *already past.*

"17. When the prophets speak of the *last* or *latter days*, they always mean the *days of the Messiah*, or the time of the Gospel dispensation. *That day* means often the same, and always some period at a distance.

"18. When places are mentioned as lying *north, south, east,* or *west*, it is generally to be understood of their situation with respect to *Judea* or *Jerusalem*, when the context does not plainly restrict the scene to some other place.

"19. By the *earth*, or the word so translated, the prophets frequently mean the *land of Judea;* and sometimes, says Sir Isaac Newton, the great continent of all Asia and Africa, to which they had access by land. By the *isles of the sea*, on the other hand, they understood the places to which they sailed, particularly all Europe, and probably the islands and seacoasts of the Mediterranean.

"20. The greatest part of the prophetic writings was first composed in *verse*, and still retains, notwithstanding all the disadvantages of a literal prose translation, much of the air and cast of the original, particularly in the division of the lines, and in that peculiarity of Hebrew poetry by which the sense of one line or couplet so frequently corresponds with that of the other. Thus:—

I will greatly rejoice in the Lord,
My soul shall be joyful in my God;
For he hath clothed me with the garments of salvation,
He hath covered me with the robe of righteousness:
As a bridegroom decketh himself with ornaments,
And as a bride adorneth herself with her jewels.

Isa. lxi. 10.

"Attention to this peculiarity in sacred poetry will frequently lead to the meaning of many passages in the poetical parts of Scripture, in which it perpetually occurs, as the one line of a couplet, or member of a sentence, is generally a commentary on the other. Thus:—

The Lord hath a sacrifice in Bozrah,
And a great slaughter in the land of Idumea.

Isa. xxxiv. 6.

"Here the metaphor in the first line is expressed in plain terms in the next: the *sacrifice in Bozrah* means the *great slaughter in Idumea*, of which Bozrah was the capital.

"It must be observed that the *parallelism* is frequently more extended. Thus:—

For I will pour out waters on the thirsty,
And flowing streams upon the dry ground;
I will pour out my Spirit on thy seed,
And my blessing on thine offspring.

Isa. xliv. 3.

"Here the two last lines explain the metaphor in the two preceding."

As the *gift of prophecy* was the greatest which God gave to men upon earth, so the *prophet*, as being the immediate instrument of revealing the will of God to the people, was the greatest, the most important, the most august, venerable, and useful person in the land of Israel. Ipsi eis exeant, says St. Augustine, philosophi ipsi sapientes, ipsi theologi, ipsi prophetæ, ipsi doctores probitatis ac pietatis; "They were to the people the philosophers, the wise men, the divines, the prophets, and the teachers of truth and godliness." By their intercourse with God, they were his mediators with the people; and their *persons*, as well as their *office*, were considered as peculiarly sacred. They did not mix with the people, and only appeared in public when they came to announce the will of God. They were also a kind of typical persons—whatever occurred to them was instructive, so that they were for signs, metaphors, and portents.

Most of the ancient prophets were *extraordinary* messengers. They were not bred up to the prophetic function; as the office was immediately from God, as well as the message they were to deliver to the people, so they had no previous education, in reference to such an office, for no man knew whom the God of Israel might please to call to announce his righteousness to the people. Several of them were taken out of the walks of *common life. Jonah* appears to have been a private person at Gath-heper, in Galilee, before God called him to prophesy against Nineveh. *Elisha* was a ploughman at Abel-meholah (1 Kings xix. 16) when called to the prophetic function. *Zechariah* appears to have been a husbandman, and a keeper of cattle, Zech. xiii. 5. *Amos* was a herdsman of Tekoa, and a gatherer of sycamore fruit; (Amos i. 1, vii. 14, 15;) and no doubt several others of the ancient prophets had an equally mean origin; but the office and the calling *dignified* the man. We know that our blessed Lord called not his disciples from the higher walks or offices of life; but out of fishermen, tax-gatherers, and tent-makers, he formed *evangelists* and *apostles*.

The prophets appear to have gone in mean clothing; either *sack-cloth, hair-cloth,* or *coats of skin* appear to have been their ordinary clothing. They spoke against the pride and vain-glory of man; and their very garb and manner gave additional weight to the solemn words they delivered. They lived in a retired manner; and, when not sent on special errands, they employed their vacant time in the instruction of youth; as this is probably what we are to understand by the *schools of the prophets,* such as those over which Elijah, Elisha, and Samuel presided; though no doubt there were some of their disciples that were made partakers of the prophetic gift.

The prophets do not appear to have been called to a life of *celibacy. Isaiah* was a married man, chap. viii. 3; and so was *Hosea,* chap. i. 2; unless we are to understand the latter case enigmatically. And that the sons of the prophets had *wives,* we learn from 2 Kings iv. 1, &c.; and from this, as well as from the case of the *apostles,* we learn that the matrimonial state was never considered, either by Moses or the prophets, Christ or his apostles, as disqualifying men from officiating in the most holy offices; as we find Moses, Aaron, Isaiah, Zechariah, and Peter, all married men, and yet the most eminent of their order.

Of Isaiah, the writer of this book, very little is known. He is supposed to have been of the *tribe of Judah,* and of the *royal family of David.* Himself says that he was *son of Amoz;* and others tell us that this *Amoz* was the son of *Joash,* and brother of *Amaziah,* king of Judah. "Of his family and tribe we know nothing," says *R. D. Kimchi,* "only our rabbins, of blessed memory, have received the tradition that Amoz and Amaziah were brothers;" and it is on this ground that he has been called the *royal prophet.* It has been also said that Isaiah gave his daughter in marriage to Manasseh, son of Hezekiah, king of Judah; and that himself was put to death by Manasseh, being sawn asunder with a wooden saw. But all these traditions stand on very slender authority, and are worthy of very little regard. Several commentators have thought that his prophecies afford presumptive evidence of his *high descent* and *elegant education:* 1. Because his *style* is more *correct* and *majestic* than any of the other prophets. 2. That his frequent use of *images* taken from *royalty* is a proof that this state was familiar to him, being much at court, as he must have been, had he been the brother of the king. These things are spoken by many with much confidence; for my own part, I had rather look to his *inspiration* for the correctness of his language and the dignity of his sentiments, than to those very inferior helps. On the other hypothesis nothing is left to the Divine Spirit, except the mere *matter* of his prophecies. Suppositions of this kind are not creditable to Divine revelation.

Isaiah appears to have had *two sons,* who were typical in their names; one, *Shear-jashub,* "a remnant shall return," chap. vii. 3; and the other *Maher-shalal-hash-baz,* "haste to the spoil; quick to the prey;" chap. viii. 3; and it is remarkable, that his wife is called a *prophetess.* Other matters relative to his character will appear in the notes on his prophecies.

In the notes on this book I have consulted throughout the commentary of *Rabbi David Kimchi,* and have made much use of *Bishop Lowth,* as the reader will perceive. His *various readings* I have re-collated with Dr. *Kennicott,* and *B. De Rossi;* in consequence of which I have been enabled in many cases to add double weight to the authorities by which the learned bishop was supported in the readings which he has either mentioned, or *received into the text*. Bishop *Lowth* could avail himself only of the *collections* of Dr. *Kennicott*—the sheets of Isaiah in the doctor's edition of the Hebrew Bible, as they passed through the press, were sent by him to the Bishop; but the Collections of *De Rossi*, more numerous and more accurate than those of Dr. *Kennicott*, were not published till *six* years after the doctor had published his Bible, and about *one* year before this most learned and pious prelate went to his reward. I have also consulted some excellent Hebrew MSS. in my own library, from *six* to *eight hundred* years old, which have afforded me additional help in estimating the worth and importance of the various readings in the above Collections of *Kennicott* and *De Rossi*, as far as they are employed in the illustration of this prophet. From the ancient English MS. Version of this prophet I have extracted several curious translations of select parts, which I have no doubt will meet with every reader's approbation. Though I have followed Bishop *Lowth* chiefly, yet I have consulted the best commentators within my reach, in order to remove doubts and clear up difficult passages, but have studied to be as brief as possible, that the sacred text might not be encumbered either with the multitude or length of the notes, nor the reader's time occupied with any thing not essentially necessary; besides, I wish to bring my work to as speedy a close as possible.

This book, according to Vitringa, is *twofold* in its *matter:* 1. *Prophetical;* 2. *Historical.*

1. The *prophetical* is divided into *five* parts: Part I. From chap. i. to chap. xiii. is directed to the Jews and Ephraimites, and contains *five* prophetic discourses. Part II. From chap. xiii. to chap. xxiv. declares the fate of the Babylonians, Philistines, Moabites, Syrians, Egyptians, Tyrians, and others; and contains *eight* prophetic discourses. Part III. From chap. xxiv. to chap. xxxvi. denounces judgments on the disobedient Jews, and consoles the true followers of God. This contains *three* discourses. Part IV. From chap. xl. to chap. xlix. refers to the Messiah and the deliverance of the Jews from the Babylonians; and contains *four* discourses. Part V. From chap. xlix. to the *end*, points out the passion, crucifixion, and glory of the Messiah, and contains *five* discourses.

2. The *historical* part begins with chap. xxxvi., and ends with chap. xxxix., and relates some of the transactions of the prophet's own times. On this analysis *Vitringa* explains the whole prophecy. For my own part I have little or no confidence in such *technical arrangements.*

Calmet takes a different view of it. He divides it into *eight* parts, viz.: Part I. he supposes to relate to Jotham, son of Uzziah, king of Judah: this is included in the first *six* chapters. The prophet inveighs against the crimes of the Jews; declares the judgments of God against them; predicts a more auspicious time, which took place under Hezekiah, who was a type of Christ. Part II. concerns the reign of Ahaz, and comprehends the six following chapters, in which he speaks of the siege of Jerusalem by Pekah and Rezin; of the birth of Immanuel, as a proof of the approaching deliverance of Judah; predicts the calamities that were to fall on the kingdoms of Syria and Israel, &c. Part III. contains many prophecies against Babylon, the Philistines, Moabites, &c. Part IV. contains prophecies against Egypt, Babylon, Kedar, Arabia, &c. Part V. concerns the reign of Hezekiah, and especially the war of Sennacherib against the Jews, &c. The *four historical chapters* inserted here contain the account of the fulfilment of the preceding prophecy. Part VI., included in chap. xl. to xlv. inclusive, contains the prophet's discourses on the existence of God, the truth and perfection of the Jewish religion, the vanity of idolatry, the return of the people from captivity, and the coming of Christ. Part VII. from chap. xlix. to chap. lvi., the prophet, personifying the Messiah, speaks of his sufferings, death, and burial; predicts the return from the Babylonish captivity, and the glory of the latter days. Part VIII. speaks of the coming of the Messiah, and the vocation of the Gentiles; the disgrace and confusion of all false prophets and teachers; and the establishment of a pure and holy Church, &c.

I might give other analyses of this book, but it is needless; from what is before the reader he will at once see how vain all attempts of this kind are, and how foolish to make divisions and subdivisions, partitions and classifications, where the Spirit of God has given no intimations of the kind, and where even the most learned men differ in their arrangement.

"God never left his work for man to mend." The prophecies were given as they were necessary, and no classification was ever intended. We should take them up as we find them; and humbly endeavour to find out their objects and meaning, and how far ourselves are interested in these denunciations of Divine wrath; and in those glorious promises of mercy and salvation through Him who was once the hope of Israel, and now is salvation to the ends of the earth.

Bishop Lowth's translation is by far the best that has ever been made of this sublime prophet: as he thoroughly understood his *language,* so he entered deeply into his spirit. Were it allowable, I should be glad to supersede what is called the *authorized version*, and put that of the learned bishop, with a few genuine alterations, in its place, as being abundantly more correct and nervous, rendering the sacred text more clearly, and consequently more intelligibly, so that the common reader can understand this text better without a comment, than he can the authorized version even with one. His *notes,* which are a treasure of learning and sound criticism, I have almost universally preserved, intermingling them with my own; but large quotations from his notes I have distinguished by the letter L.; and I have often adopted his *text,* as being vastly superior to that in common use; the catch words from which follow those from the authorized version. Should a *new translation* of the Bible be ever published by authority, I have no doubt but, with a few alterations, that of Bishop Lowth would be adopted as the standard.

A. C.

Millbrook, Sept. 24, 1823.

THE BOOK

OF THE

PROPHET ISAIAH

Chronological Notes relative to the commencement of Isaiah's prophecy

Year from the Creation of the World, according to the computation of Archbishop Usher, 3244.—Year from the Deluge, according to the generally received Hebrew text, 1588.—Year from the vocation of Abram, 1161.—Year from the foundation of Solomon's Temple, 251.—First year of the fifth Olympiad.—Year before the building of Rome, according to the Varronian computation, 7.—Fifteenth year of the reign of Thurimas, king of Macedon.—Eleventh year of the reign of Theopompus, king of Lacedæmon.—Second year of the reign of Alyattes, king of Lydia.—Eighteenth year of Æschylus, perpetual archon of the Athenians.—Second year of the reign of Pekahiah, king of Israel.—Fifty-first year of the reign of Azariah, or Uzziah, king of Judah.—Epoch of the establishment of the Ephori at Lacedæmon by Theopompus.

CHAPTER I

The prophet, with a boldness and majesty becoming the herald of the Most High, begins with calling on the whole creation to attend while Jehovah speaks, 2. *A charge of gross insensibility and ingratitude is then brought against the Jews, by contrasting their conduct with that of the* ox and ass, *the most stupid of animals,* 3. *This leads to an amplification of their guilt,* 4; *highly aggravated by their slighting the chastisements and judgments of God, though repeated till they had been left almost like* Sodom and Gomorrah, 5–9. *The incidental mention of those places leads to an address to the rulers and people of the Jews, under the character of* princes of Sodom, *and* people of Gomorrah, *which is no less spirited and severe than elegant and unexpected,* 10. *The vanity of trusting to the performance of the outward rites and ceremonies of religion is then exposed,* 11–15; *and the necessity of repentance and reformation is strongly enjoined,* 16, 17, *and urged by the most encouraging promises as well as by the most awful threatenings,* 18–20. *But neither of these producing the proper effect on that people who were the prophet's charge, he bitterly laments their degeneracy,* 21–23; *and concludes with introducing God, declaring his purpose of inflicting such heavy judgments as would entirely cut off the wicked, and excite in the righteous, who should also pass through the furnace, an everlasting shame and abhorrence of every thing connected with idolatry, the source of their misery,* 24–31.

A. M. cir. 3244
B. C. cir. 760
Anno Olymp. Quintæ I.
Ante Urbem Conditam 7

THE [a]vision of Isaiah the son of Amoz, which he saw concerning Judah and Jerusalem in the days of Uzziah, Jotham, Ahaz, *and* Hezekiah, kings of Judah.

[a]Numbers, chap. xii. 6

ISAIAH exercised the prophetical office during a long period of time, if he lived to the reign of Manasseh; for the lowest computation, beginning from the year in which Uzziah died, when some suppose him to have received his first appointment to that office, brings it to sixty-one years. But the tradition of the Jews, that he was put to death by Manasseh, is very uncertain; and one of their principal rabbins, *Aben Ezra*, Com. in Isa. i. 1, seems rather to think that he died before Hezekiah, which is indeed more probable. It is however certain that he lived at least to the fifteenth or sixteenth year of Hezekiah; this makes the least possible term of the duration of his prophetical office about forty-eight years. The time of the delivery of some of his prophecies is either expressly marked, or sufficiently clear from the history to which they relate; that of a few others may with some probability be deduced from internal marks; from expressions, descriptions, and circumstances interwoven. It may therefore be of some use in this respect, and for the better understanding of his prophecies in general, to give here a summary view of the history of his time.

The kingdom of Judah seems to have been in a more flourishing condition during the reigns of Uzziah and Jotham, than at any other time after the revolt of the ten tribes. The former recovered the port of Elath on the Red Sea, which the Edomites had taken in the reign of Joram. He was successful in his wars with the Philistines, and took from them several cities,

A. M. cir. 3244
B. C. cir. 760
Anno Olymp.
Quintæ I.
Ante Urbem
Conditam 7

2 [b]Hear, O heavens, and give
ear, O earth; for the LORD
hath spoken: [c]I have nourished and brought up children,
and they have rebelled against
me.
3 [d]The ox knoweth his owner,
and the ass his master's crib:

[b]Deut. xxxii. 1; Jer. ii. 12; vi. 19; xxii. 29; Ezek. xxxvi. 4; Mic. i. 2; vi. 1, 2——[c]Chap. v. 1, 2——[d]Jer. viii. 7

Gath, Jabneh, Ashdod; as likewise against some people of Arabia Deserta, and against the Ammonites, whom he compelled to pay him tribute. He repaired and improved the fortifications of Jerusalem; and had a great army, well appointed and disciplined. He was no less attentive to the arts of peace; and very much encouraged agriculture, and the breeding of cattle. Jotham maintained the establishments and improvements made by his father; added to what Uzziah had done in strengthening the frontier places; conquered the Ammonites, who had revolted; and exacted from them a more stated and probably a larger tribute. However, at the latter end of his time, the league between Pekah, king of Israel, and Retsin, king of Syria, was formed against Judah; and they began to carry their designs into execution.

But in the reign of Ahaz his son not only all these advantages were lost, but the kingdom of Judah was brought to the brink of destruction. Pekah king of Israel overthrew the army of Ahaz, who lost in battle *one hundred and twenty thousand* men; and the Israelites carried away captives *two hundred thousand* women and children, who however were released and sent home again upon the remonstrance of the prophet Oded. After this, as it should seem, (see *Vitringa* on chap. vii. 2,) the two kings of Israel and Syria, joining their forces, laid siege to Jerusalem; but in this attempt they failed of success. In this distress Ahaz called in the assistance of Tiglath-pileser, king of Assyria, who invaded the kingdoms of Israel and Syria, and slew Rezin; but he was more in danger than ever from his too powerful ally; to purchase whose forbearance, as he had before bought his assistance, he was forced to strip himself and his people of all the wealth he could possibly raise from his own treasury, from the temple, and from the country. About the time of the siege of Jerusalem the Syrians took Elath, which was never after recovered. The Edomites likewise, taking advantage of the distress of Ahaz, ravaged Judea, and carried away many captives. The Philistines recovered what they had before lost; and took many places in Judea, and maintained themselves there. Idolatry was established by the command of the king in Jerusalem, and throughout Judea; and the service of the temple was either intermitted, or converted into an idolatrous worship.

Hezekiah, his son, on his accession to the throne, immediately set about the restoration of the legal worship of God, both in Jerusalem and through Judea. He cleansed and repaired the temple, and held a solemn passover. He improved the city, repaired the fortification, erected magazines of all sorts, and built a new aqueduct. In the fourth year of his reign Shalmaneser, king of Assyria, invaded the kingdom of Israel, took Samaria, and carried away the Israelites into captivity, and replaced them by different people sent from his own country; and this was the final destruction of that kingdom, in the sixth year of the reign of Hezekiah.

Hezekiah was not deterred by this alarming example from refusing to pay the tribute to the king of Assyria, which had been imposed on Ahaz: this brought on the invasion of Sennacherib in the fourteenth year of his reign, an account of which is inserted among the prophecies of Isaiah. After a great and miraculous deliverance from so powerful an enemy, Hezekiah continued his reign in peace. He prospered in all his works, and left his kingdom in a flourishing state to his son Manasseh—a son in every respect unworthy of such a father. See *Lowth.*

NOTES ON CHAP. I

Verse 1. *The vision of Isaiah*] It seems doubtful whether this title belongs to the whole book, or only to the prophecy contained in this chapter. The former part of the title seems properly to belong to this particular prophecy; the latter part, which enumerates the kings of Judah under whom Isaiah exercised his prophetical office, seems to extend it to the whole collection of prophecies delivered in the course of his ministry. *Vitringa*—to whom the world is greatly indebted for his learned labours on this prophet and to whom we should have owed much more if he had not so totally devoted himself to Masoretic authority—has, I think, very judiciously resolved this doubt. He supposes that the former part of the title was originally prefixed to this single prophecy; and that, when the collection of all Isaiah's prophecies was made, the enumeration of the kings of Judah was added, to make it at the same time a proper title to the whole book. As such it is plainly taken in 2 Chron. xxxii. 32, where the book of Isaiah is cited by this title: "The vision of Isaiah the prophet, the son of Amoz."

The prophecy contained in this first chapter stands single and unconnected, making an entire piece of itself. It contains a severe remonstrance against the corruptions prevailing among the Jews of that time, powerful exhortations to repentance, grievous threatenings to the impenitent, and gracious promises of better times, when the nation shall have been reformed by the just judgments of God. The expression, upon the whole, is clear; the connection of the several parts easy; and in regard to the images, sentiments, and style, it gives a beautiful example of the prophet's elegant manner of writing; though perhaps it may not be equal in these respects to many of the following prophecies.

Verse 2. *Hear, O heavens*—"Hear, O ye heavens"] God is introduced as entering into a public action, or pleading, before the whole world, against his disobedient people. The prophet, as herald or officer to proclaim the summons to the court, calls upon all created beings, celestial and terrestrial, to attend and bear witness to the truth of his plea and the justice of his cause. The same scene is more fully displayed in the noble exordium of Psa. l., where God summons all mankind, from east to west, to

A. M. cir. 3244
B. C. cir. 760
Anno Olymp.
Quintæ I.
Ante Urbem
Conditam 7

but Israel [e]doth not know, my
people [f]doth not consider.
4 Ah sinful nation, a people
[g]laden with iniquity, [h]a seed of
evil doers, children that are corrupters! They have forsaken
the LORD, they have provoked
the Holy One of Israel unto

A. M. cir. 3244
B. C. cir. 760
Anno Olymp.
Quintæ I.
Ante Urbem
Conditam 7

---

[e]Jer. ix. 3, 6——[f]Chap. v. 12——[g]Heb. *of heaviness*——[h]Chap. lvii. 3, 4; Matt. iii. 7

---

be present to hear his appeal; and the solemnity is held on Sion, where he is attended with the same terrible pomp that accompanied him on Mount Sinai:—

"A consuming fire goes before him,
And round him rages a violent tempest:
He calleth the heavens from above.
And the earth, that he may contend in judgment with his people." Psa. l. 3, 4.

By the same bold figure, Micah calls upon the mountains, that is, the whole country of Judea, to attend to him, chap. vi. 1, 2:—

"Arise, plead thou before the mountains,
And let the hills hear thy voice.
Hear, O ye mountains, the controversy of JEHOVAH;
And ye, O ye strong foundations of the earth:
For JEHOVAH hath a controversy with his people,
And he will plead his cause against Israel."

With the like invocation, Moses introduces his sublime song, the design of which was the same as that of this prophecy, "to testify as a witness, against the Israelites," for their disobedience, Deut. xxxi. 21:—

"Give ear, O ye heavens, and I will speak;
And let the earth hear the words of my mouth." Deut. xxxii. 1.

This, in the simple yet strong oratorical style of Moses, is, "I call heaven and earth to witness against thee this day; life and death have I set before thee; the blessing and the curse: choose now life, that thou mayest live, thou and thy seed." Deut. xxx. 19. The poetical style, by an apostrophe, sets the personification in a much stronger light.

Hath spoken—"That speaketh"] I render it in the present time, pointing it דבר *dober*. There seems to be an impropriety in demanding attention to a speech already delivered. But the present reading may stand, as the prophet may be here understood to declare to the people what the Lord *had* first spoken to him.

I have nourished] The *Septuagint* have εγεννησα, "I have begotten." Instead of גדלתי *giddalti*, they read ילדתי *yaladti;* the word little differing from the other, and perhaps more proper; which the Chaldee likewise seems to favour; "vocavi eos filios." See Exod. iv. 22; Jer. xxxi. 9.

Verse 3. *The ox knoweth*] An amplification of the gross insensibility of the disobedient Jews, by comparing them with the most heavy and stupid of all animals, yet not so insensible as they. Bochart has well illustrated the comparison, and shown the peculiar force of it. "He sets them lower than the beasts, and even than the most stupid of all beasts, for there is scarcely any more so than the ox and the ass. Yet these acknowledge their master; they know the manger of their lord; by whom they are fed, not for their own, but for his good; neither are they looked upon as children, but as beasts of burden; neither are they advanced to honours, but oppressed with great and daily labours. While the Israelites, chosen by the mere favour of God, adopted as sons, promoted to the highest dignity, yet acknowledged not their Lord and their God; but despised his commandments, though in the highest degree equitable and just." Hieroz. i., col. 409.

Jeremiah's comparison to the same purpose is equally elegant, but has not so much spirit and severity as this of Isaiah.

"Even the stork in the heavens knoweth her season;
And the turtle, and the swallow, and the crane, observe the time of their coming:
But my people doth not know the judgment of JEHOVAH." Jer. viii. 7.

Hosea has given a very elegant turn to the same image, in the way of metaphor or allegory:—

"I drew them with human cords, with the bands of love:
And I was to them as he that lifteth up the yoke upon their cheek;
And I laid down their fodder before them." Hos. xi. 4.

Salomo ben Melech thus explains the middle part of the verse, which is somewhat obscure: "I was to them at their desire as they that have compassion on a heifer, lest she be overworked in ploughing; and that lift up the yoke from off her neck, and rest it upon her cheek that she may not still draw, but rest from her labour an hour or two in the day."

But *Israel*] The *Septuagint*, *Syriac*, *Aquila*, *Theodotion*, and *Vulgate*, read וישראל *veyisrael*, BUT *Israel*, adding the *conjunction*, which being rendered as an adversative, sets the opposition in a stronger light.

Doth not know] The same ancient versions agree in adding ME, which very properly answers, and indeed is almost necessarily required to answer, the words *possessor* and *lord* preceding. Ισραηλ δε ΜΕ ουκ εγνω; *Sept*. "Israel *autem* ME *non cognovit;*" *Vulg*. Ισραηλ δε ΜΟΥ ουκ εγνω; *Aquil*., *Theod*. The testimony of so scrupulous an interpreter as *Aquila* is of great weight in this case. And both his and *Theodotion's* rendering is such as shows plainly that they did not add the word ΜΟΥ to help out the sense, for it only embarrasses it. It also clearly determines what was the original reading in the old copies from which they translated. It could not be ידעני *yedani*, which most obviously answers to the version of the *Septuagint* and *Vulgate*, for it does not accord with that of *Aquila* and *Theodotion*. The version of these latter interpreters, however injudicious, clearly ascertains both the phrase, and the order of the words of the original Hebrew; it was וישראל אותי לא ידע *veyisrael*

A. M. cir. 3244
B. C. cir. 760
Anno Olymp.
Quintæ I.
Ante Urbem
Conditam 7

anger, they are [i]gone away
backward.
5 [k]Why should ye be stricken
any more? ye will [l]revolt more
and more: the whole head is sick, and the
whole heart faint.

6 From the sole of the foot
even unto the head *there is* no
soundness in it; *but* wounds,
and bruises, and putrefying
sores; [m]they have not been closed, neither
bound up, neither mollified with [n]ointment.

[i]Heb. *alienated*, or *separated;* Psa. lviii. 3——[k]Chap. ix. 13; Jer. ii. 30; v. 3

[l]Hebrew, *increase revolt*——[m]Jeremiah viii. 22
[n]Or, *oil*

othi lo yada. The word אותי *othi has been* lost out of the text. The very same phrase is used by Jeremiah, chap. iv. 22, עמי אותי לא ידעו *ammi othi lo yadau.* And the order of the words must have been as above represented; for they have joined ישראל *yisrael,* with אותי *othi,* as *in regimine;* they could not have taken it in this sense, *Israel* MEUS *non cognovit,* had either this phrase or the order of the words been different. I have endeavoured to set this matter in a clear light, as it is the first example of a *whole word* lost out of the text, of which the reader will find many other plain examples in the course of these notes. But *Rosenmüller* contends that this is unnecessary, as the pasage may be translated, "Israel knows nothing: my people have no understanding."

The *Septuagint, Syriac,* and *Vulgate,* read ועמי *veammi, "and* my people;" and so likewise sixteen MSS. of *Kennicott,* and fourteen of *De Rossi.*

Verse 4. *Ah sinful nation*—"Degenerate"] Five MSS., one of them ancient, read משחתים *moschathim,* without the first י *yod,* in *hophal corrupted,* not *corrupters.* See the same word in the same form, and in the same sense, Prov. xxv. 26.

Are corrupters—"Are estranged"] Thirty-two MSS., five ancient, and two editions, read נזורו *nazoru;* which reading determines the word to be from the root זור *zur, to alienate,* not from נזר *nazar, to separate;* so *Kimchi* understands it. See also *Annotat.* in *Noldium,* 68.

They are gone away backward—"They have turned their backs upon him."] So *Kimchi* explains it: "they have turned unto him the back, and not the face." See Jer. ii. 27; vii. 24. I have been forced to render this line paraphrastically; as the verbal translation, "they are estranged backward," would have been unintelligible.

Verse 5. *Why should ye be stricken any more*—"On what part," &c.?] The *Vulgate* renders על מה *al meh, super quo,* (see Job xxxviii. 6; 2 Chron, xxxii. 10,) *upon what* part. And so *Abendana* on *Sal. ben Melech:* "There are some who explain it thus: Upon what limb shall you be smitten, if you add defection? for already for your sins have you been smitten upon all of them; so that there is not to be found in you a whole limb on which you can be smitten." Which agrees with what follows: "From the sole of the foot even unto the head, there is no soundness in it:" and the sentiment and image is exactly the same with that of *Ovid, Pont.* ii. 7, 42:—

Vix habet in nobis jam nova plaga locum.

There is no place on you for a new stripe.

Or that still more expressive line of *Euripides;* the great force and effect of which *Longinus* ascribes to its close and compressed structure, analogous to the sense which it expresses:—

Γεμω κακων δη· κ' ουκετ' εσθ' ὁπη τιθη.

I am full of miseries: there's no room for more.

Herc. Fur. 1245, *Long.* sec. 40.

"On what part will ye strike again? will ye add correction?" This is addressed to the instruments of God's vengeance; those that inflicted the punishment, who or whatsoever they were. Ad verbum certæ personæ intelligendæ sunt, quibus ista actio quæ per verbum exprimitur competit; "The words are addressed to the persons who were the agents employed in the work expressed by the original word," as Glassius says in a similar case, *Phil. Sacr.* i. 3, 22. See chap. vii. 4.

As from ידע *yada,* דעה *deah,* knowledge; from יעץ *yaats,* עצה *etsah,* counsel; from ישן *yashan,* שנה *shenah,* sleep, &c.; so from יסר *yasar* is regularly derived סרה *sarah,* correction.

Verse 5. *The whole head is sick*] The king and the priests are equally gone away from truth and righteousness. Or, The state is oppressed by its enemies, and the Church corrupted in its rulers and in its members.

Verse 6. *They have not been closed, &c.*—"It hath not been pressed," &c.] The pharmaceutical art in the East consists chiefly in external applications: accordingly the prophet's images in this place are all taken from surgery. Sir John Chardin, in his note on Prov. iii. 8, "It shall be health to thy navel, and marrow to thy bones," observes that "the comparison is taken from the plasters, ointments, oils, and frictions, which are made use of in the East upon the belly and stomach in most maladies. Being ignorant in the villages of the art of making decoctions and potions, and of the proper doses of such things, they generally make use of external medicines."—*Harmer's Observations on Scripture,* vol. ii. p. 488. And in surgery their *materia medica* is extremely simple, oil making the principal part of it. "In India," says *Tavernier,* "they have a certain preparation of oil and melted grease, which they commonly use for the healing of wounds." Voyage Ind. So the good Samaritan poured oil and wine on the wounds of the distressed Jew: wine, cleansing and somewhat astringent, proper for a fresh wound; oil, mollifying and healing, Luke x. 34. Kimchi has a judicious remark here: "When various medicines are applied, and no healing takes place, that disorder is considered as coming immediately from God."

Of the three verbs in this sentence, one is in the singular number in the text; another is

A. M. cir. 3244 B. C. cir. 760 Anno Olymp. Quintæ I. Ante Urbem Conditam 7

7 [o]Your country *is* desolate, your cities *are* burned with fire: your land, strangers devour it in your presence, and *it is* desolate, [p]as overthrown by strangers.

8 And the daughter of Zion is left [q]as a cottage in a vineyard, as a lodge in a garden of cucumbers, [r]as a besieged city.

[o]Deut. xxviii. 51, 52——[p]Heb. *as the overthrow of strangers*——[q]Job xxvii. 18; Lam. ii. 6——[r]Jer. iv. 17

singular in two MSS., (one of them ancient,) חבשה *chubbeshah;* and the *Syriac* and *Vulgate* render all of them in the singular number.

Verses 7-9. *Your country* is *desolate*] The description of the ruined and desolate state of the country in these verses does not suit with any part of the prosperous times of Uzziah and Jotham. It very well agrees with the time of Ahaz, when Judea was ravaged by the joint invasion of the Israelites and Syrians, and by the incursions of the Philistines and Edomites. The date of this prophecy is therefore generally fixed to the time of Ahaz. But on the other hand it may be considered whether those instances of idoltary which are urged in ver. 29—the worshipping in groves and gardens—having been at all times too commonly practised, can be supposed to be the only ones which the prophet would insist upon in the time of Ahaz; who spread the grossest idolatry through the whole country, and introduced it even into the temple; and, to complete his abominations, made his son pass through the fire to Molech. It is said, 2 Kings xv. 37, that in Jotham's time "the Lord began to send against Judah Rezin—and Pekah." If we may suppose any invasion from that quarter to have been actually made at the latter end of Jotham's reign, I should choose to refer this prophecy to that time.

And *your cities* are *burned.—Nineteen* of Dr. *Kennicott's* MSS. and *twenty-two* of *De Rossi's*, some of my own, with the *Syriac* and *Arabic*, add the conjunction which makes the hemistich more complete.

Verse 7. זרים *zarim* at the end of the verse. This reading, though confirmed by all the ancient versions, gives us no good sense; for "your land is devoured by strangers; and is desolate, as if overthrown by *strangers*," is a mere tautology, or, what is as bad, an identical comparison. *Aben Ezra* thought that the word in its present form might be taken for the same with זרם *zerem, an inundation: Schultens* is of the same opinion; (see *Taylor's* Concord.;) and *Schindler* in his Lexicon explains it in the same manner: and so, says *Kimchi*, some explain it. *Abendana* endeavours to reconcile it to grammatical analogy in the following manner: "זרים *zarim* is the same with זרם *zerem;* that is, as overthrown by *an inundation of waters:* and these two words have the same analogy as קדם *kedem* and קדים *kadim.* Or it may be a concrete of the same form with שכיר *shechir;* and the meaning will be: as overthrown by rain pouring down violently, and causing a flood." On *Sal. ben Melech, in loc.* But I rather suppose the true reading to be זרם *zerem*, and have translated it accordingly: the word זרים *zerim*, in the line above, seems to have caught the transcriber's eye, and to have led him into this mistake. But this conjecture of the learned prelate is not confirmed by any MS. yet discovered.

Verse 8. *As a cottage in a vineyard*—"As a shed in a vineyard"] A little temporary hut covered with boughs, straw, turf, or the like materials, for a shelter from the heat by day, and the cold and dews by night, for the watchman that kept the garden or vineyard during the short season the fruit was ripening, (see Job xxvii. 18,) and presently removed when it had served that purpose. See *Harmer's* Observ. i. 454. They were probably obliged to have such a constant watch to defend the fruit from the jackals. "The jackal," (*chical* of the Turks,) says *Hasselquist*, (Travels, p. 227,) "is a species of mustela which is very common in Palestine, especially during the vintage; and often destroys whole vineyards, and gardens of cucumbers." "There is also plenty of the *canis vulpes*, the fox, near the convent of St. John in the desert, about vintage time; for they destroy all the vines unless they are strictly watched." Ibid. p. 184. See Cant. ii. 15.

Fruits of the gourd kind, melons, water-melons, cucumbers, &c., are much used and in great request in the Levant, on account of their cooling quality. The Israelites in the wilderness regretted the loss of the cucumbers and melons among the other good things of Egypt, Num. xi. 5. In Egypt the season of *water-melons*, which are most in request, and which the common people then chiefly live upon, lasts but three weeks. See *Hasselquist*, p. 256. *Tavernier* makes it of longer continuance: L'on y void de grands carreaux de melons et de concombres, mais beaucoup plus de derniers, dont les Levantins font leur delices. Le plus souvent, ils les mangent sans les peler, après quoi ils vont boire une verre d'eau. Dans toute l'Asie c'est la nourriture ordinaire du petit peuple pendant trois ou quatre mois; toute la famille en vit; et quand un enfant demand à manger, au lieu qu'en France ou aillieurs nous luy donnerions du pain, dans le Levant on luy presente un concombre, qu'il mange cru comme on le vient de cueillir. Les concombres dans le Levant ont une bontè particuliere; et quoiqu' on les mange crus, ils ne font jamais de mal; "There are to be seen great beds of melons and cucumbers, but a greater number of the latter, of which the Levantines are particularly fond. In general they eat them without taking off the rind, after which they drink a glass of water. In every part of Asia this is the aliment of the common people for three or four months; the whole family live on them; and when a child asks something to eat, instead of giving it a piece of bread, as is done in France and other countries, they present it with a cucumber, which it eats raw, as gathered. Cucumbers in the Levant are peculiarly excellent; and although eaten raw, they are seldom injurious." *Tavernier*, Relat. du Serrail, cap. xix.

As a lodge, &c.] That is, after the fruit was gathered; the lodge being then permitted to fall into decay. Such was the desolate, ruined state of the city.

As a lodge, &c.] That is, after the fruit was So the ὡς πολις πολιορκουμενη; *Septuagint:* see also the *Vulgate.*

A. M. cir. 3244
B. C. cir. 760
Anno Olymp.
Quintæ I.
Ante Urbem
Conditam 7

9 [s]Except the LORD of hosts
had left unto us a very small
remnant, we should have been
as [t]Sodom, *and* we should have
been like unto Gomorrah.

10 Hear the word of the LORD, ye rulers
[u]of Sodom; give ear unto the law of our God,
ye people of Gomorrah.

11 To what purpose *is* the multitude of
your [v]sacrifices unto me? saith the LORD: I
am full of the burnt-offerings of
rams, and the fat of fed beasts;
and I delight not in the blood of
bullocks, or of lambs, or of [w]he-
goats.

A. M. cir. 3244
B. C. cir. 760
Anno Olymp.
Quintæ I.
Ante Urbem
Conditam 7

12 When ye come [x]to [y]appear before me,
who hath required this at your hand, to tread
my courts?

13 Bring no more [z]vain oblations; incense
is an abomination unto me; the new moons
and Sabbaths, [a]the calling of assemblies, I

[s]Lam. iii. 22; Rom. ix. 29——[t]Gen. xix. 24——[u]Deut. xxxii. 32; Ezek. xvi. 46——[v]1 Sam. xv. 22; Psa. l. 8, 9; li. 16; Prov. xv. 8; xxi. 27; chap. lxvi. 3; Jer. vi. 20; vii. 21; Amos v. 21, 22; Mic. vi. 7——[w]Heb. *great he-goats*——[x]Heb. *to be seen*——[y]Exod. xxiii. 17; xxxiv. 23——[z]Matt. xv. 9——[a]Joel i. 14; ii. 15

Verse 9. *The Lord of hosts*—"JEHOVAH God of hosts"] As this title of God, יהוה צבאות *Yehovah tsebaoth*, "JEHOVAH of hosts, occurs here for the first time, I think it proper to note, that I translate it always, as in this place, "JEHOVAH God of hosts;" taking it as an elliptical expression for יהוה אלהי צבאות *Yehovah Elohey tsebaoth*. This title imports that JEHOVAH is the God or Lord of hosts or armies; as he is the Creator and Supreme Governor of all beings in heaven and earth, and disposeth and ruleth them all in their several orders and stations; the almighty, universal Lord.

We should have been as Sodom] As completely and finally ruined as *that* and the cities of the plain were, no vestige of which remains at this day.

Verse 10. *Ye rulers of Sodom*—"Ye princes of Sodom"] The incidental mention of Sodom and Gomorrah in the preceding verse suggested to the prophet this spirited address to the rulers and inhabitants of Jerusalem, under the character of princes of Sodom and people of Gomorrah. Two examples of a sort of elegant turn of the like kind may be observed in St. Paul's Epistle to the Romans, chap. xv. 4, 5, 12, 13. See Locke on the place; and see ver. 29, 30, of this chapter, which gives another example of the same.

AND—*like unto Gomorrah.—The* ו *vau* is added by *thirty-one* of *Kennicott's* MSS., *twenty-nine* of *De Rossi's* and one, very ancient, of my own. See on ver. 6.

Verse 11. *To what purpose, &c.*—"What have I to do."] The prophet Amos has expressed the same sentiments with great elegance:—

"I hate, I despise your feasts;
And I will not delight in the odour of your
  solemnities:
Though ye offer unto me burnt-offerings
And your meat-offerings, I will not accept:
Neither will I regard the peace-offerings of
  your fatlings.
Take away from me the noise of your songs;
And the melody of your viols I will not hear.
But let judgment roll down like waters;
And righteousness like a mighty stream."
Amos v. 21-24.

So has Persius; see Sat. ii. v. 71-75:—

"Quin damus id Superis, de magna quod dare lanæ," &c.

The two or three last pages of Plato's *Euthyphro* contain the same idea. Sacrifices and prayers are not profitable to the offerer, nor acceptable to the gods, unless accompanied with an upright life.

Verse 11. *The fat of fed beasts, &c.*] The fat and the blood are particularly mentioned, because these were in all sacrifices set apart to God. The fat was always burnt upon the altar, and the blood was partly sprinkled, differently on different occasions, and partly poured out at the bottom of the altar. See Lev. iv.

Verse 12. *When ye come to appear*] Instead of לראות *leraoth*, to *appear*, one MS. has לראות *liroth*, to *see*. See *De Rossi*. The appearing before God here refers chiefly to the three solemn annual festivals. See Exod. xxiii. 14.

Tread my courts (no more)] So the *Septuagint* divide the sentence, joining the end of this verse to the beginning of the next: *Πατειν την αυλην μου, ου προσθησεσθε*; "To tread my court ye shall not add—ye shall not be again accepted in worship."

Verse 13. *The new moons and Sabbaths*—"The fast and the day of restraint"] און ועצרה *aven vaatsarah*. These words are rendered in many different manners by different interpreters, to a good and probable sense by all; but I think by none in such a sense as can arise from the phrase itself, agreeably to the idiom of the Hebrew language. Instead of און *aven*, the *Septuagint* manifestly read צום *tsom*, *νηστειαν*, "the fast." This *Houbigant* has adopted. The prophet could not well have omitted the *fast* in the enumeration of their *solemnities*, nor the *abuse* of it among the instances of their *hyprocrisy*, which he has treated at large with such force and elegance in his *fifty-eighth chapter*. Observe, also, that the prophet Joel, (chap. i. 14, and ii. 15,) twice joins together the fast and the day of restraint:—

אצרה קראו צום קדשו
atsarah kiru tsom kaddeshu

"Sanctify a fast; proclaim a day of restraint:"

which shows how properly they are here joined together. עצרה *atsarah*, "the restraint," is rendered, both here and in other places of our English translation, "the solemn assembly." Certain holy days ordained by the law were distinguished by a particular charge that "no servile work should be done therein;" Lev. xxviii. 36; Num. xxix. 35; Deut. xvi. 8. This circumstance clearly explains the reason of the

A. M. cir. 3244
B. C. cir. 760
Anno Olymp.
Quintæ I.
Ante Urbem
Conditam 7

cannot away with; *it is* [b]iniqui-
ty, even the solemn meeting.
14 Your [c]new moons and your
[d]appointed feasts my soul hateth: they are a trouble unto me; [e]I am
weary to bear *them.*
15 And [f]when ye spread forth your hands,
I will hide mine eyes from you: [g]yea, when
ye [h]make many prayers, I will not hear:
your hands are full of [i]blood.[k]
16 [l]Wash you, make you clean; put away
the evil of your doings from before mine eyes;
[m]cease to do evil;
17 Learn to do well; [n]seek judgment, [o]re-
lieve the oppressed, judge the fatherless, plead
for the widow.

18 Come now, and [p]let us reason together, saith the LORD:
though your sins be as scarlet,
[q]they shall be as white as snow;
though they be red like crimson, they shall be
as wool.
19 If ye be willing and obedient, ye shall eat
the good of the land:
20 But if ye refuse and rebel, ye shall be
devoured with the sword: [r]for the mouth of
the LORD hath spoken *it.*
21 [s]How is the faithful city become a
harlot! it was full of judgment; righteousness lodged in it; but now murderers.
22 [t]Thy silver is become dross, thy wine
mixed with water:

[b]Or, *grief*——[c]Num. xxviii. 11——[d]Lev. xxiii. 2, &c.; Lam. ii. 6——[e]Ch. xliii. 24——[f]Job xxvii. 29; Psa. cxxxiv. 2; Prov. i. 28; ch. lix. 2; Jer. xiv. 12; Mic. iii. 4——[g]Psa. lxvi. 18; 1 Tim. ii. 8——[h]Heb *multiply prayer*——[i]Ch. lix. 3——[k]Heb. *bloods*——[l]Jer. iv. 14

[m]Psa. xxxiv. 14; xxxvii. 27; Amos v. 15; Rom. xii. 9; 1 Pet. iii. 11——[n]Jer. xxii. 3, 16; Mic. vi. 8; Zech. vii. 9; viii. 16——[o]Or, *righten*——[p]Ch. xliii. 26; Mic. vi. 2——[q]Psa. li. 7; Rev. vii. 14——[r]Num. xxiii. 19; Tit. i. 2——[s]Jer. ii. 20, 21——[t]Jer. vi. 28, 30; Ezek. xxii. 18, 19

name, *the restraint*, or *the day of restraint*, given to those days.

If I could approve of any translation of these two words which I have met with, it should be that of the Spanish version of the Old Testament, made for the use of the Spanish Jews: *Tortura y detenimento*, "it is a pain and a constraint unto me." But I still think that the reading of the *Septuagint* is more probably the truth.

Verse 15. *When ye spread*] The *Syriac*, *Septuagint*, and a MS., read בפרשכם *beparshecem*, without the conjunction ו *vau*.

Your hands—"For your hands"] Αἱ γαρ χειρες—*Sept.* *Manus* enim *vestræ*—*Vulg.* They seem to have read כי ידיכם *ki yedeychem.*

Verse 16. *Wash you*] Referring to the preceding verse, "your hands are full of blood;" and alluding to the legal washing commanded on several occasions. See Lev. xiv. 8, 9, 47.

Verse 17. *Relieve the oppressed*—"Amend *that which is corrupted*"] אשרו המוץ *asheru chamots.* In rendering this obscure phrase I follow *Bochart*, (*Hieroz.* Part i., lib. ii., cap. 7.,) though I am not perfectly satisfied with this explication of it.

Verse 18. *Though your sins be as scarlet*] שני *shani*, "scarlet or crimson," *dibaphum, twice dipped*, or *double dyed;* from שנה *shanah, iterare, to double*, or *to do a thing twice.* This derivation seems much more probable than that which *Salmasius* prefers from שנן *shanan, acuere*, to *whet*, from the *sharpness* and strength of the colour, οξυφοινικον; תלע *tela*, the same; properly the *worm, vermiculus*, (from whence *vermeil*,) for this colour was produced from a worm or insect which grew in a coccus or excrescence of a shrub of the ilex kind, (see Plin. Nat. Hist. xvi. 8,) like the cochineal worm in the opuntia of America. See Ulloa's Voyage, book v., chap. ii., note to page 342. There is a shrub of this kind that grows in Provence and Languedoc, and produces the like insect, called the *kermes oak*, (see Miller, Dict. *Quercus*,) from *kermez*, the Arabic word for this colour, whence our word *crimson* is derived.

"Neque amissos colores
Lana refert medicata fuco,"

says the poet, applying the same image to a different purpose. To discharge these strong colours is impossible to human art or power; but to the grace and power of God all things, even much more difficult, are possible and easy. Some copies have כשנים *keshanim*, "like crimson garments."

Though they be red, &c.] But the conjunction ו *vau* is added by *twenty-one* of *Kennicott's*, and by *forty-two* of *De Rossi's* MSS., by some early editions, with the *Septuagint*, *Syriac*, *Vulgate*, and *Arabic*. It makes a fuller and more emphatic sense. "AND *though they be red as crimson*," &c.

Verse 19. *Ye shall eat the good of the land*] Referring to ver. 7: it shall not be "devoured by strangers."

Verse 20. *Ye shall be devoured with the sword*—"Ye shall be food for the sword"] The *Septuagint* and *Vulgate* read תאכלכם *tochalchem*, "the sword *shall devour you;*" which is of much more easy construction than the present reading of the text.

The Chaldee seems to read בחרב אויב תאכלו *bechereb oyeb teachelu*, "ye shall be consumed *by* the sword *of the enemy.*" The *Syriac* also reads בחרב *bechereb* and renders the verb passively. And the rhythmus seems to require this addition.—Dr. JUBB.

Verse 21.—*Become a harlot*] See before, the Discourse on the Prophetic Style; and see Lowth's Comment on the place, and De Sacr. Poës. Hebr. Præl. xxxi.

Verse 22. *Wine mixed with water*] An image used for the *adulteration* of wines, with more propriety than may at first appear, if what *Thevenot* says of the people of the Levant of late times were true of them formerly. He says, "They never mingle water with their wine

A. M. cir. 3244
B. C. cir. 760
Anno Olymp. Quintæ I.
Ante Urbem Conditam 7

23 [u]Thy princes *are* rebellious,
and [v]companions of thieves:
[w]every one loveth gifts, and followeth after rewards: they
[x]judge not the fatherless, neither
doth the cause of the widow come
unto them.
24 Therefore saith the LORD,

A. M. cir. 3244
B. C. cir. 760
Anno Olymp. Quintæ I.
Anno Urbem Conditam 7

[u]Hosea ix. 15——[v]Proverbs xxix. 24——[w]Jeremiah xxii. 17; Ezekiel xxii. 12; Hosea iv. 18; Micah iii. 11; vii. 3——[x]Jeremiah v. 28; Zechariah vii. 10

to drink; but drink by itself what water they think proper for abating the strength of the wine." "Lorsque les Persans boivent du vin, ils le prennent tout pur, à la facon des Levantins, qui ne le mêlent jamais avec de l'eua; mais en beuvant du vin, de temps en temps ils prennent un pot d'eau, et en boivent de grand traits." Voyage, part ii., liv. ii., chap. 10. "Ils (les Turcs) n'y meslent jamais d'eau, et se moquent des Chrètiens qui en mettent, ce qui leur semble tout à fait ridicule." Ibid. part i., chap. 24. "The Turks never mingle water with their wine, and laugh at the Christians for doing it, which they consider altogether ridiculous."

It is remarkable that whereas the Greeks and Latins by *mixed* wine always understood wine diluted and lowered with water, the Hebrews on the contrary generally mean by it wine made stronger and more inebriating by the addition of higher and more powerful ingredients, such as honey, spices, defrutum, (or wine inspissated by boiling it down to two-thirds or one-half of the quantity,) myrrh, mandragora, opiates, and other strong drugs. Such were the exhilarating, or rather stupifying, ingredients which Helen mixed in the bowl together with the wine for her guests oppressed with grief to raise their spirits, the composition of which she had learned in Egypt:—

Αυτικ' αρ' εις οινον βαλε φαρμακον, ενθεν επινον,
Νηπενθες τ' αχολον τε, κακων επιληθον ἁπαντων.
HOMER. *Odyss.* lib. iv., ver. 220.

"Meanwhile, with genial joy to warm the soul,
Bright Helen mix'd a mirth-inspiring bowl;
Temper'd with drugs of sovereign use, to assuage
The boiling bosom of tumultuous rage:
Charm'd with that virtuous draught, the exalted mind
All sense of wo delivers to the wind."
POPE.

Such was the "spiced wine and the juice of pomegranates," mentioned Cant. viii. 2. And how much the Eastern people to this day deal in artificial liquors of prodigious strength, the use of wine being forbidden, may be seen in a curious chapter of Kempfer upon that subject. Amœn. Exot. Fasc. iii., Obs. 15.

Thus the drunkard is properly described, Prov. xxiii. 30, as one "that seeketh *mixed* wine," and "is mighty to *mingle* strong drink," Isa. v. 22. And hence the poet took that highly poetical and sublime image of the cup of God's wrath, called by Isaiah li. 17, the "cup of trembling," causing intoxication and stupefaction, (see Chappelow's note on Hariri, p. 33,) containing, as St. John expresses in Greek the Hebrew idea with the utmost precision, though with a seeming contradiction in terms, *κεκερασμενον ακρατον*, *merum mixtum*, pure wine made yet stronger by a mixture of powerful ingredients; Rev. xiv. 10. "In the hand of JEHOVAH," saith the psalmist, Psa. lxxv. 8, "there is a cup, and the wine is turbid: it is full of a mixed liquor, and he poureth out of it;" or rather, "he poureth it out of one vessel into another," to mix it perfectly, according to the reading expressed by the ancient versions, ויגר מזה אל זה *vaiyagger mizzeh al zeh*, and he pours it from this to that, "verily the dregs thereof," the thickest sediment of the strong ingredients mingled with it, "all the ungodly of the earth shall wring them out, and drink them."

R. D. Kimchi says, "The current coin was adulterated with brass, tin, and other metals, and yet was circulated as good money. The wine also was adulterated with water in the taverns, and sold notwithstanding for pure wine."

Verse 23. *Companions of thieves*—"Associates"] The *Septuagint*, *Vulgate*, and four MSS., read חברי *chabrey* without the conjunction ו *vau*.

Verse 24. *Ah, I will ease me*—"Aha! I will be eased"] Anger, arising from a sense of injury and affront, especially from those who, from every consideration of duty and gratitude, ought to have behaved far otherwise, is an uneasy and painful sensation: and revenge, executed to the full on the offenders, removes that uneasiness, and consequently is pleasing and quieting, at least for the present. Ezekiel, chap. v. 13, introduces God expressing himself in the same manner:—

"And mine anger shall be fully accomplished;
And I will make my fury rest upon them;
And I will give myself ease."

This is a strong instance of the metaphor called anthropopathia, by which, throughout the Scriptures, as well the historical as the poetical parts, the sentiments, sensations, and affections, the bodily faculties, qualities, and members, of men, and even of brute animals, are attributed to God, and that with the utmost liberty and latitude of application. The foundation of this is obvious; it arises from necessity; we have no idea of the natural attributes of God, of his pure essence, of his manner of existence, of his manner of acting: when therefore we would treat on these subjects, we find ourselves forced to express them by sensible images. But necessity leads to beauty; this is true of metaphor in general, and in particular of this kind of metaphor, which is used with great elegance and sublimity in the sacred poetry; and what is very remarkable, in the grossest instances of the application of it, it is generally the most striking and the most sublime. The reason seems to be this: when the images are taken from the superior faculties of the human nature, from the purer and more generous affections, and applied to God, we are apt to acquiesce in the notion; we overlook the metaphor, and take it as a proper attribute; but when the idea is gross and offensive, as in this passage of Isaiah, where the impatience of anger and the pleasure of revenge is attributed to God, we are immediately shocked at the application; the impropriety

A. M. cir. 3244
B. C. cir. 760
Anno Olymp. Quintæ I.
Ante Urbem Conditam 7

the Lord of hosts, the mighty
one of Israel, Ah, [y]I will ease
me of mine adversaries, and
avenge me of mine enemies:
25 And I will turn my hand upon thee, and
[z]purely [a]purge away thy dross, and take away
all thy tin:
26 And I will restore thy judges [b]as at the
first, and thy counsellors as at the beginning:
afterward [c]thou shalt be called, The city
of righteousness, the faithful
city.
27 Zion shall be redeemed
with judgments, and [d]her converts with righteousness.
28 And the [e]destruction [f]of the transgressors and of the sinners *shall be* together, and
they that forsake the Lord shall be consumed.
29 For they shall be ashamed of [g]the oaks

A. M. cir. 3244
B. C. cir. 760
Anno Olymp. Quintæ I.
Ante Urbem Conditam 7

[y]Deut. xxviii. 63; Ezek. v. 13——[z]Heb. *according to pureness*——[a]Jer. vi. 29; ix. 7; Mal. iii. 3——[b]Jer. xxxiii. 7——[c]Zech. viii. 3

[d]Or, *they that return of her*——[e]Job xxxi. 3; Psa. i. 6; v. 6; lxxiii. 27; xcii. 9; civ. 35——[f]Heb. *breaking* [g]Chap. lvii. 5.

strikes us at once; and the mind, casting about for something in the Divine nature analogous to the image, lays hold on some great, obscure, vague idea, which she endeavours to comprehend, and is lost in immensity and astonishment. See De Sacr. Poesi. Hebr. Præel. xvi. *sub. fin.*, where this matter is treated and illustrated by examples.

Verse 25. *I will turn my hand upon thee*] So the common version; and this seems to be a metaphor taken from the custom of those who, when the metal is melted, strike off the scoriæ with their hand previously to its being poured out into the mould. I have seen this done with the naked hand, and no injury whatever sustained.

Purge away thy dross—"In the furnace"] The text has כבר *cabbor*, which some render "as with soap;" as if it were the same with כברית *keborith;* so *Kimchi;* but soap can have nothing to do with the purifying of metals. Others, "according to purity," or "purely," as our version. *Le Clerc* conjectured that the true reading is ככור *kechur*, "as in the furnace;" see Ezek. xxii. 18, 20. Dr. *Durell* proposes only a transposition of letters בכר to the same sense; and so likewise Archbishop *Secker*. That this is the true reading is highly probable.

Verse 26. *I will restore*] "This," says *Kimchi*, "shall be in the days of the Messiah, in which all the wicked shall cease, and the remnant of Israel shall neither do iniquity, nor speak lies." What a change must this be among *Jews!*

Afterward—"And after this"] The *Septuagint*, *Syriac*, *Chaldee*, and *eighteen* MSS., and one of my own, very ancient, add the *conjunction* ו *vau*, AND.

Verse 27. *With judgment*—"In judgment"] By the exercise of God's strict justice in destroying the obdurate, (see ver. 28,) and delivering the penitent *in righteousness;* by the truth and faithfulness of God in performing his promises."

Verse 29. *For they shall be ashamed of the oaks*—"For ye shall be ashamed of the ilexes"] Sacred groves were a very ancient and favourite appendage of idolatry. They were furnished with the temple of the god to whom they were dedicated, with altars, images, and every thing necessary for performing the various rites of worship offered there; and were the scenes of many impure ceremonies, and of much abominable superstition. They made a principal part of the religion of the old inhabitants of Canaan; and the Israelites were commanded to destroy their groves, among other monuments of their false worship. The Israelites themselves became afterwards very much addicted to this species of idolatry.

"When I had brought them into the land,
Which I swore that I would give unto them;
Then they saw every high hill and every thick tree;
And there they slew their victims;
And there they presented the provocation of their offerings;
And there they placed their sweet savour;
And there they poured out their libations."
Ezek. xx. 28.

"On the tops of the mountains they sacrifice;
And on the hills they burn incense;
Under the oak and the poplar;
And the ilex, because her shade is pleasant."
Hos. iv. 13.

Of what particular kinds the trees here mentioned are, cannot be determined with certainty. In regard to אלה *ellah*, in this place of Isaiah, as well as in Hosea, *Celsius* (Hierobot.) understands it of the terebinth, because the most ancient interpreters render it so; in the first place the *Septuagint*. He quotes eight places; but in three of these eight places the copies vary, some having δρυς, *the oak*, instead of τερεβινθος, the *terebinth* or *turpentine tree*. And he should have told us, that these same *seventy* render it in sixteen other places by δρυς, *the oak;* so that their authority is really against him; and the *Septuagint*, "stant pro quercu," contrary to what he says at first setting out. Add to this that *Symmachus*, *Theodotion*, and *Aquila*, generally render it by δρυς, *the oak;* the latter only once rendering it by τερεβινθος, *the terebinth*. His other arguments seem to me not very conclusive; he says, that all the qualities of אלה *ellah* agree to the terebinth, that it grows in mountainous countries, that it is a strong tree, long-lived, large and high, and deciduous. All these qualities agree just as well to the *oak*, against which he contends; and he actually attributes them to the oak in the very next section. But I think neither the oak nor the terebinth will do in this place of Isaiah, from the last circumstance which he mentions, their being deciduous, where the prophet's design seems to me to require an evergreen, otherwise the casting of its leaves would be nothing out of the common established course of nature, and no proper

A. M. cir. 3244
B. C. cir. 760
Anno Olymp. Quintæ I.
Ante Urbem Conditam 7

which ye have desired, [h]and
ye shall be confounded for the
gardens that ye have chosen.
30 For ye shall be as an oak
whose leaf fadeth, and as a garden that hath
no water.

31 [i]And the strong shall be
[k]as tow, [l]and the maker of it as
a spark, and they shall both burn
together, and none shall quench
them.

[h]Chap. lxv. 3; lxvi. 17——[i]Ezek. xxxii. 21

[k]Chap. xliii. 17——[l]Or, *and his work*

image of extreme distress and total desolation, parallel to that of a garden without water, that is, wholly burnt up and destroyed. An ancient, who was an inhabitant and a native of this country, understands it in like manner of a tree blasted with uncommon and immoderate heat; *velut arbores, cum frondes æstu torrente decusserunt. Ephrem Syr.* in loc., edit. Assemani. Compare Psa. i. 4; Jer. xvii. 8. Upon the whole I have chosen to make it the ilex, which word *Vossius*, Etymolog., derives from the Hebrew אלה *ellah*, that whether the word itself be rightly rendered or not, I might at least preserve the propriety of the poetic image.—L.

By the *ilex* the learned prelate means the *holly*, which, though it generally appears as a sort of shrub, grows, in a good soil, where it is unmolested, to a considerable height. I have one in my own garden, rising *three* stems from the root, and between *twenty* and *thirty* feet in height. It is an evergreen.

Verse 29. *For they shall be ashamed*—"For ye shall be ashamed"] תבושו *teboshu*, in the second person, *Vulgate, Chaldee, three* MSS., one of my own, ancient, and one edition; and in agreement with the rest of the sentence.

Verse 30. *Whose leaf*—"Whose leaves"] *Twenty-six* of *Kennicott's*, *twenty-four* of *De Rossi's*, one ancient, of my own, and *seven* editions, read אליה *aleyha*, in its full and regular form. This is worth remarking, as it accounts for a great number of anomalies of the like kind, which want only the same authority to rectify them.

As a garden that hath no water—"A garden wherein is no water."] In the hotter parts of the Eastern countries, a constant supply of water is so absolutely necessary for the cultivation and even for the preservation and existence of a garden, that should it want water but for a few days, every thing in it would be burnt up with the heat, and totally destroyed. There is therefore no garden whatever in those countries but what has such a certain supply, either from some neighbouring river, or from a reservoir of water collected from springs, or filled with rain water in the proper season, in sufficient quantity to afford ample provision for the rest of the year.

Moses, having described the habitation of man newly created as a garden planted with every tree pleasant to the sight and good for food, adds, as a circumstance necessary to complete the idea of a garden, that it was well supplied with water, "And a river went out of Eden to water the garden;" Gen. ii. 10: see also xiii. 10.

That the reader may have a clear notion of this matter, it will be necessary to give some account of the management of their gardens in this respect.

"Damascus," says *Maundrell*, p. 122, "is encompassed with gardens, extending no less, according to common estimation, than thirty miles round; which makes it look like a city in a vast wood. The gardens are thick set with fruit trees of all kinds, kept fresh and verdant by the waters of the Barrady, (the Chrysorrhoas of the ancients,) which supply both the gardens and city in great abundance. This river, as soon as it issues out from between the cleft of the mountain before mentioned into the plain, is immediately divided into three streams; of which the middlemost and biggest runs directly to Damascus, and is distributed to all the cisterns and fountains of the city. The other two (which I take to be the work of art) are drawn round, one to the right hand, and the other to the left, on the borders of the gardens, into which they are let as they pass, by little currents, and so dispersed all over the vast wood, insomuch that there is not a garden but has a fine quick stream running through it. The Barrady is almost wholly drunk up by the city and gardens. What small part of it escapes is united, as I was informed, in one channel again on the southeast side of the city; and, after about three or four hours' course finally loses itself in a bog there, without ever arriving at the sea." This was likewise the case in former times, as *Strabo*, lib. xvi., Pliny, lib. v. 18, testify; who say, "that this river was expended in canals, and drunk up by watering the place."

"The best sight," says the same *Maundrell*, p. 39, "that the palace of the emir of Beroot, anciently Berytus, affords, and the worthiest to be remembered, is the orange garden. It contains a large quadrangular plat of ground, divided into sixteen lesser squares, four in a row, with walks between them. The walks are shaded with orange trees of a large spreading size. Every one of these sixteen lesser squares in the garden was bordered with stone; and in the stone work were troughs, very artificially contrived, for conveying the water all over the garden; there being little outlets cut at every tree for the stream as it passed by to flow out and water it." The royal gardens at Ispahan are watered just in the same manner, according to *Kempfer's* description, Amœn. Exot., p. 193.

This gives us a clear idea of the פלגי מים *palgey mayim*, mentioned in the first Psalm, and other places of Scripture, "the divisions of waters," the waters distributed in artificial canals; for so the phrase properly signifies. The prophet Jeremith, chap. xvii. 8, has imitated, and elegantly amplified, the passage of the psalmist above referred to:—

"He shall be like a tree planted by the water side,
And which sendeth forth her roots to the aqueduct.
She shall not fear, when the heat cometh;
But her leaf shall be green;
And in the year of drought she shall not be anxious,
Neither shall she cease from bearing fruit."

From this image the son of Sirach, Ecclus. xxiv. 30, 31, has most beautifully illustrated the influence and the increase of religious wisdom in a well prepared heart.

"I also come forth as a canal from a river,
And as a conduit flowing into a paradise.
I said, I will water my garden,
And I will abundantly moisten my border:
And, lo! my canal became a river,
And my river became a sea."

This gives us the true meaning of the following elegant proverb, Prov. xxi. 1:—

"The heart of the king is like the canals of waters in the hand of JEHOVAH;
Whithersoever it pleaseth him, he inclineth it."

The direction of it is in the hand of JEHOVAH, as the distribution of the water of the reservoir through the garden by different canals is at the will of the gardener.

"Et, cum exustus ager morientibus æstuat herbis,
Ecce supercilio clivosi tramitis undam
Elicit: illa cadens raucum per levia murmur
Saxa ciet, scatebrisque arentia temperat arva."
Virg., Georg. i. 107.

"Then, when the fiery suns too fiercely play,
And shrivelled herbs on withering stems decay,
The wary ploughman on the mountain's brow
Undams his watery stores; huge torrents flow;
And, rattling down the rocks, large moisture yield,
Tempering the thirsty fever of the field."
DRYDEN.

Solomon, Eccles. ii. 5, 6, mentions his own works of this kind:—

"I made me gardens, and paradises;
And I planted in them all kinds of fruit trees.
I made me pools of water,
To water with them the grove flourishing with trees."

Maundrell, p. 88, has given a description of the remains, as they are said to be, of these very pools made by Solomon, for the reception and preservation of the waters of a spring, rising at a little distance from them; which will give us a perfect notion of the contrivance and design of such reservoirs. "As for the pools, they are three in number, lying in a row above each other; being so disposed that the waters of the uppermost may descend into the second, and those of the second into the third. Their figure is quadrangular, the breadth is the same in all, amounting to about ninety paces. In their length there is some difference between them; the first being about *one hundred and sixty* paces long, the second, *two hundred*, and the third, *two hundred and twenty*. They are all lined with wall and plastered; and contain a great depth of water."

The immense works which were made by the ancient kings of Egypt for recovering the waters of the Nile, when it overflowed, for such uses, are well known. But there never was a more stupendous work of this kind than the reservoir of Saba, or Merab, in Arabia Felix. According to the tradition of the country, it was the work of Balkis, that queen of Sheba who visited Solomon. It was a vast lake formed by the collection of the waters of a torrent in a valley, where, at a narrow pass between two mountains, a very high mole or dam was built. The water of the lake so formed had near *twenty* fathoms depth; and there were *three* sluices at different heights, by which, at whatever height the lake stood, the plain below might be watered. By conduits and canals from these sluices the water was constantly distributed in due proportion to the several lands; so that the whole country for many miles became a perfect paradise. The city of Saba, or Merab, was situated immediately below the great dam; a great flood came, and raised the lake above its usual height; the dam gave way in the middle of the night; the waters burst forth at once, and overwhelmed the whole city, with the neighbouring towns and people. The remains of eight tribes were forced to abandon their dwellings, and the beautiful valley became a morass and a desert. This fatal catastrophe happened long before the time of Mohammed, who mentions it in the Koran, chap. xxxiv. ver. 15. See also *Sale*, Prelim. s. i. p. 10, and *Michaelis*, Quest. aux Voyag. Dan. No. 94. *Niebuhr*, Descrip. de l'Arabie. p. 240.—L.

CHAPTER II

Prophecy concerning the kingdom of the Messiah, and the conversion of the Gentile world, 1–5. *Great wickedness and idolatry of the unbelieving Jews*, 6–9. *Terrible consternation that will seize the wicked, who shall in vain seek for rocks and mountains to hide them from the face of God in the day of his judgments*, 10–17. *Total destruction of idolatry in consequence of the establishment of Messiah's kingdom*, 18–21. *An exhortation to put no confidence in man*, 22.

A. M. cir. 3244
B. C. cir. 760
Anno Olymp. Quintæ I.
Ante Urbem Conditam 7

THE word that Isaiah the son of Amoz saw concerning
Judah and Jerusalem.
2 And [a]it shall come to pass [b]in the last days [c]*that* the mountain of the LORD's house shall [d]be established in the top of the mountains, and shall be exalted

[a]Mic. iv. 1, &c.——[b]Gen. xlix. 1; Jer. xxiii. 30 [c]Psa. lxviii. 15, 16——[d]Or, *prepared*

The prophecy contained in the second, third, and fourth chapters, makes one continued discourse. The first five verses of chap. ii. foretell the kingdom of Messiah, the conversion of the Gentiles, and their admission into it. From the sixth verse to the end of the second chapter is foretold the punishment of the unbelieving Jews for their idolatrous practices, their confidence in their own strength, and distrust of God's protection; and moreover the destruction of idolatry, in consequence of the establishment of Messiah's kingdom. The whole of the third chapter, with the first verse of the fourth, is a prophecy of the calamities of the Babylonian invasion and captivity; with a particular amplification of the distress of the proud

A. M. cir. 3244 B. C. cir. 760 Anno Olymp. Quintæ I. Ante Urbem Conditam 7

above the hills; [e]and all nations
shall flow unto it.
3 And many people shall go
and say, [f]Come ye and let us go
up to the mountain of the LORD,
to the house of the God of Jacob;
and he will teach us of his ways,
and we will walk in his paths:

[e]Psa. lxxii. 8; chap. xxvii. 13

[f]Jer. xxxi. 6; l. 5; Zech. viii. 21, 23

and luxurious daughters of Sion; chap. iv. 2-6 promises to the remnant, which shall have escaped this severe purgation, a future restoration to the favour and protection of God.

This prophecy was probably delivered in the time of Jotham, or perhaps in that of Uzziah, as Isaiah is said to have prophesied in his reign; to which time not any of his prophecies is so applicable as that of these chapters. The seventh verse of the second, and the latter part of the third chapter, plainly point out times in which riches abounded, and luxury and delicacy prevailed. Plenty of silver and gold could only arise from their commerce; particularly from that part of it which was carried on by the Red Sea. This circumstance seems to confine the prophecy within the limits above mentioned, while the port of Elath was in their hands: it was lost under Ahaz, and never recovered.

NOTES ON CHAP. II

Verse 2. *In the last days*—"In the latter days"] "Wherever the latter times are mentioned in Scripture, the days of the Messiah are always meant," says *Kimchi* on this place: and, in regard to this place, nothing can be more clear and certain. And *the mountain of the Lord's house*, says the same author, is Mount *Moriah*, on which the temple was built. The prophet Micah, chap. iv. 1-4, has repeated this prophecy of the establishment of the kingdom of Christ, and of its progress to universality and perfection, in the same words, with little and hardly any material variation: for as he did not begin to prophesy till Jotham's time, and this seems to be one of the first of Isaiah's prophecies, I suppose Micah to have taken it from hence. The variations, as I said, are of no great importance. Ver. 2. הוא *hu*, after ונשא *venissa*, a word of some emphasis, may be supplied from Micah, if dropped in Isaiah. An ancient MS. has it here in the margin. It has in like manner been lost in chap. liii. 4, (see note on the place,) and in Psa. xxii. 29, where it is supplied by the *Syriac* and *Septuagint*. Instead of כל הגוים *col haggoyim, all the nations*, Micah has only עמים *ammim, peoples;* where the *Syriac* has כל עמים *col ammim, all peoples*, as probably it ought to be. Ver. 3. For the second אל *el*, read ואל *veel*, seventeen MSS., one of my own, ancient, two editions, the *Septuagint*, *Vulgate*, *Syriac*, *Chaldee*, and so Micah, iv. 2. Ver. 4. Micah adds עד רחק *ad rachok, afar off*, which the *Syriac* also reads in this parallel place of Isaiah. It is also to be observed that Micah has improved the passage by adding a verse, or sentence, for imagery and expression worthy even of the elegance of Isaiah:—

"And they shall sit every man under his vine,
And under his fig tree, and none shall affright them:
For the mouth of JEHOVAH, God of hosts, hath spoken it."

The description of well established peace, by the image of "beating their swords into ploughshares, and their spears into pruning-hooks," is very poetical. The Roman poets have employed the same image, *Martial*, xiv. 34. "Falx ex ense."

"Pax me certa ducis placidos curvavit in usus:
Agricolæ nunc sum; militis ante fui."

"Sweet peace has transformed me. I was once the property of the soldier, and am now the property of the husbandman."

The prophet Joel, chap. iii. 10, hath reversed it, and applied it to war prevailing over peace:—

"Beat your ploughshares into swords,
And your pruning-hooks into spears."

And so likewise the Roman poets:—

———————— Non ullus aratro
Dignus honos: squalent abductis arva colonis,
Et curvæ rigidum falces conflantur in ensem.
Virg., Georg. i. 506.

"Agriculture has now no honour: the husbandmen being taken away to the wars, the fields are overgrown with weeds, and the crooked sickles are straightened into swords."

Bella diu tenuere viros: erat aptior ensis
Vomere: cedebat taurus arator equo
Sarcula cessabant; versique in pila ligones;
Factaque de rastri pondere cassis erat.
Ovid, Fast. i. 697.

"War has lasted long, and the sword is preferred to the plough. The bull has given place to the war-horse; the weeding-hooks to pikes; and the harrow-pins have been manufactured into helmets."

The prophet Ezekiel, chap. xvii. 22-24, has presignified the same great event with equal clearness, though in a more abstruse form, in an allegory; from an image, suggested by the former part of the prophecy, happily introduced, and well pursued:—

"Thus saith the Lord JEHOVAH:
I myself will take from the shoot of the lofty cedar,
Even a tender scion from the top of his scions will I pluck off:
And I myself will plant it on a mountain high and eminent.
On the lofty mountain of Israel will I plant it;
And it shall exalt its branch, and bring forth fruit,
And it shall become a majestic cedar:
And under it shall dwell all fowl of every wing;
In the shadow of its branches shall they dwell:
And all the trees of the field shall know,
That I JEHOVAH have brought low the high tree;

A. M. cir. 3244 B. C. cir. 760 Anno Olymp. Quintæ I. Ante Urbem Conditam 7

[g]for out of Zion shall go forth
the law, and the word of the
LORD from Jerusalem.
4 And he shall judge among
the nations, and shall rebuke many people:
and [h]they shall beat their swords into plowshares, and their spears into [i]pruning-hooks:
nation shall not lift up sword against nation,
[k]neither shall they learn war any more.

5 O house of Jacob, come ye,
and let us [l]walk in the light of
the LORD.
6 Therefore thou hast forsaken
thy people the house of Jacob, because they be
replenished [m]from [n]the east, and [o]*are* soothsayers like the Philistines, [p]and they [q]please
themselves in the children of strangers.
7 [r]Their land also is full of silver and gold,

A. M. cir. 3244 B. C. cir. 760 Anno Olymp. Quintæ I. Ante Urbem Conditam 7

[g]Luke xxiv. 47——[h]Psa. xlvi. 9; Hos. ii. 18; Zech. ix. 10——[i]Or, *scythes*——[k]Psa. lxii. 3, 7——[l]Eph. v. 8
[m]Or, *more than the east*

[n]Num. xxiii. 7——[o]Deut. xviii. 14——[p]Psa. cvi. 35; Jer. x. 2——[q]Or, *abound with the children*, &c.
[r]Deut. xvii. 16, 17

Have exalted the low tree;
Have dried up the green tree;
And have made the dry tree to flourish:
I JEHOVAH have spoken it, and will do it."

The word ונתתי *venathatti*, in this passage, ver. 22, as the sentence now stands, appears incapable of being reduced to any proper construction or sense. None of the ancient versions acknowledge it, except *Theodotion*, and the *Vulgate;* and all but the latter vary very much from the present reading of this clause. *Houbigant's* correction of the passage, by reading instead of ונתתי *venathatti*, ויונקת *veyoneketh, and a tender scion*—which is not very unlike it, perhaps better ויונק *veyonek*, with which the adjective רך *rach* will agree without alteration—is ingenious and probable; and I have adopted it in the above translation.—L.

Verse 3. *To the house*] The conjunction ו *vau* is added by nineteen of *Kennicott's*, thirteen of *De Rossi's* MSS., one of my own, and two editions, the *Septuagint, Syriac, Vulgate, Arabic*, and some copies of the *Targum;* AND *to the house.* It makes the sentence more emphatic.

He will teach us of his ways] Unless God grant a revelation of his will, what can we know?

We will walk in his paths] Unless we purpose to walk in the light, of what use can that light be to us?

For out of Zion shall go forth the law] In the house of God, and in his ordinances only, can we expect to hear the pure doctrines of revelation preached. 1. God alone can give a revelation of his own will. 2. We must use the proper means in order to know this will. 3. We should *know* it in order to *do* it. 4. We should *do* it in order to profit by it. 5. He who will not walk in the light when God vouchsafes it, shall be shut up in everlasting darkness. 6. Every man should help his neighbour to attain that light, life, and felicity: "Come ye, and let us walk in the light of the Lord."

Verse 4. *Neither shall they learn war any more.*] If wars are *necessary*, how deep must that *fall* be that renders them so! But what a reproach to humanity is the *trade of war!* Men are regularly instructed in it, as in any of the necessary arts.

"How to dislodge most souls from their frail shrines
By bomb, sword, ball, and bayonet, is the art
Which some call great and glorious!"

And is this a necessary part of a finished education in civilized society? O Earth! Earth! Earth!

Verse 6. *They be replenished*—"And they multiply"] Seven MSS. and one edition, for ישפיקו *yaspiku*, read יספיחו *yaspichu*, "and have joined themselves to the children of strangers;" that is, in marriage or worship.—Dr. JUBB. So *Vulg., adhœserunt.* Compare chap. xiv. 1. But the very learned professor Chevalier *Michaelis* has explained the word יספחו *yesupachu*, Job xxx. 7, (German translation, note on the place,) in another manner; which perfectly well agrees with that place, and perhaps will be found to give as good a sense here. ספיח *saphiach*, the noun, means corn springing up, not from the seed regularly sown on cultivated land, but in the untilled field, from the scattered grains of the former harvest. This, by an easy metaphor, is applied to a spurious brood of children irregularly and casually begotten. The *Septuagint* seem to have understood the verb here in this sense, reading it as the *Vulgate* seems to have done. This justifies their version, which it is hard to account for in any other manner: *και τεκνα πολλα αλλοφυλα εγενηθη αυτοις.* Compare Hos. v. 7, and the *Septuagint* there. But instead of ובילדי *ubeyaldey*, "and in the children," two of *Kennicott's* and eight of *De Rossi's* MSS. have וכילדי *ucheyaldey*, "and as the children." And they sin impudently as the children of strangers. See *De Rossi.*

And are soothsayers—"They are filled with diviners"] Heb. "They are filled from the east;" or "more than the east." The sentence is manifestly imperfect. The *Septuagint, Vulgate*, and *Chaldee*, seem to have read כמקדם *kemikkedem;* and the latter, with another word before it, signifying *idols;* "they are filled with idols as from of old." *Houbigant*, for מקדם *mikkedem*, reads מקסם *mikkesem*, as *Brentius* had proposed long ago. I rather think that both words together give us the true reading: מקדם *mikkedem*, מקסם *mikkesem*, "with divination from the east;" and that the first word has been by mistake omitted, from its similitude to the second.

Verse 7. *Their land is also full of horses*—"And his land is filled with horses"] This was in direct contradiction to God's command in the law: "But he (the king) shall not multiply horses to himself; nor cause the people to return to Egypt, to the end that he should multiply horses; neither shall he greatly multiply to himself silver and gold," Deut. xvii. 16, 17. Uzziah seems to have followed the

A. M. cir. 3244
B. C. cir. 760
Anno Olymp.
Quintæ I.
Ante Urbem
Conditam 7

neither *is there any* end of their
treasures; their land is also full
of horses, neither *is there any*
end of their chariots:
8 [s]Their land also is full of idols; they
worship the work of their own hands, that
which their own fingers have made:
9 And the mean man boweth down, and the
great man humbleth himself: therefore forgive them not.
10 [t]Enter into the rock, and hide thee in
the dust, for fear of the LORD, and for the
glory of his majesty.
11 The [u]lofty looks of man shall be humbled,
and the haughtiness of men shall be bowed
down, and the LORD alone shall
be exalted [v]in that day.
12 For the day of the LORD
of hosts *shall be* upon every *one*
that is proud and lofty, and upon every *one*
that is lifted up; and he shall be brought low:
13 And upon all [w]the cedars of Lebanon,
that are high and lifted up, and upon all the
oaks of Bashan,
14 And [x]upon all the high mountains, and
upon all the hills *that are* lifted up,
15 And upon every high tower, and upon
every fenced wall,
16 [y]And upon all the ships of Tarshish,
and upon all [z]pleasant pictures.

A. M. cir. 3244
B. C. cir. 760
Anno Olymp.
Quintæ I.
Ante Urbem
Conditam 7

[s]Jer. ii. 28——[t]Ver. 19, 21; Rev. vi. 15——[u]Ver. 17; chap. v. 15, 16; xiii. 11——[v]Chap. iv. 1; xi. 10, 11; xii. 1, 4; xxiv. 21; xxv. 9; xxvi. 1; xxvii. 1, 2, 12, 13; xxviii. 5; xxix. 18; xxx. 23; lii. 6; Jer. xxx. 7, 8; Ezek. xxxviii. 14, 19; xxxix. 11, 22; Hos. ii. 16, 18, 21; Joel iii. 18; Amos ix. 11; Obad. 8; Mic. iv. 6; v. 10; vii. 11, 12; Zeph. iii. 11, 16; Zech. ix. 16——[w]Chap. xiv. 8; xxxvii. 24; Ezek. xxx. i. 3; Zech. xi. 1, 2——[x]Chap. xxx. 25——[y]1 Kings x. 22——[z]Heb. *pictures of desire*

example of Solomon, see 1 Kings x. 26-29, who first transgressed in these particulars; he recovered the port of Elath on the Red Sea, and with it that commerce which in Solomon's days had "made silver and gold as plenteous at Jerusalem as stones," 2 Chron. i. 15. He had an army of 307,500 men, in which, as we may infer from the testimony of Isaiah, the chariots and horse made a considerable part. "The law above mentioned was to be a standing trial of prince and people, whether they had trust and confidence in God their deliverer." See *Bp. Sherlock's* Discourses on Prophecy. Dissert. iv., where he has excellently explained the reason and effect of the law, and the influence which the observance or neglect of it had on the affairs of the Israelites.

Verse 8. *Their land also is full of idols*—"And his land is filled with idols"] Uzziah and Jotham are both said, 2 Kings xv. 3, 4, 34, 35, "to have done that which was right in the sight of the Lord;" that is, to have adhered to and maintained the legal worship of God, in opposition to idolatry and all irregular worship; for to this sense the meaning of that phrase is commonly to be restrained; "save that the high places were not removed where the people still sacrificed and burned incense." There was hardly any time when they were quite free from this irregular and unlawful practice, which they seem to have looked upon as very consistent with the true worship of God; and which seems in some measure to have been tolerated, while the tabernacle was removed from place to place, and before the temple was built. Even after the conversion of Manasseh, when he had removed the strange gods, commanded Judah to serve JEHOVAH the God of Israel, it is added, "Nevertheless the people did sacrifice still on the high places, yet unto JEHOVAH their God only," 2 Chron, xxxiii. 17. The worshipping on the high places therefore does not necessarily imply idolatry; and from what is said of these two kings, Uzziah and Jotham, we may presume that the public exercise of idolatrous worship was not permitted in their time. The idols therefore here spoken of must have been such as were designed for a private and secret use. Such probably were the teraphim so often mentioned in Scripture; a kind of household gods, of human form, as it should seem, (see 1 Sam. xix. 13, and compare Gen. xxxi. 34,) of different magnitude, used for idolatrous and superstitious purposes, particularly for divination, and as oracles, which they consulted for direction in their affairs.

Verse 9. *Boweth down*—"Shall he bowed down"] This has reference to the preceding verse. They bowed themselves down to their idols, therefore shall they be bowed down and brought low under the avenging hand of God.

Therefore forgive them not.] "And thou wilt not forgive them."—L.

Verse 10. "When he ariseth to strike the earth with terror."] On the authority of the *Septuagint*, confirmed by the *Arabic* and an ancient MS., I have added here to the text a line, which in the 19th and 21st verses is repeated together with the preceding line, and has, I think, evidently been omitted by mistake in this place. The MS. here varies only in one letter from the reading of the other two verses; it has בארץ *baarets*, instead of הארץ *haarets*. None of *De Rossi's* MSS. confirm this addition. The line added is, *When he ariseth to strike the earth with terror*.

Verse 11. *Be humbled*] "שפל ושח *shaphel veshach*, read שפלו שח *shaphelu shach*."—Dr. *Durell*. Which rectifies the grammatical construction. No MS. or version confirms this reading.

Verses 13-16. *And upon all the cedars*—"Even against all the cedars"] Princes, potentates, rulers, captains, rich men, &c.—So *Kimchi*. These verses afford us a striking example of that peculiar way of writing, which makes a principal characteristic of the parabolical or poetical style of the Hebrews, and in which the prophets deal so largely, namely, their manner of exhibiting things Divine, spiritual, moral, and political, by a set of images taken from things natural, artificial, religious, historical,

A. M. cir. 3244
B. C. cir. 760
Anno Olymp.
Quintæ I.
Ante Urbem
Conditam 7

17 [a]And the loftiness of man
shall be bowed down, and the
haughtiness of men shall be made
low: and the LORD alone shall
be exalted [b]in that day.
18 And [c]the idols he shall utterly abolish.
19 And they shall go into the [d]holes of the
rocks, and into the caves of [e]the earth, [f]for
fear of the LORD, and for the glory of his majesty, when he ariseth [g]to shake terribly the
earth.

[a]Ver. 11——[b]Ver. 11——[c]Or, *the idols shall utterly pass away*——[d]Ver. 10; Hos. x. 8; Luke xxiii. 30; Rev. vi. 16; ix. 6——[e]Heb. *the dust*——[f]2 Thess. i. 9——[g]Chap. xxx. 32; Hag. ii. 6, 21; Heb. xii. 26

20 [h]In that day a man shall
cast [i]his idols of silver, and his
idols of gold, [k]which they made
each one for himself to worship,
to the moles and to the bats;
21 [l]To go into the clefts of the rocks, and
into the tops of the ragged rocks, [m]for fear of
the LORD, and for the glory of his majesty,
when he ariseth to shake terribly the earth.
22 [n]Cease ye from man, whose [o]breath *is* in his
nostrils: for wherein is he to be accounted of?

[h]Chap. xxx. 22; xxxi. 27——[i]Heb. *the idols of his silver, &c.*——[k]Or, *which they made for him*——[l]Ver. 19——[m]Ver. 10, 19——[n]Psa. cxlvi. 3; Jer. xvii. 5——[o]Job xxvii. 3

in the way of metaphor or allegory. Of these nature furnishes much the largest and the most pleasing share; and all poetry has chiefly recourse to natural images, as the richest and most powerful source of illustration. But it may be observed of the Hebrew poetry in particular, that in the use of such images, and in the application of them in the way of illustration and ornament, it is more regular and constant than any other poetry whatever; that it has for the most part a set of images appropriated in a manner to the explication of certain subjects. Thus you will find, in many other places besides this before us, that *cedars of Lebanon* and *oaks of Bashan*, are used in the way of metaphor and allegory for kings, princes, potentates of the highest rank; *high mountains* and *lofty hills*, for kingdoms, republics, states, cities; towers and fortresses, for defenders and protectors, whether by counsel or strength, in peace or war; *ships of Tarshish* and works of art, and invention employed in adorning them, for merchants, men enriched by commerce, and abounding in all the luxuries and elegances of life, such as those of Tyre and Sidon; for it appears from the course of the whole passage, and from the train of ideas, that the fortresses and the ships are to be taken metaphorically, as well as the high trees and the lofty mountains.

Ships of Tarshish] Are in Scripture frequently used by a metonymy for ships in general, especially such as are employed in carrying on traffic between distant countries, as Tarshish was the most celebrated mart of those times, frequented of old by the Phœnicians, and the principal source of wealth to Judea and the neighbouring countries. The learned seem now to be perfectly well agreed that Tarshish is Tartessus, a city of Spain, at the mouth of the river Bætis, whence the Phœnicians, who first opened this trade, brought silver and gold, (Jer. x. 9; Ezek. xxvii. 12,) in which that country then abounded; and, pursuing their voyage still farther to the Cassiterides, (*Bochart*, Canaan, i. c. 39; *Huet*, Hist. de Commerce, p. 194,) the islands of Scilly and Cornwall, they brought from thence lead and tin.

Tarshish is celebrated in Scripture, 2 Chron. viii. 17, 18, ix. 21, for the trade which Solomon carried on thither, in conjunction with the Tyrians. Jehoshaphat, 1 Kings xxii. 48, 2 Chron. xx. 36, attempted afterwards to renew their trade. And from the account given of his attempt it appears that his fleet was to sail to Ezion-geber on the Red Sea; they must therefore have designed to sail round Africa, as Solomon's fleet had done before, (see *Huet*, Histoire de Commerce, p. 32,) for it was a three years' voyage, (2 Chron. ix. 21,) and they brought gold from Ophir, probably on the coast of Arabia; silver from Tartessus; and ivory, apes, and peacocks, from Africa. "אופרי *Afri*, Africa, the Roman termination, *Africa terra*. תרשיש *Tarshish*, some city or country in Africa. So the *Chaldee* on 1 Kings xxii. 49, where it renders תרשיש *Tarshish* by אפריקה *Aphricah;* and compare 2 Chron. xx. 36, from whence it appears, to go to Ophir and to Tarshish is one and the same thing."—Dr. *Jubb*. It is certain that under Pharaoh Necho, about *two hundred* years afterwards, this voyage was made by the Egyptians; *Herodot*. iv. 42. They sailed from the Red Sea, and returned by the Mediterranean, and they performed it in three years, just the same time that the voyage under Solomon had taken up. It appears likewise from *Pliny*, Nat. Hist., ii. 67, that the passage round the Cape of Good Hope was known and frequently practised before his time, by Hanno the Carthaginian, when Carthage was in its glory; by one Eudoxus, in the time of Ptolemy Lathyrus, king of Egypt; and *Cœlus Antipater*, a historian of good credit, somewhat earlier than *Pliny*, testifies that he had seen a merchant who had made the voyage from Gades to Ethiopia. The Portuguese under Vasco de Gama, near *three hundred* years ago, recovered this navigation, after it had been intermitted and lost for many centuries.—L.

Verse 18. *Shall utterly abolish*—"Shall disappear"] The ancient versions and an ancient MS. read יחלפו *yachalpu*, plural. One of my MSS. reads יחלוף *yachaloph*, probably a mistake for יחלפו *yachalpu*.

Verses 19-21. *Into the holes of the rocks*—"Into caverns of rocks"] The country of Judea being mountainous and rocky, is full of caverns, as appears from the history of David's persecution under Saul. At En-gedi, in particular, there was a cave so large that David with *six hundred* men hid themselves in the sides of it; and Saul entered the mouth of the cave without perceiving that any one was there, 1 Sam. xxiv. *Josephus*, Antiq., lib. xiv., c. 15, and Bell. Jud., lib. 1, c. 16, tells us of a numerous gang of banditti, who, having infested the country, and being pursued by Herod with his army, retired into certain caverns almost inaccessible, near Arbela in Galilee, where they were with great difficulty subdued. Some of these were natural, others artificial. "Beyond Damascus," says *Strabo*, lib. xvi., "are two mountains called Trachones; from which the country has the name of Trachonitis; and from hence towards Arabia and Iturea, are certain rugged mountains, in which there are deep caverns, one of which will hold *four thousand* men." *Tavernier*, Voyage de Perse, part ii., chap. 4, speaks of a grot, between Aleppo and Bir, that would hold near *three thousand* horse. "*Three* hours distant from Sidon, about a mile from the sea, there runs along a high rocky mountain, in the sides of which are hewn a multitude of grots, all very little differing from each other. They have entrances about two feet square: on the inside you find in most or all of them a room of about four yards square. There are of these subterraneous caverns *two hundred* in number. It may, with probability at least, be concluded that these places were contrived for the use of the living, and not of the dead. *Strabo* describes the habitations of the Troglodytæ to have been somewhat of this kind."—*Maundrell*, p. 118. The Horites, who dwelt in Mount Seir, were Troglodytæ, as their name הרים *horim*, imports. But those mentioned by *Strabo* were on each side of the Arabian gulf. Mohammed (Koran, chap. xv. xxvi.) speaks of a tribe of Arabians, the tribe of Thamud, "who hewed houses out of the mountains, to secure themselves." Thus, "because of the Midianites, the children of Israel made them the dens which are in the mountains, and caves and strong holds," Judg. vi. 2. To these they betook themselves for refuge in times of distress and hostile invasion: "When the men of Israel saw that they were in a strait, for the people were distressed, then the people did hide themselves in caves, and in thickets, and in rocks, and in high places, and in pits," 1 Sam. xiii. 6, and see Jer. xli. 9. Therefore "to enter into the rock, to go into the holes of the rocks, and into the caves of the earth," was to them a very proper and familiar image to express terror and consternation. The prophet Hosea, chap. x. 8, hath carried the same image farther, and added great strength and spirit to it:

"They shall say to the mountains, Cover us;
And to the hills, Fall on us;"

which image, together with these of Isaiah, is adopted by the sublime author of the Revelation, chap. vi. 15, 16, who frequently borrows his imagery from our prophet.—L.

Verse 20. *Which they made* each one *for himself to worship*—"Which they have made to worship"] The word לו *lo, for himself*, is omitted by two ancient MSS., and is unnecessary. It does not appear that any copy of the *Septuagint* has it, except MS. *Pachom*, and MS. I. D. II., and they have ἑαυτοις, להם *lahem, to themselves.*

To the moles] They shall carry their idols with them into the dark caverns, old ruins, or desolate places, to which they shall flee for refuge; and so shall give them up, and relinquish them to the filthy animals that frequent such places, and have taken possession of them as their proper habitation. *Bellonius*, *Greaves*, *P. Lucas*, and many other travellers, speak of bats of an enormous size, as inhabiting the Great Pyramid. See *Harmer*, Obs., vol. ii., 455. Three MSS. express חפרפרות *chapharperoth, the moles*, as one word.

Verse 22. *Cease ye from man*] Trust neither in him, nor in the gods that he has invented. Neither he, nor they, can either save or destroy.

CHAPTER III

The whole of this chapter, with the first verse of the next, is a prophecy of those calamities that should be occasioned by the Babylonish invasion and captivity. These calamities are represented as so great and so general, that even royal honours, in such a state, are so far from being desirable, that hardly any can be got to accept them, 1–7. *This visitation is declared to be the consequence of their profanity and guilt; for which the prophet farther reproves and threatens them,* 8–15. *Particular amplification of the distress of the delicate and luxurious daughters of Zion; whose deplorable situation is finely contrasted with their former prosperity and ease,* 16–26.

A. M. cir. 3244 B. C. cir. 760 Anno Olymp. Quintæ I. Ante Urbem Conditam 7

FOR, behold, the Lord, the
LORD of hosts, [a]doth take
away from Jerusalem and from
Judah [b]the stay and the staff, the
whole stay of bread, and the
whole stay of water,
2 [c]The mighty man, and the
man of war, the judge, and the

[a]Jer. xxxvii. 21; xxxviii. 9——[b]Lev. xxvi. 26

[c]See 2 Kings xxiv. 14; Psa. xxiv. 8; xxix. 1

NOTES ON CHAP. III

Verse 1. *The stay and the staff*—"Every stay and support"] *Hebrew*, "the support masculine, and the support feminine:" that is, every kind of support, whether great or small, strong or weak. "*Al Kanitz, wal-kanitzah;* the wild beasts, male and female. Proverbially applied both to fishing and hunting: i. e., I seized the prey, great or little, good or bad. From hence, as *Schultens* observes, is explained Isa. iii. 1, literally, the *male and female stay:* i. e., the strong and weak, the great and small."—*Chappelow*, note on *Hariri*, Assembly I. Compare Eccles. ii. 8.

The Hebrew words משען ומשענה *mashen umashenah* come from the same root שען *shaan*, to lean against, to incline, to support; and here, being masculine and feminine, they may signify all things necessary for the support both of *man* and *woman*. My old MS. understands the staff and stay as meaning particular persons, and translates the verse thus:—**Lo forsoth, the Lordschip Lord of Hoostis schal don awey fro Jerusalem and fro Juda the stalworth and the stronge.**

A. M. cir. 3244 B. C. cir. 760 Anno Olymp. Quintæ I. Ante Urbem Conditam 7

prophet, and the prudent, and
the ancient.
3 The captain of fifty, and the
[d]honourable man, and the counsellor, and the cunning artificer, and the [e]eloquent orator.
4 And I will give [f]children *to be* their
princes, and babes shall rule over them.
5 And the people shall be oppressed, every
one by another, and every one by his neighbour: the child shall behave himself proudly
against the ancient, and the base
against the honourable.
6 When a man shall take hold
of his brother of the house of his
father, *saying,* Thou hast clothing, be thou
our ruler, and *let* this ruin *be* under thy hand:
7 In that day shall he [g]swear, saying, I will
not be a [h]healer; for in my house *is* neither
bread nor clothing: make me not a ruler of
the people.
8 For Jerusalem [i]is ruined, and Judah is

A. M. cir. 3244 B. C. cir. 760 Anno Olymp. Quintæ I. Ante Urbem Conditam 7

[d]Heb. *a man eminent in countenance*——[e]Or, *skilful of speech*——[f]Eccles. x. 16

[g]Heb. *lift up* the hand; Gen. xiv. 22——[h]Heb. *binder up*——[i]Mic. iii. 12

The two following verses, 2, 3, are very clearly explained by the sacred historian's account of the event, the captivity of Jehoiachin by Nebuchadnezzar king of Babylon: "And he carried away all Jerusalem, and all the princes, and all the mighty men of valour, even ten thousand captives, and all the craftsmen and smiths; none remained save the poorest sort of the people of the land," 2 Kings xxiv. 14. Which is supplied by our version.

Verse 4. *I will give children* to be *their princes*—"I will make boys their princes"] This also was fully accomplished in the succession of weak and wicked princes, from the death of Josiah to the destruction of the city and temple, and the taking of Zedekiah, the last of them, by Nebuchadnezzar.

Babes shall rule over them.] **Dymennysche men schul lordschipen to hem.**—Old MS. Bible.

Verse 6. *Of the house of his father*—"Of his father's house"] For בית *beith, the house*, the ancient interpreters seem to have read מבית *mibbeith, from the house; του οικειου του πατρος αυτου, Septuagint; domesticum patris sui, Vulgate;* which gives no good sense. But the *Septuagint* MS. I. D. II. for οικειου has οικου. And, *his brother, of his father's house*, is little better than a tautology. The case seems to require that the man should apply to a person of some sort of rank and eminence; one that was the head of his father's house, (see Josh. xii. 14,) whether of the house of him who applies to him, or of any other; ראש בית אביו *rosh beith abaiv*, the chief, or head of his father's house. I cannot help suspecting, therefore, that the word ראש *rosh, head, chief*, has been lost out of the text.

Saying] Before שמלה *simlah, garment*, two MSS., one ancient, and the Babylonish *Talmud* have the word לאמר *lemor*, saying; and so the *Septuagint, Vulgate, Syriac* and *Chaldee.* I place it with *Houbigant, after* שמלה *simlah.*

Thou hast clothing—"Take by the garment"] That is, shall entreat him in an humble and supplicating manner. "Ten men shall take hold of the skirt of him that is a Jew, saying, Let us go with you; for we have heard that God is with you," Zech. viii. 23. And so in Isa. iv. 1, the same gesture is used to express earnest and humble entreaty. The behaviour of Saul towards Samuel was of the same kind, when he laid hold on the skirt of his raiment, 1 Sam. xv. 27. The preceding and following verses show, that his whole deportment, in regard to the prophet, was full of submission and humility.

And let *this ruin* be *under thy hand*—"And let thy hand support"] Before תחת ידך *tachath yadecha*, a MS. adds תהיה *tihyeh*, "let it be;" another MS. adds in the same place, תקח בידך *takach beyadecha*, which latter seems to be a various reading of the two preceding words, making a very good sense: "Take into thy hand our ruinous state." *Twenty-one* MSS. of *Kennicott's, thirteen* of *De Rossi's*, one of my own, ancient, and *three* editions of the *Babylonish Talmud* have ידיך *yadeycha*, plural, "thy hands."

Verse 7. *In that day shall he swear*—"Then shall he openly declare"] The *Septuagint, Syriac* and *Jerome*, read וישא *veyissa*, adding the conjunction, which seems necessary in this place.

I will not be a healer] **I am not a leche.**—Old MS. Bible. *Leech* was the ancient English word for a *physician.*

For in my house is *neither bread nor clothing*—"For in my house is neither bread nor raiment"] "It is customary through all the East," says Sir *J. Chardin*, "to gather together an immense quantity of furniture and clothes; for their fashions never alter." Princes and great men are obliged to have a great stock of such things in readiness for presents upon all occasions. "The kings of Persia," says the same author, "have great wardrobes, where there are always many hundreds of habits ready, designed for presents, and sorted," *Harmer*, Observ., II. 11 and 88. A great quantity of provision for the table was equally necessary. The daily provision for Solomon's household, whose attendants were exceedingly numerous, was proportionately great, 1 Kings iv. 22, 23. Even Nehemiah, in his strait circumstances, had a large supply daily for his table; at which he received a *hundred and fifty* of the Jews and rulers, besides those that came from among the neighbouring heathen, Neh. v. 17, 18.

This explains the meaning of the excuse made by him that is desired to undertake the government. He alleges that he has not wherewithal to support the dignity of the station, by such acts of liberality and hospitality as the law of custom required of persons of superior rank. See *Harmer's* Observations, I. 340, II. 88.

Verse 8. *The eyes*—"The cloud"] This word appears to be of very doubtful form, from the printed editions, the MSS., and the ancient versions. The first yod in עיני *eyney*, which is

A. M. cir. 3244
B. C. cir. 760
Anno Olymp.
Quintæ I.
Ante Urbem
Conditam 7

fallen: because their tongue and
their doings *are* against the
LORD, to provoke the eyes of his
glory.
9 The show of their countenance doth witness against them; and they declare their sin
as [k]Sodom, they hide *it* not. Wo unto their
soul! for they have rewarded evil unto themselves.
10 Say ye to the righteous, [l]that *it shall be*
well *with him:* [m]for they shall eat the fruit
of their doings:
11 Wo unto the wicked! [n]*it shall be* ill
with him: for the reward of his
hands shall be [o]given him.
12 *As for* my people, [p]children
are their oppressors, and women
rule over them. O my people, [q]they [r]which
lead thee cause *thee* to err, and [s]destroy the
way of thy paths.
13 The LORD standeth up [t]to plead, and
standeth to judge the people.
14 The LORD will enter into judgment with
the ancients of his people, and the princes
thereof: for ye have [u]eaten [v]up the vineyard;
the spoil of the poor *is* in your houses.

[k]Gen. xiii. 13; xviii. 20, 21; xix. 5——[l]Eccles. viii. 12——[m]Psa. cxxviii. 2——[n]Psa. xi. 6; Eccles. viii. 13——[o]Heb. *done to him*——[p]Ver. 4

[q]Chap. ix. 16——[r]Or, *they which call thee blessed*——[s]Heb. *swallow up*——[t]Mic. vi. 2——[u]Or, *burnt*——[v]Chap. v. 7; Matt. xxi. 33

necessary according to the common interpretation, is in many of them omitted; the two last letters are upon a rasure in *two* MSS. I think it should be ענן *anan*, "a cloud," as the *Syriac* reads; and the allusion is to the cloud in in which the glory of the Lord appeared above the tabernacle; see Exod. xvi. 9, 10; xl. 34-38; Num. xvi. 41, 42.

Either of the readings gives a very good sense. The allusion may be to the cloud of the Divine presence in the wilderness: or the *eyes of the Lord* may be meant, as they *are in every place beholding the evil and the good.* And he cannot look upon iniquity but with abhorrence; therefore, *the eyes of his glory* might be well provoked by their crimes.

Verse 9. *The show of their countenance*] Bishop Lowth has it *the steadfastness of their countenance*—they appear to be bent on iniquity, their eyes tell the wickedness of their hearts. The *eye* is the index of the mind. Envy, hatred, malice, malevolence, concupiscence, and murder, when in the heart, look most intelligently out at the eye. They tell the innocent to be on their guard; and serve the same purpose as the *sonorous rings* in the tail of the *rattlesnake*—they announce the presence of the destroyer.

They declare their sin as Sodom] Impure propensities are particularly legible in the eyes: whoever has beheld the face of a *debauchee* or a *prostitute* knows this; of these it may be said, they wish to appear what they really are. They glory in their iniquity. This is the highest pitch of ungodliness.

They have rewarded evil unto themselves.] Every man's sin is against his own soul. Evil awaiteth sinners—and he that offends his God injures himself.

Verse 10. *Say ye to the righteous*] לצדיק *letsaddik;* the ל *lamed* is added here by one MS. and the *Chaldee.* The righteous is the person, 1. Who fears God. 2. Departs from evil. 3. Walks according to the testimony of God. 4. And expects and prepares for a glorious immortality.

"Pronounce ye."—The reading of this verse is very dubious. The *Septuagint* for אמרו *imru* read נאסר *neasor*, or both, אמרו נאסר *imru neasor*, and כי לא טוב לנו *ki lo tob lanu.* Δησωμεν τον δικαιον, ὁτι δυσχρηστος ἡμιν εστι. Perhaps, for אמרו *imru*, the true reading may be אשרו *ashsheru*, "bless you;" or אמרו אשרי *imru ashrey*, "say ye, blessed is." The *Vulgate* and an ancient MS. read in the singular number, יאכל *yochel, comedat*, "he shall eat."

"It shall be *well* with him:"—כי טוב *ki tob*, "that good." Say nothing to such but *good.* He is a *good man*, he does nothing but *good*, and has a *good* God to deal with, from whom he expects nothing but *goodness.* It shall be well with such in all circumstances of life. 1. In prosperity. 2. In adversity. 3. In sickness. 4. In health. 5. In death. 6. In judgment. And, 7. Through eternity. In every case, occurrence, and circumstance, he *shall eat the fruit of his doings*—he shall derive benefit from being a righteous man, and walking in a righteous way.

Verse 11. *Wo unto the wicked*] לרשע *lerasha*, the man who is, 1. Evil in his heart. 2. Evil in his purposes. 3. Evil in his life. As he is *wicked*, he does that which is *wicked;* and is influenced by the *wicked one*, of whom he is the *servant* and the *son.* It shall be *ill* with him, רע *ra;* in a single word say to him—*evil! Of* him you can speak no good; and *to* him you can speak no good—all is *evil, in* him—*before* him—*after* him—*round about* him—*above* him—*below* him. Evil in *time*—evil through *eternity!*

The reward of his hands.] What he has deserved he shall get. He shall be paid that for which he has laboured, and his reward shall be in proportion to his work. O, what a lot is that of the wicked! Cursed in time, and accursed through eternity!

Verse 12. *Err*—"Pervert"] בלעו *billeu*, "swallow." Among many unsatisfactory methods of accounting for the unusual meaning of this word in this place, I choose Jarchi's explication, as making the best sense. "Read בללו *billalu*, 'confound.' *Syriac*."—Dr. *Judd.* "Read בהלו *beholu*, 'disturb or trouble.'"—*Secker.* So *Septuagint.*

This verse might be read, "The collectors of grapes shall be their oppressors; and usurers (*noshim*, instead of *nashim*, women) shall rule over them."

Verse 13. *The people*—"His people"] עמו *ammo, Septuagint.*

Verse 14. *The vineyard.*—"My vineyard"] כרמי *carmi, Septuagint, Chaldee, Jerome.*

A. M. cir. 3244
B. C. cir. 760
Anno Olymp. Quintæ I.
Ante Urbem Conditam 7

15 What mean ye *that* ye
[w]beat my people to pieces, and
grind the faces of the poor? saith
the Lord GOD of hosts.
16 Moreover the LORD saith, Because the
daughters of Zion are haughty,
and walk with stretched forth
necks and [x]wanton eyes, walking and [y]mincing *as* they go,
and making a tinkling with their feet:

A. M. cir. 3244
B. C. cir. 760
Anno Olymp. Quintæ I.
Ante Urbem Conditam 7

[w]Chap. lviii. 4; Mic. iii. 2, 3

[x]Heb. *deceiving with their eyes*——[y]Or, *tripping nicely*

Verse 15. *And grind the faces*] The expression and the image is strong, to denote grievous oppression but is exceeded by the prophet Micah, chap. iii. 1-3:—

"Hear, I pray you, ye chiefs of Jacob,
And ye princes of the house of Israel:
Is it not yours to know what is right?
Ye that hate good and love evil:
Who tear their skins from off them,
And their flesh from off their bones;
Who devour the flesh of my people;
And flay from off them their skin;
And their bones they dash in pieces;
And chop them asunder, as morsels for the pot:
And as flesh thrown into the midst of the caldron."

In the last line but one, for כאשר *keasher*, read, by the transposition of a letter, כשאר *kisher*, with the *Septuagint* and *Chaldee*.

Verse 16. *And wanton eyes*—"And falsely setting off their eyes with paint"] Hebrew, *falsifying* their eyes. I take this to be the true meaning and literal rendering of the word; from שקר *shakar*. The Masoretes have pointed it, as if it were from שקר *sakar*, a different word. This arose, as I imagine, from their supposing that the word was the same with סקר *sakar*, *Chaldee*, "intueri, innuere oculis;" or that it had an affinity with the noun סיקרא *sikra*, which the Chaldeans, or the rabbins at least, use for *stibium*, the mineral which was commonly used in colouring the eyes. See *Jarchi's* comment on the place. Though the colouring of the eyes with stibium be not particularly here expressed, yet I suppose it to be implied; and so the Chaldee paraphrase explains it; stibio linitis oculis, "with eyes dressed with stibium." This fashion seems to have prevailed very generally among the Eastern people in ancient times; and they retain the very same to this day.

Pietro della Valle, giving a description of his wife, an Assyrian lady born in Mesopotamia, and educated at Bagdad, whom he married in that country, (*Viaggi*, Tom. I., Lettera 17,) says, "Her eyelashes, which are long, and, according to the custom of the East, dressed with stibium, (as we often read in the Holy Scriptures of the Hebrew women of old, Jer. iv. 30; Ezek. xxiii. 40; and in Xenophon, of Astyages the grandfather of Cyrus, and of the Medes of that time, *Cyropæd.* lib. i.,) give a dark, and at the same time a majestic, shade to the eyes." "Great eyes," says *Sandys*, Travels, p. 67, speaking of the Turkish women, "they have in principal repute; and of those the blacker they be the more amiable; insomuch that they put between the eyelids and the eye a certain black powder, with a fine long pencil, made of a mineral, brought from the kingdom of Fez, and called *Alcohole;* which by the not disagreeable staining of the lids doth better set forth the whiteness of the eye; and though it be troublesome for a time, yet it comforteth the sight, and repelleth ill humours." Vis ejus (stibii) astringe ac refrigerare, principalis autem circa oculos; namque ideo etiam plerique Platyophthalmon id appellavere, quoniam in calliblepharis mulierum dilatat oculos; et fluxiones inhibet oculorum exulcerationesque. "It is astringent in its virtue, and refrigerant, and to be chiefly employed about the eyes, and it is called *Platyophthalmon*, for being put into those ointments with which women *beautify their eyes*, it dilates them, removes defluxions, and heals any ulcerations that may be about the eyelids."—*Pliny*, Nat. Hist. xxxiii. 6.

Ille supercilium madida fuligine tactum
Obliqua producit acu, pingitque trementes
Attollens oculos Juv. Sat. ii. 93.

One his eyebrows, tinged with black soot,
Lengthens with an oblique bodkin, and paints,
Lifting up his winking eyes.

"But none of those [Moorish] ladies," says Dr. *Shaw*, Travels, p. 294, fol., "take themselves to be completely dressed, till they have tinged the hair and edges of their eyelids with *alkahol*, the powder of lead ore. This operation is performed by dipping first into the powder a small wooden bodkin of the thickness of a quill; and then drawing it afterwards through the eyelids, over the ball of the eye." Ezekiel, chap. xxiii. 40, uses the same word in the form of a verb, כחלת עניך *cachalt eynayik*, "thou didst dress thine eyes with *alcahol;*" which the *Septuagint* render εστιβιζου τους οφθαλμους σου, "thou didst dress thine eyes with *stibium;*" just as they do when the word פוך *phuch* is employed: compare 2 Kings ix. 30; Jer. iv. 30. They supposed, therefore, that פוך *phuch* and כחל *cachal*, or in the Arabic form, *alcahol*, meant the same thing; and probably the mineral used of old for this purpose was the same that is used now; which Dr. *Shaw* (*ibid.* note) says is "a rich lead ore, pounded into an impalpable powder." *Alcoholados;* the word משקרות *meshakkeroth* in this place is thus rendered in an old Spanish translation.—*Sanctius*. See also *Russell's* Nat. Hist. of Aleppo, p. 102.

The following inventory, as one may call it, of the wardrobe of a Hebrew lady, must, from its antiquity, and the nature of the subject, have been very obscure even to the most ancient interpreters which we have of it; and from its obscurity must have been also peculiarly liable to the mistakes of transcribers. However, it is rather matter of curiosity than of importance; and is indeed, upon the whole, more intelligible and less corrupted than one might have reasonably expected. *Clemens Alexandrinus*, Pædag. lib. ii., c. 12, and *Julius Pollux*, lib. vii., c 22, have each of them preserved from a comedy of *Aristophanes*, now lost, a similar catalogue of the several parts of the dress and ornaments of a Grecian lady; which, though much more capable of illustration from other writers, though of

A. M. cir. 3244
B. C. cir. 760
Anno Olymp. Quintæ I.
Ante Urbem Conditam 7

17 Therefore the LORD will
smite with [z]a scab the crown of
the head of the daughters of
Zion, and the LORD will [a]dis-
cover [b]their secret parts.

18 In that day the LORD will
take away the bravery of *their*
tinkling ornaments *about their*
feet, and *their* [c]cauls, and *their*
[d]round tires like the moon,

[z]Deuteronomy xxviii. 24——[a]Hebrew, *make naked*——[b]Chapter xlvii. 2, 3; Jeremiah xiii. 22; Nahum ii. 5——[c]Or, *net-works*——[d]Judges viii. 21

later date, and quoted and transmitted down to us by two different authors, yet seems to be much less intelligible, and considerably more corrupted, than this passage of Isaiah. *Salmasius* has endeavoured, by comparing the two quotations, and by much critical conjecture and learned disquisition, to restore the true reading, and to explain the particulars; with what success, I leave to the determination of the learned reader, whose curiosity shall lead him to compare the passage of the comedian with this of the prophet, and to examine the critic's learned labours upon it. *Exercit. Plinian*, p. 1148; or see *Clem. Alex.* as cited above, edit. Potter, where the passage, as corrected by *Salmasius*, is given.

Nich. Guel. Schroederus, professor of oriental languages in the University of Marpurg, has published a very learned and judicious treatise upon this passage of Isaiah. The title of it is, "Commentarius Philologico-Criticus de Vestitu Mulierum Hebræarum ad Iesai iii. ver. 16-24. Lugd. Bat. 1745." 4to. As I think no one has handled this subject with so much judgment and ability as this author, I have for the most part followed him, in giving the explanation of the several terms denoting the different parts of dress, of which this passage consists; signifying the reasons of my dissent, where he does not give me full satisfaction.

Bishop Lowth's translation of these verses is the following:—

18. In that day will the Lord take from them the ornaments,
Of the feet-rings, and the net-works, and the crescents;
19. The pendants, and the bracelets, and the veils;
20. The tires, and the fetters, and the zones,
And the perfume-boxes, and the amulets;
21. The rings, and the jewels of the nostrils;
22. The embroidered robes, and the tunics,
And the cloaks, and the little purses,
23. The transparent garments, and the fine linen vests,
And the turbans, and the mantles.
24. And there shall be instead of perfume, a putrid ulcer;
And instead of well-girt raiment, rags;
And instead of high-dressed hair, baldness;
And instead of a zone, a girdle of sackcloth;
And sun-burnt skin, instead of beauty.

The daughters of Zion—walk] What is meant by these several kinds of action and articles of dress cannot be well conjectured. How our ancestors understood them will appear from the following, which is the translation of these verses in my old MS. Bible:—

16. **The doughteris of Syon wenten with stright out necks, and in beckes** (winking) **of eegen, geeden and flappeden with hondis for joye, and geeden; and with theire feet in curyous goying geeden;**—17. **the Lord schall fully make ballid the top of the doughtris of Syon: and the Lord the her of hem schal naken. And for ournemente schal be schenschip.**

18. **In that day, the Lord schal don awey the ournement of Schoon and hoosis;** 19. **and beegis, and brochis, and armeerclis, and mytris;** 20. **and coombis, and rybanys and reversis at the hemmys, and oynment boris and ereringis;** 21. **and ryngis and jemmys in the frount hongynge;** 22. **and chaunginge clothis, and litil pallis, and scheetis, and prynys;** 23. **and scheweris, and necke kercheuys, and fyletis, and roketis;** 24. **and ther schal be for swot smel, stynke, and for gyrdil, a litil coord; and for crisp her, ballidnesse; and for brest boond and heyr.**

Some of these things are hard to be understood, though I think this version as good as that of the very learned bishop: but there is little doubt that articles of clothing and dress bore these names in the fourteenth century.

Verse 17. *The Lord will smite*—"Will the Lord humble"] ταπεινωσει, *Septuagint;* and so *Syriac* and *Chaldee*. For שפח *sippach* they read שפל *shaphal*. Instead of יהוה *Yehovah*, many MSS. have אדני *Adonai*.

Will discover their secret parts—"Expose their nakedness"] It was the barbarous custom of the conquerors of those times to strip their captives naked, and to make them travel in that condition, exposed to the inclemency of the weather; and the worst of all, to the intolerable heat of the sun. But this to the women was the height of cruelty and indignity; and especially to such as those here described, who had indulged themselves in all manner of delicacies of living, and all the superfluities of ornamental dress; and even whose faces had hardly ever been exposed to the sight of man. This is always mentioned as the hardest part of the lot of captives. Nahum, chap. iii. 5, 6, denouncing the fate of Nineveh, paints it in very strong colours:—

"Behold, I am against thee, saith JEHOVAH, God of hosts:
And I will discover thy skirts upon thy face;
And I will expose thy nakedness to the nations;
And to the kingdoms thy shame.
And I will throw ordures upon thee;
And I will make thee vile, and set thee as a gazing-stock."

Verse 18. *Ornaments* about their feet—"The ornaments of the feet rings"] The late learned Dr. *Hunt*, professor of Hebrew and Arabic in the University of Oxford, has very well explained the word עכס both verb and noun, in his very ingenious Dissertation on Prov. vii. 22, 23. The verb means to *skip*, to *bound*, to *dance along;* and the noun, those *ornaments* of the *feet* which the Eastern ladies wore; *chains* or *rings*, which made a tinkling sound as they moved nimbly in walking. *Eugene Roger*, Description de la Terre Sainte, Liv. ii. ch. 2,

A. M. cir. 3244 B. C. cir. 760 Anno Olymp. Quintæ I. Ante Urbem Conditam 7

19 The [e]chains, and the bracelets, and the [f]mufflers,
20 The bonnets, and the ornaments of the legs, and the head-
bands, and the [g]tablets, and the ear-rings,
21 The rings, and nose-
jewels,
22 The changeable suits of
apparel, [h]and the mantles, and
the wimples, and the crisping-pins,

A. M. cir. 3244 B. C. cir. 760 Anno Olymp. Quintæ I. Ante Urbem Conditam 7

[e]Or, *sweet balls*——[f]Or, *spangled ornaments* [g]Heb. *houses of the soul*——[h]Dan. iii. 21, in the margin

speaking of the Arabian women, of the first rank in Palestine, says,—"Au lieu de brasselets elles ont de menottes d'argent, qu'elles portent aux poignets et aux pieds; où sont attachez quantitè de petits annelets d'argent, qui font un cliquetis comme d'une cymbale, lorsqu'elles cheminent ou se mouvent quelque peu." See Dr. *Hunt's Dissertation;* where he produces other testimonies to the same purpose from authors of travels. Hindoo women of ill fame wear loose ornaments one above another on their ankles, which at every motion make a tinkling noise. See WARD.

And their *cauls*—"the net-works"] I am obliged to differ from the learned *Schroederus* almost at first setting out. He renders the word שבישים *shebisim* by *soliculi*, little ornaments, bullæ, or studs, in shape representing the *sun*, and so answering to the following word שהרנים *saharonim, lunulæ*, crescents. He supposes the word to be the same with שמישים *shemishim*, the י *yod* in the second syllable making the word diminutive, and the letter מ *mem* being changed for ב *beth*, a letter of the same organ. How just and well founded his authorities for the transmutation of these letters in the Arabic language are, I cannot pretend to judge; but as I know of no such instance in Hebrew, it seems to me a very forced etymology. Being dissatisfied with this account of the matter, I applied to my good friend above mentioned, the late Dr. *Hunt*, who very kindly returned the following answer to my inquiries:—

"I have consulted the Arabic Lexicons, as well MS. as printed, but cannot find שביסים *shebisim* in any of them, nor any thing belonging to it; so that no help is to be had from that language towards clearing up the meaning of this difficult word. But what the *Arabic* denies, the *Syriac* perhaps may afford; in which I find the verb שבש *shabas*, to *entangle* or *interweave*, an etymology which is equally favourable to our marginal translation, *net-works*, with שבץ *shabats, to make chequer work*, or *embroider*, (the word by which *Kimchi* and others have explained שבים *shabis;*) and has moreover this advantage over it, that the letters ש *sin* and ס *samech* are very frequently put for each other, but צ *tsaddi* and ס *samech* scarcely ever. Aben Ezra joins שביסים *shebisim* and עכסים *achasim*, which immediately precedes it, together; and says that שבים *shabis* was *the ornament of the legs*, as עכס *eches* was *of the feet.* His words are, שבים תכשיט של שוקים כמו עכס של רגלים—L."

Verse 20. *The tablets*] The words בתי הנפש *bottey hannephesh*, which we translate *tablets*, and Bishop *Lowth, perfume boxes*, literally signify *houses of the soul;* and may refer to strong-scented bottles used for pleasure and against fainting; similar to bottles with *otto of roses*, worn by the ladies of the East to the present time.

Verse 21. *Nose-jewels*—"The jewels of the nostril."] נזמי האף *nizmey haaph. Schroederus* explains this, as many others do, of jewels, or strings of pearl hanging from the forehead, and reaching to the upper part of the nose; than which nothing can be more ridiculous, as such are seldom seen on an Asiatic face. But it appears from many passages of Holy Scripture that the phrase is to be literally and properly understood of nose-jewels, rings set with jewels hanging from the nostrils, as ear-rings from the ears, by holes bored to receive them.

Ezekiel, enumerating the common ornaments of women of the first rank, has not omitted this particular, and is to be understood in the same manner, chap. xvi. 11, 12. See also Gen. xxiv. 47:—

"And I decked thee with ornaments;
And I put bracelets upon thine hands,
And a chain on thy neck:
And I put a jewel on thy nose,
And ear-rings on thine ears,
And a splendid crown upon thine head."

And in an elegant proverb of Solomon, Prov. xi. 22, there is a manifest allusion to this kind of ornament, which shows it to have been used in his time:—

"As a jewel of gold in the snout of a swine;
So is a woman beautiful, but wanting discretion."

This fashion, however strange it may appear to us, was formerly and is still common in many parts of the East, among women of all ranks. *Paul Lucas*, speaking of a village or clan of wandering people, a little on this side of the Euphrates, says, (2d Voyage du Levant, tom. i., art. 24,) "The women, almost all of them, travel on foot; I saw none handsome among them. They have almost all of them the nose bored; and wear in it a great ring, which makes them still more deformed." But in regard to this custom, better authority cannot be produced than that of *Pietro della Valle*, in the account which he gives of the lady before mentioned, Signora Maani Gioerida, his own wife. The description of her dress, as to the ornamental parts of it, with which he introduces the mention of this particular, will give us some notion of the taste of the Eastern ladies for finery. "The ornaments of gold and of jewels for the head, for the neck, for the arms, for the legs, and for the feet (for they wear rings even on their toes) are indeed, unlike those of the Turks, carried to great excess, but not of great value: for in Bagdad jewels of high price are either not to be had, or are not used; and they wear such only as are of little value, as turquoises, small rubies, emeralds, carbuncles, garnets, pearls, and the like. My spouse dresses herself with all of them according to their fashion; with exception, however, of certain ugly rings of very large size, set with jewels, which, in truth, very absurdly, it is the custom to wear fastened to one of their nostrils, like buffaloes: an ancient custom, however, in the

A. M. cir. 3244 B. C. cir. 760 Anno Olymp. Quintæ I. Ante Urbem Conditam 7

23 The glasses, [i]and the fine linen, and the hoods, and the veils.

24 And it shall come to pass, *that* instead of sweet smell there shall be stink: and instead of a girdle a rent; and instead of well-set hair [k]baldness; and instead of a stomacher a girding of sackcloth; *and* burning instead of beauty.

25 Thy men shall fall by the sword, and thy [l]mighty in the war.

26 [m]And her gates shall lament and mourn; and she *being* [n]desolate [o]shall [p]sit upon the ground.

[i]Gen. xli. 42——[k]Chap. xxii. 12; Mic. i. 16——[l]Heb. *might*

[m]Jer. xiv. 2; Lam. i. 4——[n]Or, *emptied*——[o]Heb. *cleansed*——[p]Lam. ii. 10

East, which, as we find in the Holy Scriptures, prevailed among the Hebrew ladies even in the time of Solomon, Prov. xi. 22. These nose-rings, in complaisance to me, she has left off; but I have not yet been able to prevail with her cousin and her sisters to do the same; so fond are they of an old custom, be it ever so absurd, who have been long habituated to it." *Viaggi*, Tom. i., Let. 17.

It is the left nostril that is bored and ornamented with rings and jewels. More than *one hundred* drawings from life of Eastern ladies lie now before me, and scarcely *one* is without the nose-jewel: both the arms and wrists are covered with bracelets, arm-circles, &c., as also their legs and feet; the soles of their feet and palms of their hands coloured beautifully red with *henna*, and their hair plaited and ornamented superbly. These beautiful drawings are a fine comment on this chapter.

Verse 23. *The glasses*] The conjunction ו *vau, and*—AND *the glasses*, is added here by *forty-three* of *Kennicott's* and *thirty-four* of *De Rossi's* MSS., and one of my own, ancient, as well as by many *editions*.

And the veils.—"*The transparent garments.*"] Τα διαφανη Λακωνικα, *Sept.* A kind of silken dress, transparent, like gauze; worn only by the most elegant women, and such as dressed themselves elegantius quam necesse esset probis, "more elegantly than modest women should." Such garments are worn to the present day; garments that not only show the shape of every part of the body, but the very colour of the skin. This is evidently the case in some scores of drawings of Asiatic females now before me. This sort of garments was afterwards in use among the Greeks. *Prodicus*, in his celebrated fable (Xenoph. Memorab. Socr. lib. ii.) exhibits the personage of Sloth in this dress: Εσθητα δε, εξ ἡς αν μαλιστα ὡρα διαλαμποι:—

"Her robe betray'd
Through the clear texture every tender limb,
Height'ning the charms it only seem'd to shade;
And as it flow'd adown so loose and thin,
Her stature show'd more tall, more snowy white her skin."

They were called *multitia* and *coa* (*scil, vestimenta*) by the Romans, from their being invented, or rather introduced into Greece, by one *Pamphila* of the island of Cos. This, like other Grecian fashions, was received at Rome, when luxury began to prevail under the emperors. It was sometimes worn even by the men, but looked upon as a mark of extreme effeminacy. See Juvenal, Sat. ii., 65, &c. *Publius Syrus*, who lived when the fashion was first introduced, has given a humorous satirical description of it in two lines, which by chance have been preserved:—

"Æquum est, induere nuptam ventum textilem?
Palam prostare nudam in nebula linea?"

Verse 24. *Instead of sweet smell*—"perfume."] A principal part of the delicacy of the Asiatic ladies consists in the use of baths, and of the richest oils and perfumes; an attention to which is in some degree necessary in those hot countries. Frequent mention is made of the rich ointments of the spouse in the Song of Solomon, Cant. iv. 10, 11:—

"How beautiful are thy breasts, my sister, my spouse!
How much more excellent than wine;
And the odour of thine ointments than all perfumes!
Thy lips drop as the honey-comb, my spouse!
Honey and milk are under thy tongue:
And the odour of thy garments is as the odour of Lebanon."

The preparation for Esther's being introduced to King Ahasuerus was a course of bathing and perfuming for a whole year; "six months with oil of myrrh, and six months with sweet odours;" Esth. ii. 12. See the notes on this place. A diseased and loathsome habit of body, instead of a beautiful skin, softened and made agreeable with all that art could devise, and all that nature, so prodigal in those countries of the richest perfumes, could supply, must have been a punishment the most severe and the most mortifying to the delicacy of these haughty daughters of Sion.

Burning instead of beauty—"A sunburnt skin."] *Gaspar Sanctius* thinks the words כי תחת *ki thachath* an interpolation, because the *Vulgate* has omitted them. The clause כי תחת יפי *ki thachath yophi* seems to me rather to be imperfect at the end. Not to mention that כי *ki*, taken as a noun for *adustio, burning*, is without example, and very improbable. The passage ends abruptly, and seems to want a fuller conclusion.

In agreement with which opinion, of the defect of the Hebrew text in this place, the *Septuagint*, according to MSS. Pachom. and 1 D. ii., and Marchal., which are of the best authority, express it with the same evident marks of imperfection at the end of the sentence; thus: ταυτα σοι αντι καλλωπισμου— The two latter add δου. This chasm in the text, from the loss probably of three or four words, seems therefore to be of long standing.

Taking כי *ki* in its usual sense, as a particle, and supplying לך *lech* from the σοι of the *Septuagint*, it might possibly have been originally somewhat in this form:—

כי תחת יפי תהיה לך רעת מראה
marah raath lech thihyeh yophi thachath ki

"Yea, instead of beauty thou shalt have an ill-favoured countenance."

כי תחת יפי *ki thachath yophi* (q. יחת *yachath,*) "for beauty *shall be destroyed.*" *Syr.* חתת *chathath* or נחת *nachath.*—Dr. DURELL.

"May it not be כהי *cohey, 'wrinkles* instead of beauty?' as from יפה *yaphah* is formed יפי *yephi, yophi;* from מרה *marah,* מרי *meri,* &c.; so from כהה *cahah, to be wrinkled,* כהי *cohey.*" —Dr. JUBB. The כי *ki* is wanting in one MS., and has been omitted by several of the ancients.

Verse 25. *Thy mighty men.*] For גבורתך *geburathech* an ancient MS. has גבורך *gibborech.* The true reading, from the *Septuagint, Vulgate, Syriac,* and *Chaldee,* seems to be גבוריך *gibborayich.*

Verse 26. *Sit upon the ground.*] Sitting on the ground was a posture that denoted mourning and deep distress. The prophet Jeremiah (Lam. ii. 8) has given it the first place among many indications of sorrow, in the following elegant description of the same state of distress of his country:—

"The elders of the daughter of Sion sit on the ground, they are silent:
They have cast up dust on their heads; they have girded themselves with sackcloth;
The virgins of Jerusalem have bowed down their heads to the ground."

"We find Judea," says Mr. Addison, (on Medals, Dial. ii,) "on several coins of Vespasian and Titus, in a posture that denotes sorrow and captivity. I need not mention her sitting on the ground, because we have already spoken of the aptness of such a posture to represent an extreme affliction. I fancy the Romans might have an eye on the customs of the Jewish nation, as well as those of their country, in the several marks of sorrow they have set on this figure. The psalmist describes the Jews lamenting their captivity in the same pensive posture: 'By the waters of Babylon we sat down and wept, when we remembered thee, O Zion.' But what is more remarkable, we find Judea represented as a woman in sorrow sitting on the ground, in a passage of the prophet, that foretells the very captivity recorded on this medal." Mr. *Addison,* I presume, refers to this place of Isaiah; and therefore must have understood it as foretelling the destruction of Jerusalem and the Jewish nation by the Romans: whereas it seems plainly to relate, in its first and more immediate view at least, to the destruction of the city by Nebuchadnezzar, and the dissolution of the Jewish state under the captivity at Babylon.—L.

Several of the coins mentioned here by Mr. *Addison* are in my own collection: and to such I have already referred in this work. I shall describe one here. On the obverse a fine head of the emperor *Vespasian* with this legend, *Imperator Julius Cæsar Vespasianus Augustus, Pontifex Maximus, Tribunitia Potestate Pater Patriæ, Consul* VIII.

On the reverse a tall palm tree, emblem of the land of *Palestine,* the emperor standing on the left, close to the tree, with a trophy behind him; on the right, Judea under the figure of a female captive sitting on the ground, with her head resting on her hand, the elbow on her knee, weeping. Around is this legend, *Judea Capta. Senatus Consulto.* However this prediction may refer proximately to the destruction of Jerusalem by Nebuchadnezzar, I am fully of opinion that it ultimately refers to the final ruin of the Jewish state by the *Romans.* And so it has been understood by the general run of the best and most learned interpreters and critics.

CHAPTER IV

The havoc occasioned by war, and those other calamities which the prophet had been describing in the preceding chapter, are represented as so terribly great that seven women should be left to one man, 1. *Great blessedness of the remnant that shall be accounted worthy to escape these judgments,* 2–4. *The privileges of the Gospel set forth by allusions to the glory and pomp of the Mosaic dispensation,* 5, 6.

A. M. cir. 3244
B. C. cir. 760
Anno Olymp. Quintæ I.
Ante Urbem Conditam 7

AND [a]in that day seven women shall take hold of one man, Saying, We will [b]eat our own bread, and wear our own apparel: only [c]let us be called by thy name, [d]to take away [e]our reproach.

2 In that day shall [f]the branch

A. M. cir. 3244
B. C. cir. 760
Anno Olymp. Quintæ I.
Ante Urbem Conditam 7

[a]Chap. ii. 11, 17——[b]2 Thess. iii. 12——[c]Heb. *let thy name be called upon us* [d]Or, *take thou away*——[e]Luke i. 25——[f]Jer. xxiii. 5; Zech. iii. 8; vi. 12

NOTES ON CHAP. IV

Verse 1. *And seven women*] The division of the chapters has interrupted the prophet's discourse, and broken it off almost in the midst of the sentence. "The numbers slain in battle shall be so great, that seven women shall be left to one man." The prophet has described the greatness of this distress by images and adjuncts the most expressive and forcible. The young women, contrary to their natural modesty, shall become suitors to the men: they will take hold of them, and use the most pressing importunity to be married. In spite of the natural suggestions of jealousy, they will be content with a share only of the rights of marriage in common with several others; and that on hard conditions, renouncing the legal demands of the wife on the husband, (see Exod. xxi. 10,) and begging only the name and credit of wedlock, and to be freed from the reproach of celibacy. See chap. liv. 4, 5. Like Marcia,

A. M. cir. 3244 B. C. cir. 760 Anno Olymp. Quintæ I. Ante Urbem Conditam 7

of the LORD be [g]beautiful and
glorious, and the fruit of the earth
shall be excellent and comely [h]for
them that are escaped of Israel.
3 And it shall come to pass *that he that*
is left in Zion, and *he that* remaineth in
Jerusalem, [i]shall be called holy, *even* every
one that is [k]written [l]among the living in
Jerusalem.
4 When [m]the LORD shall have washed away
the filth of the daughters of Zion, and shall
have purged the blood of Jerusalem from the
midst thereof by the spirit of
judgment, and by the spirit of
burning.
5 And the LORD will create upon
every dwelling place of Mount Zion, and
upon her assemblies, [n]a cloud and smoke by
day, and [o]the shining of a flaming fire by night:
for [p]upon all the glory *shall be* [q]a defence.
6 And there shall be a tabernacle for a shadow in the day-time from the heat, and [r]for
a place of refuge, and for a covert from storm
and from rain.

[g]Heb. *beauty and glory*——[h]Heb. *for the escaping of Israel*——Chap. lx. 21——[k]Phil. iv. 3; Rev. iii. 5 [l]Or, *to life*

[m]Mal. iii. 2, 3——[n]Exod. xiii. 21——[o]Zech. ii. 5 [p]Or, *above*——[q]Heb. *a covering;* chap viii. 14——[r]Chap. xxv. 4

on a different occasion, and in other circumstances:—

> Da tantum nomen inane
> Connubii: liceat tumulo scripsisse, Catonis
> Marcia. LUCAN, ii. 342.

"This happened," says *Kimchi*, "in the days of Ahaz, when Pekah the son of Remaliah slew in Judea *one hundred and twenty thousand* men in one day; see 2 Chron. xviii. 6. The widows which were left were so numerous that the prophet said, 'They are multiplied beyond the sand of the sea,'" Jer. xv. 8.

In that day] These words are omitted in the *Septuagint*, and MSS.

Verse 2. *The branch of the Lord*—"the branch of JEHOVAH"] The Messiah of JEHOVAH, says the *Chaldee*. And *Kimchi* says, *The Messiah, the Son of David.* The branch is an appropriate title of the Messiah; and the fruit of the land means the great Person to spring from the house of Judah, and is only a parallel expression signifying the same; or perhaps the blessings consequent upon the redemption procured by him. Compare chap. xlv. 8, where the same great event is set forth under similar images, and see the note there.

Them that are escaped of Israel—"the escaped of the house of Israel."] A MS. has בית ישראל *beith yisrael*, the house of Israel.

Verse 3. *Written among the living*] That is, whose name stands in the enrolment or register of the people; or every man living, who is a citizen of Jerusalem. See Ezek. xiii. 9, where, "they shall not be written in the writing of the house of Israel," is the same with what immediately goes before, "they shall not be in the assembly of my people." Compare Psa. lxix. 28; lxxxvii. 6; Exod. xxxii. 32. To number and register the people was agreeable to the law of Moses, and probably was always practised; being, in sound policy, useful, and even necessary. David's design of numbering the people was of another kind; it was to enrol them for his army. *Michaelis Mosaisches Recht*, Part iii., p. 227. See also his *Dissert. de Censibus Hebrœorum.*

Verse 4. *The spirit of burning*] Means the fire of God's wrath, by which he will prove and purify his people; gathering them into his furnace, in order to separate the dross from the silver, the bad from the good. The severity of God's judgments, the fiery trial of his servants, Ezekiel (chap. xxii. 18-22) has set forth at large, after his manner, with great boldness of imagery and force of expression. God threatens to gather them into the midst of Jerusalem, as into the furnace; to blow the fire upon them, and to melt them. Malachi, chap. iii. 2, 3, treats the same subject, and represents the same event, under the like images:—

> "But who may abide the day of his coming?
> And who shall stand when he appeareth?
> For he is like the fire of the refiner,
> And like the soap of the fullers.
> And he shall sit refining and purifying the silver;
> And he shall purify the sons of Levi;
> And cleanse them like gold, and like silver;
> That they may be JEHOVAH's ministers,
> Presenting unto him an offering in righteousness."

This is an allusion to a chemist purifying metals. He *first judges* of the state of the ore or adulterated metal. *Secondly*, he kindles the proper degree of *fire*, and applies the requisite test; and thus *separates* the *precious* from the *vile.*

Verse 5. *And the Lord will create*—One MS., the *Septuagint*, and the *Arabic*, have יביא *yabi, He shall bring:* the cloud already exists; the Lord will bring it over. This is a blessed promise of the presence of God in all the assemblies of his people.

Every dwelling place—"the station"] The Hebrew text has, *every station:* but four MSS. (one ancient) omit כל *col, all;* very rightly, as it should seem: for the station was Mount Zion itself, and no other. See Exod. xv. 17. And the *Septuagint*, *Arabic*, and MSS., add the same word כל *col*, before מקראה *mikraeha*, probably right: the word has only changed its place by mistake. מקראיה *mikrayeh*, "the place where they were gathered together in their holy assemblies," says *Sal ben Melech.* But *twenty-five* of *Kennicott's* MSS., and *twenty-two* of *De Rossi's fifty-three* editions, besides the *Septuagint*, *Syriac*, and *Arabic*, have the word in the plural number.

A cloud and smoke by day] This is a manifest allusion to the pillar of a cloud and of fire which attended the Israelites in their passage out of Egypt, and to the glory that rested on the tabernacle, Exod. xiii. 21, xl. 38. The prophet Zechariah, chap. ii. 5, applies the same image to the same purpose:—

"And I will be unto her a wall of fire round about;
And a glory will I be in the midst of her."

That is, the visible presence of God shall protect her. Which explains the conclusion of this verse of Isaiah; where the *makkaph* between כל *col*, and כבוד *cabod*, connecting the two words in construction, which ought not to be connected, has thrown an obscurity upon the sentence, and misled most of the translators.

For upon all the glory shall be *a defence*.] Whatever God creates, he must uphold, or it will fail. Every degree of grace brings with it a degree of power to maintain itself in the soul.

Verse 6. *A tabernacle*] In countries subject to violent tempests, as well as to intolerable heat, a portable tent is a necessary part of a traveller's baggage, for defence and shelter. And to such tents the words of the text make evident allusion. They are to be met with in every part of Arabia and Egypt, and in various other places in the East.

CHAPTER V

This chapter begins with representing, in a beautiful parable, the tender care of God for his people, and their unworthy returns for his goodness, 1–7. *The parable or allegory is then dropped; and the prophet, in plain terms, reproves and threatens them for their wickedness; particularly for their covetousness,* 8–10; *intemperance,* 11; *and inattention to the warnings of Providence,* 12. *Then follows an enumeration of judgments as the necessary consequence. Captivity and famine appear with all their horrors,* 13. *Hades, or the grave, like a ravenous monster, opens wide its jaws, and swallows down its myriads,* 14. *Distress lays hold on all ranks,* 15; *and God is glorified in the execution of his judgments,* 16; *till the whole place is left desolate, a place for the flocks to range in,* 17. *The prophet then pauses; and again resumes his subject, reproving them for several other sins, and threatening them with woes and vengeance,* 18–24; *after which he sums up the whole of his awful denunciation in a very lofty and spirited* epiphonema *or conclusion. The God of armies, having hitherto corrected to no purpose, is represented with inimitable majesty, as only giving a hist, and a swarm of nations hasten to his standard,* 25–27. *Upon a guilty race, unpitied by heaven or by earth, they execute their commission; and leave the land desolate and dark, without one ray of comfort to cheer the horrid gloom,* 28–30.

A. M. cir. 3244
B. C. cir. 760
Anno Olymp. Quintæ I.
Ante Urbem Conditam 7

NOW will I sing to my well-
beloved a song of my be-
loved touching [a]his vineyard.
My well-beloved hath a vineyard
in [b]a very fruitful hill.

2 And he [c]fenced it, and gathered out the stones thereof, and
planted it with the choicest vine,
and built a tower in the midst of
it, and also [d]made a wine press therein: [e]and

[a]Psa. lxxx. 8; Cant. viii. 12; chap. xxvii. 2; Jer. ii. 21; Matt. xxi. 33; Mark xii. 1; Luke xx. 9

[b]Heb. *the horn of the son of oil*——[c]Or, *made a wall about it*——[d]Heb. *hewed*——[e]Deut. xxxii. 6; chap. i. 2, 3

This chapter likewise stands single and alone, unconnected with the preceding or following. The subject of it is nearly the same with that of the first chapter. It is a general reproof of the Jews for their wickedness; but it exceeds that chapter in force, in severity, in variety, and elegance; and it adds a more express declaration of vengeance by the Babylonian invasion.

NOTES ON CHAP. V

Verse 1. *Now will I sing to my well-beloved a song of my beloved*—"Let me sing now a song," &c.] A MS., respectable for its antiquity, adds the word שיר *shir, a song*, after נא *na;* which gives so elegant a turn to the sentence by the repetition of it in the next member, and by distinguishing the members so exactly in the style and manner in the Hebrew poetical composition, that I am much inclined to think it genuine.

A song of my beloved—"A song of loves"] דודי *dodey*, for דודים *dodim; status constructus pro absoluto*, as the grammarians say, as Mic. vi. 16; Lam. iii. 14, 66, so Archbishop *Secker*. Or rather, in all these and the like cases, a mistake of the transcribers, by not observing a small stroke, which in many MSS., is made to supply the ם *mem*, of the plural, thus, /דודי *dodi*. שירת דודים *shirath dodim* is the same with שיר ידידת *shir yedidoth*, Psa. xlv. 1. In this way of understanding it we avoid the great impropriety of making the author of the song, and the person to whom it is addressed, to be the same.

In a very fruitful hill—"On a high and fruitful hill."] Heb. בקרן בן שמן *bekeren ben shamen*, "on a horn the son of oil." The expression is highly descriptive and poetical. "He calls the land of Israel a horn, because it is higher than all lands; as the horn is higher than the whole body; and the son of oil, because it is said to be a land flowing with milk and honey."—*Kimchi* on the place. The parts of animals are, by an easy metaphor, applied to parts of the earth, both in common and poetical language. A promontory is called a cape or head; the Turks call it a nose. "Dorsum immane mari summo;" *Virgil*, a back, or ridge of rocks:—

"Hanc latus angustum jam se cogentis in arctum
Hesperiæ tenuem producit in æquora *linguam*,
Adriacas flexis claudit quæ *cornibus* undas."

A. M. cir. 3244 B. C. cir. 760 Anno Olymp. Quintæ I. Ante Urbem Conditam 7

he looked that it should bring forth grapes, and it brought forth wild grapes.

3 And now, O inhabitants of Jerusalem, and men of Judah, [f]judge, I pray you, betwixt me and my vineyard.

4 What could have been done

[f]Romans, chap. iii. 4

Lucan, ii. 612, of *Brundusium*, i. e., Βρεντεσιον, which, in the ancient language of that country, signifies stag's head, says *Strabo*. A horn is a proper and obvious image for a mountain or mountainous country. *Solinus*, cap. viii., says, "Italiam, ubi longius processerit, in *cornua* duo scindi;" that is, the high ridge of the Alps, which runs through the whole length of it, divides at last into two ridges, one going through Calabria, the other through the country of the Brutii. "Cornwall is called by the inhabitants in the British tongue *Kernaw*, as lessening by degrees like a horn, running out into promontories like so many horns. For the Britons call a horn *corn*, in the plural *kern*."—*Camden*. "And *Sammes* is of opinion, that the country had this name originally from the Phœnicians, who traded hither for tin; *keren*, in their language, being a *horn*."—*Gibson*.

Here the precise idea seems to be that of a high mountain standing by itself; "vertex montis, aut pars montis ad aliis divisa;" which signification, says *I. H. Michaelis*, Bibl. *Hallens*., Not. in loc., the word has in Arabic.

Judea was in general a mountainous country, whence Moses sometimes calls it The Mountain, "Thou shalt plant them in the mountain of thine inheritance;" Exod. xv. 17. "I pray thee, let me go over, and see the good land beyond Jordan; that goodly mountain, and Lebanon;" Deut. iii. 25. And in a political and religious view it was detached and separated from all the nations round it. Whoever has considered the descriptions given of Mount Tabor, (see *Reland*, Palæstin.; *Eugene Roger*, Terre Sainte, p. 64,) and the views of it which are to be seen in books of travels, (*Maundrell*, p. 114; *Egmont* and *Heyman*, vol. ii., p. 25; *Thevenot*, vol. i., p. 429,) its regular conic form rising singly in a plain to a great height, from a base small in proportion, and its beauty and fertility to the very top, will have a good idea of "a horn the son of oil;" and will perhaps be induced to think that the prophet took his image from that mountain.

Verse 2. *And gathered out the stones*—"And he cleared it from the stones"] This was agreeable to the husbandry: "Saxa, summa parte terræ, et vites et arbores lædunt; ima parte refrigerant;" *Columell.* de arb. iii. "Saxosum facile est expedire lectione lapidum;" *Id.* ii. 2. "Lapides, qui supersunt, [al. insuper sunt,] hieme rigent, æstate fervescunt; idcirco satis, arbustis, et vitibus nocent;" *Pallad.* i. 6. A piece of ground thus cleared of the stones *Persius*, in his hard way of metaphor, calls "exossatus ager," *an unboned field;* Sat. vi. 52.

The choicest vine—"Sorek"] Many of the ancient interpreters, the *Septuagint*, *Aquila*, and *Theod.*, have retained this word as a proper name; I think very rightly. Sorek was a valley lying between Ascalon and Gaza, and running far up eastward in the tribe of Judah. Both Ascalon and Gaza were anciently famous for wine; the former is mentioned as such by *Alexander Trallianus;* the latter by several authors, quoted by *Reland*, Palæst., p. 589 and 986. And it seems that the upper part of the valley of Sorek, and that of Eshcol, where the spies gathered the single cluster of grapes, which they were obliged to bear between two upon a staff, being both near to Hebron were in the same neighbourhood, and that all this part of the country abounded with rich vineyards. Compare Num. xiii. 22, 23; Judg. xvi. 3, 4. *P. Nau* supposes Eshcol and Sorek to be only different names for the same valley. Voyage Noveau de la Terre Sainte, lib. iv., chap. 18. See likewise *De Lisle's* posthumous map of the Holy Land. Paris, 1763. See *Bochart*, Hieroz. ii., col. 725. *Thevenot*, i, p. 406. *Michaelis* (note on Judg. xvi. 4, German translation) thinks it probable, from some circumstances of the history there given, that Sorek was in the tribe of Judah, not in the country of the Philistines.

The vine of Sorek was known to the Israelites, being mentioned by Moses, Gen. xlix. 11, before their coming out of Egypt. Egypt was not a wine country. "Throughout this country there are no wines;" *Sandys*, p. 101. At least in very ancient times they had none. *Herodotus*, ii. 77, says it had no vines and therefore used an artificial wine made of barley. That is not strictly true, for the vines of Egypt are spoken of in Scripture, Psa. lxxviii. 47; cv. 33; and see Gen. xl. 11, by which it should seem that they drank only the fresh juice pressed from the grape, which was called οινος αμπελινος; *Herodot.*, ii. 37. But they had no large vineyards, nor was the country proper for them, being little more than one large plain, annually overflowed by the Nile. The Mareotic in later times is, I think, the only celebrated Egyptian wine which we meet with in history. The vine was formerly, as *Hasselquist* tells us it is now, "cultivated in Egypt for the sake of eating the grapes, not for wine, which is brought from Candia," &c. "They were supplied with wine from Greece, and likewise from Phœnicia," *Herodot.*, iii. 6. The vine and the wine of Sorek therefore, which lay near at hand for importation into Egypt, must in all probability have been well known to the Israelites, when they sojourned there. There is something remarkable in the manner in which Moses, Gen. xlix. 11, makes mention of it, which, for want of considering this matter, has not been attended to; it is in Jacob's prophecy of the future prosperity of the tribe of Judah:—

"Binding his foal to the vine,
And his ass's colt to his own sorek;
He washeth his raiment in wine,
And his cloak in the blood of grapes."

I take the liberty of rendering שרקה *sorekah*, for שרקו *soreko*, his sorek, as the Masoretes *do by pointing* עירה *iroh*, for עירו *iro*, his foal. עיר *ir*, might naturally enough appear in the feminine form; but it is not at all probable that שרק *sorek* ever should. By naming particularly the vine of Sorek, and as the vine

A. M. cir. 3244
B. C. cir. 760
Anno Olymp. Quintæ I.
Ante Urbem Conditam 7

more to my [g]vineyard, that I
have not done in it? wherefore,
when I looked that it should
bring forth grapes, brought it
forth wild grapes?

5 And now go to; I will tell
you what I will do to my
vineyard: [h]I will take away
the hedge thereof, and it shall
be eaten up; *and* break down [i]the wall

[g]Luke xiii. 6, 7, 8, 9, 10

[h]Psa. lxxx. 12——[i]Lam. ii. 8

belonging to Judah, the prophecy intimates the very part of the country which was to fall to the lot of that tribe. Sir *John Chardin* says, "that at Casbin, a city of Persia, they turn their cattle into the vineyards after the vintage, to browse on the vines." He speaks also of vines in that country so large that he could hardly compass the trunks of them with his arms. Voyages, tom. iii., p. 12, 12mo. This shows that the ass might be securely bound to the vine, and without danger of damaging the tree by browsing on it.

And built a tower in the midst of it] Our Saviour, who has taken the general idea of one of his parables, Matt. xxi. 33, Mark xii. 1, from this of Isaiah, has likewise inserted this circumstance of building a tower; which is generally explained by commentators as designed for the keeper of the vineyard to watch and defend the fruits. But for this purpose it was usual to make a little temporary hut, (Isa. i. 8,) which might serve for the short season while the fruit was ripening, and which was removed afterwards. The tower therefore should rather mean a building of a more permanent nature and use; the farm, as we may call it, of the vineyard, containing all the offices and implements, and the whole apparatus necessary for the culture of the vineyard, and the making of the wine. To which image in the allegory, the situation, the manner of building, the use, and the whole service of the temple, exactly answered. And so the *Chaldee* paraphrast very rightly expounds it: Et statui eos (Israelitas) ut plantam vineæ selectæ et ædificavi *Sanctuarium* meum in medio illorum. "And I have appointed the Israelites as a plant of a chosen vine, and I have built my *sanctuary* in the midst of them." So also *Hieron.* in loc. Ædificavit quoque turrim in medio ejus; templum videlicet in media civitate. "He built also a tower in the midst of it, viz., his *own temple* in the midst of the city." That they have still such towers or buildings for use or pleasure, in their gardens in the East, see *Harmer's* Observations, ii. p. 241.

And also made a wine-press therein.—"And hewed out a lake therein."] This image also our Saviour has preserved in his parable. יקב *yekeb;* the *Septuagint* render it here προληνιον, and in four other places ὑποληνιον, Isa. xvi. 10; Joel iii. 13; Hag. ii. 17; Zech. xiv. 10, I think more properly; and this latter word St. Mark uses. It means not the wine-press itself, or *calcatorium*, which is called גת *gath,* or פורה *purah;* but what the Romans called *lacus,* the *lake;* the large open place or vessel, which by a conduit or spout received the *must* from the wine-press. In very hot countries it was perhaps necessary, or at least very convenient, to have the lake under ground, or in a cave hewed out of the side of the rock, for coolness, that the heat might not cause too great a fermentation, and sour the must. Vini confectio instituitur in cella, vel intimæ domus camera quadam a ventorum ingressu remota. *Kempfer*, of Shiras wine. *Amœn. Exot.* p. 376. For the wind, to which that country is subject, would injure the wine. "The wine-presses in Persia," says Sir *John Chardin*, "are formed by making hollow places in the ground, lined with masons' work." *Harmer's* Observations, i., p. 392. See a print of one in *Kempfer*, p. 377. *Nonnus* describes at large Bacchus hollowing the inside of a rock, and hewing out a place for the wine-press, or rather the lake:—

Και σκοπελους ελαχηνε· πεδοσκαφεος δε σιδηρου
Θηγαλεῃ γλωχινι μυχον κοιληνατο πετρης·
Λειηνας δε μετωπα βαθυνομενων κενεωνων
Αφρον [f. ακρον] εΰστραφυλοιο τυπον ποιησατο λενου.
DIONYSIAC. lib. xii., l. 331.

"He pierced the rock; and with the sharpen'd tool
Of steel well-temper'd scoop'd its inmost depth:
Then smooth'd the front, and form'd the dark recess
In just dimensions for the foaming lake."

And he looked—"And he expected"] Jeremiah, chap. ii. 21, uses the same image, and applies it to the same purpose, in an elegant paraphrase of this part of Isaiah's parable, in his flowing and plaintive manner:—

"But I planted thee a sorek, a scion perfectly genuine:
How then art thou changed, and become to me the degenerate shoots of the strange vine!"

Wild grapes—"poisonous berries."] באשים *beushim*, not merely useless, unprofitable grapes, such as wild grapes; but grapes offensive to the smell, noxious, poisonous. By the force and intent of the allegory, to good grapes ought to be opposed fruit of a dangerous and pernicious quality; as, in the explication of it, to judgment is opposed tyranny, and to righteousness, oppression. גפן *gephen*, the vine, is a common name or genus, including several species under it; and Moses, to distinguish the true vine, or that from which wine is made, from the rest, calls it, Num. vi. 4, גפן היין *gephen haiyayin*, the wine-vine. Some of the other sorts were of a poisonous quality, as appears from the story related among the miraculous acts of Elisha, 2 Kings iv. 39-41. "And one went out into the field to gather potherbs; and he found a field vine, and he gathered from it wild fruit, his lapful; and he went and shred them into the pot of pottage, for they knew them not. And they poured it out for the men to eat: and it came to pass, as they were eating of the pottage, that they cried out and said, There is death in the pot, O man of God; and they could not eat of it. And he said, Bring meal, (leg. קחו *kechu*, *nine* MSS., *one* edition,) and he threw it into the pot. And he said, Pour out for the people,

A. M. cir. 3244
B. C. cir. 760
Anno Olymp.
Quintæ I.
Ante Urbem
Conditam 7

thereof, and it shall be [k]trodden
down.
6 And I will lay it waste: it
shall not be pruned nor digged;
but there shall come up briers and thorns: I
will also command the clouds that they
rain no rain upon it.
7 For the vineyard of the LORD of hosts *is*
the house of Israel, and the men of Judah
[l]his pleasant plant: and he looked for judgment, but behold [m]oppression; for righteousness, but behold a cry.
8 Wo unto them that join [n]house to house,
that lay field to field, till *there be* no place,
that [o]they may be placed alone in the midst
of the earth!

9 [p]In [q]mine ears, *said* the
LORD of hosts, [r]Of a truth many
houses shall be desolate, *even*
great and fair, without inhabitant.
10 Yea, ten acres of vineyard shall yield
one [s]bath, and the seed of a homer shall yield
an ephah.
11 [t]Wo unto them that rise up early in the
morning, *that* they may follow strong drink;
that continue until night, *till* wine [u]inflame
them!
12 And [v]the harp, and the viol, the tabret,
and pipe, and wine, are in their feasts: but
[w]they regard not the work of the LORD,
neither consider the operation of his hands.

A. M. cir. 3244
B. C. cir. 760
Anno Olymp.
Quintæ I.
Ante Urbem
Conditam 7

---

[k]Heb. *for a trading*——[l]Heb. *plant of his pleasures*——[m]Heb. *a scab*——[n]Mic. ii. 2——[o]Heb. *ye*——[p]Chap. xxii. 14——[q]Or, *This* is *in mine ears,* saith *the LORD,* &c.

[r]Heb. *If not,* &c.——[s]See Ezek. xlv. 11——[t]Prov. xxiii. 29, 30; Eccles. x. 16; ver. 22——[u]Or, *pursue them*——[v]Amos vi. 5, 6——[w]Job xxxiv. 27; Psalm xxviii. 5

---

that they may eat. And there was nothing hurtful in the pot."

From some such sorts of poisonous fruits of the grape kind Moses has taken these strong and highly poetical images, with which he has set forth the future corruption and extreme degeneracy of the Israelites, in an allegory which has a near relation, both in its subject and imagery, to this of Isaiah: Deut. xxxii. 32, 33.

"Their vine is from the vine of Sodom,
And from the fields of Gomorrah:
Their grapes are grapes of gall;
Their clusters are bitter:
Their wine is the poison of dragons,
And the cruel venom of aspics."

"I am inclined to believe," says *Hasselquist,* "that the prophet here, Isa. v. 2-4, means the hoary nightshade, *solanum incanum;* because it is common in Egypt, Palestine, and the East; and the Arabian name agrees well with it. The Arabs call it *anab el dib,* i. e., *wolf grapes.* The באושים *beushim,* says Rab. *Chai.,* is a well known species of the vine, and the worst of all sorts. The prophet could not have found a plant more opposite to the vine than this; for it grows much in the vineyards, and is very pernicious to them; wherefore they root it out: it likewise resembles a vine by its shrubby stalk;" Travels, p. 289. See also *Michaelis,* Questions aux Voyageurs Danois, No. 64.

Verse 3. *Inhabitants*] ישבי *yoshebey,* in the plural number; *three* MSS., (*two* ancient,) and so likewise the *Septuagint* and *Vulgate.*

Verse 6. *There shall come up briers and thorns*—"The thorn shall spring up in it"] *One* MS. has בשמיר *beshamir.* The true reading seems to be בו שמיר *bo shamir,* which is confirmed by the *Septuagint, Syriac,* and *Vulgate.*

Verse 7. *And he looked for judgment*] The *paronomasia,* or play on the words, in this place, is very remarkable; *mishpat, mishpach, tsedakah, tseakah.* There are many examples of it in the other prophets, but Isaiah seems peculiarly fond of it. See chap. xiii. 6, xxiv. 17, xxxii. 7, xxviii. 1, lvii. 6, lxi. 3, lxv. 11, 12. Rabbi *David Kimchi* has noticed the *paronomasia* here: he expected משפט *mishpat, judgment,* but behold משפח *mishpach, oppression;* he expected צדקה *tsedakah, righteousness,* but behold צעקה *tseakah, a cry.* The rabbins esteem it a great beauty; their term for it is צחות הלשון *tsachoth hallashon, elegance of language.*

Oppression—"tyranny."] משפח *mishpach,* from שפח *shaphach,* servum fecit, *Arab. Houbigant:* שפחה *shiphchah* is *serva,* a handmaid, or female slave. משפח *mispach,* eighteen MSS.

Verse 8. *Wo unto them that—lay field to field*—"You who lay field unto field"] Read תקריבו *takribu,* in the second person; to answer to the verb following. So *Vulgate.*

Verse 9. *In mine ears.*—"To mine ear"] The sentence in the Hebrew text seems to be imperfect in this place; as likewise in chap. xxii. 14, where the very same sense seems to be required as here. See the note there; and compare 1 Sam. ix. 15. In this place the *Septuagint* supply the word ηκουσθη, and the *Syriac* אשתמע *eshtama,* auditus est JEHOVAH in auribus meis, i. e., נגלה *niglah,* as in chap. xxii. 14.

Many houses] This has reference to what was said in the preceding verse: "In vain are ye so intent upon joining house to house, and field to field; your houses shall be left uninhabited, and your fields shall become desolate and barren; so that a vineyard of ten acres shall produce but one bath (not eight gallons) of wine, and the husbandman shall reap but a tenth part of the seed which he has sown." *Kimchi* says this means such an extent of vineyard as would require ten yoke of oxen to plough in one day.

Verse 11. *Wo unto them that rise up early*] There is a likeness between this and the following passage of the prophet Amos, chap. vi. 3-6, who probably wrote before Isaiah. If the latter be the copier, he seems hardly to have equalled the elegance of the original:—

A. M. cir. 3244
B. C. cir. 760
Anno Olymp.
Quintæ I.
Ante Urbem
Conditam 7

13 [x]Therefore my people are
gone into captivity, [y]because
they have no knowledge: and
[z]their honourable men *are* famished, and their multitude dried up with
thirst.
14 Therefore hell hath enlarged herself, and
opened her mouth without measure: and their
glory, and their multitude, and their pomp,
and he that rejoiceth, shall descend into it.
15 And [a]the mean man shall be brought
down, and the mighty man shall be humbled,
and the eyes of the lofty shall
be humbled:

A. M. cir. 3244
B. C. cir. 760
Anno Olymp.
Quintæ I.
Ante Urbem
Conditam 7

16 But the LORD of hosts
shall be exalted in judgment,
and [b]God [c]that is holy shall be sanctified
in righteousness.
17 Then shall the lambs feed after their
manner, and the waste places of [d]the fat ones
shall strangers eat.
18 Wo unto them that draw iniquity with
cords of vanity, and sin as it were with a cart-
rope:

[x]Hos. iv. 6——[y]Chap. i. 3; Luke xix. 44——[z]Heb. *their glory* are *men of famine*

[a]Chap. ii. 9, 11, 17——[b]Or, *the holy God*——[c]Heb. *the God the holy*——[d]Chap. x. 16

"Ye that put far away the evil day,
 And affect the seat of violence;
 Who lie upon beds of ivory,
 And stretch yourselves upon your couches;
 And eat the lambs from the flock,
 And calves from the midst of the stall;
 Who chant to the sound of the viol,
 And like David invent for yourselves instruments of music;
 Who quaff wine in large bowls,
 And are anointed with the choicest ointments:
 But are not grieved for the affliction of Joseph."

Kimchi says, "they consider not the heavens nor their hosts: they pray not the morning nor the evening prayer unto the Lord."

Follow strong drink] *Theodoret* and *Chrysostom* on this place, both Syrians, and unexceptionable witnesses in what belongs to their own country, inform us that שכר *shechar* (σικερα in the Greek of both Testaments, rendered by us by the general term *strong drink*) meant properly *palm wine*, or date wine, which was and is still much in use in the Eastern countries. Judea was famous for the abundance and excellence of its palm trees; and consequently had plenty of this wine. "Fiunt (vina) et e pomis; primumque e palmis, quo Parthi et Indi utuntur, et oriens totus: maturarum modio in aquæ congiis tribus macerato expressoque." Plin. lib. xiv. 19. "Ab his *cariotæ* [palmæ] maxime celebrantur; et cibo quidem, sed et succo, uberrimæ. Ex quibus præcipua vina orienti; iniqua *capiti*, unde pomo nomen." Id. xiii. 9. Καρος signifies *stupefaction:* and in Hebrew likewise the wine has its name from its remarkably *inebriating* quality.

Verse 13. *And their honourable men*—"And the nobles"] These verses have likewise a reference to the two preceding. They that indulged in feasting and drinking shall perish with hunger and thirst; and Hades shall indulge his appetite as much as they had done, and devour them all. The image is strong and expressive in the highest degree. Habakkuk, chap. ii. 5, uses the same image with great force:—the ambitious and avaricious conqueror.

"Enlargeth his appetite like Hades;
 And he is like Death, and will never be satisfied."

But, in Isaiah, Hades is introduced to much greater advantage, in person; and placed before our eyes in the form of a ravenous monster, opening wide his immeasurable jaws, and swallowing them all together: "Therefore Shoel hath dilated her soul, she hath opened her mouth beyond limit." Destruction expects more than a common meal, when God visits Jerusalem for her iniquities. This seems to refer to the ruin brought on the Jews by the Romans. Our blessed Lord repeats this parable, and applies it to this very transaction, Matt. xxi. 33.

Verse 17. *The lambs*—"And the kids"] גרים *gerim*, "strangers." The *Septuagint* read, more agreeably to the design of the prophet, כרים *carim*, αρνες, "the lambs." גדים *gedayim*, "the kids," Dr. *Durell;* nearer to the present reading: and so Archbishop *Secker*. The meaning is, their luxurious habitations shall be so entirely destroyed as to become a pasture for flocks.

After their manner—"Without restraint"] כדברם *kedobram*, secundum ductum eorum; i. e., suo ipsorum ductu; as their own will shall lead them.

Verse 18. *With a cart-rope*—"As a long cable"] The *Septuagint, Aquila, Sym.*, and *Theod.*, for בחבלי *bechabley*, read כחבלי *kechabley*, ὡς σχοινιῳ, or σχοινιοις; and the *Septuagint*, instead of שוא *shav*, read some other word signifying *long;* ὡς σχοινιῳ μακρῳ; and so likewise the *Syriac*, אריכא *arecha*. *Houbigant* conjectures that the word which the *Septuagint* had in their copies was שרוע *sarua*, which is used Lev. xxi. 18, xxii. 23, for something in an animal body superfluous, lengthened beyond its natural measure. And he explains it of sin added to sin, and one sin drawing on another, till the whole comes to an enormous length and magnitude; compared to the work of a rope-maker still increasing and lengthening his rope, with the continued addition of new materials. "Eos propheta similes facit homini restiario, qui funem torquet, cannabe addita et contorta, eadem iterans, donec funem in longum duxerit, neque eum liceat protrahi longius." "An evil inclination," says *Kimchi* on this place, from the ancient rabbins, "is at the beginning like a fine hair-string, but at the finishing like a thick cart-rope." By a long progression in iniquity, and a continued accumulation of sin, men arrive at length to the highest degree of wickedness; bidding open defiance to God, and scoffing at his threatened judgments, as it is finely expressed in the next verse. The *Chaldee* paraphrast explains it in the same manner, of

A. M. cir. 3244
B. C. cir. 760
Anno Olymp. Quintæ I.
Ante Urbem Conditam 7

19 [e]That say, Let him make speed, *and* hasten his work, that we may see *it:* and let the counsel of the Holy One of Israel draw nigh and come, that we may know *it!*

20 Wo unto them [f]that call evil good, and good evil; that put darkness for light, and light for darkness; that put bitter for sweet, and sweet for bitter!

21 Wo unto *them that are* [g]wise in their own eyes, and prudent [h]in their own sight!

22 [i]Wo unto *them that are* mighty to drink wine, and men of strength to mingle strong drink:

23 Which [k]justify the wicked for reward, and take away the righteousness of the righteous from him!

A. M. cir. 3244
B. C. cir. 760
Anno Olymp. Quintæ I.
Ante Urbem Conditam 7

24 Therefore [l]as [m]the fire devoureth the stubble, and the flame consumeth the chaff, *so* [n]their root shall be as rottenness, and their blossom shall go up as dust: because they have cast away the law of the LORD of hosts, and despised the word of the Holy One of Israel.

25 [o]Therefore is the anger of the LORD kindled against his people, and he hath stretched forth his hand against them, and hath smitten them: and [p]the hills did tremble, and their carcasses *were* [q]torn in the midst of the streets. [r]For all this his anger is not turned away, but his hand *is* stretched out still.

[e]Chap. lxvi. 5; Jer. xvii. 15; Amos v. 18; 2 Pet. iii. 3, 4——[f]Heb. *that say concerning evil,* It is *good,* &c.——[g]Prov. iii. 7; Rom. i. 22; xii. 16——[h]Heb. *before their face*——[i]Verse 11——[k]Prov. xvii. 15; xxiv. 24

[l]Exod. xv. 7——[m]Heb. *the tongue of fire*——[n]Job xviii. 16; Hos. ix. 16; Amos ii. 9——[o]2 Kings xxii. 13, 17——[p]Jer. iv. 24——[q]Or, *as dung*——[r]Lev. xxvi. 14, &c.; chap. ix. 12, 17, 21; x. 4

wickedness increasing from small beginnings, till it arrives to a great magnitude.—L.

I believe neither the rabbins nor Bishop *Lowth* have hit on the true meaning of this place; the prophet seems to refer to *idol sacrifices.* The victims they offered were splendidly decked out for the sacrifice. Their horns and hoofs were often gilded, and their heads dressed out with fillets and garlands. The *cords of vanity* may refer to the silken strings by which they were led to the altar, some of which were unusually thick. The offering for iniquity was adorned with fillets and garlands; the sin-offering with silken cords, like unto cart-ropes. *Pride,* in their acts of *humiliation,* had the upper hand.

Verse 19. *Let the counsel of the Holy One*] *Tryphiodorus* has an expression something like this:—

—— επει Διος ηλυθε βουλη.

TRYPH. *Il Excid.* 239.

Because the counsel of Jupiter was come.

"This expression, ηλυθε βουλη, is, I believe, something uncommon; but it is exactly paralleled and explained by a passage in Isaiah, chap. v. 19. The *Septuagint* has expressed it in the very same words with *Tryphiodorus:* και ελθοι ἡ βουλ η του ἁγιου Ισραηλ, ἱνα γνωμεν."—*Merrick's note, ad loc.*

Verse 22. *Mighty to drink wine*] "They show not," says *Kimchi,* "their strength in combating their enemies, but in drunkenness and debauchery."

Verse 23. *The righteous*] צדיק *tsaddik,* singular, *Sept., Vulg.,* and two editions.

Verse 24. *The flame*—"The tongue of fire"] "The flame, because it is in the shape of a tongue; and so it is called metaphorically." *Sal. ben Melec.* The metaphor is so exceedingly obvious, as well as beautiful, that one may wonder that it has not been more frequently used. Virgil very elegantly intimates, rather than expresses, the image:—

Ecce levis summo de vertice visus Iüli
Fundere lumen apex; tactuque innoxia molli
Lambere flamma comas, et circum tempora pasci.

Æn. ii. 682.

"Strange to relate! from young Iulus' head
A *lambent flame* arose, which gently spread
Around his brows, and on his temples fed."

And more boldly of Ætna darting out flames from its top:—

Interdumque atram prorumpit ad æthera nubem,
Turbine fumantem piceo, et candente favilla:
Attollitque globos flammarum, et sidera *lambit.*

Æn. iii. 574.

"By turns a pitchy cloud she rolls on high,
By turns hot embers from her entrails fly,
And flakes of mountain flames, that *lick* the sky."

The disparted tongues, as it were of fire, Acts ii. 3, which appeared at the descent of the Holy Spirit, on the apostles, give the same idea; that is, of flames shooting diversely into pyramidal forms, or points, like tongues. It may be farther observed that the prophet in this place has given the metaphor its full force, in applying it to the action of fire in eating up and devouring whatever comes in its way, like a ravenous animal whose tongue is principally employed in taking in his food or prey; which image Moses has strongly exhibited in an expressive comparison: "And Moab said to the elders of Midian, Now shall this collection of people lick up all that are around about us, as the ox licketh up the grass of the field," Num. xxii. 4. See also 1 Kings xviii. 38.

Their root shall be as rottenness] כמק *cammak, like mak;* whence probably our word *muck,* dung, was derived.

Verse 25. *The hills did tremble*—"And the mountains trembled"] Probably referring to the great earthquakes in the days of Uzziah

A. M. cir. 3244
B. C. cir. 760
Anno Olymp. Quintæ I.
Ante Urbem Conditam 7

26 [s]And he will lift up an
ensign to the nations from far,
and will [t]hiss unto them from
[u]the end of the earth: and,
behold, [v]they shall come with speed
swiftly:
27 None shall be weary nor stumble among
them; none shall slumber nor sleep; neither
[w]shall the girdle of their loins be loosed, nor
the latchet of their shoes be broken:
28 [x]Whose arrows *are* sharp, and all their
bows bent, their horses' hoofs shall be counted
like flint, and their wheels like
a whirlwind:
29 Their roaring *shall be* like
a lion, they shall roar like young
lions: yea, they shall roar, and lay hold of the
prey, and shall carry *it* away safe, and none
shall deliver *it*.
30 And in that day they shall roar against
them like the roaring of the sea: and if *one*
[y]look unto the land, behold darkness *and*
[z]sorrow, [a]and the [b]light is darkened in the
heavens thereof.

[s]Chap. xi. 12——[t]Chap. vii. 18——[u]Deut. xxviii. 49; Psa. lxxii. 8; Mal. i. 11——[v]Joel ii. 7——[w]Dan. v. 6 [x]Jer. v. 16

[y]Chap. viii. 22; Jer. iv. 23; Lam. iii. 2; Ezek. xxxii. 7, 8 [z]Or, *distress*——[a]Or, *when it is light it shall be dark in the destructions thereof*——[b]Ezek. xxxii. 8, in the margin

king of Judah, in or not long before the time of the prophet himself, recorded as a remarkable era in the title of the prophecies of Amos., chap. i. 1, and by Zechariah, chap. xiv. 5.

Verse 26. *He will—hiss*—"He will hist"] "The metaphor is taken from the practice of those that keep bees, who draw them out of their hives into the fields, and lead them back again, συρισμασι, by a hiss or a whistle."—*Cyril*, on this place; and to the same purpose *Theodoret*, ib. In chap. vii. 18, the metaphor is more apparent, by being carried farther, where the hostile armies are expressed by the fly and the bee:—

"JEHOVAH shall hist the fly
That is in the utmost parts of Egypt;
And the bee, that is in the land of Assyria."

On which place see Deut. i. 44; Psa. cxviii. 12; and God calls the locusts his great army, Joel ii. 25; Exod. xxiii. 28. See Huet, Quest. Alnet. ii. 12. שרק *sharak* or *shrak*, he shall *whistle* for them, call loud and *shrill;* he shall *shriek*, and they (their enemies) shall come at his call.

With speed] This refers to the *nineteenth* verse. As the scoffers had challenged God to make speed, and to hasten his work of vengeance, so now God assures them that with speed and swiftly it shall come.

Verse 27. *None—among them*] *Kimchi* has well illustrated this continued exaggeration or hyperbole, as he rightly calls it, to the following effect: "Through the greatness of their courage, they shall not be fatigued with their march; nor shall they stumble though they march with the utmost speed: they shall not slumber by day, nor sleep by night; neither shall they ungird their armour, or put off their sandals to take their rest. Their arms shall be always in readiness, their arrows sharpened, and their bows bent. The hoofs of their horses are hard as a rock. They shall not fail, or need to be shod with iron: the wheels of their carriages shall move as rapidly as a whirlwind."

Neither shall the girdle] The Eastern people, wearing long and loose garments, were unfit for action or business of any kind, without girding their clothes about them. When their business was finished they took off their girdles. A girdle therefore denotes strength and activity; and to unloose the girdle is to deprive of strength, to render unfit for action. God promises to unloose the loins of kings before Cyrus, chap. xlv. 1. The girdle is so essential a part of a soldier's accoutrement, being the last that he puts on to make himself ready for action, that *to be girded*, ζωννυσθαι, with the Greeks means to be completely armed and ready for battle:—

Ατρειδης δ εβοησεν, ιδε ζωννυσθαι ανωγεν
Αργειους. Iliad, xi. 15.

Το *δε ενδυναι τα ὁπλα εκαλουν οἱ παλαιοι ζωννυσθαι.* Pausan. Bœot. It is used in the same manner by the Hebrews: "Let not him that girdeth himself boast as he that unlooseth his girdle," 1 Kings xx. 11; that is, triumph not before the war is finished.

Verse 28. *Their horses' hoofs shall be counted like flint*—"The hoofs of their horses shall be counted as adamant"] The shoeing of horses with iron plates nailed to the hoof is quite a modern practice, and was unknown to the ancients, as appears from the silence of the Greek and Roman writers, especially those that treat of horse medicine, who could not have passed over a matter so obvious and of such importance that now the whole science takes its name from it, being called by us farriery. The horseshoes of leather and iron which are mentioned; the silver and gold shoes with which Nero and Poppæa shod their mules, used occasionally to preserve the hoofs of delicate cattle, or for vanity, were of a very different kind; they enclosed the whole hoof as in a case, or as a shoe does a man's foot, and were bound or tied on. For this reason the strength, firmness and solidity of a horse's hoof was of much greater importance with them than with us, and was esteemed one of the first praises of a fine horse. Xenophon says that a good horse's hoof is hard, hollow, and sounds upon the ground like a cymbal. Hence the χαλκοποδες ἱπποι, of Homer, and Virgil's *solido graviter sonat ungula cornu.* And Xenophon gives directions for hardening the horses' hoofs by making the pavement on which he stands in the stable with round-headed stones. For want of this artificial defence to the foot which our horses have Amos, chap. vi. 12, speaks of it as a thing as much impracticable to make horses run upon a hard rock as to plough up the same rock with oxen:—

"Shall horses run upon a rock?
Shall one plough it up with oxen?"

These circumstances must be taken into consideration in order to give us a full notion of the propriety and force of the image by which the prophet sets forth the strength and excellence of the Babylonish cavalry, which made a great part of the strength of the Assyrian army. Xenop. Cyrop. lib. ii.

Like a whirlwind] כסופה *cassuphah, like the stormy blast.* Here *sense* and *sound* are well connected.

Verse 30. *If* one *look unto the land, &c.*—"And these shall look to the heaven upward, and down to the earth"] ונבט לארץ *venibbat laarets.* Και εμβλεψονται εις την γην. So the *Septuagint*, according to the Vatican and Alexandrian copies; but the Complutensian and Aldine editions have it more fully, thus:—Και εμβλεψονται εις τον ουρανον ανω, και κατω; and the *Arabic* from the *Septuagint*, as if it had stood thus:—Και εμβλεψονται εις τον ουρανον, και εις την γην κατω, both of which are plainly defective; the words εις την γην, *unto the earth*, being wanted in the former, and the word ανω, *above*, in the latter. But an ancient *Coptic* version from the *Septuagint*, supposed to be of the second century, some fragments of which are preserved in the library of St. Germain des Prez at Paris, completes the sentence; for, according to this version, it stood thus in the *Septuagint*:—Και εμβλεψονται εις τον ουρανον ανω, και εις την γην κατω; "And they shall look unto the heavens above and unto the earth beneath," and so it stands in the *Septuagint* MSS., Pachom. and I. D. II., according to which they must have read their Hebrew text in this manner:—ונבט לשמים למעלה ולארץ למטה. This is probably the true reading, with which I have made the translation agree. Compare chap. viii. 22; where the same sense is expressed in regard to both particulars, which are here equally and highly proper, the looking *upwards*, as well as *down to the earth:* but the form of expression is varied. I believe the Hebrew text in that place to be right, though not so full as I suppose it was originally here; and that of the *Septuagint* there to be redundant, being as full as the *Coptic* version and MSS. Pachom. and I. D. II. represent it in this place, from which I suppose it has been interpolated.

Darkness—"The gloomy vapour"] The *Syriac* and *Vulgate* seem to have read בערפלה *bearphalach;* but *Jarchi* explains the present reading as signifying *darkness;* and possibly the *Syriac* and *Vulgate* may have understood it in the same manner.

CHAPTER VI

This chapter, by a particular designation of Isaiah to the prophetic office, 1–8, *introduces, with great solemnity, a declaration of the whole tenor of the Divine conduct in reference to his people, who, on account of their unbelief and impenitence, should for a very long period be given up to a judicial blindness and hardness of heart,* 9, 10; *and visited with such calamities as would issue in the total desolation of their country, and their general dispersion,* 11, 12. *The prophet adds, however, that under their repeated dispersions, (by the Chaldeans, Romans, &c.,) a small remnant would be preserved as a seed from which will be raised a people, in whom will be fulfilled all the Divine promises,* 13.

A. M. 3245
B. C. 759
Anno Olymp.
Quintæ 2
Ante Urbem
Conditam 6

IN the year that [a]King Uzziah
died I [b]saw also the Lord
sitting upon a throne, high and
lifted up, and [c]his train filled
the temple.

2 Above it stood the seraphims;
each one had six wings; with
twain he covered his face, and
[d]with twain he covered his feet,
and with twain he did fly.

[a]2 Kings xv. 7——[b]1 Kings xxii. 19; John xii. 41; Rev. iv. 2——[c]Or, *the skirts thereof*——[d]Ezek. i. 11

As this vision seems to contain a solemn designation of Isaiah to the prophetic office, it is by most interpreters thought to be the first in order of his prophecies. But this perhaps may not be so; for Isaiah is said, in the general title of his prophecies, to have prophesied in the time of Uzziah, whose acts, first and last, he wrote, 2 Chron. xxvi. 22; which is usually done by a contemporary prophet; and the phrase, *in the year that Uzziah died*, probably means after the death of Uzziah; as the same phrase (chap. xiv. 28) means after the death of Ahaz. Not that Isaiah's prophecies are placed in exact order of time. Chapters ii., iii., iv., v., seem by internal marks to be antecedent to chap. i.; they suit the time of Uzziah, or the former part of Jotham's reign; whereas chap. i. can hardly be earlier than the last years of Jotham. See note on chap. i. 7, and ii. 1. This might be a new designation, to introduce more solemnly a general dedication of the whole course of God's dispensations in regard to his people and the fates of the nation; which are even now still depending, and will not be fully accomplished till the final restoration of Israel.

In this vision the ideas are taken in general from royal majesty, as displayed by the monarchs of the East; for the prophet could not represent the ineffable presence of God by any other than sensible and earthly images. The particular scenery of it is taken from the temple. God is represented as seated on his throne above the ark, in the most holy place, where the glory appeared above the cherubim, surrounded by his attendant ministers. This is called by God himself "the place of his throne, and the place of the soles of his feet," Ezek. xliii. 7. "A glorious throne exalted of old, is the place of our sanctuary," saith the prophet Jeremiah, chap, xvii. 12. The very posture of sitting is a mark of state and solemnity: Sed et ipsum verbum *sedere* regni significat potestatem, saith *Jerome*, Comment. in Eph. i. 20. See note on chap. iii. 2. St. John, who has taken

A. M. 3245
B. C. 759
Anno Olymp.
Quintæ 2
Ante Urbem
Conditam 6

3 And [e]one cried unto another, and said, [f]Holy, holy,
holy, *is* the LORD of hosts:
[g]the [h]whole earth *is* full of
his glory.

4 And the posts of the [i]door
moved at the voice of him that
cried, and [k]the house was filled
with smoke.
5 [l]Then said I, Wo *is* me! for I am

A. M. 3245
B. C. 759
Anno Olymp.
Quintæ 2
Ante Urbem
Conditam 6

[e]Heb. *this cried to this*——[f]Rev. iv. 8——[g]Heb. *his glory* is *the fulness of the whole earth*——[h]Psa. lxxii. 19

[i]Heb. *thresholds*——[k]Exod. xl. 34; 1 Kings viii. 10
[l]Exod. iv. 10; vi. 30; Judg. vi. 22; xiii. 22; Jer. i. 6

many sublime images from the prophets of the Old Testament, and in particular from Isaiah, hath exhibited the same scenery, drawn out into a greater number of particulars; Rev. iv.

The veil, separating the most holy place from the holy or outermost part of the temple, is here supposed to be taken away; for the prophet, to whom the whole is exhibited, is manifestly placed by the altar of burnt-offering, at the entrance of the temple, (compare Ezek. xliii. 5, 6,) which was filled with the train of the robe, the spreading and overflowing of the Divine glory. The Lord upon the throne, according to St. John (chap. xii. 41,) was Christ; and the vision related to his future kingdom, when the veil of separation was to be removed, and the whole earth was to be filled with the glory of God, revealed to all mankind: which is likewise implied in the hymn of the seraphim, the design of which is, saith *Jerome* on the place, Ut mysterium Trinitatis in una Divinitate demonstrent; et nequaquam templum Judaicum, sicut prius, sed omnem terram illius gloria plenam esse testentur; "That they may point out the mystery of the Trinity in one Godhead; and that the Jewish temple alone should not be, as formerly, the place of the Divine glory, for the whole earth should be filled with it." It relates, indeed, primarily to the prophet's own time, and the obduration of the Jews of that age, and their punishment by the Babylonish captivity; but extends in its full attitude to the age of Messiah, and the blindness of the Jews to the Gospel, (see Matt. xiii. 14; John xii. 40; Acts xxviii. 26; Rom. xi. 8,) the desolation of their country by the Romans, and their being rejected by God. That nevertheless a holy seed—a remnant, should be preserved; and that the nation should spread out and flourish again from the old stock.—L.

NOTES ON CHAP. VI

Verse 1. *The Lord*] *Fifty-one* MSS. of *Kennicott's*, and *fifty-four* of *De Rossi's*, and *one* edition; in the 8th verse, *forty-four* MSS. of *Kennicott's*, and *forty-six* of *De Rossi's*, and *one* edition; and in the 11th verse *thirty-three* MSS. of *Kennicott's*, and many of *De Rossi's*, and *one* edition, for אדני *Adonai*, "the Lord" read יהוה "JEHOVAH," which is probably the true reading; (compare ver. 6;) as in many other places, in which the superstition of the Jews has substituted אדני *Adonai* for יהוה *Yehovah.* One of my own MSS., a very ancient and large folio, to which the points and the masora have been added by a later hand, has יהוה *Yehovah* in the 1st and 8th verses, in the teeth of the masora, which orders it in both places to be read אדני *Adonai.*

Verse 2. *Above it stood the seraphim*] שרפים *seraphim*, from שרף *seraph*, to *burn.* He saw says *Kimchi*, the angels as flames of fire, that the depravity of that generation might be exhibited, which was worthy of being totally burnt up.

He covered his feet—"He covereth his feet"] By the *feet* the Hebrews mean all the lower parts of the body. But the people of the East generally wearing long robes, reaching to the ground, and covering the lower parts of the body down to the feet, it may hence have been thought want of respect and decency to appear in public and on solemn occasions with even the feet themselves uncovered. *Kempfer*, speaking of the king of Persia giving audience, says, Rex in medio supremi atrii cruribus more patrio inflexis sedebat: corpus tunica investiebat flava, ad suras cum staret protensa; discumbentis vero *pedes discalceatos pro urbanitate patria operiens.*—Amœn. Exot. p. 227. "The king sat on the floor cross-legged, as is the custom of the country. He was covered with a yellow garment, which reached down to the feet when standing, but covered the feet for decency when sitting with his slippers off." Sir *John Chardin's* MS. note on this place of Isaiah is as follows: Grande marque de respect en orient de se cacher les pieds, quand on est assis, et de baisser le visage. Quand le souvrain se monstre en Chine et à Japon, chacun se jette le visage contre terre, et il n'est pas permis de regarder le roi; "It is a great mark of respect in the East to cover the feet, and to bow down the head in the presence of the king."

Verse 3. *Holy, holy, holy*] This hymn, performed by the seraphim, divided into two choirs, the one singing responsively to the other, which *Gregory Nazian.*, Carm. 18, very elegantly calls *Συμφωνον, αντιφωνον, αγγελων στασιν*, is formed upon the practice of alternate singing, which prevailed in the Jewish Church from the time of Moses, whose ode at the Red Sea was thus performed, (see Exod. xv. 20, 21,) to that of Ezra, under whom the priests and Levites sung alternately,

"O praise JEHOVAH, for he is gracious;
For his mercy endureth for ever;"

Ezra iii. 11. See De Sac. Poes. Hebr. Præl. xix., at the beginning.

Verse 5. *Wo* is *me! for I am undone*] נדמיתי *nidmeythi*, I am become dumb. There is something exceedingly affecting in this complaint. I am a man of unclean lips; I cannot say, Holy, holy, holy! which the seraphs exclaim. They are holy; I am not so: they see God, and live; I have seen him, and must die, because I am unholy. Only the pure in heart shall see God; and they only can live in his presence for ever. Reader, lay this to heart; and instead of boasting of thy excellence, and trusting in thy might, or comforting thyself in thy comparative innocence, thou wilt also be dumb before him, because thou hast been a man of unclean lips, and because thou hast still an unclean heart.

I am undone—"I am struck dumb"] נדמיתי

A. M. 3245
B. C. 759
Anno Olymp.
Quintæ 2
Ante Urbem
Conditam 6

[m]undone; because I *am* a
man of unclean lips, and I dwell
in the midst of a people of unclean lips; for mine eyes have
seen the King, the LORD of hosts.
6 Then flew one of the seraphims unto
me, [n]having a live coal in his hand, *which*
he had taken with the tongs from off [o]the
altar:
7 And he [p]laid [q]*it* upon my mouth, and
said, Lo, this hath touched thy lips; and
thine iniquity is taken away, and thy sin
purged.
8 Also I heard the voice of the Lord, saying, Whom shall I send, and who will go for
[r]us? Then said I, [s]Here *am* I;
send me.
9 And he said, Go, and tell
this people, [t]Hear ye [u]indeed,
[v]but understand not; and see ye [w]indeed,
but perceive not.
10 Make [x]the heart of this people fat, and
make their ears heavy, and shut their eyes;
[y]lest they see with their eyes, and hear with
their ears, and understand with their heart,
and convert, and be healed.
11 Then said I, Lord, how long? And he
answered, [z]Until the cities be wasted without
inhabitant, and the houses without man, and
the land be [a]utterly desolate,

[m]Heb. *cut off*——[n]Heb. *and in his hand a live coal*——[o]Rev. viii. 3——[p]Heb. *caused* it *to touch*——[q]See Jer. i. 9; Dan. x. 16——[r]Gen. i. 26; iii. 22; xi. 7——[s]Heb. *Behold me*——[t]Chap. xliii. 8; Matt. xiii. 14; Mark iv. 12; Luke viii. 10; John xii. 40; Acts xxviii. 26; Romans xi. 8——[u]Or, *without ceasing*, &c.——[v]Hebrew, *hear ye in hearing*, &c.——[w]Hebrew, *in seeing*——[x]Psalm cxix. 70; chapter lxiii. 17——[y]Jeremiah v. 21——[z]Micah iii. 12——[a]Hebrew, *desolate with desolation*

nidmeythi, twenty-eight MSS. (*five* ancient) and *three* editions.——I understand it as from דום *dum* or דמם *damam, silere*, "to be silent;" and so it is rendered by the *Syriac, Vulgate, Symmachus*, and by some of the Jewish interpreters, *apud* Sal. b. Melec. The rendering of the Syriac is תויר אני *tavir ani, stupens, attonitus sum*, "I am amazed." He immediately gives the reason why he was struck dumb: because he was a man of polluted lips, and dwelt among a people of polluted lips; and was unworthy, cither to join the seraphim in singing praises to God, or to be the messenger of God to his people. Compare Exod. iv. 10; vi. 12; Jer. i. 6.

Verse 6. *A live coal*] The word of prophecy, which was put into the mouth of the prophet.

From off the altar] That is, from the altar of burnt-offerings, before the door of the temple, on which the fire that came down at first from heaven (Lev. ix. 24; 2 Chron. vii. 1) was perpetually burning. It was never to be extinguished, Lev. vi. 12, 13,

Verse 9. *And he said*] לי *li, to me, two* MSS. and the *Syriac. Thirteen* MSS. have ראה *raah*, in the regular form.

Verse 10. *Make the heart of this people fat*—"Gross"] The prophet speaks of the event, the fact as it would actually happen, not of God's purpose and act by his ministry. The prophets are in other places said to perform the thing which they only foretell:—

"Lo! I have given thee a charge this day
Over the nations, and over the kingdoms;
To pluck up, and to pull down;
To destroy, and to demolish;
To build, and to plant." Jer. i. 10.

And Ezekiel says, "When I came to destroy the city;" that is, as it is rendered in the margin of our version, "when I came to prophesy that the city should be destroyed;" chap. xliii. 3. To hear, and not understand; to see, and not perceive; is a common saying in many languages. *Demosthenes* uses it, and expressly calls it a proverb: *ὡστε το της παροιμιας ὁρωντας μη ὁρᾳν, και ακουοντας μη ακουειν*; *Contra Aristogit.* I., *sub fin.* The prophet, by the bold figure in the sentiment above mentioned, and the elegant form and construction of the sentence, has raised it from a common proverb into a beautiful *mashal*, and given it the sublime air of poetry.

Or the words may be understood thus, according to the Hebrew idiom: "Ye certainly hear, but do not understand; ye certainly see, but do not acknowledge." Seeing this is the case, make the heart of this people fat—declare it to be stupid and senseless; and remove from them the means of salvation, which they have so long abused.

There is a saying precisely like this in *Æschylus*:—

——————— *βλεποντες εβλεπον ματην,*
Κλυοντες ουκ ηκουον. ÆSCH. *Prom. Vinct.* 456.

"Seeing, they saw in vain; and hearing, they did not understand."

And shut—"Close up"] השע *hasha*. This word *Sal. ben Melec* explains to this sense, in which it is hardly used elsewhere, on the authority of *Onkelos*. He says it means closing up the eyes, so that one cannot see; that the root is שוע *shava*, by which word the *Targum* has rendered the word טח *tach*, Lev. xiv. 42, וטח את בית *vetach eth beith*, "and shall plaster the house." And the word טח *tach* is used in the same sense, Isa. xliv. 18. So that it signifies to close up the eyes by some matter spread upon the lids. Mr. *Harmer* very ingeniously applies to this passage a practice of sealing up the eyes as a ceremony, or as a kind of punishment used in the East, from which the image may possibly be taken. Observ. ii. 278.

With their heart—"With their hearts"] ובלבבו *ubilebabo, fifteen* MSS. of *Kennicott's* and *fourteen* of *De Rossi's*, and *two* editions, with the *Septuagint, Syriac, Chaldee*, and *Vulgate*.

And be healed—"And I should heal"] ואר פא *veer pa, Septuagint, Vulgate.* So likewise Matt. xiii. 14; John xii. 40; Acts xxviii. 27.

Verse 11. *Be utterly desolate*—"Be left"] For תשאה *tishaeh*, the *Septuagint* and *Vulgate* read תשאר *tishshaer*.

A. M. 3245
B. C. 759
Anno Olymp. Quintæ 2
Ante Urbem Conditam 6

12 [b]And the LORD have removed men far away, and *there*
be a great forsaking in the midst
of the land.
13 But yet in it *shall be* a tenth, [c]and *it*
shall return, and shall be eaten:
as a teil tree, and as an oak,
whose [d]substance *is* in them,
when they cast *their leaves: so*
[e]the holy seed *shall be* the substance thereof.

A. M. 3245
B. C. 759
Anno Olymp. Quintæ 2
Ante Urbem Conditam 6

[b]2 Kings xxv. 21——[c]Or, *when it is returned, and hath been broused*

[d]Or, *stock* or *stem*——[e]Ezra ix. 2; Mal. ii. 15; Romans xi. 5

Verse 13. *A tenth*] This passage, though somewhat obscure, and variously explained by various interpreters, has, I think, been made so clear by the accomplishment of the prophecy, that there remains little room to doubt of the sense of it. When Nebuchadnezzar had carried away the greater and better part of the people into captivity, there was yet a *tenth* remaining in the land, the poorer sort left to be vinedressers and husbandmen, under Gedaliah, 2 Kings xxv. 12, 22, and the dispersed Jews gathered themselves together, and returned to him, Jer. xl. 12; yet even these, fleeing into Egypt after the death of Gedaliah, contrary to the warning of God given by the prophet Jeremiah, miserably perished there. Again, in the subsequent and more remarkable completion of the prophecy in the destruction of Jerusalem, and the dissolution of the commonwealth by the Romans, when the Jews, after the loss of above a million of men, had increased from the scanty residue that was left of them, and had become very numerous again in their country; Hadrian, provoked by their rebellious behaviour, slew above half a million more of them, and a second time almost extirpated the nation. Yet after these signal and almost universal destructions of that nation, and after so many other repeated exterminations and massacres of them in different times and on various occasions since, we yet see, with astonishment, that the stock still remains, from which God, according to his promise frequently given by his prophets, will cause his people to shoot forth again, and to flourish.—L.

A tenth, עשיריה *asiriyah.* The meaning, says *Kimchi*, of this word is, there shall yet be in the land *ten kings* from the time of declaring this prophecy. The names of the ten kings are *Jotham, Ahaz, Hezekiah, Manasseh, Amon, Josiah, Jehoahaz, Jehoiachin, Jehoiakim,* and *Zedekiah;* then there shall be a general consumption, the people shall be carried into captivity, and Jerusalem shall b- destroyed.

For בם *bam, in them*, above seventy MSS., *eleven* of *Kennicott's*, and *thirty-four* of *De Rossi's*, read בה *bah, in it;* and so the *Septuagint.*

CHAPTER VII

The king of Judah and the royal family being in the utmost consternation on receiving accounts of the invasion of the kings of Syria and Israel, the prophet is sent to assure them that God would make good his promises to David and his house; so that, although they might be corrected, *they could not be* destroyed, *while these prophecies remained to be accomplished,* 1–9. *The Lord gives Ahaz a sign that the confederacy against Judah shall be broken, which sign strikingly points out the miraculous conception of the Messiah, who was to spring from the tribe of Judah,* 10–16. *Prediction of very heavy calamities which the Assyrians would inflict upon the land of Judea,* 17–25.

A. M. cir. 3262
B. C. cir. 742
Anno Olymp. Nonæ 3
Ante Urbem Conditam 12

AND it came to pass in the
days of [a]Ahaz the son of
Jotham, the son of Uzziah, king
of Judah, *that* Rezin the king of
Syria, and [b]Pekah the son of
Remaliah, king of Israel, went up
toward Jerusalem to war against
it, but could not prevail against it.

A. M. cir. 3262
B. C. cir. 742
Anno Olymp. Nonæ 3
Ante Urbem Conditam 12

[a]2 Kings xvi. 5; 2 Chron. xxiii. 5, 6

[b]2 Kings xv. 25, 30, 37

The confederacy of *Rezin*, king of Syria, and *Pekah*, king of Israel, against the kingdom of Judah, was formed in the time of Jotham; and perhaps the effects of it were felt in the latter part of his *reign;* see 2 Kings xv. 37, and note on chap. i. 7-9. However, in the very beginning of the reign of *Ahaz*, they jointly invaded Judah with a powerful army, and threatened to destroy or to dethrone the house of David. The king and royal family being in the utmost consternation on receiving advices of their designs, Isaiah is sent to them to support and comfort them in their present distress, by assuring them that God would make good his promises to David and his house. This makes the subject of this, and the following, and the beginning of the ninth chapters, in which there are many and great difficulties.

Chap. vii. begins with an historical account of the occasion of this prophecy; and then follows, ver. 4-16, a prediction of the ill success of the designs of the Israelites and Syrians against Judah; and from thence to the end of the chapter, a denunciation of the calamities to be brought upon the king and people of Judah by the Assyrians, whom they had now hired to assist them. Chap. viii. has a pretty close connection with the foregoing; it contains a con-

A. M. cir. 3262
B. C. cir. 742
Anno Olymp.
Nonæ 3
Ante Urbem
Conditam 12

2 And it was told the house of
David, saying, Syria [c]is confederate with Ephraim. And his
heart was moved, and the heart
of his people, as the trees of the wood are
moved with the wind.
3 Then said the LORD unto Isaiah, Go forth
now to meet Ahaz, thou, [d]and [e]Shearjashub
thy son, at the end of the [f]conduit of the
upper pool in the [g]highway of the fuller's field;
4 And say unto him, Take heed and be
quiet; fear not, [h]neither be faint-hearted for
the two tails of these smoking firebrands, for
the fierce anger of Rezin with Syria, and of
the son of Remaliah.
5 Because Syria, Ephraim, and the son of
Remaliah, have taken evil counsel against thee, saying,
6 Let us go up against Judah,
and [i]vex it, and let us make a
breach therein for us, and set a king in the
midst of it, *even* the son of Tabeal;
7 Thus saith the Lord GOD, [k]It shall not
stand, neither shall it come to pass.
8 [l]For the head of Syria *is* Damascus, and
the head of Damascus *is* Rezin: and within
threescore and five years shall Ephraim be
broken, [m]that it be not a people.
9 And the head of Ephraim *is* Samaria, and
the head of Samaria *is* Remaliah's son. [n]If
[o]ye will not believe, surely ye shall not be
established.

A. M. cir. 3262
B. C. cir. 742
Anno Olymp.
Nonæ 3
Ante Urbem
Conditam 12

[c]Heb. *resteth on Ephraim*——[d]Chap. x. 21——[e]That is, *The remnant shall return;* see chap. vi. 13; x. 21——[f]2 Kings xviii. 17; chap. xxxvi. 2——[g]Or, *causeway*——[h]Hebrew, *let not thy heart be tender*——[i]Or, *waken*——[k]Proverbs xxi. 30; chapter viii. 10——[l]2 Samuel viii. 6——[m]Hebrew, *from a people*——[n]See 2 Chronicles xx. 20——[o]Or, *Do ye not believe?* it is *because ye are not stable*

firmation of the prophecy before given of the approaching destruction of the kingdoms of Israel and Syria by the Assyrians, of the denunciation of the invasion of Judah by the same Assyrians. Verses 9, 10, give a repeated general assurance, that all the designs of the enemies of God's people shall be in the end disappointed, and brought to naught; ver. 11, &c., admonitions and threatenings, (I do not attempt a more particular explanation of this very difficult part,) concluding with an illustrious prophecy, chap. ix. 1-6, of the manifestation of Messiah, the transcendent dignity of his character, and the universality and eternal duration of his kingdom.

NOTES ON CHAP. VII

Verse 3. *Now*] נא *na,* is omitted by *two* MSS., the *Septuagint, Syriac, Arabic,* and *Vulgate.*

Verse 4. The *Syriac* omits וארם *vearam,* "and Syria;" the *Vulgate* reads מלך ארם *melech aram,* "king of Syria:" one or the other seems to be the true reading. I prefer the former: or, instead of וארם ובן *vearam uben,* read ופקח בן *vepekach ben, and pekah son,* MS.

Verse 5. *Because—Remaliah*] All these words are omitted by one MS. and the *Syriac;* a part of them also by the *Septuagint.*

Verses 8, 9. *For the head of Syria, &c.*]

"Though the head of Syria be Damascus,
And the head of Damascus Retsin;
Yet within *threescore* and *five* years
Ephraim shall be broken, that he be no more a people:
And the head of Ephraim be Samaria;
And the head of Samaria Remaliah's son.

"Here are *six* lines, or *three* distichs, the order of which seems to have been disturbed by a transposition, occasioned by three of the lines beginning with the same word וראש *verosh,* "and the head," which three lines ought not to have been separated by any other line intervening; but a copyist, having written the first of them, and casting his eye on the *third,* might easily proceed to write after the *first* line beginning with וראש *verosh,* that which ought to have followed the third line beginning with וראש *verosh.* Then finding his mistake, to preserve the beauty of his copy, added at the end the distich which should have been in the middle; making that the second distich, which ought to have been the third. For the order as it now stands is preposterous: the destruction of Ephraim is denounced, and then their grandeur is set forth; whereas naturally the representation of the grandeur of Ephraim should precede that of their destruction. And the destruction of Ephraim has no coherence with the grandeur of Syria, simply as such, which it now follows: but it naturally and properly follows the grandeur of Ephraim, joined to that of Syria their ally.

"The arrangement then of the whole sentence seems originally to have been thus:—

Though the head of Syria be Damascus,
And the head of Damascus Retsin;
And the head of Ephraim be Samaria;
And the head of Samaria Remaliah's son:
Yet within *threescore* and *five* years
Ephraim shall be broken that he be no more a people."

DR. JUBB.

Threescore and five years] It was *sixty-five* years from the beginning of the reign of Ahaz, when this prophecy was delivered, to the total depopulation of the kingdom of Israel by Esarhaddon, who carried away the remains of the *ten* tribes which had been left by Tiglath-pileser, and Shalmaneser, and who planted the country with new inhabitants. That the country was not wholly stripped of its inhabitants by Shalmaneser appears from many passages of the history of Josiah, where Israelites are mentioned as still remaining there, 2 Chron. xxxiv. 6, 7, 33; xxxv. 18; 2 Kings xxiii. 19, 20. This seems to be the best explanation of the chronological difficulty in this place, which has much embarrassed the commentators: see *Usserii*

A. M. cir. 3262
B. C. cir. 742
Anno Olymp. Nonæ 3
Ante Urbem Conditam 12

10 [p]Moreover the LORD spake
again unto Ahaz, saying,
11 [q]Ask thee a sign of the
LORD thy God; [r]ask it either in
the depth, or in the height above.
12 But Ahaz said, I will not ask, neither
will I tempt the LORD.
13 And he said, Hear ye now, O house of
David, *Is it* a small thing for you to weary
men, but will ye weary my God
also?
14 Therefore the LORD himself
shall give you a sign; [s]Behold, a
virgin shall conceive, and bear [t]a son, and
[u]shall call his name [v]Immanuel.
15 Butter and honey shall he eat, that he
may know to refuse the evil, and choose the
good.

A. M. cir. 3262
B. C. cir. 742
Anno Olymp. Nonæ 3
Ante Urbem Conditam 12

[p]Heb. *And the LORD added to speak*——[q]Judg. vi. 36, &c.; Matt. xii. 33——[r]Or, *make* thy *petition deep* [s]Matt. i. 23; Luke i. 31, 34

[t]Chap. ix. 6——[u]Or, *thou*, O virgin, *shalt call;* see Genesis iv. 1, 25; xvi. 11; xxix. 32; xxx. 6, 8; 1 Sam. iv. 21——[v]Chap. viii. 8

Annal. V. T. *ad an.* 3327, and Sir *I. Newton*, Chronol. p. 283.

"That the last deportation of Israel by Esarhaddon was in the *sixty-fifth* year after the *second* of Ahaz, is probable for the following reasons: The Jews, in *Seder Olam Rabba*, and the Talmudists, in *D. Kimchi* on Ezek. iv., say, that Manasseh king of Judah was carried to Babylon by the king of Assyria's captains, 2 Chron. xxxiii. 11, in the *twenty-second* year of his reign; that is, before Christ 676, according to Dr. *Blair's* tables. And they are probably right in this. It could not be much earlier; as the king of Assyria was not king of Babylon till 680, ibid. As Esarhaddon was then in the neighbourhood of Samaria, it is highly probable that he did then carry away the last remains of Israel, and brought those strangers thither who mention him as their founder, Ezra iv. 2. But this year is just the *sixty-fifth* from the *second* of Ahaz, which was 740 before Christ. Now the carrying away the remains of Israel, who, till then, though their kingdom was destroyed *forty-five* years before, and though small in number, might yet keep up some form of being a people, by living according to their own laws, entirely put an end to the people of Israel, as a people separate from all others: for from this time they never returned to their own country in a body, but were confounded with the people of Judah in the captivity; and the whole people, the *ten tribes* included, were called Jews."—DR. JUBB. *Two* MSS. have *twenty-five* instead of *sixty-five;* and *two* others omit the word *five*, reading only *sixty*.

If ye will not believe—"If ye believe not"] "This clause is very much illustrated by considering the captivity of Manasseh as happening at the same time with this predicted final ruin of Ephraim as a people. The near connection of the *two* facts makes the prediction of the one naturally to cohere with the prediction of the other. And the words are well suited to this event in the history of the people of Judah: 'If ye believe not, ye shall not be established;' that is, unless ye believe this prophecy of the destruction of Israel, ye Jews also, as well as the people of Israel, shall not remain established as a kingdom and people; ye also shall be visited with punishment at the same time: as our Saviour told the Jews in his time, 'Unless ye repent, ye shall all likewise perish;' intimating their destruction by the Romans; to which also, as well as to the captivity of Manasseh, and to the Babylonish captivity, the views of the prophet might here extend. The close connection of this threat to the Jews with the prophecy of the destruction of Israel, is another strong proof that the order of the preceding lines above proposed is right."—DR. JUBB.

"If ye believe not in me."—The exhortation of Jehoshaphat, 2 Chron. xx. 20, to his people, when God had promised to them, by the prophet Jahaziel, victory over the Moabites and Ammonites, is very like this both in sense and expression, and seems to be delivered in verse:

"Hear me, O Judah; and ye inhabitants of Jerusalem;
Believe in JEHOVAH your God, and ye shall be established:
Believe his prophets, and ye shall prosper."

Where both the sense and construction render very probable a conjecture of Archbishop *Secker* on this place; that instead of כי *ki*, we should read בי *bi*. "If ye will not believe *in me*, ye shall not be established." So likewise Dr. *Durell*. The *Chaldee* has, "If ye will not believe in the words of the prophet;" which seems to be a paraphrase of the reading here proposed. In favour of which it may be farther observed, that in one MS. כי *ki* is upon a rasure; and another for the last לא *lo* reads ולא *velo*, which would properly follow בי *bi*, but could not follow כי *ki*.

Some translate thus, and paraphrase thus: If ye will not believe, surely ye shall not be established. Or, If ye do not give credit, it is because ye are unfaithful. Ye have not been faithful to the grace already given: therefore ye are now incapable of crediting my promises.

Verse 11. *In the depth*—"Go deep to the grave"] So *Aquila*, *Symmachus*, *Theodotion*, and the *Vulgate*.

Verse. 14. *The Lord*—"JEHOVAH"] For אדני *Adonai*, *twenty-five* of *Kennicott's* MSS., *nine* ancient, and *fourteen* of *De Rossi's*, read יהוה *Yehovah*. And so ver. 20, *eighteen* MSS.

Immanuel.] For עמנואל *Immanuel*, many MSS. and editions have עמנו אל *immanu El*, God with us.

Verse 15. *That he may know*—"When he shall know"] "Though so much has been written on this important passage, there is an obscurity and inconsequence which still attends it, in the general run of all the interpretations given to it by the most learned. And this obscure incoherence is given to it by the false rendering of a Hebrew particle, viz., ל *le*, in לדעתו *ledato*. This has been generally rendered, either 'that he may know,' or 'till he know.' It

A. M. cir. 3262
B. C. cir. 742
Anno Olymp. Nonæ 3
Ante Urbem Conditam 12

16 [w]For before the child shall
know to refuse the evil, and
choose the good, the land that
thou abhorrest shall be forsaken
of [x]both her kings.

17 [y]The LORD shall bring
upon thee, and upon thy people, and upon thy father's house,
days that have not come from
the day that [z]Ephraim departed from

[w]See chap. viii. 4——[x]2 Kings xv. 30; xvi. 9

[y]2 Chron. xxviii. 19——[z]1 Kings xii. 16

is capable of either version, without doubt; but either of these versions makes ver. 15 incoherent and inconsistent with ver. 16. For ver. 16 plainly means to give a reason for the assertion in ver. 15, because it is subjoined to it by the particle כי *ki, for.* But it is no reason why a child should eat butter and honey *till* he was at an age to distinguish, that *before* that time the land of his nativity should be free from its enemies. This latter supposition indeed implies, what is inconsistent with the preceding assertion. For it implies, that in part of that time of the infancy spoken of the land should not be free from enemies, and consequently these species of delicate food could not be attainable, as they are in times of peace. The other version, 'that he may know,' has no meaning at all; for what sense is there in asserting, that a child shall eat butter and honey *that* he may know to refuse evil and choose good? Is there any such effect in this food? Surely not. Besides, the child is thus represented to eat those things, which only a state of peace produces, during its whole infancy, inconsistently with ver. 16, which promises a relief from enemies only before the *end* of this infancy: implying plainly, that part of it would be passed in distressful times of war and siege, which was the state of things when the prophecy was delivered.

"But all these objections are cut off, and a clear, coherent sense is given to this passage, by giving another sense to the particle ל *le,* which never occurred to me till I saw it in *Harmer's* Observat., vol. i., p. 299. See how coherent the words of the prophet run, with how natural a connection one clause follows another, by properly rendering this one particle: 'Behold this Virgin shall conceive and bear a Son, and thou shalt call his name Immanuel; butter and honey, shall he eat, *when* he shall know to refuse evil, and choose good. For before this child shall know to refuse evil and choose good, the land shall be desolate, by whose two kings thou art distressed.' Thus ver. 16 subjoins a plain reason why the child should eat butter and honey, the food of plentiful times, *when* he came to a distinguishing age; viz., because before that time the country of the two kings, who now distressed Judea, should be desolated; and so Judea should recover that plenty which attends peace. That this rendering, which gives perspicuity and rational connection to the passage, is according to the use of the Hebrew particle, is certain. Thus לפנות בקר *liphnoth boker,* '*at* the appearing of morning, or *when* morning appeared,' Exod. xiv. 27; לעת האכל *leeth haochel,* '*at* mealtime, or *when* it was time to eat,' Ruth ii. 14. In the same manner, לדעתו *ledato,* '*at* his knowing, that is, *when* he knows.'

"*Harmer* (*ibid.*) has clearly shown that these articles of food are delicacies in the East, and, as such, denote a state of plenty. See also Josh. v. 6. They therefore naturally express the plenty of the country, as a mark of peace restored to it. Indeed, in ver. 22 it expresses a plenty arising from the thinness of the people; but that it signifies, ver. 15, a plenty arising from deliverance from war then present, is evident; because otherwise there is no expression of this deliverance. And that a deliverance was intended to be here expressed is plain, from calling the child which should be born *Immanuel,* God with us. It is plain, also, because it is before given to the prophet in charge to make a declaration of the deliverance, ver. 3-7; and it is there made; and this prophecy must undoubtedly be conformable to that in this matter."—Dr. *Jubb.*

The circumstance of the child's eating butter and honey is explained by *Jarchi,* as denoting a state of plenty: "Butter and honey shall this child eat, because our land shall be full of all good." *Comment in locum.* The infant Jupiter, says *Callimachus,* was tenderly nursed with goat's milk and honey. Hymn, in Jov. 48. *Homer,* of the orphan daughters of Pandareus:—

Κομισσε δε δι' Αφροδιτη
Τυρῳ και μελιτι γλυκερῳ, και ἡδει οινῳ.
ODYSS. XX., 68.

"Venus in tender delicacy rears
With honey, milk, and wine, their infant years." POPE.

Τρυφης εστιν ενδειξις; "This is a description of delicate food," says *Eustathius* on the place.

Agreeably to the observations communicated by the learned person above mentioned, which perfectly well explain the historical sense of this much disputed passage, not excluding a higher secondary sense, the obvious and literal meaning of the prophecy is this: "that within the time that a young woman, now a virgin, should conceive and bring forth a child, and that child should arrive at such an age as to distinguish between good and evil, that is, within a few years, (compare chap. viii. 4,) the enemies of Judah should be destroyed." But the prophecy is introduced in so solemn a manner; the sign is so marked, as a sign selected and given by God himself, after Ahaz had rejected the offer of any sign of his own choosing out of the whole compass of nature; the terms of the prophecy are so peculiar, and the name of the child so expressive, containing in them much more than the circumstances of the birth of a common child required, or even admitted; that we may easily suppose that, in minds prepared by the general expectation of a great Deliverer to spring from the house of David, they raised hopes far beyond what the present occasion suggested; especially when it was found, that in the subsequent prophecy, delivered immediately afterward, this child, called Immanuel, is treated as the Lord and

A. M. cir. 3262
B. C. cir. 742
Anno Olymp. Nonæ 3
Ante Urbem Conditam 12

Judah; *even* the king of Assyria.
18 And it shall come to pass
in that day, *that* the LORD [a]shall
hiss for the fly that *is* in the
uttermost part of the rivers of
Egypt, and for the bee that *is* in
the land of Assyria.

A. M. cir. 3262
B. C. cir. 742
Anno Olymp. Nonæ 3
Ante Urbem Conditam 12

[a]Isaiah, chap. v. 26

Prince of the land of Judah. Who could this be, other than the heir of the throne of David; under which character a great and even a Divine person had been promised? No one of that age answered to this character except Hezekiah; but he was certainly born nine or ten years before the delivery of this prophecy. That this was so understood at that time is collected, I think, with great probability, from a passage of Micah, a prophet contemporary with Isaiah, but who began to prophesy after him; and who, as I have already observed, imitated him, and sometimes used his expressions. Micah, having delivered that remarkable prophecy which determines the place of the birth of Messiah, "the Ruler of God's people, whose goings forth have been of old, from everlasting;" that it should be Bethlehem Ephratah; adds immediately, that nevertheless, in the mean time, God would deliver his people into the hands of their enemies: "He will give them up, till she, who is to bear a child, shall bring forth," Mic. v. 3. This obviously and plainly refers to some known prophecy concerning a woman to bring forth a child; and seems much more properly applicable to this passage of Isaiah than to any others of the same prophet, to which some interpreters have applied it. St. Matthew, therefore, in applying this prophecy to the birth of Christ, does it, not merely in the way of accommodating the words of the prophet to a suitable case not in the prophet's view, but takes it in its strictest, clearest, and most important sense; and applies it according to the original design and principal intention of the prophet.—L.

After all this learned criticism, I think something is still wanting to diffuse the proper light over this important prophecy. On Matt. i. 23 I have given what I judge to be the true meaning and right application of the whole passage, as there quoted by the evangelist, the substance of which it will be necessary to repeat here:—

At the time referred to, the kingdom of Judah, under the government of Ahaz, was reduced very low. *Pekah*, king of Israel, had slain in Judea *one hundred and twenty thousand* persons in one day; and carried away captives *two hundred thousand*, including women and children, together with much spoil. To add to their distress, *Rezin*, king of Syria, being confederate with *Pekah*, had taken *Elath*, a fortified city of Judah, and carried the inhabitants away captive to Damascus. In this critical conjuncture, need we wonder that Ahaz was afraid that the enemies who were now united against him must prevail, destroy Jerusalem, end the kingdom of Judah, and annihilate the family of David? To meet and remove this fear, apparently well grounded, Isaiah is sent from the Lord to Ahaz, swallowed up now both by sorrow and by unbelief, in order to assure him that the counsels of his enemies should not stand; and that they should be utterly discomfited. To encourage Ahaz, he commands him to *ask a sign* or *miracle*, which should be a pledge in hand, that God should, in due time, fulfill the predictions of his servant, as related in the context. On Ahaz humbly refusing to ask any sign, it is immediately added, "Therefore the Lord himself shall give you a sign; Behold, a virgin shall conceive and bear a son; and shall call his name Immanuel. Butter and honey shall he eat," &c. Both the *Divine* and *human* nature of our Lord, as well as the miraculous conception, appear to be pointed out in the prophecy quoted here by the evangelist: He shall be called עמנואל IMMANU-EL; literally, *The* STRONG GOD WITH US: similar to those words in the New Testament: *The word* which *was God—was made flesh, and dwelt among us, full of grace and truth;* John i. 1, 14. And *God was manifested in the flesh*, 1 Tim. iii. 16. So that we are to understand *God with us* to imply, God *incarnated*—God in *human nature*. This seems farther evident from the words of the prophet, ver. 15: *Butter and honey shall he eat*—he shall be truly *man*—grow up and be nourished in a *human natural way;* which refers to his being WITH US, i. e., incarnated. To which the prophet adds, *That he may know to refuse the evil, and choose the good;* or rather, *According to his knowledge*, לדעתו *ledato, reprobating the evil, and choosing the good;* this refers to him as GOD, and is the same idea given by this prophet, chap. liii. 11: *By* (or in) *his knowledge*, בדעתו *bedato*, (the knowledge of Christ crucified,) *shall my righteous servant justify many; for he shall bear their offences.* Now this *union* of the Divine and human nature is termed a *sign* or *miracle*, אות *oth*, i. e., something which exceeds the power of nature to produce. And this *miraculous union* was to be brought about in a *miraculous way: Behold, a* VIRGIN *shall conceive:* the word is very emphatic, העלמה *haalmah*, THE *virgin;* the only one that ever was, or ever shall be, a *mother* in this way. But the *Jews*, and some called *Christians*, who have espoused their desperate cause, assert that "the word עלמה *almah* does not signify a VIRGIN *only;* for it is applied Prov. xxx. 19 to signify a young *married* woman." I answer, that this latter text is no proof of the contrary doctrine: the words דרך גבר בעלמה *derech geber bealmah, the way of a man with a maid*, cannot be proved to mean *that* for which it is produced. Besides, one of De Rossi's MSS. reads בעלמיו *bealmaiv*, the *way of a strong* or stout *man* (גבר *geber*) IN HIS YOUTH; and in this reading the *Syriac, Septuagint, Vulgate*, and *Arabic* agree; which are followed by the *first version* in the *English* language, as it stands in a MS. in my own possession: **the weie of a man in his waxing youth:** so that this place, the only one that can with any *probability* of *success* be produced, were the interpretation contended for correct, which I am by no means disposed to admit, proves nothing. Besides, the consent of so many *versions* in the opposite meaning deprives it of much of its influence in this question.

A. M. cir. 3262
B. C. cir. 742
Anno Olymp.
Nonæ 3
Ante Urbem
Conditam 12

19 And they shall come, and
shall rest all of them in the
desolate valleys, and in [b]the
holes of the rocks, and upon
all thorns, and upon all
[c]bushes.
20 In the same day shall the
Lord shave with a [d]razor that is

A. M. cir. 3262
B. C. cir. 742
Anno Olymp.
Nonæ 3
Ante Urbem
Conditam 12

[b]Chap. ii. 19; Jer. xvi. 16——[c]Or, *commendable trees*

[d]2 Kings xvi. 7, 8; 2 Chron. xxviii. 20, 21; see Ezek. v. 1

The word עלמה *almah*, comes from עלם *alam*, to *lie hid*, be *concealed:* and we are told, that "virgins were so called, because they were *concealed* or *closely kept up* in their father's houses till the time of their marriage." This is not correct: see the case of Rebecca, Gen. xxiv. 43, and my note there; that of Rachel, Gen. xxix. 6, 9, and the note there also; and see the case of Miriam, the sister of Moses, Exod. ii. 8, and also the Chaldee paraphrase on Lam. i. 4, where the *virgins* are represented as *going out* in the dance. And see also the whole history of *Ruth*. This being *concealed* or *kept at home*, on which so much stress is laid, is purely fanciful; for we find that young *unmarried* women drew water, kept sheep, gleaned publicly in the fields, &c., &c., and the same works they perform among the Turcomans to the present day. This reason, therefore, does not account for the radical meaning of the word; and we must seek it elsewhere. Another well-known and often-used root in the Hebrew tongue will cast light on this subject. This is גלה *galah*, which signifies to *reveal*, *make manifest*, or *uncover;* and is often applied to matrimonial connections in different parts of the Mosaic law: עלם *alam*, therefore, may be considered as implying the *concealment* of the *virgin*, as *such*, till lawful, marriage had taken place. A virgin was not called עלמה *almah*, because she was concealed by being kept at home in her father's house, which is not true; but, *literally* and *physically*, because as a *woman* she had not been *uncovered*—she had not known man. This fully applies to the blessed virgin, see Luke i. 34. "How can this be, seeing *I know no man?*" And this text throws much light on the subject before us. This also is in perfect agreement with the ancient prophecy, "The seed of the woman shall bruise the head of the serpent," Gen. iii. 15; for the person who was to destroy the work of the devil was to be the progeny of the *woman*, without any concurrence of the *man*. And hence the text in Genesis speaks as fully of the *virgin state* of the person from whom *Christ*, according to the flesh, should come, as that in the *prophet*, or this in the *evangelist*. According to the original promise there was to be a *seed*, a *human being*, who should destroy sin: but this *seed* or *human being*, must come from the *woman* ALONE; and no *woman* ALONE could produce such a human being without being a *virgin*. Hence, *A virgin shall bear a son*, is the very spirit and meaning of the original text, independently of the *illustration* given by the prophet; and the *fact* recorded by the evangelist is the proof of the whole. But how could that be a *sign* to *Ahaz*, which was to take place so many hundreds of years after? I answer, the meaning of the prophet is plain: not only Rezin and Pekah should be unsuccessful against Jerusalem at *that time*, which was the fact; but Jerusalem, Judea, and the house of David should be both preserved, notwithstanding their depressed state, and the multitude of their adversaries, till the time should come when a VIRGIN *should bear a son*. This is a most remarkable circumstance—the house of David could never fail, till a virgin should conceive and bear a son—nor did it: but when that incredible and miraculous fact did take place, the kingdom and house of David became extinct! This is an irrefragable confutation of every argument a Jew can offer in vindication of his opposition to the Gospel of Christ. Either the prophecy in Isaiah has been fulfilled, or the kingdom and house of David are yet standing. But the kingdom of David, we know, is destroyed: and where is the man, Jew or Gentile, that can show us a single descendant of David on the face of the earth? The prophecy could not fail: the kingdom and house of David have failed; the *virgin*, therefore, must have brought forth her son, and this son is Jesus, the Christ. Thus Moses, Isaiah, and Matthew concur; and facts the most unequivocal have confirmed the whole! Behold the wisdom and providence of God!

Notwithstanding what has been said above, it may be asked, In what sense could this name, *Immanuel*, be applied to Jesus Christ, if he be not truly and properly GOD? Could the Spirit of truth ever design that Christians should receive him as an *angel* or a *mere man;* and yet, in the very beginning of the Gospel history, apply a character to him which belongs only to the most high God? Surely *no*. In what sense, then, is Christ GOD WITH US? Jesus is called Immanuel, or *God with us*, in his *incarnation;* God united to our nature; *God with man*, God *in* man; *God with us*, by his continual *protection; God with us*, by the *influences* of his *Holy Spirit*, in the *holy sacrament*, in the *preaching* of his *word*, in *private prayer*. And *God with us*, through every *action* of our life, that we begin, continue, and end in his name. He is *God with us*, to *comfort*, *enlighten*, *protect*, and *defend* us, in every time of *temptation* and *trial*, in the hour of *death*, in the day of *judgment;* and *God with us* and *in* us, and we *with* and *in* him, to all eternity.

Verse 17. *The Lord shall bring*—"But JEHOVAH will bring"] *Houbigant* reads יביא *vaiyabi*, from the *Septuagint*, αλλα επαξει ὁ Θεος, to mark the transition to a new subject.

Even *the king of Assyria*.] *Houbigant* supposes these words to have been a marginal gloss, brought into the text by mistake; and so likewise Archbishop *Secker*. Besides their having no force or effect here, they do not join well in construction with the words preceding, as may be seen by the strange manner in which the ancient interpreters have taken them; and they very inelegantly forestall the mention of the king of Assyria, which comes in with great propriety in the 20th verse. I have therefore taken the liberty of omitting them in the translation.

Verse 18. *Hiss for the fly*—"Hist the fly"] See note on chap. v. 26.

Egypt, and—Assyria.] Sennacherib, Esar-

A. M. cir. 3262
B. C. cir. 742
Anno Olymp.
Nonæ 3
Ante Urbem
Conditam 12

hired, *namely,* by them beyond
the river, by the king of Assyria,
the head, and the hair of the
feet: and it shall also consume the beard.

21 And it shall come to pass in that day,
that a man shall nourish a young cow, and
two sheep:

22 And it shall come to pass, for the abundance of milk *that* they shall give that he shall
eat [e]butter: for butter and honey shall every
one eat that is left [f]in the land.

23 And it shall come to pass in that day,
that every place shall be, where
there were a thousand vines
at a thousand silverlings, [g]it
shall *even* be for briers and
thorns.

A. M. cir. 3262
B. C. cir. 742
Anno Olymp.
Nonæ 3
Ante Urbem
Conditam 12

24 With [h]arrows and with bows shall *men*
come thither; because all the land shall become briers and thorns.

25 And *on* all hills that shall be digged with
the mattock, there shall not come thither the
fear of briers and thorns: but it shall be for
the sending forth of oxen, and for the treading of lesser cattle.

---

[e]Deut. xxxii. 14——[f]Heb. *in the midst of the land*

[g]Chap. v. 6——[h]Jer. l. 14

---

haddon, Pharaoh-necho, and Nebuchadnezzar, who one after another desolated Judea.

Verse 19. *Holes of the rocks*—"Caverns"] So the *Septuagint, Syriac,* and *Vulgate,* whence *Houbigant* supposes the true reading to be הנחללים *hannachalolim.* One of my oldest MSS. reads הנחלולים *hannachalolim.*

Verse 20. *The river*] That is, the Euphrates: הנהר *hanahar.* So read the *Septuagint* and two MSS.

Shall the Lord shave with a razor that is hired—"JEHOVAH shall shave by the hired razor"] To shave with the hired razor the head, the feet, and the beard, is an expression highly parabolical, to denote the utter devastation of the country from one end to the other; and the plundering of the people, from the highest to the lowest, by the Assyrians, whom God employed as his instrument to punish the Jews. Ahaz himself, in the first place, hired the king of Assyria to come to help him against the Syrians, by a present made to him of all the treasures of the temple, as well as his own. And God himself considered the great nations, whom he thus employed as his mercenaries; and paid them their wages. Thus he paid Nebuchadnezzar for his services against Tyre, by the conquest of Egypt, Ezek. xxix. 18-20. The hairs of the head are those of the highest order in the state; those of the feet, or the lower parts, are the common people; the beard is the king, the high priest, the very supreme in dignity and majesty. The Eastern people have always held the beard in the highest veneration, and have been extremely jealous of its honour. To pluck a man's beard is an instance of the greatest indignity that can be offered. See Isa. l. 6. The king of the Ammonites, to show the utmost contempt of David, "cut off half the beards of his servants, and the men were greatly ashamed; and David bade them tarry at Jericho till their beards were grown," 2 Sam. x. 4, 5. *Niebuhr,* Arabie, p. 275, gives a modern instance of the very same kind of insult. "The Turks," says *Thevenot,* "greatly esteem a man who has a fine beard; it is a very great affront to take a man by his beard, unless it be to kiss it; they swear by the beard." Voyages, i., p. 57. *D'Arvieux* gives a remarkable instance of an Arab, who, having received a wound in his jaw, chose to hazard his life, rather than suffer his surgeon to take off his beard. Memoires, tom. iii., p. 214. See also *Niebuhr,* Arabie, p. 61.

The remaining verses of this chapter, 21-25, contain an elegant and very expressive description of a country depopulated, and left to run wild, from its adjuncts and circumstances: the vineyards and cornfields, before well cultivated, now overrun with briers and thorns; much grass, so that the few cattle that are left, a young cow and two sheep, have their full range, and abundant pasture, so as to yield milk in plenty to the scanty family of the owner; the thinly scattered people living, not on corn, wine, and oil, the produce of cultivation; but on milk and honey, the gifts of nature; and the whole land given up to the wild beasts, so that the miserable inhabitants are forced to go out armed with bows and arrows, either to defend themselves against the wild beasts, or to supply themselves with necessary food by hunting.

A VERY judicious friend has sent me the following observations on the preceding prophecy, which I think worthy of being laid before the reader; though they are in some respects different from my own view of the subject.

"To establish the primary and literal meaning of a passage of Scripture is evidently laying the true foundation for any subsequent views or improvements from it.

"The kingdom of Judah, under the government of Ahaz, was reduced very low. Pekah, king of Israel, had slain in Judea *one hundred and twenty thousand* in one day; and carried away captive *two hundred thousand,* including women and children, with much spoil. To add to this distress, Rezin, king of Syria, being confederate with Pekah, had taken Elath, a fortified city of Judah, and carried the inhabitants to Damascus. I think it may also be gathered from the *sixth* verse of chap. viii., that the kings of Syria and Israel had a considerable party in the land of Judea, who, regardless of the Divine appointment and promises, were disposed to favour the elevation of Tabeal, a stranger, to the throne of David.

"In this critical conjuncture of affairs, Isaiah was sent with a message of mercy, and a promise of deliverance, to Ahaz. He was commanded to take with him *Shearjashub,* his son, whose *name* contained a *promise* respecting the captives lately made by Pekah, whose *return* from Samaria, effected by the expostulation of the prophet Oded and the concurrence of the princes of Ephraim, was now promised as a pledge of the Divine interposition offered to Ahaz in favour of the house of David. And as a farther token of this preservation, notwithstanding the incredulity of Ahaz, Isaiah was directed to predict the birth of *another* son which should be born to him within the space of a year, and to be named *Immanuel*, signifying thereby the protection of God to the land of Judah and family of David at this present conjuncture, with reference to the promise of the Messiah who was to spring from that family, and be born in that land. Compare chap. viii. 8. Hence Isaiah testifies, chap. viii. 18: 'Behold, I and the children whom the Lord hath given me are for signs and for *types* in Israel.' Compare Zech. iii. 8: 'Thy companions are men of sign and type:' see Dr. *Lowth* on this verse. The message of Divine displeasure against Israel is in like manner expressed by the *names* the prophet Hosea was directed to give *his* children; see Hos. i. and ii.

"Concerning *this child*, who was to be named Immanuel, the prophet was commissioned to declare, that notwithstanding the present scarcity prevailing in the land from its being harassed by war, yet within the space of time wherein this child should be of age to discern good and evil, both these hostile kings, viz., of Israel and Syria, should be cut off; and the country enjoy such plenty, that butter and honey, food accounted of peculiar delicacy, should be a *common* repast. See *Harmer's* Observations, p. 299.

"To this it may be objected that Isaiah's son was *not* named Immanuel, but *Maher-shalal-hash-baz;* the signification of which bore a threatening aspect, instead of a consolatory one. To this I think a satisfactory answer may be given. Ahaz, by his unbelief and disregard of the message of mercy sent to him from God, (for instead of depending upon it he sent and made a treaty with the king of Assyria,) drew upon himself the Divine displeasure, which was expressed by the *change of the child's name*, and the declaration that *though* Damascus and Samaria should, according to the former prediction, fall before the king of Assyria, yet that this very power, i. e., Assyria, in whom Ahaz trusted for deliverance, (see 2 Kings xvi. 7, &c.,) should afterwards come against *Judah*, and 'fill the breadth of the land,' which was accomplished in the following reign, when Jerusalem was so endangered as to be delivered only by miracle. The *sixth* and *seventh* verses of chap. viii. indicate, I think, as I before observed, that the kings of Syria and Israel had many adherents in Judah, who are said to *refuse* the peaceful waters of Shiloah or Siloam, *him that is to be sent*, who ought to have been their confidence, typified by the fountain at the foot of Mount Zion, whose stream watered the city of Jerusalem; and therefore, since the splendour of victory, rather than the blessings of peace, was the object of their admiration, compared to a swelling river which overflowed its banks, God threatens to chastise them by the victorious armies of Ashur. The prophet at the same time addresses words of consolation to such of the people who yet feared and trusted in Jehovah, whom he instructs and comforts with the assurance (ver. 10) that they shall prove the fulfilment of the promise contained in the name Immanuel.

"But it may still be objected, that according to this interpretation of the *fourteenth* verse of chap. vii. nothing *miraculous* occurs, which is readily admitted; but the objection rests upon the supposition that something miraculous was intended; whereas the word אות *oth*, 'sign,' does by no means generally imply a miracle, but most commonly an *emblematic representation*, (see Ezek. iv. 3-12; xi.; xx. 20; Zech. vi. 14,) either by actions or names, of some future event either promised or threatened. Exod. iii. 12; 1 Sam. ii. 34; 2 Kings xix. 29; Jer. xliv. 29, 30, are all examples of a *future event* given as a sign or token of something else which is also future. The birth of Isaiah's son was indeed typical of him whose name he was, at first, appointed to bear, viz., Immanuel, even as Oshea the son of Nun had his name changed to Jehoshua, the same with Jesus, of whom *he* was an eminent type. Hence the prophet, in the *ninth* chapter, breaks forth into a strain of exultation: 'To us a child is born;' after which follow denunciations against Rezin and the kingdom of Israel, which are succeeded by declarations, that when *Assyria* had completed the appointed chastisement upon Judah and Jerusalem, that empire should be destroyed. The whole of the *tenth* chapter is a very remarkable prophecy, and was probably delivered about the time of Sennacherib's invasion.

"But still it will be urged, that St. Matthew, when relating the miraculous conception of our Lord, says, 'Now all this was done that it might be fulfilled which was spoken of the Lord by the prophet,' &c. To this it may readily be answered, that what was spoken by the prophet was indeed now fulfilled in a higher, more important, and also in a more literal sense, than the primary fulfilment could afford, which derived all its value from its connection with this event, to which it ultimately referred.

"In like manner the prophecy of Isaiah, contained in the *second* chapter, received a *complete* fulfilment in our Saviour's honouring Capernaum with his residence, and preaching throughout Galilee; though there appears reason to interpret the passage as having a primary respect to the reformation wrought by Hezekiah and which, at the eve of the dissolution of the kingdom of Israel by the captivity of the ten tribes, extended to the tribes of Asher and Zebulun, and many of the inhabitants of Ephraim and Manasseh, who were hereby stirred up to destroy idolatry in their country. See 2 Chron. xxxi. 1. And without doubt the great deliverance wrought afterwards for Judah by the miraculous destruction of Sennacherib's army, and the recovery of Hezekiah in so critical a conjuncture from a sickness which had been declared to be unto death, contributed not a little to revive the fear of God in that part of Israel which, through their defection from the house of David, had grievously departed from the temple and worship of the true God; and as Galilee lay contiguous to countries inhabited by Gentiles, they had probably sunk deeper into idolatry than the southern part of Israel.

"In several passages of St. Matthew's Gospel, our translation conveys the idea of things being done *in order to fulfil certain prophecies;* but I apprehend that if the words ἱνα και ὁπως were rendered as simply denoting the event, *so that* and *thus* was fulfilled, the sense would be much clearer. For it is obvious that our Lord did not speak in parables or ride into Jerusalem previously to his last passover, simply for the purpose of fulfilling the predictions recorded, but also from other motives; and in chap. ii. the evangelist only remarks that the circumstance of our Lord's *return from Egypt* corresponded with the prophet Hosea's relation of that part of the history of the Israelites. So in the *twenty-third* verse Joseph dwelt at Nazareth *because* he was directed so to do by God himself; and the sacred historian, having respect to the effect afterwards produced, (see John vii. 41, 42, 52,) remarks that this abode in Nazareth was a means of fulfilling those predictions of the prophets which indicate the contempt and neglect with which by many the Messiah should be treated. Galilee was considered by the inhabitants of Judea as a degraded place, chiefly from its vicinity to the Gentiles; and Nazareth seems to have been *proverbially contemptible;* and from the account given of the spirit and conduct of the inhabitants by the evangelists, not without reason."—E. M. B.

To my correspondent, as well as to many learned men, there appears some difficulty in the text; but I really think this is quite done away by that mode of interpretation which I have already adopted; and as far as the miraculous conception is concerned, the whole is set in the clearest and strongest light, and the objections and cavils of the Jews entirely destroyed.

CHAPTER VIII

Prediction respecting the conquest of Syria and Israel by the Assyrians, 1–4. *Israel, for rejecting the* gentle stream *of Shiloah, near Jerusalem, is threatened to be overflowed by the* great river *of Assyria, manifestly alluding by this strong figure to the conquests of Tiglath-pileser and Shalmaneser over that kingdom,* 5–7. *The invasion of the kingdom of Judah by the Assyrians under Sennacherib foretold,* 8. *The prophet assures the Israelites and Syrians that their hostile attempts against Judah shall be frustrated,* 9, 10. *Exhortation not to be afraid of the wrath of man, but to fear the displeasure of God,* 11–13. *Judgments which shall overtake those who put no confidence in Jehovah,* 14, 15. *The prophet proceeds to warn his countrymen against idolatry, divination, and the like sinful practices, exhorting them to seek direction from the word of God, professing in a beautiful apostrophe that this was his own pious resolution. And to enforce this counsel, and strengthen their faith, he points to his children, whose symbolic names were signs or pledges of the Divine promises,* 16–20. *Judgments of God against the finally impenitent,* 21, 22.

A. M. cir. 3262
B. C. cir. 742
Anno Olymp. Nonæ 3
A. U. C. 12

MOREOVER the LORD said
unto me, Take thee a great
roll, and [a]write in it with a man's
pen concerning [b]Maher-shalal-
hash-baz.

2 And I took unto me faithful

[a]Chap. xxx. 8; Hab. ii. 2——[b]Heb. *in making speed to the spoil he hasteneth the prey,* or *make speed, &c.*

The prophecy of the foregoing chapter relates directly to the kingdom of Judah only: the first part of it promises them deliverance from the united invasion of the Israelites and Syrians; the latter part, from ver. 17, denounces the desolation to be brought upon the kingdom of Judah by the Assyrians. The *sixth, seventh,* and *eighth* verses of this chapter seem to take in both the kingdoms of Israel and Judah. "This people that refuseth the waters of Shiloah," may be meant of both: the Israelites despised the kingdom of Judah, which they had deserted, and now attempted to destroy; the people of Judah, from a consideration of their own weakness, and a distrust of God's promises, being reduced to despair, applied to the Assyrians for assistance against the two confederate kings. But how could it be said of Judah, that they rejoiced in Rezin, and the son of Remaliah, the enemies confederated against them? If some of the people were inclined to revolt to the enemy, (which however does not clearly appear from any part of the history or the prophecy,) yet there was nothing like a tendency to a general defection. This, therefore, must be understood of Israel. The prophet denounces the Assyrian invasion, which should overwhelm the whole kingdom of Israel under Tiglath-pileser, and Shalmaneser; and the subsequent invasion of Judah by the same power under Sennacherib, which would bring them into the most imminent danger, like a flood reaching to the neck, in which a man can but just keep his head above water. The two next verses, 9 and 10, are addressed by the prophet, as a subject of the kingdom of Judah, to the Israelites and Syrians, and perhaps to all the enemies of God's people; assuring them that their attempts against that kingdom shall be fruitless; for that the promised Immanuel, to whom he alludes by using his name to express the signification of it, *for God is with us,* shall be the defence of the house of David, and deliver the kingdom of Judah out of their hands. He then proceeds to warn the people of Judah against idolatry, divination, and the like forbidden practices; to which they were much inclined, and which would soon bring down God's judgments upon Israel. The prophecy concludes at the *sixth* verse of chap. ix. with promises of blessings in future times by the coming of the great deliverer already pointed out by the name of Immanuel, whose person and character is set forth in terms the most ample and magnificent.

And here it may be observed that it is almost the constant practice of the prophet to connect in like manner deliverances temporal with spiritual. Thus the *eleventh* chapter, setting forth the kingdom of Messiah, is closely connected with the *tenth,* which foretells the destruction of Sennacherib. So likewise the destruction of nations, enemies to God, in the *thirty-fourth*

A. M. cir. 3262 witnesses to record, [c]Uriah the
B. C. cir. 742 priest, and Zechariah the son of
Anno Olymp. Nonæ 3 Jeberechiah.
Ante Urbem Conditam 12 3 And I [d]went unto the prophetess; and she conceived, and bare a son.
Then said the LORD to me, Call his name
Maher-shalal-hash-baz.
4 [e]For before the child shall have knowledge to cry, My father and my mother, [f]the
[g]riches of Damascus and the spoil of Samaria
shall be taken away before the king of Assyria.
5 The LORD spake also unto A. M. cir. 3263
me again, saying, B. C. cir. 741
6 Forasmuch as this people Olymp. IX. 4
refuseth the waters of [h]Shiloah cir. annum Romuli, Regis Roman., 13
that go softly, and rejoice [i]in Rezin and Re-
maliah's son;
7 Now therefore, behold, the LORD bringeth
up upon them the waters of the river, strong
and many, *even* [k]the king of Assyria, and all
his glory: and he shall come up over all his
channels, and go over all his banks:

---

[c]2 Kings xvi. 10——[d]Hebrew, *approached unto*——[e]See chap. vii. 16——[f]Or, he that is *before the king of Assyria shall take away the riches*, &c.——[g]2 Kings xv. 29; xvi. 9; chapter xvii. 3——[h]Nehemiah iii. 15; John ix. 7——[i]Chapter vii. 1, 2, 6——[k]Chapter x. 12

---

chapter, introduces the flourishing state of the kingdom of Christ in the *thirty-fifth*. And thus the chapters from xl. to xlix. inclusive, plainly relating to the deliverance from the captivity of Babylon, do in some parts plainly relate to the greater deliverance by Christ.

NOTES ON CHAP. VIII

Verse 1. *Take thee a great roll*—"Take unto thee a large mirror"] The word גליון *gillayon* is not regularly formed from גלל *galal, to roll*, but from גלה *galah*, as פדיון *pidyon* from פדה *padah*, כליון *killayon* from כלה *calah*, נקיון *nikkayon* from נקה *nakah*, עליון *elyon* from עלה *alah*, &c., the י *yod* supplying the place of the radical ה *he*. גלה *galah* signifies to *show, to reveal;* properly, as *Schroederus* says, (De Vestitu Mulier. Hebr. p. 294,) *to render clear and bright by rubbing; to polish.* גליון *gillayon*, therefore, according to this derivation, is not a roll or volume: but may very well signify *a polished tablet of metal*, such as was anciently used for a *mirror*. The *Chaldee* paraphrast renders it by לוח *luach, a tablet*, and the same word, though somewhat differently pointed, the Chaldee paraphrast and the rabbins render *a mirror*, chap. iii. 23. The mirrors of the Israelitish women were made of brass finely polished, Exod. xxxviii. 8, from which place it likewise appears that what they used were little hand mirrors which they carried with them even when they assembled at the door of the tabernacle. I have a metalline mirror found in Herculaneum, which is not above three inches square. The prophet is commanded to take a mirror, or brazen polished tablet, not like these little hand mirrors, but a large one; large enough for him to engrave upon it in deep and lasting characters, בחרט אנוש *becheret enosh*, with a workman's graving tool, the prophecy which he was to deliver. חרט *cheret* in this place certainly signifies an *instrument* to *write* or *engrave* with: but חריט *charit*, the same word, only differing a little in the form, means something belonging to a lady's dress, chap. iii. 22, (where however *five* MSS. leave out the י *yod*, whereby only it differs from the word in this place,) either a crisping-pin, which might be not unlike a graving tool, as some will have it, or a purse, as others infer from 2 Kings v. 23. It may therefore be called here חרט אנוש *cheret enosh, a workman's instrument*, to distinguish it from חרט אשה *cheret ishshah, an instrument* of the same name, *used by the women.* In this manner he was to record the prophecy of the destruction of Damascus and Samaria by the Assyrians; the subject and sum of which prophecy is here expressed with great brevity in four words, מהר שלל הש בז *maher shalal hash baz;* i. e., *to hasten the spoil, to take quickly the prey;* which are afterwards applied as the name of the prophet's son, who was made a sign of the speedy completion of it; Maher-shalal-hash-baz; *Haste-to-the-spoil, Quick-to-the-prey.* And that it might be done with the greater solemnity, and to preclude all doubt of the real delivery of the prophecy before the event, he calls witnesses to attest the recording of it.

The prophet is commanded to take a great roll, and yet *four words* only are to be written in it, מהר שלל הש בז *maher shalal hash baz, Make haste to the spoil; fall upon the prey.* The great volume points out the land of Judea; and the few words the small number of inhabitants, after the *ten* tribes were carried into captivity.

The words were to be written with a *man's pen;* i. e., though the prophecy be given in the *visions* of God, yet the writing must be real; the words must be transcribed on the great roll, that they may be read and publicly consulted. Or, חרט אנוש *cherot enosh, the pen* or *graver* of the weak miserable man, may refer to the already condemned Assyrians, who though they should be the instruments of chastening Damascus and Samaria, should themselves shortly be overthrown. The four words may be considered as the commission given to the Assyrians to destroy and spoil the cities. *Make haste to the spoil; Fall upon the prey*, &c.

Verse 4. *For before the child*] For *my father and my mother*, one MS. and the *Vulgate* have *his father and his mother.* The prophecy was accordingly accomplished within three years; when Tiglath-pileser, king of Assyria, went up against Damascus and took it, and carried the people of it captive to Kir, and slew Rezin, and also took the Reubenites and the Gadites, and the half-tribe of Manasseh, and carried them captive to Assyria, 2 Kings xv. 29; xvi. 9; 1 Chron. v. 26.

Verse 6. *Forasmuch as this people refuseth*—

A. M. cir. 3263
B. C. cir. 741
Olymp. IX. 4
cir. annum
Romuli, Regis
Roman., 13

8 And he shall pass through
Judah; he shall overflow and go
over, [l]he shall reach *even* to the
neck; and [m]the stretching out
of his wings shall fill the breadth of thy
land, O [n]Immanuel.

9 [o]Associate yourselves, O ye people, [p]and
ye shall be broken in pieces; and give ear, all
ye of far countries: gird yourselves, and ye
shall be broken in pieces; gird yourselves,
and ye shall be broken in pieces.

[l]Chap. xxx. 28——[m]Heb. *the fulness of the breadth of thy land shall be the stretchings out of his wings* [n]Chapter viii. 14——[o]Joel iii. 9, 11——[p]Or, *yet*

10 [q]Take counsel together,
and it shall come to naught;
speak the word, [r]and it shall
not stand: [s]for God *is* with
us.

A. M. cir. 3263
B. C. cir. 741
Olymp. IX. 4
cir. annum
Romuli, Regis
Roman., 13

11 For the LORD spake thus to me [t]with a
strong hand, and instructed me that I should
not walk in the way of this people, saying,

12 Say ye not, A confederacy, to all *them
to* whom [u]this people shall say, A confederacy; [v]neither fear ye their fear, nor be afraid.

[q]Job v. 12——[r]Chap. vii. 7——[s]Chap. vii. 14; Acts v. 38, 39; Rom. viii. 13——[t]Heb. *in strength of hand* [u]Chap. vii. 2——[v]1 Pet. iii. 14, 15

"Because this people have rejected"] The gentle waters of Shiloah, a small fountain and brook just without Jerusalem, which supplied a pool within the city for the use of the inhabitants, is an apt emblem of the state of the kingdom and house of David, much reduced in its apparent strength, yet supported by the blessing of God; and is finely contrasted with the waters of the Euphrates, great, rapid, and impetuous; the image of the Babylonian empire, which God threatens to bring down like a mighty flood upon all these apostates of both kingdoms, as punishment for their manifold iniquities, and their contemptuous disregard of his promises. The brook and the river are put for the kingdoms to which they belong, and the different states of which respectively they most aptly represent. *Juvenal*, inveighing against the corruption of Rome by the importation of Asiatic manners, says, with great elegance, that "the Orontes has been long discharging itself into the Tiber:"—

Jampridem Syrus in Tiberim defluxit Orontes.

And *Virgil*, to express the submission of some of the Eastern countries to the Roman arms, says:—

Euphrates ibat jam mollior undis.
Æn. viii. 726.

"The waters of the Euphrates now flowed more humbly and gently."

But the happy contrast between the brook and the river gives a peculiar beauty to this passage of the prophet, with which the simple figure in the Roman poets, however beautiful, yet uncontrasted, cannot contend.

Verse 8. *He shall reach* even *to the neck*] He compares Jerusalem, says *Kimchi*, to the head of the human body. As when the waters come up to a man's neck, he is very near drowning, (for a little increase of them would go over his head,) so the king of Assyria coming up to Jerusalem was like a flood reaching to the neck—the whole country was overflowed, and the capital was in imminent danger. Accordingly the *Chaldee* renders *reaching to the neck* by *reaching to Jerusalem.*

Verse 9. *Associate yourselves*—"Know ye this"] God by his prophet plainly declares to the confederate adversaries of Judah, and bids them regard and attend to his declaration, that all their efforts shall be in vain. The present reading, רעו *rou*, is subject to many difficulties; I follow that of the *Septuagint*, דעו *deu*, γνωτε. Archbishop *Secker* approves this reading. דעו *deu, know ye this*, is parallel and synonymous to האזינו *haazinu, give ear to it*, in the next line. The *Septuagint* have likewise very well paraphrased the conclusion of this verse: "*When ye have strengthened yourselves, ye shall be broken; and though ye again strengthen yourselves, again shall ye be broken;*" taking חתו *chottu* as meaning the same with נשברו, *ye shall be broken.*

Verse 11. *With a strong hand*—"As taking me by the hand"] *Eleven* MSS., (*two* ancient,) of *Kennicott's*, *thirty-four* of *De Rossi's*, and *seven* editions, read כחזקת *kechezkath;* and so *Symmachus*, the *Syriac*, and *Vulgate*. Or rather *with a strong hand*, that is, with a strong and powerful influence of the prophetic Spirit.

Verse 12. *Say ye not, A confederacy*—"Say ye not, It is holy"] קשר *kesher*. Both the reading and the sense of this word are doubtful. The *Septuagint* manifestly read קשה *kashah;* for they render it by σκληρον, *hard*. The *Syriac* and *Chaldee* render it מרדא *merda*, and מרוד *merod, rebellion*. How they came by this sense of the word, or what they read in their copies, is not so clear. But the worst of it is, that neither of these readings or renderings gives any clear sense in this place. For why should God forbid his faithful servants to say with the unbelieving Jews, It is *hard;* or, There is a *rebellion;* or, as our translators render it, a *confederacy?* And how can this be called "walking in the way of this people?" ver. 11, which usually means, following their example, joining with them in religious worship. Or what confederacy do they mean? The union of the kingdoms of Syria and Israel against Judah? That was properly a league between two independent states, not an unlawful conspiracy of one part against another in the same state; this is the meaning of the word קשר *kesher*. For want of any satisfactory interpretation of this place that I can meet with, I adopt a conjecture of Archbishop *Secker*, which he proposes with great diffidence, and even seems immediately to give up, as being destitute of any authority to support it. I will give it in his own words:—"Videri potest ex cap. v. 16, et hujus cap. 13, 14, 19, legendum קרש vel קדוש *kadosh*, eadem sententia, qua אלהינו *Eloheynu*, Hos. xiv. 3. Sed nihil necesse est. Vide enim Jer. xi. 9; Ezek. xxii. 25. Optime tamen sic responderent huic

A. M. cir. 3263
B. C. cir. 741
Olymp. IX. 4
cir. annum
Romuli, Regis
Roman., 13

13 [w]Sanctify the LORD of
hosts himself; and [x]*let* him *be*
your fear, and *let* him *be* your
dread.

14 And [y]he shall be for a sanctuary; but
for [z]a stone of stumbling and for a rock of
offence to both the houses of Israel, for a gin
and for a snare to the inhabitants of Jerusalem.

15 And many among them shall [a]stumble,
and fall, and be broken, and be snared, and be
taken.

16 Bind up the testimony, seal the law among
my disciples.

17 And I will wait upon the LORD, that
[b]hideth his face from the house of
Jacob, and I [c]will look for him.

18 [d]Behold, I and the children
whom the LORD hath given me
[e]*are* for signs and for wonders in Israel from
the LORD of hosts, which dwelleth in Mount
Zion.

19 And when they shall say unto you,
[f]Seek unto them that have familiar spirits,
and unto wizards [g]that peep, and that mutter:
should not a people seek unto their God? for
the living [h]to the dead?

20 [i]To the law and to the testimony: if
they speak not according to this word, *it is*
because [k]*there is* [l]no light in them.

[w]Num. xx. 12——[x]Psa. lxxvi. 7; Luke xii. 5——[y]Ezek. xi. 16——[z]Chap. xxviii. 16; Luke ii. 34; Rom. ix. 33; 1 Pet. ii. 8——[a]Matt. xxi. 44; Luke xx. 18; Rom. ix. 32; xi. 25——[b]Chap. liv. 8

[c]Hab. ii. 3; Luke ii. 25, 38——[d]Heb. ii. 13——[e]Psa. lxxi. 7; Zech. iii. 8——[f]1 Sam. xxviii. 8; chap. xix. 3——[g]Chap. xxix. 4——[h]Psa. cvi. 28——[i]Luke xvi. 29——[k]Mic. iii. 6——[l]Heb. *no morning*

versiculo versiculi 13, 14." The passages of Jeremiah and Ezekiel above referred to seem to me not at all to clear up the sense of the word קשר *kesher* in this place. But the context greatly favours the conjecture here given, and makes it highly probable: "Walk not in the way of this people; call not their idols holy, nor fear ye the object of their fear:" (that is, the *σεβασματα*, or *gods* of the idolaters; for so *fear* here signifies, to wit, the thing feared. So God is called "The fear of Isaac," Gen. xxxi. 42, 53:) "but look up to JEHOVAH as your Holy One; and let him be your fear, and let him be your dread; and he shall be a holy Refuge unto you." Here there is a harmony and consistency running through the whole sentence; and the latter part naturally arises out of the former, and answers to it. Idolatry, however, is full of *fears*. The superstitious fears of the Hindoos are very numerous. They fear death, bad spirits generally, and *hobgoblins* of all descriptions. They fear also the cries of *jackalls, owls, crows, cats, asses, vultures, dogs, lizards,* &c. They also dread different *sights* in the air, and are alarmed at various dreams. See WARD'S Customs. Observe that the difference between קשר *kesher* and קדש *kadosh* is chiefly in the transposition of the two last letters, for the letters ר *resh* and ד *daleth* are hardly distinguishable in some copies, printed as well as MS.; so that the mistake, in respect of the letters themselves, is a very easy and a very common one.—L.

Verse 14. *And he shall be for a sanctuary*—"And he shall be unto you a sanctuary"] The word לכם *lachem, unto you,* absolutely necessary, as I conceive, to the sense, is lost in this place: it is preserved by the *Vulgate*, "et erit *vobis* in sanctificationem." The *Septuagint* have it in the singular number: *εσται σοι εις ἁγιασμον, it shall be to* THEE. Or else, instead of מקדש *mikdash, a sanctuary,* we must read מוקש *mokesh, a snare,* which would then be repeated without any propriety or elegance, at the end of the verse. The *Chaldee* reads instead of it משפט *mishpat, judgment;* for he renders it by פורען *purean*, which word frequently answers to משפט *mishpat* in his paraphrase. *One* MS. has instead of מקדש ולאבן *mikdash uleeben*, להם לאבן *lahem leeben*, which clears the sense and construction. But the reading of the *Vulgate* is, I think, the best remedy to this difficulty; and is in some degree authorized by להם *lahem*, the reading of the MS. above mentioned.

Verse 16. *Among my disciples.*] בלמדי *belimmudai*. The *Septuagint* render it *του μη μαθειν*. Bishop *Chandler*, Defence of Christianity, p. 308, thinks they read מלמד, *that it be not understood*, and approves of this reading.—Abp. *Secker*.

Verse 18. *Lord of hosts*] *One* MS. reads אלהי צבאות *Elohey tsebaoth, God of hosts.*

Verse 19. *Should not a people seek*—"Should they seek"] After ידרש *yidrosh*, the *Septuagint*, repeating the word, read הידרש *hayidrosh: Ουκ εθνος προς Θεον αυτου εκζητησουσι; τι εκζητησουσι περι των ζωντων τους νεκρους; Should not a nation seek unto its God? Why should you seek unto the dead concerning the living?* and this repetition of the verb seems necessary to the sense; and, as *Procopius* on the place observes, it strongly expresses the prophet's indignation at their folly.

Verse 20. *To the law and to the testimony*—"Unto the command, and unto the testimony."] "Is not תעודה *teudah* here the attested prophecy, ver. 1-4? and perhaps תורה *torah* the command, ver. 11-15? for it means sometimes a particular, and even a human, command; see Prov. vi. 20, and vii. 1, 2, where it is ordered to be hid, that is, secretly kept."—Abp. *Secker*. So *Deschamps*, in his translation, or rather paraphrase, understands it: "Tenons nous à l'instrument authentique mis en dèpôt par ordre du Seigneur," "Let us stick to the authentic instrument, laid up by the command of the Lord." If this be right, the *sixteenth* verse must be understood in the same manner.

Because there is *no light in them*—"In which there is no obscurity."] שחר *shachor*, as an adjective, frequently signifies *dark, obscure;* and the noun שחר *shachar* signifies *darkness, gloominess*, Joel ii. 2, if we may judge by the context:—

A. M. cir. 3263 B. C. cir. 741 Olymp. IX. 4 cir. annum Romuli, Regis Roman., 13

21 And they shall pass through
it, hardly bestead and hungry:
and it shall come to pass, that
when they shall be hungry, they
shall fret themselves, and [m]curse their king
and their God, and look upward.
22 And [n]they shall look unto
the earth; and behold trouble
and darkness, [o]dimness of an-
guish; and *they shall be* driven to darkness.

[m]Rev. xvi. 11 — [n]Chap. v. 30 — [o]Chap. ix. 1

"A day of darkness and obscurity;
Of cloud, and of thick vapour;
As the gloom spread upon the mountains:
A people mighty and numerous."

Where the *gloom*, שחר *shachar*, seems to be the same with the cloud and thick vapour mentioned in the line prceding. See Lam. iv. 8, and Job xxx. 30. See this meaning of the word שחר *shachar* well supported in *Christ. Muller.* Sat. Observat. Phil. p. 53, Lugd. Bat. 1752. The *morning* seems to have been an idea wholly incongruous in the passage of Joel; and in this of Isaiah the words *in which there is no morning* (for so it ought to be rendered if שחר *shachar* in this place signifies, according to its usual sense, *morning*) seem to give no meaning at all. "It is because there is no light in them," says our translation. If there be any sense in these words, it is not the sense of the original; which cannot justly be so translated. *Qui n'a rien d'obscur*, "which has no obscurity."—*Deschamps*. The reading of the *Septuagint* and *Syriac*, שחד *shochad*, *gift*, affords no assistance towards the clearing up of any of this difficult place. *R. D. Kimchi* says this was the form of an oath: "By the law and by the testimony such and such things are so." Now if they had sworn this falsely, it is because there is no *light*, no *illumination*, שחר *shachar*, no scruple of conscience, in them.

Ver. 21. *Hardly bestead*—"Distressed"] Instead of נקשה *niksheh*, *distressed*, the *Vulgate*, *Chaldee*, and *Symmachus* manifestly read נכשל *nichshal*, *stumbling*, *tottering through weakness*, *ready to fall;* a sense which suits very well with the place.

And look upward—"And he shall cast his eyes upward."] The learned professor *Michaelis*, treating of this place (Not. in de Sacr. Poës. Hebr. Præl. ix.) refers to a passage in the Koran which is similar to it. As it is a very celebrated passage, and on many accounts remarkable, I shall give it here at large, with the same author's farther remarks upon it in another place of his writings. It must be noted here that the learned professor renders נבט *nibbat*, הביט *hibbit*, in this and the parallel place, chap. v. 30, which I translate *he looketh*, by *it thundereth*, from *Schultens*, Orig. Ling. Hebr. Lib. i. cap. 2, of the justness of which rendering I much doubt. This brings the image of Isaiah more near in one circumstance to that of *Mohammed* than it appears to be in my translation:—

"*Labid*, contemporary with *Mohammed*, the last of the seven Arabian poets who had the honour of having their poems, one of each, hung up in the entrance of the temple of Mecca, struck with the sublimity of a passage in the Koran, became a convert to Mohammedism; for he concluded that no man could write in such a manner unless he were Divinely inspired.

"One must have a curiosity to examine a passage which had so great an effect upon *Labid*. It is, I must own, the finest that I know in the whole Koran: but I do not think it will have a second time the like effect, so as to tempt any one of my readers to submit to circumcision. It is in the second chapter, where he is speaking of certain apostates from the faith. 'They are like,' saith he, 'to a man who kindles a light. As soon as it begins to shine, God takes from them the light, and leaves them in darkness that they see nothing. They are deaf, dumb, and blind; and return not into the right way. Or they fare as when a cloud, full of darkness, thunder, and lightning, covers the heaven. When it bursteth, they stop their ears with their fingers, with deadly fear; and God hath the unbelievers in his power. The lightning almost robbeth them of their eyes: as often as it flasheth they go on by its light; and when it vanisheth in darkness, they stand still. If God pleased, they would retain neither hearing nor sight.' That the thought is beautiful, no one will deny; and *Labid*, who had probably a mind to flatter *Mohammed*, was lucky in finding a passage in the Koran so little abounding in poetical beauties, to which his conversion might with any propriety be ascribed. It was well that he went no farther; otherwise his taste for poetry might have made him again an infidel." *Michaelis*, Erpenii Arabische Grammatik abgekurzt, Vorrede, s. 32.

CHAPTER IX

This chapter contains an illustrious prophecy of the Messiah. He is represented under the glorious figure of the sun, or light, rising on a benighted world, and diffusing joy and gladness wherever he sheds his beams, 1–3. *His conquests are astonishing and miraculous, as in the day of Midian; and the peace which they procure is to be permanent, as denoted by the burning of all the implements of war,* 4, 5. *The person and character of this great Deliverer are then set forth in the most magnificent terms which the language of mankind could furnish,* 6. *The extent of his kingdom is declared to be universal, and the duration of it eternal,* 7. *The prophet foretells most awful calamities which were ready to fall upon the Israelites on account of their manifold impieties,* 8–21.

A. M. cir. 3264 B. C. cir. 740 Olymp. X. 1 cir. annum Romuli, Regis Roman., 14

NEVERTHELESS [a]the dim-
ness *shall* not *be* such as
was in her vexation, when at the
[b]first he lightly afflicted the land
of Zebulun, and the land of Naphtali, and
[c]afterward did more grievously afflict *her by*
the way of the sea, beyond Jordan, in Galilee
[d]of the nations.

2 [e]The people that walked in darkness have
seen a great light: they that dwell in the land
of the shadow of death, upon them hath the
light shined.

3 Thou hast multiplied the
nation, *and* [f]not increased the
joy: they joy before thee according to the joy in harvest, *and* as
men rejoice [g]when they divide the spoil.

4 [h]For thou hast broken the yoke of his
burden, and the [i]staff of his shoulder, the rod
of his oppressor, as in the day of [k]Midian.

5 [l]For every battle of the warrior *is* with
confused noise, and garments rolled in blood;
[m]but [n]*this* shall be with burning *and* [o]fuel
of fire.

---

[a]Chap. viii. 22——[b]2 Kings xv. 29; 2 Chron. xvi. 4——[c]Lev. xxvi. 24; 2 Kings xvii. 5, 6; 1 Chron. v. 26——[d]Or, *populous*——[e]Matt. iv. 16; Eph. v. 8, 14——[f]Or, *to him*——[g]Judg. v. 30

[h]Or, *When thou brakest*——[i]Chap. x. 5; xiv. 5——[k]Judg. vii. 22; Psa. lxxxiii. 9; chap. x. 26——[l]Or, *When the whole battle of the warrior was, &c.*——[m]Chap. lxvi. 15, 16——[n]Or, *and it was, &c.*——[o]Heb. *meat*

NOTES ON CHAP. IX

Verse 1. *Dimness*—"Accumulated darkness"] Either מנדחה *menuddechah*, fem. to agree with אפלה *aphelah;* or אפל המנדח *aphel hammenuddach*, alluding perhaps to the palpable Egyptian darkness, Exod. x. 21.

The land of Zebulun] Zebulun, Naphtali, Manasseh, that is, the country of Galilee all round the sea of Gennesareth, were the parts that principally suffered in the first Assyrian invasion under Tiglath-pileser; see 2 Kings xv. 29; 1 Chron. v. 26. And they were the first that enjoyed the blessings of Christ's preaching the Gospel, and exhibiting his miraculous works among them. See *Mede's* Works, p. 101, and 457. This, which makes the *twenty-third* verse of chap. viii. in the Hebrew, is the *first* verse in chap. ix. in our authorized version. Bishop *Lowth* follows the division in the Hebrew.

Verse 3. And *not increased the joy*—"Thou hast increased their joy"] *Eleven* MSS. of *Kennicott's* and *six* of *De Rossi's*, *two* ancient, read לו *lo, it*, according to the Masoretical correction, instead of לא *lo, not.* To the same purpose the *Targum* and *Syriac.*

The joy in harvest] כשמחת בקציר *kesimchath bakkatsir.* For בקציר *bakkatsir one* MS. of *Kennicott's* and *one* of *De Rossi's* have קציר *katsir*, and another הקציר *hakkatsir*, "the harvest;" one of which seems to be the true reading, as the noun preceding is *in regimine.*

Verse 5. *Every battle of the warrior*—"The greaves of the armed warrior"] סאון סאן *seon soen.* This word, occurring only in this place, is of very doubtful signification. *Schindler* fairly tells us that we may guess at it by the context. The Jews have explained it, by guess I believe, as signifying *battle, conflict:* the *Vulgate* renders it *violenta prædatio.* But it seems as if something was rather meant which was capable of becoming fuel for the fire, together with the garments mentioned in the same sentence. In *Syriac* the word, as a noun, signifies a *shoe*, or a *sandal*, as a learned friend suggested to me some years ago. See Luke xv. 22; Acts xii. 8. I take it, therefore, to mean that part of the armour which covered the legs and feet; and I would render the two words in Latin by *caliga caligati.* The burning of heaps of armour, gathered from the field of battle, as an offering made to the god supposed to be the giver of victory, was a custom that prevailed among some heathen nations; and the Romans used it as an emblem of peace, which perfectly well suits with the design of the prophet in this place. A medal struck by *Vespasian* on finishing his wars both at home and abroad represents the goddess Peace holding an olive branch in one hand, and, with a lighted torch in the other, setting fire to a heap of armour. *Virgil* mentions the custom:—

"—Cum primam aciem Præneste sub ipsa
Stravi, scutorumque incendi victor acervos."
Æn. lib. viii., ver. 561.

"Would heaven, (said he,) my strength and youth recall,
Such as I was beneath Præneste's wall—
Then when I made the foremost foes retire,
And set *whole heaps of conquered shields on fire.*"
DRYDEN.

See *Addison* on Medals, Series ii. 18. And there are notices of some such practice among the Israelites, and other nations of the most early times. God promises to Joshua victory over the kings of Canaan. "To-morrow I will deliver them up all slain before Israel: thou shalt hough their horses, and burn their chariots with fire," Josh. xi. 6. See also Nahum ii. 13. And the psalmist employs this image to express complete victory, and the perfect establishment of peace:—

"He maketh wars to cease, even to the end of the land:
He breaketh the bow, and cutteth the spear in sunder;
And burneth the chariots in the fire."
—Psa. xlvi. 9.

עגלות *agaloth*, properly *plaustra, impedimenta*, the *baggage-wagons:* which however the *Septuagint* and *Vulgate* render *scuta*, "shields;" and the *Chaldee*, "round shields," to show the propriety of that sense of the word from the etymology; which, if admitted, makes the image the same with that used by the Romans.

Ezekiel, chap xxxix. 8-10, in his bold manner, has carried this image to a degree of amplification which I think hardly any other of the Hebrew poets would have attempted. He describes the burning of the arms of the enemy,

A. M. cir. 3264
B. C. cir. 740
Olymp. X. 1
cir. annum
Romuli, Regis
Roman., 14

6 [p]For unto us a child is born,
unto us a [q]son is given: and
[r]the government shall be upon
his shoulder: and his name shall
be called [s]Wonderful, Counsellor, [t]The
mighty God, The everlasting Father, The
[u]Prince of Peace.

7 Of the increase of *his* government and peace [v]*there shall be* no
end, upon the throne of David,
and upon his kingdom, to order
it, and to establish it with judgment and with
justice from henceforth even for ever. The
[w]zeal of the LORD of hosts will perform this.

A. M. cir. 3264
B. C. cir. 740
Olymp. X. 1
cir. annum
Romuli, Regis
Roman., 14

[p]Chap. vii. 14; Luke ii. 11——[q]John iii. 16——[r]Matt. xxviii. 18; 1 Cor. xv. 25——[s]Judg. xiii. 18

[t]Tit. ii. 13——[u]Eph. ii. 14——[v]Dan. ii. 44; Luke i. 32, 33——[w]2 Kings xix. 31; chap. xxxvii. 32

in consequence of the complete victory to be obtained by the Israelites over Gog and Magog:—

"Behold, it is come to pass, and it is done,
Saith the Lord JEHOVAH.
This is the day of which I spoke:
And the inhabitants of the cities of Israel shall go forth.
And shall set on fire the armour, and the shield,
And the buckler, and the bow, and the arrows,
And the clubs, and the lances;
And they shall set them on fire for seven years.
And they shall not bear wood from the field;
Neither shall they hew from the forest:
For of the armour shall they make their fires;
And they shall spoil their spoilers,
And they shall plunder their plunderers."

R. D. Kimchi, on this verse says this refers simply to the destruction of the Assyrians. Other battles are fought man against man, and spear against spear; and the garments are rolled in blood through the wounds given and received: but this was with burning, for the angel of the Lord smote them by night, and there was neither sword nor violent commotion, nor blood; they were food for the fire, for the angel of the Lord consumed them.

Verse 6. The government shall *be upon his shoulder*] That is, the ensign of government; the sceptre, the sword, the key, or the like, which was borne upon or hung from the shoulder. See note on chap. xxii. 22.

And his name shall be called] אל גבור *El gibbor*, the prevailing or conquering God.

The everlasting Father—"The Father of the everlasting age"] Or אבי עד *Abi ad*, the Father of eternity. The *Septuagint* have μεγαλης βουλης Αγγελος, "the Messenger of the Great Counsel." But instead of אבי עד *Abi ad*, a MS. of *De Rossi* has אבעזר *Abezer*, the *helping Father;* evidently the corruption of some Jew, who did not like such an evidence in favour of the Christian Messiah.

Prince of Peace] שר שלום *sar shalom*, the Prince of prosperity, the Giver of all blessings.

A MS. of the *thirteenth* century in *Kennicott's* collection has a remarkable addition here. "He shall be a *stumbling-block*, המכשלה; the government is on his shoulder." This reading is nowhere else acknowledged, as far as I know.

Verse 7. *Of the increase*] In the common *Hebrew* Bibles, and in many MSS., this word is written with the *close* or final ם למרבה. But in *twelve* of *Kennicott's* MSS., and *twelve* of *De Rossi's*, it is written with the open מ *mem;* but here it is supposed to contain mysteries, viz., that Jerusalem shall be *shut up, closed*, and *confined*, till the days of the Messiah.

This is an ilustrious prophecy of the *incarnation* of Christ, with an enumeration of those *characters* in which he stands most nearly related to mankind as their Saviour; and of others by which his infinite *majesty* and *Godhead* are shown. He shall appear as a *child, born of a woman*, born as a Jew, *under the law*, but not in the way of ordinary generation. He is a *Son given*—the human nature, in which the fulness of the Godhead was to dwell, being produced by the creative energy of the Holy Ghost in the womb of the Virgin. See Matt. i. 20, 21, 23, 25, and Luke i. 35, and Isa. vii. 14, and the notes on those passages. As being *God manifested in the flesh*, he was *wonderful* in his conception, birth, preaching, miracles, sufferings, death, resurrection, and ascension; *wonderful* in his person, and *wonderful* in his working. He is the *Counsellor* that expounds the law; shows its origin, nature, and claims; instructs, pleads for the guilty; and ever appears in the presence of God for men. He is the *mighty God;* God essentially and *efficiently prevailing* against his enemies, and destroying ours. He is the *Father of eternity;* the Origin of all being, and the Cause of the existence, and particularly the Father, of the spirits of all flesh. The *Prince of peace*—not only the *Author* of peace, and the Dispenser of peace, but also he that *rules* by *peace*, whose rule tends always to *perfection*, and produces *prosperity*. *Of the increase of his government*—this Prince has a *government*, for he has all power both in heaven and in earth: and his government *increases*, and is daily more and more *extended*, and will continue till all things are put under his feet. His kingdom is *ordered*—every act of government regulated according to wisdom and goodness; is *established* so securely as not to be overthrown; and administered in *judgment* and *justice*, so as to manifest his wisdom, righteousness, goodness, and truth. Reader, *such* is that Jesus who came into the world to save sinners! Trust in HIM!

Chap. ix. 8-chap. x. 4. This whole passage reduced to its proper and entire form, and healed of the dislocation which it suffers by the absurd division of the chapters, makes a distinct prophecy, and a just poem, remarkable for the regularity of its disposition and the elegance of its plan. It has no relation to the preceding or following prophecy; though the parts, violently torn asunder, have been, on the one side and the other, patched on to them. Those relate principally to the kingdom of Judah; this is addressed exclusively to the kingdom of Israel. The subject of it is a denunciation of vengeance awaiting their crimes. It is divided

A. M. cir. 3266 B. C. cir. 738 Olymp. X. 3 cir. annum Romuli, Regis Roman., 16

8 The Lord sent a word into
Jacob, and it hath lighted upon
Israel.
9 And all the people shall
know, *even* Ephraim and the inhabitant of
Samaria, that say in the pride and stoutness
of heart,
10 The bricks are fallen down, but we will
build with hewn stones: the sycamores are
cut down, but we will change *them into* cedars.
11 Therefore the LORD shall set up the
adversaries of Rezin against him,
and [x]join his enemies together;
12 The Syrians before and the
Philistines behind; and they
shall devour Israel [y]with open mouth. [z]For
all this his anger is not turned away, but his
hand *is* stretched out still.
13 For [a]the people turneth not unto him
that smiteth them, neither do they seek the
LORD of hosts.
14 Therefore the LORD will cut off from

[x]Heb. *mingle*——[y]Heb. *with whole mouth*

[z]Chap. v. 25; x. 4; Jer. iv. 8——[a]Jer. v. 3; Hos. vii. 10

into *four* parts, each threatening the particular punishment of some grievous offence—of their pride, of their perseverance in their vices, of their impiety, and of their injustice. To which is added a general denunciation of a farther reserve of Divine wrath, contained in a distich, before used by the prophet on a like occasion, chap. v. 25, and here repeated after each part. This makes the intercalary verse of the poem; or, as we call it, the burden of the song.

"Post hoc comma (cap. ix. 4) interponitur spatium unius lineæ, in Cod. 2 et 3: idemque observatur in 245. in quo nullum est spatium ad finem capitis ix." *Kennicott*, Var. Lect.

"After this clause (chap. ix. 4) is interposed the space of one line in Cod. 2 and 3. The same is likewise observed in Cod. 245, in which no space exists at the end of chap. ix."

Verse 8. *Lord*—"JEHOVAH"] For אדני *Adonai*, *thirty* MSS. of *Kennicott's*, and many of *De Rossi's*, and *three* editions, read יהוה *Yehovah*.

Verse 9. *Pride and stoutness of heart*—"Carry themselves haughtily"] וידעו *veyadeu*, "and they shall know;" so ours and the Versions in general. But what is it that they shall know? The verb stands destitute of its object; and the sense is imperfect. The *Chaldee* is the only one, as far as I can find, that expresses it otherwise. He renders the verb in this place by ואתרברבו *veithrabrabu*, "they exalt themselves, or carry themselves haughtily; the same word by which he renders גבהו *gabehu*, chap. iii. 16. He seems, therefore, in this place to have read ויגבהו *vaiyigbehu*, which agrees perfectly well with what follows, and clears up the difficulty. Archbishop *Secker* conjectured וידברו *vayedabberu*, referring it to לאמר *lemor*, in the next verse, which shows that he was not satisfied with the present reading. *Houbigant* reads וירעו *vaiyereu, et pravi facti sunt*, they are become wicked, which is found in a MS.; but I prefer the reading of the *Chaldee*, which suits much better with the context.

Houbigant approves of this reading; but it is utterly unsupported by any evidence from antiquity: it is a mere mistake of ר *resh* for ד *daleth;* and I am surprised that it should be favoured by *Houbigant*.

Verse 10. *The bricks*] "The eastern bricks," says Sir *John Chardin*, (see *Harmer's* Observ. I., p. 176,) "are only clay well moistened with water, and mixed with straw, and dried in the sun." So that their walls are commonly no better than our mud walls; see *Maundrell*, p. 124. That straw was a necessary part in the composition of this sort of bricks, to make the parts of the clay adhere together, appears from Exod. v. These bricks are properly opposed to hewn stone, so greatly superior in beauty and durableness. The sycamores, which, as *Jerome* on the place says, are timber of little worth, with equal propriety are opposed to the cedars. "As the grain and texture of the sycamore is remarkably coarse and spongy, it could therefore stand in no competition at all (as it is observed, Isa. ix. 10) with the cedar, for beauty and ornament."—*Shaw*, Supplement to Travels, p. 96. We meet with the same opposition of cedars to sycamores, 1 Kings x. 27, where Solomon is said to have made silver as the stones, and cedars as the sycamores in the vale for abundance. By this *mashal*, or figurative and sententious speech, they boast that they shall easily be able to repair their present losses, suffered perhaps by the first Assyrian invasion under Tiglath-pileser; and to bring their affairs to a more flourishing condition than ever.

Some of the *bricks* mentioned above lie before me. They were brought from the site of ancient Babylon. The *straw* is *visible, kneaded with the clay;* they are very *hard*, and evidently were *dried in the sun;* for they are very easily *dissolved* in *water*.

Verse 11. *The adversaries of Rezin against him*—"The princes of Retsin against him"] For צרי *tsarey*, *enemies*, *Houbigant*, by conjecture, reads שרי *sarey*, *princes;* which is confirmed by *thirty* of *Kennicott's* and *De Rossi's* MSS., (two ancient,) one of my own, ancient; and *nine* more have צ *tsaddi*, upon a rasure, and therefore had probably at first שרי *sarey*. The princes of Retsin, the late ally of Israel, that is, the Syrians, expressly named in the next verse, shall now be excited against Israel.

The *Septuagint* in this place give us another variation; for רצין *Retsin*, they read הר ציון *har tsiyon*, ορος Σιων, *Mount Sion*, of which this may be the sense; but JEHOVAH shall set up the adversaries of Mount Sion against him, (i. e., against Israel,) and will *strengthen* his enemies together; the Syrians, the Philistines, who are called the adversaries of Mount Sion. See *Simonis* Lex. in voce סכך *sachach*.

Verse 12. *With open mouth*—"On every side"] בכל פה *bechol peh*, in every corner, in every part of their country, pursuing them to the remotest extremities, and the most retired parts. So the *Chaldee* בכל אתר *bechol athar*, in every place.

Verse 14. *In one day*.] *Thirteen* MSS. of

A. M. cir. 3266
B. C. cir. 738
Olymp. X. 3
cir. annum
Romuli, Regis
Roman., 16

Israel head and tail, branch and
rush, [b]in one day.
15 The ancient and honourable, he *is* the head; and the prophet that teacheth lies, he *is* the tail.
16 For [c]the [d]leaders of this people cause *them* to err; and [e]*they that are* led of them *are* [f]destroyed.
17 Therefore the Lord [g]shall have no joy in their young men, neither shall have mercy on their fatherless and widows: [h]for every one *is* a hypocrite and an evil doer, and every mouth speaketh [i]folly. [k]For all this his anger is not turned away, but his hand *is* stretched out still.
18 For wickedness [l]burneth as the fire: it shall devour the briers and thorns, and shall kindle in the thickets of the forest, and they shall mount up *like* the lifting up of smoke.
19 Through the wrath of the LORD of hosts is [m]the land darkened, and the people shall be as the [n]fuel of the fire: [o]no man shall spare his brother.
20 And he shall [p]snatch on the right hand, and be hungry; and he shall eat on the left hand, [q]and they shall not be satisfied: [r]they shall eat every man the flesh of his own arm:
21 Manasseh, Ephraim; and Ephraim, Manasseh: *and* they together *shall be* against Judah. [s]For all this his anger is not turned away, but his hand *is* stretched out still.

[b]Chap. x. 17; Rev. xviii. 8——[c]Chap. iii. 12——[d]Or, *they that call them blessed*——[e]Or, *they that are called blessed of them*——[f]Heb. *swallowed up*——[g]Psa. cxlvii. 10, 11——[h]Mic. vii. 2——[i]Or, *villany*

[k]Ver. 12, 21; chap. v. 25; x. 4——[l]Chap. x. 17; Mal. iv. 1——[m]Chap. viii. 22——[n]Heb. *meat*——[o]Mic. vii. 2, 6——[p]Heb. *cut*——[q]Lev. xxvi. 26——[r]Chap. xlix. 26; Jer. xix. 9——[s]Ver. 12, 17; chap. v. 25; x. 4

Kennicott and *De Rossi* read ביום *beyom*, in a day; and another has a rasure in the place of the letter ב *beth*.

Verse 17. *The Lord*—"JEHOVAH"] For אדני *Adonai*, a great number of MSS. read יהוה *Yehovah*.

Verse 18. *For wickedness*] Wickedness rageth like a fire, destroying and laying waste the nation: but it shall be its own destruction, by bringing down the fire of God's wrath, which shall burn up the briers and the thorns; that is, the wicked themselves. Briers and thorns are an image frequently applied in Scripture, when set on fire, to the rage of the wicked; violent, yet impotent, and of no long continuance. "They are extinct as the fire of thorns," Psa. cxviii. 12. To the wicked themselves, as useless and unprofitable, proper objects of God's wrath, to be burned up, or driven away by the wind. "As thorns cut up they shall be consumed in the fire," Isa. xxxiii. 12. Both these ideas seem to be joined in Psa. lviii. 9:—

"Before your pots shall feel the thorn,
As well the green as the dry, the tempest shall bear them away."

The green and the dry is a proverbial expression, meaning all sorts of them, good and bad, great and small, &c. So Ezekiel: "Behold, I will kindle a fire, and it shall devour every green tree, and every dry tree," chap. xx. 47. *D'Herbelot* quotes a Persian poet describing a pestilence under the image of a conflagration: "This was a lightning that, falling upon a forest, consumed there the green wood with the dry." See *Harmer's* Observations, Vol. II., p. 187.

Verse 20. *The flesh of his own arm*—"The flesh of his neighbour"] "Του βραχιονος του αδελφου αυτου, the *Septuagint Alexand. Duplex versio, quarum altera legit* רעו *reo, quæ vox extat*, Jer. vi. 21. *Nam* רע *rea*, αδελφος, Gen. xliii. 33. *Recte ni fallor*."—SECKER. I add to this excellent remark, that the *Chaldee* manifestly reads רעו *reo, his neighbour*, not זרעו *zeroo, his arm;* for he renders it by קריביה *karibeyh, his neighbour*. And Jeremiah has the very same expression: ואיש בשר רעהו יאכלו *veish besar reehu yochelu*, "and every one shall eat the flesh of his neighbour," chap. xix. 9. This observation, I think, gives the true reading and sense of this place: and the context strongly confirms it by explaining the general idea by particular instances, in the following verse: "Every man shall devour the flesh of his neighbour;" that is, they shall harass and destroy one another. "Manasseh shall destroy Ephraim, and Ephraim, Manasseh;" which two tribes were most closely connected both in blood and situation as brothers and neighbours; "and both of them in the midst of their own dissensions shall agree in preying upon Judah." The common reading, "shall devour the flesh of his own *arm*," in connexion with what follows, seems to make either an inconsistency, or an anticlimax; whereas by this correction the following verse becomes an elegant illustration of the foregoing.—L.

CHAPTER X

God's judgments against oppressive rulers, 1–4. *The prophet foretells the invasion of Sennacherib, and the destruction of his army. That mighty monarch is represented as a rod in the hand of God to correct his people for their sins; and his ambitious purposes, contrary to his own intentions, are made subservient to the great designs of Providence*, 5–11. *Having accomplished this work, the Almighty takes account of his impious vauntings*, 12–14; *and threatens utter destruction to the small and great of his army, represented by the thorns, and the glory of the forest*, 15–19. *This leads the prophet to comfort his countrymen with the promise of this signal interposition of God in their favour*, 20–27. *Brief description of the march of Sennacherib towards*

Jerusalem, and of the alarm and terror which he spread every where as he hastened forward, 28–32. *The spirit and rapidity of the description is admirably suited to the subject. The affrighted people are seen fleeing, and the eager invader pursuing; the cries of one city are heard by those of another; and groan swiftly succeeds to groan, till at length the rod is lifted over the last citadel. In this critical situation, however, the promise of a Divine interposition is seasonably renewed. The scene instantly changes; the uplifted arm of this mighty conqueror is at once arrested and laid low by the hand of heaven; the forest of Lebanon, (a figure by which the immense Assyrian host is elegantly pointed out, is hewn down by the axe of the Divine vengeance; and the mind is equally pleased with the equity of the judgment, and the beauty and majesty of the description,* 33, 34.

A. M. cir. 3291
B. C. cir. 713
Olymp. XVI. 4
cir. annum
NumæPompilii,
R. Roman., 3

WO unto them that [a]decree
unrighteous decrees, and
[b]that write grievousness *which*
they have prescribed;
2 To turn aside the needy from judgment,
and to take away the right from the poor of
my people, that widows may be their prey, and
that they may rob the fatherless!
3 And [c]what will ye do in [d]the day of
visitation, and in the desolation *which* shall
come from far? to whom will ye flee for help?
and where will ye leave your glory?
4 Without me they shall bow down under
the prisoners, and they shall fall under the
slain. [e]For all this his anger is not turned
away, but his hand *is* stretched out still.
5 [f]O [g]Assyrian, [h]the rod of mine anger, [i]and
the staff in their hand is mine indignation.
6 I will send him against [k]a hypocritical
nation, and against the people of my wrath
will I [l]give him a charge, to take the spoil, and
to take the prey, and [m]to tread them down
like the mire of the streets.
7 [n]Howbeit he meaneth not so,
neither doth his heart think so;
but *it is* in his heart to destroy
and cut off nations not a few.

A. M. cir. 3291
B. C. cir. 713
Olymp. XVI. 4
cir. annum
NumæPompilii,
R. Roman., 3

8 [o]For he saith, *Are* not my princes altogether kings?
9 *Is* not [p]Calno [q]as Carchemish? *is* not
Hamath as Arpad? *is* not Samaria as [r]Da-
mascus?
10 As my hand hath found the kingdoms of
the idols, and whose graven images did excel
them of Jerusalem and of Samaria;
11 Shall I not, as I have done unto Samaria and her idols, so do to Jerusalem and her
idols?
12 Wherefore it shall come to pass, *that*
when the Lord hath performed his whole
work [s]upon Mount Zion, and on Jerusalem,
[t]I will [u]punish the fruit [v]of the stout heart
of the king of Assyria, and the glory of his
high looks.
13 [w]For he saith, By the strength of my
hand I have done *it,* and by my wisdom; for

[a]Psa. lviii. 2; xciv. 20——[b]Or, *to the writers that write grievousness*——[c]Job xxxi. 14——[d]Hos. ix. 7; Luke xix. 44——[e]Chap. v. 25; ix. 12, 17, 21——[f]Or, *Wo to the Assyrian*——[g]Heb. *Asshur*——[h]Jer. li. 20——[i]Or, *though*——[k]Chap. xix. 17——[l]Jer. xxxiv. 22——[m]Heb. *to lay them a treading*

[n]Gen. l. 20; Mic. iv. 12——[o]2 Kings xviii. 24, 33, &c.; xix. 10, &c.——[p]Amos vi. 2——[q]2 Chron. xxxv. 20——[r]2 Kings xvi. 9——[s]2 Kings xix. 31——[t]Jer. l. 18——[u]Heb. *visit upon*——[v]Heb. *of the greatness of the heart*——[w]Isa. xxxvii. 24; Ezek. xxviii. 4, &c.; Dan. iv. 30

NOTES ON CHAP. X

Verse 2. *My people*] Instead of עמי *ammi,* my people, many MSS., and one of my own, ancient, read עמו *ammo,* his people. But this is manifestly a corruption.

Verse 4. *Without me*] That is, without my aid: they shall be taken captive even by the captives, and shall be subdued even by the vanquished. "The י *yod* in בלתי *bilti* is a pronoun, as in Hos. xiii. 4."—*Kimchi* on the place. One MS. has לבלתי *lebilti.*

As the people had hitherto lived *without God* in worship and obedience; so they should now be *without* his help, and should perish in their transgressions.

Verse 5. *O Assyrian*—"Ho to the Assyrian"] Here begins a new and distinct prophecy, continued to the end of the *twelfth* chapter: and it appears from ver. 9-11 of this chapter, that this prophecy was delivered after the taking of Samaria by Shalmaneser; which was in the sixth year of the reign of Hezekiah: and as the former part of it foretells the invasion of Sennacherib, and the destruction of his army, which makes the whole subject of this chapter, it must have been delivered before the *fourteenth* of the same reign.

The staff in their hand—"The staff in whose hand"] The word הוא *hu,* the staff *itself,* in this place seems to embarrass the sentence. I omit it on the authority of the Alexandrine copy of the *Septuagint: nine* MSS., (*two* ancient,) and one of my own, ancient, for ומטה הוא *umatteh hu,* read מטהו *mattehu, his staff.* Archbishop *Secker* was not satisfied with the present reading. He proposes another method of clearing up the sense, by reading ביום *beyom, in the day,* instead of בידם *beyadam, in their hand:* "And he is a staff *in the day* of mine indignation."

Verse 12. *The Lord*—"JEHOVAH"] For אדני *Adonai, fourteen* MSS. and *three editions* read יהוה *Yehovah.*

The fruit—"The effect"] "פרי *peri,* f. צבי *tsebi,* vid. xiii. 19, *sed confer,* Prov. i. 31; xxxi. 16, 31."—SECKER. The *Chaldee* renders the word פרי *peri* by עיבדי *obadey, works;* which seems to be the true sense; and I have followed it.—L.

Verse 13. *Like a valiant* man—"Strongly

A. M. cir. 3291 B. C. cir. 713 Olymp. XVI. 4 cir. annum NumæPompilii, R. Roman., 3

I am prudent: and I have removed the bounds of the people, and have robbed their treasures, and I have put down the inhabitants [x]like a valiant *man:*

14 And [y]my hand hath found as a nest the riches of the people: and as one gathereth eggs *that are* left, have I gathered all the earth; and there was none that moved the wing, or opened the mouth, or peeped.

15 Shall [z]the axe boast itself against him that heweth therewith? *or* shall the saw magnify itself against him that shaketh it? [a]as if the rod should shake *itself* against them that lift it up, *or* as if the staff should lift up [b]*itself, as if it were* no wood.

16 Therefore shall the Lord, the Lord of hosts, send among his [c]fat ones leanness; and under his glory he shall kindle a burning like the burning of a fire.

17 And the light of Israel shall be for a fire, and his Holy One for a flame: [d]and it shall burn and devour his thorns and his briers in one day;

A. M. cir. 3291 B. C. cir. 713 Olymp. XVI. 4 cir. annum NumæPompilii, R. Roman., 3

18 And shall consume the glory of his forest, and of [e]his fruitful field, [f]both soul and body; and they shall be as when a standard bearer fainteth.

19 And the rest of the trees of his forest shall be [g]few, that a child may write them.

20 And it shall come to pass in that day, *that* the remnant of Israel, and such as are escaped of the house of Jacob, [h]shall no more again stay upon him that smote them; but shall stay upon the LORD, the Holy One of Israel, in truth.

21 [i]The remnant shall return, *even* the remnant of Jacob, unto the mighty God.

22 [k]For though thy people Israel be as the

[x]Or, *like many people*——[y]Job xxxi. 25——[z]Jer. li. 20 [a]Or, *as if a rod should shake them that lift it up*——[b]Or, that which is *not wood*——[c]Chap. v. 17——[d]Chap. ix. 18; xxvii. 4

[e]2 Kings xix. 23——[f]Heb. *from the soul, and even to the flesh*——[g]Heb. *number*——[h]See 2 Kings xvi. 7; 2 Chronicles xxviii. 20——[i]Chapter vii. 3——[k]Rom. ix. 27

seated." *Twelve* MSS. agree with the Keri in reading כביר *kabbir*, without the א *aleph*. And *Sal. ben Melec* and *Kimchi* thus explain it: "them who dwelled in a great and strong place I have brought down to the ground."

Verse 15. *No wood*—"Its master."] I have here given the meaning, without attempting to keep to the expression of the original, לא עץ *lo ets*, "the no-wood;" that which is not wood like itself, but of a quite different and superior nature. The Hebrews have a peculiar way of joining the negative particle לא *lo* to a noun, to signify in a strong manner a total negation of the thing expressed by the noun.

"How hast thou given help (ללא כח *lelo choach*) to the no-strength?
And saved the arm (לא עז *lo oz*) of the no-power?
How hast, thou given counsel (ללא חכמה *lelo chochmah*) to the no-wisdom?"
Job xxvi. 2, 3.

That is, to the man totally deprived of strength, power, and wisdom.

"Ye that rejoice (ללא דבר *lelo dabar*) in nothing." Amos vi. 13.

That is, in your fancied strength, which is none at all, a mere nonentity.

"For I am God, (ולא איש *velo ish,*) and no-man;
The Holy One in the midst of thee, yet do not frequent cities." Hos. xi. 9.

"And the Assyrian shall fall by a sword (לא איש *lo ish*) of no-man;
And a sword of (לא אדם *lo adam*) no-mortal, shall devour him." Isa. xxxi. 8.

"Wherefore do ye weigh out your silver (בלוא לחם *belo lechem*) for the no-bread."
Isa. lv. 2.

So here לא עץ *lo ets* means him who is far from being an inert piece of wood, but is an animated and active being; not an instrument, but an agent.

Verse 16. *The Lord*—"JEHOVAH."] For אדני *Adonai*, *fifty-two* MSS., *eleven* editions, and two of my own, ancient, read יהוה *Yehovah*, as in other cases.

And under his glory] That is, all that he could boast of as great and strong in his army, (*Sal. ben Melec in loc.,*) expressed afterwards, ver. 18, by the glory of his forest, and of his fruitful field.

Verse 17. *And it shall burn and devour his thorns*—"And he shall burn and consume his thorn."] The briers and thorns are the common people; the glory of his forest are the nobles and those of highest rank and importance. See note on chap. ix. 17, and compare Ezek. xx. 47. The fire of God's wrath shall destroy them, both great and small; it shall consume them *from the soul to the flesh;* a proverbial expression; *soul and body*, as we say; it shall consume them entirely and altogether; and the few that escape shall be looked upon as having escaped from the most imminent danger; "as a firebrand plucked out of the fire," Amos iv. 11; ὡς δια πυρος, *so as by fire*, 1 Cor. iii. 15; as a man when a house is burning is forced to make his escape by running through the midst of the fire.

I follow here the reading of the *Septuagint*, כמאש נסס *kemash noses*, ὡς ὁ φευγων απω φλογος χαιομενης, *as he who flees from the burning flame. Symmachus* also renders the latter word by φευγων, *flying*.

Verse 21. *The remnant shall return—unto*

A. M. cir. 3291
B. C. cir. 713
Olymp. XVI. 4
cir. annum
NumæPompilii,
R. Roman., 3

sand of the sea, [l]*yet* a remnant
[m]of them shall return: [n]the consumption decreed shall overflow
[o]with righteousness.

23 [p]For the Lord GOD of hosts shall make
a consumption, even determined, in the midst
of all the land.

24 Therefore thus saith the Lord GOD of
hosts, O my people that dwellest in Zion, [q]be
not afraid of the Assyrian: he shall smite
thee with a rod, [r]and shall lift up his staff
against thee, after the manner of [s]Egypt.

25 [t]For yet a very little while, [u]and the indignation shall cease, and mine
anger in their destruction.

A. M. cir. 3291
B. C. cir. 713
Olymp. XVI. 4
cir. annum
NumæPompilii,
R. Roman., 3

26 And the LORD of hosts shall
stir up [v]a scourge for him according to the slaughter of [w]Midian at the
rock of Oreb: and [x]*as* his rod *was* upon
the sea, so shall he lift it up after the manner of Egypt.

27 And it shall come to pass in that day,
that [y]his burden [z]shall be taken away from
off thy shoulder, and his yoke from off thy
neck, and the yoke shall be destroyed because of [a]the anointing.

---

[l]Chap. vi. 13——[m]Heb. *in* or *among*——[n]Chap. xxviii. 22——[o]Or, *in*——[p]Chap. xxviii. 22; Dan. ix. 27; Rom. ix. 28——[q]Chap. xxxvii. 6——[r]Or, *but he shall lift up his staff for thee*——[s]Exod. xiv

[t]Chap. liv. 7——[u]Dan. xi. 36——[v]2 Kings xix. 35 [w]Judg. vii. 25; chap. ix. 4——[x]Exod. xiv. 26, 27 [y]Chap. xiv. 25——[z]Heb. *shall remove*——[a]Psa. cv. 15; Dan. ix. 24; 1 John ii. 20

---

the mighty God.] אל גבור *El gibbor*, the *mighty* or *conquering God;* the Messiah, the same person mentioned in ver. 6 of the preceding chapter.

Verse 22. *For though thy people Israel*] I have endeavoured to keep to the letter of the text as nearly as I can in this obscure passage; but it is remarkable that neither the *Septuagint*, nor St. *Paul*, Rom. ix. 28, who, except in a few words of no great importance, follows them nearly in this place, nor any one of the ancient Versions, take any notice of the word שטף *shoteph, overflowing;* which seems to give an idea not easily reconcilable with those with which it is here joined. *I. S. Mœrlius* (Schol. Philolog. ad Selecta S. Cod. loca) conjectures that the two last letters of this word are by mistake transposed, and that the true reading is שפט *shophet, judging*, with strict justice. The *Septuagint* might think this sufficiently expressed by *εν δικαιοσυνῃ, in righteousness.* One MS., with St. *Paul* and *Septuagint Alex.*, omits בו *bo* in ver. 22; *sixty-nine* of *Kennicott's* and *seventeen* of *De Rossi's* MSS. and *eight* editions, omit כל *col, all*, in ver. 23; and so St. *Paul*, Rom. ix. 28.

The learned Dr. *Bagot*, dean of Christ Church, Oxford, afterwards Bishop of Bristol and Norwich, in some observations on this place, which he has been so kind as to communicate to me, and which will appear in their proper light when he himself shall give them to the public, renders the word כליון *kilayon* by *accomplishment*, and makes it refer to the predictions of Moses; the blessing and the curse which he laid before the people; both conditional, and depending on their future conduct. They had by their disobedience incurred those judgments which were now to be fully executed upon them. His translation is, *The accomplishment determined overflows with justice; for it is accomplished, and that which is determined the Lord God of hosts doeth in the midst of the land.*—L. Some think that the words might be paraphrased thus: The determined destruction of the Jews shall overflow with righteousness, (צדקה *tsedakah,*) justification, the consequence of the Gospel of Christ being preached and believed on in the world. After the destruction of Jerusalem this word or doctrine of the Lord had free course,—did *run*, and was glorified.

Verse 24. *After the manner of Egypt*—"In the way of Egypt."] I think there is a designed ambiguity in these words. Sennacherib, soon after his return from his Egyptian expedition, which, I imagine, took him up three years, invested Jerusalem. He is represented by the prophet as lifting up his rod in his march from Egypt, and threatening the people of God, as Pharaoh and the Egyptians had done when they pursued them to the Red Sea. But God in his turn will lift up his rod over the sea, as he did at that time, in the way, or after the manner, of Egypt; and as Sennacherib has imitated the Egyptians in his threats, and came full of rage against them from the same quarter; so God will act over again the same part that he had taken formerly in Egypt, and overthrow their enemies in as signal a manner. It was all to be, both the attack and the deliverance, בדרך *bederech*, or כדרך *kederech*, as a MS. has it in each place, *in the way*, or *after the manner*, of Egypt.

Verse 25. *The indignation*—"Mine indignation."] *Indignatio mea, Vulg.* ἡ οργη, *Sept.* Μου ἡ οργη ἡ κατα σου, MS. *Pachom.* Μου ἡ οργη κατα σου, MS. I. D. II. So that זעמי *zaami*, or הזעם *hazzaam*, as one MS. has it, seems to be the true reading.

Verse 26. *And* as *his rod* was *upon the sea*—"And like his rod which he lifted up over the sea"] The Jewish interpreters suppose here an ellipsis of כ *ke*, the particle of similitude, before מטהו *mattehu*, to be supplied from the line above; so that here are two similitudes, one comparing the destruction of the Assyrians to the slaughter of the Midianites at the rock of Oreb; the other to that of the Egyptians at the Red Sea. *Aben Ezra, Kimchi, Sal. ben Melec.*

Verse 27. *From off thy shoulder*] Bishop *Lowth* translates the whole verse thus:—

"And it shall come to pass in that day,
His burden shall be removed from off thy shoulder;
And his yoke off thy neck:
Yea, the yoke shall perish from off your shoulders."

A. M. cir. 3291
B. C. cir. 713
Olymp. XVI. 4
cir. annum
NumæPompilii,
R. Roman., 3

28 He is come to Aiath, he is
passed to Migron; at Michmash
he hath laid up his carriages:
29 They are gone over the
[b]passage: they have taken up their lodging at
Geba; Ramah is afraid; [c]Gibeah of Saul
is fled.
30 [d]Lift up thy voice, O daughter [e]of Gallim:
cause it to be heard unto [f]Laish, [g]O
poor Anathoth.
31 [h]Madmenah is removed; the inhabitants
of Gebim gather themselves to flee.

[b]1 Sam. xiii. 23——[c]1 Sam. xi. 4——[d]Heb. *cry shrill with thy voice*——[e]1 Sam. xxv. 44——[f]Judg. xviii. 7——[g]Josh. xxi. 18

32 As yet shall he remain [i]at
Nob that day: he shall [k]shake
his hand *against* the mount of
[l]the daughter of Zion, the hill
of Jerusalem.
33 Behold, the Lord, the LORD of hosts,
shall lop the bough with terror: and [m]the
high ones of stature *shall be* hewn down, and
the haughty shall be humbled.
34 And he shall cut down the thickets of
the forest with iron, and Lebanon shall fall
[n]by a mighty one.

[h]Josh. xv. 31——[i]1 Sam. xxi. 1; xxii. 19; Neh. xi. 32——[k]Chap. xiii. 2——[l]Chap. xxxvii. 22——[m]See Amos ii. 9——[n]Or, *mightily*

On which he gives us the following note: I follow here the *Septuagint,* who for מפני שמן *mippeney shamen* read משכמיכם *mishshichmeychem*, *απο των ωμων ὑμων*, *from your shoulders*, not being able to make any good sense out of the present reading. I will add here the marginal conjectures of Archbishop *Secker*, who appears, like all others, to have been at a loss for a probable interpretation of the text as it now stands. "ô. *leg.* שכם shakam; *forte legend.* מבני שמן mibbeney shamen, *vide* cap. v. 1. Zech. iv. 14: *Et possunt intelligi Judæi uncti Dei*, Psa. cv. 15, *vel Assyrii,* משמנים mishmannim, *hic* ver. 16, *ut dicat propheta depulsum iri jugum ab his impositum: sed hoc durius. Vel potest legi* מפני שמי mippeney shami."

Verse 28. *He is come to Aiath*] A description of the march of Sennacherib's army approaching Jerusalem in order to invest it, and of the terror and confusion spreading and increasing through the several places as he advanced; expressed with great brevity, but finely diversified. The places here mentioned are all in the neighbourhood of Jerusalem; from *Ai* northward, to *Nob* westward of it; from which last place he might probably have a prospect of Mount *Sion*. *Anathoth* was within three Roman miles of Jerusalem, according to *Eusebius*, *Jerome* and *Josephus*. Onomast. Loc. Hebr. et Antiq. Jud. x. 7, 3. *Nob* was probably still nearer. And it should seem from this passage of Isaiah that Sennacherib's army was destroyed near the latter of these places. In coming out of Egypt he might perhaps join the rest of his army at *Ashdod*, after the taking of that place, which happened about that time, (see chap. xx.;) and march from thence near the coast by *Lachish* and *Libnah*, which lay in his way from south to north, and both which he invested till he came to the north-west of Jerusalem, crossing over to the north of it, perhaps by *Joppa* and *Lydda;* or still more north through the plain of *Esdraelon.*

Verse 29. *They are gone over the passage*—"They have passed the strait"] The strait here mentioned is that of Michmas, a very narrow passage between two sharp hills or rocks, (see 1 Sam. xiv. 4, 5,) where a great army might have been opposed with advantage by a very inferior force. The author of the Book of Judith might perhaps mean this pass, at least among others: "Charging them to keep the passages of the hill country, for by them there was an entrance into Judea; and it was easy to stop them that would come up, because the passage was strait for two men at the most," Judith iv. 7. The enemies having passed the strait without opposition, shows that all thoughts of making a stand in the open country were given up, and that their only resource was in the strength of the city.

Their lodging] The sense seems necessarily to require that we read למו *lamo, to them,* instead of לנו *lanu, to us.* These two words are in other places mistaken one for the other. Thus chap. xliv. 7, for למו *lamo,* read לנו *lanu.* with the *Chaldee;* and in the same manner Psa. lxiv. 6, with the *Syriac*, and Psa. lxxx. 7, on the authority of the *Septuagint* and *Syriac*, besides the necessity of the sense.

Verse 30. *Cause it to be heard unto Laish, O poor Anathoth*—"Hearken unto her, O Laish; answer her, O Anathoth!"] I follow in this the *Syriac* Version. The prophet plainly alludes to the name of the place, and with a peculiar propriety, if it had its name from its remarkable echo. "ענתות anathoth, *responsiones: eadem ratio nominis, quæ in* בית ענת beith anath, *locus echus; nam hodienum ejus rudera ostenduntur in valle, scil. in medio montium, ut referunt Robertus in Itiner.* p. 70, *et Monconnysius*, p. 301." *Simonis Onomasticon Vet. Test.*—L. *Anathoth*—Answers, replies; for the same reason that Bethany, בית ענת *beith anath,* had its name, *the house of echo;* the remains of which are still shown in the valley, i. e., among the mountains.

Verse 33. *Shall lop the bough with terror*] פארה *purah;* but פורה *purah, wine-press,* is the reading of *twenty-six* of *Kennicott's* and *twenty-three* of *De Rossi's* MSS., *four* ancient editions, with *Symmachus, Theodotion,* and the *Chaldee.*

Verse 34. *Lebanon shall fall by a mighty one*] באדיר *beaddir*, the angel of the Lord, who smote them, *Kimchi.* And so *Vitringa* understands it. Others translate, "The high cedars of Lebanon shall fall:" but the king of Assyria is the person who shall be overthrown.

CHAPTER XI

The Messiah represented as a slender twig shooting up from the root of an old withered stem, which tender plant, so extremely weak in its first appearance, should nevertheless become fruitful and mighty, 1–4. *Great equity of the Messiah's government,* 5. *Beautiful assemblages of images by which the great peace and happiness of his kingdom are set forth,* 6–8. *The extent of his dominion shall be ultimately that of the whole habitable globe,* 9. *The prophet, borrowing his imagery from the exodus from Egypt, predicts, with great majesty of language, the future restoration* of the outcasts of Israel and the dispersed of Judah, (*viz., the whole of the* twelve *tribes of Israel,*) *from their several dispersions, and also that blessed period when both* Jews *and* Gentiles *shall assemble under the banner of Jesus, and zealously unite in extending the limits of his kingdom,* 10–16.

A. M. cir. 3291 B. C. cir. 713 Olymp. XVI. 4 cir. annum NumæPompilii, R. Roman., 3

AND [a]there shall come forth
a rod out of the stem of
[b]Jesse, and [c]a Branch shall grow
out of his roots:

2 [d]And the Spirit of the LORD shall rest
upon him, the spirit of wisdom and understanding, the spirit of counsel and might, the
spirit of knowledge and of the fear of the
LORD;

3 And shall make him of quick [e]under-
standing in the fear of the LORD: and he shall
not judge after the sight of his eyes, neither
reprove after the hearing of his ears;

4 But [f]with righteousness shall
he judge the poor, and [g]reprove
with equity for the meek of the
earth: and he shall [h]smite the
earth with the rod of his mouth, and with
the breath of his lips shall he slay the
wicked.

5 And [i]righteousness shall be the girdle of
his loins, and faithfulness the girdle of his reins.

6 [k]The wolf also shall dwell with the lamb,
and the leopard shall lie down with the kid;
and the calf and the young lion and the fatling
together; and a little child shall lead them.

A. M. cir. 3291 B. C. cir. 713 Olymp. XVI. 4 cir. annum NumæPompilii, R. Roman., 3

[a]Chap. liii. 2; Zech. vi. 12; Rev. v. 5——[b]Acts xiii. 23; ver. 10——[c]Chap. iv. 2; Jer. xxiii. 5——[d]Chap. lxi. 1; Matt. iii. 16; John i. 32, 33; iii. 34——[e]Heb. *scent* or *smell*

[f]Psa. lxxii. 2, 4; Rev. xix. 11——[g]Or, *argue*——[h]Job iv. 9; Mal. iv. 6; 2 Thess. ii. 8; Rev. i. 16; ii. 16; xix. 15 [i]See Psa. xl. 9; li. 14; lxv. 5; lxxii. 19; Eph. vi. 14 [k]Chap. lxv. 25; Ezek. xxxiv. 25; Hos. ii. 18

NOTES ON CHAP. XI

The prophet had described the destruction of the Assyrian army under the image of a mighty forest, consisting of flourishing trees growing thick together, and of a great height; of Lebanon itself crowned with lofty cedars, but cut down and laid level with the ground by the axe wielded by the hand of some powerful and illustrious agent. In opposition to this image he represents the great Person who makes the subject of this chapter as a slender twig shooting out from the trunk of an old tree, cut down, lopped to the very root, and decayed; which tender plant, so weak in appearance, should nevertheless become fruitful and prosper. This contrast shows plainly the connexion between this and the preceding chapter, which is moreover expressed by the connecting particle; and we have here a remarkable instance of that method so common with the prophets, and particularly with Isaiah, of taking occasion, from the mention of some great temporal deliverance, to launch out into the display of the spiritual deliverance of God's people by the Messiah; for that this prophecy relates to the Messiah we have the express authority of St. Paul, Rom. xv. 12. "He joins this paragraph, with respect to the days of the Messiah, with the fidelity that was in the days of Hezekiah."—*Kimchi,* in ver. 1. Thus in the latter part of Isaiah's prophecies the subject of the great redemption, and of the glories of the Messiah's kingdom, arises out of the restoration of Judah by the deliverance from the captivity of Babylon, and is all along connected and intermixed with it.

Verse 4. *With the rod of his mouth*—"By the blast of his mouth"] For בשבט *beshebet,* by the *rod, Houbigant* reads בשבת *beshebeth,* by the *blast* of his mouth, from נשב *nashab, to blow.* The conjecture is ingenious and probable; and seems to be confirmed by the *Septuagint* and *Chaldee,* who render it by the *word* of his mouth, which answers much better to the correction than to the present reading. Add to this, that the *blast of his mouth* is perfectly parallel to *the breath of his lips* in the next line.

Verse 5. *The girdle*—"The cincture"] All the ancient Versions, except that of *Symmachus,* have two different words for *girdle* in the two hemistichs. It is not probable that Isaiah would have repeated אזור *azer,* when a synonymous word so obvious as חגור *chagor* occurred. The tautology seems to have arisen from the mistake of some transcriber. The meaning of this verse is, that a zeal for justice and truth shall make him active and strong in executing the great work which he shall undertake. See note on chap. v. 27.

Verse 6. *The wolf also shall, &c.*—"Then shall the wolf," &c.] The idea of the renewal of the golden age, as it is called, is much the same in the Oriental writers with that of the Greeks and Romans:—the wild beasts grow tame; serpents and poisonous herbs become harmless; all is peace and harmony, plenty and happiness:—

Occidet et serpens, et fallax herba veneni
Occidet. VIRG. *Eclog.* iv. 24.

"The serpent's brood shall die. The sacred ground
Shall weeds and noxious plants refuse to bear."

A. M. cir. 3291 B. C. cir. 713 Olymp. XVI. 4 cir. annum NumæPompilii, R. Roman., 3

7 And the cow and the bear
shall feed; their young ones
shall lie down together: and the
lion shall eat straw like the ox.
8 And the sucking child shall play on the
hole of the asp, and the weaned child shall put
his hand on the [l]cockatrice' den.
9 [m]They shall not hurt nor destroy in all
my holy mountain: for [n]the earth shall be full
of the knowledge of the LORD,
as the waters cover the sea.
10 [o]And in that day [p]there
shall be a root of Jesse, which
shall stand for an ensign of the people; to
it shall the [q]Gentiles seek: and [r]his rest
shall be [s]glorious.
11 And it shall come to pass [t]in that day,
that the LORD shall set his hand again the

[l]Or, *adder's*——[m]Job v. 23; ch. ii. 4; xxxv. 9——[n]Hab. ii. 14——[o]Chap. ii. 11

[p]Ver. 1; Rom. xv. 12——[q]Rom. xv. 10——[r]Heb. iv. 1, &c.——[s]Heb. *glory*——[t]Chap. ii. 11

——Nec magnos metuent armenta leones.
VIRG. *Eclog.* iv. 22.

"Nor shall the flocks fear the great lions."

Non lupus insidias explorat ovilia circum,
Nec gregibus nocturnus obambulat: acrior illum
Cura domat: timidæ damæ cervique fugaces
Nunc interque canes, et circum tecta vagantur.
VIRG. *Georg.* iii. 537.

"The nightly wolf that round the enclosure prowled,
To leap the fence, now plots not on the fold:
Tamed with a sharper pain, the fearful doe
And flying stag amidst the greyhounds go;
And round the dwellings roam, of man, their former foe." DRYDEN.

Nec vespertinus circumgemit ursus ovile,
Nec intumescit alta viperis humus.
HOR. *Epod.* xvi. 51.

"Nor evening bears the sheepfold growl around,
Nor mining vipers heave the tainted ground."
DRYDEN.

Εσται δη τουτ' αμαρ, ὁπηνικα νεβρον εν ευνᾳ
Καρχαροδων δινεσθαι ιδων λυκος ουκ εθελησει.
THEOC. *Idyl.* xxiv. 84.

There shall be a time when the ravenous wolf shall see the kid lying at ease, and shall feel no desire to do it an injury.

I have laid before the reader these common passages from the most elegant of the ancient poets, that he may see how greatly the prophet on the same subject has the advantage upon the comparison; how much the former fall short of that beauty and elegance, and variety of imagery, with which Isaiah has set forth the very same ideas. The wolf and the leopard not only forbear to destroy the lamb and the kid, but even take their abode and lie down together with them. The calf, and the young lion, and the fatling, not only come together, but are led quietly in the same band, and that by a little child. The heifer and the she-bear not only feed together, but even lodge their young ones, for whom they used to be most jealously fearful, in the same place. All the serpent kind is so perfectly harmless, that the sucking infant and the newly weaned child puts his hand on the basilisk's den, and plays upon the hole of the aspic. The lion not only abstains from preying on the weaker animals, but becomes tame and domestic, and feeds on straw like the ox. These are all beautiful circumstances, not one of which has been touched upon by the ancient poets. The Arabian and Persian poets elegantly apply the same ideas to show the effects of justice impartially administered, and firmly supported, by a great and good king:—

"Mahmoud the powerful king, the ruler of the world,
To whose tank the wolf and the lamb come together to drink." FERDUSI.

"Through the influence of righteousness, the hungry wolf
Becomes mild, though in the presence of the white kid." IBN ONEIN.
JONES, *Poes. Asiat. Comment.*, p. 380.

The application is extremely ingenious and beautiful: but the exquisite imagery of Isaiah is not equalled.

Verse 7. In this verse a word is omitted in the text, יחדו *yachdav, together;* which ought to be repeated in the second hemistich, being quite necessary to the sense. It is accordingly twice expressed by the *Septuagint* and *Syriac*.

Verse 8. *The cockatrice' den.*] This is supposed, both by the *Targum* and by *Kimchi*, to mean the pupil of this serpent's eye. "When," says *Kimchi*, "he is in the mouth of his den, in an obscure place, then his eyes *sparkle* exceedingly: the child, seeing this, and supposing it to be a piece of *crystal*, or *precious stone*, puts forth his hand to take it. What would be very dangerous at another time, shall be safe in the days of the Messiah; for the serpent will not hurt the child."

Verse 10. *A root of Jesse, which shall stand,* &c.—"The root of Jesse, which standeth," &c.] St. John hath taken this expression from Isaiah, Rev. v. 5, and xxii. 16, where Christ hath twice applied it to himself. Seven MSS. have עומד *omed, standing*, the present participle. Radix Isæi dicitur jam stare, et aliquantum stetisse, in signum populorum.—VITRINGA. "The root of Jesse is said to *stand*, and for some time to *have stood*, for an ensign to the people." Which rightly explains either of the two readings. The *one hundred and tenth* psalm is a good comment on this verse. See the notes there.

Verse 11. *And it shall come to pass in that day*] This part of the chapter contains a prophecy which certainly remains yet to be accomplished.

The Lord—"JEHOVAH"] For אדני *Adonai*, thirty-three MSS. of *Kennicott's*, and many of *De Rossi's*, and two editions, read יהוה *Yehovah.*

The islands of the sea.] The Roman and Turkish empires, say *Kimchi*.

A. M. cir. 3291
B. C. cir. 713
Olymp. XVI. 4
cir. annum
NumæPompilii,
R. Roman., 3

second time to recover the remnant of his people, which shall
be left, [u]from Assyria, and from
Egypt, and from Pathros, and
from Cush, and from Elam, and from Shinar,
and from Hamath, and from the islands of
the sea.
12 And he shall set up an ensign for the
nations, and shall assemble the outcasts of
Israel, and gather together [v]the dispersed of
Judah from the four [w]corners of the earth.
13 [x]The envy also of Ephraim shall depart,
and the adversaries of Judah shall be cut off:
Ephraim shall not envy Judah, and Judah
shall not vex Ephraim.
14 But they shall fly upon the shoulders of
the Philistines toward the west;
they shall spoil [y]them of the
east together: [z]they [a]shall lay
their hand upon Edom and
Moab; [b]and the children of Ammon [c]shall
obey them.
15 And the LORD [d]shall utterly destroy the
tongue of the Egyptian Sea; and with his
mighty wind shall he shake his hand over the
river, and shall smite it in the seven streams
[e]and make *men* go over [f]dry shod.
16 [g]And there shall be a highway for the
remnant of his people, which shall be left,
from Assyria; [h]like as it was to Israel in the
day that he came up out of the land of
Egypt.

[u]Zech. x. 10——[v]John vii. 35; James i. 1——[w]Heb. *wings*——[x]Jer. iii. 18; Ezek. xxxvii. 16, 17, 22; Hos. i. 11——[y]Heb. *the children of the east*——[z]Dan. xi. 41——[a]Heb. *Edom and Moab* shall be *the laying on of their hand*——[b]Heb. *the children of Ammon their obedience*——[c]Chap. lx. 14——[d]Zech. x. 11——[e]Rev. xvi. 12——[f]Heb. *in shoes*——[g]Chap. xix. 23——[h]Exod. xiv. 29; chap. li. 10; lxiii. 12, 13

Verse 13. *The adversaries of Judah*—"And the enmity of Judah"] צ֗ירים *tsorerim*. Postulat pars posterior versus, ut intelligantur *inimicitiæ* Judæ in Ephraimum: et potest (צררים *tsorerim*) inimicitiam notare, ut (נחומים *nichumim*) pœnitentiam, Hos. xi. 8.—SECKER.

Verse 15. *The Lord—shall smite it in the seven streams*—"Smite with a drought"] The *Chaldee* reads החריב *hecherib;* and so perhaps the *Septuagint*, who have ερημωσει, the word by which they commonly render it. Vulg. *desolabit;* "shall desolate." The *Septuagint, Vulgate*, and *Chaldee* read הדריכהו *hidrichahu*, "shall make *it* passable," adding the pronoun, which is necessary: but this reading is not confirmed by any MS.

Here is a plain allusion to the passage of the Red Sea. And the Lord's shaking his hand over the river with his vehement wind, refers to a particular circumstance of the same miracle: for "he caused the sea to go back by a strong east wind all that night, and made the sea dry land," Exod. xiv. 21. The *tongue;* a very apposite and descriptive expression for a bay such as that of the Red Sea. It is used in the same sense, Josh. xv. 2, 5; xviii. 19. The Latins gave the same name to a narrow strip of land running into the sea: *tenuem producit in æquora linguam.* LUCAN. ii. 613. *He shall smite the river in its seven streams.* This has been supposed to refer to the *Nile*, because it falls into the Mediterranean Sea by *seven mouths:* but *R. Kimchi* understands it of the *Euphrates*, which is the opinion of some good judges. See the *Targum.* See below.

Herodotus, lib. i. 189, tells a story of his Cyrus, (a very different character from that of the Cyrus of the Scriptures and Xenophon,) which may somewhat illustrate this passage, in which it is said that God would inflict a kind of punishment and judgment on the Euphrates, and render it fordable by dividing it into seven streams. "Cyrus, being impeded in his march to Babylon by the Gyndes, a deep and rapid river which falls into the Tigris, and having lost one of his sacred white horses that attempted to pass it, was so enraged against the river that he threatened to reduce it, and make it so shallow that it should be easily fordable even by women, who should not be up to their knees in passing it. Accordingly he set his whole army to work, and cutting three hundred and sixty trenches, from both sides of the river, turned the waters into them, and drained them off."

CHAPTER XII

Prophetic hymn of praise for the great mercies vouchsafed to the children of Israel in their deliverance from the great Babylonish captivity, and for redemption by the Messiah, 1–6.

A. M. cir. 3291
B. C. cir. 713
Olymp. XVI. 4
cir. annum
NumæPompilii,
R. Roman., 3

AND [a]in that day thou shalt
say, O LORD, I will praise
thee: though thou wast angry
with me, thine anger is turned
away, and thou comfortedst
me.
2 Behold, God *is* my salvation;
I will trust, and not be afraid: for

[a]Isaiah, chap. ii. 11

This hymn seems, by its whole tenor, and by many expressions in it, much better calculated for the use of the Christian Church than for the Jewish, in any circumstances, or at any

A. M. cir. 3291
B. C. cir. 713
Olymp. XVI. 4
cir. annum
NumæPompilii,
R. Roman., 3

the LORD [b]JEHOVAH *is* my
[c]strength and *my* song; he also
is become my salvation.
3 Therefore with joy shall
ye draw [d]water out of the wells of salvation.
4 And in that day shall ye say, [e]Praise the
LORD, [f]call upon his name, [g]declare his
doings among the people, make
mention that his [h]name is exalted.
5 [i]Sing unto the LORD; for he
hath done excellent things: this
is known in all the earth.
6 [k]Cry out and shout, thou [l]inhabitant of
Zion: for great *is* [m]the Holy One of Israel in
the midst of thee.

[b]Psa. lxxxiii. 18——[c]Exod. xv. 2——[d]John iv. 10, 14; vii. 37, 38——[e]1 Chron. xvi. 8; Psa. cv. 1——[f]Or, *proclaim his name*——[g]Psa. cxlv. 4, 5, 6——[h]Psa. xxxiv. 3

[i]Exod. xv. 1, 21; Psa. lxviii. 32; xcviii. 1——[k]Chap. liv. 1; Zeph. iii. 14——[l]Heb. *inhabitress*——[m]Psa. lxxi. 22; lxxxix. 18; chap. xli. 14, 16

time that can be assigned. The Jews themselves seem to have applied it to the times of Messiah. On the last day of the feast of tabernacles they fetched water in a golden pitcher from the fountain of Shiloah, springing at the foot of Mount Sion without the city: they brought it through the water-gate into the temple, and poured it, mixed with wine, on the sacrifice as it lay upon the altar, with great rejoicing. They seem to have taken up this custom, for it is not ordained in the law of Moses, as an emblem of future blessings, in allusion to this passage of Isaiah, "Ye shall draw waters with joy from the fountains of salvation," expressions that can hardly be understood of any benefits afforded by the Mosaic dispensation. Our Saviour applied the ceremony, and the intention of it, to himself, and the effusion of the Holy Spirit, promised, and to be given, by him. The sense of the Jews in this matter is plainly shown by the following passage of the Jerusalem Talmud: "Why is it called the place or house of drawing?" (for that was the term for this ceremony, or for the place where the water was taken up) "Because from thence they draw the Holy Spirit; as it is written, And ye shall draw water with joy from the fountains of salvation." See Wolf. Curæ Philol. in N. T. on John vii. 37, 39.—L. The *water* is Divine knowledge, says *Kimchi*, and the *wells* the teachers of righteousness. The *Targum* renders this in a very remarkable manner: "Ye shall receive with joy (אולפן חדת *ulephan chadath*) a new doctrine from the chosen among the righteous." Does not this mean the *Gospel*, the *new covenant?* And did not the Targumist speak as a *prophet?*

NOTES ON CHAP. XII

Verse 1. *Though thou wast angry*—"For though thou hast been angry"] The Hebrew phrase, to which the *Septuagint* and *Vulgate* have too closely adhered, is exactly the same with that of St. Paul, Rom. vi. 17: "But thanks be to God, that ye were the slaves of sin; but have obeyed from the heart;" that is, "that whereas, or though, ye were the slaves of sin, yet ye have now obeyed from the heart the doctrine on the model of which ye were formed."

Verse 2. *The Lord JEHOVAH*] The word יה *Yah* read here is probably a mistake; and arose originally from the custom of the Jewish scribes, who, when they found a line too short for the word, wrote as many letters as filled it, and then began the next line with the whole word. In writing the word יהוה *Yehovah*, the line might terminate with יה *Yah*, the two first letters; and then at the beginning of the next line the whole word יהוה *Yehovah* would be written. This might give rise to יה יהוה *Yah Yehovah*. The *Yah* is wanting here in two of Dr. *Kennicott's* MSS., in one ancient MS. of my own, and in the *Septuagint*, *Vulgate*, *Syriac*, and *Arabic*. See *Houbigant* and *De Rossi*.

My *song*] The pronoun is here necessary; and it is added by the *Septuagint*, *Vulgate*, and *Syriac*, who read וזמרתי *zimrathi*, as it is in a MS. Two MSS. omit יה *Yah*, see *Houbigant*, not. in loc. Another MS. has it in one word, זמרתיה *zimrathyah*. Seven others omit יהוה *Yehovah*. See Exod. xv. 2, with Var. Lect. *Kennicott*.

Verse 4. *Call upon his name*] קראו בשמו *kiru bishmo*, *invoke his name*. Make him your *Mediator*, or *call* the people *in his name*. Preach him who is the *Root of Jesse*, and *who stands as an ensign for the nations*. Call on the people to believe in him; as in him alone salvation is to be found.

Verse 6. *Thou inhabitant of Zion*] Not only the *Jewish people*, to whom his word of salvation was to be sent first; but also all members of the Church of Christ: as in *them*, and in his *Church*, the Holy One of Israel *dwells*. St. Paul, speaking of the *mystery* which had been proclaimed among the Gentiles, sums it up in these words: "which is CHRIST IN YOU, the hope of glory; whom we preach, warning every man, and teaching every man in all wisdom, that we may present every man perfect in Christ Jesus;" Col. i. 27, 28. Well, therefore, may the inhabitant of Zion *cry out and shout*, and proclaim the greatness of her Redeemer.

CHAPTER XIII

God mustereth the armies of his wrath against the inhabitants of Babylon, 1–6. The dreadful consequences of this visitation, and the terror and dismay of those who are the objects of it, 7–16. The horrid cruelties that shall be inflicted upon the Babylonians by the Medes, 17, 18. Total and irrecoverable desolation of Babylon, 19–22.

A. M. cir. 3292
B. C. cir. 712
Olymp. XVII. 1
cir. annum
NumæPompilii,
R. Roman., 4

THE [a]burden of Babylon,
which Isaiah the son of
Amoz did see.
2 [b]Lift ye up a banner [c]upon
the high mountain, exalt the
voice unto them, [d]shake the hand,
that they may go into the gates
of the nobles.

A. M. cir. 3292
B. C. cir. 712
Olymp. XVII. 1
cir. annum
NumæPompilii,
R. Roman., 4

[a]Chap. xxi. 1; xlvii. 1; Jer. l., li——[b]Ch. v. 26; xviii. 3; Jer. l. 2——[c]Jer. li. 25——[d]Ch. x. 32

This and the following chapter,—striking off the *five* last verses of the latter, which belong to a quite different subject,—contain one entire prophecy, foretelling the destruction of Babylon by the Medes and Persians; delivered probably in the reign of Ahaz, (see *Vitringa*, i. 380,) about *two hundred* years before its accomplishment. The captivity itself of the Jews at Babylon, which the prophet does not expressly foretell, but supposes, in the spirit of prophecy, as what was actually to be effected, did not fully take place till about *one hundred and thirty* years after the delivery of this prophecy: and the Medes, who are expressly mentioned chap. xiii. 17, as the principal agents in the overthrow of the Babylonian monarchy, by which the Jews were released from that captivity, were at this time an inconsiderable people; having been in a state of anarchy ever since the fall of the great Assyrian empire, of which they had made a part, under Sardanapalus; and did not become a kingdom under Deioces till about the *seventeenth* of Hezekiah.

The former part of this prophecy is one of the most beautiful examples that can be given of elegance of composition, variety of imagery, and sublimity of sentiment and diction, in the prophetic style; and the latter part consists of an ode of supreme and singular excellence.

The prophecy opens with the command of God to gather together the forces which he had destined to this service, ver. 2, 3. Upon which the prophet immediately hears the tumultuous noise of the different nations crowding together to his standard; he sees them advancing, prepared to execute the Divine wrath, ver. 4, 5. He proceeds to describe the dreadful consequences of this visitation, the consternation which will seize those who are the objects of it; and, transferring unawares the speech from himself to God, ver. 11, sets forth, under a variety of the most striking images, the dreadful destruction of the inhabitants of Babylon which will follow, ver. 11-16, and the everlasting desolation to which that great city is doomed, ver. 17-22.

The deliverance of Judah from captivity, the immediate consequence of this great revolution, is then set forth, without being much enlarged upon, or greatly amplified, chap. xiv. 1, 2. This introduces, with the greatest ease and the utmost propriety, the triumphant song on that subject, ver. 4-28. The beauties of which, the various images, scenes, persons introduced, and the elegant transitions from one to another, I shall here endeavour to point out in their order, leaving a few remarks upon particular passages of these two chapters to be given after these general observations on the whole.

A chorus of Jews is introduced, expressing their surprise and astonishment at the sudden downfall of Babylon; and the great reverse of fortune that had befallen the tyrant, who, like his predecessors, had oppressed his own, and harassed the neighbouring kingdoms. These oppressed kingdoms, or their rulers, are represented under the image of the fir trees and the cedars of Libanus, frequently used to express any thing in the political or religious world that is super-eminently great and majestic: the whole earth shouteth for joy; the cedars of Libanus utter a severe taunt over the fallen tyrant, and boast their security now he is no more.

The scene is immediately changed, and a new set of persons is introduced. The regions of the dead are laid open, and Hades is represented as rousing up the shades of the departed monarchs: they rise from their thrones to meet the king of Babylon at his coming; and insult him on his being reduced to the same low estate of impotence and dissolution with themselves. This is one of the boldest prosopopœias that ever was attempted in poetry; and is executed with astonishing brevity and perspicuity, and with that peculiar force which in a great subject naturally results from both. The image of the state of the dead, or the *infernum poeticum* of the Hebrews, is taken from their custom of burying, those at least of the higher rank, in large sepulchral vaults hewn in the rock. Of this kind of sepulchres there are remains at Jerusalem now extant; and some that are said to be the sepulchres of the kings of Judah. See *Maundrell*, p. 76. You are to form to yourself an idea of an immense subterranean vault, a vast gloomy cavern, all round the sides of which there are cells to receive the dead bodies; here the deceased monarchs lie in a distinguished sort of state, suitable to their former rank, each on his own couch, with his arms beside him, his sword at his head, and the bodies of his chiefs and companions round about him. See Ezek. xxxii. 27. On which place Sir John Chardin's MS. note is as follows: "En Mingrelie ils dorment tous leurs epées sous leurs têtes, et leurs autres armes à leur cotè; et on les enterre de mesme, leurs armes posées de cette façon." In Mingrelia they always sleep with their swords under their heads, and their other arms by their sides; and they bury their dead with their arms placed in the same manner. These illustrious shades rise at once from their couches, as from their thrones; and advance to the entrance of the cavern to meet the king of Babylon, and to receive him with insults on his fall.

The Jews now resume the speech; they address the king of Babylon as the morning-star fallen from heaven, as the first in splendour and dignity in the political world, fallen from his high state; they introduce him as uttering the most extravagant vaunts of his power and ambitious designs in his former glory. These are strongly contrasted in the close with his present low and abject condition.

Immediately follows a different scene, and a most happy image, to diversify the same subject, to give it a new turn, and an additional force. Certain persons are introduced who light upon the corpse of the king of Babylon, cast out and lying naked on the bare ground, among the com-

A. M. cir. 3292
B. C. cir. 712
Olymp. XVII. 1
cir. annum
NumæPompilii,
R. Roman., 4

3 I have commanded my sanctified ones, I have also called
[e]my mighty ones for mine anger,
even them that [f]rejoice in my
highness.
4 The noise of a multitude in the mountains [g]like as of a great people; a tumultuous
noise of the kingdoms of nations gathered together; the LORD of hosts mustereth the host
of the battle.
5 They come from a far country, from the
end of heaven, *even* the LORD, and the weapons
of his indignation, to destroy the whole land.
6 Howl ye; [h]for the day of the LORD *is* at
hand; [i]it shall come as a destruction from the
Almighty.
7 Therefore shall all hands [k]be
faint, and every man's heart
shall melt.
8 And they shall be afraid;
[l]pangs and sorrows shall take hold of them;
they shall be in pain as a woman that travaileth: they shall [m]be amazed [n]one at
another; their faces *shall be as* [o]flames.
9 Behold, [p]the day of the LORD cometh,
cruel both with wrath and fierce anger, to lay
the land desolate: and he shall destroy [q]the
sinners thereof out of it.
10 For the stars of heaven and the constellations thereof shall not give their light:
the sun shall be [r]darkened in his going forth,
and the moon shall not cause her light to shine.

[e]Joel iii. 11——[f]Psa. cxlix. 2, 5, 6——[g]Heb. *the likeness of*——[h]Zeph. i. 7; Rev. vi. 17——[i]Job xxxi. 23; Joel i. 15——[k]Or, *fall down*——[l]Psa. xlviii. 6; chap. xxi. 3——[m]Heb. *wonder*

[n]Heb. *every man at his neighbour*——[o]Heb. *faces of the flames*——[p]Mal. iv. 1——[q]Psa. civ. 35; Prov. ii. 22 [r]Chap. xxiv. 21, 23; Ezek. xxxii. 7; Joel ii. 31; iii. 15; Matt. xxiv. 29; Mark xiii. 24; Luke xxi. 25

mon slain, just after the taking of the city; covered with wounds, and so disfigured, that it is some time before they know him. They accost him with the severest taunts; and bitterly reproach him with his destructive ambition, and his cruel usage of the conquered; which have deservedly brought him this ignominious treatment, so different from that which those of his rank usually meet with, and which shall cover his posterity with disgrace.

To complete the whole, God is introduced, declaring the fate of Babylon, the utter extirpation of the royal family, and the total desolation of the city; the deliverance of his people, and the destruction of their enemies; confirming the irreversible decree by the awful sanction of his oath.

I believe it may with truth be affirmed, that there is no poem of its kind extant in any language, in which the subject is so well laid out, and so happily conducted, with such a richness of invention, with such variety of images, persons, and distinct actions, with such rapidity and ease of transition, in so small a compass, as in this ode of Isaiah. For beauty of disposition, strength of colouring, greatness of sentiment, brevity, perspicuity, and force of expression, it stands, among all the monuments of antiquity, unrivalled.—L.

NOTES ON CHAP. XIII.

Verse 1. *The burden of Babylon*] The prophecy that foretells its destruction by the Medes and Persians: see the preceding observations.

Verse 2. *Exalt the voice*] The word להם *lahem*, "to them," which is of no use, and rather weakens the sentence, is omitted by an ancient MS., and the *Vulgate*.

Verse 3. *I have commanded my sanctified ones*] מקדשי *mekuddashai*, the persons *consecrated* to this very purpose. Nothing can be plainer than that the verb קדש *kadash*, "to make holy," signifies also to *consecrate* or *appoint* to a particular purpose. Bishop *Lowth* translates, "my enrolled warriors." This is the *sense*.

Verse 4. *Of the battle*—"For the battle."] The *Bodleian* MS. has למלחמה *lemilchamah*. Cyrus's army was made up of many different nations. Jeremiah calls it an "assembly of great nations from the north country," chap. l. 9. And afterwards mentions the kingdoms of "Ararat, Minni, and Ashchenaz, (i. e. Armenia, Corduene, Pontus or Phrygia, Vitring.,) with the kings of the Medes," chap. li. 27, 28. See Xenophon. Cyrop.

Verse 5. *They come from a far country*] The word מארץ *meerets* is wanting in *one* MS. and in the *Syriac:* "They come from afar."

From the end of heaven] *Kimchi* says, *Media*, "the end of heaven," in Scripture phrase, means, the EAST.

Verse 8. *And they shall be afraid*—"And they shall be terrified"] I join this verb, ונבהלו *venibhalu*, to the preceding verse, with the *Syriac* and *Vulgate*.

Pangs and sorrows shall take hold of them—"Pangs shall seize them"] The *Septuagint*, *Syriac*, and *Chaldee* read יאחזום *yochezum*, instead of יאחזון *yochezun*, which does not express the pronoun *them*, necessary to the sense.

Verse 10. *For the stars of heaven*—"Yea, the stars of heaven"] The Hebrew poets, to express happiness, prosperity, the instauration and advancement of states, kingdoms, and potentates, make use of images taken from the most striking parts of nature, from the heavenly bodies, from the sun, moon, and stars: which they describe as shining with increased splendour, and never setting. The moon becomes like the meridian sun, and the sun's light is augmented sevenfold; (see Isa. xxx. 26;) new heavens and a new earth are created, and a brighter age commences. On the contrary, the overflow and destruction of kingdoms is represented by opposite images. The stars are obscured, the moon withdraws her light, and the sun shines no more! The earth quakes, and the heavens tremble; and all things seem tending to their original chaos. See Joel ii. 10, iii. 15,

A. M. cir. 3292
B. C. cir. 712
Olymp. XVII. 1
cir. annum
Numæ Pompilii,
R. Roman., 4

11 And I will punish the world
for *their* evil, and the wicked for
their iniquity; [s]and I will cause
the arrogancy of the proud to
cease, and will lay low the haughtiness of
the terrible.
12 I will make a man more precious than
fine gold; even a man than the golden wedge
of Ophir.
13 [t]Therefore I will shake the heavens, and
the earth shall remove out of her place, in the
wrath of the LORD of hosts, and in [u]the day
of his fierce anger.
14 And it shall be as the chased roe, and as
a sheep that no man taketh up:
[v]they shall every man turn to his
own people, and flee every one
into his own land.
15 Every one that is found shall be thrust
through; and every one that is joined *unto
them* shall fall by the sword.
16 Their children also shall be [w]dashed to
pieces before their eyes; their houses shall
be spoiled, and their wives ravished.
17 [x]Behold, I will stir up the Medes
against them, which shall not regard silver;
and *as for* gold, they shall not delight
in it.

A. M. cir. 3292
B. C. cir. 712
Olymp. XVII. 1
cir. annum
Numæ Pompilii,
R. Roman., 4

[s]Chap. ii. 17——[t]Hag. ii. 6——[u]Psa. cx. 5; Lam. i. 12
[v]Jer. l. 16; li. 9

[w]Psa. cxxxvii. 9; Nah. iii. 10; Zech. xiv. 2——[x]Chap. xxi. 2; Jer. li. 11, 28; Dan. v. 28, 31

16; Amos viii. 9; Matt. xxiv. 29; and De S. Poës. Herb. Præl. VI. et IX.

And the moon shall not cause her light to shine] This in its farther reference may belong to the Jewish polity, both in Church and state, which should be totally eclipsed, and perhaps shine no more in its distinct state for ever.

Verse 11. *I will punish the world*—"I will visit the world"] That is, the Babylonish empire; as η οικουμενη, for the Roman empire, or for Judea, Luke ii. 1; Acts xi. 28. So the *universus orbis Romanus*, for the Roman empire; *Salvian.* lib. v. *Minos* calls Crete his world: "Creten, quæ meus est orbis;" *Ovid. Metamorph.* viii. 9.

Verse 12. *I will make a man more precious than fine gold—wedge of Ophir.*] The Medes and Persians will not be satisfied with the *spoils* of the Babylonians. They seek either to destroy or enslave them; and they will accept no *ransom* for any man—either for אנוש *enosh*, the poor man, or for אדם *adam*, the more honourable person. All must fall by the sword, or go into captivity together; for *the Medes*, (ver. 17,) *regard not silver, and delight not in gold.*

Verse 14. "And the remnant"] Here is plainly a defect in this sentence, as it stands in the *Hebrew* text; the subject of the proposition is lost. What is it that shall be like a roe chased? The *Septuagint* happily supply it, οἱ καταλελειμμενοι, שאר *shear, the remnant.* A MS. here supplies the word יושב *yosheb, the inhabitant;* which makes a tolerably good sense; but I much prefer the reading of the *Septuagint.*

They shall—turn—"They shall look"] That is, the forces of the king of Babylon, destitute of their leader, and all his auxiliaries, collected from Asia Minor, and other distant countries, shall disperse and flee to their respective homes.

Verse 15. *Every one that is found*—"Every one that is overtaken"] That is, none shall escape from the slaughter; neither they who flee singly, dispersed and in confusion; nor they who endeavour to make their retreat in a more regular manner, by forming compact bodies: they shall all be equally cut off by the sword of the enemy. The *Septuagint* have understood it in this sense, which they have well expressed:—

Ὁς γαρ αν ἁλῳ ἡττηθησεται,
Και οἱτινες συνηγμενοι εισι πεσουνται μαχαιρα.

"Whosoever is caught shall be overthrown,
And all that are collected together shall fall by the sword."

Where, for ἡττηθησεται, MS. Pachom has εκκενθησεται, et οἱ Γ Cod. Marchal. in margine, et MS. I. D. II. εκκεντηθησεται, which seems to be right, being properly expressive of the *Hebrew*.

Verse 17. *Which shall not regard silver*—"Who shall hold silver of no account"] That is, who shall not be induced, by large offers of gold and silver for ransom, to spare the lives of those whom they have subdued in battle; their rage and cruelty will get the better of all such motives. We have many examples in the Iliad and in the Æneid of addresses of the vanquished to the pity and avarice of the vanquishers, to induce them to spare their lives.

Est domus alta: jacent penitus defossa talenta
Cælati argenti: sunt auri pondera facti
Infectique mihi: non hic victoria Teucrum
Vertitur; aut anima una dabit discrimina tanta.
Dixerat: Æneas contra cui talia reddit:
Argenti atque auri memoras quæ multa talenta
Gnatis parce tuis. *Æn.* x. 526.

"High in my dome are silver talents rolled,
With piles of laboured and unlaboured gold.
These, to procure my ransom, I resign;
The war depends not on a life like mine:
One, one poor life can no such difference yield,
Nor turn the mighty balance of the field.
Thy talents, (cried the prince,) thy treasured store
Keep for thy sons." *Pitt.*

It is remarkable that Xenophon makes Cyrus open a speech to his army, and in particular to the Medes, who made the principal part of it, with praising them for their disregard of riches. Ανδρες Μηδοι, και παντες οἱ παροντες, εγω ὑμας οιδα σαφως, ὁτι ουτε χρηματων δεομενοι συν εμοι εξελθετε· "Ye Medes, and others who now hear me, I well know that you have not accompanied me in this

A. M. cir. 3292
B. C. cir. 712
Olymp. XVII. 1
cir. annum
Numæ Pompilii,
R. Roman., 4

18 *Their* bows also shall dash
the young men to pieces; and
they shall have no pity on the
fruit of the womb; their eye shall
not spare children.
19 [y]And Babylon, the glory of kingdoms,
the beauty of the Chaldees' excellency, shall
be [z]as when God overthrew
[a]Sodom and Gomorrah.
20 [b]It shall never be inhabited,
neither shall it be dwelt in from
generation to generation: neither shall the
Arabian pitch tent there; neither shall the
shepherds make their fold there.

[y]Chapter xiv. 4, 22——[z]Hebrew *as the overthrowing*——[a]Genesis xix. 24, 26; Deuteronomy xxix. 23; Jeremiah xlix. 18; l. 40——[b]Jeremiah l. 3, 39; li. 29, 62

---

expedition with a view of acquiring wealth."—*Cyrop.* lib. v.

Verse 18. Their *bows also shall dash*—"Their bows shall dash"] Both Herodotus, i. 61, and Xenophon, Anab. iii., mention, that the Persians used large bows τοξα μεγαλα: and the latter says particularly that their bows were *three* cubits long, Anab. iv. They were celebrated for their archers, see chap xxii. 6; Jer. xlix. 35. Probably their neighbours and allies, the Medes, dealt much in the same sort of arms. In Psa. xviii. 34, and Job xx. 24, mention is made of a bow of steel; if the Persian bows were of metal, we may easily conceive that with a metalline bow of *three* cubits' length, and proportionably strong, the soldiers might dash and slay the young men, the weaker and unresisting of the inhabitants (for they are joined with the fruit of the womb and the children) in the general carnage on taking the city. תרתשנה *terattashnah*, shall be broken or shivered to pieces. This seems to refer, not to נערים *nearim*, young *men*, but to קשתות *keshathoth*, their *bows*. *The bows of the young men shall be broken to pieces.*

On the fruit, &c.—"And on the fruit," &c.] A MS. of Dr. *Kennicott's* reads ועל פרי *veal peri, and on the fruit*. And *nine* MSS. (*three* ancient) and *two* editions, with the *Septuagint*, *Vulgate*, and *Syriac*, add likewise the conjunction ו *vau, and*, to על *al, upon*, afterwards.

Verse 19. *And Babylon*] The great city of Babylon was at this time rising to its height of glory, while the Prophet Isaiah was repeatedly denouncing its utter destruction. From the first of Hezekiah to the first of Nebuchadnezzar, under whom it was brought to the highest degree of strength and splendour, are about *one hundred and twenty years.* I will here very briefly mention some particulars of the greatness of the place, and note the several steps by which this remarkable prophecy was at length accomplished in the total ruin of it.

It was, according to the lowest account given of it by ancient historians, a regular square, *forty-five* miles in compass, inclosed by a wall *two hundred* feet high and *fifty* broad; in which there were a *hundred* gates of brass. Its principal ornaments were the temple of Belus, in the middle of which was a tower of *eight* stories of building, upon a base of a quarter of a mile square, a most magnificent palace, and the famous hanging gardens, which were an artificial mountain, raised upon arches, and planted with trees of the largest as well as the most beautiful sorts.

Cyrus took the city by diverting the waters of the Euphrates which ran through the midst of it, and entering the place at night by the dry channel. The river being never restored afterward to its proper course, overflowed the whole country, and made it little better than a great morass; this and the great slaughter of the inhabitants, with other bad consequences of the taking of the city, was the first step to the ruin of the place. The Persian monarchs ever regarded it with a jealous eye; they kept it under, and took care to prevent its recovering its former greatness. Darius Hystaspes not long afterward most severely punished it for a revolt, greatly depopulated the place, lowered the walls, and demolished the gates. Xerxes destroyed the temples, and with the rest the great temple of Belus, Herod. iii. 159, Arrian, Exp. Alexandri, lib. vii. The building of Seleucia on the Tigris exhausted Babylon by its neighbourhood, as well as by the immediate loss of inhabitants taken away by Seleucus to people his new city, *Strabo*, lib. xvi. A king of the Parthians soon after carried away into slavery a great number of the inhabitants, and burned and destroyed the most beautiful parts of the city, *Valesii Excerpt. Diodori*, p. 377. Strabo (ibid.) says that in his time great part of it was a mere desert; that the Persians had partly destroyed it; and that time and the neglect of the Macedonians, while they were masters of it, had nearly completed its destruction. Jerome (*in loc.*) says that in his time it was quite in ruins, and that the walls served only for the inclosure for a park or forest for the king's hunting. Modern travellers, who have endeavoured to find the remains of it, have given but a very unsatisfactory account of their success. What Benjamin of Tudela and Pietro della Valle supposed to have been some of its ruins, Tavernier thinks are the remains of some late Arabian building. Upon the whole, Babylon is so utterly annihilated, that even the place where this wonder of the world stood cannot now be determined with any certainty! See also note on chap. xliii. 14.

We are astonished at the accounts which ancient historians of the best credit give of the immense extent, height, and thickness of the walls of Nineveh and Babylon; nor are we less astonished when we are assured, by the concurrent testimony of modern travellers, that no remains, not the least traces, of these prodigious works are now to be found. Scattered fragments of its *tiles* and *bricks* are yet to be found. Proud Babylon reduced now to a few brick-bats! Our wonder will, I think, be moderated in both respects, if we consider the fabric of these celebrated walls, and the nature of the materials of which they consisted. Buildings in the east have always been, and are to this day, made of earth or clay, mixed or beat up with straw to make the parts cohere, and dried only in the sun. This is their method of making bricks; see on chap. ix. 9. The walls of the city were built of the earth digged out on the spot, and

A. M. cir. 3292 B. C. cir. 712 Olymp. XVII. 1 cir. annum NumæPompilii, R. Roman., 4

21 [c]But [d]wild beasts of the
desert shall lie there; and their
houses shall be full of [e]doleful
creatures; [f]and [g]owls shall
dwell there, and satyrs shall dance there.

22 And [h]the wild beasts of the
islands shall cry in their [i]desolate
houses, and dragons in *their* pleasant palaces: [k]and her time *is* near
to come, and her days shall not be prolonged.

A. M. cir. 3292 B. C. cir. 712 Olymp. XVII. 1 cir. annum NumæPompilii, R. Roman., 4

[c]Chap. xxxiv. 11–15; Rev. xviii. 2——[d]Heb. *Ziim*——[e]Heb. *Ochim*——[f]Or, *ostriches*——[g]Heb. *daughters of the owl*——[h]Heb. *Iim*——[i]Or, *palaces*——[k]Jer. li. 33

dried upon the place, by which means both the ditch and the wall were at once formed, the former furnishing materials for the latter. That the walls of Babylon were of this kind is well known; and *Berosus* expressly says, (*apud Joseph.* Antiq. x. 11,) that Nebuchadnezzar added three new walls both to the old and new city, partly of brick and bitumen, and partly of brick alone. A wall of this sort must have a great thickness in proportion to its height, otherwise it cannot stand. The thickness of the walls of Babylon is said to have been one-fourth of their height, which seems to have been no more than was absolutely necessary. *Maundrell*, speaking of the garden walls of Damascus, says, "They are of a very singular structure. They are built of great pieces of earth, made in the fashion of brick, and hardened in the sun. In their dimensions they are two yards long each, and somewhat more than one broad, and half a yard thick." And afterward, speaking of the walls of the houses, he says, "From this dirty way of building they have this amongst other inconveniences, that upon any violent rain the whole city becomes, by the washing of the houses, as it were a quagmire;" p. 124. And see note on chap. xxx. 13. When a wall of this sort comes to be out of repair, and is neglected, it is easy to conceive the necessary consequences, namely, that in no long course of ages it must be totally destroyed by the heavy rains, and at length washed away, and reduced to its original earth.—L.

Verse 21. *Satyrs*] A kind of beast like to man, which is called מרמוטי *marmots, a monkey.—Rabbi Parchon.*

Verse 22. *In their pleasant palaces*—"In their palaces"] באלמנותיו *bealmenothaiv;* a plain mistake, I presume, for בארמנתיו *bearmenothaiv.* It is so corrected in *two* MSS., the *Syriac*, *Chaldee*, and *Vulgate.*

> Πουλυποδες δ' εν εμοι θαλαμασ φωκαι τε μελαιναι
> Οικια ποιησονται ακηδεα, χητεϊ λαων.
>
> Hom. *Hymn. in Apol.* 77.

Of which the following passage of *Milton* may be taken for a translation, though not so designed:—

> "And in their palaces,
> Where luxury late reigned, sea monsters whelped,
> And stabled." *Par. Lost*, xi. 750.

This image of desolation is handled with great propriety and force by some of the Persian poets:—

> پرده داري ميکند در قصر قيصر عنکبوت
> بومي نوبت ميزند بر گنبد افراسياب

> "The spider holds the veil in the palace of Cæsar;
> The owl stands centinel on the watch-tower of Afrasiab."

On this quotation Sir *W. Jones* observes, نوبت *noubet* is an Arabic word, signifying a *turn*, a *change*, a *watch;* hence نوبت زدن *noubet zudun* in Persian signifies to *relieve the guards by the sounds of drums and trumpets.* Their office is given by the poet to the *owl;* as that of پرده دار *purdeh dar*, or chamberlain, is elegantly assigned to the *spider.*

CHAPTER XIV

Deliverance of Israel from captivity, which shall follow the downfall of the great Babylonish empire, 1, 2. *Triumphant ode or song of the children of Jacob, for the signal manifestation of Divine vengeance againsi their oppressors,* 3–23. *Prophecy against the Assyrians,* 24, 25. *Certainty of the prophecy, and immutability of the Divine counsels,* 26, 27. *Palestine severely threatened,* 28–31. *God shall establish Zion in these troublous times,* 32.

A. M. cir. 3292 B. C. cir. 712 Olymp. XVII. 1 cir. annum NumæPompilii, R. Roman., 4

FOR the Lord [a]will have
mercy on Jacob, and [b]will
yet choose Israel, and set them
in their own land: [c]and the
strangers shall be joined with
them, and they shall cleave to
the house of Jacob.
2 And the people shall take

A. M. cir. 3292 B. C. cir. 712 Olymp. XVII. 1 cir. annum NumæPompilii, R. Roman., 4

[a]Psa. cii. 13——[b]Zech. i. 17; ii. 12——[c]Chap. lx. 4, 5, 10; Eph. ii. 12, 13, &c.

NOTES ON CHAP. XIV

Verse 1. *And will yet choose Israel.*] That is, will still regard Israel as his chosen people; however he may seem to desert them, by giving them up to their enemies, and scattering them among the nations. Judah is sometimes called Israel; see Ezek. xiii. 16; Mal. i. 1; ii. 11: but the name of Jacob and of Israel, used apparently with design in this place, each of which names

A. M. cir. 3292 B. C. cir. 712 them, [d]and bring them to their
Olymp. XVII.1 place: and the house of Israel
cir. annum NumæPompilii, shall possess them in the land
R. Roman., 4 of the LORD for servants and
handmaids: and they shall take them captives, [e]whose captives they were; [f]and they
shall rule over their oppressors.
3 And it shall come to pass in the day that
the LORD shall give thee rest from thy sorrow,
and from thy fear, and from the hard bondage
wherein thou wast made to serve,
4 That thou [g]shalt take up this [h]proverb
against the king of Babylon, and say, How
hath the oppressor ceased! and [i]golden [k]city
ceased!
5 The LORD hath broken [l]the staff of the
wicked, *and* the sceptre of the rulers.
6 He who smote the people in A. M. cir. 3292 B. C. cir. 712
wrath with [m]a continual stroke, Olymp. XVII.1
he that ruled the nations in anger, cir. annum NumæPompilii,
is persecuted, *and* none hindereth. R. Roman., 4
7 The whole earth is at rest, *and* is quiet:
they break forth into singing.
8 [n]Yea, the fir trees rejoice at thee, *and* the
cedars of Lebanon, *saying,* Since thou art laid
down, no feller is come up against us.
9 [o]Hell [p]from beneath is moved for thee to
meet *thee* at thy coming: it stirreth up the
dead for thee, *even* all the [q]chief [r]ones of the
earth; it hath raised up from their thrones
all the kings of the nations.
10 All they shall speak and say unto thee,
Art thou also become weak as we? art thou
become like unto us?

---

[d]Chap. xlix. 22; lx. 9; lxvi. 20——[e]Heb. *that had taken them captives*——[f]Chap. lx. 14——[g]Chap. xiii. 19; Hab. ii. 6——[h]Or, *taunting speech*——[i]Or, *exactress of gold*

[k]Rev. xviii. 16——[l]Psa. cxxv. 3——[m]Heb. *a stroke without removing*——[n]Chap. lv. 12; Ezek. xxxi. 16 [o]Ezek. xxxii. 21——[p]Or, *The grave*——[q]Heb. *leaders* [r]Or, *great goats*

---

includes the twelve tribes, and the other circumstances mentioned in this and the next verse, which did not in any complete sense accompany the return from the captivity of Babylon, seem to intimate that this whole prophecy extends its views beyond that event.

Verse 2. *For servants and handmaids*] **For thrallis and thrallesses.**—OLD BIBLE. Male and female slaves.

Verse 3. *In the day*—"In that day"] ביום ההוא *bayom hahu.* The word ההוא *hahu* is added in *two* MSS. of *Kennicott's,* and was in the copies from which the *Septuagint* and *Vulgate* translated: *εν τῃ ἡμερᾳ εκεινῃ, in die illa,* (*ᾗ αναπαυσει,* MS. Pachom. adding *ᾗ,*) in that day. This is a matter of no great consequence: however, it restores the text to the common form, almost constantly used on such occasions; and is one among many instances of a word apparently lost out of the printed copies.

Verse 4. *This proverb*—"This parable"] משל *mashal.* I take this to be the general name for poetic style among the Hebrews, including every sort of it, as ranging under one or other, or all of the characters, of sententious, figurative, and sublime; which are all contained in the original notion, or in the use and application of the word *mashal.* Parables or proverbs, such as those of Solomon, are always expressed in short pointed sentences; frequently figurative, being formed on some comparison; generally forcible and authoritative, both in the matter and the form. And such in general is the style of the Hebrew poetry. The verb *mashal* signifies to rule; to exercise authority; to make equal; to compare one thing with another; to utter parables, or acute, weighty, and powerful speeches, in the form and manner of parables, though not properly such. Thus Balaam's first prophecy, (Num. xxiii. 7-10,) is called his *mashal;* though it has hardly any thing figurative in it: but it is beautifully sententious, and, from the very form and manner of it, has great spirit, force, and energy. Thus Job's last speeches, in answer to his three friends, chap. xxvii.-xxxi., are called *mashals;* from no one particular character, which discriminates them from the rest of the poem, but from the sublime, the figurative, the sententious manner which equally prevails through the whole poem, and makes it one of the first and most eminent examples extant of the truly great and beautiful in poetic style. See the note on Prov. i. 1.

The *Septuagint* in this place render the word by *θρηνος, a lamentation.* They plainly consider the speech here introduced as a piece of poetry, and of that species of poetry which we call the elegiac; either from the subject, it being a poem on the fall and death of the king of Babylon, or from the form of the composition, which is of the longer sort of Hebrew verse, in which the Lamentations of Jeremiah, called by the *Septuagint* Θρηνοι, are written.

The golden city ceased] מדהבה *madhebah,* which is here translated *golden city,* is a Chaldee word. Probably it means that *golden coin* or *ingot* which was given to the Babylonians by way of tribute. So the word is understood by the *Vulgate,* where it is rendered *tributum;* and by Montanus, who translates it *aurea pensio,* the golden pension. *Kimchi* seems to have understood the word in the same sense. *De Rossi* translates it *auri dives,* rich in gold, or *auri exactrix,* the exactor of gold; the same as the exactor of tribute.

Verse 9. *Hell from beneath is moved for thee to meet* thee] That is, *Nebuchadnezzar.* "*It* (hell) hath raised up from their thrones all the kings of the earth;—the *ghosts* (*rephaim*) of all the *mighty ones,* or *goats,* (עתודי *attudey,*) of the earth—all the oppressors of mankind." What a most terrible idea is here! Tyrannical kings who have oppressed and spoiled mankind, are here represented as *enthroned in hell;* and as taking a Satanic pleasure in seeing others of the same description enter those abodes of misery!

A. M. cir. 3292
B. C. cir. 712
Olymp. XVII. 1
cir. annum
NumæPompilii,
R. Roman., 4

11 Thy pomp is brought down
to the grave, *and* the noise of
thy viols: the worm is spread
under thee and the worms
cover thee.
12 [s]How art thou fallen from heaven, [t]O
Lucifer, son of the morning! *how* art thou
cut down to the ground, which didst weaken
the nations!
13 For thou hast said in thine heart, [u]I will
ascend into heaven, [v]I will exalt my throne
above the stars of God: I will sit also upon
the mount of the congregation, [w]in the sides
of the north:
14 I will ascend above the heights of the
clouds; [x]I will be like the Most High.
15 Yet thou [y]shalt be brought
down to hell, to the sides of
the pit.
16 They that see thee shall nar-
rowly look upon thee, *and* consider thee, *say-*
ing, Is this the man that made the earth to
tremble, that did shake kingdoms?
17 *That* made the world as a wilderness,
and destroyed the cities thereof; *that* [z]opened
not the house of his prisoners.
18 All the kings of the nations, *even* all
of them, lie in glory, every one in his own
house.
19 But thou art cast out of thy grave like
an abominable branch, *and as* the raiment of
those that are slain, thrust through with a

[s]Chap. xxxiv. 4——[t]Or, *O day star*——[u]Matt. xi. 23——[v]Dan. viii. 10——[w]Psa. xlviii. 2

[x]Chap. xlvii. 8; 2 Thess. ii. 4——[y]Matt. xi. 23——[z]Or, *did not let his prisoners loose homeward*

Verse 11. *Cover thee*—"Thy covering."] *Twenty-eight* MSS. (*ten* ancient) of *Kennicott's*, *thirty-nine* of *De Rossi's*, *twelve* editions, with the *Septuagint* and *Vulgate*, read ומכסך *umechassecha*, in the singular number.

Verse 12. *O Lucifer, son of the morning*] The *Versions* in general agree in this translation, and render הילל *heilel* as signifying *Lucifer*, *Φωσφωρος*, the *morning star*, whether *Jupiter* or *Venus;* as these are both *bringers of the morning light*, or *morning stars*, annually in their turn. And although the context speaks explicitly concerning Nebuchadnezzar, yet this has been, I know not why, applied to the chief of the fallen angels, who is most incongruously denominated *Lucifer*, (the bringer of light!) an epithet as common to him as those of *Satan* and *Devil*. That the Holy Spirit by his prophets should call this arch-enemy of God and man the *light-bringer*, would be strange indeed. But the truth is, the text speaks nothing at all concerning *Satan* nor his *fall*, nor the *occasion* of that fall, which many divines have with great confidence deduced from this text. O how necessary it is to understand the literal meaning of Scripture, that preposterous comments may be prevented! Besides, I doubt much whether our translation be correct. הילל *heilel*, which we translate *Lucifer*, comes from ילל *yalal, yell, howl*, or *shriek*, and should be translated, "Howl, son of the morning;" and so the *Syriac* has understood it; and for this meaning *Michaelis* contends: see his reasons in *Parkhurst*, under הלל *halal*.

Verse 13. *I will ascend into heaven*] I will get the empire of the whole world. *I will exalt my throne above the stars of God*—above the Israelites, who are here termed the stars of God. So the *Targum* of Jonathan, and *R. D. Kimchi*. This chapter speaks not of the ambition and fall of Satan, but of the pride, arrogance, and fall of Nebuchadnezzar.

The mount of the congregation—"The mount of the Divine Presence"] It appears plainly from Exod. xxv. 22, and xxix. 42, 43, where God appoints the place of meeting with Moses, and promises to meet with him before the ark to commune with him, and to speak unto him; and to meet the children of Israel at the door of the tabernacle; that the tabernacle, and afterwards the door of the tabernacle, and Mount Zion, (or Moriah, which is reckoned a part of Mount Zion,) whereon it stood, was called the tabernacle, and the mount of convention or of appointment; not from the people's assembling there to perform the services of their religion, (which is what our translation expresses by calling it the tabernacle of the congregation,) but because God appointed that for the place where he himself would meet with Moses, and commune with him, and would meet with the people. Therefore הר מועד *har moed*, the "mountain of the assembly," or אהל מועד *ohel moed*, the "tabernacle of the assembly," means the place appointed by God, where he would present himself; agreeably to which I have rendered it in this place, *the mount of the Divine Presence*.

Verse 19. *Like an abominable branch*—"Like the tree abominated"] That is, as an object of abomination and detestation; such as the tree is on which a malefactor has been hanged. "It is written," saith St. Paul, Gal. iii. 13, "Cursed is every man that hangeth on a tree," from Deut. xxi. 23. The Jews therefore held also as accursed and polluted the tree itself on which a malefactor had been executed, or on which he had been hanged after having been put to death by stoning. "Non suspendunt super arbore, quæ radicibus solo adhæreat; sed super ligno eradicato, ut ne sit excisio molesta: nam lignum, super quo fuit aliquis suspensus, cum suspendioso sepelitur; ne maneat illi malum nomen, et dicant homines, Istud est lignum, in quo suspensus est ille, ὁ δεινα. Sic lapis, quo aliquis fuit lapidatus; et gladius, quo fuit occisus is qui est occisus; et sudarium sive mantile, quo fuit aliquis strangulatus; omnia hæc cum iis, qui perierunt, sepeliuntur." *Maimonides, apud Casaub. in Baron. Exercitat.* xvi. An. 34, Num. 134. "Cum itaque homo suspensu maximæ esset abominationi,—Judæi quoque præ cæteris abominabantur lignum

A. M. cir. 3292
B. C. cir. 712
Olymp. XVII.1
cir. annum
NumæPompilii,
R. Roman, 4

sword, that go down to the stones of the pit; as a carcass trodden under feet.

20 Thou shalt not be joined with them in burial, because thou hast destroyed thy land *and* slain thy people: [a]the seed of evil-doers shall never be renowned.

21 Prepare slaughter for his children [b]for the iniquity of their fathers; that they do not rise, nor possess the land, nor fill the face of the world with cities.

22 For I will rise up against them, saith the LORD of hosts, and cut off from Babylon [c]the name, and [d]remnant, [e]and son, and nephew, saith the LORD.

23 [f]I will also make it a possession for the bittern, and pools of water: and I will sweep it with the besom of destruction, saith the LORD of hosts.

24 The LORD of hosts hath sworn, saying, Surely as I have thought, so shall it come to pass; and as I have purposed, *so* shall it stand:

A. M. cir. 3292
B. C. cir. 712
Olymp. XVII.1
cir. annum
NumæPompilii,
R. Roman., 4

25 That I will break the Assyrian in my land, and upon my mountains tread him under foot: then shall [g]his yoke depart from off them, and his burden depart from off their shoulders.

26 This *is* the purpose that is purposed upon the whole earth: and this *is* the hand that is stretched out upon all the nations.

27 For the LORD of hosts hath [h]purposed, and who shall disannul *it?* and his hand *is* stretched out, and who shall turn it back?

A. M. cir. 3278
B. C. cir. 726
Olymp. XIII. 3
cir. annum
Romuli,
R. Roman., 28

28 In the year that [i]king Ahaz died was this burden.

[a]Job xviii. 19; Psa. xxi. 10; xxxvii. 28; cix. 13 [b]Exod. xx. 5; Matt. xxiii. 35——[c]Prov. x. 7; Jer. li 62 [d]1 Kings xiv. 10——[e]Job xviii. 19——[f]Chap. xxxiv. 11; Zeph. ii. 14

[g]Chapter x. 27——[h]2 Chronicles xx. 6; Job ix. 12; xxiii. 13; Psalm xxxiii. 11; Proverbs xix. 21; xxi. 30; chapter xliii. 13; Daniel iv. 31, 35——[i]2 Kings xvi. 20

quo fuerat suspensus, ita ut illud quoque terra tegerent, tanquam rem abominabilem. Unde interpres Chaldæus hæc verba transtulit כחת טמיר *kechat temir*, sicut virgultum absconditum, sive sepultum." *Kalinski, Vaticinia Observationibus Illustrata*, p. 342.

"The Jews never hang any malefactor upon a tree that is *growing in the earth*, but upon a post fixed in the ground, that it might never be said, 'That is the tree on which such a one was hanged;' for custom required that the tree should be *buried* with the *malefactor*. In like manner the *stone* by which a criminal was *stoned to death*, or the *sword* by which he was *beheaded*, or the *napkin* or *handkerchief* by which he was *strangled*, should be buried with him in the same grave." "For as the hanged man was considered the *greatest abomination*, so the very *post* or *wood* on which he was hanged was deemed a most abominable thing, and therefore buried under the earth."

Agreeably to which *Theodoret*, *Hist. Ecclesiast.* i. 17, 18, in his account of the finding of the cross by Helena, says, "That the three crosses were buried in the earth near the place of our Lord's sepulchre." And this circumstance seems to confirm the relation of the discovery of the cross of Christ. The crosses were found where the custom required they should be buried.

The raiment of those that are slain—"Clothed with the slain"] *Thirty-five* MSS., (*ten* ancient,) and *three* editions, have the word fully written, לבוש *lebush*. It is not a noun, but the participle passive; thrown out among the common slain, and covered with the dead bodies. So ver. 11, the earth-worm is said to be his bed-covering. This reading is confirmed by two ancient MSS. in my own collection.

Verse 20. *Because thou hast destroyed thy land,* &c.—"Because thou hast destroyed thy country; thou hast slain thy people"] Xenophon gives an instance of this king's wanton cruelty in killing the son of Gobrias, on no other provocation than that, in hunting, he struck a boar and a lion which the king had missed. *Cyrop.* iv. 309.

Verse 23. *I will sweep it with the besom of destruction*—"I will plunge it in the miry gulf of destruction"] I have here very nearly followed the Version of the *Septuagint;* the reasons for which see in the last note on De Poësi Hebr. Prælect. xxviii.

The besom of destruction, as our Version renders it. במטאטא *bematate.* This, says *Kimchi*, is a *Chaldee* word: and it is worthy of remark that the prophet, writing to the *Chaldeans*, uses several words peculiar to their own language to point out the *nature* of the Divine judgments, and the *causes* of them. See the note on Jer. x. 11. *Sixteen* of *Kennicott's* MSS., and *seventeen* of *De Rossi's*, and *one* ancient of my own, have the word במטאטי *bematatey*, in the plural. "I will sweep her with the besoms of destruction."

Verse 25. *I will break the Assyrian—upon my mountains*—"To crush the Assyrian—on my mountains"] The Assyrians and Babylonians are the same people, Herod. i. 199, 200. Babylon is reckoned the principal city in Assyria, *ibid.* 178. Strabo says the same thing, lib. xvi. *sub init.* The circumstance of this judgment being to be executed on God's mountains is of importance; it may mean the destruction of Sennacherib's army near Jerusalem, and have a still farther view: compare Ezek. xxxix. 4; and see Lowth on this place of Isaiah.

Verse 28. *In the year that king Ahaz died was this burden*] Uzziah had subdued the Philistines, 2 Chron. xxvi. 6, 7; but, taking advantage of the weak reign of Ahaz, they invaded Judea, and took, and held in possession, some cities in the southern part of the kingdom. On

A. M. cir. 3278 B. C. cir. 726 Olymp. XIII. 3 cir annum Romuli, R. Roman., 28

29 Rejoice not thou, whole Palestina, [k]because the rod of him that smote thee is broken: for out of the serpent's root shall come forth a [l]cockatrice, [m]and his fruit *shall be* a fiery flying serpent.

30 And the first-born of the poor shall feed, and the needy shall lie down in safety: and I will kill thy root with famine, and he shall slay thy remnant.

31 Howl, O gate; cry, O city; thou, whole Palestina, *art* dissolved: for there shall come from the north a smoke, and [n]none *shall be* alone in his [o]appointed times.

32 What shall *one* then answer the messengers of the nation? that [p]the LORD hath founded Zion, and [q]the poor of his people shall [r]trust in it.

[k]2 Chron. xxvi. 6——[l]Or, *adder*——[m]2 Kings xviii. 8 [n]Or, he shall *not* be *alone*

[o]Or, *assemblies*——[p]Psa. lxxxvii. 1, 5; cii. 16——[q]Zeph. iii. 12; Zech. xi. 11——[r]Or, *betake themselves unto it*

the death of Ahaz, Isaiah delivers this prophecy, threatening them with the destruction that Hezekiah, his son, and great-grandson of Uzziah, should bring upon them: which he effected; for "he smote the Philistines, even unto Gaza, and the borders thereof," 2 Kings xviii. 8. Uzziah, therefore, must be meant by the rod that smote them, and by the serpent from whom should spring the flying fiery serpent, ver. 29, that is, Hezekiah, a much more terrible enemy than even Uzziah had been.

The *Targum* renders the *twenty-ninth* verse in a singular way. "For, from the sons of Jesse shall come forth the Messiah; and his works among you shall be as the flying serpent."

Verse 30. *And the first-born of the poor*, &c.] The *Targum* goes on applying all to the *Messiah*. "And the poor of the people shall he feed, and the humble shall dwell securely in his days: and he shall kill thy children with famine, and the remnant of thy people shall he slay."

I will kill—"He will slay"] The *Septuagint* reads המית *hemith, in the third person*, ανελει; and so the *Chaldee*. The *Vulgate* remedies the confusion of persons in the present text, by reading both the verbs in the first person.

Verse 31. *There shall come from the north a smoke*—"From the north cometh a smoke"] That is, a cloud of dust raised by the march of Hezekiah's army against Philistia; which lay to the south-west from Jerusalem. A great dust raised has, at a distance, the appearance of smoke: *Fumantes pulvere campi;* "The fields *smoking* with dust."—VIRG. Æn. xi. 908.

Verse 32. *The messengers of the nation*—"The ambassadors of the nations"] The *Septuagint* read גוים *goyim*, εθνων, plural; and so the *Chaldee*, and one MS. The ambassadors of the neighbouring nations, that send to congratulate Hezekiah on his success; which in his answer he will ascribe to the protection of God. See 2 Chron. xxxii. 23. Or, if גוי *goi singular*, the reading of the text, be preferred, the ambassadors sent by the Philistines to demand peace. —L.

The Lord hath founded Zion] *Kimchi* refers this to the state of *Zion* under Hezekiah, when the rest of the cities of Judea had been taken, and this only was left for a *hope* to the poor of God's people: and God so defended it that Rabshakeh could not prevail against it.

The true Church of God is a place of safety; for as all its members are devoted to God, and walk in his testimonies, so they are continually defended and supported by him. In the congregations of his people, God dispenses his light and salvation; hence his *poor* or humble ones expect in his ordinances the blessings they need.

CHAPTER XV

Prediction of very heavy calamities about to fall upon the Moabites, 1–9.

A. M. cir. 3278 B. C. cir. 726 Olymp. XIII. 3 cir. annum Romuli, R. Roman., 28

THE [a]burden of Moab. Because in the night [b]Ar of Moab is laid waste *and* [c]brought to silence; because in the night Kir of Moab is laid waste, *and* brought to silence:

2 [d]He is gone to Bajith, and to Dibon, the high places, to

[a]Jer. xlviii. 1, &c.; Ezek. xxv. 8–11; Amos ii. 1

[b]Num. xxi. 28——[c]Or, *cut off*——[d]Chap. xvi. 12

This and the following chapter, taken together, make one entire prophecy, very improperly divided into two parts. The time of its delivery, and consequently of its accomplishment, which was to be in three years from that time, is uncertain; the former not being marked in the prophecy itself, nor the latter recorded in history. But the most probable account is, that it was delivered soon after the foregoing, in the first year of Hezekiah; and that it was accomplished in his fourth year, when Shalmaneser invaded the kingdom of Israel. He might probably march through Moab; and to secure every thing behind him, possess himself of the whole country, by taking their principal strong places, Ar and Kirhares.—L. The authorized Version, which we have followed in the margin, places the prophecy in this chapter *fourteen* years earlier than that contained in the *two* preceding.

A. M. cir. 3278
B. C. cir. 726
Olymp. XIII. 3
cir. annum
Romuli,
R. Roman., 28

weep: Moab shall howl over
Nebo, and over Medeba: [e]on
all their heads *shall be* baldness,
and every beard cut off.

3 In their streets they shall gird themselves
with sackcloth: [f]on the tops of their houses,
and in their streets, every one shall howl,
[g]weeping abundantly.

4 And Heshbon shall cry, [h]and Elealeh:
their voice shall be heard *even* unto Jahaz:
therefore the armed soldiers
of Moab shall cry out; his
life shall be grievous unto
him.

5 [i]My heart shall cry out for Moab; [k]his
fugitives *shall flee* unto Zoar, a [l]heifer of
three years old: for [m]by the mounting up of
Luhith with weeping shall they go it up; for
in the way of Horonaim they shall raise up a
cry of [n]destruction.

[e]See Lev. xxi. 5; chap. iii. 24; xxii. 12; Jer. xlvii. 5; xlviii. 1, 37, 38; Ezek. vii. 18——[f]Jer. xlviii. 38——[g]Heb. *descending into weeping*, or *coming down with weeping*——[h]Chap. xvi. 9——[i]Chap. xvi. 11; Jer. xlviii. 31——[k]Or, *to the borders thereof, even as a heifer*——[l]Chap. xvi. 14; Jer. xlviii. 34——[m]Jer. xlviii. 5——[n]Heb. *breaking*

Jeremiah has happily introduced much of this prophecy of Isaiah into his own larger prophecy against the same people in his *forty-eighth* chapter, denouncing God's judgment on Moab, subsequent to the calamity here foretold, and to be executed by Nebuchadnezzar; by which means several mistakes of transcribers in the present text of both prophets may be rectified.

NOTES ON CHAP. XV

Verse 1. *Because in the night*] בליל *beleil.* That both these cities should be taken in the *night* is a circumstance somewhat unusual; but not so material as to deserve to be so strongly insisted upon. *Vitringa*, by his remark on this word, shows that he was dissatisfied with it in its plain and obvious meaning, and is forced to have recourse to a very hard metaphorical interpretation of it. Noctu vel nocturno impetu; vel metaphorice, repente, subito, inexpectata destructione: placet posterius. *Calmet* conjectures, and I think it probable, that the true reading is כליל *keleil, as the night.* There are many mistakes in the *Hebrew* text arising from the very great similitude of the letters ב *beth*, and כ *caph*, which in many MSS., and some printed editions, are hardly distinguishable. Admitting this reading, the translation will be,—

"Because Ar is utterly destroyed, Moab is undone!
Because Kir is utterly destroyed, Moab is undone!"

Verse 2. *He is gone to Bajith, and to Dibon*] עלה הבית *alah habbayith*, should be rendered, *he is gone to the* HOUSE, i. e., to their chief temple, where they practised idolatry. Dibon was the name of a tower where also was an idolatrous temple; thither they went to weep and pray before their idols, that they might interpose and save them from their calamities. So *R. D. Kimchi. He is gone to Bajith and to Dibon:* but Bishop *Lowth* reads *Beth Dibon;* this is the name of *one* place; and the two words are to be joined together, without the ו *vau* intervening. So the *Chaldee* and *Syriac.* This reading is not supported by any MS. or Version: but some MSS., instead of ער *ar*, have עיר *ir*, *a city*, others have עד *ad*, *unto*, and some editions have על *al, upon.* But all these help little, though they show that the place puzzled both the *scribes* and the *editors.*

On all their heads shall be *baldness*, &c.—"On every head there is baldness," &c.] Herodotus, ii. 36, speaks of it as a general practice among all men, except the Egyptians, to cut off their hair as a token of mourning. "Cut off thy hair, and cast it away," says Jeremiah, vii. 29, "and take up a lamentation."

Τουτο νυ και γερας οιον οἰζυροισι βροτοισι
Κειρασθαι τε κομην, βαλεειν τ' απο δακρυ παρειων.
HOM. *Odyss.* iv. 197.

"The rites of wo
Are all, alas! the living can bestow;
O'er the congenial dust enjoined to shear
The graceful curl, and drop the tender tear."
POPE.

On every head.—For ראשיו *roshaiv*, read ראש *rosh.* So the parallel place, Jer. xlviii. 37, and so *three* MSS., *one* ancient. An ancient MS. reads על כל ראש *al col rosh. Five* read בכל ראש *bechol rosh, on every head*, with the *Septuagint* and *Arabic.* AND *every head.* The ו *vau, and*, is found in *thirty* MSS., in *three* editions, and in the *Syriac, Vulgate*, and *Chaldee.*

Cut off—"Shorn."] The printed editions, as well as the MSS., are divided on the reading of this word. Some have גדועה *geduah, shorn*, others גרעה *geruah, diminished.* The similitude of the letters ד *daleth* and ר *resh* has likewise occasioned many mistakes. In the present case, the sense is pretty much the same with either reading. The text of Jer. xlviii. 37 has the latter, *diminished.* The former reading is found in *twelve* of Dr. *Kennicott's* MSS., *forty* of *De Rossi's*, and *two* of my own. A great number of *editions* have the same reading.

Verse 3. *With sackcloth*] שק *sak.* The word is in the plural שקים *sakkim, sacks*, in one of *De Rossi's* MSS.

Verse 4. *The armed soldiers*—"The very loins"] So the *Septuagint*, ἡ οσφυς, and the *Syriac.* They cry out violently, with their utmost force.

Verse 5. *My heart shall cry out for Moab*—"The heart of Moab crieth within her"] For לבי *libbi, my heart*, the *Septuagint* reads לבו *libbo, his heart*, or לב *leb;* the *Chaldee*, לבו *libbo.* For בריחיה *bericheyha*, the *Syriac* reads ברוחה *berocheh;* and so likewise the *Septuagint*, rendering it εν αυτῃ, *Edit. Vat:* or εν ἑαυτῃ, *Edit. Alex.* and MSS. I. D. II.

A heifer of three years old—"A young heifer."] *Hebrew*, a heifer *three years* old, in full strength; as *Horace* uses *equa trima*, for a

A. M. cir. 3278
B. C. cir. 726
Olymp. XIII. 3
cir. annum
Romuli,
R. Roman., 28

6 For the waters [o]of Nimrim
shall be [p]desolate: for the hay
is withered away, the grass faileth, there is no green thing.
7 Therefore the abundance they have gotten,
and that which they have laid up, shall they
carry away to the [q]brook of the willows.
8 For the cry is gone round about the borders of Moab; the howling
thereof unto Eglaim, and the
howling thereof unto Beer-
elim.
9 For the waters of Dimon shall be full of
blood: for I will bring [r]more upon Dimon,
[s]lions upon him that escapeth of Moab, and
upon the remnant of the land.

[o]Num. xxxii. 36——[p]Heb. *desolations*——[q]Or, *valley of the Arabians*——[r]Heb. *additions*——[s]2 Kings xvii. 25

young mare just coming to her prime. *Bochart* observes, from *Aristotle*, Hist. Animal. lib. iv., that in this kind of animals alone the voice of the female is deeper than that of the male; therefore the lowing of the heifer, rather than of the bullock, is chosen by the prophet, as the more proper image to express the mourning of Moab. But I must add that the expression here is very short and obscure; and the opinions of interpreters are various in regard to the meaning. Compare Jer. xlviii. 34.

Shall they go it up—"They shall ascend"] For יעלה *yaaleh*, the *Septuagint* and a MS. read in the plural, יעלו *yaalu*. And from this passage the parallel place in Jer. xlviii. 5 must be corrected; where, for יעלה בכי *yaaleh bechi*, which gives no good sense, read יעלה בו *yaaleh bo*.

Verse 7. "Shall perish"] אבדו *abadu or* אבדה *abadeh*. This word seems to have been lost out of the text: it is supplied by the parallel place, Jer. xlviii. 36. The *Syriac* expresses it by עבר *aber*, *præteriit*, "he hath passed;" and the *Chaldee* by יתבזזון *yithbazezun*, *diripientur*.

To the brook of the willows—"To the valley of willows"] That is, to Babylon. *Hieron.* and *Jarchi in loc.*; both referring to Psa. cxxxvii. 2. So likewise *Prideaux*, *Le Clerc*, &c.

Verse 9. *The waters of Dimon*] Some have *Dibon*, others have *Ribon* and *Rimon*. *St. Jerome* observes that the same town was called both *Dibon* and *Dimon*. The reading is therefore indifferent.

Upon him that escapeth of Moab, &c.—"Upon the escaped of Moab, and Ariel, and the remnant of Admah."] The *Septuagint* for עריה *aryeh* read אריאל *ariel*. Ar Moab was called also Ariel or Areopolis, *Hieron.* and *Theodoret*. See *Cellarius*. They make ארמה *Admah* also a proper name. Michaelis thinks that the Moabites might be called the remnant of Admah, as sprung from Lot and his daughters, escaped from the destruction of that and the other cities; or, metaphorically, as the Jews are called princes of Sodom, and people of Gomorrah, chap. i. 10. Bibliotheque Orient. Part v., p. 195. The reading of this verse is very doubtful; and the sense, in every way in which it can be read, very obscure.—L. *Calmet* thinks there may be a reference to 1 Chron. xi. 22, where it is said, "Benaiah slew two lion-like men of Moab," or the *two Ariels* of Moab, and would therefore translate, "I will bring down the remnant of Moab like Ariel, (which Benaiah smote,) and them that are escaped like Adamah." They shall be exterminated, as were the inhabitants of those two cities. Ariel was a double city—the river Arnon dividing it in two. This is the two Ariels of Moab—not *two lion-like men*, much less *two lions*. See *Calmet* on this place.

CHAPTER XVI

The distress of Moab pathetically described by the son of the prince, or ruler of the land, being forced to flee for his life through the desert, that he may escape to Judea; and the young women, like young birds scared from their nest, wade helpless through the fords of Arnon, the boundary of their country, to seek protection in some foreign land, 1, 2. *The prophet addresses Sion, exhorting her to show mercy to her enemies in their distress, that her throne may be established in righteousness,* 3–5. *Exceeding great pride of Moab,* 6. *The terrible calamities about to fall upon Moab farther described by the languishing of the vine, the ceasing of the vintage, the sound of the prophet's bowels quivering like a harp, &c.,* 7–13. *Awful nearness of the full accomplishment of the prophecy,* 14.

A. M. cir. 3278
B. C. cir. 726
Olymp. XIII. 3
cir. annum
Romuli,
R. Roman., 28

SEND [a]ye the lamb to the
ruler of the land [b]from
[c]Sela[d] to the wilderness, unto the
mount of the daughter of Zion.
2 For it shall be, *that*, as a
wandering bird [e]cast out of the
nest, *so* the daughters of Moab
shall be at the fords of [f]Arnon.

[a]2 Kings iii. 4——[b]2 Kings xiv. 7——[c]Or, *Petra*——[d]Heb. *a rock*——[e]Or, *a nest forsaken*——[f]Num. xxi. 13

NOTES ON CHAP. XVI

Verse 1. *Send ye the lamb, &c.*—"I will send forth the son, &c."] Both the reading and meaning of this verse are still more doubtful than those of the preceding. The *Septuagint* and *Syriac* read אשלח *eshlach*, *I will send*, in the first person singular, future tense: the *Vulgate* and *Talmud Babylon.*, read שלח *shelach*,

A. M. cir. 3278
B. C. cir. 726
Olymp. XIII. 3
cir. annum
Romuli,
R. Roman., 28

3 [g]Take counsel, execute judgment; make thy shadow as the
night in the midst of the noonday; hide the outcasts; bewray
not him that wandereth.
4 Let mine outcasts dwell with thee, Moab;
be thou a covert to them from the face of the
spoiler: for the [h]extortioner is at an end, the
spoiler ceaseth, [i]the oppressors are consumed
out of the land.

5 And in mercy [k]shall the
throne be [l]established; and he
shall sit upon it in truth in the tabernacle of David, [m]judging, and
seeking judgment, and hasting righteousness.
6 We have heard of the [n]pride of Moab;
he is very proud; *even* of his haughtiness,
and his pride, and his wrath; [o]*but* his lies
shall not *be* so.
7 Therefore shall Moab [p]howl for Moab,

[g]Heb. *Bring*——[h]Heb. *wringer*——[i]Heb. *the treaders down*——[k]Dan. vii. 14, 27; Mic. iv. 7; Luke i. 33——[l]Or, *prepared*

[m]Psa. lxxii. 2; xcvi. 13; xcviii. 9——[n]Jer. xlviii 29; Zeph. ii. 10——[o]Chapter xxviii. 15——[p]Jeremiah xlviii. 20

send, singular imperative: some read שלחו *shilchu*, *send ye forth*, or *shalechu*, *they send forth*. The *Syriac*, for כר *car*, *a lamb*, reads בר *bar*, *a son*, which is confirmed by five MSS. of *Kennicott* and *De Rossi*. The two first verses describe the distress of Moab on the Assyrian invasion; in which even the son of the prince of the country is represented as forced to flee for his life through the desert, that he may escape to Judea; and the young women are driven forth like young birds cast out of the nest, and endeavouring to wade through the fords of the river Arnon. Perhaps there is not so much difficulty in this verse as appears at first view. "Send the lamb to the ruler of the land," may receive light from 2 Kings iii. 4, 5: "And Mesha, king of Moab, was a sheepmaster, and rendered unto the king of Israel *one hundred thousand* lambs with their wool, and *one hundred thousand* rams: but when Ahab was dead, the king of Moab rebelled against Israel." Now the prophet exhorts them to begin paying the tribute as formerly, that their punishment might be averted or mitigated.

Verse 3. *Take counsel*—"Impart counsel"] The *Vulgate* renders the verbs in the beginning of this verse in the singular number. So the *Keri;* and so likewise *sixty-one* MSS. of *Kennicott's* and *De Rossi's* have it, and *nineteen* editions, and the *Syriac*. The verbs throughout the verse are also in the feminine gender; agreeing with Zion, which I suppose to be understood.

Verse 4. *Let mine outcasts dwell with thee, Moab*—"Let the outcasts of Moab sojourn with thee, O Zion"] Setting the points aside, this is by much the most obvious construction of the *Hebrew*, as well as most agreeable to the context, and the design of the prophet. And it is confirmed by the *Septuagint* οἱ φυγαδες Μωαβ, and *Syriac*.

The oppressors—"The oppressor"] Perhaps the Israelites, who in the time of Ahaz invaded Judah, defeated his army, slaying *one hundred and twenty thousand* men, and brought the kingdom to the brink of destruction. Judah, being now in a more prosperous condition, is represented as able to receive and to protect the fugitive Moabites. And with those former times of distress the security and flourishing state of the kingdom under the government of Hezekiah is contrasted.

Verse 5. *In mercy shall the throne be established*] May not this refer to the throne of Hezekiah? Here we have the character of such a king as cannot fail to be a blessing to the people. 1. "He sitteth on the throne in truth"—He does not merely *profess* to be the *father* and protector of his people: but he is actually such. 2. He is *judging*. He is not a man of war or blood, who wastes his subjects' lives and treasures in contentions with neighbouring nations, in order to satisfy his ambition by the extension of his territory. On the contrary, his whole life is occupied in the distribution of justice. 3. *He seeketh judgment*. He seeks out the poor distressed ones who cannot make their way to him, and avenges them on their oppressors. 4. *He hastens righteousness*. He does not suffer any of the courts of justice to delay the determination of the causes brought before them: he so orders that the point in litigation be fairly, fully, and speedily heard; and then judgment pronounced. *Delays* in the execution of justice answer little end but the enriching of unprincipled lawyers.

Verse 6. *We have heard of the pride of Moab*—"We have heard the pride of Moab"] For נא *ge*, read גאה *geah;* two MSS., one ancient, and Jer. xlviii. 29. Zephaniah, chap. ii. 8-10, in his prophecy against Moab, the subject of which is the same with that of Jeremiah in his *forty-eighth* chapter, (see the note on chap. xv. 1,) enlarges much on the pride of Moab, and their insolent behaviour towards the Jews:—

"I have heard the reproach of Moab;
And the revilings of the sons of Ammon:
Who have reproached my people;
And have magnified themselves against their borders.
Therefore, as I live, saith Jehovah God of hosts, the God of Israel:
Surely Moab shall be as Sodom,
And the sons of Ammon as Gomorrah:
A possession of nettles, and pits of salt,
And a desolation for ever.
The residue of my people shall spoil them,
And the remnant of my nation shall dispossess them:
This shall they have for their pride;
Because they have raised a reproach, and have magnified themselves
Against the people of Jehovah God of hosts."

Verse 7. *For the foundations of Kir-hareseth*—"For the men of Kirhares."] A palpable mistake in this place is happily corrected by the parallel text of Jer. xlviii. 31, where, instead of אשישי *ashishey*, *foundations* or *flagons*, we read אנשי *anshey*, *men*. In the same place of Jeremiah, and in ver. 36, and here in ver. 11, the name of the city is Kirhares, not Kirhareseth.

A. M. cir. 3278 B. C. cir. 726 Olymp. XIII. 3 cir. annum Romuli, R. Roman., 28

every one shall howl: for the
foundations [q]of Kir-hareseth
shall ye [r]mourn; surely *they are*
stricken.
8 For [s]the fields of Heshbon languish, *and*
[t]the vine of Shibmah: the lords of the heathen
have broken down the principal plants thereof, they are come *even* unto Jazer, they wandered *through* the wilderness: her branches
are [u]stretched out, they are gone over the
sea.
9 Therefore [v]I will bewail with the weeping
of Jazer the vine of Sibmah: I will water
thee with my tears, [w]O Heshbon, and Elealeh:
for [x]the shouting for thy summer
fruits and for thy harvest is fallen.
10 And [y]gladness is taken
away, and joy out of the plentiful
field; and in the vineyards there shall be no
singing, neither shall there be shouting: the
treaders shall tread out no wine in *their*
presses; I have made *their vintage*-shouting
to cease.
11 Wherefore [z]my bowels shall sound like
a harp for Moab, and mine inward parts for
Kir-haresh.
12 And it shall come to pass, when it is seen
that Moab is weary on [a]the high place, that

A. M. cir. 3278 B. C. cir. 726 Olymp. XIII. 3 cir. annum Romuli, R. Roman., 28

[q]2 Kings iii. 25——[r]Or, *mutter*——[s]Chap. xxiv. 7——[t]Ver. 9——[u]Or, *plucked up*——[v]Jer. xlviii. 32——[w]Ch. xv. 4

[x]Or, *the alarm is fallen upon*, &c.——[y]Chap. xxiv. 8; Jer. xlviii. 33——[z]Chap. xv. 5; lxiii. 15; Jer. xlviii. 36——[a]Chap. xv. 2

Verse 8. *Languish*—"Are put to shame"] Here the text of Jeremiah leaves us much at a loss, in a place that seems to be greatly corrupted. The *Septuagint* join the two last words of this verse with the beginning of the following. Their rendering is: *και ουκ εντραπησῃ, τα πεδια Εσεβων*. For אך *ach* they must have read אל *al;* otherwise, how came they by the negative, which seems not to belong to this place? Neither is it easy to make sense of the rest without a small alteration, by reading, instead of *εντραπησῃ τα*, *εντραπησεται*. In a word, the *Arabic* version, taken from the *Septuagint*, plainly authorizes this reading of the *Septuagint*, and without the negative; and it is fully confirmed by MSS. *Pachom.* and I. D. II., which have both of them *εντραπησεται πεδια Εσεβων*, without the negative; which makes an excellent sense, and, I think, gives us the true reading of the *Hebrew* text; אך נכלמו שדמות חשבון *ak nichlemu shadmoth cheshbon*. They frequently render the verb נכלם *nichlam* by *εντρεπομαι*. And נכלמו *nichlemu* answers perfectly well to אמלל *umlal*, the parallel word in the next line. The MSS. vary in expressing the word נכאים *nechaim*, which gives no tolerable sense in this place; one reads נוכאים *nochaim;* two others בכאים *bechaim;* in another the כ *caph* is upon a rasure of two letters; and the *Vulgate* instead of it reads מכותם *mecotham, plagas suas*.—L.

For the men of Kirhares ye shall make a moan. For the fields of Heshbon are put to shame. This is Bp. *Lowth's* sense of the passage.

Her branches are stretched out—"Her branches extended themselves."] For נטשו *nitteshu*, a MS. has נגשו *niggeshu;* which may perhaps be right. Compare Jer. xlviii. 32, which has in this part of the sentence the synonymous word נגעו *nagau*.

The meaning of this verse is, that the wines of Sibmah and Heshbon were greatly celebrated, and in high repute with all the great men and princes of that and the neighbouring countries; who indulged themselves even to intemperance in the use of them. So that their vines were so much in request as not only to be propagated all over the country of Moab to the sea of Sodom, but to have scions of them sent even beyond the sea into foreign countries. הלמו *halemu, knocked down, demolished;* that is overpowered, intoxicated. The drunkards of Ephraim are called by the prophet, chap. xxviii. 1, הלומי יין *halumey yayin, drinkers of wine.* See Schultens on Prov. xxiii. 25. Gratius, speaking of the Mareotic wine, says of it,

Pharios quæ fregit noxia reges. CYNEG. 312.

Verse 9. *With the weeping*—"As with the weeping"] For בבכי *bibechi*, a MS. reads בכי *bechi*. In Jer. xlviii. 32, it is מבכי *mibbechi*. The *Septuagint* read כבכי *kibeki, as with weeping*, which I follow.

For thy summer fruits and for thy harvest is fallen—"And upon thy vintage the destroyer hath fallen."] ועל קצירך הידד נפל *veal ketsirech heidad naphal*. In these few words there are two great mistakes, which the text of Jer. xviii. 32 rectifies. For קצירך *ketsirech*, it has בצירך *betsirech;* and for הידד *heidad*, שדד *shoded;* both which corrections the *Chaldee* in this place confirms. As to the first,

"Hesebon and Eleale, and
The flowery dale of Sibmah, clad with vines,"

were never celebrated for their *harvests;* it was the *vintage* that suffered by the irruption of the enemy; and so read the *Septuagint* and *Syriac*. הידד *heidad* is the noisy acclamation of the treaders of the grapes. And see what sense this makes in the literal rendering of the *Vulgate:* super messem tuam *vox calcantium irruit*, "upon thy harvest the voice of the treaders rushes." The reading in Jer. xlviii. 32 is certainly right, שדד נפל *shoded naphal*, "the destroyer hath fallen." The shout of the treaders does not come in till the next verse; in which the text of Isaiah in its turn mends that of Jeremiah, xlviii. 33, where instead of the first חידד *heidad*, "the shout," we ought undoubtedly to read, as here, הדרך *haddorech*, "the treader."

Verse 10. *Neither shall there be shouting*—"An end is put to the shouting"] The *Septuagint* read השבת *hishbeth*, passive, and in the third person; rightly, for God is not the speaker in this place. The rendering of the *Septuagint* is *πεπαυται γαρ κελευσμα*, "the cry ceaseth;" which last word, necessary to the rendering of the

A. M. cir. 3278
B. C. cir. 726
Olymp. XIII. 3
cir. annum
Romuli,
R. Roman., 28

he shall come to his sanctuary
to pray; but he shall not prevail.
13 This *is* the word that the
LORD hath spoken concerning
Moab since that time.
14 But now the LORD hath spoken, saying,
Within three years, [b]as the
years of a hireling, and the glory
of Moab shall be contemned,
with all that great multitude;
and the remnant *shall be* very small *and*
[c]feeble.

[b]Chap. xxi. 16 —— [c]Or, *not many*

Hebrew and to the sense, is supplied by MSS. *Pachom.* and I. D. II., having been lost out of the other copies.

Verse 12. *When it is seen that Moab, &c.*—"When Moab shall see," &c.] For נראה *nirah*, a MS. reads ראה *raah*, and so the *Syriac* and *Chaldee*. "Perhaps כי נראה *ki nirah* is only a various reading of כי נלאה *ki nilah*." SECKER. A very probable conjecture.

Verse 14. *Within three years*] בשלש *beshalish* כשלש *keshalish, according*, or *in or about three years*, is the reading of nine of *Kennicott's* and *De Rossi's* MSS., and *two* ancient editions.

But the *present reading* may well stand: "Now, the Lord hath spoken, saying, Within three years, as the years of a hireling." It seems as if this prophecy had been delivered before, without any time specified for its fulfilment; but now the time is determined—"in three years, as the years of a hireling"—for, as a *hireling* counts even to a single day, and will not abide with his employer an hour beyond the time agreed on; so, in *three years*, even to a day, from the delivery of this prophecy, shall destruction come upon Moab. This is the import of the present text; but if we take כשלש *keshalish*, AS in three years, or *in about three years' time*, the prophecy is not so definite.

These three years, says *Calmet*, are mentioned from the death of Ahaz, see chap. xiv. 28, and end the third year of Hezekiah, three years before the taking of Samaria by Shalmaneser. This conqueror did not ruin Moab so completely as not to leave a man in the land; the final desolation of Moab was reserved for Nebuchadnezzar, five years after the taking of Jerusalem.

Feeble—"And without strength."] An ancient MS., with the *Septuagint*, reads ולא *velo*, "and not."

CHAPTER XVII

Judgments of God upon Damascus, 1–3; *and upon Israel,* 4–6. *Good effects of these judgments on the small remnant or gleaning that should escape them,* 7, 8. *The same judgments represented in other but stronger terms, and imputed to irreligion and neglect of God,* 9–11. *The remaining verses are a distinct prophecy, a beautiful detached piece, worked up with the greatest elegance, sublimity, and propriety; and forming a noble description of the formidable invasion and sudden overthrow of Sennacherib, exactly suitable to the event,* 12–14.

A. M. cir. 3263
B. C. cir. 741
Olymp. IX. 4
cir. annum
Romuli,
R. Roman., 13

THE [a]burden of Damascus.
Behold, Damascus is taken
away from *being* a city, and it
shall be a ruinous heap.
2 The cities of Aroer *are* forsaken: they shall be for flocks,
which shall lie down, and [b]none
shall make *them* afraid.

[a]Jer. xlix 23; Amos i. 3; Zech. ix. 1; 2 Kings xvi. 9—[b]Jer. vii. 33

This prophecy by its title should relate only to Damascus; but it full as much concerns, and more largely treats of, the kingdom of Samaria and the Israelites, confederated with Damascus and the Syrians against the kingdom of Judah. It was delivered probably soon after the prophecies of the seventh and eighth chapters, in the beginning of the reign of Ahaz; and was fulfilled by Tiglath-pileser's taking Damascus, and carrying the people captives to Kir, (2 Kings xvi. 9,) and overrunning great part of the kingdom of Israel, and carrying a great number of the Israelites also captives to Assyria; and still more fully in regard to Israel, by the conquest of the kingdom, and the captivity of the people, effected a few years after by Shalmaneser.—L.

NOTES ON CHAP. XVII

Verse 1. *The burden of Damascus.*] Which is, according to the common version, *The cities of Aroer are forsaken.* It has already been observed by the learned prelate that the prophecy, as it relates to Damascus, was executed in the beginning of the reign of Ahaz, probably about the *third* year. If we credit *Midrash*, the *Damascenes* were the most *extensive* and flagrant of all idolaters. "There were in Damascus *three hundred and sixty-five* streets, in each of these was an idol, and each idol had his peculiar day of worship; so that the whole were worshipped in the course of the year." This, or any thing like this, was a sufficient reason for this city's destruction.

A ruinous heap] For מעי *mei*, "a ruinous heap," the *Septuagint* reads לעי *lei*, "for a ruin," the *Vulgate* כעי *kei*, "as a ruin." I follow the former.

Verse 2. *The cities of Aroer* are *forsaken*—"The cities are deserted for ever"] What has Aroer on the river Arnon to do with Damascus? and if there be another Aroer on the northern border of the tribe of Gad, as Reland seems to

A. M. cir. 3263
B. C. cir. 741
Olymp. IX. 4
cir. annum
Romuli,
R. Roman., 13

3 [c]The fortress also shall cease from Ephraim, and the kingdom from Damascus, and the remnant of Syria: they shall be as the glory of the children of Israel, saith the LORD of hosts.

4 And in that day it shall come to pass, *that* the glory of Jacob shall be made thin, and [d]the fatness of his flesh shall wax lean.

5 [e]And it shall be as when the harvestman gathereth the corn, and reapeth the ears with his arm; and it shall be as he that gathereth ears in the valley of Rephaim.

6 [f]Yet gleaning grapes shall be left in it, as the shaking of an olive tree, two *or* three berries in the top of the uppermost bough, four *or* five in the outmost fruitful branches thereof, saith the LORD God of Israel.

7 At that day shall a man [g]look to his Maker, and his eyes shall have respect to the Holy One of Israel.

A. M. cir. 3263
B. C. cir. 741
Olymp. IX. 4
cir. annum
Romuli,
R. Roman., 13

8 And he shall not look to the altars, the work of his hands, neither shall respect *that* which his fingers have made, either the groves, or the [h]images.

9 In that day shall his strong cities be as a forsaken bough, and an uppermost branch, which they left because of the children of Israel: and there shall be desolation.

10 Because thou hast forgotten [i]the God of thy salvation, and hast not been mindful of the rock of thy strength, therefore shalt thou plant pleasant plants, and shalt set it with strange slips:

11 In the day shalt thou make thy plant to grow, and in the morning shalt thou make thy seed to flourish: *but* the harvest *shall be*

---

[c]Chap. vii. 16; viii. 4——[d]Chap. x. 16——[e]Jer. li. 33 [f]Chap. xxiv. 13

[g]Micah vii. 7——[h]Or, *sun images*——[i]Psalm lxviii. 19

---

think there might be, this is not much more to the purpose. Besides, *the cities of Aroer*, if Aroer itself is a city, makes no good sense. The *Septuagint*, for ערער *aroer*, read עדי עד *adey ad*, εις τον αιωνα, *for ever*, or for a long duration. The *Chaldee* takes the word for a verb from ערה *arah*, translating it חרבו *cherebu*, devastabuntur, "they shall be wasted." The *Syriac* read עדועיר *adoeir*. So that the reading is very doubtful. I follow the *Septuagint* as making the plainest sense.

Verse 3. *The remnant of Syria*—"The pride of Syria."] For שאר *shear*, "remnant," *Houbigant* reads שאת *seeth*, "pride," answering, as the sentence seems evidently to require, to כבוד *cabod*, "the glory of Israel." The conjecture is so very probable that I venture to follow it.

As the glory] בכבוד *bichbod*, "IN the glory," is the reading of *eight* MSS., and *ten* editions.

Verse 4. *In that day*] That is, says *Kimchi*, the time when the ten tribes of Israel, which were *the glory of Jacob*, should be carried into captivity.

Verse 5. *As when the harvestman gathereth*—"As when one gathereth"] That is, the king of Assyria shall sweep away the whole body of the people, as the reaper strippeth off the whole crop of corn; and the remnant shall be no more in proportion than the scattered ears left to the gleaner. The valley of Rephaim near Jerusalem was celebrated for its plentiful harvest; it is here used poetically for any fruitful country. *One* MS., and *one* ancient edition, has באסף *beesoph*, "IN gathering," instead of כאסף *keesoph*, "AS the gathering."

Verse 8. *The altars, the work of his hands*—"The altars dedicated to the work of his hands"] The construction of the words, and the meaning of the sentence, in this place, are not obvious; all the ancient Versions, and most of the modern, have mistaken it. The word מעשה *maaseh*, "the work," stands *in regimine* with מזבחות *mizbechoth*, "altars," not in opposition to it; it means the altars *of* the work of their hand; that is *of* the idols, which *are* the work of their hands. Thus *Kimchi* has explained it, and *Le Clerc* has followed him.

Verse 9. *As a forsaken bough, and an uppermost branch*—"the Hivites and the Amorites"] החרש והאמיר *hachoresh vehaamir*. No one has ever yet been able to make any tolerable sense of these words. The translation of the *Septuagint* has happily preserved what seems to be the true reading of the text, as it stood in the copies of their time; though the words are now transposed, either in the text or in their Version; οἱ Αμαρραιοι και οἱ Ευαιοι, "the Amorites and the Hivites." It is remarkable that many commentators, who never thought of admitting the reading of the *Septuagint*, understand the passage as referring to that very event which their Version expresses; so that it is plain that nothing can be more suitable to the context. "My father," says Bishop Lowth, "saw the necessity of admitting this variation at a time when it was not usual to make so free with the Hebrew text." Mr. Parkhurst is not satisfied with the prelate's adoption of the reading of the *Septuagint*, "the Hivites and the Amorites." He thinks the difficult words should be thus rendered; he takes the whole verse: "And his fortified cities shall be like the leaving, or what is left כעזובת *caazubath*, of or in a ploughed field, החרש *hachoresh*, or on a branch which they leave *coram*, before, the children of Israel." Which he considers a plain reference to the Mosaic laws relative to the *not gleaning of their ploughed fields, vineyards, and oliveyards*, but *leaving* עזב *ozeb*, somewhat of the fruits, for the poor of the land; Lev. ix. 9, 10; Deut. xxiv. 19-21, in the *Hebrew*. I fear that the text is taken by storm on both interpretations. One MS. has כל ערי *col arey*, "all the cities;" and instead of החלש *hachalash*, "of the branch," six MSS. have החדש *hachodesh*, "of the month." But this is probably a mistake.

Verse 10. *Strange slips*—"Shoots from a for-

A. M. cir. 3263
B. C. cir. 741
Olymp. IX. 4
cir. annum
Romuli,
R. Roman., 13

[k]a heap in the day of grief and
of desperate sorrow.
12 Wo to the [l]multitude of
many people, *which* make a noise
[m]like the noise of the seas; and to the rushing of nations, *that* make a rushing like the
rushing of [n]mighty waters!
13 The nations shall rush like the rushing
of many waters: but *God* shall [o]rebuke them,
and they shall flee far off, and
[p]shall be chased as the chaff of
the mountains before the wind,
and like [q]a rolling thing before
the whirlwind.
14 And behold at evening-tide trouble; *and*
before the morning he *is* not. This *is* the
portion of them that spoil us, and the lot of
them that rob us.

A. M. cir. 3263
B. C. cir. 741
Olymp. IX. 4
cir. annum
Romuli,
R. Roman., 13

[k]Or, *removed in the day of inheritance, and* there shall be *deadly sorrow*——[l]Or, *noise*——[m]Jer. vi. 23

[n]Or, *many*——[o]Psa. ix. 5——[p]Psa. lxxxiii. 13; Hos. xiii. 3——[q]Or, *thistle down*

eign soil."] The pleasant plants, and shoots from a foreign soil, are allegorical expressions for strange and idolatrous worship; vicious and abominable practices connected with it; reliance on human aid, and on alliances entered into with the neighbouring nations, especially Egypt; to all which the Israelites were greatly addicted, and in their expectations from which they should be grievously disappointed.

Verse 12. *Wo to the multitude*] The three last verses of this chapter seem to have no relation to the foregoing prophecy, to which they are joined. It is a beautiful piece, standing singly and by itself; for neither has it any connexion with what follows: whether it stands in its right place, or not, I cannot say. It is a noble description of the formidable invasion and the sudden overthrow of Sennacherib; which is intimated in the strongest terms and the most expressive images, exactly suitable to the event.

Like the rushing of mighty waters!] Five words, three at the end of the *twelfth* verse, and two at the beginning of the *thirteenth*, are omitted in eight MSS., with the *Syriac;* that is, in effect, the repetition contained in the first line of ver. 13 in this translation, is not made. After having observed that it is equally easy to account for the omission of these words by a transcriber if they are genuine, or their insertion if they are not genuine, occasioned by his carrying his eye backwards to the word לאמים *leammim*, or forwards to ישאון *yeshaon*, I shall leave it to the reader's judgment to determine whether they are genuine or not. Instead of כהמות *cahamoth*, "as the roaring," five MSS. and the *Vulgate* have כהמון *kehamon*, "as the multitude."

Verse 14. *He is not*—"He is no more."] For איננו *einennu* ten MSS. of Dr. *Kennicott's*, (three ancient,) ten of *De Rossi's*, and two editions, and the *Septuagint*, *Syriac*, *Chaldee*, *Vulgate*, and *Arabic*, have ואיננו *veeinenno*. This particle, authenticated by so many good vouchers, restores the sentence to its true poetical form implying a repetition of some part of the parallel line preceding, thus:—

"At the season of evening, behold terror!
Before the morning, and [behold] he is no more!"

That spoil us] For שוסינו *shoseynu*, *them* that spoil us, fifteen MSS., one edition, and the *Syriac* have שוסנו *shosenu*, *him* that spoileth us. And for לבוזינו *lebozezeynu*, *them* that rob us, six MSS. and the *Syriac* have לבוזנו *lebozzeno*, *him* that robbeth us: and these readings make the place answer better to *Sennacherib*, according to Lowth's conjecture. Though God may permit the wicked to prevail for a time against his people, yet in the end those shall be overthrown, and the glory of the Lord shall shine brightly on them that fear him; for the earth shall be subdued, and the universe filled with his glory. Amen, and Amen!

CHAPTER XVIII

This chapter contains a very obscure prophecy; possibly designed to give the Jews, and perhaps the Egyptians, whose country is supposed to be meant, 1, 2, *and with whom many Jews resided, an intimation of God's interposition in favour of Sion,* 3, 4; *and of his counsels in regard to the destruction of their common enemy, Sennacherib, whose vast army, just as he thought his projects ripe, and ready to be crowned with success,* 5, *should become a prey to the beasts of the field, and to the fowls of heaven,* 6; *and that Egypt should be grateful to God for the deliverance vouchsafed her,* 7.

A. M. cir. 3290
B. C. cir. 714
Olymp. XVI. 3
cir. annum
NumæPompilii,
R. Roman., 2

WO [a]to the land shadowing
with wings, which *is* beyond the rivers of Ethiopia:
2 That sendeth ambassadors by
the sea, even in vessels of bulrushes upon the waters, *saying,*
Go, ye swift messengers, to [b]a
nation [c]scattered and peeled, to

A. M. cir. 3290
B. C. cir. 714
Olymp. XVI. 3
cir. annum
NumæPompilii
R. Roman., 2

[a]Chap. xx. 4, 5; Ezek. xxx. 4, 5, 9; Zeph. ii. 12; iii. 10

[b]Ver. 7——[c]Or, *outspread and polished*

This is one of the most obscure prophecies in the whole Book of Isaiah. The *subject* of it, the *end* and *design* of it, the *people* to whom it is addressed, the *history* to which it belongs, the

A. M. cir. 3290 B. C. cir. 714 Olymp. XVI. 3 cir. annum NumæPompilii, R. Roman., 2

a people terrible from their beginning hitherto; [d]a [e]nation meted
out and trodden down, [f]whose
land the rivers have spoiled!

3 All ye [g]inhabitants of the
world, and dwellers on the earth,
see ye, [h]when he lifteth up an
ensign on the mountains; and

A. M. cir. 3290 B. C. cir. 714 Olymp. XVI. 3 cir. annum NumæPompilii, R. Roman., 2

[d]Or, *a nation that meteth out, and treadeth down*——[e]Heb. *a nation of line, and treading under foot*

[f]Or, *whose land the rivers despise*——[g]Jer. i. 14; x. 18; xlvii. 2; Hos. iv. 1; Joel ii. 1; Zech. xi. 6——[h]Ch. v. 26

person who sends the messengers, and the *nation* to whom the messengers are sent, are all obscure and doubtful.—L.

NOTES ON CHAP. XVIII

Verse 1. *Wo to the land*] הוי ארץ *hoi arets!* This interjection should be translated *ho!* for it is properly a particle of calling: Ho, land! Attend! Give ear!

Shadowing with wings—"The winged cymbal] צלצל כנפים *tsiltsal kenaphayim.* I adopt this as the most probable of the many interpretations that have been given of these words. It is *Bochart's:* see Phaleg, iv. 2. The Egyptian sistrum is expressed by a periphrasis; the Hebrews had no name for it in their language, not having in use the instrument itself. The cymbal they had was an instrument in its use and sound not much unlike the sistrum; and to distinguish it from the sistrum, they called it the cymbal with wings. The cymbal was a round hollow piece of metal, which, being struck against another, gave a ringing sound: the sistrum was a *round* instrument, consisting of a broad rim of metal, through which from side to side ran several loose laminæ or small rods of metal, which being shaken, gave a like sound. These, projecting on each side, had somewhat the appearance of wings; or might be very properly expressed by the same word which the Hebrews used for wings, or for the extremity, or a part of any thing projecting. The sistrum is given in a medal of Adrian, as the proper attribute of Egypt. See *Addison* on Medals, Series iii. No. 4; where the figure of it may be seen. The frame of the sistrum was in shape rather like the ancient *lyre;* it was not *round.*

If we translate *shadowing with wings*, it may allude to the multitude of its vessels, whose *sails* may be represented under the notion of *wings.* The *second* verse seems to support this interpretation. Vessels of bulrushes, גמא *gome,* or rather the flag *papyrus,* so much celebrated as the substance on which people *wrote* in ancient times, and from which our *paper* is denominated. The sails might have been made of this flag: but whole *canoes* were constructed from it. *Mat* sails are used to the present day in China. The *Vulgate* fully understood the meaning of the word, and has accordingly translated, *in vasis papyri,* "in vessels of papyrus." **Reshi vesselis.**—Old MS. Bib. This interpretation does not please Bp. *Lowth,* and for his dissent he gives the following reasons:—

In opposition to other interpretations of these words which have prevailed, it may be briefly observed that צלצל *tsiltsel* is never used to signify *shadow,* nor is כנף *canaph* applied to the sails of ships. If, therefore, the words are rightly interpreted *the winged cymbal,* meaning the sistrum, Egypt must be the country to which the prophecy is addressed. And upon this hypothesis the version and explanation must proceed. I farther suppose, that the prophecy was delivered before Sennacherib's return from his Egyptian expedition, which took up three years; and that it was designed to give to the Jews, and perhaps likewise to the Egyptians, an intimation of God's counsels in regard to the destruction of their great and powerful enemy.

Which is *beyond the rivers of Ethiopia*—"Which borders on the rivers of Cush"] What are the rivers of Cush? whether the eastern branches of the lower Nile, the boundary of Egypt towards Arabia, or the parts of the upper Nile towards Ethiopia, it is not easy to determine. The word מעבר *meeber* signifies either *on this side* or *on the farther side:* I have made use of the same kind of ambiguous expression in the translation.

Verse 2. *In vessels of bulrushes*—"In vessels of papyrus"] This circumstance agrees perfectly well with Egypt. It is well known that the Egyptians commonly used on the Nile a light sort of ships, or boats, made of the reed papyrus. Ex ipso quidem papyro navigia texunt. PLINY, xiii. 11.

Conseritur bibula Memphitis cymba papyro.
LUCAN, iv. 136.

Go, ye swift messengers] To this nation before mentioned, who, by the Nile, and by their numerous canals, have the means of spreading the report in the most expeditious manner through the whole country: go, ye swift messengers, and carry this notice of God's designs in regard to them. By the swift messengers are meant, not any particular persons specially appointed to this office, but any of the usual conveyers of news whatsoever, travellers, merchants, and the like, the instruments and agents of common fame. These are ordered to publish this declaration made by the prophet throughout Egypt, and to all the world; and to excite their attention to the promised visible interposition of God.

Scattered—"Stretched out in length"] Egypt, that is, the fruitful part, exclusive of the deserts on each side, is one long vale, through the middle of which runs the Nile, bounded on each side to the east and west by a chain of mountains seven hundred and fifty miles in length; in breadth from one to two or three days' journey: even at the widest part of the Delta, from Pelusium to Alexandria, not above two hundred and fifty miles broad. *Egmont* and *Hayman,* and *Pococke.*

Peeled—"Smoothed"] Either relating to the practice of the Egyptian priests, who made their bodies smooth by shaving off their hair, (see *Herod.* ii. 37;) or rather to their country's being made smooth, perfectly plain and level, by the overflowing of the Nile.

Meted out—"Meted out by line"] It is generally referred to the frequent necessity of having recourse to mensuration in Egypt, in order to determine the boundaries after the inundations of the Nile; to which even the origin of the science of geometry is by some ascribed. *Strabo,* lib. xvii. *sub init.*

Trodden down] Supposed to allude to a

A. M. cir. 3290 B. C. cir. 714 Olymp. XVI. 3 cir. annum NumæPompilii, R. Roman., 2

when he bloweth a trumpet,
hear ye.
4 For so the LORD said unto
me, I will take my rest, and I
will [i]consider in my dwelling
place like a clear heat [k]upon
herbs, *and* like a cloud of dew
in the heat of harvest.

A. M. cir. 3290 B. C. cir. 714 Olymp. XVI. 3 cir. annum NumæPompilii, R. Roman., 2

[i]Or, *regard my set dwelling* — [k]Or, *after rain*

peculiar method of tillage in use among the Egyptians. Both Herodotus, (lib. ii.,) and Diodorus, (lib. i.,) say that when the Nile had retired within its banks, and the ground became somewhat dry, they sowed their land, and then sent in their cattle, (their hogs, says the former,) to tread in the seed; and without any farther care expected the harvest.

The rivers have spoiled—"The rivers have nourished"] The word בזאו *bazeu* is generally taken to be an irregular form for בזזו *bazezu*, "have spoiled," as four MSS. have it in this place; and so most of the Versions, both ancient and modern, understand it. On which Schultens, Gram. Heb. p. 491, has the following remark:—"Ne minimam quidem speciem veri habet בזאו *bazau*, Esai. xviii. 2, elatum pro בזזו *bazazu, deripiunt.* Hæc esset anomalia, cui nihil simile in toto linguæ ambitu. In talibus nil finire, vel fateri ex mera agi conjectura, tutius justiusque. Radicem בזא *baza* olim extare potuisse, quis neget? Si cognatum quid sectandum erat, ad בזה *bazah*, contemsit, potius decurrendum fuisset; ut בזאו *bazeu*, pro בזו *bazu*, sit enuntiatum, vel בזיו *baziv*. Digna phrasis, flumina contemmunt terram, i. e., inundant." "בזא *baza*, Arab. extulit se superbius, *item* subjecit sibi: *unde præt. pl.* בזאו *bazeu*, subjecerunt sibi, i. e., inundarunt."—*Simonis*' Lexic. Heb.

A learned friend has suggested to me another explanation of the word. בזא *baza*, *Syr.*, and ביזא *beiza*, *Chald.*, signifies *uber*, "a dug," *mamma*, "a breast;" agreeably to which the verb signifies *to nourish.* This would perfectly well suit with the Nile: whereas nothing can be more discordant than the idea of spoiling and plundering; for to the inundation of the Nile Egypt owed every thing; the fertility of the soil, and the very soil itself. Besides, the overflowing of the Nile came on by gentle degrees, covering without laying waste the country: "Mira æque natura fluminis, quod cum cæteri omnes abluant terras et eviscerent, Nilus tanto cæteris major adeo nihil exedit, nec abradit, ut contra adjiciat vires; minimumque in eo sit, quod solum temperet. Illato enim limo arenas saturat ac jungit; debetque illi Ægyptus non tantum fertilitatem terrarum, sed ipsas.—*Seneca*, Nat. Quæst., iv. 2. I take the liberty, therefore, which Schultens seems to think allowable in this place, of hazarding a conjectural interpretation. It is a fact that the *Ganges* changes its course, and overruns and lays barren whole districts, from which it was a few years back several miles distant. Such changes do not *nourish* but *spoil* the ground.

Verse 3. *When he lifteth up an ensign*—"When the standard is lifted up"] I take God to be the Agent in this verse; and that by the standard and the trumpet are meant the meteors, the thunder, the lightning, the storm, earthquake, and tempest, by which Sennacherib's army shall be destroyed, or by which at least the destruction of it shall be accompanied; as it is described in chap. x. 16, 17, xxix. 6, and xxx. 30, 31. See also Psa. lxxvi., and the title of it, according to the *Septuagint*, *Vulgate* and *Æthiopic*. They are called, by a bold metaphor, the standard lifted up, and the trumpet sounded. The latter is used by Homer, I think with great force, in his introduction to the battle of the gods; though I find it has disgusted some of the minor critics:—

Βραχε δ' ευρεια χθων,
Αμφι δε σαλπιγξεν μεγας ουρανος.
Il. xxi. 388.

"Heaven in loud thunders bids the trumpet sound,
And wide beneath them groans the rending ground." POPE.

Verse 4. *For so the Lord said unto me*—"For thus hath JEHOVAH said unto me"] The subject of the remaining part of this chapter is, that God would comfort and support his own people, though threatened with immediate destruction by the Assyrians; that Sennacherib's great designs and mighty efforts against them should be frustrated; and that his vast expectations should be rendered abortive, when he thought them mature, and just ready to be crowned with success; that the chief part of his army should be made a prey for the beasts of the field and the fowls of the air, (for this is the meaning of the allegory continued through the *fifth* and *sixth* verses;) and that Egypt, being delivered from his oppression, and avenged by the hand of God of the wrongs which she had suffered, should return thanks for the wonderful deliverance, both of herself and of the Jews, from this most powerful adversary.

Like a clear heat—"Like the clear heat"] The same images are employed by an Arabian poet:—

Solis more fervens, dum frigus; quumque ardet
Sirius, tum vero frigus ipse et umbra.

Which is illustrated in the note by a like passage from another Arabian poet:—

Calor est hyeme, refrigerium æstate.

Excerpta ex Hamasa; published by Schultens, at the end of Erpenius's Arabic Grammar, p. 425.

Upon herbs—"After rain"] "אור *aur* here signifies *rain*, according to what is said Job xxxvi. 11: 'The cloud scatters his rain.'"—*Kimchi.* In which place of Job the *Chaldee* paraphrast does indeed explain אורו *auro* by מטריה *matereyh;* and so again ver. 21 and chap. xxxvi. 30. This meaning of the word seems to make the best sense in this place; it is to be wished that it were better supported.

In the heat of harvest—"In the day of harvest."] For בחם *bechom, in the heat, fourteen* MSS., (several ancient,) the *Septuagint*, *Syriac*, *Arabic*, and *Vulgate* read ביום *beyom, in the day.* The mistake seems to have arisen from כחם *kechom* in the line above.

A. M. cir. 3290 B. C. cir. 714 Olymp. XVI. 3 cir. annum NumæPompilii, R. Roman., 2

5 For afore the harvest,
when the bud is perfect,
and the sour grape is ripening in the flower, he shall
both cut off the sprigs with pruning
hooks, and take away *and* cut down the
branches.
6 They shall be left together unto the fowls
of the mountains, and to the beasts of the
earth: and the fowls shall summer upon them,
and all the beasts of the earth
shall winter upon them.
7 In that time [l]shall the present
be brought unto the LORD of hosts
of a people [m]scattered and peeled, and from a
people terrible from their beginning hitherto;
a nation meted out and trodden under foot,
whose land the rivers have spoiled, to the place
of the name of the LORD of hosts, the mount
Zion.

A. M. cir. 3290 B. C. cir. 714 Olymp. XVI. 3 cir. annum NumæPompilii, R. Roman., 2

[l]See Psa. lxviii. 31; lxxii. 10; chap. xvi. 1; Zeph. iii. 10; Mal. i. 11——[m]Or, *outspread and polished;* see ver. 2

Verse 5. *The flower*—"The blossom"] Heb. *her* blossom; נצה *nitstsah,* that is, *the blossom of the vine,* גפן *gephen, vine,* understood, which is of the common gender. See Gen. xl. 10. Note, that by the defective punctuation of this word, many interpreters, and our translators among the rest, have been led into a grievous mistake, (for how can the swelling grape become a blossom?) taking the word נצה *nitstsah* for the predicate; whereas it is the subject of the proposition, or the nominative case to the verb.

Verse 7. *The present*—"A gift"] The Egyptians were in alliance with the kingdom of Judah, and were fellow-sufferers with the Jews under the invasion of their common enemy Sennacherib; and so were very nearly interested in the great and miraculous deliverance of that kingdom, by the destruction of the Assyrian army. Upon which wonderful event it is said, 2 Chron. xxxii. 23, that "many brought gifts unto Jehovah to Jerusalem, and presents to Hezekiah king of Judah; so that he was magnified of all nations from henceforth." It is not to be doubted, that among these the Egyptians distinguished themselves in their acknowledgments on this occasion.

Of a people—"From a people"] Instead of עם *am, a people,* the *Septuagint* and *Vulgate* read מעם *meam, from a people,* which is confirmed by the repetition of it in the next line. The difference is of importance; for if this be the true reading, the prediction of the admission of Egypt into the true Church of God is not so explicit as it might otherwise seem to be. However, that event is clearly foretold at the end of the next chapter.—L.

CHAPTER XIX

Prophecy concerning Egypt, in which her lamentable condition under the Babylonians, Persians, &c., is forcibly pointed out, 1–17. *The true religion shall be propagated in Egypt; referring primarily to the great spread of Judaism in that country in the reign of the Ptolemies, and ultimately to its reception of the Gospel in the latter days,* 18–22. *Profound peace between Egypt, Assyria, and Israel, and their blessed condition under the Gospel,* 23–25.

A. M. cir. 3290 B. C. cir. 714 Olymp. XVI. 3 cir. annum NumæPompilii, R. Roman., 2

THE [a]burden of Egypt. Behold, the LORD [b]rideth upon
a swift cloud, and shall come
into Egypt: and [c]the idols
of Egypt shall be moved at
his presence, and the heart
of Egypt shall melt in the midst
of it.

A. M. cir. 3290 B. C. cir. 714 Olymp. XVI. 3 cir. annum NumæPompilii, R. Roman., 2

[a]Jer. xlvi. 13; Ezek. xxix., xxx ——[b]Psa. xviii. 10; civ. 3——[c]Exod. xii. 12; Jer. xliii. 12

Not many years after the destruction of Sennacherib's army before Jerusalem, by which the Egyptians were freed from the yoke with which they were threatened by so powerful an enemy, who had carried on a successful war of three years' continuance against them; the affairs of Egypt were again thrown into confusion by intestine broils among themselves, which ended in a perfect anarchy, that lasted some few years. This was followed by an aristocracy, or rather tyranny, of twelve princes, who divided the country between them, and at last by the sole dominion of Psammitichus, which he held for fifty-four years. Not long after that followed the invasion and conquest of Egypt by Nebuchadnezzar, and then by the Persians under Cambyses, the son of Cyrus. The yoke of the Persians was so grievous, that the conquest of the Persians by Alexander may well be considered as a deliverance to Egypt; especially as he and his successors greatly favoured the people and improved the country. To all these events the prophet seems to have had a view in this chapter; and in particular, from ver. 18, the prophecy of the propagation of the true religion in Egypt seems to point to the flourishing state of Judaism in that country, in consequence of the great favour shown to the Jews by the Ptolemies. Alexander himself settled a great many Jews in his new city Alexandria, granting them privileges equal to those of the Macedonians. The first Ptolemy, called Soter, carried great numbers of them thither, and gave them such encouragement that still more of them were collected there from different parts; so that Philo reckons that in his

A. M. cir. 3290 B. C. cir. 714 Olymp. XVI. 3 cir. annum NumæPompilii, R. Roman., 2

2 And I will [d]set [e]the Egyptians against the Egyptians:
and [f]they shall fight every one
against his brother, and every
one against his neighbour; city against city,
and kingdom against kingdom.
3 And the spirit of Egypt [g]shall fail in the
midst thereof; and I will [h]destroy the counsel
thereof: and they shall [i]seek to the idols, and
to the charmers, and to them that have familiar spirits, and to the wizards.
4 And the Egyptians will I [k]give over [l]into
the hand of a cruel lord; and a fierce king
shall rule over them, saith the Lord, the LORD
of hosts.
5 [m]And the waters shall fail from the sea,
and the river shall be wasted and dried up.
6 And they shall turn the rivers far away;
and the brooks [n]of defence shall
be emptied and dried up: the
reeds and flags shall wither.
7 The paper reeds by the
brooks, by the mouth of the brooks, and every
thing sown by the brooks, shall wither, be
driven away, [o]and be no *more*.
8 The fishers also shall mourn, and all they
that cast angle into the brooks shall lament,
and they that spread nets upon the waters
shall languish.
9 Moreover they that work in [p]fine flax,
and they that weave [q]networks, shall be confounded.
10 And they shall be broken in the [r]pur-
poses thereof, all that make sluices *and* ponds
[s]for fish.
11 Surely the princes of [t]Zoan *are* fools,

A. M. cir. 3290 B. C. cir. 714 Olymp. XVI. 3 cir. annum NumæPompilii, R. Roman., 2

[d]Heb. *mingle*——[e]Judg. vii. 22; 1 Sam. xiv. 16, 20; 2 Chron. xx. 23——[f]Ezek. xxxix. 21——[g]Heb. *shall be emptied*——[h]Heb. *swallow up*——[i]Chap. viii. 19; xlvii. 12——[k]Or, *shut up*——[l]Chap. xx. 4; Jer. xlvi. 26; Ezek. xxix. 19

[m]Jeremiah li. 36; Ezekiel xxx. 12——[n]2 Kings xix. 24——[o]Hebrew, *and shall not be*——[p]1 Kings x. 28; Proverbs vii. 16——[q]Or, *white works*——[r]Hebrew, *foundations*——[s]Hebrew, *of living things*——[t]Num. xiii. 22

time there were a million of Jews in that country. These worshipped the God of their fathers; and their example and influence must have had a great effect in spreading the knowledge and worship of the true God through the whole country. See Bp. *Newton* on the Prophecies, Dissert. xii.

NOTES ON CHAP. XIX

Verse 1. *The burden of Egypt.*] That is, the prophet's declaration concerning Egypt.

Verse 3. *They shall seek to the idols, and to the charmers, and to them that have familiar spirits, and to the wizards.*] **And thei schul asken their symulacres, and their debynouris, and their debyl cleperis, and their debyl sacristers.**—Old Bible. The import of the original words has already been given where they occur in the Pentateuch. See Deut. xviii. 10, &c.

Verse 4. *A cruel lord*—"Cruel lords"] Nebuchadnezzar in the first place, and afterwards the whole succession of Persian kings, who in general were hard masters, and grievously oppressed the country. Note, that for קשה *kasheh, lord*, a MS. reads קשים *kashim, lords*, agreeable to which is the rendering of the *Septuagint, Syriac*, and *Vulgate*.

Verse 5. *The river shall be wasted and dried up.*] The Nile shall not overflow its banks; and if no inundation, the land must become barren. For, as there is little or no rain in Egypt, its fertility depends on the *overflowing* of the Nile.

Verse 6. *Shall turn the rivers far away*—"Shall become putrid"] האזניחו *heeznichu*. This sense of the word, which Simonis gives in his Lexicon, from the meaning of it in Arabic, suits the place much better than any other interpretation hitherto given; and that the word in Hebrew had some such signification, is probable from 2 Chron. xxix. 19, where the *Vulgate* renders it by *polluit, polluted*, and the *Targum*, by *profaned*, and *made abominable*, which the context in that place seems plainly to require. The form of the verb here is very irregular; and the rabbins and grammarians seem to give no probable account of it.

Verse 8. *The fishers also*—"And the fishers"] There was great plenty of fish in Egypt; see Num. xi. 5. "The Nile," says *Diodorus*, lib. i., "abounds with incredible numbers of all sorts of fish." And much more the lakes. So *Egmont, Pococke*, &c.

Verse 9. *They that work in fine flax*] פשתים שריקות *pishtim sericoth, heckled flax*, i. e., flax dressed on the heckle, or comb used for that purpose. The *Vulgate* uses the word *pectentes*, combing.

They that weave networks shall be confounded—**And confounden schul ben that wrogten flax, plattinge and webynge sotel thingis.**—Old MS. Bible.

Verse 10. *And they shall be broken*, &c.—"Her stores"] שתתיה *shathotheyha*, αποθηκαι, *granaries.*—*Aquila.*

All that make sluices and *ponds for fish*—"All that make a gain of pools for fish."] This obscure line is rendered by different interpreters in very different manners. *Kimchi* explains אגמי *agmey* as if it were the same with אגמה *agemah*, from Job xxx. 25, in which he is followed by some of the rabbins, and supported by the *Septuagint:* and שכר *secher*, which I translate *gain*, and which some take for *nets* or *inclosures*, the *Septuagint* render by ζυθον, *strong drink* or *beer*, which it is well known was much used in Egypt; and so likewise the *Syriac*, retaining the Hebrew word שכרא *sekra.* I submit these very different interpretations to the reader's judgment. The Version of the *Septuagint* is as follows: Και παντες οἱ ποιουντες τον ζυθον λυπηθησονται, και τας ψυχας πονεσουσι· "And all they that make barley wine shall mourn, and be grieved in soul."

Verse 11. *The counsel of the wise counsellors of Pharaoh is become brutish*—"Have coun-

A. M. cir. 3290
B. C. cir. 714
Olymp. XVI. 3
cir. annum
NumæPompilii,
R. Roman., 2

the counsel of the wise counsellors of Pharaoh is become brutish: how say ye unto Pharaoh,
I *am* the son of the wise, the
son of ancient kings?
12 [u]Where *are* they? where *are* thy wise
men? and let them tell thee now, and let
them know what the LORD of hosts hath purposed upon Egypt.
13 The princes of Zoan are become fools,
[v]the princes of Noph are deceived; they have
also seduced Egypt, *even* [w]*they* [x]*that are* the
stay of the tribes thereof.
14 The LORD hath mingled [y]a [z]perverse
spirit in the midst thereof: and they have
caused Egypt to err in every work thereof, as
a drunken *man* staggereth in his vomit.

15 Neither shall there be *any*
work for Egypt, which [a]the head
or tail, branch or rush, may do.
16 In that day shall Egypt
[b]be like unto women: and it shall be afraid
and fear because of the shaking of the hand
of the LORD of hosts, [c]which he shaketh
over it.
17 And the land of Judah shall be a terror
unto Egypt, every one that maketh mention
thereof shall be afraid in himself, because of
the counsel of the LORD of hosts, which he
hath determined against it.
18 In that day shall five cities in the land
of Egypt [d]speak [e]the language of Canaan,
and swear to the LORD of hosts; one shall
be called, The city [f]of destruction.

A. M. cir. 3290
B. C. cir. 714
Olymp. XVI. 3
cir. annum
NumæPompilii,
R. Roman., 2

---

[u]1 Cor. i. 20——[v]Jer. ii. 16——[w]Or, *governors* [x]Heb. *corners*——[y]Heb. *a spirit of perverseness*——[z]1 Kings xxii. 22; chap. xxix. 10

[a]Chap. ix. 14——[b]Jer. li. 30; Nah. iii. 13——[c]Chap. xi. 15——[d]Zeph. iii. 9——[e]Heb. *the lip*——[f]Or, *of Heres*, or *of the sun*

---

selled a brutish counsel"] The sentence as it now stands in the Hebrew, is imperfect: it wants the verb. Archbishop *Secker* conjectures that the words יועצי פרעה *yoatsey pharoh* should be transposed; which would in some degree remove the difficulty. But it is to be observed, that the translator of the *Vulgate* seems to have found in his copy the verb יעצו *yaatsu* added after פרעה *pharoh:* Sapientes consiliarii Pharaonis *dederunt* consilium insipiens, "The wise counsellors of Pharaoh gave unwise counsel." This is probably the true reading: it is perfectly agreeable to the Hebrew idiom, makes the construction of the sentence clear, and renders the transposition of the words above mentioned unnecessary.—L.

Verse 12. "Let them come"] Here too a word seems to have been left out of the text. After חכמיך *chachameycha, thy wise men, two* MSS., *one* ancient, add יבאו *yibu, let them come;* which, if we consider the form and construction of the sentence, has very much the appearance of being genuine: otherwise the connective conjunction at the beginning of the next member is not only superfluous but embarrassing. See also the Version of the *Septuagint*, in which the same deficiency is manifest.

Let them tell thee now—"And let them declare"] For ידעו *yidu, let them know*, perhaps we ought to read יודיעו *yodiu, let them make known.—Secker.* The *Septuagint* and *Vulgate* favour this reading, *ειπατωσαν, let them declare.*

Verse 13. *Are deceived*—"They have caused," &c.] The text has והתעו *vehithu*, AND *they have caused to err. Fifty* of *Kennicott's* MSS., *fifty-three* of *De Rossi's*, and *one* of my own, ancient, *thirty-two* editions, and the *Vulgate* and *Chaldee*, omit the ו *vau, and.*

Stay—"Pillars"] פנת *pinnath*, to be pointed as plural *pinnoth*, without doubt. So *Grotius*, and so the *Chaldee.*

Verse 14. *In the midst thereof*] "בקרבם *bekirbam;* so the *Septuagint*, and perhaps more correctly."—*Secker.* So likewise the *Chaldee.*

Verse 15. *The head or tail, branch or rush*] *R. D. Kimchi* says, there are some who suppose that these words mean the dragon's head and tail; and refer to all those who are conversant in astronomy, astrology, &c.

Verse 16. *Shall Egypt be*—"The Egyptians shall be"] יהיו *yihyu, they shall be*, plural, MS. Bodl. *Septuagint*, and *Chaldee.* This is not proposed as an emendation, for either form is proper.

Verse 17. *And the land of Judah*] The threatening hand of God will be held out and shaken over Egypt, from the side of Judea; through which the Assyrians will march to invade it. It signifies that kind of terror that drives one to his wit's end, that causes him to *reel* like a drunken man, to be giddy through astonishment. Such is the import of חג *chag*, and חגה *chagah. Five* MSS. and *two* editions have לחגה *lechagah.*

Verse 18. *The city of destruction*—"The city of the sun"] עיר החרס *ir hacheres.* This passage is attended with much difficulty and obscurity. First, in regard to the true reading. It is well known that Onias applied it to his own views, either to procure from the king of Egypt permission to build his temple in the Hieropolitan Nome, or to gain credit and authority to it when built; from the notion which he industriously propagated, that Isaiah had in this place prophesied of the building of such a temple. He pretended that the very place where it should be built was expressly named by the prophet, עיר החרס *ir hacheres, the city of the sun.* This possibly may have been the original reading. The present text has עיר ההרס *ir haheres, the city of destruction;* which some suppose to have been introduced into the text by the Jews of Palestine afterwards, to express their detestation of the place, being much offended with this schismatical temple in Egypt. Some think the latter to have been the true reading; and that the prophet himself gave this turn to the name out of contempt, and to inti-

A. M. cir. 3290
B. C. cir. 714
Olymp. XVI. 3
cir. annum
NumæPompilii,
R. Roman., 2

19 In that day [g]shall there be an altar to the LORD in the midst of the land of Egypt, and a pillar at the border thereof to the LORD.

20 And [h]it shall be for a sign and for a witness unto the LORD of hosts in the land of Egypt: for they shall cry unto the LORD because of the oppressors, and he shall send them a Saviour, and a great one, and he shall deliver them.

21 And the LORD shall be known to Egypt, and the Egyptians shall know the LORD in that day, and [i]shall do sacrifice and oblation; yea, they shall vow a vow unto the LORD, and perform *it*.

22 And the LORD shall smite Egypt: he shall smite and heal *it:* and they shall return *even* to the LORD, and he shall be intreated of them, and shall heal them.

A. M. cir. 3290
B. C. cir. 714
Olymp. XVI. 3
cir. annum
NumæPompilii,
R. Roman., 2

23 In that day [k]shall there be a highway out of Egypt to Assyria, and the Assyrian shall come into Egypt, and the Egyptian into Assyria, and the Egyptians shall serve with the Assyrians.

24 In that day shall Israel be the third with Egypt and with Assyria, *even* a blessing in the midst of the land:

25 Whom the LORD of hosts shall bless, saying, Blessed *be* Egypt my people, and Assyria [l]the work of my hands, and Israel mine inheritance.

---

[g]Gen. xxviii. 18; Exod. xxiv. 4; Josh. xxii. 10, 26, 27 — [h]See Josh. iv. 20; xxii. 27

[i]Mal. i. 11——[k]Chap. xi. 16——[l]Psa. c. 3; chap. xxix. 23; Hos. ii. 23; Eph. ii. 10

---

mate the demolition of this Hieropolitan temple; which in effect was destroyed by Vespasian's orders, after that of Jerusalem, "Videtur propheta consulto scripsisse הרם *heres, pro* חרם *cheres*, ut alibi scribitur בית און *beith aven* pro בית אל *beith El:* איש בשת *ish bosheth* pro איש בעל *ish baal*, &c. Vide *Lowth* in loc."—*Secker*. "It seems that the prophet designedly wrote הרם *heres, destruction*, for חרם *cheres, the sun:* as elsewhere בית און *beith aven, the house of iniquity*, is written for בית אל *beith El, the house of God;* איש בשת *ish bosheth* for איש בעל *ish baal*," &c. But on the supposition that עיר ההרם *air haheres* is the true reading, others understand it differently. The word הרם *heres* in Arabic signifies *a lion;* and Conrad Ikenius has written a dissertation (Dissert. Philol. Theol. XVI.) to prove that the place here mentioned is not Heliopolis, as it is commonly supposed to be, but Leontopolis in the Heliopolitan Nome, as it is indeed called in the letter, whether real or pretended, of Onias to Ptolemy, which Josephus has inserted in his Jewish Antiquities, lib. xiii. c. 3. And I find that several persons of great learning and judgment think that Ikenius has proved the point beyond contradiction. See *Christian. Muller.* Satura Observ. Philolog. *Michaelis* Bibliotheque Oriental, Part v., p. 171. But, after all, I believe that neither Onias, Heliopolis, nor Leontopolis has any thing to do with this subject. The application of this place of Isaiah to Onias's purpose seems to have been a mere invention, and in consequence of it there may perhaps have been some unfair management to accommodate the text to that purpose; which has been carried even farther than the Hebrew text; for the Greek version has here been either translated from a corrupted text, or wilfully mistranslated or corrupted, to serve the same cause. The place is there called πολις Ασεδεκ, *the city of righteousness;* a name apparently contrived by Onias's party to give credit to their temple, which was to rival that of Jerusalem. Upon the whole, the true reading of the Hebrew text in this place is very uncertain; *fifteen* MSS. and *seven* editions have חרם *cheres, the city of Hacheres*, or, *of the sun.* So likewise *Symmachus*, the *Vulgate*, *Arabic*, *Septuagint*, and *Complutensian.* On the other hand, *Aquila*, *Theodotion*, and the *Syriac* read הרם *heres, destruction;* the *Chaldee* paraphrase takes in both readings.

The reading of the text being so uncertain, no one can pretend to determine what the city was that is here mentioned by name; much less to determine what the four other cities were which the prophet does not name. I take the whole passage from the 18th verse to the end of the chapter, to contain a general intimation of the future propagation of the knowledge of the true God in Egypt and Syria, under the successors of Alexander; and, in consequence of this propagation, of the early reception of the Gospel in the same countries, when it should be published to the world. See more on this subject in *Prideaux's* Connect. An. 145; Dr. *Owen's* Inquiry into the present state of the *Septuagint* Version, p. 41; and *Bryant's* Observations on Ancient History, p. 124.—L.

Verse 19. *An altar to the Lord*] צבאות *tsebaoth*, "of hosts," or *Yehovah tsebaoth*, is added by *eight* MSS. of good repute, and the *Syriac* Version.

Verse 23. *Shall there be a highway*] Under the latter kings of Persia, and under Alexander, Egypt, Judea, and Assyria lived peaceably under the same government, and were on such friendly terms that there was a regular, uninterrupted intercourse between them, so that the Assyrian came into Egypt and the Egyptian into Assyria, and *Israel* became *the third*, i. e., was in strict union with the other two; and was a *blessing* to both, as affording them some knowledge of the true God, ver. 24.

Verse 25. *Blessed* be *Egypt—Assyria—and Israel*] All these countries shall be converted to the Lord. Concerning Egypt, it was said, chap. xviii. 7, that it should bring gifts to the Lord at Jerusalem. Here it is predicted, ver. 19, that there shall be an altar to the Lord in Egypt itself; and that they, with the Assyrians, shall become the people of God with the Is-

raelites. This remains partly to be fulfilled. These countries shall be all, and perhaps at no very distant time from this, converted to the faith of our Lord Jesus Christ.

CHAPTER XX

The Prophet Isaiah a sign to Egypt and Cush or Ethiopia, that the captives and exiles of these countries shall be indignantly treated by the king of Assyria, 1–6.

A. M. cir. 3290
B. C. cir. 714
Olymp. XVI. 3
cir. annum
NumæPompilii,
R. Roman., 2

IN the year that [a]Tartan came unto Ashdod, (when Sargon the king of Assyria sent him,) and fought against Ashdod, and took it;

2 At the same time spake the LORD [b]by Isaiah the son of Amoz, saying, Go and loose the [c]sackcloth from off thy loins, and put off thy shoe from thy foot. And he did so, [d]walking naked and barefoot.

3 And the LORD said, Like as my servant Isaiah hath walked naked and barefoot three years [e]*for* a sign and wonder upon Egypt and upon Ethiopia;

[a]2 Kings xviii. 17——[b]Heb. *by the hand of Isaiah* [c]Zech. xiii. 4——[d]1 Sam. xix. 24; Mic. i. 8, 11——[e]Ch. viii. 18——[f]Heb. *the captivity of Egypt*

4 So shall the king of Assyria lead away [f]the Egyptians prisoners, and the Ethiopians captives, young and old, naked and barefoot, [g]even with *their* buttocks uncovered, to the [h]shame of Egypt.

A. M. cir. 3290
B. C. cir. 714
Olymp. XVI. 3
cir. annum
NumæPompilii,
R. Roman., 2

5 [i]And they shall be afraid and ashamed of Ethiopia their expectation, and of Egypt their glory.

6 And the inhabitant of this [k]isle shall say in that day, Behold, such *is* our expectation, whither we flee for help to be delivered from the king of Assyria: and how shall we escape?

[g]2 Sam. x. 4; chap. iii. 17; Jer. xiii. 22, 26; Mic. i. 11 [h]Heb. *nakedness*——[i]2 Kings xviii. 21; chap. xxx. 3, 5, 7; xxxvi. 6——[k]Or, *country;* Jer. xlvii. 4

NOTES ON CHAP. XX

Tartan besieged Ashdod or Azotus, which probably belonged at this time to Hezekiah's dominions; see 2 Kings xviii. 8. The people expected to be relieved by the Cushites of Arabia and by the Egyptians. Isaiah was ordered to go uncovered, that is, without his upper garment, the rough mantle commonly worn by the prophets, (see Zech. xiii. 4,) probably three days to show that within three years the town should be taken, after the defeat of the Cushites and Egyptians by the king of Assyria, which event should make their case desperate, and induce them to surrender. Azotus was a strong place; it afterwards held out twenty-nine years against Psammitichus, king of Egypt, *Herod.* ii. 157. Tartan was one of Sennacherib's generals, 2 Kings xviii. 17, and Tirhakah, king of the Cushites, was in alliance with the king of Egypt against Sennacherib. These circumstances make it probable that by Sargon is meant Sennacherib. It might be one of the seven names by which Jerome, on this place, says he was called. He is called Sacherdonus and Sacherdan in the book of Tobit. The taking of Azotus must have happened before Sennacherib's attempt on Jerusalem; when he boasted of his late conquests, chap. xxxvii. 25. And the warning of the prophet had a principal respect to the Jews also, who were too much inclined to depend upon the assistance of Egypt. As to the rest history and chronology affording us no light, it may be impossible to clear either this or any other hypothesis, which takes Sargon to be Shalmaneser or Asarhaddon, &c., from all difficulties.—L. *Kimchi* says, this happened in the *fourteenth* year of Hezekiah.

Verse 2. *Walking naked and barefoot.*] It is not probable that the prophet walked uncovered and barefoot for three years; his appearing in that manner was a sign that within three years the Egyptians and Cushites should be in the same condition, being conquered and made captives by the king of Assyria. The time was denoted as well as the event; but his appearing in that manner for three whole years could give no premonition of the time at all. It is probable, therefore, that the prophet was ordered to walk so for *three days* to denote the accomplishment of the event in *three years;* a *day* for a *year*, according to the prophetical rule, Num. xiv. 34; Ezek. iv. 6. The words שלש ימים *shalosh yamim, three days*, may possibly have been lost out of the text, at the end of the second verse, after יחף *yacheph, barefoot;* or after the same word in the third verse, where, in the Alexandrine and Vatican copies of the *Septuagint*, and in MSS. *Pachom.* and I. D. II. the words *τρια ετη, three years*, are twice expressed. Perhaps, instead of שלש ימים *shalosh yamim, three days*, the Greek translator might read שלש שנים *shalosh shanim, three years*, by his own mistake, or by that of his copy, after יחף *yacheph* in the third verse, for which stands the first *τρια ετη, three years*, in the Alexandrine and Vatican *Septuagint*, and in the two MSS. above mentioned. It is most likely that Isaiah's walking naked and barefoot was done in a *vision;* as was probably that of the Prophet Hosea taking a *wife of whoredoms*. None of these things can well be taken *literally*.

From thy foot] רגליך *ragleycha*, thy *feet*, is the reading of *thirty-four* of *Kennicott's* and *De Rossi's* MSS., *four* ancient editions, with the *Septuagint, Syriac, Vulgate*, and *Arabic*

CHAPTER XXI

Prediction of the taking of Babylon by the Medes and Persians at the time of a great festival, 1–9. *Short application of the prophecy to the Jews, partly in the person of God, and partly in his own,* 10. *Obscure prophecy respecting Dumah,* 11, 12. *Prophecy concerning the Arabians to be fulfilled in a very short time after its delivery,* 13–17.

A. M. cir. 3290
B. C. cir. 714
Olymp. XVI. 3
cir. annum
NumæPompilii,
R. Roman., 2

THE burden of the desert of
the sea. As [a]whirlwinds in
the south pass through; *so* it
cometh from the desert, from a
terrible land.
2 A [b]grievous vision is declared unto me;
[c]the treacherous dealer dealeth treacherously,
and the spoiler spoileth. [d]Go
up, O Elam: besiege, O Media;
all the sighing thereof have I
made to cease.

A. M. cir. 3290
B. C. cir. 714
Olymp. XVI. 3
cir. annum
NumæPompilii,
R. Roman., 2

3 Therefore are [e]my loins filled with pain:
[f]pangs have taken hold upon me, as the pangs
of a woman that travaileth: I was bowed down

[a]Zech. ix. 14——[b]Heb. *hard*——[c]Ch. xxxiii. 1——[d]Ch. xiii. 17; Jer. xlix. 34——[e]Ch. xv. 5; xvi. 11——[f]Ch. xiii. 8

The first *ten* verses of this chapter contain a prediction of the taking of Babylon by the Medes and Persians. It is a passage singular in its kind for its brevity and force, for the variety and rapidity of the movements, and for the strength and energy of colouring with which the action and event are painted. It opens with the prophet's seeing at a distance the dreadful storm that is gathering and ready to burst upon Babylon. The event is intimated in general terms, and God's orders are issued to the Persians and Medes to set forth upon the expedition which he has given them in charge. Upon this the prophet enters into the midst of the action; and in the person of Babylon expresses, in the strongest terms, the astonishment and horror that seizes her on the sudden surprise of the city at the very season dedicated to pleasure and festivity, ver. 3, 4. Then, in his own person, describes the situation of things there, the security of the Babylonians, and in the midst of their feasting the sudden alarm of war, ver. 5. The event is then declared in a very singular manner. God orders the prophet to set a watchman to look out, and to report what he sees; he sees two companies marching onward, representing by their appearance the two nations that were to execute God's orders, who declare that Babylon is fallen, ver. 6-9.

But what is this to the prophet, and to the Jews, the object of his ministry? The application, the end, and design of the prophecy are admirably given in a short, expressive address to the Jews, partly in the person of God, partly in that of the prophet: "O my threshing—" "O my people, whom for your punishment I shall make subject to the Babylonians, to try and to prove you, and to separate the chaff from the corn, the bad from the good, among you; hear this for your consolation: your punishment, your slavery, and oppression will have an end in the destruction of your oppressors."—L.

NOTES ON CHAP. XXI

Verse 1. *The desert of the sea*] This plainly means Babylon, which is the subject of the prophecy. The country about Babylon, and especially below it towards the sea, was a great flat morass, overflowed by the Euphrates and Tigris. It became habitable by being drained by the many canals that were made in it.

Herodotus, lib. i. 184, says that "Semiramis confined the Euphrates within its channel by raising great dams against it; for before it overflowed the whole country like a sea." And Abydenus, (quoting Megasthenes, *apud Euseb.* Præp. Evang. IX. 41,) speaking of the building of Babylon by Nebuchadonosor, says, "it is reported that all this part was covered with water, and was called the sea; and that Belus drew off the waters, conveying them into proper receptacles, and surrounded Babylon with a wall." When the Euphrates was turned out of its channel by Cyrus, it was suffered still to drown the neighbouring country; and, the Persian government, which did not favour the place, taking no care to remedy this inconvenience, it became in time a great barren morassy desert, which event the title of the prophecy may perhaps intimate. Such it was originally; such it became after the taking of the city by Cyrus; and such it continues to this day.

As whirlwinds in the south—"Like the southern tempests"] The most vehement storms to which Judea was subject came from the desert country to the south of it. "Out of the south cometh the whirlwind," Job xxxvii. 9. "And there came a great wind from the wilderness, and smote the four corners of the house," Job i. 19. For the situation of Idumea, the country (as I suppose) of Job, see Lam. iv. 21 compared with Job i. 1, was the same in this respect with that of Judea:—

"And JEHOVAH shall appear over them,
And his arrow shall go forth as the lightning;
And the Lord JEHOVAH shall sound the trumpet;
And shall march in the whirlwinds of the south." Zech. ix. 14.

Verse 2. *The treacherous dealer dealeth treacherously, and the spoiler spoileth*—"The plunderer is plundered, and the destroyer is destroyed."] הבוגד בוגד והשודד שודד *habboged boged vehashshoded shoded.* The MSS. vary in expressing or omitting the ו *vau,* in these four words. *Ten* MSS. of *Kennicott* are without the ו *vau* in the *second* word, and *eight* MSS. are without the ו *vau* in the *fourth* word; which justifies *Symmachus,* who has rendered them passively: ὁ αθετων αθετειται και ὁ ταλαιπωριζων ταλαιπωρει. He read בגוד שדוד *bagud shadud. Cocceius* (Lexicon *in voce*) observes that the *Chaldee* very often renders the verb בגד *bagad,* by בזז *bazaz, he spoiled;* and in this place, and in xxxiii. 1, by the equivalent word אנס *anas, to press, give trouble;* and in chap. xxiv. 16 both by אנס *anas* and בזז *bazaz;* and the *Syriac* in this place renders it by טלם *talam, he oppressed.*

All the sighing thereof have I made to cease—

A. M. cir. 3290 B. C. cir. 714 Olymp. XVI. 3 cir. annum NumæPompilii, R. Roman., 2

at the hearing *of it;* I was dismayed at the seeing *of it.*

4 [g]My heart panted, fearfulness affrighted me: [h]the night
of my pleasure hath he [i]turned into fear
unto me.

5 [k]Prepare the table, watch in the watchtower, eat, drink: arise, ye princes, *and*
anoint the shield.

6 For thus hath the LORD said unto me, Go,
set a watchman, let him declare what he
seeth.

7 [l]And he saw a chariot *with* a couple of
horsemen, a chariot of asses, *and* a chariot of
camels; and he hearkened diligently with
much heed:

8 And [m]he cried, a lion: My
lord, I stand continually upon the
[n]watchtower in the day-time, and
I am set in my ward [o]whole nights:

A. M. cir. 3290 B. C. cir. 714 Olymp. XVI. 3 cir. annum NumæPompilii, R. Roman., 2

9 And, behold, here cometh a chariot of men,
with a couple of horsemen. And he answered
and said, [p]Babylon is fallen, is fallen; and
[q]all the graven images of her gods he hath
broken unto the ground.

10 [r]O my threshing, and the [s]corn of my
floor: that which I have heard of the LORD of
hosts, the God of Israel, have I declared unto
you.

11 [t]The burden of Dumah. He calleth to
me out of Seir, Watchman, what of the night?
Watchman, what of the night?

[g]Or, *my mind wandered*——[h]Deut. xxviii. 67——[i]Heb. *put*——[k]Dan. v. 5——[l]Ver. 9——[m]Or, *cried as a lion* [n]2 Chron. xx. 24; ver. 5; Hab. ii. 1——[o]Or, *every night*

[p]Jer. li. 8; Rev. xiv. 8; xviii. 2——[q]Chap. xlvi. 1; Jer. l. 2; li. 44——[r]Jer. li. 33——[s]Heb. *son*——[t]1 Chron. i. 30; Jer. xlix. 7, 8; Ezek. xxxv. 2; Obad. 1

"I have put an end to all her vexations"] *Heb.* "Her sighing; that is, the sighing caused by her." So *Kimchi* on the place: "It means those who groaned through fear of him: for the suffixes of the nouns refer both to the agent and the patient. All those who groaned before the face of the king of Babylon he caused to rest;" *Chald.* And so likewise *Ephrem Syr.* in loc., edit. Assemani: "His groans, viz., the grief and tears which the Chaldeans occasioned through the rest of the nations."

Verse 5. *Prepare the table*—"The table is prepared"] In *Hebrew* the verbs are in the infinitive mood absolute, as in Ezek. i. 14: "And the animals ran and returned, רצוא ושוב *ratso veshob*, like the appearance of the lightning;" just as the Latins say, *currere et reverti*, for *currebant et revertebantur*. See chap. xxxii. 11, and the note there.

Arise, ye princes, and *anoint the shield.*] *Kimchi* observes that several of the rabbins understood this of Belshazzar's impious feast and death. The king of a people is termed *the shield*, because he is their *defence*. The command, *Anoint the shield*, is the same with *Anoint a new king.* Belshazzar being now suddenly slain, while they were all eating and drinking, he advises the princes, whose business it was, to make speed and anoint another in his stead.

Verse 7. *And he saw a chariot, &c.*—"And he saw a chariot with two riders; a rider on an ass, a rider on a camel"] This passage is extremely obscure from the ambiguity of the term רכב *recheb*, which is used three times, and which signifies a chariot, or any other vehicle, or the rider in it; or a rider on a horse, or any other animal; or a company of chariots, or riders. The prophet may possibly mean a cavalry in two parts, with two sorts of riders; riders on asses or mules, and riders on camels; or led on by two riders, one on an ass, and one on a camel. However, so far it is pretty clear, that Darius and Cyrus, the Medes and the Persians, are intended to be distinguished by the two riders on the two sorts of cattle. It appears from *Herodotus*, i. 80, that the baggage of Cyrus' army was carried on camels. In his engagement with Crœsus, he took off the baggage from the camels, and mounted his horsemen upon them; the enemy's horses, offended with the smell of the camels, turned back and fled.—L.

Verse 8. *And he cried, A lion*—"He that looked out on the watch"] The present reading, אריה *aryeh, a lion*, is so unintelligible, and the mistake so obvious, that I make no doubt that the true reading is הראה *haroeh, the seer;* as the *Syriac* translator manifestly found it in his copy, who renders it by דוקא *duka, a watchman.*

Verse 9. *Here cometh a chariot of men, &c.*—"A man, one of the two riders"] So the *Syriac* understands it, and Ephrem Syr.

Verse 10. *O my threshing*] "O thou, the object upon which I shall exercise the severity of my discipline; that shalt lie under my afflicting hand, like corn spread upon the floor to be threshed out and winnowed, to separate the chaff from the wheat!" The image of threshing is frequently used by the Hebrew poets, with great elegance and force, to express the punishment of the wicked and the trial of the good, or the utter dispersion and destruction of God's enemies. Of the different ways of threshing in use among the Hebrews, and the manner of performing them, see the note on chap. xxviii. 27.

Our translators have taken the liberty of using the word *threshing* in a passive sense, to express the object or matter that is threshed; in which I have followed them, not being able to express it more properly, without departing too much from the form and letter of the original. "*Son* of my floor," *Heb.* It is an idiom of the *Hebrew* language to call the effect, the object, the adjunct, any thing that belongs in almost any way to another, the *son* of it. "O my threshing." The prophet abruptly breaks off the speech of God; and instead of continuing it in the form in which he had begun, and in the person of God, "This I declare unto you by my prophet," he changes the form of address, and adds, in his own person, "This I declare unto you from God."

Verse 11. *The burden of Dumah*—"The oracle

A. M. cir. 3290 B. C. cir. 714 Olymp. XVI. 3 cir. annum NumæPompilii, R. Roman., 2
12 The watchman said, The
morning cometh, and also the
night: if ye will inquire, inquire
ye: return, come.
13 [u]The burden upon Arabia. In the forest
in Arabia shall ye lodge, O ye
travelling companies [v]of De-
danim.
14 The inhabitants of the land
of Tema [w]brought water to him that was

[u]Jer. xlix. 28——[v]1 Chron. i. 9, 32

[w]Or, *bring ye*

concerning Dumah."] Pro דומה *Dumah*, Codex R. Meiri habet אדום *Edom;* and so the *Septuagint*, Vid. *Kimchi* ad h. l. Biblia Michaelis, Halæ, 1720, not. ad l. See also *De Rossi*. Bishop *Lowth* translates the prophecy thus:—

11. The oracle concerning Dumah.
A voice crieth to me from Seir:
Watchman, what from the night?
Watchman, what from the night?
12. The watchman replieth:—
The morning cometh, and also the night.
If ye will inquire, inquire ye: come again.

This differs very little from our common Version. One of *Kennicott's* MSS., and one of my own, omit the repetition, "Watchman, what from the night?"

This prophecy, from the uncertainty of the occasion on which it was uttered, and from the brevity of the expression, is extremely obscure. The Edomites as well as the Jews were subdued by the Babylonians. They inquire of the prophet how long their subjection is to last: he intimates that the Jews should be delivered from their captivity; not so the Edomites. Thus far the interpretation seems to carry with it some degree of probability. What the meaning of the last line may be, I cannot pretend to divine. In this difficulty the *Hebrew* MSS. give no assistance. The MSS. of the *Septuagint*, and the fragments of the other *Greek* Versions, give some variations, but no light. This being the case, I thought it best to give an exact literal translation of the whole two verses, which may serve to enable the English reader to judge in some measure of the foundation of the various interpretations that have been given of them.

The burden of Dumah.—R. D. Kimchi says, "His father understood this of the destruction of *Dumah* (one of the cities of the Ishmaelites) by the inhabitants of *Seir;* and that they inquired of the prophet to know the particular time in which God had given them a commission against it. The prophet answered: The *morning*—the time of *success* to you, cometh, is just at hand; and the *night*—the time of *utter destruction* to the inhabitants of Dumah, is also ready."

I have heard the words applied in the way of general exhortation. 1. Every minister of God is a *watchman*. He is continually *watching* for the *safety* and *interests* of his people, and looking for the counsel of God that he may be properly qualified to *warn* and to *comfort*. 2. Such are often called to denounce *heavy judgments;* they have the *burden* of the word of the Lord to denounce against the impenitent, the backslider, the lukewarm, and the careless. 3. When the watchman threatens judgments, some are *awakened*, and some *mock: Watchman, what of the night?* "*What* are the judgments thou threatenest, and *when* are they to take place?" 4. To this question, whether *seriously* or *tauntingly* proposed, the watchman answers: 1. *The morning cometh*—there is a *time of repentance* granted; a *morning* of God's *long-suffering kindness* now appears: and *also the night*—the time in which God will no longer wait to be gracious, but will cut you off as cumberers of the ground. 2. But *if you will inquire* seriously how you are to escape God's judgments, *inquire ye.* 3. There is still a door of hope; *continue* to pray for mercy. 4. *Return* from your iniquities. 5. *Come* to God, through Christ, that ye may obtain salvation.

Verse 13. *The burden upon Arabia*—"The oracle concerning Arabia"] This title is of doubtful authority. In the first place, because it is not in many of the MSS. of the *Septuagint;* it is in MSS. *Pachom.* and I. D. II. only, as far as I can find with certainty. Secondly, from the singularity of the phraseology; for משא *massa* is generally prefixed to its object without a preposition, as משא בבל *massa babel;* and never but in this place with the preposition ב *beth.* Besides, as the word בערב *baarab* occurs at the very beginning of the prophecy itself, the first word but one, it is much to be suspected that some one, taking it for a proper name and the object of the prophecy, might note it as such by the words משא בערב *massa baarab* written in the margin, which he might easily transfer to the text. The *Septuagint* did not take it for a proper name, but render it εν τῳ δρυμῳ ἑσπερας, "in the forest, in the evening," and so the *Chaldee*, which I follow; for otherwise, the forest *in Arabia* is so indeterminate and vague a description, that in effect it means nothing at all. This observation might have been of good use in clearing up the foregoing very obscure prophecy, if any light had arisen from joining the two together by removing the separating title; but I see no connexion between them. The *Arabic* Version has, "The prophecy concerning the Arabians, and the children of Chedar."

This prophecy was to have been fulfilled within a year of the time of its delivery, see ver. 16; and it was probably delivered about the same time with the rest in this part of the book, that is, soon before or after the 14th of Hezekiah, the year of Sennacherib's invasion. In his first march into Judea, or in his return from the Egyptian expedition, he might perhaps overrun these several clans of Arabians; their distress on some such occasion is the subject of this prophecy.—L.

Verse 14. *The land of Tema*—"The southern country"] Θαιμαν, *Sept.;* Austri, *Vulg.* They read תימן *teiman*, which seems to be right; for probably the inhabitants of Tema might be involved in the same calamity with their brethren and neighbours of Kedar, and not in a condition to give them assistance, and to relieve them, in their flight before the enemy, with bread and water. To bring forth bread and water is an instance of common humanity in such cases of distress; especially in those desert countries in which the common necessaries of life, more particularly water, are not easily to be met with or procured. Moses forbids the Ammonite and Moabite to be admitted into the congregation of the Lord to the tenth generation. One reason

A. M. cir. 3290 B. C. cir. 714 Olymp. XVI. 3 cir. annum NumæPompilii, R. Roman., 2

thirsty, they prevented with
their bread him that fled.
15 For they fled [x]from [y]the
swords, from the drawn sword,
and from the bent bow, and from the grievousness of war.
16 For thus hath the LORD said unto me,
Within a year, [z]according to the
years of a hireling, and all the
glory of [a]Kedar shall fail:
17 And the residue of the
number of [b]archers, the mighty men of the
children of Kedar, shall be diminished: for
the LORD God of Israel hath spoken *it*.

[x]Or, *for fear*——[y]Heb. *from the face*——[z]Chap. xvi. 14

[a]Psa. cxx. 5; chap. lx. 7——[b]Heb. *bows*

which he gives for this reprobation is their omission of the common offices of humanity towards the Israelites; "because they met them not with bread and water in the way, when they came forth out of Egypt," Deut. xxiii. 4.

Verse 17. *The archers, the mighty men of the children of Kedar*—"The mighty bowmen of the sons of Kedar"] *Sagittariorum fortium, Vulg.;* transposing the two words, and reading נבורי קשת *gibborey kesheth;* which seems to be right. The strong men of the bow, the most excellent archers.

For the Lord—hath spoken it—"For JEHOVAH hath spoken it."] The prophetic Carmina of Marcius, foretelling the battle of Cannæ, lib. xxv. 12, conclude with the same kind of solemn form: *Nam mihi ita Jupiter fatus est;* "Thus hath Jupiter spoken to me." Observe that the word נאם *naam, to pronounce, to declare,* is the solemn word appropriated to the delivering of prophecies: "Behold, I am against the prophets, saith (נאם *naam, pronounceth*) JEHOVAH, who use their tongues, וינאמו נאם *vaiyinamu neum, and solemnly pronounce,* He hath pronounced it;" Jer. xxiii. 31. What God says shall most assuredly come to pass; he cannot be deceived.

CHAPTER XXII

Prophecy concerning Jerusalem, 1–14. *Sentence against Shebna, who was over the household,* 15–19. *Prophecy concerning Eliakim, the son of Hilkiah,* 20, 21. *From Eliakim, Isaiah, (agreeably to the mode universally adopted in the prophetical writings, of making the things then present, or which were shortly to be accomplished,* types *or* representations *of things to be fulfilled upon a larger scale in distant futurity,) makes a transition to the Messiah, of whom Eliakim was a type, to whom the words will best apply, and to whom some passages in the prophecy must be solely restrained,* 20–24. *The sentence against Shebna again confirmed,* 25.

A. M. cir. 3292 B. C. cir. 712 Olymp. XVII. 1 cir. annum NumæPompilii, R. Roman., 4

THE burden of the valley of
vision. What aileth thee
now, that thou art wholly gone
up to the housetops?
2 Thou that art full of stirs, a
tumultuous city, [a]a joyous city:
thy slain *men are* not slain with
the sword, nor dead in battle.

[a]Isaiah, chap. xxxii. 13

This prophecy, ending with the *fourteenth* verse of this chapter, is entitled, "The oracle concerning the valley of vision," by which is meant Jerusalem, because, says *Sal. ben Melech,* it was the place of prophecy. Jerusalem, according to Josephus, was built upon two opposite hills, Sion and Acra, separated by a valley in the midst. He speaks of another broad valley between Acra and Moriah, *Bell. Jud.* v. 13, vi. 6. It was the seat of Divine revelation; the place where chiefly prophetic vision was given, and where God manifested himself visibly in the holy place. The prophecy foretells the invasion of Jerusalem by the Assyrians under Sennacherib; or by the Chaldeans under Nebuchadnezzar. *Vitringa* is of opinion that the prophet has both in view: that of the Chaldeans in the first part, ver. 1-5, which he thinks relates to the flight of Zedekiah, 2 Kings xxv. 4, 5; and that of the Assyrians in the latter part, which agrees with the circumstances of that time, and particularly describes the preparations made by Hezekiah for the defence of the city, ver. 8-11. Compare 2 Chron. xxxii. 2-5.—L.

NOTES ON CHAP. XXII

Verse 1. *Art—gone up to the house-tops*—"Are gone up to the house-tops"] The houses in the east were in ancient times, as they are still, generally, built in one and the same uniform manner. The roof or top of the house is always flat, covered with broad stones, or a strong plaster of terrace, and guarded on every side with a low parapet wall; see Deut. xxii. 8. The terrace is frequented as much as any part of the house. On this, as the season favours, they walk, they eat, they sleep, they transact business, (1 Sam. ix. 25, see also the *Septuagint* in that place,) they perform their devotions, Acts x. 9. The house is built with a court within, into which chiefly the windows open: those that open to the street are so obstructed with lattice-work that no one either without or within can see through them. Whenever, therefore, any thing is to be seen or heard in the

A. M. cir. 3292 B. C. cir. 712 Olymp. XVII. 1 cir. annum NumæPompilii, R. Roman., 4

3 All thy rulers are fled together, they are bound [b]by the archers: all that are found in thee, are bound together, *which* have fled from far.

4 Therefore, said I, Look away from me; [c]I [d]will weep bitterly, labour not to comfort me, because of the spoiling of the daughter of my people.

5 [e]For *it is* a day of trouble, and of treading down, and of perplexity [f]by the Lord GOD of hosts in the valley of vision, breaking down the walls, and of crying to the mountains.

6 [g]And Elam bare the quiver with chariots of men *and* horsemen, and [h]Kir [i]uncovered the shield.

7 And it shall come to pass, *that* [k]thy choicest valleys shall be full of chariots, and the horsemen shall set themselves in array [l]at the gate.

8 And he discovered the covering of Judah, and thou didst look in that day to the armour [m]of the house of the forest.

9 [n]Ye have seen also the breaches of the city of David, that they are many: and ye gathered together the waters of the lower pool.

10 And ye have numbered the houses of Jerusalem, and the houses have ye broken down, to fortify the wall.

11 [o]Ye made also a ditch between the two

[b]Heb. *of the bow*——[c]Jer. iv. 19; ix. 1——[d]Heb. *I will be bitter in weeping*——[e]Chap. xxxvii. 3——[f]Lam. i. 5; ii. 2——[g]Jer. xlix. 35——[h]Chap. xv. 1

[i]Heb. *made naked*——[k]Heb. *the choice of thy valleys* [l]Or, *toward*——[m]1 Kings vii. 2; x. 17——[n]2 Kings xx. 20; 2 Chron. xxxii. 4, 5, 30——[o]Neh. iii. 16

streets, any public spectacle, any alarm of a public nature, every one immediately goes up to the house-top to satisfy his curiosity. In the same manner, when any one has occasion to make any thing public, the readiest and most effectual way of doing it is to proclaim it from the house-tops to the people in the streets. "What ye hear in the ear, that publish ye on the house-top," saith our Saviour, Matt. x. 27. The people running all to the tops of their houses gives a lively image of a sudden general alarm. Sir *John Chardin's* MS. note on this place is as follows: "Dans les festes pour voir passer quelque chose, et dans les maladies pour les annoncer aux voisins en allumant des lumieres, le peuple monte sur les terrasses." "In festivals, in order to see what is going forward, and in times of sickness, in order to indicate them to neighbours by lighting of candles, the people go up to the house-tops."

Verse 3. *All thy rulers—are bound by the archers*—"All thy leaders—are fled from the bow"] There seems to be somewhat of an inconsistency in the sense according to the present reading. If the leaders were bound, אסרו *usseru*, how could they flee away? for their being bound, according to the obvious construction and course of the sentence, is a circumstance prior to their flight. I therefore follow *Houbigant*, who reads הסרו *huseru, remoti sunt*, "they are gone off." גלו *galu, transmigraverunt, Chaldee;* which seems to confirm this emendation.

Verse 6. *Chariots of men*—"The Syrian"] It is not easy to say what רכב אדם *recheb adam*, a *chariot of men*, can mean. It seems by the form of the sentence, which consists of three members, the first and the third mentioning a particular people, that the second should do so likewise. Thus ברכב ארם ופרשים *berecheb aram uparashim*, "with chariots the Syrian, and with horsemen:" the similitude of the letters ד *daleth* and ר *resh* is so great, and the mistakes arising from it are so frequent, that I readily adopt the correction of *Houbigant*, ארם *aram, Syria*, instead of אדם *adam, man;* which seems to me extremely probable. The conjunction ו *vau, and*, prefixed to פרשים *parashim, horsemen*, seems necessary in whatever way the sentence may be taken; and it is confirmed by *five* MSS., (one ancient,) *four* of *De Rossi's*, and two ancient of my own; one by correction of Dr. *Kennicott's*, and *three* editions. Kir was a city belonging to the Medes. The Medes were subject to the Assyrians in Hezekiah's time, (see 2 Kings xvi. 9, and xvii. 6;) and so perhaps might Elam (the Persians) likewise be, or auxiliaries to them.

Verse 8. *The armour*—"The arsenal"] Built by Solomon within the city, and called the house of the forest of Lebanon; probably from the great quantity of cedar from Lebanon which was employed in the building. See 1 Kings vii. 2, 3.

Verse 9. *Ye gathered together the waters*—"And ye shall collect the waters"] There were two pools in or near Jerusalem, supplied by springs: the upper pool, or the old pool, supplied by the spring called Gihon, 2 Chron. xxxii. 30, towards the higher part of the city, near Sion, or the city of David, and the lower pool, probably supplied by Siloam, towards the lower part. When Hezekiah was threatened with a siege by Sennacherib, he stopped up all the waters of the fountains without the city; and brought them into the city by a conduit, or subterranean passage cut through the rock; those of the old pool, to the place where he had a double wall, so that the pool was between the two walls. This he did in order to distress the enemy, and to supply the city during the siege. This was so great a work that not only the historians have made particular mention of it, 2 Kings xx. 20; 2 Chron. xxxii. 2, 3, 5, 30; but the son of Sirach also has celebrated it in his encomium on Hezekiah. "Hezekiah fortified his city, and brought in water into the midst thereof: he digged the hard rock with iron, and made wells for water," Ecclus. xlviii.

Verse 11. *Unto the maker thereof*—"To him that hath disposed this"] That is, to God the Author and Disposer of this visitation, the invasion with which he now threatens you. The

A. M. cir. 3292
B. C. cir. 712
Olymp. XVII. 1
cir. annum
NumæPompilii,
R. Roman., 4

walls for the water of the old
pool: but ye have not looked
unto [p]the maker thereof, neither had respect unto him that
fashioned it long ago.
12 And in that day did the Lord God of
hosts [q]call to weeping, and to mourning, and
[r]to baldness, and to girding with sackcloth:
13 And behold joy and gladness, slaying
oxen, and killing sheep, eating flesh, and
drinking wine; [s]let us eat and
drink, for to-morrow we shall
die.
14 [t]And it was revealed in
mine ears by the Lord of hosts, Surely this
iniquity [u]shall not be purged from you till
ye die, saith the Lord God of hosts.
15 Thus saith the Lord God of Hosts, Go,
get thee unto this treasurer, *even* unto [v]Sheb-
na, [w]which *is* over the house, *and say,*

[p]See ch. xxxvii. 26——[q]Joel i. 13——[r]See Ezra ix. 3; ch. xv. 2; Mic. i. 16——[s]Ch. lvi. 12; Wisd. ii. 6; 1 Cor, xv. 32——[t]Ch. v. 9——[u]1 Sam. iii. 14; Ezek. xxiv. 13 [v]2 Kings xviii. 37; ch. xxxvi. 3——[w]1 Kings iv. 6

very same expressions are applied to God, and upon the same occasion, chap. xxxvii. 26:—

"Hast thou not heard of old, that I have disposed it;
And of ancient times, that I have formed it?"

Verse 13. *Let us eat and drink, for to-morrow we shall die.*] This has been the language of all those who have sought their portion in this life, since the foundation of the world. So the poet:—

Heu, heu nos miseri! quam totus homuncio nil est!
Sic erimus cuncti, postquam nos auferet orcus.
Ergo vivamus, dum licet esse, bene.

Alas, alas! what miserable creatures are we, only the semblances of men! And so shall we be all when we come to die. Therefore let us live joyfully while we may.

Domitian had an image of death hung up in his dining-room, to show his guests that as life was uncertain, they should make the best of it by indulging themselves. On this *Martial*, to flatter the emperor, whom he styles *god*, wrote the following epigram:—

Frange thoros, pete vina, tingere nardo.
Ipse jubet mortis te meminisse Deus.

Sit down to table—drink heartily—anoint thyself with spikenard; for God himself commands thee to remember death.

So the *adage:*—

Ede, bibe, lude: post mortem nulla voluptas.

"Eat, drink, and play, while here ye may:
No revelry after your dying day."

St. Paul quotes the same heathen sentiment, 1 Cor. xv. 32: "Let us eat and drink, for to-morrow we die."

Anacreon is full in point, and from him nothing better can be expected:—

'Ως ουν ετ' ευδι' εστιν,
Και πινε και κυβευε
Και σπενδε τῳ Λυαιῳ·
Μη νουσος, ην τις ελθῃ,
Λεγῃ, σε μη δει πινειν.

Anac. *Od.* xv., l. 11.

"While no tempest blots your sky,
Drink, and throw the sportful dye:
But to Bacchus drench the ground,
Ere you push the goblet round;
Lest some fatal illness cry,
'Drink no more the cup of joy.'"

Addison.

Verse 14. *It was revealed in mine ears*—"The voice of Jehovah"] The *Vulgate* has *vox Domini;* as if in his copy he had read קול יהוה *kol Yehovah;* and in truth, without the word קול *kol, voice,* it is not easy to make out the sense of the passage; as appears from the strange versions which the rest of the ancients, (except the *Chaldee,*) and many of the moderns, have given of it; as if the matter were revealed in or to the ears of Jehovah: εν τοις ωσι Κυριου, *in the ears of the Lord,* Septuagint. *Vitringa* translates it, Revelatus est in auribus meis Jehovah, "Jehovah hath revealed it in mine ears;" and refers to 1 Sam. ii. 27; iii. 21: but the construction in those places is different, and there is no speech of God added; which here seems to want something more than the verb נגלה *nigleh* to introduce it. Compare chap. v. 9, where the text is still more imperfect.

The Lord God of hosts] אדני יהוה צבאות *Adonai Yehovah tsebaoth.* But אדני *Adonai, Lord,* is omitted by *two* of *Kennicott's* and *De Rossi's* MSS., and by *two* of my own; by *three* editions, and the *Septuagint, Syriac* and *Arabic.*

Verse 15. *Go—unto Shebna*] The following prophecy concerning Shebna seems to have very little relation to the foregoing, except that it might have been delivered about the same time; and Shebna might be a principal person among those whose luxury and profaneness is severely reprehended by the prophet in the conclusion of that prophecy, ver. 11-14.

Shebna the scribe, mentioned in the history of Hezekiah, chap. xxxvi., seems to have been a different person from this Shebna, the treasurer or steward of the household, to whom this prophecy relates. The Eliakim here mentioned was probably the person who, at the time of Sennacherib's invasion, was actually treasurer, the son of Hilkiah. If so, this prophecy was delivered, as the preceding, (which makes the former part of the chapter,) plainly was, some time before the invasion of Sennacherib. As to the rest, history affords us no information.

"And say unto him"] Here are two words lost out of the text, which are supplied by *two* of Dr. *Kennicott's* MSS., *one* ancient, which read ואמרת אליו *veamarta elaiv, and thou shalt say unto him;* by the *Septuagint,* και ειπον αυτῳ, and in the same manner by all the ancient versions. It is to be observed that this passage is

A. M. cir. 3292
B. C. cir. 712
Olymp. XVII. 1
cir. annum
NumæPompilii,
R. Roman., 4

16 What hast thou here? and
whom hast thou here, that thou
hast hewed thee out a sepulchre
here, [x]*as* he [y]that heweth him
out a sepulchre on high, *and* that graveth a
habitation for himself in a rock?
17 Behold, [z]the LORD will carry thee away
with [a]a mighty captivity, [b]and will surely
cover thee.
18 He will surely violently turn and toss
thee *like* a ball into a [c]large country: there
shalt thou die, and there the chariots of thy
glory *shall be* the shame of thy lord's house.
19 And I will drive thee from thy station,
and from thy state shall he pull
thee down.
20 And it shall come to pass
in that day, that I will call my
servant [d]Eliakim the son of Hilkiah:
21 And I will clothe him with thy robe, and
strengthen him with thy girdle, and I will
commit thy government into his hand: and
he shall be a father to the inhabitants of Jerusalem, and to the house of Judah.
22 And the key of the house of David will
I lay upon his shoulder; so he shall [e]open,
and none shall shut: and he shall shut, and
none shall open.

A. M. cir. 3292
B. C. cir. 712
Olymp. XVII. 1
cir. annum
NumæPompilii,
R. Roman., 4

[x]Or, *O he*——[y]2 Sam. xviii. 18; Matt. xxvii. 60——[z]Or, *the LORD who covered thee with an excellent covering, and clothed thee gorgeously, shall surely*, &c.; ver. 18——[a]Heb. *the captivity of a man*——[b]Esth. vii. 8——[c]Heb. *large of spaces*——[d]2 Kings xviii. 18——[e]Job xii. 14; Rev. iii. 7

merely historical, and does not admit of that sort of ellipsis by which in the poetical parts a person is frequently introduced speaking, without the usual notice, that what follows was delivered by him.

Verse 16. *A sepulchre on high—in a rock*] It has been observed before, on chap. xiv., that persons of high rank in Judea, and in most parts of the east, were generally buried in large sepulchral vaults, hewn out in the rock for the use of themselves and their families. The vanity of Shebna is set forth by his being so studious and careful to have his sepulchre on high—in a lofty vault; and that probably in a high situation, that it might be more conspicuous. Hezekiah was buried, למעלה *lemalah*, εν αναβασει, *Sept.:* in the chiefest, says our translation; rather, in the highest part of the sepulchres of the sons of David, to do him the more honour, 2 Chron. xxxii. 33. There are some monuments still remaining in Persia of great antiquity, called *Naksi Rustam*, which give one a clear idea of Shebna's pompous design for his sepulchre. They consist of several sepulchres, each of them hewn in a high rock near the top; the front of the rock to the valley below is adorned with carved work in relievo, being the outside of the sepulchre. Some of these sepulchres are about thirty feet in the perpendicular from the valley, which is itself perhaps raised above half as much by the accumulation of the earth since they were made. See the description of them in Chardin, Pietro della Valle, Thevenot, and Kempfer. Diodorus Siculus, lib. xvii., mentions these ancient monuments, and calls them the sepulchres of the kings of Persia.—L.

Verse 17. *Cover thee*] That is, thy face. This was the condition of mourners in general, and particularly of condemned persons. See Esther vi. 12; vii. 8.

Verse 19. *I will drive thee*] אהרסך *ehersecha*, in the first person, *Syr. Vulg.*

Verse 21. *To the inhabitants*] ליושבי *leyoshebey*, in the plural number, four of Dr. *Kennicott's* MSS., (two ancient,) and two of *De Rossi's*, with the *Septuagint*, *Syriac*, and *Vulgate*.

Verse 22. *And the key of the house of David will I lay upon his shoulder*] As the robe and the baldric, mentioned in the preceding verse, were the ensigns of power and authority, so likewise was the key the mark of office, either sacred or civil. The priestess of Juno is said to be the key-bearer of the goddess, κλειδουχος 'Ηρας· *Æschyl.* Suppl. 299. A female high in office under a great queen has the same title:—

Καλλιθοη κλειδουχος Ολυμπιαδος βασιλειης.

"Callithoe was the key-bearer of the Olympian queen."

Auctor Phoronidis ap. Clem. Alex. p. 418, edit. Potter. This mark of office was likewise among the Greeks, as here in Isaiah, borne on the shoulder; the priestess of Ceres, κατωμαδιαν εχε κλαιδα, *had the key on her shoulder. Callim.* Ceres, ver. 45. To comprehend how the key could be borne on the shoulder, it will be necessary to say something of the form of it: but without entering into a long disquisition, and a great deal of obscure learning, concerning the locks and keys of the ancients, it will be sufficient to observe, that one sort of keys, and that probably the most ancient, was of considerable magnitude, and as to the shape, very much bent and crooked. *Aratus*, to give his reader an idea of the form of the constellation Cassiopeia, compares it to a *key*. It must be owned that the passage is very obscure; but the learned Huetius has bestowed a great deal of pains in explaining it, Animadvers. in Manilii, lib. i. 355; and I think has succeeded very well in it. *Homer*, Odyss. xxi. 6, describes the key of Ulysses' storehouse as ευκαμπης, of a large curvature; which Eustathius explains by saying it was δρεπανοειδης, in shape like a *reaphook.* Huetius says the constellation Cassiopeia answers to this description; the stars to the north making the curve part, that is, the principal part of the key; the southern stars, the handle. The curve part was introduced into the key-hole; and, being properly directed by the handle, took hold of the bolts within, and moved them from their places. We may easily collect from this account, that such a key would lie very well upon the shoulder; that it must be of some considerable size and weight, and could hardly be commodiously carried otherwise.

A. M. cir. 3292 B. C. cir. 712 Olymp. XVII. 1 cir. annum NumæPompilii, R. Roman., 4

23 And I will fasten him *as* [f]a nail in a sure place; and he shall be for a glorious throne to his father's house.

24 And they shall hang upon him all the glory of his father's house, the offspring and the issue, all vessels of small quantity, from the vessels of cups, even to all the [g]vessels of flagons.

25 In that day, saith the LORD of hosts, shall the [h]nail that is fastened in the sure place be removed, and be cut down, and fall; and the burden that *was* upon it shall be cut off: for the LORD hath spoken *it.*

[f]Ezra ix. 8 — [g]Or, *instruments of viols*——[h]Ver. 23

Ulysses' key was of brass, and the handle of ivory: but this was a royal key. The more common ones were probably of wood. In Egypt they have no other than wooden locks and keys to this day; even the gates of Cairo have no better. *Baumgarten*, Peregr. i. 18. *Thevenot*, part ii., chap. 10. But was it not the *representation* of a *key*, either cut out in *cloth* and *sewed* on the *shoulder* of the garment, or *embroidered* on that part of the garment itself? The idea of a *huge* key of a gate, in any kind of *metal*, laid across the shoulder, is to me very ridiculous.

In allusion to the image of the key as the ensign of power, the unlimited extent of that power is expressed with great clearness as well as force by the sole and exclusive authority to open and shut. Our Saviour, therefore, has upon a similar occasion made use of a like manner of expression, Matt. xvi. 19; and in Rev. iii. 7 has applied to himself the very words of the prophet.

Verse 23. *A nail*] In ancient times, and in the eastern countries, as the way of life, so the houses, were much more simple than ours at present. They had not that quantity and variety of furniture, nor those accommodations of all sorts, with which we abound. It was convenient and even necessary for them, and it made an essential part in the building of a house, to furnish the inside of the several apartments with sets of spikes, nails, or large pegs, upon which to dispose of and hang up the several movables and utensils in common use, and proper to the apartment. These spikes they worked into the walls at the first erection of them, the walls being of such materials that they could not bear their being driven in afterwards; and they were contrived so as to strengthen the walls by binding the parts together, as well as to serve for convenience. Sir John Chardin's account of this matter is this:—"They do not drive with a hammer the nails that are put into the eastern walls. The walls are too hard, being of brick; or, if they are of clay, too mouldering: but they fix them in the brick-work as they are building. They are large nails, with square heads like dice, well made, the ends being bent so as to make them cramp-irons. They commonly place them at the windows and doors, in order to hang upon them, when they like, veils and curtains." *Harmer's* Observ. i. p. 191. And we may add, that they were put in other places too, in order to hang up other things of various kinds; as appears from this place of Isaiah, and from Ezek. xv. 3, who speaks of a pin or nail, "to hang any vessel thereon." The word used here for a nail of this sort is the same by which they express that instrument, the stake, or large pin of iron, with which they fastened down to the ground the cords of their tents. We see, therefore, that these nails were of necessary and common use, and of no small importance in all their apartments; conspicuous, and much exposed to observation: and if they seem to us mean and insignificant, it is because we are not acquainted with the thing itself, and have no name to express it but by what conveys to us a low and contemptible idea. "Grace hath been showed from the Lord our God," saith Ezra, chap. ix. 8, "to leave us a remnant to escape, and to give us a nail in his holy place:" that is, as the margin of our Bible explains it, "a constant and sure abode."

"He that doth lodge near her (Wisdom's) house,
Shall also fasten a pin in her walls."
Ecclus. xiv. 24.

The dignity and propriety of the metaphor appears from the Prophet Zechariah's use of it:—

"From him shall be the corner-stone, from him the nail,
From him the battle-bow,
From him every ruler together." Zech. x. 4.

And Mohammed, using the same word, calls Pharaoh the lord or master of the *nails*, that is, well attended by nobles and officers capable of administering his affairs. Koran, Sur. xxxviii. 11, and lxxxix. 9. So some understand this passage of the Koran. Mr. Sale seems to prefer another interpretation.

Taylor, in his Concordance, thinks יתד *yathed* means the *pillar* or *post* that stands in the middle, and supports the tent, in which such pegs are fixed to hang their arms, &c., upon; referring to *Shaw's* Travels, p. 287. But יתד *yathed* is never used, as far as appears to me, in that sense. It was indeed necessary that the pillar of the tent should have such pegs on it for that purpose; but the hanging of such things in this manner upon this pillar does not prove that יתד *yathed* was the pillar itself.

A glorious throne—"A glorious seat"] That is, his father's house and all his own family shall be gloriously seated, shall flourish in honour and prosperity; and shall depend upon him, and be supported by him.

Verse 24. *All the glory*] One considerable part of the magnificence of the eastern princes consisted in the great quantity of gold and silver vessels which they had for various uses. "Solomon's drinking vessels were of gold, and all the vessels of the house of the forest of Lebanon were of pure gold; none were of silver; it was nothing accounted of in Solomon's days;" 1 Kings x. 21. "The vessels in the house of the forest of Lebanon," the armoury of Jerusalem so called, "were two hundred targets, and three hundred shields of beaten gold." Ibid. ver. 16, 17. These were ranged in order upon the walls of the armoury, (see Cant. iv. 4,) upon pins worked into the walls on purpose, as above mentioned. Eliakim is considered as a principal stake of this sort, immovably fastened in the wall for the support of all vessels destined for common or sacred uses; that is, as the principal support of the whole civil and ecclesiastical polity. And the consequence of his continued power will be the promotion and flourishing condition of his family and dependants, from the highest to the lowest.

Vessels of flagons—"Meaner vessels"] נבלים *nebalim* seems to mean earthen vessels of common use, brittle, and of little value, (see Lam. iv. 2; Jer. xlviii. 12,) in opposition to אגנות *aganoth*, goblets of gold and silver used in the sacrifices. Exod. xxiv. 6.

Verse 25. *The nail that is fastened*] This must be understood of Shebna, as a repetition and confirmation of the sentence above denounced against him.

What is said of Eliakim the son of Hilkiah, ver. 20-24, is very remarkable; and the literal meaning is not easy to be understood. From chap. ix. 6, and from Rev. iii. 7, it seems to belong to our Lord alone. The *removal* of *Shebna* from being *over the treasure* of the *Lord's house*, ver. 19, and the *investiture of Eliakim* with his *robe*, *girdle*, *office*, and *government*, ver. 20, &c., probably point out the *change* of the Jewish priesthood, and the proclaiming of the unchangeable priesthood of Christ. See Psa. cx. 4. *Eliakim* signifies *The resurrection of the Lord;* or, *My God, he shall arise. Hilkiah* signifies *The Lord my portion* or *lot.* The *key of David, shutting and opening*, &c., may intend the way of salvation through Christ alone. For the hope of salvation and eternal *life* comes only through *Eliakim*, the *resurrection* of Jesus Christ from the *dead.*

It is said, ver. 24, "They shall hang upon him all the glory of his father's house"—for, in Jesus Christ *dwells all the fulness of the Godhead bodily; and the offspring and the issue*, הצאצאים *hatstseetsaim* from יצא *yatsa*, *to go out*,—the *suckers from the root;* the *sideshoots*, the *apostles* and *primitive ministers* of his word. The *issue*, הצפיעות *hatstsephioth*, probably means the *issue's issue;* so the Targum. The *grandchildren*, all those who believe on the Lord Jesus through their word.

"The nail that is fastened in the sure place shall be removed," ver. 25, *Kimchi* refers not to *Eliakim*, but to *Shebna*, ver. 17-19. By, "They shall hang upon him all vessels of small quantity and large quantity," has been understood the *dependence* of *all souls*, of *all capacities*, from the *lowest* in *intellect* to the most *exalted*, on the Lord Jesus, as the only Saviour of all lost human spirits.

As the literal interpretation of this prophecy has not been found out, we are justified from *parallel texts* to consider the whole as referring to Jesus Christ, and the government of the Church, and the redemption of the world by him. Nor are there many prophecies which relate to him more clearly than this, taken in the above sense.

CHAPTER XXIII

Prophecy denouncing the destruction of Tyre by Nebuchadnezzar, delivered upwards of one hundred and twenty *years before its accomplishment, at a period when the Tyrians were in great prosperity, and the Babylonians in abject subjection to the Assyrian empire; and, consequently, when an event of so great magnitude was improbable in the highest degree,* 1–14. *Tyre shall recover its splendour at the termination of* seventy years, the days of one king, *or kingdom, by which must be meant the time allotted for the duration of the Babylonish empire, as otherwise the prophecy cannot be accommodated to the event,* 15–17. *Supposed reference to the early conversion of Tyre to Christianity,* 18.

A. M. cir. 3289 B. C. cir. 715 Olymp. XVI. 2 cir. annum NumæPompilii, R. Roman., 1

THE [a]burden of Tyre. Howl,
ye ships of Tarshish; for it
is laid waste, so that there is no
house, no entering in: [b]from the
land of Chittim it is revealed
to them.
2 Be [c]still, ye inhabitants of
the isle; thou whom the mer-

A. M. cir. 3289 B. C. cir. 715 Olymp. XVI. 2 cir. annum NumæPompilii, R. Roman., 1

[a]Jer. xxv. 22; xlvii. 4; Ezek. xxvi., xxvii., xxviii; Amos i. 9; Zech. ix. 2, 4——[b]Ver. 12——[c]Heb. *silent*

NOTES ON CHAP. XXIII

Verse 1. *The burden of Tyre*] Tyre, a city on the coast of Syria, about lat. 32° N. was built *two thousand seven hundred and sixty* years before Christ. There were *two* cities of this name; *one* on the *continent*, and the other on an *island*, about half a mile from the shore; the city on the island was about four miles in circumference. *Old* Tyre resisted Nebuchadnezzar for thirteen years; then the inhabitants carried, so to speak, the city to the forementioned island, ver. 4. This *new* city held out against Alexander the Great for seven months; who, in order to take it, was obliged to fill up the channel which separated it from the main land. In A. D. 1289 it was totally destroyed by the sultan of Egypt; and now contains only a few huts, in which about fifty or sixty wretched families exist. This desolation was foretold by this prophet and by Ezekiel, *one thousand nine hundred* years before it took place!

Howl, ye ships of Tarshish] This prophecy denounces the destruction of Tyre by Nebuchadnezzar. It opens with an address to the Tyrian negotiators and sailors at Tarshish, (Tartessus, in Spain,) a place which, in the course of their trade, they greatly frequented. The news of the destruction of Tyre by Nebuchadnezzar is said to be brought to them from Chittim, the islands

A. M. cir. 3289 B. C. cir. 715 Olymp. XVI. 2 cir. annum NumæPompilii, R. Roman., 1

chants of Zidon, that pass over
the sea, have replenished.
3 And by great waters the seed
of Sihor, the harvest of the river,
is her revenue; and [d]she is a mart of nations.
4 Be thou ashamed, O Zidon: for the sea
hath spoken, *even* the strength of the sea,
saying, I travail not, nor bring forth children,
neither do I nourish up young men, *nor* bring
up virgins.
5 [e]As at the report concerning Egypt, *so*
shall they be sorely pained at the report of
Tyre.
6 Pass ye over to Tarshish; howl, ye inhabitants of the isle.
7 *Is* this your [f]joyous *city,*
whose antiquity *is* of ancient
days? her own feet shall carry
her [g]afar off to sojourn.
8 Who hath taken this counsel against Tyre,
[h]the crowning *city,* whose merchants *are*
princes, whose traffickers *are* the honourable
of the earth.
9 The LORD of hosts hath purposed it, [i]to
stain the pride of all glory, *and* to bring into
contempt all the honourable of the earth.
10 Pass through thy land as a river, O
daughter of Tarshish: *there is* no more
[k]strength.
11 He stretched out his hand over the sea,

[d]Ezek. xxvii. 3——[e]Chap. xix. 16——[f]Chap. xxii. 2——[g]Heb. *from afar off*——[h]See Ezek. xxviii. 2, 12——[i]Heb. *to pollute*——[k]Heb. *girdle*

and coasts of the Mediterranean; "for the Tyrians," says Jerome on ver. 6, "when they saw they had no other means of escaping, fled in their ships, and took refuge in Carthage and in the islands of the Ionian and Ægean sea." From whence the news would spread and reach Tarshish; so also *Jarchi* on the same place. This seems to be the most probable interpretation of this verse.

Verse 2. *Be still*—"Be silent"] Silence is a mark of grief and consternation. See chap. xlvii. 5. Jeremiah has finely expressed this image:—

"The elders of the daughter of Zion sit on the ground, they are silent:
They have cast up dust on their heads, they have girded themselves with sackcloth.
The virgins of Jerusalem hang down their heads to the ground." Lam. ii. 10.

Verse 3. *The seed of Sihor*—"The seed of the Nile"] The Nile is called here *Shichor*, as it is Jer. ii. 18, and 1 Chron. xiii. 5. It had this name from the *blackness* of its waters, charged with the mud which it brings down from Ethiopia when it overflows, *Et viridem Ægyptum nigra fecundat arena;* as it was called by the Greeks *Melas*, and by the Latins *Melo*, for the same reason. See *Servius* on the above line of Virgil, Georg. iv. 291. It was called *Siris* by the Ethiopians, by some supposed to be the same with *Shichor*. Egypt by its extraordinary fertility, caused by the overflowing of the Nile, supplied the neighbouring nations with corn, by which branch of trade the Tyrians gained great wealth.

Verse 4. *Be thou ashamed, O Zidon*] Tyre is called ver. 12, the daughter of Sidon. "The Sidonians," says *Justin*, xviii. 3, "when their city was taken by the king of Ascalon, betook themselves to their ships, and landed, and built by Tyre." Sidon, as the mother city is supposed to be deeply affected with the calamity of her daughter.

Nor *bring up virgins*—"*Nor* educated virgins."] ורוממתי *veromamti;* so an ancient MS. of Dr. *Kennicott's* prefixing the ו *vau,* which refers to the negative preceding, and is equivalent to ולא *velo.* See Deut. xxiii. 6; Prov. xxx. 3. Two of my own MSS. have ו *vau* in the margin.

Verse 7. *Whose antiquity* is *of ancient days*—"Whose antiquity is of the earliest date"] Justin, in the passage above quoted, had dated the building of Tyre at a certain number of years before the taking of Troy; but the number is lost in the present copies. Tyre, though not so old as Sidon, was yet of very high antiquity: it was a strong city even in the time of Joshua. It is called עיר מבצר צר *ir mibtsar tsor*, "the city of the fortress of Sor," Josh. xix. 29. Interpreters raise difficulties in regard to this passage, and will not allow it to have been so ancient; with what good reason I do not see, for it is called by the same name, "the fortress of Sor," in the history of David, 2 Sam. xxiv. 7, and the circumstances of the history determine the place to be the very same. See on ver. 1.

Whose antiquity is of ancient days, may refer to *Palæeyrus*, or *Old Tyre.*

Her own feet shall carry her afar off to sojourn.] This may belong to the *new* or insular *Tyre; her own feet*, that is, her own inhabitants, *shall carry her*—shall transport the city, from the continent to the island. "But the text says, it shall be carried *far off;* and the new city was founded only half a mile distant from the other." I answer, מרחוק *merachok* does not always signify a *great distance*, but distance or interval in general; for in Josh. iii. 4 רחוק *rachok* is used to express the *space* between the camp and the ark, which we know to have been only *two thousand* cubits. Some refer the *sojourning afar off* to the extent of the commercial voyages undertaken by the Tyrians and their foreign connexions.

Verse 10. *O daughter of Tarshish*] Tyre is called the daughter of Tarshish; perhaps because, Tyre being ruined, Tarshish was become the superior city, and might be considered as the metropolis of the Tyrian people; or rather because of the close connexion and perpetual intercourse between them, according to that latitude of signification in which the Hebrews use the words *son* and *daughter* to express any sort of conjunction and dependence whatever. מזח *mezach, a girdle*, which collects, binds, and keeps together the loose raiment, when applied

A. M. cir. 3289 B. C. cir. 715 Olymp. XVI. 2 cir. annum NumæPompilii, R. Roman., 1

he shook the kingdoms: the
LORD hath given a commandment
[l]against [m]the merchant *city*, to
destroy the [n]strong holds thereof.
12 And he said, [o]Thou shalt no more rejoice, O thou oppressed virgin, daughter of
Zidon: arise, [p]pass over to Chittim; there
also shalt thou have no rest.
13 Behold the land of the Chaldeans; this
people was not, *till* the Assyrian
founded it for [q]them that dwell
in the wilderness: they set up
the towers thereof, they raised
up the palaces thereof; *and* he brought it
to ruin.
14 [r]Howl, ye ships of Tarshish: for your
strength is laid waste.
15 And it shall come to pass in that day,

[l]Or, *concerning a merchantman*——[m]Heb. *Canaan* [n]Or, *strengths*

[o]Rev. xviii. 22——[p]Ver. 1——[q]Psa. lxxii. 9——[r]Ver. 1; Ezek. xxvii. 25, 30

to a river, may mean a mound, mole, or artificial dam, which contains the waters, and prevents them from spreading abroad. A city taken by siege and destroyed, whose walls are demolished, whose policy is dissolved, whose wealth is dissipated, whose people is scattered over the wide country, is compared to a river whose banks are broken down, and whose waters, let loose and overflowing all the neighbouring plains, are wasted and lost. This may possibly be the meaning of this very obscure verse, of which I can find no other interpretation that is at all satisfactory.—L.

Verse 13. *Behold the land of the Chaldeans*] This verse is extremely obscure; the obscurity arises from the ambiguity of the agents, which belong to the verbs, and of the objects expressed by the pronouns; from the change of number of the verbs, and of gender in the pronouns. The MSS. give us no assistance, and the ancient Versions very little. The *Chaldee* and *Vulgate* read שמוה *samoah*, in the plural number. I have followed the interpretation which, among many different ones, seemed to be most probable, that of Perizonius and Vitringa.

The Chaldeans, *Chasdim*, are supposed to have had their origin, and to have taken their name, from *Chesed*, the son of Nachor, the brother of Abraham. They were known by that name in the time of Moses, who calls Ur in Mesopotamia, from whence Abraham came, to distinguish it from other places of the same name, *Ur* of the *Chaldeans*. And Jeremiah calls them an ancient nation. This is not inconsistent with what Isaiah here says of them: "This people was not," that is, they were of no account, (see Deut. xxxii. 21;) they were not reckoned among the great and potent nations of the world till of later times; they were a rude, uncivilized, barbarous people, without laws, without settled habitations; wandering in a wide desert country (ציים *tsiyim*) and addicted to rapine like the wild Arabians. Such they are represented to have been in the time of Job, chap. i. 17, and such they continued to be till Assur, some powerful king of Assyria, gathered them together, and settled them in Babylon in the neighbouring country. This probably was Ninus, whom I suppose to have lived in the time of the Judges. In this, with many eminent chronologers, I follow the authority of Herodotus, who says that the Assyrian monarchy lasted but *five hundred and twenty* years. Ninus got possession of Babylon from the Cuthean Arabians; the successors of Nimrod in that empire collected the Chaldeans, and settled a colony of them there to secure the possession of the city, which he and his successors greatly enlarged and ornamented. They had perhaps been useful to him in his wars, and might be likely to be farther useful in keeping under the old inhabitants of that city, and of the country belonging to it; according to the policy of the Assyrian kings, who generally brought new people into the conquered countries; see Isa. xxxvi. 17; 2 Kings xvii. 6, 24. The testimony of Dicæarchus, a Greek historian contemporary with Alexander, (*apud.* Steph. de Urbibus, in voc. Χαλδαιος,) in regard to the fact is remarkable, though he is mistaken in the name of the king he speaks of. He says that "a certain king of Assyria, the *fourteenth* in succession from Ninus, (as he might be, if Ninus is placed, as in the common chronology, *eight hundred* years higher than we have above set him,) named, as it is said, *Chaldæus*, having gathered together and united all the people called Chaldeans, built the famous city, Babylon, upon the Euphrates."—L.

Verse 14. *Howl, ye ships*] The Prophet Ezekiel hath enlarged upon this part of the same subject with great force and elegance:—

"Thus saith the Lord JEHOVAH concerning Tyre:—
At the sound of thy fall, at the cry of the wounded,
At the great slaughter in the midst of thee, shall not the islands tremble?
And shall not all the princes of the sea descend from their thrones,
And lay aside their robes, and strip off their embroidered garments?
They shall clothe themselves with trembling, they shall sit on the ground;
They shall tremble every moment, they shall be astonished at thee.
And they shall utter a lamentation over thee, and shall say unto thee:
How art thou lost, thou that wast inhabited from the seas!
The renowned city, that was strong in the sea, she and her inhabitants!
That struck with terror all her neighbours!
Now shall the coasts tremble in the day of thy fall,
And the isles that are in the sea shall be troubled at thy departure."
Ezek. xxvi. 15-18.

Verse 15. *According to the days of one king*] That is, of one *kingdom*; see Dan. vii. 17, viii. 20. Nebuchadnezzar began his conquests in the first year of his reign; from thence to the taking of Babylon by Cyrus are *seventy* years, at which time the nations subdued by Nebuchadnezzar were to be restored to liberty. These

A. M. cir. 3289 B. C. cir. 715 Olymp. XVI. 2 cir. annum NumæPompilii, R. Roman., 1

that Tyre shall be forgotten
seventy years, according to the
days of one king: after the end
of seventy years [s]shall Tyre
sing as a harlot.

16 Take a harp, go about the city, thou
harlot that hast been forgotten; make sweet
melody, sing many songs, that thou mayest be
remembered.

17 And it shall come to pass after the end
of seventy years, that the LORD
will visit Tyre, and she shall turn
to her hire, and [t]shall commit
fornication with all the king-
doms of the world upon the face of the earth.

18 And her merchandise and her hire [u]shall
be holiness to the LORD: it shall not be treasured nor laid up; for her merchandise shall
be for them that dwell before the LORD, to
eat sufficiently, and for [v]durable clothing.

[s]Heb. *it shall be unto Tyre as the song of a harlot*

[t]Rev. xvii. 2——[u]Zech. xiv. 20, 21——[v]Heb. *old*

seventy years limit the duration of the Babylonish monarchy. Tyre was taken by him towards the middle of that period; so did not serve the king of Babylon during the whole period, but only for the remaining part of it. This seems to be the meaning of Isaiah; the days allotted to the one king or kingdom, are seventy years; Tyre, with the rest of the conquered nations, shall continue in a state of subjection and desolation to the end of that period. Not from the beginning and through the whole of the period; for, by being one of the latest conquests, the duration of that state of subjection in regard to her, was not much more than half of it. "All these nations," saith Jeremiah, xxv. 11, "shall serve the king of Babylon seventy years." Some of them were conquered sooner, some later; but the end of this period was the common term for the deliverance of them *all*.

There is another way of computing the *seventy years*, from the year in which Tyre was actually taken to the nineteenth of Darius Hystaspis; whom the Phœnicians, or Tyrians, assisted against the Ionians, and probably on that account might then be restored to their former liberties and privileges. But I think the former the more probable interpretation.—L.

Sing as a harlot] Fidicinam esse meretricum est, says *Donatus* in Terent. Eunuch. iii. 2, 4.

> Nec meretrix tibicina, cujus
> Ad strepitum salias.
>
> HOR. I. Epist. xiv. 25.

> "Nor harlot minstrel sings, when the rude sound
> Tempts you with heavy heels to thump the ground."
>
> FRANCIS.

Sir John Chardin, in his MS. note on this place, says:—C'est que les vielles prostituées,—ne font que chanter quand les jeunes dancent, et les animer par l'instrument et par la voix. "The old prostitutes do nothing but sing, while the young ones dance; and animate them both by vocal and instrumental music."

Verse 17. *After the end of seventy years*] Tyre, after its destruction by Nebuchadnezzar, recovered, as it is here foretold, its ancient trade, wealth, and grandeur; as it did likewise after a second destruction by Alexander. It became Christian early with the rest of the neighbouring countries. St. Paul himself found many Christians there, Acts xxi. 4. It suffered much in the Diocletian persecution. It was an archbishopric under the patriarchate of Jerusalem, with fourteen bishoprics under its jurisdiction. It continued Christian till it was taken by the Saracens in 639; was recovered by the Christians in 1124; but in 1280 was conquered by the Mamelukes, and afterwards taken from them by the Turks in 1517. Since that time it has sunk into utter decay; is now a mere ruin, a bare rock, "a place to spread nets upon," as the Prophet Ezekiel foretold it should be, chap. xxvi. 14. See *Sandy's* Travels; *Vitringa* on the place; Bp. *Newton* on the Prophecies, Dissert. xi.

CHAPTER XXIV

Dreadful judgments impending over the people of God, 1–4. Particular enumeration of the horrid impieties which provoked the Divine vengeance, 5, 6. Great political wretchedness of the transgressors, 7–12. The calamities shall be so great that only a small remnant shall be left in the land, as it were the gleanings of the vintage, 13. The rest, scattered over the different countries, spread there the knowledge of God, 14–16. Strong figures by which the great distress and long captivity of the transgressors are set forth, 17–22. Gracious promise of a redemption from captivity; and of an extension of the kingdom of God in the latter days, attended with such glorious circumstances as totally to eclipse the light and splendour of the previous dispensation, 23.

A. M. cir. 3292 B. C. cir. 712 Olymp. XVII. 1 cir. annum NumæPompilii, R. Roman., 4

BEHOLD, the LORD maketh
the earth empty, and mak-
eth it waste, and [a]turneth
it upside down, and scattereth abroad the inhabitants
thereof.

2 And it shall be, as with the
people, so with the [b]priest; [c]as

[a]Heb. *perverteth the face thereof*

[b]Or, *prince*——[c]Hos. iv. 9

From the thirteenth chapter to the twenty-third inclusive, the fate of several cities and nations is denounced: of Babylon, of the Philistines, Moab, Damascus, Egypt, Tyre. After having foretold the destruction of the foreign nations, enemies of Judah, the prophet declares

A. M. cir. 3292
B. C. cir. 712
Olymp. XVII. 1
cir. annum
NumæPompilii,
R. Roman., 4

with the servant, so with his master; as with the maid, so with
her mistress; [d]as with the buyer,
so with the seller; as with the
lender, so with the borrower; as with the taker
of usury, so with the giver of usury to him.
3 The land shall be utterly emptied, and
utterly spoiled: for the LORD hath spoken
this word.
4 The earth mourneth *and* fadeth away,
the world languisheth *and* fadeth away, [e]the
haughty people of the earth do languish.
5 [f]The earth also is defiled under the inhabitants thereof; because they have transgressed the laws, changed the ordinance,
broken the everlasting covenant.
6 Therefore hath [g]the curse devoured the
earth, and they that dwell therein are desolate: therefore the inhabitants of the earth are
burned, and few men left.
7 [h]The new wine mourneth, the vine languisheth, all the merry-hearted do sigh.

A. M. cir. 3292
B. C. cir. 712
Olymp. XVII. 1
cir. annum
NumæPompilii,
R. Roman., 4

8 The mirth [i]of tabrets ceaseth, the noise of them that rejoice endeth, the joy of the harp
ceaseth.
9 They shall not drink wine with a song;
strong drink shall be bitter to them that
drink it.
10 The city of confusion is broken down:
every house is shut up, that no man may
come in.
11 *There is* a crying for wine in the streets;
all joy is darkened, the mirth of the land is
gone.
12 In the city is left desolation, and the gate
is smitten with destruction.
13 When thus it shall be in the midst of
the land among the people, [k]*there shall be* as
the shaking of an olive tree, *and* as the gleaning grapes when the vintage is done.
14 They shall lift up their voice, they shall
sing for the majesty of the LORD, they shall
cry aloud from the sea.

---

[d]Ezek. vii. 12, 13——[e]Heb. *the height of the people*——[f]Gen. iii. 17; Num. xxxi. 35——[g]Mal. iv. 6——[h]Ch. xvi. 8, 9; Joel i. 10, 12——[i]Jer. vii. 34; xvi. 9; xxv. 10; Ezek. xxvi. 13; Hos. ii. 11; Rev. xviii. 22——[k]Ch. xvii. 5, 6

---

the judgments impending on the people of God themselves for their wickedness and apostasy, and the desolation that shall be brought on their whole country.

The twenty-fourth and the three following chapters seem to have been delivered about the same time: before the destruction of Moab by Shalmaneser; see chap. xxv. 10, consequently, before the destruction of Samaria; probably in the beginning of Hezekiah's reign. But concerning the particular subject of the twenty-fourth chapter interpreters are not at all agreed: some refer it to the desolation caused by the invasion of Shalmaneser; others to the invasion of Nebuchadnezzar; and others to the destruction of the city and nation by the Romans. Vitringa is singular in his opinion, who applies it to the persecution of Antiochus Epiphanes. Perhaps it may have a view to all of the three great desolations of the country, by Shalmaneser, by Nebuchadnezzar, and by the Romans; especially the last, to which some parts of it may seem more peculiarly applicable. However, the prophet chiefly employs general images; such as set forth the greatness and universality of the ruin and desolation that is to be brought upon the country by these great revolutions, involving all orders and degrees of men, changing entirely the face of things, and destroying the whole polity, both religious and civil; without entering into minute circumstances, or necessarily restraining it by particular marks to one great event, exclusive of others of the same kind.—L.

NOTES ON CHAP. XXIV

Verse 4. *The world languisheth*] The world is the same with the land; that is, the kingdoms of Judah and Israel; *orbis Israeliticus.* See note on chap. xiii. 11.

Verse 5. *The laws*—"The law"] תורה *torah.* singular: so read the *Septuagint, Syriac,* and *Chaldee.*

Verse 6. *Are burned*—"Are destroyed"] For חרו *charu,* read חרבו *charebu.* See the *Septuagint, Syriac, Chaldee,* and *Symmachus.*

Verse 8. *The mirth,* &c.] שאון *sheon, the noise.* גאון *geon, the pride,* is the reading of *three* of *De Rossi's* MSS., with the *Septuagint* and *Arabic.*

Verse 9. *Strong drink*—"Palm wine"] This is the proper meaning of the word שכר *shechar,* σικερα. See note on chap. v. 11. All enjoyment shall cease: the sweetest wine shall become bitter to their taste.

Verse 11. *All joy is darkened*—"All gladness is passed away"] For ערבה *arebah, darkened,* read עברה *aberah, passed away,* transposing a letter. *Houbigant, Secker. Five* of *Dr. Kennicott's* and *five* of *De Rossi's* MSS., several ancient, add כל *col, all,* after משוש *mesos:* the *Septuagint* adds the same word before it.

Verse 14. *They shall lift up their voice*—"But these shall lift up their voice"] That is, they that escaped out of these calamities. The great distresses brought upon Israel and Judah drove the people away, and dispersed them all over the neighbouring countries: they fled to Egypt, to Asia Minor, to the islands and the coasts of Greece. They were to be found in great numbers in most of the principal cities of these countries. Alexandria was in a great measure peopled by them. They had synagogues for their worship in many places, and were greatly instrumental in propagating the knowledge of the true God among these heathen nations, and

A. M. cir. 3292
B. C. cir. 712
Olymp. XVII. 1
cir. annum
NumæPompilii,
R. Roman., 4

15 Wherefore glorify ye the
LORD in the [l]fires *even* [m]the
name of the LORD God of Israel
in the isles of the sea.
16 From the [n]uttermost part of the earth
have we heard songs, *even* glory to the righteous. But I said, [o]My leanness, my leanness,
wo unto me! [p]the treacherous
dealers have dealt treacherously;
yea, the treacherous dealers have
dealt very treacherously.
17 [q]Fear, and the pit, and the [r]snare, *are*
upon thee, O inhabitant of the earth.
18 And it shall come to pass, *that* he who

A. M. cir. 3292
B. C. cir. 712
Olymp. XVII. 1
cir. annum
NumæPumpilii,
R. Roman., 4

[l]Or, *valleys*——[m]Mal. i. 11——[n]Heb. *wing*——[o]Heb. *Leanness to me*, or *My secret to me*

[p]Jer. v. 11——[q]See 1 Kings xix. 17; Jer. xlviii. 43, 44; Amos v. 19——[r]Psa. lxix. 22

preparing them for the reception of Christianity. This it what the prophet seems to mean by the celebration of the name of JEHOVAH in the waters, in the distant coasts, and in the uttermost parts of the land. מים *mayim, the waters; ὑδωρ, Sept.; ὑδατα, Theod.;* not מים *miyam from the sea.*

Verse 15. *In the isles of the sea*—"In the distant coasts of the sea."] For בארים *beurim, in the valleys*, I suppose we ought to read באיים *beiyim, in the isles*, which is in a great degree justified by the repetition of the word in the next member of the sentence, with the addition of הים *haiyam, the sea*, to vary the phrase, exactly in the manner of the prophet. איים *iyim* is a word chiefly applied to any distant countries, especially those lying on the Mediterranean Sea. Others conjecture ביארים *biorim*. בהרים *beharim*, באמים *beummim*, בעמים *beammim*, בחורים *.bechorim*, באורים *beurim*, a באר *bar*, illustrati.—*Le Clerc. Twenty-three* MSS. of *Kennicott's*, many of *De Rossi's*, and some of my own, read באורים *beorim, in the valleys.* The *Septuagint* do not acknowledge the reading of the text, expressing here only the word איים *iyim*, *εν ταις νησοις, in the islands*, and that not repeated. But MSS. Pachom. and I. D. II. supply in this place the defect in the other copies of the *Septuagint* thus, *Δια τουτο ἡ δοξα Κυριου εσται εν ταις νησοις της θαλασσης· εν ταις νησοις το ονομα του Κυριου Θεου Ισραηλ ενδοξον εσται·* "Therefore the glory of the Lord shall be in the isles of the sea: in the islands shall the name of the Lord God of Israel be glorified." *Kimchi* says, that by באורים *beurim, in the valleys*, is meant *the cities*, because they were generally built *in valleys.* The *Vulgate* has *in doctrinis*, and so my old MS., **in techingis**. *Coverdale* translates, *Praise the name of the Lord God of Israel* in the *valleys and in the floodis.* It should not be rendered *in the fires;* none of the ancient Versions understood it thus. According to which the *Septuagint* had in their Hebrew copy באיים *beiyim*, repeated afterwards, not בארים *beurim.*

Verse 16. *But I said*] The prophet speaks in the person of the inhabitants of the land still remaining there, who should be pursued by Divine vengeance, and suffer repeated distresses from the inroads and depredations of their powerful enemies. Agreeably to what he said before in a general denunciation of these calamities:—

"Though there be a tenth part remaining in it;
Even this shall undergo a repeated destruction."

Chap. vi. 13. See the note there.—L.

My leanness, my leanness—Or, *my secret;* so the *Vulgate, Montanus*, and my old MS. רזן *razan* has this meaning in *Chaldee;* but in *Hebrew* it signifies to *make lean*, to *waste.* This sentence in the *Hebrew* has a strange connexion of uncouth sounds: ואמר רזי לי רזי לי אוי לי בונדים בגדו ובגד בגדים בגדו *Vaomer, razi li razi li, oi li, bogedim bagadu, ubeged bogedim bagadu.* This may be equalled by the translation in my Old MS. Bible: **And I seide, my priveye thinge to me: my priveye thinge to me: woo to me: The lawe breykynge thei breken: and in lawe brekynge of the overdon thingis, they breken the lawe.**

The treacherous dealers have dealt treacherously—"The plunderers plunder"] See note on chap. xxi. 2.

Verse 17. *Fear, and the pit*—"The terror, the pit"] If they escape one calamity, another shall overtake them.

"As if a man should flee from a lion, and a bear should overtake him:
Or should betake himself to his house, and lean his hand on the wall,
And a serpent should bite him."

Amos v. 19.

"For," as our Saviour expressed it in a like parabolical manner, "wheresoever the carcass is, there shall the eagles be gathered together," Matt. xxiv. 28. The images are taken from the different methods of hunting and taking wild beasts, which were anciently in use. The *terror* was a line strung with feathers of all colours, which fluttering in the air scared and frightened the beasts into the toils, or into the pit which was prepared for them. Nec est mirum, cum maximos ferarum greges linea pennis distincta contineat, et in insidias agat, ab ipso effectu dicta *formido. Seneca* de Ira, ii. 12. The *pit* or pitfall, *fovea;* digged deep in the ground, and covered over with green boughs, turf, &c., in order to deceive them, that they might fall into it unawares. The *snare*, or toils, *indago;* a series of nets, inclosing at first a great space of ground, in which the wild beasts were known to be; and then drawn in by degrees into a narrower compass, till they were at last closely shut up, and entangled in them.—L.

For מכול *mikkol*, a MS. reads מפני *mippeney*, as it is in Jer. xlviii. 44, and so the *Vulgate* and *Chaldee.* But perhaps it is only, like the latter, a *Hebraism*, and means no more than the simple preposition מ *mem.* See Psa. cii. 6. For it does not appear that the terror was intended to scare the wild beasts by its noise. The paronomasia is very remarkable; פחד *pachad*, פחת *pachath*, פך *pach:* and that it was a common proverbial form, appears from Jeremiah's repeating it in the same words, chap. xlviii. 43, 44.

Verse 18. *Out of the midst of the pit*—"From the pit"] For מתוך *mittoch, from the midst of*, a MS. reads מן *min, from*, as it is in Jer. xlviii.

A. M. cir. 3292 B. C. cir. 712 Olymp. XVII. 1 cir. annum NumæPompilii, R. Roman., 4

fleeth from the noise of the fear
shall fall into the pit; and he
that cometh up out of the midst
of the pit shall be taken in the
snare: for [s]the windows from on high are open,
and [t]the foundations of the earth do shake.
19 [u]The earth is utterly broken down, the
earth is clean dissolved, the earth is moved
exceedingly.
20 The earth shall [v]reel to and fro like a
drunkard, and shall be removed like a cottage;
and the transgression thereof shall be heavy
upon it; and it shall fall, and not rise again.
21 And it shall come to pass
in that day, *that* the LORD shall
[w]punish the host of the high
ones *that are* on high, [x]and the
kings of the earth upon the earth.
22 And they shall be gathered together,
[y]*as* prisoners are gathered in the [z]pit, and
shall be shut up in the prison, and after many
days shall they be [a]visited.
23 Then the [b]moon shall be confounded,
and the sun ashamed, when the LORD of hosts
shall [c]reign [d]in Mount Zion, and in Jerusalem,
and [e]before his ancients gloriously.

A. M. cir. 3292 B. C., cir. 712 Olymp. XVII. 1 cir. annum NumæPompilii, R. Roman., 4

[s]Gen. vii. 11——[t]Psa. xviii. 7——[u]Jer. iv. 23——[v]Chap. xix. 14——[w]Heb. *visit upon*——[x]Psa. lxxvi. 12——[y]Heb. *with the gathering of prisoners*——[z]Or, *dungeon*

[a]Or, *found wanting*——[b]Chap. xiii. 10; lx. 19; Ezek. xxxii. 7; Joel ii. 31; iii. 15——[c]Rev. xix. 4, 6——[d]Heb. xii. 22——[e]Or, there shall be *glory before his ancients*

44; and so likewise the *Septuagint*, *Syriac*, and *Vulgate*.

Verse 19. *The earth*—"The land"] הארץ *haarets, forte delendum* ה *he, ut ex præcedente ortum.* Vid. seqq.—*Secker*. "Probably the ה *he*, in הארץ *haarets*, should be blotted out, as having arisen from the preceding."

Verse 20. *Like a cottage*—"Like a lodge for a night"] See note on chap. i. 8.

Verse 21. *On high—upon the earth.*] That is, the ecclesiastical and civil polity of the Jews, which shall be destroyed. The nation shall continue in a state of depression and dereliction for a long time. The image seems to be taken from the practice of the great monarchs of that time; who, when they had thrown their wretched captives into a dungeon, never gave themselves the trouble of inquiring about them; but let them lie a long time in that miserable condition, wholly destitute of relief, and disregarded. God shall at length revisit and restore his people in the last age: and then the kingdom of God shall be established in such perfection, as wholly to obscure and eclipse the glory of the temporary, typical, preparative kingdom now subsisting.

Verse 23. *Before his ancients gloriously*] **In the sigt of their olde men he schal ben glorified.** Old MS. BIBLE.

"The figurative language of the prophets is taken from the analogy between the *world natural* and an empire or kingdom considered as a *world politic.* Accordingly the whole world natural, consisting of *heaven* and *earth*, signifies the whole world politic, consisting of thrones and people; or so much of it as is considered in prophecy: and the things in that world signify the analogous things in this. For the *heavens* and the *things therein* signify *thrones* and *dignities*, and *those* who *enjoy them;* and the *earth* with the *things thereon*, the *inferior people;* and the *lowest parts* of the *earth*, called *hades* or *hell*, the *lowest* or most *miserable part of them.* Great *earthquakes*, and the *shaking of heaven* and *earth*, are put for the *shaking of kingdoms*, so as to *distract* and *overthrow* them; the *creating a new heaven* and *earth*, and the *passing away of an old one*, or the *beginning and end of a world*, for the *rise* and *ruin* of a *body politic* signified thereby. The *sun*, for the whole species and race of *kings*, in the kingdoms of the world politic; the *moon*, for the body of the common people, considered as the king's wife; the *stars*, for subordinate princes and great men; or for bishops and rulers of the people of God, when the sun is Christ: *setting* of the *sun*, *moon*, and *stars*, *darkening* the *sun*, turning the *moon* into *blood*, and *falling* of the *stars*, for the ceasing of a kingdom." Sir *I. Newton's* Observations on the Prophecies, Part I., chap. 2.

These observations are of great consequence and use, in explaining the phraseology of the prophets.

CHAPTER XXV

The short glance which the prophet gave at the promised restoration of the people of God and the Messiah's kingdom, in the close of the preceding chapter, makes him break out into a rapturous song of praise in this, where although he alludes to temporal mercies, such as the destruction of the cities which had been at war with Zion, the ruin of Moab, and other signal interpositions of Divine Providence in behalf of the Jews; yet he is evidently impressed with a more lively sense of future and much higher blessings under the Gospel dispensation, in the plenitude of its revelation, of which the temporal deliverances vouchsafed at various times to the primitive kingdoms of Israel and Judah were the prototypes, 1–5. *These blessings are described under the figure of a feast made for all nations,* 6; *the removing of a veil from their faces,* 7; *the total extinction of the empire of death by the resurrection from the dead, the exclusion of all sorrow, and the final overthrow of all the enemies of the people of God,* 8–12.

A. M. cir. 3292
B. C. cir. 712
Olymp. XVII. 1
cir. annum
NumæPompilii,
R. Roman., 4

O LORD, thou *art* my God; [a]I
will exalt thee, I will praise
thy name; [b]for thou hast done
wonderful *things;* [c]*thy* counsels
of old *are* faithfulness *and* truth.
2 For thou hast made [d]of a city a heap;
of a defenced city a ruin: a palace of strangers
to be no city; it shall never be built.
3 Therefore shall the strong people [e]glorify
thee, the city of the terrible nations shall fear
thee.
4 For thou hast been a strength to the poor,
a strength to the needy in his distress, [f]a refuge
from the storm, a shadow
from the heat, when the blast of
the terrible one *is* as a storm
against the wall.
5 Thou shalt bring down the noise of
strangers, as the heat in a dry place; *even* the
heat with the shadow of a cloud: the branch
of the terrible ones shall be brought low.
6 And in [g]this mountain shall [h]the LORD
of hosts make unto [i]all people a feast of fat
things, a feast of wines on the lees, of fat
things full of marrow, of wines on the lees
well refined.

[a]Exod. xv. 2; Psalm cxviii. 28——[b]Psalm xcviii. 1——[c]Num. xxiii. 19——[d]Chap. xxi. 9; xxiii. 13; Jer. li. 37

[e]Rev. xi. 13——[f]Chap. iv. 6——[g]Chap. ii. 2, 3 [h]Prov. ix. 2; Matt. xxii. 4——[i]Dan. vii. 14; Matt. viii. 11

It does not appear to me that this chapter has any close and particular connexion with the chapter immediately preceding, taken separately, and by itself. The subject of that was the desolation of the land of Israel and Judah, by the just judgment of God, for the wickedness and disobedience of the people: which, taken by itself, seems not with any propriety to introduce a hymn of thanksgiving to God for his mercies to his people in delivering them from their enemies. But taking the whole course of prophecies, from the *thirteenth* to the *twenty-fourth* chapter inclusive, in which the prophet foretells the destruction of several cities and nations, enemies to the Jews, and of the land of Judah itself, yet with intimations of a remnant to be saved, and a restoration to be at length effected by a glorious establishment of the kingdom of God: with a view to this extensive scene of God's providence in all its parts, and in all its consequences, the prophet may well be supposed to break out into this song of praise; in which his mind seems to be more possessed with the prospect of future mercies than with the recollection of the past.—L.

NOTES ON CHAP. XXV

Verse 1. Thy *counsels of old* are *faithfulness* and *truth.*] That is, All thy past declarations by the prophets shall be fulfilled in their proper time.

Verse 2. *A city*—"The city"] Nineveh, Babylon, Ar, Moab, or any other strong fortress possessed by the enemies of the people of God.

For the first מעיר *meir, of a city,* the *Syriac* and *Vulgate* read העיר *hair, the city;* the *Septuagint* and *Chaldee* read ערים *arim, cities,* in the plural, transposing the letters. After the second מעיר *meir,* a MS. adds לגל *lagol, for a heap.*

A palace of strangers—"The palace of the proud ones"] For זרים *zarim, strangers,* MS. *Bodl.* and another read זדים *zedim, the proud:* so likewise the *Septuagint;* for they render it ασεβων here, and in ver. 5, as they do in some other places: see Deut. xviii. 20, 22. Another MS. reads צרים *tsarim, adversaries;* which also makes a good sense. But זרים *zarim, strangers,* and זדים *zedim, the proud,* are often confounded by the great similitude of the letters ד *daleth* and ר *resh.* See Mal. iii. 15, iv. 1; Psa. xix. 14, in the *Septuagint;* and Psa. liv. 5, where the *Chaldee* reads זדים *zedim,* compared with Psa. lxxxvi. 16.

Verse 4. *As a storm* against *the wall*—"Like a winter-storm."] For קיר *kir,* read קור *kor:* or, as עיר *ir* from ערר *arar,* so קיר *kir* from קרר *karar.*—Capellus.

Verse 5. *Of strangers*—"Of the proud"] The same mistake here as in ver. 2: see the note there. Here זדים *zedim, the proud,* is parallel to עריצים *aritsim, the formidable:* as in Psa. liv. 5, and lxxxvi. 14.

The heat with the shadow of a cloud—"As the heat by a thick cloud"] For חרב *choreb,* the *Syriac, Chaldee, Vulgate,* and two MSS. read כחרב *kechoreb;* which is a repetition of the beginning of the foregoing parallel line; and the verse taken out of the parallel form, and more fully expressed, would run thus: "As a thick cloud interposing tempers the heat of the sun on the burnt soil; so shalt thou, by the interposition of thy power, bring low and abate the tumult of the proud, and the triumph of the formidable."

Verse 6. *In this mountain*] Zion, at Jerusalem. In his Church.

Shall the Lord of hosts make unto all people a feast] Salvation by Jesus Christ. A feast is a proper and usual expression of joy in consequence of victory, or any other great success. The feast here spoken of is to be celebrated on Mount Sion; and all people, without distinction, are to be invited to it. This can be no other than the celebration of the establishment of Christ's kingdom, which is frequently represented in the Gospel under the image of a feast; "where many shall come from the east and west, and shall sit down at table with Abraham, Isaac, and Jacob, in the kingdom of heaven;" Matt. viii. 11. See also Luke xiv. 16; xxiv. 29, 30. This sense is fully confirmed by the concomitants of this feast expressed in the next verse; the removing of the veil from the face of the nations, and the abolition of death: the first of which is obviously and clearly explained of the preaching of the Gospel; and the second must mean the blessing of immortality procured for us by Christ, "who hath abolished death, and through death hath destroyed him that had the power of death."

Of wines on the lees—"Of old wines"] Heb. *lees;* that is, of wines kept long on the lees.

A. M. cir. 3292 B. C. cir. 712 Olymp. XVII. 1 cir. annum NumæPompilii, R. Roman., 4

7 And he will [k]destroy in this mountain the face of the covering [l]cast over all people, and [m]the vail that is spread over all nations.

8 He will [n]swallow up death in victory; and the Lord GOD will [o]wipe away tears from off all faces; and the rebuke of his people shall he take away from off all the earth: for the LORD hath spoken *it*.

9 And it shall be said in that day, Lo, this *is* our God; [p]we have waited for him,

[k]Heb. *swallow up*——[l]Heb. *covered*——[m]2 Cor. iii. 15; Eph. iv. 18

[n]Hos. xiii. 14; 1 Cor. xv. 54; Rev. xx. 14; xxi. 4——[o]Rev. vii. 17; xxi. 4——[p]Gen. xlix. 18; Tit. ii. 13

The word used to express the lees in the original signifies the *preservers;* because they preserve the strength and flavour of the wine. "All recent wines, after the fermentation has ceased, ought to be kept on their lees for a certain time, which greatly contributes to increase their strength and flavour. Whenever this first fermentation has been deficient, they will retain a more rich and sweet taste than is natural to them in a recent true vinous state; and unless farther fermentation is promoted by their lying longer on their own lees, they will never attain their genuine strength and flavour, but run into repeated and ineffectual fermentations, and soon degenerate into a liquor of an acetous kind.—All wines of a light and austere kind, by a fermentation too great, or too long continued, certainly degenerate into a weak sort of vinegar; while the stronger not only require, but will safely bear a stronger and often-repeated fermentation; and are more apt to degenerate from a defect than excess of fermentation into a vapid, ropy, and at length into a putrescent state." Sir *Edward Barry*, Observations on the Wines of the Ancients, p. 9, 10.

Thevenot observes particularly of the Shiras wine, that, after it is refined from the lees, it is apt to grow sour. "Il a beaucoup de lie; c'est pourquoi il donne puissemment dans la teste; et pour le rendre plus traitable on le passe par un chausse d'hypocras; après quoi il est fort clair, et moins fumeux. Ils mettent ce vin dans des grandes jarres de terres qui tiennent dix ou douze jusqu'à quatorze carabas: mais quand l'on a entamé une jarre, il faut la vuider au plutost, et mettre le vin qu'on en tire dans des bouteilles ou carabas; car si l'on y manque en le laissant quelque tems après que la jarre est entamée il se gâte et s'aigrit." Voyages, Tom. ii. p. 245.—"It has much sediment, and therefore is intoxicating. In order to make it more mellow, they strain it through a hypocrates' sleeve, after which it is very clear and less heady. They lay up this wine in great earthen jars, which hold from ten to fourteen *carabas:* but when a jar is unstopped, it is necessary to empty it immediately, and put the wine into bottles, or carabas; for if it be left thus in the jar, it will spoil and become acid."

The *caraba*, or *girba*, is a goat's skin drawn off from the animal, having no apertures but those occasioned by the *tail*, the *feet*, and the *neck*. One opening is left, to pour in and draw off the liquor. This skin goes through a sort of tanning process, and is often beautifully ornamented, as is the case with one of these girbas now lying before me.

This clearly explains the very elegant comparison, or rather allegory, of Jeremiah, chap. xlviii. 11; where the reader will find a remarkable example of the mixture of the proper with the allegorical, not uncommon with the Hebrew poets:—

"Moab hath been at ease from his youth,
And he hath settled upon his lees;
Nor hath he been drawn off from vessel to vessel,
Neither hath he gone into captivity:
Wherefore his taste remaineth in him,
And his flavour is not changed."

Sir *John Chardin's* MS. note on this place of Jeremiah is as follows: "On change ainsi le vin de coupe en coupe en Orient; et quand on en entame une, il faut la vuider en petites coupes ou bouteilles, sans quoy il s'aigrit. "They change the wine from vessel to vessel in the east; and when they unstop a large one, it is necessary to empty it into small vessels, as otherwise it will grow sour."

Verse 7. *The face of the covering cast over all people*—"The covering that covered the face of all the peoples"] MS. *Bodl.* reads על פני כל *al peney chol.* The word פני *peney, face*, has been removed from its right place into the line above, where it makes no sense; as *Houbigant* conjectured. "The face of the covering," &c. He will unveil all the Mosaic ritual, and show by his apostles that it referred to, and was accomplished in, the sacrificial offering of Jesus Christ.

Verse 8. *He will swallow up death*] He, by the grace of God, will taste death for every man. Heb. ii. 9. Probably, *swallow up death*, and *taste death*, in both these verses, refer to the same thing: Jesus dying instead of a guilty world. These forms of speech may refer to the punishment of certain criminals; they were obliged to drink a cup of poison. That *cup* which every criminal in the world must have drunk, Jesus Christ drank for them; and thus he *swallowed up death:* but as he rose again from the dead, complete *victory* was gained.

From these *three* verses we learn:—

I. That the Gospel is a plenteous provision "I will make a feast for all people."

II. That it is a source of light and salvation "I will destroy the veil. I will abolish death, and bring life and immortality to light."

III. That it is a source of comfort and happiness: "I will wipe away all tears from off all faces."

As in the Arabic countries a *covering* was put over the face of him who was condemned to suffer death, it is probable that the words in ver. 7 may refer to this. The whole world was condemned to death, and about to be led out to execution, when the gracious Lord interposed, and, by a glorious sacrifice, procured a general pardon.

Verse 9. *It shall be said*—"Shall they say"] So the *Septuagint* and *Vulgate*, in the plural number. They read ואמרו *veameru*, the *Syriac* reads ואמרת *veamarta, thou shalt say. They shall say*, i. e., the Jews and the Gentiles—Lo,

A. M. cir. 3292
B. C. cir. 712
Olymp. XVII. 1
cir. annum
NumæPompilii,
R. Roman., 4

and he will save us: this *is* the
LORD; we have waited for him,
[q]we will be glad and rejoice in
his salvation:

10 For in this mountain shall the hand of the LORD rest, and Moab shall be [r]trodden down under him, even as straw is [s]trodden down for the dunghill.

11 And he shall spread forth his hands in the midst of them, as he that swimmeth spreadeth forth *his hands* to swim: and he shall bring down their pride together with the spoils of their hands.

12 And the [t]fortress of the high fort of thy walls shall he bring down, lay low, *and* bring to the ground, *even* to the dust.

[q]Psa. xx. 5——[r]Or, *threshed*

[s]Or, *threshed in Madmenah*——[t]Chap. xxvi. 5

this [Jesus Christ] is our God: we have waited for him, according to the predictions of the prophets. We have expected him, and we have not been disappointed; therefore will we be glad, and rejoice in his salvation.

Verse 10. *Shall the hand of the Lord rest*—"The hand of JEHOVAH shall give rest"] Heb. תנוח *tenuach, quiescet.* Annon תניח *taniach,* quietem dabit, *shall rest; shall give rest,* ut Græci, *αναπαυσιν δωσει,* et Copt.?—Mr. WOIDE. That is, "shall give peace and quiet to Sion, by destroying the enemy;" as it follows.

As straw is trodden down—"As the straw is threshed"] Hoc juxta ritum loquitur Palæstinæ et multarum Orientis provinciarum, quæ ob pratorum et fœni penuriam paleas preparant esui animantium. Sunt autem carpenta ferrata rotis per medium in serrarum modum se volventibus, quæ stipulam conterunt; et comminuunt in paleas. Quomodo igitur plaustris ferratis paleæ conteruntur, sic conteretur Moab sub eo; sive sub Dei potentia, sive in semetipso, ut nihil in eo integri remaneat. "This is spoken in reference to the mode of threshing in Palestine, and various other Asiatic provinces. Because of the scarcity of meadow land and hay, they make chopped straw for the cattle. They have large wheels studded over with iron teeth or nails, by which, on the out-of-door threshing-floors, they pound and reduce the straw into chaff. As, therefore, the straw is reduced to chaff by bringing the iron-shod wheel over it; so shall Moab be bruised by the power of God, that nothing *whole* shall remain."—*Hieron.* in loc. See the note on chap. xxviii. 27.

For the dunghill—"Under the wheels of the car."] For מדמנה *madmenah,* the *Septuagint, Syriac,* and *Vulgate* read מרכבה *mercabah,* which I have followed. See Joshua xv. 31, compared with xix. 5, where there is a mistake very nearly the same. The keri, במי *bemi,* is confirmed by twenty-eight MSS., seven ancient, and three editions.

Verse 11. *As he that swimmeth spreadeth forth* his hands *to swim*—"As he that sinketh stretcheth out his hands to swim"] There is great obscurity in this place: some understand God as the agent; others, Moab. I have chosen the latter sense, as I cannot conceive that the stretching out of the hands of a swimmer in swimming can be any illustration of the action of God stretching out his hands over Moab to destroy it. I take השחה *hashshocheh,* altering the point on the ש *sin,* on the authority of the *Septuagint,* to be the participle of שחה *shachah,* the same with שוח *shuach,* and שחח *shachach, to bow down, to be depressed;* and that the prophet designed a paronomasia here, a figure which he frequently uses between the similar words שחה *shachah,* and שחות *shechoth.* As תחתיו *tachtaiv, in his place,* or *on the spot,* as we say in the preceding verse, gives us an idea of the sudden and complete destruction of Moab; so בקרבו *bekirbo, in the midst of him,* means that this destruction shall be open, and exposed to the view of all: the neighbouring nations shall plainly see him struggling against it, as a man in the midst of the deep waters exerts all his efforts by swimming, to save himself from drowning.—L.

CHAPTER XXVI

This chapter, like the foregoing, is a song of praise, in which thanksgivings for temporal and spiritual mercies are beautifully mingled, though the latter still predominate. Even the sublime and evangelical doctrine of the resurrection seems here to be hinted at, and made to typify the deliverance of the people of God from a state of the lowest misery; the captivity, the general dispersion, or both. This hymn too, like the preceding, is beautifully diversified by the frequent change of speakers. It opens with a chorus of the Church, celebrating the protection vouchsafed by God to his people; and the happiness of the righteous, whom he guards, contrasted with the misery of the wicked, whom he punishes, 1–7. *To this succeeds their own pious resolution of obeying, trusting, and delighting in God,* 8. *Here the prophet breaks in, in his own person, eagerly catching the last words of the chorus, which were perfectly in unison with the feelings of his own soul, and which he beautifully repeats, as one musical instrument reverberates the sound of another on the same key with it. He makes likewise a suitable response to what had been said on the judgments of God, and observes their different effects on the good and the bad; improving the one, and hardening the other,* 9–11. *After this, a chorus of Jews express their gratitude to God for past deliverances, make confession of their sins, and supplicate his power, which they*

***had been long expecting,* 12–18. *To this God makes a gracious reply, promising deliverance that should be as life from the dead,* 19. *And the prophet, (apparently alluding to the command of Moses to the Israelites, when the destroying angel was to go through the land of Egypt,) concludes with exhorting his people to patience and resignation, till God sends the deliverance he has promised,* 20, 21.**

A. M. cir. 3292
B. C. cir. 712
Olymp. XVII. 1
cir. annum
NumæPompilii,
R. Roman., 4

IN [a]that day shall this song be sung in the land of Judah; We have a strong city; [b]salvation will *God* appoint *for* walls and bulwarks.

2 [c]Open ye the gates, that the righteous nation which keepeth the [d]truth may enter in.

3 Thou wilt keep *him* [e]in perfect peace, *whose* [f]mind *is* stayed *on thee;* because he trusteth in thee.

4 Trust ye in the LORD for ever: [g]for in the LORD JEHOVAH *is* [h]everlasting strength.

5 For he bringeth down them that dwell on high; [i]the lofty city, he layeth it low; he layeth it low, *even* to the ground; he bringeth it *even* to the dust.

6 The foot shall tread it down, *even* the feet of the poor, *and* the steps of the needy.

7 The way of the just *is* uprightness: [k]thou most upright, dost weigh the path of the just.

8 Yea, [l]in the way of thy judgments, O LORD, have we waited for thee; the desire of *our* soul *is* to thy name, and to the remembrance of thee.

A. M. cir. 3292
B. C. cir. 712
Olymp. XVII. 1
cir. annum
NumæPompilii,
R. Roman., 4

9 [m]With my soul have I desired thee in the night; yea, with my spirit within me will I seek thee early: for when thy judgments *are* in the earth, the inhabitants of the world will learn righteousness.

10 [n]Let favour be showed to the wicked, *yet* will he not learn righteousness: in [o]the land of uprightness will he deal unjustly, and will not behold the majesty of the LORD.

11 LORD, *when* thy hand is lifted up, [p]they will not see: *but* they shall see, and be ashamed for *their* envy [q]at the people; yea, the fire of thine enemies shall devour them.

12 LORD, thou wilt ordain peace for us: for thou also hast wrought all our works [r]in us.

13 O LORD our God, [s]*other* lords beside thee have had dominion over us: *but* by thee

[a]Chap. ii. 11——[b]Chap. lx. 18——[c]Psa. cxviii. 19, 20 [d]Heb. *truths*——[e]Heb. *peace, peace;* chap. lvii. 19 [f]Or, *thought,* or *imagination*——[g]Chap. xlv. 17——[h]Heb. *the rock of ages;* Deut. xxxii. 4——[i]Chap. xxv. 12; xxxii. 19——[k]Psa. xxxvii. 23

[l]Chapter lxiv. 5——[m]Psalm lxiii. 6; Cant. iii. 1 [n]Ecclesiastes viii. 12; Romans ii. 4——[o]Psalm cxliii. 10——[p]Job xxxiv. 27; Psalm xxviii. 5; chapter v. 12 [q]Or, *toward* thy *people*——[r]Or, *for us*——[s]2 Chron. xii. 8

NOTES ON CHAP. XXVI

Verse 1. *We have a strong city*] In opposition to the city of the enemy, which God hath destroyed, chap. xxv. See the note there.

Salvation—for *walls and bulwarks*] חומת וחל *chomoth vachel, walls and redoubts,* or the *walls and the ditch.* חל *chel* properly signifies the *ditch* or *trench* without the wall; see *Kimchi.* The same rabbin says, This song refers to the time of salvation, *i. e.,* the days of the Messiah.

Verse 2. *The righteous nation*] The converted Gentiles shall have the *gates opened*—a full entrance into all the glories and privileges of the Gospel; being fellow heirs with the converted Jews. The Jewish peculiarity is destroyed, for the middle wall of partition is broken down.

The truth] The Gospel itself—as the fulfilment of all the ancient types, shadows, and ceremonies; and therefore termed *the truth,* in opposition to all those shadowy rites and ceremonies. "The law was given by Moses; *but* grace *and* TRUTH came by Jesus Christ;" John i. 17, and see the note there.

Verse 3. *In perfect peace*] שלום שלום *shalom, shalom,* "peace, peace," *i. e.,* peace upon peace—all kinds of *prosperity*—happiness in this world and in the world to come.

Because he trusteth in thee—"Because they have trusted in thee"] So the *Chaldee,* בטחו *betacho.* The *Syriac* and *Vulgate* read בטחנו *batachnu,* "we have trusted." *Schroeder,* Gram. Heb. p. 360, explains the present reading בטוח *batuach,* impersonally, *confisum est.*

Verse 4. *In the Lord JEHOVAH*—"In JEHOVAH"] In JAH JEHOVAH, Heb.; but see *Houbigant,* and the note on chap. xii. 2.

Everlasting strength] צור עולמים *tsur olamim,* "the rock of ages;" or, according to Rab. *Maimon,*—the *eternal Fountain, Source,* or *Spring.* Does not this refer to the lasting streams from the rock in the desert? And that rock was Christ. **Ȝe han hoped in the Lord fro the everlastinge worldis.**—Old MS. BIBLE.

Verse 8. *Have we waited for thee*—"We have placed our confidence in thy name"] The *Septuagint, Syriac,* and *Chaldee* read קוינו *kavinu,* without the pronoun annexed.

Verse 9. *Have I desired thee*] *Forty-one* MSS. of Dr. *Kennicott's* and many of *De Rossi's,* (nine ancient,) and *five* editions read אויתיך *ivvithicha.* It is proper to note this; because the second י *yod* being omitted in the text, the *Vulgate* and many others have rendered it in the third person.

When thy judgments, &c.] It would be better to read, When thy judgments were in the earth, the inhabitants of the world have learned (למדו *lamedu*) *righteousness.* Men seldom seek God in *prosperity;* they are apt to rest in an earthly portion; but God in mercy embitters this by ad-

A. M. cir. 3292 B. C. cir. 712 Olymp. XVII. 1 cir. annum NumæPompilii, R. Roman., 4

only will we make mention of
thy name.
14 *They are* dead, they shall
not live; *they are* deceased, they
shall not rise: therefore hast thou visited and
destroyed them, and made all their memory
to perish.
15 Thou hast increased the nation, O LORD,
thou hast increased the nation: thou art
glorified: thou hadst removed *it* far *unto* all
the ends of the earth.
16 LORD, [t]in trouble have they visited thee,
they poured out a [u]prayer *when* thy chastening
was upon them.
17 Like as a [v]woman with child, *that* draweth
near the time of her delivery,
is in pain, *and* crieth out in her
pangs; so have we been in thy
sight, O LORD.

A. M. cir. 3292 B. C. cir. 712 Olymp. XVII. 1 cir. annum NumæPompilii, R. Roman., 4

18 We have been with child, we have been
in pain, we have as it were brought forth
wind; we have not wrought any deliverance
in the earth; neither have [w]the inhabitants of
the world fallen.
19 [x]Thy dead *men* shall live, *together with*
my dead body shall they arise. [y]Awake and
sing, ye that dwell in dust: for thy dew *is as*
a dew of herbs, and the earth shall cast out
the dead.
20 Come, my people, [z]enter thou into thy

[t]Hos. v. 15.——[u]Heb. *secret speech*.——[v]Chap. xiii. 8; John xvi. 21

[w]Psa. xvii. 14.——[x]Ezek. xxxvii. 1, &c.——[y]Dan. xii. 2.——[z]Exod. xii. 22, 23

versity; then there is a general cry after himself as our chief, solid, and only permanent good.

Verse 16. *Lord, in trouble have they visited thee*—"O JEHOVAH, in affliction we have sought thee"] So the *Septuagint* and two MSS. have פקדנוך *pekadnucha*, in the first person plural. And so perhaps it should be צקנו *tsaknu*, in the first person; but how the *Septuagint* read this word is not clear; and this last member of the verse is extremely obscure.

For למו *lamo*, "on them," the *Septuagint* read לנו *lanu*, "on us," in the first person likewise; a frequent mistake; see note on chap. x. 29.

Verse 18. *We have—brought forth wind*] The learned Professor *Michaelis* explains this image in the following manner: "Rariorem morbum describi, empneumatosin, aut ventosam molam, dictum; quo quæ laborant diu et sibi et peritis medicis gravidæ videntur, tandemque post omnes veræ graviditatis molestias et labores ventum ex utero emittunt: quem morbum passim describunt medici." Syntagma Comment., vol. ii., p. 165. The *empneumatosis*, or windy inflation of the womb, is a disorder to which females are liable. Some have had this in such wise, for a long time together, that they have appeared to themselves, and even to very skilful medical men, to be pregnant; and after having endured much pain, and even the throes of apparent childbearing, they have been eased and restored to health by the emission of a great quantity of wind from the uterus. This disorder is well known to medical men." The *Syriac* translator seems to have understood it in this manner: Enixi sumus, ut illæ quæ ventos pariunt. "We have brought forth as they who bring forth wind."

In the earth—"In the land"] בארץ *bearets;* so a MS., the *Septuagint*, *Syriac*, and *Vulgate*.

Verse 19. *My dead body*—"My deceased"] All the ancient Versions render it in the plural; they read נבלותי *niblothai*, my *dead bodies*. The *Syriac* and *Chaldee* read נבלותיהם *niblotheyhem*, their *dead bodies*. No MS. yet found confirms this reading.

The dew of herbs—"The dew of the dawn"] *Lucis*, according to the *Vulgate;* so also the *Syriac* and *Chaldee*.

The deliverance of the people of God from a state of the lowest depression is explained by images plainly taken from the resurrection of the dead. In the same manner the Prophet Ezekiel represents the restoration of the Jewish nation from a state of utter dissolution by the restoring of the dry bones to life, exhibited to him in a vision, chap. xxxvii., which is directly thus applied and explained, ver. 11-13. And this deliverance is expressed with a manifest opposition to what is here said above, ver. 14, of the great lords and tyrants, under whom they had groaned:—

"They are dead, they shall not live;
They are deceased tyrants, they shall not rise:"

that they should be destroyed utterly, and should never be restored to their former power and glory. It appears from hence, that the doctrine of the resurrection of the dead was at that time *a popular and common doctrine;* for an image which is assumed in order to express or represent any thing in the way of allegory or metaphor, whether poetical or prophetical, must be an image *commonly known and understood;* otherwise it will not answer the purpose for which it is assumed.—L.

Kimchi refers these words to the days of the Messiah, and says, "Then many of the saints shall rise from the dead." And quotes Dan. xii. 2. Do not these words speak of the *resurrection* of our blessed Lord; and of that resurrection of the *bodies of men*, which shall be the consequence of *his body* being raised from the dead? *Thy dead* men *shall live,*—with *my dead body shall they arise.*] This seems very express.

Verse 20. *Come, my people, enter thou into thy chambers*] An exhortation to patience and resignation under oppression, with a confident expectation of deliverance by the power of God manifestly to be exerted in the destruction of the oppressor. It seems to be an allusion to the command of Moses to the Israelites, when the destroying angel was to go through the land of Egypt, "not to go out at the door of their houses until the morning;" Exod. xii. 22. And before the passage of the Red Sea: "Fear

A. M. cir. 3292 B. C. cir. 712 Olymp. XVII. 1 cir. annum NumæPompilii, R. Roman., 4

chambers, and shut thy doors
about thee: hide thyself as it
were [a]for a little moment, until
the indignation be overpast.
21 For, behold, the LORD [b]cometh out of
his place to punish the inhabitants of the earth for their iniquity: the earth also shall disclose her [c]blood, and shall no more cover her slain.

[a]Psa. xxx. 5; chap. liv. 7, 8; 2 Cor. iv. 17 — [b]Mic. i. 3; Jude 14 — [c]Heb. *bloods*

ye not, stand still, and see the salvation of JEHOVAH. JEHOVAH shall fight for you, and ye shall hold your peace," Exod. xiv. 13, 14.

Verse 21. *The earth also shall disclose her blood*] Crimes of cruelty and oppression, which have passed away from the eyes of men, God will bring into judgment, and exact punishment for them. O what a reckoning will the kingdoms of the earth have with God, for the torrents of blood which they have shed for the gratification of the lust of power and ambition! Who shall live when he doeth this?

CHAPTER XXVII

Destruction of the enemies of the Church, 1. *God's care of his vineyard,* 2–11. *Prosperity of the descendants of Abraham in the latter days,* 12, 13.

A. M. cir. 3292 B. C. cir. 712 Olymp. XVII. 1 cir. annum NumæPompilii, R. Roman., 4

IN that day the LORD with his
sore and great and strong
sword shall punish leviathan the
[a]piercing serpent, [b]even leviathan
that crooked serpent; and he shall
slay [c]the dragon that *is* in the sea.
2 In that day [d]sing ye unto her,
[e]A vineyard of red wine.

[a]Or, *crossing like a bar* — [b]Psa. lxxiv. 13, 14 — [c]Chap. li. 9; Ezek. xxix. 3; xxxii. 2 — [d]Chapter v. 1 — [e]Psalm lxxx. 8; Jeremiah ii. 21

The subject of this chapter seems to be the nature, the measure, and the design of God's dealings with his people. 1. His judgments inflicted on their great and powerful enemies, ver. 1. 2. His constant care and protection of his favourite vineyard, in the form of a dialogue, ver. 2. 3. The moderation and lenity with which the severity of his judgments have been tempered, ver. 7. 4. The end and design of them, to recover them from idolatry, ver. 9. And, 5. The recalling of them, on their repentance, from their several dispersions, ver. 12. The first verse seems connected with the two last verses of the preceding chapter.—L.

NOTES ON CHAP. XXVII

Verse 1. *Leviathan*] The animals here mentioned seem to be the *crocodile*, rigid by the stiffness of the backbone, so that he cannot readily turn himself when he pursues his prey; hence the easiest way of escaping from him is by making frequent and short turnings: the *serpent* or *dragon*, flexible and winding, which coils himself up in a circular form: and the *sea-monster*, or *whale*. These are used allegorically, without doubt for great potentates, enemies and persecutors of the people of God: but to specify the particular persons or states designed by the prophet under these images, is a matter of great difficulty, and comes not necessarily within the design of these notes. *R. D. Kimchi* says, *leviathan* is a parable concerning the kings of the Gentiles: it is the largest fish in the sea, called also תנין *tannin, the dragon,* or rather the *whale.* By these names the Grecian, Turkish, and Roman empires are intended. The *dragon of the sea* seems to mean some nation having a strong naval force and extensive commerce. See *Kimchi* on the place.

Verse 2. *Sing ye unto her*] אנו לה *anu lah.* Bishop *Lowth* translates this, *Sing ye a responsive song;* and says that ענה *anah, to answer*, signifies occasionally to sing responsively; and that this mode of singing was frequently practised among the ancient Hebrews. See *De Pöes. Sac. Heb. Præl.* xix., at the beginning.

This, indeed, was the ancient method of singing in various nations. The song was divided into distinct portions, and the singers sang *alternately.* There is a fine specimen of this in the song of Deborah and Barak; and also in the Idyls of Theocritus, and the Eclogues of Virgil.

This kind of singing was properly a dialogue in verse, sung to a particular tune, or in the mode which is now termed *recitativo.* I have seen it often practised on funeral occasions among the descendants of the aboriginal Irish. The poems of Ossian are of this kind.

The learned *Bishop* distinguishes the parts of this dialogue thus:—

3. JEHOVAH. It is I, JEHOVAH, that preserve her;
I will water her every moment;
I will take care of her by night;
And by day I will keep guard over her.

4. VINEYARD. I have no wall for my defence:
O that I had a fence of the thorn and brier!

JEHOVAH. Against them should I march in battle,
I should burn them up together.

5. Ah! let her rather take hold of my protection.

VINEYARD. Let him make peace with me!
Peace let him make with me!

A. M. cir. 3292
B. C. cir. 712
Olymp. XVII. 1
cir. annum
NumæPompilii,
R. Roman., 4

3 [f]I the LORD do keep it; I
will water it every moment: lest
any hurt it, I will keep it night
and day.
4 Fury *is* not in me: who would set [g]the
briers *and* thorns against me in battle? I
would [h]go through them, I would burn them
together.
5 Or let him take hold [i]of my strength, *that*
he may [k]make peace with me; *and* he shall
make peace with me.

6 He shall cause them that come
of Jacob [l]to take root: Israel
shall blossom and bud, and fill
the face of the world with fruit,
7 Hath he smitten him, [m]as he smote those
that smote him? *or* is he slain according to
the slaughter of them that are slain by him?
8 [n]In measure, [o]when it shooteth forth, thou
wilt debate with it: [p]he [q]stayeth his rough
wind in the day of the east wind.
9 By this therefore shall the iniquity of

A. M. cir. 3292
B. C. cir. 712
Olymp. XVII. 1
cir. annum
NumæPompilii,
R. Roman., 4

[f]Psa. cxxi. 4, 5——[g]2 Sam. xxiii. 6; ch. ix. 18——[h]Or, *march against*——[i]Ch. xxv. 4——[k]Job xxii. 21——[l]Ch. xxxvii. 31; Hos. xiv. 5, 6——[m]Heb. *according to the stroke of those*

[n]Job xxiii. 6; Psalm vi. 1; Jeremiah x. 24; xxx. 11; xlvi. 28; 1 Corinthians x. 13——[o]Or, *when thou sendest it forth*——[p]Or, *when he removeth it*——[q]Psalm lxxviii. 38

6. JEHOVAH. They that come from the root of Jacob shall flourish, Israel shall bud forth;
And they shall fill the face of the world with fruit.

A vineyard of red wine] The redder the wine, the more it was valued, says *Kimchi*.

Bishop *Lowth* translates, *To the beloved vineyard.* For חמר *chemer, red*, a multitude of MSS. and editions have חמד *chemed, desirable.* This is supported by the *Septuagint* and *Chaldee*.

Verse 3. *Lest* any *hurt it, I will keep it night and day*—"I will take care of her by night; and by day I will keep guard over her"] For פן יפקד *pen yiphkod, lest any visit it*, the *Syriac* read ואפקד *veephkod, and I will visit it.* Twenty MSS. of *Kennicott's*, fourteen of *De Rossi's*, and two of my own, and six editions read אפקד *ephkod, I will visit*, in the first person.

Verse 4. *Fury* is *not in me*—"I have no wall"] For חמה *chemah, anger*, the *Septuagint* and *Syriac* read חומה *chomah, wall.* An ancient MS. has חימה *cheimah.* For בה *bah, in her*, two MSS. read בם *bam, in them*, plural. The vineyard wishes for a wall and a fence of thorns—human strength and protection, (as the Jews were too apt to apply to their powerful neighbours for assistance, and to trust to the shadow of Egypt:) JEHOVAH replies, that this would not avail her, nor defend her against his wrath. He counsels her, therefore, to betake herself to his protection. On which she entreats him to make peace with her.

From the above note it appears that the bishop reads חומה *chomah, wall*, for חמה *chemah, anger* or *fury*, in accordance with the *Syriac* and *Septuagint.* The letter ו *vau* makes the only difference, which letter is frequently absent from many words where its place is supplied by the point . *cholem:* it might have been so here formerly; and in process of time both *vau* and *cholem* might have been lost. The *Syriac* supports the learned bishop's criticism, as the word ܫܘܪܐ *shora* is there used; which word in the plural is found, Heb. xi. 30: "By faith the *walls* of Jericho." The bishop thinks the *Septuagint* is on his side: to me, it seems neither *for* nor *against* the criticism. The words in the *Vatican copy* are εγω πολις οχυρα, *I am a fortified city;* which the *Arabic* follows: but instead of οχυρα, the *Codex Alexandrinus* has ισχυρα, *I am a* STRONG *city*.

The word חומה *chomah, wall*, is not found in any MS. in the collections of *Kennicott* and *De Rossi*, nor in any of my own MSS.

However, one of Dr. *Kennicott's* MSS. has חימה *cheimah;* but probably that which now appears to be a י *yod* was formerly a ו *vau*, and now partially obliterated.

This song receives much light from being collated with that in chap. v.; and perhaps the bishop's criticism will find its best support from such a collation. In ver. 5 of that chapter, God threatens to take away the *wall* of his vineyard: this *was* done; and here the vineyard complains, *I have no wall*, and wishes for any kind of defence rather than be thus naked. This is the only *natural* support of the above criticism.

"About Tripoli there are abundance of vineyards and gardens, inclosed, for the most part, with hedges, which chiefly consist of the rhamnus, paliurus, oxyacantha," &c. *Rawolf*, p. 21, 22. A fence of thorns is esteemed equal to a wall for strength, being commonly represented as impenetrable. See Mic. vii. 4; Hos. ii. 6.

Who would set the briers and *thorns against me*—"O that I had a fence of the thorn and brier"] *Seven* MSS., (*two* ancient,) and *one* edition, with the *Syriac*, *Vulgate*, and Aquila, read ושית *veshayith*, with the conjunction ו *vau* prefixed: *Who would set the briers and thorns.* מי יתנני שמיר שית *mi yitteneni shamir shayith, Who shall give me the brier and thorn*, i. e., for a defence: but hear *Kimchi:* "*Who* (the vineyard) *hath given me* (Jehovah) *the brier and the thorn* instead of good grapes."

Verse 5. *Or*—"Ah"] For או *o* I read אוי *oi*, as it was at first in a MS. The י *yod* was easily lost, being followed by another י *yod.*

Verse 6. *To take root*—"From the root"] For ישרש *yashresh*, I read, with the *Syriac*, משרש *mishshoresh.* And for יציץ ופרח *yatsits uparach*, יציצו פרח *yatsitsu parach*, joining the ו *vau* to the first word, and taking that into construction with the first part of the sentence, *Israel shall bud forth.* I suppose the dialogue to be continued in this verse, which pursues the same image of the allegory, but in the way of metaphor.

Verse 9. *The groves*—"And if the groves"] ולא *velo. Four* MSS., *two* ancient, of *Kennicott's*, and *one* ancient of my own, with the *Septuagint;* this makes a fuller sense.

A. M. cir. 3292
B. C. cir. 712
Olymp. XVII. 1
cir. annum
NumæPompilii,
R. Roman., 4

Jacob be purged; and this *is* all
the fruit to take away his sin;
when he maketh all the stones
of the altar as chalk-stones that
are beaten in sunder, the groves and [r]images
shall not stand up.

10 Yet the defenced city *shall be* desolate,
and the habitation forsaken, and left like a
wilderness: [s]there shall the calf feed, and
there shall he lie down, and consume the
branches thereof.

11 When the boughs thereof are withered,
they shall be broken off: the women come,
and set them on fire: for [t]it *is* a people of no
understanding: therefore he that
made them will not have mercy
on them, and [u]he that formed
them will show them no favour.

12 And it shall come to pass in that day, *that*
the LORD shall beat off from the channel of the
river unto the stream of Egypt, and ye shall be
gathered one by one, O ye children of Israel.

13 [v]And it shall come to pass in that day,
[w]*that* the great trumpet shall be blown, and
they shall come which were ready to perish
in the land of Assyria, and the outcasts in the
land of Egypt, and shall worship the LORD in
the holy mount at Jerusalem.

---

[r]Or, *sun images*——[s]See chapter xvii. 2; xxxii. 14 [t]Deut. xxxii. 28; chap. i. 3; Jer. viii. 7

[u]Deut. xxxii. 18; chapter xliii. 1, 7; xliv. 2, 21, 24 [v]Chap. ii. 11——[w]Matt. xxiv. 31; Rev. xi. 15

Verse 10. *There shall the calf feed*] That is, the king of Egypt, says *Kimchi*.

Verse 11. *The boughs thereof*—"Her boughs"] קציריה *ketsireyha*, MS. and Vulg.; that is, the boughs of the *vineyard*, referring still to the subject of the dialogue above.

The scarcity of fuel, especially wood, in most parts of the east is so great, that they supply it with every thing capable of burning; cow-dung dried, roots, parings of fruit, withered stalks of herbs and flowers; see Matt. vi. 21-30. Vine-twigs are particularly mentioned as used for fuel in dressing their food, by D'Arvieux; *La Roque*, Palestine, p. 198. Ezekiel says, in his parable of the vine, used figuratively for the people of God, as the vineyard is here: "Shall wood be taken thereof to do any work? or will men take a pin of it to hang any vessel thereon? Behold, it is cast into the fire for fuel;" chap. xv. 3, 4. "If a man abide not in me," saith our Lord, "he is cast forth as a branch of the vine and is withered; and men gather them, and cast them into the fire, and they are burned;" John xv. 6. They employed women and children to gather these things, and they laid them up in store for use. The dressing and pruning their vines afforded a good supply of the last sort of fuel; but the prophet says that the vines themselves of the beloved vineyard shall be blasted, withered, and broken, and the women shall come and gather them up, and carry away the whole of them to make their fires for domestic uses. See *Harmer's* Observations, vol. i., p. 254, &c.

Verse 12. *The channel of the river*] The river *Sabbation*, beyond which the Israelites were carried captive.—*Kimchi*.

Verse 13. *The great trumpet shall be blown*] Does not this refer to the time spoken of by our Lord, Matt. xxiv. 31: *He shall send forth his angels*—the preachers of his Gospel *with a great sound of a trumpet*—the earnest invitation to be saved by Jesus Christ; *and shall gather his elect*—the Jews, his ancient *chosen* people, *from the four winds*—from all parts of the habitable globe in which they have been dispersed.

In this prophet there are several predictions relative to the conversion of Egypt to the true faith, which have not yet been fulfilled, and which *must* be fulfilled, for the truth of God cannot fail. Should Egypt ever succeed in casting off the *Ottoman* yoke, and fully establish its independence, it is most likely that the Gospel of Christ would have a speedy entrance into it; and, according to these prophecies, a wide and permanent diffusion. At present the Mohammedan power is a genuine antichrist. This also the Lord will remove in due time.

CHAPTER XXVIII

This chapter begins with a denunciation of the approaching ruin of the Israelites by Shalmaneser, whose power is compared to a tempest or flood, and his keenness to the avidity with which one plucks and swallows the grape that is soonest ripe, 1–4. *It then turns to the two tribes of Judah and Benjamin, who were to continue a kingdom after the final captivity of their brethren; and gives first a favourable prognostication of their affairs under Hezekiah,* 5, 6; *but soon changes to reproofs and threatenings for their intemperance and their profaneness,* 7, 8. *They are introduced as not only scornfully rejecting, but also mocking and ridiculing, the instructions of the prophet,* 9, 10. *To this God immediately retorts in terms alluding to their own mocking, but differently applied,* 11–13. *The prophet then addresses these scoffers,* 14; *who considered themselves as perfectly secure from every evil,* 15; *and assures them that there was no method under heaven but one, by which they could be saved,* 16; *that every other vain resource should fail in the day of visitation,* 17, 18. *He then farther adds, that the judgments of God were particularly levelled against them; and that all the means to which they trusted for warding them off should be to no purpose,* 19, 20; *as the Almighty, who, on account of his patience and long-*

***suffering, is amiably described as unacquainted with punishing, had nevertheless determined to punish them,* 21, 22. *The prophet then concludes with a beautiful parable in explanation and defence of God's dealing with his people,* 23–29.**

A. M. cir. 3279
B. C. cir. 725
Olymp. XIII. 4
cir. annum
Romuli,
R. Roman., 29

WO to [a]the crown of pride, to the drunkards of Ephraim, whose [b]glorious beauty *is* a fading flower, which *are* on the head of the fat valleys of them that are [c]overcome with wine!

2 Behold, the Lord hath a mighty and strong one, [d]*which* as a tempest of hail *and* a destroying storm, as a flood of mighty waters overflowing, shall cast down to the earth with the hand.

3 [e]The crown of pride, the drunkards of Ephraim, shall be trodden [f]under feet:

A. M. cir. 3279
B. C. cir. 725
Olymp. XIII. 4
cir. annum
Romuli,
R. Roman., 29

4 And [g]the glorious beauty, which *is* on the head of the fat valley, shall be a fading flower, *and* as the hasty fruit before the summer; which *when* he that looketh upon it seeth, while it is yet in his hand he [h]eateth it up.

5 In that day shall the LORD of hosts be for a crown of glory, and for a diadem of beauty, unto the residue of his people,

[a]Ver. 3——[b]Ver. 4——[c]Heb. *broken*——[d]Chap. xxx. 30; Ezek. xiii. 11

[e]Ver. 1——[f]Heb. *with feet*——[g]Ver. 1——[h]Heb. *swalloweth*

NOTES ON CHAP. XXVIII

Verse 1. *Wo to the crown of pride*] By the crown of pride, &c., *Samaria* is primarily understood. "Sebaste, the ancient Samaria, is situated on a long mount of an oval figure, having first a fruitful valley, and then a ring of hills running round about it;" *Maundrell*, p. 58. "E regione horum ruderum mons est peramœnus, planitie admodum frugifera circumseptus, super quem olim Samaria urbs condita fuit;" Fureri Itinerarium, p. 93. The city, beautifully situated on the top of a round hill, and surrounded immediately with a rich valley and a circle of other hills beyond it, suggested the idea of a chaplet or wreath of flowers worn upon their heads on occasions of festivity, expressed by *the proud crown* and the *fading flower of the drunkards.* That this custom of wearing chaplets in their banquets prevailed among the Jews, as well as among the Greeks and Romans, appears from the following passage of the book of Wisdom:—

"Let us fill ourselves with costly wine and ointments,
And let no flower of the spring pass by us:
Let us crown ourselves with rose-buds before they are withered."

Wisd. ii. 7, 8.

Verse 2. *Behold the Lord hath a mighty and strong one*—"Behold the mighty one, the exceedingly strong one"] אמץ לאדני *ammits ladonai, fortis Domino,* i. e., *fortissimus,* a Hebraism. For לאדני *ladonai, to the Lord, thirty-eight* MSS. of Dr. *Kennicott's* and many of *De Rossi's,* with some of my own, and *two* editions, read ליהוה *laihovah, to* JEHOVAH.

Verse 3. *The crown of pride, the drunkards of Ephraim*—"The proud crown of the drunkards of Ephraim"] I read עטרות *ataroth, crowns,* plural, to agree with the verb תרמסנה *teramasnah,* "shall be trodden down."

Verse 4. *The hasty fruit before the summer*—"The early fruit before the summer"] "No sooner doth the *boccore,* (the early fig,) draw near to perfection in the middle or latter end of June, than the *kermez* or summer fig begins to be formed, though it rarely ripens before August; about which time the same tree frequently throws out a third crop, or the winter fig, as we may call it. This is usually of a much longer shape and darker complexion than the kermez, hanging and ripening upon the tree even after the leaves are shed; and, provided the winter proves mild and temperate, is gathered as a delicious morsel in the spring;" *Shaw,* Travels, p. 370, fol. The image was very obvious to the inhabitants of Judea and the neighbouring countries, and is frequently applied by the prophets to express a desirable object; by none more elegantly than by Hosea, chap. ix. 10:—

"Like grapes in the wilderness I found Israel;
Like the first ripe fig in her prime, I saw your fathers."

Which when he that looketh upon it seeth—"Which whoso seeth, he plucketh it immediately"] For יראה *yireh,* which with הראה *haroeh* makes a miserable tautology, read, by a transposition of a letter, יארה *yoreh;* a happy conjecture of Houbigant. The image expresses in the strongest manner the great ease with which the Assyrians shall take the city and the whole kingdom, and the avidity with which they shall seize the rich prey without resistance.

Verse 5. *In that day*] Thus far the prophecy relates to the Israelites, and manifestly denounces their approaching destruction by Shalmaneser. Here it turns to the two tribes of Judah and Benjamin, the remnant of God's people who were to continue a kingdom after the final captivity of the Israelites. It begins with a favourable prognostication of their affairs under Hezekiah; but soon changes to reproofs and threatenings for their intemperance, disobedience, and profaneness.

Jonathan's Targum on this verse is worthy of notice: "In that time Messiah, the Lord of hosts משיחא דיי צבאות *meshicha dayai tsebaoth,* shall be a crown of joy and a diadem of praise to the residue of his people." Kimchi says the rabbins in general are of this opinion. Here then the rabbins, and their most celebrated Targum, give the incommunicable name, יהוה צבאות *Yehovah tsebaoth, the Lord of hosts,* to our ever blessed Redeemer, Jesus Christ.

A. M. cir. 3279
B. C. cir. 725
Olymp. XIII. 4
cir. annum
Romuli,
Roman., 29

6 And for a spirit of judgment
to him that sitteth in judgment,
and for strength to them that
turn the battle to the gate.
7 But they also [i]have erred through wine,
and through strong drink are out of the way;
[k]the priest and the prophet have erred through
strong drink, they are swallowed up of wine,
they are out of the way through strong drink;
they err in vision, they stumble *in* judgment.
8 For all tables are full of vomit *and* filthiness, *so that there is* no place
clean.
9 [l]Whom shall he teach knowledge? and whom shall he make
to understand [m]doctrine? *them that are* weaned
from the milk, *and* drawn from the breasts.
10 For precept [n]*must be* upon precept, precept upon precept; line upon line, line upon
line; here a little, *and* there a little:
11 For with [o]stammering [p]lips and another
tongue [q]will he speak to this people.

A. M. cir. 3279
B. C. cir. 725
Olymp. XIII. 4
cir. annum
Romuli,
R. Roman., 29

---

[i]Prov. xx. 1; Hos. iv. 11——[k]Chap. lvi. 10, 12——[l]Jer. vi. 10——[m]Heb. *the hearing*

[n]Or, hath been——[o]Heb. *stammerings of lips*——[p]1 Cor. xiv. 21——[q]Or, *he hath spoken*

Verse 6. *The battle to the gate*—"The war to the gate *of the enemy*."] That is, who pursue the fleeing enemy even to the very gates of their own city. "But we were upon them even unto the entering of the gate," 2 Sam. xi. 23; that is, we drove the enemy back to their own gates. See also 1 Sam. xvii. 52. The *Targum* says, The Messiah shall give the victory to those who go out to battle, that he may bring them back to their own houses in peace.

Verse 9. *Whom shall he teach knowledge?*—"Whom, say they, would he teach knowledge?"] The scoffers mentioned below, ver. 14, are here introduced as uttering their sententious speeches; they treat God's method of dealing with them, and warning them by his prophets, with contempt and derision. What, say they, doth he treat us as mere infants just weaned? doth he teach us like little children, perpetually inculcating the same elementary lessons, the mere rudiments of knowledge; precept after precept, line after line, here and there, by little and little? imitating at the same time, and ridiculing, in ver. 10, the concise prophetical manner. God, by his prophet, retorts upon them with great severity their own contemptuous mockery, turning it to a sense quite different from what they intended. Yes, saith he, it shall be in fact as you say; ye shall be taught by a strange tongue and a stammering lip; in a strange country; ye shall be carried into captivity by a people whose language shall be unintelligible to you, and which ye shall be forced to learn like children. And my dealing with you shall be according to your own words: it shall be command upon command for your punishment; it shall be line upon line, stretched over you to mark your destruction, (compare 2 Kings xxi. 13;) it shall come upon you at different times, and by different degrees, till the judgments, with which from time to time I have threatened you, shall have their full accomplishment.

Jerome seems to have rightly understood the general design of this passage as expressing the manner in which the scoffers, by their sententious speeches, turned into ridicule the warnings of God by his prophets, though he has not so well explained the meaning of the repetition of their speech in ver. 13. His words are on ver. 9—"Solebant hoc ex persona prophetarum ludentes dicere:" and on ver. 14—"Quod supra diximus, cum irrisione solitos principes Judæorum prophetis dicere, *manda*, *remanda*, et cætera his similia, per quæ ostenditur, nequaquam eos prophetarum credidisse sermonibus, sed prophetiam habuisse despectui, præsens ostendit capitulum, per quod appellantur viri illusores." *Hieron. in loc.*

And so Jarchi interprets the word משלים *mishelim* in the next verse: Qui dicunt verba irrisionis parabolicè." And the *Chaldee* paraphrases ver. 11 to the same purpose, understanding it as spoken, not of God, but of the people deriding his prophets: "Quoniam in mutatione loquelæ et in lingua subsannationis irridebant contra prophetas, qui prophetabant populo huic."—L.

Verse 10. *For precept* must be *upon precept*] The original is remarkably abrupt and sententious. The hemistichs are these:—

כי צו לצו צו לצו
latsav tsav latsav tsav ki

קו לקו קו לקו
lakav kav lakav kav

זעיר שם זעיר שם
sham zeeir sham zeeir

For,—Command to command, command to command.
Line to line, line to line.
A little there, a little there.

Kimchi says צו *tsav*, *precept*, is used here for מצוה *mitsvah*, *command*, and is used in no other place for it but here. צו *tsav* signifies a *little precept*, such as is suited to the capacity of a child; see ver. 9. קו *kav* signifies the *line* that a mason stretches out to build a layer of stones by. After one layer or course is placed, he raises the line and builds another; thus the building is by degrees regularly completed. This is the method of teaching children, giving them such information as their narrow capacities can receive; and thus the prophet dealt with the Israelites. See *Kimchi in loc.*, and see a fine parallel passage, Heb. v. 12-14, by which this may be well illustrated.

My old MS. Bible translates oddly:—

For sende efter sende, sende efter sende:
Abiide efter abiide, abiide efter abiide:
Lityl ther, lytyl ther.

Coverdale is also singular:—

Commande that may be commanded;
Byd that maye be bydden:
Forbyd that maye be forbydden;
Kepe backe that maye be kepte backe:
Here a litle, there a litle.

A. M. cir. 3279
B. C. cir. 725
Olymp. XIII. 4
cir. annum
Romuli,
R. Roman., 29

12 To whom he said, This *is* the rest *wherewith* ye may cause the weary to rest; and this *is* the refreshing: yet they would not hear.

13 But the word of the LORD was unto them, precept upon precept, precept upon precept; line upon line, line upon line; here a little, *and* there a little; that they might go, and fall backward, and be broken, and snared, and taken.

14 Wherefore hear the word of the LORD, ye scornful men, that rule this people which *is* in Jerusalem.

15 Because ye have said, We have made a covenant with death, and with hell are we at agreement; when the overflowing scourge shall pass through, it shall not come unto us: [r]for we have made lies our refuge, and under falsehood have we hid ourselves:

16 Therefore thus saith the Lord GOD, Behold, I lay in Zion for a foundation [s]a stone, a tried stone, a precious corner *stone,* a sure foundation: he that believeth shall not make haste.

17 Judgment also will I lay to the line, and righteousness to the plummet: and the hail shall sweep away [t]the refuge of lies, and the waters shall overflow the hiding place.

18 And your covenant with death shall be disannulled, and your agreement with hell shall not stand; when the overflowing scourge shall pass through, then ye shall be [u]trodden down by it.

19 From the time that it goeth forth it shall take you: for morning by morning shall it pass over, by day and by night: and it shall be a vexation only [v]*to* understand the report.

20 For the bed is shorter than that *a man* can stretch himself *on it:* and the covering

[r]Amos ii. 4——[s]Gen. xlix. 42; Psa. cxviii. 22; Matt. xxi. 42; Acts iv. 11; Rom. ix. 33; x. 11; Eph. ii. 20; 1 Pet. ii. 6, 7, 8——[t]Ver. 15——[u]Heb. *a treading down to it* [v]Or, when *he shall make* you *to understand doctrine*

Verse 12. *This* is *the rest*—"This is the true rest"] The sense of this verse is: God had warned them by his prophets that their safety and security, their deliverance from their present calamities and from the apprehensions of still greater approaching, depended wholly on their trust in God, their faith and obedience; but they rejected this gracious warning with contempt and mockery.

Verse 15. *A covenant with death*] To be in covenant with, is a kind of proverbial expression to denote *perfect security* from evil and mischief of any sort:—

"For thou shalt be in league with the stones of the field;
And the beasts of the field shall be at peace with thee." Job v. 23.

"And I will make a covenant for them with the beasts of the field,
And with the fowls of heaven, and with the creeping things of the ground."
Hos. ii. 18.

That is, none of these shall hurt them. But Lucan, speaking of the Psylli, whose peculiar property it was to be unhurt by the bite of serpents, with which their country abounded, comes still nearer to the expression of Isaiah in this place:—

Gens unica terras
Incolit a sævo serpentum innoxia morsu
Marmaridæ Psylli.——
Pax illis cum morte data est.
Pharsal. ix. 891.

"Of all who scorching Afric's sun endure,
None like the swarthy Psyllians are secure:
With healing gifts and privileges graced,
Well in the land of serpents were they placed:
Truce with the dreadful tyrant death they have,
And border safely on his realm the grave."
ROWE.

We have made a covenant with death, and with hell are we at agreement] עשינו חזה *asinu chozeh,* we have made a *vision,* we have had an *interview,* struck a bargain, and settled all preliminaries. So they had made a *covenant with hell* by *diabolic sacrifice,* כרתנו ברית *carathnu berith,* "We have cut the covenant sacrifice;" they divided it for the contracting parties to *pass between* the separated victim; for the victim was split exactly down the middle, so that even the *spinal marrow was exactly divided* through its whole length; and being set opposite to each other, the contracting parties entered, one at the head part, the other at the feet; and, meeting in the centre, took the covenant oath. Thus, it is intimated, these bad people made an agreement with שאול *sheol,* with *demons,* with whom they had an *interview; i. e.,* meeting them in the covenant sacrifice! To such a pitch had the Israelitish idolatry reached at that time!

Verse 16. *Behold, I lay in Zion*] See the notes on the parallel places in the margin. *Kimchi* understands this of *Hezekiah;* but it most undoubtedly belongs to Jesus Christ alone; and his application of it to himself, even the Jews could not contest. See the margin as above.

Verse 18. *Your covenant with death shall be disannulled*—"Your covenant with death shall be broken"] For כפר *caphar,* which seems not to belong to this place, the *Chaldee* reads תפר *taphar,* which is approved by *Houbigant* and *Secker.* See Jer. xxxiii. 21, where the very same phrase is used. See Prelim. Dissert. p. l.

Verse 20. *For the bed is shorter*] A *mashal* or proverbial saying, the meaning of which is, that

A. M. cir. 3279
B. C. cir. 725
Olymp. XIII. 4
cir. annum
Romuli,
R. Roman., 29

narrower than that he can wrap
himself *in it.*
21 For the LORD shall rise up
as *in* Mount [w]Perazim, he shall
be wroth as *in* the valley of [x]Gibeon, that he
may do his work, [y]his strange work; and
bring to pass his act, his strange act.
22 Now therefore be ye not mockers, lest
your bands be made strong: for I have heard
from the Lord GOD of hosts [z]a consumption,
even determined upon the whole earth.
23 Give ye ear, and hear my voice; hearken,
and hear my speech.
24 Doth the ploughman plough all day to
sow? doth he open and break the clods of his
ground?
25 When he hath made plain the face thereof, doth he not cast abroad the fitches, and
scatter the cummin, and cast in
[a]the principal wheat and the appointed barley and the [b]rye in
their [c]place?

A. M. cir. 3279
B. C. cir. 725
Olymp. XIII. 4
cir. annum
Romuli,
R. Roman., 29

26 [d]For [e]his God doth instruct him to discretion, *and* doth teach him.
27 For the fitches are not threshed with a
threshing instrument, neither is a cart wheel
turned about upon the cummin; but the
fitches are beaten out with a staff, and the
cummin with a rod.
28 Bread *corn* is bruised; because he will
not ever be threshing it, nor break *it with* the
wheel of his cart, nor bruise it *with* his horsemen.
29 This also cometh forth from the LORD
of hosts, [f]*which* is wonderful in counsel, *and*
excellent in working.

---

[w]2 Samuel v. 20; 1 Chronicles xiv. 11——[x]Joshua x. 10, 12; 2 Samuel v. 25; 1 Chronicles xiv. 16——[y]Lamentations iii. 33——[z]Chap. x. 22, 23; Daniel ix. 27——[a]Or, *the wheat in the principal* place, *and barley in the appointed* place——[b]Or, *spelt*——[c]Heb. *border?*——[d]Or, *And he bindeth it in such sort as his God doth teach him*——[e]Ecclesiasticus vii. 15——[f]Psalm xcii. 5; Jeremiah xxxii. 19

---

they will find all means of defence and protection insufficient to secure them, and cover them from the evils coming upon them. מסך *massek*, chap. xxii. 8, the *covering*, is used for the outworks of defence, the barrier of the country; and here, in the allegorical sense, it means much the same thing. Their beds were only mattresses laid on the floor; and the coverlet a sheet, or in the winter a carpet, laid over it, in which the person wrapped himself. For כהתכנס *kehithcannes*, it ought probably to be מהתכנס *mehithcannes*. *Houbigant, Secker.*

Verse 21. *As in Mount Perazim*] כהר *kehar;* but בהר *bahar*, IN *the mount*, is the reading of two of *Kennicott's*, one of *De Rossi's*, and one of my own MSS.

Verse 22. *The Lord God*] אדני יהוה *Adonai Yehovah.* Adonai is omitted by four of *Kennicott's* MSS., and in the *Septuagint*, *Syriac*, and *Arabic.*

Verse 23. *Give ye ear, and hear my voice*—"Listen ye, and hear my voice"] The foregoing discourse, consisting of severe reproofs, and threatenings of dreadful judgments impending on the Jews for their vices, and their profane contempt of God's warnings by his messengers, the prophet concludes with an explanation and defence of God's method of dealing with his people in an elegant parable or allegory; in which he employs a variety of images, all taken from the science of agriculture. As the *husbandman* uses various methods in preparing his land, and adapting it to the several kinds of seeds to be sown, with a due observation of times and seasons; and when he hath gathered in his harvest, employs methods as various in separating the corn from the straw and the chaff by different instruments, according to the nature of the different sorts of grain; so God, with unerring wisdom, and with strict justice, instructs, admonishes, and corrects his people; chastises and punishes them in various ways, as the exigence of the case requires; now more moderately, now more severely; always tempering justice with mercy; in order to reclaim the wicked, to improve the good, and, finally, to separate the one from the other.

Verse 26. *For his God doth instruct him*] All nations have agreed in attributing agriculture, the most useful and the most necessary of all sciences, to the invention and to the suggestions of their deities. "The Most High hath ordained husbandry," saith the son of Sirach, Ecclus. vii. 15.

Namque Ceres fertur fruges, Liberque liquoris
Vitigeni laticem mortalibus instituisse.
LUCRETIUS, v. 14.

"Ceres has taught mortals how to produce fruits; and Bacchus has taught them how to cultivate the vine."

'Ο δ' ηπιος ανθρωποισι
Δεξια σημαινει, λαους δ' επι εργον εγειρει
Μιμνησκων βιοτοιο· λεγει δ' ότε βωλος αριστη
Βουσι τε και μακελῃσι· λεγει δ' ότε δεξιαι ὡραι
Και φυτα γυρωσαι, και σπερματα παντα βαλεσθαι.
ARATUS, *Phænom.* v.

"He, Jupiter, to the human race
Indulgent, prompts to necessary toil
Man provident of life; with kindly signs
The seasons marks, when best to turn the glebe
With spade and plough, to nurse the tender plant,
And cast o'er fostering earth the seeds abroad."

Verses 27, 28. Four methods of threshing are here mentioned, by different instruments; the *flail*, the *drag*, the *wain*, and the *treading of the cattle.* The *staff* or *flail* was used for the *infirmiora semina*, says Jerome, the grain that was *too tender* to be treated in the other methods. The *drag* consisted of a sort of strong planks, made rough at the bottom, with hard stones or iron; it was drawn by horses or oxen over the corn sheaves spread on the floor, the driver sitting upon it. Kempfer has given a print representing the manner of using this instrument, *Amœn. Exot.* p. 682, fig. 3. The *wain* was much like the former; but had *wheels* with *iron teeth,* or *edges* like a *saw:* Ferrata carpenta rotis per medium in serrarum modum se volventibus. Hieron. in loc. From this it would seem that the axle was armed with irŏn teeth or *serrated wheels* throughout. See a description and print of such a machine used at present in Egypt for the same purpose in *Niebuhr's* Voyage en Arabie, Tab. xvii. p. 123; it moves upon three rollers armed with iron teeth or wheels to cut the straw. In Syria they make use of the *drag,* constructed in the very same manner as above described; *Niebuhr,* Description de l'Arabie, p. 140. This not only forced out the grain, but cut the straw in pieces for fodder for the cattle; for in the eastern countries they have no *hay.* See *Harmer's* Observ. I. p. 425. The last method is well known from the law of Moses, which "forbids the ox to be muzzled, when he treadeth out the corn;" Deut. xxv. 4.

Verse 28. *The bread*-corn] I read ולחם *velahem,* on the authority of the *Vulgate* and *Symmachus;* the former expresses the conjunction ו *vau,* omitted in the text, by *autem;* the latter by δε.

Bruise it with *his horsemen*—"Bruise it with the hoofs of his cattle."] For פרשיו *parashaiv, horsemen* or *teeth,* read פרסיו *perasaiv, hoofs.* So the *Syriac, Symmachus, Theodotion,* and the *Vulgate.* The first is read with ש *shin,* the latter with ס *samech,* the pronunciation is nearly the same.

CHAPTER XXIX

Distress of Ariel, or Jerusalem, on Sennacherib's invasion, with manifest allusion, however, to the still greater distress which it suffered from the Romans, 1–4. *Disappointment and fall of Sennacherib described in terms, like the event, the most awful and terrible,* 5–8. *Stupidity and hypocrisy of the Jews,* 9–16. *Rejection of the Jews, and calling of the Gentiles,* 17. *The chapter concludes by a recurrence to the favourite topics of the prophet, viz., the great extension of the Messiah's kingdom in the latter days, and the future restoration of Israel,* 18–24.

A. M. cir. 3292
B. C. cir. 712
Olymp. XVII. 1
cir. annum
NumæPompilii,
R. Roman., 4

WO [a]to[b] Ariel, to Ariel, [c]the
city [d]*where* David dwelt!
add ye year to year; let them
[e]kill sacrifices.

2 Yet I will distress Ariel, and
there shall be heaviness and sorrow: and it shall be unto me as
Ariel.

A. M. cir. 3292
B. C. cir. 712
Olymp. XVII. 1
cir. annum
NumæPompilii,
R. Roman., 4

[a]Or, *O Ariel,* that is, *the lion of God*——[b]Ezek. xliii. 15, 16——[c]Or, *of the city*——[d]2 Sam. v. 9——[e]Heb. *cut off the heads*

The subject of this and the four following chapters is the invasion of Sennacherib; the great distress of the Jews while it continued; their sudden and unexpected deliverance by God's immediate interposition in their favour; the subsequent prosperous state of the kingdom under Hezekiah; interspersed with severe reproofs, and threats of punishment, for their hypocrisy, stupidity, infidelity, their want of trust in God, and their vain reliance on the assistance of Egypt; and with promises of better times, both immediately to succeed, and to be expected in the future age. The whole making, not one continued discourse, but rather a collection of different discourses upon the same subject; which is treated with great elegance and variety. Though the matter is various, and the transitions sudden, yet the prophet seldom goes far from his subject. It is properly enough divided by the chapters in the common translation.—L.

NOTES ON CHAP. XXIX

Verse 1. *Ariel*] That Jerusalem is here called by this name is very certain: but the reason of this name, and the meaning of it as applied to Jerusalem, is very obscure and doubtful. Some, with the Chaldee, suppose it to be taken from the hearth of the great altar of burnt-offerings, which Ezekiel plainly calls by the same name; and that Jerusalem is here considered as the seat of the fire of God, אור אל *ur el* which should issue from thence to consume his enemies: compare chap. xxxi. 9. Some, according to the common derivation of the word, ארי אל *ari el,* the lion of God, or the strong lion, suppose it to signify the strength of the place, by which it was enabled to resist and overcome all its enemies. Τινες δε φασι την πολιν ούτως ειρησθαι· επει, δια Θεου, λεοντος δικην εσπαραττε τους ανταιροντας. *Procop.* in loc. There are other explanations of this name given: but none that seems to be perfectly satisfactory.—*Lowth.*

From Ezekiel xliii. 15, we learn that Ari-el was the name of the altar of burnt-offerings, put here for the *city* itself in which that altar was. In the second verse it is said, I will distress Ari-el, and it shall be unto me as Ari-el. The first *Ari-el* here seems to mean *Jerusalem,* which should be distressed by the Assyrians: the second *Ari-el* seems to mean the *altar of burnt-offerings.* But why is it said, "Ari-el shall be unto me as Ari-el?" As the altar of burnt-offerings was surrounded daily by the victims which were offered: so the walls of Jerusalem shall be surrounded by the *dead bodies* of those who had rebelled against the Lord, and who should be victims to his justice. The translation of Bishop Lowth appears to embrace both meanings: "I will bring distress upon Ari-el; and it shall be to me as the hearth of the great altar."

Add ye year to year] Ironically. Go on year after year, keep your solemn feasts; yet know, that God will punish you for your hypocritical worship, consisting of mere form destitute of true piety. Probably delivered at the time of some great feast, when they were thus employed.

Verse 2. *There shall be heaviness and sorrow* —"There shall be continual mourning and sor-

A. M. cir. 3292 B. C. cir. 712 Olymp. XVII. 1 cir. annum NumæPompilii, R. Roman., 4

3 And I will camp against thee
round about, and will lay siege
against thee with a mount, and I
will raise forts against thee.
4 And thou shalt be brought down, *and*
shalt speak out of the ground, and thy speech
shall be low out of the dust, and thy voice
shall be, as of one that hath a familiar spirit,
[f]out of the ground, and thy speech shall
[g]whisper out of the dust.
5 Moreover the multitude of thy [h]strangers
shall be like small dust, and the multitude of
the terrible ones *shall be* [i]as
chaff that passeth away: yea,
it shall be [k]at an instant suddenly.
6 [l]Thou shalt be visited of the LORD of
hosts with thunder, and with earthquake, and
great noise, with storm and tempest, and the
flame of devouring fire.
7 [m]And the multitude of all the nations that
fight against Ariel, even all that fight against
her and her munition, and that distress her,
shall be [n]as a dream of a night vision.

---

[f]Ch. viii. 19——[g]Heb. *peep* or *chirp*——[h]Ch. xxv. 5——[i]Job xxi. 18; chap. xvii. 13——[k]Chap. xxx. 13——[l]Chap. xxviii. 2; xxx. 30——[m]Chap. xxxvii. 36——[n]Job xx. 8

---

row"] Instead of your present joy and festivity.

And it shall be unto me as Ariel—"And it shall be unto me as the hearth of the great altar."] That is, it shall be the seat of the fire of God; which shall issue from thence to consume his enemies. See note on ver. 1. Or, perhaps, all on flame; as it was when taken by the Chaldeans; or covered with carcasses and blood, as when taken by the Romans: an intimation of which more distant events, though not immediate subjects of the prophecy, may perhaps be given in this obscure passage.

Verse 3. *And I will camp against thee round about*—"And I will encamp against thee like David"] For כדור *caddur*, some kind of military engine, כדוד *kedavid, like David*, is the reading of the *Septuagint*, two MSS. of *Kennicott's*, if not two more: but though Bishop Lowth adopts this reading, I think it harsh and unnecessary.

Forts—"Towers"] For מצרת *metsuroth*, read מצדות *metsudoth:* so the *Septuagint* and five MSS. of Dr. *Kennicott's*, one of them ancient, and four of *De Rossi's*.

Verse 4. *And thy speech shall be low out of the dust*—"And from out of the dust thou shalt utter a feeble speech"] That the souls of the dead uttered a feeble stridulous sound, very different from the natural human voice, was a popular notion among the heathens as well as among the Jews. This appears from several passages of their poets; Homer, Virgil, Horace. The pretenders to the art of necromancy, who were chiefly women, had an art of speaking with a feigned voice, so as to deceive those who applied to them, by making them believe that it was the voice of the ghost. They had a way of uttering sounds, as if they were formed, not by the organs of speech, but deep in the chest, or in the belly; and were thence called εγγαστριμυθοι, *ventriloqui:* they could make the voice seem to come from beneath the ground, from a distant part, in another direction, and not from themselves; the better to impose upon those who consulted them. Εξεπιτηδες το γενος τουτο τον αμυδρον ηχον επιτηδευονται, ἱνα δια την ασαφειαν της φωνης τον του ψευδους αποδιδρασκωσιν ελεγχον. *Psellus* De Dæmonibus, apud *Bochart*, i. p. 731. "These people studiously acquire, and affect on purpose, this sort of obscure sound; that by the uncertainty of the voice they may the better escape being detected in the cheat." From these arts of the necromancers the popular notion seems to have arisen, that the ghost's voice was a weak, stridulous, almost inarticulate sort of sound, very different from the speech of the living.

Verse 5. *The multitude of thy strangers*—"The multitude of the proud"] For זריך *zarayich, thy strangers*, read זדים *zedim, the proud*, according to the *Septuagint;* parallel to and synonymous with עריצים *aritsim, the terrible*, in the next line: the ר *resh* was at first ד *daleth* in a MS. See note on chap. xxv. 2.

The fifth, sixth, and seventh verses contain an admirable description of the destruction of Sennacherib's army, with a beautiful variety of the most expressive and sublime images: perhaps more adapted to show the greatness, the suddenness, and horror of the event, than the means and manner by which it was effected. Compare chap. xxx. 30-33.

Verse 7. *As a dream*] This is the beginning of the comparison, which is pursued and applied in the next verse. Sennacherib and his mighty army are not compared to a dream because of their sudden disappearance; but the disappointment of their eager hopes is compared to what happens to a hungry and thirsty man, when he awakes from a dream in which fancy had presented to him meat and drink in abundance, and finds it nothing but a vain illusion. The comparison is elegant and beautiful in the highest degree, well wrought up, and perfectly suited to the end proposed. The image is extremely natural, but not obvious: it appeals to our inward feelings, not to our outward senses; and is applied to an event in its concomitant circumstances exactly similar, but in its nature totally different. See *De S. Poës. Hebr.* Prælect. xii. For beauty and ingenuity it may fairly come in competition with one of the most elegant of Virgil, greatly improved from Homer, Iliad xxii. 199, where he has applied to a different purpose, but not so happily, the same image of the ineffectual working of imagination in a dream:—

Ac veluti in somnis, oculos ubi languida pressit
Nocte quies, necquicquam avidos extendere cursus
Velle videmur, et in mediis conatibus ægri
Succidimus; non lingua valet, non corpore notæ
Sufficiunt vires, nec vox, nec verba sequuntur.
Æn., xii. 908.

A. M. cir. 3292
B. C. cir. 712
Olymp. XVII. 1
cir. annum
NumæPompilii,
R. Roman., 4

8 [o]It shall even be as when a
hungry *man* dreameth, and, behold, he eateth; but he awaketh,
and his soul is empty: or as
when a thirsty man dreameth, and, behold, he
drinketh; but he awaketh, and, behold, *he is*
faint, and his soul hath appetite: so shall the
multitude of all the nations be, that fight
against Mount Zion.
9 Stay yourselves, and wonder; [p]cry ye out,
and cry: [q]they are drunken, [r]but not with
wine; they stagger, but not with strong
drink.
10 For [s]the LORD hath poured out upon
you the spirit of deep sleep, and hath [t]closed
your eyes: the prophets and your [u]rulers,
[v]the seers hath he covered.
11 And the vision of all is become unto
you as the words of a [w]book [x]that is sealed,
which *men* deliver to one that is learned, saying, Read this, I pray thee: [y]and he saith, I
cannot; for it *is* sealed.
12 And the book is delivered to him that is
not learned, saying, Read this, I pray
thee; and he saith, I am not
learned.

A. M. cir. 3292
B. C. cir. 712
Olymp. XVII. 1
cir. annum
NumæPompilii,
R. Roman., 4

13 Wherefore the LORD said,
[z]Forasmuch as this people draw
near *me* with their mouth, and with their lips
do honour me, but have removed their heart
far from me, and their fear toward me is
taught by [a]the precept of men:
14 [b]Therefore, behold, [c]I will proceed to
do a marvellous work among this people, *even*
a marvellous work and a wonder: [d]for the
wisdom of their wise *men* shall perish, and the
understanding of their prudent *men* shall be
hid.
15 [e]Wo unto them that seek deep to hide
their counsel from the LORD, and their works
are in the dark, and [f]they say, [g]Who seeth
us? and who knoweth us?
16 Surely your turning of things upside
down shall be esteemed as the potter's clay:
for shall the [h]work say of him that made it,
He made me not? or shall the thing framed
say of him that framed it, He had no understanding?

---

[o]Psa. lxxiii. 20——[p]Or, *take your pleasure and riot*——[q]See chap. xxviii. 7, 8——[r]Chap. li. 21——[s]Rom. xi. 8——[t]Psa. lxix. 23; chap. vi. 10——[u]Heb. *heads;* see chap. iii. 2; Jer. xxvi. 8——[v]1 Samuel ix. 9——[w]Or, *letter*——[x]Chap. viii. 16

[y]Dan. xii. 4, 9; Rev. v. 1–5, 9; vi. 1——[z]Ezek. xxxiii. 31; Matt. xv. 8, 9; Mark vii. 6, 7——[a]Col. ii. 22——[b]Hab. i. 5——[c]Heb. *I will add*——[d]Jer. xlix. 7; Obad. 8; 1 Cor. i. 19——[e]Chap. xxx. 1——[f]Psalm xciv. 7——[g]Ecclus. xxiii. 18——[h]Chap. xlv. 9; Rom. ix. 20

"And as, when slumber seals the closing sight,
The sick wild fancy labours in the night;
Some dreadful visionary foe we shun
With airy strides, but strive in vain to run;
In vain our baffled limbs their powers essay;
We faint, we struggle, sink, and fall away;
Drain'd of our strength, we neither fight nor fly,
And on the tongue the struggling accents die."

PITT.

Lucretius expresses the very same image with Isaiah:—

Ut bibere in somnis sitiens quum quærit, et humor
Non datur, ardorem in membris qui stinguere possit;
Sed laticum simulacra petit, frustraque laborat,
In medioque sitit torrenti flumine potans.

iv. 1091.

As a thirsty man desires to drink in his sleep,
And has no fluid to allay the heat within,
But vainly labours to catch the image of rivers,
And is parched up while fancying that he is drinking at a full stream.

Bishop *Stock's* translation of the prophet's text is both elegant and just:—

"As when a hungry man dreameth; and, lo! he is eating:
And he awaketh; and his appetite is unsatisfied.
And as a thirsty man dreameth; and, lo! he is drinking:
And he awaketh; and, lo! he is faint,
And his appetite craveth."

Lucretius almost copies the original.

All that fight against her and her munition—"And all their armies and their towers"] For צביה ומצדתה *tsobeyha umetsodathah*, I read, with the *Chaldee*, צבאם ומצדתם *tsebaam umetsodatham.*

Verse 9. *Stay yourselves, and wonder*] התמהמהו *hithmahmehu, go on what-what-whatting*, in a state of mental indetermination, till the overflowing scourge take you away. See the note on Psa. cxix. 60.

They are drunken, but not with wine] See note on chap. li. 21.

Verse 11. *I cannot; for it* is *sealed*—"I cannot read it; for it is sealed up."] An ancient MS. and the *Septuagint* have preserved a word here, lost out of the text; לקרות *likroth*, (for לקראות,) αναγνωναι, *read it.*

Verse 13. *The Lord*—"JEHOVAH"] For אדני *Adonai*, sixty-three MSS. of *Kennicott's*, and many of *De Rossi's*, and four editions, read יהוה *Yehovah*, and five MSS. add יהוה.

Kimchi makes some just observations on this verse. *The vision*, meaning the Divine revelation of all the prophets, *is a book or letter that is sealed*—is not easily understood. *This is delivered to one that is learned*—instructed in the law. *Read this; and he saith, I cannot, for it is sealed;* a full proof that he does not wish to know the contents, else he would apply to the prophet to get it explained. See *Kimchi* on the place.

A. M. cir. 3292
B. C. cir. 712
Olymp. XVII. 1
cir. annum
NumæPompilii,
R. Roman., 4

17 *Is* it not yet a very little
while, and [i]Lebanon shall be
turned into a fruitful field, and
the fruitful field shall be esteemed as a forest?
18 And [k]in that day shall the deaf hear
the words of the book, and the eyes of the
blind shall see out of obscurity, and out of
darkness.
19 [l]The meek also [m]shall increase *their*
joy in the LORD, and [n]the poor among men
shall rejoice in the Holy One of Israel.
20 For the terrible one is brought to nought,
and [o]the scorner is consumed, and all that
[p]watch for iniquity are cut off:
21 That make a man an offender for a word,
and [q]lay a snare for him that reproveth in the gate, and turn
aside the just [r]for a thing of
nought.
22 Therefore thus saith the LORD, [s]who
redeemed Abraham, concerning the house of
Jacob, Jacob shall not now be ashamed, neither shall his face now wax pale.
23 But when he seeth his children, [t]the
work of mine hands, in the midst of him,
they shall sanctify my name, and sanctify the
Holy One of Jacob, and shall fear the God
of Israel.
24 They [u]also that erred in spirit [v]shall
come to understanding, and they that murmured shall learn doctrine.

[i]Chap. xxxii. 15——[k]Chap. xxxv. 5——[l]Chap. lxi. 1 [m]Heb. *shall add*——[n]James ii. 5——[o]Chap. xxviii. 14, 22——[p]Mic. ii. 1——[q]Amos v. 10, 12

[r]Prov. xxviii. 21——[s]Josh. xxiv. 3——[t]Chap. xix. 25; xlv. 11; lx. 21; Eph. ii. 10——[u]Chap. xxviii. 7——[v]Heb. *shall know understanding*

And their fear toward me is taught by the precept of men—"And vain is their fear of me, teaching the commandments of men"] I read, for ותהי *vattehi*, ותהו *vethohu*, with the *Septuagint*, Matt. xv. 9; Mark viii. 7; and for מלמדה *melummedah*, מלמדים *melummedim*, with the *Chaldee*.

Verse 17. *And Lebanon shall be turned into a fruitful field*—"Ere Lebanon become like Carmel"] A mashal, or proverbial saying, expressing any great revolution of things; and, when respecting two subjects, an entire reciprocal change: explained here by some interpreters, I think with great probability, as having its principal view beyond the revolutions then near at hand, to the rejection of the Jews, and the calling of the Gentiles. The first were the vineyard of God, כרם אל *kerem El*, (if the prophet, who loves an allusion to words of like sounds, may be supposed to have intended one here,) cultivated and watered by him in vain, to be given up, and to become a wilderness: compare chap. v. 1-7. The last had been hitherto barren; but were, by the grace of God, to be rendered fruitful. See Matt. xxi. 43; Rom. xi. 30, 31. Carmel stands here opposed to Lebanon, and therefore is to be taken as a proper name.

Verse 21. *Him that reproveth in the gate*—"Him that pleaded in the gate"] "They are heard by the treasurer, master of the horse, and other principal officers of the regency of Algiers, who sit constantly in the gate of the palace for that purpose:" that is, the distribution of justice.—*Shaw's* Travels, p. 315, fol. He adds in the note, "That we read of the *elders in the gate*. Deut. xxi. 15; xxv. 7; and, Isa. xxix. 21; Amos v. 10, of *him that reproveth* and *rebuketh in the gate*. The Ottoman court likewise seems to have been called *the Porte*, from the distribution of justice and the despatch of public business that is carried on in the gates of it."

Verse 22. *Who redeemed Abraham*] As God redeemed Abraham from among idolaters and workers of iniquity, so will he redeem those who hear the words of the Book, and are humbled before him, ver. 18, 19.

Concerning the house of Jacob—"The God of the house of Jacob"] I read אל *El* as a noun, not a preposition: the parallel line favours this sense; and there is no address to the house of Jacob to justify the other.

Neither shall his face now wax pale—"His face shall no more be covered with confusion."] "יחורו *yechoro*, Chald. *ut* ὁ *μεταβαλει*, Theod. *εντραπησεται*, Syr. נחפרו *necaphro, videtur legendum* יחפרו *yechepheru: hic enim solum legitur verbum*, חור *chavar, nec in linguis affinibus habet pudoris significationem*."—SECKER. "Here alone is the verb חור *chavar* read; nor has it in the cognate languages the signification of *shame*."

Verse 23. *But when he seeth his children, the work of mine hands*—"For when his children shall see the work of my hands"] For בראותו *birotho* I read בראות *biroth*, with the *Septuagint* and *Syriac*.

CHAPTER XXX

The Jews reproved for their reliance on Egypt, 1–7. *Threatened for their obstinate adherence to this alliance*, 8–17. *Images the most elegant and lofty, by which the intense gloriousness of Messiah's reign at the period when* all Israel *shall be added to the Church is beautifully set forth*, 18–26. *Dreadful fall of Sennacherib's army, an event most manifestly typical of the terrible and sudden overthrow of Antichrist; as, unless this typical reference be admitted, no possible connexion can be imagined between the stupendous events which took place in Hezekiah's reign, and the very remote and inconceivably more glorious displays of Divine vengeance and mercy in the days of the Messiah*, 27–33.

A. M. cir. 3291
B. C. cir. 713
Olymp. XVI. 4
cir. annum
NumæPompilii,
R. Roman., 3

WO to the rebellious children, saith the LORD, [a]that take counsel, but not of me; and that cover with a covering, but not of my spirit, [b]that they may add sin to sin:

2 [c]That walk to go down into Egypt, and [d]have not asked at my mouth; to strengthen themselves in the strength of Pharaoh, and to trust in the shadow of Egypt!

3 [e]Therefore shall the strength of Pharaoh be your shame, and the trust in the shadow of Egypt *your* confusion.

4 For his princes were at [f]Zoan, and his ambassadors came to Hanes.

5 [g]They were all ashamed of a people *that* could not profit them, nor be a help nor profit, but a shame, and also a reproach.

6 [h]The burden of the beasts of the south: into the land of trouble and anguish, from whence *come* the young and old lion, [i]the viper and fiery flying serpent, they will carry their riches upon the shoulders of young asses, and their treasures upon the bunches of camels, to a people *that* shall not profit *them.*

A. M. cir. 3291
B. C. cir. 713
Olymp. XVI. 4
cir. annum
NumæPompilii,
R. Roman., 3

7 [k]For the Egyptians shall help in vain, and to no purpose: therefore have I cried [l]concerning this, [m]Their strength *is* to sit still.

8 Now go, [n]write it before them in a table, and note it in a book, that it may be for [o]the time to come for ever and ever:

9 That [p]this *is* a rebellious people, lying children, children *that* will not hear the law of the LORD:

10 [q]Which say to the seers, See not; and to the prophets, Prophesy not unto us right things, [r]speak unto us smooth things, prophesy deceits:

11 Get you out of the way, turn aside out of the path, cause the Holy One of Israel to cease from before us.

12 Wherefore thus saith the Holy One of Israel, Because ye despise this word, and trust in [s]oppression and perverseness, and stay thereon:

[a]Chap. xxix. 15——[b]Deut. xxix. 19——[c]Chap. xxxi. 1 [d]Num. xxvii. 21; Josh. ix. 14; 1 Kings xxii. 7; Jer. xxi. 2; xlii. 2, 20——[e]Chap. xx. 5; Jer. xxxvii. 5, 7——[f]Chap. xix. 11——[g]Jer. ii. 36——[h]Chap. lvii. 9; Hos. viii. 9; xii. 1——[i]Deut. viii. 15

[k]Jeremiah xxxvii. 7——[l]Or, *to her*——[m]Verse 15; chapter vii. 4——[n]Habakkuk ii. 2——[o]Hebrew, *the latter day*——[p]Deuteronomy xxxii. 20; chapter i. 4; verse 1——[q]Jeremiah xi. 21; Amos ii. 12; vii. 13; Mic. ii. 6——[r]1 Kings xxii. 13; Mic. ii. 11——[s]Or, *fraud*

NOTES ON CHAP. XXX

Verse 1. *And that cover with a covering*—"Who ratify covenants"] Heb. "Who pour out a libation." Sacrifice and libation were ceremonies constantly used, in ancient times by most nations in the ratifying of covenants: a libation therefore is used for a covenant, as in Greek the word σπονδη, for the same reason, stands for both. This seems to be the most easy explication of the Hebrew phrase, and it has the authority of the *Septuagint*, εποιησατε συνθηκας.

Verse 4. *Hanes*] Six MSS. of *Kennicott's*, and perhaps six others, with four of *De Rossi's*, read חנם *chinnam, in vain*, for הנם *Hanes;* and so also the *Septuagint*, who read likewise יגעו *yageu, laboured*, for יגיעו *yaggiu, arrived at.*

Verse 5. *Were—ashamed*] Eight MSS. (one ancient) of *Kennicott's*, and ten of *De Rossi's*, read הביש *hobish*, without א *aleph.* So the *Chaldee* and *Vulgate.*

But a shame—"But proved even a shame"] Four MSS. (three ancient) after כי *ki*, add אם *im, unless*, which seems wanted to complete the phrase in its usual form.

Verse 6. *The burden*] משא *massa* seems here to be taken in its proper sense; the *load*, not the *oracle.* The same subject is continued; and there seems to be no place here for a new title to a distinct prophecy.

Does not *burden of the beasts of the South* in this place relate to the *presents* sent by Hoshea king of Israel to the *South*—to Egypt, which lay *south* of Judea, to engage the Egyptians to succour him against the king of Assyria?

Into the land of trouble and anguish—"Through a land of distress and difficulty"] The same deserts are here spoken of which the Israelites passed through when they came out of Egypt, which Moses describes, Deut. viii. 15, as "that great and terrible wilderness wherein were fiery serpents, and scorpions, and drought; where there was no water." And which was designed to be a kind of barrier between them and Egypt, of which the Lord had said, "Ye shall henceforth return no more that way," Deut. xvii. 16.

Shall not profit them] A MS. adds in the margin the word למו *lamo, them*, which seems to have been lost out of the text: it is authorized by the *Septuagint* and *Vulgate.*

Verse 7. *Their strength is to sit still*—"Rahab the Inactive."] The two last words, הם שבת *hem shabeth*, joined into one, make the participle pihel המשבת *hammeshabbeth.* I find the learned Professor Doederlein, in his version of Isaiah, and note on this place, has given the same conjecture; which he speaks of as having been formerly published by him. A concurrence of different persons in the same conjecture adds to it a greater degree of probability.

Verse 8. *For ever and ever*—"For a testimony for ever"] לעד *leed.* So the *Syriac, Chaldee, Vulgate*, and *Septuagint*, in MSS. Pachom. and I. D. II. εις μαρτυριον, which two words have been lost out of the other copies of the *Septuagint.*

Verse 12. *In oppression*—"In obliquity"] בעקש *beakesh*, transposing the two last letters of בעשק *beoshek, in oppression*, which seems not to belong to this place: a very probable conjecture of Houbigant.

A. M. cir. 3291 B. C. cir. 713 Olymp. XVI. 4 cir. annum NumæPompilii, R. Roman., 3

13 Therefore this iniquity shall
be to you [t]as a breach ready to
fall, swelling out in a high wall,
whose breaking [u]cometh suddenly at an instant.

14 And [v]he shall break it as the breaking
of [w]the potters' vessel that is broken in pieces; he shall not spare: so that there shall
not be found in the bursting of it a shred to
take fire from the hearth, or to take water
withal out of the pit.

15 For thus saith the Lord GOD, the Holy
One of Israel; [x]In returning and rest shall ye
be saved; in quietness and in confidence shall
be your strength: [y]and ye would not.

16 But ye said, No; for we will flee upon
horses; therefore shall ye flee: and, We will
ride upon the swift; therefore shall they that
pursue you be swift.

17 [z]One thousand *shall flee* at the rebuke
of one; at the rebuke of five shall ye flee:
till ye be left as [a]a beacon upon
the top of a mountain, and as an
ensign on a hill.

A. M. cir. 3291 B. C. cir. 713 Olymp. XVI. 4 cir. annum NumæPompilii, R. Roman., 3

18 And therefore will the LORD
wait, that he may be gracious unto you, and
therefore will he be exalted, that he may have
mercy upon you: for the LORD *is* a God of
judgment: [b]blessed *are* all they that wait
for him.

19 For the people [c]shall dwell in Zion at
Jerusalem: thou shalt weep no more: he will
be very gracious unto thee at the voice of thy
cry; when he shall hear it, he will answer
thee.

20 And *though* the LORD give you [d]the bread
of adversity, and the water of [e]affliction, yet
shall not thy [f]teachers be removed into a
corner any more, but thine eyes shall see thy
teachers:

21 And thine ears shall hear a word behind
thee, saying, This *is* the way, walk ye in it,

---

[t]Psa. lxii. 3——[u]Chap. xxix. 5——[v]Psa. ii. 9; Jer. xix. 11——[w]Heb. *the bottle of potters*——[x]Ver. 7; chap. vii. 4——[y]Matt. xxiii. 37——[z]Rev. xxvi. 8; Deut. xxviii. 25; xxxii. 30; Josh. xxiii. 10

[a]Or, *a tree bereft of branches* or *boughs;* or, *a mast*
[b]Psa. ii. 12; xxxiv. 8; Prov. xvi. 20; Jer. xvii. 7——[c]Ch. lxv. 9——[d]1 Kings xxii. 27; Psa. cxxvii. 2——[e]Or, *oppression*——[f]Psa. lxxiv. 9; Amos viii. 11

Verse 13. *Swelling out in a high wall*—"A swelling in a high wall"] It has been observed before, that the buildings of Asia generally consist of little better than what we call mud walls. "All the houses at Ispahan," says Thevenot, Vol. II., p. 159, "are built of bricks made of clay and straw, and dried in the sun; and covered with a plaster made of a fine white stone. In other places in Persia the houses are built with nothing else but such bricks, made with tempered clay and chopped straw, well mingled together, and dried in the sun, and then used: but the least rain dissolves them." Sir John Chardin's MS. remark on this place of Isaiah is very apposite: Murs en Asie etant faits de terre se fendent ainsi par milieu et de haut en bas. "The walls in Asia being made of earth often cleave from top to bottom." This shows clearly how obvious and expressive the image is. The psalmist has in the same manner made use of it, to express sudden and utter destruction:—

"Ye shall be slain all of you;
Ye shall be like an inclining wall, like a shattered fence." Psa. lxii. 4.

Verse 14. *He shall not spare*—"And spareth it not"] Five MSS. add the conjunction ו *vau* to the negative; ולא *velo.*

Verse 17. *At the rebuke of five shall ye flee*—"At the rebuke of five, ten thousand of you shall flee"] In the second line of this verse a word is manifestly omitted, which should answer to *one thousand* in the first: the *Septuagint* supply πολλοι, רבים *rabbim.* But the true word is רבבה *rebabah,* as I am persuaded any one will be convinced, who will compare the following passages with this place:—

"How should one chase a thousand;
And two put ten thousand (רבבה) to flight?" Deut. xxxii. 30.

"And five of you shall chase a hundred;
And a hundred of you shall chase (רבבה) ten thousand." Lev. xxvi. 8.

Verse 18. *And therefore will he be exalted*—"Even for this shall he expect in silence"] For ירום *yarum, he shall be exalted,* which belongs not to this place, Houbigant reads ידום *yadum, he shall be silent:* and so it seems to be in a MS. Another MS. instead of it reads ישוב *yashub, he shall return.* The mistakes occasioned by the similitude of the letters ד *daleth* and ר *resh* are very frequent, as the reader may have already observed.

Verse 19. *For the people shall dwell in Zion*—"When a holy people shall dwell in Sion"] Λαος ἁγιος, *Septuagint;* עם קדוש *am kadosh.* The word קדוש *kadosh,* lost out of the text, but happily supplied by the *Septuagint,* clears up the sense, otherwise extremely obscure. When the rest of the cities of the land were taken by the king of Assyria, Zion was preserved, and all that were in it.

Thou shalt weep no more—"Thou shalt implore him with weeping"] The negative particle לא *lo* is not acknowledged by the *Septuagint.* It may perhaps have been written by mistake for לו *lo, to him,* of which there are many examples.

Verse 20. Though *the Lord*—"Though JEHOVAH"] For אדני *Adonai,* sixteen MSS. and three editions have יהוה *Yehovah;* many of *De Rossi's* have the same reading; all my own have יהוה *Yehovah.*

Verse 21. *When ye turn to the right hand,*

A. M. cir. 3291 B. C. cir. 713 Olymp. XVI. 4 cir. annum NumæPompilii, R. Roman., 3

when ye [g]turn to the right hand, and when ye turn to the left.

22 [h]Ye shall defile also the covering of [i]thy graven images of silver, and the ornament of thy molten images of gold: thou shalt [k]cast them away as a menstruous cloth; [l]thou shalt say unto it, Get thee hence.

23 [m]Then shall he give the rain of thy seed, that thou shalt sow the ground withal; and bread of the increase of the earth, and it shall be fat and plenteous: in that day shall thy cattle feed in large pastures.

24 The oxen likewise and the young asses that ear the ground shall eat [n]clean [o]provender, which hath been winnowed with the shovel and with the fan.

25 And there shall be [p]upon every high mountain, and upon every [q]high hill, rivers *and* streams of waters in the day of the great slaughter, when the towers fall.

A. M. cir. 3291 B. C. cir. 713 Olymp. XVI. 4 cir. annum NumæPompilii, R. Roman., 3

26 Moreover [r]the light of the moon shall be as the light of the sun, and the light of the sun shall be sevenfold, as the light of seven days, in the day that the LORD bindeth up the breach of his people, and healeth the stroke of their wound.

27 Behold, the name of the LORD cometh from far, burning *with* his anger, [s]and the burden *thereof is* [t]heavy: his lips are full of indignation, and his tongue as a devouring fire:

28 And [u]his breath, as an overflowing stream, [v]shall reach to the midst of the neck, to sift the nations with the sieve of vanity: and *there shall be* [w]a bridle in the jaws of the people, causing *them* to err.

---

[g]Josh. i. 7——[h]2 Chron. xxxi. 1; chap. ii. 20; xxxi. 7 [i]Heb. *the graven images of thy silver*——[k]Heb. *scatter* [l]Hos. xiv. 8——[m]Matt. vi. 33; 1 Tim. iv. 8——[n]Or, *savoury*——[o]Heb. *leavened*

[p]Chap. ii. 14, 15; xliv. 3——[q]Heb. *lifted up*——[r]Ch. lx. 19, 20——[s]Or, *and the grievousness of flame*——[t]Heb. *heaviness*——[u]Chap. xi. 4; 2 Thess. ii. 8——[v]Chap. viii. 8——[w]Chap. xxxvii. 29

---

and when ye turn to the left—"Turn not aside, to the right or to the left."] The *Syriac*, *Chaldee*, and *Vulgate*, translate as if, instead of כי—וכי *ki—vechi*, they read לא—ולא *lo—velo*.

Verse 22. *Ye shall defile*—"Ye shall treat as defiled"] The very prohibition of Moses, Deut. vii. 25, only thrown out of the prose into the poetical form: "The graven images of their gods ye shall burn with fire: thou shalt not desire the silver or the gold that is on them; nor take it unto thee, lest thou be snared therein; for it is an abomination to JEHOVAH thy God."

Verse 25. *When the towers fall*—"When the mighty fall."] מגדלים *migdalim*, *μεγαλους*, *Sym.; μεγαλυνομενους*, *Aquila;* רברבין *rabrebin*, *Chald.;* all signifying *mighty ones*.

Verse 26. *Shall be sevenfold*] The text adds כאור שבעת הימים *keor shibath haiyamayim*, "as the light of seven days," a manifest gloss, taken in from the margin; it is not in most of the copies of the *Septuagint*. It interrupts the rhythmical construction, and obscures the sense by a false, or at least an unnecessary, interpretation.

By *moon, sun, light*, are to be understood the abundance of spiritual and temporal felicity, with which God should bless them in the days of the Messiah, which should be sevenfold, i. e., vastly exceed all that they had ever before possessed.

Verse 27. *And the burden* thereof is *heavy*—"And the flame raged violently"] משאה *massaah;* this word seems to be rightly rendered in our translation, *the flame*, Judg. xx. 38, 40, &c.; a sign of *fire*, Jer. vi. 1; called properly משאת *masseeth*, *an elevation*, from its tending upwards.

Verse 28. *To sift the nations with a sieve of vanity*—"To toss the nations with the van of perdition"] The word להנפה *lahanaphah* is in its form very irregular. *Kimchi* says it is for להניף *lehaniph*. *Houbigant* supposes it to be a mistake, and shows the cause of it; the joining it to the ה *he*, which should begin the following word. The true reading is להניף הגוים *lehaniph haggoyim*, "to sift the nations."

The *Vulgate* seems to be the only one of the ancient interpreters who has explained rightly the sense; but he has dropped the image: ad perdendas gentes in nihilum, "to reduce the nations to nothing." *Kimchi's* explanation is to the following effect: "נפה *naphah* is a van with which they winnow corn; and its use is to cleanse the corn from the chaff and straw: but the van with which God will winnow the nations will be the van of emptiness or perdition; for nothing useful shall remain behind, but all shall come to nothing, and perish. In like manner, a bridle is designed to guide the horse in the right way; but the bridle which God will put in the jaws of the people shall not direct them aright, but shall make them err, and lead them into destruction." This latter image the prophet has applied to the same subject afterwards, ch. xxxvii. 29:—

"I will put my bridle in thy jaws,
And turn thee back by the way in which thou camest."

And as for the former it is to be observed, that the van of the ancients was a large instrument, somewhat like a shovel, with a long handle, with which they tossed the corn mixed with the chaff and chopped straw into the air, that the wind might separate them. See *Hammond* on Matt. iii. 12.

There shall be *a bridle in the jaws*] A metaphor taken from a headstrong, unruly horse: the bridle checks, restrains, and directs him.

A. M. cir. 3291 B. C. cir. 713 Olymp. XVI. 4 cir. annum NumæPompilii, R. Roman., 3

29 Ye shall have a song, as
in the night [x]*when* a holy solemnity is kept; and gladness of
heart, as when one goeth with
a pipe to come into the [y]mountain of the
LORD, to the [z]mighty One of Israel.

30 [a]And the LORD shall cause [b]his glorious
voice to be heard, and shall show the lighting
down of his arm, with the indignation of *his*
anger, and *with* the flame of a devouring fire,
with scattering, and tempest, [c]and hailstones.

31 For [d]through the voice of the LORD shall
the Assyrian be beaten down,
[e]*which* smote with a rod.

32 And [f]*in* every place where
the grounded staff shall pass,
which the LORD shall [g]lay upon him, *it* shall
be with tabrets and harps: and in battles of
[h]shaking will he fight [i]with it.

33 [k]For Tophet *is* ordained [l]of old; yea,
for the king it is prepared; he hath made *it*
deep *and* large; the pile thereof *is* fire and
much wood: the breath of the LORD, like a
stream of brimstone, doth kindle it.

---

[x]Psa. xlii. 4——[y]Chap. ii. 3——[z]Heb. *Rock;* Deut. xxxii. 4——[a]Chap. xxix. 6——[b]Heb. *the glory of his voice* [c]Chap. xxviii. 2; xxxii. 19——[d]Chap. xxxvii. 36 [e]Chap. x. 5, 24

[f]Heb. *every passing of the rod founded*——[g]Heb. *cause to rest upon him*——[h]Chap. xi. 15; xix. 16——[i]Or, *against them*——[k]Jeremiah vii. 31; xix. 6, &c.——[l]Heb. *from yesterday*

What the true God does in restraining sinners, has been also attributed to the false gods of the heathen. Thus *Æschylus*, prom. Vinct. 691:—

αλλ' επηναγκαζε νιν
Διος χαλινος προς βιαν πρασσειν ταδε.

"But the bridle of Jupiter violently constrained him to do these things."

Verse 30. *The Lord shall cause his glorious voice to be heard*] *Kimchi* understands this of the great destruction of the Assyrian host by the angel of the Lord. Instead of בזעף אץ *bezaaph ats*, "with swift anger," five of Dr. *Kennicott's* MSS. and one of my own, read בזעם אף *bezaam aph*, "with detestation indignant." For אץ *ats*, "swift," which is the common reading, forty-two of *Kennicott's*, forty-three of *De Rossi's*, and two of my own, have אף *aph*, "wrath or fury." The former reading, אץ *ats*, is not found in any Bible previously to that of *Van der Hooght*, in 1705; and there it seems to be a typographical mistake.

Verse 31. Which *smote with a rod*—"He that was ready to smite with his staff"] "Post אשור *ashshur*, forte excidit אשר *asher*."—SECKER. After אשור *ashshur*, probably אשר *asher*, "which," has been omitted.

Verse 32. *The grounded staff*—"The rod of his correction"] For מוסדה *musadah*, the *grounded* staff, of which no one yet has been able to make any tolerable sense, Le Clerc conjectured מוסרה *musarah, of correction;* (see Prov. xxii. 15;) and so it is in two MSS., (one of them ancient,) and seems to be so in the Bodleian MS. The *Syriac* has דשועבדה *deshuebedah, virgo domans, vel subjectionis,*—"the taming rod, or rod of subjection."

With tabrets and harps] With every demonstration of joy and thanksgiving for the destruction of the enemy in so wonderful a manner: with hymns of praise, accompanied with musical instruments. See ver. 29.

With it—"Against them."] For בה *bah, against her*, fifty-two MSS. and five editions read בם *bam, against them.*

Verse 33. *For Tophet* is *ordained*] Tophet is a valley very near to Jerusalem, to the southeast, called also the valley of Hinnom or Gehenna; where the Canaanites, and afterwards the Israelites, sacrificed their children, by making them pass through the fire, that is, by burning them in the fire, to Molech, as some suppose. It is therefore used for a place of punishment by fire; and by our blessed Saviour in the Gospel for hell-fire, as the Jews themselves had applied it. See Chald. on Isa. xxxiii. 14, where מוקדי עלם *mokedey olam* is rendered "the Gehenna of everlasting fire." Here the place where the Assyrian army was destroyed is called Tophet by a metonymy; for the Assyrian army was destroyed probably at a greater distance from Jerusalem, and quite on the opposite side of it: for Nob is mentioned as the last station, from which the king of Assyria should threaten Jerusalem, chap. x. 32, where the prophet seems to have given a very exact chorographical description of his march in order to attack the city; which however he never reached.—L.

CHAPTER XXXI

The Jews again reproved for their confidence in Egypt, finely contrasted with their neglect of the power and protection of God, 1–3. *Deliverance and protection are, notwithstanding, promised, expressed by two similes; the first remarkably lofty and poetical, the latter singularly beautiful and tender,* 4, 5. *Exhortation to repentance, joined with the prediction of a more reformed period,* 6, 7. *This chapter concludes like the preceding, with a prophecy of the fall of Sennacherib,* 8, 9.

A. M. cir. 3291
B. C. cir. 713
Olymp. XVI. 4
cir. annum
NumæPompilii,
R. Roman., 3

WO to them [a]that go down to
Egypt for help; and [b]stay
on horses, and trust in chariots,
because *they are* many; and in
horsemen, because they are very strong; but
they look not unto the Holy One of Israel,
[c]neither seek the LORD!
2 Yet he also *is* wise, and will bring evil,
and [d]will not [e]call back his words: but will
arise against the house of the evil-doers, and
against the help of them that work iniquity.
3 Now the Egyptians *are* [f]men, and not
God; and their horses flesh, and not spirit.
When the LORD shall stretch out his hand,
both he that helpeth shall fall,
and he that is holpen shall fall
down, and they all shall fail
together.

A. M. cir. 3291
B. C. cir. 713
Olymp. XVI. 4
cir. annum
NumæPompilii,
R. Roman., 3

4 For thus hath the LORD spoken unto me,
[g]Like as the lion, and the young lion roaring
on his prey, when a multitude of shepherds
is called forth against him, *he* will not be
afraid of their voice, nor abase himself for the
[h]noise of them: [i]so shall the LORD of hosts
come down to fight for Mount Zion, and for
the hill thereof.
5 [k]As birds flying, so will the LORD of hosts
defend Jerusalem; defending [l]also he will

[a]Chap. xxx. 2; xxxvi. 6; Ezek. xvii. 15——[b]Psa. xx. 7; chap. xxxvi. 9——[c]Dan. ix. 13; Hos. vii. 7——[d]Num. xxiii. 19——[e]Heb. *remove*

[f]Psa. cxlvi. 3, 5——[g]Hos. xi. 10; Amos iii. 8——[h]Or, *multitude*——[i]Chap. xlii. 13——[k]Deut. xxxii. 11; Psa. xci. 4——[l]Psa. xxxvii. 40

NOTES ON CHAP. XXXI

Verse 1. *Wo to them that go down to Egypt*] This is a reproof to the Israelites for forming an alliance with the Egyptians, and not trusting in the Lord.

And stay on horses—"Who trust in horses"] For ועל *veal, and upon,* first twenty MSS. of *Kennicott's*, thirty of *De Rossi's*, one of my own, and the *Septuagint*, *Arabic*, and *Vulgate*, read על *al, upon,* without the conjunction, which disturbs the sense.

Verse 2. *His words*—"His word"] דברו *debaro, singular,* without י *yod,* two MSS. of Dr. *Kennicott's*, the *Septuagint*, and *Targ. Hieros.* דרכיו *derachaiv, his ways,* is found in one MS.

Verse 3. *He that helpeth* (the Egyptians) *shall fall, and he that is holpen* (the Israelites) *shall fall down—together.*

Verse 4. *Like as the lion*] This comparison is exactly in the spirit and manner, and very nearly approaching to the expression, of *Homer.*

Βη ρ' ιμεν, ὡστε λεων ορεσιτροφος, ὁστ' επιδευης
Δηρον εῃ κρειων, κελεται δε ἑ θυμος αγηνωρ,
Μηλων πειρησοντα, και ες πυκινον δομον ελθειν·
Ειπερ γαρ χ' εὑρῃσι παρ' αυτοψι βωτορας ανδρας
Συν κυσι και δουρεσσι φυλασσοντας περι μηλα,
Ου ρα τ' απειρητος μεμονε σταθμοιο διεσθαι.
Αλλ' ὁγ' αῥ η ἡρπαξε μεταλμενος, ηε και αυτος
Εβλητ' εν πρωτοισι θοης απο χειρος ακοντι.
Iliad xii. 299.

As the bold lion, mountain-bred, now long
Famished, with courage and with hunger stung
Attempts the thronged fold: him nought appals,
Though dogs and armed shepherds stand in guard
Collected; he nathless undaunted springs
O'er the high fence, and rends the trembling prey;
Or, rushing onward, in his breast receives
The well-aimed spear.

Of metaphors, allegories, and comparisons of the Hebrew poets, in which the Divine nature and attributes are represented under images taken from brutes and other low objects; of their effect, their sublimity, and the causes of it; see *De Sac. Poës. Heb.*, Prælect. xvi. sub. fin.

Verse 5. *Passing over*—"Leaping forward"] The generality of interpreters observe in this place an allusion to the deliverance which God vouchsafed to his people when he destroyed the first-born of the Egyptians, and exempted those of the Israelites sojourning among them by a peculiar interposition. The same word is made use of here which is used upon that occasion, and which gave the name to the feast which was instituted in commemoration of that deliverance, פסח *pesach.* But the difficulty is to reconcile the commonly received meaning of that word with the circumstances of the similitude here used to illustrate the deliverance represented as parallel to the deliverance in Egypt.

"As the mother birds hovering over their young,
So shall JEHOVAH God of hosts protect Jerusalem;
Protecting and delivering, *passing over,* and rescuing her."

This difficulty is, I think, well solved by Vitringa, whose remark is the more worthy of observation, as it leads to the true meaning of an important word, which hitherto seems greatly to have been misunderstood, though Vitringa himself, as it appears to me, has not exactly enough defined the precise meaning of it. He says, "פסח *pasach* signifies *to cover, to protect by covering; σκεπασω ὑμας, Septuagint.* JEHOVAH *obteget ostium;* 'The Lord will cover or protect the door:'" whereas it means that particular action or motion by which God at that time placed himself in such a situation as to protect the house of the Israelite against the destroying angel; to spring forward, to throw one's self in the way, in order to cover and protect. *Cocceius* comes nearer to the true meaning than Vitringa, by rendering it *gradum facere,* to march, to step forward; *Lexicon* in voc. The common meaning of the word פסח *pasach* upon other occasions is *to halt, to be lame, to leap,* as in a rude manner of dancing, (as the prophets of Baal did, 1 Kings xviii. 26,) all which agrees very well together; for the motion of a lame person is a perpetual springing forward,

A. M. cir. 3291 B. C. cir. 713 Olymp. XVI. 4 cir. annum NumæPompilii, R. Roman., 3

deliver *it; and* passing over he
will preserve *it*.
6 Turn ye unto *him from*
whom the children of Israel have
[m]deeply revolted.
7 For in that day every man shall [n]cast away
his idols of silver, and [o]his idols of gold,
which your own hands have made unto you
for [p]a sin.
8 Then shall the Assyrian [q]fall with the
sword, not of a mighty man;
and the sword, not of a mean
man, shall devour him: but he
shall flee [r]from the sword, and
his young men shall be [s]discomfited.[t]
9 And [u]he [v]shall pass over to [w]his
strong hold for fear, and his princes shall
be afraid of the ensign, saith the LORD,
whose fire *is* in Zion, and his furnace in
Jerusalem.

[m]Hos. ix. 9——[n]Chap. ii. 20; xxx. 22——[o]Heb. *the idols of his gold*——[p]1 Kings xii. 30——[q]See 2 Kings xix. 35, 36; ch. xxxvii. 36——[r]Or, *for fear of the sword*

[s]Or, *tributary*——[t]Heb. *for melting* or *tribute*——[u]Ch. xxxvii. 37; Deut. xxii. 25, in the margin——[v]Heb. *his rock shall pass away for fear*——[w]Or, *his strength*

by throwing himself from the weaker upon the stronger leg. The common notion of God's passage over the houses of the Israelites is, that in going through the land of Egypt to smite the first-born, seeing the blood on the door of the houses of the Israelites, he passed over, or skipped, those houses, and forbore to smite them. But that this is not the true notion of the thing, will be plain from considering the words of the sacred historian, where he describes very explicitly the action: "For JEHOVAH will pass through to smite the Egyptians; and when he seeth the blood on the lintels and on the two side posts, JEHOVAH will spring forward over (or before) the door, ופסח יהוה על הפתח *upasach Yehovah al happethach*, and will not suffer the destroyer to come into your houses to smite *you*," Exod. xii. 23. Here are manifestly two distinct agents, with which the notion of *passing over* is not consistent, for that supposes but one agent. The two agents are the destroying angel passing through to smite every house, and JEHOVAH the Protector keeping pace with him; and who, seeing the door of the Israelite marked with the blood, the token prescribed, *leaps forward, throws himself with a sudden motion in the way*, opposes the destroying angel, and *covers* and *protects* that house against the destroying angel, nor suffers him to smite it. In this way of considering the action, the beautiful similitude of the bird protecting her young answers exactly to the application by the allusion to the deliverance in Egypt. As the mother bird spreads her wings to cover her young, throws herself before them, and opposes the rapacious bird that assaults them, so shall JEHOVAH protect, as with a shield, Jerusalem from the enemy, protecting and delivering, *springing forward* and rescuing her; ὑπερβαινων, as the three other Greek interpreters, *Aquila*, *Symmachus*, and *Theodotion*, render it. The *Septuagint*, περιποιησεται· instead of which MS. *Pachom.* has περιβησεται, circumeundo proteget, "in going about he shall protect," which I think is the true reading.—*Homer*, Il. viii. 329, expresses the very same image by this word:—

Αιας δ' ουκ αμελησε κασιγνητοιο πεσοντος,
Αλλα θεων περιβη, και οἱ σακος αμφεκαλυψε:

"——But Ajax his broad shield displayed,
And screened his brother with a mighty shade."

——'Ος Χρυσην αμφιβεβηκας. Il. i. 37.

Which the scholiast explains by περιβεβηκας, ὑπερμαχεις, i. e., "Thou who *strictly guardest* Chryses."—L. On this verse *Kimchi* says, "The angel of the Lord which destroyed the Assyrians is compared to a *lion*, ver. 4, for his *strength;* and here (ver. 5) to *flying birds*, for his *swiftness*.

Verse 6. *Have deeply revolted*—"Have so deeply engaged in revolt."] All the ancient Versions read תעמיקו *taamiku*, in the second person, instead of העמיקו *heemiku, they have deeply revolted*, &c.

Verse 7. *Which your own hands have made unto you* for *a sin*—"The sin, which their own hands have made."] The construction of the word חטא *chet*, *sin*, in this place is not easy. The *Septuagint* have omitted it: MSS. *Pachom.* and I. D. II. and *Cod. Marchal.* in margine, supply the omission by the word ἁμαρτιαν, *sin*, or ἁμαρτημα, said to be from Aquila's Version, which I have followed. The learned Professor *Schroeder*, Institut. Ling. Heb. p. 298, makes it to be *in regimine* with ידיכם *yedeychem*, as an epithet, your *sinful hands*. The *Septuagint* render the pronoun in the third person, αἱ χειρες αυτων, *their hands;* and an ancient MS. has, agreeable to that rendering, להם *lahem, to them*, for לכם *lachem, to you;* which word they have likewise omitted, as not necessary to complete the sense.

Verse 8. *Then shall the Assyrian fall, &c.*] Because he was to be discomfited by the angel of the Lord, destroying in his camp, in one night, upwards of *one hundred and eighty thousand* men; and Sennacherib himself fell by the hands of the princes, his own sons. Not *mighty men*, for they were not soldiers; not *mean men*, for they were *princes*.

CHAPTER XXXII

Prophecy of great prosperity under Hezekiah; but, in its highest sense, applicable to Christ, 1–8. *Description of impending calamities*, 9–14. *Rejection of the Jews, and calling of the Gentiles*, 15. *The future prosperity of the Church*, 16–20.

A. M. cir. 3291
B. C. cir. 713
Olymp. XVI. 4
cir. annum
NumæPompilii,
R. Roman., 3

BEHOLD, a [a]king shall reign
in righteousness, and princes
shall rule in judgment.
2 And a man shall be as a hiding-place from the wind, and [b]a covert from
the tempest; as rivers of water in a dry place,
as the shadow of a [c]great rock in a weary land.
3 And [d]the eyes of them that see shall not be
dim, and the ears of them that hear shall
hearken.
4 The heart also of the [e]rash shall understand knowledge, and the tongue of the stam-
merers shall be ready to speak [f]plainly.
5 The vile person shall be no
more called liberal, nor the churl
said *to be* bountiful.
6 For the vile person will
speak villany, and his heart will work iniquity,
to practise hypocrisy, and to utter error
against the LORD, to make empty the soul of
the hungry, and he will cause the drink of
the thirsty to fail.
7 The instruments also of the churl *are* evil:
he deviseth wicked devices to destroy the poor
with lying words, even [g]when the needy
speaketh right.

A. M. cir. 3291
B. C. cir. 713
Olymp. XVI. 4
cir. annum
NumæPompilii,
R. Roman., 3

---

[a]Psa. xlv. 1, &c.; Jer. xxiii. 5; Hos. iii. 5; Zech. ix. 9 [b]Chap. iv. 6; xxv. 4——[c]Heb. *heavy*——[d]Chap. xxix. 18; xxxv. 5, 6——[e]Heb. *hasty*——[f]Or, *elegantly* [g]Or, *when he speaketh* against *the poor in judgment*

NOTES ON CHAP. XXXII

Verse 1. *Behold, a king shall reign in righteousness*] If King Hezekiah were a type of Christ, then this prophecy may refer to his time; but otherwise it seems to have Hezekiah primarily in view. It is evident, however, that in the fullest sense these words cannot be applied to any man; GOD alone can do all that is promised here.

And princes] ושרים *ve-sarim*, without ל *lamed, to;* so the ancient Versions. An ancient MS. has ושריו *vesaraiv, and* his *princes.*

Verse 2. *As the shadow of a great rock*] The shadow of a great projecting rock is the most refreshing that is possible in a hot country, not only as most perfectly excluding the rays of the sun, but also as having in itself a natural coolness, which it reflects and communicates to every thing about it.

Speluncæque tegant, et saxea procubet umbra.
VIRG. *Georg.* iii. 145.

"Let the cool cave and shady rock protect them."

Επει κεφαλην και γουνατα Σειριος αζει,
Αυαλεος δε τε χρως απο καυματος· αλλα τοτ' ηδη
Ειη πετραιη τε σκιη, και Βιβλινος οινος.
HESIOD. ii. 206.

"When Sirius rages, and thine aching head,
Parched skin, and feeble knees refreshment need;
Then to the rock's projected shade retire,
With Biblin wine recruit thy wasted powers."

Verse 3. *And the eyes of them that see shall not be dim*—"And him the eyes of those that see shall regard"] For ולא *velo, and not, Le Clerc* reads ולו *velo, and to him,* of which mistake the Masoretes acknowledge there are *fifteen* instances; and many more are reckoned by others. The removal of the *negative* restores to the verb its true and usual sense.

Verse 5. *The vile person shall no more be called liberal*] The different epithets here employed require minute explanation.

The vile person—נבל *nabal,* the pampered, fattened, brainless fellow, who eats to live, and lives to eat; who will scarcely part with any thing, and that which he does give he gives with an evil eye and a grudging heart.

Liberal—נדיב *nadib;* the generous, openhearted, princely man, who writes on all his possessions, *For myself and mankind,* and lives only to *get* and to *do* good.

The churl—כילי *kilai,* the avaricious man; he who starves himself amidst his plenty, and will not take the necessaries of life for fear of lessening his stock.

Thus he differs from נבל *nabal,* who feeds himself to the full, and regards no one else; like the rich man in the Gospel. The avaricious man is called כילי *kilai,* from כי *ki, for,* and לי *li, myself;* or contracted from כל *col, all,* and לי *li, to myself:* all is mine; all I have is *my own;* and all I can get is *for myself:* and yet this man enjoys nothing; he withholds

From back and belly too their proper fare:—
O cursed lust of gold, when for thy sake
The wretch throws up his interest in both worlds,
First *starved* in *this,* then *damned* in *that* to come!

Bountiful—שוע *shoa,* he who is abundantly rich; who *rejoices* in his plenty, and deals out to the distressed with a liberal hand.

Verse 6. *The vile person will speak villany*—"The fool will still utter folly"] A sort of proverbial saying, which *Euripides* (Bacchæ, 369) has expressed in the very same manner and words: Μωρα γαρ μωρος λεγει· "The fool speaks folly." Of this kind of simple and unadorned proverb or parable, see *De S. Poës,* Hebr. Prælect. xxiv.

Against the Lord—"Against JEHOVAH"] For אל *El,* two MSS. read על *al,* more properly; but both are of nearly the same meaning.

Verse 7. *The instruments also of the churl are evil*—"As for the niggard, his instruments are evil"] His machinations, his designs. The paronomasia, which the prophet frequently deals in, suggested this expression וכלי כליו *vechelai kelaiv.* The first word is expressed with some variety in the MSS. Seven MSS. read וכילי *vekili,* one וכל *vechol,* another וכולי *vecoli.*

To destroy the poor with lying words—"To

A. M. cir. 3291 B. C. cir. 713 Olymp. XVI. 4 cir. annum NumæPompilii, R. Roman., 3

8 But the liberal deviseth liberal things; and by liberal things shall he [h]stand.

9 Rise up, ye women [i]that are at ease; hear my voice, ye careless daughters; give ear unto my speech.

10 [k]Many days and years shall ye be troubled, ye careless women: for the vintage shall fail, the gathering shall not come.

11 Tremble, ye women that are at ease; be troubled, ye careless ones; strip you, and make you bare, and gird *sackcloth* upon *your* loins.

12 They shall lament for the teats, for [l]the pleasant fields, for the fruitful vine.

13 [m]Upon the land of my people shall come up thorns *and* briers; [n]yea, upon all the houses of joy *in* [o]the joyous city:

14 [p]Because the palaces shall be forsaken; the multitude of the city shall be left; the [q]forts and towers shall be for dens for ever, a joy of wild asses, a pasture of flocks;

15 Until [r]the spirit be poured upon us from on high, and [s]the wilderness be a fruitful field, and the fruitful field be counted for a forest.

16 Then judgment shall dwell in the wilderness, and righteousness remain in the fruitful field.

17 [t]And the work of righteousness shall be peace; and the effect of righteousness quietness and assurance for ever.

18 And my people shall dwell in a peaceable habitation, and in sure dwellings, and in quiet resting places;

[h]Or, *be established*——[i]Amos vi. 1——[k]Heb. *Days above a year*——[l]Heb. *the fields of desire*——[m]Chap. xxxiv. 13; Hos. ix. 6

[n]Or, *burning upon, &c.*——[o]Chap. xxii. 22——[p]Chap. xxvii. 10——[q]Or, *clifts and watch-towers*——[r]Psa. civ. 30; Joel ii. 28——[s]Ch. xxix. 17; xxxv. 2——[t]James iii. 18

defeat the assertions of the poor in judgment"] A word seems to have been lost here, and two others to have suffered a small alteration, which has made the sentence very obscure. The *Septuagint* have happily retained the rendering of the lost word, and restored the sentence in all its parts: Και διασκεδασαι λογους ταπεινων εν κρισει· ולהפר דברי אביון במשפט *ulehapher dibrey ebyon bemishpat*, "And disperse the words of the poor in judgment." They frequently render the verb הפר *haphar* by διασκεδασαι, A MS. reads ולדבר *uledabber*, which gives authority for the preposition ל *lamed, to*, necessary to the sense; and the *Septuagint*, *Syriac*, and *Chaldee* read במשפט *bemishpat*, IN *judgment*.

Verse 8. *Liberal things*—"Generous purposes"] "Of the four sorts of persons mentioned ver. 5, three are described, ver. 6, 7, and 8, but not the fourth."—SECKER. Perhaps for והוא *vehu, and he*, we ought to read ושוע *veshoa, the bountiful*.

Verse 9. *Rise up, ye women*—"ye provinces." *Ye careless daughters*—"ye cities."—*Targum*.

From this verse to the end of the *fourteenth*, the desolation of Judea by the Chaldeans appears to be foretold.

Verse 11. *Gird* sackcloth] שק *sak, sackcloth*, a word necessary to the sense, is here lost, but preserved by the *Septuagint*, MSS. *Alex.* and *Pachom.*, and I. D. II., and edit. *Ald.* and *Comp.*, and the *Arabic* and *Syriac*.

Tremble—be troubled—strip you] פשטה *peshotah*, רגזה *regazah*, &c. These are infinitives, with a paragogic ה *he*, according to *Schultens*, Institut. Ling. Hebr. p. 453, and are to be taken in an imperative sense.

Verse 12. *They shall lament—for the pleasant fields*—"Mourn ye for the pleasant field"] The *Septuagint*, *Syriac*, and *Vulgate* read ספדו *siphdu, mourn ye*, imperative; twelve MSS., (five ancient,) two editions, the *Septuagint*, *Aquila*, *Symmachus*, *Theodotion*, *Syriac*, and *Vulgate*, all read שדה *sadeh, a field;* not שדי *shedey, breasts*.

Verse 13. *Shall come up thorns* and *briers*—"The thorn and the brier shall come up"] All the ancient Versions read ושמיר *veshamir*, with the conjunction. And an ancient MS. has תעלה בו *taaleh bo*, "shall come up in it," which seems to be right; or rather בה *bah:* and there is a rasure in the place of בו *bo* in another ancient MS.

Yea, upon all the houses of joy] For כי *ki*, the ancient Versions, except the *Vulgate*, seem to have read ו *ve.* כי *ki* may perhaps be a mistake for בו *bo*, or בה *bah, in it*, above mentioned. It is not necessary in this place.

The description of impending distress which begins at ver. 13 belongs to other times than that of Sennacherib's invasion, from which they were so soon delivered. It must at least extend to the ruin of the country and city by the Chaldeans. And the promise of blessings which follows was not fulfilled under the Mosaic dispensation; they belong to the KINGDOM of Messiah. Compare ver. 15 with chap. xxix. 17, and see the note there.

Verse 14. *The palaces shall be forsaken*] The house of the sanctuary (the temple) shall be destroyed.—*Targum*.

The forts—"Ophel"] It was a part of Mount Zion, rising higher than the rest, at the eastern extremity, near to the temple, a little to the south of it; called by Micah, chap. iv. 8, "Ophel of the daughter of Zion." It was naturally strong by its situation; and had a wall of its own, by which it was separated from the rest of Zion.

Verse 15. *And the fruitful field*] והכרמל *vehaccarmel*. So *fifteen* MSS., *six* ancient, and *two* editions; which seems to make the noun an appellative.

Verse 17. *The work of righteousness*] Righteousness works and produces peace.

The effect of righteousness] עבדת *abodath, the*

A. M. cir. 3291 B. C. cir. 713 Olymp. XVI. 4 cir. annum NumæPompilii, R. Roman., 3

19 [u]When it shall hail, coming down [v]on the forest; [w]and the city shall be low in a low place.

20 Blessed *are* ye that sow beside all waters, that send forth *thither* the feet of [x]the ox and the ass.

[u]Chap. xxx. 30——[v]Zech. xi. 2——[w]Or, *and the city shall be utterly abased*——[x]Ch. xxx. 24

culture. Righteousness, *cultivated* by peace, produces tranquillity of mind and permanent security. Reader, hast thou the principle? If so, dost thou cultivate it? If thou dost, thou hast peace of conscience, joy in the Holy Ghost, and a sure and certain hope of everlasting life.

Verse 19. *The city shall be low in a low place.*—"The city shall be laid level with the plain."] For ובשפלה *ubashephelah*, the *Syriac* reads וכשפלה *ukeshephelah. The city*—probably Nineveh or Babylon: but this verse is very obscure. Saltus; Assyriorum regnum: civitas; magnifica Assyriorum castra. Ephrem Syr. *in loc.* For וברד *ubarad*, a MS. has ויירד *vaiyered;* and so conjectured Abp. *Secker*, referring to Zech. xi. 2.

Verse 20. *That sow beside all waters*—"Who sow your seed in every well-watered place"] Sir John Chardin's note on this place is:—"This exactly answers the manner of planting rice; for they sow it upon the water, and before sowing, while the earth is covered with water, they cause the ground to be trodden by oxen, horses, and asses, who go mid-leg deep; and this is the way of preparing the ground for sowing. As they sow the rice on the water, they transplant it in the water." *Harmer's* Observ. vol. i. p. 280. "Rice is the food of two-thirds of mankind." Dr. *Arbuthnot.* "It is cultivated in most of the eastern countries." *Miller.* "It is good for all, and at all times." Sir *J. Chardin*, ib. "Le ris, qui est leur principal aliment et leur froment (i. e., des Siamois,) n'est jamais assez arrosé; il croit au milieu de l'eau, et les campagnes ou on le cultive ressemblent plutôt à de marèts que non pas à des terres qu'on laboure avec la charue. Le ris a bien cette force, que quoy qu'il y ait six ou sept pieds d'eau sur lui, il pousse toujours sa tige au dessus; et le tuyau qui le porte s'eleve et croit à proportion de la hauteur de l'eau qui noye son champ. Voyage de l'Evêque de *Beryte*, p. 144. Paris, 1666.—L. "*Rice*, which is the principal grain and aliment of the *Siamese*, can never be too much watered. It grows in the water, and the fields where it is sown resemble *marshes* rather than fields cultivated by ploughing. Rice has that property that although it be covered with water six or seven feet deep, yet it raises its stalk above it; and this grows long in proportion to the depth of the water by which the field is inundated."

CHAPTER XXXIII

This chapter contains the sequel of the prophecy respecting Sennacherib. The prophet addresses himself to the Assyrian monarch, 1–4. The mercy and power of God acknowledged by the Jews, 5, 6. Distress and despair of the Jews at the approach of Sennacherib, 7–9. Gracious promise of deliverance, 10–13. Dreadful apprehensions of the wicked, and security of the righteous, 14–17. The security of the Jews under the reign of Hezekiah, and the wretched condition of Sennacherib and his army, 18–24.

A. M. cir. 3291 B. C. cir. 713 Olymp. XVI. 4 cir. annum NumæPompilii, R. Roman., 3

WO to thee [a]that spoilest, and thou *wast* not spoiled; and dealest treacherously, and they dealt not treacherously with thee! [b]when thou shalt cease to spoil, thou shalt be spoiled; *and* when thou shalt make an end to deal treacherously, they

[a]Chap. xxi. 2; Hab. ii. 8——[b]Rev. xiii. 10

The plan of the prophecy continued in this chapter, and which is manifestly distinct from the foregoing, is peculiarly elegant. To set it in a proper light, it will be necessary to mark the transitions from one part of it to another.

In ver. 1, the prophet addresses himself to Sennacherib, briefly, but strongly and elegantly, expressing the injustice of his ambitious designs, and the sudden disappointments of them.

In ver. 2, the Jews are introduced offering up their earnest supplications to God in their present distressful condition; with expressions of their trust and confidence in his protection.

In verses 3 and 4 the prophet in the name of God, or rather God himself, is introduced addressing himself to Sennacherib, and threatening him that, notwithstanding the terror which he had occasioned in the invaded countries, yet he should fall, and become an easy prey to those whom he had intended to subdue.

In verses 5 and 6, a chorus of Jews is introduced, acknowledging the mercy and power of God, who had undertaken to protect them; extolling it with direct opposition to the boasted power of their enemies, and celebrating the wisdom and piety of their king Hezekiah, who had placed his confidence in the favour of God.

Then follows, in verses 7, 8, and 9, a description of the distress and despair of the Jews, upon the king of Assyria's marching against Jerusalem, and sending his summons to them to surrender, after the treaty he had made with Hezekiah on the conditions of his paying, as he actually did pay to him, three hundred talents of silver and thirty talents of gold. 2 Kings xviii. 14-16.

A. M. cir. 3291 B. C. cir. 713 Olymp. XVI. 4 cir. annum NumæPompilii, R. Roman., 3

shall deal treacherously with
thee.
2 O Lord, be gracious unto
us; [c]we have waited for thee:
be thou their arm every morning, our salvation also in the time of trouble.
3 At the noise of the tumult the people fled;
at the lifting up of thyself the nations were
scattered.
4 And your spoil shall be gathered *like* the
gathering of the caterpillar: as the running to
and fro of locusts shall he run upon them.
5 [d]The Lord is exalted; for he dwelleth on
high: he hath filled Zion with
judgment and righteousness.
6 And wisdom and knowledge
shall be the stability of thy times,
and strength of [e]salvation: the fear of the
Lord *is* his treasure.
7 Behold, their [f]valiant ones shall cry without: [g]the ambassadors of peace shall weep
bitterly.
8 [h]The highways lie waste, the wayfaring
man ceaseth: [i]he hath broken the covenant,
he hath despised the cities, he regardeth no
man.

A. M. cir. 3291 B. C. cir. 713 Olymp. XVI. 4 cir. annum NumæPompilii, R. Roman., 3

[c]Chap. xxv. 9——[d]Psa. xcvii. 9——[e]Heb. *salvations* [f]Or, *messengers*

[g]2 Kings xviii. 18, 37——[h]Judg. v. 6——[i]2 Kings xviii. 14, 15, 16, 17

In ver. 10, God himself is again introduced, declaring that he will interpose in this critical situation of affairs, and disappoint the vain designs of the enemies of his people, by discomfiting and utterly consuming them.

Then follows, ver. 11-22, still in the person of God, which however falls at last into that of the prophet, a description of the dreadful apprehensions of the wicked in those times of distress and imminent danger; finely contrasted with the confidence and security of the righteous, and their trust in the promises of God that he will be their never-failing strength and protector.

The whole concludes, in the person of the prophet, with a description of the security of the Jews under the protection of God, and of the wretched state of Sennacherib and his army, wholly discomfited, and exposed to be plundered even by the weakest of the enemy.

Much of the beauty of this passage depends on the explanation above given of ver. 3 and 4, as addressed by the prophet, or by God himself, to Sennacherib; not as it is usually taken, as addressed by the Jews to God, ver. 3, and then ver. 4, as addressed to the Assyrians. To set this in a clear light, it may be of use to compare it with a passage of the Prophet Joel; where, speaking of the destruction caused by the locusts, he sets in the same strong light of opposition as Isaiah does here, the power of the enemy, and the power of Jehovah, who would destroy that enemy. Thus Isaiah to Sennacherib:—

"When thou didst raise thyself up, the nations
were dispersed"— Ver. 3.

"But now will I arise, saith Jehovah;
Now will I be exalted." Ver. 10.

And thus Joel, chap. ii. 20, 21:—

"His stink shall come up, and his ill savour
shall ascend;
Though he hath done great things.
Fear not, O land; be glad and rejoice;
For Jehovah will do great things."—L.

NOTES ON CHAP. XXXIII

Verse 1. *And dealest treacherously*—"Thou plunderer"] See note on chap. xxi. 2.

When thou shalt make an end to deal treacherously—"When thou art weary of plundering"] "כנלתך *cannelothecha, alibi non extat in s. s. nisi f.* Job xv. 29—*simplicius est legere* ככלתך *kechallothecha. Vid.* Capell.; *nec repugnat* Vitringa. *Vid.* Dan. ix. 24. כלה *calah* התים *hatim.*"—Secker.

Verse 2. *Be thou their arm every morning*—"Be thou our strength every morning"] For זרעם *zeroam, their arm*, the *Syriac, Chaldee*, and *Vulgate* read זרענו *zeroenu, our arm*, in the first person of the pronoun, not the third: the edition of Felix Pratensis has זרעתינו *zerootheynu* in the margin.

The prophet is here praying against the enemies of God's people; and yet this part of the prayer seems to be in their behalf: but from the above authorities it appears that our *arm* is the true reading, though I do not find it confirmed by any of *Kennicott's*, *De Rossi's*, or my own MSS. My old MS. Bible has,—**Be thou oure arm in erly.**

Verse 3. *At the noise of the tumult*—"From thy terrible voice"] For המון *hamon*, "multitude," the *Septuagint* and *Syriac* read אמיך *amica*, "terrible," whom I follow.

Verse 6. *His treasure*—"Thy treasure."] 'C θησαυρος σου, *Sym.* He had in his copy אצרך *otsarcha*, "thy treasure," not אצרו *otsaro*, "his treasure."

Verse 7. *Their valiant ones shall cry without*—"The mighty men raise a grievous cry"] *Three* MSS. read אראלים *erelim*, that is, *lions of God*, or *strong lions.* So they called valiant men heroes; which appellation the Arabians and Persians still use. See *Bochart.* Hieroz. Part I. lib. iii. cap. 1. "Mahomet, ayant reconnu Hamzeh son oncle pour homme de courage et de valeur, lui donne le titre ou surnom d'Assad Allah, qui signifie le lion de Dieu." *D'Herbelot*, p. 427. And for חצה *chatsah*, the *Syriac* and *Chaldee*, read קשה *kashah*, whom I follow. The *Chaldee*, *Syriac*, *Aquila*, *Symmachus*, and *Theodotion* read אראה להם *ereh lahem*, or יראה *yireh*, with what meaning is not clear.

The word אראלם *erellam*, which we translate *valiant ones*, is very difficult; no man knows what it means. *Kimchi* supposes that it is the name of the angel that smote the Assyrian camp! The *Vulgate*, and my old MS., translate

A. M. cir. 3291
B. C. cir. 713
Olymp. XVI. 4
cir. annum
NumæPompilii,
R. Roman., 3

9 [k]The earth mourneth *and* languisheth: Lebanon is ashamed *and* [l]hewn down: Sharon is like a wilderness; and Bashan and Carmel shake off *their fruits.*

10 [m]Now will I rise, saith the LORD; now will I be exalted; now will I lift up myself.

11 [n]Ye shall conceive chaff, ye shall bring forth stubble: your breath, *as* fire, shall devour you.

12 And the people shall be *as* the burnings of lime: [o]*as* thorns cut up shall they be burned in the fire.

13 Hear, [p]ye *that are* far off, what I have done; and, ye *that are* near, acknowledge my might.

14 The sinners in Zion are afraid; fearfulness hath surprised the hypocrites. Who among us shall dwell with the devouring fire? who among us shall dwell with everlasting burnings?

15 He that [q]walketh [r]righteously, and speaketh [s]uprightly; he that despiseth the gain of [t]oppressions, that shaketh his hands from holding of bribes, that stoppeth his ears from hearing of [u]blood, and [v]shutteth his eyes from seeing evil;

A. M. cir. 3291
B. C. cir. 713
Olymp. XVI. 4
cir. annum
NumæPompilii,
R. Roman., 3

16 He shall dwell on [w]high: his place of defence *shall be* the munitions of rocks: bread shall be given him; his waters *shall be* sure.

17 Thine eyes shall see the king in his beauty: they shall behold [x]the land that is very far off.

18 Thine heart shall meditate terror. [y]Where *is* the scribe? where *is* the [z]receiver? where *is* he that counted the towers?

19 [a]Thou shalt not see a fierce people, [b]a people of deeper speech than thou canst perceive; of a [c]stammering tongue, *that thou canst* not understand.

20 [d]Look upon Zion, the city of our solemnities: thine eyes shall see [e]Jerusalem a quiet habitation, a tabernacle *that* shall not be taken down; [f]not one of [g]the stakes thereof shall ever be removed, neither shall any of the cords thereof be broken.

---

[k]Chap. xxiv. 4——[l]Or, *withered away*——[m]Psa. xii. 5——[n]Psa. vii. 14; chap. lix. 4——[o]Chap. ix. 18——[p]Chap. xlix. 1——[q]Psa. xv. 2; xxiv. 4——[r]Heb. *in righteousnesses*——[s]Heb. *uprightnesses*——[t]Or, *deceits*——[u]Heb. *bloods*——[v]Psa. cxix. 37

[w]Heb. *heights* or *high places*——[x]Heb. *the land of far distances*——[y]1 Cor. i. 20——[z]Heb. *weigher*——[a]2 Kings xix. 32——[b]Deut. xxviii. 49, 50; Jer. v. 15——[c]Or, *ridiculous*——[d]Psa. xlviii. 12——[e]Psa. xlvi. 5; cxxv. 1, 2——[f]Chap. xxxvii. 33——[g]Chap. liv. 2

---

it *seers;* and most of the Versions understand it in this way. None of the MSS. give us any help, but as we see above in *Lowth.*

Verse 9. *Bashan and Carmel shake off* their fruits—"Bashan and Carmel are stripped of their beauty."] Φανερα εσται, *made manifest. Sept.* They read ונערה *veneerah.*

Verse 11. *Your breath*—"And my spirit"] "For רוחכם *ruchechem, your spirit,* read רוחי כמו *ruchi kemo.*" *Secker.* Which reading is confirmed by the *Chaldee,* where מימרי *meymri,* "my word," answers to רוחי *ruchi,* "my spirit."

Verse 14. *The sinners in Zion are afraid*] Zion has been generally considered as a type of the Church of God. Now all the members of God's Church should be holy, and given to good works; sinners in *Zion,* therefore, are portentous beings! but, alas! where are they not? The *Targum* on this verse is worthy of notice: "The sinners in Zion are broken down; fear hath seized the ungodly, who are suffering for their ways. They say, Who among us shall dwell in Zion, where the splendour of the Divine Majesty is like a consuming fire? Who of us shall dwell in Jerusalem, where the ungodly are judged and delivered into hell for an eternal burning?" **Everdurynge brennyngis.** Old MS. Bible.

Verse 15. *That stoppeth his ears from hearing of blood*—"Who stoppeth his ears to the proposal of bloodshed"] A MS. reads בדמים *bedamim,* "in blood."

Verse 18. *Where is the scribe?*] The person appointed by the king of Assyria to estimate their number and property in reference to their being heavily taxed.

Where is the receiver?] Or he who was to have collected this tribute.

Where is he that counted the towers?] That is, the commander of the enemy's forces, who surveyed the fortifications of the city, and took an account of the height, strength, and situation of the walls and towers, that he might know where to make the assault with the greatest advantage; as Capaneus before Thebes is represented in a passage of the Phœnissæ of Euripides, which *Grotius* has applied as an illustration of this place:—

Εκεινος ἑπτα προσβασεις τεκμαιρεται
Πυργων, ανω τε και κατω τειχη μετρων.

Ver. 187.

"To these seven turrets each approach he marks;
The walls from their proud summit to their base
Measuring with eager eye."

He that counted the towers—"Those who were ordered to review the fortified places in Judea, that they might be manned and provisioned for the king of Assyria. So sure was he of gaining Jerusalem and subduing the whole of Judea, that he had already formed all these arrangements."—*Dodd's* notes.

Verse 20. *Look upon Zion*—"Thou shalt see

A. M. cir. 3291
B. C. cir. 713
Olymp. XVI. 4
cir. annum
NumæPompilii,
R. Roman., 3

21 But there the glorious
LORD *will be* unto us a place
[h]of broad rivers *and* streams;
wherein shall go no galley with
oars, neither shall gallant ship pass thereby.
22 For the LORD *is* our judge, the LORD *is*
our [i]lawgiver,[k] [l]the LORD *is* our king; he
will save us.

[h]Heb. *broad of spaces* or *hands*——[i]James iv. 12
[k]Heb. *statute maker*

23 [m]Thy tacklings are loosed;
they could not well strengthen
their mast, they could not spread
the sail: then is the prey of a
great spoil divided; the lame take the prey.
24 And the inhabitant shall not say, I am
sick: [n]the people that dwell therein *shall be*
forgiven *their* iniquity.

A. M. cir. 3291
B. C. cir. 713
Olymp. XVI. 4
cir. annum
NumæPompilii,
R. Roman., 3

[l]Psa. lxxxix. 18——[m]Or, *they have forsaken thy tacklings*
[n]Jer. l. 20

Zion"] For חזה *chazeh*, "see," read תחזה *techezeh*, "thou shalt see," with the *Chaldee*.—*Houbigant*. At the end of this verse we find in the Masoretic Bibles this note, חצי הספר *chatsi hassepher*, "the middle of the book;" that is, the middle of the book of Isaiah.

Verse 21. *The glorious Lord*—"The glorious name of JEHOVAH"] I take שם *shem* for a noun, with the *Septuagint* and *Syriac*. See Psa. xx. 1; Prov. xviii. 10.

Verse 23. *Thy tacklings are loosed*] Here the Assyrians are represented under the figure of a *ship* wrecked by a violent storm; and the people on the beach, young, old, feeble, and diseased, gathering the spoil without any to hinder them. *Kimchi*, who understands the whole of this chapter of Hezekiah and the king of Assyria, says, "There are others of our rabbins who apply it all to the days of the Messiah."

Their mast—"Thy mast"] For תרנם *tornam*, "their mast," the *Syriac* reads תרניך *torneycha*, "thy mast;" the *Septuagint* and *Vulgate*, תרנך *tornecha*, ὁ ιστος σου εκλινεν, "thy mast is fallen aside."—*Septuagint*. They seem to have read נטה *natah* or פנה *panah*, תרנך *tornecha*, or rather, לא כן *lo cun*, "is not firm," the negative having been omitted in the present text by mistake. However, I have followed their sense, which seems very probable, as the present reading is to me extremely obscure.

Verse 24. *And the inhabitant shall not say*] This verse is somewhat obscure. The meaning of it seems to be, that the army of Sennacherib shall by the stroke of God be reduced to so shattered and so weak a condition, that the Jews shall fall upon the remains of them, and plunder them without resistance; that the most infirm and disabled of the people of Jerusalem shall come in for their share of the spoil; the lame shall seize the prey; even the sick and the diseased shall throw aside their infirmities, and recover strength enough to hasten to the general plunder. See above.

The last line of the verse is parallel to the first, and expresses the same sense in other words. Sickness being considered as a visitation from God, a punishment of sin; the forgiveness of sin is equivalent to the removal of a disease. Thus the psalmist:—

"Who forgiveth all thy sin;
And healeth all thine infirmities."
Psa. ciii. 3.

Where the latter line only varies the expression of the former. And our blessed Saviour reasons with the Jews on the same principle: "Whether is it easier to say to the sick of the palsy, Thy sins are forgiven thee; or to say, Arise, and take up thy bed, and walk?" Mark ii. 9. See also Matt. viii. 17; Isa. liii. 4. Qui locus Isaiæ, 1 Pet. ii. 24, refertur ad remissionem peccatorum: hic vero ad sanationem morborum, quia ejusdem potentiæ et bonitatis est utrumque præstare; et, quia peccatis remissis, et morbi, qui fructus sunt peccatorum, pelluntur. "Which passage of Isaiah has reference, in 1 Pet. ii. 24, to *the remission of sins*, and here to *the healing of diseases*, because both are effects of the same power and goodness; and because with the remission of sins was associated the removal of disorders, the fruits of sin."—*Wetstein* on Matt. viii. 17.

That this prophecy was exactly fulfilled, I think we may gather from the history of this great event given by the prophet himself. It is plain that Hezekiah, by his treaty with Sennacherib, by which he agreed to pay him *three hundred* talents of silver and thirty talents of gold, had stripped himself of his whole treasure. He not only gave him all the silver and gold that was in his own treasury and in that of the temple, but was even forced to cut off the gold from the doors of the temple and from the pillars, with which he had himself overlaid them, to satisfy the demands of the king of Assyria: but after the destruction of the Assyrian army, we find that he "had exceeding much riches, and that he made himself treasuries for silver, and for gold, and for precious stones," &c. 2 Chron. xxxii. 27. He was so rich, that out of pride and vanity he displayed his wealth to the ambassadors from Babylon. This cannot be otherwise accounted for, than by the prodigious spoil that was taken on the destruction of the Assyrian army.—L. And thus, in the providence of God, he had the wealth which was exacted from him restored.

CHAPTER XXXIV

The prophet earnestly exhorts all nations to attend to the communication which he has received from Jehovah, as the matter is of the highest importance, and of universal concern, 1. *The wrath of God is denounced against all the nations that had provoked to anger the Defender of the cause of Zion,* 2, 3. *Great crowd of images, by which the final overthrow and utter extermination of every thing that opposes the spread of true religion in the earth are forcibly and majestically set forth; images so very bold and expressive as to render it impossible, without doing great violence to symbolical language, to restrain their import to the calamities which befell the Edomites in the reign of Nebuchadnezzar, or in that of any other potentate, or even to the calamities which the enemies of the Church have yet suffered since the delivery of the prophecy. Edom must therefore be a type of Antichrist, the last grand adversary of the people of God; and consequently this most awful prophecy, in its ultimate signification, remains to be accomplished,* 4–15. *The Churches of God, at the period of the consummation, commanded to consult the book of Jehovah, and note the exact fulfilment of these terrible predictions in their minutest details. Not one jot or tittle relative even to the circumstances shadowed forth by the impure animals shall be found to fail; for what the mouth of the Lord has declared necessary to satisfy the Divine justice, his Spirit will accomplish,* 16, 17.

A. M. cir. 3291 B. C. cir. 713 Olymp. XVI. 4 cir. annum NumæPompilii, R. Roman., 3

COME [a]near, ye nations, to
hear; and hearken, ye
people: [b]let the earth hear, and
[c]all that is therein; the world,
and all things that come forth of it.
2 For the indignation of the LORD *is* upon
all nations, and *his* fury upon all their armies:
he hath utterly destroyed them,
he hath delivered them to the
slaughter.
3 Their slain also shall be cast
out, and [d]their stink shall come up out of
their carcasses, and the mountains shall be
melted with their blood.

[a]Psa. xlix. 1——[b]Deut. xxxii. 1

[c]Heb. *the fulness thereof*——[d]Joel ii. 20

This and the following chapter make one distinct prophecy; an entire, regular, and beautiful poem, consisting of two parts: the first containing a denunciation of Divine vengeance against the enemies of the people or Church of God; the second describing the flourishing state of the Church of God consequent upon the execution of those judgments. The event foretold is represented as of the highest importance, and of universal concern: ALL *nations* are called upon to attend to the declaration of it; and the wrath of God is denounced against all the nations, that is, all those that had provoked to anger the Defender of the cause of Zion. Among those, Edom is particularly specified. The principal provocation of Edom was their insulting the Jews in their distress, and joining against them with their enemies, the Chaldeans; see Amos i. 11; Ezek. xxv. 12; xxxv. 15; Psa. cxxxvii. 7. Accordingly the Edomites were, together with the rest of the neighbouring nations, ravaged and laid waste by Nebuchadnezzar; see Jer. xxv. 15-26; Mal. i. 3, 4, and see *Marsham*, Can. Chron. Sæc. xviii., who calls this the age of the destruction of cities. The general devastation spread through all these countries by Nebuchadnezzar may be the event which the prophet has primarily in view in the *thirty-fourth* chapter: but this event, as far as we have any account of it in history, seems by no means to come up to the terms of the prophecy, or to justify so highly wrought and terrible a description; and it is not easy to discover what connexion the extremely flourishing state of the Church or people of God, described in the next chapter, could have with those events, and how the former could be the consequence of the latter, as it is there represented to be. By a figure, very common in the prophetical writings, any city or people, remarkably distinguished as enemies of the people and kingdom of God, is put for those enemies in general. This seems here to be the case with Edom and Botsra. It seems, therefore, reasonable to suppose, with many learned expositors, that this prophecy has a farther view to events still *future;* to some great revolutions to be effected in later times, *antecedent* to that more perfect state of the kingdom of God upon earth, and serving to introduce it, which the Holy Scriptures warrant us to expect.

That the *thirty-fifth* chapter has a view beyond any thing that could be the immediate consequence of those events, is plain from every part, especially from the middle of it, ver. 5, 6; where the miraculous works wrought by our blessed Saviour are so clearly specified, that we cannot avoid making the application: and our Saviour himself has moreover plainly referred to this very passage, as speaking of him and his works, Matt. xi. 4, 5. He bids the disciples of John to go and report to their master the things which they heard and saw; that the blind received their sight, the lame walked, and the deaf heard; and leaves it to him to draw the conclusion in answer to his inquiry, whether he who performed the very works which the prophets foretold should be performed by the Messiah, was not indeed the Messiah himself. And where are these works so distinctly marked by any of the prophets as in this place? and how could they be marked more distinctly? To these the strictly literal interpretation of the prophet's words directs us. According to the allegorical interpretation, they may have a farther view: this part of the prophecy may run parallel with the former, and relate to the future advent of Christ; to the conversion of the Jews, and their restitution to their land; to the extension and purification of the Christian faith; events predicted in the Holy Scriptures as preparatory to it. *Kimchi* says, "This chapter points out the future destruction of Rome, which is here called Bosra; for Bosra was a great city of the Edomites. Now the major part of the *Romans* are Edomites, who profess the law of Jesus. The Emperor Cæsar (qy. Constantine) was an Edomite, and so were all the emperors after him. *The destruction of the Turkish empire is also comprehended in this prophecy.*"—L. As to the last, I say, Amen!

NOTES ON CHAP. XXXIV

Verse 1. *Hearken*—"Attend unto me"] A MS. adds in this line the word אלי *ali, unto me,* after לאמים *leummim;* which seems to be genuine.

A. M. cir. 3291 B. C. cir. 713 Olymp. XVI. 4 cir. annum NumæPompilii, R. Roman., 3

4 And [e]all the hosts of heaven
shall be dissolved, and the heavens shall be [f]rolled together as
a scroll: [g]and all their host shall
fall down as the leaf falleth off from the vine,
and as a [h]falling *fig* from the fig-tree.
5 [i]For my sword shall be bathed in heaven:
behold, [k]it shall come down upon Idumea, and
upon the people of my curse, to judgment.
6 The sword of the LORD is filled with
blood, it is made fat with fatness, *and* with
the blood of lambs and goats, with the fat of
the kidneys of rams: for [l]the LORD hath a
sacrifice in Bozrah, and a great slaughter in
the land of Idumea.
7 And the [m]unicorns shall come down
with them, and the bullocks with the bulls;
and their land shall be [n]soaked with blood,
and their dust made fat with
fatness.
8 For *it is* the day of the LORD'S
[o]vengeance, *and* the year of recompenses for the controversy of Zion.
9 [p]And the streams thereof shall be turned
into pitch, and the dust thereof into brimstone, and the land thereof shall become burning pitch.
10 It shall not be quenched night nor day;
[q]the smoke thereof shall go up for ever: [r]from
generation to generation it shall lie waste;
none shall pass through it for ever and ever.
11 [s]But the [t]cormorant and the bittern shall
possess it; the owl also and the raven shall
dwell in it: and [u]he shall stretch out upon
it the line of confusion, and the stones of
emptiness.

[e]Psa. cii. 36; Ezek. xxxii. 7, 8; Joel ii. 31; iii. 15; Matt. xxiv. 29; 2 Pet. iii. 10——[f]Rev. vi. 14——[g]Chap. xiv. 12——[h]Rev. vi. 13——[i]Jer. xlvi. 10——[k]Jer. xlix. 7, &c.; Mal. i. 4——[l]Ch. lxiii. 1; Jer. xlix. 13; Zeph. i. 7

[m]Or, *rhinoceros*——[n]Or, *drunken*——[o]Ch. lxiii. 4——[p]See Deut. xxix. 23——[q]Rev. xiv. 11; xviii. 18; xix. 3——[r]Mal. i. 4——[s]Ch. xiv. 23; Zeph. ii. 14; Rev. xviii. 2——[t]Or, *pelican*——[u]2 Kings xxi. 13; Lam. ii. 8

Verse 4. *And all the host of heaven*] See note on chap. xxiv. 21, and *De Sacra Poësi Hebræorum*, Præl. ix.

Verse 5. *For my sword shall be bathed in heaven*—"For my sword is made bare in the heavens"] There seems to be some impropriety in this, according to the present reading: "My sword is made drunken, or is bathed in the heavens;" which forestalls, and expresses not in its proper place, what belongs to the next verse: for the sword of JEHOVAH was not to be bathed or glutted with blood in the heavens, but in Botsra and the land of Edom. In the heavens it was only prepared for slaughter. To remedy this, Archbishop *Secker* proposes to read, for בשמים *bashshamayim*, בדמם *bedamim;* referring to Jer. xlvi. 10. But even this is premature, and not in its proper place. The *Chaldee*, for רותה *rivvethah*, has תתגלי *tithgalli*, shall be *revealed* or *disclosed:* perhaps he read תראה *teraeh* or נראתה *nirathah*. Whatever reading, different I presume from the present, he might find in his copy, I follow the sense which he has given of it.

Verse 6. *The Lord hath a sacrifice*—"For JEHOVAH celebrateth a sacrifice"] Ezekiel, chap. xxxix. 16, 17, has manifestly imitated this place of Isaiah. He hath set forth the great leaders and princes of the adverse powers under the same emblems of goats, bulls, rams, fatlings, &c., and has added to the boldness of the imagery, by introducing God as summoning all the fowls of the air, and all the beasts of the field; and bidding them to the feast which he has prepared for them by the slaughter of the enemies of his people:—

"And thou, son of man,
Thus saith the Lord JEHOVAH,
Say to the bird of every wing,
And to every beast of the field:
Assemble yourselves, and come;
Gather together from every side,
To the sacrifice which I make for you,
A great slaughter on the mountains of Israel.
And ye shall eat flesh and drink blood:
The flesh of the mighty shall ye eat,
And the blood of the lofty of the earth shall ye drink;
Of rams, of lambs, and of goats,
Of bullocks, all of them the fat ones of Bashan;
And ye shall eat fat, till ye are cloyed,
And drink blood, till ye are drunken;
Of my slaughter, which I have slain for you."

The sublime author of the Revelation, chap. xix. 17, 18, has taken this image from Ezekiel, rather than from Isaiah.

Verse 7. *The unicorns shall come down*] ראמים *reemim*, translated *wild goats* by Bishop *Lowth*. The ראם *reem Bochart* thinks to be a species of wild goat in the deserts of Arabia. It seems generally to mean the rhinoceros.

With blood—"With their blood"] מדמם *middamam;* so two ancient MSS. of *Kennicott's*, the *Syriac*, and *Chaldee*.

Verse 8. *The year of recompenses for the controversy of Zion*—"The year of recompense to the defender of the cause of Zion"] As from דון *dun*, דין *din, a judge;* so from רוב *rub*, ריב *rib, an advocate*, or *defender; Judici* Sionis: *Syriac*.

Verse 11. *The cormorant*] קאת *kaath, the pelican*, from the root קיא *ki, to vomit*, because it is said she swallows shell-fish, and when the heat of her stomach has killed the fish, she vomits the shells, takes out the dead fish, and eats them.

The bittern] קפד *kippod*, the *hedge-hog*, or *porcupine*.

The owl] ינשוף *yanshoph*, the *bittern*, from נשף *nashaph*, to *blow*, because of the *blowing* noise it makes, almost like the *lowing of an ox*. My old MS. Bible renders the words thus:—**The foule in face like an asse, and the yrchoun, and the snyte** (snipe.)

A. M. cir. 3291 B. C. cir. 713 Olymp. XVI. 4 cir. annum NumæPompilii, R. Roman., 3

12 They shall call the nobles thereof to the kingdom, but none *shall be* there, and all her princes shall be nothing.

13 And [v]thorns shall come up in her palaces, nettles and brambles in the fortresses thereof: and [w]it shall be a habitation of dragons, *and* a court for [x]owls.[y]

14 [z]The wild beasts of the desert shall also meet with [a]the wild beasts of the island, and the satyr shall cry to his fellow; the [b]screech owl also shall rest there, and find for herself a place of rest.

15 There shall the great owl make her nest, and lay, and hatch, and gather under her shadow: there shall the vultures also be gathered, every one with her mate.

16 Seek ye out of [c]the book of the LORD and read; no one of these shall fail, none shall want her mate, for my mouth it hath commanded, and his spirit it hath gathered them.

17 And he hath cast the lot for them, and his hand hath divided it unto them by line: they shall possess it for ever, from generation to generation shall they dwell therein.

[v]Chap. xxxii. 13; Hos. ix. 6——[w]Chap. xiii. 21, &c. [x]Or, *ostriches*

[y]Heb. *daughters of the owl*——[z]Heb. *Ziim*——[a]Heb. *Ijim*——[b]Or, *night monster*——[c]Mal. iii. 16

The line of confusion, and the stones of emptiness—"The plummet of emptiness over her scorched plains."] The word חריה *choreyha*, joined to the 12th verse, embarrasses it, and makes it inexplicable. At least I do not know that any one has yet made out the construction, or given any tolerable explication of it. I join it to the 11th verse, and supply a letter or two, which seem to have been lost. *Fifteen* MSS., five ancient, and two editions, read חוריה *choreyha;* the first printed edition of 1486, I think nearer to the truth, חור חריה *chor choreyha.* I read בחרריה *bechrereyha*, or על חרריה *al chorereyha;* see Jer. xvii. 6. A MS. has חדיה *chodiah*, and the *Syriac* reads חדוה *chaduah, gaudium*, joining it to the two preceding words; which he likewise reads differently, but without improving the sense. However, his authority is clear for dividing the verses as they are here divided. I read שם *shem*, as a noun. They shall boast, יקראו *yikreu;* see Prov. xx. 6.

Verse 13. *And thorns shall come up in her palaces*] ועלו בארמנותיה *vealu bearmenotheyha;* so read all the ancient versions.

A court for owls.] יענה *yaanah*, the *ostrich*, from ענה *anah*, to *cry*, because of the noise it makes. "They *roar*," says Dr. *Shaw*, "sometimes like a *lion*—sometimes like a *bull*. I have often heard them *groan* as if in the utmost distress."

Verse 14. *The wild beasts of the desert*] ציים *tsiyim*, the *mountain cats.*—Bochart.

Wild beasts of the island] איים *aiyim*, the *jackals*.

The satyr] שעיר *seir*, the *hairy one*, probably the *he-goat*.

The screech owl] לילית *lilith*, the *night-bird*, the *night-raven, nyctycorax*, from ליל *layil*, or לילה *lailah*, the *night*.

Verse 15. *The great owl*] קפוז *kippoz*, the *ακοντιας*, or *darter*, a serpent so called because of its suddenly leaping up or *darting* on its prey. Probably the *mongoz* or *ichneumon* may be intended.

The vultures] דיות *daiyoth*, the *black vultures*. My old MS. Bible renders these names curiously: **And ageyn cumen schul devylis: the beste, party of an asse, and party of a man: and the wodwose, the tother schal crien to the tother. There schal ben lamya, that is, thrisse, or a beste havynge the body liic a woman, and hors feet. Ther hadde dichis, the yrchoun, and nurshide out littil chittis. There ben gadred kiitis, the top to the top.** What language!

Every one with her mate.] A MS. adds אל *el* after אשה *ishshah*, which seems necessary to the construction; and so the *Syriac* and *Vulgate*. Another MS. adds in the same place את *eth*, which is equivalent.

Verse 16. *My mouth*—"For the mouth of JEHOVAH"] For הוא *hu*, five MSS., (three ancient,) read יהוה *Yehovah*, and another is so corrected; so likewise the *Septuagint*. Two editions have צום *tsivam;* and so the *Septuagint, Vulgate*, and *Arabic*, with the edition of 1486, and a MS. has קבצם *kebatsam*, with the masculine pronoun instead of the feminine: and so in the next verses it is להם *lahem*, instead of להן *lahen*, in fourteen MSS., six of them ancient.—L. To see the importance of these various readings, the Hebrew Bible must be consulted.

CHAPTER XXXV

Flourishing state of the Church of God consequent *to the awful judgments predicted in the preceding chapter. The images employed in the description are so very consolatory and sublime as to oblige us to extend their fulfilment to that period of the Gospel dispensation when Messiah shall take unto himself his great power and reign. The* fifth *and* sixth *verses were* literally *accomplished by our Saviour and his apostles: but that the miracles wrought in the first century were not the only import of the language used by the prophet, is sufficiently plain from the context. They, therefore, have a farther application; and are contemporary with, or rather a consequence of, the judgments of God upon the enemies of the Church in the latter days; and so relate to the greater influence and extension of the Christian faith, the conversion of the Jews, their restoration to their own land, and the second advent of Christ. Much of the imagery of this chapter seems to have been borrowed from the exodus from Egypt: but it is greatly enlivened by the life, sentiments, and passions ascribed to inanimate objects; all nature being represented as rejoicing with the people of God in consequence of their deliverance; and administering in such an unusual manner to their relief and comfort, as to induce some commentators to extend the meaning of the prophecy to the blessedness of the saints in heaven,* 1–10.

A. M. cir. 3291
B. C. cir. 713
Olymp. XVI. 4
cir. annum
NumæPompilii,
R. Roman., 3

THE [a]wilderness and the solitary place shall be glad for
them; and the desert shall rejoice and blossom as the rose.
2 [b]It shall blossom abundantly, and rejoice
even with joy and singing: the glory of Lebanon shall be given unto it, the excellency
of Carmel and Sharon, they shall see the glory
of the LORD, *and* the excellency of our God.
3 [c]Strengthen ye the weak hands, and confirm the feeble knees.
4 Say to them *that are* of a [d]fearful heart,
Be strong, fear not: behold,
your God will come *with* vengeance, *even* God *with* a recompense; he will come and
save you.
5 Then the [e]eyes of the blind shall be opened,
and [f]the ears of the deaf shall be unstopped.
6 Then shall the [g]lame *man* leap as a hart,
and the [h]tongue of the dumb sing: for in
the wilderness shall [i]waters break out, and
streams in the desert.
7 And the parched ground shall become a

[a]Chap. lv. 12——[b]Chap. xxxii. 15——[c]Job iv. 3, 4; Heb. xii. 12——[d]Heb. *hasty*——[e]Chap. xxix.1 8; xxxii. 3, 4; xlii. 7; Matt. ix. 27, &c.; xi. 5; xii. 22; xx. 30, &c.; xxi. 14; John ix. 6, 7

[f]Matt. xi. 5; Mark vii. 32, &c.——[g]Matt. xi. 5; xv. 30; xxi. 14; John v. 8, 9; Acts iii. 2, &c.; viii. 7; xiv. 8, &c.——[h]Chap. xxxii. 4; Matt. ix. 32, 33; xii. 22; xv. 30
[i]Chap. xli. 18; xliii. 19; John vii. 38, 39

The various miracles our Lord wrought are the best comment on this chapter, which predicts those wondrous works and the glorious state of the Christian Church. See the parallel texts in the margin.

On this chapter Bishop Lowth has offered some important emendations. I shall introduce his translation, as the best yet given of this singular prophecy:—

1. The desert and the waste shall be glad;
And the wilderness shall rejoice, and flourish:
2. Like the rose shall it beautifully flourish;
And the well-watered plain of Jordan shall also rejoice:
The glory of Lebanon shall be given unto it,
The beauty of Carmel and of Sharon;
These shall behold the glory of JEHOVAH,
The majesty of our God.
3. Strengthen ye the feeble hands,
And confirm ye the tottering knees.
4. Say ye to the faint-hearted, Be ye strong;
Fear ye not; behold your God!
Vengeance will come; the retribution of God:
He himself will come, and will deliver you.
5. Then shall be unclosed the eyes of the blind;
And the ears of the deaf shall be opened:
6. Then shall the lame bound like the hart,
And the tongue of the dumb shall sing;
For in the wilderness shall burst forth waters,
And torrents in the desert:
7. And the glowing sand shall become a pool,
And the thirsty soil bubbling springs:
And in the haunt of dragons shall spring forth
The grass with the reed and the bulrush.
8. And a highway shall be there;
And it shall be called The way of holiness:
No unclean person shall pass through it:
But he himself shall be with them, walking in the way,
And the foolish shall not err therein:
9. No lion shall be there;
Nor shall the tyrant of the beasts come up thither:
Neither shall he be found there;
But the redeemed shall walk in it.
10. Yea, the ransomed of JEHOVAH shall return;
They shall come to Sion with triumph;
And perpetual gladness shall crown their heads.
Joy and gladness shall they obtain;
And sorrow and sighing shall flee away.

NOTES ON CHAP. XXXV

Verse 1. *Shall be glad*] ישׂשׂום *yesusum;* in one MS. the מ *mem* seems to have been added; and שום *sum* is upon a rasure in another. None of the ancient versions acknowledge it; it seems to have been a mistake, arising from the next word beginning with the same letter. *Seventeen* MSS. have ישושום *yesusum,* both *vaus* expressed; and *five* MSS. ישׂשׂם *yesusum,* without the *vaus.* Probably the true reading is, "The wilderness and the dry place shall be glad." Not *for them.*

Verse 2. *Rejoice even with joy and singing* —"The well-watered plain of Jordan shall also rejoice"] For ורנן *veranen,* the *Septuagint* read ירדן *yarden,* τα ερημα του Ιορδανου, "the deserts of Jordan." *Four* MSS. read גלת *gulath;* see Josh. xv. 19: "Irrigua Jordani;" *Houbigant.* גידת *gidoth,* Ripæ Jordani, "the banks of Jordan;" *Kennicott.* See De S. Poësi Hebr. Prælect. xx. note.

Unto it] For לה *lah, to it, nine* MSS. of *Kennicott's* and *four* of *De Rossi's* read לך *lecha, to thee.* See ibid.

Verse 7. *The parched ground*—"The glowing sand"] שרב *sharab;* this word is Arabic, سراب as well as Hebrew, expressing in both languages the same thing, the *glowing sandy plain,* which in the hot countries at a distance has the appearance of water. It occurs in the Koran, chap. xxiv.: "But as to the unbelievers, their works are like a vapour in a plain, which the

A. M. cir. 3291
B. C. cir. 713
Olymp. XVI. 4
cir. annum
NumæPompilii,
R. Roman., 3

pool, and the thirsty land
springs of water: in [k]the habitation of dragons, where each
lay, *shall be* [l]grass with reeds
and rushes.
8 And a highway shall be there, and a way,
and it shall be called, The way of holiness;
[m]the unclean shall not pass over it; [n]but it
shall be for those: the way-faring men, though
fools, shall not err *therein.*
9 [o]No lion shall be there, nor
any ravenous beast shall go up
thereon, it shall not be found
there; but the redeemed shall
walk *there:*
10 And the [p]ransomed of the LORD shall
return, and come to Zion with songs and everlasting joy upon their heads: they shall obtain joy and gladness, and [q]sorrow and
sighing shall flee away.

A. M. cir. 3291
B. C. cir. 713
Olymp. XVI. 4
cir. annum
NumæPompilii,
R. Roman., 3

[k]Ch. xxxiv. 13——[l]Or, *a court for reeds, &c.*——[m]Ch. lii. 1; Joel iii. 17; Rev. xxi. 27——[n]Or, *for he* shall be *with them*——[o]Lev. xxvi. 6; ch. xi. 9; Ezek. xxxiv. 25——[p]Ch. li. 11——[q]Ch. xxv. 8; lxv. 19; Rev. vii. 17; xxi. 4

thirsty traveller thinketh to be water, until, when he cometh thereto, he findeth it to be nothing." Mr. Sale's note on this place is, "The Arabic word *serab* signifies that false appearance which in the eastern countries is often seen on sandy plains about noon, resembling a large lake of water in motion, and is occasioned by the reverberation of the sun beams: 'by the quivering undulating motion of that quick succession of vapours and exhalations which are extracted by the powerful influence of the sun.'—*Shaw*, Trav. p. 378. It sometimes tempts thirsty travellers out of their way; but deceives them when they come near, either going forward, (for it always appears at the same distance,) or quite vanishing." Q. Curtius has mentioned it: "Arenas vapor æstivi solis accendit; camporumque non alia, quam vasti et profundi æquoris species est."—Lib. vii., c. 5. Dr. Hyde gives us the precise meaning and derivation of the word. "Dictum nomen *Barca* הברקה *habberakah, splendorem,* seu *splendentem regionem* notat; cum ea regio radiis solaribus tam copiose collustretur, ut reflexum ab arenis lumen adeo intensè fulgens, a longinquo spectantibus, ad instar corporis solaris, aquarum speciem referat; et hinc arenarum splendor et radiatio, (et linguâ Persicâ petito nomine,) dicitur سراب *serab,* i. e., aquæ superficies seu superficialis aquarum species." Annot. in Peritsol., cap. ii.

"Shall spring forth"] The ה *he* in רבצה *rebitseh* seems to have been at first ם *mem* in MS. Bodl., whence Dr. *Kennicott* concludes it should be רבצים *rebitsim.* But instead of this word the *Syriac, Vulgate,* and *Chaldee* read some word signifying *to grow, spring up,* or *abound.* Perhaps פרצה *paretsah,* or פרצו *paretsu,* or פרץ החציר *parats hachatsir,* as Houbigant reads.—L.

Verse 8. *And a highway*] The word ודרך *vederech* is by mistake added to the first member of the sentence from the beginning of the following member. *Sixteen* MSS. of Dr. *Kennicott's, seven* ancient, and *two* of *De Rossi's,* have it but once; so likewise the *Syriac, Septuagint,* and *Arabic.*

Err therein.] A MS. of Dr. *Kennicott's* adds בו *bo, in it,* which seems necessary to the sense; and so the *Vulgate, per eam,* "by it." One of *De Rossi's* has שם *sham, there.*

But it shall be *for those*—"But he himself shall be with them, walking in the way."] That is, God; see ver. 4. "Who shall dwell among them, and set them an example that they should follow his steps." Our old English Version translated the place to this purpose; our last translators were misled by the authority of the Jews, who have absurdly made a division of the verses in the midst of the sentence, thereby destroying the construction and the sense.

Verse 9. *It shall not be found there*—"Neither shall he be found there"] *Three* MSS. read ולא *velo,* adding the conjunction; and so likewise the *Septuagint* and *Vulgate.* And *four* MSS., *one* ancient, read ימצא *yimmatsa,* the verb, as it certainly ought to be, in the masculine form.

The redeemed shall walk there] גאולים *geulim.* Those whose forfeited inheritances are brought back by the *kinsman,* גואל *goel,* the nearest of kin to the family. This has been considered by all orthodox divines as referring to the incarnation of our Lord, and his sacrificial offering. After גאולים *geulim,* one of *De Rossi's* MSS. adds עד עולם *ad olam, for ever,* "The redeemed shall walk there for ever."

Verse 10. *The ransomed*] פדויי *peduyey,* from פדה *padah,* "to redeem by paying a price." Those for whom a price was paid down to redeem them from bondage and death.

Sighing shall flee away.] אנחה *anachah.* Never was a sorrowful accent better expressed than in this strong guttural word, *an-ach-ah;* nearly the same with the Irish in their funeral wailings, *och-och-on.* The whole nation express all their mournful accents by these *three* monosyllables.

THIS chapter contains the following parts:—

1. We have here blessed promises of the latter-day glory.
2. The prophet may be considered as addressing the teachers of the Gospel, to show them that it was their business to encourage and direct the people in their expectation of redemption.
3. A promise of the manifestation of God among men is given.
4. The miracles which Christ should work are explicitly mentioned.
5. The privileges of Christianity are specified; there shall be, 1. Thorough teaching; 2. Holy walking.
6. Perfect safety.
7. Complete happiness. And—
8. Final glory.

The chapter shows also that no impurity should be tolerated in the Church of God; for as that is the mystical body of Christ, it should be like himself, without spot or wrinkle, or any such thing.

CHAPTER XXXVI

Sennacherib, king of Assyria, comes against Judah, and takes all the fenced cities, 1. *He afterwards sends a great host against Jerusalem; and his general Rabshakeh delivers an insulting and blasphemous message to Hezekiah,* 2–20. *Hezekiah and his people are greatly afflicted at the words of Rabshakeh,* 21, 22.

A. M. cir. 3291 B. C. cir. 713 Olymp. XVI. 4 cir. annum NumæPompilii, R. Roman., 3

NOW [a]it came to pass in the fourteenth year of king Hezekiah, *that* Sennacherib king of Assyria came up against all the defenced cities of Judah, and took them.

A. M. cir. 3294 B. C. cir. 710 Olymp. XVII. 3 cir. annum NumæPompilii, R. Roman., 6

2 And the king of Assyria sent Rabshakeh from Lachish to Jerusalem unto king Hezekiah with a great army. And he stood by the conduit of the upper pool in the highway of the fuller's field.

3 Then came forth unto him Eliakim, Hilkiah's son, which was over the house, and Shebna the [b]scribe, and Joah, Asaph's son, the recorder.

4 [c]And Rabshakeh said unto them, Say ye now to Hezekiah, Thus saith the great king, the king of Assyria, What confidence *is* this wherein thou trustest?

5 I say, *sayest thou,* (but *they are but* [d]vain words) [e]*I have* counsel and strength for war: now on whom dost thou trust, that thou rebellest against me?

A. M. cir. 3294 B. C. cir. 710 Olymp. XVII. 3 cir. annum NumæPompilii, R. Roman., 6

6 Lo, thou trustest in the [f]staff of this broken reed, on Egypt; whereon if a man lean, it will go into his hand, and pierce it: so *is* Pharaoh king of Egypt to all that trust in him.

7 But if thou say to me, We trust in the LORD our God: *is it* not he, whose high places and whose altars Hezekiah hath taken away, and said to Judah and to Jerusalem, Ye shall worship before this altar?

8 Now therefore give [g]pledges, I pray thee, to my master the king of Assyria, and I will give thee two thousand horses, if thou be able on thy part to set riders upon them.

9 How then wilt thou turn away the face of one captain of the least of my master's servants, and put thy trust on Egypt for chariots and for horsemen?

10 And am I now come up without the LORD against this land to destroy it? the LORD said unto me, Go up against this land, and destroy it.

11 Then said Eliakim and Shebna and Joah

[a]2 Kings xviii. 13, 17; 2 Chron. xxxii. 1——[b]Or, *secretary* [c]2 Kings xviii. 19, &c.——[d]Heb. *a word of lips*

[e]Or, but *counsel and strength* are *for the war*——[f]Ezek. xxix. 6, 7——[g]Or, *hostages*

The history of the invasion of Sennacherib, and of the miraculous destruction of his army, which makes the subject of so many of Isaiah's prophecies, is very properly inserted here as affording the best light to many parts of those prophecies, and as almost necessary to introduce the prophecy in the *thirty-seventh* chapter, being the answer of God to Hezekiah's prayer, which could not be properly understood without it. We find the same narrative in the Second Book of Kings, chaps. xviii., xix., xx.; and these chapters of Isaiah, xxxvi., xxxvii., xxxviii., xxxix., for much the greater part, (the account of the sickness of Hezekiah only excepted,) are but a different copy of that narration. The difference of the two copies is little more than what has manifestly arisen from the mistakes of transcribers; they mutually correct each other, and most of the mistakes may be perfectly rectified by a collation of the two copies with the assistance of the ancient versions. Some few sentences, or members of sentences, are omitted in this copy of Isaiah, which are found in the other copy in the Book of Kings. Whether these omissions were made by design or mistake may be doubted.—L.

NOTES ON CHAP. XXXVI

Verse 3. *Then came forth unto him*] Before these words the other copy, 2 Kings xviii. 18, adds, ויקראו אל המלך *vaiyikreu el hammelech,* "And they demanded audience of the king."

Verse 5. *I say*—"Thou hast said"] *Fourteen* MSS. (*three* ancient) of *Kennicott's* and *De Rossi's* have it in the second person, אמרת *amarta;* and so the other copy, 2 Kings xviii. 20.

But they are but *vain words*] דבר שפתים *debar sephathayim, a word of the lips.* Thou dost talk about *counsels,* but thou hast none; about *strength,* but there is none with thee.

Verse 6. *The staff of this broken reed*] A weakened, faithless ally.

On Egypt] The Bodl. MS. adds מלך *melech, the king* of Egypt; and so perhaps the *Chaldee* might read.

It will go into his hand, and pierce it] Will take subsidy after subsidy, and do nothing for it.

Verse 7. *But if thou say*—"But if ye say"] *Two* ancient MSS. have תאמרו *tomeru* in the plural number; so likewise the *Septuagint, Chaldee,* and the other copy, 2 Kings xviii. 22.

Ye shall worship before this altar—"To worship only before this altar"] See 2 Chron. xxxii. 12.

Verse 10. *Am I now come up without the Lord*] Probably some apostate Israelitish priest might have encouraged the king of Assyria by telling him that JEHOVAH had given him a commission against Jerusalem.

A. M. cir. 3294
B. C. cir. 710
Olymp. XVII. 3
cir. innum
NumæPompilii,
R. Roman., 6

unto Rabshakeh, Speak, I pray thee, unto thy servants in the Syrian language; for we understand *it:* and speak not to us in the Jews' language, in the ears of the people that *are* on the wall.

12 But Rabshakeh said, Hath my master sent me to thy master and to thee to speak these words? *hath he* not *sent me* to the men that sit upon the wall, that they may eat their own dung, and drink their own piss with you?

13 Then Rabshakeh stood, and cried with a loud voice in the Jews' language, and said, Hear ye the words of the great king, the king of Assyria.

14 Thus saith the king, Let not Hezekiah deceive you: for he shall not be able to deliver you.

15 Neither let Hezekiah make you trust in the LORD, saying, The LORD will surely deliver us: this city shall not be delivered into the hand of the king of Assyria.

16 Hearken not to Hezekiah: for thus saith the king of Assyria, [h]Make [i]*an agreement* with me *by* a present, and come out to me: [k]and eat ye every one of his vine, and every one of his fig-tree; and drink ye every one the waters of his own cistern;

A. M. cir. 3294
B. C. cir. 710
Olymp. XVII. 3
cir. annum
NumæPompilii,
R. Roman., 6

17 Until I come and take you away to a land like your own land, a land of corn and wine, a land of bread and vineyards.

18 *Beware* lest Hezekiah persuade you, saying, The LORD will deliver us. Hath any of the gods of the nations delivered his land out of the hand of the king of Assyria?

19 Where *are* the gods of Hamath and Arphad? where *are* the gods of Sepharvaim? and have they delivered Samaria out of my hand?

20 Who *are they* among all the gods of these lands, that have delivered their land out of my hand, that the LORD should deliver Jerusalem out of my hand?

21 But they held their peace, and answered him not a word: for the king's commandment was, saying, Answer him not.

22 Then came Eliakim, the son of Hilkiah, that *was* over the household, and Shebna the scribe, and Joah, the son of Asaph, the recorder, to Hezekiah with *their* clothes rent and told him the words of Rabshakeh.

---

[h]Or, *Seek my favour by a present* [i]Heb. *Make with me a blessing*——[k]Zech. iii. 10

Verse 12. *That they may eat their own dung*—"Destined to eat their own dung"] לאכל *leechol, that they may eat,* as our translation literally renders it. But the *Syriac* reads מאכל *meechol, that they may not eat,* perhaps rightly, and afterward ומשתות *umishshethoth,* or ושתות *ushethoth,* to the same purpose. *Seventeen* of Dr. *Kennicott's* MSS., *ten* of *De Rossi's* and *two* of my own, read מימי *meymey, the water;* mine have מימי שניהם *meymey sheneyhem,* and write in the margin מימי רגליהם *meymey regaleyhem, the water of their feet,* a modest way of expressing *urine.*

Verse 15. *This city shall not be delivered*] ולא *ve-lo,* AND *this city. Ten* of *Kennicott's* MSS., and *nine* of *De Rossi's,* with *one* (ancient) of my own, add the *conjunction.*

Verse 16. *Make* an agreement] ברכה *berachah, make a blessing with me;* i. e., Give me a ransom for the city, and I will not destroy it; give me the yearly tribute thou hast promised.

Verse 17. *And vineyards*] The other copy, 2 Kings xviii. 32, adds here: "A land of oil-olive, and of honey; that ye may live, and not die: and hearken not unto Hezekiah when he seduceth you."

Verse 19. *Where* are *the gods*] Many MSS. add the conjunction here also: *And,* or *But, where* are *the gods,* &c.

For other matters relative to this chapter, see the notes on 2 Kings xviii. 13, &c.

Of Sepharvaim] The other copy, 2 Kings xviii. 34, adds, of "Henah and Ivah."

Have they delivered] וכי *vechi.* The copulative is not expressed here by the *Septuagint, Syriac, Vulgate,* and *three* MSS.; nor is it in any other copy. Ib. Houbigant reads הכי *hachi,* with the interrogative particle; a probable conjecture, which the ancient Versions above quoted seem to favour.

Verse 21. *But they held their peace*—"But the people held their peace"] The word העם *haam, the people,* is supplied from the other copy, and is authorized by a MS. which inserts it after אתו *otho.*

CHAPTER XXXVII

Hezekiah is greatly distressed, and sends to Isaiah the prophet to pray for him,* 1–4. *Isaiah returns a comfortable answer, and predicts the destruction of the king of Assyria and his army,* 5–7. *Sennacherib, hearing that his kingdom was invaded by the Ethiopians, sends a terrible letter to Hezekiah, to induce him to surrender,

9–13. *Hezekiah goes to the temple, spreads the letter before the Lord, and makes a most affecting prayer,* 14–20. *Isaiah is sent to him to assure him that his prayer is heard; that Jerusalem shall be delivered; and that the Assyrians shall be destroyed,* 21–35. *That very night* a messenger of God *slays one hundred and eighty-five thousand Assyrians,* 36. *Sennacherib returns to Nineveh, and is slain by his own sons,* 37, 38.

A. M. cir. 3294
B. C. cir. 710
Olymp. XVII. 3
cir. annum
NumæPompilii,
R. Roman., 6

AND [a]it came to pass, when king Hezekiah heard *it,* that he rent his clothes, and covered himself with sackcloth, and went into the house of the LORD.

2 And he sent Eliakim, who *was* over the household, and Shebna the scribe, and the elders of the priests covered with sackcloth, unto Isaiah the prophet the son of Amoz.

3 And they said unto him, Thus saith Hezekiah, This day *is* a day of trouble, and of rebuke, and of [b]blasphemy: for the children are come to the birth, and *there is* not strength to bring forth.

4 It may be the LORD thy God will hear the words of Rabshakeh, whom the king of Assyria his master hath sent to reproach the living God, and will reprove the words which the LORD thy God hath heard: wherefore lift up *thy* prayer for the remnant that is [c]left.

5 So the servants of king Hezekiah came to Isaiah.

6 And Isaiah said unto them, Thus shall ye say unto your master, Thus saith the LORD, Be not afraid of the words that thou hast heard, wherewith the servants of the king of Assyria have blasphemed me.

A. M. cir. 3294
B. C. cir. 710
Olymp. XVII. 3
cir. annum
NumæPompilii,
R. Roman., 6

7 Behold, I will [d]send a blast upon him, and he shall hear a rumour, and return to his own land; and I will cause him to fall by the sword in his own land.

8 So Rabshakeh returned, and found the king of Assyria warring against Libnah: for he had heard that he was departed from Lachish.

9 And he heard say concerning Tirhakah king of Ethiopia, He is come forth to make war with thee. And when he heard *it,* he sent messengers to Hezekiah, saying,

10 Thus shall ye speak to Hezekiah king of Judah, saying, Let not thy God, in whom thou trustest, deceive thee, saying, Jerusalem shall not be given into the hand of the king of Assyria.

11 Behold, thou hast heard what the kings of Assyria have done to all lands by destroying them utterly; and shalt thou be delivered?

12 Have the gods of the nations delivered

[a]2 Kings xix. 1, &c.——[b]Or, *provocation*

[c]Heb. *found*——[d]Or, *put a spirit into him*

NOTES ON CHAP. XXXVII

Verse 6. *Thus shall ye say*] כה תאמרון *ko tomerun,* "thus shall ye (*explicitly, earnestly,* and *positively*) say." The paragogic ן *nun* deepens and increases the sense.

Verse 7. *I will send a blast*—"I will infuse a spirit into him"] "נותי בו רוח *nothen bo ruach* never signifies any thing but putting a spirit into a person: this was πνευμα δειλιας, *the spirit of deceit.*"—*Secker.* "I will send a blast"—I do not think that Archbishop Secker has hit the true meaning of these words. I believe רוח *ruach* means here a pestilential *wind,* such as the Arabs call *simoom,* that instantly suffocates both man and beast; and is what is termed "the angel of the Lord," God's messenger of death to the Assyrians, ver. 36.

Verse 8. *Rabshakeh returned*] From chap. xxxvi. 2, we learn that the king of Assyria had sent Rabshakeh from Lachish to Jerusalem; now it is likely that Rabshakeh had besieged that place, and that the king of Assyria had taken his station before this city, and despatched Rabshakeh against Jerusalem. But, as in the verse above it is said, "he had departed from Lachish," probably he had been obliged to raise the siege, and sat down before *Libnah,* which promised an easier conquest.

Verse 9. *He heard say concerning Tirhakah king of Ethiopia*] When he heard that Tirhakah king of Ethiopia had come out against him, then he sent that blasphemous *manifesto* which is contained in ver. 10-13, to terrify Hezekiah into submission. How much was this like, in words and spirit, to the manifesto sent to the *Parisians* by the late *Duke of Brunswick,* from the plains of *Champaigne,* in 1792, which was the forerunner of the mighty torrents of human blood which was shed in the French revolution! And what a blast of God fell upon *him* and his *army*—nearly like that which fell on the army of Sennacherib!

He sent messengers—"He sent messengers again"] The word וישמע *vaiyishma,* "and he heard," which occurs the second time in this verse, is repeated by mistake from the beginning of the verse. It is omitted in an ancient MS. It is a mere tautology, and embarrasses the sense. The true reading instead of it is, וישב *veyesheb,* "and he returned," which the *Septuagint* read in this place, απεστρεψε, and which is preserved in the other copy, 2 Kings xix. 9: "He returned and sent," that is, according to the Hebrew idiom, "he sent again."

Verse 12. As *Gozan, and Haran*] חרן *Charan:* but הרן *Haran* is the reading of *four* of *Kennicott's* MSS. and *one* of *De Rossi's.*

A. M. cir. 3294 B. C. cir. 710 Olymp. XVII. 3 cir. annum NumæPompilii, R. Roman., 6

them which my fathers have
destroyed, *as* Gozan, and Haran,
and Rezeph, and the children of
Eden which *were* in Telassar?
13 Where *is* the king of [e]Hamath, and the
king of Arphad, and the king of the city of
Sepharvaim, Hena, and Ivah?
14 And Hezekiah received the letter from
the hand of the messengers, and read it: and
Hezekiah went up unto the house of the LORD,
and spread it before the LORD.
15 And Hezekiah prayed unto the LORD,
saying,
16 O LORD of hosts, God of Israel, that
dwellest *between* the cherubims, thou *art* the
God, *even* thou alone, of all the kingdoms of
the earth: thou hast made heaven and earth.
17 [f]Incline thine ear, O LORD, and hear:
open thine eyes, O LORD, and see: and hear
all the words of Sennacherib, which hath sent
to reproach the living God.
18 Of a truth, LORD, the kings of Assyria
have laid waste all the [g]nations, and their
countries,
19 And have [h]cast their gods
into the fire: for they *were* no
gods, but the work of men's
hands, wood and stone: therefore they have destroyed them.
20 Now therefore, O LORD our God, save
us from his hand, that all the kingdoms of the
earth may know that thou *art* the LORD, *even*
thou only.
21 Then Isaiah the son of Amoz sent unto
Hezekiah, saying, Thus saith the LORD God
of Israel, Whereas thou hast prayed to me
against Sennacherib king of Assyria:
22 This *is* the word which the LORD hath
spoken concerning him; The virgin, the
daughter of Zion, hath despised thee, *and*
laughed thee to scorn; the daughter of Jerusalem hath shaken her head at thee.
23 Whom hast thou reproached and blasphemed; and against whom hast thou exalted
thy voice, and lifted up thine eyes on high?
even against the Holy One of Israel.
24 [i]By thy servants hast thou reproached
the Lord, and hast said, By the multitude of

A. M. cir. 3294 B. C. cir. 710 Olymp. XVII. 3 cir. annum NumæPompilii, R. Roman., 6

---

[e]Jer. xlix. 23——[f]Dan. ix. 18——[g]Heb. *lands*

[h]Heb. *given*——[i]Heb. *By the hand of thy servants*

Verse 14. *And read it*—"And read them"] ויקראם *vayikraem*. So MS. Bodl. in this place; and so the other copy; instead of ויקראהו *vaiyikraehu*, "and read IT."

And spread it—"And spread them"] ויפרשהו *vaiyiphresehu*. הו *hu* is upon a rasure in a MS., which probably was at first ם *mem*. The same mistake as in the foregoing note.

Verse 15. *Unto the Lord*—"Before JEHOVAH"] That is, in the sanctuary. For אל *el*, the *Syriac*, *Chaldee*, and the other copy, 2 Kings xix. 15, read לפני *liphney*, "before the face."

Verse 18. *The nations*] הארצות *haratsoth*, "the lands;" instead of this word, which destroys the sense, *ten* of *Kennicott's* and *five* of *De Rossi's* MSS. (*one* ancient) have here גוים *goyim*, "nations;" which is undoubtedly the true reading, being preserved also in the other copy; 2 Kings xix. 17. Another MS. suggests another method of rectifying the sense in this place, by reading מלכם *malcam*, "their king," instead of ארצם *artsam*, "their land;" but it ought to be מלכיהם *malcheyhem*, "all the countries and their kings."

Verse 20. *Save us*—"Save us, we beseech thee"] The supplicating particle, נא *na*, is supplied here from *eighteen* MSS., *three* ancient, of *Dr. Kennicott*, and *ten* of *De Rossi*, and from the other copy; 2 Kings xix. 19.

That thou art *the Lord*, even *thou only*—"That thou JEHOVAH art the only God."] The word אלהים *Elohim*, "God," is lost here in the Hebrew text, but preserved in the other copy; 2 Kings xix. 19. The *Syriac* and *Septuagint* seem here to have had in their copies אלהים *Elohim*, instead of יהוה *Yehovah*.

Verse 21. *Then Isaiah—sent unto Hezekiah*] The *Syriac* and *Septuagint* understand and render the verb passively, *was sent*.

Whereas thou hast prayed to me against Sennacherib—"Thy prayer unto me concerning Sennacherib—*I have heard*"] שמעתי *shamati;* this word, necessary to the sense, is lost in this place out of the Hebrew text. *One* MS. of *Dr. Kennicott's* and *one* of *De Rossi's* have it written above the line in a later hand. The *Septuagint* and *Syriac* found it in their copies; and it is preserved in the other copy; 2 Kings xix. 20.

Verse 23. *Against the Holy One of Israel.*] For אל *el, to*, the other copy has על *al, against*, rather more properly.

Verse 24. *By thy servants*—"By thy messengers"] The text has עבדיך *abdeycha, thy servants;* but the true reading seems to be מלאכיך *malacheycha, thy messengers*, as in the other copy, 2 Kings xix. 23; and as the *Septuagint* and *Syriac* found it in their copies in this place.

Reproached the Lord] אדני *Adonai:* but *one* of my MSS. has יהוה אדני *Yehovah Adonai, Jehovah the Lord.* This reading is not found, I think, in any other MS., but several have יהוה *Yehovah* for אדני *Adonai*.

I will enter into the height of his border—"I will penetrate into his extreme retreats"] The text has מרום *marom, the height* which seems to have been taken by mistake from the line but one above. *Two* MSS. have here מלון *malon*, the *lodge* or *retreat;* which is the word

A. M. cir. 3294 my chariots am I come up to
B. C. cir. 710
Olymp. XVII. 3 the height of the mountains, to
cir. annum
NumæPompilii, the sides of Lebanon; and I
R. Roman., 6 will cut down [k]the tall cedars
thereof, *and* the choice fir trees thereof: and I will enter into the height of his border, *and* [l]the forest of his Carmel.

25 I have digged, and drunk water; and with the sole of my feet have I dried up all the rivers of the [m]besieged places.

26 [n]Hast thou not heard long ago, *how* I have done it; *and* of ancient times, that I have formed it? now have I brought it to pass, that thou shouldest be to lay waste defenced cities *into* ruinous heaps.

27 Therefore their inhabitants *were* [o]of small power, they were dismayed and confounded: they were *as* the grass of the field, and *as* the green herb, *as* the grass on the housetops, and *as corn* blasted before it be grown up.

28 But I know thy [p]abode, and thy going out, and thy coming in, and thy rage against me.

29 Because thy rage against A. M. cir. 3291
B. C. cir. 713
me, and thy tumult, is come up Olymp. XVI. 4
cir. annum
into mine ears, therefore [q]will I NumæPompilii,
put my hook in thy nose, and my R. Roman., 3
bridle in thy lips, and I will turn thee back by the way by which thou camest.

30 And this *shall be* a sign unto thee, Ye shall eat *this* year such as groweth of itself: and the second year that which springeth of the same: and in the third year sow ye, and reap, and plant vineyards, and eat the fruit thereof.

31 And [r]the remnant that is escaped of the house of Judah shall again take root downward, and bear fruit upward:

32 For out of Jerusalem shall go forth a remnant, and [s]they that escape out of Mount Zion: the [t]zeal of the LORD of hosts shall do this.

33 Therefore thus saith the LORD concerning the king of Assyria, He shall not come into this city, nor shoot an arrow there, nor come before it with [u]shields, nor cast a bank against it.

---

[k]Heb. *the tallness of the cedars thereof*, and *the choice of the fir-trees thereof*——[l]Or, *the forest* and *his fruitful field* [m]Or, *fenced and closed*——[n]Or, *Hast thou not heard* how *I have made it long ago*, and *formed it of ancient times? should I now bring it to be laid waste*, and *defenced cities* to be *ruinous heaps?* as 2 Kings xix. 25——[o]Heb. *short of hand*——[p]Or, *sitting*——[q]Ch. xxx. 28; Ezek. xxxviii. 4 [r]Heb. *the escaping of the house of Judah that remaineth* [s]Heb. *the escaping*——[t]2 Kings xix. 31; chap. ix. 7 [u]Heb. *shield*

---

in the other copy, 2 Kings xix. 23, and I think is the true reading.

The forest of his Carmel.] The forest and his fruitful field; that is, I will possess myself of the *whole country*.

Verse 25. *Water*—"Strange waters"] The word זרים *zarim*, *strange*, lost out of the Hebrew text in this place, is supplied from the other copy. A MS. supplies the word רבים *rabbim*, *many*, instead of it.

With the sole of my feet] With my *infantry*.

All the rivers of the besieged places—"All the canals of fenced places."] The principal cities of Egypt, the scene of his late exploits, were chiefly defended by deep moats, canals, or large lakes, made by labour and art, with which they were surrounded. See *Harmer's* Observ. ii. p. 304. Claudian introduces Alaric boasting of his conquests in the same extravagant manner:—

"Subsidere nostris
Sub pedibus montes; arescere vidimus amnes.—
Fregi Alpes, galeisque Padum victricibus hausi."
De Bello Getic. 526.

"The mountains have passed away under our feet; we have seen the rivers dried up. I have broken the Alps, and laden out the Po with our victorious helmets."

Verse 26. *Lay waste defenced cities* into *ruinous heaps*—"Lay waste warlike nations. strong fenced cities."] גלים נצים *gallim nitstsim.* It is not easy to give a satisfactory account of these two words, which have greatly embarrassed all the interpreters, ancient and modern. For גלים *gallim* I read גוים *goyim*, as the *Septuagint* do in this place, εθνη. The word נצים *netsim* the *Vulgate* renders in this place *compugnantium;* in the parallel place, 2 Kings xix. 25, *pugnantium;* and the *Septuagint* μαχιμων, *fighting, warlike.* This rendering is as well authorized as any other that I know of; and, with the reading of the *Septuagint*, perfectly clears up the construction. See the *margin* on all the preceding verses.

Verse 27. Corn *blasted*] שדמה *shedemah, parched:* it does not appear that there is any good authority for this word. The true reading seems to be שדפה *shedephah, blasted*, as it is in six MSS. (two ancient) here, and in the other copy.

Verse 29. *Will I put my hook in thy nose*] Et frænum meum: *Jonathan* vocem מתג *metheg*, interpretatus est זמם *zemam*, i. e., annulum, sive uncum, eumque ferreum, quem infigunt naribus camelæ: eoque trahitur, quoniam illa feris motibus agitur: et hoc est, quod discimus in Talmude; et camela cum annulo narium: scilicet, egreditur die sabbathi. "*And my bridle: Jonathan* interprets the word *metheg* by *zemam*, a ring, or that iron hook which they put in the nostrils of a camel to lead her about, check her in her restiveness, &c. And this is what we mean in the *Talmud*, when we say,

A. M. cir. 3291
B. C. cir. 713
Olymp. XVI. 4
cir. annum
NumæPompilii,
R. Roman., 3

34 By the way that he came,
by the same shall he return, and
shall not come into this city,
saith the LORD.
35 For I will [v]defend this city to save it
for mine own sake, and for my servant David's
sake.
36 Then the [w]angel of the LORD went
forth, and smote in the camp of the Assyrians
a hundred and fourscore and five thousand:
and when they arose early in the morning,
behold, they *were* all dead
corpses.
37 So Sennacherib king of Assyria departed, and went and returned, and dwelt at Nineveh.
38 And it came to pass, as he was worshipping in the house of Nisroch his god, that
Adrammelech and Sharezer his sons smote
him with the sword; and they escaped into
the land of [x]Armenia: and Esar-haddon his
son reigned in his stead.

A. M. cir. 3291
B. C. cir. 713
Olymp. XVI. 4
cir. annum
NumæPompilii,
R. Roman., 3

[v]2 Kings xx. 6; chap. xxxviii. 6 — [w]2 Kings xix. 35 — [x]Heb. *Ararat*

And the camel with the ring of her nostrils shall go out on the Sabbath day."—*Jarchi* in 2 Kings xix. 28. Ponam circulum in naribus tuis. "I will put a ring in thy nostrils."—*Jerome*. Just as at this day they put a ring into the nose of the bear, the buffalo, and other wild beasts, to lead them, and to govern them when they are unruly. Bulls are often ringed thus in several parts of England. The Hindoos compare a person who is the *slave of his wife* to a *cow* led by the *ring* in her nose.

Verse 36. *Then the angel*] Before "the angel," the other copy, 2 Kings xix. 35, adds, "it came to pass the same night, that"——

The Prophet Hosea, chap. i. 7, has given a plain prediction of the miraculous deliverance of the kingdom of Judah:—

"And to the house of Judah I will be tenderly merciful:
And I will save them by JEHOVAH their God.
And I will not save them by the bow;
Nor by sword, nor by battle;
By horses, nor by horsemen."—L.

Verse 38. *His sons smote him*] What an awful punishment of his blasphemy! Who can harden his neck against God, and be successful? God does not lightly pass by blasphemy against himself, his government, his word, his Son, or his people. Let the profligate take care!

CHAPTER XXXVIII

Account of Hezekiah's dangerous sickness and miraculous recovery, 1–9. *Tender and beautiful song of thanksgiving, in which this pious king breathed out the sentiments of a grateful heart, when his life was, as it were, restored. This ode may be adapted to other cases; and will always afford profit and pleasure to those who are not void of feeling and piety,* 10–22.

A. M. cir. 3291
B. C. cir. 713
Olymp. XVI. 4
cir. annum
NumæPompilii,
R. Roman., 3

IN [a]those days was Hezekiah
sick unto death. And Isaiah
the prophet the son of Amoz
came unto him, and said unto
him, Thus saith the LORD, [b]Set[c] thine
house in order: for thou shalt
die, and not live.
2 Then Hezekiah turned his
face toward the wall, and prayed
unto the LORD.

A. M. cir. 3291
B. C. cir. 713
Olymp. XVI. 4
cir. annum
NumæPompilii,
R. Roman., 3

[a]2 Kings xx. 1, &c.; 2 Chron. xxxii. 24 — [b]2 Sam. xvii. 23; 1 Mac. ix. 55 — [c]Heb. *Give charge concerning thy house*

NOTES ON CHAP. XXXVIII

Verse 1. *In those days*] The reader is requested to consult the notes on 2 Kings xx. in reference to the principal parts of this chapter.

Verse 2. *Then Hezekiah turned his face toward the wall*] The furniture of an eastern divan or chamber, either for the reception of company or for private use, consists chiefly of carpets spread on the floor in the middle; and of sofas, or couches ranged on one or more sides of the room, on a part raised somewhat above the floor. On these they repose themselves in the day, and sleep at night. It is to be observed that the corner of the room is the place of honour. Dr. *Pococke*, when he was introduced to the Sheikh of Furshout, found him sitting in the corner of his room. He describes another Arab Sheikh "as sitting in the corner of a large green tent, pitched in the middle of an encampment of Arabs; and the Bey of Girge as placed on a sofa in a corner to the right as one entered the room."—*Harmer's* Observ. ii. p. 60. Lady Mary Montague, giving an account of a visit which she made to the Kahya's lady at Adrianople, says, "She ordered cushions to be given me; and took care to place me in the corner, which is the place of honour." —Letter xxxiii. The reason of this seems to be, that the person so placed is distinguished, and in a manner separated, from the rest of the company, and as it were guarded by the wall on each side. We are to suppose Hezekiah's couch placed in the same situation; in which, turning on either side, he must turn his face to the wall; by which he would withdraw himself from those who were attending upon him in his apartment, in order to address his private prayer to God.

A. M. cir. 3291
B. C. cir. 713
Olymp. XVI. 4
cir. annum
NumæPompilii,
R. Roman., 3

3 And said, [d]Remember now,
O LORD, I beseech thee, how I
have walked before thee in truth
and with a perfect heart, and
have done *that which is* good in thy sight.
And Hezekiah wept [e]sore.
4 Then came the word of the LORD to
Isaiah, saying,
5 Go, and say to Hezekiah, Thus saith the
LORD, the God of David thy father, I have
heard thy prayer, I have seen thy tears: behold I will add unto thy days fifteen years.
6 And I will deliver thee and this city out
of the hand of the king of Assyria: and [f]I
will defend this city.
7 And this *shall be* [g]a sign unto thee from
the LORD, that the LORD will do this thing
that he hath spoken;
8 Behold, I will bring again the
shadow of the degrees, which is
gone down in the [h]sun dial of
Ahaz, ten degrees backward. So
the sun returned ten degrees, by which degrees
it was gone down.
9 The writing of Hezekiah king of Judah,
when he had been sick, and was recovered of
his sickness:
10 I said in the cutting off of my days, I
shall go to the gates of the grave: I am deprived of the residue of my years.
11 I said, I shall not see the LORD, *even*
the LORD, [i]in the land of the living: I shall
behold man no more with the inhabitants of
the world.
12 [k]Mine age is departed, and is removed
from me as a shepherd's tent: I have cut off

A. M. cir. 3291
B. C. cir. 713
Olymp. XVI. 4
cir. annum
NumæPompilii,
R. Roman., 3

[d]Neh. xiii. 14——[e]Heb. *with great weeping*——[f]Chap. xxxvii. 35——[g]2 Kings xx. 8, &c.; chap. vii. 11

[h]Heb. *degrees by* or *with the sun*——[i]Psa. xxvii. 13; cxvi. 9——[k]Job vii. 6

Ver. 3. And he said, I beseech thee, O JEHOVAH, remember now how I have endeavoured to walk before thee in truth, and with a perfect heart; and have done that which is good in thine eyes. And Hezekiah wept, and lamented grievously.—L.

Ver. 4. Now [before Isaiah was gone out into the middle court] the word of JEHOVAH came unto him, saying, Go [back,] and say unto Hezekiah, Thus saith JEHOVAH the God of David thy father, I have heard thy supplication; I have seen thy tears. Behold [I will heal thee; and on the third day thou shalt go up into the house of JEHOVAH.

Ver. 5. And] I will add unto thy days fifteen years. And I will deliver thee, and this city, from the hand of the king of Assyria; and I will protect this city. And [Hezekiah said, By what sign shall I know that I shall go up into the house of JEHOVAH?

Ver. 7. And Isaiah said,] This shall be the sign unto thee from JEHOVAH, that JEHOVAH will bring to effect this word which he hath spoken.

The words in the translation included within crotchets are supplied from the parallel place, 2 Kings xx. 4, 5, to make the narration more perfect. I have also taken the liberty, with *Houbigant*, of bringing forward the two last verses of this chapter, and inserting them in their proper places of the narration with the same mark. *Kimchi's* note on these two verses is as follows: "This and the following verse belong not to the writing of Hezekiah; and I see no reason why they are written here after the writing; for their right place is above, after *And I will protect this city*, ver. 6. And so they stand in the book of Kings," 2 Kings xx. 7, 8. The narration of this chapter seems to be in some parts an abridgment of that of 2 Kings xx. The abridger, having finished his extract here with the eleventh verse, seems to have observed, that the seventh and eighth verses of 2 Kings xx. were wanted to complete the narration: he therefore added them at the end of the chapter, after he had inserted the song of Hezekiah, probably with marks for their insertion in their proper places; which marks were afterwards neglected by transcribers. Or a transcriber might omit them by mistake, and add them at the end of the chapter with such marks. Many transpositions are, with great probability, to be accounted for in the same way.

Verse 6. *I will defend this city.*] The other copy, 2 Kings xx. 6, adds: "for mine own sake, and for the sake of David my servant;" and the sentence seems somewhat abrupt without it.

Verse 8. *Which is gone down*—"By which the sun is gone down"] For בשמש *bashshemesh*, the *Septuagint*, *Syriac*, and *Chaldee* read השמש *hashshemesh*.—*Houbigant*. In the history of this miracle in the book of Kings, (2 Kings xx. 9-11,) there is no mention at all made of the sun, but only of the going backward of the shadow: which might be effected by a supernatural refraction. The first ὁ ἥλιος, *the sun*, in this verse is omitted in the *Septuagint*, MS. Pachom.

Verse 9. *The writing of Hezekiah*] Here the book of Kings deserts us, the song of Hezekiah not being inserted in it. Another copy of this very obscure passage (obscure not only from the concise poetical style, but because it is probably very incorrect) would have been of great service. The MSS. and ancient Versions, especially the latter, will help us to get through some of the many difficulties which we meet with in it.

Verse 11. *The Lord*—"JEHOVAH"] יה *Yah*, יה *Yah*, seems to be יהוה *Yehovah*, in MS. Bodl., and it was so at first written in another. So the *Syriac*. See *Houbigant*. I believe יהוה *Yehovah* was the original reading. See the note on chap. xii. 2.

Verse 12. *Mine age—is removed from me as a shepherd's tent*] רעי *roi* is put for רעה *roeh*, say the rabbins; (*Sal. ben Melec* on the place;) but much more probably is written imperfectly for רעים *roim*, *shepherds*. See note on chap. v. 1.

I shall be removed from this state to another,

A. M. cir. 3291
B. C. cir. 713
Olymp. XVI. 4
cir. annum
NumæPompilii,
R. Roman., 3

like a weaver my life: he will cut me off [l]with pining sickness: from day *even* to night wilt thou make an end of me.

13 I reckoned till morning, *that,* as a lion, so will he break all my bones: from day *even* to night wilt thou make an end of me.

14 Like a crane *or* a swallow, so did I chatter: [m]I did mourn as a dove: mine eyes fail *with looking* upward: O LORD, I am oppressed; [n]undertake for me.

15 What shall I say? he hath both spoken unto me, and himself hath done *it:* I shall go softly all my years [o]in the bitterness of my soul.

16 O LORD, by these *things* *men* live, and in all these *things* *is* the life of my spirit; so wilt thou recover me, and make me to live.

17 Behold [p]for peace I had great bitterness: but [q]thou hast in love to my soul *delivered it* from the pit of corruption: for thou hast cast all my sins behind thy back.

18 For [r]the grave cannot praise thee, death can *not* celebrate thee: they that go down into the pit cannot hope for thy truth.

19 The living, the living, he shall praise thee, as I *do* this day: [s]the father to the children shall make known thy truth.

[l]Or, *from the* thrum——[m]Chap. lix. 11——[n]Or, *ease me*——[o]Job vii. 11; x. 1——[p]Or, *on my peace* came *great bitterness*

[q]Heb. *thou hast loved my soul from the pit*——[r]Psa. vi. 5; xxx. 9; lxxxviii. 11; cxv. 17; Eccles. ix. 10——[s]Deut. iv. 9; vi. 7; Psa. lxxviii. 3, 4

as a shepherd removes his *tent* from one place to another for the sake of his flock. Is not this a strong intimation of his belief in a future state?

I have cut off like a weaver my life—"My life is cut off as by the weaver"] קפדתי *kippadti.* This verb is rendered passively, and in the third person, by the *Syriac, Chaldee,* and *Vulgate.*

Verse 13. The last line of the foregoing verse מיום עד לילה תשלימני *miyom ad layelah tashlimeni,* "In the course of the day thou wilt finish my web;" or, as the common version has it, "From day *even* to night wilt thou make an end of me," is not repeated at the end of this verse in the Syriac version; and a MS. omits it. It seems to have been inserted a second time in the Hebrew text by mistake.

I reckoned till morning, &c.—"I roared until the morning like the lion"] For שויתי *shivvithi,* the Chaldee has נהמית *nihameith:* he read שאגתי *shaagti,* the proper term for the roaring of a lion; often applied to the deep groaning of men in sickness. See Psa. xxii., xxxii. 3, xxxviii. 9; Job iii. 24. The Masoretes divide the sentence, as I have done; taking כארי *caari, like a lion,* into the first member; and so likewise the *Septuagint.*

Verse 14. *Like—a swallow*—"Like the swallow"] כסים *kesis;* so read two MSS., *Theodot.,* and *Hieron.*

Mine eyes fail] For דלו *dallu* the *Septuagint* read כלו *calu,* εξελιπον. Compare Psa. lxix. 4, cxix. 82, 123; Lam. ii. 11, iv. 17, in the *Hebrew* and in the *Septuagint.*

O LORD—"O Lord"] For יהוה *Yehovah,* thirty MSS. and eight editions read אדני *Adonai.*

Undertake for me—"Contend for me"] עשקה *ashekah,* with ש *shin, Jarchi:* this sense of the word is established by Gen. xxvi. 20: "He called the name of the well עשק *esek,* because they *strove* with him:" התעשקו *hithasseku,* equivalent to יריבו *yaribu,* at the beginning of the verse.

Verse 15. *I shall go softly all my years in the bitterness of my soul*—"Through the rest of my years will I reflect on this bitterness of my soul"] אדדה *eddaddeh; recogitabo,* Vulg., *reputabo,* Hieron. in loc.

Verse 16. *By these* things men *live*—"For this cause shall it be declared"] Περι αυτης γαρ ανηγγελη σοι, και εξηγειρας μου την πνοην, Sept. They read in their copies עליה יחוו לך ותחיי רוחי not very different from the present text, from which all the ancient Versions vary. They entirely omit two words, ולכל בהן *ulecol bahen;* as to which there is some variation in the MSS. One MS. has ובכל *ubechol, and in all;* two others וכל *vechol, and all,* and ten MSS. have בהם *bahem, in them,* in the masculine gender.

Taking this as in the common Version, we may observe, it is not an unfrequent case, that afflictions, and especially such as tend to a speedy death, become the means, not only of saving the *soul,* but also of lengthening the *life.*

Make me to live—"Hast prolonged my life."] A MSS. and the Babylonish Talmud read ותחיני *vetachayeni,* and so the ancient Versions. It must necessarily be in the second person.

Verse 17. *For peace I had great bitterness*—"My anguish is changed into ease"] מר לי מר *mar li mar,* "mutata mihi est amaritudo." Paronomasia; a figure which the prophet frequently admits. I do not always note it, because it cannot ever be preserved in the translation, and the sense seldom depends upon it. But here it perfectly clears up the great obscurity of the passage. See Lowth on the place.

Thou hast rescued] חשכת *chashachta,* with כ *caph,* instead of ק *koph;* so the *Septuagint* and *Vulgate; Houbigant.* See *Chappelow* on Job xxxiii. 18.

From perdition] משחת בלי *mishshachath beli,* ινα μη αποληται, *Sept. ut non periret,* "that it may not perish." *Vulg.* Perhaps inverting the order of the words. See *Houbigant.*

Thou hast in love to my soul] חשקת *chashakta,* "thou hast lovingly embraced" or kissed "my soul out of the pit of corruption."

Verse 19. *Thy truth*] אל אמתך *el amittecha.*

A. M. cir. 3291
B. C. cir. 713
Olymp. XVI. 4
cir. annum
NumæPompilii,
R. Roman., 3

20 The LORD *was ready* to
save me: therefore we will sing
my songs to the stringed instruments all the days of our life in
the house of the LORD.
21 For [t]Isaiah had said, Let them take a
lump of figs, and lay *it* for a
plaster upon the boil, and he
shall recover.
22 [u]Hezekiah also had said,
What *is* the sign that I shall go up to the
house of the LORD?

[t]2 Kings xx. 7

[u]2 Kings xx. 8

A MS. omits אל *el;* and instead of אל *el*, an ancient MS. and one edition read את *eth.* The same mistake as in Psa. ii. 7.

Verse 21. *Let them take a lump of figs, &c.*] God, in effecting this miraculous cure, was pleased to order the use of means not improper for that end. "Folia, et, quæ non maturuere, fici, strumis illinuntur omnibusque quæ emollienda sunt discutiendave."—PLIN. *Nat. Hist.* xxiii. 7. "Ad discutienda ea, quæ in corporis parte aliqua coierunt, maxime possunt—ficus arida," &c.—CELSUS, v. 11. See the note on 2 Kings xx. 7. *Philemon Holland* translates the passage as a *medical* man:—"The milke or white juice that the figge tree yieldeth is of the same nature that vinegre: and therefore it will cruddle milke as well as rennet, or rendles. The right season of gathering this milkie substance is before that the figs be ripe upon the tree; and then it must be dried in the shadow: thus prepared, *it is good to break impostumes, and keepe ulcer open.*"

CHAPTER XXXIX

The Babylonish monarch sends letters of congratulation and a present to Hezekiah, on account of his recovery from his late dangerous illness, 1. *The king of Judah shows the messengers of Merodach-baladan all the treasures of his house and kingdom,* 2. *The prophet takes occasion from this ostentatious display of the king to predict the captivity of the royal family, and of the people, by the Babylonians,* 3–8.

A. M. cir. 3292
B. C. cir. 712
Olymp. XVII. 1
cir. annum
NumæPompilii,
R. Roman., 4

AT [a]that time Merodach-baladan, the son of Baladan, king
of Babylon, sent letters and a
present to Hezekiah: for he had
heard that he had been sick, and was recovered.
2 [b]And Hezekiah was glad of them, and
showed them the house of his [c]precious things,
the silver, and the gold, and the spices, and
the precious ointment, and all the house of
his [d]armour, [e]and all that was found in his
treasures: there was nothing in his house, nor
in all his dominion, that Hezekiah showed
them not.
3 Then came Isaiah the prophet unto king
Hezekiah, and said unto him, What said these
men? and from whence came they unto thee?
And Hezekiah said, They are
come from a far country unto
me, *even* from Babylon.
4 Then said he, What have
they seen in thine house? And Hezekiah
answered, All that *is* in mine house have they
seen: there is nothing among my treasures
that I have not showed them.
5 Then said Isaiah to Hezekiah, Hear the
word of the LORD of hosts:
6 Behold, the days come, [f]that all that *is*
in thine house, and *that* which thy fathers
have laid up in store until this day, shall be
carried to Babylon: nothing shall be left, saith
the LORD.
7 And of thy sons that shall issue from thee,

[a]2 Kings xx. 12, &c.——[b]2 Chron. xxxii. 31
[c]Or, *spicery*

[d]Or, *jewels*——[e]Heb. *vessels* or *instruments*
[f]Jer. xx. 5

NOTES ON CHAP. XXXIX

Hitherto the copy of this history in the second book of Kings has been much the most correct; in this chapter that in Isaiah has the advantage. In the two first verses two mistakes in the other copy are to be corrected from this: for הזקיהו *hizkiyahu*, read ויחזק *vayechezek, and was recovered;* and for וישמע *vaiyishma, he heard*, read וישמח *vaiyismach, he rejoiced.*

Verse 1. *At that time Merodach-baladan*] This name is variously written in the MSS. *Berodach, Medorach, Medarech*, and *Medurach.*

"And ambassadors"] The *Septuagint* add here *και πρεσβεις;* that is, ומלאכים *umalachim, and ambassadors;* which word seems to be necessary to the sense, though omitted in the Hebrew text both here and in the other copy, 2 Kings xx. 12. For the subsequent narration refers to them all along, "these men, whence came they?" &c.; plainly supposing them to have been personally mentioned before. See *Houbigant.*

Verse 6. *To Babylon*] בבלה *babelah*, so two MSS., (one ancient;) rightly, without doubt, as the other copy (2 Kings xx. 17) has it. This prediction was fulfilled about one hundred and fifty years after it was spoken: see Dan. i. 2, 3-7. What a proof of Divine omniscience!

A. M. cir. 3292 B. C. cir. 712 Olymp. XVII. 1 cir. annum NumæPompilii, R. Roman., 4

which thou shalt beget, shall
they take away; and [g]they shall
be eunuchs in the palace of the
king of Babylon.
8 Then said Hezekiah to Isaiah, [h]Good
is the word of the LORD
which thou hast spoken. He
said moreover, For there shall
be peace and truth in my
days.

[g]Fulfilled, Dan. i. 2, 3, 7

[h]1 Sam. iii. 18

Verse 8. *Then said Hezekiah*] The nature of Hezekiah's crime, and his humiliation on the message of God to him by the prophet, is more expressly declared by the author of the book of the Chronicles: "But Hezekiah rendered not again according to the benefit done unto him; for his heart was lifted up; therefore there was wrath upon him, and upon Judah and Jerusalem. Notwithstanding, Hezekiah humbled himself for the pride of his heart, both he and the inhabitants of Jerusalem, so that the wrath of the Lord came not upon them in the days of Hezekiah. And Hezekiah prospered in all his works. Howbeit, in the business of the ambassadors of the princes of Babylon, who sent unto him to inquire of the wonder that was done in the land, God left him, to try him, that he might know all that was in his heart." 2 Chron. xxxii. 25, 26, 30, 31.

There shall be peace and truth in my days.] I rather think these words should be understood as an humble inquiry of the king, addressed to the prophet. "Shall there be prosperity, שלום *shalom*, and truth in MY days?—Shall *I* escape the evil which thou predictest?" Understood otherwise, they manifest a pitiful unconcern both for his own family and for the nation. "So *I* be well, I care not how it may go with others." This is the view I have taken of the passage in 2 Kings xxi. 19. Let the reader judge whether *this*, or the *former*, should be preferred. See the concluding notes on 2 Kings xx.

CHAPTER XL

In this chapter the prophet opens the subject respecting the restoration of the Church with great force and elegance; declaring God's command to his messengers the prophets to comfort his people in their captivity, and to impart to them the glad tidings that the time of favour and deliverance was at hand, 1, 2. *Immediately a harbinger is introduced giving orders, as usual in the march of eastern monarchs, to remove every obstacle, and to prepare the way for their return to their own land,* 3–5. *The same words, however, the New Testament Scriptures authorize us to refer to the opening of the Gospel dispensation. Accordingly, this subject, coming once in view, is principally attended to in the sequel. Of this the prophet gives us sufficient notice by introducing a voice commanding another proclamation, which calls off our attention from all temporary, fading things to the spiritual and eternal things of the Gospel,* 6–11. *And to remove every obstacle in the way of the prophecy in either sense, or perhaps to give a farther display of the character of the Redeemer, he enlarges on the power and wisdom of God, as the Creator and Disposer of all things. It is impossible to read this description of God, the most sublime that ever was penned, without being struck with inexpressible reverence and self-abasement. The contrast between the great Jehovah and every thing reputed great in this world, how admirably imagined, how exquisitely finished! What atoms and inanities are they all before* HIM *who sitteth on the circle of the immense heavens, and views the potentates of the earth in the light of* grasshoppers,—*those poor insects that wander over the barren heath for sustenance, spend the day in continual chirpings, and take up their humble lodging at night on a blade of grass!* 12–26. *The prophet concludes with a most comfortable application of the whole, by showing that all this infinite power and unsearchable wisdom is unweariedly and everlastingly engaged in strengthening, comforting, and saving his people,* 27–31.

A. M. cir. 3292 B. C. cir. 712 Olymp. XVII. 1 cir. annum NumæPompilii, R. Roman., 4

COMFORT ye, comfort ye my
people, saith your God.
2 Speak ye [a]comfortably to
Jerusalem, and cry unto her, that
her [b]warfare is accomplished, that
her iniquity is pardoned: [c]for
she hath received of the LORD'S
hand double for all her sins.

[a]Heb. *to the heart*——[b]Or, *appointed time*

[c]See Job xlii. 10; chap. lxi. 7

The course of prophecies which follow, from hence to the end of the book, and which taken together constitute the most elegant part of the sacred writings of the Old Testament, interspersed also with many passages of the highest sublimity, was probably delivered in the latter part of the reign of Hezekiah. The prophet in the foregoing chapter had delivered a very explicit declaration of the impending dissolution of the kingdom, and of the captivity of the royal house of David, and of the people, under the kings of Babylon. As the subject of his subsequent prophecies was to be chiefly of the consolatory kind, he opens them with giving a promise of the restoration of the kingdom, and the return of the people from that captivity, by the merciful interposition of God in their favour. But the views of the prophet are not confined to this event. As the restoration of the royal family, and of the tribe of Judah, which would otherwise have soon become undistinguished, and have been irrecoverably lost, was necessary, in the design and order of Providence, for the fulfilling of God's promises of

A. M. cir. 3292
B. C. cir. 712
Olymp. XVII. 1
cir. annum
Numæ Pompilii,
R. Roman., 4

3 [d]The voice of him that crieth
in the wilderness, [e]Prepare ye
the way of the LORD, [f]make
straight in the desert a highway
for our God.

4 Every valley shall be exalted,
and every mountain and hill
shall be made low: [g]and the
crooked shall be made [h]straight,
and the rough places [i]plain:

[d]Matt. iii. 3; Mark i. 3; Luke iii. 4; John i. 23——[e]Mal. iii. 1

[f]Psa. lxviii. 4; chap. xlix. 11——[g]Ch. xlv. 2——[h]Or, *a straight place*——[i]Or, *a plain place*

establishing a more glorious and an everlasting kingdom, under the Messiah to be born of the tribe of Judah, and of the family of David, the prophet connects these two events together, and hardly ever treats of the former without throwing in some intimations of the latter; and sometimes is so fully possessed with the glories of the future and more remote kingdom, that he seems to leave the more immediate subject of his commission almost out of the question.

Indeed this evangelical sense of the prophecy is so apparent, and stands forth in so strong a light, that some interpreters cannot see that it has any other; and will not allow the prophecy to have any relation at all to the return from the captivity of Babylon. It may therefore be useful to examine more attentively the train of the prophet's ideas, and to consider carefully the images under which he displays his subject. He hears a crier giving orders, by solemn proclamation, to prepare the way of the Lord in the wilderness; to remove all obstructions before JEHOVAH marching through the desert; through the wild, uninhabited, impassable country. The deliverance of God's people from the Babylonish captivity is considered by him as parallel to the former deliverance of them from the Egyptian bondage. God was then represented as their king leading them in person through the vast deserts which lay in their way to the promised land of Canaan. It is not merely for JEHOVAH himself that in both cases the way was to be prepared, and all obstructions to be removed; but for JEHOVAH marching in person at the head of his people. Let us first see how this idea is pursued by the sacred poets who treat of the exodus, which is a favourite subject with them, and affords great choice of examples:—

"When Israel came out of Egypt,
The house of Jacob from the barbarous people;
Judah was his sanctuary,
Israel his dominion." Psa. cxiv. 1, 2.

"JEHOVAH his God is with him;
And the shout of a king is among them:
God brought them out of Egypt"——
Num. xxiii. 21, 22.

"Make a highway for him that rideth through the deserts:
O God, when thou wentest forth before thy people,
When thou marchedst through the wilderness,
The heavens dropped"—— Psa. lxviii. 4, 7.

Let us now see how Isaiah treats the subject of the return of the people from Babylon. They were to march through the wilderness with JEHOVAH at their head, who was to lead them, to smooth the way before them, and to supply them with water in the thirsty desert; with perpetual allusion to the exodus:—

"Come ye forth from Babylon, flee ye from the land of the Chaldeans with the voice of joy:
Publish ye this, and make it heard; utter it forth even to the end of the earth;
Say ye, JEHOVAH hath redeemed his servant Jacob:
They thirsted not in the deserts, through which he made them go;
Waters from the rock he caused to flow for them;
Yea, he clave the rock, and forth gushed the waters."
Chap. xlviii. 20, 21.

"Remember not the former things;
And the things of ancient times regard not:"

(That is, the deliverance from Egypt:)

"Behold, I make a new thing;
Even now shall it spring forth; will ye not regard it?
Yea, I will make in the wilderness a way;
In the desert streams of water."
Chap. xliii. 18, 19.

"But he that trusteth in me shall inherit the land,
And shall possses my holy mountain.
Then will I say: Cast up, cast up the causeway; make clear the way;
Remove every obstruction from the road of my people." Chap. lvii. 13, 14.

"How beautiful appear on the mountains
The feet of the joyful messenger, of him that announceth peace;
Of the joyful messenger of good tidings, of him that announceth salvation;
Of him that saith to Sion, Thy God reigneth!
All thy watchmen lift up their voice, they shout together;
For face to face shall they see, when JEHOVAH returneth to Sion.
Verily not in haste shall ye go forth,
And not by flight shall ye march along:
For JEHOVAH shall march in your front;
And the God of Israel shall bring up your rear." Chap. lii. 7, 8, 12.

Babylon was separated from Judea by an immense tract of country which was one continued desert; that large part of Arabia called very properly Deserta. It is mentioned in history as a remarkable occurrence, that Nebuchadnezzar, having received the news of the death of his father, in order to make the utmost expedition in his journey to Babylon from Egypt and Phœnicia, set out with a few attendants, and passed through this desert. *Berosus apud Joseph.*, Antiq. x. 11. This was the nearest way homewards for the Jews; and whether they actually returned by this way or not, the first thing that would occur on the proposal or thought of their return would be

A. M. cir. 3292
B. C. cir. 712
Olymp. XVII. 1
cir. annum
NumæPompilii,
R. Roman., 4

5 And the [k]glory of the LORD shall be revealed, and all flesh shall see *it* together; for the mouth of the LORD hath spoken *it*.

6 The voice said, Cry. And he said, What shall I cry? [l]All flesh *is* grass, and all the goodliness thereof *is* as the flower of the field.

[k]Chap. xxxv. 2; lviii. 8; lx. 1; Exod. xvi. 7; Lev. ix. 23; Num. xiv. 10; xxiv. 16; 1 Kings viii. 11

[l]Job xiv. 2; Psa. xc. 5; cii. 11; ciii. 15; James i. 10; 1 Pet. i. 24

the difficulty of this almost impracticable passage. Accordingly the proclamation for the preparation of the way is the most natural idea, and the most obvious circumstance, by which the prophet could have opened his subject.

These things considered, I have not the least doubt that the return of the Jews from the captivity of Babylon is the first, though not the principal, thing in the prophet's view. The redemption from Babylon is clearly foretold, and at the same time is employed as an image to shadow out a redemption of an infinitely higher and more important nature. I should not have thought it necessary to employ so many words in endeavouring to establish what is called the *literal sense* of this prophecy, which I think cannot be rightly understood without it, had I not observed that many interpreters of the first authority, in particular the very learned Vitringa, have excluded it entirely.

Yet obvious and plain as I think this literal sense is, we have nevertheless the irrefragable authority of John the Baptist, and of our blessed Saviour himself, as recorded by all the Evangelists, for explaining this exordium of the prophecy of the opening of the Gospel by the preaching of John, and of the introduction of the kingdom of Messiah; who was to effect a much greater deliverance of the people of God, Gentiles as well as Jews, from the captivity of sin and the dominion of death. And this we shall find to be the case in many subsequent parts also of this prophecy, where passages manifestly relating to the deliverance of the Jewish nation, effected by Cyrus, are, with good reason, and upon undoubted authority, to be understood of the redemption wrought for mankind by Christ.

If the literal sense of this prophecy, as above explained, cannot be questioned, much less surely can the spiritual; which, I think, is allowed on all hands, even by Grotius himself. If both are to be admitted, here is a plain example of the mystical allegory, or double sense, as it is commonly called, of prophecy; which the sacred writers of the New Testament clearly suppose, and according to which they frequently frame their interpretation of passages from the Old Testament. Of the foundation and properties of this sort of allegory, see *De S. Poës. Hebr.* Prælect. xi.

NOTES ON CHAP. XL

Verse 1. *Comfort ye, comfort ye*] "The whole of this prophecy," says *Kimchi*, "belongs to the days of the Messiah."

Verse 2. *Double for all her sins*—"Blessings double to the punishment."] It does not seem reconcilable to our notions of the Divine justice, which always punishes less than our iniquities deserve, to suppose that God had punished the sins of the Jews in double proportion; and it is more agreeable to the tenor of this consolatory message to understand it as a promise of ample recompense for the effects of past displeasure, on the reconciliation of God to his returning people. To express this sense of the passage, which the words of the original will very well bear, it was necessary to add a word or two in the version to supply the elliptical expression of the Hebrew. Compare chap. lxi. 7; Job xlii. 10; Zech. ix. 12. חטאה *chattaah* signifies punishment for sin, Lam. iii. 39; Zech. xiv. 19. But *Kimchi* says, "*Double* here means the *two captivities* and *emigrations* suffered by the Israelites. The *first*, the Babylonish captivity; the *second*, that which they *now* endure." This is not a bad conjecture.

Verse 3. *The voice of him that crieth in the wilderness*—"A voice crieth, In the wilderness"] The idea is taken from the practice of eastern monarchs, who, whenever they entered upon an expedition or took a journey, especially through desert and unpractised countries, sent harbingers before them to prepare all things for their passage, and pioneers to open the passes, to level the ways, and to remove all impediments. The officers appointed to superintend such preparations the Latins call *stratores.* Ipse (Johannes Baptista) se *stratorem* vocat Messiæ, cujus esset alta et elata voce homines in desertis locis habitantes ad itinera et vias Regi mox venturo sternendas et reficiendas hortari.—Mosheim, Instituta, Majora, p. 96. "He (John the Baptist) calls himself the pioneer of the Messiah, whose business it was with a loud voice to call upon the people dwelling in the deserts to level and prepare the roads by which the King was about to march."

Diodorus's account of the marches of Semiramis into Media and Persia will give us a clear notion of the preparation of the way for a royal expedition: "In her march to Ecbatana she came to the Zarcean mountain, which, extending many furlongs, and being full of craggy precipices and deep hollows, could not be passed without taking a great compass about. Being therefore desirous of leaving an everlasting memorial of herself, as well as of shortening the way, she ordered the precipices to be digged down, and the hollows to be filled up; and at a great expense she made a shorter and more expeditious road, which to this day is called from her the road of Semiramis. Afterward she went into Persia, and all the other countries of Asia subject to her dominion; and wherever she went, she ordered the mountains and precipices to be levelled, raised causeways in the plain country, and at a great expense made the ways passable."—*Diod. Sic.* lib. ii.

The writer of the apocryphal book called *Baruch* expresses the same subject by the same images, either taking them from this place of Isaiah, or from the common notions of his countrymen: "For God hath appointed that every high hill, and banks of long continuance, should be cast down, and valleys filled up, to make even the ground, that Israel may go safely in the glory of God." Chap. v. 7.

A. M. cir. 3292 B. C. cir. 712 Olymp. XVII. 1 cir. annum NumæPompilii, R. Roman., 4

7 The grass withereth, the flower fadeth: because the [m]spirit of the LORD bloweth upon it: surely the people *is* grass.

8 The grass withereth, the flower fadeth: but the [n]word of our God shall stand for ever.

[m]Psa. ciii. 16

[n]John xii. 34; 1 Pet. i. 25

The Jewish Church, to which John was sent to announce the coming of Messiah, was at that time in a barren and desert condition, unfit, without reformation, for the reception of her King. It was in this desert country, destitute at that time of all religious cultivation, in true piety and good works unfruitful, that John was sent to prepare the way of the Lord by preaching repentance. I have distinguished the parts of the sentence according to the punctuation of the Masoretes, which agrees best both with the literal and the spiritual sense; which the construction and parallelism of the distich in the Hebrew plainly favours, and of which the Greek of the Septuagint and of the evangelists is equally susceptible.

John was born in the desert of Judea, and passed his whole life in it, till the time of his being manifested to Israel. He preached in the same desert: it was a mountainous country; however not entirely and properly a desert; for though less cultivated than other parts of Judea, yet it was not uninhabited. Joshua (chap. xv. 61, 62) reckons six cities in it. We are so prepossessed with the idea of John's living and preaching in the desert, that we are apt to consider this particular scene of his preaching as a very important and essential part of history: whereas I apprehend this circumstance to be no otherwise important, than as giving us a strong idea of the rough character of the man, which was answerable to the place of his education; and as affording a proper emblem of the rude state of the Jewish Church at that time, which was the true wilderness meant by the prophet, in which John was to prepare the way for the coming of the Messiah.

Verse 4. *Crooked*] The word עקב *akob* is very generally rendered *crooked:* but this sense of the word seems not to be supported by any good authority. *Ludolphus*, Comment. ad Hist. Æthiop. p. 206, says "that in the Ethiopic language it signifies *clivus, locus editus:*" and so the *Syriac* Version renders it in this place, ערמא *arama: Hebrew*, ערמה *aramah, tumulus, acervus*. Thus the parallelism would be more perfect: "the hilly country shall be made level, and the precipices a smooth plain."

Verse 5. "The salvation of our God."] These words are added here by the *Septuagint: το σωτηριον του Θεου*, את ישועת אלהינו *eth yesuath Eloheynu*, as it is in the parallel place, chap. lii. 10. The sentence is abrupt without it, the verb wanting its object; and I think it is genuine. Our English translation has supplied the word *it*, which is equivalent to this addition, from the *Septuagint*.

This omission in the *Hebrew* text is ancient, being prior to the *Chaldee, Syriac*, and *Vulgate* Versions: but the words stand in all the copies of the *Septuagint*, and they are acknowledged by Luke, chap. iii. 6. The whole of this verse is wanting in one of my oldest MSS.

Verse 6. *The voice said, Cry*—"A voice saith, Proclaim"] To understand rightly this passage is a matter of importance; for it seems designed to give us the true key to the remaining part of Isaiah's prophecies, the general subject of which is the restoration of the people and Church of God. The prophet opens the subject with great clearness and elegance: he declares at once God's command to his messengers, (his prophets, as the *Chaldee* rightly explains it,) to comfort his people in captivity, to impart to them the joyful tidings, that their punishment has now satisfied the Divine justice, and the time of reconciliation and favour is at hand. He then introduces a harbinger giving orders to prepare the way for God, leading his people from Babylon, as he did formerly from Egypt, through the wilderness; to remove all obstacles, and to clear the way for their passage. Thus far nothing more appears to be intended than a return from the Babylonish captivity; but the next words seem to intimate something much greater:—

"And the glory of JEHOVAH shall be revealed;
And all flesh shall see together the salvation
of our God."

He then introduces a voice commanding him to make a solemn proclamation. And what is the import of it? that the people—the flesh, is of a vain temporary nature; that all its glory fadeth, and is soon gone; but that the word of God endureth for ever. What is this, but a plain opposition of the flesh to the spirit; of the carnal Israel to the spiritual; of the temporary Mosaic economy to the eternal Christian dispensation? You may be ready to conclude, (the prophet may be disposed to say,) by this introduction to my discourse, that my commission is only to comfort you with a promise of the restoration of your religion and polity, of Jerusalem, of the temple, and its services and worship in all its ancient splendour. These are earthly, temporary, shadowy, fading things, which shall soon pass away, and be destroyed for ever; these are not worthy to engage your attention in comparison of the greater blessings, the spiritual redemption, the eternal inheritance, covered under the veil of the former, which I have it in charge to unfold unto you. The law has only a shadow of good things; the substance is the Gospel. I promise you a restoration of the former, which, however, is only for a time, and shall be done away, according to God's original appointment: but under that image I give you a view of the latter, which shall never be done away, but shall endure for ever. This I take to be agreeable to St. Peter's interpretation of this passage of the prophet, quoted by him, 1 Pet. i. 24, 25: "All flesh is as grass, and all the glory of man as the flower of grass. The grass withereth, and the flower thereof falleth away; but the word of the Lord endureth for ever. And this is the word which by the Gospel is preached unto you." This is the same word of the Lord of which Isaiah speaks, which hath now been preached unto you by the Gospel. The law and the Gospel are frequently opposed to one an-

A. M. cir. 3292
B. C. cir. 712
Olymp. XVII. 4
cir. annum
NumæPompilii,
R. Roman., 4

9 [o]O Zion, that bringest good tidings, get thee up into the high mountain; [p]O Jerusalem, that bringest good tidings, lift up thy voice with strength; lift *it* up, be not afraid; say unto the cities of Judah, Behold your God!

10 Behold, the Lord GOD will come [q]with strong *hand,* and [r]his arm shall rule for him: behold, [s]his reward *is* with him, and [t]his work before him.

11 He shall [u]feed his flock like a shepherd: he shall gather the lambs with his arm, and carry *them* in his bosom, *and* shall gently lead those [v]that are with young.

A. M. cir. 3292
B. C. cir. 712
Olymp. XVII. 1
cir. annum
NumæPompilii,
R. Roman., 4

12 [w]Who hath measured the waters in the hollow of his hand, and meted out heaven with the span, and comprehended the dust of the earth in [x]a measure, and weighed the mountains in scales, and the hills in a balance?

[o]Or, *O thou that tellest good tidings to Zion;* chap. xli. 27; lii. 7——[p]Or, *O thou that tellest good tidings to Jerusalem*——[q]Or, *against the strong*——[r]Chap. lix. 16——[s]Chap. lxii. 11; Rev. xxii. 12

[t]Or, *recompense for his work;* chap. xlix. 4——[u]Chap. xlix. 10; Ezek. xxxiv. 23; xxxvii. 24; John x. 11; Heb. xiii. 20; 1 Pet. ii. 25; v. 4; Rev. vii. 17——[v]Or, *that give suck*——[w]Prov. xxx. 4——[x]Heb. *a tierce*

other by St. Paul, under the images of flesh and spirit: "Having begun in the spirit, are ye now made perfect by the flesh?" Gal. iii. 3.—L.

All the goodliness thereof—"All its glory"] For חסדו *chasdo* read חדו *chadu;* the *Septuagint* and *Vulgate,* and 1 Pet. i. 24.

Verse 7. *The grass withereth*] The whole of this verse is wanting in three of *Kennicott's* and five of *De Rossi's* MSS., and in a very correct and ancient MS. of my own, and also in the *Septuagint* and *Arabic.*

Surely the people—"Verily this people"] So the *Syriac;* who perhaps read העם הזה *haam hazzeh.*

Because the spirit of the Lord—"When the wind of JEHOVAH"] רוח יהוה *ruach Yehovah,* a wind of JEHOVAH, is a Hebraism, meaning no more than a strong wind. It is well known that a hot wind in the east destroys every green thing. Compare Psa. ciii. 16. Two MSS. omit the word יהוה *Yehovah, Jehovah.*

Verse 9. *O Zion, that bringest good tidings*—"O daughter, that bringest glad tidings to Zion"] That the true construction of the sentence is this, which makes Zion the receiver, not the publisher, of the glad tidings, which latter has been the most prevailing interpretation, will, I think, very clearly appear, if we rightly consider the image itself, and the custom and common practice from which it is taken. I have added the word *daughter* to express the feminine gender of the Hebrew participle, which I know not how to do otherwise in our language; and this is absolutely necessary in order to ascertain the image. For the office of announcing and celebrating such glad tidings as are here spoken of, belongs peculiarly to the women. On occasion of any great public success, a signal victory, or any other joyful event, it was usual for the women to gather together, and with music, dances, and songs, to publish and celebrate the happy news. Thus after the passage of the Red Sea, Miriam, and all the women, with timbrels in their hands, formed a chorus, and joined the men in their triumphant song, dancing, and throwing in alternately the refrain or burden of the song:—

"Sing ye to JEHOVAH, for he is greatly exalted;
The horse and his rider hath he cast into the sea." Exod. xv. 20, 21.

So Jephthah's daughter collected a chorus of virgins, and with dances and songs came out to meet her father, and to celebrate his victory, Judg. xi. 34. After David's conquest of Goliath, "all the women came out of the cities of Israel singing and dancing to meet Saul, with tabrets, with joy, and with instruments of music;" and, forming themselves into two choruses, they sang alternately:—

"Saul has slain his thousands:
And David his ten thousands."
1 Sam. xviii. 6, 7.

And this gives us the true sense of a passage in the sixty-eighth Psalm, which has frequently been misunderstood:—

"JEHOVAH gave the word, (that is, the joyful news,)
The women, who published the glad tidings, were a great company;
The kings of mighty armies did flee, did flee:
And even the matron, who stayed at home, shared the spoil."

The word signifying *the publishers of glad tidings* is the same, and expressed in the same form by the feminine participle, as in this place, and the last distich is the song which they sang. So in this place, JEHOVAH having given the word by his prophet, the joyful tidings of the restoration of Zion, and of God's returning to Jerusalem, (see chap. lii. 8,) the women are exhorted by the prophet to publish the joyful news with a loud voice from eminences, whence they might best be heard all over the country; and the matter and burden of their song was to be, "Behold your God!" See on Psalm lxviii. 11.

Verse 10. *His reward* is *with him, and his work before him.*—"His reward is with him, and the recompense of his work before him."] That is, the reward and the recompense which he bestows, and which he will pay to his faithful servants; this he has ready at hand with him, and holds it out before him, to encourage those who trust in him and wait for him.

Verse 11. *Shall gently lead those that are with young*—"The nursing ewes shall he gently lead."] A beautiful image, expressing, with the utmost propriety as well as elegance, the tender attention of the shepherd to his flock. That the greatest care in driving the cattle in regard to the dams and their young was necessary, appears clearly from Jacob's apology to his brother Esau, Gen. xxxiii. 13: "The flocks and the herds giving suck to their young are

A. M. cir. 3292
B. C. cir. 712
Olymp. XVII. 1
cir. annum
NumæPompilii,
R. Roman., 4

13 [y]Who hath directed the Spirit of the LORD, or *being* [z]his counsellor hath taught him.

14 With whom took he counsel, and *who* [a]instructed him, and taught him in the path of judgment, and taught him knowledge, and showed to him the way of [b]understanding?

15 Behold, the nations *are* as a drop of a bucket, and are counted as the small dust of the balance: behold, he taketh up the isles as a very little thing.

16 And Lebanon *is* not sufficient to burn, nor the beasts thereof sufficient for a burnt-offering.

17 All nations before him *are* as [c]nothing; and [d]they are counted to him less than nothing, and vanity.

[y]Job xxi. 22; xxxvi. 22, 23; Wisd. ix. 13; Rom. xi. 34; 1 Cor. ii. 16——[z]Heb. *man of his counsel*——[a]Heb. *made him understand*——[b]Hebrew, *understandings?* [c]Dan. iv. 34——[d]Psa. lxii. 9

18 To whom then will ye [e]liken God? or what likeness will ye compare unto him?

A. M. cir. 3292
B. C. cir. 712
Olymp. XVII. 1
cir. annum
NumæPompilii,
R. Roman., 4

19 [f]The workman melteth a graven image, and the goldsmith spreadeth it over with gold, and casteth silver chains.

20 He that [g]*is* so impoverished that he hath no oblation chooseth a tree *that* will not rot; he seeketh unto him a cunning workman [h]to prepare a graven image *that* shall not be moved.

21 [i]Have ye not known? have ye not heard? hath it not been told you from the beginning? have ye not understood from the foundations of the earth?

22 [k]*It is* he that sitteth upon the circle of the earth, and the inhabitants thereof *are* as

[e]Ver. 25; chap. xlvi. 5; Acts xvii. 29——[f]Chap. xli. 6, 7; xliv. 12, &c.; Jer. x. 3, &c.——[g]Heb. *is poor of oblation*——[h]Chap. xli. 7; Jer. x. 4——[i]Psa. xix. 1; Acts xiv. 17; Rom. i. 19, 20——[k]Or, *Him that sitteth*, &c.

with me; and if they should be overdriven, all the flock will die." Which is set in a still stronger light by the following remark of Sir John Chardin: "Their flocks," says he, speaking of those who now live in the east after the patriarchal manner, "feed down the places of their encampments so quick, by the great numbers that they have, that they are obliged to remove them too often, which is very destructive to their flocks, on account of the young ones, who have not strength enough to follow." *Harmer's* Observ. i., p. 126.

Verse 16. *And Lebanon* is *not sufficient*] The image is beautiful and uncommon. It has been imitated by an apocryphal writer, who however comes far short of the original:—

"For all sacrifice is too little for a sweet savour unto thee:
And all the fat is not sufficient for thy burnt-offering." Judith xvi. 16.

Does not the prophet mean here that all the burnt-offerings and sacrifices that could be offered were insufficient to atone for sin? That the nations were as nothing before him, not merely because of his immensity, but because of their insufficiency to make any atonement by their oblations for the iniquities which they had committed? Therefore the Redeemer was to come to Zion, &c.

Verse 19. *And casteth silver chains*—"And forgeth for it chains of silver."] For צורף *tsoreph*, the participle, twenty-seven MSS., five ancient, and three editions, read צרף *tsaraph*, pret. third person.

Verse 20. *Chooseth a tree* that *will not rot*] For what? To make a god out of it! The *rich* we find made theirs of *gold* and *silver;* the *poor man* was obliged to put up with a *wooden god!* From the words "he that hath no oblation chooseth a tree," we may learn that the gold and silver necessary to make the graven image was first *dedicated*, and then formed into a god! How stupid is idolatry! Strange that these people did not perceive that there could be no help in these molten and wooden idols!

Verse 21. *Have ye not known?*] On this verse *Kimchi* has a very interesting comment, an extract of which I subjoin. "The whole world may be considered as a house built up; *heaven* its roof; the *stars* its lamps; and the fruits of the earth its table spread. The *Master* of the house is God, blessed for ever; and *man* is the steward into whose hand all the business of the house is given. If he always consider in his heart that the Master of the house is continually over him, and that he keeps his eye upon his work, and if in consequence he acts wisely, he shall find favour in the eyes of the Master of the house. But if he find wickedness in the house, then will he remove him מן פקידתו *min pekidutho*, 'from his stewardship.' The foolish steward does not think of this; for as his eyes do not see the *Master* of the house, he saith in his heart, 'I will eat and drink what I find in this house, and will take my pleasure in it; nor shall I be careful whether there be a master over this house or not.' When the Lord of the house marks this, he comes and expels him from the house speedily, and with great anger; therefore it is said, ver. 23, *He bringeth the princes to nothing.*" It seems that this parable had been long in use among the Jews, as our blessed Lord alludes to it in his parable of the unjust steward. Or did the rabbin, finding it to his purpose, steal the parable from the Gospel? In both places it has great and peculiar beauties.

Have ye not understood from the foundations of the earth—"Have ye not understood it from the foundations of the earth?"] The true reading seems to be ממוסדות *mimmosedoth*, to answer to מראש *merosh* in the foregoing line. It follows a word ending with מ *mem*, and out of three *mems* concurring, it was an easy mistake to drop the middle one.

Verse 22. *As a curtain*—"As a thin veil"] "It

A. M. cir. 3292
B. C. cir. 712
Olymp. XVII. 1
cir. annum
NumæPompilii,
R. Roman., 4

grasshoppers; that [l]stretcheth
out the heavens as a curtain, and
spreadeth them out as a tent to
dwell in:
23 That bringeth the [m]princes to nothing;
he maketh the judges of the earth as vanity.
24 Yea, they shall not be planted: yea, they
shall not be sown: yea, their stock shall not
take root in the earth: and he shall also blow
upon them, and they shall wither, and the
whirlwind shall take them away as stubble.
25 [n]To whom then will ye liken me, or shall
I be equal? saith the Holy One.
26 Lift up your eyes on high, and behold
who hath created these *things*, that bringeth
out their host by number: [o]he calleth them
all by names by the greatness of his might,
for that *he is* strong in power; not one faileth.
27 Why sayest thou, O Jacob,
and speakest, O Israel, My way
is hid from the LORD, and my
judgment is passed over from
my God?
28 Hast thou not known? hast thou not
heard, *that* the everlasting God, the LORD,
the creator of the ends of the earth, fainteth
not, neither is weary? [p]*there is* no searching
of his understanding.
29 He giveth power to the faint; and to *them*
that have no might he increaseth strength.
30 Even the youths shall faint and be weary,
and the young men shall utterly fall;
31 But they that wait upon the LORD [q]shall
[r]renew *their* strength; they shall mount up
with wings as eagles; they shall run, and not
be weary; *and* they shall walk, and not faint.

A. M. cir. 3292
B. C. cir. 712
Olymp. XVII. 1
cir. annum
NumæPompilii,
R. Roman., 4

---

[l]Job ix. 8; Psa. civ. 2; chap. xlii. 5; xliv. 24; li. 13; Jer. x. 12——[m]Job xii. 21; Psa. cvii. 40——[n]Ver. 18; Deut. iv. 15, &c.——[o]Psa. cxlvii. 4——[p]Psa. cxlvii. 5; Rom. xi. 33——[q]Psa. ciii. 5——[r]Heb. *change*

---

is usual in the summer season, and upon all occasions when a large company is to be received, to have the court sheltered from heat or inclemency of the weather by a *velum*, umbrella, or veil, as I shall call it; which being expanded on ropes from one side of the parapet wall to the other, may be folded or unfolded at pleasure. The psalmist seems to allude to some covering of this kind in that beautiful expression of spreading out the heavens like a curtain."—*Shaw's* Travels, p. 274.

Verse 24. *And he shall also blow upon them*—"And if he but blow upon them"] The *Septuagint*, *Syriac*, *Vulgate*, and MS. *Bodl.*, with another, have גם *gam, only*, without the conjunction ו *vau, and.*

Verse 26. *Lift up your eyes on high*] The rabbins say, He who is capable of meditating on the revolutions of the heavenly bodies, and does not meditate on them, is not worthy to have his name mentioned among men.

Verse 28. There is *no searching of his understanding*—"And that his understanding is unsearchable."] Twenty-four MSS., two editions, the *Septuagint* and *Vulgate*, read ואין *veein*, with the conjunction ו *vau*.

Verse 31. *They shall mount up with wings as eagles*—"They shall put forth fresh feathers like the moulting eagle"] It has been a common and popular opinion that the eagle lives and retains his vigour to a great age; and that, beyond the common lot of other birds, he moults in his old age, and renews his feathers, and with them his youth. "Thou shalt renew thy youth like the eagle," says the psalmist, ciii. 5; on which place St. Ambrose notes, Aquila longam ætatem ducit, dum, vetustis plumis fatiscentibus, nova pennarum successione juvenescit:—"The eagle lives to a very advanced age; and in moulting his youth is renewed with his new feathers."

Phile, De Animalibus, treating of the eagle, and addressing himself to the emperor Michael Palæologus junior, raises his compliment upon the same notion:—

Τουτον συ, βασιλευ, τον πολυν ζωοις βιον,
Αει νεουργων, και κρατυνων την φυσιν.

"Long may'st thou live, O king; still like the eagle
Renew thy youth, and still retain thy vigour."

To this many fabulous and absurd circumstances are added by several ancient writers and commentators on Scripture; see *Bochart*, Hieroz. II. ii. 1. Rabbi Saadias says, Every *tenth* year the eagle flies near the sun; and when not able any longer to bear the burning heat, she falls down into the sea, and soon loses her feathers, and thus renews her vigour. This she does every *tenth* year till the *hundredth*, when, after she has ascended near the sun, and fallen into the sea, she rises no more. How much proof do such stories require! Whether the notion of the eagle's renewing his youth is in any degree well founded or not, I need not inquire; it is enough for a poet, whether profane or sacred, to have the authority of popular opinion to support an image introduced for illustration or ornament.—L.

CHAPTER XLI

The prophet, having intimated the deliverance from Babylon, and the still greater redemption couched under it, resumes the subject. He begins with the Divine vocation of Abraham, the root of the Israelitish family, and his successful exploits against the idolaters, 1–7. *He then recurs to the Babylonish captivity, and encourages the seed of Abraham, the friend of God, not to fear, as all their enemies would be ultimately subdued under them,* 8–16; *and every thing furnished necessary to refresh and comfort them in their passage homewards through the desert,* 17–20. *The prophet then takes occasion to celebrate the prescience of God, from his knowledge of events so very distant, as instanced in the prediction concerning the* messenger of glad tidings *which should be given to Jerusalem to deliver her from all her enemies; and challenges the idols of the heathen to produce the like proof of their pretended divinity,* 21–27. *But they are all vanity, and accursed are they that choose them,* 28, 29.

A. M. cir. 3292 B. C. cir. 712 Olymp. XVII. 1 cir. annum NumæPompilii, R. Roman., 4

KEEP [a]silence before me, O
islands; and let the people
renew *their* strength: let them
come near; then let them speak:
let us come near together to judgment.
2 Who raised up [b]the righteous *man* [c]from
the east, called him to his foot, [d]gave the nations before him, and made *him* rule over
kings? he gave *them* as the dust to his sword,
and as driven stubble to his
bow.
3 He pursued them, *and* passed
[e]safely; *even* by the way *that*
he had not gone with his feet.
4 [f]Who hath wrought and done *it,* calling
the generations from the beginning? I
the LORD, the [g]first, and with the last; I
am he.

[a]Zech. ii. 13——[b]Heb. *righteousness*——[c]Ch. xlvi. 11 [d]See Gen. xiv. 14, &c.; ver. 25; chap. xlv. 1

[e]Heb. *in peace*——[f]Ver. 26; ch. xliv. 7; xlvi. 10——[g]Ch. xliii. 10; xliv. 6; xlviii. 12; Rev. i. 17; xxii. 13

NOTES ON CHAP. XLI

Verse 1. *Keep silence before me, O islands*—"Let the distant nations repair to me with new force of mind"] Εγκαινιζεσθε, *Septuagint.* For החרישו *hacharishu, be silent,* they certainly read in their copy החדישו *hachadishu, be renewed;* which is parallel and synonymous with יחלפו כח *yechalephu coach,* "recover their strength;" that is, their strength of mind, their powers of reason; that they may overcome those prejudices by which they have been so long held enslaved to idolatry. A MS. has הר *har,* upon a rasure. The same mistake seems to have been made in this word, Zeph. iii. 17. For יחריש באהבתו *yacharish beahabatho, silebit in directione sua,* as the *Vulgate* renders it; which seems not consistent with what immediately follows, *exultabit super te in laude;* the *Septuagint* and *Syriac* read יחדיש באהבתו *yachadish beahabatho,* "he shall be renewed in his love." אלי *elai, to me,* is wanting in one of *De Rossi's* MSS. and in the *Syriac.*

Verse 2. *The righteous* man] The *Chaldee* and *Vulgate* seem to have read צדיק *tsaddik.* But Jerome, though his translation has *justum,* appears to have read צדק *tsedek;* for in his comment he expresses it by *justum, sive justitiam.* However, I think all interpreters understand it of a person. So the *Septuagint* in MS. *Pachom.* εκάλεσεν αυτον, "he hath called him;" but the other copies have *αυτην, her.* They are divided in ascertaining this person; some explain it of Abraham, others of Cyrus. I rather think that the former is meant; because the character of the righteous man, or righteousness, agrees better with Abraham than with Cyrus. Besides, immediately after the description of the success given by God to Abraham and his posterity, (who, I presume, are to be taken into the account,) the idolaters are introduced as greatly alarmed at this event. Abraham was called out of the east; and his posterity were introduced into the land of Canaan, in order to destroy the idolaters of that country, and they were established there on purpose to stand as a barrier against the idolatry then prevailing, and threatening to overrun the whole face of the earth. Cyrus, though not properly an idolater or worshipper of images, yet had nothing in his character to cause such an alarm among the idolaters, ver. 5-7. Farther, after having just touched upon that circumstance, the prophet with great ease returns to his former subject, and resumes Abraham and the Israelites; and assures them that as God had called them, and chosen them for this purpose, he would uphold and support them to the utmost, and at length give them victory over all the heathen nations, their enemies; ver. 8-16. *Kimchi* is of the same mind and gives the same reasons.

He gave them *as the dust to his sword*—"Hath made them like the dust before his sword"] The image is strong and beautiful; it is often made use of by the sacred poets; see Psa. i. 4; xxxv. 5; Job xxi. 18, and by Isaiah himself in other places, chap. xvii. 13; xxix. 5. But there is great difficulty in making out the construction. The *Septuagint* read קשתם חרבם *kashtam, charbam, their sword, their bow,* understanding it of the sword and bow of the conquered kings: but this is not so agreeable to the analogy of the image, as employed in other places. The *Chaldee* paraphrast and *Kimchi* solve the difficulty by supposing an ellipsis of לפני *liphney* before those words. It must be owned that the ellipsis is hard and unusual: but I choose rather to submit to this, than, by adhering with *Vitringa* to the more obvious construction, to destroy entirely both the image and the sense. But the *Vulgate* by *gladio ejus,* to his sword, and *arcui ejus,* to his bow, seems to express לחרבו *lecharbo, to his sword,* and לקשתו *lekashto, to his bow,* the admission of which reading may perhaps be thought preferable to *Kimchi's* ellipsis.

Verse 3. And *passed safely*—"He passeth in safety"] The preposition seems to have been omitted in the text by mistake; the *Septuagint* and *Vulgate* seem to have had it in their copies; *εν ειρηνῃ, in pace,* בשלום *beshalom,* "prosperously." It is so in one of *De Rossi's* MSS.

Verse 4. *Who hath wrought and done* it—"Who hath performed and made these things"] A word is here lost out of the text. It is supplied by an ancient MS., אלה *elleh,* "these

A. M. cir. 3292
B. C. cir. 712
Olymp. XVII. 1
cir. annum
NumæPompilii,
R. Roman., 4

5 The isles saw *it*, and feared;
the ends of the earth were afraid,
drew near, and came.
6 [h]They helped every one his
neighbour; and *every one* said to his brother,
[i]Be of good courage.
7 [k]So the carpenter encouraged the [l]gold-
smith, *and* he that smootheth *with* the hammer
[m]him that smote the anvil, [n]saying, It *is* ready
for the soddering: and he fastened it with
nails, [o]*that* it should not be moved.
8 But thou, Israel, *art* my servant, Jacob
whom I have [p]chosen, the seed of Abraham
my [q]friend.
9 *Thou* whom I have taken from the ends of
the earth, and called thee from the chief men
thereof, and said unto thee, Thou *art* my servant; I have chosen thee, and not cast thee
away.
10 [r]Fear thou not; [s]for I *am* with thee: be
not dismayed; for I *am* thy God: I will
strengthen thee; yea, I will help thee; yea,
I will uphold thee with the right hand of my
righteousness.
11 Behold, all they that were incensed
against thee shall be [t]ashamed and confounded: they shall be as nothing; and [u]they
that strive with thee shall perish.
12 Thou shalt seek them, and shalt not find
them, *even* [v]them that contended with thee:
[w]they that war against thee shall
be as nothing, and as a thing of
nought.
13 For I the LORD thy God
will hold thy right hand, saying unto thee,
[x]Fear not; I will help thee.
14 Fear not, thou worm Jacob, *and* ye [y]men
of Israel; I will help thee, saith the LORD,
and thy Redeemer, the Holy One of Israel.
15 Behold, [z]I will make thee a new sharp
threshing instrument having [a]teeth: thou
shalt thresh the mountains, and beat *them*
small, and shalt make the hills as chaff.
16 Thou shalt [b]fan them, and the wind shall
carry them away, and the whirlwind shall
scatter them: and thou shalt rejoice in the
LORD, *and* [c]shalt glory in the Holy One of
Israel.
17 *When* the poor and needy seek water, and
there is none, *and* their tongue faileth for
thirst, I the LORD will hear them, *I* the God
of Israel will not forsake them.
18 I will open [d]rivers in high places, and
fountains in the midst of the valleys: I will
make the [e]wilderness a pool of water, and the
dry land springs of water.
19 I will plant in the wilderness the cedar,
the shittah tree, and the myrtle, and the oil
tree; I will set in the desert the fir tree, *and*
the pine, and the box tree together:

A. M. cir. 3292
B. C. cir. 712
Olymp. XVII. 1
cir. annum
NumæPompilii,
R. Roman., 4

[h]Chap. xl. 19; xliv. 12——[i]Heb. *Be strong*——[k]Chap. xl. 19——[l]Or, *founder*——[m]Or, *the smiting*——[n]Or, *saying of the sodder, It is good*——[o]Chap. xl. 20——[p]Deut. vii. 6; x. 15; xiv. 2; Psa. cxxxv. 4; chap. xliii. 1; xliv. 1 [q]2 Chron. xx. 7; James ii. 23——[r]Ver. 13, 14; chap. xliii. 5——[s]Deut. xxxi. 6, 8

[t]Exod. xxiii. 22; chap. xlv. 24; lx. 12; Zech. xii. 3 [u]Heb. *the men of thy strife*——[v]Heb. *the men of thy contention*——[w]Heb. *the men of thy war*——[x]Ver. 10 [y]Or, *few men*——[z]Mic. iv. 13; 2 Cor. x. 4, 5——[a]Heb. *mouths*——[b]Jer. li. 2——[c]Chap. xlv. 25——[d]Chap. xxxv. 6, 7; xliii. 19; xliv. 3——[e]Psa. cvii. 35

things;" and by the *Septuagint*, ταυτα; and by the *Vulgate*, *hæc;* and by the *Chaldee*, אלן *elin;* all of the same meaning.

Verse 5. *Were afraid*—"And they were terrified"] Three MSS. have ויחרדו *vaiyecheridu*, adding the conjunction ו *vau*, which restores the second member of the sentence to its true poetical form.

Verse 7. That *it should not be moved*—"That it shall not move."] Five MSS., (two ancient,) and the ancient Versions, add the conjunction ו *vau*, "and," reading ולא *velo*, "and not," which seems to be right.

Verse 9. *And called thee from the chief men thereof*—"And called from the extremities thereof"] אציל מאציליה *atsil meatsileyha*, signifies *the arm, axilla, ala;* and is used like כנף *canaph*, "the wing," for any thing extended from the extremity of another, or joined on to it. It is here parallel with and synonymous to מקצות *mikkatsoth*, "from the ends," in the preceding member.

Verse 10. *Be not dismayed*—ואל תשתע *veal tishta*, "AND be not dismayed." The ו *vau* is added by twenty-one of Dr. *Kennicott's* MSS., thirty of *De Rossi's*, and one of my own, and three editions. It makes the sense more complete.

Verse 14. *Fear not, thou worm Jacob*] In the rabbinical commentary on the five books of Moses, *Yelamedenu*, it is asked, Why are the Israelites called a *worm?* To signify, that as the worm does not smite, that is, *gnaw* the cedars, but with its mouth, which is very tender, yet it nevertheless destroys the hard wood; so all the strength of the Israelites is in prayer, by which they smite the wicked of this world, though strong like the cedars, to which they are compared, Ezek. xxxi. 3.

Verse 15. *A new sharp threshing instrument having teeth*—"A threshing wain; a new corn-drag armed with pointed teeth"] See note on chap. xxviii. 27, 28.

Thou shalt thresh the mountains] Mountains and hills are here used metaphorically for the kings and princes of the Gentiles.—*Kimchi*.

Verse 19. *I will plant in the wilderness the cedar*] The two preceding verses express God's

A. M. cir. 3292 B. C. cir. 712 Olymp. XVII. 1 cir. annum Numæ Pompilii, R. Roman., 4

20 [f]That they may see, and
know, and consider, and understand together, that the hand
of the LORD hath done this, and
the Holy One of Israel hath created it.
21 [g]Produce your cause, saith the LORD;
bring forth your strong *reasons,* saith the
King of Jacob.
22 [h]Let them bring *them* forth, and show us
what shall happen: let them show the former
things, what they *be,* that we may [i]consider
them, and know the latter end of them; or
declare us things for to come.
23 [k]Show the things that are to come hereafter, that we may know that ye *are* gods:
yea, [l]do good, or do evil, that we may be dismayed, and behold *it* together.
24 Behold, [m]ye *are* [n]of nothing, and your
work [o]of naught: an abomination *is he that*
chooseth you.

25 I have raised up *one* from
the north, and he shall come:
from the rising of the sun [p]shall
he call upon my name: [q]and he
shall come upon princes as *upon* mortar, and
as the potter treadeth clay.
26 [r]Who hath declared from the beginning,
that we may know? and beforetime, that we
may say, *He is* righteous? yea, *there is* none
that showeth, yea, *there is* none that declareth,
yea, *there is* none that heareth your words.
27 [s]The first [t]*shall say* to Zion, Behold,
behold them: and I will give to Jerusalem
one that bringeth good tidings.
28 [u]For I beheld, and *there was* no man; even
among them, and *there was* no counsellor, that,
when I asked of them, could [v]answer a word.
29 [w]Behold, they *are* all vanity; their works
are nothing: their molten images *are* wind
and confusion.

A. M. cir. 3292 B. C. cir. 712 Olymp. XVII. 1 cir. annum Numæ Pompilii, R. Roman., 4

[f]Job xii. 9——[g]Heb. *Cause to come near*——[h]Chap. xlv. 21——[i]Heb. *set our heart* upon them——[k]Chap. xlii. 9; xliv. 7, 8; xlv. 3; John xiii. 19——[l]Jer. x. 5 [m]Psa. cxv. 8; chap. xliv. 9, 1 Cor. viii. 4

[n]Or, worse *than nothing*——[o]Or, worse *than of a viper* [p]Ezra i. 2——[q]Verse 2——[r]Chapter xliii. 9——[s]Verse 4——[t]Chapter xl. 9——[u]Chapter lxix. 5——[v]Heb. *return*——[w]Ver. 24

mercy to them in their passage through the dry deserts, in supplying them with abundant water, when distressed with thirst, in allusion to the exodus. This verse expresses the relief afforded to them, fainting with heat in their journey through that hot country, destitute of shelter, by causing shady trees, and those of the tallest and most beautiful kinds, to spring up for their defence. The apocryphal Baruch, speaking of the return from Babylon, expresses God's protection of his people by the same image: "Even the woods and every sweet-smelling tree shall overshadow Israel by the commandment of God." Chap. v. 8.

The oil tree] This, *Kimchi* says, is not to be understood of the *olive tree*, for the olive is distinguished, Neh. viii. 15; but it means the pine or fir, from which pitch is extracted.

Verse 20. *And consider*] The verb ישימו *yasimu,* without לב *leb* added, cannot signify *to apply the heart,* or *to attend* to a thing, as *Houbigant* has observed; he therefore reads ישמו *yashshemu,* they shall *wonder.* The conjecture is ingenious; but it is much more probable that the word לב *leb* is lost out of the text; for all the ancient versions render the phrase to the same sense, as if it were fully expressed, ישימו לב *yasimu leb;* and the *Chaldee* renders it paraphrastically, yet still retaining the very words in his paraphrase, וישוון דחלתי על לבהון *vishavvun dechalti al lebehon,* "that they may put my fear in their heart." See also ver. 22, where the same phrase is used.

Verse 21. *Bring forth your strong* reasons—"Produce these your mighty powers"] "Let your idols come forward which you consider to be so very strong." *Hieron.* in loc. I prefer this to all other interpretations of this place; and to *Jerome's* own translation of it, which he adds immediately after, Afferte, si quid forte habetis. "Bring it forward, if haply ye have any thing." The false gods are called upon to come forth and appear in person; and to give evident demonstration of their foreknowledge and power by foretelling future events, and exerting their power in doing good or evil.

Verse 23. *That we may be dismayed, and behold* it *together*—"Then shall we be struck at once with admiration and terror."] The word ונרא *venere* is written imperfectly in the *Hebrew* text; the Masoretes supply ה *he* at the end; and so it is read in *twenty-two* MSS. and *four* editions; that is, ונראה *venireh,* and we shall *see.* But the true reading seems to be ונירא *venira,* and we shall *fear,* with י *yod* supplied, from ירא *yara.*

Verse 24. *Your work of naught*—"Your operation is less than naught"] For מאפע *meepha,* read מאפס *meephes;* so the *Chaldee* and *Vulgate.* A manifest error of the text; compare chap. xl. 17. The rabbins acknowledge no such error, but say that the former word signifies the same with the latter, by a change of the two letters ס *samech* and ע *ain.*—*Sal ben Melec* in loc.

Verse 25. *I have raised up* one *from the north*] "That is," says *Kimchi,* "the Messiah. The king of Assyria placed the ten tribes in Chalach and Chabar by the river Gozan, and in the cities of the Medes, 2 Kings xvii. 6, which lands lie northerly and easterly."

He shall come upon princes—"He shall trample on princes"] For יבא *yabo, Le Clerc* reads יבס *yebes,* from the *Chaldee,* who seems to read both words. "*Forte legend.* ויבס *vaiyebes* vel וירמס *vaiyirmos: sequitur* ס." "This should perhaps be read ויבס *vaiyebes,* or וירמס *vaiyirmos:* a ס *samech* follows."—*Secker.* See Nah. iii. 14.

Verse 26. *Your words*] אמרתיכם *imrathey-*

chem; but, instead of this, one of my most ancient MSS. has דבריכם *dibreychem.* The meaning is nearly the same: but in this reading this MS. is singular.

Verse 27. *The first* shall say *to Zion, Behold, behold them*—"I first to Zion *gave the word*, Behold they are here"] This verse is somewhat obscure by the transposition of the parts of the sentence, and the peculiar manner in which it is divided into two parallel lines. The verb at the end of the sentence belongs to both parts; and the phrase, *Behold, they are here!* is parallel to *the messenger of glad tidings;* and stands like it, as the accusative case to the verb. The following paraphrase will explain the form and the sense of it. "I first, by my prophets, give notice of these events, saying, Behold, they are at hand! and I give to Jerusalem a messenger of glad tidings."

Verse 28. *Among them*—"Among the idols"] For ומאלה *umeelleh,* I read ומאלים *umeellim,* with the *Septuagint*, και απο των ειδωλων, "*and from* or among the *idols*." See Exod. xv. 11; Isa. lvii. 5.

R. D. Kimchi has many good observations on this chapter. Bishop *Lowth* follows him in applying it to Abraham, and not to Cyrus; the whole being spoken in the past tense, which is not used, or rarely, in such a case for the future. Almost the whole of the rabbins understand it of Abraham. On *Kimchi's* plan, the following is a paraphrase.

The righteous man—Abram, *from the east*—the land of his nativity, called the land of the children of the east, Gen. xxix. 1.

Brought him to his feet—Whithersoever his feet went, he preached righteousness and truth; as it is written, "There he proclaimed in the name of JEHOVAH," Gen. xxi. 31. And he called it ויקראהו *vaiyikraehu*—that is, צדק *tsedek,* righteousness, to his feet, enabled him to hold it forth wherever he went.

He called the nations—To leave their idols, and worship him who made the universe. He taught them the way of righteousness, truth, and faith. Was there ever a prodigy like to this? A man who had been an idolater, rising up against all the nations of the earth, reproving their faith, and not fearing before them nor their kings! Who stirred up his heart to do this? Was it not the Lord?

Gave the nations before him—And made him rule over kings—Chedorlaomer, and the kings which were with him: whom the Lord *gave as dust to his sword, and stubble to his bow.*

He pursued them—He and his *three hundred and eighteen* servants.

He passed safely—שלום *shalom* for בשלום *beshalom, in safety;* so said, because he lost not one of his men in this expedition. See *Kimchi.*

CHAPTER XLII

The prophet sets forth the meekness of Messiah's character, and the extent and blessings of his kingdom, particularly among the Gentiles, 1–9. *In consequence of this he calls on the whole creation to join him in one song of praise to God,* 10–12. *After which he seems again to glance at the deliverance from the captivity; although the words may full as well apply to the deliverance vouchsafed to the Church; to the overthrow of her most powerful enemies; and to the prevalency of true religion over idolatry and error,* 13–17. *The prophet then reproves the Jews for their blindness and infidelity in rejecting the Messiah, and gives intimations of those judgments which their guilt would draw on them,* 18–25.

A. M. cir. 3292
B. C. cir. 712
Olymp. XVII. 1
cir. annum
NumæPompilii,
R. Roman., 4

BEHOLD [a]my servant, whom I uphold; mine elect, *in whom* my soul [b]delighteth; [c]I have put my spirit upon him: he shall bring forth judgment to the Gentiles.

2 He shall not cry, nor lift up, nor cause his voice to be heard in the street.

3 A bruised reed shall he not break, and the [d]smoking flax shall he not

A. M. cir. 3292
B. C. cir. 712
Olymp. XVII. 1
cir. annum
NumæPompilii,
R. Roman., 4

[a]Chap. xliii. 10; xlix. 3, 6; lii. 13; liii. 11; Matt. xii. 18, 19, 20; Phil. ii. 7 —— [b]Matt. iii. 17; xvii. 5; Eph. i. 6 —— [c]Chap. xi. 2; John iii. 34 —— [d]Or, *dimly burning*

The prophet, having opened his subject with the preparation for the return from captivity at Babylon, and intimated that a much greater deliverance was covered under the veil of that event, proceeded to vindicate the power of God, as Creator and disposer of all things; and his infinite knowledge, from his prediction of future events, and in particular of that deliverance. He went still farther, and pointed out the instrument by which he should effect the redemption of his people the Jews from slavery; namely, a great conqueror, whom he would call forth from the north and the east to execute his orders. In this chapter he proceeds to the greater deliverance; and at once brings forth into full view, without throwing any veil of allegory over the subject, the Messiah. "Behold my servant, Messiah," says the *Chaldee.* St. Matthew has applied it directly to Christ; nor can it with any justice or propriety be applied to any other person or character whatever.—L.

NOTES ON CHAP. XLII

Verse 1. *Behold my servant, whom I uphold*] אתמך בו *ethmach bo, on whom I lean.* Alluding to the custom of kings leaning on the arm of their most beloved and faithful servant. All, both Jews and Christians, agree, that the seven first verses of this chapter belong to Christ. Now, as they are evidently a continuation of the prophecy in the preceding chapter, that prophecy cannot belong to Cyrus, but to Christ.

He shall bring forth judgment to the Gentiles—"He shall publish judgment to the nations"]

A. M. cir. 3292
B. C. cir. 712
Olymp. XVII. 1
cir. annum
NumæPompilii,
R. Roman., 4

[e]quench: he shall bring forth
judgment unto truth.
4 He shall not fail nor be
[f]discouraged, till he have set
judgment in the earth: [g]and the isles shall
wait for his law.
5 Thus saith God the LORD, [h]he that created
the heavens, and stretched them out; [i]he that
spread forth the earth, and that which cometh
out of it; [k]he that giveth breath unto the
people upon it, and spirit to them that walk
therein:
6 [l]I the LORD have called thee in righteousness, and will hold thine hand, and will keep
thee, [m]and give thee for a covenant of the
people, for [n]a light of the Gentiles;
7 [o]To open the blind eyes, to [p]bring out
the prisoners from the prison, *and* them that
sit in [q]darkness out of the
prison house.
8 I *am* the LORD: that *is* my
name: and my [r]glory will I not
give to another, neither my praise to graven
images.
9 Behold, the former things are come to
pass, and new things do I declare: before
they spring forth I tell you of them.
10 [s]Sing unto the LORD a new song, *and*
his praise from the end of the earth, [t]ye that
go down to the sea, and [u]all that is therein;
the isles, and the inhabitants thereof.
11 Let the wilderness and the cities thereof
lift up *their voice,* the villages *that* Kedar
doth inhabit: let the inhabitants of the rock
sing, let them shout from the top of the mountains.

A. M. cir. 3292
B. C. cir. 712
Olymp. XVII. 1
cir. annum
NumæPompilii,
R. Roman., 4

[e]Heb. *quench it*——[f]Heb. *broken*——[g]Gen. xlix. 10——[h]Chap. xliv. 24; Zech. xii. 1——[i]Psa. cxxxvi. 6——[k]Acts xvii. 25——[l]Chap. xliii. 1——[m]Chap. xlix. 8——[n]Chap. xlix. 6; Luke ii. 32; Acts xiii. 47

[o]Chap. xxxv. 5——[p]Chap. lxi. 1; Luke iv. 18; 2 Tim. ii. 26; Heb. ii. 14, 15——[q]Chap. ix. 2——[r]Chap. xlviii. 11——[s]Psa. xxxiii. 3; xl. 3; xcviii. 1——[t]Psa. cvii. 23——[u]Heb. *the fulness thereof*

Four MSS. two ancient, add the conjunction ומשפט *vemishpat.* See Matt. xii. 18.

The word משפט *mishpat, judgment,* like צדקה *tsedakah, righteousness,* is taken in a great latitude of signification. It means *rule, form, order, model, plan; rule of right,* or of *religion;* an *ordinance, institution; judicial process, cause, trial, sentence, condemnation, acquittal, deliverance, mercy,* &c. It certainly means in this place the law to be published by Messiah, the institution of the Gospel.

Verse 4. *He shall not fail nor be discouraged*—"His force shall not be abated nor broken"] Rabbi Meir ita citat locum istum, ut post ירוץ *yaruts,* addat כוחו *cocho, robur ejus,* quod hodie non comparet in textu Hebræo, sed addendum videtur, ut sensus fiat planior. "Rabbi Meir cites this passage so as to add after ירוץ *yaruts* כוחו *cocho, his force,* which word is not found in the present Hebrew text, but seems necessary to be added to make the sense more distinct." *Capell.* Crit. Sac. p. 382. For which reason I had added it in the translation, before I observed this remark of *Capellus.*—L.

Verse 6. *A covenant of the people*—"A covenant to the people"] For עם *am,* two MSS. of *Dr. Kennicott's,* and of my own, read עולם *olam,* the covenant *of the age to come,* or *the everlasting* covenant; which seems to give a clearer and better sense. But I think the word ברית *berith,* here, should not be translated *covenant,* but *covenant sacrifice,* which meaning it often has; and undoubtedly in this place. This gives a still stronger and clearer sense.

Verse 7. *To open the blind eyes*] In this verse the prophet seems to set forth the spiritual redemption, under images borrowed from the temporal deliverance.

Out of the prison house—"*And* from the dungeon."] The *Septuagint, Syriac,* and four MSS., one ancient, add the conjunction ו *vau,* ומבית *umibbeith, and from the house.*

Verse 8. *I am the Lord*] אני יהוה *ani Yehovah.* This is the famous tetragrammaton, or name of *four letters,* which we write *Jehovah, Yehovah, Yehveh, Yeveh, Jhuh, Javah,* &c. The letters are Y H U H. The Jews never pronounce it, and the true pronunciation is utterly unknown.

That is *my name*] A name peculiar to myself.

Verse 10. *Ye that go down to the sea*] This seems not to belong to this place; it does not well consist with what follows, "and the fulness thereof." They that go down upon the sea means navigators, sailors, traders, such as do business in great waters; an idea much too confined for the prophet, who means the sea in general, as it is used by the Hebrews, for the distant nations, the islands, the dwellers on the sea-coasts all over the world. I suspect that some transcriber had the 23d verse of Psalm cvii. running in his head, יורדי הים באניות *yoredey haiyam booniyoth,* and wrote in this place יורדי הים *yoredey haiyam* instead of ירעם הים *yiram haiyam,* or יריע *yari,* or ירן *yaran;* "let the sea roar, or shout, or exult." But as this is so different in appearance from the present reading, I do not take the liberty of introducing it into the translation. Conjeceram legendum יגידו *yegidu,* ut ver. 12; sed non favent Versiones. "I would propose to read יגידו *yegidu,* as in ver. 12; but this is not supported by the Versions."—*Secker.*

Verse 11. *Let the wilderness*] The most uncultivated countries, and the most rude and uncivilized people, shall confess and celebrate with thanksgiving the blessing of the knowledge of God graciously imparted to them. By the *desert* is meant Arabia Deserta; by the *rocky country,* Arabia Petræa; by the *mountains,* probably those celebrated ones, Paran, Horeb, Sinai, in the same country; to which also belonged *Kedar,* a clan of Arabians, dwelling for the most part in tents; but there were

A. M. cir. 3292 B. C. cir. 712 Olymp. XVII. 1 cir. annum NumæPompilii, R. Roman., 4

12 Let them give glory unto
the LORD, and declare his praise
in the islands.
13 The LORD shall go forth as
a mighty man, he shall stir up jealousy like
a man of war: he shall cry, [v]yea, roar; he
[w]shall prevail against his enemies.
14 I have long time holden my peace; I
have been still, *and* refrained myself: *now*
will I cry like a travailing woman; I will destroy and [x]devour at once.
15 I will make waste mountains
and hills, and dry up all their
herbs; and I will make the rivers
islands, and I will dry up the
pools.
16 And I will bring the blind by a way *that*
they knew not; I will lead them in paths *that*
they have not known: I will make darkness
light before them, and crooked things
[y]straight. These things will I do unto them,
and not forsake them.
17 They shall be [z]turned back, they shall

[v]Chapter xxxi. 4——[w]Or, *behave himself mightily*——[x]Heb. *swallow* or *sup up*

[y]Heb. *into straightness*——[z]Psa. xcvii. 7; chap. i. 29; xliv. 11; xlv. 16

others of them who inhabited or frequented *cities* and *villages*, as may be collected from this place of the prophet. *Pietro della Valle*, speaking of the people of Arabia Deserta, says: "There is a sort of Arabs of that country called Maédi, who with their herds, of buffaloes for the most part, sometimes live in the *deserts*, and sometimes in *cities;* from whence they have their name, which signifies *wandering*, going from place to place. They have no professed houses; nor are they properly *Bedaui*, or *Beduui*, that is, *Deserticoli*, who are the most noble among them, and never abide within walls, but always go wandering through the open country with their *black tents;* nor are they properly called *Hhadesi*, as they call those who dwell in cities, and lands with fixed houses. These by the latter are esteemed ignoble and base; but both are considered as of low condition." *Viaggi*, Parte III. lett. ii.

The villages that *Kedar doth inhabit*] The *Arabs*, according to the *Targum*.

The inhabitants of the rock] They who dwell in fortified places. The *Vulgate* has *habitatores Petrææ*, "the inhabitants of Arabia Petræa." Those who make the *rock* Jesus Christ, the *inhabitants of the rock*, true believers in him; the *singing*, rejoicing for the salvation they have received; *abuse* and *disgrace* the *passage* and the *pulpit.* I have heard a clergyman, a magistrate, a justice of the quorum, spend an hour in showing from these words, 1. That they meant Jesus Christ, and none other. 2. That he might be fully compared to a *rock*, as the *foundation* on which his Church was built, and on which all true believers rested for their salvation. 3. A *rock*, because of his *strength* and *might* in destroying his enemies, and supporting his friends. 4. A *refreshing rock*, like that in the *wilderness;* and *that rock was Christ.* 5. A *perspective rock*, from which true believers could discover their heavenly inheritance: "When my heart is overwhelmed, lead me to the *rock* that is higher than I," &c. Now all this is true in itself; but false in respect to the words on which it was professedly built, for they have no such meaning.

Verse 14. *I have been still*—"Shall I keep silence for ever"] After מעולם *meolam*, in the copy which the *Septuagint* had before them, followed the word הלעולם *haleolam*, εσιωπησα απ' αιωνος· Μη και αει σιωπησομαι· according to MSS. *Pachom.* and I. D. II. and Edit. *Complut.;* which word, הלעולם *haleolam*, has been omitted in the text by an easy mistake of a transcriber, because of the similitude of the word preceding. *Shall I always keep silence?* like that of *Juvenal:* Semper ego auditor tantum? *Shall I always be a hearer only?*

Verse 15. *I will make the rivers islands*—"I will make the rivers dry deserts"] Instead of איים *iyim, islands*, read ציים *tsiim;* a very probable conjecture of *Houbigant.*

Verse 16. *In paths*] The *Septuagint*, *Syriac*, *Vulgate*, and nine MSS., (two ancient,) read ובנתיבות *ubenotiboth.*

Will I do unto them] עשיתם *asitem.* This word, so written as it is in the text, means "thou wilt do," in the second person. The Masoretes have indeed pointed it for the first person; but the י *yod* in the last syllable is absolutely necessary to distinguish the first person; and so it is written in forty MSS., עשיתים *asithim.*

Jarchi, *Kimchi*, *Sal. ben Melec*, &c., agree that the past time is here put for the future, עשיתי *asithi* for אעשה; and indeed the context necessarily requires that interpretation. Farther it is to be observed that עשיתים *asithim* is put for עשיתי להם *asithi lahem*, "I have done them," for "I have done for them;" as עשיתני *asitheni* is for עשיתי לי *asiti li*, "I have made myself," for "I have made for myself," Ezek. xxix. 2; and in the celebrated passage of Jephthah's vow, Judges xi. 31, והעליתיהו עולה *veheelitihu olah* for העליתי לו עולה *heelithi lo olah*, "I will offer him a burnt-offering," for "I will offer unto him (that is, unto JEHOVAH) a burnt-offering;" by an ellipsis of the preposition of which Buxtorf gives many other examples, Thes. Grammat. lib. ii. 17. See also note on chap. lxv. 5. A late happy application of this grammatical remark to that much disputed passage has perfectly cleared up a difficulty which for *two thousand* years had puzzled all the translators and expositors, had given occasion to dissertations without number, and caused endless disputes among the learned on the question, whether Jephthah sacrificed his daughter or not; in which both parties have been equally ignorant of the meaning of the place, of the state of the fact, and of the very terms of the vow; which now at last has been

A. M. cir. 3292 B. C. cir. 712 Olymp. XVII. 1 cir. annum NumæPompilii, R. Roman., 4

be greatly ashamed, that trust in
graven images, that say to the
molten images, Ye *are* our gods.
18 Hear, ye deaf; and look, ye
blind that ye may see.
19 [a]Who *is* blind, but my servant? or
deaf, as my messenger *that* I sent? who *is*
blind as *he that is* perfect, and blind as the
LORD'S servant?
20 Seeing many things, [b]but thou observest
not; opening the ears, but he heareth not.
21 The LORD is well pleased for his righteousness' sake; he will magnify the law, and
make [c]*it* honourable.
22 But this *is* a people robbed and spoiled;
[d]*they are* all of them snared in holes, and they
are hid in prison houses: they
are for a prey, and none delivereth; for [e]a spoil, and none saith,
Restore.
23 Who among you will give ear to this? *who*
will hearken and hear [f]for the time to come?
24 Who gave Jacob for a spoil, and Israel
to the robbers? did not the LORD, he against
whom we have sinned? for they would not
walk in his ways, neither were they obedient
unto his law.
25 Therefore he hath poured upon him the
fury of his anger, and the strength of battle:
[g]and it hath set him on fire round about, [h]yet
he knew not; and [i]it burned him, yet he laid
it not to heart.

[a]Ch. xliii. 8; Ezek. xii. 2; see John ix. 39, 41——[b]Rom. ii. 21——[c]Or, him——[d]Or, *in snaring all the young men of them*——[e]Heb. *a treading*——[f]Heb. *for the after time?* [g]2 Kings xxv. 9——[h]Hos. vii. 9——[i]Jer. iv. 4; xxi. 12

cleared up beyond all doubt by my learned friend Dr. Randolph, Margaret Professor of Divinity in the University of Oxford, in his Sermon on Jephthah's Vow, Oxford, 1766.—L.

Verse 19. *As my messenger* that *I sent*—"As he to whom I have sent my messengers"] כמלאכי אשלח *kemalachey eshlach*, ut ad quem nuncios meos misi. The *Vulgate* and *Chaldee* are almost the only interpreters who render it rightly, in consistence with the rest of the sentence, and in perfect agreement with the Hebrew idiom; according to which the ellipsis is to be thus supplied: כלאשר מלאכי אשלח *kelaasher malachey eshlach;* "As he to whom I have sent my messengers."

As he that is *perfect*—"As he who is perfectly instructed"] See note on chap. xliv. 2.

And blind as the Lord's servant—"And deaf, as the servant of JEHOVAH"] For ועור *veivver, and blind*, we must read וחרש *vecheresh, and deaf: κωφος, Symmachus*, and so a MS. The mistake is palpable, and the correction self-evident, and admissible though there had been no authority for it.

Verse 20. *Seeing many things*—"Thou hast seen indeed"] The text has ראית רבית *raith rabith*, which the Masoretes in the marginal Keri have corrected to ראות רבות *reoth rabboth;* as indeed *one hundred and seven* MSS., and *five* editions, now have it in the text. This was probably the reading of most of the MSS. of their time; which, though they approved of it, out of some superstition they would not admit into their standard text. But these wretched critics, though they perceived there was some fault, yet did not know where the fault lay, nor consequently how to amend it; and yet it was open enough to a judicious eye: "רבות *rabboth*, sic veteres; et tamen forte legendum, ראות *reoth*, vide cap. vi. 9."—*Secker*. That is, ראית ראות *raith, reoth, seeing, thou shalt see.* I believe no one will doubt of admitting this as the true reading.

But he heareth not—"Yet thou wilt not hear"] For ישמע *yishma*, read תשמע *tishma*, in the second person; so all the ancient Versions and *forty* MSS. of *Kennicott's*, (four of them ancient,) and *seventeen* of *De Rossi's*, and perhaps *five* more. *Two* others have תשמעו *tishmeu*, second person plural.

Verse 21. *He will magnify the law*—"He hath exalted his own praise"] For תורה *torah, the law*, the *Septuagint* read תודה *todah, praise.*

Verse 22. They are *all of them snared in holes*—"All their chosen youths are taken in the toils"] For הפח *hapheach* read הופחו *huphachu*, in the plural number, hophal; as החבאו *hochbau*, which answers to it in the following member of the sentence. *Le Clerc, Houbigant.* הפח *huppach, Secker.*

Verse 24. *We have sinned*—"They have sinned"] For חטאנו *chatanu*, "we have sinned," first person; the *Septuagint* and *Chaldee* read חטאו *chateu*, "they have sinned," in the third person.

Verse 25. *The fury of his anger*—"The heat of his wrath"] For חמה *chammah*, the Bodl. MS. has חמת *chammath*, in *regimine*, more regularly.

It hath set him on fire round about] So thoroughly hardened are the Jewish people, that they are represented as being in a house on fire, and even scorched with the flames, without perceiving their danger, or feeling that they are hurt! What a picture of mental induration! and this is their state to the present day. But by whom shall Jacob arise? for in this sense he is small indeed. Many efforts have been made to Christianize them, but without effect; and is this to be wondered at, while we tell them how great they are, how learned, how wise, how much we owe to them, that they are still the peculiar people of God, &c., &c.? If all this be true, what can they gain by becoming Christians? Whereas a more stupid, proud, hardened, ignorant people can scarcely be found in the civilized world, and they are most grossly ignorant of their own Scriptures.

CHAPTER XLIII

Prediction of that blessed period when God should gather the posterity of Abraham, with tender care, from their several dispersions in every quarter under heaven, and bring them safely to their own land, 1–7. *Struck with astonishment at so clear a display of an event so very remote, the prophet again challenges all the blinded nations and their idols to produce an instance of such foreknowledge,* 8, 9; *and intimates that the Jews should remain, (as at this day,) a singular monument to witness the truth of the prediction, till it should at length be fulfilled by the irresistible power of God,* 10–13. *He then returns to the nearer deliverance—that from the captivity of Babylon,* 14, 15; *with which, however, he immediately connects another deliverance described by allusions to that from Egypt, but represented as much more wonderful than that; a character which will not at all apply to the deliverance from Babylon, and must therefore be understood of the restoration from the mystical Babylon,* 16–18. *On this occasion the prophet, with peculiar elegance, and by a very strong poetic figure, represents the tender care of God in comforting and refreshing his people on their way through the desert, to be so great as to make even the wild beasts haunting those parched places so sensible of the blessing of those copious streams then provided by him, as to join their hissing and howling notes with one consent to praise God,* 19–21. *This leads to a beautiful contrast of the ingratitude of the Jews, and a vindication of God's dealings with regard to them,* 22–28.

A. M. cir. 3292
B. C. cir. 712
Olymp. XVII. 1
cir. annum
NumæPompilii,
R. Roman., 4

BUT now thus saith the LORD
[a]that created thee, O Jacob,
[b]and he that formed thee, O Israel, Fear not: [c]for I have re-
deemed thee, [d]I have called *thee* by thy name;
thou *art* mine.
2 [e]When thou passest through the waters,
[f]I *will be* with thee; and through the rivers,
they shall not overflow thee: when thou
[g]walkest through the fire, thou shalt not be
burned; neither shall the flame kindle upon
thee.
3 For I *am* the LORD thy God, the Holy
One of Israel, thy Saviour: [h]I gave Egypt
for thy ransom, Ethiopia and
Seba for thee.
4 Since thou wast precious in
my sight, thou hast been honoura-
ble, and I have loved thee: therefore will I
give men for thee, and people for thy [i]life.
5 [k]Fear not: for I *am* with thee: I will
bring thy seed from the east, and gather thee
from the west;
6 I will say to the north, Give up; and to the
south, Keep not back: bring my sons from
far, and my daughters from the ends of the
earth;
7 *Even* every one that is [l]called by my

A. M. cir. 3292
B. C. cir. 712
Olymp. XVII. 1
cir. annum
NumæPompilii,
R. Roman., 4

[a]Ver. 7.——[b]Ver. 21; chap. xliv. 2, 21, 24——[c]Chap. xliv. 6——[d]Chap. xlii. 6; xlv. 4——[e]Psa. lxvi. 12; xci. 3, &c.——[f]Deut. xxxi. 6, 8

[g]Dan. iii. 25, 27——[h]Prov. xi. 8; xxi. 18——[i]Or, *person*——[k]Chap. xli. 10, 14; xliv. 2; Jer. xxx. 10, 11; xlvi. 27, 28——[l]Chap. lxiii. 19; James ii. 7

NOTES ON CHAP. XLIII

Verse 1. *I have called* thee *by thy name*] "קראתי בשמך *karathi beshimcha.* So all the Versions. But it seems from the seventh verse, and from the thing itself, that we should read קראתיך בשמי *karathicha bishmi,* 'I have called thee by my name;' for this form of speech often occurs—the other never. For chap. xlv. 24, concerning Cyrus, is another matter; but when God calls Jacob Israel, he calls him by the name of God. See Exod. xxxi. 2."—*Secker.*

Verse 3. *I gave Egypt* for *thy ransom*] This is commonly supposed to refer to the time of Sennacherib's invasion; who, when he was just ready to fall upon Jerusalem, soon after his entering Judea, was providentially diverted from that design, and turned his arms against the Egyptians, and their allies the Cushean Arabians, with their neighbours the Sabeans, probably joined with them under Tirhakah. See chap. xx. and chap. xxxvii. 9. Or as there are some reasonable objections to this opinion, perhaps it may mean more generally that God has often saved his people at the expense of other nations, whom he had, as it were in their stead, given up to destruction. Vitringa explains this of Shalmaneser's designs upon the kingdom of Judea after he had destroyed that of Samaria, from which he was diverted by carrying the war against the Egyptians, Cusheans, and Sabeans; but of this I think he has no clear proof in history. It is not to be wondered at that many things of this kind should remain very obscure for the want of the light of history, which in regard to these times is extremely deficient.

"Did not Cyrus overcome these nations? and might they not be given for releasing the Jews? It seems to have been so from chap. xlv. 14."—*Secker.*

Kimchi refers all this to the deliverance of Jerusalem from the invasion of Sennacherib. Tirhakah, king of Ethiopia, had come out to war against the king of Assyria, who was thereupon obliged to raise the siege of Jerusalem. Thus the Ethiopians, Egyptians, and Sabeans were delivered into the hands of the Assyrians as a ransom for Israel.—*Kimchi.* I cannot help thinking this to be a very rational solution of the text.

Verse 7. *Every one that is called by my name*] All who worship the true God, and are obedient to his laws.

I have created him] בראתיו *berathiv.* I have produced him out of nothing.

For my glory] *Ten* MSS., *three* ancient, and the *Syriac* and *Vulgate,* read לכבודי *licabodi,* without the conjunction ו *vau, and.*

A. M. cir. 3292
B. C. cir. 712
Olymp. XVII. 1
cir. annum
Numæ Pompilii,
R. Roman., 4

name: for [m]I have created him
for my glory, [n]I have formed
him; yea, I have made him.
8 [o]Bring forth the blind people
that have eyes, and the deaf that have ears.
9 Let all the nations be gathered together,
and let the people be assembled: [p]who among
them can declare this, and show us former
things? let them bring forth their witnesses,
that they may be justified: or let them hear,
and say, *It is* truth.
10 [q]Ye *are* my witnesses, saith the LORD,
[r]and my servant whom I have chosen: that
ye may know and believe me, and understand that I *am* he: [s]before me there was [t]no
God formed, neither shall there be after me.

11 I, *even* I, [u]*am* the LORD;
and beside me *there is* no Saviour.
12 I have declared, and have
saved, and I have showed, when *there was*
no [v]strange *god* among you: [w]therefore ye
are my witnesses, saith the LORD, that I
am God.
13 [x]Yea, before the day *was* I *am* he; and
there is none that can deliver out of my hand:
I will work, and who shall [y]let [z]it?
14 Thus saith the LORD, your Redeemer,
the Holy One of Israel; for your sake I
have sent to Babylon, and have brought down
all their [a]nobles, and the Chaldeans, whose
cry *is* in the ships.

A. M. cir. 3292
B. C. cir. 712
Olymp. XVII. 1
cir. annum
Numæ Pompilii,
R. Roman., 4

[m]Psa. c. 3; chap. xxix. 23; John iii. 3, 5; 2 Cor. v. 17; Eph. ii. 10——[n]Ver. 1——[o]Chap. vi. 9; xlii. 19; Ezek. xii. 2——[p]Chap. xli. 21, 22, 26——[q]Chap. xliv. 8 [r]Chap. xlii. 1; lv. 4——[s]Chap. xli. 4; xliv. 6

[t]Or, *nothing formed of God*——[u]Chap. xlv. 21; Hos. xiii. 4——[v]Deut. xxxii. 16; Psa. lxxxi. 9——[w]Chap. xliv. 8; ver. 10——[x]Psa. xc. 2; John viii. 58——[y]Heb. *turn it back?*——[z]Job ix. 12; chap. xiv. 27——[a]Heb. *bars*

I have formed him] יצרתיו *yetsartiv*. I have given him that particular form and shape which are best suited to his station in life.

I have made him] עשיתיו *asithiv*. I have adapted him to the accomplishment of my counsels and designs.

Verse 8. *Bring forth the blind people that have eyes*—"Bring forth the people, blind, although they have eyes"] I understand this of the Gentiles, as the verse following, not of the Jews. Their natural faculties, if they had made a proper use of them, must have led them to the knowledge of the being and attributes of the one true God; "for his eternal power and Godhead," if well attended to, are clearly seen in his works, (Rom. i. 20,) and would have preserved them from running into the folly and absurdity of worshipping idols. They are here challenged to produce the evidence of the power and foreknowledge of their idol gods; and the Jews are just afterwards, ver. 10, appealed to as witnesses for God in this cause, therefore these latter cannot here be meant by the people blind with eyes and deaf with ears.

Verse 9. *Who among them*] *Seven* MSS., *three* ancient, and the first edition, 1486, with the *Syriac* and *Vulgate*, read בכם *bechem*, who among *you;* the present reading is preferable.

Verse 10. *Ye* (the Israelites) are *my witnesses—and my servant* (the prophet) *whom I have chosen*, that whatever has been said before concerning Sennacherib has been literally fulfilled. The *prophet* had predicted it; the *Israelites* saw it accomplished.

Before me there was no God formed, neither shall there be after me.] This is a most difficult place. Was there a time when God was not? No! Yet he says, *before* me. Will there be a time in which God will not exist? No! Yet he says, *after* me. Are not all these words to be referred to his creation? *Before* me, no god created any thing, nor was there any thing pre-existent but myself. And *after* me, *i. e.*, after my creation, such as now exists, there shall be no other class of beings formed. This mode of interpretation frees the passage from all embarrassment, and the context perfectly agrees with it. The words *my servant*, in this verse, the *Targum* understands of *the Messiah*.

Verse 12. *I have declared, and have saved*] My prophets have always predicted your deliverances before they took place; and I have fulfilled their words to the uttermost.

Verse 14. *The Chaldeans, whose cry* is *in the ships*—"The Chaldeans exulting in their ships."] Babylon was very advantageously situated both in respect to commerce, and as a naval power. It was open to the Persian Gulf by the Euphrates, which was navigable by large vessels; and being joined to the Tigris above Babylon by the canal called *Naharmalca* or the Royal River, supplied the city with the produce of the whole country to the north of it, as far as the Euxine and Caspian seas, *Herod.* i. 194. Semiramis was the foundress of this part also of the Babylonian greatness. She improved the navigation of the Euphrates, *Herod.* i. 184; *Strabo*, lib. xvi.; and is said to have had a fleet of three thousand galleys, *Huet*, Hist. du Commerce, chap. xi. We are not to wonder that in later times we hear little of the commerce and naval power of Babylon; for, after the taking of the city by Cyrus, the Euphrates was not only rendered less fit for navigation by being on that occasion diverted from its course and left to spread over the whole country; but the Persian monarchs, residing in their own country, to prevent any invasion by sea on that part of their empire, purposely obstructed the navigation of both the rivers by making cataracts in them, *Strabo*, ib., that is, by raising dams across the channel, and making artificial falls in them, that no vessel of any size or force could possibly come up. Alexander began to restore the navigation of the rivers by demolishing the cataracts upon the Tigris as far up as Seleucia, *Arrian*, lib. vii., but he did not live to finish his great designs; those upon the Euphrates still continued. Ammianus, xxiv. 1, mentions them as subsisting in his time.

The prophet therefore might very justly speak of the Chaldeans as glorying in their naval

A. M. cir. 3292 B. C. cir. 712 Olymp. XVII. 1 cir. annum NumæPompilii, R. Roman., 4

15 I *am* the LORD, your Holy One, the Creator of Israel, your King.

16 Thus saith the LORD, which [b]maketh a way in the sea, and [c]a path in the mighty waters;

17 Which [d]bringeth forth the chariot and horse, the army and the power; they shall lie down together, they shall not rise: they are extinct, they are quenched as tow.

18 [e]Remember ye not the former things, neither consider the things of old.

19 Behold, I will do a [f]new thing; now it shall spring forth; shall ye not know it? [g]I will even make a way in the wilderness, *and* rivers in the desert.

20 The beast of the field shall honour me, the dragons and the [h]owls[i]: because [k]I give waters in the wilderness, *and* rivers in the desert, to give drink to my people, my chosen.

21 [l]This people have I formed for myself; they shall show forth my praise.

A. M. cir. 3292 B. C. cir. 712 Olymp. XVII. 1 cir. annum NumæPompilii, R. Roman., 4

22 But thou hast not called upon me, O Jacob; but thou [m]hast been weary of me, O Israel.

23 [n]Thou hast not brought me the [o]small cattle of thy burnt-offerings; neither hast thou honoured me with thy sacrifices. I have not caused thee to serve with an offering, nor wearied thee with incense.

24 Thou hast bought me no sweet cane with money, neither hast thou [p]filled me with the fat of thy sacrifices: but thou hast made me to serve with thy sins, thou hast [q]wearied me with thine iniquities.

25 I, *even* I, *am* he that [r]blotteth out thy transgressions [s]for mine own sake, [t]and will not remember thy sins.

26 Put me in remembrance: let us plead

---

[b]Exod. xiv. 16, 22; Psa. lxxvii. 19; chap. li. 10——[c]Josh. iii. 13, 16——[d]Exod. xiv. 4–9, 25——[e]Jer. xvi. 14; xxiii. 7——[f]2 Cor. v. 17; Rev. xxi. 5——[g]Exod. xvii. 6; Num. xx. 11; Deut. viii. 15; Psa. lxxviii. 16; chap. xxxv. 6; xli. 18——[h]Or, *ostriches*——[i]Heb. *daughters of the owl*——[k]Chap. xlviii. 21

[l]Psa. cii. 18; ver. 1, 7; Luke i. 74, 75; Eph. i. 5, 6——[m]Mal. i. 13——[n]Amos v. 25——[o]Heb. *lambs* or *kids*——[p]Heb. *made me drunk*, or *abundantly moistened*——[q]Ch. i. 14; Mal. ii. 17——[r]Chap. xliv. 22; xlviii. 9; Jer. l. 20; Acts iii. 19——[s]Ezek. xxxvi. 22, &c.——[t]Chap. i. 18; Jer. xxxi. 34

---

power in his time; though afterwards they had no foundation for making any such boast.

Verse 15. *The Creator*] For בורא *bore*, "Creator," six MSS. (two ancient) have אלהי *Elohey*, "God."

Verse 19. *Behold, I will do a new thing*] At ver. 16, the prophet had referred to the deliverance from Egypt and the passage through the Red Sea; here he promises that the same power shall be employed in their redemption and return from the Babylonish captivity. This was to be a *new* prodigy.

Verse 20. *The beast of the field shall honour me*—"The wild beast of the field shall glorify me"] The image is elegant and highly poetical. God will give such an abundant miraculous supply of water to his people traversing the dry desert in their return to their country, that even the wild beasts, the serpents, the ostriches, and other animals that haunt those arid regions, shall be sensible of the blessing, and shall break forth into thanksgiving and praises to him for the unusual refreshment which they receive from his so plentifully watering the sandy wastes of Arabia Deserta, for the benefit of his people passing through them.

Verse 22. *But thou hast not called upon me*] The connexion is: But thou, Israel, whom I have chosen, whom I have formed for myself to be my witness against the false gods of the nations; even thou hast revolted from me, hast neglected my worship, and hast been perpetually running after strange gods. The emphasis of this and the following parts of the sentence, on which the sense depends, is laid on the words ME, on MY ACCOUNT, &c. The Jews were diligent in performing the external services of religion; in offering prayers, incense, sacrifices, oblations; but their prayers were not offered with faith; and their oblations were made more frequently to their idols than to the God of their fathers. The Hebrew idiom excludes with a general negative, in a comparative sense, one of two objects opposed to one another: thus, "I will have mercy, and *not* sacrifice," Hos. vi. 6. "For I spoke *not* to your fathers, *nor* commanded them, concerning burnt-offerings or sacrifices; but this thing I commanded them, saying, Obey my voice," Jer. vii. 22, 23. And the meaning of this place of Isaiah seems to be much the same with that of Amos; who however has explained at large both parts of the comparison, and specified the false service opposed to the true:—

"Have ye offered unto me sacrifices and offerings,
In the wilderness forty years, O house of Israel?
Nay, but you have borne the tabernacle of your Moloch,
And Chiun, your images;
The star of your god, which you made to yourselves." Amos v. 25, 26.

But thou hast been weary of me, O Israel—"Neither on my account hast thou laboured, O Israel."] For כי יגעת *ki yagata*, the *Septuagint* and *Vulgate* read ויגעת *veyagata.—Houbigant.* The negative is repeated or referred to by the conjunction ו *vau;* as in many other places. See note on chap. xxiii. 4.

Verse 25. *I, even I, am he*] The original is extremely abrupt: אנכי אנכי הוא *anochi anochi hu*, "I, I, He." Is there any mystery in this form? Does it refer to a plurality of persons in the Godhead?

For mine own sake] In the pardon of sin

A. M. cir. 3292 B. C. cir. 712 Olymp. XVII. 1 cir. annum NumæPompilii, R. Roman., 4

together: declare thou, that thou
mayest be justified.
27 Thy first father hath sinned,
and thy [u]teachers have transgressed against me.
28 Therefore [v]I have profaned the [w]princes of the sanctuary, [x]and have given Jacob to the curse, and Israel to reproaches.

[u]Heb. *interpreters;* Mal. ii. 7, 8——[v]Chap. xlvii. 6; Lam. ii. 2, 6, 7——[w]Or, *holy princes*——[x]Psa. lxxix. 4; Jer. xxiv. 9; Dan. ix. 11; Zech. viii. 13

God can draw no reason but from his own infinite goodness.

Verse 27. *Thy first father hath sinned*] On this *Kimchi* speaks well: "How can ye say that ye have not sinned, seeing your first father, Adam, sinned; and man hath sin impressed on him through natural generation?"

Verse 28. *I have profaned the princes of the sanctuary*—"Thy princes have profaned my sanctuary"] Instead of ואחלל שרי *vaachallel sarey*, read ויחללו שריך *vayechalelu sareycha*. So the *Syriac* and *Septuagint*, και εμιαναν οἱ αρχοντες τα ἁγια μου, "the rulers have defiled my holy things." קדשי *kodshi, Houbigant*. Οἱ αρχοντες σου, "thy rulers," MSS. Pachom. and I. D. II. and Marchal.

To reproaches—"To reproach"] לגדופה *ligeduphah*, in the singular number; so an ancient MS. and the *Septuagint, Syriac*, and *Vulgate*. And, alas! what a curse do they still bear, and what reproach do they still suffer! No national crimes have ever equalled those of the Jewish nation, for no nation ever had such privileges to neglect, despise, sin against. When shall this severity of God towards this people have an end? *Answ.* Whenever, with one heart, they turn to him, and receive the doctrine of the Lord Jesus; and not till *then*.

CHAPTER XLIV

This chapter, besides promises of redemption, of the effusion of the Spirit, and success of the Gospel, 1–5, *sets forth, in a very sublime manner, the supreme power and foreknowledge, and absolute eternity, of the one true God; and exposes the folly and absurdity of idolatry with admirable force and elegance,* 6–20. *And to show that the knowledge of future events belongs only to Jehovah, whom all creation is again called to adore for the deliverance and reconciliation granted to his people,* 21–23, *the prophet concludes with setting in a very strong point of view the absolute impotence of every thing considered great and insurmountable in the sight of men, when standing in the way of the Divine counsel; and mentions the future deliverer of the Jewish nation expressly by name, nearly* two hundred years *before his birth,* 24–28.

A. M. cir. 3292 B. C. cir. 712 Olymp. XVII. 1 cir. annum NumæPompilii, R. Roman., 4

YET now hear, [a]O Jacob my servant; and Israel, whom I have chosen.
2 Thus saith the LORD that made thee, [b]and formed thee from the womb, *which* will help thee; Fear not, O Jacob, my servant; and thou, [c]Jesurun, whom I have chosen.
3 For I will [d]pour water upon him that is thirsty, and floods upon the dry ground: I will pour my spirit upon thy seed, and my blessing upon thine offspring:
4 And they shall spring up *as* among the grass, as willows by the water courses.

[a]Ver. 21; chap. xli. 8; xliii. 1; Jer. xxx. 10; xlvi. 27, 28——[b]Chap. xliii. 1, 7——[c]Deut. xxxii. 15——[d]Chap. xxxv. 7; Joel ii. 28; John vii. 38; Acts ii. 13

NOTES ON CHAP. XLIV

Verse 2. *Jesurun*] Jeshurun means Israel. This name was given to that people by Moses, Deut. xxxii. 15; xxxiii. 5, 26. The most probable account of it seems to be that in which the Jewish commentators agree; namely, that it is derived from ישר *yashar*, and signifies *upright*. In the same manner, Israel, as a people, is called משלם *meshullam, perfect*, chap. xlii. 19. They were taught of God, and abundantly furnished with the means of rectitude and perfection in his service and worship. *Grotius* thinks that ישרון *yeshurun* is a diminutive of ישראל *yishrael, Israel;* expressing peculiar fondness and affection; Ισραηλιδιον, *O little Israel*.

Verse 4. *They shall spring up* as *among the grass*—"They shall spring up as the grass among the waters"] בבין חציר *bebeyn chatsir*. "They shall spring up *in the midst of*, or rather, *in among, the grass*." This cannot be right: *eleven* MSS., and *thirteen* editions, have כבין *kebeyn*, or כבן *keben*. Twenty-four MSS. read it without the י *yod*, בבן *beben, in the son of the grass;* and so reads the *Chaldee;* בבן *beben, in the son* of the grass. *Twenty-four* MSS. of Dr. *Kennicott's, thirty-three* of *De Rossi's*, and one of my own, with *six* editions, have this reading. The *Syriac*, מבין *mibbeyn*. The true reading is in all probability כבין *kebeyn;* and the word מים *mayim*, which should have followed it, is lost out of the text: but it is happily supplied by the *Septuagint;* ὡς ανα μεσον ὑδατος, *as among the water*. "In every place where there is water, there is always grass; for water makes every thing grow in the east." Sir *John Chardin's* note on 1 Kings xvii. 5. *Harmer's* Observations, i. 54.

A. M. cir. 3292
B. C. cir. 712
Olymp. XVII. 1
cir. annum
NumæPompilii,
R. Roman., 4

5 One shall say, I *am* the LORD'S; and another shall call *himself* by the name of Jacob; and another shall subscribe *with* his hand unto the LORD, and surname *himself* by the name of Israel.

6 Thus saith the LORD, the King of Israel, [e]and his Redeemer the LORD of hosts; [f]I *am* the first, and I *am* the last: and beside me *there is* no God.

7 And [g]who, as I, shall call, and shall declare it, and set it in order for me, since I appointed the ancient people? and the things that are coming, and shall come, let them show unto them.

A. M. cir. 3292
B. C. cir. 712
Olymp. XVII. 1
cir. annum
NumæPompilii,
R. Roman., 4

8 Fear ye not, neither be afraid: [h]have not I told thee from that time, and have declared *it?* [i]ye *are* even my witnesses. Is there a God beside me? yea [k]*there is* no [l]God; I know not *any.*

9 They [m]that make a graven image *are* all of them vanity; and their [n]delectable things shall not profit; and they *are* their own witnesses; [o]they see not, nor know; that they may be ashamed.

10 Who hath formed a god, or molten a graven image [p]*that* is profitable for nothing?

11 Behold, all his fellows shall be [q]ashamed; and the workmen, they *are* of men: let them

[e]Ver. 24; chap. xliii. 1, 14——[f]Chap. xli. 4; xlviii. 12; Rev. i. 8, 17; xxii. 13——[g]Chap. xli. 4, 22; xlv. 21 [h]Chap. xli. 22——[i]Chap. xliii. 10, 12——[k]Deut. iv. 35, 39; xxxii. 39; 1 Sam. ii. 2——2 Sam. xxii. 32; chap. xlv. 5——[l]Heb. *rock;* Deut. xxxii. 4——[m]Chap. xli. 24, 29——[n]Heb. *desirable*——[o]Psalm cxv. 4, &c. [p]Jeremiah x. 5; Habakkuk ii. 18——[q]Psalm xcvii. 7; chap. i. 29; xlii. 17; xlv. 16

Verse 5. *Shall call* himself—"Shall be called"] Passive, יקרא *yikkare;* κληθησεται, *Symmachus.*

Another shall subscribe with his hand unto the Lord—"This shall inscribe his hand to JEHOVAH"] Και ἑτερος επιγραψει χειρι (χειρα, *Aq., Sym.*) αυτου, Του Θεου ειμι· "And another shall write upon his hand, I belong to God."—*Sept.* They seem to have read here, as before, ליהוה אני *laihovah ani, I belong to* JEHOVAH. But the repetition of the same phrase without any variation is not elegant. However, they seem to have understood it rightly, as an allusion to the marks, which were made by punctures rendered indelible, by fire or by staining, upon the hand or some other part of the body, signifying the state or character of the person, and to whom he belonged. The slave was marked with the name of his master; the soldier, of his commander; the idolater, with the name or ensign of his god: Στιγματα επιγραφομενα δια των στρατευομενων εν ταις χερσιν· "Punctural inscriptions made by the soldiers on their hands." Aetius apud Turnebum Advers. xxiv. 12. Victuris in cute punctis milites scripti et matriculis inserti jurare solent. "The soldiers having indelible inscriptions on their skin, and inserted in the muster-rolls, are accustomed to make oath." *Vigetius,* ii. 5. And the Christians seem to have imitated this practice, by what *Procopius* says on this place of Isaiah: Το δε ΤΗ ΧΕΙΡΙ, δια το στιζειν ισως πολλους επι καρπων, η βραχιονων, η τον σταυρον το σημειον, η την Χριστου προσηγοριαν. "Because many marked their wrists, or their arms, with the sign of the cross, or with the name of Christ." See Rev. xx. 4; *Spencer,* De Leg. Hebr. lib. ii., cap. 20.

Verse 7. *Let them show unto them*—"Let them declare unto us."] For למו *lamo,* unto *them,* the *Chaldee* reads לנו *lanu,* unto *us.* The *Septuagint* read לכם *lachem,* unto *you;* which is preferable to the reading of the text. But למו *lamo,* and לנו *lanu,* are frequently mistaken one for the other, see chap. x. 29; Psa. lxxx. 7; lxiv. 6.

Verse 8. *Fear ye not*] תרהו *tirehu* never occurs. Perhaps it should be תיראו *tireu, fear ye.* Two MSS. read תירהו *tirehu,* and one of mine תהרו *taharu.*

Verses 9, 10. *That they may be ashamed. Who hath formed a god*—"That every one may be ashamed, that he hath formed a god"] The *Bodleian* MS., one of the first extant for its antiquity and authority, instead of מי *mi,* at the beginning of the *tenth* verse, has כי *ki,* which greatly clears up the construction of a very obscure passage. *Doederlein* approves of this reading. The *Septuagint* likewise closely connect in construction the end of ver. 9 with the beginning of ver. 10; and wholly omit the interrogative מי *mi,* which embarrasses the sentence: Αισχυνθησονται οἱ πλασσοντες Θεον, και γλυφοντες παντες ανωφελη· "But they shall be confounded that make a god; and they who engrave unprofitable things;" agreeably to the reading of the MS. above mentioned.

Verse 11. *His fellows*] חבריו *chaberaiv:* but עבדיו *abadaiv, his servants* or *worshippers,* is the reading of one of *De Rossi's* MSS., and of the *Chaldee.*

And the workmen, they are *of men*—"Even the workmen themselves shall blush"] I do not know that any one has ever yet interpreted these words to any tolerably good sense: וחרשים המה מאדם *vecharashim hemmah meadam.* The *Vulgate* and our translators, have rendered them very fairly, as they are written and pointed in the text: Fabri enim sunt ex hominibus. "And the workmen they are of men." Out of which the commentators have not been able to extract any thing worthy of the prophet. I have given another explanation of the place; agreeable enough to the context, if it can be deduced from the words themselves. I presume that אדם *adam, rubuit,* may signify *erubuit,* to be red through shame, as well as from any other cause; though I cannot produce any example of it in that particular sense; and the word in the text I would point מאדם *meoddam;* or if any one should object to the irregularity of the number, I would read מאדמים *meoddamim.* But I rather think that the irregularity of the construction has been the cause of the obscurity, and has given occasion to the mistaken punctuation. The singular is sometimes put for the plural. See Psa. lxviii. 31; and the par-

A. M. cir. 3292
B. C. cir. 712
Olymp. XVII. 1
cir. annum
NumæPompilii,
R. Roman., 4

all be gathered together, let them stand up; *yet* they shall fear, *and* they shall be ashamed together.

12 [r]The smith [s]with the tongs both worketh in the coals, and fashioneth it with hammers, and worketh it with the strength of his arms: yea, he is hungry, and his strength faileth: he drinketh no water, and is faint.

13 The carpenter stretcheth out *his* rule; he marketh it out with a line; he fitteth it with planes, and he marketh it out with the compass, and maketh it after the figure of a man, according to the beauty of a man: that it may remain in the house.

14 He heweth him down cedars, and taketh the cypress and the oak, which he [t]strengtheneth for himself among the trees of the forest: he planteth an ash, and the rain doth nourish *it*.

15 Then shall it be for a man to burn: for he will take thereof, and warm himself; yea, he kindleth *it*, and baketh bread; yea, he maketh a god, and worshippeth *it;* he maketh it a graven image, and falleth down thereto.

16 He burneth part thereof in the fire; with part thereof he eateth flesh; he roasteth roast, and is satisfied: yea, he warmeth *himself,* and saith, Aha, I am warm, I have seen the fire:

A. M. cir. 3292
B. C. cir. 712
Olymp. XVII. 1
cir. annum
NumæPompilii,
R. Roman., 4

17 And the residue thereof he maketh a god, *even* his graven image: he falleth down unto it, and worshippeth *it,* and prayeth unto it, and saith, Deliver me; for thou *art* my god.

18 [u]They have not known nor understood: for [v]he hath [w]shut their eyes, that they cannot see; *and* their hearts, that they cannot understand.

19 And none [x]considereth [y]in his heart, neither *is there* knowledge nor understanding to say, I have burned part of it in the fire: yea, also I have baked bread upon the coals thereof; I have roasted flesh and eaten *it:* and shall I make the residue thereof an abomination? shall I fall down to [z]the stock of a tree?

20 He feedeth on ashes: [a]a deceived heart hath turned him aside, that he cannot deliver his soul, nor say, *Is there* not a lie in my right hand?

21 Remember these, O Jacob and Israel; for [b]thou *art* my servant: I have formed

[r]Chap. xl. 19; xli. 6; Jer. x. 3, &c.; Wisd. xiii. 11, &c. [s]Or, *with an axe*——[t]Or, *taketh courage*——[u]Chap. xlv. 20——[v]2 Thess. ii. 11

[w]Heb. *daubed*——[x]Heb. *setteth to his heart*——[y]Chap. xlvi. 8——[z]Heb. *that which comes of a tree?*——[a]Hos. iv. 11; Rom. i. 21; 2 Thess. ii. 11——[b]Ver. 1. 2

ticiple for the future tense, see Isa. xl. 11.—L.

Verse 12. *The smith with the tongs, &c.*—"The smith cutteth off a portion of iron"] מעצד *meatstsed,* Participium Pihel of עצד *atsad, to cut;* still used in that sense in the *Arabic.* See *Simonis* Lex. Heb. The *Septuagint* and *Syriac* take the word in this form: but they render it *sharpeneth* the iron. See *Castell.* Lex. in voce.

The sacred writers are generally large and eloquent upon the subject of idolatry; they treat it with great severity, and set forth the absurdity of it in the strongest light. But this passage of Isaiah, ver. 12-20, far exceeds any thing that ever was written upon the subject, in force of argument, energy of expression, and elegance of composition. One or two of the apocryphal writers have attempted to imitate the prophet, but with very ill success; Wisd. xiii. 11-19; xv. 7, &c.; Baruch vi., especially the latter, who, injudiciously dilating his matter, and introducing a number of minute circumstances, has very much weakened the force and effect of his invective. On the contrary a heathen author, in the ludicrous way, has, in a line or two, given idolatry one of the severest strokes it ever received:—

Olim truncus eram ficulnus, inutile lignum,
Cum faber incertus, scamnum faceretne Priapum,
Maluit esse Deum. Deus inde ego.

HORAT. *Satyr,* lib. 1. sat. viii.

"Formerly I was the stump of a fig tree, a useless log; when the carpenter, after hesitating whether to make me a *god* or a *stool,* at last determined to make me a *god.* Thus I became a god!"

From the *tenth* to the *seventeenth* verse, a most beautiful strain of irony is carried on against idolatry. And we may naturally think that every idolater, who either read or heard it, must have been for ever ashamed of his own devices.—L.

Verse 14. *He heweth him down*—"He heweth down"] For לכרת *lichroth,* the *Septuagint* and *Vulgate* read כרת *carath* or יכרת *yichroth.*

Verse 16. *With part*—"AND with part"] *Twenty-three* MSS., the *Septuagint,* and *Vulgate* add the conjunction ו *vau,* and ועל *veal.*

Verse 17. *He falleth down unto it*] There were *four* forms of adoration used among the Hebrews: 1. השתחוה HISHTACHAVAH, The prostration of the whole body. 2. קדד KADAD, The bowing of the head. 3. כרע CARA, The bending of the upper part of the body down to the knees. 4. ברך BARACH, Bowing the knee, or kneeling. See on chap. xlix. 23.

Verse 18. *He hath shut their eyes*—"Their eyes are closed up"] The *Septuagint, Chaldee,* and *Vulgate,* for טח *tach,* read טחו *tachu.* See note on chap. vi. 10.

Verse 20. *He feedeth on ashes*] He feedeth

A. M. cir. 3292 B. C. cir. 712 Olymp. XVII. 1 cir. annum NumæPompilii, R. Roman., 4

thee; thou *art* my servant: O
Israel, thou shalt not be forgotten of me.

22 [c]I have blotted out, as a
thick cloud, thy transgressions, and, as a
cloud, thy sins: return unto me; for [d]I have
redeemed thee.

23 [e]Sing, O ye heavens; for the LORD hath
done *it:* shout, ye lower parts of the earth:
break forth into singing, ye mountains, O
forest, and every tree therein: for the LORD
hath redeemed Jacob, and glorified himself
in Israel.

24 Thus saith the LORD, [f]thy Redeemer,
and [g]he that formed thee from the womb, I
am the LORD that maketh all *things;* [h]that
stretcheth forth the heavens alone; that
spreadeth abroad the earth by
myself:

25 That [i]frustrateth the tokens
[k]of the liars, and maketh diviners mad; that turneth wise *men* backward,
[l]and maketh their knowledge foolish;

26 [m]That confirmeth the word of his servant,
and performeth the counsel of his messengers;
that saith to Jerusalem, Thou shalt be inhabited; and to the cities of Judah, Ye shall be
built, and I will raise up the [n]decayed places
thereof:

27 [o]That saith to the deep, Be dry, and I
will dry up thy rivers:

28 That saith of Cyrus, *He is* my shepherd,
and shall perform all my pleasure: even saying to Jerusalem, [p]Thou shalt be built; and
to the temple, Thy foundation shall be laid.

[c]Chap. xliii. 25——[d]Chap. xliii. 1; xlviii. 20; 1 Cor. vi. 20; 1 Pet. i. 18, 19——[e]Psa. lxix. 34; xcvi. 11, 12; chap. xlii. 10; xlix. 13; Jer. li. 48; Rev. xviii. 20——[f]Ch. xliii. 14; Ver. 6——[g]Chap. xliii. 1

[h]Job ix. 8; Psa. civ. 2; chap. xl. 22; xlii. 5; xlv. 12; li. 13——[i]Chap. xlvii. 13——[k]Jer. l. 36——[l]1 Cor. i. 20——[m]Zech. i. 6——[n]Heb. *wastes*——[o]See Jer. l. 38; li. 32, 36——[p]2 Chron. xxxvi. 22, 23; Ezra i. 1, &c.; chap. xlv. 13

on that which affordeth no nourishment; a proverbial expression for using ineffectual means, and bestowing labour to no purpose. In the same sense Hosea says, "Ephraim feedeth on wind." Chap. xii. 1.

Verse 22. *I have blotted out, as a thick cloud, thy transgressions, and, as a cloud, thy sins*—"I have made thy transgressions vanish away like a cloud, and thy sins like a vapour"] *Longinus* admired the sublimity of the sentiment, as well as the harmony of the numbers, in the following sentence of *Demosthenes:* Τουτο το ψηφισμα τον τοτε τῃ πολει τεριστατα κινδυνον παρελθειν εποιησεν ὡσπερ νεφος. "This decree made the danger then hanging over the city pass away like a cloud." Probably Isaiah alludes here to the smoke rising up from the sin-offering, dispersed speedily by the wind and rendered invisible. He who offered his sacrifice aright was as sure that the sin for which he offered it was blotted out, as that the smoke of the sacrifice was dispersed by the wind, and was no longer discernible.

Verse 24. *By myself*] *Thirteen* MSS., six ancient, confirm the reading of the *Keri*, מאתי *meittai.*

Verse 27. *That saith to the deep, Be dry*—"Who saith to the deep, Be thou wasted"] Cyrus took Babylon by laying the bed of the Euphrates dry, and leading his army into the city by night through the empty channel of the river. This remarkable circumstance, in which the event so exactly corresponded with the prophecy, was also noted by Jeremiah, chap. l. 38, li. 36.

"A drought shall be upon her waters, and they
shall be dried up:—
I will lay her sea dry;
And I will scorch up her springs."

It is proper here to give some account of the means and method by which the stratagem of Cyrus was effected.

The Euphrates, in the middle of the summer, from the melting of the snows on the mountains of Armenia, like the Nile, overflows the country. In order to diminish the inundation, and to carry off the waters, two canals were made by Nebuchadnezzar a hundred miles above the city; the first on the eastern side called Naharmalca, or the Royal River, by which the Euphrates was let into the Tigris; the other on the western side, called Pallacopas, or Naharaga, (נהר אגם *nahar agam*, The river of the pool,) by which the redundant waters were carried into a vast lake, forty miles square, contrived, not only to lessen the inundation, but for a reservoir, with sluices, to water the barren country on the Arabian side. Cyrus, by turning the whole river into the lake by the Pallacopas, laid the channel, where it ran through the city, almost dry; so that his army entered it, both above and below, by the bed of the river, the water not reaching above the middle of the thigh. By the great quantity of water let into the lake, the sluices and dams were destroyed; and being never repaired afterwards, the waters spread over the whole country below, and reduced it to a morass, in which the river is lost. Ingens modo et navigabilis, inde tenuis rivus, despectus emoritur; et nusquam manifesto exitit effluit, ut alii omnes, sed deficit. "And thus a navigable river has been totally lost, it having no exit from this morass. No wonder then that the geographical face of this country is completely changed;" MELA iii. 8; HEROD. i. 185, 190; XENOPHON, *Cyrop.* vii.; ARRIAN vii.

Verse 28. *That saith of Cyrus, He* is *my shepherd*—"Who saith to Cyrus, Thou art my shepherd"] *Pastor meus* es; *Vulg.* The true reading seems to be רעי אתה *roi attah;* the word אתה *attah*, has probably been dropped out of the text. The same word is lost out of the text, Psa. cxix. 57. It is supplied in the *Septuagint* by the word ει, *thou art.*

Saying to Jerusalem] For ולאמר *velemor*, the *Septuagint* and *Vulgate* read האומר *haomer.*

And to the temple] ולהיכל *uleheychal*, as לירושלם *lirushalayim*, before; the preposition is necessary, and the *Vulgate* seems to read so.—*Houbigant.*

That saith of CYRUS, *He is*, or thou art, *my shepherd—Saying to* JERUSALEM, "Thou shalt be built;" *and to the* TEMPLE, "Thy foundation shall be laid."—There is a remarkable beauty and propriety in this verse.

1. Cyrus is called God's shepherd. Shepherd was an epithet which Cyrus took to himself; and what he gave to all good kings.

2. This Cyrus should say to the temple: "Thy foundation shall be laid." Not—thou shalt be *built.* The fact is, only the *foundation* was laid in the days of Cyrus, the *Ammonites* having prevented the building; nor was it resumed till the *second* year of Darius, one of his successors. There is often a precision in the expressions of the prophets which is as honourable to truth, as it is unnoticed by careless readers.

CHAPTER XLV

Prophecy concerning Cyrus, the first king of the Persians. Every obstruction shall be removed out of his way, and the treasures taken from his enemies shall be immense, 1–3. *To whom, and on what account, Cyrus was indebted for his wonderful success,* 4–6. *The prophet refutes the absurd opinion of the Persians, that there were two supreme beings, an* evil *and a* good *one, represented by* light *and* darkness, *here declared to be only the operation of the* ONE *true God,* 7; *and makes a transition to the still greater* work *of God displayed in the dispensation of the Gospel,* 8. *Great impiety of those who call in question the mysterious providence of God towards his children,* 9–12. *The remaining part of this chapter, interspersed with strictures on the absurdity of idolatry and some allusions to the dark lying oracles of the heathens, may partly refer to the deliverance begun by Cyrus, but chiefly to the salvation by the Messiah, which, it is declared, shall be of universal extent and everlasting duration,* 13–25.

A. M. cir. 3292 B. C. cir. 712 Olymp. XVII. 1 cir. annum NumæPompilii, R. Roman., 4

THUS saith the LORD to his
anointed, to Cyrus, whose
[a]right hand I [b]have holden [c]to
subdue nations before him; and
I will loose the loins of kings, to open before
him the two leaved gates; and the gates shall
not be shut;

2 I will go before thee, [d]and
make the crooked places
straight: [e]I will break in pieces
the gates of brass, and cut in
sunder the bars of iron:

3 And I will give thee the treasures of darkness, and hidden riches of secret places, [f]that

[a]Chap. xli. 13——[b]Or, *strengthened*——[c]Chap. xli. 2; Dan. v. 30

[d]Chapter xl. 4——[e]Psalm cvii. 16——[f]Chapter xli. 23

NOTES ON CHAP. XLV

Verse 1. *Loose the loins of kings*—"ungird the loins of kings"] See the note on chap. v. 27. *Xenophon* gives the following list of the nations conquered by Cyrus: the Syrians, Assyrians, Arabians, Cappadocians, both the Phrygians, Lydians, Carians, Phœnicians, Babylonians. He moreover reigned over the Bactrians, Indians, Cilicians, the Sacæ Paphlagones, and Mariandyni.—*Cyrop.*, lib. i. p. 4, Edit. *Hutchinson*, Quarto. All these kingdoms he acknowledges, in his decree for the restoration of the Jews, to have been given to him by JEHOVAH, the God of heaven. Ezra i. 2.

To open before him the two leaved gates, &c.—"That I may open before him the valves; and the gates shall not be shut"] The gates of Babylon within the city leading from the streets to the river, were providentially left open, when Cyrus's forces entered the city in the night through the channel of the river, in the general disorder occasioned by the great feast which was then celebrated; otherwise, says *Herodotus*, i. 191, the Persians would have been shut up in the bed of the river, and taken as in a net, and all destroyed. And the gates of the palace were opened imprudently by the king's orders, to inquire what was the cause of the tumult without; when the two parties under Gobrias and Gadatas rushed in, got possession of the palace, and slew the king.—XENOPH., *Cyrop.* vii. p. 528.

Verse 2. *The crooked places*—"The mountains"] For הדורים *hadurim, crooked places*, a word not easily accounted for in this place, the *Septuagint* read הררים *hararim*, τα ορη, *the mountains.* Two MSS. have הדרים *hadarim*, without the ו *vau*, which is hardly distinguishable from the reading of the *Septuagint.* The Divine protection that attended Cyrus, and rendered his expedition against Babylon easy and prosperous, is finely expressed by God's going before him, and making the mountains level. The image is highly poetical:—

At vos, qua veniet, tumidi subsidite montes,
Et faciles curvis vallibus este viæ.
OVID, Amor. ii. 16.

"Let the lofty mountains fall down, and make level paths in the crooked valleys."

The gates of brass—"The valves of brass"] Abydenus, *apud, Euseb.* Præp. Evang. ix. 41, says, that the wall of Babylon had brazen gates. And *Herodotus*, i, 179, more particularly: "In the wall all round there are a hundred gates, all of brass; and so in like manner are the sides and the lintels." The gates likewise within the city, opening to the river from the several streets, were of brass; as were those also of the temple of Belus.—*Herod.* i., 180, 181.

Verse 3. *I will give thee the treasures of darkness*] Sardes and Babylon, when taken by Cyrus, were the wealthiest cities in the world. Crœsus, celebrated beyond all the kings of that age for his riches, gave up his treasures to Cyrus, with an exact account in writing of the whole, containing the particulars with

A. M. cir. 3292
B. C. cir. 712
Olymp. XVII. 1
cir. annum
NumæPompilii,
R. Roman., 4

thou mayest know that I, the
LORD, which [g]call *thee* by thy
name, *am* the God of Israel.
4 For [h]Jacob my servant's sake,
and Israel mine elect, I have even called thee
by thy name: I have surnamed thee, though
thou hast [i]not known me.
5 I [k]*am* the LORD, and [l]*there is* none else,
there is no God beside me: [m]I girded thee,
though thou hast not known
me:
6 [n]That they may know from
the rising of the sun, and from
the west, that *there is* none beside me. I *am*
the LORD, and *there is* none else.
7 I form the light, and create darkness: I
make peace, and [o]create evil: I the LORD do
all these *things*.

A. M. cir. 3292
B. C. cir. 712
Olymp. XVII. 1
cir. annum
NumæPompilii,
R. Roman., 4

---

[g]Exod. xxxiii. 12, 17; chap. xliii. 1; xlix. 1——[h]Chap. xliv. 1——[i]1 Thess. iv. 5——[k]Deuteronomy iv. 35, 39; xxxii. 39; chapter xliv. 8; xlvi. 9——[l]Verse 14, 18, 21, 22——[m]Psalm xviii. 32, 39——[n]Psalm cii. 15; chapter xxxvii. 20; Malachi i. 11——[o]Amos iii. 6

---

which each wagon was loaded when they were carried away; and they were delivered to Cyrus at the palace of Babylon.—*Xenoph.* Cyrop. lib. vii. p. 503, 515, 540.

Pliny gives the following account of the wealth taken by Cyrus in Asia. Jam Cyrus, devicta Asia, pondo xxxiv. millia auri invenerat; præter vasa aurea, aurumque factum, et in eo folia, ac platanum, vitemque. Qua victoria argenti quii genta millia talentorum reportavit; et craterem Semiramidis, cujus pondus quindecim talents colligebat. Talentum autem Ægyptium pondo lxxx. patere l. capere Varro tradit.—Nat. Hist. xxxiii. 15. "When Cyrus conquered Asia, he found *thirty-four* thousand pounds weight of gold, besides golden vessels and articles in gold; and leaves, (*folia*, perhaps *solia*, bathing vessels, *Hol.*,) a plane, and vine tree, (of gold.) By which victory he carried away *fifteen thousand* talents of silver; and the cup of Semiramis, the weight of which was *fifteen talents*. The Egyptian talent, according to Varro, was *eighty* pounds." This cup was the *crater*, or large vessel, out of which they filled the drinking cups at great entertainments. Evidently it could not be a *drinking vessel*, which, according to what *Varro* and *Pliny* say, must have weighed 1,200 pounds!

The gold and silver estimated by weight in this account, being converted into pounds sterling, amount to *one hundred and twenty-six millions two hundred and twenty-four thousand* pounds.—*Brerewood*, De Ponderibus, cap. x.

Treasures of darkness may refer to the custom of burying their jewels and money under the ground in their house floors, fearing robbers.

Verse 7. *I form the light, and create darkness*] It was the great principle of the Magian religion, which prevailed in Persia in the time of Cyrus, and in which probably he was educated, that there are two supreme, co-eternal, and independent causes always acting in opposition one to the other; one the author of all good, the other of all evil. The good being they called LIGHT; the evil being, DARKNESS. That when LIGHT had the ascendant, then *good* and *happiness* prevailed among men; when DARKNESS had the superiority, then *evil* and *misery* abounded. An opinion that contradicts the clearest evidence of our reason, which plainly leads us to the acknowledgment of one only Supreme Being, infinitely good as well as powerful. With reference to this absurd opinion, held by the person to whom this prophecy is addressed, God, by his prophet, in the most significant terms, asserts his omnipotence and absolute supremacy:—

"I am JEHOVAH, and none else;
Forming light, and creating darkness,
Making peace, and creating evil:
I JEHOVAH am the author of all these things."

Declaring that those powers whom the Persians held to be the original authors of good and evil to mankind, representing them by *light* and *darkness*, as their proper emblems, are no other than creatures of God, the instruments which he employs in his government of the world, ordained or permitted by him in order to execute his wise and just decrees; and that there is no power, either of good or evil, independent of the one supreme God, infinite in power and in goodness.

There were, however, some among the Persians whose sentiments were more moderate as to this matter; who held the evil principle to be in some measure subordinate to the good; and that the former would at length be wholly subdued by the latter. See *Hyde*, De Relig. Vet. Pers. cap. xxii.

That this opinion prevailed among the Persians as early as the time of Cyrus we may, I think, infer not only from this passage of Isaiah, which has a manifest reference to it, but likewise from a passage in Xenophon's Cyropædia, where the same doctrine is applied to the human mind. Araspes, a noble young Persian, had fallen in love with the fair captive Panthea, committed to his charge by Cyrus. After all his boasting that he was superior to the assaults of that passion, he yielded so far to it as even to threaten violence if she would not comply with his desires. Awed by the reproof of Cyrus, fearing his displeasure, and having by cool reflection recovered his reason; in his discourse with him on this subject he says: "O Cyrus, I have certainly two souls; and this piece of philosophy I have learned from that wicked sophist, Love. For if I had but one soul, it would not be at the same time good and evil; it would not at the same time approve of honourable and base actions; and at once desire to do, and refuse to do, the very same things. But it is plain that I am animated by two souls; and when the good soul prevails, I do what is virtuous; and when the evil one prevails, I attempt what is vicious. But now the good soul prevails, having gotten you for her assistant, and has clearly gained the superiority." Lib. vi. p. 424.

I make peace, and create evil] *Evil* is here evidently put for *war* and its attendant miseries. I will procure *peace* for the Israelites, and destroy Babylon by *war*. *I form light, and create darkness*. Now, as darkness is only the priva-

A. M. cir. 3292
B. C. cir. 712
Olymp. XVII. 1
cir. annum
NumæPompilii,
R. Roman., 4

8 [p]Drop down, ye heavens,
from above, and let the skies
pour down righteousness: let the
earth open, and let them bring
forth salvation, and let righteousness spring
up together; I the Lord have created it.
9 Wo unto him that striveth with [q]his
Maker! *Let* the potsherd *strive* with the
potsherds of the earth. [r]Shall the clay say to
him that fashioneth it, What makest thou?
or thy work, He hath no hands?
10 Wo unto him that saith unto *his* father,
What begettest thou? or to the
woman, What hast thou brought
forth?

A. M. cir. 3292
B. C. cir. 712
Olymp. XVII. 1
cir. annum
NumæPompilii,
R. Roman., 4

11 Thus saith the Lord, the
Holy One of Israel, and his Maker, Ask me
of things to come concerning [s]my sons, and
concerning [t]the work of my hands command
ye me.
12 [u]I have made the earth, and [v]created man
upon it: I, *even* my hands, have stretched out
the heavens, and [w]all their host have I commanded.

[p]Psa. lxxii. 3; xxxv. 11——[q]Chap. lxiv. 8——[r]Chap. xxix. 16; Jer. xviii. 6; Rom. ix. 20

[s]Jer. xxxi. 9——[t]Isa. xxix. 23——[u]Chap. xlii. 5; Jer. xxvii. 5——[v]Gen. i. 26, 27——[w]Gen. ii. 1

tion of light, so the evil of *war* is the privation of *peace.*

Verse 8. *Drop down, ye heavens*] The *eighty-fifth* psalm is a very elegant ode on the same subject with this part of Isaiah's prophecies, the restoration of Judah from captivity; and is, in the most beautiful part of it, a manifest imitation of this passage of the prophet:—

"Verily his salvation is nigh unto them that fear him,
That glory may dwell in our land.
Mercy and truth have met together;
Righteousness and peace have kissed each other.
Truth shall spring from the earth,
And righteousness shall look down from heaven.
Even Jehovah will give that which is good,
And our land shall yield her produce.
Righteousness shall go before him,
And shall direct his footsteps in the way."
Psa. lxxxv. 10-14.

See the notes on these verses.

These images of the dew and the rain descending from heaven and making the earth fruitful, employed by the prophet, and some of those nearly of the same kind which are used by the psalmist, may perhaps be primarily understood as designed to set forth in a splendid manner the happy state of God's people restored to their country, and flourishing in peace and plenty, in piety and virtue; but justice and salvation, mercy and truth, righteousness and peace, and glory dwelling in the land, cannot with any sort of propriety, in the one or the other, be interpreted as the consequences of that event; they must mean the blessings of the great redemption by Messiah.

Let the earth open, &c.] Jonathan, in his Targum, refers this to the resurrection of the dead; the earth shall be opened, ויחון מיתיא *veyechon meiteiya,* and the dead shall revive. A plain proof that the ancient Jews believed in a future state, and acknowledged the resurrection of the dead.

Let them bring forth salvation—"Let salvation produce her fruit"] For ויפרו *vaiyiphru,* the *Septuagint, Vulgate,* and *Syriac* read ויפרה *vaiyiphrah;* and one MS. has a rasure close after the latter ו *vau,* which probably was ה *he* at first.

Verse 9. *Wo unto him that striveth with his Maker*—"Wo unto him that contendeth with the power that formed him"] The prophet answers or prevents the objections and cavils of the unbelieving Jews, disposed to murmur against God, and to arraign the wisdom and justice of his dispensations in regard to them; in permitting them to be oppressed by their enemies, and in promising them deliverance instead of preventing their captivity. St. Paul has borrowed the image, and has applied it to the like purpose with equal force and elegance: "Nay, but, O man! who art thou that repliest against God? Shall the thing formed say to him that formed it, Why hast thou made me thus? Hath not the potter power over the clay, out of the same lump to make one vessel to honour, and another to dishonour?" Rom. ix. 20, 21. This is spoken, says *Kimchi,* against the king of Babylon, who insulted the Most High, bringing forth the sacred vessels, drinking out of them, and magnifying himself against God.

Or thy work, He hath no hands—"And to the workman, Thou hast no hands"] The *Syriac* renders, as if he had read, ולא היתי פעל ידיך *velo hayithi pheal yadeycha,* "neither am I the work of thy hands;" the *Septuagint,* as if they had read, ולא פעלת ואין ידים לך *velo phaalta veeyn yadim lecha,* "neither hast thou made me; and thou hast no hands." But the fault seems to be in the transposition of the two pronouns; for ופעלך *uphoolcha,* read ופעלו *uphoolo:* and for לו *lo,* read לך *lecha.* So Houbigant corrects it; reading also ופעלו *uphoolo;* which last correction seems not altogether necessary. The *Septuagint,* in MSS. Pachom. and I. D. II. have it thus, *και το εργον ουκ εχεις χειρας,* which favours the reading here proposed.

Verse 11. *Ask me of things to come*—"And he that formeth the things which are to come"] I read ויוצר *veyotser,* without the ו *vau* suffixed; from the *Septuagint,* who join it in construction with the following word, *ὁ ποιησας τα επερχομενα.*

"Do ye question me."—תשאלוני *tishaluni, Chald.* recte; præcedit ת *tau;* et sic forte legerunt reliqui Intt.—*Secker.* "The Chaldee has, more properly, תשאלוני *tishaluni,* with a ת *tau* preceding; and thus the other interpreters probably read." The learned bishop therefore reads the passage thus:—

"Thus saith Jehovah, the Holy One of Israel;
And he that formeth the things which are to come;

A. M. cir. 3292 B. C. cir. 712 Olymp. XVII. 1 cir. annum NumæPompilii, R. Roman., 4
13 [x]I have raised him up in
righteousness, and I will [y]direct
all his ways: he shall [z]build
my city, and he shall let go my
captives, [a]not for price nor reward, saith the
LORD of hosts.
14 Thus saith the LORD, [b]The labour of
Egypt, and merchandise of Ethiopia and of
the Sabeans, men of stature, shall come over
unto thee, and they shall be thine: they shall
come after thee; [c]in chains they shall come
over, and they shall fall down unto thee, they
shall make supplication unto thee, *saying,*
[d]Surely God *is* in thee; and [e]*there is* none
else, *there is* no God.
15 Verily thou *art* a God [f]that hidest thyself, O God of Israel, the Saviour.

16 They shall be ashamed, and A. M. cir. 3292 B. C. cir. 712
also confounded, all of them: Olymp. XVII. 1
they shall go to confusion to- cir. annum NumæPompilii,
gether *that are* [g]makers of idols. R. Roman., 4
17 [h]*But* Israel shall be saved in the LORD
with an everlasting salvation: ye shall not be
ashamed nor confounded world without end.
18 For thus saith the LORD [i]that created the
heavens; God himself that formed the earth
and made it; he hath established it, he created
it not in vain, he formed it to be inhabited:
[k]I *am* the LORD; and *there is* none else.
19 I have not spoken in [l]secret, in a dark
place of the earth: I said not unto the seed
of Jacob, Seek ye me in vain: [m]I the LORD
speak righteousness, I declare things that are
right.

[x]Ch. xli. 2——[y]Or, *make straight*——[z]2 Chron. xxxvi. 22, 23; Ezra i. 1, &c.; ch. xliv. 28——[a]Ch. lii. 3; see Rom. iii. 24——[b]Psa. lxviii. 31; lxxii. 10, 11; ch. xlix. 23; lx. 9, 10, 14, 16; Zech. viii. 22, 23——[c]Psa. cxlix. 8

[d]1 Cor. xiv. 25——[e]Ver. 5——[f]Psa. xliv. 24; ch. viii. 17; lvii. 17——[g]Ch. xiiv. 11——[h]Ch. xxvi. 4; ver. 25; Rom. xi. 26——[i]Ch. xlii. 5——[k]Ver. 5——[l]Deut. xxx. 11; ch. xlviii. 16——[m]Psa. xix. 8; cxix. 137, 138

Do ye question me concerning my children?
And do ye give me directions concerning the
work of my hands?"

Verse 13. *I have raised him up*] This evidently refers to Cyrus, and to what he did for the Jews; and informs us by *whom* he was excited to do it.

Verse 14. *The labour of Egypt*—"The wealth of Egypt"] This seems to relate to the future admission of the Gentiles into the Church of God. Compare Psa. lxviii. 32; lxxii. 10; chap. lx. 6-9. And perhaps these particular nations may be named, by a metonymy common in all poetry, for powerful and wealthy nations in general. See note on chap. lx. 1.

The Sabeans, men of stature—"The Sabeans, tall of stature"] That the Sabeans were of a more majestic appearance than common, is particularly remarked by Agatharchides, an ancient Greek historian quoted by Bochart, Phaleg, ii. 26, *τα σωματα εστι των κατοικουντων αξιολογωτερα.* So also the *Septuagint* understand it, rendering it *ανδρες ὑψηλοι*, "tall men." And the same phrase, אנשי מדה *anshey middah*, is used for persons of extraordinary stature, Num. xiii. 32, and 1 Chron. xx. 6.

They shall make supplication unto thee—"They shall in suppliant guise address thee"] The conjunction ו *vau* is supplied by the ancient Versions, and confirmed by *fifteen* MSS. of *Kennicott's*, (*seven* ancient,) *thirteen* of *De Rossi's*, and *six* editions, ואליך *veelayich. Three* MSS. (*two* ancient) omit the ו *vau* before אליך *elayich* at the beginning of the line.

Verse 15. *Verily thou* art *a God that hidest thyself*] At present, from the nations of the world.

O God of Israel, the Saviour] While thou revealest thyself to the *Israelites* and *savest* them.

Verse 16. *They shall be ashamed*—"They are ashamed"] The reader cannot but observe the sudden transition from the solemn adoration of the secret and mysterious nature of God's counsels in regard to his people, to the spirited denunciation of the confusion of idolaters, and the final destruction of idolatry; contrasted with the salvation of Israel, not from temporal captivity, but the *eternal* salvation by the Messiah, strongly marked by the repetition and augmentation of the phrase, *to the ages of eternity.* But there is not only a sudden change in the sentiment, the change is equally observable in the construction of the sentences; which, from the usual short measure, runs out at once into two distichs of the longer sort of verse. See Prelim. Dissert. p. 66, &c. There is another instance of the same kind, and very like to this, of a sudden transition in regard both to the sentiment and construction in chap. xlii. 17.

"His adversaries"] This line, to the great diminution of the beauty of the distich, is imperfect in the present text: the subject of the proposition is not particularly expressed, as it is in the line following. The version of the *Septuagint* happily supplies the word that is lost: *οἱ αντικειμενοι αυτῳ*, "his adversaries," the original word was צריו *tsaraiv.*—L.

Verse 18. *He formed it to be inhabited*—"For he formed it to be inhabited"] An ancient MS. has כי *ki* before לשבת *lashebeth;* and so the ancient Versions.

Verse 19. *I have not spoken in secret, in a dark place of the earth*] In opposition to the manner in which the heathen oracles gave their answers, which were generally delivered from some deep and obscure cavern. Such was the seat of the Cumean Sybil:—

Excisum Euboicæ latus ingens rupis in antrum.
VIRG. *Æn.* vi. 42.

"A cave cut in the side of a huge rock."

Such was that of the famous oracle at Delphi; of which, says Strabo, lib. ix., *φασι δ' ειναι το μαντειον αντρον κοιλον μετα βαθους, ου μαλα ευρυστομον.* "The oracle is said to be a hollow cavern of considerable depth, with an opening not very

A. M. cir. 3292
B. C. cir. 712
Olymp. XVII. 1
cir. annum
NumæPompilii,
R. Roman., 4

20 Assemble yourselves and come; draw near together, ye *that are* escaped of the nations: [n]they have no knowledge that set up the wood of their graven image, and pray unto a god *that* cannot save.

21 Tell ye, and bring *them* near; yea, let them take counsel together: [o]who hath declared this from ancient time? *who* hath told it from that time? *have* not I the LORD? [p]and *there is* no God else beside me; a just God and a Saviour: *there is* none beside me.

22 [q]Look unto me, and be ye saved, [r]all the ends of the earth: for I *am* God, and *there is* none else.

23 [s]I have sworn by myself, the word is gone out of my mouth *in* righteousness, and shall not return, That unto me every [t]knee shall bow, [u]every tongue shall swear.

24 [v]Surely, shall *one* say, In the LORD have I [w]righteousness[x] and strength: *even* to him shall *men* come; and [y]all that are incensed against him shall be ashamed.

25 [z]In the LORD shall all the seed of Israel be justified, and [a]shall glory.

[n]Ch. xliv. 17, 18, 19; xlvi. 7; xlviii. 7; Rom. i. 22, 23——[o]Ch. xli. 22; xliii. 9; xliv. 7; xlvi. 10; xlviii. 14——[p]Ver. 5, 14, 18; ch. xliv. 8; xlvi. 9; xlviii. 3, &c.——[q]Psa. xxii. 27; lxv. 5——[r]Psa. lxv. 3; xcviii. 3——[s]Gen. xxii. 16; Jer. xlix. 13; li. 14; Amos vi. 8; Heb. vi. 13

[t]Rom. xiv. 11; Phil. ii. 10——[u]Gen. xxxi. 53; Deut. vi. 13; Psa. lxiii. 11; ch. lxv. 16——[v]Or, *Surely he shall say of me, In the LORD is all righteousness and strength*——[w]Jer. xxiii. 5; 1 Cor. i. 30——[x]Heb. *righteousnesses*——[y]Ch. xli. 11——[z]Ver. 17——[a]1 Cor. i. 31

wide." And Diodorus, giving an account of the origin of this oracle, says "that there was in that place a great chasm or cleft in the earth; in which very place is now situated what is called the Adytum of the temple." *Αδυτον· σπηλαιον, η το αποκρυφον μερος του ιερου. Hesych.* "Adytum means a cavern, or the hidden part of the temple."

I the Lord speak righteousness, I declare things that are right—"I am JEHOVAH, who speak truth, who give direct answers."] This also is said in opposition to the false and ambiguous answers given by the heathen oracles, of which there are many noted examples; none more so than that of the answer given to Crœsus when he marched against Cyrus, which piece of history has some connexion with this part of Isaiah's prophecies. Let us hear Cicero's account of the Delphic answers in general, and of this in particular: Sed jam ad te venio,

O sancte Apollo, qui umbilicum certum terrarum obsides,
Unde superstitiosa primum sæva evasit vox fera.

Tuis enim oraculis Chrysippus totum volumen implevit, partim falsis, ut ego opinor; partim casu veris, ut fit in omni oratione sæpissime; partim flexiloquis et obscuris, ut interpres egeat interprete, et sors ipsa ad sortes referenda sit; partim ambiguis, et quæ ad dialecticum deferenda sint. Nam cum sors illa edita est opulentissimo regi Asiæ,

Crœsus Halym penetrans magnam pervertet opum vim: hostium vim sese perversurum putavit; pervertit autem suam. Utrum igitur eorum accidisset, verum oraculum fuisset. *De Divinat.* ii. 56. Mountainous countries, and those which abounded in chasms, caves, and grottos, were the places in which oracles were most frequent. The horror and gloom inspired by such places were useful to the lying priests in their system of deception. The terms in which those oracles were conceived, (they were always ambiguous, or equivocal, or false, or illusory,) sometimes the turn of a phrase, or a peculiarity in idiom or construction which might be turned *pro* or *con*, contained the essence of the oracular declaration. Sometimes, in the multitude of guesses, one turned out to be true; at other times, so equivocal was the oracle, that, however the thing fell out, the declaration could be interpreted in that way; as in the above to Crœsus, from the oracle at Delphi, which was: *If Crœsus march against Cyrus, he shall overthrow a great empire:* he, supposing that this promised him success, fought, and lost his own, while he expected to destroy that of his enemy. Here the quack demon took refuge in his designed ambiguity. He predicted the destruction of a great empire, but did not say which it was; and therefore he was safe, howsoever the case fell out. Not one of the predictions of God's prophets is conceived in this way.

Verse 21. *Bring* them *near; yea, let them take counsel together*] For יועצו *yoatsu* or *yivvaatsu*, *let them consult*, the *Septuagint* read ידעו *yedau*, *let them know:* but an ancient MS. has יועדו *yoedu*, *let them come together by appointment;* which may probably be the true reading.

Verse 22. *Look unto me, and be ye saved, &c.*] This verse and the following contain a plain prediction of the universal spread of the knowledge of God through Christ; and so the *Targum* appears to have understood it; see Rom. xiv. 11; Phil. ii. 10. The reading of the *Targum* is remarkable, viz., אתפנו למימרי *ithpeno lemeymri*, *look to my* WORD, ὁ Λογος, the Lord Jesus.

Verse 23. *I have sworn by myself*] במימרי *bemeymri*, *by my* WORD: and *the word*—פתגם *pithgam*, or *saying*, to distinguish it from the *personal substantial* WORD *meymra*, mentioned before. See the *Targum*.

The word is gone out of my mouth—"Truth is gone forth from my mouth; the word"] So the *Septuagint* distinguish the members of the sentence, preserving the elegance of the construction and the clearness of the sense.

Verse 24. *Surely, shall* one *say, In the Lord have I righteousness and strength*—"Saying, Only to JEHOVAH belongeth salvation and power"] A MS. omits לי *li, unto me;* and instead of לי אמר *li amar, he said* or *shall say unto me*, the *Septuagint* read, in the copy which they used, לאמר *lemor, saying.* For יבא *yabo*, HE *shall come*, in the singular, twelve MSS.

(three ancient) read יבאו *yabeu*, plural; and a letter is erased at the end of the word in two others: and so the Alexandrine copy of the *Septuagint*, *Syriac*, and *Vulgate* read it. For צדקות *tsedakoth*, plural, two MSS. read צדקת *tsidkath*, singular; and so the *Septuagint*, *Syriac*, and *Chaldee*.

Probably these are the words of Cyrus, who acknowledged that all his success came from Jehovah. And this sentiment is in effect contained in his decree or proclamation, Ezra i. 2: "Thus saith Cyrus, king of Persia, The Lord God of heaven hath given me all the kingdoms of the earth," &c.

CHAPTER XLVI

The idols of Babylon represented as so far from being able to bear the burden of their votaries, that they themselves are borne by beasts of burden into captivity, 1, 2. *This beautifully contrasted with the tender care of God, in bearing his people from first to last in his arms, and delivering them from their distress,* 3, 4. *The prophet, then, with his usual force and elegance, goes on to show the folly of idolatry, and the utter inability of idols,* 5–7. *From which he passes with great ease to the contemplation of the attributes and perfections of the true God,* 8–10. *Particularly that prescience which foretold the deliverance of the Jews from the Babylonish captivity, with all its leading circumstances; and also that very remote event of which it is the type in the days of the Messiah,* 11–13.

A. M. cir. 3292
B. C. cir. 712
Olymp. XVII. 1
cir. annum
NumæPompilii,
R. Roman., 4

BEL [a]boweth down, Nebo
stoopeth, their idols were
upon the beasts, and upon the
cattle: your carriages *were* heavy
loaden; [b]*they are* a burden to the weary *beast.*
2 They stoop, they bow down together;
they could not deliver the burden, [c]but [d]them-
selves are gone into captivity.
3 Hearken unto me, O house of Jacob, and
all the remnant of the house of Israel, [e]which
are borne *by me* from the belly, which are
carried from the womb:
4 And *even* to *your* old age [f]I *am* he; and
even to hoar hairs [g]will I carry *you:* I have
made, and I will bear; even I
will carry, and will deliver *you.*
5 [h]To whom will ye liken me,
and make *me* equal, and compare
me, that we may be like?
6 [i]They lavish gold out of the bag, and
weigh silver in the balance, *and* hire a goldsmith; and he maketh it a god: they fall
down, yea, they worship.
7 [k]They bear him upon the shoulder, they
carry him, and set him in his place, and he
standeth; from his place shall he not remove;
yea, [l]*one* shall cry unto him, yet can he not
answer, nor save him out of his trouble.

A. M. cir. 3292
B. C. cir. 712
Olymp. XVII. 1
cir. annum
NumæPompilii,
R. Roman., 4

[a]Chap. xxi. 9; Jer. l. 2; li. 44——[b]Jer. x. 5——[c]Jer. xlviii. 7——[d]Heb. *their soul*——[e]Exod. xix. 4; Deut. i. 31; xxxii. 11; Psa. lxxi. 6; chap. lxiii. 9

[f]Psa. cii. 27; Mal. iii. 6——[g]Psa. xlviii. 14; lxxi. 18
[h]Ch. xl. 18, 25——[i]Ch. xl. 19; xli. 6; xliv. 12, 19; Jer. x. 3——[k]Jer. x. 5——[l]Chap. xlv. 20

NOTES ON CHAP. XLVI

Verse 1. *Their carriages* were *heavy loaden*—"Their burdens are heavy"] For נשאתיכם *nesuotheychem, your burdens*, the *Septuagint* had in their copy נשאתיהם *nesuotheyhem, their burdens.*

Verse 2. *They could not deliver the burden*—"They could not deliver their own charge"] That is, their worshippers, who ought to have been borne by them. See the two next verses. The *Chaldee* and *Syriac* Versions render it in effect to the same purpose, *those that bear them*, meaning their worshippers; but how they can render משא *massa* in an active sense, I do not understand.

For לא *lo, not,* ולא *velo, and they could not,* is the reading of twenty-four of *Kennicott's*, sixteen of *De Rossi's*, and two of my own MSS. The added ו *vau* gives more elegance to the passage.

But themselves—"Even they themselves"] For ונפשם *venaphsham*, an ancient MS. has כי נפשם *ki naphsham*, with more force.

Verse 3. *Which are borne* by me *from the belly*—"Ye that have been borne by me from the birth"] The prophet very ingeniously, and with great force, contrasts the power of God, and his tender goodness effectually exerted towards his people, with the inability of the false gods of the heathen. He like an indulgent father had carried his people in his arms, "as a man carrieth his son," Deut. i. 31. He had protected them, and delivered them from their distresses: whereas the idols of the heathen are forced to be carried about themselves, and removed from place to place, with great labour and fatigue, by their worshippers; nor can they answer, or deliver their votaries, when they cry unto them.

Moses, expostulating with God on the weight of the charge laid upon him as leader of his people, expresses that charge under the same image of a parent's carrying his children, in very strong terms: "Have I conceived all this people? have I begotten them? that thou shouldest say unto me, Carry them in thy bosom, as a nursing father beareth the sucking child, unto the land which thou swarest unto their fathers;" Num. xi. 12.

Verse 7. *They bear him upon the shoulder—and set him in his place*] This is the way in which the Hindoos carry their gods; and indeed so exact a picture is this of the *idolatrous procession* of this people, that the prophet might almost be supposed to have been sitting among the Hindoos when he delivered this prophecy.—WARD'S *Customs.*

A. M. cir. 3292
B. C. cir. 712
Olymp. XVII. 1
cir. annum
NumæPompilii,
R. Roman., 4

8 Remember this, and show
yourselves men: [m]bring *it* again
to mind, O ye transgressors.
9 [n]Remember the former
things of old: for I *am* God, and [o]*there is* none
else: *I am* God, and *there is* none like me,
10 [p]Declaring the end from the beginning,
and from ancient times *the things* that are not
yet done, saying, [q]My counsel shall stand,
and I will do all my pleasure:
11 Calling a ravenous bird [r]from the east,
[s]the man [t]that executeth my
counsel from a far country: yea,
[u]I have spoken *it*, I will also
bring it to pass; I have purposed *it*, I will also do it.
12 Hearken unto me, ye [v]stout-hearted,
[w]that *are* far from righteousness:
13 [x]I bring near my righteousness; it shall
not be far off, and my salvation [y]shall not
tarry: and I will place [z]salvation in Zion for
Israel my glory.

[m]Ch. xliv. 19; xlvii. 7——[n]Deut. xxxii. 7——[o]Ch. xlv. 5, 21——[p]Ch. xlv. 21——[q]Psa. xxxiii. 11; Prov. xix. 21; xxi. 30; Acts v. 39; Heb. vi. 17——[r]Ch. xli. 2, 25

[s]Heb. *the man of my counsel*——[t]Ch. xliv. 28; xlv. 13——[u]Num. xxiii. 19——[v]Psa. lxxvi. 5——[w]Rom. x. 3——[x]Ch. li. 5; Rom. i. 17; iii. 21——[y]Hab. ii. 3——[z]Ch. lxii. 11

Pindar has treated with a just and very elegant ridicule the work of the statuary even in comparison with his own poetry, from this circumstance of its being fixed to a certain station. "The friends of Pytheas," says the Scholiast, "came to the poet, desiring him to write an ode on his victory. Pindar demanded three drachms, (*minæ*, I suppose it should be,) for the ode. No, say they, we can have a brazen statue for that money, which will be better than a poem. However, changing their minds afterwards, they came and offered him what he had demanded." This gave him the hint of the following ingenious exordium of his ode:—

Ουκ ανδριαντοποιος ειμ'
'Ωστ' ελινυσσοντα μ' εργαζε-
σθαι αγαλματ' επ' αυτας βαθμιδος
'Εσταοτ'. Αλλ' επι πασας
'Ολκαδος εν τ' ακατῳ γλυκει' αοιδα
Στειχ' απ' Αιγινας διαγγελ-
λοισ' ὁτι Λαμπωνος ὑιος
Πυθεας ευρυσθενης
Νικῃ Νεμειοις παγκρατιου στεφανον. Nem. v.

Thus elegantly translated by Mr. *Francis* in a note to *Hor. Carm.* iv. 2. 19.

"It is not mine with forming hand
To bid a lifeless image stand
For ever on its base:
But fly, my verses, and proclaim
To distant realms, with deathless fame,
That Pytheas conquered in the rapid race."

Jeremiah, chap. x. 3-5, seems to be indebted to Isaiah for most of the following passage:—

"The practices of the people are altogether vanity:
For they cut down a tree from the forest;
The work of the artificer's hand with the axe;
With silver and with gold it is adorned;
With nails and with hammers it is fastened, that it may not totter.
Like the palm-tree they stand stiff, and cannot speak;
They are carried about, for they cannot go:
Fear them not, for they cannot do harm;
Neither is it in them to do good."

Verse 8. *Show yourselves men*] התאששו *hithoshashu*. This word is rather of doubtful derivation and signification. It occurs only in this place: and some of the ancient interpreters seem to have had something different in their copies. The *Vulgate* read התבששו *hithbosheshu*, *take shame to yourselves;* the *Syriac* התבוננו *hithbonenu*, *consider with yourselves;* the *Septuagint* στεναξετε· *perhaps* התאבלו *hithabbelu*, *groan* or *mourn*, *within yourselves*. Several MSS. read התאוששו *hithosheshu*, but without any help to the sense.

Verse 11. *Calling a ravenous bird from the east*—"Calling from the east the eagle"] A very proper emblem for Cyrus, as in other respects, so particularly because the ensign of Cyrus was a golden eagle, ΑΕΤΟΣ χρυσους, the very word עיט *ayit*, which the prophet uses here, expressed as near as may be in Greek letters. Xenoph. *Cyrop.* lib. vii. *sub. init.* *Kimchi* says his father understood this, not of Cyrus, but of the Messiah.

From a far country—"From a land far distant"] Two MSS. add the conjunction ו *vau*, ומארץ *umeerets;* and so the *Septuagint*, *Syriac*, and *Vulgate*.

Verse 12. *Hearken unto me, ye stout-hearted*—This is an address to the Babylonians, stubbornly bent on the practice of injustice towards the Israelites.

CHAPTER XLVII

The destruction of Babylon is denounced by a beautiful selection of circumstances, in which her prosperous is contrasted with her adverse condition. She is represented as a tender and delicate female reduced to the work and abject condition of a slave, and bereaved of every consolation, 1–4. *And that on account of her cruelty, particularly to God's people, her pride, voluptuousness, sorceries, and incantations,* 5–11. *The folly of these last practices elegantly exposed by the prophet,* 12–15. *It is worthy of observation that almost all the imagery of this chapter is applied in the book of the Revelation, (in nearly the same words,) to the antitype of the illustrious capital of the Chaldean empire, viz.,* Babylon the Great.

A. M. cir. 3292
B. C. cir. 712
Olymp. XVII. 1
cir. annum
NumæPompilii,
R. Roman., 4

COME [a]down, and [b]sit in the
dust, O virgin daughter of
Babylon; sit on the ground:
there is no throne, O daughter
of the Chaldeans: for thou shalt no more be
called tender and delicate.
2 [c]Take the millstones, and grind meal:
uncover thy locks, make bare the leg, uncover
the thigh, pass over the rivers.
3 [d]Thy nakedness shall be uncovered, yea,
thy shame shall be seen: [e]I will take vengeance, and I will not meet *thee as* a man.
4 *As for* [f]our Redeemer, the LORD of hosts
is his name, the Holy One of Israel.
5 Sit thou [g]silent, and get thee into darkness, O daughter of the Chaldeans: [h]for thou
shalt no more be called, The lady
of kingdoms.
6 [i]I was wroth with my people, [k]I have polluted mine inheritance, and given them into thine hand: thou
didst show them no mercy; [l]upon the ancient
hast thou very heavily laid thy yoke.
7 And thou saidst, I shall be [m]a lady for
ever: *so* that thou didst not [n]lay these *things*
to thy heart, [o]neither didst remember the latter end of it.
8 Therefore hear now this, *thou that art* given
to pleasures, that dwellest carelessly, that
sayest in thine heart, [p]I *am,* and none else
beside me; [q]I shall not sit *as* a widow,
neither shall I know the loss of children:

A. M. cir. 3292
B. C. cir. 712
Olymp. XVII. 1
cir. annum
NumæPompilii,
R. Roman., 4

[a]Jer. xlviii. 18——[b]Ch. iii. 26——[c]Exod. xi. 5; Judg. xvi. 21; Matt. xxiv. 41——[d]Ch. iii. 17; xx. 4; Jer. xiii. 22, 26; Nah. iii. 5——[e]Rom. xii. 19——[f]Chap. xliii. 3, 14; Jer. l. 34——[g]1 Sam. ii. 9——[h]Ver. 7; chap. xiii. 19; Dan. ii. 37——[i]See 2 Sam. xxiv. 14; 2 Chron. xxviii. 9; Zech. i. 15——[k]Ch. xliii. 28——[l]Deut. xxviii. 50——[m]Ver. 5; Rev. xviii. 7——[n]Ch. xlvi. 8——[o]Deut. xxxii. 29——[p]Ver. 10; Zeph. ii. 15——[q]Rev. xviii. 7

NOTES ON CHAP. XLVII

Verse 1. *Come down, and sit in the dust*—"Descend, and sit on the dust"] See note on chap. iii. 26, and on chap. lii. 2.

Verse 2. *Take the mill-stones, and grind meal*—"Take the mill, and grind corn"] It was the work of slaves to grind the corn. They used hand-mills: water-mills were not invented till a little before the time of Augustus, (see the Greek epigram of Antipater, which seems to celebrate it as a new invention, *Anthol. Cephalæ,* 653;) wind-mills, not until long after. It was not only the work of slaves, but the hardest work; and often inflicted upon them as a severe punishment:—

> Molendum in pistrino; vapulandum; habendæ compedes.
>
> TERENT. *Phorm.* ii. 1. 19.

> Hominem pistrino dignum.
>
> *Id. Heaut.* iii. 2. 19.

To grind in the mill, to be scourged, to be put in the stocks, were punishments for slaves. Hence a delinquent was said to be *a man worthy of the mill.* The *tread-mill,* now in use in England, is a revival of this ancient usage. But in the east grinding was the work of the female slaves. See Exod. xi. 5; xii. 29, (in the version of the *Septuagint;*) Matt. xxiv. 41; *Homer,* Odyss. xx. 105-108. And it is the same to this day. "Women alone are employed to grind their corn;" *Shaw's* Algiers and Tunis, p. 287. "They are the female slaves, that are generally employed in the east at those hand-mills for grinding corn; it is extremely laborious, and esteemed the lowest employment in the house;" Sir J. *Chardin, Harmer's* Observ. i., p. 153. The words denote that state of captivity to which the Babylonians should be reduced.

Make bare the leg, uncover the thigh] This is repeatedly seen in Bengal, where there are few bridges, and both sexes, having neither shoes nor stockings, truss up their loose garments, and walk across, where the waters are not deep. In the *deeper* water they are obliged to truss *very high,* to which there seems a reference in the *third verse: Thy nakedness shall be uncovered.*

Verse 3. *I will not meet* thee as *a man*—"Neither will I suffer man to intercede with me."] The verb should be pointed, or written, אפגיע *aphgia,* in Hiphil.

Verse 4. *Our Redeemer*—"Our Avenger"] Here a chorus breaks in upon the midst of the subject, with a change of construction, as well as sentiment, from the longer to the shorter kind of verse, for one distich only; after which the former subject and style are resumed. See note on chap. xlv. 16.

Verse 6. *I was wroth with my people*] God, in the course of his providence, makes use of great conquerors and tyrants as his instruments to execute his judgments in the earth; he employs one wicked nation to scourge another. The inflicter of the punishment may perhaps be as culpable as the sufferer; and may add to his guilt by indulging his cruelty in executing God's justice. When he has fulfilled the work to which the Divine vengeance has ordained him, he will become himself the object of it; see chap. x. 5-12. God charges the Babylonians, though employed by himself to chastise his people, with cruelty in regard to them. They exceeded the bounds of justice and humanity in oppressing and destroying them; and though they were really executing the righteous decree of God, yet, as far as it regarded themselves, they were only indulging their own ambition and violence. The Prophet Zechariah sets this matter in the same light: "I was but a little angry, and they helped forward the affliction;" chap. i. 15.—L.

Verse 7. So *that thou didst not*—"Because thou didst not"] For עד *ad,* read על *al;* so two MSS., and one edition. And for אחריתה *acharithah,* "the latter end *of it,*" read אחריתך *acharithecha, "thy* latter end;" so thirteen MSS., and two editions, and the *Vulgate.* Both the *sixth* and *seventh* verses are wanting in one of my oldest MSS.

A. M. cir. 3292
B. C. cir. 712
Olymp. XVII. 1
cir. annum
NumæPompilii,
R. Roman., 4

9 Beside [r]these two *things* shall come to thee [s]in a moment in one day, the loss of children and widowhood: they shall come upon thee in their perfection [t]for the multitude of thy sorceries, *and* for the great abundance of thine enchantments.

10 For thou [u]hast trusted in thy wickedness: [v]thou hast said, None seeth me. Thy wisdom and thy knowledge, it hath [w]perverted thee; [x]and thou hast said in thine heart, I *am,* and none else beside me.

11 Therefore shall evil come upon thee; thou shalt not know [y]from whence it riseth: and mischief shall fall upon thee; thou shalt not be able to [z]put it off: and [a]desolation shall come upon thee suddenly, *which* thou shalt not know.

12 Stand now with thine enchantments, and with the multitude of thy sorceries, wherein thou hast laboured from thy youth: if so be thou shalt be able to profit, if so be thou mayest prevail.

A. M. cir. 3292
B. C. cir. 712
Olymp. XVII. 1
cir. annum
NumæPompilii,
R. Roman., 4

13 [b]Thou art wearied in the multitude of thy counsels. Let now [c]the [d]astrologers, the stargazers, [e]the monthly prognosticators, stand up, and save thee from *these things* that shall come upon thee.

14 Behold, they shall be [f]as stubble; the fire shall burn them; they shall not deliver [g]themselves from the power of the flame: *there shall* not *be* a coal to warm at, *nor* fire to sit before it.

15 Thus shall they be unto thee with whom thou hast laboured, *even* [h]thy merchants, from thy youth: they shall wander every one to his quarter; none shall save thee.

---

[r]Chap. li. 19——[s]1 Thess. v. 3——[t]Nah. iii. 4——[u]Psa. lii. 7——[v]Chap. xxix. 15; Ezek. viii. 12; ix. 9——[w]Or, *caused thee to turn away*——[x]Ver. 8——[y]Heb. *the morning thereof*——[z]Heb. *expiate*——[a]1 Thess. v. 3

[b]Chapter lvii. 10——[c]Chapter xliv. 25; Dan. ii. 2——[d]Heb. *viewers of the heavens*——[e]Heb. *that give knowledge concerning the months*——[f]Nah. i. 10; Mal. iv. 1——[g]Heb. *their souls*——[h]Rev. xviii. 11

Verse 9. *These two* things *shall come to thee in a moment*] That is, suddenly. Belshazzar was slain; thus the city became metaphorically a *widow*, the *husband*—the governor of it, being slain. In the time in which the king was slain, the Medes and Persians took the city, and slew many of its inhabitants, see Dan. v. 30, 31. When Darius took the city, he is said to have crucified *three thousand* of its principal inhabitants.

In their perfection—"On a sudden"] Instead of בתמם *bethummam*, "in their perfection," as our translation renders it, the *Septuagint* and *Syriac* read, in the copies from which they translated, פתאם *pithom, suddenly;* parallel to רגע *rega, in a moment*, in the preceding alternate member of the sentence. The concurrent testimony of the *Septuagint* and *Syriac*, favoured by the context, may be safely opposed to the authority of the present text.

For the multitude—"Notwithstanding the multitude"] ברב *berob.* For this sense of the particle ב *beth*, see Num. xiv. 11.

Verse 11. *Thou shalt not know from whence it riseth*—"Thou shalt not know how to deprecate"] שחרה *shachrah;* so the *Chaldee* renders it, which is approved by *Jarchi* on the place; and *Michaelis* Epim. in Prælect. xix.; see Psa. lxxviii. 34.

Videtur in fine hujus commatis deese verbum, ut hoc membrum prioribus respondeat. "A word appears to be wanting at the end of this clause to connect it properly with the two preceding."—Secker.

In order to set in a proper light this judicious remark, it is necessary to give the reader an exact verbal translation of the whole verse:—

"And evil shall come upon thee, thou shalt not
know how to deprecate it;
And mischief shall fall upon thee, thou shalt
not be able to expiate it;
And destruction shall come suddenly upon
thee, thou shalt not know"—

What? how to escape, to avoid it, to be delivered from it? perhaps צאת ממנה *tseth mimmennah*, "they could not *go out from it*," Jer. xi. 11. I am persuaded that a phrase is here lost out of the text. But as the ancient versions retain no traces of it, and a wide field lies open to uncertain conjecture, I have not attempted to fill up the chasm, but have in the translation, as others have done before me, palliated and disguised the defect, which I cannot with any assurance pretend to supply.—L.

Verse 13. *From* these things—"What are the events"] For מאשר *measher*, read מה אשר *mah asher*, so the *Septuagint*, "what is to happen to thee."

Verse 15. *To his quarter*—"To his own business"] לעברו *leebro.* Expositors give no very good account of this word in this place. In a MS. it was at first לעבדו *leabdo, to his servant* or *work*, which is probably the true reading. The sense however is pretty much the same with the common interpretation: "Every one shall turn aside to his own business; none shall deliver thee."

CHAPTER XLVIII

The Jews reproved for their obstinate attachment to idols, notwithstanding their experience of the Divine providence over them; and of the Divine prescience that revealed by the prophets the most remarkable events which concerned them, that they should not have the least pretext for ascribing any portion of their success to their idols, 1–8. *The Almighty, after bringing them to the furnace for their perverseness, asserts his glorious sovereignty, and repeats his gracious promises of deliverance and consolation,* 9–11. *Prophecy concerning that individual (Cyrus) who shall be an instrument in the hand of God of executing his will on Babylon, and his power on the Chaldeans; and the idols of the people are again challenged to give a like proof of their foreknowledge,* 12–16. *Tender and passionate exclamation of Jehovah respecting the hardened condition of the Jewish nation, to which the very pathetic exclamation of the Divine Saviour when he wept over Jerusalem may be considered a striking parallel,* 17–19. *Notwithstanding the repeated provocations of the house of Israel, Jehovah will again be merciful to them. They are commanded to escape from Babylon; and God's gracious favour towards them is beautifully represented by images borrowed from the exodus from Egypt,* 20, 21. *Certain perdition of the finally impenitent,* 22. *It will be proper here to remark that many passages in this chapter, and indeed the general strain of these prophecies, have a plain aspect to a restoration of the Church in the latter days upon a scale much greater than the world has yet witnessed, when the very violent fall of Babylon the Great, mentioned in the Revelation, of which the Chaldean capital was an expressive type, shall introduce by a most tremendous political convulsion,* (Rev. xvi. 17–21,) *that glorious epoch of the Gospel, which forms so conspicuous a part of the prophecies of the Old Testament, and has been a subject of the prayers of all saints in all ages.*

A. M. cir. 3292
B. C. cir. 712
Olymp. XVII. 1
cir. annum
NumæPompilii,
R. Roman., 4

HEAR ye this, O house of Jacob, which are called by the name of Israel, and [a]are come forth out of the waters of Judah, [b]which swear by the name of the LORD, and make mention of the God of Israel, [c]*but* not in truth, nor in righteousness.

2 For they call themselves [d]of the holy city, and [e]stay themselves upon the God of Israel; The LORD of hosts *is* his name.

3 [f]I have declared the former things from the beginning; and they went forth out of my mouth, and I showed them; I did *them* suddenly, [g]and they came to pass.

4 Because I knew that thou *art* [h]obstinate, and [i]thy neck *is* an iron sinew, and thy brow brass;

5 [k]I have even from the beginning declared *it* to thee; before it came to pass I showed *it* thee: lest thou shouldest say, Mine idol hath done them; and my graven image, and my molten image, hath commanded them.

A. M. cir. 3292
B. C. cir. 712
Olymp. XVII. 1
cir. annum
NumæPompilii,
R. Roman., 4

6 Thou hast heard, see all this; and will not ye declare *it?* I have showed thee new things from this time, even hidden things, and thou didst not know them.

7 They are created now, and not from the beginning; even before the day when thou heardest them not; lest thou shouldest say, Behold, I knew them.

8 Yea, thou heardest not; yea, thou knewest not: yea, from that time *that* thine ear was not opened: for I knew that thou wouldest [l]deal very treacherously, and wast called [m]a transgressor from the womb.

9 [n]For my name's sake [o]will I defer mine anger, and for my praise will I refrain

[a]Psa. lxviii. 26——[b]Deut. vi. 13; chap. lxv. 16; Zeph. i. 5——[c]Jer. iv. 2; v. 2——[d]Ch. lii. 1——[e]Mic. iii. 11; Rom. ii. 17——[f]Ch. xli. 22; xlii. 9; xliii. 9; xliv. 7, 8; xlv. 21: xlvi. 9, 10——[g]Josh. xxi. 45——[h]Heb. *hard*

[i]Exod. lii. 9; Deut. xxxi. 27——[k]Ver. 3——[l]Chap. xxxiii. 1; Jer. iii. 20; v. 11; Hos. v. 7; vi. 7; Mal. ii. 10, 14, 15, 16——[m]Psa. lviii. 3——[n]Psa. lxxix. 9; cvi. 8; chap. xliii. 25; ver. 1; Ezek. xx. 9, 14, 22, 44——[o]Psa. lxxviii. 38

NOTES ON CHAP. XLVIII

Verse 1. *Are come forth out of the waters of Judah*—"Ye that flow from the fountain of Judah"] ממי *mimmey*, "from the *waters.*" Perhaps ממעי *mimmeey*, "from the bowels," so many others have conjectured, or מני יהודה *meni yehudah*, or מיהודה *meyhudah*, "from Judah."—*Secker.* But see *Michaelis* in Prælect, not. 22. And we have עין יעקב *eyn yaakob*, "the fountain of Jacob," Deut. xxxiii. 28, and ממקור ישראל *mimmekor yishrael*, "from the fountain of Israel," Psa. lxviii. 27. Twenty-seven MSS. of *Kennicott's*, six of *De Rossi's* and two of my own, with six editions, have מימי *meymey*, "from the *days;*" which makes no good sense.

Verse 6. *Thou hast heard, see all this*—"Thou didst hear it beforehand; behold, the whole is accomplished"] For חזה *chazeh, see*, a MS. has הזה *hazzeh, this;* thou hast heard the whole of *this:* the *Syriac* has וחזית *vechazith*, "thou hast heard, *and thou hast seen*, the whole." Perhaps it should be הנה *hinneh, behold.* In order to express the full sense, I have rendered it somewhat paraphrastically.

Verse 9. *And for my praise*—"And for the sake of my praise"] I read ולמען תהלתי *ulemaan tehillathi.* The word למען *lemaan*, though not absolutely necessary here, for it may be understood as supplied from the preceding member, yet seems to have been removed from hence to ver. 11; where it is redundant, and where it is not repeated in the *Septuagint,*

A. M. cir. 3292
B. C. cir. 712
Olymp. XVII. 1
cir. annum
NumæPompilii,
R. Roman., 4

for thee, that I cut thee
not off.
10 Behold, [p]I have refined thee,
but not [q]with silver; I have
chosen thee [r]in the furnace of affliction.
11 [s]For mine own sake, *even* for mine own
sake, will I do *it:* for how [t]should *my name*
be polluted: and [u]I will not give my glory
unto another.
12 Hearken unto me, O Jacob and Israel,
my called; [v]I *am* he; I *am* the [w]first, I also
am the last.
13 [x]Mine hand also hath laid the foundation
of the earth, and [y]my right hand
hath spanned the heavens: *when*
[z]I call unto them, they stand up
together.
14 [a]All ye, assemble yourselves, and hear;
which among them hath declared these *things?*
[b]The LORD hath loved him: [c]he will do his
pleasure on Babylon, and his arm *shall be on*
the Chaldeans.
15 I, *even* I, have spoken; yea, [d]I have
called him: I have brought him, and he shall
make his way prosperous.
16 Come ye near unto me, hear ye this; [e]I

[p]Psa. lxvi. 10——[q]Or, *for silver;* see Ezek. xxii. 20, 21, 22——[r]Ecclus. ii. 5——[s]Ver. 9——[t]See Deut. xxxii. 26, 27; Ezek. xx. 9——[u]Chap. xlii. 8——[v]Deut. xxxii. 39——[w]Chap. xli. 4; xliv. 6; Rev. i. 17; xxii. 13

[x]Psa. cii. 25——[y]Or, *the palm of my right hand hath spread out*——[z]Chap. xl. 26——[a]Chap. xli. 22; xliv. 7; xlv. 20, 21——[b]Chap. xlv. 1——[c]Chap. xliv. 28 [d]Chap. xlv. 1, 2, &c.——[e]Chap. xlv. 19

Syriac, and a MS. I have therefore omitted it in the latter place, and added it here.

Verse 10. *I have chosen thee*—"I have tried thee"] For בחרתיך *bechasrticha*, "I have *chosen* thee," a MS. has בחנתיך *bechanticha*, "I have *tried* thee." And so perhaps read the *Syriac* and *Chaldee* interpreters; they retain the same word בחרתך *bechartach;* but in those languages it signifies, I have *tried* thee. ככסף *kecheseph*, *quasi* argentum, "as silver." *Vulgate*.

I cannot think בכסף *becheseph*, WITH *silver*, is the true reading. ככסף *kecheseph*, LIKE *silver*, as the *Vulgate* evidently read it, I suppose to have been the original reading, though no MS. yet found supports this word; the similarity of the two letters, ב *beth* and כ *caph*, might have easily led to the mistake in the first instance; and it has been but too faithfully copied ever since. כור *cur*, which we translate *furnace*, should be rendered *crucible*, the vessel in which the silver is melted. The meaning of the verse seems to be this: I have purified you, but not as silver is purified; for when it is purified, no dross of any kind is left behind. Had I done this with you, I should have consumed you altogether; but I have put you in the crucible of affliction, in *captivity*, that you may acknowledge your sins, and turn unto me.

Verse 11. *For how should* my name *be polluted*—"For how would my name be blasphemed"] The word שמי *shemi, my name,* is dropped out of the text; it is supplied by a MS. which has שמי *shemi;* and by the *Septuagint*, ὁτι το εμον ονομα βεβηλουται. The *Syriac* and *Vulgate* get over the difficulty, by making the verb in the first person; that *I may not be blasphemed.*

Verse 12. *O Jacob*—"O Jacob, my servant"] After יעקב *yaakob*, a MS. of *Kennicott's*, two of *De Rossi's*, and the two old editions of 1486 and 1488, add the word עבדי *abdi*, "my servant," which is lost out of the present text; and there is a rasure in its place in another ancient MS. The Jerusalem Talmud has the same word.

I also am *the last*—"I am the last"] For אף אני *aph ani*, "even I," two ancient MSS. and the ancient Versions, read ואני *veani*, "and I;" more properly.

Verse 14. *Which among them hath declared these* things—"Who among you hath predicted these things"] For בהם *bahem*, "among *them*," twenty-one MSS., nine ancient, and two editions, one of them that of the year 1488, fourteen of *De Rossi's*, and one ancient of my own, have בכם *bachem*, "among *you;*" and so the *Syriac*.

The Lord hath loved him: he will do his pleasure on Babylon—"He, whom JEHOVAH hath loved, will execute his will on Babylon"] That is, Cyrus; so *Symmachus* has well rendered it: 'Ον ὁ Κυριος ηγαπησε ποιησει το θελημα αυτου, "He whom the Lord hath loved will perform his *will.*"

On *the Chaldeans.*] The preposition is lost; it is supplied in the edition of 1486, which has בכשדים *bechasdim*, and so the *Chaldee* and *Vulgate*.

Verse 16. *Come ye near unto me*] After the word קרבו *kirbu*, "draw near," a MS. adds גוים *goyim*, "O ye nations;" which, as this and the two preceding verses are plainly addressed to the idolatrous nations, reproaching their gods as unable to predict future events, is probably genuine.

Hear ye this—"And hear ye this"] A MS. adds the conjunction, ושמעו *vashimu;* and so the *Septuagint*, *Syriac*, and *Vulgate*.

I have not spoken in secret] The Alexandrine copy of the *Septuagint* adds here, ουδε εν τοπῳ γης σκοτεινω, "nor in a dark place of the earth," as in chap. xlv. 19. That it stands rightly, or at least stood very early, in this place of the Version of the *Septuagint*, is highly probable, because it is acknowledged by the *Arabic* Version, and by the *Coptic* MS. *St. Germain de Prez*, Paris, translated likewise from the *Septuagint*. But whether it should be inserted, as of right belonging to the *Hebrew* text, may be doubted; for a transcriber of the *Greek* Version might easily add it by memory from the parallel place; and it is not necessary to the sense.

From the time that it was—"Before the time when *it* began to exist"] An ancient MS. has היותם *heyotham*, "*they* began to exist;" and so another had it at first. From the time that the expedition of Cyrus was planned, there was God managing the whole by the economy of his providence.

A. M. cir. 3292
B. C. cir. 712
Olymp. XVII. 1
cir. annum
NumæPompilii,
R. Roman., 4

have not spoken in secret from the beginning; from the time that it was, there *am* I: and now [f]the Lord GOD, and his Spirit, hath sent me.

17 Thus saith [g]the LORD, thy Redeemer, the Holy One of Israel; I *am* the LORD thy God which teacheth thee to profit, which [h]leadeth thee by the way *that* thou shouldest go.

18 [i]O that thou hadst hearkened to my commandments! [k]then had thy peace been as a river, and thy righteousness as the waves of the sea:

19 [l]Thy seed also had been as the sand, and the offspring of thy bowels like the gravel thereof; his name should not have been cut off nor destroyed from before me.

A. M. cir. 3292
B. C. cir. 712
Olymp. XVII. 1
cir. annum
NumæPompilii,
R. Roman., 4

20 [m]Go ye forth of Babylon, flee ye from the Chaldeans, with a voice of singing declare ye, tell this, utter it *even* to the end of the earth; say ye, The LORD hath [n]redeemed his servant Jacob.

21 And they [o]thirsted not *when* he led them through the deserts: he [p]caused the waters to flow out of the rock for them: he clave the rock also, and the waters gushed out.

22 [q]*There is* no peace, saith the LORD, unto the wicked.

---

[f]Ch. lxi. 1; Zech. ii. 8, 9, 11——[g]Ch. xliii. 14; xliv. 6, 24; ver. 20——[h]Psa. xxxii. 8——[i]Deut. xxxii. 29; Psa. lxxxi. 13——[k]Psa. cxix. 165——[l]Gen. xxii. 17; Hos. i. 10

[m]Ch. lii. 11; Jer. l. 8; li. 6, 45; Zech. ii. 6, 7; Rev. xviii. 4 [n]Exod. xix. 4, 5, 6; ch. xliv. 22, 23——[o]See ch. xli. 17, 18 [p]Exod. xvii. 6; Num. xx. 11; Psa. cv. 41——[q]Ch. lvii. 21

Verse 16. *There am I*—"I had decreed it"] I take שם *sham* for a verb, not an adverb.

And now the Lord God, and his Spirit, hath sent me—"And now the Lord JEHOVAH hath sent me, and his Spirit"] Τις εστιν ὁ εν τῳ Ησαιᾳ λεγων, Και νυν Κυριος απεστειλε με και το Πνευμα αυτου; εν ᾡ, αμφιβολου οντος του ῥητου, ποτερον ὁ Πατηρ και το Ἁγιον Πνευμα απεστειλαν τον Ιησουν, η ὁ Πατηρ απεστειλε τον τε Χριστον και το Ἁγιον Πνευμα· το δευτερον εστιν αληθες. "Who is it that saith in Isaiah, And now the Lord hath sent me and his Spirit? in which, as the expression is ambiguous, is it the Father and the Holy Spirit who have sent Jesus; or the Father, who hath sent both Christ and the Holy Spirit. The latter is the true interpretation."—*Origen* cont. Cels. lib. i. I have kept to the order of the words of the original, on purpose that the ambiguity, which *Origen* remarks in the Version of the *Septuagint*, and which is the same in the *Hebrew*, might still remain; and the sense which he gives to it, be offered to the reader's judgment, which is wholly excluded in our translation.

Verse 18. *As a river*—"Like the river"] That is, the Euphrates.

Verse 19. *Like the gravel thereof*—"Like that of the bowels thereof"] בצאצאי מעי הים והם הדגים *betseetsaey meey haiyam vehem haddagim;* "As the issue of the bowels of the sea; that is, fishes."—*Salom. ben Melec.* And so likewise *Aben Ezra*, *Jarchi*, *Kimchi*, &c.

His name—"Thy name"] For שמו *shemo*, "*his* name," the *Septuagint* had in the copy from which they translated שמך *shimcha*, "*thy* name."

Verse 20. *Tell this*—"Make it heard"] *Twenty-seven* MSS. of *Kennicott's*, (*ten* ancient,) many of *De Rossi's*, and *two* ancient, of my own, with the *Septuagint*, *Syriac*, *Chaldee*, and *Arabic*, and one edition, prefix to the verb the conjunction ו *vau*, והשמיעו *vehashmiu*.

Verse 21. *They thirsted not—through the deserts*] *Kimchi* has a surprising observation upon this place: "If the prophecy," says he, "relates to the return from the Babylonish captivity, as it seems to do, it is to be wondered how it comes to pass, that in the Book of Ezra, in which he gives an account of their return, no mention is made that such miracles were wrought for them; as, for instance, that God clave the rock for them in the desert." It is really much to be wondered, that one of the most learned and judicious of the Jewish expositors of the Old Testament, having advanced so far in a large Comment on Isaiah, should appear to be totally ignorant of the prophet's manner of writing; of the parabolic style, which prevails in the writings of all the prophets, and more particularly in the prophecy of Isaiah, which abounds throughout in parabolical images from the beginning to the end; from "Hear, O heavens, and give ear, O earth," to "the worm and the fire" in the last verse. And how came he to keep his wonderment to himself so long? Why did he not expect that the historian should have related how, as they passed through the desert, cedars, pines, and olive-trees shot up at once on the side of the way to shade them; and that instead of briers and brambles the acacia and the myrtle sprung up under their feet, according to God's promises, chap. xli. 19 and lv. 13? These and a multitude of the like parabolical or poetical images, were never intended to be understood literally. All that the prophet designed in this place, and which he has executed in the most elegant manner, was an amplification and illustration of the gracious care and protection of God vouchsafed to his people in their return from Babylon, by an allusion to the miraculous exodus from Egypt. See *De S. Poësi*, Hebr. Præl. ix.

Verse 22. There is *no peace, saith the Lord, unto the wicked.*] See below, note on chap. lvii. 21. As the destruction of Babylon was determined, God commands his people to hasten out of it; for, saith the Lord, *there is no peace* (prosperity) *to the wicked;* ουκ εστι χαιρειν τοις ασεβεσιν, λεγει Κυριος.—*Sept.* "There is no rejoicing or prosperity to the wicked saith the Lord." **Their is not pese to unrytous men seith the Lord.**—Old MS. Bible.

CHAPTER XLIX

In this chapter the Messiah is introduced, declaring the full extent of his commission, which is not only to be Saviour to the Jews, but also to the Gentiles. The power and efficacy of his word is represented by apt images; the ill success of his ministry among the Jews is intimated, and the great success of the Gospel among the Gentiles, 1–12. *But the prophet, then casting his eye on the happy, though distant, period of Israel's restoration, makes a beautiful apostrophe to the whole creation to shout forth the praises of God on the prospect of this remarkable favour,* 13. *The tender mercies of God to his people, with the prosperity of the Church in general, and the final overthrow of all its enemies, make the subject of the remaining verses,* 14–26.

A. M. cir. 3292
B. C. cir. 712
Olymp. XVII. 1
cir. annum
NumæPompilii,
R. Roman., 4

LISTEN, [a]O isles, unto me;
and hearken, ye people, from
far; [b]The LORD hath called me
from the womb; from the bowels
of my mother hath he made mention of my
name.
2 And he hath made [c]my mouth like a sharp
sword; [d]in the shadow of his hand hath he
hid me, and made me [e]a polished
shaft; in his quiver hath he
hid me;
3 And said unto me, [f]Thou
art my servant, O Israel, [g]in whom I will be
glorified.
4 [h]Then I said, I have labored in vain, I
have spent my strength for nought, and in vain:

[a]Chap. xli. 1——[b]Ver. 5; Jer. i. 5; Matt. i. 20, 21; Luke i. 15, 31; John x. 36; Gal. i. 15——[c]Chap. xi. 4; li. 16; Hos. vi. 5; Heb. iv. 12; Rev. i. 16

[d]Chap. li. 16——[e]Psa. xlv. 5——[f]Chap. xlii. 1; Zech. iii. 8——[g]Chap. xliv. 23; John xiii. 31; xv. 8; Eph. i. 6 [h]Ezek. iii. 19

NOTES ON CHAP. XLIX

Verse 1. *Listen, O isles, unto me*—"Hearken unto me, O ye distant lands"] Hitherto the subject of the prophecy has been chiefly confined to the redemption from the captivity of Babylon; with strong intimations of a more important deliverance sometimes thrown in, to the refutation of idolatry, and the demonstration of the infinite power, wisdom, and foreknowledge of God. The character and office of the Messiah was exhibited in general terms at the beginning of chap. xlii.; but here he is introduced in person, declaring the full extent of his commission, which is not only to restore the Israelites, and reconcile them to their Lord and Father, from whom they had so often revolted, but to be a light to lighten the Gentiles, to call them to the knowledge and obedience of the true God, and to bring them to be one Church together with the Israelites, and to partake with them of the same common salvation procured for all by the great Redeemer and Reconciler of man to God.

Verse 2. *And he hath made my mouth like a sharp sword*—"And he hath made my mouth a sharp sword"] The servant of God, who speaks in the former part of this chapter, must be the Messiah. If any part of this character can in any sense belong to the prophet, yet in some parts it must belong exclusively to Christ; and in all parts to him in a much fuller and more proper sense. Isaiah's mission was to the Jews, not to the distant nations, to whom the speaker in this place addresses himself. "He hath made my mouth a sharp sword;" "to reprove the wicked, and to denounce unto them punishment," says Jarchi, understanding it of Isaiah. But how much better does it suit him who is represented as having "a sharp two-edged sword going out of his mouth," Rev. i. 16; who is himself the Word of God; which word is "quick and powerful, and sharper than any two-edged sword, piercing even to the dividing asunder of soul and spirit, and of the joints and marrow, and is a discerner of the thoughts and intents of the heart;" Heb. iv. 12. This mighty Agent and Instrument of God, "long laid up in store with him, and sealed up among his treasures," is at last revealed and produced by his power, and under his protection, to execute his great and holy purposes. He is compared to a polished shaft stored in his quiver for use in his due time. The polished shaft denotes the same efficacious word which is before represented by the sharp sword. The doctrine of the Gospel pierced the hearts of its hearers, "bringing into captivity every thought to the obedience of Christ." The metaphor of the sword and the arrow, applied to powerful speech, is bold, yet just. It has been employed by the most ingenious heathen writers, if with equal elegance, not with equal force. It is said of Pericles by Aristophanes, (see *Cicero*, Epist. ad Atticum, xii. 6:)—

Οὑτως εκηλει, και μονος των ῥητορων
Το κεντρον εγκατελειπε τοις ακροωμενοις.
Apud. Diod. lib. xii.

His powerful speech
Pierced the hearer's soul, and left behind
Deep in his bosom its keen point infixed.

Pindar is particularly fond of this metaphor, and frequently applies it to his own poetry:—

Επεχε νυν σκοπῳ τοξον,
Αγε, θυμε. τινα βαλλομεν
Εκ μαλθακας αυτε φρε-
νος ευκλεας οϊστους
'Ιεντες—; *Olymp.* ii. 160.

"Come on! thy brightest shafts prepare,
And bend, O Muse, thy sounding bow;
Say, through what paths of liquid air
Our arrows shall we throw?" WEST.

See also ver. 149 of the same ode, and *Olymp.* ix. 17, on the former of which places the *Scholiast* says, *τροπικος ὁ λογος· βελη δε τους λογους ειρηκε, δια το οξυ και καιριον των εγκωμιων.* "He calls his verses

A. M. cir. 3292 B. C. cir. 712 Olymp. XVII. 1 cir. annum NumæPompilii, R. Roman., 4

yet surely my judgment *is* with
the LORD, and [i]my work with
my God.
5 And now, saith the LORD
[k]that formed me from the womb *to be* his servant, to bring Jacob again to him, [l]Though
Israel [m]be not gathered, yet shall I be glorious
in the eyes of the LORD, and my God shall be
my strength.
6 And he said, [n]It is a light thing that thou
shouldest be my servant to raise up the tribes
of Jacob, and to restore the [o]preserved of
Israel: I will also give thee for a [p]light to
the Gentiles, that thou mayest be my salvation
unto the end of the earth.
7 Thus saith the LORD, the Redeemer of
Israel, *and* his Holy One, [q]to [r]him whom
man despiseth, to him whom the nation abhorreth, to a servant of rulers, [s]kings shall
see and arise, princes also shall worship, because of the LORD that is faithful, *and* the
Holy One of Israel, and he shall choose thee.
8 Thus saith the LORD, [t]In an
acceptable time have I heard
thee, and in a day of salvation
have I helped thee: and I will
preserve thee, [u]and give thee for a covenant of the people, to [v]establish the earth
to cause to inherit the desolate heritages;
9 That thou mayest say [w]to the prisoners,
Go forth; to them that *are* in darkness,
Show yourselves. They shall feed in the
ways, and their pastures *shall be* in all high
places.
10 They shall not [x]hunger nor thirst; [y]nei-
ther shall the heat nor sun smite them: for
he that hath mercy on them [z]shall lead them,
even by the springs of water shall he guide
them.
11 [a]And I will make all my mountains a
way, and my highways shall be exalted.
12 Behold, [b]these shall come from far: and,
lo, these from the north and from the west;
and these from the land of Sinim.

A. M. cir. 3292 B. C. cir. 712 Olymp. XVII. 1 cir annum NumæPompilii, R. Roman., 4

---

[i]Or, *my reward;* ch. xl. 10; lxii. 11——[k]Ver. 1——[l]Or, *That Israel may be gathered to him, and I may,* &c. [m]Matt. xxiii. 37——[n]Or, Art thou *lighter than that thou shouldest,* &c.——[o]Or, *desolations*——[p]Ch. xlii. 6; lx. 3; Luke ii. 32; Acts xiii. 47; xxvi. 18——[q]Chap. liii. 3; Matt. xxvi. 67

[r]Or, *to him that is despised in soul*——[s]Psa. lxxii. 10, 11; verse 23——[t]See Psalm lxix. 13; 2 Corinthians vi. 2——[u]Chapter xlii. 6——[v]Or, *raise up*——[w]Chap. xlii. 7; Zechariah ix. 12——[x]Revelation vii. 16——[y]Psa. cxxi. 6——[z]Psalm xxiii. 2——[a]Chapter xl. 4——[b]Chap. xliii. 5, 6

---

shafts, by a metaphor, signifying the acuteness and the apposite application of his panegyric."

This person, who is (ver. 3) called *Israel*, cannot in any sense be Isaiah. That name, in its original design and full import, can only belong to him who *contended powerfully with God* in behalf of mankind, and prevailed, Gen. xxxii. 28. After all that *Vitringa*, Bp. *Lowth*, and others have said in proof of this chapter speaking of the Messiah, and of him alone, I have my doubts whether sometimes Isaiah, sometimes Cyrus, and sometimes the Messiah, be not intended; the former shadowing out the latter, of whom, in certain respects, they may be considered the *types*. The literal sense should be sought out *first;* this is of the utmost importance both in reading and interpreting the oracles of God.

Verse 5. *And now, saith the Lord*—"And now, thus saith JEHOVAH"] The word כה *coh*, before אמר *amar*, is dropped out of the text: it is supplied by eight MSS. (two ancient) of Dr. *Kennicott's*, two of *De Rossi's*, and the *Septuagint*, *Syriac*, and *Vulgate*.

Though Israel be not gathered—"And that Israel unto him might be gathered"] Five MSS. (two ancient) confirm the *Keri*, or marginal correction of the Masoretes, לו *lo, unto him*, instead of לא *lo, not*, in the text; and so read *Aquila;* and the *Chaldee*, *Septuagint*, and *Arabic* omit the negative. But the *Septuagint*, MSS. *Pachom*, and I. D. II. express also the *Keri* לו *lo* by προς αυτον, *to him.*

Verse 6. *And to restore the preserved of Israel*—"And to restore the branches of Israel"] נצירי *netsirey*, or נצורי *netsurey*, as the Masoretes correct it in the marginal reading. This word has been matter of great doubt with interpreters: the *Syriac* renders it *the branch*, taking it for the same with נצר *netser*, chap. xi. 1. See *Michaelis* Epim. in Prælect. xix.

Verse 7. *The Redeemer of Israel*, and *his Holy One*—"The Redeemer of Israel, his Holy One"] "Perhaps we should read לקדושו *likdosho*," SECKER: that is, *to his Holy One*. The preceding word ends with a ל *lamed*, which might occasion that letter's being lost here. The *Talmud* of Babylon has וקדושו *ukedosho*, *and his Holy One.*

To him whom man despiseth—"To him whose person is despised"] "Perhaps we should read נבזה *nibzeh*," SECKER; or בזוי *bazui*, *Le Clerc;* that is, instead of the active, the passive form, which seems here to be required.

Verse 9. *To them that* are *in darkness*—"And to those that are in darkness"] Fifteen MSS. (five ancient) of Dr. *Kennicott's*, eleven of *De Rossi's*, and one ancient of my own, and the two old editions of 1486 and 1488, and three others, add the conjunction ו *vau* at the beginning of this member. Another MS. had it so at first, and two others have a rasure at the place: and it is expressed by the *Septuagint*, *Syriac*, *Chaldee*, and *Vulgate*.

Verse 12. *Behold, these shall come from far*] "Babylon was far and east, ממזרח *mimmizrach*, (*non sic Vett.*,) Sinim, Pelusians, to the south." —SECKER.

The land of Sinim.] Prof. *Doederlein* thought of Syene, the southern limit of Egypt, but does

A. M. cir. 3292 B. C. cir. 712 Olymp. XVII. 1 cir. annum NumæPompilii, R. Roman., 4

13 [c]Sing, O heavens; and be
joyful, O earth; and break forth
into singing, O mountains: for
the LORD hath comforted his
people, and will have mercy upon his afflicted.
14 [d]But Zion said, The LORD hath forsaken
me, and my Lord hath forgotten me.
15 [e]Can a woman forget her sucking child,
[f]that she should not have compassion on the
son of her womb? yea, they may forget, [g]yet
will I not forget thee.
16 Behold, [h]I have graven thee upon the
palms of *my* hands; thy walls *are*
continually before me.
17 Thy children shall make
haste; [i]thy destroyers and
they that made thee waste shall go forth of
thee.
18 [k]Lift up thine eyes round about, and behold:
all these gather themselves together,
and come to thee. *As* I live, saith the LORD,
thou shalt surely clothe thee with them all, [l]as
with an ornament, and bind them *on thee,*
as a bride *doeth.*

A. M. cir. 3292 B. C. cir. 712 Olymp. XVII. 1 cir. annum NumæPompilii, R. Roman., 4

[c]Ch. xliv. 23——[d]See ch. xl. 27——[e]See Psa. ciii. 13; Mal. iii. 17; Matt. vii. 11——[f]Heb. *from having compassion*——[g]Rom. xi. 29——[h]See Exod. xiii. 9; Cant. viii. 6——[i]Ver. 19——[k]Ch. lx. 4——[l]Prov. xvii. 6

not abide by it. *Michaelis* thinks it is right, and promises to give his reasons for so thinking in the second part of his Spicilegium Geographiæ Hebræorum Exteræ. See *Biblioth. Oriental.* Part xi. p. 176.

סין *sin* signifies a *bush*, and סינים *sinim*, *bushes, woods*, &c. Probably this means that the land where several of the lost Jews dwell is a woodland. The ten tribes are gone, no one knows whither. On the slave coast in Africa, some Jewish rites appear among the people, and all the males are circumcised. The whole of this land, as it appears from the coast, may be emphatically called ארץ סינים *erets sinim, the land of bushes*, as it is all covered with *woods* as far as the eye can reach. Many of the Indians in North America, which is also a woodland, have a great profusion of rites, apparently in their basis *Jewish.* Is it not possible that the descendants of the *ten* lost tribes are among those in America, or among those in Africa, whom European nations *think they have a right to enslave?* It is of those lost tribes that the twenty-first verse speaks: "And these, where had they been?"

Verse 13. *Break forth into singing, O mountains*—"Ye mountains, burst forth into song"] Three ancient MSS. are without the י *yod* or the conjunction ו *vau* before the verb: and so the *Septuagint, Syriac*, and *Vulgate.*

Verse 14. *The Lord* (יהוה *Yehovah*) *hath forsaken me, and my Lord* (אדני *Adonai*) *hath forgotten me.*] But a multitude of MSS. and several ancient editions read יהוה *Yehovah* in both places.

Verse 16. *Behold, I have graven thee upon the palms of* my *hands*—"Behold, on the palms of my hands have I delineated thee"] This is certainly an allusion to some practice, common among the Jews at that time, of making marks on their hands or arms by punctures on the skin, with some sort of sign or representation of the city or temple, to show their affection and zeal for it. They had a method of making such punctures indelible by fire, or by staining. See note on chap. xliv. 5. It is well known, that the pilgrims at the holy sepulchre get themselves marked in this manner with what are called the ensigns of Jerusalem. See *Maundrell*, p. 75, where he tells us how it is performed: and this art is practised by travelling Jews all over the world at this day.

Verse 17. *Thy children shall make haste*—"They that destroyed thee shall soon become thy builders"] Auctor Vulgatæ pro בניך *banayich*, videtur legisse בוניך *bonayich*, unde vertit, *structores tui;* cui et Septuaginta fere consentiunt, qui verterunt ῳκοδομηθης, *ædificata es*, prout in Plantiniana editione habetur; in Vaticana sive Romana legitur, οικοδομηθηση, *ædificaberis.* Hisce etiam Targum Jonathanis aliquatenus consentit, ubi, *et ædificabunt.* Confer infra Esai. liv. 13, ad quem locum rabbini quoque notarunt ex tractatu Talmudico Berachot, c. ix., quod non legendum sit בניך *banayich*, id est, *filii tui;* sed בניך *bonayich, ædificatores tui.* Confer not. ad librum Prec. Jud. part ii., p. 226, ut et D Wagenseil Sot. p. 253, n. 9. "The author of the *Vulgate* appears to have read בוניך *bonayich* for בניך *banayich*, as he translates it by *structores tui*, 'thy builders.' The *Septuagint* is almost the same with the *Vulgate*, having ῳκοδομηθης, *art built*, as in the *Plantin* edition: but the *Vatican* or *Roman* copy reads οικοδομηθηση, *thou shalt be built.* To these readings the *Targum* of *Jonathan* has some sort of correspondence, translating *et ædificabunt*, 'and they shall build.' See chap. liv. 13; on which place the rabbins also remark, in the Talmudic tract *Berachoth*, c. 9, that we should not read בניך *banayich, thy sons*, but בניך *bonayich, thy builders.* See the note in *Prec. Jud.* part ii., p. 226, and also *D. Wagenseil, Sot.* p. 253, n. 9." See also *Breithaupt.* not. ad *Jarchi* in loc.; and the note on this place in De Sac. Poës. Hebr. Prælect. xxxi. Instead of בוניך or בניך *bonayich, thy builders*, several MSS. read בניך *baneycha, thy sons.* So also the *Syriac:* see the above note.

Shall go forth of thee—"Shall become thine offspring."] ממך יצאו *mimmech yetseu*, shall *proceed, spring, issue, from thee*, as thy children. The phrase is frequently used in this sense: see chap. xi. 1; Mic. v. 2; Nah. i. 11. The accession of the Gentiles to the Church of God is considered as an addition made to the number of the family and children of Sion: see ver. 21, 22, and chap. lx. 4. The common rendering, "shall go forth of thee, or depart from thee," is very flat, after their zeal had been expressed by "shall become thy builders:" and as the opposition is kept up in one part of the sentence, one has reason to expect it in the other, which should be parallel to it.

Verse 18. *Bind them* on thee, *as a bride* doeth —"Bind them about thee, as a bride *her jewels.*"] The end of the sentence is manifestly

A. M. cir. 3292
B. C. cir. 712
Olymp. XVII. 1
cir. annum
NumæPompilii,
R. Roman., 4

19 For thy waste and thy desolate places, and the land of thy destruction, [m]shall even now be too narrow by reason of the inhabitants, and they that swallowed thee up shall be far away.

20 [n]The children which thou shalt have, [o]after thou hast lost the other, shall say again in thine ears, The place *is* too strait for me: give place to me that I may dwell.

21 Then shalt thou say in thine heart, Who hath begotten me these, seeing I have lost my children, and am desolate, a captive, and removing to and fro? and who hath brought up these? Behold, I was left alone; these, where *had* they *been?*

22 [p]Thus saith the Lord GOD, Behold, I will lift up mine hand to the Gentiles, and set up my standard to the people: and they shall bring thy sons in *their* [q]arms, and thy daughters shall be carried upon *their* shoulders.

A. M. cir. 3292
B. C. cir. 712
Olymp. XVII. 1
cir. annum
NumæPompilii,
R. Roman., 4

23 [r]And kings shall be thy [s]nursing fathers, and their [t]queens thy nursing mothers: they shall bow down to thee with *their* face toward the earth, and [u]lick up the dust of thy feet; and thou shalt know that I *am* the LORD: for [v]they shall not be ashamed that wait for me.

24 [w]Shall the prey be taken from the mighty, or [x]the lawful captive delivered?

25 But thus saith the LORD, Even the [y]captives of the mighty shall be taken away, and the prey of the terrible shall be delivered: for I will contend with him that contendeth with thee, and I will save thy children.

26 And I will [z]feed them that oppress thee with their own flesh; and they shall be drunken with their own [a]blood, as with [b]sweet wine: and all flesh [c]shall know that I the LORD am thy Saviour and thy Redeemer, the Mighty One of Jacob.

[m]See ch. liv. 1, 2; Zech. ii. 4; x. 10——[n]Ch. lx. 4——[o]Matt. iii. 9; Rom. xi. 11, 12, &c.——[p]Ch. lx. 4; lxvi. 20——[q]Heb. *bosom*——[r]Psa. lxxii. 11; ver. 7; ch. lii. 15; lx. 16——[s]Heb. *nourishers*——[t]Heb. *princesses*——[u]Psa. lxxii. 9; Mic. vii. 17——[v]Psa. xxxiv. 22; Rom. v. 5; ix. 33; x. 11——[w]Matt. xii. 29; Luke xi. 21, 22——[x]Heb. *the captivity of the just*——[y]Heb. *captivity*——[z]Ch. ix. 20——[a]Rev. xiv. 20; xvi. 6——[b]Or, *new wine*——[c]Psa. ix. 16; ch. lx. 16

imperfect. Does a bride bind her children, or her new subjects, about her? Sion clothes herself with her children, as a bride clothes herself,—with what? some other thing certainly. The *Septuagint* help us out in this difficulty, and supply the lost word: ὡς κοσμον νυμφη· *as a bride her ornaments.* ככליה כלה *kichleyha callah*, or ככלה כליה *kecallah keleyha.* The great similitude of the two words has occasioned the omission of one of them. See chap. lxi. 10.

Verse 21. *These, where* had *they* been—"These then, where were they?"] The conjunction is added before אלה *elleh*, that is, ואלה *veelleh*, in thirty-two MSS. (nine ancient) of *Kennicott's*, and fifty-four of *De Rossi's;* and so the *Septuagint*, *Chaldee*, and *Vulgate.* See on ver. 12.

Verse 22. *Thus saith the Lord God*—אדני יהוה *Adonai Yehovah.* Adonai is wanting in one MS., in the Alexandrine copy of the *Septuagint*, and in the *Arabic.*

Verse 23. *With* their *face toward the earth*—"With their faces to the earth"] It is well known that expressions of submission, homage, and reverence always have been and are still carried to a great degree of extravagance in the eastern countries. When Joseph's brethren were introduced to him, "they bowed down themselves before him with their faces to the earth," Gen. xlii. 6. The kings of Persia never admitted any one to their presence without exacting this act of adoration; for that was the proper term for it. Necesse est, says the Persian courtier to Conon, si in conspectum veneris, venerari te regem; quod προσκυνειν illi vocant. "It is necessary, if thou shouldest come in sight, to venerate thee as king; which they call *worshipping.*"—NEPOS in Conone. Alexander, intoxicated with success, affected this piece of oriental pride: Itaque more Persarum Macedonas venerabundos ipsum salutare, prosternentes humi corpora. "The Macedonians, after the manner of the Persians, saluted their monarch with the ceremony of prostration."—CURTIUS, lib. viii. The insolence of eastern monarchs to conquered princes, and the submission of the latter, is astonishing. Mr. *Harmer*, Observ. ii. 43, gives the following instance of it from D'Herbelot: "This prince threw himself one day on the ground, and kissed the prints that his victorious enemy's horse had made there; reciting some verses in Persian, which he had composed, to this effect:—

"'The mark that the foot of your horse has left upon the dust, serves me now for a crown.

"'The ring which I wear as the badge of my slavery, is become my richest ornament.

"'While I shall have the happiness to kiss the dust of your feet, I shall think that fortune favours me with its tenderest caresses, and its sweetest kisses.'"

These expressions therefore of the prophet are only general poetical images, taken from the manners of the country, to denote great respect and reverence: and such splendid poetical images, which frequently occur in the prophetical writings, were intended only as general amplifications of the subject, not as predictions to be understood and fulfilled precisely according to the letter. For the different kinds of adoration in the east, see the note on chap. xliv. 17.

Verse 24. *Shall the prey be taken from the mighty*—"Shall the prey seized by the terrible be rescued"] For צדיק *tsaddik*, read עריץ

arits. A palpable mistake, like that in chap. xlii. 19. The correction is self-evident from the very terms of the sentence; from the necessity of the strict correspondence in the expressions between the question and the answer made to it,—and it is apparent to the blindest and most prejudiced eye. However, if authority is also necessary, there is that of the *Syriac* and *Vulgate* for it; who plainly read עריץ *arits,* in ver. 24 as well as in ver. 25, rendering it in the former place by the same word as in the latter.—L.

These two last verses contain a glorious promise of deliverance to the persecuted Church of Christ from the *terrible one*—Satan, and all his representatives and vicegerents, persecuting antichristian rulers. They shall at last cease from destroying the Church of God, and destroy one another.

CHAPTER L

In this chapter God vindicates his dealings with his people, whose alienation is owing to themselves, 1. *And, by allusion to the temporal deliverances connected with the drying up of the Red Sea and the Euphrates, asserts his power to save,* 2, 3; *namely, by the obedience and sufferings of the Messiah,* 4–6; *who was at length to prove victorious over all his enemies,* 7–9. *The two last verses exhort to faith and trust in God in the most disconsolate circumstances; with a denunciation of vengeance on those who should trust to their own devices,* 10, 11.

A. M. cir. 3292
B. C. cir. 712
Olymp. XVII. 1
cir. annum
NumæPompilii,
R. Roman., 4

THUS saith the LORD, Where
is [a]the bill of your mother's
divorcement, whom I have put
away? or which of my [b]creditors
is it to whom I have sold you? Behold, for
your iniquities [c]have ye sold yourselves, and
for your transgressions is your mother put
away.
2 Wherefore, when I came, *was there* no
man? [d]when I called, *was there* none to answer? [e]Is my hand shortened at all, that it
cannot redeem? or have I no power to deliver? behold, [f]at my rebuke I [g]dry up the
sea, I make the [h]rivers a wilderness: [i]their
fish stinketh, because *there is* no
water, and dieth for thirst.
3 [k]I clothe the heavens with
blackness, [l]and I make sackcloth
their covering.
4 [m]The Lord GOD hath given me the tongue
of the learned, that I should know how to
speak a word in season to *him that is* [n]weary:
he wakeneth morning by morning, he wakeneth mine ear to hear as the learned.
5 The Lord GOD [o]hath opened mine ear,
and I was not [p]rebellious, neither turned
away back.
6 [q]I gave my back to the smiters, and [r]my

A. M. cir. 3292
B. C. cir. 712
Olymp. XVII. 1
cir. annum
NumæPompilii,
R. Roman., 4

[a]Deut. xxiv. 1; Jer. iii. 8; Hos. ii. 2——[b]See 2 Kings iv. 1; Matt. xviii. 25——[c]Chap. lii. 3——[d]Prov. i. 24; chap. lxv. 12; lxvi. 4; Jer. vii. 13; xxxv. 15——[e]Num. xi. 23; chap. lix. 1——[f]Psa. cvi. 9; Nah. i. 4——[g]Exod. xiv. 21——[h]Josh. iii. 16

[i]Exod. vii. 18, 21——[k]Exod. x. 21——[l]Rev. vi. 12——[m]Exod. iv. 11——[n]Matt. xi. 28——[o]Psa. xl. 6, 7, 8——[p]Matt. xxvi. 39; John xiv. 31; Phil. ii. 8; Heb. x. 5, &c.——[q]Matt. xxvi. 67; xxvii. 26; John xviii. 22——[r]Lam. iii. 30

NOTES ON CHAP. L

Verse 1. *Thus saith the Lord*] This chapter has been understood of the prophet himself; but it certainly speaks more clearly about Jesus of Nazareth than of Isaiah, the son of Amos.

Where is *the bill*—"Where is this bill"] Husbands, through moroseness or levity of temper, often sent bills of divorcement to their wives on slight occasions, as they were permitted to do by the law of Moses, Deut. xxiv. 1. And fathers, being oppressed with debt, often sold their children, which they might do for a time, till the year of release, Exod. xxi. 7. That this was frequently practised, appears from many passages of Scripture, and that the persons and the liberty of the children were answerable for the debts of the father. The widow, 2 Kings iv. 1, complains "that the creditor is come to take unto him her two sons to be bondmen." And in the parable, Matt xviii. 25: "The lord, forasmuch as his servant had not to pay, commands him to be sold, and his wife and children, and all that he had, and payment to be made." Sir John Chardin's MS. note on this place of Isaiah is as follows: En Orient on paye ses dettes avec ses esclaves, car ils sont des principaux meubles; et en plusieurs lieux on les paye aussi de ses enfans. "In the east they pay their debts by giving up their slaves, for these are their chief property of a disposable kind; and in many places they give their children to their creditors." But this, saith God, cannot be my case; I am not governed by any such motives, neither am I urged by any such necessity. Your captivity therefore and your afflictions are to be imputed to yourselves, and to your own folly and wickedness.

Verse 2. *Their fish stinketh*—"Their fish is dried up"] For תבאש *tibaosh, stinketh,* read תיבש *tibash, is dried up;* so it stands in the Bodl. MS., and it is confirmed by the *Septuagint,* ξηρανθησονται, *they shall be dried up.*

Verse 5. *Neither turned away back*—"Neither did I withdraw myself backward"] Eleven MSS. and the oldest edition prefix the conjunction ו *vau;* and so also the *Septuagint* and *Syriac.*

Verse 6. *And my cheeks to them that plucked off the hair*] The greatest indignity that could possibly be offered. See the note on chap. vii. 20.

I hid not my face from shame and spitting.]

A. M. cir. 3292
B. C. cir. 712
Olymp. XVII. 1
cir. annum
NumæPompilii,
R. Roman., 4

cheeks to them that plucked off
the hair: I hid not my face from
shame and spitting.
7 For the Lord GOD will help
me; therefore shall I not be confounded:
therefore have [s]I set my face like a flint, and
I know that I shall not be ashamed.
8 [t]*He is* near that justifieth me; who will
contend with me? let us stand together: who
is [u]mine adversary? let him come near to me.
9 Behold, the Lord GOD will help me; who
is he *that* shall condemn me? [v]lo, they all
shall wax old as a garment;
[w]the moth shall eat them up.
10 Who *is* among you that feareth the LORD, that obeyeth the
voice of his servant, that [x]walketh *in* darkness, and hath no light? [y]let him trust in the
name of the LORD, and stay upon his God.
11 Behold, all ye that kindle a fire, that compass *yourselves* about with sparks: walk in
the light of your fire, and in the sparks *that*
ye have kindled. [z]This shall ye have of mine
hand; ye shall lie down [a]in sorrow.

[s]Ezek. iii. 8, 9——[t]Rom. viii. 32, 33, 34——[u]Heb. *the master of my cause*——[v]Job xiii. 28; Psa. cii. 26; ch. li. 6

[w]Chap. li. 8——[x]Psa. xxiii. 4——[y]2 Chron. xx. 20; Psa. xx. 7——[z]John ix. 19——[a]Psa. xvi. 4

Another instance of the utmost contempt and detestation. It was ordered by the law of Moses as a severe punishment, carrying with it a lasting disgrace; Deut. xxv. 9. Among the Medes it was highly offensive to spit in any one's presence, *Herod.* i. 99; and so likewise among the Persians, *Xenophon*, Cyrop. Lib. i., p. 18.

"They abhor me; they flee far from me;
They forbear not to spit in my face."
Job xxx. 10.

"And JEHOVAH said unto Moses, If her father had but spit in her face, should she not be ashamed seven days?" Num. xxii. 14. On which place Sir John Chardin remarks, that "spitting before any one, or spitting upon the ground in speaking of any one's actions, is through the east an expression of extreme detestation."—*Harmer's* Observ. ii. 509. See also, of the same notions of the Arabs in this respect, *Niebuhr*, Description de l'Arabie, p. 26. It so evidently appears that in those countries spitting has ever been an expression of the utmost detestation, that the learned doubt whether in the passages of Scripture above quoted any thing more is meant than spitting,—not in the face, which perhaps the words do not necessarily imply,—but only in the presence of the person affronted. But in this place it certainly means spitting *in the face;* so it is understood in St. Luke, where our Lord plainly refers to this prophecy: "All things that are written by the prophets concerning the Son of man shall be accomplished; for he shall be delivered to the Gentiles, and shall be mocked and spitefully entreated, and spitted on, εμπτυσθησεται," xviii. 31, 32, which was in fact fulfilled; *και ηρξαντο τινες εμπτυειν αυτῳ*, "and some began to spit on him," Mark xiv. 65, xv. 19. If spitting in a person's presence was such an indignity, how much more spitting in his face?

Verse 7. *Therefore have I set my face like a flint*] The Prophet Ezekiel, chap. ii. 8, 9, has expressed this with great force in his bold and vehement manner:

"Behold, I have made thy face strong against their faces,
And thy forehead strong against their foreheads:
As an adamant, harder than a rock, have I made thy forehead;
Fear them not, neither be dismayed at their looks,
Though they be a rebellious house."

Verse 8. *Who will contend with me*] The Bodleian MS. and another add the word הוא *hu;* מי הוא יריב *mi hu yarib*, as in the like phrase in the next verse; and in the very same phrase Job xiii. 19, and so likewise in many other places, Job xvii. 3, xli. 1. Sometimes on the like occasions it is מי זה *mi zeh*, and מי הוא זה *mi hu zeh*, "Who is this one?" The word has probably been lost out of the present text; and the reading of the MSS. above mentioned seems to be genuine.

Verse 10. *Who is among you that feareth the Lord*] I believe this passage has been generally, if not *dangerously*, misunderstood. It has been *quoted*, and *preached upon*, to prove that "a man might conscientiously fear God, and be obedient to the words of the law and the prophets; *obey the voice of his servant*—of Jesus Christ himself, that is, be sincerely and regularly obedient to the moral law and the commands of our blessed Lord, and yet *walk in darkness* and *have no light*, no sense of God's approbation, and no evidence of the safety of his state." This is utterly impossible; for Jesus hath said, "He that followeth me shall not walk in darkness, but shall have the light of life." If there be some religious persons who, under the influence of morbid melancholy, are continually writing bitter things against themselves, the word of God should not be bent down to their state. There are other modes of spiritual and Scriptural comfort. But does not the text speak of such a case? And are not the words precise in reference to it? I think not: and Bishop Lowth's translation has set the whole in the clearest light, though he does not appear to have been apprehensive that the *bad use* I mention had been made of the text as it stands in our common Version. The text contains *two questions*, to each of which a particular answer is given:—

Q. 1. "Who is there among you that feareth JEHOVAH?
Ans. *Let him hearken unto the voice of his servant.*
Q. 2. *Who* that walketh in darkness and hath no light?
Ans. *Let him trust in the name of Jehovah;*
And lean himself (prop himself) *upon his God.*"

Now, a man awakened to a sense of his sin and misery, may have a *dread of* JEHOVAH, and *tremble at his word;* and what should such a person do? Why he should hear what God's servant saith: "Come unto me, all ye who labour and are heavy laden; and I will give you rest." There may be a sincere *penitent*, walking in darkness, having no light of salvation; for this is the case of all when they first begin to turn to God. What should such do? They should *trust, believe on, the Lord Jesus*, who died for them, and *lean upon* his all-sufficient merits for the light of salvation which God has promised. Thus acting, they will soon have a sure trust and confidence that God for Christ's sake has forgiven them their sin, and thus they shall have the light of life.

Verse 10. *That obeyeth the voice of his servant*—"Let him hearken unto the voice of his servant"] For שמע *shomea*, pointed as the participle, the *Septuagint* and *Syriac* read ישמע *yishma*, future or imperative. This gives a much more elegant turn and distribution to the sentence.

Verse 11. *Ye that kindle a fire*] The fire of their own kindling, by the light of which they walk with security and satisfaction, is an image designed to express, in general, human devices and mere worldly policy, exclusive of faith, and trust in God; which, though they flatter themselves for a while with pleasing expectations and some appearance of success, shall in the end turn to the confusion of the authors. Or more particularly, as Vitringa explains it, it may mean the designs of the turbulent and factious Jews in the times succeeding those of Christ, who, in pursuit of their own desperate schemes, stirred up the war against the Romans, and kindled a fire which consumed their city and nation.

That compass yourselves *about with sparks*—"Who heap the fuel round about"] "מגוזלי *megozeley, accendentes, Syr.; forte legerunt pro* מאזרי *meazzerey* מאירי *meirey; nam sequitur* אור *ur.*"—*Secker*. Lud. Capellus, in his criticism on this place, thinks it should be מאזרי *meazzerey*, from the *Septuagint*, κατισχυοντες.

There are others who are widely different from those already described. Without faith, repentance, or a holy life, they are bold in their professed confidence in God—presumptuous in their trust in the mercy of God; and, while destitute of all preparation for and right to the kingdom of heaven, would think it criminal to doubt their final salvation! Living in this way, what can they have at the hand of God but an endless bed of sorrow! *Ye shall lie down in sorrow.*

But there is a general sense, and accordant to the design of the prophecy, in which these words may be understood and paraphrased: *Behold, all ye that kindle a fire*—provoke war and contention; *compass yourselves about with sparks*—stirring up seditions and rebellions: *walk in the light of your fire*—go on in your lust of power and restless ambition. *Ye shall lie down in sorrow*—it will turn to your own perdition. See the *Targum.* This seems to refer to the restless spirit of the Jews, always stirring up confusion and strife; rebelling against and provoking the Romans, till at last their city was taken, their temple burnt to the ground, and upwards of a million of themselves destroyed, and the rest led into captivity!

CHAPTER LI

The prophet exhorts the children of Abraham to trust in the Lord; and briefly, but beautifully, describes the great blessedness which should be the consequence, 1–3. *Then, turning to the Gentiles, encourages them to look for a portion in the same salvation,* 4, 5; *the everlasting duration of which is majestically described,* 6. *And as it is everlasting, so is it sure to the righteous, notwithstanding all the machinations of their enemies,* 7, 8. *The faithful, then, with exultation and joy, lift their voices, reminding God of his wondrous works of old, which encourage them to look now for the like glorious accomplishment of these promises,* 9–11. *In answer to this the Divinity is introduced comforting them under their trials, and telling them that the deliverer was already on his way to save and to establish them,* 12–16. *On this the prophet turns to Jerusalem to comfort and congratulate her on so joyful a prospect. She is represented, by a bold image, as a person lying in the streets, under the intoxicating effects of the cup of the Divine wrath, without a single person from among her own people appointed to give her consolation, and trodden under the feet of her enemies; but, in the time allotted by the Divine providence,* the cup of trembling *shall be taken out of her hand, and put into that of her oppressors; and she shall drink it no more again for ever,* 17–22.

A. M. cir. 3292 B. C. cir. 712 Olymp. XVII. 1 cir. annum NumæPompilii, R. Roman., 4

HEARKEN [a]to me, [b]ye that
follow after righteousness,
ye that seek the LORD: look
unto the rock *whence* ye are
hewn, and to the hole of the pit *whence* ye
are digged.

2 [c]Look unto Abraham your
father, and unto Sarah *that* bare
you: [d]for I called him alone,
and [e]blessed him, and increased him.

A. M. cir. 3292 B. C. cir. 712 Olymp. XVII. 1 cir. annum NumæPompilii, R. Roman., 4

3 For the LORD [f]shall comfort Zion: he

[a]Ver. 7——[b]Rom. ix. 30, 31, 32——[c]Rom. iv. 1, 16; Heb. xi. 11, 12——[d]Gen. xii. 1, 2

[e]Gen. xxiv. 1, 35——[f]Psa. cii. 13; chap. xl. 1; lii. 9; lxi. 2; lxvi. 13; Zech. i. 17; ver. 12

NOTES ON CHAP. LI

Verse 1. *Ye that follow after righteousness*] The people who, feeling the want of salvation, seek the Lord in order to be justified.

The rock] Abraham.

The hole of the pit] Sarah; as explained in ver. 2.

Verse 2. *I called him alone*] As I have made out of one a great nation; so, although ye are

A. M. cir. 3292
B. C. cir. 712
Olymp. XVII. 1
cir. annum
NumæPompilii,
R. Roman., 4

will comfort all her waste places; and he will make her wilderness like Eden, and her desert [g]like the garden of the LORD: joy and gladness shall be found therein, thanksgiving and the voice of melody.

4 Hearken unto me, my people; and give ear unto me, O my nation: [h]for a law shall proceed from me, and I will make my judgment to rest [i]for a light of the people.

5 [k]My righteousness *is* near; my salvation is gone forth, [l]and mine arms shall judge the people: [m]the isles shall wait upon me, and [n]on mine arm shall they trust.

6 [o]Lift up your eyes to the heavens, and look upon the earth beneath: for [p]the heavens shall vanish away like smoke, [q]and the earth shall wax old like a garment, and they that dwell therein shall die in like manner: but my salvation shall be for ever, and my righteousness shall not be abolished.

7 [r]Hearken unto me, ye that know righteousness, the people [s]in whose heart *is* my law; [t]fear ye not the reproach of men, neither be ye afraid of their revilings.

8 For [u]the moth shall eat them up like a garment, and the worm shall eat them like wool: but my righteousness shall be for ever, and my salvation from generation to generation.

A. M. cir. 3292
B. C. cir. 712
Olymp. XVII. 1
cir. annum
NumæPompilii,
R. Roman., 4

9 [v]Awake, awake, [w]put on strength, O arm of the LORD; awake, [x]as in the ancient days, in the generations of old. [y]*Art* thou not it that hath cut [z]Rahab, *and* wounded the [a]dragon?

10 *Art* thou not it which hath [b]dried the sea, the waters of the great deep; that hath made the depths of the sea a way for the ransomed to pass over?

11 Therefore [c]the redeemed of the LORD shall return, and come with singing unto Zion; and everlasting joy *shall be* upon their head: they shall obtain gladness and joy: *and* sorrow and mourning shall flee away.

12 I, *even* I, *am* he [d]that comforteth you: who *art* thou, that thou shouldest be afraid [e]of a man *that* shall die, and of the son of man *which* shall be made [f]*as* grass;

13 And forgettest the LORD thy Maker, [g]that hath stretched forth the heavens, and laid the

[g]Gen. xiii. 10; Joel ii. 3——[h]Ch. ii. 3; xlii. 4——[i]Ch. xlii. 6——[k]Ch. xlvi. 13; lvi. 1; Rom. i. 16, 17——[l]Psa. lxvii. 4; xcviii. 9——[m]Ch. lx. 9——[n]Rom. i. 16——[o]Ch. xl. 26——[p]Psa. cii. 26; Matt. xxiv. 35; 2 Pet. iii. 10, 12 [q]Ch. l. 9——[r]Ver. 1——[s]Psa. xxxvii. 31——[t]Matt. x. 28; Acts v. 41——[u]Ch. l. 9——[v]Psa. xliv. 23; ch. lii. 1

[w]Psa. xciii. 1; Rev. xi. 17——[x]Psa. xliv. 1——[y]Job xxvi. 12——[z]Psa. lxxxvii. 4; lxxxix. 10——[a]Psa. lxxiv. 13, 14; ch. xxvii. 1; Ezek. xxix. 3——[b]Exod. xiv. 21; ch. xliii. 16——[c]Ch. xxxv. 10——[d]Ver. 3; 2 Cor. i. 3 [e]Psa. cxviii. 6——[f]Ch. xl. 6; 1 Pet. i. 24——[g]Job ix. 8; Psa. civ. 2; ch. xl. 22; xlii. 5; xliv. 24

brought low and minished, yet I can restore you to happiness, and greatly multiply your number.

Verse 4. *My people—O my nation*—"O ye peoples—O ye nations"] For עמי *ammi, my people*, the Bodleian MS. and another read עמים *ammim, ye peoples;* and for לאומי *leumi, my nation*, the Bodleian MS. and *eight* others, (*two* of them ancient,) and *four* of *De Rossi's*, read לאמים *leummim, ye nations;* and so the *Syriac* in both words. The difference is very material; for in this case the address is made, not to the Jews, but to the Gentiles, as in all reason it ought to be; for this and the two following verses express the call of the Gentiles, the islands, or the distant lands on the coasts of the Mediterranean and other seas. It is also to be observed that God in no other place calls his people לאמי *leummi, my nation.* It has been before remarked that transcribers frequently omitted the final ם *mem* of nouns plural, and supplied it, for brevity's sake, and sometimes for want of room at the end of a line, by a small stroke thus עמי/; which mark, being effaced or overlooked, has been the occasion of many mistakes of this kind.

A law shall proceed from me] The new law, the Gospel of our Lord Jesus. *Kimchi* says, "After the war with Gog and Magog the King Messiah will teach the people to walk in the ways of the Lord."

Verse 5. *My righteousness* is *near*] The word צדק *tsedek, righteousness*, is used in such a great latitude of signification, for justice, truth, faithfulness, goodness, mercy, deliverance, salvation, &c., that it is not easy sometimes to give the precise meaning of it without much circumlocution; it means here the faithful completion of God's promises to deliver his people.

Verse 6. *My salvation shall be for ever*] Aben Ezra says, From this verse divines have learnt the immortality of the soul. Men shall perish as the earth does, because they are formed from it; but they who are filled with the salvation of God shall remain for ever. See *Kimchi*.

Verse 11. *They shall obtain gladness and joy;* and *sorrow and mourning shall flee away.*] *Nineteen* MSS. and the *two* oldest editions have ישגו *yasigu;* and *forty-six* MSS. of *Kennicott's* and *ten* of *De Rossi's*, and the same *two* editions, and agreeably to them the *Chaldee* and *Syriac*, have ונסו *venasu;* and so both words are expressed, chap. xxxv. 10, of which place this is a repetition. And from comparing both together it appears that the ו *vau* in this place is become by mistake in the present text final ן *nun* of the preceding word.

Verse 13. *Of the oppressor, as if he, &c.*]

A. M. cir. 3292
B. C. cir. 712
Olymp. XVII. 1
cir. annum
NumæPompilii,
R. Roman., 4

foundations of the earth; and hast feared continually every day because of the fury of the oppressor, as if he [h]were ready to destroy? [i]and where *is* the fury of the oppressor?

14 The captive exile hasteneth that he may be loosed, [k]and that he should not die in the pit, nor that his bread should fail.

15 But I *am* the LORD thy God, that [l]divided the sea, whose waves roared: The LORD of hosts *is* his name.

16 And [m]I have put my words in thy mouth, and [n]I have covered thee in the shadow of mine hand, [o]that I may plant the heavens, and lay the foundations of the earth, and say unto Zion, Thou *art* my people.

17 [p]Awake, awake, stand up, O Jerusalem, which [q]hast drunk at the hand of the LORD the cup of his fury; [r]thou hast drunken the dregs of the cup of trembling, *and* wrung *them* out.

A. M. cir. 3292
B. C. cir. 712
Olymp. XVII. 1
cir. annum
NumæPompilii,
R. Roman., 4

18 *There is* none to guide her among all the sons *whom* she hath brought forth; neither *is there any* that taketh her by the hand of all the sons *that* she hath brought up.

19 [s]These two *things* [t]are come unto thee; who shall be sorry for thee? desolation, and [u]destruction, and the famine, and the sword: [v]by whom shall I comfort thee?

20 [w]Thy sons have fainted, they lie at the head of all the streets, as a wild bull in a net: they are full of the fury of the LORD, the rebuke of thy God.

21 Therefore hear now this, thou afflicted, and drunken, [x]but not with wine.

---

[h]Or, *made* himself *ready*——[i]Job xx. 7——[k]Zech. ix. 11——[l]Psa. lxxiv. 13; Job xxvi. 12; Jer. xxxi. 35 [m]Deut. xviii. 18; chap. lix. 21; John iii. 34——[n]Chap. xlix. 2——[o]Chap. lxv. 17; lxvi. 22——[p]Chap. lii. 1 [q]Job xxi. 20; Jer. xxi. 15, 16

[r]See Deut. xxviii. 28, 34; Psa. lx. 3; lxxv. 8; Ezek. xxiii. 32, 33, 34; Zech. xii. 2; Rev. xiv. 10——[s]Chap. xlvii. 9——[t]Hebrew, *happened*——[u]Hebrew, *breaking*——[v]Amos vii. 2——[w]Lam. ii. 11, 12——[x]See ver. 17; Lam. iii. 15

"The כ *caph* in כאשר *keasher* seems clearly to have changed its situation from the end of the preceding word to the beginning of this; or rather, to have been omitted by mistake there, because it was here. That it was there the *Septuagint* show by rendering המציקך *hammetsikech* θλιβοντος σε, *of him that oppressed* thee. And so they render this word in both its places in this verse. The *Vulgate* also has the pronoun in the first instance; *furoris ejus qui* te *tribulabat*." Dr. *Jubb*. The correction seems well founded; I have not conformed the translation to it, because it makes little difference in the sense.

Verse 14. *The captive exile hasteneth that he may be loosed*—"He marcheth on with speed, who cometh to set free the captive"] Cyrus, if understood of the temporal redemption from the captivity of Babylon; in the spiritual sense, the Messiah, who comes to open the prison to them that are bound.

Verse 16. *That I may plant the heavens*—"To stretch out the heavens"] In the present text it is לנטע *lintoa, "to plant* the heavens:" the phrase is certainly very obscure, and in all probability is a mistake for לנטות *lintoth*. This latter is the word used in ver. 13 just before, in the very same sentence; and this phrase occurs very frequently in Isaiah, chap. xl. 22, xlii. 5, xliv. 24, xlv. 12; the former in no other place. It is also very remarkable, that in the Samaritan text, Num. xxiv. 6, these two words are twice changed by mistake, one for the other, in the same verse.

Verse 17. *The cup of trembling*] כוס התרעלה *cos hattarelah*, "the cup of mortal poison," veneni mortiferi.—MONTAN. This may also allude to the ancient custom of taking off criminals by a cup of poison. Socrates is well known to have been sentenced by the Areopagus to drink a cup of the juice of hemlock, which occasioned his death. See the note on Heb. ii. 9, and see also Bishop Lowth's note on ver. 21.

Verse 19. *These two* things—*desolation, and destruction, and the famine, and the sword*] That is, desolation by famine, and destruction by the sword, taking the terms alternately: of which form of construction see other examples. *De S. Poësi*, Heb. Præl. xix., and Prelim. Dissert. p. xxx. The *Chaldee* paraphrast, not rightly understanding this, has had recourse to the following expedient: "Two afflictions are come upon thee, and when *four* shall come upon thee, *depredation*, and *destruction*, and the *famine*, and the *sword*—" Five MSS. have הרעב *haraab*, without the conjunction ו *vau;* and so the *Septuagint* and *Syriac*.

By whom shall I comfort thee—"Who shall comfort thee"] A MS., the *Septuagint*, *Syriac*, *Chaldee*, and *Vulgate* have it in the third person, ינחמך *yenachamech*, which is evidently right.

Verse 20. *As a wild bull in a net: they are full, &c.*—"Like the oryx taken in the toils; drenched to the full"] "Perhaps מכמרה מלאים *michmerah meleim*." SECKER. The demonstrative ה *he*, prefixed to מלאים *meleim, full*, seems improper in this place.

Verse 21. *Drunken, but not with wine*] *Æschylus* has the same expression:—

Αοινοις εμμανεις θυμωμασι· *Eumen.* 863.

Intoxicated with passion, not with wine.

Schultens thinks that this circumlocution, as he calls it, gradum adfert incomparabiliter majorem; and that it means, not simply *without wine*, but *much more than with wine*. *Gram. Heb.* p. 182. See his note on Job xxx. 38.

The bold image of the cup of God's wrath, often employed by the sacred writers, (see note

A. M. cir. 3292 B. C. cir. 712 Olymp. XVII. 1 cir. annum NumæPompilii, R. Roman., 4

22 Thus saith thy Lord the
LORD, and thy God [y]*that* pleadeth
the cause of his people, Behold I
have taken out of thine hand the
cup of trembling, *even* the dregs of the cup of
my fury; thou shalt no more drink it again:

23 But [z]I will put it into the
hand of them that afflict thee;
which have [a]said to thy soul,
Bow down, that we may go over:
and thou hast laid thy body as the ground,
and as the street, to them that went over.

[y]Jer. l. 34——[z]Jer. xxv. 17, 26, 28; Zech. xii. 2

[a]Psa. lxvi. 11, 12

on chap. i. 22,) is nowhere handled with greater force and sublimity than in this passage of Isaiah, ver. 17-23. Jerusalem is represented in person as staggering under the effects of it, destitute of that assistance which she might expect from her children; not one of them being able to support or to lead her. They, abject and amazed, lie at the head of every street, overwhelmed with the greatness of their distress; like the oryx entangled in a net, in vain struggling to rend it, and extricate himself. This is poetry of the first order, sublimity of the highest character.

Plato had an idea something like this: "Suppose," says he, "God had given to men a medicating potion inducing fear, so that the more any one should drink of it, so much the more miserable he should find himself at every draught, and become fearful of every thing both present and future; and at last, though the most courageous of men, should be totally possessed by fear: and afterwards, having slept off the effects of it, should become himself again." *De Leg.* i., near the end. He pursues at large this hypothesis, applying it to his own purpose, which has no relation to the present subject. *Homer* places two vessels at the disposal of Jupiter, one of good, the other of evil. He gives to some a potion mixed of both; to others from the evil vessel only: these are completely miserable. Iliad xxiv. 527-533.

Δοιοι γαρ τε πιθοι κατακειαται εν Διος ουδει
Δωρων, οἱα διδωσι, κακων, ἑτερος δε εαων.
Ὡ μεν καμμιξας δῳη Ζευς τερπικεραυνος,
Αλλοτε μεν τε κακῳ ὁγε κυρεται, αλλοτε δ' εσθλῳ·
Ὡ δε κε των λυγρων δῳη, λωβητον εθηκε.
Και ἑ κακη βουβρωστις επι χθονα διαν ελαυνει·
Φοιτᾳ δ' ουτε θεοισι τετιμενος, ουτι βροτοισιν.

"*Two urns* by Jove's high throne have ever stood,
The source of *evil* one, and one of *good;*
From thence the cup of mortal man he fills,
Blessings to *these*, to *those* distributes *ills;*
To most he *mingles both:* the wretch decreed
To taste the *bad unmixed*, is cursed indeed:
Pursued by wrongs, by meagre famine driven,
He wanders outcast both of earth and heaven."

POPE.

Verse 23. *Them that afflict thee*—"Them who oppress thee"] The *Septuagint, Chaldee, Syriac*, and *Vulgate* appear to have read מוניך *monayich*, as in chap. xl. 26."—SECKER.

Which have said to thy soul, Bow down—"Who say to thee, Bow down thy body"] A very strong and most expressive description of the insolent pride of eastern conquerors; which, though it may seem greatly exaggerated, yet hardly exceeds the strict truth. An example has already been given of it in the note to chap. xlix. 23. I will here add one or two more. "Joshua called for all the men of Israel; and said unto the captains of the men of war that went with him, Come near, put your feet upon the necks of these kings," Josh. x. 24. "Adonibezek said, Threescore and ten kings, having their thumbs and their great toes cut off, gathered their meat under my table: As I have done, so hath God requited me," Judg. i. 7. The Emperor Valerianus, being through treachery taken prisoner by Sapor king of Persia, was treated by him as the basest and most abject slave: for the Persian monarch commanded the unhappy Roman to bow himself down, and offer him his back, on which he set his foot, in order to mount his chariot or horse, whenever he had occasion.—LACTANTIUS, *De Mort. Persec.* cap. v. AUREL. VICTOR. *Epitome*, cap. xxxii.—L.

CHAPTER LII

Jerusalem, in manifest allusion to the strong figure employed in the close of the preceding chapter, is represented as fallen asleep in the dust, and in that helpless state bound by her enemies. The prophet, with all the ardour natural to one who had such joyful news to communicate, bids her awake, arise, put on her best attire, (holiness to the Lord,) and ascend her lofty seat; and then he delivers the message he had in charge, a very consolatory part of which was, that "no more should enter into her the uncircumcised and the polluted," 1–6. Awaking from her stupefaction, Jerusalem sees the messenger *of such joyful tidings on the eminence from which he spied the coming deliverance. She expresses, in beautiful terms, her joy at the news, repeating with peculiar elegance the words of the crier, 7. The rapturous intelligence, that Jehovah was returning to resume his residence on his holy mountain, immediately spreads to others on the watch, who all join in the glad acclamation, 8; and, in the ardour of their joy, they call to the very ruins of Jerusalem to sing along with them, because Jehovah maketh bare his holy arm in the sight of all the nations, and all the ends of the earth are about to see the salvation of Israel's God, 9, 10. To complete the deliverance, they are commanded to march in triumph out of Babylon, earnestly exhorted to have nothing to do with any of her abominations, and assured that Jehovah will guide them in all their way, 11, 12. The prophet then passes to the procuring cause of this great blessedness to the house of Israel in particular, and to the world in general, viz., the humiliation, sufferings, death, burial, resurrection, and ascension of Jesus Christ; a very celebrated and clear prophecy, which takes up the remainder of this and the whole of the following chapter.*

A. M. cir. 3292 B. C. cir. 712 Olymp. XVII. 1 cir. annum NumæPompilii, R. Roman., 4

AWAKE, [a]awake; put on thy
strength, O Zion; put on thy
beautiful garments, O Jerusalem, [b]the holy city: for [c]hence-
forth there shall no more come into thee the
uncircumcised [d]and the unclean.
2 [e]Shake thyself from the dust; arise, *and*
sit down, O Jerusalem: [f]loose thyself from the
bands of thy neck, O captive daughter of Zion.
3 For thus saith the LORD, [g]ye have sold
yourselves for nought; and ye shall be redeemed without money.
4 For thus saith the Lord GOD,
My people went down aforetime
into [h]Egypt to sojourn there;
and the Assyrian oppressed them
without cause.
5 Now therefore, what have I here, saith the
LORD, that my people is taken away for
nought? they that rule over them make them
to howl, saith the LORD; and my name continually every day *is* [i]blasphemed.
6 Therefore my people shall know my name:
therefore *they shall know* in that day that I

[a]Chap. li. 9, 17——[b]Neh. xi. 1; chap. xlviii. 2; Matt. iv. 5; Rev. xxi. 2——[c]Chap. xxxv. 8; lx. 21; Nah. i. 15 [d]Rev. xxi. 27——[e]See chap. iii. 26; li. 23

[f]Zech. ii. 7——[g]Psa. xliv. 12; chap. xlv. 13; Jer. xv. 13——[h]Gen. xlvi. 6; Acts vii. 14——[i]Ezek. xx. 27; Rom. ii. 24

NOTES ON CHAP. LII

Verse 1. *There shall no more come into thee*—For יבא *yabo*, "shall come," לבא *lebo*, "to come," is the reading of *five* of *Kennicott's* and *two* of *De Rossi's* MSS. This is the better reading, כי לא יוסיף לבא *ki lo yosiph lebo*, "There shall not add to come."

The uncircumcised and the unclean.] Christians have turned many passages of the prophets against the Jews; and it is not to be wondered at, that in support of their obstinate and hopeless cause, they should press a prophecy into their service, and make it speak against the Christians. This *Kimchi* does in this place; for he says, by the uncircumcised, the *Christians* are meant; and by the unclean, the *Turks*. The *Christians* are *uncircumcised;* and the *Turks*, though circumcised, and using many ablutions, are *unclean* in their works.

Verse 2. *Sit down, O Jerusalem*—"Ascend thy lofty seat, O Jerusalem"] The literal rendering here is, according to our English translation, "arise, sit;" on which a very learned person remarks: "So the old versions. But sitting is an expression of mourning in Scripture and the ancients; and doth not well agree with the rising just before." It does not indeed agree, according to our ideas; but, considered in an oriental light, it is perfectly consistent. The common manner of sitting in the eastern countries is upon the ground or the floor with the legs crossed. The people of better condition have the floors of their chambers or divans covered with carpets for this purpose; and round the chamber broad couches, raised a little above the floor, spread with mattresses handsomely covered, which are called sofas. When sitting is spoken of as a posture of more than ordinary state, it is quite of a different kind; and means sitting on high, on a chair of state or throne called the *musnud;* for which a footstool was necessary, both in order that the person might raise himself up to it, and for supporting the legs when he was placed in it. "Chairs," says Sir *John Chardin*, "are never used in Persia, but at the coronation of their kings. The king is seated in a chair of gold set with jewels, three feet high. The chairs which are used by the people in the east are always so high as to make a footstool necessary. And this proves the propriety of the style of Scripture, which always joins the footstool to the throne." (Isa. lxvi. 1; Psa. cx. 1.) *Voyages*, tom. ix. p. 85, 12mo. Besides the six steps to Solomon's throne, there was a footstool of gold fastened to the seat, 2 Chron. ix. 18, which would otherwise have been too high for the king to reach, or to sit on conveniently.

When Thetis comes to wait on Vulcan to request armour for her son, she is received with great respect, and seated on a silver-studded throne, a chair of ceremony, with a footstool:—

> Την μεν επειτα καθεισεν επι θρονου αργυροηλου,
> Καλου, δαιδαλεου· ὑπο δε θρηνυς ποσιν ηεν.
> *Iliad* xviii. 389.

> "High on a throne, with stars of silver graced,
> And various artifice, the queen she placed;
> A footstool at her feet." POPE.

Ὁ γαρ θρονος αυτος μονον ελευθεριος εστι καθεδρα συν ὑποποδιῳ. *Athenæus*, v. 4. "A throne is nothing more than a handsome sort of chair with a footstool."—L.

Verse 4. *Thus saith the Lord God*] אדני יהוה *Adonai Yehovah;* but *Adonai* is wanting in *twelve* of *Kennicott's*, *five* of *De Rossi's*, and two of my own MSS.; and by the *Septuagint* and *Arabic*. Some MSS. have יהוה צבאות *Yehovah tsebaoth*, "Lord of hosts;" and others have יהוה אלהים *Yehovah Elohim*, "Lord God."

Verse 5. *They that rule over them*—"They that are lords over them"] For משלו *moshelo*, singular, in the text, more than a hundred and twenty MSS. (*De Rossi* says, codices innumeri, "numberless copies") have משליו *moshelaiv*, plural, according to the Masoretical correction in the margin; which shows that the Masoretes often superstitiously retained apparent mistakes in the text, even when they had sufficient evidence to authorize the introduction of the true reading.

Make them to howl—"Make their boast of it"] For יהילילו *yeheililu*, "make them to howl," five MSS., (two ancient,) have יהללו *yehalelu*, "make their boast;" which is confirmed by the *Chaldee* paraphrast, *who renders it* משתבחין *mishtabbechin*. *Ulaloo* is not only the cry itself, but also the name of the funeral song of the *Irish*. The *Arabs* have a cry very much resembling this.

Verse 6. *Therefore my people shall know*]

A. M. cir. 3292 B. C. cir. 712 Olymp. XVII. 1 cir. annum NumæPompilii, R. Roman., 4

am he that doth speak: behold, *it is* I.

7 [k]How beautiful upon the
mountains are the feet of him that bringeth good tidings, that publisheth peace; that bringeth good tidings of good, that publisheth salvation; that saith unto Zion, [l]Thy God reigneth!

8 Thy watchmen shall lift up
the voice; with the voice together shall they sing: for they shall see eye to eye, when the LORD shall bring again Zion.

9 Break forth into joy, sing together, ye waste places of Jerusalem: [m]for the LORD hath comforted his people, [n]he hath redeemed Jerusalem.

[k]Nah. i. 15; Rom. x. 15——[l]Psa. xciii. 1; xcvi. 10; xcvii. 1——[m]Chap. li. 3——[n]Chap. xlviii. 20

The word לכן *lachen*, occurring the second time in this verse, seems to be repeated by mistake. It has no force nor emphasis as a repetition; it only embarrasses the construction and the sense. It was not in the copies from which the *Septuagint*, *Syriac*, and *Vulgate* were translated; it was not in the copy of the *Septuagint* from which the *Arabic* was translated; but in the *Aldine* and *Complutensian* editions *δια τουτο* is repeated; probably so corrected, in order to make it conformable with the Hebrew text.

I am he that doth speak—"I am he, JEHOVAH, that promised"] For הוא *hu*, the Bodleian MS. and another have יהוה *Yehovah;* "For I am JEHOVAH that promised;" and another ancient MS. adds יהוה *Yehovah* after הוא *hu*. The addition of JEHOVAH seems to be right in consequence of what was said in the preceding line, "My people shall know my *name*."

Verse 7. *How beautiful*] The watchmen discover afar off, on the mountains, the messenger bringing the expected and much-wished-for news of the deliverance from the Babylonish captivity. They immediately spread the joyful tidings, ver. 8, and with a loud voice proclaim that JEHOVAH is returning to Zion, to resume his residence on his holy mountain, which for some time he seemed to have deserted. This is the *literal* sense of the place.

"How beautiful on the mountains are the feet of the joyful messenger," is an expression highly poetical: for, how welcome is his arrival! how agreeable are the tidings which he brings!

Nahum, chap. i. 15, who is generally supposed to have lived after Isaiah, has manifestly taken from him this very pleasing image; but the imitation does not equal the beauty of the original:—

"Behold upon the mountain the feet of the joyful messenger,
Of him that announceth peace!
Celebrate, O Judah, thy festivals; perform thy vows:
For no more shall pass through thee the wicked one;
He is utterly cut off."

But it must at the same time be observed that Isaiah's subject is infinitely more interesting and more sublime than that of Nahum; the latter denounces the destruction of the capital of the Assyrian empire, the most formidable enemy of Judah; the ideas of the former are in their full extent evangelical; and accordingly St. Paul has, with the utmost propriety, applied this passage to the preaching of the Gospel, Rom. x. 15. The joyful tidings here to be proclaimed, "Thy God, O Zion, reigneth," are the same that John the Baptist, the messenger of Christ, and Christ himself, published: "The kingdom of heaven is at hand."

From the use made of this by our Lord and the apostles, we may rest assured that the preachers of the Gospel are particularly intended. *Mountains* are put for the whole land of Judea, where the Gospel was first preached. There seems to be an allusion to a battle fought, and the messengers coming to announce the victory, which was so decisive that a *peace* was the consequence, and the king's throne established in the land.

There appear to have been two sorts of *messengers* among the Jews: one sort always employed to bring evil tidings; the other to bring good. The names also and persons of these different messengers appear to have been well known; so that at a distance they could tell, from seeing the messenger, what sort of tidings he was bringing. See a case in point, 2 Sam. xviii. 19-27. Ahimaaz and Cushi running to bring tidings of the defeat of Absalom and his rebel army. *Ahimaaz is a* GOOD *man, and bringeth* GOOD *tidings*.

Verse 8. *Thy watchmen lift up the voice*—"All thy watchmen lift up their voice"] There is a difficulty in the construction of this place which, I think, none of the ancient versions or modern interpreters have cleared up satisfactorily. Rendered word for word it stands thus: "The voice of thy watchmen: they lift up their voice." The sense of the first member, considered as elliptical, is variously supplied by various expositors; by none, as it seems to me, in any way that is easy and natural. I am persuaded there is a mistake in the present text, and that the true reading is כל צפיך *col tsophayich, all thy watchmen*, instead of קול צפיך *kol tsophayich, the voice of thy watchmen*. The mistake was easy from the similitude in sound of the two letters כ *caph* and ק *koph*. And in one MS. the ק *koph* is upon a rasure. This correction perfectly rectifies the sense and the construction.—L.

They shall see eye to eye] May not this be applied to the prophets and apostles; the one predicting, and the other discovering in the prediction the truth of the prophecy. The meaning of both Testaments is best understood by bringing them *face to face*.

When the Lord shall bring again Zion—"When JEHOVAH returneth to Zion"] So the *Chaldee:* כד יתיב שכנתיה לציון *cad yethib shechinteih letsiyon*, "when he shall place the shechinah in Zion." God is considered as having deserted his people during the captivity; and at the restoration, as returning himself with them to Zion, his former habitation. See Psa. lx. 1; Isa. xl. 9, and note.

Verse 9. *He hath redeemed Jerusalem*—"He

A. M. cir. 3292
B. C. cir. 712
Olymp. XVII. 1
cir. annum
NumæPompilii,
R. Roman., 4

10 [o]The LORD hath made bare
his holy arm in the eyes of all
the nations; and [p]all the ends
of the earth shall see the salvation of our God.
11 [q]Depart ye, depart ye, go ye out from
thence, touch no unclean *thing;* go ye out
of the midst of her; [r]be ye clean,
that bear the vessels of the LORD.
12 For [s]ye shall not go out
with haste, nor go by flight: [t]for
the LORD will go before you; and [u]the God
of Israel *will* [v]*be* your rereward.
13 Behold, [w]my servant shall [x]deal pru-

A. M. cir. 3292
B. C. cir. 712
Olymp. XVII. 1
cir. annum
NumæPompilii,
R. Roman., 4

[o]Psa. xcviii. 2, 3——[p]Luke iii. 6——[q]Chap. xlviii. 20; Jer. l. 8; li. 6, 45; Zech. ii. 6, 7; 2 Cor. vi. 17; Rev. xviii. 4——[r]Lev. xxii. 2, &c.——[s]See Exod. xii. 33, 39

[t]Mic. ii. 13——[u]Num. x. 25; chap. lviii. 8; see Exod. xiv. 19——[v]Heb. *gather you up*——[w]Chap. xlii. 1——[x]Or, *prosper;* chap. liii. 10; Jer. xxiii. 5

hath redeemed Israel."] For the word ירושלם *yerushalaim*, which occurs the second time in this verse, MS. Bodleian and another read ישראל *yisrael.* It is upon a rasure in a third; and left unpointed at first, as suspected, in a fourth. It was an easy mistake, by the transcriber casting his eye on the line above: and the propriety of the correction, both in regard to sense and elegance, is evident.

Verse 11. *Depart ye, depart ye, go ye out from thence*] The Prophet Jeremiah seems to have had his eye on this passage of Isaiah, and to have applied it to a subject directly opposite. It is here addressed by the prophet in a way of encouragement and exhortation to the Jews coming out of Babylon. Jeremiah has given it a different turn, and has thrown it out, as a reproach of the heathen upon the Jews when they were driven from Jerusalem into captivity:—

"Depart; ye are polluted, depart; depart ye,
forbear to touch.
Yea, they are fled, they are removed: they
shall dwell here no more." Lam. iv. 15.

Of the metrical distribution of these lines, see the Prelim. Dissert., p. lviii. note.

Verse 13. *My servant shall deal prudently*] ישכיל *yaskil, shall prosper*, or *act prosperously.* The subject of Isaiah's prophecy, from the fortieth chapter inclusive, has hitherto been, in general, the deliverance of the people of God. This includes in it *three distinct parts;* which, however, have a close connexion with one another; that is, 1. The deliverance of the Jews from the captivity of Babylon; 2. The deliverance of the Gentiles from their miserable state of ignorance and idolatry; and, 3. The deliverance of mankind from the captivity of sin and death. These *three subjects* are subordinate to one another; and the *two* latter are shadowed out under the image of the former. They are covered by it as by a veil; which however is transparent, and suffers them to appear through it. *Cyrus* is expressly named as the immediate agent of God in effecting the first deliverance. A *greater person* is spoken of as the Agent who is to effect the two latter deliverances, called the *servant*, the *elect, of God*, in whom his soul delighteth; *Israel*, in whom God will be glorified. Now these three subjects have a very near relation to one another; for as the *Agent* who was to effect the *two latter* deliverances,—that is, the Messiah,—was to be born a Jew, with particular limitations of *time, family*, and *other circumstances;* the *first deliverance* was necessary in the order of providence, and according to the determinate counsel of God, to the accomplishment of the *two latter deliverances;* and the *second deliverance* was necessary to the *third*, or rather was involved in it, and made an essential part of it. This being the case, Isaiah has not treated the *three subjects* as quite *distinct* and *separate* in a methodical and orderly manner, like a philosopher or a logician, but has taken them in their connective veiw. He has handled them as a prophet and a *poet;* he has *allegorized the former*, and under the image of it has *shadowed out the two latter:* he has thrown them all together, has mixed one with another, has passed from this to that with rapid transitions, and has painted the whole with the strongest and boldest imagery. The *restoration of the Jews* from captivity, the *call of the Gentiles*, the *redemption by Messiah*, have hitherto been handled interchangeably and alternately. *Babylon* has hitherto been kept pretty much in sight; at the same time, that strong intimations of something *much greater* have frequently been thrown in. But here *Babylon* is at once dropped, and I think hardly ever comes in sight again; unless perhaps in chap. lv. 12, and lvii. 14. The prophet's views are almost wholly engrossed by the *superior part* of his subject. He introduces the *Messiah* as appearing at first in the *lowest state of humiliation*, which he had just touched upon before, (chap. l. 5, 6,) and obviates the offence which would be occasioned by it, by declaring the *important* and *necessary cause* of it, and foreshowing the glory which should follow it.

This seems to me to be the nature and the true design of this part of Isaiah's prophecies; and this view of them seems to afford the best method of resolving difficulties, in which expositors are frequently engaged, being much divided between what is called the *literal* and the *mystical sense*, not very properly; for the *mystical* or *spiritual* sense is very often the *most literal* sense of all.

Abarbanel seems to have had an idea of this kind, as he is quoted by Vitringa on chap. xlix. 1, who thus represents his sentiments: Censet Abarbanel prophetam hic *transitum* facere a *liberatione ex exilio Babylonico* ad *liberationem ex exilio Romano;* et, quod hic animadversu dignum est, observat liberationem ex exilio Babylonico esse אות וראיה *oth veraayah*, signum et argumentum liberationis futuræ; atque adeo orationem prophetæ de duabus hisce liberationibus in superioribus concionibus sæpe inter se permisceri. Verba ejus: "Et propterea verba, sive res, in prophetia superiore inter se permixtæ occurrunt; modo *de liberatione Babylonica*, modo *de liberatione extrema* accipiendæ, ut orationis necessitas exigit." Nullum hic vitium, nisi quod redemptionem veram et spiritualem a Messia vero Jesu adductam, non agnoscat. "Abarbanel supposes that the prophet here makes a transition from the de-

A. M. cir. 3292 B. C. cir. 712 Olymp. XVII. 1 cir. annum NumæPompilii, R. Roman., 4

dently, [y]he shall be exalted and extolled, and be very high.

14 As many were astonished at thee; his [z]visage was so marred more than any man, and his form more than the sons of men.

15 [a]So shall he sprinkle many nations; [b]the kings shall shut their mouths at him: for *that* [c]which had not been told them shall they see; and *that* which they had not heard shall they consider.

[y]Phil. ii. 9——[z]Psa. xxii. 6, 7; ch. liii. 2, 3——[a]Ezek. xxxvi. 25; Acts ii. 33; Heb. ix. 13, 14

[b]Chap. xlix. 7, 23——[c]Chap. lv. 5; Rom. xv. 21; xvi. 25, 26; Eph. iii. 5, 9

liverance from the *Babylonish* captivity to the deliverance from the *Roman* captivity; and (which is worthy of particular note) he observes that the deliverance from the Babylonish captivity is a *sign* and *pledge* of the future redemption; and that on this account it is we find in the preceding prophecies the circumstances of the two captivities intimately blended together. His words are the following: 'And, therefore, the words or subjects in the foregoing prophecy are very much intermixed; in one passage the redemption from the Babylonish captivity being treated of, in another the redemption from the general dispersion, as may be collected from the obvious import of the words.' No fault can be found with the above remark, except that the true and spiritual redemption procured by Jesus the Messiah is not acknowledged."—L.

Verse 14. *As many were astonished at thee*—"As many were astonished at him"] For עליך *aleicha* read עליו *alaiv.* So the *Syriac, Chaldee,* and *Vulgate* in a MS.; and so likewise two ancient MSS.

His visage was so marred more than any man] Most interpreters understand this of the indignities offered to our blessed Lord: but *Kimchi* gives it another turn, and says, "It means the Jewish people, who are considered by most nations as having an appearance different from all the people of the earth." Poor Jews! they have in general a very disagreeable look, partly affected, and partly through neglect of neatness and cleanliness. Most Christians think they carry the impress of their reprobation on every feature of their face. However this may be, it should never be forgotten that the greatest men that ever flourished as kings, judges, magistrates, lawgivers, heroes, and poets, were of Jewish extraction. *Isaiah* was a Jew; so was *Paul;* and so was Jesus of *Nazareth.*

Verse 15. *So shall he sprinkle many nations*] I retain the common rendering, though I am by no means satisfied with it. "יזה *yazzeh,* frequent in the law, means only to sprinkle: but the water sprinkled is the accusative case; the thing on which has על *al* or אל *el.* θαυμασονται, ὁ, makes the best apodosis. ינהג *yenahag* would do. ינהרו *yinharu* is used chap. ii. 2, Jer. xxxi. 12, chap. li. 14, but is unlike. 'Kings shall shut,' &c., is good, but seems to want a first part."—Secker. Munster translates it, *faciet loqui, (de se;)* and in his note thus explains it: יזה *yazzeh proprie significat* spargere *et* stillas disseminare; *hic vero capitur pro* loqui, *et verbum disseminare.* "יזה *yazzeh* properly signifies *to sprinkle,* and *to scatter about drops;* but it here means *to speak,* and *to disseminate the word.*" This is pretty much as the *Rabbins Kimchi* and *Sal. ben Melec* explain it, referring to the expression of "dropping the word." But the same objection lies to this as to the common rendering; it ought to be יזה (דבר) על גוים *yazzeh (debar) al goyim.* Bishop *Chandler,* Defence, p. 148, says, "that to sprinkle is used for to surprise and astonish, as people are that have much water thrown upon them. And this sense is followed by the *Septuagint.*" This is ingenious, but rather too refined. Dr. *Durell* conjectures that the true reading may be יחזו *yechezu, they shall regard,* which comes near to the θαυμασονται of the *Septuagint,* who seem to give the best sense of any to this place.

"I find in my papers the same conjecture which Dr. *Durell* made from θαυμασονται in the *Septuagint.* And it may be added that חזה *chazah* is used to express 'looking on any thing with admiration,' Psa. xi. 7; xvii. 15; xxvii. 4; lxiii. 2; Cant. vi. 13. It is particularly applied to 'looking on God,' Exod. xxiv. 11, and Job xix. 26. *Gisbert Cuper,* in Observ. lib. ii. 1, though treating on another subject, has some observations which show how nearly ὁραω and θαυμαζω are allied, which, with the peculiar sense of the verb חזה *chazah* above noted, add to the probability of θαυμασονται being the version of יחזו *yechezu* in the text: οἱ δε νυ λαοι Παντες ες αυτον ὁρωσι. *Hesiod., id est, cum veneratione quadam admirantur. Hinc* ὁραω *et* θαυμαζω *junxit Themistius* Or. i. Ειτα παυσονται οἱ ανθρωποι προς σε μονον ὁρωντες, και σε μονον θαυμαζοντες. *Theophrastus in Charact.* c. 3. Ενθυμη ὡς αποβλεπουσιν εις σε οἱ ανθρωποι. Hence the rendering of this verse seems to be—

"So many nations shall look on him with admiration;
Kings shall stop their mouths—" Dr. Jubb.

Does not sprinkling the nations refer to the conversion and baptism of the Gentiles? Many nations shall become proselytes to his religion.

Kings shall shut their mouths at him] His Gospel shall so prevail that all opposition shall be finally overcome; and kings and potentates shall be overwhelmed with confusion, and become speechless before the doctrines of his truth. When they hear these *declared* they shall attentively *consider* them, and their conviction of their truth shall be the consequence.

For that which had not been told them] The mystery of the Gospel so long concealed. See Rom. xv. 21; xvi. 25.

Shall they see] With the eyes of their faith; God enlightening both *organ* and *object.*

And that which they had not heard] The redemption of the world by Jesus Christ; the conversion of the Gentiles, and making them one flock with the converted Jews.—Trapp.

CHAPTER LIII

This chapter foretells the sufferings of the Messiah, the end for which he was to die, and the advantages resulting to mankind from that illustrious event. It begins with a complaint of the infidelity of the Jews, 1; *the offence they took at his mean and humble appearance,* 2; *and the contempt with which they treated him,* 3. *The prophet then shows that the Messiah was to suffer for sins not his own; but that our iniquities were laid on him, and the punishment of them exacted of him, which is the meritorious cause of our obtaining pardon and salvation,* 4–6. *He shows the meekness and placid submission with which he suffered a violent and unjust death, with the circumstances of his dying with the wicked, and being buried with the great,* 7–9; *and that, in consequence of his atonement, death, resurrection, and intercession, he should procure pardon and salvation to the multitudes, insure increasing prosperity to his Church, and ultimately triumph over all his foes,* 10, 11. *This chapter contains a beautiful summary of the most peculiar and distinguishing doctrines of Christianity.*

A. M. cir. 3292
B. C. cir. 712
Olymp. XVII. 1
cir. annum
NumæPompilii,
R. Roman., 4

WHO [a]hath believed our [b]re-
port?[c] and to whom is [d]the
arm of the LORD revealed?
2 For [e]he shall grow up before
him as a tender plant, and as a root out of a
dry ground: [f]he hath no form
nor comeliness; and when we
shall see him, *there is* no beauty
that we should desire him.
3 [g]He is despised and rejected of men; a

A. M. cir. 3292
B. C. cir. 712
Olymp. XVII. 1
cir. annum
NumæPompilii,
R. Roman., 4

[a]John xii. 38; Rom. x. 16——[b]Or, *doctrine*——[c]Heb. *hearing*——[d]Chap. li. 9; Rom. i. 16; 1 Cor. i. 18

[e]Chap. xi. 1——[f]Chap. lii. 14; Mark ix. 12——[g]Psa. xxii. 6; chap. xlix. 7

NOTES ON CHAP. LIII

That this chapter speaks of none but JESUS must be evident to every unprejudiced reader who has ever heard the history of his sufferings and death. The Jews have endeavoured to apply it to their sufferings in captivity; but, alas for their cause! they can make nothing out in this way. Allowing that it belongs to our blessed Lord, (and the best men and the best scholars agree in this,) then who can read verses 4, 5, 6, 8, 10, without being convinced that his death was a vicarious sacrifice for the sins of mankind? On the *first* and *second* verses of this chapter I have received the following remarks from an unknown hand.

"Verse 1. *Who hath believed our report?*] The report of the *prophets*, of *John the Baptist*, and *Christ's own report of himself*. The Jews did not *receive the report*, and for this reason he was not manifested to them as the promised Messiah. 'He came unto his own, but his own received him not.' Before the FATHER *he grew up as a tender plant:* but to the JEWS he was as *a root out of a dry ground*. 'He hath no form nor comeliness; and when we shall see him, there is no beauty that we should desire him.'

"Verse 2. *For he shall grow up*] Supposes something to have preceded; as it might be asked, what or who shall 'grow up before him,' &c. As the translation now stands, no correct answer can be given to this question. The translation then is wrong, the connexion broken, and the sense obscured. זרוע *zeroa*, translated *the arm*, from the root *zara*. 1. *To sow*, or *plant;* also *seed*, &c. 2. The *limb* which reaches from the shoulder to the hand, called the *arm;* or more properly beginning at the shoulder and ending at the elbow. The translator has given the wrong sense of the word. It would be very improper to say, *the arm of the Lord should grow up before him;* but by taking the word in its former sense, the connexion and metaphor would be restored, and the true sense given to the text. זרע *zera* signifies, not only the *seed of herbs*, but *children, offspring*, or *posterity*. The same word we find Gen. iii. 15, where CHRIST is the Seed promised. See also Gen. xxii. 17, 18; xxvi. 4; xxviii. 14. Hence the SEED of the *woman*, the SEED promised to the patriarchs is, according to Isaiah, the *Seed of the Lord*, the Child born, and the Son given; and according to St. John, 'the Son of God, the only-begotten of the Father, full of grace and truth.' זרע then, in this place, should be understood to mean JESUS CHRIST, and him alone. To speak here of the *manifestation of the arm* or *power* of God would be irregular; but to suppose the text to speak of the *manifestation of Jesus Christ* would be very proper, as the whole of the chapter is written concerning him; particularly his humiliation and sufferings, and the reception he should meet with from the Jewish nation.

"The first verse of this chapter is quoted John xii. 38, and the former part of the same verse Rom. x. 16. But no objection of importance can be brought forward from either of these quotations against the above explanation, as they are quoted to show the unbelief of the Jews in not receiving Christ as the promised Messiah."

He hath no form nor comeliness—"He hath no form nor any beauty"] Ουκ ειδος αυτῳ, ουδε αξιωμα, ἱνα ειδωμεν αυτον· ουδε θεωρια, ἱνα επιθυμωμεν αυτον. "He hath no form, nor any beauty, that we should regard him; nor is his countenance such that we should desire him." *Symmachus;* the only one of the ancients that has translated it rightly.

Verse 3. *Acquainted with grief*] For וידוע *vidua, familiar with grief*, eight MSS. and one edition have וידע *veyada, and knowing grief;* the *Septuagint*, *Syriac*, and *Vulgate* read it ויודע *veyodea*.

We hid as it were our faces from him—"As one that hideth his face from us"] For וכמסתר *uchemaster, four* MSS. (*two* ancient) have וכמסתיר *uchemastir, one* MS. ומסתיר *umastir*. For פנים *panim, two* MSS. have פניו *panaiv;* so likewise the *Septuagint* and *Vulgate*. Mourners covered up the lower part of their faces, and their heads, 2 Sam. xv. 30; Ezek. xxix. 17; and lepers were commanded by the law, Lev. xii. 45, to cover their upper lip. From which circumstance it seems that the *Vulgate*, *Aquila*, *Symmachus*, and the Jewish commenta-

A. M. cir. 3292 B. C. cir. 712 Olymp. XVII. 1 cir. annum NumæPompilii, R. Roman., 4

man of sorrows, and [h]acquainted
with grief: and [i]we [k]hid as it
were *our* faces from him; he
was despised, and [l]we esteemed
him not.

4 Surely [m]he hath borne our griefs, and
carried our sorrows: yet we did esteem him
stricken, smitten of God, and afflicted.

5 But he *was* [n]wounded [o]for our transgressions, *he was* bruised for our iniquities: the
chastisement of our peace *was* upon him; and
with his [p]stripes [q]we are healed.

6 [r]All we like sheep have gone
astray; we have turned every one
to his own way; and the LORD [s]hath
laid on him the iniquity of us all.

A. M. cir. 3292 B. C. cir. 712 Olymp. XVII. 1 cir. annum NumæPompilii, R. Roman., 4

7 He was oppressed, and he was afflicted,
yet [t]he opened not his mouth: [u]he is
brought as a lamb to the slaughter, and as a
sheep before her shearers is dumb, so he
openeth not his mouth.

8 [v]He was taken from prison and from judgment: and who shall declare his generation?
for [w]he was cut off out of the land of the

[h]Heb. iv. 15——[i]Or, *he hid as it were* his *face from us* [k]Heb. *as a hiding of faces from him*, or *from us*——[l]John i. 10, 11——[m]Matt. viii. 17; Heb. ix. 28; 1 Pet. ii. 24 [n]Or, *tormented*——[o]Rom. iv. 25; 1 Cor. xv. 3; 1 Pet. iii. 18——[p]1 Pet. ii. 24

[q]Heb. *bruise*——[r]Psa. cxix. 176; 1 Pet. ii. 25——[s]Heb. *hath made the iniquities of us all to meet on him*——[t]Matt. xxvi. 63; xxvii. 12, 14; Mark xiv. 61; xv. 5; 1 Pet. ii. 23 [u]Acts viii. 32——[v]Or, *He was taken away by distress and judgment; but*, &c.——[w]Dan. ix. 26

tors have taken the word נגוע *nagua, stricken*, in the next verse, as meaning stricken with the *leprosy: εν αφῃ οντα, Sym.; αφημενον, Aq.; leprosum, Vulg.* So my old MS. Bible. I will insert the whole passage as curious:—

There is not schap to him, ne fairnesse,
And we seegen him, and he was not of sigte,
And we desiriden him dispisid; and the last of men:
Man of souaris and witing infirmitie;
And as hid his cheer and despisid;
Wherfor ne we settiden bi him:
Verili our seeknesse he toke and our sorewis he bair,
And we helden him as leprous and smyten of God, and meekid;
He forsoth wounded is for our wickednesse,
Defoulid is for our hidous giltis
The discipline of our pese upon him,
And with his wanne wound we ben helid.

Verse 4. *Surely he hath borne our griefs*—"Surely our infirmities he hath borne"] *Seven* MSS. (*two* ancient) and *three* editions have חליינו *cholayeynu* in the plural number.

And carried our sorrows—"And our sorrows, he hath carried them"] *Seventeen* MSS. (*two* ancient) of Dr. *Kennicott's*, *two* of *De Rossi's*, and *two* editions have the word הוא *hu, he*, before סבלם *sebalam*, "carrieth them," in the text; *four* other MSS. have it in the margin. This adds force to the sense, and elegance to the construction.

Verse 5. *The chastisement of our peace*—"The chastisement by which our peace is effected"] *Twenty-one* MSS. and *six* editions have the word fully and regularly expressed, שלומינו *shelomeynu;* pacificationum nostrarum, "our pacification;" that by which we are brought into a state of peace and favour with God. *Ar. Montan.*

Verse 6. *The iniquity of us all.*] For עון *avon*, "iniquity," the ancient interpreters read עונות *avonoth*, "iniquities," plural; and so the *Vulgate* in MS. Blanchini. And the Lord hath הפגיע בו *hiphgia bo*, caused to meet in him the iniquities of us all. He was the subject on which all the rays collected on the focal point fell. These fiery rays, which should have fallen on all mankind, diverged from Divine justice to the east, west, north, and south, were deflected from them, and *converged* in him. So the Lord hath caused to meet in him the punishment due to the iniquities of ALL.

Verse 8. *And who shall declare his generation*—"And his manner of life who would declare"] A learned friend has communicated to me the following passages from the Mishna, and the Gemara of Babylon, as leading to a satisfactory explication of this difficult place. It is said in the former, that before any one was punished for a capital crime, proclamation was made before the prisoner by the public crier, in these words: כל מי שיודע לו זכות יבא וילמד עליו *col mi shioda lo zachoth yabo vayilmad alaiv*, "whosoever knows any thing of this man's innocence, let him come and declare it." Tract. Sandhedrim. Surenhus. Part iv. p. 233. On which passage the Gemara of Babylon adds, that "before the death of Jesus this proclamation was made for forty days; but no defence could be found." On which words Lardner observes: "It is truly surprising to see such falsities, contrary to well-known facts." Testimonies, Vol. I. p. 198. The report is certainly false; but this false report is founded on the supposition that there was such a custom, and so far confirms the account given from the Mishna. The Mishna was composed in the middle of the second century according to Prideaux; Lardner ascribes it to the year of Christ 180.

Casaubon has a quotation from Maimonides which farther confirms this account:—Exercitat. in Baronii Annales, Art. lxxvi. Ann. 34. Num. 119. Auctor est Maimonides in Perek xiii. ejus libri ex opere Jad, solitum fieri, ut cum reus, sententiam mortis passus, a loco judicii exibat ducendus ad supplicium, præcedoret ipsum הכרוז κηρυξ, præco; et hæc verba diceret: *Ille* exit occidendus morte *illa*, quia transgressus est transgressione *illa*, in loco *illo*, tempore *illo*, et sunt ejus rei testes *ille* et *ille*. Qui noverit aliquid ad ejus innocentiam probandam, veniat, et loquatur pro eo. "It was customary when sentence of death was passed upon a criminal, and he was led out from the seat of judgment to the place of punishment, a crier went before, and spoke as follows:—'This man is going out to suffer death by —— because he has transgressed by —— such a transgression, in such a place, in such a time; and

A. M. cir. 3292 B. C. cir. 712 Olymp. XVII. 1 cir. annum NumæPompilii, R. Roman., 4

living: for the transgression
of my people [x]was he
stricken.
9 [y]And he made his grave
with the wicked, and with the
rich in his [z]death; because he
had done no violence, neither
was any [a]deceit in his mouth.

[x]Heb. was *the stroke upon him*——[y]Matt. xxvii. 57, 58, 60——[z]Heb. *deaths*——[a]1 Pet. ii. 22; 1 John iii. 5

the witnesses against him are ——. He who may know any thing relative to his innocence, let him come and speak in his behalf.' "

Now it is plain from the history of the four Evangelists, that in the trial and condemnation of Jesus no such rule was observed; though, according to the account of the Mishna, it must have been in practice at that time, no proclamation was made for any person to bear witness to the innocence and character of Jesus; nor did any one voluntarily step forth to give his attestation to it. And our Saviour seems to refer to such a custom, and to claim the benefit of it, by his answer to the high priest, when he asked him of his disciples and of his doctrine: "I spoke openly to the world; I ever taught in the synagogue and in the temple, whither the Jews always resort; and in secret have I said nothing. Why askest thou me? ask them who heard me, what I have said unto them: behold, they know what I said;" John xviii. 20, 21. This, therefore, was one remarkable instance of hardship and injustice, among others predicted by the prophet, which our Saviour underwent in his trial and sufferings.

St. Paul likewise, in similar circumstances, standing before the judgment seat of Festus, seems to complain of the same unjust treatment; that no one was called, or would appear, to vindicate his character. "My manner of life (*την βιωσιν μου*, דורי *dori*, 'my generation') from my youth, which was at the first among my own nation at Jerusalem, know all the Jews, who knew me from the beginning, *if they would testify;* that after the straitest sect of our religion I lived a Pharisee;" Acts xxvi. 4, 5.

דור *dor* signifies age, duration, the time which one man or many together pass in this world, in this place; the course, tenor, or manner of life. The verb דור *dor* signifies, according to Castell, ordinatam vitam sive ætatem egit, ordinavit, ordine constituit. "He passed a certain course of life, he ordained," &c. In Arabic, *curavit, administravit,* "he took care of, administered to."

Was he stricken—"He was smitten to death"] The *Septuagint* read למות *lemaveth, εις θανατον,* "to death." And so the *Coptic* and *Saidic* Versions, from the *Septuagint;* MSS. St. Germain de Prez.

"Origen," (*Contra* Celsum, lib. i. p. 370, edit. 1733,) after having quoted at large this prophecy concerning the Messiah, "tells us, that having once made use of this passage in a dispute against some that were accounted wise among the Jews, one of them replied, that the words did not mean one man, but *one people*, the *Jews*, who were smitten of God and dispersed among the Gentiles for their conversion; that he then urged many parts of this prophecy to show the absurdity of this interpretation, and that he seemed to press them the hardest by this sentence, *απο των ανομιων του λαου μου ηχθη εις θανατον*, 'for the iniquity of my people was he smitten to death.' " Now as Origen, the author of the Hexapla, must have understood Hebrew, we cannot suppose that he would have urged this last quotation as so decisive if the Greek Version had not agreed here with the Hebrew text; nor that these wise Jews would have been at all distressed by this quotation, unless their Hebrew text had read agreeably to *εις θανατον*, "to death," on which the argument principally depended; for, by quoting it immediately, they would have triumphed over him, and reprobated his Greek version. This, whenever they could do it, was their constant practice in their disputes with the Christians. Jerome, in his Preface to the Psalms, says, Nuper cum Hebræo disputans, quædam pro Domino Salvatore de Psalmis testimonia protulisti: volensque ille te illudere, per sermones fere singulos asserebat, non ita haberi in Hebræo, ut tu de LXX. opponebas. "Lately disputing with a Hebrew,—thou advancedst certain passages out of the Psalms which bear testimony to the Lord the Saviour; but he, to elude thy reasoning, asserted that almost all thy quotations have an import in the Hebrew text different from what they had in the Greek." And Origen himself, who laboriously compared the Hebrew text with the *Septuagint*, has recorded the necessity of arguing with the Jews from such passages only as were in the *Septuagint* agreeable to the Hebrew: *ινα προς Ιουδαιοις διαλεγομενοι μη προφερωμεν αυτοι τα μη κειμενα εν τοις αντιγραφοις αυτων, και ινα συγχρησωμεθα τοις φερομενοις παρ' εκεινοις.* See *Epist. ad African.* p. 15, 17. Wherefore as Origen had carefully compared the Greek version of the *Septuagint* with the Hebrew text, and speaks of the contempt with which the Jews treated all appeals to the Greek version where it differed from their Hebrew text; and as he puzzled and confounded the learned Jews by urging upon them the reading *εις θανατον*, "unto death," in this place; it seems almost impossible not to conclude, both from Origen's argument and the silence of his Jewish adversaries, that the Hebrew text at that time actually had למות *lemaveth,* "to death," agreeably to the version of the *Septuagint.*—Dr. *Kennicott.*

Verse 9. *With the rich in his death*—"With the rich man was his tomb"] It may be necessary to introduce Bishop *Lowth's* translation of this verse before we come to his very satisfactory criticisms:—

And his grave was appointed with the wicked;
But with the rich man was his tomb:
Although he had done no wrong,
Neither was there any guile in his mouth.

Among the various opinions which have been given on this passage, I have no doubt in giving my assent to that which makes the ב *beth* in במותיו *bemothaiv* radical, and renders it *excelsa sua.* This is mentioned by Aben Ezra as received by some in his time; and has been long since approved by Schindler, Drusius, and many other learned Christian interpreters.

The most simple tombs or monuments of old

A. M. cir. 3292
B. C. cir. 712
Olymp. XVII. 1
cir. annum
NumæPompilii,
R. Roman., 4

10 Yet it pleased the LORD to
bruise him; he hath put *him* to
grief: [b]when thou shalt make
his soul [c]an offering for sin, he
shall see *his* seed, [d]he shall prolong *his* days, and [e]the pleasure
of the LORD shall prosper in his
hand.

[b]Or, *when his soul shall make an offering*——[c]2 Cor. v. 21; 1 Pet. ii. 24——[d]Romans vi. 9——[e]Ephesians i. 5, 9; 2 Thess. i. 11

consisted of hillocks of earth heaped up over the grave; of which we have numerous examples in our own country, generally allowed to be of very high antiquity. The Romans called a monument of this sort very properly *tumulus;* and the Hebrews as properly במות *bamoth,* "high place," for that is the form of the noun in the singular number; and *sixteen* MSS. and the *two* oldest editions express the word fully in this place, במותיו *bamothaiv.* Tumulus et collem et sepulchrum fuisse significat. Potest enim tumulus sine sepulchro interpretatione collis interdum accipi. Nam et terræ congestio super ossa tumulus dicitur. "*Tumulus* signifies a sepulchre with a hillock of earth raised over it. The word is sometimes restrained to the bank of earth; for the heaping up of the earth over the bones is named the *tumulus.*"—Servius, Æn. iii. 22. And to make the tumulus still more elevated and conspicuous, a pillar or some other ornament was often erected upon it:—

Τυμβον χευαντες, και επι στηλην ερυσαντες, .
Πηξαμεν ακροτατῳ τυμβῳ ευηρες ερετμον.
Odyss. xii. 14.

"A rising tomb, the silent dead to grace,
Fast by the roarings of the main we place;
The rising tomb a *lofty column* bore,
And *high above it* rose the *tapering oar.*"
POPE.

The tomb therefore might with great propriety be called the *high place.* The Hebrews might also call such a tomb במות *bamoth,* from the situation, for they generally chose to erect them on *eminences.* The sepulchre of Joseph of Arimathea, in which the body of Christ was laid, was upon a hill, Mount Calvary. See chap. xxii. 16, and the note there.

"It should be observed that the word במותיו *bamothaiv* is not formed from במות *bamoth,* the plural of במה *bamah,* the feminine noun, but from במותים *bamothim,* the plural of a masculine noun, במות *bamoth.* This is noted because these two nouns have been negligently confounded with one another, and absurdly reduced to one by very learned men. So *Buxtorf,* lex. in voc. במה *bamah,* represents במותי *bamotey,* though plainly without any pronoun suffixed, as it governs the word ארץ *arets* following it, as only another form of במות *bamoth;* whereas the truth is, that במות *bamoth* and במותים *bamothim* are different words, and have through the whole Bible very different significations; במה *bamah,* whether occurring in the singular or plural number, always signifying a *place* or *places* of *worship;* and במותים *bamothim* always signifying *heights.* Thus in Deut. xxxii. 13; Isa. lviii. 14; Amos iv. 13; and Micah i. 3, במותי ארץ *bamothey arets* signifies 'the heights of the earth;' Isa. xiv. 14, במותי עב *bamothey ab,* 'the heights of the clouds;' and in Job ix. 8, במותי ים *bamothey yam,* 'the heights of the sea,' i. e., the high waves of the sea, as Virgil calls a wave *prœruptus aquæ mons,* 'a broken mountain of water.' These being all the places where this word occurs without a suffix, the sense of it seems nearly determined by them. It occurs in other instances with a pronoun suffixed, which confirm this signification. Unluckily, our English Bible has not distinguished the feminine noun במה *bamah* from the masculine singular noun במות *bamoth;* and has consequently always given the signification of the latter to the former, always rendering it a *high place;* whereas the true sense of the word appears plainly to be, in the very numerous passages in which it occurs, 'a place of worship,' or 'a sacred court,' or 'a sacred inclosure;' whether appropriated to the worship of idols or to that of the true God, for it is used of both, *passim.* Now as the Jewish graves are shown, from 2 Chron. xxxii. 33, and Isa. xxii. 16, to have been in high situations, to which may be added the custom of another eastern nation from *Osbeck's* Travels, who says, vol. i. p. 339, 'the Chinese graves are made on the side of hills;' 'his heights' becomes a very easy metaphor to express 'his sepulchre.'"—JUBB.

The exact completion of this prophecy will be fully shown by adding here the several circumstances of the burial of Jesus, collected from the accounts of the evangelists:—

"There was a rich man of Arimathea, named Joseph, a member of the sanhedrin, and of a respectable character, who had not consented to their counsel and act; he went to Pilate and begged the body of Jesus: and he laid it in his own new tomb, which had been hewn out of the rock, near to the place where Jesus was crucified; having first wound it in fine linen with spices, as the manner of the Jews was to bury the rich and great."

It has been supposed that קברו *kibro, his grave,* and במתיו *bemothaiv, in his death,* may have been transposed, as also the prefix ב *be* originally placed before רשעים *reshaim, the wicked.* Thus:—

ויתן ברשעים את מתיו
mothaiv eth bireshayim vaiyitten

ואת עשיר קברו
kibro ashir veeth

Yea, his death was appointed among the wicked,
And with a rich man, his tomb.

By these alterations it is supposed the text would be freed from all embarrassment. But see the preceding notes of Bishop *Lowth,* and the various readings of *De Rossi,* in loc.

Verse 10. *To grief*—"With affliction"] For החלי *hecheli,* the verb, the construction of which seems to be hard and inelegant in this place, the *Vulgate* reads בחלי *bocholi,* in infirmitate, "with infirmity."

When thou shalt make his soul—"If **his soul**

A. M. cir. 3292 B. C. cir. 712 Olymp. XVII. 1 cir. annum NumæPompilii, R. Roman., 4

11 He shall see of the travail
of his soul, *and* shall be satisfied: [f]by his knowledge
shall [g]my righteous [h]servant[i]
justify many; [k]for he shall bear their
iniquities.
12 [l]Therefore will I divide him *a portion*
with the great, [m]and he shall
divide the spoil with the strong;
because he hath poured out his
soul unto death: and he was
[n]numbered with the transgressors; and he
bare the sin of many, and [o]made intercession
for the transgressors.

[f]John xvii. 3; 2 Pet. i. 3——[g]1 John ii. 1——[h]Chap. xlii. 1; xlix. 3——[i]Rom. v. 18, 19——[k]Ver. 4, 5——[l]Psa. ii. 8; Phil. ii. 9

[m]Col. ii. 15——[n]Mark xv. 28; Luke xxii. 37——[o]Luke xxiii. 34; Rom. viii. 34; Heb. vii. 25; ix. 24; 1 John ii. 1

shall make"] For תשים *tasim*, a MS. has תשם *tasem*, which may be taken passively, "If his soul shall be made—" agreeably to some copies of the *Septuagint*, which have δωται. See likewise the *Syriac*.

When thou shalt make his soul an offering] The word נפש *nephesh, soul*, is frequently used in *Hebrew* to signify *life*. Throughout the New Testament the salvation of men is uniformly attributed to the *death* of Christ.

He shall see his *seed*] True converts, genuine Christians.

He shall prolong his *days*] Or this spiritual progeny shall prolong their days, i. e., Christianity shall endure to the end of time.

And the pleasure of the Lord] To have all men saved and brought to the knowledge of the truth.

Shall prosper in his hand.] Shall go on in a state of progressive prosperity; and so completely has this been thus far accomplished, that every succeeding century has witnessed more Christianity in the world than the preceding, or any former one.

Verse 11. *Shall be satisfied*—"And be satisfied"] The *Septuagint, Vulgate, Syriac*, and a MS. add the conjunction to the verb, וישבע *vaiyisba*.

Shall my righteous servant justify—"Shall my servant justify"] Three MSS., (two of them ancient,) omit the word צדיק *tsaddik;* it seems to be only an imperfect repetition, by mistake, of the preceding word. It makes a solecism in this place; for according to the constant usage of the Hebrew language, the adjective, in a phrase of this kind, ought to follow the substantive; and צדיק עבדי *tsaddik abdi*, in Hebrew, would be as absurd as "shall my *servant righteous* justify," in English. Add to this, that it makes the hemistich too long.

Verse 12. *He bare the sin of many*] רבים *rabbim*, the *multitudes*, the *many that* were *made sinners* by *the offences of one;* i. e., the whole human race; for *all have sinned —all have fallen;* and for all that have sinned, and for all that have fallen, Jesus Christ died. The רבים *rabbim* of the *prophet* answers to the οἱ πολλοι, of the apostle, Rom. v. 15, 19. As the πολλοι of the apostle means all that have sinned; so the רבים *rabbim* of the prophet means those for whom Christ died; i. e., all that have sinned.

And made intercession for the transgressors.] For יפגיע *yaphgia*, in the future, a MS. has הפגיע *hiphgia*, preterite, rather better, as agreeable with the other verbs immediately preceding in the sentence.

He made intercession for the transgressors.—This was literally fulfilled at his death, "Father, forgive them; they know not what they do!" Luke xxiii. 34. And to make intercession for transgressors is one part of his *mediatorial* office. Heb. vii. 25, and ix. 24.

In this chapter the *incarnation, preaching, humiliation, rejection, sufferings, death, atonement, resurrection*, and *mediation* of Jesus Christ are all predicted, together with the prevalence of his Gospel, and the *extension* of his *kingdom* through all ages.

CHAPTER LIV

Some suppose this chapter to have been addressed to the Gentiles; some, to the Jewish Church; and some, to the Christian, in its first stage. On comparing the different parts of it, particularly the seventh *and* eighth *verses, with the remainder, the most obvious import of the prophecy will be that which refers it to the future conversion of the Jews, and to the increase and prosperity of that nation, when reconciled to God after their long rejection, when their glory and security will far surpass what they were formerly in their most favoured state,* 1–17.

A. M. cir. 3292 B. C. cir. 712 Olymp. XVII. 1 cir. annum NumæPompilii, R. Roman., 4

[a]SING, O barren, thou *that*
didst not bear; break forth
into singing, and cry aloud, thou
that didst not travail with child:
for [b]more *are* the children of
the desolate than the children
of the married wife, saith the
Lord.

[a]Zeph. iii. 14; Gal. iv. 27

[b]1 Sam. ii. 5

NOTES ON CHAP. LIV

Verse 1. *Sing, O barren, thou* that *didst not bear*—"Shout for joy, O thou barren, that didst not bear"] The Church of God under the Old Testament, confined within the narrow bounds of the Jewish nation, and still more so in respect of the very small number of true be-

A. M. cir. 3292 B. C. cir. 712 Olymp. XVII. 1 cir. annum NumæPompilii, R. Roman., 4

2 [c]Enlarge the place of thy tent,
and let them stretch forth the
curtains of thine habitations;
spare not, lengthen thy cords,
and strengthen thy stakes;
3 For thou shalt break forth on the right
hand and on the left: [d]and thy seed shall inherit the Gentiles, and make the desolate
cities to be inhabited.
4 Fear not; for thou shalt not be ashamed:
neither be thou confounded; for thou shalt
not be put to shame: for thou shalt forget the
shame of thy youth, and shalt not remember
the reproach of thy widowhood any more.
5 [e]For thy Maker *is* thine Husband; the
[f]LORD of hosts *is* his name; and thy Redeemer the Holy One of Israel; [g]The God
of the whole earth shall he be called.
6 For the LORD [h]hath called thee as a woman
forsaken and grieved in spirit, and a wife of
youth, when thou wast refused, saith thy God.
7 [i]For a small moment have I forsaken
thee; but with great mercies will I gather
thee.
8 In a little wrath I hid my face from thee
for a moment; [k]but with everlasting kindness will I have
mercy on thee, saith the LORD
thy Redeemer.
9 For this *is as* the waters of [l]Noah unto
me: for *as* I have sworn that the waters of
Noah should no more go over the earth; so
have I sworn that I would not be wroth with
thee, nor rebuke thee.
10 For [m]the mountains shall depart, and the
hills be removed: [n]but my kindness shall not
depart from thee, neither shall the covenant
of my peace be removed, saith the LORD that
hath mercy on thee.
11 O thou afflicted, tossed with tempest,
and not comforted, behold, I will lay thy
stones with [o]fair colours, and lay thy foundations with sapphires.
12 And I will make thy windows of agates,
and thy gates of carbuncles, and all thy borders of pleasant stones.
13 And all thy children *shall be* [p]taught of
the LORD; and [q]great *shall be* the peace of
thy children.
14 In righteousness shalt thou be established:

[c]Ch. xlix. 19, 20——[d]Ch. lv. 5; lxi. 9——[e]Jer. iii. 14——[f]Luke i. 32——[g]Zech. xiv. 9; Rom. iii. 29——[h]Ch. lxii. 4——[i]Psa. xxx. 5; ch. xxvi. 20; lx. 10; 2 Cor. iv. 17——[k]Ch. lv. 3; Jer. xxxi. 3——[l]Gen. viii. 21; ix. 11; ch. lv. 11; see Jer. xxxi. 35, 36——[m]Psa. xlvi. 2; ch. li. 6; Matt. v. 18——[n]Psa. lxxxix. 33, 34——[o]1 Chron. xxix. 2; Rev. xxi. 18, &c.——[p]Ch. xi. 9; Jer. xxxi. 54; John vi. 45; 1 Cor. ii. 10; 1 Thess. iv. 9; 1 John ii. 20——[q]Psa. cxix. 165

lievers, and which sometimes seemed to be deserted of God her husband, is *the barren woman, that did not bear*, and was *desolate.* She is exhorted to rejoice, and to express her joy in the strongest manner, on the reconciliation of her husband, (see ver. 6,) and on the accession of the Gentiles to her family. The converted Gentiles are all along considered by the prophet as a new accession of adopted children, admitted into the original Church of God, and united with it. See chap. xlix. 20, 21.

Verse 4. *For thou shalt forget the shame of thy youth*] That is, "The bondage of Egypt: *widowhood*, the captivity of Babylon."—*Secker.*

Verse 7. *For a small moment*—"In a little anger"] So the *Chaldee* and *Syriac*, either reading רגז *regaz*, for רגע *rega;* or understanding the latter word as meaning the same with the former, which they both make use of. See Psa. xxx. 5, xxxv. 20, in the *Septuagint*, where they render רגע *rega* by οργη, *anger.*

Verse 8. *I hid my face from thee for a moment*] The word רגע *rega* is omitted by the *Septuagint*, *Syriac*, and two MSS. of *Kennicott's*, and two of *De Rossi's.* It seems to embarrass rather than to help the sentence. Forte reponi debet pro שצף *shetseph*, quod potest a קצף *ketseph* errore scribæ originem duxisse. "Perhaps it ought to be substituted for שצף *shetseph*, an error probably made by some scribe from its similarity to קצף *ketseph.*"—*Secker.*

Thy Redeemer—גאלך *goalech:* but for this word three of *De Rossi's* MSS. have מרחמך *merachamech, thy commiserator.*

Verse 9. *For this* is as *the waters of Noah unto me*—"The same will I do now, as in the days of Noah"] כימי *kimey*, in one word, in a MS., and some editions; and so the *Syriac*, *Chaldee*, *Vulgate*, *Symmachus*, *Theodotion*, *Abarbanel*, *Sal. ben Melec*, and *Kimchi* acknowledge that their copies vary in this place.

It is certain that these two words כי מי *ki mey*, were written formerly as *one.* Taken as two כי מי *ki mey*, they signify *for* as *the waters* —when as one, כימי *kimey*, they signify *as the days.* This latter reading is found in about four of *Kennicott's* and *De Rossi's* MSS. In one of my own it appears to have been intended as *one word:* but he who added the *points*, which are by a much *later hand* than the MS. itself, has pointed the letters so as to make the *two words* which are commonly found in the text. For *the waters*, *Symmachus*, *Theodotion*, the *Syriac*, *Vulgate*, and *Arabic* have *days.* The former seems to make the best sense; and the ancient *Versions*, except the *Septuagint*, support it.

Verse 11. *Behold, I will lay thy stones*—"Behold, I lay thy stones"] These seem to be general images to express beauty, magnificence, purity, strength, and solidity, agreeably to the ideas of the eastern nations; and to have never been intended to be strictly scrutinized, or minutely and particularly explained, as if they

A. M. cir. 3292
B. C. cir. 712
Olymp. XVII. 1
cir. annum
NumæPompilii,
R. Roman., 4

thou shalt be far from oppression; for thou shalt not fear: and from terror; for it shall not come near thee.

15 Behold, they shall surely gather together, *but* not by me: whosoever shall gather together against thee shall fall for thy sake.

16 Behold, I have created the smith that bloweth the coals in the fire, and that bringeth forth an instrument for his work; and I have created the waster to destroy.

17 No weapon that is formed against thee shall prosper; and every tongue *that* shall rise against thee in judgment thou shalt condemn. This *is* the heritage of the servants of the LORD, [r]and their righteousness *is* of me, saith the LORD.

[r]Chap. xlv. 24, 25; Psa. iv. 1; xxxv. 28; li. 14; lxix. 27; lxxxix. 16; cxxxii. 9

had each of them some precise, moral, or spiritual meaning. Tobit, in his prophecy of the final restoration of Israel, describes the New Jerusalem in the same oriental manner: "For Jerusalem shall be built up with sapphires, and emeralds, and precious stones; thy walls, and towers, and battlements, with pure gold. And the streets of Jerusalem shall be paved with beryl, and carbuncle, and stones of ophir." Tob. xiii. 16, 17. Compare also Rev. xxi. 18-21.

Verse 15. *Shall fall for thy sake*—"Shall come over to thy side."] For יפול *yippol*, twenty-eight MSS. (eight ancient) have יפל *yipal*, in its more common form. For the meaning of the word in this place, see Jer. xxxvii. 13.

CHAPTER LV

This chapter first displays the fulness, freeness, excellence, and everlasting nature of the blessings of the Gospel, and foretells again the enlargement of Messiah's kingdom, 1–5. *This view leads the prophet to exhort all to seize the precious opportunity of sharing in such blessings, which were not, however, to be expected without repentance and reformation,* 6, 7. *And as the things now and formerly predicted were so great as to appear incredible, the prophet points to the omnipotence of God, who would infallibly accomplish his word, and bring about those glorious deliverances which he had promised; the happy effects of which are again set forth by images beautiful and poetical in the highest degree,* 8–13.

A. M. cir. 3292
B. C. cir. 712
Olymp. XVII. 1
cir. annum
NumæPompilii,
R. Roman., 4

HO, [a]every one that thirsteth, come ye to the waters, and he that hath no money; [b]come ye, buy, and eat; yea, come, buy wine and milk without money and without price.

2 Wherefore do ye [c]spend money for *that which is* not bread? and your labour for *that which* satisfieth not? hearken diligently unto me, and eat ye *that which is* good, and let your soul delight itself in fatness.

3 Incline your ear, and [d]come unto me: hear, and your soul shall live: [e]and I will make an everlasting covenant with you, *even* the [f]sure mercies of David.

[a]John iv. 14; vii. 37; Rev. xxi. 6; xxii. 17——[b]Ecclus. li. 25; Matt. xiii. 44, 46; Rev. iii. 18——[c]Heb. *weigh*——[d]Matt. xi. 28——[e]Gen. ix. 16; xvii. 13, 19; Lev. xxiv. 8; 2 Sam. xxiii. 5; chap. liv. 8; lxi. 8; Jer. xxxii. 40——[f]2 Sam. vii. 8, &c.; Psa. lxxxix. 28; Acts xiii. 34

NOTES ON CHAP. LV

Verse 1. *Ho, every one that thirsteth*] "Water," says *Kimchi*, "is a metaphor for the *law* and *wisdom:* as the world cannot subsist without water, so it is impossible that it can subsist without *wisdom.* The *law* is also compared to *wine* and *milk:* to *wine* because *wine* rejoiceth the heart, as it is written: 'The statutes of the Lord are right, rejoicing the heart,' Psa. xix. 8. It is compared also to *milk*, because *milk* is the subsistence of the child; so are the *words of the law* the *nourishment* of his soul who walks in the Divine teaching, and grows up under it."

Come, buy wine and milk] In ancient times our forefathers used what is now called the *old third person singular*, ending in *eth*, for the *imperative mood.* We have a fine example of this in the first verses of this chapter. I shall present them as they stand in my old MS. Bible:—**Alle gee thirstinge cummeth to wateris: and gee that han not sylver, goth forth and bieth, and etith. Cummeth, bieth without silver, and without eny chaungyng, wyn and mylc. Heerith gee, heering me and etith gode thinge, and deliten schal in fattnesse your soule. Bowith in your eie and cummeth to mee, heerith and liven schal your soule. And I schal smyten with gou, everlastynge covenant, the faithful mercies of David.**

Verse 2. *Wherefore do ye spend*] Why should ye be so zealously attached to a doctrine from which your souls derive neither comfort nor nourishment?

Verse 3. *I will make an everlasting covenant*] Heb. אכרתה לכם ברית עולם *echrethah lachem berith olam*, "I will cut the old or everlasting covenant sacrifice with you." That covenant sacrifice which was pointed out of old from the very beginning; and which is to last to the con-

A. M. cir. 3292
B. C. cir. 712
Olymp. XVII. 1
cir. annum
NumæPompilii,
R. Roman., 4

4 Behold, I have given him [g]*for* a witness to the people, [h]a leader and commander to the people.

5 [i]Behold, thou shalt call a nation *that* thou knowest not, [k]and nations *that* knew not thee shall run unto thee because of the LORD thy God, and for the Holy One of Israel; [l]for he hath glorified thee.

6 [m]Seek ye the LORD while he may be found, call ye upon him while he is near:

7 [n]Let the wicked forsake his way, and [o]the unrighteous man [p]his thoughts: and let him return unto the LORD, [q]and he will have mercy upon him; and to our God, for [r]he will abundantly pardon.

8 [s]For my thoughts *are* not your thoughts, neither *are* your ways my ways, saith the LORD.

9 [t]For *as* the heavens are higher than the earth, so are my ways higher than your ways, and my thoughts than your thoughts.

A. M. cir. 3292
B. C. cir. 712
Olymp. XVII. 1
cir. annum
NumæPompilii,
R. Roman., 4

10 For [u]as the rain cometh down, and the snow from heaven, and returneth not thither, but watereth the earth, and maketh it bring forth and bud, that it may give seed to the sower, and bread to the eater:

11 [v]So shall my word be that goeth forth out of my mouth: it shall not return unto me void, but it shall accomplish that which I please, and it shall prosper *in the thing* whereto I sent it.

12 [w]For ye shall go out with joy, and be led forth with peace: the mountains and the hills shall [x]break forth before you into singing, and [y]all the trees of the field shall clap *their* hands.

13 [z]Instead of [a]the thorn shall come up the fir tree, and instead of the brier shall come up the myrtle tree: and it shall be to the LORD [b]for a name, for an everlasting sign *that* shall not be cut off.

---

[g]John xviii. 37; Rev. i. 5——[h]Jer. xxx. 9; Ezek. xxxiv. 23; Hos. iii. 5; Dan. ix. 25——[i]Chap. lii. 15; Eph. ii. 11, 12——[k]Chap. lx. 5——[l]Chap. lx. 9; Acts iii. 13——[m]Psa. xxxii. 6; Matt. v. 25; xxv. 11; John vii. 34; viii. 21; 2 Cor. vi. 1, 2; Heb. iii. 13——[n]Chap. i. 16——[o]Heb. *the man of iniquity*

[p]Zech. viii. 17——[q]Psa. cxxx. 7; Jer. iii. 12——[r]Heb. *he will multiply to pardon*——[s]2 Sam. vii. 19——[t]Psa. ciii. 11——[u]Deut. xxxii. 2——[v]Chap. liv. 9——[w]Chap. xxxv. 10; lxv. 13, 14——[x]Psa. xcvi. 12; xcviii. 8; chap. xiv. 8; xxxv. 1, 2; xlii. 11——[y]1 Chron. xvi. 33——[z]Chap. xli. 19——[a]Mic. vii. 4——[b]Jer. xiii. 11

---

summation of ages; viz., the Lamb of God that was slain from the foundation of the world.

The sure mercies of David] That is, says *Kimchi*, "The MESSIAH," called here *David;* as it is written, "David my servant shall be a prince over you."

Verse 6. *Seek ye the Lord while he may be found*] Rab. *David Kimchi* gives the true sense of this passage: "Seek ye the Lord, *because* he may be found: call upon him, *because* he is near. Repent before ye die, for after death there is no conversion of the soul."

Verse 9. *For as the heavens are higher*] I am persuaded that כ *caph*, the particle of comparison, is lost in this place, from the likeness of the particle כי *ki*, immediately preceding it. So *Houbigant* and *Secker*. And their remark is confirmed by all the ancient Versions, which express it; and by the following passage of Psa. ciii. 11, which is almost the same:—

כי כגבהה שמים על הארץ
haarets al shamayim chigboah ki

גבר חסדו על יראיו
yereaiv al chasdo gabar

"For as the heavens are high above the earth,
So high is his goodness over them that fear him."

Where, by the nature of the sentence, the verb, in the second line ought to be the same with that in the first; גבה *gabah*, not גבר *gabar:* so Archbishop *Secker* conjectured; referring however to Psa. cxvii. 2.

Verse 12. *The mountains and the hills*] These are highly poetical images to express a happy state attended with joy and exultation.

Ipsi lætitia voces ad sidera jactant
Intonsi montes: ipsæ jam carmina rupes,
Ipsa sonant arbusta. VIRG. Ecl. v. 61.

"The mountain tops unshorn, the *rocks* rejoice;
The lowly *shrubs* partake of human voice."
DRYDEN.

Verse 13. *Instead of the thorn*—"Instead of the thorny bushes"] These likewise (see note on the preceding verse, and on chap. liv. 11) are general poetical images, expressing a great and happy change for the better. The wilderness turned into a paradise, Lebanon into Carmel: the desert of the Gentiles watered with the heavenly snow and rain, which fail not to have their due effect, and becoming fruitful in piety and righteousness: or, as the *Chaldee* gives the moral sense of the emblem, "instead of the wicked shall arise the just; and instead of sinners, such as fear to sin." Compare chap. xxxv. 1, 2; xli. 19.

And instead of] The conjunction ו *vau* is added, ותחת *vetachath*, in forty-five MSS. of *Kennicott's* several of *De Rossi's*, and five editions; and it is acknowledged by all the ancient Versions. The Masoretes therefore might have safely received it into the text, and not have referred us for it to the margin. But this is no uncommon case with them. Even in our own *Version* the best reading is very often found in the *margin.*

CHAPTER LVI

Whoever would partake of the blessings of the Gospel is required to be holy in all manner of life and conversation. And he that will be so is declared to be accepted according to this gracious dispensation, the blessings of which are large as the human race, without any respect to persons or to nations, 1–8. *At the ninth verse begins a different subject, or new section of prophecy. It opens with calling on the enemies of the Jews, (the Chaldeans, or perhaps the Romans,) as beasts of prey against them, for the sins of their rulers, teachers, and other profane people among them, whose guilt drew down judgments on the nation,* 9–12.

A. M. cir. 3292
B. C. cir. 712
Olymp. XVII. 1
cir. annum
NumæPompilii,
R. Roman., 4

THUS saith the LORD, Keep
ye [a]judgment, and do jus-
tice: [b]for my salvation *is* near to
come, and my righteousness to
be revealed.
2 Blessed *is* the man *that* doeth this, and
the son of man *that* layeth hold on it; [c]that
keepeth the sabbath from polluting it, and
keepeth his hand from doing any evil.
3 Neither let [d]the son of the stranger, that
hath joined himself to the LORD, speak, saying, The LORD hath utterly separated me from
his people: neither let the eunuch say, Behold,
I *am* a dry tree.
4 For thus saith the LORD unto the eunuchs
that keep my sabbaths, and choose *the things*
that please me, and take hold of my covenant;
5 Even unto them will I give in [e]mine
house and within my walls a place [f]and a
name better than of sons and of daughters: I
will give them an everlasting
name, that shall not be cut off.

A. M. cir. 3292
B. C. cir. 712
Olymp. XVII. 1
cir. annum
NumæPompilii,
R. Roman., 4

6 Also the sons of the stranger,
that join themselves to the
LORD, to serve him, and to love the name of
the LORD, to be his servants, every one that
keepeth the sabbath from polluting it, and
taketh hold of my covenant;
7 Even them will I [g]bring to my holy
mountain, and make them joyful in my house
of prayer: [h]their burnt-offerings and their
sacrifices *shall be* accepted upon mine altar;
for [i]mine house shall be called a house of
prayer [k]for all people.
8 The LORD God [l]which gathereth the outcasts of Israel saith, [m]Yet will I gather *others*
to him, [n]beside those that are gathered unto
him.
9 [o]All ye beasts of the field, come to devour,
yea, all ye beasts in the forest.

---

[a]Or, *equity*——[b]Chap. xlvi. 13; Matt. iii. 2; iv. 17; Rom. xiii. 11, 12——[c]Chap. lviii. 13——[d]See Deut. xxiii. 1, 2, 3; Acts viii. 27; x. 1, 2, 34; xvii. 4; xviii. 7; 1 Pet. i. 1——[e]1 Tim. iii. 15——[f]John i. 12; 1 John iii. 1 [g]Chap. ii. 2; 1 Pet. i. 1, 2

[h]Rom. xii. 1; Heb. xiii. 15; 1 Pet. ii. 5——[i]Matt. xxi. 13; Mark xi. 17; Luke xix. 46——[k]Mal. i. 11 [l]Psa. cxlvii. 2; chap. xi. 12——[m]John x. 16; Eph. i. 10; ii. 14, 15, 16——[n]Hebrew, *to his gathered* [o]Jer. xii. 9

NOTES ON CHAP. LVI

Verse 2. *That keepeth the Sabbath from polluting it*] *Kimchi* has an excellent note here. "The Sabbath is sanctified when it is *distinguished in dignity;* and *separated* from *other days.* 1. As to the *body,* in meat, drink, and clean clothing. 2. As to the *soul,* that it be empty of worldly occupations, and be busily employed in the words of the law and wisdom, and in meditation on the works of the Lord." The *rabbins* say, "Jerusalem had never been destroyed, had not the Sabbaths been profaned in it."

Verse 5. *I will give them an everlasting name*] For לו *lo, him,* in the singular, it is evident that we ought to read למו *lamo, them,* in the plural: so read the *Septuagint, Syriac, Chaldee,* and *Vulgate.*

Verse 6. *The sons of the stranger*] The Gentiles.

That join themselves to the Lord] Who shall enter into the Christian covenant by baptism and faith in Christ, as the Jews and proselytes did by *circumcision.*

To serve him] To live according to the Gospel, and ever do that which is right in the sight of the Lord.

To love the name of the Lord] The name of JESUS, the Christ, the *Saviour* of sinners, the *Anointed* of God, and the Giver of the Holy Spirit to his followers.

To be his servants] To worship no other God but JEHOVAH, and to trust in none for salvation but his CHRIST.

That keepeth the Sabbath] That observes it as a type of the *rest* that remains for the people of God.

And taketh hold of my covenant] בבריתי *biberithi,* "of my covenant sacrifice;" as without this he can do nothing good; and without it nothing can be acceptable to the infinite majesty of the Most High.

Verse 7. Shall be *accepted*] A word is here lost out of the text: it is supplied from the *Septuagint,* יהיו *yihyu,* εσονται, "they shall be."—*Houbigant.*

Verse 9. *All ye beasts of the field*] Here manifestly begins a new section. The prophet in the foregoing chapters, having comforted the faithful Jews with many great promises of God's favour to be extended to them, in the restoration of their ruined state, and in the

A. M. cir. 3292 B. C. cir. 712 Olymp. XVII. 1 cir. annum NumæPompilii, R. Roman., 4

10 His watchmen *are* [p]blind:
they are all ignorant, [q]they *are*
all dumb dogs, they cannot bark;
[r]sleeping, lying down, loving to
slumber.

11 Yea, *they are* [s]greedy [t]dogs *which* [u]can
[v]never have enough, and they *are* shepherds
that cannot understand: they all
look to their own way, every one
for his gain, from his quarter.

12 Come ye, *say they*, I will
fetch wine; and we will fill ourselves with
strong drink; [w]and to-morrow shall be as this
day, *and* much more abundant.

[p]Matt. xv. 14; xxiii. 17; Luke vi. 39; xxiii. 16 —— [q]Phil. iii. 2 —— [r]Or, *dreaming*, or *talking in their sleep* —— [s]Heb. *strong of appetite* —— [t]Mic. iii. 11 —— [u]Heb. *know not to be satisfied* —— [v]Ezek. xxxiv. 2, 3 —— [w]Psa. x. 6; Prov. xxiii. 35; chap. xxii. 13; Luke xii. 19; 1 Cor. xv. 32

enlargement of his Church by the admission of the Gentiles; here on a sudden makes a transition to the more disagreeable part of the prospect, and to a sharp reproof of the wicked and unbelievers; and especially of the negligent and faithless governors and teachers, of the idolaters and hypocrites, who would still draw down his judgments upon the nation. Probably having in view the destruction of their city and polity by the Chaldeans, and perhaps by the Romans. The same subject is continued in the next chapter; in which the charge of corruption and apostasy becomes more general against the whole Jewish Church. Some expositors have made great difficulties in the 9th verse of this chapter, where there seems to be none. It is perfectly well explained by Jeremiah, chap. xii. 7, 9, where, having introduced God declaring his purpose of punishing his people, by giving them up as a prey to their enemies the Chaldeans, a charge to these his agents is given in words very nearly the same with those of Isaiah in this place:—

"I have forsaken my house; I have deserted my heritage;
I have given up the beloved of my soul into the hands of her enemies.—
Come away, be gathered together, all ye beasts of the field;
Come away to devour."

All ye beasts in the forest—"All ye beasts of the forest."] Instead of ביער *baiyaar*, three MSS. have יער *yaar*, without the preposition; which seems to be right, and is confirmed by all the ancient Versions.

Verse 10. *His watchmen* are *blind*] *Kimchi* observes, "The flock is intrusted to the care of these watchmen. The wild beasts come; these dogs bark not; and the wild beasts devour the flock. Thus they do not *profit* the flock. Yea, they *injure* it; for the owner trusts in them, that they will watch and be faithful; but they are not. These are the false teachers and careless shepherds."

Dumb dogs, they cannot bark] See note on chap. lxii. 6.

Sleeping—"Dreamers"] הזים *hozim*, ενυπνιαζομενοι, *Septuagint*. This seems to be the best authority for the meaning of this word, which occurs only in this place: but it is to be observed, that eleven MSS. of *Kennicott's* and *De Rossi's*, and four editions, have חזים *chazim*, *seers*, or *those who see;* and so the *Vulgate* seems to have read, videntes vana, "seeing vain things."

Loving to slumber.] לנום *lanum:* but six of *Kennicott's* and seven of *De Rossi's* MSS. read לנוס *lanus, to fly*, "to change their residence:" but what connexion such reading can have with the *sense* of the passage, I cannot discern. What is taken for ס *samech* here is, I have no doubt, a *narrow* formed final ם *mem*, which has been mistaken for the above. Many instances occur in my own MSS., where the final ם *mem* is similar to the *samech;* and yet no such change was intended by the scribe.

Verse 11. *Greedy dogs*] Insatiably feeding themselves with the fat, and clothing themselves with the wool, while the flock is scattered, ravaged, and starved! O what an abundance of these dumb and greedy dogs are there found hanging on and prowling about the flock of Christ! How can any careless, avaricious, hireling minister read this without agitation and dismay?

Verse 12. *I will fetch wine*—"Let us provide wine"] For אקחה *ekchah*, first person singular, an ancient MS. has נקחה *nikchah*, first person plural; and another ancient MS. has אק *ak* upon a rasure. So the *Syriac*, *Chaldee*, and *Vulgate* render it. The spirit of this epicurean sentiment is this: Let us indulge ourselves in the present time to the utmost, and instead of any gloomy forebodings of the future, let us expect nothing but increasing hilarity for every day we shall live. Thus they,

"Counting on long years of pleasure here,
Are quite unfurnished for the world to come."

CHAPTER LVII

After mentioning the removal of righteous persons as an awful symptom of the approach of Divine judgments, 1, 2, *the prophet goes on to charge the nation in general with idolatry, and with courting the unprofitable alliance of idolatrous kings,* 3–12. *In opposition to such vain confidence, the prophet enjoins trust in God, with whom the penitent and humble are sure to find acceptance, and from whom they should obtain temporal and spiritual deliverances,* 13–19. *Awful condition of the wicked and finally impenitent,* 20, 21.

A. M. cir. 3292 B. C. cir. 712 Olymp. XVII. 1 cir. annum NumæPompilii, R. Roman., 4

THE righteous perisheth, and
no man layeth *it* to heart:
and [a]merciful [b]men *are* taken
away, [c]none considering that the
righteous is taken away [d]from the evil *to*
come.
2 He shall [e]enter into peace: they shall
rest [f]in their beds, *each one* walking [g]*in* his
uprightness.
3 But draw near hither, [h]ye sons of the
sorceress, the seed of the adulterer and the whore.
4 Against whom do ye sport
yourselves? against whom make
ye a wide mouth, *and* draw out the tongue?
are ye not children of transgression, a [i]seed
of falsehood,
5 Enflaming yourselves [k]with idols [l]under
every green tree, [m]slaying the children in the
valleys under the clifts of the rocks?

A. M. cir. 3292 B. C. cir. 712 Olymp. XVII. 1 cir. annum NumæPompilii, R. Roman., 4

[a]Heb. *men of kindness,* or *godliness*——[b]Psa. xii. 1; Mic. vii. 2——[c]1 Kings xiv. 13; see 2 Kings xxii. 20; Wisd. iv. 20, &c.——[d]Or, *from that which is evil*——[e]Or, *go in peace;* Luke ii. 29——[f]2 Chron. xvi. 14

[g]Or, *before him*——[h]Matthew xvi. 4——[i]Chapter i. 4——[k]Or, *among the oaks;* chap. i. 29——[l]2 Kings xvi. 4; xvii. 10; Jer. ii. 20——[m]Lev. xviii. 21; xx. 2; 2 Kings xvi. 3, xxiii. 10; Jer. vii. 31; Ezek. xvi. 20; xx. 26

NOTES ON CHAP. LVII

I shall give Bishop *Lowth's* translation of the two first verses, and give the substance of his criticisms with additional evidence.

Ver. 1. The righteous man perisheth, and no one considereth;
And pious men are taken away, and no one understandeth,
That the righteous man is taken away because of the evil.
2. He shall go in peace: he shall rest in his bed;
Even the perfect man: he that walketh in the straight path.

Verse 1. *The righteous perisheth*—הצדק אבד *hatstsadik abad.* There is an emphasis here which seems intended to point out a particular person. See below. *Perisheth*—As the root עבד *abad* signifies the straying of cattle, their passing away from one pasture to another, I feel inclined to follow the grammatical meaning of the word "perish," *pereo.* So the *Vulgate, justus periit,* from *per,* BY or THROUGH, and *eo,* to GO. In his death the righteous man may be said to have passed *through* life, and to have passed by men, i. e., gone or passed before them into the eternal world. A similar mode of speech is used by our Saxon ancestors to express death: **geforon site.** he went out of sight; and **gefor,** he went away; and **forðforen,** to fare forth, to die.

There are very few places in Isaiah where Jesus Christ is not intended; and I am inclined to think that *He* is intended here, THAT Just One; and perhaps Stephen had this place in view, when he thus charged the Jews, "Ye denied *τον ἁγιον και δικαιον,* that HOLY and JUST One," Acts iii. 14. That his death was not laid to heart by the wicked Jewish people, needs no proof.

Merciful men] If the *first* refers to *Christ,* this may well refer to the *apostles,* and to others of the primitive Christians, who were *taken away,* some by death and martyrdom, and others by a providential escape from the city that they knew was devoted to destruction.

The evil to come.] That destruction which was to come upon this disobedient people by the Romans.

Verse 2. *He shall enter into peace*—"He shall go in peace"] יבוא שלום *yabo shalom;* the expression is elliptical, such as the prophet frequently uses. The same sense is expressed at large and in full terms, Gen. xv. 15: ואתה תבא אל אבותיך בשלום *veattah tibbo al abotheycha beshalom,* "and thou shalt go to thy fathers in peace."

They shall rest in their beds, each one *walking* in *his uprightness*—"He shall rest in his bed; even the perfect man."] This obscure sentence is reduced to a perfectly good sense, and easy construction by an ingenious remark of Dr. Durell. He reads ינוח על משכבו תם *yanuach al mishcabo tam,* "the perfect man shall rest in his bed." Two MSS. (one of them ancient) have ינוח *yanuach,* singular; and so the *Vulgate* renders it, *requiescat,* "he shall rest." The verb was probably altered to make it plural, and so consistent with what follows, after the mistake had been made in the following words, by uniting משכבו *mishcabo* and תם *tam* into one word. See *Merrick's* Annotations on the Psalms, Addenda; where the reader will find that J. S. Moerlius, by the same sort of correction, and by rescuing the adjective תם *tam,* which had been swallowed up in another word in the same manner, has restored to a clear sense a passage before absolutely unintelligible:—

כי אין חרצבות למו
lemo chartsubboth ein ki
תם ובריא אולם:
ulam ubari tham

"For no distresses happen to them;
Perfect and firm is their strength."
Psa. lxxiii. 4.

To follow on my application of this to our Lord:—HE, the JUST ONE, *shall enter into peace*—the peaceable, prosperous possession of the glorious mediatorial kingdom. *They shall rest upon their beds*—the hand of wrong and oppression can reach these persecuted followers of Christ no more. (But see below.) *The perfect man walking in his uprightness.* This may be considered as a general declaration. The separated spirit, though disunited from its body, walking in conscious existence in the paradise of God, reaping the fruit of *righteousness.* The word which we render *their beds,* משכבותם *mishkebotham,* the learned bishop supposes to be two words; and to be compounded of משכבו *mishkabo, his bed,* and תם *tam, the upright* or *perfect man.* This is the reading both of the *Syriac* and *Vulgate,* and it is favoured by the *Chaldee;* and one of *De Rossi's* MS. has משכבו

A. M. cir. 3292 B. C. cir. 712 Olymp. XVII. 1 cir. annum Numæ Pompilii, R. Roman., 4

6 Among the smooth *stones* of
the stream *is* thy portion; they,
they *are* thy lot: even to them
hast thou poured a drink-offering, thou hast offered a meat-offering.
Should I receive comfort in these?
7 ⁿUpon a lofty and high mountain hast thou
set ᵒthy bed: even thither wentest thou up to
offer sacrifice.
8 Behind the doors also and the posts hast
thou set up thy remembrance:
for thou hast discovered *thyself*
to another than me, and art gone
up; thou hast enlarged thy bed,
and ᵖmade thee *a covenant* with them; ᵠthou
lovedst their bed ʳwhere thou sawest *it*.
9 And ˢthou ᵗwentest to the king with ointment, and didst increase thy perfumes, and
didst send thy messengers far off, and didst
debase *thyself even* unto hell.

A. M. cir. 3292 B. C. cir. 712 Olymp. XVII. 1 cir. annum Numæ Pompilii, R. Roman., 4

ⁿEzek. xvi. 16, 25.——ᵒEzek. xxiii. 41.——ᵖOr, *hewed it for thyself* larger *than theirs*.——ᵠEzek. xvi. 26, 28; xxiii. 2–20.——ʳOr, *thou providest room*.——ˢOr, *thou respectedst the king*.——ᵗChap. xxx. 6; Ezek. xvi. 33; xxiii. 16; Hosea vii. 11; xii. 1.

mishkabo, his bed, without the word תם *tam*, which has been added by a later hand. Bishop *Lowth*, as we have seen, adopts this separation of the word; and for ינוחו *yanuchu, they shall rest*, reads ינוח *yanuach, he shall rest*, which is supported by two of Dr. *Kennicott's* MSS., and by the *Vulgate*, *Septuagint*, and *Arabic*. The word תם *tam*, taken from משכבותם *mishkebotham*, should begin the latter clause of the verse; and then the interpolated words, *each one*, which our translators supplied, may be very well spared. The verse may be then read and paraphrased thus:—

He shall enter into peace: he shall rest upon his bed;
The perfect man walking in his uprightness.

The *bed* must signify the *grave;* the walking in uprightness after death, the conscious existence of the happy spirit, and its eternal progression in happiness and perfection: נכחו *nechocho, straight before him;* proceeding into the unlimited extent of eternal glory, increasing in happiness, and increasing in perfection.

My old MS. Bible translates very nervously:—

The rightwise man perishith,
And there is not that bethinke in his herte.
And men of mercy ben gedrid,
For there is not that understonde:
From the face forsoth of malice,
Gedrid is the rigtwise.
Cumm pese: reste it in his bed
That geede in his rigt rewlinge.

It has been often remarked that, previously to the execution of God's judgments upon a wicked place, he has removed good men from it, that they might not suffer with the wicked. When great and good men are removed by death, or otherwise, from any place, the remaining inhabitants have much cause to tremble.

Verse 6. *Among the smooth* stones *of the stream*—"Among the smooth stones of the valley"] The Jews were extremely addicted to the practice of many superstitious and idolatrous rites, which the prophet here inveighs against with great vehemence. Of the worship of rude stones consecrated, there are many testimonials of the ancients. They were called Βαιτυλοι and Βαιτυλια· probably from the stone which Jacob erected at Beth-el, pouring oil upon the top of it. This practice was very common in different ages and places. *Arnobius*, lib. i., gives an account of his own practice in this respect before he became a Christian: Si quando conspexeram lubricatum lapidem, et ex olivi unguine sordidatum; tanquam inesset vis præsens, adulabar, affabar, et beneficia poscebam nihil sentiente de trunco.—"When I have met with a smooth stone, smeared with oil, supposing a spiritual power to be connected with it, I worshipped it, paid my addresses to it, and requested blessings," &c. *Clemens* Alex., Strom. lib. vii., speaks of a worshipper of every smooth stone in a proverbial way, to denote one given up to superstition. And accordingly Theophrastus has marked this as one strong feature in the character of the superstitious man: Και των λιπαρων λιθων των εν ταις τριοδοις παριων, εκ της ληκυθου ελαιου καταχειν, και επι γονατα πεσων και προσκυνησας απαλλαττεσθαι. "Passing by the anointed stones in the streets, he takes out his phial of oil, and pours it on them; and having fallen on his knees, and made his adorations, he departs." *Kimchi* says: "When they found a beautiful polished stone in a brook or river, they paid Divine adoration to it." This idolatry is still prevalent among the Hindoos. The stone which is the object of their adoration is called *salgram.* They are found about eighty miles from the source of the river Sown, in the viceroyalty of Bahar, on the coast of Bengal. *Ayeen Akbery* vol. ii. p. 29.

Verse 8. *Behind the doors also and the posts hast thou set up thy remembrance*—"Behind the door, and the door-posts, hast thou set up thy memorial"] That is, the image of their tutelary gods, or something dedicated to them; in direct opposition to the law of God, which commanded them to write upon the door-posts of their house, and upon their gates, the words of God's law; Deut. vi. 9; xi. 20. If they chose for them such a situation as more private, it was in defiance of a particular curse denounced in the law against the man who should make a graven or a molten image, and put it in a secret place; Deut. xxvii. 15. An ancient MS., with another, has אחר *achar*, without the conjunction ו *vau, and.*

Verse 9. *And thou wentest to the king with ointment*—"And thou hast visited the king with a present of oil"] That is, the king of Assyria, or Egypt. Hosea, chap. xii. 1, reproaches the Israelites for the same practice:—

"They make a covenant with Assyria,
And oil is carried to Egypt."

It is well known, that in all parts of the east, whoever visits a great person must carry him a present. "It is counted uncivil," says *Maundrell*, p. 26, "to visit in this country without

A. M. cir. 3292
B. C. cir. 712
Olymp. XVII. 1
cir. annum
NumæPompilii,
R. Roman., 4

10 Thou art wearied in the
greatness of thy way; [u]*yet* saidst
thou not, There is no hope:
thou hast found the [v]life of thine
hand; therefore thou wast not grieved.
11 And [w]of whom hast thou been afraid or
feared, that thou hast lied, and hast not remembered me, nor laid *it* to thy heart? [x]have
not I held my peace even of old, and thou
fearest me not?
12 I will declare thy righteousness, and thy
works; for they shall not profit thee.
13 When thou criest, let thy companies deliver thee; but the wind shall carry them all
away; vanity shall take *them*: but he that putteth his trust in me shall possess
the land, and shall inherit my
holy mountain;
14 And shall say, [y]Cast ye
up, cast ye up, prepare the way, take up
the stumbling block out of the way of my
people.
15 For thus saith the high and lofty One
that inhabiteth eternity, [z]whose name *is*
Holy; [a]I dwell in the high and holy *place*,
[b]with him also *that is* of a contrite and humble spirit, [c]to revive the spirit of the humble,
and to revive the heart of the contrite ones.
16 [d]For I will not contend for ever, neither
will I be always wroth: for the spirit should

A. M. cir. 3292
B. C. cir. 712
Olymp. XVII. 1
cir. annum
NumæPompilii,
R. Roman., 4

[u]Jeremiah ii. 25——[v]Or, *living*——[w]Chap. li. 12, 13——[x]Psalm l. 21——[y]Chap. xl. 3; lxii. 10——[z]Job vi. 10; Luke i. 49——[a]Psalm lxviii. 4; Zechariah ii. 13——[b]Psa. xxxiv. 18; li. 17; cxxxviii. 6; chap. lxvi. 2——[c]Psalm cxlvii. 3; chap. lxi. 1——[d]Psalm lxxxv. 5; ciii. 9; Mic. vii. 18

an offering in hand. All great men expect it as a tribute due to their character and authority; and look upon themselves as affronted, and indeed defrauded, when the compliment is omitted." Hence שור *shur, to visit* a person, is equivalent to making him a present; and תשורה *teshurah* signifies a *present* made on such occasions; as our translators have rightly rendered it, 1 Sam. ix. 7; on which Jarchi says, Menachem exponit תשורה *teshurah*, quod significat oblationem sive manus, ut aliquis aspiciat faciem regis, aut alicujus magnatis. "Menachem expounds תשורה *teshurah* of an offering or gift which is presented in order to be admitted into the presence of the king or some great man."

Verse 10. Yet *saidst thou not, There is no hope*—"Thou hast said, There is hope"] In one of the MSS. at Koningsberg, collated by Lilienthal, the words לא אמרת *lo amarta*, are left in the text unpointed, as suspected; and in the margin the corrector has written ותאמרי *vattomari*. Now if we compare Jer. ii. 25 and xviii. 12, we shall find that the subject is in both places quite the same with this of Isaiah; and the sentiment expressed, that of a desperate resolution to continue at all hazards in their idolatrous practices; the very thing that in all reason we might expect here. Probably, therefore, the latter is the true reading in this place.—L.

Verse 11. *Nor laid* it *to thy heart*—"Nor revolved it in thy hand"] *Eight* MSS., (*four* ancient,) and the *two* oldest editions, with another, add the conjunction ו *vau*, ולא *velo:* which is confirmed by all the ancient Versions.

Even of old—"And winked"] For ומעולם *umeolam*, which makes no good sense or construction in this place, *twenty-three* MSS. (*seven* ancient) and *three* editions have מעלם, (to be thus pointed מעלם *malim;*) Παρορω, *Septuagint; quasi non videns*, "as if not seeing," *Vulgate*. See Psa. x. 1. The truth of this reading, so confirmed, admits of no doubt. In one of my own MSS. the ו *vau* has been written, but afterwards struck out. *Is it not because I was silent, and winked?*

Verse 12. *Thy righteousness*—"My righteousness"] For צדקתך *tsidkathech*, THY *righteousness*, the *Syriac*, *Septuagint*, MSS. *Alex.* and *Pachom.*, and I. D. II., and *Marchal.* and οἱ Γ, and the *Arabic*, read צדקי *tsidki*, MY *righteousness*.

Verse 13. *Let thy companies deliver thee*—"Let thine associates deliver thee"] *Thirty-nine* MSS. (*ten* ancient) of Dr. *Kennicott's*, and *two* of my own, and the two oldest editions have יצילךו *yatstsiluchu*, plural.

Verse 14. *And shall say*—"Then will I say"] ואמר *vaomer*, to be pointed as the first person future. They are the words of God, as it is plain from the conclusion of the verse; *my* people, עמי *ammi*.

Verse 15. *For thus saith the high and lofty One*—"For thus saith JEHOVAH, the high and the lofty"] A MS. adds יהוה *Yehovah*, after אמר *amar*, and edition Prag. 1518. So the *Septuagint*, *Alex.*, and *Arabic*. An ancient MS. adds יה *Yah*.

With him also that is *of a contrite and humble spirit*] *Twelve* MSS. have את *eth*, without the conjunction ו *vau*. Pro ואת *veeth*, forte legendum ואראה *veerah:* confer Psa. cxiii. 5, *et* cxxxviii. 6.—SECKER. "We should perhaps read ואראה *veerah*, instead of ואת *veeth*. See Psa. cxiii. 5, and cxxxviii. 6."

Verse 16. *For I will not contend for ever*] The learned have taken a great deal of pains to little purpose on the latter part of this verse, which they suppose to be very obscure. After all their labours upon it, I think the best and easiest explication of it is given in the two following elegant passages of the Psalms, which I presume are exactly parallel to it, and very clearly express the same sentiment.

"But he in his tender mercy will forgive their sin,
And will not destroy them;
Yea, oftentimes will he turn away his wrath,
And will not rouse up his indignation:
For he remembereth that they are but flesh,
A breath that passeth, and returneth not."
Psa. lxxviii. 38, 39.

A. M. cir. 3292
B. C. cir. 712
Olymp. XVII. 1
cir. annum
NumæPompilii,
R. Roman., 4

fail before me, and the souls
[e]*which* I have made.
17 For the iniquity of [f]his
covetousness was I wroth, and
smote him: [g]I hid me, and was wroth, [h]and he
went on [i]frowardly in the way of his heart.
18 I have seen his ways, and [k]will heal him:
I will lead him also, and restore comforts unto
him and to [l]his mourners.

19 I create [m]the fruit of the lips;
Peace, peace [n]to *him that is* far
off, and to *him that is* near, saith
the LORD; and I will heal him.
20 [o]But the wicked *are* like the troubled
sea, when it cannot rest, whose waters cast
up mire and dirt.
21 [p]*There is* no peace, saith my God, to the
wicked.

A. M. cir. 3292
B. C. cir. 712
Olymp. XVII. 1
cir. annum
NumæPompilii,
R. Roman., 4

[e]Num. xvi. 22; Job xxxiv. 14; Heb. xii. 9——[f]Jer. vi. 13——[g]Chap. viii. 17; xlv. 15——[h]Chap. ix. 13
[i]Heb. *turning away*

[k]Jer. iii. 22——[l]Chap. lxi. 2——[m]Heb. xiii. 15
[n]Acts ii. 39; Eph. ii. 17——[o]Job xv. 20, &c.; Prov. iv. 16——[p]Chap. xlviii. 22

"He will not always contend,
Neither will he for ever hold his wrath:
As a father yearneth towards his children,
So is JEHOVAH tenderly compassionate towards them that fear him:
For he knoweth our frame;
He remembereth that we are but dust."
Psa. ciii. 9, 13, 14.

In the former of these two passages the second line seems to be defective both in measure and sense. I suppose the word אותם *otham, them,* is lost at the end; which seems to be acknowledged by the *Chaldee* and *Vulgate,* who render as if they had read ולא ישחית אותם *velo yaschith otham.*—L.

For the spirit] רוח *ruach, the animal life.*

And the souls] נשמות *neshamoth, the immortal spirits.* The *Targum* understands this of the resurrection. *I will restore the souls of the dead,* i. e., to their bodies.

Verse 17. *For the iniquity of his covetousness was I wroth*—"Because of his iniquity for a short time was I wroth"] For בצעו *bitso,* I read בצע *betsa, a little while,* from בצע *batsa, he cut off;* as the *Septuagint* read and render it, *βραχυ τι,* "a certain short space." *Propter iniquitatem* avaritiæ ejus, "because of the iniquity of his avarice," the rendering of the *Vulgate,* which our translators and I believe all others follow, is surely quite beside the purpose.

Verse 18. *I have seen his ways*] Probably these verses refer to the restoration of the Jews from captivity.

Verse 19. *I create the fruit of the lips*] "The sacrifice of praise," saith St. Paul, Heb. xiii. 15, "is the fruit of the lips." God creates this fruit of the lips, by giving new subject and cause of thanksgiving by his mercies conferred on those among his people, who acknowledge and bewail their transgressions, and return to him. The great subject of thanksgiving is peace—reconciliation and pardon, offered to them that are nigh, and to them that are afar off; not only to the Jew, but also to the Gentile, as St. Paul more than once applies those terms, Eph. ii. 13, 17. See also Acts ii. 39.

Peace to him that is *far off*—"That is, to the penitent; *and to* him that is *near,* i. e., the righteous."—*Kimchi.*

Verse 21. There is *no peace, saith my God*] For אלהי *Elohai, twenty-two* MSS. (*five* ancient) of *Kennicott's, thirty* of *De Rossi's,* and *one* ancient of my own, read יהוה *Yehovah;* the *Vulgate, Septuagint, Alex.,* and *Arabic,* and three MSS. have both. This verse has reference to the *nineteenth.* The perseveringly wicked and impenitent are excluded from all share in that peace above mentioned, that reconcilement and pardon which is promised to the *penitent* only. The forty-eighth chapter ends with the same declaration, to express the exclusion of the unbelievers and impenitent from the benefit of the foregoing promises.—L.

CHAPTER LVIII

This elegant chapter contains a severe reproof of the Jews on account of their vices, particularly their hypocrisy in practising and relying on outward ceremonies, such as fasting and bodily humiliation, without true repentance, 1–5. It then lays down a clear and comprehensive summary of the duties they owed to their fellow creatures, 6, 7. Large promises of happiness and prosperity are likewise annexed to the performance of these duties in a variety of the most beautiful and striking images, 8–12. Great temporal and spiritual blessedness of those who keep holy the Sabbath day, 13, 14.

A. M. cir. 3292
B. C. cir. 712
Olymp. XVII. 1
cir. annum
NumæPompilii,
R. Roman., 4

CRY [a]aloud, spare not, lift up
thy voice like a trumpet,
and show my people their transgression, and the house of Jacob
their sins.
2 Yet they seek me daily, and

A. M. cir. 3292
B. C. cir. 712
Olymp. XVII. 1
cir. annum
NumæPompilii,
R. Roman., 4

[a]Heb. *with the throat*

NOTES ON CHAP. LVIII

Verse 1. *Cry aloud, spare not*] Never was a louder cry against the hypocrisy, nor a more cutting reproof of the wickedness, of a people professing a national established religion, having all the forms of godliness without a particle of its power. This chapter has been often appointed to be read on political fast days for the success of wars carried on for—God *knows*

A. M. cir. 3292 B. C. cir. 712 Olymp. XVII. 1 cir. annum NumæPompilii, R. Roman., 4

delight to know my ways, as a
nation that did righteousness,
and forsook not the ordinance of
their God: they ask of me the
ordinances of justice; they take delight in approaching to God.
3 [b]Wherefore have we fasted, *say they,* and
thou seest not? *wherefore* have we [c]afflicted
our soul, and thou takest no knowledge? Behold, in the day of your fast ye find pleasure,
and exact all your [d]labours[e].
4 [f]Behold, ye fast for strife and debate, and
to smite with the fist of wickedness: [g]ye shall
not fast as *ye do this* day, to make your voice
to be heard on high.
5 Is it [h]such a fast that I have chosen?
[i]a[k] day for a man to afflict his soul? *is it* to
bow down his head as a bulrush, and [l]to
spread sackcloth and ashes *under him?* wilt
thou call this a fast, and an acceptable day to the LORD?
6 *Is* not this the fast that I
have chosen? to loose the bands
of wickedness, [m]to undo [n]the heavy burdens,
and [o]to let the [p]oppressed go free, and that
ye break every yoke?
7 *Is it* not [q]to deal thy bread to the hungry,
and that thou bring the poor that are [r]cast
out to thy house? [s]when thou seest the naked,
that thou cover him; and that thou hide not
thyself from [t]thine own flesh?
8 [u]Then shall thy light break forth as the
morning, and thine health shall spring forth
speedily: and thy righteousness shall go before thee; [v]the glory of the LORD [w]shall be
thy rereward.
9 Then shalt thou call, and the LORD shall
answer; thou shalt cry, and he shall say,

[b]Mal. iii. 14——[c]Lev. xvi. 29, 31; xxiii. 27——[d]Or, *things wherewith ye grieve others*——[e]Heb. *griefs* [f]1 Kings xxi. 9, 12, 13——[g]Or, *ye fast not as this day* [h]Zech. vii. 5——[i]Lev. xvi. 29——[k]Or, *to afflict his soul for a day*——[l]Esth. iv. 3; Job ii. 8; Dan. ix. 3; Jonah iii. 6

[m]Neh. v. 10, 11, 12——[n]Heb. *the bundles of the yoke* [o]Jer. xxxiv. 9——[p]Heb. *broken*——[q]Ezek. xviii. 7, 16; Matt. xxv. 35——[r]Or, *afflicted*——[s]Job xxxi. 19 [t]Gen. xxix. 14; Neh. v. 5——[u]Job xi. 17——[v]Exod. xiv. 19; chap. lii. 12——[w]Heb. *shall gather thee up*

what purposes, and originating in—God *knows* what motives. Politically speaking, was ever any thing more injudicious?

Verse 3. *Have we afflicted our soul*—"Have we afflicted our souls"] *Twenty-seven* MSS. (*six* ancient) of Dr. *Kennicott's*, *thirty-six* of *De Rossi's*, and *two* of my own, and the old edition of 1488 have the noun in the plural number, נפשינו *naphsheynu, our souls;* and so the *Septuagint*, *Chaldee*, and *Vulgate*. This reading is undoubtedly genuine.

In the day of your fast ye find pleasure] Fast days are generally called *holidays*, and holidays are days of idleness and pleasure. In numberless cases the *fast* is turned into a *feast*.

And exact all your labours.] Some disregard the most sacred fast, and will oblige their servant to *work* all day long; others use fast days for the purpose of settling their accounts, posting up their books, and drawing out their bills to be ready to collect their debts. These are sneaking hypocrites; the others are daringly irreligious.

Verse 4. *Ye fast for strife and debate*] How often is this the case! A whole nation are called to fast to implore God's blessing on wars carried on for the purposes of wrath and ambition.

To smite with the fist of wickedness: ye shall not fast as ye do this *day*—"To smite with the fist the poor. Wherefore fast ye unto me in this manner"] I follow the version of the *Septuagint*, which gives a much better sense than the present reading of the Hebrew. Instead of רשע לא *resha lo*, they seem to have read in their copy רש על מה לי *rash al mah lli.* The four first letters are the same, but otherwise divided in regard to the words; the four last are lost, and א *aleph* added in their place, in order to make some sort of sense with רשע ל. The version of the *Septuagint* is, *και τυπτετε πυγμαις ταπεινον· ἱνα τι μοι νηστευετε*—— as above.

Verse 6. *Let the oppressed go free*] How can any nation pretend to fast or worship God at all, or dare to profess that they believe in the existence of such a Being, while they carry on the *slave trade*, and traffic in the souls, blood, and bodies, of men! O ye most flagitious of knaves, and worst of hypocrites, cast off at once the mask of religion; and deepen not your endless perdition by professing the *faith* of our *Lord Jesus Christ*, while ye continue in this traffic!

Verse 7. *Deal thy bread to the hungry*] But this thou canst not do, if thou eat it *thyself.* When a man fasts, suppose he do it through a religious motive, he should give the food of that day, from which he abstains, to the poor and hungry, who, in the course of providence, are called to sustain many involuntary fasts, besides suffering general privations. Wo to him who saves a day's victuals by his religious fast! He should either give them or their value in money to the poor. See ver. 6.

That thou bring the poor that are cast out to thy house—"To bring the wandering poor into thy house"] *πτωχους αστεγους*, *Septuagint;* *egenos* vagosque, *Vulgate;* and מטלטלין *metaltelin, Chaldee.* They read, instead of מרודים *merudim,* הנודים *hanudim.* מר *mer* is upon a rasure in the Bodleian MS. The same MS. reads ביתה *bayethah*, in *domum*, "into the house."—L.

Verse 8. *And thine health shall spring forth speedily*—"And thy wounds shall speedily be healed over"] Et cicatrix vulneris tui cito obducetur; "And the scar of thy wounds shall be speedily removed." *Aquila's* Version, as reported by Jerome, with which agrees that of the *Chaldee*.

The glory—"And the glory"] Sixteen MSS.

A. M. cir. 3292
B. C. cir. 712
Olymp. XVII. 1
cir. annum
NumæPompilii,
R. Roman., 4

Here I *am*. If thou take away from the midst of thee the yoke, the putting forth of the finger, and [x]speaking vanity;

10 And *if* thou draw out thy soul to the hungry, and satisfy the afflicted soul; then shall thy light rise in obscurity, and thy darkness *be* as the noon day:

11 And the LORD shall guide thee continually, and satisfy thy soul in [y]drought, and make fat thy bones: and thou shalt be like a watered garden, and like a spring of water, whose waters [z]fail not.

12 And *they that shall be* of thee [a]shall build the old waste places: thou shalt raise up the foundations of many generations; and thou shalt be called, The repairer of the breach, The restorer of paths to dwell in.

A. M. cir. 3292
B. C. cir. 712
Olymp. XVII. 1
cir. annum
NumæPompilii,
R. Roman., 4

13 If [b]thou turn away thy foot from the sabbath, *from* doing thy pleasure on my holy day; and call the sabbath a delight, the holy of the LORD, honourable; and shalt honour him, not doing thine own ways, nor finding thine own pleasure, nor speaking *thine own* words;

14 [c]Then shalt thou delight thyself in the LORD; and I will cause thee to [d]ride upon the high places of the earth, and feed thee with the heritage of Jacob thy father: [e]for the mouth of the LORD hath spoken *it*.

[x]Psa. xii. 2——[y]Heb. *droughts*——[z]Heb. *lie* or *deceive* [a]Chap. lxi. 4——[b]Chap. lvi. 2

[c]Job xxii. 26——[d]Deut. xxxii. 13; xxxiii. 29——[e]Chap. i. 20; xl. 5; Mic. iv. 4

(five ancient) of Dr. *Kennicott's*, and the *Septuagint*, *Syriac*, and *Vulgate* add the conjunction ו *vau*, וכבוד *vechabod*.

Verse 10. *And if thou draw out thy soul to the hungry*—"If thou bring forth thy bread to the hungry"] "To draw out thy soul to the hungry," as our translators rightly enough express the present Hebrew text, is an obscure phrase, and without example in any other place. But instead of נפשך *naphshecha, thy soul,* eight MSS. (three ancient) of *Kennicott's* and three of *De Rossi's* read לחמך *lachmecha, thy bread;* and so the *Syriac* renders it. The *Septuagint* express both words, *τον αρτον εκ της ψυχης σου*, "thy bread from thy soul." I cannot help thinking, however, that this reading is a gloss, and should not be adopted. To *draw out the soul* in relieving the poor, is to do it, not of constraint or necessity, but cheerfully, and is both nervous and elegant. His *soul pities* and his *hand gives*.

Verse 11. *And make fat thy bones*—"And he shall renew thy strength"] Chaldæus forte legit יחליף עצמתך *yachaliph otsmathecha; confer cap.* xl. 29, 31, *et* xli. 1.—SECKER. "The *Chaldee* perhaps read יחליף עצמתך *yachaliph otsmathecha.*" The *Chaldee* has ונופך יחיי בחיי עלמא *veguphach yechaiyey bechaiyey alma*, "and he will vivify thy body in life eternal." The rest of the ancients seem not to know what to make of יחליץ *yachalits;* and the rendering of the *Vulgate*, which seems to be the only proper one, *ossa tua liberabit*, "he will deliver thy bones," makes no sense. I follow this excellent emendation; to favour which it is still farther to be observed that three MSS., instead of עצמתיך *atsmotheycha*, have עצמתך *otsmathecha*, singular.—L.

Verse 12. *The restorer of paths to dwell in*—"The restorer of paths to be frequented by inhabitants."] To this purpose it is rendered by the *Syriac*, *Symmachus*, and *Theodotion*.

Verse 13. *If thou turn away thy foot from the Sabbath*] The meaning of this seems to be, that they should be careful not to take their pleasure on the Sabbath day, by paying visits, and taking country jaunts; not going, as *Kimchi* interprets it, more than a Sabbath day's journey, which was only *two thousand* cubits beyond the city's suburbs. How vilely is this rule transgressed by the inhabitants of this land! They seem to think that the Sabbath was made only for their recreation!

From *doing thy pleasure*] The *Septuagint*, *Syriac*, and *Chaldee*, for עשות *asoth*, manifestly express מעשות *measoth*. So likewise a MS. has it, but with the omission of the words שבת רגלך *shabbath raglecha*.—L.

The holy of the Lord—"And the holy feast of JEHOVAH"] Twenty-eight MSS. (seven ancient) add the conjunction ו *vau*, ולקדוש *velikedosh;* and so the *Syriac*, *Chaldee*, and *Vulgate*. One of my own has the same reading.

Nor speaking thine own *words*—"From speaking vain words."] It is necessary to add some epithet to make out the sense; the *Septuagint* say, *angry* words; the *Chaldee*, words of violence. If any such epithet is lost here, the safest way is to supply it by the prophet's own expression, ver. 9, ודבר און *vedabar aven*, *vain words;* that is, profane, impious, injurious, &c. "The additional epithet seems unnecessary; the *Vulgate* and *Syriac* have it not; and the sense is good without it; two ways, first by taking ודבר *vedabar* for a noun, and דבר *dabur* for the participle pahul, and rendering,—

'From pursuing thy pleasure, and the thing resolved on.'

Or, secondly, by supposing the force of the preposition מ *mem* to have been continued from the verb ממצוא *mimmetso* to the verb ודבר *vedabber* immediately following; and rendering,—

'From executing thy pleasure, and from speaking words concerning it.'

But the first seems the easier rendering."—Dr. JUBB.

Verse 14. *Then shalt thou delight thyself*] If all *fasts* and religious observances be carried on in the spirit and manner recommended above, God's blessing will attend every ordinance. But in public fasts, prescribed not in the Book of God, but by the rulers of nations in general (very unfit persons) care should be taken that the *cause is good*, and that God's blessing may be *safely* implored in it.

France has lately fasted and prayed that they might be able to subjugate Spain, restore and establish the horrible inquisition, and utterly destroy all the liberties of the people! Is this such a fast as God hath chosen?—A. D. 1823.

CHAPTER LIX

This chapter contains a more general reproof of the wickedness of the Jews, 1–8. *After this they are represented confessing their sins, and deploring the unhappy consequences of them,* 9–15. *On this act of humiliation God, ever ready to pardon the penitent, promises that he will have mercy on them; that the Redeemer will come, mighty to save; and that he will deliver his people, subdue his enemies, and establish a new and everlasting covenant,* 16–21.

A. M. cir. 3292
B. C. cir. 712
Olymp. XVII. 1
cir. annum
NumæPompilii,
R. Roman., 4

BEHOLD, the LORD's hand is
not [a]shortened, that it cannot save; neither his ear heavy,
that it cannot hear:
2 But your iniquities have separated between
you and your God, and your sins [b]have hid
his face from you, that he will not hear.
3 For [c]your hands are defiled with blood,
and your fingers with iniquity; your lips have
spoken lies, your tongue hath muttered perverseness.
4 None calleth for justice, nor *any* pleadeth
for truth: they trust in vanity, and speak lies;
[d]they conceive mischief, and bring forth iniquity.

5 They hatch [e]cockatrice' eggs,
and weave the spider's web: he
that eateth of their eggs dieth,
and [f]that which is crushed
breaketh out into a viper.
6 [g]Their webs shall not become garments, neither shall they cover themselves
with their works: their works *are* works of
iniquity, and the act of violence *is* in their
hands.
7 [h]Their feet run to evil, and they make
haste to shed innocent blood: their thoughts
are thoughts of iniquity; wasting and [i]de-
struction *are* in their paths.

A. M. cir. 3292
B. C. cir. 712
Olymp. XVII. 1
cir. annum
NumæPompilii,
R. Roman., 4

---

[a]Numbers xi. 23; chap. l. 2——[b]Or, *have made him hide*——[c]Chap. i. 15——[d]Job xv. 35; Psalm vii. 14——[e]Or, *adders'*——[f]Or, *that which is sprinkled* is as if *there brake out a viper*——[g]Job viii. 14, 15——[h]Proverbs i. 16; Romans iii. 15——[i]Hebrew, *breaking*

The foregoing elegant chapter contained a severe reproof of the Jews, in particular for their hypocrisy in pretending to make themselves accepted with God by fasting and outward humiliation without true repentance; while they still continued to oppress the poor, and indulge their own passions and vices; with great promises however of God's favour on condition of their reformation. This chapter contains a more general reproof of their wickedness, bloodshed, violence, falsehood, injustice. At ver. 9 they are introduced as making, themselves, an ample confession of their sins, and deploring their wretched state in consequence of them. On this act of humiliation a promise is given that God, in his mercy and zeal for his people, will rescue them from this miserable condition; that the Redeemer will come like a mighty hero to deliver them; he will destroy his enemies, convert both Jews and Gentiles to himself, and give them a new covenant, and a law which shall never be abolished.

As this chapter is remarkable for the beauty, strength, and variety of the images with which it abounds; so is it peculiarly distinguished by the elegance of the composition, and the exact construction of the sentences. From the first verse to the two last it falls regularly into stanzas of four lines, (see Prelim. Dissert. p. xxi.,) which I have endeavoured to express as nearly as possible in the form of the original.—L.

NOTES ON CHAP. LIX

Verse 2. *His face*] For פנים *panim, faces,* I read *panaiv, his face.* So the *Syriac, Septuagint, Alexandrian, Arabic,* and *Vulgate.* פני *panai,* MS. Forte legendum פני *panai,* nam מ *mem,* sequitur, et loquitur Deus; confer cap. lviii. 14. "We should perhaps read פני *panai;* for מ *mem* follows, and God is the speaker."—SECKER. I rather think that the speech of God was closed with the last chapter, and that this chapter is delivered in the person of the prophet.—L.

Verse 3. *Your tongue*—"And your tongue"] An ancient MS., and the *Septuagint* and *Vulgate,* add the conjunction.

Verse 4. *They conceive mischief, and bring forth iniquity.*] There is a curious propriety in this mode of expression; a thought or purpose is compared to *conception;* a word or act, which is the consequence of it, to the *birth of a child.* From the *third* to the *fifteenth* verse inclusive may be considered a true statement of the then moral state of the Jewish people; and that they were, in the most proper sense of the word, guilty of the iniquities with which they are charged.

A. M. cir. 3292
B. C. cir. 712
Olymp. XVII. 1
cir. annum
NumæPompilii,
R. Roman., 4

8 The way of peace they know not; and *there is* no [k]judgment in their goings: [l]they have made them crooked paths: whosoever goeth therein shall not know peace.

9 Therefore is judgment far from us, neither doth justice overtake us: [m]we wait for light, but behold obscurity; for brightness, *but* we walk in darkness.

10 [n]We grope for the wall like the blind, and we grope as if *we had* no eyes: we stumble at noon day as in the night; *we are* in desolate places as dead *men*.

11 We roar all like bears, and [o]mourn sore like doves: we look for judgment, but *there is* none; for salvation, *but* it is far off from us.

12 For our transgressions are multiplied before thee, and our sins testify against us: for our transgressions *are* with us; and *as for* our iniquities, we know them:

13 In transgressing and lying against the LORD, and departing away from our God, speaking oppression and revolt, conceiving and uttering [p]from the heart words of falsehood.

14 And judgment is turned away backward, and justice standeth afar off: for truth is fallen in the street, and equity cannot enter.

15 Yea, truth faileth; and he *that* departeth from evil [q]maketh himself a prey: and the LORD saw *it* and [r]it displeased him that *there was* no judgment.

16 [s]And he saw that *there was* no man, and [t]wondered that *there was* no intercessor: [u]therefore his arm brought salvation unto him; and his righteousness, it sustained him.

17 [v]For he put on righteousness as a breastplate, and a helmet of salvation upon his head; and he put on the garments of ven-

---

[k]Or, *right*——[l]Psa. cxxv. 5; Prov. ii. 15——[m]Jer. viii. 15——[n]Deut. xxviii. 29; Job v. 14; Amos viii. 9——[o]Chap. xxxviii. 14; Ezek. vii. 16——[p]Matt. xii. 34——[q]Or, *is accounted mad*——[r]Hebrew, *it was evil in his eyes*——[s]Ezek. xxii. 30——[t]Mark vi. 6——[u]Psalm xcviii. 1; chapter lxiii. 5——[v]Wisd. v. 18, 19; Ephesians vi. 14, 17; 1 Thessalonians v. 8

Verse 8. *Whosoever goeth therein shall not know peace*—"Whoever goeth in them knoweth not peace"] For בה *bah*, singular, read בם *bam*, plural, with the *Septuagint*, *Syriac*, *Vulgate*, and *Chaldee*. The ה *he* is upon a rasure in one MS. Or, for נתיבתיהם *nethibotheyhem*, plural, we must read נתיבתם *nethibatham*, singular, as it is in an ancient MS., to preserve the grammatical concord.—L.

Verse 10. *We stumble at noon day as in the night*—"We stumble at mid-day, as in the twilight"] I adopt here an emendation of Houbigant, נשגגה *nishgegah*, instead of the second, נגששה *negasheshah*, the repetition of which has a poverty and inelegance extremely unworthy of the prophet, and unlike his manner. The mistake is of long standing, being prior to all the ancient versions. It was a very easy and obvious mistake, and I have little doubt of our having recovered the true reading in this ingenious correction.

Verse 11. But *it is far off from us*—"And it is far distant from us."] The conjunction ו *vau* must necessarily be prefixed to the verb, as the *Syriac*, *Chaldee*, and *Vulgate* found it in their copies; ורחקה *verachakah*, "and far off."

Verse 14. *Justice standeth afar off*] צדקה *tsedakah*, *righteousness*, put here, says Kimchi, for *alms to the poor*. This casts some light on Matt. vi. 1: "Take heed that you do not your alms," ελεημοσυνην. But the best copies have δικαιοσυνην, *righteousness;* the former having been inserted in the text at first merely as the explanation of the genuine and original word.

Verse 15. *And the Lord saw* it—"And JEHOVAH saw it ——"] This third line of the stanza appears manifestly to me to be imperfect by the loss of a phrase. The reader will perhaps more perfectly conceive my idea of the matter if I endeavour to supply the supposed defect. I imagine it might have stood originally in this manner:—

וירא יהוה ויחר לו
vaiyar Yehovah veyachar lo

וירע בעיניו כי אין משפט
veyera beeyinaiv ki ein mishpat

"And JEHOVAH saw it, and he was wroth;
And it displeased him, that there was no judgment."

We have had already many examples of mistakes of omission; this, if it be such, is very ancient, being prior to all the versions.—L.

Verse 16. *And wondered that* there was *no intercessor*] This and the following verses some of the most eminent rabbins understand as spoken of the Messiah. Kimchi says that Rabbi Joshua ben Levi proposes this objection: "It is written, 'Behold, he will come in the clouds of heaven as the son of man,' Dan. vii. 13; and elsewhere it is written, 'He cometh lowly, and riding upon an ass,' Zech. ix. 9. How can these texts be reconciled? Thus: If the Jews have merit, he will come unto them in the clouds of heaven; but if they be destitute of merit, he will come unto them riding upon an ass." Now out of their own mouth they may be condemned. They were truly destitute of all merit when Jesus Christ came into Jerusalem riding upon an ass, according to the letter of the above prophecy; and they neither acknowledged nor received him. And that they were destitute of merit their destruction by the Romans, which shortly followed their rejection of him, sufficiently proves.

Verse 17. For *clothing*—"For his clothing"] תלבשת *tilbosheth*. "I cannot but think that

A. M. cir. 3292 B. C. cir. 712 Olymp. XVII. 1 cir. annum NumæPompilii, R. Roman., 4

geance *for* clothing, and was
clad with zeal as a cloak.
18 [w]According to *their* [x]deeds,
accordingly we will repay, fury to
his adversaries, recompense to his enemies;
to the islands he will repay recompense.
19 [y]So shall they fear the name of the
LORD from the west, and his
glory from the rising of the sun.
When the enemy shall come in
[z]like a flood, the Spirit of the
LORD shall [a]lift up a standard against
him.
20 And [b]the Redeemer shall come to

[w]Chap. lxiii. 6; Psa. xxviii. 4; Jer. l. 29; Matt. xvi. 27; Rev. xx. 12; xxii. 12——[x]Heb. *recompenses*

[y]Psa. cxiii. 3; Mal. i. 11——[z]Rev. xii. 15——[a]Or, *put him to flight*——[b]Rom. xi. 26

this word, תלבשת *tilbosheth*, is an interpolation. 1. It is in no one ancient version. 2. It is redundant in the sense, as it is before expressed in בגדי *bigdey.* 3. It makes the hemistich just so much longer than it ought to be, if it is compared with the others adjoining. 4. It makes a form of construction in this clause less elegant than that in the others. 5. It might probably be in some margin a various reading for בגדי *bigdey*, and thence taken into the text. This is more probable, as its form is such as it would be if it were *in regimine*, as it must be before נקם *nakam.*"—DR. JUBB. Two sorts of armour are mentioned: a *breast-plate* and a *helmet*, to bring *righteousness* and *salvation* to those who fear him; and the *garments of vengeance* and the *cloak of zeal* for the destruction of all those who finally oppose him, and reject his Gospel.

Verse 18. *According to* their *deeds, accordingly he will repay*—"He is mighty to recompense; he that is mighty to recompense will requite"] The former part of this verse, as it stands at present in the Hebrew text, seems to me to be very imperfect, and absolutely unintelligible. The learned Vitringa has taken a great deal of pains upon it after Cocceius, who he says is the only one of all the interpreters, ancient or modern, who has at all understood it, and has opened the way for him. He thinks that both of them together have clearly made out the sense; I do not expect that any third person will ever be of that opinion. He says, Videtur sententia ad verbum sonare: quasi propter facta [adversariorum] quasi propter rependet; excandescentiam, &c., et sic reddidit Pagnimus. "According to the height of their demerits, he will repay them to the height: fury to his adversaries, recompense to his enemies," &c.—*Waterland.* This he converts, by a process which will not much edify my reader, into Secundum summe merita, secundum summe (*merita*) rependet; which is his translation. They that hold the present Hebrew text to be absolutely infallible must make their way through it as they can; but they ought surely to give us somewhat that has at least the appearance of sense. However, I hope the case here is not quite desperate; the *Chaldee* leads us very fairly to the correction of the text, which is both corrupted and defective. The paraphrase runs thus: מרי גמליא הוא גמלא ישלם *marey gumlaiya hu gimla yeshallem*, "The Lord of retribution, he will render recompense." He manifestly read בעל *baal* instead of כעל *keal.* מרי גמליא *marey gumlaiya* is בעל גמלות *baal gemuloth;* as מרי מרירותא *marey merirutha* is בעל אף *baal aph.* Prov. xxii. 24. And so in the *Chaldee* paraphrase on Isa. xxxv. 4: מרי גמליא יי הוא יתגלי *marey gamlaiya yeya hu yithgeley*, "The Lord of retribution, Jehovah himself, shall be revealed;" words very near to those of the prophet in this place. The second כעל *keal*, which the *Chaldee* has omitted, must be read בעל *baal* likewise. With this only addition to the *Chaldee*, which the Hebrew text justifies, we are supplied with the following clear reading of the passage:—

בעל גמלות הוא
hu gemuloth baal

בעל גמלות ישלם
yeshallem gemuloth baal

The Lord of retributions, he
The Lord of retributions, shall repay.

The כ *caph* in כעל *keal* twice seems to have been at first ב *beth*, in MS. This verse in the *Septuagint* is very imperfect. In the first part of it they give us no assistance: the latter part is wholly omitted in the printed copies; but it is thus supplied by MSS. Pachom. and I. D. II: Τοις ὑπεναντιοις αυτου· αμυναν τοις εχθροις αυτου· ταις νησοις αποδομα αποτισει.—L.

Verse 19. *When the enemy shall come in like a flood*] This all the rabbins refer to the coming of the Messiah. If ye see a generation which endures much tribulation, then (say they) expect him, according to what is written: "When the enemy shall come in like a flood, the Spirit of the Lord shall lift up a standard against him."

Kimchi says, he that was the standard-bearer always began the battle by first smiting at the enemy. Here then the Spirit of the Lord is the standard-bearer, and strikes the first blow. They who go against sin and Satan with the Holy Spirit at their head, are sure to win the day.

The Spirit of the Lord shall lift up a standard against him—"Which a strong wind driveth along."] Quam spiritus Domini cogit, "Which the Spirit of the Lord drives on."—*Vulg.* נוססה *nosesah*, pihel à נוס *nus* fugit. *Kimchi* says his father thus explained this word: נוססה *nosesah* interpretatur in significatione fugæ, et ait, spiritus Domini *fugabit* hostem;— nam secundum eum נוססה *nosesah* est ex conjugatione quadrata, ejusque radix est נוס *nus:* "nosesah he interpreted in the signification of *flight*,—*The Spirit of the Lord shall put the enemy to flight;* for according to him the root of the word is נוס *nus, he put to flight.*" The object of this action I explain otherwise. The conjunction ו *vau*, prefixed to רוח *ruach*, seems necessary to the sense; it is added by the corrector in one of the Koningsberg MSS., collated by Lilienthal. It is added also in one of my own.

Verse 20. *Unto them that turn from trans-*

A. M. cir. 3292
B. C. cir. 712
Olymp. XVII. 1
cir. annum
NumæPompilii,
R. Roman., 4

Zion, and unto them that turn
from transgression in Jacob,
saith the LORD.
21 [c]As for me, this *is* my covenant with them, saith the LORD; My Spirit
that *is* upon thee, and my words which I have
put in thy mouth, shall not de-
part out of thy mouth, nor out
of the mouth of thy seed, nor
out of the mouth of thy seed's
seed, saith the LORD, from henceforth and for
ever.

[c]Heb. viii. 10; x. 16

gression in Jacob—"And shall turn away iniquity from Jacob"] So the *Septuagint* and St. Paul, Rom. xi. 26, reading instead of לשבי *leshabey* and ביעקב *beyaacob*, והשיב *veheshib* and מיעקב *meyaacob*. The *Syriac* likewise reads והשיב *veheshib;* and the *Chaldee*, to the same sense, ולהשיב *ulehashib*. Our translators have expressed the sense of the present reading of the Hebrew text: "And unto them that turn from transgression in Jacob."

Verse 21. *This* is *my covenant with them*—"This is the covenant which I make with them"] For אותם *otham, them*, twenty-four MSS., (four ancient,) and nine editions have אתם *ittam, with them.*

My Spirit that is *upon thee*] This seems to be an address to the *Messiah; Kimchi* says it is to the *prophet*, informing him that the spirit of prophecy should be given to all Israelites in the days of the Messiah, as it was then given to *him*, i. e., to the prophet.

And my words which I have put in thy mouth] Whatsoever Jesus spoke was the *word* and *mind* of God himself; and must, as such, be implicitly received.

Nor out of the mouth of thy seed] The *same doctrines* which Jesus preached, all his faithful ministers preach; and his *seed*—genuine Christians, who are all *born of God*, believe; and *they* shall continue, and the doctrines remain in the *seed's seed* through all generations—for ever and ever. This is God's *covenant*, ordered in all things and sure.

CHAPTER LX

The glorious prospect displayed in this chapter seems to have elevated the prophet even above his usual majesty. The subject is the very flourishing condition of the Church of Jesus Christ at that period of the Gospel dispensation when both Jews and Gentiles shall become one fold under one Shepherd. The imagery employed is of the most consolatory and magnificent description. This blessed state of the world shall follow a time of gross darkness, 1, 2. *The universal diffusion of vital godliness beautifully set forth by a great variety of images,* 3–14. *The everlasting duration and spotless purity of this kingdom of Christ,* 15–21. *A time appointed in the counsels of Jehovah for the commencement of this happy period; and when this time arrives, the particulars of the prophecy shall have a speedy accomplishment,* 22.

A. M. cir. 3292
B. C. cir. 712
Olymp. XVII. 1
cir. annum
NumæPompilii,
R. Roman., 4

ARISE, [a]shine; [b]for thy light
is come, and [c]the glory of
the LORD is risen upon thee.
2 For, behold, the darkness
shall cover the earth, and gross
darkness the people: but the
LORD shall arise upon thee, and
his glory shall be seen upon thee.

[a]Eph. v. 14——[b]Or, *be enlightened; for thy light cometh*——[c]Mal. iv. 2

The subject of this chapter is the great increase and flourishing state of the Church of God by the conversion and accession of the heathen nations to it, which is set forth in such ample and exalted terms, as plainly show that the full completion of this prophecy is reserved for future times. This subject is displayed in the most splendid colours under a great variety of images highly poetical, designed to give a general idea of the glories of that perfect state of the Church of God which we are taught to expect in the latter times; when the fulness of the Gentiles shall come in, and the Jews shall be converted and gathered from their dispersions, and the kingdoms of this world shall become the kingdoms of our Lord and of his Christ.

Of the use in prophecy of general or common poetical images, in setting forth the greatness and importance of a future event universally, without descending to particulars, or too minutely explaining circumstances, I have already pretty largely treated in the twentieth prelection on the Hebrew poetry; and have more than once observed in these notes that such images are not always to be applied particularly to persons and things, and were never intended to be minutely explained. I shall add here the opinion of a very learned and judicious person upon this subject: "It is, I think, a mark of right understanding in the language of prophecy, and in the design of prophecy too, to keep to what appears the design and meaning of the prophecy in general, and what the whole of it laid together points out to us; and not to suffer a warm imagination to mislead us from the real intention of the spirit of prophecy, by following uncertain applications of the parts of it." *Lowman* on the Revelation, note on chap. xix. 21.—L. To this testimony I must add my own. This is one of the most glorious chapters in the whole of the Old Testament. The splendour, glory, and excellence of the Church of Christ are here pointed out in language which the Spirit of God alone is capable of using. But *when* shall this state of blessedness take place? Lord, *thou* only knowest.

NOTES ON CHAP. LX

Verse 1. *Arise*] Call upon God through Christ, for his salvation; and,

Shine] אורי *ori, be illuminated;* for till thou

A. M. cir. 3292
B. C. cir. 712
Olymp. XVII. 1
cir. annum
NumæPompilii,
R. Roman., 4

3 And the [d]Gentiles shall come
to thy light, and kings to the
brightness of thy rising.
4 [e]Lift up thine eyes round
about, and see: all they gather themselves
together, [f]they come to thee: thy sons shall
come from far, and thy daughters shall be
nursed at *thy* side.
5 Then thou shalt see, and flow together,
and thine heart shall fear, and be enlarged;
because [g]the [h]abundance of the sea
shall be converted unto thee, the [i]forces
of the Gentiles shall come unto
thee.
6 The multitude of camels shall
cover thee, the dromedaries of Midian
and [k]Ephah; all they from [l]Sheba shall
come: they shall bring [m]gold and incense; and
they shall show forth the praises of the LORD.
7 All the flocks of [n]Kedar shall be gathered
together unto thee, the rams of Nebaioth shall
minister unto thee: they shall come up with
acceptance on mine altar, and [o]I will glorify
the house of my glory.

[d]Chap. xlix. 6, 23; Rev. xxi. 24——[e]Chap. xlix. 18 [f]Chap. xlix. 20, 21, 22; lxvi. 12——[g]Rom. xi. 25 [h]Or, *noise of the sea shall be turned toward thee*

[i]Or, *wealth;* ver. 11; chap. lxi. 6——[k]Gen. xxv. 4 [l]Psa. lxxii. 10——[m]Chap. lxi. 6; Matt. ii. 11——[n]Gen. xxv. 13——[o]Hag. ii. 7, 9

arise and call upon God, thou wilt never receive true light.

For thy light is come] כי בא אורך *ki ba orech, for thy light cometh.* The Messiah is at the door; who, while he is a light to lighten the Gentiles, will be the glory—the effulgence, of his people Israel.

Verse 2. *Darkness shall cover the earth*] This is the state of the Gentile people.

Verse 3. *And the Gentiles shall come*] This has been in some sort already fulfilled. The Gentiles have received the light of the Gospel from the land of Judea, and the Gentile *kings* have embraced that Gospel; so that many nations of the earth are full of the doctrine of Christ.

Verse 4. *Shall be nursed at* thy *side*—"Shall be carried at the side."] For תאמנה *teamanah, shall be nursed,* the *Septuagint* and *Chaldee* read תנשאנה *tinnasenah, shall be carried.* A MS. has על כתף תנשאנה *al catheph tinnasenah,* "shall be carried on the shoulder;" instead of על צד תאמנה *al tsad teamanah,* "shall be nursed on the side." Another MS. has both כתף *catheph* and צד *tsad.* Another MS. has it thus: תנשאנה : תאמנה *tinnasenah : teamanah,* with a line drawn over the first word. Sir John Chardin says that it is the general custom in the east to carry their children astride upon the hip with the arm round their body. His MS. note on this place is as follows:—Coutume en Orient de porter les enfans sur le coste à califourchon sur la hanche: cette facon est generale aux Indes; les enfans se tiennent comme cela, et la personne qui les porte les embrasse et serre par le corps; parceque sont (ni) emmaillottès, ni en robes qui les embrassent. "In the east it is the custom to carry the children on the haunch, with the legs astride. This is the general custom in India. The children support themselves in this way, and the arm of the nurse goes round the body and presses the child close to the side; and this they can easily do, as the children are not swathed, nor encumbered with clothes." Non brachiis occidentalium more, sed humeris, divaricatis tibiis, impositos circumferunt. "They carry them about, not in their arms after the manner of the western nations, but on their shoulders; the children being placed astride." *Cotovic.* Iter. Syr. cap. xiv. This last quotation seems to favour the reading על כתף *al catheph, on the shoulder,* as the *Septuagint* likewise do: but upon the whole I think that על צד תנשאנה *al tsad tinnasenah* is the true reading, which the *Chaldee* favours; and I have accordingly followed it. See chap. lxvi. 12.—L. This mode of carrying children is as common in *India* as carrying them in the arms is in *Europe.*

Verse 5. *Then thou shalt see*—"Then shalt thou fear"] For תראי *tirai, thou shalt see,* as ours and much the greater number of the translators, ancient and modern, render it, forty MSS. (ten ancient) of *Kennicott's,* and twenty-eight of *De Rossi's,* with one ancient of my own, and the old edition of 1488, have תיראי *tirai, thou shalt fear:* the true reading, confirmed by the perfect parallelism of the sentences: the heart *ruffled* and *dilated* in the second line answering to the *fear* and *joy* expressed in the first. The Prophet Jeremiah, chap. xxxiii. 9, has the same natural and elegant sentiment:—

"And this city shall become to me a name of joy;
A praise and an honour for all the nations of the earth;
Which shall hear all the good that I do unto them:
And they shall fear, and they shall tremble, at all the goodness
And at all the prosperity that I procure unto her."

And David:—

"I will praise thee, for I am fearfully and wonderfully made." Psa. cxxxix. 14.

His tibi me rebus quædam divina voluptas
Percipit atque horror. LUCRET. iii. 28.

Recenti mens trepidat metu,
Plenoque Bacchi pectore turbidum
Lætatur. HOR. *Carm.* ii. 19. l. 5.—L.

Verse 6. *The praises of the Lord*—"And the praise of JEHOVAH."] Thirty-three MSS. and three editions have ותהלת *uthehillath,* in the singular number; and so read the ancient versions, and one of my own MSS.

Verse 7. *The rams of Nebaioth shall minister unto thee*] Vitringa on the place understands their ministering, and ascending or going up on the altar, as offering themselves voluntarily: ipsi se, non expectato sacerdote alio, gloriæ et

A. M. cir. 3292
B. C. cir. 712
Olymp. XVII. 1
cir. annum
NumæPompilii,
R. Roman., 4

8 Who *are* these *that* fly as a cloud, and as the doves to their windows?

9 [p]Surely the isles shall wait for me, and the ships of Tarshish first, [q]to bring thy sons from far, [r]their silver and their gold with them, [s]unto the name of the LORD thy God, and to the Holy One of Israel, [t]because he hath glorified thee.

10 And [u]the sons of strangers shall build up thy walls, [v]and their kings shall minister unto thee: for [w]in my wrath I smote thee, [x]but in my favour have I had mercy on thee.

11 Therefore thy gates [y]shall be open continually; they shall not be shut day nor night; that *men* may bring unto thee the [z]forces of the Gentiles, and *that* their kings *may be* brought.

12 [a]For the nation and kingdom that will not serve thee shall perish; yea, *those* nations shall be utterly wasted.

13 [b]The glory of Lebanon shall come unto thee, the fir tree, the pine tree, and the box together, to beautify the place of my sanctuary; and I will make [c]the place of my feet glorious.

14 The sons also of them that afflicted thee shall come bending unto thee; and all they that despised thee shall [d]bow themselves down at the soles of thy feet; and they shall call thee, The city of the LORD, [e]the Zion of the Holy One of Israel.

A. M. cir. 3292
B. C. cir. 712
Olymp. XVII. 1
cir. annum
NumæPompilii,
R. Roman., 4

15 Whereas thou hast been forsaken and hated, so that no man went through *thee,* I will make thee an eternal excellency, a joy of many generations.

16 Thou shalt also suck the milk of the Gentiles, [f]and shalt suck the breast of kings: and thou shalt know that [g]I the LORD *am* thy Saviour and thy Redeemer, the Mighty One of Jacob.

17 For brass I will bring gold, and for iron I will bring silver, and for wood brass, and for stones iron: I will also make thy officers peace, and thine exactors righteousness.

18 Violence shall no more be heard in thy land, wasting nor destruction within thy borders; but thou shalt call [h]thy walls Salvation, and thy gates Praise.

19 The [i]sun shall be no more thy light by day; neither for brightness shall the moon give light unto thee: but the LORD shall be unto thee an everlasting light, and [k]thy God thy glory.

20 [l]Thy sun shall no more go down; neither

---

[p]Psa. lxxii. 10; chap. xlii. 4; li. 5——[q]Gal. iv. 26 [r]Psa. lxviii. 30; Zech. xiv. 14——[s]Jer. iii. 17——[t]Chap. lv. 5——[u]Zech. vi. 15——[v]Chap. xlix. 23; Rev. xxi. 24 [w]Chap. lvii. 17——[x]Chap. liv. 7, 8——[y]Rev. xxi. 25 [z]Or, *wealth;* ver. 5——[a]Zech. xiv. 17, 19; Matt. xxi. 44

[b]Chap. xxxv. 2; xli. 19——[c]See 1 Chron. xxviii. 2; Psa. cxxxii. 7——[d]Chap. xlix. 23; Rev. iii. 9——[e]Heb. xii. 22; Rev. xiv. 1——[f]Chap. xlix. 23; lxi. 6; lxvi. 11, 12 [g]Chap. xliii. 3——[h]Chap. xxvi. 1——[i]Rev. xxi. 23; xxii. 5——[k]Zech. ii. 5——[l]See Amos viii. 9

---

sanctificationi divini nominis ultro ac libenter oblaturi. "They, waiting for no priest, go and freely offer themselves to the glory and sanctification of the sacred name." This gives a very elegant and poetical turn to the image. It was a general notion that prevailed with sacrificers among the heathen, that the victim's being brought without reluctance to the altar was a good omen; and the contrary a bad one. Sabinus petit aliquanto tristior; quod sacrificanti hostia aufugerat. *Sueton.* Titus, cap. x. Accessit dirum omen, profugus altaribus tauris. "It was an omen of dreadful portent when the victim fled away from the altar." *Tacit.* Hist. iii. 56.—L.

Verse 8. *And as the doves to their windows*—"And like doves upon the wing?"] Instead of אל *el, to,* forty-two MSS. of *Kennicott's,* and one of mine, have על *al, upon.* For ארבתיהם *arubboteyhem, their windows,* read אברתיהם *ebrotheyhem, their wings,* transposing a letter.—*Houbigant.* The *Septuagint* render it συν νεοσσοις, "with their young;" they read אפרחיהם *ephrocheyhem,* nearer to the latter than to the present reading.—L.

Verse 9. *The ships of Tarshish first*—"The ships of Tarshish among the first"] For בראשנה *barishonah* twenty-five MSS. and the *Syriac* read כבראשנה *kebarishonah,* "as at the first." The ships of Tarshish AS at the first; that is, *as* they brought gold and silver in the days of Solomon.

Verse 13. *And I will make the place of my feet glorious*—"And that I may glorify the place whereon I rest my feet"] The temple of Jerusalem was called the house of God, and the place of his rest or residence. The visible symbolical appearance of God, called by the Jews the schechinah, was in the most holy place, between the wings of the cherubim, above the ark. This is considered as the throne of God, presiding as King over the Jewish state; and as a footstool is a necessary appendage to a throne, (see note on chap. lii. 2,) the ark is considered as the footstool of God, and is so called, Psa. xcix. 5, 1 Chron. xxviii. 2.

The glory of Lebanon] That is, the cedar.

Verse 19. *Neither for brightness shall the moon give light unto thee*—"Nor by night shall the brightness of the moon enlighten thee"] This line, as it stands in the present text, seems to be defective. The *Septuagint* and *Chaldee* both express *the night,* which is almost necessary to answer to *day* in the preceding line, as well as to perfect the sense here. I therefore

A. M. cir. 3292
B. C. cir. 712
Olymp. XVII. 1
cir. annum
NumæPompilii,
R. Roman., 4

shall thy moon withdraw itself:
for the LORD shall be thine everlasting light, and the days of
thy mourning shall be ended.
21 [m]Thy people also *shall be* all righteous:
[n]they shall inherit the land for ever, [o]the
branch of my planting, [p]the work
of my hands, that I may be
glorified.
22 [q]A little one shall become
a thousand, and a small one a strong nation:
I the LORD will hasten it in his time.

[m]Chap. lii. 1; Rev. xxi. 27——[n]Psa. xxxvii. 11, 22; Matt. v. 5

[o]Chap. lxi. 3; Matt. xv. 13; John xv. 2——[p]Chap. xxix. 23; xlv. 11; Eph. ii. 10——[q]Matt. xiii. 31, 32

think that we ought, upon the authority of the *Septuagint and Chaldee*, to read either ולילה *velailah, and by night*, instead of ולנגה *ulenogah, and for brightness;* or ולנגה בלילה *ulenogah ballailah*, adding the word בלילה *ballailah, by night*.—L.

Verse 21. *Of my planting*] מטעי *mattai;* so, with the *Keri*, read forty-four MSS. (seven ancient) and six editions; with which agree the *Syriac, Chaldee*, and *Vulgate*.

Verse 22. *I the Lord will hasten it in his time*] There is a time set for the fulfilment of this prophecy: that time must come before it begins to take place; but when it does begin, the whole will be performed in a short space. It is not, therefore, the time determined for the event that shall be hastened, but all the circumstances of the event; all the parts of the prediction shall be speedily completed. **I the Lorde in hys tyme sodeynly schal doun thys.**—Old MS. Bible. And because it is the LORD, therefore it will be done: for although it be difficult, he is almighty.

CHAPTER LXI

The subject of the preceding chapter is continued in this; and to give it the greater solemnity, the Messiah is introduced describing his character and office, and confirming the large promises made before, 1–9. In consequence of this the Jewish Church is introduced, praising God for the honour done her by her restoration to favour, and by the accession of the Gentiles, which is beautifully described by allusions to the rich pontifical dress of the high priest; a happy similitude to express the ornaments of a restored nation and of a renewed mind, 10. Certainty of the prophecy illustrated by a figure drawn from the vegetable kingdom, 11.

A. M. cir. 3292
B. C. cir. 712
Olymp. XVII. 1
cir. annum
NumæPompilii,
R. Roman., 4

THE [a]Spirit of the Lord GOD
is upon me; because the
LORD [b]hath anointed me to
preach good tidings unto the
meek; he hath sent me [c]to bind up the
broken-hearted, to proclaim [d]liberty to the
captives, and the opening of
the prison to *them that are*
bound;
2 [e]To proclaim the acceptable
year of the LORD, and [f]the day of vengeance
of our God; [g]to comfort all that mourn;

[a]Chap. xi. 2; Luke iv. 18; John i. 32; iii. 34——[b]Psa. xlv. 7——[c]Psa. cxlvii. 3; chap. lvii. 15——[d]Chap. xlii. 7; see Jer. xxxiv. 8

[e]See Lev. xxv. 9——[f]Chap. xxxiv. 8; lxiii. 4; lxvi. 14; Mal. iv. 1, 3; 2 Thess. i. 7, 8, 9——[g]Chap. lvii. 18; Matt. v. 4

NOTES ON CHAP. LXI

Verse 1. *The Spirit of the Lord God is upon me*—"The Spirit of JEHOVAH is upon me"] The *Septuagint, Vulgate*, and St. Luke, (chap. iv. 18,) and a MS., and two old editions omit the word אדני *Adonai, the Lord;* which was probably added to the text through the superstition of the Jews, to prevent the pronunciation of the word יהוה *Yehovah* following. See *Kennicott* on the state of the printed Hebrew text, vol. i., p. 510.

In most of Isaiah's prophecies there is a primary and secondary sense, or a remote subject illustrated by one that is near. The deliverance of the Jews from their captivity in Babylon is constantly used to shadow forth the salvation of men by Jesus Christ. Even the prophet himself is a typical person, and is sometimes intended to represent the great Saviour. It is evident from Luke iv. 18 that this is a prophecy of our blessed Lord and his preaching; and yet it is as evident that it primarily refers to Isaiah preaching the glad tidings of deliverance to the Jews.

The opening of the prison—"Perfect liberty"] פקח קוח *pekach koach.* Ten MSS. of *Kennicott's*, several of *De Rossi's*, and one of my own, with the *Complutensian*, have פקחקוח *pekachkoach* in one word; and so the *Septuagint* and *Vulgate* appear to have taken it: not merely opening of prisons, but every kind of liberty—complete redemption.

The proclaiming of perfect liberty to the bound, and the year of acceptance with JEHOVAH, is a manifest allusion to the proclaiming of the year of jubilee by sound of trumpet. See Lev. xxv. 9, &c. This was a year of general release of debts and obligations, of bondmen and bondwomen, of lands and possessions which had been sold from the families and tribes to which they belonged. Our Saviour, by applying this text to himself, (Luke iv. 18, 19,) a text so manifestly relating to the institution

A. M. cir. 3292
B. C. cir. 712
Olymp. XVII. 1
cir. annum
NumæPompilii,
R. Roman., 4

3 To appoint unto them that
mourn in Zion, [h]to give unto
them beauty for ashes, the oil
of joy for mourning, the gar-
ment of praise for the spirit of heaviness;
that they might be called trees of righteousness, [i]the planting of the LORD, [k]that he might
be glorified.
4 And they shall [l]build the old wastes, they
shall raise up the former desolations, and they
shall repair the waste cities, the desolations
of many generations.
5 And [m]strangers shall stand
and feed your flocks, and the sons
of the alien *shall be* your ploughmen and your vinedressers.
6 [n]But ye shall be named the Priests of the
LORD: *men* shall call you the Ministers of
our God: [o]ye shall eat the riches of the Gentiles, and in their glory shall ye boast yourselves.
7 [p]For your shame *ye shall have* double;
and *for* confusion they shall rejoice in their
portion: therefore in their land they shall

[h]Psa. xxx. 11——[i]Chap. lx. 21——[k]John xv. 8——[l]Ch. xlix. 8; lviii. 12; Ezek. xxxvi. 33, 36——[m]Eph. ii. 12

[n]Exod. xix. 6; ch. lx. 17; lxvi. 21; 1 Pet. ii. 5, 9; Rev. i. 6; v. 10——[o]Ch. lx. 5, 11, 16——[p]Ch. xl. 2; Zech. ix. 12

above mentioned, plainly declares the typical design of that institution.

Verse 3. *To appoint unto them that mourn in Zion*—"To impart *gladness* to the mourners of Zion"] A word necessary to the sense is certainly lost in this place, of which the ancient Versions have preserved no traces. Houbigant, by conjecture, inserts the word ששון *sason, gladness*, taken from the line next but one below, where it stands opposed to אבל *ebel, sorrow* or *mourning*, as the word lost here was to אבלי *abeley, mourners:* I follow him.—L.

Beauty for ashes—"A beautiful crown instead of ashes"] In times of mourning the Jews put on sackcloth, or coarse and sordid raiment, and spread dust and ashes on their heads; on the contrary, splendid clothing and ointment poured on the head were the signs of joy. "Feign thyself to be a mourner," says Joab to the woman of Tekoah, "and put on now mourning apparel, and anoint not thyself with oil," 2 Sam. xiv. 2. These customs are at large expressed in the Book of Judith: "She pulled off the sackcloth which she had on, and put off the garments of her widowhood, and washed her body all over with water and anointed herself with precious ointment, and braided the hair of her head, and put on a tire [mitre, marg.] upon it; and put on her garments of gladness;" chap. x. 3.—L.

פאר תחת אפר *peer tachath ephar, glory for ashes;* a paronomasia which the prophet often uses: a *chaplet, crown*, or other ornament of the head (for so the *Vulgate* renders the word here and in the 10th verse; in which last place the *Septuagint* agree in the same rendering,) *instead of dust and ashes*, which before covered it; and the costly ointments used on occasions of festivity, instead of the ensigns of sorrow.—L.

Trees of righteousness—"Trees approved"] Heb. *oaks of righteousness* or *truth;* that is, such as by their flourishing condition should show that they were indeed "the scion of God's planting, and the work of his hands;" under which images, in the preceding chapter, ver. 21, the true servants of God, in a highly improved state of the Church, were represented; that is, says Vitringa on that place, "commendable for the strength of their faith, their durability, and firmness."

Verse 4. "*And they that spring from thee*"] A word is lost here likewise. After ובנו *ubanu*, "they shall build," add ממך *mimmecha*, they that spring *from thee*. Four MSS. have it so, (two of them ancient,) and one of mine has it in the margin, and it is confirmed by chap. lviii. 12, where the sentence is the very same, this word being here added. *Kimchi* makes the same remark: "the word ממך *mimmecha* is omitted here; but is found in chap. lviii. 12."

The desolations of many generations] It seems that these words cannot refer to the Jews in the Babylonish captivity, for they were not there many generations; but it may refer to their dispersions and state of ruin since the advent of our Lord; and consequently this may be a promise of the restoration of the Jewish people.

Verse 5. *Strangers shall—feed your flocks*] Gentiles shall first preach to you the salvation of Christ, and feed with Divine knowledge the Jewish congregations.

Verse 7. *For your shame*—"Instead of your shame"] The translation of this verse, which is very confused, and probably corrupted in the Hebrew, is taken from the *Syriac* Version; except that the latter has not expressed the word משנה *mishneh, double*, in the first place. Five MSS. add the conjunction ו *vau* to שמחת *simchath*. The *Syriac* reads תרנו *taronnu*, and תירשו *tirashu*, in the second person, "*ye* shall rejoice, *ye* shall inherit." And for להם *lahem, to them*, two MSS., (one of them ancient,) three of *De Rossi's*, and the *Syriac*, read לכם *lahem, to you*, in the second person likewise.

The Version of the *Septuagint* is imperfect in this place; the first half of the verse is entirely omitted in all the printed copies. It is supplied by MSS. *Pachom.* and I. D. II. in the following manner:—

Αντι της αισχυνης ὑμων της διπλης,
Και αντι της εντροπης αγαλλιασεται ἡ μερις αυτων·
Δια τουτο την γην αυτων εκ δευτερου—

"Instead of your shame *ye shall have* double,
And instead of your confusion their portion shall rejoice;
Therefore, they shall possess their land a second time."

In which the two MSS. agree, except that I. D. II. has by mistake ἡμερας, *day*, for ἡ μερις, *the part*. And *Cod. Marchal.*, in the margin, has pretty nearly the same supplement as from *Theodotion*.—L.

A. M. cir. 3292 B. C. cir. 712 Olymp. XVII. 1 cir. annum NumæPompilii, R. Roman., 4

possess the double: everlasting
joy shall be unto them.
8 For [q]I the LORD love judgment, [r]I hate robbery for burnt-
offering; and I will direct their work in truth,
[s]and I will make an everlasting covenant with
them.
9 And their seed shall be known among the
Gentiles, and their offspring among the
people: all that see them shall acknowledge
them, [t]that they *are* the seed *which* the LORD
hath blessed.
10 [u]I will greatly rejoice in the LORD, my
soul shall be joyful in my God;
for [v]he hath clothed me with the
garments of salvation, he hath
covered me with the robe of
righteousness, [w]as a bridegroom [x]decketh
himself with ornaments, and as a bride adorneth *herself* with her jewels.
11 For as the earth bringeth forth her
bud, and as the garden causeth the things
that are sown in it to spring forth; so the
Lord GOD will cause [y]righteousness and
[z]praise to spring forth before all the
nations.

[q]Psa. xi. 7——[r]Chap. i. 11, 13——[s]Chap. lv. 3 [t]Gen. xli. 7; xiii. 15; xv. 18; xvii. 8; xxiv. 7; xxvi. 3; xxviii. 4, 13; chap. lxv. 23

[u]Hab. iii. 18——[v]Psa. cxxxii. 9, 16——[w]Chap. xlix. 18; Rev. xxi. 2——[x]Heb. *decketh as priest*——[y]Psa. lxxii. 3; lxxxv. 11——[z]Chap. lx. 18; lxii. 7

Verse 8. *I hate robbery for burnt-offering*—"Who hate rapine and iniquity"] The *Syriac*, and *Chaldee* prefix the conjunction ו *vau*, instead of the preposition ב *beth*, to עולה *olah*, which they render *iniquity* or *oppression;* and so the *Septuagint*, αδικιας. The difference lies in the *punctuation;* בעולה *beolah*, in a *burnt-offering* בעולה *beavelah*, in *iniquity*. The *letters* are the same in both words. Five of *De Rossi's* MSS. confirm this reading.

Verse 9. *Their seed shall be known among the Gentiles*] Both Jews and Gentiles are to make but *one fold* under one shepherd, Christ Jesus. But still, notwithstanding this, they may retain their peculiarity and national distinction; so that though they are known to be Christians, yet they shall appear to be converted Jews. After their conversion to Christianity this will necessarily be the case for a long time. Strange nations are not so speedily amalgamated, as to lose their peculiar cast of features, and other national distinctions.

Verse 10. *I will greatly rejoice in the Lord*] These may be the words of the Jews now converted, and brought into the Church of Christ, and with the Gentiles made fellow heirs of the blessings of the new covenant.

As a bridegroom decketh himself *with ornaments*—"As the bridegroom decketh himself with a priestly crown"] An allusion to the magnificent dress of the high priest, when performing his functions; and particularly to the mitre, and crown or plate of gold on the front of it, Exod. xxix. 6. The bonnet or mitre of the priests also was made, as Moses expresses it, "for glory and for beauty," Exod. xxviii. 40. It is difficult to give its full force to the prophet's metaphor in another language. The version of *Aquila* and *Symmachus* comes nearest to it: ὡς νυμφιον ἱερατευομενον στεφανῳ· "as a bridegroom decked with a priestly crown."—L.

Verse 11. *The Lord God*—"The Lord JEHOVAH"] "אדני *Adonai, the Lord*, makes the line longer than the preceding and following; and the *Septuagint*, *Alexandrian*, (and MSS. *Pachom*. and I. D. II.,) and *Arabic*, do not so render it. Hence it seems to be interpolated."—Dr. JUBB. Three MSS. have it not. See on ver. 1 of this chapter. Both words אדני יהוה *Adonai Yehovah*, are wanting in one of my MSS.; but are supplied in the margin by a later hand.

CHAPTER LXII

The prophet opens this chapter with ardent prayers that the happy period of reconciliation just now promised, and here again foretold, may be hastened, 1–5. He then calls upon the faithful, particularly the priests and Levites, to join him, urging the promises, and even the oath, of Jehovah, as the foundation of their request, 6–9. And, relying on this oath, he goes on to speak of the general restoration promised, as already performing; and calls to the people to march forth, and to the various nations among whom they are dispersed to prepare the way for them, as God had caused the order for their return to be universally proclaimed, 10–12.

A. M. cir. 3292 B. C. cir. 712 Olymp. XVII. 1 cir. annum NumæPompilii, R. Roman., 4

FOR Zion's sake will I not hold
my peace, and for Jerusa-
lem's sake [a]I will not rest, until
the righteousness thereof go forth
as brightness, and the salvation
thereof as a lamp *that* burneth.
2 [b]And the Gentiles shall see
thy righteousness, and all kings

[a]Ver. 7

[b]Chap. lx. 3

NOTES ON CHAP. LXII

Verse 1. *For Zion's sake will I not hold my peace*] These are the words of JEHOVAH declaring his purpose relative to the events predicted in the preceding chapter.

Thou shalt be called by a new name] Viz., CHRISTIAN—or, as in the fourth verse, חפצי בה

A. M. cir. 3292
B. C. cir. 712
Olymp. XVII. 1
cir. annum
NumæPompilii,
R. Roman., 4

thy glory: [c]and thou shalt be
called by a new name, which
the mouth of the LORD shall
name.

3 Thou shalt also be [d]a crown of glory in
the hand of the LORD, and a royal diadem in
the hand of thy God.

4 [e]Thou shalt no more be termed [f]Forsaken;
neither shall thy land any more be termed
[g]Desolate: but thou shalt be called [h]Hephzi-
bah, and thy land [i]Beulah: for the LORD delighteth in thee, and thy land shall be married.

5 For *as* a young man marrieth
a virgin, *so* shall thy sons marry
thee: and [k]*as* the bridegroom rejoiceth over the bride, *so* [l]shall
thy God rejoice over thee.

A. M. cir. 3292
B. C. cir. 712
Olymp. XVII. 1
cir. annum
NumæPompilii,
R. Roman., 4

6 [m]I have set watchmen upon thy walls, O
Jerusalem, *which* shall never hold their peace
day nor night: [n]ye that make mention of the
LORD, keep not silence,

7 And give him no [o]rest, till he establish,
and till he make Jerusalem [p]a praise in the
earth.

---

[c]See verse 4, 12; chapter lxv. 15——[d]Zech. ix. 16 [e]Hos. i. 10; 1 Pet. ii. 10——[f]Chap. xlix. 14; liv. 6, 7 [g]Chap. liv. 1——[h]That is, *My delight is in her*——[i]That is, *Married*

[k]Heb. *with the joy of the bridegroom*——[l]Chap. lxv. 19——[m]Ezek. iii. 17; xxxiii. 7——[n]Or, *ye that are the LORD'S remembrancers*——[o]Heb. *silence*——[p]Chap. lxi. 11; Zeph. iii. 20

---

chephtsi bah, "my delight is in her"—because she has now received that command, "This is my beloved Son, in whom I am well pleased; HEAR HIM."

Verse 4. *Thy land Beulah*] בעולה *beulah*, *married*. In the prophets, a *desolate land* is represented under the notion of *a widow;* an *inhabited land*, under that of a *married woman*, who has both *a husband* and *children*.

Verse 5. *For as a young man*—so] The particles of comparison are not at present in the *Hebrew* Text: but the *Septuagint*, *Syriac*, and *Chaldee* seem to have read in their copies כ *caph* prefixed to the verb, כי כיבעל *ki keyibal*, which seems to have been omitted by mistake of a transcriber, occasioned by the repetition of the same two letters. And before the verb in the second line a MS. adds כן *ken, so;* which the *Septuagint*, *Syriac*, and *Chaldee* seem also to have had in their copies. In the third line of this verse the same MS. has in like manner וכמשוש *vechimsos*, and two MSS. and the *Babylonish Talmud* כמשוש *kimsos*, adding the כ *caph;* and in the fourth line, the *Babylonish Talmud* likewise adds כן *ken, so,* before the verb.

Sir *John Chardin*, in his note on this place, tells us, "that it is the custom in the east for youths, that were never married, always to marry virgins; and widowers, however young, to marry widows."—HARMER, *Observ.* ii. p. 482.

So *shall thy sons marry thee.*] For בניך *banayich, thy sons*, Bishop *Lowth* reads, *restorer* or *builder*, as he does not consider the word as the plural of בן *ben, a son*, but the participle *benoni* of the verb בנה *banah, he built.* I do not see that we gain much by this translation. *Thy sons shall dwell in thee, Vulgate;* and so the *Septuagint* and *Chaldee.*

Verse 6. *Ye that make mention of the Lord, keep not silence*] The faithful, and in particular the priests and Levites, are exhorted by the prophet to beseech God with unremitted importunity (compare Luke xviii. 1, &c.) to hasten the redemption of Sion. The image in this place is taken from the temple service; in which there was appointed a constant watch, day and night, by the Levites: and among them this seems to have belonged particularly to the singers, see 1 Chron. ix. 33. Now the watches in the east, even to this day, are performed by a loud cry from time to time of the watchmen, to mark the time, and that very frequently, and in order to show that they themselves are constantly attentive to their duty. Hence the watchmen are said by the prophet, chap. lii. 8, *to lift up their voice;* and here they are commanded, *not to keep silence;* and the greatest reproach to them is, *that they are dumb dogs; they cannot bark; dreamers; sluggards, loving to slumber*, chap. lvi. 10. "The watchmen in the camp of the caravans go their rounds crying one after another, 'God is one, he is merciful:' and often add, 'Take heed to yourselves.'" TAVERNIER, *Voyage de Perse*, Liv. i. chap. x. The hundred and thirty-fourth Psalm gives us an example of the temple watch. The whole Psalm is nothing more than the alternate cry of two different divisions of the watch. The first watch addresses the second, reminding them of their duty; the second answers by a solemn blessing. The address and the answer seem both to be a set form, which each division proclaimed, or sung aloud, at stated intervals, to notify the time of the night:—

FIRST CHORUS

"Come on now, bless ye JEHOVAH, all ye servants of JEHOVAH;
Ye that stand in the house of JEHOVAH in the nights;
Lift up your hands towards the sanctuary,
And bless ye JEHOVAH."

SECOND CHORUS

"JEHOVAH bless thee out of Sion;
He that made heaven and earth."

"Ye who stand in the *place of the watch*, in the house of the sanctuary of the Lord; and ye praise through the nights;"—says the *Chaldee* paraphrase on the second line. And this explains what is here particularly meant by proclaiming, or making remembrance of, the name of JEHOVAH: the form, which the watch made use of on these occasions, was always a short sentence, expressing some pious sentiment, of which JEHOVAH was the subject; and it is remarkable, that the custom in the east in this respect also still continues the very same; as appears by the example above given from *Tavernier*.

A. M. cir. 3292
B. C. cir. 712
Olymp. XVII. 1
cir. annum
NumæPompilii,
R. Roman., 4

8 The LORD hath sworn by his
right hand, and by the arm of his
strength, [q]Surely I will no more
[r]give thy corn *to be* meat for
thine enemies; and the sons of the stranger
shall not drink thy wine, for the which thou
hast laboured:
9 But they that have gathered it shall eat it,
and praise the LORD; and they that have
brought it together shall drink it [s]in the courts
of my holiness.
10 Go through, go through the gates; [t]pre-
pare ye the way of the people;
cast up, cast up the highway;
gather out the stones; [u]lift up a
standard for the people.
11 Behold, the LORD hath proclaimed unto
the end of the world, [v]Say ye to the daughter
of Zion, Behold, thy salvation cometh; behold,
his [w]reward *is* with him, and his [x]work before him.
12 And they shall call them, The holy people, The redeemed of the LORD: and thou shalt
be called, Sought out, A city [y]not forsaken.

A. M. cir. 3292
B. C. cir. 712
Olymp. XVII. 1
cir. annum
NumæPompilii,
R. Roman., 4

[q]Heb. *If I give*, &c.——[r]Deut. xxix. 31, &c.; Jer. v. 17——[s]See Deut. xii. 12; xiv. 23, 26; xvi. 11, 14 [t]Chap. xl. 3; lvii. 14

[u]Chap. xi. 12——[v]Zech. ix. 9; Matt. xxi. 5; John xii. 15——[w]Chap. xl. 10; Rev. xxii. 12——[x]Or, *recompense*——[y]Ver. 4

And this observation leads to the explanation of an obscure passage in the Prophet Malachi, chap. ii. 12.

"JEHOVAH will cut off the man that doeth this;
The watchman and the answerer, from the tabernacles of Jacob;
And him that presenteth an offering to JEHOVAH God of hosts."

ער וענה *er veoneh, the master and the scholar*, says our translation, after the *Vulgate: the son and the grandson*, says the *Syriac* and *Chaldee*, as little to the purpose: *Arias Montanus* has given it *vigilantem et respondentem*, "the watchman and the answerer;" that is, the Levite and "him that presenteth an offering to JEHOVAH," that is, the priest.—L. *Ye that make mention of the Lord, keep not silence.* Is not this clause an address to the ministers of Christ, to continue in supplication for the conversion of the Jewish people? *Kimchi* seems to think that the watchmen are the *interceding angels!*

Verse 9. *But they that have gathered it shall eat it, and praise the Lord*] This and the following line have reference to the law of Moses: "Thou mayest not eat within thy gates the tithe of thy corn, or of thy wine, or of thy oil; but thou must eat them before the Lord thy God, in the place which the Lord thy God shall choose," Deut. xii. 17, 18. "And when ye shall come into the land, and shall have planted all manner of trees for food, then ye shall count the fruit thereof as uncircumcised: three years it shall be as uncircumcised unto you; it shall not be eaten of. But in the fourth year all the fruit thereof shall be holy to praise the Lord withal. And in the fifth year ye shall eat the fruit thereof," Lev. xix. 23-25. This clearly explains the force of the expressions, "shall praise JEHOVAH," and "shall drink it in my sacred courts."

Five MSS., one ancient, have יאכלוהו *yocheluhu, they shall eat it*, fully expressed: and so likewise ישתוהו *yishtuhu, they shall drink it*, is found in nineteen MSS., three of them ancient.—L.

Verse 10. *Of the people*—"For the people"] Before the word העם *haam, the people*, two MSS. insert יהוה *Yehovah;* one MS. adds the same word after; and eight MSS., three ancient, instead of העם *haam*, have יהוה *Yehovah*, and so likewise one edition. But though it makes a good sense either way, I believe it to be an interpolation, as the ancient Versions do not favour it. The *Septuagint* indeed read עמי *ammi, my people.*—L.

Verse 11. *Unto the end of the world*—אל קצה הארץ *el ketseh haarets*—Instead of אל *el, to*, עד *ad*, UNTO, is the reading of two of *Kennicott's* MSS.; and one of mine has מקצה *mikketseh*, "FROM the end of the earth."

Behold, thy salvation cometh—"Lo, thy Saviour cometh"] So all the ancient Versions render the word ישעך *yishech.*

Behold, his reward] See note on chap. xl. 10, 11. This *reward* he carries as it were in his hand. *His work is before him*—he perfectly knows what is to be done; and is perfectly able to do it. He will do what God should do, and what man cannot do; and men should be *workers with him.* Let no man fear that the promise shall not be fulfilled on account of its difficulty, its greatness, the hinderances in the way, or the unworthiness of the person to whom it is made. It is God's work; he is *able* to do it, and as *willing* as he is able.

Verse 12. *They shall call them*—These characteristics seem to be put in their inverted order.—1. God will not *forsake* them. 2. They shall be *sought out.* 3. They shall be *redeemed.* And, 4. Be in consequence a *holy people.* 1. When God *calls*, it is a proof that he has not *forsaken.* 2. When he *seeks*, it is a proof he is *waiting* to be *gracious.* 3. When the *atonement* is exhibited, *all things are then ready.* 4. And when that is received, *holiness* of *heart* and *life* is then to be kept continually in view, as this is the genuine work of God's Spirit; and without *holiness* none shall see the Lord.

CHAPTER LXIII

The prophet, (or rather the Church he represents,) sees the great Deliverer, long promised and expected, making his appearance, after having crushed his enemies, like grapes in the wine-vat. The comparison suggests a lively idea of the wrath of Omnipotence, which its unhappy objects can no more resist than the grapes can resist the treader. Indeed, there is so much pathos, energy, and sublimity in this remarkable passage, as hardly any thing can be conceived to exceed. The period to which it refers must be the same with that predicted in the nineteenth *chapter of the Revelation, some parts of which are expressed in the same terms with this, and plainly enough refer to the very sudden and total overthrow of Antichrist, and of all his adherents and auxiliaries, of which the destruction of Babylon, the capital of Chaldea, and of Bozra, the chief city of the Edomites, was the prototype,* 1–6. *At the* seventh *verse commences a penitential confession and supplication of the Jews, as uttered in their present dispersion,* 7–19.

A. M. cir. 3292 B. C. cir. 712 Olymp. XVII. 1 cir. annum NumæPompilii, R. Roman., 4

WHO *is* this that cometh from
Edom, with dyed garments
from Bozrah? this *that is* [a]glo-
rious in his apparel, travelling in
the greatness of his strength? I
that speak in righteousness,
mighty to save.
2 Wherefore [b]*art thou* red in

[a]Heb. *decked*

[b]Rev. xix. 13

The very remarkable passage with which this chapter begins seems to me to be, in a manner, detached from the rest, and to stand singly by itself; having no immediate connexion with what goes before, or with what follows, otherwise than as it may pursue the general design, and stand in its proper place in the order of prophecy. It is by many learned interpreters supposed that Judas Maccabeus and his victories make the subject of it. What claim Judas can have to so great an honour will, I think, be very difficult to make out; or how the attributes of the great person introduced can possibly suit him. Could Judas call himself the *announcer of righteousness*, mighty to save? Could he talk of the *day of vengeance being in his heart*, and the *year of his redeemed being come?* or that *his own arm wrought salvation for him?* Besides, what were the great exploits of Judas in regard to the Idumeans? He overcame them in battle, and slew twenty thousand of them. And John Hyrcanus, his brother Simon's son and successor, who is called in to help out the accomplishment of the prophecy, gave them another defeat some time afterward, and compelled them by force to become proselytes to the Jewish religion, and to submit to circumcision: after which they were incorporated with the Jews, and became one people with them. Are these events adequate to the prophet's lofty prediction? Was it so great an action to win a battle with considerable slaughter of the enemy, or to force a whole nation by dint of the sword into Judaism? or was the conversion of the Idumeans, however effected, and their admission into the Church of God, equivalent to a most grievous judgment and destruction, threatened in the severest terms? But here is another very material circumstance to be considered, which, I presume, entirely excludes Judas Maccabeus, and even the Idumeans, properly so called. For the Idumea of the prophet's time was quite a different country from that which Judas conquered. For during the Babylonish captivity the Nabatheans had driven the Edomites out of their country; who upon that took possession of the southern parts of Judea, and settled themselves there; that is, in the country of the whole tribe of Simeon and in half of that of Judah. See Prideaux, ad. an. 740 and 165. And the metropolis of the Edomites, and of the country thence called Idumea, which Judas took, was *Hebron*, 1 Macc. v. 65, not Bozrah.

I conclude, therefore, that this prophecy has not the least relation to Judas Maccabeus. It may be asked, to whom, and to what event does it relate? I can only answer, that I know of no event in history to which, from its importance and circumstances, it can be applied: unless, perhaps, to the destruction of Jerusalem and the Jewish polity; which in the Gospel is called the *coming of Christ* and *the days of vengeance*, Matt. xvi. 28; Luke xxi. 22. But though this prophecy must have its accomplishment, there is no necessity for supposing that it has been already accomplished. There are prophecies, which intimate a great slaughter of the enemies of God and his people, which remain to be fulfilled; these in Ezekiel, chap. xxxviii., and in the Revelation of St. John, chap. xx., are called *Gog* and *Magog*. This prophecy of Isaiah may possibly refer to the same or the like event. We need not be at a loss to determine the person who is here introduced, as *stained with treading the wine-press*, if we consider how St. John in the Revelation has applied this image of the prophet, Rev. xix. 13, 15, 16. Compare chap. xxxiv.—L.

NOTES ON CHAP. LXIII

Verse 1. *Who is this that cometh from Edom*] Probably both Edom and Bozrah are only figurative expressions, to point out the place in which God should discomfit his enemies. *Edom* signifies *red*, and *Bozrah*, *a vintage*. *Kimchi* interprets the whole of the destruction of Rome.

I that speak in righteousness—"I who publish righteousness"] A MS. has המדבר *hammedabber*, with the demonstrative article added with greater force and emphasis: *The announcer* of righteousness. A MS. has צדקה *tsedakah*, without ב *be* prefixed; and so the *Septuagint* and *Vulgate*. And *thirty-eight* MSS. (*seven* ancient) of Dr. *Kennicott's*, and many of *De Rossi's*, and *one* of my own, add the conjunction ו *vau* to רב *rab, and mighty;* which the *Septuagint*, *Syriac*, and *Vulgate* confirm.—L.

Verse 2. *Wherefore* art thou *red in thine apparel*] For ללבושך *lilebushecha*, *twenty-nine* MSS. (*nine* ancient) of *Kennicott's*, and *thirty* of *De Rossi's*, and *one* edition, have ללבושיך

A. M. cir. 3292
B. C. cir. 712
Olymp. XVII. 1
cir. annum
NumæPompilii,
R. Roman., 4

thine apparel, and thy garments
like him that treadeth in the
winefat?
3 I have [c]trodden the wine-
press alone; and of the people *there was* none
with me: for I will tread them in mine anger,
and trample them in my fury; and their blood
shall be sprinkled upon my garments, and I
will stain all my raiment.
4 For the [d]day of vengeance *is* in mine
heart, and the year of my redeemed is
come.
5 [e]And I looked, and [f]*there was* none to
help; and I wondered that *there was* none to
uphold: therefore mine own
[g]arm brought salvation unto me;
and my fury, it upheld me.
6 And I will tread down the
people in mine anger, and [h]make them drunk
in my fury, and I will bring down their
strength to the earth.
7 I will mention the [i]loving-kindnesses of
the LORD, *and* the praises of the LORD,
according to all that the LORD hath bestowed
on us, and the great goodness toward the house
of Israel, which he hath bestowed on them
according to his mercies, and according to the
multitude of his loving-kindnesses.

[c]Lam. i. 15; Rev. xiv. 19, 20; xix. 15——[d]Chap. xxxiv. 8; lxi. 2——[e]Chap. xli. 28; lix. 16

[f]John xvi. 32——[g]Psa. xcviii. 1; chap. lix. 16——[h]Rev. xvi. 6——[i]Psa. xxv. 6; lxxxix. 49

lilebusheycha in the plural; so the *Septuagint* and *Syriac*. And all the ancient Versions read it with מ *mem*, instead of the first ל *lamed*. But the true reading is probably מלבושך *malbushecha* in the singular, as in ver. 3.—L.

Verse 3. *And of the people* there was *none with me*] I was wholly abandoned by them: but a good meaning is, No man has had any part in making the atonement; it is entirely the work of the Messiah alone. No created being could have any part in a sacrifice that was to be of infinite merit.

And I will stain—"And I have stained"] For אגאלתי *egalti*, a verb of very irregular formation, compounded, as they say, of the two forms of the preterite and future, a MS. has אגאלהו *egalehu*, the regular future with a pleonastic pronoun added to it, according to the Hebrew idiom: "And all my raiment, I have stained it." The necessity of the verb's being in the past tense seems to have given occasion to the alteration made in the end of the word. The conversive ו *vau* at the beginning of the sentence affects the verb, though not joined to it; of which there are many examples:—

anithani remim umikkarney

ומקרני רמים עניתני

"And thou wilt hear me (or hear thou me) from among the horns of the unicorns," Psa. xxii. 22.—L.

Instead of על בגדי *al begadai, upon my garments*, one of my ancient MSS. has לארץ בגדי *laarets begadai, to the earth:* but this word is partly effaced, and על *al* written in the margin by a later hand.

Verse 5. *And my fury*—"And mine indignation"] For וחמתי *vachamathi, nineteen* MSS. (*three* ancient) of *Kennicott's, nine* of *De Rossi's*, and *one* of mine, and *four* editions, have וצדקתי *vetsidkathi, and my righteousness;* from chap. lix. 16, which I suppose the transcriber retained in his memory. It is true that the Versions are in favour of the common reading; but that noticed above seems to stand on good authority, and is a reading both pleasing and impressive. Opposite, in the margin, my MS. has the common reading by a later hand.

Verse 6. *And make them drunk in my fury*—"And I crushed them in mine indignation"] For ואשכרם *vaashkerem, and I made them drunken, twenty-seven* MSS., (*three* ancient,) *twelve* of *De Rossi's*, and the old edition of 1488, have ואשברם *vaashabberem, and I crushed them:* and so the *Syriac* and *Chaldee*. The *Septuagint* have omitted this whole line.

Verse 7. *I will mention the loving-kindnesses of the Lord*] The prophet connects the preceding mercies of God to the Jews with the present prospect he has of their redemption by the Messiah; thus making a *circle* in which eternal goodness revolves. The remaining part of this chapter, with the whole chapter following, contains a penitential confession and supplication of the Israelites in their present state of dispersion, in which they have so long marvellously subsisted, and still continue to subsist, as a people; cast out of their country; without any proper form of civil polity or religious worship; their temple destroyed, their city desolated and lost to them, and their whole nation scattered over the face of the earth, apparently deserted and cast off by the God of their fathers, as no longer his peculiar people.

They begin with acknowledging God's great mercies and favours to their nation, and the ungrateful returns made to them on their part, that by their disobedience they had forfeited the protection of God, and had caused him to become their adversary. And now the prophet represents them, induced by the memory of the great things that God had done for them, as addressing their humble supplication for the renewal of his mercies. They beseech him to regard them in consideration of his former loving-kindness, they acknowledge him for their Father and Creator, they confess their wickedness and hardness of heart, they entreat his forgiveness, and deplore their present miserable condition under which they have so long suffered. It seems designed as a formulary of humiliation for the Israelites, in order to their conversion.

The whole passage is in the elegiac form, pathetic and elegant; but it has suffered much in our present copy by the mistakes of transcribers.

The praises of the Lord—"The praise of JEHOVAH"] For תהלות *tehilloth*, plural, *twenty-*

A. M. cir. 3292 B. C. cir. 712 Olymp. XVII. 1 cir. annum NumæPompilii, R. Roman., 4

8 For he said, Surely they *are*
my people, children *that* will not
lie: so he was their Saviour.
9 [k]In all their affliction he was
afflicted, [l]and the angel of his presence saved
them [m]in his love and in his pity he redeemed them; and [n]he bare them, and carried them all the days of old.

10 But they [o]rebelled, and [p]vexed his holy
Spirit: [q]therefore he was turned to be their
enemy, *and* he fought against them.

11 Then he remembered the days of old,
Moses, *and* his people, *saying,* Where *is* he
that [r]brought them up out of the sea with the
[s]shepherd of his flock? [t]where
is he that put his holy Spirit
within him?

12 That led *them* by the right
hand of Moses, [u]with his glorious arm, [v]dividing the water before them, to make himself
an everlasting name?

13 [w]That led them through the deep as a
horse in the wilderness, *that* they should not
stumble?

14 As a beast goeth down into the valley,
the Spirit of the LORD caused him to rest:
so didst thou lead thy people, [x]to make thyself a glorious name.

---

[k]Judg. x. 16; Zech. ii. 8; Acts ix. 4——[l]Exod. xiv. 19; xxiii. 20, 21; xxxiii. 14; Malachi iii. 1; Acts xii. 11——[m]Deut. vii. 7, 8——[n]Exod. xix. 4; Deut. i. 31; xxxii. 11, 12; chap. xlvi. 3, 4——[o]Exod. xv. 24; Num. xiv. 11; Psa. lxxviii. 56; xcv. 9——[p]Psa. lxxviii. 40; Acts vii. 51; Eph. iv. 30——[q]Exod. xxiii. 21——[r]Exod. xiv. 30; xxxii. 11, 12; Num. xiv. 13, 14, &c.; Jer. ii. 6——[s]Or, *shepherds*, as Psa. lxxvii. 20——[t]Num. xi. 17, 25; Neh. ix. 20; Dan. iv. 8; Hag. ii. 5——[u]Exod. xv. 6——[v]Exod. xiv. 21; Joshua iii. 16——[w]Psalm cvi. 9——[x]2 Samuel vii. 23

---

nine MSS. (*three* ancient) and *two* editions, have תהלת *tehillath*, in the singular number; and so the *Vulgate* renders it; and one of the Greek versions, in the margin of Cod. Marchal. and in the text of MSS. Pachom. and I. D. II. την αινεσιν Κυριου, "the praise of the Lord."—L.

Verses 8, 9. *So he was their Saviour. In all their affliction*—"And he became their Saviour in all their distress"] I have followed the translation of the *Septuagint* in the latter part of the *eighth*, and the former part of the *ninth* verse; which agrees with the present text, a little differently divided as to the members of the sentence. They read מכל *miccol, out of all*, instead of בכל *bechol, in all*, which makes no difference in the sense; and צר *tsar* they understand as ציר *tsir.* Και εγενετο αυτοις εις σωτηριαν εκ πασης θλιψεως αυτων· ου πρεσβυς, ουδε αγγελος· "And he was salvation to them in all their tribulation; neither an ambassador nor an angel, but himself saved them." An angel of his presence means an angel of superior order, in immediate attendance upon God. So the angel of the Lord says to Zacharias, "I am Gabriel, that stand in the presence of God," Luke i. 19. The presence of JEHOVAH, Exod. xxxiii. 14, 15, and the angel, Exod. xxxiii. 20, 21, is JEHOVAH himself; here an angel of his presence is opposed to JEHOVAH himself, as an angel is in the following passages of the same book of Exodus. After their idolatrous worshipping of the golden calf, "when God had said to Moses, I will send an angel before thee—I will not go up in the midst of thee—the people mourned," Exod. xxxiii. 2-4. God afterwards comforts Moses, by saying, "My presence (that is, I myself in person, and not by an angel) will go with thee," ver. 14. Αυτος προπορευσομαι σου, "I myself will go before thee," as the *Septuagint* render it.

The MSS. and editions are much divided between the two readings of the text and margin in the common copies, לא *lo, not,* and לו *lo, to him.* All the ancient Versions express the chetib reading, לא *lo, not.*

And he bare them and carried them all the days of old—"And he took them up, and he bore them, all the days of old."] See the note on chap. xlvi. 3.—L.

Verse 10. And *he fought against them*] *Twenty-six* MSS. (*ten* ancient) and the *first* edition, with another, add the conjunction ו *vau*, והוא *vehu, and he.*

Verse 11. *Moses* and *his people*—"Moses his servant"] For עמו *ammo, his people*, two MSS. (*one* of them ancient) and *one* of my own, (ancient,) and *one* of *De Rossi's*, and the old edition of 1488, and the *Syriac*, read עבדו *abdo, his servant.* These two words have been mistaken one for the other in other places; Psa. lxxviii. 71, and lxxx. 5, for עמו *ammo, his people*, and עמך *ammecha, thy people*, the *Septuagint* read עבדו *abdo, his servant*, and עבדך *abdecha, thy servant.*

Where is he that brought them up out of the sea with the shepherd of his flock? where &c.—"How he brought them up from the sea, with the shepherd of his flock; how," &c.] For איה *aiyeh, how*, interrogative, twice, the *Syriac* Version reads איך *eich, how*, without interrogation, as that particle is used in the *Syriac* language, and sometimes in the *Hebrew.* See Ruth iii. 18; Eccles. ii. 16.

The shepherd of his flock] That is, Moses. The MSS. and editions vary in this word; some have it רעה *roeh*, in the singular number; so the *Septuagint*, *Syriac*, and *Chaldee.* Others רעי *roey*, plural, *the shepherds.*—L.

Verses 13, 14. *That led them through the deep—As a beast goeth down into the valley*] In both these verses there is an allusion to the Israelites going through the Red Sea, in the bottom of which they found no more inconvenience than a horse would in running in the desert, where there was neither *stone* nor *mud;* nor a beast in the valley, where all was *plain* and *smooth.*

Verse 14. *The Spirit of the Lord caused him to rest*—"The Spirit of JEHOVAH conducted them"] For תניחנו *tenichennu, caused him to rest*, the *Septuagint* have ὡδηγησεν αυτους, *conducted them;* they read תנחם *tanchem.* The *Syriac, Chaldee*, and *Vulgate* read תנחנו *tan-*

A. M. cir. 3292 B. C. cir. 712 Olymp. XVII. 1 cir. annum NumæPompilii, R. Roman., 4

15 [y]Look down from heaven,
and behold [z]from the habitation
of thy holiness and of thy glory:
where *is* thy zeal and thy strength,
[a]the sounding [b]of thy bowels and of thy
mercies toward me? are they restrained?

16 [c]Doubtless thou *art* our father, though
Abraham [d]be ignorant of us, and Israel
acknowledge us not: thou, O LORD *art* our
Father, [e]our Redeemer; thy name *is* from
everlasting.

17 O LORD, why hast thou
[f]made us to err from thy ways
and [g]hardened our heart from
thy fear? [h]Return, for thy
servants' sake, the tribes of thine inheritance.

18 [i]The people of thy holiness have possessed *it* but a little while: [k]our adversaries
have trodden down thy sanctuary.

19 We are *thine:* thou never barest rule
over them: [l]they were not called by thy name.

---

[y]Deut. xxvi. 15; Psa. lxxx. 14——[z]Psa. xxxiii. 14——[a]Or, *the multitude*——[b]Jer. xxxi. 20; Hos. xi. 8——[c]Deut. xxxii. 6; 1 Chron. xxix. 10; chap. lxiv. 8——[d]Job xiv. 21; Eccles. ix. 5——[e]Or, *our Redeemer from everlasting* is *thy name*

[f]Psa. cxix. 10——[g]See chap. vi. 10, with John xii. 40; Rom. ix. 18——[h]Num. x. 36; Psa. xc. 13——[i]Deut. vii. 6; xxvi. 19; chap. lxii. 12; Dan. viii. 24——[k]Psa. lxxiv. 7——[l]Or, *thy name was not called upon them;* chap. lxv. 1

---

chennu, conducted him. Two MSS. have the word without the י *yod* in the middle.

Verse 15. *And thy strength*—"And thy mighty power"] For גבורתיך *geburotheycha,* plural, *thirty-two* MSS. (*seven* ancient) and *twenty-one* of *De Rossi's,* and *seven* editions, have גבורתך *geburathecha,* singular.

Are they restrained?] For אלי *elai, from* (or in regard to) *me,* the *Septuagint* and *Syriac* read אלינו *eleynu, from us.*—L.

Verse 16. *Our Redeemer; thy name* is *from everlasting*—"O deliver us for the sake of thy name."] The present text reads, as our translation has rendered it, "Our Redeemer, thy name is from everlasting." But instead of מעולם *meolam, from everlasting,* an ancient MS. has למען *lemaan, for the sake of,* which gives a much better sense. To show the impropriety of the present reading, it is sufficient to observe, that the *Septuagint* and *Syriac* translators thought it necessary to add עלינו *aleynu, upon us,* to make out the sense; That is, "Thy name is *upon us,* or we are called by thy name, from of old." And the *Septuagint* have rendered גאלנו *goalenu,* in the *imperative* mood, ῥυσαι ἡμας, *deliver us.*—L.

Verse 17. *Why hast thou made us to err*] A mere *Hebraism,* for why hast thou *permitted* us to err. So, *Lead us not into temptation;* do not *suffer* us to fall into that to which we are tempted.

Verse 18. *The people of thy holiness have possessed* it *but a little while*—"It is little that they have taken possession of thy holy mountain"] The difficulty of the construction in this place is acknowledged on all hands. *Vitringa* prefers that sense as the least exceptionable which our translation has expressed; in which however there seems to be a great defect; that is, the want of what in the speaker's view must have been the principal part of the proposition, the object of the verb, *the land,* or *it,* as our translators supply it, which surely ought to have been expressed, and not to have been left to be supplied by the reader. In a word, I believe there is some mistake in the text; and here the *Septuagint* help us out; they had in their copy הר *har, mountain,* instead of עם *am, people,* του ορους του ἁγιου σου, *the mountain of thy Holy One.* "Not only have our enemies taken possession of Mount Sion, and trodden down thy sanctuary; even far worse than this has befallen us; thou hast long since utterly cast us off, and dost not consider us as thy peculiar people."—L.

CHAPTER LXIV

The whole of this chapter, which is very pathetic and tender, may be considered as a formulary of prayer and humiliation intended for the Jews in order to their conversion, 1–12.

A. M. cir. 3292 B. C. cir. 712 Olymp. XVII. 1 cir. annum NumæPompilii, R. Roman., 4

O THAT thou wouldest [a]rend
the heavens, that thou
wouldest come down, that the
[b]mountains might flow down at
thy presence,

2 As *when* [c]the melting fire
burneth, the fire causeth the
waters to boil, to make thy name
known to thine adversaries, *that*
the nations may tremble at thy presence!

---

[a]Psa. cxliv. 5——[b]Judg. v. 5; Mic. i. 4

[c]Heb. *the fire of meltings*

NOTES ON CHAP. LXIV

Verse 1. *O that thou wouldest rend the heavens*—This seems to allude to the wonderful manifestation of God upon Mount Sinai.

Verse 2. *As* when *the melting fire burneth*—"As the fire kindleth the dry fuel"] המסים *hamasim.* "It means *dry stubble,* and the root is המס *hamas,*" says *Rabbi Jonah,* apud *Sal. ben Melec* in loc. Which is approved by *Schultens,* Orig. Heb. p. 30.

"The fire kindling the stubble does not seem like enough to the melting of the mountains to be brought as a simile to it. What if thus?—

A. M. cir. 3292
B. C. cir. 712
Olymp. XVII. 1
cir. annum
NumæPompilii,
R. Roman., 4

3 When [d]thou didst terrible
things *which* we look not for,
thou camest down, the mountains flowed down at thy presence.
4 For since the beginning of the world [e]*men*
have not heard, nor perceived by the ear,
neither hath the eye [f]seen, O
God, beside thee, *what* he hath
prepared for him that waiteth
for him.
5 Thou meetest him that rejoiceth [g]and
worketh righteousness, [h]*those that* remember

[d]Exod. xxxiv. 10; Judg. v. 4, 5; Psa. lxviii. 8; Hab. iii. 3, 6——[e]Psa. xxxi. 19; 1 Cor. ii. 9

[f]Or, *seen a God besides thee*, which *doeth so for him*, &c. [g]Acts x. 35——[h]Chap. xxvi. 8

'That the mountains might flow down at thy presence!
As the fire of things smelted burneth,
As the fire causeth the waters to boil—'

There is no doubt of the Hebrew words of the second line bearing that version."—Dr. JUBB.

I submit these different interpretations to the reader's judgment. For my own part I am inclined to think that the text is much corrupted in this place. The ancient Versions have not the least traces of either of the above interpretations. The *Septuagint* and *Syriac* agree exactly together in rendering this line by, "As the wax melted before the fire," which can by no means be reconciled with the present text. The *Vulgate*, for המסים *hamasim*, read ימסו *yemasu*.

That *the nations*] For גוים *goyim, the nations*, four MSS. (one of them ancient) have הרים *harim, the mountains*.—L.

Verse 4. *For since the beginning of the world men have not heard*—"For never have men heard"] St. Paul is generally supposed to have quoted this passage of Isaiah, 1 Cor. ii. 9; and Clemens Romanus in his first epistle has made the same quotation, very nearly in the same words with the apostle. But the citation is so very different both from the *Hebrew* text and the version of the *Septuagint*, that it seems very difficult, if not impossible, to reconcile them by any literal emendation, without going beyond the bounds of temperate criticism. One clause, "neither hath it entered into the heart of man," (which, by the way, is a phrase purely Hebrew, עלה על לב *alah al leb*, and should seem to belong to the prophet,) is wholly left out; and another is repeated without force or propriety; viz., "nor perceived by the ear," after, "never have heard:" and the sense and expression of the apostle is far preferable to that of the Hebrew text. Under these difficulties I am at a loss what to do better, than to offer to the reader this, perhaps disagreeable, alternative: either to consider the *Hebrew* text and *Septuagint* in this place as wilfully disguised and corrupted by the Jews; of which practice in regard to other quotations in the New Testament from the Old, they lie under strong suspicions, (see Dr. *Owen* on the version of the *Septuagint*, sect. vi.-ix.;) or to look upon St. Paul's quotation as not made from Isaiah, but from one or other of the two apocryphal books, entitled, The Ascension of Esaiah, and the Apocalypse of Elias, in both of which this passage was found; and the apostle is by some supposed in other places to have quoted such apocryphal writings. As the first of these conclusions will perhaps not easily be admitted by many, so I must fairly warn my readers that the second is treated by Jerome as little better than heresy. See his comment on this place of Isaiah.—L. I would read the whole verse thus; "Yea, from the time of old they have not heard, they have not hearkened to, an eye hath not seen a God besides thee. He shall work for that one that waiteth for him." This I really think on the whole to be the best translation of the original.

The variations on this place are as follows: for שמעו *shameu, they* have heard, a MS. and the *Septuagint* read שמענו *shamanu, we* have heard: for the second לא *lo, not, sixty-nine* MSS. and four editions have ולא *velo, and not*, and the *Syriac, Chaldee*, and *Vulgate*. And so ועין *veayin, and eye, Septuagint* and *Syriac*. את *eth, the*, (emphatic,) is added before אלהים *Elohim, God*, in MS. *Bodleian*. למחכי *limechakkey*, to them *that wait*, plural, two MSS. and all the ancient Versions.—L.

Verse 5. *Thou meetest him that rejoiceth and worketh righteousness*—"Thou meetest with joy those who work righteousness"] The *Syriac* reads פוגע אתה שש בעשי *poga attah shesh baashi*, as above.

In those is continuance, and we shall be saved—"Because of our deeds, for we have been rebellious"] בהם עולם ונושע *bahem olam venivvashea*. I am fully persuaded that these words as they stand in the present Hebrew text are utterly unintelligible; there is no doubt of the meaning of each word separately; but put together they make no sense at all. I conclude, therefore, that the copy has suffered by mistakes of transcribers in this place. The corruption is of long standing; for the ancient interpreters were as much at a loss for the meaning as the moderns, and give nothing satisfactory. The *Septuagint* render these words by δια τουτο επλανηθημεν, *therefore we have erred:* they seem to have read עליהם נפשע *aleyhem niphsha*, without helping the sense. In this difficulty what remains but to have recourse to conjecture? Archbishop *Secker* was dissatisfied with the present reading: he proposed הבט עלינו ונושע *hebet aleynu venivvashea;* "look upon us, and we shall, or that we may, be saved:" which gives a very good sense, but seems to have no sufficient foundation. Besides, the word ונושע *venivvashea*, which is attended with great difficulties, seems to be corrupted as well as the two preceding; and the true reading of it is, I think, given by the *Septuagint*, ונפשע *veniphsha*, επλανηθημεν, *we have erred*, (so they render the verb פשע *pasha*, chap. xlvi. 8, and Ezek. xxiii. 12,) parallel to ונחטא *vannecheta*, ἡμαρτομεν, *we have sinned*. For בהם עולם *bahem olam*, which means nothing, I would propose המעללינו *hammaaleleynu*, "because of our deeds; which I presume was first altered to במעלליהם *bemaaleleyhem*, an

A. M. cir. 3292 B. C. cir. 712 Olymp. XVII. 1 cir annum NumæPompilii, R. Roman., 4

thee in thy ways: behold, thou art wroth; for we have sinned: [i]in those is continuance, and we shall be saved.

6 But we are all as an unclean *thing,* and all [k]our righteousnesses *are* as filthy rags; and we all do [l]fade as a leaf: and our iniquities, like the wind, have taken us away.

7 And [m]*there is* none that calleth upon thy name, that stirreth up himself to take hold of thee: for thou hast hid thy face from us, and hast [n]consumed us, [o]because of our iniquities.

8 [p]But now, O LORD, thou *art* our Father; we *are* the clay, [q]and thou our potter; and we all *are* [r]the work of thy hand.

9 Be not [s]wroth very sore, O LORD, neither remember iniquity for ever: behold, see, we beseech thee, [t]we *are* all thy people.

10 Thy holy cities are a wilderness, Zion is a wilderness, [u]Jerusalem a desolation.

11 [v]Our holy and our beautiful house, where our fathers praised thee, is burned up with fire: and all [w]our pleasant things are laid waste.

12 [x]Wilt thou refrain thyself for these *things,* O LORD? [y]wilt thou hold thy peace and afflict us very sore?

[i]Mal. iii. 6——[k]Phil. iii. 9——[l]Psa. xc. 5, 6——[m]Hos. vii. 7——[n]Heb. *melted*——[o]Heb. *by the hand,* as Job ix. 4——[p]Chap. lxiii. 16——[q]Chap. xxix. 16; xlv. 9; Jer. xviii. 6; Rom. ix. 20, 21——[r]Eph. ii. 10

[s]Psa. lxxiv. 1, 2; lxxix. 8——[t]Psa. lxxix. 13——[u]Psa. lxxix. 1; chap. iii. 8; Jer. vi. 1; ix. 11——[v]2 Kings xxv. 9; Psa. lxxiv. 7; 2 Chron. xxxvi. 12——[w]Ezek. xxiv. 21, 25——[x]Chap. xlii. 24——[y]Psa. lxxxiii. 1

easy and common mistake of the third person plural of the pronoun for the first, (see note on chap. xxxiii. 2,) and then with some farther alteration to בהם עולם *behem olam.* The עליהם *aleyhem,* which the *Septuagint* probably found in their copy, seems to be a remnant of במעלליהם *bemaaleleyhem.*

This, it may be said, is imposing your sense upon the prophet. It may be so; for perhaps these may not be the very words of the prophet: but however it is better than to impose upon him what makes no sense at all; as they generally do, who pretend to render such corrupted passages. For instance, our own translators: "in *those* is continuance, and we shall be saved:" in those—in whom, or what? There is no antecedent to the relative. "In the ways of God," say some: "with our fathers," says *Vitringa,* joining it in construction with the verb, קצפת *katsaphta,* "thou hast been angry with them, our fathers;" and putting ונחטא *vannecheta,* "for we have sinned," in a parenthesis. But there has not been any mention of *our fathers:* and the whole sentence, thus disposed, is utterly discordant from the *Hebrew* idiom and construction. In those is *continuance;* עולם *olam* means a *destined* but hidden and *unknown* portion of time; but cannot mean continuation of time, or *continuance,* as it is here rendered. Such forced interpretations are equally conjectural with the boldest critical emendation; and generally have this farther disadvantage, that they are altogether unworthy of the sacred writers.—L.

Coverdale renders the passage thus:—**But lo, thou art angrie, for we offende, and have been ever in synne; and there is not one whole.** This is, I am afraid, *making a sense.*

After all that this very learned prelate has done to reduce these words to sense and meaning, I am afraid we are still far from the prophet's mind. Probably בהם *bahem, in them,* refers to דרכיך *deracheycha, thy ways,* above. עולם *olam* may be rendered *of old,* or during the whole of the Jewish economy; and ונושע *venivvashea,* "and shall we be saved?" Thus: —Thou art wroth, for we have sinned in them (thy ways) of old; and can we be saved? For we are all as an unclean thing, &c.

Verse 6. *As filthy rags*] עדים *iddim.* Rab. Mosheh ben Maimon interpretatur עדים *iddim,* vestes quibus mulier se abstergit post congressum cum marito suo. *Alii* pannus menstruatus. *Alii* panni mulieris parientis.—**And we ben made as unclene alle we: and as the cloth of the woman rooten blode flowing, all our rigtwisnesses.** —Old MS. Bible. If preachers knew properly the meaning of this word, would they make such a liberal use of it in their public ministry? And why should any use a word, the meaning of which he does not understand? How many in the congregation blush for the incautious man and his "filthy rags!"

Verse 7. There is *none*] Twelve MSS. have אין *ein,* without the conjunction ו *vau* prefixed; and so read the *Chaldee* and *Vulgate.*

And hast consumed us because of our iniquities—"And hast delivered us up into the hands of our iniquities."] For ותמוגנו *vattemugenu,* "hast dissolved us," the *Septuagint, Syriac,* and *Chaldee* had in their copies תמגננו *temaggenenu,* "hast delivered us up." *Houbigant. Secker.*

Verse 8. *But, now, O Lord, thou* art *our Father*—"But thou, O JEHOVAH, thou art our Father"] For ועתה *veattah, and now,* five MSS., one of them ancient, and the two oldest editions, 1486 and 1488, have ואתה *veattah, and thou;* and so the *Chaldee* seems to have read. The repetition has great force. The other word may be well spared. "But now, O Lord, thou art our Father." How very affectionate is the complaint in this and the following verses! But how does the distress increase, when they recollect the desolations of the temple, and ruin of public worship, ver. 11: "Our holy and beautiful house, where our fathers praised thee, is burnt up with fire," &c.

We all are *the work of thy hand*] Three MSS. (two of them ancient) and the *Septuagint* read מעשה *maaseh, the work,* without the conjunction ו *vau* prefixed. And for ידך *yadecha, thy hand,* the *Bodleian,* and two others MSS., the *Septuagint, Syriac,* and *Vulgate* read ידיך *yadeycha, thy hands,* in the plural number.—L.

Verse 9. *Neither remember iniquity*] For

לעד תזכר *laad tizcor*, one of my MSS. has לעד תקצף *laad tiktsoph*, "be not *angry*," as in the preceding clause. This has been partially obliterated, and תזכר *tizcor*, written in the margin by a later hand: but this MS. abounds with words of this kind, all altered by later hands.

CHAPTER LXV

We have here a vindication of God's dealings with the Jews, 1, 2. *To this end the prophet points out their great hypocrisy, and gives a particular enumeration of their dreadful abominations, many of which were committed under the specious guise of sanctity*, 3–5. *For their horrid impieties, (recorded in writing before Jehovah,) the wrath of God shall certainly come upon them to the uttermost; a prediction which was exactly fulfilled in the first and second centuries in the reigns of the Roman emperors Vespasian, Titus, and Hadrian, when the whole Jewish polity was dissolved, and the people dispersed all over the world*, 6, 7. *Though God had rejected the Jews, and called the Gentiles, who sought him not,* (Rom. ix. 24–26,) *yet a remnant from among the former shall be preserved, to whom he will in due time make good all his promises*, 8–10. *Denunciation of Divine vengeance against those idolaters who set in order a table for Gad, and fill out a libation to Meni, ancient idolatries, which, from the context, and from the chronological order of the events predicted, have a plain reference to the idolatries practised by Antichrist under the guise of Christianity*, 11, 12. *Dreadful fate which awaits these gross idolaters beautifully contrasted with the great blessedness reserved for the righteous*, 13–16. *Future restoration of the posterity of Jacob, and the happy state of the world in general from that most glorious epoch, represented by the strong figure of the creation of* NEW heavens and a NEW earth, *wherein dwelleth righteousness, and into which no distress shall be permitted to enter*, 17–19. *In this new state of things the term of human life shall be greatly protracted, and shall possess none of that uncertainty which attaches to it in "the heavens and the earth which are now." This is elegantly illustrated by the longevity of a tree; manifestly alluding to the* oak or cedar of Lebanon, *some individuals of which are known to have lived from seven to ten centuries*, 20–23. *Beautiful figures shadowing forth the profound peace and harmony of the Church of Jesus Christ, which shall immediately follow the total overthrow of Antichrist; with a most gracious promise that the great chain of Omnipotence shall be put upon every adversary, so that none will be able any longer to hurt and destroy in all God's holy mountain*, 24, 25.

A. M. cir. 3292 B. C. cir. 712 Olymp. XVII. 1 cir. annum NumæPompilii, R. Roman., 4

I [a]AM sought of *them that* asked not *for me;* I am found of *them that* sought me not: I said, Behold me, behold me, unto a nation *that* [b]was not called by my name.

2 [c]I have spread out my hands all the day unto a rebellious people, which walketh in a way *that was* not good, after their own thoughts;

3 A people [d]that provoketh me to anger

[a]Rom. ix. 24, 25, 26, 30; x. 20; Eph. ii. 12, 13 — [b]Chap. lxiii. 19 — [c]Rom. x. 21 — [d]Deut. xxxii. 21

This chapter contains a defence of God's proceedings in regard to the Jews, with reference to their complaint in the chapter preceding. God is introduced declaring that he had called the Gentiles, though they had not sought him; and had rejected his own people for their refusal to attend to his repeated call; for their obstinate disobedience, their idolatrous practices, and detestable hypocrisy. That nevertheless he would not destroy them all; but would preserve a remnant, to whom he would make good his ancient promises. Severe punishments are threatened to the apostates; and great rewards are promised to the obedient in a future flourishing state of the Church.—L.

NOTES ON CHAP. LXV

Verse 1. *I am sought of* them that *asked not* for me—"I am made known to those that asked not for me"] נדרשתי *nidrashti*, εμφανης εγενομην, the *Septuagint*, *Alexandrian*, and *St. Paul*, Rom. x. 20; who has however inverted the order of the phrases, εμφανης εγενομην, "I was made manifest," and ευρεθην, "I was found," from that which they have in the *Septuagint*. נדרשתי *nidrashti* means, "I am sought so as to be found." *Vitringa*. If this be the true meaning of the word, then שאלו *shaalu*, "that asked," which follows, should seem defective, the verb wanting its object: but two MSS., one of them ancient, have שאלוני *shealuni*, "asked me;" and another MS. שאלו לי *shealu li*, "asked for me;" one or other of which seems to be right. But *Cocceius* in Lex., and *Vitringa* in his translation, render נדרשתי *nidrashti*, by "I have answered;" and so the verb is rendered by all the ancient Versions in Ezek. xx. 3, 31. If this be right, the translation will be, 'I have answered those that asked not." I leave this to the reader's judgment; but have followed in my translation the *Septuagint* and *St. Paul*, and the MSS. above mentioned. בקשני *bikeshuni* is written regularly and fully in above a hundred MSS. and in the oldest edition, בקשוני *bikeshuni*. —L.

Verse 3. *That sacrificeth in gardens, and burneth incense upon altars of brick*—"Sacrificing in the gardens, and burning incense on the tiles"] These are instances of heathenish superstition, and idolatrous practices, to which the Jews were immoderately addicted before the

A. M. cir. 3292
B. C. cir. 712
Olymp. XVII. 1
cir. annum
NumæPompilii,
R. Roman., 4

continually to my face; [e]that
sacrificeth in gardens, and burneth incense [f]upon altars of brick;
4 [g]Which remain among the
graves, and lodge in the monuments; [h]which eat swine's flesh,
and [i]broth of abominable *things*
is in their vessels;

[e]Chap. i. 29; lxvi. 17; see Lev. xvii. 5——[f]Heb. *upon bricks*

[g]Deut. xviii. 11——[h]Chap. lxvi. 17; see Lev. xi. 7
[i]Or, *pieces*

Babylonish captivity. The heathen worshipped their idols in groves; whereas God, in opposition to this species of idolatry, commanded his people, when they should come into the promised land, to destroy all the places wherein the Canaanites had served their gods, and in particular to burn their groves with fire, Deut. xii. 2, 3. These apostate Jews sacrificed upon altars built of bricks; in opposition to the command of God in regard to his altar, which was to be of unhewn stone, Exod. xx. 25. Et pro uno altari, quod impolitis lapidibus Dei erat lege constructum, coctos lateres et agrorum cespites hostiarum sanguine cruentabant. "And instead of one altar which, according to the law of God, was to be constructed of unhewn stones, they stained the bricks and turfs of the fields with the blood of their victims." *Hieron.* in loc. Or it means, perhaps, that they sacrificed upon the roofs of their houses, which were always flat, and paved with brick, or tile, or plaster of terrace. An instance of this idolatrous practice we find in 2 Kings xxiii. 12, where it is said that Josiah "beat down the altars that were on the top of the upper chamber of Ahaz, which the kings of Judah had made." See also Zeph. i. 5. Sir *John Chardin's* MS. note on this place of Isaiah is as follows: "Ainsi font tous les Gentiles, sur les lieux elevés, et sur les terrasses, appellez *latcres*, parceque sont faits de briq." "Who dwell in the sepulchres, and lodge in the caverns," for the purposes of necromancy and divination; to obtain dreams and revelations. Another instance of heathenish superstition: so Virgil:—

Huc dona sacerdos
Cum tulit, et cæsarum ovium sub nocte silenti
Pellibus incubuit stratis, somnosque petivit:
Multa modis simulacra videt volitantia miris,
Et varias audit voces, fruiturque deorum
Colloquio, atque imis Acheronta affatur Avernis.
Æn. vii. 86.—L.

"Here in distress the Italian nations come,
Anxious, to clear their doubts, and learn their doom.
First, on the fleeces of the slaughtered sheep,
By night the sacred priest dissolves in sleep:
When in a train, before his slumbering eye,
Thin airy forms and wondrous visions fly.
He calls the powers who guard the infernal floods,
And talks inspired, familiar with the gods."
Pitt.

There was a practice exactly like this which prevailed among the Highlanders of Scotland; an authentic account of this is given by Sir Walter Scott, in a note on his poem called *The Lady of the Lake*. It is as follows:—

"The Highlanders, like all rude people, had various superstitious modes of inquiring into futurity. One of the most noted was the *Taghairm*, mentioned in the text. A person was wrapped up in the skin of a newly-slain bullock, and deposited beside a waterfall, or at the bottom of a precipice, or in some other strange, wild, and unusual situation, where the scenery around him suggested nothing but objects of horror. In this situation he revolved in his mind the question proposed; and whatever was impressed upon him by his exalted imagination passed for the inspiration of the disembodied spirits who haunt these desolate recesses. In some of the Hebrides, they attributed the same oracular power to a large black stone by the sea-shore, which they approached with certain solemnities; and considered the first fancy which came into their own minds after they did so, to be the undoubted dictate of the tutelar deity of the stone; and as such to be, if possible, punctually complied with. Martin has recorded the following curious modes of Highland augury, in which the Taghairm, and its effects upon the person who was subjected to it, may serve to illustrate the text.

"It was an ordinary thing among the over-curious to consult an invisible oracle concerning the fate of families and battles, &c. This was performed three different ways; the first was by a company of men, one of whom, being detached by lot, was afterwards carried to a river, which was the boundary between two villages. Four of the company laid hold on him; and, having shut his eyes, they took him by the legs and arms, and then, tossing him to and again, struck his hips with force against the bank. One of them cried out, What is it you have got here? Another answers, A log of birch-wood. The other cries again, Let his invisible friends appear from all quarters, and let them relieve him by giving an answer to our present demands; and in a few minutes after, a number of little creatures came from the sea, who answered the question, and disappeared suddenly. The man was then set at liberty; and they all returned home, to take their measures according to the prediction of their false prophets; but the poor deluded fools were abused; for the answer was still ambiguous. This was always practised in the night, and may literally be called the works of darkness.

"I had an account from the most intelligent and judicious men in the Isle of Skie, that, about sixty-two years ago, the oracle was thus consulted only once, and that was in the parish of Kilmartin, on the east side, by a wicked and mischievous race of people, who are now extinguished, both root and branch.

"The second way of consulting the oracle was by a party of men, who first retired to solitary places, remote from any house; and there they singled out one of their number, and wrapt him in a big cow's hide, which they folded about him. His whole body was covered with it, except his head, and so left in this posture all night, until his invisible friends relieved him, by giving a proper answer to the question in hand; which he received, as he fancied, from several persons that he found about him all that time. His consorts returned to him at the break

A. M. cir. 3292
B. C. cir. 712
Olymp. XVII. 1
cir. annum
NumæPompilii,
R. Roman., 4

5 [k]Which say, Stand by thyself, come not near to me; for I
am holier than thou. These *are*
a smoke in my [l]nose, a fire that
burneth all the day.
6 Behold, [m]*it is* written before me: [n]I will
not keep silence, [o]but will recompense, even
recompense into their bosom,
7 Your iniquities, and [p]the iniquities of your
fathers together, saith the LORD, [q]which
have burned incense upon the
mountains, [r]and blasphemed
me upon the hills: therefore
will I measure their former work
into their bosom.
8 Thus saith the LORD, As the new wine is
found in the cluster, and *one* saith, Destroy it
not; for [s]a blessing *is* in it: so will I do for
my servants' sakes, that I may not destroy
them all.

[k]See Matt. ix. 11; Luke v. 30; xviii. 11; Jude 19——[l]Or, *anger*——[m]Deut. xxxii. 34; Mal. iii. 16——[n]Psa. l. 3——[o]Psa. lxxix. 12; Jer. xvi. 18; Ezek. xi. 21——[p]Exod. xx. 5——[q]Ezek. xviii. 6——[r]Ezek. xx. 27, 28——[s]Joel ii. 14

of day, and then he communicated his news to them; which often proved fatal to those concerned in such unwarrantable inquiries.

"There was a third way of consulting, which was a confirmation of the second above mentioned. The same company who put the man into the hide took a live cat, and put him on a spit. One of the number was employed to turn the spit; and one of his consorts inquired of him, What are you doing? He answered, I roast this cat until his friends answer the question; which must be the same that was proposed by the man shut up in the hide. And afterwards, a very big cat (in allusion to the story of 'the King of the Cats,' in Lord Lyttleton's Letters, and well known in the Highlands as a nursery tale) comes, attended by a number of lesser cats, desiring to relieve the cat turned upon the spit, and then answers the question. If this answer proved the same that was given to the man in the hide, then it was taken as a confirmation of the other, which, in this case, was believed infallible.

"Mr. Alexander Cooper, present minister of North-Vist, told me that one John Erach, in the Isle of Lewis, assured him it was his fate to have been led by his curiosity with some who consulted this oracle, and that he was a night within the hide, as above-mentioned; during which time he felt and heard such terrible things, that he could not express them. The impression it made on him was such as could never go off; and he said for a thousand worlds he would never again be concerned in the like performance, for this had disordered him to a high degree. He confessed it ingenuously, and with an air of great remorse; and seemed to be very penitent under a just sense of so great a crime. He declared this about five years since, and is still living in the Lewis for any thing I know."—*Description of the Western Isles*, p. 110. See also PENNANT'S *Scottish Tour*, vol. ii. p. 361.

Verse 4. *Which remain among the graves*] "For the purpose of evoking the dead. They lodged in desert places that demons might appear to them; for demons do appear in such places, to those who do believe in them."—*Kimchi*.

In the monuments—"In the caverns"] בנצורים *bannetsurim*, a word of doubtful signification. An ancient MS. has בצורים *batstsurim*, another בצרים *batstsurim*, "in the rocks;" and *Le Clerc* thinks the *Septuagint* had it so in their copy. They render it by εν τοις σπηλαιοις, "in the caves."

Which eat swine's flesh] This was expressly forbidden by the law, Lev. xi. 7, but among the heathen was in principal request in their sacrifices and feasts. Antiochus Epiphanes compelled the Jews to eat swine's flesh, as a full proof of their renouncing their religion, 2 Mac. vi. 18 and vii. 1. "And the broth of abominable meats," for lustrations, magical arts, and other superstitious and abominable practices.

In *their vessels*] For כליהם *keleyhem*, a MS. had at first בכליהם *bichleyhem*. So the *Vulgate* and *Chaldee*, (and the preposition seems necessary to the sense,) "in their vessels."

Verse 5. *For I am holier than thou*] So the *Chaldee* renders it. קדשתיך *kedashticha* is the same with קדשתי ממך *kadashti mimmecha*. In the same manner חזקתני *chazaktani*, Jer. xx. 7, is used for חזקת ממני *chazacta mimmenni*, "thou art stronger than I."—L.

Verse 6. *Behold*, it is *written before me*] Their sin is registered in heaven, calling aloud for the punishment due to it.

I will—recompense into their bosom] The bosom is the place where the Asiatics have their pockets, and not in their skirts like the inhabitants of the west. Their loose flowing garments have scarcely any thing analogous to *skirts*.

Into their bosom] For על *al*, *ten* MSS. and *five* editions have אל *el*. So again at the end of this verse, *seventeen* MSS. and *four* editions have אל *al*.—L.

Verse 7. *Your iniquities, and the iniquities of your fathers*—"Their iniquities, and the iniquities of their fathers"] For the pronoun affixed of the second person כם *chem, your*, twice, read הם *hem, their*, in the third person; with the *Septuagint* and *Houbigant*.—L.

Verse 8. *A blessing* is *in it*] The Hebrews call all things which serve for food ברכה *berachah*, "a blessing." On this verse *Kimchi* remarks: "As the cluster of grapes contains, besides the juice, the bark, and the kernels, so the Israelites have, besides the just, sinners among them. Now as the cluster must not be destroyed because there is a *blessing*, a nutritive part in it; so Israel shall not be destroyed, because there are righteous persons in it. But as the bark and kernels are thrown away, when the wine is pressed out, so shall the sinners be purged away from among the just, and on their return from exile, shall not be permitted to enter into the land of Israel;" Ezek. xx. 38.

For my servant's sakes—"For the sake of my servant"] It is to be observed that one of the Koningsburg MSS. collated by Lilienthal points

A. M. cir. 3292
B. C. cir. 712
Olymp. XVII. 1
cir. annum
NumæPompilii,
R. Roman., 4

9 And I will bring forth a seed
out of Jacob, and out of Judah
an inheritor of my mountains:
and mine [t]elect shall inherit it,
and my servants shall dwell there.
10 And [u]Sharon shall be a fold of flocks,
and [v]the valley of Achor a place for the
herds to lie down in, for my people that have
sought me.
11 But ye *are* they that forsake the LORD,
that forget [w]my holy mountain, that prepare
[x]a table for that [y]troop, and that
furnish the drink-offering unto
that [z]number.

A. M. cir. 3292
B. C. cir. 712
Olymp. XVII. 1
cir. annum
NumæPompilii,
R. Roman., 4

12 Therefore will I number
you to the sword, and ye shall all bow down
to the slaughter: [a]because when I called, ye
did not answer; when I spake, ye did not hear;
but did evil before mine eyes, and did choose
that wherein I delighted not.
13 Therefore thus saith the Lord GOD, Behold, my servants shall eat, but ye shall be

---

[t]Ver. 15, 22; Matt. xxiv. 22; Rom. xi. 5, 7——[u]Chap. xxxiii. 9; xxxv. 2——[v]Josh. vii. 24, 26; Hos. ii. 15 [w]Chap. lvi. 7; lvii. 13; ver. 25

[x]Ezek. xxiii. 41; 1 Cor. x. 21——[y]Or, *Gad*——[z]Or, *Meni*——[a]2 Chron. xxxvi. 15, 16; Prov. i. 24, &c.; chap. lxvi. 4; Jer. vii. 13; Zech. vii. 7; Matt. xxi. 34–43

---

the word עבדי *abdi*, singular; that is, "my servant," meaning the Messiah; and so read the *Septuagint*, which gives a very good sense. In two of my old MSS. it is pointed עבדי *abadai*, and עבדי *abdi*, "my servant," this confirms the above reading.

Verse 9. *An inheritor of my mountains*—"An inheritor of my mountain"] הרי *hari*, in the singular number; so the *Septuagint* and *Syriac;* that is, of Mount Sion. See ver. 11 and chap. lvi. 7, to which Sion, the pronoun feminine singular, added to the verb in the next line, refers; ירשוה *yereshuah*, "shall inherit her."—L.

Verse 10. *Sharon—and the valley of Achor*] Two of the most fertile parts of Judea; famous for their rich pastures; the former to the west, not far from Joppa; the latter north of Jericho, near Gilgal.

Verse 11. *That prepare a table for that troop* —"Who set in order a table for Gad"] The disquisitions and conjectures of the learned concerning Gad and Meni are infinite and uncertain: perhaps the most probable may be, that Gad means good fortune, and Meni the moon. "But why should we be solicitous about it?" says Schmidius. "It appears sufficiently, from the circumstances, that they were false gods; either stars, or some natural objects; or a mere fiction. The Holy Scriptures did not deign to explain more clearly what these objects of idolatrous worship were; but chose rather, that the memory of the knowledge of them should be utterly abolished. And God be praised, that they are so totally abolished, that we are now quite at a loss to know what and what sort of things they were." Schmidius on the place, and on Jud. ii. 13, Bibl. Hallensia.

Jerome, on the place, gives an account of this idolatrous practice of the apostate Jews, of making a feast, or a lectisternium, as the Romans called it, for these pretended deities. Est in cunctis urbibus, et maxime in Ægypto, et in Alexandria, idololatriæ vetus consuetudo, ut ultimo die anni, et mensis ejus qui extremus est, ponant mensam refertam varii generis epulis, et poculum mulso mixtum; vel præteriti anni vel futuri fertilitatem auspicantes. Hoc autem faciebant et Israelitæ, omnium simulachrorum portenta venerantes; et nequaquam altari victimas, sed hujusmodi mensæ liba fundebant. "In all cities, and especially in Egypt and Alexandria, it was an ancient idolatrous custom on the last day of the year, to spread a table covered with various kinds of viands, and a goblet mixed with new wine, referring to the fertility either of the past or coming year. The Israelites did the same, worshipping all kinds of images, and pouring out libations on such tables," &c. See also *Le Clerc* on the place; and on lxvi. 17, and Dav. Millii Dissert. v.

The allusion to Meni, which signifies *number*, is obvious. If there had been the like allusion to Gad, which might have been expected, it might perhaps have helped to let us into the meaning of that word. It appears from Jerome's version of this place, that the words *τῳ δαιμονιω*, *to a demon*, (or *δαιμονι*, as some copies have it,) and *τῃ τυχῃ*, *to fortune*, stood in his time in the Greek version in an inverted order from that which they have in the present copies; the latter then answering to גד *gad*, the former to מני *meni:* by which some difficulty would be avoided; for it is commonly supposed that גד *gad* signifies *τυχη*, *fortune.* See Gen. xxx. 11, apud *Sept.* This matter is so far well cleared up by MSS. Pachom. and I. D. II., which agree in placing these two words in that order, which Jerome's version supposes.—L.

My Old MS. Bible translates: **That putten the borde of fortune; and offreden licours upon it**; and so the *Vulgate.*

Ἑτοιμαζοντες τῳ δαιμονιῳ τραπεζαν, και πληρουντες τῃ τυχῃ κερασμα. "Preparing a table for the demon, and filling up, or pouring out, a libation to fortune."—*Septuagint.*

Ye have set up an aulter unto fortune
And geven rich drink offeringes unto treasure.
COVERDALE.

Verse 12. *Therefore will I number you*] Referring to *Meni*, which signifies *number*. "Rabbi Eliezar said to his disciples, Turn to God one day before you die. His disciples said, How can a man know the day of his death? He answered, Therefore it is necessary that you should turn to God to-day, for possibly ye may die to-morrow."

Verse 13. *My servants shall eat, but ye shall be hungry*] Rabbi Joachan ben Zachai said in a parable: There was a king who invited his servants, but set them no time to come to the feast. The prudent and wary who were among them adorned themselves; and, standing at the gate of the king's house, said, Is there any thing lacking in the king's house? i. e., Is there any work to be done in it? But the foolish

A. M. cir. 3292 B. C. cir. 712 Olymp. XVII. 1 cir. annum NumæPompilii, R. Roman., 4

hungry: behold, my servants
shall drink, but ye shall be thirsty:
behold, my servants shall rejoice,
but ye shall be ashamed:
14 Behold, my servants shall sing for joy
of heart, but ye shall cry for sorrow of heart,
and [b]shall howl for [c]vexation of spirit.
15 And ye shall leave your name [d]for a
curse unto [e]my chosen: for the Lord GOD
shall slay thee, and [f]call his servants by another name:
16 [g]That he who blesseth himself in the
earth shall bless himself in the God of truth;
and [h]he that sweareth in the earth shall swear
by the God of truth; because the former
troubles are forgotten, and because they are
hid from mine eyes.
17 For, behold, I create [i]new heavens and
a new earth: and the former shall not be remembered, nor [k]come into
mind.
18 But be ye glad and rejoice
for ever *in that* which I create:
for, behold, I create Jerusalem a rejoicing,
and her people a joy.
19 And [l]I will rejoice in Jerusalem, and
joy in my people; and the [m]voice of weeping
shall be no more heard in her, nor the voice
of crying.
20 There shall be no more thence an infant
of days, nor an old man that hath not filled
his days: for the child shall die a hundred
years old; [n]but the sinner *being* a hundred
years old shall be accursed.
21 And [o]they shall build houses, and inhabit *them;* and they shall plant vineyards,
and eat the fruit of them.
22 They shall not build, and another in-

[b]Matt. viii. 12; Luke xiii. 28——[c]Heb. *breaking*——[d]See Jer. xxix. 22; Zech. viii. 13——[e]Ver. 9. 22——[f]Ch. lxii. 2; Acts xi. 26——[g]Psalm lxxii. 17; Jer. iv. 2——[h]Deut. vi. 13; Psa. lxiii. 11; chap. xix. 18; xlv. 23; Zeph. i. 5

[i]Chap. li. 16; lxvi. 22; 2 Pet. iii. 13; Rev. xxi. 1——[k]Heb. *come upon the heart*——[l]Chap. lxii. 5——[m]Chap. xxxv. 10; li. 11; Rev. vii. 17; xxi. 4——[n]Eccles. viii. 12——[o]See Lev. xxvi. 16; Deut. xxviii. 30; chap. lxii. 8; Amos ix. 14

which were among them went, and mocking said, When shall the feast be, in which there is no labour? Suddenly, the king sought out his servants: they who were adorned entered in, and they who were still polluted entered in also. The king was glad when he met the *prudent;* but he was angry when he met the *foolish.* Therefore he said, Let *those* sit down, and let them eat; but let *these* stand and look on.

This parable is very like that of the wise and foolish virgins, Matt. xxv., and that of the marriage of the king's son, Matt. xxii.

Verse 15. *Shall slay thee*—"Shall slay you"] For והמיתך *vehemithecha, shall slay thee,* the *Septuagint* and *Chaldee* read והמיתכם *vehemithechem, shall slay you,* plural.

Verse 17. *I create new heavens and a new earth*] This has been variously understood. Some Jews and some Christians understand it *literally.* God shall change the state of the atmosphere, and render the earth more fruitful. Some refer it to what they call the Millennium; others, to a glorious state of religion; others, to the re-creation of the earth after it shall have been destroyed by fire. I think it refers to the full conversion of the Jews *ultimately;* and primarily to the deliverance from the Babylonish captivity.

Verse 18. *Rejoice for ever* in that *which I create*—"Exult in the age to come which I create"] So in chap. ix. 5 אבי עד *abi ad,* πατηρ του μελλοντος αιωνος, "the father of the age to come," *Sept.* See Bishop Chandler, Defence of Christianity, p. 136.

Verse 19. *The voice of weeping,* &c.] "Because of untimely deaths shall no more be heard in thee; for natural death shall not happen till men be full of days; as it is written, ver. 20: *There shall be no more thence an infant of days,* i. e., the people shall live to *three* or *five hundred* years of age, as in the days of the patriarchs; and if one die at *one hundred* years, it is because of his sin; and even at that age he shall be reputed an *infant;* and they shall say of him, An infant is dead. These things shall happen to Israel in the days of the Messiah."—*Kimchi.*

Verse 20. *Thence*—"There"] For משם *mish-sham, thence,* the *Septuagint, Syriac,* and *Vulgate,* read שם *sham, there.*

Verse 22. *They shall not build, and another inhabit*] The reverse of the curse denounced on the disobedient, Deut. xxviii. 30: "Thou shalt build a house, and thou shalt not dwell therein; thou shalt plant a vineyard, and shalt not gather the grapes thereof."

For as the days of a tree] It is commonly supposed that the oak, one of the most long-lived of the trees, lasts about a thousand years; being five hundred years growing to full perfection, and as many decaying: which seems to be a moderate and probable computation. See *Evelyn,* Sylva, B. III. chap. iii. The present emperor of China, in his very ingenious and sensible poem entitled *Eloge de Moukden,* a translation of which in French was published at Paris, 1770, speaks of a tree in his country which lives more than a hundred ages: and another, which after fourscore ages is only in its prime, pp. 37, 38. But his imperial majesty's commentators, in their note on the place, carry the matter much farther; and quote authority, which affirms, that the tree last mentioned by the emperor, the immortal tree, after having lived ten thousand years, is still only in its prime. I suspect that the Chinese enlarge somewhat in their national chronology, as well as in that of their trees. See *Chou King,* Preface, by Mons. de Guignes. The prophet's idea seems

A. M. cir. 3292 B. C. cir. 712 Olymp. XVII. 1 cir. annum NumæPompilii, R. Roman., 4

habit; they shall not plant, and
another eat: for [p]as the days of
a tree *are* the days of my people,
and [q]mine elect [r]shall long enjoy the work of their hands.

23 They shall not labour in vain, [s]nor bring
forth for trouble; for [t]they *are* the seed of
the blessed of the LORD, and their offspring
with them.

A. M. cir. 3292 B. C. cir. 714 Olymp. XVII. 1 cir. annum NumæPompilii, R. Roman., 4

24 And it shall come to pass,
that [u]before they call, I will
answer; and while they are yet
speaking, I will hear.

25 The [v]wolf and the lamb shall feed together, and the lion shall eat straw like the
bullock: [w]and dust *shall be* the serpent's meat.
They shall not hurt nor destroy in all my holy
mountain, saith the LORD.

[p]Psa. xcii. 12——[q]Ver. 9, 15——[r]Heb. *shall make them continue long*, or *shall wear out*

[s]Deut. xxviii. 41; Hos. ix. 12——[t]Ch. lxi. 9——[u]Psa. xxxii. 5; Dan. ix. 21——[v]Ch. xi. 6, 7, 9——[w]Gen. iii. 14

to be, that they shall live to the age of the antediluvians; which seems to be very justly expressed by the days of a tree, according to our notions. The rabbins have said that this refers to the tree of life, which endures five hundred years.—L.

Verse 23. *They shall not labour in vain*—"My chosen shall not labour in vain"] I remove בחירי *bechirai, my elect*, from the end of the twenty-second to the beginning of the twenty-third verse, on the authority of the *Septuagint*, *Syriac*, and *Vulgate*, and a MS.; contrary to the division in the Masoretic text.—L. The *Septuagint* is beautiful: My chosen shall not labour in vain, neither shall they beget children for the curse; for the seed is blessed of the Lord, and their posterity with them."

Nor bring forth for trouble—"Neither shall they generate a short-lived race"] לבהלה *labbehalah, in festinationem*, "what shall soon hasten away." Εις καταραν, *for a curse, Sept.* They seem to have read לאלה *lealah*.—Grotius. But Psa. lxxviii. 33 both justifies and explains the word here:—

ויכל בהבל ימיהם

yemeyhem bahebel vayechal

ושנותם בבהלה

babbehalah ushenotham

"And he consumed their days in vanity;
And their years in haste."

μετα σπουδης, say the *Septuagint*. Jerome on this place of Isaiah explains it to the same purpose: "εις ανυπαρξιαν, *hoc est*, ut esse desistant."

Verse 24. *Before they call, I will answer*] I will give them all they crave for, and more than they can desire.

Verse 25. *The wolf and the lamb, &c.*] The glorious salvation which Jesus Christ procures is for men, and for men only: fallen spirits must still abide under the curse: "He took not on him the nature of angels, but the seed of Abraham."

Shall feed together] For כאחד *keechad, as one*, an ancient MS. has יחדו *yachdav, together;* the usual word, to the same sense, but very different in the letters. The *Septuagint*, *Syriac*, and *Vulgate* seem to agree with the MSS.—L.

CHAPTER LXVI

This chapter treats of the same subject with the foregoing. God, by his prophet, tells the Jews, who valued themselves much on their temple and pompous worship, that the Most High dwelleth not in temples made with hands; and that no outward rites of worship, while the worshippers are idolatrous and impure, can please him who looketh at the heart, 1–3. *This leads to a threatening of vengeance for their guilt, alluding to their making void the law of God by their abominable traditions, their rejection of Christ, persecution of his followers, and consequent destruction by the Romans. But as the Jewish ritual and people shadow forth the system of Christianity and its professors; so, in the prophetical writings, the idolatries of the Jews are frequently put for the idolatries afterwards practised by those bearing the Christian name. Consequently, if we would have the plenitude of meaning in this section of prophecy, which the very context requires, we must look through the type into the antitype, viz., the very gross idolatries practised by the members of Antichrist, the pompous heap of human inventions and traditions with which they have encumbered the Christian system, their most dreadful persecution of Christ's spiritual and true worshippers, and the awful judgments which shall overtake them in the great and terrible day of the Lord,* 4–6. *The mighty and sudden increase of the Church of Jesus Christ at the period of Antichrist's fall represented by the very strong figure of Sion being delivered of a man-child before the time of her travail, the meaning of which symbol the prophet immediately subjoins in a series of interrogations for the sake of greater force and emphasis,* 7–9. *Wonderful prosperity and unspeakable blessedness of the world when the posterity of Jacob, with the fulness of the Gentiles, shall be assembled to Messiah's standard,* 10–14. *All the wicked of the earth shall be gathered together to the battle of that great day of God Almighty, and the slain of Jehovah shall be many,* 15–18. *Manner of the future restoration of the Israelites from their several dispersions throughout the habitable globe,* 19–21. *Perpetuity of this new economy of grace to the house of Israel,* 22. *Righteousness shall be universally diffused in the earth; and the memory of those who have transgressed against the Lord shall be had in continual abhorrence,* 23, 24. *Thus this great prophet, after tracing the principal events of* time, *seems at length to have terminated his views in* eternity, *where all revolutions cease, where the blessedness of the righteous shall be unchangeable as the new heavens, and the misery of the wicked as the fire that shall not be quenched.*

A. M. cir. 3292
B. C. cir. 712
Olymp. XVII. 1
cir. annum
NumæPompilii,
R. Roman., 4

THUS saith the LORD, [a]The
heaven *is* my throne, and
the earth *is* my footstool: where
is the house that ye build unto
me? and where *is* the place of my rest?
2 For all those *things* hath mine hand made,
and all those *things* have been, saith the
LORD: [b]but to this *man* will I look, [c]*even* to
him that is poor and of a contrite spirit, and
[d]trembleth at my word.
3 [e]He that killeth an ox *is as if* he slew a
man; he that sacrificeth a [f]lamb, *as if* he
[g]cut off a dog's neck; he that
offereth an oblation, *as if he offer-*
ed swine's blood; he that [h]burneth
incense, *as if* he blessed an idol.
Yea, they have chosen their own ways, and
their soul delighteth in their abominations.
4 I also will choose their [i]delusions, and
will bring their fears upon them; [k]because
when I called, none did answer; when I
spake, they did not hear: but they did evil
before mine eyes, and chose *that* in which I
delighted not.

A. M. cir. 3292
B. C. cir. 712
Olymp. XVII. 1
cir. annum
NumæPompilii,
R. Roman., 4

[a]1 Kings viii. 27; 2 Chron. vi. 18; Matt. v. 34, 35; Acts vii. 48, 49; xvii. 24——[b]Chap. lvii. 15; lxi. 1——[c]Psa. xxxiv. 18; li. 17——[d]Ezra ix. 4; x. 3; Prov. xxviii. 14; ver. 5

[e]Chapter i. 11——[f]Or, *kid*——[g]Deuteronomy xxiii. 18——[h]Hebrew, *maketh a memorial of*, Lev. ii. 2——[i]Or, *devices*——[k]Proverbs i. 24; chapter lxv. 12; Jer. vii. 13

NOTES ON CHAP. LXVI

This chapter is a continuation of the subject of the foregoing. The Jews valued themselves much upon their temple, and the pompous system of services performed in it, which they supposed were to be of perpetual duration; and they assumed great confidence and merit to themselves for their strict observance of all the externals of their religion. And at the very time when the judgments denounced in verses 6 and 12 of the preceding chapter were hanging over their heads, they were rebuilding, by Herod's munificence, the temple in a most magnificent manner. God admonishes them, that "the Most High dwelleth not in temples made with hands;" and that a mere external worship, how diligently soever attended, when accompanied with wicked and idolatrous practices in the worshippers, would never be accepted by him. This their hypocrisy is set forth in strong colours, which brings the prophet again to the subject of the former chapter; and he pursues it in a different manner, with more express declaration of the new economy, and of the flourishing state of the Church under it. The increase of the Church is to be sudden and astonishing. They that escape of the Jews, that is, that become converts to the Christian faith, are to be employed in the Divine mission to the Gentiles, and are to act as priests in presenting the Gentiles as an offering to God; see Rom. xv. 16. And both, now collected into one body, shall be witnesses of the final perdition of the obstinate and irreclaimable.

These two chapters manifestly relate to the calling of the Gentiles, the establishment of the Christian dispensation, and the reprobation of the apostate Jews, and their destruction executed by the Romans.—L.

Verse 2. *And all those* things *have been*—"And all these things are mine"] A word absolutely necessary to the sense is here lost out of the text: לי *li, mine.* It is preserved by the *Septuagint* and *Syriac.*

Verse 3. *He that killeth an ox* is as if *he slew a man*—"He that slayeth an ox killeth a man"] These are instances of wickedness joined with hypocrisy; of the most flagitious crimes committed by those who at the same time affected great strictness in the performance of all the external services of religion. God, by the Prophet Ezekiel, upbraids the Jews with the same practices: "When they had slain their children to their idols, then they came the same day into my sanctuary to profane it," chap. xxiii. 39. Of the same kind was the hypocrisy of the Pharisees in our Saviour's time: "who devoured widows' houses, and for a pretence made long prayers," Matt. xxiii. 14.

The generality of interpreters, by departing from the literal rendering of the text, have totally lost the true sense of it, and have substituted in its place what makes no good sense at all; for it is not easy to show how, in any circumstances, sacrifice and murder, the presenting of legal offerings and idolatrous worship, can possibly be of the same account in the sight of God.

He that offereth an oblation, as if he offered *swine's blood*—"That maketh an oblation *offereth* swine's blood"] A word here likewise, necessary to complete the sense, is perhaps irrecoverably lost out of the text. The *Vulgate* and *Chaldee* add the word *offereth,* to make out the sense; not, as I imagine, from any different reading, (for the word wanted seems to have been lost before the time of the oldest of them, as the *Septuagint* had it not in their copy,) but from mere necessity.

Le Clerc thinks that מעלה *maaleh* is to be repeated from the beginning of this member; but that is not the case in the parallel members, which have another and a different verb in the second place. "דם *dam,* sic Versiones; putarem tamen legendum participium aliquod, et quidem זבח *zabach,* cum sequatur ח *cheth,* nisi jam præcesserat."—SECKER. *Houbigant* supplies אכל *achal, eateth.* After all, I think the most probable word is that which the *Chaldee* and *Vulgate* seem to have designed to represent; that is, מקריב *makrib, offereth.*

In their abominations.] ובשקוציהם *ubeshikkutseyhem,* "and in their abominations;" two

A. M. cir. 3292 B. C. cir. 712 Olymp. XVII. 1 cir. annum NumæPompilii, R. Roman., 4

5 Hear the word of the LORD,
[l]ye that tremble at his word;
Your brethren that hated you,
that cast you out for my name's
sake, said, [m]Let the LORD be glorified: but
[n]he shall appear to your joy, and they shall
be ashamed.

6 A voice of noise from the city, a voice
from the temple, a voice of the LORD that
rendereth recompense to his enemies.

7 Before she travailed, she brought forth;
before her pain came, she was delivered of a
man child.

8 Who hath heard such a thing? who hath
seen such things? Shall the earth be made to
bring forth in one day: *or* shall a nation be
born at once? for as soon as Zion travailed,
she brought forth her children.

9 Shall I bring to the birth, and not [o]cause
to bring forth? saith the LORD: shall I cause
to bring forth, and shut *the womb?* saith thy
God.

A. M. cir. 3292 B. C. cir. 712 Olymp. XVII. 1 cir. annum NumæPompilii, R. Roman., 4

10 Rejoice ye with Jerusalem,
and be glad with her, all ye that
love her: rejoice for joy with her,
all ye that mourn for her:

11 That ye may suck, and be satisfied with
the breasts of her consolations; that ye may
milk out, and be delighted with the [p]abun-
dance of her glory.

12 For thus saith the LORD, Behold, [q]I
will extend peace to her like a river, and the
glory of the Gentiles like a flowing stream;
then shall ye [r]suck, ye shall be [s]borne
upon *her* sides, and be dandled upon *her*
knees.

13 As one whom his mother comforteth, so
will I comfort you; and ye shall be comforted
in Jerusalem.

14 And when ye see *this*, your heart shall
rejoice, and [t]your bones shall flourish like
an herb: and the hand of the LORD shall be
known toward his servants, and *his* indignation toward his enemies.

---

[l]Ver. 1——[m]Chap. v. 19——[n]2 Thess. i. 10; Tit. ii. 13——[o]Or, *beget*——[p]Or, *brightness*

[q]Chap. xlviii. 18; lx. 5——[r]Chap. lx. 16——[s]Chap. xlix. 22; lx. 4——[t]See Ezek. xxxvii. 1, &c.

---

copies of the *Machazor*, and one of *Kennicott's* MSS. have ובגלוליהם *ubegilluleyhem*, "and in their idols." So the *Vulgate* and *Syriac*.

Verse 5. *Your brethren that hated you—said*—"Say ye to your brethren that hate you"] The *Syriac* reads אמרו לאחיכם *imru laacheychem;* and so the *Septuagint*, Edit. Comp. ειπατε αδελφοις ὑμων· and MS. Marchal. has αδελφοις· and so Cyril and Procopius read and explain it. It is not easy to make sense of the reading of the *Septuagint* in the other editions; ειπατε αδελφοι ἡμων τοις μισουσιν ὑμας· but for ἡμων, *our*, MS. I. D. II. also has ὑμων, *your*.

Verse 6. *A voice of noise from the city, a voice from the temple, a voice of the Lord*] It is very remarkable that similar words were spoken by Jesus, son of Ananias, previously to the destruction of Jerusalem. See his very affecting history related by *Josephus*, WAR, B. vi., chap. v.

Verse 8. *Who hath seen*—"And who hath seen"] Twenty MSS., (four ancient,) of *Kennicott's*, and twenty-nine of *De Rossi's*, and two ancient of my own, and the two oldest editions, with two others, have ומי *umi*, adding the conjunction ו *vau;* and so read all the ancient versions. AND *who hath seen?*

Verse 9. *Shall I bring to the birth*] האני אשביר *haani ashbir*, num ego matricem frangam; MONTANUS. The word means that which immediately precedes the appearance of the fetus—*the breaking forth* of the *liquor amnii*. This also is an expression that should be studiously avoided in prayers and sermons.

Verse 11. *With the abundance of her glory*—"From her abundant stores."] For מזיז *miz-ziz, from the splendour*, two MSS. and the old edition of 1488, have מזיו *mizziv;* and the latter ז *zain* is upon a rasure in three other MSS. It is remarkable that *Kimchi* and *Sal. ben Melec*, not being able to make any thing of the word as it stands in the text, say it means the same with מזיו *mizziv;* that is, in effect, they admit of a various reading, or an error in the text. But as *Vitringa* observes, what sense is there in sucking nourishment from the *splendour* of her glory? He therefore endeavours to deduce another sense of the word זיז *ziz;* but, as far as it appears to me, without any authority. I am more inclined to accede to the opinion of those learned rabbins, and to think that there is some mistake in the word; for that in truth is their opinion, though they disguise it by saying that the corrupted word means the very same with that which they believe to be genuine. So in chap. xli. 24 they say that אפע *apha, a viper*, means the same with אפס *ephes, nothing;* instead of acknowledging that one is written by mistake instead of the other. I would propose to read in this place מזין *mizzin* or מזן *mizzen*, which is the reading of one of *De Rossi's* MS., (instead of מזיז *meziz,*) *from the stores*, from זון *zun, to nourish, to feed;* see Gen. xlv. 23; 2 Chron. xi. 23; Psa. cxliv. 13. And this perhaps may be meant by Aquila, who renders the word by απο παντοδαπιας· with which that of the *Vulgate, ab* omnimoda *gloria*, and of Symmachus and Theodotion, nearly agree. The Chaldee follows a different reading, without improving the sense; מיין *meyin, from the wine.*—L.

Verse 12. *Like a river, and—like a flowing stream*—"Like the great river, and like the overflowing stream"] That is, the Euphrates, (it ought to have been pointed כנהר *cannahar*, ut fluvius ille, *as the river,*) and the Nile.

Then shall ye suck—"And ye shall suck at the breast"] These two words על שד *al shad, at the*

A. M. cir. 3292
B. C. cir. 712
Olymp. XVII. 1
cir. annum
NumæPompilii,
R. Roman., 4

15 [u]For, behold, the LORD
will come with fire, and with his
chariots like a whirlwind, to
render his anger with fury, and
his rebuke with flames of fire.
16 For by fire and by [v]his sword will the
LORD plead with all flesh: and the slain of
the LORD shall be many.
17 [w]They that sanctify themselves, and purify themselves in the gardens [x]behind one
tree in the midst, eating swine's flesh, and the
abomination, and the mouse,
shall be consumed together, saith
the LORD.
18 For I *know* their works and
their thoughts; it shall come that I will gather
all nations and tongues; and they shall come,
and see my glory.
19 [y]And I will set a sign among them, and
I will send those that escape of them unto the
nations, *to* Tarshish, Pul, and Lud, that draw
the bow, *to* Tubal, and Javan, *to* the isles afar

A. M. cir. 3292
B. C. cir. 712
Olymp. XVII. 1
cir. annum
NumæPompilii,
R. Roman., 4

---

[u]Chap. ix. 5; 2 Thess. i. 8——[v]Chap. xxvii. 1——[w]Ch. lxv. 3, 4——[x]Or, *one after another*——[y]Luke ii. 34

---

breast, seem to have been omitted in the present text, from their likeness to the two words following; על צד *al tsad, at the side.* A very probable conjecture of *Houbigant.* The *Chaldee* and *Vulgate* have omitted the two latter words instead of the two former. See note on chap. lx. 4.

Verse 15. *The Lord will come with fire*—"JEHOVAH shall come as a fire"] For באש *baesh, in fire*, the *Septuagint* had in their copy כאש *kaesh, as a fire;* ὡς πυρ.

To render his anger with fury—"To breathe forth his anger in a burning heat"] Instead of להשב *lehashib*, as pointed by the Masoretes, *to render*, I understand it as להשב *lehashshib, to breathe*, from נשב *nashab.*

Verse 17. *Behind one* tree—"After the rites of Achad"] The Syrians worshipped a god called Adad, *Plin.* Nat. Hist. xxxvii. 11; Macrob. Sat. i. 23. They held him to be the highest and greatest of the gods, and to be the same with Jupiter and the sun; and the name Adad, says *Macrobius*, signifies *one;* as likewise does the word Achad in Isaiah. Many learned men therefore have supposed, and with some probability, that the prophet means the same pretended deity. אחד *achad*, in the *Syrian* and *Chaldean* dialects, is חד *chad;* and perhaps by reduplication of the last letter to express perfect unity, it may have become חדד *chadad*, not improperly expressed by Macrobius *Adad*, without the aspirate. It was also pronounced by the Syrians themselves, with a weaker aspirate, הדד *hadad;* as in Benhadad, Hadadezer, names of their kings, which were certainly taken from their chief object of worship. This seems to me to be a probable account of this name.

But the Masoretes correct the text in this place. Their marginal reading is אחת *achath*, which is the same word, only in the feminine form; and so read thirty MSS. (six ancient) and the two oldest editions. This *Le Clerc* approves, and supposes it to mean Hecate, or the moon; and he supports his hypothesis by arguments not at all improbable. See his note on the place.

Whatever the particular mode of idolatry which the prophet refers to might be, the general sense of the place is perfectly clear. But the *Chaldee* and *Syriac*, and after them *Symmachus* and *Theodotion*, cut off at once all these difficulties, by taking the word אחד *achad* in its common meaning, not as a proper name; the two latter rendering the sentence thus: *Οπισω αλληλων εν μεσῳ εσθιοντων το κρεας το χοιρειον;* "One after another, in the midst of those that eat swine's flesh." I suppose they all read in their copies אחד אחד *achad achad, one by one*, or perhaps אחד אחר אחד *achad achar achad, one after another.* See a large dissertation on this subject in *Davidis Millii* Dissertationes Selectæ, Dissert. vi.—L.

I know not what to make of this place; it is certain that our translation makes no sense, and that of the learned prelate seems to me too refined. *Kimchi* interprets this of the Turks, who are remarkable for ablutions. "Behind one in the midst" he understands of a large fish-pond placed in the middle of their gardens. Others make אחד *achad a deity*, as above; and a deity of various names it is supposed to be, for it is *Achad*, and *Chad*, and *Hadad*, and *Achath*, and *Hecat*, an Assyrian idol. **Behynd the fyrst tree or the gate withine forth.**—Old MS. Bible.

Verse 18. *For I* know *their works*] A word is here lost out of the present text, leaving the text quite imperfect. The word is יודע *yodea, knowing*, supplied from the *Syriac.* The *Chaldee* had the same word in the copy before him, which he paraphrases by קדמי גלן *kedemi gelon*, their deeds *are manifest before me;* and the Aldine and Complutensian editions of the *Septuagint* acknowledge the same word επισταμαι, which is verified by MS. *Pachom.* and the *Arabic* version. I think there can be little doubt of its being genuine. The concluding verses of this chapter refer to the complete restoration of the Jews, and to the destruction of all the enemies of the Gospel of Christ, so that the earth shall be filled with the knowledge and glory of the Lord. Talia sæcla currite! Lord, hasten the time!

It shall come—"And I come"] For באה *baah*, which will not accord with any thing in the sentence, I read בא *ba*, with a MS.; the participle answering to יודע *yodea*, with which agree the *Septuagint, Syriac*, and *Vulgate.* Perhaps it ought to be ובא *veba, when* I shall come, Syr.; and so the *Septuagint*, according to Edit. Ald. and Complut., and Cod. Marchal.

Verse 19. *That draw the bow*] I much suspect that the words משכי קשת *moshechey kesheth, who draw the bow*, are a corruption of the word משך *meshek, Moschi*, the name of a nation situated between the Euxine and Caspian seas; and properly joined with תבל *tubal*, the Tibareni. See *Bochart*, Phaleg. iii. 12. The *Septuagint* have μοσοχ, without any thing of the *drawers of the bow:* the word being once taken for a participle, *the bow* was added to make

A. M. cir. 3292
B. C. cir. 712
Olymp. XVII. 1
cir. annum
NumæPompilii,
R. Roman., 4

off, that have not heard my fame, neither have seen my glory; [z]and they shall declare my glory among the Gentiles.

20 And they shall bring all your brethren [a]*for* an offering unto the LORD out of all nations upon horses, and in chariots, and in [b]litters, and upon mules, and upon swift beasts, to my holy mountain Jerusalem, saith the LORD, as the children of Israel bring an offering in a clean vessel into the house of the LORD.

21 And I will also take of them for [c]priests *and* for Levites, saith the LORD.

[z]Mal. i. 11——[a]Rom. xv. 16——[b]Or, *couches* [c]Exod. xix. 6; ch. lxi. 6; 1 Pet. ii. 9; Rev. i. 6——[d]Chap. lxv. 17; 2 Pet. iii. 13; Rev. xxi. 1——[e]Zech. xiv. 16

A. M. cir. 3292
B. C. cir. 712
Olymp. XVII. 1
cir. annum
NumæPompilii,
R. Roman., 4

22 For as [d]the new heavens and the new earth, which I will make, shall remain before me, saith the LORD, so shall your seed and your name remain.

23 And [e]it shall come to pass *that* [f]from one new moon to another, and from one sabbath to another, [g]shall all flesh come to worship before me, saith the LORD.

24 And they shall go forth, and look upon [h]the carcasses of the men that have transgressed against me: for their [i]worm shall not die, neither shall their fire be quenched; and they shall be an abhorring unto all flesh.

[f]Heb. *from new moon to his new moon, and from sab bath to his sabbath*——[g]Psa. lxv. 2; chap. xlix. 26 [h]Ver. 16——[i]Mark ix. 44, 46, 48

sense of it קשת *kesheth, the bow,* is omitted in a MS. and by the *Septuagint.*

That have not heard my fame—"Who never heard my name"] For שמעי *shimi, my fame,* I read, with the *Septuagint* and *Syriac,* שמי *shemi, my name.*

Verse 20. *And in chariots*—"And in counes"] There is a sort of vehicle much used in the east, consisting of a pair of hampers or cradles, thrown across a camel's back, one on each side; in each of which a person is carried. They have a covering to defend them from the rain and the sun. *Thevenot* calls them *counes,* i. p. 356. *Maillet* describes them as covered cages hanging on both sides of a camel. "At Aleppo," says Dr. *Russell,* "women of inferior condition in longer journeys are commonly stowed, one on each side of a mule, in a sort of covered cradles." Nat. Hist. of Aleppo, p. 89. These seem to be what the prophet means by the word צבים *tsabbim. Harmer's* Observations, i. p. 445.

Verse 21. And *for Levites*] For ללוים *laleviyim,* fifty-nine MSS., (eight ancient,) have וללוים *velaleviyim,* adding the conjunction ו *vau,* which the sense seems necessarily to require: and so read all the ancient versions. See Josh. iii. 3, and the various readings on that place in *Kennicott's* Bible.

Verse 24. *For their worm shall not die*] These words of the prophet are applied by our blessed Saviour, Mark ix. 44, to express the everlasting punishment of the wicked in Gehenna, or in hell. Gehenna, or the valley of Hinnom, was very near to Jerusalem to the south-east: it was the place where the idolatrous Jews celebrated that horrible rite of making their children pass through the fire, that is, of burning them in sacrifice to Moloch. To put a stop to this abominable practice, Josiah defiled, or desecrated, the place, by filling it with human bones, 2 Kings xxiii. 10, 14; and probably it was the custom afterwards to throw out the carcasses of animals there, when it also became the common burying place for the poorer people of Jerusalem. Our Saviour expressed the state of the blessed by sensible images; such as paradise, Abraham's bosom, or, which is the same thing, a place to recline next to Abraham at table in the kingdom of heaven. See Matt. viii. 11. Cœnabat Nerva cum paucis. Veiento *proximus,* atque etiam *in sinu* recumbebat. "The Emperor Nerva supped with few. *Veiento* was the first in his estimation, and even reclined in his bosom." *Plin. Epist.* iv. 22. Compare John xiii. 23; for we could not possibly have any conception of it, but by analogy from worldly objects. In like manner he expressed the place of torment under the image of Gehenna; and the punishment of the wicked by the worm which there preyed on the carcasses, and the fire that consumed the wretched victims. Marking however, in the strongest manner, the difference between Gehenna and the invisible place of torment; namely, that in the former the suffering is transient:—the worm itself which preys upon the body, dies; and the fire which totally consumes it, is soon extinguished:—whereas in the figurative Gehenna the instruments of punishment shall be everlasting, and the suffering without end; "for there the worm dieth not, and the fire is not quenched."

These emblematical images, expressing heaven and hell, were in use among the Jews before our Saviour's time; and in using them he complied with their notions. "Blessed is he that shall eat bread in the kingdom of God," says the Jew to our Saviour, Luke xiv. 15. And in regard to Gehenna, the Chaldee paraphrast, as I observed before on chap. xxx. 33, renders everlasting or continual burnings by "the Gehenna of everlasting fire." And before his time the son of Sirach, chap. vii. 17, had said, "The vengeance of the ungodly is fire and worms." So likewise the author of the book of Judith, chap. xvi. 17: "Wo to the nations rising up against my kindred: the Lord Almighty will take vengeance of them in the day of judgment, in putting fire and worms in their flesh;" manifestly referring to the same emblem.—L.

Kimchi's conclusion of his notes on this book is remarkable:—

"Blessed be God who hath created the mountains and the hills,
And hath endued me with strength to finish the book of salvation:
He shall rejoice us with good tidings and reports;

He shall show us a token for good;—
And the end of his miracles he shall cause to approach us."

Several of the Versions have a peculiarity in their terminations:—

And they shall be to a satiety of sight to all flesh. VULGATE.

And thei schul ben into fyllyng of sigt to all fleshe. Old MS. BIBLE.

And they shall be as a vision to all flesh. SEPTUAGINT.

And the wicked shall be punished in hell till the righteous shall say,—It is enough. CHALDEE.

They shall be an astonishment to all flesh;
So that they shall be a spectacle to all beings. SYRIAC.

The end of the prophecy of Isaiah the prophet.
Praise to God who is truly praiseworthy. ARABIC.

One of my old Hebrew MSS. after the twenty-first verse repeats the twenty-third: "And it shall come to pass that from one new moon to another, and from one Sabbath to another, shall all flesh come to worship before me, saith the Lord."

MASORETIC NOTES

Number of verses in this book, 1295.
Middle verse,—Chap. xxxiii. 21.
Masoretic sections, 26.
חזק *chazak*, Be strong.

In the course of these notes the reader will have often observed two MSS. of the *Septuagint* referred to by Bp. Lowth, and marked I. B. II., I. D. II. They are both in the British Museum. The *former* contains the prophets, and was written about the tenth or eleventh century; and because it once belonged to Pachomius, patriarch of Constantinople, in the beginning of the sixteenth century, the bishop often quotes it by the title MS. Pachom. The *other* contains many of the historical books, beginning with *Ruth*, and ending with *Ezra;* and has also the Prophet Isaiah. This MS. consists of two parts,—one apparently written in the eleventh or twelfth century; the other, in the beginning of the fourteenth. Dr. *Grabe* and Dr. *Woide*, as well as Bp. *Lowth*, considered these MSS. of great value and authority.

It may be necessary to say something of the Hebrew MSS. which I have also frequently quoted. The collations of *Kennicott* and *De Rossi* have been long before the public; and to describe them would be useless. The collections of the *latter* Bp. Lowth had never seen, else he could have strengthened his authorities: these, for the first time, I have in the preceding notes incorporated with Bishop Lowth's references, and thus added double strength to the learned prelate's authorities. But of my own I should say something, as they form no part of the above collections; and yet are among the oldest MSS. known to exist. Independently of rolls, which contain only the Megillah, Esther, and the Pentateuch, they are *ten* in number, and formerly belonged to the Rev. Cornelius Schulting, a Protestant minister of Amsterdam. After his death in 1726, they were sold by public auction, and came into the possession of the Rev. John Van der Hagen, a reformed minister of the same place.

In 1733, Jo. Christ. Wolf described these MSS. in the fourth volume of his Bibliotheca Hebræa, p. 79. A few years ago I had the singular good fortune to purchase the whole of these at Utrecht; a collection of MSS., which Dr. *Kennicott* complains that he could not by any entreaties obtain the privilege of collating. These are his own words,—"Wolfius, (Bib. Heb. iv. 79-82,) memorat codices 10. olim penes Schultingium; quorum plurimi postea erant penes Rev. Joh. Van der Hagen. Usum Codd. Hagenianorum obtinere nulla potuit à me precatio." Dissert. Gener. p. 78. sub Cod. 84. Dr. *Kennicott* supposed that three of those MSS. had been collated for him: but in this I believe he was mistaken; as he was also in supposing that only the greater part of the ten MSS. of Schulting had fallen into the hands of Mr. Van der Hagen; for the fact is, the whole ten were purchased by Van der Hagen, and the same ten are now in my library, being precisely those described by Wolfius, as above. I have collated the Prophet Isaiah throughout, in two of the most ancient of these MSS.; and have added their testimony in many places to the various readings collected by *Kennicott* and *De Rossi.* The very bad state of my health, and particularly of my eyes, prevented a more extensive collation of these very ancient and invaluable MSS. Some of the oldest are without any date. They are marked with the ten first letters of the alphabet. Cod. C. was written A. D. 1076,—D. in 1286,—G. in 1215,—H. in 1309,—I. in 1136. In most of these there is an ample harvest of important various readings.

Bishop Lowth, in giving an account of his labours on this prophet, takes a general view of the difficulties and helps he met with in his work. This being of considerable importance, I shall lay an abstract of it before the reader, as a proper supplement to the preceding sheets. He observes:—

"The Masoretic punctuation,—by which the pronunciation of the language is given, and the forms of the several parts of speech, the construction of the words, the distribution and limits of the sentences, and the connexion of the several members, are fixed,—is in effect an interpretation of the Hebrew text made by the Jews of late ages, probably not earlier than the eight century; and may be considered as *their* translation of the Old Testament. Where the words unpointed are capable of various meanings, according as they may be variously pronounced and constructed, the Jews by their pointing have determined them to one meaning and construction; and the sense which they thus give is *their* sense of the passage, just as the rendering of a translator into another language is *his* sense. The points have been considered as part of the Hebrew text, and as giving the meaning of it on no less than Divine authority. Accordingly our public translations in the modern tongues, for the use of the Church among Protestants, and so likewise the modern Latin translations, are for the most part close copies of the Hebrew pointed text, and are in reality only versions at second hand, translations of the Jews' interpretation of the Old Testament.

"To what a length an opinion lightly taken up, and embraced with a full assent without due examination, may be carried, we may see in another example of much the same kind. The learned of the Church of Rome, who have taken the liberty of giving translations of

Scripture in the modern languages, have for the most part subjected and devoted themselves to a prejudice equally groundless and absurd. The Council of Trent declared the Latin translation of the Scriptures, called the Vulgate, which had been for many ages in use in their Church, to be authentic; a very ambiguous term, which ought to have been more precisely defined than the fathers of this council chose to define it. Upon this ground many contended that the Vulgate Version was dictated by the Holy Spirit; at least was providentially guarded against all error; was consequently of Divine authority, and more to be regarded than even the original Hebrew and Greek texts.

"But a very fruitful source of error proceeded from the Jewish coypists consulting more the fair appearance of their copy than the correctness of it, by wilfully leaving mistakes uncorrected, lest by erasing they should diminish the beauty and the value of the transcript, (for instance, when they had written a word or part of a word wrong, and immediately saw their mistake, they left the mistake uncorrected, and wrote the word anew after it;) their scrupulous regard to the evenness and fulness of their lines, which induced them to cut off from the ends of lines a letter or letters for which there was not sufficient room, (for they never divided a word, so that the parts of it should belong to two lines,) and to add to the ends of lines letters wholly insignificant, by way of expletives to fill up a vacant space: their custom of writing part of a word at the end of a line, where there was not room for the whole, and then giving the whole word at the beginning of the next line.

"These circumstances considered, it would be the most astonishing of all miracles, if the Hebrew writings of the Old Testament had come down to us through their hands absolutely pure, and free from all mistakes whatsoever.

"The ancient Versions, as the principal sources of emendation, and highly useful in rectifying as well as in explaining the Hebrew text, are contained in the London Polyglot.

"The *Greek* Version, commonly called the Septuagint, or of the seventy interpreters, probably made by different hands, (the number of them uncertain,) and at different times, as the exigence of the Jewish Church at Alexandria and in other parts of Egypt required, is of the first authority, and of the greatest use in correcting the Hebrew text, as being the most ancient of all; and as the copy from which it was translated appears to have been free from many errors which afterwards by degrees got into the text. But the Greek Version of Isaiah is not so old as that of the Pentateuch by a hundred years and more, having been made in all probability after the time of Antiochus Epiphanes, when the reading of the prophets in the Jewish synagogues began to be practised; and even after the building of Onias' temple, to favour which there seems to have been some artifice employed in a certain passage of Isaiah (chap. xix. 18) in this Version. And it unfortunately happens that Isaiah has had the hard fate to meet with a Greek translator very unworthy of him, there being hardly any book of the Old Testament so ill rendered in that Version as this of Isaiah.

"The *Arabic* Version is sometimes referred to as verifying the reading of the Septuagint, being, for the most part at least, taken from that Version.

"The *Chaldee* paraphrase of Jonathan ben Uzziel, made about or before the time of our Saviour, though it often wanders from the text in a wordy allegorical explanation, yet very frequently adheres to it closely, and gives a verbal rendering of it; and accordingly is sometimes of great use in ascertaining the true reading of the Hebrew text.

"The *Syriac* Version stands next in order of time, but is superior to the Chaldee in usefulness and authority, as well in ascertaining as in explaining the Hebrew text. It is a close translation of the Hebrew language into one of near affinity to it. It is supposed to have been made as early as the first century.

"The fragments of the three Greek Versions of *Aquila*, *Symmachus*, and *Theodotion*, all made in the second century, which are collected in the Hexapla of Montfauçon, are of considerable use for the same purpose.

"The *Vulgate*, being for the most part the translation of Jerome, made in the fourth century, is of service in the same way, in proportion to its antiquity.

"In referring to Dr. Kennicott's Collections, I have given the whole number of manuscripts or editions which concur in any particular reading; what proportion that number bears to the whole number of collated copies which contain the Book of Isaiah, may be seen by comparing it with the catalogue of copies collated, which is given at the end of that book in the doctor's edition of the Hebrew Bible.

"Among the manuscripts which have been collated, I consider those of the tenth, eleventh, and twelfth centuries as ancient, comparatively and in respect of the rest. Therefore in quoting a number of manuscripts, where the variation is of some importance, I have added, that so many of that number are *ancient*, that is, are of the centuries above mentioned.

"The design of the notes is to give the reasons and authorities on which the translation is founded; to rectify or to explain the words of the text; to illustrate the ideas, the images, and the allusions of the prophet, by referring to objects, notions, and customs which peculiarly belong to his age and his country; and to point out the beauties of particular passages. If the reader would go deeper into the mystical sense, into theological, historical, and chronological disquisitions, there are many learned expositors to whom he may have recourse, who have written full commentaries on this prophet, to which title the present work has no pretensions. The sublime and spiritual uses to be made of this peculiarly evangelical prophet, must be all founded on a faithful representation of the literal sense which his words contain. This is what I have endeavoured closely and exactly to express."

In conclusion, it may be necessary to give some account of what I have ventured to superadd to the labours of this very learned prelate. After consulting the various commentators, who have spent much time and labour in their endeavours to illustrate this prophet, I found their interpretations of many of the most important prophecies strangely different, and often at variance. Former commentators have taken especial care to bring forth in the most prominent point of view all those passages which have been generally understood to refer to our blessed Lord, and the Christian dispensation. Later critics, especially those on the continent, have adopted the Jewish plan of interpretation, referring the parts belonging to the Messiah in his sufferings, &c., to the prophet himself, or to the children of the captivity in their state of *suffering;* and those passages which speak of the *redemption of the world*, and the *glorious state of the Christian Church*, they apply to the *deliverance of the Israelites from the Babylonish captivity.* It is really painful to see what labour and learning these critics spend to rob the prophet of his title of *evangelical;* and to show that even the sacred writers of the New Testament, in their application of select passages to our Lord, only followed the popular custom of *accommodating* passages of the Sacred Writings to occurrences and events, to which their leading circumstances bore some kind of resemblance, the application being only intended to convey the idea of *similitude*, and not of *identity.*

While I have cautiously handled those passages, the application of which was *dubious*, I have taken care to give my opinion with firmness on those which seem to have no other meaning than what they derive from their application to the great work of redemption by Jesus Christ, and the glory that should follow the outpouring of his Spirit. Many readers will no doubt suppose that I should have dwelt more on the *spiritual* parts of this inimitable book; but to this there would be scarcely any end. Who could exhaust the stores of this prophet! and if any thing were left unsaid, some would still be unsatisfied, to say nothing of the volume being thereby swollen beyond all reasonable bounds. I have marked enough for the reader's meditation; and have thrown out a sufficient number of hints to be improved by ministers of the word of God. To another class it may appear too *critical;* but this chiefly applies to the learned bishop, whose plan, as by far the best in my judgment, I have followed; and whose collection of various readings I felt it my duty to complete, a thing that none of his editors have attempted before. I have therefore added the various readings collected by De Rossi to those of Dr. Kennicott, which the bishop had cited as authorities, on which he built his alterations and critical conjectures.

INTRODUCTION TO THE BOOK

OF THE

PROPHET JEREMIAH

THE Prophet Jeremiah, son of Hilkiah, was of the sacerdotal race, and a native of *Anathoth,* a village in the tribe of *Benjamin,* within a few miles of Jerusalem, which had been appointed for the use of the priests, the descendants of Aaron, Josh. xxi. 18. He was called to the prophetic office when very young; probably when he was fourteen years of age, and in the thirteenth of the reign of Josiah, A. M. 3375, B. C. 629. He continued to prophesy till after the destruction of Jerusalem by the Chaldeans, which took place A. M. 3416; and it is supposed that about two years after he died in Egypt. Thus it appears that he discharged the arduous duties of the prophetic office for upwards of *forty* years.

Being very young when called to the prophetic office, he endeavoured to excuse himself on account of his youth and incapacity for the work; but, being overruled by the Divine authority, he undertook the task, and performed it with matchless zeal and fidelity in the midst of a most crooked and perverse people, by whom he was continually persecuted, and whom he boldly reproved, often at the hazard of his life.

His attachment to his country was strong and fervent; he foresaw by the light of prophecy the ruin that was coming upon it. He might have made terms with the enemy, and not only saved his life, but have gained ease and plenty; but he chose rather to continue with his people, and take his part in all the disasters that befell them.

After the destruction of Jerusalem, Nebuchadnezzar having made *Gedaliah* governor of Judea, the fractious Jews rose up against him, and put him to death; they then escaped to *Tahpanhes* in Egypt, carrying Jeremiah with them; who, continuing to testify against their wickedness and idolatry, at length fell a victim to his faithfulness: they filled up the measure of their iniquity, as tradition reports, by stoning the prophet to death. God marked this murderous outrage by his peculiar displeasure; for in a few years after they were almost all miserably destroyed by the Chaldean armies which had invaded Egypt; and even this destruction had been foretold by the prophet himself, chap. xliv: "They were consumed by the sword and by the famine until there was an end of them, a small remnant only escaping," ver. 14, 27, 28.

The pitch of desperate wickedness to which the Jews had arrived previously to their captivity was truly astonishing. They had exhausted all the means that infinite *mercy,* associated with infinite *justice,* could employ for the salvation of sinners; and they became in consequence *desperately wicked;* no wonder, therefore, that wrath fell upon them to the *uttermost.* It seems that their hardness and darkness had proceeded to such lengths that they abandoned themselves to all the abominations of idolatry to avenge themselves on God, because he would not bear with their continual profligacy. Were ever people more highly favoured, more desperately ungrateful, or more signally punished! What a lesson is their history to the nations of the earth, and especially to those who have been favoured with the light of revelation!

INTRODUCTION TO THE BOOK OF JEREMIAH

I should have entered into a particular discussion relative to the history of those times mentioned by this prophet, had they not passed already in review in the Books of *Kings* and *Chronicles;* in which much of the historical parts of this prophet has been anticipated; and to which, in order to avoid repetition, I must refer my readers. What is farther necessary to be added will be found in the following notes.

As a writer, the character of Jeremiah has been well drawn by Bishop *Lowth.* On comparing him with *Isaiah,* the learned prelate says: "Jeremiah is by no means wanting either in elegance or sublimity; although, generally speaking, inferior to Isaiah in both. St. Jerome has objected to him a certain *rusticity* in his diction; of which, I must confess, I do not discover the smallest trace. His thoughts, indeed, are somewhat less elevated, and he is commonly more large and diffuse in his sentences; but the reason of this may be, that he is mostly taken up with the gentler passions of *grief* and *pity,* for the expressing of which he has a peculiar talent. This is most evident in the *Lamentations,* where those passions altogether predominate; but it is often visible also in his *Prophecies;* in the former part of the book more especially, which is principally *poetical.* The middle parts are for the most part *historical;* but the last part, consisting of *six* chapters, is entirely *poetical;* and contains several oracles distinctly marked, in which this prophet falls very little short of the loftiest style of Isaiah."

It has often been remarked, that although several of the prophecies in this book have their *dates* distinctly noted, and most of the rest may be ascertained from collateral evidence; yet there is a strange *disorder* in the *arrangement.* "There is," says Dr. *Blayney,* "a preposterous jumbling together of the prophecies of the reigns of Jehoiakim and Zedekiah in the seventeen chapters which follow the twentieth, according to the Hebrew copies; so that, without any apparent reason, many of the *latter* reigns *precede* those of the *former;* and in the *same reign,* the *last* delivered are put *first,* and the *first, last.*" In order to prevent the confusion arising from this, Dr. *Blayney* has transposed the chapters where he thought it needful, without altering the numerals as they stand in our common Bibles.

This defect has been noticed, and attempts made to remedy it, by others. Dr. *John George Dahler,* Professor of Theology in the Protestant seminary of Strasburg, has just now published the *first volume* of a work, entitled, Jeremie, *traduit sur le Texte original, accompagnê de Notes Explicatives, Historiques, et Critiques,* 8vo., (antedated) *Strasbourg,* 1824. After a *preface,* and very judicious *historical introduction,* consisting, the first of *twenty-two,* the second of *thirty-six* pages, the *text* and *notes* follow. The poetical parts of the text are translated in the *hemistich* manner, as the original appears in the best copies; and the whole is divided into *sections;* each of which is introduced with judicious observations relative to time, place, circumstances, and the matter contained in that section. The discourses or prophecies delivered under a particular reign, are all produced under that reign in their chronological order. A table of this arrangement I shall here introduce, and refer to the use of it afterwards:—

TABLE I

Prophecies under Josiah

Chap. i. 1–19.
iv. v.–vi. 30.
ii. 1.–iii. 5.
iii. 6.–iv. 4.
xvii. 19–27.
xlvii. 1–7.

Under Jehoiakim

vii. 1.–ix. 25.
xxvi. 1–24.
xlvi. 2–12.
x. 1–16.
Chap. xiv. 1.–xv. 21.
xvi. 1.–xvii. 18.
xviii. 1–23.
xix. 1.–xx. 13.
xx. 14–18.
xxiii. 9–40.
xxxv. 1–19.
xxv. 1–38.
xxxvi. 1–32.
xlv. 1–5.
xii. 14–17.
x. 17–25.

Under Jeconiah

xiii. 1–27.

Under Zedekiah

Chap. xxiii. 1.–xxii. 8.
xi. 1–17.
xi. 18.–xii. 13.
xxiv. 1–10.
xxix. 1–32.
xxvii. 1.–xxviii. 17.
xlix. 34–39.
li. 59–64.
xxi. 1–14.
xxxiv. 1–7.
xxxvii. 1–10.
xxxiv. 8–22.
xxxvii. 11–21.
xxxviii. 1–28.

Chap. xxxix. 15–18.
xxxii. 1–44.
xxxiii. 1–26.
xxxix. 1–10.

After the destruction of Jerusalem

xxxix. 11–14.
xl. 1.–xli. 18.
xlii. 1.–xliii. 7.
xxx. 1.–xxxi. 40.

Prophecies delivered in Egypt

Chap. xliii. 8–13.
xliv. 1–30.
xlvi. 13–28.

Prophecies relative to strange nations

xlvi. 1, and xlix. 1–6.

Chap. xlviii. 1–47.
xlix. 7–22.
xlix. 23–27.
xlix. 28–33.
l. 1.–li. 58–64.

Historical Appendix

lii. 1–34.

The kings under whom Jeremiah prophesied succeeded each other in the following order: 1. Josiah; 2. Jehoahaz; 3. Jehoiachin, or Jeconiah; 4. Jehoiakim; 5. Zedekiah.

To render the *transpositions* evident which have taken place in these prophetical discourses, we have only to look at those which bear the date of their delivery.

TABLE II

Chap.	
i. 1.	Delivered the thirteenth year of Josiah.
iii. 6.	Under Josiah.
xxi. 1.	Under Zedekiah.
xxiv. 1.	After the carrying away of Jeconiah, son of Jehoiakim.
xxv. 1.	The fourth year of Jehoiakim.
xxvi. 1.	The beginning of the reign of Jehoiakim.
xxviii. 1.	The beginning of the reign of Zedekiah.
xxix. 1.	After the carrying away of Jeconiah.
xxxii. 1.	The tenth year of Zedekiah.
xxxiv. 1.	(Under Zedekiah) during the siege of Jerusalem.
xxxiv. 8.	(Under Zedekiah) when he had obliged his subjects to give liberty to the Israelites whom they had reduced to slavery.
xxxv. 1.	Under Jehoiakim.
xxxvi. 1.	Under Jehoiakim.
xxxvii. 1.	Under Zedekiah during the siege of Jerusalem.
xxxvii. 11.	Under Zedekiah.
xxxviii. 1.	Under Zedekiah.
xxxix. 15.	Under Zedekiah while Jeremiah was in prison.
xlv. 1.	The fourth year of Jehoiakim.
xlvi. 2.	The fourth year of Jehoiakim.
xlix. 34.	In the beginning of the reign of Zedekiah.
li. 59.	The fourth year of Zedekiah.

Taking into consideration the order of the reigns, a child may perceive that the above prophecies are not in the order of the times of their delivery; and that the *sheets* or *skins* on which the text of that MS. was written, from which the present copies have derived their origin, have been pitifully interchanged, huddled and tacked together, without connexion or arrangement.

To remedy this defect, Dr. *Blayney* has arranged the chapters in the following order which he terms a new arrangement of the chapters in Jeremiah, from chap. xx. to chap. xlvi., inclusive: xx., xxii., xxiii., xxv., xxvi., xxxv., xxxvi., xlv., xxiv., xxix., xxx., xxxi., xxvii., xxviii., xxi., xxxiv., xxxvii., xxxii., xxxiii., xxxviii., xxxix. 15–18, xxxix. 1–14, xl., xli., xlii., xliii., xliv., xlvi., &c.

The preceding and subsequent chapters Dr. *Blayney* thought sufficiently correct for all the general purposes of chronology; and it is according to this order that he prints the text in his edition and translation of this prophet.

Dr. *Dahler*, as we have seen, is more circumstantial. Where he has *dates*, as are shown in the preceding table, he produces the text in that order; where there are not *positive* dates, he ascertains several by circumstantial intimations, which bear great evidence of accuracy; but there is a numerous class of discourses which he is obliged to insert in this work by *critical conjecture*. In such a case as this, when the *arrangement* of the common text is so evidently *defective*, and in many respects *absurd*, this procedure is quite allowable; for although the present text as to its arrangement has the sanction of *antiquity*, yet when a remedy is found, it would be absurd, if not sinful, to follow an order which we may rest satisfied never did proceed from the inspired writer.

I hope none will suppose that these observations detract any thing from the Divine inspiration of the book. The prophet delivered his discourses at particular times in *select portions*, during *forty* or *forty-three* years; these were afterwards gathered together and stitched up without any attention to chronological arrangement. Though the Spirit of the Lord directed the prophet, yet it would be absurd to suppose that it guided the hand of every *collector* or *scribe* into whose custody these several parcels might come. Suppose a man buy a copy of the Bible *in sheets*, and not knowing how to collate them, stitches the whole confusedly together, so that in many places the sense cannot be made out from a preceding to a following sheet, would it not be singularly foolish for any person to say, "As God is the Fountain of wisdom and Author of reason, such incongruities cannot proceed from him, therefore this book was not given by Divine revelation." A child in a printer's office might reply, "Cut the stitching asunder, that is man's work; collate the sheets and put them in their proper order, and you will soon see that every paragraph is in harmony with the rest, and contains the words of Divine wisdom."

Many an ancient MS., which appeared mutilated and imperfect, I have restored to order and perfection by cutting the binding asunder, and restoring the sheets and leaves to those places from which the ignorance and unskilfulness of the binder had detached them. May we not be allowed to treat the dislocations in the writings of a prophet in the same way, when it is evident that in the lapse of time his work has suffered by the hand of the careless and ignorant.

But it may be asked, "After all the evidence I have, and the concessions I have made, why I have not transposed those disjointed chapters, and produced them in the order in which I think they should be read?" I answer, Were I to give a new translation with notes of this prophet separately, as Drs. *Blayney* and *Dahler* have done, I should feel it my duty to do what the objection states; but as my province as a general commentator requires me to take up all the *books* of the sacred volume in the *order* in which I find them in the present authorized version, though convinced that this arrangement is neither correct nor convenient; so I take up the *parts* of each, however transposed, in the same manner, directing the reader by *tables* and *notes* to regulate his use of the work so as to produce general edification with as little embarrassment as possible.

For general purposes, Dr. *Blayney's* chronological arrangement may be sufficient; but for greater accuracy Table I. may be preferred. These may at least be considered in the light of *helps* to a better understanding of these several prophecies; but no man is bound to follow either, farther than he is convinced that it follows what is specifically set down by the prophet himself, or fairly deducible from strong circumstantial evidence.

In my notes on this prophet I have availed myself, as far as my plan would permit, of the best helps within my reach. The *various readings* of *Kennicott* and *De Rossi* I have carefully consulted, and occasionally strengthened the evidence in behalf of those readings, more particularly recommended by collations from my own MSS. I regret that I have not been able, for the reasons mentioned at the conclusion of the notes on Isaiah, to produce all the various readings of importance found in these ancient MSS., and especially in the Book of *Lamentations*, which is contained in *five* of them; but like the woman in the Gospels, *I have done what I could*, and must leave the rest to those who, with better abilities, may possess the greater advantages of youth and strength, with unimpaired sight.

Reader! God designs thee a blessing by every portion of his word: in thy reading seek for *this;* and if these notes be helpful to thee, give Him the glory.

A. C.

Eastcott, Nov. 1, 1824.

THE BOOK
OF THE
PROPHET JEREMIAH

Chronological notes relative to the commencement of Jeremiah's prophesying

Year from the Creation, according to Archbishop Usher, 3375.—Year from the Deluge, according to the generally received Hebrew text, conferred with Acts vii. 4, 1719.—Fourth year of the *thirty-seventh* Olympiad.—Year from the building of Rome according to the Varronian account, 125.—Year before the vulgar era of Christ's nativity, 629.—Twelfth year of Ancus Martius, the fourth king of the Romans: this was the *one hundred and twentieth* year before the expulsion of the Tarquins.—Nineteenth year of Phraortes, the second king of Media.—Twenty-third year of Archidamus, king of Lacedæmon, of the family of the Proclidæ.—Sixteenth year of Eurycrates II., king of Lacedæmon, of the family of the Eurysthenidæ.—Third year of Sadyattes, king of Lydia, which was the *eighty-second* year before the conquest of this kingdom by Cyrus.—Twelfth year of Philip, the sixth king of Macedon, or the *two hundred and ninety-third* before the commencement of the reign of Alexander the Great.—Thirteenth year of Josiah, king of Judah.—Epoch of the building of Cyrene by Battus, according to some chronologers.

CHAPTER I

General title to the whole Book, 1–3. *Jeremiah receives a commission to prophesy concerning nations and kingdoms, a work to which in the Divine purpose he had been appointed before his birth*, 4–10. *The vision of* the rod of an almond tree *and of the* seething pot, *with their significaiion*, 11–16. *Promises of Divine protection to Jeremiah in the discharge of the arduous duties of his prophetical office*, 17–19.

A. M. 3375
B. C. 629
Ol. XXXVII. 4
Anci Martii, R. Roman., 12

THE words of Jeremiah the
son of Hilkiah, of the priests
that *were* [a]in Anathoth in the
land of Benjamin:
2 To whom the word of the LORD came in
the days of Josiah the son of Amon king of
Judah, [b]in the thirteenth year of his reign.

A. M. cir. 3394—3416
B. C. cir. 610—588
Ol. XLII. 3—XLVIII. 1

3 It came also in the days of
Jehoiakim the son of Josiah king
of Judah, [c]unto the end of the
eleventh year of Zedekiah the
son of Josiah king of Judah,
[d]unto the carrying away of Jerusalem captive [e]in the fifth
month.

A. M. 3375
B. C. 629
Ol. XXXVII. 4
Anci Martii, R. Roman., 12

4 Then the word of the LORD
came unto me, saying,
5 Before I [f]formed thee in the
belly [g]I knew thee; and before
thou camest forth out of the womb I [h]sancti-
fied thee, *and* I [i]ordained thee a prophet unto
the nations.

---

[a]Joshua xxi. 18; 1 Chronicles vi. 60; chapter xxxii. 7, 8, 9——[b]Chap. xxv. 3——[c]Chap. xxxix. 2——[d]Chap. lii. 12, 15——[e]2 Kings xxv. 8——[f]Isaiah xlix. 1, 5; Ecclesiasticus xlix. 7——[g]Exodus xxxiii. 12, 17——[h]Luke i. 15, 41; Galatians i. 15, 16——[i]Hebrew, *gave*

NOTES ON CHAP. I

Verse 1-3. *The words of Jeremiah*] These three verses are the *title* of the Book; and were probably added by Ezra when he collected and arranged the sacred books, and put them in that order in which they are found in Hebrew Bibles in general. For particulars relative to this prophet, the times of his prophesying, and the arrangement of his discourses, see the *introduction*.

Eleventh year of Zedekiah] That is, the last year of his reign; for he was made prisoner by the Chaldeans in the fourth month of that year, and the *carrying away of the inhabitants of Jerusalem* was in the fifth month of the same year.

Verse 4. *The word of the Lord came unto me*] Then I first felt the inspiring influence of the Divine Spirit, not only revealing to me the subjects which he would have me to declare to the people, but also the *words* which I should use in these declarations.

Verse 5. *Before I formed thee*] I had destined thee to the prophetic office before thou wert born: I had formed my plan, and appointed thee to be my envoy to his people. St. Paul speaks of his own call to preach the Gospel to the Gentiles in similar terms, Gal. i. 15, 16.

A. M. 3375 B. C. 629 Ol. XXXVII. 4 Anci Martii, R. Roman., 12

6 Then said I, [k]Ah, Lord GOD!
behold, I cannot speak: for I *am*
a child.
7 But the LORD said unto me,
Say not, I *am* a child; for thou shalt go to all
that I shall send thee, and [l]whatsoever I command thee thou shalt speak.
8 [m]Be not afraid of their faces; for [n]I *am*
with thee to deliver thee, saith the LORD.
9 Then the LORD put forth his hand, and
[o]touched my mouth. And the LORD said unto
me, Behold, I have [p]put my words in thy
mouth.
10 [q]See, I have this day set thee over the
nations and over the kingdoms, to [r]root out,
and to pull down, and to destroy, and to
throw down, to build, and to
plant.
11 Moreover the word of the
LORD came unto me, saying, Je-
remiah, what seest thou? And I said, I see a
rod of an almond tree.
12 Then said the LORD unto me, Thou hast
well seen: for I will hasten my word to perform it.
13 And the word of the LORD came unto
me the second time, saying, What seest thou?
And I said, I see [s]a seething pot; and the
face thereof *is* [t]toward the north.
14 Then the LORD said unto me, Out of the
[u]north an evil [v]shall break forth upon all the
inhabitants of the land.

A. M. 3375 B. C. 629 Ol. XXXVII. 4 Anci Martii, R. Roman., 12

[k]Exod. iv. 10; vi. 12, 30; Isa. vi. 5——[l]Num. xxii. 20, 38; Matt. xxviii. 20——[m]Ezek. ii. 6; iii. 9; ver. 17——[n]Exod. iii. 12; Deut. xxxi. 6, 8; Josh. i. 5; chap. xv. 20; Acts xxvi. 17; Heb. xiii. 6

[o]Isa. vi. 7——[p]Isa. li. 16; chap. v. 14——[q]1 Kings xix. 17——[r]Ch. xviii. 7, 8, 9, 10; 2 Cor. x. 4, 5——[s]Ezek. xi. 3, 7; xxiv. 3——[t]Heb. *from the face of the north*——[u]Chap. iv. 6; vi. 1——[v]Heb. *shall be opened*

Verse 6. *I cannot speak*] Being very young, and wholly inexperienced, I am utterly incapable of conceiving aright, or of clothing these Divine subjects in suitable language. Those who are really *called of God* to the sacred ministry are such as have been brought to a deep acquaintance with themselves, feel their own ignorance, and know their own weakness. They know also the awful responsibility that attaches to the work; and nothing but the authority of God can induce such to undertake it. They whom God never called *run*, because of worldly honour and emolument: the others hear the call with *fear* and *trembling*, and can go only in the strength of Jehovah.

"How *ready* is the man to *go*,
Whom God hath never sent!
How *timorous, diffident,* and *slow,*
God's chosen instrument!"

Verse 7. *Whatsoever I command thee*] It is my words and message, not thine own, that thou shalt deliver. I shall teach thee; therefore thy youth and inexperience can be no hinderance.

Verse 8. *Be not afraid of their faces*] That is, the *Jews*, whom he knew would persecute him because of the message which he brought. To be *fore*-warned is to be half armed. He knew what he was to expect from the disobedient and the rebellious, and must now be prepared to meet it.

Verse 10. *I have—set thee over the nations*] God represents his messengers the prophets as *doing* what he commanded them to declare *should be done.* In this sense they *rooted up, pulled down,* and *destroyed*—declared God's judgments; they *builded up* and *planted*—declared the promises of his *mercy.* Thus God says to Isaiah, chap. vi. 10: "Make the heart of this people fat—and shut their eyes." Show them that they are *stupid* and *blind;* and that, because they have shut their eyes and hardened their hearts, God will in his judgments leave them to their hardness and darkness.

Verse 11. *A rod of an almond tree.*] שקד *shaked*, from שקד *shakad*, "to be ready," "to hasten," "to *watch* for an opportunity to do a thing," to *awake;* because the almond tree is the *first* to flower and bring forth fruit. *Pliny* says, Floret prima omnium amygdala mense Januario; Martio vero pomum maturat. It blossoms in *January*, when other trees are locked up in their winter's repose; and it bears fruit in *March*, just at the commencement of spring, when other trees only begin to *bud.* It was here the symbol of that *promptitude* with which God was about to fulfil his promises and threatenings. As a *rod*, says *Dahler*, is an instrument of punishment, the rod of the almond may be intended here as the symbol of that punishment which the prophet was about to announce.

Verse 12. *I will hasten my word*] Here is a paronomasia. *What dost thou see?* I see שקד *shaked,* "an almond," the *hastening* tree: that which first *awakes. Thou hast well seen, for* (שקד *shoked*) *I will hasten my word.* I will awake, or watch over my word for the first opportunity to inflict the judgments which I threaten. The judgment shall come speedily; it shall soon *flourish*, and come to *maturity.*

Verse 13. *A seething pot—toward the north.*] We find, from Ezekiel xxiv. 3, &c., that a *boiling pot* was an emblem of *war*, and the desolations it produces. Some have thought that by the seething pot *Judea* is intended, *agitated* by the invasion of the Chaldeans, whose land lay *north* of Judea. But Dr. *Blayney* contends that מפני צפונה *mippeney tsaphonah* should be translated, *From the face of the north*, as it is in the margin; for, from the next verse, it appears that the evil was to come *from the north;* and therefore the *steam*, which was designed as an emblem of that evil, must have arisen from that quarter also. The pot denotes the empire of the Babylonians and Chaldeans lying to the north of Judea, and pouring forth its multitudes like a *thick vapour*, to overspread the land. Either of these interpretations will suit the text.

Verse 14. *Shall break forth*] תפתח *tippath-*

A. M. 3375
B. C. 629
Ol. XXXVII. 4
Anci Martii, R. Roman., 12

15 For, lo, I will [w]call all the families of the kingdoms of the north, saith the LORD; and they shall come, and they shall [x]set every one his throne at the entering of the gates of Jerusalem, and against all the walls thereof round about, and against all the cities of Judah.

16 And I will utter my judgments against them touching all their wickedness, [y]who have forsaken me, and have burned incense unto other gods, and worshipped the works of their own hands.

17 Thou therefore [z]gird up thy loins, and arise, and speak unto them all that I command thee: [a]be not dismayed at their faces, lest I [b]confound thee before them.

A. M. 3375
B. C. 629
Ol. XXXVII. 4
Anci Martii, R. Roman., 12

18 For, behold, I have made thee this day [c]a defenced city, and an iron pillar, and brazen walls against the whole land, against the kings of Judah, against the princes thereof, against the priests thereof, and against the people of the land.

19 And they shall fight against thee; but they shall not prevail against thee; [d]for I *am* with thee, saith the LORD, to deliver thee.

---

[w]Chap. v. 15; vi. 22; x. 22; xxv. 9——[x]Chap. xxxix. 3; xliii. 10——[y]Deut. xxviii. 20; chap. xvii. 13——[z]1 Kings xviii. 46; 2 Kings iv. 29; ix. 1; Job xxxviii. 3; Luke xii. 35; 1 Pet. i. 18——[a]Exod. iii. 12; ver. 8; Ezek. ii. 6——[b]Or, *break to pieces*——[c]Isa. l. 7; chap. vi. 27; xv. 20——[d]Ver. 8

---

ach, shall be opened. The door shall be thrown abroad, that these calamities may pass out freely.

Verse 15. *Shall set every one his throne at the entering of the gates*] As the gates of the cities were the ordinary places where justice was administered, so the enemies of Jerusalem are here represented as conquering the whole land, assuming the reins of government, and laying the whole country under their own laws; so that the Jews should no longer possess any *political power:* they should be wholly subjugated by their enemies.

Verse 16. *I will utter my judgments*] God denounced his judgments: the conquest of their cities, and the destruction of the realm, were the facts to which these judgments referred; and these facts prove that the threatening was fulfilled.

Worshipped the works of their own hands.] *Idolatry* was the source of all their wickedness, and was the cause of their desolations. For למעשי *lemaasey, the works*, more than a hundred MSS. of *Kennicott's* and *De Rossi's*, with many editions, have למעשה *lemaaseh, the work.* Idolatry was their ONE great WORK, the *business* of their *life*, their *trade.*

Verse 17. *Gird up thy loins*] Take courage and be ready, lest I confound thee; take courage and be resolute, פן *pen*, lest by their opposition thou be terrified and confounded. God is often represented as *doing* or *causing to be done*, what he only *permits* or *suffers* to be done. Or, do not fear them, I will not suffer thee to be confounded. So *Dahler*, Ne crains pas que je te confonde a leurs yeux, "Do not fear that I shall confound thee before them." It is well known that the phrase, *gird up thy reins*, is a metaphor taken from the *long robes* of the Asiatics; which, on going a journey, or performing their ordinary work, they were obliged to truss up under their girdles, that the motions of the body might not be impeded.

Verse 18. *I have made thee this day a defenced city, and an iron pillar, and brazen walls*] Though thou shalt be exposed to persecutions and various indignities, they shall not prevail against thee. To their attacks thou shalt be as an *impregnable city;* as *unshaken* as an *iron pillar;* and as *imperishable* as a *wall of brass.* None, therefore, can have less cause to apprehend danger than thou hast. The issue proved the truth of this promise: he outlived all their insults; and saw Jerusalem destroyed, and his enemies, and the enemies of his Lord, carried into captivity. Instead of חמות *chomoth, walls*, many MSS. and editions read חמת *chomath, a wall*, which corresponds with the singular nouns preceding.

Verse 19. *They shall not prevail against thee*] Because I am determined to defend and support thee against all thy enemies. One of the ancients has said, Θεου θελοντος, και επι ῥιπος πλεῃ Σωζῃ· Thestius, apud Theophil. ad Autolyc. lib. ii. "God protecting thee, though thou wert at sea upon a twig, thou shouldst be safe."

CHAPTER II

God expresses his continued regard for his people, long since chosen, 1–3. He then expostulates with them on their ungrateful and worse than heathen return to his regard, 4–11; at which even the inanimate creation must be astonished, 12, 13. After this their guilt is declared to be the sole cause of the calamities which their enemies had power to inflict on them, 14–17. They are upbraided for their alliances with idolatrous countries, 18, 19; and for their strong propensity to idolatry, notwithstanding all the care and tender mercy of God, 20–29. Even the chastenings of the Almighty have produced in this people no repentance, 30. The chapter concludes with compassionately remonstrating against their folly and ingratitude in revolting so deeply from God, and with warning them of the fearful consequences, 31, 37.

A. M. 3375
B. C. 629
Ol. XXXVII. 4
Anci Martii,
R. Roman.,
12

MOREOVER the word of the
LORD came to me, saying,
2 Go and cry in the ears of
Jerusalem, saying, Thus saith
the LORD; I remember [a]thee, the kindness of
thy [b]youth, the love of thine espousals, [c]when
thou wentest after me in the wilderness, in a
land *that was* not sown.
3 [d]Israel *was* holiness unto the LORD, *and*
[e]the first-fruits of his increase: [f]all that devour him shall offend; evil shall come upon
them, saith the LORD.
4 Hear ye the word of the LORD, O house
of Jacob, and all the families of the house of
Israel:
5 Thus saith the LORD, [g]What iniquity
have your fathers found in me, that they are
gone far from me, [h]and have walked after
vanity, and are become vain?
6 Neither said they, Where *is* the LORD
that [i]brought us up out of the
land of Egypt, that led us through
the [k]wilderness, through a land
of deserts and of pits, through a
land of drought, and of the shadow of death,
through a land that no man passed through,
and where no man dwelt?
7 And I brought you into [l]a [m]plentiful country, to eat the fruit thereof and the goodness
thereof; but when ye entered, ye [n]defiled my
land, and made mine heritage an abomination.
8 The priests said not, Where *is* the LORD?
and they that handle the [o]law knew me not:
the pastors also transgressed against me, [p]and
the prophets prophesied by Baal, and walked
after *things that* [q]do not profit.
9 Wherefore [r]I will yet plead with you, saith
the LORD, and [s]with your children's children
will I plead.
10 For pass [t]over the isles of Chittim, and

A. M. 3375
B. C. 629
Ol. XXXVII. 4
Anci Martii,
R. Roman.,
12

[a]Or, *for thy sake*——[b]Ezek. xvi. 8, 22, 60; xxiii. 3, 8, 19; Hos. ii. 15——[c]Deut. ii. 7——[d]Exod. xix. 5, 6——[e]James i. 18; Rev. xiv. 4——[f]Chap. xii. 14; see chap. l. 7——[g]Isa. v. 4; Mic. vi. 3——[h]2 Kings xvii. 15; Jonah ii. 8——[i]Isa. lxiii. 9, 11, 13; Hos. xiii. 4——[k]Deut. viii. 15; xxxii. 10——[l]Or, *the land of Carmel*

[m]Num. xiii. 27; xiv. 7, 8; Deut. viii. 7, 8, 9——[n]Lev. xviii. 25, 27, 28; Num. xxxv. 33, 34; Psa. lxxviii. 58, 59; cvi. 38; chap. iii. 1; xvi. 18——[o]Mal. ii. 6, 7; Rom. ii. 20——[p]Chap. xxiii. 13——[q]Ver. 11; Hab. ii. 18——[r]Ezek. xx. 35, 36; Mic. vi. 2——[s]Exod. xx. 5; Lev. xx. 5——[t]Or, *over to*

NOTES ON CHAP. II

Verse 2. *I remember thee*] The *youth* here refers to their *infant political state* when they came out of Egypt; they just then began to be a *people.* Their *espousals* refer to their receiving the law at Mount Sinai, which they solemnly accepted, Exod. xxiv. 6-8, and which acceptance was compared to a *betrothing* or *espousal.* Previously to this they were no *people,* for they had no *constitution* nor *form of government.* When they received the *law,* and an *establishment in the Promised Land,* then they became a *people* and a *nation.*

Wentest after me] Receivedst my law, and wert obedient to it; confiding thyself wholly to my guidance, and being conscientiously attached to my worship. The *kindness* was that which God showed them by taking *them* to be his people, not *their kindness* to *him.*

Verse 3. *Israel* was *holiness unto the Lord*] Fully *consecrated* to his service.

The first fruits of his increase] They were as wholly the Lord's, as the first fruits were the property of the priests according to the law, Num. xviii. 13. These the priests alone had a right to devote to their own use.

All that devour him shall offend] As they were *betrothed* to the Lord, they were considered his *especial property;* they therefore who injured them were considered as laying violent hands on the property of God. They who persecute God's children have a grevious burden to bear, an awful account to give.

Verse 5. *What iniquity have your fathers found in me*] Have they ever discovered any thing *cruel, unjust, oppressive* in my *laws?* Any thing *unkind* or *tyrannical* in my *government?* Why then have they become *idolaters?*

Verse 6. *Through the wilderness*] Egypt was the *house of their bondage:* the *desert* through which they passed after they came out of Egypt, was a place where the *means of life* were not to be found; where no one family could subsist, much less a company of 600,000 men. God mentions these things to show that it was by the bounty of an *especial providence* that they were fed and preserved alive. Previously to this, it was a *land through which no man passed, and in which no man dwelt.* And why? because it did not produce the means of life; it was the *shadow of death* in its appearance, and the *grave* to those who committed themselves to it.

Verse 7. *And I brought you into a plentiful country*] The land of *Canaan.*

My land] The *particular property of God,* which he gave to them as an inheritance, they being his peculiar people.

Verse 8. *They that handle the law*] ותפשי *vethophe shey, they that draw out the law;* they whose office it is to *explain* it, *draw out* its spiritual meanings, and show to what its testimonies refer.

The pastors also] Kings, political and civil rulers.

Prophesied by Baal] Became his prophets, and were inspired with the words of *lying spirits.*

Verse 9. *I will yet plead with you*] אריב *arib,* I will maintain my *process,* vindicate my own conduct, and prove the wickedness of yours.

Verse 10. *The isles of Chittim*] This is the island of *Cyprus,* according to Josephus. In 1 Maccabees, chap. viii. 5, it is taken for *Macedonia. Besides this, how they* (the Romans) *had discomfited in battle Philip* and *Perseus,*

A. M. 3375 B. C. 629 Ol. XXXVII. 4 Anci Martii, R. Roman., 12

see; and send unto Kedar, and
consider diligently, and see if
there be such a thing:
11 [u]Hath a nation changed
their gods, which *are* [v]yet no gods? [w]but my
people have changed their glory for [x]*that*
which doth not profit.
12 [y]Be astonished, O ye heavens, at this, and
be horribly afraid, be ye very desolate, saith
the LORD.
13 For my people have committed two evils;
they have forsaken me the [z]Fountain of living
waters, *and* hewed them out cisterns, broken
cisterns that can hold no water.
14 *Is* Israel [a]a servant? *is* he a home-born
slave? why is he [b]spoiled?
15 [c]The young lions roared upon him, *and*
[d]yelled, and they made his land waste: his
cities are burned without inhabitant.
16 Also the children of Noph
and [e]Tahapanes, [f]have broken
the crown of thy head.
17 [g]Hast thou not procured this
unto thyself, in that thou hast forsaken the
LORD thy God, when [h]he led thee by the
way?
18 And now what hast thou to do [i]in the
way of Egypt, to drink the waters of [k]Sihor?
or what hast thou to do in the way of Assyria,
to drink the waters of the river?
19 Thine own [l]wickedness shall correct
thee, and thy backslidings shall reprove thee:
know therefore and see that *it is* an evil *thing*
and bitter, that thou hast forsaken the LORD
thy God, and that my fear *is* not in thee,
saith the Lord GOD of hosts.
20 For of old time I have broken thy yoke,
and burst thy bands; and [m]thou saidst, I will

A. M. 3375 B. C. 629 Ol. XXXVII. 4 Anci Martii, R. Roman., 12

---

[u]Mic. iv. 5——[v]Psa. cxv. 4; Isa. xxxvii. 19; chap. xvi. 20——[w]Psa. cvi. 20; Rom. i. 23——[x]Ver. 8——[y]Isa. i. 2; chap. vi. 19——[z]Psa. xxxvi. 9; chap. xvii. 13; xviii. 14; John iv. 14——[a]See Exod. iv. 22——[b]Heb. *become a spoil?*——[c]Isa. i. 7; chap. iv. 7

[d]Heb. *gave out their voice*——[e]Chap. xliii. 7, 8, 9 [f]Or, *feed on thy crown;* Deut. xxxiii. 20; Isa. viii. 8 [g]Chap. iv. 18——[h]Deut. xxxii. 10——[i]Isa. xxx. 1, 2 [k]Josh. xiii. 3——[l]Isa. iii. 9; Hos. v. 5——[m]Exod. xix. 8; Josh. xxiv. 18; Judg. x. 16; 1 Sam. xii. 10

---

king of the Chittims. Chittim was the grandson of Japhet; and *Bochart* has made it appear that the countries inhabited by the *Chittim* were *Italy* and the adjacent provinces of *Europe*, lying along the coast of the Mediterranean Sea; and probably this is the prophet's meaning.

Send unto Kedar] The name of an *Arabian tribe.* See if nations either near or remote, cultivated or stupid, have acted with such fickleness and ingratitude as you have done! *They* have *retained* their gods to whom they had no obligation; ye have *abandoned* your God, to whom ye owe your life, breath, and all things!

Verse 12. *Be astonished, O ye heavens*] Or, *the heavens are astonished.* The original will admit either sense. The conduct of this people was so altogether bad, that among all the iniquities of mankind, neither heaven nor earth had witnessed any thing so excessively sinful and profligate.

Verse 13. *Two evils*] *First,* they *forsook God,* the Fountain of life, light, prosperity, and happiness. *Secondly,* they hewed out broken cisterns; they *joined themselves to idols,* from whom they could receive neither temporal nor spiritual good! Their conduct was the excess of folly and blindness. What we call here *broken cisterns,* means more properly such vessels as were *ill made, not staunch, ill put together,* so that the water *leaked through them.*

Verse 14. Is *Israel a servant?*] Is he a *slave* purchased with money, or a *servant born in the family?* He is a *son* himself. If so, then, *why is he spoiled?* Not because God has not shown him love and kindness; but because he forsook God, turned to and is joined with idols.

Verse 15. *The young lions roared upon him*] The Assyrians, who have sacked and destroyed the kingdom of Israel, with a fierceness like that of pouncing upon their prey.

Verse 16. *The children of Noph and Tahapanes*] Noph and Tahapanes were two cities of Egypt, otherwise called *Memphis* and *Daphni.* It is well known that the good king was defeated by the Egyptians, and slain in battle. Thus was the *crown of Judah's head broken.*

Verse 18. *What hast thou to do in the way of Egypt*] Why dost thou *make alliances* with Egypt?

To drink the waters of Sihor?] This means the *Nile.* See on Isa. xxiii. 3.

The way of Assyria] Why *make alliances* with the Assyrians? All such connexions will only expedite thy ruin.

To drink the waters of the river?] The *Euphrates,* as נהר *nahar* or הנהר *hannahar* always means *Euphrates,* the country between the *Tigris* and *Euphrates,* is termed to this day *Maher alnahar,* "the country beyond the river," i. e., *Mesopotamia.*

Instead of cleaving to the Lord, they joined affinity and made alliances with those two nations, who were ever jealous of them, and sought their ruin. *Egypt* was to them a *broken reed* instead of a *staff; Assyria* was a *leaky cistern,* from which they could derive no *help.*

Verse 20. *Of old time I have broken thy yoke*] It is thought by able critics that the verbs should be read in the *second person singular,* THOU *hast broken thy yoke,* THOU *hast burst thy bonds;* and thus the *Septuagint,* *συντριψας τον ζυγον σου,* "thou hast broken thy yoke." And the *Vulgate,* Confregisti jugum meum, rupisti, vincula mea; "Thou hast broken my yoke; thou hast burst my bonds;" and so the *Arabic.* But the *Chaldee* gives it a meaning which removes the difficulty: "I have broken the yoke of the people from thy neck; I have cut your bonds asunder." And when this was done, they did promise fair; for "thou saidst, I will not trans-

A. M. 3375
B. C. 629
Ol. XXXVII. 4
Anci Martii,
R. Roman., 12

not [n]transgress; when [o]upon
every high hill and under every
green tree thou wanderest,
[p]playing the harlot.
21 Yet I had [q]planted thee a noble vine,
wholly a right seed: how then art thou turned
into [r]the degenerate plant of a strange vine
unto me?
22 For though thou [s]wash thee with nitre,
and take thee much soap, *yet* [t]thine iniquity
is marked before me, saith the Lord God.
23 [u]How canst thou say, I am not polluted,
I have not gone after Baalim? see thy way
[v]in the valley, know what thou hast done:
[w]*thou art* a swift dromedary traversing her
ways;
24 [x]A[y] wild ass [z]used to the
wilderness, *that* snuffeth up the
wind at [a]her pleasure; in her
occasion who can [b]turn her
away? all they that seek her will not weary
themselves; in her mouth they shall
find her.
25 Withhold thy foot from being unshod,
and thy throat from thirst: but
[c]thou saidst, [d]There is no hope; no; for
I have loved [e]strangers, and after them
will I go.
26 As the thief is ashamed when he is found,
so is the house of Israel ashamed; they, their
kings, their princes, and their priests, and
their prophets,

A. M. 3375
B. C. 629
Ol. XXXVII. 4
Anci Martii,
R. Roman., 12

---

[n]Or, *serve*——[o]Deut. xii. 2; Isa. lvii. 5, 7; chap. iii. 6——[p]Exod. xxxiv. 15, 16——[q]Exod. xv. 17; Psa. xliv. 2; lxxx. 8; Isa. v. 1, &c.; lx. 21; Matt. xxi. 33; Mark xii. 1; Luke xx. 9——[r]Deut. xxxii. 32; Isa. i. 21; v. 4——[s]Job ix. 30——[t]Deut. xxxii. 34; Job xiv. 17; Hos. xiii. 12

[u]Prov. xxx. 12——[v]Chap. vii. 31——[w]Or, *O swift dromedary*——[x]Job xxxix. 5, &c.; chap. xiv. 6——[y]Or, *O wild ass, &c.*——[z]Heb. *taught*——[a]Heb. *the desire of her heart*——[b]Or, *reverse it*——[c]Chap. xviii. 12——[d]Or, *is the case desperate?*——[e]Deut. xxxii. 16; chap. iii. 13

---

gress;" but still *they played the harlot*—committed idolatrous acts in the high places, where the heathen had built their altars, pretending that *elevation* of this kind assisted their devotion.

Verse 21. *I had planted thee a noble vine*] I gave thee the fullest instruction, the purest ordinances, the highest privileges; and reason would that I should expect thee to *live suitably to such advantages;* but instead of this thou *art become degenerate;* the *tree* is deteriorated, and the *fruit* is *bad.* Instead of being true worshippers, and of a holy life and conversation, ye are become idolaters of the most corrupt and profligate kind. See Isa. v. 1, &c., where the same image is used.

Verse 22. *For though thou wash thee with nitre*] It should be rendered *natar* or *natron,* a substance totally different from our *nitre.* It comes from the root נתר *nathar,* to dissolve, loosen, because a solution of it in water is abstersive, taking *out spots,* &c., from clothes. It is still used in the *east* for the purpose of *washing.* If *vinegar* be poured on it, Dr. *Shaw* says, a strong effervescence is the immediate consequence, which illustrates Prov. xxv. 20: "The singing of songs to a heavy heart is like vinegar upon natron;" that is, there is no affinity between them; opposition and strife are occasioned by any attempt to unite them.

Thine iniquity is marked before me] No washing will take out *thy spots;* the *marks* of thy idolatry and corruption are too deeply rooted to be extracted by any human means.

Verse 23. *See thy way in the valley*] The *valley of Hinnom,* where they offered their own children to Moloch, an idol of the Ammonites.

A swift dromedary traversing her ways] Dr. *Blayney* translates, "A fleet dromedary that hath taken to company with her."

Dr. *Dahler* rather paraphrases, thus:—

Semblable a une dromedaire en chaleur,
Qui court d'une cote a l'autre.

"Like to a dromedary in her desire for the male,
Which runs hither and thither."

This is an energetic comparison; and shows the unbridled attachment of those bad people to idolatry, and the abominable practices by which it was usually accompanied.

Verse 24. *A wild ass used to the wilderness*] Another comparison to express the same thing.

Snuffeth up the wind] In a high fever from the inward heat felt at such times, these animals open their mouths and nostrils as wide as possible, to take in large draughts of fresh air, in order to cool them.

In her mouth they shall find her.] The meaning is, that although such animals are exceedingly fierce and dangerous when they are in this state; yet, as soon as they have found the male, the desire is satisfied, and they become quiet and governable as before. But it was not so with this idolatrous people: their desires were ever fierce and furious; they were never satiated, one indulgence always leading to another. The brute beasts had only a short season in which this appetite prevailed; but *they* acted without restraint or limit.

Verse 25. *Withhold thy foot from being unshod*] When it was said to them, "Cease from discovering thy feet; prostitute thyself no more to thy idols."

And thy throat from thirst] Drink no more of their libations, nor use those potions which tend only to increase thy appetite for pollution. Thou didst say, There is no hope: it is useless to advise me thus; I am determined; I have loved *these strange gods,* and to them will I cleave.

Verse 26. *As the thief is ashamed*] As the pilferer is confounded when he is caught in the fact; so shalt thou, thy kings, princes, priests, and prophets, be confounded, when God shall arrest thee in thy idolatries, and deliver thee into the hands of thine enemies.

A. M. 3375
B. C. 629
Ol. XXXVII. 4
Anci Martii,
R. Roman.,
12

27 Saying to a stock, Thou *art* my father; and to a stone, Thou hast [f]brought me forth: for they have turned [g]*their* back unto me, and not *their* face: but in the time of their [h]trouble they will say, Arise, and save us.

28 But [i]where *are* thy gods that thou hast made thee? let them arise, if they [k]can save thee in the time of thy [l]trouble: for [m]*according to* the number of thy cities are thy gods, O Judah.

29 [n]Wherefore will ye plead with me? ye all have transgressed against me, saith the LORD.

30 In vain have I [o]smitten your children; they received no correction: your own sword hath [p]devoured your prophets, like a destroying lion.

31 O generation, see ye the word of the LORD. [q]Have I been a wilderness unto Israel? a land of darkness? wherefore say my people, [r]We [s]are lords; [t]we will come no more unto thee?

32 Can a maid forget her ornaments, *or* a bride her attire? yet my people [u]have forgotten me days without number.

33 Why trimmest thou thy way to seek love? therefore hast thou also taught the wicked ones thy ways.

34 Also in thy skirts is found [v]the blood of the souls of the poor innocents: I have not found it by [w]secret search, but upon all these.

35 [x]Yet thou sayest, Because I am innocent, surely his anger shall turn from me. Behold, [y]I will plead with thee, [z]because thou sayest, I have not sinned.

36 [a]Why gaddest thou about so much to change thy way? [b]thou also shalt be ashamed of Egypt, [c]as thou wast ashamed of Assyria.

37 Yea, thou shalt go forth from him, and [d]thine hands upon thine head: for the LORD hath rejected thy confidences, and thou shalt not prosper in them.

[f]Or, *begotten me*——[g]Heb. *the hinder part of the neck*——[h]Judg. x. 10; Psa. lxxviii. 34; Isa. xxvi. 16——[i]Deut. xxxii. 37; Judg. x. 14——[k]Isa. xlv. 20——[l]Heb. *evil*——[m]Chap. xi. 13——[n]Ver. 23, 35——[o]Isa. i. 5 ix. 13; chap. v. 3——[p]2 Chron. xxxvi. 16; Neh. ix. 26; Matt. xxiii. 29, &c.; Acts vii. 52; 1 Thess. ii. 15——[q]Ver. 5

[r]Heb. *We have dominion*——[s]Psa. xii. 4——[t]Deut. xxxii. 15——[u]Psa. cvi. 21; chap. xiii. 25; Hos. viii. 14——[v]Psa. cvi. 38; chap. xix. 4——[w]Heb. *digging*——[x]Ver. 23, 29——[y]Ver. 9——[z]Prov. xxviii. 13; 1 John i. 8, 10——[a]Ver. 18; chap. xxxi. 22; Hos. v. 13; xii. 1——[b]Isa. xxx. 3; chap. xxxvii. 7——[c]2 Chron. xxviii. 16, 20, 21——[d]2 Sam. xiii. 19

Verse 27. *Thou* art *my father*] By thee we have been produced, and by thee we are sustained. This was the property of the true God; for he is the *Author* and *Supporter* of *being*. How deeply fallen and brutishly ignorant must they be when they could attribute this to the stock of a tree!

Verse 28. According *to the number of thy cities are thy gods*] Among heathen nations every city had its *tutelary deity*. Judah, far sunk in idolatry, had adopted this custom. The Church of Rome has refined it a little: every city has its *tutelary saint*, and this saint has a procession and worship peculiar to himself. So here; not much of the old idolatry is lost.

Verse 31. *Have I been a wilderness unto Israel?*] Have I ever withheld from you any of the blessings necessary for your support?

A land of darkness] Have you, since you passed through the wilderness, and came out of the darkness of Egypt, ever been brought into similar circumstances? You have had food and all the necessaries of life for your bodies; and my ordinances and word to enlighten and cheer your souls. I have neither *been a wilderness* nor *a land of darkness to you*.

We are lords] We wish to be our own masters; we will neither brook religious nor civil restraint; we will regard no laws, human or Divine. It was this disposition that caused them to fall in so fully with the whole system of idolatry.

Verse 32. *Can a maid forget her ornaments*] This people has not so much attachment to me as young females have to their dress and ornaments. They never forget them; and even when arrived at old age, look with pleasure on the dress and ornaments which they have worn in their youth.

Days without number.] That is, for many years; during the whole reign of Manasses, which was *fifty-five* years, the land was deluged with idolatry, from which the *reform* by good King Josiah his grandson had not yet purified it.

Verse 33. *Why trimmest thou thy way*] Ye have used a multitude of artifices to gain alliances with the neighbouring idolatrous nations.

Hast thou also taught the wicked ones thy ways.] Ye have made even these idolaters worse than they were before. Dr. *Blayney* translates, "Therefore have I taught calamity thy ways." A prosopopœia: "I have instructed calamity where to find thee." Thou shalt not escape punishment.

Verse 34. *The blood of the souls of the poor innocents*] We find from the sacred history that Manasseh had filled Jerusalem with innocent blood; see 2 Kings xxi. 16, and Ezek. xxxiv. 10.

I have not found it by secret search, but upon all these.] Such deeds of darkness and profligacy are found only in Israel. Dr. *Blayney* translates, "I have not found it in a digged hole, but upon every oak." Others cover the blood that it may not appear; but ye have shed it openly, and sprinkled it upon your consecrated oaks, and gloried in it.

Verse 35. *Because I am innocent*] They continued to assert their innocence, and therefore expected that God's judgments would be speedily removed!

I will plead with thee] I will maintain my *process*, follow it up to conviction, and inflict the deserved punishment.

Verse 36. *Why gaddest thou about*] When they had departed from the Lord, they sought foreign alliances for support. 1. The *Assyrians*, 2 Chron. xxviii. 13-21; but they injured instead of helping them. 2. The *Egyptians:* but in this they were utterly disappointed, and were ashamed of their confidence. See chap. xxxvii. 7, 8, for the fulfilment of this prediction.

Verse 37. *Thou shalt go forth from him, and thine hands upon thine head*] Thou shalt find all thy confidence in vain,—thy hope disappointed,—and thy state reduced to desperation. *The hand being placed on the head* was the evidence of deep sorrow, occasioned by utter desolation. See the case of Tamar, when ruined and abandoned by her brother Amnon, 2 Sam. xiii. 19.

Thou shalt not prosper in them.] They shall all turn to thy disadvantage; and this, as we shall see in the history of this people, was literally fulfilled. O what a grievous and bitter thing it is to sin against the Lord, and have him for an enemy!

CHAPTER III

The first five verses of this chapter allude to the subject of the last; and contain earnest exhortations to repentance, with gracious promises of pardon, notwithstanding every aggravation of guilt, 1–5. *At the* sixth *verse a new section of prophecy commences, opening with a complaint against Judah for having exceeded in guilt her sister Israel, already cast off for her idolatry,* 6–11. *She is cast off, but not forever; for to this same Israel, whose place of captivity (Assyria) lay to the north of Judea, pardon is promised on her repentance, together with a restoration to the Church of God, along with her sister Judah, in the latter days,* 12–20. *The prophet foretells the sorrow and repentance of the children of Israel under the Gospel dispensation,* 21. *God renews his gracious promises,* 22; *and they again confess their sins. In this confession their not deigning to name the idol Baal, the source of their calamities, but calling him in the abstract* shame, *or a* thing of shame, *is a nice touch of the pencil, extremely beautiful and natural,* 22–25.

A. M. 3375 B. C. 629 Ol. XXXVII. 4 Anci Martii, R. Roman., 12

THEY [a]say, If a man put
away his wife, and she go
from him, and become another
man's, [b]shall he return unto her
again? shall not that [c]land be greatly polluted? but thou hast [d]played the harlot with
many lovers; [e]yet return again to me, saith
the LORD.
2 Lift up thine eyes unto [f]the high places,
and see where thou hast not been lien with.
[g]In the ways hast thou sat for
them, as the Arabian in the
wilderness; [h]and thou hast
polluted the land with thy
whoredoms and with thy wickedness.
3 Therefore the [i]showers have been withholden, and there hath been no latter rain;
and thou hast a [k]whore's forehead, thou re-
fusedst to be ashamed.
4 Wilt thou not from this time cry unto me,

[a]Heb. *saying*——[b]Deut. xxiv. 4——[c]Ch. ii. 7 [d]Ch. ii. 20; Ezek. xvi. 26, 28, 29——[e]Ch. iv. 1; Zech. i. 3 [f]See Deut. xii. 2; ch. ii. 20——[g]Gen. xxxviii. 14; Prov. xxiii. 28; Ezek. xvi. 24, 25——[h]Ch. ii. 7; ver. 9——[i]Lev. xxvi. 19; Deut. xxviii. 23, 24; chap. ix. 12; xiv. 4 [k]Chap. v. 3; vi. 15; viii. 12; Ezek. iii. 7; Zeph. iii. 5

NOTES ON CHAP. III

Verse 1. *If a man put away his wife*] It was ever understood, by the law and practice of the country, that if a woman were divorced by her husband, and became the wife of another man, the first husband could never take her again. Now Israel had been married unto the Lord; joined in solemn covenant to him to worship and serve him only. Israel turned from following him, and became idolatrous. On this ground, considering idolatry as a *spiritual whoredom*, and the precept and practice of the law to illustrate this case, Israel could never more be restored to the Divine favour: but God, this first husband, in the plenitude of his mercy, is willing to receive this adulterous spouse, if she will abandon her idolatries and return unto him. And this and the following chapters are spent in affectionate remonstrances and loving exhortations addressed to these sinful people, to make them sensible of their own sin, and God's tender mercy in offering to receive them again into favour.

Verse 2. *As the Arabian in the wilderness*] They were as fully intent on the practice of their idolatry as the *Arab* in the desert is in lying in wait to plunder the caravans. Where they have not cover to lie in ambush, they scatter themselves about, and run hither and thither, raising themselves up on their saddles to see if they can discover, by *smoke*, *dust*, or other *token*, the approach of any travellers.

Verse 3. *There hath been no latter rain*] The *former rain*, which prepared the earth for tillage, fell in the beginning of *November*, or a little sooner; and the *latter rain* fell in the middle of *April*, after which there was scarcely any rain during the summer.

Verse 4. *Wilt thou not—cry unto me, My father*] Wilt thou not allow me to be thy Creator and Preserver, and cease thus to acknowledge idols? See on chap. ii. 27.

A. M. 3375
B. C. 629
Ol. XXXVII. 4
Anci Martii,
R. Roman.,
12

My father, thou *art* [l]the guide of
[m]my youth?
5 [n]Will he reserve *his anger*
for ever? will he keep *it* to the
end? Behold, thou hast spoken and done evil
things as thou couldest.

A. M. cir. 3392
B. C. cir. 612
Ol. cir. XLII. 1
TarquiniiPrisci,
R. Roman.,
cir. annum 5

6 The LORD said also unto me
in the days of Josiah the king,
Hast thou seen *that* which
[o]backsliding Israel hath done?
she is [p]gone up upon every high mountain
and under every green tree, and there hath
played the harlot.
7 [q]And I said, after she had done all these
things, Turn thou unto me. But she returned
not. And her treacherous [r]sister Judah saw *it.*
8 And I saw, when [s]for all the causes
whereby backsliding Israel committed adultery I had [t]put her away, and given her a bill
of divorce; [u]yet her treacherous sister Judah
feared not, but went and played the harlot
also.
9 And it came to pass through the [v]lightness
of her whoredom, that she [w]defiled the land,
and committed adultery with
[x]stones and with stocks.

A. M. cir. 3392
B. C. cir. 612
Ol. cir. XLII. 1
TarquiniiPrisci,
R. Roman.,
cir. annum 5

10 And yet for all this her
treacherous sister Judah hath
not turned unto me [y]with her whole heart,
but [z]feignedly, saith the LORD.
11 And the LORD said unto me, [a]The backsliding Israel hath justified herself more than
treacherous Judah.
12 Go and proclaim these words toward [b]the
north, and say, Return, thou backsliding Israel, saith the LORD; *and* I will not cause mine
anger to fall upon you: for I *am* [c]merciful,
saith the LORD, *and* I will not keep *anger*
for ever.
13 [d]Only acknowledge thine iniquity, that
thou hast transgressed against the LORD thy
God, and hast [e]scattered thy ways to the
[f]strangers [g]under every green tree, and ye
have not obeyed my voice, saith the LORD.
14 Turn, O backsliding children, saith the
LORD; [h]for I am married unto you: and I
will take you [i]one of a city, and two of a
family, and I will bring you to Zion:

---

[l]Prov. ii. 17——[m]Chap. ii. 2; Hos. ii. 15——[n]Psa. lxxvii. 7, &c.; ciii. 9; Isa. lvii. 16; ver. 12——[o]Ver. 11, 14; chap. vii. 24——[p]Chap. ii. 23——[q]2 Kings xvii. 13 [r]Ezek. xvi. 46; xxiii. 2, 4——[s]Ezek. xxiii. 9——[t]2 Kings xvii. 6, 18——[u]Ezek. xxiii. 11, &c.——[v]Or, *fame* [w]Chap. ii. 7; ver. 2——[x]Chap. ii. 27

[y]2 Chron. xxxiv. 33; Hos. vii. 14——[z]Heb. *in falsehood*——[a]Ezek. xvi. 51; xxiii. 11——[b]2 Kings xvii. 6 [c]Psa. lxxxvi. 15; ciii. 8, 9; ver. 5——[d]Lev. xxvi. 40, &c.; Deut. xxx. 1, 2, &c.; Prov. xxviii. 13——[e]Ver. 2; Ezek. xvi. 15, 24, 25——[f]Chap. ii. 25——[g]Deut. xii. 2 [h]Chap. xxxi. 38; Hos. ii. 19, 20——[i]Rom. xi. 5

Verse 5. *Will he reserve* his anger *for ever?*] Why should not wrath be continued against thee, as thou continuest transgression against the Lord?

Verse 6. *The Lord said also unto me in the days of Josiah the king*] This is a new discourse, and is supposed to have been delivered after the *eighteenth* year of the reign of Josiah. Here the prophet shows the people of Judah the transgressions, idolatry, obstinacy, and punishment of their brethren, the ten tribes, whom he calls to return to the Lord, with the most gracious promises of restoration to their own country, their reunion with their brethren of Judah, and every degree of prosperity in consequence. He takes occasion also to show the Jews how much more culpable they were than the Israelites, because they practised the same iniquities while they had the punishment and ruin of the others before their eyes. He there fore exhorts them to return to God with all their hearts, that they might not fall into the same condemnation. See the following verses.

Verse 7. *And I said*] By the prophets *Elijah, Elisha, Hosea, Amos,* &c.; for all these prophesied to that rebellious people, and exhorted them to return to the Lord.

Verse 8. *I had put her away*] Given them up into the hands of the Assyrians.

Verse 9. *The lightness of her whoredom*] The *grossness* of her idolatry: worshipping objects the most degrading, with rites the most impure.

Verse 11. *Backsliding Israel hath justified herself more*] She was less offensive in my eyes, and more excusable, than treacherous Judah. So it is said, Luke xviii. 14, the humbled *publican* went down to his house *justified rather than* the boasting *Pharisee.* The one was more to be pitied than the other, and more likely to receive the mercy of God.

Verse 12. *Proclaim these words toward the north*] The countries where the ten tribes were then in captivity, Mesopotamia, Assyria, Media, &c., see 2 Kings xvii. 6; these lay *north* of Judea. How tender and compassionate are the exhortations in this and the following verses! Could these people believe that God had sent the prophet and yet prefer the land of their bondage to the blessings of freedom in their own country, and the approbation of their God?

Verse 14. *I will take you one of a city, and two of a family*] If there should be but *one of a city* left, or one willing to return, and *two only of a whole tribe,* yet will I receive these, and bring them back from captivity into their own land. I have heard these words most sinfully applied to show the nature of a fancied eternal decree of election, that has appointed in several cases one only out of a whole city, and *two out of a whole family,* to be eternally saved, leaving the rest, according to the decree of reprobation, to perish everlastingly! And yet these persons, who spoke thus of the Fountain of eternal goodness and mercy, professed to be-

A. M. cir. 3392 B. C. cir. 612 Ol. cir. XLII. 1 TarquiniiPrisci, R. Roman., cir. annum 5

15 And I will give you [k]pas-
tors according to mine heart,
which shall [l]feed you with
knowledge and understanding.

16 And it shall come to pass, when ye be multiplied and increased in the land, in those
days, saith the LORD, they shall say no more,
The ark of the covenant of the LORD: [m]neither
shall it [n]come to mind: neither shall they
remember it; neither shall they visit *it;*
neither shall [o]*that* be done any more.

17 At that time they shall call Jerusalem
the throne of the LORD; and all the nations
shall be gathered unto it, [p]to the name of the
LORD, to Jerusalem: neither shall they [q]walk
any more after the [r]imagination of their evil
heart.

18 In those days [s]the house of Judah shall
walk [t]with the house of Israel, and they shall
come together out of the land of
[u]the north to [v]the land that I
have [w]given for an inheritance
unto your fathers.

A. M. cir. 3392 B. C. cir. 612 Ol. cir. XLII.1 TarquiniiPrisci, R. Roman., cir. annum 5

19 But I said, How shall I put thee among
the children, and give thee [x]a [y]pleasant land,
[z]a goodly heritage of the hosts of nations?
and I said, Thou shalt call me, [a]My father;
and shalt not turn away [b]from me.

20 Surely *as* a wife treacherously departeth
from her [c]husband, so [d]have ye dealt treacherously with me, O house of Israel, saith the
LORD.

21 A voice was heard upon [e]the high places,
weeping *and* supplications of the children of
Israel: for they have perverted their way,
and they have forgotten the LORD their God.

22 [f]Return, ye backsliding children, *and*
[g]I will heal your backslidings. Behold, we

[k]Chap. xxiii. 4; Ezek. xxxiv. 23; Eph. iv. 11——[l]Acts xx. 28——[m]Isa. lxv. 17——[n]Heb. *come upon the heart*——[o]Or, it *be magnified*——[p]Isa. lx. 9——[q]Chap. xi. 8——[r]Or, *stubbornness*——[s]See Isa. xi. 13; Ezek. xxxvii. 16-22; Hos. i. 11——[t]Or, *to*——[u]Ver. 12; chap. xxxi. 8——[v]Amos ix. 15

[w]Or, *caused your fathers to possess*——[x]Psa. cvi. 24; Ezek. xx. 6; Dan. viii. 9; xi. 16, 41, 45——[y]Heb. *land of desire*——[z]Heb. *a heritage of glory* or *beauty*——[a]Isa. lxiii. 16——[b]Heb. *from after me*——[c]Heb. *friend*——[d]Isa. xlviii. 8; chap. v. 11——[e]Isa. xv. 2——[f]Ver. 14; Hos. xiv. 1——[g]Hos. vi. 1; xiv. 4

lieve in Him who by the grace of God tasted death for every man.

Verse 15. *I will give you pastors according to mine heart*] The pastor means either the *king* or the *prophet;* and the pastors here promised may be either kings or prophets, or both. These shall be according to God's own heart; they shall be of his own choosing and shall be qualified by himself: and in consequence they shall feed the people with knowledge, דעה *deah,* that Divine truth concerning the true God and the best interests of man, which was essentially necessary to their salvation; and *understanding*—השכיל *haskeil,* the full interpretation of every point, that in receiving the truth they might become wise, holy, and happy.

Verse 16. *The ark of the covenant of the Lord*] This symbol of the Divine presence, given to the Jews as a token and pledge of God's dwelling among them, shall be no longer necessary, and shall no longer exist; for in the days of the Messiah, to which this promise seems to relate, God's worship shall not be confined either to *one place* or to *one people.* The temple of God shall be among men, and every where God be adored through Christ Jesus.

Neither shall that *be done any more.*] The ark shall be no more established, nor carried from place to place; nor shall men go to visit it. All its ceremonies and importance shall cease; and, if lost, shall never be *rebuilt.*

Verse 17. *They shall call Jerusalem the throne of the Lord*] The new Jerusalem, the universal Church of Christ, shall be God's throne: and wherever he is acknowledged as *the Lamb of God who takes away the sin of the world,* there God sits on his throne, and holds his court.

Verse 18. *The house of Judah shall walk with the house of Israel*] That is, in those days in which the Jews shall be brought in with the fulness of the Gentiles.

Out of the land of the north] From Chaldea. This prophecy has two aspects: one refers to the return from the Babylonish captivity; the other, to the glorious days of Christianity. But the words may refer to that gathering together of the Jews, not only from Chaldea, but from the countries of their dispersion over the face of the whole earth, and uniting them in the Christian Church.

Verse 19. *How shall I put thee among the children*] As if he had said, How can ye be accounted a holy seed, who are polluted? How can ye be united to the people of God, who walk in the path of sinners? How can ye be taken to heaven, who are unholy within, and unrighteous without?

And I said, Thou shalt call me, My father] This is the answer to the above question. They could *not be put among the children* unless they became legal *members* of the heavenly family: and they could not become members of this family unless they abandoned *idolatry,* and took the Lord for their portion. Nor could they be continued in the privileges of the heavenly family, unless they *no more turned away from their heavenly Father.*

Verse 21. *A voice was heard upon the high places*] Here the Israelites are represented as assembled together to bewail their idolatry and to implore mercy. While thus engaged, they hear the gracious call of Jehovah—

Verse 22. *Return, ye backsliding children*] This they gladly receive, and with one voice make their confession to him: "Behold, we come unto thee, for thou art Jehovah our God;" and thence to the end of the chapter, show the reasons why they return unto God. 1. Because he

A. M. cir. 3392
B. C. cir. 612
Ol. cir. XLII. 1
TarquiniiPrisci,
R. Roman.,
cir. annum 5

come unto thee; for thou *art* the
LORD our God.
23 [h]Truly in vain *is salvation*
hoped for from the hills, *and*
from the multitude of mountains: [i]truly in
the LORD our God *is* the salvation of Israel.
24 [k]For shame hath devoured the labour of
our fathers from our youth; their flocks and
their herds, their sons and their
daughters.
25 We lie down in our shame,
and our confusion covereth us:
[l]for we have sinned against the LORD our God,
we and our fathers, from our youth even unto
this day, and [m]have not obeyed the voice of
the LORD our God.

[h]Psa. cxxi. 1, 2——[i]Psa. iii. 8——[k]Chap. xi. 13; Hos. ix. 10——[l]Ezra ix. 7——[m]Chap. xxii. 21

is the true God. 2. Because the idols did not profit them: they could give no help in time of trouble. 3. Because it is the prerogative of God alone to give salvation. 4. Because they had no kind of prosperity since they had abandoned the worship of their Maker. And this was not only their case, but it was the case of their *forefathers*, who all suffered in consequence of their idolatry and disobedience. 5. These reasons are concluded with a hearty confession of sin, at the thought of which they are *confounded;* for the remembrance of their sin was grievous to them, and the burden was intolerable. This confession ended, God appears in the next chapter with gracious promises, and proper directions how they are to return, and how to conduct themselves in future.

Verse 24. *For shame hath devoured*] The word *shame*, here and in chap. xi. 13; Hos. ix. 10, is supposed to signify Baal, the idol which they worshipped. That thing or shame which has brought you into contempt, confusion, and ruin. Sooner or later every sinner must be *ashamed* of his conduct; next, *confounded;* and, lastly, *ruined* by it, unless by true faith and hearty repentance he returns to the Lord.

CHAPTER IV

Sequel of the exhortations and promises addressed to Israel in the preceding chapter, 1, 2. *The prophet then addresses the people of Judah and Jerusalem, exhorting to repentance and reformation, that the dreadful visitation with which they were threatened might be averted,* 3, 4. *He then sounds the alarm of war,* 5, 6. *Nebuchadnezzar, like a fierce lion, is, from the certainty of the prophecy, represented to be on his march; and the disastrous event to have been already declared,* 7–9. *And as the lying prophets had flattered the people with the hopes of peace and safety, they are now introduced, (when their predictions are falsified by the event,) excusing themselves; and, with matchless effrontery, laying the blame of the deception upon God, ("And they said," &c., so the text is corrected by Kennicott,)* 10. *The prophet immediately resumes his subject; and, in the person of God, denounces again those judgments which were shortly to be inflicted by Nebuchadnezzar,* 11–18. *The approaching desolation of Jerusalem lamented in language amazingly energetic and exquisitely tender,* 19–21. *The incorrigible wickedness of the people the sole cause of these calamities,* 22. *In the remaining verses the prophet describes the sad catastrophe of Jerusalem by such a beautiful assemblage of the most striking and afflictive circumstances as form a picture of a land "swept with the besom of destruction." The earth seems ready to return to its original chaos; every ray of light is extinguished, and succeeded by a frightful gloom; the mountains tremble, and the hills shake, under the dreadful apprehension of the wrath of Jehovah; all is one awful solitude, where not a vestige of the human race is to be seen. Even the fowls of heaven, finding no longer whereon to subsist, are compelled to migrate; the most fruitful places are become a dark and dreary desert, and every city is a ruinous heap. To complete the whole, the dolorous shrieks of Jerusalem, as of a woman in peculiar agony, break through the frightful gloom; and the appalled prophet pauses, leaving the reader to reflect on the dreadful effects of apostasy and idolatry,* 23–31.

A. M. cir. 3392
B. C. cir. 612
Ol. cir. XLII. 1
TarquiniiPrisci,
R. Roman.,
cir. annum 5

IF thou wilt return, O Israel,
saith the LORD, [a]return unto
me: and if thou wilt put away
thine abominations out of my
sight, then shalt thou not remove.
2 [b]And thou shalt swear, The
LORD liveth, [c]in truth, in judg-

[a]Chap. iii. 1, 22; Joel ii. 12——[b]Deut. x. 29; Isa. xlv. 23; lxv. 16; see chap. v. 2; Zech. viii. 8——[c]Isa. xlviii. 1

NOTES ON CHAP. IV

Verse 1. *Shalt thou not remove.*] This was spoken *before* the Babylonish captivity; and here is a promise that if they will return from their idolatry, they *shall not be led into captivity.* So, even that positively threatened judgment would have been averted had they returned to the Lord.

Verse 2. *Thou shalt swear, The Lord liveth*] Thou shalt not *bind* thyself by any false god; thou shalt acknowledge ME as the Supreme. Bind thyself BY me, and TO me; and do this *in truth*, in *judgment*, and in *righteousness*.

A. M. cir. 3392
B. C. cir. 612
Ol. cir. XLII. 1
TarquiniiPrisci, R. Roman., cir. annum 5

ment, and in righteousness; [d]and the nations shall bless themselves in him, and in him shall they [e]glory.

3 For thus saith the LORD to the men of Judah and Jerusalem, [f]Break up your fallow ground, and [g]sow not among thorns.

4 [h]Circumcise yourselves to the LORD, and take away the foreskins of your heart, ye men of Judah and inhabitants of Jerusalem: lest my fury come forth like fire, and burn that none can quench *it,* because of the evil of your doings.

5 Declare ye in Judah, and publish in Jerusalem; and say, Blow ye the trumpet in the land: cry, gather together, and say, [i]Assemble yourselves, and let us go into the defenced cities.

6 Set up the standard toward Zion: [k]retire, stay not: for I will bring evil from the [l]north, and a great [m]destruction.

7 [n]The lion is come up from his thicket, and [o]the destroyer of the Gentiles is on his way; he is gone forth from his place [p]to make thy land desolate; *and* thy cities shall be laid waste, without an inhabitant.

A. M. cir. 3392
B. C. cir. 612
Ol. cir. XLII. 1
TarquiniiPrisci, R. Roman., cir. annum 5

8 For this [q]gird you with sackcloth, lament and howl: for the fierce anger of the LORD is not turned back from us.

9 And it shall come to pass at that day saith the LORD, *that* the heart of the king shall perish, and the heart of the princes; and the priests shall be astonished, and the prophets shall wonder.

10 Then said I, Ah, Lord GOD! [r]surely thou hast greatly deceived this people and Jerusalem, [s]saying, Ye shall have peace; whereas the sword reacheth unto the soul.

11 At that time shall it be said to this people and to Jerusalem, [t]A dry wind of the high places in the wilderness toward the daughter of my people, not to fan nor to cleanse,

12 *Even* [u]a full wind from those *places* shall come unto me: now also [v]will I [w]give sentence against them.

---

[d]Gen. xxii. 18; Psa. lxxii. 17; Gal. iii. 8——[e]Isa. xlv. 25; 1 Cor. i. 31——[f]Hos. x. 12——[g]Matt. xiii. 7, 22 [h]Deut. x. 16; xxx. 6; chap. ix. 26; Col. ii. 11; Rom. ii. 28, 29——[i]Chap. viii. 14——[k]Or, *strengthen*——[l]Chap. i. 13, 14, 15; vi. 1, 22——[m]Heb. *breaking*

[n]2 Kings xxiv. 1; ch. v. 6; Dan. vii. 4——[o]Ch. xxv. 9 [p]Isa. i. 7; chap. ii. 15——[q]Isa. xxii. 12; chap. vi. 26 [r]Ezek. xiv. 9; 2 Thess. ii. 11——[s]Ch. v. 12; xiv. 13 [t]Ch. li. 1; Ezek. xvii. 10; Hos. xiii. 15——[u]Or, *a fuller wind than those*——[v]Ch. i. 16——[w]Heb. *utter judgments*

The nations shall bless themselves in him] They shall be so fully convinced of the power and goodness of Jehovah in seeing the change wrought on thee, and the mercies heaped upon thee, that their usual mode of benediction shall be, *May the God of Israel bless thee!*

Verse 3. *Break up your fallow ground*] *Fallow* ground is either that which, having been *once tilled*, has *lain long uncultivated;* or, *ground slightly ploughed*, in order to be ploughed again previously to its being sown. Ye have been long *uncultivated* in righteousness; let true repentance *break up* your fruitless and hardened hearts; and when the *seed* of the *word of life* is sown in them, take heed that worldly cares and concerns do not arise, and, like *thorns*, choke the good seed.

Verse 4. *Circumcise yourselves*] Put away every thing that has a tendency to grieve the Spirit of God, or to render your present holy resolutions unfruitful.

Verse 5. *Blow ye the trumpet*] Give full information to all parts of the land, that the people may assemble together and defend themselves against their invaders.

Verse 6. *I will bring evil from the north*] From the land of Chaldea.

Verse 7. *The lion is come up*] Nebuchadnezzar, king of Babylon. "The king (Nebuchadnezzar) is come up from his tower."—*Targum.*

The destroyer of the Gentiles] Of the *nations:* of all the people who resisted his authority. He destroyed them all.

Verse 8. *Lament and howl*] הילילו *heililu.* The aboriginal Irish had a funeral song called the *Caoinian*, still continued among their descendants, one part of which is termed the *ulaloo:* this is sung responsively or alternately, and is accompanied with a *full chorus of sighs and groans.* It has been thought that Ireland was originally peopled by the Phœnicians: if so, this will account for the similarity of many words and customs among both these people.

Verse 9. *The heart of the king shall perish*] Shall lose all courage.

Verse 10. *Ah, Lord God! surely thou hast greatly deceived this people*] The *Targum* paraphrases this verse thus: "And I said, Receive my supplication, O Lord God; for, behold, the false prophets deceive this people and the inhabitants of Jerusalem, saying, Ye shall have peace." The prophet could not reconcile this *devastation* of the country with the *promises* already made; and he appears to ask the question, Hast thou not then deceived this people in saying there shall be peace, i. e., prosperity?

Whereas the sword reacheth unto the soul.] That is, the life; the people being generally *destroyed.*

Verses 11-13. *A dry wind—a full wind—as clouds—as a whirlwind*] All these expressions appear to refer to the *pestilential winds, suffocating vapours*, and *clouds and pillars of sand* collected by *whirlwinds*, which are so common and destructive in the east, (see on Isa. xxi. 1;) and these images are employed here to

A. M. cir. 3392
B. C. cir. 612
Ol. cir. XLII. 1
TarquiniiPrisci,
R. Roman.,
cir. annum 5

13 Behold, he shall come up as clouds, and [x]his chariots *shall be* as a whirlwind: [y]his horses are swifter than eagles. Wo unto us! for we are spoiled.

14 O Jerusalem, [z]wash thine heart from wickedness, that thou mayest be saved. How long shall thy vain thoughts lodge within thee?

15 For a voice declareth [a]from Dan, and publisheth affliction from Mount Ephraim.

16 Make ye mention to the nations; behold, publish against Jerusalem, *that* watchers come [b]from a far country, and give out their voice against the cities of Judah.

17 [c]As keepers of a field, are they against her round about; because she hath been rebellious against me, saith the LORD.

18 [d]Thy way and thy doings have procured these *things* unto thee; this *is* thy wickedness, because it is bitter, because it reacheth unto thine heart.

19 My [e]bowels, my bowels! I am pained at [f]my very heart; my heart maketh a noise in me; I cannot hold my peace, because thou hast heard, O my soul, the sound of the trumpet, the alarm of war.

20 [g]Destruction upon destruction is cried; for the whole land is spoiled: suddenly are [h]my tents spoiled, *and* my curtains in a moment.

A. M. cir. 3392
B. C. cir. 612
Ol. cir. XLII. 1
TarquiniiPrisci,
R. Roman.,
cir. annum 5

21 How long shall I see the standard, *and* hear the sound of the trumpet?

22 For my people *is* foolish, they have not known me: they *are* sottish children, and they have none understanding; [i]they *are* wise to do evil, but to do good they have no knowledge.

23 [k]I beheld the earth, and, lo, *it was* [l]without form and void; and the heavens, and they *had* no light.

24 [m]I beheld the mountains, and, lo, they trembled, and all the hills moved lightly.

25 I beheld, and, lo, *there was* no man, and [n]all the birds of the heavens were fled.

26 I beheld, and, lo, the fruitful place *was* a wilderness, and all the cities thereof were broken down at the presence of the LORD, *and* by his fierce anger.

27 For thus hath the LORD said, The whole land shall be desolate; [o]yet will I not make a full end.

---

[x]Isa. v. 28——[y]Deut. xxviii. 49; Lam. iv. 19; Hos. viii. 1; Hab. i. 8——[z]Isa. i. 16; James iv. 8——[a]Chap. viii. 16——[b]Chap. v. 15——[c]2 Kings xxv. 1, 4——[d]Psa. cvii. 17; Isa. l. 1; chap. ii. 17, 19——[e]Isa. xv. 5; xvi. 11; xxi. 3; xxii. 4; chap. ix. 1, 10; see Luke xix. 42

[f]Hebrew, *the walls of my heart*——[g]Psalm xlii. 7; Ezekiel vii. 26——[h]Chap. x. 20——[i]Romans xvi. 19——[k]Isa. xxiv. 19——[l]Gen. i. 2——[m]Isa. v. 25; Ezek. xxxviii. 20——[n]Zeph. i. 3——[o]Chap. v. 10, 18; xxx. 11; xlvi. 28

---

show the overwhelming effect of the invasion of the land by the Chaldeans.

Verse 13. *Wo unto us!*] The people, deeply affected with these threatened judgments, interrupt the prophet with the lamentation—*Wo unto us, for we are spoiled!* The prophet then resumes:—

Verse 14. *O Jerusalem, wash thine heart*] Why do ye not put away *your wickedness, that ye may be saved* from these tremendous judgments? *How long shall thy vain thoughts* of safety and prosperity *lodge within thee?* Whilst thou continuest a rebel against God, and provokest him daily by thy abominations!

Verse 15. *For a voice declareth from Dan*] *Dan* was a city in the tribe of Dan, north of Jerusalem; the first city in Palestine, which occurs in the way from Babylon to Jerusalem.

Affliction from Mount Ephraim.] Between Dan and Jerusalem are the *mountains of Ephraim.* These would be the first places attacked by the Chaldeans; and the rumour from thence would show that the land was invaded.

Verse 16. *Watchers come from a far country*] Persons to besiege fortified places.

Verse 17. *As keepers of a field*] In the eastern countries grain is often sown in the *open country;* and, when nearly ripe, guards are placed at different distances round about it to preserve it from being plundered. Jerusalem was watched, like one of these fields, by guards all round about it; so that none could enter to give assistance, and none who wished to escape were permitted to go out.

Verse 19. *My bowels*] From this to the *twenty-ninth* verse the prophet describes the ruin of Jerusalem and the desolation of Judea by the Chaldeans in language and imagery scarcely paralleled in the whole Bible. At the sight of misery the *bowels* are first affected; pain is next felt by a sort of stricture in the *pericardium;* and then, the heart becoming strongly affected by irregular palpitations, a gush of tears, accompanied with wailings, is the issue.—"My bowels, my bowels! I am pained at my very heart, (the walls of my heart;) my heart maketh a noise in me; I cannot hold my peace." Here is nature, and fact also.

Verse 20. *Destruction upon destruction*] Cities burnt, and their inhabitants destroyed.

My tents spoiled] Even the solitary dwellings in the fields and open country do not escape.

Verse 23. *I beheld the earth,* (the land,) *and lo* it was *without form and void*] תהו ובהו *tohu vabohu;* the very words used in Genesis to denote the formless state of the chaotic mass before God had brought it into order.

Verse 24. *The mountains—hills*] Princes, rulers, &c., were astonished and fled.

Verse 25. *The birds of the heavens were fled.*]

A. M. cir. 3392
B. C. cir. 612
Ol. cir. XLII. 1
TarquiniiPrisci,
R. Roman.,
cir. annum 5

28 For this [p]shall the earth mourn, and [q]the heavens above be black: because I have spoken *it,* I have purposed *it,* and [r]will not repent, neither will I turn back from it.

29 The whole city shall flee for the noise of the horsemen and bowmen; they shall go into thickets, and climb up upon the rocks: every city *shall be* forsaken, and not a man dwell therein.

30 And *when* thou *art* spoiled, what wilt thou do? Though thou clothest thyself with crimson, though thou deckest thee with ornaments of gold, [s]though thou rentest thy [t]face with painting, in vain shalt thou make thyself fair; [u]*thy* lovers will despise thee, they will seek thy life.

A. M. cir. 3392
B. C. cir. 612
Ol. cir. XLII. 1
TarquiniiPrisci,
R. Roman.,
cir. annum 5

31 For I have heard a voice as of a woman in travail, *and* the anguish as of her that bringeth forth her first child, the voice of the daughter of Zion, *that* bewaileth herself, *that* [v]spreadeth her hands, *saying,* Wo *is* me now! for my soul is wearied because of murderers.

[p]Hos. iv. 3——[q]Isa. v. 30; l. 3——[r]Num. xxiii. 19; chap. vii. 16——[s]2 Kings ix. 30; Ezek. xxiii. 40

[t]Heb. *eyes*——[u]Chap. xxii. 20, 22; Lam. i. 2, 19——[v]Isa. i. 15; Lam. i. 17

The land was so desolated that even the fowls of heaven could not find meat, and therefore fled away to another region. How powerfully energetic is this description! See Zeph. i. 3.

Verse 30. *Though thou rentest thy face with painting*] This probably refers to the custom of introducing *stibium*, a preparation of antimony, between the eye and the lids, in order to produce a fine lustre, which occasions a distension of the eye-lid in the time of the operation. In order to heighten the effect from this, some may have introduced a *more than ordinary quantity*, so as nearly to *rend* the eye-lid itself. Though thou make use of every means of address, of cunning, and of solicitation, to get assistance from the neighbouring states, it will be all in vain. Reference is here particularly made to the practice of *harlots* to allure men.

Verse 31. *Bringeth forth her first child*] In such a case the fear, danger, and pain were naturally the greatest.

Spreadeth her hands] The gesture indicated by nature to signify distress, and implore help. We have met with this figure in other parts, and among the classic writers it is frequent.

CHAPTER V

The prophet, having described the judgments impending over his countrymen, enlarges on the corruptions which prevailed among them. Their profession of religion was all false and hypocritical, 1, 2. *Though corrected, they were not amended, but persisted in their guilt,* 3. *This was not the case with the low and ignorant only,* 4; *but more egregiously so with those of the higher order, from whose knowledge and opportunities better things might have been expected,* 5. *God therefore threatens them with the most cruel enemies,* 6; *and appeals to themselves if they should be permitted to practise such sins unpunished,* 7–9. *He then commands their enemies to raze the walls of Jerusalem,* 10; *that devoted city, whose inhabitants added to all their other sins the highest contempt of God's word and prophets,* 11–13. *Wherefore his word, in the mouth of his prophet, shall be as fire to consume them,* 14; *the Chaldean forces shall cruelly afflict them,* 15–17; *and farther judgments await them as the consequence of their apostasy and idolatry,* 18, 19. *The chapter closes with a most melancholy picture of the moral condition of the Jewish people at that period which immediately preceded the Babylonish captivity,* 20–31.

A. M. cir. 3392
B. C. cir. 612
Ol. cir. XLII. 1
TarquiniiPrisci,
R. Roman.,
cir. annum 5

RUN ye to and fro through the streets of Jerusalem, and see now, and know, and seek in the broad places thereof, [a]if ye can find a man, [b]if there be *any* that executeth judgment, that seeketh the truth; [c]and I will pardon it.

A. M. cir. 3392
B. C. cir. 612
Ol. cir. XLII.1
TarquiniiPrisci,
R. Roman.,
cir. annum 5

2 And [d]though they say, [e]The LORD liveth; surely they [f]swear falsely.

[a]Ezek. xxii. 30——[b]Gen. xviii. 23, &c.; Psa. xii. 1

[c]Gen. xviii. 26——[d]Tit. i. 16——[e]Chap. iv. 2——[f]Chap. vii. 9

NOTES ON CHAP. V

Verse 1. *Broad places*] Market-places, and those where there was most public resort.

If ye can find a man] A certain philosopher went through the streets of Athens with a lighted lamp in his hand; and being asked what he sought, answered, "I am seeking to find a MAN." So in Jerusalem none was found, on the most diligent search, who acted worthy the character of a rational being.

I will pardon it.] I will spare the city for the sake of *one righteous person*. So at the intercession of Abraham, God would have spared Sodom if there had been *ten* righteous persons found in it; Gen. xviii. 26.

Verse 2. *The Lord liveth*] Though they profess to *bind themselves* by Jehovah, as if they acknowledged him their God and only Lord, yet they *swore falsely;* for not believing in him, they took *a false oath;* one by which they did not believe themselves bound, not acknowledging him as their Lord. See on chap. iv. 2.

A. M. cir. 3392
B. C. cir. 612
Ol. cir. XLII. 1
TarquiniiPrisci,
R. Roman.,
cir. annum 5

3 O LORD, *are* not [g]thine eyes
upon the truth? thou hast
[h]stricken them, but they have
not grieved; thou hast consumed
them, *but* [i]they have refused to receive correction: they have made their faces harder
than a rock; they have refused to return.
4 Therefore I said, Surely these *are* poor;
they are foolish: for [k]they know not the
way of the LORD, *nor* the judgment of their
God.
5 I will get me unto the great men, and will
speak unto them; for [l]they have known the
way of the LORD, *and* the judgment of their
God: but these have altogether [m]broken the
yoke, *and* burst the bonds.
6 Wherefore [n]a lion out of the forest shall
slay them, [o]*and* a wolf of the [p]evenings shall
spoil them, [q]a leopard shall watch over their
cities: every one that goeth out thence shall
be torn in pieces: because their transgressions are many, *and* their backslidings [r]are
increased.
7 How shall I pardon thee for this? thy
children have forsaken me, and
[s]sworn by *them* [t]*that are* no
gods: [u]when I had fed them to
the full, they then committed
adultery, and assembled themselves by troops
in the harlots' houses.
8 [v]They were *as* fed horses in the morning:
every one [w]neighed after his neighbour's wife.
9 [x]Shall I not visit for these *things?* saith the
LORD: [y]and shall not my soul be avenged on
such a nation as this?
10 [z]Go ye up upon her walls, and destroy;
[a]but make not a full end: take away her battlements; for they *are* not the LORD'S.
11 For [b]the house of Israel and the house
of Judah have dealt very treacherously against
me, saith the LORD.
12 [c]They have belied the LORD, and said,
[d]*It is* not he; neither shall evil come upon
us; [e]neither shall we see sword nor famine:
13 And the prophets shall become wind, and
the word *is* not in them: thus shall it be done
unto them.
14 Wherefore thus saith the LORD God of

A. M. cir. 3392
B. C. cir. 612
Ol. cir. XLII. 1
TarquiniiPrisci,
R. Roman.,
cir. annum 5

---

[g]2 Chron. xvi. 9——[h]Isa. i. 5; ix. 13; chap. ii. 30——[i]Chap. vii. 28; Zeph. iii. 2——[k]Chap. vii. 8——[l]Mic. iii. 1——[m]Psa. ii. 3——[n]Chap. iv. 7——[o]Psa. civ. 20; Hab. i. 8; Zeph. iii. 3——[p]Or, *deserts*——[q]Hos. xiii. 7——[r]Heb. *are strong*——[s]Josh. xxiii. 7; Zeph. i. 5

[t]Deut. xxxii. 21; Gal. iv. 8——[u]Deut. xxxii. 15——[v]Ezek. xxii. 11——[w]Chap. xiii. 27——[x]Ver. 29; chap. ix. 9——[y]Chap. xliv. 22——[z]Chap. xxxix. 8——[a]Chap. iv. 27; ver. 18——[b]Chap. iii. 20——[c]2 Chron. xxxvi. 16; chap. iv. 10——[d]Isa. xxviii. 15——[e]Chap. xiv. 13

Verse 4. *These* are *poor*] They are ignorant; they have no education; they know no better.

Verse 5. *I will get me unto the great men*] Those whose circumstances and rank in life gave them opportunities of information which the others could not have, for the reasons already given.

These have altogether broken the yoke] These have cast aside all restraint, have acted above law, and have trampled all moral obligations under their feet; and into their vortex the lower classes of the people have been swept away. *Solon* said, "The laws are like cobwebs; they entangle the small fry, but the great ones go through them, and carry all away with them."

Verse 6. *Wherefore a lion*] Nebuchadnezzar, according to the general opinion; who is called here a *lion* for his courage and violence, a *bear* for his rapaciousness, and a *leopard* for his activity. *Dahler* supposes the *Scythians* to be intended, both here and in chap. iv. 7.

Verse 7. *In the harlots' houses.*] In places consecrated to idolatry. In the language of the prophets, adultery generally signifies *idolatry.* This we have often seen.

Verse 8. *After his neighbour's wife.*] This may have been *literally* true, as the abominations of idolatry, in which they were so deeply practised, would necessarily produce such a state of things as that here mentioned.

Verse 10. *Go ye up upon her walls*] This is the permission and authority given to the Chaldeans to pillage Jerusalem.

Take away her battlements] Some translate נטישות *netishoth, branches;* others, *vines.* Destroy the *branches,* cut down the *stem;* but do not damage the *root.* Leave so many of the people that the state may be regenerated. The *Septuagint, Syriac,* and *Arabic* read, "Leave her foundations, for they are the Lord's;" and this agrees with "Destroy, but make not a full end."

Verse 12. *They have belied the Lord*] כחשו *kichashu.* They have *denied* or disavowed the Lord.

It is *not he*] לוא הוא *lo hu, he is not;* there is no such being; therefore this evil shall not come upon us. On their premises, this conclusion was just. There is no judge; therefore there shall be no judgment. Thus they denied the Lord. They were atheists at heart.

Verse 13. *And the prophets shall become wind*] What are the prophets? Empty persons. Their words are wind; we hear the *sound* of their threatenings, but of the matter of the threatenings we shall hear no more.

And the word is *not in them*] There is no inspirer, but may their own predictions fall on their own heads! This seems the natural sense of this passage.

Verse 14. *Because ye speak this word*] Because ye thus treat my message, "I will make my words in thy mouth fire." They have said *they are but air;* but I will make them *fire,*

A. M. cir. 3392
B. C. cir. 612
Ol. cir. XLII. 1
TarquiniiPrisci,
R. Roman.,
cir. annum 5

hosts, Because ye speak this
word, [f]behold, I will make my
words in thy mouth fire, and this
people wood, and it shall devour them.
15 Lo, I will bring a [g]nation upon you
[h]from far, O house of Israel, saith the LORD:
it *is* a mighty nation, it *is* an ancient nation,
a nation whose language thou knowest not,
neither understandest what they say.
16 Their quiver *is* as an open sepulchre,
they *are* all mighty men.
17 And they shall eat up thine [i]harvest, and
thy bread, *which* thy sons and thy daughters
should eat: they shall eat up thy flocks and
thine herds: they shall eat up thy vines and
thy fig trees: they shall impoverish thy
fenced cities, wherein thou trustedst, with the
sword.
18 Nevertheless in those days, saith the
LORD, I [k]will not make a full end with you.
19 And it shall come to pass, when ye shall
say, [l]Wherefore doeth the LORD our God all
these *things* unto us? then shalt thou answer
them, Like as ye have [m]forsaken me, and
served strange gods in your land, so [n]shall ye
serve strangers in a land *that is*
not yours.

A. M. cir. 3392
B. C. cir. 612
Ol. cir. XLII. 1
TarquiniiPrisci,
R. Roman.,
cir. annum 5

20 Declare this in the house of
Jacob, and publish it in Judah,
saying,
21 Hear now this, O [o]foolish people, and
without [p]understanding; which have eyes, and
see not; which have ears, and hear not:
22 [q]Fear ye not me? saith the LORD: will
ye not tremble at my presence, which have
placed the sand *for* the [r]bound of the sea by
a perpetual decree, that it cannot pass it: and
though the waves thereof toss themselves, yet
can they not prevail; though they roar, yet
can they not pass over it?
23 But this people hath a revolting and a
rebellious heart; they are revolted and gone.
24 Neither say they in their heart, Let us
now fear the LORD our God, [s]that giveth rain,
both the [t]former and the latter, in his
season: [u]he reserveth unto us the appointed
weeks of the harvest.
25 [v]Your iniquities have turned away these
things, and your sins have withholden good
things from you.
26 For among my people are found wicked

[f]Ch. i. 9——[g]Deut. xxviii. 49; Isa. v. 26; ch. i. 15; vi. 22——[h]Isa. xxxix. 3; ch. iv. 16——[i]Lev. xxvi. 16; Deut. xxviii. 31, 33——[k]Ch. iv. 27——[l]Deut. xxix. 24, &c.; 1 Kings ix. 8, 9; ch. xiii. 22; xvi. 10——[m]Ch. ii. 13 [n]Deut. xxviii. 48——[o]Isa. vi. 9; Ezek. xii. 2; Matt. xiii. 14; John xii. 40; Acts xxviii. 26; Rom. xi. 8——[p]Heb. *heart;* Hos. vii. 11——[q]Rev. xv. 4——[r]Job xxvi. 10; xxxviii. 10, 11; Psa. civ. 9; Prov. viii. 29——[s]Psa. cxlvii. 8; ch. xiv. 22; Matt. v. 45; Acts xiv. 17——[t]Deut. xi. 14; Joel ii. 23——[u]Gen. viii. 22——[v]Chap. iii. 3

and a *fire* too that shall *devour them.* And how this was to be done, and by whom, is mentioned in the next verse.

Verse 15. *I will bring a nation*] The *Scythians*, says *Dahler;* the *Babylonians*, whose antiquity was great, that empire being founded by Nimrod.

Whose language thou knowest not] The Chaldee, which, though a dialect of the Hebrew, is so very different in its words and construction, that in hearing it spoken they could not possibly collect the meaning of what was said.

Verse 16. *Their quiver* is *an open sepulchre*] They are such exact archers as never to miss their mark; every arrow is sure to slay one man.

Verse 18. *I will not make a full end*] There are more evils in store for you. You shall not only be spoiled, and all your property destroyed, but ye shall be carried into *captivity; and ye shall serve strangers in a land that is not yours*, ver. 19.

Verse 22. *Which have placed the sand* for *the bound of the sea*] What can I not do, who confine the sea, that enormous mass of waters, and prevent it from overflowing the earth; not by immense *mountains* and *rocks*, but by the *sand*, no particle of which is in cohesion with another? The most tremendous waves cannot displace nor pass over this simple barrier.

Verse 23. *They are revolted and gone.*] They have abandoned me, and are gone farther and farther into transgression. They are gone *entirely* away from truth and righteousness.

Verse 24. *Giveth rain, both the former and the latter*] See the note on chap. iii. 3.

The appointed weeks of the harvest.] As the early rains fell in the northern parts of Judea about the end of *September*, in the *civil year* of the Hebrews, so the *latter rains* fell before harvest, in the months of *March* and *April*. The appointed weeks of the harvest were those which fell between the *passover* and *pentecost*. In the southern parts the harvest was earlier than in the northern. Dr. *Blayney* translates, "A sufficiency of the appointed things of harvest he secureth to us."

If the word שבעת *weeks*, be read with a שׂ *sin* instead of a שׁ *shin*, it will signify *fulness* or *sufficiency;* and thus the *Septuagint* and *Vulgate* have read it. I think the present reading is much to be preferred. God *appoints a harvest time*, and in his good providence he generally gives *harvest weather*.

Verse 25. *Your iniquities have turned away these* things] When these appointed weeks of harvest do not come, should we not examine and see whether this be not in God's judgments? Have not our iniquities turned away these good things from *us?*

Verse 26. *They lay wait, as he that setteth*

A. M. cir. 3392 B. C. cir. 612 Ol. cir. XLII. 1 TarquiniiPrisci, R. Roman., cir. annum 5

men: [w]they [x]lay wait, as he that
setteth snares; they set a trap,
they catch men.
27 As a [y]cage is full of birds,
so *are* their houses full of deceit: therefore
they are become great, and waxen rich:
28 They are waxen [z]fat, they shine: yea,
they overpass the deeds of the wicked: they
judge not [a]the cause, the cause of the fatherless, [b]yet they prosper; and the right of the
needy do they not judge.
29 [c]Shall I not visit for
these *things?* saith the LORD:
shall not my soul be avenged on such a nation as
this?
30 [d]A wonderful and [e]horrible thing is committed in the land;
31 The prophets prophesy [f]falsely, and the
priests [g]bear rule by their means; and my
people [h]love *to have it* so: and what will ye
do in the end thereof?

[w]Or, *they pry as fowlers lie in wait*——[x]Prov. i. 11, 17, 18; Hab. i. 15——[y]Or, *coop*——[z]Deut. xxxii. 15 [a]Isa. i. 23; Zech. vii. 10——[b]Job xii. 6; Psa. lxxiii. 12; chap. xii. 1

[c]Ver. 9; Mal. iii. 5——[d]Or, *Astonishment and filthiness*——[e]Chap. xxiii. 14; Hos. vi. 10——[f]Chap. xiv. 14; xxiii. 25, 26; Ezek. xiii. 6——[g]Or, *take into their hands*——[h]Mic. ii. 11

snares] A metaphor taken from *fowlers*, who, having fixed their nets, lie down and keep out of sight, that when birds come, they may be ready to draw and entangle them.

Verse 27. *As a cage is full of birds*] There is no doubt that the reference here is to a *decoy* or *trap-cage*, as Dr. *Blayney* has rendered it; in these the fowlers put several tame birds, which when the wild ones see, they come and light on the cage, and fall into the snare.

Verse 28. *They judge not the cause, yet they prosper*] Perhaps we might be justified in translating, "And shall they prosper?"

Verse 30. *A wonderful and horrible thing is committed in the land*] *Dahler* translates: "Strange crimes and horrible trespasses have been committed in the land." These have been already detailed; but this may refer to what follows.

Verse 31. *The prophets prophesy falsely*] The false prophets predict favourable things, that they may please both the princes and the people.

The priests bear rule by their means] The false prophets affording them all that their influence and power can procure, to enable them to keep their places, and feed on the riches of the Lord's house.

And my people love to have it *so*] Are perfectly satisfied with this state of things, because they are permitted to continue in their sins without reproof or restraint. The prophets and the priests united to deceive and ruin the people. The prophets gave out false predictions; by their means the priests got the government of the people into their own hands; and so infatuated were the people that they willingly abandoned themselves to those blind guides, and would not hearken to the voice of any reformer. In my Old Bible the words stand thus:—**Stonyng and merbailis ben made in the erthe, prophets prophecieden lesing; and prestis flappiden with joye with ther hondes, and my peple lobid siche thingis.** False prophets and worldly priests have been in all ages the bane of religion, and the ruin of many souls. When profligate people stand up on behalf of profligate priests, corruption must then be at its height.

CHAPTER VI

Jeremiah, in the spirit of prophecy, seeing the Chaldeans on their march, bids his people set up the usual signals of distress, and spread the general alarm to betake themselves to flight, 1. *Then, by a beautiful allusion to the custom of shepherds moving their flocks to the richest pastures, Jerusalem is singled out as a place devoted to be eaten up or trodden down by the armies of the Chaldeans, who are called up against her, and whose ardour and impatience are so great that the soldiers, when they arrive in the evening, regret they have no more day, and desire to begin the attack without waiting for the light of the morning,* 2–5. *God is then represented as animating and directing the besiegers against this guilty city, which sinned as incessantly as a fountain flows,* 6, 7, *although warned of the fatal consequence,* 8. *He intimates also, by the gleaning of the grapes, that one invasion should carry away the remains of another, till their disobedience, hypocrisy, and other sins should end in their total overthrow,* 9–15. *And to show that God is clear when he judgeth, he mentions his having in vain admonished and warned them, and calls upon the whole world to witness the equity of his proceedings,* 16–18, *in punishing this perverse and hypocritical people,* 19, 20, *by the ministry of the cruel Chaldeans,* 21–23. *Upon this a chorus of Jews is introduced expressing their fears and alarm,* 24, 25; *to which the prophet echoes a response full of sympathy and tenderness,* 26. *The concluding verses, by metaphors taken from the process of refining gold and silver, represent all the methods hitherto used to amend them as wholly ineffectual,* 27–30.

A. M. cir. 3392
B. C. cir. 612
Ol. cir. XLII. 1
TarquiniiPrisci,
R. Roman.,
cir. annum 5

O YE children of Benjamin,
gather yourselves to flee out
of the midst of Jerusalem, and
blow the trumpet in Tekoa, and
set up a sign of fire in [a]Beth-haccerem: [b]for
evil appeareth out of the north, and great
destruction.
2 I have likened the daughter of Zion to a
[c]comely and delicate *woman.*
3 The shepherds with their flocks shall come
unto her; [d]they shall pitch *their* tents against
her round about; they shall feed every one
in his place.
4 [e]Prepare ye war against her; arise, and
let us go up [f]at noon. Wo unto us! for the
day goeth away, for the shadows of the evening are stretched out.
5 Arise, and let us go by night, and let us
destroy her palaces.
6 For thus hath the LORD of hosts said,
Hew ye down trees, and [g]cast a mount against
Jerusalem: this *is* the city to be visited; she
is wholly oppression in the midst of her.
7 [h]As a fountain casteth out her waters, so
she casteth out her wickedness: [i]violence and
spoil is heard in her; before me
continually *is* grief and wounds.

A. M. cir. 3392
B. C. cir. 612
Ol. cir. XLII. 1
TarquiniiPrisci,
R. Roman.,
cir. annum 5

8 Be thou instructed, O Jerusalem, lest [k]my soul [l]depart from
thee; lest I make thee desolate, [m]a land not
inhabited.
9 Thus saith the LORD of hosts, They shall
thoroughly glean the remnant of Israel as a
vine: turn back thine hand as a grape-gatherer into the baskets.
10 To whom shall I speak, and give warning, that they may hear? behold, their [n]ear
is uncircumcised, and they cannot hearken:
behold, [o]the word of the LORD is unto them
a reproach; they have no delight in it.
11 Therefore I am full of the fury of the
LORD; [p]I am weary with holding in: I will
pour it out [q]upon the children abroad, and
upon the assembly of young men together: for
even the husband with the wife shall be taken,
the aged with *him that is* full of days.
12 And [r]their houses shall be turned unto
others, *with their* fields and wives together:
for I will stretch out my hand upon the inhabitants of the land, saith the LORD.

[a]Neh. iii. 14——[b]Chap. i. 14; iv. 6——[c]Or, *dwelling at home*——[d]1 Kings xxv. 1, 4; chap. iv. 17——[e]Ch. li. 27; Joel iii. 9——[f]Chap. xv. 8——[g]Or, *pour out the engine of shot*——[h]Isa. lvii. 20——[i]Psa. lv. 9, 10, 11; chap. xx. 8; Ezek. vii. 11, 23——[k]Ezek. xxiii. 18; Hos. ix. 12——[l]Heb. *be loosed* or *disjointed*——[m]Lev. xvi. 22; 2 Sam. xxiv. 6, in the margin——[n]Chap. vii. 26; Acts vii. 61; see Exod. vi. 12——[o]Chap. xx. 8——[p]Chap. xx. 9——[q]Chap. ix. 21——[r]Deut. xxviii. 30; chap. viii. 10

NOTES ON CHAP. VI

Verse 1. *O ye children of Benjamin, gather yourselves to flee*] As the invading armies are fast approaching, the prophet calls on the inhabitants of Jerusalem to sound an alarm, and collect all the people to arm themselves and go against the invaders. They are called the children of Benjamin, because Jerusalem was in the tribe of Benjamin.

Tekoa] Was a city about *twelve* miles to the south of Jerusalem.

Beth-haccerem] Was the name of a small village situated on an eminence between Jerusalem and Tekoa. On this they were ordered to set up a *beacon*, or *kindle a large fire*, which might be seen at a distance, and give the people to understand that an enemy was entering the land.

Out of the north] From *Babylon*. The *Scythians.—Dahler.*

Verse 3. *The shepherds with their flocks*] The chiefs and their battalions. The invading army is about to spoil and waste all the fertile fields round about the city, while engaged in the siege.

Verse 4. *Prepare ye war against her*] The words of the invaders exciting each other to the assault, and impatient lest any time should be lost; lest the besieged should have time to strengthen themselves, or get in supplies.

Verse 5. *Arise, and let us go by night*] Since we have lost the day, let us not lose the night; but, taking advantage of the darkness, let us make a powerful assault while they are under the impression of terror.

Verse 6. *Hew ye down trees*] To form machines.

And cast a mount] That may overlook the city, on which to place our engines.

This is the city to be visited] We are sure of success, for their God will deliver it into our hands; for it is full of oppression, and he has consigned it to destruction.

Verse 7. *As a fountain casteth out her waters*] The inhabitants are incessant in their acts of iniquity; they do nothing but sin.

Verse 8. *Be thou instructed*] Still there is respite: if they would even now return unto the Lord with all their heart, the advancing Chaldeans would be arrested on their march and turned back.

Verse 9. *They shall thoroughly glean the remnant of Israel as a vine: turn back thine hand*] The Chaldeans are here exhorted to *turn back* and glean up the remnant of the inhabitants that were left after the capture of Jerusalem; for even that remnant did not profit by the Divine judgments that fell on the inhabitants at large.

Verse 10. *The word of the Lord is unto them a reproach*] It is an object of *derision; they despise it.*

Verse 11. *I am full of the fury of the Lord*] God has given me a dreadful revelation of the judgments he intends to inflict: my soul is

A. M. cir. 3392
B. C. cir. 612
Ol. cir. XLII. 1
TarquiniiPrisci,
R. Roman.,
cir. annum 5

13 For from the least of them
even unto the greatest of them
every one *is* given to [s]covetous-
ness; and from the prophet even
unto the priest every one dealeth falsely.
14 They have [t]healed also the [u]hurt *of the*
daughter of my people slightly, [v]saying, Peace,
peace; when *there is* no peace.
15 Were they [w]ashamed when they had committed abomination? nay, they were not at
all ashamed, neither could they blush: therefore they shall fall among them that fall: at
the time *that* I visit them they shall be cast
down, saith the LORD.
16 Thus saith the LORD, Stand ye in the
ways, and see, and ask for the [x]old paths,
where *is* the good way, and walk therein, and
ye shall find [y]rest for your souls. But they
said, We will not walk *therein*.
17 Also I set [z]watchmen over you, *saying*,
Hearken to the sound of the trumpet. But
they said, We will not hearken.
18 Therefore hear, ye nations, and know, O
congregation, what *is* among them.
19 [a]Hear, O earth: behold, I will bring evil
upon this people, *even* [b]the fruit of their
thoughts, because they have not
hearkened unto my words, nor to
my law, but rejected it.
20 [c]To what purpose cometh
there to me incense [d]from Sheba, and the
sweet cane from a far country? [e]your burnt-
offerings *are* not acceptable, nor your sacrifices sweet unto me.
21 Therefore thus saith the LORD, Behold,
I will lay stumbling blocks before this people,
and the fathers and the sons together shall
fall upon them; the neighbour and his friends
shall perish.
22 Thus saith the LORD, Behold, a people
cometh from the [f]north country, and a great
nation shall be raised from the sides of the
earth.
23 They shall lay hold on bow and spear;
they *are* cruel, and have no mercy; their voice
[g]roareth like the sea; and they ride upon
horses, set in array as men for war against
thee, O daughter of Zion.
24 We have heard the fame thereof: our
hands wax feeble: [h]anguish hath taken hold
of us, *and* pain, as of a woman in travail.
25 Go not forth into the field, nor walk by

A. M. cir. 3392
B. C. cir. 612
Ol. cir. XLII. 1
TarquiniiPrisci,
R. Roman.,
cir. annum 5

[s]Isa. lvi. 11; chap. viii. 10; xiv. 18; xxiii. 11; Mic. iii. 5, 11——[t]Chap. viii. 11; Ezek. xiii. 10——[u]Heb. *bruise*, or *breach*——[v]Chap. iv. 10; xiv. 13; xxiii. 17 [w]Chap. iii. 3; viii. 12——[x]Isa. viii. 20; chap. xviii. 15; Mal. iv. 4; Luke xvi. 29——[y]Matt. xi. 29

[z]Isa. xxi. 11; lviii. 1; chap. xxv. 4; Ezek. iii. 17; Hab. ii. 1——[a]Isa. i. 2——[b]Prov. i. 31——[c]Psa. xl. 6; l. 7, 8, 9; Isa. i. 11; lvi. 3; Amos v. 21; Mic. vi. 6, &c.——[d]Isa. lx. 6——[e]Ch. vii. 21——[f]Ch. i. 15; v. 15; x. 22; l. 41, 42, 43——[g]Isa. v. 30——[h]Ch. iv. 31; xiii. 21; xlix. 24; l. 43

burdened with this prophecy. I have endeavoured to suppress it; but I must pour it forth upon the *children*, on the *young people*, on *husbands* and *wives*, on the *old* and the *superannuated*. All must partake in these judgments.

Verse 14. *They have healed also the hurt* of the daughter *of my people slightly*] *Of the daughter* is not in the text, and is here improperly added: it is, however, in some MSS.

Peace, peace] Ye shall have *prosperity*—when there was none; and when God had determined that there should be none. Here the *prophets prophesied falsely;* and the people continued in sin, being deceived by the priests and the prophets.

Verse 16. *Thus saith the Lord, Stand ye in the ways, and see*] Let us observe the metaphor. A *traveller* is going to a particular city; he comes to a place where the road divides into several paths, he is afraid of going astray; he stops short,—endeavours to find out the right path: he cannot fix his choice. At last he sees another traveller; he inquires of him, gets proper directions—proceeds on his journey—arrives at the desired place—and *reposes* after his fatigue. There is an excellent sermon on these words in the works of our first poet, *Geoffrey Chaucer;* it is among the Canterbury Tales, and is called *Chaucer's Tale*. The text, I find, was read by him as it appears in my old MS. Bible:—**Standith upon weies and seeth, and asketh of the olde pathes; What is the good weie? and goth in it, and gee schul fynden refresching to your soulis.** The soul needs *rest;* it can only find this by *walking in the good way*. The *good way* is that which has been *trodden* by the *saints from the beginning:* it is the *old way*, the way of *faith* and *holiness*. BELIEVE, LOVE, OBEY; be *holy*, and be *happy*. This is the *way;* let us *inquire* for it, and *walk* in it. But these bad people said, *We will not walk* in it. Then they took another way, walked over the precipice, and fell into the bottomless pit; where, instead of *rest*, they find—

——————a fiery deluge, fed
With ever-burning sulphur, unconsumed.

Verse 17. *I set watchmen*] I have sent prophets to warn you.

Verse 20. *Incense from Sheba*] Sheba was in Arabia, famous for the best incense. It was situated towards the southern extremity of the peninsula of Arabia; and was, in respect of Judea, *a far country*.

And the sweet cane from a far country] The *calamus aromaticus*, which, when dried and pulverized, yields a very fine aromatic smell; see on Isa. xliii. 24. This was employed in making the *holy anointing oil*. See Exod. xxx. 23.

Verse 23. *They shall lay hold on bow and spear*] Still pointing out the Chaldeans; or

A. M. cir. 3392 B. C. cir. 612 Ol. cir. XLII. 1 TarquiniiPrisci, R. Roman., cir. annum 5

the way; for the sword of the
enemy *and* fear *is* on every side.
26 O daughter of my people,
[i]gird *thee* with sackcloth, [k]and
wallow thyself in ashes: [l]make thee mourning,
as for an only son, most bitter lamentation:
for the spoiler shall suddenly come upon us.
27 I have set thee *for* a tower *and* [m]a fortress
among my people, that thou mayest know and
try their way.
28 [n]They *are* all grievous revolters, [o]walking with slanders:
they are [p]brass and iron; they
are all corrupters.
29 The bellows are burned, the lead is
consumed of the fire; the founder melteth
in vain: for the wicked are not plucked
away.
30 [q]Reprobate [r]silver shall *men* call them,
because the LORD hath rejected them.

[i]Chap. iv. 8——[k]Chap. xxv. 34; Mic. i. 10——[l]Zech. xii. 10——[m]Chap. i. 18; xv. 20——[n]Chap. v. 23——[o]Chap. ix. 4——[p]Ezek. xxii. 18——[q]Isa. i. 22——[r]Or, *refuse silver*

according to *Dahler*, the *Scythians*, who had before their invasion of Palestine overrun many parts of Asia, and had spread consternation wherever their name was heard.

Verse 27. *I have set thee for a tower and a fortress*] Dr. *Blayney* translates, *I have appointed thee to make an assay among my people.* The words refer to the *office of an assayer of silver and gold;* and the *manner* of *assaying* here intended is by the *cupel*, a flat broad iron ring filled with the ashes of burnt bones. To separate the alloy from the silver they add a portion of *lead;* and when all is fused together, and brought into a state of ebullition, the cupel absorbs the lead, and with it the dross or alloy, and the silver is left pure and motionless on the top of the cupel. The people are here represented under the notion of *alloyed silver*. They are full of *impurities;* and they are put into the hands of the prophet, the *assayer*, to be purified. The *bellows* are placed, the *fire* is lighted up, but all to no purpose: so intensely commixed is the alloy with the silver, that it cannot be separated. The nozzle of the *bellows* is even *melted* with the intensity of the fire used to effect the refinement; and the *lead is carried off* by the action of the heat; and the *assayer melteth in vain*, for the alloy still continues in union with the metal. The assayer gives up the process,—will not institute one more expensive or tedious—pronounces the mass unfit to be coined, and denominates it *reprobate silver*, ver. 30. Thus, the evil habits and dispositions of the Israelites were so ingrained that they would not yield to either the *ordinary* or *extraordinary* means of salvation. God pronounces them *reprobate silver*,—not sterling,—full of alloy;—having neither the image nor the superscription of the Great King either on their hearts or on their conduct. Thus he gave them up as incorrigible, and their adversaries prevailed against them. This should be a warning to other nations, and indeed to the Christian Church; for if God did not spare the natural branches, neither will he spare these.

CHAPTER VII

Here begins another section of prophecy, ending with the ninth *chapter. It opens with exhorting to amendment of life, without which the confidence of the Jews in their temple is declared vain,* 1–11. *God bids them take warning from the fate of their brethren the Israelites, who had been carried away captive on account of their sins without any regard to that sacred place,* (Shiloh,) *where the ark of God once resided,* 12–15. *The iniquities of Judah are so great in the sight of God that the prophet is commanded not to intercede for the people,* 16; *the more especially as they persisted in provoking God by their idolatrous practices,* 17–20. *The Jewish sacrifices, if not accompanied with obedience to the moral law, are of no avail,* 21–24. *Notwithstanding the numerous messages of mercy from the time of the exodus, the people revolted more and more; and have added to their other sins this horrible evil,* the setting up of their abominations in the temple of Jehovah; *or, in other words, they have encumbered the Mosaic economy, which shadowed forth the glorious truths of Christianity, with a heterogeneous admixture of the idolatrous, impure, and cruel rites of heathenism; consequently, the whole land shall be utterly desolated,* 25–34.

A. M. cir. 3394 B. C. cir. 610 Ol. cir. XLII. 3 TarquiniiPrisci, R. Roman., cir. annum 7

THE word that came to Jeremiah from the LORD, saying,
2 [a]Stand in the gate of the
LORD's house, and proclaim there
this word, and say, Hear the
word of the LORD, all *ye of* Judah, that enter in at these gates
to worship the LORD.

[a]Jeremiah, chap. xxvi. 2

NOTES ON CHAP. VII

Verse 1. *The word that came to Jeremiah*] This prophecy is supposed to have been delivered in the *first year of the reign of Jehoiakim*, son of Josiah, who, far from following the example of his pious father, restored idolatry, maintained bad priests and worse prophets, and filled Jerusalem with abominations of all kinds.

A. M. cir. 3394
B. C. cir. 610
Ol. cir. XLII. 3
TarquiniiPrisci,
R. Roman.,
cir. annum 7

3 Thus saith the LORD of hosts, the God of Israel, [b]Amend your ways and your doings, and I will cause you to dwell in this place.

4 [c]Trust ye not in lying words, saying, The temple of the LORD, The temple of the LORD, The temple of the LORD, *are* these.

5 For if ye throughly amend your ways and your doings; if ye throughly [d]execute judgment between a man and his neighbour;

6 *If* ye oppress not the stranger, the fatherless, and the widow, and shed not innocent blood in this place, [e]neither walk after other gods to your hurt:

7 [f]Then will I cause you to dwell in this place, in [g]the land that I gave to your fathers, for ever and ever.

8 Behold, [h]ye trust in [i]lying words, that cannot profit.

9 [k]Will ye steal, murder, and commit adultery, and swear falsely, and burn incense unto Baal, and [l]walk after other gods whom ye know not;

10 [m]And come and stand before me in this house, [n]which [o]is called by my name, and say, We are delivered to do all these abominations?

11 Is [p]this house, which is called by my name, become a [q]den of robbers in your eyes? Behold, even I have seen *it,* saith the LORD.

A. M. cir. 3394
B. C. cir. 610
Ol. cir. XLII. 3
TarquiniiPrisci,
R. Roman.,
cir. annum 7

12 But go ye now unto [r]my place which *was* in Shiloh, [s]where I set my name at the first, and see [t]what I did to it for the wickedness of my people Israel.

13 And now, because ye have done all these works, saith the LORD, and I spake unto you, [u]rising up early and speaking, but ye heard not; and I [v]called you, but ye answered not;

14 Therefore will I do unto *this* house, which is called by my name, wherein ye trust, and unto the place which I gave to you and to your fathers, as I have done to [w]Shiloh.

15 And I will cast you out of my sight, [x]as I have cast out all your brethren, [y]*even* the whole seed of Ephraim.

16 Therefore [z]pray not thou for this people, neither lift up cry nor prayer for them, neither make intercession to me: [a]for I will not hear thee.

17 Seest thou not what they do in the cities of Judah and in the streets of Jerusalem?

[b]Chap. xviii. 11; xxvi. 13——[c]Mic. iii. 11——[d]Chap. xxii. 3——[e]Deut. vi. 14, 15; viii. 19; xi. 28; chap. xiii. 10——[f]Deut. iv. 40——[g]Chap. iii. 18——[h]Ver. 4——[i]Chap. v. 31; xiv. 13, 14——[k]1 Kings xviii. 21; Hos. iv. 1, 2; Zeph. i. 5——[l]Exod. xx. 3; ver. 6——[m]Ezek. xxiii. 39——[n]Heb. *whereupon my name is called*——[o]Ver. 11, 14, 30; chap. xxxii. 34; xxxiv. 15——[p]Isa. lvi. 7

[q]Matt. xxi. 13; Mark xi. 17; Luke xix. 46——[r]Josh. xviii. 1; Judg. xviii. 31——[s]Deut. xii. 11——[t]1 Sam. iv. 10, 11; Psa. lxxviii. 60; chap. xxvi. 6——[u]2 Chron. xxxvi. 15; ver. 25; chap. xi. 7——[v]Prov. i. 24; Isa. lxv. 12; lxvi. 4——[w]1 Sam. iv. 10, 11; Psa. lxxviii. 60; chap. xxvi. 6——[x]2 Kings xvii. 23——[y]Psa. lxxviii. 67, 68——[z]Exod. xxxii. 10; chap. xi. 14; xiv. 11——[a]Chap. xv. 1

Verse 2. *Stand in the gate of the Lord's house*] There was a show of public worship kept up. The temple was considered God's residence; the usual ceremonies of religion restored by Josiah were still observed; and the people were led to consider the temple and its services as *sacred things*, which would be preservatives to them in case of the threatened invasion.

Verse 4. *The temple of the Lord*] In the *Chaldee* the passage stands thus:—"Do not trust in the words of lying prophets, which say, Before the temple of the Lord ye shall worship; Before the temple of the Lord ye shall sacrifice; Before the temple of the Lord ye shall adore; thrice in the year ye shall appear before it." This the *Targumist* supposes to have been the reason why the words are here *thrice* repeated. They rather seem to express the conviction which the people had, that they should be safe while their temple service continued; for they supposed that God would not give it up into profane hands. But *sacred places* and *sacred symbols* are nothing in the sight of God when the heart is not right with him.

Verse 5. *If ye throughly amend your ways*] Literally, *If in making good ye fully make good your ways.* God will no longer admit of *half-hearted* work. *Semblances* of piety cannot deceive him; he will not accept *partial* reformation; there must be a *thorough amendment.*

Verse 9. *Will ye steal, murder*] Will you continue to commit such abominations, and pretend to worship *me;* and thus defile the place that is called by my name; and so make my house a *den of robbers? I have seen this,*—and can you expect to escape condign punishment? Ye shall not escape.

Verse 12. *But go ye now unto my place which* was *in Shiloh*] See what I did to my tabernacle and ark formerly: after a long residence at Shiloh, for the iniquity of the priests and the people, I suffered it to fall into the hands of the Philistines, and to be carried captive into their land, and to be set up in the house of their idols. And because of *your* iniquities, I will deal with you and this temple in the same way; for as I spared not Shiloh, though my ark was there, but made it a victim of my wrath, so will I do to Jerusalem and her temple.

Verse 15. *The whole seed of Ephraim.*] Taken here for all the *ten* tribes, that of Ephraim being the principal.

Verse 16. *Therefore pray not thou for this people*] They have filled up the measure of their iniquity, and they must become examples of my justice. How terrible must the state of

A. M. cir. 3394 B. C. cir. 610 Ol. cir. XLII. 3 TarquiniiPrisci, R. Roman., cir. annum 7

18 [b]The children gather wood,
and the fathers kindle the fire,
and the women knead *their*
dough, to make cakes to the
[c]queen of heaven, and to [d]pour out drink-
offerings unto other gods, that they may provoke me to anger.

19 [e]Do they provoke me to anger? saith
the LORD: *do they* not *provoke* themselves to
the confusion of their own faces?

20 Therefore thus saith the Lord GOD; Behold, mine anger and my fury shall be poured
out upon this place, upon man, and upon
beast, and upon the trees of the field, and
upon the fruit of the ground; and it shall
burn, and shall not be quenched.

21 Thus saith the LORD of hosts, the God
of Israel; [f]Put your burnt-offerings unto your
sacrifices, and eat flesh.

22 [g]For I spake not unto your fathers, nor
commanded them in the day that I brought
them out of the land of Egypt, [h]concerning
burnt-offerings or sacrifices.

23 But this thing commanded I them, saying, [i]Obey my voice, and [k]I will be your
God, and ye shall be my people: and walk
ye in all the ways that I have
commanded you, that it may be
well unto you.

24 [l]But they hearkened not,
nor inclined their ear, but [m]walked in the
counsels *and* in the [n]imagination of their evil
heart, and [o]went[p] backward, and not forward.

25 Since the day that your fathers came forth
out of the land of Egypt unto this day I have
even [q]sent unto you all my servants the prophets; [r]daily rising up early and sending *them*:

26 [s]Yet they hearkened not unto me, nor
inclined their ear, but [t]hardened their neck:
[u]they did worse than their fathers.

27 Therefore [v]thou shalt speak all these
words unto them; but they will not hearken
to thee: thou shalt also call unto them; but
they will not answer thee.

28 But thou shalt say unto them, This *is* a
nation that obeyeth not the voice of the LORD
their God, [w]nor receiveth [x]correction: [y]truth
is perished, and is cut off from their mouth.

29 [z]Cut off thine hair, *O Jerusalem,* and
cast *it* away, and take up a lamentation on
high places; for the LORD hath rejected and
forsaken the generation of his wrath.

[b]Chap. xliv. 17, 19——[c]Or, *frame,* or *workmanship of heaven*——[d]Ch. xix. 13——[e]Deut. xxxii. 16, 21——[f]Isa. i. 11; ch. vi. 20; Amos v. 21; see Hos. viii. 13——[g]1 Sam. xv. 22; Psa. li. 16, 17; Hos. vi. 6——[h]Heb. *concerning the matter of*——[i]Exod. xv. 26; Deut. vi. 3; ch. xi. 4, 7 [k]Exod. xix. 5; Lev. xxvi. 12——[l]Psa. lxxxi. 11; chap. xi. 8——[m]Deut. xxix. 19; Psa. lxxxi. 12

[n]Or, *stubbornness*——[o]Heb. *were*——[p]Chap. ii. 27; xxxii. 33; Hos. iv. 16——[q]2 Chron. xxxvi. 15; chap. xxv. 4; xxix. 19——[r]Ver. 13——[s]Ver. 24; chap. xi. 8; xvii. 23; xxv. 3, 4——[t]Neh. ix. 17, 29; chap. xix. 15——[u]Ch. xvi. 12——[v]Ezek. ii. 7——[w]Chap. v. 3; xxxii. 33 [x]Or, *instruction*——[y]Chap. ix. 3——[z]Job i. 20; Isa. xv. 2; chap. xvi. 6; xlviii. 37; Mic. i. 16

that place be, where God refuses to pour out the spirit of supplication on his ministers and people in its behalf!

Verse 18. *The children gather wood*] Here is a description of a *whole family* gathered together, and acting unitedly in idolatrous worship. 1. The *children* go and collect wood, and bring it to the place of sacrifice. 2. The *fathers* lay it in order, and kindle a fire. 3. The *mother* and her *maids* knead dough, make their batch, and out of it form *cakes*, and bake them for the honour of the queen of heaven; most probably the *moon*, though perhaps not exclusive of the *sun* and *planets*, generally called the *host of heaven.* Family worship is a most amiable and becoming thing when performed according to truth. What a pity that so few families show such zeal for the worship of God as those apostate Israelites did for that of their idols!

Verse 21. *Put your burnt-offerings unto your sacrifices, and eat flesh.*] I will receive neither sacrifice nor oblation from you; therefore you may take the beasts intended for sacrifice, and slay and eat them for your *common nourishment.* See on ver. 29.

Verse 23. *This thing commanded I them—Obey my voice*] It was not *sacrifices* and *oblations* which I required of your fathers in the wilderness, but *obedience;* it was to *walk in that way* of righteousness which I have commanded; then I should have acknowledged them for *my people*, and I should have been *their God;* and then it would have *been well with them.* But to my commands, 1. *They hearkened not*—paid no regard to my word. 2. They *inclined not the ear*—showed no disposition to attend to my counsels. 3. They *walked in the imaginations of their evil heart*—followed its irregular and impure motions, rather than the holy dictates of my Spirit. 4. They *went backward and not forward.* Instead of becoming more wise, obedient, and holy, they grew more corrupt; so that they became more profligate than their fathers.

Verse 28. *Nor receiveth correction*] They have profited neither by *mercies* nor by *judgments:* blessings and corrections have been equally lost upon them.

Verse 29. *Cut off thine hair*] גזי נזרך *gozzi nizrech, shear thy nazarite.* The Nazarite was one who took upon him a particular vow, and *separated* himself from all worldly connexions for a certain time, that he might devote himself without interruption to the service of God; and during all this time no razor was to pass on his

A. M. cir. 3394 B. C. cir. 610 Ol. cir. XLII. 3 TarquiniiPrisci, R. Roman., cir. annum 7

30 For the children of Judah
have done evil in my sight, saith
the LORD: [a]they have set their
abominations in the house which
is called by my name, to pollute it.
31 And they have built the high [b]places
of Tophet, which *is* in the valley of the son of
Hinnom, to [c]burn their sons and their daughters in the fire; [d]which I commanded *them*
not, neither [e]came it into my heart.
32 Therefore, behold, [f]the days come, saith
the LORD, that it shall no more be called
Tophet, nor the valley of the son of Hinnom,
but the valley of slaughter: [g]for
they shall bury in Tophet, till
their be no place.
33 And the [h]carcasses of this
people shall be meat for the fowls of the heaven, and for the beasts of the earth; and none
shall fray *them* away.
34 Then will I cause to [i]cease from the
cities of Judah, and from the streets of Jerusalem, the voice of mirth, and the voice of
gladness, the voice of the bridegroom, and the
voice of the bride: for [k]the land shall be
desolate.

A. M. cir. 3394 B. C. cir. 610 Ol. cir. XLII. 3 TarquiniiPrisci, R. Roman., cir. annum 7

[a]2 Kings xxi. 4, 7; 2 Chron. xxxiii. 4, 5, 7; chap. xxiii. 11; xxxii. 34; Ezek. vii. 20; viii. 5, 6, &c.; Dan. ix. 27 [b]2 Kings xxiii. 10; chap. xix. 5; xxxii. 35——[c]Psa. cvi. 38——[d]See Deut. xvii. 3——[e]Heb. *came it upon my heart*——[f]Chap. xix. 6

[g]2 Kings xxiii. 10; chapter xix. 11; Ezekiel vi. 5 [h]Deut. xxviii. 26; Psa. lxxix. 2; chap. xii. 9; xvi. 4; xxxiv. 20——[i]Isa. xxiv. 7, 8; chap. xvi. 9; xxv. 10; xxxv. 11; Ezek. xxvi. 13; Hos. ii. 11; Rev. xviii. 23 [k]Lev. xxvi. 33; Isa. i. 7; iii. 26

head, for none of his hair was to be taken off. After the vow was over, he shaved his head and beard, and returned to society. See Num. vi. 2, &c., and the notes there. Jerusalem is here considered under the notion of a Nazarite, by profession devoted to the service of God: but that profession was empty; it was not accompanied with any suitable practice. God tells them here to cut off their hair; to make no vain pretensions to holiness or religion; to throw off the mask, and attempt no longer to impose upon themselves and others by their hypocritical pretensions. On the same ground he orders them, ver. 21, to devote to common use the animals destined for sacrifice; and to make no more vain shows of religion while their hearts were not right with him. Dr. *Blayney* thinks the address is to the *prophet*, who was a Nazarite by virtue of his office, and who was called to cut off his hair as a token of *mourning* for the desolations which were coming upon his people. That *cutting off the hair* was a sign of *distress* and *mourning* may be seen, Ezra ix. 3; Isa. xv. 2; Jer. xli. 5, &c. But I think the other the more natural construction.

On high places] That the lamentation may be heard to the greater distance.

The generation of his wrath.] Persons exposed to punishment: used here as *children of wrath*, Eph. ii. 3.

Verse 31. *Tophet—in the valley of the son of Hinnom*] Tophet was the place in that valley where the continual fires were kept up, in and through which they consecrated their children to Moloch.

Verse 32. *The valley of slaughter*] The place where the slaughtered thousands of this rebellious people shall be cast, in order to their being burnt, or becoming food for the beasts of the field and the fowls of the air, ver. 33. These words are repeated, and their meaning more particularly explained, chap. xix. 6-15.

Verse 34. *Then will I cause to cease—the voice of mirth*] There shall no longer be in Jerusalem any *cause of joy;* they shall neither marry nor be given in marriage, for the land shall be totally desolated. Such horrible sins required such a horrible punishment. And they must be *horrible*, when they move God to destroy the work of his own hands.

CHAPTER VIII

The judgments threatened in the last chapter are here declared to extend to the very dead, whose tombs should be opened, and the carcasses treated with every mark of indignity, 1–3. *From this the prophet returns to reprove them for their perseverance in transgression,* 4–6; *and for their thoughtless stupidity, which even the instinct of the brute creation, by a beautiful contrast, is made to upbraid,* 7–9. *This leads to farther threatenings, expressed in a variety of striking terms,* 10–13. *Upon which a chorus of Jews is introduced, expressing their terror on the news of the invasion,* 14, 15; *which is greatly heightened in the next verse by the prophet's hearing the snorting of Nebuchadnezzar's horses even from Dan, and then seeing the devastation made by his army,* 16, *whose cruelties God himself declares no entreaties will soften,* 17. *On this declaration the prophet laments most bitterly the fate of the daughter of his people, changing the scene unawares to the place of her captivity, where she is introduced answering in mournful responses to the prophet's dirge,* 18–22. *The variety of images and figures used to diversify the same subject is equally pleasing and astonishing. The dress is generally new, always elegant.*

A. M. cir. 3394
B. C. cir. 610
Ol. cir. XLII. 3
TarquiniiPrisci,
R. Roman.,
cir. annum 7

AT that time, saith the LORD, they shall bring out the bones of the kings of Judah, and the bones of his princes, and the bones of the priests, and the bones of the prophets, and the bones of the inhabitants of Jerusalem, out of their graves:

2 And they shall spread them before the sun, and the moon, and all the host of heaven, whom they have loved, and whom they have served, and after whom they have walked, and whom they have sought, and [a]whom they have worshipped: they shall not be gathered, [b]nor be buried; they shall be for [c]dung upon the face of the earth.

3 And [d]death shall be chosen rather than life by all the residue of them that remain of this evil family, which remain in all the places whither I have driven them, saith the LORD of hosts.

4 Moreover thou shalt say unto them, Thus saith the LORD; Shall they fall, and not arise? shall he turn away, and not return?

A. M. cir. 3394
B. C. cir. 610
Ol. cir. XLII. 3
TarquiniiPrisci,
R. Roman.,
cir. annum 7

5 Why *then* is this people of Jerusalem [e]slidden back by a perpetual backsliding? [f]they hold fast deceit, [g]they refuse to return.

6 [h]I hearkened and heard, *but* they spake not aright: no man repented him of his wickedness, saying, What have I done? every one turned to his course, as the horse rusheth into the battle.

7 Yea, [i]the stork in the heaven knoweth her appointed times; and [k]the turtle and the crane and the swallow observe the time of their coming; but [l]my people know not the judgment of the LORD.

8 How do ye say, We *are* wise, [m]and the

[a]2 Kings xxiii. 5; Ezek. iii. 16——[b]Chap. xxii. 19——[c]2 Kings ix. 36; Psa. lxxxiii. 10; chap. ix. 22; xvi. 4——[d]Job iii. 21, 22; vii. 15, 16; Rev. ix. 6

[e]Chap. vii. 24——[f]Chap. ix. 6——[g]Chap. v. 3——[h]2 Pet. iii. 9——[i]Isa. i. 3——[k]Cant. ii. 12——[l]Chap. v. 4, 5——[m]Rom. ii. 17

NOTES ON CHAP. VIII

Verse 1. *They shall bring out the bones*] This and the two following verses are a continuation of the preceding prophecy, and should not have been separated from the foregoing chapter.

In order to pour the utmost contempt upon the land, the victorious enemies dragged out of their graves, caves, and sepulchres, the bones of kings, princes, prophets, priests, and the principal inhabitants, and exposed them in the open air; so that they became, in the order of God's judgments, a reproach to them in the vain confidence they had in the *sun*, *moon*, and *the host of heaven*—all the planets and stars, whose worship they had set up in opposition to that of Jehovah. This custom of raising the bodies of the dead, and scattering their bones about, seems to have been general. It was the highest expression of hatred and contempt. *Horace* refers to it:—

Barbarus, heu, cineres insistet victor, et urbem
Eques sonante verberabit ungula:
Quæque carent ventis et solibus ossa Quirini
(Nefas videre) dissipabit insolens.

Epod. xvi. 11.

"Barbarians fell shall wanton with success,
Scatter the city's flaming ruins wide;
Or through her streets in vengeful triumph ride,
And her great founder's hallowed ashes spurn,
That slept uninjured in the sacred urn."

FRANCIS.

See this judgment referred to, Baruch ii. 24, 25.

Verse 4. *Moreover thou shalt say*] Dr. *Blayney* very properly observes, "In that part of the prophecy which follows next, the difference of speakers requires to be attended to; the transition being quick and sudden, but full of life and energy. The prophet at first, in the name of God, reproves the people's incorrigibility; he charges their wise ones with folly, and threatens them with grievous calamities, ver. 4-13. In the three next verses he seems to apostrophize his countrymen in his own person, and as one of the people that dwelt in the open towns, advising those that were in the like situation to retire with him into some of the fortified cities, and there wait the event with patience, since there was nothing but terror abroad, and the noise of the enemy, who had already begun to ravage the country, ver. 14-16. God speaks, ver. 17, and threatens to bring foes against them that should be irresistible. The prophet appears again in his own person, commiserating the daughter of his people, who is heard bewailing her forlorn case in a distant land; while the voice of God, like that of conscience, breaks in upon her complaints, and shows her that all this ruin is brought upon her by her own infidelities, ver. 18-20. The prophet once more resumes his discourse; he regrets that no remedy can be found to close up the wounds of his country, and pathetically weeps over the number of her slain, ver. 21, chap. ix. 1."

Shall they fall, and not arise? shall he turn away, and not return?] That is, It is as possible for sinners to return from their sin to God, for his grace is ever at hand to assist, as it is for God, who is pouring out his judgments, to return to them on their return to him. But these *held fast deceit, and refused to return;* they would not be undeceived.

Verse 6. *As the horse rusheth into the battle.*] This strongly marks the unthinking, careless desperation of their conduct.

Verse 7. *The stork in the heaven*] The *birds of passage* know the times of their going and return, and punctually observe them; they obey the dictates of nature, but my people do not obey my law.

Verse 8. *The pen of the scribes* is *in vain.*]

A. M. cir. 3394
B. C. cir. 610
Ol. cir. XLII. 3
TarquiniiPrisci, R. Roman., cir. annum 7

law of the LORD *is* with us? Lo, certainly [n]in vain made he *it;* the pen of the scribes *is* in vain.

9 [o]The [p]wise *men* are ashamed, they are dismayed and taken: lo, they have rejected the word of the LORD; and [q]what wisdom *is* in them?

10 Therefore [r]will I give their wives unto others, *and* their fields to them that shall inherit *them:* for every one from the least even unto the greatest is given to [s]covetousness, from the prophet even unto the priest every one dealeth falsely.

11 For they have [t]healed the hurt of the daughter of my people slightly, saying, [u]Peace, peace; when *there is* no peace.

12 Were they [v]ashamed when they had committed abomination; nay, they were not at all ashamed, neither could they blush: therefore shall they fall among them that fall: in the time of their visitation they shall be cast down, saith the LORD.

13 [w]I will surely consume them, saith the LORD: *there shall be* no grapes [x]on the vine, nor figs on the [y]fig tree, and the leaf shall fade; and *the things that* I have given them shall pass away from them.

14 Why do we sit still? [z]assemble yourselves, and let us enter into the defenced cities, and let us be silent there: for the LORD our God hath put us to silence, and given us [a]water of [b]gall to drink, because we have sinned against the LORD.

A. M. cir. 3394
B. C. cir. 610
Ol. cir. XLII. 3
TarquiniiPrisci, R. Roman., cir. annum 7

15 We [c]looked for peace, but no good *came; and* for a time of health, and behold trouble!

16 The snorting of his horses was heard from [d]Dan: the whole land trembled at the sound of the neighing of his [e]strong ones; for they are come, and have devoured the land, and [f]all that is in it; the city, and those that dwell therein.

17 For, behold, I will send serpents, cockatrices, among you, which *will* not *be* [g]charmed, and they shall bite you, saith the LORD.

18 *When* I would comfort myself against sorrow, my heart *is* faint [h]in me.

19 Behold the voice of the cry of the daughter of my people [i]because of them that dwell in [k]a far country: *Is* not the LORD in Zion? *is* not her king in her? Why have they [l]provoked me to anger with their graven images, *and* with strange vanities?

20 The harvest is past, the summer is ended, and we are not saved.

21 [m]For the hurt of the daughter of my people am I hurt; I am [n]black; astonishment hath taken hold on me.

22 *Is there* no [o]balm in Gilead; *is there* no physician there? why then is not the health of the daughter of my people [p]recovered?

[n]Or, *the false pen of the scribes worketh for falsehood;* Isa. x. 1——[o]Chap. vi. 15——[p]Or, *have they been ashamed,* &c.——[q]Heb. *the wisdom of what thing* [r]Deut. xxviii. 30; chap. vi. 12; Amos v. 11; Zeph. i. 13 [s]Isa. lvi. 11; chap. vi. 13——[t]Chap. vi. 14——[u]Ezek. xiii. 10——[v]Chap. iii. 3; vi. 15——[w]Or, *in gathering I will consume*——[x]Isa. v. 1, &c.; Joel i. 7——[y]Matt. xxi. 19; Luke xiii. 6, &c.——[z]Chap. iv. 5

[a]Chap. ix. 15; xxiii. 15——[b]Or, *poison*——[c]Chap. xiv. 19——[d]Chap. iv. 15——[e]Judg. v. 22; chap. xlvii. 3 [f]Heb. *the fulness thereof*——[g]Psa. lviii. 4, 5; Eccles. x. 11——[h]Heb. *upon*——[i]Heb. *because of the country of them that are far off*——[k]Isa. xxxix. 3——[l]Deut. xxxii. 21; Isa. i. 4——[m]Chap. iv. 19; ix. 1; xiv. 17 [n]Joel ii. 6; Nah. ii. 10——[o]Gen. xxxvii. 25; xliii. 11; chap. xlvi. 11; li. 8——[p]Heb. *gone up*

The *deceitful pen* of the scribes. They have written falsely, though they had the truth before them. It is too bold an assertion to say that "the Jews have never falsified the sacred oracles;" they have done it again and again. They have written falsities when they knew they were such.

Verse 10. *Therefore will I give their wives*] From this to the end of ver. 15 is repeated from chap. vi. 13-15.

Verse 16. *The snorting of his horses was* From this to the end of ver. 15 is repeated from Babylon to Jerusalem; and it was by this city, after the battle of Carchemish, that Nebuchadnezzar, in pursuing the Egyptians, entered Palestine.

The whole land trembled at the sound of the neighing of his strong ones] Of his *war horses.* This is a fine image; so terrible was the united neighing of the cavalry of the Babylonians that the reverberation of the air caused the ground to tremble. This is better, and more majestic, than the celebrated line of *Virgil:*—

Quadrupe-dante pu-trem soni-tu quatit ungula campum. It would be much easier to *shake the ground* with the *prancings* of many horses, than to cause an *earthquake* by the sound of the *neighing* of the troops of cavalry.

Verse 17. *I will send serpents*] These were symbols of the enemies that were coming against them; a foe that would rather slay them and destroy the land than get booty and ransom.

Verse 20. *The harvest is past*] The siege of Jerusalem lasted *two years;* for Nebuchadnezzar came against it in the *ninth* year of Zedekiah, and the city was taken in the *eleventh;* see 2 Kings xxv. 1-3. This seems to have been a proverb: "We expected deliverance the *first year*—none came. We hoped for it the *second year*—we are disappointed; we are not saved—no deliverance is come."

Verse 22. Is there *no balm in Gilead?*] Yes, the most excellent in the world. "Is there no physician there?" Yes, persons well skilled to apply it. "Why then is not the health of the daughter of my people recovered?" Because ye have not applied to the physician, nor used the balm. Ye die because ye will not use the remedy. But to apply this metaphor:—The *Israelites* are represented as a *man dying* through disease; and a disease for the cure of which the *balm of Gilead* was well known to be a *specific*, when judiciously applied by a physician. But though there be *balm* and a *physician*, the people are not cured; neither their spiritual nor political evils are removed. But what may all this *spiritually* mean? The people are morally diseased; they have sinned against God, and provoked him to destroy them. They are warned by the prophet to repent and turn to God: they refuse, and sin on. Destruction is come upon them. Might they not have avoided it? Yes. Was it the fault of God? No. Did he not send his prophets with the richest offers of mercy? Did he not give them time, the best instructions, and the most effectual means of returning to him? Has not *mercy*, the heavenly *balm*, been ever at hand? And has not God, the great *Physician*, been ever ready to apply it? Yes. Why then are they not converted and healed? Because they would not apply to the Divine Physician, nor receive the only remedy by which they could be spiritually healed. They, then, that sin against the only remedy must perish, because they might have had it, but would not. It is not because there is a deficiency of grace, nor of the means of grace, that men are not saved; but because they either make no use, or a bad use, of them. Jesus Christ, by the grace of God, has tasted death for every man; but few are saved, because *they* WILL NOT *come unto him that they may have life*.

In my old MS. Bible the text is rendered thus:—

Whether gumm is not in Galaad? Or a leche is not there? Why than the hid wounde of the daughter of my peple is not alle helid?

How shall they escape who neglect so great a salvation? Reader, lay this to heart; and, while there is time, apply heartily to the great Physician for thy cure.

CHAPTER IX

The prophet bitterly laments the terrible judgments about to be inflicted upon his countrymen, and points ou some of the evils which have provoked the Divine Majesty, 1–9. *Judea shall be utterly desolated, and the inhabitants transplanted into heathen countries,* 10–17. *In allusion to an ancient custom, a band of mourning women is called to lament over the ruins of Jerusalem,* 17, 18; *and even the funeral dirge is given in terms full of beauty, elegance, and pathos,* 19–22. *God is the fountain of all good; man, merely an instrument by which a portion of this good is distributed in the earth; therefore none should glory in his wisdom, might, or riches,* 23, 24. *The judgments of God shall fall, not upon the land of Judea only, but also upon many heathen nations,* 25, 26.

A. M. cir. 3394
B. C. cir. 610
Ol. cir. XLII. 3
TarquiniiPrisci, R. Roman., cir. annum 7

O [a]THAT[b] my head were
waters, and mine eyes a
fountain of tears, that I might
weep day and night for the slain
of the daughter of my people!
2 O that I had in the wilderness a lodging
place of way-faring men; that I might leave
my people, and go from them!
for [c]they *be* all adulterers, an
assembly of treacherous men.
3 And [d]they bend their tongues
like their bow *for* lies: but they are
not valiant for the truth upon the earth;
for they proceed from evil to evil, and

A. M. cir. 3394
B. C. cir. 610
Ol. cir. XLII. 3
TarquiniiPrisci, R. Roman., cir. annum 7

[a]Heb. *Who will give my head, &c.*——[b]Isa. xxii. 4; chap. iv. 19; xiii. 17; xiv. 17; Lam. ii. 11; iii. 48

[c]Chapter v. 7, 8——[d]Psalm lxiv. 3; Isaiah lix. 4 13, 15

NOTES ON CHAP. IX

Verse 1. *O that my head were waters*] מי יתן ראשי מים *mi yitten roshi mayim*, "who will give to my head waters?" My mourning for the sins and desolations of my people has already exhausted the source of tears: I wish to have a fountain opened there, that I may weep day and night for the slain of my people. This has been the sorrowful language of many a pastor who has preached long to a hardened, rebellious people, to little or no effect. This verse belongs to the preceding chapter.

Verse 2. *O that I had in the wilderness*] In the eastern countries there are no such *inns* or *houses of entertainment* as those in Europe. There are in different places public buildings called *caravanserais*, where travellers may *lodge:* but they are without *furniture* of any kind, and without food. Indeed they are often without a *roof*, being mere *walls* for a protection against the wild beasts of the desert. I wish to hide myself any where, in the most uncomfortable circumstances, that I may not be obliged any longer to witness the abominations of this people who are shortly to be visited with the most grievous punishments. Several interpreters suppose this to be the speech of God. I cannot receive this. I believe this verse to be spoken by the prophet, and that God proceeds with the next verse, and so on to the *ninth* inclusive.

Verse 3. *They bend their tongues* like *their bow for lies*] And their lies are such that they as fully *take away life* as the *keenest arrow* shot from the best strung bow. The false prophets told the people that there was no desolation at hand: the people believed them; made no preparation for their defence; did not return to the Lord; and the sword came and destroyed them.

They are not valiant for the truth] They are *bold* in sin, and *courageous* to support their

A. M. cir. 3394
B. C. cir. 610
Ol. cir. XLII. 3
TarquiniiPrisci,
R. Roman.,
cir. annum 7

they [e]know not me, saith the LORD.

4 [f]Take ye heed every one of his [g]neighbour, and trust ye not in any brother: for every brother will utterly supplant, and every neighbour will [h]walk with slanders.

5 And they will [i]deceive every one his neighbour, and will not speak the truth: they have taught their tongues to speak lies, *and* weary themselves to commit iniquity.

6 Thine habitation *is* in the midst of deceit; through deceit they refuse to know me, saith the LORD.

7 Therefore thus saith the LORD of hosts, Behold, [k]I will melt them, and try them; [l]for how shall I do for the daughter of my people?

8 Their tongue *is as* an arrow shot out; it speaketh [m]deceit: *one* speaketh [n]peaceably to his neighbour with his mouth, but [o]in heart he layeth [p]his wait.

9 [q]Shall I not visit them for these *things?* saith the LORD: shall not my soul be avenged on such a nation as this?

10 For the mountains will I take up a weeping and wailing, and [r]for the [s]habitations of the wilderness a lamentation, because they are [t]burned up, so that none can pass through *them;* neither can *men* hear the voice of the cattle; [u]both [v]the fowl of the heavens and the beast are fled; they are gone.

A. M. cir. 3394
B. C. cir. 610
Ol. cir. XLII. 3
TarquiniiPrisci,
R. Roman.,
cir. annum 7

11 And I will make Jerusalem [w]heaps, *and* [x]a den of dragons; and I will make the cities of Judah [y]desolate, without an inhabitant.

12 [z]Who *is* the wise man that may understand this? and *who is he* to whom the mouth of the LORD hath spoken, that he may declare it, for what the land perisheth *and* is burned up like a wilderness, that none passeth through?

13 And the LORD saith, Because they have forsaken my law which I set before them, and have not obeyed my voice, neither walked therein;

14 But have [a]walked after the [b]imagination of their own heart, and after Baalim, [c]which their fathers taught them:

15 Therefore thus saith the LORD of hosts, the God of Israel; Behold, I will [d]feed them, *even* this people, [e]with wormwood, and give them water of gall to drink.

16 I will [f]scatter them also among the heathen, whom neither they nor their fathers have known: [g]and I will send a sword after them till I have consumed them.

17 Thus saith the LORD of hosts, Consider ye, and call for [h]the mourning women, that

---

[e]1 Sam. ii. 12; Hos. iv. 1——[f]Chap. xii. 6; Mic. vii. 5, 6——[g]Or, *friend*——[h]Chap. vi. 28——[i]Or, *mock*
[k]Isa. i. 25; Mal. iii. 3——[l]Hos. xi. 8——[m]Psa. xii. 2; cxx. 3, ver. 3——[n]Psa. xxviii. 3; lv. 21——[o]Heb. *in the midst of him*——[p]Or, *wait for him*——[q]Ch. v. 9. 29
[r]Ch. xii. 4; xxiii. 10; Hos. iv. 3——[s]Or, *pastures*
[t]Or, *desolate*——[u]Heb. *from the fowl even to,* &c.——[v]Ch. iv. 25

[w]Isa. xxv. 2——[x]Isa. xiii. 22; xxxiv. 13; chap. x. 22
[y]Heb. *desolation*——[z]Psa. cvii. 43; Hos. xiv. 9
[a]Chap. iii. 17; vii. 43——[b]Or, *stubbornness*——[c]Gal. i. 14——[d]Psa. lxxx. 5——[e]Chap. viii. 14; xxii. 15; Lam. iii. 15, 19——[f]Lev. xxvi. 33; Deut. xxviii. 64
[g]Lev. xxvi. 33; chap. xliv. 27; Ezek. v. 2, 12——[h]2 Chron. xxxv. 25; Job iii. 8; Eccles. xii. 5; Amos v. 16; Matt. ix. 23

---

lies; but the *truth* they neither patronize nor support.

Verse 5. And *weary themselves to commit iniquity.*] O, what a drudgery is sin! and how much labour must a man take in order to get to hell! The tenth part of it, in *working together with God,* would bring him to the gate of glory.

Verse 7. *Behold, I will melt them*] I will put them in the *furnace of affliction,* and see if this will be a means of purging away their dross. See on chap. vi. 27.

Verse 10. *Both the fowl of the heavens and the beast are fled*] The land shall be so utterly devastated, that neither beast nor bird shall be able to live in it.

Verse 11. *A den of dragons*] תנים *tannim* is supposed to mean here *jackals;* the *chakal* is a beast frequent in the east, an attendant on the lion, the refuse of whose prey he devours. It is an animal that seems to have been bred originally between the *wolf* and the *dog.* The original is sometimes interpreted, *dragons, whales,* &c.

Verse 12. *Who is the wise man*] To whom has God revealed these things? He is the truly wise man. But it is to his prophet alone that God has revealed these things, and the speedy fulfilment of the predictions will show that the prophet has not spoken of himself.

Verse 15. *I will feed them—with wormwood*] They shall have the deepest sorrow and heaviest affliction. They shall have *poison* instead of *meat* and *drink.*

Verse 17. *Call for the mourning women*] Those whose office it was to make lamentations at funerals, and to bewail the dead, for which they received *pay.* This custom continues to the present in Asiatic countries. In *Ireland* this custom also prevails, which no doubt their ancestors brought from the east. I have often witnessed it, and have given a specimen of this elsewhere. See the note on Matt. ix. 23. The first lamentations for the dead consisted only in the sudden bursts of inexpressible grief, like that of David over his son Absalom, 2 Sam. xix. 4. But as men grew refined, it was not deemed

A. M. cir. 3394
B. C. cir. 610
Ol. cir. XLII. 3
TarquiniiPrisci,
R. Roman.,
cir. annum 7

they may come; and send for
cunning *women*, that they may
come:
18 And let them make haste,
and take up a wailing for us, that [i]our eyes
may run down with tears, and our eyelids gush
out with waters.
19 For a voice of wailing is heard out of
Zion, How are we spoiled! we are greatly
confounded, because we have forsaken the
land, because [k]our dwellings have cast *us* out.
20 Yet hear the word of the LORD, O ye
women, and let your ear receive the word of
his mouth, and teach your daughters wailing,
and every one her neighbour lamentation.
21 For death is come up into our windows,
and is entered into our palaces,
to cut off [l]the children from
without, *and* the young men
from the streets.
22 Speak, Thus saith the LORD, Even the
carcasses of men shall fall [m]as dung upon the
open field, and as the handful after the harvestman,
and none shall gather *them*.
23 Thus saith the LORD, [n]Let not the wise
man glory in his wisdom, neither let the
mighty *man* glory in his might, let not the
rich *man* glory in his riches:
24 But [o]let him that glorieth glory in this,
that he understandeth and knoweth me, that I
am the LORD which exercise loving-kindness,
judgment, and righteousness, in the earth:

A. M. cir. 3394
B. C. cir. 610
Ol. cir. XLII. 3
TarquiniiPrisci,
R. Roman.,
cir. annum 7

[i]Chap. xiv. 17——[k]Lev. xviii. 28; xx. 22——[l]Chap. vi. 11

[m]Chap. viii. 2; xvi. 4——[n]Eccles. ix. 11——[o]1 Cor. i. 31; 2 Cor. x. 17

sufficient for the surviving relatives to vent their sorrows in these natural, artless expressions of wo, but they endeavoured to join others as partners in their sorrows. This gave rise to the custom of *hiring persons to weep at funerals*, which the *Phrygians* and *Greeks* borrowed from the *Hebrews*. *Women* were generally employed on these occasions, because the tender passions being predominant in this sex, they succeeded better in their parts; and there were never wanting persons who would let out their services to hire on such occasions. Their lamentations were sung to the pipe as we learn from Matt. ix. 23. See the funeral ceremonies practised at the burial of Hector, as described by Homer:—

Οἱ δ' επει εισαγαγον κλυτα δωματα, τον μεν επειτα
Τρητοις εν λεχεεσσι θεσαν, παρα δ' εἱσαν αοιδους,
Θρηνων εξαρχους, οἱ τε στονοεσσαν αοιδην
Οἱ μεν αρ' εθρηνεον, επι δε στεναχοντο γυναικες.

IL. lib. xxiv., ver. 719.

"Arrived within the royal house, they stretched
The breathless Hector on a sumptuous bed,
And *singers* placed beside him, who should chant
The *strain funereal;* they with many a *groan*
The *dirge began;* and still at every close
The *female train* with *many a groan replied.*"

COWPER.

St. Jerome tells us that even to his time this custom continued in Judea; that women at funerals, with dishevelled hair and naked breasts, endeavoured in a modulated voice to invite others to lament with them. The poem before us, from the *seventeenth* to the *twenty-second* verse, is both an illustration and confirmation of what has been delivered on this subject, and worthy of the reader's frequent perusal, on account of its affecting pathos, moral sentiments, and fine images, particularly in the *twenty-first* verse, where *death* is decribed in as animated a prosopopœia as can be conceived. See *Lowth's twenty-second* Prelection, and *Dodd*. The *nineteenth* verse is supposed to be the funeral song of the women.

"How are we spoiled!
We are greatly confounded!
For we have forsaken the land;
Because they have destroyed our dwellings."

Verse 20. *Teach your daughters*] This is not a common dirge that shall last only till the body is consigned to the earth; it must last longer; teach it to your children, that it may be continued through every generation, till God turn again your captivity.

Verse 21. *For death is come up into our windows*] Here DEATH is personified, and represented as scaling their wall; and after having slain the *playful children* without, and the *vigorous youth* employed in the labours of the field, he is now come into the private houses, to destroy the aged and infirm; and into the palaces, to destroy the king and the princes.

Verse 22. *And as the handful after the harvestman*] The reapers, after having cut enough to fill their hand, threw it down; and the binders, following after, collected those handfuls, and bound them in sheaves. *Death* is represented as having *cut down* the inhabitants of the land, as the *reapers do the corn;* but so general was the *slaughter*, that there was none to *bury the dead*, to gather up these handfuls; so that they lay in a state of putrescence, *as dung upon the open field*.

Verse 23. *Let not the wise* man *glory in his wisdom*] Because God is the Fountain of all good, neither *wisdom*, nor *might*, nor *riches*, nor *prosperity* can come but *from* or *through* him. Nothing can be more rational than that the Source of all our blessings should be acknowledged. *Riches* cannot deliver in the day of death; *strength* cannot avail against him; and as a shield against him, our *wisdom* is foolishness.

Verse 24. *But let him that glorieth*] To *glory* in a thing is to depend on it as the means or cause of procuring *happiness*. But there can be no happiness but in being *experimentally acquainted* with that God *who exercises loving-kindness, judgment*, and *righteousness in the earth*. He who has God's mercy for his portion may well exult; for he need not fear the power of any adversary.

A. M. cir. 3394
B. C. cir. 610
Ol. cir. XLII. 3
TarquiniiPrisci,
R. Roman.,
cir. annum 7

[p]for in these *things* I delight,
saith the LORD.
25 Behold, the days come,
saith the LORD, that [q]I will
[r]punish all *them which are* circumcised with
the uncircumcised;
26 Egypt, and Judah, and Edom, [s]and the
children of Ammon, and Moab,
and all *that are* [t]in the [u]ut-
most corners, that dwell in the
wilderness: for all *these* na-
tions *are* uncircumcised, and all the house
of Israel *are* [v]uncircumcised, in the
heart.

[p]Mic. vi. 8; vii. 18——[q]Rom. ii. 8, 9——[r]Heb. *visit upon*——[s]Judith xiv. 10——[t]Heb. *cut off into corners*, or *having the corners* of their hair *polled*——[u]Ch. xxv. 23; xlix. 32——[v]Lev. xxvi. 41; Ezek. xliv. 7; Rom. ii. 28, 29

Sometimes the ancient heathen poets uttered sentiments of morality far beyond their dispensation. Witness PHOCYLIDES on this subject:—

> Μη γαυρου σοφιῃ, μητ' αλκῃ, μητ' ενι πλουτῳ·
> Εἰs Θεος εστι σοφος, δυνατος θ' ἁμα, και τολυολβος.

> "If *wisdom*, *strength*, or *riches* be thy lot,
> *Boast not;* but rather think thou hast them not.
> ONE GOD alone from whom those gifts proceed
> Is *wise*, is *mighty*, and is *rich indeed*."

Verse 25. *I will punish all* them which are *circumcised with the uncircumcised*] Do not imagine that *you*, because of your crimes, are the only objects of my displeasure; the *circumcised* and the *uncircumcised*, the *Jew* and the *Gentile*, shall equally feel the stroke of my justice, their transgressions being alike, after their advantages and disadvantages are duly compared. In like manner, *other nations* also were delivered into the hands of Nebuchadnezzar; these he immediately enumerates: *Egypt* and *Edom*, and the *Moabites* and the *Ammonites*, and the *Arabians of the desert*. All these nations were *uncircumcised* in that way which God required that rite to be practised as a sign of his *covenant;* and the Israelites, that did practise it as a sign of that covenant, did not attend to its spiritual meaning, for they were all *uncircumcised in heart*. And it may be remarked, that these people were in general confederated against the Chaldeans.

Verse 26. *All* that are *in the utmost corners*] כל קצוצי פאה *col ketsutsey pheah*. These words have been variously understood. The *Vulgate* translates: Omnes qui attonsi sunt in comam; "All who have their hair cut short." The *Targum*, *Septuagint*, *Syriac*, and *Arabic* have understood it nearly in the same way; and so our margin. Others think that the *insular* or *peninsular* situation of the people is referred to. Dr. *Blayney* thinks the *Arabians* are meant, who dwelt in the great desert, between Mesopotamia and Palestine. I really think our marginal reading should be preferred, as expressing the sense of all the ancient Versions.

CHAPTER X

The Jews, about to be carried into captivity, are here warned against the superstition and idolatry of that country to which they were going. Chaldea was greatly addicted to astrology, and therefore the prophet begins with warning them against it, 1, 2. *He then exposes the absurdity of idolatry in short but elegant satire; in the midst of which he turns, in a beautiful apostrophe, to the one true God, whose adorable attributes repeatedly strike in view, as he goes along, and lead him to contrast his infinite perfections with those despicable inanities which the blinded nations fear,* 3–16. *The prophet again denounces the Divine judgments,* 17, 18; *upon which Jerusalem laments her fate, and supplicates the Divine compassion in her favour,* 19–25.

A. M. cir. 3397
B. C. cir. 607
Ol. XLIII. 2
TarquiniiPrisci,
R. Roman.,
cir. annum 10

HEAR ye the word which the
LORD speaketh unto you, O
house of Israel:
2 Thus saith the LORD, [a]Learn
not the way of the heathen, and be not dismayed at the signs of heaven;
for the heathen are dismayed at
them.
3 For the [b]customs of the peo-
ple *are* vain: for [c]*one* cutteth a tree out of

[a]Lev. xviii. 3; xx. 23——[b]Heb. *statutes*, or *ordinances*, *are vanity*——[c]Isa. xl. 19, 20; xliv. 9, 10, &c.; xlv. 20

NOTES ON CHAP. X

Verse 1. *Hear ye the word which the Lord speaketh unto you*] Dr. *Dahler* supposes this discourse to have been delivered in the *fourth* year of the reign of *Jehoiakim*. It contains an invective against idolatry; showing its absurdity, and that the Creator alone should be worshipped by all mankind.

Verse 2. *Learn not the way of the heathen*] These words are more particularly addressed to the ten tribes scattered among the heathen by the Assyrians, who carried them away captive; they may also regard those in the land of Israel, who still had the customs of the former heathen settlers before their eyes.

Be not dismayed at the signs of heaven; for the heathen are dismayed] The Chaldeans and Egyptians were notoriously addicated to astrology; and the Israelites here are cautioned against it. The *signs* of the heavens may mean either the *sun, moon, planets*, and particular *stars* or *constellations;* or the *figures* or *characters* by which they represented these heavenly bodies.

Verse 3. *The customs of the people* are *vain*]

A. M. cir. 3397
B. C. cir. 607
Ol. XLIII. 2
TarquiniiPrisci,
R. Roman.,
cir. annum 10

the forest, the work of the hands
of the workman, with the axe.
4 They deck it with silver and
with gold; they [d]fasten it with
nails and with hammers, that it move not.
5 They *are* upright as the palm tree, [e]but
speak not: they must needs be [f]borne, because they cannot go. Be not afraid of them;
for [g]they cannot do evil, neither also *is it* in
them to do good.
6 Forasmuch as *there is* none [h]like unto
thee, O LORD; thou *art* great, and thy name
is great in might.
7 [i]Who would not fear thee, O King of
nations? for [k]to thee doth it appertain: forasmuch as [l]among all the wise *men* of the nations, and in all their kingdoms, *there is* none
like unto thee.
8 But they are [m]altogether
[n]brutish and foolish: the stock
is a doctrine of vanities.
9 Silver spread into plates is
brought from Tarshish, and [o]gold from Uphaz,
the work of the workman, and of the hands of
the founder: [p]blue and purple *is* their clothing: they *are* all [q]the work of cunning *men*.
10 But the LORD *is* the [r]true God, he *is*
[s]the living God, and an [t]everlasting [u]King:
at his wrath the earth shall tremble, and the nations shall not be able to abide his indignation.
11 [v]Thus shall ye say unto them, [w]The
gods that have not made the heavens and the
earth, *even* [x]they shall perish from the earth,
and from under these heavens.
12 He [y]hath made the earth by his power,
he hath [z]established the world by his wisdom,

A. M. cir. 3397
B. C. cir. 607
Ol. XLIII. 2
TarquiniiPrisci,
R. Roman.,
cir. annum 10

---

[d]Isa. xli. 7; xlvi. 7——[e]Psa. cxv. 5; cxxxv. 16; Hab. ii. 19; 1 Cor. xii. 2——[f]Psa. cxv. 7; Isa. xlvi. 1, 7——[g]Isa. xli. 23——[h]Exod. xv. 11; Psa. lxxxvi. 8, 10——[i]Rev. xv. 4——[k]Or, *it liketh thee*——[l]Psa. lxxxix. 6——[m]Heb. *in one*, or *at once*——[n]Psa. cxv. 8; Isa. xli. 29; Hab. ii. 18; Zech. x. 2; Rom. i. 21, 22

[o]Dan. x. 5——[p]Bar. vi. 12, 72——[q]Psa. cxv. 4——[r]Heb. *God of truth;* Psa. xxxi. 5——[s]1 Tim. vi. 17——[t]Heb. *king of eternity*——[u]Psa. x. 16——[v]In the Chaldean language——[w]See Psa. xcvi. 5——[x]Ver. 15; Isa. ii. 18; Zech. xiii. 2——[y]Gen. i. 1, 6, 9; Psa. cxxxvi. 5, 6; chap. li. 15, &c.——[z]Psa. xciii. 1

חקות *chukkoth;* the statutes and principles of the science are vain, empty, and illusory. They are founded in nonsense, ignorance, idolatry, and folly.

One *cutteth a tree out of the forest*] See the notes on Isa. xl. 19, and xliv. 9, &c., which are all parallel places and where this conduct is strongly ridiculed.

Verse 5. *They* are *upright as the palm tree*] As straight and as stiff as the trees out of which they are hewn.

Verse 7. *Who would not fear thee*] Who would not *worship* thee as the Author and Giver of all good? The *fear of God* is often taken for the whole of true *religion*.

Among all the wise men *of the nation*] Not even the wisest and most cultivated of the nations have ever found out any one equal to thee; but so exalted and holy art thou, that in all their wisdom and research they have never been able to find out the *true God*.

Verse 8. *The stock* is *a doctrine of vanities.*] Dr. *Blayney* translates,—"The wood itself is a rebuker of vanities." The very tree out of which the god is hewn demonstrates the vanity and folly of the idolaters; for, can all the art of man make out of a log of wood an animate and intelligent being?

Verse 9. *Brought from Tarshish*] Some suppose this to be *Tartessus* in *Spain*, from which the Phœnicians brought much silver. *Uphaz*, *Calmet* thinks to be the river *Pison;* some think *Ophir* is intended.

Blue and purple is *their clothing*] These were the most precious dyes; very rare, and of high price.

Verse 10. *But the Lord*] The original word should be preserved, however we agree to pronounce it: יהוה *Yehovah is the true God.* He is without beginning, and without end. This is *true* of no being else.

He is *the living God*] His being is underived; and he gives *life* to all. He is the very *Fountain* whence all *life* is derived.

And an everlasting king] As he has *made*, so he *governs*, all things. His *sway* is felt both in the heavens and in the earth.

At his wrath the earth shall tremble] All storms, tempests, tornadoes, and earthquakes are the effects of his power; and when the *nations* are destroyed, or turned upside down, it is the effect of his displeasure.

Verse 11. *Thus shall ye say unto them*] This is the message you shall deliver to the Chaldean idolaters.

The gods that have not made the heavens and the earth, even *they shall perish*] Both they and their worshippers shall be destroyed; and idolatry shall *finally* be destroyed from the earth; and the heavens shall look no more on so great an abomination. It is suffered for a *while:* but in the *end* shall be destroyed. This verse is written in a sort of *Hebræo-Syriaco-Chaldee;* such a dialect as I suppose was spoken at that time in Babylon, or during the captivity. As it is a message to the Babylonians, therefore, it is given in their own language. The *Chaldee* makes it the beginning of the copy of the epistle which the Prophet Jeremiah sent to the rest of the elders of the captivity who were in Babylon. All the ancient Versions acknowledge this verse; and it is found in all MSS. hitherto collated, except one of Dr. *Kennicott's* numbered 526; and he has included it between lines, as doubting its authenticity. Dr. *Blayney* supposes that some public teacher during the captivity, deducing it by direct inference from the prophet's words, had it inserted in the margin, and perhaps usually read together with this section, in the assemblies of the people, in order that they might have their answer always ready, whenever they were mo-

A. M. cir. 3397 and [a]hath stretched out the hea-
B. C. cir. 607
Ol. XLIII. 2 vens by his discretion.
TarquiniiPrisci,
R. Roman., 13 [b]When he uttereth his
cir. annum 10 voice, *there is* a [c]multitude of
waters in the heavens, and [d]he causeth the
vapours to ascend from the ends of the earth;
he maketh lightnings [e]with rain, and bringeth
forth the wind out of his treasures.
14 [f]Every man [g]is [h]brutish in *his* knowledge: [i]every founder is confounded by the
graven image: [k]for his molten image *is* falsehood, and *there is* no breath in them.
15 They *are* vanity, *and* the A. M. cir. 3397
work of errors: in the time of B. C. cir. 607
their visitation [l]they shall perish. Ol. XLIII. 2
TarquiniiPrisci, R. Roman., cir. annum 10
16 [m]The Portion of Jacob *is*
not like them: for he *is* the former of all
things; and [n]Israel *is* the rod of his inheritance: [o]The LORD of hosts *is* his name.
17 [p]Gather up thy wares out A. M. cir. 3404
of the land, O [q]inhabitant of the B. C. cir. 600
fortress. Ol. cir. XLV. 1
TarquiniiPrisci, R. Roman., cir. annum 17
18 For thus saith the LORD,
Behold, I will [r]sling out the inhabitants of

[a]Job ix. 8; Psa. civ. 2; Isa. xl. 22——[b]Job xxxviii. 34——[c]Or, *noise*——[d]Psa. cxxxv. 7——[e]Or, *for rain*
[f]Chap. li. 17, 18——[g]Or, *is more brutish than to know*
[h]Prov. xxx. 2——[i]Isa. xlii. 17; xliv. 11; xlv. 16
[k]Hab. ii. 18——[l]Verse 11——[m]Psalm xvi. 5; lxxiii. 26; cxix. 57; chap. li. 19; Lamentations iii. 24——[n]Deuteronomy xxxii. 9; Psalm lxxiv. 2——[o]Isaiah xlvii. 4; li. 15; liv. 5——chap. xxxi. 35; xxxii. 18; l. 34——[p]See chap. vi. 1; Ezek. xii. 3, &c.——[q]Heb. *inhabitress*
[r]1 Sam. xxv. 29; chap. xvi. 18

lested on the point of religion, or importuned to join the idolatrous worship of the Chaldeans.

Dahler has left it entirely out of the text, and introduces it in a note thus:—"After ver. 10 the Hebrew text is interrupted by a verse written in the Chaldean or Babylonish tongue. It is thus expressed:—

Ye shall say unto them, Let the gods perish!
Who have not made the heavens and the earth.
Let them be banished from above the earth,
and from under the heavens.

This verse can be considered only as a foreign insertion, not only on account of the difference of the language, but also because it interrupts the natural course of the ideas, and of the connexion of the *tenth* and *twelfth* verses."

As a curiosity I shall insert it in *Hebrew*, which the reader may compare with the *Chaldee* text, which I also subjoin.

כזאת תאמרו להם האלהים אשר לא עשו השמים והארץ יאבדו מן הארץ ומן תחת השמים אלה *cazoth tomeru lahem; haelohim asher lo asu hashshamayim vehaarets, yobedu min haarets, umin tachath hashshamayim elleh.* כדנא תאמרון להון אלהיא די שמיא וארקא לא עבדו יאבדו מארעא ומן תחות שמיא אלה: *kidna temerun lehon; elahaiya di shemaiya vearka la abadu, yebadu meara umin techoth shemaiya elleh.*

The *Hebrew* is the translation of *Leusden;* the *Chaldee* is that of the common text. Had not *all the ancient Versions* acknowledged it, I also, principally on account of the *strangeness* of the language, as being neither *Chaldee* nor *Syriac*, should have doubted its authenticity.

Verse 13. *When he uttereth his voice*, there is *a multitude of waters*] This is a plain allusion to a storm of thunder and lightning, and the abundance of rain which is the consequence. Water is composed of two *gases, hydrogen* and *oxygen:* the electric or galvanic spark decomposes them, and they become *air;* when recomposed, they form *water.* The lightning acts upon the *hydrogen* and *oxygen*, which are found in the atmospheric air: they are decomposed, and water or rain is the consequence; which, being heavier than the air falls down in the form of rain.

This verse and the *three* following are the same in substance, and nearly in words, as chap. li. 16, and following.

Verse 14. *Every man is brutish*] נבער *nibar*, is a boor, acts as a brute, who may suppose that a *stock* of a *tree*, formed *like a man*, may be an intellectual being; and therefore shuns the *form* as though it had *life.* See Isa. xliv. 10, 11. Of which verses, by the way, Dr. *Blayney* gives the following version to correct that of Bishop *Lowth:*—

Verse 10. Who hath formed a god?
Or set up a graven image that profiteth not?
11. Behold, all that are connected with it shall be ashamed,
And the artificers, they above all men!
They shall assemble all of them; they shall stand forth;
They shall fear; they shall be ashamed at the same time.

"That is, while they stand before the image they have set up, and worship it with a *religious dread*, the glaring absurdity of their conduct shall lead to their *shame* and *disgrace.*" With due deference to this learned man, I think this interpretation too refined.

Verse 16. *The Portion of Jacob* is *not like them*] Every nation had its tutelary god; this was its *portion;* in reference to this God says Deut. iv. 19, "He has divided the sun, moon, and stars, to all the nations under the heaven." And the Lord had taken the Israelites to be his *portion;* for "the Lord's portion is his people," Deut. xxxii. 9, and David says, "The Lord is the portion of mine inheritance," Psa. xvi. 5; cxix. 57. And hence Isaiah terms the *smooth stones of the brook*, to which Divine honours were paid, the *portion* of those idolaters, chap. lvii. 6. But in the text he says, "The PORTION, i. e., the God of Jacob is not like them; for he is the former of all things," and they are formed by their foolish worshippers.

Verse 17. *Gather up thy wares*] Pack up your goods, or what necessaries of life your enemies will permit you to carry away; for,

Verse 18. *I will sling out the inhabitants of the land*] I will *project* you with *violence* from your country. I will send you all into captivity. This discourse, from ver. 17, is supposed to have

A. M. cir. 3404
B. C. cir. 600
Ol. cir. XLV. 1
TarquiniiPrisci,
R. Roman.,
cir. annum 17

the land at this once, and will
distress them, [s]that they may
find *it so.*
19 [t]Wo is me for my hurt!
my wound is grievous: but I said, [u]Truly
this *is* a grief, and [v]I must bear it.
20 [w]My tabernacle is spoiled, and all my
cords are broken: my children are gone forth
of me, and they *are* not: *there is* none to
stretch forth my tent any more, and to set up
my curtains.
21 For the pastors are become brutish, and
have not sought the LORD: therefore they
shall not prosper, and all their flocks shall be
scattered.
22 Behold, the noise of the bruit
is come, and a great commotion
out of the [x]north country, to
make the cities of Judah desolate, *and* a [y]den of dragons.
23 O LORD, I know that the [z]way of man
is not in himself: *it is* not in man that walketh to direct his steps.
24 O LORD, [a]correct me, but with judgment;
not in thine anger, lest thou [b]bring me to
nothing.
25 [c]Pour out thy fury upon the heathen
[d]that know thee not, and upon the families
that call not on thy name: for they have eaten
up Jacob, and [e]devoured him, and consumed
him, and have made his habitation desolate.

---

[s]Ezek. vi. 10——[t]Chap. iv. 19; viii. 21; ix. 1——[u]Psa. lxxvii. 10——[v]Mic. vii. 9——[w]Chap. iv. 20——[x]Chap. i. 15; iv. 6; v. 15; vi. 22——[y]Chap. ix. 11——[z]Prov. xvi. 1; xx. 24——[a]Psa. vi. 1; xxxviii. 1; chap. xxx. 11——[b]Heb. *diminish me*——[c]Psa. lxxix. 6——[d]Job xviii. 21; 1 Thess. iv. 5; 2 Thess. i. 8——[e]Chap. viii. 16

---

been delivered in the *eleventh year* of Jehoiakim.

Verse 19. *This* is *a grief, and I must bear it.*] Oppressive as it is, I have deserved it, and worse; but even in this *judgment* God remembers *mercy.*

Verse 20. *My tabernacle is spoiled*] The city is taken, and all our villages ruined and desolated.

Verse 21. *The pastors are become brutish*] The king and his counsellors, who, by refusing to pay the promised tribute to Nebuchadnezzar, had kindled a new war.

Verse 22. *The noise of the bruit is come*] How this silly French word *bruit,* which signifies *noise,* got in here, I cannot imagine. The simple translation is this: "The voice of the report! behold, it is come; yea, great commotion from the land of the north; (Chaldea;) to make the cities of Judea a desolation, a habitation of wild beasts." That is, the *report* we had heard of the projected invasion of Judea by Nebuchadnezzar is confirmed. He has entered the land; the Chaldeans are at the doors, and the total desolation of Judea is their sole object.

Verse 23. *O Lord, I know that the way of man* is *not in himself*] I will not pretend to dispute with thee; thou dost every thing wisely and justly; we have sinned, and thou hast a right to punish; and to choose that sort of punishment thou thinkest will best answer the ends of justice. We cannot choose; thou hast appointed us to captivity; we must not repine: yet,

Verse 24. *Correct me, but with judgment*] Let not the punishment be to the uttermost of the demerit of the offence; else *we shall be brought to nothing*—totally and irrecoverably ruined.

Verse 25. *Pour out thy fury upon the heathen*] Even those who are now the executors of thy justice upon us will, in their turn, feel its scourge; for if judgment begins at us, who have been called *thy house* and *thy people,* shall they who have *not acknowledged thee* escape? It is impossible. The families and tribes which invoke thee not shall have thy fury poured out upon them, and especially they who "have eaten up Jacob and consumed him, and have made his habitation desolate." This was fulfilled in the *Chaldeans.* Nebuchadnezzar was punished with madness, his son was slain in his revels, and the city was taken and sacked by Cyrus; and the Babylonish empire was finally destroyed! This verse has been often quoted against those ungodly families who set not up the worship of God in their houses. These are spiritual *Chaldeans,* worse indeed than the Chaldeans ever were: they acknowledge God and his Christ; and yet neither worship nor serve him. How can that family expect the blessing of God, where the worship of God is not daily performed? No wonder their servants are wicked, their children profligate, and their goods cursed! What an awful reckoning shall such heads of families have with the Judge in the great day, who have refused to petition for that mercy which they might have had for the asking.

CHAPTER XI

The prophet proclaims the tenor of God's covenant with the Jews of old, 1–5; *and then reproves them for their hereditary disobedience,* 6–19. *In consequence of this the Almighty is introduced, declaring he will show them no pity,* 11–13; *forbidding Jeremiah to intercede,* 14; *rejecting their sacrifices,* 15; *and in a word, condemning this fair but unfruitful tree to the fire,* 16, 17. *In what remains of the chapter the prophet predicts evil to his neighbours of Anathoth, who had conspired against him,* 18–23. *"Let us," said they, "destroy this tree, with the fruit thereof," &c., alluding to what Jeremiah had said in the sixteenth verse.*

A. M. cir. 3406
B. C. cir. 598
Ol. cir. XLV. 3
TarquiniiPrisci,
R. Roman.,
cir. annum 19

THE word that came to Jeremiah from the LORD, saying,

2 Hear ye the words of this covenant, and speak unto the men of Judah, and to the inhabitants of Jerusalem;

3 And say thou unto them, Thus saith the LORD God of Israel; [a]Cursed *be* the man that obeyeth not the words of this covenant,

4 Which I commanded your fathers in the day *that* I brought them forth out of the land of Egypt, [b]from the iron furnace, saying, [c]Obey my voice, and do them, according to all which I command you: so shall ye be my people, and I will be your God:

5 That I may perform the [d]oath which I have sworn unto your fathers, to give them a land flowing with milk and honey, as *it is* this day. Then answered I, and said, [e]So be it, O LORD.

6 Then the LORD said unto me, Proclaim all these words in the cities of Judah, and in the streets of Jerusalem, saying, Hear ye the words of this covenant, [f]and do them.

7 For I earnestly protested unto your fathers in the day *that* I brought them up out of the land of Egypt, *even* unto this day, [g]rising early and protesting, saying, Obey my voice.

8 [h]Yet they obeyed not, nor inclined their ear, but [i]walked every one in the [k]imagination of their evil heart: therefore I will bring upon them all the words of this covenant, which I commanded *them* to do; but they did *them* not.

A. M. cir. 3406
B. C. cir. 598
Ol. cir. XLV. 3
TarquiniiPrisci,
R. Roman.,
cir. annum 19

9 And the LORD said unto me, [l]A conspiracy is found among the men of Judah, and among the inhabitants of Jerusalem.

10 They are turned back to [m]the iniquities of their forefathers, which refused to hear my words; and they went after other gods to serve them: the house of Israel and the house of Judah have broken my covenant which I made with their fathers.

11 Therefore thus saith the LORD, Behold, I will bring evil upon them, which they shall not be able [n]to escape; and [o]though they shall cry unto me, I will not hearken unto them.

12 Then shall the cities of Judah and inhabitants of Jerusalem go, and [p]cry unto the gods unto whom they offer incense: but they shall not save them at all in the time of their [q]trouble.

13 For *according to* the number of thy [r]cities were thy gods, O Judah; and *according to* the number of the streets of Jerusalem have ye set up altars to *that* [s]shameful thing, *even* altars to burn incense unto Baal.

14 Therefore [t]pray not thou for this people, neither lift up a cry or prayer for them: for

[a]Deut. xxvii. 26; Gal. iii. 10——[b]Deut. iv. 20; 1 Kings viii. 51——[c]Lev. xxvi. 3, 12; chap. vii. 23——[d]Deut. vii. 12, 13; Psa. cv. 9, 10——[e]Heb. *Amen;* Deut. xxvii. 15-26——[f]Rom. ii. 13; James i. 22——[g]Chap. vii. 13, 25; xxxv. 15——[h]Chap. vii. 26——[i]Chap. iii. 17; vii. 24; ix. 14——[k]Or, *stubbornness*

[l]Ezek. xxii. 25; Hos. vi. 9——[m]Ezek. xx. 18——[n]Heb. *to go forth of*——[o]Psa. xviii. 41; Prov. i. 28; Isa. i. 15; chap. xiv. 12; Ezek. viii. 18; Mic. iii. 4; Zech. vii. 13——[p]Deut. xxxii. 37, 38——[q]Heb. *evil*——[r]Chap. ii. 28——[s]Heb. *shame;* chap. iii. 24; Hos. ix. 10——[t]Exod. xxxii. 10; chap. vii. 16; xiv. 11; 1 John v. 16

NOTES ON CHAP. XI

Verse 1. *The word that came to Jeremiah*] This discourse is supposed to have been delivered in the first year of the reign of Zedekiah. See *Dahler*.

Verse 2. *Hear ye the words of this covenant*] It is possible that the prophet caused the words of the covenant made with their fathers in the desert (Exod. xxiv. 4-8) to be read to them on this occasion; or, at least, the *blessings and the cursings* which Moses caused to be pronounced to the people as soon as they had set foot in Canaan, Deut. xxvii., xxviii.

Verse 3. *Cursed* be *the man that obeyeth not*] After the reading, the prophet appears to *sum up* the things contained in what was read to them; as if he had said, "Ye hear what the Lord saith unto you: remember, the sum of it is this: The man is cursed who obeyeth not; and he is blessed who obeys. From these declarations God will not depart."

Verse 5. *So be it, O Lord*] Let thy promises be fulfilled; and let the incorrigible beware of thy threatenings!

Verse 6. *Proclaim all these words*] Let the same covenant, with the blessings and cursings, be read in every city of Judah, and in all the streets of Jerusalem, that all the people may know their duty, their privileges, and their danger.

Verse 9. *A conspiracy is found*] They were all *fratres conjurati*, sworn brothers, determined to cast off the Divine yoke, and no longer to have God to reign over them.

Verse 10. *They are turned back to the iniquities of their forefathers*] A great reformation had taken place under the reign of Josiah, and the public worship of idols had been abolished, and most of the high places destroyed; but under the reign of his son and his successors, they had *turned back again* to idolatry, and were become worse than ever. It required a *captivity* to cure them of this propensity; and God sent one: after that, there was no idolatry among the Jews.

Verse 12. *Go, and cry unto the gods*] See chap. ii. 28.

Verse 14. *Therefore pray not thou for this people*] I am determined to give them up into

A. M. cir. 3406
B. C. cir. 598
Ol. cir. XLV. 3
TarquiniiPrisci,
R. Roman.,
cir. annum 19

I will not hear *them* in the time
that they cry unto me for their
[u]trouble.
15 [v]What [w]hath my beloved
to do in mine house, *seeing* she hath [x]wrought
lewdness with many, and [y]the holy flesh is
passed from thee? [z]when thou doest evil,
then thou [a]rejoicest.
16 The LORD called thy name, [b]A green
olive tree, fair, *and* of goodly fruit: with the
noise of a great tumult he hath kindled fire
upon it, and the branches of it are broken.
17 For the LORD of hosts, [c]that planted
thee, hath pronounced evil against thee, for
the evil of the house of Israel and of the house
of Judah, which they have done against themselves to provoke me to anger in offering
incense unto Baal.
18 And the LORD hath given me knowledge
of it, and I know *it:* then thou showedst me
their doings.
19 But I *was* like a lamb *or* an ox *that* is
brought to the slaughter; and
I knew not that [d]they had devised devices against me, *saying,*
Let us destroy [e]the tree with the
fruit thereof, [f]and let us cut him off from
[g]the land of the living, that his name may be
no more remembered.
20 But, O LORD of hosts, that judgest righteously, that [h]triest the reins and the heart, let
me see thy vengeance on them: for unto thee
have I revealed my cause.
21 Therefore thus saith the LORD of the
men of Anathoth, [i]that seek thy life, saying,
[k]Prophesy not in the name of the LORD, that
thou die not by our hand:
22 Therefore thus saith the LORD of hosts,
Behold, I will [l]punish them: the young men
shall die by the sword; their sons and their
daughters shall die by famine:
23 And there shall be no remnant of them:
for I will bring evil upon the men of Anathoth, *even* [m]the year of their visitation.

A. M. cir. 3406
B. C. cir. 598
Ol. cir. XLV. 3
TarquiniiPrisci,
R. Roman.,
cir. annum 19

[u]Heb. *evil*——[v]Psa. l. 16; Isa. i. 11, &c.——[w]Heb. *What is to my beloved in my house?*——[x]Ezek. xvi. 25, &c.——[y]Hag. ii. 12, 13, 14; Titus i. 15——[z]Or, *when thy evil is*——[a]Prov. ii. 14——[b]Psa. lii. 8; Rom. xi. 17 [c]Isa. v. 2; chap. ii. 21——[d]Chap. xviii. 18——[e]Heb. *the stalk with his bread*

[f]Psa. lxxxiii. 4——[g]Psa. xxvii. 13; cxvi. 9; cxlii. 5 [h]1 Sam. xvi. 7; 1 Chron. xxviii. 9; Psa. vii. 9; chap. xvii. 10; xx. 12; Rev. ii. 23——[i]Chap. xii. 5, 6——[k]Isa. xxx. 10; Amos ii. 12; vii. 13, 16; Mic. ii. 6——[l]Heb. *visit upon*——[m]Chap. xxiii. 12; xlvi. 21; xlviii. 44; l. 27; Luke xix. 44

the hands of their enemies; I will neither hear thy intercession, nor regard their prayers. Their measure is *full.*

Verse 15. *What hath my beloved to do in mine house*] This has been supposed to refer to *Abraham, Moses,* or such eminent servants of God, whose intercession was very powerful. Were even *they* to appear as intercessors, their prayer should not be regarded. Others think that this is an *endearing expression,* which properly belonged to the Israelites. When God took them into covenant with himself, they were *espoused* to him, and therefore his *beloved;* but now that they have forsaken him, and *joined themselves to another,* what have they to do with his house or its ordinances, which they wish now to frequent with *vows* and *sacrifices,* when they see the evil fast coming upon them? This is probably the sense of this very obscure passage. Dr. *Blayney* translates, "What hath my beloved to do in my house whilst she practiseth wickedness? Shall vows and holy flesh (sacrifices) be allowed to come from thee? When thou art malignant, shalt thou rejoice?"

Verse 16. *The Lord called thy name, A green olive tree*] That is, he made thee like a green olive—fair, flourishing, and fruitful; but thou art degenerated, and God hath given the Chaldeans permission to burn thee up.

Verse 18. *The Lord hath given me knowledge of it*] The men of Anathoth had conspired against his life, because he reproved them for their sins, and denounced the judgments of God against them. Of this God had given him a secret warning, that he might be on his guard.

Verse 19. *I* was *like a lamb* or *an ox*] *Dahler* translates, "I was like a fattened lamb that is led to the slaughter." *Blayney,* "I was like a tame lamb that is led to slaughter." The word אלוף *alluph,* which we translate *ox,* is taken by both as an *adjective,* qualifying the noun כבש *kebes, a lamb.* It may probably signify a lamb brought up in the house—fed at home, (אלוף *alluph,*) instructed or nourished at home; perfectly innocent and unsuspecting, while leading to the slaughter. This meaning the word will bear in Arabic, for الف *alaf* signifies *accustomed, familiar,* (to or with any person or thing;) a *companion,* a *comrade,* an *intimate friend.* I therefore think that ככבש אלוף *kechebes alluph* signifies, *like the familiar lamb*—the lamb *bred up in the house,* in a state of *friendship* with the family. The people of Anathoth were Jeremiah's *townsmen;* he was *born* and *bred* among them; they were his *familiar friends;* and now they lay wait for his life! All the *Versions* understood אלוף *alluph* as an epithet of כבש *kebes,* a *chosen, simple, innocent* lamb.

Let us destroy the tree with the fruit] Let us slay the prophet, and his prophecies will come to an end. The *Targum* has, *Let us put mortal poison in his food;* and all the Versions understand it something in the same way.

Verse 20. *Let me see thy vengeance on them*] Rather, *I shall see* (אראה *ereh*) *thy punishment inflicted on them.*

Verse 22. *Behold, I will punish them*] And the punishment is, *Their young men shall die by the sword* of the Chaldeans; and *their sons and daughters shall die by the famine* that shall come on the land through the desolations occasioned by the Chaldean army.

Verse 23. *The year of their visitation.*] This punishment shall come in that year in which I shall visit their iniquities upon them.

CHAPTER XII

This chapter is connected with the foregoing. The prophet expostulates with God concerning the ways of Providence in permitting the wicked to prosper, 1–4. *It is intimated to him that he must endure still greater trials,* 5, *from his false and deceitful brethren,* 6; *but that still heavier judgments awaited the nation for their crimes,* 7–13. *That God, however, would at length have compassion on them; restore them to their land; and turn his judgments against those that oppressed them, if not prevented by their becoming converts to the true religion,* 14–17.

A. M. cir. 3406
B. C. cir. 598
Ol. cir. XLV. 3
TarquiniiPrisci, R. Roman., cir. annum 19

RIGHTEOUS [a]*art* thou, O
LORD, when I plead with
thee: yet [b]let me talk with thee
of *thy* judgments: [c]Wherefore
doth the way of the wicked prosper? *where-*
fore are all they happy that deal very treacherously?
2 Thou hast planted them, yea, they have
taken root: [d]they grow, yea, they bring forth
fruit: [e]thou *art* near in their mouth, and far
from their reins.
3 But thou, O LORD, [f]knowest me: thou
hast seen me, and [g]tried mine heart [h]toward
thee: pull them out like sheep for the slaughter, and prepare them for [i]the day of slaughter.

A. M. cir. 3406
B. C. cir. 598
Ol. cir. XLV. 3
TarquiniiPrisci, R. Roman., cir. annum 19

4 How long shall [k]the land
mourn, and the herbs of every
field wither, [l]for the wickedness of them that dwell therein?
[m]the beasts are consumed, and the birds; because they said, He shall not see our last end.
5 If thou hast run with the footmen, and
they have wearied thee, then how canst thou
contend with horses? and *if* in the land of
peace, *wherein* thou trustedst, *they wearied*
thee, then how wilt thou do in [n]the swelling
of Jordan?
6 For even [o]thy brethren, and the house
of thy father, even they have dealt treacherously with thee; yea, [p]they have called a

---

[a]Psa. li. 4——[b]Or, *let me reason the case with thee* [c]Job xii. 6; xxi. 7; Psa. xxxvii. 1, 35; lxxiii. 3, &c.; chap. v. 28; Hab. i. 4; Mal. iii. 15——[d]Heb. *they go on* [e]Isa. xxix. 13; Matt. xv. 8; Mark vii. 6——[f]Psa. xvii. 3; cxxxix. 1——[g]Chap. xi. 20

[h]Heb. *with thee*——[i]James v. 5——[k]Chap. xxiii. 10; Hos. iv. 3——[l]Psa. cvii. 34——[m]Chap. iv. 25; vii. 20; ix. 10; Hos. iv. 3——[n]Josh. iii. 15; 1 Chron. xii. 15; chap. xlix. 19; l. 44——[o]Chap. ix. 4; xi. 19, 21——[p]Or, *they cried after thee fully*

NOTES ON CHAP. XII

Verse 1. *Righteous* art *thou, O Lord, when I plead with thee*] The prophet was grieved at the prosperity of the wicked; and he wonders how, consistently with God's righteousness, vice should often be in affluence, and piety in suffering and poverty. He knows that God is righteous, that every thing is done well; but he wishes to inquire how these apparently unequal and undeserved lots take place. On this subject he wishes to reason with God, that he may receive instruction.

Verse 2. *Thou* art *near in their mouth*] They have no sincerity: they have something of the *form* of religion, but nothing of its *power*.

Verse 3. *But thou, O Lord, knowest me*] I know that the very secrets of my heart are known to thee; and I am glad of it, for *thou knowest that my heart is towards thee*—is upright and sincere.

Verse 4. *How long shall the land mourn*] These hypocrites and open sinners are a curse to the country; *pull them out, Lord,* that the land may be delivered of that which is the cause of its desolation.

Verse 5. *If thou hast run with the footmen*] If the smallest evils to which thou art exposed cause thee to make so many bitter complaints, how wilt thou feel when, in the course of thy prophetic ministry, thou shalt be exposed to much greater, from enemies much more powerful? *Footmen* may here be the symbol of *common evil events; horsemen,* of evils much more terrible. If thou have sunk under small difficulties, what wilt thou do when great ones come?

And if *in the land of peace,* wherein *thou trustedst*] I believe the meaning is this, "If in a country now enjoying peace thou scarcely thinkest thyself in safety, what wilt thou do in the swellings of Jordan? in the time when the enemy, like an overflowing torrent, shall deluge every part of the land?"

The overflowing of Jordan, which generally happened in harvest, drove the lions and other beasts of prey from their coverts among the bushes that lined its banks; who, spreading themselves through the country, made terrible havoc, slaying men, and carrying off the cattle.

Perhaps by *footmen* may be meant the *Philistines, Edomites,* &c., whose armies were composed principally of *infantry;* and by the *horses,* the *Chaldeans,* who had abundance of *cavalry* and chariots in their army. But still the words are *proverbial,* and the above is their meaning.

Verse 6. *For even thy brethren, and the house of thy father*] Thou hast none to depend on but God: even thy brethren will betray thee when they have it in their power.

A. M. cir. 3406 B. C. cir. 598 Ol. cir. XLV. 3 TarquiniiPrisci, R. Roman., cir. annum 19

multitude after thee: [q]believe
them not, though they speak
[r]fair words unto thee.
7 I have forsaken mine house,
I have left mine heritage; I have given [s]the
dearly beloved of my soul into the hand of her
enemies.
8 Mine heritage is unto me as a lion in the
forest; it [t]crieth [u]out against me: therefore
have I hated it.
9 Mine heritage *is* unto me *as* a [v]speckled
bird, the birds round about *are* against her;
come ye, assemble all the beasts of the field,
[w]come [x]to devour.
10 Many [y]pastors have destroyed [z]my
vineyard, they have [a]trodden my portion
under foot, they have made my [b]pleasant portion a desolate wilderness.
11 They have made it desolate, *and being*
desolate [c]it mourneth unto me; the whole
land is made desolate, because
[d]no man layeth *it* to heart.
12 The spoilers are come upon
all high places through the wilderness: for the sword of the LORD shall devour
from the *one* end of the land even to the *other*
end of the land: no flesh shall have peace.
13 [e]They have sown wheat, but shall reap
thorns: they have put themselves to pain,
but shall not profit: and [f]they shall be
ashamed of your revenues because of the
fierce anger of the LORD.

A. M. cir. 3401 B. C. cir. 603 Ol. XLIV. 2 TarquiniiPrisci, R. Roman., cir. annum 14

14 Thus saith the LORD against
all mine evil neighbours, that
[g]touch the inheritance which I
have caused my people Israel to
inherit; Behold, I will [h]pluck them out of
their land, and pluck out the house of Judah
from among them.
15 [i]And it shall come to pass, after that I

[q]Prov. xxvi. 25——[r]Heb. *good things*——[s]Heb. *the love*——[t]Or, *yelleth*——[u]Heb. *giveth out his voice* [v]Or, *having talons*——[w]Or, *cause them to come*——[x]Isa. lvi. 9; chap. vii. 33——[y]Chap. vi. 3——[z]Isa. v. 1, 5

[a]Isa. lxiii. 18——[b]Heb. *portion of desire*——[c]Ver. 4 [d]Isa. xlii. 25——[e]Lev. xxvi. 16; Deut. xxviii. 38; Mic. vi. 15; Hag. i. 6——[f]Or, *ye*——[g]Zech. ii. 8——[h]Deut. xxx. 3; chap. xxxii. 37——[i]Ezek. xxviii. 25

Believe them not] Do not trust to them; do not commit thyself to them; they are in heart thy enemies, and will betray thee.

Verse 7. *I have forsaken mine house*] I have abandoned my temple.

I have given the dearly beloved of my soul] The people once in covenant with me, and inexpressibly dear to me while faithful.

Into the hand of her enemies.] This was a condition in the covenant I made with them; if they forsook me, they were to be abandoned to their enemies, and cast out of the good land I gave to their fathers.

Verse 8. *Mine heritage is unto me as a lion*] The people are *enraged* against me; they *roar like a furious lion* against their God. They have proceeded to the most open acts of the most flagrant iniquity.

Verse 9. Is *unto me* as *a speckled bird*] A bird of *divers colours.* This is a people who have corrupted the worship of the true God with heathenish rites and ceremonies; therefore, the different nations, (see ver. 10,) whose gods and forms of worship they have adopted, shall come and spoil them. As far as you have followed the surrounding nations in their worship, so far shall they prevail over your state. Every one shall take that which is his own; and wherever he finds his own gods, he will consider the land consecrated to them, and take it as his property, because those very gods are the objects of his worship. The fable of the *daw* and *borrowed plumes* is no mean illustration of this passage.

Dahler translates the whole verse thus:—

Birds of prey! inundate *with blood my heritage.*
Birds of prey! come against her from all sides.
Run together in crowds, ye savage beasts!
Come to the carnage!

Verse 10. *Many pastors have destroyed my vineyard*] My people have had many kinds of enemies which have fed upon their richest pastures; the Philistines, the Moabites, Ammonites, Assyrians, Egyptians, and now the *Chaldeans.*

Verse 11. *No man layeth* it *to heart.*] Notwithstanding all these desolations, from which the land every where mourns, and which are so plainly the consequences of the people's crimes, no man layeth it to heart, or considereth that these are God's judgments; and that the only way to have them removed is to repent of their sins, and turn to God with all their hearts.

Verse 12. *The sword of the Lord shall devour*] It is the sword of the Lord that has devoured, and will devour: this is what no man layeth to heart. They think these things come in the course of events.

Verse 13. *They have sown wheat, but shall reap thorns*] All their projects shall fail: none of their enterprises shall succeed. They are enemies to God, and therefore cannot have his blessing.

Verse 14. *Against all mine evil neighbours*] All the neighbouring nations who have united in desolating Judea shall be desolated in their turn: they also are *wicked,* and they shall be punished. If I make them executors of my justice, it is to them no proof of my approbation. God often uses one wicked nation to scourge another; and afterwards scourges the scourger by some other scourge. In some places a felon who was condemned to be hanged is made the common hangman for the county; he himself being still under the sentence of death,—

Till soon some trusty brother of the trade
Shall do for *him* what *he* has done for *others.*

Verse 15. *I will return, and have compassion*

A. M. cir. 3401
B. C. cir. 603
Ol. XLIV. 2
TarquiniiPrisci,
R. Roman.,
cir. annum 14

have plucked them out I will return, and have compassion on
them, [k]and will bring them
again, every man to his heritage,
and every man to his land.
16 And it shall come to pass, if they will
diligently learn the ways of my people, [l]to
swear by my name, The LORD
liveth; (as they taught my people
to swear by Baal;) then shall they
be [m]built in the midst of my
people.
17 But if they will not [n]obey, I will utterly
pluck up and destroy that nation, saith the LORD.

A. M. cir. 3401
B. C. cir. 603
Ol. cir. XLV. 2
TarquiniiPrisci,
R. Roman.,
cir. annum 14

[k]Amos ix. 14——[l]Chap. iv. 2

[m]Eph. ii. 20, 21; 1 Pet. ii. 5——[n]Isa. lx. 12

on them] This is a promise of restoration from the captivity, and an intimation also that some of their enemies would turn to the true God with them; *learn the ways of his people;* that is, would abjure idols, and take Jehovah for their God; *and be built in the midst of his people*, that is, Jew and Gentile forming *one Church* of the Most High.

Verse 17. *I will—destroy that nation*] Several of them did not obey, and are destroyed. Of the Moabites, Ammonites, and Chaldeans, not one vestige remains. The *sixteenth* verse is supposed to be a promise of the conversion of the Gentiles. See Eph. ii. 13-22.

From the *thirteenth* verse to the end is a different discourse, and *Dahler* supposes it to have been delivered in the *seventh* or *eighth* year of the reign of *Jehoiakim.*

CHAPTER XIII

This chapter contains an entire prophecy. The symbol of the linen girdle, left to rot for a considerable time, was a type of the manner in which the glory of the Jews should be marred during the course of their long captivity, 1–11. The scene of hiding the girdle being laid near the Euphrates, intimated that the scene of the nation's distress should be Chaldea, which that river waters. The next three verses, by another emblem frequently used to represent the judgments of God, are designed to show that the calamities threatened should be extended to every rank and denomination, 12–14. This leads the prophet to a most affectionate exhortation to repentance, 15–17. But God, knowing that this happy consequence would not ensue, sends him with an awful message to the royal family particularly, and to the inhabitants of Jerusalem in general, declaring the approaching judgments in plain terms, 18–27. The ardent desire for the reformation of Jerusalem, with which the chapter concludes, beautifully displays the compassion and tender mercy of God.

A. M. cir. 3405
B. C. cir. 599
Ol. cir. XLV. 2
TarquiniiPrisci,
R. Roman.,
cir. annum 18

THUS saith the LORD unto
me, Go and get thee [a]a linen
girdle, and put it upon thy loins,
and put it not in water.
2 So I got a girdle according to the word
of the LORD, and put *it* on my [b]loins.
3 And the word of the LORD came unto
me the second time, saying,
4 Take the girdle that thou
hast got, which *is* upon thy loins,
and arise, go to Euphrates, and
hide it there in a hole of the rock.
5 So I went and hid it by Euphrates, as the
LORD commanded me.
6 And it came to pass after many days, that
the LORD said unto me, Arise, go to Euphrates,

A. M. cir. 3405
B. C. cir. 599
Ol. cir. XLV. 2
TarquiniiPrisci,
R. Roman.,
cir. annum 18

[a]Lev. vi. 10

[b]Isa. xi. 5

NOTES ON CHAP. XIII

Verse 1. *Thus saith the Lord unto me*] This discourse is supposed to have been delivered under the reign of *Jeconiah*, the son and successor of Jehoiakim, who came to the throne in the *eighteenth* year of his age; when the Chaldean generals had encamped near to Jerusalem, but did not besiege it in form till Nebuchadnezzar came up with the great body of the army. In these circumstances the prophet predicts the captivity; and, by a symbolical representation of a rotten girdle, shows the people their totally corrupt state; and by another *of bottles filled with wine*, shows the destruction and madness of their counsels, and the confusion that must ensue.

Go and get thee a linen girdle] This was either a vision, or God simply describes the thing in order that the prophet might use it in the way of illustration.

Put it not in water.] After having worn it let it not be washed, that it may more properly represent the uncleanness of the Israelites; for *they* were represented by the *girdle;* for "as the girdle cleaveth to the loins of a man, so have I caused to cleave unto me the whole house of Israel, and the whole house of Judah." And as a girdle is as well for *ornament* as *use;* God took them *for a name*, and *for a praise*, and *for a glory*, ver. 11.

Verse 4. *Go to Euphrates, and hide it there*] Intending to point out, by this distant place, the *country* into which they were to be carried away captive.

A. M. cir. 3405
B. C. cir. 599
Ol. cir. XLV. 2
TarquiniiPrisci,
R. Roman.,
cir. annum 18

and take the girdle from thence,
which I commanded thee to hide
there.
7 Then I went to Euphrates,
and digged, and took the girdle from the place
where I had hid it; and, behold, the girdle
was marred, it was profitable for nothing.
8 Then the word of the LORD came unto
me, saying,
9 Thus saith the LORD, After this manner
[c]will I mar the pride of Judah, and the great
pride of Jerusalem.
10 This evil people, which refuse to hear my
words, which [d]walk in the [e]imagination of
their heart, and walk after other gods, to serve
them, and to worship them, shall even be as
this girdle, which is good for nothing.
11 For as the girdle cleaveth to the loins of
a man, so have I caused to cleave unto me
the whole house of Israel and the whole house
of Judah, saith the LORD; that [f]they might
be unto me for a people, and [g]for a name, and
for a praise, and for a glory: but they would
not hear.
12 Therefore thou shalt speak unto them
this word; Thus saith the LORD God of Israel, Every bottle shall be filled with wine:
and they shall say unto thee, Do we not certainly know that every bottle
shall be filled with wine?
13 Then shalt thou say unto
them, Thus saith the LORD, Be-
hold, I will fill all the inhabitants of this land,
even the kings that sit upon David's throne, and
the priests, and the prophets, and all the inhabitants of Jerusalem, [h]with drunkenness.
14 And [i]I will dash them [k]one against another, even the fathers and the sons together,
saith the LORD: I will not pity, nor spare,
nor have mercy, [l]but destroy them.
15 Hear ye, and give ear; be not proud: for
the LORD hath spoken.
16 [m]Give glory to the LORD your God, before he cause [n]darkness, and before your feet
stumble upon the dark mountains, and, while
ye [o]look for light, he turn it into [p]the shadow
of death, *and* make *it* gross darkness.
17 But if ye will not hear it, my soul shall
weep in secret places for *your* pride; and
[q]mine eye shall weep sore, and run down
with tears, because the LORD's flock is carried
away captive.
18 Say unto [r]the king and to the queen,
Humble yourselves, sit down: for your [s]prin-
cipalities shall come down, *even* the crown of
your glory.

A. M. cir. 3405
B. C. cir. 599
Ol. cir. XLV. 2
TarquiniiPrisci,
R. Roman.,
cir. annum 18

---

[c]Lev. xxvi. 19——[d]Chap. ix. 14; xi. 8; xvi. 12——[e]Or, *stubbornness*——[f]Exod. xix. 5——[g]Chap. xxxiii. 9 [h]Isa. li. 17, 21; lxviii. 6; chap. xxv. 27; li. 7——[i]Psa. ii. 9——[k]Heb. *a man against his brother*

[l]Heb. *from destroying them*——[m]Josh. vii. 19——[n]Isa. v. 30, viii. 22; Amos viii. 9——[o]Isa. lix. 9——[p]Psa. xliv. 19——[q]Chap. ix. 1; xiv. 17; Lam. i. 2, 16; ii. 18——[r]See 2 Kings xxiv. 12; chap. xxii. 26——[s]Or, *head-tires*

Verse 7. *And, behold, the girdle was marred; it was profitable for nothing.*] This symbolically represented the state of the Jews: they were corrupt and abominable; and God, by sending them into captivity, "marred the pride of Judah, and the great pride of Jerusalem," ver. 9.

Verse 12. *Every bottle shall be filled with wine?*] The bottles were made for the purpose of being filled with wine; and it is likely, from the promising appearance of the *season* and the *grapes*, that there was a great likelihood of a *copious vintage;* and this made them say, "Do we not certainly know that every bottle shall be filled with wine? Have we not every prospect that it will be so? Do we need a revelation to inform us of this?"

Verse 13. *Behold, I will fill all the inhabitants of this land—with drunkenness.*] You pretend to take this *literally*, but it is a *symbol. You*, and your *kings*, and *priests*, and *prophets*, are represented by these bottles. The *wine* is God's *wrath* against you, which shall first be shown by *confounding* your deliberations, filling you with foolish plans of defence, causing you from your divided counsels to fall out among yourselves, so that like so many drunken men you shall reel about and jostle each other; defend yourselves without plan, and fight without order, till ye all fall an easy prey into the hands of your enemies. The ancient adage is here fulfilled:—

Quos Deus vult perdere, prius dementat.
"Those whom God determines to destroy, he first renders foolish."

Verse 16. *Give glory to—God*] Confess your sins and turn to him, that these sore evils may be averted.

While ye look for light] While ye expect *prosperity*, he turned it into the *shadow of death*—sent you adversity of the most *distressing* and *ruinous kind.*

Stumble upon the dark mountains] Before you meet with those great *obstacles*, which, having no *light*—no proper understanding in the matter, ye shall be utterly unable to surmount.

Verse 17. *My soul shall weep in secret places*] If you will not hearken to the Lord, there is no remedy: destruction must come; and there is nothing left for me, but to go in secret, and mourn and bewail your wretched lot.

Verse 18. *Say unto the king and to the queen*] Probably Jeconiah and his mother, under whose tutelage, being young when he began to reign, he was left, as is very likely.

A. M. cir. 3405
B. C. cir. 599
Ol. cir. XLV. 2
TarquiniiPrisci,
R. Roman.,
cir. annum 18

19 The cities of the south shall
be shut up, and none shall open
them; Judah shall be carried
away captive all of it, it shall be
wholly carried away captive.
20 Lift up your eyes, and behold them [t]that
come from the north: where *is* the flock *that*
was given thee, thy beautiful flock?
21 What wilt thou say when he shall [u]punish
thee? for thou hast taught them *to be* captains, *and* as chief over thee: shall not [v]sor-
rows take thee, as a woman in travail?
22 And if thou say in thine heart, [w]Where-
fore come these things upon me? For the
greatness of thine iniquity are [x]thy skirts
discovered, *and* thy heels [y]made bare.
23 Can the Ethiopian change his skin, or
the leopard his spots? *then* may
ye also do good, that are [z]accus-
tomed to do evil.
24 Therefore will I scatter them
[a]as the stubble that passeth away by the wind
of the wilderness.
25 [b]This *is* thy lot, the portion of thy
measures from me, saith the LORD; because
thou hast [c]forgotten me, and trusted in [d]false-
hood.
26 Therefore [e]will I discover thy skirts
upon thy face, that thy shame may appear.
27 I have seen thine adulteries, and thy
[f]neighings, the lewdness of thy whoredom,
and thine abominations [g]on the hills in the
fields. Wo unto thee, O Jerusalem! wilt thou
not be made clean? [h]when *shall it* once *be?*

A. M. cir. 3405
B. C. cir. 599
Ol. XLIII. 4
TarquiniiPrisci,
R. Roman.,
cir. annum 18

---

[t]Ch. vi. 22——[u]Heb. *visit upon*——[v]Ch. vi. 24 [w]Ch. v. 19; xvi. 10——[x]Isa. iii. 17; xlvii. 2, 3; ver. 26; Ezek. xvi. 37, 38, 39; Nah. iii. 5——[y]Or, *shall be violently taken away*——[z]Heb. *taught*——[a]Psa. i. 4; Hos. xiii. 3

[b]Job xx. 29; Psa. xi. 6——[c]Psa. l. 22; Isa. lxv. 11; chap. xxiii. 27——[d]Chap. x. 14——[e]Ver. 22; Lam. i. 8; Ezek. xvi. 37; xxiii. 29; Hos. ii. 10——[f]Chap. v. 8 [g]Isa. lxv. 7; chap. ii. 20; iii. 2, 6; Ezek. vi. 13——[h]Heb. *after when yet?*

Sit down] Show that ye have *humbled* yourselves; for your state will be destroyed, and your glorious crown taken from your heads.

Verse 19. *The cities of the south shall be shut up*] Not only the cities of the *north*, the quarter at which the Chaldeans entered, but the cities of the *south* also; for he shall proceed from one extremity of the land to the other, spreading devastation every where, and carrying off the inhabitants.

Verse 20. *Where* is *the flock—thy beautiful flock?*] Jerusalem is addressed. Where are the prosperous multitudes of men, women, and children? Alas! are they not driven before the Babylonians, who have taken them captive?

Verse 21. *Thou hast taught them* to be *captains*, and *as chief over thee*] This is said of their enemies, whether Assyrians or Chaldeans: for ever since Ahaz submitted himself to the king of Assyria, the kings of Judah never regained their *independence*. Their enemies were thus taught to be their lords and masters.

Verse 22. *Are thy skirts discovered*] Thy defenceless state is every where known; thou art not only *weak*, but ignominiously so. It is thy *scandal* to be in so depressed a condition; thou art lower than the basest of thy adversaries, and thou art so because of thy sin.

Verse 23. *Can the Ethiopian change his skin*] Can a *black*, at his own pleasure, change the *colour* of his *skin?* Can the *leopard* at will change the *variety* of his *spots?* These things are natural to them, and they cannot be altered; so sin, and especially your attachment to idolatry, is become a *second nature;* and we may as well expect the Ethiopian to change his skin, and the leopard his spots, *as you to do good, who have been accustomed to do evil.* It is a matter of the utmost difficulty to get a sinner, deeply rooted in vicious habits, brought to the knowledge of himself and God. But the expression does not imply that the thing is as impossible in a *moral* as it is in a *natural* sense: it only shows that it is *extremely difficult*, and not to be often expected; and a thousand matters of fact prove the truth of this. But still, what is impossible to man is possible to God. See on ver. 27.

Verse 24. *The wind of the wilderness.*] Some strong tempestuous wind, proverbially severe, coming from the desert to the south of Judea.

Verse 25. *Trusted in falsehood.*] In *idols*, and in *lying prophets.*

Verse 26. *Therefore will I discover thy skirts upon thy face*] It was the custom to punish lewd women by stripping them naked, and exposing them to public view; or by throwing their clothes over their heads, as here intimated. Was this the way to correct the evil?

Verse 27. *I have seen thine adulteries*] Thy *idolatries* of different kinds, practised in various ways; no doubt often accompanied with gross debauchery.

Wo unto thee, O Jerusalem! wilt thou not be made clean?] We see from this, that though the thing was difficult, yet it was not *impossible*, for these *Ethiopians* to change their *skin*, for these *leopards* to change their *spots.* It was only their obstinate refusal of the grace of God that rendered it impossible. Man cannot change himself; but he may pray to God to do it, and come to him through Christ, that he *may* do it. To enable him to pray and believe, the power is still at hand. If he will not use it, he must perish.

CHAPTER XIV

This chapter begins with foretelling a drought that should greatly distress the land of Judea, the effects of which are described in a most pathetic manner, 1–6. *The prophet then, in the people's name, makes a confession of sins, and supplication for pardon,* 7–9. *But God declares his purpose to punish, forbidding Jeremiah to pray for the people,* 10–12. *False prophets are then complained of, and threatened with destruction, as are also those who attend to them,* 13–16. *The prophet, therefore, bewails their misery,* 17, 18; *and though he had just now been forbidden to intercede for them, yet, like a tender pastor, who could not cease to be concerned for their welfare, he falls on the happy expedient of introducing themselves as supplicating in their own name that mercy which he was not allowed to ask in his,* 19–22.

A. M. cir. 3399
B. C. cir. 605
Ol. XLIII. 4
TarquiniiPrisci,
R. Roman.,
cir. annum 12

THE word of the LORD that
came to Jeremiah concern-
ing [a]the dearth.
2 Judah mourneth, and [b]the
gates thereof languish; they are [c]black unto
the ground; and [d]the cry of Jerusalem is
gone up.
3 And their nobles have sent their little ones
to the waters: they came to the pits, *and*
found no water; they returned with their
vessels empty; they were [e]ashamed and confounded, [f]and covered their heads.
4 Because the ground is chapt, for there was
no rain in the earth, the ploughmen were
ashamed, they covered their heads.
5 Yea, the hind also calved in
the field, and forsook *it,* because
there was no grass.
6 And [g]the wild asses did stand
in the high places, they snuffed up the wind
like dragons; their eyes did fail, because *there*
was no grass.
7 O LORD, though our iniquities testify
against us, do thou *it* [h]for thy name's sake:
for our backslidings are many; we have sinned
against thee.
8 [i]O the hope of Israel, the Saviour thereof
in time of trouble, why shouldest thou be as
a stranger in the land, and as a way-faring
man *that* turneth aside to tarry for a night?

A. M. cir. 3399
B. C. cir. 605
Ol. XVIII. 4
TarquiniiPrisci,
R. Roman.,
cir. annum 12

[a]Heb. *the words of the dearths,* or *restraints*——[b]Isa. iii. 26——[c]Chap. viii. 21——[d]See 1 Sam. v. 12

[e]Psa. xl. 14——[f]2 Sam. xv. 30——[g]Chap. ii. 24
[h]Psa. xxv. 11——[i]Chap. xvii. 13

NOTES ON CHAP. XIV

Verse 1. *The word—that came—concerning the dearth.*] This discourse is supposed to have been delivered, after the *fourth* year of Jehoiakim. *Concerning the dearth.* We have no historic record of any dearth that may fall in with the time of this prophecy, and perhaps it does not refer to any particular dearth: but this was a calamity to which Judea was very liable. They had ordinarily very dry summers, for scarcely any rain fell from *April* to the middle of *October;* and during much of this time, the rivers were generally either very low or entirely dry. They kept the rain of the winter in tanks and reservoirs; and if little fell in winter, a dearth was unavoidable. See an account of a dearth in the time of Elijah, 1 Kings xviii. 5, through which almost all the cattle were lost.

Verse 2. *The gates thereof languish*] The *gates* being the places of public resort, they are put here for the *people.*

They are black unto the ground] Covered from head to foot with a black garment, the emblem of sorrow and calamity.

Verse 3. *Their nobles have sent their little ones*] So general was this calamity, that the servants no longer attended to their lords, but every one was interested alone for himself; and the *nobles* of the land were obliged to employ their *own children* to scour the land, to see if any water could be found in the tanks or the pits. In the dearth in the time of Elijah, Ahab the king, and Obadiah his counsellor, were obliged to traverse the land *themselves,* in order to find out water to keep their cattle alive. This and the three following verses give a lively but distressing picture of this dearth and its effects.

Verse 4. *The ground is chapt*] The cracks in the earth before the descent of the rains are in some places a cubit wide, and deep enough to receive the greater part of a human body.

Verse 6. *Snuffed up the wind like dragons*] תנים *tannim* here probably means the *hippopotamus,* who, after feeding under the water, is obliged to come to the surface in order to take in fresh draughts of air; or it may mean the *wild asses.*

Verse 7. *O Lord, though our iniquities testify against us*] We deeply acknowledge that we have sinned, and deserve nothing but death. Yet *act for thy name's sake*—work in our behalf, that we perish not.

Verse 8. *O the hope of Israel*] O thou who art the only object of the *hope* of this people.

The Saviour thereof in time of trouble] Who hast never yet abandoned them that seek thee.

Why shouldest thou be as a stranger in the land] As one who has no interest in the prosperity and safety of the country.

And as a way-faring man] A traveller on his journey.

That *turneth aside to tarry for a night?*] Who stays the shortest time he can; and takes up his lodging in a *tent* or *caravanserai,* for the dead of the night, that he may pursue his journey by break of day. Instead of *dwelling among us,* thou hast scarcely paid the most transient visit to thy land. O come once more, and dwell among us.

A. M. cir. 3399
B. C. cir. 605
Ol. XLIII. 4
TarquiniiPrisci,
R. Roman.,
cir. annum 12

9 Why shouldest thou be as a man astonied, as a mighty man [k]*that* cannot save? yet thou, O LORD, [l]*art* in the midst of us, and [m]we are called by thy name; leave us not.

10 Thus saith the LORD unto this people, [n]Thus have they loved to wander, they have not refrained their feet, therefore the LORD doth not accept them; [o]he will now remember their iniquity, and visit their sins.

11 Then said the LORD unto me, [p]Pray not for this people for *their* good.

12 [q]When they fast, I will not hear their cry; and [r]when they offer burnt-offering and an oblation, I will not accept them: but [s]I will consume them by the sword, and by the famine, and by the pestilence.

13 [t]Then said I, Ah, Lord GOD! behold, the prophets say unto them, Ye shall not see the sword, neither shall ye have famine; but I will give you [u]assured peace in this place.

14 Then the LORD said unto me, [v]The prophets prophesy lies in my name: [w]I sent them not, neither have I commanded them, neither spake unto them: they prophesy unto you a false vision and divination, and a thing of nought, and the deceit of their heart.

A. M. cir. 3399
B. C. cir. 605
Ol. XLIII. 4
TarquiniiPrisci,
R. Roman.,
cir. annum 12

15 Therefore thus saith the LORD concerning the prophets that prophesy in my name, and I sent them not, [x]yet they say, Sword and famine shall not be in this land; By sword and famine shall those prophets be consumed.

16 And the people to whom they prophesy shall be cast out in the streets of Jerusalem because of the famine and the sword; [y]and they shall have none to bury them, them, their wives, nor their sons, nor their daughters: for I will pour their wickedness upon them.

17 Therefore thou shalt say this word unto them; [z]Let mine eyes run down with tears night and day, and let them not cease: [a]for the virgin daughter of my people is broken with a great breach, with a very grievous blow.

18 If I go forth into [b]the field, then behold the slain with the sword! and if I enter into

---

[k]Isa. lix. 1——[l]Exod. xxix. 45, 46; Lev. xxvi. 11, 12——[m]Heb. *thy name is called upon us;* Dan. ix. 18, 19——[n]See ch. ii. 23, 24, 25——[o]Hos. viii. 13; ix. 9——[p]Exod. xxxii. 10; chap. vii. 16; xi. 14——[q]Prov. i. 28; Isa. i. 15; lviii. 3; ch. xi. 11; Ezek. viii. 18; Mic. iii. 4; Zech. vii. 13——[r]Chap. vi. 20; vii. 21, 22——[s]Chap. ix. 16——[t]Chap. iv. 10——[u]Heb. *peace of truth*——[v]Chap. xxvii. 10——[w]Chap. xxiii. 21; xxvii. 15; xxix, 8. 9——[x]Chap. v. 12, 13——[y]Psa. lxxix. 3——[z]Chap. ix. 1; xiii. 17; Lam. i. 16; ii. 18——[a]Chap. viii. 21——[b]Ezek. vii. 15

Verse 9. *Yet thou, O Lord,* art *in the midst of us*] Thy ark, temple, and sacred rites, are all here; and thou thyself, who art every where present, art here also: but alas! thou dost not *reveal* thyself as the Father of mercies, who forgivest iniquity, transgression, and sin.

We are called by thy name; leave us not.] Let us call thee our Father, and say thou to us, "Ye are my sons and daughters!" O leave us not!

Verse 10. *Thus have they loved to wander*] And the measure of your iniquity being now full, ye must be punished.

Verse 11. *Pray not for this people*] They are ripe for destruction, intercede not for them. O, how dreadful is the state of that people in reference to whom the Lord says to his ministers, *Pray not for them;* or, what amounts nearly to a prohibition, withholds from his ministers the spirit of prayer and intercession in behalf of the people!

Verse 13. *Ah, Lord God! behold, the prophets say unto them*] True, Lord, they are exceedingly wicked; but the false prophets have deceived them; this is some mitigation of their offence. This plea God does not admit; and why? the people believed them, without having any proof of their Divine mission.

Verse 14. *The prophets prophesy lies*] They say they have *visions*, but they have them by *divination*, and they are false. The people should know their character, and avoid them; but they love to have it so, and will not be undeceived.

Verse 15. *By sword and famine shall those prophets be consumed.*] Jeremiah had told Jehoiakim that, if he rebelled against Nebuchadnezzar, he should be overthrown, and the land wasted by *sword* and *famine:* the false prophets said there shall be neither *sword* nor *famine*, but *peace* and *prosperity.* The king believed *them*, and withheld the *tribute.* Nebuchadnezzar, being incensed, invaded and destroyed the land; and the false prophets fell in these calamities. See 2 Kings xxv. 3; Lam. ii. 11-19.

Verse 16. *And the people—shall be cast out*] They shall be destroyed, because they preferred *their lying words* to *my truth*, proclaimed by thee.

Verse 17. *For the virgin daughter of my people is broken*] *First*, the land was sadly distressed by *Pharaoh-necho*, king of Egypt. *Secondly*, it was laid under a heavy tribute by *Nebuchadnezzar.* And, *thirdly*, it was nearly desolated by a *famine* afterwards. In a few years all these calamities fell upon them; these might be well called *a great breach, a very grievous blow.*

Verse 18. *If I go forth into the field, then behold the slain with the sword*] Every place presents frightful spectacles; the wounded, the dying, the starving, and the slain; none to bury the dead, none to commiserate the dying, none to bring either relief or consolation. Even the *prophets* and the *priests* are obliged to leave the cities, and wander about in unfrequented and unknown places, seeking for the neces-

A. M. cir. 3399 B. C. cir. 605 Ol. XLIII. 4 TarquiniiPrisci, R. Roman., cir. annum 12

the city, then behold them that
are sick with famine! yea, both
the prophet and the priest [c]go
about into a land that they
know not.
19 [d]Hast thou utterly rejected Judah?
hath thy soul loathed Zion? why hast thou
smitten us, and [e]*there is* no healing for us?
[f]we looked for peace, and *there is* no good;
and for the time of healing, and behold
trouble!
20 We acknowledge, O LORD, our wickedness, *and* the iniquity of our
fathers: for [g]we have sinned
against thee.
21 Do not abhor *us*, for thy
name's sake, do not disgrace the throne of thy
glory: [h]remember, break not thy covenant
with us.
22 [i]Are there *any* among the [k]vanities of
the Gentiles that can cause rain? or can the
heavens give showers? [l]*art* not thou he, O
LORD our God? therefore we will wait upon
thee: for thou hast made all these *things*.

[c]Or, *make merchandise against a land, and* men *acknowledge* it *not;* chap. v. 13——[d]Lam. v. 22——[e]Ch. xv. 18——[f]Ch. viii. 15——[g]Psa. cvi. 6; Dan. ix. 8

[h]Psa. lxxiv. 2, 20; cvi. 45——[i]Zech. x. 1, 2——[k]Deut. xxxii. 21——[l]Psa. cxxxv. 7; cxlvii. 8; Isa. xxx. 23; chap. v. 24; x. 13

saries of life. Dr. *Blayney* thinks that the *going about of the prophets and priests of the land*, is to be understood thus:—"They went trafficking about with their false doctrines and lying predictions, as pedlars do with their wares, seeking their own gain." I think the other sense preferable.

Verse 19. *We looked for peace*] We expected prosperity when Josiah purged the land of idolatry.

And there is *no good*] For we have relapsed into our former ways.

Verse 20. *We acknowledge, O Lord, our wickedness*] This the prophet did in behalf of the people; but, alas! they did not join him.

Verse 21. *Do not disgrace the throne of thy glory*] The temple. Let not this sacred place be profaned by impious and sacrilegious hands.

Break not thy covenant] See Exod. xxiv. 7, 8; xix. 5. *They* had already broken the covenant, and they wish God to fulfil his part. They ceased to *be his people*, for they abandoned themselves to idolatry; and yet they wished Jehovah *to be their Lord;* to defend, support, and fill them with all good things! But when the conditions of a covenant are broken by one of the contracting parties, the other party is not bound; and the covenant is necessarily annulled.

Verse 22. *Are there* any *among the vanities of the Gentiles*] Probably the dearth was now coming, as there had been a long want of rain. It was the prerogative of the true God to give rain and send showers at the prayers of his people.

Therefore we will wait upon thee] If thou do not undertake for us, we must be utterly ruined.

CHAPTER XV

God declares to Jeremiah that not even Moses and Samuel, whose prayers had been so prevalent, could divert him from his purpose of punishing so wicked a people, 1. *Accordingly their captivity is again announced in a variety of images so full of terror,* 2–9, *that the prophet complains of his own hard fate in being obliged to deliver such unwelcome messages,* 10; *for which too he is reproved,* 11–14. *Immediately he appeals to God for his sincerity, and supplicates pardon,* 15–18; *and God tempers his reproof with promising again to protect him in the faithful discharge of his duty,* 19–21.

A. M. cir. 3399 B. C. cir. 605 Ol. XLIII. 4 TarquiniiPrisci, R. Roman., cir. annum 12

THEN said the LORD unto me,
[a]Though [b]Moses and [c]Sa-
muel stood before me, *yet* my
mind *could* not *be* toward this
people: cast *them* out of my
sight, and let them go forth.
2 And it shall come to pass, if
they say unto thee, Whither shall

[a]Ezek. xiv. 14, &c.

[b]Exod. xxxii. 11, 12; Psa. xcix. 6——[c]1 Sam. vii. 9

NOTES ON CHAP. XV

Verse 1. *Though Moses and Samuel*] *Moses* had often supplicated for the people; and in consequence they were spared. See Exod. xxxii. 11 and following verses, Num. xiv. 13. *Samuel* also had prayed for the people, and God heard him, 1 Sam. vii. 9; but if these or the most holy men were now to supplicate for this people, he would not spare them.

Cast them *out of my sight, and let them go forth.*] Do not bring them into my *presence* by your prayers; *let them go forth* into captivity.

Verse 2. *Whither shall we go forth?—Such* as are *for death, to death*] Some shall be destroyed by the *pestilence*, here termed *death*. See chap. xviii. 21. Others shall be slain by the *sword* in battle, and in the sackage of cities. Others shall perish by *famine*, shall be starved to death through the mere want of the necessaries of life; and the rest shall go into *captivity*. There shall be *different* sorts of punishments inflicted on them according to the nature of their transgressions. Some shall be punished in one way, and some in another.

A. M. cir. 3399 B. C. cir. 605 Ol. XLIII. 4 TarquiniiPrisci, R. Roman., cir. annum 12

we go forth? then thou shalt tell
them, Thus saith the LORD;
[d]Such as *are* for death, to death;
and such as *are* for the sword,
to the sword; and such as *are* for the famine,
to the famine; and such as *are* for the captivity, to the captivity.
3 And I will [e]appoint over them four [f]kinds,
saith the LORD: the sword to slay, and the
dogs to tear, and [g]the fowls of the heaven,
and the beasts of the earth, to devour and
destroy.
4 And [h]I will cause them to be [i]removed
into all kingdoms of the earth, because of
[k]Manasseh the son of Hezekiah king of Judah,
for *that* which he did in Jerusalem.
5 For [l]who shall have pity upon thee, O
Jerusalem? or who shall bemoan thee? or
who shall go aside [m]to ask how thou doest?
6 [n]Thou hast forsaken me, saith the LORD,
thou art [o]gone backward: therefore will I
stretch out my hand against thee, and destroy
thee; [p]I am weary with repenting.
7 And I will fan them with a fan in the
gates of the land; I will bereave *them* of
[q]children, I will destroy my people, *since* [r]they return not from
their ways.

A. M. cir. 3399 B. C. cir. 605 Ol. XLIII. 4 TarquiniiPrisci, R. Roman., cir. annum 12

8 Their widows are increased to
me above the sand of the seas: I have brought
upon them [s]against the mother of the young
men, a spoiler at noonday: I have caused *him* to
fall upon it suddenly, and terrors upon the city.
9 [t]She that hath borne seven languisheth:
she hath given up the ghost; [u]her sun is gone
down while *it was* yet day: she hath been
ashamed and confounded: and the residue of
them will I deliver to the sword before their
enemies, saith the LORD.
10 [v]Wo is me, my mother, that thou hast
borne me a man of strife and a man of contention to the whole earth! I have neither
lent on usury, nor men have lent to me on
usury; *yet* every one of them doth curse me.
11 The LORD said, Verily it shall be well
with thy remnant, verily [w]I will cause [x]the
enemy to entreat thee *well* in the time of evil
and in the time of affliction.
12 Shall iron break the northern iron and the
steel?

---

[d]Ch. xliii. 11; Ezek. v. 2, 12; Zech. xi. 9——[e]Lev. xxvi. 16, &c.——[f]Heb. *families*——[g]Ch. vii. 33; Deut. xxviii. 26——[h]Heb. *I will give them for a removing* [i]Deut. xxviii. 25; ch. xxiv. 9; Ezek. xxiii. 46——[k]2 Kings xxi. 11, &c.; xxiii. 26; xxiv. 3, 4——[l]Isa. li. 19 [m]Heb. *to ask of thy peace*——[n]Ch. ii. 13——[o]Ch. vii. 24

[p]Hos. xiii. 14——[q]Or, *whatsoever is dear*——[r]Isa. ix. 13; ch. v. 3; Amos iv. 10, 11——[s]Or, *against the mother city a young man spoiling*, &c.; or *against the mother* and *the young men*——[t]1 Sam. ii. 5——[u]Amos viii. 9 [v]Job iii. 1, &c.; ch. xx. 14——[w]Or, *I will entreat the enemy for thee*——[x]Ch. xxxix. 11, 12; xl. 3, 4, 5

Verse 3. *I will appoint over them four kinds*] There shall appear *four* instruments of my justice. 1. The *sword* to slay. 2. The *dogs* to tear what is slain. 3. The *fowls* of the heaven to feed on the dead carcasses. And, 4. The wild *beasts* to destroy all that the fowls have left.

Verse 4. *I will cause them to be removed into all kingdoms of the earth*] This seems to have respect to the *succeeding* state of the Jews in their *different generations;* and never was there a prophecy more literally fulfilled; and it is still a standing monument of Divine truth. Let *infidelity* cast its eyes on the scattered Jews whom it may meet with in every civilized nation of the world; and then let it deny the truth of this prophecy, if it can. The Jews are scattered through every nation, and yet *are not a nation;* nor do they form even *a colony* on any part of the face of the earth. Behold the truth and the justice of God!

Verse 5. *Who shall go aside to ask how thou doest?*] Perhaps there is not a more despised nor a more degraded people under the sun. Scarcely any one thinks himself called upon to do a kind office for a Jew. Their character is bad in society, and they are not at all solicitous to redeem it.

Verse 6. *I am weary with repenting.*] With repeatedly *changing my purpose.* I have often, after purposing to punish, showed them mercy. I will do it no longer; it is useless. I took them often at their promise, and in every instance they have failed.

Verse 7. *I will fan them with a fan*] There is no pure grain; all is chaff.

In the gates of the land] The places of public justice: and there it shall be seen that the judgments that have fallen upon them have been highly merited. And from these places of fanning they shall go out into their captivity.

Verse 8. *The mother of the young men*] The *metropolis* or mother city, *Jerusalem.*

Verse 9. *She that hath borne seven*] She that hath had a numerous offspring; Jerusalem, the parent of so many cities, villages, and families in the land. *Seven* signifies a *complete* or *full* number.

Verse 10. *A man of contention to the whole earth!*] To the whole LAND, to all his countrymen; though he had done nothing to merit their displeasure.

Verse 11. *I will cause the enemy to entreat thee* well *in the time of evil*] This was literally fulfilled; see chap. xxxix. 11, &c. Nebuchadnezzar had given strict charge to Nebuzar-adan, commander in chief, to look well to Jeremiah, to do him no harm, and to grant him all the privileges he was pleased to ask.

Verse 12. *Shall iron break the northern iron and the steel?*] Shall our weak forces be able to oppose and overcome the powers of the Chal-

A. M. cir. 3399
B. C. cir. 605
Ol. XLIII. 4
TarquiniiPrisci,
R. Roman.,
cir. annum 12

13 Thy substance and thy treasures will I give to the [y]spoil without price, and *that* for all thy sins, even in all thy borders.

14 And I will make *thee* to pass with thine enemies [z]into a land *which* thou knowest not: for a [a]fire is kindled in mine anger, *which* shall burn upon you.

15 O LORD, [b]thou knowest: remember me, and visit me, and [c]revenge me of my persecutors, take me not away in thy long-suffering: know that [d]for thy sake I have suffered rebuke.

16 Thy words were found, and I did [e]eat them; and [f]thy word was unto me the joy and rejoicing of mine heart: for [g]I am called by thy name, O LORD God of hosts.

17 [h]I sat not in the assembly of the mockers, nor rejoiced; I sat alone because of thy hand: for thou hast filled me with indignation.

A. M. cir. 3399
B. C. cir 605
Ol. XLIV. 4
TarquiniiPrisci,
R. Roman.,
cir. annum 12

18 Why is my [i]pain perpetual, and my wound incurable, *which* refuseth to be healed? wilt thou be altogether unto me [k]as a liar, *and as* waters *that* [m]fail?

19 Therefore thus saith the LORD, [n]If thou return, then will I bring thee again, *and* thou shalt [o]stand before me: and if thou [p]take forth the precious from the vile, thou shalt be as my mouth: let them return unto thee; but return not thou unto them.

20 And I will make thee unto this people a fenced brazen [q]wall: and they shall fight against thee, [r]but they shall not prevail against thee: for I *am* with thee to save thee and to deliver thee, saith the LORD.

21 And I will deliver thee out of the hand of the wicked, and I will redeem thee out of the hand of the terrible.

---

[y]Psa. xliv. 12; chap. xvii. 3——[z]Chap. xvi. 13; xvii. 4——[a]Deut. xxxii. 22——[b]Chap. xii. 3——[c]Chap. xi. 20; xx. 12——[d]Psa. lxix. 7——[e]Ezek. iii. 1, 3; Rev. x. 9, 10——[f]Job xxiii. 12; Psa. cxix. 72, 111

[g]Heb. *thy name is called upon me*——[h]Psa. i. 1; xxvi. 4, 5——[i]Ch. xxx. 15——[k]See ch. i. 18, 19——[l]Job vi. 15, &c.——[m]Heb. *be not sure*——[n]Zech. iii. 7——[o]Ver. 1——[p]Ezek. xxii. 26; xliv. 23——[q]Ch. i. 18; vi. 27——[r]Ch. xx. 11, 12

---

deans? נחשת *nechasheth*, which we here translate *steel*, properly signifies brass or copper united with tin, which gives it much hardness, and enables it to bear a good edge.

Verse 13. *Thy substance—will I give to the spoil without price*] *Invaluable property* shall be given up to thy adversaries. Or, *without price*—thou shalt have nothing for it in return.

Verse 15. *O Lord—remember me, and visit me*] Let me not be carried away into captivity; and it does not appear that he had ever been taken to Babylon. After the capture of the city he went into Egypt; and either died there, or was put to death by his countrymen.

Verse 16. *Thy word was—the joy and rejoicing of mine heart*] When I did receive the prophetic message, I did rejoice in the honour thou hadst done me; and I faithfully testified thy will to them. They have become mine enemies; not because there was any evil in me, but because I was faithful to thee.

Verse 18. *Wilt thou be altogether unto me as—waters* that *fail?*] Meaning either springs, which in the height of summer grow dry; or, like that phenomenon in the sandy desert, where, by a peculiar action of the air on the rising vapours, the resemblance of water is produced, so that the traveller, deceived, rejoices that he is come, in the sandy desert, to the verge of a beautiful lake; but the farther he travels, it is still at the same distance, and at last vanishes; and he finds the whole was an illusion, for the waters have *failed*. Nothing can exceed the disappointment of the farmer whose subsistence absolutely depends on the periodical rains, when these *fail*, or fall short of their usual *quantity*. Some times the *rice* is sown and springs up in the most promising manner; but the latter rains *fail*, and whole fields of young rice wither and perish.

Verse 19. *If thou return*] By repentance unto me,—

Then will I bring thee again] Restore thee to thy own country. But some think the words are spoken to the prophet in reference to his ministry. He had greatly repined because of the persecutions which he endured. The Lord reprehends him, and is about to take from him the prophetic gift; but exhorts him first to take the *precious* from the *vile*—not to attend to the deceitful words of the people, but boldly declare the message he had given him; not to return unto the people, but let the people return unto him. And then he should be as *God's mouth*—his words should appear to be what they were, the genuine words of God; and the people should be obliged to acknowledge them as such.

Verse 20. *I will make thee—a fenced brazen wall*] While thou art faithful to me, none of them shall be able to prevail against thee.

Verse 21. *I will deliver thee out of the hand of the wicked*] From the power of this evil people.

And I will redeem thee out of the hand of the terrible.] Out of the power of the Chaldean armies. Every thing took place as God had promised, for no word of his can ever fall to the ground.

CHAPTER XVI

On account of the evils which threatened his country, the prophet is forbidden to encumber himself with a wife and family, or to bear any share in the little joys and sorrows of his neighbours, which were to be forgotten and absorbed in those public calamities, 1–9, *which their sins should draw on them,* 10–13. *A future restoration however is intimated,* 14, 15, *after those calamities should be endured,* 16–18; *and the conversion of the Gentiles is foretold,* 19–21.

A. M. cir. 3400
B. C. cir. 604
Ol. XLIV. 1
TarquiniiPrisci,
R. Roman.,
cir. annum 13

THE word of the LORD came also unto me, saying,

2 Thou shalt [a]not take thee a wife, neither shalt thou have sons or daughters in this place.

3 For thus saith the LORD concerning the sons and concerning the daughters that are born in this place, and concerning their mothers that bare them, and concerning their fathers that begat them in this land;

4 They shall die of [b]grievous deaths; they shall not be [c]lamented; neither shall they be buried; *but* they shall be [d]as dung upon the face of the earth: and they shall be consumed by the sword, and by famine; and their [e]carcasses shall be meat for the fowls of heaven, and for the beasts of the earth.

5 For thus saith the LORD, [f]Enter not into the house of [g]mourning, neither go to lament nor bemoan them: for I have taken away my peace from this people, saith the LORD, *even* loving-kindness and mercies.

6 Both the great and the small shall die in this land: they shall not be buried, [h]neither shall *men* lament for them, nor [i]cut themselves, nor [k]make themselves bald for them:

A. M. cir. 3400
B. C. cir. 604
Ol. XLIV. 1
TarquiniiPrisci,
R. Roman.,
cir. annum 13

7 Neither shall *men* [l]tear *themselves* for them in mourning, to comfort them for the dead; neither shall *men* give them the cup of consolation to [m]drink for their father or for their mother.

8 Thou shalt not also go into the house of feasting, to sit with them to eat and to drink.

9 For thus saith the LORD of hosts, the God of Israel; Behold, [n]I will cause to cease out of this place in your eyes, and in your days, the voice of mirth, and the voice of gladness, the voice of the bridegroom, and the voice of the bride.

10 And it shall come to pass, when thou shalt show this people all these words, and they shall say unto thee, [o]Wherefore hath the LORD pronounced all this great evil against us? or what *is* our iniquity? or what *is* our sin that we have committed against the LORD our God?

11 Then shalt thou say unto them, [p]Because your fathers have forsaken me, saith the LORD, and have walked after other gods, and

[a]1 Cor. vii. 26——[b]Chap. xv. 2——[c]Chap. xxii. 18, 19; xxv. 33——[d]Psa. lxxxiii. 10; chap. viii. 2; ix. 22 [e]Psa. lxxix. 2; chap. vii. 33; xxxiv. 20——[f]Ezek. xxiv. 17, 22, 23——[g]Or, *mourning feast*——[h]Chap. xxii. 18 [i]Lev. xix. 28; Deut. xiv. 1; chap. xli. 5; xlvii. 5——[k]Isa. xxii. 12; chap. vii. 29

[l]Or, *break bread for them*, as Ezek. xxiv. 17; Hos. ix. 4; see Deut. xxvi. 14; Job xlii. 11——[m]Prov. xxxi. 6, 7 [n]Isa. xxiv. 7, 8; chap. vii. 34; xxv. 10; Ezek. xxvi. 13; Hos. ii. 11; Rev. xviii. 23——[o]Deut. xxix. 24; chap. v. 19; xiii. 22; xxii. 8——[p]Deuteronomy xxix. 25; chap. xxii. 9

NOTES ON CHAP. XVI

Verse 1. *The word of the Lord came also unto me*] This discourse *Dahler* supposes to have been delivered some time in the *reign of Jehoiakim.*

Verse 2. *Thou shalt not take thee a wife*] As it would be very inconvenient to have a family when the threatened desolations should come on the place. The reason is given in the following verses.

Verse 4. *They shall die of grievous deaths*] All *prematurely;* see chap. xiv. 16.

As dung upon the face of the earth] See chap. viii. 2.

Be meat for the fowls] See chap. vii. 33.

Verse 5. *Enter not into the house of mourning*] The public calamities are too great to permit individual losses to come into consideration.

Verse 6. *Nor cut themselves*] A custom of the heathen forbidden to the Jews, Lev. xix. 28, Deut. xiv. 1, and which appears now to have prevailed among them; because, having become idolaters, they conformed to all the customs of the heathen. They *tore their hair, rent their garments, cut their hands, arms,* and *faces.* These were not only *signs of sorrow,* but were even supposed to give ease to the dead, and appease the angry deities. The *Hindoos,* on the death of a relation, express their grief by loud lamentations, and not unfrequently *bruise* themselves in an agony of grief with whatever they can lay hold on.

Verse 8. *Thou shalt not also go into the house of feasting*] *Funeral banquets* were made to commemorate the dead, and comfort the surviving relatives; and *the cup of consolation,* strong mingled wine, was given to those who were deepest in distress, to divert their minds and to soothe their sorrows. These kinds of ceremonies were common among almost all the nations of the world on funeral occasions. The *Canaanites,* the *Jews,* the *Persians, Arabians, New Zealanders, Huns,* &c., &c.

A. M. cir. 3400
B. C. cir. 604
Ol. XLIV. 1
TarquiniiPrisci,
R. Roman.,
cir. annum 13

have served them, and have worshipped them, and have forsaken me, and have not kept my law;

12 And ye have done [q]worse than your fathers; for, behold, [r]ye walk every one after the [s]imagination of his evil heart, that they may not hearken unto me:

13 [t]Therefore will I cast you out of this land [u]into a land that ye know not, *neither* ye nor your fathers; and there shall ye serve other gods day and night; where I will not show you favour.

14 Therefore, behold, the [v]days come, saith the LORD, that it shall no more be said, The LORD liveth, that brought up the children of Israel out of the land of Egypt;

15 But, The LORD liveth, that brought up the children of Israel from the land of the north, and from all the lands whither he had driven them: and [w]I will bring them again into their land that I gave unto their fathers.

16 Behold, I will send for many [x]fishers, saith the LORD, and they shall fish them; and after will I send for many hunters, and they shall hunt them from every mountain, and from every hill, and out of the holes of the rocks.

A. M. cir. 3400
B. C. cir. 604
Ol. XLIV. 1
TarquiniiPrisci,
R. Roman.,
cir. annum 13

17 For mine [y]eyes *are* upon all their ways: they are not hid from my face, neither is their iniquity hid from mine eyes.

18 And first I will recompense their iniquity and their sin [z]double; because [a]they have defiled my land, they have filled mine inheritance with the carcasses of their detestable and abominable things.

19 O LORD, [b]my strength, and my fortress, and [c]my refuge in the day of affliction, the Gentiles shall come unto thee from the ends of the earth, and shall say, Surely our fathers have inherited lies, vanity, and *things* [d]wherein *there is* no profit.

20 Shall a man make gods unto himself, and [e]they *are* no gods?

21 Therefore, behold, I will this once cause them to know, I will cause them to know mine hand and my might; and they shall know that [f]my name *is* [g]The LORD.

[q]Ch. vii. 26——[r]Ch. xiii. 10——[s]Or, *stubbornness* [t]Deut. iv. 26, 27, 28; xxviii. 36, 63, 64, 65——[u]Ch. xv. 14 [v]Isa. xliii. 18; ch. xxiii. 7, 8——[w]Ch. xxiv. 6; xxx. 3; xxxii. 37——[x]Amos iv. 2; Hab. i. 15——[y]Job xxxiv. 21; Prov. v. 21; xv. 3; chap. xxxii. 19

[z]Isa. xl. 2; ch. xvii. 18——[a]Ezek. xliii. 7, 9——[b]Psa. xviii. 2——[c]Ch. xvii. 17——[d]Isa. xliv. 10; ch. ii. 11; x. 5 [e]Isa. xxxvii. 19; ch. ii. 11; Gal. iv. 8——[f]Exod. xv. 3; chap. xxxiii. 2; Amos v. 8——[g]Or, *JEHOVAH;* Psa. lxxxiii. 18

Verse 12. *And ye have done worse than your fathers*] The sins of the fathers would not have been visited on the children, had they not followed their example, and become even worse than they.

Verse 13. *Will I cast you out of this land*] See chap. vii. 15, and ix. 15.

Verse 14. *The Lord liveth, that brought up*] See Isa. xliii. 18.

Verse 15. *The land of the north*] Chaldea: and their deliverance thence will be as remarkable as the deliverance of their fathers from the land of Egypt.

Verse 16. *I will send for many fishers—for many hunters*] I shall raise up enemies against them some of whom shall destroy them by *wiles*, and others shall ruin them by *violence*. This seems to be the meaning of these symbolical *fishers* and *hunters*.

Verse 18. *The carcasses of their detestable—things.*] Either meaning the *idols* themselves, which were only *carcasses* without life; or the *sacrifices* which were made to them.

Verse 19. *The Gentiles shall come*] Even the days shall come when the Gentiles themselves, ashamed of their confidence, shall renounce their idols, and acknowledge that their fathers had believed lies, and worshipped vanities. This may be a prediction of the *calling of the Gentiles* by the Gospel of Christ; if so, it is a *light* amidst much *darkness*. In such dismal accounts there is need of some gracious promise relative to an amended state of the world.

Verse 20. *Shall a man make gods unto himself?*] Can any be so silly, and so preposterously absurd? Yes, fallen man is capable of any thing that is base, mean, vile, and wicked, till influenced and converted by the grace of Christ.

Verse 21. *Therefore, behold, I will this once*] I will not now change my purpose. They shall be visited and carried into captivity; nothing shall prevent this: and they shall know that my name is JEHOVAH. Since they would not receive the abundance of my *mercies*, they shall know what the true God can do in the way of *judgment*.

CHAPTER XVII

This chapter begins with setting forth the very strong bias which the people of Judah had to idolatry, with the fatal consequences, 1–4. *The happiness of the man that trusteth in Jehovah is then beautifully contrasted with the opposite character,* 5–8. *God alone knows the deceitfulness and wretchedness of the heart of man,* 9, 10. *The comparison of a bird's hatching the eggs of another of a different species, which will soon forsake*

***her, is highly expressive of the vanity of ill-acquired riches, which often disappoint the owner,* 11. *The prophet continues the same subject in his own person, appeals to God for his sincerity, and prays that the evil intended him by his enemies may revert on their own heads,* 12–18. *The remaining part of the chapter is a distinct prophecy relating to the due observance of the Sabbath, enforced both by promises and threatenings,* 19–27.**

A. M. cir. 3400
B. C. cir. 604
Ol. XLIV. 1
TarquiniiPrisci,
R. Roman.,
cir. annum 13

THE sin of Judah *is* written with a [a]pen of iron, *and* with the [b]point of a diamond: *it is* [c]graven upon the table of their heart, and upon the horns of your altars;

2 Whilst their children remember their altars and their [d]groves by the green trees upon the high hills.

3 O my mountain in the field, [e]I will give thy substance *and* all thy treasures to the spoil, *and* thy high places for sin, throughout all thy borders.

4 And thou, even [f]thyself, shalt discontinue from thine heritage that I gave thee; and I will cause thee to serve thine enemies in [g]the land which thou knowest not: for [h]ye have kindled a fire in mine anger, *which* shall burn for ever.

A. M. cir. 3400
B. C. cir. 604
Ol. XLIV. 1
TarquiniiPrisci,
R. Roman.,
cir. annum 13

5 Thus saith the LORD; [i]Cursed *be* the man that trusteth in man, and maketh [k]flesh his arm, and whose heart departeth from the LORD.

6 For he shall be [l]like the heath in the desert, and [m]shall not see when good cometh; but shall inhabit the parched places in the wilderness, [n]*in* a salt land and not inhabited.

7 [o]Blessed *is* the man that trusteth in the LORD, and whose hope the LORD is.

8 For he shall be [p]as a tree planted by the waters, and *that* spreadeth out her roots by the river, and shall not see when heat cometh, but her leaf shall be green; and shall not be careful in the year of [q]drought, neither shall cease from yielding fruit.

9 The heart *is* deceitful above all *things*,

[a]Job xix. 24——[b]Heb. *nail*——[c]Prov. iii. 3; 2 Cor. iii. 3——[d]Judg. iii. 7; 2 Chron. xxiv. 18; xxxiii. 3, 19; Isa. i. 29; xvii. 8; ch. ii. 20——[e]Ch. xv. 13——[f]Heb. *in thyself* [g]Ch. xvi. 13——[h]Ch. xv. 14——[i]Isa. xxx. 1, 2; xxxi. 1

[k]See Isa. xxxi. 3——[l]Chap. xlviii. 6——[m]Job xx. 17 [n]Deut. xxix. 23——[o]Psa. ii. 12; xxxiv. 8; cxxv. 1; cxlvi. 5; Prov. xvi. 20; Isa. xxx. 18——[p]Job viii. 16; Psa. i. 3——[q]Or, *restraint*

NOTES ON CHAP. XVII

Verse 1. *The sin of Judah*] Idolatry.

Is *written with a pen of iron*] It is deeply and indelibly written in their *heart*, and shall be as indelibly written in their *punishment*. Writing with the *point of a diamond* must refer to *glass*, or some *vitrified* substance, as it is distinguished here from engraving with a *steel burine*, or *graver*. Their altars show what the deities are which they worship. There may be reference here to the different methods of recording events in those days:—1. A pen or stile of iron, for engraving on lead or wood. 2. A point of a diamond, for writing on vitreous substances. 3. Writing on tables of brass or copper. 4. Writing on the horns of the altars the names of the deities worshipped there. This is probable.

In several parts of India, and all through Ceylon, an *iron* or *steel pen* is used universally; with these the natives form the letters by incisions on the outer rind of the palm leaf. Books written in this way are very durable. This pen is *broad* at the *top*, has a very *fine sharp point*, and is *sharp* at *one side* as a knife, to shave and prepare the palm leaf. A pen of this description now lies before me.

Verse 2. *Whilst their children remember*] Even the rising generation have their *imagination* stocked with *idol images*, and their *memories* with the frantic rites and ceremonies which they saw their parents observe in this abominable worship.

Verse 3. *O my mountain in the field*] The prophet here addresses the *land of Judea*, which was a *mountainous* country, Deut. iii. 25; but *Jerusalem* itself may be meant, which is partly built upon *hills* which, like itself, are elevated above the rest of the country.

Verse 5. *Cursed* be *the man that trusteth in man*] This reprehends their vain confidence in trusting in *Egypt*, which was *too feeble* itself to help, and, had it been otherwise, too ill disposed towards them to help them *heartily*. An *arm of flesh* is put here for a *weak* and *ineffectual support*. And he who, in reference to the salvation of his soul, trusts in an *arm of flesh*—in *himself* or *others*, or in any thing he has *done* or *suffered*, will inherit a curse instead of a blessing.

Verse 6. *He shall be like the heath in the desert*] כערער *kearar;* or, like a blasted *tree*, without moisture, parched and withered.

Shall not see when good cometh] Shall not be sensible of it: the previous drought having rendered it incapable of absorbing any more vegetable juices.

A salt land] Barren; and therefore unfit to be *inhabited*.

Verse 8. *As a tree planted by the waters*] Which is sufficiently supplied with *moisture*, though the heat be intense, and there be no rain; for the roots being spread out by the river, they absorb from it all the moisture requisite for the flourishing vegetation of the tree.

Shall not see when heat cometh] Shall not feel any damage by *drought*, for the reason already assigned. It shall be strong and vigorous, its *leaf* always *green;* and shall produce plenty of fruit in its season.

Verse 9. *The heart* is *deceitful*] עקב הלב *akob halleb*, "the heart is supplanting—tortuous—full of windings—insidious;" lying ever at the catch; striving to avail itself of every

A. M. cir. 3400
B. C. cir. 604
Ol. XLIV. 1
TarquiniiPrisci,
R. Roman.,
cir. annum 13

and desperately wicked: who
can know it?
10 I the LORD [r]search the
heart, *I* try the reins, [s]even to
give every man according to his ways, *and*
according to the fruit of his doings.
11 *As* the partridge [t]sitteth *on eggs,* and
hatcheth *them* not; *so* he that getteth riches,
and not by right, [u]shall leave them in the
midst of his days, and at his end shall be [v]a
fool.
12 A glorious high throne from the beginning *is* the place of our sanctuary.
13 O LORD, [w]the hope of Israel, [x]all that
forsake thee shall be ashamed, *and* they that
depart from me shall be [y]written
in the earth, because they have
forsaken the LORD, the [z]Foun-
tain of living waters.

A. M. cir. 3400
B. C. cir. 604
Ol. XLIV. 1
TarquiniiPrisci,
R. Roman.,
cir. annum 13

14 Heal me, O LORD, and I shall be healed;
save me, and I shall be saved: for [a]thou *art*
my praise.
15 Behold, they say unto me, [b]Where *is*
the word of the LORD? let it come now.
16 As for me, [c]I have not hastened from
being a pastor [d]to follow thee: neither have
I desired the woful day; thou knowest: that
which came out of my lips was *right* before
thee.
17 Be not a terror unto me: [e]thou *art*

---

[r]1 Sam. xvi. 7; 1 Chron. xxviii. 9; Psa. vii. 9; cxxxix. 23, 24; Prov. xvii. 3; chap. xi. 20; xx. 12; Rom. viii. 27; Rev. ii. 23——[s]Psa. lxii. 12; chap. xxxii. 19; Rom. ii. 6
[t]Or, *gathereth* young *which she hath not brought forth*
[u]Psa. lv. 23——[v]Luke xii. 20

[w]Chap. xiv. 8——[x]Psa. lxxiii. 27; Isa. i. 21——[y]See Luke x. 20——[z]Chap. ii. 13——[a]Deut. x. 28; Psa. cix. 1; cxlviii. 14——[b]Isa. v. 19; Ezek. xii. 22; Amos v. 18; 2 Pet. iii. 4——[c]Chap. i. 4, &c.——[d]Heb. *after thee*——[e]Chap. xvi. 19

---

favourable circumstance to gratify its propensities to pride, ambition, evil desire, and corruption of all kinds.

And desperately wicked] ואנש הוא *veanush hu*, and is *wretched*, or *feeble; distressed beyond all things*, in consequence of the wickedness that is in it. I am quite of Mr. *Parkhurst's* opinion, that this word is here badly translated, as אנש *anash* is never used in Scripture to denote *wickedness* of any kind. My old MS. Bible translates thus:—**Schrewid is the herte of a man; and unserchable: who schal knowen it?**

Who can know it?] It even hides itself from itself; so that its owner does not know it. A corrupt heart is the worst enemy the fallen creature can have; it is full of evil devices,—of deceit, of folly, and abomination; and its owner knows not what is in him till it boils over, and is often past remedy before the evil is perceived. Therefore, trust not in man, whose purposes are continually changing, and who is actuated only by motives of *self-interest.*

Verse 10. *I the Lord search the heart*] The Lord is called by his apostles, Acts i. 24, Καρδιωγνωστης, *the Knower of the heart.* To him alone can this epithet be applied; and it is from him alone that we can derive that *instruction* by which we can in any measure *know ourselves.*

Verse 11. As *the partridge*] קרא *kore.* It is very likely that this was a bird different from our partridge. The text Dr. *Blayney* translates thus:—

(As) the koré that hatcheth what it doth not
lay,
(So is) he who getteth riches, and not according to right.

"The covetous man," says *Dahler*, "who heaps up riches by unjust ways, is compared to a bird which hatches the eggs of other fowls. And as the young, when hatched, and able at all to shift for themselves, abandon her who is not their mother, and leave her nothing to compensate her trouble, so the covetous man loses those unjustly-gotten treasures, and the fruit of his labour."

And at his end shall be a fool.] Shall be reputed as such. He was a fool all the way through; he lost his soul to get wealth, and this wealth he never enjoyed. To him also are applicable those strong words of the poet:—

"O cursed lust of gold! when for *thy* sake
The wretch throws up his interest in *both*
worlds.
First *starved* in *this*, then *damned* in *that to*
come."
BLAIR.

Verse 12. *A glorious high throne*] As he is *cursed* who trusts in *man*, so he is *blessed* who trusts in GOD. He is here represented as on a *throne* in his temple; to him in the *means of grace* all should resort. He is the support, and a *glorious support*, of all them that trust in him.

Verse 13. *Written in the earth*] They shall never come to true honour. Their names shall be written in the dust; and the first wind that blows over it shall mar every letter, and render it illegible.

Verse 14. *Heal me—and I shall be healed*] That is, I shall be *thoroughly* healed, and *effectually* saved, if thou undertake for me.

Thou art *my praise.*] The whole glory of the work of salvation belongs to thee alone.

Verse 15. *Where is the word of the Lord?*] Where is the accomplishment of his *threatenings?* Thou hast said that the city and the temple should both be destroyed. No such events have yet taken place. But they did take place, and every tittle of the menace was strictly fulfilled.

Verse 16. *I have not hastened from* being *a pastor*] Dr. *Blayney* translates thus: "But I have not been in haste to outrun thy guidance." I was obliged to utter thy prediction; but I have not hastened the evil day. For the credit of my prophecy I have not desired the calamity to come speedily; I have rather pleaded for *respite.* I have followed thy steps, and proclaimed thy truth. I did not desire to be a prophet; but thou hast commanded, and I obeyed.

Verse 17. *Be not a terror unto me*] Do not

A. M. cir. 3400
B. C. cir. 604
Ol. cir. XLII. 2
TarquiniiPrisci,
R. Roman.,
cir. annum 13

my hope in the day of evil.

18 [f]Let them be confounded that persecute me, but [g]let not me be confounded: let them be dismayed, but let not me be dismayed: bring upon them the day of evil, and [h]destroy[i] them with double destruction.

A. M. cir. 3393
B. C. cir. 611
Ol. cir. XLII. 2
TarquiniiPrisci,
R. Roman.,
cir. annum 6

19 Thus saith the LORD unto me; Go and stand in the gate of the children of the people, whereby the kings of Judah come in, and by the which they go out, and in all the gates of Jerusalem;

20 And say unto them, [k]Hear ye the word of the LORD, ye kings of Judah, and all Judah, and all the inhabitants of Jerusalem, that enter in by these gates:

21 Thus saith the LORD; [l]Take heed to yourselves, and bear no burden on the sabbath day, nor bring *it* in by the gates of Jerusalem;

22 Neither carry forth a burden out of your houses on the sabbath day, neither do ye any work, but hallow ye the sabbath day, as I [m]commanded your fathers.

23 [n]But they obeyed not, neither inclined their ear, but made their neck stiff, that they might nor hear, nor receive instruction.

A. M. cir. 3393
B. C. cir. 611
Ol. cir. XLII. 2
TarquiniiPrisci,
R. Roman.,
cir. annum 6

24 And it shall come to pass, if ye diligently hearken unto me, saith the LORD, to bring in no burden through the gates of this city on the sabbath day, but hallow the sabbath day, to do no work therein;

25 [o]Then shall there enter into the gates of this city kings and princes sitting upon the throne of David, riding in chariots and on horses, they, and their princes, the men of Judah, and the inhabitants of Jerusalem: and this city shall remain for ever.

26 And they shall come from the cities of Judah, and from [p]the places about Jerusalem, and from the land of Benjamin, and from [q]the plain, and from the mountains, and from [r]the south, bringing burnt-offerings, and sacrifices, and meat-offerings, and incense, and bringing [s]sacrifices of praise, unto the house of the LORD.

27 But if ye will not hearken unto me to hallow the sabbath day, and not to bear a burden, even entering in at the gates of Jerusalem on the sabbath day; then [t]will I kindle a fire in the gates thereof, [u]and it shall devour the palaces of Jerusalem, and it shall not be quenched.

---

[f]Psa. xxxv. 4; xl. 14; lxx. 2——[g]Psa. xxv. 2——[h]Heb. *break them with a double breach*——[i]Ch. xi. 20——[k]Ch. xix. 8; xxii. 2——[l]Num. xv. 32, &c.; Neh. xiii. 19 [m]Exod. xx. 8; xxiii. 12; xxxi. 13; Ezek. xx. 12

[n]Ch. vii. 24, 26; xi. 10——[o]Ch. xxii. 4——[p]Ch. xxxii. 44; xxxiii. 13——[q]Zech. vii. 7——[r]Zech. vii. 7——[s]Psa. cvii. 22; cxvi. 17——[t]Ch. xxi. 14; xlix. 27; Lam. iv. 11; Amos i. 4, 7, 10, 12; ii. 2, 5——[u]2 Kings xxv. 9; ch. lii. 13

---

command me to predict miseries, and abandon me to them and to my enemies.

Verse 18. *Let them be confounded*] They shall be confounded. These words are to be understood as simple *predictions*, rather than *prayers*.

Verse 19. *The gate of the children of the people*] I suppose the most *public gate* is meant; that through which there was the greatest thoroughfare.

Verse 20. *Ye kings of Judah, and all Judah*] This last clause is wanting in eight of *Kennicott's* and *De Rossi's* MSS., in the *Arabic*, and some copies of the *Septuagint*.

Verse 21. *Take heed to yourselves and bear no burden*] From this and the following verses we find the ruin of the Jews attributed to the breach of the Sabbath; as this led to a neglect of sacrifice, the ordinances of religion, and all public worship, so it necessarily brought with it all immorality. This *breach* of the *Sabbath* was that which let in upon them all the *waters of God's wrath*.

Verse 24. *If ye diligently hearken unto me*] So we find that though their destruction was *positively* threatened, yet still there was an unexpressed proviso that, *if they did return to the Lord*, the calamities should be averted, and a succession of princes would have been continued on the throne of David, ver. 25, 26.

Verse 27. *But if ye will not hearken*] Then their sin lay at their own door. How fully were they warned; and how basely did they reject the counsel of God against themselves!

CHAPTER XVIII

The type of the potter's vessel, and its signification, 1–10. *The inhabitants of Judah and Jerusalem exhorted to repentance,* 11; *but on their refusal, (which is represented to be as unnatural as if a man should prefer the snowy Lebanon or barren rock to a fruitful plain, or other waters to the cool stream of the fountain,) their destruction is predicted,* 12–17. *In consequence of these plain reproofs and warnings of Jeremiah, a conspiracy is formed against him,* 18. *This leads him to appeal to God for his integrity,* 19, 20; *who puts a most dreadful curse in the mouth of his prophet, strongly indicative of the terrible fate of his enemies,* 21–23.

A. M. cir. 3396
B. C. cir. 608
Ol. XLIII. 1
TarquiniiPrisci,
R. Roman.,
cir. annum 9

THE word which came to
Jeremiah from the LORD,
saying,
2 Arise, and go down to the
potter's house, and there I will cause thee to
hear my words.
3 Then I went down to the potter's house,
and, behold, he wrought a work on the
[a]wheels.
4 And the vessel [b]that he made of clay was
marred in the hand of the potter: so he [c]made
it again another vessel, as seemed good to
the potter to make *it*.
5 Then the word of the LORD
came to me, saying,
6 O house of Israel, [d]cannot I
do with you as this potter? saith
the LORD. Behold, [e]as the clay *is* in the
potter's hand, so *are* ye in mine hand, O house
of Israel.
7 *At what* instant I shall speak concerning
a nation, and concerning a kingdom, to [f]pluck
up, and to pull down, and to destroy *it;*
8 [g]If that nation, against whom I have pronounced, turn from their evil, [h]I will repent
of the evil that I thought to do unto them.

[a]Or, *frames* or *seats*——[b]Or, *that he made was marred, as clay in the hand of the potter*——[c]Heb. *returned and made*

[d]Isa. xlv. 9; Wisd. xv. 7; Rom. ix. 20, 21——[e]Isa. lxi. 8——[f]Chap. i. 10——[g]Ezek. xviii. 21; xxxiii. 11
[h]Chap. xxvi. 3; Jonah iii. 10

NOTES ON CHAP. XVIII

Verse 1. *The word which came to Jeremiah*] This discourse is supposed to have been delivered some time in the reign of Jehoiakim, probably within the first three years.

Verse 2. *Go down to the potter's house*] By this similitude God shows the absolute state of dependence on himself in which he has placed mankind. They are as clay in the hands of the potter; and in reference to every thing *here below*, he can shape their destinies as he pleases. Again; though while under the providential care of God they may go *morally astray*, and *pervert themselves*, yet they can be reclaimed by the almighty and all-wise Operator, and become such vessels as *seemeth good for him to make*. In considering this parable we must take heed that in running parallels we do not *destroy* the *free agency* of man, nor *disgrace* the *goodness* and *supremacy* of God.

Verse 3. *He wrought a work on the wheels.*] אל האבנים *al haabnayim, upon the stones*, the potter's wheel being usually made of such; the spindle of the moving stone being placed on a stone below, on which it turned, and supported the stone above, on which the vessel was manufactured, and which alone had a rotatory motion. The potter's wheel in the present day seems to differ very little from that which was in use between *two* and *three thousand* years ago.

Verse 4. *The vessel—was marred in the hands of the potter*] It did not stand in the working; it got out of shape; or some *gravel* or *small stone* having been incorporated with the mass of clay, made a breach in that part where it was found, so that the potter was obliged to knead up the clay afresh, place it on the wheel, and form it anew; and then it was *such a vessel as seemed good to the potter* to make it.

Verse 6. *Cannot I do with you as this potter?*] Have I not a right to do with a people whom I have created as reason and justice may require? If they do not answer my intentions, may I not reject and destroy them; and act as this potter, make a new vessel out of that which at first did not succeed in his hands?

It is generally supposed that St. Paul has made a very different use of this similitude from that mentioned above. See Rom. ix. 20, &c. His words are, "Hath not the potter power over the clay, of the same lump to make one vessel unto honour, and another unto dishonour?" To this every sensible and pious man will answer, *Undoubtedly he has.* But would any potter make an exceedingly fair and good vessel on purpose to dash it to pieces when he had done? Surely no! And would, or could, the God of infinite perfection and love make millions of immortal souls on purpose for eternal perdition, as the horrible decree of reprobation states? No! This is a lie against all the attributes of God. But does not the text state that he can, out of the same lump, the same mass of human nature, make one vessel to honour, and another to dishonour? Yes. But the text does not say, what the horrible decree says, that he makes one part, and indeed the greater, for eternal perdition. But what then is the meaning of the text? Why evidently this: As out of the *same* mass of clay a potter may make a *flagon* for the table and a certain utensil for the chamber, the one for a more honourable, the other for a less honourable use, though both equally necessary to the owner; so God, out of the same *flesh and blood*, may make the *tiller of the field* and the *prophet of the Most High;* the one in a more honourable, the other in a less honourable employ; yet both equally necessary in the world, and equally capable of bringing glory to God in their respective places. But if the vessel be marred in his hand, under his providential and gracious dealings, he may reject it as he did the *Jews*, and make another vessel, such as he is pleased with, of the *Gentiles;* yet even these *marred vessels*, the *reprobate Jews*, are not finally rejected; for all Israel shall be saved in (through) the Lord, *i. e.*, Jesus Christ. And should the *Gentiles* act as the *Jews* have done, then *they* also shall be cut off, and God will call his Church by another name. See on Rom. ix. 22, and below.

Verses 7-10. At what *instant I shall speak concerning a nation*, &c.—*If that nation, against whom*, &c.—*And* at what *instant*, &c.—*If it do evil*, &c.] These verses contain what may be called *God's decree* by which the whole of his conduct towards man is regulated. If he purpose destruction against an offending person, if that person repent and turn to God, he shall *live* and not *die*.

A. M. cir. 3396
B. C. cir. 608
Ol. XLIII. 1
TarquiniiPrisci,
R. Roman.,
cir. annum 9

9 And *at what* instant I shall speak concerning a nation, and concerning a kingdom, to build and to plant *it;*

10 If it do evil in my sight, that it obey not my voice, then I will repent of the good, wherewith I said I would benefit them.

11 Now therefore go to, speak to the men of Judah, and to the inhabitants of Jerusalem, saying, Thus saith the LORD; Behold, I frame evil against you, and devise a device against you: [i]return ye now, every one from his evil way, and make your ways and your doings good.

12 And they said, [k]There is no hope: but we will walk after our own devices, and we will every one do the imagination of his evil heart.

13 Therefore thus saith the LORD; [l]Ask ye now among the heathen, who hath heard such things: the virgin of Israel hath done [m]a very horrible thing.

14 Will *a man* leave [n]the snow of Lebanon *which cometh* from the rock of the field? *or* shall the cold flowing waters that come from another place be forsaken?

15 Because my people hath forgotten [o]me, they have burned incense to [p]vanity, and they have caused them to stumble in their ways *from* the [q]ancient paths, to walk in paths, *in* a way not cast up;

16 To make their land [r]desolate, *and* a perpetual [s]hissing; every one that passeth thereby shall be astonished, and wag his head.

[i]2 Kings xxvii. 13; ch. vii. 3; xxv. 5; xxvi. 13; xxxv. 15 —— [k]Ch. ii. 25 —— [l]Ch. ii. 10; 1 Cor. v. 1 —— [m]Ch. v. 30 —— [n]Or, *my fields for a rock,* or for *the snow of Lebanon? shall the running waters be forsaken for the strange cold* waters? —— [o]Ch. ii. 13, 32; iii. 21; xiii. 25; xvii. 13 —— [p]Ch. x. 15; xvi. 19 —— [q]Ch. vi. 16 —— [r]Ch. xix. 8; xlix. 13; l. 13

A. M. cir. 3396
B. C. cir. 608
Ol. XLIII. 1
TarquiniiPrisci,
R. Roman.,
cir. annum 9

17 [t]I will scatter them [u]as with an east wind before the enemy; [v]I will show them the back, and not the face, in the day of their calamity.

18 Then said they, [w]Come, and let us devise devices against Jeremiah; [x]for the law shall not perish from the priest, nor counsel from the wise, nor the word from the prophet. Come, and let us smite him [y]with the tongue, and let us not give heed to any of his words.

19 Give heed to me, O LORD, and hearken to the voice of them that contend with me.

20 [z]Shall evil be recompensed for good? for [a]they have digged a pit for my soul. Remember that I stood before thee to speak good for them, *and* to turn away thy wrath from them.

21 Therefore [b]deliver up their children to the famine, and [c]pour out their *blood* by the force of the sword; and let their wives be bereaved of their children, and *be* widows; and let their men be put to death; *let* their young men *be* slain by the sword in battle.

22 Let a cry be heard from their houses, when thou shalt bring a troop suddenly upon them: for [d]they have digged a pit to take me, and hid snares for my feet.

23 Yet, LORD, thou knowest all their counsel against me [e]to slay *me:* [f]forgive not their iniquity, neither blot out their sin from thy sight, but let them be overthrown before thee; deal *thus* with them in the time of thine anger.

[s]1 Kings ix. 8; Lam. ii. 15; Mic. vi. 16 —— [t]Ch. xiii. 24 —— [u]Psa. xlviii. 7 —— [v]See ch. ii. 27 —— [w]Ch. xi. 19 —— [x]Lev. x. 11; Mal. ii. 7; John vii. 48, 49 —— [y]Or, *for the tongue* —— [z]Psa. cix. 4, 5 —— [a]Psa. xxxv. 7; lvii. 6; ver. 22 —— [b]Psa. cix. 9, 10 —— [c]Heb. *pour them out* —— [d]Ver. 20 —— [e]Heb. *for death* —— [f]Psa. xxxv. 4; cix. 14; ch. xi. 20; xv. 15

If he purpose peace and salvation to him that walketh uprightly, if he turn from God to the world and sin, he shall *die* and not *live.*

Verse 12. *There is no hope*] See chap. ii. 25.

Verse 13. *The virgin of Israel*] Instead of ישראל *Yisrael, three* of *Kennicott's* and *De Rossi's* MSS., with the Alexandrian copy of the *Septuagint,* have ירושלם *Yerushalem, Jerusalem.*

Verse 14. *Will* a man *leave the snow of Lebanon*] Lebanon was the highest mountain in Judea. Would any man in his senses abandon a *farm* that was always watered by the melted snows of Lebanon, and take a *barren rock* in its place? How stupid therefore and absurd are my people, who abandon the everlasting God for the worship of idols!

Verse 16. *A perpetual hissing*] שריקות *sherikoth,* a *shrieking, hissing;* an expression of contempt.

Verse 17. *I will scatter them as with an east wind*] It is the property of this wind, almost every where, to parch up, blast, and destroy grain and trees, and even cattle and men suffer from it. Hence the old metrical proverb:—

"When the wind blows from the east,
'Tis good for neither man nor beast."

Verse 18. *Come, and let us devise devices*] Let us form a conspiracy against him, accuse him of being a *false prophet,* and a contradicter of the words of God, for God has promised us protection, and *he* says we shall be destroyed, and that God will forsake his people.

Let us smite him with the tongue] ON *the tongue;* so it should be rendered. Lying and false testimony are punished in the eastern countries, to the present day, by smiting the person on the mouth with a strong piece of leather like the sole of a shoe. Sometimes a bodkin is run through the tongue. Blasphemy, calumny, and cursing of parents, are usually punished in that way among the Chinese.

Verse 20. *They have digged a pit for my soul.*] For my *life;* this they wish to take away.

Stood before thee to speak good for them] I was their continual intercessor.

Verse 21. *Therefore deliver up their children*] The execrations in these verses should be considered as simply *prophetic declarations* of the judgments which God was about to pour out on them.

If we consider them in their *grammatical* meaning, then they are not directions to us, to whom our Lawgiver has said, "Love your *enemies.*"

CHAPTER XIX

By the significant type of breaking a potter's vessel, Jeremiah is directed to predict the utter desolation of Judah and Jerusalem, 1–15. *The prophets taught frequently by* symbolic actions *as well as by* words.

A. M. cir. 3397
B. C. cir. 607
Ol. XLIII. 2
TarquiniiPrisci,
R. Roman.,
cir. annum 10

THUS saith the LORD, Go and
get a potter's earthen bottle,
and *take* of the ancients of the
people, and of the ancients of
the priests;
2 And go forth unto [a]the valley of the son
of Hinnom, which *is* by the entry of [b]the
east gate, and proclaim there the words that
I shall tell thee,
3 [c]And say, Hear ye the word of the LORD,
O kings of Judah, and inhabitants of Jerusalem;
Thus saith the LORD of hosts, the
God of Israel; Behold, I will bring evil upon
this place, the which whosoever heareth, his
ears shall [d]tingle.
4 Because they [e]have forsaken me, and have
estranged this place, and have burned incense
in it unto other gods, whom neither they nor
their fathers have known, nor the kings of
Judah, and have filled this place with [f]the
blood of innocents;
5 [g]They have built also the high places of
Baal, to burn their sons with fire *for* burnt-
offerings unto Baal, [h]which I commanded not,
nor spake *it,* neither came *it* into my mind:
6 Therefore, behold, the days
come, saith the LORD, that this
place shall no more be called
Tophet, nor [i]The valley of
the son of Hinnom, but The valley of
slaughter.

A. M. cir. 3397
B. C. cir. 607
Ol. XLIII. 2
TarquiniiPrisci,
R. Roman.,
cir. annum 10

7 And I will make void the counsel of Judah and Jerusalem in this place; [k]and I will
cause them to fall by the sword before their
enemies, and by the hands of them that seek
their lives: and their [l]carcasses will I give
to be meat for the fowls of the heaven, and
for the beasts of the earth.
8 And I will make this city [m]desolate, and
a hissing: every one that passeth thereby
shall be astonished and hiss because of all
the plagues thereof.
9 And I will cause them to eat the [n]flesh of
their sons and the flesh of their daughters,
and they shall eat every one the flesh of his
friend in the siege and straitness, wherewith
their enemies, and they that seek their lives,
shall straiten them.
10 [o]Then shalt thou break the bottle in the
sight of the men that go with thee,

---

[a]Josh. xv. 8; 2 Kings xxiii. 10; chap. vii. 31——[b]Heb. *the sun gate*——[c]Chap. xvii. 20——[d]1 Sam. iii. 11; 2 Kings xxi. 12——[e]Deut. xxviii. 20; Isa. lxv. 11; chap. ii. 13, 17, 19; xv. 6; xvii. 13——[f]2 Kings xxi. 16; chap. ii. 34——[g]Chap. vii. 31, 32; xxxii. 35

[h]Lev. xviii. 21——[i]Josh. xv. 8——[k]Lev. xxvi. 17; Deut. xxviii. 25——[l]Psa. lxxix. 2; chap. vii. 33; xvi. 4; xxxiv. 20——[m]Chap. xviii. 16; xlix. 13; l. 13——[n]Lev. xxvi. 29; Deut. xxviii. 53; Isa. ix. 20; Lam. iv. 10
[o]So chap. li. 63, 64

NOTES ON CHAP. XIX

Verse 1. *Go and get a potter's earthen bottle*] This discourse was also delivered some time in the reign of *Jehoiakim.* Under the type of breaking a potter's earthen bottle or jug, Jeremiah shows his enemies that the word of the Lord should stand, that Jerusalem should be taken and sacked, and they all carried into captivity.

Ancients of the priests] The chiefs of the *twenty-four* classes which David had established. See 1 Chron. xxiv. 4.

Verse 4. *Estranged this place*] Ye have devoted my temple to a widely different purpose from that for which it was erected.

Verse 5. *Offerings unto Baal*] A general name for all the popular idols; Baal, Moloch, Ashtaroth, &c.

Verse 7. *I will make void the counsel of Judah*] Probably this refers to some determination made to proclaim themselves *independent,* and pay no more tribute to the Chaldeans.

To be meat for the fowls] See on chap. vii. 33.

Verse 9. *I will cause them to eat the flesh of their sons*] This was literally fulfilled when Jerusalem was besieged by the Romans. This also the prophet might have had in view.

A. M. cir. 3397
B. C. cir. 607
Ol. XLIII. 2
TarquiniiPrisci,
R. Roman.,
cir. annum 10

11 And shalt say unto them,
Thus saith the LORD of hosts;
[p]Even so will I break this people and this city, as *one* breaketh
a potter's vessel, that cannot [q]be made whole
again: and they shall [r]bury *them* in Tophet,
till *there be* no place to bury.
12 Thus will I do unto this place, saith the
LORD, and to the inhabitants thereof, and
even make this city as Tophet:
13 And the houses of Jerusalem, and the
houses of the kings of Judah, shall be defiled
[s]as the place of Tophet, because of all the
houses upon whose [t]roofs they have burned
incense unto all the host
of heaven, and [u]have poured
out drink-offerings unto other
gods.

A. M. cir. 3397
B. C. cir. 607
Ol. XLIII. 2
TarquiniiPrisci,
R. Roman.,
cir. annum 10

14 Then came Jeremiah from Tophet, whither the LORD had sent him to prophesy;
and he stood in [v]the court of the LORD'S
house, and said to all the people,
15 Thus saith the LORD of hosts, the God
of Israel; Behold, I will bring upon this city
and upon all her towns all the evil that I have
pronounced against it, because [w]they have
hardened their necks, that they might not
hear my words.

[p]Psa. ii. 9; Isa. xxx. 14; Lam. iv. 2——[q]Heb. *be healed* [r]Chap. vii. 32——[s]2 Kings xxiii. 10

[t]2 Kings xxiii. 12; ch. xxxii. 29; Zeph. i. 5——[u]Ch. vii. 18——[v]See 2 Chron. xx. 5——[w]Ch. vii. 26; xvii. 23

Verse 11. *Even so will I break this people and this city*] The breaking of the bottle was the symbolical representation of the destruction of the city and of the state.

That cannot be made whole again] This seems to refer rather to the final destruction of Jerusalem by the Romans, than to what was done by the Chaldeans. Jerusalem was *healed* after 70 years: but nearly 1800 years have elapsed since Jerusalem was taken and destroyed by the Romans; and it was then so broken, *that it could not be made whole again.*

Verse 12. *And even make this city as Tophet*] A place of slaughter and destruction.

Verse 14. *Then came Jeremiah from Tophet*] He had probably gone to the *valley of Hinnom*, and there repeated the discourse which he had a little before delivered to the chief priests and elders.

Verse 15. *Because they have hardened their necks*] A metaphor taken from unruly and unbroken oxen, who resist the yoke, break and run away with their gears. So this people had broken and destroyed the yoke of the law.

CHAPTER XX

Jeremiah, on account of his prophesying evil concerning Judah and Jerusalem, is beaten and imprisoned by Pashur, chief governor of the temple, 1, 2. *On the following day the prophet is released, who denounces the awful judgments of God which should fall upon the governor and all his house, as well as upon the whole land of Judah, in the approaching Babylonish captivity,* 3–6. *Jeremiah then bitterly complains of the reproaches continually heaped upon him by his enemies; and, in his haste, resolves to speak no more in the name of Jehovah; but the word of the Lord is in his heart as a burning flame, so that he is not able to forbear,* 7–10. *The prophet professes his trust in God, whom he praises for his late deliverance,* 11–13. *The remaining verses, which appear to be out of their place, contain Jeremiah's regret that he was ever born to a life of so much sorrow and trouble,* 14–18. *This complaint resembles that of Job; only it is milder and more dolorous. This excites our pity, that our horror. Both are highly poetical, and embellished with every circumstance that can heighten the colouring. But such circumstances are not always to be too literally understood or explained. We must often make allowances for the strong figures of eastern poetry.*

A. M. cir. 3397
B. C. cir. 607
Ol. XLIII. 2
TarquiniiPrisci,
R. Roman.,
cir. annum 10

NOW Pashur the son of [a]Im-
mur the priest, who *was*
also chief governor in the house
of the LORD, heard that Jeremiah
prophesied these things.
2 Then Pashur smote Jeremiah the prophet,
and put him in the stocks that
were in the high gate of Benjamin, which *was* by the house of
the LORD.
3 And it came to pass on the morrow, that
Pashur brought forth Jeremiah out of the

[a]1 Chronicles, chap. xxiv. 14

NOTES ON CHAP. XX

Verse 1. *Pashur—chief governor*] Pashur was probably one of the chief priests of the *twenty-four* classes.

Verse 2. *Put him in the stocks*] Probably such a place near the gate as we term the *lock-up*, the *coal-hole;* or it may mean a sort of *dungeon.*

Verse 3. *The Lord hath not called thy name Pashur*]—Security on all sides. This name thou hast had, but not by Divine appointment.

A. M. cir. 3397
B. C. cir. 607
Ol. XLIII. 2
TarquiniiPrisci,
R. Roman.,
cir. annum 10

stocks. Then said Jeremiah unto him, The LORD hath not called thy name Pashur, but [b]Magor-missabib.

4 For thus saith the LORD, Behold, I will make thee a terror to thyself, and to all thy friends: and they shall fall by the sword of their enemies, and thine eyes shall behold *it:* and I will give all Judah into the hand of the king of Babylon, and he shall carry them captive into Babylon, and shall slay them with the sword.

5 Moreover I [c]will deliver all the strength of this city, and all the labours thereof, and all the precious things thereof, and all the treasures of the kings of Judah will I give into the hand of their enemies, which shall spoil them, and take them, and carry them to Babylon.

6 And thou, Pashur, and all that dwell in thine house, shall go into captivity: and thou shalt come to Babylon, and there thou shalt die, and shalt be buried there, thou, and all thy friends, to whom thou hast [d]prophesied lies.

7 O LORD, thou hast deceived me, and I was [e]deceived: [f]thou art stronger than I, and hast prevailed: [g]I am in derision daily, every one mocketh me.

A. M. cir. 3397
B. C. cir. 607
Ol. XLIII. 2
TarquiniiPrisci,
R. Roman.,
cir. annum 10

8 For since I spake, I cried out, [h]I cried violence and spoil; because the word of the LORD was made a reproach unto me, and a derision, daily.

9 Then I said, I will not make mention of him, nor speak any more in his name. But *his word* was in mine heart as a [i]burning fire shut up in my bones, and I was weary with forbearing, and [k]I could not *stay.*

10 [l]For I heard the defaming of many, fear on every side. Report, *say they,* and we will report it. [m]All [n]my familiars watched for my halting, *saying,* Peradventure he will be enticed, and we shall prevail against him, and we shall take our revenge on him.

11 But [o]the LORD *is* with me as a mighty terrible one: therefore my persecutors shall stumble, and they shall not [p]prevail: they shall be greatly ashamed; for they shall not prosper: *their* [q]everlasting confusion shall never be forgotten.

12 But, O LORD of hosts, that [r]triest the righteous, *and* seest the reins and the heart, [s]let me see thy vengeance on them: for unto thee have I opened my cause.

13 Sing unto the LORD, praise ye the LORD:

[b]That is, *fear round about;* Psa. xxxi. 13; ver. 10; ch. vi. 25; xlvi. 5; xlix. 29——[c]2 Kings xx. 17; xxiv. 12-16; xxv. 13, &c.; ch. iii. 24——[d]Ch. xiv. 13, 14; xxviii. 15; xxix. 21——[e]Or, *enticed*——[f]Ch. i. 6, 7——[g]Lam. iii. 14 [h]Ch. vi. 7——[i]Job xxxii. 18, 19; Psa. xxxix. 3

[k]Job xxxii. 18; Acts xviii. 5——[l]Psa. xxxi. 13 [m]Heb. *every man of my peace*——[n]Job xix. 19; Psa. xli. 9; lv. 13, 14; Luke xi. 53, 54——[o]Ch. i. 8, 19——[p]Ch. xv. 20; xvii. 18——[q]Chap. xxiii. 40——[r]Chap. xi. 20; xvii. 10——[s]Psa. liv. 7; lix. 10

But Magor-missabib—Fear on every side. This name hath God given thee; because, in the course of his providence, thou shalt be placed in the circumstances signified by it: *thou shalt be a terror to thyself.*

Verse 6. *And thou, Pashur—shall go into captivity.* Thou shalt suffer for the false prophecies which thou hast delivered, and for thy insults to my prophet.

Verse 7. *O Lord, thou hast deceived me*] Thou hast promised me protection; and, lo! I am now delivered into the hands of my enemies. These words were probably spoken when Pashur smote him, and put him in prison.

I think our translation of this passage is very exceptionable. My old Bible reads, **Thou laddist me aside Lord; and I was lad aside.** The original word is פתיתני *pittithani,* thou hast *persuaded me,* i. e., to go and prophesy to this people. I went, faithfully declared thy message, and now I am likely to perish by their cruelty. As the root פתה *pathah* signifies to *persuade* and *allure,* as well as to *deceive,* the above must be its meaning in this place. Taken as in our Version, it is highly irreverent. It is used in the same sense here as in Gen. ix. 27: *God shall enlarge* (*persuade,* margin) *Japheth; and he shall dwell in the tents of Shem.*

Verse 8. *I cried violence and spoil*] This was the burden of the message thou didst give me.

Verse 9. *I will not make mention of him*] I will renounce the prophetic office, and return to my house.

As a burning fire shut up in my bones] He felt stings of conscience for the hasty and disobedient resolution he had formed; he felt ashamed of his own weakness, that did not confide in the promise and strength of God; and God's word was in him as a strongly raging fire, and he was obliged to deliver it, in order to get rid of the tortures which he felt from suppressing the solemn message which God had given. It is as dangerous to refuse to go when called, as it is to run without a call. On this subject, see on chap. i. 6.

Verse 10. *Report—and we will report it.*] Let us spread calumnies against him every where; or let us spread reports of dangers coming upon him, that we may intimidate him, and cause him to desist.

Verse 11. *But the Lord* is *with me as a mighty terrible one*] Thus was he, by his strong confidence in the strong God, delivered from all his fears, and enabled to go on comfortably with his work.

A. M. cir. 3398
B. C. cir. 606
Ol. XLIII. 3
TarquiniiPrisci,
R. Roman.,
cir. annum 11

for [t]he hath delivered the soul
of the poor from the hand of evil
doers.
14 [u]Cursed *be* the day wherein
I was born: let not the day wherein my
mother bare me be blessed.
15 Cursed *be* the man who brought tidings
to my father, saying, A man child is born
unto thee; making him very glad.
16 And let that man be as the cities which
the LORD [v]overthrew, and repented not: and let him [w]hear the
cry in the morning, and the
shouting at noontide;
17 [x]Because he slew me not from the womb
or that my mother might have been my grave
and her womb *to be* always great *with me.*
18 [y]Wherefore came I forth out of the
womb to [z]see labour and sorrow, that my
days should be consumed with shame?

A. M. cir. 3398
B. C. cir. 606
Ol. XLIII. 3
TarquiniiPrisci,
R. Roman.,
cir. annum 11

[t]Psa. xxxv. 9, 10; cix. 30, 31——[u]Job iii. 3; chap. xv. 10 [v]Gen. xix. 25

[w]Chap. xviii. 22——[x]Job iii. 10, 11——[y]Job iii. 20 [z]Lam. iii. 1

Verse 13. *Sing unto the Lord*] He was so completely delivered from all fear, that although he remained in the same circumstances, yet he exults in the Divine protection, and does not fear the face of any adversary.

Verse 14. *Cursed* be *the day wherein I was born*] If we take these words *literally*, and suppose them to be in their proper place, they are utterly inconsistent with that state of confidence in which he exulted a few minutes before. If they are the language of Jeremiah, they must have been spoken on a prior occasion, when probably he had given way to a passionate hastiness. They might well comport with the state he was in ver. 9. I really believe these verses have got out of their proper place, which I conjecture to be between the *eighth* and *ninth* verses. There they will come in very properly; and might have been a part of his complaint in those moments when he had purposed to flee from God as did Jonah, and prophesy no more in his name. Transpositions in this prophet are frequent; therefore place these *five* verses after the *eighth*, and let the chapter end with the *thirteenth*, and the whole will form a piece of exquisite poetry; where the state of *despair*, and the *hasty resolutions* he had formed while under its influence, and the state of *confidence* to which he was raised by the succouring influence of God, will appear to be both illustrative of each other, and are touched with a delicacy and fervour which even a cold heart must admire. See Job iii. 3, and the notes there. The two passages are very similar.

Verse 15. *A man child is born*] **Borun is to thee a knave child.**—Old MS. Bible. This is the old English word for *man* or *servant;* and is so used by *Wiclif*, Rev. xii. 5.

Verse 16. *And let him hear the cry*] Let him be in continual alarms.

Verse 18. *Wherefore came I forth*] It would have been well had I never been born, as I have neither comfort in my life, nor comfort in my work.

CHAPTER XXI

Nebuchadnezzar being come up against Jerusalem, Zedekiah sends Pashur and Zephaniah to the prophet to request him to intercede with God in behalf of his people, 1, 2. *But he is declared to be against Jerusalem, and the whole land of Judah; and the only mitigation of their punishment must proceed from their surrendering to the king of Babylon*, 3–10. *Prophecy concerning the house of the king of Judah*, 11, 12. *Notwithstanding the amazing fortifications round about Jerusalem, in which the people vainly trust, the Lord will most assuredly visit them for their iniquities; the city shall be taken by the Chaldeans*, 13, 14.

A. M. cir. 3415
B. C. cir. 589
Ol. XLVII. 4
TarquiniiPrisci,
R. Roman.,
cir. annum 28

THE word which came unto
Jeremiah from the LORD,
when king Zedekiah sent unto
him [a]Pashur the son of Melchiah, and [b]Zephaniah the son
of Maaseiah the priest, saying,
2 [c]Inquire, I pray thee, of
the LORD for us; (for Nebuchad-

A. M. cir. 3415
B. C. cir. 589
Ol. XLVII. 4
TarquiniiPrisci,
R. Roman.,
cir. annum 28

[a]Chap. xxxviii. 1——[b]2 Kings xxv. 18; chap. xxix. 25; xxxvii. 3——[c]Chap. xxxvii. 3, 7

NOTES ON CHAP. XXI

Verse 1. *The word which came unto Jeremiah*] The chapters in the remaining parts of this prophecy seem strangely *interchanged.* This subject has been mentioned in the *introduction*, and some *tables* given; and to these the critical reader is requested to refer. The discourse here was delivered about the *ninth* year of the reign of Zedekiah. This chapter, observes Dr. *Blayney*, contains the first of those prophecies which were delivered by Jeremiah, *subsequent* to the revolt of Zedekiah, and the breaking out of the war thereupon; and which are continued on to the *taking of Jerusalem*, related in chap. xxix., in the following order:—ch. xxi., xxxiv., xxxvii., xxxii., xxxiii., xxxviii., xxxix.

Pashur the son of Melchiah] There can be little doubt that this Pashur was a different person from him who was called the son of *Immur* in the preceding chapter.

Verse 2. *Inquire, I pray thee*] See whether

A. M. cir. 3415 B. C. cir. 589 Ol. XLVII. 4 TarquiniiPrisci, R. Roman., cir. annum 28

rezzar king of Babylon maketh
war against us; if so be that the
LORD will deal with us according
to all his wondrous works, that
he may go up from us.
3 Then said Jeremiah unto them, Thus shall
ye say to Zedekiah:
4 Thus saith the LORD God of Israel; Behold, I will turn back the weapons of war that
are in your hands, wherewith ye fight against
the king of Babylon, and *against* the Chaldeans, which besiege you without the walls,
and [d]I will assemble them into the midst of
this city.
5 And I myself will fight against you with
an [e]outstretched hand and with a strong arm,
even in anger, and in fury, and in great
wrath.
6 And I will smite the inhabitants of this
city, both man and beast: they shall die of a
great pestilence.
7 And afterward, saith the LORD, [f]I will deliver Zedekiah king of Judah, and his servants,
and the people, and such as are left in this
city from the pestilence, from the sword, and
from the famine, into the hand of Nebuchadrezzar king of Babylon, and into the hand of
their enemies, and into the hand of those that
seek their life: and he shall smite them with
the edge of the sword; [g]he shall not spare
them, neither have pity, nor have mercy.

A. M. cir. 3415 B. C. cir. 589 Ol. XLVII. 4 TarquiniiPrisci, R. Roman., cir. annum 28

8 And unto this people thou
shalt say, Thus saith the LORD;
Behold, [h]I set before you the
way of life, and the way of death.
9 He that [i]abideth in this city shall die by
the sword, and by the famine, and by the
pestilence: but he that goeth out, and falleth
to the Chaldeans that besiege you, he shall
live, and [k]his life shall be unto him for a prey.
10 For I have [l]set my face against this city
for evil, and not for good, saith the LORD;
[m]it shall be given into the hand of the king of
Babylon, and he shall [n]burn it with fire.
11 And touching the house of the king
of Judah, *say,* Hear ye the word of the
LORD;
12 O house of David, thus saith the LORD;
[o]Execute [p]judgment [q]in the morning, and
deliver *him that is* spoiled out of the hand of
the oppressor, lest my fury go out like fire,
and burn that none can quench *it,* because of
the evil of your doings.
13 Behold, [r]I *am* against thee, O [s]in-
habitant of the valley, *and* rock of the plain,
saith the LORD; which say, [t]Who shall come
down against us? or who shall enter into our
habitations?
14 But I will [u]punish you according to the
[v]fruit of your doings, saith the LORD: and I
will kindle a fire in the forest thereof, and [w]it
shall devour all things round about it.

---

[d]Isa. xiii. 4——[e]Exod. vi. 6——[f]Chap. xxxvii. 17; xxxix. 5; lii. 9——[g]Deut. xxiii. 50; 2 Chron. xxxvi. 17 [h]Deut. xxx. 19——[i]Chap. xxxviii. 2, 17, 18——[k]Chap. xxxix. 18; xlv. 5——[l]Lev. xvii. 10; chap. xliv. 11; Amos ix. 4——[m]Chap. xxxviii. 3

[n]Chap. xxxiv. 2, 22; xxxvii. 10; xxxviii. 18, 23; lii. 13 [o]Chap. xxii. 3; Zech. vii. 9——[p]Heb. *Judge*——[q]Psa. ci. 8——[r]Ezek. xiii. 8——[s]Heb. *inhabitress*——[t]Chap. xlix. 4——[u]Heb. *visit upon*——[v]Prov. i. 31; Isa. iii. 10, 11——[w]2 Chron. xxxvi. 19; chap. lii. 13

God intends to deliver us *into* or *out of* the hand of the Chaldeans.

Verse 4. *I will turn back the weapons*] Every attempt you make to repel the Chaldeans shall be unsuccessful.

I will assemble them into the midst of this city.] I will deliver the city into their hands.

Verse 6. *They shall die of a great pestilence.*] The *sword* may appear to be that of *man,* though I have given the Chaldeans their commission; but the *pestilence* shall appear to be the immediate act of GOD.

Verse 7. *Nebuchadrezzar*] This name is spelt as above in *twenty-six* places of this book; and in *ten* places it is spelt *Nebuchadnezzar,* which is the common orthography. The difference is only a ר *resh* for a נ *nun;* but the MSS. are various on this point. It is the same person who is intended by both names; and here all the *Versions,* except the *Arabic,* which omits the name, have it in the usual form.

Verse 8. *Behold, I set before you the way of life, and the way of death.*] Meaning *escape* or *destruction* in the *present* instance. This is explained in the next verse.

Verse 10. *He shall burn it with fire.*] What a heavy message to all; and especially to them who had any fear of God, or reverence for the temple and its sacred services!

Verse 12. *Execute judgment in the morning*] Probably the time for dispensing judgment was *the morning,* when the people were going to their work; but the words may mean, Do justice *promptly,* do not *delay.* Let justice be administered *as soon* as required.

Verse 13. *O inhabitant of the valley,* and *rock of the plain*] Dr. *Blayney* translates: "O thou inhabitant of the levelled hollow of a rock." With all his explanation I cannot see the good sense of this translation. Jerusalem itself, though partly on *two hills,* was also extended in the valley; and *Zion,* the *city of David,* was properly *a rock,* strongly fortified both by nature and art; and by its ancient possessors, the *Jebusites,* was deemed impregnable.

Who shall come down against us?] Probably

the words of those *courtiers* who had persuaded Zedekiah to rebel against the king of Babylon.

Verse 14. *I will kindle a fire in the forest thereof*] I will send destruction into its *centre,* that shall spread to every part of the *circumference,* and so consume the whole.

The beginning of the *thirty-fourth* chapter should follow here. See the arrangement on ver. 1.

CHAPTER XXII

This section of prophecy, extending to the end of the eighth verse of the next chapter, is addressed to the king of Judah and his people. It enjoins on them the practice of justice and equity, as they would hope to prosper, 1–4; *but threatens them, in case of disobedience, with utter destruction,* 5–9. *The captivity of Shallum, the son of Josiah, is declared to be irreversible,* 10–12; *and the miserable and unlamented end of Jeconiah, contemptuously called Coniah, is foretold,* 13–19. *His family is threatened with the like captivity, and his seed declared to be for ever excluded from the throne,* 20–30.

A. M. cir. 3406
B. C. cir. 598
Ol. cir. XLV. 3
TarquiniiPrisci, R. Roman., cir. annum 19

THUS saith the LORD; Go down to the house of the king of Judah, and speak there this word,

2 And say, Hear the word of the LORD, O king of Judah, that sittest upon the throne of David, thou, and thy servants, and thy people that enter in by these gates:

3 Thus saith the LORD; [b]Execute ye judgment and righteousness, and deliver the spoiled out of the hand of the oppressor: and [c]do no wrong, do no violence to the stranger, the fatherless, nor the widow, neither shed innocent blood in this place.

4 For if ye do this thing indeed, [d]then shall there enter in by the gates of this house kings sitting [e]upon the throne of David, riding in chariots and on horses, he, and his servants, and his people.

5 But if ye will not hear these words, [f]I swear by myself, saith the LORD, that this house shall become a desolation.

A. M. cir. 3406
B. C. cir. 598
Ol. cir. XLV. 3
TarquiniiPrisci, R. Roman., cir. annum 19

6 For thus saith the LORD unto the king's house of Judah; Thou *art* Gilead unto me, *and* the head of Lebanon: *yet* surely I will make thee a wilderness, *and* cities *which* are not inhabited.

7 And I will prepare destroyers against thee, every one with his weapons: and they shall cut down [g]thy choice cedars, [h]and cast *them* into the fire.

8 And many nations shall pass by this city, and they shall say every man to his neighbour, [i]Wherefore hath the LORD done thus unto this great city?

9 Then they shall answer, [k]Because they have forsaken the covenant of the LORD their God, and worshipped other gods, and served them.

10 Weep ye not for [l]the dead, neither bemoan him: *but* weep sore for him [m]that goeth away: for he shall return no more, nor see his native country.

---

[a]Chap. xvii. 20——[b]Chap. xxi. 12——[c]See ver. 17
[d]Chap. xvii. 25——[e]Heb. *for David upon his throne*
[f]Heb. vi. 13, 17——[g]Isa. xxxvii. 24

[h]Chap. xxi. 14——[i]Deut. xxix. 24, 25; 1 Kings ix. 8, 9——[k]2 Kings xxii. 17; 2 Chron. xxxiv. 25——[l]2 Kings xxii. 20——[m]Ver. 11

NOTES ON CHAP. XXII

Verse 1. *Go down to the house of the king of Judah, and speak there this word*] This is supposed by *Dahler* to have been published in the *first* year of the reign of Zedekiah.

Verse 2. *O king of Judah—thou, and thy servants*] His *ministers* are here addressed, as chiefly governing the nation; and who had counselled Zedekiah to rebel.

Verse 6. *Thou* art *Gilead unto me,* and *the head of Lebanon*] Perhaps in allusion, says *Dahler,* to the *oaks* of *Gilead,* and the *cedars* of Mount *Lebanon,* of which the palace was constructed. *Lebanon* was the highest mountain in Israel, and *Gilead* the richest and most fertile part of the country; and were, therefore, proper emblems of the reigning *family.* Though thou art the richest and most powerful, I, who raised thee up, can bring thee down and make thee a wilderness.

Verse 7. *They shall cut down thy choice cedars*] The destruction of the country is expressed under the symbol of the destruction of a *fine forest;* a multitude of fellers come against it, each with his axe; and, there being no resistance, every tree is soon *felled* to the earth. "These destroyers," God says, "I have prepared, קדשתי *kiddashti, I have sanctified*—consecrated, to this work. They have their commission from me."

Verse 8. *Many nations shall pass*] These words seem borrowed from Deut. xxix. 22, &c.

Verse 10. *Weep ye not for the dead*] Josiah, dead in consequence of the wound he had received at Megiddo, in a battle with Pharaoh-necho, king of Egypt; but he died in peace with God.

But *weep sore for him that goeth away*] Namely, Jehoahaz, the son of Josiah, called below *Shallum,* whom Pharaoh-necho had carried captive into Egypt from which it was proph-

A. M. cir. 3406 B. C. cir. 598 Ol. cir. XLV. 3 TarquiniiPrisci, R. Roman., cir. annum 19

11 For thus saith the LORD touching [n]Shallum the son of Josiah king of Judah, which reigned instead of Josiah his father, [o]which went forth out of this place; He shall not return thither any more:

12 But he shall die in the place whither they have led him captive, and shall see this land no more.

13 [p]Wo unto him that buildeth his house by unrighteousness, and his chambers by wrong; [q]*that* useth his neighbour's service without wages, and giveth him not for his work;

14 That saith, I will build me a wide house and [r]large chambers, and cutteth him out [s]windows; and *it is* ceiled with cedar, and painted with vermilion.

A. M. cir. 3406 B. C. cir. 598 Ol. cir. XLV. 3 TarquiniiPrisci, R. Roman., cir. annum 19

15 Shalt thou reign, because thou closest *thyself* in cedar? [t]did not thy father eat and drink, and do judgment and justice, *and* then [u]*it was* well with him?

16 He judged the cause of the poor and needy; then *it was* well *with him: was* not this to know me? saith the LORD.

17 [v]But thine eyes and thine heart *are* not but for thy covetousness, and for to shed innocent blood, and for oppression, and for [w]violence, to do *it*.

18 Therefore thus saith the LORD concerning Jehoiakim the son of Josiah king of Judah; [x]They shall not lament for him, *saying,* [y]Ah my brother! or, Ah sister! they shall not lament for him, *saying,* Ah lord! or, Ah his glory!

---

[n]See 1 Chron. iii. 15, with 2 Kings xxiii. 30——[o]2 Kings xxiii. 34——[p]2 Kings xxiii. 35; ver. 18——[q]Lev. xix. 13; Deut. xxiv. 14, 15; Mic. iii. 10; Hab. ii. 9; James v. 4

[r]Heb. *thorough-aired*——[s]Or, *my windows*——[t]2 Kings xxiii. 25——[u]Psa. cxxviii. 2; Isa. iii. 10——[v]Ezek. xix. 6——[w]Or, *incursion*——[x]Chap. xvi. 4, 6——[y]See 1 Kings xiii. 30

---

esied he should never return, 2 Kings xxiii. 30-34. He was called *Shallum* before he ascended the throne, and *Jehoahaz* afterwards; so his brother *Eliakim* changed his name to *Jehoiakim,* and *Mattaniah* to *Zedekiah.*

Verse 13. *Wo unto him that buildeth his house*] These evils, charged against Jehoiakim, are nowhere else *circumstantially* related. We learn from 2 Kings xxiii. 35-37, that he taxed his subjects heavily, to give to Pharaoh-necho, king of Egypt: "He exacted the silver and gold of the people of the land, and did that which was evil in the sight of the Lord." The *mode* of taxation is here intimated; he took the *wages of the hirelings*, and caused the *people to work without wages* in his *own buildings*, &c.

Verse 15. *Shalt thou reign, &c.*] Dost thou think thou art a great king, because thou dwellest in a splendid palace?

Verse 18. *They shall not lament for him,* saying, *Ah my brother!*] These words were no doubt the burden of some *funeral dirge. Alas!* a *brother*, who was our *lord* or *governor*, is gone. *Alas, our sister!* his QUEEN, who has lost her *glory* in losing her husband. הדה *hodah* is feminine, and must refer to the *glory* of the queen.

The mournings in the east, and lamentations for the dead, are loud, vehement, and distressing. For a *child* or a *parent* grief is expressed in a variety of impassioned sentences, each ending with a *burden* like that in the text, "Ah my child!" "Ah my mother!" as the prophet in this place: הוי אחי *hoi achi*, "Ah my brother!" הוי אחות *hoi achoth*, "Ah sister!" הוי אדון *hoi adon*, "Ah lord!" הוי הדה *hoi hodah*, "Ah the glory."

Mr. *Ward*, in his Manners and Customs of the Hindoos, gives two examples of lamentation; one of a *mother* for the death of her *son*, one of a *daughter* for her departed *mother*. "When a woman," says he, "is overwhelmed with grief for the death of her child, she utters her grief in some such language as the following:—

Ah, my Hureedas, where is he gone?—'Ah my child, my child!'
My golden image, Hureedas, who has taken? —'Ah my child, my child!'
I nourished and reared him, where is he gone?—'Ah my child, my child!'
Take me with thee.—'Ah my child my child!'
He played round me, like a golden top.—'Ah my child, my child!'
Like his face I never saw one.—'Ah my child, my child!'
The infant continually cried, *Ma Ma!*—'Ah my child, my child!'
Ah my child, crying, *Ma!* come into my lap.—'Ah my child, my child!'
Who shall now drink milk?—'Ah my child, my child!'
Who shall now stay in my lap?—'Ah my child, my child!'
Our support is gone!—'Ah my child, my child!'

"The lamentations for a mother are in some such strains as these:—

Mother! where is she gone?—'Ah my mother, my mother!'
You are gone, but what have you left for me? —'Ah my mother, my mother!'
Whom shall I now call mother, mother?—'Ah my mother, my mother!'
Where shall I find such a mother?—'Ah my mother, my mother!' "

From the above we may conclude that the funeral lamentations, to which the prophet refers, generally ended in this way, in each of the verses or interrogatories.

There is another intimation of this ancient and universal custom in 1 Kings xiii. 30, where the *old prophet*, who had deceived the *man of God*, and who was afterwards slain by a lion, is represented as mourning over him, and saying, הוי אחי *hoi achi*, "Alas, my brother!" this being the *burden* of the lamentation which he

A. M. cir. 3406 B. C. cir. 598 Ol. cir. XLV. 3 TarquiniiPrisci, R. Roman., cir. annum 19

19 [z]He shall be buried with
the burial of an ass, drawn and
cast forth beyond the gates of
Jerusalem.

20 Go up to Lebanon, and cry; and lift up
thy voice in Bashan, and cry from the passages: for all thy lovers are destroyed.

21 I spake unto thee in thy [a]prosperity; *but*
thou saidst, I will not hear. [b]This *hath been*
thy manner from thy youth, that thou obey-
edst not my voice.

22 The wind shall eat up all [c]thy pastors,
and [d]thy lovers shall go into captivity; surely
then shalt thou be ashamed and confounded
for all thy wickedness.

23 O [e]inhabitant of Lebanon, that makest
thy nest in the cedars, how gracious shalt thou
be when pangs come upon thee, [f]the pain
as of a woman in travail!

24 *As* I live, saith the LORD, [g]though
Coniah the son of Jehoiakim king of Judah
[h]were the signet upon my right hand, yet
would I pluck thee thence;

25 And I will give thee into
the hand of them that seek
thy life, and into the hand *of*
them whose face thou fearest,
even into the hand of Nebuchadrezzar king
of Babylon, and into the hand of the Chaldeans.

A. M. cir. 3406 B. C. cir. 598 Ol. cir. XLV. 3 TarquiniiPrisci, R. Roman., cir. annum 19

26 [i]And I will cast thee out, and thy mother
that bare thee, into another country, where
ye were not born; and there shall ye die.

27 But to the land whereunto they [k]desire
to return, thither shall they not return.

28 *Is* this man Coniah a despised broken
idol? *is he* [l]a vessel wherein *is* no pleasure?
wherefore are they cast out, he and his seed,
and are cast into a land which they know not?

29 [m]O earth, earth, earth, hear the word of
the LORD.

30 Thus saith the LORD, Write ye this man
[n]childless, a man *that* shall not prosper in his
days: for no man of his seed shall prosper,
[o]sitting upon the throne of David, and ruling
any more in Judah.

[z]2 Chron. xxxvi. 6; chap. xxxvi. 30——[a]Heb. *prosperities*——[b]Chap. iii. 25; vii. 23, &c.——[c]Chap. xxiii. 1 [d]Ver. 20——[e]Heb. *inhabitress*——[f]Chap. vi. 24 [g]See 2 Kings xxiv. 6, 8; 1 Chron. iii. 16; chap. xxxvii. 1 [h]Cant. viii. 6

[i]2 Kings xxiv. 15; 2 Chron. xxxvi. 10——[k]Heb. *lift up their mind;* chap. xliv. 14——[l]Psa. xxxi. 12; chap. xlviii. 38; Hos. viii. 8——[m]Deut. xxxii. 1; Isa. i. 2; xxxiv. 1; Mic. i. 2——[n]See 1 Chron. iii. 16, 17; Matt. i. 12——[o]Chap. xxxvi. 30

had used on this occasion. Similar instances may be seen in other places, Jer. xxx. 7; Ezek. vi. 11; Joel i. 15; and particularly Amos v. 16, 17, and Rev. xviii. 10-19.

Verse 19. *With the burial of an ass*] Cast out, and left unburied, or buried without any *funeral solemnities*, and without such lamentations as the above.

Verse 20. *Go up to Lebanon*] Probably *Anti-Libanus*, which, together with *Bashan* and *Abarim*, which we here translate *passages*, were on the way by which the captives should be led out of their own country.

Verse 21. *I spake unto thee in thy prosperity*] In all states and circumstances I warned thee by my prophets; and thou wilt only be *ashamed* of thy conduct when thou shalt be stripped of all thy excellencies, and reduced to poverty and disgrace, ver. 22.

Verse 22. *The wind shall eat up all thy pastors*] A *blast* from God's mouth shall carry off thy kings, princes, prophets, and priests.

Verse 23. *How gracious shalt thou be*] A strong irony.

Verse 24. *Though Coniah*] Called *Jeconiah*, probably on ascending the throne. See on ver. 10.

The signet upon my right hand] The most precious seal, ring, or armlet. Though dearer to me than the most splendid gem to its possessor.

Verse 26. *I will cast thee out, and thy mother*] See all this fulfilled, 2 Kings xxiv. 12, 13. All were carried by Nebuchadnezzar into captivity together.

Verse 28. Is *this man Coniah a despised broken idol?*] These are probably the exclamations of the *people*, when they heard those solemn denunciations against their *king* and their *country*.

Verse 29. *O earth*] These are the words of the *prophet* in reply: O land! unhappy land! desolated land! *Hear the judgment of the Lord!*

Verse 30. *Write ye this man childless*] Though he had *seven* sons, 1 Chron. iii. 17, yet, having no *successor*, he is to be entered on the *genealogical tables* as one *without children*, for none of his posterity ever sat on the throne of David.

CHAPTER XXIII

Sequel of the discourse which commenced in the preceding chapter. The prophet denounces vengeance against the pastors of Israel who have scattered and destroyed the flock of the Lord, 1, 2. *He concludes with gracious promises of deliverance from the Babylonish captivity, and of better times under the Messiah, when the converts to Christianity, who are the true Israel of God, shadowed forth by the old dispensation, shall be delivered, by the glorious light of the Gospel, from worse than Chaldean bondage, from the captivity of sin and death. But this prophecy will not have its fullest accomplishment till that period arrives which is fixed in the Divine counsel for the restoration of Israel and Judah from their various dispersions, of which their deliverance from the Chaldean domination was a type; when Jesus the Christ, the righteous Branch, the Root and Offspring of David, and the only legitimate Heir to the throne, shall take unto himself his great power, and reign gloriously over the whole house of Jacob,* 3–8. *At the* ninth *verse a new discourse commences. Jeremiah expresses his horror at the great wickedness of the priests and prophets of Judah, and declares that the Divine vengeance is hanging over them. He exhorts the people not to listen to their false promises,* 9–22; *and predicts the utter ruin that shall fall upon all pretenders to inspiration,* 23–32, *as well as upon all scoffers at true prophecy,* 33–40.

A. M. cir 3406
B. C. cir. 598
Ol. cir. XLV. 3
TarquiniiPrisci,
R. Roman.,
cir. annum 19

WO [a]be unto the pastors that
destroy and scatter the
sheep of my pasture! saith the
LORD.

2 Therefore thus saith the LORD God of
Israel against the pastors that feed my people;
Ye have scattered my flock, and driven them
away, and have not visited them: [b]behold, I
will visit upon you the evil of your doings,
saith the LORD.

3 And [c]I will gather the remnant of my
flock out of all countries whither I have driven
them, and will bring them again
to their folds; and they shall be
fruitful and increase.

A. M. cir. 3406
B. C. cir. 598
Ol. cir. XLV. 3
TarquiniiPrisci,
R. Roman,
cir. annum 19

4 And I will set up [d]shepherds
over them which shall feed them: and they
shall fear no more, nor be dismayed, neither
shall they be lacking, saith the LORD.

5 Behold, [e]the days come, saith the LORD,
that I will raise unto David a righteous Branch,
and a King shall reign and prosper, [f]and shall
execute judgment and justice in the earth.

6 [g]In his days Judah shall be saved, and

[a]Chap. x. 21; xxii. 22; Ezek. xxxiv. 2——[b]Exod. xxxii. 34——[c]Chap. xxxii. 37; Ezek. xxxiv. 13, &c. [d]Chap. iii. 15; Ezek. xxxiv. 23, &c.

[e]Isa. iv. 2; xi. 1; xl. 10, 11; ch. xxxiii. 14, 15, 16; Dan. ix. 24; Zech. iii. 8; vi. 12; John i. 45——[f]Psa. lxxii. 2; Isa. xxxii. 1, 18; ix. 7——[g]Deut. xxxiii. 28; Zech. xiv. 11

NOTES ON CHAP. XXIII

Verse 1. *Wo be unto the pastors*] There shall a curse fall on the kings, princes, priests, and prophets; who, by their vicious conduct and example, have brought desolation upon the people.

Verse 2. *Ye have scattered my flock*] The bad government both in Church and State was a principal cause of the people's profligacy.

Verse 5. *I will raise unto David a righteous Branch*] As there has been no *age*, from the Babylonish captivity to the destruction of Jerusalem by the Romans, in which such a state of prosperity existed, and no *king* or *governor* who could answer at all to the character here given, the passage has been understood to refer to our blessed Lord, Jesus Christ, who was a *branch* out of the *stem of Jesse;* a *righteous king;* by the power of his Spirit and influence of his religion *reigning, prospering,* and *executing judgment* and *justice in the earth.*

Verse 6. *In his days Judah shall be saved*] The real *Jew* is not one who has his circumcision in the flesh, but in the spirit. The real *Israel* are true believers in Christ Jesus; and the genuine *Jerusalem* is the Church of the first-born, and made free, with all her children, from the bondage of sin, Satan, death, and hell. All these exist only in the *days of the Messiah.* All that went before were the *types* or *significators* of these glorious Gospel excellencies.

And this is his name whereby he shall be called, THE LORD OUR RIGHTEOUSNESS.] I shall give the *Hebrew* text of this important passage: וזה שמו אשר יקראו יהוה צדקנו *vezeh shemo asher yikreo Yehovah tsidkenu,* which the *Septuagint* translate as follows, Και τουτο το ονομα αυτου ὁ καλεσει αυτον Κυριος, Ιωσεδεκ, "And this is his name which the Lord shall call him, Josedek."

Dahler translates the text thus:—

Et voici le nom dont on l'appellera:
L'Eternel, *Auteur de* notre felicité.

"And this is the name by which he shall be called; The Lord, *the Author of* our happiness."

Dr. *Blayney* seems to follow the *Septuagint;* he translates thus, "And this is the name by which Jehovah shall call him, OUR RIGHTEOUSNESS."

In my old MS. Bible, the first English translation ever made, it is thus:—**And this is the name that thei schul clepen him: oure rigtwise Lord.**

Coverdale's, the first complete English translation of the Scriptures ever *printed,* (1535,) has given it thus:—**And this is the name that they shall call him: euen the Lorde oure rightuous Maker.**

Matthews (1549) and *Becke* (1549) follow *Coverdale* literally; but our present translation of the clause is borrowed from *Cardmarden,* (Rouen, 1566,) "Even the Lord our righteousness."

A. M. cir. 3406
B. C. cir. 598
Ol. cir. XLV. 3
TarquiniiPrisci,
R. Roman.,
cir. annum 19

Israel [h]shall dwell safely: and
[i]this *is* his name whereby he
shall be called, [k]THE LORD
OUR RIGHTEOUSNESS.

7 Therefore, behold, [l]the days come, saith
the LORD, that they shall no more say, The
LORD liveth, which brought up the children of
Israel out of the land of Egypt;

8 But, The LORD liveth, which brought up
and which led the seed of the house of Israel
out of the north country, [m]and from all countries whither I have driven them; and they
shall dwell in their own land.

A. M cir 3406
B. C. cir. 598
Ol. cir. XLV. 3
TarquiniiPrisci,
R. Roman.,
cir. annum 19

9 Mine heart within me is
broken because of the prophets;
[n]all my bones shake; I am like
a drunken man, and like a man
whom wine hath overcome, because of the
LORD, and because of the words of his holiness.

A. M. cir. 3399
B. C. cir. 605
Ol. cir. XLV. 4
TarquiniiPrisci,
R. Roman.,
cir. annum 12

10 For [o]the land is full of
adulterers; for [p]because of
[q]swearing the land mourneth;
[r]the pleasant places of the wilderness are dried up, and their [s]course is evil,
and their force *is* not right.

11 For [t]both prophet and priest are profane;
yea, [u]in my house have I found their wickedness, saith the LORD.

12 [v]Wherefore their way shall be unto them
as slippery *ways* in the darkness: they shall
be driven on, and fall therein: for I [w]will
bring evil upon them, *even* the year of their
visitation, saith the LORD.

13 And I have seen [x]folly [y]in the prophets
of Samaria; [z]they prophesied in Baal, and
[a]caused my people Israel to err.

14 I have seen also in the prophets of
Jerusalem [b]a horrible thing: [c]they commit

---

[h]Chap. xxxii. 37——[i]Chap. xxxiii. 16; 1 Cor. i. 30——[k]Heb. *Jehovah-tsidkenu*——[l]Chap. xvi. 14, 15——[m]Isa. xliii. 5, 6; ver. 3——[n]See Hab. iii. 16——[o]Chap. v. 7, 8; ix. 2——[p]Hos. iv. 2, 3——[q]Or, *cursing*——[r]Chap. ix. 10; xii. 4——[s]Or, *violence*

[t]Chap. vi. 13; viii. 10; Zeph. iii. 4——[u]Chap. vii. 30; xi. 15; xxxii. 34; Ezek. viii. 11; xxiii. 39——[v]Psa. xxxv. 6; Prov. iv. 19; chap. xiii. 16——[w]Chap. xi. 23——[x]Or *an absurd thing*——[y]Heb. *unsavoury*——[z]Chap. ii. 8——[a]Isa. ix. 16——[b]Or, *filthiness*——[c]Chap. xxix. 23

Dr. *Blayney* thus accounts for his translation:—"Literally, according to the Hebrew idiom,—'And this is his name by which Jehovah shall call, Our Righteousness;' a phrase exactly the same as, 'And Jehovah shall call him so;' which implies that God would make him such as he called him, that is, *our Righteousness*, or the author and means of our salvation and acceptance. So that by the same metonymy Christ is said to 'have been made of God unto us wisdom, and righteousness, and sanctification, and redemption,' 1 Cor. i. 30.

"I doubt not that some persons will be offended with me for depriving them, by this translation, of a favourite argument for proving the Divinity of our Saviour from the Old Testament. But I cannot help it; I have done it with no ill design, but purely because I think, and am morally sure, that the text, as it stands, will not properly admit of any other construction. The *Septuagint* have so translated before me, in an age when there could not possibly be any bias or prejudice either *for* or *against* the fore-mentioned doctrine, a doctrine which draws its *decisive* proofs from the New Testament only."

Dahler paraphrases,—"This Prince shall be surnamed by his people, 'The Lord, the author of our happiness.' The people shall feel themselves happy under him; and shall express their gratitude to him."

I am satisfied that both the *translation* from *Cardmarden* downwards, and the *meaning* put on these words, are incorrect. I prefer the translation of *Blayney* to all others; and that it speaks any thing about the *imputed* righteousness of Christ, cannot possibly be proved by any man who understands the original text. As to those who put the *sense* of their *creed* upon the words, they must be content to stand out of the list of Hebrew critics. I believe *Jesus* to be *Jehovah;* but I doubt much whether this text calls him so. No doctrine so vitally important should be rested on an interpretation so dubious and unsupported by the text. That all our righteousness, holiness, and goodness, as well as the whole of our salvation, come *by* HIM, *from* HIM, and *through* HIM, is fully evident from the Scriptures; but this is not one of the passages that support this most important truth. See on chap. xxxiii.

Verse 7. *The Lord liveth which brought up*] See on chap. xvi. 14, 15.

Verse 9. *Mine heart within me is broken because of the prophets*] The first word of this clause is לנבאים *lannebiim,* which we incorporate with the whole clause, and translate, "Because of the prophets." But as a new prophecy begins here, it is evident that the word is the *title* to this prophecy; and is thus distinguished both by *Blayney* and *Dahler*, CONCERNING THE PROPHETS. This discourse was delivered probably in the reign of *Jehoiakim.*

All my bones shake] He was terrified even by his own message, and shocked at the profanity of the false prophets.

Verse 10. *The land is full of adulterers*] Of idolaters. Of persons who *break their faith* to ME, as an *impure wife* does to her *husband.*

The pleasant places of the wilderness are dried up] He speaks here, most probably, in reference to *dearth.* Profane oaths, false swearing, evil courses, violence, &c., had provoked God to send this among other judgments; see ver. 19.

Verse 11. *In my house*] They had even introduced idolatry into the Temple of God!

Verse 13. *I have seen folly in the prophets of Samaria*] This was not to be wondered at, for their religion was a system of corruption.

Verse 14. *I have seen also in the prophets of Jerusalem*] That is, the prophets of Jerusalem,

A. M. cir. 3399
B. C. cir 605
Ol. XLIII. 4
TarquiniiPrisci,
R. Roman.,
cir. annum 12

adultery, and [d]walk in lies: they
[e]strengthen also the hands of
evil doers, that none doth return
from his wickedness: they are
all of them unto me as [f]Sodom, and the inhabitants thereof as Gomorrah.
15 Therefore thus saith the LORD of hosts
concerning the prophets; Behold, I will feed
them with [g]wormwood, and make them drink
the water of gall: for from the prophets of
Jerusalem is [h]profaneness gone forth into all
the land.
16 Thus saith the LORD of hosts, Hearken
not unto the words of the prophets that prophesy unto you: they make you vain: [i]they
speak a vision of their own heart, *and* not
out of the mouth of the LORD.
17 They say still unto them that despise me,
The LORD hath said, [k]Ye shall have peace;
and they say unto every one that walketh
after the [l]imagination of his own heart, [m]No
evil shall come upon you.
18 For [n]who hath stood in the [o]counsel of
the LORD, and hath perceived and heard his
word? who hath marked his word, and heard *it?*
19 Behold, a [p]whirlwind of the LORD is
gone forth in fury, even a grievous whirlwind:
it shall fall grievously upon the
head of the wicked.
20 The [q]anger of the LORD
shall not return until he have
executed, and till he have performed the
thoughts of his heart: [r]in the latter days ye
shall consider it perfectly.
21 [s]I have not sent these prophets, yet they
ran: I have not spoken to them, yet they
prophesied.
22 But if they had [t]stood in my counsel,
and had caused my people to hear my words,
then they should have [u]turned them from their
evil way, and from the evil of their doings.
23 *Am* I a God at hand, saith the LORD,
and not a God afar off?
24 Can any [v]hide himself in secret places
that I shall not see him? saith the LORD. [w]Do
not I fill heaven and earth? saith the LORD.
25 I have heard what the prophets said,
that prophesy lies in my name, saying, I have
dreamed, I have dreamed.
26 How long shall *this* be in the heart of
the prophets that prophesy lies? yea, *they are*
prophets of the deceit of their own heart;
27 Which think to cause my people to forget
my name by their dreams which they tell

A. M. cir. 3399
B. C. cir. 605
Ol. XLIII. 4
TarquiniiPrisci,
R. Roman.,
cir. annum 12

[d]Ver. 26——[e]Ezek. xiii. 23——[f]Deut. xxxii. 32; Isa. i. 9, 10——[g]Chap. viii. 14; ix. 15——[h]Or, *hypocrisy* [i]Chap. xiv. 14; ver. 21——[k]Chap. vi. 14; viii. 11; Ezek. xiii. 10; Zech. x. 2——[l]Or, *stubbornness;* chap. xiii. 10 [m]Mic. iii. 11

[n]Job xv. 8; 1 Cor. ii. 16——[o]Or, *secret*——[p]Chap. xxv. 32; xxx. 23——[q]Chap. xxx. 24——[r]Gen. xlix. 1 [s]Chap. xiv. 14; xxvii. 15; xxix. 9——[t]Ver. 18——[u]Jer. xxv. 5——[v]Psa. cxxxix. 7, &c.; Amos ix. 2, 3——[w]1 Kings viii. 27; Psa. cxxxix. 7

while professing a pure *faith*, have followed the ways, and become as corrupt as the prophets of *Samaria.*

They are all of them unto me as Sodom] Incorrigible, brutish sinners, who will as surely be destroyed as *Sodom* and *Gomorrah* were.

Verse 16. *Hearken not unto the words of the prophets*] That is, of those who promise you *safety*, without requiring you to forsake your sins and turn unto the Lord; see ver. 17.

Verse 18. *Who hath stood in the counsel of the Lord*] Who of *them* has ever received a word of prophecy from me? *My word* is not *in them.*

Verse 19. *Behold, a whirlwind*] The *simoom:* the hot pestilential wind blowing from the south, frequently mentioned or referred to in the sacred writings; see ver. 10.

Verse 20. *In the latter days ye shall consider it*] I give you warning: and this punishment which I now threaten shall surely take place; a short time will determine it; ye shall not escape.

Verse 21. *I have not sent these prophets, yet they ran*] Not to save souls, but to profit themselves.

I have not spoken to them, yet they prophesied.] They never received the word at my mouth; yet they went, publishing their own deceits, and pretending them to be revelations from God. The churches which have *legal emoluments* are ever in danger of being overrun and ruined by worldly and self-interested priests.

Verse 23. Am *I a God at hand,—and not a God afar off?*] You act as if you thought I could not see you! Am I not omnipresent? *Do not I fill the heavens and the earth?* ver. 24.

Verse 27. *By their dreams*] Dreams were anciently reputed as a species of inspiration; see Num. xii. 6; 1 Sam. xxviii. 6; Joel iii. 1; Dan. vii. 1. In the Book of *Genesis* we find many examples; and although many mistook the workings of their own vain *imaginations* in sleep for *revelations* from God, yet he has often revealed himself in this way: but such dreams were easily distinguished from the others. They were always such as had no connexion with the *gratification of the flesh;* they were such as contained *warnings against sin*, and *excitements* to *holiness;* they were always *consecutive—well connected*, with a proper *beginning* and *ending;* such as possessed the *intellect* more than the *imagination*. Of such dreams the Lord says, (ver. 28:) *The prophet that hath a dream, let him tell a dream*—permit him to show what he has thus received from the Lord: but let him tell it as a *dream*, and speak

A. M. cir. 3399 B. C. cir. 605 Ol. XLIII. 4 TarquiniiPrisci, R. Roman., cir. annum 12

every man to his neighbour, [x]as
their fathers have forgotten my
name for Baal.
28 The prophet [y]that hath a
dream, let him tell a dream; and he that hath
my word, let him speak my word faithfully.
What *is* the chaff to the wheat? saith the
LORD.
29 *Is* not my word like as a fire? saith the
LORD; and like a hammer *that* breaketh the
rock in pieces?
30 Therefore, behold, [z]I *am* against the
prophets, saith the LORD, that steal my words
every one from his neighbour.
31 Behold, I *am* against the prophets, saith
the LORD, [a]that use their tongues, and say,
He saith.

32 Behold, I *am* against them
that prophesy false dreams, saith
the LORD, and do tell them, and
cause my people to err by their
lies, and by [b]their lightness; yet I sent
them not, nor commanded them: therefore
they shall not profit this people at all, saith
the LORD.
33 And when this people, or the prophet, or
a priest, shall ask thee, saying, What *is* [c]the
burden of the LORD? thou shalt then say unto
them, what burden? [d]I will even forsake you,
saith the LORD.
34 And *as for* the prophet, and the priest,
and the people, that shall say, The burden of
the LORD, I will even [e]punish that man and
his house.

A. M. cir. 3399 B. C. cir. 605 Ol. XLIII. 4 TarquiniiPrisci, R. Roman., cir. annum 12

[x]Judg. iii. 7; viii. 33, 34——[y]Heb. *with whom is*——[z]Deut. xviii. 20; chap. xiv. 14, 15

[a]Or, *that smooth their tongues*——[b]Zeph. iii. 4——[c]Mal. i. 1——[d]Ver. 39——[e]Heb. *visit upon*

my word faithfully, lest he may have been deceived.

Verse 28. *What* is *the chaff to the wheat? saith the Lord.*] Do not mingle these *equivocal matters* with *positive revelations.* Do not consider a *dream,* even from a prophet, as that *positive inspiration* which my prophets receive when their *reason, judgment,* and *spiritual feelings* are all in full and in regular exercise. Mix none of your *own devices* with my *doctrines.*

Verse 29. Is *not my word like as a fire?*] It enlightens, warms, and penetrates every part. When it is communicated to the true prophet, it is *like a fire* shut up in his bones; he cannot retain it, he must publish it: and when published, it is like a *hammer* that breaks the rock in pieces; it is ever accompanied by a *Divine power,* that causes both sinner and saint to *feel* its *weight* and *importance.*

In the original words there is something singular: הלוא כה דברי כאש *halo coh debari kaesh,* "Is not thus my word like fire?" I suspect, with Dr. *Blayney,* that כה *coh, thus,* was formerly written כח *coach, strength* or *power;* and so it was understood by the *Targumist:* "Are not all my words strong, like fire?" and probably the author of the Epistle to the Hebrews read it thus, and had it in view when he wrote: "For the word of God is quick and powerful, and sharper than any two-edged sword," Heb. iv. 12. This admitted, the text would read, "Is not my word powerful, like fire?" or, "Is not the power of my word like fire?" But however we understand the words, let us take heed lest we think, as some have thought and affirmed, that the sacred writings are quite sufficient of themselves to enlighten, convince, and convert the soul, and that there is no need of the Holy Spirit. *Fire itself* must be *applied* by an *agent* in order to produce its effects; and surely the *hammer* cannot *break the rock in pieces,* unless *wielded* by an *able workman.* And it is God's *Spirit* alone that can thus *apply* it; for we find it frequently *read* and frequently *spoken,* without producing any salutary effects. And by this very thing the true preachers of the word of God may be distinguished from the *false, non-commissioned ones;* those who run, though they are not sent, ver. 21. The word of him who has his commission from heaven shall be as a *fire* and as a *hammer;* sinners shall be convinced and converted to God by it. But the others, though they steal the word from their neighbour—borrow or pilfer a good sermon, yet they do not profit the people at all, because God did not send them, ver. 32; for the *power* of God does not in their ministry accompany the word.

There may be an allusion to the practice in some mining countries, of *roasting stones* containing ore, before they are subjected to the *hammer,* in order to *pulverize* them. In Cornwall I have seen them *roast the tin stones* in the fire, before they placed them under the action of the *hammers* in the *stamp mill.* The fire separated the *arsenic* from the ore, and then they were easily reduced to powder by the hammers of the mill; afterwards, *washing* the mass with water, the grains of *tin* sank to the bottom, while the lighter parts went off with the water, and thus the metal was procured clean and pure. If this be the allusion, it is very appropriate.

Verse 30. *I* am *against the prophets*] Three cases are mentioned here which excited God's disapprobation: 1. The prophets who *stole the word* from their neighbour; who associated with the true prophets, got some intelligence from them, and then went and published it as a revelation which themselves had received, ver. 30. 2. The prophets who used their *tongues;* הלקחים לשונם *hallokechim leshonam, who lick* or *smooth with their tongues*—gave their own counsels as Divine revelations, flattering them in their sins, and promising peace, when God had not spoken; and prefaced them, "Thus saith the Lord," ver. 31. 3. The prophets who made up false stories, which they termed prophecies, revealed to them in *dreams;* and thus *caused the people to err,* ver. 32.

Verse 33. *What* is *the burden of the Lord?*] The word משא *massa,* here used, signifies *burden, oracle, prophetic discourse;* and is used by almost every prophet. But the persons in the

A. M. cir. 3399 B. C. cir. 605 Ol. XLIII. 4 TarquiniiPrisci, R. Roman., cir. annum 12

35 Thus shall ye say every
one to his neighbour, and every
one to his brother, What hath
the LORD answered? and, What
hath the LORD spoken?
36 And the burden of the LORD shall ye
mention no more: for every man's word shall
be his burden; for ye have perverted the words
of the living God, of the LORD of hosts our God.
37 Thus shalt thou say to the prophet, What
hath the LORD answered thee? and, What hath
the LORD spoken?
38 But since ye say, The burden of the
LORD; therefore thus saith the
LORD; Because ye say this
word, The burden of the LORD,
and I have sent unto you, saying,
Ye shall not say, The burden of the
LORD;
39 Therefore, behold, I, even I, [f]will utterly
forget you, and [g]I will forsake you, and the
city that I gave you and your fathers, *and cast
you* out of my presence:
40 And I will bring [h]an everlasting reproach
upon you, and a perpetual shame, which shall
not be forgotten.

A. M. cir. 3399 B. C cir 605 Ol. XLIII. 4 TarquiniiPrisci, R. Roman., cir. annum 12

[f]Hos. iv. 6——[g]Ver. 33

[h]Chap. xx. 11

text appear to have been *mockers*. "Where is this *burden* of the Lord?"—"What is the *burden* now?" To this insolent question the prophet answers in the following verses.

I will even forsake you] I will punish the prophet, the priest, and the people, that speak thus, ver. 34. Here are *burdens*.

Verse 36. *Every man's word shall be his burden*] Ye say that all God's messages are *burdens*, and to *you* they shall be such: whereas, had you used them as you ought, they would have been *blessings* to you.

For ye have perverted the words of the living God] And thus have sinned against your own souls.

Verse 39. *I will utterly forget you, and I will forsake you and the city*] Dr. *Blayney* translates:—*I will both take you up altogether, and will cast you off together with the city.* Ye are a *burden* to me: but I will take you up, and then cast you off. I will do with you as a man weary with his burden will do; cast it off his shoulders, and bear it no more.

Verse 40. *I will bring an everlasting reproach upon you*] And this reproach of having rebelled against so good a God, and rejected so powerful a Saviour, follows them to this day through all their dispersions, in every part of the habitable earth. The word of the Lord cannot fail.

CHAPTER XXIV

Under the emblem of the good and bad figs is represented the fate of the Jews already gone into captivity with Jeconiah, and of those that remained still in their own country with Zedekiah. It is likewise intimated that God would deal kindly with the former, but that his wrath would still pursue the latter, 1–10.

A. M. cir. 3406 B. C. 598 Ol. XLV. 3 Anno TarquiniiPrisci, R. Roman., 19

THE [a]LORD showed me, and,
behold, two baskets of figs
were set before the temple of the
LORD, after that Nebuchadrezzar
[b]king of Babylon had carried away captive
[c]Jeconiah the son of Jehoiakim king of Judah,
and the princes of Judah, with
the carpenters and smiths from
Jerusalem, and had brought
them to Babylon.
2 One basket *had* very good figs, *even* like
the figs *that are* first ripe; and the other basket

A. M. cir. 3406 B. C. 598 Ol. XLV. 3 Anno TarquiniiPrisci, R. Roman., 19

[a]Amos vii. 1, 4; viii. 1——[b]2 Kings xxiv. 12, &c.; 2 Chron. xxxvi. 10——[c]See chap. xxii. 24, &c.; xxix. 2

NOTES ON CHAP. XXIV

Verse 1. *The Lord showed me, and, behold, two baskets of figs*] Besides the *transposition* of *whole chapters* in this book, there is not unfrequently a transposition of *verses*, and *parts of verses*. Of this we have an instance in the verse before us; the first clause of which should be the last. Thus:—

"After that Nebuchadrezzar king of Babylon had carried away captive Jeconiah, the son of Jehoiakim king of Judah, with the carpenters and smiths from Jerusalem, and had brought them to Babylon, the Lord showed me, and, behold, two baskets of figs *were* set before the temple of the Lord."

Verse 2. "One basket *had* very good figs, *even* like the figs *that are* first ripe; and the other basket *had* very naughty figs, which could not be eaten, they were so bad."

This arrangement restores these verses to a better sense, by restoring the *natural connexion*.

This prophecy was undoubtedly delivered in the first year of the reign of Zedekiah.

Under the type of *good* and *bad figs*, God represents the state of the persons who had already been carried captives into Babylon, with their king Jeconiah, compared with the state of those who should be carried away with Zedekiah. Those already carried away, being the *choice* of the people, are represented by the *good figs:* those now remaining, and soon to be carried into captivity, are represented by the *bad figs, that were good for nothing.* The *state*

A. M. 3406
B. C. 598
Ol. XLV. 3
Anno
TarquiniiPrisci,
R. Roman., 19

had very naughty figs, which could not be eaten, [d]they were so bad.

3 Then said the LORD unto me, What seest thou, Jeremiah? And I said, Figs; the good figs, very good; and the evil, very evil, that cannot be eaten, they are so evil.

4 Again the word of the Lord came unto me, saying,

5 Thus saith the LORD, the God of Israel; Like these good figs, so will I acknowledge [e]them that are carried away captive of Judah, whom I have sent out of this place into the land of the Chaldeans for *their* good.

6 For I will set mine eyes upon them for good, and [f]I will bring them again to this land: and [g]I will build them, and not pull *them* down; and I will plant them, and not pluck *them* up.

A. M. 3406
B. C. 598
Ol. XLV. 3
Anno
TarquiniiPrisci,
R. Roman., 19

7 And I will give them [h]a heart to know me, that I *am* the LORD: and they shall be [i]my people, and I will be their God: for they shall return unto me [k]with their whole heart.

8 And as the evil [l]figs, which cannot be eaten, they are so evil; surely thus saith the LORD, So will I give Zedekiah the king of Judah, and his princes, and the residue of Jerusalem, that remain in this land, and [m]them that dwell in the land of Egypt:

9 And I will deliver them [n]to [o]be removed into all the kingdoms of the earth for *their* hurt, [p]*to be* a reproach and a proverb, a taunt [q]and a curse, in all places whither I shall drive them.

10 And I will send the sword, the famine, and the pestilence, among them, till they be consumed from off the land that I gave unto them and to their fathers.

[d]Heb. *for badness*——[e]Heb. *the captivity*——[f]Ch. xii. 15; xxix. 10——[g]Chap. xxxii. 41; xxxiii. 7; xlii. 10
[h]Deut. xxx. 6; ch. xxxii. 39; Ezek. xi. 19; xxxvi. 26, 27
[i]Chap. xxx. 22; xxxi. 33; xxxii. 38——[k]Chap. xxix. 13

[l]Ch. xxix. 17——[m]See chap. xliii. xliv——[n]Heb. *for removing*, or *vexation*——[o]Deut. xxviii. 25, 37; 1 Kings ix. 7; 2 Chron. vii. 20; chap. xv. 4; xxix. 18; xxxiv. 17
[p]Psa. xliv. 13, 14——[q]Chap. xxix. 18, 22

also of the *former* in their captivity was vastly preferable to the *state* of *those* who were now about to be delivered into the hand of the king of Babylon. The *latter* would be treated as *double rebels;* the *former*, being the most respectable of the inhabitants, were treated well; and even in captivity, a marked distinction would be made between them, God ordering it so. But the prophet sufficiently explains his own meaning.

Set before the temple]—As an offering of the first-fruits of that kind.

Verse 2. *Very good figs*] Or, figs of the *early sort.* The fig-trees in Palestine, says Dr. *Shaw*, produce fruit thrice each year. The first sort, called *boccore*, those here mentioned, come to perfection about the middle or end of June. The *second* sort, called *kermez*, or summer fig, is seldom ripe before August. And the *third*, which is called the *winter* fig, which is larger, and of a darker complexion than the preceding, hangs all the winter on the tree, ripening even when the leaves are shed, and is fit for gathering in the beginning of *spring.*

Could not be eaten] The *winter fig*,—then in its *crude* or unripe state; the spring not being yet come.

Verse 5. *Like these good figs, so will I acknowledge*] Those already carried away into captivity, I esteem as far more excellent than those who still remain in the land. They have not sinned so deeply, and they are now penitent; and, therefore, *I will set mine eyes upon them for good*, ver. 6. I will watch over them by an especial providence, and they shall be restored to their own land.

Verse 7. *They shall be my people*] I will renew my *covenant* with them, for *they will return to me with thei· whole heart.*

Verse 8. *So will I give Zedekiah*] I will treat these as they deserve. They shall be carried into captivity, and scattered through all nations. Multitudes of those never returned to Judea; the others returned at the end of *seventy years.*

Verse 10. *I will send the sword*] Many of them fell by sword and famine in the war with the Chaldeans, and many more by such means afterwards. The first received their captivity as a correction, and turned to God; the latter still hardened their hearts more and more, and probably very many of them never returned: perhaps they are now amalgamated with heathen nations. Lord, how long?

CHAPTER XXV

This chapter contains a summary of the judgments denounced by Jeremiah against Judah, Babylon, and many other nations. It begins with reproving the Jews for disobeying the calls of God to repentance, 1–7; on which account their captivity, with that of other neighbouring nations, during seventy *years, is foretold, 8–11. At the expiration of that period, (computing from the invasion of Nebuchadnezzar in the fourth year of Jehoiakim, to the famous edict of the first year of Cyrus,) an end was to be put to the Babylonian empire, 12–14. All this is again declared by the emblem of that cup of wrath which the prophet, as it should seem in a vision, tendered to all the nations which he enumerates,* 15–29. *And for farther confirmation, it is a third time repeated in a very beautiful and elevated strain of poetry,* 30–38. *The talent of diversifying the ideas, images, and language, even when the subject is the same, or nearly so, appears no where in such perfection as among the sacred poets.*

A. M. 3397
B. C. 607
Ol. XLV. 2
Anno
TarquiniiPrisci,
R. Roman., 10

THE word that came to Jeremiah concerning all the people of Judah [a]in the fourth year of Jehoiakim the son of Josiah king of Judah, that *was* the first year of Nebuchadrezzar king of Babylon.

2 The which Jeremiah the prophet spake unto all the people of Judah, and to all the inhabitants of Jerusalem, saying,

3 [b]From the thirteenth year of Josiah the son of Amon king of Judah, even unto this day, that *is* the three and twentieth year, the word of the LORD hath come unto me, and I have spoken unto you, rising early and speaking; [c]but ye have not hearkened.

4 And the LORD hath sent unto you all his servants the prophets, [d]rising early and sending *them;* but ye have not hearkened, nor inclined your ear to hear.

5 They said, [e]Turn ye again now every one from his evil way, and from the evil of your doings, and dwell in the land that the LORD hath given unto you and to your fathers for ever and ever:

6 And go not after other gods to serve them, and to worship them, and provoke me not to anger with the works of your hands; and I will do you no hurt.

A. M. 3397
B. C. 607
Ol. XLV. 2
Anno
TarquiniiPrisci,
R. Roman., 10

7 Yet ye have not hearkened unto me, saith the LORD; that ye might [f]provoke me to anger with the works of your hands to your own hurt.

8 Therefore thus saith the LORD of hosts; Because ye have not heard my words,

9 Behold, I will send and take [g]all the families of the north, saith the LORD, and Nebuchadrezzar the king of Babylon, [h]my servant, and will bring them against this land, and against the inhabitants thereof, and against all these nations round about, and will utterly destroy them, and [i]make them an astonishment, and a hissing, and perpetual desolations.

10 Moreover [k]I will take from them the [l]voice of mirth, and the voice of gladness, the voice of the bridegroom, and the voice of the bride, [m]the sound of the millstones, and the light of the candle.

11 And this whole land shall be a desolation, *and* an astonishment; and these nations shall serve the king of Babylon seventy years.

---

[a]Chap. xxxvi. 1——[b]Chap. i. 2——[c]Chap. vii. 13; xi. 7, 8, 10; xiii. 10, 11; xvi. 12; xvii. 23; xviii. 12; xix. 15; xxii. 21——[d]Ch. vii. 13, 25; xxvi. 5; xxix. 19——[e]2 Kings xvii. 13; ch. xviii. 11; xxxv. 15; Jonah iii. 8 [f]Deut. xxxii. 21; chap. vii. 19; xxxii. 30

[g]Chap. i. 15——[h]Chap. xxvii. 6; xliii. 10; see Isa. xliv. 28; xlv. 1; chap. xl. 2——[i]Chap. xviii. 16——[k]Heb. *I will cause to perish from them*——[l]Isa. xxiv. 7; chap. vii. 34; xvi. 9; Ezek. xxvi. 13; Hos. ii. 11; Rev. xviii. 23 [m]Eccles. xii. 4

NOTES ON CHAP. XXV

Verse 1. *The word that came to Jeremiah—in the fourth year*] This prophecy, we see, was delivered in the *fourth* year of Jehoiakim, and the chapter that contains it is utterly out of its place. It should be between chapters xxxv. and xxxvi.

The defeat of the Egyptians by Nebuchadnezzar at Carchemish, and the subsequent taking of Jerusalem, occurred in this year, *viz.*, the fourth year of *Jehoiakim.*

The first year of Nebuchadrezzar] This king was associated with his father *two years* before the death of the latter. The Jews reckon his reign from this time, and this was the *first* of those two years; but the Chaldeans date the commencement of his reign two years later, *viz.*, at the death of his father.

Verse 7. *That ye might provoke*] Ye would not hearken; but chose to provoke me with anger.

Verse 9. *Behold, I will send*] At this time Nebuchadrezzar had not invaded the land, according to this Version; but the Hebrew may be translated, "Behold I am sending, and have taken all the families;" that is, all the *allies* of the king of Babylon.

Instead of ואל *veel, "and* TO Nebuchadrezzar," as in the common Hebrew Bible, *seven* MSS. of *Kennicott's* and *De Rossi's,* and *one* of my own, have ואת *veeth,* "AND Nebuchadrezzar," which is undoubtedly the true reading.

Verse 10. *I will take from them*] See chap. vii. 34, and xvi. 9.

The sound of the mill-stones, and the light of the candle.] These two are conjoined, because they generally ground the corn *before day,* by the light of the candle. Sir J. *Chardin* has remarked, that every where in the morning may be heard the *noise of the mills;* for they generally grind *every day* just as much as is necessary for the day's consumption. Where then the *noise of the mill* is not *heard,* nor the *light of the candle seen,* there must be desolation; because these things are heard and seen in every inhabited country.

Verse 11. *Shall serve the king of Babylon seventy years.*] As this prophecy was delivered in the *fourth* year of Jehoiakim, and in the *first* of Nebuchadnezzar, and began to be accomplished in the same year, (for then Nebuchadnezzar invaded Judea, and took Jerusalem,)

A. M. 3397
B. C. 607
Ol. XLIII. 2
Anno
TarquiniiPrisci,
R. Roman., 10

12 And it shall come to pass,
[n]when seventy years are accomplished, *that* I will [o]punish the
king of Babylon, and that nation,
saith the LORD, for their iniquity, and the land
of the Chaldeans, [p]and will make it perpetual
desolations.
13 And I will bring upon that land all my
words which I have pronounced against it,
even all that is written in this book, which
Jeremiah hath prophesied against all the
nations.
14 [q]For many nations [r]and great kings shall
[s]serve themselves of them also: [t]and I will
recompense them according to their deeds,
and according to the works of their own
hands.
15 For thus saith the LORD God of Israel
unto me; Take the [u]wine cup of this fury at
my hand, and cause all the nations, to whom
I send thee, to drink it.
16 And [v]they shall drink, and be moved,
and be mad, because of the sword that I will
send among them.
17 Then took I the cup at the LORD's hand,
and made all the nations to
drink, unto whom the LORD had
sent me:

A. M. 3397
B. C. 607
Ol. XLIII. 2
Anno
TarquiniiPrisci,
R. Roman., 10

18 *To wit,* Jerusalem, and the
cities of Judah, and the kings thereof, and the
princes thereof, to make them [w]a desolation,
an astonishment, a hissing, and [x]a curse; as
it is this day;
19 [y]Pharaoh king of Egypt, and his servants, and his princes, and all his people;
20 And all [z]the mingled people, and all the
kings of [a]the land of Uz, [b]and all the kings
of the land of the Philistines, and Ashkelon,
and Azzah, and Ekron, and [c]the remnant of
Ashdod,
21 [d]Edom, and [e]Moab, and the children of
[f]Ammon,
22 And all the kings of [g]Tyrus, and all the
kings of Zidon, and the kings of the [h]isles
which *are* beyond the [i]sea,
23 [k]Dedan, and Tema, and Buz, and all
[l]*that are* in the utmost corners,
24 And [m]all the kings of Arabia, and all
the kings of the [n]mingled people that dwell
in the desert,

---

[n]2 Chron. xxxvi. 21, 22; Ezra i. 1; ch. xxix. 10; Dan. ix. 2; 2 Kings xxiv. 1——[o]Heb. *visit upon*——[p]Isa. xiii. 19; xiv. 23; xxi. 1, &c.; xlvii. 1; ch. l. 3, 13, 23, 39, 40, 45; li. 25, 26——[q]Ch. l. 9; li. 27, 28——[r]Ch. l. 41; li. 27 [s]Ch. xxvii. 7——[t]Ch. l. 29; li. 6, 24——[u]Job xxi. 20; Psa. lxxv. 8; Isa. li. 17; Rev. xiv. 10——[v]Ch. li. 7; Ezek. xxiii. 34; Nah. iii. 11——[w]Ver. 9, 11——[x]Ch. xxiv. 9

[y]Ch. xlvi. 2, 25——[z]Ver. 24——[a]Job i. 1——[b]Ch. xlvii. 1, 5, 7——[c]See Isa. xx. 1——[d]Ch. xlix. 7, &c. [e]Ch. xlviii. 1——[f]Ch. xlix. 1——[g]Ch. xlvii. 4——[h]Or, *region by the sea side*——[i]Ch. xlix. 23——[k]Ch. xlix. 8 [l]Heb. *cut off into corners*, or *having the corners* of the hair *polled;* ch. ix. 26; xlix. 32——[m]2 Chron. ix. 14——[n]See ver. 20; ch. xlix. 31; l. 3; Ezek. xxx. 5

---

seventy years from this time will reach down to the first year of Cyrus, when he made his proclamation for the restoration of the Jews, and the rebuilding of Jerusalem. See the note on Isa. xiii. 19, where the subject is farther considered in relation to the reign of Nebuchadnezzar, and the city of Babylon.

Verse 12. *And that nation*] הגוי ההוא *haggoi hahu.* Dr. *Blayney* contends that this should be translated *his nation,* and that ההוא *hahu* is the substantive pronoun used in the genitive case. It is certainly more clear and definite to read, "I will punish the king of Babylon, and HIS nation."

Will make it perpetual desolations] See the note on Isa. xiii. 19, where the fulfilment of this prophecy is distinctly marked.

Verse 14. *Many nations and great kings*] The *Medes* and the *Persians,* under Cyrus; and several princes, his vassals or allies.

Verse 15. *Take the wine cup of this fury*] For an ample illustration of this passage and simile, see the note on Isa. li. 21.

Verse 17. *Then took I the cup—and made all the nations to drink*] This *cup of God's wrath* is merely symbolical, and simply means that the prophet should declare to all these people that they shall fall under the Chaldean yoke, and that this is a punishment inflicted on them by God for their iniquities. "Then I took the cup;" I declared publicly the tribulation that God was about to bring on Jerusalem, the cities of Judah, and all the nations.

Verse 19. *Pharaoh king of Egypt*] This was *Pharaoh-necho,* who was the principal cause of instigating the neighbouring nations to form a league against the Chaldeans.

Verse 20. *All the mingled people*] The strangers and foreigners; Abyssinians and others who had settled in Egypt.

Land of Uz] A part of Arabia near to Idumea. See on Job. i. 1.

Verse 22. *Tyrus and—Zidon*] The most ancient of all the cities of the Phœnicians.

Kings of the isles which are *beyond the sea.*] As the *Mediterranean* Sea is most probably meant, and the Phœnicians had numerous colonies on its *coasts,* I prefer the *marginal* reading, *the kings of the region by the sea side.*

Verse 23. *Dedan*] Was son of Abraham, by Keturah, Gen. xxv. 3.

Tema] Was one of the sons of Ishmael, in the north of Arabia, Gen. xxxvi. 15.

Buz] Brother of *Uz,* descendants of Nahor, brother of Abraham, settled in Arabia Deserta, Gen. xxii. 21.

Verse 24. *The mingled people*] Probably the *Scenite Arabians.*

A. M. 3397
B. C. 607
Ol. XLIII. 2
Anno
TarquiniiPrisci,
R. Roman., 10

25 And all the kings of Zimri, and all the kings of [o]Elam, and all the kings of the Medes,

26 [p]And all the kings of the north, far and near, one with another, and all the kingdoms of the world, which *are* upon the face of the earth: [q]and the king of Sheshach shall drink after them.

27 Therefore thou shalt say unto them, Thus saith the LORD of hosts, the God of Israel; [r]Drink ye, and [s]be drunken, and spue, and fall, and rise no more, because of the sword which I will send among you.

28 And it shall be, if they refuse to take the cup at thine hand to drink, then shalt thou say unto them, Thus saith the LORD of hosts; Ye shall certainly drink.

29 For, lo, [t]I begin to bring evil on the city [u]which [v]is called by my name, and should ye be utterly unpunished? Ye shall not be unpunished: for [w]I will call for a sword upon all the inhabitants of the earth, saith the LORD of hosts.

30 Therefore prophesy thou against them all these words, and say unto them, The LORD shall [x]roar from on high, and utter his voice from [y]his holy habitation; he shall mightily roar upon [z]his habitation; he shall give [a]a shout, as they that tread *the grapes,* against all the inhabitants of the earth.

31 A noise shall come *even* to the ends of the earth; for the LORD hath [b]a controversy with the nations, [c]he will plead with all flesh; he will give them *that are* wicked to the sword, saith the LORD.

A. M. 3397
B. C. 607
Ol. XLIII. 2
Anno
TarquiniiPrisci,
R. Roman., 10

32 Thus saith the LORD of hosts, Behold, evil shall go forth from nation to nation, and [d]a great whirlwind shall be raised up from the coasts of the earth.

33 [e]And the slain of the LORD shall be at that day from *one* end of the earth even unto the *other* end of the earth: they shall not be [f]lamented, [g]neither gathered, nor buried; they shall be dung upon the ground.

34 [h]Howl, ye shepherds, and cry; and wallow yourselves *in the ashes,* ye principal of the flock: for [i]the days of your slaughter and of your dispersions are accomplished; and ye shall fall like [k] a pleasant vessel.

35 And [l]the shepherds shall have no way to flee, nor the principal of the flock to escape.

36 A voice of the cry of the shepherds, and a howling of the principal of the flock, *shall be heard:* for the LORD hath spoiled their pasture.

37 And the peaceable habitations are cut down because of the fierce anger of the LORD.

38 He hath forsaken [m]his covert, as the lion: for their land is [n]desolate because of the fierceness of the oppressor, and because of his fierce anger.

---

[o]Ch. xlix. 34——[p]Ch. l. 9——[q]Ch. li. 41——[r]Hab. ii. 16——[s]Isa. li. 21; lxiii. 6——[t]Prov. xi. 31; ch. xlix. 12; Ezek. ix. 6; Obad. 16; Luke xxiii. 31; 1 Pet. iv. 17
[u]Heb. *upon which my name is called*——[v]Dan. ix. 18, 19
[w]Ezek. xxxviii. 21——[x]Isa. xlii. 13; Joel iii. 16; Amos i. 2——[y]Psa. xi. 4; ch. xvii. 12——[z]1 Kings ix. 3; Psa. cxxxii. 14——[a]Isa. xvi. 9; chap. xlviii. 33

[b]Hos. iv. 1; Mic. vi. 2——[c]Isa. lxvi. 16; Joel iii. 2
[d]Ch. xxiii. 19; xxx. 23——[e]Isa. lxvi. 16——[f]Ch. xvi. 4, 6
[g]Psa. lxxix. 3; ch. viii. 2; Rev. xi. 9——[h]Ch. iv. 8; vi. 26
[i]Heb. *your days for slaughter*——[k]Heb. *a vessel of desire*
[l]Heb. *flight shall perish from the shepherds, and escaping from,* &c.; Amos ii. 14——[m]Psa. lxxvi. 2——[n]Heb. *a desolation*

Verse 25. *Zimri*] Descendants of Abraham, by Keturah, Gen. xxv. 2, 6.

Elam] Called Elymais by the Greeks, was on the south frontier of Media, to the north of Susiana, not far from Babylon.

Verse 26. *The kings of the north, far and near*] The *first* may mean Syria; the *latter*, the *Hyrcanians* and *Bactrians*.

And the king of Sheshach shall drink after them.] *Sheshach* was an ancient king of Babylon, who was deified after his death. Here it means either *Babylon*, or *Nebuchadnezzar* the king of it. After it has been the occasion of ruin to so many other nations, Babylon itself shall be destroyed by the *Medo-Persians*.

Verse 27. *Be drunken, and spue*] Why did we not use the word *vomit*, less offensive than the other, and yet of the same signification?

Verse 29. *The city which is called by my name*] Jerusalem, which should be *first* given up to the destruction.

Verse 32. *Evil shall go forth from nation to nation*] One nation after another shall fall before the Chaldeans.

Verse 33. *From* one *end of the earth*] From one end of the *land* to the other. All *Palestine* shall be desolated by it.

Verse 34. *Howl, ye shepherds*] Ye kings and chiefs of the people.

Ye shall fall like a pleasant vessel.] As a fall will break and utterly ruin a precious vessel of crystal, agate, &c., so your overthrow will be to you irreparable ruin.

Verse 38. *As the lion*] Leaving the banks of Jordan when overflowed, and coming with ravening fierceness to the champaign country.

CHAPTER XXVI

Jeremiah, by the command of God, goes into the court of the Lord's house; and foretells the destruction of the temple and city, if not prevented by the speedy repentance of the people, 1–7. By this unwelcome prophecy his life was in great danger; although saved by the influence of Ahikam, the son of Shaphan, who makes a masterly defence for the prophet, 8–18. Urijah is condemned, but escapes to Egypt; whence he is brought back by Jehoiakim, and slain, 20–23. Ahikam befriends Jeremiah, 24.

A. M. 3394 B. C. 610 Ol. XLII. 3 Anno TarquiniiPrisci, R. Roman., 7

IN the beginning of the reign of
Jehoiakim the son of Josiah
king of Judah came this word
from the LORD, saying,
2 Thus saith the LORD; Stand in [a]the
court of the LORD's house, and speak unto all
the cities of Judah, which come to worship in
the LORD's house, [b]all the words that I command thee to speak unto them; [c]diminish not
a word:
3 [d]If so be they will hearken, and turn
every man from his evil way, that I may [e]re-
pent me of the evil, which I purpose to do unto
them, because of the evil of their doings.
4 And thou shalt say unto them, Thus saith
the LORD; [f]If ye will not hearken to me
to walk in my law, which I have set before
you,
5 To hearken to the words of my servants
the prophets, [g]whom I sent unto you, both
rising up early, and sending *them*, but ye have
not hearkened;
6 Then will I make this house like [h]Shiloh,
and will make this city [i]a curse to all the
nations of the earth.
7 So the priests and the prophets and all the
people heard Jeremiah speaking these words
in the house of the LORD.
8 Now it came to pass, when Jeremiah had
made an end of speaking all that the LORD
had commanded *him* to speak unto all the
people, that the priests and the
prophets and all the people took
him, saying, Thou shalt surely
die.

A. M. 3394 B. C. 610 Ol. XLII. 3 Anno TarquiniiPrisci, R. Roman., 7

9 Why hast thou prophesied in the name of
the LORD, saying, This house shall be like
Shiloh, and this city shall be desolate without
an inhabitant? And all the people were
gathered against Jeremiah in the house of the
LORD.
10 When the princes of Judah heard these
things, then they came up from the king's
house unto the house of the LORD, and sat
down [k]in the entry of the new gate of the
LORD's *house*.
11 Then spake the priests and the prophets
unto the princes and to all the people, saying,
[l]This man *is* worthy to die; [m]for he hath
prophesied against this city, as ye have heard
with your ears.
12 Then spake Jeremiah unto all the princes
and to all the people, saying, The LORD sent
me to prophesy against this house and against
this city all the words that ye have heard.
13 Therefore now [n]amend your ways and
your doings, and obey the voice of the LORD
your God; and the LORD will [o]repent him of
the evil that he hath pronounced against you.
14 As for me, behold, [p]I *am* in your hand:
do with me [q]as seemeth good and meet unto
you.

[a]Chap. xix. 14——[b]Ezek. iii. 10; Matt. xxviii. 20——[c]Acts xx. 27——[d]Chap. xxxvi. 3——[e]Chap. xviii. 8; Jonah iii. 8, 9——[f]Lev. xxvi. 14, &c.; Deut. xxviii. 15——[g]Chap. vii. 13, 25; xi. 7; xxv. 3, 4——[h]1 Sam. iv. 10, 11; Psa. lxxviii. 60; chap. vii. 12, 14——[i]Isa. lxv. 15; chap. xxiv. 9——[k]Or, *at the door*——[l]Heb. *The judgment of death is for this man*——[m]Chap. xxxviii. 4——[n]Chap. vii. 3——[o]Ver. 3, 19——[p]Chap. xxxviii. 5——[q]Hebrew, *as it is good and right in your eyes*

NOTES ON CHAP. XXVI

Verse 1. *In the beginning of the reign of Jehoiakim*] As this prophecy must have been delivered in the *first* or *second* year of the reign of Jehoiakim, it is totally out of its place here. Dr. *Blayney* puts it before chap. xxxvi.; and Dr. *Dahler* immediately after chap. ix., and before chap. xlvi.

Verse 4. *If ye will not hearken*] This and several of the following verses are nearly the same with those in chap. vii. 13, &c., where see the notes.

Verse 8. *And all the people*] That were in company with the priests and the prophets.

Verse 10. *The princes of Judah*] The king's court; his cabinet counsellors.

Verse 12. *The Lord sent me to prophesy*] My commission is from him, and my words are his own. I sought not this painful office. I did not run before I was sent.

Verse 13. *Therefore now amend your ways*] If ye wish to escape the judgment which I have predicted, turn to God, and iniquity shall not be your ruin.

Verse 14. *As for me, behold, I* am *in your hand*] I am the messenger of God; you may do with me what you please; but if you slay me, you will bring innocent blood upon yourselves.

A. M. 3394
B. C. 610
Ol. XLII. 3
Anno
TarquiniiPrisci,
R. Roman., 7

15 But know ye for certain, that if ye put me to death, ye shall surely bring innocent blood upon yourselves, and upon this city, and upon the inhabitants thereof: for of a truth the LORD hath sent me unto you to speak all these words in your ears.

16 Then said the princes and all the people unto the priests and to the prophets; This man *is* not worthy to die: for he hath spoken to us in the name of the LORD our God.

17 [r]Then rose up certain of the elders of the land, and spake to all the assembly of the people, saying,

18 [s]Micah the Morasthite prophesied in the days of Hezekiah king of Judah, and spake to all the people of Judah, saying, Thus saith the LORD of hosts; [t]Zion shall be ploughed *like* a field, and Jerusalem shall become heaps, and the mountain of the house as the high places of a forest.

19 Did Hezekiah king of Judah and all Judah put him at all to death? [u]did he not fear the LORD, and besought [v]the LORD, and the LORD [w]repented him of the evil which he had pronounced against them? [x]Thus might we procure great evil against our souls.

A. M. 3394
B. C. 610
Ol. XLII. 3
Anno
TarquiniiPrisci,
R. Roman., 7

20 And there was also a man that prophesied in the name of the LORD, Urijah the son of Shemaiah of Kirjath-jearim, who prophesied against this city and against this land according to all the words of Jeremiah:

21 And when Jehoiakim the king, with all his mighty men, and all the princes, heard his words, the king sought to put him to death: but when Urijah heard it, he was afraid, and fled, and went into Egypt;

22 And Jehoiakim the king sent men into Egypt, *namely,* Elnathan the son of Achbor, and *certain* men with him into Egypt.

23 And they fetched forth Urijah out of Egypt, and brought him unto Jehoiakim the king; who slew him with the sword, and cast his dead body into the graves of the [y]common people.

24 Nevertheless [z]the hand of Ahikam the son of Shaphan was with Jeremiah, that they should not give him into the hand of the people to put him to death.

---

[r]See Acts v. 34, &c.——[s]Mic. i. 1——[t]Mic. iii. 12
[u]2 Chronicles xxxii. 26——[v]Hebrew, *the face of the LORD*
[w]Exod. xxxii. 14; 2 Sam. xxiv. 16——[x]Acts v. 39
[y]Heb. *sons of the people*——[z]2 Kings xxii. 12, 14; chap. xxxix. 14

Verse 16. *This man* is *not worthy to die*] The whole court acquitted him.

Verse 17. *Certain of the elders*] This is really a fine defence, and the argument was perfectly conclusive. Some think that it was Ahikam who undertook the prophet's defence.

Verse 18. *Micah the Morasthite*] The same as stands among the prophets. Now all these prophesied as hard things against the land as Jeremiah has done; yet they were not put to death, for the people saw that they were sent of God.

Verse 20. *Urijah—who prophesied*] The process against Jeremiah is finished at the *nineteenth* verse; and the case of Urijah is next brought on, for he was also to be tried for his life; but hearing of it he fled to Egypt. He was however condemned in his absence; and the king sent to Egypt, and brought him thence and slew him, and caused him to have an ignominious burial, ver. 21-23.

Verse 24. *The hand of Ahikam—was with Jeremiah*] And it was probably by his influence that Jeremiah did not share the same fate with Urijah. The Ahikam mentioned here was probably the father of Gedaliah, who, after the capture of Jerusalem, was appointed governor of the country by Nebuchadnezzar, chap. xl. 5. Of the Prophet *Urijah*, whether he was true or false, we know nothing but what we learn from this place.

That they should not give him into the hand of the people] Though acquitted in the supreme court, he was not out of danger; there was a popular prejudice against him, and it is likely that Ahikam was obliged to conceal him, that they might not put him to death. The genuine ministers of God have no favour to expect from those who are HIS enemies.

CHAPTER XXVII

Ambassadors being come from several neighbouring nations to solicit the king of Judah to join in a confederacy against the king of Babylon, Jeremiah is commanded to put bands and yokes upon his neck, (the emblems of subjection and slavery,) and to send them afterwards by those ambassadors to their respective princes; intimating by this significant type that God had decreed their subjection to the Babylonian empire, and that it was their wisdom to submit. It is farther declared that all the conquered nations shall remain in subjection to the Chaldeans during the reign of Nebuchadnezzar, and those of his son and grandson, even till the arrival of that period in which the Babylonians shall have filled up the measure of their iniquities; and that then the mighty Chaldean monarchy itself, for a certain period the paramount power of the habitable globe, shall be visited with a dreadful storm of Divine wrath, through the violence of which it shall be dashed to pieces like a potter's vessel, the fragments falling into the hands of many nations and great kings, 1–11. *Zedekiah, particularly, is admonished not to join in the revolt against Nebuchadnezzar, and warned against trusting to the suggestions of false prophets,* 11–18. *The chapter concludes with foretelling that what still remained of the sacred vessels of the temple should be carried to Babylon, and not restored till after the destruction of the Chaldean empire,* 19–22.

A. M. 3409 B. C. 595 Ol. XLVI. 2 Anno TarquiniiPrisci, R. Roman., 22

IN the beginning of the reign
of Jehoiakim the son of Josiah [a]king of Judah came this
word unto Jeremiah from the
LORD, saying,
2 Thus [b]saith the LORD to me; Make thee
bonds and yokes, [c]and put them upon thy
neck,
3 And send them to the king of Edom, and
to the king of Moab, and to the king of the
Ammonites, and to the king of Tyrus, and to
the king of Zidon, by the hand of the messengers which come to Jerusalem unto Zedekiah
king of Judah;
4 And command them [d]to say unto their
masters, Thus saith the LORD of hosts, the
God of Israel; Thus shall ye say unto your
masters;
5 [e]I have made the earth, the man and the
beast that *are* upon the ground, by my great
power and by my outstretched arm, and [f]have
given it unto whom it seemed meet unto me.
6 [g]And now have I given all
these lands into the hand of Nebuchadnezzar, the king of Babylon,
[h]my servant; and [i]the beasts of
the field have I given him also to serve him.
7 [k]And all nations shall serve him, and his
son, and his son's son, [l]until the very time of
his land come: [m]and then many nations and
great kings shall serve themselves of him.
8 And it shall come to pass, *that* the nation
and kingdom which will not serve the same
Nebuchadnezzar the king of Babylon, and that
will not put their neck under the yoke of the
king of Babylon, that nation will I punish,
saith the LORD, with the sword, and with the
famine, and with the pestilence, until I have
consumed them by his hand.
9 Therefore hearken not ye to your prophets,
nor to your diviners, nor to your [n]dreamers,
nor to your enchanters, nor to your sorcerers,
which speak unto you, saying, Ye shall not
serve the king of Babylon:

[a]See ver. 3, 12, 19, 20; chap. xxviii. 1——[b]Or, *hath the LORD said*——[c]Chap. xxviii. 10, 12; so Ezek. iv. 1; xii. 3; xxiv. 3, &c.——[d]Or, *concerning their masters, saying*——[e]Psa. cxv. 15; cxlvi. 6; Isa. xlv. 12

[f]Psa. cxv. 16; Dan. iv. 17, 25, 32——[g]Ch. xxviii. 14——[h]Ch. xxv. 9; xliii. 10; Ezek. xxix. 18, 20——[i]Ch. xxviii. 14; Dan. ii. 38——[k]2 Chron. xxxvi. 20——[l]Ch. xxv. 12; l. 27; Dan. v. 26——[m]Ch. xxv. 14——[n]Heb. *dreams*

NOTES ON CHAP. XXVII

Verse 1. *In the beginning of the reign of Jehoiakim*] It is most evident that his prophecy was delivered about the *fourth* year of ZEDEKIAH, and not *Jehoiakim*, as in the text. See chap. xxviii. 1. *Three* of *Kennicott's* MSS. (*one* in the text, a *second* in the margin, and the *third* upon a rasure) have *Zedekiah;* so likewise have the *Syriac* and the *Arabic*. *Houbigant*, *Lowth*, *Blayney*, *Dahler*, and others declare for this reading against that in the present text. And it is clear from the *third* and *twelfth* verses, where *Zedekiah* is expressly mentioned, that this is the true reading.

Verse 2. *Make thee bonds and yokes*] Probably *yokes* with *straps*, by which they were attached to the neck. This was a symbolical action, to show that the several kings mentioned below should be brought under the dominion of the Chaldeans.

Verse 5. *I have made the earth*] I am the Creator and Governor of all things, and I dispose of the several kingdoms of the world as seemeth best to me.

Verse 6. *And now have I given*] These kingdoms are at my sovereign disposal; and at present, for the punishment of their rulers and people, I shall give them into the hands of Nebuchadnezzar, king of Babylon.

Verse 7. *And all nations shall serve him,* (Nebuchadnezzar,) *and his son,* (Evil-merodach, chap. lii. 31,) *and his son's son,* (Belshazzar, Dan. v. 11.) All which was literally fulfilled.

Verse 9. *Therefore hearken not ye to your prophets*] Who pretend to have a revelation from heaven.

Nor to your diviners] קסמיכם *kosemeychem, from* קסם *kasam*, to *presage* or *prognosticate.* Persons who *guessed* at futurity by certain signs in the animate or inanimate creation.

Nor to your dreamers] חלמתיכם *chalomotheychem,* from חלם *chalam*, to *break in pieces;* hence חלום *chalom, a dream*, because it consists of *broken fragments*. Dream-interpreters, who, from these *broken shreds* patch up a meaning by their own interpolations.

Nor to your enchanters] ענניכם *oneneychem,* from ענן *anan, a cloud*—cloud-mongers. Diviners by the flight, colour, density, rarity, and shape of clouds.

Nor to your sorcerers] כשפיכם *cashshapheychem*, from כשף *kashaph*, to *discover;* the discoverers, the finders out of hidden things, stolen

A. M. 3409
B. C. 595
Ol. XLVI. 2
Anno
TarquiniiPrisci,
R. Roman., 22

10 [o]For they prophesy a lie unto you, to [p]remove you far from your land; and that I should drive you out, and ye should perish.

11 But the nations that bring their neck under the yoke of the king of Babylon, and serve him, those will I let remain still in their own land, saith the LORD; and they shall till it, and dwell therein.

12 I spake also to [q]Zedekiah king of Judah according to all these words, saying, Bring your necks under the yoke of the king of Babylon, and serve him and his people, and live.

13 [r]Why will ye die, thou and thy people, by the sword, by the famine, and by the pestilence, as the LORD hath spoken against the nation that will not serve the king of Babylon?

14 Therefore hearken not unto the words of the prophets that speak unto you, saying, Ye shall not serve the king of Babylon: for they prophesy [s]a lie unto you.

15 For I have not sent them, saith the LORD, yet they prophesy [t]a lie in my name; that I may drive you out, and that ye might perish, ye, and the prophets that prophesy unto you.

16 Also I spake to the priests and to all this people, saying, Thus saith the LORD; Hearken not to the words of your prophets that prophesy unto you, saying, Behold, [u]the vessels of the LORD's house shall now shortly be brought again from Babylon: for they prophesy a lie unto you.

A. M. 3409
B. C. 595
Ol. XLVI. 2
Anno
TarquiniiPrisci,
R. Roman., 22

17 Hearken not unto them; serve the king of Babylon, and live: wherefore should this city be laid waste?

18 But if they *be* prophets, and if the word of the LORD be with them, let them now make intercession to the LORD of hosts, that the vessels which are left in the house of the LORD, and *in* the house of the king of Judah, and at Jerusalem, go not to Babylon.

19 For thus saith the LORD of hosts [v]concerning the pillars, and concerning the sea, and concerning the bases, and concerning the residue of the vessels that remain in this city,

20 Which Nebuchadnezzar king of Babylon took not, when he carried away [w]captive Jeconiah the son of Jehoiakim king of Judah from Jerusalem to Babylon, and all the nobles of Judah and Jerusalem;

21 Yea, thus saith the LORD of hosts, the God of Israel, concerning the vessels that remain *in* the house of the LORD, and *in* the house of the king of Judah and of Jerusalem;

22 They shall be [x]carried to Babylon, and there shall they be until the day that I [y]visit them, saith the LORD; then [z]will I bring them up, and restore them to this place.

---

[o]Ver. 14——[p]Ch. xxxii. 31; Deut. xxviii. 25; Ezek. xii. 3——[q]Ch. xxviii. 1; xxxviii. 17——[r]Ezek. xviii. 31——[s]Ch. xiv. 14; xxiii. 21; xxix. 8, 9——[t]Heb. *in a lie*, or *lyingly*——[u]2 Chron. xxxvi. 7, 10; ch. xxviii. 3; Dan. i. 2

[v]2 Kings xxv. 13, &c.; ch. lii. 17, 20, 21——[w]2 Kings xxiv. 14, 15; chap. xxiv. 1——[x]2 Kings xxv. 13; 2 Chron. xxxvi. 18——[y]2 Chron. xxxvi. 21; chap. xxix. 10; xxxii. 5——[z]Ezra i. 7; vii. 19

---

goods, &c. Persons also who use *incantations*, and either by *spells* or *drugs* pretend to find out mysteries, or produce supernatural effects. Every nation in the world had persons who pretended to find out hidden things, or foretell future events; and such were gladly encouraged by the ignorant multitude; and many of them were mere apes of the prophets of God. Man knows that he is *short-sighted*, feels pain at the uncertainty of futurity, and wishes to have his doubts resolved by such persons as the above, to put an end to his uncertainty.

Verse 13. *Why will ye die*] If ye resist the king of Babylon, to whom I have given a commission against you, ye shall be destroyed by the sword and by famine; but if ye submit, ye shall escape all these evils.

Verse 16. *The vessels of the Lord's house*] Which had been carried away by Nebuchadnezzar under the reigns of Jehoiakim and Jeconiah, 2 Chron. xxxvi. 7-10.

Shall now shortly be brought again] This is a lie. They shall not be restored till I bring them up, ver. 22, which was after the captivity, when they were sent back by Cyrus, the Lord inclining his heart to do it, Ezra i. 7, and vii. 19.

Verse 19. *Concerning the pillars*] Two brazen columns placed by Solomon in the pronaos or portico of the temple, *eighteen* cubits high, and *twelve* in circumference, 1 Kings vii. 15-22; Jer. lii. 11.

The sea] The brazen sea, *ten* cubits in diameter, and *thirty* in circumference. It contained water for different washings in the Divine worship, and was supported on *twelve* brazen oxen. Perhaps these are what are called the *bases* here. See the parallel places in the margin, and the notes on them.

Verse 22. *They shall be carried to Babylon*] Far from those already taken being brought back, those which now remain shall be carried thither, unless ye submit to the Chaldeans. They did not submit, and the prophecy was literally fulfilled; see chap. lii. 17-23; 2 Kings xxv. 13, and the other places in the *margin*.

CHAPTER XXVIII

One of those pretended prophets spoken of in the preceding chapter, having contradicted and opposed Jeremiah, receives an awful declaration that, as a proof to the people of his having spoken without commission, he should die in the then current year; which accordingly came to pass in the seventh month, 1–17.

A. M. 3409 B. C. 595 Ol. XLVI. 2 Anno TarquiniiPrisci, R. Roman., 22

AND [a]it came to pass the
same year, in the beginning
of the reign of Zedekiah king of
Judah, in the fourth year, *and* in
the fifth month, *that* Hananiah the son of Azur
the prophet, which *was* of Gibeon, spake unto
me in the house of the LORD, in the presence
of the priests and of all the people, saying,
2 Thus speaketh the LORD of hosts, the
God of Israel, saying, I have broken [b]the
yoke of the king of Babylon.
3 [c]Within [d]two full years will I bring again
into this place all the vessels of the LORD'S
house, that Nebuchadnezzar king of Babylon
took away from this place, and carried them
to Babylon:
4 And I will bring again to this place Jeconiah the son of Jehoiakim king of Judah, with
all the [e]captives of Judah, that went into
Babylon, saith the LORD: for I will break the
yoke of the king of Babylon.
5 Then the prophet Jeremiah said unto the
prophet Hananiah in the presence of the
priests, and in the presence of all the people
that stood in the house of the LORD,
6 Even the prophet Jeremiah said, [f]Amen:
the LORD do so: the LORD per-
form thy words which thou hast
prophesied, to bring again the
vessels of the LORD'S house,
and all that is carried away captive, from
Babylon into this place.
7 Nevertheless hear thou now this word that
I speak in thine ears, and in the ears of all
the people;
8 The prophets that have been before me and
before thee of old prophesied both against
many countries, and against great kingdoms,
of war, and of evil, and of pestilence.
9 [g]The prophet which prophesieth of peace,
when the word of the prophet shall come to
pass, *then* shall the prophet be known, that
the LORD hath truly sent him.
10 Then Hananiah the prophet took the
[h]yoke from off the prophet Jeremiah's neck,
and brake it.
11 And Hananiah spake in the presence of
all the people, saying, Thus saith the LORD;
Even so will I break the yoke of Nebuchadnezzar king of Babylon [i]from the neck of all
nations within the space of two full years.
And the prophet Jeremiah went his way.

A. M. 3409 B. C. 595 Ol. XLVI. 2 Anno TarquiniiPrisci, R. Roman., 22

[a]Chap. xxvii. 1——[b]Chap. xxvii. 12——[c]Chap. xxvii. 16——[d]Heb. *two years of days*——[e]Heb. *captivity*——[f]1 Kings i. 36——[g]Deut. xviii. 22——[h]Chap. xxvii. 2——[i]Chap. xxvii. 7

NOTES ON CHAP. XXVIII

Verse 1. *And it came to pass the same year—the fifth month*] Which commenced with the first new moon of *August*, according to our calendar. This verse gives the *precise date* of the prophecy in the preceding chapter; and proves that *Zedekiah*, not *Jehoiakim*, is the name that should be read in the *first* verse of that chapter.

Hananiah the son of Azur the prophet] One who called himself a prophet; who pretended to be in commerce with the Lord, and to receive revelations from him. He was probably a *priest;* for he was of Gibeon, a sacerdotal city in the tribe of Benjamin.

Verse 2. *Thus speaketh the Lord*] What awful impudence! when he knew in his conscience that God had given him no such commission.

Verse 3. *Within two full years*] Time sufficient for the Chaldeans to destroy the city, and carry away the rest of the sacred vessels; but he did not live to see the end of this short period.

Verse 6. *Amen; the Lord do so*] O that it might be according to thy word! May the people find this to be true!

Verse 8. *The prophets that have been before me*] Namely, Joel, Amos, Hosea, Micah, Zephaniah, Nahum, Habakkuk, and others; all of whom denounced similar evils against a corrupt people.

Verse 9. *When the word of the prophet shall come to pass*] Here is the criterion. . He is a true prophet who specifies things that he says shall happen, and also fixes the *time* of the event; and the things do happen, and in that time.

You say that Nebuchadnezzar shall not overthrow this city; and that in *two years* from this time, not only the sacred vessels *already taken away* shall be restored, but also that *Jeconiah* and *all the Jewish captives* shall be restored, and the *Babylonish yoke* broken, see verses 2, 3, 4. Now *I* say that Nebuchadnezzar will come *this year*, and destroy this city, and lead away the rest of the people into captivity, and the rest of the sacred vessels; and that there will be no restoration of any kind till *seventy* years from this time.

Verse 10. *Then Hananiah—took the yoke—and brake it.*] He endeavoured by this symbolical act to persuade them of the truth of his prediction.

A. M. 3409 B. C. 595 Ol. XLVI. 2 Anno TarquiniiPrisci, R. Roman., 22

12 Then the word of the LORD came unto Jeremiah *the prophet,* (after that Hananiah the prophet had broken the yoke from off the neck of the prophet Jeremiah,) saying,

13 Go and tell Hananiah, saying, Thus saith the LORD; Thou hast broken the yokes of wood; but thou shalt make for them yokes of iron.

14 For thus saith the LORD of hosts, the God of Israel; [k]I have put a yoke of iron upon the neck of all these nations, that they may serve Nebuchadnezzar king of Babylon; and they shall serve him: and [l]I have given him the beasts of the field also.

15 Then said the prophet Jeremiah unto Hananiah the prophet, Hear now, Hananiah; The LORD hath not sent thee; but [m]thou makest this people to trust in a lie.

16 Therefore thus saith the LORD; Behold, I will cast thee from off the face of the earth: this year thou shalt die, because thou hast taught [n]rebellion [o]against the LORD.

17 So Hananiah the prophet died the same year in the seventh month.

[k]Deut. xxviii. 48; chap. xxvii. 4, 7——[l]Chap. xxvii. 6 [m]Chap. xxix. 31; Ezek. xiii. 22

[n]Deuteronomy xiii. 5; chapter xxix. 32——[o]Hebrew, *revolt*

Verse 13. *Yokes of iron.*] Instead of Nebuchadnezzar's yoke *being broken,* this captivity shall be more *severe* than the *preceding.* All these nations shall have a *yoke of iron* on their neck. He shall *subdue them,* and take all *their property,* even the *beasts of the field.*

Verse 15. *Hear now, Hananiah; the Lord hath not sent thee*] This was a bold speech in the presence of those priests and people who were prejudiced in favour of this false prophet, who prophesied to them smooth things. In such cases men wish to be *deceived.*

Verse 16. *This year thou shalt die*] By this shall the people know *who* is the *true prophet.* Thou hast taught *rebellion against the Lord,* and God will cut thee off; and this shall take place, not within *seventy years,* or *two years,* but in *this very year,* and within *two months* from this time.

Verse 17. *So Hananiah—died the same year in the seventh month.*] The prophecy was delivered in the *fifth month,* (ver. 1,) and Hananiah died in the *seventh month.* And thus God, in mercy, gave him about *two months,* in which he might prepare to meet his Judge. Here, then, the *true prophet* was *demonstrated,* and the *false prophet detected.* The death of Hananiah, thus predicted, was God's *seal* to the words of his prophet; and must have gained his other predictions great credit among the people.

CHAPTER XXIX

This chapter contains the substance of two letters sent by the prophet to the captives in Babylon. In the first he recommends to them patience and composure under their present circumstances, which were to endure for seventy *years,* 1–14; *in which, however, they should fare better than their brethren who remained behind,* 15–19. *But, finding little credit given to this message, on account of the suggestions of the false prophets, Ahab the son of Kolaiah, and Zedekiah, the son of Maaseiah, who flattered them with the hopes of a speedy end to their captivity, he sends a second, in which he denounces heavy judgments against those false prophets that deceived them,* 20–23; *as he did afterwards against Shemaiah the Nehelamite, who had sent a letter of complaint against Jeremiah, in consequence of his message,* 24–32.

A. M. cir. 3407 B. C. cir. 597 Ol. cir. XLV. 4 TarquiniiPrisci, R. Roman., cir. annum 20

NOW these *are* the words of the letter that Jeremiah the prophet sent from Jerusalem unto the residue of the [a]elders which were carried away captives, and to the priests, and to the prophets, and to all the people whom Nebuchadnezzar had [b]carried away captive from Jerusalem to Babylon;

2 (After that [c]Jeconiah the king and the queen, and the [d]eunuchs, the princes of Judah and Jerusalem, and the car-

[a]Ezra x. 14——[b]2 Kings xxv. 21——[c]2 Kings xxiv. 12, &c.; chap. xxii. 26; xxviii. 4——[d]Or, *chamberlains*

NOTES ON CHAP. XXIX

Verse 1. *Now these* are *the words of the letter*] This transaction took place in the *first* or *second* year of Zedekiah. It appears that the prophet had been informed that the Jews who had already been carried into captivity had, through the instigations of false prophets, been led to believe that they were to be brought out of their captivity speedily. Jeremiah, fearing that this delusion might induce them to take some hasty steps, ill comporting with their present state, wrote a letter to them, which he entrusted to an embassy which Zedekiah had sent on some political concerns to Nebuchadnezzar. The letter was directed to the elders, priests, prophets, and people who had been carried away captives to Babylon.

A. M. cir. 3407 penters, and the smiths, were
B. C. cir. 597
Ol. cir. XLV. 4 departed from Jerusalem;)
TarquiniiPrisci, R. Roman., 3 By the hand of Elasah the
cir. annum 20 son of Shaphan, and Gemariah
the son of Hilkiah, (whom Zedekiah king of
Judah sent unto Babylon to Nebuchadnezzar
king of Babylon) saying,
4 Thus saith the LORD of hosts, the God of
Israel, unto all that are carried away captives,
whom I have caused to be carried away from
Jerusalem unto Babylon;
5 [e]Build ye houses, and dwell *in them,* and
plant gardens, and eat the fruit of them;
6 Take ye wives, and beget sons and daughters; and take wives for your sons, and give
your daughters to husbands, that they may
bear sons and daughters; that ye may be increased there, and not diminished.
7 And seek the peace of the city whither I
have caused you to be carried away captives,
[f]and pray unto the LORD for it: for in the
peace thereof shall ye have peace.
8 For thus saith the LORD of hosts, the
God of Israel; Let not your prophets and
your diviners, that *be* in the midst of
you, [g]deceive you, neither hearken to your
dreams which ye cause to be A. M. cir. 3407
dreamed. B. C. cir. 597
Ol. cir. XLV. 4
9 [h]For they prophesy [i]falsely TarquiniiPrisci,
R. Roman.,
unto you in my name: I have cir. annum 20
not sent them, saith the LORD.
10 For thus saith the LORD, That after
[k]seventy years be accomplished at Babylon I
will visit you, and perform my good word toward you, in causing you to return to this
place.
11 For I know the thoughts that I think toward you, saith the LORD, thoughts of peace,
and not of evil, to give you an [l]expect-
ed end.
12 Then shall ye [m]call upon me, and ye
shall go and pray unto me, and I will hearken
unto you.
13 And [n]ye shall seek me, and find *me,* when
ye shall search for me [o]with all your heart.
14 And [p]I will be found of you, saith the
LORD: and I will turn away your captivity,
and [q]I will gather you from all the nations,
and from all the places whither I have driven
you, saith the LORD; and I will bring you
again into the place whence I caused you to
be carried away captive.

---

[e]Ver. 28——[f]Ezra vi. 10; 1 Mac. xii. 11; 1 Tim. ii. 2——[g]Ch. xiv. 14; xxiii. 21; xxvii. 14, 15; Eph. v. 6——[h]Ver. 31——[i]Heb. *in a lie*——[k]2 Chron. xxxvi. 21, 22; Ezra i. 1; chap. xxv. 12; xxvii. 22; Dan. ix. 2

[l]Heb. *end and expectation*——[m]Dan. ix. 3, &c.——[n]Lev. xxvi. 39, 40, &c.; Deut. xxx. 1, &c.——[o]Chap. xxiv. 7——[p]Deut. iv. 7; Psa. xxxii. 6; xlvi. 1; Isa. lv. 6——[q]Chap. xxiii. 3, 8; xxx. 3; xxxii. 37

Verse 4. *Thus saith the Lord of hosts*] This was the commencement of the letter.

Verse 5. *Build ye houses*] Prepare for a long continuance in your present captivity. Provide yourselves with the *necessaries* of life, and multiply in the land, that ye may become a powerful people.

Verse 7. *Seek the peace of the city*] Endeavour to promote, as far as you can, the *prosperity* of the places in which ye sojourn. Let no disaffection appear in word or act. Nothing can be more reasonable than this. Wherever a man lives and has his nourishment and support, that is his country as long as he resides in it. If things go well with that country, his interest is promoted by the general prosperity, he lives at comparative ease, and has the necessaries of life cheaper; and unless he is in a state of cruel servitude, which does not appear to have been the case with those Israelites to whom the prophet writes, (those of the first captivity,) they must be nearly, if not altogether, in as good a state as if they had been in the country that gave them birth. And in this case they were much better off than their brethren now in Judea, who had to contend with *famine* and *war*, and scarcely any thing before them but God's curse and extermination.

Verse 8. *Neither hearken to your dreams*] Rather, *dreamers;* for it appears there was a class of such persons, who not only had acquired a facility of dreaming themselves, but who undertook to interpret the dreams of others.

Verse 10. *For thus saith the Lord*] It has been supposed that a very serious *transposition* of verses has taken place here; and it has been proposed to read after ver. 9 the *sixteenth* to the *nineteenth* inclusive; then the *tenth*, and on to the *fourteenth* inclusive; then the *twentieth*, the *fifteenth*, the *twenty-first*, and the rest regularly to the end.

That after seventy years be accomplished] לפי מלאת *lephi meloth*, "at the mouth of the accomplishment," or "fill to the mouth." Seventy years is the *measure* which must be *filled;* —*fill this to the brim;*—complete this measure, and then you shall be visited and released. The whole *seventy* must be completed; expect no enlargement before that time.

Verse 11. *Thoughts of peace*] Here God gives them to understand, 1. That his love was moved towards them. 2. That he would perform his good word, his promises often repeated, to them. 3. That for the fulfilment of these they must *pray*, *seek*, and *search.* 4. That he would *hearken*, and they should *find* him; provided, 5. They *sought* him with their *whole heart*, ver. 10-13.

Verse 14. *I will gather you from all the na-*

A. M. cir. 3407 B. C. cir. 597 Ol. cir. XLV. 4 TarquiniiPrisci, R. Roman., cir. annum 20

15 Because ye have said, The LORD hath raised us up prophets in Babylon;

16 *Know* that thus saith the LORD of the king that sitteth upon the throne of David, and of all the people that dwelleth in this city, *and* of your brethren that are not gone forth with you into captivity;

17 Thus saith the LORD of hosts; Behold, I will send upon them the [r]sword, the famine, and the pestilence, and will make them like [s]vile figs, that cannot be eaten, they are so evil.

18 And I will persecute them with the sword, with the famine, and with the pestilence, and [t]will deliver them to be removed to all the kingdoms of the earth, [u]to be [v]a curse, and an astonishment, and a hissing, and a reproach, among all the nations whither I have driven them:

19 Because they have not hearkened to my words, saith the LORD, which [w]I sent unto them by my servants the prophets, rising up early and sending *them;* but ye would not hear, saith the LORD.

20 Hear ye therefore the word of the LORD, all ye of the captivity, whom I have sent from Jerusalem to Babylon:

A. M. cir. 3407 B. C. cir. 597 Ol. cir. XLV. 4 TarquiniiPrisci, R. Roman., cir. annum 20

21 Thus saith the LORD of hosts, the God of Israel, of Ahab the son of Kolaiah, and of Zedekiah the son of Maaseiah, which prophesy a lie unto you in my name; Behold, I will deliver them into the hand of Nebuchadnezzar king of Babylon; and he shall slay them before your eyes;

22 [x]And of them shall be taken up a curse by all the captivity of Judah which *are* in Babylon, saying, The LORD make thee like Zedekiah, and like Ahab, [y]whom the king of Babylon roasted in the fire;

23 Because [z]they have committed villany in Israel, and have committed adultery with their neighbours' wives, and have spoken lying words in my name, which I have not commanded them; even I know, and *am* a Witness, saith the LORD.

24 *Thus* shalt thou also speak to Shemaiah the [a]Nehelamite, saying,

25 Thus speaketh the LORD of hosts, the God of Israel, saying, Because thou hast sent letters in thy name unto all the people that *are* at Jerusalem, [b]and to Zephaniah the son

---

[r]Chap. xxiv. 10——[s]Chap. xxiv. 8——[t]Deut. xxviii. 25; 2 Chron. xxix. 8; chap. xv. 4; xxiv. 9; xxxiv. 17 [u]Heb. *for a curse*——[v]Chap. xxvi. 6; chap. xlii. 18

[w]Chap. xxv. 4; xxxii. 33——[x]See Gen. xlviii. 20; Isa. lxv. 15——[y]Dan. iii. 6——[z]Chap. xxiii. 14——[a]Or, *dreamer*——[b]2 Kings xxv. 18; chap. xxi. 1

---

tions] A quotation from Deut. xxx. 3, and see also Deut. iv. 7.

Verse 15. *Because ye have said*] The *Septuagint* very properly insert this verse between the *twentieth* and the *twenty-first*, and thus the *connexion* here is not disturbed, and the connexion below completed.

Verse 17. *Behold, I will send upon them the sword*] Do not envy the state of *Zedekiah* who sits on the throne of David, nor that of the *people* who are now in the land whence ye have been carried captive, (ver. 16,) for "I will send the sword, the pestilence, and the famine upon them;" and afterwards shall cause them to be carried into a miserable captivity *in all nations*, (ver. 18;) but *ye* see the worst of *your own* case, and you have God's promise of enlargement when the proper time is come. The reader will not forget that the prophet is addressing the captives in Babylon.

Verse 20. *Hear ye therefore the word*] Dr. *Blayney* thinks there were *two letters* written by the prophet to the captives in Babylon, and that the *first* ends with this verse. That having heard, on the return of the embassy (Elasah and Gemariah, whom Zedekiah had sent to Babylon, and to whom the prophet entrusted the above letter, ver. 3,) that the captives had not received his advices favourably, because they were deceived by false prophets among them, who promised them a *speedier* deliverance, he therefore wrote a *second letter*, beginning with the *fifteenth* verse, and going on with the *twenty-first*, &c., in which he denounces God's judgments on three of the chief of those, Ahab, Zedekiah, and Shemaiah.

Verse 21. *He shall slay them before your eyes.*] Nebuchadnezzar would be led by political reasons to punish these pretended prophets, as their predictions tended to make his Israelitish subjects uneasy and disaffected, and might excite them to rebellion. He therefore slew them; two of them, it appears, he *burnt alive*, viz., *Ahab* and *Zedekiah*, who are supposed by the rabbins to be the *two elders* who endeavoured to seduce *Susanna*, see ver. 23. Burning *alive* was a Chaldean punishment, Dan. iii. 6, and Amos. ii. 1. From them other nations borrowed it.

Verse 23. *Have committed adultery with their neighbours' wives*] This is supposed to refer to the case of *Susanna*. See above.

Verse 24. *Speak to Shemaiah*] Zephaniah was the *second priest*, *sagan*, or chief priest's deputy, and Seraiah, high priest, when Jerusalem was taken. See chap. lii. 24. Shemaiah directs his letter to the former, and tells him that God had appointed him to supply the place of the high priest, who was probably then absent. His name was either *Azariah* or *Seraiah* his son, but called *Jehoiada* from the remarkable zeal and courage of that pontiff. See the passages in the margin.—*Dodd*. After the taking of Jerusalem, Zephaniah was put to death by

A. M. cir. 3407
B. C. cir. 597
Ol. cir. XLV. 4
TarquiniiPrisci,
R. Roman.,
cir. annum 20

of Maaseiah the priest, and to all
the priests, saying,
26 The LORD hath made thee
priest in the stead of Jehoiada
the priest, that ye should be [c]officers in the
house of the LORD, for every man *that is*
[d]mad, and maketh himself a prophet, that
thou shouldest [e]put him in prison, and in the
stocks.
27 Now therefore why hast thou not reproved
Jeremiah of Anathoth, which maketh himself
a prophet to you?
28 For therefore he sent unto us *in* Babylon,
saying, This *captivity is* long: [f]build ye
houses, and dwell *in them;* and plant gardens,
and eat the fruit of them.
29 And Zephaniah the priest read this letter
in the ears of Jeremiah the
prophet.
30 Then came the word of the
LORD unto Jeremiah, saying,
31 Send to all them of the captivity, saying, Thus saith the LORD concerning Shemaiah the Nehelamite; Because that Shemaiah hath prophesied unto you, [g]and I
sent him not, and he caused you to trust in
a lie:
32 Therefore thus saith the LORD; Behold
I will punish Shemaiah the Nehelamite, and
his seed: he shall not have a man to dwell
among this people: neither shall he behold the
good that I will do for my people, saith the
LORD; [h]because he hath taught [i]rebellion
against the LORD.

[c]Chap. xx. 1——[d]2 Kings ix. 11; Acts xxvi. 24——[e]Chap. xx. 2

[f]Ver. 5——[g]Chap. xxviii. 15——[h]Chap. xxviii. 16——[i]Heb. *revolt*

Nebuchadnezzar at Riblah; see chap. xxxvii. 3. The history of Jehoiada may be seen 2 Kings xi. 3, &c.

Verse 26. *For every man* that is *mad, and maketh himself a prophet*] *Mad,* משגע *meshugga, in ecstatic rapture;* such as appeared in the prophets, whether *true* or *false,* when under the influence, the one of God, the other of a demon. See 2 Kings ix. 11; Hos. ix. 7.

Verse 32. *I will punish Shemaiah*] 1. He shall have no posterity to succeed him. 2. His family, *i. e., relations,* &c., shall not be found among those whom I shall bring back from captivity. 3. Nor shall *he* himself see the good that I shall do for my people. And all this shall come upon him and his because he hath taught rebellion against the Lord. He excited the people to reject Jeremiah, and to receive the lying words of the *false prophets;* and these led them to rebel.

CHAPTER XXX

This and the following chapter must relate to a still future restoration of the posterity of Jacob from their several dispersions, as no deliverance hitherto afforded them comes up to the terms of it; for, after the return from Babylon, they were again enslaved by the Greeks and Romans, contrary to the prediction in the eighth verse; in every papistical country they have laboured under great civil disabilities, and in some of them have been horribly persecuted; upon the ancient people has this mystic Babylon very heavily laid her yoke; and in no place in the world are they at present their own masters; so that this prophecy remains to be fulfilled in the reign of David, i. e., *the Messiah; the type, according to the general structure of the prophetical writings, being put for the* antitype. *The prophecy opens by an easy transition from the temporal deliverance spoken of before, and describes the mighty revolutions that shall precede the restoration of the descendants of Israel,* 1–9, *who are encouraged to trust in the promises of God,* 10, 11. *They are, however, to expect corrections; which shall have a happy issue in a future period,* 12–17. *The great blessings of Messiah's reign are enumerated,* 18–22; *and the wicked and impenitent declared to have no share in them,* 23, 24.

A. M. cir. 3417
B. C. cir. 587
Ol. XLVIII. 2
TarquiniiPrisci,
R. Roman.,
cir. annum 30

THE word that came to Jeremiah from the LORD, saying,
2 Thus speaketh the LORD God
of Israel, saying, Write thee all
the words that I have spoken
unto thee in a book.
3 For, lo, the days come, saith
the LORD, that [a]I will bring again

[a]Ver. 18; chap. xxxii. 44; Ezek. xxxix. 25; Amos ix. 14, 15

NOTES ON CHAP. XXX

Verse 1. *The word that came to Jeremiah from the Lord*] This prophecy was delivered about *a year after the taking of Jerusalem;* so *Dahler.* Dr. *Blayney* supposes it and the following chapter to refer to the *future restoration* of both *Jews* and *Israelites* in the times of the Gospel; though also touching at the restoration from the *Babylonish captivity,* at the end of

A. M. cir. 3417
B. C. cir. 587
Ol. XLVIII. 2
TarquiniiPrisci,
R. Roman.,
cir. annum 30

the captivity of my people Israel and Judah, saith the LORD: [b]and I will cause them to return to the land that I gave to their fathers, and they shall possess it.

4 And these *are* the words that the LORD spake concerning Israel and concerning Judah.

5 For thus saith the LORD; We have heard a voice of trembling, [c]of fear, and not of peace.

6 Ask ye now, and see whether [d]a man doth travail with child? wherefore do I see every man with his hands on his loins, [e]as a woman in travail, and all faces are turned into paleness?

7 [f]Alas! for that day *is* great, [g]so that none *is* like it: it *is* even the time of Jacob's trouble; but he shall be saved out of it.

8 For it shall come to pass in that day, saith the LORD of hosts, *that* I will break his yoke from off thy neck, and will burst thy bonds, and strangers shall no more serve themselves of him.

9 But they shall serve the LORD their God, and [h]David their King, whom I will [i]raise up unto them.

10 Therefore [k]fear thou not, O my servant Jacob, saith the LORD; neither be dismayed, O Israel: for, lo, I will save thee from afar, and thy seed [l]from the land of their captivity; and Jacob shall return, and shall be in rest, and be quiet, and none shall make *him* afraid.

11 For I *am* with thee, saith the LORD, to save thee: [m]though I make a full end of all nations whither I have scattered thee, [n]yet will I not make a full end of thee: but I will correct thee [o]in measure, and will not leave thee altogether unpunished.

12 For thus saith the LORD, [p]Thy bruise *is* incurable, *and* thy wound *is* grievous.

[b]Chap. xvi. 15——[c]Or, there is *fear, and not peace*——[d]Heb. *a male*——[e]Chap. iv. 31; vi. 24——[f]Joel ii. 11, 31; Amos v. 18; Zeph. i. 14, &c.——[g]Dan. xii. 1——[h]Isa. lv. 3, 4; Ezek. xxxiv. 23; xxxvii. 24; Hos. iii. 5

[i]Luke i. 69; Acts ii. 30; xiii. 23——[k]Isa. xli. 13; xliii. 5; xliv. 2; chap. xlvi. 27, 28——[l]Chap. iii. 18——[m]Amos ix. 8——[n]Ch. iv. 27——[o]Psa. vi. 1; Isa. xxvii. 8; ch. x. 24; xlvi. 28——[p]2 Chron. xxxvi. 16; chap. xv. 18

seventy years. Supposing these two chapters to be penned after the taking of Jerusalem, which appears the most natural, they will refer to the same events, *one captivity* shadowing forth *another*, and *one restoration* being the *type* or *pledge* of the *second*.

Verse 2. *Write thee all the words that I have spoken unto thee in a book.*] The *book* here recommended I believe to be the *thirtieth* and *thirty-first* chapters; for among the Hebrews any portion of writing, in which the subject was *finished*, however small, was termed ספר *sepher*, a BOOK, a *treatise* or *discourse*.

Verse 3. *The days come*] *First*, After the conclusion of the *seventy* years. *Secondly*, Under the *Messiah*.

That I will bring again the captivity of Israel] The *ten tribes*, led captive by the king of *Assyria*, and dispersed among the *nations*.

And Judah] The people carried into *Babylon* at *two different times;* first, under *Jeconiah*, and, secondly, under *Zedekiah*, by Nebuchadnezzar.

Verse 5. *We have heard a voice of trembling*] This may refer to the state and feelings of the people during the war which Cyrus carried on against the Babylonians. *Trembling* and *terror* would no doubt affect them, and put an end to *peace* and all prosperity; as they could not tell what would be the issue of the struggle, and whether their state would be better or worse should their present masters fall in the conflict. This is well described in the next verse, where *men* are represented as being, through pain and anguish, like *women in travail*. See the same comparison Isa. xiii. 6-8.

Verse 7. *Alas! for that day* is *great*] When the Medes and Persians, with all their forces shall come on the Chaldeans, it will be *the day of Jacob's trouble*—trial, dismay, and uncertainty; but *he shall be delivered out of it*—the Chaldean empire shall fall, but the Jews shall be delivered by Cyrus. Jerusalem shall be destroyed by the Romans, but the *Israel of God* shall be delivered from its ruin. Not one that had embraced Christianity perished in the sackage of that city.

Verse 8. *I will break his yoke*] That is, the yoke of *Nebuchadnezzar*.

Of him.] Of *Jacob*, (ver. 7,) viz., the then captive Jews.

Verse 9. *But they shall serve the Lord their God, and David their King*] This must refer to the *times of the Messiah;* and hence the *Chaldee* has, "They shall obey the Lord their God, וישת מאון למשיחה בר דוד *veyishta meun limschicha bar David*, and they shall obey the Messiah, the Son of David." This is a very remarkable version; and shows that it was a version, not according to the *letter*, but according to their *doctrine* and their *expectation.* David was long since dead; and none of his descendants ever reigned over them after the Babylonish captivity, nor have they since been a *regal nation. Zerubbabel*, under the Persians, and the *Asmoneans*, can be no exception to this. They have been *no nation* since; they are no nation now; and it is only in the *latter days* that they can expect to be a *nation*, and that must be a *Christian nation.*

Christ is promised under the name of his progenitor, *David*, Isa. lv. 3, 4; Ezek. xxxiv. 23, 24, xxxvii. 24, 25; Hos. iii. 5.

Verse 11. *Though I make a full end of all nations*] Though the Persians destroy the nations whom they vanquish, yet they shall not destroy *thee*.

Verse 12. *Thy bruise* is *incurable*] אנוש *anush, desperate*, not *incurable;* for the *cure* is promised in ver. 17, *I will restore health unto thee. and I will heal thee of thy wounds.*

A. M. cir. 3417 B. C. cir. 587 Ol. XLVIII. 2 TarquiniiPrisci, R. Roman., cir. annum 30

13 *There is* none to plead thy
cause, [q]that thou mayest be
bound up: [r]thou hast no healing medicines.

14 [s]All thy lovers have forgotten thee; they
seek thee not; for I have wounded thee with
the wound [t]of an enemy, with the chastisement [u]of a cruel one, for the multitude of
thine iniquity; [v]*because* thy sins were increased.

15 Why [w]criest thou for thine affliction? thy
sorrow *is* incurable for the multitude of thine
iniquity: *because* thy sins were increased, I
have done these things unto thee.

16 Therefore all they that devour thee [x]shall
be devoured; and all thine adversaries, every
one of them shall go into captivity; and they
that spoil thee shall be a spoil, and all that
prey upon thee will I give for a prey.

17 [y]For I will restore health unto thee, and
I will heal thee of thy wounds, saith the LORD;
because they called thee an Outcast, *saying,*
This *is* Zion, whom no man seeketh after.

18 Thus saith the LORD; Behold, [z]I will
bring again the captivity of Jacob's tents, and
[a]have mercy on his dwelling-places; and the
city shall be builded upon her own [b]heap, and
the palace shall remain after the
manner thereof.

19 And [c]out of them shall proceed thanksgiving and the voice
of them that make merry: [d]and I will multiply
them, and they shall not be few; I will also
glorify them, and they shall not be small.

20 Their children also shall be [e]as aforetime,
and their congregation shall be established before me, and I will punish all that oppress
them.

21 And their nobles shall be of themselves,
[f]and their governor shall proceed from the
midst of them: and I will [g]cause him to draw
near, and he shall approach unto me: for who
is this that engaged his heart to approach unto
me? saith the LORD.

22 And ye shall be [h]my people, and I will be
your God.

23 Behold, the [i]whirlwind of the LORD goeth
forth with fury, a [k]continuing whirlwind: it
shall [l]fall with pain upon the head of the
wicked.

24 The fierce anger of the LORD shall not
return, until he have done *it,* and until he
have performed the intents of his heart: [m]in
the latter days ye shall consider it.

[q]Heb. *for binding up,* or *pressing*——[r]Chap. viii. 22——[s]Lam. i. 2——[t]Job xiii. 24; xvi. 9; xix. 11——[u]Job xxx. 21——[v]Ch. v. 6——[w]Ch. xv. 18——[x]Exod. xxiii. 22; Isa. xxxiii. 1; xli. 11; ch. x. 25——[y]Ch. xxxiii. 6——[z]Ver. 3; chap. xxxiii. 7, 11——[a]Psa. cii. 13——[b]Or, *little hill*

[c]Isa. xxxv. 10; li. 11; ch. xxxi. 4, 12, 13; xxxiii. 10, 11——[d]Zech. x. 8——[e]Isa. i. 26——[f]Gen. xlix. 10——[g]Num. xvi. 5——[h]Ch. xxiv. 7; xxxi. 1, 33; xxxii. 38; Ezek. xi. 20; xxxvi. 28; xxxvii. 27——[i]Ch. xxiii. 19, 20; xxv. 32——[k]Heb. *cutting*——[l]Or, *remain*——[m]Gen. xlix. 1

Verse 13. There is *none to plead thy cause*] All thy friends and allies have forsaken thee.

Verse 15. *Thy sorrow* is *incurable*] אנוש *anush, desperate.* See ver. 12.

Verse 16. *They that devour thee*] The Chaldeans,

Shall be devoured] By the *Medes* and *Persians.*

All that prey upon thee will I give for a prey.] The *Assyrians* were destroyed by the *Babylonians;* the *Babylonians,* by the *Medes* and *Persians;* the *Egyptians* and *Persians* were destroyed by the *Greeks,* under Alexander. All these nations are now *extinct;* but the *Jews,* as a distinct people, still exist.

Verse 18. *The city shall be builded upon her own heap*] Be re-edified from its own *ruins.* See the book of *Nehemiah, passim.*

And the palace shall remain] Meaning, the *king's house* shall be restored; or, more probably, the *temple shall be rebuilt;* which was true, for after the Babylonish captivity it was rebuilt by Nehemiah, &c. By the *tents,* distinguished from the *dwelling-places of Jacob,* we may understand all *the minor dispersions of the Jews,* as well as those *numerous synagogues* found in large cities.

Verse 19. *I will multiply them*] They shall be *very numerous;* even where at present they have but *tents.*

I will also glorify them] I will put *honour* upon them every where, so that they shall be no longer *contemptible.* This will be a very great *change,* for they are now *despised* all over the earth.

Verse 20. *Their children also*] They shall have the education of their own children as formerly.

And their congregation] Their religious *assemblies.*

Shall be established] Being, in the latter days, incorporated with those "who serve the Lord their God, and worship the Messiah, the son of David."

Verse 21. *Their nobles shall be of themselves*] *Strangers* shall not rule over them; and—

Their governor shall proceed from the midst of them] Both *Nehemiah* and *Zerubbabel,* their nobles and governors after the return from Babylon, were *Jews.*

Verse 22. *Ye shall be my people*] The *old covenant* shall be renewed.

Verse 23. *The whirlwind of the Lord*] A grievous tempest of desolation,—

Shall fall with pain upon the head of the wicked.] On Nebuchadnezzar and the Chaldeans.

Verse 24. *In the latter days ye shall consider it.*] By the *latter days* the Gospel dispensation is generally meant; and that restoration which is the principal topic in this and the succeeding chapter refers to this time. Had the Jews properly *considered* this subject, they would long ere this have been brought into the liberty of the Gospel, and saved from the maledictions under which they now groan. Why do not the Jews read their own prophets more conscientiously?

CHAPTER XXXI

This chapter continues the subject of the preceding in a beautiful vision represented at a distant period. God is introduced expressing his continual regard for Israel, and promising to restore them to their land and liberty, 1–5. *Immediately heralds appear, proclaiming on Mount Ephraim the arrival of the great year of jubilee, and summoning the people to gather unto Zion,* 6. *Upon which God resumes the speech; and makes such gracious promises both of leading them tenderly by the way, and making them happy in their own land, that all the nations of the world are called upon to consider with deep attention this great salvation,* 7–14. *The scene is then diversified by a very happy invention. Rachel, the mother of Joseph and Benjamin, is represented as risen from her tomb, in a city of Benjamin near Jerusalem, looking about for her children, and bitterly lamenting their fate, as none of them are to be seen in the land of their fathers,* 15. *But she is consoled with the assurance that they are not lost, and that they shall in due time be restored,* 16, 17. *To this another tender and beautiful scene immediately succeeds. Ephraim, (often put for the* TEN *tribes,) comes in view. He laments his past errors, and expresses the most earnest desires of reconciliation; upon which God, as a tender parent, immediately forgives him,* 18–20. *The virgin of Israel is then directed to prepare for returning home,* 21, 22; *and the vision closes with a promise of abundant peace and security to Israel and Judah in the latter days,* 23–26. *The blessed condition of Israel under the Messiah's reign is then beautifully contrasted with their afflicted state during the general dispersion,* 27, 28. *In the remaining part of the chapter the promises to the posterity of Jacob of the impartial administration of justice, increasing peace and prosperity, the universal diffusion of righteousness, and stability in their own land after a general restoration in Gospel times, are repeated, enlarged on, and illustrated by a variety of beautiful figures,* 29–40.

A. M. cir. 3417
B. C. cir. 587
Ol. XLVIII. 2
TarquiniiPrisci, R. Roman., cir. annum 30

AT [a]the same time, saith the LORD, [b]will I be the God of all the families of Israel, and they shall be my people.

2 Thus saith the LORD, The people *which were* left of the sword found grace in the wilderness; *even* Israel,

[a]Chap. xxx. 24 [b]Chap. xxx. 22

NOTES ON CHAP. XXXI

Dr. *Blayney* has introduced this and the preceding chapter with the following excellent observations:—

"There are many prophecies," says he, "in various parts of the Old Testament, which announce the future restoration of Israel to their own land, and the complete re-establishment of both their civil and religious constitution in the latter days, meaning the times of the Gospel dispensation. These two chapters contain a prophecy of this kind; which must necessarily be referred to these times, because it points out circumstances which certainly were not fulfilled at the return of the Jews from the Babylonish captivity, nor have hitherto had their completion. For the people who returned from Babylon were the people of Judah only, who had been carried away captive by Nebuchadnezzar; but here it is foretold, that not only should the captivity of Judah be restored, but the captivity of Israel also, meaning those ten tribes which were carried away before, by Shalmaneser king of Assyria; and who still remain in their several dispersions, having never returned, in a national capacity at least, to their own land, whatever some few individuals have done. But the terms of the prophecy entitle us to expect, not an obscure and partial, but a complete and universal, restoration; when God will manifest himself, as formerly, the God and Patron of all the families of Israel, and not of a few only. Again it is promised that, after this restoration, they should no more fall under the dominion of foreigners, but be governed by princes and magistrates of their own nation, independently of any but God, and David their king. But this was not the case with the Jews who returned from Babylon. They then indeed had a leader, Zerubbabel, one of their own nation, and also of the family of David; but both the nation and their leader continued still in a state of vassalage, and the most servile dependence upon the Persian monarchy. And when the Grecian monarchy succeeded, they changed their masters only, but not their condition; till at length under the Asmonean princes they had for a while an independent government of their own, but without any title to the name of David. At last they fell under the Roman yoke; since which time their situation has been such as not to afford the least ground to pretend that the promised restoration has yet taken place. It remains therefore to be brought about in future under the reign of the Messiah, emphatically distinguished by the name of David; when every particular circumstance predicted concerning it will no doubt be verified by a distinct and unequivocal accomplishment. There is no particular date annexed to this prophecy, whereby to ascertain the precise time of its delivery.

A. M. cir. 3417
B. C. cir. 587
Ol. XLVIII. 2
TarquiniiPrisci,
R. Roman.,
cir. annum. 30

when [c]I went to cause him to
rest.
3 The LORD hath appeared
[d]of old unto me, *saying,* Yea,
[e]I have loved thee with [f]an
everlasting love: therefore [g]with
loving-kindness have I [h]drawn
thee.

[c]Num. x. 33; Deut. i. 33; Psa. xcv. 11; Isa. lxiii. 14 —— [d]Heb. *from afar* —— [e]Mal. i. 2

[f]Rom. xi. 28, 29 —— [g]Or, *have I extended loving-kindness unto thee* —— [h]Hos. xi. 4

But it may not unreasonably be presumed to have followed immediately after the preceding one, in which the restoration of the people from their Babylonish captivity is in direct terms foretold. From hence the transition is natural and easy to the more glorious and general restoration which was to take place in a more distant period, and was designed for the ultimate object of the national hopes and expectations. Both events are frequently thus connected together in the prophetic writings; and perhaps with this design, that when that which was nearest at hand should be accomplished, it might afford the clearest, and strongest, and most satisfactory kind of evidence that the latter, how remote soever its period, would in like manner be brought about by the interposition of Providence in its due season. But though this prophecy relates wholly to one single subject, it seems naturally to divide itself into three distinct parts. The first part, after a short preface, in which the prophet is required to commit to writing the matters revealed to him, commences with representing, in a style of awe and energy, the consternation and distress which, in some future day of visitation, should fall upon all nations, preparatory to the scene of Jacob's deliverance, ver. 5-9. Israel is encouraged to confide in the Divine assurance of restoration and protection, ver. 10, 11. He is prepared previously to expect a severe chastisement for the multitude of his sins; but consoled with the prospect of a happy termination, ver. 12-17. This is followed by an enumeration at large of the blessings and privileges to which the Jews should be restored upon their re-admission into God's favour, ver. 18-22. Again, however, it is declared that the anger of JEHOVAH would not subside till his purposed vengeance against the wicked should have been fully executed; and then, but not till then, an entire reconciliation would take place between him and all the families of Israel, ver. 23, chap. xxxi. 1. The second part of this prophecy begins chap. xxxi. 2, and is marked by a sudden transition to a distant period of time, represented in a vision, and embellished with a variety of beautiful scenes and images. God announces the renewal of his ancient love for Israel; and promises, in consequence thereof, a speedy restoration of their former privileges and happiness, ver. 2-5. Already the heralds have proclaimed on Mount Ephraim the arrival of the joyful day; they summon the people to re-assemble once more in Zion; and promulge by special command the glad tidings of salvation which God had accomplished for them. God himself declares his readiness to conduct home the remnant of Israel from all parts of their dispersion, to compassionate and relieve their infirmities, and to provide them with all necessary accommodations by the way, ver. 6-9. The news is carried into distant lands; and the nations are summoned to attend to the display of God's power and goodness in rescuing his people from their stronger enemies, and in supplying them after their return with all manner of good things to the full extent of their wants and desires, ver. 10-14. Here the scene changes; and two new personages are successively introduced, in order to diversify the same subject, and to impress it more strongly. Rachel first; who is represented as just risen from the grave, and bitterly bewailing the loss of her children; for whom she anxiously looks about, but none are to be seen. Her tears are dried up; and she is consoled with the assurance that they are not lost for ever, but shall in time be brought back to their ancient borders, ver. 15-17. Ephraim comes next. He laments his past undutifulness with great contrition and penitence, and professes an earnest desire of amendment. These symptoms of returning duty are no sooner discerned in him, than God acknowledges him once more as a darling child and resolves with mercy to receive him, ver. 18-20. The virgin of Israel is then earnestly exhorted to hasten the preparations for their return; and encouraged with having the prospect of a signal miracle wrought in her favour, ver. 21, 22. And the vision closes at last with a promise that the Divine blessing should again rest upon the land of Judah; and that the men of Judah should once more dwell there, cultivating it according to the simplicity of ancient institutions, and fully discharged from every want, ver. 23-26. In the third part, by way of appendix to the vision, the following gracious promises are specifically annexed: That God would in time to come supply all the deficiencies of Israel and Judah; and would be as diligent to restore as he had ever been to destroy them; and would not any more visit the offences of the fathers upon the children, ver. 27-30. That he would make with them a better covenant than he had made with their forefathers, ver. 31-34. That they should continue his people by an ordinance as firm and as lasting as that of the heavens, ver. 35-37. And that Jerusalem should again be built, enlarged in its extent, and secure from future desolation, ver. 38-40."

Verse 1. *At the same time*] This discourse was delivered at the same time with the former; and, with that, constitutes the *Book* which God ordered the prophet to write.

Will I be the God of all the families of Israel] I shall bring back the *ten tribes*, as well as their brethren the *Jews*. The restoration of the *Israelites* is the principal subject of this chapter.

Verse 2. *The people* which were *left of the sword*] Those of the *ten tribes* that had escaped death by the sword of the Assyrians.

Found grace in the wilderness] The place of their exile; a *wilderness*, compared to their own land.—*Dahler*. See Isa. xl. 3.

Verse 3. *I have loved thee with an everlasting love*] ואהבת עולם אהבתיך *veahabath olam ahabtich*, "and with the old love I have loved thee." "Also, with a love of long standing have

A. M. cir. 3417
B. C. cir. 587
Ol. XLVIII. 2
TarquiniiPrisci,
R. Roman.,
cir. annum 30

4 Again, [i]I will build thee, and thou shalt be built, O virgin of Israel: thou shalt again be adorned with thy [k]tabrets, [l]and shalt go forth in the dances of them that make merry.

5 [m]Thou shalt yet plant vines upon the mountains of Samaria: the planters shall plant, and shall [n]eat *them* as common things.

6 For there shall be a day, *that* the watchmen upon the mount Ephraim shall cry, [o]Arise ye, and let us go up to Zion unto the LORD our God.

7 For thus saith the LORD; [p]Sing with gladness for Jacob, and shout among the chief of the nations: publish ye, praise ye, and say, O LORD, save thy people, the remnant of Israel.

A. M. cir. 3417
B. C. cir. 587
Ol. XLVIII. 2
TarquiniiPrisci,
R. Roman.,
cir. annum 30

8 Behold, I will bring them [q]from the north country, and [r]gather them from the coasts of the earth, *and* with them the blind and the lame, the woman with child and her that travaileth with child together: a great company shall return thither.

9 [s]They shall come with weeping, and with [t]supplications will I lead them: I will cause them to walk [u]by the rivers of waters in a straight way, wherein they shall not stumble: for I am a father to Israel, and Ephraim *is* my [v]first-born.

10 Hear the word of the LORD, O ye nations, and declare *it* in the isles afar off, and

[i]Chap. xxxiii. 7——[k]Exod. xv. 20; Judg. xi. 34; Psa. cxlix. 3——[l]Or, *timbrels*——[m]Isa. lxv. 21; Amos ix. 14——[n]Heb. *profane* them; Deut. xx. 6; xxviii. 30——[o]Isa. ii. 3; Mic. iv. 2——[p]Isa. xii. 5, 6

[q]Chap. iii. 12, 18; xxiii. 8——[r]Ezek. xx. 34, 41; xxxiv. 13——[s]Psa. cxxvi. 5, 6; chap. l. 4——[t]Or, *favours;* Zech. xii. 10——[u]Isa. xxxv. 8; xliii. 19; xlix. 10, 11——[v]Exod. iv. 22

I loved thee."—*Blayney*. "But I love thee always."—*Dahler*. I still bear to the Jewish people that love which I showed to their fathers in Egypt, in the wilderness, and in the promised land. Can it be supposed, by any person seriously considering the context, that these words are spoken of *God's decree of election* in behalf of the Jews? Those who make it such, act most injudiciously on their own principle; for, how few of the Jews have ever given evidence that they were the *children of God*, from their restoration from Babylon to the present day! The words refer simply to their state as a people, most wondrously preserved by the providence and mercy of God, as a *standing* proof of the Divine authority of the Scriptures, and as an evidence of God's displeasure against sin.

Therefore with loving-kindness have I drawn thee.] "Therefore have I lengthened out mercy to thee."—*Blayney*.

C'est pourquoi je t'ai conservé ma grace.—*Dahler*.

"Therefore I have preserved my grace to thee."

The exiles, who had not for a long time received any proofs of the Divine protection, are represented as deploring their state; but God answers, that though this may seem to be the case, he has *always* loved them; and this *continued* love he will show by bringing them out of their captivity. However *creeds* may fare, this is the sense of the passage; all the context proves this.

Verse 4. *O virgin of Israel*] Israelites in general; now called *virgin*, because restored to their ancient *purity*.

With thy tabrets] Women in general played on these; they were used in times of *rejoicing*, and accompanied with *dancing*. To these customs, still preserved, the prophet alludes.

Verse 5. *Thou shalt yet plant vines upon the mountains of Samaria*] This was the regal city of the Israelites, as *Jerusalem* was of the Jews.

Shall eat them *as common things.*] By the law of Moses no man was permitted to eat of the fruit of his vineyard till the fifth year after planting. For the first *three* years it was considered uncircumcised, unclean, not fit to be eaten; in the *fourth* year it was *holy to the Lord*, the fruit belonged to Him; in the *fifth* year he might use it for himself, Lev. xix. 23-25. But in the time here mentioned the fruit should be considered *common*—lawful at all times to be eaten.

Verse 6. *For there shall be a day*] Literally, *for this is the day*, or *the day is come*. The *watchmen*—the prophets.

Arise ye, and let us go up to Zion] Let both *Israelites* and *Jews* join together in the worship of the Lord.

Verse 7. *The chief of the nations*] The same as Jacob or Israel; for most certainly this people was once the *most honourable* on the face of the earth.

O Lord, save thy people] Let the Jews earnestly intercede in behalf of their Israelitish brethren; or let them rejoice and praise the Lord, who *hath saved* the remnant of Israel. So Dr. *Blayney* thinks the clause should be understood.

Verse 8. *I will bring them from the north country*] From Babylon.

From the coasts of the earth] The ten tribes were carried away partly into Assyria by Tiglath-pileser, and partly into Mesopotamia and Media by Shalmaneser, 2 Kings xv. 29; xvii. 6. Assyria and Media, being very distant from Palestine, might have been called, in prophetic language, *the coasts of the earth*.

The blind and the lame] I will so effectually remove all difficulties out of the way, so provide for them on the journey, so supernaturally support their bodies and minds, that the veriest invalids shall safely proceed to, and happily arrive at, the end of their journey.

Verse 9. *They shall come with weeping*] Duly penetrated with a sense of their sins, they shall deeply deplore them; and, while weeping for them, earnestly *supplicate* God to have mercy upon them.

By the rivers of waters] I will so guide and provide for them in the arid deserts, that they

A. M. cir. 3417
B. C. cir. 587
Ol. XLVIII. 2
TarquiniiPrisci,
R. Roman.,
cir. annum 30

say, He that scattered Israel
[w]will gather him, and keep him,
as a shepherd *doth* his flock.
11 For [x]the LORD hath redeem-
ed Jacob, and ransomed him [y]from the hand
of *him that was* stronger than he.
12 Therefore they shall come and sing in
[z]the height of Zion, and shall flow together to
[a]the goodness of the LORD, for wheat, and for
wine, and for oil, and for the young of the flock
and of the herd: and their soul shall be as a
[b]watered garden; [c]and they shall not sorrow
any more at all.
13 Then shall the virgin rejoice in the dance,
both young men and old together: for I will
turn their mourning into joy, and will comfort
them, and make them rejoice from their sorrow.
14 And I will satiate the soul of the priests
with fatness, and my people shall be satisfied
with my goodness, saith the LORD.
15 Thus saith the LORD; [d]A voice was
heard in [e]Ramah, lamentation, *and* bitter
weeping; Rachel weeping for her
children refused to be comforted
for her children, because [f]they
were not.

A. M. cir. 3417
B. C. cir. 587
Ol. XLVIII. 2
TarquiniiPrisci,
R. Roman.,
cir. annum 30

16 Thus saith the LORD; Refrain thy voice
from weeping, and thine eyes from tears: for
thy work shall be rewarded, saith the LORD;
and [g]they shall come again from the land of
the enemy.
17 And there is hope in thine end, saith the
LORD, that thy children shall come again to
their own border.
18 I have surely heard Ephraim bemoaning
himself *thus;* Thou hast chastised me, and I
was chastised, as a bullock unaccustomed *to
the yoke:* [h]turn thou me, and I shall be
turned; for thou *art* the LORD my God.
19 Surely [i]after that I was turned, I repented; and after that I was instructed, I smote
upon *my* thigh: I was ashamed, yea, even
confounded, because I did bear the reproach
of my youth.

---

[w]Isa. xl. 11; Ezek. xxxiv. 12, 13, 14——[x]Isa. xliv. 23 xlviii. 20——[y]Isa. xlii. 24, 25——[z]Ezek. xvii. 23; xx. 40 [a]Hos. iii. 5——[b]Isa. lviii. 11

[c]Isa. xxxv. 10; lxv. 19; Rev. xxi. 4——[d]Matt. ii. 17, 18——[e]Josh. xviii. 25——[f]Gen. xlii. 13——[g]Ver. 4, 5; Ezra i. 5; Hos. i. 11——[h]Lam. v. 21——[i]Deut. xxx. 2

---

shall find streams of water whenever necessary. Every one knows of how much consequence water is to travellers in the eastern deserts.

Ephraim is *my first-born.*] Ephraim, being the most considerable, is often put for the whole of the *ten tribes.*

Verse 12. *And shall flow together*] Perhaps this may refer to their assembling at the *three* great national feasts, the passover, pentecost, and tabernacles.

Their soul shall be as a watered garden] Full of the light, life, and power of God; so that they shall rejoice evermore, pray without ceasing, and give thanks in every thing.

Verse 14. *And I will satiate the soul of the priests*] The worship of God being restored, they shall have their proper share of the victims brought to the temple.

Verse 15. *A voice was heard in Ramah*] The Ramah mentioned here, (for there were several towns of this name,) was situated in the tribe of Benjamin, about *six* or *seven* miles from Jerusalem. Near this place *Rachel* was buried; who is here, in a beautiful figure of poetry, represented as coming out of her grave, and lamenting bitterly for the loss of her children, none of whom presented themselves to her view, all being slain or gone into exile. St. Matthew, who is ever fond of accommodation, applies these words, chap. ii. 17, 18, to the massacre of the children at Bethlehem. That is, they were suitable to that occasion, and therefore he so applied them; but they are not a prediction of that event.

Verse 16. *They shall come again from the land of the enemy.*] This could not be said of the *murdered innocents* at Bethlehem; they never came again; but the Jews, who had gone into captivity, did come again from the *land of their enemy* to *their own border.*

Verse 18. *I have surely heard Ephraim bemoaning himself*] The exiled Israelites are in a state of deep repentance.

Thou hast chastised me, and I was chastised] I was at first like an unbroken and untoward steer, the more I was chastised the more I rebelled; but now I have benefited by thy correction.

Turn thou me] I am now *willing* to take thy yoke upon me, but I have no *power.* I can only *will* and *pray.* Take the matter into thy own hand, and fully convert my soul.

Verse 19. *After that I was turned*] Converted from my sin, folly, and idolatry.

I repented] To *conviction of sin,* I now added *contrition for sin.* Conviction, in this sense of the word, must precede contrition or repentance. As soon as a man sees himself lost and undone, he is *convicted* of sin; when *convicted,* he begins to *mourn.* Thus *contrition* follows *conviction.*

I smote upon my *thigh*] My sorrow grew deeper and deeper; I smote upon my thigh through the extremity of my distress. This was a usual sign of deep affliction. See Ezek. xxi. 12. It was the same among the ancient Greeks. So Homer:—

Ως εφατ'· αυταρ Αρης θαλερω πεπληγετο μηρω
Χερσι καταπρηνεσσ', ολοφυρομενος δε προσηυδα.
IL. lib. xv. 113.

"She spake; and with expanded arms, his *thighs*
Smiting, thus *sorrowful,* the god exclaimed."
COWPER.

A. M. cir. 3417
B. C. cir. 587
Ol. XLVIII. 2
TarquiniiPrisci,
R. Roman.,
cir. annum 30

20 *Is* Ephraim my dear son? *is*
he a pleasant child? for since I
spake against him, I do earnestly remember him still:
[k]therefore my bowels [l]are troubled for him;
[m]I will surely have mercy upon him, saith
the LORD.

21 Set thee up waymarks, make thee high
heaps: [n]set thine heart toward the highway,
even the way *which* thou wentest: turn again,
O virgin of Israel, turn again to these thy cities.

22 How long wilt thou [o]go
about, O thou [p]backsliding
daughter? for the LORD hath
created a new thing in the earth,
A woman shall compass a man.

A. M. cir. 3417
B. C. cir. 587
Ol. XLVIII. 2
TarquiniiPrisci
R. Roman.,
cir. annum 30

23 Thus saith the LORD of hosts, the God
of Israel; As yet they shall use this speech
in the line of Judah and in the cities thereof,
when I shall bring again their captivity; [q]The
LORD bless thee, O habitation of justice, *and*
[r]mountain of holiness.

---

[k]Deut. xxxii. 36; Isa. lxiii. 15; Hos. xi. 8——[l]Heb. *sound*
[m]Isa. lvii. 18; Hos. xiv. 4——[n]Chap. l. 5

[o]Chap. ii. 18, 23, 36——[p]Chap. iii. 6, 8, 11, 12, 14, 22
[q]Psa. cxxii. 5, 6, 7, 8; Isa. i. 26——[r]Zech. viii. 3

——— *αυταρ Αχιλλευς*
Μηρω πληξαμενος Πατροκληα προσεειπεν.
IL. lib. xvi. 124.

"Achilles saw it, *smote his thigh*, and said——."
COWPER.

I have often seen persons in deep grief act thus.

Verse 20. Is *Ephraim my dear son?*] It is impossible to conceive any thing more *tenderly affectionate* than this. Let us consider the whole account. The *ten tribes*, called here *Ephraim*, for the reason before alleged, are represented as acknowledging their sins. I have heard Ephraim bemoaning himself; and in his lamentation he says, 1. *Thou hast chastised me.* 2. Though he at first rebelled against the chastisement, yet at last he submitted and acknowledged his offences. 3. He turned from all his offences; he was *converted.* 4. After his conversion, (שובי *shubi*,) he *repented;* after conviction came *contrition*, as before stated. 5. Being in a state of godly sorrow, he was instructed, הודעי *hivvadei*, he got a thorough *knowledge* of the desperate wickedness of his heart and life. 6. Having received this *instruction*, he was filled with *excessive grief;* which is signified here by *smiting on his thigh.* See above. 7. He finds that from his *youth up* he had been sinning against God; and although his youthful sins had long passed from his memory, yet the light of God brought them back, and he was ashamed and confounded at the sight of them. 8. In this state of confusion and distress God sees him; and, commiserating his state, thus speaks:—

1. *Is Ephraim my dear son?* Bad as he is in his own sight, and in the sight of my justice, he is now a *penitent*, and to me is *precious.* 2. However loathsome and disfigured he may be with sin and sorrow, he is to me a *pleasant child*—a *child of delights;* one in whose conversion I delight, and my angels rejoice. 3. I did speak against him: כי מדי דברי בו *ki middey dabberi bo*, for "from the abundance of my speaking in him;" accusing, threatening, promising, exhorting, encouraging; "I do still earnestly remember him." God has taken much pains with him, and is unwilling to give him up; but now that he repents, he has not received the grace of God utterly in vain. 4. God feels a *yearning* desire towards him; המו מעי לו *hamu meai lo*, "my bowels are agitated for him." I feel nothing towards him but *pity* and *love.* When a sinner turns to God, God ceases to be angry with him. 5. God expresses his determination to save him; רחם ארחמנו *rachem arachamennu*, "I will be affectionately merciful to him, with tender mercy, saith the Lord." He shall find that I treat him as a *father* does a returning prodigal son. So every penitent is sure to find mercy at the hand of God.

Verse 21. *Set thee up waymarks*] Alluding to stones, or *heaps of stones*, which travellers in the desert set up to ascertain the way, that they may know how to return. Mark the way to Babylon: thither *ye shall certainly go;* but *from it* ye shall as certainly *return.*

Verse 22. *A woman shall compass a man*] נקבה תסובב גבר *nekebah tesobeb gaber*, "A weak woman shall compass or circumvent a strong man." This place has given much trouble to Biblical critics. By many Christian writers it is considered a prophecy of the *miraculous conception of the holy virgin;* but as I am sure no such meaning is in the *words*, nor in the *context*, so I am satisfied no such meaning can be fairly brought out of them. *Houbigant* thinks there is a small error in the text, i. e., תשובב *teshobeb*, shall *return*, and not תסובב *tesobeb*, shall *compass.* This reading is found in *two* of *Kennicott's* MSS., and *he* contends that the passage should be read, "The wife shall return to her husband;" alluding to the conversion of the Jewish people, called above a *backsliding daughter.* This makes a good sense; but I do not see why this should be called *a new thing in the earth.* After all, I think it likely that the Jews in their present distressed circumstances are represented under the similitude of a *weak defenceless female* נקבה *nekebah;* and the *Chaldeans* under that of a *fierce strong man*, גבר *gaber*, who had prevailed over and oppressed this *weak woman.* But, notwithstanding the disparity between them, God would cause the *woman*—the *weak defenceless Jews*, to *compass*—to overcome, the *strong man*—the *powerful Babylonians.* And this the prophet says would be *a new thing in the land;* for in such a case the lame would take the prey. The context favours both these meanings. Dr. *Blayney* gives a sense very near to this: "A weak woman shall repulse a strong or mighty man." It is most likely a proverbial expression.

Verse 23. *The Lord bless thee, O habitation of justice*] After their return they shall be remarkably prosperous. *Piety* and *industry* shall go hand in hand; they shall have their *husbandmen*, their *shepherds*, and *neatherds*,

A. M. cir. 3417
B. C. cir. 587
Ol. XLVIII. 2
TarquiniiPrisci,
R. Roman.,
cir. annum 30

24 And there shall dwell in Judah itself, and [s]in all the cities thereof together, husbandmen, and they *that* go forth with flocks.

25 For I have satiated the weary soul, and I have replenished every sorrowful soul.

26 Upon this I awaked, and beheld; and my sleep was sweet unto me.

27 Behold, the days come, saith the LORD, that [t]I will sow the house of Israel and the house of Judah, with the seed of man, and with the seed of beast.

28 And it shall come to pass, *that* like as I have [u]watched over them, [v]to pluck up, and to break down, and to throw down, and to destroy, and to afflict; so will I watch over them, [w]to build, and to plant, saith the LORD.

29 [x]In those days they shall say no more, The fathers have eaten a sour grape, and the children's teeth are set on edge.

30 [y]But every one shall die for his own iniquity: every man that eateth the sour grape, his teeth shall be set on edge.

31 Behold, the [z]days come, saith the LORD, that I will make a new covenant with the house of Israel, and with the house of Judah:

A. M. cir. 3417
B. C. cir. 587
Ol. XLVIII. 2
TarquiniiPrisci,
R. Roman.,
cir. annum 30

32 Not according to the covenant that I made with their fathers, in the day *that* [a]I took them by the hand, to bring them out of the land of Egypt; which my covenant they brake, [b]although I was a husband unto them, saith the LORD.

33 [c]But this shall *be* the covenant that I will make with the house of Israel; After those days, saith the LORD, [d]I will put my law in their inward parts, and write it in their hearts; [e]and will be their God, and they shall be my people.

34 And they shall teach no more every man his neighbour, and every man his brother, saying, Know the LORD: for [f]they shall all know me, from the least of them unto the greatest of them, saith the LORD: for [g]I will forgive their iniquity, and I will remember their sin no more.

35 Thus saith the LORD; [h]which giveth the sun for a light by day, *and* the ordinances of the moon and of the stars for a light by night, which divideth [i]the sea when the waves thereof roar; [k]The LORD of hosts *is* his name:

---

[s]Ch. xxxiii. 12, 13——[t]Ezek. xxxvi. 9, 10, 11; Hos. ii. 23; Zech. x. 9——[u]Ch. xliv. 27——[v]Ch. i. 10; xviii. 7——[w]Ch. xxiv. 6——[x]Ezek. xviii. 2, 3——[y]Gal. vi. 5, 7——[z]Ch. xxxii. 40; xxxiii. 14; Ezek. xxxvii. 26; Heb. viii. 8–12; x. 16, 17——[a]Deut. i. 31——[b]Or, *should I have continued a husband unto them?*——[c]Chap. xxxii. 40

[d]Psa. xl. 8; Ezek. xi. 19, 20; xxxvi. 26, 27; 2 Cor. iii. 3——[e]Chap. xxiv. 7; xxx. 22; xxxii. 38——[f]Isa. liv. 13; John vi. 45; 1 Cor. ii. 10; 1 John ii. 20——[g]Chap. xxxiii. 8; l. 20; Mic. vii. 18; Acts x. 43; xiii. 39; Rom. xi. 27——[h]Gen. i. 16; Psa. lxxii. 5, 17; lxxxix. 2, 36, 37; cxix. 89——[i]Isa. li. 15——[k]Chap. x. 16

---

ver. 24. And Jerusalem shall become a *righteous city*, and the *temple* shall be a *place of holiness;* so the weary there shall have *rest*, and the *sorrowful* shall be abundantly *comforted*, ver. 24, 25.

Verse 26. *Upon this I awaked*] It appears that the prophecy, commencing with chap. xxx. 2 and ending with ver. 25 of this chapter, was delivered to the prophet in a dream. *Dahler* supposes it to be a *wish;* that the prophet, though he could not hope to live to that time, might be permitted to awake up from his tomb; and, having seen this prosperity, would be content to return to his grave.

Verse 27. *I will sow—with the seed of man and with the seed of beast.*] I will multiply both men and cattle.

Verse 29. *The fathers have eaten a sour grape*] A proverbial expression for, "The children suffer for the offences of their parents." This is explained in the next verse: "Every one shall die for his own iniquity." No child shall suffer Divine punition for the sin of his father; only so far as he acts in the same way can he be said to bear the sins of his parents.

Verse 31. *A new covenant*] The Christian dispensation.

Verse 33. *After those days*] When vision and prophecy shall be sealed up, and Jesus have assumed that *body which was prepared for him*, and have laid down his life for the redemption of a lost world, and, having ascended on high, shall have obtained the gift of the Holy Spirit to purify the heart; then God's law shall, by it, be *put in their inward parts, and written on their hearts;* so that all *within* and all *without* shall be holiness to the Lord. Then God will be truly *their God*, received and acknowledged as their *portion*, and the sole object of their devotion; and they shall be *his people*, filled with holiness, and made partakers of the Divine nature, so that they shall perfectly love him and worthily magnify his name.

Verse 34. *And they shall teach no more*] It shall be a time of universal *light* and *knowledge;* all shall *know God in Christ, from the least to the greatest;* the *children* shall be taught to *read the New Covenant*, and to *understand* the *terms* of their salvation.

I will forgive their iniquity] It shall be a time of GENERAL PARDON; multitudes shall be daily in the Christian Church receiving the witness of God's Spirit, and in their life and conversation witnessing a good confession. How wonderfully is this prophecy fulfilled in the age of *Bibles, Sunday schools*, and *village preaching.*

A. M. cir. 3417
B. C. cir. 587
Ol. XLVIII. 2
TarquiniiPrisci,
R. Roman.,
cir. annum 30

36 [l]If those ordinances depart
from before me, saith the LORD,
then the seed of Israel also shall
cease from being a nation before
me for ever.
37 Thus saith the LORD; [m]If heaven above
can be measured, and the foundations of the
earth searched out beneath, I will also cast off
all the seed of Israel for all that they have
done, saith the LORD.
38 Behold, the days come, saith the LORD,
that the city shall be built to the LORD, [n]from
the tower of Hananeel unto the
gate of the corner.

A. M. cir. 3417
B. C. cir. 587
Ol. XLVIII. 2
TarquiniiPrisci,
R. Roman.,
cir. annum 30

39 And [o]the measuring line
shall yet go forth over against
it upon the hill Gareb, and shall compass
about to Goath.
40 And the whole valley of the dead bodies,
and of the ashes, and all the fields unto the
brook of Kidron, [p]unto the corner of the
horse-gate toward the east, [q]*shall be* holy unto
the LORD; it shall not be plucked up, nor
thrown down any more for ever.

[l]Psa. cxlviii. 6; Isa. liv. 9, 10; ch. xxxiii. 20——[m]Ch. xxxiii. 22——[n]Neh. iii. 1; Zech. xiv. 10

[o]Ezek. xl. 8; Zech. ii. 1——[p]2 Chron. xxiii. 15; Neh. iii. 28——[q]Joel iii. 17

Verse 36. *If those ordinances*] As sure as the *sun* shall give light to the *day*, and the *moon* to the *night*, so surely shall the Jews continue to be a distinct people. The same thing is expressed in other words in the next verse. Hitherto this prophecy has been literally fulfilled; the Jews are still a distinct people from all the dwellers upon earth. Every attempt that has been made in any country to *naturalize* and unite them with the people of that country, has proved abortive. The well-circumstanced attempt made this year (1830) in England, when the strongest interest was excited in their behalf, has also utterly failed. And why? Because of God's *purpose* expressed in chap. xxxi. 35-37 of the BOOK *of the Prophet* JEREMIAH.

Verse 38. *The city shall be built to the Lord*] This cannot mean the city built after the return from Babylon, for two reasons: 1. This is to be much *greater* in *extent;* 2. It is to be *permanent*, never to be *thrown down*, ver. 40. It must therefore mean, if taken literally at all, the city that is to be built by them when they are brought in with the fulness of the Gentiles.

The tower of Hananeel] This stood in the *northeast* part of the city; from thence the wall proceeded to the *corner gate*, (probably the same as the *old gate*,) thus named from its running out into an *angle* in that part.

Verse 39. *Upon the hill Gareb*] *Gareb* and *Goath* are out of the limits of this city. The latter is supposed to be *Golgotha;* that is, the *heap of Gotha*, which, being the place where our Lord was crucified, was *without the city*. These hills were a little to the north-west of the old city walls: but are destined to be *within* the new city. See Dr. *Blayney* on all these verses.

Verse 40. *The whole valley of the dead bodies*] The valley of the son of *Hinnom*.

And all the fields unto the brook of Kidron, unto the corner of the horse-gate toward the east] All these places, the *fuller's field*, &c., shall be consecrated to the Lord, and become a part of this new city; so that this will appear to be a city much more extensive than the city of Jerusalem ever was; and to be suited to that time, when the people shall have the law written in their hearts, and God shall have filled the land with the seed of man, and with the seed of beast. Talia sæcla currite! "Make speed, ye happy times!"

CHAPTER XXXII

Jeremiah, now confined for his faithful admonitions, foretells the fate of the king and city, 1–5. *According to the direction of God, he buys of his cousin Hanameel a field in Anathoth; the contract, or deed of sale, being subscribed, sealed, and witnessed, and delivered to Baruch, together with a duplicate not sealed, who is commanded to put them into an earthern vessel that they may remain there for many days,* 6–14. *This transaction of the prophet, which is entered and subscribed in the public register, God constitutes a* sign *or* pledge *of the Jews' return from the Babylonish captivity, and of their again possessing houses, fields, and vineyards, in their own land, and by their own right, according to their tribes and families,* 15. *Jeremiah's prayer, in which he recounts God's marvellous acts towards the children of Israel, and deeply deplores the lamentable state of the country, and the numerous provocations which have led to it,* 16–25. *After which God is introduced declaring his purpose of giving up his people into the hands of their enemies,* 26–35; *promising, however, to restore them in due time to their ancient possessions, and to make with them an everlasting covenant,* 36–44.

A. M. 3415
B. C. 589
Ol. XLVII. 4
Anno
TarquiniiPrisci,
R. Roman., 28

THE word that came to Jeremiah from the LORD [a]in the
tenth year of Zedekiah king of
Judah, which *was* the eighteenth
year of Nebuchadrezzar.
2 For then the king of Babylon's army besieged Jerusalem: and Jeremiah the prophet
was shut up [b]in the court of the prison, which
was in the king of Judah's house.
3 For Zedekiah king of Judah had shut him
up, saying, Wherefore dost thou prophesy,
and say, Thus saith the LORD, [c]Behold, I will
give this city into the hand of the king of
Babylon, and he shall take it;
4 And Zedekiah king of Judah [d]shall not
escape out of the hand of the Chaldeans, but
shall surely be delivered into the hand of the
king of Babylon, and shall speak with him
mouth to mouth, and his eyes shall behold
his eyes;
5 And he shall lead Zedekiah to Babylon,
and there shall he be [e]until I visit him, saith
the LORD: [f]though ye fight with
the Chaldeans, ye shall not
prosper.
6 And Jeremiah said, The
word of the LORD came unto me, saying,
7 Behold, Hanameel the son of Shallum
thine uncle shall come unto thee, saying, Buy
thee my field that *is* in Anathoth: for the
[g]right of redemption *is* thine to buy *it*.
8 So Hanameel mine uncle's son came to
me in the court of the prison according to the
word of the LORD, and said unto me, Buy my
field, I pray thee, that *is* in Anathoth, which
is in the country of Benjamin: for the right
of inheritance *is* thine, and the redemption *is*
thine; buy *it* for thyself. Then I knew that
this *was* the word of the LORD.
9 And I bought the field of Hanameel
my uncle's son, that *was* in Anathoth, and
[h]weighed him the money, *even* [i]seventeen
shekels of silver.
10 And I [k]subscribed the evidence, and

A. M. 3415
B. C. 589
Ol. XLVII. 4
Anno
TarquiniiPrisci,
R. Roman., 28

[a]2 Kings xxv. 1, 2; Jer. xxxix. 1——[b]Neh. iii. 25; chap. xxxiii. 1; xxxvii. 21; xxxviii. 6; xxxix. 14——[c]Ch. xxxiv. 2——[d]Ch. xxxiv. 3; xxxviii. 18, 23; xxxix. 5; lii. 9——[e]Ch. xxvii. 22——[f]Ch. xxi. 4; xxxiii. 5——[g]Leviticus xxv. 24, 25, 32; Ruth iv. 4——[h]Gen. xxiii. 16; Zech. xi. 12——[i]Or, *seven shekels and ten* pieces *of silver*——[k]Heb. *wrote in the book*

NOTES ON CHAP. XXXII

Verse 1. *The word that came*] This prophecy bears its own *date:* it was delivered in the *tenth* year of *Zedekiah,* which answered to the *eighteenth* of Nebuchadnezzar. It appears from 2 Kings xxv. 8, that the *eleventh* year of Zedekiah was the *nineteenth* of Nebuchadnezzar; and consequently, that the *eighteenth* of that monarch must have been the *tenth* of the Jewish king.

Verse 2. *Then the king of Babylon's army besieged Jerusalem*] The siege had commenced the *year before,* and continued a *year after,* ending in the *fifth* month of the following year; consequently, the siege must have lasted about *eighteen* months and *twenty-seven* days. See 2 Kings xxv. 18.

Verse 4. *And shall speak with him mouth to mouth*] He shall be reduced to a state of the most abject servitude. The *slave* was obliged to fix his eyes on every motion of the master whilst giving his orders, who often condescended to give them only by *dumb signs.*

Verse 7. *The right of redemption* is *thine*] The law had established that the estates of a family should never be alienated. If, therefore, a man through poverty was obliged to sell his patrimony, the *nearest relative* had a right to purchase it before all others, and even to redeem it, if it had been sold to another. This is what is called the *right of goel,* or *kinsman,* Lev. xxv. 25. And in the year of jubilee the whole reverted to its ancient master, Lev. xxv. 13.

Verse 8. *This* was *the word of the Lord.*] It was by his appointment that I was to make this purchase. The whole was designed as a symbolical act, to show the people that there would be a *return* from Babylon, that each family should re-enter on its former possessions, and that a man might safely purchase on the certainty of this event.

Verse 9. *Weighed him the money*] It does not appear that there was any *coined* or *stamped* money among the Jews before the captivity; the Scripture, therefore, never speaks of *counting* money, but of *weighing* it.

Seventeen shekels of silver.] The shekel at this time must have been a *nominal* coin; it was a thing of a certain *weight,* or a certain *worth. Seventeen* shekels was the *weight* of the silver paid: but it might have been in *one ingot,* or piece. The shekel has been valued at from *two shillings and threepence* to *two shillings and sixpence,* and even at *three shillings;* taking the purchase-money at a *medium* of the value of the shekel, it would amount only to about *two pounds two shillings and sixpence.* But as estates bore value only in proportion to the *number of years before the jubilee,* and the field in question was then in the hands of the *Chaldeans,* and this cousin of Jeremiah was not likely to come back to enjoy it after *seventy* years, (nor could he then have it, as a jubilee would intervene and restore it to the original family,) and money must now be very scarce and high in its value, the *seventeen* shekels might have been a sufficient sum for a field in those circumstances, and one probably not large in its dimensions.

Verse 10. *I subscribed the evidence*] We have here all the circumstances of this legal act: 1. An offer is made of the reversion of the ground, till the jubilee, to him who would then of right come into possession. 2. The price is agreed on, and the silver *weighed* in the balances. 3. A *contract* or *deed* of sale is drawn

A. M. 3415
B. C. 589
Ol. XLVII. 4
Anno TarquiniiPrisci, R. Roman., 28

sealed *it,* and took witnesses, and weighed *him* the money in the balances.

11 So I took the evidence of the purchase, *both* that which was sealed *according* to the law and custom, and that which was open:

12 And I gave the evidence of the purchase unto [l]Baruch the son of Neriah, the son of Maaseiah, in the sight of Hanameel mine uncle's *son,* and in the presence of the [m]witnesses that subscribed the book of the purchase, before all the Jews that sat in the court of the prison.

13 And I charged Baruch before them, saying,

14 Thus saith the LORD of hosts, the God of Israel; Take these evidences, this evidence of the purchase, both which is sealed, and this evidence which is open; and put them in an earthen vessel, that they may continue many days.

15 For thus saith the LORD of hosts, the God of Israel; Houses and fields and vineyards [n]shall be possessed again in this land.

16 Now when I had delivered the evidence of the purchase unto Baruch the son of Neriah, I prayed unto the LORD, saying,

17 Ah Lord GOD! behold, [o]thou hast made the heaven and the earth by thy great power and stretched-out arm, *and* [p]there is nothing [q]too hard for thee:

18 Thou showest [r]loving-kindness unto thousands, and recompensest the iniquity of the fathers into the bosom of their children after them: the Great, [s]the Mighty God, [t]the LORD of hosts, *is* his name,

A. M. 3415
B. C. 589
Ol. XLVII. 4
Anno TarquiniiPrisci, R. Roman., 28

19 [u]Great in counsel, and mighty in [v]work: for thine [w]eyes *are* open upon all the ways of the sons of men: [x]to give every one according to his ways, and according to the fruit of his doings:

20 Which hast set signs and wonders in the land of Egypt, *even* unto this day, and in Israel, and among *other* men; and hast made thee [y]a name, as at this day;

21 And [z]hast brought forth thy people Israel out of the land of Egypt with signs, and with wonders, and with a strong hand, and with a stretched-out arm, and with great terror;

22 And hast given them this land, which thou didst swear to their fathers to give them, [a]a land flowing with milk and honey;

23 And they came in, and possessed it; but [b]they obeyed not thy voice, neither walked in thy law; they have done nothing of all that thou commandedst them to do: therefore thou hast caused all this evil to come upon them:

24 Behold the [c]mounts, they are come unto the city to take it; and the city [d]is given into the hand of the Chaldeans, that fight against

[l]Ch. xxxvi. 4——[m]See Isa. viii. 2——[n]Ver. 37, 43——[o]2 Kings xix. 15——[p]Gen. xviii. 14; ver. 27; Luke i. 37 [q]Or, *hid from thee*——[r]Exod. xx. 6; xxxiv. 7; Deut. v. 9, 10 [s]Isa. ix. 6——[t]Ch. x. 16——[u]Isa. xxviii. 29——[v]Heb. *doing* [w]Job xxxiv. 21; Psa. xxxiii. 13; Prov. v. 21; chap. xvi. 17

[x]Ch. xvii. 10——[y]Exod. ix. 16; 1 Chron. xvii. 21; Isa. lxiii. 12; Dan. ix. 15——[z]Exod. vi. 6; 2 Sam. vii. 23; 1 Chron. xvii. 21; Psa. cxxxvi. 11, 12——[a]Exod. iii. 8, 17; chap. xi. 5——[b]Neh. ix. 26; ch. xi. 8; Dan. ix. 10–14 [c]Or, *engines of shot;* chap. xxxiii. 4——[d]Ver. 25, 36

up; to which both parties agreeing, 4. *Witnesses* are brought forward to see it *signed* and *sealed;* for the contract was both *subscribed* and *sealed.* 5. A *duplicate* of the deed was drawn, which was not to be *sealed,* but to lie *open* for the inspection of those concerned, in some public place where it might be safe, and always to be seen. 6. The original, which was *sealed up,* was put in an *earthen pitcher,* in order to be preserved from accidents. 7. This was delivered by the purchaser into the hands of a third party, to be preserved for the use of the purchaser, and *witnesses* were called to attest this *delivery.* 8. They subscribed the *book of the purchase,* perhaps a *town book,* or *register,* where such purchases were entered. *Baruch* was a *scribe* by profession; and the deeds were delivered into his hands, before witnesses, to be preserved as above. Perhaps the *law,* in this case, required that the *instrument* should be thus lodged. But, in the present case, *both the deeds,* the *orignal* and the *duplicate,* were put into the earthen pitcher, because the city was about to be burnt; and, if lodged as *usual,* they would be destroyed in the general conflagration. See ver. 14.

Verse 15. *Houses and fields—shall be possessed again*] That is, this is an evidence that the captivity shall not last long: houses, &c., shall here be possessed again, either by their present owners or immediate descendants. The *young* might return; at least, all *under ten years* of age: there was no natural impossibility that *they* should not live till they should be *fourscore.*

Verse 16. *I prayed unto the Lord*] And what a prayer! What weight of matter, sublimity of expression, profound veneration, just conception, Divine unction, powerful pleading, and strength of faith! Historical, without flatness; condensed, without obscurity; confessing the greatest of crimes against the most righteous of Beings, without despairing of his mercy, or presuming on his goodness: a confession that, in fact, acknowledges that God's *justice should* smite and destroy, had not his infinite goodness said, I will pardon and spare.

Verse 19. *Thine eyes* are *open upon all the*

A. M. 3415
B. C. 589
Ol. XLVII. 4
Anno
TarquiniiPrisci,
R. Roman., 28

it, because of [e]the sword, and
of the famine, and of the pestilence: and what thou hast spoken is come to pass; and, behold,
thou seest *it*.
25 And thou hast said unto me, O Lord
GOD, Buy thee the field for money, and take
witnesses; [f]for [g]the city is given into the
hand of the Chaldeans.
26 Then came the word of the LORD unto
Jeremiah, saying,
27 Behold, I *am* the LORD, the [h]God of all
flesh: [i]is there any thing too hard for me?
28 Therefore thus saith the LORD; Behold,
[k]I will give this city into the hand of the
Chaldeans, and into the hand of Nebuchadrezzar king of Babylon, and he shall take it:
29 And the Chaldeans, that fight against
this city, shall come, and [l]set fire on this city,
and burn it with the houses, [m]upon whose
roofs they have offered incense unto Baal, and
poured out drink-offerings unto other gods,
to provoke me to anger.
30 For the children of Israel and the children of Judah [n]have only done evil before me
from their youth: for the children of Israel
have only provoked me to anger with the work
of their hands, saith the LORD.
31 For this city hath been to me *as* [o]a provocation of mine anger and of my fury from
the day that they built it even unto this day;
[p]that I should remove it from before my face.
32 Because of all the evil of the children
of Israel, and of the children of Judah, which
they have done to provoke me to
anger, [q]they, their kings, their
princes, their priests, and their
prophets, and the men of Judah,
and the inhabitants of Jerusalem.

A. M. 3415
B. C. 589
Ol. XLVII. 4
Anno
TarquiniiPrisci,
R. Roman., 28

33 And they have turned unto me the [r]back,[s]
and not the face: though I taught them, [t]ris-
ing up early and teaching *them*, yet they have
not hearkened to receive instruction.
34 But they [u]set their abominations in the
house, which is called by my name, to defile it.
35 And they built the high places of Baal,
which *are* in the valley of the son of Hinnom,
to [v]cause their sons and their daughters to
pass through *the fire* unto [w]Molech; [x]which
I commanded them not, neither came it into
my mind, that they should do this abomination, to cause Judah to sin.
36 And now therefore thus saith the LORD,
the God of Israel, concerning this city,
whereof ye say, [y]It shall be delivered into the
hand of the king of Babylon by the sword,
and by the famine, and by the pestilence;
37 Behold, I will [z]gather them out of all
countries, whither I have driven them in mine
anger, and in my fury, and in great wrath;
and I will bring them again unto this place,
and I will cause them [a]to dwell safely:
38 And they shall [b]be my people, and I
will be their God:
39 And I will [c]give them one heart, and
one way, that they may fear me [d]for ever,
for the good of them, and of their children
after them:

[e]Ch. xiv. 12——[f]Or, *though*——[g]Ver. 24——[h]Num. xvi. 22——[i]Ver. 17——[k]Ver. 3——[l]Ch. xxi. 10; xxxvii. 8, 10; lii. 13——[m]Ch. xix. 13——[n]Ch. ii. 7; iii. 25; vii. 22–26; xxii. 21; Ezek. xx. 28——[o]Heb. *for my anger* [p]2 Kings xxiii. 27; xxiv. 3——[q]Isa. i. 4, 6; Dan. ix. 8 [r]Heb. *neck*——[s]Ch. ii. 27; vii. 24——[t]Ch. vii. 13

[u]Ch. vii. 30, 31; xxiii. 11; Ezek. viii. 5, 6——[v]Ch. vii. 31; xix. 5——[w]Lev. xviii. 21; 1 Kings xi. 33——[x]Chap. vii. 31——[y]Ver. 24——[z]Deut. xxx. 3; ch. xxiii. 3; xxix. 14; xxxi. 10; Ezek. xxxvii. 21——[a]Ch. xxiii. 6; xxxiii. 16 [b]Ch. xxiv. 7; xxx. 22; xxxi. 33——[c]Chap. xxiv. 7; Ezek. xi. 19, 20——[d]Heb. *all days*

ways of—men] Thou art omniscient, and knowest all things; thou art omnipresent, and seest all things.

Verse 24. *Behold the mounts*] The huge terraces raised up to plant their engines on, that they might throw darts, stones, &c., into the city.

Because of the sword, and of the famine, and of the pestilence] The city was now reduced to extreme necessity; and from the siege continuing nearly a year longer, we may conclude that the besieged made a noble defence.

Verse 29. *With the houses, upon whose roofs*] As it is most probable that *Baal* was the *sun*, they might have chosen the *tops* of the houses, which were always flat, with battlements around, to offer incense and sacrifice to him at his *rising*, and while he was *in sight* above the horizon.

Verse 30. *For the children of Israel and the children of Judah have only done evil*] They have all been transgressors from their earliest history.

For the children of Israel] The ten tribes.

Have only provoked me to anger with the work of their hands] They have been sinners beyond all others, being *excessive idolaters*. Their *hands* have formed the *objects* of their *worship*.

Verse 33. *Though I taught them, rising up early and teaching* them] From the frequent reference to this, we may naturally conclude that *morning preaching* prevailed much in Judea.

Verse 37. *Behold, I will gather them out of all countries*] A promise often repeated. See chap. xxix. 14, and the notes on chap. xxxi. 8, &c.

Verse 39. *I will give them one heart*] And that a *clean one*.

A. M. 3415
B. C. 589
Ol. XLVII. 4
Anno
TarquiniiPrisci,
R. Roman., 28

40 And [e]I will make an everlasting covenant with them, that I will not turn away [f]from them, to do them good; but [g]I will put my fear in their hearts, that they shall not depart from me.

41 Yea, [h]I will rejoice over them to do them good, and [i]I will plant them in this land [k]assuredly with my whole heart and with my whole soul.

42 For thus saith the LORD; [l]Like as I have brought all this great evil upon this people, so will I bring upon them all the good that I have promised them.

43 And [m]fields shall be bought in this land, [n]whereof ye say, *It is* desolate without man or beast; it is given into the hand of the Chaldeans.

44 Men shall buy fields for money, and subscribe evidences, and seal *them,* and take witnesses in [o]the land of Benjamin, and in the places about Jerusalem, and in the cities of Judah, and in the cities of the mountains, and in the cities of the valley, and in the cities of the south: for [p]I will cause their captivity to return, saith the LORD.

[e]Isa. lv. 3; chap. xxxi. 31——[f]Heb, *from after them* [g]Chap. xxxi. 33——[h]Deut. xxx. 9; Zeph. iii. 17——[i]Ch. xxiv. 6; xxxi. 28; Amos ix. 15

[k]Heb. *in truth,* or *stability*——[l]Chap. xxxi. 28 [m]Ver. 15——[n]Chap. xxxiii. 10——[o]Chap. xvii. 26 [p]Chap. xxxiii. 7, 11, 26

And one way] And that a *holy and safe one:* and to have this *clean heart,* and to *walk in this good way, will be for the good of them and their children after them.* God's blessing is a profitable inheritance. They shall have but *one object* of *worship,* and *one way* of salvation; and being saved from sin, idolatry, and destruction, they must necessarily be happy within and happy without.

Verse 41. *Yea, I will rejoice over them to do them good*] Nothing can please God better than our coming to him to receive the good which, *with his whole heart* and *his whole soul,* he is ready to impart. How exceedingly condescending are these words of God!

Verse 42. *Will I bring upon them all the good that I have promised*] God's word cannot fail. The Jews have never yet received the good that God has promised. Nothing like the fulfilment of these promises took place after their return from Babylon; therefore there remaineth yet a *rest* for these ancient people of God; and it is under the *Christian* dispensation that they are to have it.

Verse 44. *Men shall buy fields for money*] This is a reference to the symbolical purchase mentioned at the beginning of the chapter; *that* may be considered by them as a sure sign of their restoration, not only to the *same land,* but to their respective inheritances in that land. This the power of God could alone perform.

CHAPTER XXXIII

In this chapter the prophet predicts a restoration of Israel and Judah to the favour of God, attended with such glorious circumstances as shall astonish all the world, 1–9. *Their prosperity from that period is then described by a beautiful enumeration of circumstances,* 10–13. *This leads to the promise of the Messiah, the grand subject of the prophetical writings, and the happiness and stability which the children of Israel shall enjoy under his government; promises which, in so far as they respect the great body of the Jews, remain still to be fulfilled,* 14–26.

A. M. 3416
B. C. 588
Ol. XLVIII. 1
Anno
TarquiniiPrisci,
R. Roman., 29

MOREOVER the word of the LORD came unto Jeremiah the second time, (while he was yet [a]shut up in the court of the prison,) saying,

2 Thus saith the LORD the [b]Maker thereof, the LORD that formed it, to establish it; [c]the[d] LORD *is* his name;

3 [e]Call unto me, and I will answer thee, and

[a]Ch. xxxii. 2, 3——[b]Isa. xxxvii. 26——[c]Or, *JEHOVAH*

[d]Exod. xv. 3; Amos v. 8; ix. 6——[e]Psa. xci. 15; ch. xxix

NOTES ON CHAP. XXXIII

Verse 1. *Moreover the word of the Lord*] This was in the *eleventh* year of the reign of Zedekiah, Jeremiah being still *shut up in prison:* but he was now in the *court of the prison,* where the elders and the king's officers, &c., might consult him with the greater ease; for they continued to inquire, foolishly thinking, that if he would but prophesy good things, that these must come; or that he had sufficient power with God to induce him to alter his mind,—destroy the Chaldeans, and deliver the city.

Verse 2. *Thus saith the Lord the Maker thereof*] עשה *osah, the doer of it.* That is, he who is to perform *that* which he is now about to promise. Thus translated by *Dahler:*—Voici ce que dit l'Eternel, qui *fait* ce qu'il a *dit.*—"Thus saith the Lord, who doth that which he hath said." The word *Jehovah,* not *Lord,* should be used in all such places as this.

Verse 3. *Call unto me, and I will answer thee*] To me alone it belongs to reveal what is future; and the stupendous things which are now coming are known only to myself. These idolaters go to their gods to get information

A. M. 3416
B. C. 588
Ol. XLVIII. 1
Anno
TarquiniiPrisci,
R. Roman., 29

show thee great and [f]mighty things which thou knowest not.

4 For thus saith the LORD, the God of Israel, concerning the houses of this city, and concerning the houses of the kings of Judah, which are thrown down by [g]the mounts, and by the sword;

5 [h]They come to fight with the Chaldeans, but *it is* to fill them with the dead bodies of men, whom I have slain in mine anger and in my fury, and for all whose wickedness I have hid my face from this city.

6 Behold, [i]I will bring it health and cure, and I will cure them, and will reveal unto them the abundance of peace and truth.

7 And [k]I will cause the captivity of Judah and the captivity of Israel to return, and will build them, [l]as at the first.

8 And I will [m]cleanse them from all their iniquity, whereby they have sinned against me; and I will [n]pardon all their iniquities, whereby they have sinned, and whereby they have transgressed against me.

9 [o]And it shall be to me a name of joy, a praise and an honour before all the nations of the earth, which shall hear all the good that I do unto them: and they shall [p]fear and tremble for all the goodness and for all the prosperity that I procure unto it.

10 Thus saith the LORD; Again there shall be heard in this place, [q]which ye say *shall be* desolate without man and without beast, *even* in the cities of Judah, and in the streets of Jerusalem, that are desolate, without man, and without inhabitant, and without beast,

A. M. 3416
B. C. 588
Ol. XLVIII. 1
Anno
TarquiniiPrisci
R. Roman., 29

11 The [r]voice of joy, and the voice of gladness, the voice of the bridegroom, and the voice of the bride, the voice of them that shall say, [s]Praise the LORD of hosts: for the LORD *is* good; for his mercy *endureth* for ever: *and* of them that shall bring [t]the sacrifice of praise into the house of the LORD. For [u]I will cause to return the captivity of the land, as at the first, saith the LORD.

12 Thus saith the LORD of hosts; [v]Again in this place, which is desolate without man and without beast, and in all the cities thereof, shall be a habitation of shepherds causing *their* flocks to lie down.

13 [w]In the cities of the mountains, in the cities of the vale, and in the cities of the south, and in the land of Benjamin, and in the places about Jerusalem, and in the cities of Judah, shall the flocks [x]pass again under the hands of him that telleth *them*, saith the LORD.

14 [y]Behold, the days come, saith the LORD, that [z]I will perform that good thing which

[f]Or, *hidden;* Isa. xlviii. 6——[g]Ch. xxxii. 24——[h]Ch. xxxii. 5——[i]Ch. xxx. 17——[k]Ch. xxx. 3; xxxii. 44; ver. 11——[l]Isa. i. 26; chap. xxiv. 6; xxx. 20; xxxi. 4, 28; xlii. 10——[m]Ezek. xxxvi. 25; Zech. xiii. 1; Heb. ix. 13, 14——[n]Chap. xxxi. 34; Mic. vii. 18——[o]Isa. lxii. 7; chap. xiii. 11——[p]Isa. lx. 5

[q]Ch. xxxii. 43——[r]Ch. vii. 34; xvi. 9; xxv. 10; Rev. xviii. 23——[s]1 Chron. xvi. 8, 34; 2 Chron. v. 13; vii. 3; Ezra iii. 11; Psa. cxxxvi. 1; Isa. xii. 4——[t]Lev. vii. 12; Psa. cvii. 22; cxvi. 17——[u]Ver. 7——[v]Isa. lxv. 10; ch. xxxi. 24; l. 19——[w]Ch. xvii. 26; xxxii. 44——[x]Lev. xxvii 32——[y]Ch. xxiii. 5; xxxi. 27, 31——[z]Ch. xxix. 10

relative to the issue of the present commotions; but there is no light in them. Ask *thou*, O Jeremiah, and I will tell *thee* the great and mighty things which *even thou* knowest not.

Verse 4. *Thus saith the Lord*] This is a new confirmation of what has already been said, viz., The city shall fall, a number of the inhabitants shall perish, the rest shall be carried into captivity; but the *nation* shall be preserved, and the people return from their captivity.

Verse 6. *Behold I will bring it health and cure*] ארכה *aruchah*, an *extensive plaister;* or, as we phrase it, *a plaister as large as the sore.* I will repair the losses of families by numerous births, and bless the land with fertility.

Verse 7. *The captivity of Judah and the captivity of Israel*] This must respect the latter times, for the *ten tribes* did not return with the Jews at the termination of the *seventy* years.

Verse 8. *I will cleanse them*] These promises of pardon and holiness must be referred to their state under the Gospel, when they shall have received Jesus as the promised Messiah.

Verse 9. *They shall fear and tremble*] The surrounding nations shall be persuaded that it is the hand of the Almighty that has wrought this change in your behalf; and shall *fear* to molest you, and *tremble* lest they should incur the displeasure of your God by doing you any kind of evil.

Verse 11. *The voice of them that shall say, Praise the Lord of hosts*] That is, the voice of the *Levites* in the sacred service: intimating that the temple should be rebuilt, and the public service restored.

Verse 12. *A habitation of shepherds*] See on chap. xxxi. 12.

Verse 14. *Behold, the days come*] See chap. xxiii. 5, and xxxi. 31.

That good thing which I have promised] By my prophets: for those who have predicted the captivity have also foretold its conclusion, though not in such express terms as Jeremiah did. See Hos. i. 10, &c.; ii. 15, &c.; vi. 11, &c.; Amos ix. 14, &c., and Jer. iii. 12, &c. The *end* of the captivity has been foretold by Micah, chap. vii. 9, &c.; Zephaniah, iii. 10, &c.; and by Jeremiah, chap. xvi. 15; xxiii. 3; xxix. 10;

A. M. 3416 B. C. 588 Ol. XLVIII. 1 Anno TarquiniiPrisci, R. Roman., 29

I have promised unto the house
of Israel and to the house of
Judah.

15 In those days, and at that
time, will I cause the [a]Branch of righteousness to grow up unto David; and he shall execute judgment and righteousness in the land.

16 [b]In those days shall Judah be saved, and
Jerusalem shall dwell safely: and this *is the
name* wherewith she shall be called, [c]The LORD
our Righteousness.

17 For thus saith the LORD; [d]David shall
never [e]want a man to sit upon the throne of
the house of Israel;

18 Neither shall the priests the Levites
want a man before me to [f]offer burnt-offerings,
and to kindle meat-offerings, and to do sacrifice continually.

19 And the word of the LORD came unto
Jeremiah, saying,

20 Thus saith the LORD; [g]If ye can break
my covenant of the day, and my covenant of
the night, and that there should not be day
and night in their season;

21 *Then* may also [h]my covenant be broken
with David my servant, that he
should not have a son to reign
upon his throne; and with the
Levites, the priests, my ministers.

A. M. 3416 B. C. 588 Ol. XLVIII. 1 Anno TarquiniiPrisci. R. Roman., 29

22 As [i]the host of heaven cannot be numbered, neither the sand of the sea measured:
so will I multiply the seed of David my servant, and the Levites that minister unto me.

23 Moreover the word of the LORD came to
Jeremiah, saying,

24 Considerest thou not what this people
have spoken, saying, [k]The two families which
the LORD hath chosen, he hath even cast them
off? thus they have despised my people, that
they should be no more a nation before them.

25 Thus saith the LORD; If [l]my covenant
be not with day and night, *and if* I have not
[m]appointed the ordinances of heaven and
earth;

26 [n]Then will I cast away the seed of Jacob,
and David my servant, *so* that I will not take
any of his seed *to be* rulers over the seed of
Abraham, Isaac, and Jacob: for [o]I will cause
their captivity to return, and have mercy on
them.

---

[a]Isa. iv. 2; xi. 1; chap. xxiii. 5——[b]Chap. xxiii. 6
[c]Heb. *Jehovah-tsidkenu*——[d]Heb. *there shall not be cut off from David*——[e]2 Sam. vii. 16; 1 Kings ii. 4; Psa. lxxxix. 29, 36; Luke i. 32, 33——[f]Rom. xii. 1; xv. 16; 1 Pet. ii. 5, 9; Rev. i. 6

[g]Psa. lxxxix. 37; Isa. liv. 9; chap. xxxi. 36; ver. 25
[h]Psa. lxxxix. 34——[i]Gen. xiii. 16; xv. 5; xxii. 17; chap. xxxi. 37——[k]Ver. 21, 22——[l]Ver. 20; Gen. viii. 22
[m]Psa. lxxiv. 16, 17; civ. 19; chap. xxxi. 35, 36——[n]Ch. xxxi. 37——[o]Ver. 7, 11; Ezra ii. 1

---

xxxii. 37. The *Targum* explains verses 14, 15, and 16 of the Messiah.

Verse 16. *And this* is the name *wherewith she shall be called, The Lord our Righteousness.*] See what has been said on chap. xxiii. 6, which is generally supposed to be a strictly parallel passage: but they are very different, and I doubt whether they mean exactly the same thing. As to our translation here, it is ignorant, and almost impious; it says that *Jerusalem*, for that is the antecedent, shall be called *The Lord our Righteousness.* The pronoun לה *lah*, which is translated *her*, is the *masculine* affix, in the *Chaldaic* form, which frequently occurs; and Dr. *Blayney* translates, "And this is He whom Jehovah shall call our righteousness," or Justification. Perhaps there is a sense which these words will bear far more congenial to the scope of the place. I will give the original, as before: וזה אשר יקרא לה יהוה צדקנו *vezeh asher yikra lah, Yehovah tsidkenu*, "And this one who shall call to her *is* the Lord our Justification;" that is, the salvation of the Jews shall take place when Jesus Christ is proclaimed to them as their Justifier, and they receive him as such.

Instead of לה *lah, her* or *him*, Chaldaice, the *Vulgate, Chaldee*, and *Syriac* have read לו *lo, him*, less ambiguously; and this reading is supported by one or two MSS. This emendation renders the passage here more conformable to that in chap. xxiii. 6; but if the translation above be admitted, all embarrassment is gone. One of my own MSS. has לה *loh*, with the masculine points, and no mappik on the ה *he;* and for *tsidkenu* has צדקינו *tsidkeynu*, the contracted plural form, *our righteousness:* but this may be a mistake. The passages in this and the *twenty-third* chapter were not, I am satisfied, intended to express the same thing. I suppose that above refers to the preaching or proclaiming Christ crucified to the Jews, when the time shall arrive in which they shall be incorporated with the Gentile Church. *Dahler* translates this as he did that in chap. xxiii., which is a perfect oversight: but paraphrastic renderings are too often introduced by this learned foreigner.

Verse 18. *Neither shall the priests the Levites want a man*] This is a repetition of the promise made to Phinehas, Num. xxv. 13.

Verse 20. *If ye can break my covenant of the day*] See the note on chap. xxxi. 36.

Verse 22. *So will I multiply the seed of David*] This must be understood of the spiritual David, Jesus Christ, and his progeny, genuine Christians. The two families which God chose for the priesthood, that of Aaron and Phinehas, or, on its being taken away from him, that of Ithamar, 1 Sam. ii. 35, are both extinct. Nor has the office of high priest, or priest of any kind offering sacrifice, been exercised among the Jews for nearly *eighteen hundred* years; therefore what is said here of the priesthood must refer to the spiritual priesthood, at the head of which is Jesus Christ.

Verse 24. *The two families which the Lord hath chosen*] Some think these refer to the two kingdoms of Israel and Judah; but they never can be considered as two distinct families, being of one and the same race. Others think that the families of Jacob and David are intended; but neither were these distinct. If the two families which had the priesthood be not meant, then the regal family of David, and the sacerdotal family of Jacob through Levi, may be designed. See ver. 26. Following the spiritual interpretation, neither the regal nor sacerdotal family has failed; for Jesus is a King and a Priest, and all true believers in him are kings and priests unto God and the Lamb. And the highest King that ever reigned is He who is the seed of David, King of kings and Lord of lords, who has all power in heaven and in earth.

CHAPTER XXXIV

This chapter contains two prophecies: the first, delivered during the siege of Jerusalem, predicts to Zedekiah the taking and burning of the city, with his own peaceful death and honourable burial, 1–7. The second was delivered when the Chaldeans had for some time broken up the siege. It reproves the Jews for their conduct towards their brethren of the poorer sort, whom they released, by a solemn covenant, from bondage, in the extremity of their danger; but compelled to return to it when they thought that danger over, 8–11. For this God threatens them with the sword, pestilence, and famine; and with the return of the Chaldeans, who should take the city, destroy it and the other cities by fire, and make an utter desolation of the whole land of Judea, 12–22.

A. M. 3415
B. C. 589
Ol. XLVII. 4
Anno
TarquiniiPrisci,
R. Roman., 28

THE word which came unto
Jeremiah from the LORD,
([a]when Nebuchadnezzar king of
Babylon, and all his army, and
[b]all the kingdoms of the earth [c]of his dominion,
and all the people, fought against Jerusalem,
and against all the cities thereof,) saying,
2 Thus saith the LORD, the God of Israel;
Go and speak to Zedekiah king of Judah,
and tell him, Thus saith the LORD; Behold
[d]I will give this city into the hand of the king
of Babylon, and [e]he shall burn it with fire:
3 And [f]thou shalt not escape out of his
hand, but shalt surely be taken, and delivered
into his hand; and thine eyes
shall behold the eyes of the king
of Babylon, and [g]he shall speak
with thee mouth to mouth, and
thou shalt go to Babylon.
4 Yet hear the word of the LORD, O Zedekiah king of Judah; Thus saith the LORD of
thee, Thou shalt not die by the sword:
5 *But* thou shalt die in peace: and with
[h]the burnings of thy fathers, the former kings
which were before thee, [i]so shall they burn
odours for thee; and [k]they will lament thee,
saying, Ah lord! for I have pronounced the
word, saith the LORD.

A. M. 3415
B. C. 589
Ol. XLVII. 4
Anno
TarquiniiPrisci,
R. Roman., 28

---

[a]2 Kings xxv. 1, &c.; chap. xxxix. 1; lii. 4——[b]Chap. i. 15——[c]Heb. *the dominion of his hand*——[d]Chap. xxi. 10; xxxii. 3, 28——[e]Chap. xxxii. 29; ver. 22

[f]Chap. xxxii. 4——[g]Heb. *his mouth shall speak to thy mouth*——[h]See 2 Chron. xvi. 14; xxi. 19——[i]Dan ii. 46 [k]See chap. xxii. 18

NOTES ON CHAP. XXXIV

Verse 1. *The word which came unto Jeremiah*] This discourse was delivered in the *tenth* year of the reign of Zedekiah. The chapter contains two discourses; one, ver. 1-7, which concerns the taking of the city, and Zedekiah's captivity and death; the other, ver. 8-22, which is an invective against the inhabitants of Jerusalem for having Hebrew male and female slaves. These, having been manumitted at the instance of the prophet, were afterwards brought back by their old masters, and put in the same thraldom; for which God threatens them with severe judgments.

Nebuchadnezzar—and all his army, and all the kingdoms of the earth of his dominion] That is, his army was composed of soldiers gathered out of Babylon, and out of all his tributary dominions: one hundred and twenty provinces.

Verse 2. *He shall burn it with fire*] This was a newly-added circumstance. Among many ancient nations they burned the bodies of the more illustrious dead. Odours were used in the burning: they then gathered the ashes, and put them into an urn or pitcher, sometimes into a strong vessel, and buried them. Many of these have been digged up in different parts of England, where the Romans had stations.

Verse 3. *Thou shalt not escape*] This, however, he had attempted, but was taken in his flight. See chap. xxxix. 4, and lii. 7, &c.

Verse 5. *Thou shalt die in peace*] Thou shalt not die a *violent* death; and at thy death thou shalt have all those funereal solemnities which were usual at the demise of kings. See 2 Chron. xvi. 14.

So shall they burn odours *for thee*] Scented wood and other odoriferous substances are placed on the funeral pile of the rich Hindoos, and burned with the body.

And they will lament thee, saying, *Ah lord!*] They will recite the funeral dirge that begins with those words. See the note on chap. xxii. 18.

A. M. 3415 B. C. 589 Ol. XLVII. 4 Anno TarquiniiPrisci, R. Roman., 28

6 Then Jeremiah the prophet spake all these words unto Zedekiah king of Judah in Jerusalem,

7 When the king of Babylon's army fought against Jerusalem, and against all the cities of Judah that were left, against Lachish, and against Azekah: for [l]these defenced cities remained of the cities of Judah.

A. M. cir. 3415 B. C. cir. 589 Ol. XLVII. 4 TarquiniiPrisci, R. Roman., cir. annum 28

8 *This is* the word that came unto Jeremiah from the LORD, after that the king Zedekiah had made a covenant with all the people which *were* at Jerusalem, to proclaim [m]liberty unto them;

9 [n]That every man shauld let his man-servant, and every man his maid-servant, *being* a Hebrew or a Hebrewess, go free; [o]that none should serve himself of them, *to wit,* of a Jew his brother.

10 Now when all the princes, and all the people, which had entered into the covenant, heard that every one should let his man-servant, and every one his maid-servant, go free, that none should serve themselves of them any more, then they obeyed, and let *them* go.

11 But [p]afterward they turned, and caused the servants and the handmaids, whom they had let go free, to return, and brought them into subjection for servants and for handmaids.

A. M. cir. 3415 B. C. cir. 589 Ol. XLVII. 4 TarquiniiPrisci, R. Roman., cir. annum 28

12 Therefore the word of the LORD came to Jeremiah from the LORD, saying,

13 Thus saith the LORD, the God of Israel; I made a covenant with your fathers in the day that I brought them forth out of the land of Egypt, out of the house of bondmen, saying,

14 At the end of [q]seven years let ye go every man his brother a Hebrew, which [r]hath been sold unto thee; and when he hath served thee six years, thou shalt let him go free from thee: but your fathers hearkened not unto me, neither inclined their ear.

15 And ye were [s]now turned, and had done right in my sight, in proclaiming liberty every man to his neighbour; and ye had [t]made a covenant before me [u]in the house [v]which is called by my name:

16 But ye turned and [w]polluted my name, and caused every man his servant, and every man his handmaid, whom he had set at liberty at their pleasure, to return, and brought them into subjection, to be unto you for servants and for handmaids.

17 Therefore thus saith the LORD; Ye have not hearkened unto me, in proclaiming liberty, every one to his brother, and every man to his neighbour: [x]behold, I proclaim a liberty for you, saith the LORD, [y]to the sword, to the pes-

---

[l]2 Kings xviii. 13; xix. 8; 2 Chron. xi. 5, 9——[m]Exod. xxi. 2; Lev. xxv. 10; ver. 14——[n]Neh. v. 11——[o]Lev. xxv. 39-46——[p]See ver. 21; chap. xxxvii. 5——[q]Exod. xxi. 2; xxiii. 10; Deut. xv. 12——[r]Or, *hath sold himself*

[s]Heb. *to-day*——[t]So 2 Kings xxiii. 3; Neh. x. 29 [u]Chap. vii. 10——[v]Heb. *whereupon my name is called* [w]Exod. xx. 7; Lev. xix. 42——[x]Matt. vii. 2; Gal. vi. 7; James ii. 13——[y]Chap. xxxii. 24, 36

Verse 6. *Spake all these words unto Zedekiah*] He delivered this message at the hazard of his life. Jeremiah feared God, and had no other fear.

Verse 7. *Against Lachish, and against Azekah*] These were two cities of Judah of considerable importance: they had been strongly fortified by Rehoboam, 2 Chron. xi. 9-11; 2 Chron. xxxii. 9.

Verse 8. *The word that came unto Jeremiah*] Here the *second* discourse begins, which was delivered probably a short time, even a few days, after the former.

Zedekiah had made a covenant] We find no account elsewhere of this covenant: "Every man should let his man-servant and his maid-servant go free;" i. e., as we learn from ver. 14, on the *sabbatical year;* for the *seventh* year was the *year of release.* See Deut. xv. 12.

Verse 11. *But afterward they turned*] They had agreed to manumit them at the end of the *seventh* year; but when the *seventh* year was ended, they recalled their engagement, and detained their servants. This, I believe, is what is here meant.

Verse 16. *Ye—polluted my name*] Had made the covenant in my name, calling me to witness it; now ye have dishonoured my name, by breaking that covenant, and acting contrary to my law.

Verse 17. *I proclaim a liberty for you*] Ye proclaimed *liberty* to your slaves, and afterward resumed your *authority* over them; and I had in consequence *restrained* the sword from cutting you off: but now I give *liberty* to the *sword,* to the *pestilence,* and to the *famine,* and to the *captivity,* to destroy and consume you, and *enslave* you: for ye shall be removed to all the kingdoms of the earth. The prophet loves to express the *conformity* between the *crime* and its *punishment.* You promised to give *liberty* to your *enslaved* brethren; I was pleased, and *bound* the sword in its sheath. You broke your promise, and brought them again into *bondage;* I gave *liberty* to the sword, pestilence, and famine, to destroy multitudes of you, and *captivity* to take the rest. Thus you are punished *according* to your crimes, and in the *punishment* you may see the *crime.* Sword, pestilence, and famine are frequently joined together, as

A. M. cir. 3415
B. C. cir. 589
Ol. XLVII. 4
TarquiniiPrisci,
R. Roman.,
cir. annum 28

tilence, and to the famine; and I will make you [z]to be [a]removed into all the kingdoms of the earth.

18 And I will give the men that have transgressed my covenant, which have not performed the words of the covenant which they had made before me, when [b]they cut the calf in twain, and passed between the parts thereof,

19 The princes of Judah, and the princes of Jerusalem, the eunuchs, and the priests, and all the people of the land, which passed between the parts of the calf;

20 I will even give them into the hand of their enemies, and into the hand of them that seek their life: and their [c]dead bodies shall be for meat unto the fowls of the heaven, and to the beasts of the earth.

A. M. cir. 3415
B. C. cir. 589
Ol. XLVII. 4
TarquiniiPrisci,
R. Roman.,
cir. annum 28

21 And Zedekiah king of Judah, and his princes, will I give into the hand of their enemies, and into the hand of them that seek their life, and into the hand of the king of Babylon's army, [d]which are gone up from you.

22 [e]Behold, I will command, saith the LORD, and cause them to return to this city; and they shall fight against it, [f]and take it, and burn it with fire: and [g]I will make the cities of Judah a desolation without an inhabitant.

[z]Heb. *for a removing*——[a]Deut. xxviii. 25, 64; chap. xxix. 18——[b]See Gen. xv. 10, 17——[c]Chap. vii. 33; xvi. 4; xix. 7

[d]See chap. xxxvii. 5, 11——[e]Chap. xxxvii. 8, 10 [f]Chap. xxxviii. 3; xxxix. 1, 2, 8; lii. 7, 13——[g]Chap. ix. 11; xliv. 2, 6

being often the effects of each other. The *sword* or *war* produces *famine; famine*, the *pestilence.*

Verse 18. *When they cut the calf in twain, and passed between the parts thereof*] This was the ancient and most solemn way of making a covenant. 1. A calf as sacrifice was offered to God to secure his approbation and support. 2. The *victim* was then *exactly divided* from the nose to the rump; the *spinal marrow* being divided longitudinally, in the most careful manner, that the *half* of it might remain on *each side.* 3. These divided parts were laid opposite to each other, a passage being left between them. 4. The contracting parties entered this passage at each end, met in the middle, and there took the covenant oath; adjudging themselves to death should they break this covenant. 5. Then they both feasted on the victim. In reference to this last circumstance, God says he *will give their bodies* for *meat to the fowls of heaven* and *to the beasts.* This is a farther conformity between the crime and the punishment. See my notes on Gen. xv. 9-17.

Verse 21. *The king of Babylon's army, which are gone up from you.*] Nebuchadnezzar, hearing that there was an Egyptian army coming to the relief of Jerusalem, raised the siege, went out, and met and defeated the Egyptians. It was in the interim this prophecy was delivered.

Verse 22. *I will—cause them to return*] They did return; re-invested the city; and, after an obstinate defence, took it, plundered it, and burned it to the ground, taking *Zedekiah* and his *princes* captive.

CHAPTER XXXV

Jeremiah is commanded to go to the Rechabites, who, on the approach of the Chaldean army, took refuge in Jerusalem; and to try their obedience to the command of Jonadab, (*or Jehonadab,* 2 Kings x. 15, 16,) *their great progenitor, who lived in the reign of Jehu, king of Israel, upwards of* two hundred and fifty *years before this time, offers them wine to drink, which they refuse,* 1–11. *Hence occasion is taken to upbraid the Jews with their disobedience to God, their heavenly Father,* 12–17; *and a blessing is pronounced on the Rechabites,* 18, 19.

A. M. cir. 3397
B. C. cir. 607
Ol. XLIII. 2
TarquiniiPrisci,
R. Roman.,
cir. annum 10

THE word which came unto Jeremiah from the LORD in the days of Jehoiakim the son of Josiah king of Judah, saying,

2 Go unto the house of the [a]Rechabites, and speak unto them, and bring them into the house of the LORD, into one of

A. M. cir. 3397
B. C. cir. 607
Ol. XLIII. 2
TarquiniiPrisci,
R. Roman.,
cir. annum 10

[a]2 Kings x. 15; 1 Chron. ii. 55

NOTES ON CHAP. XXXV

Verse 1. *The word which came—in the days of Jehoiakim*] What strange confusion in the placing of these chapters! Who could have expected to hear of *Jehoiakim* again, whom we have long ago buried; and we have now arrived in the history at the very last year of the last Jewish king.

This discourse was probably delivered in the *fourth* or *fifth* year of Jehoiakim's reign.

Verse 2. *The house of the Rechabites*] The *Rechabites* were not descendants of *Jacob;* they were *Kenites,* 1 Chron. ii. 55, a people originally settled in that part of *Arabia Petræa,* called the *land of Midian;* and most probably the descendants of *Jethro,* the father-in-law of Moses. Compare Num. x. 29-32, with Judg. i. 16; iv. 11.

A. M. cir. 3397
B. C. cir. 607
Ol. XLIII. 2
TarquiniiPrisci,
R. Roman.,
cir. annum 10

[b]the chambers, and give them wine to drink.

3 Then I took Jaazaniah the son of Jeremiah, the son of Habaziniah, and his brethren, and all his sons, and the whole house of the Rechabites;

4 And I brought them into the house of the LORD, into the chamber of the sons of Hanan, the son of Igdaliah, a man of God which *was* by the chamber of the princes, which *was* above the chamber of Maaseiah the son of Shallum, [c]the keeper of the [d]door:

5 And I set before the sons of the house of the Rechabites pots full of wine, and cups, and I said unto them, Drink ye wine.

6 But they said, We will drink no wine: for [e]Jonadab the son of Rechab our father commanded us, saying, Ye shall drink no wine, *neither* ye, nor your sons for ever:

A. M. cir. 3397
B. C. cir. 607
Ol. XLIII. 2
TarquiniiPrisci,
R. Roman.,
cir. annum. 10

7 Neither shall ye build house, nor sow seed, nor plant vineyard, nor have *any:* but all your days ye shall dwell in tents; [f]that ye may live many days in the land where ye *be* strangers.

8 Thus have we obeyed the voice of Jonadab the son of Rechab our father in all that he hath charged us, to drink no wine all our days, we, our wives, our sons, nor our daughters;

9 Nor to build houses for us to dwell in: neither have we vineyard, nor field, nor seed:

10 But we have dwelt in tents, and have obeyed, and done according to all that Jonadab our father commanded us.

---

[b]1 Kings vi. 5——[c]2 Kings xii. 9; xxv. 18; 1 Chron. ix. 18, 19——[d]Heb. *threshold*, or *vessel*——[e]2 Kings x. 15——[f]Exod. xx. 12; Eph. vi. 2, 3

Those mentioned here seem to have been a tribe of Nomades or Scenite Arabs, who fed their flocks in the deserts of Judea; they preserved the simple manners of their ancestors, considering the life of the *inhabitants of cities* and *large towns* as the death of *liberty;* believing that they would dishonour themselves by using that *sort of food* that would oblige them to live a *sedentary* life. Jonadab, one of their ancestors, had required his children and descendants to abide faithful to the customs of their forefathers; to continue to live in *tents*, and to nourish themselves on the produce of their *flocks;* to abstain from the *cultivation* of the *ground*, and from that particularly of the *vine* and its produce. His descendants religiously observed this rule, till the time when the armies of the Chaldeans had entered Judea; when, to preserve their lives, they retired within the walls of Jerusalem. But even there we find, from the account in this chapter, they did not quit their frugal manner of life: but most scrupulously observed the law of Jonadab their ancestor, and probably of this family.

When the children of *Hobab*, or *Jethro*, the father-in-law of Moses, were invited by him to accompany them in their journeying to the Promised Land, it is very likely that they continued their ancient usages, and lived a *patriarchal life*. Their property, consisting in nothing but their *cattle* and *tents*, was easily removable from place to place; and their manner of living was not likely to excite the *envy* or *jealousy* of those who had learnt to relish the luxuries of life; and therefore we may naturally conclude that as they were enemies to none, so they had no enemies themselves. Nature has few wants. Most of those which we feel are *factitious;* and howsoever what we call civilization may furnish us with the *conveniences* and *comforts* of *life*, let us not deceive ourselves by supposing that these very things do not create the very wants which they are called in to supply; and most certainly do not contribute to the comfort of life, when the term of life is considerably abridged by their use.

But it is time to return to the case of the Rechabites before us.

Verse 3. *The whole house of the Rechabites*] That is, the *family*—the chiefs of which are here specified.

Verse 4. *Igdaliah, a man of God*] A prophet or holy man, having some office in the temple.

Verse 5. *Pots full of wine, and cups*] The *cups* were to draw the wine out of the *pots*, in order to drink it.

Verse 6. *We will drink no wine*] The reason is given above. Their whole religious and political institution consisted in obedience to *three* simple precepts, each of which has an appropriate spiritual meaning:—

1. *Ye shall drink no wine*] Ye shall preserve your bodies in temperance, shall use nothing that would deprive you of the exercise of your sober reason at any time; lest in such a time ye should do what might be prejudicial to yourselves, injurious to your neighbour, or dishonourable to your God.

2. *Neither shall ye build house*] Ye shall not become residents in any place; ye shall not court earthly possessions; ye shall live free from ambition and from envy, that ye may be free from contention and strife.

3. *But—ye shall dwell in tents*] Ye shall imitate your forefathers, Abraham, Isaac, and Jacob, and the rest of the patriarchs, *who dwelt in tents*, being *strangers and pilgrims* upon earth, looking for a heavenly country, and being determined to have nothing here that would indispose their minds towards that place of endless rest, or prevent them from passing through *temporal* things so as not to lose those that are *eternal*.

There must necessarily be more in these injunctions than meets the eye in the *letter* of this account.

Verse 8. *Thus have we obeyed the voice*] We have considered these precepts so very *reasonable*, so very *useful*, so *conducive* to the *health of both body and mind*, and sanctioned by such a respectable *antiquity* that we scrupulously and religiously observe them.

A. M. cir. 3397
B. C. cir. 607
Ol. XLIII. 2
TarquiniiPrisci,
R. Roman.,
cir. annum 10

11 But it came to pass, when
Nebuchadrezzar king of Babylon
came up into the land, that we
said, Come, and let us go to Jerusalem for fear of the army of the Chaldeans,
and for fear of the army of the Syrians: so
we dwell at Jerusalem.
12 Then came the word of the LORD unto
Jeremiah, saying,
13 Thus saith the LORD of hosts, the God of
Israel; Go and tell the men of Judah and the
inhabitants of Jerusalem, Will ye not [g]receive
instruction to hearken to my words? saith the
LORD.
14 The words of Jonadab the son of Rechab,
that he commanded his sons not to drink wine,
are performed; for unto this day they drink
none, but obey their father's commandment:
[h]notwithstanding I have spoken unto you,
[i]rising early and speaking; but ye hearkened
not unto me:
15 [k]I have sent also unto you all my servants the prophets, rising up early and sending
them, saying, [l]Return ye now every man from
his evil way, and amend your doings, and go
not after other gods to serve them, and ye shall
dwell in the land which I have
given to you and to your fathers:
but ye have not inclined your
ear, nor hearkened unto me.
16 Because the sons of Jonadab the son of
Rechab have performed the commandment of
their father, which he commanded them; but
this people hath not hearkened unto me:
17 Therefore thus saith the LORD God of
hosts, the God of Israel; Behold, I will bring
upon Judah and upon all the inhabitants of
Jerusalem all the evil that I have pronounced
against them: [m]because I have spoken
unto them, but they have not heard; and
I have called unto them, but they have not
answered.
18 And Jeremiah said unto the house of the
Rechabites, Thus saith the LORD of hosts, the
God of Israel; Because ye have obeyed the
commandment of Jonadab your father, and
kept all his precepts, and done according unto
all that he hath commanded you:
19 Therefore thus saith the LORD of hosts,
the God of Israel; [n]Jonadab the son of Rechab shall not want a man to [o]stand before me
for ever.

[g]Chap. xxxii. 33——[h]2 Chron. xxxvi. 15——[i]Chap. vii. 13; xxv. 3——[k]Chap. vii. 25; xxv. 4——[l]Chap. xviii. 11; xxv. 5, 6

[m]Prov. i. 24; Isa. lxv. 12; lxvi. 4; chap. vii. 13
[n]Heb. *There shall not a man be cut off from Jonadab the son of Rechab to stand,* &c.——[o]Chap. xv. 19

Verse 11. *But—when Nebuchadnezzar—came up*] If at present we appear to be acting contrary in any respect to our institutions, in being found in the city, *necessity* alone has induced us to take this temporary step. We have sought the *shelter of the city* for the *preservation of our lives; so now we dwell at Jerusalem.*

Verse 14. *The words of Jonadab—are performed—but ye hearkened not unto me.*] The Lord, knowing the fidelity of this people, chose to try them in this way, that he might, by their conscientious obedience to the precepts of their forefathers, show the Jews, to their confusion, their ingratitude to him, and their neglect of his precepts, which if a man do, he shall live by them.

Verse 17. *I will bring upon Judah and upon all the inhabitants of Jerusalem all the evil*] Having, by the conduct of the Rechabites, clearly and fully convicted them of *ingratitude* and *rebellion,* he now proceeds to pronounce sentence against them.

Verse 19. *Thus saith the Lord—Jonadab—shall not want a man to stand before me for ever.*] His name shall ever be honourable, and his posterity shall enjoy my continual protection; and there shall never be found a time in which men of his spirit shall be wanting as patterns of genuine simplicity, filial obedience, purity of manners, and deadness to the world. True Christians may be considered as the genuine *successors* of these ancient *Rechabites;* and some suppose that the *Essenes,* in our Lord's time, were literally their *descendants,* and that these were they who followed our Lord particularly, and became the *first converts* to the Gospel. If so, the prophecy is *literally* fulfilled: *they shall never want a man to stand before God,* to proclaim his salvation, and minister to the edification and salvation of others, as long as the earth shall endure.

CHAPTER XXXVI

God commands Jeremiah to write down in one roll or volume all the predictions he had uttered against Israel and Judah, and all the surrounding nations, from the day of his vocation to the prophetic office, that the house of Judah might have abundant warning of the dreadful calamities with which their country was about to be visited, if not prevented by a timely repentance, 1–3. *The prophet employs Baruch the scribe, the son of Neriah, to write from his mouth all the words of the Lord, and then to read them publicly upon a fast day in the Lord's house,* 4–8. *A general fast is proclaimed in the following year, viz., the* fifth *year of the reign of Jehoiakim; upon which occasion Baruch, in obedience to the prophet's command, reads the words of Jeremiah to all the people at the entry of the new gate of the temple,* 9, 10. *The princes, hearing of this, send for Baruch, who reads the roll to them; at the contents of which they are greatly alarmed, and solemnly resolve to give information to the king, at the same time advising both the prophet and his scribe to hide themselves,* 11–19. *Jehoiakim likewise having sent for the roll, Jehudi reads to him a part; and then the king, though advised to the contrary by some of his princes, having cut the leaves, throws the whole into the fire,* 20–25, *and orders Jeremiah and Baruch to be seized; but they could not be found, because a special providence of God had concealed them,* 26. *Jeremiah is commanded to re-write his prophecies, and to denounce the judgments of God against the king who had destroyed the first roll,* 27–31. *Baruch accordingly writes from the mouth of Jeremiah a new copy, with numerous additions,* 32.

A. M. 3397
B. C. 607
Ol. XLIII. 2
Anno
TarquiniiPrisci,
R. Roman., 10

AND it came to pass in the
fourth year of Jehoiakim,
the son of Josiah king of Judah,
that this word came unto Jeremiah from the LORD, saying,
2 Take thee a [a]roll of a book, and [b]write
therein all the words that I have spoken unto
thee against Israel, and against Judah, and
against [c]all the nations, from the day I spake
unto thee, from the days of [d]Josiah, even
unto this day.
3 [e]It may be that the house of Judah will
hear all the evil which I purpose to do unto
them; that they may [f]return every man from
his evil way; that I may forgive their iniquity and their sin.
4 Then Jeremiah [g]called Baruch the son of
Neriah: and [h]Baruch wrote from the mouth
of Jeremiah all the words of the LORD, which
he had spoken unto him, upon a roll of a book.
5 And Jeremiah commanded Baruch, saying,
I *am* shut up; I cannot go into
the house of the LORD:

A. M. 3397
B. C. 607
Ol. XLIII. 2
Anno
TarquiniiPrisci,
R. Roman., 10

6 Therefore go thou, and read
in the roll, which thou hast written from my mouth, the words of the LORD
in the ears of the people in the LORD'S house
upon [i]the fasting day: and also thou shalt
read them in the ears of all Judah that come
out of their cities.
7 [k]It may be [l]they will present their supplication before the LORD, and will return
every one from his evil way: for great *is* the
anger and the fury that the LORD hath pronounced against this people.
8 And Baruch the son of Neriah did according to all that Jeremiah the prophet commanded him, reading in the book the words of
the LORD in the LORD'S house.
9 And it came to pass in the fifth year of
Jehoiakim the son of Josiah king of Judah,
in the ninth month, *that* they proclaimed

[a]Isa. viii. 1; Ezek. ii. 9; Zech. v. 1——[b]Chap. xxx. 2——[c]Chap. xxv. 15, &c.——[d]Chap. xxv. 3——[e]Ver. 7; chap. xxvi. 3——[f]Chap. xviii. 8; Jonah iii. 8

[g]Chap. xxxii. 12——[h]See chap. xlv. 1——[i]Lev. xvi. 29; xxii. 27, 32; Acts xxvii. 9——[k]Ver. 3——[l]Heb. *their supplication shall fall*

NOTES ON CHAP. XXXVI

Verse 1. *And it came to pass in the fourth year*] About the end of this year, see ver. 9. This discourse also bears its own *date*, and was probably delivered at a time when the people enjoyed peace, and were about to celebrate one of their annual fasts.

Verse 2. *Take thee a roll of a book*] Take a sufficient quantity of parchment; cut and stitch it together, that it may make a roll on which to write the words that I have already spoken, that they may serve for a testimony to future generations. The *Jewish rolls*, several of which now lie before me, were made of vellum, or of *sheep-skins* dressed in the *half-tanned* or Basil manner. These were cut into certain lengths, and those parts were all stitched together, and rolled upon a roller. The *matter* was written on these skins in *columns* or *pages*. Sometimes *two rollers* are used, that as the matter is read from the roll in the left hand, the reader may coil it on the roller in his right. In this form the *Pentateuch* is written which is read in the synagogues.

Verse 3. *It may be that the house of Judah will hear*] It was yet possible to avert the judgments which had been so often denounced against them. But in order to this they must—1. *Hear* what God has spoken. 2. Every man *turn* from his evil way. 3. If they do so, God graciously promises to *forgive their iniquity and their sin.*

Verse 4. *Then Jeremiah called Baruch*] This man, so useful to the prophet, and so faithfully attached to him, was by office a *scribe;* which signifies, not only a writer, but also a man in office; a chancellor, secretary, &c., a learned man; one acquainted with laws and customs.

Verse 6. *Upon the fasting day*] A day when multitudes of people would be gathered together from all parts to implore the mercy of God. This was a favourable time to read these tremendous prophecies.

Verse 7. *Present their supplication*] "Let their supplication fall," that they may fall down before God, and deplore their sins.

Verse 9. *In the ninth month*] Answering tc a part of our *December*.

A. M. 3398 B. C. 606 Ol. XLIII. 3 Anno TarquiniiPrisci, R. Roman., 11

a fast before the LORD to all the
people in Jerusalem, and to all
the people that came from the
cities of Judah unto Jerusalem.

10 Then read Baruch in the book the words
of Jeremiah in the house of the LORD, in the
chamber of Gemariah the son of Shaphan the
scribe, in the higher court, at the [m]entry [n]of
the new gate of the LORD's house, in the ears
of all the people.

11 When Michaiah the son of Gemariah, the
son of Shaphan, had heard out of the book all
the words of the LORD,

12 Then he went down into the king's
house, into the scribe's chamber: and, lo, all
the princes sat there, *even* Elishama the
scribe, and Delaiah the son of Shemaiah, and
Elnathan the son of Achbor, and Gemariah
the son of Shaphan, and Zedekiah the son of
Hananiah, and all the princes.

13 Then Michaiah declared unto them all
the words that he had heard, when Baruch
read the book in the ears of the people.

14 Therefore all the princes sent Jehudi
the son of Nethaniah, the son of Shelemiah,
the son of Cushi, unto Baruch, saying, Take
in thine hand the roll wherein thou hast read
in the ears of the people, and come. So
Baruch the son of Neriah took the roll in his
hand, and came unto them.

15 And they said unto him, Sit down now,
and read it in our ears. So Baruch read *it* in
their ears.

16 Now it came to pass, when they had
heard all the words, they were afraid both
one and other, and said unto
Baruch, We will surely tell the
king of all these words.

A. M. 3398 B. C. 606 Ol. XLIII. 3 Anno TarquiniiPrisci, R. Roman., 11

17 And they asked Baruch,
saying, Tell us now, How didst thou write all
these words at his mouth?

18 Then Baruch answered them, He pronounced all these words unto me with his
mouth, and I wrote *them* with ink in the
book.

19 Then said the princes unto Baruch, Go,
hide thee, thou and Jeremiah; and let no man
know where ye be.

20 And they went in to the king into the
court, but they laid up the roll in the chamber
of Elishama the scribe, and told all the words
in the ears of the king.

21 So the king sent Jehudi to fetch the roll:
and he took it out of Elishama the scribe's
chamber. And Jehudi read it in the ears of
the king, and in the ears of all the princes
which stood beside the king.

22 Now the king sat in [o]the winterhouse in
the ninth month: and *there was a fire* on the
hearth burning before him.

23 And it came to pass, *that* when Jehudi
had read three or four leaves, he cut it with
the penknife, and cast *it* into the fire that *was*
on the hearth, until all the roll was consumed
in the fire that *was* on the hearth.

24 Yet they were not afraid, nor [p]rent their
garments, *neither* the king, nor any of his
servants that heard all these words.

25 Nevertheless Elnathan and Delaiah and
Gemariah had made intercession to the king

[m]Or, *door*——[n]Chap. xxvi. 10——[o]See Amos iii. 15

[p]2 Kings xxii. 11; Isa. xxxvi. 22; xxxvii. 1

Verse 10. *In the chamber of Gemariah*] He was one of the princes of Judah. See ver. 12.

Verse 17. *How didst thou write all these words?—At his mouth?*] So the text should be pointed. They wished to know whether he had not copied them, or whether he wrote as Jeremiah prophesied.

Verse 19. *Go, hide thee, thou and Jeremiah*] They saw that the king would be displeased, and most probably seek their lives; and as they believed the prophecy was from God, they wished to save both the prophet and his scribe; but they were obliged to inform the king of what they had heard.

Verse 22. *Winterhouse*] A warm apartment suited to the season of the year, (*December*,) when in Palestine there is often snow upon the ground, though it does not last long. *A fire on the hearth*—a *pan* or *brazier* of burning coals. This is the case to the present day. In cold weather the rich burn wood in brass or earthen pans, placed in any part of the room; the indigent burn sticks on the floor.

Verse 23. *When Jehudi had read three or four leaves*] Rather columns; for the law, and the sacred Hebrew Books, are written in *columns* of a certain breadth. דלתות *delathoth*, signifies *gates* or *openings* between column and column, or between section and section.

He cut it with the penknife] בתער הספר *bethaar hassopher*, "the knife of the scribe," properly enough *penknife*.

And cast it *into the fire*] To show his contempt for God's words.

Verse 25. *Elnathan and Delaiah and Gemariah*] Three of the princes wished to *save the roll*, and entreated the king that it might not be burnt. They would have saved it *out of the fire*, but the king would not permit it to be done.

A. M. 3398
B. C. 606
Ol. XLIII. 3
Anno
TarquiniiPrisci,
R. Roman., 11

that he would not burn the roll: but he would not hear them.

26 But the king commanded Jerahmeel the son [q]of Hammelech, and Seraiah the son of Azriel, and Shelemiah the son of Abdeel, to take Baruch the scribe and Jeremiah the prophet: but the LORD hid them.

A. M. cir. 3399
B. C. cir. 605
Ol. XLIII. 4
TarquiniiPrisci,
R. Roman.,
cir. annum 12

27 Then the word of the LORD came to Jeremiah, after that the king had burned the roll, and the words which Baruch wrote at the mouth of Jeremiah, saying,

28 Take thee again another roll, and write in it all the former words that were in the first roll, which Jehoiakim the king of Judah hath burned.

29 And thou shalt say to Jehoiakim king of Judah, Thus saith the LORD; Thou hast burned this roll, saying, Why hast thou written therein, saying, The king of Babylon shall certainly come and destroy this land, and shall cause to cease from thence man and beast?

A. M. cir. 3399
B. C. cir. 605
Ol. XLIII. 4
TarquiniiPrisci,
R. Roman.,
cir. annum 12

30 Therefore thus saith the LORD of Jehoiakim king of Judah; [r]He shall have none to sit upon the throne of David: and his dead body shall be [s]cast out in the day to the heat, and in the night to the frost.

31 And I will [t]punish him and his seed and his servants for their iniquity; and I will bring upon them, and upon the inhabitants of Jerusalem, and upon the men of Judah, all the evil that I have pronounced against them; but they hearkened not.

32 Then took Jeremiah another roll, and gave it to Baruch the scribe, the son of Neriah; who wrote therein from the mouth of Jeremiah all the words of the book which Jehoiakim king of Judah had burned in the fire: and there were added besides unto them many [u]like words.

[q]Or, *of the king*——[r]Chap. xxii. 30——[s]Chap. xxii. 19

[t]Heb. *visit upon;* chap. xxiii. 34——[u]Heb. *as they*

Verse 26. *But the Lord hid them.*] They had, at the counsel of some of the princes, hidden themselves, ver. 19. And now, though a diligent search was made, the Lord did not permit them to be found.

Verse 28. *Take thee again another roll*] There was no duplicate of the former preserved; and now God inspired the prophet with the same matter that he had given him before; and there is to be added the heavy judgment that is to fall on Jehoiakim and his courtiers.

Verse 30. *He shall have none to sit upon the throne of David*] He shall have no *successor*, and himself shall have an untimely end, and shall not even be buried, but his body be exposed to the open air, both night and day. He who wishes to hide his crimes, or take away the evidence which is against him, adds thereby to his iniquities, and is sure in consequence to double his punishment. See the threatening against Jehoiakim, chap. xxii. 19, and the note there.

Verse 32. *There were added—many like words.*] All the first roll, with many other threatenings, and perhaps more minute declarations which were merely of a temporary importance and local application; and the Holy Spirit did not think proper to record them here.

CHAPTER XXXVII

Zedekiah succeeds Coniah, the son of Jehoiakim, in the Jewish throne, and does that which is evil in the sight of the Lord, 1, 2. *The king sends a message to Jeremiah,* 3–5. *God suggests an answer; and foretells the return of the Chaldean army, who should most assuredly take and burn the city,* 6–10. *Jeremiah, in attempting to leave this devoted city, and retire to his possession in the country, is seized as a deserter, and cast into a dungeon,* 11–15. *The king, after a conference with him, abates the rigour of his confinement,* 16–21.

A. M. 3406
—3416
B. C. 598
—588
Ol. XLV. 3—
XLVIII. 1

AND king [a]Zedekiah the son of Josiah reigned instead of Coniah the son of Jehoiakim, whom Nebuchadrezzar king of Babylon made king in the land of Judah.

2 [b]But neither he, nor his servants, nor the people of the land, did hearken unto the words of the LORD, which he spake [c]by the prophet Jeremiah.

3 And Zedekiah the king sent Jehucal the

[a]2 Kings xxiv. 17; 2 Chron. xxxvi. 10; chap. xxii. 24

[b]2 Chron. xxxvi. 12, 14——[c]Heb. *by the hand of the prophet*

NOTES ON CHAP. XXXVII

Verse 1. *And king Zedekiah the son of Josiah*] Of the siege and taking of Jerusalem referred to here, and the making of Zedekiah king instead of Jeconiah, see 2 Kings xxiv. 1, &c., and the notes there.

Verse 3. *Zedekiah—to the prophet Jeremiah*]

A. M. cir. 3414
B. C. cir. 590
Ol. XLVII. 3
TarquiniiPrisci, R. Roman., cir. annum 27

son of Shelemiah and [d]Zephaniah the son of Maaseiah the priest to the prophet Jeremiah, saying, Pray now unto the LORD our God for us.

4 Now Jeremiah came in and went out among the people: for they had not put him into prison.

5 Then [e]Pharaoh's army was come forth out of Egypt: [f]and when the Chaldeans that besieged Jerusalem heard tidings of them, they departed from Jerusalem.

6 Then came the word of the LORD unto the prophet Jeremiah, saying,

7 Thus saith the LORD, the God of Israel; Thus shall ye say to the king of Judah, [g]that sent you unto me to inquire of me; Behold, Pharaoh's army, which is come forth to help you, shall return to Egypt into their own land.

8 [h]And the Chaldeans shall come again, and fight against this city, and take it, and burn it with fire.

9 Thus saith the LORD; Deceive not [i]yourselves, saying, The Chaldeans shall surely depart from us: for they shall not depart.

10 [k]For though ye had smitten the whole army of the Chaldeans that fight against you, and there remained *but* [l]wounded men among them, *yet* should they rise up every man in his tent, and burn this city with fire.

A. M. cir. 3414
B. C. cir. 590
Ol. XLVII. 3
TarquiniiPrisci, R. Roman. cir. annum 27

11 [m]And it came to pass, that when the army of the Chaldeans was [n]broken up from Jerusalem for fear of Pharaoh's army,

12 Then Jeremiah went forth out of Jerusalem to go into the land of Benjamin, [o]to separate himself thence in the midst of the people.

13 And when he was in the gate of Benjamin, a captain of the ward *was* there, whose name *was* Irijah, the son of Shelemiah, the son of Hananiah; and he took Jeremiah the prophet, saying, Thou fallest away to the Chaldeans.

14 Then said Jeremiah, *It is* [p]false; I fall not away to the Chaldeans. But he hearkened not to him: so Irijah took Jeremiah, and brought him to the princes.

15 Wherefore the princes were wroth with Jeremiah, and smote him, [q]and put him in prison in the house of Jonathan the scribe: for they had made that the prison.

---

[d]Ch. xxi. 1, 2; xxix. 25; lii. 24——[e]See 2 Kings xxiv.; Ezek. xvii. 15——[f]Ver. 11; ch. xxxiv. 21——[g]Ch. xxi. 2——[h]Chap. xxxiv. 22——[i]Heb. *souls*——[k]Chap. xxi. 4, 5

[l]Heb. *thrust through*——[m]Ver. 5——[n]Heb. *made to ascend*——[o]Or, *to slip away from thence in the midst of the people*——[p]Heb. *falsehood*, or *a lie*——[q]Chap. xxxviii. 26

He was willing to hear a message from the Lord, provided it were according to his own mind. He did not fully trust in his own prophets.

Verse 4. *Now Jeremiah came in and went out*] After the siege was raised, he had a measure of liberty; he was not *closely confined*, as he afterwards was. See ver. 16.

Verse 5. *Then Pharaoh's army*] This was *Pharaoh-hophra* or *Apries*, who then reigned in Egypt in place of his father *Necho*. See Ezek. xxix. 6, &c. Nebuchadnezzar, hearing that the Egyptian army, on which the Jews so much depended, was on their march to relieve the city, suddenly raised the siege, and went to meet them. In the interim Zedekiah sent to Jeremiah to inquire of the Lord to know whether they might consider themselves in safety.

Verse 7. *Pharaoh's army—shall return to Egypt*] They were defeated by the Chaldeans; and, not being hearty in the cause, returned immediately to Egypt, leaving Nebuchadnezzar unmolested to recommence the siege.

Verse 10. *For though ye had smitten the whole army*] Strong words; but they show how fully God was determined to give up this city to fire and sword, and how fully he had instructed his prophet on this point.

Verse 12. *Jeremiah went forth*] At the time that Nebuchadnezzar had raised the siege, and gone to meet the Egyptian army.

Go into the land of Benjamin] To *Anathoth*, his native city.

To separate himself thence] "To receive a portion thereof among the people;"—*Blayney:* who supposes that Jeremiah went to receive a portion of the proceeds of his patrimony at *Anathoth*, which had, previously to the siege, been in the hands of the Chaldeans. The siege being now raised, he thought of looking thus after his own affairs. The *Chaldee* is to the same sense. "He went that he might divide the inheritance which he had there among the people."

Dahler translates, "He went to withdraw himself from *the siege*, as many others *of the inhabitants*." I believe he went to withdraw himself from a city devoted to destruction, and in which he could no longer do any good.

Verse 13. *Thou fallest away to the Chaldeans.*] Thou art a deserter, and a traitor to thy country. As he had always declared that the Chaldeans should take the city, &c., his enemies took occasion from this to say he was in the interest of the Chaldeans, and that he wished now to go to them, and betray the place.

Verse 15. *And smote him*] Without any *proof* of the alleged treachery, without any form of *justice*.

In prison in the house of Jonathan] In Asiatic countries there is an apartment in the houses of the officers of the law, to confine all

A. M. cir. 3415
B. C. cir. 589
Ol. XLVII. 4
TarquiniiPrisci,
R. Roman.,
cir. annum 28

16 When Jeremiah was entered
into [r]the dungeon, and into the
[s]cabins, and Jeremiah had remained there many days;
17 Then Zedekiah the king sent, and took
him out: and the king asked him secretly in
his house, and said, Is there *any* word from
the LORD? And Jeremiah said, There is:
for, said he, thou shalt be delivered into the
hand of the king of Babylon.
18 Moreover Jeremiah said unto king Zedekiah, What have I offended against thee, or
against thy servants, or against this people,
that ye have put me in prison?
19 Where *are* now your prophets which
prophesied unto you, saying, The
king of Babylon shall not come
against you, nor against this land?
20 Therefore hear now, I pray
thee, O my lord the king: [t]let my supplication, I pray thee, be accepted before thee;
that thou cause me not to return to the house
of Jonathan the scribe, lest I die there.
21 Then Zedekiah the king commanded that
they should commit Jeremiah [u]into the court
of the prison, and that they should give him
daily a piece of bread out of the bakers' street,
[v]until all the bread in the city were spent.
Thus Jeremiah remained in the court of the
prison.

[r]Gen. xl. 15; xli. 14; Exod. xii. 29; chap. xxxviii. 6 —— [s]Or, *cells*

[t]Heb. *let my supplication fall* —— [u]Chap. xxxii. 2; xxxviii. 13, 28 —— [v]Chap. xxxviii. 9; lii. 6

the accused that are brought before them. Jonathan was a *scribe* or *secretary*, and had a prison of this kind in his house.

Verse 16. *Entered into the dungeon, and into the cabins*] The dungeon was probably a deep pit; and the cabins or *cells*, niches in the sides, where different malefactors were confined. See *Blayney*.

Verse 17. *Is there* any *word from the Lord?*] Is there any farther revelation?

There is:—thou shalt be delivered] What bold faithfulness! And to a king, in whose hands his life now lay.

Verse 19. *Where* are *now your prophets*] *They* told you that the Chaldeans should *not* come; I told you they *would*. According to my word the Chaldeans *are come*, and are departed only for a short time.

Verse 20. *Cause me not to return to the house of Jonathan*] He had been ill used in this man's custody, so as to endanger his life, the place being cold, and probably unhealthy.

Verse 21. *Then Zedekiah—the court of the prison*] Was contiguous to the king's house, where the prisoners could readily see their friends.

Give him daily a piece of bread out of the bakers' street] From the public stores; which he received till all the provisions were spent.

CHAPTER XXXVIII

The princes of Judah, taking offence at Jeremiah on account of his predicting the destruction of Jerusalem and the temple by the Chaldeans, cause him to be cast into a deep and miry dungeon, 1–6. *Ebed-melech, an Ethiopian, gets the king's permission to take him out,* 7–13. *Jeremiah advises the king, who consulted him privately, to surrender to the Chaldeans,* 14–23. *The king promises the prophet that he will not put him to death, and requires him not to reveal what had passed to the princes; to whom he accordingly gives an evasive answer, telling them only so much of the conference as related to his request for his life,* 24–28.

A. M. cir. 3415
B. C. cir. 589
Ol. XLVII. 4
TarquiniiPrisci,
R. Roman.,
cir. annum 28

THEN Shephatiah the son of
Mattan, and Gedaliah the
son of Pashur, and [a]Jucal the
son of Shelemiah, and [b]Pashur
the son of Malchiah, [c]heard the words that
Jeremiah had spoken unto all the people,
saying,
2 Thus saith the LORD, [d]He
that remaineth in this city shall
die by the sword, by the famine,
and by the pestilence: but he that
goeth forth to the Chaldeans shall live; for
he shall have his life for a prey, and shall live.
3 Thus saith the LORD, [e]This city shall

[a]Chap. xxxvii. 3 —— [b]Chap. xxi. 1 —— [c]Chap. xxi. 8 —— [d]Chap. xxi. 9 —— [e]Chap. xxi. 10; xxxii. 3

NOTES ON CHAP. XXXVIII

Verse 1. *Then Shephatiah*] This was the *faction*—what *Dahler* terms the *Antitheocratic faction*—who were enemies to Jeremiah, and sought his life.

Verse 3. *This city shall surely be given*] This was a testimony that he constantly bore: he

A. M. cir. 3415
B. C. cir. 589
Ol. XLVII. 4
TarquiniiPrisci,
R. Roman.,
cir. annum 28

surely be given into the hand of the king of Babylon's army, which shall take it.

4 Therefore the princes said unto the king, We beseech thee, [f]let this man be put to death: for thus he weakeneth the hands of the men of war that remain in this city, and the hands of all the people, in speaking such words unto them: for this man seeketh not the [g]welfare of this people, but the hurt.

5 Then Zedekiah the king said, Behold, he *is* in your hand: for the king *is* not *he that* can do *any* thing against you.

6 [h]Then took they Jeremiah, and cast him into the dungeon of Malchiah the son [i]of Hammelech, that *was* in the court of the prison: and they let down Jeremiah with cords. And in the dungeon *there was* no water, but mire: so Jeremiah sunk in the mire.

7 [k]Now when Ebed-melech the Ethiopian, one of the eunuchs which was in the king's house, heard that they had put Jeremiah in the dungeon (the king then sitting in the gate of Benjamin;)

8 Ebed-melech went forth out of the king's house, and spake to the king, saying,

9 My lord the king, these men have done evil in all that they have done to Jeremiah the prophet, whom they have cast into the dungeon; and [l]he is like to die for hunger in the place where he is: for *there is* no more bread in the city.

A. M. cir. 3415
B. C. cir. 589
Ol. XLVII. 4
TarquiniiPrisci,
R. Roman.,
cir. annum 28

10 Then the king commanded Ebed-melech the Ethiopian, saying, Take from hence thirty men [m]with thee, and take up Jeremiah the prophet out of the dungeon, before he die.

11 So Ebed-melech took the men with him, and went into the house of the king under the treasury, and took thence old cast clouts and old rotten rags, and let them down by cords into the dungeon to Jeremiah.

12 And Ebed-melech the Ethiopian said unto Jeremiah, Put now *these* old cast clouts and rotten rags under thine armholes under the cords. And Jeremiah did so.

13 [n]So they drew up Jeremiah with cords, and took him up out of the dungeon: and Jeremiah remained [o]in the court of the prison.

14 Then Zedekiah the king sent, and took Jeremiah the prophet unto him into the [p]third entry that *is* in the house of the LORD: and the king said unto Jeremiah, I will ask thee a thing; hide nothing from me.

15 Then Jeremiah said unto Zedekiah, If I declare *it* unto thee, wilt thou not surely put me to death? and if I give thee counsel, wilt thou not hearken unto me?

[f]See chap. xxvi. 11——[g]Heb. *peace*——[h]Chap. xxxvii. 21——[i]Or, *of the king*

[k]Chap. xxxix. 16——[l]Heb. *he will die*——[m]Heb. *in thine hand*——[n]Ver. 6——[o]Ch. xxxvii. 21——[p]Or, *principal*

had the authority of God for it. He knew it was true, and he never wavered nor equivocated.

Verse 4. *Let this man be put to death*] And they gave their reasons plain enough: but the *proof* was wanting.

Verse 5. *He* is *in your hand*] Ye have power to do as you please; I must act by your counsel. Poor weak prince! you respect the prophet, you fear the cabal, and you sacrifice an innocent man to your own weakness and their malice!

Verse 6. *So Jeremiah sunk in the mire.*] Their obvious design was, that he might be stifled in that place.

Verse 7. *Ebed-melech*] *The servant of the king*, one of the eunuchs who belonged to the palace. Perhaps it should be read, "Now, a servant of the king, a Cushite, one of the eunuchs," &c.

The king then sitting in the gate of Benjamin] To give audience, and to administer justice. We have often seen that the *gates* of cities were the places of public judicature.

Verse 9. *My lord the king, these men have done evil*] He must have been much in the king's confidence, and a humane and noble spirited man, thus to have raised his voice against the powerful cabal already mentioned.

There is *no more bread in the city.*] They had defended it to the last extremity; and it appears that bread had been afforded to the prophet according to the king's commandment, as long as there was any remaining. See chap. xxxvi. 21.

Verse 10. *Take from hence thirty men*] The king was determined that he should be rescued by force, if the princes opposed.

Verse 11. *Went into the house of the king—and took thence*] The eastern kings had their wardrobes always well furnished; as garments were a usual present to ambassadors, &c. I cannot think that, in the proper acceptation of the words, these were in any part of the king's house.

Old cast clouts, and old rotten rags] The fact seems to be this: there were several garments that had been *used*, and would not be used again; and there were others which, through continuing long there, had by *insects*, &c., been rendered *useless*. These he took, tied to the cord, let down to the prophet, that he might roll them round the ropes, and place them under his arm-pits, so that in being hauled up he might not suffer injury from the ropes, which in this case must sustain the whole weight of his body.

Verse 14. *Into the third entry*] A place

A. M. cir. 3415
B. C. cir. 589
Ol. XLVII. 4
TarquiniiPrisci,
R. Roman.,
cir. annum 28

16 So Zedekiah the king sware
secretly unto Jeremiah, saying,
As the LORD liveth, [q]that made
us this soul, I will not put thee
to death, neither will I give thee into the hand
of these men that seek thy life.
17 Then said Jeremiah unto Zedekiah, Thus
saith the LORD, the God of hosts, the God of
Israel; If thou wilt assuredly [r]go forth [s]unto
the king of Babylon's princes, then thy soul
shall live, and this city shall not be burned
with fire; and thou shalt live, and thine
house:
18 But if thou wilt not go forth to the king
of Babylon's princes, then shall this city be
given into the hand of the Chaldeans, and they
shall burn it with fire, and [t]thou shalt not
escape out of their hand.
19 And Zedekiah the king said unto Jeremiah, I am afraid of the Jews that are fallen
to the Chaldeans, lest they deliver me into
their hand, and they [u]mock me.
20 But Jeremiah said, They shall not deliver
thee. Obey, I beseech thee, the voice of the
LORD, which I speak unto thee: so it shall be
well unto thee, and thy soul shall live.
21 But if thou refuse to go forth, this *is* the
word that the LORD hath showed me:
22 And, behold, all the women that are left
in the king of Judah's house *shall be* brought
forth to the king of Babylon's princes, and
those *women* shall say, [v]Thy friends have set
thee on, and have prevailed against thee: thy
feet are sunk in the mire, *and*
they are turned away back.
23 So they shall bring out
all thy wives and [w]thy children
to the Chaldeans: and [x]thou shalt not
escape out of their hand, but shalt be taken
by the hand of the king of Babylon: and
[y]thou shalt cause this city to be burned
with fire.
24 Then said Zedekiah unto Jeremiah, Let
no man know of these words, and thou shalt
not die.
25 But if the princes hear that I have talked
with thee, and they come unto thee, and say
unto thee, Declare unto us now what thou hast
said unto the king, hide it not from us, and we
will not put thee to death; and also what the
king said unto thee:
26 Then thou shalt say unto them, [z]I presented my supplication before the king, that
he would not cause me to return [a]to Jonathan's house, to die there.
27 Then came all the princes unto Jeremiah, and asked him: and he told them
according to all these words that the king
had commanded. So [b]they left off speaking
with him; for the matter was not perceived.

A. M. 3415
—3416
B. C. 589
—588
Ol. XLVII. 4
—XLVIII. 1

28 So [c]Jeremiah abode in the
court of the prison until the day
that Jerusalem was taken: and
he was *there* when Jerusalem
was taken.

[q]Isa. lvii. 16——[r]2 Kings xxiv. 12——[s]Chap. xxxix. 3——[t]Chap. xxxii. 4; xxxiv. 3; ver. 23——[u]1 Sam. xxxi. 4——[v]Heb. *Men of thy peace*——[w]Chap. xxxix. 6; xli. 10——[x]Ver. 18——[y]Heb. *thou shalt burn,* &c. [z]Chap. xxxvii. 28——[a]Chap. xxxvii. 15——[b]Heb. *they were silent from him*——[c]Ch. xxxvii. 21; xxxix. 14

to enter which *two* others must be passed through.

Verse 16. *As the Lord liveth, that made us this soul*] He is the *living* God, and he is the Author of that *life* which each of us possesses; and as sure as he *lives*, and we *live* by him, I will not put thee to *death*, nor give thee into the hands of those men who seek thy *life*. A very solemn oath; and the first instance on record of the profane custom of swearing *by the soul.*

Verse 17. *Wilt assuredly go*] On the king's obedience to the advice of the prophet the safety of the city depended.

Unto the king of Babylon's princes] The generals of the army then returning to the siege from the defeat of the Egyptians; for Nebuchadnezzar himself was then at Riblah, in Syria, chap. xxxix. 5, 6.

Verse 19. *They mock me.*] Insult me, and exhibit me in triumph.

Verse 22. *All the women—brought forth*] I think this place speaks of a kind of defection among the women of the harem; many of whom had already *gone forth* privately to the principal officers of the Chaldean army, and made the report mentioned in the end of this verse. These were the *concubines* or women of the second rank.

Verse 23. *They shall bring out all thy wives and thy children*] These were the women of the *first rank*, by whom the king had children. These had no temptation to go out to the Chaldeans, nor would they have been made welcome; but the others being young, and without children, would be well received by the Chaldean princes.

Verse 26. *I presented my supplication*] This was telling the *truth*, and *nothing* but the truth, but not the *whole* truth. The king did not wish him to defile his conscience, nor did he propose any thing that was not consistent with the truth.

Verse 27. *The matter was not perceived.*]

They did not question him farther; and the king's commandment to remove him from the house of Jonathan being well known, they took for granted that they had all the information that they sought. And he was most certainly not obliged to relate any thing that might embroil this weak king with his factious but powerful princes, or affect his own life. He related simply what was necessary, and no more.

CHAPTER XXXIX

This chapter gives an account of the siege and taking of Jerusalem; the flight, capture, and punishment of Zedekiah; the burning of the city; and the carrying away of the people, (a few of the meanest excepted,) to Babylon, 1–10; *also of the release of Jeremiah, and the special orders of Nebuchadnezzar concerning him,* 11–14. *The remaining verses relate to the subject of the preceding chapter; and contain promises of personal safety to Ebed-melech the Ethiopian amidst the public calamities, on account of his piety, and his humanity to the prophet,* 15–18.

A. M. 3414 B. C. 590 Ol. XLVII. 3 Anno TarquiniiPrisci, R. Roman., 27

IN the [a]ninth year of Zedekiah
king of Judah, in the tenth
month, came Nebuchadrezzar
king of Babylon and all his army
against Jerusalem, and they besieged it.

A. M. 3416 B. C. 588 Ol. XLVIII. 1 Anno TarquiniiPrisci, R. Roman., 29

2 *And* in the eleventh year of
Zedekiah, in the fourth month,
the ninth *day* of the month, the
city was broken up.
3 [b]And all the princes of the king of Babylon came in, and sat in the middle gate, *even*
Nergal-sharezer, Samgar-nebo, Sarsechim,
Rab-saris, Nergal-sharezer, Rab-mag, with all
the residue of the princes of the king of Babylon.

A. M. 3416 B. C. 588 Ol. XLVIII. 1 Anno TarquiniiPrisci, R. Roman., 29

4 [c]And it came to pass, *that*
when Zedekiah the king of Judah
saw them, and all the men of war,
then they fled, and went forth
out of the city by night, by the way of the
king's garden, by the gate betwixt the two
walls: and he went out the way of the plain.
5 But the Chaldeans' army pursued after
them, and [d]overtook Zedekiah in the plains of
Jericho: and when they had taken him, they
brought him up to Nebuchadnezzar king of
Babylon to [e]Riblah in the land of Hamath,
where he [f]gave judgment upon him.
6 Then the king of Babylon slew the sons
of Zedekiah in Riblah before his eyes: also the

---

[a]2 Kings xv. 1–4; chap. lii. 4–7——[b]Chap. xxxviii. 17——[c]2 Kings xxv. 4, &c.; chap. lii. 7, &c.

[d]Chap. xxxii. 4; xxxviii. 18, 23——[e]2 Kings xxiii. 33——[f]Heb. *spake with him judgments;* chap. iv. 12

NOTES ON CHAP. XXXIX

Verse 1 *In the ninth year of Zedekiah—in the tenth month*] This month is called *Tebeth* in Esther ii. 16. It began with the first new moon of our *January*, and it was on the tenth day of this month that Nebuchadnezzar invested the city.

Verse 2. *The eleventh year—in the fourth month*] This month in the Hebrew calendar is called *Thammuz*, and commences with the first new moon of our *July*. The siege had lasted just *eighteen* months.

The city was broken up.] A breach was made in the wall by which the Chaldeans entered.

Verse 3. *Sat in the middle gate*] The city of Jerusalem stood upon *two* hills, *Sion* to the south, and *Acra* to the north, with a deep valley between them. The *gate of the centre*, as the term seems plainly to import, was a gate of communication in the middle of the valley, between the *two* parts of the city, sometimes called the *higher* and the *lower* city. The Chaldeans entered the city on the *north* side by a breach in the walls, and rushing forward and posting themselves in this gate, in the very heart or centre of the city, became thereby masters at will of the whole. Zedekiah with his troop, perceiving this, fled out of the opposite gate on the *south* side. See *Blayney*. This is likely; but we know nothing positively on this subject.

Nergal-sharezer] These were the principal commanders; but Dr. *Blayney* thinks that instead of *six* persons, we have in reality but *three*, as the name that follows each is a *title* of office. Thus, *Nergal-sharezer*, who was *Samgar; Nebusarsechim*, who was *Rab-saris;* and *Nergal-sharezer*, who was *Rab-mag*. As *Nergal-sharezer* occurs *twice* here, and we know that *Nebuzaradan* was general-in-chief, the first Nergal-sharezer is probably a mistake for Nebuzar-adan, or some other of the commanders. But these things are as uncertain as they are unimportant.

Verse 4. *Went forth out of the city by night*] Probably there was a *private passage under ground*, leading without the walls, by which Zedekiah and his followers might escape unperceived, till they had got some way from the city.

The way of the plain.] There were two roads from Jerusalem to Jericho. One passed over the mount of Olives; but, as this might have retarded his flight, he chose *the way of the plain*, and was overtaken near Jericho, perhaps about sixteen or eighteen miles from Jerusalem. He had probably intended to have passed the Jordan, in order to escape to Egypt, as the Egyptians were then his professed allies.

Verse 5. *To Riblah*] This city was situated on the northern frontier of Palestine, and Hamath was a large city belonging also to Syria. See Gen. x. 18.

A. M. 3416
B. C. 588
Ol. XLVIII. 1
Anno
TarquiniiPrisci,
R. Roman., 29

king of Babylon slew all the nobles of Judah.

7 Moreover [g]he put out Zedekiah's eyes, and bound him [h]with chains, to carry him to Babylon.

8 [i]And the Chaldeans burnt the king's house, and the houses of the people, with fire, and brake down the walls of Jerusalem.

9 [k]Then Nebuzar-adan the [l]captain [m]of the guard carried away captive into Babylon the remnant of the people that remained in the city, and those that fell away, that fell to him, with the rest of the people that remained.

10 But Nebuzar-adan the captain of the guard left of the poor of the people, which had nothing, in the land of Judah, and gave them vineyards and fields [n]at the same time.

11 Now Nebuchadrezzar king of Babylon gave charge concerning Jeremiah [o]to Nebuzaradan the captain of the guard, saying,

12 Take him, and [p]look well to him, and do him no harm; but do unto him even as he shall say unto thee.

13 So Nebuzar-adan the captain of the guard sent, and Nebushasban, Rab-saris, and Nergal-sharezer Rab-mag, and all the king of Babylon's princes;

A. M. 3416
B. C. 588
Ol. XLVIII. 1
Anno
TarquiniiPrisci,
R. Roman., 29

14 Even they sent, [q]and took Jeremiah out of the court of the prison, and committed him [r]unto Gedaliah the son of [s]Ahikam the son of Shaphan, that he should carry him home: so he dwelt among the people.

15 Now the word of the LORD came unto Jeremiah, while he was shut up in the court of the prison, saying,

16 Go and speak to [t]Ebed-melech the Ethiopian, saying, Thus saith the LORD of hosts, the God of Israel; Behold [u]I will bring my words upon this city for evil, and not for good; and they shall be *accomplished* in that day before thee.

17 But I will deliver thee in that day, saith the LORD: and thou shalt not be given into the hand of the men of whom thou *art* afraid.

18 For I will surely deliver thee, and thou shalt not fall by the sword, but [v]thy life shall be for a prey unto thee: [w]because thou hast put thy trust in me, saith the LORD.

---

[g]Ezek. xii. 13, compared with chap. xxxii. 4——[h]Heb. *with two brazen chains* or *fetters*——[i]2 Kings xxv. 9; chap. xxxviii. 18; lii. 13——[k]2 Kings xxv. 11, &c.; chap. lii. 15, &c.——[l]Or, *chief marshal*——[m]Heb. *chief of the executioners*, or *slaughtermen;* and so ver. 10, 11, &c.; see Gen. xxxvii. 26

[n]Hebrew, *in that day*——[o]Hebrew, *by the hand of*——[p]Hebrew, *set thine eyes upon him*——[q]Chapter xxxviii. 28——[r]Chapter xl. 5——[s]Chapter xxvi. 24——[t]Chapter xxxviii. 7, 12——[u]Daniel ix. 12 [v]Chapter xxi. 9; xlv. 5——[w]1 Chron. v. 20; Psalm xxxvii. 40

Verse 7. ***Bound him with chains*****] Margin: "Two brazen chains;" one for his hands, and the other for his feet.**

Verse 9. ***Those that fell away*****] That deserted to the Chaldeans during the siege.**

Verse 10. ***Left of the poor of the people*****] The very refuse of the inhabitants, who were not worthy of being carried away; and among them he divided the fields and vineyards of those whom he took away.**

Verse 12. ***Take him—look well to him*****] Nebuchadnezzar had heard that this prophet had foretold his capture of the city, and had frequently used all his influence to induce Zedekiah to pay the tribute, and not rebel against him; and on this account would be inclined to show the prophet especial favour.**

Verse 16. ***Go and speak to Ebed-melech*****] The king's servant, the Cushite.**

Verse 18. ***I will surely deliver thee*****] Thou hast feared the Lord, and not the king, nor his princes, and thou hast taken the part of the prophet, and become his intercessor. Thou shalt not be slain. Thou hast put thy trust in me; thou shalt therefore be safe whithersoever thou goest. They that fear God need fear nothing besides.**

CHAPTER XL

This and the four following chapters contain a distinct account of what passed in the land of Judah from the taking of Jerusalem to the retreat of the remnant of the people to Egypt; together with the prophecies of Jeremiah concerning that place, whither he himself accompanied them. In this chapter we have an account of the enlargement of Jeremiah by Nebuzar-adan, the captain of the guard, who advises him to put himself under the jurisdiction of Gedaliah, the son of Ahikam, whom the king of Babylon had made governor over the land of Judea, 1–5. The prophet and many of the dispersed Jews repair to Gedaliah, 6–12. Johanan acquaints the governor of a conspiracy against him, but is not believed, 13–16.

A. M. 3416
B. C. 588
Ol. XLVIII. 1
Anno
TarquiniiPrisci,
R. Roman., 29

THE word that came to Jeremiah from the LORD, [a]after that Nebuzar-adan the captain of the guard had let him go from Ramah, when he had taken him being bound in [b]chains among all that were carried away captive of Jerusalem and Judah, which were carried away captive unto Babylon.

2 And the captain of the guard took Jeremiah, and [c]said unto him, The LORD thy God hath pronounced this evil upon this place.

3 Now the LORD hath brought *it,* and done according as he hath said: [d]because ye have sinned against the LORD, and have not obeyed his voice, therefore this thing is come upon you.

4 And now, behold, I loose thee this day from the chains which [e]*were* upon thine hand. [f]If it seem good unto thee to come with me into Babylon, come; and [g]I will look well unto thee: but if it seem ill unto thee to come with me into Babylon, forbear: behold, [h]all the land *is* before thee: whither it seemeth good and convenient for thee to go, thither go.

5 Now while he was not yet gone back, *he said,* Go back also to Gedaliah the son of Ahikam the son of Shaphan, [i]whom the king of Babylon hath made governor over the cities of Judah, and dwell with him among the people: or go wheresoever it seemeth convenient unto thee to go. So the captain of the guard gave him victuals and a reward, and let him go.

6 [k]Then went Jeremiah unto Gedaliah the son of Ahikam to [l]Mizpah, and dwelt with him among the people that were left in the land.

A. M. 3416
B. C. 588
Ol. XLVIII. 1
Anno
TarquiniiPrisci,
R. Roman., 29

7 [m]Now when all the captains of the forces which *were* in the fields, *even* they and their men, heard that the king of Babylon had made Gedaliah the son of Ahikam governor in the land, and had committed unto him men, and women, and children, and of [n]the poor of the land, of them that were not carried away captive to Babylon;

8 Then they came to Gedaliah to Mizpah, [o]even Ishmael the son of Nethaniah, and Johanan and Jonathan the sons of Kareah, and Seraiah the son of Tanhumeth, and the sons of Ephai the Netophathite, and Jezaniah the son of a Maachathite, they and their men.

9 And Gedaliah the son of Ahikam the son of Shaphan sware unto them and to their men, saying, Fear not to serve the Chaldeans: dwell in the land, and serve the king of Babylon, and it shall be well with you.

10 As for me, behold, I will dwell at Mizpah, [p]to serve the Chaldeans, which will come unto us: but ye, gather ye wine, and summer fruits, and oil, and put *them* in your vessels, and dwell in your cities that ye have taken.

11 Likewise when all the Jews that *were* in Moab, and among the Ammonites, and in Edom, and that *were* in all the countries, heard that the king of Babylon had left a

[a]Chap. xxxix. 14——[b]Or, *manacles*——[c]Chap. l. 7——[d]Deut. xxix. 24, 25; Dan. ix. 11——[e]Or, are *upon thine hand*——[f]Chap. xxxix. 12——[g]Heb. *I will set mine eye upon thee*

[h]Gen. xx. 15——[i]2 Kings xxv. 22, &c.——[k]Chap. xxxix. 14——[l]Judg. xx. 1——[m]2 Kings xxv. 23, &c.——[n]Chap. xxxix. 10——[o]Chap. xli. 1——[p]Heb. *to stand before;* Deut. i. 38

NOTES ON CHAP. XL.

Verse 1. *The word that came to Jeremiah*] This and the four following chapters contain a particular account of what passed in the land of Judea from the taking of the city to the retreat of the people into Egypt, and the prophecies of Jeremiah concerning them there.

Had let him go from Ramah] This has embarrassed most of the commentators. Dr. *Blayney* has thrown much light upon it by his translation and note:—

"The word that came to Jeremiah from Jehovah, after that Nebu-Zaradan captain of the guards had taken him, and let him go from Ramah: for he had been bound with chains among all the captives of Jerusalem and Judah, who were carried away captive to Babylon."

"HAD TAKEN HIM, AND LET HIM GO.—Most interpreters have understood בקחתו אתו *bekachto otho* of Nebuchadnezzar's having first taken Jeremiah as a captive unto Ramah. But if the order of the sentence be well observed, as well as the more common use of the verb לקח *lakach,* it will, I think, rather appear that those words relate to his *taking* or having him brought to him, in order to give him his discharge."

Verse 2. *The Lord thy God hath pronounced*] I know that thou art a true prophet, for what thou hast predicted from thy God is come to pass.

Verse 4. *Come; and I will look well unto thee*] Thou art now at full liberty to do as thou pleasest; either to come to Babylon or to stay in thy own land.

Verse 5. *Go back also to Gedaliah*] If thou wilt stay in thy own land, thou hadst best put thyself under the protection of thy countryman Gedaliah, whom the King of Babylon has made governor of the land.

Verse 8. *Ishmael the son of Nethaniah*] This is he who afterwards murdered Gedaliah. He had

A. M. 3416
B. C. 588
Ol. XLVIII. 1
Anno
TarquiniiPrisci,
R. Roman., 29

remnant of Judah, and that he had set over them Gedaliah the son of Ahikam the son of Shaphan;

12 Even all the Jews returned out of all places whither they were driven, and came to the land of Judah, to Gedaliah, unto Mizpah, and gathered wine and summer fruits very much.

13 Moreover Johanan the son of Kareah, and all the captains of the forces that *were* in the fields, came to Gedaliah to Mizpah,

14 And said unto him, Dost thou certainly know that [q]Baalis the king of the Ammonites hath sent Ishmael the son of Nethaniah [r]to slay thee? But Gedaliah the son of Ahikam believed them not.

15 Then Johanan the son of Kareah spake to Gedaliah in Mizpah secretly, saying, Let me go, I pray thee, and I will slay Ishmael the son of Nethaniah, and no man shall know *it:* wherefore should he slay thee, that all the Jews which are gathered unto thee should be scattered, and the remnant in Judah perish?

16 But Gedaliah the son of Ahikam said unto Johanan the son of Kareah, Thou shalt not do this thing: for thou speakest falsely of Ishmael.

[q]See chap. xli. 10 — [r]Heb. *to strike thee in soul?*

been employed to do this by Baalis, king of the Ammonites, with whom he appears to have taken refuge during the siege. See ver. 14.

Verse 14. *But Gedaliah the son of Ahikam believed them not.*] The account given of this man proves him to have been a person of uncommon greatness of soul. Conscious of his own integrity and benevolence, he took the portrait of others from his own mind; and therefore believed evil of no man, because he felt none towards any in his own breast. He may be reproached for being too credulous and confident: but any thing of this kind that may be justly charged against him serves only to show the greatness of his mind. A *little soul* is ever suspicious, and ready to believe the worst of every person and thing. A great mind acts always on the contrary.

Verse 16. *Thou shalt not do this thing*] He cannot be so base.

***Thou speakest falsely of Ishmael.*] He thought it quite possible that the man who was capable of becoming an *assassin* was capable of telling a *lie;* and therefore he would not credit what he said. Had he been a little more distrustful, he would have saved his own life. The next chapter shows that Johanan's information was too true. So noble Gedaliah lost his life by not believing that evil of others of which he himself was incapable.**

CHAPTER XLI

Ishmael executes his conspiracy against Gedaliah the governor and his companions, and attempts to carry away the Jews who were with him captives to the Ammonites, 1–10; *but Johanan recovers them, and purposes to flee into Egypt,* 11–18.

A. M. 3416
B. C. 588
Ol. XLVIII. 1
Anno
TarquiniiPrisci,
R. Roman., 29

NOW it came to pass in the seventh month, [a]*that* Ishmael the son of Nethaniah the son of Elishama, of the seed royal, and the princes of the king, even ten men with him, came unto Gedaliah the son of Ahikam to Mizpah; and there they did eat bread together in Mizpah.

2 Then arose Ishmael the son of Nethaniah, and the ten men that were with him, and [b]smote Gedaliah the son of Ahikam the son of Shaphan with the sword, and slew him, whom the king of Babylon had made governor over the land.

3 Ishmael also slew all the Jews that were with him, *even* with Gedaliah, at Mizpah, and the Chaldeans that were found there, *and* the men of war.

4 And it came to pass the second day after he had slain Gedaliah, and no man knew *it,*

5 That there came certain from Shechem, from Shiloh, and from Samaria, *even* fourscore men, [c]having their beards shaven, and their clothes rent, and having cut themselves,

[a]2 Kings xxv. 25; chap. xl. 6, 8——[b]2 Kings xxv. 25 — [c]Lev. xix. 27, 28; Deut. xiv. 1; Isa. xv. 2

NOTES ON CHAP XLI

Verse 1. *Now—in the seventh month*] Answering to the first new moon in our month of *October.*

There they did eat bread together*] This was the same as making a solemn covenant; for he who *ate bread* with another was ever reputed a *friend.

Verse 2. *Smote Gedaliah*] See the preceding chapter, ver. 14.

Verse 5. *Having their beards shaven*] All these were signs of deep mourning, probably on account of the destruction of the city.

A. M. 3416
B. C. 588
Ol. XLVIII. 1
Anno
TarquiniiPrisci,
R. Roman., 29

with offerings and incense in their hand, to bring *them* to [d]the house of the LORD.

6 And Ishmael the son of Nethaniah went forth from Mizpah to meet them, [e]weeping all along as he went: and it came to pass, as he met them, he said unto them, Come to Gedaliah the son of Ahikam.

7 And it was *so,* when they came into the midst of the city, that Ishmael the son of Nethaniah slew them, *and* [f]*cast them* into the midst of the pit, he, and the men that *were* with him.

8 But ten men were found among them that said unto Ishmael, Slay us not: for we have treasures in the field, of wheat, and of barley, and of oil, and of honey. So he forbare, and slew them not among their brethren.

9 Now the pit wherein Ishmael had cast all the dead bodies of the men, whom he had slain [g]because [h]of Gedaliah, *was* it [i]which Asa the king had made for fear of Baasha king of Israel: *and* Ishmael the son of Nethaniah filled it with *them that were* slain.

10 Then Ishmael carried away captive all the residue of the people that *were* in Mizpah, [k]*even* the king's daughters, and all the people that remained in Mizpah, [l]whom Nebuzar-adan the captain of the guard had committed to Gedaliah the son of Ahikam: and Ishmael the son of Nethaniah carried them away captive, and departed to go over to [m]the Ammonites.

11 But when Johanan the son of Kareah, and all [n]the captains of the forces that *were* with him, heard of all the evil that Ishmael the son of Nethaniah had done,

A. M. 3416
B. C. 588
Ol. XLVIII. 1
Anno
TarquiniiPrisci,
R. Roman., 29

12 Then they took all the men, and went to fight with Ishmael the son of Nethaniah, and found him by [o]the great waters that *are* in Gibeon.

13 Now it came to pass *that* when all the people which *were* with Ishmael saw Johanan the son of Kareah, and all the captains of the forces that *were* with him, then they were glad.

14 So all the people that Ishmael had carried away captive from Mizpah cast about and returned, and went unto Johanan the son of Kareah.

15 But Ishmael the son of Nethaniah escaped from Johanan with eight men, and went to the Ammonites.

16 Then took Johanan the son of Kareah, and all the captains of the forces that *were* with him, all the remnant of the people whom he had recovered from Ishmael the son of Nethaniah, from Mizpah, after *that* he had slain Gedaliah the son of Ahikam, *even* mighty men of war, and the women, and the children, and the eunuchs, whom he had brought again from Gibeon:

17 And they departed, and dwelt in the habitation of [p]Chimham, which is by Beth-lehem, to go to enter into Egypt,

18 Because of the Chaldeans: for they were afraid of them, because Ishmael the son of Nethaniah had slain Gedaliah the son of Ahikam, [q]whom the king of Babylon made governor in the land.

---

[d]See 2 Kings xxv. 9; 1 Sam. i. 7——[e]Heb. *in going and weeping*——[f]So 1 Mac. vii. 19——[g]Or, *near Gedaliah* [h]Heb. *by the hand,* or *by the side of Gedaliah*

[i]1 Kings xv. 22; 2 Chron. xvi. 6——[k]Chap. xliii. 6 [l]Chap. xl. 7——[m]Chap. xl. 14——[n]Chap. xl. 7, 8, 13 [o]2 Sam. ii. 13——[p]2 Sam. xix. 37, 38——[q]Chap. xl. 5

Verse 6. *Weeping all along as he went*] This felonious hypocrite pretended that he also was deeply afflicted, and wished to bear them company in their sorrow.

Come to Gedaliah] He will appoint you vineyards and fields.

Verse 7. *Slew them*] He kept the murder of Gedaliah secret, and no doubt had a band of his assassins lodged in Mizpah; and he decoyed these fourscore men thither that he might have strength to slay them. He kept *ten* alive because they told him they had treasures hidden in a field, which they would show him. Whether he kept his word with them is not recorded. He could do nothing good or great; and it is likely that, when he had possessed himself of those treasures, he served them as he had served their companions. *Grain* is preserved to the present day in subterranean pits, called *mattamores,* in different parts of the east.

Verse 9. *Now the pit—was it which Asa the king had made for fear of Baasha*] See 1 Kings xv. 22. Asa made this cistern as a reservoir for water for the supply of the place; for he built and fortified *Mizpah* at the time that he was at war with Baasha, king of Israel.

Verse 10. *Carried away captive*] He took all these that he might sell them for slaves among the Ammonites.

Verse 14. *Went unto Johanan*] They were weary of the tyranny of Ishmael, and were glad of an opportunity to abandon him.

Verse 16. *The women,—children, and the eunuchs*] These were all, most probably, persons who belonged to the palace and harem of Zedekiah: some of them his own concubines and their children.

Verse 17. *Dwelt in the habitation of Chimham*] The estate that David gave Chimham, the son of Barzillai. See 2 Sam. xix. 37, &c. He took this merely as a resting-place; as he designed to carry all into Egypt, fearing the *Chaldeans*, who would endeavour to revenge the death of Gedaliah.

CHAPTER XLII

Johanan and the remnant of the people desire Jeremiah to ask counsel of God what they should do, 1–3. *The prophet assures them of safety in Judea, but destruction in Egypt,* 4–18; *and reproves their hypocrisy in asking counsel with which they had no intention to comply,* 19–22.

A. M. 3416 B. C. 588 Ol. XLVIII. 1 Anno TarquiniiPrisci, R. Roman., 29

THEN all the captains of the
forces, [a]and Johanan the
son of Kareah, and Jezaniah the
son of Hoshaiah, and all the
people, from the least even unto the greatest,
came near,
2 And said unto Jeremiah the prophet, [b]Let,
we beseech thee, our supplication be accepted
before thee, and [c]pray for us unto the LORD
thy God, *even* for all this remnant; (for we
are left *but* [d]a few of many, as thine eyes do
behold us:)
3 That the LORD thy God may show us
[e]the way wherein we may walk, and the thing
that we may do.
4 Then Jeremiah the prophet said unto them,
I have heard *you;* behold, I will pray unto the
LORD your God according to your words; and
it shall come to pass, *that* [f]whatsoever thing
the LORD shall answer you, I will declare it unto you; I will [g]keep nothing back from you.
5 Then they said to Jeremiah, [h]The LORD
be a true and faithful Witness between us, if
we do not even according to all things for the
which the LORD thy God shall send thee to us.
6 Whether *it be* good, or whether *it be* evil,
we will obey the voice of the
LORD our God, to whom we send
thee; [i]that it may be well with
us, when we obey the voice of
the LORD our God.

A. M. 3416 B. C. 588 Ol. XLVIII. 1 Anno TarquiniiPrisci, R. Roman., 29

7 And it came to pass after ten days, that
the word of the LORD came unto Jeremiah.
8 Then called he Johanan the son of Kareah, and all the captains of the forces which
were with him, and all the people from the
least even to the greatest,
9 And said unto them, Thus saith the LORD,
the God of Israel, unto whom ye sent me to
present your supplication before him;
10 If ye will still abide in this land, then
[k]will I build you, and not pull *you* down;
and I will plant you, and not pluck *you* up:
for [l]I repent me of the evil that I have done
unto you.
11 Be not afraid of the king of Babylon,
of whom ye are afraid; be not afraid of him,
saith the LORD: [m]for I *am* with you to save
you, and to deliver you from his hand.
12 And [n]I will show mercies unto you, that
he may have mercy upon you, and cause you
to return to your own land.

---

[a]Chap. xl. 8, 13; xli. 11——[b]Or, *Let our supplication fall before thee*——[c]1 Sam. vii. 8; xii. 19; Isa. xxxvii. 4; James v. 16——[d]Lev. xxvi. 22——[e]Ezra viii. 21 [f]1 Kings xxii. 14

[g]1 Sam. iii. 18; Acts xx. 20——[h]Gen. xxxi. 50 [i]Deut. vi. 3; chap. vii. 23——[k]Chap. xxiv. 6; xxxi. 28; xxxiii. 7;——[l]Deut. xxxii. 36; chap. xviii. 8——[m]Isa. xliii. 5; Rom. viii. 31——[n]Psa. cvi. 45, 46

NOTES ON CHAP. XLII

Verse 1. *The captains of the forces*] The different leaders of the small bands or companies, collected from different parts of the land. The principal are those here named.

Verse 3. *That the Lord thy God may show us*] They all thought there was no safety in Jerusalem or in Judea, and therefore determined to leave the land: but they did not know which might be the safest direction to take; for though they inclined to Egypt, yet they wished to know the mind of God on that point.

Verse 5. *The Lord be a true and faithful Witness*] The Lord is such; and as ye have bound yourselves to obey his voice, he will register the covenant, and bless or curse according as ye shall conduct yourselves in this matter.

Verse 7. *After ten days*] All this time he was waiting upon God; for it is evident the prophets could not prophesy when they pleased, any more than the disciples of our Lord could work miracles when they wished. The gift of prophecy and the gift of miracles were both dependent on the will of the Most High, and each of them was given only for the moment; and when the necessity was over, the influence ceased.

Verse 10. *For I repent me of the evil*] The meaning is, As I have punished you only because you continued to be rebellious, I will arrest this punishment as soon as you become

A. M. 3416
B. C. 588
Ol. XLVIII. 1
Anno
TarquiniiPrisci,
R. Roman., 29

13 But if [o]ye say, We will not dwell in this land, neither obey the voice of the LORD your God,

14 Saying, No; but we will go into the land of Egypt, where we shall see no war, nor hear the sound of the trumpet, nor have hunger of bread; and there will we dwell:

15 And now therefore hear the word of the LORD, ye remnant of Judah, Thus saith the LORD of hosts, the God of Israel; If ye [p]wholly set [q]your faces to enter into Egypt, and go to sojourn there;

16 Then it shall come to pass, *that* the sword, [r]which ye feared, shall overtake you there in the land of Egypt, and the famine, whereof ye were afraid, [s]shall follow close after you there in Egypt; and there ye shall die.

17 [t]So shall it be with all the men that set their faces to go into Egypt to sojourn there; they shall die [u]by the sword, by the famine, and by the pestilence: and [v]none of them shall remain or escape from the evil that I will bring upon them.

18 For thus saith the LORD of hosts, the God of Israel; As mine anger and my fury hath been [w]poured forth upon the inhabitants of Jerusalem; so shall my fury be poured forth upon you, when ye shall enter into Egypt: and [x]ye shall be an execration, and an astonishment, and a curse, and a reproach; and ye shall see this place no more.

19 The LORD hath said concerning you, O ye remnant of Judah; [y]Go ye not into Egypt: know certainly that I have [z]admonished you this day.

20 For [a]ye dissembled in your hearts, when ye sent me unto the LORD your God, saying, [b]Pray for us unto the LORD our God: and according unto all that the LORD our God shall say, so declare unto us, and we will do *it*.

21 And *now* I have this day declared *it* to you; but ye have not obeyed the voice of the LORD your God, nor any *thing* for the which he hath sent me unto you.

22 Now therefore know certainly that [c]ye shall die by the sword, by the famine, and by the pestilence, in the place whither ye desire [d]to go *and* to sojourn.

[o]Ch. xliv. 16——[p]Deut. xvii. 16; ch. xliv. 12, 13, 14——[q]Luke ix. 51——[r]Ezek. xi. 8——[s]Heb. *shall cleave after you*——[t]Heb. *So shall all the men be*——[u]Chap. xxiv. 10; ver. 22——[v]See ch. xliv. 14, 28——[w]Ch. vii. 20——[x]Ch. xviii. 16; xxiv. 9; xxvi. 6; xxix. 18, 22; xliv. 12; Zech. viii. 13——[y]Deut. xvii. 16——[z]Heb. *testified against you*——[a]Or, *ye have used deceit against your souls*——[b]Ver. 2——[c]Ver. 17; Ezek. vi. 11——[d]Or, *to go to sojourn*

obedient to my word. You need not fear the king of Babylon if you have me for your helper; and I will so show mercy to you that he shall see it, and cease from afflicting you, as he shall see that I am on your side.

Verse 15. *If ye—set your faces to enter into Egypt, &c.*] Every evil that ye dreaded by staying in your own land shall come upon you in Egypt.

Verse 16. *The sword—and the famine—shall follow close after you*] Shall be at your heels; shall overtake and destroy you; *for there ye shall die.*

Verse 19. *Go ye not into Egypt*] Why? Because God knew, such was their miserable propensity to idolatry, that they would there adopt the worship of the country, and serve idols.

Verse 20. *For ye dissembled in your hearts*] What a most miserable and incorrigible people! Ingratitude, hypocrisy, rebellion, and cruelty seem to have been enthroned in their hearts! And what are they still? Just what their fathers were, except in the mere article of *idolatry;* and that they do not practise because they are indifferent to their own religion and to that of all others. Examine their devotions and their lives, and see whether Charity herself can say they believe in the God of Abraham!

Verse 21. *Ye have not obeyed the voice*] Though ye have requested to have this particular revelation of the Divine will, and promised obedience, yet have ye not done one thing for which ye sent me to inquire of the Lord.

Verse 22. *Now therefore know certainly*] As ye have determined to disobey, God has determined to punish. Ye may now follow the full bent of your wicked devices, and I will follow the requisitions of my justice. Ye shall die by the sword, by the pestilence, and by the famine, in the place whither ye desire to go to sojourn. Thus was their doom *sealed.*

With such dispositions and with such rebellion of heart, it is strange that they should put themselves to any trouble to inquire of the Lord relative to their future operations. They did not intend to obey; but as a matter of curiosity they would inquire to hear what the prophet might say; and if according to their own inclination, they would obey.

CHAPTER XLIII

The leading men, discrediting Jeremiah's prophecy, carry the people into Egypt, 1–7. Jeremiah, by a type, foretells the conquest of Egypt by Nebuchadnezzar, 8–13. This mode of conveying instruction by actions was very expressive, and frequently practised by the prophets. The image of Nebuchadnezzar arraying himself

with Egypt, as a shepherd puts on his garment, is very noble. Egypt at this time contended with Babylon for the empire of the east; yet this mighty kingdom, when God appoints the revolution, shifts its owner with as much ease as a shepherd removes his tent or garment, which the new proprietor has only to spread over him. **See ver. 12.**

A. M. 3416
B. C. 588
Ol. XLVIII. 1
Anno
TarquiniiPrisci,
R. Roman., 29

AND it came to pass, *that* when Jeremiah had made an end of speaking unto all the people all the words of the LORD their God, for which the LORD their God had sent him to them, *even* all these words,

2 [a]Then spake Azariah the son of Hoshaiah, and Johanan the son of Kareah, and all the proud men, saying unto Jeremiah, Thou speakest falsely: the LORD our God hath not sent thee to say, Go not into Egypt to sojourn there:

3 But Baruch the son of Neriah setteth thee on against us, for to deliver us into the hand of the Chaldeans, that they might put us to death, and carry us away captives into Babylon.

4 So Johanan the son of Kareah, and all the captains of the forces, and all the people, obeyed not the voice of the LORD, to dwell in the land of Judah.

5 But Johanan the son of Kareah, and all the captains of the forces, took [b]all the remnant of Judah, that were returned from all nations, whither they had been driven to dwell in the land of Judah;

6 *Even* men, and women, and children, [c]and the king's daughters, [d]and every person that Nebuzar-adan the captain of the guard had left with Gedaliah the son of Ahikam the son of Shaphan, and Jeremiah the prophet, and Baruch the son of Neriah.

A. M. 3416
B. C. 588
Ol. XLVIII. 1
Anno
TarquiniiPrisci,
R. Roman., 29

7 So they came into the land of Egypt: for they obeyed not the voice of the LORD: thus came they *even* to [e]Tahpanhes.

A. M. 3417
B. C. 587
Ol. XLVIII. 2
TarquiniiPrisci,
R. Roman.,
cir. annum 30

8 Then came the word of the LORD unto Jeremiah in Tahpanhes, saying,

9 Take great stones in thine hand, and hide them in the clay in the brickkiln, which *is* at the entry of Pharaoh's house in Tahpanhes, in the sight of the men of Judah;

10 And say unto them, Thus saith the LORD of hosts, the God of Israel; Behold, I will send and take Nebuchadrezzar the king of Babylon, [f]my servant, and will set his throne upon these stones that I have hid; and he shall spread his royal pavilion over them.

11 [g]And when he cometh, he shall smite the land of Egypt, *and deliver* [h]such *as are* for death to death; and such *as are* for captivity to captivity; and such *as are* for the sword to the sword.

12 And I will kindle a fire in the houses of [i]the gods of Egypt; and he shall burn them

[a]Chap. xlii. 1——[b]Chap. xl. 11, 12——[c]Chap. xli. 10 [d]Chap. xxxix. 10; xl. 7——[e]Chap. ii. 16; xliv. 1, called *Hanes;* Isa. xxx. 4

[f]Chap. xxv. 9; xxvii. 6; see Ezek. xxix. 18, 20——[g]Ch. xliv. 13; xlvi. 13——[h]Chap. xv. 2; Zech. xi. 9——[i]Chap. xlvi. 25

NOTES ON CHAP. XLIII

Verse 2. ***Thou speakest falsely*]** **They had no other colour for their rebellion than *flatly to deny* that God had spoken what the prophet related.**

Verse 6. ***Men, and women, and children, and the king's daughters*]** **See the note on chap. xli. 10. It is truly surprising that the Chaldeans should have left behind any of the royal family of Judah! But, 1. Perhaps they knew not there were any. 2. If they did know, they might think, being children of *concubines*, they could not inherit. Or, 3. That being females, they were not eligible. And they had taken care to seize all Zedekiah's sons, and slay them before his eyes.**

Verse 7. ***Came they* even *to Tahpanhes*]** **This city was called *Daphne* by the Greeks, and was situated at the extremity of Lower Egypt, near to Heliopolis. It was called *Daphne Pelusiaca*. They halted at this place, most probably for the purpose of obtaining the king's permission to penetrate farther into Egypt. It was at this place that, according to St. Jerome, tradition says the faithful Jeremiah was stoned to death by these rebellious wretches; for whose welfare he had watched, prayed, gone through many indignities, and suffered every kind of hardship. And now he sealed the truth of his Divine mission with his blood.**

Verse 9. ***Take great stones*]** **This discourse seems to have been delivered about a year after the destruction of Jerusalem. They pretended that they dared not stay in *Judea* for fear of the *Chaldeans*. The prophet here assures them that *Nebuchadnezzar* shall come to Egypt, extend his conquests in that kingdom, and place his tent over the very place where these stones were laid up, and destroy them. How these prophecies were fulfilled, see at the end of chap. xliv.**

Verse 11. ***Such* as are *for death to death*]** **See the note on chap. xv. 2.**

Verse 12. ***He shall burn them, and carry them away captives*]** **Some of these gods, such as were of *wood*, he will burn; those of *metal* he will carry away. Some of them were of *gold*. See below.**

***Shall array himself with the land of Egypt*]**

A. M. cir. 3417
B. C. cir. 587
Ol. XLVIII. 2
Anno
TarquiniiPrisci,
R. Roman., 30

and carry them away captives:
and he shall array himself with
the land of Egypt, as a shepherd
putteth on his garment; and he
shall go forth from thence in peace.

13 He shall break also the
[k]images of [l]Bethshemesh, that *is*
in the land of Egypt; and the
houses of the gods of the Egyptians shall he burn with fire.

A. M. cir. 3417
B. C. cir. 587
Ol. XLVIII. 2
Anno
TarquiniiPrisci,
R. Roman., 30

[k]Heb. *statues*, or *standing images* — [l]Or, *the house of the sun*

Shall take all its wealth, and all its grandeur; shall take all its spoils.

***As a shepherd putteth on his garment*] With as much ease, and with as little opposition; and with as full a confidence that it is now his own.**

***He shall go forth from thence in peace.*] He shall suffer no interruption, nor endure any disaster in his return from his Egyptian expedition. See the proof of all this in the notes at the end of chap. xliv.**

Verse 13. *He shall break also the images of Beth-shemesh*] בית שמש *beith shemesh* is, literally, *the house* or *temple of the sun;* which was worshipped here, and whose images are said to have been of *solid gold.* These Nebuchadnezzar was to break and carry away; and the *houses of the gods*—all the temples of Egypt, he was to burn with fire. Beth-shemesh is the same as Heliopolis.

CHAPTER XLIV

Jeremiah reproves the Jews in Egypt for continuing in idolatry after the exemplary judgments inflicted by God on their nation for that sin, 1–14; *and, upon their refusing to reform, denounces destruction to them, and to that kingdom wherein they sought protection,* 15–30.

A. M. cir. 3433
B. C. cir. 571
Ol. cir. LII. 2
Servii Tullii,
R. Roman.,
cir. annum 8

THE word that came to Jeremiah concerning all the
Jews which dwell in the land of
Egypt, which dwell at [a]Migdol,
and at [b]Tahpanhes, and at [c]Noph, and in the
country of Pathros, saying,
2 Thus saith the LORD of hosts, the God of
Israel; Ye have seen all the evil that I have
brought upon Jerusalem, and upon all the
cities of Judah; and, behold, this day they *are*
[d]a desolation, and no man dwelleth therein,
3 Because of their wickedness which they
have committed to provoke me to anger, in
that they went [e]to burn incense, *and* to [f]serve
other gods, whom they knew not,
neither they, ye, nor your fathers.
4 Howbeit [g]I sent unto you all
my servants the prophets, rising early and
sending *them,* saying, O, do not this abominable thing that I hate.
5 But they hearkened not, nor inclined their
ear to turn from their wickedness, to burn no
incense unto other gods.
6 Wherefore [h]my fury and mine anger was
poured forth, and was kindled in the cities of
Judah and in the streets of Jerusalem; and
they are wasted *and* desolate, as at this day.

A. M. cir. 3433
B. C. cir. 571
Ol. cir. LII. 2
Servi Tullii,
R. Roman.,
cir. annum 8

[a]Exod. xiv. 2; ch. xlvi. 14——[b]Ch. xliii. 7——[c]Isa. xix. 13——[d]Chap. ix. 11; xxxiv. 22——[e]Chap. xix. 4

[f]Deut. xiii. 6; xxxii. 17——[g]2 Chron. xxxvi. 15; chap. vii. 25; xxv. 4; xxvi. 5; xxix. 19——[h]Chap. xlii. 18

NOTES ON CHAP. XLIV

Verse 1. *The word that came to Jeremiah concerning all the Jews*] *Dahler* supposes this discourse to have been delivered in the *seventeenth* or *eighteenth* year after the taking of Jerusalem.

***Which dwell at Migdol*] A city of Lower Egypt, not far from Pelusium.**

***Tahpanhes*] *Daphne Pelusiaca*, the place to which the emigrant Jews first went.**

***Noph*] מפס *Maphes*, Targum. *Memphis*, a celebrated city of Middle Egypt, and the capital of its district.**

***The country of Pathros*] A district of Upper Egypt, known by the name of the *Thebais.* See *Bochart*, Lib. Phaleg, lib. iv., c. 22. Thus we find that the Jews were scattered over the principal parts of Egypt.**

Verse 2. *No man dwelleth therein*] The desolation of the land of Judea must have been exceedingly great when this, in almost any sense, could be spoken of it.

Verse 4. *O, do not this abominable thing*] A strong specimen of affectionate entreaty. One of the finest figures of poetry, when judiciously managed, the *anthropopathia*, the ascribing *human passions* to God, is often used by this prophet: so God is said to *grieve*, to *mourn*, to have his *bowels moved* with compassion, to *repent*, to be *angry*, &c. Here he is represented as *tenderly expostulating: O, do not;* or, *I entreat you, do not that abominable thing which I hate.* 1. *Do it not:* your *God* commands. 2. *O, do it not:* your *Father entreats.* 3. It is *an abominable* thing, and should *not be done.* 4. *I hate it*, and on that account ye should abstain from it.

Verse 5. *But they hearkened not*] 1. They disregarded the *authority* of their God. 2. They were not *moved* by the *entreaties* of their most affectionate Father. 3. In abominations they

A. M. cir. 3433
B. C. cir. 571
Ol. cir. LII. 2
Servii Tullii,
R. Roman.,
cir. annum 8

7 Therefore now thus saith the LORD, the God of hosts, the God of Israel; Wherefore commit ye *this* great evil [i]against your souls, to cut off from you man and woman, child and suckling, [k]out of Judah, to leave you none to remain;

8 In that ye [l]provoke me unto wrath with the works of your hands, burning incense unto other gods in the land of Egypt, whither ye be gone to dwell, that ye might cut yourselves off, and that ye might be [m]a curse and a reproach among all the nations of the earth?

9 Have ye forgotten the [n]wickedness of your fathers, and the wickedness of the kings of Judah, and the wickedness of their wives, and your own wickedness, and the wickedness of your wives, which they have committed in the land of Judah, and in the streets of Jerusalem?

10 They are not [o]humbled *even* unto this day, neither have they [p]feared, nor walked in my law, nor in my statutes, that I set before you and before your fathers.

11 Therefore thus saith the LORD of hosts, the God of Israel; Behold [q]I will set my face against you for evil, and to cut off all Judah.

12 And I will take the remnant of Judah, that have set their faces to go into the land of Egypt to sojourn there, and [r]they shall all be consumed, *and* fall in the land of Egypt; they shall *even* be consumed by the sword *and* by the famine: they shall die, from the least even unto the greatest, by the sword and by the famine: and [s]they shall be an execration, *and* an astonishment, and a curse, and a reproach.

A. M. cir. 3433
B. C. cir 571
Ol. cir. LII. 2
Servii Tullii,
R. Roman.,
cir. annum 8

13 [t]For I will punish them that dwell in the land of Egypt, as I have punished Jerusalem, by the sword, by the famine, and by the pestilence:

14 So that none of the remnant of Judah, which are gone into the land of Egypt to sojourn there, shall escape or remain, that they should return into the land of Judah, to the which they [u]have a desire to return to dwell there: for [v]none shall return but such as shall escape.

15 Then all the men which knew that their wives had burned incense unto other gods, and all the women that stood by, a great multitude, even all the people that dwelt in the land of Egypt, in Pathros, answered Jeremiah, saying,

16 *As for* the word that thou hast spoken unto us in the name of the LORD, [w]we will not hearken unto thee.

17 But we will certainly do [x]whatsoever thing goeth forth out of our own mouth, to burn incense unto the [y]queen [z]of heaven, and to pour out drink-offerings unto her, as we have done, we, and our fathers, our kings, and our princes, in the cities of Judah, and in the streets of Jerusalem: for *then* had we plenty of [a]victuals, and were well, and saw no evil.

18 But since we left off to burn incense to the queen of heaven, and to pour out drink-offerings unto her, we have wanted all *things*, and have been consumed by the sword and by the famine.

19 [b]And when we burned incense to the queen of heaven, and poured out drink-offerings unto her, did we make her cakes to worship

[i]Num. xvi. 38; chap. vii. 19——[k]Heb. *out of the midst of Judah*——[l]Chap. xxv. 6, 7——[m]Chap. xlii. 18; ver. 12——[n]Heb. *wickedness*, or *punishments*, &c.——[o]Heb. *contrite;* Psa. li. 17——[p]Prov. xxviii. 14——[q]Lev. xvii. 10; xx. 5, 6; chap. xxi. 10; Amos ix. 4

[r]Chap. xlii. 15, 16, 17, 22——[s]Chap. xlii. 18——[t]Ch. xliii. 11——[u]Heb. *lift up their soul*——[v]Ver. 28——[w]So chap. vi. 16——[x]Num. xxx. 12; Deut. xxiii. 23; Judg. xi. 36; see ver. 25——[y]Or, *frame of heaven*——[z]Chap. vii. 18——[a]Heb. *bread*——[b]Chap. vii. 18

delighted. And, 4. They *loved that* which *God hated;* and, apparently, *because* he hated it.

Verse 7. This *great evil against your souls*] Will not *self-interest* weigh with you? See what ruin your conduct has brought upon your country. Your fathers sinned as you are doing; and where are they now? Either destroyed, or in captivity. And you are now taking the same way to your own destruction.

Verse 9. *Have ye forgotten the wickedness of your fathers*] It seems that the *women* were principal agents in idolatrous practices; for the *queens*—the *wives*, of rulers and of common people, burnt incense to the *queen of heaven*, (the moon,) ver. 17, and poured out drink-offerings to her.

Verse 15. *Then all the men—and all the women*] We have not seen the women in determined rebellion before. Here they make a common cause with their idolatrous husbands.

Verse 19. *And when we burned incense to the queen of heaven*] The MOON seems to have been called מלכת *melecheth*, as the SUN was called מלך *molech*. The Hindoos pour out water to the sun thrice a day; and to the moon whenever they worship her.

The idolatrous worship of these people was a sort of imitation of the worship of the true God; only sacrifice was not common in it. The factious women here tell us in what it consisted. 1. They burnt incense to the moon, and perhaps

A. M. cir. 3433 B. C. cir. 571 Ol. cir. LII. 2 Servii Tullii, R. Roman., cir. annum. 8

her, and pour out drink-offerings unto her, without our [c]men?
20 Then Jeremiah said unto
all the people, to the men, and to
the women, and to all the people which had
given him *that* answer, saying,
21 The incense that ye burned in the cities
of Judah, and in the streets of Jerusalem, ye,
and your fathers, your kings, and your princes,
and the people of the land, did not the LORD
remember them, and came it *not* into his mind?
22 So that the LORD could no longer bear,
because of the evil of your doings *and* because
of the abominations which ye have committed;
therefore is your land [d]a desolation, and an
astonishment, and a curse, without an inhabitant, [e]as at this day.
23 Because ye have burned incense, and because ye have sinned against the LORD, and
have not obeyed the voice of the LORD, nor
walked in his law, nor in his statutes, nor in
his testimonies; [f]therefore this evil is happened unto you, as at this day.
24 Moreover Jeremiah said unto all the people, and to all the women, Hear the word of the
LORD, all Judah [g]that *are* in the land of Egypt:
25 Thus saith the LORD of hosts, the God
of Israel, saying; [h]Ye and your wives have
both spoken with your mouths, and fulfilled
with your hand, saying, We will surely perform
our vows that we have vowed, to burn incense
to the queen of heaven, and to pour out drink-
offerings unto her: ye will surely
accomplish your vows, and surely
perform your vows.

A. M. cir. 3433 B. C. cir. 571 Ol. cir. LII. 2 Servii Tullii, R. Roman., cir. annum 8

26 Therefore hear ye the word
of the LORD, all Judah that dwell in the land
of Egypt; Behold, [i]I have sworn by my great
name, saith the LORD, that [k]my name shall no
more be named in the mouth of any man of
Judah in all the land of Egypt, saying, The
Lord GOD liveth.
27 [l]Behold, I will watch over them for evil,
and not for good; and all the men of Judah
that *are* in the land of Egypt [m]shall be consumed by the sword and by the famine, until
there be an end of them.
28 Yet [n]a small number that escape the
sword shall return out of the land of Egypt
into the land of Judah, and all the remnant
of Judah, that are gone into the land of Egypt
to sojourn there, shall know whose [o]words
shall stand, [p]mine or theirs.
29 And this *shall be* a sign unto you, saith
the LORD, that I will punish you in this place,
that ye may know that my words shall [q]surely
stand against you for evil:
30 Thus saith the LORD; Behold, [r]I will
give Pharaoh-hophra king of Egypt into the
hand of his enemies, and into the hand of
them that seek his life; as I gave [s]Zedekiah
king of Judah into the hand of Nebuchadrezzar king of Babylon, his enemy, and that
sought his life.

---

[c]Or, *husbands*——[d]Chap. xxv. 11, 18, 38——[e]Ver. 6——[f]Dan. ix. 11, 12——[g]Chap. xliii. 7; ver. 15——[h]Ver. 15 &c.——[i]Gen. xxii. 16——[k]Ezek. xx. 39——[l]Chap. i. 10; xxxi. 28; Ezek. vii. 6——[m]Ver. 12——[n]Ver. 14; Isa. xxvii. 13——[o]Ver. 17, 25, 26——[p]Heb. *from me*, or *them*——[q]Psa. xxxiii. 11——[r]Chap. xlvi. 25, 26; Ezek. xxix. 3, &c.; xxx. 21, &c.——[s]Chap. xxxix. 5

---

to the sun and the planets. 2. They poured out libations to her. 3. They made and consecrated cakes to her. All these were prescribed in the worship of the true GOD. See, among others, Exod. xxix. 23, &c.; Lev. ii. 4; xxiii. 16; and Num. vi. 15. And the women vindicate their conduct by asserting that they did all this by the consent of their husbands: "Did we worship her without our men?"

Verse 22. *Therefore is your land a desolation*] I grant that ye and your husbands have joined together in these abominations; and what is the consequence? "The Lord could no longer bear because of your evil doings; and therefore is your land a desolation, and an astonishment, and a curse, without an inhabitant, this day."

Verse 30. *Behold I will give Pharaoh-hophra*] That is, *Pharaoh Apries*. How this and the prophecies in the preceding chapter were fulfilled, we learn from ancient historians. The sum of such information is this: the subjects of *Pharaoh Apries* rebelling, he sent *Amasis*, one of his generals, to reduce them to their duty. But no sooner had *Amasis* begun to make his speech, than they fixed a helmet on his head, and proclaimed him king. *Amasis* accepted the title, and confirmed the Egyptians in their revolt; and the greater part of the nation declaring for him, *Apries* was obliged to retire into Upper Egypt; and the country being thus weakened by intestine war, was attacked and easily overcome by Nebuchadnezzar, who on quitting it left *Amasis* his viceroy. After Nebuchadnezzar's departure, *Apries* marched against *Amasis;* but, being defeated at *Memphis*, was taken prisoner, carried to *Sais*, and was strangled in his own palace, thus verifying this prophecy. See *Herodotus* in Euterpe.

Thus Nebuchadnezzar made an easy conquest of the land. He conquered it as easily as "a shepherd puts on his cloak: he went thence in peace," having clothed himself with its spoils; and left all quiet under a viceroy of his own choosing. The rebellion of Pharaoh's subjects was the "fire that God kindled in Egypt," chap. xliii. 12. And thus was he "delivered into the hands of his enemies," his revolted people; and "into the hand of him who sought his life," i. e., *Amasis* his general. And thus the whole prophecy was literally fulfilled.

CHAPTER XLV

This chapter is evidently connected with the subject treated of in the thirty-sixth. *Baruch, who had written the prophecies of Jeremiah, and read them publicly in the temple, and afterwards to many of the princes, is in great affliction because of the awful judgments with which the land of Judah was about to be visited; and also on account of the imminent danger to which his own life was exposed, in publishing such unwelcome tidings,* 1–3. *To remove Baruch's fear with respect to this latter circumstance, the prophet assures him that though the total destruction of Judea was determined because of the great wickedness of the inhabitants, yet his life should be preserved amidst the general desolation,* 4, 5.

A. M. cir. 3397 B. C. cir. 607 Ol. XLIII. 2 Anno TarquiniiPrisci, R. Roman., 10

THE [a]word that Jeremiah the prophet spake unto Baruch the son of Neriah, when he had written these words in a book at the mouth of Jeremiah, in the fourth year of Jehoiakim [b]the son of Josiah king of Judah, saying,

2 Thus saith the LORD, the God of Israel, unto thee, O Baruch,

3 Thou didst say, Wo is me now! for the LORD hath added grief to my sorrow; I fainted in my sighing, and I find no rest.

4 Thus shalt thou say unto him, The LORD saith thus; Behold, [c]*that* which I have built will I break down, and that which I have planted I will pluck up, even this whole land.

5 And seekest thou great things for thyself? seek *them* not: for, behold, [d]I will bring evil upon all flesh, saith the LORD: but thy life will I give unto thee [e]for a prey in all places whither thou goest.

[a]Ch. xxxvi. 1, 4, 32——[b]2 Kings xxiii. 34——[c]Isa. v. 5

[d]Chap. xxv. 26——[e]Chap. xxi. 9; xxxviii. 2; xxxix. 18

NOTES ON CHAP. XLV

Verse 1. *The word that Jeremiah—spake unto Baruch*] This is another instance of shameless transposition. This discourse was delivered in the *fourth* year of Jehoiakim, several years before Jerusalem was taken by the Chaldeans. It is a simple appendage to chap. xxxvi., and there it should have been inserted.

Verse 3. *Thou didst say, Wo is me now!*] All that were the enemies of Jeremiah became his enemies too; and he needed these promises of support.

The Lord hath added grief to my sorrow] He had mourned for the desolations that were coming on his country, and now he mourns for the dangers to which he feels his own life exposed; for we find, from chap. xxxvi. 26, that the king had given commandment to take both Baruch and Jeremiah, in order that they might be put to death at the instance of his nobles.

Verse 4. *Behold*, that *which I have built*] I most certainly will fulfil all those threatenings contained in the roll thou hast written; for I will destroy this whole land.

Verse 5. *And seekest thou great things for thyself?*] Nothing better can be expected of this people: thy hopes in reference to *them* are vain. Expect no national amendment, till national judgments have taken place. And as for any *benefit* to *thyself*, think it sufficient that God has determined to preserve thy life amidst all these dangers.

But thy life will I give unto thee for a prey] This is a proverbial expression. We have met with it before, chap. xxi. 9, xxxviii. 2, xxxix. 18; and it appears to have this meaning. As a *prey* or *spoil* is that which is gained from a vanquished enemy, so it is preserved with pleasure as the proof and reward of a man's own valour. So Baruch's life should be doubly precious unto him, not only on account of the dangers through which God had caused him to pass safely, but also on account of those services he had been enabled to render, the consolations he had received, and the continual and very evident interposition of God in his behalf. All these would be dearer to him than the *spoils* of a vanquished foe to the hero who had overcome in battle.

Spoil may signify *unlooked-for gain.* The preservation of his life, in such circumstances, must be more than he could reasonably expect; but his life should be safe, and he should have it as a *spoil*, whithersoever he should go. This assurance must have quieted all his fears.

CHAPTER XLVI

The difference between the preceding and the subsequent prophecies in point of composition is very remarkable; the last excelling much in majesty and elegance. This chapter (of which the first *verse forms a general title to this and the five chapters following) contains two distinct prophecies relating to Egypt. The* first *was delivered previous to an engagement between Pharaoh-necho, king of Egypt, and Nebuchadnezzar, king of Babylon; in which the Egyptians were routed in Carchemish with great slaughter, as here predicted. The prophet sees the mighty preparations; but they are all declared to be of no avail, as God had decreed their fall,* 1–6. *The king of Egypt, however, is represented as marching with all the confidence of victory, like a river overflowing its banks, and threatening all around with its inundation,* 7, 8. *But this immense armament of Pharaoh-necho, consisting of various nations, shall, by a righteous judgment of God, receive such a signal overthrow near the river Euphrates, that the political consequence of Egypt shall be thereby irretrievably ruined, and its remaining power become contemptible in the sight of the nations,* 9–12. *The other prophecy, beginning at the* thirteenth *verse, relates to the memorable overthrow of the Egyptians by Nebuchadnezzar, subsequent to his siege of Tyre, in the* sixteenth *year after the destruction of Jerusalem,* 13–26. *The promise, in the conclusion of the chapter, of preservation to the Jews, (who have for many ages continued a distinct people, when the various nations of antiquity who oppressed them, or with whom they had any intercourse, have long ago ceased to have any separate and visible existence,) has been most remarkably fulfilled; and is a very signal act of providence, and a pledge of the restoration of Israel to the Divine favour, when the time of the Gentiles shall be fulfilled,* 27, 28.

A. M. cir. 3397
B. C. cir. 607
Ol. XLIII. 2
TarquiniiPrisci,
R. Roman.,
cir. annum 10

THE word of the LORD which
came to Jeremiah the
prophet against [a]the Gentiles;
2 Against Egypt, [b]against the
army of Pharaoh-necho king of Egypt, which
was by the river Euphrates in Carchemish,
which Nebuchadrezzar king of Babylon smote
in the fourth year of Jehoiakim the son of
Josiah king of Judah.
3 [c]Order ye the buckler and shield, and
draw near to battle.
4 Harness the horses; and get up, ye horsemen, and stand forth with *your* helmets; furbish the spears, *and* put on the brigandines.
5 Wherefore have I seen them dismayed
and turned away back? and their
mighty ones are [d]beaten down,
and are [e]fled apace, and look not
back: *for* [f]fear *was* round about,
saith the LORD.
6 Let not the swift flee away, nor the mighty
man escape; they shall [g]stumble, and fall
toward the north by the river Euphrates.
7 Who *is* this *that* cometh up [h]as a flood,
whose waters are moved as the rivers?
8 Egypt riseth up like a flood, and *his*
waters are moved like the rivers; and he saith,
I will go up, *and* will cover the earth; I will
destroy the city and the inhabitants thereof.
9 Come up, ye horses; and rage, ye chariots;

[a]Chap. xxv. 15, &c.——[b]2 Kings xxiii. 29; 2 Chron. xxxv. 20——[c]So chap. li. 11, 12; Nah. ii. 1; iii. 14
[d]Heb. *broken in pieces*

[e]Heb. *fled a flight*——[f]Chap. vi. 25; xlix. 29——[g]Dan. xi. 19——[h]See Isaiah viii. 7, 8; chap. xlvi. 2; Daniel xi. 22

NOTES ON CHAP. XLVI

Verse 1. *The word of the Lord—against the Gentiles*] This is a general title to the following collection of prophecies, written concerning different nations, which had less or more connexion with the Jews, either as *enemies, neighbours,* or *allies.*

They were not written at the same time; and though some of them bear dates, yet it would be difficult to give them any chronological arrangement. *Dahler's* mode of ascertaining the times of their delivery may be seen in the table in the *introduction.*

Verse 2. *Pharaoh-necho*] This was the person who defeated the army of Josiah, in which engagement Josiah received a mortal wound, of which he died, greatly regretted, soon after at *Megiddo.* After this victory, he defeated the Babylonians, and took Carchemish; and, having fortified it, returned to his own country. *Nabopolassar* sent his son *Nebuchadnezzar* with an army against him, defeated him with immense slaughter near the river Euphrates, retook *Carchemish,* and subdued all the revolted provinces, according to the following prophecies.

Verse 3. *Order ye the buckler*] This is the call to the general armament of the people against the Chaldeans.

Verse 4. *Furbish the spears*] Cleanse, brighten, and sharpen them; from the Franco-Gallic *fourbir,* to polish, brighten.

Brigandines.] A coat of mail, especially that which was made *scale fashion;* one plate overlapping the other, like the scales of fish.

Verse 5. *Wherefore have I seen them dismayed*] What! such a numerous, formidable, and well-appointed army panic-struck? So that they have *turned back—fled apace,* and *looked not round;* while their *mighty ones*—their generals and commanders, striving to rally them, are *beaten down.*

Verse 6. *Let not the swift flee away*] Even the swiftest shall not be able to escape.

They shall—fall toward the north] By the *Euphrates,* which was northward of Judea. Here the Egyptian army was routed with great slaughter.

Verse 7. *Who* is *this* that *cometh up as a flood*] The vast concourse of people is here represented as a *river:* for instance, the Jordan, suddenly swollen with the rains in harvest, rolling its waters along, and overflowing the whole country. A fine image to represent the incursions of vast armies carrying all before them. Such was the army of Pharaoh-necho in its march to Carchemish.

Verse 9. *The Ethiopians*] Heb. *Cush, Phut,* and the *Ludim.* This army was composed of many nations. *Cush,* which we translate *Ethiopians,* almost invariably means the *Arabians;* and here, those *Arabs* that bordered on Egypt near the Red Sea. *Phut* probably means the *Libyans;* for *Phut* settled in *Libya,* according

A. M. cir. 3397 B. C. cir. 607 Ol. XLIII. 2 TarquiniiPrisci, R. Roman., cir. annum 10

and let the mighty men come
forth; [i]the Ethiopians and [k]the
Libyans, that handle the shield;
and the Lydians, [l]that handle
and bend the bow.

10 For this *is* [m]the day of the Lord GOD of
hosts, a day of vengeance, that he may avenge
him of his adversaries: and [n]the sword shall
devour, and it shall be satiate and made drunk
with their blood: for the Lord GOD of hosts
[o]hath a sacrifice in the north country by the
river Euphrates.

11 [p]Go up into Gilead, and take balm, [q]O
virgin, the daughter of Egypt: in vain shalt
thou use many medicines; *for* [r]thou [s]shalt
not be cured.

12 The nations have heard of thy shame,
and thy cry hath filled the land: for
the mighty man hath stumbled against
the mighty, *and* they are fallen both together.

13 The word that the LORD spake to Jeremiah the prophet, how Nebuchadrezzar king
of Babylon should come *and*
[t]smite the land of Egypt.

14 Declare ye in Egypt, and
publish in Migdol, and publish
in Noph and in Tahpanhes: say ye, [u]Stand
fast, and prepare thee; for [v]the sword shall
devour round about thee.

15 Why are thy valiant *men* swept away?
they stood not, because the LORD did drive
them.

16 He [w]made many to fall, yea, [x]one fell
upon another: and they said, Arise, and let
us go again to our own people, and to the land
of our nativity, from the oppressing sword.

17 They did cry there, Pharaoh king of
Egypt *is but* a noise; he hath passed the time
appointed.

18 *As* I live, saith the King, [y]whose name
is the LORD of hosts, Surely as Tabor *is*
among the mountains, and as Carmel by the
sea, *so* shall he come.

19 O [z]thou daughter dwelling in Egypt,
[a]furnish thyself [b]to go into captivity: for

[i]Heb. *Cush*——[k]Heb. *Put*——[l]Isa. lxvi. 19——[m]Isa. xiii. 6; Joel i. 15; ii. 1——[n]Deut. xxxii. 42; Isa. xxxiv. 6——[o]Isa. xxxiv. 6; Zeph. i. 7; see Ezek. xxxix. 17——[p]Chap. viii. 22; li. 8——[q]Isa. xlvii. 1——[r]Heb. *no cure* shall be *unto thee*——[s]Ezek. xxx. 21

[t]Isa. xix. 1; chap. xliii. 10, 11; Ezek. xxix., xxx., xxxii.——[u]Ver. 3, 4——[v]Ver. 10——[w]Heb. *multiplied the faller*——[x]Lev. xxvi. 37——[y]Isa. xlvii. 4; xlviii. 2; chap. xlviii. 15——[z]See chap. xlviii. 18——[a]Heb. *make thee instruments of captivity*——[b]Isa. xx. 4

to Josephus. *Phut* and *Cush* were two of the sons of *Ham*, and brothers to *Mitsraim*, the father of the Egyptians, Gen. x. 6; and the *Ludim* were descended from *Mitsraim;* see Gen. x. 13. *Bochart* contends that the *Ludim* were *Ethiopians*, and that they were famous for the *use of the bow*. *Phaleg*, lib. iv. 26.

Verse 10. *For this is the day of the Lord God of hosts*] The prophet represents this as a *mighty sacrifice*, where innumerable victims were slain.

Verse 11. *Go up into Gilead, and take balm*] An irony. Egypt is so completely enfeebled by this overthrow, that her political wound is utterly incurable. This figure is used with the more propriety here, as the Egyptians have been celebrated from the remotest antiquity for their *knowledge of medicine*.

Verse 12. *The nations have heard of thy shame*] Of thy disgrace, by this prodigious slaughter of thy troops.

Verse 13. *How Nebuchadrezzar—should come* and *smite the land of Egypt.*] See on chap. xliv. This was after Amasis had driven Pharaoh-necho into Upper Egypt. See chap. xliv. 30.

Verse 14. *Migdol*] Magdolum, a city of Lower Egypt. *Noph*, Memphis. *Tahpanhes*, Daphne. See before, chap. xliv. 1.

Round about thee.] The Phœnicians, Philistines, Ammonites, Moabites, and Edomites, all prostrated by the arms of the Chaldeans.

Verse 15. *They stood not, because the Lord did drive them.*] The Lord panic-struck them, and *drove* them back.

Verse 16. *One fell upon another*] In their terror and confusion ranks fell on ranks, and overturned each other.

Let us go again to our own people] Let us flee to our own country with all possible speed. These were the auxiliaries.

Verse 17. *They did cry there*] Dr. *Blayney* translates this cry thus:—

——— "O Pharaoh, king of Egypt,
A tumult hath frustrated the appointed meeting."

These allies sent their excuse to Pharaoh, that the disasters they had met with had prevented them from joining him as they had intended.

Verse 18. *As Tabor is among the mountains*] This mountain is situated in the plain of Esdraelon in Galilee, on the confines of the tribes of Zebulun and Issachar, Josh. xix. 22. It stood by itself, separated from all the other mountains by deep valleys, and is the highest of the whole.

And as Carmel by the sea] Carmel is a mountain on the coast of the Mediterranean Sea, on the southern frontier of the tribe of Asher. Were the Egyptians as distinguished for valour and strength as the mountains Tabor and Carmel are for height among the other mountains in their vicinity, they should not be able to stand the shock of the Chaldean army.

Verse 19. *Furnish thyself to go into captivity*] The thing is unavoidable; prepare for this calamity.

A. M. cir. 3398 B. C. cir. 606 Ol. XLIII. 3 TarquiniiPrisci, R. Roman., cir. annum 11

Noph shall be waste and desolate
without an inhabitant.
20 Egypt *is like* a very fair
[c]heifer, *but* destruction cometh;
it cometh [d]out of the north.
21 Also her hired men *are* in the midst of
her like [e]fatted bullocks; for they also are
turned back, *and* are fled away together: they
did not stand, because [f]the day of their calamity was come upon them, *and* the time of
their visitation.
22 [g]The voice thereof shall go like a serpent; for they shall march with an army, and
come against her with axes, as hewers of wood.
23 They shall [h]cut down her forest, saith
the LORD, though it cannot be searched; because they are more than [i]the grasshoppers,
and *are* innumerable.
24 The daughter of Egypt shall be confounded: she shall be delivered into the hand
of [k]the people of the north.
25 The LORD of hosts, the God of Israel,
saith; Behold, I will punish the [l]multitude[m]
of [n]No, and Pharaoh, and Egypt,
[o]with their gods, and their kings;
even Pharaoh, and *all* them that
trust in him:
26 [p]And I will deliver them into the hand
of those that seek their lives, and into the hand
of Nebuchadrezzar king of Babylon, and into
the hand of his servants: and [q]afterward it
shall be inhabited, as in the days of old, saith
the LORD.
27 [r]But fear not thou, O my servant Jacob,
and be not dismayed, O Israel; for, behold, I
will save thee from afar off, and thy seed from
the land of their captivity; and Jacob shall
return, and be in rest and at ease, and none
shall make *him* afraid.
28 Fear thou not, O Jacob my servant, saith
the LORD: for I *am* with thee; for I will
make a full end of all the nations whither
I have driven thee: but I will not make
[s]a full end of thee, but correct thee in measure, yet will I [t]not leave thee wholly unpunished.

[c]So Hos. x. 11——[d]Ch. i. 14; xlvii. 2; ver. 6, 10 [e]Heb. *bullocks of the stall*——[f]Psa. xxxvii. 13; ch. l. 27 [g]See Isa. xxix. 4——[h]Isa. x. 34——[i]Judg. vi. 5——[k]Ch. i. 15——[l]Or, *nourisher*——[m]Heb. *Amon*——[n]Ezek. xxx. 14, 15, 16; Nah. iii. 8——[o]Ch. xliii. 12, 13; Ezek. xxx. 13 [p]Ch. xliv. 30; Ezek. xxxii. 11——[q]Ezek. xxix. 11, 13, 14 [r]Isa. xli. 13, 14; xliii. 5; xliv. 2; ch. xxx. 10, 11——[s]Ch. x. 24; xxx. 11——[t]Or, *not utterly cut thee off*

Verse 20. *Egypt* is like *a very fair heifer*] Fruitful and useful; but destruction cometh out of the north, from Chaldea. It may be that there is an allusion here to *Isis*, worshipped in Egypt under the form of a beautiful cow.

Verse 21. *Are fled away together*] Perhaps there is a reference here to the case of a cow stung with gnats. She runs hither and thither, not knowing where to go; so shall it be with this scattered people.

Verse 22. *The voice—shall go like a serpent*] See Isa. xxix. 4, and the note there.

Verse 23. *They shall cut down her forest*] Supposed to mean her cities, of which Egypt had no fewer than *one thousand* and *twenty*.

Verse 24. *The hand of the people of the north*] The Chaldeans.

Verse 25. *The multitude of No*] אמון מנא *Amon minno*, the Amon of No, called by the Greeks Διοσπολις, or *Jupiter's city*. It was the famous *Thebes*, celebrated anciently for its hundred gates. *Amon* was the name by which the Egyptians called Jupiter, who had a famous temple at Thebes.

The word Pharaoh is twice repeated here; and Dr. *Dahler* thinks that one may design *Pharaoh Hophrah*, and the other *Amasis*, the new king.

Verse 26. *Afterward it shall be inhabited*] That is, within *forty years*, as Ezekiel had predicted, chap. xxix. 13.

Verse 27. *Fear not—my servant Jacob*] In the midst of wrath God remembers mercy. Though Judah shall be destroyed, Jerusalem taken, the temple burnt to the ground, and the people carried into captivity, yet the *nation* shall not be destroyed. A seed shall be preserved, out of which the nation shall revive.

Verse 28. *I will make a full end of all the nations whither I have driven thee; but I will not make a full end of thee*] The Jews still remain as a *distinct people*, while the *Assyrians*, *Chaldeans*, *Egyptians*, &c., are no more!

ON this subject, I cannot withhold from my readers the following very judicious remarks of Bp. *Newton*, in his Dissertations on the Prophecies.

"The preservation of the Jews through so many ages, and the total destruction of their enemies, are wonderful events; and are made still more wonderful by being signified beforehand by the spirit of prophecy, as particularly in the passage before us. Their preservation is really one of the most illustrious acts of Divine Providence. They are dispersed among all nations, yet not confounded with any. The drops of rain which fall, nay the great rivers which flow into the ocean, are soon mingled with and lost in that immense body of waters. And the same, in all human probability, would have been the fate of the Jews; they would have been mingled and lost in the common mass of mankind: but, on the contrary, they flow into all parts of the world, mix with all nations, and yet keep separate from all. They still live as a distinct people; and yet they nowhere live according to their own laws, nowhere elect their own magistrates, nowhere enjoy the full exercise of their religion. Their solemn feasts and sacrifices are limited to one certain place; and that hath been now for many ages in the hands of strangers and aliens, who will not suffer them to come thither. No people have continued unmixed so long as they have done; not only of those who have sent colonies into foreign countries, but even of those who have remained in their own country. The northern nations have come in swarms into the more southern parts of Europe: but where are they now to be discerned and distinguished? The Gauls went forth in great bodies to seek their fortune in foreign parts; but what traces or footsteps of them are now remaining any where? In France, who can separate the race of the ancient Gauls from the various other people who from time to time have settled there? In Spain, who can distinguish between the first possessors, the Spaniards, and the Goths and Moors, who conquered and kept possession of the country for some ages? In England, who can pretend to say certainly which families are derived from the ancient Britons, and which from the Romans, Saxons, Danes, and Normans? The most ancient and honourable pedigrees can be traced up only to a certain period; and beyond that there is nothing but conjecture and uncertainty, obscurity and ignorance. But the Jews can go up higher than any nation; they can even deduce their pedigree from the beginning of the world. They may not know from what particular tribe or family they are descended; but they know certainly that they all sprang from the stock of Abraham. And yet the contempt with which they have been treated, and the hardships they have undergone in almost all countries, should, one would think, have made them desirous to forget or renounce their original: but they profess it; they glory in it; and after so many wars, massacres, and persecutions, they still subsist; they are still very numerous. And what but a supernatural power could have preserved them in such a manner as no other nation upon earth has been preserved? Nor is the providence of God less remarkable in the destruction of their enemies, than in their own preservation. For, from the beginning, who have been the great enemies and oppressors of the Jewish nation, removed them from their own land, and compelled them into captivity and slavery? The Egyptians afflicted them much, and detained them in bondage several years. The Assyrians carried away captive the ten tribes of Israel; and the Babylonians, afterwards, the two remaining tribes of Judah and Benjamin. The Syro-Macedonians, especially Antiochus Epiphanes, cruelly persecuted them; and the Romans utterly dissolved the Jewish state, and dispersed the people so as that they have never been able to recover their city and country again. And where are now those great and famous monarchies, which in their turn subdued and oppressed the people of God? Are they not vanished as a dream; and not only their power, but their very names, lost in the earth? The Egyptians, Assyrians, and Babylonians were overthrown and entirely subjugated by the Persians; and the Persians, it is remarkable, were the restorers of the Jews as well as the destroyers of their enemies. The Syro-Macedonians were swallowed up by the Romans; and the Roman empire, great and powerful as it was, was broken into pieces by the incursions of the northern nations; while the Jews are subsisting as a distinct people at this day. And what a wonder of providence is it, that the vanquished should so many ages survive the victors; and the former be spread all over the world, while the latter are no more! Nay, not only nations have been punished for their cruelties to the Jews, but Divine vengeance has pursued even single persons who have been their persecutors and oppressors. The first-born of Pharaoh was destroyed; and he himself, with his host, drowned in the sea. Nebuchadnezzar was stricken with madness, and the crown was transferred from his family to strangers. Antiochus Epiphanes and Herod died in great agonies, with ulcers and vermin issuing from them. Flaccus, governor of Egypt, who barbarously plundered and oppressed the Jews of Alexandria, was afterwards banished and slain; and Caligula, who persecuted the Jews for refusing to do Divine honours to his statue, was murdered in the flower of his age, after a short and wicked reign. But where are now,—since they have absolutely rejected the Gospel. and been no longer the peculiar people of God, —where are now such visible manifestations of a Divine interposition in their favour? The Jews would do well to consider this point; for, rightly considered, it may be an effectual means of opening their eyes, and of turning them to Christ our Saviour." See Bp. *Newton* on the prophecies, dissert. viii. sect. 2. And see the notes on Ezekiel, where the calamities of these miserable people are largely detailed.

CHAPTER XLVII

Among the nations doomed to suffer from the hostilities of Nebuchadnezzar are the Philistines, (see chap. xxv. 20.) *And the calamities predicted in this chapter befell them probably during the long siege of Tyre, when their country was desolated to prevent their giving Tyre or Sidon any assistance,* 1–5. *The whole of this chapter is remarkably elegant. The address to the sword of Jehovah, at the close of it, is particularly a very beautiful and bold personification,* 6, 7.

A. M. cir. 3387
B. C. cir. 617
Ol. cir. XL. 4
Anci Martii,
R. Roman.,
cir. annum 24

THE word of the LORD that
came to Jeremiah the pro-
phet [a]against the Philistines, [b]be-
fore that Pharaoh smote [c]Gaza.
2 Thus saith the LORD; Behold, [d]waters rise
up [e]out of the north, and shall be an overflowing flood, and shall overflow the land, and [f]all
that is therein; the city and them that dwell
therein: then the men shall cry, and all the
inhabitants of the land shall howl.
3 At the [g]noise of the stamping of the hoofs
of his strong *horses, at* the rushing of his
chariots, *and at* the rumbling of his wheels,
the fathers shall not look back to *their* children for feebleness of hands;
4 Because of the day that cometh to spoil all the Philistines,
and to cut off from [h]Tyrus and
Zidon every helper that remain-
eth: for the LORD will spoil the Philistines,
[i]the remnant of [k]the country of [l]Caphtor.
5 [m]Baldness is come upon Gaza; [n]Ashkelon
is cut off *with* the remnant of their valley:
how long wilt thou [o]cut thyself?
6 O thou [p]sword of the LORD, how long *will
it be* ere thou be quiet? [q]put up thyself into
thy scabbard, rest, and be still.
7 [r]How can it be quiet, seeing the LORD hath
[s]given it a charge against Ashkelon, and against
the sea shore? there hath he [t]appointed it.

A. M. cir. 3387
B. C. cir. 617
Ol. cir. XL. 4
Anci Martii,
R. Roman.,
cir. annum 24

[a]Chap. xxv. 20; Ezek. xxv. 15, 16; Zeph. ii. 4, 5 [b]Amos i. 6, 7, 8——[c]Heb. *Azzah*——[d]Isa. viii. 7; chap. xlvi. 7, 8——[e]Ch. i. 14; xlvi. 20——[f]Heb. *the fulness thereof*——[g]Ch. viii. 16; Nah. iii. 2——[h]Ch. xxv. 2 [i]Ezek. xxv. 16; Amos i. 8; ix. 7

[k]Heb. *the isle*——[l]Gen. x. 14——[m]Amos i. 7; Mic. i. 16; Zeph. ii. 4, 7; Zech. ix. 5——[n]Ch. xxv. 20——[o]Ch. xvi. 6; xli. 5; xlviii. 37——[p]Deut. xxxii. 41; Ezek. xxi. 3, 4, 5——[q]Heb. *gather thyself*——[r]Heb. *how canst thou?* [s]Ezek. xiv. 17——[t]Mic. vi. 9

NOTES ON CHAP. XLVII

Verse 1. *The word of the Lord—against the Philistines*] The *date* of this prophecy cannot be easily ascertained. Dr. *Blayney* thinks it was delivered about the *fourth year* of *Zedekiah*, while *Dahler* assigns it some time in the reign of *Josiah*.

Before that Pharaoh smote Gaza.] We have no historical relation of any Egyptian king smiting Gaza. It was no doubt smitten by some of them; but *when*, and by *whom*, does not appear either from sacred or profane history.

Verse 2. *Waters rise up out of the north*] *Waters* is a common prophetic image for a *multitude of people*. The *north* here, as in other places of this prophecy, means *Chaldea*.

Verse 3. *The stamping of the hoofs*] At the *galloping sound*,—

Quadrupedante putrem sonitu quatit ungula campum,

is a line of *Virgil*, (Æn. viii. 596,) much celebrated; and quoted here by *Blayney*, where the galloping sound of the horses' hoofs is *heard*. In the *stamping* of the *horses*, the *rushing* of the *chariots*, and the *rumbling* of the *wheels*, our translators intended to convey the *sense* by the *sound* of the words; and they have not been unsuccessful. Their translation of the original is at the same time sufficiently literal.

The fathers shall not look back] Though their children are left behind, they have neither *strength* nor *courage* to go back to bring them off.

Verse 4. *To spoil all the Philistines*] These people, of whom there were *five seignories*, occupied the coast of the Mediterranean Sea, to the south of the Phœnicians.

Tyrus and Zidon] Places sufficiently remarkable both in the Old and New Testament, and in profane history. They belonged to the Phœnicians; and at this time were depending on the succour of their allies, the Philistines. But their expectation was cut off.

The remnant of the country of Caphtor.] *Crete*, or *Cyprus*. Some think it was a district along the coast of the Mediterranean, belonging to the Philistines; others, that the *Cappadocians* are meant.

Verse 5. *Baldness is come upon Gaza*] They have *cut off their hair* in token of deep sorrow and distress.

Ashkelon is cut off] Or *put to silence;* another mark of the deepest sorrow. Ashkelon was one of the *five seignories* of the Philistines, *Gaza* was another.

The remnant of their valley] Or *plain;* for the whole land of the Philistines was a *vast plain*, which extended along the coast of the Mediterranean Sea from Phœnicia to the frontiers of Egypt. The whole of this plain, the territory of the Philistines, shall be desolated.

Verse 6. *O thou sword of the Lord*] This is a most grand prosopopœia—a dialogue between the sword of the Lord and the prophet. Nothing can be imagined more sublime.

Put up thyself into thy scabbard, rest, and be still.] Shed no more blood, destroy no more lives, erase no more cities, desolate no more countries. *Rest:*—hast thou not been long enough at this work of judgment? *O be still:* —let wars and desolations cease for ever.

Verse 7. *How can it be quiet*] This is the *answer* of the *Sword*. I am the officer of God's judgments, and he has given me a commission against Ashkelon, and against the sea shore; all the coast where the Philistines have their territories. The measure of their iniquities is full; and these God hath appointed this sword to ravage. The Philistines were ever the implacable enemies of the Jews, and the basest and worst of all idolaters. On these accounts the sword of the Lord had its commission against them; and it did its office most fearfully and effectually by the hand of the Chaldeans.

CHAPTER XLVIII

The following prophecy concerning the Moabites is supposed to have had its accomplishment during the long siege of Tyre in the reign of Nebuchadnezzar. The whole of this chapter is poetry of the first order. The distress of the cities of Moab, with which it opens, is finely described. The cries of one ruined city resound to those of another, 1–3. *The doleful helpless cry of the children is heard,* 4; *the highways, on either hand, resound with the voice of weeping,* 5; *and the few that remain resemble a blasted tree in the wide howling waste,* 6. *Chemosh, the chief god of the Moabites, and the capital figure in the triumph, is represented as carried off in chains, with all his trumpery of priests and officers,* 7. *The desolation of the country shall be so general and sudden that, by a strong figure, it is intimated that there shall be no possibility of escape, except it be in the speediest flight,* 8, 9. *And some idea may be formed of the dreadful wickedness of this people from the consideration that the prophet, under the immediate inspiration of the Almighty, pronounces a curse on those who do the work of the Lord negligently, in not proceeding to their utter extermination,* 10. *The subject is then diversified by an elegant and well-supported comparison, importing that the Moabites increased in insolence and pride in proportion to the duration of their prosperity,* 11; *but this prosperity is declared to be nearly at an end; the destroyer is already commissioned against Moab, and his neighbours called to sing the usual lamentation at his funeral,* 13–18. *The prophet then represents some of the women of Aroer and Ammon, (the extreme borders of Moab,) standing in the highways, and asking the fugitives of Moab, What intelligence? They inform him of the complete discomfiture of Moab,* 19–24, *and of the total annihilation of its political existence,* 25. *The Divine judgments about to fall upon Moab are farther represented under the expressive metaphor of a cup of intoxicating liquor, by which he should become an object of derision because of his intolerable pride, his magnifying himself against Jehovah, and his great contempt for the children of Israel in the day of their calamity,* 26, 27. *The prophet then points out the great distress of Moab by a variety of striking figures, viz., by the failure of the customary rejoicings at the end of harvest, by the mournful sort of music used at funerals, by the signs which were expressive among the ancients of deep mourning, as shaving the head, clipping the beard, cutting the flesh, and wearing sackcloth; and by the methods of catching wild beasts in toils, and by the terror and pitfall,* 28–46. *In the close of the chapter it is intimated that a remnant shall be preserved from this general calamity whose descendants shall be prosperous in the latter days,* 47.

A. M. cir. 3420
B. C. cir. 584
Ol. XLIX. 1
TarquiniiPrisci,
R. Roman.,
cir. annum 33

AGAINST [a]Moab thus saith
the LORD of hosts, the God
of Israel; Wo unto [b]Nebo! for
it is spoiled: [c]Kiriathaim is confounded *and* taken: [d]Misgab is confounded
and dismayed.

2 [e]*There shall be* no more praise of Moab:
in [f]Heshbon they have devised evil against it;
come, and let us cut it off from *being* a nation. Also thou shalt [g]be cut down, O
Madmen; the sword shall [h]pursue thee.

3 [i]A voice of crying *shall be*
from Horonaim, spoiling and
great destruction.

A. M. cir. 3420
B. C. cir. 584
Ol. XLIX. 1
TarquiniiPrisci,
R. Roman.,
cir. annum 33

4 Moab is destroyed; her little
ones have caused a cry to be heard.

5 [k]For in the going up of Luhith [l]continual
weeping shall go up; for in the going down of
Horonaim the enemies have heard a cry of
destruction.

6 [m]Flee, save your lives, and be like [n]the
[o]heath in the wilderness.

[a]Isa. xv., xvi.; chap. xxv. 21; xxvii. 3; Ezek. xxv. 9; Amos ii. 1, 2——[b]Num. xxxii. 38; xxxiii. 47; Isa. xv. 2——[c]Num. xxxii. 37——[d]Or, *The high place*——[e]Isa. xvi. 14——[f]Isa. xv. 4

[g]Or, *be brought to silence;* Isa. xv. 1——[h]Heb. *go after thee*——[i]Ver. 5——[k]Isa. xv. 5——[l]Heb. *weeping with weeping*——[m]Chap. li. 6——[n]Or, *a naked tree*——[o]Ch. xvii. 6

NOTES ON CHAP. XLVIII

Verse 1. *Against Moab*] This was delivered some time after the destruction of Jerusalem. The Moabites were in the neighbourhood of the Ammonites, and whatever evils fell on the one would naturally involve the other. See Isa. xv. and xvi. on this same subject.

Wo unto Nebo! for it is spoiled] This was a city in the tribe of Reuben, afterwards possessed by the Moabites. It probably had its name from *Nebo*, one of the principal idols of the Moabites.

Kiriathaim] Another city of the Moabites.

Misgab is confounded] There is no place of this name known; and therefore several learned men translate המשגב *hammisgab*, literally, *The high tower*, or *fortress*, which may apply to *Kiriathaim*, or any other high and well-fortified place.

Verse 2. *No more praise of Moab*] "The glory of Moab, that it had never been conquered," (*Dahler*,) is now at an end. Dr. *Blayney* translates:—

"Moab shall have no more glorying in Heshbon;
They have devised evil against her (saying.)"

And this most certainly is the best translation of the original. He has marked also a double *paronomasia* in this and the next verse, a figure in which the prophets delight; בחשבון חשבו *becheshbon chashebu*, "in Cheshbon they have devised," and מדמן תדמי *madmen tiddommi*, "Madmena, thou shalt be dumb."

Verse 3. *Horonaim*] Another city of Moab, near to Luhith. At this latter place the *hill country* of Moab commenced. "It is a place," says *Dahler*, "situated upon a height between *Areopolis* and *Zoar*."

A. M. cir. 3420
B. C. cir. 584
Ol. XLIX. 1
TarquiniiPrisci,
R. Roman.,
cir. annum 33

7 For because thou hast trusted in thy works and in thy treasures, thou shalt also be taken: and [p]Chemosh shall go forth into captivity *with* his [q]priests and his princes together.

8 And [r]the spoiler shall come upon every city, and no city shall escape: the valley also shall perish, and the plain shall be destroyed, as the LORD hath spoken.

9 [s]Give wings unto Moab, that it may flee and get away: for the cities thereof shall be desolate, without any to dwell therein.

10 [t]Cursed *be* he that doeth the work of the LORD [u]deceitfully, and cursed *be* he that keepeth back his sword from blood.

11 Moab hath been at ease from his youth, and he [v]hath settled on his lees, and hath not been emptied from vessel to vessel, neither hath he gone into captivity: therefore his taste [w]remained in him, and his scent is not changed.

12 Therefore, behold, the days come, saith the LORD, that I will send unto him wanderers, that shall cause him to wander, and shall empty his vessels, and break their bottles.

A. M. cir. 3420
B. C. cir. 584
Ol. XLIX. 1
TarquiniiPrisci,
R. Roman.,
cir. annum 33

13 And Moab shall be ashamed of [x]Chemosh. as the house of Israel [y]was ashamed of [z]Beth-el their confidence.

14 How say ye, [a]We *are* mighty and strong men for the war?

15 [b]Moab is spoiled, and gone up *out of* her cities, and [c]his chosen young men are [d]gone down to the slaughter, saith [e]the King, whose name *is* the LORD of hosts.

16 The calamity of Moab *is* near to come, and his affliction hasteth fast.

17 All ye that are about him, bemoan him; and all ye that know his name, say, [f]How is the strong staff broken, *and* the beautiful rod!

18 [g]Thou daughter that dost inhabit [h]Dibon, come down from *thy* glory, and sit in thirst; for [i]the spoiler of Moab shall come upon thee, *and* he shall destroy thy strong holds.

---

[p]Num. xxi. 29; Judg. xi. 24; see Isa. xlvi. 1, 2; chap. xliii. 12——[q]Chap. xlix. 3——[r]Chap. vi. 26; ver. 18 [s]Psa. lv. 6; ver. 28——[t]See Judg. v. 23; 1 Sam. xv. 3, 9; 1 Kings xx. 42——[u]Or, *negligently*——[v]Zeph. i. 12 [w]Heb. *stood*

[x]Judg. xi. 24; 1 Kings xi. 7——[y]Hos. x. 6——[z]1 Kings xii. 29——[a]Isa. xvi. 6——[b]Ver. 8, 9, 18——[c]Heb. *the choice of*——[d]Chap. l. 27——[e]Chap. xlvi. 18; li. 57 [f]See Isa. ix. 4; xiv. 4, 5——[g]Isa. xlvii. 1; chap. xlvi. 19 [h]Num. xxi. 30; Isa. xv. 2——[i]Ver. 8

Verse 6. *Flee, save your lives*] The enemy is in full pursuit of you.

Be like the heath] כערוער *caaroer*, "like Aroer;" which some take for a *city*, others for a *blasted* or *withered tree*. It is supposed that a place of this name lay towards the north, in the land of the Ammonites, on a branch of the river Jabbok; surrounded by *deserts*. Save yourselves by getting into the wilderness, where the pursuing foe will scarcely think it worth his while to follow you, as the wilderness itself must soon destroy you.

Verse 7. *Chemosh shall go forth into captivity*] The grand national idol of the Moabites, Num. xxi. 29; Judg. xi. 24. Ancient idolaters used to take their gods with them to the field of battle. This was probably in imitation of the Israelites, who took the *ark* with them in such cases.

Verse 9. *Give wings unto Moab*] There is no hope in resistance, and to escape requires the *speediest* flight. I cannot conceive how *Dahler* came to translate thus: Tirez Moab par les chevaux, "Drag Moab away by the hair of the head."

Verse 10. *Cursed* be *he that doeth the work of the Lord deceitfully*] Moab is doomed to destruction, and the Lord pronounces a curse on their enemies if they do not proceed to utter extirpation. God is the Author of life, and has a sovereign right to dispose of it as he pleases; and these had forfeited theirs long ago by their idolatry and other crimes.

Verse 11. *Moab hath been at ease*] The metaphor here is taken from the mode of preserving wines. They let them rest upon their lees for a considerable time, as this improves them both in strength and flavour; and when this is sufficiently done, they rack, or pour them off into other vessels. Moab had been very little molested by war since he was a nation; he had never gone out of his own land. Though some had been carried away by Shalmaneser forty years before this, he has had neither wars nor captivity.

Therefore his taste remained in him] Still carrying on the allusion to the curing of wines; by resting long upon the *lees*, the *taste* and *smell* are both improved. See the note on Isa. xxv. 6.

Verse 12. *I will send unto him wanderers, that shall cause him to wander*] Dr. *Blayney* renders צעים *tsaim, tilters;* those who elevate one end of the wine cask when nearly run out, that the remains of the liquor may be the more effectually drawn off at the cock. And this seems to be well supported by the following words,—

And shall empty his vessels] I will send such as will carry the whole nation into captivity.

Verse 13. *Beth-el their confidence.*] Alluding to the golden calves which Jeroboam had there set up, and commanded all the Israelites to worship.

Verse 17. *How is the strong staff broken*] The *sceptre*. The sovereignty of Moab is destroyed.

Verse 18. *That dost inhabit Dibon*] This was anciently a city of the Reubenites, afterwards inhabited by the Moabites, about two leagues north of the river Arnon, and about six to the east of the Dead Sea.—*Dahler.*

A. M. cir. 3420
B. C. cir. 584
Ol. XLIX. 1
TarquiniiPrisci,
R. Roman.,
cir. annum 33

19 O [k]inhabitant of [l]Aroer,
[m]stand by the way, and espy;
ask him that fleeth, and her that
escapeth, *and* say, What is done?
20 Moab is confounded; for it is broken
down: [n]howl and cry; tell ye it in [o]Arnon,
that Moab is spoiled,
21 And judgment is come upon [p]the plain
country; upon Holon, and upon Jahazah, and
upon Mephaath,
22 And upon Dibon, and upon Nebo, and
upon Beth-diblathaim,
23 And upon Kiriathaim, and upon Beth-ga-
mul, and upon Beth-meon,
24 And upon [q]Kerioth, and upon Bozrah,
and upon all the cities of the land of Moab,
far or near.
25 [r]The horn of Moab is cut off, and his
[s]arm is broken, saith the LORD.
26 [t]Make ye him drunken: for he magnified
himself against the LORD: Moab also shall wallow in his vomit, and he also shall be in derision.
27 For [u]was not Israel a derision unto thee?
[v]was he found among thieves? for since thou
spakest of him, thou [w]skippedst for joy.
28 O ye that dwell in Moab, leave the
cities, and [x]dwell in the rock, and be like
[y]the dove *that* maketh her nest in the sides
of the hole's mouth.
29 We have heard the [z]pride of Moab, (he
is exceeding proud,) his loftiness, and his
arrogancy, and his pride, and the haughtiness of his heart.
30 I know his wrath, saith
the LORD; but *it shall* not *be* so;
[a]his [b]lies shall not so effect *it*.
31 Therefore [c]will I howl for
Moab, and I will cry out for all Moab; *mine*
heart shall mourn for the men of Kir-heres.
32 [d]O vine of Sibmah, I will weep for thee
with the weeping of Jazer: thy plants are
gone over the sea, they reach *even* to the sea
of Jazer: the spoiler is fallen upon thy summer fruits and upon thy vintage.
33 And [e]joy and gladness is taken from the
plentiful field, and from the land of Moab;
and I have caused wine to fail from the wine-
presses: none shall tread with shouting; *their*
shouting *shall be* no shouting.
34 [f]From the cry of Heshbon *even* unto
Elealeh, *and even* unto Jahaz, have they
uttered their voice, [g]from Zoar *even* unto Horonaim, *as* a heifer of three years old: for the
waters also of Nimrim shall be [h]desolate.
35 Moreover I will cause to cease in Moab,
saith the LORD, [i]him that offereth in the high
places, and him that burneth incense to his gods.
36 Therefore [k]mine heart shall sound for
Moab like pipes, and mine heart shall sound
like pipes for the men of Kir-heres: because
[l]the riches *that* he hath gotten are perished.
37 For [m]every head *shall be* bald, and every
beard [n]clipped: upon all the hands *shall be*
cuttings, and [o]upon the loins sackcloth.
38 *There shall be* lamentation generally
upon all the housetops of Moab, and in the

A. M. cir. 3420
B. C. cir. 584
Ol. XLIX. 1
TarquiniiPrisci
R. Roman.,
cir. annum 33

[k]Heb. *inhabitress*——[l]Deut. ii. 36——[m]1 Sam. iv. 13, 16——[n]Isa. xiv. 7——[o]See Num. xxi. 13——[p]Ver. 8 [q]Ver. 41; Amos ii. 2——[r]Psa. lxxv. 10——[s]See Ezek. xxx. 21——[t]Chap. xxv. 15, 27——[u]Zeph. ii. 8——[v]See chap. ii. 26——[w]Or, *movedst thyself*——[x]Psa. lv. 6, 7; ver. 9——[y]Cant. ii. 14——[z]Isa. xvi. 6, &c.——[a]Isa. xvi. 6; chap. l. 36

[b]Or, *those on whom he stayeth* (Heb. *his bars*) *do not right*——[c]Isa. xv. 2; xvi. 7, 11——[d]Isa. xvi. 8, 9 [e]Isa. xvi. 10; Joel i. 12——[f]Isa. xv. 4, 5, 6——[g]Isa. xv. 5, 6; ver. 5——[h]Heb. *desolations*——[i]Isa. xv. 2; xvi. 12 [k]Isa. xv. 5; xvi. 11——[l]Isa. xv. 7——[m]Isa. xv. 2, 3; chapter xlvii. 5——[n]Hebrew, *diminished*——[o]Genesis xxxvii. 34

Verse 19. *O inhabitant of Aroer*] See the note on ver. 6. This place, being at a greater distance, is counselled to watch for its own safety, and inquire of every passenger, *What is done?* that it may know when to pack up and be gone.

Verse 20. *Tell ye it in Arnon*] Apprize the inhabitants there that the territories of Moab are invaded, and the country about to be destroyed, that they may provide for their own safety.

Verse 21. *Upon Holon, &c.*] All these were cities of the Moabites, but several of them are mentioned in no other place.

Verse 25. *The horn of Moab is cut off, and his arm is broken*] His political and physical powers are no more.

Verse 27. *Was not Israel a derision unto thee?*] Didst thou not mock my people, and say their God was no better than the gods of other nations? See Ezek. xxv. 8.

Was he found among thieves?] Did the Israelites come to *rob* and *plunder* you? Why then mock them, and rejoice at their desolation, when their enemies prevailed over them? This the Lord particularly resents.

Verse 28. *Dwell in the rock*] Go to the most inaccessible places in the mountains.

The hole's mouth.] And into the most secret caves and holes of the earth.

Verse 29. *The pride of Moab*] See on Isa. xvi. 1.

Verse 32. *O vine of Sibmah*] See on Isa. xvi. 8.

Verse 34. As *a heifer of three years old*] Which runs lowing from place to place in search of her calf, which is lost or taken from her.

Verse 37. *For every head* shall be *bald*]

A. M. cir. 3420
B. C. cir. 584
Ol. XLIX. 1
TarquiniiPrisci,
R. Roman.,
cir. annum 33

streets thereof: for I have broken
Moab like [p]a vessel wherein *is*
no pleasure, saith the LORD.
39 They shall howl, *saying,*
How is it broken down! how hath Moab
turned the [q]back with shame! so shall Moab
be a derision and a dismaying to all them
about him.
40 For thus saith the LORD; Behold, [r]he shall
fly as an eagle, and shall [s]spread his wings
over Moab.
41 [t]Kerioth [u]is taken, and the strong holds
are surprised, and [v]the mighty men's hearts in
Moab at that day shall be as the heart of a
woman in her pangs.
42 And Moab shall be destroyed [w]from
being a people, because he hath magnified
himself against the LORD.
43 [x]Fear, and the pit, and the snare, *shall be*
upon thee, O inhabitant of Moab,
saith the LORD.
44 He that fleeth from the fear
shall fall into the pit; and he that
getteth up out of the pit shall be taken in the
snare: for [y]I will bring upon it, *even* upon
Moab, the year of their visitation, saith the
LORD.
45 They that fled stood under the shadow of
Heshbon because of the force: but [z]a fire shall
come forth out of Heshbon, and a flame from
the midst of Sihon, and [a]shall devour the corner of Moab, and the crown of the head of the
[b]tumultuous ones.
46 [c]Wo be unto thee, O Moab! the people
of Chemosh perisheth: for thy sons are taken
[d]captives, and thy daughters captives.
47 Yet will I bring again the captivity of
Moab [e]in the latter days, saith the LORD.
Thus far *is* the judgment of Moab.

A. M. cir. 3420
B. C. cir. 584
Ol. XLIX. 1
TarquiniiPrisci
R. Roman.,
cir. annum 33

---

[p]Chap. xxii. 28——[q]Heb. *neck*——[r]Deut. xxviii. 49; chap. xlix. 22; Dan. vii. 4; Hos. viii. 1; Hab. i. 8——[s]Isa. viii. 8——[t]Ver. 24——[u]Or, *The cities*——[v]Isa. xiii. 8; xxi. 3; chap. xxx. 6; xlix. 22, 24; l. 43; li. 30; Mic. iv. 9

[w]Psa. lxxxiii. 4; Isa. vii. 8——[x]Isa. xxiv. 17, 18——[y]See chap. xi. 23——[z]Num. xxi. 28——[a]Num. xxiv. 17——[b]Heb. *children of noise*——[c]Num. xxi. 29——[d]Heb. *in captivity*——[e]Chap. xlix. 6, 39

These, as we have seen before, were signs of the deepest distress and desolation.

Verse 40. *He shall fly as an eagle*] The enemy will pounce upon him, carry him off, and tear him to pieces.

Verse 42. *Moab shall be destroyed from* being *a people*] They shall not have a king or *civil governor:* and I doubt whether there be any evidence that they were ever reinstated in their *national character.* They were captivated by the Chaldeans; and probably many returned with the Jews on the edict of Cyrus: but as to their being an *independent nation* after this, where is the positive proof?

Verse 43. *Fear, and the pit, and the snare*] See the note on Isa. xxiv. 17, 18.

Verse 45. *They that fled stood under the shadow of Heshbon*] Heshbon being a fortified place, they who were worsted in the fight fled to it, and rallied under its walls; but, instead of safety, they found themselves disappointed, betrayed, and ruined. See ver. 2, and the note there.

But a fire shall come forth out of Heshbon] Jeremiah has borrowed this part of his discourse from an ancient poet quoted by Moses, Num. xxi. 28; where see the notes.

The crown of the head] The choicest persons of the whole nation.

Verse 46. *The people of Chemosh*] The Moabites, who worshipped *Chemosh* as their supreme god.

Verse 47. *Will I bring again the captivity of Moab in the latter days*] I have already expressed doubts (see ver. 42) whether the Moabites were ever restored to their national distinction. The expressions in this chapter, relative to their total destruction as a people, are so strong and so frequent, that they leave little room for a limited interpretation. That many of them returned on the edict of Cyrus, by virtue of which the Jews were restored, I doubt not; but neither the *Ammonites, Moabites, Philistines*, nor even the *Jews* themselves, were ever restored to their national consequence. Perhaps the restoration spoken of here, which was to take place in the *latter days*, may mean the conversion of these people, in their existing remnants, to the faith of the Gospel. Several judicious interpreters are of this opinion. The Moabites were partially restored; but never, as far as I have been able to learn, to their national consequence. Their conversion to the Christian faith must be the main end designed by this prophecy.

CHAPTER XLIX

This chapter is a collection of prophecies relating to several nations in the neighbourhood of Judea; and, like those preceding, are supposed to have been fulfilled by the ministry of Nebuchadnezzar during the thirteen years' siege of Tyre. The chapter opens with a prophecy concerning the Ammonites, whose chief city, Rabbah, shall be destroyed; and Malcom, the supreme divinity of the people, with all his retinue of priests and officers, carried into captivity, 1–5. *Promise that the Ammonites shall be restored to their liberty,* 6. *Prophecy against the Edomites, (very like that most dreadful one in the thirty-fourth chapter of Isaiah against the same people,) who shall be utterly exterminated, after the similitude of Sodom and Gomorrah,* 7–22. *Prophecy against Damas-*

cus, 23–27; and against Kedar, 28, 29. Utter desolation of the kingdoms of Hazor foretold, 30–33. The polity of the Elamites shall be completely dissolved, and the people dispersed throughout the nations, 34–38. The Elamites shall be delivered from their captivity in the latter days, 39. It will be proper here to observe that these predictions should not be so explained as if they admitted of merely a private interpretation; for, as Bishop Lowth remarks upon Isaiah's prophecy concerning the Idumeans, "by a figure very common in the prophetical writings, any city or people, remarkably distinguished as enemies of the people and kingdom of God, is put for those enemies in general;" therefore, it is under the Gospel dispensation that these prophecies shall be accomplished to their fullest extent upon all the antichristian nations that have sinned after the similitude *of the ancient enemies of the people of God under the Mosaic economy.*

A. M. cir. 3421
B. C. cir. 583
Ol. XLIX. 2
TarquiniiPrisci,
R. Roman.,
cir. annum 34

[a]CONCERNING [b]the Am-
monites, thus saith the
LORD; Hath Israel no sons? hath
he no heir? why *then* doth [c]their
king inherit [d]Gad, and his people dwell in his
cities?
2 Therefore, behold, the days come, saith
the LORD, that I will cause an alarm of war
to be heard in [q]Rabbah of the Ammonites;
and it shall be a desolate heap, and her
daughters shall be burned with fire: then
shall Israel be heir unto them that were his
heirs, saith the LORD.
3 Howl, O Heshbon, for Ai is spoiled: cry,
ye daughters of Rabbah, [f]gird you with sackcloth; lament, and run to and fro by the
hedges; for [g]their king shall go into captivity,
and his [h]priests and his princes together.
4 Wherefore gloriest thou in the valleys, [i]thy
flowing valley, [o]O [k]backsliding
daughter? that trusted in her
treasures, [l]*saying,* Who shall
come unto me?
5 Behold, I will bring a fear upon thee,
saith the Lord GOD of hosts, from all those
that be about thee; and ye shall be driven
out every man right forth; and none shall
gather up him that wandereth.
6 And [m]afterward I will bring again the
captivity of the children of Ammon, saith the
LORD.

A. M. cir. 3417
B. C. cir. 587
Ol. XLVIII. 2
TarquiniiPrisci,
R. Roman.,
cir. annum 30

7 [n]Concerning Edom, thus
saith the LORD of hosts; [o]*Is*
wisdom no more in Teman?
[p]is counsel perished from the
prudent? is their wisdom vanished?
8 [q]Flee ye, [r]turn back, dwell deep, O inhabitants of [s]Dedan; for I will bring the cala-

[a]Or, *Against*——[b]Ezek. xxi. 28; xxv. 2; Amos i. 13; Zeph. ii. 8, 9——[c]Or, *Melcom*——[d]Amos i. 13 [e]Ezek. xxv. 5; Amos i. 14——[f]Isa. xxxii. 11; chap. iv. 8; vi. 26——[g]Or, *Melcom;* 1 Kings xi. 5, 33——[h]Chap. xlviii. 7; Amos i. 15

[i]Or, *thy valley floweth away*——[k]Chap. iii. 14; vii. 24 [l]Chap. xxi. 13——[m]So ver. 39; chap. xlviii. 47 [n]Ezek. xxv. 12; Amos i. 11——[o]Obad. 8——[p]See Isa. xix. 11——[q]Ver. 30——[r]Or, *they are turned back* [s]Chap. xxv. 23

NOTES ON CHAP. XLIX

Verse 1. CONCERNING THE AMMONITES] This prophetic discourse was also delivered *after* the capture of Jerusalem.

Hath Israel no sons?—no heir?] The Ammonites, it appears, took advantage of the depressed state of Israel, and invaded their territories in the tribe of Gad, hoping to make them their own for ever. But the prophet intimates that God will preserve the descendants of Israel, and will bring them back to their forfeited inheritances.

Why then *doth their king*] מלכם *Malcom* or *Milcom*, the chief idol of the Ammonites. That the idol *Milcom* is here meant is sufficiently evident from ver. 3, where it is said: "Milcom (not *their king*) shall go into captivity; his PRIESTS and his princes together." *Milcom* is also called *Molech. Malcom* is put here for the *Ammonites*, as the *people of Chemosh* in the preceding chapter are put for the *Moabites* in general.

Verse 3. *Run to and fro by the hedges*] It is supposed that this may refer to the women making lamentations for the dead, that were in general buried by the walls of their *gardens;* but others think that it refers to the *smaller cities* or *villages*, called here the *daughters of Rabbah*, the metropolis; the inhabitants of which are exhorted to seek safety somewhere else, as none can be expected from them, now that the enemy is at hand.

Verse 4. *Wherefore gloriest thou*] Though thy valleys be fruitful, yet glory not in them. Though thou have much political and military power, do not trust in them, nor in the multitude of thy cities; a stronger than thou is coming against thee.

Verse 6. *Afterward I will bring again*] The *Ammonites* are supposed to have returned with the Moabites and Israelites, on permission given by the edict of Cyrus.

Verse 7. CONCERNING EDOM] This is a new and separate discourse.

Teman] A part of Idumea, put here for the whole country.

Verse 8. *Dwell deep*] An allusion to the custom of the Arabs, who, when about to be attacked by a powerful foe, strike their tents, pack up their utensils, lade their camels, which they can do in *a couple of hours*, and set off to the great desert, and so *bury themselves in it* that no enemy either will or can pursue, as it is the Arabs alone that know the deserts, and can find *water* and *provender* for their support.

Dedan] Was a city of Idumea, not far from Teman.

A. M. cir. 3417 B. C. cir. 587 Ol. XLVIII. 2 TarquiniiPrisci, R. Roman., cir. annum 30

mity of Esau upon him, the time
that I will visit him.
9 If [t]grape-gatherers come to
thee, would they not leave *some*
gleaning grapes? if thieves by night, they
will destroy [u]till they have enough.
10 [v]But I have made Esau bare, I have
uncovered his secret places, and he shall not
be able to hide himself: his seed is spoiled,
and his brethren, and his neighbours, and
[w]he *is* not.
11 Leave thy fatherless children, I will preserve *them* alive; and let thy widows trust
in me.
12 For thus saith the LORD; Behold, [x]they
whose judgment *was* not to drink of the cup
have assuredly drunken; and *art* thou he *that*
shall altogether go unpunished? thou shalt
not go unpunished, but thou shalt surely
drink *of it*.
13 For [y]I have sworn by myself, saith the
LORD, that [z]Bozrah shall become a desolation,
a reproach, a waste, and a curse; and all the
cities thereof shall be perpetual wastes.
14 I have heard a [a]rumour from the LORD,
and an ambassador is sent unto the heathen,
saying, Gather ye together, and
come against her, and rise up to
the battle.
15 For, lo, I will make thee small
among the heathen, *and* despised among men.
16 Thy terribleness hath deceived thee, *and*
the pride of thine heart, O thou that dwellest
in the clefts of the rock, that holdest the
height of the hill: [b]though thou shouldest
make thy [c]nest as high as the eagle, [d]I will
bring thee down from thence, saith the LORD.
17 Also Edom shall be a desolation: [e]every
one that goeth by it shall be astonished, and
shall hiss at all the plagues thereof.
18 [f]As in the overthrow of Sodom and
Gomorrah and the neighbour *cities* thereof,
saith the LORD, no man shall abide there,
neither shall a son of man dwell in it.
19 [g]Behold, he shall come up like a lion
from [h]the swelling of Jordan against the habitation of the strong: but I will suddenly
make him run away from her: and who *is* a
chosen *man, that* I may appoint over her?
for [i]who *is* like me? and who will [k]appoint me
the time? and [l]who *is* that shepherd that will
stand before me?

[t]Obad. 5——[u]Heb. *their sufficiency*——[v]Mal. i. 3——[w]Isa. xvii. 14——[x]Chap. xxv. 29; Obad. 16——[y]Gen. xxii. 16; Isa. xlv. 23; Amos vi. 8——[z]Isa. xxxiv. 6; lxiii. 1——[a]Obad. 1, 2, 3——[b]Obad. 4

[c]Job xxxix. 27——[d]Amos ix. 2——[e]Ch. xviii. 16; l. 13——[f]Gen. xix. 25; Deut. xxix. 23; chap. l. 40; Amos iv. 11——[g]Chap. l. 44, &c.——[h]Chap. xii. 5——[i]Exod. xv. 11——[k]Or, *convent me in judgment*——[l]Job xli. 10

Verse 9. *If grape-gatherers*] Both in vintage and harvest every grape and every stalk are not gathered; hence the gleaners get something for their pains: but your enemies shall not leave one of you behind; all shall be carried into captivity.

Verse 10. *I have made Esau bare*] I have stripped him of all defence, and have discovered his hiding-places to his enemies.

Verse 11. *Leave thy fatherless children*] The connexion of this with the context is not easy to be discerned; but, as a general maxim, it is of great importance. *Widows* and *orphans* are the peculiar care of God. He is as the best of fathers to the one, and the most loving of husbands to the other. Even the widows and orphans of Esau, who escape the general destruction, shall be taken care of by the Lord.

Verse 12. Art *thou he* that *shall altogether go unpunished?*] A similar form of speech appears, chap. xxv. 29. Others, less wicked than thou, have been punished; and canst *thou* expect to escape? Thou shalt not escape.

Verse 13. *Bozrah shall become a desolation*] *Bozrah*, a city of Idumea, is here put for the whole country.

Verse 14. *I have heard a rumour*] The Lord has revealed to me what he is about to do to the Edomites.

An ambassador is sent] I believe this means only that God has given *permission*, and has *stirred up* the hearts of these nations to go against those whom he has doomed to destruction.

Verse 16. *O thou that dwellest*] All *Idumea* is full of *mountains* and *rocks*, and these rocks and mountains full of caves, where, in time of great heats, and in time of war, the people take shelter.

Verse 18. *As in the overthrow of Sodom*] The destruction of Sodom and Gomorrah and the neighbouring cities was so terrible, that, when God denounces judgments against incorrigible sinners, he tells them they shall be like Sodom and Gomorrah.

No man shall abide there] It shall be so desolate as not to be habitable. Travellers may lodge on the ground for a night; but it cannot become a permanent dwelling.

Verse 19. *Behold, he shall come up like a lion*] See the note on chap. xii. 5. The similitude used here is well illustrated by Dr. *Blayney:* "When I shall occasion a like commotion in her (Idumea) as a fierce and strong lion may be supposed to do in the sheep-folds, then I will cause him (the man of whom it is said in the preceding verse that he should not dwell in it) to run away from her as the affrighted shepherds and their flocks run from the lion."

A chosen man] Nebuchadnezzar. That is, God has *chosen* this man, and given him a commission against Idumea.

A. M. cir. 3417 B. C. cir. 587 Ol. XLVIII. 2 TarquiniiPrisci, R. Roman., cir. annum 30

20 [m]Therefore hear the counsel of the LORD, that he hath
taken against Edom; and his
purposes, that he hath purposed
against the inhabitants of Teman: Surely the
least of the flock shall draw them out: surely
he shall make their habitations desolate with
them.

21 [n]The earth is moved at the noise of their
fall, at the cry the noise thereof was heard
in the [o]Red Sea.

22 Behold, [p]he shall come up and fly as the
eagle, and spread his wings over Bozrah: and
at that day shall the heart of the mighty men
of Edom be as the heart of a woman in her
pangs.

A. M. cir. 3404 B. C. cir. 600 Ol. cir. XLV. 1 TarquiniiPrisci, R. Roman., cir. annum 17

23 [q]Concerning Damascus.
Hamath is confounded, and
Arpad: for they have heard evil
tidings: they [r]are faint-hearted;
[s]*there is* sorrow [t]on the sea; it cannot be
quiet.

24 Damascus is waxed feeble, *and* turneth
herself to flee, and fear hath seized on *her:*
[u]anguish and sorrows have taken
her, as a woman in travail.

A. M. cir. 3404 B. C. cir. 600 Ol. cir. XLV. 1 TarquiniiPrisci, R. Roman., cir. annum 17

25 How is [v]the city of praise
not left, the city of my joy!

26 [w]Therefore her young men shall fall in
her streets, and all the men of war shall be cut
off in that day, saith the LORD of hosts.

27 And I will kindle a [x]fire in the wall of
Damascus, and it shall consume the palaces
of Ben-hadad.

A. M. cir. 3403 B. C. cir. 601 Ol. XLIV. 4 TarquiniiPrisci, R. Roman., cir. annum 16

28 [y]Concerning Kedar, and
concerning the kingdoms of
Hazor, which Nebuchadrezzar
king of Babylon shall smite, thus
saith the LORD; Arise ye, go up to Kedar,
and spoil [z]the men of the east.

29 Their [a]tents and their flocks shall they
take away: they shall take to themselves their
curtains, and all their vessels, and their
camels, and they shall cry unto them, [b]Fear
is on every side.

30 [c]Flee, [d]get you far off, dwell deep, O ye
inhabitants of Hazor, saith the LORD; for Nebuchadrezzar king of Babylon hath taken coun-

---

[m]Chap. l. 45——[n]Chap. l. 46——[o]Heb. *weedy sea*
[p]Chap. iv. 13; xlviii. 40, 41——[q]Isa. xvii. 1; xxxvii. 13; Amos i. 3; Zeph. ix. 1, 2——[r]Heb. *melted*——[s]Isa. lvii. 20——[t]Or, *as on the sea*

[u]Isa. xiii. 8; ch. 31; vi. 24; xxx. 6; xlviii. 41; ver. 22
[v]Ch. xxxiii. 9; li. 41——[w]Ch. l. 30; li. 4——[x]Amos i. 4
[y]Isa. xxi. 13——[z]Judg. vi. 5; Job i. 3——[a]Psa. cxx. 5
[b]Ch. vi. 25; xlvi. 5——[c]Ver. 8——[d]Heb. *flit greatly*

Verse 20. *The inhabitants of Teman*] Taken here for the whole of Idumea. These are a kind of synonyms which prevent monotony, and give variety to the poet's versification.

Surely the least of the flock shall draw them out] They shall be like timid sheep; the weakest foe shall overcome them.

Verse 21. *The earth is moved*] The whole state is represented here as a *vast building* suddenly thrown down, so as to cause the earth to tremble, and the noise to be heard at a great distance.

Verse 22. *He shall come up and fly as the eagle*] Nebuchadnezzar. See chap. xlviii. 40.

Verse 23. CONCERNING DAMASCUS.] This is the *head* or *title* of another prophecy. *Damascus* was one of the principal cities of Syria. It was taken by David, 2 Sam. viii. 6, was retaken in the reign of Solomon, 1 Kings xi. 24, &c., and regained its independence. Its kings were often at war with the ten tribes, and once it joined with them for the destruction of Judah. To defend himself against these powerful enemies Ahaz made a league with the king of Assyria, who besieged Damascus, took, and demolished it. From that time we hear nothing of Damascus till we meet with it in this prophecy. It appears to have been rebuilt and restored to some consequence. It made an obstinate resistance to Nebuchadnezzar; but was at last taken and sacked by him. At present it is both a large and populous city, with considerable commerce.

Hamath is confounded] This is a city of Syria, on the *Orontes*. The Greeks called it *Epiphania*.

Arpad] Not far from Damascus.

Sorrow on the sea] They are like the troubled sea, that cannot rest.

Verse 25. *How is the city of praise not left*] Damascus is so ruined that she can no more be called a *praiseworthy* or *happy city*.

Verse 27. *The palaces of Ben-hadad.*] Damascus was a seat of the Syrian kings, and *Ben-hadad* was a name common to several of its kings.

Verse 28. CONCERNING KEDAR, AND CONCERNING THE KINGDOMS OF HAZOR] This is the *title* of another new prophecy.

Kedar was the name of one of the sons of Ishmael (Gen. xxv. 13) who settled in Arabia, and who gave name to a powerful tribe of Arabs who used to traffic with the Tyrians in cattle. It appears from this prophecy that Nebuchadnezzar got a commission to go against and reduce them to great misery.

Verse 29. *Their tents and their flocks*] This description of *property* shows that they were *Scenite* or *Nomad Arabs;* persons who dwell in *tents*, and whose principal property was *cattle*, especially *camels*, of the whole of which they were plundered by the Chaldeans.

Verse 30. *Dwell deep*] Retire into the depths of the *desert*. See on ver. 8.

Inhabitants of Hazor] I cannot find this place. It was no doubt in Arabia, and a place of considerable importance; but it is now no more

A. M. cir. 3403
B. C. cir. 601
Ol. XLIV. 4
TarquiniiPrisci,
R. Roman.,
cir. annum 16

sel against you, and hath conceived a purpose against you.
31 Arise, get you up unto [e]the
[f]wealthy nation, that dwelleth
without care, saith the LORD, which have neither gates nor bars, *which* [g]dwell alone.
32 And their camels shall be a booty, and
the multitude of their cattle a spoil; and I will
[h]scatter into all winds [i]them *that are* [k]in
the utmost corners, and I will bring their
calamity from all sides thereof, saith the
LORD.
33 And Hazor [l]shall be a dwelling for
dragons, *and* a desolation for ever: [m]there
shall no man abide there, nor *any* son of man
dwell in it.

A. M. cir. 3406
B. C. cir. 598
Ol. cir. XLV. 3
TarquiniiPrisci,
R. Roman.,
cir. annum 19

34 The word of the LORD that
came to Jeremiah the prophet
against [n]Elam in the beginning
of the reign of Zedekiah king of
Judah, saying,
35 Thus saith the LORD of
hosts; Behold, I will break [o]the
bow of Elam, the chief of their
might.
36 And upon Elam will I bring the four
winds from the four quarters of heaven, and
[p]will scatter them toward all those winds; and
there shall be no nation whither the outcasts
of Elam shall not come.
37 For I will cause Elam to be dismayed
before their enemies, and before them that
seek their life: and I will bring evil upon
them, *even* my fierce anger, saith the LORD;
[q]and I will send the sword after them, till I
have consumed them:
38 And I will [r]set my throne in Elam, and
will destroy from thence the king and the
princes, saith the LORD.
39 But it shall come to pass [s]in the latter
days, *that* I will bring again the captivity of
Elam, saith the LORD.

---

[e]Ezek. xxxviii. 11——[f]Or, *that is at ease*——[g]Num. xxiii. 9; Deut. xxxiii. 28; Mic. vii. 14——[h]Ezek. v. 10; ver. 36——[i]Chap. ix. 26; xxv. 23——[k]Heb. *cut off into corners*, or *that have the corners* of their hair *polled*

[l]Chap. ix. 11; x. 22; Mal. i. 3——[m]Ver. 18——[n]Chap. xxv. 25——[o]See Isa. xxii. 6——[p]Ver. 32——[q]Chap. ix. 16; xlviii. 2——[r]See chap. xliii. 10——[s]Chap. xlviii. 47; ver. 6

Verse 31. *The wealthy nation*] גוי שליו *goi sheleiv*, "the peaceable nation"—

Have neither gates nor bars] The Arabs, who had nothing but their tents; no cities, nor even *permanent villages*.

Verse 32. *The utmost corners*] Even in these utmost inaccessible recesses the sword and pillage shall reach them. "'The utmost corners;' insulated coasts; the peninsula of Arabia."—*Blayney*.

Verse 33. *Hazor shall be a dwelling for dragons*] Shall be turned into a *wilderness*.

A desolation for ever] Never to be re-peopled.

There shall no man abide there] It may occasionally be *visited*, but never made a permanent abode.

Verse 34. THE WORD—AGAINST ELAM] Another new head of prophecy. As this was delivered in the beginning of the reign of Zedekiah, it can have no natural nor historical connexion with the other prophecies in this various chapter. Some think that by *Elam* Persia is always meant; but this is not at all likely. It was a part of the Babylonian empire in the time of Daniel, (chap. viii. 2,) and is most probably what is called *Elymais* by the Greeks. This, with Susiana, Nebuchadnezzar subdued, and took from Astyages, king of Media.

Verse 35. I *will break the bow of Elam*] They were eminent archers; and had acquired their power and eminence by their dexterity in the use of the bow. See Isa. xxii. 6. *Strabo*, *Livy*, and others speak of their eminence in archery.

Verse 36. *Will I bring the four winds*] Nebuchadnezzar and his armies, gathered out of different provinces, and attacking this people at all points in the same time.

There shall be no nation, &c.] They shall be scattered through the *one hundred* and *twenty-seven* provinces of which the Babylonish empire is composed.

Verse 38. *I will set my throne in Elam*] This is spoken either of *Nebuchadnezzar* or *Cyrus*. It is certain that Cyrus did render himself master of *Elymais* and *Media*, which are in the land of Elam.

Verse 39. *I will bring again the captivity of Elam*] As this is to be in *the latter days*, probably it may mean the *spiritual freedom* which these people would receive under the Gospel dispensation. Under Cyrus, the *Elamites*, collected out of all quarters, were united with the *Persians*, their neighbours, and became, with them, masters of the east. See *Calmet* and *Dahler*. There are still, however, difficulties on this subject. Who the *Elamites* were is still a question. That which appears to be nearest the truth is, that the *Elamites* and *Persians* were two *distinct people*, and continued so till blended together under Cyrus. It is in this light that I have considered the subject in the preceding notes. Neighbouring people are frequently confounded in history, and sometimes the name of a people is given to those who have the same *character*.

CHAPTER L

This and the following chapter contain a prophecy relating to the fall of Babylon, interspersed with several predictions relative to the restoration of Israel and Judah, who were to survive their oppressors, and, on their repentance, to be pardoned and brought to their own land. This chapter opens with a prediction of the complete destruction of all the Babylonish idols, and the utter desolation of Chaldea, through the instrumentality of a great northern nation, 1–3. *Israel and Judah shall be reinstated in the land of their forefathers after the total overthrow of the great Babylonish empire,* 4, 5. *Very oppressive and cruel bondage of the Jewish people during the captivity,* 6, 7. *The people of God are commanded to remove speedily from Babylon, because an assembly of great nations are coming out of the north to desolate the whole land,* 8–10. *Babylon, the hammer of the whole earth, the great desolator of nations, shall itself become a desolation on account of its intolerable pride, and because of the iron yoke it has rejoiced to put upon a people whom a mysterious Providence had placed under its domination,* 11–34. *The judgments which shall fall upon Chaldea, a country addicted to the grossest idolatry, and to every species of superstition, shall be most awful and general, as when God overthrew Sodom and Gomorrah,* 35–40. *Character of the people appointed to execute the Divine judgments upon the oppressors of Israel,* 41–45. *Great sensation among the nations at the very terrible and sudden fall of Babylon,* 46.

A. M. 3409
B. C. 595
Ol. XLVI. 2
Anno
TarquiniiPrisci,
R. Roman., 22

THE word that the LORD
spake [a]against Babylon *and*
against the land of the Chaldeans
[b]by Jeremiah the prophet.

2 Declare ye among the nations, and publish,
and [c]set up a standard; publish, *and* conceal
not: say, Babylon is taken, [d]Bel is confounded,
Merodach is broken in pieces; [e]her idols
are confounded, her images are broken in
pieces.

3 [f]For out of the north there cometh up [g]a
nation against her, which shall make her land
desolate, and none shall dwell
therein: they shall remove, they
shall depart, both man and beast.

A. M. 3409
B. C. 595
Ol. XLVI. 2
Anno
TarquiniiPrisci,
R. Roman., 22

4 In those days, and in that
time, saith the LORD, the children of Israel
shall come, [h]they and the children of Judah
together, [i]going and weeping: they shall go,
[k]and seek the LORD their God.

5 They shall ask the way to Zion with their
faces thitherward, *saying,* Come, and let us
join ourselves to the LORD in [l]a perpetual covenant *that* shall not be forgotten.

---

[a]Isa. xiii. 1; xxi. 1; xlvii. 1——[b]Heb. *by the hand of Jeremiah*——[c]Heb. *lift up*——[d]Isa. xlvi. 1; chap. li. 44
[e]See chap. xliii. 12, 13——[f]Chap. li. 48

[g]Isa. xiii. 17, 18, 20; ver. 39, 40——[h]Hos. i. 11
[i]Ezra iii. 12, 13; Psa. cxxvi. 5, 6; chap. xxxi. 9; Zech. xii. 10——[k]Hos. iii. 5——[l]Chap. xxxi. 31, &c.; xxxii. 40

NOTES ON CHAP. L

Verse 1. THE WORD THAT THE LORD SPAKE AGAINST BABYLON] This is also a new head of discourse.

The prophecy contained in this and the following chapter was sent to the captives in Babylon in the *fourth* year of the reign of Zedekiah. They are very important; they predict the total destruction of the Babylonish empire, and the return of the Jews from their captivity. These chapters were probably composed, with several additions, out of the book that was then sent by Jeremiah to the captives by the hand of Seraiah. See chap. li. 59-64.

Verse 2. *Declare ye among the nations*] God's determination relative to this empire.

Set up a standard] Show the people where they are to assemble.

Say, Babylon is taken] It is a thing so firmly determined, that it is as good as already done.

Bel] The tutelar deity of Babylon *is confounded,* because it cannot save its own city.

Merodach] Another of their idols, *is broken to pieces;* it was not able to save *itself,* much less the whole empire.

Her idols are confounded] It is a reproach to have acknowledged them.

Her images] Great and small, golden and wooden, *are broken to pieces;* even the *form* of them no longer appears.

Verse 3. *Out of the north there cometh up a nation*] The *Medes,* who formed the chief part of the army of Cyrus, lay to the *north* or *north-east* of Babylon.

Shall make her land desolate] This war, and the consequent taking of the city, *began* those disasters that brought Babylon in process of time to *complete desolation;* so that now it is not known where it stood, the whole country being a total solitude.

Verse 4. *In those days, and in that time*] In the times in which Babylon shall be opposed by the Medes and Persians, both Israel and Judah, seeing the commencement of the fulfilling of the prophecies, shall begin to seek the Lord with much prayer, and broken and contrite hearts. When the decree of Cyrus comes, they shall be ready to set off for their own country, deploring their offences, yet rejoicing in the mercy of God which has given them this reviving in their bondage.

Verse 5. *Let us join ourselves to the Lord in a perpetual covenant*] All our *former covenants* have been *broken;* let us now make one that shall *last for ever.* He shall be the LORD OUR GOD, and WE will no more worship *idols.* This covenant they have kept to the present day; whatever their present moral and spiritual state may be, they are no idolaters, in the gross sense of the term.

The description that is here given of the

A. M. 3409
B. C. 595
Ol. XLVI. 2
Anno
TarquiniiPrisci,
R. Roman., 22

6 My people hath been [m]lost
sheep: their shepherds have
caused them to go astray, they
have turned them away *on* [n]the
mountains: they have gone from mountain to
hill, they have forgotten their [o]resting place.
7 All that found them have [p]devoured them:
and [q]their adversaries said, [r]We offend not,
because they have sinned against the LORD,
[s]the habitation of justice, even the LORD, [t]the
Hope of their fathers.
8 [u]Remove out of the midst of Babylon, and
go forth out of the land of the
Chaldeans, and be as the he-goats
before the flocks.
9 [v]For, lo, I will raise and
cause to come up against Babylon an assembly
of great nations from the north country: and
they shall [w]set themselves in array against
her; from thence she shall be taken: their
arrows *shall be* as of a mighty [x]expert man;
[y]none shall return in vain.
10 And Chaldea shall be a spoil: [z]all that
spoil her shall be satisfied, saith the LORD.

A. M. 3409
B. C. 595
Ol. XLVI. 2
Anno
TarquiniiPrisci,
R. Roman., 22

[m]Isa. liii. 6; ver. 17; 1 Pet. ii. 25——[n]Chap. ii. 20; iii. 6, 23——[o]Heb. *place to lie down in*——[p]Psa. lxxix. 7 [q]Chap. xl. 2, 3; Zech. xi. 5——[r]See chap. ii. 3; Dan. ix. 16——[s]Psa. xc. 1; xci. 1

[t]Psa. xxii. 4——[u]Isa. xlviii. 20; chap. li. 6, 45; Zech. ii. 6, 7; Rev. xviii. 4——[v]Chap. xv. 14; li. 27; Ver. 3, 41——[w]Ver. 14, 29——[x]Or, *destroyer*——[y]2 Sam. i. 22——[z]Rev. xvii. 16

state of this people, their feelings and their conduct, finely exhibit the state of *real penitents*, who are fervently seeking the salvation of their souls.

1. *In those days*, when Jesus Christ is manifested in the flesh; *and in that time*, when through him is preached the remission of sins, and the people who hear are pricked in their conscience.

2. *The children of Israel and the children of Judah together.*—No distinctions being then felt or attended to; for all feel themselves *sinners*, who have come short of the glory of God. Even national distinctions and religious differences, which bind men fastest, and hold them longest, are absorbed in the deep and overpowering concern they feel for their eternal interests.

3. *Going and weeping shall they go.*—Religious *sorrow* does not preclude *activity* and *diligence.* While they are *weeping* for their sins, they are *going on* in the path of duty, seeking the Lord while he may be found, and calling upon him while he is near.

4. *They shall ask the way to Zion.—Real penitents* are the most *inquisitive* of all mortals; but their inquiries are limited to one object, *they ask the way to Zion.* What shall we do to be saved? How shall we shun the perdition of ungodly men, &c.

5. *With their faces thitherward.*—They have *turned* FROM *sin*, and *turned* TO *God.* They have left the paths of the destroyer, and their hearts are towards God, and the remembrance of his name. Thus they are profiting by that light which has convinced them of sin, righteousness, and judgment.

6. *Come, and let us join ourselves to the Lord.*—Religion is a *social principle*, and begets a *social feeling* in the soul. No man who feels his own sore, and the plague of his heart, wishes to venture *alone* in the way to heaven. He feels he wants counsel, support, comfort, and the company of those who will watch over him in love. Like David, the true penitent is a companion of all those who fear the Lord. These heavenly feelings come from one and the same Spirit, and lead to the same end; hence they say,—

7. *Let us join ourselves to the Lord in a perpetual covenant.* It is said, that *to be undecided, is to be decided.* They who are not *determined* to go to heaven, will never reach it. If the heart be not *laid under obligation*, it will do nothing. "I hope I am in earnest; I trust I shall be in earnest about the salvation of my soul; it is very proper I should be so;" and such like, show an *irresolute* soul. Such persons are ever learning, and never able to come to the knowledge of the truth.

Let us therefore bind ourselves. We have trifled too long; been *indecisive* too long; have *halted* too long between two opinions. We know now that *Jehovah* is God; let us, therefore, enter into a *covenant* with him. Let this covenant be a *perpetual* one: let us not make it for a *day*, for any *particular time*, but *for ever;* and let it never be *broken.* Let *our part* be kept inviolable: *we* ARE *and* WILL BE *thy people;* and God's part will never fail, I AM *and* WILL BE *your God.*

The covenant requires a *sacrifice.*—Hence ברית *berith* signifies *both.* Christ crucified is the great covenant sacrifice. By him God becomes united to us, and through him we become united to God.

Verse 6. *My people hath been lost sheep*] He pities them; for their pastors, kings, and prophets have caused them to err.

They have gone from mountain to hill] In all *high places* they have practised idolatry.

Verse 7. *Their adversaries said, We offend not*] God has abandoned them; we are only fulfilling his designs in plaguing them.

Verse 8. *Remove out of the midst of Babylon*] The sentence of destruction is gone out against it; prepare for your flight, that ye be not overwhelmed in its ruin.

Be as the he-goats before the flocks.] Who always run to the head of the flock, giving the example for others to follow. This may be addressed to the elders and persons of authority among the people.

Verse 9. *An assembly of great nations*] The army of Cyrus was composed of Medes, Persians, Armenians, Caducians, Sacæ, &c. Though all these did not come from the *north;* yet they were arranged under the *Medes*, who did come from the north, in reference to Babylon.

Their arrows] They are such expert archers, that they shall never miss their mark.

Verse 10. *Chaldea shall be a spoil*] She has been a spoiler, and she shall be spoiled. They had destroyed Judea, God's *heritage;* and now God shall cause her to be destroyed.

A. M. 3409
B. C. 595
Ol. XLVI. 2
Anno
TarquiniiPrisci,
R. Roman., 22

11 [a]Because ye were glad, because ye rejoiced, O ye destroyers of mine heritage, because ye
are grown [b]fat [c]as the heifer at
grass, and [d]bellow as bulls;
12 Your mother shall be sore confounded;
she that bare you shall be ashamed: *behold,*
the hindermost of the nations *shall be* a
wilderness, a dry land, and a desert.
13 Because of the wrath of the LORD it
shall not be inhabited, [e]but it shall be wholly
desolate: [f]every one that goeth by Babylon shall be astonished, and hiss at all her
plagues.
14 [g]Put yourselves in array against Babylon
round about: all ye [h]that bend the bow, shoot
at her, spare no arrows: for she hath sinned
against the LORD.
15 Shout against her round about: she hath
[i]given her hand: her foundations are fallen,
[k]her walls are thrown down: for [l]it *is* the
vengeance of the LORD: take vengeance upon
her; [m]as she hath done, do unto her.
16 Cut off the sower from Babylon, and him
that handleth the [n]sickle in the time of harvest: for fear of the oppressing sword [o]they
shall turn every one to his peo-
ple, and they shall flee every one
to his own land.
17 Israel *is* [p]a scattered sheep;
[q]the lions have driven *him* away: first [r]the
king of Assyria hath devoured him; and last
this [s]Nebuchadrezzar king of Babylon hath
broken his bones.
18 Therefore thus saith the LORD of hosts,
the God of Israel; Behold, I will punish the
king of Babylon and his land, as I have
punished the king of Assyria.
19 [t]And I will bring Israel again to his
habitation, and he shall feed on Carmel and
Bashan, and his soul shall be satisfied upon
Mount Ephraim and Gilead.
20 In those days, and in that time, saith the
LORD, [u]the iniquity of Israel shall be sought
for, and *there shall be* none; and the sins of
Judah, and they shall not be found: for I will
pardon them [v]whom I reserve.
21 Go up against the land [w]of Merathaim,
even against it, and against the inhabitants of
[x]Pekod:[y] waste and utterly destroy after
them, saith the LORD, and do [z]according to
all that I have commanded thee.

A. M. 3409
B. C. 595
Ol. XLVI. 2
Anno
TarquiniiPrisci,
R. Roman., 22

[a]Isa. xlvii. 6——[b]Heb. *big,* or *corpulent*——[c]Hos. x. 11——[d]Or, *neigh as steeds*——[e]Chap. xxv. 12——[f]Ch. xlix. 17——[g]Ver. 9; chap. li. 2——[h]Chap. xlix. 35; ver. 29——[i]1 Chron. xxix. 24; 2 Chron. xxx. 8; Lam. v. 6; Ezek. xvii. 18——[k]Chap. li. 58——[l]Chap. li. 6, 11——[m]Psa. cxxxvii. 8; ver. 29; Rev. xviii. 6——[n]Or, *scythe*

[o]Isa. xiii. 14; chap. li. 9——[p]Ver. 6——[q]Chap. ii. 15——[r]2 Kings xvii. 6——[s]2 Kings xxiv. 10, 14——[t]Isa. lxv. 10; chap. xxxiii. 12; Ezek. xxxiv. 13, 14——[u]Chap. xxxi. 34——[v]Isa. i. 9——[w]Or, *of the rebels*——[x]Ezek. xxiii. 23——[y]Or, *visitation*——[z]See 2 Sam. xvi. 11; 2 Kings xviii. 25; 2 Chron. xxxvi. 23; Isa. x. 6; xliv. 28; xlviii. 14; chap. xxxiv. 22

Verse 11. *As the heifer at grass*] Ye were wanton in the desolations ye brought upon Judea.

Verse 12. *Your mother*] Speaking to the Chaldeans: BABYLON, the *metropolis,* or mother city, shall be a wilderness, a dry land, a desert, neither fit for man nor beast.

Verse 15. *Shout against her round about*] Encompass her with lines and with troops; let none *go in* with relief, none *come out* to escape from her ruin.

Verse 16. *Cut off the sower*] Destroy the gardens and the fields, that there may be neither fruits nor tillage.

Verse 17. *Israel*] All the descendants of Jacob have been harassed and spoiled, first by the Assyrians, and afterwards by the Chaldeans. They acted towards them as a lion to a sheep which he has caught; first he devours all the flesh, next he breaks all the bones to extract the marrow.

Verse 18. *As I have punished the king of Assyria.*] The Assyrians were overthrown by the *Medes* and the *Chaldeans.* The *king* is here taken for all their kings, generals, &c., Tiglathpileser, Shalmaneser, Sennacherib, Esar-haddon, &c. To them succeeded the Chaldean or Babylonish kings. Nebuchadnezzar came against Judea several times; and at last took the city and burnt it, profaned and demolished the temple, wasted the land, and carried the princes and people into captivity.

Verse 19. *I will bring Israel again*] This seems to refer wholly to the ten tribes; for Carmel, Bashan, Mount Ephraim, and Gilead, were in their territories.

Verse 20. *In those days and in that time*] This phrase appears to take in the whole of an epoch, from its commencement to its end. See ver. 4.

I will pardon them] So as to deliver them from their captivity, and exact no more *punishment* from *them whom I reserve;* namely, the *remnant* left in the Babylonish captivity.

Verse 21. *Go up against the land of Merathaim—and against the inhabitants of Pekod*] No such *places* as these are to be found any where else; and it is not likely that *places* are at all meant. The ancient *Versions* agree in rendering the first as an *appellative,* and the last as a *verb,* except the Chaldee, which has *Pekod* as a proper name. Dr. *Blayney* translates:—

"Against the land of bitternesses, go up:
Upon it, and upon its inhabitants, visit, O sword!"

Dr. *Dahler* renders thus:—

A. M. 3409
B. C. 595
Ol. XLVI. 2
Anno
TarquiniiPrisci,
R. Roman., 22

22 [a]A sound of battle *is* in the land, and of great destruction.

23 How is [b]the hammer of the whole earth cut asunder and broken! how is Babylon become a desolation among the nations!

24 I have laid a snare for thee, and thou art also taken, O Babylon, [c]and thou wast not aware: thou art found, and also caught, because thou hast striven against the LORD.

25 The LORD hath opened his armoury, and hath brought forth [d]the weapons of his indignation: for this *is* the work of the Lord GOD of hosts in the land of the Chaldeans.

26 Come against her [e]from the utmost border, open her storehouses: [f]cast her up as heaps, and destroy her utterly: let nothing of her be left.

27 Slay all her [g]bullocks; let them go down to the slaughter: wo unto them! for their day is come, the time of [h]their visitation.

28 The voice of them that flee and escape out of the land of Babylon, [i]to declare in Zion the vengeance of the LORD our God, the vengeance of his temple.

29 Call together the archers against Babylon: [k]all ye that bend the bow, camp against it round about; let none thereof escape: [l]recompense her according to her work; according to all that she hath done, do unto her: [m]for she hath been proud against the LORD, against the Holy One of Israel.

A. M. 3409
B. C. 595
Ol. XLVI. 2
Anno
TarquiniiPrisci,
R. Roman., 22

30 [n]Therefore shall her young men fall in the streets, and all her men of war shall be cut off in that day, saith the LORD.

31 Behold, I *am* against thee, *O thou* [o]most proud, saith the Lord GOD of hosts: for [p]thy day is come, the time *that* I will visit thee.

32 And [q]the most proud shall stumble and fall, and none shall raise him up: and [r]I will kindle a fire in his cities, and it shall devour all round about him.

33 Thus saith the LORD of hosts; The children of Israel and the children of Judah *were* oppressed together: and all that took them captives held them fast; they refused to let them go.

34 [s]Their Redeemer *is* strong; [t]the LORD of hosts *is* his name: he shall thoroughly plead their cause, that he may give rest to the land, and disquiet the inhabitants of Babylon.

35 A sword *is* upon the Chaldeans, saith the LORD, and upon the inhabitants of Babylon, and [u]upon her princes, and upon [v]her wise *men*.

---

[a]Ch. li. 54——[b]Isa. xiv. 6; ch. li. 20——[c]Ch. li. 8, 31, 39, 57; Dan. v. 30, 31——[d]Isa. xiii. 5——[e]Heb. *from the end*——[f]Or, *tread her*——[g]Psa. xxii. 12; Isa. xxxiv. 7; ch. xlvi. 21——[h]Ch. xlviii. 44; ver. 31——[i]Ch. li. 10, 11

[k]Ver. 14——[l]Ver. 15; ch. li. 56; Rev. xviii. 6——[m]Isa. xlvii. 10——[n]Ch. xlix. 26; li. 4——[o]Heb. *pride*——[p]Ver. 27——[q]Heb. *pride*——[r]Ch. xxi. 14——[s]Rev. xviii. 8 [t]Isa. xlvii. 4——[u]Dan. v. 30——[v]Isa. xlvii. 13

"March against the country doubly rebellious,
And against its inhabitants *worthy* of punishment."

The latter of these two versions I take to be the most literal. The words are addressed to the *Medes* and *Persians;* and the country is *Chaldea,* doubly rebellious by its *idolatry* and its insufferable *pride.* In these *two,* it was exceeded by no other land.

Verse 23. *The hammer of the whole earth*] Nebuchadnezzar dashed to pieces the nations against whom he warred. He was the scourge of the Lord.

Verse 24. *I have laid a snare for thee*] It was not by *storm* that Cyrus took the city. The *Euphrates* ran through it; he dug a channel for the river in another direction, to divert its stream; he waited for that time in which the inhabitants had delivered themselves up to debauchery: in the dead of the night he turned off the stream, and he and his army entered by the *old channel,* now void of its waters. This was the *snare* of which the prophet here speaks. See *Herodotus,* lib. i., c. 191.

Verse 26. *Open her store-houses*] At the time that Cyrus took the city, it was full of provisions and treasures of all kinds; the walls had suffered no injury; and when the inhabitants heard that the enemy was *within,* they thought they must have *arisen out of the earth* in the centre of the city!

Verse 27. *Slay all her bullocks*] Princes, magistrates, &c., &c.

Verse 28. *Declare in Zion the vengeance of the Lord*] Zion was desolated by Babylon; tell Zion that God hath desolated the desolator.

The vengeance of his temple.] Which Nebuchadnezzar had pillaged, profaned, and demolished, transporting its sacred vessels to Babylon, and putting them in the temple of his god Bel.

Verse 29. *Call together the archers*] The preceding verses are the prediction: here, God calls the *Medes* and *Persians* to fulfil it.

Verse 31. O thou *most proud*] זדון *zadon.* PRIDE in the abstract; proudest of all people.

Verse 32. *And the most proud*] זדון *zadon,* as before. Here *pride* is personified and addressed, as if possessing a being and rational powers.

Verse 34. *Their Redeemer* is *strong*] And it was not that he *wanted power,* and that Nebuchadnezzar had *much,* that Jerusalem was taken; but because the people had *sinned,* and would *not return;* and therefore *national sins* called for *national punishments.* These have

A. M. 3409
B. C. 595
Ol. XLVI. 2
Anno
TarquiniiPrisci,
R. Roman., 22

36 A sword *is* [w]upon the [x]liars; [y]and they shall dote: a sword *is* upon her mighty men; and they shall be dismayed.

37 A sword *is* upon their horses, and upon their chariots, and upon all [z]the mingled people that *are* in the midst of her; and [a]they shall become as women: a sword *is* upon her treasures; and they shall be robbed.

38 [b]A drought *is* upon her waters; and they shall be dried up: for it *is* the land of [c]graven images, and they are mad upon *their* idols.

39 [d]Therefore the wild beasts of the desert with the wild beasts of the islands shall dwell *there*, and the owls shall dwell therein: [e]and it shall be no more inhabited for ever; neither shall it be dwelt in from generation to generation.

40 [f]As God overthrew Sodom and Gomorrah and the neighbour *cities* thereof, saith the LORD; *so* shall no man abide there, neither shall any son of man dwell therein.

41 [g]Behold, a people shall come from the north, and a great nation, and many kings shall be raised up from the coasts of the earth.

42 [h]They shall hold the bow and the lance: [i]they *are* cruel, and will not show mercy: [k]their voice shall roar like the sea, and they shall ride upon horses, *every one* put in array, like a man to the battle, against thee, O daughter of Babylon.

A. M. 3409
B. C. 595
Ol. XLVI. 2
Anno
TarquiniiPrisci,
R. Roman., 22

43 The king of Babylon hath heard the report of them, and his hands waxed feeble: [l]anguish took hold of him, *and* pangs as of a woman in travail.

44 [m]Behold, he shall come up like a lion from the swelling of Jordan unto the habitation of the strong: but I will make them suddenly run away from her: and who *is* a chosen *man, that* I may appoint over her? for who *is* like me? and who will [n]appoint me the time? and [o]who *is* that shepherd that will stand before me?

45 Therefore hear ye [p]the counsel of the LORD, that he hath taken against Babylon; and his purposes, that he hath purposed against the land of the Chaldeans: Surely the least of the flock shall draw them out: surely he shall make *their* habitation desolate with them.

46 [q]At the noise of the taking of Babylon the earth is moved, and the cry is heard among the nations.

[w]Isa. xliv. 25; chap. xlviii. 30——[x]Or, *chief stays*——[y]Heb. *bars*——[z]Chap. xxv. 20, 24; Ezek. xxx. 5——[a]Ch. li. 30; Nah. iii. 13——[b]Isa. xliv. 27; chap. li. 32, 36; Rev. xvi. 12——[c]Ver. 2; chap. li. 44, 47, 52——[d]Isa. xiii. 21, 22; xxxiv. 14; chap. li. 37; Rev. xviii. 2——[e]Isa. xiii. 20; chap. xxv. 12——[f]Gen. xiii. 10; xix. 24, 25, 28; Deut. xxix. 23; Isa. i. 9; xiii. 19; ch. xlix. 18; Lam. iv. 6; Amos iv. 11; Zeph. ii. 9; 2 Pet. ii. 6; Jude 7——[g]Ver. 9; ch. vi. 22; xxv. 14; li. 27; Rev. xvii. 16——[h]Ch. vi. 22——[i]Isa. xiii. 18——[k]Isa. v. 30——[l]Ch. xlix. 24——[m]Ch. xlix. 19, &c.——[n]Or, *convent me to plead*——[o]Job xli. 10; ch. xlix. 19——[p]Isa. xiv. 24, &c.; ch. li. 11——[q]Rev. xviii. 9

taken place; and now the Lord of hosts shows them that the *power of the Chaldeans* is mere *weakness* against his *might.*

Verse 35. *A sword*] War and its calamities, or any grievous plague; and so in the following verses.

Verse 38. *A drought* is *upon her waters*] May not this refer to the *draining of the channel of the Euphrates*, by which the army of Cyrus entered the city. See on ver. 24. The original is, however, חרב *chereb*, a sword, as in the preceding verses, which signifies war, or any calamity by which the thing on which it falls is ruined.

Verse 39. *The wild beasts of the desert*] *Dahler* translates these various terms, "The wild cats, the jackals, and the ostriches." And *Blayney* the same. *Wicklif*, "Dragons, woodewoses, and ostriches." *Coverdale*, "Wild beestes, apes, and estriches."

Verse 40. *As God overthrew Sodom*] As the very *ground* on which these cities stood, with all the *plain*, now lies under the *Dead Sea;* so *Babylon* and the *adjacent country* shall be rendered totally barren and unfruitful, and utterly incapable of being inhabited. And this is the *fact* concerning both countries. See chap. xlix. 18.

Verse 41. *Behold, a people shall come from the north*] This and the two following verses are nearly the same with chap. vi. 22-24. But *here*, destroyers against *Babylon* are intended; *there*, destroyers against *Jerusalem.*

Verse 44. *Behold, he shall came up like a lion*] The same words as in chap. xlix. 19, &c., where see the note.

Verse 46. *At the noise of the taking of Babylon*] See the note on the parallel place, chap. xlix. 21. In the *forty-ninth* chapter, these words are spoken of *Nebuchadnezzar; here*, of *Cyrus.* The taking of Babylon was a wonder to all the surrounding nations. It was thought to be impregnable.

CHAPTER LI

Sequel of the prophecies of Jeremiah against Babylon. The dreadful, sudden, and final ruin that shall fall upon the Chaldeans, who have compelled the nations to receive their idolatrous rites, (see an instance in the third chapter of Daniel,) set forth by a variety of beautiful figures; with a command to the people of God, (who have made continual intercession for the conversion of their heathen rulers,) to flee from the impending vengeance, 1–14. *Jehovah, Israel's God, whose infinite power, wisdom, and understanding are every where visible in the works of creation, elegantly contrasted with the utterly contemptible objects of the Chaldean worship,* 15–19. *Because of their great oppression of God's people, the Babylonians shall be visited with cruel enemies from the north, whose innumerable hosts shall fill the land, and utterly extirpate the original inhabitants,* 20–44. *One of the figures by which this formidable invasion is represented is awfully sublime. "The* SEA *is come up upon Babylon; she is covered with the multitude of the waves thereof." And the account of the sudden desolation produced by this great armament of a multitude of nations, (which the prophet, dropping the figure, immediately subjoins,) is deeply afflictive. "Her cities are a desolation, a dry land, and a wilderness; a land wherein no man dwelleth, neither doth any son of man pass thereby." The people of God a third time admonished to escape from Babylon, lest they be overtaken with her plagues,* 45, 46. *Other figures setting forth in a variety of lights the awful judgments with which the Chaldeans shall be visited on account of their very gross idolatries,* 47–58. *The significant emblem with which the chapter concludes, of Seraiah, after having read the book of the Prophet Jeremiah against Babylon, binding a stone to it, and casting it into the river Euphrates, thereby prefiguring the very sudden downfall of the Chaldean city and empire,* 59–64, *is beautifully improved by the writer of the Apocalypse,* chap. xviii. 21, *in speaking of* Babylon the GREAT, *of which the other was a most expressive type; and to which many of the passages interspersed throughout the Old Testament Scriptures relative to Babylon must be ultimately referred, if we would give an interpretation in every respect equal to the terrible import of the language in which these prophecies are conceived.*

A. M. 3409
B. C. 595
Ol. XLVI. 2
Anno
TarquiniiPrisci,
R. Roman., 22

THUS saith the LORD; Behold, I will raise up against
Babylon, and against them that
dwell in the [a]midst of them that
rise up against me, [b]a destroying wind;
2 And will send unto Babylon [c]fanners that
shall fan her, and shall empty her land; [d]for
in the day of trouble they shall be against her
round about.
3 Against *him that* bendeth [e]let the archer
bend his bow, and against *him that* lifteth himself up in his brigandine: and spare ye not her
young men; [f]destroy ye utterly all her host.
4 Thus the slain shall fall in the land of the
Chaldeans, [g]and *they that are* thrust through
in her streets.
5 For Israel *hath* not *been* forsaken, nor
Judah of his God, of the LORD of hosts;
though their land was filled with
sin against the Holy One of
Israel.

A. M. 3409
B. C. 595
Ol. XLVI. 2
Anno
TarquiniiPrisci,
R. Roman., 22

6 [h]Flee out of the midst of
Babylon, and deliver every man his soul; be
not cut off in her iniquity; for [i]this *is* the
time of the LORD's vengeance; [k]he will
render unto her a recompense.
7 [l]Babylon *hath been* a golden cup in the
LORD's hand, that made all the earth
drunken: [m]the nations have drunken of her
wine; therefore the nations [n]are mad.
8 Babylon is suddenly [o]fallen and destroyed:
[p]howl for her; [q]take balm for her pain, if so
be she may be healed.
9 We would have healed Babylon, but she
is not healed: forsake her, and [r]let us go
every one into his own country: [s]for her

[a]Heb. *heart*——[b]2 Kings xix. 7; chap. iv. 11——[c]Ch. xv. 7——[d]Chap. l. 14——[e]Chap. l. 14——[f]Chap. l. 21
[g]Chap. xlix. 26; l. 30, 37——[h]Chap. l. 8; Rev. xviii. 4
[i]Chap. l. 15, 28——[k]Chap. xxv. 14

[l]Rev. xvii. 4——[m]Rev. xiv. 8——[n]Chap. xxv. 16
[o]Isa. xxi. 9; Rev. xiv. 8; xviii. 2——[p]Chap. xlviii. 20; Rev. xviii. 9, 11, 19——[q]Chap. xlvi. 11——[r]Isa. xiii. 4; chap. l. 16——[s]Rev. xviii. 5

NOTES ON CHAP. LI

Verse 1. *Thus saith the Lord*] This chapter is a continuation of the preceding prophecy.

A destroying wind.] Such as the *pestilential winds* in the east; and here the emblem of a *destroying army*, carrying all before them, and wasting with fire and sword.

Verse 2. *And will send—fanners*] When the corn is trodden out with the feet of cattle, or crushed out with a heavy wheel armed with iron, with a shovel they throw it up against the wind, that the chaff and broken straw may be separated from it. This is the image used by the prophet; these people shall be trodden, crushed, and fanned by their enemies.

Verse 5. *For Israel* hath *not* been *forsaken*] God still continued his prophets among them; he had never cast them wholly off. Even in the midst of *wrath*—highly deserved and inflicted *punishment*, he has remembered *mercy;* and is now about to crown what he has done by restoring them to their own land. I conceive אשם *asham*, which we translate *sin*, as rather signifying *punishment*, which meaning it often has.

Verse 7. *Made all the earth drunken*] The cup of God's wrath is the *plenitude of punishment*, that he inflicts on transgressors. It is represented as *intoxicating* and making them *mad.*

Verse 8. *Babylon is suddenly fallen and destroyed*] These appear to be the words of some of the spectators of Babylon's misery.

Verse 9. *We would have healed Babylon*] Had it been in our power, we would have saved her; but we could not turn away the judgment of God.

A. M. 3409 B. C. 595 Ol. XLVI. 2 Anno TarquiniiPrisci, R. Roman., 22

judgment reacheth unto heaven, and is lifted up *even* to the skies.

10 The LORD hath [t]brought forth our righteousness: come, and let us [u]declare in Zion the work of the LORD our God.

11 [v]Make [w]bright the arrows; gather the shields: [x]the LORD hath raised up the spirit of the kings of the Medes: [y]for his device *is* against Babylon, to destroy it; because it *is* [z]the vengeance of the LORD, the vengeance of his temple.

12 [a]Set up the standard upon the walls of Babylon, make the watch strong, set up the watchmen, prepare the [b]ambushes: for the LORD hath both devised and done that which he spake against the inhabitants of Babylon.

13 [c]O thou that dwellest upon many waters, abundant in treasures, thine end is come, *and* the measure of thy covetousness.

14 [d]The LORD of hosts hath sworn [e]by himself, *saying,* Surely I will fill thee with men, [f]as with caterpillars; and they shall [g]lift [h]up a shout against thee.

A. M. 3409 B. C. 595 Ol. XLVI. 2 Anno TarquiniiPrisci R. Roman., 22

15 [i]He hath made the earth by his power, he hath established the world by his wisdom, and [k]hath stretched out the heaven by his understanding.

16 [l]When he uttereth *his* voice, *there is* a [m]multitude of waters in the heavens; and [n]he causeth the vapours to ascend from the ends of the earth: he maketh lightnings with rain, and bringeth forth the wind out of his treasures.

17 [o]Every man [p]is brutish by *his* knowledge; every founder is confounded by the graven image: [q]for his molten image *is* falsehood, and *there is* no breath in them.

18 [r]They *are* vanity, the work of errors: in the time of their visitation they shall perish.

19 [s]The Portion of Jacob *is* not like them; for he *is* the former of all things: and *Israel is* the rod of his inheritance: the LORD of hosts *is* his name.

---

[t]Psa. xxxvii. 6——[u]Chap. l. 28——[v]Chap. xlvi. 4 [w]Heb. *pure*——[x]Isa. xiii. 17; ver. 28——[y]Chap. l. 45 [z]Chap. l. 28——[a]Nah. ii. 1; iii. 14——[b]Heb. *liers in wait*——[c]Rev. xvii. 1, 15——[d]Chap. xlix. 13; Amos vi. 8——[e]Heb. *by his soul*——[f]Nah. iii. 15

[g]Heb. *utter*——[h]Chap. l. 15——[i]Gen. i. 1, 6; chap. x. 12, &c.——[k]Job ix. 8; Psa. civ. 2; Isa. xl. 22——[l]Chap. x. 13——[m]Or, *noise*——[n]Psa. cxxxv. 7——[o]Chap. x. 14 [p]Or, *is more brutish than to know*——[q]Chap. l. 2 [r]Chap. x. 15——[s]Chap. x. 16

Verse 10. *The Lord hath brought forth our righteousness.*] This is the answer of the Jews. God has vindicated our cause.

Verse 11. *Make bright the arrows*] This is the prophet's address to Babylon.

The Lord hath raised up the spirit of the kings of the Medes] Of Cyaxares king of Media, called *Darius the Mede* in Scripture; and of Cyrus king of Persia, presumptive heir of the throne of Cyaxares, his uncle. Cambyses, his father, sent him, Cyrus, with 30,000 men to assist his uncle Cyaxares, against Neriglissar king of Babylon, and by these was Babylon overthrown.

Verse 12. *Set up the standard*] A call to the enemies of Babylon to invest the city and press the siege.

Verse 13. *O thou that dwellest upon many waters*] Thou who hast an abundant supply of waters. It was built on the confluence of the Tigris and Euphrates; the latter running through the city. But the *many waters* may mean the many nations which belonged to the Babylonish empire; nations and people are frequently so called in Scripture.

Verse 14. *I will fill thee with men*] By means of these very waters through the channel of thy boasted river, thou shalt be filled with men, suddenly appearing as an army of *locusts;* and, without being expected, shall lift up a terrific cry, as soon as they have risen from the channel of the river.

Verse 15. *He hath made the earth by his power*] The *omnipotence* of God is particularly manifested in the works of *creation.*

He hath established the world by his wisdom] The *omniscience* of God is particularly seen in the *government* of תבל *tebel,* the inhabited surface of the globe. What a profusion of wisdom and skill is apparent in that wondrous *system of providence* by which he governs and provides for every living thing.

And hath stretched out the heaven by his understanding.] Deep thought, comprehensive design, and consummate skill are especially seen in the formation, magnitudes, distances, revolutions, and various affections of the heavenly bodies.

Verse 16. *When he uttereth* his *voice*] Sends *thunder.*

There is *a multitude of waters*] For the *electric spark,* by decomposing atmospheric air, converts the *hydrogen* and *oxygen* gases, of which it is composed, into *water;* which falls down in the form of *rain.*

Causeth the vapours to ascend] He is the Author of that power of *evaporation* by which the water is *rarified,* and, being lighter than the air, ascends in form of *vapour,* forms clouds, and is ready to be sent down again to water the earth by the action of his *lightnings,* as before. And by those same lightnings, and the agency of heat in general, *currents of air* are formed, moving in various directions, which we call *winds.*

Verse 17. *Every man is brutish by* his *knowledge*] He is brutish for want of real knowledge; and he is brutish when he acknowledges that an idol is any thing in the world. These verses, from *fifteen* to *nineteen,* are transcribed from chap. x. 12-16.

A. M. 3409
B. C. 595
Ol. XLVI. 2
Anno
TarquiniiPrisci,
R. Roman., 22

20 [t]Thou *art* my battle axe *and* weapons of war: for [u]with thee will I break in pieces the nations, and with thee will I destroy kingdoms;

21 And with thee will I break in pieces the horse and his rider; and with thee will I break in pieces the chariot and his rider;

22 With thee also will I break in pieces man and woman; and with thee will I break in pieces [v]old and young; and with thee will I break in pieces the young man and the maid;

23 I will also break in pieces with thee the shepherd and his flock; and with thee will I break in pieces the husbandman and his yoke of oxen; and with thee will I break in pieces captains and rulers.

24 [w]And I will render unto Babylon and to all the inhabitants of Chaldea all their evil that they have done in Zion in your sight, saith the LORD.

25 Behold, I *am* against thee, [x]O destroying mountain, saith the LORD, which destroyest all the earth: and I will stretch out mine hand upon thee, and roll thee down from the rocks, [y]and will make thee a burnt mountain.

26 And they shall not take of thee a stone for a corner, nor a stone for foundations; but [z]thou shalt be [a]desolate for ever, saith the LORD.

A. M. 3409
B. C. 595
Ol. XLVI. 2
Anno
TarquiniiPrisci,
R. Roman., 22

27 [b]Set ye up a standard in the land, blow the trumpet among the nations, [c]prepare the nations against her, call together against her [d]the kingdoms of Ararat, Minni, and Ashchenaz; appoint a captain against her; cause the horses to come up as the rough caterpillars.

28 Prepare against her the nations with [e]the kings of the Medes, the captains thereof, and all the rulers thereof, and all the land of his dominion.

29 And the land shall tremble and sorrow, for every purpose of the LORD shall be performed against Babylon, [f]to make the land of Babylon a desolation without an inhabitant.

30 The mighty men of Babylon have forborne to fight, they have remained in *their* holds: their might hath failed; [g]they became as women: they have burned her dwelling-places; [h]her bars are broken.

31 [i]One post shall run to meet another, and one messenger to meet another, to show the king of Babylon that his city is taken at *one* end,

[t]Isa. x. 5, 15; chap. l. 23——[u]Or, *in thee*, or *by thee* [v]So 2 Chron. xxxvi. 17——[w]Chap. l. 15, 29——[x]Isa. xiii. 2; Zech. iv. 7——[y]Rev. viii. 8——[z]Chap. l. 40 [a]Heb. *everlasting desolations*

[b]Isa. xiii. 2——[c]Chap. xxv. 14——[d]Chap. l. 41 [e]Ver. 11——[f]Chap. l. 13, 39, 40; ver. 43——[g]Isa. xix. 16; chap. xlviii. 41; l. 37——[h]Lam. ii. 9; Amos i. 5; Nah. iii. 13——[i]Chap. l. 24

Verse 20. *Thou* art *my battle axe*] I believe *Nebuchadnezzar* is meant, who is called, chap. l. 23, the *hammer* of the whole earth. Others think the words are spoken of *Cyrus*. All the verbs are in the past tense: "With thee have I broken in pieces," &c., &c.

Verse 24. *And I will render*] The ו *vau* should be translated *but*, of which it has here the full power: "*But* I will render unto Babylon."

Verse 25. *O destroying mountain*] An epithet which he applies to the Babylonish government; it is like a *burning mountain*, which, by vomiting continual streams of *burning lava*, inundates and destroys all towns, villages, fields, &c., in its vicinity.

And roll thee down from the rocks] I will tumble thee from the rocky base on which thou restest. The combustible matter in thy bowels being exhausted, thou shalt appear as an *extinguished* crater; and the *stony matter* which thou castest out shall not be of sufficient substance to make a *foundation stone* for solidity, or a *corner stone* for beauty, ver. 26. Under this beautiful and most expressive metaphor, the prophet shows the nature of the Babylonish government; setting the nations on fire, deluging and destroying them by its troops, till at last, exhausted, it tumbles down, is extinguished, and leaves nothing as a basis to erect a new form of government on; but is altogether *useless*, like the cooled lava, which is, properly speaking, fit for no human purpose.

Verse 27. *Set ye up a standard*] Another summons to the *Medes* and *Persians* to attack Babylon.

Ararat, Minni] The Greater and Lesser Armenia.

And Ashchenaz] A part of Phrygia, near the Hellespont. So *Bochart*, Phaleg, lib. i. c. 3, lib. iii. c. 9. Concerning *Ashchenaz Homer* seems to speak, Il. ii. 370, 371:—

Φορκυς αυ Φρυγας ηγε, και Ασκανιος θεοειδης,
Τηλ' εξ Ασκανιης.

"Ascanius, godlike youth, and Phorcys led
The Phrygians from Ascania's distant land."

Calmet thinks that the *Ascantes*, who dwelt in the vicinity of the Tanais, are meant.

Verse 29. *And the land shall tremble*] It is represented here as trembling under the numerous armies that are passing over it, and the prancing of their horses.

Verse 30. *The mighty men—have forborne to fight*] They were panic-struck when they found the Medes and Persians within their walls, and at once saw that resistance was useless.

Verse 31. *One post shall run to meet another*] As the city was taken by *surprise*, in the manner already related, so now messengers, one

A. M. 3409
B. C. 595
Ol. XLVI. 2
Anno
TarquiniiPrisci,
R. Roman., 22

32 And that [k]the passages are stopped, and the reeds they have burned with fire, and the men of war are affrighted.

33 For thus saith the LORD of hosts, the God of Israel; The daughter of Babylon *is* [l]like a threshing-floor, [m]*it* [n]*is* time to thresh her: yet a little while, [o]and the time of her harvest shall come.

34 Nebuchadrezzar the king of Babylon hath [p]devoured me, he hath crushed me, he hath made me an empty vessel, he hath swallowed me up like a dragon, he hath filled his belly with my delicates, he hath cast me out.

35 [q]The violence done to me and to my [r]flesh *be* upon Babylon, shall the [s]inhabitant of Zion say: and my blood upon the inhabitants of Chaldea, shall Jerusalem say.

36 Therefore thus saith the LORD; Behold, [t]I will plead thy cause, and take vengeance for thee; [u]and I will dry up her sea, and make her springs dry.

A. M. 3409
B. C. 595
Ol. XLVI. 2
Anno
TarquiniiPrisci,
R. Roman., 22

37 [v]And Babylon shall become heaps, a dwelling-place for dragons, [w]an astonishment, and a hissing, without an inhabitant.

38 They shall roar together like lions: they shall [x]yell as lions' whelps.

39 In their heat I will make their feasts, and [y]I will make them drunken, that they may rejoice, and sleep a perpetual sleep, and not wake, saith the LORD.

40 I will bring them down like lambs to the slaughter, like rams with he-goats.

41 How is [z]Sheshach taken! and how is [a]the praise of the whole earth surprised! how is Babylon become an astonishment among the nations!

[k]Ch. l. 38——[l]Isa. xxi. 10; Mic. iv. 13; Amos i. 3——[m]Isa. xli. 15; Hab. iii. 12——[n]Or, *in the time that he thresheth her*——[o]Isa. xvii. 5, &c.; Hos. vi. 11; Joel iii. 13; Rev. xiv. 15, 18——[p]Ch. l. 17——[q]Heb. *My violence*

[r]Or, *remainder*——[s]Heb. *inhabitress*——[t]Ch. l. 34——[u]Ch. l. 38——[v]Isa. xiii. 22; ch. l. 39; Rev. xviii. 2——[w]Ch. xxv. 9, 18——[x]Or, *shake themselves*——[y]Ver. 57——[z]Ch. xxv. 26——[a]Isa. xiii. 19; ch. xlix. 25; Dan. iv. 30

after another, were despatched to give the king information of what was done; viz., that the city was taken at *one end*. *Herodotus* tells us that the *extreme parts* of the city were taken, before those of the *centre* knew any thing of the invasion. *Herodot.* lib. i. c. 191.

Verse 32. *That the passages are stopped*] Either the *bridges* or *slips* for boats, by which the inhabitants passed from one side to the other, and may mean the principal gates or passes in the city, which the victorious army would immediately seize, that they might prevent all communication between the inhabitants.

The reeds they have burned with fire] What this means I cannot tell, unless it refer to something done *after* the taking of the city. *Setting fire to the reeds* in the marshy ground, in order the better to clear the places, and give a freer passage to the water, that it may neither stagnate nor turn the solid ground into a marsh. Dr. *Blayney* thinks it refers to the *firing of the houses*, in order to throw the inhabitants into the greater confusion; but no historian makes any mention of *burning the city*, except what is said ver. 30, "They have burned her dwelling places;" and this may be a poetical expression. That they burnt nothing before they took the city must be evident from the circumstance of their taking the city by *surprise*, in the night time, with the greatest *secrecy*. Still there might have been some gates, barricadoes, or wooden works, serving for barracks or such like, which obstructed some of the great passages, which, when they had entered, they were obliged to *burn*, in order to get themselves a ready passage through the city. This is the more likely because this *burning of reeds* is connected with the *stopping of the passages*, *burning the dwelling places*, and *breaking the bars*.

Verse 33. *The daughter of Babylon* is *like a threshing floor*] The threshing wheel is gone over her; she is trodden under foot.

Verse 34. *Nebuchadrezzar—hath devoured me*] These are the words of Judea; he has taken away all my riches.

He hath cast me out.] He shall vomit all up; i. e., they shall be regained.

Verse 35. *The violence done to me*—be *upon Babylon,—and my blood upon the inhabitants of Chaldea*] Zion begins to speak, ver. 34, and ends with this verse. The answer of Jehovah begins with the next verse. Though the Chaldeans have been the instrument of God to punish the Jews, yet in return they, being themselves exceedingly wicked, shall suffer for all the carnage they have made, and for all the blood they have shed.

Verse 36. *I will dry up her sea*] Exhaust all her treasures.

Verse 37. *Without an inhabitant.*] See chap. l. 39.

Verse 39. *In their heat I will make their feasts*] It was on the night of a feast day, while their hearts were *heated* with wine and revelry, that Babylon was taken; see Dan. v. 1-3. This feast was held in honour of the goddess *Sheshach*, (or perhaps of *Bel*,) who is mentioned, ver. 41, as being taken with her worshippers. As it was in the *night* the city was taken, many had retired to rest, and *never awoke;* slain in their beds, *they slept a perpetual sleep.*

Verse 41. *How is Sheshach taken!*] Perhaps the city is here called by the name of its idol.

The praise of the whole earth] One of the *seven wonders* of the world; superexcellent for the height, breadth, and compass of its *walls*, its *hanging gardens*, the *temple of Belus*, &c., &c.

Verse 42. *The sea is come up*] A multitude of foes have inundated the city.

A. M. 3409
B. C. 595
Ol. XLVI. 2
Anno
TarquiniiPrisci,
R. Roman., 22

42 [b]The sea is come up upon Babylon: she is covered with the multitude of the waves thereof.

43 [c]Her cities are a desolation, a dry land, and a wilderness, a land wherein no man dwelleth, neither doth *any* son of man pass thereby.

44 [d]And I will punish Bel in Babylon, and I will bring forth out of his mouth that which he hath swallowed up: and the nations shall not flow together any more unto him: yea, [e]the wall of Babylon shall fall.

45 [f]My people, go ye out of the midst of her, and deliver ye every man his soul from the fierce anger of the LORD.

46 And [g]lest your heart faint, and ye fear [h]for the rumour that shall be heard in the land; a rumour shall both come *one* year, and after that in *another* year *shall come* a rumour, and violence in the land, ruler against ruler.

47 Therefore, behold, the days come, that [i]I will [k]do judgment upon the graven images of Babylon: and her whole land shall be confounded, and all her slain shall fall in the midst of her.

48 Then [l]the heaven and the earth, and all that *is* therein, shall sing for Babylon: [m]for the spoilers shall come unto her from the north, saith the LORD.

49 [n]As Babylon *hath caused* the slain of Israel to fall, so at Babylon shall fall the slain of all [o]the earth.

A. M. 3409
B. C. 595
Ol. XLVI. 2
Anno
TarquiniiPrisci,
R. Roman , 22

50 [p]Ye that have escaped the sword, go away, stand not still: remember the LORD afar off, and let Jerusalem come into your mind.

51 [q]We are confounded, because we have heard reproach; shame hath covered our faces: for strangers are come into the sanctuaries of the LORD's house.

52 Wherefore, behold, the days come, saith the LORD, [r]that I will do judgment upon her graven images: and through all her land the wounded shall groan.

53 [s]Though Babylon should mount up to heaven, and though she should fortify the height of her strength, *yet* from me shall spoilers come unto her, saith the LORD.

54 [t]A sound of a cry *cometh* from Babylon, and great destruction from the land of the Chaldeans:

55 Because the LORD hath spoiled Babylon, and destroyed out of her the great voice; when her waves do roar like great waters, a noise of their voice is uttered:

56 Because the spoiler is come upon her, *even* upon Babylon, and her mighty men are taken, every one of their bows is broken: [u]for the LORD God of recompenses shall surely requite.

57 [v]And I will make drunk her princes, and her wise *men*, her captains, and her rulers, and her mighty men: and they shall sleep a perpetual sleep, and not wake, saith [w]the King,

[b]See Isa. viii. 7, 8——[c]Chap. l. 39, 40; ver. 29——[d]Isa. xlvi. 1; chap. l. 2——[e]Ver. 58——[f]Ver. 6; chap. l. 8; Rev. xviii. 4——[g]Or, *let not*——[h]2 Kings xix. 7——[i]Chap. l. 2; ver. 52——[k]Heb. *visit upon*——[l]Isa. xliv. 23; xlix. 43; Rev. xviii. 20——[m]Chap. l. 3, 41

[n]Or, *Both Babylon is to fall, O ye slain of Israel, and with Babylon, &c.*——[o]Or, *the country*——[p]Ch. xliv. 28——[q]Psa. xliv. 15, 16; lxxix. 4——[r]Ver. 47——[s]Ch. xlix. 16; Amos ix. 2; Obad. 4——[t]Ch. l. 22——[u]Psa. xciv. 1; ch. lvi. 29; ver. 24——[v]Ver. 39——[w]Ch. xlvi. 18; xlviii. 15

Verse 44. *I will punish Bel in Babylon*] Bel or Belus was their supreme deity.

That which he hath swallowed up] The sacred vessels of the temple of Jerusalem, which were taken thence by Nebuchadnezzar, and dedicated to him in his temple at Babylon.

The wall of Babylon shall fall.] It shall cease to be a defence; and shall moulder away until, in process of time, it shall not be discernible.

Verse 45. *My people, go ye out*] A warning to all the Jews in Babylon to leave the city, and escape for their lives.

Verse 46. *A rumour shall—come one year*] A year before the capture of the city there shall be a rumour of war,—and in that year Belshazzar was defeated by Cyrus. In the *following year* the city was taken.

Verse 48. *The heaven and the earth—shall sing for Babylon*] Its fall shall be a subject of universal rejoicing.

Verse 50. *Ye that have escaped the sword*] The Jews.

Let Jerusalem come into your mind.] Pray for its restoration; and embrace the first opportunity offered of returning thither.

Verse 51. *Strangers are come into the sanctuaries*] The lamentation of the pious Jews for the profanation of the temple by the Chaldeans.

Verse 53. *Though Babylon should mount up to heaven*] Though it were fortified even to the skies, it shall fall by the enemies that I will send against it.

Verse 55. *The great voice*] Its *pride* and insufferable boasting.

Verse 56. *The Lord God of recompenses*] The fall of Babylon is an act of Divine justice; whatever it suffers, it is in consequence of its crimes.

Verse 57. *I will make drunk her princes*] See on ver. 39.

A. M. 3409
B. C. 595
Ol. XLVI. 2
Anno
TarquiniiPrisci,
R. Roman., 22

whose name *is* the LORD of
hosts.
58 Thus saith the LORD of
hosts; [x]The [y]broad walls of
Babylon shall be utterly [z]broken, and her high
gates shall be burned with fire; and [a]the people shall labour in vain, and the folk in the
fire, and they shall be weary.
59 The word which Jeremiah the prophet
commanded Seraiah the son of Neriah, the
son of Maaseiah, when he went [b]with Zedekiah the king of Judah into Babylon in the
fourth year of his reign. And *this* Seraiah
was a [c]quiet prince.
60 So Jeremiah wrote in a book all the evil
that should come upon Babylon, *even* all these
words that are written against Babylon.
61 And Jeremiah said to
Seraiah, When thou comest to
Babylon, and shalt see, and shalt
read all these words;
62 Then shalt thou say, O LORD, thou hast
spoken against this place, to cut it off, that
[d]none shall remain in it, neither man nor
beast, but that it shall be [e]desolate for ever.
63 And it shall be, when thou hast made an
end of reading this book, [f]*that* thou shalt bind
a stone to it, and cast it into the midst of
Euphrates:
64 And thou shalt say, Thus shall Babylon sink, and shall not rise from the evil
that I will bring upon her: [g]and they shall
be weary. Thus far *are* the words of Jeremiah.

A. M. 3409
B. C. 595
Ol. XLVI. 2
Anno
TarquiniiPrisci,
R. Roman., 22

[x]Or, *The walls of broad Babylon*——[y]Verse 44——[z]Or, *made naked*——[a]Habakkuk ii. 13——[b]Or, *on the behalf of*——[c]Or, *prince of Menucha*, or *chief chamberlain*——[d]Ch. l. 3, 39; verse 29——[e]Heb. *desolations*——[f]See Rev. xviii. 21——[g]Ver. 58

Verse 58. *The broad walls of Babylon*] Herodotus, who saw these walls, says, "The city was a regular square, each side of which was *one hundred and twenty* stadia, the circumference *four hundred and eighty* stadia. It was surrounded by a wall *fifty* cubits broad, and *two hundred* cubits high; and each side had *twenty-five* brazen gates."—*Herod.*, lib. i. c. 178. Had not Cyrus resorted to *stratagem*, humanly speaking, he could not have taken this city. For the destruction of this wall and its very vestiges, see on Isa. xiii. 19.

Verse 59. *The word which Jeremiah*] On account of the message sent by Jeremiah to the Jewish captives in Babylon.

Verse 60. *Wrote in a book*] Whether this book contained any more than is recorded in this place we do not know; probably it contained no more than what is found in verses 62-64. A *book*, ספר *sepher*, signifies, in Hebrew, any writing, *great* or *small*.

Verse 64. *Thus shall Babylon sink, &c.*] This is the emblem of its overthrow and irretrievable ruin. See Rev. xviii. 21, where we find that this is an emblem of the total ruin of *mystical Babylon*.

Herodotus relates a similar action of the *Phocæans*, who, having resolved to leave their country, and never return to it again, *μυδρον σιδηρεον κατεποντωσαν, και ωμοσαν μη πριν ες Φωκαιην ἡξειν, πριν η τον μυδρον τουτον αναφηναι·* "threw a mass of iron into the sea, and swore that they would never return to Phocæa till that iron mass should rise and swim on the top." The story is this: The Phocæans, being besieged by Harpagus, general of the Persians, demanded one day's truce to deliberate on the propositions he had made to them relative to their surrendering their city; and begged that in the mean while he would take off his army from the walls. Harpagus having consented, they carried their wives, children, and their most valuable effects, aboard their ships; then, throwing a mass of iron into the sea, bound themselves by an oath never to return till that iron should rise to the top and swim. See *Herodotus*, lib. i. c. 165.

Horace refers to this in his epode *Ad Populum Romanum*, Epode xvi. ver. 25:—

Sed juremus in hæc: simul imis saxa renarint
Vadis levata, ne redire sit nefas.

"As the Phocæans oft for freedom bled,
At length with imprecated curses fled."
FRANCIS.

Thus far are *the words of Jeremiah.*] It appears that the following chapter is not the work of this prophet: it is not his style. The author of it writes *Jehoiachin;* Jeremiah writes him always *Jeconiah*, or *Coniah*. It is merely historical, and is very similar to 2 Kings xxiv. 18-xxv. 30. The author, whoever he was, relates the capture of Jerusalem, the fate of Zedekiah, the pillage and burning of the city and the temple. He mentions also certain persons of distinction who were slain by the Chaldeans. He mentions the number of the captives that were carried to Babylon at three different times; and concludes with the deliverance of King Jehoiachin from prison in Babylon, in which he had been for thirty-seven years. It is very likely that the whole chapter has been compiled from some chronicle of that time; or it was designed as a *preface* to the Book of the *Lamentations;* and would stand with great propriety before it, as it contains the *facts* on which that inimitable poem is built. Were it allowable, I would remove it to that place.

CHAPTER LII

This chapter was added after Jeremiah's time probably by Ezra, after the return from the captivity, of which it gives a short account, nearly the same as in 2 Kings xxiv. 18–20, *and* xxv. *It is very properly subjoined to the preceding prophecies, in order to show how exactly they were fulfilled. It likewise forms a proper introduction to the following Lamentations, as it gives an account of the mournful events which gave rise to them. Zedekiah's evil reign and rebellion against Nebuchadnezzar,* 1–3. *Jerusalem is taken by the Chaldeans after a siege of* eighteen *months,* 4–7. *Zedekiah pursued and taken in the plains of Jericho, and his whole army dispersed,* 8, 9. *The king's sons and all the princes of Judah slain in Riblah,* 10. *Zedekiah has his eyes put out by order of the Chaldean monarch; and is afterward bound in chains, carried to Babylon, and imprisoned for life,* 11. *Nebuzar-adan, the captain of the guard, burns and spoils the city and temple,* 12–19. *The two pillars of the temple, with their dimensions and ornaments,* 20–23. *The officers of the temple, and several others, carried away captives into Babylon, and then slain by order of Nebuchadnezzar,* 24–27. *The number of Jews that Nebuchadnezzar carried away captive in the* seventh *year of his reign,* 28; *in his* eighteenth *year,* 29; *and in his* twenty-third *year* 30. *Evil-merodach, the son of Nebuchadnezzar, in the year of his accession to the throne of Babylon, (which was in the* thirty-seventh *year of the captivity, and the* one hundred and ninety-first *from the building of Rome, according to the computation of Varro,) orders Jehoiachin to be taken out of prison, and treats him kindly for the remainder of his life,* 31–34.

A. M. 3406—3416 B. C. 598—588 Ol. XLV. 3—XLVIII. 1

ZEDEKIAH *was* [a]one and twenty years old when he [b]began to reign, and he reigned eleven years in Jerusalem. And his mother's name *was* Hamutal the daughter of Jeremiah of Libnah.

2 And he did *that which was* evil in the eyes of the LORD, according to all that Jehoiakim had done.

A. M. cir. 3411 B. C. cir. 593 Ol. XLVI. 4 TarquiniiPrisci, R. Roman., cir. annum 24

3 For through the anger of the LORD it came to pass in Jerusalem and Judah, till he had cast them out from his presence, that Zedekiah rebelled against the king of Babylon.

A. M. 3414 B. C. 590 Ol. XLVII. 3 Anno TarquiniiPrisci, R. Roman., 27

4 And it came to pass in the [c]ninth year of his reign, in the tenth month, in the tenth *day* of the month, *that* Nebuchadrezzar king of Babylon came, he and all his army, against Jerusalem, and pitched against it, and built forts against it round about.

A. M. 3414—3416 B. C. 590–588 Ol. XLVII. 3—XLVIII. 1

5 So the city was besieged unto the eleventh year of king Zedekiah.

A. M. 3416 B. C. 588 Ol. XLVIII. 1 Anno TarquiniiPrisci, R. Roman., 29

6 And in the fourth month, in the ninth *day* of the month, the famine was sore in the city, so that there was no bread for the people of the land.

7 Then the city was broken up, and all the men of war fled, and went forth out of the city by night by the way of the gate between the two walls, which *was* by the king's garden; (now the Chaldeans *were* by the city round about:) and they went by the way of the plain.

8 But the army of the Chaldeans pursued after the king, and overtook Zedekiah in the plains of Jericho; and all his army was scattered from him.

9 [d]Then they took the king, and carried him up unto the king of Babylon to Riblah in the land of Hamath; where he gave judgment upon him.

10 [e]And the king of Babylon slew the sons of Zedekiah before his eyes: he slew also all the princes of Judah in Riblah.

11 Then he [f]put out the eyes of Zedekiah; and the king of Babylon bound him in [g]chains,

[a]2 Kings xxiv. 18——[b]Heb. *reigned*——[c]2 Kings xxv. 1–27; chap. xxxix. 1; Zech. viii. 19

[d]Chap. xxxii. 4——[e]Ezek. xii. 13——[f]Heb. *blinded*——[g]Or, *fetters*

NOTES ON CHAP. LII

Verse 1. *Zedekiah* was *one and twenty years old*] See 2 Kings xxiv. 18.

Verse 2. *And he did—evil*] This and the following verse are the same as 2 Kings xxiv. 19.

Verse 3. *Through the anger of the Lord*] Here is a king given to a people in God's anger, and taken away in his displeasure.

Verse 4. *Ninth year—tenth month*] Answering nearly to our January.

Verse 5. *So the city was besieged*] It held out *one year and six months.*

Verse 6. *And in the fourth month*] See the notes on chap. xxxix. 1, &c. The *fourth* month answers nearly to our July.

Verse 8. *The army of the Chaldeans pursued*] See on 2 Kings xxv. 5.

Verse 9. *King of Babylon to Riblah*] See the note on chap. xxxix. 5.

Verse 11. *He put out the eyes of Zedekiah*] See on chap. xxxix. 7.

A. M. 3416
B. C. 588
Ol. XLVIII. 1
Anno
TarquiniiPrisci,
R. Roman., 29

and carried him to Babylon, and put him in [h]prison till the day of his death.

12 [i]Now in the fifth month, in the tenth *day* of the month, [k]which *was* the nineteenth year of Nebuchadrezzar king of Babylon, [l]came Nebuzar-adan, [m]captain[n] of the guard, *which* [o]served the king of Babylon, into Jerusalem,

13 And burned the house of the LORD, and the king's house; and all the houses of Jerusalem, and all the houses of the great *men,* burned he with fire:

14 And all the army of the Chaldeans, that *were* with the captain of the guard, brake down all the walls of Jerusalem round about.

15 [p]Then Nebuzar-adan the captain of the guard carried away captive *certain* of the poor of the people, and the residue of the people that remained in the city, and those that fell away, that fell to the king of Babylon, and the rest of the multitude.

16 But Nebuzar-adan the captain of the guard left *certain* of the poor of the land for vinedressers and for husbandmen.

17 [q]Also the [r]pillars of brass that *were* in the house of the LORD, and the bases, and the brazen sea that *was* in the house of the LORD the Chaldeans brake, and carried all the brass of them to Babylon.

18 [s]The caldrons also, and the [t]shovels, and the snuffers, and the [u]bowls, and the spoons, and all the vessels of brass wherewith they ministered, took they away.

19 And the basins, and the [v]firepans, and the bowls, and the caldrons, and the candlesticks, and the spoons, and the cups; *that* which *was* of gold *in* gold, and *that* which *was* of silver *in* silver, took the captain of the guard away.

A. M. 3416
B. C. 588
Ol. XLVIII. 1
Anno
TarquiniiPrisci,
R. Roman., 29

20 The two pillars, one sea, and twelve brazen bulls that were under the bases, which king Solomon had made in the house of the LORD: [w]the [x]brass of all these vessels was without weight.

21 And *concerning* the [y]pillars, the height of one pillar *was* eighteen cubits; and a [z]fillet of twelve cubits did compass it; and the thickness thereof *was* four fingers: *it was* hollow.

22 And a chapiter of brass *was* upon it; and the height of one chapiter *was* five cubits, with network and pomegranates upon the chapiters round about, all *of* brass. The second pillar also and the pomegranates *were* like unto these.

23 And there were ninety and six pomegranates on a side; *and* [a]all the pomegranates upon the network *were* a hundred round about.

24 And [b]the captain of the guard took Seraiah the chief priest, [c]and Zephaniah the second priest, and the three keepers of the [d]door:

25 He took also out of the city an eunuch, which had the charge of the men of war; and seven men of them that [e]were near the king's person, which were found in the city; and the [f]principal scribe of the host, who mustered the people of the land; and threescore men of the people of the land, that were found in the midst of the city.

26 So Nebuzar-adan the captain of the guard took them, and brought them to the king of Babylon to Riblah.

27 And the king of Babylon smote them, and put them to death in Riblah in the land of Hamath. Thus [g]Judah was carried away captive out of his own land.

---

[h]Heb. *house of the wards*——[i]Zech. vii. 5; viii. 19——[k]See ver. 29——[l]Chap. xxxix. 9——[m]Or, *chief marshal*——[n]Heb. *chief of the executioners,* or *slaughtermen;* and so ver. 14, &c.——[o]Heb. *stood before*——[p]Chap. xxxix. 8, 9——[q]Chap. xxvii. 19——[r]See 1 Kings vii. 15, 23, 27, 50——[s]Exod. xxvii. 3; 2 Kings xxv. 14, 15, 16——[t]Or, *instruments to remove the ashes*

[u]Or, *basins*——[v]Or, *censers*——[w]1 Kings vii. 47——[x]Heb. *their brass*——[y]1 Kings vii. 15; 2 Kings xxv. 17; 2 Chronicles iii. 15——[z]Hebrews, *thread*——[a]See 1 Kings vii. 20——[b]2 Kings xxv. 18——[c]Chap. xxi. 1; xxix. 25——[d]Hebrew, *threshold*——[e]Hebrew, *saw the face of the king*——[f]Or, *scribe of the captain of the host*——[g]Lam. i. 3

Verse 12. *Now in the fifth month*] Answering nearly to our August.

Verse 13. *And burned the house of the Lord*] Thus perished this magnificent structure, after it had stood *four hundred and twenty-four* years *three* months and *eight* days. It was built A. M. 2992, and destroyed A. M. 3416.

Verse 15. *Those that fell away*] The deserters to the Chaldeans during the siege.

Verse 16. *The poor of the land*] See on chap. xxxix. 1.

Verse 17. *Also the pillars*] See on chap. xxvii. 19.

Verses 18-23. In reference to these verses see the parallel texts in the margin, the various readings there, and the notes.

Verse 24. *The second priest*] See the note on 2 Kings xxv. 18.

The three keepers] The priests who stood at the door to receive the offerings of the people, see 2 Kings xx. 9, and xxiii. 4.

Verse 25. *Seven men—that were near the*

A. M. 3404 B. C. 600 Ol. XLV. 1 Anno TarquiniiPrisci, R. Roman., 17
28 [h]This *is* the people whom
Nebuchadrezzar carried away
captive: in the [i]seventh year
[k]three thousand Jews and three
and twenty:

A. M. 3415 B. C. 589 Ol. XLVII. 4 Anno TarquiniiPrisci, R. Roman., 28
29 [l]In the eighteenth year of
Nebuchadrezzar he carried away
captive from Jerusalem eight
hundred thirty and two [m]persons:

A. M. 3420 B. C. 584 Ol. XLIX. 1 Anno TarquiniiPrisci, R. Roman., 33
30 In the three and twentieth
year of Nebuchadrezzar Nebuzar-adan the captain of the guard
carried away captive of the Jews
seven hundred forty and five persons: all the
persons *were* four thousand and
six hundred.

A. M. 3442 B. C. 562 Ol. LIV. 3 Anno Servii Tullii, R. Roman., 17
31 [n]And it came to pass in the
seven and thirtieth year of the
captivity of Jehoiachin king of Judah, in the
twelfth month, in the five and twentieth *day*
of the month, *that* Evil-merodach king of
Babylon in the *first* year of his reign [o]lifted
up the head of Jehoiachin king of Judah, and
brought him forth out of prison,
32 And spake [p]kindly unto him, and set his
throne above the throne of the kings that *were*
with him in Babylon,
33 And changed his prison garments: [q]and

---

[h]2 Kings xxiv. 2——[i]See 2 Kings xxiv. 12——[k]See 2 Kings xxiv. 14——[l]See ver. 12; ch. xxxix. 9——[m]Heb. *souls*——[n]2 Kings xxv. 27, 28, 29, 30——[o]Gen. xiv. 13, 20——[p]Heb. *good things with him*——[q]2 Sam. ix. 13

---

king's person] These were privy counsellors.

Verses 28-30. On these verses Dr. *Blayney* has some sensible remarks; I will extract the substance. These verses are not inserted in 2 Kings xxv. Are we to conclude from these verses that the whole number of the Jews which Nebuchadnezzar, in all his expeditions, carried away, was no more than *four thousand six hundred?* This cannot be true; for he carried away more than twice that number at one time; and this is expressly said to have been in the *eighth* year of his reign, 2 Kings xxiv. 12-16. Before that time he had carried off a number of captives from Jerusalem, in the *first* year of his reign, among whom were *Daniel* and his companions, Dan. i. 3-6. These are confessedly not noticed here. And as the taking and burning of Jerusalem is in this very chapter said to have been in the *fourth* and *fifth* months of the *nineteenth* year of the reign of Nebuchadnezzar, those who were carried into captivity at the date of those events cannot possibly be the same with those that are said to be carried away either in the *eighteenth* or *twenty-third* year of that prince. Nor, indeed, is it credible that the number carried away at the time that the city was taken, and the whole country reduced, could be so few as *eight hundred and thirty-two*, (see ver. 29;) supposing a mistake in the date of the year, which some are willing to do without sufficient grounds.

Here then we have *three* deportations, and those the most considerable ones, in the *first*, in the *eighth*, and *nineteenth* years of Nebuchadnezzar, sufficiently distinguished from those in the *seventh*, *eighteenth*, and *twenty-third* years. So that it seems most reasonable to conclude with Abp. *Usher*, in *Chronologia Sacra*, that by the latter *three* the historian meant to point out deportations of a minor kind, not elsewhere noticed in direct terms in Scripture.

The *first* of these, said to have been in the *seventh* year of Nebuchadnezzar, was one of those that had been picked up in several parts of Judah by the band of Chaldeans, Syrians, and others, whom the king of Babylon sent against the land previously to his own coming, 2 Kings xxiv. 2.

That in the *eighteenth* year corresponds with the time when the Chaldean army broke off the siege before Jerusalem, and marched to meet the Egyptian army, at which time they might think it proper to send off the prisoners that were in camp, under a guard to Babylon.

And the *last*, in the *twenty-third* year of Nebuchadnezzar, was when that monarch, being engaged in the siege of Tyre, sent off Nebuzar-adan against the Moabites, Ammonites, and other neighbouring nations, who at the same time carried away the gleanings of Jews that remained in their own land, amounting in all to no more than *seven hundred* and *forty-five.*

Josephus speaks of this expedition against the Moabites and Ammonites, which he places in the *twenty-third* year of Nebuchadnezzar; but mentions nothing done in the land of Israel at that time. Only he says that after the conquest of those nations, Nebuchadnezzar carried his victorious arms against Egypt, which he in some measure reduced, and carried the Jews whom he found there captives to Babylon. But the Egyptian expedition was not till the *twenty-seventh* year of Jehoiachin's captivity, i. e., the *thirty-fifth* of Nebuchadnezzar, as may be collected from Ezek. xxix. 17; so that those who were carried away in the *twenty-third* year were not from Egypt, but were, as before observed, the few Jews that remained in the land of Judah.

Verse 31. *In the twelfth month*] Answering nearly to our *twenty-fifth* of *April*, A. M. 3442.

Lifted up the head of Jehoiachin] This phrase is taken from Gen. xl. 13. It is founded on the observation that those who are in sorrow *hold down* their heads, and when they are comforted, or the cause of their sorrow removed, *they lift up their heads.* The Hebrew phrase, *lift up the head*, signifies to *comfort*, *cheer*, *make happy.*

Verse 32. *Spake kindly*] Conversed freely with him.

Set his throne] Gave him a more respectable *seat* than any of the captive princes, or better than even his own princes had, probably near his person.

Verse 33. *And changed his prison garments*] That is, Jehoiachin changed his own garments, that he might be suited in that respect to the state of his elevation. Kings also, in token of

A. M. 3442 B. C. 562 Ol. LIV. 3 Anno Servii Tullii, R. Roman., 17

he did continually eat bread before him all the days of his life.
34 And *for* his diet, there was a continual diet given him of the king of Babylon, [r]every day a portion until the day of his death, all the days of his life.

[r]Heb. *the matter of the day in his day*

favour, gave caftans or robes to those whom they wish to honour.

And he did continually eat bread before him] Was a constant guest at the king's table.

Verse 34. *And—there was a continual diet given him*] This was probably a ration allowed by the king for the support of Jehoiachin's household. For other particulars, see the note on 2 Kings xxv. 30.

All the days of his life.] I believe these words have been by mistake added from the preceding verse. *There*, they are proper; *here*, they are tautological. They are wanting in the *Septuagint* and in the *Arabic*.

The preceding words, עד יום מותו *ad yom motho*, "to the day of his death," are wanting in two of *De Rossi's* and one of *Kennicott's* MSS.

Coverdale ends thus: **All the days of his life untill he died.** This is better than the common Version.

Immediately after this verse my old MS. Bible adds the following words: **And done is aftir that into caitifte is brougt Israel, and Jerusalem is destroide, satte Jeremye the prophet weepund, and weiled with this lamentation Jerusalem; and with bitter inwit sighand and criand weilawai, seide.** Then follows in red letters: **Here beginneth the Lamentation of Jeremye, that is intitle Cenoth; with the sortynge out of Ebrue letters.** ALEPH: **How sittith aloon the city**, &c. See something of a similar kind from other authorities, at the beginning of Lamentations.

MASORETIC NOTES.

Number of verses in this Book, 1365.

Middle verse, chap. xxviii. 11.

Masoretic sections, 31.

INTRODUCTION
TO THE
LAMENTATIONS
OF
JEREMIAH

THIS book, like the several books of the Pentateuch, is denominated in Hebrew איכה *eicah, how*, from its first word; and sometimes קינות *kinnoth, lamentations*, from its subject. In the *Septuagint* it is termed ΘΡΗΝΟΙ ΤΟΥ ΙΕΡΕΜΙΟΥ, for the same reason. The *Syriac* and *Arabic* copy or follow the *Septuagint;* and so does the *Vulgate*, from the *Lamentationes* of which, the book has that name which it bears in our language. In the *Chaldee* it has no name; and in it, and perhaps anciently in the *Hebrew*, it was written consecutively with the last chapter of Jeremiah.

It is one of the books of the מגילות *Megilloth*, or Roll, among the Jews; and because it relates to the ruin of their affairs, and contains promises of restoration, it is peculiarly prized, and frequently read. The five Megilloth are: *Ecclesiastes, Canticles, Lamentations, Ruth*, and *Esther*.

There has been little difference among learned men concerning the *author* of this book. The whole current of antiquity and modern times has pointed out Jeremiah as the writer: of this the style is a sufficient evidence. Mr. *John Henry Pareau*, in a Dissertation prefixed to his Translation and Notes on this book, (8vo. Lugd. Bat. 1790,) has proved this point amply from a general collation of the prophecy of Jeremiah with select passages in this book. I have heard of but one learned man who has entertained serious doubts on the subject, Mr. *Herman Van der Hardt*, who has supposed the five chapters were written by *Daniel, Shadrach, Meshach, Abednego*, and *Jeconiah*. To this opinion I suppose none has ever been converted.

There has been more difference of opinion relative to the *subject* and *occasion*. Some have thought the book was composed on the *death of Josiah;* others that it was composed on occasion of the *destruction of Jerusalem*, and the *various desolations* connected with it. To *this* all its parts and its general phraseology seem best to apply; and this is the sentiment most generally embraced at present. This will receive much proof from a minute consideration of the book itself.

The *composition* of this poem is what may be called very technical. Every chapter, except the last, is an *acrostic*. Of the *two first*, each verse begins with a several letter of the Hebrew alphabet, in the order of the letters, with this exception, that in the *second, third*, and *fourth* chapters, the פ *phe* is put before the ע *ain;* whereas in all the acrostic Psalms the latter preceded the former, as it does in all *grammars* of the Hebrew language. In the *first* and *second* chapters each verse is composed of *three hemistichs* or half verses, except the *seventh* verse of the *first*, and the *nineteenth* of the *second* chapter, which have each *four* hemistichs.

The *third* chapter contains *sixty-four* verses, each, as before, formed of *three hemistichs*, but with this difference, that each hemistich begins with the same letter, so that the whole alphabet is *thrice* repeated in this chapter.

The *fourth* chapter is made up of *twenty-two* verses, according to the number of the Hebrew letters; but the composition is different from all the rest, for each verse consists of only *two* hemistichs, and those much shorter than any in the preceding chapters.

I have called this an inimitable poem; better judges are of the same opinion. "Never," says Bishop *Lowth*, "was there a more rich and elegant variety of beautiful images and adjuncts arranged together within so small a compass, nor more happily chosen and applied."

"One would think," says Dr. *South*, "that every letter was written with a tear; every word, the sound of a breaking heart: that the author was compacted of sorrows; disciplined to grief from his infancy; one who never breathed but in sighs, nor spoke but in a groan."

"Nor can we too much admire," says Dr. *Blayney*, "the full and graceful flow of that pathetic eloquence in which the author pours forth the effusions of a patriotic heart, and piously weeps over the ruins of his venerable country. But it was observed before that the prophet's peculiar talent lay in working up and expressing the passions of grief and *pity;* and, unhappily for him as a man and a citizen, he met with a subject but too well calculated to give his genius its full display."

David in several places has forcibly depicted the sorrows of a heart oppressed with penitential sorrow; but where, in a composition of such length, have bodily misery and mental agony been more successfully painted? All the expressions and images of sorrow are here exhibited in various combinations, and in various points of view. *Misery* has no expression that the author of the *Lamentations* has not employed. Patriots! you who tell us you burn for your country's welfare, look at the prophecies and history of this extraordinary man; look at his *Lamentations;* take him through his life to his death, and learn from him what true patriotism means! The man who watched, prayed, and lived for the welfare of his country; who choose to share her adversities, her sorrows, her wants, her afflictions, and disgrace, where he might have been a companion of princes, and have sat at the table of kings; who only ceased to live for his country when he ceased to breathe;—that was a patriot, in comparison with whom almost all others are obscured, minished, and brought low, or are totally annihilated!

THE
LAMENTATIONS
OF
JEREMIAH

Chronological notes relative to the Book of the Lamentations

Year from the Creation, according to Archbishop Usher, 3416.—Year of the Jewish era of the world, 3173.—Year from the Deluge, 1760.—First year of the *forty-eighth* Olympiad.—Year from the building of Rome, according to the Varronian account, 166.—Year before the birth of Christ, 584.—Year before the vulgar era of Christ's nativity, 588.—Year of the Julian Period, 4126.—Year of the era of Nabonassar, 160.—Cycle of the Sun, 10.—Cycle of the Moon, 3.—Second year after the fourth Sabbatic year after the *seventeenth* Jewish jubilee, according to Helvicus.—Twenty-ninth year of Tarquinius Priscus, the fifth king of the Romans: this was the *seventy-ninth* year before the commencement of the consular government.—Thirty-eighth year of Cyaxares or Cyaraxes, the fourth king of Media.—Eighteenth year of Agasicles, king of Lacedæmon, of the family of the Proclidæ.—Twentieth year of Leon, king of Lacedæmon, of the family of the Eurysthenidæ. Thirty-second year of Alyattes II., king of Lydia. This was the father of the celebrated Crœsus.—Fifteenth year of Æropas, the seventh king of Macedon.—Nineteenth year of Nebuchadnezzar, king of Babylon.—Eleventh year of Zedekiah, the last king of Judah.

CHAPTER I

The prophet begins with lamenting the dismal reverse of fortune that befell his country, confessing at the same time that her calamities were the just consequence of her sins, 1–6. Jerusalem herself is then personified and brought forward to continue the sad complaint, and to solicit the mercy of God, 7–22.

A. M. cir. 3416
B. C. cir. 588
Ol. XLVIII. 1
TarquiniiPrisci,
R. Roman.,
cir. annum 29

HOW doth the city sit solitary,
that was full of people:
[a]*how* is she become as a widow!
she *that was* great among the
nations, *and* [b]princess among the
provinces, *how* is she become
tributary!
2 She [c]weepeth sore in the

[a]Isa. xlvii. 7, 8——[b]Ezra iv. 20

[c]Jer. xiii. 17

In all copies of the *Septuagint*, whether of the Roman or Alexandrian editions, the following words are found as a part of the text: Και εγενετο μετα το αιχμαλωτισθηναι τον Ισραηλ, και Ιερουσαλημ ερημωθηναι, εκαθισεν Ιερεμιας κλαιων, και εθρηνησεν τον θρηνον τουτον επι Ιερουσαλημ, και ειπεν·—"And it came to pass after Israel had been carried away captive, and Jerusalem was become desolate, that Jeremiah sat weeping: and he lamented with this lamentation over Jerusalem; and he said."

The *Vulgate* has the same, with some variations:—"Et factum est, postquam in captivitatem redactus est Israel, et Jerusalem deserta est, sedit Jeremias propheta flens, et planxit lamentatione hac in Jerusalem, et amaro animo suspirans et ejulans, dixit." The translation of this, as given in the *first translation* of the Bible into English, may be found at the end of Jeremiah, taken from an ancient MS. in my own possession.

I subjoin another taken from the *first* PRINTED *edition* of the English Bible, that by *Coverdale*, 1535. "And it came to passe, (after Israel was brought into captyvitie, and Jerusalem destroyed;) that Jeremy the prophet sat weeping, mournynge, and makinge his mone in Jerusalem; so that with an hevy herte he sighed and sobbed, sayenge."

Matthew's Bible, printed in 1549, refines upon this: "It happened after Israell was brought into captyvite, and Jerusalem destroyed, that Jeremy the prophet sate wepyng, and sorrowfully bewayled Jerusalem; and syghynge and hewlynge with an hevy and wooful hert, sayde."

Becke's Bible of the same date, and *Cardmarden's* of 1566, have the same, with a trifling change in the *orthography*.

On this *Becke* and others have the following note:—"These words are read in the LXX. interpreters: but not in the Hebrue."

All these show that it was the ancient opinion

A. M. cir. 3416 B. C. cir. 588 Ol. XLVIII 1. TarquiniiPrisci, R. Roman., cir. annum 29

[d]night, and her tears are on her
cheeks: [e]among all her lovers
[f]she hath none to comfort *her:*
all her friends have dealt treacherously with her, they are become her enemies.
3 [g]Judah is gone into captivity because of
affliction, and [h]because of great servitude:
[i]she dwelleth among the heathen, she findeth
no rest: all her persecutors overtook her between the straits.
4 The ways of Zion do mourn, because none
come to the solemn feasts: all her gates are
desolate: her priests sigh, her
virgins are afflicted, and she *is*
in bitterness.
5 Her adversaries [k]are the
chief, her enemies prosper; for the LORD hath
afflicted her [l]for the multitude of her transgressions: her [m]children are gone into captivity before the enemy.
6 And from the daughter of Zion all her
beauty is departed: her princes are become
like harts *that* find no pasture, and they are
gone without strength before the pursuer.

A. M. cir. 3416 B. C. cir. 588 Ol. XLVIII 1. TarquiniiPrisci, R. Roman., cir. annum 29

---

[d]Job vii. 3; Psalm vi. 6——[e]Jeremiah iv. 30; xxx. 14; ver. 19——[f]Verses 9, 16, 17, 21——[g]Jeremiah lii. 27——[h]Hebrew, *for the greatness of servitude*

[i]Deuteronomy xxviii. 64, 65; chapter ii. 9——[k]Deuteronomy xxviii. 43, 44——[l]Jeremiah xxx. 14, 15; Daniel ix. 7, 16——[m]Jer. lii. 28

---

that the Book of Lamentations was composed, not over the death of *Josiah*, but on account of the *desolations of Israel and Jerusalem.*

The *Arabic* copies the *Septuagint.* The *Syriac* does not acknowledge it; and the *Chaldee* has these words only: "Jeremiah the great priest and prophet said."

NOTES ON CHAP. I

Verse 1. *How doth the city sit solitary*]. Sitting down, with the elbow on the knee, and the head supported by the hand, without any company, unless an oppressor near,—all these were signs of mourning and distress. The coin struck by Vespasian on the capture of Jerusalem, on the obverse of which there is a *palm-tree*, the emblem of Judea, and under it a woman, the emblem of Jerusalem, sitting, leaning as before described, with the legend *Judea capta*, illustrates this expression as well as that in Isa. xlvii. 1. See the note on Isa. iii. 26, where the subject is farther explained.

Become as a widow] Having lost her *king. Cities* are commonly described as the *mothers* of their *inhabitants*, the *kings* as *husbands*, and the *princes* as *children.* When therefore they are bereaved of these, they are represented as *widows*, and *childless.*

The *Hindoo* widow, as well as the *Jewish*, is considered the most destitute and wretched of all human beings. She has her hair cut short, throws off all ornaments, eats the coarsest food, fasts often, and is all but an outcast in the family of her late husband.

Is she become tributary!] Having no longer the political form of a nation; and the remnant that is left paying tribute to a foreign and heathen conqueror.

Verse 2. *Among all her lovers*] Her allies; her *friends*, instead of helping her, have helped her enemies. Several who sought her friendship when she was in prosperity, in the time of David and Solomon, are now among her enemies.

Verse 3. *Between the straits.*] She has been brought into such difficulties, that it was impossible for her to escape. Has this any reference to the circumstances in which Zedekiah and the princes of Judah endeavoured to escape from Jerusalem, *by the way of the gates between the two walls?* Jer. lii. 7.

Verse 4. *The ways of Zion do mourn*] A fine prosopopœia. The ways in which the people trod coming to the sacred solemnities, being now no longer frequented, are represented as *shedding tears;* and the *gates* themselves partake of the general distress. All poets of eminence among the Greeks and Romans have recourse to this image. So *Moschus*, in his Epitaph on *Bion*, ver. 1-3:—

Αιλινα μοι στροναχειτε ναπαι, και Δωριον ὑδωρ
Και ποταμοι κλαιοιτε τον ἱμεροεντα Βιωνα.
Νυν φυτα μοι μυρεσθε, και αλσεα νυν γοαοισθε, κ. τ. λ.

"Ye winds, with grief your waving summits bow,
Ye Dorian fountains, murmur as ye flow;
From weeping urns your copious sorrows shed,
And bid the rivers mourn for Bion dead.
Ye shady groves, in robes of sable hue,
Bewail, ye plants, in pearly drops of dew;
Ye drooping flowers, diffuse a languid breath,
And die with sorrow, at sweet Bion's death."

FAWKES.

So *Virgil*, Æn. vii., ver. 759:—

Te nemus Anguitiæ, vitrea te Fucinus unda
Te liquidi flevere lacus.

"For thee, wide echoing, sighed th' Anguitian woods;
For thee, in murmurs, wept thy native floods."

And more particularly on the *death of Daphnis*, Eclog. v. ver. 24:—

Non ulli pastos illis egere diebus
Frigida, Daphni, boves ad flumina: nulla neque amnem
Libavit quadrupes, nec graminis attigit herbam.
Daphni, tuum Pœnos etiam ingemuisse leones
Interitum, montesque feri, sylvæque loquuntur.

"The swains forgot their sheep, nor near the brink
Of running waters brought their herds to drink:
The thirsty cattle of themselves abstained
From water, and their grassy fare disdained.
The death of Daphnis woods and hills deplore;
The Libyan lions hear, and hearing roar."

DRYDEN.

Verse 5. *Her adversaries are the chief*] They have now *supreme dominion* over the whole land.

A. M. cir. 3416
B. C. cir. 588
Ol. XLVIII. 1
TarquiniiPrisci,
R. Roman.,
cir. annum 29

7 Jerusalem remembered in
the days of her affliction and of
her miseries all [n]her pleasant
things that she had in the days
of old, when her people fell into the hand of
the enemy, and none did help her: the adversaries saw her, *and* did mock at her sabbaths.
8 [o]Jerusalem hath grievously sinned; therefore she [p]is removed: all that honoured her
despise her, because [q]they have seen her nakedness: yea, she sigheth, and turneth backward.
9 Her filthiness *is* in her skirts; she [r]re-
membereth not her last end; therefore she
came down wonderfully: [s]she had no comforter. O LORD, behold my affliction: for the
enemy hath magnified *himself*.
10 The adversary hath spread out his hand
upon [t]all her [u]pleasant things: for she hath
seen *that* [v]the heathen entered into her sanctuary, whom thou didst command *that* [w]they
should not enter into thy congregation.
11 All her people sigh, [x]they seek bread;
they have given their pleasant things for meat
[y]to relieve the soul: see, O LORD, and consider; for I am become vile.
12 [z]*Is it* nothing to you, all ye that [a]pass
by? behold, and see [b]if there be
any sorrow like unto my sorrow,
which is done unto me, wherewith the LORD hath afflicted *me*
in the day of his fierce anger.

A. M. cir. 3416
B. C. cir. 588
Ol. XLVIII. 1
TarquiniiPrisci,
R. Roman.,
cir. annum 29

13 From above hath he sent fire into my
bones, and it prevaileth against them: he hath
[c]spread a net for my feet, he hath turned me
back: he hath made me desolate *and* faint all
the day.
14 [d]The yoke of my transgressions is bound
by his hand: they are wreathed, *and* come up
upon my neck: he hath made my strength
to fall, the LORD hath delivered me into
their hands, *from whom* I am not able to
rise up.
15 The LORD hath trodden under foot all my
mighty *men* in the midst of me: he hath called
an assembly against me to crush my young
men: [e]the LORD hath trodden [f]the virgin, the
daughter of Judah, *as* in a wine-press.
16 For these *things* I weep; [g]mine eye,
mine eye runneth down with water, because
[h]the comforter that should [i]relieve my soul
is far from me: my children are desolate, because the enemy prevailed.

---

[n]Or, *desirable;* ver. 10——[o]1 Kings viii. 46——[p]Heb. *is become a removing*, or *wandering*——[q]Jer. xiii. 22, 26; Ezek. xvi. 37; xxiii. 29; Hos. ii. 10——[r]Deut. xxxii. 29; Isa. xlvii. 7——[s]Ver. 2, 17, 21——[t]Ver. 7——[u]Or, *desirable*——[v]Jer. li. 51——[w]Deut. xxiii. 3; Neh. xiii. 1 [x]Jer. xxxviii. 9; lii. 6; chap. ii. 12; iv. 4

[y]Or, *to make the soul to come again*——[z]Or, It is *nothing*——[a]Heb. *pass by the way*——[b]Dan. ix. 12 [c]Ezek. xii. 13; xvii. 20——[d]Deut. xxviii. 48——[e]Isa. lxiii. 3; Rev. xiv. 19, 20; xix. 15——[f]Or, *the winepress of the virgin*, &c.——[g]Jer. xiii. 17; xiv. 17; chap. ii. 18 [h]Ver. 2. 9——[i]Heb. *bring back*

Verse 7. *Did mock at her Sabbaths.*] משבתה *mishbatteha.* Some contend that *Sabbaths* are not intended here. The *Septuagint* has κατοικεσια αυτης, "her habitation;" the *Chaldee*, על טובהא *al tubaha*, "her good things;" the *Syriac*, ܥܠ ܬܒܪܗ *al toboroh*, "her breach." The *Vulgate* and *Arabic* agree with the Hebrew. Some of my oldest MSS. have the word in the plural number, משבתיה *mishbatteyha*, "her Sabbaths." A multitude of *Kennicott's* MSS. have the same reading. The Jews were despised by the heathen for *keeping the Sabbath. Juvenal* mocks them on that account:—

> —— cui septima quæque fuit lux
> Ignava et partem vitæ non attigit ullam.
> *Sat.* v.

"To whom every seventh day was a blank, and formed not any part of their life."

St. Augustine represents *Seneca* as doing the same:—Inutiliter id eos facere affirmans, quod septimani ferme partem ætatis suæ perdent vacando, et multa in tempore urgentia non agendo lædantur. "That they lost the seventh part of their life in keeping their Sabbaths; and injured themselves by abstaining from the performance of many necessary things in such times." He did not consider that the Roman calendar and customs gave them many more idle days than God had prescribed in Sabbaths to the Jews. The Sabbath is a most wise and beneficent ordinance.

Verse 9. *She remembereth not her last end*] Although evident marks of her pollution appeared about her, and the land was defiled by her sinfulness even to its utmost borders, she had no thought or consideration of what must be the consequence of all this at the last.—*Blayney.*

Verse 11. *They have given their pleasant things*] Jerusalem is compared to a woman brought into great straits, who parts with her jewels and trinkets in order to purchase by them the necessaries of life.

Verse 12. Is it *nothing to you, all ye that pass by?*] The desolations and distress brought upon this city and its inhabitants had scarcely any parallel. Excessive abuse of God's accumulated mercies calls for singular and exemplary punishment.

Verse 14. *The yoke of my transgressions*] I am now tied and bound by the chain of my sins; and it is so *wreathed*, so *doubled* and *twisted* round me, that I cannot free myself. A fine representation of the miseries of a penitent soul, which feels that nothing but the pitifulness of God's mercy can loose it.

Verse 15. *Called an assembly*] The Chaldean

A. M. cir. 3416
B. C. cir. 588
Ol. XLVIII. 1
TarquiniiPrisci,
R. Roman.,
cir. annum 29

17 [k]Zion spreadeth forth her hands, *and* [l]*there is* none to comfort her: the LORD hath commanded concerning Jacob, *that* his adversaries *should be* round about him: Jerusalem is as a menstruous woman among them.

18 The LORD is [m]righteous; for I have [n]rebelled against his [o]commandment: hear, I pray you, all people, and behold my sorrow: my virgins and my young men are gone into captivity.

19 I called for my lovers, *but* [p]they deceived me: my priests and mine elders gave up the ghost in the city, [q]while they sought their meat to relieve their souls.

20 Behold, O LORD; for I *am* in distress: my [r]bowels are troubled: mine heart is turned within me; for I have grievously rebelled: [s]abroad the sword bereaveth, at home *there is* as death.

A. M. cir. 3416
B. C. cir. 588
Ol. XLVIII. 1
TarquiniiPrisci,
R. Roman.,
cir. annum 29

21 They have heard that I sigh: [t]*there is* none to comfort me: all mine enemies have heard of my trouble; they are glad that thou hast done *it:* thou wilt bring [u]the day *that* thou hast [v]called, and they shall be like unto me.

22 [w]Let all their wickedness come before thee; and do unto them, as thou hast done unto me for all my transgressions: for my sighs *are* many, and [x]my heart *is* faint.

---

[k]Jer. iv. 31——[l]Ver. 2, 9——[m]Neh. ix. 33; Dan. ix. 7, 14 [n]1 Sam. xii. 14, 15——[o]Heb. *mouth*——[p]Ver. 2; Jer. xxx. 14——[q]Ver. 11——[r]Job xxx. 27; Isa. xvi. 11; Jer. iv. 19; xlviii. 36; ch. ii. 11; Hos. xi. 8——[s]Deut. xxxii. 25; Ezek. vii. 15——[t]Ver. 2——[u]Isa. xiii. &c.; Jer. xlvi. &c. [v]Or, *proclaimed*——[w]Psa. cix. 15——[x]Chap. v. 17

---

army, composed of various nations, which God commissioned to destroy Jerusalem.

Verse 17. *Zion spreadeth forth her hands*] Extending the hands is the form in supplication.

Jerusalem is as a menstruous woman] To whom none dared to approach, either to help or comfort, because of the law, Lev. xv. 19-27.

Verse 19. *I called for my lovers*] My allies; the *Egyptians* and others.

Verse 20. *Abroad the sword bereaveth*] WAR is through the *country; and at home death;* the pestilence and famine rage in the city; calamity in every shape is fallen upon me.

Virgil represents the calamities of Troy under the same image:—

——— Nec soli pœnas dant sanguine Teucri:
Quondam etiam victis redit in præcordia virtus;
Victoresque cadunt Danai. Crudelis ubique
Luctus, ubique *Pavor*, et *plurima mortis imago.*
Æneid. lib. ii. 366.

"Not only Trojans fall; but, in their turn,
The vanquished triumph, and the victors mourn.
Ours take new courage from despair and night;
Confused the fortune is, confused the fight.
All parts resound with *tumults*, *plaints*, and *fears;*
And grisly death in *sundry shapes* appears."
DRYDEN.

So Milton—

"—————Despair
Tended the sick, busiest from couch to couch;
And over them triumphant Death his dart
Shook." *Par. Lost*, B. xi. 489.

Jeremiah, chap. ix. 21, uses the same image:—

Death is come up into our windows:
He hath entered our palaces,
To cut off the infants without,
And the young men in our streets.

So *Silius Italicus*, II. 548:—

Mors graditur, vasto pandens cava guttura rictu,
Casuroque inhians populo.

"Death stalks along, and opens his hideous throat to gulp down the people."

Verse 21. *They have heard that I sigh*] My affliction is public enough; but no one comes to comfort me.

They are glad that thou hast done it] On the contrary, they exult in my misery; and they see that THOU hast done what *they* were incapable of performing.

Thou wilt bring the day that *thou hast called, and they shall be like unto me.*] Babylon shall be visited in her turn; and thy judgments poured out upon her shall equal her state with my own. See the last six chapters of the preceding prophecy for the accomplishment of this prediction.

Verse 22. *Let all their wickedness come before thee*] That is, Thou wilt call their crimes also into remembrance; and thou wilt do unto them by siege, sword, famine, and captivity, what thou hast done to me. Though thy judgments, because of thy long-suffering, are slow; yet, because of thy righteousness, they are sure.

For my sighs are *many*] My desolations continue; and *my heart* is *faint*—my political and physical strength almost totally destroyed.

Imprecations in the sacred writings are generally to be understood as *declarative* of the evils they indicate; or, that such evils will take place. No prophet of God ever wished desolation on those against whom he was directed to prophesy.

CHAPTER II

***The prophet shows the dire effects of the Divine anger in the miseries brought on his country; the unparalleled calamities of which he charges, in a great measure, on the false prophets,* 1–14. *In this desperate condition, the astonishment and by-word of all who see her, Jerusalem is directed to sue earnestly for mercy and pardon,* 15–22.**

A. M. cir. 3416
B. C. cir. 588
Ol. XLVIII. 1
TarquiniiPrisci,
R. Roman.,
cir. annum 29

HOW hath the LORD covered
the daughter of Zion with a
cloud in his anger, [a]*and* cast
down from heaven unto the earth
[b]the beauty of Israel, and remembered not
[c]his footstool in the day of his anger!
2 The LORD hath swallowed up all the
habitations of Jacob, [d]and hath not pitied:
he hath thrown down in his wrath the strong
holds of the daughter of Judah; he hath
[e]brought *them* down to the ground: [f]he
hath polluted the kingdom and the princes
thereof.
3 He hath cut off in *his* fierce anger all the
horn of Israel: [g]he hath drawn back his right
hand from before the enemy, [h]and he burned
against Jacob like a flaming fire, *which* devoureth round about.
4 [i]He hath bent his bow like an enemy:
he stood with his right hand as an adversary,
and slew [k]all [l]*that were* pleasant to the eye
in the tabernacle of the daughter of Zion: he
poured out his fury like fire.
5 [m]The LORD was as an enemy: he hath
swallowed up Israel, [n]he hath
swallowed up all her palaces:
he hath destroyed his strong
holds, and hath increased in the
daughter of Judah mourning and lamentation.
6 And he hath violently [o]taken away his
[p]tabernacle, [q]as *if it were of* a garden: he
hath destroyed his places of the assembly:
[r]the LORD hath caused the solemn feasts and
sabbaths to be forgotten in Zion, and hath
despised in the indignation of his anger the
king and the priest.
7 The LORD hath cast off his altar, he hath
abhorred his sanctuary, he hath [s]given up
into the hand of the enemy the walls of her
palaces; [t]they have made a noise in the house
of the LORD, as in the day of a solemn feast.
8 The LORD hath purposed to destroy the
wall of the daughter of Zion: [u]he hath
stretched out a line, he hath not withdrawn
his hand from [v]destroying: therefore he made
the rampart and the wall to lament; they
languished together.

A. M. cir. 3416
B. C. cir. 588
Ol. XLVIII. 1
TarquiniiPrisci,
R. Roman.,
cir. annum 29

[a]Matt. xi. 23——[b]2 Sam. i. 19——[c]1 Chron. xxviii. 2; Psa. xcix. 5; cxxxii. 7——[d]Ver. 17, 21; chap. iii. 43——[e]Heb. *made to touch*——[f]Psa. lxxxix. 39——[g]Psa. lxxiv. 11——[h]Psa. xxxix. 46——[i]Isa. lxiii. 10; ver. 5——[k]Heb. *all the desirable of the eye*

[l]Ezek. xxiv. 25——[m]Ver. 4; Jer. xxx. 14——[n]2 Kings xxv. 9; Jer. lii. 13——[o]Psa. lxxx. 12; lxxxix. 40; Isa. v. 5——[p]Or, *hedge*——[q]Isa. i. 8——[r]Chap. i. 4; Zeph. iii. 18——[s]Heb. *shut up*——[t]Psa. lxxiv. 4——[u]2 Kings xxi. 13; Isa. xxxiv. 11——[v]Heb. *swallowing up*

NOTES ON CHAP. II

Verse 1. *How hath the Lord covered the daughter of Zion with a cloud*] The women in the eastern countries wear *veils*, and often very costly ones. Here, Zion is represented as being *veiled* by the hand of God's judgment. And what is the veil? A *dark cloud*, by which she is entirely obscured.

Instead of אדני *Adonai, lord, twenty-four* of Dr. *Kennicott's* MSS., and some of the most ancient of my own, read יהוה *Yehovah*, LORD, as in ver. 2.

The beauty of Israel] His *Temple*.

His footstool] The ark of the covenant, often so called. The rendering of my old MS. Bible is curious:—**And record not of his litil steging-stole of his feet, in the dai of his woodnesse.** To be *wood* signifies, in our ancient language, to be *mad*.

Verse 2. *The Lord hath swallowed up*] It is a strange figure when thus applied: but Jehovah is here represented as having swallowed down Jerusalem and all the cities and fortifications in the land: that is, he has permitted them to be destroyed. See ver. 5.

Verse 3. *The horn of Israel*] His *power* and *strength*. It is a metaphor taken from cattle, whose principal strength lies in their *horns*.

Hath drawn back his right hand] He did not support us when our enemies came against us.

Verse 4. *He hath bent his bow—he stood with his right hand*] This is the attitude of the archer. He first bends his bow; then sets his arrow upon the string; and, lastly, placing his right hand on the lower end of the arrow, in connexion with the string, takes his aim, and prepares to let fly.

Verse 6. *As* if it were of *a garden*] "As it were the garden of his own hedging."—*Blayney.*

The Lord hath caused the solemn feasts] By delivering us up into the hands of the enemy our religious worship is not only suspended, but all Divine ordinances are destroyed.

Verse 7. *They have made a noise in the house of the Lord*] Instead of the silver trumpets of the sanctuary, nothing but the sounds of warlike instruments are to be heard.

Verse 8. *He hath stretched out a line*] The *line of devastation;* marking what was to be pulled down and demolished.

A. M. cir. 3416
B. C. cir. 588
Ol. XLVIII. 1
TarquiniiPrisci,
R. Roman.,
cir. annum 29

9 Her gates are sunk into the
ground; he hath destroyed and
[w]broken her bars: [x]her king
and her princes *are* among the
Gentiles: [y]the law *is* no *more;* her [z]prophets
also find no vision from the LORD.
10 The elders of the daughter of Zion [a]sit
upon the ground, *and* keep silence: they have
[b]cast up dust upon their heads; they have
[c]girded themselves with sackcloth: the virgins
of Jerusalem hang down their heads to the
ground.
11 [d]Mine eyes do fail with tears, [e]my bowels
are troubled, [f]my liver is poured upon the
earth, for the destruction of the daughter of
my people; because [g]the children and the
sucklings [h]swoon in the streets of the city.
12 They say to their mothers, Where *is*
corn and wine? when they swooned as the
wounded in the streets of the city, when their
soul was poured out into their mothers' bosom.
13 What thing shall I take to witness for
thee? [i]what thing shall I liken to thee, O
daughter of Jerusalem? what shall I equal to
thee, that I may comfort thee, O virgin
daughter of Zion? for thy breach
is great like the sea: who can
heal thee?
14 Thy [k]prophets have seen
vain and foolish things for thee: and they have
not [l]discovered thine iniquity, to turn away
thy captivity; but have seen for thee false
burdens and causes of banishment.
15 [m]All that pass [n]by [o]clap *their* hands at
thee; they hiss [p]and wag their head at the
daughter of Jerusalem, *saying, Is* this the
city that *men* call [q]The perfection of beauty,
The joy of the whole earth?
16 [r]All thine enemies have opened their
mouth against thee: they hiss and gnash the
teeth: they say, [s]We have swallowed *her* up:
certainly this *is* the day that we looked for;
we have found, [t]we have seen *it.*
17 The LORD hath done *that* which he had
[u]devised; he hath fulfilled his word that he
had commanded in the days of old: [v]he hath
thrown down, and hath not pitied: and he
hath caused *thine* enemy to [w]rejoice over thee,
he hath set up the horn of thine adversaries.
18 Their heart cried unto the LORD, O

A. M. cir. 3416
B. C. cir. 588
Ol. XLVIII. 1
TarquiniiPrisci,
R. Roman.,
cir. annum 29

[w]Jer. li. 30——[x]Deut. xxviii. 36; 2 Kings xxiv. 15; xxv. 7; chap. i. 3; iv. 20——[y]2 Chron. xv. 3——[z]Psa. lxxiv. 9; Ezek. vii. 26——[a]Job ii. 13; Isa. iii. 26; chap. iii. 28——[b]Job ii. 12——[c]Isa. xv. 3; Ezek vii. 18; xxvii. 31——[d]Psa. vi. 7; chap. iii. 48, &c. [e]Chap. i. 20——[f]Job xvi. 13; Psa. xxii. 14——[g]Ver. 19; chapter iv. 4——[h]Or, *faint*——[i]Chapter i. 12; Dan. ix. 12

[k]Jer. ii. 8; v. 31; xiv. 14; xxiii. 16; xxvii. 14; xxix. 8, 9; Ezek. xiii. 2——[l]Isa. lviii. 1——[m]1 Kings ix. 8; Jer. xviii. 16; Nah. iii. 19; Ecclus. xii. 18——[n]Heb. *by the way*——[o]Ezek. xxv. 6——[p]2 Kings xix. 21; Psa. xliv. 14 [q]Psa. xlviii. 2; l. 2——[r]Job xvi. 9, 10; Psa. xxii. 13; chap. iii. 46——[s]Psa. lvi. 2——[t]Psa. xxxv. 21——[u]Lev. xxvi. 16, &c.; Deut. xxviii. 15, &c.——[v]Ver. 2——[w]Psa. xxxviii. 16; lxxxix. 42

Verse 9. *Her gates are sunk into the ground*] The consequence of their being long thrown down and neglected. From this it appears that the captivity had already lasted a considerable time.

Her king and her princes are *among the Gentiles*] Zedekiah and many of the princes were then prisoners in Babylon, another proof that the captivity had endured some time; unless all this be spoken *prophetically*, of what *should be done.*

Verse 10. *Sit upon the ground*] See the note on chap. i. 1.

Keep silence] No words can express their sorrows: small griefs are eloquent, great ones dumb.

Verse 11. *Swoon in the streets of the city.*] Through the excess of the famine.

Verse 12. *When their soul was poured out into their mothers' bosom.*] When, in endeavouring to draw nourishment from the breasts of their exhausted mothers, they breathed their last in their bosoms! How dreadfully afflicting was this!

Verse 13. *What thing shall I take*] Or, rather, as Dr. *Blayney*, "What shall I urge to thee?" How shall I comfort thee?

Thy breach is *great like the sea*] Thou hast a *flood* of *afflictions*, a *sea* of *troubles*, an *ocean* of *miseries.*

Verse 14. *They have not discovered thine iniquity*] They did not reprove for sin; they flattered them in their transgressions; and instead of turning away thy captivity, by turning thee from thy sins, they have pretended visions of good in thy favour, and false burdens for thy enemies.

Verse 15. *The perfection of beauty*] This probably only applied to the *temple.* Jerusalem never was a fine or splendid city; but the temple was most assuredly the most splendid building in the world.

Verse 16. *This* is *the day that we looked for*] Jerusalem was the envy of the surrounding nations: they longed for its destruction, and rejoiced when it took place.

Verse 17. *The Lord hath done* that] This and the *sixteenth* verse should be interchanged, to follow the order of the letters in the Hebrew alphabet; as the *sixteenth* has **פ** *phe* for its acrostic letter, and the *seventeenth* has **ע** *ain*, which should precede the other in the order of the alphabet.

Verse 18. *O wall of the daughter of Zion*] חומת בת ציון *chomath bath tsiyon, wall of the daughter of Zion.* These words are probably those of the passengers, who appear to be affected by the desolations of the land; and they address the people, and urge them to plead with God day and night for their restoration.

A. M. cir. 3416 B. C. cir. 588 Ol. XLVIII. 1 TarquiniiPrisci, R. Roman., cir. annum 29

[x]wall of the daughter of Zion,
[y]let tears run down like a river
day and night: give thyself no
rest; let not the apple of thine
eye cease.
19 Arise, [z]cry out in the night: in the beginning of the watches [a]pour out thine heart
like water before the face of the LORD: lift
up thy hands toward him for the life of thy
young children, [b]that faint for hunger [c]in the
top of every street.
20 Behold, O LORD, and consider to whom
thou hast done this. [d]Shall the women eat
their fruit, *and* children [e]of a span long?
[f]shall the priest and the pro-
phet be slain in the sanctuary
of the LORD?
21 [g]The young and the old
lie on the ground in the streets: my virgins and my young men are fallen by the
sword; thou hast slain *them* in the day of
thine anger; [h]thou hast killed, *and* not
pitied.
22 Thou hast called as in a solemn day
[i]my terrors round about, so that in the day
of the LORD's anger none escaped nor remained: [k]those that I have swaddled and
brought up hath mine enemy consumed.

---

[x]Ver. 8——[y]Jer. xiv. 17; ch. i. 16——[z]Psa. cxix. 147——[a]Psa. lxii. 8——[b]Ver. 11——[c]Isa. li. 20; ch. iv. 1; Nah. iii. 10——[d]Lev. xxvi. 29; Deut. xxviii. 53; Jer. xix. 9; ch. iv. 10; Ezek. v. 10——[e]Or, *swaddled with their hands*——[f]Ch. iv. 13, 16——[g]2 Chron. xxxvi. 17——[h]Ch. iii. 43——[i]Psa. xxxi. 13; Jer. vi. 25; xliv. 5——[k]Hos. ix. 12, 13

But what is the meaning of *wall of the daughter of Zion?* I answer, I do not know. It is certainly harsh to say, "O wall of the daughter of Zion, let tears run down like a river day and night." Zion's *ways* may *lament*, and her *streets mourn;* but how the *walls* can be said to *weep* is not so easy to be understood, because there is no parallel for it. One of my most ancient MSS. *omits* the three words; and in it the text stands thus: "Their heart cried unto the Lord, Let tears run down like a river day and night; give thyself no rest," &c.

Let not the apple of thine eye cease.] בת עין *bath ayin* means either the *pupil* of the *eye*, or the *tears*. Tears are the produce of the eye, and are here elegantly termed *the daughter of the eye*. Let not thy tears cease. But with what propriety can we say to the *apple* or *pupil* of the eye, *Do not cease?* *Tears* are most certainly meant.

Verse 19. *Arise, cry out in the night*] This seems to refer to Jerusalem besieged. Ye who keep the night watches, pour out your hearts before the Lord, instead of calling the time of night, &c.; or, when you call it, send up a fervent prayer to God for the safety and relief of the place.

Verse 20. *Consider to whom thou hast done this*] Perhaps the best sense of this difficult verse is this: "Thou art our *Father*, we are thy *children;* wilt thou *destroy thy own offspring?* Was it ever heard that a mother devoured her own child, a helpless infant of a span long?" That it was foretold that there should be such distress in the siege,—that mothers should be obliged to eat their own children, is evident enough from Lev. xxvi. 29; Deut. xxviii. 53, 56, 57; but the former view of the subject seems the most natural, and is best supported by the *context*. The *priest* and the *prophet* are slain; the *young* and *old* lie on the ground in the streets; the *virgins* and *young men* are fallen by the sword. "THOU hast slain them in the day of thine anger; THOU hast killed, and not pitied." See chap. iv. 10.

Verse 22. *Thou hast called as in a solemn day*] It is by thy influence alone that so many enemies are called together at one time; and they have so hemmed us in that none could escape, and none remained unslain or uncaptivated. Perhaps the figure is the collecting of the people in Jerusalem on one of the solemn annual festivals. God has called terrors together to feast on Jerusalem, similar to the convocation of the people from all parts of the land to one of those annual festivals. The indiscriminate slaughter of young and old, priest and prophet, all ranks and conditions, may be illustrated by the following verses from *Lucan*, which appear as if a translation of the *nineteenth*, *twentieth*, and *twenty-first* verses of this chapter:—

Nobilitas cum plebe perit; lateque vagatur
Ensis, et a nullo revocatum est pectore ferrum.
Stat cruor in Templis; multaque rubentia cæde
Lubrica saxa madent. Nulli sua profuit ætas.
Non senes extremum piguit vergentibus annis
Præcipitasse diem; nec primo in limine vitæ,
Infanti miseri nascentia rumpere fata.

Pharsal. lib. ii., 101.

"With what a slide devouring slaughter passed,
And swept promiscuous orders in her haste;
O'er noble and plebeian ranged the sword,
Nor pity nor remorse one pause afford!
The sliding streets with blood were clotted o'er,
And sacred temples stood in pools of gore.
The ruthless steel, impatient of delay,
Forbade the sire to linger out his day:
It struck the bending father to the earth,
And cropped the wailing infant at its birth."

ROWE.

CHAPTER III

The prophet, by enumerating his own severe trials, 1–20, *and showing his trust in God,* 21, *encourages his people to the like resignation and trust in the Divine and never-failing mercy,* 22–27. *He vindicates the goodness of God in all his dispensations, and the unreasonableness of murmuring under them,* 28–39. *He recommends self-examination and repentance; and then, from their experience of former deliverances from God, encourages them to look for pardon for their sins, and retribution to their enemies,* 40–66.

A. M. cir. 3416 B. C. cir. 588 Ol. XLVIII. 1 TarquiniiPrisci, R. Roman., cir. annum 29

I AM the man *that* hath seen
affliction by the rod of his
wrath.
2 He hath led me, and brought
me into darkness, but not *into* light.
3 Surely against me is he turned; he turneth
his hand *against me* all the day.
4 [a]My flesh and my skin hath he made old;
he hath [b]broken my bones.
5 He hath builded against me, and compassed *me* with gall and travail.
6 [c]He hath set me in dark places, as *they*
that be dead of old.
7 [d]He hath hedged me about, that I cannot
get out: he hath made my chain heavy.
8 Also [e]when I cry and shout, he shutteth
out my prayer.

[a]Job xvi. 3——[b]Psa. li. 8; Isa. xxxviii. 13; Jer. l. 17——[c]Psa. lxxxviii. 5, 6; cxliii. 3——[d]Job iii. 23; xix. 8; Hos. ii. 6——[e]Job xxx. 20; Psa. xxii. 2——[f]Job x. 16; Isa. xxxviii. 13; Hos. v. 14; xiii. 7, 8

9 He hath inclosed my ways
with hewn stone, he hath made
my paths crooked.
10 [f]He *was* unto me *as* a bear
lying in wait, *and as* a lion in secret places.
11 He hath turned aside my ways, and
[g]pulled me in pieces: he hath made me desolate.
12 He hath bent his bow, and [h]set me as a
mark for the arrow.
13 He hath caused [i]the [k]arrows of his
quiver to enter into my reins.
14 I was a [l]derision to all my people; *and*
[m]their song all the day.
15 [n]He hath filled me with [o]bitterness, he
hath made me drunken with wormwood.
16 He hath also broken my teeth [p]with

A. M. cir. 3416 B. C. cir. 588 Ol. XLVIII. 1 TarquiniiPrisci, R. Roman., cir. annum 29

[g]Hos. vi. 1——[h]Job vii. 20; xvi. 12; Psa. xxxviii. 2——[i]Job vi. 4——[k]Heb. *sons*——[l]Jer. xx. 7——[m]Job xxx. 9; Psa. lxix. 12; ver. 63——[n]Jer. ix. 15——[o]Heb. *bitternesses*——[p]Prov. xx. 17

NOTES ON CHAP. III

Verse 1. *I* am *the man* that *hath seen affliction*] Either the prophet speaks here of himself, or he is personating his miserable countrymen. This and other passages in this poem have been applied to Jesus Christ's passion; but, in my opinion, without any foundation.

Verse 2. *He hath—brought* me into *darkness*] In the sacred writings, *darkness* is often taken for *calamity; light,* for *prosperity.*

Verse 5. *He hath builded against me*] Perhaps there is a reference here to the *mounds* and *ramparts* raised by the Chaldeans in order to take the city.

Verse 7. *He hath hedged me about*] This also may refer to the lines drawn round the city during the siege. But these and similar expressions in the following verses may be merely metaphorical, to point out their *straitened, oppressed,* and *distressed* state.

Verse 9. *He hath inclosed my ways with hewn stone*] He has put insuperable obstacles in my way; and confounded all my projects of deliverance, and all my expectations of prosperity.

Verse 12. *He hath bent his bow, and set me as a mark for the arrow.*] One might conjecture that the following thought in the *Toozek i Teemour* was borrowed from this:—

"One addressed the caliph Aaly, and said, 'If the *heavens* were a *bow,* and the *earth* the *cord* thereof; if *calamities* were *arrows, man* the *butt* for those arrows; and the holy blessed *God* the unerring *marksman;* where could the sons of Adam flee for succour?' The caliph replied, 'The children of Adam must flee unto the Lord.'" This was the state of poor Jerusalem. It seemed as a *butt* for all God's *arrows;* and each *arrow* of *calamity* entered into the soul, for God was the *unerring marksman.*

Verse 13. *The arrows of his quiver*] בני אשפתו *beney ashpatho,* "The sons of his quiver." The *issue* or *effect;* the subject, adjunct, or accident, or produce of a thing, is frequently denominated its *son* or *child.* So *arrows* that *issue* from a *quiver* are here termed *the sons of the quiver.*

Verse 15. *He hath filled me with bitterness*] במרורים *bimrorim,* with bitternesses, bitter upon bitter.

He hath made me drunken with wormwood.] I have drunk the cup of misery till I am intoxicated with it. Almost in all countries, and in all languages, *bitterness* is a metaphor to express *trouble* and *affliction.* The reason is, there is nothing more disagreeable to the *taste* than the one; and nothing more distressing to the *mind* than the other. An Arabic poet, *Amralkeis,* one of the writers of the *Moallakat,* terms a man grievously afflicted ناقع حنظل *a pounder of wormwood.*

Verse 16. *He hath also broken my teeth with gravel stones*] What a figure to express *disgust, pain,* and the consequent incapacity of *taking food* for the support of life; a man, instead of bread, being obliged to eat *small pebbles,* till all his teeth are *broken to pieces* by endeavouring to grind them. One can scarcely read this description without feeling the *toothache.* The next figure is not less expressive.

A. M. cir. 3416
B. C. cir. 588
Ol. XLVIII. 1
TarquiniiPrisci,
R. Roman.,
cir. annum 29

gravel stones, he hath [q]covered
me with ashes.
17 And thou hast removed my
soul far off from peace: I forgat
[r]prosperity.
18 [s]And I said, My strength and my hope
is perished from the LORD:
19 [t]Remembering mine affliction and my
misery, [u]the wormwood and the gall.
20 My soul hath *them* still in remembrance,
and is [v]humbled in me.
21 This I [w]recall to my mind, therefore have
I hope.
22 [x]*It is of* the LORD's mercies that we are
not consumed, because his compassions fail
not.
23 *They are* new [y]every morning: great *is*
thy faithfulness.

[q]Or, *rolled me in the ashes*——[r]Heb. *good*——[s]Psa. xxxi. 22——[t]Or, *Remember*——[u]Jer. ix. 15——[v]Heb. *bowed*——[w]Heb. *make to return to my heart*——[x]Mal. iii. 6——[y]Isa. xxxiii. 2——[z]Psa. xvi. 5; lxxiii. 26; cxix. 57; Jer. x. 16

24 The LORD *is* my [z]portion,
saith my soul: therefore will I
hope in him.
25 The LORD *is* good unto
them that [a]wait for him, to the soul *that*
seeketh him.
26 *It is* good that *a man* should both hope
[b]and quietly wait for the salvation of the
LORD.
27 [c]*It is* good for a man that he bear the
yoke in his youth.
28 [d]He sitteth alone and keepeth silence,
because he hath borne *it* upon him.
29 [e]He putteth his mouth in the dust; if
so be there may be hope.
30 [f]He giveth *his* cheek to him that smiteth
him: he is filled full with reproach.
31 [g]For the LORD will not cast off for ever:

[a]Psalm cxxx. 6; Isaiah xxx. 18; Micah vii. 7——[b]Psa. xxxvii. 7——[c]Psalm xc. 12; cxix. 71——[d]Jeremiah xv. 17; chapter ii. 10——[e]Job xlii. 6——[f]Isaiah l. 6; Matthew v. 39——[g]Psalm xciv. 14

He hath covered me with ashes.] הכפישני באפר *hichphishani beepher*, "he hath plunged me into the dust." To be thrown into a mass or bed of perfect *dust*, where the eyes are blinded by it, the ears stopped, and the mouth and lungs filled at the very first attempt to respire after having been thrown into it—what a horrible idea of *suffocation* and *drowning!* One can scarcely read this without feeling a suppression of breath, or a stricture upon the lungs! Did ever man paint sorrow like this man?

Verse 17. *Thou hast removed my soul*] Prosperity is at such an utter distance from me, that it is impossible I should ever reach it; and as to *happiness*, I have forgotten whether I have ever tasted of it.

Verse 18. *And my hope*] That first, that last support of the miserable—it is gone! it is perished! The sovereign God alone can revive it.

Verse 20. *My soul—is humbled in me.*] It is evident that in the preceding verses there is a *bitterness* of *complaint* against the *bitterness* of *adversity*, that is not becoming to *man* when under the chastising hand of God; and, while indulging this feeling, all *hope* fled. Here we find a different feeling; he *humbles* himself under the mighty hand of God, and then his *hope* revives, ver. 21.

Verse 22. It is of *the Lord's mercies that we are not consumed*] Being thus *humbled*, and seeing *himself* and his *sinfulness* in a proper point of view, he finds that God, instead of dealing with him in *judgment*, has dealt with him in *mercy;* and that though the affliction was excessive, yet it was less than his iniquity deserved. If, indeed, any sinner be kept out of hell, it is because God's *compassion* faileth not.

Verse 23. They are *new every morning*] Day and night proclaim the mercy and compassion of God. Who could exist throughout the *day*, if there were not a continual superintending Providence? Who could be preserved in the *night*, if the Watchman of Israel ever slumbered or slept?

Verse 24. *The Lord* is *my portion*] See on Psa. cxix. 57.

Verse 26. It is *good that* a man *should both hope*] *Hope* is essentially necessary to *faith;* he that *hopes not*, *cannot believe;* if there be no *expectation*, there can be no *confidence*. When a man *hopes* for salvation, he should not only *wait* for it, but use every means that may lead to it; for *hope* cannot live, if there be no *exercise*. If *hope* become *impatient*, *faith* will be impossible: for who can believe for his salvation when his mind is *agitated?* He must therefore *quietly wait*. He must *expect*, and yet be *dumb*, as the words imply; ever feeling his *utter unworthiness;* and, without *murmuring*, struggle into life.

Verse 27. *That he bear the yoke in his youth.*] Early *habits*, when good, are invaluable. Early *discipline* is equally so. He who has not got under wholesome restraint in youth will never make a useful man, a good man, nor a happy man.

Verse 28. *He sitteth alone*] He has learned that necessary lesson of *independence*, that shows him how *he is to serve himself;* to *give no trouble to others;* and *keep his troubles*, as far as possible, *in his own bosom.*

Verse 29. *He putteth his mouth in the dust*] Lives in a state of deep humility.

If so be there may be hope.] Because there is room for hope.

Verse 30. *He giveth* his *cheek to him that smiteth*] He has that love that is not provoked. He is not quarrelsome, nor apt to resent injuries; he suffers long and is kind. Or, it may be rendered, "let him give his cheek."

He is filled full with reproach.] Though all this take place, yet let his "trust be in God, who will not cast off for ever." God will take his part, and bring him safely through all hardships.

Verse 31. *The Lord*] אדני *Adonai;* but one

A. M. cir. 3416
B. C. cir. 588
Ol. XLVIII. 1
TarquiniiPrisci,
R. Roman.,
cir. annum 29

32 But though he cause grief,
yet will he have compassion according to the multitude of his
mercies.

33 For [h]he doth not afflict [i]willingly, nor grieve the children of men.

34 To crush under his feet all the prisoners of the earth,

35 To turn aside the right of a man before the face of [k]the Most High,

36 To subvert a man in his cause, [l]the LORD [m]approveth not.

37 Who *is* he [n]*that* saith, and it cometh to pass, *when* the LORD commanded *it* not?

38 Out of the mouth of the Most High proceedeth not [o]evil and good?

39 [p]Wherefore doth a living man [q]complain, a man for the punishment of his sins?

40 Let us search and try our
ways, and turn again to the
LORD.

41 [s]Let us lift up our heart
with *our* hands unto God in the heavens.

42 [t]We have transgressed and have rebelled: thou hast not pardoned.

43 Thou hast covered with anger, and persecuted us: [u]thou hast slain, thou hast not pitied.

44 Thou hast covered thyself with a cloud, [v]that *our* prayer should not pass through.

45 Thou hast made us *as* the [w]offscouring and refuse in the midst of the people.

46 [x]All our enemies have opened their mouths against us.

47 [y]Fear and a snare is come upon us, [z]desolation and destruction.

---

[h]Ezek. xxxiii. 11; Heb. xii. 10——[i]Heb. *from his heart*——[k]Or, *a superior*——[l]Hab. i. 13——[m]Or, *seeth not*——[n]Psa. xxxiii. 9——[o]Job ii. 10; Isa. xlv. 7; Amos iii. 6——[p]Prov. xix. 3

[q]Or, *murmur*——[r]Mic. vii. 9——[s]Psa. lxxxvi. 4——[t]Dan. ix. 5——[u]Chap. ii. 17, 21——[v]Ver. 8——[w]1 Cor. iv. 13——[x]Chap. ii. 16——[y]Isa. xxiv. 17; Jer. xlviii. 43——[z]Isa. li. 19

---

of my ancient MSS. has יהוה *Yehovah.* The above verse is quoted in reference to our Lord's passion, by Matt. xxvi. 62.

Verse 33. *For he doth not afflict willingly*] It is no pleasure to God to afflict men. He takes no delight in our pain and misery: yet, like a tender and intelligent parent, he uses the rod; not to gratify himself, but to profit and save us.

Verse 34. *To crush under his feet*] He can neither gain credit nor pleasure in trampling upon those who are already *bound*, and in suffering; such he knows to be the state of man here below. From which it most assuredly follows, that God never afflicts us but for our good, nor chastises but that we may be partakers of his holiness.

All the prisoners of the earth] By the *prisoners of the earth*, or *land*, Dr. *Blayney* understands those insolvent debtors who were put in prison, and there obliged to work out the debt. Yet this is mercy in comparison with those who put them in prison, and keep them there, when they know that it is impossible, from the state of the laws, to lessen the debt by their confinement.

In verses 34, 35, and 36, certain acts of tyranny, malice, and injustice are specified, which men often indulge themselves in the practice of towards one another, but which the Divine goodness is far from countenancing or approving by any similar conduct.—*Blayney.*

Verse 35. *To turn aside the right of a man*] To make a man lose his right, because one of the higher orders opposes him. Dr. *Blayney* thinks that עליון *elyon*, instead of being referred to *God*, should be considered as pointing out one of the *chief* of the people. I do not see that we gain any thing by this. The evil fact is, *turning aside the right of a man;* and the aggravation of it is, doing it *before the face of the Most High;* that is, in a court of justice, where God is ever considered to be present.

Verse 36. *To subvert a man in his cause*] To prevent his having justice done him in a lawsuit, &c., by undue interference, as by suborning false witnesses, or exerting any kind of influence in opposition to truth and right.—*Blayney.*

The Lord approveth not.] Instead of אדני *Adonai*, seventeen MSS., of *Kennicott's*, and one ancient of my own, have יהוה *Yehovah. Approveth not*, לא ראה *lo raah*, doth not see, turns away his face from it, abhors it.

Verse 39. *Wherefore doth a living man complain*] He who has his life still lent to him has small cause of complaint. How great soever his affliction may be, he is still *alive;* therefore, he may seek and find mercy unto eternal life. Of this, *death* would deprive him; therefore let not a *living* man complain.

Verse 40. *Let us search*] How are we to get the pardon of our sins? The prophet tells us: 1. Let us examine ourselves. 2. "Let us turn again to the Lord." 3. "Let us lift up our heart;" let us make fervent prayer and supplication for mercy. 4. "Let us lift up our hand;" let us solemnly promise to be his, and bind ourselves in a covenant to be the Lord's only: so much *lifting up the hand to God* implies. Or, let us put our heart on our hand, and offer it to God; so some have translated this clause. 5. "We have transgressed;" let our confession of sin be fervent and sincere. 6. And to us who profess *Christianity* it may be added, *Believe on the Lord Jesus Christ* as having *died for thee;* and thou shalt not perish, but have everlasting life. Verses 46, 47, 48, beginning with פ *phe*, should, as to the order of the alphabet, follow 49, 50, 51, which begin with ע *ain*, which in its grammatical position precedes the former.

Verse 47. *Fear and a snare*] See on Jer. xlviii. 13.

A. M. cir. 3416
B. C. cir. 588
Ol. XLVIII. 1
TarquiniiPrisci,
R. Roman.,
cir. annum 29

48 [a]Mine eye runneth down with rivers of water for the destruction of the daughter of my people.

49 [b]Mine eye trickleth down, and ceaseth not, without any intermission.

50 Till the LORD [c]look down, and behold from heaven.

51 Mine eye affecteth [d]mine heart [e]because of all the daughters of my city.

52 Mine enemies chased me sore, like a bird, [f]without cause.

53 They have cut off my life [g]in the dungeon, and [h]cast a stone upon me.

54 [i]Waters flowed over mine head; *then* [k]I said, I am cut off.

55 [l]I called upon thy name, O LORD, out of the low dungeon.

56 [m]Thou hast heard my voice: hide not thine ear at my breathing, at my cry.

57 Thou [n]drewest near in the day *that* I called upon thee: thou saidst, Fear not.

A. M. cir. 3416
B. C. cir. 588
Ol. XLVIII. 1
TarquiniiPrisci,
R. Roman.,
cir. annum 29

58 O LORD, thou hast [o]pleaded the causes of my soul; [p]thou hast redeemed my life.

59 O LORD, thou hast seen my wrong: [q]judge thou my cause.

60 Thou hast seen all their vengeance *and* all their [r]imaginations against me.

61 Thou hast heard their reproach, O LORD, *and* all their imaginations against me;

62 The lips of those that rose up against me, and their device against me all the day.

63 Behold their [s]sitting down, and their rising up; [t]I *am* their music.

64 [u]Render unto them a recompense, O LORD, according to the work of their hands.

65 Give them [v]sorrow of heart, thy curse unto them.

66 Persecute and destroy them in anger [w]from under the [x]heavens of the LORD.

---

[a]Jer. iv. 19; ix. 1; xiv. 17; ch. ii. 11——[b]Psa. lxxvii. 2; ch. i. 16——[c]Isa. lxiii. 15——[d]Heb. *my soul*——[e]Or, *more than all*——[f]Psa. xxxv. 7, 19; lxix. 4; cix. 3; cxix. 161——[g]Jer. xxxvii. 16; xxxviii. 6, 9, 10——[h]Dan. vi. 17 [i]Psa. lxix. 2; cxxiv. 4, 5——[k]Psa. xxxi. 22; Isa. xxxviii. 10, 11; ver. 18——[l]Psa. cxxx. 1; Jonah ii. 2

[m]Psa. iii. 4; vi. 8; xviii. 6; lxvi. 19; cxvi. 1——[n]James iv. 8——[o]Psa. xxxv. 1; Jer. li. 36——[p]Psa. lxxi. 23 [q]Psa. ix. 4; xxxv. 23——[r]Jer. xi. 19——[s]Psa. cxxxix. 2 [t]Ver. 14——[u]Psa. xxviii. 4; see Jer. xi. 20; 2 Tim. iv. 14 [v]Or, *obstinacy of heart*——[w]Deut. xxv. 19; Jer. x. 11 [x]Psa. viii. 3

Verse 48. *Mine eye runneth down*] I weep incessantly.

Verse 51. *Mine eye affecteth mine heart*] What I *see* I *feel*. I *see* nothing but *misery;* and I *feel*, in consequence, nothing but *pain*. There have been various translations of the original: but they all amount to this.

The daughters of my city.] The villages about Jerusalem.

Verse 52. *Mine enemies chased me*] From this to the end of the chapter the prophet speaks of his own personal sufferings, and especially of those which he endured in the *dungeon*. See Jer. xxxviii. 6, &c.

Verse 56. *Hide not thine ear at my breathing*] He dared not even to *complain*, nor to *cry*, nor to *pray aloud:* he was obliged to *whisper* his prayer to God. It was only a *breathing*.

Verse 57. *Fear not.*] How powerful is this word when spoken by the Spirit of the Lord to a disconsolate heart. To *every mourner* we may say, on the authority of God, *Fear not!* God will plead thy cause, and redeem thy soul.

Verse 60. *Thou hast seen—all their imaginations*] Every thing is open to the eye of God. Distressed soul! though *thou* knowest not *what* thy enemies *meditate* against thee; yet he who *loves thee* does, and will infallibly defeat all *their* plots, and save *thee*.

Verse 65. *Give them sorrow of heart*] They shall have a *callous* heart, *covered* with *obstinacy*, and thy *execration*. The former is their *state*, the latter their *fate*. This is the consequence of their hardening their hearts from thy fear. *Blayney* translates, "Thou wilt give with a hearty concordance thy curse unto them." That is, Thou wilt give it to them freely, and without reserve; intimating that God felt no longer any bowels of compassion for them. Formerly he inflicted punishments with reluctance, while there was any hope of amendment: but, in the instance before us, the case was so hopeless, that God acts according to the simple principle of vindictive justice. The prophet therefore considers them on the utmost verge of final reprobation: another plunge, and they are lost for ever.

Verse 66. *Persecute and destroy them*] Thou wilt pursue them with destruction. These are all *declaratory*, not *imprecatory*.

From under the heavens of the Lord.] This verse seems to allude to the Chaldaic prediction, in Jer. x. 11. By their conduct they will bring on themselves the curse denounced against their enemies.

The *Septuagint* and *Vulgate* seem to have read "From under heaven, O Jehovah:" and the *Syriac* reads, "Thy heavens, O Jehovah!" None of these makes any material change in the meaning of the words.

It has already been noticed in the *introduction*, that this chapter contains a *triple acrostic*, *three* lines always beginning with the same letter; so that the Hebrew alphabet is thrice repeated in this chapter, *twenty-two* multiplied by *three* being equal to *sixty-six*.

CHAPTER IV

The present deplorable state of the nation is now contrasted with its ancient prosperity, 1–12; *and the unhappy change ascribed, in a great degree, to the profligacy of the priests and prophets,* 13–16. *The national calamities are tenderly lamented,* 17–20. *The ruin of the Edomites also, who had insulted the Jews in their distress, is ironically predicted,* 21. See Psa. cxxxvii. 7, and Obadiah 10–12. *The chapter closes with a gracious promise of deliverance from the Babylonish captivity,* 22.

A. M. cir. 3416
B. C. cir. 588
Ol. XLVIII. 1
TarquiniiPrisci,
R. Roman.,
cir. annum 29

HOW is the gold become dim!
how is the most fine gold
changed! the stones of the sanctuary are poured out [a]in the
top of every street.
2 The precious sons of Zion, comparable to
fine gold, how are they esteemed [b]as earthen
pitchers, the work of the hands of the potter!
3 Even the [c]sea monsters draw out the
breast, they give suck to their young ones:
the daughter of my people *is become* cruel,
[d]like the ostriches in the wilderness.
4 [e]The tongue of the suckling child cleaveth
to the roof of his mouth for
thirst: [f]the young children ask
bread, *and* no man breaketh *it*
unto them.
5 They that did feed delicately are desolate
in the streets: they that were brought up in
scarlet [g]embrace dunghills.
6 For the [h]punishment of the iniquity of
the daughter of my people is greater than the
punishment of the sin of Sodom, that was
[i]overthrown as in a moment, and no hands
stayed on her.
7 Her Nazarites were purer than snow, they

A. M. cir. 3416
B. C. cir. 588
Ol. XLVIII. 1
TarquiniiPrisci,
R. Roman.,
cir. annum 29

[a]Chap. ii. 19——[b]Isa. xxx. 14; Jer. xix. 11; 2 Cor. iv. 7——[c]Or, *sea calves*——[d]Job xxxix. 14, 16

[e]Psa. xxii. 15——[f]See chap. ii. 11, 12——[g]Job xxiv. 8——[h]Or, *iniquity*——[i]Gen. xix. 25

NOTES ON CHAP. IV

Verse 1. *How is the gold become dim*] The prophet contrasts, in various affecting instances, the wretched circumstances of the Jewish nation, with the flourishing state of their affairs in former times. Here they are compared to gold, זהב *zahab*, native gold from the mine, which, contrary to its nature, is become *dim*, is tarnished; and even the *fine*, the *sterling gold*, כתם *kethem*, that which was stamped to make it *current*, is *changed* or *adulterated*, so as to be no longer passable. This might be applied to the *temple*, but particularly to the fallen *priests* and apostate *prophets*.

The stones of the sanctuary] אבני קדש *abney kodesh*, the *holy stones;* the Jewish godly men, who were even then the *living stones* of which God *built his Church*.

Verse 2. *The precious sons of Zion*] The Jewish priests and Jewish believers.

Comparable to fine gold] Who were of the *pure standard* of holiness; holy, because God who called them is holy; but now esteemed no better than *earthen pitchers*—vessels of dishonour in comparison of what they once were.

Verse 3. *Even the sea monsters draw out the breast*] The *whales* give suck to their young ones. The word תנין *tannin*, signifies all *large* and *cruel* creatures, whether *aquatic* or *terrestrial;* and need not here be restrained to the *former* sort. My Old MS. Bible translates curiously: **Bot and the cruel bestis that ben clepid Lampa, and thei nakeden ther tetis, gebe ther whelpis souken.**

Like the ostriches in the wilderness.] For her carelessness about her *eggs*, and her inattention to her *young*, the ostrich is proverbial.

Verse 4. *The tongue of the sucking child*] See the note on chap. ii. 12.

Verse 5. *Embrace dunghills.*] Lie on *straw* or *rubbish*, instead of the costly carpets and sofas on which they formerly stretched themselves.

Verse 6. *For the punishment*] He thinks the punishment of *Jerusalem* far greater than that of *Sodom*. That was destroyed *in a moment*, while all her inhabitants were in *health* and *strength;* Jerusalem fell by the most *lingering* calamities; her men *partly destroyed by the sword*, and *partly by the famine*.

Instead of *no hands stayed on her*, *Blayney* translates, "Nor were hands weakened in her." Perhaps the meaning is, "Sodom was destroyed in a moment without any human labour." It was a judgment from *God himself:* so the sacred text: "The LORD rained down fire and brimstone from the Lord out of heaven." See Gen. xix. 24.

Verse 7. *Her Nazarites were purer than snow*] נזיר *nazir* does not always signify a *person separated* under a *religious vow;* it sometimes denotes what is *chief* or *eminent*. It is applied to *Joseph*, Gen. xlix. 26. *Blayney* therefore translates here, HER NOBLES.

"Her nobles were purer than snow, they were
whiter than milk;
They were ruddier on the bone than rubies;
their veining was the sapphires."

On which he remarks:—"In the first line the *whiteness* of their skin is described; and in the second, their flesh;" and as נזר *gazar* signifies to *divide* and *intersect*, as the *blue veins* do on the surface of the body, these are without doubt intended.

Milk will most certainly well apply to the *whiteness* of the *skin;* the beautiful *ruby* to the *ruddiness* of the *flesh;* and the *sapphire*, in its clear transcendent *purple*, to the *veins* in a fine complexion. The reverse of this state, as described in the following verse, needs no explanation. The *face* was a dismal *dark brown*, the

A. M. cir. 3416 B. C. cir. 588 Ol. XLVIII. 1 TarquiniiPrisci, R. Roman., cir. annum 29

were whiter than milk, they were
more ruddy in body than rubies,
their polishing *was* of sapphire:

8 Their visage is [k]blacker [l]than a coal;
they are not known in the streets: [m]their
skin cleaveth to their bones; it is withered, it
is become like a stick.

9 *They that be* slain with the sword are
better than *they that be* slain with hunger:
for these [n]pine away, stricken through for
want of the fruits of the field.

10 [o]The hands of the [p]pitiful women have
sodden their own children: they were their
[q]meat in the destruction of the daughter of
my people.

11 The LORD hath accomplished his fury;
[r]he hath poured out his fierce anger, and
[s]hath kindled a fire in Zion, and it hath devoured the foundations thereof.

12 The kings of the earth, and all the
inhabitants of the world, would not have believed that the adversary and the enemy should
have entered into the gates of Jerusalem.

13 [t]For the sins of her prophets, *and* the iniquities of her
priests, [u]that have shed the
blood of the just in the midst
of her,

A. M. cir. 3416 B. C. cir. 588 Ol. XLVIII. 1 TarquiniiPrisci, R. Roman., cir. annum 29

14 They have wandered *as* blind *men* in the
streets, [v]they have polluted themselves with
blood, [w]so [x]that men could not touch their
garments.

15 They cried unto them, Depart ye; [y]*it is*
[z]unclean; depart, depart, touch not: when
they fled away and wandered, they said
among the heathen, They shall no more sojourn *there*.

16 The [a]anger of the LORD hath divided
them; he will no more regard them: [b]they
respected not the persons of the priests, they
favoured not the elders.

17 As for us, [c]our eyes as yet failed for
our vain help: in our watching we have
watched for a nation *that* could not save *us*.

18 [d]They hunt our steps, that we cannot go
in our streets: our end is near, our days are
fulfilled; for [e]our end is come.

---

[k]Heb. *darker than blackness*——[l]Chap. v. 10; Joel ii. 6; Nah. ii. 10——[m]Psa. cii. 5——[n]Heb. *flow out*
[o]Chap. ii. 20——[p]Isa. xlix. 15——[q]Deut. xxviii. 57; 2 Kings vi. 29——[r]Jer. vii. 20——[s]Deut. xxxii. 22; Jer. xxi. 14——[t]Jer. v. 31; vi. 13; xiv. 14; xxiii. 11, 21; Ezek. xxii. 26, 28; Zeph. iii. 4

[u]Matt. xxiii. 31, 37——[v]Jer. ii. 34——[w]Or, *in that they could not but touch*——[x]Num. xix. 16——[y]Or, *ye polluted*——[z]Lev. xiii. 45——[a]Or, *face*——[b]Chap. v. 12
[c]2 Kings xxiv. 7; Isa. xx. 5; xxx. 6, 7; Jer. xxxvii. 7; Ezek. xxix. 16——[d]2 Kings xxv. 4, 5——[e]Ezek. vii. 2, 3, 6; Amos viii. 2

---

flesh gone, the *skin* shrivelled, and apparently wrapped round the *bones*.

Verse 10. *The hands of the pitiful women have sodden their own children*] See on chap. ii. 20. But here there is a reference to mothers eating their own children; and this was done, not by mothers cruel and brutal, but by נשים רחמניות *nashim rachmaniyoth*, the *compassionate*, the *tender-hearted mothers*. From these horrible scenes it is well to pass with as hasty a step as possible.

Verse 12. *The kings of the earth*] Jerusalem was so well fortified, both by nature and art, that it appeared as a miracle that it should be taken at all.

Verse 13. *For the sins of her prophets*, and *the iniquities of her priests*] These most wretched beings, under the pretence of *zeal for the true religion*, persecuted the *genuine prophets*, *priests*, and *people of God*, and caused their blood to be shed in the midst of the city, in the most open and public manner; exactly as the murderous priests, and blood-thirsty preachers, under the reign of bloody Queen Mary, did in England. However, the profligate priests and idolatrous prophets in Jerusalem, only *shed* the blood of the saints of God there: but the sanguinary papists, in the above reign, *burnt* the blood here, for they *burnt the people alive;* and at the same time, in their worse than Molochean cruelty, consigned, with all the fervour peculiar to their then ruthless Church, the *souls* of those whom they thus massacred, to the bitter pains of eternal death! O earth, cover not thou their blood!

Verse 14. *They have wandered* as *blind* men *in the streets*] Rather, "They ran frantic through the streets, they were stained with blood." This was in their pretended zeal for their cause. Bishop *Bonner*, who was at the head of those sanguinary executions in England, was accustomed to *buffet* the poor Protestants, when on their examinations they were too powerful for him in argument:—

> "He proved his doctrine orthodox,
> By apostolic blows and knocks."

Just as his *elder brethren*, the false priests and prophets of Jerusalem.

Verse 15. *When they fled away*] These priests and prophets were so *bad*, that the very *heathen* did not like to permit them to sojourn among them. The prophet now resumes the history of the siege.

Verse 17. *We have watched for a nation*] Viz., the Egyptians, who were their pretended allies, but were neither *able* nor *willing* to help them against the Chaldeans.

Verse 18. *We cannot go in our streets*] Supposed to refer to the *darts* and other *missiles* cast from the mounds which they had raised on the outside of the walls, by which those who walked in the streets were grievously annoyed, and could not shield themselves.

A. M. cir. 3416
B. C. cir. 588
Ol. XLVIII. 1
TarquiniiPrisci,
R. Roman.,
cir. annum 29

19 Our persecutors are [f]swifter
than the eagles of the heaven:
they pursued us upon the mountains, they laid wait for us in the
wilderness.
20 The [g]breath of our nostrils, the anointed
of the LORD, [h]was taken in their pits, of whom
we said, Under his shadow we shall live among
the heathen.
21 [i]Rejoice and be glad, O daughter of
Edom, that dwellest in the land
of Uz; [k]the cup also shall pass
through unto thee: thou shalt be
drunken, and shalt make thyself
naked.
22 [l]The [m]punishment of thine iniquity is
accomplished, O daughter of Zion; he will
no more carry thee away into captivity: [n]he
will visit thine iniquity, O daughter of Edom;
he will [o]discover thy sins.

A. M. cir. 3416
B. C. cir. 588
Ol. XLVIII. 1
TarquiniiPrisci,
R. Roman.,
cir. annum 29

[f]Deut. xxviii. 49; Jer. iv. 13——[g]Gen. ii. 7; chap. ii. 9——[h]Jer. lii. 9; Ezek. xii. 13; xix. 4, 8——[i]Like Eccles. xi. 9

[k]Jer. xxv. 15, 16, 21; Obad. 10——[l]Isa. xl. 2——[m]Or, *Thine iniquity*——[n]Psa. cxxxvii. 7——[o]Or, *carry* thee *captive for thy sins*

Verse 19. *They pursued us upon the mountains*] They hunted down the poor Jews like wild beasts in every part of the country by their marauding parties, whilst the great army besieged Jerusalem. But this may apply to the pursuit of Zedekiah. See what follows.

Verse 20. *The breath of our nostrils, the anointed of the Lord*] That is, Zedekiah the king, who was as *the life of the city*, was taken in his flight by the Chaldeans, and his eyes were put out; so that he was wholly unfit to perform any function of government; though they had fondly hoped that if they surrendered and should be led captives, yet they should be permitted to live under their own laws and king in the land of their bondage.

Verse 21. *Rejoice and be glad, O daughter of Edom*] A strong irony.

The cup also shall pass through unto thee] Thou who hast triumphed in our disasters shalt shortly have enough of thy own. They had joined themselves to the Chaldeans, (see Psa. cxxxvii. 7,) and therefore they should share in the desolations of Babylon.

Verse 22. *The punishment of thine iniquity is accomplished, O daughter of Zion*] On the contrary: Rejoice, O Jerusalem, for thy captivity will soon end; thy sufferings are nearly completed; thou shalt soon return to thy own land: but he will *visit thy iniquity, O Edom; he will discover thy sins.* When sin is *pardoned*, it is said to be *covered:* here, God says he will *not cover the sins of Edom*—he will not *pardon them;* they shall drink the cup of wrath.

The promise in this last verse may refer to Jerusalem under the Gospel. When they receive Christ crucified, they shall be gathered from all nations, become one with the Church among the Gentiles, be one flock under one and the same Shepherd, and shall be *carried no more into captivity.*

CHAPTER V

This chapter is, as it were, an epiphonema, *or conclusion to the four preceding, representing the nation as groaning under their calamities, and humbly supplicating the Divine favour,* 1–22.

A. M. cir. 3416
B. C. cir. 588
Ol. XLVIII. 1
TarquiniiPrisci,
R. Roman.,
cir. annum 29

[a]REMEMBER, O LORD, what
is come upon us: consider,
and behold [b]our reproach.
2 [c]Our inheritance is turned to
strangers, our houses to aliens.
3 We are orphans and fatherless, our mothers *are* as widows.
4 We have drunken our water
for money; our wood [d]is sold
unto us.

A. M. cir. 3416
B. C. cir. 588
Ol. XLVIII. 1
TarquiniiPrisci,
R. Roman.,
cir. annum 29

[a]Psa. lxxxix. 50, 51——[b]Chap. ii. 15; Psa. lxxix. 4

[c]Psa. lxxix. 1——[d]Heb. *cometh for price*

NOTES ON CHAP. V

Verse 1. *Remember, O Lord*] In the *Vulgate, Syriac,* and *Arabic*, this is headed, "The prayer of Jeremiah." In my old MS. Bible: **Here bigynneth the orison of Jeremye the prophete.**

Though this chapter consists of exactly *twenty-two* verses, the *number of letters* in the *Hebrew alphabet*, yet the *acrostic* form is no longer observed. Perhaps any thing so technical was not thought proper when in agony and distress (under a sense of God's displeasure on account of sin) they prostrated themselves before him to ask for mercy. Be this as it may, no attempt appears to have been made to throw these verses into the form of the preceding chapters. It is properly a *solemn prayer of all the people*, stating their past and present sufferings, and praying for God's mercy.

Behold our reproach.] הביט *hebita.* But many MSS. of *Kennicott's*, and the oldest of my own, add the ה *he paragogic,* הביטה *hebitah,* "Look down earnestly with commiseration;" for *paragogic letters* always *increase* the sense.

Verse 2. *Our inheritance is turned to strangers*] The greater part of the Jews were either slain or carried away captive; and even those who were left under *Gedaliah* were not *free*, for they were vassals to the *Chaldeans*.

Verse 4. *We have drunken our water for money*] I suppose the meaning of this is, that every thing was taxed by the Chaldeans, and that they kept the management in their own

A. M. cir. 3416 B. C. cir. 588 Ol. XLVIII. 1 TarquiniiPrisci, R. Roman., cir. annum 29

5 [e]Our [f]necks *are* under persecution: we labour, *and* have
no rest.
6 [g]We have given the hand
[h]*to* the Egyptians, *and to* the Assyrians, to be
satisfied with bread.
7 [i]Our fathers have sinned, *and* [k]*are* not;
and we have borne their iniquities.
8 [l]Servants have ruled over us: *there is*
none that doth deliver *us* out of their hand.
9 We gat our bread with *the peril of* our
lives because of the sword of the wilderness.
10 Our [m]skin was black like an oven because of the[n] terrible famine.
11 [o]They ravished the women in Zion, *and*
the maids in the cities of Judah.
12 Princes are hanged up by
their hand: [p]the faces of elders
were not honoured.
13 They took the young men
[q]to grind, and the children fell under the
wood.
14 The elders have ceased from the gate,
the young men from their music.
15 The joy of our heart is ceased; our
dance is turned into mourning.
16 [r]The [s]crown is fallen *from* our head:
wo unto us, that we have sinned!
17 For this [t]our heart is faint; [u]for these
things our eyes are dim.
18 Because of the mountain of Zion, which
is desolate, the foxes walk upon it.

[e]Deut. xxviii. 48; Jer. xxviii. 14——[f]Heb. *On our necks are we persecuted*——[g]Gen. xxiv. 2; Jer. l. 15——[h]Hos. xii. 1——[i]Jer. xxxi. 29; Ezek. xviii. 2——[k]Gen. xlii. 13; Zech. i. 5——[l]Neh. v. 15——[m]Job xxx. 30; Psa. cxix. 83; chap. iv. 8

[n]Or, *terrors* or *storms*——[o]Isa. xiii. 16; Zech. xiv. 2——[p]Isa. xlvii. 6; chap. iv. 16——[q]Judg. xvi. 21——[r]Job xix. 9; Psa. lxxxix. 39——[s]Heb. *The crown of our head is fallen*——[t]Chap. i. 22——[u]Psalm vi. 7; chapter ii. 11

hands, so that *wood* and *water* were both sold, the people not being permitted to help themselves. They were now so lowly reduced by servitude, that they were obliged to pay dearly for those things which formerly were *common* and of *no price.* A poor *Hindoo* in the country never buys *fire-wood,* but when he comes to the city he is obliged to purchase his fuel, and considers it as a matter of great hardship.

Verse 5. *Our necks* are *under persecution*] We feel the yoke of our bondage; we are driven to our work like the *bullock,* which has a yoke upon his neck.

Verse 6. *We have given the hand* to *the Egyptians*] We have sought alliances both with the Egyptians and Assyrians, and made covenants with them in order to get the necessaries of life. Or, wherever we are now driven, we are obliged to submit to the people of the countries in order to the preservation of our lives.

Verse 7. *Our fathers have sinned,* and are *not*] *Nations,* as such, cannot be punished in the *other world;* therefore national judgments are to be looked for only in this life. The punishment which the Jewish nation had been meriting for a series of years came now upon them, because they copied and increased the sins of their fathers, and the cup of their iniquity was full. Thus the *children* might be said to *bear the sins of the fathers,* that is, in *temporal punishment,* for in no other way does God visit these upon the children. See Ezek. xviii. 1, &c.

Verse 8. *Servants have ruled over us*] To be subject to such is the most painful and dishonourable bondage:—

Quio domini faciant, audent cum talia fures?
Virg. Ecl. iii. 16.

"Since slaves so insolent are grown,
What may not masters do?"

Perhaps he here alludes to the Chaldean *soldiers,* whose will the wretched Jews were obliged to obey.

Verse 9. *We gat our bread with* the peril of *our lives*] They could not go into the wilderness to feed their cattle, or to get the necessaries of life, without being harassed and plundered by marauding parties, and by these were often exposed to the peril of their lives. This was predicted by Moses, Deut. xxviii. 31.

Verse 10. *Our skin was black—because of the terrible famine.*] Because of the *searching winds* that burnt up every green thing, destroying vegetation, and in consequence producing a famine.

Verse 11. *They ravished the women in Zion,* and *the maids in the cities of Judah.*] The evil mentioned here was predicted by Moses, Deut. xxviii. 30, 32, and by Jeremiah, chap. vi. 12.

Verse 12. *Princes are hanged up by their hand*] It is very probable that this was a species of punishment. They were suspended from hooks in the wall by their hands till they died through torture and exhaustion. The body of Saul was fastened to the wall of Bethshan, probably in the same way; but his head had already been taken off. They were hung in this way that they might be devoured by the fowls of the air. It was a custom with the Persians after they had slain, strangled, or beheaded their enemies, to hang their bodies upon poles, or empale them. In this way they treated *Histiæus* of Miletum, and *Leonidas* of Lacedæmon. See *Herodot.* lib. vi. c. 30, lib. vii. c. 238.

Verse 13. *They took the young men to grind*] This was the work of female slaves. See the note on Isa. xlvii. 2.

Verse 14. *The elders have ceased from the gate*] There is now no more justice administered to the people; they are under military law, or disposed of in every sense according to the caprice of their masters.

Verse 16. *The crown is fallen* from *our head*] At feasts, marriages, &c., they used to crown themselves with garlands of flowers; all festivity of this kind was now at an end. Or it may refer to their having lost all *sovereignty,* being made *slaves.*

Verse 18. *The foxes walk upon it.*] *Foxes*

A. M. cir. 3416 B. C. cir. 588 Ol. XLVIII. 1 TarquiniiPrisci, R. Roman., cir. annum 29

19 Thou, O LORD, [v]remain-
est for ever; [w]thy throne from
generation to generation.
20 [x]Wherefore dost thou forget
us for ever, *and* forsake us [y]so long time?

21 [z]Turn thou us unto thee,
O LORD, *and* we shall be turned;
renew our days as of old.
22 [a]But thou hast utterly rejected us; thou art very wroth against us.

[v]Psa. ix. 7; x. 16; xxix. 10; xc. 2; cii. 12, 26, 27; cxlv. 13; Hab. i. 12——[w]Psa. xlv. 6——[x]Psa. xiii. 1

[y]Heb. *for length of days?*——[z]Psa. lxxx. 3, 7, 19; Jer. xxxi. 18——[a]Or, *For wilt thou utterly reject us?*

are very numerous in Palestine, see on Judges xv. 4. It was usual among the Hebrews to consider all desolated land to be the resort of wild beasts; which is, in fact, the case every where when the inhabitants are removed from a country.

Verse 19. *Thou, O Lord, remainest for ever*] THOU sufferest no *change.* Thou didst once *love* us; O let that love be renewed towards us!

Verse 21. *Renew our days as of old.*] Restore us to our former state. Let us regain our country, our temple, and all the Divine offices of our religion; but, more especially, thy favour.

Verse 22. *But thou hast utterly rejected us*] It appears as if thou hadst sealed our final reprobation, because thou showest against us *exceeding great wrath.* But *convert us, O Lord, unto thee, and we shall be converted.* We are now greatly humbled, *feel* our *sin*, and *see* our *folly:* once more restore us, and we shall never again forsake thee! He heard the prayer; and at the end of *seventy* years they were restored to their own land.

This last verse is well rendered in the first printed edition of our Bible, 1535:—**Renue our daies as in olde tyme, for thou hast now banished us longe ynough, and bene sore displeased at us.**

My old MS. Bible is not less nervous:—**Newe thou our dais as fro the begynnyng: bot castand aweie thou hast put us out: thou wrathedist ugein us hugely.**

Dr. *Blayney* translates, "For surely thou hast cast us off altogether:" and adds, "כי *ki* ought certainly to be rendered as *causal;* God's having rejected his people, and expressed great indignation against them, being the *cause* and *ground* of the preceding application, in which they pray to be restored to his favour, and the enjoyment of their ancient privileges."

Pareau thinks no good sense can be made of this place unless we translate interrogatively, as in Jer. xiv. 19,—

"Hast thou utterly rejected Judah?
Hath thy soul loathed Sion?"

On this ground he translates here,

An enim prorsus nos rejecisses?
Nobis iratus esses usque adeo?

"Hast thou indeed utterly cast us off?
Wilt thou be angry with us for ever?"

Wilt thou extend thy wrath against us so as to show us no more mercy? This agrees well with the *state* and *feelings* of the complainants.

MASORETIC NOTES

Number of verses in this Book, 154.
Middle verse, chap. iii. 34.

In one of my oldest MSS., the *twenty-first* verse is repeated at the conclusion of the *twenty-second* verse. In another, yet older, there is only the first word of it, השיבנו *hashibenu, Convert us!*

Having given in the preceding *preface* and *notes* what I judge necessary to explain the principal difficulties in this very fine and affecting poem, very fitly termed THE LAMENTATIONS, as it justly stands at the *head* of every composition of the kind, I shall add but a few words, and these shall be by way of recapitulation chiefly.

The Hebrews were accustomed to make *lamentations* or *mourning songs* upon the death of great men, princes, and heroes, who had distinguished themselves in arms; and upon any *occasion of public miseries and calamities. Calmet* thinks they had *collections* of these sorts of Lamentations: and refers in proof to 2 Chron. xxxv. 25: "And Jeremiah lamented for Josiah; and all the singing men and the singing women spake of Josiah in their lamentations, to this day; and made them an ordinance in Israel: and, behold, they are written in the Lamentations."

From this verse it is evident, that Jeremiah had composed a funeral elegy on *Josiah:* but, from the complexion of *this Book*, it is most evident that *it* was not composed on the death of *Josiah*, but upon the *desolations of Jerusalem*, &c., as has already been noted. His *lamentation for Josiah* is therefore lost. It appears also, that on particular occasions, perhaps *anniversaries*, these *lamentations* were sung by men and women singers, who performed their *several parts;* for these were all *alternate* or *responsive songs.* And it is very likely, that this book was sung in the same way; the *men* commencing with א *aleph*, the *women* responding with ב *beth*, and so on. Several of this sort of songs are still extant. We have those which *David* composed on the death of his son *Absalom*, and on the death of his friend *Jonathan.* And we have those made by *Isaiah*, *Jeremiah*, and *Ezekiel*, on the desolation of *Egypt*, *Tyre*, *Sidon*, and *Babylon.* See Isa. xiv. 4, 5; xv.; xvi.; Jer. vii. 29; ix. 10; xlviii. 32; Ezek. xix. 1; xxviii. 11; xxxii. 2; Jer. ix. 17. Besides these, we have *fragments* of others in different places; and references to some, which are now finally lost.

In the *two* first *chapters* of this book, the prophet describes, principally, the calamities of the siege of Jerusalem.

In the *third*, he deplores the persecutions which he himself had suffered; though he may in this be *personifying* the city and state; many of his own sufferings being illustrative of the calamities that fell generally upon the city and people at large.

The *fourth* chapter is employed chiefly on the ruin and desolation of the city and temple; and upon the misfortunes of *Zedekiah*, of whom he speaks in a most respectful, tender, and affecting manner:—

"The anointed of Jehovah, the breadth of our
nostrils, was taken in their toils,
Under whose shadow we said, We shall live
among the nations."

At the end he speaks of the cruelty of the Edomites, who had insulted Jerusalem in her miseries, and contributed to its demolition. These he threatens with the wrath of God.

The *fifth* chapter is a kind of *form of prayer* for the Jews, in their dispersions and captivity. In the conclusion of it, he speaks of their fallen royalty; attributes all their calamities to their rebellion and wickedness; and acknowledges that there can be no end to their misery, but in their restoration to the Divine favour.

This last chapter was probably written some considerable time *after* the rest: for it supposes the temple to be so deserted, that the *foxes walked undisturbed among its ruins*, and that the people were already in captivity.

The poem is a monument of the *people's* iniquity and rebellion; of the displeasure and judgment of God against them; and of the piety, eloquence, and incomparable ability of the *poet*.

INTRODUCTION TO THE BOOK

OF THE

PROPHET EZEKIEL

EZEKIEL the prophet was the son of *Buzi;* and was of the sacerdotal race, as himself informs us, chap. i. 3, and was born at a place called *Saresa,* as the *pseudo-Epiphanius* tells us in his Lives of the Prophets. He was carried captive by Nebuchadnezzar into Babylon, with Jeconiah king of Judah, and *three thousand* other captives of the principal inhabitants, and was sent into Mesopotamia, where he received the prophetic gift; which is supposed, from an obscure expression in his prophecies, chap. i. 1, to have taken place in the *thirtieth* year of his age. He had then been in captivity *five* years; and continued to prophesy about *twenty-two* years, from A. M. 3409 to A. M. 3430, which answers to the *fourteenth* year after the destruction of Jerusalem.

About *three* months and *ten* days after this conquest of Jerusalem, Nebuchadnezzar made another descent, and again besieged the city; and Jehoiachin, who succeeded his father Jehoiakim, was obliged to surrender. The victorious Chaldeans carried off all the inhabitants of note into Babylon, leaving none behind but the very poorest of the people. See 2 Kings xxiv. 8–16. These captives were fixed at *Tel-abib,* and other places on the river Chebar, which flows into the east side of the Euphrates at Carchemish, nearly *two hundred* miles northward of Babylon. There, as Archbishop *Newcome* observes, he was present in body, though, in visionary representation, he was sometimes taken to Jerusalem.

With this same learned writer I am of opinion that, the better to understand the propriety and force of these Divine revelations, the circumstances and dispositions of the Jews in their own country, and in their state of banishment, and the chief historical events of that period, should be stated and considered. Most writers on this Prophet have adopted this plan; and Archbishop *Newcome's* abstract of this history is sufficient for every purpose.

"Zedekiah, uncle to the captive king Jehoiachin, was advanced by Nebuchadnezzar to the kingdom of Judah; and the tributary king bound himself to subjection by a solemn oath in the name of Jehovah, Ezek. xvii. 18. But notwithstanding the Divine judgments which had overwhelmed Judah during the reigns of his two immediate predecessors, he did evil in the sight of God, 2 Chron. xxxvi. 12. Jerusalem became so idolatrous, impure, oppressive, and blood-thirsty, that God is represented as smiting his hands together through astonishment at such a scene of iniquity, chap. xxii. 13. The Prophet Jeremiah was insulted, rejected, and persecuted; false prophets abounded, whose language was, 'Ye shall not serve the king of Babylon,' Jer. xxvii. 9. 'I have broken the yoke of the king of Babylon,' Jer. xxviii. 2. They even limited the restoration of the sacred vessels, and the return of Jehoiachin and his fellow captives, to so short an interval as *two years,* Jer. xxviii. 3, 4. Zedekiah, blinded by his vices and these delusions, flattered by the embassies which he had received from Edom, Moab, Ammon, Tyre, and Sidon, Jer. xxvii. 3, and probably submitting with his accustomed timidity to the advice of evil counsellors, Jer. xxviii. 25, rebelled against his powerful conquerors, and sent ambassadors into Egypt for assistance, Ezek. xvii. 15. Hence arose a third invasion of the Chaldeans. Pharaoh-hophra, king of Egypt, did not advance to the assistance of Zedekiah till Jerusalem was besieged, Jer. xxxvii. 5. The Babylonians raised the siege with the design of distressing the Egyptians in their march, and of giving battle when advantage offered: but Pharaoh, with perfidy and pusillanimity, returned to his own country; and left the rebellious and perjured king of Judah to the rage of his enemies, Jer. xxxvii. 7. Before the siege was thus interrupted, Zedekiah endeavoured to conciliate the favour of God by complying so far with the Mosaic law as to proclaim the sabbatical year a year of liberty to Hebrew servants, Exod. xxi. 2. But such was his impiety and so irresolute and fluctuating were his counsels, that, on the departure of the Chaldeans, he revoked his edict, Jer. xxxiv. 11; upon which God, by the Prophet Jeremiah, proclaimed liberty to the sword, to the pestilence, and to the famine; and commissioned these messengers of his wrath to avenge himself on his people, Jer. xxxiv. 17. When the siege was resumed, we have a farther instance of Zedekiah's extreme infatuation; his rejection of Jeremiah's counsel, given him by the authority of God, to preserve himself, his family, and his city, by a surrender to the Chaldeans. Thus, after a siege of *eighteen* months, Jerusalem was stormed and burnt, Jer. xxxix. 1, 2; Zedekiah was taken in his flight; his sons were slain before his eyes; his eyes were afterwards put out, agreeably to the savage custom of eastern conquerors; and he was carried in chains to Babylon, Jer. xxxix. 5–7.

"The exiles on the river Chebar were far from being awakened to a devout acknowledgment of God's justice by the punishment inflicted on them: they continued rebellious and idolatrous, Ezek. ii. 3; xx. 39, they hearkened to false prophets and prophetesses, Ezek. xiii. 2, 17; and they were so alienated that he refused to be inquired of by them. In vain did Ezekiel endeavour to attract and win them by the charms of his flowing and insinuating eloquence; in vain did he assume a more vehement tone to awe and alarm them by heightened scenes of calamity and terror.

"We know few particulars concerning the Jews at Babylon. They enjoyed the instruction and example of the Prophet Daniel, who was carried away captive to that city in the *third* year of Jehoiakim, *eight* years before the captivity of Ezekiel, Dan. i. 1. Jeremiah cautioned them not to be deceived by their false prophets and diviners, Jer. xxix. 8, 9, 15, 21; against some of whom he denounced fearful judgments. He exhorted them to seek the peace of the city where they dwelt; to take wives, build houses, and plant gardens, till their restoration after *seventy* years, Jer. xxix. 5, 6, 7, 10. He also comforted them by a prediction of all the evil which God designed to inflict on Babylon: he assured them that *none should remain* in that proud city, but that it should be *desolate for ever*. The messenger, when he had read the book containing these denunciations, was commanded 'to bind a stone to it, and cast it into the Euphrates, and say, Thus shall Babylon sink, and shall not rise from the evil which I will bring on her,' Jer. li. 59–64. It farther appears, by Divine hymns now extant, see Psa. lxxix., cii., cvi., and cxxxvii., that God vouchsafed to inspire some of these Babylonian captives with his Holy Spirit. Nebuchadnezzar appointed Gedaliah ruler of the people that remained in Judea, 2 Kings xxv. 23; Jer. xl. 5; and the scattered military commanders and their men, together with other Jews who had taken refuge in the neighbouring countries, Jer. xl. 7, 11, submitted to his government on the departure of the Chaldeans. The Jews employed themselves in gathering the fruits of the earth, Jer. xl. 12, and a calm succeeded the tempest of war: but it was soon interrupted by the turbulence of this devoted people. Ishmael slew Gedaliah; and compelled the wretched remains of the Jews in Mizpah, the seat of Gedaliah's government, to retire with him towards the country of the Ammonites, Jer. xli. 10; a people hostile to the Chaldeans, Jer. xxvii. 3. Johanan raised a force to revenge this mad and cruel act, Jer. xli. 11–15; pursued Ishmael, overtook him, and recovered from him the people whom he had forced to follow him: but the assassin himself escaped with *eight* men to his place of refuge. The succeeding event furnishes another signal instance of human infatuation. Johanan, through fear of the Chaldeans, many of whom Ishmael had massacred, together with Gedaliah, Jer. xli. 3, conceived a design of retreating to Egypt, Jer. xli. 17; but before he executed this resolution, he formally consulted the Prophet Jeremiah. The prophet answered him in the name of Jehovah,

Jer. xlii., that if Johanan and the people abode in Judea, God would 'build them, and not pull them down: would plant them, and not pluck them up;' but if they went to sojourn in Egypt, they should 'die by the sword, by famine, and by pestilence;' and should become an 'execration, and an astonishment, and a curse, and a reproach.' Notwithstanding this awful assurance, and the many prophecies of Jeremiah, which the most calamitous events had lately verified, Johanan defied the living God and his prophet, and madly adhered to his determination. Not long after the destruction of Jerusalem, the siege of Tyre was undertaken by Nebuchadnezzar. It continued for the space of *thirteen* years; and many think that the conquest of the Sidonians, Philistines, Ammonites, Moabites, and Idumeans, coincided with this period, the Chaldean being able to make powerful detachments from his vast forces. See the prophecies, Jer. xxvii. 2, 3; xlviii., xlix., and Ezek. xxv. After the reduction of that famous city, Nebuchadnezzar made his descent on Egypt, which he subdued and ravaged throughout; and at this time Johanan and his Jewish colonists experienced the vengeance of the conqueror, together with the Egyptians. So widely did Nebuchadnezzar spread his victories and devastations, that, according to the learned chronologer *Marsham*, Lond. edit. 1672, fol. p. 556, s. 18, this might justly be called the era of the subversion of cities.

> ——— Omnis eo terrore Ægyptus, et Indi,
> Omnis Arabs, omnes vertebant terga Sabæi. VIRG. *Æn*. viii. 705.
>
> 'The trembling Indians and Egyptians yield:
> Arabs and soft Sabæans quit the field.' "

I may add that the stroke fell upon no people so heavily as upon the Jews, for no other nation possessed privileges like them, and no other nation had sinned so deeply against God. Their crimes were seen in their punishment.

The principal design of this prophet was to comfort his companions in tribulation during their captivity, and to render it light by the most positive promises of their restoration to their own land, the re-building of the temple, and the re-establishment of the Divine worship, all their enemies being finally destroyed.

That Ezekiel is a very *obscure* writer, all have allowed who have attempted to explain his prophecies. The Jews considered him inexplicable. There is a tradition that the rabbins held a consultation whether they should admit Ezekiel into the sacred canon. And it was likely to be carried in the negative, when Rabbi *Ananias* rose up and said he would undertake to remove every difficulty from the account of *Jehovah's chariot,* chap. i., which is confessedly the most difficult part in the whole book. His proposal was received; and to assist him in his work, and that he might complete it to his credit, they furnished him with *three hundred barrels of oil* to light his lamp during the time he might be employed in the study of this part of his subject! This extravagant grant proved at once the conviction the rabbins had of the difficulty of the work; and it is not even intimated that Rabbi *Ananias* succeeded in any tolerable degree, if indeed he undertook the task; and they believe that to this hour the *chariot* mentioned in chap. i., and the account of the *temple* described at the conclusion of the book, have not been explained.

I believe it may be affirmed with truth that these parts of the prophecy have had as many *different explanations* as there have been *expositors!* Yet each has been sanguine in the hope that he had removed all difficulties; while every successor felt that the whole work was yet to be done, and that the *Gordian knot* was not likely to be untied unless by himself. And it is to be lamented that in these circumstances the work still remains as to its principal difficulties; and I certainly do not attempt to add another to Ezekiel's commentators with the most distant hope of being able to solve those particular difficulties.

After all, with the exception of the *chariot, Gog and Magog,* the peculiarities in the description of the *temple,* and some matters of this kind, the major part of the prophecy is very intelligible, and highly edifying; and does not present more difficulties than have been found in the preceding prophets, and may be found in those which follow. I have in the following notes done what I could, as a help to a better understanding of this part of the sacred writings.

The ancient *Versions* give some help; but it is astonishing how difficult it is to settle the text by a collation of MSS. This has not yet been properly done; and we cannot know the *true meaning* till we can ascertain the *true reading*. But after having laboured in this way, I must express myself as the learned professor of the oriental tongues at Parma, *J. B. De Rossi:* Tanta hic in suffixis præsertim pronominibus codicum inconstantia ac varietas, ut tæduerit me laboris mei, ac verius ego quod olim de uno Zachariæ versu (xi. 5) dolens inquiebat *Norzius*, de toto Ezechielis libro usurpare possim, angustiatam fuisse animam meam ob varietates multas, et avertisse faciem meam ab eis. "That there is so much inconstancy and variation among the MSS., especially in the *suffixed pronouns*, that I was weary of my labour; and I could more truly say of the whole book of Ezekiel, than *Norzius* did relative to one passage in Zechariah, who, bitterly complaining of the many variations he met with, said, 'My soul was perplexed with them, and I turned away my face from them.' " As most of our printed editions have been taken from a very inadequate collation of MSS., especially of this prophet, much remains to be done to restore the text to a proper state of purity. When this is done it is presumed that several of the difficulties in this book will be removed. In many instances Abp. *Newcome* has been very successful.

On the famous controversy relative to GOG and MAGOG, I must refer the reader to the notes on chap. xxxviii. and xxxix., where the best accounts I have met with are detailed. There are only *two schemes* that appear at all probable; that which makes Gog *Antiochus Epiphanes*, king of Assyria, and that which makes him *Cambyses*, king of Persia. The former, as being the most probable, and the best supported in all its parts by the marks given in the prophecy, I have in a certain measure adopted, for want of one more satisfactory to my own mind.

The character of Ezekiel as a poet has been drawn at large by some of the most eminent critics of these and other countries. *Lowth*, *Michaelis*, and *Eichhorn*, are the chief. Abp. *Newcome* has quoted largely from the latter; and from his work, which is now very scarce and extremely dear, I shall present my readers with the following extracts:—

"The two first visions are so accurately polished, chap. i.–vii., viii.–xi., and demanded so much art to give them their last perfection and proportion, that they cannot possibly be an unpremeditated work. And if, according to the commonly received opinion, they were publicly read by Ezekiel as we read them now, he must have seriously designed them as a picture, and finished them in form. The intention of his visions might make this necessary. He designed no doubt to make deep impressions upon the people whom he was to guide; and by highly labouring the Divine appearances, to open their ears for his future oracles and representations. The more complete, divine, and majestic the Divine appearances were which he represented, the deeper veneration was impressed upon the mind towards the prophet to whom such high visions were communicated. Most of the parts which compose Ezekiel, as they are generally works of art, are full of artificial and elaborate plans.

"The peculiarities of language in the first chapter are to be found in the middle and end of the book. The same enthusiasm which in the beginning of his prophecies produced the magnificent Divine appearances, must also have built the temple of God at the conclusion. As in the beginning every thing is first proposed in high allegorical images, and afterwards the same ideas are repeated in plain words, thus also in the middle and at the end in every piece, allegorical representation is succeeded by literal. Throughout the style is rather prose than verse; and rough, hard, and mixed with the Chaldee.

"The division of Ezekiel into two parts has been adopted by several writers. They continue the former part to the *thirty-ninth* chapter, and consider the last *nine* chapters from the *fortieth* as a separate book. This division is possible. From the *eleventh* chapter a new elevated scene commences. Before there was nothing but oracles, full of misfortunes, punishments, death, and ruin; visions concerning the destruction of the government, and concerning the flight and state of the last king; and pictures of the universal corruption, idolatry, and superstition of Israel. From the *fortieth* chapter a new temple rises before the eyes of the holy seer; he walks round about it in Palestine; he measures the city and country for their new inhabitants; he orders sacrifices, feasts, and customs. In short, a Magna Charta is planned for priests, kings, and people, in future and better times. Lastly, from hence prosaic expressions predominate; at least the prophet elevates himself by poetical colouring much more rarely than before.

"A generally acknowledged character of Ezekiel is, that he minutely distinguishes every thing in its smallest parts. What the more ancient prophets brought together in one single picture, and to which they only alluded, and what they explained with the utmost brevity, and showed only from one side, *that* he explains and unfolds formally, and represents from all possible sides.

"Another character, and a principal one, which distinguishes his oracle is, that no other prophet has given so free a course to his imagination. Almost every thing is dressed in symbolical actions, in fables, narrations, allegories, or in the still higher poetry of visions. And as they are very complicate, there resound from all sides complaints of darkness. Whoever can look on these things with the eye of an eagle, and is not disturbed from the principal object by what is not essential; he alone is able to comprehend the sense of the whole composition, and he scarcely conceives how any one can complain of obscurity. Meanwhile, how different soever the species of composition are which he hazards, they are all worked out in the same general form. What he represents in one image, picture, or vision, in allegory, parable, or narration, is explained in a short speech, which God, who is at his right hand, enables him to pronounce.

"It is evident that he has shown an inexhaustible imagination and power of invention throughout all the pages of his book. He uses all sorts of prophetical poetry to appear always great and magnificent; and it cannot be denied that he has given all kinds, excellent pieces, both in design and execution. Particularly, he is so used to ecstasies and visions that he adopts the language proper to these, where he has no visions to describe.

"If the dress of vision fitted any prophet, it was certainly Ezekiel: he was even naturally led to it by his situation, and by the subjects which he was to represent. He was to describe and foretell to his fellow captives several facts which happened in Palestine, in Jerusalem, and in the king's palace. A narration and description in simple prose could not possibly suit a prophet; he must give his object the requisite prophetic dignity, by a particular dress.

"He therefore brought the scene of events nearer. For this purpose he chose high ecstasies, such as the Greek and Roman poets pretended to in their flights of enthusiasm; the hand of Jehovah came upon him, and carried him to that place where what he intended to propose to his countrymen in their exile might be seen and considered. All ecstasies in my opinion are nothing but dresses, nothing but poetical fictions; and a poet of another age, and of another tone, of an inferior imagination and poetical endowments, would have given the same ideas quite another dress.

"Accustomed to this kind of poetry, he represented the restitution of the Jewish state in a sublime vision. His imagination placed him upon graves, where he stood on the dried bones of the dead. He saw how the graves opened, the bones were clothed with flesh, and the dead came forth by a new creation. Could there be a more lively fiction for this case? Another poet would have represented the restoration of the Jews in simple words; and would only have compared it to a resurrection, or give it some other ornamental delineation. To view this intuitively in an example, compare Ezek. xxxvii. 1–14 and Isa. xxvi. 19.

INTRODUCTION TO THE BOOK OF EZEKIEL

'Thy dead shall live, their dead bodies shall rise:
Awake and sing, ye that dwell in dust:
For thy dew is as the dew of herbs,
And the earth shall cast forth the mighty dead.'

"And, however numerous the fictions of Ezekiel are, they all appear in magnificent dress, and each in its peculiar splendid one. Lustre shines in him on every side; and if the poet has here and there overloaded his subject with ornaments, we shall be unable to refuse our admiration to his genius, notwithstanding these defects.

"The first part of his book may be an instance. The barren genius of Moses was gone when God appeared only in a fiery bush in the wilderness; and as the world improved in cultivation, a more luxuriant one succeeded in his place, which in process of time demanded wonderful figures and giant forms, that the representation of the Divine appearance might please. Isaiah had already appeared in a higher style than Moses. To him God manifested himself in the pomp of an oriental king; and this piece makes a strong impression by its unity and gains on us by its elevated simplicity, majesty, and dignity, Isa. vi. But Ezekiel differs widely. Before him stands the chariot-throne of God, with wonderful forms; he summons all the pomp which nature and art can furnish; he abundantly employs fiction and composition to give his Divine appearance dignity, elevation, and majesty; and thus to make a suitable expression. The whole creation must lend him its most noble forms. Men, oxen, lions, and eagles support the throne: the Hebrew history must furnish all its most wonderful scenes, to surround the chariot-throne with the greatest pomp imaginable. I admire the master-hand of the artist, who knew how to compose in such a manner. I am astonished at the richness of *his* imagination, that could give dignity to all the exalted scenes of the Hebrew history, and could combine them in one body. But, notwithstanding this, the scene in Ezekiel is far from making the same deep and heart-striking impression with that of Isaiah. A short view of the whole in Isaiah does wonders; in Ezekiel the prospect is dispersed; and as it is not rounded, it astonishes rather than impresses. In Isaiah there is a majestic silence, which is only interrupted by the heavenly cry of the seraphs, Isa. vi. 3; in Ezekiel, the noise of the restless wheels and moving wings confounds us. In Isaiah, the eye is delighted with artless majesty; in Ezekiel, it is consumed by the brightness of the fire which shines round about the chariot-throne.

"The author of the Revelation, whose poetry is in the same style with that of Ezekiel, and full of imagination, has for the most part avoided the rocks upon which his predecessor struck; and, happily for the most part, has cut off the wild shoots of a heated imagination. He also has fictions of wonders and giant forms; but he has produced them only so far as to give the reader a full image before his eyes. He does not pursue them minutely, and he does not distract or pain his reader.

"On the contrary, it was a happy invention that his lofty poems are sometimes interrupted by short speeches; they are not only useful for the illustration of his symbols, but also for the repose of the mind. By this change, his readers are agreeably entertained; and their imagination finds resting places, so as to soar more easily after the imagination of the poet.

"Ezekiel is a great poet, full of originality; and, in my opinion, whoever censures him as if he were only an imitator of the old prophets, can never have felt his power. He must not in general be compared with Isaiah and the rest of the old prophets. Those are great, Ezekiel is also great; those in *their* manner of poetry, Ezekiel in *his;* which he had invented for himself, if we may form our judgment from the Hebrew monuments still extant." Thus far a judicious critic, who but indirectly admits the prophet's *inspiration.*

Bp. *Lowth*, who has done so much to elucidate the Hebrew *poetry*, has also given fine critical judgments on the comparative merits of the *prophets. Isaiah* is his favorite and him he places always at the *head*, and with *him* all others are compared. Of *Ezekiel*, his character is very high and accurately drawn; and my readers will naturally expect that I should produce what he says on this subject, rather than attempt any thing of my own; for this would resemble the attempt *to write an Iliad after Homer*.

"*Ezekiel*," says this learned prelate, "is inferior to *Jeremiah* in *elegance*, but is equal to *Isaiah* in SUBLIMITY, though in a different species of the *sublime*. He is *bold, vehement, tragical*, and deals very much in *amplification*. His SENTIMENTS are *lofty, animated, poignant*, and full of *indignation*. His IMAGES are *fertile, magnificent*, and sometimes rather bordering on *indelicacy*. His DICTION is *grand, weighty, austere, rough*, and sometimes *uncultivated*. He abounds in *repetitions*, not for the sake of *beauty* or *grace*, but from *vehemence* and *indignation*. Whatever his *subject* be, he keeps it always in his eye, without the least deviation, and is so much taken up with it that he has scarcely any regard to *order* or *connection*. In other things he may be perhaps *exceeded* by the other prophets, but in that species for which he was particularly turned, that is, *force, impetuosity, weight*, and *grandeur*, no writer ever equalled him. His *diction* is *clear* enough; almost all his *obscurity* arises from his *subjects*. His VISIONS are particularly *obscure;* which, however, as in *Hosea, Amos*, and *Zechariah*, are delivered in a *plain historical narration*.

"The greater part of the book, particularly the middle of it, is *poetical;* whether we regard the *matter* or the *language*. But some passages are so *rough* and *unpolished*, that we are frequently at a loss to what species of writing we ought to refer them. As to STYLE, *Isaiah, Jeremiah*, and *Ezekiel* may be placed with propriety enough in the same rank among the *Hebrews*, as *Homer, Simonides*, and *Æschylus* among the *Greeks*."

Nothing need be added, and indeed nothing can be added, to this character; it is as fairly as it is fully drawn; and every paragraph in the book will show its propriety. But could we satisfactorily fathom the prophet's meaning in those places where he is *peculiarly obscure*, we should feel the force and propriety of the bishop's character still more, as in those very places the prophet is *peculiarly sublime*. The prophecy was delivered that it might be understood and be profitable; and no doubt it was fully apprehended by those to whom it was originally given, and for whose sake it was sent from heaven. As to the portions which respect a very *remote futurity*, they will be understood when the events take place; which will, in such times, be an additional argument in favour of Divine revelation, when it is seen with what precision and accuracy prophets have foreseen and described such very remote and apparently contingent events.

To the general reader the following table, taken from *Calmet*, may be useful:—

A Chronological Table of the Prophecies of Ezekiel

A. M.

3405. Ezekiel is led captive to Babylon with King Jeconiah. From this year the epoch of these prophecies must be taken.

3409. The first *vision* by the river Chebar, chap. i. The circumstances which followed Ezekiel's vocation to the prophetic office, chap. i., ii.

He draws upon a tile or bed of clay the plan of Jerusalem, and the siege that it was about to endure; and he remains lying on this plan, on his left side, *three hundred* and *ninety* days, chap. iv. See under A. M. 3420.

3410. He turns on his right side, and lies *forty* days, which point out the *forty* years of the sins of Judah, To this time chap. v., vi., vii. refer.

About the month of *September*, this being the *sixth* year of the captivity of Jeconiah, he had the visions related, chap. viii., ix., x., xi.

3411. Prophecies and figurative actions by which he points out the flight, capture, and blinding of Zedekiah, chap. xii. and the *seven* following.

Zedekiah rebels against Nebuchadnezzar, chap. xvii. 15, 17.

The prophet charges the elders of Judah with hypocrisy, who came to consult him, chap. xx., xxi.. xxii., xxiii.

3414. The siege of *Jerusalem* by Nebuchadnezzar. This was a sabbatic year, Jer. xxiv. 8, &c. The siege did not begin till about the middle of the winter, 2 Kings xxv. 1. The prophet's wife dies on the same day of the siege, and he is forbidden to mourn for her, chap. xxiv. 1, 2.

3415. Predictions against EGYPT, chap. xxix. 16. Nebuchadnezzar puts to flight Pharaoh-hophra, and returns to the siege of Jerusalem *three hundred* and *ninety* days before it was taken.

3416. Predictions against *Tyre*, chap. xxvi.–xxviii., the *first* day of the *first* month.

In the *seventh* day of the same month, God shows the prophet the miseries to be brought on Egypt by Nebuchadnezzar, chap. xxx.

In the *third* month of the same year, the prophet had another vision against *Egypt*, chap. xxxi.

Jerusalem is taken the *ninth* of the *fourth* month. Zedekiah was taken prisoner near Jericho. He is brought to Riblah, where, after seeing his children slain, his eyes are put out, he is laden with chains and led to Babylon. Thus were fulfilled and reconciled the seemingly contradictory prophecies concerning him.

3417. Ezekiel being informed of the taking of Jerusalem the *fifth* day of the *tenth* month, he predicts the ruin of the remnant that was left there under Gedaliah, chap. xxxiv. 21–29.

He afterwards foretells the ruin of *Egypt*, chap. xxxii. 1, 16, 32; and that of the *Idumeans*, chap. xxv. 12.

3419. The commencement of the siege of *Tyre*, which lasted *thirteen* years.

To the same time we must refer the miseries of the Sidonians, the Amalekites, the Moabites, and the Idumeans, pointed out by Jeremiah, chap. xxvii., xlviii., xlix.; Ezek. xxv.

3420. End of the *forty* years mentioned chap. iv. 5, 6, and of the *three hundred* and *ninety* years from the separation of Israel and Judah. The *forty* years commence with the renewal of the covenant under Josiah.

3430. The vision in which God showed the prophet the rebuilding of the city and the temple, and the restoration of the kingdom of Israel, chap. xl. 1 to the end of the book.

This vision took place on the *tenth* of the *first* month, *fourteen* years after the taking of Jerusalem.

3432. Taking of the city of *Tyre*, by Nebuchadnezzar, to whom God promises the spoils of Egypt, as a compensation for the trouble and loss he sustained before Tyre, chap. xxix. 17–20.

Nebuchadnezzar enters *Egypt*. Amasis had been made king by the Cyrenians, who had rebelled against Pharaoh-hophra. *Herodotus*, lib. iv. c. 159, and lib. ii. cc. 161, 162.

3433. The king of Babylon overruns and subdues the whole of Egypt; commits the greatest outrages; and carries off captives the inhabitants, the Jews, and others whom he found there. See Jer. xliii., xliv., xlvi.; Ezek. xxix., xxx., xxxi.

Nebuchadnezzar leaves *Amasis* king of Lower Egypt; *Hophra*, or *Apries*, having escaped to the Thebais.

3442. Death of Nebuchadnezzar.

Evil-merodach succeeds him; and sets Jeconiah at liberty, and makes him his companion, 2 Kings xv. 27 and Jer. lii. 31.

THE BOOK

OF THE

PROPHET EZEKIEL

Chronological Notes relative to the commencement of Ezekiel's prophesying

Year from the Creation, according to Archbishop Usher, 3409.—Year of the Jewish era of the world, 3166.—Year from the Deluge, 1753.—Second year of the *forty-sixth* Olympiad.—Year from the building of Rome, according to the Varronian or generally received account, 159.—Year from the building of Rome, according to Cato and the Fasti Consulares, 158.—Year from the building of Rome, according to Polybius the historian, 157.—Year from the building of Rome, according to Fabius Pictor, 153.—Year of the Julian Period, 4119.—Year of the era of Nabonassar, 153.—Year from the foundation of Solomon's temple, 409.—Year since the destruction of the kingdom of Israel by Shalmaneser, king of Assyria, 126.—Second year after the third Sabbatic year after the *seventeenth* Jewish jubilee, according to Helvicus. Year before the birth of Christ, 591.—Year before the vulgar era of Christ's nativity, 595.—Cycle of the Sun, 3.—Cycle of the Moon, 15.—Twenty-second year of Tarquinius Priscus, the fifth king of the Romans: this was the *eighty-sixth* year before the consulship of Lucius Junius Brutus, and Publius Valerius Poplicola.—Thirty-first year of Cyaxares, or Cyaraxes, the fourth king of Media.—Eleventh year of Agasicles, king of Lacedæmon, of the family of the Proclidæ.—Thirteenth year of Leon, king of Lucedæmon, of the family of the Eurysthenidæ.—Twenty-fifth year of Alyattes II., king of Lydia, and father of the celebrated Crœsus.—Eighth year of Æropas, the seventh king of Macedon.—Sixth and last year of Psammis, king of Egypt, according to Helvicus, an accurate chronologer. This Egyptian king was the immediate predecessor of the celebrated Apries, called Vaphres by Eusebius, and Pharaoh-hophra by Jeremiah, chap. xliv. 30.—First year of Baal, king of the Tyrians. Twelfth year of Nebuchadnezzar, king of Babylon.—Fourth year of Zedekiah, the last king of Judah.

CHAPTER I

This chapter contains that extraordinary vision of the Divine glory with which the prophet was favoured when he received the commission and instructions respecting the discharge of his office, which are contained in the two following chapters. The time of this Divine manifestation to the prophet, 1–3. *The vision of the four living creatures, and of the four wheels,* 4–25. *Description of the firmament that was spread over them, and of the throne upon which one sat in appearance as a man,* 26–28. *This vision, proceeding in a whirlwind from the* NORTH, *seems to indicate the dreadful judgments that were coming upon the whole land of Judah through the instrumentality of the cruel Chaldeans, who lay to the north of it.* See Jer. i. 14; iv. 6; and vi. 1.

A. M. 3409 B. C. 595 Ol. XLVI. 2 Anno TarquiniiPrisci, R. Roman., 22

NOW it came to pass in the thirtieth year, in the fourth *month,* in the fifth *day* of the month, as I *was* among the [a]captives [b]by the river of Chebar, *that* [c]the heavens were opened, and I saw [d]visions of God.

[a]Heb. *captivity*——[b]Ver. 3; chap. iii. 15, 23; x. 15, 20, 22; xliii. 3

[c]So Matt. iii. 16; Acts vii. 56; x. 11; Rev. xix. 11——[d]Chap. viii. 3

NOTES ON CHAP. I

Verse 1. *In the thirtieth year*] We know not what this date refers to. Some think it was the *age of the prophet;* others think the date is taken from the *time* that Josiah *renewed the covenant* with the people, 2 Kings xxii. 3, from which *Usher, Prideaux,* and *Calmet* compute the *forty* years of *Judah's transgression,* mentioned chap. iv. 6.

Abp. *Newcome* thinks there is an error in the text, and that instead of בשלשים *bisheloshim,* in the *thirtieth,* we should read בחמישית *bachamishith,* in the *fifth,* as in the *second* verse. "Now it came to pass in the fifth year, in the fourth month, in the fifth day of the month," &c. But this is supported by none of the ancient *Versions,* nor by any MS. The *Chaldee* paraphrases the verse, "And it came to pass *thirty* years after the high priest Hilkiah had found the book of the law, in the house of the sanctuary," &c. This was in the *twelfth* year of

A. M. 3409 B. C. 595 Ol. XLVI. 2 Anno TarquiniiPrisci, R. Roman., 22

2 In the fifth *day* of the month,
which *was* the fifth year of [e]king
Jehoiachin's captivity.
3 The word of the LORD came
expressly unto [f]Ezekiel the priest, the son
of Buzi, in the land of the Chaldeans by the
river Chebar; and [g]the hand of the LORD was
there upon him.
4 And I looked, and, behold, [h]a whirlwind
came [i]out of the north, a great cloud, and a
fire [k]infolding itself, and a brightness *was*
about it, and out of the midst thereof as the
colour of amber, out of the midst of the fire.

[e]2 Kings xxiv. 12, 15——[f]Heb. *Jehezkel*——[g]1 Kings xviii. 46; 2 Kings iii. 15; ch. iii. 14, 22; viii. 1; xl. 1——[h]Jer. xxiii. 19; xxv. 32——[i]Jer. i. 14; iv. 6; vi. 1

A. M. 3409 B. C. 595 Ol. XLVI. 2 Anno TarquiniiPrisci, R. Roman., 22

5 [l]Also out of the midst thereof *came* the likeness of four
living creatures. And [m]this *was*
their appearance; they had [n]the
likeness of a man.
6 And every one had four faces, and every
one had four wings.
7 And their feet *were* [o]straight feet; the
sole of their feet *was* like the sole of a calf's
foot: and they sparkled [p]like the colour of
burnished brass.
8 [q]And *they had* the hands of a man under
their wings on their four sides; and they

[k]Heb. *catching itself*——[l]Rev. iv. 6, &c.——[m]Ch. x. 8, &c.——[n]Ver. 10; ch. x. 14, 21——[o]Heb. *a straight foot*——[p]Dan. x. 6; Rev. i. 15——[q]Chap. x. 18, 21

Josiah's reign. The *thirtieth* year, computed as above, comes to A. M. 3409, the *fourth* year from the captivity of Jeconiah, and the *fifth* of the reign of Zedekiah. Ezekiel was then among the captives who had been carried way with Jeconiah, and had his dwelling near the river *Chebar*, *Chaborus*, or *Aboras*, a river of Mesopotamia, which falls into the *Euphrates* a little above *Thapsacus*, after having run through Mesopotamia from east to west.—*Calmet.*

Fourth month] *Thammuz*, answering nearly to our *July*.

I saw visions of God.] Emblems and symbols of the Divine Majesty. He particularly refers to those in this chapter.

Verse 2. *Jehoiachin's captivity*] Called also Jeconiah and Coniah; see 2 Kings xxiv. 12. He was carried away by Nebuchadnezzar; see 2 Kings xxiv. 14.

Verse 3. *The hand of the Lord*] I was filled with his power, and with the influence of the prophetic spirit.

Verse 4. *A whirlwind came out of the north*] Nebuchadnezzar, whose land, Babylonia, lay north of Judea. *Chaldea* is thus frequently denominated by Jeremiah.

A great cloud, and a fire infolding itself] A mass of fire concentrated in a *vast cloud*, that the flames might be more distinctly observable, the fire never escaping from the cloud, but issuing, and then returning in upon itself. It was in a state of powerful agitation; but always involving itself, or returning back to the centre whence it appeared to issue.

A brightness was *about it*] A fine tinge of light surrounded the cloud, in order to make its limits the more discernible; beyond which verge the turmoiling fire did not proceed.

The colour of amber] This was in the centre of the cloud; and this amber-coloured substance was the centre of the labouring flame. The word ηλεκτρον, which we translate *amber*, was used to signify a compound metal, very bright, made of gold and brass.

Verse 5. *Also out of the midst thereof* came—*four living creatures.*] As the amber-coloured body was the *centre* of the *fire*, and this *fire* was in the *centre* of the *cloud;* so out of this amber-coloured igneous centre came the *living creatures* just mentioned.

Verse 6. *Every one had four faces*] There were *four* several figures of these living creatures, and each of these figures had *four* distinct faces: but as the face of the *man* was that which was presented to the prophet's view, so that he saw it more plainly than any of the others; hence it is said, ver. 5, that each of these figures had *the likeness of a man;* and the whole of this compound image bore a general resemblance to the human figure.

Verse 7. *Their feet* were *straight feet*] There did not seem to be any flexure at the knee, nor were the legs separated in that way as to indicate progression by walking. I have before me several ancient *Egyptian* images of *Isis*, *Osiris*, *Anubis*, &c., where the legs are *not separated*, nor is there any bend at the knees; so that if there was any motion at all, it must have been by *gliding*, not progressive walking. It is a remark of *Ælian*, that the gods are never represented as *walking*, but always *gliding;* and he gives this as a criterion to discern common angelic appearances from those of the *gods:* all other spiritual beings *walked progressively*, rising on one foot, while they stretched out the other; but the deities always *glided* without *gradual* progressive motions. And *Heliodorus* in his Romance of *Theogines* and *Charicha*, gives the same reason for the *united feet of the gods*, &c., and describes the same appearances.

Like the sole of a calf's foot] Before it is stated to be a *straight foot;* one that did not lay down a *flat horizontal sole*, like that of the human foot.

And they sparkled like the colour of burnished brass.] I suppose this refers rather to the *hoof* of the calf's foot, than to the whole appearance of the *leg*. There is scarcely any thing that gives a higher lustre than highly *polished* or *burnished brass*. Our blessed Lord is represented with legs like *burnished brass*, Rev. i. 15.

Verse 8. They had *the hands of a man under their wings*] I doubt much whether the arms be not here represented as all covered with feathers, so that they had the appearance of wings, only the hand was bare; and I rather think that this is the meaning of their having "the hands of a man under their wings."

A. M. 3409
B. C. 595
Ol. XLVI. 2
Anno
TarquiniiPrisci,
R. Roman., 22

four had their faces and their
wings.
9 [r]Their wings *were* joined
one to another; [s]they turned not
when they went; they went every one straight
forward.
10 As for [t]the likeness of their faces, they
four [u]had the face of a man, [v]and the face of
a lion, on the right side: [w]and they four had
the face of an ox on the left side; [x]they four
also had the face of an eagle.
11 Thus *were* their faces: and their wings
were [y]stretched upward; two *wings* of every
one *were* joined one to another, and [z]two
covered their bodies.
12 And [a]they went every one straight forward:
[b]whither the spirit was to go, they
went; *and* [c]they turned not when they
went.
13 As for the likeness of the living creatures,
their appearance *was* like burning
coals of fire, [d]*and* like the
appearance of lamps: it went up
and down among the living creatures;
and the fire was bright, and out of the
fire went forth lightning.
14 And the living creatures [e]ran and returned
[f]as the appearance of a flash of
lightning.
15 Now as I beheld the living creatures,
behold [g]one wheel upon the earth by the
living creatures, with his four faces.
16 [h]The appearance of the wheels and their
work *was* [i]like unto the colour of a beryl:
and they four had one likeness: and their appearance
and their work *was* as it were a
wheel in the middle of a wheel.
17 When they went, they went upon their
four sides: [k]*and* they turned not when they
went.

[r]Ver. 11.——[s]Ver. 12; chap. x. 11——[t]See Rev. iv. 7——[u]Num. ii. 10——[v]Num. ii. 3——[w]Num. ii. 18——[x]Num. ii. 25——[y]Or, *divided above*——[z]Isa. vi. 2

[a]Ver. 9; chap. x. 22——[b]Ver. 20——[c]Ver. 9, 17——[d]Rev. iv. 5——[e]Zech. iv. 10——[f]Matt. xxiv. 27——[g]Ch. x. 9——[h]Chap. x. 9, 10——[i]Dan. x. 6——[k]Ver. 12

Verse 9. *Their wings* were *joined one to another*] When their wings were extended, they formed a sort of canopy level with their own heads or shoulders; and on this canopy was the throne, and the "likeness of the man" upon it, ver. 26.

They turned not when they went] The wings did not flap in flying, or move in the manner of oars, or of the hands of a man in swimming, in order to their passing through the air; as they *glided* in reference to their *feet*, so they *soared* in reference to their *wings*.

Verse 10. *As for the likeness of their faces*] There was but one body to each of those compound animals: but each body had four faces; the face of a *man* and of a *lion* on the right side; the face of an *ox* and an *eagle* on the left side. Many of these compound images appear in the Asiatic idols. Many are now before me: some with the head and feet of a *monkey*, with the body, arms, and *legs* of a *man*. Others with the head of the *dog;* body, arms, and legs human. Some with the head of an *ape;* all the rest human. Some with one head and eight arms; others with six heads or faces, with twelve arms. The head of a lion and the head of a cock often appear; and some with the head of a cock, the whole body human, and the legs terminating in *snakes*. All these were symbolical, and each had its own appropriate meaning. Those in the text had theirs also, could we but find it out.

Verse 12. *They went every one straight forward*] Not by *progressive stepping*, but by *gliding*.

Whither the spirit was to go] Whither that *whirlwind* blew, they went, being borne on by the wind, see ver. 4.

Verse 13. *Like burning coals of fire*] The whole substance appeared to be of flame; and among them frequent coruscations of fire, like vibrating lamps, often emitting lightning, or rather sparks of fire, as we have seen struck out of strongly ignited iron in a forge. The flames might be something like what is called *warring wheels* in pyrotechny. They seemed to conflict together.

Verse 14. *The living creatures ran and returned*] They had a circular movement; they were in rapid motion, but did not increase their distance from the spectator. So I think this should be understood.

Verse 15. *One wheel upon the earth*] It seems at first view there were *four wheels*, one for each of the living creatures; that is, the creatures were compound, so were the wheels, for there was "a wheel in the middle of a wheel." And it is generally supposed that these wheels cut each other at right angles up and down: and this is the manner in which they are generally represented; but most probably the *wheel within* means merely the *nave* in which the spokes are inserted, in reference to the *ring*, *rim*, or *periphery*, where these *spokes* terminate from the centre or nave. I do think this is what is meant by the wheel within a wheel; and I am the more inclined to this opinion, by some fine Chinese drawings now before me, where their *deities* are represented as *walking upon wheels*, the wheels themselves *encompassed with fire*. The wheel is simply by itself, having a projecting axis; so of *these* it is said, "their appearance and their work was, as it were, a wheel within a wheel." There were either two peripheries or rims with their spokes, or the *nave* answered for the wheel within. I have examined models of what are called Ezekiel's wheels, which are designed to move equally in all directions: but I plainly saw that this was impossible; nor can any kind of complex wheel move in this way.

Verse 18. *As for their rings*] The *strakes* which form the *rim* or *periphery*.

A. M. 3409
B. C. 595
Ol. XLVI. 2
Anno
TarquiniiPrisci,
R. Roman., 22

18 As for their rings, they were so high that they were dreadful; and their [l]rings *were* [m]full of eyes round about them four.

19 And [n]when the living creatures went, the wheels went by them: and when the living creatures were lifted up from the earth, the wheels were lifted up.

20 [o]Whithersoever the spirit was to go, they went, thither *was their* spirit to go; and the wheels were lifted up over against them: [p]for the spirit [q]of the living creature *was* in the wheels.

21 [r]When those went, *these* went; and when those stood, *these* stood; and when those were lifted up from the earth, the wheels were lifted up over against them: for the spirit [s]of the living creature *was* in the wheels.

22 [t]And the likeness of the firmament upon the heads of the living creature *was* as the colour of the terrible crystal, stretched forth over their heads above.

23 And under the firmament *were* their wings straight, the one toward the other: every one had two, which covered on this side, and every one had two, which covered on that side, their bodies.

A. M. 3409
B. C. 595
Ol. XLVI. 2
Anno
TarquiniiPrisci,
R. Roman., 22

24 [u]And when they went, I heard the noise of their wings, [v]like the noise of great waters, as [w]the voice of the Almighty, the voice of speech, as the noise of a host: when they stood, they let down their wings.

25 And there was a voice from the firmament that *was* over their heads, when they stood, *and* had let down their wings.

26 [x]And above the firmament that *was* over their heads *was* the likeness of a throne, [y]as the appearance of a sapphire stone: and upon the likeness of the throne *was* the likeness as the appearance of a man above upon it.

27 [z]And I saw as the colour of amber, as the appearance of fire round about within it, from the appearance of his loins even upward, and from the appearance of his loins even downward, I saw as it were the appearance of fire, and it had brightness round about.

28 [a]As the appearance of the bow that is in the cloud in the day of rain, so *was* the appearance of the brightness round about. [b]This *was* the appearance of the likeness of the glory of the LORD. And when I saw *it*, [c]I fell upon my face, and I heard a voice of one that spake.

---

[l]Or, *strakes*——[m]Ch. x. 12; Zech. iv. 10——[n]Ch. x. 16, 17——[o]Ver. 12——[p]Ch. x. 17——[q]Or, *of life* [r]Ver. 19, 20; chap. x. 17——[s]Or, *of life*——[t]Chap. x. 1 [u]Chap. x. 5——[v]Chap. xliii. 2; Dan. x. 6; Rev. i. 15

[w]Job xxxvii. 4, 5; Psa. xxix. 3, 4; lxviii. 33——[x]Chap. x. 1——[y]Exod. xxiv. 10——[z]Chap. viii. 2——[a]Rev. iv. 3; x. 1——[b]Chap. iii. 23; viii. 4——[c]Chap. iii. 23; Dan. viii. 17; Acts ix. 4; Rev. i. 17

They were dreadful] They were exceedingly great in their diameter, so that it was tremendous to look from the part that touched the ground to that which was opposite above.

Were *full of eyes*] Does not this refer to the appearance of *nails* keeping on the spokes, or strakes or bands upon the rim?

Verse 19. *When the living creatures went, the wheels went*] The *wheels* were attached to the living creatures, so that, in progress, they had the same motion.

Verse 20. *The spirit of the living creature* was *in the wheels*.] That is, the wheels were *instinct with a vital spirit;* the wheels were *alive*, they also were *animals*, or endued with *animal life*, as the creatures were that stood upon them. Here then is the *chariot of Jehovah*. There are *four wheels*, on each of which one of the *compound animals* stands; the four compound animals form the *body* of the *chariot*, their wings spread horizontally above, forming the canopy or covering of this chariot; on the top of which, or upon the extended wings of the four living creatures, was the throne, on which was the appearance of a man, ver. 26.

Verse 22. *The colour of the terrible crystal*] Like a *crystal*, well cut and well polished, with various *faces*, by which rays of light were refracted, assuming either a variety of prismatic colours, or an insufferably brilliant splendour. This seems to be the meaning of the *terrible crystal*. *Newcome* translates, *fearful ice*. The common translation is preferable.

Verse 23. *Every one had two, which covered on this side*] While they employed two of their wings to form a foundation for the *firmament* to rest on, two other wings were let down to cover the lower part of their bodies: but this they did only when they *stood*, ver. 24.

Verse 24. *The noise of their wings*] When the whirlwind drove the wheels, the wind rustling among the wings was like the noise of *many waters;* like a *waterfall*, or *waters dashing continually against the rocks*, or *rushing down precipices*.

As the voice of the Almighty] Like distant thunder; for this is termed the *voice of God*, Psa. xviii. 13; Exod. ix. 23, 28, 29; xx. 18.

Verse 26. *A sapphire*] The pure oriental sapphire, a large well cut specimen of which is now before me, is one of the most beautiful and resplendent blues that can be conceived. I have sometimes seen the heavens assume this illustrious hue. The human form above this canopy is supposed to represent Him who, in the fulness of time, was manifested in the flesh.

Verse 27. *The colour of amber*] There are

specimens of amber which are very pure and beautifully transparent. One which I now hold up to the light gives a most beautiful *bright yellow* colour. Such a splendid appearance had the august Being who sat upon this throne from the reins upward; but from thence downward he had the appearance of *fire*, burning with a clear and brilliant flame. For farther particulars see the notes on chap. x.

Verse 28. *As the appearance of the bow*] Over the canopy on which this glorious personage sat there was a fine *rainbow*, which, from the description here, had all its colours vivid, distinct, and in perfection—red, orange, yellow, green, blue, indigo, and violet. In all this description we must understand every *metal*, every *colour*, and every *natural appearance*, to be in their utmost perfection of *shape*, *colour*, and *splendour*. "And this," as above described, "was the appearance of the likeness of the glory of the Lord." Splendid and glorious as it was, it was only the "appearance of the likeness," a faint representation of the real thing.

I have endeavoured to explain these appearances as correctly as possible; to show their forms, positions, colours, &c. But who can explain their meaning? We have conjectures in abundance; and can it be of any use to mankind to increase the number of those conjectures? I think not. I doubt whether the whole does not point out the state of the Jews, who were about to be subdued by Nebuchadnezzar, and carried into captivity. And I am inclined to think that the "living creatures, wheels, fires, whirlwinds," &c., which are introduced here, point out, emblematically, the various means, sword, fire, pestilence, famine, &c., which were employed in their destruction; and that *God appears* in all this to show that Nebuchadnezzar is only his *instrument* to inflict all these calamities. What is in the following chapter appears to me to confirm this supposition. But we have the *rainbow*, the token of God's covenant, to show that though there should be a destruction of the city, temple, &c., and sore tribulation among the people, yet there should not be a total ruin; after a long captivity they should be restored. The rainbow is an illustrious token of mercy and love.

CHAPTER II

The prophet, having been overwhelmed with the glorious vision in the preceding chapter, is here strengthened and comforted, 1, 2; *and then commissioned to declare to the rebellious house of Israel the terrible judgments that would very shortly come upon the whole land, if they repented not; with a gracious assurance to Ezekiel that God would be constantly with him while executing the duties of his office,* 3–5. *The prophet is also commanded to be fearless, resolute, and faithful in the discharge of it,* 6–8, *as he must be the messenger of very unpleasing tidings, which will expose him to great persecution,* 9, 10.

A. M. 3409
B. C. 595
Ol. XLVI. 2
Anno
TarquiniiPrisci,
R. Roman., 22

AND he said unto me, Son of
man, [a]stand upon thy feet,
and I will speak unto thee.
2 And [b]the spirit entered into
me when he spake unto me, and set me upon
my feet, that I heard him that spake unto me.
3 And he said unto me, Son of
man, I send thee to the children
of Israel, to a rebellious [c]nation
that hath rebelled against me:
[d]they and their fathers have transgressed
against me, *even* unto this very day.

A. M. 3409
B. C. 595
Ol. XLVI. 2
Anno
TarquiniiPrisci,
R. Roman., 22

[a]Dan. x. 11——[b]Chap. iii. 24——[c]Heb. *nations*

[d]Jer. iii. 25; chap. xx. 18, 21, 30

NOTES ON CHAP. II

Verse 1. *And he said unto me*] In the last verse of the preceding chapter we find that the prophet was so penetrated with awe at the sight of the glory of God in the mystical chariot, that "he fell upon his face;" and, while he was in this posture of adoration, he heard the voice mentioned here. It is evident, therefore, that the present division of these chapters is wrong. Either the *first* should end with the words, "This was the appearance of the likeness of the glory of the Lord," ver. 28; or the *first verse* of this chapter should be added to the preceding, and this begin with the *second* verse.

Verse 2. *And the spirit entered into me*] This *spirit* was different to that mentioned above, by which the wheels, &c., were moved. The *spirit of prophecy* is here intended; whose office was not merely to enable him to *foresee* and *foretell* future events, but to purify and refine his heart, and qualify him to be a successful preacher of the word of life.

He who is sent by the God of all grace to convert sinners must be influenced by the Holy Ghost; otherwise he can neither be saved himself, nor become the instrument of salvation to others.

And set me upon my feet] That he might *stand* as a servant before his master, to receive his orders.

Verse 3. *Son of man*] This appellative, so often mentioned in this book, seems to have been given first to this *prophet;* afterwards to *Daniel;* and after that to the MAN *Christ Jesus.* Perhaps it was given to the two former to remind them of their frailty, and that they should not be exalted in their own minds by the extraordinary revelations granted to them; and that they should feel themselves of the same nature with those to whom they were sent; and, from the common principle of *humanity*, deeply interest themselves in the welfare of their unhappy countrymen. To the *latter* it might have been appropriated merely to show that though all his actions demonstrated him to be GOD, yet that he was also really MAN; and that in the *man* Christ Jesus dwelt all the fulness of the

A. M. 3409
B. C. 595
Ol. XLVI. 2
Anno
TarquiniiPrisci,
R. Roman., 22

4 [e]For *they are* [f]impudent
children and stiff-hearted. I do
send thee unto them; and thou
shalt say unto them, Thus saith
the Lord God.
5 [g]And they, whether they will hear, or
whether they will forbear, (for they *are* a
rebellious house,) yet [h]shall know that there
hath been a prophet among them.
6 And thou, son of man, [i]be not afraid
of them, neither be afraid of their words,
though [k]briers [l]and thorns *be* with thee,
and thou dost dwell among scorpions: [m]be
not afraid of their words, nor be dismayed
at their looks, [n]though they *be* a rebellious
house.
7 [o]And thou shalt speak my
words unto them, [p]whether they
will hear, or whether they will
forbear: for they *are* [q]most rebellious.
8 But thou, son of man, hear what I say
unto thee; Be not thou rebellious like that
rebellious house: open thy mouth, and [r]eat
that I give thee.
9 And when I looked, behold, [s]a hand *was*
sent unto me; and, lo, [t]a roll of a book *was*
therein:
10 And he spread it before me; and it *was*
written within and without: and *there was*
written therein lamentations, and mourning,
and wo.

[e]Chap. iii. 7——[f]Heb. *hard of face*——[g]Chap. iii. 11, 26, 27——[h]Ch. xxxiii. 33——[i]Jer. i. 8, 17; Luke xii. 4——[k]Or, *rebels*——[l]Isa. ix. 18; Jer. vi. 28; Mic. vii. 4

[m]Chap. iii. 9; 1 Pet. iii. 14——[n]Chap. iii. 9, 26, 27——[o]Jer. i. 7, 17——[p]Ver. 5——[q]Heb. *rebellion*——[r]Rev. x. 9——[s]Chap. viii. 3; Jer. i. 9——[t]Chap. iii. 1

Godhead bodily. When the *acts* of Christ are considered, it is more easy to believe his *eternal Godhead*, than to be convinced that the person we hear speaking, and see working, is also a *man* like unto ourselves.

I send thee to the children of Israel] To those who were now in captivity, in Chaldea particularly; and to the Jews in general, both far and near.

Verse 4. *Thou shalt say unto them, Thus saith the Lord*] Let them know that what thou hast to declare is the message of the Lord, that they may receive it with reverence.

Every preacher of God's word should take heed that it is God's message he delivers to the people. Let him not suppose, because it is according to his own *creed* or *confession of faith*, that therefore it is God's word. False doctrines and fallacies without end are foisted on the world in this way. Bring the *creed* first to the *Word of God*, and scrupulously try whether it be right; and when this is done, leave it where you please; take the Bible, and warn them from God's word recorded there.

Verse 5. *Yet shall know that there hath been a prophet among them.*] By this they shall be assured of *two* things: 1. That God in his mercy had given them due warning. 2. That themselves were inexcusable, for not taking it.

Verse 6. *Be not afraid of them*] They will maltreat thee for thy message; but let not the apprehension of this induce thee to suppress it. Though they be *rebels*, fear them not; I will sustain and preserve thee.

Verse 7. *Whether they will hear*] Whether they receive the message, or persecute thee for it, declare it to them, that they may be without excuse.

Verse 8. *Open thy mouth and eat that I give thee.*] Take *my word* as thou wouldst take thy *proper food;* receive it into thy heart; ponder it there, that it may be the means of *strengthening* and *preserving thy soul*, as proper nourishment will strengthen the body, and preserve from death. And the people to whom such messages of God may come should so hear it, read, mark, learn, and *inwardly digest* it, that it may become efficient nourishment to their souls.

Verse 9. *A hand* was *sent*] Here the *hand* signifies not only the instrument of conveyance, but an *emblem* of the Divine *power*, which the *hand of God* always signifies.

A roll of a book] מגלת ספר *megillath sepher*. All ancient books were written so as to be *rolled up;* hence *volumen*, a *volume*, from *volvo, I roll*.

Verse 10. *It* was *written within and without*] Contrary to the state of rolls in general, which are written on the *inside* only. The *Hebrew rolls* are generally written in this way. There are several of such Hebrew rolls before me, all written on the *inside* only, consisting of skins of vellum, or parchment, or basil, a sort of half-tanned sheep or goat skin, sewed together, extending to several yards in length. Other Asiatic books were written in the same way. A Sanscrit roll of *sixty* feet in length, also before me, is written all on the *inside;* and a *Koran*, written in exceedingly small characters, about two inches broad and twelve feet long, and weighing but about half an ounce. But the *roll* presented to the prophet was written on *both sides*, because the prophecy was long, and to the same effect; that they might see the mind of God wherever they looked.

There was *written therein lamentations, and mourning, and wo.*] What an awful assemblage! קינים והגה והי *kinim, vahegeh, vehi, lamentations*, and a *groan*, and *alas! Lamentations* on all hands; *a groan* from the dying; and *alas*, or *Wo is me!* from the survivors. It was the *letter* that killeth, and is the ministration of death. What a mercy to have that which is emphatically called Το Ευαγγελιον, The *glad tidings*, the *good news! Christ Jesus is come into the world to save sinners;* and he wills that *all men should be saved and come to the knowledge of the truth.* Here are *rejoicings, thanksgivings*, and *exultation.*

CHAPTER III

This chapter contains more particular instructions to the prophet. It begins with repeating his appointment to his office, 1–3. *Ezekiel is then informed that his commission is, at this time, to the house of Israel exclusively,* 4–6; *that his countrymen would pay little regard to him,* 7; *that he must persevere in his duty notwithstanding such great discouragement; and he is endued with extraordinary courage and intrepidity to enable him fearlessly to declare to a disobedient and gainsaying people the whole counsel of God,* 8–11. *The prophet is afterwards carried by the spirit that animated the cherubim and wheels, and by which he received the gift of prophecy, to a colony of his brethren in the neighbourhood, where he remained seven days overwhelmed with astonishment,* 12–15. *He is then warned of the awful importance of being faithful in his office,* 16–21; *commanded to go forth into the plain that he may have a visible manifestation of the Divine Presence,* 22; *and is again favoured with a vision of that most magnificent set of symbols described in the first chapter, by which the glorious majesty of the God of Israel was in some measure represented,* 23. *See also* Isa. vi. 1–18; Dan. x. 5–19; *and* Rev. i. 10–16; iv. 1–11, *for other manifestations of the Divine glory, in all of which some of the imagery is very similar. The prophet receives directions relative to his future conduct,* 24–27.

A. M. 3409
B. C. 595
Ol. XLVI. 2
Anno
TarquiniiPrisci,
R. Roman., 22

MOREOVER he said unto me, Son of man, eat that thou findest; [a]eat this roll, and go speak unto the house of Israel.

2 So I opened my mouth, and he caused me to eat that roll.

3 And he said unto me, Son of man, cause thy belly to eat, and fill thy bowels with this roll that I give thee. Then did I [b]eat *it;* and it was in my mouth [c]as honey for sweetness.

4 And he said unto me, Son of man, go, get thee unto the house of Israel, and speak with my words unto them.

5 For thou *art* not sent to a people [d]of a strange speech and of a hard language, *but* to the house of Israel;

6 Not to many people [e]of a strange speech and of a hard language, whose words thou canst not understand. [f]Surely, [g]had I sent thee to them, they would have hearkened unto thee.

[a]Chap. ii. 8, 9——[b]Rev. x. 9; see Jer. xv. 16——[c]Psa. xix. 10; cxix. 103——[d]Heb. *deep of lip, and heavy of tongue;* and so ver. 6——[e]Heb. *deep of lip and heavy of language*——[f]Or, *If I had sent thee, &c., would they not have hearkened unto thee?*

7 But the house of Israel will not hearken unto thee; [h]for they will not hearken unto me: [i]for all the house of Israel *are* [k]impudent and hard-hearted.

A. M. 3409
B. C. 595
Ol. XLVI. 2
Anno
TarquiniiPrisci,
R. Roman., 22

8 Behold, I have made thy face strong against their faces, and thy forehead strong against their foreheads.

9 [l]As an adamant harder than flint have I made thy forehead: [m]fear them not, neither be dismayed at their looks, though they *be* a rebellious house.

10 Moreover he said unto me, Son of man, all my words that I shall speak unto thee, receive in thine heart, and hear with thine ears.

11 And go, get thee to them of the captivity, unto the children of thy people, and speak unto them, and tell them, [n]Thus saith the Lord GOD; whether they will hear, or whether they will forbear.

12 Then [o]the spirit took me up, and I

[g]Matt. xi. 21, 23——[h]John xv. 20——[i]Ch. ii. 4 [k]Heb. *stiff of forehead, and hard of heart*——[l]Isa. l. 7; Jer. i. 18; xv. 20; Mic. iii. 8——[m]Jer. i. 8, 17; ch. ii. 6 [n]Chap. ii. 5, 7; ver. 27——[o]Ver. 14; chap. viii. 3; see 1 Kings xviii. 12; 2 Kings ii. 16; Acts viii. 39

NOTES ON CHAP. III

Verse 1. *Eat this roll, and go speak*] This must have passed in vision; but the meaning is plain. Receive my word—let it enter into thy soul; *digest* it—let it be thy *nourishment;* and let it be thy meat and drink to do the will of thy Father who is in heaven.

Verse 3. *It was in my mouth as honey*] It was joyous to me to receive the Divine message, to be thus let into the secrets of the Divine counsel, and I promised myself much comfort in that intimate acquaintance with which I was favoured by the Supreme Being. In Rev. x. 10 we find St. John receiving a little book, which he ate, and found it sweet as *honey* in his *mouth*, but after he had eaten it, it made his *belly bitter*, signifying that a deep consideration of the awful matter contained in God's word against sinners, which multitudes of them will turn to their endless confusion, must deeply afflict those who know any thing of the worth of an immortal spirit.

Verse 5. *Thou* art *not sent to a people of a strange speech*] I neither send thee to thy adversaries, the *Chaldeans*, nor to the *Medes* and *Persians*, their enemies. Even these would more likely have hearkened unto thee than thy own countrymen.

Verse 7. *Impudent and hard-hearted.*] "Stiff of forehead, and hard of heart."—*Margin.* The marginal readings on several verses here are very nervous and very correct.

Verse 12. *Then the Spirit took me up*] This, as *Calmet* remarks, has been variously understood. 1. An impetuous *wind* carried him to the place where his brethren sojourned. 2. The *Holy Spirit*, which filled his heart, transported

A. M. 3409
B. C. 595
Ol. XLVI. 2
Anno
TarquiniiPrisci,
R. Roman., 22

heard behind me a voice of a
great rushing, *saying,* Blessed
be the glory of the LORD from
his place.
13 *I heard* also the noise of the wings of
the living creatures that [p]touched one another, and the noise of the wheels over against
them, and a noise of a great rushing.
14 So [q]the spirit lifted me up and took me
away, and I went [r]in bitterness, in the [s]heat
of my spirit; but the [t]hand of the LORD was
strong upon me.
15 Then I came to them of the captivity at
Tel-abib, that dwelt by the river of Chebar,
and [u]I sat where they sat, and remained
there astonished among them seven days.
16 And it came to pass at the end of seven
days, that the word of the LORD
came unto me, saying,
17 [v]Son of man, I have made
thee a [w]watchman unto the
house of Israel: therefore hear the word at
my mouth, and give them warning from me.
18 When I say unto the wicked, Thou
shalt surely die; and thou givest him not
warning, nor speakest to warn the wicked
from his wicked way, to save his life; the
same wicked *man* [x]shall die in his iniquity;
but his blood will I require at thine
hand.
19 Yet if thou warn the wicked, and he
turn not from his wickedness, nor from his
wicked way, he shall die in his iniquity; [y]but
thou hast delivered thy soul.

[p]Heb. *kissed*——[q]Ver. 12; chap. viii. 3——[r]Heb. *bitter*——[s]Heb. *hot anger*——[t]2 Kings iii. 15; ch. i. 3; viii. 1; xxxvii. 1——[u]Job ii. 13; Psa. cxxxvii. 1

[v]Chap. xxxiii. 7, 8, 9——[w]Isa. lii. 8; lvi. 10; lxii. 6; Jer. vi. 17——[x]Chap. xxxiii. 6; John viii. 21, 24 [y]Isa. xlix. 4, 5; Acts xx. 26

him in a moment to the place where the captives were. 3. Or, he was so *transported* with heavenly ardour in his mind, that he ran immediately off, and seemed to fly to the place where God commanded him to go. The promptitude and impetuosity of his spirit seemed to furnish him with *wings* on the occasion. However this may be understood, the going to the captives was *real.*

A voice of a great rushing] This was the noise made by the wings of the living creatures that formed the chariot of Jehovah. See the notes on chap. i. and x.

Blessed be *the glory of the Lord*] Probably the acclamation of the living creatures: "Let God be blessed from the throne of his glory! He deserves the praises of his creatures in all the dispensations of his mercy and justice, of his providence and grace."

Verse 13. *A great rushing.*] All the living *creatures* and the *wheels* being then in motion.

Verse 14. *I went in bitterness*] Being filled with indignation at the wickedness and obstinacy of my people, I went, determining to speak the word of God without disguise, and to reprove them *sharply* for their rebellion; and yet I was greatly distressed because of the heavy message which I was commanded to deliver.

Verse 15. *I came to them of the captivity*] Because the hand of the Lord was strong upon him and supported him, he soon reached the place.

Tel-abib] תל אביב "a heap of corn." So the *Vulgate: acervum novarum frugum,* "a heap of new fruits." ܠܬܠܐ ܟܒ *letola chib,* "to the hill Chib," or *the hill of grief.—Syriac.*

Seven days.] Perhaps God kept him all this time without an immediate revelation, that the *bitterness* and *heat of spirit* of which he speaks above might be *subdued,* and that he might speak God's words in God's own Spirit. Had he gone in a better spirit he had probably been employed in his work as soon as he had gained the place of labour.

Verse 17. *I have made thee a watchman*] The care and welfare of all this people I have laid on thee. Thou must *watch* for their *safety, preach* for their *edification,* and *pray* for their *eternal welfare.* And that thou mayest be successful, *receive the word at my mouth, and warn them from me.*

God is particularly jealous lest *any words* but *his own* be taught for *Divinc doctrines.* He will not have human *creeds,* no more than TRADITIONS, taught instead of his own word. No word can be successful in the salvation of sinners but that which comes from God. Every minister of the Gospel should be familiar with his Maker by *faith* and *prayer;* God will then hold communion with his spirit; otherwise, what he preaches will be destitute of spirit and life, and his *hackneyed texts* and *sermons,* instead of being the bread from heaven, will be like the dry mouldy Gibeonitish crusts.

Verse 18. *Thou shalt surely die*] That is, If he turn not from his wickedness, *and thou givest him not warning,* as above, *he shall die in his iniquity,* which he should not have committed; *but his blood will I require at thy hand*—I will visit *thy soul* for the loss of *his.* O how awful is this! Hear it, ye *priests,* ye *preachers,* ye *ministers* of the Gospel; ye, especially, who have entered into the ministry *for a living;* ye who *gather a congregation* to yourselves that ye may feed upon their fat, and clothe yourselves with their wool; in whose parishes and in whose congregations souls are dying unconverted from day to day, who have never been solemnly warned by you, and to whom you have never shown the way of salvation, probably because ye know nothing of it yourselves! O what a perdition awaits *you!* To have the blood of every soul that has died in your parishes or in your congregations unconverted laid at your door! To suffer a common damnation for *every* soul that perishes through your neglect! How *many loads* of endless wo must such have to bear! Ye take your *tithes,* your *stipends,* or your *rents,* to the last

A. M. 3409
B. C. 595
Ol. XLVI. 2
Anno
TarquiniiPrisci,
R. Roman., 22

20 Again, When a [z]righteous
man doth turn from his [a]righte-
ousness, and commit iniquity,
and I lay a stumbling-block be-
fore him, he shall die: because thou hast not
given him warning, he shall die in his sin,
and his righteousness which he hath done
shall not be remembered; but his blood will
I require at thine hand.
21 Nevertheless if thou warn the righteous
man, that the righteous sin not, and he doth
not sin, he shall surely live, because he
is warned; also thou hast delivered thy
soul.
22 [b]And the hand of the LORD was there
upon me; and he said unto me, Arise, go
forth [c]into the plain, and I will there talk
with thee.
23 Then I arose, and went forth into the
plain: and, behold, [d]the glory of the LORD
stood there, as the glory which
I [e]saw by the river of Chebar:
[f]and I fell on my face.
24 Then [g]the spirit entered
into me, and set me upon my feet, and spake
with me, and said unto me, Go, shut thyself
within thine house.
25 But thou, O son of man, behold, [h]they
shall put bands upon thee, and shall bind
thee with them, and thou shalt not go out
among them:
26 And [i]I will make thy tongue cleave to
the roof of thy mouth, that thou shalt be
dumb, and shalt not be to them [k]a reprover:
[l]for they *are* a rebellious house.
27 [m]But when I speak with thee, I will open
thy mouth, and thou shalt say unto them,
[n]Thus saith the Lord GOD; he that heareth,
let him hear; and he that forbeareth, let him
forbear: [o]for they *are* a rebellious house.

A. M. 3409
B. C. 595
Ol. XLVI. 2
Anno
TarquiniiPrisci.
R. Roman., 22

---

[z]Ch. xviii. 24; xxxiii. 12, 13——[a]Heb. *righteousnesses*——[b]Ver. 14; chap. i. 3——[c]Chap. viii. 4——[d]Chap. i. 28——[e]Chap. i. 1——[f]Chap. i. 28——[g]Chap. ii. 2

[h]Ch. iv. 8——[i]Ch. xxiv. 27; Luke i. 20, 22——[k]Heb. *a man reproving*——[l]Ch. ii. 5, 6, 7——[m]Ch. xxiv. 27; xxxiii. 22——[n]Ver. 11——[o]Ver. 9, 26; chap. xii. 2, 3

---

grain, and the last *penny;* while the souls over whom you made yourselves watchmen have perished, and are perishing, through *your* neglect. O worthless and hapless men! better for you had ye never been born! Vain is your boast of *apostolical authority,* while ye do not the *work of apostles!* Vain your boast of *orthodoxy,* while ye neither *show* nor *know* the *way of salvation!* Vain your pretensions to a *Divine call,* when ye do not the work of *evangelists!* The state of the most wretched of the human race is enviable to that of such ministers, pastors, teachers, and preachers.

But let not this discourage the *faithful minister* who *teaches every man,* and *warns every man, in all wisdom, that he may present every man perfect in Christ Jesus.* If after such teaching and warning they will sin on, and die in their sins, their blood will be upon themselves; but *thou,* O man of God, *hast delivered thine own soul.*

Verse 20. *When a righteous* man *doth turn from his righteousness*] Which these words plainly state he may do, *and commit iniquity,* and die in his sin; and consequently die eternally, which is also here granted; if he have not been warned, though he die in his sin, the *blood*—the life and salvation, of this person also will God require at the watchman's hand. Pastor hunc occidit, quia eum tacendo morti tradidit. "This man the pastor kills; for in being silent, he delivers him over to death."—GREGORY. From these passages we see that a *righteous man* may *fall from grace,* and *perish everlastingly.* Should it be said that it means the *self-righteous,* I reply, this is absurd; for self-righteousness is a *fall* itself, and the sooner a man falls from it the better for himself. Real, genuine righteousness of heart and life is that which is meant. Let him that standeth take heed lest he fall.

And I lay a stumbling-block before him] That is, I permit him to be tried, and he fall in the trial. God is repeatedly represented as doing things which he only *permits* to be done. He lays a stumbling-block, *i. e.,* he permits one to be laid.

Verse 22. *Arise, go forth into the plain*] Into a place remote from observation and noise; a place where the glory of God might have sufficient room to manifest itself, that the prophet might see all its movements distinctly.

Verse 24. *The spirit—said unto me, Go, shut thyself within thine house.*] Hide thyself for the present. The reason is immediately subjoined.

Verse 25. *They shall put bands upon thee*] Thy countrymen will rise up against thee; and, to prevent thy prophesying, will confine thee.

Verse 26. *I will make thy tongue cleave to the roof of thy mouth*] I will not give thee any message to deliver to them. They are so rebellious, it is useless to give them farther warning.

Verse 27. *I will open thy mouth*] When it is necessary to address them again, thou shalt sum up what thou hast said in this one speech: *Thus saith the Lord,* "He that heareth, let him hear; and he that forbeareth, let him forbear." Let him who feels obedience to the voice of God his interest, be steadfast. Let him who disregards the Divine monition go in his own way, and abide the consequences.

CHAPTER IV

Ezekiel delineates Jerusalem, and lays siege to it, as a type of the manner in which the Chaldean army should surround that city, 1–3. *The prophet commanded to lie on his left side* three hundred and ninety *days, and on his right side* forty *days, with the signification,* 4–8. *The scanty and coarse provision allowed the prophet during his symbolical siege, consisting chiefly of the worst kinds of grain, and likewise ill-prepared, as he had only cow's dung for fuel, tended all to denote the scarcity of provision, fuel, and every necessary of life, which the Jews should experience during the siege of Jerusalem,* 9–17.

A. M. 3409 B. C. 595 Ol. XLVI. 2 Anno TarquiniiPrisci, R. Roman., 22

THOU also, son of man, take
thee a tile, and lay it before
thee, and pourtray upon it the
city, *even* Jerusalem:

2 And lay siege against it, and build a fort
against it, and cast a mount against it; set
the camp also against it, and set [a]*battering*
rams against it round about.

3 Moreover take thou unto
thee [b]an iron pan, and set it *for*
a wall of iron between thee and
the city: and set thy face against
it, and it shall be besieged, and thou shalt
lay siege against it. [c]This *shall be* a sign to
the house of Israel.

4 Lie thou also upon thy left side, and lay

[a]Or, *chief leaders;* chap. xxi. 22——[b]Or, *a flat plate,* or *slice*——[c]Chap. xii. 6, 11; xiv. 24, 27

NOTES ON CHAP. IV

Verse 1. *Take thee a tile*] A *tile*, such as we use in covering houses, will give us but a very inadequate notion of those used anciently; and also appear very insufficient for the figures which the prophet was commanded to pourtray on it. A *brick* is most undoubtedly meant; yet, even the larger dimensions here, as to *thickness*, will not help us through the difficulty, unless we have recourse to the ancients, who have spoken of the dimensions of the bricks commonly used in building. *Palladius*, De Re Rustica, lib. vi. c. 12, is very particular on this subject:—Sint vero lateres longitudine pedum duorum, latitudine unius, altitudine quatuor unciarum. "Let the bricks be two feet long, one foot broad, and four inches thick." Edit. *Gesner*, vol. iii. p. 144. On such a surface as this the whole siege might be easily pourtrayed. There are some *brick-bats* before me which were brought from the ruins of ancient *Babylon*, which have been made of clay and straw kneaded together and *baked in the sun;* one has been more than *four inches* thick, and on one side it is *deeply impressed* with characters; others are smaller, well made, and finely impressed on one side with Persepolitan characters. These have been for *inside* or *ornamental* work; to such bricks the prophet most probably alludes.

But the tempered clay out of which the bricks were made might be meant here; of this substance he might *spread out* a sufficient quantity to receive all his figures. The figures were, 1. Jerusalem. 2. A fort. 3. A mount. 4. The camp of the enemy. 5. Battering rams, and such like engines, round about. 6. A wall round about the city, between it and the besieging army.

Verse 2. Battering *rams*] כרים *carim.* This is the earliest account we have of this military engine. It was a long beam with a head of brass, like the head and horns of a *ram*, whence its name. It was hung by chains or ropes, between two beams, or *three legs*, so that it could admit of being drawn backward and forward some yards. Several stout men, by means of ropes, pulled it as far back as it could go; and then, suddenly letting it loose, it struck with great force against the wall which it was intended to batter and bring down. This machine was not known in the time of *Homer*, as in the siege of Troy there is not the slightest mention of such. And the first notice we have of it is *here*, where we see that it was employed by Nebuchadnezzar in the siege of Jerusalem, A. M. 3416. It was afterwards used by the *Carthaginians* at the siege of *Gades*, as *Vitruvius* notes, lib. x. c. 19, in which he gives a circumstantial account of the invention, fabrication, use, and improvement of this machine. It was for the want of a machine of this kind, that the ancient sieges lasted so long; they had nothing with which to beat down or undermine the walls.

Verse 3. *Take thou unto thee an iron pan*] מחבת *machabath*, a *flat plate* or *slice*, as the margin properly renders it: such as are used in some countries to bake bread on, called a *griddle* or *girdle*, being suspended above the fire, and kept in a proper degree of heat for the purpose. A *plate* like this, stuck perpendicularly in the earth, would show the nature of a *wall* much better than any *pan* could do. The Chaldeans threw such a wall round Jerusalem, to prevent the besieged from receiving any succours, and from escaping from the city.

This shall be *a sign to the house of Israel.*] This shall be an emblematical representation of what shall actually take place.

Verse 4. *Lie thou also upon thy left side*] It appears that all that is mentioned here and in the following verses was done, not in *idea*, but in *fact.* The prophet lay down on *his left side* upon a couch to which he was *chained*, ver. 5, for *three hundred and ninety days;* and afterwards he lay in the same manner, upon his *right side*, for *forty days.* And thus was signified the state of the Jews, and the punishment that was coming upon them. 1. The *prophet* himself represents the Jews. 2. His *lying*, their state of depression. 3. His being *bound*, their helplessness and captivity. 4. The *days* signify *years*, a *day for a year;* during which they were to bear their iniquity, or the temporal punishment due to their sins. 5. The *three hundred and ninety days*, during which he was to lie on his left side, and bear the iniquity of the house of Israel, point out *two*

A. M. 3409
B. C. 595
Ol. XLVI. 2
Anno TarquiniiPrisci,
R. Roman., 22

the iniquity of the house of
Israel upon it: *according* to the
number of the days that thou
shalt lie upon it thou shalt bear
their iniquity.
5 For I have laid upon thee the years of
their iniquity, according to the number of
the days, three hundred and ninety days:
[d]so shalt thou bear the iniquity of the house
of Israel.
6 And when thou hast accomplished them,
lie again on thy right side, and thou shalt bear
the iniquity of the house of Judah forty days:
I have appointed thee [e]each day for a year.
7 Therefore thou shalt set thy face toward
the siege of Jerusalem, and thine arm *shall be*
uncovered, and thou shalt prophesy against it.
8 [f]And, behold, I will lay bands upon thee,
and thou shalt not turn thee [g]from one side
to another, till thou hast ended
the days of thy siege.
9 Take thou also unto thee
wheat, and barley, and beans,
and lentiles, and millet, and [h]fitches, and
put them in one vessel, and make thee bread
thereof, *according* to the number of the
days that thou shalt lie upon thy side,
three hundred and ninety days shalt thou eat
thereof.
10 And thy meat which thou shalt eat *shall
be* by weight, twenty shekels a day: from
time to time shalt thou eat it.
11 Thou shalt drink also water by measure,
the sixth part of a hin: from time to time
shalt thou drink.
12 And thou shalt eat it *as* barley cakes,
and thou shalt bake it with dung that cometh
out of man, in their sight.

[d]Num. xiv. 34——[e]Heb. *a day for a year, a day for a year*

[f]Chap. iii. 25——[g]Heb. *from thy side to thy side*——[h]Or, *spelt*

things: the *first*, The *duration* of the *siege* of Jerusalem. *Secondly*, The *duration* of the *captivity* of the *ten* tribes, and that of Judah. 6. The prophet lay *three hundred and ninety days* upon his left side, and *forty* days upon his right side, in all *four hundred and thirty* days. Now Jerusalem was besieged the *ninth* year of the reign of Zedekiah, 2 Kings xxv. 1, 2, and was not taken till the *eleventh* year of the same prince, 2 Kings xxv. 2. But properly speaking, the siege did not continue the *whole* of that time; it was interrupted; for Nebuchadnezzar was obliged to *raise* it, and go and meet the Egyptians, who were coming to its succour. This consumed a considerable portion of time. After he had defeated the Egyptians, he returned and recommenced the siege, and did not leave it till the city was taken. We may, therefore, conclude that the *four hundred and thirty days* only comprise the time in which the city was *actually besieged*, when the city was encompassed with walls of circumvallation, so that the besieged were reduced to a state of the utmost distress. The siege commenced the *tenth* day of the *tenth* month of the *ninth* year of Zedekiah; and it was taken on the *ninth* day of the *fourth* month of the *eleventh* year of the same king. Thus the siege had lasted, in the whole, *eighteen months*, or *five hundred and ten days*. Subtract for the time that Nebuchadnezzar was obliged to interrupt the siege, in order to go against the Egyptians, *four months and twenty days*, or *one hundred and forty days*, and there will remain *four hundred and thirty days*, composed of 390+40=430. See *Calmet* on this place. See also at the end of this chapter.

Verse 6. *Forty days*] Reckon, says Archbishop Newcome, near *fifteen* years and *six* months in the reign of Manasseh, *two* years in that of Amon, *three* months in that of Jehoahaz, *eleven* years in that of Jehoiakim, *three* months and *ten* days in that of Jehoiachin, and *eleven* years in that of Zedekiah; and there arises a period of *forty* years, during which gross idolatry was practised in the kingdom of Judah. *Forty days* may have been employed in spoiling and desolating the city and the temple.

Verse 9. *Take thou also unto thee wheat*] In times of *scarcity*, it is customary in all countries to mix several kinds of coarser grain with the finer, to make it last the longer. This *mashlin*, which the prophet is commanded to take, of wheat, barley, beans, lentiles, millet, and fitches, was intended to show how scarce the necessaries of life should be during the siege.

Verse 10. *Twenty shekels a day*] The whole of the above grain, being ground, was to be formed into one *mass*, out of which he was to make *three hundred and ninety loaves; one loaf* for *each day;* and this loaf was to be of *twenty shekels* in weight. Now a *shekel*, being in weight about half an ounce, this would be *ten* ounces of bread for each day; and with this *water* to the amount of one *sixth* part of a *hin*, which is about a pint and a half of our measure. All this shows that so reduced should provisions be during the siege, that they should be obliged to eat the *meanest* sort of aliment, and that by *weight*, and their *water* by *measure;* each man's allowance being scarcely a *pint and a half*, and *ten ounces*, a little more than *half a pound* of *bread*, for each day's support.

Verse 12. *Thou shalt bake it with dung*] Dried ox and cow dung is a common fuel in the east; and with this, for want of wood and coals, they are obliged to prepare their food. Indeed, dried excrement of every kind is gathered. Here, the prophet is to prepare his bread with *dry human excrement*. And when we know that this did not come in contact with the bread, and was only used to warm the plate, (see ver. 3,) on which the bread was laid over the fire, it removes all the horror and much of the disgust. This was required to show the extreme

A. M. 3409 B. C. 595 Ol. XLVI. 2 Anno TarquiniiPrisci, R. Roman., 22

13 And the LORD said, Even
thus [i]shall the children of Israel
eat their defiled bread among
the Gentiles, whither I will
drive them.
14 Then said I, [k]Ah Lord GOD! behold,
my soul hath not been polluted: for from my
youth up even till now have I not eaten of
[l]that which dieth of itself, or is torn in
pieces; neither came there [m]abominable flesh
into my mouth.
15 Then he said unto me, Lo, I have given
thee cow's dung for man's dung,
and thou shalt prepare thy
bread therewith.
16 Moreover he said unto me,
Son of man, behold, I will break the [n]staff of
bread in Jerusalem: and they shall [o]eat bread
by weight, and with care; and they shall
[p]drink water by measure, and with astonishment:
17 That they may want bread and water,
and be astonied one with another, and [q]con-
sume away for their iniquity.

[i]Hos. ix. 3——[k]Acts x. 14——[l]Exod. xxii. 31; Lev. xi. 40; xvii. 15——[m]Deut. xiv. 3; Isa. lxv. 4——[n]Lev. xxvi. 26; Psa. cv. 16; Isa. iii. 1; ch. v. 16; xiv. 13——[o]Ver. 10; ch. xii. 19——[p]Ver. 11——[q]Lev. xxvi. 39; ch. xxiv. 23

degree of wretchedness to which they should be exposed; for, not being able to *leave the city* to collect the dried excrements of beasts, the inhabitants during the siege would be obliged, literally, to use dried human ordure for fuel. The very circumstances show that this was the plain fact of the case. However, we find that the prophet was relieved from using this kind of fuel, for *cows' dung* was substituted at his request. See ver. 15.

Verse 14. *My soul hath not been polluted*] There is a remarkable similarity between this expostulation of the prophet and that of St. Peter, Acts x. 14.

Verse 16. *I will break the staff of bread*] They shall be besieged till all the bread is consumed, till the famine becomes *absolute;* see 2 Kings xxv. 3: "And on the ninth of the *fourth* month, the famine prevailed in the city; and THERE WAS NO BREAD for the people of the land." All this was accurately foretold, and as accurately fulfilled.

Abp. *Newcome* on ver. 6 observes: "This number of years will take us back, with sufficient exactness, from the year in which Jerusalem was sacked by Nebuchadnezzar to the first year of Jeroboam's reign, when national idolatry began in Israel. The period of days seems to predict the duration of the siege by the Babylonians, ver. 9, deducting from the year *five months and twenty-nine days,* mentioned 2 Kings xxv. 1-4, the time during which the Chaldeans were on their expedition against the Egyptians; see Jer. xxxvii. 5." This amounts nearly to the same as that mentioned above.

CHAPTER V

In this chapter the prophet shows, under the type of hair, *the judgments which God was about to execute on the inhabitants of Jerusalem by famine, sword, and dispersion,* 1–4. *The type or allegory is then dropped, and God is introduced declaring in plain terms the vengeance that was coming on the whole nation which had proved so unworthy of those mercies with which they had hitherto been distinguished,* 5–17.

A. M. cir. 3410 B. C. cir. 594 Ol. XLVI. 3 TarquiniiPrisci, R. Roman., cir. annum 23

AND thou, son of man, take
thee a sharp knife, take thee
a barber's razor, [a]and cause *it*
to pass upon thine head and
upon thy beard: then take thee balances to
weigh, and divide the *hair.*
2 [b]Thou shalt burn with fire a third part in
the midst of [c]the city, when [d]the days of the siege
are fulfilled: and thou shalt take
a third part, *and* smite about it
with a knife: and a third part
thou shalt scatter in the wind;
and I will draw out a sword after them.
3 [e]Thou shalt also take thereof a few in
number, and bind them in thy [f]skirts.
4 Then take of them again, and [g]cast them

[a]See Lev. xxi. 5; Isa. vii. 20; chap. xliv. 20——[b]Ver. 12——[c]Chap. iv. 1——[d]Chap. iv. 8, 9——[e]Jer. xl. 6; lii. 16——[f]Heb. *wings*——[g]Jer. xli. 1, 2, &c.; xliv. 14

NOTES ON CHAP. V

Verses 1-4. *Take thee a sharp knife*] Among the Israelites, and indeed among most ancient nations, there were very few *edge-tools.* The *sword* was the chief; and this was used as a *knife,* a *razor,* &c., according to its different *length* and *sharpness.* It is likely that only *one* kind of instrument is here intended; a *knife* or short *sword,* to be employed as a *razor.*

Here is a new emblem produced, in order to mark out the coming evils. 1. The *prophet* represents the Jewish *nation.* 2. His *hair,* the *people.* 3. The *razor,* the *Chaldeans.* 4. The *cutting* the *beard* and *hair,* the *calamities, sorrows,* and *disgrace* coming upon the people. *Cutting off the hair* was a sign of *mourning;* see on Jer. xlv. 5; xlviii. 37; and also a sign of great *disgrace;* see 2 Sam. x. 4. 5. He is ordered to divide the hair, ver. 2, into *three equal* parts, to intimate the *different degrees* and *kinds of punishment* which should fall upon the people. 6. The *balances,* ver. 1, were to represent the Divine justice, and the exactness with which

A. M. cir. 3410
B. C. cir. 594
Ol. XLVI. 3
TarquiniiPrisci,
R. Roman.,
cir. annum 23

into the midst of the fire, and burn them in the fire; *for* thereof shall a fire come forth into all the house of Israel.

5 Thus saith the Lord GOD; This *is* Jerusalem: I have set it in the midst of the nations and countries *that are* round about her.

6 And she hath changed my judgments into wickedness more than the nations, and my statutes more than the countries that *are* round about her: for they have refused my judgments and my statutes, they have not walked in them.

7 Therefore thus saith the Lord GOD; Because ye multiplied more than the nations that *are* round about you, *and* have not walked in my statutes, neither have kept my judgments, [h]neither have done according to the judgments of the nations that *are* round about you;

8 Therefore thus saith the Lord GOD; Behold, I, even I, *am* against thee, and will execute judgments in the midst of thee in the sight of the nations.

A. M. cir. 3410
B. C. cir. 594
Ol. XLVI. 3
TarquiniiPrisci,
R. Roman.,
cir. annum 23

9 [i]And I will do in thee that which I have not done, and whereunto I will not do any more the like, because of all thine abominations.

10 Therefore the fathers [k]shall eat the sons in the midst of thee, and the sons shall eat their fathers; and I will execute judgments in thee, and the whole remnant of thee will I [l]scatter into all the winds.

11 Wherefore, *as* I live, saith the Lord GOD; Surely, because thou hast [m]defiled my sanctuary with all thy [n]detestable things, and with all thine abominations, therefore will I also diminish *thee;* [o]neither shall mine eye spare, neither will I have any pity.

12 [p]A third part of thee shall die with the pestilence, and with famine shall they be con-

[h]Jer. ii. 10, 11; chap. xvi. 47——[i]Lam. iv. 6; Dan. ix. 12; Amos iii. 2——[k]Lev. xxvi. 29; Deut. xxviii. 53 2 Kings vi. 29; Jer. xix. 9; Lam. ii. 20; iv. 10; Bar. ii. 3 [l]Ver. 12; Lev. xxvi. 33; Deut. xxviii. 64; chap. xii. 14; Zech. ii. 6——[m]2 Chronicles xxxvi. 14; chap. vii. 20; viii. 5, &c.; xxiii. 38——[n]Chap. xi. 21——[o]Chap. vii. 4, 9; viii. 18; ix. 10——[p]See ver. 2; Jer. xv. 2; xxi. 9; chap. vi. 12

God's judgments should be distributed among the offenders. 7. This *hair,* divided into *three parts,* is to be disposed of thus: 1. A *third* part is to be *burnt* in the midst of the city, to show that so many should perish by famine and pestilence during the siege. 2. Another third part he was to *cut in small portions* about the city, (that figure which he had pourtrayed upon the brick,) to signify those who should perish in different *sorties,* and in *defending* the *walls.* 3. And the remaining third part he was to *scatter* in the *wind,* to point out those who should be driven into *captivity.* And, 4. The *sword following* them was intended to show that their lives should be at the will of their captors, and that many of them should perish by the *sword* in their dispersions. 5. The *few hairs* which he was to take in his skirts, ver. 3, was intended to represent those few Jews that should be left in the land under *Gedaliah,* after the taking of the city. 6. The throwing a part of these last into the fire, ver. 4, was intended to show the miseries that these suffered in *Judea,* in *Egypt,* and finally in their being also carried away into *Babylon* on the conquest of Egypt by Nebuchadnezzar. See these transactions particularly pointed out in the notes on Jeremiah, chapters xl., xli., xlii. Some think that this prophecy may refer to the persecution of the Jews by *Antiochus Epiphanes.*

Verse 5. *This* is *Jerusalem: I have set it in the midst of the nations*] I have made this city the most eminent and the most illustrious in the world. Some think that these words refer to its *geographical situation,* as being equally in *the centre of the habitable world.* But any point on a globe is its centre, no matter where laid down; and it would not be difficult to show that even this *literal sense* is tolerably correct. But the point which is the *centre* of the greatest portion of land that can be exhibited on one hemisphere is the capital of the *British empire.* See my *Sermon on the universal spread of the Gospel.*

Verse 6. *She hath changed my judgments*] God shows the reason why he deals with Jerusalem in greater severity than with the surrounding nations; because she was more wicked than they. Bad and idolatrous as they were, they had a greater degree of *morality* among them than the Jews had. Having fallen from the true God, they became *more abominable* than others in proportion to the height, eminence, and glory from which they had fallen. This is the common case of *backsliders;* they frequently, in their fall, become tenfold more the children of wrath than they were before.

Verse 9. *I will do in thee that which I have not done*] The destruction of Jerusalem by *Nebuchadnezzar* was one of the greatest calamities that ever fell on any nation or place *before;* and that by the *Romans* under Titus exceeded all that has taken place *since.* These two sackages of that city have no parallel in the history of mankind.

Verse 10. *The fathers shall eat the sons*] Though we have not this fact so particularly stated in *history,* yet we cannot doubt of it, considering the extremities to which they were reduced during the siege. The same is referred to by Jeremiah, Lam. iv. 10. Even the *women,* who were remarkable for *kindness* and *humanity, boiled* their own children, and ate them during the siege.

Will I scatter into all the winds.] Disperse you, by captivity, among all the nations of the earth.

Verse 12. *A third part of thee*] See the note on ver. 1-4.

A. M. cir. 3410 B. C. cir. 594 Ol. XLVI. 3 TarquiniiPrisci, R. Roman., cir. annum 23

sumed in the midst of thee: and a third part shall fall by the sword round about thee; and [q]I will scatter a third part into all the winds, and [r]I will draw out a sword after them.

13 Thus shall mine anger [s]be accomplished, and I will [t]cause my fury to rest upon them, [u]and I will be comforted: [v]and they shall know that I the LORD have spoken *it* in my zeal, when I have accomplished my fury in them.

14 Moreover [w]I will make thee waste, and a reproach among the nations that *are* round about thee, in the sight of all that pass by.

15 So it shall be a [x]reproach and a taunt, an instruction and an astonishment unto the nations that *are* round about thee, when I shall execute judgments in thee in anger and in fury and in [y]furious rebukes. I the LORD have spoken *it*.

A. M. cir. 3410 B. C. cir. 594 Ol. XLVI. 3 TarquiniiPrisci, R. Roman., cir. annum 23

16 When I shall [z]send upon them the evil arrows of famine, which shall be for *their* destruction, *and* which I will send to destroy you: and I will increase the famine upon you, and will break your [a]staff of bread.

17 So will I send upon you famine and [b]evil beasts, and they shall bereave thee; and [c]pestilence and blood shall pass through thee; and I will bring the sword upon thee. I the LORD have spoken *it*.

---

[q]Jeremiah ix. 16; verse 2, 10; chapter vi. 8——[r]Leviticus xxvi. 33; verse 2; chapter xii. 14——[s]Lamentations iv. 11; chapter vi. 12; vii. 8——[t]Chap. xxi. 17——[u]Deuteronomy xxxii. 36; Isaiah i. 24——[v]Chapter xxxvi. 6; xxxviii. 19——[w]Leviticus xxvi. 31, 32; Nehemiah ii. 17——[x]Deut. xxviii. 37; 1 Kings ix. 7; Psa. lxxix. 4; Jer. xxiv. 9; Lam. ii. 15——[y]Chap. xxv. 17——[z]Deut. xxxii. 23, 24——[a]Lev. xxvi. 26; ch. iv. 16; xiv. 13——[b]Lev. xxvi. 22; Deut. xxxii. 24; chap. xiv. 21; xxxiii. 27; xxxiv. 25——[c]Chap. xxxviii. 22

Verse 13. *I will cause my fury to rest*] My displeasure, and the evidences of it, shall not be *transient;* they shall be *permanent* upon you, and among you. And is not this dreadfully true to the present day?

Verse 16. *The evil arrows of famine*] Famine and pestilence are represented as *poisoned arrows,* inflicting death wherever they *wound.* The ancients represented them in the same way.

Verse 17. *So will I send upon you famine and evil beasts, and they shall bereave thee*] Wild beasts always multiply in depopulated countries. In England, *wolves* abounded when the country was thinly peopled, it is now full of inhabitants, and there is not one wolf in the land. Nebuchadnezzar and his Chaldeans may be called here *evil beasts.* He is often compared to a *lion,* Jer. iv. 7; Dan. vii. 14; on account of the ravages made by him and his Chaldean armies.

CHAPTER VI

In this chapter, which forms a distinct section, the prophet denounces the judgments of God against the Jews for their idolatry, 1–7; *but tells them that a remnant shall be saved, and brought to a sense of their sins by their severe afflictions,* 8–14.

A. M. cir. 3410 B. C. cir. 594 Ol. XLVI. 3 TarquiniiPrisci, R. Roman., cir. annum 23

AND the word of the LORD came unto me, saying,

2 Son of man, [a]set thy face toward the [b]mountains of Israel, and prophesy against them,

3 And say, Ye mountains of Israel, hear the word of the Lord GOD; Thus saith the Lord GOD to the mountains, and to the hills, to the rivers, and to the valleys; Behold, I, *even* I, will bring a sword upon you, and [c]I will destroy your high places.

A. M. cir. 3410 B. C. cir. 594 Ol. XLVI. 3 TarquiniiPrisci, R. Roman., cir. annum 23

4 And your altars shall be desolate, and your [d]images shall be broken: and [e]I will cast down your slain *men* before your idols.

5 And I will [f]lay the dead carcasses of the

---

[a]Chap. xx. 46; xxi. 2; xxv. 2——[b]Chap. xxxvi. 1——[c]Lev. xxvi. 30

[d]Or, *sun images;* and so ver. 6——[e]Lev. xxvi. 30——[f]Heb. *give*

NOTES ON CHAP. VI

Verse 2. *Set thy face toward the mountains of Israel*] This is a new prophecy, and was most probably given after the *four hundred and thirty* days of his lying on his left and right side were accomplished. By *Israel* here, Judea is simply meant; not the *ten tribes,* who had long before been carried into captivity. Ezekiel uses this term in reference to the Jews only.

The *mountains* may be addressed here particularly, because it was on them the chief scenes of idolatry were exhibited.

Verse 4. *Your images shall be broken*] Literally, your *sun images;* representations of the sun, which they worshipped. See the margin.

Verse 5. *Will scatter your bones round about*

A. M. cir. 3410
B. C. cir. 594
Ol. XLVI. 3
TarquiniiPrisci,
R. Roman.,
cir. annum 23

children of Israel before their
idols; and I will scatter your
bones round about your altars.
6 In all your dwelling-places
the cities shall be laid waste, and the high
places shall be desolate; that your altars may
be laid waste and made desolate, and your
idols may be broken and cease, and your
images may be cut down, and your works
may be abolished.
7 And the slain shall fall in the midst of
you, and [g]ye shall know that I *am* the LORD.
8 [h]Yet will I leave a remnant, that ye may
have *some* that shall escape the sword among
the nations, when ye shall be scattered
through the countries.
9 And they that escape of you shall remember me among the nations whither they shall
be carried captives, because [i]I am broken
with their whorish heart, which hath departed from me, and [k]with their eyes, which
go a whoring after their idols: and [l]they shall
loathe themselves for the evils which they
have committed in all their abominations.
10 And they shall know that I *am* the LORD,
and that I have not said in vain
that I would do this evil unto them.
11 Thus saith the Lord GOD;
Smite [m]with thine hand, and
stamp with thy foot, and say, Alas for all the
evil abominations of the house of Israel! [n]for
they shall fall by the sword, by the famine,
and by the pestilence.
12 He that is far off shall die of the pestilence; and he that is near shall fall by the
sword; and he that remaineth and is besieged
shall die by the famine: [o]thus will I accomplish my fury upon them.
13 Then [p]shall ye know that I *am* the
LORD, when their slain *men* shall be among
their idols round about their altars, [q]upon
every high hill, [r]in all the tops of the mountains, and [s]under every green tree, and under
every thick oak, the place where they did
offer sweet savour to all their idols.
14 So will I [t]stretch out my hand upon
them, and make the land desolate, yea, [u]more
desolate than the wilderness toward [v]Diblath,
in all their habitations: and they shall know
that I *am* the LORD.

[g]Ver. 13; ch. vii. 4, 9; xi. 10, 12; xii. 15——[h]Jer. xliv. 28; ch. v. 2, 12; xii. 16; xiv. 22——[i]Psa. lxxviii. 40; Isa. vii. 13; xliii. 24; lxiii. 10——[k]Num. xv. 39; ch. xx. 7, 24 [l]Lev. xxvi. 39; Job xlii. 6; ch. xx. 43; xxxvi. 31

[m]Chap. xxi. 14——[n]Chap. v. 12——[o]Chap. v. 13 [p]Ver. 7——[q]Jer. ii. 20——[r]Hos. iv. 13——[s]Isa. lvii. 5 [t]Isa. v. 25——[u]Or, *desolate from the wilderness* [v]Num. xxxiii. 46; Jer. xlviii. 22

your altars.] This was literally fulfilled by the Chaldeans. According to *Baruch*, chap. ii. 24, 25, they opened the sepulchres of the principal people, and threw the bones about on every side.

Verse 9. *They that escape of you shall remember me*] Those that escape the sword, the pestilence, and the famine, and shall be led into captivity, shall plainly see that it is God who has done this; and shall humble themselves on account of their abominations, leave their idolatry, and worship me alone. And this they have done from the Babylonish captivity to the present day.

Verse 11. *Smite with thine hand, and stamp with thy foot*] Show the utmost marks of thy astonishment and indignation, and dread of the evils that are coming upon them. Some have contended for the propriety of *clapping* and *stamping* in public worship from these words! It is scarcely a breach of charity to think that such persons are themselves incapable either of attending on or conducting the worship of God. To be consistent, they should copy the prophet in his other typical actions as well as these; and then we shall hear of their *lying on their left side* for *three hundred and ninety* days, and on *their right side* for *forty* days; *shaving their heads, burning their hair, baking their bread with dung*, &c. Now all these things, because they were typical and commanded, were proper in the prophet: in such persons as the above they would be evidences of insanity. Such extravagant acts are no part of God's worship.

Verse 14. *And make the land—more desolate than the wilderness toward Diblath*] *Diblath* or *Diblathayim* is situated in the land of Moab. It is mentioned Num. xxxiii. 46, *Almon-Diblathaim;* and in Jer. xlviii. 22, *Beth-Diblathaim.* It was a part of that horrible wilderness mentioned by Moses, Deut. viii. 15, "wherein were fiery serpents, and scorpions, and drought." The precise reason why it is mentioned here is not very evident. Some think it is the same as *Riblah*, where Nebuchadnezzar slew the princes of Israel, and put out Zedekiah's eyes; the principal difference lying between the ד *daleth* and the ר *resh*, which in MSS. is often scarcely discernible; and hence vast multitudes of *various readings. Five*, probably *six*, of *Kennicott's* MSS. have רבלתה *riblathah*, as likewise *two* of my oldest MSS.; though in the margin of one a later hand directs the word to be read בדלת *bedaleth, with daleth.* But all the *Versions* read the word with a D. This may appear a matter of little importance, but we should take pains to recover even one lost *letter* of the *word* of God.

CHAPTER VII

This chapter, which also forms a distinct prophecy, foretells the dreadful destruction of the land of Israel, or Judah, (for after the captivity of the ten tribes these terms are often used indiscriminately for the Jews in general,) on account of the heinous sins of its inhabitants, 1–15; *and the great distress of the small remnant that should escape,* 16–19. *The temple itself, which they had polluted with idolatry, is devoted to destruction,* 20–22; *and the prophet is directed to make a chain, as a type of that captivity, in which both king and people should be led in bonds to Babylon,* 23–27. *The whole chapter abounds in bold and beautiful figures, flowing in an easy and forcible language.*

A. M. cir. 3410 B. C. cir. 594 Ol. XLVI. 3 TarquiniiPrisci, R. Roman., cir. annum 23

MOREOVER the word of the
LORD came unto me, saying,
2 Also, thou son of man, thus
saith the Lord GOD unto the
land of Israel; [a]An end, the end is come
upon the four corners of the land.
3 Now *is* the end *come* upon thee, and I
will send mine anger upon thee, and [b]will
judge thee according to thy ways, and will
[c]recompense upon thee all thine abominations.
4 And [d]mine eye shall not spare thee, neither will I have pity: but I will recompense
thy ways upon thee, and thine abominations
shall be in the midst of thee: [e]and ye shall
know that I *am* the LORD.

A. M. cir. 3410 B. C. cir. 594 Ol. XLVI. 3 TarquiniiPrisci, R. Roman., cir. annum 23

5 Thus saith the Lord GOD; An
evil, an only evil, behold, is come.
6 An end is come, the end is
come: it [f]watcheth for thee;
behold, it is come.
7 [g]The morning is come unto thee, O thou
that dwellest in the land: [h]the time is come,
the day of trouble *is* near, and not the
[i]sounding again of the mountains.
8 Now will I shortly [k]pour out my fury
upon thee, and accomplish mine anger upon
thee: [l]and I will judge thee according to thy
ways, and will recompense thee for all thine
abominations.
9 And [m]mine eye shall not spare, neither will

[a]Ver. 3, 6; Amos viii. 2; Matt. xxiv. 6, 13, 14——[b]Ver. 8, 9——[c]Heb. *give*——[d]Ver. 9; chap. v. 11; viii. 18; ix. 10——[e]Ver. 27; chap. vi. 7; xii. 20

[f]Heb. *awaketh against thee*——[g]Ver. 10——[h]Ver. 12; Zeph. i. 14, 15——[i]Or, *echo*——[k]Chap. xx. 8, 21 [l]Ver. 3——[m]Ver. 4

NOTES ON CHAP. VII

Verse 2. *An end, the end is come*] Instead of קץ בא הקץ *kets ba hakkets, one* MS. of *Kennicott's one* of *De Rossi's*, and *one* of *my own*, read קץ בא בא הקץ *kets ba, ba hakkets*, "The end cometh, come is the end." This reading is supported by all the ancient Versions, and is undoubtedly genuine. *The end* COMETH: the termination of the Jewish state *is coming*, and while I am speaking, it *is come*. The destruction is at the door. The *later* hand, who put the *vowel points* to the ancient MS. that has the above reading, did not put the points to the first בא *ba*, but struck his pen gently across it, and by a mark in the margin intimated that it should be blotted out. All my ancient MSS. were without the points originally; but they have been added by modern hands, with a different ink; and they have in multitudes of instances corrected, or rather changed, important readings, to make them quadrate with the *masora*. But the original reading, in almost every case, is discernible.

The end is come upon the four corners of the land.] This is not a *partial* calamity; it shall cover and sweep the whole land. The cup of your iniquity is full, and my forbearing is at an end. This whole chapter is *poetical*.

Verse 4. *Thine abominations shall be in the midst of thee*] They shall ever stare thee in the face, upbraid thee with thy ingratitude and disobedience, and be witnesses against thee.

Verse 5. *An evil, an only evil*] The great, the sovereign, the last exterminating evil, is come: the sword, the pestilence, the famine, and the captivity. Many MSS. read אחר *achar, after*. So evil cometh after evil; one instantly succeeds another.

Verse 6. *An end is come, the end is come: it watcheth for thee*] This is similar to the *second* verse; but there is a *paronomasia*, or play upon letters and words, which is worthy of note. קץ בא בא הקץ הקץ אליך *kets ba, ba hakkets, hekits elayich*. קצה *katsah* signifies to make an *end* or *extremity*, by cutting off something, and יקץ *yakats* signifies to *awake from sleep:* hence קיץ *kits*, the *summer*, as the earth and its productions seem then to awake from the sleep of winter. The *end* or final destruction is here *personified;* and represented as an *executioner* who has *arisen early* from his sleep, and is *waiting* for his orders to execute judgment upon these offenders. Hence it is said—

Verse 7. *The morning is come unto thee*] Every note of *time* is used in order to show the *certainty* of the thing. The *morning* that the executioner has *watched* for is come; the *time* of that *morning*, in which it should take place, and the *day* to which that *time, precise hour* of that *morning*, belongs, in which judgment shall be executed. All, all is come.

And not the sounding again of the mountains.] The hostile troops are advancing! Ye hear a *sound*, a *tumultuous noise;* do not suppose that this proceeds from festivals upon *the mountains;* from the joy of *harvestmen*, or the treaders *of the wine-press*. It is the *noise* of those by whom ye and your country are to fall. ולא הד הרים *velo hed harim*, and not the reverberation of sound, or reflected sound, or *re-*

A. M. cir. 3410
B. C. cir. 594
Ol. XLVI. 3
TarquiniiPrisci,
R. Roman.,
cir. annum 23

I have pity: I will recompense
[n]thee according to thy ways and
thine abominations *that* are in
the midst of thee; [o]and ye shall
know that I *am* the LORD that smiteth.
10 Behold the day, behold, it is come: [p]the
morning is gone forth; the rod hath blossomed, pride hath budded.
11 [q]Violence is risen up into a rod of wickedness: none of them *shall remain,* nor of
their [r]multitude, nor of any of [s]theirs; [t]nei-
ther *shall there be* wailing for them.
12 [u]The time is come, the day draweth near:
let not the buyer rejoice, nor the seller mourn:
for wrath *is* upon all the multitude thereof.
13 For the seller shall not return to that
which is sold, [v]although they were yet alive:
for the vision *is* touching the
whole multitude thereof, *which*
shall not return; neither shall
any strengthen himself [w]in [x]the
iniquity of his life.
14 They have blown the trumpet, even to
make all ready: but none goeth to the battle:
for my wrath *is* upon all the multitude thereof.
15 [y]The sword *is* without, and the pestilence and the famine within: he that *is* in the
field shall die with the sword; and he that *is* in
the city, famine and pestilence shall devour him.
16 But [z]they that escape of them shall
escape, and shall be on the mountains like
doves of the valleys, all of them mourning,
every one for his iniquity.
17 All [a]hands shall be feeble, and all

A. M. cir. 3410
B. C. cir. 594
Ol. XLVI. 3
TarquiniiPrisci,
R. Roman.,
cir. annum 23

[n]Heb. *upon thee*——[o]Ver. 4——[p]Ver. 7——[q]Jer. vi. 7——[r]Or, *tumult*——[s]Or, *their tumultuous persons* [t]Jer. xvi. 5, 6; ch. xxiv. 16, 22——[u]Ver. 7——[v]Heb. *though their life* were *yet among the living*——[w]Or, *whose life* is *in his iniquity*——[x]Hebrew, *his iniquity*——[y]Deut. xxxii. 25; Lam. i. 20; chap. v. 12——[z]Chap. vi. 8——[a]Isa. xiii. 7; Jer. vi. 24; chap. xxi. 7

echoing from the mountains. "Now will I shortly pour out," ver. 8. Here they come!

Verse 10. *Behold the day*] The same words are repeated, sometimes varied, and pressed on the attention with *new figures* and *new circumstances*, in order to alarm this infatuated people. Look at the *day!* It is come!

The morning is gone forth] It will wait no longer. The *rod* that is to chastise you hath *blossomed;* it is quite ready.

Pride hath budded.] Your insolence, obstinacy, and daring opposition to God have brought forth their proper fruits.

Verse 11. *Violence is risen up into a rod of wickedness*] The prophet continues his metaphor: "Pride has budded."—And what has it brought forth? *Violence* and *iniquity*. To meet these, the *rod of God* cometh. There is such a vast rapidity of succession in the ideas of the prophet that he cannot wait to find language to clothe each. Hence we have broken sentences; and, consequently, *obscurity*. Something must be *supplied* to get the sense, and most critics alter words in the text. *Houbigant*, who rarely acknowledges himself to be puzzled, appears here completely nonplussed. He has given a meaning; it is this: "Violence hath burst forth from the rod; salvation shall not proceed from them, nor from their riches, nor from their turbulence: there shall be no respite for them." *Calmet* has given no less than *five* interpretations to this verse. The simple meaning seems to be, that such and so great is their wickedness that it must be punished; and from this punishment, neither their multitude nor struggles shall set them free. They may strive to evade the threatened stroke; but they shall not succeed, nor shall they have any respite. Our *Version* is to be understood as saying,—None of the people shall be left; all shall be slain, or carried into captivity: nor shall any of theirs, their princes, priests, wives, or children, escape. And so deserved shall their desolation appear, that none shall *lament* them. This may be as good a sense as any, and it is nearest to the letter.

Verse 12. *Let not the buyer rejoice, nor the seller mourn*] Such is now the state of public affairs, that he who through want has been obliged to *sell his inheritance*, need not *mourn* on the account; as of this the enemy would soon have deprived him. And he who *has bought it* need not *rejoice* in his bargain, as he shall soon be stripped of his purchase, and either fall by the sword, or be glad to flee for his life.

Verse 13. *For the seller shall not return*] In the sale of all heritages among the Jews, it was always understood that the heritage must return to the family on the *year of jubilee*, which was every *fiftieth* year; but in this case the *seller* should not return to possess it, as it was not likely that he should be *alive* when the next jubilee should come; and if he were even to live till that time, he could not possess it, as he would then be in captivity. And the reason is particularly given; *for the vision*—the prophetic declaration of a *seventy* years' captivity, regards the whole multitude of the people; and *it shall not return,* i. e., it will be found to be strictly true, without any abatement.

Verse 14. *They have blown the trumpet*] Vain are all the efforts you make to collect and arm the people, and stand on your own defence; for all shall be dispirited, and none *go to the battle.*

Verse 15. *The sword* is *without*] *War* through all the *country*, and *pestilence* and *famine* within the city, shall destroy the whole, except a small remnant. He who endeavours to flee from the one shall fall by the other.

Verse 16. *They—shall be on the mountains like doves of the valleys*] Rather, *like mourning doves* הגאיות *haggeayoth,* chased from their dove-cotes, and separated from their mates.

Verse 17. *All knees shall be weak* as *water.*] *Calmet* understands this curiously: La frayeur dont on sera saisi, fera qu'on ne pourra retenir

A. M. cir. 3410 B. C. cir. 594 Ol. XLVI. 3 Tarquinii Prisci, R. Roman., cir. annum 23

knees shall [b]be weak *as* water.

18 They shall also [c]gird *themselves* with sackcloth, and [d]horror shall cover them; and shame *shall be* upon all faces, and baldness upon all their heads.

19 They shall cast their silver in the streets, and their gold shall be [e]removed: their [f]silver and their gold shall not be able to deliver them in the day of the wrath of the LORD: they shall not satisfy their souls, neither fill their bowels: [g]because it is [h]the stumbling-block of their iniquity.

20 As for the beauty of his ornament, he set it in majesty: [i]but they made the images of their abominations *and* of their detestable things therein: therefore have I [k]set it far from them.

21 And I will give it into the hands of the strangers for a prey, and to the wicked of the earth for a spoil; and they shall pollute it.

22 My face will I turn also from them, and they shall pollute my secret *place:* for the [l]robbers shall enter into it, and defile it.

A. M. cir. 3410 B. C. cir. 594 Ol. XLVI. 3 Tarquinii Prisci, R. Roman., cir. annum 23

23 Make a chain: for [m]the land is full of bloody crimes, and the city is full of violence.

24 Wherefore I will bring the worst of the heathen, and they shall possess their houses: I will also make the pomp of the strong to cease; and [n]their holy places shall be defiled.

25 [o]Destruction cometh; and they shall seek peace, and *there shall be* none.

26 [p]Mischief shall come upon mischief, and rumour shall be upon rumour; [q]then shall they seek a vision of the prophet; but the law shall perish from the priest, and counsel from the ancients.

27 The king shall mourn, and the prince shall be clothed with desolation, and the hands of the people of the land shall be troubled: I will do unto them after their way, and [r]according to their deserts will I judge them; [s]and they shall know that I *am* the LORD.

---

[b]Heb. *go into water*——[c]Isa. iii. 24; xv. 2, 3; Jer. xlviii. 37; Amos viii. 10——[d]Psa. lv. 5——[e]Heb. *for a separation,* or *uncleanness*——[f]Prov. xi. 4; Zeph. i. 18; Ecclus. v. 8——[g]Or, *because their iniquity* is their *stumbling block*——[h]Chap. xiv. 3, 4; xliv. 12

[i]Jer. vii. 30——[k]Or, *made it unto them an unclean thing*——[l]Or, *burglars*——[m]2 Kings xxi. 16; ch. ix. 9; xi. 6——[n]Or, *they shall inherit their holy places*——[o]Heb. *Cutting off*——[p]Deut. xxxii. 23; Jer. iv. 20——[q]Psa. lxxiv. 9; Lam. ii. 9; chap. xx. 1, 3——[r]Heb. *with their judgments*——[s]Ver. 4

---

son urine. D'autres l'expliquent d'une autre soüillure plus honteuse. I believe him to be nearly about right. *St. Jerome* is exactly the same: Pavoris magnitudine, urina polluet genua, nec valebit profluentes aquas vesica prohibere. This and other malretentions are often the natural effect of extreme fear or terror.

Verse 19. *They shall cast their silver in the streets*] Their riches can be of no use; as in a time of *famine* there is no necessary of life to be *purchased,* and *gold* and *silver cannot fill their bowels.*

It is the stumbling-block of their iniquity.] They loved riches, and placed in the possession of them their supreme happiness. Now they find a *pound* of *gold* not worth an *ounce* of *bread.*

Verse 20. *As for the beauty of his ornament*] Their *beautiful temple* was their highest *ornament,* and God made it *majestic* by his presence. But they have even taken its riches to make their *idols,* which they have brought into the very courts of the Lord's house; and therefore God hath *set it*—the temple, *from him*—given it up to pillage. Some say it means, "They took their ornaments, which were their pride, and made them into images to worship."

Verse 22. *The robbers shall enter into it*] The Chaldeans shall not only destroy the city; but they shall enter the temple, deface it, plunder it, and burn it to the ground.

Verse 23. *Make a chain*] Point out the *captivity;* show them that it shall come, and show them the reason: "Because the land is full of bloody crimes," &c.

Verse 24. *The worst of the heathen*] The Chaldeans; the most cruel and idolatrous of all nations.

Verse 25. *They shall seek peace*] They see now that their ceasing to pay the tribute to the king of Babylon has brought the Chaldeans against them; and now *they sue for peace* in vain. He will not hear: he is resolved on their destruction.

Verse 26. *Then shall they seek a vision*] Vision shall perish from the prophet, the law from the priest, and counsel from the ancients. Previously to great national judgments, God restrains the influences of his Spirit. His word is not accompanied with the usual unction; and the *wise men* of the land, the *senators* and celebrated *statesmen,* devise foolish schemes; and thus, in endeavouring to avert it, they hasten on the national ruin. How true is the saying, Quem Deus vult perdere, prius dementat. "Those whom God designs to destroy, he first infatuates."

CHAPTER VIII

Here begins a section of prophecy extending to the twelfth *chapter. In this chapter the prophet is carried in vision to Jerusalem,* 1–4; *and there shown the idolatries committed by the rulers of the Jews, even within the temple. In the beginning of this vision, by the noblest stretch of an inspired imagination,* idolatry *itself is personified, and made an* idol; *and the image sublimely called, from the provocation it gave God, the* Image of Jealousy, 5. *The prophet then proceeds to describe the three principal superstitions of this unhappy people: the* Egyptian, 6–12, *the* Phœnician, 13, 14, *and the* Persian, 15, 16; *giving the striking features of each, and concluding with a declaration of the heinousness of their sins in the sight of God, and the consequent greatness of their punishment,* 17, 18.

A. M. 3410
B. C. 594
Ol. XLVI. 3
Anno
Tarquinii Prisci,
R. Roman., 23

AND it came to pass in
the sixth year, in the
sixth *month,* in the fifth *day*
of the month, *as* I sat in mine
house, and [a]the elders of Judah sat before
me, that [b]the hand of the Lord God fell
there upon me.
2 [c]Then I beheld, and lo a likeness as the
appearance of fire: from the
appearance of his loins even
downward, fire; and from his
loins even upward, as the appearance of brightness, [d]as the colour of
amber.
3 And he [e]put forth the form of a hand,
and took me by a lock of mine head; and

[a]Chap. xiv. 1; xx. 1; xxxiii. 31——[b]Chap. i. 3; iii. 22

[c]Chap. i. 26, 27——[d]Chap. i. 4——[e]Dan. v. 5

NOTES ON CHAP. VIII

Verse 1. *In the sixth year, in the sixth* month, *in the fifth* day *of the month*] This, according to Abp. *Usher*, was the *sixth* year of Ezekiel's captivity. The *sixth* day of the *fifth* month of the *ecclesiastical year*, which answers to August, A. M. 3410.

This chapter and the *three* following contain but *one vision*, of which I judge it necessary, with *Calmet*, to give a general idea, that the attention of the reader may not be too much divided.

The prophet, in the visions of God, is carried to Jerusalem, to the northern gate of the temple, which leads by the north side to the court of the priests. There he sees the glory of the Lord in the same manner as he did by the river Chebar. At one side he sees the *image of jealousy*. Going thence to the court of the people, he sees through an opening in the wall *seventy* elders of the people, who were worshipping all sorts of beasts and reptiles, which were painted on the wall. Being brought thence to the gate of the door of the house, he saw women weeping for *Tammuz* or *Adonis*. As he returned to the court of the priests, between the porch and the altar, he saw *twenty-five* men with their backs to the sanctuary and their faces towards the east, worshipping the *rising sun*. This is the substance of the vision contained in the *eighth* chapter.

About the same time he saw *six men* come from the higher gate with *swords* in their hands; and among them, one with an *ink-horn*. Then the Divine Presence left the cherubim, and took post at the entrance of the temple, and gave orders to the man with the *ink-horn* to put a *mark* on the foreheads of those who sighed and prayed because of the abominations of the land; and then commanded the men with the *swords* to go forward, and slay every person who had not this mark. The prophet, being left alone among the dead, fell on his face, and made intercession for the people. The Lord gives him the reason of his conduct; and the man with the ink-horn returns, and reports to the Lord what was done. These are the general contents of the *ninth* chapter.

The Lord commands the same person to go in between the *wheels* of the cherubim, and take his hand full of live coals, and scatter them over the city. He went as commanded, and one of the cherubim gave him the coals; at the same time the glory of the Lord, that had removed to the threshold of the house, now returned, and stood over the cherubim. The cherubim, wheels, wings, &c., are here described as in the *first* chapter. This is the substance of the *tenth* chapter.

The prophet then finds himself transported to the east gate of the temple, where he saw *twenty-five* men, and among them *Jaazaniah* the son of Azur, and *Pelatiah* the son of Benaiah, princes of the people, against whom the Lord commands him to prophesy, and to threaten them with the utmost calamities, because of their crimes. Afterwards God himself speaks, and shows that the Jews who should be left in the land should be driven out because of their iniquities, and that those who had been led captive, and who acknowledged their sins and repented of them, should be restored to their own land. Then the glory of the Lord arose out of the city, and rested for a time on one of the mountains on the east of Jerusalem, and the prophet being carried in vision by the Spirit to Chaldea, lost sight of the chariot of the Divine glory, and began to show to the captivity what the Lord had shown to him. This is the substance of the *eleventh* chapter.

We may see from all this what induced the Lord to abandon his people, his city, and his temple; the abominations of the people in public and in private. But because those carried away captives with Jeconiah acknowledged their sins, and their hearts turned to the Lord, God informs them that they shall be brought back and restored to a happy state both in temporal and spiritual matters, while the others, who had filled up the measure of their iniquities, should be speedily brought into a state of desolation and ruin. This is the sum and intent of the vision in these *four* chapters.

Verse 2. *The appearance of fire*] See the note on chap. i. 27.

Verse 3. *The image of jealousy*] סמל הקנאה

A. M. 3410
B. C. 594
Ol. XLVI. 3
Anno
Tarquinii Prisci,
R. Roman., 23

[f]the spirit lifted me up between the earth and the
heaven, and [g]brought me in
the visions of God to Jerusa-
lem, to the door of the inner gate that looketh
toward the north; [h]where *was* the seat of the
image of jealousy, which [i]provoketh to jealousy.
4 And, behold, the glory of the God of
Israel *was* there, according to the vision that
I [k]saw in the plain.
5 Then said he unto me, Son of man, lift
up thine eyes now the way toward the north.
So I lifted up mine eyes the way toward the
north, and behold northward at the gate of
the altar this image of jealousy in the entry.
6 He said furthermore unto me, Son of
man, seest thou what they do? *even* the great
abominations that the house of Israel committeth here, that I should go far off from
my sanctuary? but turn thee yet again, *and*
thou shalt see greater abominations.
7 And he brought me to the door of the
court; and when I looked, behold a hole in
the wall.
8 Then said he unto me, Son of man, dig
now in the wall: and when I
had digged in the wall, behold
a door.
9 And he said unto me, Go
in, and behold the wicked abominations that
they do here.
10 So I went in and saw; and behold
every form of creeping things, and abominable beasts, and all the idols of the house of
Israel, pourtrayed upon the wall round about.
11 And there stood before them seventy men
of the ancients of the house of Israel, and in
the midst of them stood Jaazaniah the son of
Shaphan, with every man his censer in his
hand; and a thick cloud of incense went up.
12 Then said he unto me, Son of man, hast
thou seen what the ancients of the house of
Israel do in the dark, every man in the chambers of his imagery? for they say, [l]The LORD
seeth us not; the LORD hath forsaken the
earth.
13 He said also unto me, Turn thee yet
again, *and* [m]thou shalt see greater abominations that they do.
14 Then he brought me to the door of the
gate of the LORD's house which *was* toward

A. M. 3410
B. C. 594
Ol. XLVI. 3
Anno
Tarquinii Prisci,
R. Roman., 23

[f]Chap. iii. 14——[g]Gen. xlvi. 2; 2 Chron. xxvi. 5; ch. xi. 1, 24; xl. 2——[h]Jer. vii. 30; xxxii. 34; chap. v. 11

[i]Deut. xxxii. 16, 21——[k]Chap. i. 28; iii. 22, 23——[l]Ch. ix. 9——[m]Ver. 6, 15

semel hakkinah. We do not know certainly of what *form* this image was, nor what *god* it represented. Some say it was the image of Baal, which was placed in the temple by Manasses; others, that it was the image of *Mars;* and others, that it was the image of *Tammuz* or *Adonis. Calmet* supports this opinion by the following reasons:—1. The *name* agrees perfectly with him. He was represented as a beautiful youth, beloved by Venus; at which Mars, her paramour, being incensed and filled with *jealousy,* sent a large boar against Adonis, which killed him with his tusks. Hence it was the image of him who fell a victim to *jealousy.* 2. The prophet being returned towards the northern gate, where he had seen the *image of jealousy,* ver. 14, there saw the *women lamenting for Tammuz.* Now *Tammuz,* all agree, signifies *Adonis;* it was that therefore which was called the *image of jealousy.* 3. The Scripture often gives to the heathen idols names of degradation; as Baal-zebub, *god of flies;* Baalzebul, *god of dung.* It is likely that it was *Adonis* who is called *The dead,* Lev. xix. 27, 28; Deut. xiv. 9, because he was worshipped as one *dead.* And the women represented as worshipping him were probably *adulteresses,* and had suffered through the *jealousy* of their husbands. And this worship of the *image of jealousy provoked God to jealousy,* to destroy this bad people.

Verse 4. *The vision that I saw in the plain.*] See the note on chap. iii. 23; see also chap. i. 3.

Verse 7. *A hole in the wall.*] This we find was not large enough to see what was doing within; and the prophet is directed to dig, and make it larger, ver. 8; and when he had done so and entered, he says,—

Verse 10. *And saw—every form of creeping things*] It is very likely that these images pourtrayed on the wall were the objects of *Egyptian* adoration: the *ox,* the *ape,* the *dog,* the *crocodile,* the *ibis,* the *scarabæus* or *beetle,* and various other things. It appears that these were privately worshipped by the sanhedrin or great Jewish council, consisting of *seventy* or *seventy-two* persons, *six* chosen out of every tribe, as representatives of the people. The images were pourtrayed upon the wall, as we find those ancient idols are on the walls of the *tombs of the kings and nobles of Egypt.* See the plates to *Belzoni's* Travels, the *Isaic Tomb* in the Bodleian Library, and the *Egyptian hieroglyphics* in general. *Virgil* speaks of these, *Æn.* lib. viii.:—

Omnigenumque Deum monstra, et latrator
Anubis.

"All kinds of gods, monsters, and barking dogs."

Verse 11. *Jaazaniah the son of Shaphan*] Shaphan was a scribe, or what some call comptroller of the temple, in the days of Josiah; and *Jaazaniah* his son probably succeeded him in this office. He was at the head of this band of idolaters.

Verse 14. *There sat women weeping for Tammuz.*] This was *Adonis,* as we have already

A. M. 3410
B. C. 594
Ol. XVLI. 3
Anno
Tarquinii Prisci,
R. Roman., 23

the north; and, behold, there sat women weeping for Tammuz.

15 Then said he unto me, Hast thou seen *this,* O son of man? turn thee yet again, *and* thou shalt see greater abominations than these.

16 And he brought me into the inner court of the LORD'S house, and, behold, at the door of the temple of the LORD,[n]between the porch and the altar, [o]*were* about five and twenty men, [p]with their backs toward the temple of the LORD, and their faces toward the east; and they worshipped [q]the sun toward the east.

A. M. 3410
B. C. 594
Ol. XLVI. 3
Anno
Tarquinii Prisci,
R. Roman., 23

17 Then he said unto me, Hast thou seen *this,* O son of man? [r]Is it a light thing to the house of Judah that they commit the abominations which they commit here? for they have [s]filled the land with violence, and have returned to provoke me to anger: and, lo, they put the branch to their nose.

18 [t]Therefore will I also deal in fury: mine [u]eye shall not spare, neither will I have pity; and though they [v]cry in mine ears with a loud voice, *yet* will I not hear them.

---

[n]Joel ii. 17——[o]Ch. xi. 1——[p]Jer. ii. 27; xxxii. 33 [q]Deut. iv. 19; 2 Kings xxiii. 5, 11; Job xxxi. 26; Jer. xliv. 17——[r]Or, *Is there any thing lighter than to commit*

[s]Chap. ix. 9——[t]Chap. v. 13; xvi. 42; xxiv. 13 [u]Chap. v. 11; vii. 4, 9; ix. 5, 10——[v]Prov. i. 28; Isa. i. 15; Jer. xi. 11; xiv. 12; Mic. iii. 4; Zech. vii. 13

---

seen; and so the *Vulgate* here translates. My old MS. Bible reads, **There saten women, mornynge a mawmete of lecherye that is cleped Adonydes.** He is fabled to have been a beautiful youth beloved by Venus, and killed by a wild boar in Mount Lebanon, whence springs the river *Adonis,* which was fabled to *run blood* at his festival in August. The women of Phœnicia, Assyria, and Judea worshipped him as *dead,* with deep lamentation, wearing *priapi* and other obscene images all the while, and they prostituted themselves in honour of this idol. Having for some time mourned him as *dead,* they then supposed him revivified, and broke out into the most extravagant rejoicings. Of the appearance of the river at this season, Mr. *Maundrell* thus speaks: "We had the good fortune to see what is the foundation of the opinion which *Lucian* relates, viz., that this stream at certain seasons of the year, especially about the feast of Adonis, is of a *bloody colour,* proceeding from a kind of sympathy, as the heathens imagined, for the death of Adonis, who was killed by a wild boar in the mountain out of which this stream issues. Something like this we saw actually come to pass, for the water was stained to a surprising redness; and, as we observed in travelling, had stained the sea a great way into a reddish hue." This was no doubt occasioned by a red ochre, over which the river ran with violence at this time of its increase. *Milton* works all this up in these fine lines:—

"Thammuz came next behind,
Whose annual *wound* in Lebanon allured
The Syrian damsels to lament his fate,
In amorous ditties all a summer's day;
While smooth Adonis, from his native rock,
Ran *purple* to the sea. *suffused with blood*
Of Thammuz, yearly wounded. The love tale
Infected *Sion's daughters* with like heat:
Whose wanton passions in the sacred porch
Ezekiel saw, when by the vision led,
His eye surveyed the dark idolatries
Of alienated Judah." *Par. Lost,* b. i. 446.

Tammuz signifies *hidden* or *obscure,* and hence the worship of his image was in some *secret place.*

Verse 16. *Five and twenty men*] These most probably represented the *twenty-four courses* of the *priests,* with the *high priest* for the *twenty-fifth.* This was the *Persian* worship, as their turning their faces to the east plainly shows they were worshipping the *rising sun.*

Verse 17. *They put the branch to their nose.*] This is supposed to mean some branch or branches, which they carried in succession in honour of the idol, and with which they covered their faces, or from which they inhaled a pleasant smell, the branches being odoriferous. That the heathens carried branches of trees in their sacred ceremonies is well known to all persons acquainted with classic antiquity; and it is probable that the heathen borrowed those from the use of such branches in the Jewish feast of tabernacles. There are many strange, and some filthy, interpretations given of this clause; but the former are not worth repeating, and I abominate the latter too much to submit to defile my paper with them. Probably the Brahminic *Linga* is here intended.

It really seems that at this time the Jews had incorporated every species of idolatry in their impure worship,—*Phœnician, Egyptian,* and *Persian.* I might add that some imagine the *image of jealousy* to be a personification of *idolatry* itself.

CHAPTER IX

The vision in this chapter seems intended to denote the general destruction of the inhabitants of Jerusalem, excepting a few pious individuals that were distressed at the abominations that were committed in the land; who in order to be delivered from the general calamity, were MARKED, *in allusion, perhaps, to the custom of eastern princes, who marked their servants in the forehead, or rather to the custom very frequent among the Pagan*

worshippers, of indelibly imprinting on different parts of their body the marks of their idols. To indicate, likewise, that God was soon to forsake the temple, the shechinah, or glorious symbol of his presence, is seen to remove from the inner sanctuary to the threshold or door of the temple, 1–7. The prophet intercedes for his people; but God, on account of the greatness of their sins, will not be entreated, 8–11.

A. M. 3410
B. C. 594
Ol. XLVI. 3
Anno
Tarquinii Prisci,
R. Roman., 23

HE cried also in mine ears with a loud voice, saying, Cause them that have charge over the city to draw near, even every man *with* his [a]destroying weapon in his hand.

2 And, behold, six men came from the way of the higher gate, [b]which lieth toward the north, and every man [c]a slaughter weapon in his hand; [d]and one man among them *was* clothed with linen, with a writer's inkhorn [e]by his side: and they went in, and stood beside the brazen altar.

3 And [f]the glory of the God of Israel was gone up from the cherub, whereupon he was, to the threshold of the house. And he called to the man clothed with linen, which *had* the writer's inkhorn by his side;

A. M. 3410
B. C. 594
Ol. XLVI. 3
Anno
Tarquinii Prisci,
R. Roman., 23

4 And the LORD said unto him, Go through the midst of the city, through the midst of Jerusalem, and [g]set [h]a mark upon the foreheads of the men [i]that sigh and that cry for all the abominations that be done in the midst thereof.

5 And to the others he said in [k]mine hearing, Go ye after him through the city, and smite: [l]let not your eye spare, neither have ye pity:

6 [m]Slay [n]utterly old *and* young, both maids,

[a]Jer. xxii. 7——[b]Heb. *which is turned*——[c]Heb. *a weapon of his breaking in pieces*——[d]Lev. xvi. 4; ch. x. 6, 7; Rev. xv. 6——[e]Heb. *upon his loins*——[f]See ch. iii. 23; viii. 4; x. 4, 18; xi. 22, 23——[g]Heb. *mark a mark*

[h]Exod. xii. 7; Rev. vii. 3; ix. 4; xiii. 16, 17; xx. 4——[i]Psa. cxix. 53, 136; Jer. xiii. 17; 2 Cor. xii. 21; 2 Pet. ii 8——[k]Heb. *mine ears*——[l]Ver. 10; chap. v. 11——[m]2 Chron. xxxvi. 17——[n]Heb. *to destruction*

NOTES ON CHAP. IX

Verse 1. *Cause them that have charge over the city*] By those *six* men with destroying weapons the *Chaldeans* are represented, who had received commission to destroy the city; and when the *north* is mentioned in such cases, *Chaldea* and the *Chaldean armies* are generally intended. There appears to have been *six men* with a sort of *slaughter-bills*, and *one man* with an *inkhorn*. These may represent the *seven* counsellors of the eastern monarchs, who always saw the king's face, and knew all the secrets of the government. One of them was that *minister* who had the office of *reporting* concerning *criminals*, who carried *the book of death* and the *book of life* into the presence of the king, where the names were entered of criminals who were *destined* to *suffer*, and of those who were either considered as *innocent* or *recommended to mercy;* those of the *former* in the *book of death*, those of the *latter* in the *book of life*. This person with the inkhorn might be termed, in our phrase, the *recorder*.

Verse 2. *Stood beside the brazen altar.*] To signify that the people against whom they had their commission were, for their crimes, to be sacrificed to the demands of Divine justice.

Verse 3. *And he called to the man*] The person here who called was that who sat on the chariot of the Divine glory. See chap. i. 26.

Verse 4. *Set a mark upon the foreheads of the men that sigh*] This is in allusion to the ancient every-where-used custom of setting marks on servants and slaves, to distinguish them from others. It was also common for the worshippers of particular idols to have their idol's *mark* upon their *foreheads*, *arms*, &c. These are called *sectarian marks* to the present day among the *Hindoos* and others in India. Hence by this mark we can easily know who is a follower of *Vishnoo*, who of *Siva*, who of *Bramah*, &c. The original words, והתוית תו *vehithvitha tau*, have been translated by the Vulgate, *et signa thau*, "and mark thou tau on the foreheads," &c. St. Jerome and many others have thought that the letter *tau* was that which was ordered to be placed on the foreheads of those mourners; and Jerome says, that this Hebrew letter ת *tau* was formerly written like a *cross*. So then the people were to be *signed with the sign of the cross!* It is certain that on the ancient Samaritan coins, which are yet extant, the letter ת *tau* is in the form +, which is what we term St. *Andrew's cross*. The sense derived from this by many commentators is, that God, having ordered those penitents to be marked with this figure, which is the sign of the cross, intimated that there is no redemption nor saving of life but by the cross of Christ, and that this will avail none but the real penitent. All this is true in itself, but it is not true in respect to this place. The Hebrew words signify literally, *thou shalt make a mark*, or *sign a sign*, but give no intimation what that *mark* or *sign* was. It was intended here to be what the sprinkling of the blood of the paschal lamb on the lintels and door-posts of the Israelites was, namely, a notice to the destroying angel what house he should spare. As the whole of this matter only passed in *vision* we are bound to neither *letter*, nor any other kind of *figure*. The symbolical action teaches us that God, in general judgments, will make a distinction between the *innocent* and the *guilty*, between the *penitent* and the *hardened sinner*.

Verse 6. *Begin at my sanctuary.*] Let those who have sinned against most mercy, and most privileges, be the first victims of justice. Those who know their Lord's will, and do it not, shall be beaten with many stripes. The unfaithful

A. M. 3410
B. C. 594
Ol. XLVI. 3
Anno
Tarquinii Prisci,
R. Roman., 23

and little children, and women: but [o]come not near any man upon whom *is* the mark; and [p]begin at my sanctuary. [q]Then they began at the ancient men which *were* before the house.

7 And he said unto them, Defile the house, and fill the courts with the slain: go ye forth. And they went forth, and slew in the city.

8 And it came to pass, while they were slaying them, and I was left, that I [r]fell upon my face, and cried, and said, [s]Ah Lord GOD! wilt thou destroy all the residue of Israel in thy pouring out of thy fury upon Jerusalem?

9 Then said he unto me, The iniquity of the house of Israel and Judah *is* exceeding great, and [t]the land is [u]full of blood, and the city full of [v]perverseness: for they say, [w]The LORD hath forsaken the earth, and [x]the LORD seeth not.

10 And as for me also, mine [y]eye shall not spare, neither will I have pity, *but* [z]I will recompense their way upon their head.

11 And, behold, the man clothed with linen, which *had* the inkhorn by his side, [a]reported the matter, saying, I have done as thou hast commanded me.

[o]Rev. ix. 4——[p]Jer. xxv. 29; 1 Pet. iv. 17——[q]Chap. viii. 11, 12, 16——[r]Num. xiv. 5; xvi. 4, 22, 45; Josh. vii. 6——[s]Ch. xi. 13——[t]2 Kings xxi. 16; chap. viii. 17

[u]Heb. *filled with*——[v]Or, *wresting* of judgment [w]Ch. viii. 12——[x]Psa. x. 11; Isa. xxix. 15——[y]Ch. v. 11. vii. 4; viii. 18——[z]Ch. xi. 21——[a]Heb. *returned the word*

members of Christ's church will be first visited and most punished. But let not those who belong to the *synagogue of Satan* exult in this; for if judgment begin at the house of God, what will the end be of them who obey not the Gospel! However, the truly *penitent* of all descriptions in such cases shall be safe. The command of God is, "Set a mark on all them that sigh and cry;" and his command to the destroyers is, "Come not near any man on whom is the mark."

Verse 7. *Defile the house*] A dreadful sentence, Let it be polluted, I will no more dwell in it; I now utterly forsake it.

Verse 8. *Wilt thou destroy all the residue of Israel, in thy pouring out of thy fury upon Jerusalem?*] These destroyers had slain the *seventy* elders, the *twenty-five* adorers of the sun, and the women that mourned for Tammuz; and on seeing this slaughter the prophet fell on his face, and began to make intercession.

Verse 9. *For they say, The Lord hath forsaken the earth*] את הארץ *eth haarets,* "this land." He has no more place in Israel; he has quite abandoned it; he neither sees nor cares, and he can be no longer the object of worship to any man in Israel. This seems to be the meaning; and God highly resents it, because it was bringing him on a level with idols and provincial deities, who had, according to supposition, regency only in some one place.

Verse 10. *Mine eye shall not spare*] They say, *the Lord seeth not:* this is false; I have seen all their iniquities, and do see all their abominations; and I will bring deserved judgment upon them, and then that eye which now sees will neither pity nor spare.

Verse 11. *I have done as thou hast commanded me.*] Angels and men must all give account of their conduct to God; for although he is every where, and his eye sees all things, yet they must personally account for all that they have done. *I have done as thou hast commanded me.* The penitents are all signed; the penitents are all safe. This is good news for them that mourn.

CHAPTER X

The same august vision which appeared to the prophet at first, is repeated here; and coals of fire are scattered over the city to intimate that it was to be burned. The symbol of the Divine presence is likewise represented as removing farther and farther from the temple, to signify that God's protection was about to be withdrawn from it, 1–22. It may not be improper to remark, that whatever is particularly intended by the cherubim, wheels, firmament, throne, &c., described in this and the first chapter, the prophet several times informs us (chap. i. 28; iii. 25; viii. 4; x. 4, 18,) *that his vision was a manifestation or similitude of the* GLORY *of Jehovah; or, in other words, consisted of a set of hieroglyphics by which this glory was in some measure represented. It is also worthy of observation, that the faces of the living creatures, of which we have an account in the* fourth *chapter of the Apocalypse, are precisely the same with those of Ezekiel's cherubim; and we may readily collect, as Mr. Mede remarks, the quarter of the heavens in which each cherub was situated in reference to the other three, from the consideration that as Ezekiel saw the vision proceeding from the* NORTH, *(see chap. i. 4, 10,) the human face of the cherubim was towards him, or the* south; *on his right hand, or the* east, *was the face of a lion; on his left hand, or the* west, *the face of an ox; and towards the* north, *the face of an eagle.*

A. M. 3410
B. C. 594
Ol. XLVI. 3
Anno
Tarquinii Prisci,
R. Roman., 23

THEN I looked, and, behold, in the [a]firmament that was above the head of the cherubims there appeared over them as it were a sapphire stone, as the appearance of the likeness of a throne.

2 [b]And he spake unto the man clothed with linen, and said, Go in between the wheels, even under the cherub, and fill [c]thine hand with [d]coals of fire from between the cherubims, and [e]scatter *them* over the city. And he went in my sight.

3 Now the cherubims stood on the right side of the house, when the man went in; and the cloud filled the inner court.

4 [f]Then the glory of the LORD [g]went up from the cherub, *and stood* over the threshold of the house; and [h]the house was filled with the cloud, and the court was full of the brightness of the LORD's glory.

5 And the [i]sound of the cherubims' wings was heard *even* to the outer court, as [k]the voice of the Almighty God when he speaketh.

A. M. 3410
B. C. 594
Ol. XLVI. 3
Anno
Tarquinii Prisci,
R. Roman., 23

6 And it came to pass, *that* when he had commanded the man clothed with linen, saying, Take fire from between the wheels, from between the cherubims; then he went in, and stood beside the wheels.

7 And *one* cherub [l]stretched forth his hand from between the cherubims unto the fire that *was* between the cherubims, and took *thereof,* and put *it* into the hands of *him that was* clothed with linen: who took *it,* and went out.

8 [m]And there appeared in the cherubims the form of a man's hand under their wings.

9 [n]And when I looked, behold the four wheels by the cherubims, one wheel by one cherub, and another wheel by another cherub: and the appearance of the wheels *was* as the colour of a [o]beryl stone.

10 And *as for* their appearances, they four had one likeness, as if a wheel had been in the midst of a wheel.

[a]Ch. i. 22, 26——[b]Ch. ix. 2, 3——[c]Heb. *the hollow of thine hand*——[d]Ch. i. 13——[e]See Rev. viii. 5——[f]See ver. 18; chap. i. 28; ix. 3——[g]Heb. *was lifted up*

[h]1 Kings viii. 10, 11; chap. xliii. 5——[i]Chap. i. 24——[k]Psa. xxix. 3, &c.——[l]Heb. *sent forth*——[m]Chap. i. 8; ver. 21——[n]Chap. i. 15——[o]Chap. i. 16

NOTES ON CHAP. X

Verse 1. *As it were a sapphire stone*] See the note on chap. i. 22, 26. The *chariot,* here mentioned by the prophet, was precisely the same as that which he saw at the river *Chebar,* as himself tells us, ver. 15, of which see the description in chap. i.

Verse 2. *Coals of fire*] These were to signify the burning of the city by the Chaldeans. It seems that the space between the *four* wheels, which was all on fire, was that from which those coals were taken.

Verse 3. *On the right side of the house*] The right hand always marked the *south* among the Hebrews.

Verse 4. *The glory of the Lord went up*] This is repeated from chap. ix. 3.

The house was filled with the cloud] This is a fact similar to what occurred frequently at the *tabernacle* in the wilderness, and in the *dedication of the temple* by Solomon. What is mentioned here was the *Divine shechinah,* the symbolical representation of the majesty of God.

Verse 5. *As the voice of the Almighty God*] That is, as *thunder;* for this was called the *voice of God.*

Verse 8. *The form of a man's hand under their wings.*] I am still of opinion that the *hands* and *wings* were not distinct. The *arms* were *feathered like wings,* and the *hand* terminated the arm; but as the long front feathers of the wings would extend much beyond the fingers, hence the *hands* would appear to *be under the wings.* See on chap. i. 8. The *human hand* might be intended to show that God helps and punishes *man* by *man;* and that, in the general operations of his providence, he makes use of *human agency.*

Verse 9. *The colour of a beryl stone.*] אבן תרשיש *eben Tarshish,* "the stone of Tarshish." The *Vulgate* translates it *chrysolith; Symmachus,* the *jacinct;* the *Septuagint,* the *carbuncle.* In the parallel place, chap. i. 16, it is כעין תרשיש *keeyn Tarshish,* "like the eye of Tarshish;" i. e., the *colour* of tarshish, or the stone so called, which the *Vulgate* translates *visio maris,* "like the sea," i. e., *azure.* The *beryl* is a gem of a *green* colour, passing from one side into *blue,* on the other side into *yellow.* The *chrysolith* is also *green,* what is called *pistachio green;* but the *chrysolith* of the ancients was our *topaz,* which is of a fine *wine yellow.* The *beryl,* or *chrysolith,* is most likely what is here meant by *tarshish.* One name among the ancients served for several kinds of gems that were nearly of the *same colour.* The moderns go more by *chemical characters* than by *colour.*

Verse 10. *A wheel had been in the midst of a wheel.*] It is difficult to comprehend this description. It is generally supposed to mean one wheel within another, cutting each other at right angles. This, in my opinion, will not account for the *motions* attributed to these wheels; nor can I see how, on this supposition, they could have any motion; for if one was moved on its axis, the other must be dragged contrary to its axis. I have conjectured it rather to mean a wheel within a wheel, or a wheel with two rims, working on the same axis. See on chap. i. 16-18. It is however no matter of *faith;* and the reader may judge as he thinks proper. For other matters relative to this *chariot, wheels, cherubim, wings,* &c., I

A. M. 3410
B. C. 594
Ol. XLVI. 3
Anno
Tarquinii Prisci,
R. Roman., 23

11 [p]When they went, they went upon their four sides; they turned not as they went, but to the place whither the head looked they followed it; they turned not as they went.

12 And their whole [q]body, and their backs, and their hands, and their wings, and [r]the wheels, *were* full of eyes round about, *even* the wheels that they four had.

13 As for the wheels, [s]it was cried unto them in my hearing, O wheel.

14 [t]And every one had four faces: the first face *was* the face of a cherub, and the second face *was* the face of a man, and the third the face of a lion, and the fourth the face of an eagle.

15 And the cherubims were lifted up. This *is* [u]the living creature that I saw by the river of Chebar.

16 [v]And when the cherubims went, the wheels went by them: and when the cherubims lifted up their wings to mount up from the earth, the same wheels also turned not from beside them.

17 [w]When they stood, *these* stood; and when they were lifted up, *these* lifted up themselves *also:* for the spirit [x]of the living creature *was* in them.

A. M. 3410
B. C. 594
Ol. XLVI. 3
Anno
Tarquinii Prisci,
R. Roman., 23

18 Then [y]the glory of the LORD [z]departed from off the threshold of the house, and stood over the cherubims.

19 And [a]the cherubims lifted up their wings, and mounted up from the earth in my sight: when they went out, the wheels also *were* beside them, and *every one* stood at the door of the east gate of the LORD's house; and the glory of the God of Israel was over them above.

20 [b]This *is* the living creature that I saw under the God of Israel [c]by the river of Chebar; and I knew that they *were* the cherubims.

21 [d]Every one had four faces apiece, and every one four wings; [e]and the likeness of the hands of a man *was* under their wings.

22 And [f]the likeness of their faces *was* the same faces which I saw by the river of Chebar, their appearances and themselves: [g]they went every one straight forward.

[p]Ch. i. 17——[q]Heb. *flesh*——[r]Ch. i. 18——[s]Or, *they were called in my hearing, wheel,* or, *galgal*——[t]Ch. i. 6, 10——[u]Ch. i. 5——[v]Ch. i. 19——[w]Ch. i. 12, 20, 21

[x]Or, *of life*——[y]Ver. 4——[z]Hos. ix. 12——[a]Ch. xi. 22
[b]Ch. i. 22; ver. 15——[c]Ch. i. 1——[d]Ch. i. 6; ver. 14
[e]Chap. i. 8; ver. 8——[f]Chap. i. 10——[g]Chap. i. 12

must refer to the notes on the *first* chapter. And perhaps from the whole of this vision and its difficulties, he will see the propriety of the council of rabbins ordering Rabbi Ananias *three hundred* barrels of oil to light his lamp during the time it would be necessary for him to employ in explaining this one vision.

Verse 13. *As for the wheels, it was cried unto them—O wheel.*] Never was there a more unfortunate and unmeaning translation. The word הגלגל *haggalgal*, may signify, simply, *the roller*, or *a chariot*, or *roll on*, or *the swift roller.* **And he clepide ilke wheelis volible, or turninge about.** Old MS. Bible. Any of these will do: "and as to the wheels," לאופנים *laophannim*, "they were called in my hearing" הגלגל *haggalgal*, "the chariot." The gentleman who took for his text "O wheel!" and made God's decree of eternal predestination out of it, must have borrowed some of Rabbi Ananias's *three hundred* barrels of oil! But such working of God's word cannot be too severely reprehended.

As these wheels are supposed to represent Divine *Providence*, bringing about the *designs* of the Most High, how like is the above הגלגל *haggalgal*, taken as a verb, "roll on," to those words of Virgil in his Pollio:—

Talia sæcla, suis dixerunt, *currite*, fusis,
Concordes stabili fatorum numine Parcæ.

"The Fates, when they this happy web have spun,
Shall bless the sacred clue, and bid it *swiftly run.*"

Verse 14. *The first—*was *the face of a cherub*] In chap. i. 10, this is called the "face of an ox;" here, the "face of a cherub:" hence, a *cherub* was in the likeness of an *ox*, at least, as to its *head.* כרוב *kerub* never occurs as a verb; and its meaning cannot be precisely ascertained. *Parkhurst* thinks the כ *caph* to be here the note of *similitude;* and then translates כ *ke*, "like," רב *rab* or רוב *rob*, "the mighty one;" and, in consequence, makes the *cherubim* an emblem of the *Holy Trinity.* See his *lengthy* Dissertation under כרב in his Hebrew and English Lexicon.

Verse 20. *And I knew that they* were *the cherubims.*] This formation of the plural is quite improper. In general, Hebrew nouns of the masculine gender end in ים *im*, in the plural; the *s*, therefore, should never be added to such. *Cherub* is singular; *cherubim* is plural. The *s* should be uniformly expunged.

I have already referred to the *end of this chapter* for farther information relative to this glorious chariot of Jehovah; but I must say that I have met with nothing on the subject that entirely satisfies myself. In the preceding notes I have endeavoured to make the literal meaning as plain as possible; and have occasionally given some intimations relative to the *general design* of this sublime vision. My readers are already apprised that I do not like *conjectures* on *Divine things;* many points, that had originally no other origin, are now incorporated with *creeds* of which it is deemed sinful to doubt. Because some learned and pious men have written to prove that this symbolical compound figure is a representation of the *Holy Trinity;* therefore, the sentiment now passes current. Now this is not *proved;* and I suppose never can be proved. The continuator of the *Historical Discourses of Saurin* has made some sensible remarks on the subject of this vision; and these I shall lay here before the intelligent reader. They deserve attention.

THIS intelligent writer observes: "For the right interpretation of this vision, the following rules should be laid down:—

"The *first* rule is this:—An explanation, which accounts for all the parts contained in the vision, is much more probable than those which explain only one part.

"The *second* is this:—An explanation which is conformable to the present circumstances of the prophet, and of the people to whom he is sent, as well as to the nature of the things which he is called upon to say to them, is incomparably more probable than those explanations which go in quest of past or future events, which have no connexion with the immediate circumstances of the prophet, nor with the end of his mission. These rules, which appear incontestable, being laid down, we observe, that their opinion who think that God here draws out a plan of the government of his providence, applied to the present state of the Jews, accounts for all that Ezekiel saw; and that in a manner which refers to the end of the prophet's mission, and all that he had to say to this rebellious people. Why wish God to represent to his prophet the future state of the Christian Church, which was not to be founded till after a series of time, rather than the state of the Jewish Church, and the chastisements which hung over the heads of that hardened people? The people having revolted from God, and persevering obstinately in that revolt, notwithstanding the menaces of the prophet, it was proper to show to Ezekiel, in order that he might declare it to the rebellious, that Providence had its eyes open to all that had been done, all that had hitherto happened, and that it had seized upon the rod to smite. The people imagined, but too much according to the errors of infidelity, that God saw every thing with indifference and had given the world up to chance. It was necessary, therefore, to divest them of these fatal prejudices; and to teach them that the Supreme Being did not behold with the same eye order and disorder, contempt of his laws and submission to his will; and that all the revolutions of states are directed by a superior intelligence, which cannot be imposed upon. The Jewish people imagined but too much that the prophets exaggerated when they threatened them with the severest chastisements. They repeated with emphasis and complacency the promises of God made to the patriarchs; that their posterity should not only be more numerous than the stars of heaven, and the sand which covers the sea-shore; but that it should subsist for ever and ever. God had declared to Abraham, 'I will establish my covenant between me and thee, and thy seed after thee, in their generations, for an everlasting covenant, to be a God unto thee and thy seed after thee,' Gen. xvii. 7. It was proper, therefore, to show this stiff-necked people that the threatenings of God and his promises were not contradictory. That the people, conformable to the promises given by God to the patriarchs, should not be destroyed; but that, notwithstanding, they should be severely chastised, to correct them for their propensity to idolatry, and their scandalous irregularities.

"These suppositions, which are reasonable, being granted, we shall have no difficulty to perceive the sense of this celebrated vision. We shall not follow the order observed by Ezekiel, in the description of what he saw; he raises himself from the nearest to the most distant objects, going back from effects to their general cause. We will begin with the First Cause which gives motion to all that happens, traces out the plan, and procures the execution, according to the rules of his ineffable wisdom, and agreeably to the nature of those creatures which are the object of his agency. Next, we will proceed to consider the effects of this universal Providence, and the intelligent secondary causes which he frequently employs in the administration of the government of the universe.

" 'Ezekiel saw a firmament which was above the heads of the animals; there was the resemblance of a throne like a sapphire stone; and over the resemblance of the throne, there was, as it were, the resemblance of a man.' This vast transparent *firmament* represents to us the heaven, the peculiar residence of the Lord of the earth; and where he hath established the throne of his empire. This 'appearance of a man' was the emblem of Providence or God; considered as taking care of all the creatures whom he hath made. Man is the symbol of intelligence. The mind of man, with respect to his knowledge and wisdom, is a weak sketch of that mind which knows all things, and whose wisdom is unbounded. And yet, of all sublunary beings, there is none that approaches so near to the Divine nature as man. Under this emblem also it is that God, considered as seeing all things, and directing all, would be represented. This resemblance of man was *seated* upon a *throne*, to show that God governs all things as Lord, and that without agitation and without labour.

"The *shining metal*, and the *fire* which surrounded him who sat on the throne, were the symbol of his glory and his judgments, which are poured upon the wicked as a fire which nothing can withstand; agreeably to Isaiah, chap. xxxiii. 14.

"The Jews acknowledged that there was a Providence which governs the whole universe with infinite wisdom. The psalmist gives us a description of it, equally just and pathetic, in Psa. civ. 27, &c. Christians, no less than Jews, admit this important truth; and the Gospel establishes it no less strongly than the law. See Matt. vi. 26; x. 29, 30. To raise the mind of the prophet up to the first Mover of those events which strike and admonish us in all the revolutions which happen to individuals, families, and states, God shows him *four wheels* above the firmament, over which the emblem of Providence was placed on a throne. These wheels are a symbol of those perpetual revolutions, which are observed in the earth; and which, by turns, lift up and abase individuals and nations. They are of a prodigious *height*, to show that man cannot fathom or know all that is great, wonderful, and astonishing, in the ways of Providence. See Job xi. 7, 8; Rom. xi.

33, 34; Isa. lv. 8, 9. These wheels move themselves every way, and are full of eyes in the vast circle of their felloes. This shows, that all which God does he effects without pain; and that the eye of his wisdom ordereth all events. The wheels did not move of themselves; but they followed the impulse of the four living creatures; 'when the living creatures went, they went.' This shows that, in the government of the world, all the living creatures are subject to Providence; and that God subordinates the creatures one to another. He directs what those holy intelligences ought to do, who serve him as ministers, and are here represented by the four animals. And these intelligences, enlightened and supported by the Supreme Wisdom, contribute, as far as is suitable, to all that happens to mankind. The angels whom Ezekiel saw were in number *four*, in reference to the *four* cardinal points of the world; to show that their ministry extends every where, and that there is no part of the universe which the Providence of God does not govern in an immediate manner, or by the means of his ministers. The extraordinary shape of these angels, which appeared to the prophet in vision, is symbolical; for it is not to be supposed that those heavenly ministers are really thus formed. The 'four faces, wings, and arms of a man,' denote the sublime qualities of these immediate ministers of the Deity; qualities entirely essential to fill up the extent of their duty. The face of a *man* denotes their intelligence; of a *lion*, their intrepid courage; of an *ox*, their patience and perseverance in labour; and of an *eagle*, their great penetration, their sublime sight into heavenly things, and their readiness to rise up into all that is great and Divine. The 'wings being stretched out,' signifies that they are always ready to set forward, and run with rapidity wherever the commands of their great Master call them. The 'wings bent down,' are a symbol of that profound respect in which these heavenly ministers stand before the Lord of the universe. Under the wings there were men's arms, to show that zeal produces application and labour. Labour, without zeal, can never be supported; and zeal, without application, is only a hypocritical ardour, which amounts to nothing with that supreme Master who requires sincere homage from those who serve him. If God chose to make known to Ezekiel that his providence extends to all things, and that even in this life it often takes up the rod to chastise nations and individuals, he would also show beforehand that he wished not the destruction of the Jewish people, whom he was about to visit in his anger, but only its correction and amendment. This is signified by the 'precious metal,' which the prophet found unmelted in the midst of the fiery cloud. This cloud of fire, urged on by a whirlwind, and involving on all sides the metal, represented the judgments of God which were about to fall upon this rebellious nation, not to destroy, but to humble and purify it. Nothing is more proper than afflictions to bring men back to their duty. As fire purifies metals, so the paternal chastisements of God have a tendency to purify the soul and heart, if the man be not entirely incorrigible. The people upon whom God was about to pour the vials of his anger, were not worthy of his lenity. But that great God, who is firm in his promises, remembers the covenant of peace he had made with the patriarchs. This covenant is made sensible to the prophet under the image of a *rainbow*, which was round about him who appeared upon the throne. Every one knows, that this splendid phenomenon, which seems to join heaven and earth together, was given to Noah and his posterity as a symbol of the covenant which God then made with mankind, and by which he declared to them that the earth should undergo a deluge no more. Thus, the Pagans considered the *Iris* as the messenger of the gods. See *Virgil*, *Æn.* lib. iv. ver. 694. But whereas the rainbow to the Jews was a symbol of peace, the *Iris* of the Pagans was a messenger of trouble. On the sight of this bow, the symbol of grace, Ezekiel was to be encouraged; and persuaded that his people were not threatened with an utter destruction. The event fully justified all that the prophet had contemplated, with surprise, in this enigmatical picture. The Chaldeans, the rod of the Lord's just severity, ravaged Judea; the people were carried away captive; they groaned for *seventy* years in a foreign land; but they were protected in a miraculous manner against the bloody designs of the cruel Haman; and at length, favoured with various decrees of the kings of Persia, they had permission, not only to return to their own country, but also to rebuild Jerusalem and the temple." See Dr. *Dodd's* notes on this place.

CHAPTER XI

This chapter denounces the judgments of God against those wicked persons who remained in Jerusalem, and made a mock of the types and predictions of the prophets, 1–13; *compare* ver. 3 *with* Jer. i. 13. *God promises to favour those who were gone into captivity, and intimates their restoration from the Babylonish yoke*, 14–21. *Then the shechinah, or symbol of the Divine Presence, is represented forsaking the city, as in the foregoing chapter it did the temple*, 22, 23; *and the prophet returns in vision to the place from which he set out*, (chap. viii. 1, &c.,) *in order to communicate his instructions to his brethren of the captivity*, 24, 25.

A. M. 3410
B. C. 594
Ol. XLVI. 3
Anno
Tarquinii Prisci,
R. Roman., 23

MOREOVER [a]the spirit lifted me up, and brought me unto [b]the east gate of the LORD's house, which looketh eastward: and behold [c]at the door of the gate five and

[a]Chap. iii. 12, 14; viii. 3; ver. 24 — [b]Chap. x. 19 — [c]See chap. viii. 16

NOTES ON CHAP. XI

Verse 1. *At the door of the gate five and twenty men*] The same persons, no doubt, who appear, chap. viii. 16, worshipping the sun.

Jaazaniah the son of Azur] In chap. viii. 16, we find a *Jaazaniah* the son of *Shaphan*. If *Shaphan* was also called *Azur*, they may be the same person. But it is most likely that

A. M. 3410
B. C. 594
Ol. XLVI. 3
Anno
Tarquinii Prisci,
R. Roman., 23

twenty men; among whom I
saw Jaazaniah the son of
Azur, and Pelatiah the son of
Benaiah, princes of the people.
2 Then said he unto me, Son of man, these
are the men that devise mischief, and give
wicked counsel in this city:
3 Which say, [d]*It is* not [e]near; let us build
houses: [f]this *city is* the caldron, and we *be*
the flesh.
4 Therefore prophesy against them, prophesy, O son of man.
5 And [g]the Spirit of the LORD fell upon me,
and said unto me, Speak; Thus saith the
LORD; Thus have ye said, O house of Israel:
for I know the things that come into your
mind, *every one of* them.
6 [h]Ye have multiplied your slain in this
city, and ye have filled the streets thereof
with the slain.
7 Therefore thus saith the Lord GOD; [i]Your
slain whom ye have laid in the midst of it,
they *are* the flesh, and this *city is* the caldron:
[k]but I will bring you forth out of the midst
of it.
8 Ye have feared the sword, and I will bring
a sword upon you, saith the Lord GOD.
9 And I will bring you out of the midst
thereof, and deliver you into the hands of
strangers, and [l]will execute judgments among
you.
10 [m]Ye shall fall by the sword; I will judge
you in [n]the border of Israel;
[o]and ye shall know that I *am*
the LORD.
11 [p]This *city* shall not be
your caldron, neither shall ye be the flesh in
the midst thereof; *but* I will judge you in the
border of Israel:
12 And [q]ye shall know that I *am* the LORD:
[r]for ye have not walked in my statutes, neither executed my judgments, but [s]have done
after the manners of the heathen that *are*
round about you.
13 And it came to pass, when I prophesied,
that [t]Pelatiah the son of Benaiah died. Then
[u]fell I down upon my face, and cried with a
loud voice, and said, Ah, Lord GOD! wilt thou
make a full end of the remnant of Israel?
14 Again the word of the LORD came unto
me, saying,
15 Son of man, thy brethren, *even* thy
brethren, the men of thy kindred, and all the
house of Israel wholly, *are* they unto whom
the inhabitants of Jerusalem have said, Get
you far from the LORD: unto us is this land
given in possession.
16 Therefore say, Thus saith the Lord GOD;
Although I have cast them far off among the
heathen, and although I have scattered them
among the countries, [v]yet will I be to them
as a little sanctuary in the countries where
they shall come.
17 Therefore say, Thus saith the Lord

A. M. 3410
B. C. 594
Ol. XLVI. 3
Anno
Tarquinii Prisci,
R. Roman., 23

[d]Or, It is *not* for us *to build houses near*——[e]Ch. xii. 22, 27; 2 Pet. iii. 4——[f]See Jer. i. 13; ch. xxiv. 3, &c. [g]Ch. ii. 2; iii. 24——[h]Ch. vii. 23; xxii. 3, 4——[i]Ch. xxiv. 3, 6, 10, 11; Mic. iii. 3——[k]Ver. 9——[l]Ch. v. 8——[m]2 Kings xxv. 19, 20, 21; Jer. xxxix. 6; lii. 10

[n]1 Kings viii. 65; 2 Kings xiv. 25——[o]Psa. ix. 16; ch. vi. 7; xiii. 9, 14, 21, 23——[p]See ver. 3——[q]Ver. 10 [r]Or, *which have not walked*——[s]Lev. xviii. 3, 24, &c.; Deut. xii. 30, 31; ch. viii. 10, 14, 16——[t]Ver. 1; Acts v. 5 [u]Chap. ix. 8——[v]Psa. xc. 1; xci. 9; Isa. viii. 14

there were two of this name, and both chiefs among the people.

Verse 3. It is *not near*] That is, the threatened invasion.

This city is *the caldron, and we* be *the flesh.*] See the vision of the *seething pot,* Jer. i. 13. These infidels seem to say: "We will run all risks, we will abide in the city. Though it be the *caldron,* and we the *flesh,* yet we will share its fate: if it perish, we will perish with it." Or they may allude to the above prediction of Jeremiah, in order to ridicule it: "We were to have been *boiled* long ago: but the fulfilment of that prediction is not near yet."

Verse 7. *Your slain—they* are *the flesh*] Jerusalem is the *caldron,* and those who have been slain in it, they are the flesh; and though ye purpose to stay and share its fate, ye shall not be permitted to do so; ye shall be carried into captivity.

Verse 9. *And deliver you into the hands of strangers*] This seems to refer chiefly to Zedekiah and his family.

Verse 11. *I will judge you in the border of Israel.*] Though *Riblah* was in Syria, yet it was on the very *frontiers* of Israel; and it was here that Zedekiah's sons were slain, and his own eyes put out.

Verse 13. *Pelatiah the son of Benaiah died.*] Most probably he was struck dead the very hour in which Ezekiel prophesied against him. His death appears to have resembled that of Ananias and Sapphira, Acts v. 1, &c.

Verse 15. *Get you far from the Lord*] These are the words of the inhabitants of Jerusalem, against those of Israel who had been carried away to Babylon with Jeconiah. *Go ye far from the Lord:* but as for us, the land of Israel is given to us for a possession; *we* shall never be removed from it, and *they* shall never return to it.

Verse 16. *Yet will I be to them as a little*

A. M. 3410
B. C. 594
Ol. XLVI. 3
Anno
Tarquinii Prisci,
R. Roman., 23

GOD; I will even gather you
from the people, and assemble
you out of the countries where
ye have been scattered, and I
will give you the land of Israel.

18 And they shall come thither, and [x]they
shall take away all the detestable things
thereof and all the abominations thereof from
thence.

19 And [y]I will give them one heart, and I
will put [z]a new spirit within you; and I will
take [a]the stony heart out of their flesh, and
will give them a heart of flesh:

20 [b]That they may walk in my statutes,
and keep mine ordinances, and do them:
[c]and they shall be my people, and I will be
their God.

21 But *as for them* whose heart walketh
after the heart of their detestable things and their abominations, [d]I will recompense their way upon their own heads, saith the Lord GOD.

22 Then did the cherubims [e]lift up their
wings, and the wheels beside them; and the
glory of the God of Israel *was* over them above.

23 And [f]the glory of the LORD went up
from the midst of the city, and stood [g]upon
the mountain [h]which *is* on the east side of
the city.

24 Afterwards [i]the spirit took me up, and
brought me in a vision by the Spirit of God
into Chaldea, to them of the captivity. So
the vision that I had seen went up from me.

25 Then I spake unto them of the captivity
all the things that the LORD had showed me.

---

[w]Jer. xxiv. 5; chap. xxviii. 25; xxxiv. 13; xxxvi. 24 —— [x]Chap. xxxvii. 23 —— [y]Jer. xxxii. 39; chap. xxxvi. 26, 27; see Zeph. iii. 9 —— [z]Psa. li. 10; Jer. xxxi. 33; xxxii. 39; chap. xviii. 31 —— [a]Zech. vii. 12

[b]Psa. cv. 45 —— [c]Jer. xxiv. 7; ch. xiv. 11; xxxvi. 28; xxxvii. 27 —— [d]Chap. ix. 10; xxii. 31 —— [e]Chap. i. 19; x. 19 —— [f]Chap. viii. 4; ix. 3; x. 4, 18; xliii. 4 —— [g]See Zech. xiv. 4 —— [h]Chap. xliii. 2 —— [i]Chap. viii. 3

---

sanctuary] Though thus exiled from their own land, yet not forgotten by their God. While in their captivity, I will dispense many blessings to them; and I will restore them to their own land, ver. 17, from which they shall put away all idolatry, ver. 18.

Verse 19. *And I will give them one heart*] A whole system of *renewed affections*.

And I will put a new spirit within you] To direct and influence these new affections.

And I will take the stony heart out of their flesh] That which would not receive the impressions of my Spirit.

And will give them a heart of flesh] One that is capable of receiving and retaining these impressions.

Verse 20. *That they may walk in my statutes*] The holiness of their lives shall prove the work of God upon their hearts. Then it shall appear that *I am their God*, because I have done such things *in* them and *for* them; and their *holy conduct* shall show that they are *my people*. See on chap. xxxvi. 25, &c.

Verse 21. *But* as for them *whose heart walketh*] Them whose affections are attached to idolatry, they shall have such reward as their idols can give them, and such a recompense as Divine justice shall award them.

Verse 23. *The glory of the Lord went up from the midst of the city*] This vision is no mean proof of the *long-suffering of God*. He did not abandon this people *all at once;* he departed by *little and little*. FIRST, he left the *temple*. SECONDLY, he stopped a little at the gate of the city. THIRDLY, he departed entirely from the city and went to the *Mount of Olives*, which lay on the *east* side of the city. Having tarried there for some time to see if they would repent and turn to him,—FOURTHLY, he departed to *heaven*. The vision being now concluded, the prophet is taken away by the Spirit of God into Chaldea, and there announces to the captive Israelites what God had showed him in the preceding visions, and the good that he had spoken concerning them; who at first did not seem to profit much by them, which the prophet severely reproves.

CHAPTER XII

The prophet proceeds, by a variety of types and parables, to convince those of the captivity that their brethren who were left behind to sustain the miseries of a siege and the insults of a conqueror, would be in a much worse condition than they who were already settled in a foreign land. In the beginning of this chapter he foretells the approaching captivity of Judah by action instead of words, 1–7. He predicts particularly the flight, capture, captivity, and sufferings of Zedekiah and his followers, 8–16, compared with Jer. lii. 11. *He is to eat his food with trembling and signs of terror, as an emblem of the consternation of the Jews when surrounded by their enemies, 17–20; and then he answers the objections and bywords of scoffers and infidels, who either disbelieved his threatenings, or supposed the accomplishment of them very distant, 21–28. Josephus* (Antiq. xi. 10) *tells us that Zedekiah thought the prophecy of Ezekiel in the* thirteenth *verse inconsistent with that of Jeremiah,* (chap. xxxiv. 3,) *and resolved to believe neither. Both, however, were literally fulfilled; and the event convinced him that they were not irreconcilable. Thus, blinded by infidelity, sinners rush on to that destruction against which they are sufficiently warned.*

A. M. 3410
B. C. 594
Ol. XLVI. 3
Anno
Tarquinii Prisci,
R. Roman., 23

THE word of the LORD also came unto me, saying,

2 Son of man, thou dwellest in the midst of [a]a rebellious house, which [b]have eyes to see, and see not; they have ears to hear, and hear not: [c]for they *are* a rebellious house.

3 Therefore, thou son of man, prepare thee [d]stuff for removing, and remove by day in their sight; and thou shalt remove from thy place to another place in their sight: it may be they will consider, though they *be* a rebellious house.

4 Then shalt thou bring forth thy stuff by day in their sight, as stuff for removing: and thou shalt go forth at even in their sight, [e]as they that go forth into captivity.

5 [f]Dig thou through the wall in their sight, and carry out thereby.

6 In their sight shalt thou bear *it* upon *thy* shoulders, *and* carry *it* forth in the twilight: thou shalt cover thy face, that thou see not the ground: [g]for I have set thee *for* a sign unto the house of Israel.

7 And I did so as I was commanded: I brought forth my stuff by day, as stuff for captivity, and in the even I [h]digged through the wall with mine hand; I brought *it* forth in the twilight, *and* I bare *it* upon *my* shoulder in their sight.

A. M. 3410
B. C. 594
Ol. XLVI. 3
Anno
Tarquinii Prisci,
R. Roman., 23

8 And in the morning came the word of the LORD unto me, saying,

9 Son of man, hath not the house of Israel, [i]the rebellious house, said unto thee, [k]What doest thou?

10 Say thou unto them, Thus saith the Lord GOD; This [l]burden *concerneth* the prince in Jerusalem, and all the house of Israel that *are* among them.

11 Say, [m]I *am* your sign: like as I have done, so shall it be done unto them: [n]they[o] shall remove *and* go into captivity.

12 And [p]the prince that *is* among them shall bear upon *his* shoulder in the twilight, and shall go forth; they shall dig through the wall to carry out thereby: he shall cover his face, that he see not the ground with *his* eyes.

13 My [q]net also will I spread upon him, and he shall be taken in my snare: and [r]I will bring him to Babylon *to* the land of the Chaldeans; yet shall he not see it, though he shall die there.

14 And [s]I will scatter toward every wind all that *are* about him to help him, and all his bands; and [t]I will draw out the sword after them.

15 [u]And they shall know that I *am* the LORD, when I shall scatter them among the nations, and disperse them in the countries.

[a]Chap. ii. 3, 6, 7, 8; iii. 26, 27——[b]Isa. vi. 9; xlii. 20; Jer. v. 21; Matt. xiii. 13, 14——[c]Chap. ii. 5——[d]Or, *instruments*——[e]Heb. *as the goings forth of captivity* [f]Heb. *Dig for thee*——[g]Isa. viii. 18; chap. iv. 3; xxiv. 24; ver. 11——[h]Heb. *digged for me*——[i]Chap. ii. 5——[k]Ch. xvii. 12; xxiv. 19——[l]Mal. i. 1

[m]Ver. 6——[n]Heb. *by removing go into captivity*——[o]2 Kings xxv. 4, 5, 7——[p]Jer. xxxix. 4——[q]Job xix. 6; Lam. i. 13; Jer. lii. 9; chap. xvii. 20——[r]2 Kings xxv. 7; Jer. lii. 11; chap. xvii. 16——[s]2 Kings xxv. 4, 5; chap. v. 10——[t]Chap. v. 2, 12——[u]Psa. ix. 16; chap. vi. 7, 14; xi. 10; ver. 16, 20

NOTES ON CHAP. XII

Verse 2. *Which have eyes to see, and see not*] It is not want of *grace* that brings them to destruction. *They have eyes to see*, but they will not *use* them. No man is lost because he had not *sufficient grace to save him*, but because he abused that grace.

Verse 3. *Prepare thee stuff for removing*] Get carriages to transport thy goods to another place; signifying by this the *captivity* that was at hand.

Verse 5. *Dig thou through the wall*] This refers to the manner in which Zedekiah and his family would escape from the city. They escaped by night through a *breach in the wall.* See Jer. xxxix. 2-4; and 2 Kings xxv. 4.

Verse 6. *Thou shalt cover thy face, that thou see not the ground*] Referring to the blinding of Zedekiah: even the *covering of the face* might be intended to signify that in this way Zedekiah should be carried to Babylon *on men's shoulders* in some sort of *palanquin*, with a *cloth tied over his eyes*, because of the recent wounds made by extracting them. All the prophecies from this to the *twentieth* chapter are supposed to have been delivered in the *sixth* year of Zedekiah, *five* years before the taking of Jerusalem. How accurate the prediction! and how exactly fulfilled!

Verse 10. *This burden*] This prediction concerning the *prince*. By this I point out the capture, misery, and ruin of *Zedekiah.*

Verse 13. *I will bring him to Babylon—yet shall he not see it*] Because Nebuchadnezzar caused him to have his eyes put out at *Riblah*. To Babylon he was carried in his blind state, and there he died. In saying, *My net also will I spread upon him*, there is probably a reference to an ancient manner of fighting. One, who was called the *retiarius*, had a small casting net, which if he could throw over his antagonist's head, he then despatched him with his sword; if he missed his throw, he was obliged to run in order to get his net once more adjusted for another throw. In the mean time the other pursued him with all his speed to prevent this, and to despatch *him;* hence he

A. M. 3410
B. C. 594
Ol. XLVI. 3
Anno
Tarquinii Prisci,
R. Roman., 23

16 [v]But I will leave [w]a few
men of them from the sword,
from the famine, and from the
pestilence; that they may declare all their abominations among the
heathen whither they come; and they shall
know that I *am* the LORD.
17 Moreover the word of the LORD came to
me, saying,
18 Son of man, [x]eat thy bread with quaking, and drink thy water with trembling and
with carefulness;
19 And say unto the people of the land,
Thus saith the Lord GOD of the inhabitants
of Jerusalem, *and* of the land of Israel; They
shall eat their bread with carefulness, and
drink their water with astonishment, that her
land may [y]be desolate from [z]all that is therein,
[a]because of the violence of all them that dwell
therein.
20 And the cities that are inhabited shall be
laid waste, and the land shall be desolate;
and ye shall know that I *am* the LORD.
21 And the word of the LORD came unto me,
saying,
22 Son of man, what *is* that proverb *that*
ye have in the land of Israel, saying, [b]The
days are prolonged, and every
vision faileth?
23 Tell them, therefore,
Thus saith the Lord GOD; I
will make this proverb to cease, and they shall
no more use it as a proverb in Israel; but say
unto them, [c]The days are at hand, and the
effect of every vision.
24 For [d]there shall be no more any [e]vain
vision nor flattering divination within the
house of Israel.
25 For I *am* the LORD: I will speak, and
[f]the word that I shall speak shall come to
pass; it shall be no more prolonged: for in
your days, O rebellious house, will I say the
word, and will perform it, saith the Lord GOD.
26 Again the word of the LORD came to
me, saying,
27 [g]Son of man, behold, *they of* the house
of Israel say, The vision that he seeth *is* [h]for
many days *to come,* and he prophesieth of the
times *that are* far off.
28 [i]Therefore say unto them, Thus saith
the Lord GOD; There shall none of my words
be prolonged any more, but the word which
I have spoken shall be done, saith the Lord
GOD.

[v]Ch. vi. 8, 9, 10——[w]Heb. *men of number*——[x]Ch. iv. 16——[y]Zech. vii. 14——[z]Heb. *the fulness thereof*——[a]Psa. cvii. 34——[b]Ver. 27; chap. xi. 3; Amos vi. 3; 2 Pet. iii. 4

[c]Joel ii. 1——Zeph. i. 14——[d]Chapter xiii. 23——[e]Lam. ii. 14——[f]Isaiah lv. 11; ver. 28; Daniel ix. 12; Luke xxi. 33——[g]Ver. 22——[h]2 Peter iii. 4——[i]Ver. 23, 25

was called *secutor:* the *first* the *netman,* the *second* the *pursuer.*

Verse 18. *Eat thy bread with quaking*] Assume the manner of a person who is every moment afraid of his life, who has nothing but a morsel of bread to eat, and a little water to drink. Thus signifying the *siege,* and the *straits* to which they should be reduced. See this explained, ver. 19.

Verse 22. *The days are prolonged, and every vision faileth?*] These are the words of the infidels and scoffers, who, because vengeance was not speedily executed on an evil work, set their heart to do iniquity. "These predictions either will not come in our days, or will wholly fail; why then should *we* disquiet ourselves about them?" Strange, that the very means used by the most gracious God to bring sinners to repentance, should be made by them the very instruments of their own destruction! See 2 Pet. iii. 4.

Verse 23. *The days are at hand*] Far from *failing* or being *prolonged,* time is posting on, and the destruction threatened is at the door.

Verse 25. *In your days—will I say the word, and will perform it*] Even these mockers shall *live* to see and *feel* this desolation. This is more particularly intimated in the following verses.

Verse 28. *There shall none of my words be prolonged any more*] He had waited to be gracious; they abused his mercy; and at last the protracted wrath rushed upon them with irresistible force.

CHAPTER XIII

This chapter denounces heavy judgments against the lying prophets who flattered the people, in the midst of their sin and danger, with false hopes of peace and security, 19. *The work of these deceivers is beautifully compared to a frail and insufficient piece of building, which can never stand against the battering elements of heaven, (the Chaldean forces,) which God will commission against it,* 10–16. *In the remaining part of the chapter woes are denounced against false prophetesses who practised vain rites and divinations, with the view of promoting their own gain by deceiving the people,* 17–23.

A. M. 3410
B. C. 594
Ol. XLVI. 3
Anno
Tarquinii Prisci,
R. Roman., 23

AND the word of the LORD
came unto me, saying,
2 Son of man, prophesy
against the prophets of Israel
that prophesy, and say thou unto [a]them [b]that
prophesy out of their own [c]hearts, Hear ye
the word of the LORD;
3 Thus saith the Lord GOD; Wo unto the
foolish prophets, that [d]follow their own spirit,
[e]and have seen nothing!
4 O Israel, thy prophets are [f]like the foxes
in the deserts.
5 Ye [g]have not gone up into the [h]gaps,
neither [i]made up the hedge for the house of
Israel to stand in the battle in the day of the
LORD.
6 [k]They have seen vanity and lying divination, saying, The LORD saith: and the LORD
hath not sent them: and they have made
others to hope that they would confirm the
word.
7 Have ye not seen a vain vision, and have
ye not spoken a lying divination, whereas ye
say, The LORD saith *it;* albeit I have not
spoken?
8 Therefore thus saith the
Lord GOD; Because ye have
spoken vanity, and seen lies,
therefore, behold, I *am* against
you, saith the Lord GOD.
9 And mine hand shall be upon the prophets
that see vanity, and that divine lies: they
shall not be in the [l]assembly of my people,
[m]neither shall they be written in the writing
of the house of Israel, [n]neither shall they enter
into the land of Israel; [o]and ye shall know that
I *am* the Lord GOD.
10 Because, even because they have seduced
my people, saying, [p]Peace; and *there was*
no peace; and one built up [q]a wall, and, lo,
others [r]daubed it with untempered *mortar:*
11 Say unto them which daub *it* with untempered *mortar,* that it shall fall: [s]there
shall be an overflowing shower; and ye, O
great hailstones, shall fall; and a stormy wind
shall rend *it.*
12 Lo, when the wall is fallen, shall it not
be said unto you, Where *is* the daubing wherewith ye have daubed *it?*
13 Therefore thus saith the Lord GOD; I

A. M. 3410
B. C. 594
Ol. XLVI. 3
Anno
Tarquinii Prisci,
R. Roman., 23

[a]Ver. 17——[b]Heb. *them that are prophets out of their own hearts*——[c]Jer. xiv. 14; xxiii. 16, 26——[d]Heb. *walk after*——[e]Or, *and* things which *they have not seen* [f]Cant. ii. 15——[g]Psa. cvi. 23, 30; ch. xxii. 30——[h]Or, *breaches*——[i]Heb. *hedged the hedge*

[k]Ver. 23; chap. xii. 24; xxii. 28——[l]Or, *secret,* or *council*——[m]Ezra ii. 59, 62; Neh. vii. 5; Psa. lxix. 28 [n]Chap. xx. 38——[o]Chap. xi. 10, 12——[p]Jer. vi. 14; viii. 11——[q]Or, *a slight wall*——[r]Chap. xxii. 28 [s]Chap. xxxviii. 22; Ecclus. xlix. 9

NOTES ON CHAP. XIII

Verse 2. *That prophesy out of their own hearts*] Who are *neither inspired* nor *sent* by ME. *They are prophets out of their own hearts.* They have their mission from their own *assumption*, and proceed in it from their own *presumption.* Such either go of *themselves*, or are sent by *man.* Such prophets, ministers, preachers, and clergy have been a curse to the Church and to the world for some thousands of years.

Verse 4. *Thy prophets are like the foxes in the deserts.*] The cunning of the *fox* in obtaining his prey has been long proverbial. These false prophets are represented as the foxes who, having got their prey by great subtlety, run to the desert to hide both themselves and it. So the false prophets, when the event did not answer to their prediction, *got out of the way*, that they might not be overwhelmed with the reproaches and indignation of the people.

Verse 5. *Ye have not gone up into the gaps*] Far from opposing sinners, who are bringing down the wrath of God upon the place, you prevent their repentance by your flattering promises and false predictions. Ye have neither by prayers, example, nor advice, contributed any thing for the preservation of the place, or the salvation of the people's souls.

Verse 9. *They shall not be in the assembly of my people*] They shall not be reputed members of my Church. They shall not be reckoned in the genealogy of true Israelites that return from captivity; and they shall never have a possession in the land; they shall be exhereditated and expatriated. They shall all perish in the siege, by the sword, the famine, and the pestilence.

Verse 10. *One built up a wall*] A true prophet is as *a wall of defence* to the people. These false prophets pretend to *be a wall of defence;* but their *wall* is bad, and their *mortar* is worse. One gives a *lying vision*, another pledges himself that it is *true;* and the people believe what *they* say, and trust not in God, nor turn from their sins. The city is about to be besieged; it needs stronger fortifications than what it possesses. The prophet should be as a *brazen wall* for its defence; and such my prophets would have been had the people received the word from my mouth. But ye have prevented this by your *lying vanities;* and when you have perverted the people, you pretend to raise up a *rampart* of specious prophecy, full of fine promises, for their *defence.* What one false prophet says, another confirms; and this is like daubing over a *bad wall* with *bad mortar*, which prevents its blemishes and weaknesses being discovered, though it has no tendency to strengthen the building.

Verse 11. *There shall be an overflowing shower*] That shall wash off this bad mortar; sweep away the ground on which the wall

A. M. 3410
B. C. 594
Ol. XLVI. 3
Anno
Tarquinii Prisci,
R. Roman., 23

will even rend *it* with a stormy wind in my fury; and there shall be an overflowing shower in mine anger, and great hailstones in *my* fury to consume *it*.

14 So will I break down the wall that ye have daubed with untempered *mortar,* and bring it down to the ground, so that the foundation thereof shall be discovered, and it shall fall, and ye shall be consumed in the midst thereof: [t]and ye shall know that I *am* the LORD.

15 Thus will I accomplish my wrath upon the wall, and upon them that have daubed it with untempered *mortar,* and will say unto you, The wall *is* no *more,* neither they that daubed it;

16 *To wit,* the prophets of Israel which prophesy concerning Jerusalem, and which [u]see visions of peace for her, and *there is* no peace, saith the Lord GOD.

17 Likewise, thou son of man, [v]set thy face against the daughters of thy people, [w]which prophesy out of their own heart; and prophesy thou against them,

A. M. 3410
B. C. 594
Ol. XLVI. 3
Anno
Tarquinii Prisci,
R. Roman., 23

18 And say, Thus saith the Lord GOD; Wo to the *women* that sew pillows to all [x]arm holes, and make kerchiefs upon the head of every stature to hunt souls! Will ye [y]hunt the souls of my people, and will ye save the souls alive *that come* unto you?

19 And will ye pollute me among my people [z]for handfuls of barley and for pieces of bread, to slay the souls that should not die, and to save the souls alive that should not live, by your lying to my people that hear *your* lies?

20 Wherefore thus saith the Lord GOD; Behold, I *am* against your pillows, wherewith ye there hunt the souls [a]to make *them* fly, and I will tear them from your arms, and will let the souls go, *even* the souls that ye hunt to make *them* fly.

21 Your kerchiefs also will I tear, and deliver my people out of your hand, and they shall be no more in your hand to be hunted;

[t]Ver. 9, 21, 23; ch. xiv. 8——[u]Jer. vi. 14; xxviii. 9——[v]Chap. xx. 46; xxi. 2——[w]Ver. 2——[x]Or, *elbows*——[y]2 Pet. ii. 14——[z]See Prov. xxviii. 21; Micah iii. 5——[a]Or, *into gardens*

stands, and level it with the earth. In the eastern countries, where the walls are built with *unbaked bricks*, desolations of this kind are often occasioned by tempestuous rains. Of this sort of materials were the walls of ancient cities made, and hence the reason why no vestige of them remains. Witness Babylon, which was thus built. See the note on chap. iv. 1.

Verse 17. *Set thy face against the daughters of thy people, which prophesy*] From this it appears that there were *prophetesses* in the land of Israel, that were really *inspired* by the Lord: for as a *false religion* necessarily implies a *true one*, of which it is the *ape;* so *false prophetesses* necessarily imply *true ones*, whom they endeavoured to imitate.

That there were *true prophetesses* among the Jews is evident enough from such being mentioned in the sacred writings. *Miriam*, the sister of Moses, Exod. xv. 20; Num. xii. 2; *Deborah*, Judg. iv. 4; *Huldah*, 2 Kings xxii. 14; *Anna*, the daughter of Phanuel, Luke ii. 36; the *four daughters* of Philip the deacon, Acts xxi. 9.

Calmet observes that there was scarcely a heresy in the primitive Church that was not supported and fomented by seducing women.

Verse 18. *That sew pillows to all arm holes*] I believe this refers to those *cushions* which are so copiously provided in the eastern countries for the apartments of women; on which they sit, lean, rest their heads, and prop up their arms. I have several drawings of eastern ladies, who are represented on *sofas;* and often with their *arm thrown over a pillow*, which is thereby pressed close to their side, and against which they thus recline. The prophet's discourse seems to point out that state of softness and effeminacy to which the predictions of those false prophetesses allured the inhabitants of Jerusalem. A careless voluptuous life is that which is here particularly reprehended.

And make kerchiefs] The word *kerchief* is French, *couvre chef,* that which *covers the head;* hence *handkerchief* and *neck handkerchief*, and *pocket handkerchief*, are pitifully improper; because none of them is used to *cover the head,* from which *alone,* that article of dress has its name. But what are we to understand by *kerchiefs* here? Probably some kind of *ornamental dress* which rendered women more enticing, so that they could the more successfully hunt or inveigle souls (men) into the worship of their false gods. These they put on heads of every *stature—women of all ages,* קומה *komah,* of every *woman* that *rose up* to inveigle men to idolatry.

The word מספחות *mispachoth,* translated here *kerchiefs*, and by the *Vulgate cervicalia, bolsters, Calmet* contends, means a sort of *nets* used in hunting, and in every place where it occurs it will bear this meaning; and hence the *use* to which it is here said to be applied, to *hunt souls.*

Verse 20. *The souls that ye hunt to make them fly.*] לפרחות *lephorechoth,* into the *flower gardens,* says *Parkhurst.* These false prophetesses decoyed men into these gardens, where probably some impure rites of worship were performed, as in that of אשרה *Asherah* or *Venus.* See *Parkhurst* under פרח.

Verse 21. *Your kerchiefs*] *Nets,* or *amulets,* as some think.

A. M. 3410
B. C. 594
Ol. XLVI. 3
Anno
Tarquinii Prisci,
R. Roman., 23

[b]and ye shall know that I *am*
the LORD.
22 Because with lies ye
have made the heart of the
righteous sad, whom I have not made
sad: and [c]strengthened the hands of the
wicked, that he should not return from his
wicked way, [d]by [e]promising
him life:
23 Therefore [f]ye shall see no
more vanity, nor divine divinations: for I will deliver my people out
of your hand: [g]and ye shall know that I *am*
the LORD.

A. M. 3410
B. C. 594
Ol. XLVI. 3
Anno
Tarquinii Prisci,
R. Roman., 23

[b]Ver. 9——[c]Jer. xxiii. 14——[d]Or, *that I should save his life*——[e]Heb. *by quickening him*

[f]Ver. 6, &c.; chap. xii. 24; Mic. iii. 6——[g]Ver. 9; chap. xiv. 8; xv. 7

Verse 22. *With lies ye have made the heart of the righteous sad*] Here is the *ministry* of these false prophetesses, and its effects. *They told lies:* they would *speak*, and they had no *truth* to tell; and therefore spoke *falsities*. They "saddened the souls of the righteous, and strengthened the hands of the wicked." They promised them life, and prevented them from repenting and turning from their sins.

Verse 23. *Ye shall see no more vanity*] They pretended *visions;* but they were *empty* of *reality.*

Nor divine divinations] As God would not speak to them, they employed *demons.* Where God is not, because of the iniquity of the people, the *devil* is, to strengthen and support that iniquity. And if he cannot have his *priests*, he will have his *priestesses;* and these will have a Church like themselves, full of lying doctrines, and bad works.

CHAPTER XIV

Here God threatens those hypocrites who pretended to worship him, while they loved and practised idolatry, 1–11. *He declares his irreversible purpose of punishing so guilty a nation, in behalf of which no intercession of the people of God shall be of any avail. The gross idolaters of Jerusalem and Judah shall be visited with God's four sore judgments,* famine, 12–14; wild beasts, 15, 16; *the* sword, 17, 18; *and* pestilence, 19–21. *A remnant shall be delivered from the wrath coming upon the whole land,* 22, 23.

A. M. 3410
B. C. 594
Ol. XLVI. 3
Anno
Tarquinii Prisci,
R. Roman., 23

THEN [a]came certain of the
elders of Israel unto me,
and sat before me.
2 And the word of the LORD
came unto me, saying,
3 Son of man, these men have set up their
idols in their heart, and put [b]the stumbling-
block of their iniquity before their face:
[c]should I be inquired of at all by them?
4 Therefore speak unto them, and say unto
them, Thus saith the Lord GOD; Every man
of the house of Israel that setteth up his idols
in his heart, and putteth the stumbling-block
of his iniquity before his face, and cometh to
the prophet; I the LORD will
answer him that cometh according to the multitude of his
idols:
5 That I may take the house of Israel in
their own heart, because they are all estranged
from me through their idols.
6 Therefore say unto the house of Israel,
Thus saith the Lord GOD; Repent, and turn
[d]*yourselves* from your idols; and turn away
your faces from all your abominations.
7 For every one of the house of Israel, or of
the stranger that sojourneth in Israel, which
separateth himself from me, and setteth up his

A. M. 3410
B. C. 594
Ol. XLVI. 3
Anno
Tarquinii Prisci,
R. Roman., 23

[a]Ch. viii. 1; xx. 1; xxxiii. 31——[b]Ch. vii. 19; ver. 4, 7——[c]2 Kings iii. 13——[d]Or, others

NOTES ON CHAP. XIV

Verse 1. *Then came certain of the elders of Israel unto me*] These probably came to tempt him, or get him to say something that would embroil him with the government. They were bad men, as we shall see in the third verse.

Verse 3. *These men have set up their idols in their heart*] Not only in their houses; in the *streets;* but they had them in their *hearts.* These were *stumbling-blocks* of iniquity; they *fell over them,* and broke the neck of their souls. And should God be inquired of by such miscreants as these?

Verse 4. *According to the multitude of his idols*] I will treat him as an idolater, as a flagrant idolater.

Verse 7. *And cometh to a prophet*] Generally supposed to mean a *false prophet.*

I the Lord will answer him by myself] I shall discover to him, by my own true prophet, what shall be the fruit of his ways. So, while their false prophets were assuring them of peace and prosperity, God's prophets were predicting the calamities that afterwards fell upon them. Yet they believed the *false prophets* in preference to the *true.* Ahab, about to engage with the Syrians, who had possession of Ramoth-Gilead, asked Micaiah, the prophet of the Lord, concerning the event; who told him he

A. M. 3410
B. C. 594
Ol. XLVI. 3
Anno
Tarquinii Prisci,
R. Roman., 23

idols in his heart, and putteth
the stumbling block of his iniquity before his face, and cometh to a prophet to inquire of
him concerning me; I the LORD will answer
him by myself:
8 And [e]I will set my face against that man,
and will make him a [f]sign and a proverb,
and I will cut him off from the midst of my
people; [g]and ye shall know that I *am* the
LORD.
9 And if the prophet be deceived when he
hath spoken a thing, I the LORD [h]have deceived that prophet, and I will stretch out my
hand upon him, and will destroy him from
the midst of my people Israel.
10 And they shall bear the punishment of
their iniquity: the punishment of the prophet
shall be even as the punishment of him that
seeketh *unto him;*
11 That the house of Israel may [i]go no
more astray from me, neither be polluted any
more with all their transgressions; [k]but that
they may be my people, and I may be their
God, saith the Lord GOD.
12 The word of the LORD came again to
me, saying,
13 Son of man, when the land sinneth
against me by trespassing grievously, then
will I stretch out mine hand upon it, and will
break the [l]staff of the bread
thereof, and will send famine
upon it, and will cut off man
and beast from it:

A. M. 3410
B. C. 594
Ol. XLVI. 3
Anno
Tarquinii Prisci,
R. Roman., 23

14 [m]Though these three men, Noah, Daniel,
and Job, were in it, they should deliver *but*
their own souls [n]by their righteousness, saith
the Lord GOD.
15 If I cause [o]noisome beasts to pass through
the land, and they [p]spoil it, so that it be desolate, that no man may pass through because
of the beasts:
16 [q]*Though* these three men *were* [r]in it, *as*
I live, saith the Lord GOD, they shall deliver
neither sons nor daughters; they only shall
be delivered, but the land shall be desolate.
17 Or *if* [s]I bring a sword upon that land,
and say, Sword, go through the land; so that
I [t]cut off man and beast from it:
18 [u]Though these three men *were* in it, *as*
I live, saith the Lord GOD, they shall deliver
neither sons nor daughters, but they only
shall be delivered themselves.
19 Or *if* I send [v]a pestilence into that land,
and [w]pour out my fury upon it in blood, to
cut off from it man and beast:
20 [x]Though Noah, Daniel, and Job, *were* in
it, *as* I live, saith the Lord GOD, they shall deliver neither son nor daughter; they shall *but*
deliver their own souls by their righteousness.

[e]Lev. xvii. 10; xx. 3, 5, 6; Jer. xliv. 11; chap. xv. 7 [f]Num. xxvi. 10; Deut. xxviii. 37; chap. v. 15——[g]Chap. vi. 7——[h]1 Kings xxii. 23; Job xii. 16; Jer. iv. 10; 2 Thess. ii. 11——[i]2 Pet. ii. 15——[k]Chap. xi. 20; xxxvii. 27——[l]Lev. xxvi. 26; Isa. iii. 1; chap. iv. 16; v. 16 [m]Jer. xv. 1; ver. 16, 18, 20; see Jer. vii. 16; xi. 14; xiv. 11——[n]Prov. xi. 4——[o]Lev. xxvi. 22; chap. v. 17——[p]Or, *bereave*——[q]Ver. 14, 18, 20——[r]Heb. *in the midst of it*——[s]Lev. xxvi. 25; chap. v. 12; xxi. 3, 4; xxix. 8; xxxviii. 21——[t]Chap. xxv. 13; Zeph. i. 3——[u]Ver. 14——[v]2 Sam. xxiv. 15; chap. xxxviii. 22 [w]Chap. vii. 8——[x]Ver. 14

should lose the battle. He then inquired of Zedekiah, a false prophet, who promised him a glorious victory. Ahab believed the latter, marched against the enemy, was routed, and slain in the battle, 1 Kings xxii. 10, &c.

Verse 9. *I the Lord have deceived that prophet*] That is, he ran before he was sent; he willingly became the servant of Satan's illusions; and I *suffered* this to take place, because he and his followers refused to consult and serve me. I have often had occasion to remark that it is common in the Hebrew language to state a thing as done by the Lord which he only *suffers* or *permits* to be done; for so absolute and universal is the government of God, that the smallest occurrence cannot take place without his *will* or *permission.*

Verse 10. *The punishment of the prophet*] They are both equally guilty: both have left the Lord, and both shall be equally punished.

Verse 13. *By trespassing grievously*] Having been frequently warned, and having refused to leave their sin, and so filled up the measure of their iniquity.

Verse 14. *Though—Noah, Daniel, and Job*] The intercession even of the holiest of men shall not avert my judgments. *Noah,* though a righteous man, could not by his intercession preserve the old world from being drowned. *Job,* though a righteous man, could not preserve his children from being killed by the fall of their house. Daniel, though a righteous man, could not prevent the captivity of his country. *Daniel* must have been *contemporary* with *Ezekiel.* He was taken captive in the *third* year of Jehoiakim, Dan. i. 1. After this Jehoiakim reigned *eight* years, 2 Kings xxiii. 36. And this prophecy, as appears from chap. viii. 1, was uttered in the *sixth* year of Jehoiachin's captivity, who succeeded Jehoiakim, and reigned only *three* months, 2 Kings xxiv. 6, 8. Therefore at this time Daniel had been *fourteen* years in captivity. See *Newcome.* Even at this time he had gained much public celebrity. From this account we may infer that *Job* was as *real* a *person* as *Noah* or *Daniel;* and of their identity no man has pretended to doubt. When God, as above, has determined to punish a nation,

A. M. 3410
B. C. 594
Ol. XLVI. 3
Anno
Tarquinii Prisci,
R. Roman., 23

21 For thus saith the Lord
GOD; [y]How much more when
[z]I send my four sore judgments upon Jerusalem, the
sword, and the famine, and the noisome beast,
and the pestilence, to cut off from it man and
beast?
22 [a]Yet, behold, therein shall be left a
remnant that shall be brought forth, *both* sons
and daughters: behold, they shall come forth
unto you, and [b]ye shall see
their way and their doings:
and ye shall be comforted concerning the evil that I have
brought upon Jerusalem, *even* concerning all
that I have brought upon it.
23 And they shall comfort you, when ye see
their ways and their doings: and ye shall
know that I have not done [c]without cause all
that I have done in it, saith the Lord GOD.

[y]Or, *Also when*——[z]Chap. v. 17; xxxiii. 27

[a]Chap. vi. 8——[b]Chap. xx. 43——[c]Jer. xxii. 8, 9

no intercession shall avail. *Personal holiness* alone can prevent these evils; but the holiness of any man can only avail for himself.

Verse 21. *My four sore judgments*] SWORD, *war.* FAMINE, occasioned by *drought.* PESTILENCE, epidemic diseases which sweep off a great part of the inhabitants of a land. The NOISOME BEAST, the multiplication of *wild beasts* in consequence of the general destruction of the inhabitants.

Verse 22. *Behold, they shall come forth unto you*] Though there shall be great desolations in the land of Judea, yet a *remnant shall be left that shall come here also as captives;* and their account of the abominations of the people shall prove to you with what propriety I have acted in abandoning them to such general destruction. This speech is addressed to those who were already in captivity; i. e., those who had been led to Babylon with their king Jeconiah.

Verse 23. *Ye shall know that I have not done without cause*] There is no part of the conduct of God towards man that is not dictated by the purest principles of *justice, equity,* and *truth.* He does nothing but what is *right;* and whatever is right to be done, that *ought* to be done. In God's *justice* there is no *severity;* in God's *mercy* there is no *caprice.* He alone doth all things *well;* for he is the Fountain of justice and mercy.

CHAPTER XV

The Jewish nation, about to be destroyed by the Chaldeans, compared to a barren vine which is fit for nothing but to be cast into the fire, 1–8.

A. M. 3410
B. C. 594
Ol. XLVI. 3
Anno
Tarquinii Prisci,
R. Roman., 23

AND the word of the LORD
came unto me, saying,
2 Son of man, What is the
vine tree more than any tree,
or than a branch which is among the trees
of the forest?
3 Shall wood be taken thereof to do any
work? or will men take a pin of it to hang
any vessel thereon?
4 Behold, [a]it is cast into the fire for fuel;
the fire devoureth both the
ends of it, and the midst of it
is burned. [b]Is it meet for *any*
work?
5 Behold, when it was whole, it was [c]meet
for no work: how much less shall it be meet
yet for *any* work, when the fire hath devoured
it, and it is burned?
6 Therefore thus saith the Lord GOD; As
the vine tree among the trees of the forest,

[a]John xv. 6——[b]Heb. *Will it prosper?*

[c]Heb. *made fit*

NOTES ON CHAP. XV

Verse 2. *What is the vine tree more than any tree*] It is certain that the *vine* is esteemed only on account of its *fruit.* In some countries, it is true, it grows to a considerable size and thickness: but, even then, it is not of a sufficient density to work into furniture. But whatever may be said of the *stock* of the vine, it is the *branch* that the prophet speaks of here; and I scarcely know the branch of any tree in the forest more useless than is the branch of the vine. Out of it who can even make a *pin* to drive into a mud wall, or *hang any vessel on?* A vine would never be cultivated for the sake of its *wood;* it is really *worthless* but as it bears *fruit.* What is *Israel?* Good for nothing, but as God influenced them to bring forth fruit to his glory. But now that they have ceased to be *fruitful,* they are *good* for nothing, but, like a withered branch of the vine, to be burnt.

Verse 4. *The fire devoureth both the ends of it, and the midst of it is burned.*] Judea is like a vine branch thrown into the fire, which seizes on *both the ends,* and *scorches* the *middle:* so both the extremities of the land is wasted; and the middle, Jerusalem, is now threatened with a siege, and by and by will be totally destroyed.

Verse 6. *Therefore thus saith the Lord*] As surely as I have allotted such a *vine branch,* or *vine branches,* for *fuel;* so surely have I appointed the *inhabitants of Jerusalem* to be consumed.

A. M. 3410
B. C. 594
Ol. XLVI. 3
Anno
Tarquinii Prisci,
R. Roman., 23

which I have given to the fire
for fuel, so will I give the
inhabitants of Jerusalem.
7 And [d]I will set my face
against them: [e]they shall go out from *one*
fire, and *another* fire shall devour them; [f]and
ye shall know that I *am* the
LORD, when I set my face
against them.
8 And I will make the land
desolate, because they have [g]committed a
trespass, saith the Lord GOD.

A. M. 3410
B. C. 594
Ol. XLVI. 3
Anno
Tarquinii Prisci,
R. Roman., 23

[d]Leviticus xvii. 10; chapter xiv. 8——[e]Isaiah xxiv. 18

[f]Chapter vi. 7; vii. 4; xi. 10; xx. 38, 42, 44——[g]Hebrew, *trespassed a trespass*

The design of this parable is to abate the pride of the Jews; to show them that, in their best estate, they had nothing but what they had received, and therefore deserved nothing; and now, having fallen from all righteousness, they can have no expectation of any thing but judgment unmixed with mercy.

Verse 7. *They shall go out from* one *fire, and* another *fire shall devour them*] If they escape the *sword*, they shall perish by the *famine;* if they escape the *famine*, they shall be led away *captives.* To escape will be *impossible.* It will be to them according to the proverb:—

Incidit in Scyllam, cupiens vitare Charybdim.

"Out of the scald, into the flame."

Verse 8. *They have committed a trespass*] They have *prevaricated;* they are the worst of sinners, and shall have the heaviest of punishments. Can men suppose that it is possible to hide even their dark hearts from God?

CHAPTER XVI

In this chapter the mercy of God to Jerusalem, (or the Jewish Church and nation,) is set forth by the emblem of a person that should take up an exposed infant, bring her up with great tenderness, and afterwards marry her, 1–14. *She is then upbraided with her monstrous ingratitude in departing from the worship of God, and polluting herself with the idolatries of the nations around her, under the figure of a woman that proves false to a tender and indulgent husband,* 15–52. *But, notwithstanding these her heinous provocations, God promises, after she should suffer due correction, to restore her again to his favour,* 53–63. *The mode of describing apostasy from the true religion to the worship of idols under the emblem of* adultery, *(a figure very frequent in the sacred canon,) is pursued with great force, and at considerable length, both in this and the* twenty-third *chapter; and is excellently calculated to excite in the Church of God the highest detestation of all false worship.*

A. M. 3410
B. C. 594
Ol. XLVI. 3
Anno
Tarquinii Prisci,
R. Roman., 23

AGAIN the word of the
LORD came unto me, saying,
2 Son of man, [a]cause Jerusalem to know her abominations,
3 And say, Thus saith the
Lord GOD unto Jerusalem; Thy
[b]birth [c]and thy nativity *is* of
the land of Canaan; [d]thy father *was* an Amorite, and thy mother a Hittite.

A. M. 3410
B. C. 594
Ol. XLVI. 3
Anno
Tarquinii Prisci,
R. Roman., 23

[a]Chap. xx. 4; xxii. 2; xxxiii. 7, 8, 9——[b]Heb. *cutting out*, or *habitation*——[c]Ch. xxi. 30——[d]Ver. 45

NOTES ON CHAP. XVI

Verse 2. *Cause Jerusalem to know her abominations*] And such a revelation of impurity never was seen before or since. Surely the state of the Jews, before the Babylonish captivity, was the most profligate and corrupt of all the nations of the earth. This chapter contains God's *manifesto* against this most abominable people; and although there are many *metaphors* here, yet all is not metaphorical. Where there was so much *idolatry*, there must have been adulteries, fornications, prostitutions, and lewdness of every description. The description of the prophet is sufficiently clear, except where there is a reference to ancient and obsolete *customs.* What a description of crimes! The *sixth satire of Juvenal* is its counterpart. General remarks are all that a commentator is justified in bestowing on this very long, very circumstantial, and caustic invective. For its *key,* see on the *thirteenth* and *sixty-third* verses.

Verse 3. *Thy birth and thy nativity* is *of the land of Canaan*] It would dishonour Abraham to say that you sprung from *him:* ye are rather *Canaanites* than *Israelites.* The Canaanites were accursed; so are ye.

Thy father was *an Amorite, and thy mother a Hittite.*] These tribes were the most famous, and probably the most corrupt, of all the Canaanites. So Isaiah calls the princes of Judah *rulers of Sodom*, chap. i. 10; and John the Baptist calls the Pharisees *a generation* or *brood of vipers*, Matt. iii. 7. There is a fine specimen of this kind of *catachresis* in Dido's invective against Æneas:—

Nec tibi Diva parens, generis nec Dardanus auctor,
Perfide; sed duris genuit te cautibus horrens
Caucasus, Hyrcanæque admorunt ubera tigres.
Æn. lib. iv. 365.

"False as thou art, and more than false, *forsworn;*
Not sprung from noble blood, nor goddess born:
But hewn from hardened entrails of a rock,—
And rough Hyrcanian tigers gave thee suck."
DRYDEN.

This is strong: but the invective of the prophet exceeds it far. It is the essence of

A. M. 3410
B. C. 594
Ol. XLVI. 3
Anno
Tarquinii Prisci,
R. Roman., 23

4 And *as for* thy nativity,[e]in
the day thou wast born, thy
navel was not cut, neither wast
thou washed in water [f]to
supple *thee;* thou wast not salted at all, nor
swaddled at all.
5 None eye pitied thee, to do any of these
unto thee, to have compassion upon thee;
but thou wast cast out in the open field, to
the loathing of thy person, in the day that
thou wast born.
6 And when I passed by thee, and saw thee
[g]polluted in thine own blood, I said unto
thee *when thou wast* in thy blood, Live; yea,
I said unto thee *when thou wast* in thy blood,
Live.
7 [h]I have [i]caused thee to multiply as the bud
of the field, and thou hast increased and
waxen great, and thou art come to [k]excellent
ornaments: *thy* breasts are fashioned, and
thine hair is grown, where thou *wast* naked
and bare.
8 Now when I passed by thee,
and looked upon thee, behold,
thy time *was* the time of love;
[l]and I spread my skirt over
thee, and covered thy nakedness: yea, I sware
unto thee, and entered into a covenant with
thee, saith the Lord GOD, and [m]thou becamest
mine.
9 Then washed I thee with water; yea, I
throughly washed away thy [n]blood from thee,
and I anointed thee with oil.
10 I clothed thee also with broidered work,
and shod thee with badgers' skin, and I
girded thee about with fine linen, and I covered thee with silk.
11 I decked thee also with ornaments, and
I [o]put bracelets upon thy hands, [p]and a chain
on thy neck.
12 And I put a jewel on thy [q]forehead, and
ear-rings in thine ears, and a beautiful crown
upon thine head.
13 Thus wast thou decked with gold and

A. M. 3410
B. C. 594
Ol. XLVI. 3
Anno
Tarquinii Prisci,
R. Roman., 23

[e]Hos. ii. 3——[f]Or, *when I looked* upon thee——[g]Or, *trodden under foot*——[h]Exod. i. 7——[i]Heb. *made thee a million*——[k]Heb. *ornament of ornaments*

[l]Ruth iii. 9——[m]Exod. xix. 5; Jer. ii. 2——[n]Heb. *bloods*——[o]Gen. xxiv. 22, 47——[p]Prov. i. 9——[q]Heb. *nose;* see Isa. iii. 21

degradation to its subject; and shows the Jews to be as base and contemptible as they were abominable and disgusting.

Verse 4. As for *thy nativity, &c.*] This verse refers to what is ordinarily done for every infant on its birth. The *umbilical cord,* by which it received all its nourishment while in the womb, being no longer necessary, is cut at a certain distance from the abdomen: on this part a knot is tied, which firmly uniting the sides of the tubes, they coalesce, and incarnate together. The extra part of the cord on the outside of the ligature, being cut off from the circulation by which it was originally fed, soon drops off, and the part where the ligature was is called the navel. In many places, when this was done, the infant was plunged into *cold water;* in all cases *washed,* and sometimes with a *mixture of salt and water,* in order to give a greater firmness to the skin, and constringe the pores. The last process was *swathing* the body, to support mechanically the tender muscles till they should acquire sufficient strength to support the body. But among savages this latter process is either wholly neglected, or done very slightly: and the less it is done, the better for the infant; as this kind of unnatural *compression* greatly impedes the *circulation* of the blood, the *pulsation* of the heart, and the due inflation of the lungs; respiration, in many cases, being rendered oppressive by the tightness of these bandages.

Verse 5. *Thou wast cast out in the open field*] This is an allusion to the custom of some heathen and barbarous nations, who exposed those children in the open fields to be devoured by wild beasts who had any kind of deformity, or whom they could not support.

Verse 6. *I said—Live*] I received the exposed child from the death that awaited it, while in such a state as rendered it at once an object of horror, and also of compassion.

——————Modo primos
Edere vagitus, et adhuc a matre rubentem.

Verse 8. Was *the time of love*] Thou wast marriageable.

I spread my skirt over thee] I *espoused* thee. This was one of their initiatory marriage ceremonies. See Ruth iii. 9.

I—entered into a covenant with thee] Married thee. *Espousing* preceded *marriage.*

Verse 10. *I clothed thee also with broidered work*] Cloth on which various *figures,* in various *colours,* were wrought by the needle.

With badgers' skin] See Exod. xxv. 5. The same kind of skin with which the tabernacle was covered.

Fine linen] בשש *beshesh, with cotton.* I have seen cloth of this kind enveloping the finest mummies.

I covered thee with silk.] משי *meshi.* Very probably the produce of the silk-worm.

Verse 12. *I put a jewel on thy forehead*] על אפך *al appech,* upon thy *nose.* This is one of the most common ornaments among ladies in the east. European translators, not knowing what to make of *a ring in the nose,* have rendered it, *a jewel on thy forehead* or *mouth,* (though they have sometimes a piece of *gold* or *jewel* fastened to the centre of their *forehead.*) I have already spoken of this Asiatic custom, so often referred to in the sacred writings: see Gen. xxiv. 22, 42; Exod. xxxii. 2; Job. xlii. 11; Prov. xi. 22; Isa. iii. 21; Hos. ii. 13.

Verse 13. *Thus wast thou decked, &c.*] The *Targum* understands all this of the *tabernacle*

A. M. 3410
B. C. 594
Ol. XLVI. 3
Anno
Tarquinii Prisci,
R. Roman., 23

silver; and thy raiment *was of* fine linen, and silk, and broidered work; [r]thou didst eat fine flour, and honey, and oil: and thou wast exceeding [s]beautiful, and thou didst prosper into a kingdom.

14 And [t]thy renown went forth among the heathen for thy beauty: for it *was* perfect through my comeliness, which I had put upon thee, saith the Lord GOD.

15 [u]But thou didst trust in thine own beauty, [v]and playedst the harlot because of thy renown, and pouredst out thy fornications on every one that passed by; his it was.

16 [w]And of thy garments thou didst take, and deckedst thy high places with divers colours, and playedst the harlot thereupon: *the like things* shall not come, neither shall it be *so*.

17 Thou hast also taken thy fair jewels of my gold and of my silver, which I had given thee, and madest to thyself images [x]of men, and didst commit whoredom with them,

18 And tookest thy broidered garments, and coveredst them: and thou hast set mine oil and mine incense before them.

19 [y]My meat also which I gave thee, fine flour, and oil, and honey, *wherewith* I fed thee, thou hast even set it before them for [z]a sweet savour: and *thus* it was, saith the Lord GOD.

20 [a]Moreover thou hast taken thy sons and thy daughters, whom thou hast borne unto me, and these hast thou sacrificed unto them [b]to be devoured. *Is this* of thy whoredoms a small matter,

21 That thou hast slain my children, and delivered them to cause them to pass through *the fire* for them?

22 And in all thine abominations and thy

A. M. 3410
B. C. 594
Ol. XLVI. 3
Anno
Tarquinii Prisci,
R. Roman., 23

[r]Deut. xxxii. 13, 14——[s]Psa. xlviii. 2——[t]Lam. ii. 15——[u]See Deut. xxxii. 15; Jer. vii. 4; Mic. iii. 11——[v]Isa. i. 21; lvii. 8; Jer. ii. 20; iii. 2, 6, 20; chap. xxiii. 3, 8, 11, 12; Hos. i. 2

[w]2 Kings xxiii. 7; chap. vii. 20; Hos. ii. 8——[x]Heb. *of a male*——[y]Hos. ii. 8——[z]Heb. *a savour of rest*——[a]2 Kings xvi. 3; Psa. cvi. 37, 38; Isa. lvii. 5; Jer. vii. 31; xxxii. 35; chap. xx. 26; xxiii. 37——[b]Heb. *to devour*

service, the *book of the law*, the *sacerdotal vestments*, &c.

Thou didst prosper into a kingdom.] Here the figure explains itself: by this *wretched infant*, the low estate of the Jewish nation in its *origin* is pointed out; by the *growing up of this child into woman's estate*, the increase and multiplication of the people; by her being *decked out and ornamented*, her tabernacle service, and religious ordinances; by her *betrothing* and consequent *marriage*, the *covenant* which God made with the Jews; by her *fornication* and *adulteries*, their *apostasy* from God, and the establishment of *idolatrous worship*, with all its abominable rites; by her *fornication* and *whoredoms* with the *Egyptians* and *Assyrians*, the sinful alliances which the Jews made with those nations, and the incorporation of *their* idolatrous worship with that of Jehovah; by her *lovers being brought against her*, and *stripping her naked*, the delivery of the Jews into the hands of the Egyptians, Assyrians, and Chaldeans, who stripped them of all their excellencies, and at last carried them into captivity.

This is the *key* to the whole of this long chapter of metaphors; and the reader will do well to forget the *figures*, and look at the *facts*. The *language* and *figures* may in many places appear to us exceptionable: but these are quite in conformity to those *times* and *places*, and to every reader and hearer would appear perfectly appropriate, nor would engender either a thought or passion of an irregular or improper kind. *Custom* sanctions the *mode*, and prevents the *abuse*. Among *naked savages* irregular passions and propensities are not known to predominate above those in civilized life. And why? Because such sights are *customary*, and therefore in themselves innocent. And the same may be said of the *language* by which such states and circumstances of life are described. Had Ezekiel spoken in such language as would have been called *chaste* and *unexceptionable* among *us*, it would have appeared to his auditors as a *strange dialect*, and would have lost at least one half of its *power* and *effect*. Let this be the prophet's apology for the apparent indelicacy of his metaphors; and mine, for not entering into any particular discussion concerning them. See also on ver. 63.

Verse 15. *Thou didst trust in thine own beauty*] Riches, strength, alliances, &c.; never considering that all they possessed came from God; therefore *it was his comeliness which he had put upon them*. Witness their *original abject state*, and the degree of *eminence* to which they had arrived afterwards through the protecting power of God.

Verse 17. *And madest to thyself images of men*] צלמי זכר *tsalmey zachar, male images*. *Priapi* are here meant, which were carried about in the ceremonies of Osiris, Bacchus, and Adonis; and were something like the *lingam* among the Hindoos. *Herodotus*, lib. ii, c. 48, 49, gives us an account of these *male images:* Πηχυαια αγαλματα νευροσπαστα, τα περιφορεουσι κατα κωμας ται γυναικες, νευον το αιδοιον, ου πολλῳ τεῳ ελασσον εον του αλλου σωματος. This was done at the worship of Bacchus in Egypt: and they who wish to see more may consult *Herodotus* as above. In this *phallic* worship the women were principally concerned.

Verse 18. *Hast set mine oil and mine incense before them.*] It appears that they had made use of the holy vestments, and the different kinds of offerings which belonged to the Lord, to honour their idols.

Verse 21. *To cause them to pass through* the fire] Bp. *Newcome* quotes a very apposite passage from *Dionysius Halicarnass.* Ant. Rom. lib.

A. M. 3410
B. C. 594
Ol. XLVI. 3
Anno
Tarquinii Prisci,
R. Roman., 23

whoredoms thou hast not remembered the days of thy
[c]youth, [d]when thou wast
naked and bare, *and* wast polluted in thy blood.
23 And it came to pass after all thy wickedness, (wo, wo unto thee! saith the Lord GOD;)
24 *That* [e]thou hast also built unto thee an
[f]eminent place, and [g]hast made thee a high
place in every street.
25 Thou hast built thy high place [h]at every
head of the way, and hast made thy beauty to
be abhorred, and hast opened thy feet to
every one that passed by, and multiplied thy
whoredoms.
26 Thou hast also committed fornication
with [i]the Egyptians thy neighbours, great of
flesh; and hast increased thy whoredoms, to
provoke me to anger.
27 Behold, therefore, I have stretched out
my hand over thee, and have diminished thine
ordinary *food,* and delivered thee unto the
will of them that hate thee, [k]the [l]daughters
of the Philistines, which are ashamed of thy
lewd way.
28 [m]Thou hast played the whore also with
the Assyrians, because thou wast unsatiable;
yea, thou hast played the harlot with them,
and yet couldest not be satisfied.
29 Thou hast moreover multiplied thy fornication in the land of Canaan [n]unto Chaldea;
and yet thou wast not satisfied herewith.
30 How weak is thine heart, saith the Lord
GOD, seeing thou doest all these *things,* the
work of an imperious whorish
woman;

A. M. 3410
B. C. 594
Ol. XLVI. 3
Anno
Tarquinii Prisci,
R. Roman., 23

31 [o]In that [p]thou buildest
thine eminent place in the
head of every way, and makest thine high
place in every street; and hast not been as a
harlot, in that thou scornest hire;
32 *But as* a wife that committeth adultery,
which taketh strangers instead of her husband!
33 They give gifts to all whores: but [q]thou
givest thy gifts to all thy lovers, and [r]hirest
them, that they may come unto thee on every
side for thy whoredom.
34 And the contrary is in thee from *other*
women in thy whoredoms, whereas none followeth thee to commit whoredoms: and in
that thou givest a reward, and no reward is
given unto thee, therefore thou art contrary.
35 Wherefore, O harlot, hear the word of
the LORD:
36 Thus saith the Lord GOD; Because thy
filthiness was poured out, and thy nakedness
discovered through thy whoredoms with thy
lovers, and with all the idols of thy abominations, and by [s]the blood of thy children,
which thou didst give unto them;
37 Behold, therefore [t]I will gather all thy
lovers, with whom thou hast taken pleasure,
and all *them* that thou hast loved, with all
them that thou hast hated; I will even gather
them round about against thee, and will discover thy nakedness unto them, that they may
see all thy nakedness.

---

[c]Jer. ii. 2; ver. 43, 60; Hos. xi. 1——[d]Ver. 4, 5, 6——[e]Ver. 31——[f]Or, *brothel house*——[g]Isa. lvii. 5, 7; Jer. ii. 20; iii. 2——[h]Prov. ix. 14——[i]Chap. viii. 10, 14; xx. 7, 8; xxiii. 19, 20, 21——[k]2 Chron. xxviii. 18, 19; ver. 57——[l]Or, *cities*——[m]2 Kings xvi. 7, 10; 2 Chron. xxviii. 23; Jer. ii. 18, 36——[n]Ch. xxiii. 14, &c.——[o]Or, *in thy daughters* is *thine*, &c.——[p]Ver. 24, 39——[q]Isa. xxx. 3; Hos. viii. 9——[r]Heb. *bribest*——[s]Ver. 20; Jer. ii. 34——[t]Jer. xiii. 22, 26; Lam. i. 8; chap. xxiii. 9, 10, 22, 29; Hos. ii. 10; viii. 10; Nah. iii. 5

---

i., s. 88, p. 72, and marg. p. 75, Edit. Hudson: *Μετα δε τουτο, πυρκαϊας προ των σκηνων γενεσθαι κελευσας, εξαγει τον λεων τας φλογας ὑπερθρωσκοντα, της ὁσιωσεως των μιασματων ἑνεκα.* "And after this, having ordered that fires should be made before the tents, he brings out the people to leap over the flames, for the purifying of their pollutions." This example shows that we are not always to take passing through the fire for being entirely consumed by it. Among the Israelites this appears to have been used as a rite of consecration.

Verse 24. *Thou hast also built unto thee an eminent place*] גב *gab*, a *stew* or *brothel;* Vulg. *lupanar;* Septuag. οικημα πορνικον. So my old MS. Bible, **a bordel house.** "Thou hast builded thy stewes and bordell houses in every place."—*Coverdale's* Bible, 1535. *Bordel* is an *Italian* word: how it got so early into our language I know not. Our modern word *brothel* is a corruption of it. *Diodati* translates, Tu hai edificato un bordello, "Thou hast built a brothel." Houses of this kind were of a very ancient date.

Verse 26. *Great of flesh*] The most extensive idolaters. Bene vasatis—longa mensura incognita nervi.—Juv. *Sat.* ix. 34. This is the allusion.

Verse 27. *Have diminished thine ordinary*] חקך *chukkech* means here the household provision made for a wife—food, clothing, and money.

Verse 36. *Thy filthiness was poured out*] נחשתך *nechushtech.* As this word signifies a sort of *metal,* (brass,) it is generally supposed to mean *money.* They had given *money* literally to these heathen nations to procure their friendship and assistance; but the word also

A. M. 3410
B. C. 594
Ol. XLVI. 3
Anno
Tarquinii Prisci,
R. Roman., 23

38 And I will judge thee, [u]as [v]women that break wedlock and [w]shed blood are judged; and I will give thee blood in fury and jealousy.

39 And I will also give thee into their hand, and they shall throw down [x]thine eminent place, and shall break down thy high places: [y]they shall strip thee also of thy clothes, and shall take [z]thy fair jewels, and leave thee naked and bare.

40 [a]They shall also bring up a company against thee, [b]and they shall stone thee with stones, and thrust thee through with their swords.

41 And they shall [c]burn thine houses with fire, and [d]execute judgments upon thee in the sight of many women: and I will cause thee to [e]cease from playing the harlot, and thou also shalt give no hire any more.

42 So [f]will I make my fury toward thee to rest, and my jealousy shall depart from thee, and I will be quiet, and will be no more angry.

43 Because [g]thou hast not remembered the days of thy youth, but hast fretted me in all these *things;* behold, therefore, [h]I also will recompense thy way upon *thine* head, saith the Lord GOD: and thou shalt not commit this lewdness above all thine abominations.

44 Behold, every one that useth proverbs shall use *this* proverb against thee, saying, As *is* the mother, *so is* her daughter.

A. M. 3410
B. C. 594
Ol. XLVI. 3
Anno
Tarquinii Prisci,
R. Roman., 23

45 Thou *art* thy mother's daughter, that loathed her husband and her children; and thou *art* the sister of thy sisters, which loathed their husbands and their children: [i]your mother *was* a Hittite, and your father an Amorite.

46 And thine elder sister *is* Samaria, she and her daughters that dwell at thy left hand: and [k]thy [l]younger sister, that dwelleth at thy right hand, *is* Sodom and her daughters.

47 Yet hast thou not walked after their ways, nor done after their abominations: but [m]as *if that were* a very little *thing,* [n]thou wast corrupted more than they in all thy ways.

48 *As* I live, saith the LORD GOD, [o]Sodom thy sister hath not done, she nor her daughters, as thou hast done, thou and thy daughters.

49 Behold, this was the iniquity of thy sister Sodom, pride, [p]fulness of bread, and abundance of idleness, was in her and in her daughters, neither did she strengthen the hand of the poor and needy.

50 And they were haughty, and [q]committed abomination before me: therefore [r]I took them away, as I saw *good.*

51 Neither hath Samaria committed half of thy sins; but thou hast multiplied thine abo-

---

[u]Heb. *with judgments of*——[v]Lev. xx. 10; Deut. xxii. 22; ch. xxiii. 45——[w]Gen. ix. 6; Exod. xxi. 12; see ver. 20, 36——[x]Ver. 24, 31——[y]Ch. xxiii. 26; Hos. ii. 3 [z]Heb. *instruments of thine ornament*——[a]Ch. xxiii. 10, 47 [b]John viii. 5, 7——[c]Deut. xiii. 16; 2 Kings xxv. 9; Jer. xxxix. 8; lii. 13——[d]Ch. v. 8; xxiii. 10, 48——[e]Ch. xxiii. 27

[f]Chap. v. 13——[g]Ver. 22; Psalm lxxviii. 42——[h]Ch. ix. 10, 11, 21; xxii. 31——[i]Ver. 3——[k]Deuteronomy xxxii. 32; Isaiah i. 10——[l]Hebrew, *lesser than thou* [m]Or, *that was loathed as a small* thing——[n]2 Kings xxi. 9; chap. v. 6, 7; ver. 48, 51——[o]Matt. x. 15; xi. 24 [p]Gen. xiii. 10——[q]Gen. xiii. 13; xviii. 30; xix. 5 [r]Gen. xix. 24

---

means *verdigris,* the *poisonous rust of copper* or *brass.* It is properly translated in our version *filthiness, poisonous filth.* Does it not refer to that *venereal virus* which is engendered by promiscuous connexions?

Verse 39. *They shall strip thee also of thy clothes—thy fair jewels*] Alluding to a lot common enough to prostitutes, their maintainers in the end stripping them of all they had given them.

Verse 42. *I will be quiet, and will be no more angry.*] I will completely abandon thee; have nothing more to do with thee; think no more of thee. When God in judgment ceases to reprehend, this is the severest judgment.

Verse 43. *Thou hast not remembered the days of thy youth*] Thy former low beginning, when God made thee a people, who wast no people. He who maintains not a proper recollection of past mercies is not likely to abide steadfast in the faith. Ingratitude to God is the commencement, if not the parent, of many crimes.

Verse 44. *As* is *the mother,* so is *her daughter.*] כאמה בתה *keimmah bittah,* "As the mother, her daughter." As is the *cause,* so is the *effect.* As is the *breeding,* so is the *practice.* A *silken purse* cannot be made out of a *swine's ear.* What is bred in the *bone* seldom comes out of the *flesh.* All such proverbs show the necessity of early holy *precepts,* supported by suitable *example.*

Verse 46. *Thine elder sister* is *Samaria, she and her daughters that dwell at thy left*] It is supposed that the prophet by *Sodom* in this place means the Israelites that dwelt beyond Jordan, in the land of the *Moabites* and *Ammonites;* or rather of the *Moabites* and *Ammonites* themselves. Literally, Sodom could not be called the *younger sister* of Jerusalem, as it existed before Jerusalem had a name. In looking *east* from Jerusalem, Samaria was on the *left,* and Sodom on the *right hand;* that is, the *first* was on the *north,* the *second* on the *south* of Jerusalem.

Verse 49. *This was the iniquity of thy sister Sodom*] If we are to take this place literally,

A. M. 3410
B. C. 594
Ol. XLVI. 3
Anno
Tarquinii Prisci,
R. Roman., 23

minations more than they, and [s]hast justified thy sisters in all thine abominations which thou hast done.

52 Thou also, which hast judged thy sisters, bear thine own shame for thy sins that thou hast committed more abominable than they: they are more righteous than thou: yea, be thou confounded also, and bear thy shame, in that thou hast justified thy sisters.

53 [t]When I shall bring again their captivity, [u]the captivity of Sodom and her daughters, and the captivity of Samaria and her daughters, then *will I bring again* the captivity of thy captives in the midst of them.

54 That thou mayest bear thine own shame, and mayest be confounded in all that thou hast done, in that thou art [v]a comfort unto them.

55 When thy sisters, Sodom and her daughters, shall return to their former estate, and Samaria and her daughters shall return to their former estate, then thou and thy daughters shall return to your former estate.

56 For thy sister Sodom was not [w]mentioned by thy mouth in the day of thy [x]pride,

57 Before thy wickedness was discovered, as at the time of *thy* [y]reproach of the daughters of [z]Syria, and all *that are* round about her, [a]the daughters of the Philistines, which [b]despise thee round about.

A. M. 3410
B. C. 594
Ol. XLVI. 3
Anno
Tarquinii Prisci,
R. Roman., 23

58 [c]Thou hast [d]borne thy lewdness and thine abominations, saith the LORD.

59 For thus saith the Lord GOD; I will even deal with thee as thou hast done, which hast [e]despised [f]the oath in breaking the covenant.

60 Nevertheless I will [g]remember my covenant with thee in the days of thy youth, and I will establish unto thee [h]an everlasting covenant.

61 Then [i]thou shalt remember thy ways, and be ashamed, when thou shalt receive thy sisters, thine elder and thy younger: and I will give them unto thee for [k]daughters, [l]but not by thy covenant.

62 [m]And I will establish my covenant with thee; and thou shalt know that I *am* the LORD:

63 That thou mayest [n]remember, and be confounded, [o]and never open thy mouth any more because of thy shame, when I am pacified toward thee for all that thou hast done, saith the Lord GOD.

---

[s]Jer. iii. 11; Matt. xii. 41, 42——[t]See Isa. i. 9; ver. 60, 61——[u]Jer. xx. 16——[v]Ch. xiv. 22, 23——[w]Heb. *for a report*, or *hearing*——[x]Heb. *prides*, or *excellencies* [y]2 Kings xvi. 5; 2 Chron. xxviii. 18; Isa. vii. 1; xiv. 28 [z]Heb. *Aram*.——[a]Ver. 27——[b]Or, *spoil*

[c]Chap. xxiii. 49——[d]Heb. *borne them*——[e]Chap. xvii. 13, 16——[f]Deut. xxix. 12, 14——[g]Psa. cvi. 45——[h]Jer. xxxii. 40; l. 5——[i]Ch. xx. 43; xxxvi. 31——[k]Isa. liv. 1; lx. 4; Gal. iv. 26, &c.——[l]Jer. xxxi. 31, &c.——[m]Hos. ii. 19. 20——[n]Ver. 61——[o]Rom. iii. 19

Sodom was guilty of other crimes besides that for which she appears to have been especially punished; in addition to her unnatural crime, she is charged with *pride*, *luxury*, *idleness*, and *uncharitableness;* and these were sufficient to sink any city to the bottomless pit.

Verse 52. *They are more righteous than thou*] תצדקנה ממך *tetsuddaknah mimmech*, "They shall be justified more than thou." They are less guilty in the sight of God, for their crimes were not accompanied with so many *aggravations*. This phrase casts light on Luke xviii. 14: "This man went down to his house justified rather than the other." Less blame in the sight of God was attached to him. He always had fewer advantages, and now he was a true *penitent;* while the other was boasting of what he *had done*, and what he had *not done*.

Verse 60. *I will remember my covenant*] That is, the covenant I made with Abraham *in the day of thy youth*, when in *him* thou didst *begin* to be a nation.

Verse 61. *Thy sisters, thine elder and thy younger*] The *Gentiles*, who were *before* the Jews were called, and *after* the Jews were cast off, are here termed the *elder* and *younger sister*. These were to be given to Jerusalem for *daughters;* the latter should be converted to God by the ministry of men who should spring out of the Jewish Church. The *former*, who were *patriarchs*, &c., profited by the *Lamb who was slain from the foundation of the world*. Among the latter the Gospel was preached, first by *Christ* and his *apostles*, and since by persons raised up from among themselves.

But not by thy covenant.] This was the *ancient covenant*, the conditions of which they *broke*, and the blessings of which they *forfeited;* but by that *new covenant*, or the *renewal* to the Gentiles of that *covenant* that was made *originally* with Abraham while he was a *Gentile*, promising that in *his seed all the nations of the earth should be blessed;* that *covenant* which respected the incarnation of Christ, and was ratified by the blood of his cross.

Verse 63. *When I am pacified toward thee*] This intimates that the Jews shall certainly share in the blessings of the Gospel covenant, and that they shall be restored to the favour and image of God. And *when* shall this be? Whenever *they* please. They might have enjoyed them *eighteen hundred* years ago; but they would not come, though *all things were then ready*. They may enjoy them *now;* but they still *choose* to shut their eyes against the light, and contradict and blaspheme. As they do *not turn to the Lord*, the *veil* still continues on their hearts. Let their *elder brethren* pray for them.

For a *key* to the principal metaphors in this chapter, the reader is referred to the note on the *thirteenth* verse, which, if he regard not, he will neither do justice to himself nor to the prophet. The whole chapter is a tissue of invective; sharp, cutting, and confounding; every where well sustained, in every respect richly merited; and in no case leaving any room to the delinquent for justification or response.

CHAPTER XVII

This chapter begins with a new allegory or parable, 1–10; *to which an explanation is immediately subjoined,* 11–21. *In the remaining verses the prophet, by a beautiful metaphor, makes an easy and natural transition to the Messiah, and predicts the security, increasing prosperity, and ultimate universality of his kingdom,* 22–24. *From the beauty of its images, the elegance of its composition, the perspicuity of its language, the rich variety of its matter, and the easy transition from one part of the subject to another, this chapter forms one of the most beautiful and perfect pieces of its kind that can possibly be conceived in so small a compass; and then the unexpected change from objects that presented nothing to the view but gloom and horror, to a prospect of ineffable glory and beauty, has a most happy effect. Every lowering cloud is dispelled, and the fields again smile in the beams of midday. The traveller, who this moment trembled as he looked around for shelter, now proceeds on his way rejoicing.*

A. M. 3410
B. C. 594
Ol. XLVI. 3
Anno Tarquinii Prisci, R. Roman., 23

AND the word of the LORD
came unto me, saying,
2 Son of man, put forth a
riddle, and speak a parable
unto the house of Israel;
3 And say, Thus saith the Lord GOD; [a]A
great eagle with great wings, long-winged,
full of feathers, which had [b]divers colours,
came unto Lebanon, and [c]took the highest
branch of the cedar;
4 He cropped off the top of his young
twigs, and carried it into a land of traffic:
he set it in a city of merchants.
5 He took also of the seed
of the land, and [d]planted it
in [e]a fruitful field; he placed *it* by great
waters, *and* set it [f]*as* a willow tree.
6 And it grew, and became a spreading
vine [g]of low stature, whose branches turned
toward him, and the roots thereof were under
him: so it became a vine, and brought forth
branches, and shot forth sprigs.
7 There was also another great eagle with

[a]See ver. 12, &c.——[b]Heb. *embroidering*——[c]2 Kings xxiv. 12

[d]Heb. *put it in a field of seed*——[e]Deut. viii. 7, 8, 9——[f]Isa. xliv. 4——[g]Ver. 14

NOTES ON CHAP. XVII

Verse 2. *Son of man, put forth a riddle*] Riddle, rædsel or rædels, Anglo-Saxon, from arædan, to *divine;* a thing that must be curiously *investigated* and *sifted*, to find out the meaning; and hence, *riddle*, a sort of coarse sieve to clean corn, to separate coarse chaff and straws from the pure grain. An instrument formerly used for *divination*. This is not far removed from the Hebrew חידה *chidah*, from חד *chad*, to *penetrate;* not that which *penetrates the mind*, but which *we* must *penetrate* to find out the sense.

Verse 3. *A great eagle*] Nebuchadnezzar. See Jer. xlviii. 40; xlix. 22; Dan. vii. 4. And see here, ver. 12, where it is so applied.

Great wings] Extensive empire.

Long-winged] Rapid in his conquests.

Full of feathers] Having multitudes of subjects.

Divers colours] People of various nations.

Came unto Lebanon] Came against Judea.

The highest branch] King Jehoiachin he took captive to Babylon.

The cedar] The Jewish state and king.

Verse 4. *The top of his young twigs*] The princes of Judah.

A land of traffic] Chaldea.

A city of merchants] Babylon; for which this city was the most celebrated of all the cities of the east. Its situation procured it innumerable advantages; its two rivers, the *Tigris* and *Euphrates*, and the *Persian Gulf*, gave it communication with the richest and the most distant nations.

Verse 5. *The seed of the land*] Zedekiah, brother of Jehoiachin.

Planted it in a fruitful field] Made him king of Judea in place of his brother.

Placed it by great waters] Put him under the protection of Babylon, situated on the confluence of the *Tigris* and *Euphrates*.

And *set it as a willow tree*] Made him *dependent* on this city of great waters, as the *willow* is on humidity.

Verse 6. *A spreading vine of low stature*] The Jewish state having then no height of dominion, it must abide under the wings or branches of the Chaldean king.

Whose branches turned toward him, and the roots—under him] Zedekiah was wholly dependent on Nebuchadnezzar, both for his elevation to the throne, and his support on it.

Verse 7. *Another great eagle*] Pharaoh-hophra, or Apries, king of Egypt.

With great wings] Extensive dominion.

And many feathers] Numerous subjects.

Did bend her roots] Looked to him for support in her intended rebellion against Nebuchadnezzar.

A. M. 3410
B. C. 594
Ol. XLVI. 3
Anno
Tarquinii Prisci,
R. Roman., 23

great wings and many feathers: and, behold, [h]this vine
did bend her roots toward
him, and shot forth her
branches toward him, that he might water it
by the furrows of her plantation.
8 It was planted in a good [i]soil by great
waters, that it might bring forth branches,
and that it might bear fruit, that it might
be a goodly vine.
9 Say thou, Thus saith the Lord GOD;
Shall it prosper? [k]shall he not pull up the
roots thereof, and cut off the fruit thereof,
that it wither? it shall wither in all the
leaves of her spring, even without great
power, or many people to pluck it up by the
roots thereof.
10 Yea, behold, *being* planted, shall it prosper? [l]shall it not utterly wither, when the
east wind toucheth it? it shall wither in the
furrows where it grew.
11 Moreover the word of the LORD came
unto me, saying,
12 Say now to [m]the rebellious house, Know
ye not what these *things mean?* tell *them,*
Behold, [n]the king of Babylon is come to
Jerusalem, and hath taken the king thereof,
and the princes thereof, and led them with
him to Babylon:
13 [o]And hath taken of the king's seed, and
made a covenant with him, [p]and hath [q]taken
an oath of him: he hath also taken the
mighty of the land:
14 That the kingdom might
be [r]base, that it might not
lift itself up, [s]*but* that by
keeping of his covenant it
might stand.
15 But [t]he rebelled against him in sending
his ambassadors into Egypt, [u]that they might
give him horses and much people. [v]Shall he
prosper? shall he escape that doeth such
things? or shall he break the covenant, and
be delivered?
16 *As* I live, saith the Lord GOD, surely
[w]in the place *where* the king *dwelleth* that
made him king, whose oath he despised, and
whose covenant he brake, *even* with him in
the midst of Babylon he shall die.
17 [x]Neither shall Pharaoh with *his* mighty
army and great company make for him in
the war, [y]by casting up mounts, and building
forts, to cut off many persons:
18 Seeing he despised the oath by breaking
the covenant, when, lo, he had [z]given his
hand, and hath done all these *things,* he shall
not escape.
19 Therefore thus saith the Lord GOD; *As*
I live, surely mine oath that he hath despised,
and my covenant that he hath broken, even it
will I recompense upon his own head.
20 And I will [a]spread my net upon him,
and he shall be taken in my snare, and I will
bring him to Babylon, and [b]will plead with
him there for his trespass that he hath trespassed against me.

A. M. 3410
B. C. 594
Ol. XLVI. 3
Anno
Tarquinii Prisci,
R. Roman., 23

---

[h]Ver. 15——[i]Heb. *field*——[k]2 Kings xxv. 7——[l]Ch. xix. 12; Hos. xiii. 15——[m]Ch. ii. 5; xii. 9——[n]Ver. 3; 2 Kings xxiv. 11–16——[o]2 Kings xxiv. 17——[p]2 Chron. xxxvi. 13——[q]Heb. *brought him to an oath*——[r]Ver. 6; ch. xxix. 14——[s]Heb. *to keep his covenant, to stand to it*

[t]2 Kings xxiv. 20; 2 Chron. xxxvi. 13——[u]Deut. xvii. 16; Isa. xxxi. 1, 3; xxxvi. 6, 9——[v]Ver. 9——[w]Jer. xxxii. 5; xxxiv. 3; lii. 11; ch. xii. 13——[x]Jer. xxxvii. 7 [y]Jer. lii. 4; ch. iv. 2——[z]1 Chron. xxix. 24; Lam. v. 6 [a]Chap. xii. 13; xxxii. 3——[b]Chap. xx. 36

Verse 8. *It was planted in a good soil*] Though he depended on Babylon, he lived and reigned as Nebuchadnezzar's vicegerent in the land of Judea.

Verse 9. *Shall it prosper?*] Shall Zedekiah succeed in casting off the yoke of the king of Babylon, to whom he had *sworn* fealty?

Shall he not pull up the roots] Nebuchadnezzar will come and dethrone him.

And cut off the fruit] The children of Zedekiah.

The leaves] All the nobles; all shall perish with Zedekiah.

Verse 10. *Shall—utterly wither*] The *regal* government shall be no more restored. Zedekiah shall be the *last king,* and the monarchy shall finally terminate with him.

Verse 12. *Know ye not what these* things mean?] They are explained in this and the following verses.

Verse 14. *That the kingdom might be base*] Have no political *consequence;* and at last sink into a *miserable government* under Gedaliah.

Verse 15. *Sending his ambassadors into Egypt*] Zedekiah must have sent his ambassadors into Egypt, between the *sixth* month of his *sixth* year, and the *fifth* month of his *seventh* year. Compare chap. viii. 1, with chap. xx. 1.—See *Newcome.*

Verse 16. *In the midst of Babylon he shall die.*] His eyes were put out; he was carried to Babylon, and never returned.

Verse 18. *Seeing he despised the oath*] This God particularly resents. He had bound himself by oath, in the presence of Jehovah, to be faithful to the covenant that he made with Nebuchadnezzar, and he took the first opportunity to break it; therefore he shall not escape.

Verse 20. *I will spread my net upon him*] See the note on chap. xii. 13.

A. M. 3410
B. C. 594
Ol. XLVI. 3
Anno
Tarquinii Prisci,
R. Roman., 23

21 And [c]all his fugitives
with all his bands shall fall
by the sword, and they that
remain shall be scattered
toward all winds: and ye shall know that I
the LORD have spoken *it.*
22 Thus saith the Lord GOD; I will also
take of the highest [d]branch of the high cedar,
and will set *it;* I will crop off from the top
of his young twigs [e]a tender one, and will
[f]plant *it* upon a high mountain and eminent:
23 [g]In the mountain of the height of Israel
will I plant it: and it shall
bring forth boughs, and bear
fruit, and be a goodly cedar:
and [h]under it shall dwell all
fowl of every wing; in the shadow of the
branches thereof shall they dwell.
24 And all the trees of the field shall know
that I the LORD [i]have brought down the high
tree, have exalted the low tree, have dried up
the green tree, and have made the dry tree
to flourish: [k]I the LORD have spoken and
have done *it.*

A. M. 3410
B. C. 594
Ol. XLVI. 3
Anno
Tarquinii Prisci,
R. Roman., 23

[c]Chap. xii. 14——[d]Isa. xi. 1; Jer. xxiii. 5; Zech. iii. 8——[e]Isa. liii. 2——[f]Psa. ii. 6

[g]Isa. ii. 2, 3; ch. xx. 40; Mic. iv. 1——[h]See ch. xxxi. 6; Dan. iv. 12——[i]Luke i. 52——[k]Ch. xxii. 14; xxiv. 14

Verse 21. *All his fugitives*] All who attempted to escape with him, and all that ran to Egypt, &c., shall fall by the sword.

Verse 22. *I will also take of the highest branch of the high cedar*] I will raise up *another monarchy,* which shall come in the *line of David,* namely, the *Messiah;* who shall appear as a *tender plant,* as to his incarnation; but he shall be *high and eminent;* his Church, the royal city, the highest and purest ever seen on the face of the earth.

Verse 23. *In the mountain of the height of Israel*] He shall make his appearance at the *temple,* and found his Church at *Jerusalem.*

Shall bring forth boughs] Apostles, evangelists, and their successors in the Gospel ministry.

And bear fruit] Multitudes of souls shall be converted by their preaching.

And under it shall dwell all fowl of every wing] All the nations of the earth shall receive his Gospel.

In the shadow of the branches thereof shall they dwell.] Trust in him alone for salvation, and be saved in their trusting.

Verse 24. *All the trees of the field shall know*] All the people of Israel and of Chaldea.

I the Lord have brought down the high tree] Have dethroned Jehoiachin.

Have exalted the low tree] Put Zedekiah, brother of Jehoiachin, in his place.

Have dried up the green tree] Zedekiah, who had numerous children, but who were all slain before his eyes at Riblah.

And have made the dry tree to flourish] Have raised up a rod out of the stem of Jesse, the family of David being then apparently dried up and extinct. This was the promised Messiah, of the increase and government of whose kingdom and peace there shall be no end; upon the throne of David, and upon his kingdom, to order and establish it with judgment and with justice, from henceforth, even for ever. THE ZEAL OF THE LORD OF HOSTS WILL PERFORM THIS.

The *high* and *green tree,* says *Newcome,* refers to Nebuchadnezzar; the *low* and the *dry tree,* to the Jews.

CHAPTER XVIII

The Jews, in Ezekiel's time, complained of God's dealing hardly with them in punishing them for the sins of their forefathers, 1, 2; *their* temporal *calamities having been long threatened as the consequence of the national guilt,* (Jer. xv. 4, &c.;) *and, from the general complexion of this chapter, it appears that the Jews so interpreted the second commandment of the Decalogue and other passages of like import, as if the sins of the forefathers were visited upon the children, independently of the moral conduct of the latter, not only in this world, but in that which is to come. To remove every foundation for such an unworthy idea of the Divine government, God assures them, with an oath, that he had no respect of persons,* 3, 4; *strongly intimating that the great mysteries in Providence, (mysterious only on account of the limited capacity of man,) are results of the most impartial administration of justice; and that this would be particularly manifested in the rewards and punishments of another life; when every ligament that at present connects societies and nations together shall be dissolved, and each person receive according to his work, and bear his own burden. This is illustrated by a variety of examples: such as that of a just or righteous man,* 5–9; *his wicked son,* 10–13; *and again the just son of this wicked person,* 14–20. *Then a wicked man repenting, and finding mercy, whose former wickedness shall be no impediment to his salvation,* 21–23; *and a righteous man revolting, and dying in his sins, whose former righteousness shall be of no avail,* 24. *The conduct of the Divine Providence is then vindicated,* 25–29; *and all persons, without any exception, most earnestly exhorted to repentance,* 30, 31; *because the Lord hath no pleasure in the death of the sinner,* 32. *As the whole of this chapter is taken up with the illustration of a doctrine nearly connected with the comfort of man, and the honour of the Divine government, the prophet, with great propriety, lays aside his usual mode of figure and allegory, and treats his subject with the utmost plainness and perspicuity.*

A. M. 3410
B. C. 594
Ol. XLVI. 3
Anno
Tarquinii Prisci,
R. Roman., 23

THE word of the LORD
came unto me again, say-
ing,
2 What mean ye, that ye use
this proverb concerning the land of Israel,
saying, The [a]fathers have eaten sour grapes,
and the children's teeth are set on edge?
3 *As* I live, saith the Lord GOD, ye shall
not have *occasion* any more to use this
proverb in Israel.
4 Behold, all souls are mine; as the soul of
the father, so also the soul of the son is mine:
[b]the soul that sinneth, it shall die.
5 But if a man be just, and do [c]that which
is lawful and right,
6 [d]*And* hath not eaten upon
the mountains, neither hath
lifted up his eyes to the idols
of the house of Israel, neither
hath [e]defiled his neighbour's wife, neither
hath come near to a [f]menstruous woman,
7 And hath not [g]oppressed any, *but* hath
restored to the debtor his [h]pledge, hath
spoiled none by violence, hath [i]given his
bread to the hungry, and hath covered the
naked with a garment;
8 He *that* hath not given forth upon [k]usury,
neither hath taken any increase, *that* hath
withdrawn his hand from iniquity, [l]hath executed true judgment between man and man,

[a]Jer. xxxi. 29; Lam. v. 7——[b]Ver. 20; Rom. vi. 23——[c]Heb. *judgment and justice*——[d]Ch. xxii. 9——[e]Lev. xviii. 20; xx. 10——[f]Lev. xviii. 19; xx. 18——[g]Exod. xxii. 21; Lev. xix. 15; xxv. 14——[h]Exod. xxii. 26; Deut. xxiv. 12, 13——[i]Deut. xv. 7, 8; Isa. lviii. 7; Matt. xxv. 35, 36——[k]Exod. xxii. 25; Lev. xxv. 36, 37; Deut. xxiii. 19; Neh. xv. 7; Psa. v. 5——[l]Deut. i. 16; Zech. viii. 16

NOTES ON CHAP. XVIII

Verse 2. *The fathers have eaten sour grapes, and the children's teeth are set on edge?*] We have seen this proverb already, Jer. xxxi. 29, &c., and have considered its general meaning. But the subject is here proposed in greater detail, with a variety of circumstances, to adapt it to all those cases to which it should apply. It refers simply to these questions: How far can the moral evil of the parent be extended to his offspring? And, Are the faults and evil propensities of the parents, not only transferred to the children, but punished in them? Do parents transfer their evil nature, and are their children punished for their offences?

Verse 3. As *I live, saith the Lord God, ye shall not have* occasion *any more to use this proverb in Israel.*] I will now, by this present declaration, settle this question for ever. And hence God has *sworn* to what follows. After this, who will dare to doubt the judgment pronounced?

Verse 4. *All souls are mine*] Equally so; I am the Father of the spirits of all flesh, and shall deal *impartially* with the whole.

The soul that sinneth, it shall die.] None shall *die* for *another's crimes;* none shall be saved by *another's righteousness.* Here is the *general* judgment relative to the *righteousness* and *unrighteousness* of men, and the *influence* of one *man's state* on *that of another;* particularly in respect to their moral *conduct.*

Verse 5. *If a man be just, and do that which is lawful and right*] If he be *just* or *holy* within, and do what is according to *law* and *equity.* What is meant by this, is immediately specified.

Verse 6. 1. *Hath not eaten upon the mountains*] Idolatrous worship was generally performed on *mountains* and *hills;* and those who offered sacrifices *feasted* on the sacrifice, and thus held *communion* with the idol.

2. *Neither hath lifted up his eyes to the idols*] Has paid them no religious adoration; has trusted in them for nothing, and has not made prayer nor supplication before them.

3. *Neither hath defiled his neighbour's wife*] Has had no adulterous connexion with any woman; to which idolatrous feasts and worship particularly led.

4. *Neither hath come nigh to a menstruous woman*] Has abstained from the use of the marriage-bed during the periodical indisposition of his wife. This was absolutely forbidden by the law; and both the man and the woman who disobeyed the command were to be put to death, Lev. xx. 18. For which *Calmet* gives this reason: "It has been believed, and experience confirms it, that the children conceived at such times are either leprous, or monsters, or deformed by their diminutiveness, or by the disproportion of their members." There are other reasons for this law, should those of the learned commentator be found invalid.

Verse 7. 5. *Hath not oppressed any*] Has not used his power or influence to oppress, pain, or injure another.

6. *Hath restored to the debtor his pledge*] Has carefully surrendered the pawn or pledge when its owner came to *redeem* it. As the *pledge* is generally of *more worth* than that for which it is pledged, an unprincipled man will make some pretence to keep it; which is highly abominable in the sight of God.

7. *Hath spoiled none by violence*] Either by robbery or personal insult. For a man may be spoiled both ways.

8. *Hath given his bread to the hungry*] Has been kind-hearted and charitable; especially to them that are in the deepest want.

9. *Hath covered the naked with a garment*] Has divided both his *bread* and his *clothing* with the necessitous. These are two branches of the same root.

Verse 8. 10. *Hath not given forth upon usury*] בנשך לא יתן *beneshech lo yitten.* נשך *nasach* signifies to *bite; usury* is properly so termed, because it *bites* into and *devours* the *principal.* Usury signifies, with us, exacting *unlawful interest* for money; and taking the *advantage* of a man's necessities to advance him cash on *exorbitant profit.* This *bites* the *receiver* in his *property,* and the *lender* in his *salvation.*

A. M. 3410
B. C. 594
Ol. XLVI. 3
Anno
Tarquinii Prisci,
R. Roman., 23

9 Hath walked in my stat-
utes, and hath kept my judgments, to deal truly; he *is*
just, he shall surely [m]live,
saith the Lord GOD.
10 If he beget a son *that is* a [n]robber, [o]a
shedder of blood, and [p]*that* doeth the like to
any one of these *things,*
11 And that doeth not any of those *duties,*
but even hath eaten upon the mountains, and
defiled his neighbour's wife,
12 Hath oppressed the poor and needy, hath
spoiled by violence, hath not restored the
pledge, and hath lifted up his eyes to the
idols, hath [q]committed abomination,
13 Hath given forth upon usury, and hath
taken increase: shall he then live? he shall
not live: he hath done all these abominations; he shall surely die; [r]his [s]blood shall be
upon him.
14 Now, lo, *if* he beget a son, that seeth all
his father's sins which he hath done, and
considereth, and doeth not such like,
15 [t]*That* hath not eaten upon the mountains, neither hath lifted up his eyes to the
idols of the house of Israel,
hath not defiled his neighbour's wife,

A. M. 3410
B. C. 594
Ol. XLVI. 3
Anno
Tarquinii Prisci,
R. Roman., 23

16 Neither hath oppressed
any, [u]hath not withholden the pledge, neither
hath spoiled by violence, *but* hath given his
bread to the hungry, and hath covered the
naked with a garment,
17 *That* hath taken off his hand from the
poor, *that* hath not received usury nor increase, hath executed my judgments, hath
walked in my statutes; he shall not die for
the iniquity of his father, he shall surely live.
18 *As for* his father, because he cruelly
oppressed, spoiled his brother by violence,
and did *that* which *is* not good among his
people, lo, even [v]he shall die in his iniquity.
19 Yet say ye, Why? [w]doth not the son bear
the iniquity of the father? When the son
hath done that which is lawful and right,
and hath kept all my statutes, and hath done
them, he shall surely live.
20 [x]The soul that sinneth, it shall die.
[y]The son shall not bear the iniquity of the
father, neither shall the father bear the ini-

---

[m]Chap. xx. 11; Amos v. 4——[n]Or, *breaker up of a house*——[o]Gen. ix. 6; Exod. xxi. 12; Num. xxxv. 31——[p]Or, *that doeth to his brother besides any of these*——[q]Ch. viii. 6, 17——[r]Lev. xx. 9, 11, 12, 13, 16, 27; chap. iii. 18; xxxiii. 4; Acts xviii. 6——[s]Heb. *bloods*

[t]Ver. 6, &c.——[u]Heb. *hath not pledged the pledge,* or *taken to pledge*——[v]Chap. iii. 18——[w]Exod. xx. 5; Deut. v. 9; 2 Kings xxiii. 26; xxiv. 3, 4——[x]Ver. 4——[y]Deut. xxiv. 16; 2 Kings xiv. 6; 2 Chronicles xxv. 4; Jeremiah xxxi. 29, 30

---

11. *Neither hath taken any increase*] In lending has not required more than was *lent;* and has not taken that product of the cash *lent,* which was more than the *value* for its *use.* This may be a part of the *tenth* article.

12. *That hath withdrawn his hand from iniquity*] Never *associates* with those who act contrary to *justice* and *equity;* his hand or influence being never found among *evil workers.*

13. *Hath executed true judgment between man and man*] Being neither swayed by *prejudice, fear,* nor *favour.*

These *thirteen points* concern his *social* and *civil* relations.

Verse 9. *Hath walked in my statutes*] Not only acknowledging them to be right, but acting according to them. Especially in every thing that relates to my worship, changing nothing, neglecting nothing.

And hath kept my judgments, to deal truly] Has attended to my Divine direction, both with respect to things *forbidden,* and things *commanded.* These concern men in their *religious* conduct.

He is *just*] צדיק הוא *tsaddik hu.* He is a *righteous* man; he has given to all *their due;* he has *abstained* from every appearance of evil, and done that which was *lawful* and *right* in the sight of God.

He shall surely live] He has *lived to* me, and he shall *live with* me.

Verse 10. *If he beget a son*] Who is the reverse of the above righteous character, according to the *thirteen articles* already specified and explained.

Verse 13. *Shall he then live?*] Because his father was a righteous man, shall the father's holiness be imputed to him? No!

He shall surely die; his blood shall be upon him.] He shall suffer for his own crimes.

Verse 14. *Now, lo,* if *he beget a son that seeth all his father's sins—and considereth*] Lays to heart the evil of his father's life, and the dreadful consequences of a life of rebellion against God.

And doeth not such like] Is quite a different man in moral *feeling* and *character;* and acts up to the *thirteen points* already laid down.

Verse 17. *He shall not die for the iniquity of his father*] He shall no more be affected by his father's *crimes,* than his father was *benefited* by his *grandfather's righteousness.*

Verse 20. *The soul that sinneth, it shall die.*] Hitherto we have had to do with the *simple cases* of the *righteous* and the *wicked;* of him who *lived and died a holy man,* and of him who *lived and died a wicked man.* But there are *two cases* behind: 1. That of the *wicked man,* who *repents* and *turns to God.* 2. That of the *righteous man,* who *backslides,* and *does not return to God* by repentance. On both these cases God decides thus:—

A. M. 3410
B. C. 594
Ol. XLVI. 3
Anno
Tarquinii Prisci,
R. Roman., 23

quity of the son: [z]the righteousness of the righteous shall
be upon him, [a]and the wickedness of the wicked shall be
upon him.
21 But [b]if the wicked will turn from all his
sins that he hath committed, and keep all
my statutes, and do that which is lawful
and right, he shall surely live, he shall not
die.
22 [c]All his transgressions that he hath committed, they shall not be mentioned unto
him: in his righteousness that he hath done
he shall live.
23 [d]Have I any pleasure at all that the
wicked should die? saith the Lord GOD: *and*
not that he should return from his ways, and
live?
24 But [e]when the righteous turneth away
from his righteousness, and committeth iniquity, *and* doeth according to all the abominations that the wicked *man* doeth, shall he
live? [f]All his righteousness that he hath
done shall not be mentioned: in his trespass
that he hath trespassed, and
in his sin that he hath sinned,
in them shall he die.
25 Yet ye say, [g]The way of
the LORD is not equal. Hear now, O house of
Israel; Is not my way equal? are not your
ways unequal?
26 [h]When a righteous *man* turneth away
from his righteousness, and committeth iniquity, and dieth in them; for his iniquity
that he hath done shall he die.
27 Again, [i]when the wicked *man* turneth
away from his wickedness that he hath committed, and doeth that which is lawful and
right, he shall save his soul alive.
28 Because he [k]considereth, and turneth
away from all his transgressions that he hath
committed, he shall surely live, he shall not
die.
29 [l]Yet saith the house of Israel, The way
of the LORD is not equal. O house of Israel,
are not my ways equal? are not your ways
unequal?
30 [m]Therefore I will judge you, O house of

A. M. 3410
B. C. 594
Ol. XLVI. 3
Anno
Tarquinii Prisci,
R. Roman., 23

[z]Isa. iii. 10, 11——[a]Rom. ii. 9——[b]Ver. 27; chap. xxxiii. 12, 19——[c]Chap. xxxiii. 16——[d]Ver. 32; chap. xxxiii. 11; 1 Tim. ii. 4; 2 Pet. iii. 9

[e]Chap. iii. 20; xxxiii. 12, 13, 18——[f]2 Pet. ii. 20
[g]Ver. 29; chap. xxxiii. 17, 20——[h]Ver. 24——[i]Ver. 21
[k]Ver. 14——[l]Ver. 25——[m]Chap. vii. 3; xxxiii. 20

Verse 21. *But if the wicked will turn from all his sins*] And afterwards walk according to the character of the righteous already specified; shall he find mercy, and be for ever saved? YES.

Verse 22. *All his transgressions*] Shall be so completely forgiven by God's mercy, that they *shall not be even mentioned to him;* and if he live and die in this recovered state, he shall live with God to all eternity. And why? Hear the reason:—

Verse 23. *Have I any pleasure at all that the wicked should die?*] No! That is foreign to him whose name is love, and whose nature is mercy. On the contrary he "wills that he should return from his evil ways and live."

And if God can have *no pleasure* in the *death of the wicked*, he cannot have made a *decree* to abandon him to the evil of his nature, and then damn him for what he could not avoid: for as God can *do* nothing with which he is *not pleased*, so he can *decree* nothing with which he is *not pleased.* But he is "not pleased with the death of a sinner;" therefore he cannot have *made a decree* to bring him to this *death.*

Verse 24. *When the righteous turneth away from his righteousness*] Here is the *second* case. Can a man who was once holy and pure, fall away so as to perish everlastingly? YES. For God says, "If he turn away from his righteousness;" not his *self-righteousness*, the gloss of theologians: for God never speaks of turning away from *that*, for, in his eyes, that is a *nonentity.* There is no righteousness or holiness but what himself infuses into the soul of man, and as to *self-righteousness*, i. e., a man's *supposing* himself to be *righteous* when he has not the *life of God* in his soul, it is the delusion of a dark and hardened heart; therefore it is the *real righteous principle* and *righteous practice* that God speaks of here. And he tells us, that a man may so "turn away from this," and so "commit iniquity," and "act as the wicked man," that *his righteousness shall be no more mentioned* to his account, than the *sins* of the *penitent backslider* should be *mentioned* to his condemnation; and "in the sin that he," this once righteous man, "hath sinned, and in the trespass that he hath trespassed, in them shall he die." O, how awful a termination of a life once distinguished for righteousness and true holiness! So then, God himself informs us that a *righteous man* may not only *fall foully*, but *fall finally.* But to such righteous persons the devil will ever preach, "Ye shall not surely die; ye shall be as God." Touch, taste, and handle; ye cannot ultimately fall. Thus we find, by the manner of treating these *two cases*, that *God's way is equal*, ver. 25; just, merciful, and impartial. And to prove this, he sums up his conduct in the above cases, in the following verses, 26, 27, 28, 29. And then, that the "wicked may not die in his sins," and that the "backslider may return and find mercy," he thus exhorts:—

Verse 30. *Repent, and turn yourselves from all your transgressions*] There is still life; still a God that has *no pleasure* in the death of a sinner, one who is ever ready to give his

A. M. 3410
B. C. 594
Ol. XLVI. 3
Anno
Tarquinii Prisci,
R. Roman., 23

Israel, every one according to
his ways, saith the Lord GOD.
[n]Repent, and turn [o]*yourselves*
from all your transgressions;
so iniquity shall not be your ruin.
31 [p]Cast away from you all your transgressions, whereby ye have transgressed; and
make you a [q]new heart and a
new spirit: for why will ye
die, O house of Israel?
32 For [r]I have no pleasure
in the death of him that dieth, saith the
Lord GOD: wherefore turn [s]*yourselves,* and
live ye.

[n]Matt. iii. 2; Rev. ii. 5——[o]Or, others——[p]Eph. iv. 22, 23——[q]Jer. xxxii. 39; chap. xi. 19; xxxvi. 26

[r]Lam. iii. 33; ver. 23; chap. xxxiii. 11; 2 Pet. iii. 9——[s]Or, others

Holy Spirit to all them that ask him; therefore "repent and turn, so iniquity shall not be your ruin."

Verse 31. *Cast away*] With a holy violence, dash away every transgression and incentive to it.

Make you a new heart] Call upon God for it, and he will give it: for as sure as you *earnestly call on God through Christ* to save you, so surely you shall be saved; and the *effect* will so speedily follow, that God is pleased to attribute that in some sort to *yourselves*, which is done by *his grace alone;* because ye earnestly *call* upon him for it, *come* in the right way to receive it, and are *determined* never to *rest* till you have it.

For why will ye die] Why should you go to *hell* while the kingdom of God is open to receive you? Why should you be the *devil's slaves*, when ye may be *Christ's freemen?* WHY WILL YE DIE? Every word is emphatic. *Why*—show God or man one *reason*. *Will*—obstinacy alone,—a determination not to be saved, or a *voluntary* listlessness about salvation,—can prevent you. *Ye*—children of so many mercies, fed and supported by a kind God all your life; *ye*, who are redeemed by the blood of Jesus Christ; *ye*, who have made many promises to give up yourselves to God; *ye*, who have been dedicated to the ever-blessed Trinity, and promised to renounce the devil and all his works, the pomps and vanities of this wicked world, and all the sinful lusts of the flesh; *why will* YE *die? Die!*—what is this? A separation from God and the glory of his power for ever! *Die!*—forfeiting all the purposes for which your immortal souls were made! *Die*—to know what the *worm* is that *never dieth*, and what that *fire* is which is *never quenched!* Why will ye die?

Verse 32. *For I have no pleasure*] God repeats what he had so solemnly declared before. Can ye doubt his sincerity? his ability? his willingness? the efficacy of the blood of his covenant?

Wherefore turn yourselves, *and live ye.*] Reader, now give God thy heart.

Though every man comes into the world with a *fallen nature—a soul infected with sin*, yet no man is damned on that account. He who *refuses* that grace which *pardons sin* and *heals infected nature*, who permits the *evil principle* to break out into *transgression*, and *continues* and dies in his iniquity and sin, and will not come unto Christ that he may have life; he, and he only, goes to perdition. Nor will the righteousness of a parent or relation help his sinful soul: no man can have more grace than is necessary to *save himself;* and none can have that, who does not receive it *through Christ Jesus*. It is the mercy of God in Christ which renders the *salvation of a sinner possible;* and it is that mercy alone which can *heal* the *backslider*. The atoning blood *blots out all that is past;* the same blood *cleanses from all unrighteousness*. Who believes so as to *apply* for this redemption? Who properly thanks God for having provided such a Saviour?

CHAPTER XIX

This chapter contains two beautiful examples of the parabolic kind of writing; the one lamenting the sad catastrophe of Jehoahaz and Jehoiakim, 1–9, and the other describing the desolation and captivity of the whole people, 10–14. In the first parable, the lioness is Jerusalem. The first of the young lions is Jehoahaz, deposed by the king of Egypt; and the second lion is Jehoiakim, whose rebellion drew on himself the vengeance of the king of Babylon. In the second parable the vine is the Jewish nation, which long prospered, its land being fertile, its princes powerful, and its people flourishing; but the judgments of God, in consequence of their guilt, had now destroyed a great part of the people, and doomed the rest to captivity.

A. M. 3410
B. C. 594
Ol. XLVI. 3
Anno
Tarquinii Prisci,
R. Roman., 23

MOREOVER [a]take thou up
a lamentation for the
princes of Israel,
2 And say, What *is* thy
mother? A lioness: she lay
down among lions, she nourished her whelps among young
lions.

[a]Chap. xxvi. 17; xxvii. 2

NOTES ON CHAP. XIX

Verse 1. *Moreover take thou up a lamentation*] Declare what is the great subject of sorrow in Israel. Compose a funeral dirge. Show the melancholy fate of the kings who proceeded from Josiah. The prophet deplores the misfortune of *Jehoahaz* and *Jehoiakim*, under the figure of *two lion whelps*, which were *taken by hunters*, and *confined in cages*. Next he shows the *desolation of Jerusalem* under *Zedekiah*, which he compares to a *beautiful vine* pulled up by the roots, withered, and at last burned. *Calmet* justly observes, that the style of this

A. M. 3410
B. C. 594
Ol. XLVI. 3
Anno
Tarquinii Prisci,
R. Roman., 23

3 And she brought up one of her whelps: [b]it became a young lion, and it learned to catch the prey; it devoured men.

4 The nations also heard of him; he was taken in their pit, and they brought him with chains unto the land of [c]Egypt.

5 Now when she saw that she had waited, *and* her hope was lost, then she [d]took another of her whelps, *and* made him a young lion.

6 [e]And he went up and down among the lions, [f]he became a young lion, and learned to catch the prey, *and* devoured men.

7 And he knew [g]their desolate palaces, and he laid waste their cities; and the land was desolate, and the fulness thereof, by the noise of his roaring.

8 [h]Then the nations set against him on every side from the provinces, and spread their net over him: [i]he was taken in their pit.

9 [k]And they put him in ward [l]in chains, and brought him to the king of Babylon: they brought him into holds, that his voice should no more be heard upon [m]the mountains of Israel.

10 Thy mother *is* [n]like a vine [o]in thy blood, planted by the waters: she was [p]fruitful and full of branches by reason of many waters.

11 And she had strong rods for the sceptres of them that bare rule, and her [q]stature was exalted among the thick branches, and she

[b]Ver. 6; 2 Kings xxiii. 31, 32——[c]2 Kings xxiii. 33; 2 Chron. xxxvi. 4; Jer. xxii. 11, 12——[d]2 Kings xxiii. 34——[e]Jer. xxiii. 13-17——[f]Ver. 3——[g]Or, *their widows*——[h]2 Kings xxiv. 2——[i]Ver. 4

[k]2 Chron. xxxvi. 6; Jer. xxii. 18——[l]Or, *in hooks*——[m]Ezek. vi. 2——[n]Chap. xvii. 6——[o]Or, *in thy quietness*, or *in thy likeness*——[p]Deut. viii. 7, 8, 9——[q]So chap. xxxi. 3; Dan. iv. 11

song is beautiful, and the allegory well supported throughout.

Verse 2. *What is thy mother? A lioness*] *Judea* may here be the *mother;* the *lioness*, Jerusalem. *Her lying down among lions*, her having confederacy with the neighbouring *kings;* for *lion* here means *king.*

Verse 3. *She brought up one of her whelps*] *Jehoahaz*, son of Josiah, whose father was conquered and slain by Pharaoh-necho, king of Egypt.

It learned to catch the prey] His reign was a reign of oppression and cruelty. He made his *subjects* his *prey*, and devoured their *substance.*

Verse 4. *The nations also heard of him*] The king of Egypt, whose subjects were of divers nations, marched against Jerusalem, took *Jehoahaz* prisoner, and brought him to Egypt. Thus—

He was taken in their pit] Here is an allusion to those *trap-pits* digged in forests, into which the wild beasts fall, when the huntsmen, surrounding a given portion of the forest, drive the beasts in; by degrees narrowing the inclosure, till the animals come to the place where the pits are, which, being lightly covered over with *branches* and *turf*, are not perceived, and the beasts tread on them and fall in. Jehoahaz reigned only *three* months before he was dethroned by the king of Egypt, against whom it is apparent some craft was used, here signified by the *pit*, into which he fell.

Verse 5. *When she saw that she had waited*] Being very weak, the Jews found that they could not resist with any *hope* of success; so the king of Egypt was permitted to do as he pleased.

She took another of her whelps] Jehoiakim. *And made him a young lion.*] King of Judea.

Verse 6. *And he went up and down among the lions*] He became a perfect heathen, and made Judea as idolatrous as any of the surrounding nations. He reigned *eleven* years, a monster of iniquity, 2 Kings xxiii. 30, &c.

Verse 8. *The nations set against him*] The Chaldeans, Syrians, Moabites, and Ammonites, and the king of Babylon—king of many nations.

He was taken] The city was taken by Nebuchadnezzar; and Jehoiakim was taken prisoner, and sent in *chains* to *Babylon.*

Verse 9. *That his voice should no more be heard*] He continued in prison many years, till the reign of Evil-merodach, who set him at liberty, but never suffered him to return to the *mountains of Israel.* "The unhappy fate of these princes, mentioned ver. 4, 8, 9, is a just subject of lamentation."—*Newcome.*

Verse 10. *Thy mother* (Jerusalem) is *like a vine in thy blood*] Of this expression I know not what to make. Some think the meaning is, "A vine planted by the waters to produce the *blood of the grape.*" See Deut. xxxii. 14. Others, for בדמך *bedamecha, in thy blood*, would read ברמון *berimmon, in* or *at a pomegranate;* like a vine planted by or beside a pomegranate-tree, by which it was to be supported. And so the *Septuagint* and *Arabic* appear to have read. *Calmet* reads כרמך *carmecha, thy vineyard*, instead of בדמך *bedamecha, in thy blood.* Here is no change but a ר *resh* for a ד *daleth.* This reading is supported by one of *Kennicott's* and one of *De Rossi's* MSS.: "Thy mother is like a vine in thy vineyard, planted by the waters." Though this is rather an unusual construction, yet it seems the best *emendation.* Of the textual reading no sense can be made. There is a corruption somewhere.

Full of branches] Many *princes.* See next verse.

Verse 11. *She had strong rods*] *Zedekiah*, and his many *sons.*

Her stature was exalted] Zedekiah grew *proud* of his numerous offspring and prosperity; and although he copied the example of *Jehoiakim*, yet he thought he might safely rebel against the king of Babylon.

A. M. 3410 B. C. 594 Ol. XLVI. 3 Anno Tarquinii Prisci, R. Roman., 23

appeared in her height with
the multitude of her branches.
12 But she was plucked up
in fury, she was cast down to
the ground, and the [r]east wind dried up her
fruit: her strong rods were broken and withered; the fire consumed them.
13 And now she *is* planted in the wilderness, in a dry and thirsty
ground.
14 [s]And fire is gone out of
a rod of her branches, *which*
hath devoured her fruit, so that she hath no
strong rod *to be* a sceptre to rule. [t]This
is a lamentation, and shall be for a lamentation.

A. M. 3410 B. C. 594 Ol. XLVI. 3 Anno Tarquinii Prisci, R. Roman., 23

[r]Chap. xvii. 10; Hos. xiii. 15——[s]Judg. ix. 15; 2 Kings xxiv. 20; chap. xvii. 18——[t]Lam. iv. 20

Verse 12. *But she was plucked up in fury*] Jerusalem; taken after a violent and most destructive siege; Nebuchadnezzar being violently *enraged* against Zedekiah for breaking his oath to him.

She was cast down to the ground] Jerusalem was totally ruined, by being burned to the ground.

Her strong rods were broken] The *children* of Zedekiah were slain before his eyes, and after that his *own eyes pulled out;* and he was laden with chains, and carried into Babylon.

Verse 13. *And now she* is *planted in the wilderness*] In the land of *Chaldea*, whither the people have been carried captives; and which, compared with their own land, was to them a *dreary wilderness.*

Verse 14. *Fire is gone out*] A vindictive and murderous disposition has taken hold—

Of a rod of her branches] Ishmael, son of Nethaniah, who was of the blood-royal of Judah,—

Hath devoured her fruit] Hath assassinated *Gedaliah*, slain many people, and carried off others into the country of the Ammonites. But he was pursued by Jonathan, the son of Kareah, who slew many of his adherents, and delivered much of the people.

She hath no strong rod] None of the blood-royal of Judah left. And from that time not one of her own royal race ever sat upon the throne of Israel.

This is *a lamentation*] This is a most lamentable business.

And shall be for a lamentation.] These predictions shall be so punctually fulfilled, and the catastrophe shall be so complete, that it shall ever remain as a lamentation; as this state of Jerusalem shall never be restored. Even to the present day this, to a Jew, is a subject of mourning.

CHAPTER XX

A deputation of the elders of Israel, as usual, in their distress, came to request Ezekiel to ask counsel of God, 1. *In reply to this, God commands the prophet to put them in mind of their rebellion and idolatry: In Egypt,* 2–9, *in the wilderness,* 10–27, *and in Canaan,* 28–32. *Notwithstanding which the Lord most graciously promises to restore them to their own land, after they should be purged from their dross,* 33–44. *The five last verses of this chapter ought to begin the next, as they are connected with the subject of that chapter, being a prophecy against Jerusalem, which lay to the south of Chaldea, where the prophet then was, and which here and elsewhere is represented under the emblem of a forest doomed to be destroyed by fire,* 45–49.

A. M. 3411 B. C. 594 Ol. XLVI. 4 Anno Tarquinii Prisci, R. Roman., 24

AND it came to pass in the
seventh year, in the fifth
month, the tenth *day* of the
month, *that* [a]certain of the
elders of Israel came to inquire of the LORD,
and sat before me.
2 Then came the word of the LORD unto
me, saying,
3 Son of man, speak unto
the elders of Israel, and say
unto them, Thus saith the
Lord GOD; Are ye come to
inquire of me? *As* I live, saith the Lord GOD,
[b]I will not be inquired of by you.
4 Wilt thou [c]judge [d]them, son of man, wilt
thou judge *them?* [e]cause them to know

A. M. 3411 B. C. 593 Ol. XLVI. 4 Anno Tarquinii Prisci, R. Roman., 24

[a]Chap. viii. 1; xiv. 1——[b]Ver. 31; chap. xiv. 3——[c]Or, *plead for them*——[d]Ch. xxii. 2; xxiii. 36——[e]Ch. xvi. 2

NOTES ON CHAP. XX

Verse 1. *In the seventh year*] Of the captivity of Jeconiah, (see chap. viii. 1,) and *the seventh of the reign* of Zedekiah.

The fifth month, *the tenth* day] That is, according to Abp. *Usher, Monday,* August 27, A.M. 3411.

Certain of the elders of Israel] What these came to inquire about is not known. They were doubtless hypocrites and deceivers, from the manner in which God commands the prophet to treat them. It seems to have been such a deputation of elders as those mentioned chap. viii. 1 and xiv. 1.

Verse 3. *I will not be inquired of by you.*] I will not hear you. I will have nothing to do with you.

Verse 4. *Wilt thou judge them*] If thou wilt *enter into any discussion with them,* show them *the abomination of their fathers.* The whole chapter is a consecutive history of the *unfaithfulness, ingratitude, rebellion,* and *idolatry* of the Jews, from the earliest times to that day; and vindicates the sentence which God had pronounced against them, and which he was about to execute more fully in delivering them and the city into the hands of the Chaldeans.

A. M. 3411
B. C. 593
Ol. XLVI. 4
Anno
Tarquinii Prisci,
R. Roman., 24

the abominations of their
fathers:
5 And say unto them, Thus
saith the Lord GOD; In the
day when [f]I chose Israel, and [g]lifted up mine
hand unto the seed of the house of Jacob,
and made myself [h]known unto them in the
land of Egypt, when I lifted up mine hand
unto them, saying, [i]I *am* the LORD your
God;
6 In the day *that* I lifted up mine hand
unto them, [k]to bring them forth of the land
of Egypt into a land that I had espied for
them, flowing with milk and honey, [l]which
is the glory of all lands:
7 Then said I unto them, [m]Cast ye away
every man [n]the abominations of his eyes, and
defile not yourselves with [o]the idols of Egypt:
I *am* the LORD your God.
8 But they rebelled against me, and would
not hearken unto me: they
did not every man cast away
the abominations of their
eyes, neither did they forsake
the idols of Egypt: then I said, I will [p]pour
out my fury upon them, to accomplish my
anger against them in the midst of the land
of Egypt.
9 [q]But I wrought for my name's sake, that
it should not be polluted before the heathen,
among whom they *were,* in whose sight I
made myself known unto them, in bringing
them forth out of the land of Egypt.
10 Wherefore I [r]caused them to go forth
out of the land of Egypt, and brought them
into the wilderness.
11 [s]And I gave them my statutes, and
[t]showed them my judgments, [u]which *if* a
man do, he shall even live in them.
12 Moreover also I gave them my [v]sabbaths,

A. M. 3411
B. C. 593
Ol. XLVI. 4
Anno
Tarquinii Prisci,
R. Roman., 24

[f]Exod. vi. 7; Deut. vii. 6——[g]Or, *sware;* and so ver. 6, &c.; Exod. vi. 8——[h]Exod. iii. 8; iv. 31; Deut. iv. 34 [i]Exod. xx. 2——[k]Exod. iii. 8, 17; Deut. viii. 7, 8, 9; Jer. xxxii. 22——[l]Psa. xlviii. 2; ver. 15; Dan. viii. 9; xi. 16, 41; Zech. vii. 14——[m]Chap. xviii. 31——[n]2 Chron. xv. 8 [o]Lev. xvii. 7; xviii. 3; Deut. xxix. 16, 17, 18; Josh. xxiv. 14

[p]Chap. vii. 8; ver. 13, 21——[q]See Exod. xxxii. 12; Num. xiv. 13, &c.; Deut. ix. 28; ver. 14, 22; chap. xxxvi. 21, 22——[r]Exod. xiii. 18——[s]Deut. iv.8; Neh. ix. 13, 14; Psa. cxlvii. 19, 20——[t]Heb. *made them to know* [u]Lev. xviii. 5; ver. 13, 21; Rom. x. 5; Gal. iii. 12 [v]Exod. xx. 8; xxxi. 13, &c.; xxxv. 2; Deut. v. 12; Neh. ix. 14

Verse 5. *I chose Israel*] They did not choose *me* for *their God,* till I had chosen *them* to be *my people.*

I lifted up mine hand] I bound myself in a covenant to them to continue to be their God, if they should be faithful, and continue to be my people. Among the Jews the *juror* lifted up his right hand to heaven; which explains Psa. cxliv. 8: "Their right hand is a right hand of falsehood." This is a form used in England, Scotland, and Ireland.

Verse 6. *To bring them forth of the land of Egypt*] When they had been long in a very disgraceful and oppressive bondage.

A land that I had espied for them] God represents himself as having *gone over different countries* in order to *find* a comfortable residence for these people, whom he considered as his children.

Flowing with milk and honey] These were the characteristics of a *happy and fruitful country,* producing without intense labour all the *necessaries* and *comforts* of life. Of the happiest state and happiest place, a fine poet gives the following description:—

Ver erat æternum, placidique tepentibus auris
Mulcebant Zephyri natos sine semine flores.
Mox etiam fruges tellus inarata ferebat:
Nec renovatus ager gravidis canebat aristis.
Flumina jam *lactis,* jam *flumina nectaris* ibant:
Flavaque de viridi *stillabant* ilice *mella.*
OVID'S *Metam.* lib. i., 107.

On flowers unsown soft Zephyr spreads his wing,
And time itself was one eternal spring;
Ensuing years the yellow harvest crowned,
The bearded blade sprang from the untilled ground,
And laden, unrenewed, the fields were found.
Floods were with *milk,* and *floods* with *nectar* filled,
And *honey* from the sweating *oaks* distilled.

In the flourishing state of Judea every mountain was cultivated as well as the valleys. Among the very rocks the vines grew luxuriantly.

Verse 7. *Cast ye away—the abominations*] Put away all your idols; those incentives to idolatry that ye have looked on with delight.

Verse 8. *They did not—cast away*] They continued attached to the *idolatry* of Egypt; so that, had I consulted my *justice* only, I should have consumed them *even in Egypt* itself. This is a circumstance that Moses has not mentioned, namely, their provoking God by their idolatry, *after* he had sent Moses and Aaron to them in *Egypt.*

Verse 9. *But I wrought for my name's sake*] I bare with them and did not punish them, lest the heathen, who had known my promises made to them, might suppose that I had either broken them through some caprice, or was not able to fulfil them.

Verse 10. *I caused them to go forth*] Though greatly oppressed and degraded, they were not *willing* to leave their *house of bondage.* I was obliged to *force them away.*

Verse 11. *I gave them my statutes*] I showed them what they should do in order to be safe, comfortable, wise, and happy; and what they should avoid in order to be uninjured in body, mind, and possessions. Had they attended to these things, they should have *lived by them.* They would have been holy, healthy, and happy.

Verse 12. *I gave them my Sabbaths*] The religious observance of the Sabbath was the *first statute* or *command* of God to men. This

A. M. 3411
B. C. 593
Ol. XLVI. 4
Anno
Tarquinii Prisci,
R. Roman., 24

to be a sign between me and them, that they might know that I *am* the LORD that sanctify them.

13 But the house of Israel [w]rebelled against me in the wilderness: they walked not in my statutes, and they [x]despised my judgments, which *if* a man do, he shall even live in them; and my sabbaths they greatly [y]polluted: then I said, I would pour out my fury upon them in the [z]wilderness, to consume them.

14 [a]But I wrought for my name's sake, that it should not be polluted before the heathen, in whose sight I brought them out.

15 Yet also [b]I lifted up my hand unto them in the wilderness, that I would not bring them into the land which I had given *them,* flowing with milk and honey, [c]which *is* the glory of all lands;

16 [d]Because they despised my judgments, and walked not in my statutes, but polluted my sabbaths: for [e]their heart went after their idols.

17 [f]Nevertheless mine eye spared them from destroying them, neither did I make an end of them in the wilderness.

18 But I said unto their children in the wilderness, Walk ye not in the statutes of your fathers, neither observe their judgments, nor defile yourselves with their idols:

19 I *am* the LORD your God; [g]walk in my statutes, and keep my judgments, and do them;

A. M. 3411
B. C. 593
Ol. XLVI. 4
Anno
Tarquinii Prisci,
R. Roman., 24

20 [h]And hallow my sabbaths; and they shall be a sign between me and you, that ye may know that I *am* the LORD your God.

21 Notwithstanding [i]the children rebelled against me: they walked not in my statutes, neither kept my judgments to do them, [k]which *if* a man do, he shall even live in them; they polluted my sabbaths: then I said, [l]I would pour out my fury upon them, to accomplish my anger against them in the wilderness.

22 [m]Nevertheless I withdrew mine hand, and [n]wrought for my name's sake, that it should not be polluted in the sight of the heathen, in whose sight I brought them forth.

23 I lifted up mine hand unto them also in the wilderness, that [o]I would scatter them among the heathen, and disperse them through the countries;

24 [p]Because they had not executed my judgments, but had despised my statutes, and had polluted my sabbaths, and [q]their eyes were after their fathers' idols.

25 Wherefore [r]I gave them also statutes *that were* not good, and judgments whereby they should not live;

[w]Num. xiv. 22; Psa. lxxviii. 40; xcv. 8, 9, 10——[x]Ver. 16, 24; Prov. i. 25——[y]Exod. xvi. 27——[z]Num. xiv. 29; xxvi. 65; Psa. cvi. 23——[a]Ver. 9, 22——[b]Num. xiv. 28; Psa. xcv. 11; cvi. 26——[c]Ver. 6——[d]Ver. 13, 24 [e]Num. xv. 39; Psa. lxxviii. 37; Amos v. 25, 26; Acts vii. 42, 43——[f]Psa. lxxviii. 38——[g]Deut. v. 32, 33; vi., vii., viii., x., xi., xii

[h]Ver. 12; Jer. xvii. 22——[i]Num. xxv. 1, 2; Deut. ix. 23, 24; xxxi. 27——[k]Ver. 11, 13——[l]Ver. 8, 13 [m]Psalm lxxviii. 38; ver. 17——[n]Ver. 9, 14——[o]Leviticus xxvi. 33; Deuteronomy xxviii. 64; Psalm cvi. 27; Jeremiah xv. 4——[p]Ver. 13, 16——[q]See chap. vi. 9 [r]See Psalm lxxxi. 12; ver. 39; Romans i. 24; 2 Thess. ii. 11

institution was *a sign between God and them,* to keep them in remembrance of the creation of the world, of the *rest* that he designed them in Canaan, and of the eternal inheritance among the saints in light. Of these things the Sabbath was a *type* and *pledge.*

Verse 13. *But the house of Israel rebelled*] They acted in the *wilderness* just as they had done in *Egypt;* and he spared them there for the same reason. See ver. 9.

Verse 15. *I lifted up my hand*] Their provocations in the wilderness were so great, that I vowed never to bring them into the promised land. I did not *consume* them, but I *disinherited* them. See the note on ver. 5.

Verse 18. *But I said unto their children*] These I chose in their fathers' stead; and to them I purposed to give the inheritance which their fathers by disobedience lost.

Verse 22. *I withdrew mine hand*] I had just lifted it up to crush them as in a moment; for they also were idolatrous, and walked in the steps of their fathers.

Verse 25. *I gave them also statutes* that were *not good*] What a foolish noise has been made about this verse by *critics,* believers and infidels! How is it that God can be said "to give a people statutes that were not good, and judgments whereby they could not live?" I answer, in *their sense* of the words, God never gave any such, at any time, to any people. Let any man produce *an example* of this kind if he can; or show even the *fragment* of such a law, sanctioned by the Most High! The simple meaning of this place and all such places is, that when they had rebelled against the Lord, despised his statutes, and polluted his Sabbaths—in effect cast him off, and given themselves wholly to their idols, then he *abandoned* them, and they abandoned themselves to the customs and ordinances of the heathen. That this is the meaning of the words, requires no proof to them who are the least acquainted with the *genius* and *idioms* of the Hebrew language, in which God is a thousand times said *to do,* what in the course of his *providence* or *justice* he only *permits* to be done.

A. M. 3411
B. C. 593
Ol. XLVI. 4
Anno
Tarquinii Prisci,
R. Roman., 24

26 And I polluted them in
their own gifts, in that they
caused to pass [s]through *the
fire* all that openeth the womb,
that I might make them desolate, to the end
that they [t]might know that I *am* the LORD.

27 Therefore, son of man, speak unto the
house of Israel, and say unto them, Thus
saith the Lord GOD; Yet in this your fathers
have [u]blasphemed me, in that they have
[v]committed a trespass against me.

28 *For* when I had brought them into the
land, *for* the which I lifted up mine hand to
give it to them, then [w]they saw every high
hill, and all the thick trees, and they offered
there their sacrifices, and there they presented the provocation of their offering: there
also they made their [x]sweet savour, and
poured out there their drink-offerings.

29 Then [y]I said unto them, What *is* the
high place whereunto ye go? And the name
thereof is called Bamah unto this day.

30 Wherefore say unto the house of Israel,
Thus saith the Lord GOD; Are ye polluted
after the manner of your fathers? and commit ye whoredom after their abominations?

31 For when ye offer [z]your gifts, when ye
make your sons to [a]pass through the fire, ye
pollute yourselves with all
your idols, even unto this
day: and [b]shall I be inquired
of by you, O house of Israel?
As I live, saith the Lord GOD, I will not be
inquired of by you.

A. M. 3411
B. C. 593
Ol. XLVI. 4
Anno
Tarquinii Prisci,
R. Roman., 24

32 And that [c]which cometh into your mind
shall not be at all, that ye say, We will be as
the heathen, as the families of the countries,
to serve wood and stone.

33 *As* I live, saith the Lord GOD, surely
with a mighty hand, and [d]with a stretched-
out arm, and with fury poured out, will I
rule over you:

34 And I will bring you out from the people, and will gather you out of the countries
wherein ye are scattered, with a mighty hand,
and with a stretched-out arm, and with fury
poured out.

35 And I will bring you into the wilderness
of the people, and there [e]will I plead with
you face to face.

36 [f]Like as I pleaded with your fathers in
the wilderness of the land of Egypt, so will I
plead with you, saith the Lord GOD.

37 And I will cause you to [g]pass under the
rod, and I will bring you into [h]the bond of
the covenant:

---

[s]2 Kings xvii. 17; xxi. 6; 2 Chron. xxviii. 3; xxxiii. 6; Jer. xxxii. 35; chap. xvi. 20, 21——[t]Chap. vi. 7——[u]Rom. ii. 24——[v]Heb. *trespassed a trespass*——[w]Isa. lvii. 5, &c.; chap. vi. 13——[x]Chap. xvi. 19——[y]Or, *I told them what the high place* was, or *Bamah*——[z]Ver. 26——[a]2 Kings xvi. 3; xxi. 6; xxiii. 10——[b]Ver. 3——[c]Chap. xi. 5——[d]Jer. xxi. 5——[e]Jer. ii. 9, 35; chap. xvii. 20——[f]See Numbers xiv. 21, 22, 23, 28, 29——[g]Leviticus xxvii. 32; Jeremiah xxxiii. 13——[h]Or, *a delivering*

Verse 26. *I polluted them in their own gifts*] I *permitted* them to pollute themselves by the offerings which they made to their idols. Causing their children to pass through the fire was one of those *pollutions;* but, did God ever *give them a statute* or *judgment* of *this kind?* No. He ever inveighs against such things, and they incur his heaviest displeasure and curse. See on ver. 31.

Verse 29. *What* is *the high place*] מה הבמה *mah habbamah*, "what is the high place?" What is it good for? Its being a *high place* shows it to be a *place of idolatry.* I called it במה *bamah*, to mark it with *infamy;* but ye continue to frequent it, even while it is called במה *bamah*, to the present day!

Verse 31. *Ye pollute yourselves*] This shows the sense in which God says, ver. 26, "I polluted them in their own gifts." They *chose* to pollute themselves, and I *permitted* them to do so. See on verses 25, 26.

Verse 32. *And that which cometh into your mind*] Ye wish to be naturalized among *idolaters*, and make a part of such nations. But this *shall not be at all;* you shall be preserved as a *distinct people.* Ye shall not be permitted to mingle yourselves with the people of those countries: even *they*, idolaters as they are, will *despise* and *reject you.* Besides, I will change your place, restore your captivity; yet not in *mercy*, but *in fury poured out;* and reserve you for sorer evils, ver. 34.

Verse 35. *I will bring you into the wilderness of the people*] I will bring you out of your captivity, and bring you into *your own land*, which you will find to be a *wilderness*, the consequence of your crimes.

There will I plead with you] There I will be your king, and rule you with a sovereign rule; and the dispensations of my justice and mercy shall either *end you* or *mend you.*

Verse 37. *I will cause you to pass under the rod*] This alludes to the custom of *tithing* the *sheep.* I take it from the rabbins. The sheep were all penned; and the shepherd stood at the door of the fold, where only one sheep could come out *at once.* He had in his hand a *rod* dipped in *vermillion;* and as they came out, he counted one, two, three, four, five, six, seven, eight, nine; and as the *tenth* came out, he marked it with the rod, and said, "This is the *tenth;*" and that was set apart for the Lord.

I will bring you into the bond of the covenant] You shall be placed under the same *obligations* as before, and acknowledge your-

A. M. 3411
B. C. 593
Ol. XLVI. 4
Anno
Tarquinii Prisci,
R. Roman., 24

38 And [i]I will purge out from among you the rebels, and them that transgress against me: I will bring them forth out of the country where they sojourn, and [k]they shall not enter into the land of Israel: [l]and ye shall know that I *am* the LORD.

39 As for you, O house of Israel, thus saith the Lord GOD; [m]Go ye, serve ye every one his idols, and hereafter *also,* if ye will not hearken unto me: [n]but pollute ye my holy name no more with your gifts, and with your idols.

40 For [o]in mine holy mountain, in the mountain of the height of Israel, saith the Lord GOD, there shall all the house of Israel, all of them in the land, serve me: there [p]will I accept them, and there will I require your offerings, and the [q]first-fruits of your oblations, with all your holy things.

41 I will accept you with your [r]sweet[s] savour, when I bring you out from the people, and gather you out of the countries wherein ye have been scattered; and I will be sanctified in you before the heathen.

42 [t]And ye shall know that I *am* the LORD, [u]when I shall bring you into the land of Israel, into the country *for* the which I lifted up mine hand to give it to your fathers.

A. M. 3411
B. C. 593
Ol. XLVI. 4
Anno
Tarquinii Prisci,
R. Roman., 24

43 And [v]there shall ye remember your ways, and all your doings, wherein ye have been defiled; and [w]ye shall loathe yourselves in your own sight for all your evils that ye have committed.

44 [x]And ye shall know that I *am* the LORD, when I have wrought with you [y]for my name's sake, not according to your wicked ways, nor according to your corrupt doings, O ye house of Israel, saith the Lord GOD.

45 Moreover, the word of the LORD came unto me, saying,

46 [z]Son of man, set thy face toward the south, and drop *thy word* toward the south, and prophesy against the forest of the south field;

47 And say to the forest of the south, Hear the word of the LORD; Thus saith the Lord GOD; Behold, [a]I will kindle a fire in thee, and it shall devour [b]every green tree in thee, and every dry tree: the flaming flame shall not be quenched, and all faces [c]from the south to the north shall be burned therein.

48 And all flesh shall see that I the LORD have kindled it: it shall not be quenched.

49 Then said I, Ah Lord GOD! they say of me, Doth he not speak parables?

---

[i]Chap. xxxiv. 17, 20; Matt. xxv. 32, 33——[k]Jer. xliv. 14——[l]Chap. vi. 7; xv. 7; xxiii. 49——[m]Judg. x. 14; Psa. lxxxi. 12; Amos iv. 4——[n]Isa. i. 13; chap. xxiii. 38, 39——[o]Isa. ii. 2, 3; chap. xvii. 23; Mic. iv. 1——[p]Isa. lvi. 7; lx. 7; Zech. viii. 20, &c.; Mal. iii. 4; Rom. xii. 1 [q]Or, *chief*——[r]Heb. *savour of rest*

[s]Eph. v. 2; Phil. iv. 18——[t]Ver. 38, 44; chap. xxxvi. 23; xxxviii. 23——[u]Chap. xi. 17; xxxiv. 13; xxxvi. 24 [v]Chap. xvi. 61——[w]Lev. xxvi. 39; chap. vi. 9; Hos. v. 15——[x]Ver. 38; chap. xxiv. 24——[y]Chap. xxxvi. 22 [z]Chap. vi. 2; xxi. 2——[a]Jer. xxi. 14——[b]Deut. xii. 2; Luke xxiii. 31——[c]Chap. xxi. 4

---

selves bound; ye shall feel your obligation, and live according to its nature.

Verse 38. *I will purge out from among you the rebels*] The incorrigibly wicked I will destroy; those who *will not* receive him whom I have appointed for this purpose as the Saviour of Israel. And I will gather you *who believe* out of all the countries where you sojourn, and bring you into your own land; but those of you who *will not believe*—will not receive the Son of David to reign over you, shall never enter into the land of Israel, but die in your dispersions. This is what the contradicting and blaspheming Jews of the present day have to expect. And thus, both of you *shall know that he is Jehovah*, fulfilling his *threatenings* against the one, and his *promises* to the other.

Verse 39. *Go ye, serve ye every one his idols*] Thus, God *gave* them *statutes that were not good*, and *judgments whereby they could not live*, by thus *permitting* them to take their own way, serve their gods, and follow the *maxims* and *rites* of that abominable worship.

Verse 40. *For in mine holy mountain*] The days shall come in which all *true* ISRAELITES shall receive HIM whom I have *sent* to be the *true sacrifice* for the life of the world; and shall bring to Jerusalem—the *pure Christian Church*, their offerings, which I will there accept, for they will give me thanks for my unspeakable gift.

Verse 42. *And ye shall know*] Shall acknowledge *that I am Jehovah.*

Verse 43. *And there shall ye remember your ways*] Ye shall be ashamed of your past conduct, and of your long opposition to the Gospel of your salvation.

These promises may, in a certain limited sense, be applied to the restoration from the Babylonish captivity; but they must have their proper fulfilment when the Jews shall accept Jesus as their Saviour, and in consequence be brought back from all their dispersions to their own land.

Verse 46. *Set thy face toward the south*] Towards *Judea*, which lay south from Babylon, or Mesopotamia, where the prophet then dwelt.

The forest of the south field] The *city of Jerusalem*, as full of inhabitants as the forest is of trees.

Verse 47. *I will kindle a fire*] I will send war, "and it shall devour every green tree," the most eminent and substantial of the inhabitants; and *every dry tree*, the lowest and meanest also.

The flaming flame shall not be quenched] The

fierce ravages of Nebuchadnezzar and the Chaldeans shall not be stopped till the whole land is ruined.

All faces from the south to the north shall be burned] From the one end of the land to the other there shall be nothing but fear, dismay, terror, and confusion, occasioned by the wide-wasting violence of the Chaldeans. Judea lay in length from north to south.

Verse 48. *All flesh*] All the people shall see that this war is a judgment of the Lord.

It shall not be quenched.] Till the whole land shall be utterly ruined.

Verse 49. *Ah Lord God!*] O my God, consider my situation; who will believe what I shall say? They put the evil day far from them.

Doth he not speak parables?] הלא ממשל משלים הוא *halo memashshel meshalim hu*, "Is not he a maker of parables?" Is it not his custom to deal in *enigmas?* His figures are not to be understood; we should not trouble ourselves with them. We are not obliged to fathom his meaning; and perhaps after all it does not refer to *us*, or will not be accomplished in *our time*, if it even respect the land. Thus they turned aside what might have done them good, and rejected the counsel of God against themselves.

By dividing the word with our neighbour we often lose the benefit both of threatenings and promises. They voluntarily shut their own eyes; and then God, in judgment, sealed them up in darkness.

CHAPTER XXI

The prophet goes on to denounce the fate of Jerusalem and Judea; using signs of vehement grief, to denote the greatness of the calamity, 2–7. He then changes the emblem to that of a sharp and bright sword, still denoting the same sad event, 8–17; and, becoming yet more explicit, he represents the king of Babylon, who was to be employed by God in this work, as setting out to take vengeance on both the Jews and the Ammonites, for joining with Egypt in a confederacy against him. He is described as standing at the parting of the roads leading to the respective capitals of the Jews and Ammonites; and doubting which to attack first, he commits the decision of the matter to his arts of divination, performed by mingling arrows inscribed with the names of the different nations or cities, and then marching against that whose name was written on the arrow first drawn from the quiver. In this case the name Jerusalem *comes forward; and therefore he proceeds against it, 18–24. History itself could scarcely be more explicit than this prophecy. The profane prince Zedekiah is then declared to be given up by God, and his kingdom devoted to utter destruction, for that breach of oath of which the prophet foretells he should be guilty, 25–27. The remaining verses form a distinct prophecy relating to the destruction of the Ammonites, which was fulfilled about five years after the destruction of Jerusalem, 28–32.*

A. M. 3411
B. C. 593
Ol. XLVI. 4
Anno
Tarquinii Prisci,
R. Roman., 24

AND the word of the LORD came unto me, saying,
2 [a]Son of man, set thy face toward Jerusalem, and [b]drop *thy word* toward the holy places, and prophesy against the land of Israel,
3 And say to the land of Israel, Thus saith the LORD; Behold, I *am* against thee, and will draw forth my sword out of his sheath, and will cut off from thee [c]the righteous and the wicked.

[a]Chap. xx. 46——[b]Deut. xxxii. 2; Amos vii. 16; Mic. ii. 6, 11——[c]Job ix. 22

NOTES ON CHAP. XXI

Verse 2. *Set thy face toward Jerusalem*] This is a continuation of the preceding prophecy; and in this chapter the prophet sets before them, in the *plainest language*, what the foregoing metaphors meant, so that they could not complain of his *parables*.

Verse 3. *Behold, I* am *against thee*] Dismal news! When God is *against us*, who can be *for us?*

And will draw forth my sword] War.

And will cut off from thee] The land of Judea.

The righteous and the wicked.] All shall be *removed from thee.* Some shall be *cut off*—removed by the *sword;* shall be slain in *battle*, or by the *pestilence;* and some shall be *cut off*—die by the *famine;* and some shall be *cut off*—removed from the land by *captivity.* Now, among the two latter classes there might be *many righteous* as well as *wicked.* And when all the provisions were consumed, so that there was no more bread in the city, during the siege by Nebuchadnezzar, the righteous must have suffered as well as the wicked; for they could not be preserved alive, but by miracle, when there was no bread; nor was their perishing for want any loss to them, because the Lord would take them straight to his glory. And however men in general are unwilling to die, yet there is no instance, nor can there be, of any man's complaint that he got to heaven *too soon.* Again, if God had permitted *none* to be carried off captive but the *wicked*, the case of these would be utterly hopeless, as there would be none to set a good example, to preach repentance, to reprove sin, or to show God's willingness to forgive sinners. But God, in his mercy, permitted many of the *righteous* to be carried off also, that the wicked might not be totally abandoned, or put beyond the reach of being saved. Hence, both *Ezekiel* and *Daniel*, and indeed several *others, prophets* and *righteous men*, were *thus cut off from the land*, and carried into captivity. And how much was God's glory and the good of men promoted by this! What a seed of salvation was sown, even in the heathen countries, by thus *cutting off the righteous with the wicked!* To this we owe, under God, many of the *Psalms*, the *whole of the Book of Ezekiel*, all the prophecies of *Daniel*, the

A. M. 3411
B. C. 593
Ol. XLVI. 4
Anno
Tarquinii Prisci,
R. Roman., 24

4 Seeing then that I will cut
off from thee the righteous and
the wicked, therefore shall my
sword go forth out of his
sheath against all flesh, [d]from the south to the
north:
5 That all flesh may know that I the LORD
have drawn forth my sword out of his sheath:
it [e]shall not return any more.
6 [f]Sigh therefore, thou son of man, with the
breaking of *thy* loins: and with bitterness
sigh before their eyes.
7 And it shall be, when they say unto thee,
Wherefore sighest thou? that thou shalt
answer, For the tidings; because it cometh:
and every heart shall melt, and [g]all hands
shall be feeble, and every spirit shall faint,
and all knees [h]shall be weak *as* water: behold,
it cometh, and shall be brought to pass, saith
the Lord GOD.
8 Again the word of the LORD came unto
me, saying,
9 Son of man, prophesy and say, Thus saith
the LORD; Say, [i]A sword, a
sword is sharpened, and also
furbished:
10 It is sharpened to make a
sore slaughter; it is furbished that it may
glitter: should we then make mirth? [k]it
contemneth the rod of my son, *as* every
tree.
11 And he hath given it to be furbished
that it may be handled: this sword is sharpened, and it is furbished, to give it into the
hand of [l]the slayer.
12 Cry and howl, son of man: for it shall
be upon my people, it *shall be* upon all the
princes of Israel: [m]terrors by reason of the
sword shall be upon my people: [n]smite therefore upon *thy* thigh.
13 [o]Because *it is* [p]a trial, and what if *the
sword* contemn even the rod? [q]it shall be no
more, saith the Lord GOD.
14 Thou, therefore, son of man, prophesy,
and [r]smite *thine* [s]hands together, and let the
sword be doubled the third time, the sword

A. M. 3411
B. C. 593
Ol. XLVI. 4
Anno
Tarquinii Prisci,
R. Roman., 24

[d]Chap. xx. 47——[e]So Isa. xlv. 23; lv. 11——[f]Isa. xxii. 4——[g]Chap. vii. 17——[h]Heb. *shall go into water* [i]Deut. xxxii. 41; ver. 15, 28——[k]Or, it is *the rod of my son, it despiseth every tree*——[l]Ver. 19——[m]Or, *they are thrust down to the sword with my people*

[n]Jer. xxxi. 19——[o]Or, *When the trial* hath been, *what then? shall they not also belong to the despising rod*——[p]Job ix. 23; 2 Cor. viii. 2——[q]Ver. 27 [r]Num. xxiv. 10; ver. 17; chap. vi. 11——[s]Heb. *hand to hand*

bright example of *Shadrach, Meshach,* and *Abed-nego,* the *decrees* passed *in favour of the religion of the true God* by *Nebuchadnezzar, Cyrus, Darius,* &c. And to this dispensation of God's merciful providence we owe the *Books* and *example* of *Ezra* and *Nehemiah.* Where then is the *injustice,* so loudly declaimed against, of God's thus cutting off *from the land of Judea* the *righteous* with the *wicked?* The *righteous* were not cut off for the *crimes of the wicked,* (see chap. xviii.,) nor were these crimes visited upon them; yet several of them shared in the common calamity, but none *perished.* Those that were removed by a violent death, (and I believe we shall find few such,) got a speedier entrance into eternal glory.

Verse 4. *From the south to the north*] The whole land shall be ravaged from one end to the other.

Verse 5. *It shall not return any more.*] That is, till all the work that I have designed for it is done. Nor did it; for Nebuchadnezzar never rested till he had subdued all the lands from the south to the north, from the *Euphrates* to the *Nile.*

Verse 6. *Sigh—with the breaking of* thy *loins*] Let thy mourning for this sore calamity be like that of a woman in the pains of travail.

Verse 7. *Wherefore sighest thou?*] The prophet was a *sign* unto them. His sighing and mourning showed them how *they* should act.

All knees shall be weak as *water*] See the note on chap. vii. 17.

Verse 10. *It contemneth the rod of my son*] "It," the sword of Nebuchadnezzar, "contemneth the rod," despises the power and influence *of my son*—Israel, the Jewish people: "Out of Egypt have I called MY SON."

As *every tree.*] As all the *stocks,* kindreds, and nations, over which I have already given him commission. Can the *rod of Israel* be spared, when the *trees* of *Assyria, Egypt,* &c., have been cut down?

Verse 11. *This sword is sharpened*] It is prepared for the slaughter, it is *furbished;* from the French, *fourbir,* to polish, brighten. He shall have *splendid* victories every where. Some complain of corruption in the original in this place; but I think without sufficient reason.

Verse 12. *Smite—upon* thy *thigh.*] See on Jer. xxxi. 19. So HOMER, Il. xv. ver. 113:—

Ὡς εφατ᾽· αυταρ Αρης θαλερω πεπληγετο μηρω
Χερσι καταπρηνεσσ᾽, ολοφυρομενος δε προσηυδα.

"She spake; and, with expanded arms his thighs
Smiting, thus sorrowful the god exclaimed."
COWPER.

Verse 13. *Because* it is *a trial*] This will be a trial of strength and skill between the Chaldeans and the Jews; and a *trial* of faith and patience to the righteous.

And what if the sword, (Nebuchadnezzar,) *contemn even the rod?*] Overthrow Zedekiah? It will do so; for the regal government of Judea *shall be no more.* Or, *it is tried;* that is, the *sword.* Nebuchadnezzar has already shown himself strong and skilful.

Verse 14. *Let the sword be doubled the third*

A. M. 3411
B. C. 593
Ol. XLVI. 4
Anno
Tarquinii Prisci,
R. Roman., 24

of the slain: it *is* the sword of
the great *men that are* slain,
which entereth into their
[t]privy chambers.
15 I have set the [u]point of the sword against
all their gates, that *their* heart may faint, and
their ruins be multiplied: ah! [v]*it is* made
bright, *it is* [w]wrapped up for the slaughter.
16 [x]Go thee one way or other, *either* on
the right hand, [y]*or* on the left, whithersoever
thy face *is* set.
17 I will also [z]smite mine hands together,
and [a]I will cause my fury to rest: I the LORD
have said *it*.
18 The word of the LORD came unto me
again, saying,
19 Also, thou son of man, appoint thee two
ways, that the sword of the king of Babylon
may come: both twain shall come forth out
of one land: and choose thou a
place, choose *it* at the head of
the way to the city.
20 Appoint a way, that the
sword may come to [b]Rabbath of the Ammonites, and to Judah in Jerusalem the defenced.
21 For the king of Babylon stood at the
[c]parting of the way, at the head of the two
ways, to use divination: he made *his* [d]arrows
bright, he consulted with [e]images, he looked
in the liver.
22 At his right hand was the divination for
Jerusalem, to appoint [f]captains, [g]to open the
mouth in the slaughter, to [h]lift up the voice
with shouting, [i]to appoint *battering* rams
against the gates, to cast a mount, *and* to
build a fort.
23 And it shall be unto them as a false
divination in their sight, [k]to them that [l]have

A. M. 3411
B. C. 593
Ol. XLVI. 4
Anno
Tarquinii Prisci,
R. Roman., 24

[t]1 Kings xx. 30; xxii. 25——[u]Or, *glittering*, or *fear*——[v]Ver. 10, 28——[w]Or, *sharpened*——[x]Ch. xiv. 17——[y]Heb. *set thyself, take the left hand*——[z]Ver. 14; ch. xxii. 13——[a]Ch. v. 13——[b]Jer. xlix. 2; ch. xxv. 5; Amos. i. 14

[c]Heb. *mother of the way*——[d]Or, *knives*——[e]Heb. *teraphim*——[f]Or, battering *rams;* chap. iv. 2——[g]Heb. *rams*——[h]Jer. li. 14——[i]Chap. iv. 2——[k]Or, *for the oaths made unto them*——[l]Chap. xvii. 13, 15, 16, 18

time] The sword has been *doubled*, and it shall come the *third time*. Nebuchadnezzar came against Judea THRICE. 1. Against *Jehoiakim*. 2. Against *Jeconiah*. 3. Against *Zedekiah*. The sword had already been *doubled;* it is to come now *the third time, i. e.*, against Zedekiah.

The sword of the slain] חרב חללים *chereb chalalim*, "the sword of the *soldiers*," of the *Chaldeans*. So in the next clause, היא חרב חלל הגדול *hi chereb chalal haggadol*, "it is the sword of that *great soldier*," that eminent *king* and *conqueror*. This is the meaning of the word חלל *chalal*, that is so ill rendered in almost every place of its occurrence, in our Version. See Dr. *Kennicott*.

Verse 15. *Wrapped up*] It is not a blunt sword, it is carefully sharpened and preserved for the slaughter.

Verse 16. *Go thee one way or other*] Thou shalt prosper, O sword, whithersoever thou turnest; against Ammon, or Judea, or Egypt.

Verse 19. *Appoint thee two ways*] Set off from Babylon, and lay down two ways, either of which thou mayest take; that to the *right*, which leads to *Jerusalem;* or that to the *left*, which leads to *Rabbath* of the Ammonites, ver. 20. But why against the *Ammonites?* Because both they and the Moabites were united with Zedekiah against the Chaldeans, (see Jer. xxvii. 3,) though they afterwards fought against Judea, chap. xii. 6.

Verse 21. *For the king of Babylon stood at the parting of the way*] He was in doubt which way he should first take; whether to humble the Ammonites by taking their metropolis, *Riblath*, or go at once against Jerusalem. In this case of uncertainty, he made use of *divination*. And this was of *three* kinds: 1. By *arrows*. 2. By *images* or *talismans*. 3. By inspecting the *entrails* of a sacrifice offered on the occasion.

1. *He made bright his arrows*. This might be after the manner in which the divination is still practised among the Arabs. These arrows were without head or wing. They took three. On one they wrote, *Command me, Lord*. On the second, *Forbid me, Lord*. The third was *blank*. These were put in a bag, and the querist put in his hand and took one out. If it was *Command me*, he set about the business immediately; if it was *Forbid me*, he rested for a *whole year;* if it was the *blank* one, he drew again. On all occasions the Arabs consulted futurity by such *arrows*. See *D'Herbelot*, under the word ACDAH.

2. As to the *images*, the Hebrew calls them תרפים *teraphim*. See the note on Gen. xxxi. 19.

3. And as to the *liver*, I believe it was only inspected to see whether the animal offered in sacrifice were *sound* and *healthy*, of which the state of the *liver* is the most especial indication. When the liver is sound, the animal is healthy; and it would have been a bad omen to any who offered sacrifice, to find that the animal they had offered to their gods was *diseased;* as, in that case, they would have taken for granted that the sacrifice was not accepted.

Verse 22. *At his right hand was the divination for Jerusalem*] He had probably written on *two* arrows; *one, Jerusalem;* the *other, Riblath;* the *third*, left *blank*. He drew, and that on which *Jerusalem* was written came to his hand; in consequence of which he marched immediately against that city. It was ripe for destruction; and had he marched *before* or *after*, it would have fallen; but he never considered himself as sure of the conquest till now.

Verse 23. *To them that have sworn oaths*] To Zedekiah and his *ministers*, who had bound themselves by the oath of the Lord to be faithful to the Chaldeans, and to pay them the

A. M. 3411
B. C. 593
Ol. XLVI. 4
Anno
Tarquinii Prisci,
R. Roman., 24

sworn oaths: but he will call to
remembrance the iniquity,
that they may be taken.
24 Therefore thus saith the
Lord GOD; Because ye have made your iniquity to be remembered, in that your transgressions are discovered, so that in all your doings your sins do appear; because, *I say,* that ye are come to remembrance, ye shall be taken with the hand.
25 And thou [m]profane wicked prince of Israel, [n]whose day is come, when iniquity *shall have* an end,
26 Thus saith the Lord GOD; Remove the diadem, and take off the crown: this *shall* not *be* the same: [o]exalt *him that is* low, and abase *him that is* high.
27 [p]I will overturn, overturn, overturn it: [q]and it shall be no *more,* until he come whose right it is; and I will give it *him.*
28 And thou, son of man, prophesy and say, Thus saith the Lord GOD [r]concerning the Ammonites, and concerning their reproach; even say thou, [s]The sword, the sword *is* drawn: for the slaughter *it is* furbished, to consume because of the glittering:
29 Whiles they [t]see vanity unto thee, whiles they divine a lie unto thee, to bring thee upon the necks of *them that are* slain, of the wicked, [u]whose day is come, when their iniquity *shall have* an end.
30 [v]Shall [w]I cause *it* to return into his sheath? [x]I will judge thee in the place where thou wast created, [y]in the land of thy nativity.
31 And I will [z]pour out mine indignation upon thee, I will [a]blow against thee in the fire of my wrath, and deliver thee into the hand of [b]brutish men, *and* skilful to destroy.
32 Thou shalt be for fuel to the fire; thy blood shall be in the midst of the land; [c]thou shalt be no *more* remembered: for I the LORD have spoken *it.*

[m]2 Chron. xxxvi. 13; Jer. lii. 2; chap. xvii. 19 — [n]Ver. 29; chap. xxxv. 5 — [o]Ch. xvii. 24; Luke i. 52 — [p]Heb. *perverted, perverted, perverted will I make it* — [q]Gen. xlix. 10; ver. 13; Luke i. 32, 33; John i. 49 — [r]Jer. xlix. 1; chap. xxv. 2, 3, 6; Zeph. ii. 8, 9, 10

[s]Ver. 9, 10 — [t]Chap. xii. 24; xxii. 28 — [u]Ver. 25; Job xviii. 20; Psa. xxxvii. 13 — [v]Or, *Cause* it *to return* — [w]Jer. xlvii. 6, 7 — [x]Gen. xv. 14; ch. xvi. 38 — [y]Chap. xvi. 3 — [z]Chap. vii. 8; xiv. 19; xxii. 22 — [a]Chap. xxii. 20, 21 — [b]Or, *burning* — [c]Chap. xxv. 10

promised tribute. The *oaths* may refer, farther, to the *alliances* formed with the Egyptians, Ammonites, and others. They will not believe that Nebuchadnezzar shall succeed against them, while they expect the powerful assistance of the Egyptians.

Verse 25. *And thou profane wicked prince of Israel*] Zedekiah, called here *profane*, because he had broken his oath; and *wicked*, because of his opposition to God and his prophet.

Whose day is come] Who in a short time shalt be delivered into the hands of thy enemies.

Verse 26. *Exalt* him that is *low*] Give Gedaliah the government of Judea.

Abase him that is *high.*] Depose Zedekiah—remove his diadem, and take off his crown.

Verse 27. *I will overturn*] I will utterly destroy the Jewish government. Perverted will I make it. See the margin.

Until he come whose—is] משפט *mishpat*, the judgment; *i. e.*, till the coming of the son of David, the Lord Jesus; who, in a mystic and spiritual sense, shall have the throne of Israel, and whose *right it is.* See the famous prophecy, Gen. xlix. 10, and Luke i. 32. The עוה *avah*, which we translate *overturn*, is *thrice* repeated here; to point out, say the rabbins, the *three* conquests of Jerusalem, in which *Jehoiakim*, *Jeconiah*, and *Zedekiah* were *overthrown*.

Verse 28. *Concerning the Ammonites*] They had reproached and insulted Judea in its low estate, see chap. xxv. This prophecy against them was fulfilled about *five* years after the taking of Jerusalem. See Joseph. Ant. lib. x. c. 11; and Jer. xxvii., xlviii., xlix.; Ezek. xxv.

Verse 30. *I will judge thee*] This seems to refer to Nebuchadnezzar, who, after his return from Jerusalem, became insane, and lived like a beast for *seven* years; but was afterwards restored, and acknowledged the Lord.

Verse 32. *Thou shalt be no* more *remembered*] The empire of the *Chaldeans* was destroyed, and the power transferred to the *Persians;* the Persian empire was destroyed, and given to the *Greeks;* the Grecian empire was destroyed, and given to the *Mohammedans;* and the destruction of the Mohammedans is at no great distance.

CHAPTER XXII

This chapter contains a recital of the sins of Jerusalem, 1–12; *for which God threatens it with severe judgments,* 13–16, *in order to purify it from the dross,* 17–22. *And as the corruption is general, pervading prophets, priests, princes, and people; so, it is declared, shall be the punishment,* 23–31.

A. M. cir. 3411
B. C. cir. 593
Ol. XLVI. 4
Tarquinii Prisci,
R. Roman.,
cir. annum 24

MOREOVER the word of the LORD came unto me, saying,

2 Now, thou son of man, [a]wilt thou [b]judge, wilt thou judge [c]the [d]bloody city? yea, thou shalt [e]show her all her abominations.

3 Then say thou, Thus saith the Lord GOD; The city sheddeth blood in the midst of it, that her time may come, and maketh idols against herself to defile herself.

4 Thou art become guilty in thy blood that thou hast [f]shed, and hast defiled thyself in thine idols which thou hast made; and thou hast caused thy days to draw near, and art come *even* unto thy years: [g]therefore have I made thee a reproach unto the heathen, and a mocking to all countries.

5 *Those that be* near, and *those that be* far from thee, shall mock thee, *which art* [h]infamous *and* much vexed.

6 Behold, [i]the princes of Israel, every one were in thee to their [k]power to shed blood.

7 In thee have they [l]set light by father and mother: in the midst of thee have they [m]dealt by [n]oppression with the stranger: in thee have they vexed the fatherless and the widow.

8 Thou hast [o]despised mine holy things, and hast [p]profaned my sabbaths.

9 In thee are [q]men [r]that carry tales to shed blood: [s]and in thee they eat upon the mountains: in the midst of thee they commit lewdness.

A. M. cir. 3411
B. C. cir. 593
Ol. XLVI. 4
Tarquinii Prisci,
R. Roman.,
cir. annum 24

10 In thee have they [t]discovered their father's nakedness: in thee have they humbled her that was [u]set apart for pollution.

11 And [v]one hath committed abomination [w]with his neighbour's wife; and [x]another [y]hath [z]lewdly defiled his daughter-in-law: and another in thee hath humbled his [a]sister, his father's daughter.

12 In thee [b]have they taken gifts to shed blood; [c]thou hast taken usury and increase, and thou hast greedily gained of thy neighbours by extortion, and [d]hast forgotten me, saith the Lord GOD.

13 Behold, therefore, I have [e]smitten mine hand at thy dishonest gain which thou hast made, and at thy blood which hath been in the midst of thee.

14 [f]Can thine heart endure, or can thine hands be strong, in the days that I shall deal with thee? [g]I the LORD have spoken *it,* and will do *it.*

15 And [h]I will scatter thee among the heathen, and disperse thee in the countries, and [i]will consume thy filthiness out of thee.

16 And thou [k]shalt take thine inheritance

---

[a]Chap. xx. 4; xxiii. 36——[b]Or, *plead for*——[c]Chap. xxiv. 6, 9; Nah. iii. 1——[d]Heb. *city of bloods*——[e]Heb. *make her know;* chap. xvi. 2——[f]2 Kings xxi. 16 [g]Deut. xxviii. 37; 1 Kings ix. 7; chap. v. 14; Dan. ix. 16 [h]Heb. *polluted of name, much in vexation*——[i]Isa. i. 23; Mic. iii. 1, 2, 3; Zeph. iii. 3——[k]Heb. *arm*——[l]Deut. xxvii. 16——[m]Exod. xxii. 21, 22——[n]Or, *deceit*——[o]Ver 26——[p]Lev. xix. 30; chap. xxiii. 38——[q]Heb. *men of slanders*——[r]Exod. xxiii. 1; Lev. xix. 16——[s]Chap. xviii. 6, 11——[t]Lev. xviii. 7, 8; xx. 11; 1 Cor. v. 1

[u]Lev. xviii. 19; xx. 18; chap. xviii. 6——[v]Or, *every one* [w]Lev. xviii. 20; xx. 10; Deut. xxii. 22; Jer. v. 8; chap. xviii. 11——[x]Or, *every one*——[y]Lev. xviii. 15; xx. 12 [z]Or, *by lewdness*——[a]Lev. xviii. 9; xx. 17——[b]Exod. xxiii. 8; Deut. xvi. 19; xxvii. 25——[c]Exod. xxii. 25; Lev. xxv. 36; Deut. xxiii. 19; chap. xviii. 13——[d]Deut. xxxii. 18; Jer. iii. 21; chap. xxiii. 35——[e]Chap. xxi. 17 [f]See chap. xxi. 7——[g]Chap. xvii. 24——[h]Deut. iv. 27; xxviii. 25, 64; chap. xii. 14, 15——[i]Chap. xxiii. 27, 48 [k]Or, *shalt be profaned*

NOTES ON CHAP. XXII

Verse 2. *Wilt thou judge the bloody city*] Pronounce the sentence of death against the murderers.

Show her all her abominations.] And a most revolting and dreadful catalogue of these is in consequence exhibited.

Verse 3. *Her time may come*] Till now, it was my long-suffering; she has fulfilled her days—completed the time of her probation; has not mended, but is daily worse; therefore her judgment can linger no longer.

Verse 4. *Thou art become guilty in thy blood*] Thou art guilty of blood.

Verse 5. Those that be *near*] Both *distant* as well as *neighbouring* provinces consider thee the most abandoned of characters; and through thee many have been involved in distress and ruin.

Verse 6. *Behold, the princes*] Ye are a vile and murderous people, and your princes have been of the same character. *Like people, like prince.*

Verse 7. *In thee have they set light*] The children do not reverence their parents. Parental affection and filial respect do not exist among you. The *stranger* is not only not succoured, but he is *oppressed.* The *widows* and *fatherless* are *vexed* by wrongs and exactions.

Verse 8. *Thou hast despised*] All my ordinances are not only neglected, but treated with contempt; and my Sabbaths profaned. There is not only no *power* of godliness among you, but there is no *form.*

Verse 9. *In thee are men that carry tales*] Witnesses that will swear any thing, even where life is concerned.

They eat upon the mountains] Sacrifice to *idols*, and celebrate their *festivals.*

Verse 10. *In thee have they discovered*] They are guilty of the most abominable *incest* and unnatural lust.

In thee have they humbled] In their unholy

A. M. cir. 3411
B. C. cir. 593
Ol. XLVI. 4
Tarquinii Prisci,
R. Roman.,
cir. annum 24

in thyself in the sight of the heathen, and [l]thou shalt know that I *am* the LORD.

17 And the word of the LORD came unto me, saying,

18 Son of man, [m]the house of Israel is to me become dross: all they *are* brass, and tin, and iron, and lead, in the midst of the furnace; they are *even* the [n]dross of silver.

19 Therefore thus saith the Lord GOD; Because ye are all become dross, behold, therefore I will gather you into the midst of Jerusalem.

20 [o]*As* they gather silver, and brass, and iron, and lead, and tin, into the midst of the furnace, to blow the fire upon it, to melt *it;* so will I gather *you* in mine anger and in my fury, and I will leave *you there,* and melt you.

21 Yea, I will gather you, and [p]blow upon you in the fire of my wrath, and ye shall be melted in the midst thereof.

22 As silver is melted in the midst of the furnace, so shall ye be melted in the midst thereof: and ye shall know that I the LORD have [q]poured out my fury upon you.

23 And the word of the LORD came unto me, saying,

24 Son of man, say unto her, Thou *art* the land that is not cleansed, nor rained upon in the day of indignation.

25 [r]*There is* a conspiracy of her prophets in the midst thereof, like a roaring lion ravening the prey: they [s]have devoured souls: [t]they have taken the treasure and precious things: they have made her many widows in the midst thereof.

A. M. cir. 3411
B. C. cir. 593
Ol. XLVI. 4
Tarquinii Prisci,
R. Roman.,
cir. annum 24

26 [u]Her priests have [v]violated my law, and have [w]profaned mine holy things; they have put no [x]difference between the holy and profane, neither have they showed *difference* between the unclean and the clean, and have hid their eyes from my sabbaths, and I am profaned among them.

27 [y]Her princes in the midst thereof *are* like wolves ravening the prey, to shed blood, *and* to destroy souls, to get dishonest gain.

28 And [z]her prophets have daubed them with untempered *mortar,* [a]seeing vanity, and divining lies unto them, saying, Thus saith the Lord GOD, when the LORD hath not spoken.

29 [b]The people of the land have used [c]oppression, and exercised robbery, and have vexed the poor and needy: yea, they have [d]oppressed the stranger [e]wrongfully.

30 [f]And I sought for a man among them, that should [g]make up the hedge, and [h]stand in the gap before me for the land, that I should not destroy it: but I found none.

31 Therefore have I [i]poured out mine indignation upon them; I have consumed them with the fire of my wrath: [k]their own way have I recompensed upon their heads, saith the Lord GOD.

[l]Psa. ix. 16; ch. vi. 7——[m]Isa. i. 22; Jer. vi. 28, &c.; see Psa. cxix. 119——[n]Heb. *drosses*——[o]Heb. according *to the gathering*——[p]Ch. xxii. 20, 21, 22——[q]Ch. xx. 8, 33; ver. 31——[r]Hos. vi. 9——[s]Matt. xxiii. 14——[t]Mic. iii. 11; Zeph. iii. 3, 4——[u]Mal. ii. 8——[v]Heb. *offered violence to*——[w]Lev. xxii. 2, &c.; 1 Sam. ii. 29——[x]Lev. x. 10; Jer. xv. 19; chap. xlv. 23

[y]Isa. i. 23; chap. xxii. 6; Mic. iii. 2, 3, 9, 10, 11; Zeph. iii. 3——[z]Chap. xiii. 10——[a]Chap. xiii. 6, 7; xxi. 29——[b]Jer. v. 26, 27, 28; chap. xviii. 12——[c]Or, *deceit*——[d]Exod. xxii. 21; xxiii. 9; Lev. xix. 33; chap. xxii. 7——[e]Heb. *without right*——[f]Jer. v. 1——[g]Chap. xiii. 5——[h]Psa. cvi. 23——[i]Ver. 22——[k]Chap. ix. 10; xi. 21; xvi. 43

and unnatural connexions, they have not abstained from those set apart because of their infirmities. The catalogue of crimes that follow is too plain to require comment.

Verse 16. *Thou shalt know that I* am *the Lord.*] I shall so deal with and punish thee, that thou shalt be obliged to own the vindictive hand of a sin-avenging God.

Verse 18. *The house of Israel is to me become dross*] They are all like *base metal—brass, tin, iron,* and *lead* alloyed together with *silver.* Ye must be put in the furnace, and subjected to the most intense fire, till your impurities are consumed away. No *ordinary* means will avail any thing; the most *violent* must be resorted to.

Verse 19. *I will gather you*] Jerusalem is represented here as the *fining pot;* all the people are to be gathered together in *it,* and the *Chaldean fire* is to *melt* the whole. And God will increase thy sufferings: as the refiner *blows the fire* with his bellows, so God will *blow upon you* with the *fire of his wrath,* ver. 21.

Verse 24. *Thou* art *the land that is not cleansed*] Thou art like a country where there is no *rain,* either *to cleanse* the *garments,* or *fertilize* the *ground.*

Verse 25. There is *a conspiracy*] The false prophets have united together to say and support the same things; and have been the cause of the destruction of souls, and the death of many, so that *widows,* through their means, are multiplied in thee.

Verse 26. *Her priests*] Even they whose lips should preserve knowledge, have not instructed the people: they *have violated my law,* not only in their private conduct, but in their careless and corrupt manner of serving in my temple.

Verse 27. *Her princes*] Are as bad as her *priests;* they are rapacious, and grievously oppress the people by unjust impositions in order to increase their revenues.

Verse 28. *Her prophets*] Even those who profess themselves to be my prophets, have been unfaithful in the discharge of their office; have *soothed* the people in their sins, and pretended to have oracles of *peace* and *safety* when I had not spoken to them.

Verse 29. *The people*] All that have power or authority have abused it; *vexed* and *oppressed* the *poor*, the *needy*, and the *stranger*.

Verse 30. *I sought for a man*] I saw that there was a grievous breach made in the *moral state* and *feeling* of the people, and I sought for a man that would stand in the gap; that would faithfully exhort, reprove, and counsel, with all long-suffering and doctrine. But none was to be found!

Verse 31. *Therefore*] Because of the *profligacies* already mentioned; because of the *false worship* so generally practised; because of the *false prophets* tolerated; because of the unholy and profane *priesthood;* because of the oppressive *princes;* because of the *unfaithful* and deceiving *prophets;* because of the oppressions of *petty officers;* and because of the *total corruption of manners* in all *ranks, places, offices,* &c.;—

Have I poured out mine indignation—consumed them with the fire of my wrath] Considering the above, has there not been sufficient reason why I should abandon such a people, and pour out upon them such a destructive storm of calamities?

CHAPTER XXIII

The idolatries of Samaria and Jerusalem are represented in this chapter by the bad practices of two common harlots, for which God denounces severe judgments against them, 1–49. *See the* sixteenth *chapter, where the same metaphor is enlarged upon as here, it being the prophet's view to excite the utmost detestation of the crime against which he inveighs.*

A. M. cir. 3411
B. C. cir. 593
Ol. XLVI. 4
Tarquinii Prisci,
R. Roman.,
cir. annum 24

THE word of the LORD came
again unto me, saying,
2 Son of man, there were
[a]two women, the daughters of
one mother:
3 And [b]they committed whoredoms in
Egypt; they committed whoredoms in [c]their
youth: there were their breasts pressed, and
there they bruised the teats of their virginity.
4 And the names of them *were* Aholah the
elder, and Aholibah her sister: and [d]they
were mine, and they bare sons and daughters.
Thus *were* their names; Sa-
maria *is* [e]Aholah, and Jerusalem [f]Aholibah.
5 And Aholah played the
harlot when she was mine; and she doted on
her lovers, on [g]the Assyrians *her* neighbours,
6 *Which were* clothed with blue, captains
and rulers, all of them desirable young men,
horsemen riding upon horses.
7 Thus she [h]committed her whoredoms with
them, with all them *that were* [i]the chosen men
of Assyria, and with all on whom she doted:

A. M. cir. 3411
B. C. cir. 593
Ol. XLVI. 4
Tarquinii Prisci,
R. Roman.,
cir. annum 24

[a]Jer. iii. 7, 8, 10; ch. xvi. 46——[b]Lev. xvii. 7; Josh. xxiv. 14; ch. xx. 8——[c]Ch. xvi. 22——[d]Ch. xvi. 8, 20——[e]That is, *His tent*, or *tabernacle*——[f]That is, *My tabernacle in her;* 1 Kings viii. 29——[g]2 Kings xv. 19; xvi. 7; xvii. 3; Hos. viii. 9——[h]Heb. *bestowed her whoredoms upon them*——[i]Heb. *the choice of the children of Ashur*

NOTES ON CHAP. XXIII

Verse 2. *Son of man, there were two women*] All the Hebrews were derived from *one source*, Abraham and Sarah; and, till the schism under Rehoboam, formed but one people: but as these ten tribes and a half separated from Judah and Benjamin, they became two distinct people under different kings; called the kingdom of Judah, and the kingdom of Israel. They are called here, because of their consanguinity, *two sisters*. The elder, Samaria, (for there was the *seat of government* for the kingdom of Israel,) was called אהלה *aholah*, "a tent." The younger, Judah, was called אהליבה *aholibah*, "my tent is in her," because the temple of God was in Jerusalem, the seat of the government of the kingdom of Judah.

Verse 5. *And Aholah played the harlot*] Without entering into detail here, or following the *figures*, they both became idolatrous, and received the impure rites of the Egyptians, Assyrians, and Chaldeans; of which connexion the prophet speaks here as he did in chap. xvi., which see.

In this chapter there are many of what we would call indelicate expressions, because a parallel is run between *idolatry* and *prostitution*, and the circumstances of the latter illustrate the peculiarities of the former. In such cases, perhaps, the *matter* alone was given to the prophet, and he was left to use his own language, and amplify as he saw good. *Ezekiel* was among the *Jews* what *Juvenal* was among the Romans,—a rough reprover of the most abominable vices. They both spoke of things as they found them; stripped vice naked, and scourged it publicly. The original is still more rough than the translation; and surely there is no need of a *comment* to explain imagery that is but too generally understood. I have said enough on chap. xvi., and to that I must refer the reader. It is true that there are a few things here in the shade that might be illustrated by *anatomy;* and it would not be difficult to do it: but they are not necessary to salvation, and I shall not take off the covering. They were sufficiently understood by those for whose use they were originally designed.

Verse 6. *Clothed with blue*] The *purple* dye was highly valued among the ancients, and at

A. M. cir. 3411
B. C. cir. 593
Ol. XLVI. 4
Tarquinii Prisci,
R. Roman.,
cir. annum 24

with all their idols she defiled herself.

8 Neither left she her whoredoms *brought* [k]from Egypt: for in her youth they lay with her, and they bruised the breasts of her virginity, and poured their whoredom upon her.

9 Wherefore I have delivered her into the hand of her lovers, into the hand of the [l]Assyrians, upon whom she doted.

10 These [m]discovered her nakedness: they took her sons and her daughters, and slew her with the sword: and she became [n]famous among women: for they had executed judgment upon her.

11 And [o]when her sister Aholibah saw *this*, [p]she [q]was more corrupt in her inordinate love than she, and in her whoredoms [r]more than her sister in *her* whoredoms.

12 She doted upon the [s]Assyrians *her* neighbours, [t]captains and rulers clothed most gorgeously, horsemen riding upon horses, all of them desirable young men.

13 Then I saw that she was defiled, *that* they *took* both one way,

14 And *that* she increased her whoredoms: for when she saw men pourtrayed upon the wall, the images of the Chaldeans pourtrayed with vermilion,

15 Girded with girdles upon their loins, exceeding in dyed attire upon their heads, all of them princes to look to, after the manner of the Babylonians of Chaldea, the land of their nativity:

16 [u]And [v]as soon as she saw them with her eyes, she doted upon them, and sent messengers unto them into Chaldea.

17 And the [w]Babylonians came to her into the bed of love, and they defiled her with their whoredom, and she was polluted with them, and [x]her mind was [y]alienated from them.

A. M. cir. 3411
B. C. cir. 593
Ol. XLVI. 4
Tarquinii Prisci,
R. Roman.,
cir. annum 24

18 So she discovered her whoredoms, and discovered her nakedness: then [z]my mind was alienated from her, like as my mind was alienated from her sister.

19 Yet she multiplied her whoredoms in calling to remembrance the days of her youth, [a]wherein she had played the harlot in the land of Egypt.

20 For she doted upon their paramours, [b]whose flesh *is as* the flesh of asses, and whose issue *is like* the issue of horses.

21 Thus thou calledst to remembrance the lewdness of thy youth, in bruising thy teats by the Egyptians for the paps of thy youth.

22 Therefore, O Aholibah, thus saith the Lord God; [c]Behold, I will raise up thy lovers against thee, from whom thy mind is alienated; and I will bring them against thee on every side;

23 The Babylonians, and all the Chaldeans, [d]Pekod, and Shoa, and Koa, *and* all the Assyrians with them: [e]all of them desirable young men, captains, and rulers, great lords and renowned, all of them riding upon horses.

24 And they shall come against thee with chariots, wagons, and wheels, and with an assembly of people, *which* shall set against thee buckler and shield and helmet round about: and I will set judgment before them, and they shall judge thee according to their judgments.

25 And I will set my jealousy against thee,

[k]Ver. 3——[l]2 Kings xvii. 3, 4, 5, 6, 23; xviii. 9, 10, 11——[m]Ch. xvi. 37, 41——[n]Heb. *a name*——[o]Jer. iii. 8——[p]Jer. iii. 11; ch. xvi. 47, 51——[q]Heb. *she corrupted her inordinate love more than*, &c.——[r]Heb. *more than the whoredoms of her sister*——[s]2 Kings xvi. 7, 10; 2 Chron. xxviii. 16–23; chap. xvi. 28

[t]Ver. 6, 23——[u]2 Kings xxiv. 1; chap. xvi. 29——[v]Hebrew, *at the sight of her eyes*——[w]Hebrew, *children of Babel*——[x]Ver. 22, 28——[y]Hebrew, *loosed*, or *disjointed*——[z]Jeremiah vi. 8——[a]Ver. 3——[b]Chap. xvi. 26——[c]Chap. xvi. 37; verse 28——[d]Jeremiah l. 21——[e]Ver. 12

first was only used by kings; at last it was used among the military, particularly by officers of high rank in the country.

Verse 14. *Men pourtrayed upon the wall*] See on chap. viii. 10.

Verse 20. *She doted upon their paramours*] פלגשיהם *pillagsheyhem*, their *harlots* or *concubines*. Anciently *harlot* meant in our language either the *male* or *female* prostitute.

***Whose flesh* is as *the flesh of asses*] See on chap. xvi. 25.**

Verse 23. *Pekod, and Shoa, and Koa*] פקוד ושוע וקוע. These names have been thought to designate certain people bordering on the Chaldeans; but no geographer has ever been able to find them out.

In our old translations these names were considered *appellatives—rulers*, *mighty men*, and *tyrants*. Others, following the literal import of the words, have translated, *visiting*, *shouting*, and *retreating*. Others have applied them to the *habits* of the Chaldean soldiers. *Pekod* signifying the *muster* or *review* of armies; *Shoa*, the *magnificence* of their *uniform* and

A. M. cir. 3411
B. C. cir. 593
Ol. XLVI. 4
Tarquinii Prisci,
R. Roman.,
cir. annum 24

and they shall deal furiously with thee: they shall take away thy nose and thine ears; and thy remnant shall fall by the sword: they shall take thy sons and thy daughters; and thy residue shall be devoured by the fire.

26 [f]They shall also strip thee out of thy clothes, and take away thy [g]fair jewels.

27 Thus [h]will I make thy lewdness to cease from thee, and [i]thy whoredom *brought* from the land of Egypt: so that thou shalt not lift up thine eyes unto them, nor remember Egypt any more.

28 For thus saith the Lord God; Behold, I will deliver thee into the hand *of them* [k]whom thou hatest, into the hand *of them* [l]from whom thy mind is alienated:

29 And they shall deal with thee hatefully, and shall take away all thy labour, and [m]shall leave thee naked and bare: and the nakedness of thy whoredoms shall be discovered, both thy lewdness and thy whoredoms.

30 I will do these *things* unto thee, because thou hast [n]gone a whoring after the heathen, *and* because thou art polluted with their idols.

31 Thou hast walked in the way of thy sister; therefore will I give her [o]cup into thine hand.

32 Thus saith the Lord God; Thou shalt drink of thy sister's cup deep and large: [p]thou shalt be laughed to scorn and had in derision; it containeth much.

33 Thou shalt be filled with drunkenness and sorrow, with the cup of astonishment and desolation, with the cup of thy sister Samaria.

A. M. cir. 3411
B. C. cir. 593
Ol. XLVI. 4
Tarquinii Prisci,
R. Roman.,
cir. annum 24

34 Thou shalt [q]even drink it and suck *it* out, and thou shalt break the sherds thereof, and pluck off thine own breasts: for I have spoken *it,* saith the Lord God.

35 Therefore thus saith the Lord God; Because thou [r]hast forgotten me, and [s]cast me behind thy back, therefore bear thou also thy lewdness and thy whoredoms.

36 The Lord said moreover unto me; Son of man, wilt thou [t]judge [u]Aholah and Aholibah? yea, [v]declare unto them their abominations;

37 That they have committed adultery, and [w]blood *is* in their hands, and with their idols have they committed adultery, and have also caused their sons, [x]whom they bare unto me, to pass for them through *the fire,* to devour *them.*

38 Moreover this they have done unto me: they have defiled my sanctuary in the same day, and [y]have profaned my sabbaths.

39 For when they had slain their children to their idols, then they came the same day into my sanctuary to profane it; and, lo, [z]thus have they done in the midst of mine house.

40 And furthermore, that ye have sent for men [a]to come from far, [b]unto whom a messenger *was* sent; and, lo, they came; for whom thou didst [c]wash thyself, [d]paintedst thy eyes, and deckedst thyself with ornaments.

[f]Ch. xvi. 39——[g]Heb. *instruments of thy decking* [h]Ch. xvi. 41; xxii. 15——[i]Ver. 3, 19——[k]Ch. xvi. 37 [l]Ver. 17——[m]Ch. xvi. 39; ver. 26——[n]Ch. vi. 9——[o]Jer xxv. 15, &c.——[p]Ch. xxii. 4, 5——[q]Psa. lxxv. 8; Isa. li. 17——[r]Jer. ii. 32; iii. 21; xiii. 25; ch. xxii. 12——[s]1 Kings xiv. 9; Neh. ix. 26——[t]Ch. xx. 4; xxii. 2

[u]Or, *plead for*——[v]Isa. lviii. 1——[w]Ch. xvi. 38; ver. 45——[x]Ch. xvi. 20, 21, 36, 45; xx. 26, 31——[y]Ch. xxii. 8 [z]2 Kings xxi. 4——[a]Heb. *coming*——[b]Isa. lvii. 9 [c]Ruth iii. 3——[d]2 Kings ix. 30; Jer. iv. 30——[e]Heb. *honourable*——[f]Esth. i. 6; Isa. lvii. 7; Amos ii. 8; vi. 4 [g]Prov. vii. 17; chap. xvi. 18, 19; Hos. ii. 8

arms; and *Koa*, the marks or *embroidery* of the clothes of the captains and generals. *Grotius* thought that they might be names of contiguous nations: *Pekod*, the *Bactrians; Shoa*, a people of *Armenia;* and *Koa*, the *Medes*. I have nothing to add that would satisfy myself, or be edifying to my readers.

Verse 25. *Shall take away thy nose*] A punishment frequent among the Persians and Chaldeans, as ancient authors tell. Adulteries were punished in this way; and to this *Martial* refers:—

Quis tibi persuasit nares abscindere mœcho?

"Who has counselled thee to cut off the adulterer's nose?"

Women were thus treated in Egypt. See *Calmet*.

Verse 26. *They shall also strip thee*] See on chap. xvi. 39.

Verse 32. *Thou shalt drink of thy sister's cup*] Thou shalt be ruined and desolated as Samaria was.

Verse 34. *Thou shalt—pluck off thine own breasts*] Thou shalt *tear them;* a frequent action in extreme sorrow and desolation. *Weeping, tearing the bosom, and beating the breasts.*

Tunc vero rupique sinus, et pectora planxi.
Ovid's Ep. 5.

Verse 38. *They have defiled my sanctuary*] By placing idols there.

Verse 40. *Thou didst wash thyself, paintedst thy eyes, and deckedst thyself with ornaments.*] This is exactly the way in which a loose female in Bengal adorns herself to receive guests. She first bathes, then rubs black paint around her

41 And satest upon a [e]stately [f]bed, and a table prepared before it, [g]whereupon thou hast set mine incense and mine oil.

A. M. cir. 3411
B. C. cir. 593
Ol. XLVI. 4
Tarquinii Prisci,
R. Roman.,
cir. annum 24

42 And a voice of a multitude being at ease *was* with her: and with the men [h]of the common sort *were* brought [i]Sabeans from the wilderness, which put bracelets upon their hands, and beautiful crowns upon their heads.

43 Then said I unto *her that was* old in adulteries, Will they now commit [k]whoredoms with her, and she *with them?*

44 Yet they went in unto her, as they go in unto a woman that playeth the harlot: so went they in unto Aholah and unto Aholibah, the lewd women.

45 And the righteous men, they shall [l]judge them after the manner of adulteresses, and after the manner of women that shed blood; because they *are* adulteresses, and [m]blood *is* in their hands.

A. M. cir. 3411
B. C. cir. 593
Ol. XLVI. 4
Tarquinii Prisci,
R. Roman.,
cir. annum 24

46 For thus saith the Lord God, [n]I will bring up a company upon them, and will give them [o]to be removed and spoiled.

47 [p]And the company shall stone them with stones, and [q]despatch them with their swords; they [r]shall slay their sons and their daughters, and burn up their houses with fire.

48 Thus [s]will I cause lewdness to cease out of the land, [t]that all women may be taught not to do after your lewdness.

49 And they shall recompense your lewdness upon you, and ye shall [u]bear the sins of your idols: [v]and ye shall know that I *am* the Lord God.

[h]Heb. *of the multitude of men*——[i]Or, *drunkards*——[k]Heb. *her whoredoms*——[l]Chap. xvi. 38——[m]Ver. 37——[n]Chap. xvi. 40——[o]Heb. *for a removing and spoil*——[p]Chap. xvi. 41——[q]Or, *single them out*——[r]2 Chron. xxxvi. 17, 19; chap. xxiv. 21——[s]Chap. xxii. 15; ver. 27——[t]Deut. xiii. 11; 2 Pet. ii. 6——[u]Ver. 35——[v]Chap. xx. 38, 42, 44; xxv. 5

eyes, and then covers her body with ornaments. —Ward's *Customs.*

Verse 41. *And satest upon a stately bed*] Hast raised a stately altar to thy idols; probably alluding to that which Ahaz ordered to be made, after the similitude of that which he saw at Damascus. The *bed* here is in allusion to the *sofas* on which the ancients were accustomed to recline at their meals; or to the couches on which they place Asiatic brides, with incense pots and sweetmeats on a table before them.

Verse 42. *And a voice of a multitude*] This seems to be an account of an idolatrous festival, where a riotous multitude was assembled, and fellows of the baser sort, with *bracelets* on their arms and *chaplets* on their heads, performed the religious rites.

Verse 45. *And the righteous men*] אנשים צדיקים *anashim tsaddikim.* The Chaldeans, thus called because they are appointed by God to *execute judgment* on these criminals.

Verse 47. *Shall stone them with stones*] As they did adulteresses under the law. See Lev. xx. 10, Deut. xxii. 22, compared with John viii. 3.

Verse 48. *Thus will I cause lewdness to cease*] *Idolatry;* and from that time to the present day the Jews never relapsed into idolatry.

Verse 49. *Ye shall bear the sins of your idols*] The punishment due to your adultery; your apostasy from God, and setting up idolatry in the land.

CHAPTER XXIV

The prophet now informs those of the captivity of the very day on which Nebuchadnezzar was to lay siege to Jerusalem, (compare Jer. lii. 4,) *and describes the fate of that city and its inhabitants by a very apt similitude,* 1–14. *As another sign of the greatness of those calamities, the prophet is forbidden to mourn for his wife, of whom he is to be deprived; intimating thereby that the sufferings of the Jews should be so astonishing as to surpass all expressions of grief; and that private sorrow, however affectionate and tender the object, ought to be absorbed in the public calamities,* 15–18. *The prophet, having farther expressed his prediction in plain terms, intimates that he was to speak to* them *no more till they should have the news of these prophecies having been fulfilled,* 19–27.

A. M. 3414
B. C. 590
Ol. XLVII. 3
Anno
Tarquinii Prisci,
R. Roman., 27

AGAIN in the ninth year, in the tenth month, in the tenth *day* of the month, the [a]word of the Lord came unto me, saying,

2 Son of man, write thee the name of the day, *even* of this same day: the king of Babylon set himself against Jerusalem [b]this same day.

A. M. 3414
B. C. 590
Ol. XLVII. 3
Anno
Tarquinii Prisci,
R. Roman., 27

3 [c]And utter a parable unto the rebellious

[a]Chap. xxiii. 1——[b]2 Kings xxv. 1; Jer. xxxix1; lii. 4.——[c]Chap. xvii. 12

NOTES ON CHAP. XXIV

Verse 1. *The ninth year*] This prophecy was given in the *ninth* year of Zedekiah, about *Thursday*, the *thirtieth* of *January*, A. M. 3414; the very day in which the king of Babylon commenced the siege of Jerusalem.

Verse 3. *Set on a pot*] The *pot* was Jeru-

A. M. 3414
B. C. 590
Ol. XLVII. 3
Anno
Tarquinii Prisci,
R. Roman., 27

house, and say unto them,
Thus saith the Lord GOD; [d]Set
on a pot, set *it* on, and also
pour water into it:
4 Gather the pieces thereof into it, *even*
every good piece, the thigh, and the shoulder;
fill *it* with the choice bones.
5 Take the choice of the flock, and [e]burn
also the bones under it, *and* make it boil well,
and let them seethe the bones of it therein.
6 Wherefore thus saith the Lord GOD; Wo
to [f]the bloody city, to the pot whose scum *is*
therein, and whose scum is not gone out of
it! bring it out piece by piece; let no [g]lot
fall upon it.
7 For her blood is in the midst of her; she
set it upon the top of a rock; [h]she poured it
not upon the ground, to cover it with dust;
8 That it might cause fury to come up to
take vengeance; [i]I have set her blood upon
the top of a rock, that it should not be covered.
9 Therefore thus saith the Lord GOD; [k]Wo
to the bloody city! I will even make the pile
for fire great.
10 Heap on wood, kindle the fire, consume
the flesh, and spice it well,
and let the bones be burned.
11 Then set it empty upon
the coals thereof, that the
brass of it may be hot, and may burn, and *that*
[l]the filthiness of it may be molten in it, *that*
the scum of it may be consumed.
12 She hath wearied *herself* with lies, and
her great scum went not forth out of her: her
scum *shall be* in the fire.
13 In thy filthiness *is* lewdness; because I
have purged thee, and thou wast not purged,
thou shalt not be purged from thy filthiness
any more, [m]till I have caused my fury to rest
upon thee.
14 [n]I the LORD have spoken *it:* it shall come
to pass, and I will do *it;* I will not go back;
[o]neither will I spare, neither will I repent;
according to thy ways, and according to thy
doings, shall they judge thee, saith the Lord
GOD.
15 Also the word of the LORD came unto
me, saying,
16 Son of man, behold, I take away from
thee the desire of thine eyes with a stroke:

A. M. 3414
B. C. 590
Ol. XLVII. 3
Anno
Tarquinii Prisci,
R. Roman., 27

[d]See Jer. i. 13; chap. xi. 3——[e]Or, *heap*——[f]Chap. xxii. 3; xxiii. 37; ver. 9——[g]See 2 Sam. viii. 2; Joel iii. 3; Obad. 11; Nah. iii. 10——[h]Lev. xvii. 13; Deut. xii. 16, 24——[i]Matt. vii. 2——[k]Ver. 6; Nah. iii. 1; Hab. ii. 12 [l]Chap. xxii. 15——[m]Chap. v. 13; viii. 18; xvi. 42 [n]1 Sam. xv. 29——[o]Chap. v. 11

salem; the *flesh*, the inhabitants in general; *every good piece, the thigh* and *the shoulder*, King Zedekiah and his family; the *bones*, the soldiers; and *the setting on* the *pot*, the commencement of the siege. The prophet was then in *Mesopotamia;* and he was told particularly to mark the day, &c., that it might be seen how precisely the spirit of prophecy had shown the very day in which the siege took place. Under the same image of a *boiling pot*, Jeremiah had represented the siege of Jerusalem, chap. i. 13. Ezekiel was a priest; the action of boiling pots was familiar to him, as these things were much in use in the temple service.

Verse 5. *Make it boil well*] Let it boil over, that its own scum may augment the fire, that the *bones*—the soldiers, may be *seethed therein.* Let its contentions, divided counsels, and disunion be the means of increasing its miseries, רתח רתחיה *rattach rethacheyha*, let it bubble its bubbling; something like that of the poet:—

"Bubble, bubble, toil and trouble:
Fire burn, and cauldron bubble."

Very like the noise made by ebullition, when a *pot of thick broth*, "sleek and slab," is set over a fierce fire. Such was that here represented, in which all the *flesh*, the *fat*, and the *bones* were to be boiled, and generally dissolved together.

Verse 6. *Let no lot fall upon it.*] Pull out the flesh indiscriminately; let no piece be *chosen* for *king* or *priest;* thus showing that all should be involved in one indiscriminate ruin.

Verse 7. *For her blood is in the midst of her*] She gloried in her idol sacrifices; she offered them upon a *rock*, where the blood should *remain evident;* and she poured none upon the *ground* to cover it with dust, in horror of that moral evil that required the blood of an innocent creature to be shed, in order to the atonement of the offender's guilt. To "cover the blood of the victim," was a command of the law, Lev. xvii. 13; Deut. xii. 24.

Verse 8. *That it might cause fury*] This very blood shall be against them, as the blood of *Abel* was against *Cain.*

Verse 10. *Heap on wood*] Let the siege be *severe*, the carnage great, and the ruin and catastrophe complete.

Verse 13. *In thy filthiness* is *lewdness*] זמה *zimmah*, a word that denominates the *worst kinds of impurity; adultery, incest*, &c., and the *purpose, wish, design*, and *ardent desire* to do these things. Hers were not *accidental* sins, they were *abominations by design;* and they were the worse in her, because God had *cleansed her*, had separated the Israelites from idolatry and idolatrous nations, and by his institutions removed from them all idolatrous incentives. But they formed *alliances* with the *heathen*, and adopted all their abominations; therefore God would not spare them. See ver. 14.

Verse 16. *Behold, I take away from thee the desire of thine eyes*] Here is an intimation that the stroke he was to suffer was to be above

A. M. 3414
B. C. 590
Ol. XLVII. 3
Anno
Tarquinii Prisci,
R. Roman., 27

yet neither shalt thou mourn
nor weep, neither shall thy
tears [p]run down.
17 [q]Forbear to cry, [r]make no
mourning for the dead, [s]bind the tire of thine
head upon thee, and [t]put on thy shoes upon
thy feet, and [u]cover not *thy* [v]lips, and eat not
the bread of men.
18 So I spake unto the people in the morning: and at even my wife died; and I did in
the morning as I was commanded.
19 And the people said unto me, [w]Wilt thou
not tell us what these *things are* to us, that
thou doest *so?*
20 Then I answered them, The word of the
LORD came unto me, saying,
21 Speak unto the house of Israel, Thus saith
the Lord GOD; Behold, [x]I will profane my
sanctuary, the excellency of your strength,
[y]the desire of your eyes, and [z]that which your
soul pitieth; [a]and your sons and your daughters whom ye have left, shall fall by the
sword.
22 And ye shall do as I have done: [b]ye
shall not cover *your* lips, nor
eat the bread of men.
23 And your tires *shall be*
upon your heads, and your
shoes upon your feet: [c]ye shall not mourn nor
weep; but [d]ye shall pine away for your iniquities, and mourn one toward another.
24 Thus [e]Ezekiel is unto you a sign: according to all that he hath done shall ye do:
[f]and when this cometh, [g]ye shall know that
I *am* the Lord GOD.
25 Also, thou son of man, *shall it* not *be* in
the day when I take from them [h]their
strength, the joy of their glory, the desire of
their eyes, and [i]that whereupon they set their
minds, their sons and their daughters,
26 *That* [k]he that escapeth in that day shall
come unto thee, to cause *thee* to hear *it* with
thine ears?
27 [l]In that day shall thy mouth be opened
to him which is escaped, and thou shalt speak,
and be no more dumb: and [m]thou shalt be a
sign unto them; and they shall know that I
am the LORD.

A. M. 3414
B. C. 590
Ol. XLVII. 3
Anno
Tarquinii Prisci,
R. Roman., 27

[p]Heb. *go*——[q]Heb. *Be silent*——[r]Jer. xvi. 5, 6, 7——[s]See Lev. x. 6; xxi. 10——[t]2 Sam. xv. 30——[u]Mic. iii. 7——[v]Heb. *upper lip;* and so ver. 22; Lev. xiii. 45——[w]Chap. xii. 9; xxxvii. 18——[x]Jer. vii. 14; chap. vii. 20, 21, 22——[y]Psa. xxvii. 4——[z]Heb. *the pity of your soul*——[a]Chap. xxiii. 47

[b]Jer. xvi. 6, 7; ver. 17——[c]Job xxvii. 15; Psa. lxxviii. 64——[d]Lev. xxvi. 39; ch. xxxiii. 10——[e]Isa. xx. 3; ch. iv. 3; xii. 6, 11——[f]Jer. xvii. 15; John xiii. 19; xiv. 29——[g]Chap. vi. 7; xxv. 5——[h]Ver. 21——[i]Heb. *the lifting up of their soul*——[k]Chap. iii. 21, 22——[l]Chap. iii. 26, 27; xxix. 21; xxxiii. 22——[m]Ver. 24

all grief; that it would be so great as to prevent the relief of tears.

Curæ leves loquuntur, graviores silent,

is a well-accredited maxim in such cases. Superficial griefs affect the more easily moved passions; great ones affect the soul itself, in its powers of reasoning, reflecting, comparing, recollecting, &c., when the sufferer feels all the weight of wo.

Neither shall thy tears run down.] Τουτο γαρ ιδιον των οφθαλμων εν τοις μεγαλοις κακοις· εν μεν γαρ ταις μετριαις συμφοραις αφθονως τα δακρυα καταῤῥει, ———εν δε τοις ὑπερβαλλουσι δεινοις φευγει και τα δακρυα και προδιδωσι και τους αφθαλμους· Achill. Tat. lib. 3. c. 11. For this is the case with the eyes in great calamities: in light misfortunes tears flow freely, but in heavy afflictions tears fly away, and betray the eyes.

Verse 17. *Make no mourning*] As a *priest*, he could make no public mourning, Lev. xxi. 1, &c.

Bind the tire of thine head] This seems to refer to the high priest's bonnet; or perhaps, one worn by the ordinary priests: it might have been a black veil to cover the head.

Put on thy shoes upon thy feet] Walking barefoot was a sign of grief.

Cover not thy *lips*] Mourners covered the under part of the face, from the nose to the bottom of the chin.

Eat not the bread of men.] לחם אנשים *lechem anashim*, "the bread of miserable men," i. e., *mourners;* probably, the funeral banquet.

Verse 18. *At even my wife died*] The prophet's wife was a type of the city, which was to him exceedingly dear. The *death of his wife* represented the *destruction of the city* by the Chaldeans; see ver. 21, where the *temple* is represented to be the *desire of his eyes*, as his *wife* was, ver. 16.

Verse 19. *Wilt thou not tell us*] In the following verses he explains and applies the whole of what he had *done* and *said.*

Verse 27. *In that day shall thy mouth be opened*] That is, When some one who shall have escaped from Jerusalem, having arrived among the captives, shall inform them of the destruction of the city, the temple, the royal family, and the people at large; till then he might suppress his tears and lamentations. And we find from chap. xxxiii. 21, that one did actually escape from the city, and informed the prophet and his brethren in captivity that the *city was smitten.*

Thus he was not only a prophet to foretell such things, but he was also a *sign* or *portent*, shadowing them out by circumstances in his own person and family; and thus the prediction, agreeing so perfectly with the event, proved that the previous information was from the Lord.

CHAPTER XXV

This chapter contains threatenings of the heavy judgments of God against the Ammonites, 1–7; Moabites, 8–11; Edomites, 12–14; and Philistines, 15–17; on account of their hatred to his people, and their insulting them in the time of their distress. These prophecies were fulfilled by the instrumentality of Nebuchadnezzar, about five years after the destruction of Jerusalem. The same events were predicted by several of the other prophets, as may be seen from the citation of parallel texts in the margin.

A. M. 3414
B. C. 590
Ol. XLVII. 3
Anno
Tarquinii Prisci,
R. Roman., 27

THE word of the LORD came
again unto me, saying,
2 Son of man, [a]set thy face
[b]against the Ammonites, and
prophesy against them;
3 And say unto the Ammonites, Hear the
word of the Lord GOD; Thus saith the Lord
GOD; [c]Because thou saidst, Aha, against my
sanctuary, when it was profaned; and against
the land of Israel, when it was desolate; and
against the house of Judah, when they went
into captivity;
4 Behold, therefore I will deliver thee to the
[d]men of the east for a possession, and they
shall set their palaces in thee, and make their
dwellings in thee: they shall eat thy fruit, and
they shall drink thy milk.
5 And I will make [e]Rabbah [f]a stable for
camels, and the Ammonites a couching-place
for flocks: [g]and ye shall know that I *am* the
LORD.
6 For thus saith the Lord GOD; Because
thou [h]hast clapped *thine*
[i]hands, and stamped with the
[k]feet, and [l]rejoiced in [m]heart
with all thy despite against
the land of Israel;
7 Behold, therefore I will [n]stretch out mine
hand upon thee, and will deliver thee for [o]a
spoil to the heathen; and I will cut thee off
from the people, and I will cause thee to
perish out of the countries: I will destroy
thee; and [p]thou shalt know that I *am* the
LORD.
8 Thus saith the Lord GOD; Because that
[q]Moab and [r]Seir do say, Behold, the house
of Judah *is* like unto all the heathen;
9 Therefore, behold, I will open the [s]side of
Moab from the cities, from his cities *which are*
on his frontiers, the glory of the country,
Beth-jeshimoth, Baal-meon, and Kiriathaim,
10 [t]Unto the men of the east [u]with the
Ammonites, and will give them in possession,
that the Ammonites [v]may not be remembered
among the nations.

A. M. 3414
B. C. 590
Ol. XLVII. 3
Anno
Tarquinii Prisci,
R. Roman., 27

[a]Chap. vi. 2; xxxv. 2——[b]Jer. xlix. 1, &c.; chap. xxi. 28; Amos i. 13; Zeph. ii. 9——[c]Prov. xvii. 5; chap. xxvi. 2——[d]Heb. *children*——[e]Chap. xxi. 20——[f]Isa. xvii. 2; xxxii. 14; Zeph. ii. 14, 15——[g]Chap. xxiv. 24; xxvi. 6; xxxv. 9——[h]Job xxvii. 23; Lam. ii. 15; Zeph. ii. 15
[i]Heb. *hand*

[k]Heb. *foot*——[l]Chap. xxxvi. 5; Zeph. ii. 8, 10
[m]Heb. *soul*——[n]Chap. xxxv. 3——[o]Or, *meat*——[p]Ch. xxii. 16; xxiv. 24——[q]Isa. xv., xvi.; Jer. xlviii. 1, &c.; Amos ii. 1——[r]Chap. xxxv. 2, 5, 12——[s]Heb. *shoulder of Moab*——[t]Ver. 4——[u]Or, *against the children of Ammon*——[v]Chap. xxi. 32

NOTES ON CHAP. XXV

Verse 1. *The word of the Lord*] The chronological order of this chapter is after chap. xxxiii. 21, &c. See Abp. *Newcome.*

Verse 2. *Set thy face against the Ammonites*] We have already seen, chap. xxi. 19, &c., that when Nebuchadnezzar left Babylon, he was in doubt whether he should besiege Riblath, the capital of the Ammonites, or Jerusalem, the capital of the Jews, first: and having used his divination, he was determined, by the result, to attack Jerusalem the first. He did so; and the Ammonites, seeing the success of his arms, made friends with him, and exulted in the ruin of the Jews. God resents this, and predicts their downfall with that of Edom, Moab, and the Philistines. The fulfilment of this prediction is not noted in Scripture: but *Josephus* tells us, that about *five* years after the taking of Jerusalem, Nebuchadnezzar turned his arms against the *Ammonites* and *Moabites*, and afterwards against *Egypt;* and having subdued those nations, he returned to Babylon. *Joseph.* Antiq., l. x., c. ii. *Berosus* states, as quoted by Josephus, contra App., that Nebuchadnezzar subdued Syria, Arabia, Phœnicia, and Egypt: and consequently, that he had brought under his dominion the Ammonites, Moabites, and Idumeans, who were included among the *Philistines.* See *Calmet.*

Verse 4. *Will deliver thee to the men of the east*] Probably the *Scenite Arabs, Ishmaelites,* and people of Kedar, who seized upon the provinces of the vanquished *Ammonites,* &c. The following description suits this people only, living on fruits, the milk of their flocks, using camels, &c. Some think the *people of the east* mean the *Chaldeans.*

Verse 7. *I will cause thee to perish*] Except in history, the name of the Ammonites does not now exist.

Verse 8. *Moab and Seir do say*] *Seir* means the *Idumeans.* It appears that both these, with the Ammonites, had made a league with Zedekiah, Jer. xxvii. 3, which they did not keep; and it is supposed that they even joined with the Chaldeans.

Verse 9. *I will open the side*] כתף *ketheph,* the shoulder, the strongest frontier place. *Beth-jeshimoth, Baal-meon,* and *Kiriathaim* were strong frontier towns of Moab.

Verse 10. *That the Ammonites*] The Syriac

A. M. 3414
B. C. 590
Ol. XLVII. 3
Anno
Tarquinii Prisci,
R. Roman., 27

11 And I will execute judgments upon Moab; and they
shall know that I *am* the LORD.
12 Thus saith the Lord GOD;
[w]Because that Edom hath dealt against the house of Judah [x]by taking vengeance, and hath greatly offended, and revenged himself upon them;
13 Therefore thus saith the Lord GOD; I
will also stretch out mine hand upon Edom, and will cut off man and beast from it; and I will make it desolate from Teman; and [y]they of Dedan shall fall by the sword.
14 And [z]I will lay my vengeance upon
Edom by the hand of my people Israel: and they shall do in Edom according to mine anger and according to my fury; and they shall know my vengeance, saith the Lord GOD.
15 Thus saith the Lord GOD;
[a]Because [b]the Philistines have dealt by revenge, and have taken vengeance with a despiteful heart, to destroy *it* [c]for the old hatred;
16 Therefore thus saith the Lord GOD; Be-
hold, [d]I will stretch out mine hand upon the Philistines, and I will cut off the [e]Cherethims, [f]and destroy the remnant of the [g]sea coasts.
17 And I will [h]execute great [i]vengeance
upon them with furious [k]rebukes; [l]and they shall know that I *am* the LORD, when I shall lay my vengeance upon them.

[w]2 Chron. xxviii. 17; Psa. cxxxvii. 7; Jer. xlix. 7, 8, &c.; chap. xxxv. 2, &c.; Amos i. 11; Obad. 10, &c.; &c.; 1 Esd. iv. 45——[x]Heb. *by revenging revengement*——[y]Or, *they shall fall by the sword unto Dedan*——[z]See Isa. xi. 14; Jer. xlix. 2; 1 Mac. v. 3; 2 Mac. x. 16, 17——[a]Jer. xxv. 20; xlvii. 1, &c.; Joel iii. 4, &c.; Amos i. 6——[b]2 Chron. xxviii. 18——[c]Or, *with perpetual hatred*——[d]Zeph. ii. 4, &c.——[e]1 Sam. xxx. 14——[f]Jer. xlvii. 4——[g]Or, *haven of the sea*——[h]Chap. v. 15——[i]Hebrew, *vengeances*——[k]1 Chron. xii. 17; Psa. lxviii. 30; Isa. ii. 4; xvii. 13; Micah iv. 3; Malachi iii. 11——[l]Psalm ix. 16

has, "That Rabbah of the sons of Ammon be not remembered."

Verse 12. *Because that Edom hath dealt*] The Edomites were the most inveterate enemies of the Jews from the very earliest times, and ever did all that they could to annoy them.

Verse 13. *I will make it desolate from Teman*] *Teman* and *Dedan* were both cities of the Moabites, and apparently at each extremity of the land.

Verse 14. *I will lay my vengeance upon Edom*] God will not allow men to insult those whom he has cast down. His judgment is sufficient; to add more is an insult to God.

By the hand of my people Israel] This was fulfilled by the Maccabees, who not only defeated them and brought them under complete subjection, but obliged them to receive circumcision, *Joseph.* Antiq. l. xiii., c. 17; 1 Macc. v. 65; 2 Macc. x. 16.

Verse 15. *Because the Philistines*] They were as inimical to the Jews as the Ammonites, &c., were. Nebuchadnezzar punished them because they had assisted the Tyrians during the time he was besieging their city.

I will cut off the Cherethims] See the note on 2 Sam. viii. 18.

The remnant of the sea coasts.] The different seignories of the Philistines inhabited the coast of the Mediterranean Sea, from Judea to Egypt. For other matters relative to these prophecies, see the passages in the margin.

CHAPTER XXVI

This prophecy, beginning here and ending in the twentieth verse of the twenty-eighth *chapter, is a declaration of the judgments of God against Tyre, a very famous commercial city of antiquity, which was taken by Nebuchadnezzar after an arduous siege of thirteen years. The prophet begins with introducing Tyre insulting Jerusalem, and congratulating herself on the prospect of accession to her commerce now that this city was no more,* 1, 2. *Upon which God denounces utter destruction to Tyre, and the cities depending on her,* 3–6. *We have then a particular account of the person raised up in the course of the Divine providence to accomplish this work. We see, as it were, his mighty hosts, (which are likened to the* waves *of the sea for their multitude,) raising the mounds, setting the engines, and shaking the walls; we hear the noise of the horsemen, and the sound of their cars; we see the clouds of smoke and dust; we see the sword bathed in blood, and hear the groans of the dying. Tyre, (whose buildings were very splendid and magnificent, and whose walls were* one hundred and fifty *feet in height, with a proportionable breadth,) immediately disappears; her strong (and as she thought impregnable) towers are thrown down; and her very dust is buried in the sea. Nothing remains but the bare rock,* 7–14. *The scene is then varied. The isles and adjacent regions, by a very strong and beautiful figure, are represented to be shaken, as with a mighty earthquake by violent concussion occasioned by the fall of Tyre. The groans of the dying reach the ears of the people inhabiting these regions. Their princes, alarmed for themselves and grieved for Tyre, descend from their thrones, lay aside their robes, and clothe themselves with—sackcloth?—no, but with* trembling! *Arrayed in this astonishing attire, the prophet introduces them as a chorus of mourners, lamenting Tyre in a funeral song or dirge, as customary on the death of renowned personages. And pursuing the same image still farther, in the person of God, he performs the last sad office for her. She is brought forth from her place in solemn pomp; the pit is dug for her; and she is buried, to rise no more,* 15–21. *Such is the prophecy concerning Tyre, comprehending both the city on the continent and that on the island, and most punctually fulfilled in regard to both. That on the continent was razed to the ground by Nebuchadnezzar, B. C.* 572, *and that on the island by Alexander the Great, B. C.* 332. *And at present, and for ages past, this ancient and renowned city, once the emporium of the world, and by her great naval superiority the centre of a powerful monarchy, is literally what the prophet has repeatedly foretold it should be, and what in his time was, humanly speaking, so highly improbable*—a BARE rock, a place to spread nets on!

A. M. 3416
B. C. 588
Ol. XLVIII. 1
Anno
Tarquinii Prisci,
R. Roman., 29

AND it came to pass in the eleventh year, in the first *day* of the month, *that* the word of the LORD came unto me, saying,

2 Son of man, [a]because that Tyrus hath said against Jerusalem, [b]Aha, she is broken *that was* the gates of the people: she is turned unto me: I shall be replenished, *now* she is laid waste:

3 Therefore, thus saith the Lord GOD: Behold, I *am* against thee, O Tyrus, and will cause many nations to come up against thee, as the sea causeth his waves to come up.

4 And they shall destroy the walls of Tyrus, and break down her towers: I will also scrape her dust from her, and [c]make her like the top of a rock.

5 It shall be *a place for* the spreading of nets, [d]in the midst of the sea: for I have spoken *it,* saith the Lord GOD: and it shall become a spoil to the nations.

6 And her daughters which *are* in the field shall be slain by the sword; [e]and they shall know that I *am* the LORD.

A. M. 3416
B. C. 588
Ol. XLVIII. I
Anno
Tarquinii Prisci,
R. Roman, 29

7 For thus saith the Lord GOD; Behold, I will bring upon Tyrus Nebuchadrezzar king of Babylon, [f]a king of kings, from the north, with horses, and with chariots, and with horsemen, and companies, and much people.

8 He shall slay with the sword thy daughters in the field: and he shall [g]make a fort against thee, and [h]cast a mount against thee, and lift up the buckler against thee.

9 And he shall set engines of war against thy walls, and with his axes he shall break down thy towers.

10 By reason of the abundance of his horses their dust shall cover thee: thy walls shall shake at the noise of the horsemen, and of the wheels, and of the chariots, when he shall enter into thy gates, [i]as men enter into a city wherein is made a breach.

---

[a]Isa. xxiii.; Jer. xxv. 22; xlvii. 4; Amos i. 9; Zech. ix. 2 [b]Chap. xxv. 3; xxxvi. 2——[c]Ver. 14——[d]Chap. xxvii. 32——[e]Chap. xxv. 5

[f]Ezra vii. 12; Dan. ii. 37——[g]Chap. xxi. 22——[h]Or, *pour out the engine of shot*——[i]Heb. *according to the enterings of a city broken up*

Verse 1. *The eleventh year*] This was the year in which Jerusalem was taken; the *eleventh* of the captivity of Jeconiah, and the *eleventh* of the reign of Zedekiah. What *month* we are not told, though the *day* is mentioned. There have been many conjectures about this, which are not of sufficient consequence to be detailed.

Verse 2. *Tyrus hath said*] From this it would appear that Jerusalem *had been* taken, which was on the *fourth* month of this year; but it is possible that the prophet speaks of the event beforehand.

She is broken that was *the gates of the people*] Jerusalem, a general emporium.

I shall be replenished] The merchandise that went to Jerusalem will come to me, (to Tyre.)

Verse 3. *Will cause many nations to come up against thee*] We have already seen that the empire of the Chaldeans was composed of many different provinces, and that Nebuchadnezzar's army was composed of soldiers from different nations: these may be the people meant; but I doubt whether this may not refer to the different nations which in successive ages fought against Tyre. It was at last finally destroyed in the *sixteenth* century of the Christian era.

Verse 4. *I will also scrape her dust from her*] I will totally destroy her fortifications, and leave her nothing but a barren rock, as she was before. This cannot refer to the capture of Tyre by Nebuchadnezzar. It flourished long after his time.

Verse 5. A place for *the spreading of nets*] A place for the habitation of some poor fishermen, who spent the fishing season there, and were accustomed to dry their nets upon the rocks. See on ver. 11.

Verse 6. *And her daughters*] The places dependent on Tyre. As there were *two* places called *Tyre,* one on the *main land,* and the other on a *rock* in the sea, opposite to that on the main land, sometimes the one seems to be spoken of, and sometimes the other. That on the *land, Palœtyre,* was soon taken; but that in the sea cost Nebuchadnezzar *thirteen years* of siege and blockade. The two formed only *one city,* and one state.

Verse 7. *Nebuchadrezzar—king of kings*] An ancient title among those proud Asiatic despots شاهنشاه پدشاه *shahinshah* and *padshah,* titles still in use.

Verse 8. *Thy daughters in the field*] This seems to be spoken of *Palœtyre,* or Tyre on the main land; for *forts, mounts, engines of war, horses,* and *chariots* could not be brought to act against the other.

A. M. 3416
B. C. 588
Ol. XLVIII. 1
Anno
Tarquinii Prisci,
R. Roman., 29

11 With the hoofs of his horses shall he tread down all thy streets: he shall slay thy people by the sword, and thy strong garrisons shall go down to the ground.

12 And they shall make a spoil of thy riches, and make a prey of thy merchandise: and they shall break down thy walls, and destroy [k]thy pleasant houses: and they shall lay thy stones and thy timber and thy dust in the midst of the water.

13 [l]And I will cause the noise of [m]thy songs to cease; and the sound of thy harps shall be no more heard.

14 And [n]I will make thee like the top of a rock: thou shalt be *a place* to spread nets upon; thou shalt be built no more: for I the LORD have spoken *it,* saith the Lord GOD.

15 Thus saith the Lord GOD to Tyrus; Shall not the isles [o]shake at the sound of thy fall, when the wounded cry, when the slaughter is made in the midst of thee?

16 Then all the [p]princes of the sea shall [q]come down from their thrones, and lay away their robes, and put off their broidered garments: they shall clothe themselves with [r]trembling; [s]they shall sit upon the ground, and [t]shall tremble at *every* moment, and [u]be astonished at thee.

A. M. 3416
B. C. 588
Ol. XLVIII. 1
Anno
Tarquinii Prisci,
R. Roman., 29

17 And they shall take up a [v]lamentation for thee, and say to thee, How art thou destroyed, *that wast* inhabited [w]of seafaring men, the renowned city, which wast [x]strong in the sea, she and her inhabitants, which cause their terror *to be* on all that haunt it!

18 Now shall [y]the isles tremble in the day of thy fall; yea, the isles that *are* in the sea shall be troubled at thy departure.

19 For thus saith the Lord GOD; When I shall make thee a desolate city, like the cities that are not inhabited; when I shall bring up the deep upon thee, and great waters shall cover thee;

20 When I shall bring thee down [z]with them that descend into the pit, with the people of old time, and shall set thee in the low parts of the earth, in [a]places desolate of old, with them that go down to the pit, that thou be not inhabited; and I shall set glory [b]in the land of the living;

21 [c]I will make thee [d]a terror, and thou *shalt be* no *more:* [e]though thou be sought for, yet shalt thou never be found again, saith the Lord GOD.

---

[k]Heb. *houses of thy desire*——[l]Isa. xiv. 11; xxiv. 8; Jer. vii. 34; xvi. 9; xxv. 10——[m]Isa. xxiii. 16; ch. xxviii. 13; Rev. xviii. 22——[n]Ver. 4, 5——[o]Jer. xlix. 21; ver. 18; ch. xxvii. 28; xxxi. 16——[p]Isa. xxiii. 8——[q]Jonah iii. 6——[r]Heb. *tremblings*——[s]Job ii. 13——[t]Chap. xxxii. 10——[u]Chap. xxvii. 35

[v]Jer. vii. 29; chap. xix. 1; xxvii. 2, 32; xxviii. 12; xxxii. 2; Rev. xviii. 9——[w]Heb. *of the seas*——[x]Isa. xxiii. 4——[y]Ver. 15——[z]Chap. xxxii. 18, 24——[a]Job iii. 14; Psa. cix. 10; Isa. xlix. 19; lix. 10; Amos vii. 9——[b]Chap. xxxii. 23, 26, 27, 32——[c]Chap. xxvii. 36; xxviii. 19——[d]Heb. *terrors*——[e]Psa. xxxvii. 36

Verse 12. *And they shall lay thy stones and thy timber and thy dust in the midst of the water.*] This answers to the taking of Tyre by Alexander; he actually took the timbers, stones, rubbish, &c. of *old Tyre,* and filled up the space between it and new Tyre, and thus connected the latter with the main land; and this he was obliged to do before he could take it.

Verse 14. *Thou shalt be built no more*] If this refer to Nebuchadnezzar's capture of the city, *old Tyre* must be intended: that was destroyed by him, and never rebuilt. But I doubt whether the whole of this prophecy do not refer to the taking of Tyre by Alexander, *three hundred* years after its capture by Nebuchadnezzar. Indeed it may include more recent conquests of this important city. It went through a variety of vicissitudes till 1289, when it and the neighbouring towns were sacked and ravaged by the Mamelukes. Mr. *Maundrell,* who visited this place, says, "it is a Babel of broken walls, pillars, vaults, &c., there being not so much as *one entire house left!* Its present inhabitants are only a few *poor wretches,* harbouring themselves in the *vaults,* and subsisting chiefly on *fishing;* who seem to be preserved in this place by Divine Providence as a visible argument how God has fulfilled his word concerning Tyre, that it should be *the top of a rock, a place for fishers to dry their nets on.*"

Verse 15. *The isles shake at the sound of thy fall*] All those which had traded with this city, which was the grand mart, and on which they all depended. Her ruin involved them all, and caused general wailing.

Verse 16. *The princes of the sea*] The chief maritime states, such as *Leptis, Utica, Carthage, Gades,* &c. See *Calmet.*

Verse 17. *Wast strong in the sea*] The strength of Tyre was so great, that Alexander despaired of being able to reduce it unless he could *fill up that arm of the sea that ran between it and the main land.* And this work cost his army *seven months* of labour.

Verse 20. *And I shall set glory in the land of the living.*] Judea so called, the land of the living God.

Verse 21. *Yet shalt thou never be found again*] This is literally true; there is not the smallest vestige of the *ancient Tyre,* that which was erected on the main land. Even the ground seems to have been washed away; and the new Tyre is in nearly a similar state. I think this prophecy must be extended to the whole duration of Tyre. If it now be found to be in the state here described, it is sufficient to show the truth of the prophecy. And now it is found precisely in the state which the above prophetic declarations, taken according to the letter, point out! No word of God can ever fall to the ground.

Notwithstanding the former destructions, Tyre was a place of some consequence in the time of St. Paul. There was a Church there, (see Acts xxi. 3, 4, &c.,) which afterwards became famous. *Calmet* observes, it afforded a great number of martyrs for the Christian Church.

CHAPTER XXVII

This chapter may be considered as the second part of the prophecy concerning Tyre. The prophet pursues his subject in the manner of those ancient lamentations or funeral songs, in which the præficiæ or mourning women first recounted whatever was great or praiseworthy in the deceased, and then mourned his fall. Here the riches, glory, and extensive commerce of Tyre are enlarged upon, 1–25. *Her downfall is then described in a beautiful allegory, executed in a few words, with astonishing brevity, propriety, and perspicuity,* 26; *upon which all the maritime and commercial world are represented as grieved and astonished at her fate, and greatly alarmed for their own,* 27–36. *Besides the view which this chapter gives of the conduct of Providence, and the example with which it furnishes the critic and man of taste of a very elegant and highly finished piece of composition, it likewise affords the antiquary a very curious and interesting account of the wealth and commerce of ancient times. And to the mind that looks for "a city that hath foundations," what a picture does the whole present of the mutability and inanity of all earthly things! Many of the places mentioned in ancient history have, like Tyre, long ago lost their political consequence; the geographical situation of others cannot be traced; they have sunk in the* deep waters *of oblivion; the* east wind *hath carried them away.*

A. M. 3416
B. C. 588
Ol. XLVIII. 1
Anno
Tarquinii Prisci,
R. Roman., 29

THE word of the LORD came
again unto me, saying,
2 Now, thou son of man, [a]take
up a lamentation for Tyrus;
3 And say unto Tyrus, [b]O thou that art
situate at the entry of the sea, *which art* [c]a
merchant of the people for
many isles, Thus saith the
Lord GOD; O Tyrus, thou hast
said, [d]I *am* [e]of perfect beauty.
4 Thy borders *are* in the [f]midst of the seas,
thy builders have perfected thy beauty.

A. M. 3416
B. C. 588
Ol. XLVIII. 1
Anno
Tarquinii Prisci,
R. Roman., 29

[a]Chap. xix. 1; xxvi. 17; xxviii. 12; xxxii. 2——[b]Chap. xxviii. 2——[c]Isa. xxiii. 3——[d]Chap. xxviii. 12——[e]Heb. *perfect of beauty*——[f]Heb. *heart*

NOTES ON CHAP. XXVII

Verse 2. *Take up a lamentation for Tyrus*] This is a singular and curious chapter. It gives a very circumstantial account of the trade of Tyre with different parts of the world, and the *different sorts of merchandise* in which she trafficked. The *places* and the *imports* are as regularly entered here as they could have been in a European custom-house.

Verse 3. *The entry of the sea*] Tyre was a small island, or rather rock, in the sea, at a short distance from the main land. We have already seen that there was another Tyre on the main land; but they are both considered as one city.

Verse 4. *Thy builders have perfected thy beauty.*] Under the allegory of a *beautiful ship*, the prophet, here and in the following verses, paints the glory of this ancient city. *Horace* describes the *commonwealth of Rome* by the same allegory, and is as minute in his description, *Carm.* lib. i. Od. xiv:—

O *navis*, referent in *mare* te novi
Fluctus? O quid agis? Fortiter occupa
  Portum. Nonne vides, ut
    Nudum *remigio latus*,
Et *malus* celeri saucius *Africo*,
Antennæque gemant? ac sine *funibus*
  Vix durare *carinæ*
    Possint imperiosius
Æquor? non tibi sunt *integra lintea;*
Non Di, quos iterum pressa voces malo:
  Quamvis Pontica *pinus*,
    Sylvæ filia nobilis,
Jactes et genus, et nomen inutile
Nil *pictis* timidus *navita puppibus*
  Fidit. Tu, nisi, *ventis*
    Debes ludibrium, cave.

Unhappy *vessel*, shall the *waves* again
Tumultuous bear thee to the faithless *main?*
What, would thy madness thus with *storms* to
  sport?
Cast firm your anchor in the friendly *port.*
Behold thy *naked decks*, the *wounded mast*,
And *sail-yards* groan beneath the *southern*
  blast.
Nor, without *ropes*, thy *keel* can longer brave
The rushing fury of the imperious *wave:*
Torn are thy *sails;* thy *guardian gods* are
  lost,
Whom you might call, in future *tempests* tost.
What, though majestic in your pride you
  stood,
A noble daughter of the *Pontic wood*,
You now may vainly boast an empty name,
Of birth conspicuous in the rolls of fame.
The *mariner*, when *storms* around him rise,
No longer on a *painted stern* relies.
Ah! yet take heed, lest these *new tempests*
  sweep,
In sportive rage, thy glories to the *deep*.

FRANCIS.

A. M. 3416
B. C. 588
Ol. XLVIII. 1
Anno
Tarquinii Prisci,
R. Roman., 29

5 They have [g]made all thy
ship boards of fir trees of
[h]Senir: they have taken
[i]cedars from Lebanon to make
masts for thee.
6 *Of* the oaks of Bashan have they made
thine oars: [k]the [l]company of the Ashurites
have made thy benches *of* ivory, *brought* out
of [m]the isles of Chittim.
7 Fine linen with broidered work from
Egypt was that which thou spreadest forth to
be thy sail; [n]blue and purple from the isles
of Elishah was that which covered thee.
8 The inhabitants of Zidon and Arvad were
thy mariners: thy wise *men*, O Tyrus, *that*
were in thee, were thy pilots.
9 The ancients of [o]Gebal and the wise *men*
thereof were in thee thy [p]calkers[q]; all the
ships of the sea with their mariners were in
thee to occupy thy merchandise.
10 They of Persia and of
Lud and of [r]Phut were in
thine army, thy men of war:
they hanged the shield and
helmet in thee; they set forth thy comeliness.
11 The men of Arvad with thine army *were*
upon thy walls round about, and the Gammadims were in thy towers: they hanged their
shields upon thy walls round about; they
have made [s]thy beauty perfect.
12 [t]Tarshish *was* thy merchant by reason
of the multitude of all *kind of* riches; with
silver, iron, tin, and lead, they traded in thy
fairs.
13 [u]Javan, Tubal, and Meshech, they *were*
thy merchants: they traded [v]the persons of
men and vessels of brass in thy [w]market.
14 They of the house of [x]Togarmah traded
in thy fairs with horses and horsemen and
mules.

A. M. 3416
B. C. 588
Ol. XLVIII. 1
Anno
Tarquinii Prisci,
R. Roman., 29

[g]Heb. *built*——[h]Deut. iii. 9——[i]Judg. ix. 15——[k]Or, *they have made thy hatches of ivory well trodden*——[l]Heb. *the daughter*——[m]Jer. ii. 10——[n]Or, *purple and scarlet* [o]1 Kings v. 18; Psa. lxxxiii. 7

[p]Or, *stoppers of chinks*——[q]Heb. *strengtheners* [r]Jer. xlvi. 9; chap. xxx. 5; xxxviii. 5——[s]Ver. 3——[t]Gen. x. 4; 2 Chron. xx. 36——[u]Gen. x. 2——[v]Rev. xviii. 13 [w]Or, *merchandise*——[x]Gen. x. 3; chap. xxxviii. 6

I give this as a striking parallel to many passages in this chapter.

Verse 5. *Fir trees of Senir*] *Senir* is a mountain which the Sidonians called Sirion, and the Hebrews *Hermon*, Deut. iii. 9. It was beyond Jordan, and extended from Libanus to the mountains of Gilead.

Verse 6. Of *the oaks of Bashan*] Some translate *alder*, others the *pine*.

The company of the Ashurites] The word אשרים *asherim* is by several translated *boxwood*. The *seats* or *benches* being made of this wood inlaid with *ivory*.

Isles of Chittim] The Italian islands; the islands of Greece; Cyprus. *Calmet* says *Macedonia* is meant.

Verse 7. *Fine linen*] שש *shesh*, *cotton cloth*. In this sense the word is generally to be understood.

To be thy sail] Probably the flag—*ensign* or *pennant*, is meant.

Blue and purple from the isles of Elishah] *Elis*, a part of the *Peloponnesus*.

Verse 8. *Zidon* and *Arvad*] Or *Arad*. Two powerful cities on the Phœnician coast, in the neighbourhood of Tyre, from which Tyre had her sailors; and the best instructed of her own inhabitants were her pilots or steersmen.

Verse 9. *The ancients of Gebal*] This was a city of Phœnicia, near Mount Libanus, Josh. xiii. 5. It was called *Biblos* by the Greeks.

Thy calkers] Those who repaired their vessels; *paying*, as it is termed, pitched hemp into the seams, to prevent the water from oozing through.

To occupy thy merchandise.] That is, to be thy *agents* or *factors*.

Verse 10. *They of Persia*] Lud, the Lydians; *Phut*, a people of Africa, see Gen. x. 6. From these places they had auxiliary troops; for as they traded with the then known world, were rich, and could afford to give good pay, they no doubt had soldiers and sailors from every part. Skilful and desperate men will go any where after their *price*.

Verse 11. *The Gammadims were in thy towers*] Some think these were a people of Phœnicia; others, that *tutelar images* are meant; others, that the word expresses *strong men*, who acted as *guards*. The *Vulgate* reads *Pygmæi*, the pygmies, who were fabled to be a little people of a *cubit* in height, from גמד *gomed*, a *cubit;* and we are told that this little people were celebrated for their wars with the *cranes;* but nothing of this kind can enter into this description. Probably a people inhabiting the promontories of Phœnicia are here intended; and their hanging their *shields upon the walls* is a proof that *soldiers* are meant, and persons of skill and prowess too.

Verse 12. *Tarshish* was *thy merchant*] After having given an account of the *naval* and *military* equipment of this city, he now speaks of the various *places* and *peoples* with whom the Tyrians traded, and the different kinds of merchandise imported from those places.

By *Tarshish* some understand the *Carthaginians;* some think *Tartessus*, near the straits of Gibraltar, is meant; others, *Tharsis* in Cilicia. The place was famous for all the useful metals, *silver, iron, tin*, and *lead*. All these they might have had from *Britain*.

Verse 13. *Javan, Tubal, and Meshech*] The Ionians, the Tybarenians, and the Cappadocians, or Muscovites.

They traded the persons of men] That is, they trafficked in *slaves*. The bodies and souls of men were bought and sold in those days, as in our degenerate age. With these also they traded in brazen vessels.

Verse 14. *Togarmah*] The *Sarmatians*. Some think *Cappadocia*. With these they dealt

A. M. 3416
B. C. 588
Ol. XLVIII. 1
Anno
Tarquinii Prisci,
R. Roman., 29

15 The men of [y]Dedan *were* thy merchants; many isles *were* the merchandise of thine hand: they brought thee *for* a present horns of ivory and ebony.

16 Syria *was* thy merchant by reason of the multitude of [z]the wares of thy making: they occupied in thy fairs with emeralds, purple, and broidered work, and fine linen, and coral, and [a]agate.

17 Judah, and the land of Israel, they *were* thy merchants: they traded in thy market [b]wheat of [c]Minnith, and Pannag, and honey, and oil, and [d]balm.[e]

18 Damascus *was* thy merchant in the multitude of the wares of thy making, for the multitude of all riches; in the wine of Helbon, and white wool.

19 Dan also and Javan [f]going to and fro occupied in thy fairs: bright iron, cassia, and calamus, were in thy market.

20 [g]Dedan *was* thy merchant in [h]precious clothes for chariots.

A. M. 3416
B. C. 588
Ol. XLVIII. 1
Anno
Tarquinii Prisci,
R. Roman., 29

21 Arabia, and all the princes of [i]Kedar, [k]they occupied with thee in lambs, and rams, and goats: in these *were they* thy merchants.

22 The merchants of [l]Sheba and Raamah, they *were* thy merchants: they occupied in thy fairs with chief of all spices, and with all precious stones, and gold.

23 [m]Haran, and Canneh, and Eden, the merchants of [n]Sheba, Asshur, *and* Chilmad, *were* thy merchants.

24 These *were* thy merchants in [o]all sorts *of things,* in blue [p]clothes, and broidered work, and in chests of rich apparel, bound with cords, and made of cedar, among thy merchandise.

25 [q]The ships of Tarshish did sing of thee in thy market: and thou wast replenished, and made very glorious [r]in the midst of the seas.

26 Thy rowers have brought thee into great

---

[y]Gen. x. 7——[z]Heb. *thy works*——[a]Heb. *chrysoprase* [b]1 Kings v. 9, 11; Ezra iii. 7; Acts xii. 20——[c]Judg. xi. 33——[d]Jer. viii. 22——[e]Or, *rosin*——[f]Or, *Meuzal* [g]Gen. xxv. 3——[h]Heb. *clothes of freedom*——[i]Gen. xxv. 13; Isa. lx. 7

[k]Heb. *they* were *the merchants of thy hand*——[l]Gen. x. 7; 1 Kings x. 1, 2; Psa. lxxii. 10, 15; Isa. lx. 6 [m]Gen. xi. 31; 2 Kings xix. 12——[n]Gen. xxv. 3——[o]Or, *excellent things*——[p]Heb. *foldings*——[q]Psa. xlviii. 7; Isa. ii. 16; xxiii. 14——[r]Ver. 4

---

in *horses, mules,* and *horsemen;* or probably *draught horses* and *war horses* are intended.

Verse 15. *The men of Dedan*] Dedan was one of the descendants of Abraham by Keturah, and dwelt in Arabia, Gen. xxv. 3. *Ivory* and *ebony* might come from that quarter. By way of distinction ivory is called both in Hebrew שן *shen*, and in Arabic شن *shen*, the TOOTH, as that beautiful substance is the *tooth* of the *elephant.*

Verse 16. *Syria*] These were always a mercantile people. For the precious stones mentioned here see the notes on Exod. xxviii. 17.

Verse 17. *Judah, and the land of Israel—traded in thy market wheat*] The words have been understood as articles of merchandise, not names of *places.* So the Jews traded with the Tyrians in *wheat, stacte, balsam, honey, oil,* and *resin.*

Verse 18. *Damascus—wine of Helbon*] Now called by the Turks Haleb, and by us Aleppo.

White wool.] Very fine wool: wool of a fine quality. Some think *Milesian wool* is meant.

Verse 19. *Dan also and Javan*] It is probable that both these words mean some of the Grecian islands.

Going to and fro] They both *took* and *brought—imported* and *exported:* but מאזל *meuzal,* from *uzal,* may be a proper name. What place is signified I cannot tell, unless it be *Azal,* a name, according to *Kamoos,* of the capital of Arabia Felix.

Verse 20. *Dedan*] Possibly the descendants of *Dedan,* son of *Raamah,* see Gen. x. 7.

In precious clothes for chariots.] Either fine carpets, or rich housings for horses, camels, &c., used for riding.

Verse 21. *Arabia, and all the princes of Kedar*] Arabia Deserta, on the confines of the Dead Sea. The *Kedarenes* inhabited the same country. These brought *lambs, rams,* and *goats* for the consumption of the city.

Verse 22. *Sheba and Raamah*] Inhabitants of Arabia Felix, at the entrance of the Persian Gulf, who were famous for their riches and spices.

Verse 23. *Haran*] In Mesopotamia; well known in Scripture.

Canneh] Or *Chalane;* see Gen. x. 10. It is supposed to be a cape or port of Arabia Felix, on the Indian Sea.

Eden] Equally famous: supposed to have been situated near the confluence of the *Tigris* and *Euphrates.*

Sheba] Different from that in ver. 22. This was probably near the country of the Edomites.

Asshur] Perhaps the Assyrians.

Chilmad] Possibly *Cholmadora,* on the Euphrates. *Ptol.* lib. v., cap. 15. For several of these places, and the persons from whom they derived their names, see Gen. x., and the notes there; and see *Calmet.*

Verse 24. *These* were *thy merchants in all sorts* of things] The above people traded with the Tyrians in a great variety of the most valuable merchandise: *blue* or *purple cloth, boxes of cedar, covered with skins, and bound with silken cords,* and *sealed with an engraved seal, finely cut, &c.* See the *Chaldee.*

Verse 25. *The ships of Tarshish*] The ships of *Tharsis,* in Cilicia, were the chief of those which traded with thee.

Verse 26. *Thy rowers have brought thee into great waters*] Tyre is still considered under

A. M. 3416
B. C. 588
Ol. XLVIII. 1
Anno
Tarquinii Prisci,
R. Roman., 29

waters: [s]the east wind hath
broken thee in the [t]midst of
the seas.
27 Thy [u]riches, and thy
fairs, thy merchandise, thy mariners, and
thy pilots, thy calkers, and the occupiers of
thy merchandise, and all thy men of war, that
are in thee, [v]and in all thy company which *is*
in the midst of thee, shall fall into the
[w]midst of the seas in the day of thy ruin.
28 The [x]suburbs [y]shall shake at the sound
of the cry of thy pilots.
29 And [z]all that handle the oar, the mariners, *and* all the pilots of the sea, shall come
down from their ships, they shall stand upon
the land;
30 And shall cause their voice to be
heard against thee, and shall cry bitterly,
and shall [a]cast up dust upon their heads,
they [b]shall wallow themselves in the
ashes:
31 And they shall [c]make themselves utterly
bald for thee, and gird them with sackcloth,
and they shall weep for thee
with bitterness of heart *and*
bitter wailing.
32 And in their wailing
they shall [d]take up a lamentation for thee,
and lament over thee, *saying*, [e]What *city is*
like Tyrus, like the destroyed in the midst of
the sea.
33 [f]When thy wares went forth out of the
seas, thou filledst many people; thou didst
enrich the kings of the earth with the multitude of thy riches and of thy merchandise.
34 In the time *when* [g]thou shalt be broken
by the seas in the depths of the waters, [h]thy
merchandise and all thy company in the
midst of thee shall fall.
35 [i]All the inhabitants of the isles shall be
astonished at thee, and their kings shall be
sore afraid, they shall be troubled in *their*
countenance.
36 The merchants among the people [k]shall
hiss at thee; [l]thou shalt be [m]a terror, and
[n]never *shalt be* any more.

[s]Psa. xlviii. 7——[t]Heb. *heart*——[u]Prov. xi. 4; ver. 34; Rev. xviii. 9, &c.——[v]Or, *even with all*——[w]Heb. *heart* [x]Or, *waves*——[y]Ch. xxvi. 15, 18——[z]Rev. xviii. 17, &c. [a]Job ii. 12; Rev. xviii. 19——[b]Esth. iv. 1, 3; Jer. vi. 26

[c]Jer. xvi. 6; xlvii. 5; Mic. i. 16——[d]Ch. xxvi. 17; ver. 2 [e]Rev. xviii. 18——[f]Rev. xviii. 19——[g]Ch. xxvi. 19 [h]Ver. 27——[i]Ch. xxvi. 15, 16——[k]Jer. xviii. 16——[l]Ch. xxvi. 21——[m]Heb. *terrors*——[n]Heb. shalt *not* be *for ever*

the allegory of a *ship;* and all the vessels of different nations trading with her are represented as towing her into deep waters—bringing her into great affluence. But while in this state, a stormy *east wind*, or a destructive wind, meaning the Chaldeans, arises, and dashes her to pieces! See the ode from *Horace*, already quoted on ver. 4.

Verse 27. *Thy riches*] This vast ship, laden with all kinds of valuable wares, and manned in the best manner, being wrecked, all her *valuables, sailors, officers*, &c., went to the bottom.

Verse 28. *The cry of thy pilots.*] When the ship was dashed against the rocks by the violence of the winds and the waves, and all hope of life was taken away, then a universal cry was set up by all on board. I have heard this cry, and nothing more dismal can be imagined, when the ship by a violent tempest is driving among *rocks* on a lee shore. Then "All lost! cut away the boat!" is more dreadful than the cry of *fire* at midnight.

Verse 30. *Shall cry bitterly*] All that were on the land, seeing this dreadful sight, a gallant ship perishing with all her men and goods, are represented as setting up a dismal cry at this heart-rending sight. But what must they have felt who were on board? Reader, wert thou ever *shipwrecked?* Wert thou ever in a *hurricane* on a *lee rocky shore*, where the helm had lost its power, and the sails were rendered useless? Dost thou remember that apparently last moment, when the ship drove up to the tremendous rocks, riding on the back of a mountainous surge? Then what was the universal cry? Hast thou ever heard any thing so terrific? so appalling? so death and judgment-like? No. It is impossible. These are the circumstances, this is the cry, that the prophet describes; disorder, confusion, dismay, and ruin. And this is a scene which the present writer has witnessed, himself a part of the wretched, when all hope of life was taken away, the yawning gulf opened, and nothing presented itself to support body or soul but that God who gave to both their being, and ultimately rescued him and his forlorn companions from one of the worst of deaths, by heaving the ship from the rocks by the agency of a tremendous receding wave. My soul hath these things still in remembrance, and therefore is humbled within me.

Verse 32. *What* city is *like Tyrus*] This, to the end of the chapter, is the lamentation.

Verse 36. *Shall hiss at thee*] שרקו *shareku*, shall *shriek* for thee. This powerfully expresses the sensation made on the feelings of the spectators on the shore when they saw the vessel swallowed up.

CHAPTER XXVIII

The first part of this chapter relates to a king of Tyre, probably the same who is called in the Phœnician annals Ithobalus. He seems to have been a vain man, who affected Divine honours. The prophet treats his foolish pretensions with severe irony, and predicts his doom, 1–10. *He then takes up a funeral dirge and lamentation over him, in which his former pomp and splendour are finely contrasted with his fall, in terms that seem frequently to allude to the fall of Lucifer from heaven,* (Isa. xiv.,) 11–19. *The overthrow of Sidon, the mother city of Tyre, is next announced,* 20–23; *and the chapter concludes with a promise to the Jews of deliverance from all their enemies, and particularly of their restoration from the Babylonish captivity,* 24–26.

A. M. 3416
B. C. 588
Ol. XLVIII. 1
Anno
Tarquinii Prisci,
R. Roman., 29

THE word of the LORD came again unto me, saying,

2 Son of man, say unto the prince of Tyrus, Thus saith the Lord GOD; Because thine heart *is* lifted up, and [a]thou hast said, I *am* a god, I sit *in* the seat of God, [b]in the [c]midst of the seas; [d]yet thou *art* a man, and not God, though thou set thine heart as the heart of God:

3 Behold, [e]thou *art* wiser than Daniel; there is no secret that they can hide from thee:

4 With thy wisdom and with thine understanding thou hast gotten thee riches, and hast gotten gold and silver into thy treasures:

5 [f]By [g]thy great wisdom *and* by thy traffic hast thou increased thy riches, and thine heart is lifted up because of thy riches:

6 Therefore thus saith the Lord GOD; Because thou hast set thine heart as the heart of God;

7 Behold, therefore I will bring strangers upon thee, [h]the terrible of the nations: and they shall draw their swords against the beauty of thy wisdom, and they shall defile thy brightness.

A. M. 3416
B. C. 588
Ol. XLVIII. 1
Anno
Tarquinii Prisci,
R. Roman., 29

8 They shall bring thee down to the pit, and thou shalt die the deaths of *them that are* slain in the midst of the seas.

9 Wilt thou yet [i]say before him that slayeth thee, I *am* God; but thou *shalt be* a man, and no God, in the hand of him that [k]slayeth thee.

10 Thou shalt die the deaths of [l]the uncircumcised by the hand of strangers: for I have spoken *it*, saith the Lord GOD.

11 Moreover the word of the LORD came unto me, saying,

12 Son of man, [m]take up a lamentation upon the king of Tyrus, and say unto him, Thus saith the Lord GOD; [n]Thou sealest up the sum, full of wisdom, and perfect in beauty.

13 Thou hast been in [o]Eden the garden of God; every precious stone *was* thy covering, the [p]sardius, topaz, and the diamond, the [q]beryl, the onyx, and the jasper, the sapphire, the [r]emerald, and the carbuncle, and gold:

[a]Ver. 9——[b]Chap. xxvii. 3, 4——[c]Hebrew, *heart*——[d]Isaiah xxxi. 3——[e]Zechariah ix. 2——[f]Hebrew, *By the greatness of thy wisdom*——[g]Psalm lxii. 10; Zechariah ix. 3——[h]Chap. xxx. 11; xxxi. 12; xxxii. 12

[i]Ver. 2——[k]Or, *woundeth*——[l]Chap. xxxi. 18; xxxii. 19, 21, 25, 27——[m]Chap. xxvii. 2——[n]Chap. xxvii. 3; ver. 3——[o]Chap. xxxi. 8, 9——[p]Or, *ruby*——[q]Or, *chrysolite*——[r]Or, *chrysoprase*

NOTES ON CHAP. XXVIII

Verse 2. *Say unto the prince of Tyrus*] But who was this prince of Tyrus? Some think *Hiram;* some, *Sin;* some, the *devil;* others, *Ithobaal,* with whom the chronology and circumstances best agree. *Origen* thought the guardian angel of the city was intended.

I am a god] That is, I am absolute, independent, and accountable to none. He was a man of great pride and arrogance.

Verse 3. *Thou* art *wiser than Daniel*] Daniel was at this time living, and was reputable for his great wisdom. This is said *ironically.* See chap. xiv. 14; xxvi. 1.

Verse 5. *By thy great wisdom*] He attributed every thing to himself; he did not acknowledge a Divine providence. As he got all by himself, so he believed he could keep all by himself, and had no need of any foreign help.

Verse 7. *I will bring strangers upon thee*] The Chaldeans.

Verse 9. *Wilt thou yet say before him that slayeth thee*] Wilt thou continue thy pride and arrogance when the sword is sheathed in thee, and still imagine that thou art self-sufficient and independent?

Verse 10. *The deaths of the uncircumcised*] *Two* deaths, *temporal* and *eternal.* Ithobaal was taken and killed by Nebuchadnezzar.

Verse 12. *Thou sealest up*] This has been translated, "Thou drawest thy own likeness." "Thou formest a portrait of thyself; and hast represented thyself the perfection of wisdom and beauty." I believe this to be the meaning of the place.

Verse 13. *Thou hast been in Eden*] This also is a strong irony. Thou art like *Adam,* when in his innocence and excellence he was in the garden of Eden!

Every precious stone was *thy covering*] For a description of these stones see the note on Exod. xxviii. 17.

Verse 14. *Thou* art *the anointed cherub that covereth*] The irony is continued; and here he is likened to the CHERUB that guarded the gates of Paradise, and kept the way of the tree

A. M. 3416
B. C. 588
Ol. XLVIII. 1
Anno
Tarquinii Prisci,
R. Roman., 29

the workmanship of [s]thy tabrets and of thy pipes was prepared in thee in the day that thou wast created.

14 Thou *art* the anointed [t]cherub that covereth: and I have set thee *so:* thou wast upon [u]the holy mountain of God; thou hast walked up and down in the midst of the stones of fire.

15 Thou *wast* perfect in thy ways from the day that thou wast created, till iniquity was found in thee.

16 By the multitude of thy merchandise they have filled the midst of thee with violence, and thou hast sinned: therefore I will cast thee as profane out of the mountain of God: and I will destroy thee, [v]O covering cherub, from the midst of the stones of fire.

17 [w]Thine heart was lifted up because of thy beauty, thou hast corrupted thy wisdom by reason of thy brightness: I will cast thee to the ground, I will lay thee before kings, that they may behold thee.

[s]Ch. xxvi. 13——[t]See Exod. xxv. 20; ver. 16——[u]Ch. xx. 40——[v]Ver. 14——[w]Ver. 2, 5——[x]Ch. xxvi. 21; xxvii. 36——[y]Heb. *terrors*——[z]Ch. vi. 2; xxv. 2; xxix. 2

A. M. 3416
B. C. 588
Ol. XLVIII. 1
Anno
Tarquinii Prisci,
R. Roman., 29

18 Thou hast defiled thy sanctuaries by the multitude of thine iniquities, by the iniquity of thy traffic; therefore will I bring forth a fire from the midst of thee, it shall devour thee, and I will bring thee to ashes upon the earth in the sight of all them that behold thee.

19 All they that know thee among the people shall be astonished at thee: [x]thou shalt be [y]a terror, and never *shalt* thou *be* any more.

20 Again the word of the LORD came unto me, saying,

21 Son of man, [z]set thy face [a]against Zidon, and prophesy against it,

22 And say, Thus saith the Lord GOD; [b]Behold, I *am* against thee, O Zidon; and I will be glorified in the midst of thee: and [c]they shall know that I *am* the LORD, when I shall have executed judgments in her, and shall be [d]sanctified in her.

23 [e]For I will send into her pestilence, and blood into her streets; and the wounded shall be judged in the midst of her by the sword

[a]Isa. xxiii. 4, 12; Jer. xxv. 22; xxvii. 3; ch. xxxii. 30——[b]Exod. xiv. 4, 17; ch. xxxix. 13——[c]Psa. ix. 16——[d]Ch. xx. 41; xxxvi. 23; ver. 25——[e]Ch. xxxviii. 22

of life; or to one of the cherubs whose wings, spread out, covered the mercy-seat.

Thou wast upon the holy mountain of God] The irony is still continued; and now he is compared to *Moses*, and afterwards to one of the *chief angels*, who has walked up and down among the stones of fire; that is, thy floors have been paved with precious stones, that shone and sparkled like fire.

Lucan, describing the splendour of the apartments of *Cleopatra*, queen of Egypt, speaks in nearly a similar language:—

Nec summis crustata domus, sectisque nitebat
Marmoribus, stabatque sibi non segnis *achâtes*,
Purpureusque lapis, totusque effusus in aula
Calcabatur onyx— *Pharsal.* lib. x.

Rich as some fane by slavish zealots reared,
For the proud banquet stood the hall prepared:
Thick *golden plates* the latent beams infold,
And the high roof was fretted o'er with *gold.*
Of solid *marble* all the walls were made,
And *onyx* e'en the *meaner floor* inlaid;
While *porphyry* and *agate* round the court
In massy columns rose, a proud support.
Of solid *ebony* each post was wrought,
From swarthy Meroë profusely brought.
With *ivory* was the entrance crusted o'er,
And polished *tortoise* hid each shining door;
While on the cloudy spots enchased was seen
The trusty *emerald's* never-fading green.
Within the royal beds and couches shone,
Beamy and bright with many a costly *stone*,
The glowing *purple* rich. ROWE.

Verse 15. *Thou* wast *perfect in thy ways*] The irony seems still to be kept up. Thou hast been like the angels, like Moses, like the cherubs, like Adam, like God, till thy iniquity was found out.

Verse 16. *I will cast thee as profane*] Thou shalt be cast down from thine eminence.

From the midst of the stones of fire.] Some, supposing that *stones of fire* means the *stars*, have thought that the whole refers to the *fall of Satan.*

Verse 18. *Thou hast defiled thy sanctuaries*] Irony continued. As God, as the angels, as the cherubim, thou must have had thy sanctuaries; but thou hast defiled them: and as Adam, thou hast polluted thy Eden, and hast been expelled from Paradise.

Verse 19. *Thou shalt be a terror*] Instead of being an object of *adoration* thou shalt be a subject of horror, and at last be destroyed with thy city, so that nothing but thy name shall remain. It was entirely burnt by Alexander the Great, as it had been before by Nebuchadnezzar.

Verse 22. *I am against thee, O Zidon*] Sidon for a long time had possessed the empire of the sea and of all Phœnicia, and Tyre was one of its colonies; but in process of time, the daughter became greater than the mother. It seems to have been an independent place at the time in which Tyre was taken; but it is likely that it was taken by the Chaldeans soon after the former.

Verse 23. *And the wounded*] חלל *chalal*, the *soldiery.* All its supports shall be taken away, and its defenders destroyed.

A. M. 3416
B. C. 588
Ol. XLVIII. 1
Anno
Tarquinii Prisci,
R. Roman., 29

upon her on every side; and
they shall know that I *am* the
LORD.
24 And there shall be no
more [f]a pricking brier unto the house of
Israel, nor *any* grieving thorn of all *that are*
round about them, that despised them; and
they shall know that I *am* the Lord GOD.
25 Thus saith the Lord GOD; When I shall
have [g]gathered the house of Israel from the
people among whom they are scattered, and
shall be [h]sanctified in them
in the sight of the heathen,
then shall they dwell in their
land that I have given to my
servant Jacob.
26 And they shall [i]dwell [k]safely therein,
and shall [l]build houses, and [m]plant vineyards; yea, they shall dwell with confidence,
when I have executed judgments upon all those
that [n]despise them round about them; and they
shall know that I *am* the LORD their God.

A. M. 3416
B. C. 588
Ol. XLVIII. 1
Anno
Tarquinii Prisci,
R. Roman., 29

[f]Num. xxxiii. 55; Josh. xxiii. 13——[g]Isa. xi. 12; xi. 17; xx. 41; xxxiv. 13; xxxvii. 21——[h]Ver. 22

[i]Jer. xxiii. 6; ch. xxxvi. 28——[k]Or, *with confidence*
[l]Isa. lxv. 21; Amos ix. 14——[m]Jer. xxxi. 5——[n]Or, *spoil*

Verse 24. *There shall be no more a pricking brier*] Nothing to excite Israel to idolatry when restored from their captivity. Perhaps there is an allusion to *Jezebel*, daughter of *Ethbaal*, king of Sidon, and wife to Ahab, king of Israel, who was the greatest curse to Israel, and the universal restorer of idolatry in the land, see 1 Kings xvi. 31. Sidon being destroyed, there would come no encourager of idolatry from that quarter.

Verse 25. *When I shall have gathered the house of Israel*] In their long captivity, God had been preparing the land for them so as to make it a *safe dwelling;* and hence he executed judgments on all the heathen nations round about by means of the Chaldeans. Thus Tyre and Sidon were destroyed, as were the Ammonites and others who had been the inveterate enemies of the Jews. Judgment first began at his own house, then proceeded to the heathen nations; and when they were brought down, then he visited and redeemed his people. Thus God's ways are proved to be all equal; partialities and caprices belong not to him.

CHAPTER XXIX

This and the three following chapters foretell the conquest of Egypt by Nebuchadnezzar, which he accomplished in the twenty-seventh *year of Jehoiachin's captivity. The same event is foretold by Jeremiah,* chap. xlvi. 13, &c. *The prophecy opens with God's charging the king of Egypt* (*Pharaoh-hophra*) *with the same extravagant pride and profanity which were in the preceding chapter laid to the charge of the prince of Tyre. He appears, like him, to have affected Divine honours; and boasted so much of the strength of his kingdom, that, as an ancient historian* (Herodotus) *tells us, he impiously declared that God himself could not dispossess him. Wherefore the prophet, with great majesty, addresses him under the image of one of those crocodiles or monsters which inhabited that river, of whose riches and revenue he vaunted; and assures him that, with as much ease as a fisherman drags the fish he has hooked, God would drag him and his people into captivity, and that their carcasses should fall a prey to the beasts of the field and to the fowls of heaven,* 1–7. *The figure is then dropped; and God is introduced denouncing, in plain terms, the most awful judgments against him and his nation, and declaring that the Egyptians should be subjected to the Babylonians till the fall of the Chaldean empire,* 8–12. *The prophet then foretells that Egypt, which was about to be devastated by the Babylonians, and many of the people carried into captivity, should again become a kingdom; but that it should never regain its ancient political importance; for, in the lapse of time, it should be even* the BASEST of the kingdoms, *a circumstance in the prophecy most literally fulfilled, especially under the Christian dispensation, in its government by the Mameluke slaves,* 13–16. *The prophecy, beginning at the* seventeenth *verse, is connected with the foregoing, as it relates to the same subject, though delivered about* seventeen *years later. Nebuchadnezzar and his army, after the long siege of Tyre, which made every head bald by constantly wearing their helmets, and wore the skin off every shoulder by carrying burdens to raise the fortifications, were disappointed of the spoil which they expected, by the retiring of the inhabitants to Carthage. God, therefore, promises him Egypt for his reward,* 17–20. *The chapter concludes with a prediction of the return of the Jews from the Babylonish captivity,* 21.

A. M. 3415
B. C. 589
Ol. XLVII. 4
Anno
Tarquinii Prisci,
R. Roman., 28

IN the tenth year, in the tenth
month, in the twelfth *day*
of the month, the word of the
LORD came unto me, saying,
2 Son of man, [a]set thy face against Pharaoh
king of Egypt, and prophesy against him, and
[b]against all Egypt:
3 Speak, and say, Thus saith the Lord GOD;
[c]Behold, I *am* against thee, Pharaoh king of
Egypt, the great [d]dragon that lieth in the
midst of his rivers, [e]which hath said, My
river *is* mine own, and I have made *it* for
myself.
4 But [f]I will put hooks in thy jaws, and I
will cause the fish of thy rivers to stick unto
thy scales, and I will bring thee up out of the
midst of thy rivers, and all the fish of thy
rivers shall stick unto thy scales.
5 And I will leave thee *thrown* into the
wilderness, thee and all the fish of thy rivers:
thou shalt fall upon the [g]open fields; [h]thou
shalt not be brought together, nor gathered:
[i]I have given thee for meat to the beasts of
the field and to the fowls of the heaven.
6 And all the inhabitants of Egypt shall
know that I *am* the LORD, because they have
been a [k]staff of reed to the
house of Israel.
7 [l]When they took hold of
thee by thy hand, thou didst
break, and rend all their shoulder: and
when they leaned upon thee, thou brakest,
and madest all their loins to be at a
stand.
8 Therefore thus saith the Lord GOD; Behold,
I will bring [m]a sword upon thee, and
cut off man and beast out of thee.
9 And the land of Egypt shall be desolate
and waste; and they shall know that I *am*
the LORD: because he hath said, The river *is*
mine, and I have made *it*.
10 Behold, therefore I *am* against thee, and
against thy rivers, [n]and I will make the land
of Egypt [o]utterly waste *and* desolate, [p]from[q]
the tower of [r]Syene even unto the border of
Ethiopia.
11 [s]No foot of man shall pass through it,
nor foot of beast shall pass through it, neither
shall it be inhabited forty years.
12 [t]And I will make the land of Egypt
desolate in the midst of the countries *that*
are desolate, and her cities among the cities

A. M. 3415
B. C. 589
Ol. XLVII. 4
Anno
Tarquinii Prisci
R. Roman., 28

[a]Chap. xxviii. 21——[b]Isa. xix. 1; Jer. xxv. 19; xlvi. 2, 25——[c]Jer. xliv. 30; ch. xxviii. 22; ver. 10——[d]Psa. lxxiv. 13, 14; Isa. xxvii. 1; li. 9; ch. xxxii. 2——[e]See ch. xxviii. 2——[f]Isa. xxxvii. 29; ch. xxxviii. 4——[g]Heb. *face of the field*——[h]Jer. viii. 2; xvi. 4; xxv. 33——[i]Jer. vii. 33; xxxiv. 20

[k]2 Kings xviii. 21; Isa. xxxvi. 6——[l]Jer. xxxvii. 5, 7, 11; ch. xvii. 17——[m]Ch. xiv. 17; xxxii. 11, 12, 13——[n]Ch. xxx. 12——[o]Heb. *wastes of wastes*——[p]Or, *from Migdol to Syene;* Exod. xiv. 2; Jer. xliv. 1——[q]Chap. xxx. 6——[r]Heb. *Seveneh*——[s]Chap. xxxii. 13——[t]Chap. xxx. 7, 26

NOTES ON CHAP. XXIX

Verse 1. *In the tenth year*] Of Zedekiah; and *tenth* of the captivity of Jeconiah.

The ten month, *in the twelfth* day *of the month*] Answering to *Monday*, the first of *February*, A. M. 3415.

Verse 2. *Set thy face against Pharaoh king of Egypt*] This was Pharaoh-hophra or Pharaoh-apries, whom we have so frequently met with in the prophecies of Jeremiah, and much of whose history has been given in the notes.

Verse 3. *The great dragon*] התנים *hattannim* should here be translated *crocodile*, as that is a *real* animal, and numerous in the *Nile;* whereas the *dragon* is wholly *fabulous*. The original signifies any large animal.

The midst of his rivers] This refers to the several *branches* of the Nile, by which this river empties itself into the Mediterranean. The ancients termed them septem ostia Nili, "the seven mouths of the Nile." The *crocodile* was the *emblem* of *Egypt*.

Verse 4. *I will put hooks in thy jaws*] Amasis, one of this king's generals, being proclaimed king by an insurrection of the people, dethroned *Apries*, and seized upon the kingdom; and Apries was obliged to flee to Upper Egypt for safety.

I will cause the fish—to stick unto thy scales] Most fish are sorely troubled with a species of *insect* which bury their heads in their flesh, under their *scales*, and suck out the vital juices. The allusion seems to be to this. *Pharaoh* was the *crocodile;* the *fish*, the *common people;* and the *sticking to his scales*, the *insurrection* by which he was *wasted* and despoiled of his kingdom.

Verse 5. *I will leave thee* thrown *into the wilderness*] Referring to his being obliged to take refuge in Upper Egypt. But he was afterwards taken prisoner, and strangled by Amasis. *Herod.* lib. ii. s. 169.

Verse 6. *They have been a staff of reed*] An inefficient and faithless ally. The Israelites expected assistance from them when Nebuchadnezzar came against Jerusalem; and they made a feint to help them, but retired when Nebuchadnezzar went against them. Thus were the Jews deceived and ultimately ruined, see ver. 7.

Verse 10. *From the tower of Syene*] ממגדל סונה *mimmigdol seveneh*, "from Migdol to Syene." Syene, now called *Essuan*, was the last city in Egypt, going towards Ethiopia. It was famous for a well into which the rays of the sun fell *perpendicularly* at *midday*.

Verse 12. *Shall be desolate forty years*] The country from Migdol or Magdolan, which was on the isthmus between the Mediterranean and the Red Sea, was so completely ruined, that it might well be called *desert;* and it is

A. M. 3415
B. C. 589
Ol. XLVII. 4
Anno
Tarquinii Prisci,
R. Roman., 28

that are laid waste shall be desolate forty years: and I will scatter the Egyptians among the nations, and will disperse them through the countries.

13 Yet thus saith the Lord GOD; At the [u]end of forty years will I gather the Egyptians from the people whither they were scattered:

14 And I will bring again the captivity of Egypt, and will cause them to return *into* the land of Pathros, into the land of their [v]habitation; and they shall be there a [w]base [x]kingdom.

15 It shall be the basest of the kingdoms; neither shall it exalt itself any more above the nations: for I will diminish them, that they shall no more rule over the nations.

16 And it shall be no more [y]the confidence of the house of Israel, which bringeth *their* iniquity to remembrance, when they shall look after them: but they shall know that I *am* the Lord GOD.

17 And it came to pass in the seven and twentieth year, in the first *month*, in the first *day* of the month, the word of the LORD came unto me, saying,

A. M. 3432
B. C. 572
Ol. LII. 1
Anno
Servii Tullii,
R. Roman., 7

18 Son of man, [z]Nebuchadrezzar king of Babylon caused his army to serve a great service against Tyrus: every head *was* made bald, and every shoulder *was* peeled; yet had he no wages, nor his army, for Tyrus, for the service that he had served against it:

19 Therefore thus saith the Lord GOD; Behold, I will give the land of Egypt unto Nebuchadrezzar king of Babylon; and he shall take her multitude, and [a]take her spoil, and take her prey; and it shall be the wages for his army.

20 I have given him the land of Egypt [b]*for* his labour wherewith he [c]served against it because they wrought for me, saith the Lord GOD.

21 In that day [d]will I cause the horn of the house of Israel to bud forth, and I will give thee [e]the opening of the mouth in the midst of them; and they shall know that I *am* the LORD.

[u]Isa. xix. 23; Jer. xlvi. 26——[v]Or, *birth*——[w]Heb. *low*——[x]Chapter xvii. 6, 14——[y]Isaiah xxx. 2, 3; xxxvi. 4, 6

[z]Jer. xxvii. 6; chap. xxvi. 7, 8——[a]Heb. *spoil her spoil, and prey her prey*——[b]Or, for *his hire*——[c]Jer. xxv. 9——[d]Psa. cxxxii. 17——[e]Chap. xxiv. 27

probable that this desolation continued during the whole of the *reign of Amasis*, which was just *forty years*. See *Herod.* lib. iii. c. 10; and see *Calmet*.

Verse 13. *Will I gather the Egyptians*] It is probable that Cyrus gave permission to the Egyptians brought to Babylon by Nebuchadnezzar, to return to their own country. And if we reckon from the commencement of the war against Pharaoh-hophra by Nebuchadnezzar, to the *third* or *fourth* year of Cyrus, the term will be about *forty* years.

Verse 14. Into *the land of Pathros*] Supposed to mean the *Delta*, a country included between the branches of the Nile; called Δ *delta*, from its being in the form of the Greek letter of that name. It may mean the *Pathrusim*, in Upper Egypt, near to the Thebaid. This is most likely.

Shall be there a base kingdom.] That is, it shall continue to be *tributary*. It is upwards of *two thousand* years since this prophecy was delivered, and it has been uninterruptedly fulfilling to the *present hour*. 1. Egypt became tributary to the *Babylonians*, under Amasis. 2. After the ruin of the Babylonish empire, it became subject to the *Persians*. 3. After the Persians, it came into the hands of the *Macedonians*. 4. After the Macedonians it fell into the hands of the *Romans*. 5. After the division of the Roman empire it was subdued by the *Saracens*. 6. About A. D. 1250, it came into the hands of the *Mameluke* slaves. 7. Selim, the *ninth* emperor of the Turks, conquered the Mamelukes, A. D. 1517, and annexed Egypt to the *Ottoman empire*, of which it still continues to be a province, governed by a *pacha* and *twenty-four beys*, who are always advanced from *servitude* to the administration of public affairs. So true is it that Egypt, once so glorious, is the *basest of kingdoms*. See *Newton* on the prophecies.

Verse 17. *The seven and twentieth year*] That is, of the *captivity of Jeconiah*, *fifteen* years after the taking of *Jerusalem;* about *April* 20, 3432. The *preceding* prophecy was delivered one year before the taking of Jerusalem; *this*, sixteen years after; and it is supposed to be the last which this prophet wrote.

Verse 18. *Caused his army to serve a great service against Tyrus*] He was *thirteen* years employed in the siege. See *Joseph.* Antiq. lib. x. c. 11. In this siege his soldiers endured great hardships. Being continually on duty, their *heads became bald* by wearing their helmets; and their *shoulders bruised and peeled* by carrying baskets of earth to the fortifications, and wood, &c., to build towers, &c.

Yet had he no wages, nor his army] The Tyrians, finding it at last impossible to defend their city, put all their wealth aboard their vessels, sailed out of the port, and escaped for Carthage; and thus Nebuchadnezzar lost all the spoil of one of the richest cities in the world.

Verse 20. *I have given him the land of Egypt* for *his labour*] Because he fulfilled the designs of God against Tyre, God promises to *reward* him with the spoil of Egypt.

Verse 21. *Will I cause the horn of the house of Israel to bud*] This may refer generally to the *restoration;* but particularly to *Zerubbabel,* who became one of the leaders of the people from Babylon. Or it may respect *Daniel,* or *Mordecai,* or *Jeconiah,* who, about this time, was brought out of prison by Evil-merodach, and afterwards kindly treated.

CHAPTER XXX

This chapter describes, with great force and elegance, the ruin of Egypt and all her allies by the Chaldeans under Nebuchadnezzar, 1–11; *with an amplification of the distress of the principal cities of Egypt on that occasion,* 12–19. *The remaining verses are a short prophecy relating to the same event, and therefore annexed to the longer one preceding, although this was predicted sooner,* 20–26.

A. M. 3432
B. C. 572
Olymp. LII. 1
Anno
Servii Tullii,
R. Roman., 7

THE word of the LORD came again unto me, saying,

2 Son of man, prophesy and say, Thus saith the Lord GOD; [a]Howl ye, Wo worth the day!

3 For [b]the day *is* near, even the day of the LORD *is* near, a cloudy day; it shall be the time of the heathen.

4 And the sword shall come upon Egypt, and great [c]pain shall be in Ethiopia, when the slain shall fall in Egypt, and they [d]shall take away her multitude, and [e]her foundations shall be broken down.

5 Ethiopia, and [f]Libya, and Lydia, and [g]all the mingled people, and Chub, and the [h]men of the land that is in league, shall fall with them by the sword.

6 Thus saith the LORD; They also that uphold Egypt shall fall; and the pride of her power shall come down: [i]from [k]the tower of Syene shall they fall in it by the sword, saith the Lord GOD.

7 [l]And they shall be desolate in the midst of the countries *that are* desolate, and her cities shall be in the midst of the cities *that are* wasted.

A. M. 3432
B. C. 572
Olymp. LII. 1
Anno
Servii Tullii,
R. Roman., 7

8 And they shall know that I *am* the LORD, when I have set a fire in Egypt, and *when* all her helpers shall be [m]destroyed.

9 In that day [n]shall messengers go forth from me in ships to make the careless Ethiopians afraid, and great pain shall come upon them, as in the day of Egypt: for, lo, it cometh.

10 Thus saith the Lord GOD: [o]I will also make the multitude of Egypt to cease by the hand of Nebuchadrezzar king of Babylon.

11 He and his people with him, [p]the terrible of the nations, shall be brought to destroy the land: and they shall draw their swords against Egypt, and fill the land with the slain.

12 And [q]I will make the rivers [r]dry, and [s]sell the land into the hand of the wicked: and I will make the land waste, and [t]all that is therein, by the hand of strangers: I the LORD have spoken *it.*

13 Thus saith the Lord GOD; I will also [u]destroy the idols, and I will cause *their* images to cease out of Noph; [v]and there shall be no more a prince of the land of Egypt: [w]and I will put a fear in the land of Egypt.

---

[a]Isa. xiii. 6——[b]Chap. vii. 7, 12; Joel ii. 1; Zeph. i. 7——[c]Or, *fear*——[d]Chap. xxix. 19——[e]Jer. l. 15——[f]Heb. *Phut;* chap. xxvii. 10——[g]Jer. xxv. 20, 24——[h]Heb. *children*——[i]Or, *from Migdol to Syene*——[k]Chap. xxix. 10——[l]Chap. xxix. 12

[m]Heb. *broken*——[n]Isa. xviii. 1, 2——[o]Chap. xxix. 19——[p]Chap. xxviii. 7——[q]Isa. xix. 5, 6——[r]Heb. *drought*——[s]Isa. xix. 4——[t]Heb. *the fulness thereof*——[u]Isa. xix. 1; Jer. xliii. 12; xlvi. 25; Zech. xiii. 2——[v]Zech. x. 11——[w]Isa. xix. 16

NOTES ON CHAP. XXX

Verse 2. *Howl ye, Wo worth the day!*] My Old MS. Bible,—**Houle gee, woo woo to the day!** הילילו הה ליום *heylilu, hah laiyom!* "Howl ye, Alas for the day!" The reading in our present text is taken from *Coverdale's* Bible, 1535. The expressions signify that a most dreadful calamity was about to fall on Egypt and the neighbouring countries, called here the "time of the heathen," or of the *nations;* the day of calamity to them. They are afterwards specified, Ethiopia, Libya, Lydia, and *Chub,* and the *mingled people,* probably persons from different nations, who had followed the ill fortune of Pharaoh-hophra or Pharaoh-apries, when he fled from Amasis, and settled in Upper Egypt.

Verse 5. *Lydia*] This place is not well known. The *Ludim* were contiguous to Egypt, Gen. xi. 13.

Chub] The Cubians, placed by Ptolemy in the *Mareotis.* But probably instead of וכוב *vechub,* "and Chub," we should read וכל *vechol,* "and ALL the men of the land," &c. The *Septuagint* adds "the Persians and the Cretans."

Verse 7. *Shall be desolate*] All these countries shall be desolated, and the places named shall be *chief* in these desolations.

Verse 9. *Messengers go forth from me in ships*] Ships can ascend the Nile up to Syene or Essuan, by the *cataracts;* and when Nebuchadnezzar's vessels went up, they struck terror into the Ethiopians. They are represented here as the "messengers of God."

Verse 12. *I will make the rivers dry*] As the

A. M. 3432
B. C. 572
Ol. LII. 1
Anno
Servii Tullii,
R. Roman., 7

14 And I will make [x]Path-
ros desolate, and will set fire
in [y]Zoan,[z] [a]and will execute
judgments in No.
15 And I will pour my fury upon [b]Sin, the
strength of Egypt; [c]and I will cut off the
multitude of No.
16 And I will [d]set fire in Egypt: Sin shall
have great pain, and No shall be rent asunder, and Noph *shall have* distresses daily.
17 The young men of [e]Aven and of [f]Pi-
beseth shall fall by the sword: and these
cities shall go into captivity.
18 [g]At Tehaphnehes also the day shall be
[h]darkened, when I shall break there the yokes
of Egypt: and the pomp of her strength shall
cease in her: as for her, a cloud shall cover
her, and her daughters shall go into captivity.
19 Thus will I execute judgments in Egypt:
and they shall know that I *am* the LORD.

A. M. 3416
B. C. 588
Ol. XLVIII. 1
Anno
Tarquinii Prisci,
R. Roman., 29

20 And it came to pass in
the eleventh year, in the first
month, in the seventh *day* of
the month, *that* the word of
the LORD came unto me, saying,
21 Son of man, I have [i]broken the arm of
Pharaoh king of Egypt; and lo, [k]it shall not
be bound up to be healed, to
put a roller to bind it, to
make it strong to hold the
sword.

A. M. 3416
B. C. 588
Ol. XLVIII. 1
Anno
Tarquinii Prisci,
R. Roman., 29

22 Therefore thus saith the Lord GOD; Behold, I *am* against Pharaoh king of Egypt,
and will [l]break his arms, the strong, and that
which was broken; and I will cause the
sword to fall out of his hand.
23 [m]And I will scatter the Egyptians
among the nations, and will disperse them
through the countries.
24 And I will strengthen the arms of the
king of Babylon, and put my sword in his
hand: but I will break Pharaoh's arms, and
he shall groan before him with the groanings
of a deadly wounded *man.*
25 But I will strengthen the arms of the
king of Babylon, and the arms of Pharaoh
shall fall down; and [n]they shall know that
I *am* the LORD, when I shall put my sword
into the hand of the king of Babylon, and he
shall stretch it out upon the land of Egypt.
26 [o]And I will scatter the Egyptians among
the nations, and disperse them among the
countries; and they shall know that I *am*
the LORD.

---

[x]Ch. xxix. 14——[y]Psa. lxxviii. 12, 43——[z]Or, *Tanis* [a]Nah. iii. 8, 9, 10——[b]Or, *Pelusium*——[c]Jer. xlvi. 25 [d]Ver. 8——[e]Or, *Heliopolis*——[f]Or, *Pubastum*

[g]Jer. ii. 16——[h]Or, *restrained*——[i]Jer. xlviii. 25 [k]Jer. xlvi. 11——[l]Psa. xxxvii. 17——[m]Ver. 26; ch. xxix. 12——[n]Psa. ix. 16——[o]Ver. 23; ch. xxix. 12

---

overflowing of the Nile was the grand cause of fertility to Egypt, the *drying* it up, or preventing that *annual inundation*, must be the cause of dearth, famine, &c. By *rivers*, we may understand the *various canals* cut from the Nile to carry water into the different parts of the land. When the Nile did not rise to its usual height, these canals were quite dry.

Verse 13. Their *images to cease out of Noph*] Afterwards *Memphis*, and now *Cairo* or *Kahira.* This was the seat of Egyptian idolatry; the place where *Apis* was particularly worshipped.

No more a prince of the land of Egypt] Not one, from that time to the present day. See the note on chap. xxix. 14.

Verse 14. *I will make Pathros desolate*] See the preceding chapter, ver. 14.

Zoan] *Tanis*, the ancient capital of Egypt.

No.] *Diospolis*, or *Thebes*, the city of Jupiter.

Verse 15. *My fury upon Sin*] *Pelusium*, a strong city of Egypt, on the coast of the Mediterranean Sea.

Verse 16. *Noph*] *Cairo* or *Kahira;* see ver. 13.

Verse 17. *Aven*] Or *On, the famous Heliopolis*, or city of the sun.

Pibeseth] *Bubastum* or *Bubaste*, by a slight alteration of the letters. It is situated on the eastern branch of the Nile, towards Arabia.

Verse 18. *Tehaphnehes*] Called also *Tahapanes*, Jer. ii. 16. This is the *Pelusian Daphne.*

Break there the yokes] The sceptres. Nebuchadnezzar broke the sceptre of Egypt when he confirmed the kingdom to *Amasis*, who had rebelled again t *Apries*.

Verse 20. *In the eleventh year, in the first* month, *in the seventh* day] This was the *eleventh* year of the captivity of Jeconiah, and the date here answers to April 26, A. M. 3416; a prophecy anterior by several years to that already delivered. In collecting the writings of Ezekiel, more care was taken to put all that related to *one subject* together, than to attend to *chronological arrangement.*

Verse 21. *I have broken the arm of Pharaoh*] Perhaps this may refer to his defeat by Nebuchadnezzar, when he was coming with the Egyptian army to succour Jerusalem.

Verse 22. *I will cause the sword to fall out of his hand.*] When the arm is broken, the sword will naturally fall. But these expressions show that the Egyptians would be rendered wholly useless to Zedekiah, and should never more recover their political strength. This was the case from the time of the rebellion of Amasis.

Verse 26. *I will scatter the Egyptians*] Several fled with *Apries* to Upper Egypt; and when Nebuchadnezzar wasted the country, he carried many of them to Babylon. See on chap. xxix. 12.

CHAPTER XXXI

This very beautiful chapter relates also to Egypt. The prophet describes to Pharaoh the fall of the king of Nineveh, (see the books of Nahum, Jonah, and Zephaniah,) under the image of a fair cedar of Lebanon, once exceedingly tall, flourishing, and majestic, but now cut down and withered, with its broken branches strewed around, 1–17. *He then concludes with bringing the matter home to the king of Egypt, by telling him that this was a picture of his approaching fate,* 18. *The beautiful cedar of Lebanon, remarkable for its loftiness, and in the most flourishing condition, but afterwards cut down and deserted, gives a very lively painting of the great glory and dreadful catastrophe of both the Assyrian and Egyptian monarchies. The manner in which the prophet has embellished his subject is deeply interesting; the colouring is of that kind which the mind will always contemplate with pleasure.*

A. M. 3416
B. C. 588
Ol. XLVIII. 1
Anno
Tarquinii Prisci,
R. Roman., 29

AND it came to pass in the eleventh year, in the third *month,* in the first *day* of the month, *that* the word of the LORD came unto me, saying,
2 Son of man, speak unto Pharaoh king of
Egypt, and to his multitude; [a]Whom art thou
like in thy greatness?
3 [b]Behold, the Assyrian *was* a cedar in Lebanon [c]with fair branches, and with a shadowing shroud, and of a high stature; and his top was among the thick boughs.
4 [d]The waters [e]made him great, the deep [f]set him up on high with her rivers running round about his plants, and sent out her [g]little rivers unto all the trees of the field.
5 Therefore [h]his height was exalted above all the trees of the field, and his boughs were multiplied, and his branches became long because of the multitude of waters, [i]when he shot forth.
6 All the [k]fowls of heaven made their nests in his boughs, and under his branches did all the beasts of the field bring forth their young, and under his shadow dwelt all great nations.
7 Thus was he fair in his greatness, in the
length of his branches: for his root was by great waters.
8 The cedars in the [l]garden of God could not hide him: the fir trees were not like his boughs, and the chesnut trees were not like his branches; nor any tree in the garden of God was like unto him in his beauty.
9 I have made him fair by the multitude of his branches; so that all the trees of Eden, that *were* in the garden of God, envied him.
10 Therefore thus saith the Lord GOD; Because thou hast lifted up thyself in height, and he hath shot up his top among the thick boughs, and [m]his heart is lifted up in his height;
11 I have therefore delivered him into the hand of the mighty one of the heathen; [n]he shall surely deal with him: I have driven him out for his wickedness.
12 And strangers, [o]the terrible of the nations, have cut him off, and have left him: [p]upon the mountains and in all the valleys his branches are fallen, and his boughs are broken by all the rivers of the land; and all the people of the earth are gone down from his shadow, and have left him.

A. M. 3416
B. C. 588
Ol. XLVIII. 1
Anno
Tarquinii Prisci,
R. Roman., 29

[a]Ver. 18——[b]Dan. iv. 10——[c]Heb. *fair of branches* [d]Jer. li. 36——[e]Or, *nourished*——[f]Or, *brought him up* [g]Or, *conduits*——[h]Dan. iv. 11——[i]Or, *when it sent them forth*

[k]Chap. xvii. 23; Dan. iv. 12——[l]Gen. ii. 8; xiii. 10; chap. xxviii. 13——[m]Dan. v. 20——[n]Heb. *in doing he shall do unto him*——[o]Chap. xxviii. 7——[p]Chap. xxxii. 5; xxxv. 8

NOTES ON CHAP. XXXI

Verse 1. *In the eleventh year*] On *Sunday,* June 19, A. M. 3416, according to Abp. Usher; a *month* before Jerusalem was taken by the Chaldeans.

Verse 3. *Behold, the Assyrian* was *a cedar*] Why is the *Assyrian* introduced here, when the whole chapter concerns *Egypt?* Bp. *Lowth* has shown that אשור ארז *ashshur erez* should be translated *the tall cedar, the very stately cedar;* hence there is reference to his *lofty top;* and all the following description belongs to *Egypt,* not to *Assyria.* But see on ver. 11.

Verse 4. *The waters made him great*] Alluding to the fertility of Egypt by the *overflowing of the Nile.* But *waters* often mean *peoples.* By means of the different nations under the Egyptians, that government became very opulent. These nations are represented as *fowls* and *beasts,* taking shelter under the protection of this great political Egyptian tree, ver. 6.

Verse 8. *The cedars in the garden of God*] Egypt was one of the most eminent and affluent of all the neighbouring nations.

Verse 11. *The mighty one of the heathen*] Nebuchadnezzar. It is worthy of notice, that Nebuchadnezzar, in the *first* year of his reign, rendered himself master of *Nineveh,* the capital of the *Assyrian* empire. See *Sedar Olam.* This happened about *twenty* years before Ezekiel delivered this prophecy; on this account,

A. M. 3416
B. C. 588
Ol. XLVIII. 1
Anno
Tarquinii Prisci,
R. Roman., 29

13 [q]Upon his ruin shall all the fowls of the heaven remain, and all the beasts of the field shall be upon his branches:

14 To the end that none of all the trees by the waters exalt themselves for their height, neither shoot up their top among the thick boughs, neither their trees [r]stand up in their height, all that drink water: for [s]they are all delivered unto death, [t]to the nether parts of the earth, in the midst of the children of men, with them that go down to the pit.

15 Thus saith the Lord GOD; In the day when he went down to the grave I caused a mourning: I covered the deep for him, and I restrained the floods thereof, and the great waters were stayed: and I caused Lebanon [u]to mourn for him, and all the trees of the field fainted for him.

16 I made the nations to [v]shake at the sound of his fall, when I [w]cast him down to hell with them that descend into the pit: and [x]all the trees of Eden, the choice and best of Lebanon, all that drink water, [y]shall be comforted in the nether parts of the earth.

17 They also went down into hell with him unto *them that be* slain with the sword; and *they that were* his arm, *that* [z]dwelt under his shadow in the midst of the heathen.

18 [a]To whom art thou thus like in glory and in greatness among the trees of Eden? yet shalt thou be brought down with the trees of Eden unto the nether parts of the earth: [b]thou shalt lie in the midst of the uncircumcised with *them that be* slain by the sword. This *is* Pharaoh and all his multitude, saith the Lord GOD.

[q]Isa. xviii. 6; ch. xxxii. 4——[r]Or, *stand upon themselves for their height*——[s]Psa. lxxxii. 7——[t]Ch. xxxii. 18 [u]Heb. *to be black*——[v]Chap. xxvi. 15

[w]Isa. xiv. 15——[x]Isa. xiv. 8——[y]Chap. xxxii. 31 [z]Lam. iv. 20——[a]Ver. 2; chap. xxxii. 19——[b]Chap. xxviii. 10; xxxii. 19, 21, 24, &c.

Ashshur, ver. 3, may relate to the *Assyrians*, to whom it is possible the prophet here compares the Egyptians. But see on ver. 3.

Verse 13. *Upon his ruin shall all the fowls*] The fall of Egypt is likened to the fall of a great tree; and as the fowls and beasts sheltered under its branches before, ver. 6, so they now feed upon its ruins.

Verse 14. *To the end that none of all the trees*] Let this ruin, fallen upon Egypt, teach all the nations that shall hear of it to be *humble*, because, however *elevated*, God can soon bring them down; and *pride* and *arrogance*, either in *states* or *individuals*, have the peculiar abhorrence of God. Pride does not suit the sons of men; it made devils of *angels*, and makes fiends of *men*.

Verse 15. *I caused Lebanon to mourn for him*] All the confederates of Pharaoh are represented as deploring his fall, ver. 16, 17.

Verse 17. *They also went down into hell with him*] Into *remediless destruction*.

Verse 18. *This is Pharaoh*] All that I have spoken in this allegory of the *lofty cedar* refers to *Pharaoh*, king of Egypt, his princes, confederates, and people. *Calmet* understands the whole chapter of the *king of Assyria*, under which he allows that *Egypt* is adumbrated; and hence on this verse he quotes,—

Mutato nomine, de te fabula narratur.

What is said of Assyria belongs to thee, O Egypt.

CHAPTER XXXII

The prophet goes on to predict the fall of the king of Egypt, under the figure of an animal of prey, such as a lion or crocodile, caught, slain, and his carcass left a prey to the fowls and wild beasts, 1–6. The figure is then changed; and the greatness of his fall (described by the darkening of the sun, moon, and stars) strikes terror into all the surrounding nations, 7–10. The prophet adds, that the overthrow of the then reigning Egyptian dynasty was to be effected by the instrumentality of the king of Babylon, who should leave Egypt so desolate, that its waters, (alluding to the metaphor used in the second verse,) *should run as pure and smooth as oil, without the foot of man or the hoof of a beast to disturb them, 11–16. A beautiful, nervous, and concise description of a land ruined and left utterly desolate. In the remaining part of the chapter the same event is pourtrayed by one of the boldest figures ever attempted in any composition, and which at the same time is executed with astonishing perspicuity and force. God is introduced ordering a place in the lower regions for the king of Egypt and his host, 17, 18. The prophet delivers his messsage, pronounces their fate, and commands those who buried the slain to drag him and his multitudes to the subterraneous mansions, 19, 20. At the tumult and commotion which this mighty work occasions, the infernal shades are represented as roused from their couches to learn the cause. They see and congratulate the king of Egypt, on his arrival among them, 21. Pharaoh being now introduced into this immense subterraneous cavern, (see the* fourteenth *chapter of Isaiah, where a similar imagery is employed,) the prophet leads him all around the sides of the pit; shows him the gloomy mansions of former tyrants, tells their names as he goes along; beautifully contrasts their former pomp and destructive ambition, when they were a terror to the surrounding states, with their present most abject and help-*

less condition; declares that all these oppressors of mankind have not only been cut off out of the land of the living, but have gone down into the grave uncircumcised, *that is, they have died in their sins, and therefore shall have no resurrection to eternal life; and concludes with showing Pharaoh the place destined for him in the midst of the uncircumcised, and of them that have been slain by the sword,* 22–32. *This prophetic ode may be considered as a finished model in that species of writing which is appropriated to the exciting of terror. The imagery throughout is sublime and terrible; and no reader of sensibility and taste can accompany the prophet in this funeral procession, and visit the mansions of Hades, without being impressed with a degree of awe nearly approaching to horror.*

A. M. 3417
B. C. 587
Ol. XLVIII. 2
Anno Tarquinii Prisci, R. Roman., 30

AND it came to pass in the twelfth year, in the twelfth month, in the first *day* of the month, *that* the word of the LORD came unto me, saying,

2 Son of man, [a]take up a lamentation for Pharaoh king of Egypt, and say unto him, [b]Thou art like a young lion of the nations, [c]and thou *art* as a [d]whale in the seas: and thou camest forth with thy rivers, and troubledst the waters with thy feet, and [e]fouledst their rivers:

3 Thus saith the Lord GOD; I will therefore [f]spread out my net over thee with a company of many people; and they shall bring thee up in my net.

4 Then [g]will I leave thee upon the land, I will cast thee forth upon the open field, and [h]will cause all the fowls of the heaven to remain upon thee, and I will fill the beasts of the whole earth with thee.

5 And I will lay thy flesh [i]upon the mountains, and fill the valleys with thy height.

6 I will also water with thy blood [k]the land wherein thou swimmest, *even* to the mountains; and the rivers shall be full of thee.

A. M. 3417
B. C. 587
Ol. XLVIII. 2
Anno Tarquinii Prisci, R. Roman., 30

7 And when I shall [l]put thee out, [m]I will cover the heaven, and make the stars thereof dark; I will cover the sun with a cloud, and the moon shall not give her light.

8 All the [n]bright lights of heaven will I make [o]dark over thee, and set darkness upon thy land, saith the Lord GOD.

9 I will also [p]vex the hearts of many people, when I shall bring thy destruction among the nations, into the countries which thou hast not known.

10 Yea, I will make many people [q]amazed at thee, and their kings shall be horribly afraid for thee, when I shall brandish my sword before them; and [r]they shall tremble at *every* moment, every man for his own life, in the day of thy fall.

11 [s]For thus saith the Lord GOD; The sword of the king of Babylon shall come upon thee.

12 By the swords of the mighty will I cause

[a]Chap. xxvii. 2; ver. 16——[b]Chap. xix. 3, 6; xxxviii. 13——[c]Chap. xxix. 3——[d]Or, *dragon*——[e]Chap. xxxiv. 18——[f]Chap. xii. 13; xvii. 20; Hos. vii. 12——[g]Chap. xxix. 5——[h]Chap. xxxi. 13——[i]Chap. xxxi. 12——[k]Or, *the land of thy swimming*——[l]Or, *extinguish*

[m]Isa. xiii. 10; Joel ii. 31; iii. 15; Amos viii. 9; Rev. vi. 12, 13; Matt. xxiv. 29——[n]Heb. *light of the light in heaven*——[o]Heb. *them dark*——[p]Heb. *provoke to anger*, or *grief*——[q]Chap. xxvii. 35——[r]Chap. xxvi. 16 [s]Jer. xlvi. 26; chap. xxx. 4

NOTES ON CHAP. XXXII

Verse 1. *In the twelfth year, in the twelfth month, in the first* day *of the month*] On *Wednesday*, March 22, the *twelfth* year of the captivity of Jeconiah, A. M. 3417.

Instead of the *twelfth* year, *five* of *Kennicott's* MSS., and *eight* of *De Rossi's*, *read* בעשתי עשרה *in the eleventh* year. This reading is supported by the *Syriac;* and is confirmed by an excellent MS. of my own, about *four hundred* years old.

Verse 2. *Thou art like a young lion—and thou* art *as a whale in the seas*] Thou mayest be likened to *two* of the fiercest animals in the creation; to a lion, the fiercest on the *land;* to a *crocodile*, תנים *tannim*, (see chap. xxix. 3,) the fiercest in the *waters.* It may, however, point out the *hippopotamus*, as there seems to be a reference to his mode of *feeding.* He walks deliberately into the water over head, and pursues his way in the same manner; still keeping on his feet, and feeding on the plants, &c., that grow at the bottom. Thus he *fouls the water* with his feet.

Verse 5. *And fill the valleys with thy height.*] Some translate, with *the worms*, which should proceed from the putrefaction of his flesh.

Verse 6. *The land wherein thou swimmest*] Egypt; so called, because intersected with *canals*, and *overflowed* annually by the *Nile.*

Verse 7. *I will cover the heaven*] Destroy the *empire.*

Make the stars thereof dark] Overwhelm all the *dependent states.*

I will cover the sun] The *king* himself.

And the moon shall not give her light.] The *queen* may be meant, or some *state* less than the kingdom.

Verse 8. *And set darkness upon thy land*] As I did when a former king refused to let my people go to the wilderness to worship me. I will involve *thee*, and thy *house*, and thy *people*, and the whole *land*, in desolation and wo.

Verse 9. *I will also vex the hearts*] Even the remote nations, who had no connexion with thee, shall be amazed at the judgments which have fallen upon thee.

Verse 14. *Cause their rivers to run like oil*] Bring the whole state into quietness, there being no longer a political *hippopotamus* to *foul*

A. M. 3417
B. C. 587
Ol. XLVIII. 2
Anno
Tarquinii Prisci,
R. Roman., 30

thy multitude to fall, [t]the terrible of the nations, all of
them: and [u]they shall spoil
the pomp of Egypt, and all
the multitude thereof shall be destroyed.
13 I will destroy also all the beasts thereof
from beside the great waters; [v]neither shall
the foot of man trouble them any more, nor
the hoofs of beasts trouble them.
14 Then will I make their waters deep, and
cause their rivers to run like oil, saith the
Lord GOD.
15 When I shall make the land of Egypt
desolate, and the country shall be [w]destitute
of that whereof it was full, when I shall smite
all them that dwell therein, [x]then shall they
know that I *am* the LORD.
16 This *is* the [y]lamentation wherewith they
shall lament her: the daughters of the nations
shall lament her: they shall lament for her,
even for Egypt, and for all her multitude,
saith the Lord GOD.
17 It came to pass also in the twelfth year,
in the fifteenth *day* of the month, that the
word of the LORD came unto me, saying,
18 Son of man, wail for the multitude of
Egypt, and [z]cast them down, *even* her, and
the daughters of the famous nations, unto the
nether parts of the earth, with them that go
down into the pit.
19 [a]Whom dost thou pass in beauty? [b]go
down, and be thou laid with the uncircumcised.
20 They shall fall in the
midst of *them that are* slain
by the sword: [c]she is delivered
to the sword: draw her and all
her multitudes.
21 [d]The strong among the mighty shall
speak to him out of the midst of hell with
them that help him: they are [e]gone down, they
lie uncircumcised, slain by the sword.
22 [f]Asshur *is* there and all her company:
his graves *are* about him: all of them slain,
fallen by the sword:
23 [g]Whose graves are set in the sides of the
pit, and her company is round about her
grave; all of them slain, fallen by the sword,
which [h]caused [i]terror in the land of the
living.
24 There *is* [k]Elam and all her multitude
round about her grave, all of them slain, fallen
by the sword, which are [l]gone down uncircumcised into the nether parts of the earth,
[m]which caused their terror in the land of the
living; yet have they borne their shame with
them that go down to the pit.
25 They have set her a bed in the midst of
the slain with all her multitude: her graves
are round about him: all of them uncircumcised, slain by the sword: though their terror
was caused in the land of the living, yet have
they borne their shame with them that go
down to the pit: he is put in the midst of *them
that be* slain.
26 There *is* [n]Meshech, Tubal, and all her

A. M. 3417
B. C. 587
Ol. XLVIII. 2
Anno
Tarquinii Prisci,
R. Roman., 30

---

[t]Ch. xxviii. 7——[u]Ch. xxix. 19——[v]Ch. xxix. 11
[w]Heb. *desolate from the fulness thereof*——[x]Exod. vii. 5; xiv. 4, 18; Psa. ix. 16; ch. vi. 7——[y]Ver. 2; 2 Sam. i. 17; 2 Chron. xxxv. 25; ch. xxvi. 17——[z]Ch. xxvi. 20; xxxi.14
[a]Ch. xxxi. 2, 18——[b]Ver. 21, 24, &c.; ch. xxviii. 10

[c]Or, *the sword is laid*——[d]Isa. i. 31; xiv. 9, 10; ver. 27
[e]Ver. 19, 25, &c.——[f]Ver. 24, 26, 29, 30——[g]Isa. xiv. 15
[h]Ch. xxvi. 17, 20; ver. 24, 25, 26, 27, 32——[i]Or, *dismaying*——[k]Jer. xlix. 34, &c.——[l]Ver. 21——[m]Ver. 23
[n]Gen. x. 2; chap. xxvii. 13; xxxviii. 2

---

the waters—to disturb the peace of the country.

Verse 15. *Shall be destitute of that whereof it was full*] Of *corn*, and all other necessaries of life.

Verse 17. *In the twelfth year*] Two of *Kennicott's* MSS., *one* of *De Rossi's*, and *one* of my own, (that mentioned ver. 1,) have, *in the* ELEVENTH *year;* and so has the *Syriac*, as before. This prophecy concerns the *people of Egypt*.

Verse 18. *Cast them down*] Show them that they shall be cast down. Proclaim to them a *casting down* prophecy.

Verse 19. *Whom dost thou pass in beauty?*] How little does it signify, whether a mummy be well embalmed, wrapped round with rich stuff, and beautifully painted on the outside, or not. Go down into the *tombs*, examine the *niches*, and see whether one dead carcass be preferable to another.

Verse 21. *Out of the midst of hell*] שאול *sheol*, the *catacombs*, the *place of burial*. There is something here similar to Isa. xiv. 9, where the descent of the king of Babylon to the state of the dead is described.

Verse 22. *Asshur* is *there*] The mightiest conquerors of the earth have gone down to the grave before thee; there they and their soldiers lie together, all slain by the sword.

Verse 23. *Whose graves are set in the sides of the pit*] Alluding to the *niches* in the sides of the subterranean caves or burying-places, where the bodies are laid. These are numerous in Egypt.

Verse 24. *There* is *Elam*] The Elamites, not far from the Assyrians; others think that *Persia* is meant. It was invaded by the joint forces of Cyaxares and Nebuchadnezzar.

Verse 26. *There* is *Meshech, Tubal*] See on chap. xxvii. 13.

A. M. 3417
B. C. 587
Ol. XLVIII. 2
Anno
Tarquinii Prisci,
R. Roman., 30

multitude: her graves *are* round about him: all of them [o]uncircumcised, slain by the sword, though they caused their terror in the land of the living.

27 [p]And they shall not lie with the mighty *that are* fallen of the uncircumcised, which are gone down to hell [q]with their weapons of war: and they have laid their swords under their heads, but their iniquities shall be upon their bones, though *they were* the terror of the mighty in the land of the living.

28 Yea, thou shalt be broken in the midst of the uncircumcised, and shalt lie with *them that are* slain with the sword.

29 There *is* [r]Edom, her kings, and all her princes, which with their might are [s]laid by *them that were* slain by the sword: they shall lie with the uncircumcised, and with them that go down to the pit.

30 [t]There *be* the princes of the north, all of them, and all the [u]Zidonians which are gone down with the slain; with their terror they are ashamed of their might; and they lie uncircumcised with *them that be* slain by the sword, and bear their shame with them that go down to the pit.

31 Pharaoh shall see them, and shall be [v]comforted over all his multitude, *even* Pharaoh and all his army slain by the sword, saith the Lord GOD.

32 For I have caused my terror in the land of the living: and he shall be laid in the midst of the uncircumcised with *them that are* slain with the sword, *even* Pharaoh and all his multitude, saith the Lord GOD.

[o]Ver. 19, 20, &c.——[p]Ver. 21; Isa. xiv. 18, 19——[q]Heb. *with weapons of their war*——[r]Chap. xxv. 12, &c.

[s]Heb. *given*, or *put*——[t]Chap. xxxviii. 6, 15; xxxix. 2——[u]Chap. xxviii. 21——[v]Chap. xxxi. 16

Verse 27. *Gone down to hell with their weapons of war*] Are buried in their armour, and with their weapons lying by their sides. It was a very ancient practice, in different nations, to bury a warrior's weapons in the same grave with himself.

Verse 29. *There* is *Edom*] All the glory and pomp of the *Idumean* kings, who also helped to oppress the Israelites, are gone down into the grave. Their kings, princes, and all their mighty men lie mingled with the *uncircumcised*, not distinguished from the *common dead:*

"Where they an equal honour share,
Who buried or unburied are.
Where Agamemnon knows no more
Than Irus, he condemned before.
Where fair Achilles and Thersites lie,
Equally naked, poor, and dry."

Verse 30. *There be the princes of the north*] The kings of Media and Assyria, and all the *Zidonians*—the kings of *Tyre*, *Sidon*, and *Damascus*. See *Calmet*.

Verse 31. *Pharaoh shall see them*] Pharaoh also, who said he was *a god*, shall be found among the vulgar dead.

And shall be comforted] Shall console himself, on finding that all other proud boasters are in the same circumstances with himself. Here is a reference to a *consciousness* after death.

Verse 32. *I have caused my terror in the land of the living*] I have spread dismay through Judea, the land of the *living God*, where the *living oracles* were delivered, and where the upright *live* by faith. When Pharaoh-necho came against Josiah, defeated, and slew him at Megiddo, fear and terror were spread through all the land of Judea; and the allusion here is probably to that circumstance. But even he is now laid with the *uncircumcised*, and is no more to be distinguished from the common dead.

Much of the phraseology of this chapter may be illustrated by comparing it with Isa. xiv., where see the notes, which the intelligent reader will do well to consult.

CHAPTER XXXIII

The prophet, after having addressed several other nations, returns now to his own; previously to which he is told, as on a former occasion, the duty of a watchman, the salvation or ruin of whose soul depends on the manner in which he discharges it. An awful passage indeed; full of important instruction both to such as speak, and to such as hear, the word of God, 1–9. *The prophet is then directed what answer to make to the cavils of infidelity and impiety; and to vindicate the equity of the Divine government by declaring the general terms of acceptance with God to be* (as told before, chap. xviii.) *without respect of persons; so that the ruin of the finally impenitent must be entirely owing to themselves,* 10–20. *The prophet receives the news of the destruction of Jerusalem by the Chaldeans, about a year and four months after it happened, according to the opinion of some, who have been led to this conjecture by the date given to this prophecy in the* twenty-first *verse, as it stands in our common Version: but some of the manuscripts of this prophet consulted by Dr. Kennicott have in this place* the ELEVENTH year, *which is probably the genuine reading. To check the vain confidence of those who expected to hold out by possessing themselves of its other fastnesses, the utter desolation of all Judea is foretold,* 21–29. *Ezekiel is informed that among those that attended his instructions were a great number of hypocrites,*

***against whom he delivers a most awful message. When the Lord is destroying these hypocrites, then shall they know that there hath been a prophet among them,* 30–33.**

A. M. cir. 3416
B. C. cir. 588
Ol. XLVIII. 1
Tarquinii Prisci,
R. Roman.,
cir. annum 29

AGAIN the word of the LORD came unto me, saying,

2 Son of man, speak [a]to the children of thy people, and say unto them, [b]When [c]I bring the sword upon a land, if the people of the land take a man of their coasts, and set him for their [d]watchman:

3 If when he seeth the sword come upon the land, he blow the trumpet, and warn the people;

4 Then [e]whosoever heareth the sound of the trumpet and taketh not warning; if the sword come, and take him away, [f]his blood shall be upon his own head.

5 He heard the sound of the trumpet, and took not warning; his blood shall be upon him. But he that taketh warning shall deliver his soul.

6 But if the watchman see the sword come, and blow not the trumpet, and the people be not warned; if the sword come, and take *any* person from among them, [g]he is taken away in his iniquity; but his blood will I require at the watchman's hand.

7 [h]So thou, O son of man, I have set thee a watchman unto the house of Israel; therefore thou shalt hear the word at my mouth, and warn them from me.

8 When I say unto the wicked, O wicked *man,* thou shalt surely die; if thou dost not speak to warn the wicked from his way, that wicked *man* shall die in his iniquity; but his blood will I require at thine hand.

9 Nevertheless, if thou warn the wicked of his way to turn from it; if he do not turn from his way, he shall die in his iniquity; but thou hast delivered thy soul.

A. M. cir. 3416
B. C. cir. 588
Ol. XLVIII. 1
Tarquinii Prisci,
R. Roman.,
cir. annum 29

10 Therefore, O thou son of man, speak unto the house of Israel; Thus ye speak, saying, If our transgressions and our sins *be* upon us, and we [i]pine away in them, [k]how should we then live?

11 Say unto them, *As* I live, saith the Lord GOD, [l]I have no pleasure in the death of the wicked; but that the wicked turn from his way and live: turn ye, turn ye from your evil ways; for [m]why will ye die, O house of Israel?

12 Therefore, thou son of man, say unto the children of thy people, [n]The righteousness of the righteous shall not deliver him in the day of his transgression: as for the wickedness of the wicked, [o]he shall not fall thereby in the day that he turneth from his wickedness; neither shall the righteous be able to live for his *righteousness* in the day that he sinneth.

13 When I shall say to the righteous, *that* he shall surely live; [p]if he trust to his own righteousness, and commit iniquity, all his righteousness shall not be remembered; but for his iniquity that he hath committed he shall die for it.

14 Again, [q]when I say unto the wicked, Thou shalt surely die; if he turn from his sin, and do [r]that which is lawful and right;

15 *If* the wicked [s]restore the pledge, [t]give again that he had robbed, walked in [u]the sta-

[a]Chap. iii. 11——[b]Chap. xiv. 17——[c]Heb. *A land when I bring a sword upon her*——[d]2 Sam. xviii. 24, 25; 2 Kings ix. 17; ver. 7; Hos. ix. 8——[e]Heb. *he that hearing heareth*——[f]Chap. xviii. 13——[g]Ver. 8 [h]Chap. iii. 17, &c.——[i]Chap. xxiv. 23——[k]So Isa. xlix. 14; chap. xxxvii. 11——[l]2 Sam. xiv. 14; chap. xviii. 23, 32; 2 Pet. iii. 9——[m]Chap. xviii. 31——[n]Chap. iii. 20; xviii. 24, 26, 27——[o]2 Chron. vii. 14——[p]Chap. iii. 20; xviii. 24——[q]Chap. iii. 18, 19; xviii. 27——[r]Heb. *judgment and justice*——[s]Chap. xviii. 7——[t]Exod. xxii. 1, 4; Lev. vi. 2, 4, 5; Num. v. 6, 7; Luke xix. 8——[u]Lev. xviii. 5; chap. xx. 11, 13, 21

NOTES ON CHAP. XXXIII

Verse 2. *Son of man—if the people of the land take a man*] The first *ten* verses of this chapter are the same with chap. iii. 17-22; and to what is said there on this most important and awful subject I must refer the reader. *Here* the PEOPLE *choose* the *watchman; there,* the Lord appoints him. When God chooses, the people should approve.

Verse 10. *If our transgressions and our sins* be *upon us*] They *are* upon us, as a grievous burden, too weighty for us to bear: how then can we *live* under such a load?

We pine away in them] In such circumstances how consoling is that word: "Come unto me, all ye who are heavy laden, and I will give you rest!"

Verse 11. As *I live, saith the Lord God, I have no pleasure in the death of the wicked*] From this to the twentieth verse inclusive is nearly the same with chap. xviii., on which I wish the reader to consult the notes.

Verse 13. *If he trust to his own righteousness, and commit iniquity*] If he trust in his *acting according to the statutes and ordinances of religion,* and according to the *laws relative to rights and wrongs among men,* and in

A. M. cir. 3416
B. C. cir. 588
Ol. XLVIII. 1
Tarquinii Prisci,
R. Roman.,
cir. annum 29

tutes of life, without commit-
ting iniquity; he shall surely
live, he shall not die.
16 [v]None of his sins that he
hath committed shall be mentioned unto him:
he hath done that which is lawful and right;
he shall surely live.
17 [w]Yet the children of thy people say, The
way of the Lord is not equal: but as for them,
their way is not equal.
18 [x]When the righteous turneth from his
righteousness, and committeth iniquity, he
shall even die thereby.
19 But if the wicked turn from his wickedness, and do that which is lawful and right, he
shall live thereby.
20 Yet ye say, [y]The way of the Lord is not
equal. O ye house of Israel, I will judge you
every one after his ways.
21 And it came to pass in the twelfth year
[z]of our captivity, in the tenth *month,* in the
fifth *day* of the month, [a]*that* one that had
escaped out of Jerusalem came unto me, saying, [b]The city is smitten.
22 Now [c]the hand of the LORD was upon
me in the evening, afore he that was escaped
came; and had opened my mouth, until
he came to me in the morning; [d]and my
mouth was opened, and I was no more
dumb.

23 Then the word of the
LORD came unto me, saying,
24 Son of man, [e]they that inhabit those [f]wastes of the land
of Israel speak, saying, [g]Abraham was one,
and he inherited the land: [h]but we *are* many;
the land is given us for inheritance.
25 Wherefore say unto them, Thus saith the
Lord GOD; [i]Ye eat with the blood, and [k]lift
up your eyes towards your idols, and [l]shed
blood: and shall ye possess the land?
26 [m]Ye stand upon your sword, ye work
abomination, and ye [n]defile every one his
neighbour's wife: and shall ye possess the
land?
27 Say thou thus unto them, Thus saith the
Lord GOD; *As* I live, surely [o]they that *are* in
the wastes shall fall by the sword, and him
that *is* in the open field [p]will I give to the
beasts [q]to be devoured, and they that *be* in the
forts and [r]in the caves shall die of the pestilence.
28 [s]For I will lay the land [t]most desolate,
and the [u]pomp of her strength shall cease;
and the [v]mountains of Israel shall be desolate,
that none shall pass through.
29 Then shall they know that I *am* the
LORD, when I have laid the land most desolate because of all their abominations which
they have committed.

A. M. 3416
B. C. 588
Ol. XLVIII. 1
Anno
Tarquinii Prisci,
R. Roman., 29

[v]Chap. xviii. 22——[w]Ver. 20; chap. xviii. 25, 29——[x]Chap. xviii. 26, 27——[y]Ver. 17; chap. xviii. 25, 29——[z]Chap. i. 2——[a]Chap. xxiv. 26——[b]2 Kings xxv. 4——[c]Chap. i. 3——[d]Chap. xxiv. 27——[e]Chap. xxxiv. 2——[f]Ver. 27; chap. xxxvi. 4——[g]Isaiah li. 2; Acts vii. 5——[h]See Micah iii. 11; Matthew iii. 9; John viii. 39

[i]Gen. ix. 4; Lev. iii. 17; vii. 26; xvii. 10; xix. 26; Deut. xii. 16——[k]Ch. xviii. 6——[l]Ch. xxii. 6, 9——[m]Wisd. ii. 11——[n]Chap. xviii. 6; xxii. 11——[o]Ver. 24——[p]Ch. xxxix. 4——[q]Heb. *to devour him*——[r]Judg. vi. 2; 1 Sam. xiii. 6——[s]Jer. xliv. 2, 6, 22; chap. xxxvi. 34, 35——[t]Heb. *desolation and desolation*——[u]Chap. vii. 24; xxiv. 21; xxx. 6, 7——[v]Chap. vi. 2, 3, 6

other respects commit iniquity, *he shall die for it.*

Verse 19. *He shall live thereby*] "The *wages* of sin is death;" the "gift of God is eternal life." It is a miserable trade by which a man *cannot live;* such a trade is *sin.*

Verse 21. *In the twelfth year of our captivity, in the tenth* month, *in the fifth* day *of the month*] Instead of the *twelfth year,* the *eleventh* is the reading of *seven* of *Kennicott's* MSS., *one* of *De Rossi's*, and the *Syriac.* My own, mentioned in the preceding chapter, reads with the present text. This was on *Wednesday, Jan.* 25, A. M. 3416 or 3417.

One that had escaped out of Jerusalem] After it had been taken by the Chaldeans.

Came unto me, saying, THE CITY IS SMITTEN.] This very message God had promised to the prophet, chap. xxiv. 26.

Verse 22. *My mouth was opened*] They had now the fullest evidence that I had spoken from the Lord. I therefore spoke freely and fully what God delivered to me, chap. xxiv. 27.

Verse 24. *Abraham was one*] If he was called to inherit the land when he was alone, and had the whole to himself, why may we not expect to be established here, who are his posterity, and are *many?* They wished to remain in the land and be happy after the Chaldeans had carried the rest away captives.

Verse 25. *Ye eat with the blood*] Abraham was *righteous*, ye are *unrighteous.* Eating of *blood*, in any way dressed, or of *flesh* from which the blood had not been *extracted*, was and is in the sight of God abominable. All such practices he has absolutely and for ever forbidden. Let the vile blood-eaters hear and tremble. See the note on Acts xv. 20, and the passages in the margin.

Verse 26. *Ye stand upon your sword*] Ye live by plunder, rapine, and murder. Ye are every way impure; and shall ye possess the land? No.

Verse 27. *They that* are *in the wastes*] He seems to speak of those Jews who had fled to *rocks*, *caves*, and *fortresses*, in the *mountains;*

A. M. 3416
B. C. 588
Ol. XLVIII. 1
Anno
Tarquinii Prisci,
R. Roman., 29

30 Also, thou son of man,
the children of thy people
still are talking [w]against thee
by the walls and in the doors
of the houses, and [x]speak one to another,
every one to his brother, saying, Come, I pray
you, and hear what is the word that cometh
forth from the LORD.

31 And [y]they come unto thee [z]as the people
cometh, and [a]they [b]sit before thee *as* my people, and they hear thy words, but they will
not do them: for [c]with their
mouth [d]they show much love,
but [e]their heart goeth after
their covetousness.

32 And, lo, thou *art* unto them as [f]a very
lovely song of one that hath a pleasant voice,
and can play well on an instrument: for they
hear thy words, but they do them not.

33 [g]And when this cometh to pass, (lo, it
will come,) then [h]shall they know that a
prophet hath been among them.

[w]Or, *of thee*——[x]Isa. xxix. 13——[y]Chap. xiv. 1; xx. 1, &c.——[z]Heb. *according to the coming of the people*
[a]Or, *my people set before thee*
[b]Ch. viii. 1——[c]Psa. lxxviii. 36, 37; Isa. xxix. 13
[d]Heb. *they make loves*, or *jests*——[e]Matt. xiii. 22
[f]Heb. *a song of loves*——[g]1 Sam. iii. 20——[h]Chap. ii. 5

whose death he predicts, partly by the *sword*, partly by *wild beasts*, and partly by *famine*.

Verse 30. *The people still are talking against thee*] בך *bach* should be rather translated, "concerning thee," than "against thee;" for the following verses show that the prophet was much respected. The *Vulgate* translates, *de te;* the *Septuagint*, περι σου, "concerning thee;" both right.

Talking by the walls and in the doors of the houses is not a custom peculiar to the *Copts*, mentioned by Bp. *Pococke;* it is a practice among *idle people*, and among those who are *resting from their work*, in *every country*, when the *weather permits*. Gossiping *in the inside of the house* is not less frequent, and much more blamable.

Verse 31. *As the people cometh*] As they are accustomed to come on public days, Sabbaths, &c.

With their mouth they show much love] They respected the prophet, but would not bend themselves to follow his precepts. They loved *earthly things*, and did not relish those of *heaven*.

Verse 32. *As a very lovely song*] They admired the *fine voice* and *correct delivery* of the prophet; this was *their religion*, and this is the *whole* of the religion of thousands to the present day; for never were *itching ears* so multiplied as now.

Verse 33. *When this cometh to pass—then shall they know that a prophet hath been among them.*] What I have predicted, (and it is even now at the doors,) then they will be convinced that there was a prophet among them, by whose ministry they did not profit as they ought.

CHAPTER XXXIV

The prophet is commanded to declare the dreadful judgments of God against the covetous shepherds of Israel, who feed themselves, and not their flocks; by which emblem the priests and Levites are intended, who in Ezekiel's time were very corrupt, and the chief cause of Israel's apostasy and ruin, 1–10. *From this gloomy subject the prophet passes to the blessedness of the true Israel of God under the reign of* DAVID, *the Great Shepherd of the sheep, our Lord Jesus Christ being named after this prince by a figure exceedingly frequent in the sacred oracles, of putting the type for the antitype,* 11–31.

A. M. cir. 3417
B. C. cir. 587
Ol. XLVIII. 2
Tarquinii Prisci,
R. Roman.,
cir. annum 30

AND the word of the LORD
came unto me, saying,

2 Son of man, prophesy
against the [a]shepherds of Isra-
el, prophesy, and say unto them, Thus saith
the Lord GOD unto the shepherds, [b]Wo *be* to
the shepherds of Israel that do
feed themselves! should not
the shepherds feed the flocks?

3 [c]Ye eat the fat, and ye
clothe you with the wool, [d]ye kill them that
are fed: *but* ye feed not the flock.

[a]Chap. xxxiii. 24——[b]Jer. xxiii. 1; Zech. xi. 17——[c]Isa. lvi. 11; Zech. xi. 16
[d]Chapter xxxiii. 25, 26; Micah iii. 1, 2, 3; Zechariah xi. 5

NOTES ON CHAP. XXXIV

Verse 2. *Prophesy against the shepherds of Israel*] The *shepherds* include, first, the *priests* and *Levites;* secondly, the *kings*, *princes*, and *magistrates*. The *flock* means the whole of the *people*. The *fat* and the *wool*, the *tithes* and *offerings*, the *taxes* and *imposts*. The reprehensible *feeding* and *clothing* with these, as to the priests and Levites, the using these *tithes* and *offerings*, not to enable them the better to fulfil the work of the *ministry*, but to pamper their own bodies, and support them in an idle voluptuous life; and in reference to the *state*, the employing the *taxes* and *imposts*, not for the support and administration of *justice* and good *government*, but to subsidize heathen powers, and maintain their own luxury and idolatrous prodigality.

Verse 3. *Ye eat the fat*] I think החלב *hacheleb* should be translated *the milk;* and so most of the Versions understand it. Or they lived on the *fat sheep*, and took the *wool* of all.

"The *priests*," says *Calmet*, "ate the tithes,

A. M. cir. 3417
B. C. cir. 587
Ol. XLVIII. 2
Tarquinii Prisci,
R. Roman.,
cir. annum 30

4 [e]The diseased have ye not
strengthened, neither have ye
healed that which was sick,
neither have ye bound up *that
which was* broken, neither have ye brought
again that which was driven away, neither
have ye [f]sought that which was lost; but with
[g]force and with cruelty have ye ruled them.

5 [h]And they were [i]scattered,
[k]because *there is* no shepherd:
[l]and they became meat to all
the beasts of the field, when
they were scattered.

6 My sheep wandered through all the mountains, and upon every high hill: yea, my flock
was scattered upon all the face of the earth,

[e]Ver. 16; Zech. xi. 16——[f]Luke xv. 4——[g]1 Pet. v. 3
[h]Chap. xxxiii. 21, 28

[i]1 Kings xxii. 17; Matt. ix. 36——[k]Or, *without a shepherd;* and so ver. 8——[l]Isa. lvi. 9; Jer. xii. 9; ver. 8

the first-fruits, and the offerings of the people; the *princes* received the tributes and imposts; and instead of instructing and protecting them, the latter took away their *lives* by the cruelties they practised against them: the former destroyed their *souls* by the poison of their doctrine, and by their bad example. The *fat sheep* point out the *rich*, to whom these pastors often disguised the truth, by a cruel condescension and complaisance."

Verse 4. *The diseased have ye not strengthened*] No person is fit for the office of a shepherd, who does not *well understand* the *diseases* to which sheep are incident, and the *mode of cure.* And is any man fit for the *pastoral office*, or to be a shepherd of souls, who is not well acquainted with the *disease of sin* in all its *varieties*, and the *remedy* for this disease, and the proper mode of administering it, in those various cases? He who does not know Jesus Christ as his *own Saviour*, never can recommend him to others. He who is not saved, will not save.

Neither have ye healed that which was sick] The prophet first speaks of the *general disease;* next, of the different kinds of spiritual infirmity.

Neither have ye bound up that which was *broken*] If a sheep have broken a leg, a proper shepherd knows how to *set the bones*, and splint and bind it till the bones knit and become strong. And the *skilful* spiritual pastor knows, if one of the flock be overtaken in a fault, how to restore such. Those *sudden falls*, where there was not a strong propensity to sin, are, to the soul, as a *broken bone* to the body.

Neither have ye brought again] A proper shepherd *loves* his sheep: he feels *interested* for their welfare; he acquaints himself with them all, so that he knows and can distinguish each. He knows also their *number*, and frequently counts to see that none is missing; if one be *lost* or *strayed*, he goes immediately and *seeks* it; and as he is constantly on the *watch*, it cannot have strayed *far* before he is apprised of its absence from the flock; and the *less* it has strayed, the *sooner* it is found and brought back to the fold.

The shepherds of Israel knew nothing about their flock; they might have been *diseased, infirm, bruised, maimed,* their *limbs broken, strayed,* and *lost;* for they *watched not* over them. When they got *fat sheep* and *wool* for their *table* and their *clothing*, they regarded nothing else; as they considered the flock *given them* for their *own use*, and scarcely ever supposed that they were to give any thing in return for the milk and the wool.

But with force and with cruelty] *Exacting tithes* and dues by the strong arm of the law, with the most *ungodly feeling;* and with a *cruelty* of *disposition* that proved it was the *fat* and the *wool* they sought, and not the safety or comfort of the flock.

Verse 5. *And they were scattered*] There was no discipline kept up; and the flock, the Church, became disorganized, and separated from each other, both in affection and fellowship. And the consequence was, the grievous wolves, false and worldly interested teachers, seized on and made a prey of them. Of the *communion of saints* such shepherds know nothing, farther than that it makes a part of the common *creed.*

Verse 6. *My sheep wandered through all the mountains*] They all became idolaters, and lost the knowledge of the true God. And could it be otherwise while they had such pastors?

"Himself a wanderer from the narrow way;
His silly sheep, no wonder that they stray!"

Reader, if thou be a *minister*, a *preacher*, or a person in *holy orders*, or *pretended holy orders*, or art one *pretending to holy orders*, look at the qualifications of a good shepherd as laid down by the prophet.

1. He professes to be a *shepherd*, and to be *qualified* for the office.

2. In consequence he *undertakes the care of a flock.* This supposes that he believes the great Bishop of souls has *called him* to the pastoral office; and that office implies that he is to give all diligence to *save the souls of them that hear him.*

HIS QUALIFICATIONS

1. He is *skilful;* he knows the *disease of sin* and its consequences; for the Eternal Spirit, by whom he is called, has convinced him of sin, of righteousness, and of judgment.

2. He knows well the *great remedy* for this disease, the passion and sacrificial death of the Lord Jesus Christ.

3. He is skilful, and knows *how to apply* this remedy.

4. The flock over which he watches is, in its *individuals*, either,—1. *Healthy* and *sound.* 2. Or, in a *state* of *convalescence,* returning to health. 3. Or, still under the *whole power* of the *general disease.* 4. Or, some are *dying* in a state of *spiritual weakness.* 5. Or, some are *fallen into sin*, and sorely bruised and broken in their souls by that fall. 6. Or, some have been *driven away* by some sore *temptation* or *cruel usage.* 7. Or, some have *wandered* from the flock, are got into strange pastures, and are perverted by erroneous doctrines. Or, 8. Some

A. M. cir. 3417
B. C. cir. 587
Ol. XLVIII. 2
Tarquinii Prisci,
R. Roman.,
cir. annum 30

and none did search or seek
after them.
7 Therefore, ye shepherds,
hear the word of the LORD;
8 *As* I live, saith the Lord GOD, surely because my flock became a prey, and my flock
[m]became meat to every beast of the field, because *there was* no shepherd, neither did my
shepherds search for my flock, [n]but the shepherds fed themselves, and fed not my flock;
9 Therefore, O ye shepherds, hear the word
of the LORD;
10 Thus saith the Lord GOD; Behold, I *am*
against the shepherds; and [o]I will require
my flock at their hand, and cause them to
cease from feeding the flock; neither shall
the shepherds [p]feed themselves any more:
for I will deliver my flock from their mouth,
that they may not be meat for them.
11 For thus saith the Lord GOD; Behold,
I, *even* I, will both search my
sheep, and seek them out.
12 [q]As a shepherd seeketh
out his flock in the day that
he is among his sheep *that are* scattered; so
will I seek out my sheep, and will deliver
them out of all places where they have been
scattered in [r]the cloudy and dark day.
13 And [s]I will bring them out from the
people, and gather them from the countries,
and will bring them to their own land, and
feed them upon the mountains of Israel by
the rivers, and in all the inhabited places of
the country.
14 [t]I will feed them in a good pasture, and
upon the high mountains of Israel shall their
fold be: [u]there shall they lie in a good fold,
and *in* a fat pasture shall they feed upon the
mountains of Israel.
15 I will feed my flock, and I will cause

A. M. cir. 3417
B. C. cir. 587
Ol. XLVIII. 2
Tarquinii Prisci,
R. Roman.,
cir. annum 30

[m]Ver. 5, 6——[n]Ver. 2, 10——[o]Chap. iii. 18; Hebrews xiii. 17——[p]Ver. 2. 8——[q]Hebrew, *According to the seeking*——[r]Chap. xxx. 3; Joel ii. 2——[s]Isaiah lxv. 9, 10; Jeremiah xxiii. 3; chap. xxviii. 25; xxxvi. 24; xxxvii. 21, 22——[t]Psalm xxiii. 2——[u]Jeremiah xxxiii. 12

wolf has got among them, and scattered the whole flock. Now, the true shepherd, the pastor of God's choosing, knows—

1. How to keep the *healthy* in health; and cause them to grow in grace, and in the knowledge of Jesus Christ.
2. How to *nourish, feed,* and *care for* the *convalescent,* that they may be brought into a state of spiritual *soundness.*
3. How to *reprove,* instruct, and awaken those who are still under the *full power* of the *disease of sin.*
4. How to *find out* and *remove* the cause of all that *spiritual weakness* of which he sees some slowly *dying.*
5. How to deal with those who have *fallen into some scandalous sin,* and restore them from their *fall.*
6. How to *find out* and *turn aside* the *sore temptation* or *cruel usage* by which some have been *driven away.*
7. How to *seek* and *bring back* to the fold those who have *strayed* into strange pastures, and have had their souls perverted by *erroneous doctrines;* and knows also how, by a godly *discipline,* to preserve him in the flock, and keep the flock honourably together.
8. How to *oppose, confound,* and *expel* the *grievous wolf,* who has got among the flock, and is *scattering* them from each other, and from God. He knows how to *preach, explain,* and *defend* the truth. He is well acquainted with the *weapons* he is to use, and the *spirit* in which he is to employ them.

In a word, the true shepherd gives up his life *to* the sheep; spends and is spent for the glory of God; and gives up his life *for* the sheep, in defence of them, and in labouring for their welfare. And while he is thus employed, it is the duty of the flock to feed and clothe him; and see that neither he nor his family lack the *necessaries* and *conveniencies* of life. The *labourer* is worthy of his meat. He who does not *labour,* or, because of his *ignorance* of God and salvation, *cannot labour,* in the word and doctrine, deserves neither meat nor drink; and if he exact that by law, which he has not honestly earned by a proper discharge of the *pastoral function,* let him read this chapter, and learn from it what a fearful *account* he shall have to give to the chief Shepherd at the great day; and what a dreadful *punishment* shall be inflicted on him, when the blood of the souls lost through his neglect or inefficiency is visited upon him! See the notes on chap. iii. 17, &c.

Verse 7. *Therefore, ye shepherds,* (ye *bad* and *wicked shepherds,*) *hear the word of the Lord*] In the preceding character of the *good shepherd* the reader will find, by reversing the particulars, the character of a *bad shepherd;* and therefore I may be excused from entering into farther detail.

Verse 10. *I will—cause them to cease from feeding the flock*] God, in this country, *unpriested* a whole hierarchy who fed not the flock, but *ruled them with force and cruelty;* and he raised up a new set of shepherds better qualified, both by sound doctrine and learning, to feed the flock. Let these be faithful, lest God cause *them to cease,* and raise up other feeders.

Verse 12. *Cloudy and dark day.*] Times of general distress and persecution; in such times the shepherd should be especially watchful.

Verse 13. *I will—feed them upon the mountains*] When I bring back the people from their captivity, I will raise up to them a holy and diligent priesthood, who shall in all places give them sound instruction. But this, and some of the following promises, belong to the *Christian Church,* as we shall find below.

A. M. cir. 3417
B. C. cir. 587
Ol. XLVIII. 2
Tarquinii Prisci,
R. Roman.,
cir. annum 30

them to lie down, saith the
Lord God.
16 [v]I will seek that which
was lost, and bring again that
which was driven away, and will bind up *that*
which was broken, and will strengthen that
which was sick: but I will destroy [w]the fat and
the strong; I will feed them [x]with judgment.
17 And *as for* you, O my flock, thus saith
the Lord God: [y]Behold, I judge between
[z]cattle and cattle, between the rams and the
[a]he-goats.
18 *Seemeth it* a small thing unto you to
have eaten up the good pasture, but ye must
tread down with your feet the residue of
your pastures? and to have drunk of the deep
waters, but ye must foul the residue with
your feet?
19 And *as for* my flock, they eat that which
ye have trodden with your feet; and they
drink that which ye have
fouled with your feet.
20 Therefore thus saith the
Lord God unto them; [b]Be-
hold, I, even I, will judge between the fat
cattle and between the lean cattle.
21 Because ye have thrust with side and
with shoulder, and pushed all the diseased
with your horns, till ye have scattered them
abroad;
22 Therefore will I save my flock, and they
shall no more be a prey; and [c]I will judge
between cattle and cattle.
23 And I will set up one [d]Shepherd over
them, and he shall feed them, [e]*even* my servant David; he shall feed them, and he shall
be their Shepherd.
24 And [f]I the Lord will be their God, and
my Servant David [g]a Prince among them; I
the Lord have spoken *it*.

A. M. cir. 3417
B. C. cir. 587
Ol. XLVIII. 2
Tarquinii Prisci,
R. Roman.,
cir. annum 30

---

[v]See ver. 4; Isa. xl. 11; Mic. iv. 6; Matt. xviii. 11; Mark ii. 17; Luke v. 32——[w]Isa. x. 16; Amos iv. 1——[x]Jer. x. 24——[y]Chap. xx. 37, 38; ver. 20, 22; Zech. x. 3; Matt. xxv. 32, 33——[z]Heb. *small cattle of lambs and kids*——[a]Heb. *great he-goats*

[b]Ver. 17——[c]Ver. 17——[d]Isa. xl. 11; Jer. xxiii. 4, 5; John x. 11; Heb. xiii. 20; 1 Pet. ii. 25; v. 4——[e]Jer. xxx. 9; chap. xxxvii. 24, 25; Hos. iii. 5——[f]Ver. 30; Exod. xxix. 45; chap. xxxvii. 27——[g]Chap. xxxvii. 22; Luke i. 32, 33

Verse 16. *I will destroy the fat and the strong*] I will destroy those cruel and imperious shepherds who abuse their authority, and tyrannize over the flock.

Verse 17. *And* as for *you, O my flock*] After having spoken to the *shepherds*, he now addresses the *flock*.

I judge between cattle and cattle] Between *false* and *true* professors; between them that have only the *form* and them that have the *power* of godliness; between the *backslider in heart* and the *upright man*.

Verse 18. *Have eaten up the good pasture*] Arrogate to yourselves all the promises of God, and will hardly permit the simple believer to claim or possess any token of God's favour.

Ye must foul the residue with your feet?] Ye abuse God's mercies; you *consume much* upon yourselves, and ye *spoil more*, on which the *poor* would have been glad to *feed*. There are some who would rather give food to their *sporting dogs* than to the *poor* around them, who are ready to starve, and who would be glad of the crumbs that fall from the table of those *masters!*

Verse 20. *I will judge between the fat cattle and between the lean cattle.*] Between the *rich* and the *poor;* those who *fare sumptuously* every day and those who have not the *necessaries of life*.

Verse 23. *I will set up one Shepherd—my servant David*] David, king of Israel, had been dead upwards of *four hundred years;* and from that time till now there never was a ruler of any kind, either in the Jewish *Church* or *state*, of the name of *David*. This, then, must be some *typical person;* and from the texts marked in the margin we understand that *Jesus Christ* alone is meant, as both *Old* and *New* Testaments agree in this. And from this one *Shepherd* all Christian *ministers* must derive their authority to teach, and their grace to teach effectually.

By the kind providence of God it appears that he has not permitted any *apostolic succession* to be preserved, lest the members of his Church should seek that in an *uninterrupted succession* which must be found in the Head *alone*. The *papists* or *Roman Catholics*, who boast of an *uninterrupted succession*, which is a mere fable that never was and never can be proved, have raised up *another head*, the pope. And I appeal to themselves, in the fear of God, whether they do not in *heart* and in *speech* trace up all their *authority* to *him*, and only compliment Christ as having appointed *Peter* to be the first bishop of Rome, (which is an *utter falsity*, for he was never appointed to such an office there, nor ever held such an office in that city, nor, in their sense, *any where else;*) and they hold also that the popes of Rome are not so much *Peter's successors* as *God's vicars;* and thus both God and Peter are nearly *lost sight of* in their *papal enumerations*. With them the *authority of the Church* is all in all; the *authority of Christ* is seldom mentioned.

Verse 24. *I the Lord will be their God, and my Servant David a Prince*] Here we find God and his Christ are *all in all* in his Church, and Jesus is still Prince *among them;* and to him the *call* and *qualifications* of all genuine pastors belong, and *from* him they must be derived. And he has blotted out what is called *uninterrupted succession*, that every Christian minister may seek and receive credentials from himself. Here is the grand reason why the *uninterrupted succession cannot be made out*. And here is the proof also that the Church that *pretends to*

A. M. cir. 3417
B. C. cir. 587
Ol. XLVIII. 2
Tarquinii Prisci,
R. Roman.,
cir. annum 30

25 And [h]I will make with them a covenant of peace, and [i]will cause the evil beasts to cease out of the land: and they [k]shall dwell safely in the wilderness, and sleep in the woods.

26 And I will make them and the places round about [l]my hill [m]a blessing: and I will [n]cause the shower to come down in his season; there shall be [o]showers of blessing.

27 And [p]the tree of the field shall yield her fruit, and the earth shall yield her increase, and they shall be safe in their land, and shall know that I *am* the LORD, when I have [q]broken the bands of their yoke, and delivered them out of the hand of those that [r]served themselves of them.

28 And they shall no more [s]be a prey to the heathen, neither shall the beast of the land devour them; but [t]they shall dwell safely, and none shall make *them* afraid.

A. M. cir. 3417
B. C. cir. 587
Ol. XLVIII. 2
Tarquinii Prisci,
R. Roman.,
cir. annum 30

29 And I will raise up for them a [u]plant [v]of renown, and they shall be no more [w]consumed with hunger in the land, [x]neither bear the shame of the heathen any more.

30 Thus shall they know that [y]I the LORD their God *am* with them, and *that* they, *even* the house of Israel, *are* my people, saith the Lord GOD.

31 And ye my [z]flock, the flock of my pasture, *are* men, *and* I *am* your God, saith the Lord GOD.

[h]Ch. xxxvii. 26——[i]Lev. xxvi. 6; Isa. xi. 6–9; xxxv. 9; Hos. ii. 18——[k]Ver. 28; Jer. xxiii. 6——[l]Isa. lvi. 7; chap. xx. 40——[m]Gen. xii. 2; Isa. xix. 24; Zech. viii. 13——[n]Lev. xxvi. 4——[o]Psa. lxviii. 9; Mal. iii. 10——[p]Lev. xxvi. 4; Psa. lxxxv. 12; Isa. iv. 2

[q]Lev. xxvi. 13; Jer. ii. 20——[r]Jer. xxv. 14——[s]See ver. 8——chap. xxxvi. 4——[t]Ver. 25; Jer. xxx. 10; xlvi. 27——[u]Isa. xi. 1; Jer. xxiii. 5——[v]Or, *for renown;*——[w]Heb. *taken away*——[x]Ch. xxxvi. 3, 6, 15——[y]Ver. 24; chap. xxxvii. 27——[z]Psa. c. 3; John x. 11

it, and builds upon it, must be a *false Church;* for it is founded on a falsity; an *uninterrupted succession* which does not exist either in *history* or in *fact*.

Verse 25. *I will make with them a covenant of peace*] The original is emphatic: וכרתי להם ברית שלום *vecharatti lahem berith shalom*, "And I will cut with them the peace covenant;" that is, a *covenant sacrifice*, procuring and establishing peace between God and man, and between man and his fellows. I need not tell the reader that the *cutting* refers to the ancient mode of *making covenants*. The blood was poured out; the animal was divided from mouth to tail, exactly in *two;* the divisions placed *opposite to each other;* the contracting parties entered into the space, going in at each end, and met in the *middle*, and *there* took the *covenant oath*. He is the *Prince of peace*, and through him come glory to God in the highest, and *peace* and good will to men upon earth.

And will cause the evil beasts to cease] These *false* and *ravenous pastors*. Christ purges them out of his Church, and destroys that *power* by which they lorded it over God's heritage.

Verse 26. *The shower to come down*] The Holy Spirit's influence.

There shall be showers of blessing.] Light, life, joy, peace, and power shall be manifest in all the *assemblies of Christ's people*.

Verse 29. *I will raise up—a plant of renown*] מטע לשם *matta leshem*, "a plantation to the name;" to the name of CHRIST. A *Christian Church* composed of men who are *Christians*, who have the spirit of *Christ* in them, and do not bear his *name* in vain. I believe the words might be applied to the *Christian Church;* but that Christ may be called a *plant* or *plantation* here,—as he is elsewhere called a *branch* and a *rod*, Isa. iv. 2; xi. 1; so Jer. xxiii. 5; xxxv. 15,—is most probable. He is the Person of *name*, לשם *leshem*, JESUS; the *Saviour*, CHRIST; the *Anointer*, long *spoken* of before he was manifested in the flesh, and since the *daily theme* in the Church militant. It is he who hath loved us, and washed us from our sins in his own blood, no other *name* being given under heaven among men by which we can be saved; he who has a *name* above every *name*, and at whose *name* every knee shall bow; through whose *name*, by faith in his *name*, the diseased are healed; and in whose *name* all our prayers and supplications must be presented to God to make them acceptable. This is the Person of NAME!

They shall be no more consumed with hunger] For this glorious *plant of name* is the *Bread of life;* and this is broken in all the assemblies of his people where his *name* is properly proclaimed.

Verse 31. *And ye my flock*] That is, under the allegory of a *flock* of *sheep*, I point out *men;* under that of a *pasture*, my *Church;* and under that of a *shepherd*, the *Messiah*, through whom I am become *your God*. And he who is your God is אדני יהוה *Adonai Yehovah*, the self-existent Being; the *Governor* and *Director*, as well as the *Saviour* and *Judge* of men.

CHAPTER XXXV

The prophet having formerly predicted the ruin of Edom, the same with Seir, (chap. xxv. 12,) *now resumes and pursues the subject at greater length, intimating, as did also Isaiah,* (chap. xxi. 11, 12,) *that though other nations should recover their liberty after the fall of the Babylonian monarchy, the Edomites should continue in bondage for their very despiteful behaviour towards the children of Israel in the day of their calamity,* 1–15.

A. M. cir. 3417
B. C. cir. 587
Ol. XLVIII. 2
Tarquinii Prisci,
R. Roman.,
cir. annum 30

MOREOVER the word of
the LORD came unto me,
saying,
2 Son of man, [a]set thy face
against [b]Mount Seir, and [c]prophesy against it.
3 And say unto it, Thus saith the Lord
GOD; Behold, O Mount Seir, I *am* against
thee, and [d]I will stretch out mine hand against
thee, and I will make thee [e]most desolate.
4 [f]I will lay thy cities waste, and thou shalt
be desolate, and thou shalt know that I *am*
the LORD.
5 [g]Because thou hast had a [h]perpetual
hatred, and hast [i]shed *the blood of* the children of Israel, by the [k]force of the sword in
the time of their calamity, [l]in the time *that*
their iniquity *had* an end:
6 Therefore, *as* I live, saith the Lord GOD,
I will prepare thee unto blood, and blood
shall pursue thee: [m]sith thou hast not hated
blood, even blood shall pursue thee.
7 Thus will I make Mount Seir [n]most desolate, and cut off from it [o]him that passeth
out and him that returneth.
8 [p]And I will fill his mountains with his slain *men:* in
thy hills, and in thy valleys,
and in all thy rivers, shall
they fall that are slain with the sword.
9 [q]I will make thee perpetual desolations,
and thy cities shall not return: [r]and ye shall
know that I *am* the LORD.
10 Because thou hast said, These two nations and these two countries shall be mine,
and we will [s]possess it; [t]whereas [u]the LORD
was there:
11 Therefore, *as* I live, saith the Lord GOD,
I will even do, [v]according to thine anger, and
according to thine envy which thou hast used
out of thy hatred against them; and I will
make myself known among them, when I
have judged thee.
12 [w]And thou shalt know that I *am* the
LORD, *and that* I have heard all thy blasphemies which thou hast spoken against
the mountains of Israel, saying, They are
laid desolate, they are given us [x]to consume.

A. M. cir. 3417
B. C. cir. 587
Ol. XLVIII. 2
Tarquinii Prisci,
R. Roman.,
cir. annum 30

[a]Chap. vi. 2——[b]Deut. ii. 5——[c]Jer. xlix. 7, 8; chap. xxv. 12; Amos i. 11; Obad. 10, &c.——[d]Chap. vi. 14 [e]Heb. *desolation and desolation;* so ver. 7——[f]Ver. 9 [g]Chap. xxv. 12; Obad. 10——[h]Or, *hatred of old;* chap. xxv. 15——[i]Heb. *poured out the children*——[k]Heb. *hands*——[l]Psa. cxxxvii. 7; chap. xxi. 25, 29; Dan. ix. 24; Obad. 11——[m]Psa. cix. 17——[n]Heb. *desolation and desolation;* ver. 3

[o]Judg. v. 6; chap. xxix. 11——[p]Chap. xxxi. 12; xxxii. 5——[q]Jer. xlix. 17, 18; ver. 4; chap. xxv. 13; Mal. i. 3, 4——[r]Chap. vi. 7; vii. 4, 9; xxxvi. 11——[s]Psa. lxxxiii. 4, 12; chap. xxxvi. 5; Obad. 13——[t]Or, *though the LORD was there*——[u]Psa. xlviii. 1, 3; cxxxii. 13, 14; chap. xlviii. 35——[v]Matt. vii. 2; James ii. 13 [w]Chap. vi. 7; Psa. ix. 16——[x]Heb. *to devour*——[y]1 Sam. ii. 3; Rev. xiii. 6——[z]Heb. *magnified*

NOTES ON CHAP. XXXV

Verse 2. *Set thy face against Mount Seir*] That is, against the *Edomites.* This prophecy was probably delivered about the time of the preceding, and before the destruction of Idumea by Nebuchadnezzar, which took place about *five years after.*

Calmet supposes that *two destructions of Idumea* are here foretold; one by Nebuchadnezzar, and the other by the *Jews* after their return from their captivity.

Verse 3. *Most desolate.*] Literally, "A desolation and a wilderness."

Verse 5. *A perpetual hatred*] The Edomites were the descendants of *Esau;* the Israelites, the descendants of *Jacob.* Both these were brothers; and between them there was contention even in the womb, and they lived generally in a state of enmity. Their descendants kept up the ancient feud: but the Edomites were implacable; they had not only a *rooted* but *perpetual enmity* to the Israelites, harassing and distressing them by all possible means; and they seized the opportunity, when the Israelites were most harassed by other enemies, to make inroads upon them, and cut them off wherever they found them.

To afflict the afflicted is cruel. This is scarcely of man, bad as he is. He must be possessed by the *malignant spirit* of the *devil,* when he wounds the wounded, insults over the miseries of the afflicted, and seeks opportunities to add affliction to those who are already under the rod of God.

Verse 6. *Blood shall pursue thee*] Thou lovest blood, and thou shalt have blood. It is said that Cyrus and *two hundred thousand* men were slain in an ambush by Thomyris, queen of the Scythians, and that she cut off his head, and threw it into a vessel filled with blood, with this severe sarcasm:—

Satia te sanguine quem sitisti, Cyre.
"O Cyrus, now satisfy thyself with blood."

Hence, the *figure:*—

"*Sarcasmus,* with this biting taunt doth kill:
Cyrus, thy thirst was blood, now drink thy fill."

Verse 9. *Perpetual desolations*] Thou shalt have perpetual desolation for thy perpetual hatred.

Verse 10. *These two nations*] Israel and Judah. The Idumeans thought of conquering and possessing both; and they would have succeeded, but only *the Lord was there;* and this spoiled their projects, and blasted their hopes.

Verse 12. *They are laid desolate, they are given us to consume.*] They exulted in seeing Judea overrun; and they rejoiced in the prospect of completing the ruin, when the Chaldeans had withdrawn from the land.

Verse 13. *Thus with your mouth ye have*

A. M. cir. 3417
B. C. cir. 587
Ol. XLVIII. 2
Tarquinii Prisci,
R. Roman.,
cir. annum 30

13 Thus [y]with your mouth ye
have [z]boasted against me, and
have multiplied your words
against me: I have heard *them.*
14 Thus saith the Lord GOD; [a]When the
whole earth rejoiceth, I will make thee
desolate.

15 [b]As thou didst rejoice at
the inheritance of the house
of Israel, because it was desolate, so will I do unto thee:
[c]thou shalt be desolate, O Mount Seir, and
all Idumea, *even* all of it: and they shall
know that I *am* the LORD.

A. M. cir. 3417
B. C. cir. 587
Ol. XLVIII. 2
Tarquinii Prisci,
R. Roman.,
cir annum 30

---

[a]Isa. lxv. 13, 14

[b]Obad. xii. 15——[c]Ver. 3, 4

---

boasted against me] Ye have said you would enter into those lands, and take them for your inheritance; though ye knew that God had promised them to the Israelites, and that you should never have them for your portion.

Verse 14. *When the whole earth rejoiceth*] When the whole *land* shall rejoice in the restoration of the Jews, I will make thee desolate. Probably this refers to the time of the *Maccabees.*

Verse 15. *So will I do unto thee*] Others shall rejoice in thy downfall as thou hast rejoiced at their downfall.

This whole chapter strongly inculcates this maxim: Do as thou wouldst be done by; and what thou wouldst not have done to thee, do not to others. And from it we learn that every man may, in some sort, be said to make his own temporal good or evil; for as he does to others, God will take care to do to him, whether it be evil or good, weal or wo. Would you not be slandered or backbitten? Then do not slander nor backbite. Wouldst thou wish to live in peace? Then do not disturb the peace of others. Be merciful, and thou shalt obtain mercy.

CHAPTER XXXVI

The Edomites or Idumeans, during the Babylonish captivity, took possession of the mountainous parts of Judea, and the fortresses which commanded the country, intending to exclude the Jews if ever they should return from their captivity. The prophet therefore, by a beautiful personification, addresses the mountains of Israel; and, ascribing to them passions and emotions similar to those of his own breast, consoles them with the prospect of being soon rid of those usurping foes; of being freed from the dishonour of idols under which they groaned; and of flourishing again in their ancient glory under their rightful owners, 1–15. *The idolatry and other sins of the Jews are then declared to be the cause of their captivity and dispersion,* 16–20; *from which however they are promised a deliverance in terms of great force and beauty,* 21–38. *This chapter contains also, under the type of the happy condition of the Israelites after their restoration from the Babylonish captivity, a glorious prophecy of the rich blessings of the Gospel dispensation.*

A. M. cir. 3417
B. C. cir. 587
Ol. XLVIII. 2
Tarquinii Prisci,
R. Roman.,
cir. annum 30

ALSO, thou son of man,
prophesy unto the [a]moun-
tains of Israel, and say, Ye
mountains of Israel, hear the
word of the LORD:
2 Thus saith the Lord GOD; Because [b]the
enemy hath said against you, Aha, [c]even the
ancient high places [d]are ours in possession:
3 Therefore prophesy and say, Thus saith
the Lord GOD; [e]Because they have made *you*
desolate, and swallowed you up on every side,
that ye might be a possession unto the residue
of the heathen, [f]and [g]ye are taken up in the lips of talkers, and
are an infamy of the people:
4 Therefore, ye mountains of
Israel, hear the word of the Lord GOD; Thus
saith the Lord GOD to the mountains, and to
the hills, to the [h]rivers, and to the valleys, to the
desolate wastes, and to the cities that are forsaken, which [i]became a prey and [k]derision to the
residue of the heathen that *are* round about;
5 Therefore thus saith the Lord GOD;
[l]Surely in the fire of my jealousy have I

A. M. cir. 3417
B. C. cir. 587
Ol. XLVIII. 2
Tarquinii Prisci,
R. Roman.,
cir. annum 30

---

[a]Ch. vi. 2, 3——[b]Ch. xxv. 3; xxvi. 2——[c]Deut. xxxii. 13——[d]Ch. xxxv. 10——[e]Heb. *Because for because* ——[f]Deut. xxviii. 37; 1 Kings ix. 7; Lam. ii. 15; Dan. ix. 16

[g]Or, *ye are made to come upon the lip of the tongue* ——[h]Or, *bottoms,* or *dales*——[i]Ch. xxxiv. 28——[k]Psa. lxxix. 4——[l]Deut. iv. 24; chap. xxxviii. 19

NOTES ON CHAP. XXXVI

Verse 1. *Prophesy unto the mountains of Israel*] This is a part of the preceding prophecy, though it chiefly concerns the Jews. In it they are encouraged to expect a glorious restoration; and that none of the evil wishes of their adversaries should take place against them.

Verse 2. *Because the enemy hath said*] The Idumeans thought they would shortly be put in possession of all the strong places of Israel; *the ancient high places shall be ours.*

Verse 4. *Therefore—thus saith the Lord God to the mountains, &c.*] They shall neither possess *mountain* nor *valley, hill* nor *dale, fountain* nor *river;* for though in my justice I made you desolate, yet they shall not profit by your disasters. See ver. 5, 6, and 7.

A. M. cir. 3417
B. C. cir. 587
Ol. XLVIII. 2
Tarquinii Prisci,
R. Roman.,
cir. annum 30

spoken against the residue of the heathen, and against all Idumea, [m]which have appointed my land into their possession with the joy of all *their* heart, with despiteful minds, to cast it out for a prey.

6 Prophesy therefore concerning the land of Israel, and say unto the mountains, and to the hills, to the rivers, and to the valleys, Thus saith the Lord GOD; Behold, I have spoken in my jealousy and in my fury, because ye have [n]borne the shame of the heathen:

7 Therefore thus saith the Lord GOD; I have [o]lifted up mine hand, Surely the heathen that *are* about you, they shall bear their shame.

8 But ye, O mountains of Israel, ye shall shoot forth your branches, and yield your fruit to my people of Israel; for they are at hand to come.

9 For, behold, I *am* for you, and I will turn unto you, and ye shall be tilled and sown:

10 And I will multiply men upon you, all the house of Israel, *even* all of it: and the cities shall be inhabited, and [p]the wastes shall be builded:

11 And [q]I will multiply upon you man and beast: and they shall increase and bring fruit: and I will settle you after your old estates, and will do better *unto you* than at your beginnings: [r]and ye shall know that I *am* the LORD.

12 Yea, I will cause men to walk upon you, *even* my people Israel; [s]and they shall possess thee, and thou shalt be their inheritance, and thou shalt no more henceforth [t]bereave them *of men*.

13 Thus saith the Lord GOD; Because they say unto you, [u]Thou *land* devourest up men, and hast bereaved thy nations;

A. M. cir. 3417
B. C. cir. 587
Ol. XLVIII. 2
Tarquinii Prisci,
R. Roman.,
cir. annum 30

14 Therefore thou shalt devour men no more, neither [v]bereave thy nations any more, saith the Lord GOD.

15 [w]Neither will I cause *men* to hear in thee the shame of the heathen any more, neither shalt thou bear the reproach of the people any more, neither shalt thou cause thy nations to fall any more, saith the Lord GOD.

16 Moreover the word of the LORD came unto me, saying,

17 Son of man, when the house of Israel dwelt in their own land, [x]they defiled it by their own way and by their doings: their way was before me as [y]the uncleanness of a removed woman.

18 Wherefore I poured my fury upon them [z]for the blood that they had shed upon the land, and for their idols *wherewith* they had polluted it:

19 And I [a]scattered them among the heathen and they were dispersed through the countries: [b]according to their way and according to their doings I judged them.

20 And when they entered unto the heathen, whither they went, they [c]profaned my holy name, when they said to them, These *are* the people of the LORD, and are gone forth out of his land.

21 But I had pity [d]for mine holy name, which the house of Israel had profaned among the heathen, whither they went.

22 Therefore say unto the house of Israel,

[m]Chap. xxxv. 10, 12——[n]Psa. cxxiii. 3, 4; chap. xxxiv. 29; ver. 15——[o]Ch. xx. 5——[p]Ver. 33; Isa. lviii. 12; lxi. 4; Amos ix 14——[q]Jer. xxxi. 27; xxxiii. 12 [r]Chap. xxxv. 9; xxxvii. 6, 13——[s]Obad. 17, &c.——[t]See Jer. xv. 7

[u]Num. xiii. 32——[v]Or, *cause to fall*——[w]Chap. xxxiv. 29——[x]Lev. xviii. 25, 27, 28; Jer. ii. 7——[y]Lev. xv. 19, &c.——[z]Chap. xvi. 36, 38; xxiii. 37——[a]Chap. xxii. 15——[b]Chap. vii. 3; xviii. 30; xxxix. 24——[c]Isa. lii. 5; Rom. ii. 24——[d]Chap. xx. 9, 14

Verse 8. *For they are at hand to come.*] The restoration of the Jews is so absolutely determined that you may rest assured it will take place; and be as confident relative to it, as if you saw the different families entering into the Israelitish borders. It was near at hand in God's determination, though there were about *fifty-eight* of the *seventy* years unelapsed.

Verse 9. *Ye shall be tilled and sown*] The land shall be *cultivated* as it formerly was, when *best peopled* and at *peace*.

Verse 11. *I will multiply upon you man and beast*] The *agriculturalist* and the *beast of burden*.

And will do better unto you *than at your beginnings*] I agree with *Calmet*, that it would be difficult to show the literal fulfilment of this prophecy from the days of Zerubbabel to the birth of Christ. The colouring is too high for that period; and the whole falls in better with Gospel than with Jewish times.

Verse 17. *When the house of Israel dwelt in their own land*] Had they continued faithful to me, they had never been removed from it: but they polluted it with their crimes; and I abhorred the land on that account, and gave both them and it up to the destroyers.

Verse 20. *And when they entered unto the heathen*] So bad were they, and so deeply fallen, that they *profaned the Lord's name among the heathen;* and, on their account, the true God was blasphemed. *These*, say they, *are the people*

A. M. cir. 3417
B. C. cir. 587
Ol. XLVIII. 2
Tarquinii Prisci,
R. Roman.,
cir. annum 30

Thus saith the Lord GOD; I do
not *this* for your sakes, O
house of Israel, [e]but for mine
holy name's sake, which ye
have profaned among the heathen, whither ye
went.
23 And I will sanctify my great name,
which was profaned among the heathen,
which ye have profaned in the midst of
them; and the heathen shall know that I *am*
the LORD, saith the Lord GOD, when I shall
be [f]sanctified in you before [g]their eyes.
24 For [h]I will take you from among the
heathen, and gather you out of all countries,
and will bring you into your
own land.
25 [i]Then will I sprinkle clean
water upon you, and ye shall
be clean: [k]from all your filthiness, and from
all your idols, will I cleanse you.
26 A [l]new heart also will I give you, and
a new spirit will I put within you: and I will
take away the stony heart out of your flesh:
and I will give you a heart of flesh.
27 And I will put my [m]Spirit within
you, and cause you to walk in my statutes,
and ye shall keep my judgments, and do
them.

[e]Psa. cvi. 8——[f]Chap. xx. 41; xxviii. 22——[g]Or, *your*——[h]Chap. xxxiv. 13; xxxvii. 21

[i]Isa. lii. 15; Heb. x. 22——[k]Jer. xxxiii. 8——[l]Jer. xxxii. 39; chap. xi. 19——[m]Chap. xi. 19; xxxvii. 14

of Jehovah! O what an abominable people are these! and what a being must that God be who can have and own such for his people!

Verse 23. *I will sanctify my great name*] By changing your hearts and your conduct, I shall show my hatred to vice, and my love to holiness: but it is not *for your sakes*, but for *my holy name's sake*, that I shall do you good in your latter days.

Verse 24. *I will take you from among the heathen*] This does not relate to the restoration from Babylon merely. The Jews are at this day scattered in all *Heathen, Mohammedan*, and *Christian countries*. From these they are to be gathered, and brought to repossess their own land.

Verse 25. *Then*—at the time of this great restoration—*will I sprinkle clean water upon you*—the *truly cleansing water;* the influences of the HOLY SPIRIT typified by *water*, whose property it is to *cleanse, whiten, purify, refresh*, render *healthy* and *fruitful*.

From all your filthiness] From every sort of external and internal abomination and pollution.

And from all your idols] False gods, false worship, false opinions, and false hopes.

Will I cleanse you.] Entirely separate you.

Verse 26. *A new heart also will I give you*] I will change the whole of your infected nature; and give you new appetites, new passions; or, at least, the old ones *purified* and *refined*. The *heart* is generally understood to mean all the *affections* and *passions*.

And a new spirit will I put within you] I will renew your *minds*, also *enlighten* your *understanding, correct* your *judgment*, and *refine* your *will;* so that you shall have a *new spirit* to actuate your new *heart*.

I will take away the stony heart] That heart that is *hard, impenetrable*, and *cold;* the affections and passions that are unyielding, frozen to good, unaffected by heavenly things; that are slow to credit the words of God. I will entirely remove this heart: it is the opposite to that which I have promised you; and you cannot have the *new heart* and the *old heart* at the same time.

And I will give you a heart of flesh.] One that can *feel*, and that can *enjoy;* that can feel *love to God* and to *all men*, and be a proper habitation for the living God.

Verse 27. *And I will put my Spirit within you*] To keep the *heart of flesh alive*, the *feeling heart* still *sensible*, the *loving heart* still *happy*. I will *put my Spirit*, the *great principle* of light, life, and love, within you, to actuate the *new spirit*, and to influence the *new affections* and *passions;* that the *animal* spirit may not become *brutish*, that the *mental* powers become not *foolish*. I will put my Spirit within you, so that as the *new spirit* may influence the *new heart*, so will MY SPIRIT influence YOUR *new spirit*, that each may have a proper *mover;* and then all will be pure, regular, and harmonious, when *passion* is influenced by *reason*, and *reason* by the *Holy Ghost*.

And the *cause* shall be evidenced by the *effects;* for I will *cause you to walk in my statutes*—not only to *believe* and *reverence* my appointments relative to what I command you to *perform;* but ye shall *walk in them*, your *conduct* shall be regulated by them. "And ye shall keep my judgments;" whatsoever I enjoin you to avoid. And ye shall *do them*—ye shall not only *avoid* every appearance of *evil*, but keep all my ordinances and commandments unblamably.

Here is the salvation that God promises to give to restored Israel; and here is the salvation that is the birthright of every *Christian believer: the complete destruction of all sin in the soul, and the complete renewal of the heart;* no *sin* having any place *within*, and no *unrighteousness* having any place *without*.

"But where are they that are thus saved?" *Ans.* Wherever *true Christians* are to be found. "But I know many *true Christians* that have not this salvation, but daily mourn over their evil hearts?" *Ans.* They may be *sincere*, but they are not *true Christians;* i. e., such as are saved from their sins; the true Christians are those who are *filled* with the *nature* and *Spirit of Christ*. But I will ask a question in my turn: "Do those you mention think it a *virtue* to be always *mourning* over their *impurities?*" Most certainly. Then it is a pity they were not *better instructed*. It is right they should *mourn* while they feel an *impure heart;* but why do they not apply to that *blood which cleanses from all unrighteousness*, and to that *Spirit* which *cleanses the very thoughts of the heart by his inspiration?* Many employ that time in *brooding* and

A. M. cir. 3417
B. C. cir. 587
Ol. XLVIII. 2
Tarquinii Prisci,
R. Roman.,
cir. annum 30

28 [n]And ye shall dwell in
the land that I gave to your
fathers; [o]and ye shall be my
people, and I will be your God.
29 I will also [p]save you from all your uncleannesses: and [q]I will call for the corn, and
will increase it, and [r]lay no famine upon you.
30 [s]And I will multiply the fruit of the
tree, and the increase of the field, that ye
shall receive no more reproach of famine
among the heathen.
31 Then [t]shall ye remember your own evil
ways, and your doings that *were* not good,
and [u]shall loathe yourselves in your own sight
for your iniquities and for your abominations.
32 [v]Not for your sakes do I *this,* saith the
Lord GOD, be it known unto you: be ashamed
and confounded for your own ways, O house
of Israel.
33 Thus saith the Lord GOD; In the day
that I shall have cleansed you from all your
iniquities I will also cause *you* to dwell in
the cities, [w]and the wastes
shall be builded.
34 And the desolate land
shall be tilled, whereas it lay
desolate in the sight of all that passed by.
35 And they shall say, This land that was
desolate is become like the garden of [x]Eden;
and the waste and desolate and ruined cities
are become fenced, *and* are inhabited.
36 Then the heathen that are left round
about you shall know that I the LORD build
the ruined *places, and* plant that that was
desolate: [y]I the LORD have spoken *it,* and I
will do *it.*
37 Thus saith the Lord GOD; [z]I will yet
for this be inquired of by the house of Israel,
to do *it* for them; I will [a]increase them with
men like a flock.
38 As the [b]holy flock, as the flock of Jerusalem in her solemn feasts; so shall the waste
cities be filled with flocks of men: and they
shall know that I *am* the LORD.

A. M. cir. 3417
B. C. cir. 587
Ol. XLVIII. 2
Tarquinii Prisci,
R. Roman.,
cir. annum 30

[n]Chap. xxviii. 25; xxxvii. 25——[o]Jer. xxx. 22; chap. xi. 20; xxxvii. 27——[p]Matt. i. 21; Rom. xi. 26——[q]See Psa. cv. 16——[r]Chap. xxxiv. 29——[s]Chap. xxxiv. 27 [t]Ch. xvi. 61, 63——[u]Lev. xxvi. 39; ch. vi. 9; xx. 43

[v]Deut. ix. 5; ver. 22——[w]Ver. 10——[x]Isa. li. 3; chap. xxviii. 13; Joel ii. 3——[y]Chap. xvii. 24; xxii. 14; xxxvii. 14——[z]See chap. xiv. 3; xx. 3, 31——[a]Ver. 10 [b]Heb. *flock of holy things*

mourning over their impure hearts, which should be spent in prayer and faith before God, that their impurities might be washed away. In what a state of nonage are many members of the Christian Church!

Verse 28. *Ye shall be my people*] Wholly given up to me in body, soul, and spirit.

And I will be your God.] To fill you with love, joy, peace, meekness, gentleness, long-suffering, fidelity, and goodness, to *occupy* your *whole soul,* and *gratify* your *every desire.*

Verse 29. *I will also save you from all your uncleannesses*] I repeat it; "I WILL save you from all your sins."

Verse 30. *Ye shall receive no more reproach of famine*] Ye shall be daily and hourly fed with the *bread that endures unto eternal life.* "But will not those get *proud,* who are *thus saved,* if there be any such? and will they not *undervalue* the *blood of the covenant,* for then they shall *not need it?*" *Ans.* Hear what the Lord saith,—

Verse 31. *Then shall ye remember your own evil ways*] Ye shall never forget that ye were once *slaves of sin,* and *sold under sin; children of the wicked one; heirs to all God's curses,* with no *hope* beyond *hell.* Such cleansed people never forget *the horrible pit* and the *miry clay* out of which they have been brought. And can they then be *proud?* No; *they loathe themselves in their own sight.* They never *forgive themselves* for having sinned against so *good a God,* and so *loving a Saviour.* And can they *undervalue* HIM by whose blood they were bought, and by whose blood they were cleansed? No! That is impossible: they *now see Jesus* as they *ought to see him;* they see him *in his splendour,* because they *feel him* in his *victory* and *triumph* over sin. To them *that thus believe he is precious,* and he was never *so precious* as *now.* As to their not *needing him* when thus saved from their sins, we may as well say, as soon may the *creation* not need the *sustaining hand of God,* because the *works are finished!* Learn this, that *as* it requires the *same power* to *sustain* creation as to *produce* it, so it requires the *same Jesus* who *cleansed* to *keep clean.* They feel that it is only through his *continued indwelling,* that they are kept *holy,* and *happy,* and *useful.* Were he to leave them the original darkness and kingdom of death would soon be restored.

Verse 35. *This land that was desolate* by sin, *is become like the garden of Eden* by righteousness.—Satan's blast is removed; God's blessing has taken place.

Verse 36. *Then the heathen*] They shall see how powerful Jehovah is, and how *fully he saves* those who come unto and worship him.

Verse 37. *Thus saith the Lord God*] In answer to the question, "Who shall have such blessings?" we say, they that *pray,* that *seek* earnestly, that *strive* to enter in at the strait gate. "Thus saith the Lord, I will yet for this be inquired of by the house of Israel." Neither *Jew* nor *Gentile* shall be thus saved who do not *earnestly pray* to God; and for *this thing;* for this *complete salvation;* this setting up of the kingdom of Christ upon earth, and particularly in their *own souls.*

Verse 38. *As the holy flock*] The *Church of Christ,* without spot, or wrinkle, or any such thing.

The flock of Jerusalem] The Jerusalem that is *from above, the city of the living God,* the *place* where *his Majesty dwells.* As they came in ancient times to the solemn national feasts, so shall they come when they have fully returned unto the Lord, and received his salvation by Christ Jesus.

I do not ask my reader's pardon for having considered this most beautiful chapter as relating, not to the restoration from the Babylonish captivity, but to the redemption under the new covenant by Jesus Christ. There is no period of the Jewish history from that time until now, to which it can be applied. It must belong to the *Gospel dispensation;* and if the *Jews* will still refuse, contradict, and blaspheme, let no *Christian* have any fellowship with them in their opposition to this *Almighty Saviour.* Let none be *indifferent* to his *salvation;* let all *plead* his *promises;* and let the *messengers of the Churches* proclaim to the Christian world a FREE, a FULL, and a PRESENT SALVATION! And may great grace rest upon themselves, and upon all their flocks!

CHAPTER XXXVII

This chapter treats of the same subject with the preceding, in a beautiful and significant vision. Under the emblem of the open valley being thickly strewed with very dry bones is represented the hopeless state of the Jews when dispersed throughout the provinces of the Chaldean empire. But God, contrary to every human probability, restores these bones to life, thereby prefiguring the restoration of that people from the Babylonish captivity, and their resettlement in the land of their forefathers, 1–14. *The prophet then makes an easy and elegant transition to the blessedness of the people of God under the Gospel dispensation, in the plenitude of its manifestation; when the genuine converts to Christianity, the* spiritual *Israel, shall be no longer under the domination of heathen and anti-christian rulers, but shall be collected together into one visible kingdom, and constitute but one flock under one Shepherd,* 15–28. *The vision of the dry bones reviving is considered by some as having a remote view to the general resurrection.*

A. M. cir. 3417
B. C. cir. 587
Ol. XLVIII. 2
Tarquinii Prisci, R. Roman., cir. annum 30

THE [a]hand of the LORD
was upon me, and carried me out [b]in the spirit of
the LORD, and set me down in
the midst of the valley which *was* full of bones,
2 And caused me to pass by them round
about: and, behold, *there were* very many in
the open [c]valley; and, lo, *they were* very dry.
3 And he said unto me, Son of man, can
these bones live? And I answered, O Lord
GOD, [d]thou knowest.
4 Again he said unto me, Prophesy upon
these bones, and say unto them, O ye dry
bones, hear the word of the LORD.
5 Thus saith the Lord GOD unto these
bones; Behold, I will [e]cause
breath to enter into you, and
ye shall live:
6 And I will lay sinews upon
you, and will bring up flesh upon you, and
cover you with skin, and put breath in you,
and ye shall live; [f]and ye shall know that I
am the LORD.
7 So I prophesied as I was commanded;
and as I prophesied, there was a noise, and
behold a shaking, and the bones came together, bone to his bone.
8 And when I beheld, lo, the sinews and the
flesh came up upon them, and the skin covered
them above: but *there was* no breath in them.

A. M. cir. 3417
B. C. cir. 587
Ol. XLVIII. 2
Tarquinii Prisci, R. Roman., cir. annum 30

---

[a]Ch. i. 3——[b]Ch. iii. 14; viii. 3; xi. 24; Luke iv. 1 [c]Or, *champaign*——[d]Deut. xxxii. 36; 1 Sam. ii. 6; John v. 21; Rom. iv. 17; 2 Cor. i. 9——[e]Psa. civ. 30; ver. 9 [f]Chap. vi. 7; xxxv. 12; Joel ii. 27; iii. 17

NOTES ON CHAP. XXXVII

Verse 1. *The hand of the Lord was upon me*] The prophetic influence was communicated.

And carried me out in the spirit] Or, And the Lord brought me out in the spirit; that is, a spiritual vision, in which all these things were doubtless transacted.

The valley which was *full of bones*] This vision of the *dry bones* was designed, *first,* as an emblem of the then *wretched* state of the Jews; *secondly,* of the general resurrection of the body.

Verse 3. *Can these bones live?*] Is it possible that the persons whose bones these are can return to life?

Verse 4. *Prophesy upon these bones*] Declare to your miserable countrymen the gracious designs of the Lord; show them that their state, however deplorable, is not hopeless.

Verse 5. *Behold, I will cause breath*] רוח *ruach* signifies both *soul, breath,* and *wind;* and sometimes the *Spirit of God. Soul* is its proper meaning in this vision, where it refers to the bones: "I will cause the SOUL to enter into you."

Verse 6. *I will lay sinews upon you*] Observe the progress: 1. Here are the *bones.* 2. The *ligaments,* called here *sinews,* are to be added in order to *unite* the bones, that the *skeleton* might be complete. 3. The *flesh* (the whole *muscular system,* the *subjacent* and *superjacent muscles,* including the *arterial* and *venous system*) clothes this skeleton. 4. The *skin* (the *dermis* and *epidermis,* or *cutis* and *cuticle*) envelopes the whole of these muscles or flesh; and now these bodies are in the state that the body of Adam was before it received the animal and intellectual principle from God. 5. *There was no breath in them*—they had not yet received their *souls.* 6. The *wind,* רוח *ruach,* the *soul,* came into them. They were endued with animal and intellectual life; and they *arose* and evidenced a complete restoration to life, and began to perform its functions, ver. 10.

A. M. cir. 3417
B. C. cir. 587
Ol. XLVIII. 2
Tarquinii Prisci,
R. Roman.,
cir. annum 30

9 Then said he unto me,
Prophesy unto the [g]wind, prophesy, son of man, and say to
the wind, Thus saith the Lord
GOD; [h]Come from the four winds, O breath,
and breathe upon these slain, that they may
live.
10 So I prophesied as he commanded me,
[i]and the breath came into them, and they
lived, and stood up upon their feet, an exceeding great army.
11 Then he said unto me, Son of man,
these bones are the whole house of Israel: behold, they say, [k]Our bones are dried, and our
hope is lost: we are cut off for our parts.
12 Therefore prophesy and say unto them,
Thus saith the Lord GOD; Behold, [l]O my
people, I will open your graves, and cause
you to come up out of your
graves, and [m]bring you into
the land of Israel.
13 And ye shall know that I
am the LORD, when I have opened your
graves, O my people, and brought you up out
of your graves,
14 And [n]shall put my Spirit in you, and ye
shall live, and I shall place you in your own
land: then shall ye know that I the LORD
have spoken *it*, and performed *it*, saith the
LORD.
15 The word of the LORD came again unto
me, saying,
16 Moreover, thou son of man, [o]take thee
one stick, and write upon it, For Judah,
and for [p]the children of Israel his companions: then take another stick, and write

A. M. cir. 3417
B. C. cir. 587
Ol. XLVIII. 3
Tarquinii Prisci,
R. Roman.,
cir. annum 30

[g]Or, *breath*——[h]Psa. civ. 30; ver. 5——[i]Rev. xi. 11——[k]Psalm cxli. 7; Isa. xlix. 14——[l]Isa. xxvi. 19; Hos. xiii. 14

[m]Chap. xxxvi. 24; ver. 25——[n]Chap. xxxvi. 27——[o]See Num. xvii. 2——[p]2 Chron. xi. 12, 13, 16; xv. 9; xxx. 11, 18

Verse 9. *Prophesy unto the wind*] רוח *ruach.* Address thyself to the *soul*, and command it to enter into these well-organized bodies, that they may live.

Come from the four winds] SOULS, *come from all parts* where ye are scattered; and reanimate these bodies from which ye have been so long separated. The *four winds* signify *all parts*—in *every direction*. Literally it is, "Souls, come from the four souls;" "Breath, come from the four breaths;" or, "Wind, come from the four winds." But here רוח *ruach* has both of its most general meanings, *wind* or *breath*, and *soul*.

Verse 11. *These bones are the whole house of Israel*] That is, their state is represented by *these bones;* and their restoration to their own land is represented by the *revivification* of these bones.

Verse 12. *I will open your graves*] Here is a pointed allusion to the *general resurrection;* a doctrine properly credited and understood by the Jews, and to which our Lord refers, John v. 25, 28, 29: "The hour is coming when they that are in their graves shall hear his voice, and come forth."

And cause you to come up out of your graves] I am determined that ye shall be restored; so that were ye even *in your graves*, as mankind at the general resurrection, yet my all-powerful *voice* shall *call you forth*.

Verse 13. *When I have opened your graves*] When I shall have done for you what was *beyond* your *hope*, and deemed *impossible*, then shall ye know that I am *Jehovah*.

Verse 14. *And shall put my Spirit*] רוחי *ruchi.* Here רוח *ruach* is taken for the *Holy Ghost.* They were *living souls, animal* and *intellectual beings*, when they had received their souls, as mentioned above: but they could only become *spiritual, holy*, and *obedient* creatures by the *Spirit of God* actuating *their spirits.* See the notes on chap. xxxvi. 25, 26, 27.

THREE *degrees* or *processes* have been remarked in this mystic vision. When the prophet was commanded to *prophesy*—to foretell, on the authority of God, that there should be a restoration to their own land,—

1. There was a *noise*, which was followed by a general *shaking*, during which the *bones* became arranged and united.

2. The *flesh* and *skin* came upon them, so that the *dry bones* were no longer seen.

3. The *spirit* or *soul* came into them, and they *stood up* perfectly vivified.

Perhaps these might be illustrated by *three* periods of time, which marked the *regeneration* of the *Jewish polity.*

1. The *publication* of the *edict of Cyrus* in behalf of the Jews, which caused a *general shaking* or *stir* among the people, so that the *several families* began to *approach each other*, and prepare for their return to Judea, Ezra i. 2, 3. But though partially restored, they were obliged to discontinue the rebuilding of their temple.

2. The *edict* published by *Darius* in the *second* year of his reign, Ezra iv. 23, 24, which removed the impediments thrown in the way of the Jews. Ezra vi. 6, 7, &c.

3. The *mission of Nehemiah*, with orders from Artaxerxes to complete the building of the temple and the city, Neh. ii. 7, &c. Then the Jews *became a great army*, and found themselves in sufficient force to defend themselves and city against all their enemies.

As to the *spiritual uses* of this curious vision, I must leave them to preachers. I have given the *literal* meaning, and what the different parts refer to; and if they found their observations on these, they may profit their hearers.

Verse 16. *Son of man, take thee one stick*] The *two sticks* mentioned in this symbolical transaction represented, as the text declares, the two kingdoms of Israel and Judah, which were formed in the days of Rehoboam, and continued distinct till the time of the captivity. The kingdom of *Judah* was composed of the tribes of *Judah* and *Benjamin*, with the *Levites;* all the rest went off in the schism with Jero-

A. M. cir. 3417
B. C. cir. 587
Ol. XLVIII. 2
Tarquinii Prisci,
R. Roman.,
cir. annum 30

upon it, For Joseph, the stick of Ephraim, and *for* all the house of Israel his companions:

17 And [q]join the one to another into one stick, and they shall become one in thine hand.

18 And when the children of thy people shall speak unto thee, saying, [r]Wilt thou not show us what thou *meanest* by these?

19 [s]Say unto them, Thus saith the Lord GOD; Behold, I will take [t]the stick of Joseph, which *is* in the hand of Ephraim, and the tribes of Israel his fellows, and will put them with him, *even* with the stick of Judah, and make them one stick, and they shall be one in mine hand.

20 And the sticks whereon thou writest shall be in thine hand [u]before their eyes.

21 And say unto them, Thus saith the Lord GOD; Behold, [v]I will take the children of Israel from among the heathen, whither they be gone, and will gather them on every side, and bring them into their own land:

22 And I[w]will make them one nation in the land upon the mountains of Israel; and [x]one king shall be king to them all: and they shall be no more two nations, neither shall they be divided into two kingdoms any more at all:

23 [y]Neither shall they defile themselves any more with their idols, nor with their detestable things, nor with any of their transgressions: but[z]I will save them out of all their dwelling-places, wherein they have sinned, and will cleanse them: so shall they be my people, and I will be their God.

24 And [a]David my servant *shall be* king over them; and [b]they all shall have one shepherd: [c]they shall also walk in my judgments, and observe my statutes, and do them.

25 [d]And they shall dwell in the land that I have given unto Jacob my servant, wherein your fathers have dwelt; and they shall dwell therein, *even* they, and their children, and their children's children [e]for ever: and [f]my servant David *shall be* their prince for ever.

26 Moreover I will make a [g]covenant of peace with them; it shall be an everlasting covenant with them: and I will place them, and [h]multiply them, and will set my [i]sanctuary in the midst of them for evermore.

27 [k]My tabernacle also shall be with them: yea, I will be [l]their God, and they shall be my people.

28 [m]And the heathen shall know that I the LORD do [n]sanctify Israel, when my sanctuary shall be in the midst of them for evermore.

[q]See ver. 22, 24——[r]Ch. xii. 9; xxiv. 19——[s]Zech. x. 6 [t]Ver. 16, 17——[u]Ch. xii. 3——[v]Ch. xxxvi. 24——[w]Isa. xi. 13; Jer. iii. 18; l. 4; Hos. i. 11——[x]Ch. xxxiv. 23, 24; John x. 16——[y]Ch. xxxvi. 25——[z]Ch. xxxvi. 28, 29 [a]Isa. xl. 11; Jer. xxiii. 5; xxx. 9; ch. xxxiv. 23, 24; Hosea iii. 5; Luke i. 32——[b]Ver. 22; John x. 16

[c]Ch. xxxvi. 27——[d]Ch. xxxvi. 28——[e]Isa. lx. 21; Joel iii. 20; Amos ix. 15——[f]Ver. 24; John xii. 34——[g]Psa. lxxxix. 3; Isa. lv. 3; Jer. xxxii. 40; ch. xxxiv. 25——[h]Ch. xxxvi. 10, 37——[i]2 Cor. vi. 16——[k]Lev. xxvi. 11, 12; chap. xliii. 7; John i. 14——[l]Chap. xi. 20; xiv. 11; xxxvi. 28——[m]Chap. xxxvi. 23——[n]Chap. xx. 12

boam, and formed the kingdom of Israel. Though some out of those tribes did rejoin themselves to Judah, yet no *whole tribe* ever returned to that kingdom. Common sufferings in their captivity became the means of reviving a kinder feeling; and to encourage this, God promises that he will reunite them, and restore them to their own land; and that there shall no more be any divisions or feuds among them. To represent this in such a way as would make it a subject of *thought*, *reflection*, and *inquiry*, the prophet is ordered to take the *two sticks* mentioned above, to *write on them* the distinguishing names of the divided kingdoms, and then by a *notch*, *dovetail*, *glue*, or some such method, to unite them both before the people. He did so; and on their inquiry, showed them the full meaning of this symbolical action.

Verse 19. *The stick of Joseph, which* is *in the hand of Ephraim*] Jeroboam, the first king of the ten tribes, was an *Ephraimite*. *Joseph* represents the ten tribes in general; they were in the hand of *Ephraim*, that is, *under the government of Jeroboam*.

Verse 22. *I will make them one nation*] There was no distinction after the return from Babylon.

And one king shall be king to them all] Politically speaking, they never had a *king* from that day to this; and the grand junction and government spoken of here must refer to another time—to that in which they shall be brought into the Christian Church with the fulness of the Gentiles; when JESUS, the *King of kings* and *Lord of lords*, shall rule over all.

Verse 24. *And David my servant* shall be *King*] That this refers to *Jesus Christ*, see proved, chap. xxxiv. 23.

Verse 25. *The land that I have given unto Jacob my servant*] Jacob means here the *twelve tribes;* and the *land given to them* was the whole land of *Palestine;* consequently, the promise states that, when they return, they are to possess the whole of the *Promised Land.*

Verse 26. *Covenant of peace*] See this explained chap. xxxiv. 25.

Verse 27. *My tabernacle*] Jesus Christ, the true tabernacle, in whom dwelt all the fulness of the Godhead bodily.

CHAPTER XXXVIII

The sublime prophecy contained in this and the following chapter relates to Israel's victory over Gog, and is very obscure. It begins with representing a prodigious armament of many nations combined together under the conduct of Gog, with the intention of overwhelming the Jews, after having been for some time resettled in their land subsequent to their return from the Babylonish captivity, 1–9. *These enemies are farther represented as making themselves sure of the spoil,* 10–13. *But in this critical conjuncture when Israel, to all human appearance, was about to be swallowed up by her enemies, God most graciously appears, to execute by terrible judgments the vengeance threatened against these formidable adversaries of his people,* 14–16. *The prophet, in terms borrowed from human passions, describes, with awful emphasis, the fury of Jehovah as coming up to his face; and the effects of it so dreadful, as to make all the animate and inanimate creation tremble, and even to convulse with terror the whole frame of nature,* 17–23.

A. M. cir. 3417
B. C. cir. 587
Ol. XLVIII. 2
Tarquinii Prisci,
R. Roman.,
cir. annum 30

AND the word of the LORD
came unto me, saying,
2 [a]Son of man, [b]set thy face
against [c]Gog, the land of Magog,
[d]the chief prince of [e]Meshech and Tubal,
and prophesy against him,
3 And say, Thus saith the Lord GOD; Behold,
I *am* against thee, O Gog, the chief
prince of Meshech and Tubal:
4 And [f]I will turn thee back, and put hooks
into thy jaws, and I will bring thee forth,
and all thine army, horses and horsemen, [g]all
of them clothed with all sorts *of armour, even*
a great company *with* bucklers
and shields, all of them
handling swords:
5 Persia, Ethiopia, and [h]Libya
with them; all of them with shield and helmet.
6 [i]Gomer, and all his bands; the house of
[k]Togarmah of the north quarters, and all his
bands: *and* many people with thee.
7 [l]Be thou prepared, and prepare for thyself,
thou, and all thy company that are assembled
unto thee, and be thou a guard unto them.
8 [m]After many [n]days thou shalt be visited:
in the latter years thou shalt come into the

[a]Chap. xxxix. 1——[b]Chap. xxxv. 2, 3——[c]Rev. xx. 8——[d]Or, *prince of the chief*——[e]Chap. xxxii. 26——[f]2 Kings xix. 28; chap. xxix. 4; xxxix. 2——[g]Ch. xxiii. 12

[h]Or, *Phut;* chap. xxvii. 10; xxx. 5——[i]Gen. x. 2 [k]Chap. xxvii. 14——[l]Like Isa. viii. 9, 10; Jer. xlvi. 3, 4, 14; li. 12——[m]Gen. xlix. 1; Deut. iv. 30; ver. 16 [n]Isa. xxix. 6

NOTES ON CHAP. XXXVIII

Verse 2. *Son of man, set thy face against Gog, the land of Magog*] This is allowed to be the most difficult prophecy in the Old Testament. It is difficult to us, because we know not the *king* nor *people* intended by it: but I am satisfied they were well known by these names in the time that the prophet wrote.

I have already remarked in the *introduction* to this book that there are but *two* opinions on this subject that appear to be at all probable: 1. That which makes GOG *Cambyses,* king of *Persia;* and, 2. That which makes him ANTIOCHUS EPIPHANES, king of *Syria.* And between these *two* (for one or other is supposed to be the person intended) men are much divided.

Calmet, one of the most judicious commentators that ever wrote on the Bible, declares for *Cambyses;* and supports his opinion, in opposition to all others, by many arguments.

Mr. *Mede* supposes the *Americans* are meant, who were originally colonies of the Scythians, who were descendants of *Magog,* son of *Japheth. Houbigant* declares for the *Scythians,* whose neighbours were the people of *Rosh, Meshech,* and *Tubal,* that is the *Russians, Muscovites,* and *Tybareni* or *Cappadocians.* Several eminent critics espouse this opinion. *Rabbi David Kimchi* says the *Christians* and *Turks* are meant: and of later opinions there are several, founded in the ocean of conjecture. *Calmet* says expressly, that GOG is *Cambyses,* king of Persia, who on his return from the land of Egypt, died in *Judea.* The Rev. *David Martin,* pastor of the Waloon church at Utrecht, concludes, after examining all previous opinions, that *Antiochus Epiphanes,* the great enemy of the Israelites, is alone intended here; and that *Gog,* which signifies *covered,* is an allusion to the well-known *character* of Antiochus, whom historians describe as an *artful, cunning,* and *dissembling* man. See Dan. viii. 23, 25; xi. 23, 27, 32. *Magog* he supposes to mean the country of *Syria.* Of this opinion the following quotation from *Pliny,* Hist. Nat., lib. v., c. 23, seems a proof; who, speaking of Cœle-Syria, says: Cœle habet Apamiam Marsyia amne divisam a Nazarinorum Tetrarchia. Bambycem quam alio nomine Hierapolis vocatur, Syris vero Magog. "Cœle-Syria has Apamia separated from the tetrarchy of the Nazarenes by the river Marsyia; and Bambyce, otherwise called Hierapolis; but by the Syrians, MAGOG."

I shall at present examine the text by this latter opinion.

Chief prince of Meshech and Tubal] These probably mean the auxiliary forces, over whom Antiochus was supreme; they were the *Muscovites* and *Cappadocians.*

Verse 4. *I will turn thee back*] Thy enterprise shall fail.

Verse 5. *Persia*] That a part of this country was tributary to *Antiochus,* see 1 Macc. iii. 31.

Ethiopia, and Libya] That these were auxiliaries of Antiochus is evident from Dan. xi. 43: "The Libyans and Ethiopians shall be at his steps."

Verse 6. *Gomer, and all his bands; the house of Togarmah*] The *Cimmerians* and *Turcomanians,* and other northern nations.— *Calmet.*

Verse 8. *In the latter years thou shalt come*] This was fulfilled about *four hundred* years after.—*Martin.* The expedition of *Cambyses* against Egypt was about *twelve* years after the return of the Jews from Babylon.—*Calmet.*

A. M. cir. 3417
B. C. cir. 587
Ol. XLVIII. 2
Tarquinii Prisci,
R. Roman.,
cir. annum 30

land *that is* brought back from the sword, [n]*and is* gathered out of many people, against [o]the mountains of Israel, which have been always waste: but it is brought forth out of the nations, and they shall [p]dwell safely all of them.

9 Thou shalt ascend and come [q]like a storm, thou shalt be [r]like a cloud to cover the land, thou, and all thy bands, and many people with thee.

10 Thus saith the Lord GOD; It shall also come to pass *that* at the same time shall things come into thy mind, and thou shalt [s]think an evil thought:

11 And thou shalt say, I will go up to the land of unwalled villages; I will [t]go to them that are at rest, [u]that dwell [v]safely, all of them dwelling without walls, and having neither bars nor gates,

12 [w]To take a spoil, and to take a prey, to turn thine hand upon [x]the desolate places *that are now* inhabited, [y]and upon the people *that are* gathered out of the nations, which have gotten cattle and goods, that dwell in the [z]midst of the land.

13 [a]Sheba, and [b]Dedan, and the merchants [c]of Tarshish, with all [d]the young lions thereof, shall say unto thee, Art thou come to take a spoil? hast thou gathered thy company to take a prey? to carry away silver and gold, to take away cattle and goods, to take a great spoil?

14 Therefore, son of man, prophesy and say unto Gog, Thus saith the Lord GOD; [e]In that day when my people of Israel [f]dwelleth safely, shalt thou not know *it?*

A. M. cir. 3417
B. C. cir 587
Ol. XLVIII. 2
Tarquinii Prisci,
R. Roman.,
cir. annum 30

15 [g]And thou shalt come from thy place out of the north parts, thou, [h]and many people with thee, all of them riding upon horses, a great company, and a mighty army:

16 [i]And thou shalt come up against my people of Israel, as a cloud to cover the land; [k]it shall be in the latter days, and I will bring thee against my land, [l]that the heathen may know me, when I shall be sanctified in thee, O Gog, before their eyes.

17 Thus saith the Lord GOD; *Art* thou he of whom I have spoken in old time, [m]by my servants the prophets of Israel, which prophesied in those days *many* years that I would bring thee against them?

18 And it shall come to pass at the same time when Gog shall come against the land of Israel, saith the Lord GOD, *that* my fury shall come up in my face.

19 For [n]in my jealousy [o]*and* in the fire of my wrath have I spoken, [p]Surely in that day there shall be a great shaking in the land of Israel;

20 So that [q]the fishes of the sea, and the fowls of the heaven, and the beasts of the field, and all creeping things that creep upon the earth, and all the men that *are* upon the face of the earth, shall shake at my presence, [r]and the mountains shall be thrown down, and

---

[n]Ver. 12; chap. xxxiv. 13——[o]Chap. xxxvi. 1, 4, 8——[p]Jer. xxiii. 6; chap. xxviii. 26; xxxiv. 25, 28; ver. 11——[q]Isa. xxviii. 2——[r]Jer. iv. 13; ver. 16——[s]Or, *conceive a mischievous purpose*——[t]Jer. xlix. 31——[u]Ver. 8——[v]Or, *confidently*——[w]Heb. *To spoil the spoil, and to prey the prey;* chap. xxix. 19——[x]Chap. xxxvi. 34, 35——[y]Ver. 8——[z]Heb. *navel;* Judg. ix. 37

[a]Chap. xxvii. 22, 23——[b]Chap. xxvii. 15, 20——[c]Ch. xxvii. 12——[d]See chap. x. 3, 5——[e]Isa. iv. 1——[f]Ver. 8——[g]Chap. xxxix. 2——[h]Ver. 6——[i]Ver. 9——[k]Ver. 8——[l]Exod. xiv. 4; chap. xxxvi. 23; xxxix. 21——[m]Heb. *by the hands*——[n]Chap. xxxvi. 5, 6; xxxix. 25——[o]Psa. lxxxix. 46——[p]Hag. ii. 6, 7; Rev. xvi. 18——[q]Hos. iv. 3——[r]Jer. iv. 24; Nah. i. 5, 6

Verse 9. *Thou shalt ascend and come like a storm*] It is observable that Antiochus is thus spoken of by Daniel, chap. xi. 40: *The king of the north*—Antiochus, *shall come against him* (the king of the south is the king of Egypt) *like a whirlwind.*

Verse 10. *Shall things come into thy mind, and thou shalt think an evil thought*] Antiochus purposed to invade and destroy *Egypt*, as well as *Judea;* see Dan. xi. 31, 32, 36. This *Calmet* interprets of Cambyses, his cruelties in Egypt, and his evil design to destroy the Israelites.

Verse 12. *To take a spoil—and a prey*] When Antiochus took Jerusalem he gave the pillage of it to his soldiers, and spoiled the temple of its riches, which were immense. See *Joseph.* WAR, B. i. c. 1.

Verse 13. *Sheba, and Dedan*] The Arabians, anciently great plunderers; and *Tarshish*, the inhabitants of the famous isle of Tartessus, the most noted merchants of the time. They are here represented as coming to Antiochus before he undertook the expedition, and *bargaining for the spoils of the Jews. Art thou come to take a spoil, to carry away silver and gold, cattle and goods?*

Verse 16. *When I shall be sanctified in thee, O Gog*] By the defeat of his troops under *Lysias*, his general. 1 Mac. iii. 32, 33, &c., and chap. vi. 6.

Verse 17. Art *thou he of whom I have spoken in old time*] This prophecy concerning Antiochus and the Jews was delievered about *four hundred* years before the events took place.—*Martin. Calmet* maintains that Cambyses is spoken of, and refers to ancient prophecies, especially Isa. xiv., xv., xvi. 20, 21.

A. M. cir. 3417
B. C. cir. 587
Ol. XLVIII. 2
Tarquinii Prisci,
R. Roman.,
cir. annum 30

the [s]steep places shall fall,
and every wall shall fall to
the ground.
21 And I will [t]call for [u]a
sword against him throughout all my mountains, saith the Lord GOD: [v]every man's sword
shall be against his brother.
22 And I will [w]plead against him with [x]pes-
tilence and with blood; and [y]I will rain upon
him, and upon his bands, and
upon the many people that
are with him, an overflowing
rain, and [z]great hailstones,
fire, and brimstone.
23 Thus will I magnify myself, and [a]sanc-
tify myself; [b]and I will be known in the eyes
of many nations, and they shall know that I
am the LORD.

A. M. cir. 3417
B. C. cir. 587
Ol. XLVIII. 2
Tarquinii Prisci,
R. Roman.,
cir. annum 30

[s]Or, *towers*, or *stairs*——[t]Psa. cv. 16——[u]Chap. xiv. 17——[v]Judg. vii. 22; 1 Sam. xiv. 20; 2 Chron. xx. 23——[w]Isa. lxvi. 16; Jer. xxv. 31——[x]Ch. v. 17——[y]Psa. xi. 6; Isa. xxix. 6; xxx. 30——[z]Chap. xiii. 11; Rev. xvi. 21——[a]Chap. xxxvi. 23——[b]Psa. ix. 16; chap. xxxvii. 28; xxxix. 7; ver. 16

Verse 21. *I will call for a sword against him*] Meaning *Judas Maccabeus*, who defeated his army under Lysias, making a horrible carnage.—*Martin*. Cambyses had no wars in the mountains of Israel.

Verse 22. *Great hailstones, fire, and brimstone.*] These are probably figurative expressions, to signify that the whole tide of the war should be against him, and that his defeat and slaughter should be great. Abp. *Newcome* supposes all the above prophecy remains yet to be fulfilled. Where such eminent scribes are divided, who shall decide!

CHAPTER XXXIX

The prophet goes on to denounce the Divine judgments against Gog and his army, 1–7; *and describes their dreadful slaughter,* 8–10, *and burial,* 11–16, *in terms so very lofty and comprehensive, as must certainly denote some very extraordinary interposition of Providence in behalf of the Jews. And to amplify the matter still more, the prophet, with peculiar art and propriety, delays the summoning of all the birds and beasts of prey in nature to feast on the slain, (in allusion to the custom of feasting on the remainder of sacrifices,) till after the greater multitudes are buried; to intimate that even the remainder, and as it were the stragglers of such mighty hosts, would be more than sufficient to satisfy their utmost rapacity,* 17–20. *The remaining verses contain a prediction of the great blessedness of the people of God in Gospel times, and of the stability of the kingdom of Christ,* 21–29. *It will be proper to remark that the great northern expedition against the natural Israel, described in this and the preceding chapter, is, from its striking resemblance in the main particulars, put by the writer of the Apocalypse,* (chap. xx. 7–10,) *for a much more formidable armament of a multitude of nations in the four quarters of the earth against the pure Christian Church,* the MYSTICAL Israel; *an event still extremely remote, and which it is thought shall immediately precede the destruction of the world by fire, and the general judgment.*

A. M. cir. 3417
B. C. cir. 587
Ol. XLVIII. 2
Tarquinii Prisci,
R. Roman.,
cir. annum 30

THEREFORE, [a]thou son
of man, prophesy against
Gog, and say, Thus saith
the Lord GOD; Behold, I *am*
against thee, O Gog, the chief prince of
Meshech and Tubal;
2 And I will turn thee back, and [b]leave but
the sixth part of thee, [c]and will cause thee
to come up from [d]the north parts, and
will bring thee upon the mountains of
Israel:
3 And I will smite thy bow out of thy left
hand, and will cause thine
arrows to fall out of thy right
hand.
4 [e]Thou shalt fall upon the
mountains of Israel, thou, and
all thy bands, and the people that *is* with
thee: [f]I will give thee unto the ravenous
birds of every [g]sort, and *to* the beasts of the
field [h]to be devoured.
5 Thou shalt fall upon [i]the open field: for
I have spoken *it,* saith the Lord GOD.
6 [k]And I will send a fire on Magog, and

A. M. cir. 3417
B. C. cir. 587
Ol. XLVIII. 2
Tarquinii Prisci,
R. Roman.,
cir. annum 30

[a]Ch. xxxviii. 2, 3——[b]Or, *strike thee with six plagues;* or, *draw thee back with a hook of six teeth,* as chap. xxxviii. 4——[c]Chap. xxxviii. 15——[d]Heb. *the sides of the north*——[e]Chap. xxxviii. 21; ver. 17——[f]Chap. xxxiii. 27——[g]Heb. *wing*——[h]Heb. *to devour*——[i]Heb. *the face of the field*——[k]Chap. xxxviii. 22; Amos i. 4

NOTES ON CHAP. XXXIX

Verse 2. *And leave but the sixth part of thee*] The margin has, *strike thee with six plagues;* or, *draw thee back with a hook of six teeth.*

Verse 3. *I will smite thy bow out of thy left hand*] The *Persians* whom Antiochus had in his army, chap. xxxviii. 5, were famous as *archers,* and they may be intended here. The *bow* is held by the *left hand;* the *arrow* is pulled and discharged by the *right.*

Verse 6. *I will send a fire on Magog*] On Syria. I will destroy the Syrian troops.

And among them that dwell carelessly in the isles] The auxiliary troops that came to Antiochus from the borders of the Euxine Sea.—*Martin.*

A. M. cir. 3417
B. C. cir. 587
Ol. XLVIII. 2
Tarquinii Prisci,
R. Roman.,
cir. annum 30

among them that dwell [l]carelessly in [m]the isles: and they shall know that I *am* the LORD.

7 [n]So will I make my holy name known in the midst of my people Israel; and I will not *let them* [o]pollute my holy name any more: [p]and the heathen shall know that I *am* the LORD, the Holy One in Israel.

8 [q]Behold, it is come, and it is done, saith the Lord GOD; this *is* the day [r]whereof I have spoken.

9 And they that dwell in the cities of Israel shall go forth, and shall set on fire and burn the weapons, both the shields and the bucklers, the bows and the arrows, and the [s]handstaves, and the spears, and they shall [t]burn them with fire seven years:

10 So that they shall take no wood out of the field, neither cut down *any* out of the forests; for they shall burn the weapons with fire: [u]and they shall spoil those that spoiled them, and rob those that robbed them, saith the Lord GOD.

11 And it shall come to pass in that day, *that* I will give unto Gog a place there of graves in Israel, the valley of the passengers on the east of the sea; and it shall stop the [v]*noses* of the passengers: and there shall they bury Gog and all his multitude: and they shall call *it* The valley of [w]Hamon-gog.

12 And seven months shall the house of Israel be burying of them, [x]that they may cleanse the land.

13 Yea, all the people of the land shall

[l]Or, *confidently*——[m]Psa. lxxii. 10——[n]Ver. 22——[o]Lev. xviii. 21; chap. xx. 39——[p]Chap. xxxviii. 16, 23——[q]Rev. xvi. 17; xxi. 6——[r]Chap. xxxviii. 17

[s]Or, *javelins*——[t]Or, *make a fire of them*——[u]Isa. xiv. 2——[v]Or, *mouths*——[w]That is, *The multitude of Gog*——[x]Deut. xxi. 23; ver. 14, 16

Verse 7. *In the midst of my people Israel*] This defeat of Gog is to be in Israel: and it was *there* according to this prophecy, that the immense army of Antiochus was so completely defeated.

And I will not let them *pollute my holy name any more*] See on 1 Macc. i. 11, &c., how Antiochus had *profaned the temple, insulted Jehovah and his worship*, &c. God permitted that as a scourge to his disobedient people; but now the scourger shall be scourged, and he shall *pollute the sanctuary no more*.

Verse 9. *And shall set on fire—the weapons*] The Israelites shall make bonfires and fuel of the weapons, tents, &c., which the defeated Syrians shall leave behind them, as expressive of the joy which they shall feel for the destruction of their enemies; and to keep up, in their *culinary consumption*, the memory of this great event.

They shall burn them with fire seven years] These may be *figurative* expressions, after the manner of the Asiatics, whose language abounds with such descriptions. They occur every where in the prophets. As to the number *seven*, it is only a certain for an indeterminate number. But as the slaughter was great, and the *bows, arrows, quivers, shields, bucklers, handstaves*, and *spears* were in vast multitudes, it must have taken a long time to gather them up in the different parts of the *fields* of battle, and the *roads* in which the Syrians had *retreated*, throwing away their *arms* as they proceeded; so there might have been a long time employed in collecting and burning them. And as all seem to have been doomed to the fire, there might have been some found at different intervals and burned, during the *seven years* here mentioned. *Mariana*, in his History of Spain, lib. xi., c. 24, says, that after the Spaniards had given that signal overthrow to the Saracens, A. D. 1212, they found such a vast quantity of lances, javelins, and such like, that they served them for *four years* for fuel. And probably these instruments obtained by the Israelites were used in general for *culinary firewood*, and might *literally* have served them for *seven years;* so that during that time *they should take no wood out of the fields, nor out of the forests* for the purpose of *fuel*, ver. 10.

Verse 11. *The valley of the passengers on the east of the sea*] That is, of *Gennesareth*, according to the *Targum*. The valley near this lake or sea is called *the Valley of the Passengers*, because it was a great road by which the merchants and traders from Syria and other eastern countries went into Egypt; see Gen. xxxvii. 17, 25. See *Calmet* here.

There shall they bury Gog and all his multitude] Some read, "There shall they bury Gog, that is, all his multitude." Not Gog, or Antiochus himself, for he was not in this battle; but his *generals, captains*, and *soldiers*, by whom he was represented. As to *Hamon-gog*, we know no valley of this name but here. But we may understand the words thus: the place where this great slaughter was, and where the multitudes of the slain were buried, might be better called *Hamon-gog*, the *valley of the multitude of Gog*, than the *valley of passengers;* for so great was the carnage there, that the way of the passengers shall be stopped by it. See the text.

Verse 12. *And seven months*] It shall require a long time to bury the dead. This is another figurative expression; which, however, may admit of a good deal of *literal* meaning. Many of the Syrian soldiers had secreted themselves in different places during the pursuit after the battle, where they died of their wounds, of hunger, and of fatigue; so that they were not all found and buried till *seven months* after the defeat of the Syrian army. This slow process of burying is distinctly related in the three following verses, and extended even to a *bone*, ver. 15; which, when it was found by a passenger, the place was marked, that the buriers might see and *inter* it. *Seven months* was little time enough for all this work; and in that country putrescency does not easily take place; the

A. M. cir. 3417
B. C. cir. 587
Ol. XLVIII. 2
Tarquinii Prisci,
R. Roman.,
cir. annum 30

bury *them;* and it shall be to them a renown, the day that [y]I shall be glorified, saith the Lord GOD.

14 And they shall sever out [z]men of continual employment, passing through the land to bury with the passengers those that remain upon the face of the earth,[a]to cleanse it: after the end of seven months shall they search.

15 And the passengers *that* pass through the land, when *any* seeth a man's bone, then shall he [b]set up a sign by it, till the buriers have buried it in the valley of Hamon-gog.

16 And also the name of the city *shall be* [c]Hamonah. Thus shall they [d]cleanse the land.

17 And, thou son of man, thus saith the Lord GOD; [e]Speak [f]unto every feathered fowl, and to every beast of the field, [g]Assemble yourselves, and come; gather yourselves on every side to my [h]sacrifice that I do sacrifice for you, *even* a great sacrifice [i]upon the mountains of Israel, that ye may eat flesh, and drink blood.

18 [k]Ye shall eat the flesh of the mighty, and drink the blood of the princes of the earth, of rams, of lambs, and of [l]goats, of bullocks, all of them [m]fatlings of Bashan.

19 And ye shall eat fat till ye be full, and drink blood till ye be drunken, of my sacrifice which I have sacrificed for you.

20 [n]Thus ye shall be filled at my table with horses and chariots, [o]with mighty men, and with all men of war, saith the Lord GOD.

A. M. cir. 3417
B. C. cir. 587
Ol. XLVIII. 2
Tarquinii Prisci,
R. Roman.,
cir. annum 30

21 [p]And I will set my glory among the heathen, and all the heathen shall see my judgment that I have executed, and [q]my hand that I have laid upon them.

22 [r]So the house of Israel shall know that I *am* the LORD their God from that day and forward.

23 [s]And the heathen shall know that the house of Israel went into captivity for their iniquity: because they trespassed against me, therefore [t]hid I my face from them, and [u]gave them into the hand of their enemies: so fell they all by the sword.

24 [v]According to their uncleanness and according to their transgressions have I done unto them, and hid my face from them.

25 Therefore thus saith the Lord GOD; [w]Now will I bring again the captivity of Jacob, and have mercy upon the [x]whole house of Israel, and will be jealous for my holy name;

26 [y]After that they have borne their shame, and all their trespasses whereby they have trespassed against me, when they [z]dwelt safely in their land, and none made *them* afraid.

27 [a]When I have brought them again from the people, and gathered them out of their

[y]Ch. xxviii. 22——[z]Heb. *men of continuance*——[a]Ver. 12——[b]Heb. *build*——[c]That is, *the multitude*——[d]Ver. 12——[e]Rev. xix. 17; [f]Heb. *to the fowl of every wing* [g]Isa. xviii. 6; xxxiv. 6; Jer. xii. 9; Zeph. i. 7——[h]Or, *slaughter*——[i]Ver. 4——[k]Rev. xix. 18——[l]Heb. *great goats*——[m]Deut. xxxii. 14; Psa. xxii. 12——[n]Psa. lxxvi. 6; chap. xxxviii. 4

[o]Rev. xix. 18——[p]Chap. xxxviii. 16, 23——[q]Exod. vii. 4——[r]Ver. 7, 28——[s]Chap. xxxvi. 18, 19, 20, 23——[t]Deut. xxxi. 17; Isa. lix. 2——[u]Lev. xxvi. 25——[v]Chap. xxxvi. 19——[w]Jer. xxx. 3, 18; chap. xxxiv. 13; xxxvi. 21——[x]Chap. xx. 40; Hos. i. 11 [y]Dan. ix. 16——[z]Lev. xxvi. 5, 6——[a]Chap. xxviii. 25, 26

scorching winds serving to desiccate the flesh, and preserve it from decomposition.

Verse 17. *Gather yourselves—to my sacrifice*] This is an allusion to a custom common in the east: when a sacrifice is made, the friends and neighbours of the party sacrificing are invited to come and feast on the sacrifice.

Verse 18. *Ye shall—drink the blood of the princes of the earth*] I need not mention the custom of the Scandinavians: they were accustomed to drink the blood of their enemies out of the skulls of the dead. But this is spoken of *fowls* and *beasts* here—*rams, lambs*, and *goats.* The feast shall be as grateful and as plenteous to the *fowls* and *beasts*, as one made of the above animals, the fattest and best of their kind, (because fed in the fertile fields of Bashan,) would be to the guests of him who makes a sacrifice.

Verse 19. *And ye shall eat fat—and drink blood*] *Who* shall eat and drink, &c.? Not the *Jews;* though *Voltaire* says they ate *human flesh*, and are invited here by the prophet to *eat the flesh and drink the blood of their enemies;* which is a most unprincipled falsehood. It is the *fowls* and the *beasts* that God invites, ver. 17: "Speak to every feathered fowl, and to every beast of the field, assemble yourselves—that ye may eat flesh and drink blood;" nor are the persons altered in all these verses, 17, 18, 19, 20: so the assertion of *Voltaire* is either through *brutish ignorance* or *Satanic malice.*

Verse 25. *Now will I bring again the captivity of Jacob*] Both *they* and the *heathen* shall know that it was for their iniquity that I gave them into the hands of their enemies: and now I will redeem them from those hands in such a way as to prove that I am a *merciful God*, as well as a *just God.*

Verse 26. *After that they have borne their shame*] After they shall have borne the *punishment* due to a line of conduct which is their *shame* and reproach, viz. *idolatry.*

Verse 27. *When I have—gathered them*]

A. M. cir. 3417
B. C. cir. 587
Ol. XLVIII. 2
Tarquinii Prisci,
R. Roman.,
cir. annum 30

enemies' lands, and [b]am sanctified in them in the sight of many nations;

28 [c]Then shall they know
that I *am* the Lord their God, [d]which caused them to be led into captivity among the heathen: but I have gathered them unto their own land, and have left none of them any more there.

29 [e]Neither will I hide my face any more
from them, for I have [f]poured out my Spirit
upon the house of Israel, saith the Lord God.

[b]Chap. xxxvi. 23, 24; xxxviii. 16——[c]Chap. xxxiv. 30; ver. 22

[d]Heb. *by my causing of them*, &c.——[e]Isa. liv. 8——[f]Joel ii. 28; Zech. xii. 10; Acts ii. 17

Antiochus had before captured many of the Jews, and sold them for *slaves;* see Dan. xi. 33.

Verse 28. *And have left none of them any more there.*] All that *chose* had liberty to return; but many remained behind. This promise may therefore refer to a *greater restoration*, when not a Jew shall be left behind. This, the next verse intimates, will be in the *Gospel dispensation.*

Verse 29. *For I have poured out my Spirit*] That is, I will pour out my Spirit; see the notes on chap. xxxvi. 25-29, where this subject is largely considered. This *Spirit* is to enlighten, quicken, purify, and cleanse their hearts; so that, being completely changed, they shall become God's people, and be a praise in the earth. Now, they are a proverb of reproach; then, they shall be eminently distinguished.

A NEW PLAN OF THE TEMPLE AT JERUSALEM

[*For an explanation of this plan, and of the accompanying map of the division of the Land of Canaan, see at the end of chap.* xlviii.]

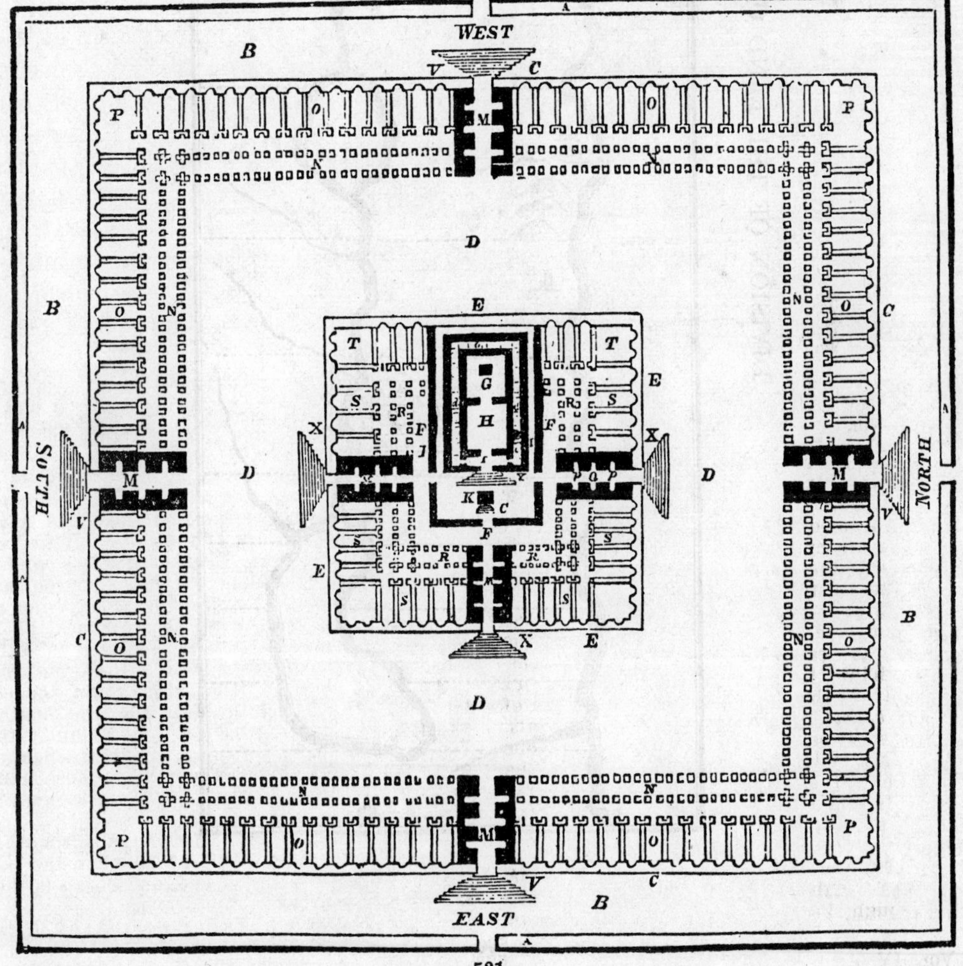

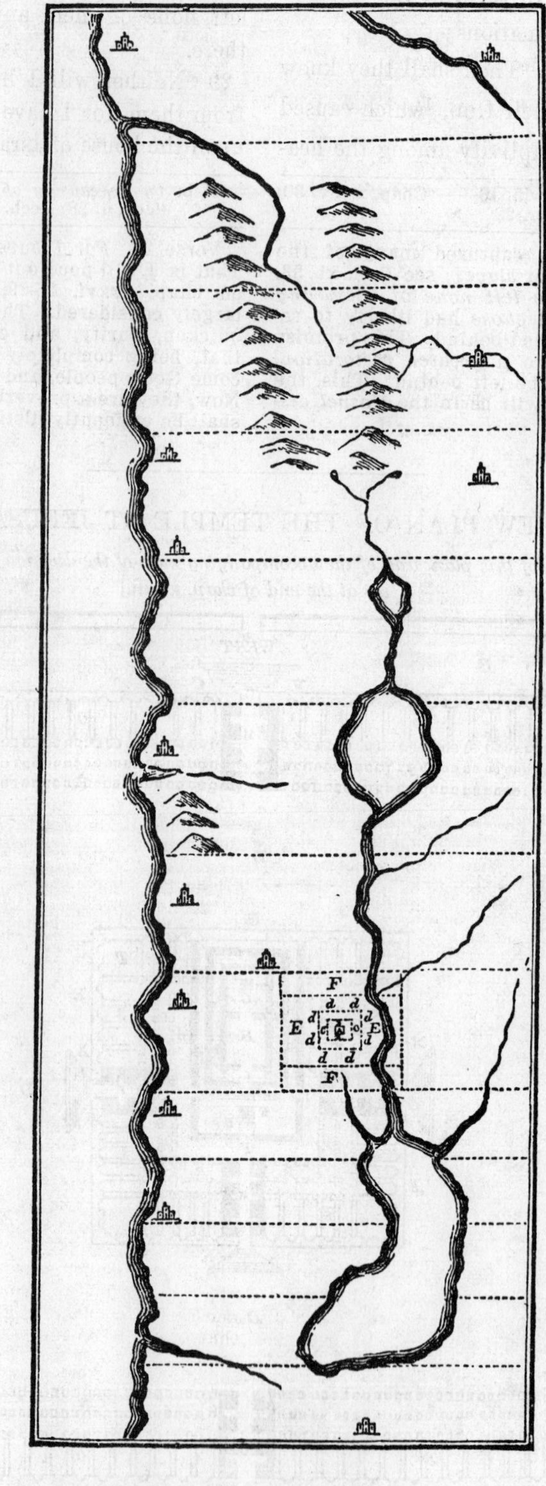
DIVISION OF THE LAND OF CANAAN
F
d d
E
d d
E
d d
F

CHAPTER XL

The prophecy or vision, which begins here, continues to the end of the Book. The Temple of Jerusalem lying in ruins when Ezekiel had this vision, (for its date is the fourteenth *year after the destruction of Jerusalem by Nebuchadnezzar,) the Jews needed consolation. If they were not promised a restoration of the temple, they would not feel so great an interest in returning home. It is thought by some that no model of Solomon's Temple had remained. To direct them, therefore, in the dimensions, parts, order, and rules of their new temple might be one reason why Ezekiel is so particular in the description of the old; to which the new was conformable in figure and parts, though inferior in magnificence, on account of the poverty of the nation at the time. Whatever was august or illustrious in the prophetic figures, and not literally fulfilled in or near their own times, the ancient Jews properly considered as belonging to the time of the Messiah. Accordingly, upon finding that the latter temple fell short of the model of the temple here described by Ezekiel, they supposed the prophecy to refer, at least in part, to the period now mentioned. And we, who live under the Gospel dispensation, have apostolical authority for the assertion that the temple and temple worship were emblematic of Christ's Church, frequently represented in the New Testament under the metaphor of a temple, in allusion to the symmetry, beauty, and firmness of that of Solomon; to its orderly worship; and to the manifestations it had of the Divine Presence. This chapter commences with the time, manner, and end of the vision,* 1–5. *We have next a description of the east gate,* 6–19, *the north gate,* 20–22, *and the south gate,* 24–31. *A farther description of the east gate,* 32–34, *and of the north gate,* 35–38. *Account of the eight tables,* 39–43; *of the chambers,* 44–47; *and of the porch of the temple,* 48, 49.

A. M. 3430 B. C. 574 Olymp. LI. 3 Anno Servii Tullii, R. Roman., 5

IN the five and twentieth year of our captivity, in the beginning of the year, in the tenth *day* of the month, in the fourteenth year after that [a]the city was smitten, in the selfsame day [b]the hand of the LORD was upon me, and brought me thither.

[a]Chap. xxxiii. 21 — [b]Chap. i. 3

NOTES ON CHAP. XL

Verse 1. *In the five and twentieth year of our captivity*] According to the date here given, this prophecy was delivered on Tuesday, April 20, A. M. 3430, in the *twenty-fifth* year of the captivity of *Jeconiah,* and *fourteen* years after the taking of Jerusalem.

The temple here described by Ezekiel is, in all probability, the same which he saw before his captivity, and which had been burned by the Chaldeans *fourteen* years before this vision. On comparing the Books of Kings and Chronicles with this prophet, we shall find the same dimensions in the parts described by both; for instance, the temple, or place which comprehended the sanctuary, the holy place, and the vestibule or porch before the temple, is found to measure equally the same both in Ezekiel and the Kings. Compare 1 Kings vi. 3-16, with chap. xli. 2, &c. The inside ornaments of the temple are entirely the same; in both we see two courts; an inner one for the priests, and an outer one for the people. Compare 1 Kings vi. 29-36; 2 Chron. iv. 9; and Ezek. xli. 16, 17, and xlviii. 7-10. So that there is room to suppose that, in all the rest, the temple of Ezekiel resembled the old one; and that God's design in retracing these ideas in the prophet's memory was to preserve the remembrance of the plan, the dimensions, the ornaments, and whole structure of this Divine edifice; and that at the return from captivity the people might more easily repair it, agreeably to this model. The prophet's applying himself to describe this edifice was a motive of hope to the Jews of seeing themselves one day delivered from captivity, the temple rebuilt, and their nation restored to its ancient inheritance. Ezekiel touches very slightly upon the description of the temple or house of the Lord, which comprehended the holy place or sanctuary, and which are so exactly described in the Books of Kings. He dwells more largely upon the gates, the galleries, and apartments, of the temple, concerning which the history of the kings had not spoken, or only just taken notice of by the way.

This is the judgment of *Calmet;* and although every Biblical critic is of the same opinion, yet more labour is spent on *rebuilding* this temple of *Ezekiel* than was spent on that built by Solomon! The Jesuits, *Prada* and *Villalpand,* have given *three* folio volumes on this temple, with abundance of cuts, where the different parts are exhibited after the finest models of *Grecian* and *Roman* architecture! But still the building is incomplete. Now, of what consequence is all this to the Christian, or to any other reader? I confess I see not. While, then, we have the exact dimensions and accurate description in 1 Kings and 2 Chronicles, of that built by Solomon, in imitation of which this *plan by Ezekiel* was drawn, we need not be very solicitous about the *manner of measuring* and *describing* used by the prophet; as, when we have laboured through the whole, we have only the measurements and description of that built by Solomon, and delineated by a hand not less faithful in the First Book of Kings, chap. vi., and 2 Chron. ii., iii., iv., v. and vi.

As the prophet knew that the Chaldeans had utterly destroyed the temple, he thought it necessary to preserve an *exact description* of it, that on their restoration the people might build one on the same model. As to *allegorical meanings* relative to this temple, I can say nothing: God has given no *data* by which any thing of this kind can be known or applied; and as to those who have laboured in this way, perhaps "Solomon's Temple Spiritualized, by *John Bunyan,*" is equally good with their well-intended inventions. Those who wish to enter much into the particulars of this temple must have recourse to the more voluminous expositors, who

A. M. 3430
B. C. 574
Olymp. LI. 3
Anno
Servii Tullii,
R. Roman., 5

2 [c]In the visions of God
brought he me into the land
of Israel, [d]and set me upon
a very high mountain, [e]by
which *was* as the frame of a city on the
south.
3 And he brought me thither, and, behold,
there was a man, whose appearance *was* [f]like
the appearance of brass, [g]with a line of flax
in his hand, [h]and a measuring reed; and he
stood in the gate.
4 And the man said unto me, [i]Son of man,
behold with thine eyes, and hear with thine
ears, and set thine heart upon all that I shall
show thee; for to the intent that I might
show *them* unto thee *art* thou brought
hither: [k]declare all that thou seest to the
house of Israel.
5 And behold [l]a wall on the outside of the
house round about, and in the man's hand a
measuring reed of six cubits *long* by the
cubit and a hand breadth: so he measured
the breadth of the building, one reed; and
the height, one reed.
6 Then came he unto the gate [m]which looketh toward the east, and went up the stairs
thereof, and measured the threshold of the
gate, *which was* one reed broad; and the
other threshold *of the gate, which was* one
reed broad.
7 And *every* little chamber *was* one reed
long, and one reed broad; and between the
little chambers *were* five cubits;
and the threshold of the gate by
the porch of the gate within
was one reed.
8 He measured also the porch of the gate
within, one reed.
9 Then measured he the porch of the gate,
eight cubits: and the posts thereof, two
cubits; and the porch of the gate *was* inward.
10 And the little chambers of the gate eastward *were* three on this side, and three on
that side; they three *were* of one measure:
and the posts had one measure on this side
and on that side.
11 And he measured the breadth of the
entry of the gate, ten cubits; *and* the length
of the gate, thirteen cubits.
12 The [n]space also before the little chambers *was* one cubit *on this side,* and the space
was one cubit on that side: and the little
chambers *were* six cubits on this side, and six
cubits on that side.
13 He measured then the gate from the
roof of *one* little chamber to the roof of another: the breadth *was* five and twenty
cubits, door against door,
14 He made also posts of threescore cubits,
even unto the posts of the court round about
the gate.
15 And from the face of the gate of the
entrance unto the face of the porch of the
inner gate *were* fifty cubits.

[c]Chap. viii.——[d]Rev. xxi. 10——[e]Or, *upon which*
[f]Chap. i. 7; Dan. x. 6——[g]Chap. xlvii. 3——[h]Rev.
xi. 1; xxi. 15

[i]Chap. xliv. 5——[k]Chap. xliii. 10——[l]Chap. xlii. 20
[m]Heb. *whose face was the way toward the east*——[n]Heb.
limit, or *bound*

on this subject seem to have thought that they could never say enough. See also the accompanying *map.*

Verse 2. *Set me upon a very high mountain*] Mount *Moriah,* the mount on which Solomon's temple was built, 2 Chron. iii. 1.

Verse 3. *A man, whose appearance* was *like—brass*] Like *bright polished brass,* which strongly reflected the rays of light. Probably he had what we would term a *nimbus* or *glory* round his head. This was either an *angel;* or, as some think, a personal appearance of our blessed Lord.

Verse 4. *Declare all that thou seest to the house of Israel*] That they may know how to build the second temple, when they shall be restored from their captivity.

Verse 5. *A measuring reed of six cubits* long] The Hebrew cubit is supposed to be about *twenty and a half* inches; and a palm, about *three* inches more; the length of the rod about *ten* feet *six* inches.

The breadth—one reed; and the height, one reed.] As this *wall* was as *broad* as it was *high,* it must have been a kind of *parapet,* which was carried, of the same dimensions, all round the temple. See AAAA in the plan.

Verse 6. *Went up the stairs thereof*] As the temple was built upon an eminence, there must have been steps on the outside, opposite to each door, to ascend by. And it appears there were *steps* to go up from *one court* to *another,* see ver. 22, 26, 34, 37; and also from the *court of the priests* to the *sanctuary,* ver. 49. See MMMMM in the plan.

Verse 7. *And* every *little chamber* was *one reed*] These were the chambers of the buildings which were within the inclosure of the temple round the court, and these chambers appear to have been numerous. See the map, which has been carefully copied from that of *Calmet.*

Verse 9. *The porch of the gate*] See account of the *gates* in the plan.

Verse 15. *Fifty cubits.*] The length of the building. See MMMMM in the plan.

A. M. 3430 B. C. 574 Olymp. LI. 3 Anno Servii Tullii, R. Roman., 5

16 And *there were* [o]narrow[p]
windows to the little chambers,
and to their posts within the gate
round about, and likewise to the
[q]arches: and windows *were* round about [r]inward: and upon *each* post *were* palm trees.

17 Then brought he me into [s]the outward court, and, lo, *there were* [t]chambers, and a pavement made for the court round about: [u]thirty chambers *were* upon the pavement.

18 And the pavement by the side of the gates over against the length of the gates *was* the lower pavement.

19 Then he measured the breadth from the forefront of the lower gate unto the forefront of the inner court [v]without, a hundred cubits eastward and northward.

20 And the gate of the outward court [w]that looked toward the north, he measured the length thereof, and the breadth thereof.

21 And the little chambers thereof *were* three on this side, and three on that side; and the posts thereof and the [x]arches thereof were after the measure of the first gate: the length thereof *was* fifty cubits, and the breadth five and twenty cubits.

22 And their windows, and their arches, and their palm trees, *were* after the measure of the gate that looketh toward the east: and they went up unto it by seven steps; and the arches thereof *were* before them.

23 And the gate of the inner court *was* over against the gate toward the north, and toward the east; and he measured from gate to gate a hundred cubits.

24 After that he brought me toward the south, and behold a gate toward the south: and he measured the posts thereof and the arches thereof according to these measures.

25 And *there were* windows in it and in the arches thereof round about, like those windows: the length *was* fifty cubits, and the breadth five and twenty cubits.

A. M. 3430 B. C. 574 Olymp. LI. 3 Anno Servii Tullii, R. Roman., 5

26 And *there were* seven steps to go up to it, and the arches thereof *were* before them: and it had palm trees, one on this side, and another on that side, upon the posts thereof.

27 And *there was* a gate in the inner court toward the south: and he measured from gate to gate toward the south a hundred cubits.

28 And he brought me to the inner court by the south gate: and he measured the south gate according to these measures;

29 And the little chambers thereof, and the posts thereof, and the arches thereof, according to these measures: and *there were* windows in it, and in the arches thereof round about: *it was* fifty cubits long, and five and twenty cubits broad.

30 And the arches round about *were* [y]five and twenty cubits long, and five cubits [z]broad.

31 And the arches thereof *were* toward the utter court; and palm trees *were* upon the posts thereof: and the going up to it *had* eight steps.

32 And he brought me into the inner court toward the east: and he measured the gate according to these measures.

33 And the little chambers thereof, and the posts thereof, and the arches thereof, *were* according to these measures: and *there were* windows therein and in the arches thereof round about: *it was* fifty cubits long, and five and twenty cubits broad.

34 And the arches thereof *were* toward the outward court; and palm trees *were* upon the posts thereof, on this side, and on that side: and the going up to it *had* eight steps.

35 And he brought me to the north gate, and measured *it* according to these measures;

[o]1 Kings vi. 4——[p]Heb. *closed*——[q]Or, *galleries*, or *porches*——[r]Or, *within*——[s]Rev. xi. 2——[t]1 Kings vi. 5 [u]Chap. xlv. 5

[v]Or, *from without*——[w]Heb. *whose face* was——[x]Or, *galleries*, or *porches*——[y]See verses 21, 25, 33, 36 [z]Hebrew, *breadth*

Verse 17. *The outward court*] This was the court of the people.

Verse 21. *And the little chambers thereof* were *three, &c.*] See the plan.

Arches] Porch. The arch was not known at this period.

Verse 24. *According to these measures.*] The same measures that had been used at the eastern court.

Verse 30. *And the arches round about* were *five and twenty cubits long*] That the *five cubits broad* should be *read twenty-five* is evident from verses 21, 25, 29, 33, and 36. The word ועשרים *veesrim, twenty,* has probably been lost out of the text. Indeed the whole verse is wanting in *two* of *Kennicott's* MSS., *one* of *De Rossi's*, and *one* of mine, (Cod. B.) It has been added in the margin of mine by a later hand. It is reported to have been anciently wanting in many MSS.

A. M. 3430
B. C. 574
Olymp. LI. 3
Anno
Servii Tullii,
R. Roman., 5

36 The little chambers thereof, the posts thereof, and the arches thereof, and the windows to it round about: the length *was* fifty cubits, and the breadth five and twenty cubits.

37 And the posts thereof *were* toward the utter court; and palm trees *were* upon the posts thereof, on this side, and on that side: and the going up to it *had* eight steps.

38 And the chambers and the entries thereof *were* by the posts of the gates, where they washed the burnt-offering.

39 And in the porch of the gate *were* two tables on this side, and two tables on that side, to slay thereon the burnt-offering and [a]the sin-offering and [b]the trespass-offering.

40 And at the side without, [c]as one goeth up to the entry of the north gate, *were* two tables; and on the other side, which *was* at the porch of the gate, *were* two tables.

41 Four tables *were* on this side, and four tables on that side, by the side of the gate; eight tables, whereupon they slew *their sacrifices.*

42 And the four tables *were* of hewn stone for the burnt-offering, of a cubit and a half long, and a cubit and a half broad, and one cubit high: whereupon also they laid the instruments wherewith they slew the burnt-offering and the sacrifice.

43 And within *were* [d]hooks, a hand broad, fastened round about: and upon the tables *was* the flesh of the offering.

44 And without the inner gate *were* the chambers of [e]the singers in the inner court, which *was* at the side of the north gate; and their prospect *was* toward the south: one at the side of the east gate *having* the prospect toward the north.

45 And he said unto me, This chamber, whose prospect *is* toward the south, *is* for the priests, [f]the keepers of the [g]charge of the house.

46 And the chamber whose prospect *is* toward the north *is* for the priests, [h]the keepers of the charge of the altar: these *are* the sons of [i]Zadok among the sons of Levi, which come near to the LORD to minister unto him.

47 So he measured the court, a hundred cubits long, and a hundred cubits broad, foursquare; and the altar *that was* before the house.

48 And he brought me to the porch of the house, and measured *each* post of the porch, five cubits on this side, and five cubits on that side: and the breadth of the gate *was* three cubits on this side, and three cubits on that side.

49 [k]The length of the porch *was* twenty cubits, and the breadth eleven cubits; and *he brought me* by the steps whereby they went up to it: and *there were* [l]pillars by the posts, one on this side, and another on that side.

[a]Lev. iv. 2, 3——[b]Lev. v. 6; vi. 6; vii. 1——[c]Or, *at the step*——[d]Or, *endirons,* or *the two hearthstones* [e]1 Chron. vi. 31——[f]Lev. viii. 35; Num. iii. 27, 28, 32, 38; xviii. 5; 1 Chron. ix. 23; 2 Chron. xiii. 11; Psa. cxxxiv. 1——[g]Or, *ward,* or *ordinance;* and so ver. 46——[h]Num. xviii. 5; chap. xliv. 15——[i]1 Kings ii. 35; chap. xliii. 19; xliv. 15, 16——[k]1 Kings vi. 3 [l]1 Kings vii. 21

Verse 39. *The porch of the gate*] The north gate of the court of the priests. See Q in the plan.

Two tables] Some say of *marble.* See *dddd* in the plan.

Verse 41. *Four tables*] These were in the porch of the north gate, in the court of the priests: on them they slew, flayed, and cut up the victims. See *dddd* in the plan.

Verse 47. *He measured the court*] This was the court of the priests. See FFF in the plan.

Verse 48. *Breadth of the gate*] It is evident that the gate was a bivalve, or had folding doors. The length of the porch was *twenty* cubits. *Josephus* says the vestibule was *twenty* cubits long and *ten* broad. Antiq. lib. viii. 3, 2.

Verse 49. *By the steps*] This was a flight of steps that led to the temple; there were *eight* steps in each flight. See YY in the plan.

CHAPTER XLI

In this chapter the prophet gives us a circumstantial account of the measures, parts, chambers, and ornaments of the temple, 1–26.

A. M. 3430
B. C. 574
Olymp. LI. 3
Anno
Servii Tullii,
R. Roman., 5

AFTERWARD he brought
me to the temple, and
measured the posts, six cubits
broad on the one side, and six
cubits broad on the other side, *which was* the
breadth of the tabernacle.
2 And the breadth of the [a]door *was* ten
cubits; and the sides of the door *were* five
cubits on the one side, and five cubits on the
other side: and he measured the length
thereof, forty cubits: and the breadth,
[b]twenty cubits.
3 Then went he inward, and measured the
post of the door, two cubits; and the door six
cubits; and the breadth of the door, seven
cubits.
4 So [c]he measured the length thereof,
twenty cubits; and the breadth, twenty
cubits, before the temple: and he said unto
me, This *is* the most holy *place.*
5 After he measured the wall of the house,
six cubits; and the breadth of *every* side
chamber, four cubits, round about the house
on every side.
6 [d]And the side chambers *were* three, [e]one
over another, and [f]thirty in order; and they
entered into the wall which *was* of the house
for the side chambers round about, that they
might [g]have hold, but they had not hold in
the wall of the house.

[a]Or, *entrance*——[b]1 Kings vi. 2——[c]1 Kings vi. 20; 2 Chron. iii. 8——[d]1 Kings vi. 5, 6——[e]Heb. *side chamber over side chamber*

A. M. 3430
B. C. 574
Olymp. LI. 3
Anno
Servii Tullii,
R. Roman., 5

7 And [h]*there* [i]*was* an enlarging, and a winding about still
upward to the side chambers:
for the winding about of the
house went still upward round about the
house: therefore the breadth of the house *was*
still upward, and so increased *from* the lowest *chamber* to the highest by the midst.
8. I saw also the height of the house round
about: the foundations of the side chambers
were [k]a full reed of six great cubits.
9 The thickness of the wall, which *was* for
the side chamber without, *was* five cubits:
and *that* which *was* left *was* the place of the
side chambers that *were* within.
10 And between the chambers *was* the
wideness of twenty cubits round about the
house on every side.
11 And the doors of the side chambers
were toward *the place that was* left, one door
toward the north, and another door toward
the south: and the breadth of the place that
was left *was* five cubits round about.
12 Now the building that *was* before the
separate place at the end toward the west
was seventy cubits broad; and the wall of the
building *was* five cubits thick round about,
and the length thereof ninety cubits.
13 So he measured the house, a hundred
cubits long: and the separate place, and the

[f]Or, *three and thirty times*, or *foot*——[g]Heb. *be holden*——[h]Heb. it was *made broader, and went round* [i]1 Kings vi. 8——[k]Chap. xl. 5

NOTES ON CHAP. XLI

Verse 1. *To the temple*] He had first described the courts and the porch. See chap. xl.

Verse 2. *The breadth of the door*] This was the door, or gate, of the sanctuary, (see *gates*, 3, in the plan,) and this *doorway* was filled up with folding gates. The measurements are exactly the same as those of Solomon's temple. See 1 Kings vi. 2, 17.

Verse 4. *The length thereof, twenty cubits*] This is the measurement of the sanctuary, or holy of holies. See G in the plan. This also was the exact measurement of Solomon's temple, see 1 Kings vi. 20. This, and the other resemblances here, sufficiently prove that Ezekiel's temple and that of Solomon were on the same plan; and that the latter temple was intended to be an exact resemblance of the former.

Verse 6. *The side chambers* were *three*] We find by *Joseph*. Antiq. viii. 3, 2, that round Solomon's temple were chambers *three* stories high, each story consisting of *thirty* chambers. It is supposed that *twelve* were placed to the *north* of the temple, *twelve* to the *south*, and *six* to the *east*.

Entered into the wall] The beams were admitted into the outer wall, but they rested on projections of the inner wall.

Verse 7. *An enlarging, and a winding about*] Perhaps a winding staircase that widened upward as the inner wall decreased in thickness; this wall being six cubits thick as high as the first story, five from the floor of the second story to that of the third, and four from the floor to the ceiling of the third story: and thus there was a rest of one cubit in breadth to support the stories.—*Newcome.*

Verse 9. *The thickness of the wall*] See LLL in the plan.

The place of the side chambers] A walk, or gallery of communication along the chambers, *five* cubits broad, ver. 11.

Verse 11. *And the doors*] See the plan, *aa. bb.*

Verse 12. *The length thereof ninety cubits.*] The temple, with the buildings which surrounded it, was *eighty-one* cubits long; add *ten* cubits for the vestibule, or *five* for the breadth of the separate place, and five for its wall; in all, *ninety* cubits. See the plan, LHIL. By the *separate place* I suppose the temple itself is meant.

Verse 13. *So he measured the house*] The

A. M. 3430
B. C. 574
Olymp. LI. 3
Anno
Servii Tullii,
R. Roman., 5

building, with the walls thereof,
a hundred cubits long;
14 Also the breadth of the face
of the house, and of the separate
place toward the east, a hundred cubits.
15 And he measured the length of the
building over against the separate place
which *was* behind it, and the [l]galleries thereof on the one side and on the other side, a
hundred cubits, with the inner temple, and
the porches of the court;
16 The door posts, and [m]the narrow window, and the galleries round about on their
three stories, over against the door, [n]ceiled
with wood round about, [o]and from the ground
up to the windows, and the windows *were*
covered;
17 To that above the door, even unto the
inner house, and without, and by all the wall
round about within and without, by [p]measure.
18 And *it was* made [q]with cherubims and
palm trees, so that a palm tree *was* between a
cherub and a cherub; and *every* cherub had
two faces;
19 [r]So that the face of a man *was* toward
the palm tree on the one side, and the face
of a young lion toward the palm tree on the
other side: *it was* made through all the house
round about.
20 From the ground unto
above the door *were* cherubims
and palm trees made, and *on*
the wall of the temple.
21 The [s]posts of the temple *were* squared
and the face of the sanctuary; the appearance *of the one* as the appearance *of the*
other.
22 [t]The altar of wood *was* three cubits
high, and the length thereof two cubits; and
the corners thereof, and the length thereof,
and the walls thereof, *were* of wood: and he
said unto me, This *is* [u]the table that *is* [v]be-
fore the LORD.
23 [w]And the temple and the sanctuary had
two doors.
24 And the doors had two leaves *apiece,*
two turning leaves; two *leaves* for the one
door, and two leaves for the other *door.*
25 And *there were* made on them, on the
doors of the temple, cherubims and palm
trees, like as *were* made upon the walls; and
there were thick planks upon the face of the
porch without.
26 And *there were* [x]narrow windows and
palm trees on the one side and on the other
side, on the sides of the porch, and *upon*
the side chambers of the house, and thick
planks.

[l]Or, *several walks,* or, *walks with pillars*——[m]Chap. xl. 16; ver. 26——[n]Heb. *ceiling of wood*——[o]Or, *and the ground unto the windows*——[p]Heb. *measures*

[q]1 Kings vi. 29——[r]See chap. i. 10——[s]Heb. *post*
[t]Exod. xxx. 1——[u]Ch. xliv. 16; Mal. i. 7, 12——[v]Exod. xxx. 8——[w]1 Kings vi. 31-35——[x]Ch. xl. 16; ver. 16

temple, taken from the wall which encompassed it from the western side to the vestibule, was *one hundred and one* cubits; *five* for the separate place, *nine* for the wall and the chambers attached to the temple, *sixty* for the sanctuary and the holy place, *ten* for the vestibule, and *twelve* for the two great walls on the west and east of the temple; in all, *one hundred and one cubits.* See the plan, GHI.

Verse 14. *The breadth of the face of the house*] That is, the front. See the plan, FRR.

Verse 18. *A palm tree* was *between a cherub and a cherub*] That is, the palm trees and the cherubs were alternated; and each cherub had two faces, one of a *lion,* and the other of a *man;* one of which was turned to the palm tree on the right, the other to the palm tree on the left.

Verse 20. *From the ground unto above the door*] The temple was *thirty* cubits high, 1 Kings vi. 2, the gate was *fourteen* cubits, chap. xl. 48. The *palm trees* and the *cherubim* were the same height as the *gate* or *door.* The windows were above the door.

Verse 22. *The altar of wood*] This was the altar of incense, and was covered with plates of gold.

Verse 25. There were *thick planks*] The wood, or planks, were thick and strong; for the cherubim and palm trees were carved in *relief,* out of their substance, and unless they had been of considerable thickness, this could not have been done.

CHAPTER XLII

This chapter gives us a description of the priests' chambers and their use, with the dimensions of the holy mount on which the temple stood, 1-20.

A. M. 3430 B. C. 574 Olymp. LI. 3 Anno Servii Tullii, R. Roman., 5

THEN he brought me forth into the utter court, the way toward the north: and he brought me into [a]the chamber that *was* over against the [b]separate place, and which *was* before the building toward the north.

2 Before the length of a hundred cubits *was* the north door, and the breadth *was* fifty cubits.

3 Over against the twenty *cubits* which *were* for the inner court, and over against the pavement which *was* for the utter court, *was* [c]gallery against gallery in three *stories.*

4 And before the chambers *was* a walk of ten cubits' breadth inward, a way of one cubit; and their doors toward the north.

5 Now the upper chambers *were* shorter: for the galleries [d]were higher than these, [e]than the lower, and than the middlemost of the building.

6 For they *were* in three *stories,* but had not pillars as the pillars of the courts: therefore *the building* was straitened more than the lowest and the middlemost from the ground.

7 And the wall that *was* without over against the chambers, toward the utter court on the forepart of the chambers, the length thereof *was* fifty cubits.

8 For the length of the chambers that *were* in the utter court *was* fifty cubits: and, lo, before the temple *were* a hundred cubits.

9 And [f]from under these chambers *was* [g]the entry on the east side, [h]as one goeth into them from the utter court.

10 The chambers *were* in the thickness of the wall of the court toward the east, over against the separate place, and over against the building.

11 And [i]the way before them *was* like the appearance of the chambers which *were* toward the north, as long as they, *and* as broad as they: and all their goings out *were* both according to their fashions, and according to their doors.

A. M. 3430 B. C. 574 Olymp. LI. 3 Anno Servii Tullii, R. Roman., 5

12 And according to the doors of the chambers that *were* toward the south *was* a door in the head of the way *even* the way directly before the wall toward the east, as one entereth into them.

13 Then said he unto me, The north chambers *and* the south chambers, which *are* before the separate place, they *be* holy chambers, where the priests that approach unto the LORD [k]shall eat the most holy things: there shall they lay the most holy things, and [l]the meat-offering, and the sin-offering, and the trespass-offering; for the place *is* holy.

14 [m]When the priests enter therein, then shall they not go out of the holy *place* into the utter court, but there they shall lay their garments wherein they minister; for they *are* holy; and shall put on other garments, and shall approach to *those things* which *are* for the people.

15 Now when he had made an end of measuring the inner house, he brought me forth toward the gate whose prospect *is* toward the east, and measured it round about.

16 He measured the east [n]side with the measuring reed, five hundred reeds, with the measuring reed round about.

17 He measured the north side, five hundred reeds, with the measuring reed round about.

18 He measured the south side five hundred reeds, with the measuring reed.

19 He turned about to the west side, *and* measured five hundred reeds, with the measuring reed.

20 He measured it by the four sides: [o]it had a wall round about, [p]five hundred *reeds* long, and five hundred broad, to make a separation between the sanctuary and the profane place.

[a]Chap. xli. 12, 15——[b]Chap. xli. 12, 13, 14; xlii. 10, 13——[c]Chap. xli. 16——[d]Or, *did eat of these*——[e]Or, and *the building* consisted *of the lower and the middlemost*——[f]Or, *from the place*——[g]Or, *he that brought me* [h]Or, *as he came*——[i]Ver. 4——[k]Lev. vi. 16, 26; xxiv. 9——[l]Lev. ii. 3, 10; vi. 14, 17, 25, 29; vii. 1; x. 13, 14; Num. xviii. 9, 10——[m]Chap. xliv. 19——[n]Heb. *wind*——[o]Chap. xl. 5——[p]Chap. xlv. 2

NOTES ON CHAP. XLII

Verse 1. *He brought me forth into the utter court*] He brought him out from the temple into the *court of the priests.* This, in reference to the temple, was called the *outer court;* but the *court of the people* was beyond this.

Verse 4. *A walk of ten cubits' breadth inward*] This seems to have been a sort of *parapet.*

Verse 14. *They shall lay their garments wherein they minister*] The priests were not permitted to wear their *robes* in the *outer court.* These vestments were to be used *only when they ministered;* and when they had done, they were to deposit them in one of the chambers mentioned in the *thirteenth* verse.

Verses 16-19. *He measured the east—north—south—west side*] Each of which was *five hundred* reeds: and, as the building was square, the *area* must have been nearly *thirteen thousand* paces. No wonder this was called a city. See chap. xl. 2.

Verse 20. *It had a wall round about—to make a separation between the sanctuary and the profane place.*] The *holy place* was that which was consecrated to the Lord; into which no heathen, nor stranger, nor any in a state of impurity, might enter. The *profane place* was that in which men, women, Gentiles, pure or impure, might be admitted. *Josephus* says *War*, lib. vi., c. 14, that in his time there was a wall built before the entrance *three* cubits high, on which there were posts fixed at certain distances, with inscriptions on them in *Latin* and *Greek*, containing the laws which enjoined *purity* on those that entered; and forbidding all strangers to enter, on pain of death. See *Calmet*.

CHAPTER XLIII

The glory of the Lord is represented as returning to the temple, 1–6; *where God promises to fix his residence, if the people repent and forsake those sins which caused him to depart from them,* 7–12. *Then the measures of the altar, and the ordinances relating to it, are set down,* 13–27.

A. M. 3430
B. C. 574
Olymp. LI. 3
Anno
Servii Tullii,
R. Roman., 5

AFTERWARD he brought me
to the gate, *even* the gate
[a]that looketh toward the east:
2 [b]And behold, the glory of the
God of Israel came from the way of the east:
and [c]his voice *was* like a noise of many
waters: [d]and the earth shined with his glory.
3 And *it was* [e]according to the appearance
of the vision which I saw, *even* according to
the vision that I saw [f]when I came [g]to destroy the city: and the visions *were* like the
vision that I saw [h]by the river Chebar; and
I fell upon my face.
4 [i]And the glory of the LORD came into the
house by the way of the gate
whose prospect *is* toward the east.
5 [k]So the spirit took me up,
and brought me into the inner
court; and, behold, [l]the glory of the LORD
filled the house.
6 And I heard *him* speaking unto me out
of the house; and [m]the man stood by me.
7 And he said unto me, Son of man, [n]the
place of my throne, and [o]the place of the soles
of my feet, [p]where I will dwell in the midst
of the children of Israel for ever, and my
holy name shall the house of Israel [q]no more
defile, *neither* they, nor their kings, by their

A. M. 3430
B. C. 574
Olymp. LI. 3
Anno
Servii Tullii,
R. Roman., 5

[a]Chap. x. 19; xliv. 1; xlvi. 1——[b]Chap. xi. 23——[c]Chap. i. 24; Rev. i. 15; xiv. 2; xix. 1, 6——[d]Chap. x. 4; Rev. xviii. 1——[e]Chap. i. 4, 28; viii. 4——[f]Or, *when I came to* prophesy *that the city should be destroyed;* see ch. ix. 1 5——[g]So Jer. i. 10——[h]Chap. i. 3; iii. 23

[i]See chap. x. 19; xliv. 2——[k]Chap. iii. 12, 14; viii. 3——[l]1 Kings viii. 10, 11; chap. xliv. 4——[m]Chap. xl. 3——[n]Psa. xcix. 1——[o]1 Chron. xxviii. 2; Psa. xcix. 5——[p]Exod. xxix. 45; Psa. lxviii. 16; cxxxii. 14; Joel iii. 17; John i. 14; 2 Cor. vi. 16——[q]Chap. xxxix. 7

NOTES ON CHAP. XLIII

Verse 2. *The glory of the God of Israel came from the way of the east*] This was the *chariot of cherubim, wheels,* &c., which he saw at the river Chebar. And this glory, coming from the east, is going to enter into the *eastern gate* of the temple, and thence to shine out upon the whole earth. Is there not a *mystery* here? All knowledge, all religion, and all arts and sciences, have travelled, according to the *course of the sun,* FROM EAST TO WEST! From that quarter the Divine glory at first came; and thence the rays of Divine light continue to diffuse themselves over the face of the earth. From thence came the *Bible*, and through that the *new covenant*. From thence came the *prophets*, the *apostles*, and the *first missionaries*, that brought the knowledge of God to *Europe*, to the *isles of the sea*, and to the *west first*, and afterwards to these *northern regions*.

Verse 5. *The spirit took me up*] And, to follow this thought for a moment, how many men has this heavenly *Spirit taken up;* filled them with his own *influence*, and sent them to every country, and nation, and tongue, and people, to testify the Gospel of the grace of God, and to preach among the Gentiles the unsearchable riches of Christ! What spiritual *temples* have been raised, beautified, and filled with the *glory of God!* And this light is shining and burning more and more unto the perfect day, when the whole earth shall be filled with the glory of God!

Verse 7. *Son of man, the place of my throne*] The *throne* refers to his *majesty;* the *soles of his feet*, to his *condescension* in *dwelling among men.*

Where I will dwell in the midst of the children of Israel] The *tabernacle* and *temple* were types of the *incarnation* of *Jesus Christ:* "Destroy THIS TEMPLE, and after three days I will raise it up;—but this he spake of the temple of his body;" John ii. 19, 21. And in THAT TEMPLE "dwelt all the fulness of the Godhead bodily." Into this *immaculate humanity* did the *glory* of the Supreme God enter; and thus, "God was in Christ reconciling the world unto himself." And this Jesus is *Immanuel*, GOD *with* US. In him we find united the *ineffable majesty* of God, with the *abjectness of man.* He humbled himself in human nature, not only to bear the *form of a servant*, but to *suffer death upon the cross* as a malefactor *slave!* But by these means he has purchased *eternal redemption* for us; and the *spiritual Israel*, who find redemption in his blood, shall be raised up wherever his *holy name* shall be proclaimed; and shall not, like the old apostate Israel, *defile* that *great name* by idolatry or a life of wickedness, but

A. M. 3430
B. C. 574
Olymp. LI. 3
Anno
Servii Tullii,
R. Roman., 5

whoredom, nor by the [r]carcasses of their kings in their high places.

8 [s]In their setting of their threshold by my thresholds, and their posts by my posts, [t]and the wall between me and them, they have even defiled my holy name by their abominations that they have committed: wherefore I have consumed them in mine anger.

9 Now let them put away their whoredom, and [u]the carcasses of their kings, far from me, [v]and I will dwell in the midst of them for ever.

10 Thou son of man, [w]show the house to the house of Israel, that they may be ashamed of their iniquities: and let them measure the [x]pattern.

11 And if they be ashamed of all that they have done, show them the form of the house, and the fashion thereof, and the goings out thereof, and the comings in thereof, and all the forms thereof, and all the ordinances thereof, and all the forms thereof, and all the laws thereof: and write *it* in their sight, that they may keep the whole form thereof, and all the ordinances thereof, and do them.

A. M. 3430
B. C. 574
Olymp. LI. 3
Anno
Servii Tullii,
R. Roman., 5

12 This *is* the law of the house; Upon [y]the top of the mountain the whole limit thereof round about *shall be* most holy. Behold, this *is* the law of the house.

13 And these *are* the measures of the altar after the cubits: [z]The cubit *is* a cubit and a hand breadth; even the [a]bottom *shall be* a cubit, and the breadth a cubit, and the border thereof by the [b]edge thereof round about *shall be* a span: and this *shall be* the higher place of the altar.

14 And from the bottom *upon* the ground *even* to the lower settle *shall be* two cubits, and the breadth one cubit; and from the lesser settle *even* to the greater settle *shall be* four cubits, and the breadth *one* cubit.

15 So [c]the altar *shall be* four cubits; and from [d]the altar and upward *shall be* four horns.

16 And the altar *shall be* twelve *cubits* long, twelve broad, square in the four squares thereof.

17 And the settle *shall be* fourteen *cubits*

[r]Lev. xxvi. 30; Jer. xvi. 18——[s]See 2 Kings xvi. 14; xxi. 4, 5, 7; chap. viii. 3; xxiii. 39; xliv. 7——[t]Or, *for there was but a wall between me and them*——[u]Ver. 7——[v]Ver. 7——[w]Chap. xl. 4

[x]Or, *sum*, or *number*——[y]Chap. xl. 2——[z]Chap. xl. 5; xli. 8——[a]Heb. *bosom*——[b]Heb. *lip*——[c]Heb. *Harel*, that is, *the mountain of God*——[d]Heb. *Ariel*, that is, *the lion of God;* Isa. xxix. 1

they shall show forth the virtues of Him who has called them from darkness into his marvellous light.

Verse 8. *In their setting of their threshold*] They had even gone so far as to set up their idol altars by those of Jehovah; so that their abominable idols were found in the very house of God! therefore, "he consumed them in his anger."

Verse 9. *Now let them put away their whoredom*] Their *idolatry.*

And the carcasses of their kings] It appears that God was displeased with their *bringing their kings so near his temple.* David was buried in the *city of David,* which was on *Mount Zion,* near to the temple; and so were almost all the kings of Judah; but God requires that the place of his temple and its vicinity shall be kept unpolluted; and when they *put away* all kinds of defilement, then will he *dwell among them.*

Verse 10. *Show the house to the house of Israel*] Show them this holy house where the holy God dwells, that they may be *ashamed of their iniquities.* Their name, their profession, their temple, their religious services, all bound them to a holy life; all within them, all without them, should have been *holiness unto the Lord.* But alas! they have been bound by no ties, and they have sinned against all their obligations; nevertheless, *let them measure the pattern,* let them see the rule by which they should have walked, and let them measure themselves by this standard, and walk accordingly.

Verse 11. *And if they be ashamed*] If, in a spirit of true repentance, they acknowledge their past transgressions, and purpose in his help never more to offend their God, then teach them every thing that concerns my worship, and their profiting by it.

Verse 12. *This* is *the law of the house*] From the top of the mountain on which it stands, to the bottom, *all round about,* all shall be holy; no buildings shall be erected in any part, nor place nor spot be appropriated to a common use; all shall be considered as being *most holy.*

Verse 13. *The cubit* is *a cubit and a hand breadth*] It is the same cubit by which all the previous admeasurements were made, and was a hand breadth or *four* inches longer than the Babylonian cubit.

Verse 15. *So the altar*] ההראל *haharel,* "the mount of God."

And from the altar] ומהאריאל *umihaariel,* "and from the lion of God." Perhaps the first was a name given to the *altar* when *elevated* to the honour of God, and on which the victims were offered to him; and the second, the *lion of God,* may mean the *hearth,* which might have been thus called, because it *devoured* and consumed the burnt-offerings, as a lion does his prey. See on Isa. xxix. 1.

Verse 17. *And the settle*] The *ledge* on

A. M. 3430
B. C. 574
Olymp. LI. 3
Anno
Servii Tullii,
R. Roman., 5

long and fourteen broad in the
four squares thereof; and the
border about it *shall be* half a
cubit; and the bottom thereof
shall be a cubit about; and [e]his stairs shall
look toward the east.
18 And he said unto me, Son of man, thus
saith the Lord GOD; These *are* the ordinances of the altar in the day when they
shall make it, to offer burnt-offerings thereon, and to [f]sprinkle blood thereon.
19 And thou shalt give to [g]the priests the
Levites that be of the seed of Zadok, which
approach unto me, to minister unto me, saith
the Lord GOD, [h]a young bullock for a sin-
offering.
20 And thou shalt take of the blood thereof,
and put *it* on the four horns of it, and on
the four corners of the settle, and upon the
border round about: thus shalt thou cleanse
and purge it.
21 Thou shalt take the bullock also of the
sin-offering, and he [i]shall burn it in the appointed place of the house, [k]without the sanctuary.
22 And on the second day thou
shalt offer a kid of the goats
without blemish for a sin-offering; and they shall cleanse the
altar, as they did cleanse *it* with the bullock.
23 When thou hast made an end of cleansing *it,* thou shalt offer a young bullock without blemish, and a ram out of the flock without blemish.
24 And thou shalt offer them before the
LORD, [l]and the priests shall cast salt upon
them, and they shall offer them up *for* a
burnt-offering unto the LORD.
25 [m]Seven days shalt thou prepare every
day a goat *for* a sin-offering: they shall also
prepare a young bullock, and a ram out of
the flock, without blemish.
26 Seven days shall they purge the altar
and purify it; and they shall [n]consecrate
themselves.
27 And when these days are expired, it shall
be, *that* upon the [o]eighth day, and *so* forward,
the priests shall make your burnt-offerings
upon the altar, and your [p]peace-offerings;
and I will [q]accept you, saith the Lord GOD.

A. M. 3430
B. C. 574
Olymp. LI. 3
Anno
Servii Tullii,
R. Roman., 5

---

[e]See Exodus xx. 26——[f]Leviticus i. 5——[g]Chap. xliv. 15——[h]Exodus xxix. 10, 12; Leviticus viii. 14, 15; chap. xlv. 18, 19——[i]Exodus xxix. 14——[k]Hebrew xiii. 11——[l]Leviticus ii. 13——[m]Exodus xxix. 35, 36; Leviticus viii. 33——[n]Hebrew, *fill their hands;* Exodus xxix. 24——[o]Leviticus ix. 1——[p]Or, *thank-offerings*——[q]Job xlii. 8; chapter xx. 40, 41; xliii. 27; Romans xii. 1; 1 Peter ii. 5, 20

---

which the priests walked round the altar, see ver. 14. By these settles or ledges the altar was narrowed towards the top. "The ascent shall look toward the east;" this ascent was an inclined plane. But these *settles,* or more properly *ledges,* as Bp. *Newcome* translates, may be thus computed. The altar itself was *ten* feet high and *twenty* broad; the same as that of Solomon, 2 Chron. iv. 1.

	Cubits
For the base, ver. 13, is in height - - -	1
From the surface of the base to the first ledge, ver. 14, is - - - - - - - -	1
From the lower ledge to the upper, ver. 14, are - - - - - - - - - - - - -	4
From the upper ledge to the ariel or hearth, ver. 15, are - - - - - - - -	4
In all - - -	10

	Cubits
And as to the breadth, the upper ledge, ver. 17, was - - - - - - - - - - -	14
Add a cubit on each side for the higher ledge, ver. 14, latter part - - - - - - - -	2
Add a cubit on each side for the lower ledge, ver. 14, former part - - - - -	2
Add a cubit on each side for the base, ver. 13,	2
In all - - -	20

The altar of burnt-offerings, described Exod. xxvii. 1, xxxviii. 1, was smaller than this, because it was to be removed from place to place with the tabernacle. This was designed for a permanent temple. See Bp. *Newcome* on this chapter.

Verse 19. *The priests—that be of the seed of Zadok*] It was this Zadok that was put in the place of Abiathar, by Solomon, 1 Kings ii. 35, in whose family the priesthood had continued ever since.

Verse 25. *Seven days shalt thou prepare*] These are, in general, ordinances of the LAW: and may be seen by consulting the parallel passages. All these directions are given that they might follow them, when they should be put in possession of their own land. For in several cases the prophet enters into particulars, as if he had supposed that the book of the law had perished.

CHAPTER XLIV

This chapter gives an account of the glory of God having returned to the temple, 1–4. *The Jews reproved for suffering idolatrous priests to pollute it with their ministrations,* 5–8. *Ordinances respecting the conduct of the priests, and the maintenance due to them,* 9–31.

A. M. 3430
B. C. 574
Olymp. LI. 3
Anno
Servii Tullii,
R. Roman., 5

THEN he brought me back
the way of the gate of the
outward sanctuary [a]which looketh toward the east; and it *was*
shut.
2 Then said the LORD unto me; This gate
shall be shut, it shall not be opened, and no
man shall enter in by it; [b]because the LORD,
the GOD of Israel, hath entered in by it,
therefore it shall be shut.
3 *It is* for the prince; the prince, he shall
sit in it to [c]eat bread before the LORD; [d]he
shall enter by the way of the porch of *that*
gate, and shall go out by the way of the
same.
4 Then brought he me the way of the north
gate before the house: and I looked, and,
[e]behold, the glory of the LORD filled the house
of the LORD: [f]and I fell upon my face.
5 And the LORD said unto me, [g]Son of man,
[h]mark well, and behold with thine eyes, and
hear with thine ears all that I say unto thee
concerning all the ordinances of the house of
the LORD, and all the laws thereof; and mark
well the entering in of the house, with every
going forth of the sanctuary.
6 And thou shalt say to the [i]rebellious, *even*
to the house of Israel, Thus saith the Lord
GOD; O ye house of Israel, [k]let
it suffice you of all your abominations.
7 [l]In that ye have brought *into*
my sanctuary [m]strangers,[n] [o]uncircumcised in
heart, and uncircumcised in flesh, to be in
my sanctuary, to pollute it, *even* my house,
when ye offer [p]my bread, [q]the fat and the
blood, and they have broken my covenant because of all your abominations.
8 And ye have not [r]kept the charge of mine
holy things; but ye have set keepers of my
[s]charge in my sanctuary for yourselves.
9 Thus saith the Lord GOD; [t]No stranger,
uncircumcised in heart, nor uncircumcised in
flesh, shall enter into my sanctuary, of any
stranger that *is* among the children of Israel.
10 [u]And the Levites that are gone away
far from me, when Israel went astray, which
went astray away from me after their idols;
they shall even bear their iniquity.
11 Yet they shall be ministers in my sanctuary, [v]*having* charge at the gates of the
house, and ministering to the house: [w]they
shall slay the burnt-offering and the sacrifice
for the people, and [x]they shall stand before
them to minister unto them.
12 Because they ministered unto them before

[a]Chap. xliii. 1——[b]Chap. xliii. 4——[c]Gen. xxxi. 54; 1 Cor. x. 18——[d]Chap. xlvi. 2, 8——[e]Chap. iii. 23; xliii. 5——[f]Chap. i. 28——[g]Chap. xl. 4——[h]Heb. *set thine heart*——[i]Chap. ii. 5——[k]Chap. xlv. 9; 1 Pet. iv. 3 [l]Chap. xliii. 8; ver. 9; Acts xxi. 28——[m]Heb. *children of a stranger*——[n]Lev. xxii. 25

[o]Lev. xxvi. 41; Deut. x. 16; Acts vii.5 1——[p]Lev. xxi. 6, 8, 17, 21——[q]Lev. iii. 16; xvii. 11——[r]Lev. xxii. 2, &c.——[s]Or, *ward*, or *ordinance;* and so ver. 14, 16; chap. xl. 45——[t]Ver. 7——[u]See 2 Kings xxiii. 8, &c.; 2 Chron. xxix. 4, ‘; chap. xlviii. 11——[v]1 Chron. xxvi. 1 [w]2 Chron. xxix. 34; [x]Num. xvi. 9

NOTES ON CHAP. XLIV

Verse 1. *The outward sanctuary*] In opposition to the temple itself, which was the inner sanctuary.

Verse 2. *This gate shall be shut*] It was not to be opened on *ordinary occasions*, nor at all on the *week days:* but only on the *Sabbaths* and the *new moons*. See the account of the *gates* (4) in the explanation of the plan.

This verse has been adduced by the Roman Catholics to prove the *perpetual virginity* of the mother of our Lord; and it may be allowed to be as much to the purpose as any other that has been brought to prove this very precarious point, on which no stress should ever be laid by any man. Mary was a virgin when she brought forth Jesus.

Verse 5. *Mark well, and behold*] Take notice of every thing; register all so fully that thou shalt be able to give the most minute information to the children of Israel.

Verse 7. *The fat and the blood*] These never went into common use; they were wholly offered to God. The *blood* was poured out; the *fat* consumed.

Because of all your abominations.] Several MSS. of *Kennicott's* and *De Rossi's* read *their abominations*, referring to the *strangers* mentioned before.

Verse 10. *And the Levites that are gone away far from me*] This refers to the schism of Jeroboam, who, when he set up a new worship, got as many of the priests and Levites to join him in his idolatry as he could. These, on the return from the captivity, should not be permitted to perform the functions of *priests* in the new temple; but they might be continued as *keepers of all the charge of the house*—be treasurers, guards of the temple, porters, &c.; see

A. M. 3430
B. C. 574
Olymp. LI. 3
Anno
Servii Tullii,
R. Roman., 5

their idols, and [y]caused [z]the house of Israel to fall into iniquity; therefore have I [a]lifted up mine hand against them, saith the Lord GOD, and they shall bear their iniquity.

13 [b]And they shall not come near unto me, to do the office of a priest unto me, nor to come near to any of my holy things, in the most holy *place:* but they shall [c]bear their shame, and their abominations which they have committed.

14 But I will make them [d]keepers of the charge of the house, for all the service thereof, and for all that shall be done therein.

15 [e]But the priests the Levites, [f]the sons of Zadok, that kept the charge of my sanctuary [g]when the children of Israel went astray from me, they shall come near to me to minister unto me, and they [h]shall stand before me to offer unto me [i]the fat and the blood, saith the Lord GOD:

16 They shall enter into my sanctuary, and they shall come near to [k]my table, to minister unto me, and they shall keep my charge.

17 And it shall come to pass, *that* when they enter in at the gates of the inner court, [l]they shall be clothed with linen garments; and no wool shall come upon them, whiles they minister in the gates of the inner court, and within.

18 [m]They shall have linen bonnets upon their heads, and shall have linen breeches upon their loins; they shall not gird *themselves* [n]with [o]any thing that causeth sweat.

19 And when they go forth into the utter court, *even* into the utter court of the people, [p]they shall put off their garments wherein they ministered, and lay them in the holy chambers, and they shall put on other garments; and they shall [q]not sanctify the people with their garments.

A. M. 3430
B. C. 574
Olymp. LI. 3
Anno
Servii Tullii,
R. Roman., 5

20 [r]Neither shall they shave their heads, nor suffer their locks to grow long; they shall only poll their heads.

21 [s]Neither shall any priest drink wine, when they enter into the inner court.

22 Neither shall they take for their wives a [t]widow, nor her that is [u]put away: but they shall take maidens of the seed of the house of Israel, or a widow [v]that had a priest before.

23 And [w]they shall teach my people *the difference* between the holy and profane, and cause them to discern between the unclean and the clean.

24 And [x]in controversy they shall stand in judgment; *and* they shall judge it according to my judgments; and they shall keep my laws and my statutes in all mine assemblies; [y]and they shall hallow my sabbaths.

25 And they shall come at no [z]dead person to defile themselves: but for father, or for mother, or for son, or for daughter, for brother, or for sister that hath had no husband, they may defile themselves.

26 And [a]after he is cleansed, they shall reckon unto him seven days.

27 And in the day that he goeth into the

[y]Isa. ix. 16; Mal. ii. 8——[z]Heb. *were for a stumbling block of iniquity unto,* &c.; ch xiv 3, 4——[a]Psa. cvi. 26
[b]2 Kings xxiii. 9; Num. xviii. 3——[c]Ch. xxxii. 30; xxxvi. 7——[d]Num. xviii. 4; 1 Chron. xxiii. 28, 32——[e]Ch. xl. 46; xliii. 19——[f]1 Sam. ii. 35——[g]Ver. 10——[h]Deut. x. 8——[i]Ver. 7——[k]Ch. xli. 22——[l]Exod. xxviii. 39, 40, 43; xxxix. 27, 28——[m]Exod. xxviii. 40, 42; xxxix. 28

[n]Or, *in sweating* places——[o]Heb. *in,* or *with sweat.*
[p]Ch. xlii. 14——[q]Ch. xlvi. 20; see Exod. xxix. 37; xxx 29; Lev. vi. 27; Matt. xxiii. 17, 19——[r]Lev. xxi. 5
[s]Lev. x. 9——[t]Lev. xxi. 7, 13, 14——[u]Heb. *thrust forth*
[v]Heb. *from a priest*——[w]Lev. x. 10, 11; ch. xxii. 26; Mal. ii. 7——[x]Deut. xvii. 8, &c.; 2 Chron. xix. 8, 10——[y]See ch. xxii. 26——[z]Lev. xxi. 1, &c.——[a]Num. vi. 10; xix. 11, &c.

ver. 11-15. The whole of these passages refer to the period of time when the second temple was built.

Verse 16. *Come near to my table*] To place the *shew-bread* there, and to burn incense on the golden altar in the holy of holies.

Verse 17. *No wool shall come upon them*] The reason is plain; wool is more apt than *linen* to contract *dirt* and breed *insects;* linen breeds none; besides, this is a *vegetable,* and the other an *animal* substance. It was an ancient maxim, that whatever was taken from a *dead body* was impure in matters of religion, and should not be permitted to enter into the temple. The Egyptian priests always wore *linen* on their bodies, and shoes of *matting* or *rushes* on their feet. The Mohammedans never write the Koran upon *vellum* or *skin* of any kind, as they would consider that as a defilement.

Verse 20. *Neither shall they shave their heads*] The priests of *Isis* shaved their heads close to the skin; the priests of *Budhoo* do so still; their ordinances oblige them to shave their heads every *tenth day.* To let the hair grow *long* would have been improper; therefore the Lord commands them to *poll*—cut the hair *short,* but not to shave.

Verse 22. *Neither shall they take for their wives a widow*] This was prohibited to the *high priest* only, by Moses, Lev. xxi. 13, 14.

Verse 25. *And they shall come at no dead person to defile themselves*] Touching the dead defiles a *Hindoo* now, as it formerly did a *Jew;* and they must bathe to become clean again.

A. M. 3430
B. C. 574
Olymp. LI. 3
Anno
Servii Tullii,
R. Roman., 5

sanctuary, [b]unto the inner
court, to minister in the sanctuary, [c]he shall offer his sin-
offering, saith the Lord GOD.
28 And it shall be unto them for an inheritance: I [d]*am* their inheritance: and ye
shall give them no possession in Israel: I *am*
their possession.
29 [e]They shall eat the meat-offering, and the
sin-offering, and the trespass-offering; and [f]ev-
ery [g]dedicated thing in Israel shall be theirs.
30 And the [h]first[i] of all the
first-fruits of all *things,* and
every oblation of all, of every
sort of your oblations, shall be
the priest's: [k]ye shall also give unto the
priest the first of your dough, [l]that he
may cause the blessing to rest in thine
house.
31 The priest shall not eat of any thing
that is [m]dead of itself, or torn, whether it be
fowl or beast.

[b]Ver. 17——[c]Lev. iv. 3——[d]Num. xviii. 20; Deut. x. 9; xviii. 1, 2; Josh. xiii. 14, 33——[e]Lev. vi. 18, 29; vii. 6——[f]Lev. xxvii. 21, 28, compared with Num. xviii. 14——[g]Or, *devoted*

[h]Or, *chief*——[i]Exod. xiii. 2; xxii. 29, 30; xxiii. 19; Num. iii. 13; xviii. 12, 13——[k]Num. xv. 20; Neh. x. 37 [l]Prov. iii. 9, 10; Mal. iii. 10——[m]Exod. xxii. 31; Lev. xxii. 8

Verse 28. *I* am *their inheritance*] Those who affect to form their ecclesiastical matters on the model of the Jewish Church have with one consent left this out of the question. They will not live on the *free-will offerings of the people;* but must have vast revenues, and these secured to them by *law.* That every minister of God should be supported by the altar I grant; but I think, instead of that method of paying the parochial clergy which I see is so much objected to, and breeds so much dissension between the pastors and their flocks, it would be better, *on these accounts,* to assign them a portion of land adequate to their supply, or let the state maintain them as it does its other officers. In Israel God was their *inheritance* and their *possession;* but *they* had the *breast* and *shoulder* of all sin-offerings and trespass-offerings, and all *dedicated things* were theirs; and they had a portion of all the *dough* that was prepared for bread. These were considered as the *Lord's property,* and these he gave to *them;* and this is always implied in the *Lord's being their inheritance* and their *possession.* They had a plentiful support.

Hitherto *tithes* have been thought the best mode of paying the *clergy,* and providing for the *poor* of each parish; but these matters have undergone such *alterations* since the time of their institution, that some emendation of the system is at present absolutely necessary.

There should be a public acknowledgment of God in every nation, and this should be provided for by the *state* in a way the least burdensome to the *people,* that all may rejoice in the benefit. Happy the nations that have a Bible so correct, and a *Liturgy* so pure, as those in the British empire! In such cases, a religion established by the state is an unutterable blessing to the nation; only keep it to the Bible, and to the Liturgy, and all, under God, will be well; but when the sermon is against these, all is bad.

CHAPTER XLV

The several portions of land appointed for the sanctuary, 1–5, *the city,* 6, *and the prince,* 7, 8. *Regulations concerning the weights and measures,* 9–12; *with ordinances respecting the provisions for the ordinary and extraordinary sacrifices,* 13–25.

A. M. 3430
B. C. 574
Olymp. LI. 3
Anno
Servii Tullii,
R. Roman., 5

MOREOVER, [a]when ye shall
[b]divide by lot the land for
inheritance, ye shall [c]offer an
oblation unto the LORD, [d]a holy
portion of the land: the length *shall be* the
length of five and twenty thousand *reeds,*
and the breadth *shall be* ten thousand. This
shall be holy in all the borders
thereof round about.
2 Of this there shall be for the
sanctuary [e]five hundred *in*
length, with five hundred *in breadth,* square
round about; and fifty cubits round about
for the [f]suburbs thereof.

[a]Heb. *when ye cause the land to fall*——[b]Chap. xlvii. 22 [c]Chap. xlviii. 8

[d]Hebrew, *holiness*——[e]Chapter xlii. 20——[f]Or, *void places*

NOTES ON CHAP. XLV

Verse 1. *When ye shall divide by lot*] That is, when on your repossessing your land, every family settles according to the allotment which they *formerly* had; for it is certain that the *land* was not divided afresh by lot after the Babylonish captivity. The allotment mentioned and described here was merely for the *service* of the *temple,* the use of the *priests,* and the *prince* or governor of the people. A division of the *whole land* is not intended.

Verse 2. *Of this there shall be for the sanctuary*] See the plan, A.

A. M. 3430
B. C. 574
Olymp. LI. 3
Anno
Servii Tullii,
R. Roman., 5

3 And of this measure shalt thou
measure the length of five and
twenty thousand, and the breadth
of ten thousand: [g]and in it shall
be the sanctuary *and* the most holy *place*.
4 [h]The holy *portion* of the land shall be for
the priests the ministers of the sanctuary,
which shall come near to minister unto the
LORD: and it shall be a place for their
houses, and a holy place for the sanctuary.
5 [i]And the five and twenty thousand of
length, and the ten thousand of breadth,
shall also the Levites, the ministers of the
house, have for themselves, for a possession
for [k]twenty chambers.
6 And [l]ye shall appoint the possession of
the city five thousand broad, and five and
twenty thousand long, over against the oblation of the holy *portion:* it shall be for the
whole house of Israel.
7 [m]And *a portion shall be* for the prince on
the one side and on the other side of the oblation of the holy portion, and of the possession of the city, before the oblation of the
holy *portion,* and before the possession of the
city, from the west side westward, and from
the east side eastward: and the length *shall
be* over against one of the portions, from the
west border unto the east border.
8 In the land shall be his possession in
Israel: and [n]my princes shall no more oppress my people; and *the rest of* the land
shall they give to the house of Israel according to their tribes.
9 Thus saith the Lord GOD; [o]Let it suffice
you, O princes of Israel: [p]remove violence
and spoil, and execute judgment and justice,
take away your [q]exactions from
my people, saith the Lord
GOD.
10 Ye shall have just [r]bal-
ances, and a just ephah, and a just bath.
11 The ephah and the bath shall be of one
measure, that the bath may contain the tenth
part of an homer, and the ephah the tenth
part of an homer: the measure thereof shall
be after the homer.
12 And the [s]shekel *shall be* twenty gerahs:
twenty shekels, five and twenty shekels,
fifteen shekels shall be your maneh.
13 This *is* the oblation that ye shall offer:
the sixth part of an ephah of an homer of
wheat, and ye shall give the sixth part of an
ephah of an homer of barley:
14 Concerning the ordinance of oil, the
bath of oil, *ye shall offer* the tenth part of a
bath out of the cor, *which is* an homer of ten
baths; for ten baths *are* an homer:
15 And one [t]lamb out of the flock, out of
two hundred, out of the fat pastures of
Israel; for a meat-offering, and for a burnt-
offering, and for [u]peace-offerings, [v]to make
reconciliation for them, saith the Lord
GOD.
16 All the people of the land [w]shall give
this oblation [x]for the prince in Israel.
17 And it shall be the prince's part *to give*
burnt-offerings, and meat-offerings, and
drink-offerings, in the feasts, and in the new
moons, and in the sabbaths, in all solemnities
of the house of Israel: he shall prepare the
sin-offering, and the meat-offering, and the
burnt-offering, and the [y]peace-offerings, to
make reconciliation for the house of Israel.

[g]Chap. xlviii. 10——[h]Ver. 1; chap. xlviii. 10, &c. [i]Ch. xlviii. 13——[k]See ch. xl. 17——[l]Ch. xlviii. 15 [m]Chap. xlviii. 21——[n]Chap. xlvi. 18; see Jer. xxii. 17; chap. xxii. 27——[o]Chap. xliv. 6——[p]Jer. xxii. 3

[q]Heb. *expulsions*——[r]Lev. xix. 35, 36; Prov. xi. 1 [s]Exod. xxx. 13; Lev. xxvii. 25; Num. iii. 47——[t]Or, *kid* [u]Or, *thank-offerings*——[v]Lev. i. 4——[w]Heb. *shall be for* [x]Or, *with*——[y]Or, *thank-offerings*

Verse 3. *And of this measure*] See the plan, A, B, C, D, E.

Verse 4. *The holy* portion] See the plan, A.

Verse 5. *And the five and twenty thousand*] See the plan, B.

Verse 6. *Ye shall appoint*] See the plan, FF.

Verse 7. A portion shall be *for the prince*] נשיא *nasi*, he who had the authority of *chief magistrate;* for there was neither *king* nor *prince* among the Jews after the Babylonish captivity. For these allotments and divisions, see the plan, EE, FF, GG.

Verse 8. *My princes shall no more oppress my people*] By exorbitant taxes to maintain profligate courts, or subsidize other powers to help to keep up a system of tyranny in the earth. The former princes even robbed the temple of God to give subsidies to other states.

Verse 9. *Take away your exactions from my people*] This is the voice of God to all the rulers of the earth.

Take away your exactions; do not oppress the people; they are *mine.* Abolish all oppressive taxes.

Verse 10. *Ye shall have just balances*] This appreciation of *weights, measures,* and *money* was intended to show them that they must not

A. M. 3430
B. C. 574
Olymp. LI. 3
Anno
Servii Tullii,
R. Roman., 5

18 Thus saith the Lord God:
In the first *month,* in the first
day of the month, thou shalt
take a young bullock without
blemish, and [z]cleanse the sanctuary.
19 [a]And the priest shall take of the blood
of the sin-offering, and put *it* upon the posts
of the house, and upon the four corners of
the settle of the altar, and upon the posts of
the gate of the inner court.
20 And so thou shalt do the seventh *day* of
the month [b]for every one that erreth, and for
him that is simple: so shall ye reconcile the
house.
21 [c]In the first *month,* in the fourteenth
day of the month, ye shall have the passover,
a feast of seven days; unleavened bread shall
be eaten.
22 And upon that day shall the
prince prepare for himself and
for all the people of the land
[d]a bullock *for* a sin-offering.
23 And [e]seven days of the feast he shall
prepare a burnt-offering to the Lord, seven
bullocks and seven rams without blemish
daily the seven days; [f]and a kid of the goats
daily *for* a sin-offering.
24 [g]And he shall prepare a meat-offering of
an ephah for a bullock, and an ephah for a
ram, and a hin of oil for an ephah.
25 In the seventh *month,* in the fifteen day
of the month, shall he do the like in the
[h]feast of the seven days, according to the
sin-offering, according to the burnt-offering,
and according to the meat-offering, and according to the oil.

[z]Lev. xvi. 16——[a]Chap. xliii. 20——[b]Lev. iv. 27
[c]Exod. xii. 18; Lev. xxiii. 5, 6; Num. ix. 2, 3; xxviii. 16, 17; Deut. xvi. 1, &c.

[d]Lev. iv. 14——[e]Lev. xxiii. 8——[f]See Num. xxviii. 15, 22, 30; xxix. 5, 11, 16, 19, &c.——[g]Ch. xlvi. 5, 7
[h]Lev. xxiii. 34; Num. xxix. 12; Deut. xvi. 13

introduce those to which they had been accustomed in the captivity, but those which God had prescribed to their forefathers. See the notes on the parallel places.

Verse 16. *All—this oblation for the prince*] A present or offering to the prince.

Verse 18. *Thou shalt take a young bullock —and cleanse the sanctuary.*] There is nothing of this in the Mosaic law; it seems to have been a new ceremony. An *annual* purification of the sanctuary may be intended.

Verse 20. *For* him that is *simple*] That wants understanding to conduct himself properly.

Verse 25. *In the seventh* month] He shall do at the feast of tabernacles the same things that he was desired to do on the *passover.* The prince should offer the same number of victims, of the same quality, and with the same ceremonies, as during the above *seven* days. The offerings were, sin-offerings, burnt-offerings, and peace-offerings.

CHAPTER XLVI

Ordinances of worship prescribed for the prince and for the people, 1–15; *and the gifts he may bestow on his sons and servants,* 16–18. *A description of the courts appointed for boiling or baking any part of the holy oblations,* 19–24.

A. M. 3430
B. C. 574
Olymp. LI. 3
Anno
Servii Tullii,
R. Roman., 5

THUS saith the Lord God;
The gate of the inner court
that looketh toward the east
shall be shut the six working
days; but on the sabbath it shall be opened,
and in the day of the new moon it shall be
opened.
2 [a]And the prince shall enter by the way of
the porch of *that* gate without, and shall
stand by the post of the gate, and the priest
shall prepare his burnt-offering and his
peace-offerings, and he shall worship at the
threshold of the gate: then he
shall go forth: but the gate
shall not be shut until the evening.
3 Likewise the people of the land shall
worship at the door of this gate before the
Lord in the sabbaths and in the new
moons.
4 And the burnt-offering that [b]the prince
shall offer unto the Lord in the sabbath day
shall be six lambs without blemish, and a
ram without blemish.

[a]Chap. xliv. 3; ver. 8

[b]Chap. xlv. 17

NOTES ON CHAP. XLVI

Verse 4. *The burnt-offerings that the prince shall offer*] The *chief magistrate* was always obliged to *attend the public worship of God,* as well as the *priest,* to show that the *civil* and *ecclesiastical* states were both under the same government of the Lord; and that no one was capable of being *prince* or *priest,* who did not acknowledge God in all his ways. It is no wonder that those lands mourn, where neither the *established priest* nor the *civil magistrate*

A. M. 3430
B. C. 574
Olymp. LI. 3
Anno
Servii Tullii,
R. Roman., 5

5 [c]And the meat-offering *shall be* an ephah for a ram, and the meat-offering for the lambs [d]as he shall be able to give, and a hin of oil to an ephah.

6 And in the day of the new moon *it shall be* a young bullock without blemish, and six lambs, and a ram: they shall be without blemish.

7 And he shall prepare a meat-offering, an ephah for a bullock, and an ephah for a ram, and for the lambs according as his hand shall attain unto, and a hin of oil to an ephah.

8 [e]And when the prince shall enter, he shall go in by the way of the porch of *that* gate, and he shall go forth by the way thereof.

9 But when the people of the land [f]shall come before the LORD in the solemn feasts, he that entereth in by the way of the north gate to worship shall go out by the way of the south gate; and he that entereth by the way of the south gate shall go forth by the way of the north gate: he shall not return by the way of the gate whereby he came in, but shall go forth over against it.

10 And the prince in the midst of them, when they go in, shall go in; and when they go forth, shall go forth.

11 And in the feasts and in the solemnities [g]the meat-offering shall be an ephah to a bullock, and an ephah to a ram, and to the lambs as he is able to give, and a hin of oil to an ephah.

12 Now when the prince shall prepare a voluntary burnt-offering or peace-offerings voluntarily unto the LORD, [h]*one* shall then open him the gate that looketh toward the east, and he shall prepare his burnt offering and his peace-offerings, as he did on the sabbath day: then he shall go forth; and after his going forth *one* shall shut the gate.

A. M. 3430
B. C. 574
Olymp. LI. 3
Anno
Servii Tullii,
R. Roman., 5

13 [i]Thou shalt daily prepare a burnt-offering unto the LORD *of* a lamb [k]of the first year without blemish: thou shalt prepare it [l]every morning.

14 And thou shalt prepare a meat-offering for it every morning, the sixth part of an ephah, and the third part of a hin of oil, to temper with the fine flour; a meat-offering continually by a perpetual ordinance unto the LORD.

15 Thus shall they prepare the lamb, and the meat-offering, and the oil, every morning *for* a continual burnt-offering.

16 Thus saith the Lord GOD; If the prince give a gift unto any of his sons, the inheritance thereof shall be his sons'; it *shall be* their possession by inheritance.

17 But if he give a gift of his inheritance to one of his servants, then it shall be his to [m]the year of liberty; after it shall return to the prince; but his inheritance shall be his sons' for them.

18 Moreover [n]the prince shall not take of the people's inheritance by oppression, to thrust them out of their possession; *but* he shall give his sons' inheritance out of his own possession: that my people be not scattered every man from his possession.

---

[c]Chap. xlv. 29; ver. 7, 11——[d]Heb. *the gift of his hand;* Deut. xvi. 17——[e]Ver. 2——[f]Exod. xxiii. 14-17; Deut. xvi. 16——[g]Ver. 5

[h]Chap. xliv. 3; ver. 2——[i]Exod. xxix. 38; Num. xxviii. 3——[k]Heb. *a son of his year*——[l]Heb. *morning by morning*——[m]Lev. xxv. 10——[n]Chap. xlv. 8

---

either fear or love God. Ungodly priests and profligate magistrates are a curse to any land. In no country have I found *both* so exemplary for uprightness, as in Britain.

Verse 7. *According as his hand shall attain unto*] According to his ability, to what the providence of God has put in his hand, i. e., his power. This proportion of offerings is different from that prescribed by the Mosaic law, Num. xv. 4-12.

Verse 9. *He that entereth in by the way of the north, &c.*] As the *north* and the *south* gates were opposite to each other, he that came in at the north must go out at the south; he that came in at the south must go out at the north. No person was to come in at the *east* gate, because there was no gate at the *west;* and the people were not permitted to *turn round* and go out at the same place by which they came in; for this was like turning their backs on God, and the decorum and reverence with which public worship was to be conducted would not admit of this. Besides, returning by the same way must have occasioned a great deal of confusion, where so many people must have jostled each other, in their meetings in different parts of this space.

Verse 10. *And the prince in the midst of them*] Even *he* shall act in the same way: he must also go straight forward, and never turn his back to go out at the same gate by which he entered. The prince and the people were to begin and end their worship at the same time.

Verse 13. *Thou shalt prepare it every morning.*] The *evening* offering is entirely omitted, which makes an important difference between this and the old laws. See Exod. xxix. 31-46.

Verse 17. *To the year of liberty*] That is,

A. M. 3430
B. C. 574
Olymp. LI. 3
Anno
Servii Tullii,
R. Roman., 5

19 After he brought me
through the entry, which *was* at
the side of the gate, into the
holy chambers of the priests,
which looked toward the north: and, behold,
there *was* a place on the two sides westward.
20 Then said he unto me, This *is* the place
where the priests shall [o]boil the trespass-
offering and the sin-offering, where they shall
[p]bake the meat-offering; that they bear *them*
not out into the utter court, [q]to sanctify the
people.
21 Then he brought me forth into the utter
court, and caused me to pass by the four corners of the court; and, behold,
[r]in every corner of the court
there was a court.
22 In the four corners of the
court *there were* courts [s]joined of forty
cubits long and thirty broad: these four
[t]corners *were* of one measure.
23 And *there was* a row *of building* round
about in them, round about them four, and
it was made with boiling places under the
rows round about.
24 Then said he unto me, These *are* the
places of them that boil, where the ministers of
the house shall [u]boil the sacrifice of the people.

[o]2 Chron. xxxv. 13——[p]Lev. ii. 4, 5, 7——[q]Chap. xliv. 19——[r]Heb. *a court in a corner of a court, and a court in a corner of a court*

[s]Or, *made with chimneys*——[t]Hebrew, *cornered*
[u]See verse 20; Leviticus viii. 31; 1 Kings xix. 21; 2 Kings vi. 29

to the year of *jubilee*, called the *year of liberty*, because there was then a general release. All servants had their liberty, and all alienated estates returned to their former owners.

Verse 19. *He brought me through the entry*] The prophet had entered by the north gate of the court of the priests, where he had seen, a little before, the glory of the Lord, and where he had received all those directions from chap. xliv. 4, 5, to this chapter. From that gate, (see plan Q,) he entered the vestibule by a gate which was by the side of the apartments of the priests, which were along this aisle, (see S,) to the right of the vestibule towards the west. At the extremity of a row of chambers, he remarked, at the west, the place where they *boiled the flesh* of the sin-offerings, (see T.) They did not boil there the flesh of *all sorts* of victims, there were other kitchens appointed for that, (see PP:) but that only which could not be eaten but in the *outer court*, and by the *priests* which were sanctified; such were the parts of the offerings for sins of commission and ignorance, and the offerings of *flour* with which they were accompanied.

Verse 20. *The trespass-offering*] Part of this, and of the sin-offering, and the flour-offering, was the portion of the priests. See Num. xviii. 9, 10.

Verse 23. It was *made with boiling places*] These were uncovered apartments, where they kept fires for dressing those parts of the peace-offerings, which were made in the temple by individuals through a principle of devotion. On these their families and their friends feasted; and portions were sent to the poor, the widows, and the orphans. And thus the spirit of devotion was the means of preserving the spirit of mercy, charity, and benevolence in the land. How true is that word, "Godliness is profitable for all things."

CHAPTER XLVII

The vision of the holy waters issuing out of the temple, and their virtue; an emblem of the power of God's grace under the Gospel, capable of healing all but the incorrigibly impenitent, represented by the marshy ground that cannot be healed, 1–12. Also a description of the several divisions of the Holy Land indiscriminately shared betwixt Jews and proselytes; to denote that in after times the privileges now enjoyed by the Jews should be also extended to the Gentiles, 13–23.

A. M. 3430
B. C. 574
Olymp. LI. 3
Anno
Servii Tullii,
R. Roman., 5

AFTERWARD he brought me
again unto the door of the
house; and, behold, [a]waters issued out from under the [b]thresh-
old of the house eastward: for the fore front
of the house *stood toward* the
east, and the waters came down
from under from the right side
of the house, at the south *side*
of the altar.

[a]Joel iii. 18; Zech. xiii. 1; xiv. 8; Rev. xxii. 1

[b]Psa. lxxxiv. 10, in the margin

NOTES ON CHAP. XLVII

Verse 1. *Behold, waters issued out from under the threshold*] Ezekiel, after having made the whole compass of the *court of the people*, is brought back by the *north gate* into the *courts of the priests;* and, having reached the gate of the temple, he saw waters which had their spring under the threshold of that gate, that looked towards the east; and which, passing to the south of the altar of burnt-offerings on the right of the temple, ran from the west to the east, that they might fall into the brook Kidron, and thence be carried into the Dead Sea. Literally, no such waters were ever in the temple; and because there were none, Solomon had what is called the *brazen sea* made, which held water for the use of the

A. M. 3430
B. C. 574
Olymp. LI. 3
Anno
Servii Tullii,
R. Roman., 5

2 Then brought he me out of
the way of the gate northward,
and led me about the way without unto the utter gate by the
way that looketh eastward; and, behold,
there ran out waters on the right side.
3 And when [c]the man that had the line in
his hand went forth eastward, he measured a
thousand cubits, and he brought me through
the waters; the [d]waters *were* to the ankles.
4 Again he measured a thousand, and
brought me through the waters; the waters
were to the knees. Again he measured a
thousand, and brought me through; the
waters *were* to the loins.
5 Afterward he measured a thousand; *and
it was a* river that I could not pass over: for
the waters were risen, [e]waters
to swim in, a river that could
not be passed over.
6 And he said unto me, Son
of man, hast thou seen *this?* Then he
brought me, and caused me to return to the
brink of the river.
7 Now when I had returned, behold, at the
[f]bank of the river *were* very many [g]trees on
the one side and on the other.
8 Then said he unto me, These waters issue
out toward the east country, and go down
into the [h]desert, and go into the sea: *which
being* brought forth into the sea, the waters
shall be healed.
9 And it shall come to pass, *that* every
thing that liveth, which moveth, whither-

A. M. 3430
B. C. 574
Olymp. LI. 3
Anno
Servii Tullii,
R. Roman., 5

[c]Chap. xl. 3——[d]Heb. *waters of the ankles*——[e]Heb. *waters of swimming*——[f]Heb. *lip*

[g]Ver. 12; Rev. xxii. 2——[h]Or, *plain;* see Deut. iii. 17; iv. 49; Josh. iii. 16

temple. It is true that the water which supplied this *sea* might have been brought by pipes to the place: but a fountain producing *abundance of water* was not there, and could not be there, on the top of such a hill; and consequently these waters, as well as those spoken of in Joel iii. 18, and in Zech. xiv. 8, are to be understood *spiritually* or *typically;* and indeed the whole complexion of the place here shows, that they are thus to be understood. Taken in this view, I shall proceed to apply the whole of this vision to the effusion of light and salvation by the outpouring of the Spirit of God under the Gospel dispensation, by which the knowledge of the true God was multiplied in the earth; and have only one previous remark to make, that the farther the waters flowed from the temple, the deeper they grew.

With respect to the *phraseology* of this chapter, it may be said that *St. John* had it particularly in view while he wrote his celebrated description of the paradise of God, Rev. xxii. The *prophet* may therefore be referring to the same thing which the *apostle* describes, viz., the *grace* of the *Gospel*, and its *effects* in the world.

Verse 2. *There ran out waters*] מים מפכים *mayim mephaccim*, the waters seem to have been at first *in small quantity;* for the words imply that they *oozed* or *dropped out.* They were at first so small that they came *guttatim, drop by drop;* but they increased so, that they became a river in which one could swim.

Verses 3-5. *He measured a thousand cubits,—the waters were to the* ANKLES; *a thousand more,—the waters were to the* KNEES; *a thousand more,—they became a* RIVER that could *not be forded.* The *waters were risen*, and they *were waters to* SWIM *in.*

I. This may be applied to the *gradual* discoveries of the *plan* of *salvation*,—1. In the *patriarchal* ages. 2. In the giving of the *law.* 3. In the *ministry* of *John the Baptist.* And, 4. In the *full manifestation* of *Christ* by the communication of the *Holy Ghost.*

II. This vision may be applied also to the *growth* of a *believer* in the grace and knowledge of God. There is—1. The *seed* of the kingdom. 2. The *blade* from that seed. 3. The *ear* out of that blade. And, 4. The *full corn* in that *ear.*

III. It may be applied to the discoveries a penitent believer receives of the *mercy* of God in his salvation. He is—1. *A little child*, born of God, born from above, and begins to *taste the bread of life*, and live on the *heavenly food.* 2. He grows up and increases in stature and strength, and becomes a *young man.* 3. He becomes *matured* in the *Divine life*, and has his spiritual senses exercised so as to become a *father* in Christ. In other words, the grace of God appears to come *drop by drop;* it is given as it can be used; it is a *seed of light*, and multiplies itself. The penitent at first can scarcely believe the infinite goodness of his Maker; he however ventures to follow on with the conducting angel, the minister of the Gospel, in his descriptions of the plenitude of that salvation, provided in that *living Temple* in which alone the *well-spring* of life is to be found. 4. In thus following on to know the Lord he finds a continual increase of light and life, till at last he is carried by the *streams* of *grace* to the *ocean* of *eternal mercy;* then

"Plunged in the Godhead's deepest sea,
And lost in his immensity."

IV. These waters may be considered as a type of the progress which Christianity shall make in the world. 1. There were only a few poor fishermen. 2. Afterwards many Jews. 3. Then the Gentiles of Asia Minor and Greece. 4. The continent and isles of Europe. And, 5. Now spreading through Africa, Asia, and America, at present these waters are no longer a river, but an immense sea; and the Gospel fishers are daily bringing multitudes of souls to Christ.

Verse 9. *Every thing—whithersoever the rivers shall come, shall live*] *Life* and *salvation* shall continually accompany the *preaching* of the Gospel; the *death of sin* being removed, the life of righteousness shall be brought in.

There shall be a very great multitude of fish] On the above plan this must refer to *genuine converts* to the Christian faith; true believers, who have got life and salvation by the streams

A. M. 3430
B. C. 574
Olymp. LI. 3
Anno
Servii Tullii,
R. Roman., 5

soever the [l]rivers shall come,
shall live: and there shall be
a very great multitude of fish,
because these waters shall
come thither: for they shall be healed;
and every thing shall live whither the river
cometh.
10 And it shall come to pass, *that* the fishers shall stand upon it from En-gedi even
unto En-eglaim; they shall be a *place* to
spread forth nets; their fish shall be according to their kinds, as the fish [k]of the great
sea, exceeding many.
11 But the miry places thereof and the
marshes thereof [l]shall not be healed; they
shall be given to salt.
12 And [m]by the river upon the bank thereof,
on this side and on that side, [n]shall grow all
trees for meat, [o]whose leaf shall not fade,
neither shall the fruit thereof be consumed:
it shall bring forth [p]new fruit according to
his months, because their waters
they issued out of the sanctuary; and the fruit thereof
shall be for meat, and the leaf
thereof [q]for [r]medicine.

A. M. 3430
B. C. 574
Olymp. LI. 3
Anno
Servii Tullii,
R. Roman., 5

13 Thus saith the Lord God; This *shall be*
the border, whereby ye shall inherit the land
according to the twelve tribes of Israel:
[s]Joseph *shall have* two portions.
14 And ye shall inherit it, one as well as
another: *concerning* the which I [t]lifted [u]up
mine hand to give it unto your fathers: and
this land shall [v]fall unto you for inheritance.
15 And this *shall be* the border of the land
toward the north side, from the great sea,
[w]the way of Hethlon, as men go to [x]Zedad;
16 [y]Hamath, [z]Berothah, Sibraim, which *is*
between the border of Damascus and the
border of Hamath; [a]Hazar-hatticon, which
is by the coast of Hauran.
17 And the border from the sea shall be

[i]Heb. *two rivers*——[k]Num. xxxiv. 6; Josh. xxiii. 4; chap. xlviii. 28——[l]Or, *and* that which *shall not be healed*——[m]Ver. 7——[n]Heb. *shall come up*——[o]Job viii. 16; Psa. i. 3; Jer. xvii. 8——[p]Or, *principal*——[q]Or, *for bruises and sores*——[r]Rev. xxii. 2

[s]Gen. xlviii. 5; 1 Chron. v. 1; chap. xlviii. 4, 5——[t]Or, *swore*——[u]Gen. xii. 7; xiii. 15; xv. 7; xvii. 8; xxvi. 3; xxviii. 13; chap. xx. 5, 6, 28, 42——[v]Chap. xlviii. 29 [w]Chap. xlviii. 1——[x]Num. xxxiv. 8——[y]Num. xxxiv. 8 [z]2 Sam. viii. 8——[a]Or, *the middle village*

of God's grace. The *apostles* were *fishers of men; converts* were *the fish* caught. See below. As the waters flow into the Dead *Sea*, where no fish, it is said, can live, *its* waters must be healed, that is, made capable of preserving life; and so its nature be thus far most surprisingly altered.

Verse 10. *The fishers shall stand upon it*] On the above plan of interpretation these must mean—1. The *apostles* of our Lord Jesus. 2. The *preachers* of the everlasting Gospel. See Matt. iv. 19.

From En-gedi] At the southern extremity of the Dead Sea.

Unto En-eglaim] At the northern extremity of the same.

Their fish shall be according to their kinds] Every kind of fish, and the fish all excellent of their kinds. All *nations*, and *kindreds*, and *people* shall be called by the Gospel; it shall not be an excluding system like that of Judaism, for its Author tasted death for every man.

Verse 11. *The miry places*] "Point out," says *Calmet*, "the schismatics and heretics who do not live by the Spirit of Jesus Christ, but separate from his Church; and the evil Christians who dishonour that Church, of which they are corrupt members." A description applicable to the Roman Catholic Church, that is both schismatic and heretic from the Church of Jesus Christ, which is built on the *foundation of the prophets and apostles, Jesus himself being the chief corner stone;* for the Church of Rome, leaving this foundation, is now built on the foundation of councils and traditions, and lying miracles; the popes in their succession being its only corner stones.

Verse 12. *Shall grow all trees for meat, whose leaf shall not fade*] A description that suits the righteous, who are still producing—1. The *fruits* of *faith.* 2. The *fruits* of the *Spirit.* 3. The *fruits* of *love* to God, obedience to his holy will, and love to all men. Benevolence, mercy, charity, kindness, &c.

The leaf thereof for medicine.] See Rev. xxii. 1-5. Even the *leaves*, the holy *profession* of the righteous, is a spiritual medicine. Righteousness is thus encouraged in the world. The *profession* points out the salvation, as it shows the nature and sufficiency of that salvation; for a just creed contains all the articles of the Christian faith.

Verse 13. *Joseph* shall have two *portions.*] That is, In *Ephraim* and *Manasseh*, his two sons, who each had a separate inheritance.

Verse 15. *The way of Hethlon, as men go to Zedad.*] Probably Hethlon is the same as Cuthlon, a city of Syria, between Antioch and Laodicea, according to Antoninus. Some of these places are not known; but see the same kind of division, Num. xxxiv. 7-12.

Verse 16. *Hamath*] Emesa or Amesa, in Syria.—*Calmet.*

Berothah] Berytus, now Baruth or Beeroth, which David took from Hadarezer, king of Syria, 2 Sam. viii. 8; but these things are very uncertain.

Sibraim] Sabarim or Sepharvaim, according to the Syriac, between Hamath and Damascus.

Hazar-hatticon] The middle Hazar; or *middle village*, as the *margin.*

Hauran.] The city Aurana, and the district Auranitis, are in the north-east limit of the Holy Land.

Verse 17. *The border from the sea*] The north border *eastward* is ascertained ver. 15, 16;

A. M. 3430
B. C. 574
Olymp. LI. 3
Anno
Servii Tullii,
R. Roman., 5

[b]Hazar-enan, the border of Damascus, and the north northward, and the border of Hamath. And *this is* the north side.

18 And the east side ye shall measure [c]from Hauran, and from Damascus, and from Gilead, and from the land of Israel *by* Jordan, from the border unto the east sea. And *this is* the east side.

19 And the south side southward, from Tamar *even* to [d]the waters of [e]strife *in* Kadesh, the [f]river to the great sea. And *this is* the south side [g]southward.

20 The west side also *shall be* the great sea from the border, till a man come over against [h]Hamath. This *is* the west side.

21 So shall ye divide this land unto you according to the tribes of Israel.

22 And it shall come to pass, *that* ye shall divide it by lot for an inheritance unto you, [i]and to the strangers that sojourn among you, which shall beget children among you: [k]and they shall be unto you as born in the country among the children of Israel; they shall have inheritance with you among the tribes of Israel.

23 And it shall come to pass, *that* in what tribe the stranger sojourneth, there shall ye give *him* his inheritance, saith the Lord GOD.

[b]Num. xxxiv. 9; chap. xlviii. 1——[c]Heb. *from between*——[d]Num. xx. 13; Deut. xxxii. 51; Psa. lxxxi. 7; chap. xlviii. 28——[e]Or, *Meribah*——[f]Or, *valley*——[g]Or, *toward Teman*——[h]Num. xiii. 21; xxxiv. 8; Josh. xiii. 5——[i]See Eph. iii. 6; Rev. vii. 9, 10——[k]Rom. x. 12; Gal. iii. 28; Col. iii. 11

here it is shown how far it extends itself *northward.*

Hazar-enan] The village of Enan, Num. xxxiv. 9, placed to the north of Cæsarea Philippi. *Ziphron*, see Num. xxxiv. 9, called *Zaphion* by the Syriac.

Verse 18. *The east sea*] The same as the *Dead Sea.*

Verse 19. *Tamar*] Called *Hazazon Tamar*, or *Engedi*, 2 Chron. xx. 2.

The river] Besor, which runs into the sea near Gaza.

Verse 20. *The great sea*] The Mediterranean.

From the border] The southern border, mentioned ver. 19.

Verse 22. *And to the strangers that sojourn*] In former divisions of the land, no place was given to *strangers;* but in this division, (which seems to have no other reference than to the Gospel, for literally such a division never took place,) the *strangers* are to have an *inheritance;* intimating the calling of the Gentiles into the Church of Christ, to an inheritance that is incorruptible, undefiled, and that fadeth not away. Glory be to God for his unspeakable gift! Amen. Amen.

CHAPTER XLVIII

This chapter contains a description of the several portions of the land belonging to each tribe, together with the portion allotted to the sanctuary, city, suburb, and prince, 1–29; *as also the measure and gates of the new city,* 30–35.

A. M. 3430
B. C. 574
Olymp. LI. 3
Anno
Servii Tullii,
R. Roman., 5

NOW these *are* the names of the tribes. [a]From the north end to the coast of the way of Hethlon, as one goeth to Hamath, Hazar-enan, the border of Damascus northward, to the coast of Hamath; for these are his sides east *and* west; [b]a *portion for* Dan.

2 And by the border of Dan, from the east side unto the west side, a *portion for* Asher.

3 And by the border of Asher, from the east side even unto the west side, a *portion for* Naphtali.

4 And by the border of Naphtali, from the east side unto the west side, a *portion for* Manasseh.

5 And by the border of Manasseh, from the east side unto the west side, a *portion for* Ephraim.

6 And by the border of Ephraim, from the east side even unto the west side, a *portion for* Reuben.

7 And by the border of Reuben, from the east side unto the west side, a *portion for* Judah.

8 And by the border of Judah, from the east side unto the west side, shall be [c]the

[a]Chap. xlvii. 15, &c.——[b]Heb. *one* portion——[c]Chap. xlv. 1–6

NOTES ON CHAP. XLVIII

Verse 1. *Now these* are *the names of the tribes.*] See the division mentioned Num. xxxiv. 7-12, which casts much light upon this.

Verse 9. *The oblation*] This was a portion of land *twenty-five thousand* cubits in length, by *ten thousand* broad; in the centre of which was the temple, which must be destined for the use of the priests, the Levites, and the prince

A. M. 3430 B. C. 574 Olymp. LI. 3 Anno Servii Tullii, R. Roman., 5

offering which ye shall offer of five and twenty thousand *reeds* *in* breadth, and *in* length as one of the *other* parts, from the east side unto the west side: and the sanctuary shall be in the midst of it.

9 The oblation that ye shall offer unto the LORD *shall be* of five and twenty thousand in length, and of ten thousand in breadth.

10 And for them, *even* for the priests, shall be *this* holy oblation; toward the north five and twenty thousand *in length,* and toward the west ten thousand in breadth, and toward the east ten thousand in breadth, and toward the south five and twenty thousand in length: and the sanctuary of the LORD shall be in the midst thereof.

11 [d]*It* [e]*shall be* for the priests that are sanctified of the sons of Zadok; which have kept my [f]charge, which went not astray when the children of Israel went astray, [g]as the Levites went astray.

12 And *this* oblation of the land that is offered shall be unto them a thing most holy by the border of the Levites.

13 And over against the border of the priests the Levites *shall have* five and twenty thousand in length, and ten thousand in breadth: all the length *shall be* five and twenty thousand, and the breadth ten thousand.

14 [h]And they shall not sell of it, neither exchange nor alienate the first-fruits of the land: for *it is* holy unto the LORD.

15 [i]And the five thousand that are left in the breadth over against the five and twenty thousand, shall be [k]a profane *place* for the city, for dwelling, and for suburbs: and the city shall be in the midst thereof.

16 And these *shall be* the measures thereof; the north side four thousand and five hundred, and the south side four thousand and five hundred, and on the east side four thousand and five hundred, and the west side four thousand and five hundred.

A. M. 3430 B. C. 574 Olymp. LI. 3 Anno Servii Tullii, R. Roman., 5

17 And the suburbs of the city shall be toward the north two hundred and fifty, and toward the south two hundred and fifty, and toward the east two hundred and fifty, and toward the west two hundred and fifty.

18 And the residue in length over against the oblation of the holy *portion shall be* ten thousand eastward, and ten thousand westward: and it shall be over against the oblation of the holy *portion;* and the increase thereof shall be for food unto them that serve the city.

19 [l]And they that serve the city shall serve it out of all the tribes of Israel.

20 All the oblation *shall be* five and twenty thousand by five and twenty thousand: ye shall offer the holy oblation foursquare, with the possession of the city.

21 [m]And the residue *shall be* for the prince, on the one side and on the other of the holy oblation, and of the possession of the city, over against the five and twenty thousand of the oblation toward the east border, and westward over against the five and twenty thousand toward the west border, over against the portions for the prince: and it shall be the holy oblation; [n]and the sanctuary of the house *shall be* in the midst thereof.

22 Moreover from the possession of the Levites, and from the possession of the city *being* in the midst *of that* which is the prince's between the border of Judah and the border of Benjamin, shall be for the prince.

23 As for the rest of the tribes from the

[d]Chap. xliv. 15——[e]Or, *The sanctified* portion shall be *for the priests*——[f]Or, *ward*, or *ordinance*——[g]Chap. xliv. 10

[h]Exod. xxii. 29; Lev. xxvii. 10, 28, 33——[i]Chap. xlv. 6——[k]Chap. xlii. 20——[l]Chap. xlv. 6——[m]Chap. xlv. 7——[n]Ver 8, 10

Verse 15. *And the five thousand that are left*] The territory of the Levites was *twenty-five thousand* square cubits, ver. 20. But their city was only *four thousand five hundred* square cubits, see ver. 13 and 16; there remained, therefore, *ten thousand* cubits square to be divided, of which *five thousand* cubits in breadth, by *twenty-five thousand* in length, on the east and west sides, were reserved for a sort of *second city;* or for suburbs where laymen might dwell who were employed by those priests and Levites who lodged in the temple and in the city, ver. 18. And another space of *one thousand* cubits in breadth, by *twenty-five thousand* in length, which extended only from north to south, was for fields and gardens appointed for the support of those lay servants. On which we may remark, there was no cultivated land between the portion of the Levites and that of the prince, but only on the east and west sides. See chap. xlv. 6, and the map FF.

Verse 21. *And the residue—for the prince*] His portion was alongside that of the Levites, from west to east; these were on each side *twenty-five thousand* cubits in length, from the east to the west, by *twelve thousand five hun-*

A. M. 3430
B. C. 574
Olymp. LI. 3
Anno
Servii Tullii
R. Roman., 5

east side unto the west side,
Benjamin *shall have* [o]a *portion.*
24 And by the border of Benjamin, from the east side unto
the west side, Simeon *shall have* a *portion.*
25 And by the border of Simeon, from the
east side unto the west side, Issachar a *portion.*
26 And by the border of Issachar, from the
east side unto the west side, Zebulun a *portion.*
27 And by the border of Zebulun, from the
east side unto the west side, Gad a *portion.*
28 And by the border of Gad, at the south
side southward, the border shall be even from
Tamar *unto* [p]the waters of [q]strife *in* Kadesh,
and to the river toward the great sea.
29 [r]This *is* the land which ye shall divide
by lots unto the tribes of Israel for inheritance, and these *are* their portions, saith the
Lord GOD.
30 And these *are* the goings out of the city
on the north side, four thousand and five hundred measures.
31 [s]And the gates of the city
shall be after the names of the
tribes of Israel: three gates northward; one
gate of Reuben, one gate of Judah, one gate
of Levi.
32 And at the east side four thousand and
five hundred: and three gates; and one gate of
Joseph, one gate of Benjamin, one gate of
Dan.
33 And at the south side four thousand and
five hundred measures: and three gates; one
gate of Simeon, one gate of Issachar, one gate
of Zebulun.
34 At the west side four thousand and five
hundred, *with* their three gates; one gate of
Gad, one gate of Asher, one gate of Naphtali.
35 *It was* round about eighteen thousand
measures: [t]and the name of the city from
that day *shall be,* [u]The [v]LORD *is* there.

A. M. 3430
B. C. 574
Olymp. LI. 3
Anno
Servii Tullii,
R. Roman., 5

[o]Heb. *one* portion——[p]Chap. xlvii. 19——[q]Heb. *Meribah-kadesh*——[r]Chap. xlvii. 14, 21, 22——[s]Rev. xxi. 12, &c.——[t]Jer. xxxiii. 16

[u]Heb. *Jehovah-shammah;* see Exod. xvii. 15; Judg. vi. 24——[v]Psa. ii. 6; ix. 11; lxxvi. 2; xcix. 2; Jer. iii. 17; Joel iii. 21; Zech. ii. 10; Rev. xxi. 3; xxii. 3

dred cubits in breadth from north to south. The space both above and below was equal, between the tribe of Judah and that of Benjamin to north and south; and the portion of the Levites, which had Judah and Benjamin to the north and south, and the portion of the *prince* to the east and to the west. See the *map.*

Verse 28. *From Tamar—in Kadesh*] The former was on the *south* of the Dead Sea; and the latter, or Kadesh-Barnea, was still farther south, and at the extremity of the portion of *Gad,* which was the most *southern* tribe, as *Dan* was the most *northern.*

Verse 30. *These* are *the goings out*] Each of the four sides of the city was *four thousand five hundred* cubits long. There were three gates on each side, as mentioned below; and the whole circumference of the city was *eighteen thousand* cubits. See the map, plan B, *dddd.*

The rector of New Haven College, in New England, supposes the preceding representations to refer to the happy state of the Church in what is called the Millennium. Leaving this period out of the question, the following observations are worthy of notice:—"The Jews, for whom this vision was intended, would conceive their country to be divided to the *twelve tribes,* in lots of a regular and mathematical form; and not confused or intermixed, as in Joshua's time. Their city laid out larger than before; and exactly *four-square,* with regular suburbs; the temple and appendages much more commodious for their sacrifices, and the habitations of the priests and Levites regularly formed round about the temple. So that this whole plan of the division of the country, laying out of the city, temple, and all the appendages, appears to be perfectly regular and uniform, as if it were drawn all at one time, and by one hand, who had power to effect it; and therefore conveyed to the Jews the most complete idea they were capable of conceiving of the most perfect church, commonwealth, city, temple, and conveniences, for Divine worship. I. The Holy Land, as described chap. xlvii. and xlviii., according to the original grant, being about *two hundred and fifty* miles long, north and south, and about *one hundred and fifty* miles wide, is divided, by parallel lines east and west, to the twelve tribes, each of them having a portion *twenty* miles wide. Only between Judah and Benjamin there is a *holy portion* near *ten* miles wide; in the middle of which is the *holy oblation, twenty-five thousand* cubits; that is, about *ten* miles square for the priests, Levites, city, and temple, chap. xlv. 1; xlviii. 8; the two ends are for the prince, chap. xlv. 7, &c. II. The *holy oblation,* lying in the middle of the *holy portion,* is *twenty-five thousand* cubits square, which is near *ten* miles; of which *ten thousand* cubits, or *four* miles, are taken off from the north side for a habitation for the priests, and as much for the Levites on the south side, chap. xlv. 4, 5, and xlviii. 20; and *five thousand* cubits in the middle for the city portion, chap. xlv. 6; in the middle of which is the city, *four thousand five hundred* cubits square, which is nearly *two* miles, chap. xlviii. 15, 16. Round about this is left *two hundred and fifty* cubits, near *thirty* rods, for suburbs, ver. 17. The remaining *ten thousand* cubits on the east side, and the *ten thousand* cubits on the west side, are for the profit of those who serve the city, out of all the tribes, ver. 18, 19. The sanctuary is in the midst of the city, chap.

xlviii. 8. III. The *sanctuary* or temple, and its appendages, were entirely surrounded with a wall *six* cubits high and *six* cubits thick, chap. xl. 5; and *five hundred* cubits long on each side, chap. xlii. 15, &c., and xlv. 2. In the middle square stands the temple, which was surrounded by a wall *one hundred* cubits long on each side, chap. xli. 13, and *six* cubits thick, chap. xli. 6. The side-chambers on the outside *four* cubits, ver. 6. The Holy of Holies, at the west end, was *twenty* cubits square on the inside, ver. 4. The holy place, or outer court at the east end, was *forty* cubits, ver. 12. The length of the porch on the north side was *twenty* cubits; the breadth was *eleven* cubits, chap. xl. 49; and the width of the separate place on the south side *twenty* cubits. On each side of the temple, towards the *four* gates in the outer wall, stood *two* courts, *eight* in the whole, each *one hundred* cubits square, chap. xl. 19, 23, 27. In each of these were *thirty-six* little chambers or buildings, about *six* cubits square, viz., *six* at the entrance of the gate, chap. xl. 7, 17, 20, &c., and *thirty* on the pavement, ver. 17, &c., which were for lodgings for the priests, for hanging up their garments, and their part of the sacrifices, chap. xlii. 13."

Calmet has constructed a map to show the position of the tribes, and the *quantum* of space each was to possess. As this will give a better view of the subject than any written description can, I have inserted one constructed for this work, which, consulting the places said to be connected with the possessions of the different tribes, shows that the tribes did not all possess the same *quantum* of space, *five* of the southern tribes possessing only one half as much as those of the north.

Verse 35. *The name of the city from that day* shall be, *The Lord is there.*] It would have been better to have retained the original words:—

יהוה שמה YEHOVAH SHAMMAH.

This is an allusion to the *shechinah*, or symbol of the Divine Presence, which was in the *first*, but most certainly was *not* in the *second* temple; but Ezekiel tells us that the Divine Presence should be in the *city* of which he speaks; and should be there so fully and so powerfully, that it should give name to the city itself; and that the very name, *Jehovah shammah*, should remind all men of the supereminently glorious Being who had condescended to make this city his habitation.

Two points must be considered here:—1. That the prophet intended that, when they should be restored, they should build the temple, and divide the land as he here directs, if the thing could be found to be practicable. 2. That he had *another temple*, another *holy city*, another *Promised Land*, in view. The land of Immanuel, the city of the New Jerusalem; and his temple, the Christian Church, which is the house of the living God, 1 Tim. iii. 15, in which the presence of Christ shall ever be found; and all its inhabitants, all that believe on his name, shall be temples of the Holy Ghost. Nor can there be any reasonable doubt that the prophet here, by the Spirit of God, not only points out the return of the Israelites from the Babylonish captivity, and what was to befall them previously to the advent of Jesus Christ; but also the glorious spread of the Gospel in the earth, and the final conversion of the tribes of Israel by the preaching of that Gospel.

In conclusion, I think it necessary to state, that there are but few of the prophets of the Old Testament who have left a more valuable treasure to the Church of God than Ezekiel. It is true, he is in several places obscure; but there is a great proportion of the work that is in the highest degree edifying; and several portions that for the depth of the salvation predicted, and the accuracy and minuteness of the description, have nothing equal to them in the Old Testament Scriptures. On such portions, I have felt it my duty to be very particular, that I might be able to point out spiritual beauties and excellencies in this book which are beyond all praise; while I passed slightly over prophecies and symbols which I did not fully understand; but have left to time, by the fulfilment of the events, to prove to successive generations with what heavenly wisdom this *much neglected* prophet has spoken. And I take this opportunity to recommend this book to the serious perusal of every pious man; and while he wonders at the extent of the wisdom by which Ezekiel has fathomed the depth of so many Divine mysteries, let him give God the glory for this additional testimony to the unsearchable riches of Christ, and that plenary salvation which he has purchased for, and freely offers to, the vilest of the vile, and to the whole of the descendants of Adam.

MASORETIC NOTES.—Number of verses, 1,273. Middle verse, chap. xxvi. 1. Masoretic sections, 29.

DESCRIPTION OF THE PLAN OF EZEKIEL'S TEMPLE

As I utterly despair of making the prophet's description of this temple intelligible without a plan, I have introduced one drawn up with great labour and skill by *Dom. August. Calmet*, where the measurements, distances, gates, chambers, courts, inclosures, &c., are all carefully entered as far as they could possibly be ascertained from Ezekiel's description; which, it must be allowed, though wondrously circumstantial, is in several respects obscure. But by referring to the places, both in Kings and Chronicles, as well as in this prophet, where the same things are mentioned, this obscurity will be considerably diminished, if not entirely removed. At the same time, for a description of the temple in general, I beg leave to refer the reader to 1 Kings vi., at the end, where this subject is considered at large.

THE PLAN

[Let it be observed that the Hebrew cubit is about twenty inches and a half.]

AAAA The first inclosure, or wall of *six hundred* cubits, i. e., *one thousand and twenty-five* royal feet in length on each side, chap. xlv. 2; and *six* cubits or *ten* feet *three* inches high, and as many in breadth, chap. xl. 5.

BBBB The court of the Gentiles, or first court, *fifty* cubits in breadth, or *eighty-five* feet *five* inches, chap. xl. 2.

CCCC The outward wall of the court of Israel, or inclosure, *five hundred* cubits square, i. e., *eight hundred and fifty-four* feet *two* inches. This wall might be *thirty* cubits high, taken from the level of the threshold of the gate.

DDDD The court of Israel, *one hundred* cubits, or *one hundred and seventy* feet *ten* inches broad, chap. xl. 19.

EEEE The outer wall, or inclosure of the court of the priests, *two hundred* cubits, or *three hundred and forty-one* feet *eight* inches square, is supposed to be *thirty* cubits, or *fifty-one* feet *three* inches in height.

FFF The court of the priests, *one hundred* cubits, or *one hundred and seventy* feet *ten* inches square, chap. xl. 7; xli. 14, 15.

G The Sanctuary, or Holy of Holies, *twenty* cubits, or *thirty-four* feet *two* inches square, chap. xli. 4; 1 Kings vi. 2.

H The holy place, *forty* cubits long by *twenty* broad, or *sixty-eight* feet *two* inches long by *thirty-four* feet *two* inches broad, chap. xli. 2, and 1 Kings vi. 2.

I The vestibule or porch, *twenty* cubits in breadth, by *ten* (or according to Ezekiel, *eleven*) cubits in length, i. e., *thirty-four* feet *two* inches long by *seventeen* feet *one* inch broad, chap. xl. 48; 1 Kings vi. 3.

K The altar of burnt-offerings, *twelve* cubits, or *twenty* feet *six* inches square, according to Ezekiel, chap. xliii. 12, 13, &c., or *ten* cubits high by *twenty* broad, i. e., *seventeen* feet *one* inch high, and *thirty-four* feet *two* inches broad, according to 2 Chron. iv. 1.

LLL The wall of separation which encompassed the Temple, and the altar of burnt-offerings, of which the Scriptures do not give the dimensions. It was *twenty* cubits from the buildings in the court of the priests, and *five* from the Temple, chap. xli. 9, 10. *Josephus* makes it *three* cubits high, *Antiq.* lib. viii. c. 2.

MMMMMM Gates of the court of Israel, and of the court of the priests, all of the same dimensions, chap. xl. 1, 22, 36. Each of the porches was *fifty* cubits long, i. e., *eighty-five* feet *five* inches (as much as the depth of the aisles, chap. xl. 15) and *twenty-five* cubits, or *forty-two* feet *eight* inches and a *half* in breadth in the opening, and *sixty* cubits high, i. e., *one hundred and two* feet *six* inches, chap. xl. 14. On each side of the porches there were *three* chambers, each *six* cubits square, chap. xl. 6. And the separations between the *three* chambers were *five* cubits in thickness, chap. xl. 6.

NNNNNNNN Galleries around the court of Israel, chap. xl. I place there *thirty* pillars on a line of *two hundred* cubits in length, which is the same proportion as those given for *one hundred* cubits long, 1 Kings vii. 2, 3, 4, for the court of the palace of Solomon.

OOOOOOOO Chambers or apartments round the court of Israel; there were *thirty* on both sides of the gate, or *fifteen* on each side, chap. xl. 17.

PPPP The kitchens of the Temple, *forty* cubits, or *sixty-eight* feet *four* inches long by *thirty* cubits, or *fifty-one* feet *three* inches broad, chap. xlv. 21, 22, 23, 24.

Q The north gate of the court of the priests, where the victims were prepared, and where they slew the animals designed for sacrifice, chap. xl. 38, 39.

RRRR Galleries around the court of the priests, chap. xlii. 3.

SSSSSS Apartments continued round the court of the priests. The aisle, which was to the south of the eastern gate, was for the priests employed as *guards* of the Temple, chap. xl. 45. The aisle on the north side of the said gate was appointed for the *singers*, chap. xl. 44; the aisle that was on the eastern side of the south gate was for the *priests* employed about the *altar*, chap. xl. 46; the aisles which were to the west of the north gate and of the south gate, contained the halls where the priests ate, chap. xlii. 13.

TT The kitchens of the court of the priests were those where they dressed the trespass-offering, sin-offering, and the meat-offerings, *forty* cubits, or *sixty-eight* feet *four* inches long, and *thirty* cubits, or *fifty-one* feet *five* inches broad, chap. xlvi. 20. He speaks only of that on the *north*.

VVVV Flights of steps which led to the court of the people. In each flight there were *seven steps*, chap. xl. 22-26.

XXX Flights of steps which led to the court of the priests; in each there were *eighty steps*, chap. xl. 31, 34, 37.

YY A flight of steps which led to the porch of the Temple, *eight steps* in each, chap. xl. 49.

aaa Chambers about the Temple, *thirty-three* in number, Ezekiel makes them *four* cubits in breadth, chap. xli. 5; but in 1 Kings vi. 5, 6, they are stated to be *five* cubits in the *lower* stage, *six* in the *second*, and *seven* in the *third*.

bb Flights of steps opposite to the chambers, which were continued round the temple, chap. xli. 7, and 1 Kings vi. 8.

c The steps of the altar of burnt-offerings turned toward the east, chap. xliii. 15, 16.

dddd Tables of hewn stone, which were in the portico of the north gate of the priests' court, where they slew, flayed, and cut up the victims. Each table was *one and a half* cubits square, chap. xl. 38, 39-41.

The great walls of the temple were all *six* cubits, or *ten* feet *three* inches thick. These walls were: 1. That which formed the first inclosure; 2. The wall of the court of Israel: 3. The wall of the court of the priests; and, 4. The walls of the Temple. But the outward wall of the *thirty-three* chambers, which were round the holy place and the sanctuary, was only *five* cubits broad, and *fifteen* high; i. e., *eight* feet *six* inches *and a half* in thickness, and *twenty-five* feet *seven* inches *and a half* in height, chap. xli. 9, 12.

All the gates of the two courts, that of Israel and that of the priests, are of the same dimensions. The wall where was the opening was *six* cubits, or *ten* feet *three* inches in thickness. The gate was *eight* cubits, or *thirteen* feet *eight* inches wide; and the opening of the gate was one cubit, and the gate was *thirteen* cubits, or *twenty-two* feet *two* inches *and a half* high, chap. xl. 9, 11.

The *western* gate of the Temple is not mentioned by Ezekiel, because, according to his plan, the king's palace was not to be near the temple; and consequently this gate, which was the gate of the king, did not exist. But this was not followed, as we find that, after the return from Babylon, there were gates on the *western* side of the Temple, according to *Josephus;* and *before* the captivity the *western* gate did most certainly exist, see chap. xliii. 8; 2 Kings xi. 6; xvi. 18; 1 Chron. ix. 24; xxvi. 16, 18.

1. The gate of the porch of the holy place was *fourteen* cubits wide, i. e., *twenty-three* feet *eleven* inches, chap. xl. 48; 1 Kings vi. 3.

2. The gate of the holy place was *ten* cubits, or *seventeen* feet *one* inch wide, chap. xli. 1, 2.

3. The gate of the *sanctuary* was *six* cubits, or *ten* feet *three* inches wide. The wall of the separation was only *two* cubits, chap. xli. 1, 3.

4. The *east* gate of the court of the priests was shut all the week, and was not opened but

on the Sabbath and new moons, according to Ezekiel. It was there that the king had his *seat*, a sort of tribunal, chap. xliv. 2-4; xlvi. 1, 2, &c.

Calmet observes, with respect to his plan, that he assigns only *two* galleries to the apartments which were around the court of Israel; but those which were around the court of the priests had *three*, chap. xlii. 3, 5, 6. There is another difference between the palace (atrium) of the court of the priests, and that of the court of Israel. The walls of the first were built with *three* rows of hewn stones and one of cedar alternately, 1 Kings vi. 36; but this is not said to be the same in the structure of the outward court, or that of the people.

In the Old Testament we find no mention of the *court of the Gentiles*. Only *two* courts are mentioned there, one of the *priests*, the other of the *people;* one the *inner*, the other the *outer* court; but it is certain that such a court did exist, and is here marked BBBB.

The height of the aisles, or apartments that were around the *two* courts, is not mentioned any where in the Scriptures; but they are here fixed at *thirty* cubits; for the temple was not higher, neither was Solomon's palace. See 1 Kings vii. 2.

Explanation of the plan for the division of the land of Canaan, according to Ezekiel's vision, chap. xlviii.

A The Temple of the Lord, *five hundred* cubits square, chap. xlv. 2.

BB The city of the Levites, *four thousand five hundred* cubits square, and *eighteen thousand* in compass, chap. xlviii. 16.

cccc Suburbs of the city of the Levites, *two hundred and fifty* cubits in breadth, chap. xlviii. 17.

dddd The *twelve* gates of the Levitical city, *four* on each side, chap. xlviii. 31-34.

EE City of the lay persons or workmen employed in the service of the priests and of the Levites, *five thousand* broad by *twenty-five thousand* cubits long, chap. xlv. 6.

FF Cultivated ground for the maintenance of the lay artisans, chap. xlviii. 15.

GG Portion of the prince of Israel, *tweny-five thousand* cubits long by *twelve thousand five hundred* broad, chap. xlviii. 21.

The whole extent of the land from Kadesh-barnea south to Hethlon or Hamath north, was about *two hundred and twenty* miles, its mean breadth about *one* hundred.

INTRODUCTION TO THE BOOK

OF THE

PROPHET DANIEL

DANIEL is said to have descended from the royal family of David; and he appears to have been carried into Babylon when very young, in the *fourth* year of Jehoiakim king of Judah, A. M. 3398, B. C. 602, or 606 before the vulgar era. He and his three fellow-captives, *Hananiah*, *Mishael*, and *Azariah*, being likely youths, were chosen to be about the king's court, and were appointed to have an education suitable to the employments for which they were destined. As they had been carefully bred up in the Mosaic institutions, they regulated their conduct by them, even in the court of a heathen king, where they were in the capacity of *slaves;* hence, though ordered to be fed from the royal table, they would not touch that food, because the Chaldeans ate of meat forbidden by the Mosaic law, and probably even that which might be dominated *clean* became defiled by having been *sacrificed to idols* before it was prepared for common use. At their earnest request, the officer under whose care they were placed permitted them to use *vegetables* only; and finding that they grew healthy and strong by this aliment, did not oblige them to use the portion sent from the king's table.

Daniel appears to have been instructed in all the wisdom of the Chaldeans, which was at that time greatly superior to the learning of the ancient Egyptians; and he was soon distinguished in the Babylonish court, as well for his wisdom and strong understanding as for his deep and steady piety.

His interpretation of Nebuchadnezzar's dream of the *variously compounded metallic image* raised his credit so high at the court that he was established governor of the province of Babylon, and made chief of all the *Magians,* or wise men in that country. The chief facts and incidents of his history are so particularly woven throughout the book bearing his name, and undoubtedly written by himself, that they need not be detailed here.

The reputation of Daniel was so great, even in his *lifetime,* that it became a proverb. "*Thou art wiser than Daniel,*" said Ezekiel ironically to the king of Tyre, chap. xxviii. 3; and by the same prophet God ranks him among the most holy and exemplary of men, when he declares, speaking relative to Jerusalem, which had been condemned to destruction, "Though these three men, Noah, Daniel, and Job, were in it, they should deliver but their own lives by their righteousness," chap. xiv. 14, 20.

Josephus, Ant. lib. x., c. 12, says that God bestowed many favours on him: that he was advanced to the rank of the most considerable prophets; that he enjoyed the favour of princes, and the affection of the people during his life; and that after his death his memory became immortal. He observes also that, in the complexion of his predictions, he differs widely from all other prophets; they foretold scarcely any thing but *disastrous* events; on the contrary, he predicts the most *joyous* events, and *fixes the times of accomplishment* with more circumstantial precision than they did. And this is so true, that we cannot help thinking that God had given this eminent man a greater degree of light to fix the times when his predictions should issue, than he had given in general to all his predecessors, who simply declared the mind of God in relation to things *future*, without attempting to indicate the *distance of time* in which they should be fulfilled. There are but very few exceptions to this either in *Isaiah* or *Jeremiah*. And in this respect the prophecy of the *seventy weeks* of Daniel exceeds all that have gone before, as the incidents and transactions relative to its fulfilment were so various, and yet so fixed and declared *six hundred* years before the time, that when the time came in which they were predicted to take place, they were *expected,* and occurred exactly according to the *prediction,* and the *expectations* founded upon it. This prophet therefore, far from occupying a lower place among divinely inspired men, deserves to be placed in the front rank with all those who have been most distinguished among the men who have partaken most largely of the prophetic gift.

The rabbins have endeavoured to degrade Daniel, and have placed his prophecies among the *hagiographa,* books which they consider to possess a *minor degree of inspiration;* and it is probable that he meets with this treatment from them because his prophecies are proofs too evident that *Jesus Christ* is the true *Messiah,* and that he came at the very time that Daniel said the *Prince Messiah* should come. But the testimony and sayings of such men are infinitely overpowered by the testimony of *Ezekiel,* which has been produced above; and the testimony of our LORD, who gives him the title of *prophet,* Matt. xxiv. 15, without the slightest intimation that he was to wear this title with abatement.

It is very probable that Daniel did not return at the general restoration from the Babylonish captivity. At that time, if alive, he must have been an old man; and it is most likely that he finished his days in Babylon, though some Asiatic authors hold that he returned to Judea with Ezra, came back afterward to Persia, and died in the city of *Susa.*

Josephus speaks of his skill in *architecture,* Antiq. lib. x., c. 12, and that he built a famous tower at *Ecbatane* or *Susa,* which remained to his time, and was so exquisitely finished that it always appeared as if newly built. In this tower or palace the kings of Persia were interred; and in consideration of its *founder,* the guard of it was always chosen from the *Jews.*

Daniel is famous among the orientalists. The author of the *Tareekh Muntekheb* says that Daniel flourished in the time of *Lohorasp,* king of Persia; and consequently in that of *Ceresh,* or Cyrus, who gave him the government of Syria; that he taught these two princes the knowledge of the true God; that he preached the true faith through the whole of the Babylonian Irak; and was, on the death of Nebuchadnezzar, sent by Bahman, (Artaxerxes Longimanus,) son of Asfendiar, who then reigned in Persia, into Judea; and that, having returned, he died at *Shouster,* or *Susa,* the capital of Persia, where he lies interred.

Some have supposed that the Zoroaster or Zeradusht of the Persians is a confused picture of the Prophet Daniel. The account given by Abul Pharaje, in his *fifth* dynasty, may be considered favourable to this opinion. He says, "Zeradusht, author of the Magiouseiah *Magism,* or sect of the worshippers of fire, flourished in the reign of *Cambasous,* (Cambyses;) that he was a native of the province of Adherbigian, or Media, or, according to others, of Assyria; that he foretold to his disciples the coming of the Messiah, who should be pointed out by a *star* which should appear in the day time at his birth; that they should have the first information of his advent; that he should be born of a virgin; and that they should present him with gifts; because he is the WORD that made the heavens." See *Pococke's* Abul Pharajius, p. 83 of the *Arabic,* and 54 of the *Latin.*

D'Herbelot, on this account, makes the following remark: "We may see by these words of the historian, that the prophecy of Balaam was pretty generally known throughout the east, and that the *Magi,* who came to worship our Lord, were the true *Magians* of Persia, and not Arab kings."

The account given by Abul Pharaje makes Daniel and Zeradusht contemporary, and thus far is favourable to the opinion that the history of the former may be disguised under that of the latter. There have been several Zoroasters, of whom many fables are told; and no wonder, when the persons themselves are generally fabulous.

The Asiatics make him the *inventor* of رمل *remel,* or *geomancy;* and among them he passes for the author of a work entitled *Assoul ol Tabeer,* "The Principles of the Interpretation of Dreams." I have in my own library a very ancient work which pretends to be drawn from this, and is entitled *Somnia Daniel;* it was printed in the infancy of printing, but without date; small 4to. There is an Arabic work in the French king's library, No. 410, entitled *Odhmet al Mancoul, an Danial an Nabi*, "The Traditionary Predictions of Daniel the Prophet;" which is said to contain many falsities, built on the foundation of Daniel's prophecies; but it has never been given to the public, and I have no other notice of it than the above from *D'Herbelot*. But although all these are curious from their *antiquity*, yet they are doubtless impostures.

Abul Pharaje, in his history of the dynasties, says, that the *seventy weeks* of Daniel are to be dated from the *twentieth* year of اردشير درازدست *Ardsheer Dirazdest*, the *Artaxerxes Longimanus* of the Greeks, (called *Bahman* above,) and the same to whom Nehemiah was ساقي *sakee*, or cup-bearer. Other orientalists are of the same opinion. This shall be considered more at large when we come to the prophecy itself. Artaxerxes had the name of *Longimanus*, or Long-handed, from the great extent of his dominions.

Daniel cannot be ranked among the Hebrew *poets:* his book is all in *prose;* and it is written partly in *Hebrew*, and partly in *Chaldee*. The Chaldee, or Syro-Chaldaic part, begins with מלכא לעלמין חיי *malka lealmin chei*, "O king, live for ever!" and continues to the end of the *seventh* chapter.

In the interpretation of his prophecies I have endeavoured to follow the best critics and chronologists; and, without an extended comment, to give in as short a space as possible the meaning of every place. On the *metallic images* and *seventy weeks* I have been obliged to be more prolix, as these are of too much importance to be slightly handled. It is not my province to enter into the controversy about the date when the seventy weeks commence; even they who disagree so much from each other on this point come so near to the general issue that the difference is immaterial.

The chronology of the several events mentioned in this book *Calmet* endeavours to fix as follows:—

A. M.

3398. Daniel led captive to Babylon, chap. i. 1–7.
3399. Death of Nabopolassar, father of Nebuchadnezzar.
3401. Jehoiakim revolts against Nebuchadnezzar, 2 Kings xxiv. 1.
3402. Dream of the compound statue, Dan. ii. 1, &c.
Daniel and his companions promoted to honour at court.
Birth of Cyrus, son of Cambyses and Mandane.
3405. Jehoiakim is taken and put to death by the Chaldeans.
Jeconiah is raised to his throne, but reigns only *three* months and *ten* days.
Zedekiah, last king of Judah, succeeds; and reigns *eleven* years.
3416. Taking of Jerusalem, and destruction of the temple, 1 Chron. xxxvi.
3434. Return of Nebuchadnezzar to Babylon after his great conquests in Phœnicia, Judea, Egypt, &c.
His dream of the great tree, chap. iv. 7, &c.
3435. He becomes insane, which lasts for *seven* years, chap. iv. 32, 33.
3442. He becomes sane, and re-ascends the throne.
The golden image set up. The *three* Hebrews cast into the fiery furnace, chap. iii.
Death of Nebuchadnezzar after a reign of *forty-three* years, according to *Berosus*.
Evil-Merodach succeeds him, and reigns *two* years.—*Berosus*.
He sets Jeconiah at liberty, Jer. lii. 31.
3444. Belshazzar his son succeeds, Dan. vii. 1.
Daniel's vision of the *four* beasts, representing the *four* great empires, chap. vii.
3447. Vision of the ram and he-goat, chap. viii.
The death of Belshazzar, chap. v.
3449. Darius the Mede, called *Cyaxares* by Xenophon, and *Astyages* in the Apocrypha, son of Astyages, king of the Medes, and maternal great uncle to Belshazzar, succeeds him in the government of Chaldea, chap. v. 30, 31. See Isa. xiii. 1, &c.
The visions of Daniel related, chap. ix., x., xi., xii.
Cyrus attacks the Medes in the *first* or *second* year of Darius the Mede, chap. x. 1.

A. M.
3455. Daniel is cast into the den of lions, chap. vi.
3456. Death of Darius. Cyrus succeeds him.
3457. End of the Babylonish captivity *declared* by *Cyrus*, in the *first* year of his reign, 2 Chron. xxxvi. 22, and Ezra i. 1; but afterward interrupted. See below.
3485. Termination of Jeremiah's *seventy* years under *Darius Hystaspes*, who gives orders to *continue* the rebuilding of the temple.
3550. Commencement of the *seventy* weeks, chap. ix. 24.
Nehemiah returns to Jerusalem, Neh. ii. 1–6.

In this chronology *Calmet* differs from *Usher*.

As a writer, this prophet is simple, yet pure and correct: and he is so conscientious that he relates the very words of those persons whom he introduces as speaking. He writes *Hebrew* where what he delivers is a bare narrative; but he relates in *Chaldee* the conversations which he had with the wise men and the kings; and in the same language he relates Nebuchadnezzar's edict, which he made after Daniel had interpreted his dream concerning the great metalline image. This is a proof of his great and conscientious accuracy; and exhibits this prophet in a most advantageous point of view. Daniel writes both *Hebrew* and *Chaldee* with great purity.

This book divides itself into two parts. Part I is *historical*, and is contained in the six former chapters. Part II. is *prophetical*, and occupies the other six.

THE BOOK

OF THE

PROPHET DANIEL

Chronological Notes relative to the commencement of Daniel's prophesying

Year from the Creation, according to Archbishop Usher, 3397.—Year of the Jewish era of the world, 3154. —Year from the Deluge, 1741.—Second year of the *forty-third* Olympiad.—Year from the building of Rome, according to the Varronian or generally received account, 147.—Year from the building of Rome, according to Cato and the Fasti Consulares, 146.—Year from the building of Rome, according to Polybius the historian, 145.—Year from the building of Rome, according to Fabius Pictor, 411.—Year of the Julian Period, 4107.—Year of the era of Nabonassar, 141.—Year from the foundation of Solomon's temple, 397.—Year since the destruction of the kingdom of Israel by Shalmaneser, king of Assyria, 114. —Fourth year after the first Sabbatic year after the *seventeenth* Jewish jubilee, according to Helvicus.— Year before the birth of Christ, 603.—Year before the vulgar era of Christ's nativity, 607.—Cycle of the Sun, 19.—Cycle of the Moon, 3.—Tenth year of Tarquinius Priscus, the fifth king of the Romans.— Nineteenth year of Cyaxares or Cyaraxes, the fourth king of Media.—Forty-fourth year of Archidamus, king of Lacedæmon, of the family of the Proclidæ.—First year of Leon, king of Lacedæmon, of the family of Eurysthenidæ.—Thirteenth year of Alyattes II., king of Lydia, and father of the celebrated Crœsus. —Thirty-fourth year of Philip, the sixth king of Macedon.—Eleventh year of Pharaoh-necho, called Necus by Herodotus. This king was the immediate predecessor of Psammis; and Psammis was succeeded by the celebrated Pharaoh-hophra, called also Apries.—Eighth year of Ithobalus, king of the Tyrains, according to Helvicus.—Third year (ending) of Jehoiakim, king of Judah; for the principal part of A. M. 3397 corresponded to the *fourth* year of this prince.

CHAPTER I

This chapter begins with giving a short account of Nebuchadnezzar's conquest of Judea, when Jehoiakim became tributary to him; and consequently the seventy years' captivity and vassalage began, 1, 2. *On this expedition (taking Egypt in his way) the king of Babylon set out towards the end of the third year of Jehoiakim, but did not take Jerusalem before the* ninth *month of the year following. Hence the seeming discrepancy between Daniel and Jeremiah,* (chap. xxv. 1,) *the one computing from the time of his setting out on the expedition, and the other from the time in which the purpose of it was accomplished. We have next an account of the manner in which Daniel and his companions were brought up at the king's court,* 3–7. *They reject the daily provision of meat granted by the king, lest they should be defiled, and are allowed to live on pulse,* 8–16. *Their great proficiency in the wisdom of that time,* 17–20. *Daniel flourishes till the reign of Cyrus the Persian,* 21.

A. M. 3397 B. C. 607 Ol. XLIII. 2 Anno TarquiniiPrisci, R. Roman., 10

IN the third year of the reign
of Jehoiakim king of Judah
[a]came Nebuchadnezzar king of
Babylon unto Jerusalem, and
besieged it.

A. M. cir. 3398 B. C. cir. 606 Ol. XLIII. 3 TarquiniiPrisci. R. Roman., cir. annum 11

2 And the LORD gave Jehoiakim king of Judah into his
hand, with [b]part of the vessels
of the house of God: which he
carried [c]into the land of Shinar to the house

[a]2 Kings xxiv. 1; 2 Chron. xxxvi. 6——[b]Jer. xxvii. 19, 20——[c]Gen. x. 10; xi. 2; Isa. xi. 11; Zech. v. 11

NOTES ON CHAP. I

Verse 1. *In the third year of the reign of Jehoiakim*] This king was raised to the throne of Judea in the place of his brother *Jehoahaz*, by *Pharaoh-necho*, king of Egypt, 2 Kings xxiii. 34-36, and continued tributary to him during the first *three* years of his reign; but in the *fourth*, which was the *first* of Nebuchadnezzar, Jer. xxv. 1, Nebuchadnezzar completely defeated the Egyptian army near the Euphrates, Jer. xlvi. 2; and this victory put the neighbouring countries of Syria, among which *Judea* was the chief, under the Chaldean government. Thus Jehoiakim, who had *first* been tributary to Egypt, became now the vassal of the king of Babylon, 2 Kings xxiv. 1.

At the end of three years Jehoiakim rebelled

A. M. cir. 3398
B. C. cir. 606
Ol. XLIII. 3
TarquiniiPrisci,
R. Roman.,
cir. annum 11

of his god; [d]and he brought the
vessels into the treasure house of
his god.
3 And the king spake unto
Ashpenaz the master of his eunuchs, that
he should bring *certain* of the children of
Israel, and of the king's seed, and of the
princes;
4 Children [e]in whom *was* no blemish, but
well favoured, and skilful in all wisdom, and
cunning in knowledge, and understanding
science, and such as *had* ability in them to
stand in the king's palace, and [f]whom they

[d]2 Chron. xxxvi. 7——[e]See Lev. xxiv. 19, 20——[f]Acts vii. 22——[g]Heb. *the wine of his drink*

might teach the learning and
the tongue of the Chaldeans.
5 And the king appointed them
a daily provision of the king's
meat, and of [g]the wine which he drank: so
nourishing them three years, that at the end
thereof they might [h]stand before the king.
6 Now among these were of the children of
Judah, Daniel Hananiah, Mishael, and
Azariah:
7 [i]Unto whom the prince of the eunuchs
gave names: [k]for he gave unto Daniel *the
name* of Belteshazzar; and to Hananiah, of

[h]Ver. 19; Gen. xli. 46; 1 Kings x. 8——[i]Gen. xli. 45; 2 Kings xxiv. 17——[k]Chap. iv. 8; v. 12

against Nebuchadnezzar, who, then occupied with other wars, did not proceed against Jerusalem till *three years after*, which was the *eleventh* and last of Jehoiakim, 2 Kings xxiii. 36.

There are some difficulties in the chronology of this place. *Calmet* takes rather a different view of these transactions. He connects the history thus: Nabopolassar, king of Babylon, finding that one of his lords whom he had made governor of Cœlesyria and Phœnicia had revolted from him, and formed an alliance with the king of Egypt, sent Neubuchadnezzar his son, whom he invested with the authority of *king*, to reduce those provinces, as was customary among the easterns when the heir presumptive was sent on any important expedition or embassy. This young prince, having quelled the insurrection in those parts, marched against Jerusalem about the *end* of the *third* or *beginning* of the *fourth* year of the reign of Jehoiakim, king of Judah. He soon took the city, and put Jehoiakim in chains with the design of carrying him to Babylon; but, changing his mind, he permitted him to resume the reins of government under certain oppressive conditions. At this year, which was A. M. 3398, the *seventy years* of the Babylonish captivity commence. Nabopolassar dying in the interim, Nebuchadnezzar was obliged to return speedily to Babylon, leaving his generals to conduct the Jewish captives to Babylon, among whom were Daniel and his companions.

Verse 2. *Part of the vessels of the house of God*] He took the richest and finest of them for the service of his god *Bel*, and left what were necessary for carrying on the public worship of *Jehovah*, (for he did not attempt to alter the civil or religious constitution of Judea;) for leaving Jehoiakim on the throne, he only laid the land under tribute. The Chaldeans carried these sacred vessels away at *three* different times. 1. In the war spoken of in this place. 2. In the taking of Jerusalem and Jeconiah a few months after, 2 Kings xxiv. 13. 3. *Eleven years* after, under the reign of Zedekiah, when the city and temple were totally destroyed, and the land ruined, 2 Kings xxv. 8-15.

The land of Shinar] This was the ancient name of Babylon. See Gen. xi. 2.

The treasure house of his god.] This was *Bel*, who had a splendid temple in Babylon, and was the tutelar god of the city and empire.

Verse 3. *Master of his eunuchs*] This word *eunuchs* signifies officers about or in the palace, whether literally eunuchs or not.

Verse 4. *Children*] ילדים *yeladim*, *youths*, *young men;* and so the word should be rendered throughout this book.

Skilful in all wisdom] Rather, persons capable of every kind of literary accomplishment, that they might be put under proper instruction. And as *children of the blood* and of the *nobles* were most likely, from the care usually taken of their initiatory education, to profit most by the elaborate instruction here designed, the master of the eunuchs, the king's chamberlain, was commanded to choose the youths in question out of such.

Verse 5. *A daily provision*] *Athenæus*, lib. iv., c. 10, says: The kings of Persia, (who succeeded the kings of Babylon, on whose empire they had seized,) were accustomed to order the food left at their own tables to be delivered to their courtiers.

So nourishing them three years] This was deemed a sufficient time to acquire the *Chaldee language*, and the *sciences* peculiar to that people. I suppose they had good *introductory books*, *able teachers*, and a *proper method;* else they would have been obliged, like us, to send their children *seven years* to *school*, and *as many* to the *university*, to teach them any tolerable measure of useful and ornamental literature! O how reproachful to the nations of Europe, and particularly to our own, is this *backward* mode of instruction. And what is generally learned after this vast expense of *time* and *money?* A little *Latin*, *Greek*, and *mathematics;* perhaps a little *moral philosophy;* and by this they are *entitled*, not *qualified*, to teach others, and especially to teach the people the important *science of salvation!* To such shepherds, (and there are many such,) the hungry sheep look up, and are not fed; and if all are not such, no thanks to our plan of national education.

Verse 6. *Now among these*] There were no doubt several noble youths from other provinces: but the four mentioned here were Jews, and are supposed to have all been of royal extraction.

Verse 7. *Unto whom the prince of the eunuchs gave names*] This change of names, *Calmet* properly remarks, was a mark of dominion and authority. It was customary for

A. M. cir. 3398 B. C. cir. 606 Ol. XLIII. 3 TarquiniiPrisci, R. Roman., cir. annum 11

Shadrach; and to Mishael, of Meshach; and to Azariah, of Abed-nego.

8 But Daniel purposed in his heart that he would not defile himself [l]with the portion of the king's meat, nor with the wine which he drank: therefore he requested of the prince of the eunuchs that he might not defile himself.

9 Now [m]God had brought Daniel into favour and tender love with the prince of the eunuchs.

10 And the prince of the eunuchs said unto Daniel, I fear my lord the king who hath appointed your meat and your drink: for why should he see your faces [n]worse liking than the children which *are* of your [o]sort? then shall ye make *me* endanger my head to the king.

11 Then said Daniel to [p]Melzar, whom the prince of the [q]eunuchs had set over Daniel, Hananiah, Mishael, and Azariah,

12 Prove thy servants, I beseech thee, ten days; and let them give us [r]pulse [s]to eat, and water to drink.

A. M. cir. 3398 B. C. cir. 606 Ol. XLIII. 3 TarquiniiPrisci, R. Roman., cir. annum 11

13 Then let our countenances be looked upon before thee, and the countenance of the children that eat of the portion of the king's meat: and as thou seest, deal with thy servants.

14 So he consented to them in this matter, and proved them ten days.

15 And at the end of ten days their countenances appeared fairer and fatter in flesh than all the children which did eat the portion of the king's meat.

16 Thus Melzar took away the portion of their meat, and the wine that they should drink; and gave them pulse.

17 As for these four children, [t]God gave them [u]knowledge and skill in all learning and wisdom; and [v]Daniel had [w]understanding in all visions and dreams.

[l]Deut. xxxii. 38; Ezek. iv. 13; Hos. ix. 3——[m]See Gen. xxxix. 21; Psa. cvi. 46; Prov. xvi 7——[n]Heb. *sadder*——[o]Or, *term*, or *continuance*——[p]Or, *the steward* [q]2 Kings ix. 32; xx. 18; Isa. xxxix. 7; Acts viii. 27

[r]Heb. *of pulse*——[s]Heb. *that we may eat*, &c.——[t]1 Kings iii. 12; James i. 5, 17——[u]Acts vii. 22——[v]Or, *he made Daniel understand*——[w]Num. xii. 6; 2 Chron. xxvi. 5; chap. v. 11, 12, 14; x. 1

masters to impose new names upon their slaves; and rulers often, on their ascending the throne, assumed a name different from that which they had before.

דניאל Daniel signifies "God is my Judge." This name they changed into בלטשאצר Belteshatstsar; in Chaldee, "The treasure of Bel," or "The despository of the secrets (or *treasure*) of Bel."

הנניה Hananiah signifies, "The Lord has been gracious to me;" cr "He to whom the Lord is gracious." This name was changed into שדרך Shadrach, Chaldee, which has been variously translated: "The inspiration of the sun;" "God, the author of evil, be propitious to us;" "Let God preserve us from evil."

מישאל Mishael signifies, "He who comes from God." Him they called מישך Meshach, which in Chaldee signifies, "He who belongs to the goddess Sheshach," a celebrated deity of the Babylonians, mentioned by Jeremiah, chap. xxv. 26.

עזריה Azariah, which signifies "The Lord is my Helper," they changed into אבד נגו Abed-nego, which in Chaldee is "the servant of Nego," who was one of their divinities; by which they meant either the *sun*, or the *morning star;* whether *Jupiter* or *Venus*.

The vicious pronunciation of this name should be carefully avoided; I mean that which lays the accent on the first syllable, and hurries to the end, without attending to the natural division of the word *Abed-Nego*.

Verse 8. *But Daniel—would not defile himself*] I have spoken of this resolution in the introduction. The chief reasons why Daniel would not eat meat from the royal table were probably these three:—1. Because they ate unclean beasts, which were forbidden by the Jewish law. 2. Because they ate, as did the heathens in general, beasts which had been strangled, or not properly blooded. 3. Because the animals that were eaten were first offered as victims to their gods. It is on this account that Athenæus calls the beasts which were served up at the tables of the Persian kings, *ιερια, victims*, lib. iv. c. 10, p. 145.

Verse 11. *Then said Daniel to Melzar*] Melzar was an officer under Ashpenaz, whose office it was to attend to the food, clothing, &c., of these royal captives. Others think מלצר *meltsar*, master of the inn or hotel, the name of an *office*.

Verse 12. *Give us pulse to eat*] הזרעים *hazzeraim*, seeds or grain, such as barley, wheat, rye, and peas, &c. Though a vegetable diet might have produced that healthiness of the system in general, and of the countenance particularly, as mentioned here; yet we are to understand that there was an especial blessing of God in this, because this spare diet was taken on a religious account.

Verse 17. *As for these four children*] *Young men* or *youths*. Our translation gives a false idea.

In all visions and dreams.] That is, such as are *Divine;* for as to dreams in general, they have as much signification as they have connexion, being the effects of the state of the *body*, of the *mind*, or of the *circumstances* of the dreamer. A dream may be considered *supernatural*, if it have nothing preposterous,

A. M. cir. 3401
B. C. cir. 603
Ol. XLIV. 2
TarquiniiPrisci,
R. Roman.,
cir. annum 14

18 Now at the end of the days that the king had said he should bring them in, then the prince of the eunuchs brought them in before Nebuchadnezzar.

19 And the king communed with them; and among them all was found none like Daniel, Hananiah, Mishael, and Azariah: therefore [x]stood they before the king.

20 [y]And in all matters of [z]wisdom *and* understanding, that the king inquired of them, he found them ten times better than all the magicians *and* astrologers that *were* in all his realm.

21 [a]And Daniel continued *even* unto the first year of king Cyrus.

[x]Genesis xli. 46; ver. 5——[y]1 Kings x. 1——[z]Hebrew, *wisdom of understanding*——[a]Chap. vi. 28; x. 1 He lived to see that glorious time of the return of his people from the Babylonian captivity, though he did not die then; so *till* is used, Psalm cx. 1; cxii. 8

nothing monstrous, and nothing irregular. If the whole order and consequences of the things be preserved in them, from beginning to end, then we may presume they are supernatural. In such dreams Daniel had understanding.

Verse 18. *Now at the end of the days*] That is, at the end of *three years*, ver. 5.

Verse 19. *And among them all*] All the young noble captives from different nations.

Therefore stood they before the king.] It appears that only *four* were wanting.

Verse 20. *Magicians* and *astrologers*] Probably the same as *philosophers* and *astronomers* among us.

Verse 21. *The first year of king Cyrus.*] That is, to the *end of the Chaldean empire.* And we find Daniel alive in the *third* year of Cyrus, see chap. x. 1.

CHAPTER II

Nebuchadnezzar, in the second year of his reign, (*or in the fourth, according to the Jewish account, which takes in the first two years in which he reigned conjointly with his father,*) *had a dream which greatly troubled him; but of which nothing remained in the morning but the uneasy impression. Hence the diviners, when brought in before the king, could give no interpretation, as they were not in possession of the dream,* 1–13. *Daniel then, having obtained favour from God, is made acquainted with the dream, and its interpretation,* 14–19; *for which he blesses God in a lofty and beautiful ode,* 20–23; *and reveals both unto the king, telling him first the particulars of the dream,* 24–35, *and then interpreting it of the four great monarchies. The then existing* Chaldean *empire, represented by the head of gold, is the first; the next is the* Medo-Persian; *the third, the* Macedonian *or* Grecian; *the fourth, the* Roman, *which should break every other kingdom in pieces, but which in its last stage, should be divided into ten kingdoms, represented by the ten toes of the image, as they are in another vision* (chap. vii.) *by the ten horns of the fourth beast. He likewise informs the king that in the time of this last monarchy, viz., the Roman, God would set up the kingdom of the Messiah; which, though small in its commencement, should ultimately be extended over the whole earth,* 36–45. *Daniel and his three friends, Hananiah, Mishael, and Azariah,* (*named by the prince of the eunuchs, Shadrach, Meshach, and Abed-nego,*) *are then promoted by the king to great honour,* 46–49.

A. M. 3401
B. C. 603
Ol. XLIV. 2
Anno
TarquiniiPrisci,
R. Roman., 14

AND in the second year of the reign of Nebuchadnezzar, Nebuchadnezzar dreamed dreams, [a]wherewith his spirit was troubled, and [b]his sleep brake from him.

2 [c]Then the king commanded to call the magicians, and the

[a]Gen. xli. 8; chap. iv. 5——[b]Esth. vi. 1; chap. vi. 18——[c]Gen. xli. 8; Exod. vii. 11; chap. v. 7

NOTES ON CHAP. II

Verse 1. *The second year of the reign of Nebuchadnezzar*] That is, the *second* year of his reigning *alone*, for he was king *two* years before his father's death. See the notes on chap. i. 1. This was therefore the *fifth* year of his reign, and the *fourth* of the captivity of Daniel.

Nebuchadnezzar dreamed dreams wherewith his spirit was troubled] The dream had made a deep and solemn impression upon his mind; and, having forgotten all but general circumstances, his mind was distressed.

Verse 2. *The magicians*] חרטמים *chartummim.* See the note on Gen. xli. 8.

The astrologers] אשפים *ashshaphim.* Perhaps from נשף *nashaph*, to *breathe*, because they laid claim to Divine *inspiration;* but probably the persons in question were the *philosophers* and *astronomers* among the Babylonians.

The sorcerers] מכשפים *mechashshephim.* See the note on Deut. xviii. 10, and on Exod. xxii. 18, and Lev. xix. 31, where several of these *arts* are explained.

The Chaldeans] Who these were is difficult to be ascertained. They might be a college of learned men, where all arts and sciences were professed and taught. The Chaldeans were the most ancient philosophers of the world; they might have been originally inhabitants of the

A. M. 3401
B. C. 603
Ol. XLIV. 2
Anno
TarquiniiPrisci,
R. Roman., 14

astrologers, and the sorcerers, and the Chaldeans, for to show the king his dreams. So they came and stood before the king.

3 And the king said unto them, I have dreamed a dream, and my spirit was troubled to know the dream.

4 Then spake the Chaldeans to the king in Syriac, [d]O king, live for ever: tell thy servants the dream, and we will show the interpretation.

5 The king answered and said to the Chaldeans, The thing is gone from me: if ye will not make known unto me the dream, with the interpretation thereof, ye shall be [e]cut [f]in pieces, and your houses shall be made a dunghill.

6 [g]But if ye show the dream, and the interpretation thereof, ye shall receive of me gifts and [h]rewards and great honour: therefore show me the dream, and the interpretation thereof.

7 They answered again and said, Let the king tell his servants the dream, and we will show the interpretation of it.

8 The king answered and said, I know of certainty that ye would [i]gain the time, because ye see the thing is gone from me.

9 But if ye will not make known unto me the dream, [k]*there is but* one decree for you: for ye have prepared [l]lying and corrupt words to speak before me, till the time be changed: therefore tell me the dream, and I shall know that ye can show me the interpretation thereof.

A. M. 3401
B. C. 603
Ol. XLIV. 2
Anno
TarquiniiPrisci,
R. Roman., 14

10 The Chaldeans answered before the king, and said, There is not a man upon the earth that can show the king's matter: therefore *there is* no king, lord, nor ruler, *that* asked such things at any magician, or astrologer, or Chaldean.

11 And *it is* a rare thing that the king requireth, and there is none other that can show it before the king, [m]except the gods, whose dwelling is not with flesh.

12 For this cause the king was angry and very furious, and commanded to destroy all the wise *men* of Babylon.

13 And the decree went forth that the wise *men* should be slain; and they sought Daniel and his fellows to be slain.

14 Then Daniel [n]answered with counsel and wisdom to Arioch the [o]captain [p]of the king's guard, which was gone forth to slay the wise *men* of Babylon:

---

[d]1 Kings i. 31; chap. iii. 9; v. 10; vi. 6, 21——[e]Ezra vi. 11; 2 Kings x. 27; chap. iii. 29——[f]Chald. *made pieces*——[g]Chap. v. 16——[h]Or, *fee;* chap. v. 17; ver. 48——[i]Chald. *buy;* Eph. v. 16

[k]Esth. iii. 15; iv. 11; ix. 14——[l]Prov. vi. 17; xii. 19; xxi. 6; xxvi. 28——[m]Ver. 28; chap. v. 11——[n]Chald. *returned*——[o]Or, *chief marshal*——[p]Chald. *chief of the executioners,* or *slaughtermen;* Gen. xxxvii. 36

Babylonian Irak; and still have preserved to themselves exclusively the name of *Chaldeans,* to distinguish themselves from other nations and peoples who inhabited the *one hundred and twenty* provinces of which the Babylonish government was composed.

Verse 4. *Then spake the Chaldeans to the king in Syriac*] ארמית *aramith,* the language of *Aram* or *Syria.* What has been generally called the Chaldee.

O king, live for ever] מלכא לעלמין חיי *Malca leolmin cheyi.* With these words the *Chaldee* part of Daniel commences; and continues to the end of the *seventh* chapter. These kinds of compliments are still in use in the East Indies. A superior gives a blessing to an inferior by saying to him, when the latter is in the act of doing him reverence, *"Long life to thee."* A poor man, going into the presence of a king to solicit a favour, uses the same kind of address: *O father,* thou art the support of the destitute; *mayest thou live to old age!*—Ward's *Customs.*

Verse 5. *Ye shall be cut in pieces*] This was arbitrary and tyrannical in the extreme; but, in the order of God's providence, it was overruled to serve the most important purpose.

Verse 8. *That ye would gain the time*] The king means either that they wished to prolong the time that he might recollect it, or get indifferent about it; or that they might invent something in the place of it; or make their escape to save their lives, after having packed up their valuables. See ver. 9.

Verse 10. *There is not a man upon the earth*] The thing is utterly impossible to man. This was their decision: and when Daniel gave the dream, with its interpretation, they knew that the *spirit of the holy gods was in him.* So, even according to their own theology, he was immeasurably greater than the wisest in Babylon or in the world.

Verse 13. *They sought Daniel and his fellows*] As the decree stated that all the wise men of Babylon should be slain, the *four* young Hebrews, being reputed among the *wisest,* were considered as sentenced to death also.

Verse 14. *Captain of the king's guard*] Chief of the *king's executioners* or *slaughter men.* Margin, רב טבחיא *rab tabachaiya,* chief of the butchers, he that took off the heads of those whom the king ordered to be slain, because they had in any case displeased him. "Go and bring me the head of Giaffer." The honourable butcher went and brought the head in a bag on a dish. It was Herod's chief butcher that brought the head of John the Baptist in a dish

A. M. 3401 B. C. 603 Ol. XLIV. 2 Anno TarquiniiPrisci, R. Roman., 14

15 He answered and said to Arioch the king's captain, Why *is* the decree *so* hasty from the king? Then Arioch made the thing known to Daniel.

16 Then Daniel went in, and desired of the king that he would give him time, and that he would show the king the interpretation.

17 Then Daniel went to his house, and made the thing known to Hananiah, Mishael, and Azariah, his companions:

18 [q]That they would desire mercies [r]of the God of heaven concerning this secret; [s]that Daniel and his fellows should not perish with the rest of the wise *men* of Babylon.

19 Then was the secret revealed unto Daniel [t]in a night vision. Then Daniel blessed the God of heaven.

20 Daniel answered and said, [u]Blessed be the name of God for ever and ever: [v]for wisdom and might are his:

21 And he changeth [w]the times and the seasons: [x]he removeth kings, and setteth up kings: [y]he giveth wisdom unto the wise, and knowledge to them that know understanding:

22 [z]He revealeth the deep and secret things: [a]he knoweth what *is* in the darkness, and [b]the light dwelleth with him.

23 I thank thee, and praise thee, O thou God of my fathers, who hast given me wisdom and might, and hast made known unto me now what we [c]desired of thee: for thou hast *now* made known unto us the king's matter.

24 Therefore Daniel went in unto Arioch, whom the king had ordained to destroy the wise *men* of Babylon: he went and said thus unto him: Destroy not the wise *men* of Babylon: bring me in before the king, and I will show unto the king the interpretation.

25 Then Arioch brought in Daniel before the king in haste, and said thus unto him, [d]I have found a man of the [e]captives of Judah, that will make known unto the king the interpretation.

26 The king answered and said to Daniel, whose name *was* Belteshazzar, Art thou able to make known unto me the dream which I have seen, and the interpretation thereof?

27 Daniel answered in the presence of the king, and said, The secret which the king hath demanded cannot the wise *men*, the astrologers, the magicians, the soothsayers, show unto the king;

[q]Matt. xviii. 12——[r]Chald. *from before God*——[s]Or, *that they should not destroy Daniel*, &c.——[t]Num. xii. 6 Job xxxiii. 15, 16——[u]Psa. cxiii. 2; cxv. 18——[v]Jer. xxxii. 19——[w]Esth. i. 13; 1 Chron. xxix. 30; chap. vii. 25; xi. 6

[x]Job xii. 18; Psa. lxxv. 6, 7; Jer. xxvii. 5; chap. iv. 17 [y]James i. 5——[z]Job xii. 22; Psa. xxv. 14; ver. 28, 29 [a]Psa. cxxxix. 11, 12; Heb. iv. 13——[b]Chap. v. 11, 14; James i. 17——[c]Ver. 18——[d]Chald. *That I have found* [e]Chald. *children of the captivity of Judah*

to the delicate daughter of Herodias. This was the custom of the country. No law, no judge, no jury. The will or caprice of the king governed all things. Happy England! know and value thy excellent privileges!

Verse 16. *That he would give him time*] That is, that he might seek unto God for a revelation of the thing. The Chaldeans dared not even to promise *this;* they would only pledge themselves for the *interpretation*, provided the king would furnish the *dream*. Daniel engages both to find the *lost dream*, and to give the proper *interpretation.*

Verse 18. *That they would desire mercies*] For this Daniel had requested a little time; and doubtless both he and his *three* companions prayed incessantly till God gave the wished for revelation; but whether it was given that *same night*, we do not know.

Verse 19. *Then was the secret revealed—in a night vision.*] Daniel either dreamed it, or it was represented to his mind by an immediate inspiration.

Verse 20. *Wisdom and might are his*] He knows all things, and can do all things.

Verse 21. *He changeth the times*] Time, duration, succession are his, and under his dominion. It is in the course of his providence that one king is put down, and another raised up; and therefore he can distinctly tell what he has purposed to do in the great empires of the earth.

Verse 23. *I thank thee and praise thee*] No wonder he should feel gratitude, when God by this merciful interference had saved both the life of him and his fellows; and was about to reflect the highest credit on the God of the Jews, and on the people themselves.

Verse 24. *Destroy not the wise* men] The decree was suspended till it should be seen whether Daniel could tell the dream, and give its interpretation.

Verse 27. *Cannot the wise* men] Cannot your own able men, aided by your gods, tell you the secret? This question was necessary in order that the king might see the foolishness of depending on the one, or worshipping the other.

The soothsayers] One of our old words: "The tellers of truth:" but גזרין *gazerin* is the name of *another class* of those curious artists, unless we suppose it to mean the same as the CHALDEANS, ver. 2. They are supposed to be persons who divined by *numbers, amulets*, &c. There are many conjectures about them, which, whatever learning they show, cast little light upon this place.

A. M. 3401 B. C. 603 Ol XLIV. 2 Anno TarquiniiPrisci, R. Roman., 14

28 [f]But there is a God in heaven that revealeth secrets, and [g]maketh known to the king Nebuchadnezzar [h]what shall be in the latter days. Thy dream, and the visions of thy head upon thy bed, are these;

29 As for thee, O king, thy thoughts [i]came *into thy mind* upon thy bed, what should come to pass hereafter: [k]and he that revealeth secrets maketh known unto thee what shall come to pass.

30 [l]But as for me, this secret is not revealed to me for *any* wisdom that I have more than any living, [m]but for *their* sakes that shall make known the interpretation to the king, [n]and that thou mightest know the thoughts of thy heart.

31 Thou, O king, [o]sawest, and behold a great image. This great image, whose brightness *was* excellent, stood before thee; and the form thereof *was* terrible.

32 [p]This image's head *was* of fine gold, his breast and his arms of silver, his belly and his [q]thighs of brass,

33 His legs of iron, his feet part of iron and part of clay.

34 Thou sawest till that a stone was cut out [r]without [s]hands, which smote the image upon his feet *that were* of iron and clay, and brake them to pieces.

35 Then was the iron, the clay, the brass, the silver, and the gold, broken to pieces together, and became [t]like the chaff of the summer threshing-floors; and the wind carried them away, that [u]no place was found for them: and the stone that smote the image [v]became a great mountain, [w]and filled the whole earth.

A. M. 3401 B. C. 603 Ol. XLIV. 2 Anno TarquiniiPrisci, R. Roman., 14

36 This *is* the dream; and we will tell the interpretation thereof before the king.

37 [x]Thou, O king, *art* a king of kings: [y]for the God of heaven hath given thee a kingdom, power, and strength, and glory.

38 [z]And wheresoever the children of men dwell, the beasts of the field and the fowls of the heaven hath he given into thine hand, and hath made thee ruler over them all. [a]Thou *art* this head of gold.

39 And after thee shall arise [b]another kingdom [c]inferior to thee, and another third kingdom of brass, [d]which shall bear rule over all the earth.

40 And [e]the fourth kingdom shall be strong as iron: forasmuch as iron breaketh in pieces and subdueth all *things:* and as iron that breaketh all these, shall it break in pieces and bruise.

41 And whereas thou sawest [f]the feet and toes, part of potters' clay, and part of iron,

---

[f]Gen. xl. 8; xli. 16; ver. 18, 47; Amos iv. 13——[g]Chald. *hath made known*——[h]Gen. xlix. 1——[i]Chald. *came up*——[k]Ver. 22, 28——[l]So Gen. xli. 16; Acts iii. 12 [m]Or, *but for the intent that the interpretation may be made known to the king*——[n]Ver. 47——[o]Chald. *wast seeing* [p]See ver. 38, &c.——[q]Or, *sides*——[r]Or, *which* was *not in hands;* as ver. 45

[s]Chap. viii. 25; Zech. iv. 6; 2 Cor. v. 1; Heb. ix. 24 [t]Psa. i. 4; Hos. xiii. 3——[u]Psa. xxxvii. 10, 36——[v]Isa. ii. 2, 3——[w]Psa. lxxx. 9——[x]Ezra vii. 12; Isa. xlvii. 5; Jer. xxvii. 6, 7; Ezek. xxvi. 7; Hos. viii. 10——[y]Ezra i. 2 [z]Chap. iv. 21, 22; Jer. xxvii. 6——[a]Ver. 32——[b]Chap. v. 28, 31——[c]Ver. 32——[d]1 Mac. i. 3——[e]Chap. vii. 7, 23——[f]Ver. 33

Verse 28. *There is a God in heaven*] To distinguish him from those idols, the works of men's hands; and from the false gods in which the Chaldeans trusted.

In the latter days.] A phrase which, in the prophets, generally means the *times of the Messiah.* God is about to show what shall take place from this time to the latest ages of the world. And the vision most certainly contains a very extensive and consecutive prophecy; which I shall treat more largely at the close of the chapter, giving in the mean time a short exposition.

Verse 31. *A great image*] Representing the *four great monarchies.*

Verse 32. *Head* was *of fine gold*] The *Babylonish empire*, the first and greatest.

Breast and his arms of silver] The *Medo-Persian empire*, under Cyrus, &c.

His belly and his thighs of brass] The *Macedonian empire*, under Alexander the Great, and his successors.

Verse 33. *His legs of iron*] The *Roman government.*

His feet part of iron and part of clay.] The same, mixed with the barbaric nations, and divided into *ten* kingdoms. See at the end of the chapter.

Verse 34. *A stone was cut out*] The *fifth* monarchy; the spiritual kingdom of the Lord Jesus, which is to last for ever, and diffuse itself over the whole earth.

Verse 35. *The stone—became a great mountain*] There is the kingdom אבן *eben*, of the *stone*, and the kingdom of the *mountain.* See at the end of the chapter.

Verse 37. *The God of heaven*] Not given by thy own gods, nor acquired by thy own skill and prowess; it is a Divine gift.

Power] To rule this kingdom.

And strength] To defend it against all foes.

And glory.] Great honour and dignity.

Verse 38. *Thou* art *this head of gold*] See on ver. 31-34, and at the end.

A. M. 3401
B. C. 603
Ol. XLIV. 2
Anno Tarquinii Prisci, R. Roman., 14

the kingdom shall be divided; but there shall be in it of the strength of the iron, forasmuch as thou sawest the iron mixed with miry clay.

42 And *as* the toes of the feet *were* part of iron, and part of clay, *so* the kingdom shall be partly strong, and partly [g]broken.

43 And whereas thou sawest iron mixed with miry clay, they shall mingle themselves with the seed of men: but they shall not cleave [h]one to another, even as iron is not mixed with clay.

44 And in [i]the days of these kings [k]shall the God of heaven set up a kingdom, [l]which shall never be destroyed: and the [m]kingdom shall not be left to other people, [n]*but* it shall break in pieces and consume all these kingdoms, and it shall stand for ever.

45 [o]Forasmuch as thou sawest that the stone was cut out of the mountain [p]without hands, and that it brake in pieces the iron, the brass, the clay, the silver, and the gold; the great God hath made known to the king what shall come to pass [q]hereafter: and the dream *is* certain, and the interpretation thereof sure.

A. M. 3401
B. C. 603
Ol. XLIV. 2
Anno Tarquinii Prisci, R. Roman., 14

46 [r]Then the king Nebuchadnezzar fell upon his face, and worshipped Daniel, and commanded that they should offer an oblation [s]and sweet odours unto him.

47 The king answered unto Daniel, and said, Of a truth *it is,* that your God *is* a God of gods, and a Lord of kings, [t]and a revealer of secrets, seeing thou couldest reveal this secret.

48 Then the king made Daniel a great man, [u]and gave him many great gifts, and made him ruler over the whole province of Babylon, and [v]chief of the governors over all the wise *men* of Babylon.

49 Then Daniel requested of the king, [w]and he set Shadrach, Meshach, and Abed-nego over the affairs of the province of Babylon: but Daniel [x]*sat* in the gate of the king.

[g]Or, *brittle*——[h]Chald. *this with this*——[i]Chald. *their days*——[k]Ver. 28——[l]Chap. iv. 3, 34; vi. 26; vii. 14, 27; Mic. iv. 7; Luke i. 32, 33——[m]Chald. *kingdom thereof* [n]Psa. ii. 9; Isa. lx. 12; 1 Cor. xv. 24——[o]Ver. 35; Isa. xxviii. 16——[p]Or, *which* was *not in hand*——[q]Chald. *after this*——[r]See Acts x. 25; xiv. 13; xxviii. 6 [s]Ezra vi. 10——[t]Ver. 28——[u]Ver. 6——[v]Chap. iv. 9; v. 11——[w]Chap. iii. 12——[x]Esth. ii. 19, 21; iii. 2

Verse 44. *A kingdom which shall never be destroyed*] The extensive and extending empire of Christ.

Shall not be left to other people] All the preceding empires have swallowed up each other successively; but this shall remain to the end of the world.

Verse 45. *The dream* is *certain*] It contains a *just representation* of things as they shall be.

And the interpretation thereof sure.] The parts of the dream being truly explained.

Verse 46. *The king—fell upon his face*] Prostrated himself: this was the fullest act of adoration among the ancients.

Worshipped Daniel] Supposing him to be a god, or Divine being. No doubt Daniel forbade him; for to receive this would have been gross idolatry.

Verse 47. *Your God* is *a God of gods*] He is greater than all others.

And a Lord of kings] He governs both in heaven and earth.

Verse 48. *Made Daniel a great man*] By, 1. Giving him many rich gifts. 2. By making him *governor* over the whole province of Babylon. And, 3. By making him the *chief* or *president* over all the *wise men.*

Verse 49. *Daniel requested of the king, and he set Shadrach, Meshach, and Abed-nego over the affairs of the province of Babylon*] He wished his *three* companions promoted, who had shared his anxieties, and helped him by their prayers. They all had places of trust, in which they could do much good, and prevent much evil.

Daniel sat *in the gate of the king.*] That is, was the chief officer in the palace; and the greatest confidant and counsellor of the king. But whatever his influence and that of his friends was, it extended only over the province of Babylon; not through the empire.

A DISCOURSE ON NEBUCHADNEZZAR'S DREAM, chap. ii. 41-45.

I shall now consider this most important vision more at large, and connect it with a portion of the previous history of the Jewish people.

The kingdoms of Israel and Judah after a series of the most unparalleled ingratitude and rebellion, against displays of mercy and benevolence, only equalled by their rebellions, were at last, according to repeated threatenings, given over into the hands of their enemies. The inhabitants of the former country were subdued and carried away captives by the Assyrians; and those of the latter, by the Chaldeans.

The people of Israel never recovered their ancient territories; and were so disposed of by their conquerors, that they either became amalgamated with the heathen nations, so as to be utterly undistinguishable; or they were transported to some foreign and recluse place of settlement, that the land of their residence, though repeatedly sought for and guessed at, has for more than *two thousand* years been totally unknown.

Judah, after having been harassed by the Chaldeans, Egyptians, and others, was at last invaded by Nebuchadnezzar, king of Babylon; Jerusalem besieged and taken; and Jehoiachin the king, who had before become tributary to the Babylonians, with his mother, wives, officers of state, and chief military commanders, princes, and mighty men of valour, to the amount of *ten thousand;* and all the *artificers, smiths,* &c., to the number of *one thousand,* with all that were *fit for war,* he carried captives to Babylon; leaving only the poorest of the people behind, under the government of *Mattaniah,* son of the late king Josiah, and uncle to Jehoiachin; and, having changed his name to *Zedekiah,* gave him a nominal authority as king over the wretched remains of the people. Zedekiah, after having reigned *nine* years, rebelled against Nebuchadnezzar, who, coming against Jerusalem with all his forces, besieged it; and having reduced it to the last extremity by famine, and made a breach in the walls, took the city, pillaged and destroyed the temple by fire, slew the sons of Zedekiah before his face, then put out his eyes, and carried him *bound in brazen fetters* to Babylon, 2 Kings, chap. xxiv. and xxv. Thus, the *temple* of God, the most glorious building ever laid on the face of the earth, was profaned, pillaged, and burnt, with the king's palace, and all the houses of the Jewish nobility, in the *eleventh* year of *Zedekiah,*—the *nineteenth* of *Nebuchadnezzar,*—the *first* of the *forty-eight Olympiad,*—the *one hundred and sixtieth* current year of the era of *Nabonassar,*—*four hundred and twenty-four* years, *three* months, and *eight* days from the time in which *Solomon* laid its *foundation stone!*

In the same month in which the city was taken, and the temple burnt, *Nebuzar-adan,* commander in chief of the Babylonish forces, carried off the spoils of the temple, with the Jewish treasures, and the principal part of the residue of the people; and brought them also to Babylon. And thus *Judah* was carried away out of her own land, *four hundred and sixty-eight* years after *David* began to reign over it; from the *division* under *Rehoboam, three hundred and eighty-eight* years; from the *destruction* of the *kingdom* of *Israel, one hundred and thirty-four* years; in the year of the world, *three thousand four hundred and sixteen;* and before the *nativity* of our Lord, *five hundred and eighty-eight.*

In the *fourth* year of Jehoiakim, king of Judah, A. M. 3397, B. C. 607, Nebuchadnezzar, having besieged Jerusalem, and made its king tributary, carried away a number of captives; and among them was the Prophet *Daniel,* then in his youth, who became, for his wisdom, and knowledge of future events, very eminent at Babylon; and, with some other Jewish captives, great favourites of Nebuchadnezzar the king; who made *Daniel* president of all the wise men of his city. It was in the *second* year of the reign of this king, that a circumstance occurred which, though at first it threatened the destruction of the prophet, finally issued in the increase of his reputation and celebrity.

As prophecy is one of the strongest proofs of the authenticity of what professes to be a *Divine revelation,* God endued this man with a large portion of his Spirit, so that he clearly predicted some of the most astonishing political occurrences and changes which have ever taken place on the earth; no less than the rise, distinguishing characteristics, and termination of the FOUR *great monarchies* or *empires,* which have been so celebrated in all the histories of the world. And as the Babylonian, under which he then lived, was one of these monarchies, and was shortly to be absorbed by the *Medo-Persian,* which was to succeed it, he made Nebuchadnezzar, the then reigning monarch, by means of a most singular *dream,* the particulars of which he had forgotten, the instrument that appeared to give birth to a prediction, in which the ruin of his own empire was foretold; as well as other mighty changes which should take place in the political state of the world, for at least the term of *one thousand* years next ensuing. Nor did the prophetic Spirit in this eminent man limit his predictions to these; but showed at the same time the origin and nature of that FIFTH *monarchy,* which, under the great King of kings, should be administered and prevail to the end of time.

The dream itself, with its interpretation, and the exact and impressive manner in which the predictions relative to the *four* great monarchies have been fulfilled, and those which regard the *fifth* monarchy are in the course of being accomplished, are the subjects to which I wish to call the reader's most serious and deliberate attention.

This image, so circumstantially described from the *thirty-eighth* to the *forty-fourth* verse, was, as we learn from the prophet's general solution, intended to point out the rise and fall of *four* different *empires* and *states;* and the final prevalence and establishment of a *fifth* empire, that shall never have an end, and which shall commence *in the last days,* ver. 28; a phrase commonly used in the *prophets* to signify the *times of the Messiah,* and in the New Testament, his *advent* to judge the world.

Before we proceed to particular parts, we may remark in general, that the whole account strongly indicates:—

1. The especial *providence* of God in behalf of the Jews at that time. For, although suffering grievously because of their sins, being deprived of both their political and personal liberty, God shows them that he has not *abandoned* them; and the existence of a *prophet* among them is a proof of his fatherly care and unremitted attention to their eternal welfare.

2. The particular *interference* of God to manifest the superiority of his truth, to wean an idolatrous nation from their vanity and superstition, and lead them to that God who is the fountain of truth, the revealer of secrets, and the governor of all things.

And, 3. The direct *inspiration* of God immediately teaching his servant things which could be known only to God himself, and thus showing the Babylonians that his prophets had spoken by an unerring Spirit; that the *Jews* were the depositaries of the true religion; that HE was the only true God; and as he was *omniscient,* so he was *omnipotent;* and the things which his *wisdom* had *predicted,* his *power* could and *would* accomplish.

The sum of the account given in this chapter is the following:—

1. Nebuchadnezzar, king of Babylon, in the *second* year of his reign, about A. M. 3401, and B. C. 603, had a remarkable dream, which, although it made a deep impression on his mind, yet, on his awakening, he found it impossible to recollect; the general impression only remaining.

2. He summoned his wise men, astrologers, &c., told them that he had a dream or vision, which he had forgotten; and commanded them

to tell him the dream, and give its interpretation.

3. They request the king to tell them the dream; and promise, then, to make known the meaning. This he could not do, having forgotten it; yet he insists on their compliance on pain of death.

4. To tell the king his dream they find impossible; and a decree for the destruction of the wise men of Babylon is issued, in which Daniel and his fellows are included.

5. Daniel, hearing of it, speaks to *Arioch*, captain of the king's guard or the royal executioner; desires to be brought before the king; and promises to tell the dream, &c.

6. He is introduced; and immediately tells the king what he had dreamed, and shows him its interpretation.

THE DREAM

A vast image, exceedingly luminous, of terrible form, and composed of different substances, appears in a night vision to the king, of which the following is the description:—

I. Its *head* was of fine *gold*.

II. Its *breast* and *arms* of *silver*.

III. Its *belly* and *thighs* of *brass*.

IV. Its *legs* of *iron*, and its *feet* and *toes* of *iron* and *clay*. While gazing on this image he sees,—

V. A *stone* cut out of a mountain without hands, which smites the image on its feet, and dashes it all to pieces; and the gold, and silver, brass, iron, and clay become as small and as light as chaff.

VI. A *wind* carries the whole away, so that no place is found for them.

VII. The *stone* becomes a *great mountain*, and fills the earth.

In order to explain this, certain DATA must be laid down.

1. This image is considered a political representation of as many different governments, as it was composed of materials; and as all these materials are successively inferior to each other, so are the governments in a descending ratio.

2. The *human figure* has been used, both by *historians* and *geographers*, to represent the rise, progress, establishment, and decay of empires, as well as the *relative situation* and importance of the different parts of the government. Thus *Florus*, in the *prooemium* to his Roman history, represents the Romans under the form of a *human being*, in its different stages, from infancy to old age, *viz*.

Si quis ergo populum Romanum quasi *hominem* consideret, totamque ejus *ætatem* percenseat, ut CŒPERIT, utque ADOLEVERIT, ut quasi ad quemdam JUVENTÆ florem pervenerit; ut postea velut CONSENUERIT, quatuor gradus progressusque ejus inveniet.

1. *Prima ætas* sub *Regibus* fuit, prope ducentos quinquaginta per annos, quibus circum ipsam matrem suam cum finitimis luctatus est. Hæc erit ejus INFANTIA.

2. Sequens a Bruto, Collatinoque *consulibus*, in Appium Claudium, Quinctiumque Fulvium consules, ducentos quinquaginta annos habet, quibus Italiam subegit. Hoc fuit tempus viris armisque exercitatissi mum! ideo quis ADOLESCENTIAM dixerit.

3. Dehinc ad Cæsarem Augustum, ducenti quinquaginta anni, quibus totum orbem pacavit. Hic jam ipsa JUVENTA Imperii, et quasi quædam robusta MATURITAS.

4. A Cæsare Augusto in sæculum, nostrum, sunt non multo minus anni ducenti, quibus inertia Cæsarum quasi CONSENUIT atque DECOXIT. *L. An. Flori* PROŒM.

1. INFANCY; *first stage*—under KINGS, from Romulus to Tarquinius Superbus; about *two hundred and fifty* years.

2. YOUTH; *second stage*—under CONSULS, from Brutus and Collatinus to Appius Claudius and M. Fulvius; about *two hundred and fifty* years.

3. MANHOOD; *third stage*—the empire from the conquest of Italy to Cæsar Augustus; about *two hundred and fifty* years.

4. OLD AGE; *fourth stage*—from Augustus, through the *twelve* Cæsars, down to A. D. 200; about *two hundred* years.

Geographers have made similar representations. The *Germanic* empire, in the totality of its dependent states, has been represented by a *map* in the *form of a man;* different parts being pointed out by *head, breast, arm, belly, thighs, legs, feet*, &c., according to their geographical and political relation to the empire in general.

3. Different *metals* are used to express different *degrees of political strength*, excellence, durability, &c.

4. *Clay, earth, dust*, are emblems of *weakness, instability*, &c.

5. *Mountains* express, in Scripture, *mighty empires, kingdoms*, and *states*.

6. *Stone* signifies Jesus Christ, Gen. xlix. 24; "From thence" (of the posterity of Jacob) "is the Shepherd, the Stone of Israel." That our blessed Lord, "the good shepherd," John x. 11-17, is here intended, will appear most plainly from the following passages; Isa. viii. 14: "And he shall be for a sanctuary; but for a STONE of stumbling and for a ROCK of offence to both the houses of Israel." Isa. xxviii. 16: "Thus saith the Lord God, Behold, I lay in Zion for a foundation a STONE, a tried STONE, a precious corner STONE, a sure foundation; he that believeth shall not make haste." 1 Peter ii. 4, 6, 8. Collate these with Psa. cxviii. 22: "The STONE which the builders refused is become the head STONE of the corner." Matt. xxi. 42; Mark xii. 10; Luke xx. 17; Acts iv. 11; in which latter quotations the whole is positively applied to Christ; as also 1 Peter ii. 4-8: "To whom coming as unto a living STONE," &c.; who seems to have all the preceding passages in view. See also Isa. ii. 2: "The mountain of the Lord's house shall be established in the top of the mountains," &c.

7. This stone is said to be cut out without hands, ver. 34. *Without hands* signifies that which is *spiritual*. So 2 Cor. v. 1, *a house not made with hands* means a *spiritual* building.

EXPLANATION

The *Chaldean* empire, called the *Assyrian* in its commencement, the *Chaldean* from the country, the *Babylonish* from its chief city.

I. HEAD OF GOLD. This was the first monarchy, begun by *Nimrod*, A. M. 1771, B. C. 2233, and ending with the death of Belshazzar, A. M. 3466, B. C. 538, after having lasted nearly *seventeen hundred* years. In the time of Nebuchadnezzar it extended over *Chaldea, Assyria, Arabia, Syria*, and *Palestine*. HE, Nebuchadnezzar, was *the head of gold*.

II. BREASTS AND ARMS OF SILVER. The *Medo-Persian* empire; which properly began under *Darius* the *Mede*, allowing him tc be the same with *Cyaxares*, son of *Astyages*, and uncle to Cyrus the great, son of *Cambyses*. He first fought under his uncle Cyaxares; defeated *Neriglissar*, king of the Assyrians, and *Crœsus*, king of the Lydians; and, by the capture of Babylon, B. C. 538, terminated the Chaldean empire. On the death of his father Cambyses, and his uncle Cyaxares, B. C. 536, he became sole governor of the Medes and Persians, and thus established a potent empire on the ruins of that of the *Chaldeans*.

III. BELLY AND THIGHS OF BRASS. The *Macedonian* or *Greek* empire, founded by *Alexander the Great*. He subdued *Greece*, penetrated into *Asia*, took *Tyre*, reduced *Egypt*, overthrew *Darius Codomanus* at *Arbela*, Oct. 2, A. M. 3673, B. C. 331, and thus terminated the *Persian* monarchy. He crossed the *Caucasus*, subdued *Hyrcania*, and penetrated *India* as far as the *Ganges;* and having conquered all the countries that lay between the *Adriatic sea* and this *river*, the Ganges, he died A. M. 3681, B. C. 323; and after his death his empire became divided among his generals, *Cassander*, *Lysimachus*, *Ptolemy*, and *Seleucus*. CASSANDER had *Macedon* and *Greece;* LYSIMACHUS had *Thrace*, and those parts of *Asia* which lay on the *Hellespont* and *Bosphorus;* PTOLEMY had *Egypt*, *Lybia*, *Arabia*, *Palestine*, and *Cœlesyria;* SELEUCUS had *Babylon*, *Media*, *Susiana*, *Persia*, *Assyria*, *Bactria*, *Hyrcania*, and all other provinces, even to the *Ganges*. Thus this empire, founded on the ruin of that of the Persians, "had rule over all the earth."

IV. LEGS OF IRON, AND FEET AND TOES OF IRON AND CLAY. I think this means, in the first place, the *kingdom* of the LAGIDÆ, in *Egypt;* and the *kingdom* of the SELEUCIDÆ, in *Syria*. And, *secondly*, the ROMAN *empire*, which was properly composed of them.

1. PTOLEMY LAGUS, one of Alexander's generals, began the new kingdom of *Egypt*, A. M. 3692, B. C. 312, which was continued through a long race of sovereigns, till A. M. 3974, B. C. 30; when *Octavius Cæsar* took Alexandria, having in the preceding year defeated *Anthony* and *Cleopatra* at the battle of *Actium*, and so Egypt became a *Roman province*. Thus ended the kingdom of the *Lagidæ*, after it had lasted *two hundred and eighty-two* years.

2. SELEUCUS NICATOR, another of Alexander's generals, began the new kingdom of *Syria*, A. M. 3692, B. C. 312, which continued through a long race of sovereigns, till A. M. 3939, B. C. 65, when *Pompey* dethroned *Antiochus Asiaticus*, and Syria became a Roman province after it had lasted *two hundred and forty-seven* years.

That the *two legs of iron* meant the kingdom of the *Lagidæ* and that of the *Seleucidæ*, seems strongly intimated by the characters given in the text. "And the fourth kingdom shall be strong as iron. Forasmuch as iron breaketh in pieces and subdueth all things; and as iron that breaketh all these, shall it break in pieces and bruise," ver. 40. 1. The *iron* here not only marks the *strength* of these kingdoms, but also their *violence* and *cruelty* towards the people of God. History is full of the miseries which the kings of *Egypt* and *Syria* inflicted on the Jews. 2. It is said that these *legs* should *break in pieces and bruise*. How many generals and princes were destroyed by *Seleucus Nicator*, and by *Ptolemy*, son of *Lagus! Seleucus*, particularly, could not consider himself secure on his throne till he had destroyed Antigonus, Nicanor, and Demetrius; and *Ptolemy* endeavoured to secure himself by the ruin of *Perdiccas*, and the rest of his enemies. 3. The *dividing of the kingdom*, the *iron and clayey mixture* of the *feet*, point out the continual divisions which prevailed in those empires; and the *mixture of the good and evil qualities* which appeared in the successors of *Seleucus* and *Ptolemy;* none of them possessing the good qualities of the founders of those monarchies; neither their valour, wisdom, nor prudence. 4. The efforts which these princes made to *strengthen* their respective governments by *alliances*, which all proved not only *useless* but *injurious*, are here pointed out by their *mingling themselves with the seed of men*. "But they shall not cleave one to another," ver. 43. *Antiochus Theos*, king of Syria, married both *Laodice* and *Berenice*, daughters of *Ptolemy Philadelphus*, king of Egypt. *Antiochus Magnus*, king of Syria, gave his daughter *Cleopatra* to *Ptolemy Epiphanes*, king of Egypt; but these marriages, instead of being the means of consolidating the *union* between those kingdoms, contributed more than any thing else to *divide* them, and excite the most bloody and destructive wars.

In chap. vii. 7, the prophet, having the same subject in view, says, "I saw in the night visions, and behold a fourth beast, dreadful and terrible, and strong exceedingly; and it had great iron teeth: it devoured and brake in pieces, and stamped the residue with the feet of it;" and in chap. viii. 22: "Now that being broken," the horn of the *rough goat*, the *Grecian monarchy*, "whereas four stood up for it, four kingdoms shall stand up out of the nation, but not in his power." These and other declarations point out those peculiar circumstances that distinctly mark the kingdom of the *Seleucidæ*, and that of the *Lagidæ;* both of which rose out of the Macedonian or Grecian empire, and both terminated in that of the *Romans*.

2. These TWO LEGS OF IRON became absorbed in the Roman government, which also partook of the *iron* nature; strong, military, and extensive in its victories; and by its various conquests united to and amalgamated with itself various nations, some *strong*, and some *weak*, so as to be fitly represented in the *symbolical image* by *feet* and *toes*, partly of *iron* and partly of *clay*. Thus, as the *Lagidæ* and *Seleucidæ* arose out of the wreck of the *Grecian empire;* so the *Roman empire* arose out of their ruin. But the empire became *weakened* by its *conquests;* and although, by mingling themselves *with the seed* of men, that is, by strong leagues, and *matrimonial alliances*, as mentioned above, they endeavoured to secure a perpetual sovereignty, yet they did not *cleave to each other*, and they also were swallowed up by the *barbarous northern nations;* and thus terminated those *four* most powerful monarchies.

V. "A stone cut out of the mountain without hands."

1. That Jesus Christ has been represented by a *stone*, we have already seen; but *this stone* refers chiefly to his *Church*, which is represented as a *spiritual building*, which he supports as a *foundation stone*, *connects* and strengthens as a *corner stone*, and finishes and *adorns* as a *top stone*. He is called a *stone* also in reference to the prejudice conceived against him by his countrymen. Because he did not come in *worldly pomp* they therefore refused to receive him; and to them he is

represented as a *stone of stumbling, and rock of offence.*

2. But *here* he is represented under another notion, viz., that of a *stone projected from a catapult, or some military engine*, which smote the image on its feet; that is, it smote the then *existing government* at its *foundation*, or principles of support; and by destroying these, brought the whole into ruin.

3. By this *stroke* the *clay*, the *iron*, the *brass*, the *silver*, and the *gold* were *broken to pieces, and became like chaff which the wind carried away.* Now we have already seen that the *Roman empire*, which had absorbed the kingdoms of the *Lagidæ* and *Seleucidæ*, was represented by the *legs of iron, and feet and toes of iron and clay;* but as we find that not only the *iron and clay*, but also the *brass*, *silver*, and *gold* were confounded and destroyed by that stroke, it follows that there was then remaining in and compacted with the Roman government, something of the distinguishing marks and principles of all the *preceding empires;* not only as to their *territorial possessions*, but also as to their distinctive *characteristics.* There were at the time here referred to in the Roman empire, the *splendour* of the CHALDEANS, the *riches* of the PERSIANS, the *discipline* of the GREEKS, and the *strength* of the EGYPTIAN and SYRIAN governments, mingled with the *incoherence* and imbecility of those empires, kingdoms, and states which the Romans had subdued. In short, with every political excellence, it contains the principles of its own destruction, and its persecution of the Church of Christ accelerated its ruin.

4. As the *stone* represents *Christ* and his *governing influence*, it is here said to be a *kingdom*, that is, a state of *prevailing rule* and *government;* and was to arise *in the days of those kings* or kingdoms, ver. 44. And this is *literally* true; for its rise was when the Roman government, partaking of all the characteristics of the preceding empires, was at its *zenith of imperial splendour*, military glory, legislative authority, and literary eminence. It took place a few years after the battle of Actium, and when Rome was at peace with the whole world, *September* 2, B. C. 31.

5. This *stone* or government was *cut out of the mountain*, arose *in* and *under* the *Roman government*, Judea being, at the time of the birth of Christ, a *Roman province.*

6. It was *cut out without hands;* probably alluding to the miraculous birth of our Lord, but particularly to the *spiritual* nature of his kingdom and government, in which no *worldly policy*, *human maxims*, or *military force* were employed; for it was not *by might nor power, but by the Spirit of the Lord of hosts.*

Two things may be here distinguished: 1. The government or *kingdom* of the STONE. 2. The government or kingdom of the MOUNTAIN.

1. The *kingdom* of the STONE *smites*, *breaks to pieces*, and *destroys* all the other kingdoms, till no vestige of them remains, and till the whole earth is subdued by it.

2. The *kingdom* of the MOUNTAIN fills, and continues to govern, all that has been thus subdued, maintaining endless peace and righteousness in the earth.

First, The stone began to *strike the image*, when the *apostles* went out into every part of the Roman empire, pulling down idolatry, and founding Christian Churches.

Secondly, But the great blow was given to the heathen Roman empire by the *conversion of Constantine*, just at the time when it was an epitome of the *four great monarchies*, being under the government of FOUR EMPERORS *at once*, A. D. 308: CONSTANTIUS, who governed *Gaul*, *Spain*, and *Britain;* GALERIUS, who had *Illyricum*, *Thrace*, and *Asia;* SEVERUS, who had *Italy* and *Africa;* and MAXIMIN, who had the *East* and *Egypt.*

1. The conversion of Constantine took place while he was in Gaul, A. D. 312, by the appearance of a *luminous cross* in the sky above the sun, a little after *noon-day*, with this inscription, Εν τουτῳ νικα, "By this conquer;" *Euseb.* De Vit. Const. lib. i. cap. 28. In A. D. 324 he totally defeated *Licinius*, who had shared the empire with him, and became sole emperor. He terminated the reign of idolatry in A. D. 331, by an edict ordering the destruction of all the heathen temples. This made CHRISTIANITY the religion of the *empire.*

2. The *stroke* which thus destroyed idolatry in the Roman empire is continual in its *effects;* and must be so till idolatry be destroyed over the face of the earth, and the universe filled with the knowledge of Christ.

3. This *smiting* has been continued by all the means which God in his providence and mercy has used for the dissemination of Christianity, from the time of *Constantine* to the present: and particularly *now*, by means of the *British and Foreign Bible Society*, and its countless ramifications, and by the numerous *missionaries* sent by Christian societies to almost every part of the globe. Thus far the kingdom of the *stone.*

In ver. 44, the *kingdom of the stone*, grown into a *great mountain* and filling the whole earth, is particularly described by various characters.

1. It is a *kingdom* which the *God of heaven sets up.* That this means the *whole dispensation of the Gospel*, and the *moral effects* produced by it in the *souls of men* and in the *world*, needs little proof; for our Lord, referring to *this* and other prophecies in this book, calls its influence and his Gospel *the kingdom of God*, and *the kingdom of heaven;* showing thereby that it is a kingdom *not of this world*—not raised by human *ambition*, the *lust of rule*, or *military conquest;* but a *spiritual kingdom*, raised and maintained by the *grace of God* himself, in which he *himself lives and rules*, governing by his own laws, influencing and directing by his own Spirit; producing, not *wars and contentions*, but *glory to God in the highest*, and *on earth peace and good will among men.*

2. This is called the *kingdom of heaven*, because it is to be a counterpart of the *kingdom of glory. The kingdom of God*, says the apostle, is *righteousness*, *peace*, and *joy in the Holy Ghost*, (Rom. xiv. 17;) *righteousness*, without any *sin; peace*, without inward *disturbance; joy*, without any mental *unhappiness.* An *eternity* of righteousness, peace, and spiritual joy constitutes HEAVEN; nor can we conceive in that state any thing higher or more excellent than these.

3. This kingdom *shall never be destroyed:* it is the *everlasting Gospel*, and the work of the *everlasting* GOD. As it neither originates in nor is dependent on the *passions* of men, it cannot be *destroyed.* All other governments, from the imperfection of their nature, contain in them the seeds of their own destruction. *Kings* die, *ministers* change, *subjects* are not permanent;

new relations arise, and with them *new measures, new passions*, and *new projects;* and these produce *political changes*, and often *political ruin*. But *this* government, being the government of God, cannot be affected by the changes and chances to which mortal things are exposed.

4. *This kingdom shall not be left to other people.* Every dispensation of God, prior to Christianity, supposed another by which it was to be succeeded. 1. Holy *patriarchs* and their *families* were the *first* people among whom the kingdom of God was found. 2. *Hebrews*, in *Egypt* and in the *wilderness*, were the *next*. 3. *Jews*, in the *promised land*, were a *third* denomination. 4. And after the division of the kingdoms, captivity, and dispersion of the Jews, the *Israel of God* became a *fourth* denomination. 5. Under the Gospel, CHRISTIAN is the name of the *people of this kingdom*. Every thing in the construction of the Gospel system, as well as its own declarations, shows that it is not to be *succeeded* by any other dispensation: its *name* can never be changed; and CHRISTIAN will be the only denomination of the *people of God* while sun and moon endure. All former *empires* have changed, and the very *names* of the people have changed with them. The *Assyrians* were lost in the *Chaldeans* and *Babylonians;* the *Babylonians* were lost in the *Medes;* the *Medes* in the *Persians;* the *Persians* in the *Greeks;* and the *Greeks* in the *Syrians* and *Egyptians;* these in the *Romans;* and the *Romans* in the *Goths*, and a variety of other nations. Nor does the *name* of those ancient governments, nor the people who lived under them, remain on the face of the earth in the present day! They are only found in the *page of history*. This spiritual kingdom shall never be *transferred*, and the name of its *subjects* shall never be changed.

5. *It shall break in pieces and consume all these kingdoms;* that is, the preaching and influence of Christianity shall destroy *idolatry* universally. They did so in the Roman empire, which was the epitome of all the rest. But this was not done by the *sword*, nor by any *secular influence*. Christians wage no wars for the propagation of Christianity; for the religion of Christ breathes nothing but *love to God, and peace and good will to all mankind*. The sum of the Gospel is contained in these words of Christ: "God so loved the world that he gave his only-begotten Son, that whosoever believeth on him should not perish, but have everlasting life;—for the Son of man is not come to destroy men's lives, but to save."

For his own cause, God fights in the course of his providence. He depresses one, and exalts another; but permits not his own people to join with him in the *infliction of judgments*. It is by his own Spirit and energy that his kingdom is propagated and maintained in the world; and by the same his enemies are confounded. All *false religions*, as well as falsified and corrupted systems of Christianity, have had recourse to the *sword*, because they were conscious they had NO GOD, no influence but what was merely *human*.

6. The kingdom of Christ *breaks in pieces and consumes all other kingdoms;* that is, it destroys every thing in every earthly government where it is received, that is opposed to the glory of God and the peace and happiness of men, and yet in such a way as to leave all political governments unchanged. No law or principle in Christianity is directed against the *political code* of any country. *Britain* is Christian without the alteration of her *Magna Charta* or her constitution. All the other empires, kingdoms, and states on the face of the earth, may become Christian *and preserve their characteristic forms of political government*. If there be in them any thing hostile to Christianity, and the peace and happiness of the subject, the WIND of *God*—the *Divine Spirit*, will *fan* or *winnow* it away, so that *no more place shall be found* for it. But this he will do in the way of his ordinary *providence;* and by his influence on their hearts, dispose truly Christianized rulers to alter or abrogate whatever their laws contain inimical to the mild sway of the sceptre of Christ.

7. *And it shall stand for ever.* This is its final characteristic. It shall prevail over the whole world; it shall pervade every government; it shall be the basis of every code of laws; it shall be professed by every people of the earth: "The *Gentiles* shall come to its light, and *kings* to the brightness of its rising." The whole earth shall be subdued by its influence, and the whole earth filled with its glory.

8. The actual constitution, establishment, and maintenance of this kingdom belong to the LORD; yet he will use *human means* in the whole administration of his government. His WORD must be *distributed*, and that word must be PREACHED. Hence, under God, BIBLES and MISSIONARIES are the grand means to be employed in things *concerning* his kingdom. BIBLES must be printed, sent out, and dispersed; MISSIONARIES, called of God to the work, and filled with the Divine Spirit, must be *equipped, sent out*, and *maintained;* therefore *expenses* must necessarily be incurred. Here the people *now* of the kingdom must be helpers. It is the duty, therefore, of every soul professing Christianity to lend a helping hand to send forth the *Bible;* and wherever the Bible is sent, to send a missionary, full of faith and of the Holy Ghost, to enforce its truths.

9. The *duration* of the *kingdom of the mountain* upon *earth*. The world has now lasted nearly *six thousand* years, and a very ancient tradition has predicted its termination at the close of that period. Its duration has been divided into *three* grand periods, each comprising *two thousand years*, which should be closed by a period *without terminating* limits; and these have been supposed to have their *types* in the *six days' work of the creation*, and the *seventh* day, called *Sabbath* or *rest*.

1. There have been *two thousand* years from the creation *without any written revelation* from God; this was called the *patriarchal dispensation*.

2. There have been *two thousand* years *under the law*, where there has been a *written revelation*, a *succession of prophets*, and a Divine *ecclesiastical establishment*. This has been termed the *Mosaic dispensation*.

3. *One thousand eight hundred and twenty-nine* years have passed since the true epoch of the nativity of our blessed Lord; and this is called the *Gospel* or *Christian dispensation*, which is now within *one hundred and seventy-one years* of closing its *two thousand!*

According to the ancient tradition there were, 1. *Two thousand* years *void;* that is, without the law. 2. *Two thousand* years under the law. And, 3. *Two thousand* years under the Messiah. And at the termination of the *third* the endless

Sabbath should commence. The comments on this ancient tradition go on to state, that at the termination of each day's work of the creation it was said, *The evening and the morning were the first, second, third, fourth, fifth*, and *sixth day;* but when the *Sabbath* is introduced, and God is said to *rest from his work*, and to have *hallowed this day*, there is no mention of *the evening and the morning* being the *seventh* day. That is left without termination; and therefore a proper type of the *eternal Sabbath*, that *rest which remains for the people of God.*

And are we indeed so near that time when the elements of all things shall be dissolved by fervent heat; when the heavens shall be shrivelled up like a scroll, and the earth and all it contains be burned up? Is the *fifth empire*, the *kingdom of the stone* and *the kingdom of the mountain*, so near its termination? Are all vision and prophecy about to be sealed up, and the whole earth to be illuminated with the bright beams of the Sun of righteousness? Are the finally incorrigible and impenitent about to be swept off the face of the earth by the besom of destruction, while the righteous shall be able to lift up their heads with ineffable joy, knowing their final redemption is at hand? Are we so near the eve of that period when "they who turn many to righteousness shall shine as the stars for ever and ever?" What sort of persons should we then be in all holy conversation and godliness? Where is our zeal for God? Where the sounding of our bowels over the perishing nations who have not yet come under the yoke of the Gospel? Multitudes of whom are not under the yoke, because they have never heard of it; and they have not heard of it, because those who enjoy the blessings of the Gospel of Jesus have not felt (or have not obeyed the feeling) the imperious duty of dividing their *heavenly bread* with those who are famishing with *hunger*, and giving the *water of life* to those who are dying of *thirst*. How shall they appear in that great day when the conquests of the Lion of the tribe of Judah are ended; when the mediatorial kingdom is delivered up unto the Father, and the Judge of quick and dead sits on the great white throne, and to those on his left hand says, "I was hungry, and ye gave me no meat; I was thirsty, and ye gave me no drink." I say, How shall they appear who have made no exertions to tell the lost nations of the earth the necessity for *preparing to meet their God;* and showing them the *means* of doing it, by affording them the blessings of the Gospel of the grace of God? Let us beware lest the *stone* that struck the motley image, and dashed it to pieces, *fall* on us, and *grind us to powder.*

Bibles are sent out by millions into heathen countries; but *how shall they hear without a preacher;* and *how shall they understand the things which they read, unless* those who know the things of God teach them? Let us haste, then, and send *missionaries* after the *Bibles.* God is mightily at work in the earth: let us be *workers together with him, that we receive not the grace of God in vain.* He that giveth to those *poor* (emphatically POOR, for they are without God in the world, and consequently without the *true riches*) lendeth unto the Lord; and let him look what he layeth out, and it shall be paid unto him again. For "he that *converteth a sinner* from the error of his ways shall *save a soul from death*, and hide a multitude of sins." God does not call on *us* to shake hands with all secular, social, and family comfort, and bid farewell to the whole; and go to the heathen with the glad tidings of great joy: but he loudly calls on us to assist in sending *those* who, in the true spirit of sacrifice, the love of Christ constraining them, say, "Here are we! O Lord, send us." Let these servants of God run to and fro; that by their ministry knowledge may be increased. Amen.

CHAPTER III

Nebuchadnezzar, having erected an image, whose height (*including probably a very high pedestal*) *was sixty cubits, and the breadth six, ordered a numerous assembly, which he had convened, to fall down and worship it; threatening, at the same time, that whosoever refused should be cast into a fiery furnace*, 1–7; *a punishment not uncommon in that country*, (see Jer. xxix. 22.) *Daniel's three companions, Shadrach, Meshach, and Abed-nego, who were present, being observed to refrain from this idolatrous worship, were accused before the king; who, in great wrath, commanded them to comply with his orders on pain of death*, 8–15. *But these holy men, with the greatest composure and serenity, expressed their firm resolution not to worship his gods or his images, whatever might be the consequence*, 16–18. *Upon which the king, unaccustomed to have his will opposed, in the height of his wrath, ordered the furnace to be made seven times hotter than usual, and these men to be cast into it, bound by the most mighty of his army, who were killed by the flame in the execution of this service*, 19–23. *On this occasion God* literally *performed his promise by Isaiah*, (chap. xliii. 2:) *"When thou walkest through the fire, thou shalt not be burnt; neither shall the flame kindle upon thee;" for an angel of God, ap-*

pearing in the furnace, protected these young men, and counteracted the natural violence of the fire; which, only consuming the cords with which they were bound, left them to walk at liberty, and in perfect safety, in the midst of the furnace. The king, astonished at this prodigy, called to them to come out of the furnace, and blessed God for sending an angel to deliver his servants; and commanded all his subjects, upon pain of death, not to speak irreverently of the God of Shadrach, Meshach, and Abed-nego, who were promoted to great power and honour, 24–30. A striking example of the interposition of Providence in favour of true and inflexible piety.

A. M. cir. 3424 B. C. cir. 580 Ol. cir. L. 1 TarquiniiPrisci, R. Roman., cir. annum 37

NEBUCHADNEZZAR the king made [a]an image of gold, whose height *was* threescore cubits, *and* the breadth thereof six cubits: he set it up in the plain of Dura, in the [b]province of Babylon.
2 Then Nebuchadnezzar the king sent to gather together the princes, the governors, and the captains, the judges, the treasurers, the counsellors, the sheriffs, and all the rulers of the provinces, to come to the dedication of the image which Nebuchadnezzar the king had set up.

A. M. cir. 3424 B. C. cir. 580 Ol. cir. L. 1 TarquiniiPrisci, R. Roman., cir. annum 37

[a]Ver. 5, 7, 10, 12, 14 — [b]Chap. ii. 48

NOTES ON CHAP. III

Verse 1. *Nebuchadnezzar the king made an image of gold*] It is supposed that the history given here did not occur till the close, or near the end, of Nebuchadnezzar's reign. For it was after his insanity, as we see chap. iv. 33-36, and this happened near the close of his reign. The authorized version, which is followed in the margin, fixes the date of this event *seventeen* years earlier, and *ten* years before the king's insanity. A few observations on this image may be necessary:—

1. It is not likely that this image was in *human* form—the dimensions show the improbability of this; for what proportion is there between *sixty* cubits (*ninety* feet) in length, and *six* cubits (*nine* feet) in breadth?

2. It is not likely that this image was *all of gold;* for this would have required more of this precious metal than the whole *province* of Babylon could produce; for as I suppose the *sixty* cubits apply to the perpendicular *altitude*, so I take it for granted that the *six* cubits intend the *diameter*. Now a column of gold of this height in diameter, upon the supposition that the pillar was circular, contains *five thousand seven hundred and twenty-five and a half* cubic feet; and as there are *nineteen thousand* avoirdupois ounces in a cubic foot, the weight of the whole pillar would be *eight million two hundred and sixty-two thousand eight hundred and six* pounds *ten ounces* of gold.

3. It might have been a *pillar* on which an *image* of the god *Bel* was erected. The image itself might be of *gold*, or more probably *gilt*, that is, covered with *thin plates* of gold, and on this account it might be called the *golden image;* and most probably the height of the image may be confounded with the height of the pillar. Or perhaps it was no more than a pillar, on the sides of which their gods and sacred emblems were engraven, surmounted with *Bel* on the top.

The plain of Dura] The situation of this place is not exactly known; there was a town or city called *Dura*, or *Doura*, in Mesopotamia, near the Tigris.

Verse 2. *Sent to gather together the princes*] It is not easy to show what these different offices were, as it is difficult to ascertain the meaning of the *Chaldee* words. *Parkhurst* analyzes them thus:—

The PRINCES] אחשדרפניא *achashdarpenaiya*, from אחש *achash*, *great* or *eminent*, and דר *dar*, "to go about freely," and פנים *panim*, "the presence." Satraps or privy counsellors who had free access to the presence of the king.

The GOVERNORS] סגניא *signaiya*, *lieutenants* or *viceroys*, for סגן *sagan*, among the Hebrews, was the name of the high priest's *deputy*.

The CAPTAINS] פחותא *pachavatha*, from פח *pach*, *to extend*, because set over those provinces that had been *annexed* to the kingdom by conquest. *Pashas*—This word and office are still in use in Asiatic countries. By corruption we pronounce *bashaw*.

The JUDGES] אדרגזריא *adargazeraiya*, from אדר *adar*, *noble* or *magnificent*, and גזר *gazar*, *to decree*. The nobles, the assistants to the king in making laws, statutes, &c. The same probably in Babylon, as the *House of Lords* in England.

The TREASURERS] גדבריא *gedaberaiya*, from גנז *ganaz*, (the ז *zain* being changed into ד *daleth*, according to the custom of the *Chaldee*,) to *treasure up*, and בר *bar*, *pure*. Those who kept the current coin, or were over the *mint;* the treasurers of the exchequer in Babylon.

The COUNSELLORS] דתבריא *dethaberaiya*, from דת *dath*, a *statute*, and בר *bar*, "to declare the meaning of the law;" for in all ages and countries there has been what is termed *the glorious uncertainty of the law;* and therefore there must be a class of men whose business it is to explain it. What a pity that law cannot be tendered to the people as other sciences are, in plain, unsophisticated, and intelligible terms, and by persons whose business it is to show what is *just* and *right*, and not pervert *truth*, *righteousness*, and *judgment*.

The SHERIFFS] תפתיא *tiphtaye*, from תפת *taphath*, in Hebrew, שפת *shaphath*, "to set in order." Probably civil magistrates.

And all the rulers of the provinces] All other state or civil officers, not only to grace the solemnity, but to maintain order. My old Bible renders them: **Satrapis, or wiise men. Magistratis. Jugis. Duykis, Tyrauntis, or stronge men. Prefectis, and alle the Princes of Cuntreese.**

A. M. cir. 3424
B. C. cir. 580
Ol. cir. L. 1
TarquiniiPrisci,
R. Roman.,
cir. annum 37

3 Then the princes, the governors and captains, the judges,
the treasurers, the counsellors,
the sheriffs, and all the rulers of
the provinces, were gathered together unto the
dedication of the image that Nebuchadnezzar
the king had set up; and they stood before
the image that Nebuchadnezzar had set up.
4 Then a herald cried [c]aloud, To you [d]it
is commanded, [e]O people, nations, and languages,
5 *That* at what time ye hear the sound of
the cornet, flute, harp, sackbut, psaltery, [f]dul-
cimer, [g]and all kinds of music, ye fall down
and worship the golden image that Nebuchadnezzar the king hath set up:
6 And whoso falleth not down and worshippeth shall the same hour [h]be cast into
the midst of a burning fiery furnace.
7 Therefore at that time, when all the people
heard the sound of the cornet, flute, harp,
sackbut, psaltery, and all kinds of music, all
the people, the nations, and the languages,
fell down *and* worshipped the golden image
that Nebuchadnezzar the king had set up.
8 Wherefore at that time certain Chaldeans [i]came near, and
accused the Jews.
9 They spake and said to the
king Nebuchadnezzar, [k]O king, live for
ever.
10 Thou, O king, hast made a decree, that
every man that shall hear the sound of the
cornet, flute, harp, sackbut, psaltery, and dulcimer, and all kinds of music, shall fall down
and worship the golden image:
11 And whoso falleth not down and worshippeth, *that* he should be cast into the midst
of a burning fiery furnace.
12 [l]There are certain Jews whom thou hast
set over the affairs of the province of Babylon,
Shadrach, Meshach, and Abed-nego; these
men, O king, [m]have not regarded thee: they
serve not thy gods, nor worship the golden
image which thou hast set up.
13 Then Nebuchadnezzar in *his* rage and
fury commanded to bring Shadrach, Meshach,
and Abed-nego. Then they brought these
men before the king.
14 Nebuchadnezzar spake and said unto

A. M. cir. 3424
B. C. cir. 580
Ol. cir. L. 1
TarquiniiPrisci,
R. Roman.,
cir. annum 37

---

[c]Chald. *with might*——[d]Chald. *they command*——[e]Chap. iv. 1; vi. 25——[f]Or, *singing*——[g]Chald. *symphony*——[h]Jer. xxix. 22; Rev. xiii. 15

[i]Chapter vi. 12——[k]Chapter ii. 4; v. 10; vi. 6, 21——[l]Chapter ii. 49——[m]Chald. *have set no regard upon thee*

Verse 4. *Then a herald cried aloud*] כרווא קרא בחיל *caroza kara bechayil*, "a crier called with might." **A bedel cried mightili.**—Old MS. Bible.

Verse 5. *The sound of the* CORNET] There is not less difficulty in ascertaining the precise meaning of these *musical instruments* than there is in the *offices* in ver. 2. קרנא *karna*, here translated *cornet*, is the common *blowing horn*, which makes a deep and hollow sound, as well as one shrill and piercing.

FLUTE] משרוקיתא *mashrokitha*, from שרק *sharak, to whistle, shriek*. A wind instrument which made a strong and shrill noise, such as the *hautbois* or *clarionet*.

HARP] קיתרס *kithros, cytharus; κιθαρα*. Some kind of stringed instrument. It seems to be formed from the Greek word.

SACKBUT] סבכא *sabbecha*. The Greek has it *σαμβυκη*, from which our word *sackbut*, from סבך *sabach*, to *interweave;* probably on account of the number of chords, for it seems to have been a species of harp.

PSALTERY] פסנתרין *pesanterin;* Greek, *ψαλτηριον*. A stringed instrument, struck with a plectrum; that called *santeer* in Egypt is probably the same. Dr. *Russel* says: "It is a large triangle, and has two bottoms two inches from each other, with about twenty catguts of different sizes." It was the ancient *psalterium*, and most probably the same as *David's harp*.

DULCIMER] סומפניה *sumponeyah;* Greek, *συμφωνεια*. Probably a kind of *tamboor, tambourine*, or *tomtom drum*. It does not mean the same as the Greek *symphonia*, which signifies a *concert* or *harmony of many instruments*, for here one kind of instrument only is intended.

All kinds of music] כל זני זמרא *col zeney zemara, the whole stock*, or *band, of music;* the preceding being the chief, the most common, and the most sonorous. My old MS. Bible has, **Trumpe, and Pipe, and Harpe: Sambuke, Santrie, and Synfonye, and al kynde of musykes.**

Verse 6. *Shall the same hour*] This is the first place in the Old Testament where we find the division of time into *hours*. The Greeks say that *Anaximander* was the inventor. He had it probably from the Chaldeans, among whom this division was in use long before Anaximander was born.

Be cast into the midst of a burning fiery furnace.] This was an ancient mode of punishment among the Chaldeans, if we may credit the tradition that Abram was cast into such a fire by this idolatrous people because he would not worship their idols.

Verse 8. *Accused the Jews.*] That is, Shadrach, Meshach, and Abed-nego. The other Jews were left unnoticed; and probably at this time Daniel was too high to be touched; but we may rest assured that he was not found among these idolaters, see ver. 12.

A. M. cir. 3424
B. C. cir. 580
Ol. cir. L. 1
TarquiniiPrisci,
R. Roman.,
cir. annum 37

them, *Is it* [n]true, O Shadrach, Meshach, and Abed-nego, do not ye serve my gods, nor worship the golden image which I have set up?

15 Now if ye be ready that at what time ye hear the sound of the cornet, flute, harp, sackbut, psaltery, and dulcimer, and all kinds of music, ye fall down and worship the image which I have made; [o]*well:* but if ye worship not, ye shall be cast the same hour into the midst of a burning fiery furnace: [p]and who *is* that God that shall deliver you out of my hands?

16 Shadrach, Meshach, and Abed-nego, answered and said to the king, O Nebuchadnezzar, [q]we *are* not careful to answer thee in this matter.

17 If it be *so,* our God whom we serve is able to deliver us from the burning fiery furnace, and he will deliver *us* out of thine hand, O king.

18 [r]But if not, be it known unto thee, O king, that we will not serve thy gods, nor worship the golden image which thou hast set up.

A. M. cir. 3424
B. C. cir. 580
Ol. cir. L. 1.
TarquiniiPrisci
R. Roman.,
cir. annum 37

19 Then was Nebuchadnezzar [s]full of fury, and the form of his visage was changed against Shadrach, Meshach, and Abed-nego: *therefore* he spake, and commanded that they should heat the furnace one seven times more than it was wont to be heated.

20 And he commanded the [t]most mighty men that *were* in his army to bind Shadrach, Meshach, and Abed-nego, *and* to cast *them* into the burning fiery furnace.

21 Then these men were bound in their [u]coats, their hosen, and their [v]hats, and their *other* garments, and were cast into the midst of the burning fiery furnace.

22 Therefore because the king's [w]commandment was urgent, and the furnace exceeding hot, the [x]flame of the fire slew those men that took up Shadrach, Meshach, and Abed-nego.

23 And these three men, Shadrach, Meshach, and Abed-nego, fell down bound into the midst of the burning fiery furnace.

---

[n]Or, *of purpose,* as Exod. xxi. 13——[o]As Exod. xxxii. 32; Luke xiii. 9——[p]Exod. v. 2; 2 Kings xviii. 35 [q]Matt. x. 19

[r]2 Mac. vii. 2——[s]Chald. *filled*——[t]Chald. *mighty of strength*——[u]Or, *mantles*——[v]Or, *turbans*——[w]Chald. *word*——[x]Or, *sparks*

Verse 16. *We are not careful*] We have no need to put thee to any farther trouble; we have made up our minds on this subject, and have our answer ready: *Be it known unto thee,* WE WILL NOT SERVE THY GODS. This was as honest as it was decisive.

Verse 17. *If it be so*] Thou mayest cast us into the furnace; the terror of it has no effect on our minds to induce us to alter the resolution we have taken, nor shall the fire change our purpose. We serve a God who is able to deliver us. Should he not, we are equally determined; but we are satisfied that in some way or other he will deliver us out of thy hand. Thy power cannot affect us in the kingdom of our God to which we shall ascend from thy furnace, should he permit the fire to kindle upon us. "Render to Cæsar the things which are Cæsar's," is a maxim of Jesus Christ; but when Cæsar arrogates to himself the things that are the Lord's, then, and in such cases, his authority is to be resisted. God does not desire Cæsar's things; Cæsar's must not have the things of God.

Verse 19. *Then was Nebuchadnezzar full of fury*] How strange is this, after having had so many proofs of the supremacy of Jehovah! He had seen how God poured contempt upon his authority in the case of the *three* Hebrews, and yet he will try his strength once more! How infatuated is man!

Seven times more] As hot as it could be made. *Seven* expresses the great intensity of the heat.

Verse 20. *The most mighty men*] The generals, or chief officers of his army; not *strong* men; there was no need of such.

Verse 21. *Their hats*] This word, *hat,* is found only in this place in the Old Testament. The word סרבל *sarbal* properly means an outer garment. *Herodotus,* who lived about *one hundred* years after Daniel, says, "the dress of the Babylonians consisted of a tunic of linen reaching down to the feet; over this a tunic of woollen; and over all a white short cloak or mantle, χλανιδιον; and on their heads they wore *turbans,* μιτρησι." Following this, Mr. *Parkhurst* translates the verse thus: "Then these three men were bound [בסרבליהון *besarbaleyhon*] in their CLOAKS, [פטישיהון *patesheyhon*] their TURBANS, [וכרבלתהון *vecharbelathehon*] and in their UPPER (woollen) TUNICS, [ולבושיהון *ulebushehon*] and their UNDER (linen) TUNICS." And as, according to this interpretation, their סרבלי *sarbaley* were their *outermost garments,* we see the propriety with which it is observed at ver. 27 that these *were not changed* by the fire.

Verse 23. *And these three men—fell down bound*] There is a most evident want of connexion between this and the following verse; and it is between these verses that the apocryphal Song of the Three Children, as it is called, has been inserted by St. Jerome and others; but with this note: Quæ sequuntur in Hebræis voluminibus non reperi; "What follows I have not found in the Hebrew books." And then begins, "They walked in the midst of the flame, praising God, and blessing the Lord." The

A. M. cir. 3424 B. C. cir. 580 Ol. cir. L. 1 TarquiniiPrisci, R. Roman., cir. annum 37

24 Then Nebuchadnezzar the
king was astonied, and rose up
in haste, *and* spake, and said
unto his [y]counsellors, Did not
we cast three men bound into the midst of
the fire? They answered and said unto the
king, True, O king.

25 He answered and said, Lo, I see four
men loose, [z]walking in the midst of the fire,
and [a]they have no hurt; and the form of the
fourth is like [b]the Son of God.

26 Then Nebuchadnezzar came near to the
[c]mouth of the burning fiery furnace, *and*
spake, and said, Shadrach, Meshach, and
Abed-nego, ye servants of the most high God,
come forth, and come *hither*. Then Shadrach,
Meshach, and Abed-nego, came forth of the
midst of the fire.

27 And the princes, governors, and captains,
and the king's counsellors, being gathered
together, saw these men, [d]upon whose bodies
the fire had no power, nor was a
hair of their head singed, neither
were their coats changed, nor the
smell of fire had passed on them.

28 *Then* Nebuchadnezzar spake, and said,
Blessed *be* the God of Shadrach, Meshach,
and Abed-nego, who hath sent his angel, and
delivered his servants that [e]trusted in him,
and have changed the king's word, and
yielded their bodies, that they might not serve
nor worship any god, except their own God.

29 [f]Therefore [g]I make a decree, That
every people, nation, and language, which
speak [h]any thing amiss against the God of
Shadrach, Meshach, and Abed-nego, shall be
[i]cut [k]in pieces, and their houses shall be made
a dunghill: [l]because there is no other god
that can deliver after this sort.

30 Then the king [m]promoted Shadrach,
Meshach, and Abed-nego, in the province of
Babylon.

[y]Or, *governors*—[z]Isa. xliii. 2—[a]Chald. *there is no hurt in them*—[b]Job i. 6; xxxviii. 7; Psa. xxxiv. 7; ver. 28—[c]Chald. *door*—[d]Heb. xi. 34—[e]Psa. xxxiv. 7, 8; Jer. xvii. 7; ch. vi. 22, 23—[f]Ch. vi. 26—[g]Chald. *a decree is made by me*—[h]Chald. *error*—[i]Chap. ii. 5—[k]Chald. *made pieces*—[l]Chap. vi. 27—[m]Chald. *made to prosper*

Septuagint and *Arabic* read the *twenty-fourth* verse thus: "Then Nebuchadnezzar heard them singing praise, and was astonished." To connect the two verses *Houbigant* adds two verses found in the *Vulgate*, which are the *forty-ninth* and the *twenty-third:* "But an angel of the Lord went down with Azariah and his companions into the furnace, and drove out the flame of fire from the furnace; and they walked in the midst of the furnace." This verse (the *forty-ninth*) has been added to show the *reason* of Nebuchadnezzar's *astonishment*, and also to account for the appearance of a *fourth* person in the furnace, as in ver. 25.

Verse 25. *Is like the Son of God.*] A most improper translation. What notion could this idolatrous king have of the *Lord Jesus Christ?* for so the place is understood by thousands. בר אלהין *bar elahin* signifies *a son of the gods*, that is, a Divine person or *angel;* and so the king calls him in ver. 28: "God hath sent his ANGEL, and delivered his servants." And though even from this some still contend that it was the *Angel of the covenant*, yet the Babylonish king knew just as much of the one as he did of the other. No other ministration was necessary; a single angel from heaven was quite sufficient to answer this purpose, as that which stopped the mouths of the lions when Daniel was cast into their den.

Verse 27. *Upon whose bodies the fire had no power*] The heathens boasted that their priests could walk on burning coals unhurt; and *Virgil* mentions this of the priests of Apollo of Soracte:—

Summe Deum, sancti custos Soractis Apollo!
Quem primi colimus, cui pineus ardor acervo
Pascitur; et medium, freti pietate, per ignem
Cultores multa premimus vestigia pruna.
VIRG. *Æn.* xi. 785.

O Phœbus, guardian of Soracte's woods
And shady hills; a god above the gods;
To whom our natives pay the rites divine,
And burn whole crackling groves of hallowed pine;
Walk through the fire in honour of thy name,
Unhurt, unsinged, and *sacred from the flame.*
PITTS.

But *Varro* tells us that they anointed the soles of their feet with a species of unguent that preserved them from being burnt. Very lately a female showed many feats of this kind, putting red hot iron upon her arms, breasts, &c., and passing it over her hair without the slightest inconvenience; but in the case of the three Hebrews all was supernatural, and the king and his officers well knew it.

Verse 28. *Blessed* be *the God of Shadrach, &c.*] Here is a noble testimony from a heathen. And what produced it? The intrepidly pious conduct of these three noble Jews. Had they been time-servers, the name of the true God had not been known in Babylon. What honour does the Lord put on them that are steadfast in the faith!

Verse 29. *Speak any thing amiss*] Though by the decree the king does not oblige the people to worship the true God, yet he obliges them to treat him with reverence.

Verse 30. *Then the king promoted, &c.*] He restored them to the offices which they held before the charge of disobedience and treason was brought against them.

At the end of this verse the *Septuagint* add, "And he advanced them to be governors over all the Jews that were in his kingdom." This may be the meaning of the latter verse. They were more likely to be set over the *Jews* than over the *Chaldeans.*

CHAPTER IV

Nebuchadnezzar, after having subdued all the neighbouring countries, and greatly enriched and adorned his own, became so intoxicated with his prosperity, as to draw down upon himself a very remarkable judgment, of which this chapter gives a particular account, in the very words of the edict or proclamation which the Babylonish monarch issued on his restoration to the throne. This state document begins with Nebuchadnezzar's acknowledging the hand of God in his late malady, 1–3. *It then gives an account of the dream of Nebuchadnezzar, which portended the loss of his kingdom and reason for seven years, on account of his pride and arrogance,* 4–18. *So it was explained by Daniel,* 19–27, *and so it was verified by the event,* 28–33. *It then recites how, at the end of the period fixed by the God of heaven for the duration of his malady, the Chaldean monarch became sensible of his dependence on the Supreme Being, and lifted up his eyes to heaven in devout acknowledgment of the sovereign majesty of the King of kings, the Ruler of the earth, whose dominion alone is universal, unchangeable, and everlasting,* 34–37.

A. M. cir. 3434
B. C. cir. 570
Ol. cir. LII. 3
Servii Tullii,
R. Roman.,
cir. annum 9

NEBUCHADNEZZAR the
king, [a]unto all people, nations, and languages, that dwell
in all the earth; Peace be multiplied unto you.
2 [b]I thought it good to show the signs and
wonders [c]that the high God hath wrought
toward me.
3 [d]How great *are* his signs! and how mighty
are his wonders! his kingdom *is* [e]an everlasting kingdom, and his dominion *is* from
generation to generation.
4 I Nebuchadnezzar was at rest in mine
house, and flourishing in my palace:
5 I saw a dream which made me afraid,
[f]and the thoughts upon my bed and the
visions of my head [g]troubled me.
6 Therefore made I a decree to bring in all
the wise *men* of Babylon before me, that they
might make known unto me the interpretation of the dream.
7 [h]Then came in the magicians, the astrologers, the Chaldeans, and the
soothsayers: and I told the
dream before them; but they did
not make known unto me the
interpretation thereof.

A. M. cir. 3434
B. C. cir. 570
Ol. cir. LII. 3
Servii Tullii,
R. Roman.,
cir. annum 9

8 But at the last Daniel came in before me,
[i]whose name *was* Belteshazzar, according to
the name of my god, [k]and in whom *is* the
spirit of the holy gods: and before him I told
the dream, *saying,*
9 O Belteshazzar, [l]master of the magicians,
because I know that the spirit of the holy
gods *is* in thee, and no secret troubleth thee,
tell me the visions of my dream that I have
seen, and the interpretation thereof.
10 Thus *were* the visions of mine head in
my bed; [m]I saw, and behold [n]a tree in the
midst of the earth, and the height thereof *was*
great.
11 The tree grew, and was strong, and the
height thereof reached unto heaven, and the
sight thereof to the end of all the earth:

---

[a]Chap. iii. 4; vi. 25——[b]Chald. *It was seemly before me*——[c]Chap. iii. 26——[d]Chap. vi. 27——[e]Ver. 34; chap. ii. 44; vi. 26——[f]Chap. ii. 28, 29——[g]Chap. ii. 1

[h]Chap. ii. 2——[i]Chap. i. 7——[k]Isa. lxiii. 11; ver. 18; chap. ii. 11; v. 11, 14——[l]Chap. ii. 48; v. 11——[m]Chald. *I was seeing*——[n]Ezek. xxxi. 3, &c.; ver. 20

NOTES ON CHAP. IV

Verse 1. *Nebuchadnezzar the king, unto all people*] This is a regular *decree*, and is one of the most ancient on record; and no doubt was copied from the *state papers* of Babylon. Daniel has preserved it in the *original language.*

Verse 2. *I thought it good to show*] A part of the decree was a recital of the wonders wrought by the hand of the true God in his kingdom and on his person.

Verse 3. *How great* are *his signs!*] There are no preternatural signs like his! His *wonders*—miraculous interferences, are mighty—they surpass all human power. He is the *Sovereign of all kings*, and his *dominion is everlasting;* and *every generation* is a proof of his all-governing influence. These are very fine sentiments, and show how deeply his mind was impressed with the majesty of God.

Verse 4. *I—was at rest*] I had returned to my palace in Babylon after having subdued Syria, Phœnicia, Judea, Egypt, and Arabia. It was probably these great conquests that puffed him up with pride, and brought that chastisement upon him which he afterwards describes. See the dream of the *emblematical tree* explained.

Verse 5. *I saw a dream*] See this dream circumstantially explained in the following verses.

Verse 10. *I saw—a tree*] This vision Nebuchadnezzar says *made him afraid.* What a mercy it is that God has hidden futurity from us! Were he to show every man the lot that is before him, the misery of the human race would be complete.

Great men and princes are often represented, in the language of the prophets, under the similitude of *trees;* see Ezek. xvii. 5, 6; xxxi. 3, &c.; Jer. xxii. 15; Psa. i. 3; xxxvii. 35.

A. M. cir. 3434 B. C. cir. 570 Ol. cir. LII. 3 Servii Tullii, R. Roman., cir. annum 9

12 The leaves thereof *were* fair, and the fruit thereof much, and in it *was* meat for all: [o]the beasts of the field had shadow under it, and the fowls of the heaven dwelt in the boughs thereof, and all flesh was fed of it.

13 I saw in the visions of my head upon my bed, and, behold, [p]a watcher and [q]a holy one came down from heaven;

14 He cried [r]aloud, and said thus, [s]Hew down the tree, and cut off his branches, shake off his leaves, and scatter his fruit: [t]let the beasts get away from under it, and the fowls from his branches.

15 Nevertheless leave the stump of his roots in the earth, even with a band of iron and brass, in the tender grass of the field; and let it be wet with the dew of heaven, and *let* his portion *be* with the beasts in the grass of the earth:

16 Let his heart be changed from man's, and let a beast's heart be given unto him; and let seven [u]times pass over him.

17 This matter *is* by the decree of the watchers, and the demand by the word of the holy ones: to the intent [v]that the living may know [w]that the Most High ruleth in the kingdom of men, and giveth it to whomsoever he will, and setteth up over it the basest of men.

A. M. cir. 3434 B. C. cir. 570 Ol. cir. LII. 3 Servii Tullii R. Roman., cir. annum 9

18 This dream I king Nebuchadnezzar have seen. Now thou, O Belteshazzar, declare the interpretation thereof, [x]forasmuch as all the wise *men* of my kingdom are not able to make known unto me the interpretation: but thou *art* able; [y]for the spirit of the holy gods *is* in thee.

19 Then Daniel, [z]whose name *was* Belteshazzar, was astonied for one hour, and his thoughts troubled him. The king spake, and said, Belteshazzar, let not the dream, or the interpretation thereof, trouble thee. Belteshazzar answered and said, My lord, [a]the dream *be* to them that hate thee, and the interpretation thereof to thine enemies.

20 [b]The tree that thou sawest, which grew, and was strong, whose height reached unto the heaven, and the sight thereof to all the earth;

21 Whose leaves *were* fair, and the fruit thereof much, and in it *was* meat for all; under which the beasts of the field dwelt,

---

[o]Ezek. xvii. 23; xxxi. 6; see Lam. iv. 20——[p]Psa. ciii. 20; ver. 17, 23——[q]Deut. xxxiii. 2; chap. viii. 13; Zech. xiv. 5; Jude 14——[r]Chald. *with might*——[s]Matt. iii. 10——[t]Ezek. xxxi. 12

[u]Chap. xi. 13; xii. 7——[v]Psa. ix. 16——[w]Chap. ii. 21; v. 21; ver. 25, 32——[x]Gen. xli. 8, 15; chap. v. 8, 15 [y]Ver. 8——[z]Ver. 8——[a]See 2 Sam. xviii. 32; Jer. xxix. 7 [b]Ver. 10, 11, 12

Verse 13. *A watcher and a holy one*] These are both *angels;* but, according to the Chaldean oracles, of *different orders.* They appear, according to their opinions, to be a kind of *judges* of *human actions* who had the power of *determining the lot* of men; see ver. 17.

Verse 14. *Hew down the tree*] As the tree was to be cut down, the beasts are commanded to *flee away from under his branches.* His courtiers, officers, &c., all abandoned him as soon as his insanity appeared; but he soon fled from the society of men.

Verse 15. *Leave the stump*] Let him not be destroyed, nor his kingdom alienated.

Verse 16. *Let his heart be changed*] Let him conceive himself to be a *beast,* and act as such, herding among the beasts of the field.

Let seven times pass over him.] Let him continue in this state for *seven years.* I knew a man who was thus changed in his heart—in his imagination. He believed himself to be a *bear,* and would imitate the ursal growl, &c.; and the case did not appear to be hypochondriacal. Whether he ever came to sound mind, I know not.

Verse 17. *This matter* is *by the decree of the watchers*] See on ver. 13.

The Most High ruleth] He never leaves the government of the world to man, to second causes, or to fortuitous occurrences. What are thus called are his *agents;* they are no *moving causes.*

And setteth up—the basest of men.]

"Tyrants and kings from Jove proceed
Those are permitted, these decreed."

The *throne* ennobles no man: to be properly filled, the *man* must be *noble.* Some of the *greatest* and some of the *meanest* of men have sat on the throne. Kings differ in *education,* seldom in *intellect,* from the common mass of men; the *power* and *authority* are from God. The king himself may be given either in *mercy* or in *wrath.* When *James* II. ruled this kingdom, it might well be said, God hath *set up over it the basest of men.* His *successor* was one of the best. The *former* nearly ruined it both in a civil and religious point of view; the *latter* was the means of restoring it in both these respects.

Verse 19. *Daniel—was astonied for one hour*] He saw the design of the dream, and he felt the great delicacy of interpreting it. He was not puzzled by the difficulties of it. He felt for the king, and for the nation; and with what force and delicacy does he express the general portent; "The dream to them that hate thee, and the interpretation thereof to thine enemies!"

Verse 20. *The tree that thou sawest*] The

A. M. cir. 3434
B. C. cir. 570
Ol. cir. LII. 3
Servii Tullii,
R. Roman.,
cir. annum 9

and upon whose branches the fowls of the heaven had their habitation:

22 [c]It *is* thou, O king, that art grown and become strong: for thy greatness is grown, and reacheth unto heaven, [d]and thy dominion to the end of the earth.

23 [e]And whereas the king saw a watcher and a holy one coming down from heaven, and saying, Hew the tree down, and destroy it; yet leave the stump of the roots thereof in the earth, even with a band of iron and brass, in the tender grass of the field; and let it be wet with the dew of heaven, [f]and *let* his portion *be* with the beasts of the field, till seven times pass over him;

24 This *is* the interpretation, O king, and this *is* the decree of the Most High, which is come upon my lord the king:

25 That they shall [g]drive thee from men, and thy dwelling shall be with the beasts of the field, and they shall make thee [h]to eat grass as oxen, and they shall wet thee with the dew of heaven, and seven times shall pass over thee, [i]till thou know that the Most High ruleth in the kingdom of men, and [k]giveth it to whomsoever he will.

26 And whereas they commanded to leave the stump of the tree roots; thy kingdom shall be sure unto thee, after that thou shalt have known that the [l]heavens do rule.

27 Wherefore, O king, let my counsel be acceptable unto thee, and [m]break off thy sins by righteousness, and thine iniquities by showing mercy to the poor; [n]if it may be [o]a[p] lengthening of thy tranquillity.

28 All this came upon the king Nebuchadnezzar.

A. M. cir. 3434
B. C. cir. 570
Ol. cir. LII. 3
Servii Tullii,
R. Roman.,
cir. annum 9

29 At the end of twelve months he walked [q]in the palace of the kingdom of Babylon.

30 The king [r]spake, and said, Is not this great Babylon, that I have built for the house of the kingdom by the might of my power, and for the honour of my majesty?

31 [s]While the word *was* in the king's mouth, there fell [t]a voice from heaven, *saying,* O king Nebuchadnezzar, to thee it is spoken; The kingdom is departed from thee.

32 And [u]they shall drive thee from men, and thy dwelling *shall be* with the beasts of the field: they shall make thee to eat grass as oxen, and seven times shall pass over thee, until thou know that the Most High ruleth in the kingdom of men, and giveth it to whomsoever he will.

33 The same hour was the thing fulfilled upon Nebuchadnezzar: and he was driven from men, and did eat grass as oxen, and his body was wet with the dew of heaven, till his hairs were grown like eagles' *feathers,* and his nails like birds' *claws.*

A. M. cir. 3441
B. C. cir. 563
Ol. LIV. 2
Servii Tullii,
R. Roman.,
cir. annum 16

34 And [v]at the end of the days I Nebuchadnezzar lifted up mine eyes unto heaven, and mine understanding returned unto me, and I blessed the Most High, and I praised and honoured him [w]that liveth for ever, whose dominion *is* [x]an everlasting dominion, and his kingdom *is* from generation to generation:

35 And [y]all the inhabitants of the earth *are* reputed as nothing: and [z]he doeth according

[c]Chap. ii. 38——[d]Jer. xxvii. 6, 7, 8——[e]Ver. 13
[f]Chap. v. 21——[g]Ver. 32; chap. v. 21, &c.——[h]Psa. cvi. 20——[i]Ver. 17, 32; Psa. lxxxiii. 18——[k]Jer. xxvii. 5
[l]Matt. xxi. 25; Luke xv. 18, 21——[m]1 Pet. iv. 8
[n]Psa. xli. 1, &c.——[o]Or, *a healing of thine error*

[p]1 Kings xxi. 29——[q]Or, *upon*——[r]Prov. xvi. 18; chap. v. 20——[s]Chap. v. 5; Luke xii. 20——[t]Ver. 24
[u]Ver. 25——[v]Ver. 26——[w]Chap. xii. 7; Rev. iv. 10
[x]Psa. x. 16; chap. ii. 44; vii. 14; Mic. iv. 7; Luke i. 33
[y]Isa. xl. 15, 17——[z]Psa. cxv. 3; cxxxv. 6

dream is so fully interpreted in the following verses that it needs no comment.

Verse 26. *Thy kingdom shall be sure unto thee*] No new king was set up; Evil-merodach his son was regent during his father's insanity.

Verse 27. *Break off thy sins by righteousness*] Do *justice.* Thou hast been an *oppressive* man; *show mercy to the poor,* many of whom have been made such by thyself: witness the whole nation of the Jews. He was to cease from his *sins—repent, and bring forth fruits meet for repentance,* in order that he might find mercy at the hand of God.

Verse 30. *Is not this great Babylon*] Here his heart was inflated with pride; he attributed every thing to himself, and acknowledged God in nothing. The *walls, hanging gardens, temple of Bel,* and the *royal palace,* all built by Nebuchadnezzar, made it the greatest city in the world.

Verse 31. *While the word* was *in the king's mouth*] How awful to a victorious and proud king: "Thy kingdom is departed from thee!" All thy goods and gods are gone in a moment!

Verse 32. *They shall make thee, &c.*] Thou shalt be made *to eat grass as oxen.* The madness that fell upon him induced him to forsake society, and to run to the woods and deserts,

A. M. cir. 3441
B. C. cir. 563
Ol. LIV. 2
Servii Tullii,
R. Roman.,
cir. annum 16

to his will in the army of
heaven, and *among* the inhabitants of the earth: and [a]none
can stay his hand, or say unto
him, [b]What doest thou?
36 At the same time my reason returned
unto me; [c]and for the glory of my kingdom,
mine honour and brightness returned unto
me; and my counsellors and my lords sought
unto me; and I was established
in my kingdom, and excel-
lent majesty was [d]added unto
me.
37 Now I Nebuchadnezzar praise and extol
and honour the king of heaven, [e]all whose
works *are* truth, and his ways judgment:
[f]and those that walk in pride he is able to
abase.

[a]Job xxxiv. 29——[b]Job ix. 12; Isa. xlv. 9; Rom. ii. 20
[c]Ver. 26——[d]Job xlii. 12; Prov. xxii. 4; Matt. vi. 33
[e]Psa. xxxiii. 4; Rev. xv. 3; xvi. 7——[f]Exod. xviii. 11; chap. v. 20

where he lived like a wild beast, his *hairs* growing long and thick, so as to be a substitute for clothing; and his *nails* strong and hooked, that he might the better climb trees and grub up the ground, in order to get *roots* and *earth-nuts.* It was the *mercy* of God that thus *clothed* and *accoutred* him. His case seems much like that of the maniac in the Gospel, whose dwelling was among the tombs and in the mountains, and who shunned the society of men.

Verse 36. *My reason returned*] Every thing was fulfilled that was exhibited by the *dream* and its *interpretation.* It is very likely that this unfortunate king had so concealed himself that the place of his retreat was not found out; and the providence of God had so watched over every thing, that, on his return to his palace, he found his *counsellors* and his *lords*, who received him gladly, and cleaved to and served him as they had formerly done.

Verse 37. *Now I—praise and extol*] It is very probable that Nebuchadnezzar was a true convert; that he relapsed no more into idolatry, and died in the faith of the God of Israel. It is supposed that he lived *seventeen* years after his restoration. But the authorized Version, which is followed in the margin, states the date of this decree to be B. C. 563, the year preceding Nebuchadnezzar's death.

CHAPTER V

In the commencement of this chapter we are informed how Belshazzar, the grandson of Nebuchadnezzar, when rioting in his palace, and profaning the sacred vessels of the temple, 1–4, *was suddenly terrified with the appearance of the fingers of a man's hand, which wrote a few words on the wall before him,* 5, 6. *The wise men and astrologers were immediately called in to show the king the interpretation; but they could not so much as read the writing, because (as Houbigant and others have conjectured) though the words are in the Chaldee tongue, yet they were written in the Samaritan or ancient Hebrew characters, with which the wise men of Babylon were very probably unacquainted, as the Jews were at that time a despised people, and the knowledge of their language not a fashionable attainment,* 7–9. *Daniel, who had been so highly esteemed by Nebuchadnezzar for his superior wisdom, appears to have been altogether unknown to Belshazzar, till the queen (the same who had been the wife of Nebuchadnezzar according to the general opinion, or the queen consort according to others) had informed him,* 10–12. *Upon the queen's recommendation, Daniel is called in,* 13–16; *who boldly tells this despotic king, that as he had not benefited by the judgments inflicted on his grandfather, but gave himself up to pride and profanity, and had added to his other sins an utter contempt for the God of the Jews by drinking wine out of the sacred vessels of Jehovah in honour of his idols,* 17–23; *the Supreme Being, the Ruler of heaven and earth, had written his condemnation in three words,* MENE, TEKEL, PERES, 24, 25; *the first of which is repeated in the copies containing the Chaldean original; but all the ancient Versions, except the Syriac, are without this repetition. Daniel then gives the king and his lords the fearful import of the writing,* viz., *that the period allotted for the duration of the Chaldean empire was now completed,* (see Jer. xxv. 12–14,) *and that the kingdom was about to be transferred to the Medes and Persians,* 26–28. *However unwelcome such an interpretation must have been to Belshazzar, yet the monarch, overwhelmed with its clearness and certainty, commanded the prophet to be honoured,* 29. *And that very night the prediction was fulfilled, for the king was slain,* 30, *and the city taken by the Medes and Persians,* 31. *This great event was also predicted by Isaiah and Jeremiah; and the manner in which it was accomplished is recorded by Herodotus and Xenophon.*

A. M. cir. 3466
B. C. cir. 538
Ol. cir. LX. 3
Servii Tullii,
R. Roman.,
cir. annum 41

BELSHAZZAR the king
[a]made a great feast to a
thousand of his lords, and
drank wine before the thousand.
2 Belshazzar, whiles he tasted

[a]Esther, chap. i. 3

NOTES ON CHAP. V.

Verse 1. *Belshazzar the king made a great feast*] This chapter is out of its place, and should come in after the *seventh* and *eighth.* There are difficulties in the *chronology.* After the death of *Nebuchadnezzar, Evil-merodach* his son ascended the throne of Babylon. Having reigned about *two* years, he was slain by his brother-in-law, *Neriglissar.* He reigned *four*

A. M. cir. 3466 B. C. cir. 538 Ol. cir. LX. 3 Servii Tullii, R. Roman., cir. annum 41

the wine, commanded to bring the [b]golden and silver vessels [c]which his [d]father Nebuchadnezzar had [e]taken out of the temple which *was* in Jerusalem; that the king, and his princes, his wives, and his concubines, might drink therein.

3 Then they brought the golden vessels that were taken out of the temple of the house of God which *was* at Jerusalem; and the king, and his princes, his wives, and his concubines, drank in them.

4 They drank wine, [f]and praised the gods of gold, and of silver, of brass, of iron, of wood, and of stone.

5 [g]In the same hour came forth fingers of a man's hand, and wrote over against the candlestick upon the plaster of the wall of the king's palace: and the king saw the part of the hand that wrote.

A. M. cir. 3466 B. C. cir. 538 Ol. cir. LX. 3 Servii Tullii, R. Roman., cir. annum 41

6 Then the king's [h]countenance [i]was changed, and his thoughts troubled him, so that the [k]joints[l] of his loins were loosed, and his [m]knees smote one against another.

7 [n]The king cried [o]aloud to bring in [p]the astrologers, the Chaldeans, and the soothsayers. *And* the king spake, and said to the wise *men* of Babylon, Whosoever shall read this writing, and show me the interpretation

[b]1 Chron. xxviii. 17; Ezra vi. 5; ver. 3, 23——[c]Chap. i. 2; Jer. lii. 19——[d]Or, *grandfather;* as Jer. xxvii. 7; 2 Sam. ix. 7; 2 Chron. xv. 16; ver. 11, 13——[e]Chald. *brought forth*——[f]Rev. ix. 20——[g]Chap. iv. 31

[h]Chald. *brightnesses;* ver. 9——[i]Chald. *changed it* [k]Or, *girdles;* Isa. v. 27——[l]Chald. *bindings,* or *knots* [m]Nah. ii. 10——[n]Chap. ii. 2; iv. 6——[o]Chald. *with might*——[p]Isa. xlvii. 13

years, and was succeeded by his son *Laborosoarchod,* who reigned only *nine months.* At his death *Belshazzar,* the son of *Evil-merodach,* was raised to the throne, and reigned *seventeen years,* and was slain, as we read here, by Cyrus, who surprised and took the city on the night of this festivity. This is the chronology on which Archbishop *Usher,* and other learned chronologists, agree; but the Scripture mentions only *Nebuchadnezzar, Evil-merodach,* and *Belshazzar,* by name; and Jeremiah, chap. xxvii. 7, expressly says, "All nations shall serve him (Nebuchadnezzar,) and his son (Evil-merodach,) and his son's son (Belshazzar,) until the very time of his land come;" i. e., till the time in which the empire should be seized by Cyrus. Here there is no mention of *Neriglissar* nor *Laborosoarchod;* but as they were *usurpers,* they might have been purposely passed by. But there remains one difficulty still: *Belshazzar* is expressly called the *son of Nebuchadnezzar* by the queen mother, ver. 11: "There is a man in thy kingdom, in whom is the spirit of the holy gods: and in the days of THY FATHER light and understanding and wisdom, like the wisdom of the gods, was found in him: whom the king NEBUCHADNEZZAR THY FATHER, the king, I say, thy father, made master of the magicians." The solution of this difficulty is, that in Scripture the name of *son* is indifferently given to *sons* and *grandsons,* and even to *great grandsons.* And perhaps the *repetition* in the above verse may imply this: "The king, Nebuchadnezzar thy father, the king thy father." The king thy father's father, and consequently thy grandfather. If it have not some such meaning as this, it must be considered an *idle repetition.* As to the *two other kings, Neriglissar* and *Laborosoarchod,* mentioned by *Josephus* and *Berosus,* and by whom the chronology is so much puzzled, they might have been some *petty kings,* or *viceroys,* or *satraps,* who affected the kingdom, and produced disturbances, one for *four years,* and the other for *nine months;* and would in consequence not be acknowledged in the Babylonish chronology, nor by the sacred writers, any more than finally unsuccessful rebels are numbered among the kings of those nations which they have disturbed. I believe the only sovereigns we can acknowledge here are the following: 1. *Nabopolassar;* 2. *Nebuchadnezzar;* 3. *Evil-merodach;* 4. *Belshazzar;* and with this last the Chaldean empire ended.

To a thousand of his lords] Perhaps this means *lords* or *satraps,* that were each over *one thousand men.* But we learn from antiquity that the *Persian* kings were very profuse in their entertainments; but it does not follow that the *Chaldeans* were so too. Besides, *one thousand lords* and their appropriate attendants would have been very inconvenient in a *nocturnal assembly.* The text, however, supports the common translation. Literally, "Belshazzar the king made bread for his lords a thousand; and against the thousand he drank wine." That is, say some, he was a very great drinker.

Verse 2. *Whiles he tasted the wine*] He relished it, got heated by it, and when WINE got *fully in,* WIT went *wholly out;* and in consequence he acted the profane part of which we immediately read.

Verse 4. *And praised the gods of gold*] They had gods of *all sorts,* and of *all metals;* with *wooden* gods, and *stone* gods, beside!

Verse 5. *Fingers of a man's hand*] The fingers were collected about the *style* or *pen* as in the act of writing.

Verse 6. *The king's countenance was changed*] Here is a very natural description of fear and terror. 1. The face grows pale; 2. The mind becomes greatly agitated; 3. Pains seize on the lower part of the back and kidneys; 4. A universal tremor takes place, so that the knees smite against each other; 5. And lastly, either a *syncope* takes place, or the *cry of distress* is uttered, ver. 7: "The king cried."

Verse 7. *Whosoever shall read this writing*] He knew it must be some awful portent, and wished to know what.

Verse 8. *They could not read the writing*] Because it was in the *pure Hebrew,* not the *Chaldean, character.* See below.

Verse 10. *The queen—came*] This is generally allowed to have been the *widow* of Nebu-

A. M. cir. 3466
B. C. cir. 538
Ol. cir. LX. 3
Servii Tullii, R. Roman., cir. annum 41

thereof, shall be clothed with [q]scarlet, and *have* a chain of gold about his neck, [r]and shall be the third ruler in the kingdom.

8 Then came in all the king's wise *men:* [s]but they could not read the writing, nor make known to the king the interpretation thereof.

9 Then was king Belshazzar greatly [t]troubled, and his [u]countenance was changed in him, and his lords were astonied.

10 *Now* the queen by reason of the words of the king and his lords came into the banquet house: *and* the queen spake and said, [v]O king, live for ever: let not thy thoughts trouble thee, nor let thy countenance be changed:

11 [w]There is a man in thy kingdom, in whom *is* the spirit of the holy gods; and in the days of thy [x]father light and understanding wisdom, like the wisdom of the gods, was found in him; whom the king Nebuchadnezzar thy [y]father, the king, *I say,* thy father, made [z]master of the magicians, astrologers, Chaldeans, *and* soothsayers;

12 [a]Forasmuch as an excellent spirit, and knowledge, and understanding, [b]interpreting of dreams, and showing of hard sentences, and [c]dissolving of [d]doubts, were found in the same Daniel, [e]whom the king named Belteshazzar: now let Daniel be called, and he will show the interpretation.

13 Then was Daniel brought in before the king. *And* the king spake and said unto Daniel, *Art* thou that Daniel, which *art* of the children of the captivity of Judah, whom the king my [f]father brought out of Jewry?

A. M. cir. 3466
B. C. cir. 538
Ol. cir. LX. 3
Servii Tullii, R. Roman., cir. annum 41

14 I have even heard of thee, that [g]the spirit of the gods *is* in thee, and *that* light and understanding and excellent wisdom is found in thee.

15 And now [h]the wise *men,* the astrologers, have been brought in before me, that they should read this writing, and make known unto me the interpretation thereof: but they could not show the interpretation of the thing:

16 And I have heard of thee, that thou canst [i]make interpretations, and dissolve doubts: [k]now if thou canst read the writing, and make known to me the interpretation thereof, thou shalt be clothed with scarlet, and *have* a chain of gold about thy neck, and shalt be the third ruler in the kingdom.

17 Then Daniel answered and said before the king, Let thy gifts be to thyself, and give thy [l]rewards to another; yet I will read the writing unto the king, and make known to him the interpretation.

18 O thou king, [m]the most high God gave Nebuchadnezzar thy father a kingdom, and majesty, and glory, and honour:

19 And for the majesty that he gave him, [n]all people, nations, and languages, trembled and feared before him: whom he would he slew; and whom he would he kept alive; and whom he would he set up; and whom he would he put down.

20 [o]But when his heart was lifted up, and his mind hardened [p]in pride, he was [q]deposed

[q]Or, *purple*——[r]Chap. vi. 2——[s]Chap. ii. 27; iv. 7——[t]Chap. ii. 1——[u]Chald. *brightnesses;* ver. 6——[v]Chap. ii. 4; iii. 9——[w]Chap. ii. 48; iv. 8, 9, 18——[x]Or, *grandfather;* ver. 2——[y]Or, *grandfather;* ver. 2——[z]Chap. iv. 9——[a]Chap. vi. 3——[b]Or, *of an interpreter,* &c.——[c]Or, *of a dissolver*

[d]Chald. *knots*——[e]Chap. i. 7——[f]Or, *grandfather*——[g]Ver. 11, 12——[h]Ver. 7, 8——[i]Chald. *interpret*——[k]Ver. 7——[l]Or, *fee,* as chap. ii. 6——[m]Chap. ii. 37, 38; iv. 17, 22, 25——[n]Jer. xxvii. 7; chap. iii. 4——[o]Chap. iv. 30, 37——[p]Or, *to deal proudly;* Exod. xviii. 11——[q]Chald. *made to come down*

chadnezzar; if so, she was the queen *Amiyt,* daughter of *Astyages,* sister of *Darius* the Mede, and aunt of *Cyrus,* according to *Polyhistor,* cited by *Cedrenus.* See *Calmet.* Others think that *Nitocris* was the person who is said to be queen when Cyrus took the city; and is stated to have been a lady of eminent wisdom and discretion, and to have had the chief direction of the public affairs. She was the mother of *Labynithus;* and, if this be the same as *Belshazzar,* she must be the person here introduced.

Verse 11. *Nebuchadnezzar thy father*] See the note on ver. 1.

Verse 16. *Dissolve doubts*] *Untie knots—unbind what is bound.* An expression used in the east to signify a *judge* of eminent wisdom and skill.

Verse 17. *Let thy gifts be to thyself*] They could be of little use to any, as the city was *in a few hours* to be taken and pillaged.

Verse 18. *Nebuchadnezzar thy father*] Or *grandfather,* as the *margin* reads, ver. 2. See the notes on ver. 1.

Verse 19. *Whom he would he slew*] The genuine character of a *despot,* whose *will* is the only *rule* of his conduct.

Verse 20. *He was deposed from his kingly throne*] Became insane; and the reins of government were taken out of his hands.

A. M. cir. 3466
B. C. cir. 538
Ol. cir. LX. 3
Servii Tullii,
R. Roman.,
cir. annum 41

from his kingly throne, and they
took his glory from him:
21 And he was [r]driven from
the sons of men; and [s]his heart
was made like the beasts, and his dwelling
was with the wild asses: they fed him with
grass like oxen, and his body was wet with the
dew of heaven; [t]till he knew that the most
high God ruled in the kingdom of men, and
that he appointeth over it whomsoever he will.
22 And thou his son, O Belshazzar, [u]hast
not humbled thine heart, though thou knewest all this;
23 [v]But hast lifted up thyself against the
Lord of heaven; and they have brought the
vessels of his house before thee, and thou,
and thy lords, thy wives, and thy concubines,
have drunk wine in them; and thou hast
praised the gods of silver, and gold, of brass,
iron, wood, and stone, [w]which see not, nor
hear, nor know: and the God in whose hand
thy breath *is,* [x]and whose *are* all thy ways,
hast thou not glorified:

24 Then was the part of the
hand sent from him; and this
writing was written.
25 And this *is* the writing that
was written, MENE, MENE, TEKEL,
UPHARSIN.
26 This *is* the interpretation of the thing:
MENE; God hath numbered thy kingdom,
and finished it.
27 TEKEL; [y]Thou art weighed in the
balances, and art found wanting.
28 PERES; Thy kingdom is divided, and
given to the [z]Medes and [a]Persians.
29 Then commanded Belshazzar, and they
clothed Daniel with scarlet, and *put* a chain
of gold about his neck, and made a proclamation concerning him, [b]that he should be the
third ruler in the kingdom.
30 [c]In that night was Belshazzar the king
of the Chaldeans slain.
31 [d]And Darius the Median took the kingdom, [e]*being* [f]about threescore and two
years old.

A. M. cir. 3466
B. C. cir. 538
Ol. cir. LX. 3
Servii Tullii,
R. Roman.,
cir. annum 41

---

[r]Chap. iv. 32, &c.——[s]Or, *he made his heart equal,* &c.——[t]Chap. iv. 17, 25——[u]2 Chronicles xxxiii. 23; xxxvi. 12——[v]Ver. 3, 4——[w]Psalm cxv. 5, 6——[x]Jeremiah x. 23——[y]Job xxxi. 6; Psalm lxii. 9; Jeremiah vi. 30——[z]Foretold, Isa. xxi. 2; ver. 31; chap. ix. 1——[a]Chap. vi. 28——[b]Ver. 7——[c]Jeremiah li. 31, 39, 57——[d]Chap. vi. 1, 6, 9, 25, 28; ix. 1, 2; xi. 1——[e]Chald. he as *the son of,* &c.——[f]Or, *now*

Verse 22. *Hast not humbled thine heart*] These *judgments* and **mercies** have had no good effect upon thee.

Verse 23. *But hast lifted up thyself against the Lord*] And the highest evidence of this rebellion was, the profaning the sacred vessels of the Lord's house.

Verse 24. *Then was the part of the hand sent*] This was the filling up of the cup of thy iniquity; **this** last act made thee ripe for destruction.

Verse 25. *And this* is *the writing*] Had the words been written in the *Chaldean* character, every wise man there, every one that could read the *alphabet of his own language*, could have read and interpreted them. Let it be observed, —1. That the *character* which we now call *Hebrew* is the *Chaldean* character. 2. That the true *Hebrew* character is that which we call the *Samaritan*. 3. Daniel could easily read this, for it was the character used by the Jews previously to the *Babylonish* captivity. 4. It appears that it was simply on account of the strangeness of the *character* that the Chaldeans could not read it.

I shall set down the words in both characters, by which the least learned reader may see that it was quite possible that one might be well known, while the other might be unintelligible.

Hebrew

מנא מנא תקל ופרסין

Samaritan

ࠌࠍࠀ ࠌࠍࠀ ࠕࠒࠋ ࠅࠐࠓࠎࠉࠍ

In ancient times, no doubt, these letters differed more from each other than they appear to do now; for we know that the Samaritan on *ancient coins,* though radically the same, differs very much from that now used in printing.

It should be observed, that *each word* stands for a *short sentence;* מנא *mene* signifies NUMERATION; תקל *tekel,* WEIGHING; and פרס *peres,* DIVISION. And so the *Arabic* translates them. مقيسن *mokeeson*, measured; موزون *mewzonon*, weighed; مقسوم *mokesoomon*, divided. All the ancient Versions, except the *Syriac*, read the words simply *Mene*, *Tekel*, *Phares*, as they are explained in the following verses; without the repetition of *Mene*, and without the *conjunction* ו *vau*, and *plural termination,* ין *in*, in *Peres.*

Verse 29. *Clothed Daniel with scarlet*] ארגונא *argevana*, more probably with *purple*. The *gold chain* about the neck was an emblem of magisterial authority. It is often thus mentioned in Scripture.

Verse 30. *In that night was Belshazzar—slain.*] Xenophon says, he was despatched by two lords, *Gadatas* and *Gobrias*, who went over to Cyrus, to avenge themselves of certain wrongs which Belshazzar had done them. We have already seen that Cyrus entered the city by the bed of the Euphrates, which he had emptied, by cutting a channel for the waters, and directing them into the marshy country.

Verse 31. *Darius the Median took the kingdom*] This is supposed to be the same as *Cyaxares*, son of *Astyages* and maternal uncle of *Cyrus*, to whom he gave the throne of Babylon, after himself had had the honour of taking the city.

Daniel speaks nothing of the war that raged between the *Babylonians* and the *Medes;* but Isaiah speaks particularly of it, chap. xiii., xiv., xlv., xlvi., xlvii.; and so does Jeremiah, chap. l., li. I need not add, that it is largely spoken of by profane authors. The Medes and Persians were confederates in the war; the former under *Darius*, the latter under *Cyrus*. Both princes are supposed to have been present at the taking of this city. *Mandane*, daughter of Astyages, was mother of Cyrus, and sister to Cyaxares.

CHAPTER VI

Darius the Median, who succeeded Belshazzar in the kingdom of Babylon, having heard of Daniel's extraordinary wisdom and understanding, constitutes him the chief of the three presidents who were over the whole empire, and purposed also to make him prime minister or viceroy, 1–3. *This great partiality of the king towards a stranger of Jewish extraction, and who had been carried captive into Chaldea, raised up a great many enemies to Daniel; and a scheme was even contrived by the presidents and princes to ruin him,* 4–15; *which succeeded so far that he was cast into a den of lions, but was miraculously delivered,* 16–23. *Darius, who was greatly displeased with himself for having been entrapped by the governors of the provinces to the prejudice of his faithful minister, is pleased and astonished at this deliverance; punished Daniel's enemies with the same kind of death which they had designed for the prophet; and made a decree that, throughout his dominions, the God of Daniel should be had in the greatest veneration,* 24–38.

A. M. cir. 3466
B. C. cir. 538
Ol. cir. LX. 3
Servii Tullii,
R. Roman.,
cir. annum 41

IT pleased Darius to set [a]over
the kingdom a hundred and
twenty princes, which should be
over the whole kingdom;
2 And over these three presidents; of whom
Daniel *was* first: that the princes might give
accounts unto them, and the king should have
no damage.
3 Then this Daniel was preferred above the
presidents and princes, [b]because an excellent
spirit *was* in him; and the king thought to
set him over the whole realm.

A. M. cir. 3467
B. C. cir. 537
Ol. cir. LX. 4
Servii Tullii,
R. Roman.,
cir. annum 42

4 [c]Then the presidents and
princes sought to find occasion
against Daniel concerning the
kingdom; but they could find
none occasion nor fault; forasmuch as he *was*
faithful, neither was there any
error or fault found in him.
5 Then said these men, We
shall not find any occasion
against this Daniel, except we find *it* against
him concerning the law of his God.
6 Then these presidents and princes [d]assem-
bled together to the king, and said thus unto
him, [e]King Darius, live for ever.
7 All the presidents of the kingdom, the
governors, and the princes, the counsellors,
and the captains, have consulted together to
establish a royal statute, and to make a firm
[f]decree, that whosoever shall ask a petition of
any god or man for thirty days, save of thee,
O king, he shall be cast into the den of lions.
8 Now, O king, establish the decree, and

---

[a]Esther i. 1——[b]Chap. v. 12——[c]Eccles. iv. 4——[d]Or, *came tumultuously*——[e]Nehemiah ii. 3; verse 21; chapter ii. 4——[f]Or, *interdict*

NOTES ON CHAP. VI

Verse 1. *A hundred and twenty princes*] A chief or *satrap* over every province which belonged to the Medo-Persian empire. Afterwards we find it enlarged to *one hundred and twenty-seven* provinces, by the victories of *Cambyses* and *Darius Hystaspes*. See Esth. i. 1. *Josephus* reckons *three hundred and sixty* satrapies or lordships; but this is most probably an exaggeration or mistake.

Verse 2. *Three presidents*] Each having *forty* of these presidents accountable to him for their administration.

Daniel was *first*] As being established over that part where was the seat of government. He was confirmed in his offices by Darius.

Verse 3. *The king thought to set him over the whole realm*] Intended to make him *grand vizier* or *emir ul amrim*. This partiality of the king made Daniel the object of the other presidents, and the grandees of the kingdom.

Verse 4. *Sought to find occasion against Daniel*] But they found no blemish in his administration, for he was *faithful to his king:* this was a *virtue*. But he was also *faithful to his God:* this they hoped to construe into a *crime*, and make it the cause of his ruin.

Verse 7. *Whosoever shall ask a petition*] What pretence could they urge for so silly an ordinance? Probably to *flatter* the ambition of the king, they pretend to make him *a god* for *thirty* days; so that the whole empire should make prayer and supplication to him, and pay him Divine honours! This was the bait; but their real object was to destroy Daniel.

Verse 8. *According to the law of the Medes and Persians*] I do not think that this is to be understood so as to imply that whatever laws or ordinances the Medes or Persians once enacted, they never changed them. This would argue extreme folly in legislators in any country. Nothing more appears to be meant than that the decree should be enacted, written, and

A. M. cir. 3467
B. C. cir. 537
Ol. cir. LX. 4
Servii Tullii,
R. Roman.,
cir. annum 42

sign the writing, that it be not changed, according to the [g]law of the Medes and Persians, which [h]altereth not.

9 Wherefore king Darius signed the writing and the decree.

10 Now when Daniel knew that the writing was signed, he went into his house; and his windows being open in his chamber [i]toward Jerusalem, he kneeled upon his knees [k]three times a day, and prayed, and gave thanks before his God, as he did aforetime.

11 Then these men assembled, and found Daniel praying and making supplication before his God.

12 [l]Then they came near, and spake before the king concerning the king's decree; Hast thou not signed a decree, that every man that shall ask *a petition* of any god or man within thirty days, save of thee, O king, shall be cast into the den of lions? The king answered and said, The thing *is* true, [m]according to the law of the Medes and Persians, which altereth not.

13 Then answered they and said before the king, That Daniel, [n]which *is* of the children of the captivity of Judah, [o]regardeth not thee, O king, nor the decree that thou hast signed, but maketh his petition three times a day.

A. M. cir. 3467
B. C. cir. 537
Ol. cir. LX. 4
Servii Tullii,
R. Roman.,
cir. annum 42

14 Then the king, when he heard *these* words, [p]was sore displeased with himself, and set *his* heart on Daniel to deliver him: and he laboured till the going down of the sun to deliver him.

15 Then these men assembled unto the king, and said unto the king, Know, O king, that [q]the law of the Medes and Persians *is*, That no decree nor statute which the king establisheth may be changed.

16 Then the king commanded, and they brought Daniel, and cast *him* into the den of lions. *Now* the king spake and said unto Daniel, Thy God, whom thou servest continually, he will deliver thee.

17 [r]And a stone was brought, and laid upon the mouth of the den; [s]and the king sealed it with his own signet, and with the signet of his

[g]Esth. i. 19; viii. 8; ver. 12, 15——[h]Chald. *passeth not* [i]1 Kings viii. 44, 48; Psa. v. 7; Jonah ii. 4——[k]Psa. lv. 17; Acts ii. 1, 2, 15; iii. 1; x. 9

[l]Chap. iii. 8——[m]Ver. 8——[n]Chap. i. 6; v. 13 [o]Chap. iii. 12——[p]So Mark vi. 26——[q]Ver. 8——[r]Lam. iii. 53——[s]So Matt. xxvii. 66

registered, according to the legal forms among the Medes and Persians; and this one to be made absolute for *thirty* days. The laws were such among this people, that, when once passed with the usual formalities, the *king* could not change them at his own will. This is the utmost that can be meant by the law of the Medes and Persians that could not be changed.

Verse 10. *Now when Daniel knew that the writing was signed*] He saw *what* was *designed*, and he knew *whom* he *served*.

His windows being open] He would not shut them to conceal himself, but "kneeled down with his face turned toward Jerusalem, and prayed thrice each day, giving thanks to God as usual." When the Jews were in distant countries, in prayer they turned their faces towards *Jerusalem;* and when in Jerusalem, they turned their faces towards the *temple.* Solomon, in his prayer at the dedication of the temple, 1 Kings viii. 48, had entreated God to hear the prayers of those who might be in strange lands, or in captivity, when they should *turn their faces towards their own land*, which *God gave unto their fathers;* and towards *the city which he had chosen*, and *the house which was dedicated to his name.* It was in reference to this that Daniel turned his face towards Jerusalem when he prayed.

Verse 12. *Shall be cast into the den of lions*] Either this was the royal *menagerie*, like that place in the *Tower* of London, where wild beasts are kept for the king's pleasure, and the public amusement; or they were kept for the purpose of devouring certain criminals, which the laws might consign to that kind of death. This is most likely, from the case before us.

Verse 14. *The king—was sore displeased with himself*] And well he might, when through his excessive folly he passed a law that, for its ostensible object, would have been a disgrace almost to an idiot.

And set his *heart on Daniel*] He strove by every means to get the law annulled. He had no doubt spoken to several of his lords in private, and had gone from *one* to *another* till the going down of the sun.

Verse 15. *Then these men assembled*] Having got favourable answers, as we may presume, from many individuals, he called a *parliament;* but they now collectively joined to urge the *execution* of the law, not its *repeal.*

Verse 16. *Then the king commanded*] With a heavy heart he was obliged to warrant this murderous conspiracy. But when passing sentence his last words were affecting: "Thy God, whom thou servest continually, he will deliver thee." He is *thy* God: *thou servest him*, not occasionally, but *continually;* therefore "he will deliver thee." Daniel had now the same kind of opportunity of showing his fidelity to God, as his *three* Hebrew companions before. The *lions* were not less terrible than the *fiery furnace.*

Verse 17. *A stone was brought*] All this *precaution* served the purposes of the Divine Providence. There could be no trick nor collusion here; if Daniel be preserved, it must be by the power of the Supreme God. The same precaution was taken by the Jews, in the case

A. M. cir. 3467
B. C. cir. 537
Ol. cir. LX. 4
Servii Tullii,
R. Roman.,
cir. annum 42

lords; that the purpose might not
be changed concerning Daniel.
18 Then the king went to his
palace and passed the night
fasting: neither were [t]instruments of music
brought before him: [u]and his sleep went
from him.
19 Then the king arose very early in the
morning, and went in haste unto the den of
lions.
20 And when he came to the den, he cried
with a lamentable voice unto Daniel: *and* the
king spake and said to Daniel, O Daniel,
servant of the living God, [v]is thy God, whom
thou servest continually, able to deliver thee
from the lions
21 Then said Daniel unto the king, [w]O
king, live for ever.
22 [x]My God hath sent his angel, and hath
[y]shut the lions' mouths, that they have not
hurt me: forasmuch as before him innocency
was found in me; and also before thee, O
king, have I done no hurt.
23 Then was the king exceeding glad for
him, and commanded that they should take
Daniel up out of the den. So Daniel was
taken up out of the den, and no manner of
hurt was found upon him, [z]be-
cause he believed in his God.
24 And the king commanded,
[a]and they brought those men
which had accused Daniel, and they cast *them*
into the den of lions, them, [b]their children,
and their wives; and the lions had the
mastery of them, and brake all their bones
in pieces or ever they came at the bottom of
the den.
25 [c]Then king Darius wrote unto all people, nations, and languages, that dwell in
all the earth; Peace be multiplied unto
you.
26 [d]I make a decree, That in every dominion
of my kingdom men [e]tremble and fear before
the God of Daniel: [f]for he *is* the living God,
and steadfast for ever, and his kingdom *that*
which shall not be [g]destroyed, and his dominion *shall be even* unto the end.
27 He delivereth and rescueth, [h]and he
worketh signs and wonders in heaven and in
earth, who hath delivered Daniel from the
[i]power of the lions.
28 So this Daniel prospered in the reign of
Darius, [k]and in the reign of [l]Cyrus the
Persian.

A. M. cir. 3467
B. C. cir. 537
Ol. cir. LX. 4
Servii Tullii,
R. Roman.,
cir. annum 42

---

[t]Or, *table*——[u]Chap. ii. 1——[v]Chap. iii. 15——[w]Ch. ii. 4——[x]Chap. iii. 28——[y]Heb. xi. 33——[z]Heb. xi. 33 [a]Deut. xix. 19——[b]Esth. ix. 10; see Deut. xxiv. 16; 2 Kings xiv. 6

[c]Chap. iv. 1——[d]Chap. iii. 29——[e]Psa. xcix. 1 [f]Chap. iv. 34——[g]Chap. ii. 44; iv. 3, 34; vii. 14, 27; Luke i. 33——[h]Chap. iv. 3——[i]Heb. *hand*——[k]Chap. i. 21——[l]Ezra i. 1, 2

---

of the *burial of our blessed Lord;* and this very thing has served as one of the strongest proofs of the certainty of his resurrection and their unmixed wickedness.

Verse 18. *Passed the night fasting*] He neither ate nor drank, had no music to solace, nor sweet odours burnt or brought before him, and he passed the night without sleep. All this points out his great sincerity; and when it is considered that Darius could not be less than *sixty-two* or *sixty-three* years of age at this time, it shows more fully the depth of his concern.

Verse 19. *The king arose very early*] By the break of day.

Verse 20. *He cried with a lamentable voice*] His heart, full of grief, affected his speech.

Servant of the living God] The king was convinced that, unless his God saved him, his destruction was inevitable.

Verse 22. *My God hath sent his angel*] Such a one as that who attended Shadrach, Meshach, and Abed-nego, in the fiery furnace, and blew aside the flames, so that they could not hurt them.

Before him innocency was found in me] Because I was innocent God has preserved me; and now that I am preserved, my innocence is fully proved.

Verse 23. *No manner of hurt was found upon him*] And why? *Because he believed in his God.* How mighty is *faith?* It interests that power in the behalf of the believer by which the sea is dried up, the mountains removed, the dead raised to life, sin forgiven, the heart purified, Satan vanquished, death conquered, and God himself delighted and glorified! See Heb. xi.

Verse 24. *They brought those men*] It was perfectly just that they should suffer that death to which they had endeavoured to subject the innocent; but it was savage cruelty to destroy the *women* and *children* who had no part in the transgression.

Verse 25. *Then king Darius wrote*] And the substance of this *decree,* which was made by a heathen king, was to point out the *perfections* of the *true God,* and the *fidelity* of his devoted servant.

Verse 26. *I make a decree that—men tremble and fear before the God of Daniel*] As in the case of the *three* Hebrews, chap. iii. 29. The true God was known by his servants, and by the deliverances he wrought for them. See his characters in this decree. 1. He is the *living God,* the Author and Giver of life; all others are *dead* gods. 2. He is *steadfast for ever.* All things *change;* but he is unchangeable. 3. He has a *kingdom;* for as he made all things, so he *governs* all things. 4. His *kingdom shall not be destroyed.* No human power can prevail against it, because it is upheld by his omnipotence. 5. His *dominion* is without *end.* It is an everlasting dominion, under an everlasting rule, by an everlasting God. 6. He *delivereth* them that are in danger and bondage. 7. He *rescueth* those who have fallen into the hands of their enemies, and implore his succour. 8. He *worketh signs* in the *heavens.* 9. And *wonders* upon *earth;* showing that both are under his sway, and are parts of his dominion. 10. And to complete all, *He hath delivered Daniel.* Before our own eyes he has given the fullest proof of his *power* and *goodness,* in rescuing his faithful servant from the teeth of the lions. What a fine eulogium on the great God and his faithful servant!

Verse 28. *So this Daniel prospered*] He had served *five* kings: *Nebuchadnezzar, Evil-merodach, Belshazzar, Darius,* and *Cyrus.* Few courtiers have had so long a reign, served so many masters without flattering any, been more successful in their management of public affairs, been so useful to the states where they were in office, or have been more owned of God, or have left such an example to posterity.

Where shall we find ministers like *Samuel* and *Daniel?* None so wise, so holy, so disinterested, so useful, have ever since appeared in the nations of the earth.

CHAPTER VII

The prophet having, in the preceding chapters of this book, related some remarkable events concerning himself and his brethren in the captivity, and given proof of his being enabled, by Divine assistance, to interpret the dreams of others, enters now into a detail of his own visions, returning to a period prior to the transactions recorded in the last chapter. The first in order of the prophet's visions is that of the four beasts, which arose out of a very tempestuous ocean, 1–9; *and of one like the Son of man who annihilated the dominion of the fourth beast, because of the proud and blasphemous words of one of its horns,* 9–14. *An angel deciphers the hieroglyphics contained in this chapter, declaring that the* FOUR beasts, *diverse one from another, represent the* FOUR PARAMOUNT empires *of the habitable globe, which should succeed each other; and are evidently the same which were shadowed forth to Nebuchadnezzar by another set of hieroglyphics, (see the* second *chapter,)* 15–26. *But for the consolation of the people of God, it is added that, at the time appointed in the counsel of Jehovah, "the kingdom and dominion, and the greatness of the kingdom under the whole heaven, shall be given to the saints of the Most High;" and that this kingdom shall never be destroyed or transferred to another people, as all the preceding dominations have been, but shall itself stand for ever,* 27, 28. *It will be proper to remark that the period of* a time, times, and a half, *mentioned in the twenty-fifth verse as the duration of the dominion of the little horn that made war with the saints, (generally supposed to be a symbolical representation of the papal power,) had most probably its commencement in A. D.* 755 *or* 756, *when Pepin, king of France, invested the pope with temporal power. This hypothesis will bring the conclusion of the period to about the year of Christ* 2000, *a time fixed by Jews and Christians for some remarkable revolution; when the world, as they suppose, will be renewed, the wicked cease from troubling the Church, and the saints of the Most High have dominion over the whole habitable globe. But this is all hypothesis.*

A. M. cir. 3449
B. C. cir. 555
Ol. cir. LVI. 2
Servii Tullii,
R. Roman.,
cir. annum 24

IN the first year of Belshazzar
king of Babylon [a]Daniel [b]had
a dream and [c]visions of his head
upon his bed: then he wrote the
dream, *and* told the sum of the [d]matters.

2 Daniel spake and said, I saw
in my vision by night, and, behold,
the four winds of the
heaven strove upon the great sea.
3 And four great beasts [e]came up from

[a]Num. xii. 6; Amos iii. 7——[b]Chald. *saw* [c]Chald. ii. 28——[d]Or, *words*——[e]Rev. xiii. 1

NOTES ON CHAP. VII

Verse 1. *In the first year of Belshazzar*] This is the same Belshazzar who was slain at the taking of Babylon, as we have seen at the conclusion of chap. v. That chapter should have followed both this and the succeeding. The reason why the *fifth* chapter was put in an improper place was, that all the *historic parts* might be together, and the *prophetic* be by themselves; and, accordingly, the former end with the preceding chapter, and the latter with this. The division therefore is not *chronological* but merely *artificial.*

Told the sum of the matters.] That he might not forget this extraordinary dream, he wrote down the leading particulars when he arose.

Verse 2. *The four winds of the heaven strove upon the great sea*] The idea of *strife* is taken here from the effects that must be produced, were the east, the west, the north, and the south winds to rise tempestuously, and *meet* on the surface of the sea. By the *great sea,* the Mediterranean is meant; and is so called to distinguish it from those *lakes* called *seas* by the Hebrews; such as the *Sea* of *Galilee, Dead Sea, Sea* of *Tiberias,* &c.; but even that may refer to *Asia,* the scene of all these contentions. This dream is the same in meaning, under *different emblems,* as that of Nebuchadnezzar's metallic image; but in Daniel's dream several circumstances are added. It is supposed that Daniel had this dream about *forty-eight* years after Nebuchadnezzar had the vision of the great image.

Verse 3. *Four great beasts came up from the*

A. M. cir. 3449 B. C. cir. 555 Ol. cir. LVI. 2 Servii Tullii, R. Roman., cir. annum 24

the sea, diverse one from another.

4 The first *was* [f]like a lion,
and had eagle's wings: I beheld
till the wings thereof were plucked, [g]and it
was lifted up from the earth, and made stand
upon the feet as a man, and a
man's heart was given to it.

5 [h]And behold another beast,
a second, like to a bear, and [i]it
raised up itself on one side, and *it had* three
ribs in the mouth of it between the teeth of it:

[f]Deut. xxviii. 49; 2 Sam. i. 23; Jer. iv. 7, 13; xlviii. 40; Ezek. xvii. 3; Hab. i. 8

[g]Or, *wherewith*——[h]Chap. ii. 39——[i]Or, *it raised up one dominion*

sea] The term *sea*, in Hebrew ים *yam*, from המה *hamah, to be tumultuous, agitated*, &c., seems to be used here to point out the then known *terraqueous globe*, because of its generally agitated state; and the *four winds striving*, point out those predatory wars that prevailed almost universally among men, from the days of Nimrod, the founder of the Assyrian or Babylonish monarchy, down to that time, and in the end gave birth to the *four great monarchies* which are the subject of this vision.

Diverse one from another.] The *people* were *different;* the *laws* and *customs* different; and the *administration* of each differently executed.

Verse 4. *The first* was *like a lion, and had eagle's wings*] Bp. *Newton* well remarks, that these *great beasts*, as explained by the angel, ver. 17, are *kingdoms.* They arise out of a stormy and tempestuous sea; that is, out of the *wars* and commotions of the world; and they are called *great* in comparison of other states and kingdoms, and are denominated *beasts* for their tyrannical and cruel oppression.

These *four beasts* are indeed monstrous productions; a *lion with eagle's wings;* a *bear with three ribs* in its mouth; a *leopard with four wings, and four heads;* and a *beast with ten horns.* But such emblems and hieroglyphics were usual among the eastern nations, as may be seen in the monuments of antiquity. A *winged lion*, and such-like fictitious animals, may be seen in many parts of the ruins of *Persepolis. Horns* are attributed to beasts which naturally have none, being used in hieroglyphic writings for symbols of *strength* and *power.* And such figures are supposed to be the symbols of different nations; and are not more strange than many that are still used in *heraldry.* I believe the science of heraldry arose out of the knowledge gained from the symbols used in the Sacred Writings; and the little acquaintance anciently obtained of the meaning of some of the Egyptian hieroglyphics. Hence our wiverons, griffins, unicorns, with a congeries of natural and unnatural things, split eagles, *two*-headed swans, &c., &c., &c.

The *beast like a lion* is the kingdom of the *Babylonians;* and the king of Babylon is compared to a *lion*, Jer. iv. 7; Isa. v. 29; and is said to fly as an *eagle*, Jer. xlviii. 40; Ezek. xvii. 3, 7. The *lion* is considered the *king of the beasts*, and the *eagle* the *king of the birds;* and therefore the kingdom of Babylon, which was signified by the *golden head* of the great image, was the first and noblest of all the kingdoms; and was the greatest then in being. The *wings* of the *eagle* denote the *rapidity* with which the *lion*—Nebuchadnezzar, made his conquests; for in a few years, by his own arms, he brought his empire to such an extent, and raised it to such a degree of eminence, as was truly surprising; and all tended to show with what propriety this *eagle-winged lion* is here made his emblem.

The wings thereof were plucked] Lydia, Media, and Persia, which had been provinces of the Babylonish empire, cast off the yoke, and put themselves under kings of their own. Besides, the rapidity of its conquests was stopped by its wars with the *Medes* and *Persians;* by whom it was at last conquered, and *divided* between Darius the Mede and Cyrus the Persian.

And it was lifted up from the earth] That is, the *wings were plucked*, rendered unfit for farther flight, *by which it had* before *been lifted up from the earth;* making its conquests almost with the rapidity of an eagle's flight. In what a short time did Nebuchadnezzar, who is here chiefly intended, conquer Syria, Phœnicia, Judea, Egypt, Arabia, &c.! But on his death the *wings were plucked;* and no farther extension of the empire took place under *Evil-merodach* or *Belshazzar*, till it was lost by the latter, and became divided as we have seen above.

And made stand upon the feet as a man] This I think refers to the taming of Nebuchadnezzar's pride. He had acted like a fierce and ravening *lion.* God struck him with insanity; he then lived the life of a beast, and had a *beast's heart*—disposition, and habits. At last God restored him.

And a man's heart was given to it.] He became *humane, humble*, and *pious;* and in this state he appears to have died.

Verse 5. *Another beast—like to a bear*] This was the *Medo-Persian* empire, represented here under the symbol of the *bear*, as the largest species of these animals was found in *Media*, a mountainous, cold, and rough country, covered with *woods.* The Medes and Persians are compared to a *bear* on account of their *cruelty* and *thirst after blood*, a bear being a most voracious and cruel animal; the *bear* is termed by Aristotle *an all-devouring animal;* and the Medo-Persians are known to have been great *robbers* and *spoilers.* See Jer. li. 48-56. The Persians were notorious for the cruelty of their punishments. See *Calmet.*

Raised up itself on one side] Cyrus arose on the borders of Chaldea, and thus the *bear* appeared to put itself in the position to attack the *lion.*

It had *three ribs in the mouth of it*] As if it had just finished its repast on some animal that it had seized. Some think *three tusks, curved* like ribs, are meant; others *three throats*, עלעין *illin*, by which it (Cyrus) had absorbed the *three* empires of the Babylonians, Medes, and Persians; for these symbolic animals do not so much denote *four empires*, as *four kings.* See ver. 17. Others think *three rows of teeth* are meant, to denote the *triple* power of the Medes, Persians, and Babylonians,

A. M. cir. 3449 B. C. cir. 555 Ol. cir. LVI. 2 Servii Tullii, R. Roman., cir. annum 24

and they said thus unto it,
Arise, devour much flesh.
6 After this I beheld, and lo
another, like a leopard, which
had upon the back of it four wings of a fowl;
the beast had also [k]four heads; and dominion
was given to it.
7 After this I saw in the night visions, and
behold [l]a fourth beast, dreadful and terrible,
and strong exceedingly; and it
had great iron teeth: it devoured
and brake in pieces, and stamped
the residue with the feet of it:
and it *was* diverse from all the beasts that
were before it; [m]and it had ten horns.
8 I considered the horns, and, behold, [n]there
came up among them another little horn, before whom there were three of the first horns

[k]Chapter viii. 8, 22——[l]Chapter ii. 40; verse 19, 23

[m]Chap. ii. 41; Rev. xiii. 1——[n]Ver. 20, 21, 24; chap. viii. 9

conjoined. Or the *east, north,* and *south,* which were subdued by the Persians. But the *ribs* being between the teeth of the *bear* may show how Babylon, Lydia, and Egypt were ground and oppressed by the *bear*—the Persians; though, as ribs strengthen the body, they were a powerful support to their conquerors.

Verse 6. *Another, like a leopard—four wings —four heads*] This was the *Macedonian* or *Greek empire;* and Alexander the Great its king. Alexander and his subjects are fitly compared to a *leopard.* 1. The leopard is remarkable for its swiftness. Alexander and the Macedonians were very rapid in their conquests. 2. The leopard is a *spotted* animal; a proper emblem of the *various nations,* with their various customs and languages, which constituted the Macedonian empire. It may refer to the *character* of Alexander himself, sometimes *mild,* at others *cruel; sober* and *drunken; continent* and *lecherous;* having a great power of self-government, and at other times being a slave to his passions. 3. The leopard, though small, is not afraid to attack the lion.

Four wings of a fowl] The *Babylonian* empire was represented with *two wings;* and they sufficiently marked the *rapidity* of Nebuchadnezzar's conquests; but the *Macedonian* has here *four wings;* for nothing, in the history of the world, was equal to the conquests of Alexander, who ran through all the countries from Illyricum and the Adriatic Sea to the Indian Ocean and the River Ganges; and in *twelve* years subdued part of Europe, and all Asia.

The beast had also four heads] Signifying the empire after the death of Alexander, divided between his *four* generals. *Cassander* reigning over *Macedon* and *Greece; Lysimachus,* over *Thrace* and *Bithynia; Ptolemy,* over *Egypt;* and *Seleucus,* over *Syria.*

Dominion was given to it.] It was not owing to the skill, courage, or valour of Alexander and his troops, that he made those wondrous conquests; the nations were *given* to him. For, as Bishop *Newton* says, had he not been assisted by the mighty power of God, how could he, with only *thirty thousand* men, have overcome Darius with *six hundred thousand;* and in so short a time have brought the countries from Greece as far as India into subjection?

Verse 7. *I saw—a fourth beast—it had great iron teeth*] This is allowed, on all hands, to be the Roman empire. It was *dreadful, terrible,* and *exceeding strong: it devoured, and brake* in pieces, and stamped the residue, that is, the remains of the former kingdoms, *with its feet.* It reduced *Macedon* into a Roman province about *one hundred and sixty-eight* years before Christ; the kingdom of *Pergamos* about *one hundred and thirty-three* years; *Syria* about *sixty-five;* and *Egypt* about *thirty* years before Christ. And, besides the remains of the Macedonian empire, it subdued many other provinces and kingdoms; so that it might, by a very usual figure, be said to *devour the whole earth, to tread it down, and break it to pieces;* and became in effect, what the Roman writers delight to call it, *the empire of the whole world.*

It (the fourth beast) was *diverse from all the beasts that* were *before it*] Not only in its *republican* form of government, but also in *power* and *greatness, extent of dominion,* and *length of duration.*

It had ten horns] The *ten* kingdoms into which the Roman empire was afterwards divided. *Calmet* says, *ten* Syrian kings: and he finds them thus:—1. Seleucus Nicator. 2. Antiochus Soter. 3. Antiochus Theos. 4. Antiochus Callinicus. 5. Seleucus Ceraunus. 6. Antiochus the Great. 7. Seleucus, surnamed Philopater, brother of Antiochus Epiphanes. 8. Laomedon of Mitylene, to whom Syria and Phœnicia had been intrusted. 9. Antigone. And, 10. His son Demetrius, who possessed those provinces, with the title of *kings.* This is too much like forced work. There are different opinions concerning these *ten* kings; or rather which they were that constituted this division of the Roman empire. They are reckoned thus:—1. The Roman senate. 2. The *Greeks,* in *Ravenna.* 3. The *Lombards* in *Lombardy.* 4. The *Huns* in *Hungary.* 5. The *Alemans,* in *Germany.* 6. The *Franks* in France. 7. The *Burgundians* in *Burgundy.* 8. The *Saracens* in Africa, and a part of Spain. 9. The *Goths,* in other parts of Spain. 10. And the *Saxons, in Britain.*

Verse 8. *Another little horn*] Among Protestant writers this is considered to be the popedom.

Before whom there were three of the first horns plucked up] These were probably, 1. The exarchate of *Ravenna.* 2. The kingdom of the *Lombards.* And, 3. The *state of Rome.* The *first* was given to the Pope, Stephen II., by Pepin, king of France, A. D. 755; and this constituted the pope's temporal princes. The *second* was given to St. Peter by Charlemagne, in 774. The *third,* the *state of Rome,* was vested in the pope, both in spirituals and temporals, and confirmed to him by *Lewis the pious.* These are the *three* horns which were *plucked up from the roots* before the *little horn.*

Were *eyes like the eyes of a man*] Intimating *cunning* and *superintendence;* for the pope calls himself *Episcopus episcoporum,* the *Overseer of overseers.*

A. M. cir. 3449 B. C. cir. 555 Ol. cir. LVI. 2 Servii Tullii, R. Roman., cir. annum 24

plucked up by the roots: and,
behold, in this horn *were* eyes
like the eyes [o]of man, [p]and a
mouth speaking great things.
9 [q]I beheld till the thrones were cast down,
and [r]the Ancient of days did sit, [s]whose garment *was* white as snow, and the hair of his
head like the pure wool: his throne *was like*
the fiery flame, [t]*and* his wheels *as* burning
fire.
10 [u]A fiery stream issued and came forth
from before him: [v]thousand thousands ministered unto him, and ten thousand times ten
thousand stood before him: [w]the judgment
was set, and the books were opened.
11 I beheld then because of the voice of the
great words which the horn spake: [x]I beheld
even till the beast was slain, and his body destroyed, and given to the burning flame.
12 As concerning the rest of the beasts, they
had their dominion taken away: yet [y]their
lives were prolonged for a season and time.
13 I saw in the night visions,
and, behold, [z]*one* like the Son
of man came with the clouds
of heaven, and came to [a]the
Ancient of days, and they brought him near
before him.
14 [b]And there was given him dominion,
and glory, and a kingdom, that all [c]people,
nations, and languages, should serve him:
his dominion *is* [d]an everlasting dominion,
which shall not pass away, and his kingdom
that which shall not be destroyed.
15 I Daniel [e]was grieved in my spirit in the
midst of *my* [f]body, and the visions of my head
troubled me.
16 I came near unto one of them that stood
by, and asked him the truth of all this. So
he told me, and made me know the interpretation of the things.
17 [g]These great beasts, which are four, *are*
four kings, *which* shall arise out of the
earth.

[o]Rev. ix. 7——[p]Psa. xii. 3; ver. 25; Rev. xiii. 5——[q]Rev. xx. 4——[r]Psa. xc. 2; ver. 13, 22——[s]Psa. civ. 2; Rev. i. 14——[t]Ezek. i. 15, 16——[u]Psa. l. 3; xcvii. 3; Isa. xxx. 33; lxvi. 15——[v]1 Kings xxii. 19; Psa. lxviii. 17; Heb. xii. 22; Rev. v. 11——[w]Rev. xx. 4, 12——[x]Rev xix. 20——[y]Chald. *a prolonging in life was given them*

[z]Ezek. iv. 26; Matt. xxiv. 30; xxvi. 64; Rev. i. 7, 13; xiv. 14——[a]Ver. 9——[b]Psa. ii. 6, 7, 8; viii. 6; cx. 1, 2; Matt. xi. 27; xxviii. 18; John iii. 35; 1 Cor. xv. 27; Eph. i. 22——[c]Chap. iii. 4——[d]Psa. cxlv. 13; ch. ii. 44; ver. 27; Mic. iv. 7; Luke i. 33; John xii. 34; Heb. xii. 28——[e]Ver. 28——[f]Chald. *sheath*——[g]Ver. 3

And a mouth speaking great things.] Full of boasting; pretending to unlimited jurisdiction; binding and loosing at pleasure; promising to absolve from all sins, present, past, and future; and threatening to send to everlasting destruction all kings, kingdoms, and individuals, who would dare to dispute his power and authority.

Verse 9. *The thrones were cast down*] דמיו might be translated *erected;* so the Vulgate, *positi sunt*, and so all the versions; but that ours is a proper translation, is sufficiently evident from chap. iii. 6, 15, 20; vi. 17, &c.; where the original word can be used in no other sense than that of *throwing* or *casting down.* There is a reference here to preparations made for a general assize, or to the convocation of the sanhedrin, where the father of the consistory sat with his assessors on each side in the form of a semicircle, and the people stood before them.

The Ancient of days] God Almighty; and this is the only place in the sacred writings where God the Father is represented in a *human form.*

Verse 10. *A fiery stream issued*] This is not spoken of the *final judgment;* but of that which he was to execute upon this *fourth beast*, the Roman empire; and the *little* boasting *horn*, which is a part of the fourth beast, and must fall when the other falls.

Verse 11. *I beheld then because of the voice* (or, *the beast will be destroyed because*) *of the great words which the horn spake—his body destroyed*] When the dominion was taken from the rest of the *beasts*, their *bodies* were not destroyed, but suffered to continue still in being; but when the dominion shall be taken away from *this beast*, his *body* shall be totally destroyed; because *other kingdoms* succeeded to those, but no other earthly kingdom shall succeed to this.—Bishop *Newton.*

Verse 13. One *like the Son of man came with the clouds of heaven*] This most certainly points out the Lord Jesus, בר אנש *bar enosh*, the Son of miserable man; who took our nature upon him that he might redeem us unto himself. To prove himself to be the Messiah he applies, before the high priests, these words of the Prophet Daniel to himself, Matt. xxiv. 30.

Near before him.] The Ancient of days.

Verse 14. *And there was given him dominion*] This also is applied to our Lord Jesus by himself, after his resurrection, Matt. xxviii. 18.

His dominion is *an everlasting dominion*] Christianity shall increase, and prevail to the end of the world. See the parallel passages in the margin.

Verse 15. *I Daniel was grieved, &c.*] The words in the original are uncommonly emphatic. *My spirit was grieved*, or *sickened*, בגו נדנה *bego nidneh, within its sheath* or *scabbard.* Which I think proves, 1. That the human *spirit* is different from the *body.* 2. That it has a proper subsistence independently of the body, which is only its *sheath* for a certain time. 3. That the spirit may exist independently of its body, as the *sword* does independently of its *sheath.*

Verse 17. *These great beasts*—are *four kings*]

A. M. cir. 3449
B. C. cir. 555
Ol. cir. LVI. 2
Servii Tullii,
R. Roman.,
cir. annum 24

18 But [h]the saints of the [i]Most High shall take the kingdom, and possess the kingdom for ever, even for ever and ever.

19 Then I would know the truth of [k]the fourth beast, which was diverse [l]from all the others, exceeding dreadful, whose teeth *were of* iron, and his nails *of* brass; *which* devoured, brake in pieces, and stamped the residue with his feet;

20 And of the ten horns that *were* in his head, and *of* the other which came up, and before whom three fell; even *of* that horn that had eyes, and a mouth that spake very great things, whose look *was* more stout than his fellows.

21 I beheld, [m]and the same horn made war with the saints and prevailed against them;

22 [n]Until the Ancient of days came, [o]and judgment was given to the saints of the Most High; and the time came that the saints possessed the kingdom.

23 Thus he said, The fourth beast shall be [p]the fourth kingdom upon earth, which shall be diverse from all kingdoms, and shall devour the whole earth, and shall tread it down, and break it in pieces.

24 [q]And the ten horns out of this kingdom *are* ten kings *that* shall arise: and another shall rise after them; and he shall be diverse from the first, and he shall subdue three kings.

25 [r]And he shall speak *great* words against the Most High, and shall [s]wear out the saints of the Most High, and [t]think to change times and laws: and [u]they shall be given into his hand [v]until a time and times and the dividing of time.

[h]Isa. lx. 12, 13, 14; ver. 22, 27; 2 Tim. ii. 11, 12; Rev. ii. 26, 27; iii. 21; xx. 4——[i]Chald. *high ones*, that is, *things* or *places*——[k]Ver. 7——[l]Chald. *from all those*——[m]Chap. viii. 12, 24; xi. 31; Rev. xi. 7; xiii. 7; xvii. 14; xix. 19——[n]Ver. 9

[o]Ver. 18; 1 Cor. vi. 2; Rev. i. 6; v. 10; xx. 4——[p]Ch. ii. 40——[q]Ver. 7, 8, 20; Rev. xvii. 12——[r]Isa. xxxvii. 23; ch. viii. 24, 25; xi. 28, 30, 31, 36; 1 Mac. i. 46; Rev. xiii. 5, 6——[s]Rev. xvii. 6; xviii. 24——[t]Ch. ii. 21——[u]Rev. xiii. 7——[v]Chap. xii. 7; Rev. xii. 14

See the preceding verses, where the following explanations are inserted and illustrated.

Verse 18. *But the saints of the Most High shall take the kingdom*] I doubt whether this be the true sense of the original *Chaldee*, ויקבלון מלכותא קדישי עליונין *vikabbelun malcutha kaddishey elyonin*, "But the supreme holy ones shall receive the kingdom;" or, "they shall receive the kingdom of the supreme saints." Properly translated by *Montanus*, Et suscipient regnum sanctorum altissimorum. Whatever we may think of the *patriarchs* and the *Jews* in their best times, there has never been so *much holiness of heart possessed*, and so much *righteousness practised*, as by the genuine disciples of Christ. Christianity alone has provided a full redemption for man. They are the *chief saints*, and to them God gives the kingdom: and this Gospel dispensation, called often *the kingdom of God, and the kingdom of heaven*, shall last for ever, during the whole lapse of time; *and for ever and ever*—throughout eternity, shall they and its blessings endure.

Verse 19. *His nails* of *brass*] This is not mentioned in the *seventh* verse, where the description of the beast is given. It might be *added*, for the first time, by the person who is now explaining the fourth beast. *Houbigant* thinks it has been lost out of the text: but such loss is not intimated by any MS.; nor does any of the *ancient Versions* acknowledge this addition in the *seventh* verse.

Verse 21. *The same horn made war with the saints, and prevailed against them.*] Those who make *Antiochus* the *little horn*, make the *saints* the *Jewish people*. Those who understand the *popedom* by it, see this as referring to the cruel persecutions of the popes of Rome against the *Waldenses* and *Albigenses*, and the *Protestant* Church in general.

Verse 22. *Saints of the Most High*] *To the supereminent saints;* see the note on ver. 18.

Verse 25. *He shall speak* great *words against the Most High*] Sermones quasi Deus loquetur; "He shall speak as if he were God." So St. *Jerome* quotes from *Symmachus*. To none can this apply so well or so fully as to the popes of Rome. They have assumed *infallibility*, which belongs only to God. They profess to forgive sins, which belongs only to God. They profess to open and shut heaven, which belongs only to God. They profess to be higher than all the kings of the earth, which belongs only to God. And they go *beyond* God in pretending to loose whole nations from their oath of allegiance to their kings, when such kings do not please them! And they go *against* God when they give *indulgences for sin*. This is the *worst* of all blasphemies!

And shall wear out the saints] By wars, crusades, massacres, inquisitions, and persecutions of all kinds. What in this way have they not done against all those who have protested against their *innovations*, and refused to submit to their *idolatrous worship?* Witness the exterminating crusades published against the *Waldenses* and *Albigenses*. Witness *John Huss*, and *Jerome* of *Prague*. Witness the *Smithfield fires* in England! Witness *God* and man against this bloody, persecuting, ruthless, and impure Church!

And think to change times and laws] Appointing fasts and feasts; canonizing persons whom he chooses to call *saints;* granting pardons and indulgences for sins; instituting new modes of worship utterly unknown to the Christian Church; new articles of faith; new rules

A. M. cir. 3449
B. C. cir. 555
Ol. cir. LVI. 2
Servii Tullii,
R. Roman.,
cir. annum 24

26 [w]But the judgment shall
sit, and they shall take away his
dominion, to consume and to
destroy *it* unto the end.
27 And the [x]kingdom and dominion, and
the greatness of the kingdom under the whole
heaven, shall be given to the people of the
saints of the Most High, [y]whose kingdom *is*
an everlasting kingdom, [z]and all
[a]dominions shall serve and obey
him.
28 Hitherto *is* the end of the
matter. As for me Daniel, [b]my cogitations
much troubled me, and my countenance
changed in me: but I [c]kept the matter in
my heart.

A. M. cir. 3449
B. C. cir. 555
Ol. cir. LVI. 2
Servii Tullii,
R. Roman.,
cir. annum 24

---

[w]Ver. 10, 22——[x]Ver. 14, 18, 22; chapter ii. 42; Obadiah 21; Matthew xxv. 34; Mark xi. 10; Luke xii. 32——[y]Chapter ii. 44; Luke i. 33; John xii. 34; Revelation xi. 15——[z]Isaiah lx. 12——[a]Or, *rulers*——[b]Ver. 15; chapter viii. 27; x. 8, 16——[c]Luke ii. 19, 51

---

of practice; and reversing, with pleasure, the laws both of God and man.—*Dodd.*

Until a time and times and the dividing of time.] In prophetic language a *time* signifies a *year;* and a *prophetic year* has a *year* for *each day. Three years and a half* (a *day* standing for a *year*, as in chap. ix. 24) will amount to *one thousand two hundred and sixty years*, if we reckon *thirty* days to each month, as the Jews do.

If we knew precisely when the papal power began to exert itself in the *antichristian* way, then we could at once fix the time of its destruction. The *end* is probably not very distant; it has already been grievously shaken by the French. In 1798 the French republican army under General *Berthier* took possession of the city of Rome, and entirely superseded the whole papal power. This was a deadly wound, though at present it appears to be healed; but it is but *skinned over*, and a dreadful cicatrice remains. The *Jesuits*, not JESUS, are now the Church's doctors.

If the papal power, as a *horn* or *temporal power*, be intended here, which is most likely, (and we know that that power was given in 755 to Pope Stephen II. by *Pepin*, king of France,) counting *one thousand two hundred and sixty* years from that, we are brought to A. D. 2015, about *one hundred and ninety* years from the present [A. D. 1825.] But I neither lay stress upon nor draw conclusions from these dates. If the Church of Rome will *reform itself*, it will then be the *true Christian* Church, and will never be destroyed. Let it throw aside all that is ritually *Jewish;* all that is *heathen;* all that which pretends to be of God, and which is only of *man;* all doctrines that are not in the Bible; and all *rites* and *ceremonies* which are not of the appointment of *Christ* and his *apostles;* and then, all hail the once Roman, but now, after such a change, the HOLY, *Catholic Church!* Every true Protestant would wish rather the *reform* than the extinction of this Church.

Verse 27. *The kingdom and dominion*] The people of the saints of the Most High, or the people who are the supereminent saints, shall have the kingdom. Whatever name they may be distinguished by among men, these are the people, and theirs is the Church, that no lapse of time shall injure, and no power be able to destroy; but shall last as long as time shall endure.

Verse 28. *The end of the matter.*] So said the expounding angel; and he said so because the purpose of God had determined it. In considering these things, and looking at the evils that shall come upon the world before those auspicious times can take place, I may say, with Daniel, *My cogitations much troubled me, and my countenance changed in me: but I keep the matter* of my conjectures and consequent feelings *in my own heart.*

CHAPTER VIII

This chapter contains Daniel's vision of the ram *and* he-goat, 1–14; *referring, as explained by the angel, to the Persian and Grecian monarchies,* 15–26. *The* little horn *mentioned in the* ninth *verse,* (or fierce king, as *interpreted in the* twenty-third,) *is supposed by some to denote Antiochus Epiphanes; but seems more properly to apply to the Roman power in general, by which the polity and temple of the Jews were destroyed, on account of the great transgressions of these ancient people of God; and particularly because of their very obstinate and unaccountable rejection of the glorious doctrines of Christianity, which had been preached among them by Jesus Christ and his apostles, and the truth of which God had attested "by signs and wonders, and by divers miracles and gifts of the Holy Ghost." Daniel is then informed of the* two thousand and three hundred *prophetic days (that is, years) which must elapse before the sanctuary be cleansed; or, in other words, before righteousness shall prevail over the whole earth. This period is supposed, with considerable probability, to have had its commencement when Alexander the Great invaded Asia, in the year before Christ* 334. *This will bring the close of it to about the end of the* SIXTH chiliad *of the world; when, as already observed, some astonishing changes are expected to take place in the moral condition of the human race; when the power of Antichrist, both Papal and Mohammedan, shall be totally annihilated, and universal dominion given to the saints of the Most High. The chapter concludes with the distress of Daniel on account of the fearful judgments with which his country should be visited in after ages,* 27.

A. M. cir. 3451
B. C. cir. 553
Ol. cir. LVI. 4
Servii Tullii,
R. Roman.,
cir. annum 26

IN the third year of the reign
of King Belshazzar a vision
appeared unto me, *even unto* me
Daniel, after that which appeared unto me [a]at the first.
2 And I saw in a vision; and it came to
pass, when I saw, that I *was* at [b]Shushan *in*
the palace, which *is* in the province of Elam;
and I saw in a vision, and I was by the river
of Ulai.
3 Then I lifted up mine eyes, and saw, and
behold, there stood before the river a ram
which had *two* horns: and the *two* horns
were high; but one *was* higher
than [c]the other, and the higher
came up last.
4 I saw the ram pushing west-
ward, and northward, and southward; so that
no beasts might stand before him, neither *was*
there any that could deliver out of his hand;
[d]but he did according to his will, and became
great.
5 And as I was considering, behold, a he-goat
came from the west on the face of the whole
earth, and [e]touched not the ground: and the
goat *had* [f]a [g]notable horn between his eyes.

[a]Chap. vii. 1——[b]Esth. i. 2——[c]Heb. *the second*——[d]Chap. v. 19; xi. 3, 16

[e]Or, *none touched* him *in the earth*——[f]Heb. *a horn of sight*——[g]Ver. 21

NOTES ON CHAP. VIII

Verse 1. *In the third year of the reign of—Belshazzar*] We now come once more to the *Hebrew*, the *Chaldee* part of the book being finished. As the Chaldeans had a particular interest both in the *history* and *prophecies* from chap. ii. 4 to the end of chap. vii., the whole is written in *Chaldee;* but as the prophecies which remain concern times posterior to the Chaldean monarchy, and principally relate to the *Church and people of God generally*, they are written in the Hebrew language, this being the tongue in which God chose to reveal all his counsels given under the *Old Testament* relative to the *New*.

Verse 2. *I saw in a vision*] Daniel was at this time in Shushan, which appears to have been a strong place, where the kings of Persia had their summer residence. It was the capital of the province of Elam or the Elymais; which province was most probably added to the Chaldean territories by Nebuchadnezzar; see Jer. xlix. 34, 35. Here was Daniel's ordinary residence; and though here at this time, he, in *vision*, saw himself on the *banks of the river Ulai*. This is the same as the river *Euleus*, which divided Shushan or Susiana from Elymais.

Verse 3. *A ram which had* two *horns*] In the former vision there were *four beasts*, pointing out *four empires;* in this we have but *two*, as only *two empires* are concerned here, *viz.*, the *Grecian* and the *Persian*. The Babylonish empire is not mentioned; its fate was before decided, and it was now at its close.

By the *ram*, the empire of the Medes and Persians was pointed out, as explained by the angel Gabriel, ver. 20; and particularly Cyrus, who was the founder of that empire. Cyrus was the son of Cambyses, king of Persia; and grandson of Astyages, king of Media, by his daughter Mandane, who had been given in marriage to Cambyses. Cyrus, marrying Roxana, the daughter and only child of his uncle Cyaxares, called in Scripture *Ahasuerus*, succeeded to both crowns, and thus united Media and Persia. A *ram* was the symbol of the Persians; and a ram's head with two horns, one higher than the other, appears as such in different parts of the ruins of *Persepolis*. See the plates of these ruins in the supplement to the seventh volume of the ancient part of the *Universal History*.

This ram had *two horns;* that is, *two kingdoms, viz., Media* and *Persia;* but one was *higher than the other;* and the higher *came up last. Media*, signified by the *shorter horn*, was the more *ancient* of the two kingdoms. *Persia*, the *higher horn*, had come up but lately, and was of little historic or political consequence till the time of Cyrus; but in the reigns of this prince and his immediate successors, Persia attained a political consequence greatly superior to that possessed at any time by the kingdom of Media; therefore, it is said to have been the *higher*, and to have come up *last*.

Verse 4. *I saw the ram pushing westward*] The Persians, who are signified by the *ram*, as well as their *founder Cyrus*, pushed their conquests *west, north* and *south*. The principal theatre of their wars, says *Calmet*, was against the SCYTHIANS, *northward;* against the GREEKS, *westward;* and against the EGYPTIANS, *southward*.

He did according to his will] There was no other nation at that time that could stay the progress of the Persian arms.

Verse 5. *Behold, a he-goat*] This was *Alexander the Great;* and a *goat* was a very proper symbol of the Grecian or Macedonian people. Bp. *Newton* very properly observes that, *two hundred* years before the time of Daniel, they were called *Ægeadæ*, the *goats' people;* the origin of which name is said to be as follows: Caranus, their first king, going with a multitude of Greeks to seek a new habitation in Macedonia, was advised by an oracle to take the *goats* for his guides; and afterwards, seeing a herd of goats flying from a violent storm, he followed them to *Edessa*, and there fixed the seat of his empire, and made the *goats* his ensigns or standards; and called the place *Æge* or *Ægea*, the *goats' town;* and the people *Ægeadæ*, the *goats' people;* names which are derived from *αιξ, αιγος*, a *goat*. The city *Æge* or *Ægea*, was the usual burying-place of the Macedonian kings; and, in reference to this origin, Alexander called his son by Roxana, *Alexander Ægus*, Alexander the *goat*. All this shows the very great propriety of the symbol here used.

Came from the west] Europe lies westward of Asia.

On the face of the whole earth] Carrying every thing before him.

A. M. cir. 3451
B. C. cir. 553
Ol. cir. LVI. 4
Servii Tullii,
R. Roman.,
cir. annum 26

6 And he came to the ram
that had *two* horns, which I had
seen standing before the river,
and ran unto him in the fury of
his power.
7 And I saw him come close unto the ram,
and he was moved with choler against him,
and smote the ram, and brake his two horns:
and there was no power in the ram to stand before him, but he cast him down to the ground,
and stamped upon him: and there was none
that could deliver the ram out of his hand.

8 Therefore the he-goat waxed
very great: and when he was
strong, the great horn was broken; and for it came up [h]four
notable ones toward the four winds of
heaven.
9 [i]And out of one of them came forth a
little horn, which vexed exceeding great,
[k]toward the south, and toward the east, and
toward the [l]pleasant *land*.
10 [m]And it waxed great, *even* [n]to [o]the host
of heaven; and [p]it cast down *some* of the

[h]Ch. vii. 6; xi. 4; ver. 22——[i]Ch. vii. 8; xi. 21——[k]Ch. xi. 25; 1 Mac. i. 16–19——[l]Psa. xlviii. 2; Ezek. xx. 6, 15; ch. xi. 16, 41, 45——[m]Ch. xi. 28——[n]Or, *against the host*——[o]So Isa. xiv. 13——[p]Rev. xii. 4

Touched not the ground] Seemed to fly from conquest to conquest. By the time Alexander was *thirty* years of age he had conquered all Asia: and, because of the rapidity of his conquests, he is represented as a *leopard* with four wings, in the preceding vision.

A notable horn between his eyes.] This, says the angel, is the *first king*, ver. 21, that is, the first kingdom of the Greeks in Asia, which was erected by Alexander; and continued some years in his brother *Philip Aridæus*, and in his two young sons, *Alexander Ægus* and *Hercules*. See *Newton*.

Verse 6. *And he came to the ram.*] This and the following verse give an account of the overthrow of the Persian empire by Alexander.

And ran unto him in the fury of his power] The conflicts between the Greeks and the Persians were excessively severe. Alexander first vanquished the generals of Darius, at the river *Granicus*, in Phrygia; he next attacked and totally routed Darius, at the straits of *Issus*, in Cilicia; and afterwards at the plains of *Arbela*, in Assyria. One can hardly read these words, says Bp. *Newton*, "the ram—which I had seen standing by the river, ran unto him in the fury of his power," without having the image of Darius' army standing and guarding the *river Granicus;* and of Alexander on the *other side*, with his forces plunging in swimming across the stream, and rushing on the enemy, with all the fire and fury that can be conceived.

Verse 7. *And brake his two horns*] Subdued Persia and Media; sacked and burnt the royal city of *Persepolis*, the capital of the Persian empire, and, even in its *ruins*, one of the wonders of the world to the present day. This he did because "he was moved with choler" against Darius, who had endeavoured to draw off his captains with bribes, and had laboured to induce some of his friends to assassinate him. Alexander, finding this, would listen to no proposals of peace; and was determined never to rest till he had destroyed Darius and his whole empire. In Media, Darius was seized and made prisoner by some of his own treacherous subjects, and afterwards basely murdered.

There was no power in the ram to stand before him] Alexander's victories over the Persians were as *easy* as they were *rapid* and *decisive*.

He cast him down to the ground, and stamped upon him] Totally destroyed the *family*, and overturned the whole *monarchy*.

Verse 8. *The he-goat waxed very strong*] He had subdued nearly the whole of the then known world.

The great horn was broken] Alexander died in the height of his conquests, when he was but about *thirty-three* years of age. His natural brother, Philip Aridæus, and his two sons, Alexander Ægus and Hercules, kept up the show and name of the Macedonian kingdom for a time; but they were all murdered within *fifteen* years; and thus *the great horn*, the Macedonian kingdom, *was broken*, Alexander's family being now cut off.

And for it came up four notable ones] The regal family being all dead, the governors of provinces usurped the title of kings; and Antigonus, one of them, being slain at the battle of *Ipsus*, they were reduced to *four*, as we have already seen. 1. SELEUCUS, who had Syria and Babylon, from whom came the *Seleucidæ*, famous in history. 2. LYSIMACHUS, who had Asia Minor. 3. PTOLEMY, son of *Lagus*, who had Egypt, from whom sprang the *Lagidæ*. And, 4. CASSANDER, who had Greece and the neighbouring countries. These held dominion *towards the four winds of heaven*. *Cassander* had the *western* parts, *Lysimachus* had the *northern* regions, *Ptolemy* possessed the *southern* countries, and *Seleucus* had the *eastern* provinces.

Verse 9. *Out of one of them came forth a little horn*] Some think that *Antiochus Epiphanes* is meant; but Bp. *Newton* contends that it is the *Roman* government that is intended; and although very *great* at its *zenith*, yet very *little* in its *rising*.

Waxed—great toward the south] The Romans made *Egypt* a province of their empire, and it continued such for some centuries.

Toward the east] They conquered *Syria*, and made it a province.

Toward the pleasant land.] *Judea*, so called Psa. cvi. 24; Jer. iii. 19; Dan. xi. 16, 41. It is well known that they took Judea, and made it a province; and afterwards burnt the city and the temple, and scattered the Jews over the face of the earth.

Verse 10. *The host of heaven*] The *Jewish hierarchy*. The *stars*, the *priests* and *Levites*. The *powers* or *host of heaven* are probably intended by our Lord, Matt. xxiv. 29, to signify the whole Jewish hierarchy.

A. M. cir. 3451
B. C. cir. 553
Ol. cir. LVI. 4
Servii Tullii,
R. Roman.,
cir. annum 26

host and of the stars to the ground, and stamped upon them.

11 Yea, [q]he magnified *himself* even [r]to [s]the prince of the host, [t]and [u]by him [v]the daily *sacrifice* was taken away, and the place of his sanctuary was cast down.

12 And [w]a [x]host was given *him* against the daily *sacrifice* [y]by reason of transgression, and it cast down [z]the truth to the ground; and [a]it practised, and prospered.

13 Then I heard [b]one saint speaking, and another saint said unto [c]that[d] certain *saint* which spake, How long *shall be* the vision *concerning* the daily *sacrifice,* and the transgression of [e]desolation, to give both the sanctuary and the host to be trodden under foot?

14 And he said unto me, Unto two thousand and three hundred [f]days; [g]then shall the sanctuary be [h]cleansed.

15 And it came to pass, when I, *even* I Daniel, had seen the vision, and [i]sought for the meaning, then, behold, there stood before me [k]as the appearance of a man.

16 And I heard a man's voice [l]between *the banks of* Ulai, which called, and said, [m]Gabriel, make this *man* to understand the vision.

A. M. cir. 3451
B. C. cir. 553
Ol. cir. LVI. 4
Servii Tullii,
R. Roman.,
cir. annum 26

17 So he came near where I stood: and when he came, I was afraid, and [n]fell upon my face: but he said unto me, Understand, O son of man, for at the time of the end *shall be* the vision.

18 [o]Now as he was speaking with me, I was in a deep sleep on my face toward the ground: [p]but he touched me, and [q]set me upright.

19 And he said, Behold, I will make thee know what shall be in the last end of the indignation; [r]for at the time appointed the end *shall be.*

20 [s]The ram which thou sawest having *two* horns *are* the kings of Media and Persia.

21 [t]And the rough goat *is* the king of Grecia: and the great horn that *is* between his eyes [u]*is* the first king.

22 [v]Now that being broken, whereas four stood up for it, four kingdoms shall stand up out of the nation, but not in his power.

23 And in the latter time of their kingdom, [w]when the transgressors [x]are come to the full, a king [y]of fierce countenance, and understanding dark sentences, [z]shall stand up.

[q]Jer. xlviii. 26, 42; chap. xi. 36; ver. 25——[r]Or, *against*——[s]Josh. v. 14——[t]Chap. xi. 31; xii. 11; 1 Mac. i. 44–64——[u]Or, *from him*——[v]Exod. xxix. 38; Num. xxviii. 3; Ezek. xlvi. 13——[w]Chap. xi. 31——[x]Or, *the host was given over for the transgression against the daily* sacrifice——[y]1 Mac. i. 11, &c.; 2 Mac. iv. 13, 17 [z]Psa. cxix. 43, 142; Isa. lix. 14——[a]Ver. 4; chap. xi. 28, 36——[b]Chap. iv. 13; xii. 6; 1 Pet. i. 12——[c]Or, *the numberer of secrets*, or *the wonderful numberer*——[d]Hebrew, *Palmoni*

[e]Or, *making desolate;* ch. xi. 31; xii. 11; 1 Mac. i. 54 [f]Heb. *evening morning*——[g]1 Mac. iv. 36, &c.——[h]Heb. *justified*——[i]See ch. xii. 8; 1 Pet. i. 10, 11——[k]Ezek. i. 26——[l]Ch. xii. 6, 7——[m]Ch. ix. 21; Luke i. 19, 26 [n]Ezek. i. 28; Rev. i. 17——[o]Ch. x. 9, 10; Luke ix. 32 [p]Ezek. ii. 2——[q]Heb. *made me stand upon my standing* [r]Ch. ix. 27; xi. 27, 35, 36; xii. 7; Hab. ii. 3——[s]Ver. 3 [t]Ver. 5——[u]Ch. xi. 3——[v]Ver. 8; ch. xi. 4——[w]1 Mac. i. 11, &c.; ii. 15——[x]Heb. *are accomplished*——[y]Deut. xxviii. 50——[z]Ver. 6

Verse 11. *Even to the prince of the host*] They seemed, in this case, to fight against God himself.

The daily sacrifice *was taken away*] By the destruction of the city and temple; and has never been restored from that day until now.

Verse 12. *And a host was given* him] That is, *power;* or perhaps *the host of heaven*—the *priesthood*—the whole sacrificial system, by reason of *transgression.* They had filled up the measure of their iniquities, in rejecting the Lord that bought them; and the *daily sacrifice*, being no longer of use, was given up with the rest to destruction.

Cast down the truth] Probably the whole Jewish ritual and religion.

Practised, and prospered.] Prosperity or success followed all their acts.

Verse 13. *One saint speaking, and another saint said*] One *angel* asked another how long the sanctuary was to be trodden down?

Verse 14. *Unto two thousand and three hundred days*] Though literally it be *two thousand three hundred evenings and mornings*, yet I think the *prophetic day* should be understood here, as in other parts of this prophet, and must signify so many *years.* If we date these years from the vision of the he-goat, (Alexander's invading Asia,) this was A. M. 3670, B. C. 334; and *two thousand three hundred* years from that time will reach to A. D. 1966, or *one hundred and forty-one* years from the present A. D. 1825. This will bring it near to the time mentioned chap. vii. 25, where see the note.

Verse 15. *As the appearance of a man.*] Supposed to be the *Messiah.*

Verse 17. *At the time of the end* shall be *the vision.*] Or, as *Houbigant,* "The vision shall have an end at the proper time."

Verse 20. *The ram which thou sawest*] See this explained under the vision itself, ver. 3, &c.

Verse 22. *But not in his power.*] The *four kingdoms* which shall arise out of the Macedonian empire shall not be of Alexander's power or *family*, nor have his strength and dignity.

Verse 23. *When the transgressors are come to the full*] When the utmost degradation has taken place, by the *buying* and *selling* of the *high priesthood;* for *Onias* was ejected for a

A. M. cir. 3451 B. C. cir. 553 Ol. cir. LVI. 4 Servii Tullii, R. Roman., cir. annum 26

24 And his power shall be mighty, [a]but not by his own power: and he shall destroy wonderfully, [b]and shall prosper, and practise, [c]and shall destroy the mighty and the [d]holy people.

25 And [e]through his policy also he shall cause craft to prosper in his hand; [f]and he shall magnify *himself* in his heart, [g]and by [h]peace shall destroy many: [i]he shall also stand up against the Prince of princes; but he shall be [k]broken without hand.

26 [l]And the vision of the evening and the morning which was told *is* true: [m]wherefore shut thou up the vision; for it *shall be* for many days.

27 [n]And I Daniel fainted, and was sick *certain* days; afterward I rose up, [o]and did the king's busines and I was astonished at the vision, [p]but none understood *it*.

[a]Rev. xvii. 13, 17——[b]Ver. 12; chap. xi. 36——[c]Ver. 10; chap. vii. 25——[d]Heb. *people of the holy ones* [e]Chap. xi. 21, 23, 24——[f]Ver. 11; chap. xi. 36; 2 Mac. ix. 4, 7, 8, 11——[g]1 Mac. i. 30, &c.——[h]Or, *prosperity*

[i]Ver. 11; ch. xi. 36——[k]Job xxxiv. 20; Lam. iv. 6; ch. ii. 34, 45; 1 Mac. vi. 8–13; 2 Mac. ix. 9, &c.——[l]Ch. x. 1——[m]Ezek. xii. 27; ch. x. 14; xii. 4, 9; Rev. xxii. 10 [n]Ch. vii. 28; x. 8, 16——[o]Ch. vi. 2, 3——[p]See ver. 16

sum of money, to make room for wicked *Jason;* and Jason again was supplanted for a greater sum by a worse man, if possible, than himself, *Menelaus;* and the golden vessels of the temple were sold to pay for this sacrilegious purchase. Thus transgressions were come to the full, before the Romans had commission to destroy Jerusalem and its temple, &c.

A king of fierce countenance] The *Roman government*, as before; for *king* is often taken for *kingdom* or *empire.*

Understanding dark sentences] Very learned and skilful in all things relating to government and its intrigues. The *learning* of Rome is proverbial to the present time.

Verse 24. *But not by his own power*] The strength of the other kingdoms consisted in themselves; but the Roman empire, as a *horn* or *kingdom* of the *goat*, was *not mighty by its own power*—was not strong by virtue of the *goat*, but drew its nourishment and strength from Rome and Italy. There grew the trunk and body of the tree; though the branches extended over Greece, Asia, Syria, and Egypt.—Bp. *Newton.*

Shall destroy wonderfully] In the taking of Jerusalem by the Romans *ninety-seven thousand* Jews were made captives, and *eleven hundred thousand* were slain. So they destroyed this once mighty and holy people!

Verse 25. *He shall cause craft to prosper*] They subdued as many by their *diplomatic skill* and *political intrigues* as they did by the *sword.*

He shall also stand up against the Prince of princes] Against *Christ;* for it was by the *Roman* authority that he was condemned to death and crucified; and their persecutions had nearly destroyed the Christian religion; but the house was founded on a *rock.*

But he shall be broken without hand.] The tide was turned by the invisible hand of God; and thus heathen Rome was overcome, and converted to Christianity.

Verse 26. *The vision of the evening and the morning which was told* is *true*] That mentioned in ver. 14.

For it shall be *for many days.*] Not less than *two thousand three hundred* years!

Verse 27. *Daniel fainted*] To foresee the desolations that were coming on the land, the city, the temple, and the people.

Did the king's business] Transacted the affairs of state that belonged to my department, after having been sick for certain days through the effects of this vision. He had a pious and feeling heart; and he was distressed for the desolations that were coming upon his people.

CHAPTER IX

Daniel, understanding from the prophecies of Jeremiah that the seventy *years' captivity was now terminating, pours out his soul in fervent prayer to God, and earnestly supplicates pardon and restoration for his captive people,* 1–12. *When thus supplicating God in behalf of Israel, the angel Gabriel is sent to inform him of the* seventy *prophetic weeks, or* four hundred and ninety *natural years, which should elapse from the date of the edict to rebuild Jerusalem and the temple to the death of the Messiah,* 20–27; *a prophecy most exactly fulfilled by the event, according to the computation of the best chronologers. Dean Prideaux states the commencement of these* seventy *prophetic weeks to have been in the month Nisan, in the year of the Julian period* 4256, *which corresponds with* A. M. 3546, B. C. 458, *according to the Usherian account. How awfully are the Jews blinded, who, in contradiction to so clear a prophecy, still expect the Messiah who was cut off, and, after suffering, is entered into his glory!*

A. M. cir. 3466
B. C. cir. 538
Ol. cir. LX. 3
Servii Tullii,
R. Roman.,
cir. annum 41

IN the first year [a]of Darius the son of Ahasuerus, of the seed of the Medes, [b]which was made king over the realm of the Chaldeans;

2 In the first year of his reign I Daniel understood by books the number of the years, whereof the word of the LORD came to [c]Jeremiah the prophet, that he would accomplish seventy years in the desolations of Jerusalem.

3 [d]And I set my face unto the Lord GOD, to seek by prayer and supplications, with fasting, and sackcloth, and ashes:

4 And I prayed unto the LORD my God, and made my confession, and said, O [e]Lord, the great and dreadful God, keeping the covenant and mercy to them that love him, and to them that keep his commandments;

5 [f]We have sinned, and have committed iniquity, and have done wickedly, and have rebelled, even by departing from thy precepts and from thy judgments:

6 [g]Neither have we hearkened unto thy servants the prophets, which spake in thy name to our kings, our princes, and our fathers, and to all the people of the land.

7 O Lord, [h]righteousness [i]*belongeth* unto thee, but unto us confusion of faces, as at this day; to the men of Judah, and to the inhabitants of Jerusalem, and unto all Israel, *that are* near, and *that are* far off, through all the countries whither thou hast driven them, because of their trespass that they have trespassed against thee.

A. M. cir. 3466
B. C. cir. 538
Ol. cir. LX. 3
Servii Tullii,
R. Roman.,
cir. annum 41

8 O Lord, to us *belongeth* [k]confusion of face to our kings, to our princes, and to our fathers, because we have sinned against thee.

9 [l]To the Lord our God *belong* mercies and forgivenesses, though we have rebelled against him;

10 [m]Neither have we obeyed the voice of the LORD our God, to walk in his laws, which he set before us by his servants the prophets.

11 Yea, [n]all Israel have transgressed thy law, even by departing, that they might not obey thy voice; therefore the curse is poured upon us, and the oath that *is* written in the [o]law of Moses the servant of God, because we have sinned against him.

12 And he hath [p]confirmed his words, which he spake against us, and against our judges that judged us, by bringing upon us a great evil: [q]for under the whole heaven hath not been done as hath been done upon Jerusalem.

13 [r]As *it is* written in the law of Moses, all this evil is come upon us: [s]yet [t]made we not our prayer before the LORD our God, that we might turn from our iniquities, and understand thy truth.

---

[a]Chap. i. 21; v. 31; vi. 28——[b]Or, *in which he*, &c. [c]2 Chron. xxxvi. 21; Jer. xxv. 11, 12; xxix. 10——[d]Neh. i. 4; chap. vi. 10; Jer. xxix. 12, 13; James iv. 8, 9, 10 [e]Exod. xx. 6; Deut. vii. 9; Neh. i. 5; ix. 32——[f]1 Kings viii. 47, 48; Neh. i. 6, 7; ix. 33, 34; Psa. cvi. 6; Isa. lxiv. 5, 6, 7; Jer. xiv. 7; ver. 15; Bar. i. 17, 18——[g]2 Chron. xxxvi. 15, 16; ver. 10——[h]Neh. ix. 33; Bar. i. 15 [i]Or, *thou* hast, &c.

[k]Ver. 7; Bar. i. 15——[l]Neh. ix. 17; Psa. cxxx. 4, 7 [m]Ver. 6——[n]Isa. i. 4, 5, 6; Jer. viii. 5, 10——[o]Lev. xxvi. 14, &c.; Deut. xxvii. 15, &c.; xxviii. 15, &c.; xxix. 20, &c.; xxx. 17, 18; xxxi. 17, &c.; xxxii. 19, &c.; Lam. ii. 17 [p]Zech. i. 6——[q]Lam. i. 12; ii. 13; Ezek. v. 9; Amos iii. 2 [r]Lev. xxvi. 14, &c.; Deut. xxviii. 15; Lam. ii. 17 [s]Isa. ix. 13; Jer. ii. 30; v. 3; Hos. vii. 7, 10——[t]Heb. *intreated we not the face of the*, &c.

NOTES ON CHAP. IX

Verse 1. *In the first year of Darius*] This is the same Darius the *Mede*, spoken of before, who succeeded Belshazzar, king of the Chaldeans. See chap. v. 31.

Verse 2. *I Daniel understood by books*] The prophecy referred to here is found Jer. xxv. 12; xxix. 10. The people must have been satisfied of the Divine inspiration of Jeremiah, or his prophecies would not have been so speedily collected nor so carefully preserved. It appears that there was a copy of them then in Daniel's hands.

Verse 3. *I set my face—to seek by prayer*] He found that the time of the promised deliverance could not be at any great distance; and as he saw nothing that indicated a speedy termination of their oppressive captivity, he was very much afflicted, and earnestly besought God to put a speedy end to it; and how earnestly he seeks, his own words show. He *prayed*, he *supplicated*, he *fasted*, he put *sackcloth* upon his body, and he put *ashes* upon his head. He uses that kind of prayer prescribed by Solomon in his prayer at the dedication of the temple. See 1 Kings viii. 47, 48.

Verse 4. *Keeping the covenant*] Fidelity and truth are characteristics of God. He had never yet broken his engagements to his followers, and was ever showing *mercy* to men.

Verse 7. *All Israel*, that are *near, and* that are *far off*] He prays both for *Judah* and *Israel*. The latter were more dispersed, and had been much longer in captivity.

Verse 9. *Mercies and forgivenesses*] From God's *goodness* flow God's *mercies;* from his *mercies, forgivenesses.*

Verse 11. *Therefore the curse is poured upon us*] It is probable that he alludes here to the punishment of certain criminals by pouring *melted metal* upon them; therefore he uses the word תתך *tittach, it is poured out,* like melted

A. M. cir. 3466
B. C. cir. 538
Ol. cir. LX. 3
Servii Tullii,
R. Roman.,
cir. annum 41

14 Therefore hath the LORD
[u]watched upon the evil, and
brought it upon us: for [v]the
LORD our God *is* righteous in
all his works which he doeth: [w]for we obeyed
not his voice.
15 And now, O Lord our God, [x]that hast
brought thy people forth out of the land of
Egypt with a mighty hand, and hast [y]gotten
thee [z]renown, as at this day; [a]we have sinned,
we have done wickedly.
16 O Lord, [b]according to all thy righteousness, I beseech thee, let thine anger and thy
fury be turned away from thy city Jerusalem,
[c]thy holy mountain: because for our sins,
[d]and for the iniquities of our fathers, [e]Jeru-
salem and thy people [f]*are become* a reproach
to all *that are* about us.
17 Now therefore, O our God, hear the
prayer of thy servant, and his supplications,
[g]and cause thy face to shine upon thy sanctuary [h]that is desolate, [i]for the Lord's sake.
18 [k]O my God, incline thine ear, and hear;
open thine eyes, [l]and behold our desolations,
and the city [m]which [n]is called by thy name:
for we do not [o]present our supplications before thee for our righteousnesses, but for thy
great mercies.
19 O Lord, hear; O Lord, forgive; O Lord,
hearken and do; defer not, [p]for
thine own sake, O my God: for
thy city and thy people are
called by thy name.
20 [q]And whiles I was speaking, and praying, and confessing my sin and the sin of my
people Israel, and presenting my supplication before the LORD my God for the holy
mountain of my God;
21 Yea, whiles I *was* speaking in prayer,
even the man [r]Gabriel, whom I had seen in
the vision at the beginning, being caused to
fly [s]swiftly, [t]touched me [u]about the time of
the evening oblation.
22 And he informed *me,* and talked with
me, and said, O Daniel, I am now come forth
[v]to give thee skill and understanding.
23 At the begining of thy supplications the
[w]commandment came forth, and [x]I am come
to show *thee;* [y]for thou *art* [z]greatly beloved:
therefore [a]understand the matter, and consider the vision.
24 Seventy weeks are determined upon thy
people and upon thy holy city, [b]to finish the
transgression, and [c]to make an end of sins,
[d]and to make reconciliation for iniquity, and
to bring in everlasting righteousness, and to
seal up the vision [e]and [f]prophecy, [g]and to
anoint the Most Holy.

A. M. cir. 3466
B. C. cir. 538
Ol. cir. LX. 3
Servii Tullii,
R. Roman.,
cir. annum 41

---

[u]Jer. xxxi. 28; xliv. 27——[v]Neh. ix. 33; ver. 7——[w]Ver. 10——[x]Exod. vi. 1, 6; xxxii. 11; 1 Kings viii. 51; Neh. i. 10——Jer. xxxii. 21——[y]Heb. *made thee a name*——[z]Exod. xiv. 18; Neh. ix. 10; Jer. xxxii. 20——[a]Ver. 5——[b]1 Sam. xii. 7; Psa. xxxi. 1; lxxi. 2; Mic. vi. 4, 5——[c]Ver. 20; Zech. viii. 3——[d]Exod. xx. 5——[e]Lam. ii. 15, 16——[f]Psa. xliv. 13, 14; lxxix. 4——[g]Num. vi. 25; Psa. lxvii. 1; lxxx. 3, 7, 19——[h]Lam. v. 18——[i]Ver. 19; John xvi. 24——[k]Isa. xxxvii. 17——[l]Exod. iii. 7; Psa. lxxx. 14, &c.——[m]Jer. xxv. 29——[n]Heb. *whereupon thy name is called*

[o]Heb. *cause to fall;* Jer. xxxvi. 7——[p]Psa. lxxix. 9, 10; cii. 15, 16——[q]Psa. xxxii. 5; Isa. lxv. 24——[r]Chap. viii. 16——[s]Heb. *with weariness*, or *flight*——[t]Chap. viii. 18; x. 10, 16——[u]1 Kings xviii. 36——[v]Heb. *to make thee skilful of understanding*——[w]Heb. *word*——[x]Chap. x. 12——[y]Chap. x. 11, 19——[z]Heb. a man *of desires*——[a]Matt. xxiv. 15——[b]Or, *to restrain*——[c]Or, *to seal up;* Lam. iv. 22——[d]Isa. liii. 10——[e]Isa. liii. 11; Jer. xxiii. 5, 6; Heb. ix. 12; Rev. xiv. 6——[f]Heb. *prophet*——[g]Psalm xlv. 7; Luke i. 35; John i. 41; Hebrews ix. 11

---

metal, for this is the proper meaning of the root נתך *nathach.*

Verse 14. *The Lord watched upon the evil*] In consequence of our manifold rebellions he hath now watched for an opportunity to bring these calamities upon us.

Verse 17. *And cause thy face to shine*] Give us proof that thou art reconciled to us.

Verse 19. *Thy city and thy people are called by thy name.*] The *holy city,* the *city of the great King.* I think it scarcely possible for any serious man to read these impressive and pleading words without feeling a measure of the prophet's earnestness.

Verse 21. *The man Gabriel*] Or the angel Gabriel, who had appeared to me as a *man.* איש *ish* is the same here as *person*—the person *Gabriel.*

Being caused to fly swiftly] God hears with delight such earnest, humble, urgent prayers; and sends the *speediest* answer. Gabriel himself was ordered on this occasion to make *more than usual speed.*

Verse 24. *Seventy weeks are determined*] This is a most important prophecy, and has given rise to a variety of opinions relative to the proper mode of explanation; but the chief difficulty, if not the only one, is to find out the *time* from which these *seventy weeks* should be *dated.* What is here said by the angel is not a direct answer to Daniel's prayer. He prays to know when the *seventy weeks of the captivity* are to *end.* Gabriel shows him that there are *seventy weeks determined* relative to a *redemption* from *another sort of captivity,* which shall commence with the *going forth of the edict to restore and rebuild Jerusalem,* and shall terminate with the *death of Messiah the Prince,* and the total *abolition of the Jewish sacrifices.* In the four following verses he enters into the particulars of this most important *determination,* and leaves them with Dan-

A. M. cir. 3466
B. C. cir. 538
Ol. cir. LX. 3
Servii Tullii,
R. Roman.,
cir. annum 41

25 [h]Know therefore and understand, *that* [i]from the going forth of the commandment [k]to restore and to build Jerusalem unto [l]the Messiah [m]the Prince *shall be* seven weeks, and threescore and two weeks: the street [n]shall be built again, and the [o]wall, [p]even [q]in troublous times.

[h]Ver. 23; Matt. xxiv. 15——[i]Ezra iv. 24; vi. 1, 15; vii. 1; Neh. ii. 1, 3, 5, 6, 8——[k]Or, *to build again Jerusalem;* as 2 Sam. xv. 25; Psa. lxxi. 20

[l]John i. 41; iv. 25——[m]Isa. lv. 4——[n]Heb. *shall return and be builded*——[o]Or, *breach*, or *ditch*——[p]Neh. iv. 8, 16, 17, 18——[q]Heb. *in strait of times;* Neh. vi. 15

iel for his comfort, who has left them to the Church of God for the *confirmation* of its faith, and a *testimony* to the truth of Divine revelation. They contain the fullest confirmation of Christianity, and a complete refutation of the Jewish cavils and blasphemies on this subject.

Of all the writers I have consulted on this most noble prophecy, Dean *Prideaux* appears to me the most clear and satisfactory. I shall therefore follow his method in my explanation, and often borrow his words.

Seventy weeks are determined—The Jews had *Sabbatic years*, Lev. xxv. 8, by which their years were divided into weeks of years, as in this important prophecy, each week containing *seven* years. The *seventy weeks* therefore here spoken of amount to *four hundred and ninety* years.

In ver. 24 there are *six events* mentioned which should be the consequences of the incarnation of our Lord:—

I. *To finish* (לכלא *lechalle, to restrain,*) *the transgression*, which was effected by the preaching of the Gospel, and pouring out of the Holy Ghost among men.

II. *To make an end of sins;* rather ולהתם חטאות *ulehathem chataoth*, "to make an end of *sin-offerings;*" which our Lord did when he offered his spotless soul and body on the cross *once* for all.

III. *To make reconciliation* (ולכפר *ulechapper*, "to make atonement or expiation") *for iniquity;* which he did by the once offering up of himself.

IV. *To bring in everlasting righteousness*, צדק עלמים *tsedek olamim*, that is, "the righteousness, or righteous ONE, of ages;" that person who had been the object of the faith of mankind, and the subject of the predictions of the prophets through all the ages of the world.

V. *To seal up* (ולחתם *velachtom*, "to finish or complete") *the vision and prophecy;* that is, to put an end to the necessity of any farther revelations, by completing the canon of Scripture, and fulfilling the prophecies which related to his person, sacrifice, and the glory that should follow.

VI. *And to anoint the Most Holy*, קדש קדשים *kodesh kodashim*, "the Holy of holies." משח *mashach, to anoint*, (from which comes משיח *mashiach, the Messiah*, the anointed one,) signifies in general, to consecrate or appoint to some special office. Here it means the consecration or appointment of our blessed Lord, the Holy One of Israel, to be the Prophet, Priest, and King of mankind.

Verse 25. *From the going forth of the commandment to restore and to build Jerusalem*] The foregoing events being all accomplished by Jesus Christ, they of course determine the prophecy to him. And if we reckon back *four hundred and ninety* years, we shall find the time of the going forth of this command.

Most learned men agree that the death of Christ happened at the passover in the month *Nisan*, in the *four thousand seven hundred and forty-sixth* year of the Julian period. *Four hundred and ninety* years, reckoned back from the above year, leads us directly to the month *Nisan* in the *four thousand two hundred and fifty-sixth* year of the same period; the very month and year in which *Ezra* had his commission from *Artaxerxes Longimanus*, king of Persia, (see Ezra vii. 9,) to restore and rebuild Jerusalem. See the commission in *Ezra*, chap. vii. 11-26, and *Prideaux's* Connexions, vol. ii. p. 380.

The above *seventy* weeks, or *four hundred and ninety* years, are divided, in ver. 25, into *three distinct periods*, to each of which particular events are assigned. The three periods are,—

I. *Seven* weeks, that is, *forty-nine* years.

II. *Sixty-two* weeks, that is, *four hundred and thirty-four* years.

III. *One* week, that is, *seven* years.

To the *first* period of seven *weeks* the restoration and repairing of Jerusalem are referred; and so long were *Ezra* and *Nehemiah* employed in restoring the sacred constitutions and civil establishments of the Jews, for this work lasted *forty-nine* years after the commission was given by Artaxerxes.

From the above *seven* weeks the *second* period of *sixty-two* weeks, or *four hundred and thirty-four* years more, commences, at the end of which the prophecy says, *Messiah the Prince should come*, that is, *seven* weeks, or *forty-nine* years, should be allowed for the restoration of the Jewish state; from which time till the public entrance of the Messiah on the work of the ministry should be *sixty-two weeks*, or *four hundred and thirty-four years*, in all *four hundred and eighty-three* years.

From the coming of our Lord, the *third period* is to be dated, viz., "He shall confirm the covenant with many for one week," that is, *seven* years, ver. 27.

This confirmation of the covenant must take in the ministry of *John the Baptist* with that of our Lord, comprehending the term of *seven* years, during the whole of which he might be well said to confirm or ratify the new covenant with mankind. Our Lord says, "The law was until John;" but from his first public preaching *the kingdom of God*, or Gospel dispensation, commenced.

These *seven* years, added to the *four hundred and eighty-three*, complete the *four hundred and ninety* years, or *seventy* prophetic weeks; so that the whole of this prophecy, from the times and corresponding events, has been fulfilled to the very letter.

Some imagine that the *half* of the last *seven years* is to be referred to the total destruction of the Jews by *Titus*, when the daily sacrifice for ever ceased to be offered; and that the

A. M. cir. 3466
B. C. cir. 538
Ol. cir. LX. 3
Servii Tullii,
R. Roman.,
cir. annum 41

26 And after threescore and two weeks [r]shall Messiah be cut off, [s]but[t] not for himself: [u]and [v]the people of the prince that shall come [w]shall destroy the city [x]and the sanctuary; [y]and the end thereof *shall be* [z]with a flood, and unto the end of the war [a]desolations are determined.

27 And he shall confirm [b]the [c]covenant with [d]many for one week: and in the midst of the week he shall cause the sacrifice and the oblation to cease, [e]and for the overspreading of [f]abominations he shall make *it* desolate, [g]even until the consummation, and that determined shall be poured [h]upon the desolate.

A. M. cir. 3466
B. C. cir. 538
Ol. cir. LX. 3
Servii Tullii,
R. Roman.,
cir. annum 41

[r]Isa. liii. 8; Mark ix. 12; Luke xxiv. 26, 46——[s]1 Pet. ii. 21; iii. 18——[t]Or, *and shall have nothing;* John xiv. 30 [u]Or, *and* [*the Jews*] *they shall be no more his people;* chap. xi. 17, or, and the *Prince's* [*Messiah's*, ver. 25] *future people*——[v]Matt. xxii. 7——[w]Luke xix. 44——[x]Matt. xxiv. 2——[y]Matt. xxiv. 6, 14——[z]Isa. viii. 7, 8; chap. xi. 10, 22; Nah. i. 8

[a]Or, *it shall be cut off by desolations*——[b]Or, *a* [c]Isa. xlii. 6; lv. 3; Jer. xxxi. 31; Ezek. xvi. 60, 61, 62 [d]Isa. liii. 11; Matt. xxvi. 28; Rom. v. 15, 19; Heb. ix. 28 [e]Or, *and upon the battlements shall be the idols of the desolator*——[f]Matt. xxiv. 15; Mark xiii. 14; Luke xxi. 20 [g]See Isa. x. 22, 23; xxviii. 22; chap. xi. 36; Luke xxi. 24; Rom. xi. 26——[h]Or, *upon the desolator*

intermediate space of *thirty-seven* years, from our Lord's death till the destruction of the city, is passed over as being of no account in relation to the prophecy, and that it was on this account that the last seven years are *divided*. But Dean *Prideaux* thinks that the whole refers to our Lord's preaching connected with that of the Baptist. וחצי *vachatsi*, says he, signifies in the *half part* of the week; that is, in the latter three years and a half in which he exercised himself in the public ministry, he caused, by the sacrifice of himself, all other sacrifices and oblations to cease, which were instituted to signify his.

In the latter parts of ver. 26 and 27 we find the THIRD PART of this great prophecy, which refers to what should be done *after* the completion of these *seventy* weeks.

Verse 26. *And the people of the prince that shall come shall destroy the city and the sanctuary*] By the "prince" *Titus*, the son of *Vespasian*, is plainly intended; and "the people of that prince" are no other than the *Romans*, who, according to the prophecy, *destroyed the sanctuary*, הקדש *hakkodesh*, the *holy place* or temple, and, as a *flood*, swept away all, till the total destruction of that obstinate people finished the war.

Verse 27. *And for the overspreading of abominations he shall make* it *desolate*] This clause is remarkably obscure. כנף שקוצים משמם *kenaph shikkutsim meshomem*, "And upon the wing of abominations causing amazement." This is a literal translation of the place; but still there is no determinate sense. A *Hebrew* MS., written in the *thirteenth* century, has preserved a very remarkable reading here, which frees the place from all embarrassment. Instead of the above reading, this valuable MS. has ובהיכל יהיה שיקוץ *ubeheychal yihyey shikkuts;* that is, "And in the temple (of the Lord) there shall be abomination." This makes the passage plain, and is strictly conformable to the facts themselves, for the temple was profaned; and it agrees with the prediction of our Lord, who said that *the abomination that maketh desolate should stand in the holy place*, Matt. xxiv. 15, and quotes the words as *spoken* δια Δανιηλ του φροφητου, *by Daniel the prophet*. That the above reading gives the true sense, there can be little doubt, because it is countenanced by the most eminent ancient *versions*.

The *Vulgate* reads, Et erit in templo abominatio, "And in the temple there shall be abomination."

The *Septuagint*, Και επι το ἱερον βδελυγμα των ερημωσεων, "And upon the temple there shall be the abomination of desolation."

The *Arabic*, "And upon the sanctuary there shall be the abomination of ruin."

The above reading is celebrated by *J. D. Michaelis*, Epist. De Ebdom. Dan., p. 120: Vix insignius exemplum reperiri posse autumem, ostensuro in codicibus Hebræis latere lectiones dignissimas quæ eruantur, &c. "A more illustrious example can, I think, hardly be found, to show that various readings lie hid in Hebrew MSS., which are most worthy of being exhibited." Vid. *Bib. Heb.* KENNICOTT, *Dis. Gen.*

I have only to add that this mode of reckoning years and periods by *weeks* is not solely Jewish. *Macrobius*, in his book on Scipio's dream, has these remarkable words: Sed a sexta usque ad *septimam septimanam* fit quidem diminutio, sed occulta, et quæ detrimentum suum aperta defectione non prodat: ideo nonnullarum rerumpublicarum hic mos est, ut post *sextam* ad militiam nemo cogatur; Somn. Scip., lib. i. c. vi., *in fine*. "From the *sixth* to the *seventh week*, there is a diminution of strength; but it is hidden, and does not manifest itself by any outward defect. Hence it was the custom in some republics not to oblige a man to go to the wars after the *sixth week*, i. e., after *forty-two* years of age."

Having now gone through the whole of this important prophecy, and given that interpretation which the original seemed best to warrant, I shall next proceed to notice the principal various readings found in the Collections of *Kennicott* and *De Rossi*, with those from my own MSS., which the reader may collate with the words of the common printed text.

Verse 24. שבעים שבעים נחתך על עמך ועל עיר קדשך
לכלא הפשע ולחתם חטאות
ולכפר עון ולהביא צדק עלמים
ולחתם חזון ונביא ולמשח קדש קדשים:

Verse 25. ותדע ותשכל
מן מצא דבר להשיב ולבנות ירושלם
ער משיח נגיד שבעים שבעה
ושבעים ששים ושנים תשוב
ונבנתה רחוב וחרוץ ובצוק העתים:

Verse 26. ואחרי השבעים ששים ושנים
יכרת משיח ואין לו.
והעיר והקדש ישחית עם נגיד הבא
וקצו בשטף.
ועד קץ מלחמה נחרצת שממות:
Verse 27. והגביר ברית לרבים שבוע אחד.
והצי השבוע ישבית זבח ומנחה.
ועל כנף שקוצים משמם.
ועד כלה ונחרצה תתך על שומם:

Of the whole passage *Houbigant* gives the following translation:—

Verse 24. Seventy weeks are determined upon thy people, and the city of thy sanctuary:
That sin may be restrained, and transgressions have an end;
That iniquity may be expiated, and an everlasting righteousness brought in;
That visions and prophecies may be sealed up, and the Holy of holies anointed.
Verse 25. Know therefore and understand:—
From the edict which shall be promulgated, to return and rebuild Jerusalem, there shall be seven weeks.
Then it shall be fully rebuilt, with anxiety, in difficult times.
Thence, to the Prince Messiah, there shall be sixty-two weeks.
Verse 26. And after sixty-two weeks the Messiah shall be slain, and have no justice.
Afterwards he shall waste the city and the sanctuary, by the prince that is to come.
And his end shall be in straits; and to the end of the war desolation is appointed.
Verse 27. And for one week he shall confirm a covenant with many;
And in the middle of the week he shall abrogate sacrifice and offering;
And in the temple there shall be the abomination of desolation,
Until the ruin which is decreed rush on after the desolation.

In this translation there are some peculiarities.

Instead of "the street shall be built again, and the wall," ver. 25, he translates רחוב וחרוץ (with the prefix ב *beth* instead of ו *vau* in the latter word,) "it shall be fully (the city and all its walls) rebuilt with anxiety."

Instead of ואין לו "but not for himself," he translates, "Nor shall justice be done him;" supposing that דין "justice" was originally in the verse.

Instead of "the people of the prince," ver. 26, he translates "by the prince," using עם *im* as a preposition, instead of עם *am*, "the people."

Instead of "and for the overspreading," he translates ועל כנף "in the temple;" following the Septuagint, και επι το ιερον. This rendering is at least as good as ours: but see the *marginal* readings here, and the preceding notes.

Houbigant contends also that the arrangement of the several members in these passages is confused. He proposes one alteration, which is important, *viz.*, From the promulgation of the decree to rebuild Jerusalem shall be seven weeks; and unto Messiah the prince, sixty-two weeks. All these alterations he vindicates in his notes at the end of this chapter. In the text I have inserted Houbigant's dots, or marks of distinction between the different members of the verses.

Various Readings

Verse 24. שבעים, שבועים *weeks* written *full*, so to prevent mistakes, in *thirteen* of *Kennicott's*, *four* of *De Rossi's*, and *one* ancient of my own.

שבעים *Seventy-one* of *Kennicott's*, and *one* of *De Rossi's*, have שבועים "weeks, weeks, weeks;" that is, "many weeks:" but this is a mere mistake.

לכלא "to restrain." לכלה "to consume," is the reading of *twenty-nine* of *Kennicott's*, *thirteen* of *De Rossi's*, and *one* ancient of my own.

ולחתם "and to seal up." *Forty-three* of *Kennicott's twelve* of *De Rossi's*, and *one* of my own, have ולהתם "to make an end." One reads ולחתום, more *full*.

חטאות "sins." חטאת "sin," in the singular, is the reading of *twenty-six* of *De Rossi's;* and so, in the second instance where this word occurs, *two* of my MSS.

עלמים "everlasting." *Two* of my oldest MSS. read שלמים, and so in the next instance.

ונביא "and the prophet." The conjunction is omitted by *two* of *Kennicott's*.

ותשכל "and understand." *One* of my MSS. has ותשכיל.

Verse 25. מן מוצא "from the publication." One MS. of *De Rossi's* omits the מן "from," and instead of either, *one* of my oldest MSS. has למוצא "to the publication."

משיח "Messiah." *Nine* MSS. read the word with the point *sheva*, which makes it read, in regimine, "the anointed of the prince." But this is evidently the effect of carelessness, or rather design.

שבעה "seven." *Two* MSS. add the conjunction ו *vau*, "and."

ולבנות "and to build." One of mine omits the conjunction.

שבעים שבעה "seven weeks." *One* of *Kennicott's* has שבעים שנה "seventy years."

ושבעים "and weeks." *One* of *Kennicott's* has ושבוע "and a week."

ששים "sixty." A few add the conjunction ו *vau*, "*and* sixty;" and another has ששה "six;" and another שבעים "seventy." Wherever this word signifies *weeks*, *two* of my oldest MSS. write it *full* שבועים. In *one* of my MSS. השבועים ששים are omitted in the text, but added by a later hand in the margin.

וחרוץ "and the ditch." One MS. has העיר "the city." And for רחב "street," one of mine has רחוב of the same meaning, but more *full*.

ובצוק "and in straits," or *anxiety*. One MS. without *and*, as the *Vulgate* and *Septuagint*.

Verse 26. והקדש "and the holy place or sanctuary." But *two* of my most ancient MSS., and *four* of *Kennicott's*, leave out the ו *vau*, and read והעיר הקדש "and the holy city," or "city of holiness," instead of "the city and sanctuary." In one MS. ו is omitted in והעיר.

וקצו "and its end." *One* MS. omits the conjunction ו *and;* one omits the following קץ "the end;" reading thus: "and unto the war." But a more singular reading is that of one of my own MSS. written about A. D. 1136, which has וקיצו "and its summer."

ששים "sixty." But one of *Kennicott's* MSS.

has ששים שבעים "sixty weeks;" and another adds the conjunction, AND *sixty*.

ישחית "shall destroy." But one of *De Rossi's* has ישחת "shall be destroyed."

עם "the people." עם *im*, "with," is the reading of one of *Kennicott's*, with the *Septuagint*, *Theodotion*, *Syriac*, *Hexapla*, *Vulgate*, and *Arabic*.

בשטף "with a flood." *One* MS. has השטף "the flood."

ועל בנף "and upon the wing." Nearly *twenty* MSS. have ועד "and unto," &c.

Verse 27. ועד קץ "and unto the end." עד- "to the end;" and one has ועל "and upon."

קץ "the end." One has עת "the time;" and another both, עת קץ "the time of the end."

ועל כנף שקוצים "and upon the wing (or battlement) abomination." Instead of this, one of the Parisian MSS. numbered *three hundred and thirteen* in *Kennicott's*, has ובהיכל יהיה שיקוץ "and in the temple there shall be abomination." See the preceding notes. This is a similar reading to *Theodotion*, the *Vulgate*, *Septuagint*, *Syriac Hexapla*, and the *Arabic;* and is countenanced by our Lord, Matt. xxiv. 15. After all that has been said on this reading, (which may be genuine, but is less liable to suspicion, as the MS. appears to be the work of some *Christian;* it is written from the *left to the right hand*, and is accompanied by the *Vulgate Latin*,) if this be an attempt to accommodate the *Hebrew* to the *Vulgate*, it should be stated that they who have examined this MS. closely, have asserted that there is no evidence that the writer has endeavoured to conform the Hebrew to the Latin text, unless this be accounted such. The ancient versions give this reading great credit.

שקוצים "abominations." One of mine has less fully שקצים

משמם "desolation." *One* of mine has more fully משומם.

ועד "and unto," is wanting in one of mine; ועל "and upon" is the reading in *one* other.

על שומם "until the desolation." שומם "the desolation." *One* of mine has שמם without the ו *vau*. על is wanting; but is added in the margin, by a later hand, in another of these ancient MSS.

I have thus set down almost all the variations mentioned by *Kennicott* and *De Rossi*, and those furnished by *three* ancient MSS. of my own, that the learned reader may avail himself of every help to examine thoroughly this important prophecy. Upwards of *thirty* various readings in the compass of *four* verses, and several of them of great moment.

CHAPTER X

This and the two following chapters give an account of Daniel's last vision, wherein the succession of the Persian and Grecian monarchies is described, together with the wars that should take place between Syria and Egypt under the latter monarchy. The last part of the vision (from chap. xi. 36) *seems to relate chiefly to the persecutions of the Church in the times of Antichrist, till it be purified from all its pollutions; after which will follow that glorious kingdom of the saints spoken of in the* seventh *and* eighth *chapters. This chapter begins with an account of Daniel's fasting and humiliation,* 1–3. *Then we have a description of the Divine person who appeared to the prophet, not unlike him who appeared to the apostle in the isle of Patmos,* 4–21. *See* Rev. i. 10–16.

A. M. 3470 B. C. 534 Ol. LXI. 3 Anno Tarquinii Superbi, R. Roman., 1

IN the third year of Cyrus king
of Persia a thing was revealed unto Daniel, [a]whose name
was called Belteshazzar; [b]and
the thing *was* true, [c]but the time appointed
was [d]long; and [e]he understood the thing, and
had understanding of the vision.
2 In those days I Daniel was mourning
three [f]full weeks.
3 I ate no [g]pleasant bread,
neither came flesh nor wine in
my mouth, [h]neither did I anoint
myself at all, till three whole
weeks were fulfilled.
4 And in the four and twentieth day of the
first month, as I was by the side of the great
river, which *is* [i]Hiddekel;
5 Then [k]I lifted up mine eyes, and looked,

A. M. 3470 B. C. 534 Ol. LXI. 3 Anno Tarquinii Superbi, R. Roman., 1

[a]Chap. i. 7——[b]Chap. viii. 26; Rev. xix. 9——[c]Ver. 14——[d]Heb. *great*——[e]Chap. i. 17; viii. 16

[f]Heb. *weeks of days*——[g]Heb. *bread of desires*——[h]Matt. vi. 17——[i]Gen. ii. 14——[k]Josh. v. 13

NOTES ON CHAP. X

Verse 1. *In the third year of Cyrus*] Which answers to the *first* year of Darius the Mede.

The time appointed was *long*] וצבא גדול *vetsaba gadol*, but the *warfare long;* there will be many contentions and wars before these things can be accomplished.

Verse 2. *I—was mourning three full weeks.*] The weeks are most probably dated from the time of the termination of the last vision. *Calmet* proves this by several reasons.

Verse 3. *I ate no pleasant bread*] This fast was rather a general *abstinence;* living all the while on *coarse* and *unsavoury food;* drinking nothing but *water;* not using the *bath*, and most probably wearing *haircloth* next the skin, during the whole of the time.

Verse 4. *By the side of—Hiddekel*] The same as the *Tigris*, the great river of Assyria;

A. M. 3470
B. C. 534
Ol. LXI. 3
Anno Tarquinii Superbi, R. Roman., 1

and [l]behold [m]a certain man clothed in linen, whose loins *were* [n]girded with [o]fine gold of Uphaz:

6 His body also *was* [p]like the beryl, and his face [q]as the appearance of lightning, [r]and his eyes as lamps of fire, and his arms [s]and his feet like in colour to polished brass, [t]and the voice of his words like the voice of a multitude.

7 And I Daniel [u]alone saw the vision: for the men that were with me saw not the vision; but a great quaking fell upon them, so that they fled to hide themselves.

8 Therefore I was left alone, and saw this great vision, [v]and there remained no strength in me: for my [w]comeliness [x]was turned in me into corruption, and I retained no strength.

9 Yet heard I the voice of his words: [y]and when I heard the voice of his words, then was I in a deep sleep on my face, and my face toward the ground.

10 [z]And, behold, a hand touched me, which [a]set me upon my knees and *upon* the palms of my hands.

A. M. 3470
B. C. 534
Ol. LXI. 3
Anno Tarquinii Superbi, R. Roman., 1

11 And he said unto me, O Daniel, [b]a [c]man greatly beloved, understand the words that I speak unto thee, and [d]stand upright: for unto thee am I now sent. And when he had spoken this word unto me, I stood trembling.

12 Then said he unto me, [e]Fear not, Daniel: for from the first day that thou didst set thine heart to understand, and to chasten thyself before thy God, [f]thy words were heard, and I am come for thy words.

13 [g]But the prince of the kingdom of Persia withstood me one and twenty days: but, lo, [h]Michael, [i]one of the chief princes, came to help me; and I remained there with the kings of Persia.

14 Now I am come to make thee understand what shall befall thy people [k]in the latter days: [l]for yet the vision *is* for *many* days.

15 And when he had spoken such words unto me, [m]I set my face toward the ground, and I became dumb.

16 And, behold, [n]*one* like the similitude of the sons of men [o]touched my lips: then I

---

[l]Ch. xii. 6, 7——[m]Heb. *one man*——[n]Rev. i. 13, 14, 15; xv. 6——[o]Jer. x 9——[p]Ezek. i. 16——[q]Ezek. i. 14 [r]Rev. i. 14; xix. 12——[s]Ezek. i. 7; Rev. i. 15——[t]Ezek. i. 24; Rev. i. 15——[u]2 Kings vi. 17; Acts ix. 7——[v]Ch. viii. 27——[w]Or, *vigour*——[x]Ch. vii. 28——[y]Ch. viii. 18 [z]Jer. i. 9; ch. ix. 21; Rev. i. 17——[a]Heb. *moved*

[b]Ch. ix. 23——[c]Heb. *a man of desires*——[d]Heb. *stand upon thy standing*——[e]Rev. i. 17——[f]Ch. ix. 3, 4, 22, 23; Acts x. 4——[g]Ver. 20——[h]Ver. 21; ch. xii. 1; Jude 9; Rev. xii. 7——[i]Or, *the first*——[k]Gen. xlix. 1; ch. ii. 28 [l]Ch. viii. 26; ver. 1; Hab. ii. 3——[m]Ver. 9; ch. viii. 18 [n]Ch. viii. 15——[o]Ver. 10; Jer. i. 9

---

as the *Euphrates* of Syria, and the *Nile* of Egypt.

Verse 5. *Clothed in linen*] The description is intended to point out the *splendour* of the garments.

Gold of Uphaz] The same as *Ophir*.

Verse 6. *His body also* was *like the beryl*] The description of this person is very similar to that of our Lord in Rev. i. 13-15.

Verse 7. *The men that were with me saw not the vision*] An exactly parallel case with what occurred at the conversion of Saul of Tarsus, Acts ix. 7. There was a Divine influence which they all felt, but only Daniel saw the corporeal appearance.

Verse 9. *Was I in a deep sleep*] I fell into a swoon.

Verse 10. *A hand touched me*] Nothing was *apparent* or *palpable* but a *hand*. A hand had written Belshazzar's fate upon the wall; and the *hand* is frequently mentioned when the *power* or *majesty* of *God* is intended. Perhaps by *hand* God himself may be meant. It is remarkable that in a very ancient MS. of the Septuagint, more than a *thousand* years old, now in the imperial library of Vienna, adorned with paintings which have been engraved for the catalogue of Lambechius, and transferred to that of Nesselius, all the appearances of God are represented by a *hand in the clouds*.

Verse 12. *I am come for thy words*] On account of thy prayers I am sent to comfort and instruct thee.

Verse 13. *But the prince of the kingdom of Persia withstood me*] I think it would go far to make a *legend* or a precarious *tale* of this important place to endeavour to maintain that either a *good* or *evil* ANGEL is intended here. *Cyrus* alone was the *prince of Persia*, and God had destined him to be the deliverer of his people; but there were some matters, of which we are not informed, that caused him to hesitate for some time. Fearing, probably, the greatness of the work, and not being fully satisfied of his ability to execute it, he therefore for a time *resisted the secret inspirations* which God had sent him. The opposition might be in reference to the building of the temple.

But lo, Michael] Gabriel, who speaks, did not leave Cyrus till Michael came to take his place. Michael, *he who is like God*, sometimes appears to signify the *Messiah*, at other times the *highest* or *chief archangel*. Indeed there is no archangel mentioned in the whole Scripture but this *one*. See Jude 9; Rev. xii. 7.

Verse 14. *For yet the vision* is *for* many *days*.] There are many things which remain yet to be revealed, and the time of their accomplishment is very distant.

Verse 15. *I set my face toward the ground*] He was standing upright, ver. 11, and he now

A. M. 3470 B. C. 534 Olymp. LXI. 3 Anno Tarquinii Superbi, R. Roman., 1

opened my mouth, and spake, and said unto him that stood before me, O my lord, by the vision [p]my sorrows are turned upon me, and I have retained no strength.

17 For how can [q]the servant of this my lord talk with this my lord? for as for me, straightway there remained no strength in me, neither is there breath left in me.

18 Then there came again and touched me *one* like the appearance of a man, and he strengthened me,

19 [r]And said, O man greatly beloved, [s]fear not: peace *be* unto thee, be strong, yea, be strong. And when he had spoken unto me, I was strengthened, and said, Let my lord speak, for thou hast strengthened me.

20 Then said he, Knowest thou wherefore I come unto thee? and now will I return to fight [t]with the king of Persia: and when I am gone forth, lo, the prince of Grecia shall come.

21 But I will show thee that which is noted in the scripture of truth: and *there is* none that [u]holdeth with me in these things, [v]but Michael your prince.

[p]Ver. 8——[q]Or, *this servant of my lord*——[r]Ver. 11——[s]Judg. vi. 23

[t]Ver. 13——[u]Heb. *strengtheneth himself*——[v]Ver. 13; Jude 9; Rev. xii. 7

bent his body in reverence, and looked down upon the ground.

And became dumb.] Found himself unable to speak.

Verse 16. *Like the similitude of the sons of men*] I think Gabriel is here meant, who appeared to Daniel in a *human form;* and so in ver. 18, and see also chap. ix. 21.

Touched my lips] Before this he was unable to speak.

By the vision] The vision that I have already had, and of which I have not a proper knowledge has greatly afflicted me, because I see it intimates grievous calamities to my people. See chap. ix. 26.

Verse 17. *Neither is there breath*] He could not breathe freely; he was almost suffocated with sorrow.

Verse 19. *O man, greatly beloved*] איש חמדות *ish chamudoth*, man of delights; the most amiable of men.

Let my lord speak] I am now so strengthened and encouraged, that I shall be able to bear any revelation that thou mayest make.

Verse 20. *Knowest thou wherefore I come*] So high art thou in the favour of God, that he hath sent me unto thee to give thee farther satisfaction; though I was elsewhere employed upon a most important mission, and I must speedily return to accomplish it, *viz.:*—

To fight with the king of Persia] To remove all the scruples of Cyrus, and to excite him to do all that God designs him to do for the restoration of my people, and the rebuilding of the city and temple of Jerusalem. Nothing less than a supernatural agency in the mind of Cyrus can account for his decree in favour of the Jews. He had no natural, no political inclination to it; and his reluctance to obey the heavenly motions is here represented as a *fight between him and the angel.*

The prince of Grecia shall come.] I believe this refers to Alexander the Great, who was to destroy the *Persian* empire. See the *second* and *third* verses of the following chapter.

Verse 21. *Noted in the scripture of truth*] Perhaps this refers to what he had already *written* down. See the preceding visions, which Daniel did not fully understand, though a general impression from them had filled his heart with sorrow.

Michael your prince.] The archangel mentioned before, ver. 13, and who has been always supposed to be appointed by God as the guardian of the Jewish nation. It appears that God chose to make use of the ministry of angels in this work; that angels, as they could be only in *one place* at *one time*, could not produce influence where *they were* not; and that, to carry on the operation on the mind of the Persian king, it was necessary that either *Gabriel* or *Michael* should be *present* with him, and when one went on another commission another took his place; see ver. 13. But we know so little of the invisible world that we cannot safely *affirm* any thing *positively.*

CHAPTER XI

This chapter gives a more particular explanation of those events which were predicted in the eighth *chapter. The prophet had foretold the partition of Alexander's kingdom into four parts. Two of these, in which were included Egypt and Syria, the one to the* north, *the other to the* south, *in respect of Judea, appear to take up the chief attention of the prophet, as his people were particularly concerned in their fate; these being the countries in which by far the greatest number of the Jews were, and still are, dispersed. Of these countries he treats (according to the views of the most enlightened expositors) down to the conquest of Macedon, A. M.* 3836, *B. C.* 168, *when he begins to speak of the Romans,* 1–30; *and then of the Church under that power,* 31–35. *This leads him to speak of Antichrist, who was to spring up in that quarter,* 36–39; *and of those powers which* at the TIME of the end, *or the latter days of the Roman monarchy, (as this term is generally understood,) were* to push at *it, and overthrow many countries,* 40–43. *By the* king of the SOUTH, *in the fortieth verse, the dominion of the Saracens, or Arabs, is supposed to be intended, which was an exceeding great plague to the Roman empire in the east, and also to several papistical countries, for the space of* one hundred and fifty *years,* i. e.

from A. D. 612, *when Mohammed and his followers first began their depredations, to A. D.* 762, *when Bagdad was built, and made the capital of the caliphs of the house of Abbas; from which epoch the Saracens became a more settled people. By the* king of the NORTH *in the same verse the prophet is supposed by some to design that great scourge of eastern Christendom, the Ottoman or Othman empire, by which, after about a* hundred and fifty *years of almost uninterrupted hostilities, the Roman empire in the east was completely overturned, A. D.* 1453. *The chapter concludes with a prediction of the final overthrow of this northern power, and of the manner in which this great event shall be accomplished,* 44, 45. *But it should be observed that, notwithstanding the very learned observations of Bishop Newton and others upon this chapter, their scheme of interpretation presents very great and insurmountable difficulties; among which the very lengthy detail of events in the Syrian and Egyptian histories, comprising a period of less than* two hundred *years, and the rather uncouth transition to the incomparably greater transactions in Antichristian times, and of much longer duration, which are passed over with unaccountable brevity, are not the least. On all these subjects, however, the reader must judge for himself. See the notes.*

A. M. 3470
B. C. 534
Olymp. LXI. 3
Anno Tarquinii
Superbi,
R. Roman., 1

ALSO I, [a]in the first year of
[b]Darius the Mede, *even* I,
stood to confirm and to strengthen him.

2 And now will I show thee the truth. Behold, there shall stand up yet three kings in Persia; and the fourth shall be far richer than *they* all: and by his strength through his riches he shall stir up all against the realm of Grecia.

3 And [c]a mighty king shall stand up, that shall rule with great dominion, and [d]do according to his will.

4 And when he shall stand up, [e]his kingdom shall be broken, and shall be divided toward the four winds of heaven, and not to his posterity, [f]nor according to his dominion which he ruled: for his kingdom shall be plucked up, even for others beside those.

[a]Chap. ix. 1——[b]Chap. v. 31——[c]Chap. vii. 6; viii. 5

[d]Ch. viii. 4; ver. 16, 36——[e]Ch. viii. 8——[f]Ch. viii. 22

NOTES ON CHAP. XI

Verse 1. *In the first year of Darius the Mede*] This is a continuation of the preceding discourse. Bp. *Newton*, who is ever judicious and instructing, remarks: It is the usual method of the Holy Spirit to make the latter prophecies explanatory of the former; and thus revelation "is a shining light, that shineth more and more unto the perfect day." The four great empires shown to Nebuchadnezzar, under the symbol of a *great image*, were again more particularly represented to Daniel under the forms of *four great wild beasts*. In like manner, the memorable events that were revealed to Daniel in the vision of the *ram* and *he-goat*, are here more clearly revealed in this last vision by an angel; so that this latter prophecy may not improperly be said to be a comment on the former. It comprehends many signal events. The types, figures, and symbols of the things are not exhibited in this, as in most other visions, and then expounded by the angel; but the angel *relates* the whole: and, not by way of *vision*, but by *narration*, informs Daniel of that which is *noted in the Scripture of truth*, chap. x. 21.

Verse 2. *There shall stand up yet three kings*] Gabriel had already spoken of *Cyrus*, who was now reigning; and after him *three* others should arise. These were, 1. *Cambyses*, the son of Cyrus. 2. *Smerdis*, the Magian, who was an impostor, who pretended to be another son of Cyrus. And, 3. *Darius*, the son of *Hystaspes*, who married *Mandane*, the daughter of Cyrus.

Cambyses reigned *seven* years and *five* months; *Smerdis* reigned only *seven* months; and *Darius Hystaspes* reigned *thirty-six* years.

The fourth shall be far richer than they *all*] This was *Xerxes*, the son of Darius, of whom *Justin* says: "He had so great an abundance of riches in his kingdom, that although rivers were dried up by his numerous armies, yet his wealth remained unexhausted."

He shall stir up all against the realm of Grecia.] His military strength was such, that *Herodotus*, who lived in that time, informs us that his army amounted to *five* millions, *two hundred and eighty-three* thousand, *two hundred and twenty* men. Besides these, the Carthaginians furnished him with an army of *three hundred thousand* men, and a fleet of *two hundred* ships. He led an army against the Greeks of *eight hundred thousand* men, and *twelve hundred and seven* ships, with *three banks of rowers* each. As he marched along, he obliged all the people of the countries through which he passed to join him.

Verse 3. *A mighty king shall stand up*] This was *Alexander the Great*. It is not said that this mighty king shall stand up against *Xerxes*, for he was not born till *one hundred* years after that monarch; but simply that he should *stand up*, i. e., that he should reign in Greece.

Verse 4. *His kingdom shall be broken*] Shall, after his death, be *divided* among his *four* chief generals, as we have seen before. See chap. viii. 22.

And not to his posterity] The *family of Alexander* had a most tragical end: 1. His wife *Statira* was murdered soon after his death by his other wife *Roxana*. 2. His brother *Aridæus*, who succeeded him, was killed, together with his wife *Euridice*, by command of *Olympias*, Alexander's mother, after he had been king about six years and some months. 3. *Olympias* herself was killed by the soldiers in revenge. 4. *Alexander Ægus*, his son, together with *his* mother *Roxana*, was slain by order of Cassander. 5. Two years after, his other son *Hercules*, with his mother *Barsine*, was privately murdered by Polysperchon; so that in

A. M. 3470
B. C. 534
Olymp. LXI. 3
Anno Tarquinii
Superbi,
R. Roman., 1

5 And the king of the south shall be strong, and *one* of his princes; and he shall be strong above him, and have dominion; his dominion *shall be* a great dominion.

6 And in the end of years they [g]shall join themselves together: for the king's daughter of the south shall come to the king of the north to make [h]an agremeent: but she shall not retain the power of the arm; neither shall he stand, nor his arm: but she shall be given up, and they that brought her, and [i]he that begat her, and he that strengthened her in *these* times.

7 But out of a branch of her roots shall *one* stand up [k]in his estate, which shall come with an army, and shall enter into the fortress of the king of the north, and shall deal against them, and shall prevail:

8 And shall also carry captives into Egypt their gods, with their princes, *and* with [l]their precious vessels of silver and of gold; and he shall continue *more* years than the king of the north.

9 So the king of the south shall come into *his* kingdom, and shall return into his own land.

10 But his sons [m]shall be stirred up, and shall assemble a multitude of great forces:

[g]Heb. *shall associate themselves*——[h]Heb. *rights*——[i]Or, *whom she brought forth*

[k]Or, *in his place*, or *office;* ver. 20——[l]Heb. *vessels of their desire*——[m]Or, *shall war*

fifteen years after his death not one of his family or posterity remained alive!

"Blood calls for blood." He (Alexander) was the great butcher of men. He was either poisoned, or killed himself by immoderate drinking, when he was only *thirty-two* years and *eight* months old: and a retributive Providence destroyed all his posterity, so that neither *root* nor *branch* of them was left on the face of the earth. Thus ended Alexander, the great butcher; and thus ended his family and posterity.

Verse 5. *The king of the south*] This was *Ptolemy Lagus*, one of his generals, who had the government of Egypt, Libra, &c., which are on the south of Judea. He was strong, for he had added Cyprus, Phœnicia, Caria, &c., to his kingdom of Egypt.

And one *of his princes—shall be strong above him*] This was *Seleucus Nicator*, who possessed Syria, Babylon, Media, and the neighbouring countries. This was *the king of the north*, for his dominions lay *north* of Judea.

Verse 6. *In the end of years*] Several historical circumstances are here passed by.

The king's daughter of the south] *Berenice*, daughter of Ptolemy Philadelphus, king of Egypt, was married to *Antiochus Theos*, king of Syria. These two sovereigns had a bloody war for some years; and they agreed to terminate it by the above marriage, on condition that Antiochus would put away his wife *Laodice* and her children, which he did; and *Berenice* having brought an immense fortune to her husband, all things appeared to go on well for a time.

But she shall not retain the power of the arm] זרע *zaro, her posterity*, shall not reign in that kingdom.

But she shall be given up] Antiochus recalled his former wife Laodice and her children; and she, fearing that he might recall Berenice, caused him to be poisoned and her to be murdered, and set her son Callinicus upon the throne.

And they that brought her] Her Egyptian women, striving to defend their mistress, were many of them killed.

And he that begat her] Or, as the margin, "he whom she brought forth;" the son being murdered, as well as the mother, by order of Laodice.

And he that strengthened her] Probably her *father* Ptolemy, who was excessively fond of her, and who had died a few years before.

Verse 7. *But out of a branch of her roots*] A branch from the same root from which she sprang. This was *Ptolemy Euergetes*, her brother, who, to avenge his sister's death, marched with a great army against *Seleucus Callinicus*, took some of his best places, indeed all Asia, from Mount Taurus to India, and returned to Egypt with an immense booty, *forty thousand* talents of silver, precious vessels, and images of their gods *two thousand five hundred*, without Callinicus daring to offer him battle. I can but touch on these historic facts, for fear of extending these notes to an immoderate length.

Verse 8. *He shall continue* more *years*] *Seleucus Callinicus* died (an exile) by a fall from his horse; and *Ptolemy Euergetes* survived him four or five years.—Bp. *Newton.*

Verse 9. *So the king of the south*] Ptolemy Euergetes—

Shall come into his *kingdom*] That of Seleucus Callinicus.

And shall return] Having heard that a sedition had taken place in Egypt, Ptolemy Euergetes was obliged to return speedily in order to repress it; else he had wholly destroyed the kingdom of Callinicus.

Verse 10. *But his sons shall be stirred up*] That is, the sons of *Callinicus*, who were *Seleucus Ceraunus* and *Antiochus*, afterwards called *the Great.*

Shall assemble a multitude] Seleucus Ceraunus did assemble a multitude of forces in order to recover his father's dominions; but, not having money to pay them, they became mutinous, and he was poisoned by two of his own generals. His brother Antiochus was then proclaimed king; so that *one only* of the sons did *certainly come, and overflow, and pass through;* he retook Seleucia, and regained Syria. He *then returned*, and overcame Nicolaus the Egyptian general; and seemed disposed to invade Egypt, as he came even to *his fortress*, to the frontiers of Egypt.

A. M. 3470
B. C. 534
Olymp. LXI. 3
Anno Tarquinii Superbi,
R. Roman., 1

and *one* shall certainly come, [n]and overflow, and pass through: [o]then shall he return, and be stirred up, [p]*even* to his fortress.
11 And the king of the south shall be moved with choler, and shall come forth and fight with him, *even* with the king of the north: and he shall set forth a great multitude; but the multitude shall be given into his hand.
12 *And* when he hath taken away the multitude, his heart shall be lifted up; and he shall cast down *many* ten thousands: but he shall not be strengthened *by it.*
13 For the king of the north shall return, and shall set forth a multitude greater than the former, and shall certainly come [q]after certain years with a great army and with much riches.
14 And in those times there shall many stand up against the king of the south: also [r]the robbers of thy people shall exalt themselves to establish the vision; but they shall fall.
15 So the king of the north shall come, and cast up a mount, and take [s]the most fenced cities: and the arms of the south shall not withstand, neither [t]his chosen people, neither *shall there be any* strength to withstand.
16 But he that cometh against him [u]shall do according to his own will, and [v]none shall stand before him: and he shall stand in the [w]glorious [x]land, which by his hand shall be consumed.
17 He shall also [y]set his face to enter with the strength of his whole kingdom, and [z]up-

[n]Isa. viii. 8; chap. ix. 26——[o]Or, *then shall he be stirred up again*——[p]Ver. 7——[q]Heb. *at the end of times, even years;* chap. iv. 16; xii. 7——[r]Heb. *the children of robbers*——[s]Heb. *the city of munitions*

[t]Heb. *the people of his choices*——[u]Ch. viii. 4, 7: ver. 3, 36——[v]Josh. i. 5——[w]Or, *goodly land;* ch. viii .9; ver. 41, 45——[x]Heb. *the land of ornament*——[y]2 Chron. xx. 3 [z]Or, *much uprightness,* or *equal conditions*

Verse 11. *The king of the south*] Ptolemy Philopater, who succeeded his father *Euergetes.*

Shall come forth and fight with him] He did come forth to Raphia, where he was met by Antiochus, when a terrible battle was fought between these two kings.

And he (Antiochus, the king of the north) *shall set forth a great multitude*] Amounting to *sixty-two thousand* foot, *six thousand* horse, and *one hundred and two* elephants; but yet the multitude was *given into his hand,* the hand of the *king of the south;* for Ptolemy gained a complete victory. Raphia, and other neighbouring towns, declared for the victor; and Antiochus was obliged to retreat with his scattered army to Antioch, from which he sent to solicit a peace. See 3 Macc. i. 1-6, and *Polybius,* lib. v.

Verse 12. *His heart shall be lifted up*] Had Ptolemy improved his victory, he might have dispossessed Antiochus of his whole empire; but giving way to *pride,* and a criminally *sensual life,* he made peace on dishonourable terms; and though he had gained a great victory, yet his kingdom *was not strengthened by it,* for his subjects were displeased, and rebelled against him, or at least became considerably disaffected.

Verse 13. *The king of the north shall return —after certain years*] In about *fourteen* years Antiochus did return, Philopater being dead, and his son Ptolemy Epiphanes being then a minor. He brought a much larger army and more riches; these he had collected in a late eastern expedition.

Verse 14. *Many stand up against the king of the south*] Antiochus, and Philip king of Macedon, united together to overrun Egypt.

Also the robbers of thy people] The *Jews,* who revolted from their religion, and joined Ptolemy, under *Scopas,*—

Shall exalt themselves to establish the vision] That is, to build a temple like that of Jerusalem, in Egypt, hoping thereby to fulfil a prediction of Isaiah, chap. xxx. 18-25, which seemed to intimate that the Jews and the Egyptians should be one people. They now revolted from Ptolemy, and joined Antiochus; and this was the means of contributing greatly to the accomplishment of prophecies that foretold the calamities that should fall upon the Jews.

But they shall fall.] For Scopas came with a great army from Ptolemy; and, while Antiochus was engaged in other parts, reduced *Cœlesyria* and *Palestine,* subdued the Jews, placed guards on the coasts of Jerusalem, and returned with great spoils to Egypt.

Verse 15. *So the king of the north*] Antiochus came to recover Judea. Scopas was sent by Ptolemy to oppose him; but he was defeated near the fountains of Jordan, and was obliged to take refuge in *Sidon* with *ten thousand* men. Antiochus pursued and besieged him; and he was obliged by famine to surrender at discretion, and their lives only were spared. Antiochus afterwards besieged *several of the fenced cities,* and took them; in short, carried all before him; so that the king of the south, Ptolemy, and *his chosen people,* his ablest generals, were not able to oppose him.

Verse 16. *He shall stand in the glorious land*] Judea. For he reduced *Palestine;* and the Jews supplied him with provisions, and assisted him to reduce the garrison that Scopas had left in the citadel of Jerusalem.

Which by his hand shall be consumed] Or, *which shall be perfected in his hand.* For Antiochus showed the Jews great favour: he brought back those that were dispersed, and reestablished them in the land; freed the priests and Levites from all tribute, &c.

Verse 17. *He shall also set his face to enter*]

A. M. 3470
B. C. 534
Olymp. LXI. 3
Anno Tarquinii
Superbi,
R. Roman., 1

right ones with him; thus shall
he do: and he shall give him
the daughter of women, [a]cor-
rupting her: but she shall not
stand *on his side,* [b]neither be for him.
18 After this shall he turn his face unto the
isles, and shall take many: but a prince [c]for
his own behalf shall cause [d]the reproach offered by him to cease; without his own reproach he shall cause *it* to turn upon him.
19 Then he shall turn his face toward the
fort of his own land: but he
shall stumble and fall, [e]and not
be found.
20 Then shall stand up [f]in his
estate [g]a raiser of taxes *in* the glory of the
kingdom: but within few days he shall be
destroyed, neither in [h]anger, nor in battle.
21 And [i]in his estate [k]shall stand up a vile
person, to whom they shall not give the honour
of the kingdom: but he shall come in peaceably, and obtain the kingdom by flatteries.

[a]Heb. *to corrupt*——[b]Chap. ix. 26——[c]Heb. *for him* [d]Heb. *his reproach*——[e]Job xx. 8; Psa. xxxvii. 36; Ezek. xxvi. 21——[f]Or, *in his place;* ver. 7

[g]Heb. *one that causeth an exactor to pass over*——[h]Heb. *angers*——[i]Or, *in his place*——[k]Chap. vii. 8; viii. 9 23, 25

Antiochus purposed to have marched his army into Egypt; but he thought it best to proceed by *fraudulence;* and therefore proposed a treaty of marriage between him and his daughter Cleopatra, called here *the daughter of women*, because of her great beauty and accomplishments. And this he appeared to do, having "upright ones with him." Or, as the *Septuagint* have it και ευθεια παντα μετ' αυτου ποιησει, "and he will make all things straight with him;" that is, he acted as if he were influenced by nothing but the most *upright views*. But he intended his daughter to be a snare to Ptolemy, and therefore purposed to *corrupt her* that she might betray her husband.

But she shall not stand on his side] On the contrary, her husband's interests became more dear to her than her father's; and by her means Ptolemy was put upon his guard against the intentions of Antiochus.

Verse 18. *Shall he turn his face unto the isles*] Antiochus had fitted out a great fleet of *one hundred* large ships and *two hundred* smaller, and with this fleet subdued most of the *maritime places* on the *coast* of the Mediterranean, and took many of the isles, *Rhodes*, *Samos*, *Eubœa*, *Colophon*, and others.

But a prince for his own behalf] Or, *a captain.* The consul *Acilius Glabrio caused the reproach to cease;* beat and routed his army at the straits of Thermopylæ, and expelled him from Greece. So he obliged him to pay the tribute which he hoped to impose on others; for he would grant him peace only on condition of paying the expense of the war, *fifteen thousand* talents; *five hundred* on the spot,—*two thousand five hundred* when the peace should be ratified by the senate,—and the remaining *twelve thousand* in *twelve* years, each year *one thousand.* See *Polybius* in his Legations, and *Appian* in the Wars of Syria. And thus,—

Without his own reproach] Without losing a battle, or taking a false step, *Acilius* caused *the reproach* which he was bringing upon the Romans *to turn upon himself.*

Verse 19. *He shall turn his face toward the fort of his own land*] After this shameful defeat, Antiochus fled to Sardis, thence to Apamea, and the next day got into Syria, and to *Antioch*, his *own fort*, whence he sent ambassadors to treat for peace; and was obliged to engage to pay the immense sum of money mentioned above.

But he shall stumble and fall] Being under the greatest difficulties how to raise the stipulated sums, he marched into his eastern provinces to exact the arrears of taxes; and, attempting to plunder the temple of *Jupiter Belus* at Elymais, he was opposed by the populace, and he and his attendants slain. This is the account that *Diodorus Siculus*, *Strabo*, and *Justin* give of his death. But it is variously related by others; some saying that he was assassinated by some of his own people whom he had punished for being drunk at a feast.—So *Aurelius Victor*. St. *Jerome* says he lost his life in a battle against the inhabitants of Elymais. In short, the manner of his death is uncertain; and perhaps even this circumstance is referred to by the prophet, when he says, "He shall stumble and fall, and NOT BE FOUND."

Verse 20. *Then shall stand up in his estate a raiser of taxes*] *Seleucus Philopater* succeeded his father *Antiochus*. He sent his treasurer *Heliodorus* to seize the money deposited in the temple of Jerusalem, which is here called *the glory of the kingdom*, see 2 Macc. ix. 23. He was so cramped to pay the annual tax to the Romans, that he was obliged to burden his subjects with continual taxes.

He shall be destroyed, neither in anger—fighting against an enemy, *nor in battle*—at the head of his troops; but basely and treacherously, by the hand of *Heliodorus* his treasurer, who hoped to reign in his stead.

Verse 21. *In his estate shall stand up a vile person*] This was Antiochus, surnamed *Epiphanes—the Illustrious.* They *did not give him the honour of the kingdom:* he was at Athens, on his way from Rome, when his father died; and Heliodorus had declared himself king, as had several others. But *Antiochus came in peaceably*, for he obtained *the kingdom by flatteries.* He *flattered Eumenes*, king of Pergamus, and *Attalus* his brother, and got their assistance. He *flattered* the Romans, and sent ambassadors to court their favour, and pay them the arrears of the tribute. He *flattered* the Syrians, and gained their concurrence; and as he *flattered* the Syrians, so they flattered him, giving him the epithet of *Epiphanes*—the *Illustrious.* But that he was what the prophet here calls him, a *vile person*, is fully evident from what *Polybius* says of him, from *Athenæus*, lib. v.: "He was every man's companion: he resorted to the common shops, and prattled with the workmen: he frequented the common taverns, and ate and drank with the meanest fellows, singing debauched songs,"

A. M. 3470 B. C. 534 Ol. LXI. 3 Anno Tarquinii Superbi, R. Roman., 1

22 [l]And with the arms of a flood shall they be overflown from before him, and shall be broken; [m]yea, also the prince of the covenant.

23 And after the league *made* with him [n]he shall work deceitfully: for he shall come up, and shall become strong with a small people.

24 He shall enter [o]peaceably even upon the fattest places of the province; and he shall do *that* which his fathers have not done, nor his fathers' fathers; [p]he shall scatter among them the prey, and spoil, and riches: *yea,* and he shall [q]forecast his devices against the strong holds, even for a time.

A. M. 3470 B. C. 534 Olymp. LXI. 3 Anno Tarquinii Superbi, R. Roman., 1

25 And he shall stir up his power and his courage against the king of the south with a great army; and the king of the south shall be stirred up to battle with a very great and mighty army; but he shall not stand: for they shall forecast devices against him.

26 Yea, they that feed of the portion of his meat shall destroy him, and his army shall [r]overflow: and many shall fall down slain.

27 And both these kings' [s]hearts *shall be* to

[l]Ver. 10——[m]Chap. viii. 10, 11, 25——[n]Chap. viii. 25 [o]Or, *into the peaceable and fat,* &c.

[p]1 Mac. iii. 28, &c.——[q]Heb. *think his thoughts*——[r]Ver. 10, 22——[s]Heb. *their hearts*

&c., &c. On this account a contemporary writer, and others after him, instead of *Epiphanes,* called him *Epimanes*—the *Madman.*

Verse 22. *And with the arms of a flood*] The arms which were *overflown* before him were his competitors for the crown. They were vanquished by the forces of Eumenes and Attalus; and were dissipated by the arrival of Antiochus from Athens, whose presence disconcerted all their measures.

The prince of the covenant] This was *Onias,* the high priest, whom he removed, and put *Jason* in his place, who had given him a great sum of money; and then put wicked *Menelaus* in his room, who had offered him a larger sum. Thus he acted *deceitfully* in the *league* made with *Jason.*

Verse 23. *He shall come up*] From Rome, where he had been a hostage for the payment of the tax laid on his father.

Shall become strong with a small people.] At first he had but *few* to espouse his cause when he arrived at *Antioch,* the people having been greatly divided by the many claimants of the crown; but being supported by Eumenes and Attalus, his *few people* increased, and he became *strong.*

Verse 24. *He shall enter peaceably even upon the fattest places*] The very richest provinces—Cœlesyria and Palestine.

He shall do that *which his fathers have not done, nor his fathers' fathers*] He became profuse in his liberalities, and *scattered among them the prey* of his enemies, *the spoil* of temples, and *the riches* of his friends, as well as his own revenues. He spent much in public shows, and bestowed largesses among the people. We are told in 1 Macc. iii. 30, that "in the liberal giving of gifts he abounded above all the kings that went before him." These are nearly the words of the prophet; and perhaps without any design to copy them on the part of the apocryphal writer. He would sometimes go into the streets, and throw about a handful of money, crying out, "Let him take it, to whom Fortune sends it."

He shall forecast his devices] As Eulæus and Lenæus, who were the guardians of the young Egyptian king Ptolemy Philometer, demanded from Antiochus the restitution of Cœlesyria and Palestine, which he refused, he foresaw that he might have a war with that kingdom; and therefore *he forecast devices*—fixed a variety of plans to prevent this; visited the *strong holds* and frontier places to see that they were in a state of defence. And this he did *for a time*—he employed some years in hostile preparations against Egypt.

Verse 25. *He shall stir up his power*] Antiochus marched against Ptolemy, *the king of the south,* (Egypt,) with a great army; and the Egyptian generals had raised a *mighty force.*

Stirred up to battle] The two armies met between Pelusium and Mount Casius; *but he* (the king of the south) *could not stand*—the Egyptian army was defeated. The next campaign he had greater success; he routed the Egyptian army, took Memphis, and made himself master of all Egypt, except *Alexandria,* see 1 Macc. i. 16-19. And all these advantages he gained by *forecasting devices;* probably by *corrupting* his ministers and captains. Ptolemy Macron gave up Cyprus to Antiochus; and the Alexandrians were led to renounce their allegiance to Potlemy Philometer, and took *Euergetes,* or Physcon his younger brother, and made him king in his stead. All this was doubtless by the *corruptions* of Antiochus. See below.

Verse 26. *Yea, they that feed of the portion of his meat*] This is the proof of what has been last noted, that the intrigues of Antiochus, *corrupting* the *ministers* and *officers* of Ptolemy, were the cause of all the disasters that fell on the Egyptian king. They *that fed of the portion of his meat*—who were in his confidence and pay, and possessed the secrets of the state, betrayed him; and these were the means of destroying *him and his army,* so that he was defeated, as was before observed.

Verse 27. *And both these kings' hearts* shall be *to do mischief*] That is, *Antiochus,* and *Ptolemy Philometer,* who was nephew to the former, and whose interest he now pretended to have much at heart, since the Alexandrians had renounced their allegiance to him, and set his younger brother *Euergetes* upon the throne. When Antiochus came to Memphis, he and Philometer had frequent conferences at the *same table;* and at these times they *spoke lies* to each other, Antiochus professing great friendship to his nephew and concern for his interests, yet in his heart designing to ruin the

A. M. 3470
B. C. 534
Olymp. LXI. 3
Anno Tarquinii
Superbi,
R. Roman., 1

do mischief, and they shall speak
lies at one table; but it shall
not prosper: for [t]yet the end
shall be at the time appointed.

28 Then shall he return into his land [u]with
great riches; and [v]his heart *shall be* against
the holy covenant; and he shall do *exploits,*
and return to his own land.

29 At the time appointed he
shall return, and come toward
the south; [w]but it shall not be
as the former, [x]or as the latter.

30 [y]For the ships of Chittim shall come
against him: therefore he shall be grieved,
and return, and have indignation [z]against the
holy covenant: so shall he do; he shall even

[t]Ver. 29, 35, 40; chap. viii. 19——[u]1 Mac. i. 19
[v]Ver. 22; 1 Mac. i. 20, &c.; 2 Mac. v. 11, 14, &c.

[w]Ver. 23——[x]Ver. 25——[y]Num. xxiv. 24; Jer. ii. 10
[z]Ver. 28; 1 Mac. i. 30, 44, &c.; 2 Mac. v. 24, &c.

kingdom by fomenting the discords which already subsisted between the two brothers. On the other hand, Philometer professed much *gratitude* to his uncle for the interest he took in his affairs, and laid the blame of the war upon his minister Eulæus; while at the same time he *spoke lies*, determining as soon as possible to accommodate matters with his brother, and join all their strength against their deceitful uncle.

But it shall not prosper] Neither succeeded in his object; for *the end* of the *appointed time* was not yet come.

Verse 28. *Then shall he return into his land with great riches*] Antiochus did return, laden with riches, from the spoils that he took in Egypt; see 1 Macc. i. 19, 20. And hearing that there had been a report of his death, at which the citizens of Jerusalem had made great rejoicings,—

His heart shall be *against the holy covenant*] He was determined to take a severe revenge, and he had an ostensible pretext for it; for Jason, who had been deprived of the high priesthood, hearing the report of the death of Antiochus, raised forces, marched against Jerusalem, took it, and obliged Menelaus, the high priest, to shut himself up in the castle. Antiochus brought a great army against Jerusalem; took it by storm; slew *forty thousand* of the inhabitants; sold as many more for *slaves;* boiled swine's flesh, and sprinkled the temple and the altar with the broth; broke into the holy of holies; took away the golden vessels and other sacred treasures, to the value of *one thousand eight hundred* talents; restored Menelaus to his office; and made one *Philip*, a Phrygian, governor of Judea. 1 Macc. i. 24; 2 Macc. v. 21. *Prideaux* and *Newton.* These are what we term *exploits;* which having finished, *he returned to his own land.*

Verse 29. *At the time appointed he shall return*] Finding that his treachery was detected, and that the two brothers had united their counsel and strength for their mutual support, he threw off the mask; and having collected a great army early in the spring, he passed through *Cœlesyria;* entered Egypt; and the inhabitants of Memphis having submitted to him, he came by easy marches to Alexandria. But, says the prophet, "it shall not be as the former or as the latter:" he had not the *same success* as the *former*, when he overthrew the Egyptian army at *Pelusium;* nor as the *latter*, when he took *Memphis*, and subdued all Egypt, except *Alexandria.* See the reason.

Verse 30. *For the ships of Chittim shall come against him*] *Chittim* is well known to mean the *Roman empire.* Antiochus, being now in full march to besiege Alexandria, and within *seven miles* of that city, heard that ships were arrived there from Rome, with *legates* from the senate. He went to salute them. They delivered to him the letters of the senate, in which he was commanded, on pain of the displeasure of the Roman people, to put an end to the war against his nephews. Antiochus said he would go and consult his friends; on which *Popilius*, one of the legates, took his staff, and instantly drew a circle round Antiochus on the sand where he stood, and commanded him not to pass that circle till he had given a definitive answer. Antiochus, intimidated, said, *he would do whatever the senate enjoined;* and in a few days after began his march, and returned to Syria. This is confirmed by *Polybius, Livy, Velleius, Paterculus, Valerius Maximus*, and *Justin.*

Therefore he shall be grieved] "Grieving and groaning," says Polybius; both mortified, humbled, and disappointed.

Have indignation against the holy covenant] For he vented his rage against the Jews; and he sent his general, *Apollonius*, with *twenty-two thousand* men against Jerusalem, plundered and set fire to the city, pulled down the houses round about it, slew much of the people, and built a castle on an eminence that commanded the temple, and slew multitudes of the poor people who had come up to worship, polluted every place, so that the temple service was totally abandoned, and all the people fled from the city. And when he returned to Antioch he published a decree that all should conform to the *Grecian worship;* and the Jewish worship was totally abrogated, and the temple itself consecrated to *Jupiter Olympius.* How great must the wickedness of the people have been when God could tolerate this!

In the transacting of these matters *he had intelligence with them that forsake the holy covenant;* with wicked *Menelaus* the high priest; and the *apostate Jews* united with him, who gave from time to time such information to Antiochus as excited him against Jerusalem, the temple, and the people. See 1 Macc. i. 41, 62; 2 Macc. vi. 1-9; confirmed by *Josephus*, War, book i. chap. 1, s. 1. The concluding reflection of Bp. *Newton* here is excellent:—

"It may be proper to stand a little here, and reflect how particular and circumstantial this prophecy is, concerning Egypt and Syria, from the death of *Alexander* to the time of *Antiochus Epiphanes.* There is not so concise, comprehensive, and regular an account of their kings and affairs to be found in any authors of those times. The prophecy is really more perfect

A. M. 3470
B. C. 534
Olymp. LXI. 3
Anno Tarquinii Superbi,
R. Roman., 1

return, [a]and have intelligence
with them that forsake the holy
covenant.
31 And arms shall stand on his
part, [b]and they shall pollute the sanctuary of
strength, and shall take away the daily *sacrifice,* [c]and they shall place the abomination
that [d]maketh desolate.
32 [e]And such as do wickedly against the
covenant shall he [f]corrupt by flatteries: [g]but
the people that do know their God
shall be strong, and do *exploits.*
33 [h]And they that understand
among the people shall instruct
many: [i]yet they shall fall by the sword, and by
flame, by captivity, and by spoil, *many* days.
34 Now when they shall fall, they [k]shall be
holpen with a little help: [l]but many shall
cleave to them with flatteries.
35 And *some* of them of understanding shall

[a]1 Mac. i. 43, 52; 2 Mac. v. 15, 23——[b]Chap. viii. 11; xii. 11; 1 Mac. i. 37, 39, 41, 45, 46——[c]1 Mac. i. 54, 59; iv. 38——[d]Or, *astonisheth*——[e]1 Mac. i. 43, 52; 2 Mac. iv. 13, 14; v. 15

[f]Or, *cause to dissemble*——[g]1 Mac. i. 62; ii. 41, 42, 43; 2 Mac. v. 27; vi. 19, 20; vii. 1, &c.——[h]Mal. ii. 7 [i]Heb. xi. 35, &c.——[k]1 Mac. iii. 2; 2 Mac. viii. 1 [l]2 Mac. xii. 40; xiii. 21

than any *history,* and is so wonderfully exact, not only *to the time* of Antiochus Epiphanes, but likewise equally so *beyond that time,* that we may conclude in the words of the inspired writer, 'No one could thus declare *the times and seasons,* but he who *hath them in his own power.*' "

Verse 31. *And arms shall stand on his part*] After Antiochus, *arms,* that is, the Romans, *shall stand up:* for *arms* in this prophecy every where denote *military power;* and *standing up,* the power in *activity* and *conquering.* Both Sir *Isaac Newton* and Bp. *Newton* agree, that what follows is spoken of the *Romans.* Hitherto Daniel has described the actions of the kings of the *north* and of the *south,* that of the kings of *Syria* and *Egypt;* but, upon the conquest of Macedon by the Romans, he has left off describing the actions of the Greeks, and begun to describe those of the *Romans in Greece,* who conquered Macedon, Illyricum, and Epirus, in the year of the era of *Nabonassar,* 580. *Thirty-five* years after, by the *will* of *Attalus,* they inherited all Asia westward of Mount Taurus; *sixty-five* years after they conquered the kingdom of Syria, and reduced it into a province; and *thirty-four* years after they did the same to Egypt. By all these steps the Roman *arms stood up* over the Greeks; and after *ninety-five years* more, by making war upon the Jews, *they polluted the sanctuary of strength,*—the temple, (so called by reason of its *fortifications,*) *and took away the daily* sacrifice *and placed the abomination that maketh desolate,* or of the *desolator;* for that this *abomination* was thus placed *after* the time of Christ, appears from Matt. xxiv. 15.

In the *sixteenth* year of the Emperor Adrian, A. D. 132, they placed this *abomination* by building a temple to *Jupiter Capitolinus,* where the temple of God in Jerusalem stood; upon which the Jews, under *Barchocab,* rose up against the Romans. But in this war they had *fifty* cities demolished, *nine hundred and fifty* of their best towns destroyed, and *eighty thousand* men were slain by the sword; and in the end of the war, A. D. 136, were banished Judea on pain of death; and thenceforth the land *became desolate.* See Observations on Daniel, and Bp. Newton on the Prophecies.

Verse 32. *Such as do wickedly against the covenant*] This is understood of the *Christian Jews;* for the NEW had now succeeded to the OLD, the whole of the Jewish ritual having been abolished, and Jerusalem filled with heathen *temples. And he*—the Roman power, did all he could by *flatteries,* as well as threats, to *corrupt* the Christians, and cause them to sacrifice to the statues of the emperors.

But the people that do know their God] The genuine Christians.

Shall be strong] Shall be strengthened by his grace and Spirit.

And do exploits.] Continue steadfast in all temptations, hold fast their faith, and enjoy a good conscience.

Verse 33. *And they that understand*] The *apostles* and *primitive Christians* in general, who *understood* from the *prophets,* and his own *actions,* that JESUS was the true MESSIAH.

Instruct many] Preach the Gospel every where, and convert multitudes to the faith.

Yet they shall fall by the sword, and by flame, by captivity, and by spoil, many *days.*] They were exposed to the malice and fury of their enemies, during TEN STATE PERSECUTIONS, and suffered all kinds of tortures, with but little intermission, for *three hundred* years.—*Newton.*

Verse 34. *Now when they shall fall*] When the storm of the *tenth* persecution under *Diocletian,* which lasted *ten* years, *fell upon them,* they were sorely oppressed.

They shall be holpen with a little help] By Constantine; who, while he removed all persecution, and promoted the temporal prosperity of the Christian Church, yet added little to its spiritual perfection and strength. For many, now seeing the Christians in prosperity,—

Cleave to them with flatteries.] Became *Christians* BECAUSE the EMPEROR was *such.*

Verse 35. *And some of them of understanding*] Disputes on certain points of religion soon agitated the Christian Church; and now, having no outward persecution, they began to persecute each other. And many excellent men, *men of understanding, fell* victims because they would not embrace erroneous doctrines, when professed by the *state.* But this was permitted,—

To try them, and to purge, and to make them *white*] To bring all to the pure profession, possession, and practice of Christianity.

To the time of the end] To the time that God shall cause pure and undefiled religion every where to prevail. But when is the time appointed for this?

A. M. 3470
B. C. 534
Olymp. LXI. 3
Anno Tarquinii Superbi,
R. Roman., 1

fall, [m]to try [n]them, and to purge, and to make *them* white, [o]*even* to the time of the end: [p]because *it is* yet for a time appointed.

36 And the king [q]shall do according to his will; and he shall [r]exalt himself, and magnify himself above every god, and shall speak marvellous things [s]against the God of gods, and shall prosper [t]till the indignation be accomplished: for that that is determined shall be done.

A. M. 3470
B. C. 534
Olymp. XLI. 3
Anno Tarquinii Superbi,
R. Roman., 1

37 Neither shall he regard the God of his fathers, [u]nor the desire of women, [v]nor regard any god: for he shall magnify himself above all.

38 [w]But [x]in his estate shall he honour the god of [y]forces: [z]and a god whom his fathers knew not shall he honor with gold, and silver, and with precious stones, and [a]pleasant things.

39 Thus shall he do in the [b]most strong holds with a strange god, whom he shall ac-

[m]Chap. xii. 10; 1 Pet. i. 7——[n]Or, *by them*——[o]Chap. viii. 17, 19; ver. 40——[p]Ver. 29——[q]Ver. 16——[r]Chap. vii. 8, 25; viii. 25; 2 Thess. ii. 4; Rev. xiii. 5, 6——[s]Chap. viii. 11, 24, 25——[t]Chap. ix. 27——[u]1 Tim. iv. 3 [v]Isa. xiv. 13; 2 Thess. ii. 4

[w]Or, *But in his stead*——[x]Heb. *as for the Almighty God, in his seat he shall honour, yea, he shall honour a god, whom, &c.*——[y]Or, *munitions*——[z]Hebrew, *Mauzzim*, or *gods protectors*——[a]Heb. *things desired;* Isa. xliv. 9 [b]Hebrew, *fortresses of munitions*

Verse 36. *And the king shall do according to his will*] This may apply to *Antiochus*, who exalted himself above every god, called himself a god, sported with all religion, profaned the temple, &c., &c. But others think an *antichristian power* in the Church is intended; for in the language of this prophecy *king* is taken for *power*, a *kingdom*, &c. That such a power did spring up in the Church that acted in an arbitrary manner against all laws, human and Divine, is well known. This power showed itself in the *Greek emperors* in the *east*, and in the *bishops of Rome* in the *west*. And this is to continue.

Till the indignation be accomplished: for that that is determined shall be done.] This is the same as what was called in chap. viii. 19, *the last end of the indignation;* and chap. ix. 27, *the consummation;* and means the *end* or *consummation* of God's indignation against the Jews. And this seems more clearly expressed, chap. xii. 7: "When he shall have accomplished to scatter the power of the holy people." We see this still subsisting in the Church of Rome; and it was a saying of *Rabbi David Kimchi*, "When Rome shall be laid waste, then shall be redemption for Israel." For the destruction of Rome and the restoration of the Jews shall fall out about the same time.—Bp. *Newton.*

Verse 37. *Neither shall he regard the God of his fathers*] That God who sent the *evangelists* and *apostles* to preach the *pure doctrine.* These *true fathers of the Christian Church*, and their God, this Church has not regarded, but put *councils*, and *traditions*, and *apocryphal writings* in their place.

Nor the desire of women] Both the Greek and Latin Church, in their antichristian enactments, have discouraged, and in several cases *proscribed, marriage*, under the pretence of *greater chastity*, to the discredit of God's ordinance, and Christianity itself.

Nor regard any god] For the mandates and decrees of that Church have been often in defiance of God and his word; for it has magnified itself above all power and authority in heaven and on earth. It professes to hold the keys, and to open and shut heaven at pleasure, both to states and individuals.

Verse 38. *Shall he honour the god of forces*] מעזים *mauzzim*, or *gods protectors*, as in the *margin;* worshipping *saints* and *angels* as *guardians*, and *protectors*, and *mediators;* leaving out, in general, the *true God*, and the *only Mediator*, Jesus Christ.

And a god whom his fathers knew not] For these *gods guardians*, the *Virgin Mary, saints*, and *angels*, were utterly unknown as *mediators* and *invocable guardians* in the primitive apostolic Church.

Shall he honour with gold, and silver, and with precious stones] How literally does this apply to the *Church of Rome!* See the house of our lady at *Loretto;* the *shrines of saints;* the *decorated images, costly apparel, gold, jewels*, &c., profusely used about *images of saints, angels*, and the *blessed virgin*, in different popish churches. This superstition began to prevail in the *fourth* century, and was established in 787, by the *seventh* general council; for in that the *worship of images* was enacted.

Verse 39. *In the most strong holds with a strange god*] Bishop *Newton* proposed the following translation, after justly finding fault with our common Version: "Thus shall he do to the defenders of Mauzzim, together with the strange god whom he shall acknowledge: he shall multiply honour, and he shall cause him to rule over many; and the earth he shall divide for a reward." The *defenders* of *Mauzzim*, these saint and angel *gods protectors*, were the monks, priests, and bishops; of whom it may be truly said, "They were increased with honour, ruled over many, and divided the land for gain." They have been honoured and reverenced almost to adoration; their jurisdiction was extended over the *purses* and *consciences* of men; they have been enriched with the noblest buildings and largest endowments, and the *choicest lands* have been appropriated for Church *lands.* These are points of such public notoriety, that they require no proof.—*Newton.*

Verse 40. *At the time of the end shall the king of the south push at him*] These kings are to be understood in reference to the times of which the prophet speaks. While the kingdoms of *Egypt* and *Syria* were subsisting, the *king of the south and the north* applied to them exclusively: but they did not exist at the time of which the prophet speaks; therefore *other southern* and *northern* powers must be sought. These we may find in the *Saracens*, who were of the *Arabians*, who came from the *south*, headed by the false prophet *Mohammed*, who

A. M. 3470 B. C. 534 Olymp. LXI. 3 Anno Tarquinii Superbi, R. Roman., 1

knowledge *and* increase with
glory: and he shall cause them
to rule over many, and shall
divide the land for [c]gain.

40 [d]And at the time of the end shall the
king of the south push at him: and the king
of the north shall come against him [e]like a
whirlwind, with chariots, [f]and with horsemen, and with many ships; and he shall enter
into the countries, [g]and shall overflow and
pass over.

41 He shall enter also into the [h]glorious[i]
land, and many *countries* shall be overthrown: but these shall escape out of his
hands, [k]*even* Edom, and Moab, and the chief
of the children of Ammon.

42 He shall [l]stretch forth his
hand also upon the countries:
and the land of Egypt shall not
escape.

43 But he shall have power over the treasures of gold and of silver, and over all the
precious things of Egypt: and the Libyans
and the Ethiopians *shall be* [m]at his steps.

44 But tidings out of the east and out of
the north shall trouble him: therefore he shall
go forth with great fury to destroy, and
utterly to make away many.

45 And he shall plant the tabernacles of his
palaces between the seas in [n]the [o]glorious[p]
holy mountain; [q]yet he shall come to his end
and none shall help him.

[c]Heb. *a price*——[d]Ver. 35——[e]Psa. lviii. 9; Prov. i. 27; x. 25; Isa. xxi. 1; xl. 24; xli. 16; lxvi. 15; Zech. ix. 14——[f]Ezek. xxxviii. 4, 15; Rev. ix. 16——[g]Ver. 10, 22——[h]Or, *goodly land;* ver. 16——[i]Heb. *land of delight*, or *ornament*

[k]Isa. xi. 14——[l]Heb. *send forth*——[m]Exod. xi. 8; Judg. iv. 10——[n]Psa. xlviii. 2; ver. 16, 41; 2 Thess. ii. 4——[o]Or, *goodly*——[p]Hebrew, *mountain of delight of holiness*——[q]1 Mac. vi. 8–16; 2 Thess. ii. 8; Revelation xix. 20

pushed at him—made war on the *Greek emperor Heraclius*, and with amazing rapidity deprived him of Egypt, Syria, and many of his finest provinces.

And the king of the north] The *Turks*, who were originally *Scythians*, seized on the remains of the Greek empire; and in process of time rendered themselves masters of the whole. They are represented as coming like a *whirlwind, with chariots, and with horsemen;* their armies being chiefly composed of *cavalry*.

And with many ships] With these they got possession of many *islands* and *maritime countries;* and were so powerful in their fleets, that they entirely defeated the Venetians; and at last their fleets became of the utmost consequence to them in besieging, and afterwards taking, *Constantinople*, A. D. 1453, which they hold to the present day. So *they entered into the countries, and overflowed*, rendering themselves masters of all Asia Minor and Greece.

Verse 41. *He shall enter also into the glorious land*] Entirely subdue Judea.

And many countries *shall be overthrown*] Aleppo, Damascus, Gaza, and many other cities were forced to submit to them; and they hold them still.

But these shall escape—Edom and Moab, and the chief of the children of Ammon.] These and other Arabians they have never been able to subdue. They still occupy the deserts; and receive a yearly pension of *forty thousand* crowns of gold from the Ottoman emperors, to permit the caravans, with the pilgrims for Mecca, to have a free passage.

Verse 42. *He shall stretch forth his hand*] *He*—the *Ottoman emperors*, have *stretched forth the hand*, not only on *European*, but also upon *Asiatic* and *African* countries. *Egypt* has not escaped; it is a province of the Turkish government, as are also Fez, Morocco, Algiers, and many other African countries. And as the prophecy says they "got power over the silver and gold, and the precious things of Egypt," so it was; for when *Selim* conquered Egypt, A. D. 1517, he took all its spoils; and the immense sums drawn from it to the present day, and the wretchedness of the land in consequence, are almost incredible.

The Libyans and the Ethiopians] The *Cushim*—unconquered *Arabs*, all sought their friendship; and many of them are tributary to the present time.

Verse 44. *But tidings out of the east and out of the north shall trouble him*] This part of the prophecy is allowed to be yet *unfulfilled;* and what is portented, the course of prophetic events will show. Were we to understand it as applying to *Antiochus*, then the *news* might be of the *preparations* which he heard, that the provinces of the *east*, and *Artaxerxes*, king of *Armenia*, on the *north*, were intending to rise up against him. But if the *Turkish* power be understood, as in the preceding verses, it may mean that the *Persians* on the *east*, and the *Russians* on the *north*, will at some time greatly embarrass the Ottoman government. And how completely has this been fulfilled; first, by the total destruction of the Egyptian fleet, by the combined fleets of England, France, and Russia, in the Bay of Navarino; and, secondly, by the total overthrow of the Turkish army by the Russians, in the years 1828 and 1829, when the sultan was obliged to accept any conditions that the emperor of Russia was pleased to give! [N.B.—The former part of this note was written for the first edition of this work, printed in 1825.]

Verse 45. *He shall plant the tabernacles*] He shall make a last stand in *Judea*, and there shall his power be smitten.

He shall come to his end, and none shall help him.] All his confederate and tributary kingdoms, states, and provinces shall desert him, and leave that government to come to a shameful end.

In the interpretation of this chapter I have generally followed Bp. *Newton*, in his most excellent *Dissertations on the Prophecies*, consulting other eminent authors occasionally.

From the beginning of the chapter to the end of ver. 30 all is very clear and plain, relative to the Grecian, Syrian, and Egyptian histories; from the *thirty-first* verse to the end, the mode of interpretation is not so satisfactory, in its application to the times since Christ. Yet possibly these alone may be intended; though the whole might be, with considerable ease, applied to the remaining part of the *Syrian* and *Egyptian* history. It is a wonderful piece of prophecy, and of great utility to the cause of Divine revelation.

CHAPTER XII

The proper conclusion to the great revolutions predicted in this and the following chapters is the general resurrection, *of which the beginning of this chapter (if to be literally understood) gives some intimation,* 1–3. *Daniel is then commanded to shut up the words and to seal the book to the time of the end,* 4; *and is informed of the three grand symbolical periods of a* time, times, and a half, twelve hundred and ninety *days, and* thirteen hundred and thirty-five *days,* 4–12; *at the end of the last of which Daniel shall rest and stand in his lot,* 13. *It is generally thought by commentators that the termination of the last period is the epoch of the* FIRST resurrection. See Rev. xx. 4, 5.

A. M. 3470
B. C. 534
Olymp. LXI. 3
Anno Tarquinii Superbi,
R. Roman., 1

AND at that time shall [a]Michael stand up, the great
prince which standeth for the
children of thy people: [b]and
there shall be a time of trouble, such as never
was since there was a nation *even* to that
same time: and at that time thy people [c]shall
be delivered, every one that shall be found
[d]written in the book.
2 And many of them that sleep in the dust
of the earth shall awake, [e]some to everlasting
life, and some to shame [f]*and*
everlasting contempt.
3 And [g]they that be [h]wise
shall shine [i]as the brightness of
the firmament; [k]and they that turn many
to righteousness [l]as the stars for ever and
ever.
4 [m]But thou, O Daniel, [n]shut up the words,
and seal the book, *even* to [o]the time of the
end: many shall run to and fro, and knowledge shall be increased.

[a]Ch. x. 13, 21——[b]Isa. xxvi. 20, 21; Jer. xxx. 7; Matt. xxiv. 21; Rev. xvi. 18——[c]Rom. xi. 26——[d]Exod. xxxii. 32; Psa. lvi. 8; lxix. 28; Ezek. xiii. 9; Luke x. 20; Phil. iv. 3; Rev. iii. 5; xiii. 8——[e]Matt. xxv. 46; John v. 28, 29; Acts xxiv. 15

[f]Isa. lxvi. 24; Rom. ix. 21——[g]Ch. xi. 33, 35——[h]Or, *teachers*——[i]Prov. iv. 18; Wisd. iii. 7; Matt. xiii. 43——[k]James v. 20——[l]1 Cor. xv. 41, 42——[m]Chap. viii. 26; ver. 9——[n]Rev. x. 4; xxii. 10——[o]Chap. x. 1; ver. 9

NOTES ON CHAP. XII

Verse 1. *And at that time Michael shall stand up*] Michael the archangel, as has already been observed, was ever reputed the guardian of the Jewish people.

Every one that shall be found written in the book] All that truly fear, love, and obey the Lord. On the phrase, "written in the book, the book of life," &c., see the passages in the margin, and the notes on those passages.

Verse 2. *Many of them that sleep in the dust of the earth*] This prophecy has been referred to the future *restoration of the Jews.* It will be also true of the state of mankind at the general judgment.

Verse 3. *And they that be wise*] Those who are thoroughly instructed in Christ's word and doctrine, *shall shine*—shall be eminently distinguished in the Christian Church by the holiness of their lives, and the purity of their creed.

And they that turn many to righteousness] They who, by preaching Christ crucified among their brethren, shall be the means of converting them to the Christian faith; shall be *as the stars*—bright luminaries in the Gospel kingdom of Jesus Christ. This also may be applied to the case of holy and useful men, particularly the faithful ministers of the Gospel, in the day of judgment. See the parallel texts in the margin, and the notes on them.

Verse 4. *Shut up the words, and seal the book*] When a prophet received a prediction concerning what was at a considerable distance of time, he shut his book, did not communicate his revelation for some time after. This Daniel was commanded to do, chap. viii. 26. See also Isa. xxix. 10, 11; Rev. xxii. 10. Among the ancients, those were said to *seal,* who in the course of their reading stamped the places of which they were *yet doubtful,* in order to keep them in memory, that they might refer to them again, as not yet fully understood. This custom *Salmasius,* in his book *De modo Usurarum,* p. 446, proves from *Hesychius.*

Many shall run to and fro] Many shall endeavour to *search out* the sense; *and knowledge shall be increased* by these means; though the meaning shall not be *fully* known till the events take place: THEN the seal shall be broken, and the sense become plain. This seems to be the meaning of this verse, though another has been put on it, viz., "Many shall run to and fro preaching the Gospel of Christ, and therefore religious knowledge and true wisdom shall be increased." This is true in itself; but it is not the meaning of the prophet's words.

A. M. 3470
B. C. 534
Olymp. LXI. 3
Anno Tarquinii Superbi,
R. Roman., 1

5 Then I Daniel looked, and, behold, there stood other two, the one on this side of the [p]bank of the river, and the other on that side of the bank [q]of the river.

6 And *one* said to [r]the man clothed in linen, which *was* [s]upon the waters of the river, [t]How long *shall it be to* the end of these wonders?

7 And I heard the man clothed in linen, which *was* upon the waters of the river, when he [u]held up his right hand and his left hand unto heaven, and sware by him [v]that liveth for ever [w]that *it shall be* for a time, times, and [x]a half; [y]and when he shall have accomplished to scatter the power of [z]the holy people, all these *things* shall be finished.

8 And I heard, but I understood not: then said I, O my Lord, what *shall be* the end of these *things?*

9 And he said, Go thy way, Daniel: for the words *are* closed up and sealed [a]till the time of the end.

A. M. 3470
B. C. 534
Olymp. LXI. 3
Anno Tarquinii Superbi,
R. Roman., 1

10 [b]Many shall be purified, and made white, and tried; [c]but the wicked shall do wickedly: and none of the wicked shall understand; but [d]the wise shall understand.

11 And from the time [e]*that* the daily *sacrifice* shall be taken away, and [f]the abomination that [g]maketh desolate set up, *there shall be* a thousand two hundred and ninety days.

12 Blessed *is* he that waiteth, and cometh to the thousand three hundred and five and thirty days.

13 But [h]go thou thy way till the end *be:* [i]for [k]thou shalt rest, [l]and stand in thy lot at the end of the days.

---

[p]Heb. *lip*——[q]Ch. x. 4——[r]Ch. x. 5——[s]Or, *from above*——[t]Ch. viii. 13——[u]Deut. xxxii. 40; Rev. x. 5, 6 [v]Ch. iv. 34——[w]Ch. vii. 25; xi. 13; Rev. xii. 14——[x]Or, *part*——[y]Luke xxi. 24; Rev. x. 7——[z]Ch. viii. 24 [a]Ver. 4——[b]Ch. xi. 35; Zech. xiii. 9——[c]Hos. xiv. 9; Rev. ix. 20; xxii. 11——[d]Chap. xi. 33, 35; John vii. 17; viii. 47; xviii. 37——[e]Chap. viii. 11; xi. 31——[f]Hebrew, *to set up the abomination,* &c.——[g]Or, *astonisheth*——[h]Verse 9——[i]Or, *and thou,* &c.——[k]Isa. lvii. 2; Rev. xiv. 13——[l]Psa. i. 5

Verse 5. *Behold, there stood other two*] Probably two angels. We know no more of them, unless they be the same as those called *saints*, chap. viii. 13, which see. The *river* was most likely the *Tigris.*

Verse 6. *The man clothed in linen*] Gabriel, in a human form. Thus he is represented, chap. x. 5.

Verse 7. *Which* was *upon the waters*] By this description, he was standing on the water. This is very similar to the description of the angel, Rev. x. 5, 6, and in the seventh verse there seems to be a reference to this prophecy, "a time, times, and a half." See the note on chap. vii. 25.

Verse 8. *I heard, but I understand not*] Could not comprehend what the *time, times,* and *half time* should refer to. These make *three* years and *a half* of prophetic time, answering to *one thousand two hundred and sixty* years.

Verse 9. *The words* are *closed up*] The prophecy shall not be understood, but in its accomplishment; and then the depth of the wisdom and providence of God will be clearly seen in these matters. See on ver. 4. We must wait "till the time of the end;" and this, it appears from the following calculations, will not arrive before the TWENTIETH CENTURY. We here see the reason why these prophecies are at present so imperfectly understood. *God has sealed them.*

Verse 10. *Many shall be purified*] During the interim, the great work of God's providence and grace shall be carried on in the salvation of men; who, in the midst of trials, temptations, and difficulties, shall be *purified* and *made white*—be fully saved from their sins.

None of the wicked shall understand] Because they are wicked, and *will* continue in their sins, the eyes of their *understanding* shall be closed, and their hearts hardened; so that they shall not see the light of the glorious Gospel.

But the wise] Those who open their hearts to God, that he may pour in his light, shall *understand* the things that make for their peace.

Verse 11. *From the time* that *the daily* sacrifice *shall be taken away*] See the notes on chap. xi. 25-27.

The abomination that maketh desolate set up] I believe, with Bp. *Newton*, that this is a *proverbial* phrase; and may be applied to any thing substituted in the *place* of, or set up in opposition to, the ordinances of God, his worship, his truth, &c. Adrian's temple, built in the place of God's temple at Jerusalem, the church of St. Sophia turned into a Mohammedan mosque, &c., &c., may be termed *abominations that make desolate.* Perhaps Mohammedanism may be the abomination; which sprang up A. D. 612. If we reckon *one thousand two hundred and ninety* years, ver. 11, from that time, it will bring us down to A. D. 1902, when we might presume from this calculation, that the religion of the FALSE PROPHET will cease to prevail in the world; which from the present year, 1825, is distant only *seventy-seven* years.

Verse 12. *Blessed* is *he that waiteth*] He who implicitly depends on God, expecting, as his truth cannot fail, that these predictions shall be accomplished in due time.

And cometh to the thousand three hundred and five and thirty days.] This is *seventy-five* days more than what is included in the *three* years and a *half*, or the *time, times, and a half* in the *seventh* verse; and as we have met with so many instances of *prophetical days* and *years*, this undoubtedly is another instance; and as a *day* stands for a *year*, this must mean a period of *one thousand three hundred and thirty-five* years, which period is to bring *all these wonders to an end*, ver. 6. But we are left totally in the dark relative to the *time from which these one thousand three hundred and thirty-five years* are to be reckoned. If, however, we reckon them from the above epoch, A. D. 612, when *Mohammedanism* arose, they lead us to A. D. 1947, when the *fulness of the Gentiles* shall be brought in; and thus a final closure of vision and prophecy be made, as then all the great events relative to the salvation of men shall have taken place. Wars and contentions will probably then cease over the whole world; Jews and Gentiles become one fold, under one Shepherd and Bishop of souls; and the triune God be properly worshipped and glorified, from generation to generation, over the face of the whole earth. But all these conjectures may be founded in darkness. We have not chronological data; and "the times and seasons God has reserved in his own power."

Finished correcting for the press, March 1st, 1831.—A. C.

Verse 13. *But go thou thy way till the end be*] Here is proper advice for every man. 1. Thou hast a *way*—a *walk in life*, which God has assigned thee; *walk in that way*, it is *thy way*. 2. There will be an *end* to thee of all earthly things. Death is at the door, and eternity is at hand; *go on to the end*—be faithful unto death. 3. There is a *rest* provided for the people of God. Thou shalt *rest;* thy *body*, in the *grave;* thy *soul*, in the *Divine favour* here, and finally in *paradise*. 4. As in the promised land there was a *lot* for *each* of *God's people*, so in heaven there is a *lot* for *thee*. Do not *lose* it, do not *sell* it, do not let thy enemy *rob thee* of it. Be determined to *stand in thy own lot at the end of the days*. See that thou keep the faith; die in the Lord Jesus, that thou mayest rise and reign with him to all eternity. Amen.

MASORETIC NOTES

Number of verses in this book, 357

Middle verse, chap. v. 30

Masoretic sections, 7

INTRODUCTION TO THE BOOK
OF THE
PROPHET HOSEA

HOSEA, the son of *Beeri*, is the first of the minor prophets. *Epiphanius* says that he was of the town of *Belemoth*, in the tribe of *Issachar;* which is no other, in all probability, than *Beelmeon*, towards Esdraelon, in this tribe. The rabbins say that *Bura* was his father, who is mentioned in the *Chronicles*, and was prince of the tribe of *Reuben* at the time when *Tiglath-pileser* carried some of the tribes of *Israel* into captivity. But if it be so, *Hosea* must be said to be of the tribe of *Reuben;* and a native of *Beelmeon*, beyond *Jordan*. This prophet lived in the kingdom of *Samaria;* and his prophecies for the most part have a view to this state, though there are likewise some particular things which concern the kingdom of *Judah*.

We read, in the introduction to his prophecy, that he prophesied under the kings of *Judah*, *Uzziah*, *Jotham*, *Ahaz*, and *Hezekiah*, and under *Jeroboam* II., king of *Israel*. If he prophesied in the reign of all these princes, he must have lived a very long time; for there are a *hundred and twelve* years from the beginning of *Uzziah's* reign to the end of *Hezekiah's* reign. *Uzziah* began to reign A. M. 3194, and *Hezekiah's* reign ended in 3306. Add, if you please, *twenty* or *five and twenty* years, which might be the age of *Hosea* when he began to prophesy; and this will make *one hundred and thirty-two*, or *one hundred and thirty-seven* years. And if we were to take *ten* years from *Uzziah*, and as many from *Hezekiah*, during which *Hosea* might not have prophesied, there will still remain *one hundred and twelve*, or *one hundred and fifteen* years.

In the whole collection of *Hosea's* prophecies, we find nothing which proves that he prophesied so long. And, besides, why should his prophecies be dated in the title by the reigns of the kings of *Judah*, when he did not live under their dominion? It is therefore very probable that this title is not *Hosea's*, but some ancient transcriber's; and that the true beginning of this prophet's work is at these words: "The beginning of the word of the Lord by Hosea." It is our opinion that he began about the end of *Jeroboam's* reign, who was the second king of *Israel* of this name. See *Calmet*.

St. *Jerome* and many others believe *Hosea* to be the oldest prophet, whose writings are in our possession; and that he was witness to the *first* captivity of the *four* tribes carried away by *Tiglath-pileser*, and the extinction of the kingdom of *Samaria* by *Shalmaneser*. St. *Jerome* will have it that he prophesied even afterwards. The *first* verses of chap. i. have a view to the death of *Zechariah*, king of *Israel*, and son of *Jeroboam* II. From the *sixth* verse of the *first* chapter to the *third* chapter, is a prediction of the captivity of *Israel:* but after he has foretold this captivity, he declares the return and end of it. He inveighs strongly against the disorders which prevailed in the kingdom of the *ten* tribes. It appears that in his time there were idols; not only at *Dan*, *Beth-el*, and *Samaria*, but likewise at *Gilgal*, upon *Tabor*, at *Sichem*, *Beer-sheba*, and upon the mountains of *Gilead*. He speaks of the *Israelites* as of a people entirely corrupted, and the measure of whose sins was filled up; he foretells that their golden calves should be pulled down, cast upon the ground, and carried into *Assyria*.

He reflects, with the same severity, upon the irregularities which reigned in *Judah*. He stands up against those who went to worship false gods at *Gilgal*. He speaks of *Sennacherib's* invading the territories of *Judah*. He foretells that the people of *Judah* should still continue some time in their country after the captivity of the *ten* tribes; but that after this they themselves should likewise be carried captives beyond the *Euphrates*, from whence the Lord would bring them back after a certain number of years. The style of *Hosea* is obscure, and his expressions often dubious and perplexed. The things whereof he speaks contribute farther to his obscurity, by reason of their distance, and our ignorance of the history of those times.

In the beginning of *Hosea's* prophecy, we read that the Lord directed him "to take unto him a wife of whoredoms, and children of whoredoms;" that is, to marry a woman who, before her marriage, had lived a debauched life, but who, after her marriage, should retire from all bad conversation, and whose children should be legitimate, notwithstanding that, by reason of the blemish which their mother had contracted by her former life, they were called *the children of whoredoms*. This prostitute woman, and the children who were to be born of her, were a figure and a kind of real prophecy which described the idolatry and infidelity of *Samaria* and the *ten* tribes, formerly the Lord's spouse, but who afterwards became idolatrous and corrupt.

The children of this faithless woman are children of prostitution, since they imitate the idolatry of their mother. God gives these children the names of *Jezreel, God will disperse; Lo-rechamah*, or *Without mercy;* and *Lo-ammi, Thou art no longer my people;* to show,—1. That God was going to revenge upon the house of *Jehu*, king of *Israel*, the sins which he had committed at *Jezreel*, when he usurped the kingdom of the *ten* tribes. 2. That the Lord would treat his idolatrous and sinful people without mercy. 3. That he would reject them, and no more look upon them as his people.

Hosea is concise, sententious, and abrupt. It is his manner to omit the connexive and adversative particles; an observation which we should recollect when we observe them occasionally supplied by versions or manuscripts. These are among the causes of that obscurity for which he is remarkable: but the greatest difficulties arise from the corrupt readings which deform the printed text. He chiefly addresses Israel; but introduces frequent mention of Judah. He not only inveighs against the vices of the people, but sharply arraigns the conduct of their kings, princes, and priests.

Like many of the Hebrew prophets, he tempers denunciations of God's vengeance against an idolatrous and vicious people, with promises of abundant mercies in store for them; and his transitions from one of these subjects to the other are rapid and unexpected. He abounds with short and lively comparisons; and, like the best Greek and Roman writers, often omits the particle of similitude. These comparisons he sometimes accumulates in the spirit of that poetry which is most admired. See chap. vi. 3, 4, ix. 10, xi. 11, xiii. 3, xiv. 5, 6, 7. He has often a GREAT FORCE OF EXPRESSION. See chap. i. 7, ii. 3, 18, 21, 22, iv. 2, vi. 5, xi. 4, *l.* 1, xii. 1, *l.* 1. He is sometimes HIGHLY ANIMATED. See chap. iv. 14, v. 8, viii, 1, ix. 5, 14, xiii. 10, 14. Many BEAUTIFUL PASSAGES occur in this prophet, as in the SIMILES throughout; in the ALLEGORIES, chap. ii. 2, 20, vii. 11, 12, viii. 7, *l.* 2, 3, 4, x. 11, 12, 13, xiii. 15; in the PATHOS, chap. xi. 3, *l.* 1, 2, and ver. 8, 9; in the FIGURES, chap. xiii. 12, xiv. 2, *l.* 5. There are also some parts which are truly SUBLIME, as chap. v. 14. 15, viii. 7, *l.* 1, x. 8, *l.* 2, 3, xiii. 7, 8.

I have already, at the beginning of Isaiah, given a table of the chronological succession of all the prophets: that of Archbishop *Newcome* on the *twelve* minor prophets I subjoin here, because it contains some differences from the preceding.

ORDER AND TIME IN WHICH THE TWELVE MINOR PROPHETS FLOURISHED

1. JONAH prophesied between 823 B. C. and 783 B. C. in the reign of Jeroboam II., king of Israel. See 2 Kings xiv. 25.

2. AMOS prophesied from about 823 B. C. to about 785 B. C. in the reign of Uzziah, king of Judah, and in that of Jeroboam II., king of Israel. See Amos i. 1.

3. HOSEA flourished from about 809 B. C. to about 698 B. C., in the reigns of Uzziah, Jotham, Ahaz, and Hezekiah, kings of Judah, and in that of Jeroboam II., king of Israel. See Hos. i. 1. [But see the observations in the preceding page.]

4. MICAH flourished between 757 B. C. and 698 B. C., in the reigns of Jotham, Ahaz, and Hezekiah, kings of Judah. See Mic. i. 1.

5. NAHUM is supposed to have prophesied between 720 B. C. and 698 B. C., in the reign of Hezekiah.

6. JOEL is supposed to have prophesied between 697 B. C. and 660 B. C., in the reign of Manasseh.

7. ZEPHANIAH prophesied between 640 B. C. and 609 B. C., in the reign of Josiah. See Zeph. i. 1.

8. HABAKKUK is thought to have prophesied between 606 B. C. and 598 B. C., in the reign of Jehoiakim.

9. OBADIAH prophesied soon after 587 B. C., between the taking of Jerusalem by Nebuchadnezzar, and the destruction of the Edomites by the same prince.

10. HAGGAI prophesied about 520 B. C. after the return from Babylon. See Haggai i. 1.

11. ZECHARIAH prophesied from 520 B. C. to about 518 B. C.; and was contemporary with Haggai. See Zech. i. 1.

12. MALACHI is generally believed to have prophesied about 436 B. C.

THE BOOK
OF THE
PROPHET HOSEA

Chronological Notes relative to the commencement of Hosea's prophesying, upon the supposition that this event took place in the last year of the reign of Jeroboam II., king of Israel

Year of the world, according to the Usherian account, 3219.—Year of the Julian period, 3929.—Year since the Flood, 1563.—Year from the vocation of Abram, 1136.—Year from the foundation of Solomon's temple, 227.—Year before the First Olympiad, 9.—Year before the building of Rome, 32.—Year before the vulgar era of Christ's nativity, 785.—Cycle of the Sun, 9.—Cycle of the Moon, 15.—Second year of Cœnus, the second king of Macedon; which was the thirtieth from the foundation of the monarchy.—Thirteenth year of Agamestor, perpetual archon of the Athenians.—Thirteenth year of Ardysus, king of Lydia.—Twelfth year of Amulius Sylvius, king of the Albans.—Twenty-fifth year of Charilaus, king of the Lacedæmonians.—Forty-first year of Jeroboam II., king of Israel.—Twenty-sixth year of Uzziah, king of Judah.

CHAPTER I

Under the figure of a wife proving false to her marriage vows, and bearing children that would follow her example, the prophet represents the shameful idolatry of the ten tribes, which provoked God to cast them off. The whole passage is information by action instead of words. The names of the children are all emblematical. The first is intended to put Israel in mind of their unrepented guilt, and the acts of cruelty committed in their palace of Jezreel, (1 Kings xxi. 1.) *The second and third, signifying* not finding mercy, *and* not my peope, *denote that, in consequence of their guilt, they were to be rejected of God,* 1–9. *God promises, however, to repair the loss to his Church by calling in the Gentiles,* 10; *and by uniting all the children of God under one head, the Messiah, in the latter days,* 11.

A. M. cir. 3219 B. C. cir. 785 Ante U. C. 32 Amulii Sylvii, R. Alban., cir. annum 12

THE word of the LORD that came unto Hosea, the son of Beeri, in the days of [a]Uzziah, Jotham, Ahaz, *and* Hezekiah, kings of Judah, and in the days of [b]Jeroboam the son of Joash, king of Israel.
2 The beginning of the word of the LORD by Hosea. And the LORD said to Hosea, [c]Go, take unto thee a

[a]Isa. i. 1——[b]2 Kings xiv. 23

[c]So chap. iii. 1

NOTES ON CHAP. I

Verse 1. *Hosea, the son of Beeri*] See the preceding account of this prophet.

In the days of Uzziah, &c.] If we suppose, says Bp. *Newcome*, that Hosea prophesied during the course of *sixty-six* years, and place him from the year 790 before Christ to the year 724, he will have exercised his office *eight* years in the reign of *Jeroboam* the second, *thirty-three* years in the reign of *Uzziah*, the whole reigns of *Jotham* and *Ahaz*, and *three* years in the reign of *Hezekiah;* but will not have survived the taking of Samaria. But see the preceding account of this prophet.

I think the *first* verse to be a *title* to this book added by the compiler of his prophecies, and that it relates more to facts which took place *in those reigns*, and had been *predicted* by Hosea, who would only be said to have prophesied under all those kings. *by his predictions*, which were consecutively fulfilled under them. By those, though dead, he continued to speak. The prophet's work properly begins at ver. 2; hence called, "The beginning of the word of the Lord by Hosea."

Verse 2. *A wife of whoredoms*] That is, says *Newcome*, a wife from among the *Israelites*, who were remarkable for spiritual fornication, or idolatry. God calls himself the *husband* of Israel; and this chosen nation owed him the fidelity of a wife. See Exod. xxxiv. 15; Deut. xxxi. 16; Judge. ii. 17; Isa. liv. 5; Jer. iii. 14; xxxi. 32; Ezek. xvi. 17; xxiii. 5, 27; Hos. 2, 5; Rev. xvii. 1, 2. He therefore says, with indignation, Go join thyself in marriage to one of those who have committed fornication against me, and raise up children who, by the power of example, will themselves swerve to idolatry. See chap. v. 7. And thus show them that they are *radically* depraved.

A. M. cir. 3219
B. C. cir. 785
Ante U. C. 32
Amulii Sylvii,
R. Alban.,
cir. annum 12

wife of whoredoms, and children
of whoredoms: for [d]the land
hath committed great whoredom, *departing* from the LORD.
3 So he went and took Gomer the daughter
of Diblaim; which conceived, and bare him
a son.
4 And the LORD said unto him, Call his
name Jezreel; for yet a little *while*, [e]and I
will [f]avenge the blood of Jezreel upon the
house of Jehu, [g]and will cause to cease the
kingdom of the house of Israel.
5 [h]And it shall come to pass at that day,
that I will break the bow of Israel in the
valley of Jezreel.
6 And she conceived again, and bare a
daughter. And *God* said unto
him, Call her name [i]Lo-ru-
hamah: [k]for [l]I will no more have
mercy upon the house of Israel;
[m]but I will utterly take them away.
7 [n]But I will have mercy upon the house of
Judah, and will save them by the LORD their
God, and [o]will not save them by bow, nor by
sword, nor by battle, by horses, nor by horsemen.
8 Now when she had weaned Lo-ruhamah,
she conceived, and bare a son.
9 Then said *God*, call his name [p]Lo-ammi:
for ye *are* not my people, and I will not be
your *God*.
10 Yet [q]the number of the children of Israel

[d]Deut. xxxi. 16; Psa. lxxiii. 27; Jer. ii. 13; Ezek. xxiii. 3, &c.——[e]2 Kings x. 11——[f]Heb. *visit*——[g]2 Kings xv. 10, 12——[h]2 Kings xv. 29——[i]That is, *Not having obtained mercy*——[k]2 Kings xvii. 6, 23——[l]Heb. *I will not add any more to*——[m]Or, *that I should altogether pardon them*——[n]2 Kings xix. 35——[o]Zech. iv. 6; ix. 10——[p]That is, *Not my people*——[q]Gen. xxxii. 12; Romans ix. 27, 28

Verse 3. *He went and took Gomer*] All this appears to be a real transaction, though having a typical meaning. If he took an *Israelite*, he must necessarily have taken an *idolatress;* one who had worshipped the calves of Jeroboam at Dan or at Bethel.

Verse 4. *Call his name Jezreel*] יזרעאל that is, *God will disperse*. This seems to intimate that a dispersion or sowing of Israel shall take place; which happened under Shalmaneser, king of Assyria, 2 Kings xvii. 5, 6. But the word refers also to the name of *a city*, where Jehu slew Jezebel and all the children of Ahab. 2 Kings ix. 10, 36, and x. 6.

This was one of those *prophetic* names which we so often meet with in the Scriptures; *e. g.*, Japheth, Abraham, Israel, Judah, Joshua, Zerubbabel, Solomon, Sheer-jashub, &c.

The blood of Jezreel] Not Jehu's vengeance on Ahab's family, but his acts of cruelty while he resided at Jezreel, a city in the tribe of Issachar, Josh. xix. 18, where the kings of Israel had a palace, 1 Kings xxi. 1.

Will cause to cease the kingdom] Either relating to the cutting off of the kingdom of Israel by the Assyrians, see ver. 6, or to the ceasing of the kingdom of Israel from the house of *Jehu*, 2 Kings x. 30, and which was fulfilled, 2 Kings xv. 10.—*Newcome.*

Verse 5. *In the valley of Jezreel*] This also is supposed to relate either to some signal defeat of the Israelites by the Assyrians, which took place in the valley of Jezreel; or to the death of Zechariah, the fourth lineal descendant of Jehu, which may have happened here. See 2 Kings xv. 10.—*Newcome.*

Verse 6. *Call her Lo-ruhamah*] לא רחמה, "Not having obtained mercy." This also was a *prophetic* or *typical* name; and the reason of its imposition is immediately given:

For I will no more have mercy] כי לא אוסיף עוד ארחם *ki lo osiph od arachem*, "For I will no more add to have mercy upon the house of Israel." This refers to the total destruction of that kingdom.

Verse 7. *But I will have mercy upon the house of Judah*] I will spare them as a kingdom after Israel has been carried away into captivity by the Assyrians.

And will save them by the Lord their God] Remarkably fulfilled in the supernatural defeat of the army of the Assyrians, see 2 Kings xix. 35; and so they were saved not by *bow*, nor by *sword*, nor by *battle*, nor by *horses*, nor by *horsemen*. The former expression may mean, not in *war by horses*, *i. e.*, yoked to war *chariots*, nor *by horsemen*—nor by cavalry, however efficient such troops might have then been deemed.

Verse 9. *Call his name Lo-ammi*] לא עמי *Lo-ammi*, "Not my people;" for which the reason is immediately given:

Ye are not my people, and I will not be your God.] The word GOD is not added here by any of the ancient versions or MSS.; and yet the construction absolutely requires it, as *Houbigant* properly observes, who thinks the present reading לא אהיה לכם *lo eheyeh lachem*, "I will not be to you," a corruption of the word אלהיכם *eloheychem*, "your God." It is strange that no various reading occurs on this verse in any MS. yet discovered. In *two* of the oldest of mine there is a *blank* of *half a line* left after the last word; and so it is in the Masoretic Bibles, though the sense is not complete; for it is evidently continued in the following verse. Probably God refers to the words, Exod. iii. 14: אהיה אשר אהיה *I am that I am. I am*, אהיה *eheyeh*,—*I shall be*, hath sent me unto you. I will not be your *eheyeh*, *i. e.*, I will not be your God.

Verse 10. *Yet the number of the children of Israel*] God had promised that the children of Israel should be as the sand of the sea. See Gen. xxxii. 12; Rom. ix. 25, 26. And though for their iniquities he had thinned and scattered them, yet the spirit and design of his promise and covenant shall be fulfilled. An Israel there shall be. In the place of the reprobated people,

A. M. cir. 3219
B. C. cir. 785
Ante U. C. 32
Amulii Sylvii,
R. Alban.,
cir. annum 12

shall be as the sand of the sea,
which cannot be measured nor
numbered; [r]and it shall come
to pass, *that* [s]in the place where
it was said unto them, [t]Ye *are* not my people,
there it shall be said unto them, *Ye are* [u]the
sons of the living God.

11 [v]Then shall the children of Judah and the children
of Israel be gathered together,
and appoint themselves one
head, and they shall come up out of
the land: for great *shall be* the day of
Jezreel.

[r]Rom. ix. 25, 26; 1 Pet. ii. 10——[s]Or, *instead of that*——[t]Chap. ii. 23——[u]John i. 12; 1 John iii. 1——[v]Isa. xi. 12, 13; Jer. iii. 18; Ezek. xxxiv. 23; xxxvii. 16–24

who were now no longer his people, there shall be found an Israel that shall be the *children of the living God.* See the above scriptures, and 1 Pet. ii. 10. This must mean either the Israelites after their conversion to Christianity, or even the Gentiles themselves converted to God, and now become the *true Israel.*

Verse 11. *The children of Judah and the children of Israel*] After the return from Babylon, the distinction between Israel and Judah was entirely destroyed; and those of them that did return were all included under one denomination, *Jews;* and the *one head* may refer to Zerubbabel their leader, and afterwards under Ezra and Nehemiah. In the more extensive view of the prophet the *one Head* may mean *Jesus Christ*, under whom the true Israel, Jews and Gentiles, shall be finally gathered together; so that there shall be one flock, and one Shepherd over that flock.

They shall come up out of the land] Assyria and Chaldea in particular; but also from the various places of their dispersions in general.

Great shall be *the day of Jezreel.*] He alludes to the meaning of the word, the *seed of God.* God who has dispersed—*sown*, them in different lands, shall gather them together; and that day of God's power shall be great and glorious. It was a wonderful *seed time* in the Divine justice; it shall then be a wonderful *harvest* in the Divine mercy. He sowed them among the nations in his wrath; he shall reap them and gather them in his bounty.

CHAPTER II

The prophet exhorts his people to speak and to act as became those who obtained mercy of God; and to remonstrate strongly against the conduct of their mother, (Samaria,) whose captivity is threatened on account of her forsaking God, and ascribing her prosperity to idols, 1–5. *As an amplification of this threatening, the prophet enumerates a series of afflictions which were to befall her to bring her to a sense of her duty to God; and of her folly in seeking after idols, and falsely ascribing to them the blessings of Providence,* 6–13. *After these corrections, however, God promises to conduct Israel safely to their own land; perhaps alluding to their restoration from the Babylonish captivity, for this prophecy is supposed to have been delivered about* two hundred and fifty *years prior to this event,* 14, 15. *He farther engages to deal with them as a tender husband, and not as a severe master, as were the idols which they served,* 16, 17. *The rest of the chapter promises the people of God, the true Israel, security from every evil, with the possession of every blessing, under a new covenant; and that in terms full of beauty, energy, and consolation. Heaven and earth, and whatever they contain; all nature, and the God of nature, are represented as uniting to make the people of God happy; so that if they only breathe a wish, one part of nature, animate or inanimate, echoes it to another, and all join in sweet harmony to transmit it to the ear of the Almighty. "I will hear, saith the* Lord, *I will hear the heavens, and they shall hear the earth; and the earth shall hear the corn, and the wine, and the oil; and they shall hear Jezreel."*

A. M. cir. 3219
B. C. cir. 785
Ante U. C. 32
Amulii Sylvii,
R. Alban.,
cir. annum 12

SAY ye unto your brethren,
[a]Ammi; and to your sisters,
[b]Ruhamah.
2 Plead with your mother,
plead: for [c]she *is* not my wife, neither *am* I
her husband: let her there-
fore put away her [d]whore-
doms out of her sight, and her
adulteries from between her
breasts;

[a]That is, *My people*——[b]That is, *Having obtained mercy*——[c]Isa. l. 1——[d]Ezek. xvi. 25

NOTES ON CHAP. II

Verse 1. *Say ye unto your brethren, Ammi*] I prefer the interpretation of these proper names. *Say ye unto your brethren,* MY PEOPLE; *and to your sisters, who have* OBTAINED MERCY.

Verse 2. *Plead with your mother*] People of Judah, accuse your mother, (Jerusalem,) who has abandoned my worship, and is become idolatrous; convince her of her folly and wickedness, and let her return to him from whom she has so deeply revolted.

A. M. cir. 3219
B. C. cir. 785
Ante U. C. 32
Amulii Sylvii,
R. Alban.,
cir. annum 12

3 Lest [e]I strip her naked, and
set her as in the day that she
was [f]born, and make her [g]as
a wilderness, and set her like a
dry land, and slay her with [h]thirst.
4 And I will not have mercy upon her children; for they *be* the [i]children of whoredoms.
5 [k]For their mother hath played the harlot:
she that conceived them hath done shamefully: for she said, I will go after my lovers,
[l]that give *me* my bread and my water, my
wool and my flax, mine oil and my [m]drink.
6 Therefore, behold, [n]I will hedge up thy
way with thorns, and [o]make a wall, that she
shall not find her paths.
7 And she shall follow after her lovers, but
she shall not overtake them; and she shall
seek them, but shall not find *them:* then shall
she say, [p]I will go and return to my [q]first husband; for then *was it* better with me than
now.
8 For she did not [r]know that [s]I gave her
corn, and [t]wine, and oil, and
multiplied her silver and gold,
[u]*which* they prepared for Baal.
9 Therefore will I return, and
[v]take away my corn in the time thereof, and
my wine in the season thereof, and will [w]re-
cover my wool and my flax *given* to cover
her nakedness.
10 And now [x]will I discover her [y]lewdness
in the sight of her lovers, and none shall deliver her out of mine hand.
11 [z]I will also cause all her mirth to cease,
her [a]feast days, her new moons, and her Sabbaths, and all her solemn feasts.
12 And I will [b]destroy her vines and her
fig-trees, [c]whereof she hath said, These *are*
my rewards that my lovers have given me:
and [d]I will make them a forest, and the beasts
of the field shall eat them.
13 And I will visit upon her the days of
Baalim, wherein she burned incense to them,

A. M. cir. 3219
B. C. cir. 785
Ante U. C. 32
Amulii Sylvii,
R. Alban.,
cir. annum 12

[e]Jer. xiii. 22, 26; Ezekiel xvi. 37, 39——[f]Ezekiel xvi. 4 [g]Ezek. xix. 13——[h]Amos viii. 11, 13——[i]John viii. 41 [k]Isa. i. 21; Jer. iii. 1, 6, 8, 9; Ezek. xvi. 15, 16, &c. [l]Ver. 8, 12; Jer. xliv. 17——[m]Heb. *drinks*——[n]Job iii 23; xix. 8; Lam. iii. 7, 9——[o]Heb. *wall a wall*——[p]Chapter v. 15; Luke xv. 18

[q]Ezek. xvi. 8——[r]Isa. i. 3——[s]Ezek. xvi. 17, 18, 19 [t]Heb. *new wine*——[u]Or, *wherewith they made Baal;* chap. viii. 4——[v]Ver. 3——[w]Or, *take away*——[x]Ezek. xvi. 37; xxiii. 29——[y]Heb. *folly* or *villany*——[z]Amos viii. 10——[a]1 Kings xii. 32; Amos viii. 5——[b]Heb. *make desolate*——[c]Ver. 5——[d]Psa. lxxx. 12, 13; Isa. v. 5

Verse 3. *Lest I strip her naked*] Lest I expose her to infamy, want, and punishment. The punishment of an adulteress among the ancient Germans was this: "They shaved off her hair, stripped her naked in the presence of her relatives, and in this state drove her from the house of her husband." See on Isa. iii. 17; and see also Ezek. xvi. 39; xxiii. 26. However reproachful this might be to such delinquents, it had no tendency to promote their moral reformation.

And set her like a dry land] The Israelites, if obedient, were promised a land flowing with milk and honey; but, should they be disobedient, the reverse. And this is what God here threatens against disobedient Israel.

Verse 4. *They* be *the children of whoreaoms.*] They are all idolaters; and have been consecrated to idols, whose marks they bear.

Verse 5. *That give* me *my bread*] See the note on Jer. xliv. 17, 18, where nearly the same words are found and illustrated.

Verse 6. *I will hedge up thy way with thorns*] I will put it out of your power to escape the judgments I have threatened; and, in spite of all your attachment to your idols, you shall find that they can give you neither *bread*, nor *water*, nor *wool*, nor *flax*, nor *oil*, nor *drink*. And ye shall be brought into such circumstances, that the pursuit of your expensive idolatry shall be impossible. And she shall be led so deep into captivity, as never to find the road back to her own land. And this is the fact; for those who were carried away into Assyria have been lost among the nations, few of them having ever returned to Judea. And, if in being, where they are now is utterly unknown.

Verse 8. *For she did not know that I gave her corn*] How often are the gifts of God's *immediate bounty* attributed to fortuitous causes—to any cause but the right one!

Which *they prepared for Baal.*] And how often are the gifts of God's bounty perverted into means of dishonouring him! God gives us *wisdom, strength*, and *property;* and we use them to sin against him with the greater *skill, power*, and *effect!* Were the goods those of the *enemy*, in whose service they are employed, the crime would be the less. But the crime is deeply engrained, when God's property is made the instrument to dishonour himself.

Verse 9. *Therefore will I return, and take away*] In the course of my providence, I will withhold those benefits which she has prostituted to her idolatrous services. And I will neither give the land rain, nor fruitful seasons.

Verse 10. *In the sight of her lovers*] Her idols, and her faithful or faithless allies.

Verse 11. *Her feast days*] Jerusalem shall be pillaged and destroyed; and therefore all her joyous assemblies, and religious feasts, &c., shall cease.

Verse 12. *These* are *my rewards*] They attributed all the blessings of Providence as rewards received from the idols which they worshipped.

Verse 13. *Days of Baalim*] To *visit* signifies to *inflict punishment; the days* are taken for the *acts* of idolatrous worship committed on them; and *Baalim* means the *multitude* of false

A. M. cir. 3219 B. C. cir. 785 Ante U. C. 32 Amulii Sylvii, R. Alban., cir. annum 12

and she [e]decked herself with her
earrings and her jewels, and she
went after her lovers, and forgat
me, saith the LORD.
14 Therefore, behold, I will allure her, and
[f]bring her into the wilderness, and speak
[g]comfortably [h]unto her.
15 And I will give her vineyards from
thence, and [i]the valley of Achor for a door of
hope: and she shall sing there, as in [k]the days
of her youth, and [l]as in the day when she
came up out of the land of Egypt.
16 And it shall be at that day, saith the
LORD, that thou shalt call me [m]Ishi; and shalt
call me no more [n]Baali.
17 For [o]I will take away the names of
Baalim out of her mouth, and they shall no
more be remembered by their
name.
18 And in that day will I
make a [p]covenant for them with
the beasts of the field, and with the fowls of
heaven, and *with* the creeping things of the
ground: and [q]I will break the bow and the
sword, and the battle out of the earth, and
will make them to [r]lie down safely.
19 And I will betroth thee unto me for ever;
yea, I will betroth thee unto me in righteousness, and in judgment, and in lovingkindness,
and in mercies.
20 I will even betroth thee unto me in faithfulness; and [s]thou shalt know the LORD.
21 And it shall come to pass in that day, [t]I
will hear, saith the LORD, I will hear the hea-

A. M. cir. 3219 B. C. cir. 785 Ante U. C. 32 Amulii Sylvii, R. Alban., cir. annum 12

---

[e]Ezekiel xxiii. 40, 42——[f]Ezekiel xx. 35——[g]Or, *friendly*——[h]Hebrew, *to her heart*——[i]Joshua vii. 26; Isaiah lxv. 10——[k]Jeremiah ii. 2; Ezekiel xvi. 8, 22, 60——[l]Exodus xv. 1——[m]That is, *My husband* [n]That is, *My lord*

[o]Exod. xxiii. 13; Josh. xxiii. 7; Psa. xvi. 4; Zech. xiii. 2——[p]Job v. 23; Isa. xi. 6–9; Ezek. xxxiv. 25 [q]Psa. xlvi. 9; Isa. ii. 4; Ezek. xxxix. 9, 10; Zech. ix. 10 [r]Lev. xxvi. 5; Jer. xxiii. 6——[s]Jer. xxxi. 33, 34; John xvii. 3——[t]Zech. viii. 12

---

gods worshipped by them. *Baal* was a general name for a *male* idol, as *Astarte* was for a *female*. *Baalim* includes all the *male idols*, as *Ashtaroth* all those that were *female*. But the species of idol was often designated by some adjunct; as *Baal*-Zebub, *Baal*-Peor, *Baal*-Zephon, *Baal*-Berith, &c.

Her earrings] נזמה *nizmah*, signifies rather a *nose jewel*. These are worn by females in the East to the present day, in great abundance.

And her jewels] וחליתה *vechelyatah*, rings, armlets, bracelets, ankle-rings, and ornaments of this kind.

Verse 14. *I will allure her, and bring her into the wilderness, and speak comfortably unto her.*] After inflicting many judgments upon her, I will restore her again. I will deal with her as a very affectionate husband would do to an unfaithful wife. Instead of making her a *public example*, he takes her in private, talks to and reasons with her; puts her on her good behaviour; promises to pass by all, and forgive all, if she will now amend her ways. In the meantime he provides what is necessary for her wants and comfortable support; and thus, opening a *door of hope* for her, she may be fully reconciled; *rejoice* as at the beginning, when he first took her by the hand, and she became his bride. This is most probably the simple meaning of the above *metaphorical* expressions. The *valley of Achor* was very fruitful; it lay to the north of Jericho, not far from Gilgal. See Isa. lxv. 10.

Verse 15. *She shall sing there*] There she shall sing the *responsive song*, as on high festival occasions, and in marriage ceremonies. The Book of *Canticles* is of this sort.

Verse 16. *Thou shalt call me Ishi*] That is, *my man*, or *my husband;* a title of *love* and *affection; and not* BAALI, *my master*, a title exciting *fear* and *apprehension;* which, howsoever good in itself, was now rendered improper to be applied to Jehovah, having been prostituted to false gods. This intimated that they should scrupulously avoid idolatry; and they had such a full proof of the inefficacy of their idolatrous worship that, after their captivity, they never more served idols.

Verse 18. *Will I make a covenant for them*] I will make an *agreement* between them and the birds, beasts, and reptiles, so that they shall not be injured by those; their *flocks* shall not be destroyed, nor their *crops* spoiled. I will also prevent every species of *war*, that they may no more have the calamities that arise from that source. They shall also be safe from robbers and nightly alarms; for *I will make them to lie down in safety.*

Verse 19. *I will betroth thee unto me*] The people are always considered under the emblem of a *wife* unfaithful to her husband.

In righteousness] According to law, reason, and equity.

In judgment] According to what is fit and becoming.

In lovingkindness] Having the utmost affection and love for thee.

In mercies.] Forgiving and blotting out all past miscarriages. Or there may be an allusion here to the dowry given by the husband to his wife: "I will give righteousness," &c., as a dowry.

Verse 20. *In faithfulness*] Thou shalt no more prostitute thyself to idols, but be *faithful* to him who calls himself *thy husband.*

Thou shalt know the Lord.] There shall be no more *infidelity* on *thy part* nor *divorce* on *mine;* and thou shalt experience me to be the sole, present, and eternal good of thy immortal spirit: and when this conviction is fully rooted, then there can be no more idolatry, for it shall be seen that an idol is nothing in the world.

Verse 21. *I will hear, saith the Lord*] The sentence is repeated, to show how fully the thing was determined by the Almighty, and

A. M. cir. 3219
B. C. cir. 785
Ante U. C. 32
Amulii Sylvii,
R. Alban.,
cir. annum 12

vens, and they shall hear the
earth;
22 And the earth shall hear the
corn, and the wine, and the oil;
[u]and they shall hear Jezreel.
23 And [v]I will sow her unto me in the earth,
[w]and I will have mercy upon her
that had not obtained mercy;
and I [x]will say to *them which*
were not my people, Thou *art*
my people; and they shall say, *Thou art* my
God.

[u]Ch. i. 4——[v]Jer. xxxi. 27; Zech. x. 9——[w]Ch. i. 6

[x]Chap. i. 10; Zech. xiii. 9; Rom. ix. 26; 1 Pet. ii. 10

how implicitly they might depend on the Divine promise.

I will hear the heavens] The visible heavens, the atmosphere, where vapours are collected. The *clouds*, when they wish to deposit their fertilizing showers upon the earth.

They shall hear the earth] When it seems to supplicate for rain.

Verse 22. *Shall hear the corn, and the wine*] When they seem to express a desire to supply the wants of man.

And they shall hear Jezreel.] The destitute people who are in want of the necessaries of life.

This most elegant gradation in the exertion of the influences of nature, for the supply of the wants of man, may be considered thus:—

1. There is a concord, harmony, and mutual influence, which God has established in the parts of created nature, in reference to the support and preservation of the human race.

2. God alone is the author of all this; and unless he give his command, communicate his *energetic influence* to the different parts of nature, these effects will not, cannot be produced.

3. *Jezreel*, the people who have been *dispersed* for their iniquities, and now about to be *sown* or *planted* in their own land, will require the most *fostering care*. See on ver. 23.

4. They are heard in desiring *oil*, *wine*, and *corn*. These are necessary to the support and comfort of life; and to those the desire of animal life naturally aspires.

5. These products are looked for from the EARTH. *On* it, and *by* it, grass grows for the cattle, and corn for the service of man.

6. The seeds or germs, whence proceed corn, wine, and oil, live and grow in the earth; but cannot come to perfection, unless the earth be impregnated with the dews and rains from the clouds. They are therefore represented as imploring the heavens to collect their clouds, to pour down their fructifying moisture upon it.

7. The clouds, or materials of which they are composed, not being able to arrange themselves, nor aggregate themselves so as to meet those demands, prevent drought, and maintain an effective vegetation, are represented as calling upon the heavens to form, arrange, and supply them with the requisite quantity of moisture.

8. God, who is the author of all being and all bounty, dependent on nothing, comes forward and says, *I will hear the heavens*, the clouds which are gathered in the atmosphere; he will arrange the particles, saturate those that are *light*, till they become sufficiently *impregnated* with the necessary fluid; and then direct them in his providence *where* to deposit their contents. And,

9. When brought to the proper place, he will *shake* them with his *winds*, or *strike* them with his *thunder*, so as to cause them to fall down in drops to fertilize the earth with their showers.

Thus then—

1. God works upon the *heavens*.

2. In them the *clouds* are collected.

3. The *clouds* drop their moisture upon the earth.

4. The *earth* exerts its vegetative influence upon the *germs* which it contains.

5. *They* expand, increase, and become matured, under the genial influences of the *heavens*, *sun*, *air*, *water*, from the clouds, &c.

6. *Man* receives and applies those bounties of Providence, and *variously prepares* them for the support and comfort of life.

Take all this in still fewer words:—

As *Jezreel* or the *Israelites* are here considered as perishing for want of food, all inanimate nature is represented as invoking God in their behalf.

1. The *heavens* have prayed that they be stored with *clouds*, that they may drop down fatness upon the *earth*.

2. The Lord answers the heavens, and *clouds* are formed.

3. The *earth* invokes the *clouds*, that they may drop down their fatness into its bosom.

4. The *bottles of heaven* are, consequently, unstopped for this purpose.

5. Then the *corn*, *vine*, and *olive*, implore the *earth* to put forth its vegetative energy.

6. The *earth* answers; and *corn*, *wine*, and *oil* are produced.

7. *Jezreel* cries for the necessaries of life, and the abundance of the above supplies all his wants.

All these are dependent on each other, as the links are which constitute a chain; and God has the government of the whole; and he manages all for the benefit of man. How wondrous is this *providence!* How gracious is this GOD!

Here is a series of *prosopopœias* together. Corn, wine, oil, the earth, the clouds and their contents, the *heavens*, sun, moon, &c., are all represented as intelligent beings, speaking to and influencing each other. GOD is at *one end* of the *chain*, and MAN at the *other;* and by means of the *intermediate links* the *latter* is kept in a state of continued dependence upon the *former* for life, breath, and all things.

Verse 23. *I will sow her*] Alluding to the import of the name *Jezreel*, the seed of God. Then shall it appear that God *has shown mercy to them that had not obtained mercy.* Then the *covenant* of God will be renewed; for he will call them *his people* who were *not his people;* and they shall call Jehovah *their God*, who before had *him* not for the object of their worship. It does not appear that these promises have had their fulfilment among the Jews. They must either be understood of the blessings experienced by the *Gentiles* on their conversion to God by the preaching of the Gospel, or are yet to be fulfilled to the Jews on their embracing the Gospel, and being brought back to their own land.

The sentences in the latter part of this verse are very abrupt, but exceedingly expressive; leaving out those words *supplied* by the translators, and which unnerve the passage, it stands thus: *I will say to* NOT MY PEOPLE, THOU MY PEOPLE; and they shall say, MY GOD.

CHAPTER III

By the prophet's taking back his wife, for whom he (*her friend or husband*) *still retained his affection, though she had proved unfaithful; by his entering into a new contract with her; and by his giving her hopes of reconciliation, after she should for some time prove, as in a state of widowhood, the sincerity of her repentance; is represented the gracious manner in which God will restore the Jews from the Babylonish captivity,* 1–4. *It is also very strongly intimated that the whole house of Israel will be added to the Church of Christ in the latter days,* 5.

A. M. cir. 3219 B. C. cir. 785 Ante U. C. 32 Amulii Sylvii, R. Alban., cir. annum 12

THEN said the LORD unto
me, [a]Go yet, love a woman
beloved of *her* [b]friend, yet an
adulteress, according to the love
of the LORD toward the children of Israel,
who look to other gods, and love flagons [c]of
wine.
2 So I bought her to me for fifteen *pieces*
of silver, and *for* a homer of
barley, and a [d]half homer of
barley:
3 And I said unto her, Thou
shalt [e]abide for me many days; thou shalt
not play the harlot, and thou shalt not be for
another man: so *will* I also *be* for thee.
4 For the children of Israel shall abide many

A. M. cir. 3219 B. C. cir. 785 Ante U. C. 32 Amulii Sylvii, R. Alban., cir. annum 12

[a]Chap. i. 2——[b]Jer. iii. 20——[c]Heb. *of grapes*

[d]Heb. *lethech*——[e]Deut. xxi. 13

NOTES ON CHAP. III

Verse 1. *Go yet, love a woman*] This is a different command from that mentioned in the *first* chapter. *That* denoted the infidelity of the kingdom of Israel, and God's divorce of *them.* He gave them up to their *enemies,* and caused them to be *carried into captivity.* The *woman* mentioned *here* represents one who was a *lawful wife* joining herself to a *paramour;* then divorced by her *husband;* afterwards repenting, and desirous to be joined to her spouse; ceasing from her adulterous commerce, but not yet *reconciled* to him. This was the state and disposition of the Jews under the Babylonish captivity. Though separated from their own *idols,* they continued *separated from their God.* He is still represented as having affectionate feelings towards them; awaiting their *full repentance* and *contrition,* in order to renew the marriage covenant. These things are pointed out by the symbolical actions of the prophet.

Beloved of her *friend*] Or, *a lover of evil;* or, *loving another:* for the Hebrew words אהבת רע mean one who *loves evil* or a *friend:* because רע signifies a *friend,* or *evil,* according as it is *pointed.* The former seems to be its best sense here; רע *rea* is a *friend;* רע *ra* is *evil.*

According to the love of the Lord] This woman, who had proved false to her husband, was still beloved by him, though he could not acknowledge her; as the Israelites were beloved by the Lord, while they were *looking after other gods.* The *flagons of wine* were probably such as were used for *libations,* or drunk in idol feasts. Others think that the words should be translated *cakes of dried grapes, sweet cakes, consecrated wafers.*

Verse 2. *Fifteen* pieces *of silver*] If they were *shekels,* the price of this woman was about *two* pounds *five* shillings.

A homer of barley] As the homer was about *eight bushels,* or something more, the *homer and half* was about *twelve* or *thirteen* bushels.

Verse 3. *Thou shalt abide for me many days*] He did not take her home, but made a contract with her that, if she would abstain from her evil ways, he would take her to himself after a sufficient trial. In the meantime he gave her the *money* and the *barley* to subsist upon, that she might not be under the temptation of becoming again unfaithful.

So will *I also* be *for thee.*] That is, if *thou,* Israel, wilt keep thyself separate from thy idolatry, and give me proof, by thy total abstinence from idols, that thou wilt be my faithful worshipper, I will receive thee again, and in the meantime support thee with the *necessaries of life* while thou art in the land of thy captivity. This is farther illustrated in the following verses.

Verse 4. *Many days without a king*] Hitherto this prophecy has been literally fulfilled. Since the destruction of the temple by the Romans they have neither had *king* nor *prince,* nor any *civil government* of their own, but have lived in different nations of the earth as *mere exiles.* They have neither *priests* nor *sacrifices,* nor *urim* nor *thummim;* no *prophet,* no *oracle,* no *communication* of any kind from *God.*

Without an image—ephod—teraphim] The *Septuagint* read, Ουδε ουσης θυσιας, ουδε οντος θυσιαστηριου, ουδε ιερατειας, ουδε δηλων: "Without a sacrifice, without an altar, without a priesthood, and without oracles;" that is, the *urim* and *thummim.* The *Vulgate, Arabic,* and *Syriac* read nearly the same. Instead of מצבה *matstsebah,* an *image,* they have evidently read מזבח

A. M. cir. 3219
B. C. cir. 785
Ante U. C. 32
Amulii Sylvii,
R. Alban.,
cir. annum 12

days [f]without a king, and
without a prince, and without
sacrifice, and without [g]an image,
and without an [h]ephod, and
without [i]teraphim:

5 Afterward shall the children
of Israel return, and [k]seek the
LORD their God, and [l]David
their king; and shall fear the
LORD and his goodness in the [m]latter days.

A. M. cir. 3219
B. C. cir. 785
Ante U. C. 32
Amulii Sylvii,
R. Alban.,
cir. annum 12

[f]Chap. x. 3; Song of the three children, ver. 15 — [g]Heb. *a standing*, or *statue*, or *pillar;* Isa. xix. 19 — [h]Exod. xxviii. 6 — [i]Judg. xviii. 5

[k]Jer. l. 4, 5; Chap. v. 6 — [l]Jer. xxx. 9; Ezek. xxxiv. 23, 24; xxxvii. 22, 24 — [m]Isa. ii. 2; Jer. xxx. 24; Ezek. xxxviii. 8, 16; Dan. ii. 28; Mic. iv. 1

mizbeach, an *altar;* the letters of these words being very similar, and easily mistaken for each other. But instead of either, one, if not two, of *Kennicott's* MSS. has מנחה *minchah*, an *oblation.*

What is called *image* may signify any kind of *pillar*, such as God forbade them to erect, Lev. xxvi. 1, lest it should be an incitement to idolatry.

The *ephod* was the high priest's garment of ceremony; the *teraphim* were some kind of *amulets, telesms*, or *idolatrous images;* the *urim* and *thummim* belonged to the *breastplate*, which was attached to the *ephod.*

Instead of *teraphim* some would read *seraphim*, changing the ת *tau* into ש *sin;* these are an order of the celestial hierarchy. In short, all the time that the Israelites were in captivity in Babylon, they seem to have been as wholly without *forms* of *idolatrous worship* as they were without the *worship of God;* and this may be what the prophet designs: they were totally without any kind of public worship, whether *true* or *false.* As well without *images* and *teraphim*, as they were without *sacrifice* and *ephod*, though still idolaters in their hearts. They were in a state of the most miserable darkness, which was to *continue many days;* and it has continued now nearly *eighteen hundred* years, and must continue yet longer, till they acknowledge him as their *Saviour* whom they crucified as a *blasphemer.*

Verse 5. *Afterward shall the children of Israel return*] Shall *repent* of their iniquities, *and seek the Lord;* lay aside their *mock worship*, and serve the true God *in spirit and in truth.*

And David their king] Or as the *Targum*, "They shall obey the Messiah, the Son of David, their King;" and thus look believingly upon him whom they have pierced, and mourn. And then shall their long *spiritual darkness* and *dismal captivity* have an end; but not before. The *Messiah*, as *David*, is promised in Jer. xxx. 9; Ezek. xxxiv. 23; xxxvii. 22, 24, 25, (where see the notes,) and in this place of *Hosea.* Some think that the *family* of David is intended; but if we go to the rigour of the letter, the *house of Israel* was scarcely ever perfectly submissive to David. And we know that after the death of Solomon they never acknowledged the house of David till they were all carried away captive; and certainly never *since.* And to say that *Zerubbabel* is here meant, is not supportable, as the very *short* and *imperfect obedience* of the Jews to Zerubbabel can never comport with the *high terms* of this and similar prophecies. We are obliged, therefore, from the evidence of these *prophecies*, from the evidence of the above *facts*, from the evidence of the *rabbins* themselves, and from the evidence of the *New Testament*, to consider these texts as applying solely to JESUS CHRST, the promised MESSIAH, who has been a *light to lighten the Gentiles*, and will yet be the *glory of his people Israel.* There is a strange propensity in some men to deny these evidences of Christianity, while they profess to believe its doctrines.

CHAPTER IV

The prophet charges his people with their enormous sins, 1, 2; *in consequence of which they are threatened with heavy judgments*, 3–5. *God himself is then introduced complaining of the ignorance and obstinacy of Israel; and as their priests had a large share in the common guilt, it is declared that they shall be visited with a proportionable share of the common ruin*, 6–11. *The sins of idolatry and divination are then particularly reproved*, 12–14; *and Judah admonished to beware of these sins, which would leave her rebellious sister Israel helpless and desolate as a lamb in a desert*, 15, 16. *In the remaining verses the style is varied, but the subject is the same. Ephraim is given up to idolatry, and the necessary consequence declared to be a bitter draught! Immediately we see him bound in the wings of a mighty tempest, and driven as chaff before the wind, either to destruction or captivity*, 17–19.

A. M. cir. 3224
B. C. cir. 780
Ante U. C. 27
Amulii Sylvii,
R. Alban.,
cir. annum 17

HEAR the word of the LORD,
ye children of Israel: for
the LORD hath a [a]controversy
with the inhabitants of the land,
Because *there is* no truth, nor
mercy, nor [b]knowledge of God
in the land.
2 By swearing, and lying, and

A. M. cir. 3224
B. C. cir. 780
Ante U. C. 27
Amulii Sylvii,
R. Alban.,
cir. annum 17

[a]Isa. i. 18; iii. 13, 14; Jer. xxv. 31; Chap. xii. 2; Mic. vi. 2 — [b]Jer. iv. 22; v. 4

NOTES ON CHAP. IV

Verse 1. *The Lord hath a controversy*] ריב *rib*, what we should call a *lawsuit*, in which God is *plaintiff*, and the Israelites *defendants.* It is Jehovah *versus* Israel and Judah.

But *when* has God a controversy with any land?—*Answer.* When there is *no truth*, *nor*

A. M. cir. 3224 B. C. cir. 780 Ante U. C. 27 Amulii Sylvii, R. Alban., cir. annum 17

killing, and stealing, and com-
mitting adultery, they break out,
and [c]blood toucheth blood.
3 Therefore [d]shall the land
mourn, and [e]every one that dwelleth therein
shall languish, with the beasts of the field,
and with the fowls of heaven; yea, the fishes
of the sea also shall be taken away.
4 Yet let no man strive, nor reprove another: for thy people *are* as they [f]that strive
with the priest.

[c]Heb. *bloods*——[d]Jer. iv. 28; xii. 4; Amos v. 16; viii. 8 [e]Zeph. i. 3

5 Therefore shalt thou fall
[g]in the day, and the prophet
also shall fall with thee in the
night, and I will [h]destroy thy
mother.
6 [i]My people are [k]destroyed for lack of
knowledge: because thou hast rejected knowledge, I will also reject thee, that thou shalt
be no priest to me: seeing thou hast forgotten
the law of thy God, I will also forget thy children.

A. M. cir. 3224 B. C. cir. 780 Ante U. C. 27 Amulii Sylvii, R. Alban., cir. annum 17

[f]Deut. xvii. 12——[g]See Jer. vi. 4, 5; xx. 8——[h]Heb. *cut off*——[i]Isa. v. 13——[k]Heb. *cut off*

mercy, nor knowledge of God in the land. These refer to the *minds* of the people. But wherever these righteous *principles* are wanting, there will soon be a vicious *practice;* hence it is added,

Verse 2. *By swearing, and lying*] Where there is no *truth* there will be *lies and perjury;* for false swearing is brought in to confirm lying statements. And when there is no *mercy, killing, slaying,* and *murders,* will be frequent. And where there is *no knowledge of God,* no conviction of his *omnipresence* and *omniscience,* private offences, such as stealing, adulteries, &c., will prevail. These, sooner or later, *break out,* become a *flood,* and carry all before them. *Private stealing* will assume the form of a *public robbery,* and *adulteries* become *fashionable,* especially among the higher orders; and suits of *crim. con.* render them more public, scandalous, and corrupting. By the examination of *witnesses,* and reading of *infamous letters* in a court of justice, people are taught the *wiles* and *stratagems* to be used to accomplish these ends, and prevent detection; and also how to *avoid* those circumstances which have led to the detection of others. Every *report* of such matters is an *experimental lecture* on *successful debauchery.*

Blood toucheth blood.] Murders are not only frequent, but assassinations are mutual. Men go out to *kill each other;* as in our duels, the frenzy of cowards; and as there is no law regarded, and no justice in the land, the nearest akin slays the murderer. Even in our land, where *duels* are so frequent, if a man kill his antagonist, it is *murder;* and so generally brought in by an honest *coroner* and his jury. It is then brought into court; but who is *hanged* for it? The very murder is considered as an *affair of honour,* though it began in a dispute about a *prostitute;* and it is directed to be brought in manslaughter; and the murderer is slightly fined for having hurried his neighbour, perhaps once his *friend,* into the eternal world, *with all his imperfections on his head!* No wonder that a land *mourns* where these prevail; and that God should have a *controversy* with it. Such crimes as these are sufficient to bring God's curse upon any land. And how does God show his displeasure? See the following verse.

Verse 3. *Therefore shall the land mourn*] Fruitful seasons shall be denied.

That dwelleth therein shall languish] *Endemic* and *epidemic disorders* shall prevail, and multitudes shall die; so that *mourning* shall be found in all quarters.

The beasts of the field, and with the fowls] There is a death of cattle and domestic animals, in consequence of the badness of the season.

The fishes of the sea also shall be taken away.] Those immense shoals which at certain seasons frequent the coasts, which are caught in millions, and become a very useful home supply, and a branch of most profitable traffic, they shall be directed by the unseen influence of God to avoid our coasts, as has frequently been the case with herrings, mackerel, pilchards, &c.; and so this source of supply and wealth has been shut up, because of the iniquities of the land.

Verse 4. *Yet let no man strive*] Or, *no man contendeth.* All these evils stalk abroad unreproved, for all are guilty. None can say, "Let me pluck the *mote* out of thy eye," because he knows that "there is a *beam* in his own."

For thy people are] The *people* and the *priest* are alike *rebels* against the Lord; the priests having become idolaters, as well as the people. Bp. *Newcome* renders this clause, "And as *is* the provocation of the priest, *so is that of my people.*" The whole clause in the original is ועמך כמריבי כהן *veammecha kimeribey cohen,* "and thy people as the rebellions of the priest." But one of my oldest MSS. omits כהן *cohen,* "priest;" and then the text may be read, *And thy people are as rebels.* In this MS. כהן *cohen* is added in the margin by a much later hand.

Verse 5. *Therefore shalt thou fall in the day*] In the most open and public manner, without *snare* or *ambush.*

And the prophet also shall fall—in the night] The false prophet, when employed in taking prognostications from stars, meteors, &c.

And I will destroy thy mother.] The *metropolis* or *mother city. Jerusalem* or *Samaria* is meant.

Verse 6. *My people are destroyed for lack of knowledge*] They have not the knowledge of God, nor of sacred things, nor of their own interest, nor of the danger to which they are exposed. They walk on blindly, and perish.

Because thou hast rejected knowledge] So they might have become wise, had they not rejected the means of improvement.

Thou shalt be no priest to me] If this be the true reading, there must be reference to some *particular priest,* well known, to whom these words are personally addressed; unless by

A. M. cir. 3224
B. C. cir. 780
Ante U. C. 27
Amulii Sylvii,
R. Alban.,
cir. annum 17

7 [l]As they were increased, so they sinned against me: [m]*therefore* will I change their glory into shame.

8 They eat up the sin of my people, and they [n]set their heart on their iniquity.

9 And there shall be, [o]like people, like priest: and I will [p]punish them for their ways, and [q]reward them their doings.

10 For [r]they shall eat, and not have enough: they shall commit whoredom, and shall not increase: because they have left off to take heed to the LORD.

11 Whoredom and wine and new wine [s]take away the heart.

12 My people ask counsel at their [t]stocks, and their staff declareth unto them: for [u]the spirit of whoredoms hath caused *them* to err, and they have gone a whoring from under their God.

13 [v]They sacrifice upon the tops of the mountains, and burn incense upon the hills, under oaks and poplars and elms, because the shadow thereof *is* good: [w]therefore your daughters shall commit whoredom, and your spouses shall commit adultery.

A. M. cir. 3224
B. C. cir. 780
Ante U. C. 27
Amulii Sylvii,
R. Alban.,
cir. annum 17

14 [x]I will not punish your daughters when they commit whoredom, nor your spouses when they commit adultery: for themselves are separated with whores, and they sacrifice with harlots: therefore the people *that* [y]doth not understand shall [z]fall.

15 Though thou, Israel, play the harlot, *yet* let not Judah offend; [a]and come not ye unto Gilgal, neither go ye up to [b]Beth-aven, [c]nor swear, The LORD liveth.

16 For Israel [d]slideth back as a backsliding

[l]Chap. xiii. 6——[m]1 Samuel ii. 30; Malachi ii. 9; Philippians iii. 19——[n]Hebrew, *lift up their soul to their iniquity*——[o]Isa. xxiv. 2; Jer. v. 31——[p]Heb. *visit upon*——[q]Heb. *cause to return*——[r]Lev. xxvi. 26; Mic. vi. 14; Hag. i. 6——[s]Isa. xxviii. 7; See Eccles. vii. 7——[t]Jer. ii. 27; Hab. ii. 19

[u]Isa. xliv. 20; Chap. v. 4——[v]Isa. i. 29; lvii. 5, 7; Ezek. vi. 13; xx. 28——[w]Amos vii. 17; Rom. i. 28——[x]Or, *Shall I not*, &c.——[y]Ver. 1, 6——[z]Or, *be punished*——[a]Chap. ix. 15; xii. 11; Amos iv. 4; v. 5——[b]1 Kings xii. 29; Chap. x. 5——[c]Amos viii. 14; Zeph. i. 5——[d]Jer. iii. 6; vii. 24; viii. 5; Zech. vii. 11

priest the whole *priesthood* is meant, and then it may apply to the *priests of Jeroboam's calves.*

Verse 7. *Will I change their glory into shame.*] As the idolaters at Dan and Bethel have changed my glory into the similitude of an ox that eateth grass, (Rom. i. 23,) so will I change their *glory* into *shame* or ignominy. In the day of my wrath, their calf-gods shall not deliver them.

Verse 8. *They eat up the sin of my people*] חטאת *chattath*, the *sin-offering*, though it be offered contrary to the law; for their *hearts are set on iniquity*, they *wish* to do whatever is contrary to God.

Verse 9. *Like people, like priest*]

"The priest a wanderer from the narrow way;
The silly sheep, no wonder that they stray."

I will punish them] Both priest and people; both equally bad.

Verse 10. *They shall eat, and not have enough*] Whatever means they may use to *satisfy* or *gratify* themselves shall be ineffectual.

Verse 11. *Whoredom and wine*] These debaucheries go generally *together.*

Take away the heart.] Darken the understanding, deprave the judgment, pervert the will, debase all the passions, &c.

Verse 12. *At their stocks*] They consult their *wooden gods.*

And their staff declareth] They use divination by *rods;* see the note on Ezek. xxi., where this sort of divination (*rabdomancy*) is explained.

Verse 13. *Under oaks*] אלון *allon*, from אלל *alal*, he was *strong.* Hence, the *oak*, in Latin, is called *robur;* which word means also, *strength*, the oak being the *strongest* of all the trees of the forest.

The shadow thereof is *good*] Their "daughters committed whoredom, and their spouses committed adultery." 1. Their deities were worshipped by prostitution. 2. They *drank* much in their idol worship, ver. 11, and thus their passions became inflamed. 3. The *thick groves* were favourable to the whoredoms and adulteries mentioned here. In imitation of these, some nations have their public gardens.

Verse 14. *I will not punish*] Why should you be stricken any more; ye will revolt more and more. When God, in judgment, removes his judgments, the case of that people is desperate. While there is *hope*, there is *correction.*

Themselves are separated] There is a reference here to certain debaucheries which should not be described. The state of the people at this time must have been abominable beyond all precedent; animal, sensual, bestial, diabolical: women consecrating themselves to serve their idols by public prostitution; boys dismembered like the *Galli* or priests of Cybele; men and women acting unnaturally; and all conjoining to act diabolically.

Verse 15. *Let not Judah offend*] Israel was *totally* dissolute; Judah was not so. Here she is exhorted to maintain her integrity. If the former will go to what was once *Beth-el*, the *house of God*, now *Beth-aven*, the *house of iniquity*, because Jeroboam has set up his calves there, let not Judah imitate them. *Gilgal* was the place where the covenant of circumcision was renewed when the people passed over Jordan; but was rendered infamous by the worship of idols, after Jeroboam had set up his idolatry.

Verse 16. *Israel slideth back*] They are un-

A. M. cir. 3224
B. C. cir. 780
Ante U. C. 27
Amulii Sylvii,
R. Alban.,
cir. annum 17

heifer: now the LORD will feed
them as a lamb in a large place.
17 Ephraim *is* joined to idols:
[e]let him alone.
18 Their drink [f]is sour: they have
committed whoredom continually: [g]her
[h]rulers *with* shame do love,
Give ye.
19 [i]The wind hath bound
her up in her wings, and [k]they
shall be ashamed because of their sacrifices.

[e]Matt. xv. 14——[f]Heb. *is gone*——[g]Mic. iii. 11; vii. 3——[h]Heb. *shields;* Psa. lxxiv. 9

[i]Psa. i. 4; lxxxiii. 13; Isa. xi. 15; xli. 16; lvii. 13; Jer. iv. 11, 12; li. 1——[k]Isa. i. 29; Jer. ii. 26

tractable, like an unbroken heifer or steer, that *pulls back*, rather than *draw in the yoke*.

Will feed them as a lamb in a large place.] A species of irony. Ye shall go to Assyria, and be scattered among the nations; ye may *sport yourselves* in the extensive empire, wither ye shall be carried captives.

Verse 17. *Ephraim*] The ten tribes.

Is *joined to idols*] Is become incorporated with false gods.

Let him alone.] They are irreclaimable, leave them to the consequences of their vicious conduct.

Verse 18. *Their drink is sour*] Or rather, *he is gone after their wine.* The enticements of idolatry have carried them away.

Her rulers with *shame do love*] Rather, *have loved shame;* they glory in their abominations.

Give ye.] Perhaps it would be better to read, *Her rulers have committed, &c. They have loved gifts. What a shame!* These were *their rulers*, literally, *their shields.* Justice and judgment were perverted.

Verse 19. *The wind hath bound her*] A parching wind has blasted them in their *wings* —coasts, borders; or they are carried away into captivity, as with the most rapid blight. These two last verses are very obscure.

CHAPTER V

This chapter begins with threatening the Israelites for ensnaring the people to idolatry by their sacrifices and other rites on Mizpah and Tabor, 1–5. *Their sacrifices, however costly, are declared to be unacceptable,* 6; *and their substance is devoted to the locust,* 7. *Nor is judgment to stop here. The cities of Judah are called upon, in a very animated manner, to prepare for the approach of enemies. Benjamin is to be pursued; Ephraim is to be desolate; and all this is intimated to Israel, that they may by repentance avert the judgment,* 8, 9. *The following verses contain farther denunciations,* 10–13, *expressed in terms equally terrible and sublime,* 14. *The Lord afflicts not willingly the children of men; he visits them with temporal calamities that he may heal their spiritual malady,* 15.

A. M. cir. 3224
B. C. cir. 780
Ante U. C. 27
Amulii Sylvii,
R. Alban.,
cir. annum 17

HEAR ye this, O priests; and
hearken, ye house of Israel;
and give ye ear, O house of the
king; for judgment *is* toward
you, because [a]ye have been a snare on Mizpah, and a net spread upon Tabor.
2 And the revolters are [b]profound to make
slaughter, [c]though I *have been* [d]a Rebuker
of them all.
3 [e]I know Ephraim, and
Israel is not hid from me: for
now, O Ephraim, [f]thou com-
mittest whoredom, *and* Israel is
defiled.
4 [g]They [h]will not frame their doings to
turn unto their God: for [i]the spirit of whoredoms *is* in the midst of them, and they have
not known the LORD.

[a]Chap. vi. 9——[b]Isa. xxix. 15——[c]Or, *and, &c.*——[d]Heb. *a correction*——[e]Amos iii. 2

[f]Ezek. xxiii. 5, &c.; ch. iv. 17——[g]Heb. *They will not give*——[h]Or, *Their doings will not suffer* them——[i]Chap. iv. 12

NOTES ON CHAP. V

Verse 1. *Hear ye this, O priests*] A process is instituted against the *priests*, the *Israelites*, and the *house of the king;* and they are called on to appear and defend themselves. The accusation is, that they have *ensnared* the people, caused them to practise idolatry, both at *Mizpah* and *Tabor.* Mizpah was situated beyond Jordan, in the mountains of Gilead; see Judg. xi. 29. And Tabor was a beautiful mountain in the tribe of Zebulum. Both these places are said to be eminent for *hunting, &c.*; and hence the natural occurrence of the words *snare* and *net*, in speaking of them.

Verse 2. *The revolters are profound to make slaughter*] Here may be a reference to the practice of *hunters*, making *deep pits* in the ground, and lightly covering them over, that the beasts, not discovering them, might fall in, and become a prey.

Though I have been *a Rebuker*] "I will bring *chastisement* on them all." As they have made *victims* of others to their *idolatry*, I will make *victims* of them to my *justice.* Some have thought that as many as wished to depart from the idolatrous worship set up by Jeroboam, were *slaughtered;* and thus *Jeroboam the son of Nebat* MADE *Israel to sin.*

Verse 3. *I know Ephraim*] I know the whole to be idolaters.

Verse 4. *They will not frame their doings*]

A. M. cir. 3224
B. C. cir. 780
Ante U. C. 27
Amulii Sylvii,
R. Alban.,
cir. annum 17

5 And [k]the pride of Israel doth testify to his face: therefore shall Israel and Ephraim fall in their iniquity: Judah also shall fall with them.

6 [l]They shall go with their flocks and with their herds to seek the LORD; but they shall not find *him;* he hath withdrawn himself from them.

7 They have [m]dealt treacherously against the LORD: for they have begotten strange children: now shall [n]a month devour them with their portions.

8 [o]Blow ye the cornet in Gibeah, *and* the trumpet in Ramah: [p]cry aloud *at* [q]Beth-aven, [r]after thee, O Benjamin.

9 Ephraim shall be desolate in the day of rebuke: among the tribes of Israel have I made known that which shall surely be.

10 The princes of Judah were like them that [s]remove the bound: *therefore* I will pour out my wrath upon them like water.

A. M. cir. 3224
B. C. cir. 780
Ante U. C. 27
Amulii Sylvii,
R. Alban.,
cir. annum 17

11 Ephraim *is* [t]oppressed *and* broken in judgment, because he willingly walked after [u]the commandment.

12 Therefore *will* I *be* unto Ephraim as a moth, and to the house of Judah [v]as [w]rottenness.

13 When Ephraim saw his sickness, and Judah *saw* his [x]wound, then went Ephraim [y]to the Assyrian, [z]and sent [a]to King Jareb: yet could he not heal you, nor cure you of your wound.

14 For [b]I *will be* unto Ephraim as a lion, and as a [c]young lion to the house of Judah: I, *even* I, will tear and go away; I will take away, [d]and none shall rescue *him.*

15 I will go *and* return to my place, [e]till [f]they acknowledge their offence, and seek my face: [g]in their affliction they will seek me early.

---

[k]Chap. vii. 10——[l]Prov. i. 28; Isa. i. 15; Jer. xi. 11; Ezek. viii. 18; Mic. iii. 4; John vii. 34——[m]Isa. xlviii. 8; Jer. iii. 20; v. 11; Chap. vi. 7; Mal. ii. 11——[n]Zech. xi. 8——[o]Chap. viii. 1; Joel ii. 1——[p]Isa. x. 30 [q]Josh. vii. 2; chap. iv. 15——[r]Judg. v. 14——[s]Deut. xix. 14; xxvii. 17——[t]Deut. xxviii. 33——[u]1 Kings xii. 28; Mic. vi. 16

[v]Prov. xii. 4——[w]Or, *a worm*——[x]Jer. xxx. 12——[y]2 Kings xv. 19; chap. vii. 11; xii. 1——[z]Chap. x. 6——[a]Or *to the king of Jareb;* or, *to the king* that *should plead* [b]Lam. iii. 10; chap. xiii. 7, 8——[c]Isa. xxx. 6——[d]Psa. l. 22——[e]Heb. *till they be guilty*——[f]Lev. xxvi. 40, 41; Jer. xxix. 12, 13; Ezek. vi. 9; xx. 43; xxxvi. 31——[g]Psa. lxxviii. 34

They never *purpose* to turn to God, they have fully imbibed the spirit of idolatry.

Verse 5. *The pride of Israel doth testify to his face*] The effrontery with which they practise idolatry manifests, not only their insolence, but the deep depravity of their heart; but their pride and arrogance shall be humbled.

Verse 6. *They shall go with their flocks*] They shall *offer many sacrifices,* professing to *seek* and be reconciled to the Lord; but they shall not *find him.* As they still retain the spirit of their idolatry, he has withdrawn himself from them.

Verse 7. *Now shall a month devour them*] In a month's time the king of Assyria shall be upon them, and oblige them to purchase their lives and liberties by a grievous tax of *fifty* shekels per head. This Menahem, king of Israel, gave to *Pul,* king of Assyria, 2 Kings xv. 16-20. Instead of *month,* some translate the original *locust.* "The locusts shall devour them."

Verse 8. *Blow ye the cornet in Gibeah*] Gibeah and Ramah were cities of Judah, in the tribe of Benjamin.

After thee, O Benjamin] An abrupt call of warning. "Benjamin, fly for thy life! The enemy is just behind thee!" This is a prediction of the invasion of the Assyrians, and the captivity of the *ten* tribes.

Verse 9. *Among the tribes of Israel have I made known*] They have got sufficient warning; it is their own fault that they have not taken it.

Verse 10. *Like them that remove the bound*] As execrable as they who remove the *land-mark.* They have leaped over law's inclosure, and scaled all the walls of right; they have despised and broken all laws, human and Divine.

Verse 11. *Walked after the commandment.*] Jeroboam's commandment to worship his calves at Dan and Beth-el. Many of them were not *forced* to do this; they did it *willingly.*

Verse 12. *Unto Ephraim as a moth*] I will consume them by little and little, as a moth frets a garment.

Verse 13. *When Ephraim saw his sickness*] When both Israel and Judah felt their own weakness to resist their enemies, instead of calling upon and trusting in *me,* they sought sinful alliances, and trusted in their idols.

King Jareb] This name occurs nowhere in Scripture but here and in chap. x. 6. The *Vulgate* and *Targum* render ירב *yareb,* an *avenger,* a person whom they thought able to *save them* from their enemies. It is well known that *Menahem,* king of Israel, sought alliance with *Pul* and *Tiglath-pileser,* kings of Assyria, and *Ahaz,* king of Judah. These were the *protectors* that Ephraim sought after. See 2 Kings xv. and xvi. But far from *healing them* by making them tributary, the Assyrians made their *wound* more dangerous.

Verse 14. *I* will be—*as a lion*] כשחל *cashshachel,* as a *panther* or *lioness.*

Verse 15. *I will go* and *return to my place*] I will abandon them till they acknowledge their offences. This had the wished-for effect, as we shall see in the following chapter; for they repented and turned to God, and he had mercy upon them. These two verses are considered as instances of the *true sublime.*

CHAPTER VI

The prophet earnestly exhorts to repentance, 1–3. *God is then introduced as very tenderly and pathetically remonstrating against the backslidings of Ephraim and Judah,* 4–11.

A. M. cir. 3224
B. C. cir. 780
Ante U. C. 27
Amulii Sylvii,
R. Alban.,
cir. annum 17

COME, and let us return unto
the LORD: for [a]he hath torn,
and [b]he will heal us; he hath
smitten, and he will bind us up.
2 [c]After two days will he revive us: in the
third day he will raise us up, and we shall
live in his sight.
3 [d]Then shall we know, *if* we follow on to
know the LORD: his going forth is prepared
[e]as the morning; and [f]he shall
come unto us [g]as the rain, as
the latter *and* former rain unto
the earth.
4 [h]O Ephraim, what shall I do unto thee?
O Judah, what shall I do unto thee? for your
[i]goodness *is* [k]as a morning cloud, and as the
early dew it goeth away.
5 Therefore have I hewed *them* [l]by the

[a]Deuteronomy xxxii. 39; 1 Samuel ii. 6; Job. v. 18; Chapter v. 14——[b]Jeremiah xxx. 17——[c]1 Corinthians xv. 4——[d]Isaiah liv. 13——[e]2 Samuel xxiii. 4——[f]Psalm lxxii. 6——[g]Job xxix. 23——[h]Chap. xi. 8——[i]Or, *mercy,* or *kindness*——[k]Chap. xiii. 3——[l]Jer. i. 10; v. 14

NOTES ON CHAP. VI

Verse 1. *Come, and let us return unto the Lord*] When God had purposed to abandon them, and they found that he had *returned to his place*—to his temple, where alone he could be successfully sought; they, feeling their weakness, and the fickleness, weakness, and unfaithfulness of their idols and allies, now resolve to "return to the Lord;" and, referring to what he said, chap. v. 14: "I will tear and go away;" they say, he "hath torn, but he will heal us;" their allies had *torn,* but they gave them no healing. While, therefore, they acknowledge the *justice* of God in their punishment, they depend on his well-known mercy and compassion for restoration to life and health.

Verse 2. *After two days will he revive*] Such is his power that in *two* or *three* days he can restore us. He can realize all our hopes, and give us the strongest token for good.

In the third day he will raise us up] In so short a time can he give us complete deliverance. These words are supposed to refer to the *death and resurrection of our Lord;* and it is thought that the apostle refers to them, 1 Cor. xv. 4: "Christ rose again the third day, according to the Scriptures;" and this is the *only place* in the *Scriptures,* i. e., of the Old Testament, where his resurrection on the *third* day seems to be hinted at. The original, יקמנו *yekimenu,* has been translated, *he will raise him up.* Then they who trusted in him could believe that they should be *quickened* together with him.

And we shall live in his sight.] *His resurrection* being a proof of *theirs.*

Verse 3. *Then shall we know*] We shall have the fullest evidence that we have not believed in vain.

If *we follow on to know the Lord*] If we *continue* to be as much in *earnest* as we *now* are.

His going forth] The manifestation of his mercy to our souls is as certain as the *rising of the sun* at the appointed time.

And he shall come unto us as the rain] As surely as the early and the latter rain come. The first, to prepare the earth for the seed; this fell in *autumn:* the second, to prepare the full ear for the harvest; this fell in *spring.* Here is strong confidence; but not misplaced, however worthless the persons were. As surely as the *sun,* who is *now set,* is running his course to *arise* on us in the *morning,* and make a glorious *day* after a dreary *night;* so surely shall the Lord *come again from his place,* and the Sun of righteousness shall arise on our souls with healing in his wings. He is already *on his way* to save us.

Verse 4. *O Ephraim, what shall I do unto thee?*] This is the answer of the Lord to the above pious resolutions; sincere while they lasted, but frequently forgotten, because the people were fickle. Their *goodness* (for goodness it was while it endured) was *like the morning cloud that fadeth away* before the rising sun, or like the *early dew* which is speedily evaporated by heat. Ephraim and Judah had too much *goodness* in them to admit of their total rejection, and too much *evil* to admit of their being placed among the children. Speaking after the manner of men, the *justice* and *mercy* of God seem puzzled how to act toward them. When *justice* was about to *destroy* them for their iniquity, it was prevented by their *repentance* and *contrition:* when *mercy* was about to pour upon them as penitents its choicest blessings, it was prevented by their *fickleness* and *relapse!* These things induce the just and merciful God to exclaim, "O Ephraim, what shall I do unto thee? O Judah, what shall I do unto thee?" The only thing that could be done in such a case was that which God did.

Verse 5. *Therefore have I hewed* them *by the prophets*] I have sent my prophets to testify against their fickleness. They have smitten them with the most solemn and awful threatenings; they have, as it were, slain them by the words of my mouth. But to what purpose?

Thy judgments are as *the light* that *goeth forth*] Instead of ומשפטיך אור יצא *umispateycha or yetse,* "and thy judgments a light that goeth forth," the *versions* in general have read ומשפטי כאור *umishpati keor,* "and my judgment *is* as the light." The final ך *caph* in the common reading has by mistake been taken from אור *aur,* and joined to משפטי *mishpati;* and thus turned it from the *singular* to the *plural* number, with the postfix ך *cha.* The proper reading is, most probably, "And my judgment is as the light going forth." It shall be both *evident* and *swift;* alluding both to the *velocity* and *splendour* of light.

A. M. cir. 3224
B. C. cir. 780
Ante U. C. 27
Amulii Sylvii,
R. Alban.,
cir. annum 17

prophets; I have slain them by
[m]the words of my mouth: [n]and
thy judgments *are as* the light
that goeth forth.
6 For I desired [o]mercy, and [p]not sacrifice;
and the [q]knowledge of God more than burnt
offerings.
7 But they [r]like men [s]have transgressed the
covenant: there [t]have they dealt treacherously against me.
8 [u]Gilead *is* a city of them that work iniquity, *and is* [v]polluted with blood.
9 And as troops of robbers
wait for a man, *so* [w]the company
of priests murder in the way
[x]by consent: for they commit
[y]lewdness.
10 I have seen [z]a horrible thing in the house
of Israel: there *is* [a]the whoredom of Ephraim,
Israel is defiled.
11 Also, O Judah, [b]he hath set a harvest
for thee, [c]when I returned the captivity of
my people.

A. M. cir. 3224
B. C. cir. 780
Ante U. C. 27
Amulii Sylvii,
R. Alban.,
cir. annum 17

---

[m]Jer. xxiii. 29; Heb. iv. 12——[n]Or, *that thy judgments might be*, &c.——[o]1 Sam. xv. 22; Eccles. v. 1; Mic. vi. 8; Matt. ix. 13; xii. 7——[p]Psa. l. 8, 9; Prov. xxi. 3; Isa. i. 11——[q]Jer. xxii. 16; John. xvii. 3——[r]Or, *like Adam;* Job xxxi. 33——[s]Chap. viii. 1

[t]Chap. v. 7——[u]Chap. xii. 11——[v]Or, *cunning for blood*——[w]Jer. xi. 9; Ezek. xxii. 25; Chap. v. 1, 2 [x]Heb. *with* one *shoulder*, or *to Shechem*——[y]Or, *enormity*——[z]Jer. v. 31——[a]Chap. iv. 12, 13, 17——[b]Jer. li. 33; Joel iii. 13; Rev. xiv. 15——[c]Isa. cxxvi. 1

Verse 6. *I desired mercy, and not sacrifice*] I taught them righteousness by my prophets; for I desired mercy. I was more willing to *save* than to *destroy;* and would rather see them full of *penitent* and *holy resolutions*, than behold them offering the *best* and most *numerous victims* upon my altar. See Matt. ix. 13.

Verse 7. *But they like men* (כאדם *keadam*, "like Adam") *have transgressed the covenant*] They have sinned against light and knowledge as *he* did. This is *sense*, the other is scarcely so. There was a striking similarity in the two cases. *Adam, in Paradise*, transgressed the commandment, and I *cast him out: Israel*, in possession of the *promised land*, transgressed my covenant, and I cast *them* out, and sent them into captivity.

Verse 8. *Gilead* is *a city of them that work iniquity*] In this place Jacob and Laban made their covenant, and set up a *heap of stones*, which was called *Galeed*, the *heap of testimony;* and most probably idolatry was set up here. Perhaps the very *heap* became the object of superstitious adoration.

Verse 9. *As troops of robbers*] What a sad picture is this of the state of the priesthood! The country of Gilead was infamous for its robberies and murders. The idolatrous priests there formed themselves into companies, and kept possession of the roads and passes; and if they found any person going to Jerusalem to worship the true God, they put him to death. The reason is given:—

For they commit lewdness.] They are gross idolaters.

Verse 10. *I have seen a horrible thing*] That is, the idolatry that prevailed in Israel to such a degree that the whole land was defiled.

Verse 11. *O Judah, he hath set a harvest for thee*] Thou also hast transgressed; thy *harvest* will come; thou shalt be *reaped down* and sent into captivity. The *sickle* is already thrust in. That which thou *hast sowed* shalt thou *reap.* They who *sow* unto the *flesh* shall *reap corruption.*

When I returned the captivity of my people.] Bp. *Newcome* translates, "Among those who lead away the captivity of my people." There is thy harvest; they who have led Israel into captivity shall lead thee also into the same. The Assyrians and Babylonians were the same kind of people; equally idolatrous, equally oppressive, equally cruel. From the common reading some suppose this to be a *promise of return from captivity.* It is true that *Judah* was gathered together again and brought back to their own land; but the majority of the *Israelites* did not return, and are not now to be found.

CHAPTER VII

Here God complains that though he had employed every means for reforming Israel, they still persisted in their iniquity, without fearing the consequences, 1, 2; *that those who ought to check their crimes were pleased with them*, 3; *and that they all burned with adultery, as an oven when fully heated, and ready to receive the kneaded dough*, 4. *The* fifth *verse alludes to some recent enormities; the* sixth *charges them with dividing their time between inactivity and iniquity; the* seventh *alludes to their civil broils and conspiracies;* (*see* 2 Kings xv. 10, 14, 25;) *the* eighth *to their joining themselves with idolatrous nations; and the* ninth *describes the sad consequence. The* tenth *verse reproves their pride and open contempt of God's worship; the* eleventh *reproves their foolish conduct in applying for aid to their enemies;* (*see* 2 Kings xv. 19, *and* xvii. 4;) *the* twelfth *and* thirteenth *threaten them with punishments; the* fourteenth *charges them with hypocrisy in their acts of humiliation; the* fifteenth *with ingratitude; and the image of the deceitful bow, in the* sixteenth *verse, is highly expressive of their frequent apostasies; and their hard speeches against God shall be visited upon them by their becoming a reproach in the land of their enemies.*

A. M. cir. 3224
B. C. cir. 780
Ante U. C. 27
Amulii Sylvii,
R. Alban.,
cir. annum 17

WHEN I would have healed
Israel, then the iniquity
of Ephraim was discovered, and
the [a]wickedness of Samaria: for
[b]they commit falsehood; and the thief cometh
in *and* the troop of robbers [c]spoileth without.
2 And they [d]consider not in their hearts
that I [e]remember all their wickedness: now
[f]their own doings have beset them about;
they are [g]before my face.
3 They make the king glad with their wickedness, and the princes [h]with their lies.
4 [i]They *are* all adulterers, as an oven heated
by the baker, [k]*who* ceaseth [l]from raising
after he hath kneaded the dough, until it be
leavened.

A. M. cir. 3224
B. C. cir. 780
Ante U. C. 27
Amulii Sylvii,
R. Alban.,
cir. annum 17

5 In the day of our king the
princes have made *him* sick
[m]with bottles of wine; he stretched out his hand with scorners.
6 For they have [n]made ready their heart
like an oven, whiles they lie in wait: their
baker sleepeth all the night; in the morning
it burneth as a flaming fire.
7 They are all hot as an oven, and have devoured their judges; [o]all their kings [p]are
fallen: [q]*there is* none among them that calleth
unto me.
8 Ephraim, he [r]hath mixed himself among
the people; Ephraim is a cake not turned.
9 [s]Strangers have devoured his strength, and
he knoweth *it* not: yea, gray hairs are [t]here

---

[a]Heb. *evils*——[b]Chap. v. 1; vi. 10——[c]Hebrew, *strippeth*——[d]Heb. *say not to*——[e]Jer. xvii. 1——[f]Psa. ix. 16; Prov. v. 22——[g]Psa. xc. 8——[h]Rom. i. 32 [i]Jer. ix. 2——[k]Or, *the raiser will cease*

[l]Or, *from waking*——[m]Or, *with heat through wine* [n]Or, *applied*——[o]Chapter viii. 4——[p]2 Kings xv. 10, 14, 25, 30——[q]Isa. lxiv. 7——[r]Psa. cvi. 35——[s]Chap. viii. 7——[t]Hebrew, *sprinkled*

NOTES ON CHAP. VII

Verse 1. *When I would have healed Israel*] As soon as one wound was healed, another was discovered. Scarcely was one sin blotted out till another was committed.

The thief cometh in] Their own princes spoil them.

The troop of robbers spoileth without.] The Assyrians, under different leaders, waste and plunder the country.

Verse 2. *They consider not in their hearts*] They do not consider that *my eye is upon all their ways;* they do not think that I *record* all their wickedness; and they know not their *own* evil *doings* are as a *host of enemies encompassing* them about.

Verse 3. *They make the king glad*] They pleased Jeroboam by coming readily into his measures, and heartily joining with him in his idolatry. And they professed to be perfectly happy in their change, and to be greatly advantaged by their new gods; and that the religion of the state now was better than that of Jehovah. Thus, they made all their rulers, "glad with their lies."

Verse 4. *As an oven heated by the baker*] *Calmet's* paraphrase on this and the following verses expresses pretty nearly the sense: Hosea makes a twofold comparison of the Israelites; to an *oven,* and to *dough.* Jeroboam set fire to his own *oven*—his kingdom—and put the leaven in his dough; and afterwards went to rest, that the fire might have time to heat his *oven,* and the *leaven* to raise his *dough,* that the false principles which he introduced might infect the whole population. This prince, purposing to make his subjects relinquish their ancient religion, put, in a certain sense, the fire to his own oven, and mixed his dough with leaven. At first he used no violence; but was satisfied with exhorting them, and proclaiming a feast. This *fire* spread very rapidly, and the *dough* was very soon impregnated by the *leaven.* All Israel was seen running to this feast, and partaking in these innovations. But what shall become of the *oven*—the *kingdom;* and the *bread*—the *people?* The *oven* shall be consumed by these flames; the king, the princes, and the people shall be enveloped in the burning, ver. 7. Israel was *put under the ashes,* as a *loaf* well kneaded and leavened; but not being carefully *turned,* it was burnt on one side before those who prepared it could eat of it; and *enemies* and *strangers* came and carried off the loaf. See ver. 8 and 9. Their lasting captivity was the consequence of their wickedness and their apostasy from the religion of their fathers. On this explication verses 4, 5, 6, 7, 8, and 9, may be easily understood.

Verse 7. *All their kings are fallen*] There was a pitiful slaughter among the idolatrous kings of Israel; *four* of them had fallen in the time of this prophet. Zechariah was slain by Shallum; Shallum, by Menahem; Pekahiah, by Pekah; and Pekah, by Hoshea, 2 Kings xv. All were idolaters, and all came to an untimely death.

Verse 8. *A cake not turned.*] In the East, having heated the *hearth,* they sweep one corner, put the cake upon it, and cover it with embers; in a short time they *turn* it, cover it again, and continue this several times, till they find it sufficiently baked. All travellers into Asiatic countries have noted this.

Verse 9. *Gray hairs are here and there upon him, yet he knoweth not.*] The kingdom is grown old in iniquity; the time of their captivity is at hand, and they are apprehensive of no danger. They are in the state of a *silly old man,* who through age and infirmities is become nearly *bald,* and the few *remaining hairs* on his head are quite *gray.* But he does not consider his latter end; is making no provision for that eternity on the brink of which he is constantly standing; does not apply to the sovereign Physician to heal his spiritual diseases; but calls in the *doctors* to cure him of *old age* and *death!* This miserable state and preposterous conduct we witness every day. O how fast

A. M. cir. 3224
B. C. cir. 780
Ante U. C. 27
Amulii Sylvii,
R. Alban.,
cir. annum 17

and there upon him, yet he
knoweth not.
10 And the [u]pride of Israel
testified to his face: and [v]they
do not return to the LORD their God, nor seek
him for all this.
11 [w]Ephraim also is like a silly dove without heart: [x]they call to Egypt, they go to
Assyria.
12 When they shall go, [y]I will spread my
net upon them; I will bring them down as
the fowls of the heaven; I will chastise them,
[z]as their congregation hath heard.
13 Wo unto them! for they have fled from
me: [a]destruction unto them! because they have
transgressed against me: though
[b]I have redeemed them, yet they
have spoken lies against me.
14 [c]And they have not cried
unto me with their heart, when they howled
upon their beds: they assemble themselves
for corn and wine, *and* they rebel against me.
15 Though I [d]have bound *and* strengthened
their arms, yet do they imagine mischief
against me.
16 [e]They return, *but* not to the Most High:
[f]they are like a deceitful bow: their princes
shall fall by the sword for the [g]rage of their
tongue: this *shall be* their derision [h]in the
land of Egypt.

A. M. cir. 3224
B. C. cir. 780
Ante U. C. 27
Amulii Sylvii,
R. Alban.,
cir. annum 17

[u]Chap. v. 5——[v]Isa. ix. 13——[w]Chap. xi. 11——[x]See 2 Kings xv. 19; xvii. 4; chap. v. 13; ix. 3; xii. 1——[y]Ezek. xii. 13——[z]Lev. xxvi. 14, &c.; Deut. xxviii. 15, &c.; 2 Kings xvii. 13, 18

[a]Heb. *spoil*——[b]Mic. vi. 4——[c]Job xxxv. 9, 10; Psa. lxxviii. 36; Jer. iii. 10; Zech. vii. 5——[d]Or, *chastened*——[e]Chap. xi. 7——[f]Psalm lxxvii. 57——[g]Psalm lxxiii. 9——[h]Chapter ix. 3, 6

does the human being cling to his native earth! Reader, hear the voice of an old man:—

O my *coevals!* remnants of yourselves,
Shall *our* pale wither'd hands be *still stretch'd out?*
Trembling at once with *eagerness* and *age;*
With *avarice* and *ambition* grasping—fast
Grasping at *air!* For what hath *earth* beside?
We want but *little;* nor THAT LITTLE *long.*

Verse 10. *The pride of Israel*] The same words as at chap. v. 5, where see the note.

Verse 11. *Ephraim also is like a silly dove without heart*] A bird that has *little understanding;* that is *easily snared* and taken; that is careless about its *own young,* and seems to live without *any kind of thought.* It has been made, by those who, like itself, are *without heart,* the *symbol of conjugal affection.* Nothing *worse* could have been chosen, for the dove and its mate are continually quarrelling.

They call to Egypt, they go to Assyria.] They strive to make these their allies and friends; but in this they showed that they were *without heart,* had not a *sound understanding;* for these were rival nations, and Israel could not attach itself to the one without incurring the jealousy and displeasure of the other. Thus, like the *silly dove,* they were constantly falling into *snares;* sometimes of the Egyptians, at others of the Assyrians. By the former they were *betrayed;* by the latter, *ruined.*

Verse 12. *When they shall go*] To those nations for help—

I will spread my net upon them] I will cause them to be taken by those in whom they trusted.

I will bring them down] They shall no sooner set off to seek this foreign help, than *my net* shall *bring them down to the earth.* The allusion to the *dove,* and to the mode of taking the *fowls of heaven,* is still carried on.

As their congregation hath heard.] As in their *solemn assemblies* they before have heard; in the *reading of my law,* and the denunciation of my wrath against *idolaters.*

Bishop *Newcome* translates: "I will chastise them when they hearken to their assembly." That is, when they take the counsel of their elders to go down to Egypt for help, and trust in the arm of the Assyrians for succour.

Verse 13. *Wo unto them!*] They shall have *wo,* because they *have fled from me.* They shall have *destruction,* because they *have transgressed against me.*

Though I have redeemed them] Out of Egypt; and given them the fullest proof of my love and power.

Yet they have spoken lies against me.] They have represented me as rigorous and cruel; and my service as painful and unprofitable.

Verse 14. *They have not cried unto me with their heart*] They say they have sought me, but could not find me; that they have cried unto me, but I did not answer. I know they have *cried,* yea, *howled;* but could I hear them when all was forced and hypocritical, not one sigh coming from their *heart?*

They assemble themselves for corn and wine] In dearth and famine they call and howl: but they assemble themselves, not to seek ME, but to invoke their false gods for corn and wine.

Verse 15. *Though I have bound* and *strengthened their arms*] Whether I dealt with them in *judgment* or *mercy,* it was all one; in all circumstances they rebelled against me.

Verse 16. *They return,* but *not to the Most High*] They go to their idols.

They are like a deceitful bow] Which, when it is *reflexed,* in order to be strung, suddenly *springs back* into its *quiescent curve;* for the *eastern bows* stand in their quiescent state in a curve, something like ⊂⊃; and in order to be strung must be *bended back* in the *opposite direction.* This bending of the bow requires both *strength* and *skill;* and if not properly done, it will fly back, and regain its former position; and in this recoil endanger the archer—may even break an arm. I have been in this danger myself in bending the Asiatic bow. For want of this knowledge not one commentator has hit the meaning of the passage.

Shall fall by the sword] Their *tongue* has been enraged against ME; the *sword* shall be enraged against them. They have *mocked* me, (ver. 5,) and their fall is now a subject of *derision in the land of Egypt*. What they have sown, that do they now reap.

CHAPTER VIII

This chapter begins with threatening some hostile invasion in short and broken sentences, full of rapidity, and expressive of sudden danger and alarm: "The trumpet to thy mouth; he cometh as an eagle," 1. *And why? For their hypocrisy,* 2; *iniquity,* 3; *treason (see* 2 Kings xv. 13, 17) *and idolatry,* 4; *particularly the worshipping of the calves of Dan and Beth-el,* 5, 6. *The folly and unprofitableness of pursuing evil courses is then set forth in brief but very emphatic terms. The labour of the wicked is vain, like sowing of the wind; and the fruit of it destructive as the whirlwind. Like corn blighted in the bud, their toil shall have no recompense; or if it should have a little, their enemies shall devour it,* 7. *They themselves, too, shall suffer the same fate, and shall be treated by the nations of Assyria and Egypt as the vile sherds of a broken vessel,* 8, 9. *Their incorrigible idolatry is again declared to be the cause of their approaching captivity under the king of Assyria. And as they delighted in idolatrous altars, there they shall have these in abundance,* 10–14. *The last words contain a prediction of the destruction of the fenced cities of Judah, because the people trusted in these for deliverance, and not in the Lord their God.*

A. M. cir. 3244
B. C. cir. 760
Ante U. C. 7
Amulii Sylvii,
R. Alban.,
cir. annum 37

SET [a]the trumpet to [b]thy
mouth. *He shall come* [c]as
an eagle against the house of the
LORD, because [d]they have transgressed my covenant, and trespassed against
my law.
2 [e]Israel shall cry unto me, My God, [f]we
know thee.
3 Israel hath cast off *the thing that is* good:
the enemy shall pursue him.
4 [g]They have set up kings, but
not by me: they have made
princes, and I knew *it* not: [h]of
their silver and their gold have
they made them idols, that they may be cut off.
5 Thy calf, O Samaria, hath cast *thee* off;
mine anger is kindled against them: [i]how
long *will it be* ere they attain to innocency?
6 For from Israel *was* it also: the workman made it; therefore it *is* not God; but

A. M. cir. 3244
B. C. cir. 760
Ante U. C. 7
Amulii Sylvii,
R. Alban.,
cir. annum 37

---

[a]Chapter v. 8——[b]Hebrew, *the roof of thy mouth*——[c]Deuteronomy xxviii. 49; Jeremiah iv. 13; Habakkuk i. 8——[d]Chapter vi. 7——[e]Psalm lxxviii. 34; chapter v. 15——[f]Titus i. 16——[g]2 Kings xv. 13, 17, 25, Shallum, Menahem, Pekahiah——[h]Chapter ii. 8; xiii. 2——[i]Jeremiah xiii. 27

NOTES ON CHAP. VIII

Verse 1. Set *the trumpet to thy mouth*] Sound another alarm. Let them know that an enemy is fast approaching.

As an eagle against the house of the Lord] If this be a prophecy against *Judah*, as some have supposed, then by the *eagle* Nebuchadnezzar is meant, who is often compared to this king of birds. See Ezek. xvii. 3; Jer, xlviii. 40; xlix. 22; Dan. vii. 4.

But if the prophecy be against *Israel*, which is the most likely, then *Shalmaneser*, king of Assyria, is intended, who, for his rapidity, avarice, rapacity, and strength, is fitly compared to this royal bird. He is represented here as *hovering over the house of God*, as the eagle does over the prey which he has just espied, and on which he is immediately to pounce.

Verse 2. *Israel shall cry*] The rapidity of the eagle's flight is well imitated in the rapidity of the sentences in this place.

My God, we know thee.] The same sentiment, from the same sort of persons, under the same feelings, as that in the Gospel of St. Matthew, chap. vii. 22: "Lord, have we not prophesied in thy name? and in thy name have cast out devils? Then will I profess unto them, I never KNEW YOU."

Verse 4. *They have set up kings, but not by me*] Properly speaking, not one of the kings of Israel, from the defection of the ten tribes from the house of David, was the *anointed* of the Lord.

I knew it *not*] It had not my *approbation*. In this sense the word *know* is frequently understood.

That they may be cut off.] That is, They shall be cut off in consequence of their idolatry.

Verse 5. *Thy calf, O Samaria, hath cast* thee *off*] Bishop *Newcome* translates: "Remove far from thee thy calf, O Samaria!" Abandon thy idolatry; for *my anger is kindled against thee.*

How long will it be *ere they attain to innocency?*] How long will ye continue your guilty practices? When shall it be said that ye are from these vices? The *calf* or *ox*, which was the object of the idolatrous worship of the Israelites, was a supreme deity in Egypt; and it was there they learned this idolatry. A white ox was worshipped under the name of *Apis*, at Memphis; and another ox under the name of *Mnevis*, was worshipped at On, or Heliopolis. To Osiris the males of this genus were consecrated, and the females to Isis. It is a most ancient superstition, and still prevails in the East. The cow is a most sacred animal among the Hindoos.

Verse 6. *The workman made it; therefore it* is *not God*] As God signifies the supreme eternal Good, the Creator and Upholder of all things, therefore the workman cannot make

A. M. cir. 3244
B. C. cir. 760
Ante U. C. 7
Amulii Sylvii,
R. Alban.,
cir. annum 37

the calf of Samaria shall be
broken in pieces.
7 For [k]they have sown the
wind, and they shall reap the
whirlwind: it hath no [l]stalk: the bud shall
yield no meal: if so be it yield, [m]the strangers
shall swallow it up.
8 [n]Israel is swallowed up: now shall they
be among the Gentiles [o]as a vessel wherein
is no pleasure.
9 For [p]they are gone up to Assyria, [q]a wild
ass alone by himself: Ephraim [r]hath hired
[s]lovers.
10 Yea, though they have hired among the
nations, now [t]will I gather them, and they
shall [u]sorrow [v]a little for the burden of [w]the
king of princes.

[k]Prov. xxii. 8; Ch. x. 12, 13——[l]Or, *standing corn*——[m]Ch. vii. 9——[n]2 Kings xvii. 6——[o]Jer. xxii. 28; xlviii. 38——[p]2 Kings xv. 19——[q]Jer. ii. 24——[r]Isa. xxx. 6; Ezek. xvi. 33, 34——[s]Heb. *loves*——[t]Ezek. xvi. 37; Ch. x. 10——[u]Or, *begin*——[v]Or, *in a little while*, as Hag. ii. 6——[w]Isa. x. 8; Ezek. xxvi. 7; Dan. ii. 37——[x]Ch. xii. 11

A. M. cir. 3244
B. C. cir. 760
Ante U. C. 7
Amulii Sylvii,
R. Alban.,
cir. annum 37

11 Because Ephraim hath
made [x]many altars to sin,
altars shall be unto him to
sin.
12 I have written to him [y]the great things
of my law, *but* they were counted as a strange
thing.
13 [z]They [a]sacrifice flesh *for* the sacrifices
of mine offerings, and eat *it;* [b]*but* the LORD
accepteth them not; [c]now will he remember
their iniquity, and visit their sins: [d]they shall
return to Egypt.
14 [e]For Israel hath forgotten [f]his Maker,
and [g]buildeth temples: and Judah hath multiplied fenced cities: but [h]I will send a fire
upon his cities, and it shall devour the palaces
thereof.

[y]Deut. iv. 6, 8; Psa. cxix. 18; cxlvii. 19, 20——[z]Jer. vii. 21; Zech. vii. 6——[a]Or, *in the sacrifices of mine offerings they*, &c.——[b]Jer. xiv. 10, 12; Ch. v. 6; ix. 4; Amos v. 22——[c]Ch. ix. 9; Amos viii. 7——[d]Deut. xxviii. 68; ch. ix. 3, 6; xi. 5——[e]Deut. xxxii. 18——[f]Isa. xxix. 23; Eph. ii. 10——[g]1 Kings xii. 31——[h]Jer. xvii. 27; Amos ii. 5

Him who made all things. This is an overwhelming argument against all idols. Nothing need be added. *The workman has made them; therefore they are not God.*

Verse 7. *They have sown the wind, and they shall reap the whirlwind*] As the husbandman reaps the same kind of grain which he has sown, but in far greater abundance, *thirty, sixty*, or *one hundred* fold; so he who sows the wind shall have a whirlwind to reap. The *vental* seed shall be multiplied into a *tempest;* so they who sow the seed of unrighteousness shall reap a harvest of judgment. This is a fine, bold, and energetic metaphor.

It hath no stalk] Nothing that can yield a *blossom.* If it have a *blossom,* that blossom shall not yield *fruit;* if there be *fruit.* the sower shall not enjoy it, for *strangers shall eat it.* The meaning is, the labours of this people shall be utterly unprofitable and vain.

Verse 8. *Now shall they be among the Gentiles*] They shall be carried into captivity, and there be as a vessel wherein there is no pleasure; one soiled, unclean, infectious, to be despised, abhorred, not used. The allusion is to a rotten, corrupted skin-bottle; a bottle made of goat, deer, or calf hide, still commonly used in Asia and Africa. Some of them are splendidly ornamented. This is the case with one now before me made of a goat's skin well dressed, variously painted, and ornamented with leather fringes, tassels, &c. In such a bottle there might be pleasure; but the Israelites are compared to such a bottle, rough, ill-dressed, not ornamented, old, musty, and putrid. This shows the force of the comparison.

Verse 9. *They are gone up to Assyria*] For succour.

A wild ass alone by himself] Like that animal, jealous of its liberty, and suffering no rival. If we may credit *Pliny* and others, one male wild ass will keep a whole flock of females to himself, suffer no other to approach them, and even bite off the genitals of the colts, lest in process of time they should become his rivals. "Mares singuli fæminarum gregibus imperitant; timent libidinis æmulos, et ideo gravidas custodiunt, morsuque natos mares castrant."—*Hist. Nat.*, lib. viii., c. 30. The Israelites, with all this selfishness and love of liberty, took no step that did not necessarily lead to their thraldom and destruction.

Ephraim hath hired lovers.] Hath subsidized the neighbouring heathen states.

Verse 10. *For the burden of the king of princes.*] The exactions of the Assyrian king, and the princes of the provinces.

Verse 11. *Many altars to sin*] Though it does not appear that the Jews in Babylon were obliged to worship the idols of the country, except in the case mentioned by Daniel, yet it was far otherwise with the Israelites in Assyria, and the other countries of their dispersion. Because they had made many altars to sin while they were in their own land, they were obliged to *continue* in the land of their captivity a similar system of idolatry against their will. Thus they felt and saw the evil of their idolatry, without power to help themselves.

Verse 12. *I have written to him the great things of my law*] I have as it were inscribed my laws to them, and they have treated them as matters in which they had no interest.

Verse 13. *They sacrifice flesh*] Bp. *Newcome* translates thus: "They sacrifice gifts appointed unto me, and eat flesh." They offer to their idols the things which belong to Jehovah; or, while pretending to offer unto the Lord, they eat and drink idolatrously; and therefore the Lord will not accept them.

They shall return to Egypt.] Many of them did return to Egypt after the conquest of Palestine by Shalmaneser, and many after the ruin of Jerusalem by Nebuchadnezzar; but they had in effect returned to Egypt by setting up the worship of the golden calves, which were in imitation of the Egyptian *Apis*.

Verse 14. *Israel hath forgotten his Maker*] And therefore built *temples* to other gods. *Judah* had lost all confidence in the Divine protection, and therefore built many fenced cities. But the *fire* of God's anger burnt up both the temples and the fortified cities.

CHAPTER IX

The prophet reproves the Israelites for their sacrifices and rejoicings on their corn-floors, by which they ascribed to idols, as the heathen did, the praise of all their plenty, 1. *For which reason they are threatened with famine and exile,* 2, 3, *in a land where they should be polluted, and want the means of worshipping the God of their fathers, or observing the solemnities of his appointment,* 4, 5. *Nay more; they shall speedily fall before the destroyer, be buried in Egypt, and leave their own pleasant places desolate,* 6–9. *God is then introduced declaring his early favour for his people, and the delight he took in their obedience; but now they had so deeply revolted, all their glory will take wing, God will forsake them, and their offspring be devoted to destruction,* 10–16.

A. M. cir. 3244
B. C. cir. 760
Ante U. C. 7
Amulii Sylvii,
R. Alban.,
cir. annum 37

REJOICE not, O Israel, for
joy, as *other* people: for
thou [a]hast gone a whoring from
thy God, thou hast loved a [b]re-
ward [c]upon every corn-floor.
2 [d]The floor and the [e]wine-press shall not
feed them, and the new wine shall fail in her.
3 They shall not dwell in [f]the LORD'S
land; [g]but Ephraim shall return to Egypt,
and [h]they shall eat unclean *things* [i]in Assyria.
4 [k]They shall not offer wine *offerings* to
the LORD, [l]neither shall they be pleasing unto
him: [m]their sacrifices *shall be* unto them as
the bread of mourners; all that
eat thereof shall be polluted: for
their bread [n]for their soul shall
not come into the house of the
LORD.
5 What will ye do in [o]the solemn day, and
in the day of the feast of the LORD?
6 For, lo, they are gone because of [p]de-
struction: [q]Egypt shall gather them up,
Memphis shall bury them: [r]the [s]pleasant
places for their silver, [t]nettles shall possess
them: thorns *shall be* in their tabernacles.
7 The days of visitation are come, the days
of recompense are come; Israel shall know

---

[a]Chap. iv. 12; v. 4, 7——[b]Jer. xliv. 17; chap. ii. 12——[c]Or, *in*, &c.——[d]Ch. ii. 9, 12——[e]Or, *wine-fat*——[f]Lev. xxv. 23; Jer. ii. 7; xvi. 18——[g]Ch. viii. 13; xi. 5; not into Egypt itself, but into another bondage as bad as that——[h]Ezek. iv. 13; Dan. i. 8——[i]2 Kings xvii. 6; ch. xi. 11

[k]Ch. iii. 4——[l]Jer. vi. 20; ch. viii. 13——[m]Deut. xxvi. 14——[n]Lev. xvii. 11——[o]Ch. ii. 11——[p]Hebrew, *spoil*——[q]Ch. vii. 16; ver. 3——[r]Or, *their silver shall be desired, the nettle*, &c.——[s]Heb. *the desire*——[t]Isa. v. 6; xxxii. 13; xxxiv. 13; chap. x. 8

NOTES ON CHAP. IX

Verse 1. *Rejoice not*] Do not imitate the heathens, nor serve their idols. Do not *prostitute* thy soul and body in practising their impurities. Hitherto thou hast acted as a *common harlot*, who goes even to the common *threshing places;* connects herself with the meanest, in order to get a *hire* even of the *grain* there threshed out.

Verse 3. *But Ephraim shall return to Egypt*] See on chap. viii. 12.

Verse 4. *As the bread of mourners*] By the law, a dead body, and every thing that related to it, the house where it lay, and the persons who touched it, were all polluted and unclean, and whatever they touched was considered as defiled. See Deut. xxvi. 14; Num. xix. 11, 13, 14.

For their bread for their soul] The bread for the common support of *life* shall not be sanctified to them by having the *first-fruits* presented at the temple.

Verse 5. *What will ye do in the solemn day*] When ye shall be despoiled of every thing by the Assyrians; for the Israelites who remained in the land after its subjection to the Assyrians did worship the true God, and offer unto him the sacrifices appointed by the law, though in an imperfect and schismatic manner; and it was a great mortification to them to be deprived of their religious *festivals* in a land of strangers. See *Calmet*.

Verse 6. *For, lo, they are gone*] Many of them fled to Egypt to avoid the *destruction;* but they went there only to *die*.

Memphis] Now *Cairo*, or *Kahira*, found them *graves*.

The pleasant places *for their silver*] The fine estates or *villas* which they had purchased by their money, being now neglected and uninhabited, are covered with *nettles;* and even in their *tabernacles*, *thorns* and *brambles* of different kinds grow. These are the fullest marks of *utter desolation*.

Verse 7. *The days of visitation*] Of punishment *are come*.

The prophet is *a fool*] Who has pretended to foretell, on Divine authority, peace and plenty; for behold all is desolation.

A. M. cir. 3244
B. C. cir. 760
Ante U. C. 7
Amulii Sylvii,
R. Alban.,
cir. annum 37

it: the prophet *is* a fool, [u]the [v]spiritual man *is* mad, for the multitude of thine iniquity, and the great hatred.

8 The [w]watchman of Ephraim *was* with my God: *but* the prophet *is* a snare of a fowler in all his ways, *and* hatred [x]in the house of his God.

9 [y]They have deeply corrupted *themselves,* as in the days of [z]Gibeah: [a]*therefore* he will remember their iniquity, he will visit their sins.

10 I found Israel likes grapes in the wilderness; I saw your fathers as the [b]first ripe in the fig tree [c]at her first time: *but* they went to [d]Baal-peor, and [e]separated themselves [f]unto *that* shame; [g]and *their* abominations were according as they loved.

A. M. cir. 3244
B. C. cir. 760
Ante U. C. 7
Amulii Sylvii,
R. Alban.,
cir. annum 37

11 *As for* Ephraim, their glory shall fly away like a bird, from the birth, and from the womb, and from the conception.

12 [h]Though they bring up their children, yet [i]will I bereave them, *that there shall* not *be* a man *left:* yea, [k]wo also to them when I [l]depart from them!

13 Ephraim, [m]as I saw Tyrus, *is* planted in a pleasant place; [n]but Ephraim shall bring forth his children to the murderer.

14 Give them, O LORD: what wilt thou give? give them[o] a [p]miscarrying womb and dry breasts.

15 All their wickedness [q]*is* in Gilgal: for

---

[u]Heb. *man of the spirit*——[v]Ezek. xiii. 3, &c.; Mic. ii. 11; Zeph. iii. 4——[w]Jer. vi. 17; xxxi. 6; Ezek. iii. 17; xxxiii. 7——[x]Or, *against*——[y]Isa. xxxi. 6; ch. x. 9 [z]Judg. xix. 22——[a]Ch. viii. 13——[b]Isa. xxviii. 4; Mic. vii. 1——[c]See chap. ii. 15——[d]Num. xxv. 3; Psa. cvi. 28 [e]Chap. iv. 14——[f]Jer. xi. 13; see Judg. vi. 32

[g]Psa. lxxxi. 12; Ezek. xx. 8; Amos iv. 5——[h]Job xxvii. 14——[i]Deut. xxviii. 41, 62——[k]Deut. xxxi. 17; 2 Kings xvii. 18; ch. v. 6——[l]See 1 Sam. xxviii. 15, 16 [m]See Ezek. xxvi., xxvii., xxviii.——[n]Ver. 16; ch. xiii. 16 [o]Luke xxiii. 29——[p]Heb. *that casteth the fruit*——[q]Ch. iv. 15; xii. 11

The spiritual man] איש הרוח *ish haruach, the man of spirit,* who was *ever pretending* to be under a *Divine afflatus.*

Is *mad*] He is now *enraged* to see every thing falling out contrary to his prediction.

Verse 8. *The watchman of Ephraim*] The true prophet, *was with*—faithful to, *God.*

The prophet] The *false prophet* is the *snare of a fowler;* is continually deceiving the people, and leading them into *snares,* and infusing into their hearts deep hatred against God and his worship.

Verse 9. *They have deeply corrupted* themselves, *as in the days of Gibeah*] This relates to that shocking rape and murder of the Levite's wife, mentioned Judg. xix. 16, &c.

Verse 10. *I found Israel like grapes in the wilderness*] While they were faithful, they were as *acceptable* to me as *ripe grapes* would be to a *thirsty traveller* in the desert.

I saw your fathers] Abraham, Isaac, Jacob, Moses, Joshua, Caleb, Samuel, &c.

As the first ripe] Those grapes, whose bud having come first, and being exposed most to the sun, have been the *first ripe* upon the tree; which tree was now in the vigour of youth, and bore fruit for the *first time.* A metaphor of the *rising prosperity* of the Jewish state.

But *they went to Baal-peor*] The same as the Roman *Priapus,* and worshipped with the most impure rites.

And their *abominations were according as they loved.*] Or, "they became as abominable as the *object* of their love." So Bp. *Newcome.* And this was superlatively abominable.

Verse 11. *Their glory shall fly away*] It shall suddenly spring away from them, and return no more.

From the birth] "So that there shall be no birth, no carrying in the womb, no conception."—*Newcome.* They shall cease to glory in their *numbers;* for no *children* shall be *born,* no woman shall be *pregnant,* for none shall *conceive.* Here judgment blasts the very *germs* of population.

Verse 12. *Though they bring up their children*] And were they even to have children, I would *bereave them* of them; for, when I *depart from them,* they shall have all manner of wretchedness and wo.

Verse 13. *Ephraim, as I saw Tyrus*] Tyre was strongly situated on a rock in the sea; Samaria was on a mountain, both strong and pleasant. But the strength and beauty of those cities shall not save them from destruction.

Ephraim shall bring forth his children to the murderer.] The people shall be destroyed, or led into captivity by the Assyrians. Of the grandeur, wealth, power, &c., of Tyre, see the notes on Ezekiel, chap. xxvii. and xxviii.

Verse 14. *Give them, O Lord: what wilt thou give?*] There is an uncommon beauty in these words. The prophet, seeing the evils that were likely to fall upon his countrymen, begins to make intercession for them; but when he had formed the first part of his petition, "Give them, O Lord!" the prophetic light discovered to him that the petition would not be answered, and that God was about to give them something widely different. Then changing his petition, which the Divine Spirit had interrupted, by signifying that he must not proceed in his request, he asks the question, then, "What wilt thou give them?" and the answer is, "Give them a miscarrying womb, and dry breasts." And this he is commanded to announce. It is probable that the Israelites had prided themselves in the *fruitfulness* of their families, and the numerous *population* of their country. God now tells them that this shall be no more; their wives shall be barren, and their land cursed.

Verse 15. *All their wickedness* is *in Gilgal*] though we are not directly informed of the fact,

A. M. cir. 3244
B. C. cir. 760
Ante U. C. 7
Amulii Sylvii,
R. Alban.,
cir. annum 37

there I hated them; [r]for the
wickedness of their doings I will
drive them out of mine house,
I will love them no more: [s]all
their princes *are* revolters.
16 Ephraim is smitten, their root is dried
up, they shall bear no fruit: yea, [t]though
they bring forth, yet will I slay
even [u]the beloved *fruit* of their
womb.
17 My God will cast them
away, because they did not hearken unto him:
and they shall be [v]wanderers among the
nations.

A. M. cir. 3244
B. C. cir. 760
Ante U. C. 7
Amulii Sylvii,
R. Alban.,
cir. annum 37

[r]Chap. i. 6——[s]Isa. i. 23——[t]Ver. 13——[u]Heb. *the desires;* Ezek. xxiv. 21——[v]Deut. xxviii. 64, 65

yet we have reason to believe they had been guilty of some scandalous practices of idolatry in *Gilgal.* See chap. iv. 15.

For there I hated them] And therefore he determined, "for the wickedness of their doings, to drive them out of his house," so that they should cease to be a part of the heavenly family, either as *sons* or *servants;* for he would "love them no more," and bear with them no longer.

Verse 16. *Ephraim is smitten*] The thing being determined, it is considered as already done.

Their root is dried up] They shall never more be a kingdom. And they never had any political form from their captivity by the Assyrians to the present day.

Yea, though they bring forth] See the note on ver. 11, 12.

Verse 17. *My God will cast them away*] Here the prophet seems to apologize for the severity of these denunciations; and to vindicate the Divine justice, from which they proceeded. It is—

Because they did not hearken unto him] That "my God," the fountain of mercy and kindness, "will cast them away."

And they shall be wanderers among the nations.] And where they have *wandered* to, who can tell? and in what nations to be found, no man knows. *Wanderers* they are; and perhaps even now unknown to themselves. Some have thought they have found them in one country; some, in another; and a very pious writer, in a book entitled, *The Star in the West,* thinks he has found their descendants in the *American Indians;* among whom he has discovered many *customs,* apparently the same with those of the *ancient Jews,* and commanded in the *Law.* He even thinks that the word *Je-ho-vah* is found in their solemn festal cry, *Ye-ho-wa-he.* If they be this long lost people, they are utterly unknown to themselves; their origin being lost in a very remote antiquity.

CHAPTER X

This chapter treats of the same subject, but elegantly varied. It begins with comparing Israel to a fruitful vine but corrupted by too much prosperity, 1. *It next reproves and threatens them for their idolatry,* 2; *anarchy,* 3; *and breach of covenant,* 4. *Their idolatry is then enlarged on; and its fatal consequences declared in terms full of sublimity and pathos,* 5–8. *God is now introduced complaining of their excessive guilt; and threatening them with captivity in terms that bear a manifest allusion to their favourite idolatry, the worshipping the similitude of a calf or heifer,* 9–11. *Upon which the prophet, in a beautiful allegory suggested by the preceding metaphors, exhorts them to repentance; and warns them of the dreadful consequences of their evil courses, if obstinately persisted in,* 12–15.

A. M. cir. 3264
B. C. cir. 740
A. U. C. cir. 14
Romuli,
R. Roman.,
cir. annum 14

ISRAEL *is* [a]an [b]empty vine,
he bringeth forth fruit unto
himself: according to the multitude of his fruit [c]he hath increased the altars; according
to the goodness of his land
[d]they have made goodly
[e]images.

A. M. cir. 3264
B. C. cir. 740
A. U. C. cir. 14
Romuli,
R. Roman.,
cir. annum 14

[a]Nah. ii. 2——[b]Or, *a vine emptying the fruit which it giveth*——[c]Chap. viii. 11; xii. 11——[d]Chap. viii. 4——[e]Heb. *statues,* or *standing images*

NOTES ON CHAP. X

Verse 1. *Israel* is *an empty vine*] Or, *a vine that casteth its grapes.*

He bringeth forth fruit] Or, *he laid up fruit for himself.* He abused the blessings of God to the purposes of idolatry. He was prosperous; but his prosperity corrupted his heart.

According to the multitude of his fruit] He became idolatrous in proportion to his prosperity; and in proportion to their wealth was the costliness of their images, and the expensiveness of their idol worship. True is the homely saying of old *Quarles:*—

"So God's best gifts, usurp'd by wicked ones,
To poison turn, by their con-ta-gi-ons."

Another poet, of a higher order, but worse school, says:—

Effodiuntur opes, irritamenta malorum.—Ovid.

Of which the words of St. Paul are nearly a literal rendering,—

Ῥιζα γαρ παντων των κακων εστιν ἡ φιλαργυρια.

"For the love of money is the root of all these evils" 1 Tim. vi. 10. Pity that this beautiful

A. M. cir. 3264
B. C. cir. 740
A. U. C. cir. 14
Romuli,
R. Roman.,
cir. annum 14

2 [f]Their heart is [g]divided;
now shall they be found faulty:
he shall [h]break down their altars,
he shall spoil their images.
3 [i]For now they shall say, We have no
king, because we feared not the LORD; what
then should a king do to us?
4 They have spoken words, swearing falsely
in making a covenant: thus judgment springeth up [k]as hemlock in the furrows of the
field.
5 The inhabitants of Samaria shall fear because of [l]the calves of [m]Beth-aven: for the
people thereof shall mourn over it, and [n]the
priests thereof *that* rejoiced on
it, [o]for the glory thereof, because
it is departed from it.
6 It shall be also carried unto
Assyria *for* a present to [p]King Jareb:
Ephraim shall receive shame, and Israel shalt
be ashamed [q]of his own counsel.
7 [r]*As for* Samaria, her king is cut off as
the foam upon [s]the water.
8 [t]The high places also of Aven, [u]the sin of
Israel, shall be destroyed: [v]the thorn and the
thistle shall come up on their altars; [w]and
they shall say to the mountains, Cover us;
and to the hills, Fall on us.

A. M. cir. 3264
B. C. cir. 740
A. U. C. cir. 14
Romuli,
R. Roman.,
cir. annum 14

---

[f]Or, *He hath divided their heart*——[g]1 Kings xviii. 21; Matt. vi. 24——[h]Heb. *behead*——[i]Ch. iii. 4; xi. 5; Mic. iv. 9; ver. 7——[k]See Deut. xxix. 18; Amos v. 7; vi. 12; Acts viii. 23; Heb. xii. 15——[l]1 Kings xii. 28, 29; chap. viii. 5, 6——[m]Chap. iv. 15

[n]Or, *Chemarim;* 2 Kings xxiii. 5; Zeph. i. 4——[o]1 Sam. iv. 21, 22; ch. ix. 11——[p]Ch. v. 13——[q]Ch. xi. 6——[r]Ver. 3, 15——[s]Heb. *the face of the water*——[t]Ch. iv. 15——[u]Deut. ix. 21; 1 Kings xii. 30——[v]Chap. ix. 6——[w]Isa. ii. 19; Luke xxiii. 30; Rev. vi. 16; ix. 6

---

metal, on which God has bestowed such a large portion of mineral perfection, and then hid in the earth, should, on its being *digged up* by man, become the *incentive* to so many *vices*, and draw away his heart from the Creator of all things, and the fountain of ineffable perfection and goodness.

Verse 2. *Their heart is divided*] They wish to serve God and Mammon, Jehovah and Baal: but this is impossible. Now GOD will do in *judgment* what *they* should have done in *contrition*, "break down their altars, and spoil their images."

Verse 3. *We have no king*] We have rejected the King of kings; and had we any king, he would be of no service to us in this state, as he would be a captive like ourselves; nor could we have the approbation of God, as we now justly lie under his displeasure.

Verse 4. *They have spoken words*] Vain, empty, deceitful *words*.

Swearing falsely] This refers to the alliances made with strange powers, to whom they promised fidelity without intending to be faithful; and from whom they promised themselves protection and support, notwithstanding God was against them, and they knew it. All their words were vain, and in the end as *bitter as gall*.

Judgment springeth up as hemlock] As our land lies without cultivation, so that we have nothing but noxious weeds instead of crops; so we have no administration of justice. What is done in this way is a perversion of law, and is as hurtful to society as hemlock would be to animal life. All this may refer to the anarchy that was in the kingdom of Israel before Hoshea's reign, and which lasted, according to Archbishop *Usher*, *nine* years. They then, literally, "had no king."

Verse 5. *The inhabitants of Samaria shall fear*] According to *Calmet*, shall worship the calves of Beth-aven; those set up by Jeroboam, at Beth-el. *Fear* is often taken for religious reverence.

The people thereof shall mourn] On seeing the object of their worship carried into captivity, as well as themselves.

And the priests thereof] כמרים *kemarim*. The priests of Samaria, says *Calmet*, are here called *kemarim*, that is, *black coats*, or *shouters*, because they made loud cries in their sacrifices. Instead of יגילו *yagilu*, "they shall rejoice;" learned men propose ילילו *yalilu*, "shall howl," which is likely to be the true reading, but it is not supported by any of the MSS. yet discovered. But the *exigentia loci*, the necessity of the place, requires some such word.

Verse 6. *A present to King Jareb*] See on chap. v. 13. If this be a proper name, the person intended is not known in history: but it is most likely that *Pul*, king of Assyria, is intended, to whom Menahem, king of Israel, appears to have given one of the golden calves, to insure his assistance.

Verse 7. *Her king is cut off as the foam*] As lightly as a puff of wind blows off the foam that is formed below by a fall of water, so shall the kings of Israel be cut off. We have already seen that not less than *four* of them died by assassination in a very short time. See on chap. vii. 7.

Verse 8. *The high places*] Idol temples.

Of Aven] Beth-aven.

The thorn and the thistle shall come up on their altars] Owing to the uncultivated and unfrequented state of the land, and of their places of idol worship, the people being all carried away into captivity.

"And they shall say to the mountains, Cover us,
And to the hills, Fall on us."

"This sublime description of fear and distress our Lord had in view, Luke xxiii. 30, which may be a reference, and not a quotation. However, the *Septuagint*, in the *Codex Alexandrinus*, has the same order of words as occurs in the evangelist. The parallelism makes the passages more beautiful than Rev. vi. 16; and Isa. ii. 19 wants the animated dramatic form. That there is a reference to the caverns that abounded in the mountainous countries of Palestine, see the note on Isa. ii. 19."—*Newcome.*

A. M. cir. 3264
B. C. cir. 740
A. U. C. cir. 14
Romuli,
R. Roman.,
cir. annum 14

9 [x]O Israel, thou hast sinned
from the days of Gibeah: there
they stood: [y]the battle in Gibeah
against the children of iniquity
did not overtake them.
10 [z]*It is* in my desire that I should chastise
them; and [a]the people shall be gathered
against them, [b]when they shall bind themselves in their two furrows.
11 And Ephraim *is as* [c]a heifer *that is*
taught *and* loveth to tread out *the corn;* but
I passed over upon [d]her fair neck: I will
make Ephraim to ride; Judah shall plough,
and Jacob shall break his clods.
12 [e]Sow to yourselves in righteousness, reap
in mercy; [f]break up your fallow ground: for
it is time to seek the LORD, till
he come and rain righteousness
upon you.
13 [g]Ye have ploughed wicked-
ness, ye have reaped iniquity; ye have eaten
the fruit of lies: because thou didst trust
in thy way, in the multitude of thy mighty
men.
14 [h]Therefore shall a tumult arise among
thy people, and all thy fortresses shall be
spoiled, as Shalman spoiled [i]Beth-arbel in the
day of battle: [k]the mother was dashed in
pieces upon *her* children.
15 So shall Beth-el do unto you because of
[l]your great wickedness: in a morning [m]shall
the king of Israel utterly be cut off.

[x]Chap. ix. 9——[y]See Judg. xx——[z]Deut. xxviii. 63——[a]Jer. xvi. 16; Ezek. xxiii. 46, 47; chap. viii. 10——[b]Or, *when I shall bind them for their two transgressions*, or *in their two habitations*——[c]Jer. l. 11; Mic. iv. 13

[d]Heb. *the beauty of her neck*——[e]Prov. xviii. 21——[f]Jer. iv. 3——[g]Job iv. 8; Prov. xxii. 8; ch. viii. 7; Gal. vi. 7, 8——[h]Ch. xiii. 16——[i]2 Kings xviii. 34; xix. 13——[k]Ch. xiii. 16——[l]Heb. *the evil of your evil*——[m]Ver. 7

Verse 9. *Thou hast sinned from the days of Gibeah*] This is another reference to the horrible rape and murder of the Levite's wife, Judg. xix. 13, 14.

There they stood] Only one tribe was nearly destroyed, viz., that of *Benjamin*. They were *the criminals, the children of iniquity;* the others were faultless, and *stood* only for the rights of justice and mercy.

Verse 10. *When they shall bind themselves in their two furrows.*] "When they are chastised for their two iniquities," i. e., the calves in Dan and Beth-el.—*Newcome*. But this double iniquity may refer to what Jeremiah says, chap. xi. 13: "My people have committed *two* evils."—1. They have forsaken me. 2. They have joined themselves to idols.

Verse 11. *Ephraim* is as *a heifer* that is *taught*] One thoroughly broken in to the yoke.

And *loveth to tread out*] Goes peaceably in the yoke; and is pleased because, *not being muzzled*, she eats of the corn.

I passed over upon her fair neck] I brought the yoke upon it, that she should not tread out the corn merely, but draw the plough and drag the harrow. These operations of husbandry are all referred to here, with some others. *Ephraim* shall *tread out the corn*, that there may be *seed* for the fields.

Judah shall plough] That the *furrows* may receive it.

Jacob shall break his clods.] Harrow—that the seed may be covered with the mould.

Israel very frequently made great depredations on Judah; and as this heifer *loved to tread out the corn*, and not *plough*, it is therefore added that he should be made to *plough*, be *put under the yoke*, namely, that of the Assyrians. What is added, "Judah and Jacob shall plough for themselves," means, that Judah should not now plough for Israel, but for *himself;* as Israel shall no more make depredations upon him.—*Dodd*.

Verse 12. *Sow to yourselves in righteousness*] Let the seed you sow be of the best kind, and in just measure.

Reap in mercy] By the blessing of God on this ploughing, sowing, and harrowing, you may expect a good crop in harvest.

Break up your fallow ground] Do not be satisfied with a *slight furrow;* let the land that was *fallowed* (slightly ploughed) be broken up again with a *deep furrow*.

For it is time to seek the Lord] This should be immediately done: the season is passing; and if you do not get the seed in the ground, the early rain will be past, and your fields will be unfruitful.

Rain righteousness upon you.] God will give you the early rain in due time, and in proper measure. Here are the metaphors, and the application cannot be difficult. Here are *ploughing, fallowing, sowing, harrowing, watering, reaping, threshing*, and *feeding* on the produce of well-directed labour. All may be applied to the human heart, and the work of God upon it. Correction, contrition, conversion, receiving the grace of Christ, bringing forth fruit, &c.

Verse 13. *Ye have ploughed wickedness*] Ye have laboured sinfully.

Ye have reaped iniquity] The *punishment* due to your iniquity.

Ye have eaten the fruit of lies] Your *false worship* and your *false gods* have brought you into *captivity* and *misery*.

Because thou didst trust in thy way] Didst confide in thy own counsels, and in *thy mighty men*, and not in the God who made you.

Verse 14. *Shall a tumult arise*] The enemy shall soon fall upon thy people, and take all thy *fortified* places.

As Shalman spoiled Beth-arbel] Some think that this refers to *Jerubbaal*, or *Gideon's* victory over *Zalmunna*, general of the Midianites; see Judg. vii., viii. Others think that an allusion is made here to the destruction of *Arbela*, a city *of Armenia*, by *Shalmaneser*, here called *Shalman;* and this while he was only general of the Assyrian forces, and not yet *king*. I think the history to which this refers is unknown. It seems that it was distinguished by some remarkable ferocities.

The mother was dashed in pieces upon her *children.*] But *when, where, how,* and by *whom,* still remain unknown. Conjecture in such a case must be useless.

Verse 15. *So shall Beth-el do unto you*] This shall be the consequence of your *idolatry.*

In a morning shall the king of Israel utterly be cut off.] Suddenly, unexpectedly. *Hoshea,* the king of Israel, shall be cut off by the Assyrians. There are some allusions to facts in this chapter, which cannot be easily verified, as we have not sufficient acquaintance with the history of those times.

CHAPTER XI

This chapter gives a very pathetic representation of God's tender and affectionate regard for Israel, by metaphors chiefly borrowed from the conduct of mothers toward their tender offspring. From this, occasion is taken to reflect on their ungrateful return to the Divine goodness, and to denounce against them the judgments of the Almighty, 1–7. *But suddenly and unexpectedly the prospect changes. Beams of mercy break from the clouds just now fraught with vengeance. God, to speak in the language of men, feels the relentings of a tender parent; his bowels yearn; his mercy triumphs; his rebellious child shall yet be pardoned. As the lion of the tribe of Judah, he will employ his power to save his people, he will call his children from the land of their captivity; and, as doves, they will fly to him, a faithful and a holy people,* 8–12.

A. M. cir. 3264
B. C. cir. 740
A. U. C. cir. 14
Romuli,
R. Roman.,
cir. annum 14

WHEN [a]Israel *was* a child,
then I loved him, and
[b]called my [c]son out of Egypt.
2 *As* they called them, so they
went from them: [d]they sacrificed unto Baalim, and burned incense to graven images.
3 [e]I taught Ephraim also to go, taking
them by their arms; but they knew not that
[f]I healed them.
4 I drew them with cords of a man, with
bands of love: and [g]I was to
them as they that [h]take off the
yoke on their jaws, and [i]I laid
meat unto them.
5 [k]He shall not return into the land of
Egypt, but the Assyrian shall be his king,
[l]because they refused to return.
6 And the sword shall abide on his cities,
and shall consume his branches, and devour
them [m]because of their own counsels.

A. M. cir. 3264
B. C. cir. 740
A. U. C. cir. 14
Romuli,
R. Roman.,
cir. annum 14

---

[a]Chapter ii. 15——[b]Matthew ii. 15——[c]Exodus iv. 22, 23——[d]2 Kings xvii. 16; chapter ii. 13; xiii. 2 [e]Deuteronomy i. 31; xxxii. 10, 11, 12; Isaiah xlvi. 3 [f]Exod. xv. 26

[g]Lev. xxvi. 13——[h]Heb. *lift up*——[i]Psa. lxxviii. 25; chap. ii. 8——[k]See chap. viii. 13; ix. 3——[l]2 Kings xvii. 13, 14; Cir. 728, they became tributaries to Salmanasser——[m]Chap. x. 6

NOTES ON CHAP. XI

Verse 1. *When Israel* was *a child*] In the infancy of *his political existence.*

I loved him, and called my son out of Egypt.] Where he was greatly oppressed; and in this I gave the proof of my *love.* I *preserved* my people in their affliction there, and *brought* them safely out of it.

Verse 3. *I taught Ephraim also to go*] An allusion to a mother or nurse *teaching a child to walk,* directing it how to *lift and lay its feet,* and supporting it in the meantime *by the arms,* that it may use its feet with the greater ease. This is a passage truly pathetic.

Verse 4. *I drew them with cords of a man*] This is a reference to *leading strings,* one end of which is held by the child, the other by the nurse, by which the little one, feeling some support, and gaining confidence, endeavours to walk. God, their heavenly Father, made use of every means and method to teach them to walk in the right and only safe path; for, as the *Targum* says, "As beloved children are drawn, I drew them by the strength of love."

That take off the yoke on their jaws] I did every thing that mercy could suggest, and justice permit, to make their *duty* their *delight* and *profit.* There appears to be here an illusion to the *moving and pulling forward* the *collar* or *yoke of beasts* which have been hard at work, to let in the cool air between it and their neck, so as to refresh them, and prevent that *heat,* which with the *sweat* would scald their necks, and take off not only the *hair,* but the *skin.* I have often done this at the land ends, in ploughing, when at the *turnings* the cattle were permitted a few moments to draw their breath after the hard pull that terminated the furrow at either end of the field:—

And I laid meat unto them] Giving them at the same time a bite of *grass* or *hay,* to encourage them to go on afresh. The metaphor is strong and expressive; and he who ever had or saw the management of cattle in the *plough* or *cart* must admire it. Thus God acted with the people on *whose necks* was the *yoke of his law.* How many privileges, advantages, and comforts did he mingle with his precepts, to make them at once a righteous and happy people!

Verse 5. *He shall not return into—Egypt*] I have brought them thence already, with the design that the *nation* should never return thither again; but as they have sinned, and forfeited my favour and protection, they shall go *to Assyria;* and this *because they refused to return* to me. This view of the verse removes every difficulty.

Verse 6. *The sword shall abide on his cities*] Israel was agitated with external and intestine wars from the time of *Jeroboam the Second.*

A. M. cir. 3264
B. C. cir. 740
A. U. C. cir. 14
Romuli,
R. Roman.,
cir. annum 14

7 And my people are bent to
[n]backsliding from me: [o]though
they called them to the Most
High, [p]none at all would exalt
him.
8 [q]How shall I give thee up, Ephraim?
how shall I deliver thee, Israel? how shall
I make thee as [r]Admah? *how* shall I
set thee as Zeboim? [s]mine heart is turned
within me, my repentings are kindled together.
9 I will not execute the fierceness of mine
anger, I will not return to destroy Ephraim:
[t]for I *am* God, and not man; the Holy One
in the midst of thee: and I will
not enter into the city.
10 They shall walk after the
LORD: [u]he shall roar like a
lion: when he shall roar, then the children
shall tremble [v]from the west.
11 They shall tremble as a bird out of
Egypt, [w]and as a dove out of the land of Assyria: [x]and I will place them in their houses,
saith the LORD.
12 [y]Ephraim compasseth me about with
lies, and the house of Israel with deceit: but
Judah yet ruleth with God, and is faithful
[z]with the saints.

A. M. cir. 3264
B. C. cir. 740
A. U. C. cir. 14
Romuli,
R. Roman.,
cir. annum 14

---

[n]Jer. iii. 6, &c.; viii. 5; chap. iv. 16——[o]Chap. vii. 16
[p]Heb. *together they exalted not*——[q]Jer. ix. 7; ch. vi. 4
[r]Gen. xiv. 8; xix. 24, 25; Deut. xxix. 23; Amos iv. 11
[s]Deut. xxxii. 36; Isa. lxii. 15; Jer. xxxi. 20

[t]Num. xxiii. 19; Isa. lv. 8, 9; Mal. iii. 6——[u]Isa. xxxi. 4; Joel iii. 16; Amos i. 2——[v]Zech. viii. 7——[w]Isa. lx. 8; chap. vii. 11——[x]Ezek. xxviii. 25, 26; xxxvii. 21, 25
[y]Chap. xii. 1——[z]Or, *with the most holy*

Although *Zechariah* his son reigned *twelve* years, yet it was in *continual troubles;* and he was at last slain by the rebel *Shallum*, who, having reigned one month, was slain by *Menahem. Pekahiah* succeeded his father Menahem, and reigned two years, and was killed by *Pekah*, son of Remaliah. He joined Rezin, king of Syria, and made an irruption into the land of Judah; but Ahaz having obtained succour from *Tiglath-Pileser*, king of Assyria, Pekah was defeated, and the tribes of Reuben, Gad, Naphtali, and the half-tribe of Manasseh, were carried away captives by the Assyrian king; and in a short time after, *Hosea*, son of Elah, slew Pekah, and usurped the kingdom, which he could not possess without the assistance of *Shalmaneser*, who for his services imposed a tribute on the Israelitish king. Wishing to rid himself of this yoke, he applied to the king of Egypt; but this being known to Shalmaneser, he came against Samaria, and after a three years' siege took and destroyed it. Thus the sword rested on their cities; it continued in the land till all was ruined. See *Calmet*.

Verse 7. *Though they called them to the Most High*] *Newcome* is better: "*And* though *they call on him together because of the yoke, he will not raise it.* He shall receive no *refreshment*." See the metaphor, ver. 4.

Verse 8. *How shall I give thee up*] See the notes on chap. vi. 4, where we have similar words from similar feeling.

Mine heart is turned within me] *Justice* demands thy *punishment; Mercy* pleads for thy *life*. As thou *changest*, Justice resolves to *destroy*, or Mercy to *save*. My heart is oppressed, and I am weary with *repenting*—with so frequently changing my purpose. All this, though spoken after the manner of men, shows how merciful, compassionate, and loath to punish, the God of heaven is. What *sinner* or *saint* upon earth has not been a subject of these *gracious* operations?

Verse 9. *I will not execute*] Here is the *issue* of this conflict in the Divine mind. Mercy triumphs over Judgment; Ephraim shall be spared. *He is God, and not man.* He cannot be affected by human caprices. They are now *penitent*, and implore mercy; he will not, as *man* would do, punish them for former offences, when they have fallen into his hand. The *holy place* is in Ephraim, and *God is in this holy place;* and he will not *go into the cities*, as he did into Sodom and Gomorrah, to destroy them. Judgment is his strange work. How exceedingly affecting are these two verses!

Verse 10. *They shall walk after the Lord*] They shall discern the operations of his providence, when,

He shall roar like a lion] When he shall utter his majestic voice, Cyrus shall make his decree. The *people shall tremble*—be in a state of commotion; every one hurrying to avail himself of the opportunity to return to his own land.

Verse 11. *They shall tremble as a bird*] Those of them that are in *Egypt* shall also be called thence, and shall *speed* hither *as a bird*. Those in *Assyria* shall also be called to return, and they shall *flee as doves* to their windows. All shall, in the fulness of time, return to their own land. And,

I will place them in their houses, saith the Lord.] They shall have their *temple* once more, and all their holy ordinances.

Verse 12. *Ephraim compasseth me about with lies*] I think this verse does not well *unite* with the *above;* it belongs to *another subject*, and should begin the following chapter, as in the Hebrew.

Judah yet ruleth with God] There is an allusion here to Gen. xxxii. 24, where *Jacob*, having "wrestled with the Angel," had his name changed to *Israel*, one that *rules with God*. That glory the *Israelites* had lost by their idolatry; but *Judah* still retained the true worship, and alone deserved the name of Israel.

Bp. *Newcome* translates this clause thus:—"But hereafter they shall come down a people of God, even a faithful people of saints."

Even allowing this to be the most correct view of the original, I do not see what we gain by this change.

CHAPTER XII

The prophet, in very pointed terms, describes the unprofitableness and destruction attending vicious courses; particularly such as Ephraim pursued, who forsook God, and courted the alliance of idolatrous princes, 1. *Judah is also reproved,* 2. *He is reminded of the extraordinary favour of God to his father Jacob, in giving him the birthright; and exhorted, after his example, to wrestle with God (the Angel of the covenant, the same unchangeable Jehovah) for a blessing; and to love mercy and execute justice,* 3–6. *Ephraim is accused of pursuing practices that are deceitful, although pretending to integrity,* 7, 8. *God then threatens to deprive this people of their possessions,* 9, *as they had rejected every means of reformation,* 10, *and given themselves up to gross impieties,* 11. *And, as an aggravation of their guilt, they are reminded from what humble beginnings they had been raised,* 12, 13. *The Divine judgments about to fall upon Israel are declared to be the result of great provocation,* 14.

A. M. cir. 3279
B. C. cir. 725
A. U. C. cir. 29
Romuli,
R. Roman.,
cir. annum 29

EPHRAIM [a]feedeth on wind,
and followeth after the east
wind: he daily increaseth lies
and desolation; [b]and they do
make a covenant with the Assyrians, and [c]oil
is carried into Egypt.
2 [d]The LORD hath also a controversy with
Judah, and will [e]punish Jacob according to
his ways; according to his doings will he recompense him.
3 He took his brother [f]by the heel in the
womb, and by his strength he [g]had [h]power
with God:
4 Yea, he had power over the
Angel, and prevailed: he wept,
and made supplication unto
him: he found him *in* [i]Beth-el,
and there he spake with us;
5 Even the LORD God of hosts; the LORD
is his [k]memorial.
6 [l]Therefore turn thou to thy God: keep
mercy and judgment, and [m]wait on thy God
continually.
7 *He is* [n]a merchant, [o]the balances of deceit *are* in his hand: he loveth to [p]oppress.
8 And Ephraim said, [q]Yet I am become

[a]Chap. viii. 7——[b]2 Kings xvii. 4; chap. v. 13; chap. vii. 11——[c]Isa. xxx. 6; lvii. 9——[d]Chap. iv. 1; Mic. vi. 2——[e]Heb. *visit upon*——[f]Gen. xxv. 26——[g]Heb. *was a prince* or *behaved himself princely*——[h]Gen. xxxii. 24, &c.

[i]Gen. xxviii. 12, 19; xxxv. 9, 10, 15——[k]Exod. iii. 15——[l]Ch. xiv. 1; Mic. vi. 8——[m]Psa. xxxvii. 7——[n]Or, *Canaan:* see; Ezek. xvi. 3——[o]Prov. xi. 1; Amos viii. 5——[p]Or, *deceive*——[q]Zech. xi. 5; Rev. iii. 17

NOTES ON CHAP. XII

Verse 1. *Ephraim feedeth on wind*] He forms and follows empty and unstable counsels.

Followeth after the east wind] They are not only empty, but *dangerous* and *destructive.* The *east wind* was, and still is, in all countries, a *parching, wasting, injurious* wind.

He daily increaseth lies] He promises himself safety from foreign alliances. He "made a covenant with the Assyrians," and *sent* a subsidy of "oil to Egypt." The latter *abandoned* him; the *former oppressed* him.

Verse 2. *The Lord hath also a controversy with Judah*] The rest of the prophecy belongs both to Judah and Israel. He reproaches both with their ingratitude, and threatens them with God's anger. In order to make their infidelity the more hateful, and their malice the more sensible, he opposes to them the righteousness, obedience, and piety of their father Jacob. He recalls to their minds the benefits they had received since they returned from Egypt. He speaks afterwards of their kings; and how, in their ingratitude, they refused to have him for their monarch. Having mentioned this fact, he subjoins reflections, exhortations, invectives, and threatenings; and continues this subject in *this* and the *two* following *chapters.—Calmet.*

Verse 3. *He took his brother by the heel*] See on Gen. xxv. 26, and xxxii. 24, &c.

Verse 4. *He had power over the Angel*] Who represented the invisible Jehovah.

He wept, and made supplication] He entreated with tears that God would bless him; and he *prevailed.* The circumstance of his *weeping* is not mentioned in *Genesis.*

He found him in *Beth-el*] It was there that God made those glorious promises to Jacob relative to his posterity. See Gen. xxviii. 13-15.

Verse 5. *The Lord* is *his memorial.*] He is the same God as when Jacob so successfully wrestled with him.

Verse 6. *Therefore turn thou to thy God*] Because he is the same, and cannot change. Seek him as faithfully and as fervently as Jacob did, and you will find him the same merciful and compassionate Being.

Verse 7. He is *a merchant*] Or a *Canaanite;* referring to the *Phœnicians,* famous for their traffic. Ephraim is as corrupt as those heathenish traffickers were. He kept, as many in all ages have done, a *weight* and a *weight;* a *heavy* one to *buy* with and a *light* one to *sell* by.

Verse 8. *I am become rich*] They boasted in their riches, notwithstanding the *unjust manner* in which they were acquired.

In *all my labours they shall find none iniquity in me*] This is frequently the language of merchants, tradesmen, &c. None are so full of professions of equity and justice, while all the time they are endeavouring to overreach, both in buying and selling. "Sir, I cannot afford it at that price." "It is not *mine* for that money." "I assure you that it cost me more than you offer." "I am sorry I cannot take your money; but if I did, I should lose by the article," &c., &c., &c. I have heard such lan-

A. M. cir. 3279
B. C. cir. 725
A. U. C. cir. 29
Romuli,
R. Roman.,
cir. annum 29

rich, I have found me out substance: [r]*in* all my labours they
shall find none iniquity in me
[s]that *were* sin.
9 And [t]I *that am* the LORD thy God from
the land of Egypt [u]will yet make thee to
dwell in tabernacles, as in the days of the
solemn feasts.
10 [v]I have also spoken by the prophets, and
I have multiplied visions, and used similitudes, [w]by the ministry of the prophets.
11 [x]*Is there* iniquity *in* Gilead? surely they
are vanity: they sacrifice bullocks in [y]Gilgal;
yea, their [z]altars *are* as heaps
in the furrows of the fields.
12 And Jacob [a]fled into the
country of Syria, and Israel
[b]served for a wife, and for a wife he kept
sheep.
13 [c]And by a prophet the LORD brought
Israel out of Egypt, and by a prophet was he
preserved.
14 [d]Ephraim provoked *him* to anger [e]most
bitterly: therefore shall he leave his [f]blood
upon him, [g]and his [h]reproach shall his Lord
return unto him.

[r]Or, *all my labours suffice me not:* he shall have *punishment of iniquity in whom* is *sin*——[s]Heb. *which*——[t]Ch. xiii. 4——[u]Lev. xxiii. 42, 43; Neh. viii. 17; Zech. xiv. 16——[v]2 Kings xvii. 13——[w]Heb. *by the hand*——[x]Chap. v. 1; vi. 8——[y]Chap. iv. 15; ix. 15; Amos iv. 4; v. 5——[z]Ch. viii. 11; x. 1

[a]Gen. xxviii. 5; Deut. xxvi. 5——[b]Gen. xxix. 20, 28——[c]Exod. xii. 50, 51; xiii. 3; Psa. lxxvii. 20; Isa. lxiii. 11; Mic. vi. 4——[d]2 Kings xvii. 11–18——[e]Heb. *with bitterness*——[f]Heb. *bloods;* see Ezek. xviii. 13; xix. 10; xxiv. 7, 8——[g]Dan. xi. 18——[h]Deut. xxviii. 37; Lam. iii. 61–66

guage over and over, when I knew every word was false. *Truth* is a sacred thing in the sight of God; but who regards it as he should? There are, however, many noble exceptions among merchants and tradesmen. Bp. *Newcome* gives another turn to the subject, by translating:—

"All his labours shall not be found *profitable* unto him,
For the iniquity wherewith he hath sinned."

Verse 9. *And I—the Lord thy God*] I who brought thee out of the land of Egypt, will again make thee to dwell in tabernacles. This appears to be a *threatening.* I will reduce you to as miserable a state in the land of your captivity, as you often were through your transgressions in the wilderness. This was the opinion of some of the ancients on this verse; and the *context* requires it to be understood in this way. I do not think that the *feast of tabernacles* is referred to.

Verse 10. *I have also spoken*] I have used every means, and employed every method, to instruct and save you. I have sent *prophets,* who spake *plainly,* exhorting, warning, and beseeching you to return to me. They have had *Divine visions,* which they have declared and *interpreted.* They have used *similitudes, symbols, metaphors, allegories,* &c., in order to fix your attention, and bring you back to your duty and interest. And, alas! all is in vain; you have not profited by my condescension. This text *St. Paul* seems to have had full in view, when he wrote, Heb. i. 1: "God who, at SUNDRY TIMES and in DIVERS MANNERS, spake in *time past* unto the FATHERS by the PHOPHETS." See the note on the above.

Dr. *Dodd* supposes that there are *three* distinct kinds of prophecy mentioned here: 1. Immediate inspiration, when God declares the very words. 2. Vision; a representation of *external objects* to the *mind,* in as lively a manner as if there were conveyed by the *senses.* 3. Parables and apt resemblances.

Verse 11. *Iniquity* in *Gilead*] Gilgal and Gilead are equally iniquitous, and equally idolatrous. Gilead, which was beyond Jordan, had already been brought under subjection by Tiglath-Pileser. Gilgal, which was on this side Jordan, shall share the same fate; because it is now as idolatrous as the other.

Their altars are *as heaps*] They occur everywhere. The whole land is given to idolatry.

Verse 12. *Served for a wife*] Seven years for *Rachel.*

For a wife he kept sheep.] Seven years for *Leah;* having been cheated by Laban, who gave him first *Leah,* instead of *Rachel;* and afterwards made him serve seven years more before he would confirm his first engagement. Critics complain of want of connection here. Why is this isolated fact predicted? Thus, in a detached sentence, the prophet speaks of the low estate of their ancestors, and how amply the providence of God had preserved and provided for them. This is all the connection the place requires.

Verse 13. *By a prophet* (Moses) *the Lord brought Israel out of Egypt, and by a prophet* (Joshua) *was he preserved.*] Joshua succeeded Moses, and brought the Israelites into the promised land; and when they passed the Jordan at Gilgal, he received the covenant of circumcision; and yet this same place was now made by them the seat of idolatry! How blind and how ungrateful!

Verse 14. *Therefore shall he leave his blood upon him*] He will not remove his guilt. These are similar to our Lord's words, John iii. 36, ix. 41: "He that believeth not on the Son of God, shall not see life, for the wrath of God ABIDETH ON HIM"—shall not be removed by any remission, as he rejects the only way in which he can be saved. *Because ye say, We see; therefore,* YOUR SIN REMAINETH, i. e., it still stands charged against you. Your miseries and destruction are of your own procuring; your perdition is of yourselves. God is as *merciful* as he is *just.*

CHAPTER XIII

This chapter begins with observing that the fear of God leads to prosperity, but sin to ruin; a truth most visibly exemplified in the sin and punishment of Ephraim, 1–3. *As an aggravation of their guilt, God reminds them of his former favours,* 4, 5; *which they had shamefully abused,* 6; *and which now expose them to dreadful punishments,* 7, 8. *He, however, tempers these awful threatenings with gracious promises; and, on their repentance, engages to save them, when no other could protect them,* 9–11. *But, alas! instead of repenting, Ephraim is filling up the measure of his iniquity,* 12, 13. *Notwithstanding this, God promises to put forth his almighty power in behalf of his people, and, as it were, raise them from the dead,* 14; *although, in the meantime, they must be visited with great national calamities, compared first to the noxious and parching east wind,* 15, *and described immediately after in the plainest terms,* 16.

A. M. cir. 3279
B. C. cir. 725
A. U. C. cir. 29
Romuli,
R. Roman.,
cir. annum 29

WHEN Ephraim spake trem-
bling, he exalted himself
in Israel: but [a]when he offended
in Baal, he died.
2 And now [b]they sin more and more, and
[c]have made them molten images of their silver, *and* idols according to their own understanding, all of it the work of the craftsmen:
they say of them, Let [d]the men that sacrifice
[e]kiss the calves.
3 Therefore they shall be [f]as the morning
cloud, and as the early dew that passeth away,
[g]as the chaff *that* is driven with the whirlwind
out of the floor, and as the
smoke out of the chimney.
4 Yet [h]I *am* the LORD thy God
from the land of Egypt, and
thou shalt know no god but me: for [i]*there is*
no saviour beside me.
5 [k]I did know thee in the wilderness, [l]in
the land of [m]great drought.
6 [n]According to their pasture, so were they
filled; they were filled, and their heart was
exalted; therefore [o]have they forgotten me.
7 Therefore [p]I will be unto them as a lion:
as [q]a leopard by the way will I observe *them*:

A. M. cir. 3279
B. C. cir. 725
A. U. C. cir. 29
Romuli,
R. Roman.,
cir. annum 29

[a]2 Kings xvii. 16, 18; chap. xi. 2——[b]Heb. *they add to sin*——[c]Chap. ii. 8; viii. 4——[d]Or, *the sacrifices of men*——[e]1 Kings xix. 18——[f]Chap. vi. 4——[g]Dan. ii. 35——[h]Isa. xliii. 11; chap. xii. 9

[i]Isa. xliii. 11; xlv. 21——[k]Deut. ii. 7; xxxii. 10——[l]Deut. viii. 15; xxxii. 10——[m]Heb. *droughts*——[n]Deut. viii. 12, 14; xxxii. 15——[o]Chap. viii. 14——[p]Lam. iii. 10; chap. v. 14——[q]Jer. v. 6

NOTES ON CHAP. XIII

Verse 1. *When Ephraim spake trembling*] When he was meek and humble, of a broken heart and contrite spirit.

He exalted himself in Israel] He became great in God's sight; he rose in the Divine esteem in proportion as he sank in his own. But this did not continue.

He offended in Baal] He became an idolater.

He died.] The sentence of death from the Divine justice went out against him.

This has been differently understood: "As soon as Ephraim spake (To your tents, O Israel!) There was a trembling or commotion: then the kingdom was exalted in Israel." Thus taken, it refers to the division of the *ten* tribes from Rehoboam, son of Solomon, 1 Kings xii. 16, &c., and the establishment of the kingdom of Israel under Jeroboam in opposition to that of Judah; which breach was never healed.

Verse 2. *And now they sin more and more*] They increase in every kind of vice, having abandoned the great Inspirer of virtue.

Let the men that sacrifice kiss the calves.] This was the *test.* If there be a Jew that pretends to sacrifice, and whose conversion is dubious, let him come openly and *kiss the calves.* This will show what he is; no *real* Jew will do this. If he be an *idolater,* he will not scruple. This was the ancient method of *adoration.* 1. They *kissed* the idol. 2. When the statue was too high or too far off, they presented the hand, in token of alliance. 3. They brought that hand respectfully to their mouths, and kissed it. This was the genuine act of *adoration; from ad, to,* and *os, oris,* the *mouth.* So PLINY, *Hist. Nat.,* lib. xxviii., c. 1. Adorando, dexteram ad oscula referimus.

And APULEIUS, *Asin.,* lib. iv.: Admoventes oribus suis dexteram, ut ipsam prorsus deam religiosis adorationibus venerabantur. See *Calmet,* and see the note on Job xxxi. 17.

Verse 3. *Therefore they shall be as the morning* CLOUD—*as the early* DEW—*as the* CHAFF—*as the* SMOKE] *Four* things, most easy to be driven about and dissipated, are employed here to show how they should be *scattered* among the nations, and dissipated by captivity.

Verse 4. *I am the Lord thy God*] This was the first discovery I made of myself to you, and the *first commandment* I gave; and I showed you that besides me there was no Saviour. There is a remarkable addition in the Septuagint here: "But I am Jehovah thy God, who stretched out the heavens and created the earth. And I showed them not to thee, that thou shouldest walk after them. And I brought thee up out of the land of Egypt," &c. This might have been once in the Hebrew text.

Verse 5. *I did know thee*] I *approved* of thee; I *loved* thee; and by miraculously providing for thee in that land of *drought,* I demonstrated my love.

Verse 6. *According to their pasture*] They had a rich pasture, and were amply supplied with every good. They became *exalted in their heart, forgat their God,* and became a prey to their enemies. "He that exalteth himself shall be abased."

Verse 7. *I will be unto them as a lion*] שחל *shachal* is supposed to mean here the *black lion,* frequent in Ethiopia.

A. M. cir. 3279 B. C. cir. 725 A. U. C. cir. 29 Romuli, R. Roman., cir. annum 29

8 I will meet them [r]as a bear *that is* bereaved *of her whelps,* and will rend the caul of their heart, and there will I devour them like a lion: [s]the wild beast shall tear them.
9 O Israel, [t]thou hast destroyed thyself; [u]but in me [v]*is* thine help.
10 [w]I will be thy king: [x]where *is any other* that may save thee in all thy cities? and thy judges of whom [y]thou saidst, Give me a king and princes?
11 [z]I gave thee a king in mine anger, and took *him* away in my wrath.
12 [a]The iniquity of Ephraim *is* bound up; his sin *is* hid.
13 [b]The sorrows of a travailing woman shall come upon him: he *is* [c]an unwise son; for he should not [d]stay [e]long in *the place of* the breaking forth of children.
14 [f]I will ransom them from [g]the power of the grave; I will redeem them from death;

A. M. cir. 3279 B. C. cir. 725 A. U. C. cir. 29 Romuli, R. Roman., cir. annum 29

[r]2 Sam. xvii. 8; Prov. xvii. 12——[s]Heb. *the beast of the field*——[t]Prov. vi. 32; chap. xiv. 1; Mal. i. 9——[u]Ver. 4 [v]Heb. *in thy help*——[w]Rather, *Where is thy king?* King Hoshea being then in prison; 2 Kings xvii. 4——[x]Deut. xxxii. 38; chap. x. 3; ver. 4

[y]1 Sam. viii. 5, 19——[z]1 Sam. viii. 7; x. 19; xv. 22, 23; xvi. 1; chap. x. 3——[a]Deut. xxxii. 34; Job xiv. 17 [b]Isa. xiii. 8; Jer. xxx. 6——[c]Prov. xxii. 3——[d]2 Kings xix. 3——[e]Heb. *a time*——[f]Isa. xxv. 8; Ezek. xxxvii. 12 [g]Hebrew, *the hand*

As a leopard] נמר *namar*, so termed from its *spotted skin*, for *to be spotted* is the signification of the root.

Will I observe them] The leopard, tiger, and panther will hide themselves in thick bushwood, near where they expect any prey to pass; and as soon as it comes near, spring suddenly upon it. To this is the allusion in the text: "By the way will I observe them;" watch for them as the leopard does. They shall be greatly harassed even on their way to Assyria, when going into captivity.

Verse 8. *As a bear—bereaved*] This is a figure to denote excessive ferocity. See the note on 2 Sam. xvii. 8, where a remarkable instance is given.

And will rend the caul of their heart] Every savage beast goes first to the *seat of the blood* when it has seized its prey; as in this fluid they delight more than in the most delicate parts of the flesh.

There will I devour them like a lion] לביא *labi*, the *old strong lion;* drinking the blood, tearing the flesh, and breaking the bones to extract the marrow.

The wild beast shall tear them] Probably this refers to the *chakal* or *jackal*, who frequently hunts down the prey, which the lion takes the liberty to devour, while the *jackal* stands by, and afterwards picks the bones. Hence he has been called the *lion's* PROVIDER, and *the lion's waiting-man.*

Verse 9. *O Israel, thou hast destroyed thyself*] These evils come not by my *immediate infliction;* they are the consequences of *thy own crimes.* In the above terrifying figures of the ferocious beasts, the prophet only shows what they would meet with from the hand of the *Assyrians* in the war, the famine, and the captivity; God being represented as *doing* what he only *permits* to be done.

But in me is *thine help.*] "Though thou hast destroyed thyself, yet in me alone can thy help be found"—*Newcome.* And others read, *And who* will *help thee?* reading מי *mi, who,* for בי *bi, in me.* Though this is countenanced by the *Syriac,* yet there is no evidence of it in any of the MSS. yet collated, nor do I think it to be the true reading.

Verse 10. *Give me a king and princes?*] Referring to the time in which they cast off the Divine theocracy and chose *Saul* in the place of *Jehovah.*

Verse 11. *I gave thee a king in mine anger*] Such was *Saul;* for they highly offended God when they clamoured to have a king like the heathen nations that were around them.

Took him *away in my wrath.*] Permitted *him* and the *Israelites* to fall before the Philistines. Others think that *Shalmaneser* was the *king thus given,* and *Hoshea* the king thus *taken away.*

Verse 12. *The iniquity of Ephraim is bound up*] It is *registered* in my court of justice; the *death warrant* is in store, and will be produced in due time. Though there be not at present the judgment inflicted which such glaring transgressions demand, yet it will surely come. Such crimes cannot go unpunished.

Verse 13. *The sorrows of a travailing woman*] These judgments shall come suddenly and *unavoidably.*

The place of *the breaking forth of children.*] As there is a critical time in parturition in which the mother in hard labour may by skilful assistants be eased of her burden, which, if neglected, may endanger the life both of parent and child; so there was a time in which Ephraim might have returned to God, but they would not; therefore they are now in danger of being finally destroyed. And, speaking after the manner of men, he must be deemed an *unwise son,* who if he had power and consideration, would prolong his stay in the porch of life, where he must necessarily be suffocated; so is Ephraim, who, though warned of his danger, having yet power to escape, continued in his sin, and is now come to destruction. I could illustrate the allusion in the text farther, and show the accurate propriety of the original; but the subject forbids it.

Verse 14. *I will ransom them from the power of the grave*] In their captivity they are represented as *dead* and *buried,* which is a similar view to that taken of the Jews in the Babylonish captivity by Ezekiel in his *vision of the valley of dry bones.* They are now lost as to the purpose for which they were made, for which God had wrought so many miracles for them and for their ancestors; but the gracious purpose of God shall not be utterly defeated. He will bring them out of that grave, and ran-

A. M. cir. 3279 B. C. cir. 725 A. U. C. cir. 29 Romuli, R. Roman., cir. annum 29

[h]O death, I will be thy plagues;
O grave, I will be thy destruction; [i]repentance shall be hid
from mine eyes.
15 Though [k]he be fruitful among *his*
brethren, [l]an east wind shall come, the wind
of the LORD shall come up from the wilderness, and his spring shall become dry, and his
fountain shall be dried up: he
shall spoil the treasure of all
[m]pleasant vessels.
16 [n]Samaria shall become de-
solate; [o]for she hath rebelled against her
God: [p]they shall fall by the sword: their
infants shall be dashed in pieces, and their
women with child shall be ripped up.

A. M. cir. 3279 B. C. cir. 725 A. U. C. cir. 29 Romuli, R. Roman., cir. annum 29

[h]1 Cor. xv. 54, 55—[i]Jer. xv. 6; Rom. xi. 29——[k]See Gen. xli. 52; xlviii. 19——[l]Jer. iv. 11; Ezek. xvii. 10; xix. 12; ch. iv. 19——[m]Heb. *vessels of desire;* Nah. ii. 9

[n]Fulfilled, cir. 721; 2 Kings xvii. 6——[o]2 Kings xviii. 12——[p]2 Kings viii. 12; xv. 16; Isa. xiii. 16; chap. x. 14, 15; Amos i. 13; Nah. iii. 10

som them from that death; for as they have *deserved* that death and disgraceful burial, they must be *redeemed* and *ransomed* from it, or still lie under it. And who can do this but God himself? And he will do it. In the prospect of this the prophet exclaims, in the person of the universal Redeemer, "O death, I will be thy plagues;" I will bring into thy reign the principle of its destruction. The *Prince of life* shall lie for a time under thy power, that he may destroy that power.

O grave, I will be thy destruction] I will put an end to thy dreary domination by rising from the dead, and bringing life and immortality to life by my Gospel, and by finally raising from the death the whole human race in the day of the general resurrection.

שאול *sheol,* which we translate *grave,* is the *state of the dead.* מות *maveth,* which we translate *death,* is the *principle* of *corruption* that renders the body unfit to be longer the tenement of the soul, and finally decomposes it. *Sheol* shall be destroyed, for it must deliver up all its dead. *Maveth* shall be annihilated, for the *body shall be raised incorruptible.* See the use which the apostle makes of this passage, 1 Cor. xv. 54, 55; but he does not quote from the Hebrew, nor from any of the ancient versions. He had to apply the subject anew; and the Spirit, which had originally given the words, chose to adapt them to the subject then in hand, which was the *resurrection of the dead in the last day.* Instead of דבריך *debareycha, thy plagues, one* of my oldest MSS., *ninety-six* of *Kennicott's* and *thirty-two* of *De Rossi's,* have דברך *debarcha, thy plague,* that which shall *carry thee off,* as the *plague* does them who are affected by it. To *carry off, carry away,* is one of the regular meanings of the verb דבר *dabar.*

Repentance shall be hid from mine eyes.] On these points I will not *change my purpose;* this is the signification of *repentance* when attributed to God.

Verse 15. *Though he be fruitful*] יפריא *yaphri;* a paronomasia on the word אפרים *ephrayim,* which comes from the same root פרה *parah,* to be fruitful, to *sprout,* to *bud.*

An east wind shall come] As the east wind parches and blasts all vegetation, so shall *Shalmaneser* blast and destroy the Israelitish state.

Verse 16. *Samaria shall become desolate*] This was the capital of the Israelitish kingdom. What follows is a simple prophetic declaration of the cruelties which should be exercised upon this hapless people by the Assyrians in the sackage of the city.

CHAPTER XIV

By the terrible denunciation of vengeance which concludes the preceding chapter, the prophet is led to exhort Israel to repentance, furnishing them with a beautiful form of prayer, very suitable to the occasion, 1–3. *Upon which God, ever ready to pardon the penitent, is introduced making large promises of blessings, in allusion to those copious dews which refresh the green herbs, and which frequently denote, not only temporal salvation, but also the rich and refreshing comforts of the Gospel,* 4–7. *Their reformation from idolatry is foretold, and their consequent prosperity, under the emblem of a green flourishing fir tree,* 8; *but these promises are confined to those who may bring forth the fruits of righteousness, and the wicked are declared to have no share in them,* 9.

A. M. cir. 3279 B. C. cir. 725 A. U. C. cir. 29 Romuli, R. Roman., cir. annum 29

O ISRAEL, [a]return unto the
LORD thy God; [b]for thou
hast fallen by thine iniquity.
2 Take with you words, and
turn to the LORD: say unto him,
Take away all iniquity, and [c]re-
ceive *us* graciously: so will we
render [d]the calves of our lips.

A. M. cir. 3279 B. C. cir. 725 A. U. C. cir. 29 Romuli, R. Roman., cir. annum 29

[a]Chap. xii. 6; Joel ii. 13——[b]Chap. xiii. 9

[c]Or, *give good*——[d]Heb. xiii. 15

NOTES ON CHAP. XIV

Verse 1. *O Israel, return unto the Lord*] These words may be considered as addressed to the people now in captivity; suffering much, but having still much more to suffer if they did not repent. But it seems all these evils might yet be prevented, though so positively predicted, if the people would repent and return; and the very exhortation to this repent-

A. M. cir. 3279
B. C. cir. 725
A. U. C. cir. 29
Romuli,
R. Roman.,
cir. annum 29

3 [e]Asshur shall not save us;
[f]we will not ride upon horses:
[g]neither will we say any more
to the work of our hands, *Ye*
are our gods: [h]for in thee the fatherless
findeth mercy.
4 I will heal [i]their backsliding, I will love
them [k]freely: for mine anger is
turned away from him.
5 I will be as [l]the dew
unto Israel: he shall [m]grow as
the lily, and [n]cast forth his roots as Lebanon.
6 His branches [o]shall spread, and [p]his

[e]Jer. xxxi. 18, &c.; chap. v. 13; xii. 1——[f]Deut. xvii. 16; Psa. xxxiii. 17; Isa. xxx. 2, 16; xxxi. 1——[g]Chap. ii. 17; ver. 8——[h]Psa. x. 14; lxviii. 5

[i]Jer. v. 6; xiv. 7; ch. xi. 7——[k]Eph. i. 6——[l]Job xxix. 19; Prov. xix. 12——[m]Or, *blossom*——[n]Heb. *strike*——[o]Heb. *shall go*——[p]Psa. lii. 8; cxxviii. 3; Ecclus. l. 10

ance shows that they still had power to repent, and that God was ready to save them and avert all these evils. All this is easily accounted for on the doctrine of the *contingency of events*, i. e., the poising a multitude of events on the possibility of being and not being, and leaving the will of man to turn the scale; and that God will not foreknow a thing *as absolutely certain*, which his will has determined to make *contingent*. A doctrine against which some solemn men have blasphemed, and philosophic infidels declaimed; but without which fate and dire necessity must be the universal governors, *prayer* be a useless meddling, and Providence nothing but the ineluctable adamantine chain of unchangeable events; all virtue is vice, and vice virtue; or there is no distinction between them, each being eternally determined and unalterably fixed by a sovereign and uncontrollable will and unvarying necessity, from the operation of which no soul of man can escape, and no occurrence in the universe be otherwise than it is. From such blasphemy, and from the *monthly* publications which avouch it, good Lord, deliver us!

Verse 2. *Take with you words*] And you may be assured that you pray aright, when you use the words which God himself has put in your mouths. On this very ground there is a potency in the LORD'S PRAYER, when offered up believingly, beyond what can be found in any human composition. And it may be presumed that it was this consideration that induced our *reformers* to introduce it so *frequently* in the public liturgy.

See the order of God's directions here:—

1. Hearing these merciful invitations, believe them to be *true*.

2. Cast aside your idols; and return to God as your Maker, King, and Saviour.

3. *Take with you* the *words* by which you have been encouraged, and plead them before God.

4. Remember your iniquity, deeply deplore it, and beg of God to *take it all away*.

5. Let faith be in exercise to receive what God waits to impart. "Receive us graciously;" וקח טוב *vekach tob*, *receive*, or *let us receive good;* when thou has emptied us of evil, fill us with goodness.

6. Be then determined, through grace, to live to his glory, "so shall we render thee the calves" (פרים *parim*, for which the *versions* in general read פרי *peri*, *fruits*, omitting the מ *mem*) "of our lips;" the sacrifices of *praise*, *thanksgiving*, *gratitude*, and the hearty *obedience* which our *lips* have often promised.

7. Having thus determined, specify your *resolutions* to depend on God alone for all that can make you wise, useful, holy, and happy. The *resolutions* are,—

1. *Asshur shall not save us*—We will neither trust in, nor fear, this rich and powerful king. We will not look either to riches or power for true rest and peace of mind.

2. *We will not ride upon horses*—We shall no more fix our hopes on the proud Egyptian cavalry, to deliver us out of the hands of enemies to whom thy Divine justice has delivered us. We will expect no rest nor happiness in the elegances of life, and gratification of our senses.

3. *Neither will we say any more to the work of our hands*, Ye are *our gods*—We will not trust in any thing *without* us; nor even in any good thing we are able to do through thy grace; knowing we have nothing but what we have received. We will trust in thy infinite mercy for our final salvation.

4. And we will do all this from the conviction, that *in thee the fatherless findeth mercy;* for we are all alike helpless, desolate, perishing *orphans*, till translated into thy family.

Verse 4. *I will heal their backsliding*] Here is the *answer* of God to these prayers and resolutions. See its parts:—

1. Ye have backslidden and fallen, and are grievously and mortally wounded by that fall; but I, who am the Author of life, and who redeem from death, will *heal* all these wounds and spiritual diseases.

2. *I will love them freely*—נדבה *nedabah*, after a *liberal*, *princely* manner. I will love them so as to do them incessant good. It shall not be a love of *affection* merely, but shall be a *beneficial love*. A love that not only *feels delight in itself*, but fills them with *delight* who are its objects, by making them unutterably and supremely happy.

3. *For mine anger is turned away from him*—Because he has turned back to me. Thus God and man become *friends*.

Verse 5. *I will be as the dew unto Israel*] On these metaphors I gladly avail myself of the elegant and just observations of Bp. *Lowth*. "These verses (5, 6, 7) contain gracious promises of God's favour and blessings upon Israel's conversion. In the *fifth* verse, it is described by that refreshment which copious *dews* give to the grass in summer. If we consider the nature of the climate, and the necessity of *dews* in so hot a country, not only to refresh, but likewise to preserve life; if we consider also the beauty of the oriental *lilies*, the fragrance of the *cedars* which grow upon Lebanon, the beauteous appearance which the spreading *olive trees* afforded, the exhilarating coolness caused by the shade of such trees, and the *aromatic*

A. M. cir. 3279 B. C. cir. 725 A. U. C. cir. 29 Romuli, R. Roman., cir. annum 29

beauty shall be as the olive tree,
and [q]his smell as Lebanon.
7 [r]They that dwell under his
shadow shall return; they shall
revive *as* the corn, and [s]grow as the vine:
the [t]scent thereof *shall be* as the wine of
Lebanon.
8 Ephraim *shall say,* [u]What have I to do
any more with idols? [v]I have heard *him,* and
observed him: I *am* like a green
fir tree. [w]From me is thy fruit
found.
9 [x]Who *is* wise, and he shall
understand these *things?* prudent, and he
shall know them? for [y]the ways of the
LORD *are* right, and the just shall walk
in them: but the transgressors shall fall
therein.

[q]Gen. xxvii. 27; Cant. iv. 11——[r]Psa. xci. 1——[s]Or, *blossom*——[t]Or, *memorial*——[u]Ver. 3——[v]Jer. xxxi. 18 [w]James i. 17——[x]Psa. cvii. 43; Jer. ix. 12; Dan. xii. 10; Ecclus. xxxix. 24, 27; John viii. 47; xviii. 37——[y]Psa. cxix. 14, 27, 33; cxlv. 17; Prov. x. 29; Luke ii. 34; 2 Cor. ii. 16; 1 Pet. ii. 7, 8

smell exhaled by the *cedars;* we shall then partly understand the force of the metaphors here employed by the prophet; but their full energy no one can conceive, till he feels both the *want,* and enjoys the *advantage,* of the particulars referred to in that climate where the prophet wrote."—*Lowth's twelfth* and *nineteenth* prelection; and *Dodd* on the place.

What a glorious prophecy! What a wonderful prophet! How sublime, how emergetic, how just! The great master prophet, Isaiah, alone could have done this better. And these promises are not for *Israel* merely after the flesh; they are for all the people of God. *We* have a lot and portion in the matter; God also places his love upon *us.* Here the reader must feel some such sentiment as the shepherd in *Virgil,* when enraptured with the elegy which his associate had composed on their departed friend. The phraseology and metaphors are strikingly similar; and therefore I shall produce it.

Tale tuum carmen nobis, divine poeta,
Quale *sopor fessis in gramine,* quale *per æstum*
Dulcis aquæ saliente sitim restinguere rivo.
Nec calamis solum æquiparas, sed voce magistrum.
Fortunate puer! tu nunc eris *alter* ab illo.
Nos tamen hæc quocunque modo tibi nostra vicissim
Dicemus, Daphninque tuum tollemus ad astra:
Daphnin ad astra feremus: *amavit nos quoque Daphnis.*

VIRGIL. *Ecl.* v., ver. 45.

"O heavenly poet, such thy verse appears,
So sweet, so charming to my ravish'd ears,
As to the *weary swain* with cares oppress'd,
Beneath the *sylvan shade, refreshing rest;*
As to the *feverish traveller,* when first
He finds a *crystal stream* to quench his *thirst.*
In singing, as in piping, you excel;
And scarce your master could perform so well.
O fortunate young man! at least your lays
Are *next* to *his,* and claim the second praise.
Such as they are, my rural songs I join
To raise your Daphnis to the powers divine;
For Daphnis was *my friend,* as well as *thine.*"

Verse 7. *They that dwell under his shadow shall return*] The *Targum* is curious: "They shall be gathered together from the midst of their captivity; they shall dwell under the shadow of *his* CHRIST, and the dead shall revive."

They shall revive as *the corn*] The justness and beauty of this metaphor is not generally perceived. After the corn has been a short time above the earth, in a single spike, the blades begin to separate, and the stalk to spring out of the centre. The side leaves turn back to make way for the protruding stalk; and fall bending down to the earth, assuming a *withered* appearance, though still attached to the plant. To look at the corn in this state, no one, unacquainted with the circumstance, could entertain any sanguine hope of a copious *harvest.* In a short time other leaves spring out; the former freshen, and begin to stand erect; and the whole seems *to revive from a vegetative death.* This is the circumstance to which the prophet refers; "they shall revive as the corn." Of this a prudent and profitable use may be made.

1. When a soul is first "drawn by the cords of love," chap. xi. 4, every thing seems to it promising, comfortable, and delightful, like the corn in its *first state.*

2. But when the Spirit of judgment brings to the light of conscience the hidden things of iniquity, and repentance is deepened into *contrition,* the broken and the contrite heart groans, and thinks that *all is lost;* deep distress takes place, and discouragement succeeds discouragement. This answers to the corn in its *second state.*

3. By and by the pardon comes, and God's love is shed abroad in the heart by the Holy Ghost; every hope is *revived* and realized, the *full corn* in the ear becomes manifest; and this answers to the corn in its *third state.* "They shall revive as the corn." Glory be to God for his unspeakable gift!

Verse 8. *What have I to do any more with idols?*] The conversion of Ephraim is now as complete as if was sincere. God hears and observes this.

I am like a green fir tree.] Perhaps these words should be joined to the preceding, as *Newcome* has done, and be a part of God's speech to Ephraim. "I have heard him; and I have seen him as a flourishing fir tree." He is become strong and vigorous; and from his present appearance of healthiness, his future increase and prosperity may be safely anticipated.

From me is thy fruit found.] All thy goodness springs from the principle of grace which I have planted in thy soul; for as the earth cannot bring forth fruit without the blessing of God, sending the *dews* and *rains,* with the *genial rays* of the sun; so neither can the soul of man, even of the most pious, bear fruit, without a continual influence from the Most High.

Without the *former*, neither *grass* could grow for *cattle*, nor *corn* for the service of *man;* without the *latter*, no seeds of righteousness could take root, no stalk of promise could grow, no fruit of grace could be produced. And the unclean spirit, which was cast out, would soon return; and, finding his former house empty, swept, and garnished, would re-enter with seven demons of greater power and worse influence; and the latter end of that man would be worse than the first. Reader, ever consider that all *thy good* must be derived from God; and all that good must be preserved in thee by his continued influence of *light, love*, and *power* upon thy soul.

Verse 9. *Who is wise, and he shall understand these* things?] What things? Those which relate to the *backslidings, iniquity*, and *punishment* of Israel; and to the *mercy* and *kindness* of God in their promised restoration. *The things* which belong to the work of *sin* in the heart; *the things* which belong to the work of *grace* in the soul; and particularly *the things* mentioned in this wonderful chapter.

Prudent, and he shall know them?] He who endeavours to *understand* them, who lays his heart to them, such a person shall understand them.

For the ways of the Lord are *right*] This is the *conclusion* which the prophet makes from the whole. All God's conduct, both in the *dispensation of justice* and *mercy*, is right: all as it should be, all as it must be; because he is too wise to err, too good to be unkind.

The just shall walk in them] This is a truth which he will always acknowledge; and illustrate it by a righteous and godly life.

But the transgressors shall fall therein.] Howsoever good they might have been before, if they do not consider the necessity of depending upon God; of receiving all their light, life, power, and love from him; ever evidencing that *faith* which *worketh* by *love;* maintaining an obedient conduct, and having respect to all God's precepts; they shall fall, even in the "way of righteousness." When still using the *Divine ordinances*, and *associating with God's people*, they shall perish from the way; and be like Ephraim, who once "spoke trembling," and "was exalted in Israel," who was "God's beloved son," and "called out of Egypt;" yet, by "offending in Baal," giving way to "the idols of his heart," fell from God, fell into the hands of his enemies, and became a wretched thrall in a heathen land.

"Whoso is wise, let him understand these things!
Whoso is prudent, let him know them!"——

He who is well instructed will make a proper application of what he has here read; will tremble at the *threatenings*, and embrace the *promises*, of his God.

The *Targum* is worthy the most serious attention.

"The ways of the Lord are right, and the just who walk in them shall live for ever; but the ungodly, because they have not walked in them, shall be delivered into hell."

How instructive, how convincing, how awakening, and yet how consolatory, are the words of this prophecy! Reader, lay them to heart. A godly mind cannot consider them in vain; such shall know them, and know that the ways of the Lord are right.

INTRODUCTION TO THE BOOK

OF THE

PROPHET JOEL

JOEL, the son of *Pethuel*, the second of the twelve minor prophets, was, as is said, of the tribe of *Reuben*, and city of *Bethoran;* or rather *Betharan*, for *Bethoran* was on this side *Jordan*, in the tribe of *Ephraim*, and *Betharan* was on the other side of the river, in the tribe of *Reuben*. Joel prophesied in the kingdom of Judah; and it is the opinion of some critics that he did not appear there till after the removal of the ten tribes and the destruction of the kingdom of *Israel*. We do not know distinctly the year wherein he began to prophesy, nor that in which he died. He speaks of a great famine, and an inundation of locusts, which ravaged *Judea;* but as these are evils not uncommon in that country, and all sorts of events have not been registered in history, we can infer nothing from thence towards fixing the particular period of *Joel's* prophecy.

St. Jerome, followed by many others, both ancients and moderns, believed *Joel* to have been contemporary with *Hosea*, according to this rule laid down by him, that when there is no certain proof of the time wherein any prophet lived, we are to be directed in our conjectures by the time of the preceding prophet, whose epoch is better known. But this rule is not always certain, and should not hinder us from following another system, if we have good reason for doing so. The *Hebrews* maintain that *Joel* prophesied under *Manasseh;* and as collateral circumstances seem to preponderate in favour of this hypothesis, it has been accordingly followed in the margin. Under the idea of an enemy's army, the prophet represents a cloud of locusts, which in his time fell upon *Judea*, and caused great desolation. This, together with the caterpillars, and the drought, brought a terrible famine upon the land. God, being moved with the calamities and prayers of his people, scattered the locusts, and the wind blew them into the sea. These misfortunes were succeeded by plenty and fertility. After this, the prophet foretold the day of the Lord, and the vengeance he was to exercise in the valley of *Jezreel*. He speaks of the *teacher of righteousness*, whom God was to send; and of the Holy Spirit, which was to descend upon all flesh. He says that *Jerusalem* will be inhabited for ever; that salvation will come out from thence; and that whosoever shall call upon the name of the Lord shall be saved. All this relates to the new covenant, and the time of the Messiah. See *Calmet*.

Bishop *Lowth* observes that "the style of Joel differs much from that of Hosea; but, though of a different kind, is equally poetical. It is elegant, perspicuous, clear, diffusive, and flowing; and, at the same time, very sublime, nervous, and animated. He displays the whole power of poetic description in the first and second chapters; and, at the same time, his fondness for metaphors, comparisons, and allegories; nor is the connection of his subjects less remarkable than the graces of his diction. It is not to be denied that in some places he is very obscure; which every attentive reader will perceive, especially in the end of this prophecy." Præl. xxi.; and see *Dodd*. The two first chapters are inimitably beautiful; and the language, in force, and often in *sound*, well adapted to the subject. See the note on ver. 1.

THE BOOK

OF THE

PROPHET JOEL

Chronological Notes relative to the commencement of Joel's prophesying, upon the supposition that this event took place about six hundred and ninety *years before the commencement of the Christian era.*

Year from the Creation, according to Archbishop Usher, 3314.—Year of the Julian Period, 4024.—Year since the Flood, 1658.—Year from the foundation of Solomon's temple, 322.—Year since the division of Solomon's monarchy into the kingdoms of Israel and Judah, 285.—Year since the extinction of the kingdom of Israel by Shalmaneser, king of Assyria, 31.—Third year of the *twenty-second* Olympiad.—Year from the building of Rome, according to the Varronian computation, 64.—Year before the vulgar era of Christ's nativity, 690.—Cycle of the Sun, 20.—Cycle of the Moon, 15.—Third year of Eryxias, the last decennial archon of the Athenians.—First year of Anaxidamus, king of Lacedæmon, of the family of the Proclidæ.—Thirty-fifth year of Eurycrates I., king of Lacedæmon, of the family of the Eurysthenidæ.—Eleventh year of Deioces, the first king of the Medes.—Fortieth year of Perdiccas I., king of Macedon.—Twenty-ninth year of Gyges, king of Lydia.—Ninth year of Manasseh, king of Judah.

CHAPTER I

This and the beginning of the next chapter contain a double prophecy, applicable in its primary sense to a plague of locusts which was to devour the land, and to be accompanied with a severe drought and famine; and in its secondary sense it denotes the Chaldean invasion. Both senses must be admitted: for some of the expressions will apply only to the dearth by insects; others to the desolation by war. The contexture of both is beautiful and well conducted. In this chapter the distress of every order of people is strongly painted; and not only does the face of nature languish when the God of nature is displeased, 1–19; but the very beasts of the field, by a bold figure, are represented as supplicating God in their distress, and reproaching the stupidity of man, 20.

A. M. cir. 3314
B. C. cir. 690
Ol. cir. XXII. 3
NumæPompilii,
R. Roman.,
cir. annum 26

THE word of the LORD that
came to Joel the son of Pethuel.
2 Hear this, ye old men, and
give ear, all ye inhabitants of
the land. [a]Hath this been in
your days, or even in the days of
your fathers?

[a]Joel, chap. ii. 2

NOTES ON CHAP. I

Verse 1. *The word of the Lord that came to Joel*] See the *introduction* for some account of this prophet, whose history is very obscure. Bishop *Newcome* thinks that he prophesied while the kingdom of Judah subsisted, and refers to chap. ii. 1, 15, (see also chap. i. 14, and the note there,) but not long before its subversion as his words, chap. iii. 1, seem to imply that its captivity was approaching. See 2 Kings xxi. 10-15. He therefore favours the conjecture of *Drusius*, that this prophet lived under *Manasseh*, and before his conversion, 2 Chron. xxxiii. 13; that is, some time from before Christ 697 to (suppose) 660.

Verse 2. *Ye old men*] Instead of הזקנים *hazzekenim old men*, a few MSS. have הכהנים *haccohanim, ye priests*, but improperly.

Hath this been in your days] He begins very abruptly; and before he proposes his *subject*, excites attention and alarm by intimating that he is about to announce disastrous events, such as the *oldest man* among them has never seen, nor any of them learnt from the histories of ancient times.

A. M. cir. 3314
B. C. cir. 690
Ol. cir. XXII. 3
NumæPompilii,
R. Roman.,
cir. annum 26

3 [b]Tell ye your children of it, and *let* your children *tell* their children, and their children another generation.

4 [c]That[d] which the palmerworm hath left hath the locust eaten: and that which the locust hath left hath the cankerworm eaten; and that which the cankerworm hath left hath the caterpillar eaten.

5 Awake, ye drunkards, and weep; and howl, all ye drinkers of wine, because of the new wine; [e]for it is cut off from your mouth.

6 For [f]a nation is come up upon my land, strong, and without number, [g]whose teeth *are* the teeth of a lion, and he hath the cheek-teeth of a great lion.

7 He hath [h]laid my vine waste, and [i]barked my fig tree: he hath made it clean bare, and cast *it* away; the branches thereof are made white.

A. M. cir. 3314
B. C. cir. 690
Ol. cir. XXII. 3
NumæPompilii,
R. Roman.,
cir. annum 26

8 [k]Lament like a virgin girded with sackcloth for [l]the husband of her youth.

9 [m]The meat-offering and the drink-offering is cut off from the house of the LORD; the priests, the LORD's ministers, mourn.

10 The field is wasted, [n]the land mourneth; for the corn is wasted: [o]the new wine is [p]dried up, the oil languisheth.

11 [q]Be ye ashamed, O ye husbandmen; howl, O ye vine-dressers, for the wheat and for the barley; because the harvest of the field is perished.

---

[b]Psa. lxxviii. 4——[c]Deut. xxviii. 38; chap. ii. 25——[d]Heb. *The residue of the palmerworm*——[e]Isa. xxxii. 10——[f]So Prov. xxx. 25, 26, 27; chap. ii. 2, 11, 25——[g]Rev. ix. 8——[h]Isa. v. 6

[i]Heb. *laid my fig tree for a barking*——[k]Isa. xxii. 12——[l]Prov. ii. 17; Jer. iii. 4——[m]Ver. 13; chap. ii. 14——[n]Jer. xii. 11; xiv. 2——[o]Isa. xxiv. 7; ver. 12——[p]Or, *ashamed*——[q]Jer. xiv. 3, 4

Verse 3. *Tell ye your children of it*] To heighten the effect, he still conceals the subject, and informs them that it is such as should be handed down from father to son through all generations.

Verse 4. *That which the palmerworm hath left*] Here he begins to open his message, and the words he chooses show that he is going to announce a devastation of the land by *locusts*, and a *famine* consequent on their depredations. What the different *insects* may be which he specifies is not easy to determine. I shall give the words of the original, with their etymology.

The *palmerworm*, גזם *gazam*, from the same root, *to cut short;* probably the *caterpillar*, or some such *blight*, from its *cutting the leaves of the trees into pieces* for its nourishment.

The *locust*, ארבה *arbeh*, from רבה *rabah*, to *multiply*, from the immense increase and multitude of this insect.

Cankerworm, ילק *yelek*, from לק *lak*, to *lick* or *lap* with the tongue; the *reference* is uncertain.

Caterpillar, חסיל *chasil*, from חסל *chasal*, to *consume*, to *eat up;* the *consumer*. Bishop *Newcome* translates the *first grasshopper;* the *second*, *locust;* the *third*, *devouring locust;* and the *fourth*, *consuming locust*. After all that has been said by interpreters concerning these *four* animals, I am fully of opinion that the *arbeh*, or *locust* himself, is the *gazam*, the *yelek*, and the *chasil;* and that these different names are used here by the prophet to point out the locust in its different states, or progress from *embryo* to *full growth*. See the note on chap. ii. 2.

Verse 5. *Awake, ye drunkards*] The general destruction of vegetation by these devouring creatures has totally prevented both *harvest* and *vintage;* so that there shall not be *wine* even for *necessary* uses, much less for the purposes of *debauchery*. It is well known that the ruin among the vines by locusts prevents the vintage for several years after.

Verse 6. *A nation is come up upon my land*] That real *locusts* are intended there can be little doubt; but it is thought that this may be a *double prophecy*, and that the destruction by the *Chaldeans* may also be intended, and that the *four* kinds of *locusts* mentioned above may mean the *four* several attacks made on Judea by them. The *first* in the last year of Nabonassar, (father of Nebuchadnezzar,) which was the *third* of Jehoiakim; the *second* when Jehoiakim was taken prisoner in the *eleventh* year of his reign; the *third* in the *ninth* year of Zedekiah; and the *fourth three* years after, when Jerusalem was destroyed by Nebuchadnezzar. Others say that they mean *four powers* which have been enemies of the Jews: 1. The *palmerworm*, the Assyrians and Chaldeans. 2. The *locust*, the Persians and Medes. 3. The *cankerworm*, the Greeks, and particularly Antiochus Epiphanes. 4. The *caterpillar*, the Romans. Others make them *four* kings; Tiglath-pileser, Shalmaneser, Sennacherib, and Nebuchadnezzar. But of such similitudes there is no end; and the best of them is arbitrary and precarious.

Verse 7. *He hath laid my vine waste*] The locusts have eaten off both *leaves* and *bark*. חשף חשפה *chasoph chasaphah*, he hath *made it clean bare;* שדד שדה *suddad sadeh, the field is laid waste*, ver. 10; and כשד משדי *kesod mishshaddai*, a *destruction from the Almighty*, ver. 15; are all *paronomasias* in which this prophet seems to delight.

Verse 8. *Lament like a virgin—for the husband of her youth.*] *Virgin* is a very improper *version* here. The original is בתולה *bethulah*, which signifies a *young woman* or *bride* not a *virgin*, the proper Hebrew for which is עלמה *almah*. See the notes on Isa. vii. 14, and Matt. i. 23.

Verse 9. *The meat-offering and the drink-offering is cut off*] The crops and the vines being destroyed by the locusts, the total devasta-

A. M. cir. 3314
B. C. cir. 690
Ol. cir. XXII. 3
NumæPompilii,
R. Roman.,
cir. annum 26

12 [r]The vine is dried up, and the fig tree languisheth, the pomegranate tree, the palm tree also, and the apple tree, *even* all the trees of the field, are withered: because [s]joy is withered away from the sons of men.

13 [t]Gird yourselves, and lament, ye priests: howl, ye ministers of the altar; come, lie all night in sackcloth, ye ministers of my God: for [u]the meat-offering and the drink-offering is withholden from the house of your God.

14 [v]Sanctify ye a fast, call [w]a [x]solemn assembly, gather the elders *and* [y]all the inhabitants of the land *into* the house of the LORD your God, and cry unto the LORD.

15 [z]Alas for the day! for [a]the day of the LORD *is* at hand, and as a destruction from the Almighty shall it come.

16 Is not the meat cut off before our eyes, *yea,* [b]joy and gladness from the house of our God?

17 The [c]seed is rotten under their clods, the garners are laid desolate, the barns are broken down; for the corn is withered.

18 How do [d]the beasts groan! the herds of cattle are perplexed, because they have no pasture; yea, the flocks of sheep are made desolate.

19 O LORD, [e]to thee will I cry: for [f]the fire hath devoured the [g]pastures of the wilderness, and the flame hath burned all the trees of the field.

20 The beasts of the field [h]cry also unto thee: for [i]the rivers of waters are dried up, and the fire hath devoured the pastures of the wilderness.

[r]Ver. 10——[s]Isa. xxiv. 11; Jer. xlviii. 33; see Psa. iv. 7; Ias. ix. 3——[t]Ver. 8; Jer. iv. 8——[u]Ver. 9——[v]2 Chron. xx. 3, 4; chap. ii. 15, 16——[w]Lev. xxiii. 36 [x]Or, day of *restraint*——[y]2 Chron. xx. 13——[z]Jer. xxx. 7

[a]Isa. xiii. 6, 9; chap. ii. 1——[b]See Deut. xii. 6, 7; xvi. 11, 14, 15——[c]Heb. *grains*——[d]Hos. iv. 3——[e]Psa. l. 15——[f]Jer. ix. 10; chap. ii. 3——[g]Or, *habitations* [h]Job xxxviii. 41; Psa. civ. 21; cxlv. 15——[i]1 Kings xvii. 7; xviii. 5

tion in plants, trees, corn, &c., is referred to and described with a striking variety of expression in this and the following verses.

Verse 12. *The vine is dried up*] Dr. *Shaw* observes that in Barbary, in the month of June, the locusts collect themselves into compact bodies a furlong or more square, and march on, eating up every thing that is green or juicy, and letting nothing escape them, whether vegetables or *trees.*

They destroy the *pomegranate,* the *palm,* the *apple,* (תפוח *tappuach,* the *citron tree,*) the *vine,* the *fig,* and every *tree of the field.* See the note on chap. ii. 2.

Verse 14. *Call a solemn assembly*] עצרה *atsarah* signifies a time of *restraint,* as the *margin* has it. The clause should be translated—*consecrate a fast, proclaim a time of restraint;* that is, of total abstinence from *food,* and from all *secular employment.* All the elders of the land and the representatives of the people were to be collected at the *temple* to cry unto the Lord, to confess their sins, and pray for mercy. The *temple* was not yet destroyed. This prophecy was delivered before the captivity of Judah.

Verse 15. *Alas for the day!*] The *Syriac repeats* this; the *Vulgate, Septuagint,* and *Arabic,* thrice: "Alas, alas, alas, for the day!"

As a destruction from the Almighty] The destruction that is now coming is no ordinary calamity; it is as a signal judgment immediately inflicted by the Almighty.

Verse 17. *The seed is rotten under their clods*] When the sprout was cut off as low as possible by the locusts, there was no farther germination. The seed rotted away.

Verse 18. *How do the beasts groan!*] I really think that the *neighing* of horses, or *braying* of asses, is wonderfully expressed by the sound of the original: מה נאנחה בהמה *mah* NEENCHAH *behemah,* how do the horses *neigh!* how do the asses *bray!* בהמה *behemah* is a collective name for all *domestic cattle,* and those used in *husbandry.*

Cattle are perplexed] They are looking everywhere, and wandering about to find some grass, and know not which way to run.

Verse 19. *O Lord, to thee will I cry*] Let this calamity come as it may, *we have sinned,* and should humble ourselves before God; and it is such a calamity as God alone can remove, therefore unto him must we cry.

The fire hath devoured the pastures] This may either refer to a *drought,* or to the effects of the locusts; as the ground, after they have passed over it, everywhere appears as if a *sheet of flame* had not only *scorched,* but *consumed* every thing.

Verse 20. *The beasts of the field cry also unto thee*] Even the cattle, wild and tame, are represented as supplicating God to have mercy upon them, and send them provender! There is a similar affecting description of the effects of a drought in Jeremiah, chap. xiv. 6.

The rivers of waters are dried up] There must have been a *drought* as well as a *host of locusts;* as some of these expressions seem to apply to the effects of *intense heat.*

For המדבר *hammidbar,* "the wilderness," one of my oldest MSS. reads מדבר *midbar,* "wilderness" simply, as in ver. 19. *Eight* or *ten* of Dr. *Kennicott's* have the same reading.

CHAPTER II

The prophet sounds the alarm of a dreadful calamity, the description of which is most terribly worked up, 1–11. *Exhortation to repentance, fasting, and prayer, that the Divine judgments may be averted,* 12–17. *God will in due time take vengeance on all the enemies of pure and undefiled religion,* 18–20. *Great prosperity of the Jews subsequent to their return from the Babylonish captivity,* 21–27. *Joel then makes an elegant transition to the outpouring of the Holy Ghost on the day of pentecost,* 28–30; *for so these verses are explained by one of the twelve apostles of the Lamb. See* Acts ii. 16–21. *Prophecy concerning the destruction of Jerusalem, which was shortly to follow the opening of the Gospel dispensation,* 31. *Promises of safety to the faithful and penitent; promises afterwards remarkably fulfilled to the Christians in their escape to Pella from the desolating sword of the Roman army,* 32.

A. M. cir. 3314
B. C. cir. 690
Ol. cir. XXII. 3
NumæPompilii,
R. Roman.,
cir. annum 26

BLOW [a]ye the [b]trumpet in
Zion, and [c]sound an alarm
in my holy mountain: let all the
inhabitants of the land tremble:
for [d]the day of the LORD cometh, for *it is*
nigh at hand;

2 [e]A day of darkness and of
gloominess, a day of clouds and
of thick darkness, as the morning spread upon the mountains:
[f]a great people and a strong; [g]there hath
not been ever the like, neither shall be any

[a]Jer. iv. 5; Ver. 15——[b]Or, *cornet*——[c]Numbers x. 5, 9
[d]Chap. i. 15; Obad. 15; Zeph. i. 14, 15

[e]Amos v. 18, 20——[f]Ver. 5, 11, 25; Chap. i. 6
[g]Exod. x. 14

NOTES ON CHAP. II

Verse 1. *Blow ye the trumpet in Zion*] This verse also shows that the temple was still standing. All assemblies of the people were collected by the sound of the *trumpet.*

The day of the Lord cometh] This phrase generally means a day of judgment or punishment.

Verse 2. *A day of darkness, &c.*] The depredations of the locusts are described from the *second* to the *eleventh* verse, and their destruction in the *twentieth.* Dr. *Shaw,* who saw locusts in Barbary in 1724 and 1725, thus describes them:—

"I never observed the *mantes,* bald *locusts,* to be gregarious. But the *locusts,* properly so called, which are so frequently mentioned by *sacred* as well as *profane* writers, are sometimes so beyond expression. Those which I saw in 1724 and 1725 were much bigger than our common grasshopper; and had brown spotted wings, with legs and bodies of a bright yellow. Their first appearance was toward the latter end of *March,* the wind having been for some time south. In the middle of *April* their numbers were so vastly increased that, in the heat of the day, they formed themselves into large and numerous swarms; flew in the air like a succession of clouds; and, as the prophet Joel expresses it, (ii. 10,) they darkened the sun. When the wind blew briskly, so that these swarms were crowded by others, or thrown one upon another, we had a lively idea of that comparison of the psalmist, (Psa. cix. 23,) of being 'tossed up and down as the locust.' In the month of *May,* when the ovaries of those insects were ripe and turgid, each of these *swarms* began gradually to disappear; and retired into the *Mettijiah,* and other adjacent plains, where they deposited their eggs. These were no sooner hatched in June, than each of these broods collected itself into a compact body of a furlong or more in square; and, marching immediately forward in the direction of the sea, they let nothing escape them; eating up every thing that was green and juicy, not only the lesser kinds of vegetables, but the *vine* likewise; the *fig tree,* the *pomegranate,* the *palm,* and the *apple tree, even all the trees of the field,* Joel i. 12; in doing which *they kept their ranks like men of war;* climbing over, as they advanced, every tree or wall that was in their way. Nay, they entered into our very houses and bedchambers, like *so many thieves.* The inhabitants, to stop their progress, made a variety of pits and trenches all over their fields and gardens, which they filled with water; or else they heaped up in them heath, stubble, and such like combustible matter, which were severally set on fire upon the approach of the *locusts.* But this was all to no purpose, for the trenches were quickly filled up, and the fires extinguished, by infinite swarms succeeding one another; while the front was regardless of danger, and the rear pressed on so close, that a retreat was altogether impossible. A day or two after one of these broods was in motion, others were already hatched to march and glean after them; gnawing off the very bark, and the young branches, of such trees as had before escaped with the loss only of their fruit and foliage. So justly have they been compared by the prophet *Joel* (chap. ii. 3) to *a great army;* who further observes, that 'the land is as the garden of Eden before them, and behind them a desolate wilderness.'

"Having lived near a month in this manner (like a μυριοστομον ξιφος, or *sword with ten thousand edges,* to which they have been compared,) upon the ruin and destruction of every vegetable substance which came in their way, they arrived at their full growth, and threw off their *nympha state* by casting their outward skin. To prepare themselves for this change, they clung by their hinder feet to some bush, twig, or corner of a stone; and immediately, by using an undulating motion, their heads would first break out, and then the rest of their bodies. The whole transformation was performed in seven or eight minutes, after which they lay for a short time in a torpid and seemingly languishing condition; but as soon as the sun and air had hardened their wings, by drying up the moisture which remained upon them, after casting their sloughs, they reassumed their former voracity, with an addition both of strength and

A. M. cir. 3314 B. C. cir. 690 Ol. cir. XXII. 3 NumæPompilii, R. Roman., cir. annum 26

more after it, *even* to the years
[h]of many generations.
3 [i]A fire devoureth before
them; and behind them a flame
burneth: the land *is* as [k]the garden of Eden
before them, [l]and behind them a desolate
wilderness; yea, and nothing shall escape
them.
4 [m]The appearance of them *is* as the appearance of horses; and as horsemen, so shall
they run.
5 [n]Like the noise of chariots on the tops
of mountains shall they leap, like the noise of
a flame of fire that devoureth the stubble, [o]as
a strong people set in battle array.
6 Before their face the people shall be much
pained: [p]all faces shall gather [q]blackness.
7 They shall run like mighty
men; they shall climb the wall
like men of war; and they shall
march every one on his ways,
and they shall not one break their ranks.
8 Neither shall one thrust another; they
shall walk every one in his path: and *when*
they fall upon the [r]sword, they shall not be
wounded.
9 They shall run to and fro in the city; they
shall run upon the wall, they shall climb up
upon the houses: they shall [s]enter in at the
windows [t]like a thief.
10 [u]The earth shall quake before them; the
heavens shall tremble: [v]the sun and the
moon shall be dark, and the stars shall withdraw their shining:

[h]Heb. *of generation and generation*——[i]Ch. i. 19, 20——[k]Gen. ii. 8; xiii. 10; Isa. li. 3——[l]Zech. vii. 14——[m]Rev. ix. 7——[n]Rev. ix. 9——[o]Ver. 2——[p]Jer. viii. 21; Lam. iv. 8; Nah. ii. 10——[q]Heb. *pot*——[r]Or, *dart*——[s]Jer. ix. 21——[t]John x. 1——[u]Psa. xviii. 7——[v]Isa. xiii. 10; Ezek. xxxii. 7; Ver. 31; chap. iii. 15; Matt. xxiv. 29

agility. Yet they did not continue long in this state before they were entirely dispersed, as their parents were before, after they had laid their eggs; and as the direction of the marches and flights of them both was always to the northward, and not having strength, as they have sometimes had, to reach the opposite shores of *Italy*, *France*, or *Spain*, it is probable they perished in the sea, a grave which, according to these people, they have in common with other winged creatures."—*Travels*, 4to. edition, pp. 187, 188.

A day of darkness] They sometimes obscure the sun. And *Thuanus* observes of an immense crowd, that "they darkened the sun at mid-day."

As the morning spread upon the mountains] They appeared suddenly: as the sun, in rising behind the mountains, *shoots his rays* over them. *Adanson*, in his voyage to *Senegal*, says: "Suddenly there came over our heads a thick cloud which *darkened the air, and deprived us of the rays of the sun.* We soon found that it was owing to a cloud of *locusts*." Some clouds of them are said to have darkened the sun for a mile, and others for the space of *twelve miles!* See on ver. 10.

Verse 3. *A fire devoureth before them*] They consume like a general conflagration. "They destroy the ground, not only for the time, but burn trees for two years after." Sir *Hans Sloane*, Nat. Hist. of Jamaica, vol. i., p. 29.

Behind them a flame burneth] "Wherever they feed," says *Ludolf*, in his History of Ethiopia, "their leavings seem as if *parched with fire*."

Nothing shall escape them.] "After devouring the herbage," says *Adanson*, "with the fruits and leaves of trees, they attacked even the *buds* and the very *bark;* they did not so much as spare the *reeds with which the huts were thatched*."

Verse 4. *The appearance of horses*] The *head* of the locust is remarkably like that of the *horse;* and so *Ray* on Insects describes them: *Caput oblongum, equi instar, prona spectans*—"They have an oblong head, like to that of a horse, bending downward." On this account, the *Italians* call them *cavaletta*, cavalry. *Bochart* remarks, from an *Arabic writer*, that the *locusts* resemble *ten* different kinds of *animals:* 1. The HORSE in its *head.* 2. The ELEPHANT in its *eyes.* 3. The BULL in its *neck.* 4. The STAG in its *horns.* 5. The LION in its *breast.* 6. The SCORPION in its *belly.* 7. The EAGLE in its *wings.* 8. The CAMEL in its *thighs.* 9. The OSTRICH in its *feet.* And 10. The SERPENT in its *tail.* *Vid. Hieroz.*, vol. ii., p. 475, edit. 1692. But its most prominent resemblance is to the *horse*, which the prophet mentions; and which the *Arabic writer* puts in the *first place*, as being the *chief.*

Verse 5. *Like the noise of chariots*] *Bochart* also remarks:—"The locusts fly with a *great noise*, so as to be heard *six miles off*, and while they are eating the fruits of the earth, the *sound* of them is like that of a *flame driven by the wind*."—*Ibid.*, p. 478.

Verse 6. *All faces shall gather blackness.*] Universal mourning shall take place, because they know that such a plague is irresistible.

Verse 7. *Like mighty men—like men of war* (*and as horsemen*, ver. 4)] The prophet does not say *they are such*, but they *resemble.* They are *locusts;* but in their operations they are LIKE the above.

They shall not break their ranks] See the account on ver. 2, from Dr. *Shaw.*

Verse 8. *They shall not be wounded.*] They have hard scales like a coat of mail; but the expression refers to the *utter uselessness* of all means to prevent their depredations. See *Shaw's* account above.

Verse 10. *The earth shall quake—the heavens shall tremble*] Poetical expressions, to point out *universal consternation* and *distress.* The *earth quaked* to see itself deprived of its *verdure;* the *heavens trembled* to find themselves deprived of their *light.*

The sun and the moon shall be dark] *Bochart* relates that "their multitude is sometimes

A. M. cir. 3314
B. C. cir. 690
Ol. cir. XXII. 3
NumæPompilii,
R. Roman.,
cir. annum 26

11 [w]And the LORD shall utter
his voice before [x]his army: for
his camp *is* very great: [y]for *he*
is strong that executeth his
word: for the [z]day of the LORD *is* great and
very terrible; and [a]who can abide it?
12 Therefore also now, saith the LORD, [b]turn
ye *even* unto me with all your heart, and with
fasting, and with weeping, and with mourning:
13 And [c]rend your heart, and not [d]your
garments, and turn unto the LORD your God:
for he *is* [e]gracious and merciful, slow to anger, and of great kindness, and repenteth him
of the evil.
14 [f]Who knoweth *if* he will return and repent, and leave [g]a blessing behind him; *even*
[h]a meat-offering and a drink-offering unto
the LORD your God?
15 [i]Blow the trumpet in Zion, [k]sanctify a
fast, call a solemn assembly:
16 Gather the people, [l]sanctify
the congregation, [m]assemble the
elders, [n]gather the children, and
those that suck the breasts: [o]let
the bridegroom go forth of his chamber, and
the bride out of her closet.
17 Let the priests, the ministers of the
LORD, weep [p]between the porch and the
altar, and let them say, [q]Spare thy people, O
LORD, and give not thine heritage to reproach,
that the heathen should [r]rule over them:
[s]wherefore should they say among the people,
Where *is* their God?
18 Then will the LORD [t]be jealous for his
land, [u]and pity his people.
19 Yea, the LORD will answer and say unto
his people, Behold, I will send you [v]corn, and
wine, and oil, and ye shall be satisfied therewith: and I will no more make you a reproach among the heathen:

A. M. cir. 3314
B. C. cir. 690
Ol. cir. XXII. 3
NumæPompilii,
R. Roman.,
cir. annum 26

---

[w]Jer. xxv. 30; chap. iii. 16; Amos i. 2——[x]Ver. 25——[y]Jer. l. 34; Rev. xviii. 8——[z]Jer. xxx. 7; Amos v. 18; Zeph. i. 15——[a]Num. xxiv. 23; Mal. iii. 2——[b]Jer. iv. 1; Hos. xii. 6; xiv. 1——[c]Psa. xxxiv. 18; li. 17——[d]Gen. xxxvii. 34; 2 Sam. i. 11; Job i. 20——[e]Exod. xxxiv. 6; Psa. lxxxvi. 5, 15; Jonah iv. 2——[f]Josh. xiv. 12; 2 Sam. xii. 22; 2 Kings xix. 4; Amos v. 15; Jonah iii. 9; Zeph. ii. 3

[g]Isa. lxv. 8; Hag. ii. 19——[h]Chap. i. 9, 13——[i]Num. x. 3; ver. 1——[k]Chap. i. 14——[l]Exod. xix. 10, 22——[m]Chap. i. 14——[n]2 Chron. xx. 13——[o]1 Cor. vii. 5——[p]Ezek. viii. 16; Matt. xxiii. 35——[q]Exod. xxxii. 11, 12; Deut. ix. 26–29——[r]Or, *use a by-word against them*——[s]Psa. xlii. 10; lxxix. 10; cxv. 2; Mic. vii. 10——[t]Zech. i. 14; viii. 2——[u]Deut. xxxii. 36; Isa. lx. 10——[v]See chap. i. 10; Mal. iii. 10, 11, 12

---

so immense as to obscure the heavens for the space of *twelve miles!*"—*Ibid.* p. 479.

Verse 11. *The Lord shall utter his voice*] Such a *mighty force* seems as if summoned by the Almighty, and the noise they make in coming announces their approach, while yet afar off.

Verse 12. *Turn ye* even *to me*] *Three means* of turning are recommended: *Fasting, weeping, mourning,* i. e., *continued sorrow.*

Verse 13. *Rend your heart*] Let it not be merely a rending of your *garments,* but let your *hearts* be truly contrite. Merely *external* worship and *hypocritical pretensions* will only increase the evil, and cause God to meet you with heavier judgments.

For he is *gracious*] Good and benevolent in his own nature.

Merciful] Pitying and forgiving, as the effect of *goodness* and *benevolence.*

Slow to anger] He is not easily provoked to punish, because he is *gracious* and *merciful.*

Of great kindness] Exuberant goodness to all them that return to him.

And repenteth him of the evil.] Is ever ready to *change* his *purpose* to *destroy,* when he finds the culprit willing to be *saved.* See the notes on Exod. xxxiv. 6, 7.

Verse 14. *Who knoweth* if *he will return*] He may yet interpose and turn aside the calamity threatened, and so far preserve the land from these ravagers, that there will be food for *men* and *cattle,* and a sufficiency of *offerings* for the temple service. Therefore—

Verse 15. *Blow the trumpet*] Let no time be lost, let the alarm be sounded.

Verse 16. *Gather the children*] Let all share in the humiliation, for all must feel the judgment, should it come. Let no *state* nor *condition* among the people be exempted. The *elders,* the *young persons,* the *infants,* the *bridegroom,* and the *bride;* let all leave their houses, and go to the temple of God.

Verse 17. *Let the priests—weep between the porch and the altar*] The altar of burnt-offerings stood before the porch of the temple, 2 Chron. viii. 12, and between them there was an open space of *fifteen* or *twenty* cubits. It was there that the priests prostrated themselves on such occasions. It was into this place that the priests brought the *sacrifice* or *victim of atonement;* and where the high priest laid his hands on the head of the victim confessing his sins.

Let them say] The following was the form to be used on this occasion, "Spare thy people," &c. And if this be done with a rent heart, &c., "then will the Lord be jealous for his land, and pity his people," ver. 18. He will surely save, if ye seriously return to and penitently seek him.

Verse 19. *Yea, the Lord will answer*] It is not a *peradventure;* it will *surely* be done; if ye seek God as *commanded,* ye will find him as *promised.*

I will send you corn and wine] He will either prevent the *total* ravaging of the land, or so bless it with extraordinary *vegetable strength,* that ye shall have plentiful crops.

Verse 20. *I will remove far off from you the northern* army] "That is, the *locusts;* which might enter Judea by the *north,* as Circassia and Mingrelia abound with them. Or the locusts may be thus called, because they spread terror like the *Assyrian* armies, which entered

A. M. cir. 3314 B. C. cir. 690 Ol. cir. XXII. 3 NumæPompilii, R. Roman., cir. annum 26

20 But [w]I will remove far off
from you [x]the northern *army,*
and will drive him into a land
barren and desolate, with his
face [y]toward the east sea, and his hinder part
[z]toward the utmost sea, and his stink shall
come up, and his ill savour shall come up, because [a]he hath done great things.

21 Fear not, O land; be glad and rejoice:
for the LORD will do great things.

22 Be not afraid, [b]ye beasts of the field:
for [c]the pastures of the wilderness do spring,
for the tree beareth her fruit, the fig tree and
the vine do yield their strength.

23 Be glad then, ye children of Zion, and
[d]rejoice in the LORD your God: for he hath
given you [e]the former rain [f]moderately, and
he [g]will cause to come down for you [h]the
rain, the former rain, and the
latter rain in the first *month.*

A. M. cir. 3314 B. C. cir. 690 Ol. cir. XXII. 3 NumæPompilii, R. Roman., cir. annum 26

24 and the floors shall be full
of wheat, and the fats shall overflow with wine and oil.

25 And I will restore to you the years [i]that
the locust hath eaten, the cankerworm, and
the caterpillar, and the palmerworm, [k]my
great army which I sent among you.

26 And ye shall [l]eat in plenty, and be satisfied, and praise the name of the LORD your
God, that hath dealt wondrously with you:
and my people shall never be ashamed.

27 [m]And ye shall know that I *am* [n]in the
midst of Israel, and *that* [o]I *am* the LORD
your God, and none else: and my people shall
never be ashamed.

28 [p]And it shall come to pass afterward,

---

[w]See Exod. x. 19——[x]Jer. i. 14——[y]Ezek. xlvii. 18; Zech. xiv. 8——[z]Deut. xi. 24——[a]Heb. *he hath magnified to do*——[b]Chap. i. 18, 20——[c]Zech. viii. 12; See chap. i. 19——[d]Isa. xli. 16; lxi. 10; Hab. iii. 18; Zech. x. 7——[e]Or, *a teacher of righteousness* [f]Heb. *according to righteousness*——[g]Lev. xxvi. 4; Deut. xi. 14; xxviii. 12——[h]James v. 7——[i]Ch. i. 4 [k]Ver. 11——[l]Lev. xxvi. 5; Psa. xxii. 26; see Lev. xxvi. 26; Mic. vi. 14——[m]Ch. iii. 17——[n]Lev. xxvi. 11, 12; Ezek. xxxvii. 26, 27, 28——[o]Isa. xlv. 5, 21, 22; Ezek. xxxix. 22, 28——[p]Isa. xliv. 3; Ezek. xxxix. 29; Acts ii. 17

Judea by the *north*. See Zeph. ii. 13."—*Newcome.* Syria, which was *northward* of Judea, was infested with them; and it must have been a *northern* wind that brought them into Judea, in the time of *Joel;* as God promises to *change* this wind, and carry them into a *barren and desolate land*, Arabia Deserta. "And his face toward the east sea," i. e., the *Dead Sea*, which lay *eastward* of Jerusalem. "His hinder part toward the utmost sea," the *western sea*, i. e., the *Mediterranean.*

And his stink shall come up] After having been drowned by millions in the Mediterranean, the reflux of the tide has often brought them back, and thrown them in heaps upon the shore, where they putrefied in such a manner as to infect the air and produce pestilence, by which both *men* and *cattle* have died in great multitudes. See *Bochart*, Hieroz., vol. ii., p. 481.

Livy, and St. *Augustine* after him, relate that there was such an immense crowd of locusts in Africa that, having eaten up every green thing, a wind arose that carried them into the sea, where they perished; but being cast upon the shore, they putrefied, and bred such a *pestilence*, that *eighty thousand* men died of it in the kingdom of *Massinissa*, and *thirty thousand* in the garrison of *Utica*, in which only *ten* remained alive. See *Calmet* and *Livy*, lib. xc., and *August. De Civitate Dei*, lib. iv., c. 31. We have many testimonies of a similar kind.

Because he hath done great things] Or, כי *ki, although* he have done great things, or, *after* he has done them, i. e., in almost destroying the whole country.

Verse 21. *Fear not—for the Lord will do great things.*] The words are *repeated* from the preceding verse; Jehovah will do great things in *driving them away*, and supernaturally restoring the land to fertility.

Verse 23. *The former rain moderately*] המורה לצדקה *hammoreh litsedakah*, "the former rain in righteousness," that is, in *due time* and in *just proportion.* This rain fell after *autumn*, the other in *spring*. See Hosea vi. 3.

In the first month.] בראשון *barishon*, "as aforetime." So Bp. *Newcome*. In the month *Nisan.*—Syriac.

Verse 25. *I will restore—the years*] It has already been remarked that the *locusts* not only destroyed the produce of *that year*, but so completely ate up all *buds*, and *barked the trees*, that they did not recover for *some years.* Here God promises that he would either *prevent* or *remedy* that evil; for he would *restore the years* that the *locusts, cankerworm, caterpillar*, and *palmerworm* had eaten.

Verse 26. *Praise the name of the Lord your God, that hath dealt wondrously with you*] In so destroying this formidable enemy; and so *miraculously* restoring the land to *fertility*, after so great a devastation.

Verse 28. *Shall come to pass afterward*] אחרי כן *acharey ken*, "after this;" the same, says *Kimchi*, as *in the latter days*, which always refers to the *days of the Messiah;* and thus this prophecy is to be interpreted: and we have the testimony of St. Peter, Acts ii. 17, that this prophecy relates to *that mighty effusion of the Holy Spirit* which took place after the day of pentecost. Nor is there any evidence that such an *effusion* took place, nor such effects were produced, from the days of this prophet till the day of *pentecost*. And the *Spirit* was poured out then *upon all flesh*, that is, on people of different countries, speaking the languages of almost all the people of the earth; which intimated that these were the *first-fruits* of the conversion of all the nations of the world. For there was scarcely a tongue in the universe that

A. M. cir. 3314
B. C. cir. 690
Ol. cir. XXII. 3
NumæPompilii,
R. Roman.,
cir. annum 26

that I [q]will pour out my Spirit
upon all flesh; [r]and your sons
and [s]your daughters shall prophesy, your old men shall dream
dreams, your young men shall see visions:
29 And also upon [t]the servants and upon
the handmaids in those days will I pour out
my Spirit.
30 And [u]I will show wonders in the heavens
and in the earth, blood, and fire, and pillars
of smoke.
31 [v]The sun shall be turned
into darkness, and the moon into
blood, [w]before the great and
the terrible day of the LORD
come.
32 And it shall come to pass, *that* [x]whoso-
ever shall call on the name of the LORD shall
be delivered: for [y]in Mount Zion and in Jerusalem shall be deliverance, as the LORD hath
said, and in [z]the remnant whom the LORD
shall call.

A. M. cir. 3314
B. C. cir. 690
Ol. cir. XXII. 3
NumæPompilii,
R. Roman.,
cir. annum 26

[q]Zech. xii. 10; John vii. 39——[r]Isa. liv. 13——[s]Acts xxi. 9——[t]1 Cor. xii. 13; Gal. iii. 28; Col. iii. 11 [u]Matt. xxiv. 29; Mark xiii. 24; Luke xxi. 11, 25 [v]Verse 10; Isaiah xiii. 9, 10; chap. iii. 1, 15; Matthew xxiv. 29; Mark xiii. 24; Luke xxi. 25; Rev. vi. 12 [w]Malachi iv. 5——[x]Romans x. 13——[y]Isa. xlvi. 13; lix. 20; Obad. 17; Romans xi. 26——[z]Isa. xi. 11, 16; Jer. xxxi. 7; Mic. iv. 7; v. 3, 7, 8; Rom. ix. 27; xi. 5, 7

was not to be found among the *Parthians, Medes, Elamites, Mesopotamians, Jews, Cappadocians*, people of *Pontus*, of *Asia, Phrygia, Pamphylia, Egypt, Libya, Cyrene, Rome, Crete*, and *Arabia*, who were residents at Jerusalem at that time; and on whom this mighty gift was poured out, each hearing and apprehending the truths of the Gospel, in his own language wherein he was born. Thus we have Divine authority for saying, *that* was the fulfilment of *this* prophecy by *Joel*. And the mighty and rapid spread of the Gospel of Christ in the *present day*, by means of the translation of the Scriptures into almost all the regular languages of the world, and the sending *missionaries* to all nations, who preach the Gospel in those tongues, are farther proofs that the great promise is in the *fullest progress* to be speedily fulfilled, even in the utmost sense of the words.

Your sons and your daughters shall prophesy] Shall *preach*—exhort, pray, and instruct, so as to benefit the Church.

Your old men shall dream dreams] Have my will represented to them in this way, as the others by *direct inspiration*.

Your young men shall see visions] Have true representations of Divine things made upon their *imaginations* by the power of God; that they shall have as full an evidence of them as they could have of any thing that came to the *mind* through the medium of the *senses*.

Verse 29. *And also upon the servants and upon the handmaids*] The gifts of teaching and instructing men shall not be *restricted* to any one *class* or *order* of people. He shall call and qualify the men of his own choice; and shall take such out of all *ranks, orders, degrees*, and offices in society. And he will pour out his Spirit upon them; and they shall be endowed with all the gifts and graces necessary to convert sinners, and build up the Church of Christ on its most holy faith.

And this God *has done*, and is *still doing*. He left the *line of Aaron*, and took his *apostles* indiscriminately from *any tribe*. He passed by the *regular order* of the *priesthood*, and the *public schools* of the most celebrated doctors, and took his *evangelists* from among *fishermen, tent-makers*, and even the *Roman tax-gatherers*. And he, lastly, passed by the *Jewish tribes*, and took the *Gentile converts*, and made *them* preachers of righteousness to the inhabitants of the whole earth. The same practice he continues to the present day; yet he did not then pass by a man *brought up at the feet of Gamaliel*, no more than he would *now* a man *brought up in a celebrated seminary of learning*. He is ever free to use his *own gifts*, in his *own way;* and when *learning* is sanctified, by being *devoted to the service of God*, and the *possessor* is humble and pious, and has those *natural gifts* necessary for a *public teacher*, perhaps we might safely say, God would in many cases *prefer such:* but he will have *others*, as intimated in the prophecy, that we may see the conversion of men is not by *human might*, nor *power*, but *by the Spirit of the Lord of hosts*. The learned man can do nothing without his *Spirit;* the *unlearned* must have his *gifts* and *graces*, without which both their labours would be unprofitable; and thus the *excellency of the power is of God*, and no *flesh can glory in his presence*. See my sermon on this passage.

Verse 30. *Wonders in the heavens and in the earth*] This refers to those dreadful sights, dreadful portents, and destructive commotion, by which the Jewish polity was finally overthrown, and the Christian religion established in the Roman empire. See how our Lord applies this prophecy, Matt. xxiv. 29, and the parallel texts.

Verse 31. *The sun shall be turned into darkness*] The Jewish polity civil and ecclesiastical, shall be entirely destroyed.

Before the great and the terrible day of the Lord come.] In the taking and sacking of Jerusalem, and burning of the temple, by the Romans, under *Titus*, the son of Vespasian. This was, perhaps, the *greatest* and most *terrible day* of God's vengeance ever shown to the world, or that ever will be shown, till the great day of the general judgment. For a full view of this subject, I wish to refer the reader to the notes on Matt. xxiv.

Verse 32. *Whosoever shall call on the name of the Lord*] כל אשר יקרא בשם יהוה *col asher yikra beshem Yehovah*, "All who shall *invoke* in the name of Jehovah." That CHRIST is the *Jehovah* here mentioned appears plain from Rom. x. 15, where the reader had better consult the notes. "This refers," says Bp. *Newcome*, "to the safety of the Christians during the Jewish and the Roman war." It may: but it has a much more extensive meaning, as the use of it by St. Paul, as above, evidently shows. *Every man who invokes Jehovah* for mercy and salvation *by* or *in the name*, JESUS—that very name given under heaven among men for this purpose—*shall be saved.* Nor is there salvation in any other; and those who reject *him* had better lay these things to heart before it be too late.

For in Mount Zion and in Jerusalem] Our blessed Lord first began to preach the Gospel in *Mount Zion*, in the *temple*, and throughout *Jerusalem*. *There* he formed his Church, and *thence* he sent his apostles and evangelists to every part of the globe: "Go ye into all the world, and preach the Gospel to every creature." Of the Jews there was but a *remnant*, a very small number, that received the doctrine of the Gospel, here termed the remnant that the Lord should call; קרא *kore, whom he calleth.* Many were called who would not obey: but those who obeyed the call were saved; and still he *delivers* those who *call upon him;* and he is still calling on men to come to him that they may be saved.

CHAPTER III

The prophecy in this chapter is thought by some to relate to the latter times of the world, when God shall finally deliver his people from all their adversaries; and it must be confessed that the figures employed are so lofty as to render it impossible to restrain the whole of their import to any events prior to the commencement of the Christian era. The whole prophecy is delivered in a very beautiful strain of poetry; but what particular events are referred to is at present very uncertain, 1–21.

A. M. cir. 3314
B. C. cir. 690
Ol. cir. XXII. 3
NumæPompilii,
R. Roman.,
cir. annum 26

FOR, behold, [a]in those days,
and in that time, when I
shall bring again the captivity
of Judah and Jerusalem,
2 [b]I will also gather all nations, and
will bring them down into [c]the valley of
Jehoshaphat, and [d]will plead
with them there for my people and *for* my heritage Israel, whom they have scat-
tered among the nations, and parted my
land.

[a]Jer. xxx. 3; Ezek. xxxviii. 14——[b]Zech. xiv. 2, 3, 4——[c]2 Chron. xx. 26; ver. 42——[d]Isa. lxvi. 16; Ezek. xxxviii. 22

NOTES ON CHAP. III

Verse 1. *For, behold, in those days*] According to the preceding prophecy, *these days* should refer to *Gospel times*, or to such as should *immediately precede* them. But this is a part of the prophecy which is difficult to be understood. All interpreters are at *variance* upon it; some applying its principal parts to *Cambyses;* his unfortunate expedition to Egypt; the destruction of *fifty thousand* of his troops (by the moving pillars of sand) whom he had sent across the desert to plunder the rich temple of Jupiter Ammon; his return to Judea, and dying of a wound which he received from his own sword, in mounting his horse, which happened at *Ecbatane*, at the foot of Mount *Carmel*. On which his army, composed of different nations, seeing themselves without a head, fell out, and fought against each other, till the whole were destroyed. And this is supposed to be what *Ezekiel* means by *Gog* and *Magog*, and the destruction of the former. See Ezek. xxxviii. and xxxix.

Others apply this to the *victories* gained by the *Maccabees*, and to the destruction brought upon the enemies of their country; while several consider the whole as a figurative prediction of the *success of the Gospel* among the nations of the earth. It may refer to those times in which the Jews shall be brought in with the fulness of the Gentiles, and be re-established in their own land. Or there may be portions in this prophecy that refer to *all the events;* and to *others* that have not fallen yet within the range of human conjecture, and will be only known when the time of fulfilment shall take place. In this painful uncertainty, rendered still more so by the discordant opinions of many wise and learned men, it appears to be my province, as I have nothing in the form of a new conjecture to offer, to confine myself to an explanation of the *phraseology* of the chapter; and then leave the reader to apply it as may seem best to his own judgment.

I shall bring again the captivity of Judah and Jerusalem.] This may refer to the return from the Babylonish captivity; extending also to the restoration of *Israel*, or the *ten tribes*.

Verse 2. *The valley of Jehoshaphat*] There is no such valley in the land of Judea; and hence the word must be *symbolical.* It signifies the *judgment of God*, or *Jehovah judgeth;* and may mean some place (as Bp. *Newcome* imagines) where Nebuchadnezzar should gain a great battle, which would utterly discomfit the ancient enemies of the Jews, and resemble the victory which Jehoshaphat gained over the Ammonites, Moabites, and Edomites, 2 Chron. xx. 22-26.

And parted my land.] The above nations had frequently entered into the territories of Israel; and divided among themselves the lands they had thus overrun.

While the Jews were in captivity, much of the land of Israel was seized on, and occupied by the *Philistines*, and other nations that bordered on Judea.

A. M. cir. 3314
B. C. cir. 690
Ol. cir. XXII. 3
NumæPompilii,
R. Roman.,
cir. annum 26

3 And they have [e]cast lots for
my people; and have given a
boy for a harlot, and sold a girl
for wine, that they might drink.
4 Yea, and what have ye to do with me, [f]O
Tyre, and Zidon, and all the coasts of Palestine? [g]will ye render me a recompense? and
if ye recompense me, swiftly *and* speedily will
I return your recompense upon your own
head;
5 Because ye have taken my silver and my
gold, and have carried into your temples my
goodly [h]pleasant things:
6 The children also of Judah and the children of Jerusalem have ye sold unto [i]the
Grecians, that ye might remove them far
from their border.
7 Behold, [k]I will raise them out of the place
whither ye have sold them, and will return
your recompense upon your own head:
8 And I will sell your sons and your daughters into the hand of the chil-
dren of Judah, and they shall
sell them to the [l]Sabeans, to
a people [m]far off; for the LORD
hath spoken *it*.
9 [n]Proclaim ye this among the Gentiles;
[o]Prepare war, wake up the mighty men, let all
the men of war draw near; let them come up.
10 [p]Beat your ploughshares into swords, and
your [q]pruning hooks into spears: [r]let the
weak say, I *am* strong.
11 [s]Assemble yourselves, and come, all ye
heathen, and gather yourselves together round
about: thither [t]cause [u]thy mighty ones to
come down, O Lord.
12 Let the heathen be wakened, [v]and
come up to the valley of Jehoshaphat: for
there will I sit to [w]judge all the heathen
round about.
13 [x]Put ye in the sickle, for [y]the harvest is
ripe: come, get you down; for the [z]press

[e]Obad. 11; Nah. iii. 10——[f]Amos i. 6, 9——[g]Ezek. xxv. 15, 16, 17——[h]Heb. *desirable;* Dan. xi. 38——[i]Heb. *the sons of the Grecians*——[k]Isa. xliii. 5, 6; xlix. 12; Jer. xxiii. 8——[l]Ezek. xxiii. 42——[m]Jer. vi. 20——[n]See Isa. viii. 9, 10; Jer. xlvi. 3, 4; Ezek. xxxviii. 7——[o]Heb. *sanctify*

[p]See Isa. ii. 4; Mic. iv. 3——[q]Or, *scythes*——[r]Zech. xii. 8——[s]Ver. 2——[t]Or, *the LORD shall bring down* [u]Psa. ciii. 20; Isa. xiii. 3——[v]Ver. 2——[w]Psa. xcvi. 13; xcviii. 9; cx. 6; Isa. ii. 4; iii. 13; Mic. iv. 3——[x]Matt. xiii. 39; Rev. xiv. 15, 18——[y]Jeremiah li. 33; Hosea vi. 11——[z]Isa. lxiii. 3; Lam. i. 15; Rev. xiv. 19, 20

Verse 3. *Have given a boy for a harlot*] To such wretched circumstances were the poor Jews reduced in their captivity, that their children were sold by their oppressors; and both *males* and *females* used for the *basest purposes.* And they were often bartered for the necessaries or luxuries of life. Or this may refer to the issue of the Chaldean war in Judea, where the captives were divided among the victors. And being set in companies, *they cast lots for them:* and those to whom they fell sold them for various purposes; the boys to be slaves and catamites, the girls to be prostitutes; and in return for them they got *wine* and *such things.* I think this is the meaning of the text.

Verse 4. *What have ye to do with me*] Why have the *Tyrians* and *Sidonians* joined their other enemies to oppress my people? for they who touch my people touch *me.*

Will ye render me a recompense?] Do you think by this to avenge yourselves upon the Almighty? to retaliate upon God! Proceed, and speedily will I return your recompense; I will retaliate.

Verse 5. *Ye have taken my silver and my gold*] The Chaldeans had spoiled the temple, and carried away the *sacred vessels,* and put them in the temple of their own god in Babylon.

Verse 6. *Sold unto the Grecians*] These were the descendants of *Javan,* Gen. x. 2-5. And with them the *Tyrians* trafficked, Ezek. xxvii. 19.

That ye might remove them far from their border.] Intending to send them *as far off* as possible, that it might be impossible for them to get back to reclaim the land of which you had dispossessed them.

Verse 7. *I will raise them*] I shall find means to bring them back from *the place whither ye have sold them,* and they shall retaliate upon you the injuries they have sustained. It is said that Alexander and his successors set at liberty many Jews that had been sold into Greece. And it is likely that many returned from different lands, on the publication of the edict of Cyrus.—*Newcome.*

Verse 8. *I will sell your sons*] When *Alexander* took Tyre, he reduced into slavery all the lower people, and the women. *Arrian,* lib. ii., says that *thirty thousand* of them were *sold. Artaxerxes Ochus* destroyed *Sidon,* and subdued the other cities of *Phœnicia.* In all these wars, says *Calmet,* the Jews, who obeyed the Persians, did nct neglect to purchase Phœnician slaves, whom they sold again to the *Sabeans,* or *Arabs.*

Verse 9. *Prepare war*] Let all the enemies of God and of his people join together; let them even call all the tillers of the ground to their assistance, instead of labouring in the field; let every *peasant* become a *soldier.* Let them turn their *agricultural implements* into *offensive weapons,* so that *the weak,* being well armed, may confidently say, *I am strong:* yet, when thus collected and armed, *Jehovah will bring down thy mighty ones;* for so the clause in ver. 11 should be rendered.

Verse 12. *Let the heathen be wakened*] The heathen *shall be wakened.*

The valley of Jehoshaphat] Any place where God may choose to display his judgments against his enemies.

Verse 13. *Put ye in the sickle*] The destruc-

A. M. cir. 3314
B. C. cir. 690
Ol. cir. XXII. 3
NumæPompilii,
R. Roman.,
cir. annum 26

is full, and the fats overflow;
for their wickedness *is* great.
14 Multitudes, multitudes in
[a]the valley of [b]decision: for [c]the
day of the LORD *is* near in the valley of
decision.
15 The [d]sun and the moon shall be darkened,
and the stars shall withdraw their shining.
16 The LORD also shall [e]roar out of Zion,
and utter his voice from Jerusalem; and [f]the
heavens and the earth shall shake: [g]but the
LORD *will be* the [h]hope of his people, and the
strength of the children of Israel.

[a]Verse 2——[b]Or, *concision*, or *threshing*——[c]Chapter ii. 1——[d]Chapter ii. 10, 31——[e]Jeremiah xxv. 30; chapter ii. 11; Amos i. 2——[f]Haggai ii. 6——[g]Isaiah li. 5, 6——[h]Hebrew *place of repair*, or *harbour* [i]Chapter ii. 27

17 So [i]shall ye know that I
am the LORD your God dwelling
in Zion, [k]my holy mountain:
then shall Jerusalem be [l]holy,
and there shall [m]no strangers pass through
her any more.
18 And it shall come to pass in that day
that the mountains shall [n]drop down new
wine, and the hills shall flow with milk, [o]and
all the rivers of Judah shall [p]flow with
waters, and [q]a fountain shall come forth of
the house of the LORD, and shall water [r]the
valley of Shittim.

A. M. cir. 3314
B. C. cir. 690
Ol. cir. XXII. 3
NumæPompilii,
R. Roman.,
cir. annum 26

[k]Dan. xi. 45; Obad. 16; Zech. viii. 3——[l]Heb. *holiness*——[m]Isa. xxxv. 8; lii. 1; Nah. i. 15; Zech. xiv. 21; Rev. xxi. 27——[n]Amos ix. 13——[o]Psa. xxx. 25 [p]Heb. *go*——[q]Psa. xlvi. 4; Ezek. xlvii. 1; Zech. xiv. 8; Rev. xxii. 1——[r]Num. xxv. 1

tion of his enemies is represented here under the metaphor of reaping down the harvest; and of gathering the grapes, and treading them in the wine-presses.

Verse 14. *Multitudes, multitudes*] המנים המנים *hamonim, hamonim, crowds upon crowds*, in *the valley of decision*, or *excision:* the same as the valley of Jehoshaphat, the place where God is to execute judgment on his enemies.

Verse 15. *The sun and the moon shall be darkened*] High and mighty states shall be eclipsed, and brought to ruin, and the *stars*—petty states, princes, and governors—*shall withdraw their shining;* withhold their *influence* and *tribute* from the kingdoms to which they have belonged, and set up themselves as *independent governors.*

Verse 16. *The Lord also shall roar out of Zion*] His temple and worship shall be re-established there, and he will thence denounce his judgments against the nations. "The heavens and the earth shall shake." There shall be great commotions in powerful empires and their dependencies; but in all these things his own people shall be unmoved, for God shall be their *hope* and *strength.*

Verse 17. *So shall ye know*] By the judgments I execute on your enemies, and the support I give to yourselves, that I am the all-conquering Jehovah; and that I have again taken up my residence in Jerusalem. All this may refer, ultimately, to the restoration of the Jews to their own land; when *holiness to the Lord* shall be their motto; and no *strange* god, nor *impure people*, shall be permitted to enter the city, or even *pass through it;* they shall have neither civil nor religious connections with any who do not worship the true God in *spirit* and in *truth.* This, I think, must refer to Gospel times. It is a promise not ye fulfilled.

Verse 18. *In that day*] After their return from their captivities.

The mountains shall drop down new wine] A poetic expression for great fertility. Happy times: peace and plenty. The vines shall grow luxuriantly on the sides of the mountains; and the hills shall produce such rich pastures that the flocks shall yield abundance of milk.

And all the rivers of Judah] Far from being generally dry in the summer, shall have their *channels* always full of water.

And a fountain shall come forth of the house of the Lord] See the account of the *typical waters* in Ezekiel, chap. xlvii., to which this seems to have a reference; at least the subject is the same, and seems to point out the *grace of the Gospel*, the *waters of salvation*, that shall flow from Jerusalem, and water the valley of *Shittim. Shittim* was in the *plains of Moab* beyond Jordan; Num. xxxiii. 49; Josh. iii. 1; but as no stream of water could flow from the temple, pass across Jordan, or reach this plain, the *valley of Shittim* must be considered *symbolical*, as *the valley of Jehoshaphat.* But as *Shittim* may signify *thorns*, it may figuratively represent the most *uncultivated and ferocious inhabitants of the earth* receiving the Gospel of Christ, and being civilized and saved by it. We know that *briers and thorns* are emblems of *bad men;* see Ezek. ii. 6. Thus all the figures in this verse will point out the happy times of the Gospel: *the mountains shall drop down new wine; the hills flow with milk;* the *thorny valleys* become fertile, &c. Similar to those almost parallel words of the prince of poets:—

Mistaque ridenti colocasia fundet acantho.—
Ipsæ lacte domum referent destenta capellæ
Ubera: nec magnos metuent armenta leones.—
Molli paullatim flavescet campus arista,
Incultisque rubens pendebit sentibus uva:
Et duræ quercus sudabunt roscida mella.
VIRG. *Ecl.* iv. 20.

Unbidden earth shall wreathing ivy bring,
And fragrant herbs the promises of spring.
The goats with streaming dugs shall homeward speed;
And lowing herds, secure from lions, feed.
Unlabour'd harvests shall the fields adorn,
And cluster'd grapes shall grow on every thorn:
The *knotted oaks* shall *showers of honey weep.*
DRYDEN.

A. M. cir. 3314
B. C. cir. 690
Ol. cir. XXII. 3
NumæPompilii,
R. Roman.,
cir. annum 26

19 [s]Egypt shall be a desolation, and [t]Edom shall be a desolate wilderness, for the violence *against* the children of Judah, because they have shed innocent blood in their land.

20 But Judah shall [u]dwell [v]for ever, and Jerusalem from generation to generation.

21 For I will [w]cleanse their blood *that* I have not cleansed: [x]for [y]the LORD dwelleth in Zion.

A. M. cir. 3314
B. C. cir. 690
Ol. cir. XXII. 3
NumæPompilii,
R. Roman.,
cir. annum 26

[s]Isa. xix. 1, &c.——[t]Jer. xlix. 17; Ezek. xxv. 12, 13; Amos i. 11; Obad. 10——[u]Or, *abide*——[v]Amos ix. 15

[w]Isa. iv. 4——[x]Ezek. xlviii. 35; ver. 17; Rev. xxi. 3
[y]Or, *even I the LORD that dwelleth in Zion*

Verse 19. *Egypt shall be a desolation*] **While peace, plenty, and prosperity of every kind, shall crown my people, all their *enemies* shall be as a *wilderness;* and those who have *used violence* against the saints of God, and *shed the blood of innocents* (of the holy MARTYRS) *in their land,* when they had *political power;* these and all such shall fall under the just judgments of God.**

Verse 20. *But Judah shall dwell for ever*] **The true Church of Christ shall be supported, while all false and persecuting Churches shall be annihilated. The promise may also belong to the full and final restoration of the Jews, when they shall dwell at Jerusalem as a distinct people professing the faith of our Lord Jesus Christ.**

Verse 21. *For I will cleanse their blood*] **נקיתי** *nikkeythi, I will avenge* **the slaughter and martyrdom of my people, which I have not** *yet avenged.* **Persecuting** *nations* **and persecuting** *Churches* **shall all come, sooner or later, under the stroke of vindictive justice.**

For the Lord dwelleth in Zion.] **He shall be the life, soul, spirit, and defence of his Church for ever.**

THIS prophet, who has many things similar to Ezekiel, ends his prophecy nearly in the same way:

Ezekiel **says of the glory of the Church, יהוה שמה** *Yehovah shammah,* **THE LORD IS THERE.**

Joel **says, יהוה שכן בציון** *Yehovah shochen betsiyon,* **THE LORD DWELLETH IN ZION.**

Both point out the continued indwelling of Christ among his people.

INTRODUCTION TO THE BOOK

OF THE

PROPHET AMOS

AMOS, the third of the minor prophets, was, it is said, of the little town of Tekoa, in the tribe of Judah, about *four* leagues southward of Jerusalem. There is no good proof, however, that he was a native of this place; but only that he retired thither when he was driven from Beth-el, which was in the kingdom of the *ten* tribes. It is very probable that he was born within the territories of Israel, and that his mission was directed principally to this kingdom.

As he was prophesying in Beth-el, where the golden calves were, in the reign of Jeroboam the second, about the year of the world 3217; before the birth of Jesus Christ, 783; before the vulgar era, 787; Amaziah, the high priest of Beth-el, accused him before King Jeroboam, saying, "Amos hath conspired against thee in the midst of the house of Israel: the land is not able to bear all his words. For thus Amos saith, Jeroboam shall die by the sword, and Israel shall surely be led away captive out of their own land." Amaziah said therefore unto Amos, "O thou seer, go, flee thee away into the land of Judah, and there eat bread, and prophesy there: but prophesy not again any more at Beth-el; for it is the king's chapel, and it is the king's court."

Amos answered Amaziah, "I was no prophet, neither was I a prophet's son; but I was a herdman, and a gatherer of sycamore fruit. And the Lord took me as I followed the flock; and the Lord said unto me, Go, prophesy unto my people Israel. Now, therefore, hear thou the word of the Lord; Thou sayest, Prophesy not against Israel, and drop not thy word against the house of Isaac. Therefore thus saith the Lord, Thy wife shall be a harlot in the city, and thy sons and thy daughters shall fall by the sword, and thy land shall be divided by line; and thou shalt die in a polluted land, and Israel shall surely go into captivity forth of his land."

After this the prophet retired into the kingdom of Judah, and dwelt in the town of Tekoa, where he continued to prophesy. He complains in many places of the violence offered him by endeavouring to oblige him to silence, and bitterly exclaims against the disorders of Israel.

He began to prophesy the second year before the earthquake, which happened in the reign of King Uzziah; and which Josephus, with most of the ancient and modern commentators, refers to this prince's usurpation of the priest's office, when he attempted to offer incense to the Lord.

The first of his prophecies, in order of time, are those of the *seventh* chapter. The others he pronounced in the town of Tekoa, whither he retired. His two first chapters are against Damascus, the Philistines, Tyrians, Edomites, Ammonites, Moabites, the kingdom of Judah, and that of the ten tribes. The evils with which he threatens them refer to the times of Shalmaneser, Tiglath-pileser, Sennacherib, and Nebuchadnezzar, who did so much mischief to these provinces, and at last led the Israelites into captivity.

He foretold the misfortunes into which the kingdom of Israel should fall after the death of Jeroboam the Second, who was then living. He foretold the death of King Zechariah; the invasion of the lands belonging to Israel by Pul and Tiglath-pileser, kings of Assyria; and speaks of the captivity of the ten tribes, and of their return into their own country.

He makes sharp invectives against the sins of Israel; against their effeminacy and avarice, their harshness to the poor, the splendour of their buildings, and the delicacy of their tables. He reproves the people of Israel for going to Beth-el, Dan, Gilgal, and Beer-sheba, which were the most famous pilgrimages of the country; and for swearing by the gods of these places.

The time and manner of his death are not known. Some old authors relate that Amaziah, priest of Beth-el, whom we have spoken of, provoked by the discourses of the prophet, had his teeth broken in order to silence him. Others say that Hosea, or Uzziah, the son of Amaziah, struck him with a stake upon the temples, and knocked him down, and almost killed him; that in this condition he was carried to Tekoa, where he died, and was buried with his fathers. This is the account these authors give us. On the contrary, it is the opinion of others, that he prophesied a long time at Tekoa after the adventure he had with Amaziah: and the prophet taking no notice of the ill treatment which he is said to have received from Uzziah, his silence is no argument that he suffered nothing from him.

St. Jerome observes, that there is nothing great and sublime in the style of Amos. He applies these words of St. Paul to him, *rude in speech, though not in knowledge.* He says farther, that as every one chooses to speak of his own art, Amos generally makes use of comparisons taken from the country life wherein he had been brought up. St. Austin shows that there was a certain kind of eloquence in the sacred writers, directed by the spirit of wisdom, and so proportioned to the nature of the things they treated of, that even they who accuse them of rusticity and unpoliteness in their way of writing, could not choose a style more suitable, were they to have spoken on the same subject, to the same persons, and in the same circumstances.

Bishop Lowth is not satisfied with the judgment of St. Jerome. His authority, says the learned prelate, has occasioned many commentators to represent this prophet as entirely rude, void of eloquence, and wanting in all the embellishments of style; whereas any one who reads him with due attention will find him, though a herdsman, not a whit behind the very chiefest prophets; almost equal to the greatest in the loftiness of his sentiments; and not inferior to any in the splendour of his diction, and the elegance of his composition. And it is well observed, that the same heavenly Spirit which inspired Isaiah and Daniel in the palace, inspired David and Amos in their shepherds' tents; always choosing proper interpreters of his will, and sometimes perfecting praise even out of the mouths of babes: at one time using the eloquence of some; at another, making others eloquent to subserve his great purposes. See *Calmet* and *Dodd.*

Archbishop *Newcome* speaks also justly of this prophet: "Amos borrows many images from the scenes in which he was engaged; but he introduces them with skill, and gives them tone and dignity by the eloquence and grandeur of his manner. We shall find in him many affecting and pathetic, many elegant and sublime, passages. No prophet has more magnificently described the Deity; or more gravely rebuked the luxurious: or reproved injustice and oppression with greater warmth, and a more generous indignation. He is a prophet on whose model a preacher may safely form his style and manner in luxurious and profligate times."

THE BOOK

OF THE

PROPHET AMOS

Chronological Notes relative to this Book

Year from the Creation, according to Archbishop Usher, 3217.—Year of the Julian Period, 3927.—Year since the Flood, 1561.—Year from the foundation of Solomon's temple, 225.—Year since the division of Solomon's monarchy into the kingdoms of Israel and Judah, 188.—Year since the first Olympic games were celebrated in Elis by the Idæi Dactyli, 667.—Year since the restoration of the Olympic games at Elis by Lycurgus, Iphitus, and Cleosthenes, 97.—Year before the conquest of Corœbus at Olympia, vulgarly called the first Olympiad, 11.—Year before the building of Rome, according to the Varronian computation, 34.—Year before the birth of Christ, 783.—Year before the vulgar era of Christ's nativity, 787.—Cycle of the Sun, 7.—Cycle of the Moon, 13.—Twenty-eighth and last year of Caranus, the founder of the kingdom of Macedon.—Twenty-third year of Nicander, king of Lacedæmon, of the family of the Proclidæ.—Twenty-seventh year of Alcamenes, king of Lacedæmon, of the family of the Eurysthenidæ.—Eleventh year of Ardysus, king of Lydia.—Eleventh year of Agamestor, perpetual archon of the Athenians.—Tenth year of Amulius Sylvius, king of the Albans.—Fifth year of Telestus, monarch of Corinth.—Sixth year of Sosarmus, king of the Medes, according to some chronologers.—Thirty-ninth year of Jeroboam II., king of Israel.—Twenty-fourth year of Uzziah, king of Judah.

CHAPTER I

This chapter denounces judgments against the nations bordering on Palestine, enemies to the Jews, viz., the Syrians, 1–5; *Philistines,* 6–8; *Tyrians,* 9, 10; *Edomites,* 11, 12; *and Ammonites,* 13–15. *The same judgments were predicted by other prophets, and fulfilled, partly by the kings of Assyria, and partly by those of Babylon; though, like many other prophecies, they had their accomplishment by degrees, and at different periods. The prophecy against the Syrians, whose capital was Damascus, was fulfilled by Tiglath-pileser, king of Assyria; see* 2 Kings xvi. 9. *The prophecy against Gaza of the Philistines was accomplished by Hezekiah,* 2 Kings xviii. 8; *by Pharaoh,* Jer. xlvii. 1; *and by Alexander the Great; see* Quintius Curtius, lib. iv. c. 6. *The prophecy against Ashdod was fulfilled by Uzziah,* 2 Chron. xxvi. 6; *and that against Ashkelon by Pharaoh,* Jer. xlvii. 5. *All Syria was also subdued by Pharaoh-necho; and again by Nebuchadnezzar, who also took Tyre, as did afterwards Alexander. Nebuchadnezzar also subdued the Edomites,* Jer. xxv. 9, 21, *and* xxvii. 3, 6. *Judas Maccabeus routed the remains of them,* 1 Macc. v. 3; *and Hyrcanus brought them under entire subjection. The Ammonites were likewise conquered by Nebuchadnezzar. The earthquake, which the prophet takes for his era, is perhaps referred to in* Zech. xiv. 5, *and also in* Isa. v. 25. Josephus *ascribes it to Uzziah's invasion of the priestly office; see* 2 Chron. xxvi. 16.

A. M. cir. 3217
B. C. cir. 787
Ante U. C. 34
Amulii Sylvii,
R. Alban.,
cir. annum 10

THE words of Amos, [a]who
was among the herdmen of
[b]Tekoa, which he saw concerning Israel [c]in the days of
Uzziah king of Judah, and in
the days of [d]Jeroboam the son
of Joash king of Israel, two
years before the [e]earthquake.

[a]Chap. vii. 14——[b]2 Sam. xiv. 2; 2 Chron. xx. 20

[c]Hos. i. 1——[d]Chap. vii. 10——[e]Zech. xiv. 5

NOTES ON CHAP. I

Verse 1. *The words of Amos*] This person and the father of Isaiah, though named alike in our translation, were as different in their names as in their persons. The father of Isaiah, אמוץ *Amots;* the prophet before us, עמוס *Amos.* The first, *aleph, mem, vau, tsaddi;* the second, *ain, mem, vau, samech.* For some account of this prophet see the *introduction.*

Among the herdmen] He seems to have been among the very lowest orders of life, a herds-

A. M. cir. 3217
B. C. cir. 787
Ante U. C. 34
Amulii Sylvii,
R. Alban.,
cir. annum 10

2 And he said, The LORD will
[f]roar from Zion, and utter his
voice from Jerusalem; and the
habitations of the shepherds shall
mourn, and the top of [g]Carmel shall wither.
3 Thus saith the LORD; For three transgressions of [h]Damascus, [i]and for four, I will not
[k]turn away *the punishment* thereof; [l]because
they have threshed Gilead with threshing instruments of iron:

4 [m]But I will send a fire into
the house of Hazael, which shall
devour the palaces of Ben-
hadad.
5 I will break also the [n]bar of Damascus,
and cut off the inhabitants from [o]the plain of
Aven, and him that holdeth the sceptre from
[p]the house of Eden: and [q]the people of Syria
shall go into captivity [r]unto Kir, saith the
LORD.

A. M. cir. 3217
B. C. cir. 787
Ante U. C. 34
Amulii Sylvii,
R. Alban.,
cir. annum 10

---

[f]Jer. xxv. 30; Joel iii. 16——[g]1 Sam. xxv. 2; Isa. xxxiii. 9——[h]Isa. viii. 4; xvii. 1; Jer. xlix. 23; Zech. ix. 1——[i]Or, *yea, for four*——[k]Or, *convert it*, or *let it be quiet:* and so verse 6, &c.

[l]2 Kings x. 33; xiii. 7——[m]Jer. xvii. 27; xlix. 27; verse 7, 10, 12; chap. ii. 2, 5——[n]Jer. li. 30; Lam. ii. 9——[o]Or, *Bikath-aven*——[p]Or, *Beth-eden*——[q]Fulfilled, 2 Kings xvi. 9——[r]Chap. ix. 7

---

man, one who tended the flocks of *others* in the open fields, and *a gatherer of sycamore fruit.* Of whatever species this was, whether a kind of *fig*, it is evident that it was *wild fruit;* and he probably collected it for his own subsistence, or to dispose of either for the service of his employer, or to increase his scanty wages.

Before the earthquake.] Probably the same as that referred to Zech. xiv. 5, if הרעש *haraash* do not mean some *popular tumult.*

Verse 2. *The Lord will roar from Zion*] It is a pity that our translators had not followed the hemistich form of the Hebrew:—

Jehovah from Zion shall roar,
And from Jerusalem shall give forth his voice;
And the pleasant dwellings of the shepherds shall mourn,
And the top of mount Carmel shall wither.

Carmel was a very fruitful mountain in the tribe of Judah, Josh. xv. 55; Isa. xxxv. 2.

This introduction was natural in the mouth of a *herdsman* who was familiar with the roaring of lions, the bellowing of bulls, and the lowing of kine. The roaring of the lion in the forest is one of the most terrific sounds in nature; when near, it strikes terror into the heart of both man and beast.

Verse 3. *For three transgressions of Damascus, and for four*] These expressions of *three* and *four*, so often *repeated* in this chapter, mean *repetition, abundance*, and any thing that goes towards *excess. Very, very exceedingly;* and so it was used among the ancient Greek and Latin poets. See the passionate exclamation of Ulysses, in the storm, *Odyss.*, lib. v., ver. 306:—

Τρις μακαρες Δαναοι και τετρακις, οἱ τοτ' ολοντο
Τροιῃ εν ευρειῃ, χαριν Ατρειδῃσι φεροντες.

"*Thrice happy* Greeks! and *four times* who were slain
In Atreus' cause, upon the Trojan plain."

Which words *Virgil* translates, and puts in the mouth of his hero in similar circumstances, *Æn.* i. 93.

Extemplo Æneæ solvuntur frigore membra:
Ingemit; et, duplicis tendens ad sidera palmas,
Talia voce refert: *O terque quaterque beati!*
Queis ante ora patrum Trojæ sub mœnibus altis
Contigit oppetere.

"Struck with unusual fright, the Trojan chief
With lifted hands and eyes invokes relief.
And *thrice*, and *four times happy* those, he cried,
That under Ilion's walls before their parents died."

DRYDEN.

On the words, *O terque quaterque*, SERVIUS makes this remark, "Hoc est *sæpius;* finitus numerous pro infinito." "*O thrice and four times*, that is, *very often*, a finite number for an infinite." Other poets use the same form of expression. So SENECA in *Hippolyt.*, Act. ii. 694.

O ter quaterque prospero fato dati,
Quos hausit, et peremit, et leto dedit
Odium dolusque!

"O *thrice* and *four times* happy were the men
Whom hate devoured, and fraud, hard pressing on,
Gave as a prey to death."

And so the ancient oracle quoted by *Pausanias*, Achaic., lib. vii., c. 6: Τρις μακαρες κεινοι και τετρακις ανδρες εσονται; "Those men shall be *thrice* and *four times* happy."

These quotations are sufficient to show that this form of speech is neither unfrequent nor *inelegant*, being employed by the most correct writers of antiquity.

Damascus was the capital of Syria.

Verse 4. *Ben-hadad.*] He was son and successor of Hazael. See the cruelties which they exercised upon the Israelites, 2 Kings x. 32; xiii. 7, &c.; and see especially 2 Kings viii. 12, where these cruelties are predicted.

The *fire* threatened here is the *war* so successfully carried on against the Syrians by Jeroboam II., in which he took Damascus and Hamath, and reconquered all the ancient possessions of Israel. See 2 Kings xiv. 25, 26, 28.

Verse 5. *The bar of Damascus*] The *gates*, whose long traverse bars, running from wall to wall, were their strength. I will throw it open; and the *gates* were forced, and the city taken, as above.

The plain of Aven—the house of Eden] These are names, says *Bochart*, of the *valley of Damascus.* The *plain of Aven*, or *Birkath-Aven*, *Calmet* says, is a city of Syria, at present called *Baal-Bek*, and by the Greeks *Heliopolis;* and is situated at the end of that long valley

A. M. cir. 3217
B. C. cir. 787
Ante U. C. 34
Amulii Sylvii,
R. Alban.,
cir. annum 10

6 Thus saith the LORD; For
three transgressions of [s]Gaza,
and for four, I will not turn
away *the punishment* thereof;
because they [t]carried away captive the whole
captivity, [u]to deliver *them* up to Edom:
7 [v]But I will send a fire on the wall of Gaza,
which shall devour the palaces thereof:
8 And I will cut off the inhabitant [w]from
Ashdod, and him that holdeth the sceptre
from Ashkelon, and I will [x]turn mine hand
against Ekron: and [y]the remnant of the
Philistines shall perish, saith the Lord
GOD.
9 Thus saith the LORD; For three transgressions of [z]Tyrus, and for four, I will not
turn away *the punishment* thereof; [a]because
they delivered up the whole captivity to
Edom, and remembered not [b]the brotherly
covenant:
10 [c]But I will send a fire on the wall of
Tyrus, which shall devour the palaces thereof.

[s]2 Chron. xxviii. 18; Isa. xiv. 29; Jer. xlvii. 4, 5; Ezek. xxv. 15; Zeph. ii. 4——[t]Or, *carried them away with an entire captivity;* 2 Chron. xxi. 16, 17; Joel iii. 6——[u]Ver. 9——[v]Jer. xlvii. 1——[w]Zeph. ii. 4; Zech. ix. 5, 6 [x]Psa. lxxxi. 14——[y]Jer. xlvii. 4; Ezek. xxv. 16——[z]Isa. xxiii. 1; Jer. xlvii. 4; Ezek. xxvi., xxvii., xxviii.; Joel iii. 4, 5——[a]Ver. 6——[b]Heb. *the covenant of brethren;* 2 Sam. v. 11; 1 Kings v. 1; ix. 11–14——[c]Ver. 4, 7, &c.

11 Thus saith the LORD; For
three transgressions of [d]Edom,
and for four, I will not turn
away *the punishment* thereof;
because he did pursue [e]his brother [f]with the
sword, and [g]did cast off all pity, [h]and his
anger did tear perpetually, and he kept his
wrath for ever:
12 But [i]I will send a fire upon Teman,
which shall devour the palaces of Bozrah.
13 Thus saith the LORD; For three transgressions of [k]the children of Ammon, and
for four, I will not turn away *the punishment*
thereof; because they have [l]ripped [m]up the
women with child of Gilead, [n]that they might
enlarge their border:
14 But I will kindle a fire in the wall of
[o]Rabbah, and it shall devour the palaces
thereof, [p]with shouting in the day of battle,
with a tempest in the day of the whirlwind:
15 And [q]their king shall go into captivity,
he and his princes together, saith the LORD.

A. M. cir. 3217
B. C. cir. 787
Ante U. C. 34
Amulii Sylvii,
R. Alban.,
cir. annum 10

[d]Isa. xxi. 11; xxxiv. 5; Jer. xlix. 8, &c.; Ezek. xxv. 12, 13, 14; xxxv. 2, &c.; Joel iii. 19; Obad. 1, &c.; Mal. i. 4 [e]Gen. xxvii. 41; Deut. xxiii. 7; Mal. i. 2——[f]2 Chron. xxiii. 17——[g]Heb. *corrupted his compassions*——[h]Ezek. xxxv. 5——[i]Obad. 9, 10——[k]Jer. xlix. 1, 2; Ezek. xxv. 2; Zeph. ii. 9——[l]Or, *divided the mountains*——[m]Hos. xiii. 16——[n]Jer. xlix. 1——[o]Deut. iii. 11; 2 Sam. xii. 26; Jer. xlix. 2; Ezek. xxv. 5——[p]Chap. ii. 2——[q]Jer. xlix. 3

which extends from south to north, between Libanus and Anti-Libanus.

The people of Syria shall go into captivity unto Kir] KIR is supposed to be the country of *Cyrene* in Albania, on the river *Cyrus*, which empties itself into the Caspian Sea. The fulfilment of this prophecy may be seen in 2 Kings xvi. 1-9.

Verse 6. *They carried away captive*] Gaza is well known to have been one of the five lordships of the Philistines; it lay on the coast of the Mediterranean Sea, near to Egypt. Erkon, Ashdod, and Askelon, were other signories of the same people, which are here equally threatened with Gaza. The *captivity* mentioned here may refer to *inroads* and *incursions* made by the Philistines in times of peace. See 2 Chron. xxi. 16. The *margin* reads, *an entire captivity.* They took *all* away; none of them afterwards returned.

Verse 9. *Tyrus*] See an ample description of this place, and of its desolation and final ruin, in the notes on Ezek. xxvi., xxvii., and xxviii.

The brotherly covenant] This possibly refers to the very friendly league made between Solomon and Hiram, king of Tyre, 1 Kings v. 12; but some contend that the brotherly covenant refers to the *consanguinity* between the *Jews* and *Edomites.* The Tyrians, in exercising cruelties upon these, did it, in effect, on the Jews, with whom they were connected by the most intimate ties of kindred; the two people having descended from the two brothers, Jacob and Esau. See *Calmet.*

Verse 10. *I will send a fire on the wall of Tyrus*] The destructive *fire* or *siege* by Nebuchadnezzar, which lasted *thirteen* years, and ended in the destruction of this ancient city; see on Ezekiel, chap. xxvi. 7-14, as above. It was finally ruined by *Alexander*, and is now only a place for a few poor fishermen to spread their nets upon.

Verse 11. *For three transgressions of Edom*] That the *Edomites* (notwithstanding what *Calmet* observes above of the *brotherly covenant*) were always implacable enemies of the Jews, is well known; but most probably that which the prophet has in view was the part they took in distressing the Jews when Jerusalem was besieged, and finally taken, by the Chaldeans. See Obad. 11-14; Ezek. xxv. 12; xxxv. 5; Psa. cxxxvii. 7.

Verse 12. *Teman—Bozrah.*] Principal cities of Idumea.

Verse 13. *The children of Ammon*] The country of the Ammonites lay to the east of Jordan, in the neighbourhood of Gilead. *Rabbah* was its capital.

Because they have ripped up] This refers to some barbarous transaction well known in the time of this prophet, but of which we have no distinct mention in the sacred historians.

Verse 14. *With shouting in the day of battle*] They shall be totally subdued. This was done by Nebuchadnezzar. See Jer. xxvii. 3, 6.

Verse 15. *Their king shall go into captivity*] Probably מלכם *malcham* should be *Milcom*, who was a chief god of the Ammonites; and the following words, *he and his princes*, may refer to the *body of his priesthood*. See 1 Kings xi. 33, and the notes there. All these countries were subdued by Nebuchadnezzar.

CHAPTER II

The prophet goes on to declare the judgments of God against Moab, 1–3; *against Judah*, 4, 5; *and then against Israel, the particular object of his mission. He enumerates some of their sins*, 6–8, *aggravated by God's distinguishing regard to Israel*, 9–12; *and they are in consequence threatened with dreadful punishments*, 13–16. *See* 2 Kings xv. 19, *and* xvii. 6.

A. M. cir. 3217 B. C. cir. 787 Ante U. C. 34 Amulii Sylvii, R. Alban., cir. annum 10

THUS saith the LORD; For
three transgressions of
[a]Moab, and for four, I will not
turn away *the punishment*
thereof; because he [b]burned the bones of the
king of Edom into lime:
2 But I will send a fire upon Moab, and it
shall devour the palaces of [c]Kirioth: and
Moab shall die with tumult, [d]with shouting,
and with the sound of the trumpet:
3 And I will cut off [e]the judge from the
midst thereof, and will slay all the princes
thereof with him, saith the LORD.
4 Thus saith the LORD; For three transgressions of Judah, and for four, I will not
turn away *the punishment* thereof; [f]because
they have despised the law of the LORD, and
have not kept his commandments, and [g]their lies caused
them to err, [h]after the which
their fathers have walked:
5 [i]But I will send a fire upon Judah, and
it shall devour the palaces of Jerusalem.
6 Thus saith the LORD; For three transgressions of Israel, and for four, I will not
turn away *the punishment* thereof; because
[k]they sold the righteous for silver, and the
poor for a pair of shoes;
7 That pant after the dust of the earth on
the head of the poor, and [l]turn aside the way
of the meek: [m]and a man and his father will
go in unto the *same* [n]maid, [o]to profane my
holy name:
8 And they lay *themselves* down upon

---

[a]Isa. xv., xvi.; Jer. xlviii.; Ezek. xxv. 8; Zeph. ii. 8 —— [b]2 Kings iii. 27 —— [c]Jer. xlviii. 41 —— [d]Chap. i. 14 —— [e]Num. xxiv. 17; Jer. xlviii. 7 —— [f]Lev. xxvi. 14, 15; Neh. i. 7; Dan. ix. 11 —— [g]Isa. xxviii. 15; Jer. xvi. 19, 20; Rom. i. 25 —— [h]Ezek. xx. 13, 16, 18, 24, 40 —— [i]Jer. xvii. 27; Hos. viii. 14 —— [k]Isa. xxix. 21; chap. viii. 6 —— [l]Isa. x. 2; chap. v. 12 —— [m]Ezek. xxii. 11 —— [n]Or, *young woman* —— [o]Lev. xx. 3; Ezek. xxxvi. 20; Rom. ii. 24

NOTES ON CHAP. II

Verse 1. *For three transgressions of Moab, and for four*] See an explanation of this form, chap. i. 2. The land of the Moabites lay to the east of the Dead Sea. For the origin of this people, see Gen. xix. 37.

He burned the bones of the king of Edom into lime] Possibly referring to some brutality; such as opening the grave of one of the Idumean kings, and calcining his bones. It is supposed by some to refer to the fact mentioned 2 Kings iii. 26, when the kings of Judah, Israel, and Idumea, joined together to destroy Moab. The king of it, despairing to save his city, took *seven hundred* men, and made a desperate sortie on the quarter where the king of Edom was; and, though not successful, took prisoner the son of the king of Edom; and, on their return into the city, offered him as a burnt-offering upon the wall, so as to terrify the besieging armies, and cause them to raise the siege. Others understand the son that was sacrificed to be the king of Moab's own son.

Verse 2. *The palaces of Kirioth*] This was one of the principal cities of the Moabites.

Moab shall die with tumult] All these expressions seem to refer to this city's being taken by *storm*, which was followed by a total slaughter of its inhabitants.

Verse 3. *I will cut off the judge*] It shall be so destroyed, that it shall never more have any *form of government*. The *judge* here, שופט *shophet*, may signify the chief magistrate. The chief magistrates of the Carthaginians were called *suffetes;* probably taken from the Hebrew JUDGES, שופטים *shophetim*.

Verse 4. *For three transgressions of Judah*] We may take the *three* and *four* here to any latitude; for this people lived in continual hostility to their God, from the days of *David* to the time of *Uzziah*, under whom Amos prophesied. Their iniquities are *summed* up under *three* general heads: 1. They despised, or *rejected the law of the Lord*. 2. They *kept not his statutes*. 3. They followed lies, were idolaters, and followed false prophets rather than those sent by Jehovah.

Verse 5. *I will send a fire upon Judah*] This *fire* was the war made upon the Jews by *Nebuchadnezzar*, which terminated with the sackage and burning of Jerusalem and its *palace* the *temple*.

Verses 6-8. *For three transgressions of Israel, &c.*] To be satisfied of the exceeding delinquency of this people, we have only to open the

A. M. cir. 3217 B. C. cir. 787 Ante U. C. 34 Amulii Sylvii, R. Alban., cir. annum 10

clothes [p]laid to pledge [q]by every
altar, and they drink the wine
of [r]the condemned *in* the house
of their god.

9 Yet destroyed I the [s]Amorite before them,
[t]whose height *was* like the height of the
cedars, and he *was* strong as the oaks; yet I
[u]destroyed his fruit from above, and his roots
from beneath.

10 Also [v]I brought you up from the land of
Egypt, and [w]led you forty years through the
wilderness, to possess the land of the
Amorite.

11 And I raised up of your sons for prophets, and of your young men for [x]Nazarites.
Is it not even thus, O ye children of Israel?
saith the LORD.

12 But ye gave the Nazarites
wine to drink; and commanded
the prophets, [y]saying, Prophesy not.

13 [z]Behold, [a]I am pressed under you, as a
cart is pressed *that is* full of sheaves.

14 [b]Therefore the flight shall perish from
the swift, and the strong shall not strengthen
his force, [c]neither shall the mighty deliver
[d]himself.

15 Neither shall he stand that handleth the
bow; and *he that is* swift of foot shall not
deliver *himself*: [e]neither shall he that rideth
the horse deliver himself.

16 And *he that is* [f]courageous among the
mighty shall flee away naked in that day,
saith the LORD.

---

[p]Exod. xxii. 26——[q]Ezek. xxiii. 41; 1 Cor. viii. 10; x. 21——[r]Or, *such as have fined*, or *mulcted*——[s]Num. xxi. 24; Deut. ii. 31; Josh. xxiv. 8——[t]Num. xiii. 28, 32, 33——[u]Isa. v. 24; Mal. iv. 1——[v]Exod. xii. 51; Mic. vi. 4——[w]Deut. ii. 7; viii. 2——[x]Num. vi. 2; Judg. xiii. 5

[y]Isa. xxx. 10; Jer. xi. 21; chap. vii. 12, 13; Mic. ii. 6——[z]Isa. i. 14——[a]Or, *I will press your place, as a cart full of sheaves presseth*——[b]Chap. ix. 1, &c.; Jer. ix. 23——[c]Psa. xxxiii. 16——[d]Heb. *his soul*, or *life*——[e]Psa. xxxiii. 17——[f]Heb. *strong of his heart*

---

historical and prophetic books in any part; for the whole history of the Israelites is one tissue of transgression against God. Their crimes are enumerated under the following heads:—

1. Their judges were *mercenary* and *corrupt*. They took bribes to condemn the righteous; and even for articles of clothing, such as a *pair of shoes*, they condemned the poor man, and delivered him into the hands of his adversary.

2. They were unmerciful to the poor generally. *They pant after the dust of the earth on the head of the poor;* or, to put it on the head of the poor; or, they bruise the head of the poor against the dust of the earth. Howsoever the clause is understood, it shows them to have been general oppressors of the poor, showing them neither *justice* nor *mercy*.

3. They *turn aside the way of the meek*. They are peculiarly oppressive to the *weak* and *afflicted*.

4. They were licentious to the uttermost abomination; for in their idol feasts, where young women prostituted themselves publicly in honour of *Astarte*, the father and son entered into impure connections with the same female.

5. They were cruel in their oppressions of the poor; for the garments or beds which the poor had pledged they retained contrary to the law, Exod. xxii. 7-26, which required that such things should be restored before the setting of the sun.

6. They punished the people by unjust and oppressive fines, and served their tables with wine bought by such fines. Or it may be understood of their appropriating to themselves that wine which was allowed to criminals to mitigate their sufferings in the article of death; which was the excess of inhumanity and cruelty.

Verse 9. *Yet destroyed I the Amorite*] Here follow general heads of God's mercies to them, and the great things he had done for them. 1. Bringing them out of Egypt. 2. Miraculously sustaining them in the wilderness *forty* years. 3. Driving out the Canaanites before them, and giving them possession of the promised land. 4. Raising up prophets among them to declare the Divine will. 5. And forming the holy institution of the Nazarites among them, to show the spiritual nature of his holy religion, ver. 9-11.

Verse 12. *But ye gave the Nazarites wine*] This was expressly forbidden in the laws of their institution. See Num. vi. 1-3.

Prophesy not.] They would not worship God, and they would not hear the voice of his prophets.

Verse 13. *Behold, I am pressed under you*] The *marginal* reading is better: "Behold, I will press your place, as a cart full of sheaves presseth." I will bring over you the *wheel of destruction;* and it shall grind your *place*—your *city* and *temple*, as the wheel of a cart laden with sheaves presses down the ground, gravel, and stones over which it rolls.

Verse 14. *The flight shall perish from the swift*] The swiftest shall not be able to save himself from a swifter destruction. None, by might, by counsel, or by fleetness, shall be able to escape from the impending ruin. In a word, God has so fully determined to avenge the quarrel of his broken covenant, that all attempts to escape from his judgments shall be useless.

Verse 15. *Neither shall he that rideth the horse deliver himself.*] I believe all these sayings, from verse 13 to 16 inclusive, are proverbs, to show the inutility of all attempts, even in the best circumstances, to escape the doom now decreed, because the cup of their iniquity was full.

Verse 16. *Shall flee away naked*] In some cases the alarm shall be in the *night;* and even the most heroic shall start from his bed, and through terror not wait to put on his clothes.

CHAPTER III

This chapter begins with reproving the twelve tribes in general, 1, 2; *and then particularly the kingdom of Israel, whose capital was Samaria. The prophet assures them that, while they were at variance with God, it would be unreasonable in them to expect his presence or favour,* 3–8. *Other neighbouring nations are then called upon to take warning from the judgments about to be inflicted upon the house of Israel, which would be so general that only a small remnant should escape them,* 9–15. *The image used by the prophet on this occasion,* (*see verse* 12,) *and borrowed from his former calling, is very natural and significant, and not a little dignified by the inspired writer's lofty air and manner.*

A. M. cir. 3217
B. C. cir. 787
Ante U. C. 34
Amulii Sylvii,
R. Alban.,
cir. annum 10

HEAR this word that the
LORD hath spoken against
you, O children of Israel, against
the whole family which I
brought up from the land of Egypt, saying,
2 [a]You only have I known of all the families
of the earth: [b]therefore I will [c]punish you
for all your iniquities.
3 Can two walk together, except they be
agreed?
4 Will a lion roar in the forest, when he hath
no prey? will a young lion [d]cry
out of his den, if he have taken
nothing?
5 Can a bird fall in a snare
upon the earth, where no gin *is* for him? shall
one take up a snare from the earth, and have
taken nothing at all?
6 Shall a trumpet be blown in the city, and
the people [e]not be afraid? [f]shall there be
evil in a city, [g]and the LORD hath not done *it?*
7 Surely the Lord GOD will do nothing, but

A. M. cir. 3217
B. C. cir. 787
Ante U. C. 34
Amulii Sylvii,
R. Alban.,
cir. annum 10

[a]Deuteronomy vii. 6; x. 15; Psalm cxlvii. 19, 20 —— [b]See Daniel ix. 12; Matthew xi. 22; Luke xii. 47; Romans ii. 9; 1 Peter iv. 17 —— [c]Hebrew, *visit upon*

[d]Hebrew, *give forth his voice* —— [e]Or, *not run together* —— [f]Isaiah xlv. 7 —— [g]Or, *and shall not the LORD do* somewhat?

NOTES ON CHAP. III

Verse 1. *Against the whole family*] That is, all, both the kingdoms of Israel and Judah. In this all the *twelve* tribes are included.

Verse 2. *You only have I known*] I have taken no other people to be my own people. I have *approved* of you, loved you, fed, sustained, and defended you; but because you have forsaken me, have become idolatrous and polluted, therefore *will I punish you.* And the punishment shall be in proportion to the privileges you have enjoyed, and the grace you have abused.

Verse 3. *Can two walk together*] While ye loved and served me, I dwelt in you and walked among you. Now ye are become alienated from me, your nature and mine are totally opposite. I am holy, ye are unholy. We are no longer *agreed*, and can no longer *walk together.* I can no longer hold communion with you. I must cast you out. The similes in this and the *three* following verses are all chosen to express the same thing, viz., that no calamities or judgments can fall upon any people but by the express will of God, on account of their iniquities; and that whatever his prophets have foretold, they have done it by direct revelation from their Maker; and that God has the highest and most cogent reason for inflicting the threatened calamities. This correctness of the prophets' predictions shows that they and I are in communion.

Verse 4. *Will a lion roar*] Should I threaten such a judgment without cause?

Verse 5. *Can a bird fall in a snare*] Can ye, as a sinful people, fall into calamities which I have not appointed?

Shall one take up a snare—and have taken nothing] Will the *snare be removed before it has caught the expected prey?*—shall I remove my judgments till they are fully accomplished? This is a curious passage, and deserves farther consideration. The original, literally translated, is nearly as follows: "Shall the trap arise from the ground; and catching, shall it not catch?" Here is a plain allusion to such traps as we employ to catch *rats, foxes,* &c. The jaws of the trap opening backward, press strongly upon a spring so as to keep it down; and a key passing over one jaw, and hooking on a table in the centre, the trap continues with expanded jaws, till any thing touch the table, when the key, by the motion of the table, being loosened, the spring recovers all its elastic power, and throws up the jaws of the trap, and their serrated edges either close in each other, or on the prey that has moved the table of the trap. Will then the jaws of such a trap suddenly spring up from the ground, on which before they were lying flat, and catch nothing? Shall they let the prey that was within them escape? Certainly not. So my trap is laid for these offenders; and when it springs up, (and they themselves will soon by their transgressions free the key,) shall not the whole family of Israel be inclosed in it? Most certainly they shall. This is a singular and very remarkable passage, and, when properly understood, is beautifully expressive.

Verse 6. *Shall a trumpet be blown*] The sign of alarm and invasion.

And the people not be afraid?] Not take the alarm, and provide for their defence and safety?

Shall there be evil in a city] Shall there be any public calamity on the wicked, that is not an effect of my displeasure? The word does not mean *moral* evil, but punishment for sin; calamities falling on the workers of iniquity. *Natural evil* is the punishment of *moral evil:* God sends the former when the latter is persisted in.

A. M. cir. 3217
B. C. cir. 787
Ante U. C. 34
Amulii Sylvii,
R. Alban.,
cir. annum 10

[h]he revealeth his secret unto his
servants the prophets.
8 [i]The lion hath roared, who
will not fear? the Lord God
hath spoken, [k]who can but prophesy?
9 Publish in the palaces at Ashdod, and in
the palaces in the land of Egypt, and say,
Assemble yourselves upon the mountains of
Samaria, and behold the great tumults in the
midst thereof, and the [l]oppressed in the midst
thereof.
10 For they [m]know not to do right, saith
the Lord, who store up violence and [n]robbery
in their palaces.
11 Therefore thus saith the Lord God; [o]An
adversary *there shall be* even round about the
land; and he shall bring down thy strength
from thee, and thy palaces shall be spoiled.
12 Thus saith the Lord; As
the shepherd [p]taketh out of the
mouth of the lion two legs, or a
piece of an ear; so shall the
children of Israel be taken out that dwell in
Samaria in the corner of a bed, and [q]in
Damascus *in* a couch.
13 Hear ye, and testify in the house of
Jacob, saith the Lord God, the God of
hosts.
14 That in the day that I shall [r]visit the
transgressions of Israel upon him I will also
visit the altars of Beth-el: and the horns of the
altar shall be cut off, and fall to the ground.
15 And I will smite [s]the winter house with
[t]the summer house; and [u]the houses of ivory
shall perish, and the great houses shall have
an end, saith the Lord.

A. M. cir. 3217
B. C. cir. 787
Ante U. C. 34
Amulii Sylvii,
R. Alban.,
cir. annum 10

[h]Gen. vi. 13; xviii. 17; Psa. xxv. 14; John xv. 15——[i]Chap. i. 2——[k]Acts iv. 20; v. 20, 29; 1 Cor. ix. 16——[l]Or, *oppressions*——[m]Jer. iv. 22——[n]Or, *spoil*

[o]2 Kings xvii. 3, 6; xviii. 9, 10, 11——[p]Heb. *delivereth*——[q]Or, *on the bed's feet*——[r]Or, *punish Israel for*——[s]Jer. xxxvi. 22——[t]Judg. iii. 20——[u]1 Kings xxii. 39

Verse 7. *Surely the Lord God will do nothing*] In reference to the punishment, correction, or blessing of his people—

But he revealeth his secret unto his servants the prophets.] They are in strict correspondence with him, and he shows them *things to come*. Such *secrets* of God are revealed to them, that they may inform the people; that, by repentance and conversion, they may avoid the evil, and, by walking closely with God, secure the continuance of his favour.

Verse 8. *The lion hath roared*] God hath sent forth a terrible alarm, *Who will not fear?* Can any hear such denunciations of Divine wrath and not tremble?

The Lord God hath spoken] And those only who are in communion with him have heard the speech. *Who can but prophesy?* Who can help proclaiming at large the judgment threatened against the nation?

But I think נבא *naba*, here, is to be taken in its natural and ideal signification, to *pray*, *supplicate*, or *deprecate vengeance*. The Lord hath spoken of punishment—who can help *supplicating* his mercy, that his judgments may be averted?

Verse 9. *Publish in the palaces*] The housetops or flat roofs were the places from which public declarations were made. See on Isa. xxi. 1, and on Matt. x. 27. See whether in those places there be not *tumults*, *oppressions*, and *rapine* sufficient to excite my wrath against them.

Verse 10. *For they know not to do right*] So we may naturally say that they who are doing *wrong*, and to their own prejudice and ruin, must certainly be ignorant of what is *right*, and what is their own interest. But we say again, "There are none so blind as those who will not see." *Their eyes*, saith the Lord, *they have closed.*

Verse 11. *An adversary, round about the land*] Ye shall not be able to escape; wherever ye turn, ye shall meet a foe.

Verse 12. *As the shepherd taketh out of the mouth of the lion*] Scarcely any of you shall escape; and those that do shall do so with extreme difficulty, just as a shepherd, of a whole sheep carried away by a lion, can recover no more than *two* of its *legs*, or a piece of its *ear*, just enough to prove by the *marks* on those parts, that they belonged to a sheep which *was his own.*

So shall the children of Israel be taken out] Those of them that escape these judgments shall escape with as great difficulty, and be of as *little worth*, as the *two legs* and *piece of an ear* that shall be snatched out of the lion's mouth. We know that when the Babylonians carried away the people into Chaldea they left behind only a few, and those the *refuse of the land.*

In the corner of a bed] As the *corner* is the most honourable place in the East, and a *couch in the corner of a room* is the place of the *greatest distinction;* so the words in the text may mean, that even the *metropolitan cities*, which are in the *corner*—in the most honourable place—of the land, whether *Samaria* in *Israel*, or *Damascus* in *Syria*, shall not escape these judgments; and if any of the distinguished persons who dwell in them escape, it must be with as great difficulty as the fragments above-mentioned have been recovered from a lion. The passage is obscure. Mr. *Harmer* has taken great pains to illustrate it; but I fear with but little success. A general sense is all we can arrive at.

Verse 13. *Hear ye*] This is an address to the prophet.

Verse 14. *In the day that I shall visit*] When Josiah made a reformation in the land he destroyed *idolatry*, pulled down the temples and altars that had been consecrated to idol worship, and even burnt the bones of the priests of Baal and the golden calves upon their own altars. See 2 Kings xxiii. 15, 16, &c.

Verse 15. *I will smite the winter house with*

the summer house] I will not only destroy the *poor habitations* and *villages* in the country, but I will destroy those of the *nobility* and *gentry;* as well as the *lofty palaces* in the fortified cities in which they dwell in the *winter season*, as those *light* and *elegant seats* in which they spend the *summer season*. Dr. *Shaw* observes that "the hills and valleys round about Algiers are all over beautified with gardens and *country seats*, whither the inhabitants of *better fashion* retire during the *heats of the summer season*. They are *little white houses*, shaded with a variety of *fruit trees* and *evergreens*, which beside shade and retirement, afford a *gay* and *delightful prospect toward the sea*. The *gardens* are all well stocked with *melons*, fruits, and pot herbs of all kinds; and (which is chiefly regarded in these *hot countries*) each of them enjoys a great command of *water*."

And the houses of ivory] Those remarkable for their *magnificence* and their *ornaments*, not built of *ivory*, but in which *ivory* vessels, *ornaments*, and *inlaying* abounded. Thus, then, the *winter houses* and the *summer houses*, the *great houses* and the *houses of uncommon splendour*, shall all perish. There should be a total desolation in the land. No kind of house should be a refuge, and no kind of habitation should be spared. Ahab had at Samaria a house that was called the *ivory house*, 1 Kings xxii. 39. This may be particularly referred to in this place. We cannot suppose that a house constructed *entirely* of *ivory* can be intended.

CHAPTER IV

Israel reproved for their oppression, 1–3; *idolatry*, 4, 5; *and for their impenitence under the chastising hand of God*, 6–11. *The omniscience and uncontrollable power of God*, 12, 13.

A. M. cir. 3217
B. C. cir. 787
Ante U. C. 34
Amulii Sylvii,
R. Alban.,
cir. annum 10

HEAR this word, ye [a]kine of
Bashan, that *are* in the
mountain of Samaria, which
oppress the poor, which crush
the needy, which say to their masters, Bring,
and let us drink.
2 [b]The Lord GOD hath sworn by his holiness, that, lo, the days shall come upon you,
that he will take you away [c]with hooks,
and your posterity with fish-
hooks.
3 And [d]ye shall go out at the
breaches, every *cow at that
which is* before her; and [e]ye shall cast *them*
into the palace, saith the LORD.
4 [f]Come to Beth-el, and transgress; at
[g]Gilgal multiply transgression; and
[h]bring your sacrifices every morning, [i]*and*

---

[a]Psalm xxii. 12; Ezekiel xxxix. 18——[b]Psalm lxxxix. 35——[c]Jeremiah xvi. 16; Habakkuk i. 15——[d]Ezekiel xii. 5, 12

[e]Or, *ye shall cast away the things of the palace* [f]Ezek. xx. 39——[g]Hos. iv. 15; xii. 11; chap. v. 5 [h]Num. xxviii. 3, 4——[i]Deut. xiv. 28

NOTES ON CHAP. IV

Verse 1. *Hear this word, ye kine of Bashan*] Such an address was quite natural from the herdsman of Tekoa. *Bashan* was famous for the fertility of its soil, and its flocks and herds; and the prophet here represents the iniquitous, opulent, idle, lazy drones, whether men or women, under the idea of fatted bullocks, which were shortly to be led out to the slaughter.

Verse 2. *He will take you away with hooks*] Two modes of fishing are here alluded to: 1. Angling with rod, line, and baited hook. 2. That with the gaff, eel-spear, harpoon, or such like; the *first* used in catching *small fish*, by which the *common people* may be here represented; the *second*, for catching large fish, such as leave the sea, and come up the rivers to deposit their spawn; or such as are caught in the sea, as sharks, whales, dolphins, and even the hippopotamus, to which the more *powerful* and *opulent inhabitants* may be likened. But as the words in the text are generally *feminine*, it has been supposed that the prophecy is against the proud, powerful, voluptuous *women*. I rather think that the prophet speaks catachrestically; and means men of effeminate manners and idle lives. They are not the *bulls of Bashan*, but the *cows;* having little of the manly character remaining. Some understand the latter word as meaning a sort of *basket* or *wicker fish-nets*.

Verse 3. *And ye shall go out at the breaches*] Probably the metaphor is here kept up. They shall be caught by the *hooks*, or by the *nets;* and though they may make *breaches* in the latter by their flouncing when caught, they shall be taken out at these very breaches; and cast, not in the *palace*, but into a reservoir, to be kept awhile, and afterwards be taken out to be destroyed. *Samaria* itself is the *net;* your adversaries shall besiege it, and make *breaches* in its walls. At those *breaches* ye shall endeavour to *make your escape*, but ye shall be *caught* and led into *captivity*, where most of you shall be destroyed. See *Houbigant* on this passage.

Verse 4. *Come to Beth-el and transgress*] Spoken *ironically*. Go on to worship your calves at Beth-el; and *multiply* your *transgressions at Gilgal;* the very place where I *rolled away* the reproach of your fathers, by admitting them there into my covenant by circumcision. A place that should have ever been *sacred to me;* but you have now *desecrated* it by enormous idolatries. Let your *morning* and *evening*

A. M. cir. 3217
B. C. cir. 787
Ante U. C. 34
Amulii Sylvii,
R. Alban.,
cir. annum 10

your tithes after [k]three
years:
5 [l]And [m]offer a sacrifice of
thanksgiving with leaven, and
proclaim *and* publish [n]the free offerings: [o]for
[p]this liketh you, O ye children of Israel, saith
the Lord God.
6 And I also have given you cleanness of
teeth in all your cities, and want of bread in
all your places: [q]yet have ye not returned
unto me, saith the Lord.
7 And also I have withholden the rain from
you, when *there were* yet three months to the
harvest: and I caused it to rain upon one city,
and caused it not to rain upon another city:
one piece was rained upon, and the piece
whereupon it rained not withered.
8 So two *or* three cities wandered unto one
city, to drink water; but they were not satisfied: [r]yet have ye not returned
unto me, saith the Lord.
9 [s]I have smitten you with
blasting and mildew: [t]when
your gardens and your vineyards and your
fig trees and your olive trees increased,
[u]the palmerworm devoured *them:* yet
have ye not returned unto me, saith the
Lord.
10 I have sent among you the pestilence
[v]after [w]the manner of Egypt: your young
men have I slain with the sword, [x]and have
taken away your horses; and I have made the
stink of your camps to come up unto your
nostrils: [y]yet have ye not returned unto me,
saith the Lord.
11 I have overthrown *some* of you, as God
overthrew [z]Sodom and Gomorrah, [a]and ye
were as a firebrand plucked out of the burn-

[k]Hebrew, *three years of days*——[l]Leviticus vii. 13; xxiii. 17——[m]Hebrew, *offer by burning*——[n]Leviticus xxii. 18, 21; Deuteronomy xii. 6——[o]Psalm lxxxi. 12——[p]Hebrew, *so ye love*——[q]Isaiah xxvi. 11; Jeremiah v. 3; Hag. ii. 17; ver. 8, 9——[r]Ver. 6, 10, 11——[s]Deut. xxviii. 22; Hag. ii. 17——[t]Or, *the multitude of your gardens, &c., did the palmerworm, &c.*——[u]Joel i. 4; ii. 25——[v]Or, *in the way*——[w]Exod. ix. 3, 6; xii. 29; Deut. xxviii. 27, 60; Psa. lxxviii. 50——[x]Heb. *with the captivity of your horses;* 2 Kings xiii. 7——[y]Ver. 6——[z]Gen. xix. 24, 25; Isa. xiii. 19; Jer. xlix. 18——[a]Zech. iii. 2; Jude 23

sacrifices be offered still to your senseless gods; and continue to support your present vicious *priesthood* by the regular *triennial tithes* which should have been employed in my service; and,

Verse 5. *Offer a sacrifice of thanksgiving*] To the senseless *metal*, and the unfeeling *stock* and *stone* images, from which ye never did, and never could receive any help. Proceed yet farther, and bring *free-will offerings;* testify superabundant gratitude to your wooden and metallic gods, to whom ye are under such immense imaginary obligations! *Proclaim* and *publish* these offerings, and set forth the perfections of the objects of your worship; and see what they can do for you, when I, Jehovah, shall send *drought*, and *blasting*, and *famine*, and *pestilence*, and the *sword* among you.

Verse 6. *Cleanness of teeth*] Scarcity of bread, as immediately explained. Ye shall have no trouble in cleaning your teeth, for ye shall have nothing to eat.

Yet have ye not returned unto me, saith the Lord.] This reprehension is repeated *five* times in this chapter; and in it are strongly implied God's longsuffering, his various modes of fatherly chastisement, the ingratitude of the people, and their obstinate wickedness. The *famine* mentioned here is supposed to be that which is spoken of 2 Kings viii. 1; but it is most likely to have been that mentioned by Joel, chaps. i. and ii.

Verse 7. *When* there were *yet three months to the harvest*] St. Jerome says, from the end of April, when the *latter rain* falls, until harvest, there are *three* months, *May, June,* and *July*, in which no rain falls in Judea. The rain, therefore, that God had withheld from them, was that which was usual in the spring months, particularly in April.

I caused it to rain upon one city] To prove to them that this rain did not come *fortuitously* or of *necessity*, God was pleased to make these *most evident distinctions*. One city had rain, and could fill all its tanks or cisterns, while a neighbouring city had none. One *farm* or *field* was well watered, and abundant in its crops, while one contiguous to it had not a shower. In these instances a *particular providence* was most evident. "And yet, they did not return to the Lord."

Verse 9. *I have smitten you with blasting and mildew*] He sent *blasting* and *mildew* on the *crops*, and the *locust* on the *gardens, vineyards,* and *fields;* and this in such a way as to show it was a *Divine judgment*. They saw this; "yet they did not return to the Lord!"

Verse 10. *I have sent—the pestilence*] After the *blasting* and the *mildew*, the *pestilence* came; and it acted among them as one of the *plagues* of Egypt. Besides this, he had suffered their enemies to attack and prevail against them; alluding to the time in which the Syrians besieged Samaria, and reduced it to the most extreme necessity, when the head of an ass was sold for eighty pieces of silver, and the fourth part of a cab of dove's dung for five; and mothers ate the flesh of their children that had died through hunger, 2 Kings vi. 25. And the people were miraculously relieved by the total slaughter of the Syrians by the unseen hand of God, 2 Kings vii. 1, &c. And yet, after all those signal judgments, and singular mercies, "they did not return unto the Lord!"

Verse 11. *I have overthrown* some *of you*] In the destruction of your cities I have shown my judgments as signally as I did in the destruction of Sodom and Gomorrah; and those of you that did escape were as "brands plucked out of the fire;" if not *consumed*, yet *much*

A. M. cir. 3217
B. C. cir. 787
Ante U. C. 34
Amulii Sylvii,
R. Alban.,
cir. annum 10

ing: [b]yet have ye not returned
unto me, saith the LORD.
12 Therefore thus will I do
unto thee, O Israel: *and* be-
cause I will do this unto thee, [c]prepare to
meet thy God, O Israel.
13 For, lo, he that formeth the mountains,
and createth the [d]wind, [e]and
declareth unto man what *is*
his thought, [f]that maketh the
morning darkness, [g]and treadeth upon the high places of the earth,
[h]The LORD, The God of hosts, *is* his
name.

A. M. cir. 3217
B. C. cir. 787
Ante U. C. 34
Amulii Sylvii,
R. Alban.,
cir. annum 10

[b]Ver. 6——[c]See Ezek. xiii. 5; xxii. 30; Luke xiv. 31, 32——[d]Or, *spirit*——[e]Psa. cxxxix. 2; Dan. ii. 28

[f]Ch. v. 8; viii. 9——[g]Deut. xxxii. 13; xxxiii. 29; Mic. i. 3——[h]Isa. xlvii. 4; Jer. x. 16; chap. v. 8; ix. 6

scorched. And as the judgment was evidently from my hand, so was the deliverance; "and yet ye have not returned unto me, saith the Lord."

Verse 12. *Therefore thus will I do unto thee*] I will continue my judgments, I will fight against you; and, because I am thus determined,—

Prepare to meet thy God, O Israel.] This is a military phrase, and is to be understood as a challenge to come out to battle. As if the Lord had said, I will attack you immediately. Throw yourselves into a posture of defence, summon your idols to your help: and try how far your strength, and that of your gods, will avail you against the unconquerable arm of the Lord of hosts! This verse has been often painfully misapplied by public teachers; it has no particular relation to *the day of judgment*, nor to the *hour of death.* These constructions are impositions on the text.

Verse 13. *He that formeth the mountains*] Here is a powerful description of the majesty of God. He formed the earth; he created the wind; he knows the inmost thoughts of the heart; he is the Creator of darkness and light; he steps from mountain to mountain, and has all things under his feet! Who is he who hath done and can do all these things? JEHOVAH ELOHIM TSEBAOTH, *that is his name.* 1. The self-existing, eternal, and independent Being. 2. The God who is in covenant with mankind. 3. The universal Commander of all the hosts of earth and heaven. This name is farther illustrated in the following chapter. These words are full of instruction, and may be a subject of profitable meditation to every serious mind.

CHAPTER V

This chapter opens with a tender and pathetic lamentation, in the style of a funeral song, over the house of Israel, 1, 2. *The prophet then glances at the awful threatenings denounced against them,* 3; *earnestly exhorting them to renounce their idols, and seek Jehovah, of whom he gives a very magnificent description,* 4–9. *He then reproves their injustice and oppression with great warmth and indignation; exhorts them again to repentance; and enforces his exhortation with the most awful threatenings, delivered with great majesty and authority, and in images full of beauty and grandeur,* 10–24. *The chapter concludes with observing that their idolatry was of long standing, that they increased the national guilt, by adding to the sins of their fathers; and that their punishment, therefore, should be great in proportion,* 25–27. *Formerly numbers of them were brought captive to Damascus,* 2 Kings x. 32, 33; *but now they must go beyond it to Assyria,* 2 Kings xv. 29; xvii. 6.

A. M. cir. 3217
B. C. cir. 787
Ante U. C. 34
Amulii Sylvii,
R. Alban.,
cir. annum 10

HEAR ye this word which I
[a]take up against you, *even*
a lamentation, O house of Israel.
2 The virgin of Israel is fallen;
she shall no more rise: she is forsaken upon
her land; *there is* none to raise her up.
3 For thus saith the Lord GOD; The city
that went out *by* a thousand shall leave a
hundred, and that which went
forth *by* a hundred shall leave
ten, to the house of Israel.
4 For thus saith the LORD
unto the house of Israel, [b]Seek ye me, [c]and
ye shall live:
5 But seek not [d]Beth-el, nor enter into Gilgal, and pass not to [e]Beer-sheba: for Gilgal

A. M. cir. 3217
B. C. cir. 787
Ante U. C. 34
Amulii Sylvii,
R. Alban.,
cir. annum 10

[a]Jer. vii. 29; Ezek. xix. 1; xxvii. 2——[b]2 Chron. xv. 2; Jer. xxix. 13; ver. 6

[c]Isaiah lv. 3——[d]Chapter iv. 4——[e]Chap. viii. 14

NOTES ON CHAP. V

Verse 1. *Hear ye this word*] Attend to this doleful song which I make for the house of Israel.

Verse 2. *The virgin of Israel*] The kingdom of Israel, or the *ten* tribes, which were carried into captivity; and are now totally lost in the nations of the earth.

Verse 3. *The city that went out* by *a thousand*] The city that could easily have furnished, on any emergency, a *thousand* fighting men, can now produce scarcely one *hundred*—*one* in *ten* of the former number; and now of the *hundred* scarcely *ten* remain: so reduced was Israel when Shalmaneser besieged and took Samaria, and carried the residue into captivity.

Verse 4. *Seek ye me, and ye shall live*] Cease your rebellion against me; return to me with all your heart; and though consigned to *death*, ye shall be rescued and *live.* Deplorable as your case is, it is not utterly desperate.

Verse 5. *But seek not Beth-el*] *There* was

A. M. cir. 3217
B. C. cir. 787
Ante U. C. 34
Amulii Sylvii,
R. Alban.,
cir. annum 10

shall surely go into captivity, and
[f]Beth-el shall come to naught.
6 [g]Seek the LORD, and ye shall
live; lest he break out like fire
in the house of Joseph and devour *it,* and
there be none to quench *it* in Beth-el.
7 Ye who [h]turn judgment to wormwood,
and leave off righteousness in the earth.
8 *Seek him* that maketh the [i]seven stars
and Orion, and turneth the shadow of death
into the morning, [k]and maketh the day dark
with night: that [l]calleth for the waters of the
sea, and poureth them out upon the face of
the earth: [m]The LORD *is* his name:
9 That strengtheneth the [n]spoiled against
the strong, so that the spoiled shall come
against the fortress.
10 [o]They hate him that rebuketh in the
gate, and they [p]abhor him that speaketh uprightly.
11 Forasmuch therefore as
your treading *is* upon the poor,
and ye take from him burdens of
wheat: [q]ye have built houses of
hewn stone, but ye shall not dwell in them;
ye have planted [r]pleasant vineyards, but ye
shall not drink wine of them.
12 For I know your manifold transgressions, and your mighty sins: [s]they afflict the
just, they take [t]a bribe, and they [u]turn aside
the poor in the gate *from their right.*
13 Therefore [v]the prudent shall keep silence
in that time; for it *is* an evil time.
14 Seek good, and not evil, that ye may
live: and so the LORD, the God of hosts,
shall be with you, [w]as ye have spoken.
15 [x]Hate the evil, and love the good, and
establish judgment in the gate: [y]it may be
that the LORD God of hosts will be gracious
unto the remnant of Joseph.

A. M. cir. 3217
B. C. cir. 787
Ante U. C. 34
Amulii Sylvii,
R. Alban.,
cir. annum 10

[f]Hosea iv. 15; x. 3——[g]Ver. 4——[h]Chap. vi. 12——[i]Job ix. 9; xxxviii. 31——[k]Psalm civ. 20——[l]Job xxxviii. 34; chap. ix. 6——[m]Chap. iv. 13——[n]Hebrew, *spoil*——[o]Isaiah xxix. 21——[p]1 Kings xxii. 8——[q]Deuteronomy xxviii. 30, 38, 39; Mic. vi. 15; Zephaniah i. 13; Haggai i. 6——[r]Hebrew, *vineyards of desire*——[s]Chap. ii. 26——[t]Or, *a ransom*——[u]Isaiah xxix. 21; chap. ii. 7——[v]Chap. vi. 10——[w]Micah iii. 11——[x]Psa. xxxiv. 14; xcvii. 10; Rom. xii. 9——[y]Exod. xxxii. 30; 2 Kings xix. 4; Joel ii. 14

one of Jeroboam's *golden calves*, and at *Gilgal* were *carved images;* both were places in which idolatry was triumphant. The prophet shows them that all hope from those quarters is utterly vain; for Gilgal shall go into captivity, and Beth-el be brought to naught. There is a play or paronomasia on the *letters* and *words* in this clause: הגלגל גלה יגלה ובית אל יהיה לאון *haggilgal galoh yigleh, ubeith el yiheyeh leaven.* "This Gilgal shall go captive into captivity; and Beth-el (the house of God) shall be for Beth-aven," (the house of iniquity.)

Verse 6. *Seek the Lord, and ye shall live*] Repeated from ver. 4.

In the house of Joseph] The Israelites of the *ten* tribes, of whom Ephraim and Manasseh, sons of Joseph, were the chief.

Verse 7. *Ye who turn judgment to wormwood*] Who pervert judgment; causing him who obtains his suit to mourn sorely over the *expenses* he has *incurred* in gaining his *right.*

Verse 8. *That maketh the seven stars and Orion*] Or, *Hyades* and *Arcturus, Kimah* and *Kesil.* See my notes on Job ix. 9, and xxxviii. 32, where the subject of this verse is largely considered.

Turneth the shadow of death into the morning] Who makes day and night, light and darkness.

Calleth for the waters of the sea] Raising them up by evaporation, and collecting them into clouds.

And poureth them out] Causing them to drop down in showers upon the face of the earth. Who has done this? JEHOVAH *is his name.*

Verse 9. *That strengtheneth the spoiled*] Who takes the part of the poor and oppressed against the oppressor; and, in the course of his providence, sets up the former, and depresses the latter.

Verse 10. *They hate him that rebuketh in the gate*] They cannot bear an upright *magistrate,* and will not have *righteous laws* executed.

Verse 11. *Your treading is upon the poor*] You tread them under your feet; they form the road on which ye walk; and yet it was by oppressing and improverishing them that ye gained your riches.

Ye take from him burdens of wheat] Ye will have his *bread* for doing him justice.

Verse 12. *I know your manifold transgressions*] I have marked the *multitude* of your *smaller crimes,* as well as your *mighty offences.* Among their *greater offences* were, 1. Their afflicting the righteous. 2. Taking bribes to blind their eyes in judgment. And, 3. Refusing to hear the poor, who had no money to give them.

Verse 13. *The prudent shall keep silence*] A wise man will consider that it is useless to complain. He can have no justice without bribes; and he has no money to give: consequently, in such *an evil time,* it is best to keep silence.

Verse 14. *Seek good, and not evil*] Is there a greater mystery in the world, than that a man, instead of seeking *good,* will seek *evil,* knowing that it is *evil?*

And so the Lord] As God is the Fountain of good, so they who seek the supreme good seek him: and they who seek shall find him; *for the Lord, the God of hosts, shall be with him.*

Verse 15. *Hate the evil, and love the good*] What *ruins* you, *avoid;* what *helps* you, *cleave* to. And as a proof that you take this advice,

A. M. cir. 3217
B. C. cir. 787
Ante U. C. 34
Amulii Sylvii,
R. Alban.,
cir. annum 10

16 Therefore the LORD, the God of hosts, the Lord, saith thus; Wailing *shall be* in all streets; and they shall say in all the highways, Alas! alas! and they shall call the husbandman to mourning, and [z]such as are skilful of lamentation to wailing.

17 And in all vineyards *shall be* wailing: for [a]I will pass through thee, saith the LORD.

18 [b]Wo unto you that desire the day of the LORD! to what end *is* it for you? [c]the day of the LORD *is* darkness, and not light.

19 [d]As if a man did flee from a lion, and a bear met him; or went into the house and leaned his hand on the wall, and a serpent bit him.

20 *Shall* not the day of the LORD *be* darkness, and not light? even very dark, and no brightness in it?

A. M. cir. 3217
B. C. cir. 787
Ante U. C. 34
Amulii Sylvii,
R. Alban.,
cir. annum 10

21 [e]I hate, I despise your feast days, and [f]I will not [g]smell in your solemn assemblies.

22 [h]Though ye offer me burnt-offerings and your meat-offerings, I will not accept *them:* neither will I regard the [i]peace-offerings of your fat beasts.

23 Take thou away from me the noise of thy songs; for I will not hear the melody of thy viols.

24 [k]But let judgment [l]run down as waters, and righteousness as a mighty stream.

25 [m]Have ye offered unto me sacrifices

---

[z]Jer. ix. 17——[a]Exod. xii. 2; Nah. i. 12——[b]Isa. v. 19; Jer. xvii. 15; Ezek. xii. 22, 27; 2 Pet. iii. 4——[c]Jer. xxx. 7; Joel ii. 2; Zeph. i. 15——[d]Jer. xlviii. 44 [e]Prov. xxi. 27; Isa. i. 11–16; Jer. vi. 20; Hos. viii. 13

[f]Lev. xxvi. 31——[g]Or, *smell your holy days*——[h]Isa. lxvi. 3; Mic. vi. 6, 7——[i]Or, *thank-offerings*——[k]Hos. vi. 6; Mic. vi. 8——[l]Heb. *roll*——[m]Deut. xxxii. 17; Josh xxiv. 14; Ezek. xx. 8, 16, 24; Acts vii. 42, 43; See Isa. xliii. 23

---

purify the *seats of justice;* and then expect God to be gracious to the *remnant of Joseph*—to the posterity of the ten tribes.

Verse 16. *They shall call the husbandman to mourning*] Because the crops have failed, and the ground has been tilled in vain.

Such as are skilful of lamentation] See the note on Jer. ix. 17.

Verse 17. *And in all vineyards* shall be *wailing*] The places where festivity especially used to prevail.

I will pass through thee] As I passed, by the ministry of the destroying angel, through Egypt, not to *spare*, but to *destroy*.

Verse 18. *Wo unto you that desire the day of the Lord*] The prophet had often denounced the coming of *God's day*, that is, of a *time of judgment;* and the unbelievers had said, "Let his day come, that we may see it." Now the prophet tells them that that day would be to them *darkness*—calamity, and *not light*—not prosperity.

Verse 19. *As if a man did flee from a lion, and a bear met him*] They shall go from one evil to another. He who escapes from the *lion's* mouth shall fall into the *bear's* paws:—

Incidit in Scyllam, cupiens vitare Charybdim.

The Israelites, under their king *Menahem*, wishing to avoid a civil war, called in *Pul*, king of *Assyria*, to help them. This led to a series of evils inflicted by the Syrian and Assyrian kings, till at last Israel was ravaged by *Shalmaneser*, and carried into captivity. Thus, in avoiding one evil they fell into another still more grievous.

Leaned his hand on a wall, and a serpent bit him.] Snakes and venomous animals are fond of taking up their lodging in *walls of houses*, where they can either find or make *holes;* and it is dangerous to sit near them or lean against them. In the East Indies they keep the faithful *mongose*, a species of *ichneumon*, in their houses, for the purpose of destroying the snakes that infest them.

Verse 21. *I hate, I despise your feast days*] I *abominate* those sacrificial festivals where there is no *piety;* and I *despise* them because they *pretend* to be what they are not. This may refer to the *three annual festivals* which were still observed in a certain way among the Israelites.

Verse 22. *The peace-offerings of your fat beasts.*] מריאיכם *merieychem* probably means *buffaloes;* and so *Bochart*.

Verse 23. *The noise of thy songs—the melody of thy viols.*] They had both *vocal* and *instrumental music* in those sacrificial festivals; and God hated the *noise* of the *one* and *shut* his *ears* against the *melody* of the *other*. In the *first* there was nothing but *noise*, because their *hearts* were not right with God; and in the *latter* there could be nothing but (זמרת *zimrath*) cutting and scraping, because there was *no heart*—no religious sense in the thing, and nearly as little in them that used it. See on chap. vi. 5.

Verse 24. *Let judgment run down*] Let the execution of justice be everywhere like the *showers* that fall upon the land to render it fertile; and let righteousness in *heart* and *life* be like a mighty river, or the Jordan, that shall wind its course through the whole nation, and carry every abomination into the Dead Sea. Let *justice* and *righteousness* prevail everywhere, and sweep their contraries out of the land.

Verse 25. *Have ye offered unto me sacrifices*] Some have been led to think that "during the *forty years* which the Israelites spent in the wilderness, between Egypt and the promised land, they did *not offer any sacrifices*, as in their circumstances it was impossible; they offered none because they had none." But such people must have forgotten that when the covenant was made at Sinai, there were *burnt-offerings* and *peace-offerings* of *oxen* sacrificed to the Lord, Exod. xxiv. 5; and at the setting up of the tabernacle the *twelve princes* of the *twelve tribes* offered each a *young bullock*, a *ram*, and a *lamb*, for a *burnt-offering;* a *kid*

A. M. cir. 3217 B. C. cir. 787 Ante U. C. 34 Amulii Sylvii, R. Alban., cir. annum 10

and offerings in the wilderness
forty years, O house of
Israel?
26 But ye have borne [n]the
tabernacle [o]of your Moloch and Chiun
your images, the star of your god,
which ye made to your-
selves.
27 Therefore will I cause you
to go into captivity [p]beyond
Damascus, saith the LORD, [q]whose name *is*
The God of hosts.

[n]Or, *Siccuth your king*——[o]1 Kings xi. 33——[p]2 Kings xvii. 6——[q]Chap. iv. 13

for a *sin-offering;* two *oxen,* five *rams,* five *he-goats,* and five *lambs,* for a *peace-offering,* Num. vii. 12, &c.; which amounted to an immense number of victims offered in the course of the *twelve days* during which this *feast of the dedication* lasted. At the consecration of priests, *bullocks* and *rams* to a considerable number were offered, see Lev. viii. 1, &c.; but they were not offered so *regularly,* nor in *such abundance,* as they were after the settlement in the promised land. Learned men, therefore, have considered this verse as speaking thus: Did ye offer to me, during forty years in the wilderness, sacrifices in *such a way* as was *pleasing to me?* Ye did not; for your hearts were divided, and ye were generally in a spirit of insurrection or murmuring.

Verse 26. *But ye have borne*] The preceding verse spoke of their *fathers;* the present verse speaks of the *Israelites then existing,* who were so grievously addicted to idolatry, that they not only worshipped at stated public places the *idols* set up by *public authority,* but they *carried their gods about with them* everywhere.

The tabernacle of your Moloch] Probably a small portable shrine, with an image of their god in it, such as *Moloch;* and the *star* or *representative* of their god *Chiun.* For an ample exposition of this verse, see the note on Acts vii. 42; to which let me add, that from *Picart's* Religious Ceremonies, vol. iii. p. 199, we find that there was an idol named Choun worshipped among the *Peruvians* from the remotest antiquity.

Verse 27. *Will I cause you to go into captivity beyond Damascus*] That is, into *Assyria,* the way to which, from Judea, was by Damascus.

But St. *Stephen* says, Acts vii. 43, *beyond Babylon;* because the Holy Spirit that was in him chose to *extend* the meaning of the original text to that great and final captivity of the Jews in general, when Zedekiah, their last king, and the people of Judea, were carried into Mesopotamia, Armenia, and Media; see 2 Kings xvii. 7, 24. This captivity happened after the time of Amos.

CHAPTER VI

The prophet reproves his people for indulging themselves in luxurious ease, and forming alliances with their powerful idolatrous neighbours, 1. *He asks if* their *lands or* their *lot be better than their own,* 2, *that they should choose to worship the gods of the heathen, and forsake Jehovah. Then follows an amplification of the sin which the prophet reproves,* 3–6; *to which he annexes very awful threatenings, confirmed by the oath of Jehovah,* 7, 8. *He next particularly specifies the punishment of their sins by pestilence,* 9–11; *by famine, or a drought that should harden the earth so that it could not be tilled,* 12; *and by the sword of the Assyrians,* 14.

A. M. cir. 3217 B. C. cir. 787 Ante U. C. 34 Amulii Sylvii, R. Alban., cir. annum 10

WO [a]to them *that* [b]are at
ease in Zion, and trust in
the mountain of Samaria, *which*
are named [c]chief[d] of the nations,
to whom the house of Israel
came!
2 [e]Pass ye unto [f]Calneh, and
see; and from thence go ye to

[a]Luke vi. 24——[b]Or, *are secure*——[c]Exod. xix. 5——[d]Or, *first-fruits*——[e]Jer. ii. 10——[f]Isa. x. 9; taken cir. 794

NOTES ON CHAP. VI

Verse 1. *Wo to them* that are *at ease in Zion*] For השאננים *hashshaanannim,* "who dwell at ease," it has been proposed to read השעננים *hashshaanannim,* "who confidently lean," the two words differing only in *one letter,* an ע *ain* for an א *aleph.* They leaned confidently on Zion; supposing that, notwithstanding their iniquities they should be saved for *Zion's sake.* Thus the former clause will agree better with the latter, "leaning upon Zion," and "trusting in the mountain of Samaria." Those *that are at ease* may mean those who have no concern about the threatened judgments, and who have no deep concern for the salvation of their own souls. *Houbigant* would read, "Wo to them who despise Zion, and trust in Samaria." So the *Septuagint,* reading שנאים *soneim, hating,* instead of שאננים *shaanannim,* being at *rest, tranquil. Calmet* first proposed this conjecture; *Houbigant* follows him.

Are *named chief*] *Newcome* renders, "That are named after the chief of the nations;" and observes, that the Hebrew word נקבי *nekubey* is an allusion to marking a name or character by *punctures.* See on Isa. xliv. 5. They call themselves not after their ancestors, but after the *chief of the idolatrous nations* with whom they intermarry contrary to the law.

Perhaps the words here rather refer to the *mountains* and their *temples,* than to the *people.* The *mountain* of *Zion,* and the *mountain* of *Samaria,* were considered the *chief* or **most**

A. M. cir. 3217 B. C. cir. 787 Ante U. C. 34 Amulii Sylvii, R. Alban., cir. annum 10

[g]Hamath the great: then go
down to [h]Gath of the Philistines: [i]*be they* better than these
kingdoms? or their border
greater than your border?

3 Ye that [k]put far away the [l]evil day,
[m]and cause [n]the [o]seat of violence to come
near;

4 That lie upon beds of ivory, and [p]stretch
themselves upon their couches, and eat the
lambs out of the flock, and the calves out of
the midst of the stall;

5 [q]That [r]chant to the sound
of the viol, *and* invent to themselves instruments of music,
[s]like David;

A. M. cir. 3217 B. C. cir. 787 Ante U. C. 34 Amulii Sylvii, R. Alban., cir. annum 10

6 That drink [t]wine in bowls, and anoint
themselves with the chief ointments: [u]but they
are not grieved for the [v]affliction of Joseph.

7 Therefore now shall they go captive with
the first that go captive, and the banquet of
them that stretched themselves shall be removed.

8 [w]The Lord God hath sworn by himself,

[g]2 Kings xviii. 34——[h]Joshua xi. 22; 1 Samuel v. 8; 2 Chronicles xxvi. 6——[i]Nahum iii. 8——[k]Ezekiel xii. 27——[l]Chap. v. 18; ix. 10——[m]Chap. v. 12; ver. 12——[n]Psalm xciv. 20——[o]Or, *habitation*——[p]Or, *abound with superfluities*——[q]Isaiah v. 12——[r]Or, *quaver*——[s]1 Chronicles xxiii. 5——[t]Or, *in bowls of wine*——[u]Genesis xxxvii. 25——[v]Heb. *breach*——[w]Jer. li. 14; Heb. vi. 13, 17

celebrated among the nations, as the two kingdoms to which they belonged were the most distinguished on the earth.

Verse 2. *Pass ye unto Calneh*] This is, says *Calmet*, the Ctesiphon on the river Tigris.

Hamath] The same as *Emesa. Hamath* was a city on the Orontes, in Syria.

Gath] A well-known town, and head of one of the *five* seignories of the Philistines.

Be they *better*] You have no more reason to expect exemption from the consequences of your sins than they had. *They* have been punished; so shall you. Why then will ye trust in their gods, that could not save their own cities?

Verse 3. *Ye that put far away the evil day*] Wo to you who will not consider the day of approaching vengeance; but continue in your iniquity, and harden your hearts. Ye bring your iniquities nearer, and still suppose your punishment to be at a greater distance.

Verse 4. *That lie upon beds of ivory*] The word הוי *hoi, wo*, is understood at the beginning of each of the *first, third, fourth, fifth*, and *sixth* verses. The *beds* mentioned here may be either *sofas to recline on at table*, or *beds to sleep on;* and these among the ancients were ornamented with ivory inlaid. They were called *lectos eburatos* by Plautus, *lectos eburnos* by Horace, "ivory beds." Probably those ornamented with *shells*, or *mother-of-pearl*, may be intended. Several works of this kind may be still seen in Palestine and other places. I have before me a cross brought from Jerusalem, incrusted all over with *mother-of-pearl*, and various figures chased on it.

There must have been a great deal of luxury and effeminacy among the Israelites at this time; and, consequently, abundance of riches. This was in the time of Jeroboam the second, when the kingdom had enjoyed a long peace. The description in the *fourth, fifth*, and *sixth* verses, is that of an Asiatic court even in the present day.

Verse 5. And *invent to themselves instruments of music, like David*] See the note on 1 Chron. xxiii. 5; and see especially the note on 2 Chron. xxix. 25. I believe that David was not authorized by the Lord to introduce that multitude of musical instruments into the Divine worship of which we read; and I am satisfied that his conduct in this respect is most solemnly reprehended by this prophet; and I farther believe that the use of such instruments of music, in the Christian Church, is *without* the *sanction* and *against* the *will* of God; that they are subversive of the spirit of true devotion, and that they are *sinful*. If there was a *wo to them* who *invented* instruments of music, as did David under the law, is there *no wo, no curse* to them who invent them, and introduce them into the worship of God in the Christian Church? I am an old man, and an old minister; and I here declare that I never knew them productive of any good in the worship of God; and have had reason to believe that they were productive of much evil. Music, *as a science*, I esteem and admire: but instruments of music *in the house of God* I abominate and abhor. This is the abuse of music; and here I register my protest against all such corruptions in the worship of the Author of Christianity. The late venerable and most eminent divine, the Rev. *John Wesley*, who was a *lover of music*, and an *elegant poet*, when asked his opinion of instruments of music being introduced into the chapels of the Methodists said, in his terse and powerful manner, "I have no objection to instruments of music in our chapels, provided they are neither HEARD nor SEEN." I say the same, though I think the expense of purchase had better be spared.

The word הפרטים *happoretim*, which we render *chant*, and the margin *quaver*, signifies to *dance*, to *skip*, &c. In the sight of such a text, fiddlers, drummers, waltzers, &c., may well tremble, who perform to excite detestable passions.

Verse 6. *That drink wine in bowls*] Perhaps the *costliness* of the *drinking vessels*, more than the *quantity* drank, is that which is here reprehended by the prophet. Drinking vessels of the most costly materials, and of the most exquisite workmanship, are still in use; and as to *precious ointments* and *perfumes* among the Jews, we have a proof that the contents of one small box was worth *three hundred denarii*, at least *seven pounds ten shillings* sterling. See the case in the Gospel, John xii. 5, and the note there.

Verse 7. *With the first that go captive*] The house of *Israel* shall be carried into captivity *before* the house of *Judah*.

Verse 8. *The Lord God hath sworn by him-*

A. M. cir. 3217
B. C. cir. 787
Ante U. C. 34
Amulii Sylvii,
R. Alban.,
cir. annum 10

saith the LORD the God of hosts,
I abhor [x]the excellency of Jacob,
and hate his palaces: therefore
will I deliver up the city with all
[y]that is therein.
9 And it shall come to pass, if there remain
ten men in one house, that they shall die.
10 And a man's uncle shall take him up, and
he that burneth him, to bring out the bones
out of the house, and shall say unto him that
is by the sides of the house, *Is there* yet *any*
with thee? and he shall say, No. Then shall
he say, [z]Hold thy tongue: [a]for [b]we may not
make mention of the name of the LORD.
11 For, behold, [c]the LORD commandeth, [d]and
he will smite the great house
with [e]breaches, and the little
house with clefts.
12 Shall horses run upon the
rock? will *one* plough *there* with oxen? for
[f]ye have turned judgment into gall, and the
fruit of righteousness into hemlock:
13 Ye which rejoice in a thing of naught,
which say, Have we not taken to us horns by
our own strength?
14 But, behold, [g]I will raise up against you
a nation, O house of Israel, saith the LORD
the God of hosts; and they shall afflict you
from the [h]entering in of Hamath unto the
[i]river of the wilderness.

A. M. cir. 3217
B. C. cir. 787
Ante U. C. 34
Amulii Sylvii,
R. Alban.,
cir. annum 10

---

[x]Psa. xlvii. 4; Ezek. xxiv. 21; chap. viii. 7——[y]Heb. *the fulness thereof*——[z]Chap. v. 13——[a]Chap. viii. 3——[b]Or, *they will not*, or *have not*

[c]Isa. lv. 11——[d]Chap. iii. 15——[e]Or, *droppings*——[f]Hos. x. 4; chap. v. 7——[g]Jer. v. 15——[h]Num. xxxiv. 8; 1 Kings viii. 65——[i]Or, *valley*

---

self] בנפשו *benaphsho*, by his soul, his *being, existence.*

Verse 9. *Ten men—they shall die.*] ALL shall be cut off by the sword, or by captivity, or by famine.

Verse 10. *A man's uncle shall take him up*] Bp. *Newcome* says, this obscure verse seems to describe the effects of famine and pestilence during the siege of Samaria. The carcass shall be burnt; and the bones removed with no ceremony of funeral rites, and without the assistance of the nearest kinsman. Solitude shall reign in the house; and if one is left, he must be silent, (see chap. viii. 3,) and retired, lest he be plundered of his scanty provision! *Burning the body*, and then collecting the *ashes*, and putting them into an urn, was deemed the most honourable mode of burial.

Verse 11. *He will smite the great house with breaches*] The great and small shall equally suffer; no distinction shall be made; rich and poor shall fall together; death has received his commission, and he will spare none. *Horace* has a sentiment precisely like this, Carm. Lib. i., Od. iv., v. 13.

Pallida mors æquo pulsat pede pauperum TABERNAS,
Regumque TURRES.

With equal pace impartial fate
Knocks at the *palace* as the *cottage* gate.

But this may refer particularly to the houses of the poor in Eastern countries; their mud walls being frequently full of *clefts;* the earth of which they are built seldom adhering together because of its *sandiness.*

Verse 12. *Shall horses run upon the rock*] First, they *could not* do it, because they were *unshod;* for the shoeing of horses with *iron* was not then known. Secondly, If they did run on the rock, it would be *useless* to their owner, and *hurtful* to themselves. Thirdly, And it would be as useless to *plough on the rock with oxen;* for there it would be impossible to sow with any advantage. Fourthly, Just as useless and injurious would it be to put *gall* in the place of judgment, and hemlock in the place of righteousness. You have not only been labouring in vain for yourselves, but you have also been oppressive to others; and for both ye shall suffer.

Verse 13. *Ye which rejoice in a thing of naught*] In your idols: for an idol is nothing in the world.

Have we not taken to us horns] We have arrived to power and dignity by our strength. *Horns* were the symbols of *power* and *authority.* So *Horace:—*

Vina parant animos: tum pauper cornua sumet.

"Wine repairs our strength, and furnishes the poor with horns."

At such times they think themselves as great as the greatest.

Verse 14. *I will raise up against you a nation*] The *Assyrians* under *Pul, Tiglath-pileser*, and *Shalmaneser*, who subdued the Israelites at various times, and at last carried them away captive in the days of Hosea, the last king of Israel in Samaria.

From the entering in of Hamath (on the *north*) *unto the river of the wilderness.*] Besor, which empties itself into the sea, not far from Gaza, and was in the *southern* part of the tribe of Simeon.

CHAPTER VII

In this chapter God represents to Amos, by three several visions, the judgments he is about to bring on Israel. The first is a plague of locusts, *threatening to cut off the hopes of the harvest by attacking it in the time of the second growth; the first luxuriances of the crop being probably mowed for the king's horses,* 1–3. *The next vision threatens a judgment by* fire, *which would consume a great part,* 4–6; *and the third a total overthrow of Israel, levelling it as it were by a line,* 7–9. *The rest of the chapter is a denunciation of heavy judgments against Amaziah, priest of Beth-el, who had brought on accusation to the king against the prophet,* 10–17.

A. M. cir. 3217
B. C. cir. 787
Ante U. C. 34
Amulii Sylvii,
R. Alban.,
cir. annum 10

THUS hath the Lord GOD
showed unto me; and, be-
hold, he formed [a]grasshoppers
in the beginning of the shooting
up of the latter growth; and, lo, *it was* the
latter growth after the king's mowings.
2 And it came to pass, *that* when they had
made an end of eating the grass of the land,
then I said, O Lord GOD, forgive, I beseech
thee: [b]by [c]whom shall Jacob arise? for he
is small.
3 [d]The LORD repented for this: It shall not
be, saith the LORD.
4 Thus hath the Lord GOD showed unto
me: and, behold, the Lord GOD called to
contend by fire, and it devoured the great
deep, and did eat up a part.
5 Then said I, O Lord GOD, cease, I beseech thee: [e]by whom shall
Jacob arise? for he *is* small.
6 The LORD repented for this:
This also shall not be, saith the
Lord GOD.
7 Thus he showed me: and, behold, the
Lord stood upon a wall *made* by a plumbline,
with a plumbline in his hand.
8 And the LORD said unto me, Amos, what
seest thou? And I said, A plumbline. Then
said the Lord, Behold, [f]I will set a plumbline
in the midst of my people Israel: [g]I will not
again pass by them any more:
9 [h]And the high places of Isaac shall be
desolate, and the sanctuaries of Israel shall be
laid waste; and I will rise against [i]the house
of Jeroboam with the sword.
10 Then Amaziah [k]the priest of Beth-

A. M. cir. 3217
B. C. cir. 787
Ante U. C. 34
Amulii Sylvii,
R. Alban.,
cir. annum 10

[a]Or, *green worms*——[b]Isaiah li. 19; verse 5——[c]Or, *who of* or *for Jacob shall stand?*——[d]Deuteronomy xxxii. 36; verse 6; Jonah iii. 10; James v. 16——[e]Verse 2, 3——[f]See 2 Kings xxi. 13; Isa. xxviii. 17; xxxiv. 11; Lamentations ii. 8——[g]Ch. viii. 2; Micah vii. 18——[h]Beer-sheba, Gen. xxvi. 25; xlvi. 1; chap. v. 5; viii. 14——[i]1 Kings xvi. 3——[k]1 Kings xii. 32

NOTES ON CHAP. VII

Verse 1. *Behold, he formed grasshoppers*] גבי *gobai* is generally understood here to signify *locusts.* See the notes on Joel i. and ii.

The shooting up of the latter growth] The *early crop* of grass had been already mowed and housed. The *second crop* or *rowing,* as it is called in some places, was not yet begun. By the *king's mowings* we may understand the *first crop,* a portion of which the king probably claimed as being the better hay; but the words may signify simply the *prime crop,* that which is the *best of the whole. Houbigant* thinks the *shearing of the king's sheep* is meant.

Verse 2. *By whom shall Jacob arise?*] The *locusts,* the symbols of the many enemies that had impoverished Jerusalem, having devoured much of the produce of the land, were proceeding, till, at the intercession of the prophet, they were removed. Then, seeing in the light of prophecy the nation in every sense brought low, he cries, "By whom shall Jacob arise? for he is small." *Calmet* justly remarks: "After the death of Jeroboam the second, the kingdom, so flourishing and powerful before, was reduced to such weakness that it was obliged to have recourse to strangers for support. *Menahem* applied to Pul, king of Assyria, whence arose the final misery of the state.

Verse 3. *The Lord repented*] Changed his purpose of destroying them by the locusts. See ver. 6.

Verse 4. *The Lord God called to contend by fire*] Permitted *war,* both *civil* and *foreign,* to harass the land, after the death of Jeroboam the second. These wars would have totally destroyed it, had not the prophet interceded.

It devoured the great deep, and did eat up a part.] We are here to understand the partially destructive wars which afterwards took place; for the Lord causes all these things to pass before the eyes of Amos in the vision of prophecy; and intimates that, at the intercession of his prophets, *total* ruin should be prevented.

Verse 7. *With a plumbline in his hand.*] This appears to be intended as an emblem of strict justice, and intimated that God would now visit them according to their iniquities.

Verse 8. *I will set a plumbline*] I will visit them by *justice* without any mixture of *mercy.*

Verse 9. *And the high places of Isaac shall be desolate*] Their total destruction is at hand. The *high place of Isaac* was *Beer-sheba,* where Isaac had built an altar to the Lord, Gen. xxvi. 25. This high place, which had been abused to idolatrous uses, was demolished by Josiah, king of Judah, as we read in 2 Kings xxiii. 8, for *he defiled all the high places from Geba to Beer-sheba.*

I will rise against the house of Jeroboam] The Lord had promised to Jehu, the ancestor of Jeroboam, that his family should sit on the throne of Israel to the *fourth generation.* Zechariah, the son of Jeroboam, was the *fourth* in order after Jehu; and on him the threatening in this verse fell; for he was murdered by Shallum after he had reigned six months, and in him the family became extinct. See 2 Kings x. 30, and xv. 8-10.

Verse 10. *Amaziah the priest of Beth-el*] The idolatrous priest who had been established by the king to maintain the worship of the golden calves which Jeroboam the elder had set up at this place.

A. M. cir. 3217
B. C. cir. 787
Ante U. C. 34
Amulii Sylvii,
R. Alban.,
cir. annum 10

el, sent to [l]Jeroboam king of Israel, saying, Amos hath conspired against thee in the midst of the house of Israel: the land is not able to bear all his words.

11 For thus Amos saith, Jeroboam shall die by the sword, and Israel shall surely be led away captive out of their own land.

12 Also Amaziah said unto Amos, O thou seer, go flee thee away into the land of Judah, and there eat bread, and prophesy there:

13 But [m]prophesy not again any more at Beth-el: [n]for it *is* the king's [o]chapel, and it *is* the [p]king's court.

14 Then answered Amos, and said to Amaziah, I *was* no prophet, neither *was* I [q]a prophet's son; [r]but I *was* a herdman, and a gatherer of [s]sycamore fruit:

A. M. cir. 3217
B. C. cir. 787
Ante U. C. 34
Amulii Sylvii,
R. Alban.,
cir. annum 10

15 And the LORD took me [t]as I followed the flock, and the LORD said unto me, Go, prophesy unto my people Israel.

16 Now therefore hear thou the word of the LORD: Thou sayest, Prophesy not against Israel, and [u]drop not *thy word* against the house of Isaac.

17 [v]Therefore thus saith the LORD; [w]Thy wife shall be a harlot in the city, and thy sons and thy daughters shall fall by the sword, and thy land shall be divided by line; and thou shalt die in a polluted land: and Israel shall surely go into captivity forth of his land.

---

[l]2 Kings xiv. 23——[m]Chapter ii. 12——[n]1 Kings xii. 32; xiii. 1——[o]Or, *sanctuary*——[p]Hebrew, *house of the kingdom*——[q]1 Kings xx. 35; 2 Kings ii. 5; iv. 38; vi. 1——[r]Chap. i. 1; Zechariah xiii. 5——[s]Or, *wild figs*——[t]Hebrew, *from behind*——[u]Ezekiel xxi. 2; Micah ii. 6——[v]See Jeremiah xxviii. 12; xxix. 21, 25, 31, 32——[w]Isa. xiii. 16; Lam. v. 11; Hos. iv. 13; Zech. ix. 2

Amos hath conspired against thee] This was truly a *lying* prophet; there is not one word of truth in this message which he sent to Jeroboam. Amos had not conspired against the king—had not said that Jeroboam should die by the sword—and had not said that Israel should be carried away captive, though this last was implied in God's threatenings, and afterwards delivered by this prophet; see ver. 17.

Verse 12. *O thou seer*] He pretends kindness to the prophet, and counsels him to go into Judea, and prophesy there and be safe, even in the time that he had accused him of *high treason* against Jeroboam. Hireling priests of this kind have ever been the great enemies of the true prophets of God; and when they could bring no charge of false doctrine or immorality against them, have accused them of conspiring against the government; and because they have preached against *sin*, have held them up as exciting insurrection among the people.

Verse 13. *But prophesy not—at Beth-el*] He must not speak against idolatry, because that was the king's religion; and he who speaks against the king's religion must be an enemy to the state. This was the doctrine held in England by popish James II. and his insidious Jesuit hireling priests, till God in his mercy put this pitiful tyrant down, and with him his false prophets, and the degrading superstition which they endeavoured to establish in these lands.

Verse 14. *I* was *no prophet*] I am an extraordinary messenger of God. I am not called to the prophetic office but for *this occasion*. I have no message to *Judah*, and therefore need not go there. I have a message to *Israel* alone, and I must faithfully deliver it.

For the account which Amos gives here of himself, see the *introduction*.

Verse 16. *Now therefore hear thou the word of the Lord*] While he was speaking in his own vindication, God seems to have inspired him with the awful prediction which he immediately delivers.

Verse 17. *Thy wife shall be a harlot*] As this was *the word of the Lord*, so it was fulfilled; but as we have no farther account of this idolatrous priest, so we cannot tell in what circumstances these threatenings were executed. 1. His wife was to be a public prostitute; she was probably such already privately in the temple, as the wife of an idolatrous priest. 2. His sons and daughters were to fall by the sword. 3. Their *inheritance* was to be taken by strangers. 4. And himself was to die a captive in a heathen land.

Israel shall surely go into captivity] He now declares fully what he had not declared before, though Amaziah had made it a subject of accusation. This particular was probably revealed at this instant, as well as those which concerned Amaziah and his family.

CHAPTER VIII

This chapter begins with a fourth vision denoting the certainty and nearness of the destruction of Israel, 1–3. *The prophet then proceeds to reprove their oppression and injustice,* 4–7. *Strong and beautiful figures, by which is represented the complete dissolution of the Israelitish polity,* 8–10. *The people threatened with a most awful judgment; a* FAMINE *of the word of God,* 11–14.

A. M. cir. 3217
B. C. cir. 787
Ante U. C. 34
Amulii Sylvii,
R. Alban.,
cir. annum 10

THUS hath the Lord GOD
showed unto me: and be-
hold a basket of summer fruit.
2 And he said, Amos, what
seest thou? And I said, A basket of summer
fruit. Then said the LORD unto me, [a]The
end is come upon my people of Israel; [b]I
will not again pass by them any more.
3 And [c]the songs of the temple [d]shall be
howlings in that day, saith the Lord GOD:
there shall be many dead bodies in every
place; [e]they shall cast *them* forth [f]with
silence.
4 Hear this, O ye that [g]swallow up the
needy, even to make the poor
of the land to fail,
5 Saying, When will the [h]new
moon be gone, that we may sell
corn? and [i]the Sabbath, that we may [k]set
forth wheat, [l]making the ephah small, and the
shekel great, and [m]falsifying the balances by
deceit?
6 That we may buy the poor for [n]silver,
and the needy for a pair of shoes; *yea,* and
sell the refuse of the wheat?
7 The LORD hath sworn by [o]the excellency
of Jacob, Surely [p]I will never forget any of
their works.

[a]Ezek. vii. 2——[b]Chap. vii. 8——[c]Chap. v. 23——[d]Heb. *shall howl*——[e]Chap. vi. 9, 10——[f]Heb. *be silent*——[g]Psa. xiv. 4; Prov. xxx. 14——[h]Or, *month*

[i]Neh. xiii. 15, 16——[k]Heb. *open*——[l]Mic. vi. 10, 11——[m]Heb. *perverting the balances of deceit;* Hos. xii. 7——[n]Chap. ii. 6——[o]Chap. vi. 8——[p]Hos. viii. 13; ix. 9

NOTES ON CHAP. VIII

Verse 1. *A basket of summer fruit.*] As summer fruit was not proper for *preserving*, but must be eaten as soon as gathered, so the Lord intimates by this symbol that the kingdom of Israel was now *ripe* for destruction, and that punishment must descend upon it without delay. Some think the prophet means the fruits at the end of *autumn*. And as *after the autumn* no fruit could be expected, so Israel's summer is gone by, her autumn is ended, and she shall yield no more fruit. Or, the autumn of her iniquity is come; the measure is filled up, and now she shall gather the *fruit* of her sin in the abundance of her punishment.

Verse 2. *A basket of summer fruit*] כלוב קיץ *kelub kayits; the end is come*—בא הקץ *ba hakkets:* here is a paronomasia or play upon the words *kayits, summer fruit,* and *kets, the end,* both coming from similar roots. See the note on Ezek. vii. 2, where there is a similar play on the same word.

I will not again pass by them any more.] I will be no longer their Guardian.

Verse 3. *The songs of the temple*] Instead of שירות *shiroth, songs, Houbigant* reads שורות *shoroth,* the *singing women;* and *Newcome* follows him: "And the singing women of the palace shall howl in that day." Instead of joyous songs, they shall have nothing but lamentation.

They shall cast them *forth with silence.*] Every place shall be filled with the dead, and a dreadful silence shall reign universally; the few that remain being afraid either to speak or complain, or even to chant a funeral dirge for the most respectable of the dead.

Verse 4. *Hear this, O ye that swallow up the needy*] Ye that *bruise* the poor; exact from them, and *tread them under foot.*

Verse 5. *When will the new moon be gone*] This was kept as a kind of *holy day,* not by Divine command, but by *custom.* The *Sabbath* was strictly holy; and yet so covetous were they that they grudged to give to God and their own souls this seventh portion of time! But bad and execrable as *they* were, they neither *set forth their corn,* nor *their wheat,* nor *any other kind of merchandise,* on the *Sabbath.* They were *saints* then, when compared to multitudes called *Christians,* who keep their shops either *partially* or *entirely open* on the Lord's day, and *buy* and *sell* without any scruples of conscience. Conscience! alas! they have *none;* it is seared as with a hot iron. The strong man armed, in them, is quiet, for all his goods are in peace.

Making the ephah small, and the shekel great] Giving *short measure,* and taking *full price;* or, buying with a *heavy weight,* and selling with one that was *light.*

Falsifying the balances] Having *one scale light,* and the *other weighty; one end* of the *beam long,* and the *other short.* A few months ago I detected a knave with such balances; with a slip of his finger along the beam he altered the *centre,* which made *three ounces short weight in every pound.* He did it so dexterously, that though I knew he was cheating, or, as the prophet expresses it, was *falsifying the balances by deceit,* it was some time before I could detect the fraud, and not till I had been several times cheated by this accomplished knave. So we find that though the knaves of ancient Israel are dead, they have left their successors behind them.

Verse 6. *That we may buy the poor for silver*] Buying their services for such a time, with just money enough to clear them from other creditors.

And the needy for a pair of shoes] See on chap. ii. 6.

And sell the refuse of the wheat?] Selling bad wheat and damaged flour to poor people as good, knowing that such cannot afford to prosecute them.

Verse 7. *By the excellency of Jacob*] By the *state of eminence* to which he had raised the descendants of Jacob; or, by the *excellent* ONE *of Jacob,* that is, HIMSELF. The meaning is: "As surely as I have raised you to such a state of eminence, so surely will I punish you in proportion to your advantages and your crimes."

A. M. cir. 3217
B. C. cir. 787
Ante U. C. 34
Amulii Sylvii,
R. Alban.,
cir. annum 10

8 [q]Shall not the land tremble for this, and every one mourn that dwelleth therein? and it shall rise up wholly as a flood; and it shall be cast out and drowned, [r]as *by* the flood of Egypt.

9 And it shall come to pass in that day, saith the Lord GOD, [s]that I will cause the sun to go down at noon, and I will darken the earth in the clear day:

10 [t]And I will turn your feasts into mourning, and all your songs into lamentations; [u]and I will bring up sackcloth upon all loins, and baldness upon every head; [v]and I will make it as the mourning of an only *son*, and the end thereof as a bitter day.

11 Behold, the days come, saith the Lord GOD, that I will send a famine in the land, not a famine of bread, nor a thirst for water, but [w]of hearing the words of the LORD:

A. M. cir. 3217
B. C. cir. 787
Ante U. C. 34
Amulii Sylvii,
R. Alban.,
cir. annum 10

12 And they shall wander from sea to sea, and from the north even to the east, they shall run to and fro to seek the word of the LORD, and shall not find *it*.

13 In that day shall the fair virgins and young men faint for thirst.

14 They that [x]swear by [y]the sin of Samaria, and say, Thy god, O Dan, liveth; and, The [z]manner [a]of Beer-sheba liveth; even they shall fall, and never rise up again.

---

[q]Hos. iv. 3——[r]Chap. ix. 5——[s]Job v. 14; Isa. xiii. 10; lix. 9, 10; Jer. xv. 9; Mic. iii. 6——[t]Isa. i. 14; Tob. ii. 6——[u]Isa. xv. 2, 3; Jer. xlviii. 37; Ezek. vii. 18; xxvii. 31

[v]Jer. vi. 26; Zech. xii. 10——[w]1 Sam. iii. 1; Psa. lxxiv. 9; Ezek. vii. 26——[x]Hos. iv. 15——[y]Deut. ix. 2 [z]Heb. *way;* see Acts ix. 2; xviii. 25; xix. 9, 23; xxiv. 14——[a]Chap. v. 5

Verse 8. *Shall not the land tremble for this*] It is supposed that an *earthquake* is here intended, and that the *rising up* and *subsiding as a flood* refers to that *heaving motion* that takes place in an earthquake, and which the prophet here compares to the *overflowing* and *subsiding* of the *waters of the Nile.* But it may refer to commotions among the people.

Verse 9. *I will cause the sun to go down at noon*] This may either refer to that *darkness* which often precedes and accompanies *earthquakes*, or to an *eclipse*. Abp. *Usher* has shown that about eleven years after Amos prophesied there were two great *eclipses of the sun;* one at the *feast of tabernacles*, and the other some time before the *passover*. The prophet may refer to the darkness occasioned by those eclipses; yet I rather think the whole may refer to the *earthquake*.

Verse 10. *I will turn your feasts into mourning*] See on ver. 3.

A bitter day.] A time of grievous calamity.

Verse 11. *A famine in the land*] The most grievous of all famines, a famine of *the words of Jehovah;* a time in which no prophet should appear, no spiritual counsellor, no faithful reprover, none any longer who would point out the way of salvation, or would assure them of the mercy of God on their repentance and return to him. This is the severest of God's judgments on this side the worm that never dieth, and the fire that is never quenched.

Verse 12. *They shall wander from sea to sea*] From the Mediterranean to the Dead Sea or from west to east, and from north to south, *to seek the word of the Lord;* to find a prophet, or any person authorized by God to show them the end of their calamities. In this state they shall continue, because they have rejected Him who is the bread of life.

Verse 14. *By the sin of Samaria*] *Baal*, who was worshipped here.

Thy god, O Dan] The golden calf, or ox, the representative of the Egyptian god Apis, or Osiris.

The manner of Beer-sheba] The worship, or object of worship. Another of the golden calves which Jeroboam had set up there. The word דרך *derech, way*, is here taken for the *object* and *mode* of worship; see Acts xix. 9, where *way* is taken for the *creed* and *form* of Divine worship as practised by the followers of Christ, and by which they were distinguished from the Jews. See also Acts ix. 2.

CHAPTER IX

The first part of this chapter contains another vision, in which God is represented as declaring the final ruin of the kingdom of Israel, and the general dispersion of the people, 1–10. *The prophet then passes to the great blessedness of the people of God under the Gospel dispensation,* 11–15. *See* Acts xv. 15, 16.

A. M. cir. 3217
B. C. cir. 787
Ante U. C. 34
Amulii Sylvii,
R. Alban.,
cir. annum 10

I SAW the Lord standing upon
the altar: and he said, Smite
the [a]lintel of the door, that
the posts may shake: and [b]cut
[c]them in the head, all of them; and I
will slay the last of them with the sword:
[d]he that fleeth of them shall not flee away,
and he that escapeth of them shall not be
delivered.
2 [e]Though they dig into hell, thence shall
mine hand take them: [f]though they climb
up to heaven, thence will I bring them down:
3 And though they hide themselves in the
top of Carmel, I will search and take them
out thence; and though they be hid from my
sight in the bottom of the sea, thence will I
command the serpent, and he shall bite them:
4 And though they go into
captivity before their enemies,
[g]thence will I command the
sword, and it shall slay them:
and [h]I will set mine eyes upon them for evil,
and not for good.
5 And the Lord God of hosts *is* he that
toucheth the land, and it shall [i]melt, [k]and all
that dwell therein shall mourn: and it shall
rise up wholly like a flood; and shall be
drowned, as *by* the flood of Egypt.
6 *It is* he that buildeth his [l] [m] stories [n] in the
heaven, and hath founded his [o]troop in the
earth; he that [p]calleth for the waters of the
sea, and poureth them out upon the face of
the earth: [q]The Lord *is* his name.
7 *Are* ye not as children of the Ethiopians

[a]Or, *chapiter*, or *knop*——[b]Or, *wound them*——[c]Psa. lxviii. 21; Habakkuk iii. 13——[d]Chap. ii. 14——[e]Psa. cxxxix. 8, &c.——[f]Job xx. 6; Jeremiah li. 53; Obadiah 4——[g]Leviticus xxvi. 33; Deuteronomy xxviii. 65; Ezekiel v. 12——[h]Leviticus xvii. 10; Jeremiah xliv. 11——[i]Micah i. 4——[k]Chap. viii. 8——[l]Or, *spheres*——[m]Hebrew, *ascensions*——[n]Psalm civ. 3, 13——[o]Or, *bundle*——[p]Chap. v. 8——[q]Chap. iv. 13

NOTES ON CHAP. IX

Verse 1. *I saw the Lord standing upon the altar*] As this is a continuation of the preceding prophecy, the *altar* here may be one of those either at *Dan* or *Beer-sheba*.

Smite the lintel] Either the piece of timber that *binds the wall above the door*, or the *upper part* of the *door frame*, in which the *cheeks*, or side posts, are inserted, and which corresponds to the threshold, or lower part of the door frame.

And cut them in the head] Let all the lintels of all the doors of all those temples be thus cut, as a sign that the whole shall be thrown down and totally demolished. Or this may refer to their *heads—chief men*, who were principals in these transgressions. Mark their temples, their priests, their prophets, and their princes, for destruction.

He that fleeth—shall not flee away] He shall be caught before he can get out of the reach of danger.

And he that escapeth (that makes good his flight) *shall not be delivered.*] Captivity, famine, or sword, shall reach him even there.

Verse 2. *Though they dig into hell*] Though they should get into the deepest caverns; *though they climb up to heaven*—get to the most inaccessible heights; I will drag them up from the one, and pull them down from the other.

Verse 3. *Though they hide themselves*] All these are metaphorical expressions, to show the impossibility of escape.

Verse 4. *I will set mine eyes upon them for evil*] I will use that very *providence* against them which before worked for their good. Should they look upward, they shall see nothing but the terrible lightning-like eye of a sin-avenging God.

Verse 5. *The Lord God of hosts* is *he*] So powerful is he that a touch of his hand shall *melt* or dissolve *the land*, and cause all its *inhabitants to mourn*. Here is still a reference to the *earthquake*. See the note, chap. viii. 8, where the same images are used.

Verse 6. *Buildeth his stories in the heaven*] There is here an allusion to large houses, where there are *cellars*, or places dug in the ground as *repositories* for corn; *middle apartments*, or stories, for the families to live in; and the *house-top* for persons to take the air upon. There may be here a reference to the *various systems* which God has formed in illimitable space, *transcending each other*, as the *planets* do in our solar system: and thus we find Solomon speaking when addressing the Most High: "The heavens and the heaven of heavens cannot contain thee, השמים ושמי השמים *hashshamayim ushemey hashshamayim*, 1 Kings viii. 27. Six *heavens* are necessarily implied in these *three* words. According to the *points*, the *first* and *third* are in the *dual* number, and the *second* is the *contracted form* of the plural. But how many more *spheres* may be intended who can tell? There may be millions of millions of *stellar systems* in unlimited space; and then what are all these to the VAST IMMENSITY *of God!*

Hath founded his troop in the earth] אגדתו *aguddatho*, from אגד *agad*, to *bind* or *gather together*, possibly meaning the *seas* and other *collections of waters* which he has *gathered together* and *bound* by his perpetual decree, that they cannot pass; yet when *he calleth for* these very *waters*, as in the *general deluge*, he "poureth them out upon the face of the earth."

The Lord is *his name.*] This points out his *infinite essence*. But what is that essence? and what is his nature? and what his immensity and eternity? What archangel can tell?

Verse 7. *Children of the Ethiopians*] Or *Cushites*. Cush was the son of Ham, Gen. x. 6; and his descendants inhabited a part of Arabia Petræa and Arabia Felix. All this stock was universally despised. See *Bochart*.

A. M. cir. 3217
B. C. cir. 787
Ante U. C. 34
Amulii Sylvii,
R. Alban.,
cir. annum 10

unto me, O children of Israel?
saith the LORD. Have not I
brought up Israel out of the land
of Egypt? and the [r]Philistines
from [s]Caphtor, and the Syrians from [t]Kir?
8 Behold, [u]the eyes of the Lord GOD *are*
upon the sinful kingdom, and I [v]will destroy
it from off the face of the earth; saving that
I will not utterly destroy the house of Jacob,
saith the LORD.
9 For, lo, I will command, and I will [w]sift
the house of Israel among all nations, like as
corn is sifted in a sieve, yet
shall not the least [x]grain fall
upon the earth.
10 All the sinners of my people
shall die by the sword, [y]which say, The
evil shall not overtake nor prevent us.
11 [z]In that day will I raise up the tabernacle
of David that is fallen, and [a]close up
the breaches thereof; and I will raise up his
ruins, and I will build it as in the days of
old:
12 [b]That they may possess the remnant of

A. M. cir. 3217
B. C. cir. 787
Ante U. C. 34
Amulii Sylvii,
R. Alban.,
cir. annum 10

---

[r]Jer. xlvii. 4——[s]Deut. ii. 23; Jer. xlvii. 4——[t]Ch. i. 5
[u]Ver. 4——[v]Jer. xxx. 11; xxxi. 35, 36; Obad. 16, 17

[w]Heb. *cause to move*——[x]Heb. *stone*——[y]Chap. vi. 3
[z]Acts xv. 16, 17——[a]Heb. *hedge*, or *wall*——[b]Obad. 19

The Philistines from Caphtor] The island of *Crete*, the people of which were the *Cherethim*. See 1 Sam. xxx. 14; Ezek. xxv. 16; Zeph. ii. 5.

The Syrians from Kir?] Perhaps a city of the *Medes*, Isa. xxii. 6. *Aram*, from whom Syria had its name, was the son of *Shem*, Gen. x. 22. Part of his descendants settled in this city, and part in *Aram Naharaim*, "Syria of the two rivers," viz., *Mesopotamia*, included between the *Tigris* and the *Euphrates*.

The meaning of the verse is this: Do not presume on my having brought you out of the land of Egypt and house of bondage, into a land flowing with milk and honey. I have brought other nations, and some of your neighbours, who are your enemies, from comparatively barren countries, into fruitful territories; such, for instance, as the *Philistines* from *Caphtor*, and the *Syrians* from *Kir*.

Verse 8. *The eyes of the Lord God* are *upon the sinful kingdom*] The kingdom of Israel, peculiarly sinful; and therefore to be signally destroyed by the Assyrians.

I will not utterly destroy the house of Jacob] The race shall not become extinct: I will reserve them as monuments of my *justice*, and finally of my *mercy*.

Verse 9. *I will sift the house of Israel among all nations*] I will disperse them over the face of the earth; and yet I will so order it that the *good* shall not be *lost;* for though they shall be mixed among distant nations, yet there shall be a general restoration of them to their own land.

The least grain] צרור *tseror*, little stone, pebble, or gravel. Not one of them, howsoever little or contemptible, when the time comes, shall be left behind. All shall be collected in Christ, and brought into their own land.

Verse 10. *All the sinners of my people*] Those who are the boldest and most incredulous; especially they who *despise* my warnings, and *say the evil day shall not overtake nor prevent us;* they shall die by the sword. It is no evidence of a man's safety that he is *presumptuously fearless*. There is a blessing to him who *trembles at God's word*.

Verse 11. *Will I raise up the tabernacle of David*] It is well known that the *kingdom of Israel*, the most profane and idolatrous, fell first, and that the *kingdom of Judah* continued long after, and enjoyed considerable prosperity under Hezekiah and Josiah. The remnant of the Israelites that were left by the Assyrians became united to the kingdom of Judah; and of the others, many afterwards joined them: but this comparatively short prosperity and respite, previously to the Babylonish captivity, could not be *that*, as *Calmet* justly observes, which is mentioned here. This could not be called *closing up the breaches, raising up the ruins, and building it as in the days of old;* nor has any state of this kind taken place since; and, consequently, the prophecy remains to be fulfilled. It must therefore refer to *their restoration under the Gospel*, when they shall receive the Lord Jesus as their Messiah, and be by him restored to their own land. See these words quoted by James, Acts xv. 17. Then indeed it is likely that they shall possess the *remnant of Edom*, and have the whole length and breadth of Immanuel's land, ver. 12. Nor can it be supposed that the victories gained by the *Asmoneans* could be that intended by the prophet, and which he describes in such lofty terms. These victories procured only a short respite, and a very imperfect re-establishment of the tabernacle of David; and could not warrant the terms of the prediction in these verses.

Verse 12. *That they may possess the remnant of Edom*] Bp. *Newcome* translates this clause as follows: "That the residue of men may seek Jehovah, and all the heathen who are called by my name. Here, instead of אדום *Edom*, he reads אדם *Adam*, *men* or *mankind*, which is the reading of the *Arabic*, and some MSS. of the *Syriac*, and of Acts xv. 17.

The Pachomian MS. of the *Septuagint* adds here, ὅπως ἐκζητήσωσί με, *that they may seek me.* And the *Arabic* has الرب *the Lord;* and instead of יירשו *yireshu*, "they shall possess," the learned bishop seems to have read ידרשו *yidreshu*, "they may seek;" and thus the text resembles the quotation by St. James, Acts xv. 17, "That the residue of men might seek after the Lord." It is strange that not one of the MSS. collated by *Kennicott* and *De Rossi*, nor any of my *own*, favours or countenances any of these alterations. I am of opinion, therefore, that we must dismiss all these conjectural emendations, and take the *Hebrew* text as we find it. That it speaks of the *conversion of the Jews* in Gospel times, we have the authority of the New Testament as above to prove; and if

A. M. cir. 3217 B. C. cir. 787 Ante U. C. 34 Amulii Sylvii, R. Alban., cir. annum 10

[c]Edom, and of all the heathen,
[d]which are called by my name,
saith the LORD that doeth this.
13 Behold [e]the days come,
saith the LORD, that the ploughman shall
overtake the reaper, and the treader of grapes
him that [f]soweth seed; [g]and the mountains
shall drop [h]sweet wine, and all the hills shall
melt.
14 [i]And I will bring again the captivity of
my people of Israel, and [k]they
shall build the waste cities, and
inhabit *them;* and they shall
plant vineyards, and drink the
wine thereof; they shall also make gardens,
and eat the fruit of them.
15 And I will plant them upon their land,
and [l]they shall no more be pulled up out of
their land which I have given them, saith the
LORD thy God.

[c]Num. xxiv. 18——[d]Heb. *upon whom my name is called*——[e]Lev. xxvi. 5——[f]Heb. *draweth forth*——[g]Joel iii. 18——[h]Or, *new wine*

[i]Jer. xxx. 3——[k]Isa. lxi. 4; lxv. 21; Ezek. xxxvi. 33-36——[l]Isa. lx. 21; Jer. xxxii. 41; Ezek. xxxiv. 28; Joel iii. 20

we cannot make the *words*, as they stand *there*, *entirely* to agree with the words here, the *subject* is not affected by it. The Jews shall *be converted and restored*, and this text in both covenants is a proof of it.

Verse 13. *The ploughman shall overtake the reaper*] All the seasons shall succeed in due and natural order: but the crops shall be so copious in the fields and in the vineyards, that a long time shall be employed in gathering and disposing of them; so that the seasons of *ploughing, sowing, gathering the grapes, treading the wine-press*, &c., *shall press on the heels of each other;* so *vast* will be the abundance, and so *long* the time necessary to *gather* and *cure* the *grain* and *fruits.* We are informed by travellers in the Holy Land, Barbary, &c., that the vintage at Aleppo lasts from the *fifteenth* of September to the middle of November; and that the sowing season begins at the close of October, and lasts through all November. Here, then, the ploughman, sower, grape-gatherer, and operator at the wine-press, not only succeed each other, but have parts of these operations *going on at the same time.* But great fertility in the land, abundance in the crops, and regularity of the seasons, seem to be the things which the prophet especially predicts. These are all *poetical* and *prophetical* images, by which happy *times* are pointed out.

Verse 14. *They shall plant vineyards, and drink the wine*] When threatened with *great evils*, chap. v. 11, it is said, "They shall plant pleasant vineyards but shall not drink the wine of them." *Previously* to their *restoration*, they shall labour for *others; after* their restoration, they shall labour for *themselves.*

Verse 15. *I will plant them upon their land*] They shall receive a permanent establishment there.

And they shall no more be pulled up] Most certainly this prophecy has never yet been fulfilled. They were *pulled out* by the *Assyrian captivity*, and by that of *Babylon.* Many were *planted in again*, and again *pulled out* by the *Roman conquest* and *captivity*, and were *never since planted in*, but are now *scattered* among all the nations of the earth. I conclude, as the word of God cannot fail, and this has not yet been fulfilled, it therefore follows that it will and must be fulfilled to the fulness of its spirit and intention. And this is established by the conclusion: "Saith the Lord thy God." He is JEHOVAH, and cannot fail; he is THY GOD, and will do it. He *can* do it, because he is JEHOVAH; and he *will* do it, because he is THY GOD. Amen.

THE BOOK

OF THE

PROPHET OBADIAH

Chronological Notes relative to this book, upon the supposition that it was written about five hundred and eighty-seven *years before the commencement of the Christian era*

Year from the Creation, according to Archbishop Usher, 3417.—Year of the Jewish era of the world, 3174.—Year since the Flood, 1761.—Year from the vocation of Abram, 1335.—Year from the foundation of Solomon's temple, 425. Year since the division of Solomon's monarchy into the kingdoms of Israel and Judah, 389.—Year of the era of Iphitus, 298.—Second year of the *forty-eighth* Olympiad.—Year from the building of Rome, according to the Varronian or generally received computation, 167.—Year from the building of Rome, according to the Fasti Consulares, 166.—Year from the building of Rome, according to Polybius the historian, 165.—Year from the building of Rome, according to Fabius Pictor, 161.—Year since the overthrow of the kingdom of Israel by Shalmaneser, king of Assyria, 135.—Year since the destruction of the kingdom of Judah by Nebuchadnezzar, king of Babylon, 2.—Year of the Julian Period, 4127.—Year of the era of Nabonassar, 161.—Year before the birth of Christ, 583.—Year before the vulgar era of Christ's nativity, 587.—Cycle of the Sun, 11.—Cycle of the Moon, 4.—Thirtieth year of Tarquinius Priscus, the fifth king of the Romans.—Thirty-ninth year of Cyaraxes or Cyaxares, the fourth king of Media.—Nineteenth year of Agasicles, king of Lacedæmon of the family of the Proclidæ.—Twenty-first year of Leon, king of Lacedæmon, of the family of the Eurysthenidæ.—Thirty-third year of Alyattes II., king of Lydia.—Sixteenth year of Æropas, the seventh king of Macedon.—Eighth year of Apries, king of Egypt; the same with the celebrated Pharaoh-hophrah.—Ninth year of Baal, king of the Tyrians.—Twentieth year of Nebuchadnezzar, king of Babylon.

OBADIAH

God is here represented as summoning the nations against Edom, and declaring that his strongholds should not save him, 1–4; *that not a remnant, not a gleaning, should be left of him,* 5; *that the enemy would search out his people, and totally subdue them; and that none of their allies should stand by them,* 6–9. *He then enlarges on their particular offence, and threatens them with a speedy recompense,* 10–16. *The Babylonians accordingly subdued the Edomites, and expelled them from Arabia Petræa, of which they never afterwards recovered possession. The remaining verses contain a prophecy of the restoration of the Jews from the Babylonish captivity, and of their victory over all their enemies,* 17–21. *Some commentators think that these last verses were fulfilled by the conquests of the Maccabees over the Edomites. See* 1 Macc. v. 3–5, 65, &c.

A. M. cir. 3417 B. C. cir. 587 Ol. XLVIII. 2 TarquiniiPrisci, R. Roman., cir. annum 30

THE vision of Obadiah.
Thus saith the Lord GOD
[a]concerning Edom; [b]We have
heard a rumour from the LORD,
and an ambassador is sent
among the heathen, Arise ye,
and let us rise up against her in
battle.

[a]Isa. xxi. 11; xxxiv. 5; Ezek. xxv. 12, 13, 14; Joel iii. 19; Mal. i. 3——[b]Jer. xlix. 14, &c.

Who was this prophet? *where* born? of *what country?* at *what time* did he prophesy? *who* were his *parents? when* and *where* did he *die?* are questions which have been asked from the remotest antiquity; and which, to this day, have received no answer worthy of recording. There is a multitude of opinions concerning these points; and their *multitude* and *discrepancy* are the strongest proofs of their *uncertainty.* All that seems probable is, that, as he prophesied concerning the *destruction of Edom,* he flourished a little before, or a little after, the

A. M. cir. 3417
B. C. cir. 587
Ol. XLVIII. 2
TarquiniiPrisci,
R. Roman.,
cir. annum 30

2 Behold, I have made thee
small among the heathen: thou
art greatly despised.
3 The pride of thine heart hath
deceived thee, thou that dwellest in the clefts
[c]of the rock, whose habitation *is* high; [d]that
saith in his heart, Who shall bring me down
to the ground?
4 [e]Though thou exalt *thyself* as the eagle,
and though thou [f]set thy nest among the stars,
thence will I bring thee down, saith the LORD.
5 If [g]thieves came to thee, if robbers by
night, (how art thou cut off!) would they not
have stolen till they had
enough? if the grape-gatherers
came to thee, [h]would they not
leave [i]*some* grapes?
6 How are *the things* of Esau searched out!
how are his hidden things sought up!
7 All the men of thy confederacy have
brought thee *even* to the border: [k]the [l]men
that were at peace with thee have deceived
thee, *and* prevailed against thee; [m]*they
that eat* thy bread have laid a wound under
thee: [n]*there is* none understanding [o]in
him.

A. M. cir. 3417
B. C. cir. 587
Ol. XLVIII. 2
TarquiniiPrisci,
R. Roman.,
cir. annum 30

[c]2 Kings xiv. 7——[d]Isa. xiv. 13, 14, 15; Rev. xviii. 7——[e]Job xx. 6; Jer. xlix. 16; li. 53; Amos ix. 2——[f]Isa. xiv. 13; Nah. iii. 16; Hab. ii. 9——[g]Jer. xlix. 9

[h]Deut. xxiv. 21; Isa. xvii. 6; xxiv. 13——[i]Or, *gleanings*——[k]Heb. *the men of thy peace*——[l]Jer. xxxviii. 22——[m]Heb. the men *of thy bread*——[n]Isa. xix. 11, 12——[o]Or, *of it*

taking of Jerusalem by Nebuchadnezzar, which happened about *five hundred and eighty-eight* years before Christ; and the destruction of Idumea by the same monarch, which took place a short time after; probably between 588 B. C. and 575 B. C., in the interval of the *thirteen* years which Nebuchadnezzar employed in the siege of Tyre, which he undertook immediately after the capture of Jerusalem.

Obadiah foretells the subduction of the Idumeans by the Chaldeans, and finally by the Jews, whom they had used most cruelly when brought low by other enemies. These prophecies have been literally fulfilled for the Idumeans, as a nation, are totally extinct.

Whoever will be at the trouble to collate this short prophecy with the *forty-ninth* chapter of Jeremiah, will find a remarkable *similarity*, not only in the *sentiments* and *words*, but also in *whole verses*. In the above chapter Jeremiah predicts the destruction of the Idumeans. Whether he copied *Obadiah*, or *Obadiah* copied him, cannot be determined; but it would be very strange if two prophets, unacquainted with each other, should speak of the same event precisely in the same terms. See the parallel texts in the margin, and the notes on Jer. xlix. 1, &c.

NOTES ON THE BOOK OF OBADIAH

Verse 1. *We have heard a rumour*] See Jer. xlix. 14, where the same expressions are found. The prophet shows that the enemies of Idumea had confederated against it, and that Jehovah is now summoning them to march directly against it.

Verse 2. *I have made thee small among the heathen*] God ever attributes to *himself* the *rise and fall of nations*. If they be *great* and *prosperous*, it is by God's *providence;* if they be *low* and *depressed*, it is by his *justice*. Compared with the Assyrians, Chaldeans, Egyptians, Syrians, Arabs, and other neighbouring nations, the Idumeans were a small people.

Verse 3. *The pride of thine heart*] St. Jerome observes that all the southern part of Palestine, from Eleutheropolis to Petra and Aialath, was full of *caverns hewn out of the rocks*, and that the people had subterranean dwellings similar to ovens. Here they are said to *dwell in the clefts of the rock*, in reference to the caverns above mentioned. In these they conceived themselves to be *safe*, and thought that no power brought against them could dislodge them from those fastnesses. Some think that by סלע *sela*, *rock*, *Petra*, the capital of Idumea, is intended.

Verse 4. *Though thou exalt* thyself *as the eagle*] Though like this bird thou get into the *highest cliff of the highest rock*, it will not avail thee. To defend thee, when Jehovah has determined thy destruction, thy *deepest caves* and *highest rocks* will be equally useless. See Jer. xlix. 16.

Verse 5. *If thieves came to thee*] That is, if *thieves* entered thy dwellings, they would not have taken every thing; they would have laid hold on thy wealth; and carried off as much as they could escape with conveniently; if *grape-gatherers* entered thy vineyards, they would not have taken *every bunch;* some *gleanings* would have been left. But the Chaldeans have stripped thee bare; they *have searched out all thy hidden things*, ver. 6, they have left thee nothing. *How art thou cut off!* Thou art totally and irretrievably ruined! The prophet speaks of this desolation as if it had *already taken place*.

Verse 7. *All the men of thy confederacy*] The Chaldeans are here intended, to whom the Idumeans were attached, and whose agents they became in exercising cruelties upon the Jews.

Have brought thee even *to the border*] Have hemmed thee in on every side, and reduced thee to distress. Or, they have driven thee to thy border; cast thee out of thy own land into the hands of thine enemies.

The men that were at peace with thee] The men of *thy covenant*, with whom thou hadst made a *league*.

That eat *thy bread*] That professed to be thy *firmest friends*, have all joined together to destroy thee.

Have laid a wound] Placed a snare or trap *under thee*. See *Newcome*.

There is *none understanding in him*.] Private counsels and public plans are all in operation against thee; and yet thou art so foolish and infatuated as not to discern thy own danger.

A. M. cir. 3417
B. C. cir. 587
Ol. XLVIII. 2
TarquiniiPrisci,
R. Roman.,
cir. annum 30

8 [p]Shall I not in that day, saith the LORD, even destroy the wise *men* out of Edom, and understanding out of the mount of Esau?

9 And thy [q]mighty *men,* O [r]Teman, shall be dismayed, to the end that every one of the mount of Esau may be cut off by slaughter.

10 For *thy* [s]violence against thy brother Jacob shame shall cover thee, and [t]thou shalt be cut off for ever.

11 In the day that thou stoodest on the other side, in the day that the strangers [u]carried away captive his forces, and foreigners entered into his gates, and [v]cast lots upon Jerusalem, even thou *wast* as one of them.

12 But [w]thou shouldest not have [x]looked on [y]the day of thy brother in the day that he became a stranger; neither shouldest thou have [z]rejoiced over the children of Judah in the day of their destruction; neither shouldest thou have [a]spoken proudly in the day of distress.

A. M. cir. 3417
B. C. cir. 587
Ol. XLVIII. 2
TarquiniiPrisci,
R. Roman.,
cir. annum 30

13 Thou shouldest not have entered into the gate of my people in the day of their calamity; yea, thou shouldest not have looked on their affliction in the day of their calamity, nor have laid *hand* on their [b]substance in the day of their calamity.

14 Neither shouldest thou have stood in the crossway, to cut off those of his that did escape; neither shouldest thou have [c]delivered up those of his that did remain in the day of distress.

15 [d]For the day of the LORD *is* near upon all the heathen: [e]as thou hast done, it shall be done unto thee: thy reward shall return upon thine own head.

16 [f]For as ye have drunk upon my holy mountain, *so* shall all the heathen drink continually, yea, they shall drink, and they shall [g]swallow down, and they shall be as though they had not been.

17 [h]But upon Mount Zion [i]shall be [k]deliverance, and [l]there shall be holiness; and the

[p]Job v. 12, 13; Isa. xxix. 14; Jer. xlix. 7——[q]Psa. lxxvi. 5; Amos ii. 16——[r]Jer. xlix. 7——[s]Gen. xxvii. 11; Psa. cxxxvii. 7; Ezek. xxv. 12; xxxv. 5; Amos i. 11——[t]Ezek. xxxv. 9; Mal. i. 4——[u]Or, *carried away his substance*——[v]Joel iii. 3; Nah. iii. 10——[w]Or, *do not behold, &c.*——[x]Psa. xxii. 17; liv. 7; lix. 10; Mic. iv. 11; vii. 10——[y]Psa. xxxvii. 13; cxxxvii. 7

[z]Job xxxi. 29; Mic. vii. 8; Prov. xvii. 5; xxiv. 17, 18——[a]Heb. *magnified thy mouth*——[b]Or, *forces*——[c]Or, *shut up;* Psa. xxxi. 8——[d]Ezek. xxx. 3; Joel iii. 14——[e]Ezek. xxxv. 15; Hab. ii. 8——[f]Jer. xxv. 28, 29; xlix. 12; Joel iii. 17; 1 Pet. iv. 17——[g]Or, *sup up*——[h]Joel ii. 32——[i]Amos ix. 8——[k]Or, *they that escape*——[l]Or, *it shall be holy;* Joel iii. 17

Verse 8. *Shall I not—destroy the wise* men] It appears, from Jer. xlix. 7, that the Edomites were remarkable for wisdom, counsel, and prudence. See on the above place.

Verse 9. *Thy mighty* men, *O Teman*] This was one of the strongest places in Idumea; and is put here, as in Amos i. 2, and elsewhere, for *Idumea* itself.

Mount of Esau] Mount *Seir.*

Verse 10. *For* thy *violence against thy brother Jacob*] By this term the *Israelites* in general are understood; for the *two* brothers,—*Jacob*, from whom sprang the *Jews*, and *Esau*, from whom sprang the *Idumeans* or *Edomites*,—are here put for the *whole people* or descendants of both. We need not look for particular cases of the *violence* of the Edomites against the Jews. *Esau,* their founder, was not more inimical to his brother *Jacob*, who deprived him of his birthright, than the *Edomites* uniformly were to the *Jews.* See 2 Chron. xxviii. 17, 18. They had even stimulated the Chaldeans, when they took Jerusalem, to destroy the temple, and level it with the ground. See Psa. cxxxvii. 7.

Verse 11. *Thou stoodest on the other side*] Thou not only didst not help thy brother when thou mightest, but thou didst assist his foes against him.

And cast lots] When the Chaldeans cast lots on the spoils of Jerusalem, thou didst come in for a share of the booty; "thou wast as one of them."

Verse 12. *Thou shouldest not have looked*] It shows a malevolent heart to rejoice in the miseries of those who have acted unkindly or wickedly towards us. The Edomites triumphed when they saw the judgments of God fall upon the Jews. This the Lord severely reprehends in verses 12-15. If a man have acted cruelly towards us, and God punish him for this cruelty, and we rejoice in it, we make his crime our own; and then, as we have done, so shall it be done unto us; see ver. 15. All these verses point out the part the Edomites took against the Jews when the Chaldeans besieged and took Jerusalem, destroyed the temple, and divided the spoils.

Verse 14. *Neither shouldest thou have stood in the crossway*] They are represented here as having stood in the *passes* and *defiles* to prevent the poor Jews from escaping from the Chaldeans. By *stopping these passes,* they threw the poor fugitives back into the teeth of their enemies. They had gone so far in this systematic cruelty as to deliver up the few that had taken refuge among them.

Verse 15. *The day of the Lord* is *near*] God will not associate thee with him in the judgments which he inflicts. *Thou* also art *guilty*, and shalt have *thy punishment* in due course with the other sinful nations.

Verse 16. *For as ye have drunk*] This address is to the *Jews.* As ye have been visited and punished upon my holy mountain in Jerusalem, so shall other nations be punished in their respective countries. See Jer. xlix. 12.

Verse 17. *But upon Mount Zion shall be de-*

A. M. cir. 3417 B. C. cir. 587 house of Jacob shall possess
Ol. XLVIII. 2 their possessions.
TarquiniiPrisci, R. Roman., 18 And the house of Jacob
cir. annum 30 [m]shall be a fire, and the house
of Joseph a flame, and the house of Esau
for stubble, and they shall kindle in them,
and devour them; and there shall not be *any*
remaining of the house of Esau; for the
LORD hath spoken *it*.
19 And *they of* the south [n]shall possess the
mount of Esau; [o]and *they of* the plain the
Philistines: and they shall possess the fields
of Ephraim, and the fields of A. M. cir. 3417 B. C. cir. 587
Samaria: and Benjamin *shall* Ol. XLVIII. 2
possess Gilead. TarquiniiPrisci, R. Roman.,
20 And the captivity of this cir. annum 30
host of the children of Israel *shall possess*
that of the Canaanites, *even* [p]unto Zarephath;
and the captivity of Jerusalem, [q]which *is* in
Sepharad, [r]shall possess the cities of the
south.
21 And [s]saviours shall come up on Mount
Zion to judge the mount of Esau; and the
[t]kingdom shall be the LORD'S.

[m]Isa. x. 17; Zech. xii. 6——[n]Amos ix. 12——[o]Zeph. ii. 7——[p]1 Kings xvii. 9, 10——[q]Or, shall possess *that which* is *in Sepharad*

[r]Jer. xxxii. 44——[s]1 Tim. iv. 16; James v. 20——[t]Psa. xxii. 28; Dan. ii. 44; vii. 14, 27; Zech. xiv. 9; Luke i. 33; Rev. xi. 15; xix. 6

liverance] Here is a promise of the return from the Babylonish captivity. They shall come to *Zion*, and there they shall *find safety;* and it is remarkable that after their return they were greatly befriended by the Persian kings, and by Alexander the Great and his successors; so that, whilst they ravaged the neighbouring nations, the Jews were unmolested. See *Calmet*.

And there shall be holiness] They shall return to God, separate themselves from their idols, and become a better people than they were when God permitted them to be carried into captivity.

The house of Jacob shall possess] They were restored to their former possessions. But this may refer also to their future restoration under the Gospel, when they shall be truly converted, and become holiness to the Lord; for *salvation* and *holiness* shall be the characteristics of *Zion*—the *Christian Church*, for ever.

Verse 18. *The house of Jacob shall be a fire*] After their return from captivity, the *Jews*, called here the *house of Jacob* and the *house of Joseph*, did break out as a flame upon the Idumeans; they reduced them into slavery; and obliged them to receive circumcision, and practise the rites of the Jewish religion. See 1 Macc. v. 3, &c.; 2 Macc. x. 15-23; and *Joseph.* Antiq., lib. xiii. c. 17.

There shall not be any *remaining*] As a *people* and a *nation* they shall be totally destroyed. This is the meaning; it does not signify that *every individual* shall be destroyed.

Verse 19. They of *the south*] The Jews who possessed the *southern* part of *Palestine*, should render themselves masters of the mountains of Idumea which were contiguous to them.

They of *the plain*] From Eleutheropolis to the Mediterranean Sea. In this and the following verse the prophet shows the different districts which should be occupied by the Israelites after their return from Babylon.

The fields of Samaria] Alexander the Great gave Samaria to the Jews; and John Hyrcanus subdued the same country after his wars with the Syrians. See *Josephus*, contra. App. lib. ii., and Antiq. lib. xiii., c. 18.

Benjamin shall possess *Gilead.*] *Edom* lay to the *south;* the *Philistines* to the *west; Ephraim* to the *north;* and *Gilead* to the *east.* Those who returned from Babylon were to extend themselves everywhere. See *Newcome;* and see, for the fulfilment, 1 Macc. v. 9, 35, 45; and ix. 35, 36.

Verse 20. *Zarephath*] Sarepta, a city of the Sidonians, 1 Kings xvii. 9. That is, they should possess the whole city of *Phœnicia*, called here that of the *Canaanites.*

Which is *in Sepharad*] This is a difficult word. Some think the *Bosphorus* is meant; others, *Spain;* others, *France;* others, the *Euphrates;* others, some district in *Chaldea;* for there was a city called *Siphora*, in *Mesopotamia*, above the division of the Euphrates. Dr. *Lightfoot* says it was a part of *Edom.* Those who were captives among the Canaanites should possess the country of the *Canaanites;* and those whom the *Edomites* had enslaved should possess the cities of their masters. See *Newcome* and *Lowth.*

Verse 21. *And saviours shall come up*] Certain persons whom God may choose to be *deliverers* of his people; such as *Zerubbabel, Ezra, Nehemiah*, and the *Maccabees.*

Some think these *saviours*, מושיעים *moshiim*, mean the *apostles* of our Lord. Several MSS. have מושעים *mushaim*, the *preserved;* those *that are saved*, i. e., they who were *delivered* from the captivity; and *those of Mount Zion* shall *judge*, that is, shall *execute judgment* on the Edomites. And as the Asmonean princes joined the *priesthood* to the *state*, it might be what the prophet means when he says, "the kingdom shall be the Lord's," the high priest having both the *civil* and *ecclesiastical power* in his own hands. And these actually were masters of Edom, and judged and *governed* the *mountain of Esau.* And thus this prophecy appears to have had a very literal fulfilment.

But if we take the whole as referring to the *times of the Gospel*, which I believe is not its *primary* sense, it may signify the conversion and restoration of the Jews, and that under JESUS CHRIST the original *theocracy* shall be restored; and thus, once more, in the promised land, it may be said,—

והיתה ליהוה המלוכה

hammeluchah laihovah vehayethah.

"And the kingdom shall belong to Jehovah."

INTRODUCTION TO THE BOOK

OF THE

PROPHET JONAH

JONAH, the son of Amittai, the *fifth* of the minor prophets, was a Galilean, a native of Gath-hepher, which is believed to be the same as Jotapata, celebrated for the siege which Josephus the historian there maintained against the Roman army, a little before the destruction of Jerusalem. Gath-hepher was situated in the land of Zebulon, where was the canton of Ophir or Hepher. St. Jerome places it *two* miles from Sepphoris, in the way towards Tiberias. Some rabbins are of opinion that Jonah was the widow of Sarepta's son, restored to life by Elijah.

What we know with certainty of Jonah is, that God having commanded him to go to Nineveh, and there proclaim that the cry of the inhabitants' sins was come up to heaven, and they were threatened with approaching ruin; instead of obeying these orders, he resolved to flee away, and go to Tarsus in Cilicia. For this purpose he embarked at Joppa; but the Lord having sent a violent tempest while he was upon the sea, the mariners, with great fear, cried each of them to his god. In the meantime Jonah slept in the hold; whereupon the pilot wakened him; and they who were in the ship cast lots to know how this tempest was occasioned. The lot falling upon Jonah, they asked him who he was, and what he had done to bring upon them such a storm? He told them he was a Hebrew; that he worshipped the God of heaven; was one of his prophets; and fled from his presence to avoid going to Nineveh, whither he was sent. They asked him what was to be done to secure them from shipwreck? He replied: Throw me into the sea, and the tempest will cease.

God prepared a great fish to swallow up Jonah. This fish, according to some, was a whale; or, as others say, the lamia, *canis carcharias*, or the sea-dog. The prophet continued in the fish *three* days and *three* nights. He cried unto the Lord, and the Lord heard him, and commanded the fish to cast him upon the shore, as it is believed, at the foot of a mountain which projects a great way into the sea, between Berytus and Tripoli. Others think it was upon the coast of Cilicia, *two* leagues north from Alexandretta.

After this the word of the Lord came a second time to Jonah, and directed him to go to Nineveh. When he came into the city, which was three days' journey in extent, about twenty-five leagues in circumference, Jonah walked up and down a whole day, crying out, "In forty days Nineveh shall be destroyed." The Ninevites believed his word; they appointed a public fast to be observed; and, from the meanest of the people to the greatest, covered themselves with sackcloth. The king of Nineveh, supposed to have been *Sardanapalus*, known in profane authors by the name of *Anacyndaraxa* or *Anabaxarus*, descended from his throne, and covered himself with sackcloth, and sat down upon ashes. God suffered himself to be moved with their repentance, and did not execute the sentence which he had pronounced against them.

Jonah was afflicted at this; and complained to God, saying, that he had always questioned whether, as being a God of clemency and mercy, he would not be flexible to their prayers.

After this, in all probability, Jonah returned from Nineveh into Judea.

The Greeks have for a long time expressed their veneration for Jonah. There was a church dedicated to this prophet in the sixth age.

We do not know when it was that Jonah foretold how Jeroboam II., king of Israel, should restore the kingdom of Samaria to its former extent, from the entrance of Hamath to the Dead Sea. Whether this was before or after his going to Nineveh, we cannot tell.

Our Saviour makes frequent mention of Jonah in the Gospels. He says that the Ninevites shall one day rise in judgment against the Jews, and condemn them, because they repented at the preaching of Jonah, and the Jews would not hearken to Him who was greater than Jonah. And when the Pharisees required a sign of him to prove his mission, he said he would give them no other than that of the prophet Jonah, that is to say, of his resurrection, which would complete all his miracles, and render the Jews inexcusable in their hardness of heart. For a discussion of the question concerning the *three days and three nights* which Jonah lay in the belly of the fish, see Matt. xii. 40, and the notes there. And for Oriental and Jewish *legends* and *fabulous relations* relative to the history of this prophet, see *Calmet* in his preface to this book.

That there are *difficulties* in this book every man must allow; and that learned men have differed greatly in their mode of interpreting the book, and explaining these difficulties, is well known. Some have considered it an *allegory;* referring entirely to Manasseh, and what was done *before, during*, and *after* the war with Esar-haddon, king of Assyria. Manasseh being taken prisoner by the Assyrians, and thrust into a *dungeon;* where, having lain *three days and three nights*, on his earnest prayer to God in the dungeon, he was delivered, &c. Others have thought, that instead of a *fish*, a *ship* is meant, which had the image of a *whale* on the *stern*, and might be called Κητος, or the *whale*. Others have thought that the whole of the account of Jonah's being swallowed by a great fish, his praying in its belly, and being cast on dry land, was a *dream* which he had while *fast asleep* in the ship. See chap. i. 5. And others state that the whole book is a *parable*, intending to point out God's *justice* and *mercy*, and how prevalent *repentance* is to turn aside the threatened stroke of Divine wrath.

There is a *fable*, most probably of Phœnician origin, which, bearing some similitude to the history of Jonah, may have been taken from this book. Laomedon, king of Troy, having displeased Neptune, to appease him, was required to expose his daughter *Hesione* to be devoured by a *sea-monster*. She was chained to a rock, and was awaiting her fate at the next flux of the tide. In the interim *Hercules* slew the sea-monster, and delivered the princess. To this *Lycophron*, in his *Cassandra*, ver. 33, &c., is supposed to allude:—

Τριεσπερου λεοντος, ὁν ποτε γναθοις
Τριτωνος ημαλαψε καρχαρος κυων.

"Of the lion the offspring of three nights, which the fierce dog of Triton swallowed down greedily."

The scholiasts explain this in the following manner: While the princess was standing chained to the rock, expecting the greedy dog (καρχαρος κυων, the *shark*) to come and devour her, Hercules stood by ready armed; and when the monster came forward with open mouth, he jumped directly down his throat, and spent *three days* in cutting and hacking his entrails; and afterwards *came out of the monster*, with the loss of all the hair on his head. *Cyril*, in his comment, says this was occasioned by the *incredible heat* of the *monster's stomach*.

This *fable* might have been easily taken from the *true history;* though some have been ready enough to intimate that the history of the prophet was taken from the *fable*.

The appeal made to the *main facts* of this history by our Lord, proves that we are to admit of no *allegorical* exposition of these facts. 1. There was such a person as Jonah. 2. He was swallowed by a sea-monster, in whose belly he was miraculously preserved three days and three nights. 3. This same prophet preached to the Ninevites; and they repented, and turned from their sins, under his ministry. This testimony puts an end to all mythological, allegorical, and hypothetical interpretations of those great facts. And in its literal sense alone, I undertake the interpretation of this book.

THE BOOK
OF THE
PROPHET JONAH

Chronological Notes relative to this Book, upon the supposition that the repentance of the Ninevites happened in the twenty-third year of the reign of Jehu, king of Israel

Year from the Creation, according to Archbishop Usher, 3142.—Year of the Julian Period, 3852.—Year since the Flood, 1486.—Year from the foundation of Solomon's temple, 150.—Year since the division of Solomon's monarchy into the kingdoms of Israel and Judah, 114.—Year before the *first* Olympiad, 86.—Year before the building of Rome, according to the Varronian computation, 109.—Year before the birth of Jesus Christ, 858.—Year before the vulgar era of Christ's nativity, 862.—Twelfth year of Charilaus, king of Lacedæmon, of the family of the Proclidæ.—Fifty-second year of Archelaus, king of Lacedæmon, of the family of the Eurysthenidæ.—Second year of Phereclus, perpetual archon of the Athenians.—Fourteenth year of Alladius Sylvius, king of the Albans.—Twenty-third year of Jehu, king of Israel.—Seventeenth year of Joash, king of Judah.

CHAPTER I

Jonah, sent to Nineveh, flees to Tarshish, 1–3. *He is overtaken by a great tempest,* 4–14; *thrown into the sea,* 15, 16; *and swallowed by a fish, in the belly of which he is miraculously preserved alive three days and three nights,* 17.

A. M. cir. 3142
B. C. cir. 862
Ante U. C. 109
Alladii Sylvii,
R. Alban.,
cir. annum 14

NOW the word of the LORD
came unto [a]Jonah [b]the son
of Amittai, saying,
2 Arise, go to Nineveh, that
[c]great city, and cry against it;
for [d]their wickedness is come
up before me.
3 But Jonah [e]rose up to flee

[a]2 Kings xiv. 25.—[b]Called, Matt. xii. 39, *Jonas*.—[c]Gen. x. 11, 12; chap. iii. 2, 3; iv. 11.—[d]Gen. xviii. 20, 21; Ezra ix. 6; James v. 4; Rev. xviii. 5.—[e]Chap. iv. 2

NOTES ON CHAP. I

Verse 1. *Now the word of the Lord came unto Jonah*] All that is certainly known about this prophet has already been laid before the reader. He was of Gath-hepher, in the tribe of Zebulun, in lower Galilee, Josh. xix. 13; and he prophesied in the reigns of Jeroboam the Second, and Joash, kings of Israel. Jeroboam came to the throne *eight hundred and twenty-three* years before the Christian era, and reigned in Samaria *forty-one* years, 2 Kings xiv. 23-25. As a prophet, it is likely that he had but this one mission.

Verse 2. *Go to Nineveh*] This was the capital of the Assyrian empire, and one of the most *ancient* cities of the world, Gen. x. 10; and one of the *largest*, as it was *three days' journey in circumference.* Ancient writers represent it as *oblong;* being in length *one hundred and fifty* stadia, and *ninety* in breadth, the compass being *four hundred and eighty* stadia. Now as the *stadium* is allowed to have been equal to our *furlong*, eight of which make a mile, this amounts to *fifty-four* English miles: see on chap. iii. 3. But we must not suppose that all this *space* was covered with compact streets and buildings; it took in a considerable space of country, probably all the cultivated ground necessary to support all the inhabitants of that district. *Calmet* computes the measurement of the circumference to be equal to *twenty-five* French leagues. It is reported to have had walls *one hundred feet high*, and so *broad* that *three chariots* might run abreast upon them. It was situated on the *Tigris*, or a little to the *west*, or on the west *side* of that river. It was well peopled, and had at this time *one hundred and twenty thousand* persons in it reputed to be in a state of infancy, which on a moderate computation would make the whole number *six hundred thousand* persons. But some, supposing that persons not being able to distinguish their right hand from their left must mean *children under two years* of age, and reckoning *one* such child for every *twenty* persons from that age upwards, make the population amount to *two millions five hundred thousand.* Nor can this be considered an exaggerated estimate, when we know that London, not one-tenth of the size of ancient Nineveh, contains a population of upwards of *one million.* But calcula-

A. M. cir. 3142
B. C. cir. 862
Ante U. C. 109
Alladii Sylvii,
R. Alban.,
cir. annum 14

unto [f]Tarshish from the presence of the LORD, and went
down to [g]Joppa; and he found
a ship going to Tarshish: so he
paid the fare thereof, and went down into it,
to go with them unto Tarshish [h]from the presence of the LORD.
4 But [i]the LORD [k]sent out a great wind
into the sea, and there was a mighty tempest
in the sea, so that the ship [l]was like to be
broken.
5 Then the mariners were afraid, and cried
every man unto his god, and [m]cast forth the
wares that *were* in the ship into the sea, to
lighten *it* of them. But Jonah was gone
down [n]into the sides of ship; and he lay, and
was fast asleep.

6 So the shipmaster came to
him, and said unto him, What
meanest thou, O sleeper? arise,
[o]call upon thy God, [p]if so be that
God will think upon us, that we perish
not.
7 And they said every one to his fellow,
Come, and let us [q]cast lots, that we may know
for whose cause this evil *is* upon us. So they
cast lots, and the lot fell upon Jonah.
8 Then said they unto him, [r]Tell us, we
pray thee, for whose cause this evil *is* upon
us; What *is* thine occupation? and whence
comest thou? what *is* thy country? and of
what people *art* thou?
9 And he said unto them, I *am* a Hebrew;
and I fear [s]the LORD, the God of heaven,

A. M. cir. 3142
B. C. cir. 862
Ante U. C. 109
Alladii Sylvii,
R. Alban.,
cir. annum 14

---

[f]1 Kings x. 22——[g]Josh. xix. 46; 2 Chron. ii. 16; Acts ix. 36——[h]Gen. iv. 16; Job i. 12; ii. 7——[i]Psa. cvii. 25 [k]Heb. *cast forth*——[l]Heb. *thought to be broken*——[m]So Acts xxvii. 18, 19, 38

[n]1 Samuel xxiv. 3——[o]Psa. cvii. 28——[p]Joel ii. 14 [q]Joshua vii. 14, 16; 1 Samuel x. 20, 21; xiv. 41, 42: Prov. xvi. 33; Acts i. 26——[r]Joshua vii. 19; 1 Samuel xiv. 43——[s]Or, *JEHOVAH*

---

tions of this kind, relative to matters of such remote antiquity, are generally precarious, and not very useful: and ancient authors, though the only guides, are not always safe conductors. *Mosul* is generally supposed to be the same as the ancient *Nineveh.* It is in the province of Dearbekir, on the west bank of the Tigris.

Their wickedness is come up before me.] This is a *personification* of evil. It ascends from earth to heaven; and stands before the Supreme Judge, to bear witness against its own delinquency, and that of the persons whom it has seduced.

Verse 3. *To flee unto Tarshish*] Some say *Tartessus*, in Spain, near the straits of Gibralter; others, *Tarsus*, in *Cilicia;* and others, *Taprobana*, or the island of Ceylon, formerly called Taprobah; and *Tabrobavagh* in Sanscrit, to the present day.

And went down to Joppa] This place is celebrated as that where *Andromeda*, daughter of *Cepheus*, was chained to a rock, and exposed to be devoured by a sea-monster, from which she was delivered by the valour of Perseus. It is the nearest port to Jerusalem on that side of the Mediterranean.

And he found a ship] The Phœnicians carried on a considerable trade with *Tartessus*, Ezek. xxvii. 12; and it was probably in one of their ships that Jonah *embarked.*

He paid the fare thereof] He paid for his *passage.* This shows that there was *traffic* between the two places, and that each passenger paid a stated *fare.*

From the presence of the Lord.] He considered that God was peculiarly resident in Judea; and if he got out of that land, the Lord would most probably appoint another prophet to carry the message; for Jonah appears to have considered the enterprise as difficult and dangerous, and therefore wished to avoid it.

Verse 4. *A great wind*] They were overtaken with a *storm*, which appears from the sequel to have come by the immediate direction of God.

Like to be broken] They had nearly suffered *shipwreck.*

Verse 5. *Cried every man unto his god*] The *ship's crew* were all heathens; and, it is probable, heathens who had each a different object of religious worship.

Cast forth the wares] Threw the *lading overboard* to lighten the ship, hoping the better to *ride out* the storm.

Jonah was gone down] Most probably into the *hold* or *cabin* under the deck; or where they had berths for passengers in the sides of the ship; something in the manner of our *packets.*

Was fast asleep.] Probably quite exhausted and overcome with distress, which in many cases terminates in a deep sleep. So the disciples in the garden of Gethsemane.

Verse 6. *The shipmaster*] Either the *captain* or the *pilot.*

Arise, call upon thy God] He supposed that Jonah had *his* god, as well as they had *theirs;* and that, as the danger was imminent, every man should use the influence he had, as they were all equally involved in it.

Verse 7. *Come, and let us cast lots*] This was a very ancient mode of endeavouring to find out the mind of Divine Providence; and in this case it proves that they supposed the storm to have arisen on account of some hidden crime of some person *aboard.*

A philosopher being at sea in a violent storm, when the *crew* began to call earnestly to the gods for safety, he said, "Be silent, and cease your prayers; for should the gods know that *you* are here, we shall all be lost."

The lot fell upon Jonah.] In this case God *directed the lot.*

Verse 8. *Tell us—for whose cause*] A very gentle method of bringing the charge home to himself, and the several questions here asked gave the utmost latitude to make the best of his own case.

Verse 9. *I fear the Lord*] In this Jonah was *faithful.* He gave an honest testimony concern-

A. M. cir. 3142
B. C. cir. 862
Ante U. C. 109
Alladii Sylvii,
R. Alban.,
cir. annum 14

[t]which hath made the sea and
the dry *land*.
10 Then were the men [u]exceedingly afraid, and said unto
him, Why hast thou done this? For the men
knew that he fled from the presence of the
LORD, because he had told them.
11 Then said they unto him, What shall we
do unto thee, that the sea [v]may be calm unto
us? for the sea [w]wrought, [x]and was tempestuous.
12 And he said unto them, [y]Take me
up, and cast me forth into the sea; so
shall the sea be calm unto you: for I know
that for my sake this great tempest *is* upon
you.
13 Nevertheless the men [z]rowed hard to
bring *it* to the land; [a]but they could not: for
the sea wrought, and was tempestuous against them.
14 Wherefore they cried unto
the LORD, and said, We beseech
thee, O LORD, we beseech thee, let us not
perish for this man's life, and [b]lay not upon
us innocent blood: for thou, O LORD, [c]hast
done as it pleased thee.
15 So they took up Jonah, and cast him
forth into the sea: [d]and the sea [e]ceased from
her raging.
16 Then the men [f]feared the LORD exceedingly, and [g]offered a sacrifice unto the LORD,
and made vows.
17 Now the LORD had prepared a great fish
to swallow up Jonah. And [h]Jonah was in
the [i]belly of the fish three days and three
nights.

[t]Psa. cxlvi. 6; Acts xvii. 24——[u]Heb. *with great fear*——[v]Heb. *may be silent from us*——[w]Or, *grew more and more tempestuous*——[x]Heb. *went*——[y]John xi. 50——[z]Heb. *digged*——[a]Prov. xxi. 30——[b]Deut. xxi. 8

[c]Psa. cxv. 3——[d]Psa. lxxxix. 9; Luke viii. 24——[e]Heb. *stood*——[f]Mark iv. 41; Acts v. 11——[g]Heb. *sacrificed a sacrifice unto the LORD, and vowed vows*——[h]Matt. xii. 40; xvi. 4; Luke xi. 30——[i]Heb. *bowels*

ing the God he served, which placed him before the eyes of the sailors as infinitely higher than the objects of their adoration; for the God of Jonah *was the God of heaven, who made the sea and the dry land*, and governed both. He also honestly told them that he was *fleeing from the presence of this God*, whose honourable call he had refused to obey. See ver. 10.

Verse 11. *What shall we do unto thee*] In these poor men there was an uncommon degree of *humanity* and *tender feeling*.

Verse 12. *I know that for my sake*] I am not worthy to live; *throw me overboard.* God will not quiet the storm till I am cast out of the ship. Here was deep compunction; and honest avowal of sin; and a justification of the displeasure which God had now manifested.

Verse 13. *The men rowed hard*] Were very unwilling to proceed to this extremity, and thought they would risk every thing rather than cast this disobedient prophet into the great deep.

Verse 14. *They cried unto the Lord*] Under a conviction that he was the self-existing Being, the Maker of the heavens and the earth, and the author of the present storm, they put up their prayers to him.

Let us not perish for this man's life] They were now about to *cast him overboard;* but seemed to call God to witness that it was with the utmost reluctance, and only in obedience to his command. There is a parallel passage in the *Argonautics*, which has been quoted to illustrate this:—

Πολλα δε μερμηριζον ενι φρεσι πευκαλιμησι,
Η *μεν αποφθισωσι, και ιχθυσι κυρμα βαλωσιν*
Α*ινολεχη Μηδειαν, αποτρεψωσι δ' Ερινυν.*
Ver. 1171.

"And much they doubted, in their prudent minds,
Whether to kill and cast a prey to fishes
Wretched Medea, and avert their fate."

See *Newcome.*

Verse 16. *Offered a sacrifice*] The first perhaps ever offered on board a vessel since the ark floated on the waters of the great deluge; and it is most probable that these heathens, witnessing what was done, became sincere converts to the true God.

Verse 17. *Now the Lord had prepared a great fish*] דג גדול *dag gadol.* This could not have been a *whale*, for the throat of that animal can scarcely admit a man's leg; but it might have been a *shark*, which abounds in the Mediterranean, and whose mouth and stomach are exceedingly capacious. In several cases they have been known to swallow a man when thrown overboard. See the note on Matt. xii. 40, where the whole subject of this verse is considered at large. That *days and nights* do not, among the Hebrews, signify *complete* days and nights of *twenty-four* hours, see Esth. iv. 16, compared with chap. v. 1; Judg. xiv. 17, 18. Our Lord lay in the grave *one* natural day, and part of *two* others; and it is most likely that this was the precise time that Jonah was in the fish's belly.

CHAPTER II

This chapter (except the first verse and the last, which make a part of the narrative) contains a beautiful prayer or hymn, formed of those devout thoughts which Jonah had in the belly of the great fish, with a thanksgiving for his miraculous deliverance.

A. M. cir. 3142
B. C. cir. 862
Ante U. C. 109
Alladii Sylvii,
R. Alban.,
cir. annum 14

THEN Jonah prayed unto the LORD his God out of the fish's belly,

2 And said, I [a]cried [b]by reason of mine affliction unto the LORD, [c]and he heard me: out of the belly of [d]hell cried I, *and* thou heardest my voice.

3 [e]For thou hadst cast me into the deep, in the [f]midst of the seas; and the floods compassed me about: [g]all thy billows and thy waves passed over me.

4 [h]Then I said, I am cast out of thy sight; yet I will look again [i]toward thy holy temple.

5 The [k]waters compassed me about, *even* to the soul: the depth closed me round about, the weeds were wrapped about my head.

A. M. cir. 3142
B. C. cir. 862
Ante U. C. 109
Alladii Sylvii,
R. Alban.,
cir. annum 14

6 I went down to the [l]bottoms of the mountains; the earth with her bars *was* about me for ever: yet hast thou brought up my life [m]from [n]corruption, O LORD my God.

7 When my soul fainted within me I remembered the LORD: [o]and my prayer came in unto thee, into thine holy temple.

8 They that observe [p]lying vanities forsake their own mercy.

9 But I will [q]sacrifice unto thee with the voice of thanksgiving; I will pay *that* that I have vowed. [r]Salvation *is* of the LORD.

10 And the LORD spake unto the fish, and it vomited out Jonah upon the dry *land*.

[a]Psa. cxx. 1; cxxx. 1; cxlii. 1; Lam. iii. 55, 56——[b]Or, *out of mine affliction*——[c]Psa. lxv. 2——[d]Or, *the grave;* Isa. xiv. 9——[e]Psa. lxxxviii. 6——[f]Heb. *heart*——[g]Psa. xlii. 7——[h]Psa. xxxi. 22——[i]1 Kings viii. 38

[k]Psa. lxix. 1; Lam. iii. 54——[l]Heb. *cuttings off*——[m]Psa. xvi. 10——[n]Or, *the pit*——[o]Psa. xviii. 6——[p]2 Kings xvii. 15; Psa. xxxi. 6; Jer. x. 8; xvi. 19——[q]Psa. l. 14, 23; cxvi. 17, 18; Hos. xiv. 2; Heb. xiii. 15——[r]Psa. iii. 8

NOTES ON CHAP. II

Verse 1. *Then Jonah prayed—out of the fish's belly*] This verse makes the *first* of the *second* chapter in the Hebrew text.

It may be asked, "How could Jonah either pray or breathe in the stomach of the fish?" Very easily, if God so willed it. And let the reader keep this constantly in view; the whole is a *miracle*, from Jonah's being swallowed by the fish till he was cast ashore by the same animal. It was God that had *prepared the great fish.* It was the *Lord that spake to the fish, and caused it to vomit Jonah upon the dry land.* ALL is miracle.

Verse 2. *Out of the belly of hell*] Among the Hebrews שאול *sheol* means the *grave*, any *deep pit*, the *place of separate spirits*, &c. Here the prophet represents himself as in the *bottom of the sea;* for so *sheol* must be understood in this place.

Verse 3. *All thy billows and thy waves passed over me.*] This may be understood *literally;* while the fish, in whose belly he was, sought its pleasure or sustenance in the paths of the deep, the waves and billows of the sea were rolling above. This line seems borrowed from Psa. xlii. 7.

Verse 4. *I am cast out of thy sight*] See Psa. xxxi. 22.

Thy holy temple.] Then Jerusalem was not yet destroyed, for the *temple* was standing.

Verse 5. *The waters compassed me about* even *to the soul*] So as to seem to deprive me of life. I had no hope left.

The weeds were wrapped about my head.] This may be understood literally also. He found himself in the fish's stomach, together with *sea weeds*, and such like marine substances, which the fish had taken for its aliment.

Verse 6. *I went down to the bottoms of the mountains*] This also may be literally understood. The fish followed the slanting base of the mountains, till they terminated in a plain at the bottom of the great deep.

The earth with her bars] He represents himself as a prisoner in a dungeon, closed in with *bars* which he could not remove, and which at first appeared to *be for ever*, i. e., the place where his life must terminate.

Yet hast thou brought up my life] The substance of this poetic prayer was composed while in the fish's belly; but afterwards the prophet appears to have thrown it into its present poetic form, and to have added some circumstances, such as that before us; for he now speaks of his deliverance from this imminent danger of death. "Thou hast brought up my life from corruption."

Verse 7. *When my soul fainted*] When I had given up all hope of life.

My prayer came in unto thee] Here prayer is *personified*, and is represented as a *messenger* going from the *distressed*, and entering into the temple of God, and standing before him. This is a very fine and delicate image. This clause is one of those which I suppose the prophet to have added when he *penned* this prayer.

Verse 8. *They that observe lying vanities*] They that trust in idols, follow *vain predictions*, permit themselves to be influenced with *foolish fears*, so as to induce them to *leave the path of obvious duty, forsake their own mercy.* In leaving that God who is the *Fountain of mercy,* they abandon that *measure of mercy* which he had treasured up for them.

Verse 9. *But I will sacrifice unto thee*] I will make a sincere vow, which, as soon as my circumstances will permit, I will faithfully execute; and therefore he adds, "I will pay that which I have vowed."

Salvation is *of the Lord*.] All *deliverance* from *danger*, *preservation* of *life*, *recovery* from *sickness*, and *redemption* of the *soul* from the *power*, *guilt*, and *pollution* of sin, is from Jehovah. He *alone* is the *Saviour*, he *alone* is the *Deliverer;* for all *salvation* is *from the Lord*.

Verse 10. *And the Lord spake unto the fish*] That is, by his influence the fish swam to shore, and cast Jonah on the dry land. So the whole was a miracle from the beginning to the end; and we need not perplex ourselves to find out *literal* interpretations; such as, "When Jonah was thrown overboard he swam for his life, earnestly praying God to preserve him from drowning; and by his providence he was thrown into a *place of fish*—a *fishing cove*, where he was for a time *entangled among the weeds*, and hardly escaped with his life; and when safe, he composed this poetic prayer, in *metaphorical language*, which some have wrongly interpreted, by supposing that he was *swallowed by a fish;* when דג *dag* should have been understood, as a *place of fish*, or *fishing creek*," &c. Now I say the original has no such meaning in the Bible: and this gloss is plainly contrary to the *letter of the text;* to all *sober* and *rational modes of interpretation;* and to the express *purpose* for which God appears to have wrought this miracle, and to which *Jesus Christ* himself *applies* it. For as Jonah was intended for a *sign* to the Jews of the resurrection of Christ, they were to have the proof of this *semiosis*, in his lying as long in the *heart of the earth* as the prophet was in the *belly of the fish;* and all interpretations of this kind go to deny both the *sign* and the thing *signified*. Some men, because they cannot work a miracle themselves, can hardly be persuaded that God can do it.

The *text*, and the *use* made of it by Christ, most plainly teach us that the prophet was literally swallowed by a fish, by the order of God; and that by the Divine power he was *preserved alive*, for what is called *three days and three nights, in the stomach of the fish;* and at the conclusion of the above time that same fish was led by the unseen power of God to the shore, and there compelled to eject the prey that he could neither kill nor digest. And how easy is all this to the *almighty power* of the *Author* and *Sustainer* of *life*, who has a sovereign, omnipresent, and energetic sway in the heavens and in the earth. But foolish man will affect to be wise; though, in such cases, he appears as the recently born, stupid offspring of the wild ass. It is bad to follow *fancy*, where there is so much at stake. Both *ancients* and *moderns* have grievously trifled with this prophet's narrative; merely because they could not rationally account for the thing, and were unwilling (and why?) to allow any miraculous interference.

CHAPTER III

Jonah is sent again to Nineveh, a city of three days' journey, (being sixty miles in circumference, according to Diodorus Siculus,) 1–4. *The inhabitants, in consequence of the prophet's preaching, repent in dust and ashes,* 5–9. *God, seeing that they were deeply humbled on account of their sins, and that they turned away from all their iniquities, repents of the evil with which he had threatened them,* 10.

A. M. cir. 3142 B. C. cir. 862 Ante U. C. 109 Alladii Sylvii, R. Alban., cir. annum 14

AND the word of the Lord came unto Jonah the second time, saying,

2 Arise, go unto Nineveh, that great city, and preach unto it the preaching that I bid thee.

3 So Jonah arose, and went unto Nineveh, according to the

NOTES ON CHAP. III

Verse 1. *And the word of the Lord*] The same *oracle* as that before given; and which, from what he had felt and seen of the justice and mercy of the Lord, he was now prepared to obey.

Verse 2. *And preach unto it the preaching*] וקרא את הקריאה *vekera eth hakkeriah*, "And cry the cry that I bid thee." Be my herald, and faithfully deliver my message. The word κηρυξ in Greek answers to the Hebrew קורא *kore:* both signifying a *crier*, a *herald*, a *preacher;* one that *makes proclamation* with a *loud* and *earnest cry*. Such was John Baptist, Isa. xl. 3; such was Jesus Christ, John vii. 18-37; and such were all his apostles. And such earnestness becomes a ministry that has to do with immortal souls, asleep and dead in sin, hanging on the brink of perdition, and insensible of their state. The soft-speaking, gentle-toned, unmoved preacher, is never likely to awaken souls. As we preach, so the people hear; scarcely receiving any counsels that appear to have no importance by the *manner* in which they are *delivered*. But this earnestness is widely different from that noisy, blustering, screaming rant, that manifests more of the turbulence of disorderly passions, than of the real inspired influence of the Spirit of God.

Verse 3. *Nineveh was an exceeding great city, of three days' journey*.] See on chap. i. 2. *Strabo* says, lib. xvi., πολυ μειζων ην της Βαβυλωνος, "it was much larger than Babylon:" and Ninus, the builder, not only proposed to make it the *largest* city of the world, but the largest that *could be built by man*. See *Diodor*. Sic. Bib. l. ii. And as we find, from the lowest computation, that it was at least *fifty-four* or *sixty* English miles in circumference, it would take the prophet *three* days to walk round upon the walls, and announce from them the terrible

A. M. cir. 3142
B. C. cir. 862
Ante U. C. 109
Alladii Sylvii,
R. Alban.,
cir. annum 14

word of the LORD. Now Nineveh was an [a]exceeding great
city, of three days' journey.
4 And Jonah began to enter
into the city a day's journey, and [b]he cried,
and said, Yet forty days, and Nineveh shall
be overthrown.
5 So the people of Nineveh [c]believed God,
and proclaimed a fast, and put on sackcloth,
from the greatest of them even to the least of
them.
6 For word came unto the king of Nineveh,
and he arose from his throne, and he laid his
robe from him, and covered *him* with sackcloth [d]and sat in ashes.
7 [e]And he caused *it* to be proclaimed and
[f]published through Nineveh by
the decree of the king and his
[g]nobles, saying, Let neither man
nor beast, herd nor flock, taste
any thing: let them not feed, nor drink water:
8 But let man and beast be covered with
sackcloth, and cry mightily unto God: yea,
[h]let them turn every one from his evil way,
and from the [i]violence that *is* in their hands.
9 [k]Who can tell *if* God will turn and repent, and turn away from his fierce anger,
that we perish not?
10 [l]And God saw their works, that they
turned from their evil way; and God repented
of the evil, that he had said that he would do
unto them; and he did *it* not.

---

[a]Heb. *of God;* so Gen. xxx. 8; Psa. xxxvi. 6; lxxx. 10 —— [b]See Deut. xviii. 62 —— [c]Matt. xii. 41; Luke xi. 32 —— [d]Job ii. 8 —— [e]2 Chron. xx. 3; Joel ii. 15 —— [f]Heb. *said* —— [g]Heb. *great men* —— [h]Isa. lviii. 6 —— [i]Isa. lix. 6 —— [k]2 Samuel xii. 22; Joel ii. 14 —— [l]Jer. xviii. 8; Amos vii. 3, 6

---

message, "Yet *forty* days, and Nineveh will be destroyed!"

Verse 4. *Yet forty days*] Both the *Septuagint* and *Arabic* read *three days.* Probably some early copyist of the *Septuagint,* from whom our modern editions are derived, mistook the Greek numerals μ *forty* for γ *three;* or put the *three* days' *journey* in preaching instead of the *forty days* mentioned in the denunciation. One of *Kennicott's* MSS., instead of ארבעים *arbaim, forty,* has שלשים *sheloshim, thirty:* but the Hebrew text is undoubtedly the true reading; and it is followed by *all* the ancient versions, the *Septuagint* and *Vulgate* excepted. Thus God gives them time to *think, reflect, take counsel,* and *return* to him. Had they only *three days' space,* the denunciation would have so completely confounded them, as to excite nothing but terror, and prevent repentance and conversion.

Verse 5. *The people of Nineveh believed God*] They had no doubt that the threatening would be fulfilled, unless their speedy conversion prevented it; but, though not expressed, they knew that the threatening was conditional. "The promises and threatenings of God, which are merely personal, either to any particular man or number of men, are always conditional, because the wisdom of God hath thought fit to make these depend on the behaviour of men."—Dr. S. Clarke's Sermons, vol. i.

Proclaimed a fast] And never was there one so general, so deep, and so effectual. Men and women, old and young, high and low, and even the cattle themselves, all kept such a fast as the total abstinence from food implies.

Verse 6. *Word came unto the king*] This, some think, was *Pul;* others, *Sardanapalus* his son, king of Assyria, who flourished in the reign of Jeroboam the Second: but it seems more probable that the monarch here alluded to was a king of Assyria contemporary with Joash, king of Judah. It was by the decree of the king that the fast was instituted, and became general.

Verse 8. *Let man and beast be covered*] This was done that every object which they beheld might deepen the impression already made, and cause them to mourn after a godly sort. *Virgil* tells us that the mourning for the death of Julius Cæsar was so general, that the *cattle* neither *ate* nor *drank:*—

Non ulli pastos illis egere diebus
Frigida, Daphni, boves ad flumina: nulla neque amnem
Libavit quadrupes, nec graminis attigit herbam.
Ecl. v. 24.

"The swains forgot their sheep, nor near the brink
Of running waters brought their herds to drink.
The thirsty cattle of themselves abstain'd,
From water, and their grassy fare disdain'd."
DRYDEN.

And that they sometimes *changed* or *reversed* the harness and ornaments of cattle, as indicative of mourning, we have a proof in Virgil's description of the funeral procession in honour of Pallas, slain by Turnus, *Æn.* xi. ver. 89.

Post bellator equus, positis insignibus, Æthon
It lacrymans, guttisque humectat grandibus ora.

"Stripp'd of his trappings, and his head declined,
Æthon, his generous warrior-horse, behind,
Moves with a solemn, slow, majestic pace;
And the big tears come rolling down his face."

Verse 9. *Who can tell* if *God will turn and repent*] There is at least a peradventure for our salvation. God *may* turn towards us, change his purpose, and save us alive. While there is life there is hope; God has no pleasure in the death of sinners; he is gracious and compassionate. Himself has prescribed repentance; if we repent, and turn to him from our iniquities, who knows then whether God will not turn, &c.

Verse 10. *And God saw their works*] They repented, and brought forth *fruits* meet for repentance; works which showed that they did most earnestly repent. He therefore changed his purpose, and the city was saved. The purpose was: If the Ninevites do not return from their evil ways, and the violence that is in their hands, within *forty* days, I will destroy the city. The Ninevites did return, &c., and therefore escaped the threatened judgment. Thus we see that the threatening was conditional.

CHAPTER IV

Jonah, dreading to be thought a false prophet, repines at God's mercy in sparing the Ninevites, whose destruction he seems to have expected, from his retiring to a place without the city about the close of the forty days. But how does he glorify that mercy which he intends to blame! And what an amiable picture does he give of the compassion of God! 1–5. *This attribute of the Deity is still farther illustrated by his tenderness and condescension to the prophet himself, who, with all his prophetic gifts, had much of human infirmity,* 6–11.

A. M. cir. 3142
B. C. cir. 862
Ante U. C. 109
Alladii Sylvii,
R. Alban.,
cir. annum 14

BUT it displeased Jonah exceedingly, and he was very
angry.
2 And he prayed unto the
LORD, and said, I pray thee, O LORD, *was*
not this my saying, when I was yet in my
country? Therefore I [a]fled before unto Tarshish: for I knew that thou *art* a [b]gracious
God, and merciful, slow to anger, and of
great kindness, and repentest thee of the evil.
3 [c]Therefore now, O LORD, take, I beseech
thee, my life from me; for [d]*it*
is better for me to die than to
live.
4 Then said the LORD, [e]Doest
thou well to be angry?
5 So Jonah went out of the city, and sat on
the east side of the city, and there made him
a booth, and sat under it in the shadow, till
he might see what would become of the city.
6 And the Lord GOD prepared a [f]gourd,[g]
and made *it* to come up over Jonah, that it

A. M. cir. 3142
B. C. cir. 862
Ante U. C. 109
Alladii Sylvii,
R. Alban.,
cir. annum 14

---

[a]Chap. i. 3——[b]Exod. xxxiv. 6; Psa. lxxxvi. 5; Joel ii. 13——[c]1 Kings xix. 4——[d]Ver. 8

[e]Or, *Art thou greatly angry?*——[f]Or, *palmecrist*——[g]Heb. *Kikajon*

NOTES ON CHAP. IV

Verse 1. *But it displeased Jonah exceedingly*] This hasty, and indeed inconsiderate prophet, was vexed because his prediction was not fulfilled. He had more respect to his high sense of his own honour than he had to the goodness and mercy of God. He appeared to care little whether *six hundred and twenty thousand* persons were destroyed or not, so he might not pass for a deceiver, or one that denounced a falsity.

And he was very angry.] Because the prediction was not literally fulfilled; for he totally lost sight of the *condition.*

Verse 2. *I know that thou* art *a gracious God*] See the note on Exod. xxxiv. 6.

Verse 3. *Take, I beseech thee, my life from me*] קח נא את נפשי *kach na eth naphshi,* "Take, I beseech thee, even my soul." Do not let me survive this disgrace. Thou hast spared this city. I thought thou wouldst do so, because thou art *merciful* and *gracious;* and it was on this account that I refused to go at first, as I knew that thou mightest *change thy purpose,* though thou hadst commanded me to make an absolute denunciation of judgment. God has left this example on record to show that an inconsiderate man is not fit to be employed in his work; and he chose this one example that it might serve as an endless warning to his Church to employ no man in the work of the ministry that is not scripturally acquainted with God's justice and mercy.

Verse 4. *Doest thou well to be angry?*] ההיטב הרה לך *haheitib harah lac,* "Is anger good for thee?" No, anger is good for no man; but an angry preacher, minister, bishop, or prophet, is an abominable man. He who, in denouncing the word of God against sinners, joins his own *passions* with the Divine threatenings, is a cruel and bad man, and should not be an overseer in God's house. A *surly bishop,* a *peevish, passionate preacher,* will bring neither glory to God, nor good to man. Dr. Taylor renders the clause, "Art thou very much grieved?" A man may be very much grieved that a sinner is lost; but who but he who is of a fiendish nature will be grieved because God's mercy triumphs over judgment?

Verse 5. *So Jonah went out of the city*] I believe this refers to what had *already passed;* and I therefore agree with Bp. *Newcome,* who translates, "Now Jonah HAD gone out of the city, and HAD sat," &c.; for there are many instances where verbs in the preterite form have this force, the ו *vau* here turning the *future* into the *preterite.* And the passage is here to be understood thus: When he had delivered his message he left the city, and went and made himself a tent, or got under some shelter on the east side of the city, and there he was determined to remain till he should see what would become of the city. But when the *forty* days had expired, and he saw no evidence of the Divine wrath, he became angry, and expostulated with God as above. The *fifth* verse should be read in a parenthesis, or be considered as beginning the chapter.

Verse 6. *And the Lord God prepared a gourd*] I believe this should be rendered in the preterpluperfect tense. The Lord HAD prepared—this plant, קיקיון *kikayon.* It had in the course of God's providence been planted and grown up in that place, though perhaps not yet in full leaf;

A. M. cir. 3142
B. C. cir. 862
Ante U. C. 109
Alladii Sylvii,
R. Alban.,
cir. annum 14

might be a shadow over his head,
to deliver him from his grief.
So Jonah [h]was exceeding glad
of the gourd.

7 But God prepared a worm when the morning rose the next day, and it smote the gourd
that it withered.

8 And it came to pass, when the sun did
arise, that God prepared a [i]vehement east
wind; and the sun beat upon the head of
Jonah, that he fainted, and wished in himself
to die, and said, [k]*It is* better for me to die
than to live.

9 And God said to Jonah, [l]Doest thou
well to be angry for the gourd?
And he said, [m]I do well to be
angry, *even* unto death.

A. M. cir. 3142
B. C. cir. 862
Ante U. C. 109
Alladii Sylvii,
R. Alban.,
cir. annum 14

10 Then said the LORD, Thou
hast [n]had pity on the gourd, for the which
thou hast not laboured, neither madest it
grow; which [o]came up in a night, and perished in a night:

11 And should not I spare Nineveh, [p]that
great city, wherein are more than sixscore
thousand persons [q]that cannot discern between their right hand, and their left hand;
and *also* much [r]cattle?

---

[h]Heb. *rejoiced with great joy*——[i]Or, *silent*——[k]Ver. 3
[l]Or, *Art thou greatly angry*——[m]Or, *I am greatly angry*

[n]Or, *spared*——[o]Heb. *was the son of the night*——[p]Ch. i. 2; iii. 2, 3——[q]Deut. i. 39——[r]Psa. xxxvi. 6; cxlv. 9

---

and Jonah made that his tent. And its thick branches and large leaves made it an ample shelter for him; and because it was such, he *rejoiced greatly* on the account. But what was the *kikayon?* The best judges say the *ricinus* or *palma Christi*, from which we get what is vulgarly called *castor oil*, is meant. It is a tree as large as the olive, has leaves which are like those of the vine, and is also quick of growth. This in all probability was the plant in question, which had been already planted, though it had not attained its proper growth, and was not then in full leaf. *Celsus*, in his *Hierobot.*, says it grows to the height of an olive tree; the trunk and branches are hollow like a kex, and the leaves sometimes as broad as the rim of a hat. It must be of a soft or spongy substance, for it is said to grow surprisingly fast. See *Taylor* under the root קיק, 1670. But it is evident there was something *supernatural* in the growth of this plant, for it is stated to have *come up in a night;* though the Chaldee understands the passage thus: "It was here last night, and is withered this night." In one night it might have blown and expanded its leaves considerably, though the plant had existed before, but not in full bloom till the time that Jonah required it for a shelter.

Verse 7. *But God prepared a worm*] By being eaten through the root, the plant, losing its nourishment, would soon wither; and this was the case in the present instance.

Verse 8. *A vehement east wind*] Which was of itself of a *parching, withering* nature; and the *sun*, in addition, made it intolerable. These winds are both scorching and suffocating in the East, for deserts of burning sand lay to the east or south-east; and the easterly winds often brought such a multitude of *minute particles of sand* on their wings, as to add greatly to the mischief. I believe these, and the sands they carry, are the cause of the *ophthalmia* which prevails so much both in Egypt and India.

Verse 9. *I do well to be angry,* even *unto death.*] Many persons suppose that the *gifts of prophecy* and *working miracles* are the highest that can be conferred on man; but they are widely mistaken, for the gifts *change not the heart.* Jonah had the gift of prophecy, but had not received that grace which destroys the *old man* and *creates the soul anew in Christ Jesus.* This is the *love* of which St. Paul speaks, which if a man have not, though he had the gift of prophecy, and could miraculously remove mountains, yet in the sight of God, and for any good himself might reap from it, it would be as sounding brass and a tinkling cymbal. Jonah was a prophet, and yet had all his old bad tempers about him, in a shameful predominancy. *Balaam* was of the same kind. So we find that God gave the *gift of prophecy* even to *graceless* men. But many of the prophets were sanctified in their nature before their call to the prophetic office, and were the most excellent of men.

Verse 10. *Which came up in a night*] St. Jerome, speaking of this plant, the *kikayon*, assigns to it an extraordinary rapidity of growth. It delights in a sandy soil, and in a few days what was a *plant* grows into a *large shrub.* But he does not appear to have meant the *ricinus;* this however is the most likely. The expressions *coming up in a night* and *perishing in a night* are only metaphorical to express *speedy growth* and *speedy decay;* and so, as we have seen, the Chaldee interprets it, די בליליא הדין הוה ובליליא אוחרנא אבד "which existed this night, but in the next night perished;" and this I am satisfied is the true import of the Hebrew phrase.

Verse 11. *And should not I spare Nineveh*] In ver. 10 it is said, *thou hast had pity* on the gourd, אתה חסת *attah* CHASTA; and here the Lord uses the same word, ואני לא אחום *veani lo* ACHUS, "And shall not *I have pity* upon Nineveh?" How much is the *city* better than the *shrub?* But besides this there are in it *one hundred and twenty thousand* persons! And shall I destroy them, rather than thy *shade* should be withered or thy *word* apparently fail? And besides, these persons are *young*, and have *not offended*, (for they knew not the difference between their *right hand and their left*,) and should not I feel *more pity* for those innocents than thou dost for the fine *flowering plant* which is withered in a night, being itself exceedingly *short-lived?* Add to all this, they have now turned from those sins which induced me to denounce judgment against them. And should I destroy *them* who are now *fasting* and *afflicting their souls;* and, covered with sackcloth, are lying in the dust before me, bewailing their offences and supplicating for mercy? Learn, then, from this, that it is the incorrigibly wicked on whom my judgments must fall, and against whom they are threatened. And know, that to that man will I look who is of a broken and contrite spirit, and who trembles at my word. Even the *dumb beasts* are objects of my compassion; I will spare *them* for the sake of their penitent owners; and remember with the rest, *That the Lord careth for oxen.*

The great number of *cattle* to which reference is here made were for the support of the inhabitants; and probably at this time the Ninevites gathered in their cattle from the champaign pasture, expecting that some foe coming to besiege them might seize upon them for their forage, while they within might suffer the lack of all things.

No doubt that ancient Nineveh was like ancient Babylon, of which *Quintus Curtius* says, the buildings were not close to the walls, there being the space of an acre left between them; and in several parts there were within the walls portions of cultivated land, that, if besieged, they might have provisions to sustain the inhabitants.

And I suppose this to be true of all large ancient cities. They were rather *cantons* or *districts* than cities such as now are, only all the different inhabitants had joined together to wall in the districts for the sake of mutual defence.

This last expostulation of God, it is to be hoped, produced its proper effect on the mind of this irritable prophet; and that he was fully convinced that in this, as in all other cases, God had done all things well.

From this short prophecy many useful lessons may be derived. The Ninevites were on the verge of destruction, but on their repentance were respited. They did not, however, continue under the influence of good resolutions. They relapsed, and about *one hundred and fifty* years afterwards, the Prophet *Nahum* was sent to predict the miraculous discomfiture of the Assyrian king under Sennacherib, an event which took place about 710 B. C.; and also the total destruction of Nineveh by Cyaxares and his allies, which happened about 606 B. C. Several of the ancients, by allegorizing this book, have made Jonah declare the *divinity, humanity, death,* and *resurrection* of Christ. These points may be found in the Gospel history, their true repository; but *fancy* can find them any where it pleases to seek them; but he who seeks not for them will never find them here. Jonah was a type of the resurrection of Christ; nothing farther seems revealed in this prophet relative to the mysteries of Christianity.

In conclusion: while I have done the best I could to illustrate the very difficult prophet through whose work the reader has just passed, I do not pretend to say I have removed every difficulty. I am satisfied only of one thing, that I have conscientiously endeavoured to do it, and believe that I have generally succeeded; but am still fearful that several are left behind, which, though they may be accounted for from the briefness of the narrative of a great transaction, in which so many surprising particulars are included, yet, for general apprehension, might appear to have required a more distinct and circumstantial statement. I have only to add, that as several of the facts are evidently *miraculous*, and by the prophet stated as such, others may be probably of the same kind. On this ground all difficulty is removed; for God *can* do what he *pleases*. As his power is *unlimited*, it can meet with no *impossibilities*. He who gave the *commission* to Jonah to go and *preach to the Ninevites, and prepared the great fish* to swallow the disobedient prophet, could maintain his life for *three days and three nights* in the belly of this marine monster; and cause it to *eject him* at the termination of the appointed time, on *any sea-coast* he might choose; and afterwards the Divine power could carry the deeply contrite and now faithful prophet over the intervening distance between that and Nineveh, be that distance greater or less. Whatever, therefore, cannot be accounted for on mere natural principles in this book, may be referred to this *supernatural* agency; and this, on the ostensible principle of the prophecy itself, is at once a mode of interpretation as easy as it is rational. God gave the commission; he raised the storm; he prepared the fish which swallowed the prophet; he caused it to cast him forth on the dry land; he gave him a fresh commission, carried him to the place of his destination, and miraculously produced the sheltering gourd, that came to perfection in a night and withered in a night. This God therefore performed the other facts for which we cannot naturally account, as he did those already specified. This concession, for the admission of which both common sense and reason plead, at once solves all the real or seeming difficulties to be found in *the Book of the Prophet Jonah.*

INTRODUCTION TO THE BOOK

OF THE

PROPHET MICAH

MICAH, the Morasthite, or of Moresa, a village near the city Eleutheropolis, in the southern part of Judah, is the *sixth* in order of the *twelve* minor prophets. He prophesied under Jotham, Ahaz, and Hezekiah, kings of Judah, for about *fifty* years. Some have confounded him with Micaiah, son of Imlah, who lived in the kingdom of the ten tribes, under the reign of Ahab.

The spurious Dorotheus says that Micah was buried in the burying-place of the Anakim, whose habitation had been at Hebron, and round about it. This prophet appeared almost at the same time with Isaiah, and has even borrowed some expressions from him. Compare Isa. ii. 2 with Mic. iv. 1, and Isa. xli. 15 with Mic. iv. 13.

The prophecy of Micah contains but *seven* chapters. He foretells the calamities of Samaria, which was taken by Shalmaneser, and reduced to a heap of stones. Afterwards he prophesies against Judah, and declares the troubles that Sennacherib should bring upon it under the reign of Hezekiah. Then he declaims against the iniquities of Samaria. He foretells the captivity of the *ten* tribes, and their return into their own country. The *third* chapter contains a pathetic invective against the princes of the house of Jacob, and the judges of the house of Israel; which seems levelled against the chief of the kingdom of Judah, the judges, the magistrates, the priests, the false prophets, &c. He upbraids them with their avarice, their injustice, and falsehood; and tells them they will be the occasion that Jerusalem shall be reduced to a heap of rubbish, and the mountain of the temple shall be as a forest. We are informed, Jer. xxvi. 18, 19, that this prophecy was pronounced in the reign of Hezekiah; and that it saved Jeremiah from death.

After these terrible denunciations, Micah speaks of the reign of the Messiah, and of the establishment of the Christian Church. And as the peaceable times which succeeded the return from the Babylonish captivity, and which were a figure of the reign of the Messiah, were disturbed by a tempest of a short continuance, Micah foretold it in such a manner as agrees very well with what Ezekiel says of the war of Gog against the Jews. Micah speaks in particular of the birth of the Messiah; that he was to be born at Bethlehem; and that his dominion was to extend to the utmost parts of the earth. He says that God should raise *seven* shepherds, who should reign by the sword over Assyria, and in the land of Nimrod; which Calmet explains of Darius, son of Hystaspes; and of the *seven* confederates that killed the magian, and who possessed the empire of the Persians, after the extinction of the family of Cyrus. The *fifth* chapter, from ver. 7 to the end, describes the flourishing estate of the Jews in their own country, from the reign of Darius, and after the Maccabees; yet in such a manner, that he mingles several things in it that can apply only to the Church of Jesus Christ.

The two last chapters of Micah contain, first, a long invective against the iniquities of Samaria: then he foretells the fall of Babylon; the re-establishment of the cities of Israel; the greatness of the country possessed by the Israelites; their happiness; the graces wherewith God will favour them; and all this in such lofty terms, that they chiefly agree with the Christian Church. St. Jerome says that Micah was buried at Morasthi, ten furlongs from Eleutheropolis; and Sozomenes says that his tomb was revealed to Zebennus, bishop of Eleutheropolis, under the reign of Theodosius the Great. He calls the place of his burial Beretsate, which is probably the same as Morasthi, ten furlongs from Eleutheropolis.

Bishop *Newcome* observes that Micah was of the kingdom of Judah, as he only makes mention of kings who reigned over that country. It is supposed that he prophesied farther on in the reign of Hezekiah than Hosea did; although chap. v. 5 was written before the captivity of the ten tribes, which happened in the *sixth* year of Hezekiah. It is plain from chap. i. 1, 5, 9, 12, 13, that he was sent both to Israel and Judah. Like Amos and Hosea, he reproves and threatens, with great spirit and energy, a corrupt people. See chap. ii. 1, 2, 3, 8, 9, 10; iii. 2, 3, 4, 6, 10–16; vii. 2, 3, 4. And, like Hosea, he inveighs against the princes and prophets with the highest indignation. See chap. iii. 5–7, 9–12; vii. 3. The reader will observe that these similar topics are treated of by each prophet with remarkable variety, and copiousness of expression.

Some of his prophecies are distinct and illustrious ones, as chap. ii. 12, 13; iii. 12; iv. 1–4, 10; v. 2, 3, 4; vi. 13; vii. 8, 9, 10.

We may justly admire the *elegance* of his diction:—

Chap. ii. 12.—"I will surely gather, O Jacob, all of thee:
I will surely assemble the residue of Israel.
I will put them together as sheep of Bozra,
As a flock in the midst of their fold:
They shall make a tumult from the multitude of men.
13.—He that forceth a passage is come up before them:
They have forced a passage, and have passed through the gate; and are gone forth by it:
And their King passeth before them, even Jehovah at the head of them."

Chap. iv. 1.—"But it shall come to pass, in the latter days,
That the mountain of the temple of Jehovah shall be
Established on the top of the mountains,
And it shall be exalted above the hills;
And the people shall flow into it:
2.—And many nations shall go, and shall say,
Come, and let us go up unto the mountain of Jehovah,
And unto the temple of the God of Jacob:
That he may teach us of his ways, and that we may walk in his paths.
For from Sion shall go forth a law,
And the word of Jehovah from Jerusalem.
3.—And he shall judge between many people,
And he shall convince strong nations afar off:
And they shall beat their swords into ploughshares,
And their spears into pruninghooks:
Nation shall not lift up sword against nation,
Neither shall they any longer learn war."

His *animation*, chap. i. 5, lines 3, 4:—

"What is the transgression of Jacob?—is it not that of Samaria?
And what are the high places of Judah?—are they not those of Jerusalem?"

Chap. iv. 9.—"And now why dost thou cry out loudly?
Is there no king in thee?
Hath thy counsellor perished?
For pangs have seized thee, as a woman in travail."

There are few beauties of composition of which examples may not be found in this prophet. For *sublimity* and *impressiveness* in several places, he is unrivalled. The *Lord's controversy*, chap. vi. 1–8, is equal to any thing even in the prophet Isaiah. It has a powerful effect on every attentive reader.

His *strength* of *expression*:—

Chap. i. 6.—"Therefore will I make Samaria a heap of the field, a place for the plantings of a vineyard:
And I will pour down her stones into the valley, and I will discover her foundations."
iii. 2.—"Ye who hate good and love evil:
Who pluck their skin from off them,
And their flesh from off their bones.
3.—Who have also eaten the flesh of my people,
And have flayed their skin from off them,
And have broken their bones;
And have divided them asunder, as flesh in the pot:
And as meat within the caldron."
vii. 1.—"Wo is me; for I am become
As the gatherers of late figs, as the gleaners of the vintage.
There is no cluster to eat:
My soul desireth the first-ripe fig.
2.—The good man is perished from the land,
And there is none upright among men.
All of them lie in wait for blood;
They hunt every man his brother for his destruction."

His *pathos*:—

Chap. i. 16.—"Make thee bald, and cut off thine hair for thy delicate children;
Enlarge thy baldness as the eagle;
For they are gone into captivity from thee."
ii. 4.—"In that day shall a proverb be taken up against you;
And a grievous lamentation shall be made:
Saying, 'We are utterly laid waste:
He hath changed the portion of my people:
How hath he departed from me,
To bring again him that divided our fields!' "

His *sublimity*:—

Chap. i. 2.—"Hear, O ye people, all of you:
Hearken, O land, and all that are therein.
And let the Lord Jehovah be witness against you;
Even the Lord from his holy temple.
3.—For, behold, Jehovah will go forth from his place:
And he will come down, and will tread upon the high places of the earth.
4.—And the mountains shall be molten under him;
And the valleys shall cleave asunder;
As wax before the fire,
As waters poured down a steep place."
Chap. vi. 1.—"Hear ye now what Jehovah saith:
Arise, contend thou before the mountains;
And let the hills hear thy voice."
vii. 15.—"The nations shall see, and shall be confounded because of their might:
They shall lay their hand upon their mouth; their ears shall be deaf.
7.—They shall lick the dust as the serpent;
As the creeping things upon the earth, they shall tremble from their close places:
Because of Jehovah our God, they shall stand in awe; and they shall fear because of thee."

THE BOOK

OF THE

PROPHET MICAH

Chronological Notes relative to this Book

Year from the Creation, according to Archbishop Usher, 3254.—Year of the Julian Period, 3964.—Year since the Flood, 1598.—Year from the vocation of Abram, 1171.—Year since the first celebration of the Olympic games in Elis by the Idæi Dactyli, 704.—Year from the destruction of Troy, according to the general computation of chronologers, 434.—Year since the commencement of the kingdom of Israel, by the Divine appointment of Saul to the regal dignity, 346.—Year from the foundation of Solomon's temple, 262.—Year since the division of Solomon's monarchy into the kingdoms of Israel and Judah, 226. —Year since the restoration of the Olympic games at Elis by Lycurgus, Iphitus, and Cleosthenes, 135.—Year from the foundation of the kingdom of Macedon by Caranus, 65.—Year from the foundation of the kingdom of Lydia by Ardysus, 49.—All before this reign concerning Lydia is entirely fabulous.—Year since the conquest of Corœbus at Olympia, usually called the first Olympiad, 27.—Third year of the *seventh* Olympiad.—Year before the building of Rome, according to the Varronian computation, 4.—Year from the building of Rome, according to Cato and the Fasti Consulares, 3.—Year from the building of Rome, according to Polybius the historian, 2.—Year before the building of Rome, according to Fabius Pictor, 2.—Year before the commencement of the era of Nabonassar, 2.—Year before the birth of Christ, 746.—Year before the vulgar era of Christ's nativity, 750.—Cycle of the Sun, 16.—Cycle of the Moon, 12.—Twenty-first year of Theopompus, king of Lacedæmon, of the family of the Proclidæ.—Twenty-seventh year of Polydorus, king of Lacedæmon, of the family of the Eurysthenidæ.—Twelfth year of Alyattes, king of Lydia.—Fifth year of Charops, the first decennial archon of the Athenians.—Fourth year of Romulus, the first king of the Romans.—Tenth year of Pekah, king of Israel.—Ninth year of Jothan, king of Judah.

CHAPTER I

The prophet begins with calling the attention of all people to the awful descent of Jehovah, coming to execute his judgments against the kingdoms of Israel and Judah, 1–5; *first against Samaria, whose fate the prophet laments in the dress of mourners, and with the doleful cries of the fox or ostrich,* 6–8; *and then against Jerusalem, which is threatened with the invasion of Sennacherib. Other cities of Judah are likewise threatened; and their danger represented to be so great as to oblige them to have recourse for protection even to their enemies the Philistines, from whom they desired at first to conceal their situation. But all resources are declared to be vain; Israel and Judah must go into captivity,* 9–16.

A. M. cir. 3254 B. C. cir. 750 A. U. C. cir. 4 Romuli, R. Roman., cir. annum 4

THE word of the LORD that came to [a]Micah the Morasthite in the days of Jotham, Ahaz, *and* Hezekiah, kings of Judah, [b]which he saw concerning Samaria and Jerusalem.
2 [c]Hear, all ye people; [d]hearken, O earth, and [e]all

[a]Jer. xxvi. 18——[b]Amos i. 1——[c]Heb. *Hear, ye people, all of them*

[d]Deuteronomy xxxii. 1; Isa. i. 2——[e]Heb. *the fulness thereof*

NOTES ON CHAP. I

Verse 1. *The word of the Lord that came to Micah the Morasthite*] For all authentic particulars relative to this *prophet*, see the *preface*.

In the days of Jotham, Ahaz, and *Hezekiah*] These *three* kings reigned about threescore years; and Micah is supposed to have prophesied about *forty* or *fifty* years; but no more of his prophecies have reached posterity than what are contained in this book, nor is there any evidence that any more was written. His time appears to have been spent chiefly in *preaching* and *exhorting;* and he was directed to write

A. M. cir. 3254
B. C. cir. 750
A. U. C. cir. 4
Romuli,
R. Roman.,
cir. annum 4

that therein is: and let the Lord
God [f]be Witness against you,
the Lord from [g]his holy temple.
3 For, behold, [h]the Lord
cometh forth out of his [i]place, and will come
down, and tread upon the [k]high places of the
earth.
4 And [l]the mountains shall be molten under
him, and the valleys shall be cleft, as wax
before the fire, *and* as the waters *that are*
poured down [m]a steep place.
5 For the transgression of Jacob *is* all this,
and for the sins of the house of Israel. What
is the transgression of Jacob? *is it* not Samaria? and what *are* the high places of Judah?
are they not Jerusalem?

6 Therefore I will make Samaria [n]as a heap of the field,
and as plantings of a vineyard:
and I will pour down the stones
thereof into the valley, and I will [o]discover
the foundations thereof.
7 And all the graven images thereof shall
be beaten to pieces, and all the [p]hires thereof
shall be burned with the fire, and all the idols
thereof will I lay desolate: for she gathered
it of the hire of a harlot, and they shall return to the hire of a harlot.
8 Therefore [q]I will wail and howl, [r]I will
go stripped and naked: [s]I will make a wailing
like the dragons, and mourning as the [t]owls.
9 For [u]her wound *is* incurable; for [v]it is

A. M. cir. 3254
B. C. cir. 750
A. U. C. cir. 4
Romuli,
R. Roman.,
cir. annum 4

---

[f]Psa. l. 7; Mal. iii. 5——[g]Psa. xi. 4; Jonah ii. 7; Hab. ii. 20——[h]Isa. xxvi. 21——[i]Psa. cxv. 3——[k]Deut. xxxii. 13; xxxiii. 29; Amos iv. 13——[l]Judg. v. 5; Psa. xcvii. 5; Isa. lxiv. 1, 2, 3; Amos ix. 5; Hab. iii. 6, 10——[m]Heb. *a descent*——[n]2 Kings xix. 25; chap. iii. 12

[o]Ezek. xiii. 14——[p]Hos. ii. 5, 12——[q]Isa. xxi. 3; xxii. 4; Jer. iv. 19——[r]Isa. xx. 2, 3, 4——[s]Job xxx. 29; Psa. cii. 6——[t]Heb. *daughters of the owl*——[u]Or, *she is grievously sick of her wounds*——[v]2 Kings xviii. 13; Isa. viii. 7, 8

---

those parts only that were calculated to profit succeeding generations.

Verse 2. *Hear, all ye people*] The very commencement of this prophecy supposes *preceding* exhortations and predictions.

Hearken, O earth] ארץ *arets*, here, should be translated *land*, the country of the Hebrews being only intended.

And let the Lord God be Witness] Let him who has sent me with this message be witness that I have delivered it faithfully; and be a witness against you, if you take not the warning.

The Lord from his holy temple.] The place where he still remains as your King, and your Judge; and where you profess to pay your devotions. The temple was yet standing, for Jerusalem was not taken for many years after this; and these prophecies were delivered before the captivity of the *ten* tribes, as Micah appears to have been sent both to Israel and to Judah. See ver. 5-9, 12, 13.

Verse 3. *For, behold, the Lord cometh forth*] See this clause, Amos iv. 13. He represents Jehovah as a mighty conqueror, issuing from his pavilion, stepping from mountain to mountain, which rush down and fill the valleys before him; a consuming fire accompanying him, that melts and confounds every hill and dale, and blends all in universal confusion. God is here represented as doing that *himself* which other conquerors do by the multitude of their hosts; levelling the mountains, filling some of the valleys, and digging for waters in others, and pouring them from hills and dales for the use of the conquering armies, by pipes and aqueducts.

And why is all this mighty movement? Verse 5. "For the transgression of Jacob *is* all this, and for the sins of the house of Israel."

Verse 5. *What is the transgression of Jacob?*] Is it not something extremely grievous? Is it not that of *Samaria?* Samaria and Jerusalem, the chief cities, are infected with *idolatry*. Each has its *high places*, and its *idol worship*, in opposition to the worship of the true God. That there was *idolatry* practised by the *elders of Israel*, even *in the temple* of Jehovah, see Ezek. viii. 1, &c. As the royal cities in both kingdoms gave the *example* of gross idolatry, no wonder that it spread through the whole land, both of Israel and Judah.

Verse 6. *I will make Samaria*] I will bring it to desolation: and, instead of being a royal city, it shall be a *place for vineyards. Newcome* observes, that Samaria was situated on a hill, the right soil for a vineyard.

I will discover the foundations thereof.] I will cause its walls and fortifications to be razed to the ground.

Verse 7. *All the hires thereof shall be burned*] Multitudes of women gave the money they gained by their public *prostitution* at the temples for the support of the priesthood, the ornamenting of the walls, altars, and images. So that these things, and perhaps several of the images themselves, were literally the *hire of the harlots:* and God threatens here to deliver all into the hands of enemies who should seize on this wealth, and literally spend it in the *same way* in which it was acquired; so that "to the hire of a harlot these things should return."

Verse 8. *I will make a wailing like the dragons*] *Newcome* translates:—

I will make a wailing like the foxes, (or jackals,)

And mourning like the daughters of the ostrich. This beast, the *jackal* or *shiagal*, we have often met with in the prophets. Travellers inform us that its *howlings* by night are most lamentable; and as to the *ostrich*, it is remarkable for its *fearful shrieking* and *agonizing groanings* after night. Dr. Shaw says he has often heard them groan as if they were in the greatest agonies.

Verse 9. *Her wound* is *incurable*] Nothing shall prevent their utter ruin, for they have filled up the measure of their iniquity.

A. M. cir. 3254
B. C. cir. 750
A. U. C. cir. 4
Romuli,
R. Roman.,
cir. annum 4

come unto Judah; he is come
unto the gate of my people, *even*
to Jerusalem.
10 [w]Declare ye *it* not at Gath,
weep ye not at all: in the house of [x]Aphrah
[y]roll thyself in the dust.
11 Pass ye away, [z]thou [a]inhabitant of
Saphir, having thy [b]shame naked: the inhabitant of [c]Zaanan came not forth in the
mourning of [d]Beth-ezel; he shall receive of
you his standing.
12 For the inhabitant of Maroth [e]waited
carefully for good: but [f]evil came down from
the LORD unto the gate of Jerusalem.
13 O thou inhabitant of [g]Lachish, bind the
chariot to the swift beast: she
is the beginning of the sin to
the daughter of Zion: for the
transgressions of Israel were
found in thee.
14 Therefore shalt thou [h]give presents [i]to
Moresheth-gath: the houses of [k]Achzib [l]*shall*
be a lie to the kings of Israel.
15 Yet will I bring an heir unto thee, O inhabitant of [m]Mareshah: [n]he shall come unto
[o]Adullam the glory of Israel.
16 Make thee [p]bald, and poll thee for thy
[q]delicate children; enlarge thy baldness as
the eagle; for they are gone into captivity
from thee.

[w]2 Sam. i. 20——[x]That is, *dust*——[y]Jer. vi. 26——[z]Or, *thou that dwellest fairly*——[a]Heb. *inhabitress*——[b]Isa. xx. 4; xlvii. 2, 3; Jer. xiii. 22; Nah. iii. 5——[c]Or, *the country of flocks*——[d]Or, *a place near*——[e]Or, *was grieved*——[f]Amos iii. 6

[g]2 Kings xviii. 14, 17——[h]2 Sam. viii. 2; 2 Kings xviii. 14, 15, 16——[i]Or, *for*——[k]That is, *a lie*——[l]Josh. xv. 44——[m]Josh. xv. 44——[n]Or, *the glory of Israel shall come*, &c.——[o]2 Chron. xi. 7——[p]Job i. 20; Isa. xv. 2; xxii. 12; Jer. vii. 29; xvi. 6; xlvii. 5; xlviii. 37——[q]Lam. iv. 5

He is come—even to Jerusalem.] The desolation and captivity of Israel shall first take place; that of Judah shall come after.

Verse 10. *Declare ye* it *not at Gath*] Do not let this prediction be known among the *Philistines*, else they will glory over you.

House of Aphrah] Or, *Beth-aphrah.* This place is mentioned Josh. xviii. 23, as in the tribe of Benjamin. There is a paronomasia, or play on words, here: בבית לעפרה עפר *bebeith leaphrah aphar*, "Roll thyself in the dust in the house of dust."

Verse 11. *Inhabitant of Saphir*] *Sapher, Sepphoris*, or *Sephora*, was the strongest place in Galilee.—*Calmet.* It was a city in the tribe of Judah, between Eleutheropolis and Ascalon.—*Houbigant.*

Zaanan] Another city in the tribe of Judah, Josh. xv. 13.

Beth-ezel] A place near Jerusalem, Zech. xiv. 5. Some think that Jerusalem itself is intended by this word.

Verse 12. *The inhabitant of Maroth*] There was a city of a similar name in the tribe of Judah, Josh. xv. 59.

Verse 13. *Inhabitant of Lachish*] This city was in the tribe of Judah, Josh. xv. 39, and was taken by Sennacherib when he was coming against Jerusalem, 2 Kings xviii. 13, &c., and it is supposed that he wished to reduce this city first, that, possessing it, he might prevent Hezekiah's receiving any help from Egypt.

She is the beginning of the sin] This seems to intimate that Lachish was the first city in Judah which received the idolatrous worship of Israel.

Verse 14. *Give presents to Moresheth-gath*] *Calmet* says that *Moresa* or *Morashti*, and *Achzib*, were cities not far from Gath. It is possible that when Ahaz found himself pressed by *Pekah*, king of Israel, he might have sent to these places for succour, that by their assistance he might *frustrate the hopes of the king of Israel;* and this may be the meaning of "The houses of Achzib shall be a lie to the kings of Israel." In these verses there are several instances of the *paronomasia.* See ver. 10, עפר *aphar, dust*, and עפרה *aphrah*, the name of the city. Ver. 11. צאנן *tsaanan, the city*, and יצאה *yatsah, to go out.* Ver. 13, לכיש *lachish, the city*, and רכש *rechesh, the swift beast.* Ver. 14, אכזיב *achzib, the city*, and אכזב *achzab, a lie.* Such paronomasias were reputed ornaments by the prophets. They occur in Isaiah with great effect. See Isa. v. 7.

Verse 15. *Yet will I bring an heir unto thee, O—Mareshah*] Here is another instance, הירש *haiyeresh, to bring an heir*, and מרשה *mareshah, the city*, the name of which signifies *heirship.* And so of the above proper names.

Adullam the glory of Israel.] This was a fenced city in the south of Judah (see 2 Chron. xi. 7) towards the Dead Sea.

There is much obscurity in the concluding verses of this chapter. They undoubtedly refer to the *captivity* of Israel, and to *circumstances* of *distress*, &c., which are not mentioned in any of the historical books, and therefore their reference and meaning can only be conjectured.

Verse 16. *Make thee bald*] *Cutting off the hair* was a sign of great distress, and was practised on the death of near relatives; see Amos viii. 10. The desolation should be so great that Israel should feel it to her utmost extent; and the *mourning* should be like that of a mother for the death of her most delicate children.

Enlarge thy baldness as the eagle] Referring to the *moulting* of this bird, when in casting its feathers and breeding new ones, it is very sickly, and its strength wholly exhausted.

They are gone into captivity] This is a prediction of the captivity by Shalmaneser. Samaria, the chief city, is called on to deplore it, as then fast approaching.

CHAPTER II

Here the prophet denounces a wo against the plotters of wickedness, the covetous and the oppressor, 1, 2. *God is represented as devising their ruin,* 3. *An Israelite is then introduced as a mourner, personating his people, and lamenting their fate,* 4. *Their total expulsion is now threatened on account of their very numerous offences,* 5–10. *Great infatuation of the people in favour of those pretenders to Divine inspiration who prophesied to them peace and plenty,* 11. *The chapter concludes with a gracious promise of the restoration of the posterity of Jacob from captivity; possibly alluding to their deliverance from the Chaldean yoke, an event which was about* two hundred *years in futurity at the delivery of this prophecy,* 12, 13.

A. M. cir. 3274
B. C. cir. 730
A. U. C. cir. 24
Romuli,
R. Roman.,
cir. annum 24

WO to them [a]that devise
iniquity, and [b]work evil
upon their beds! when the
morning is light, they practise
it, because [c]it is in the power of their hand.
2 And they covet [d]fields, and take *them* by
violence; and houses, and take *them* away:
so they [e]oppress a man and his house, even a
man and his heritage.
3 Therefore thus saith the LORD; Behold,
against [f]this family do I devise an evil, from
which ye shall not remove your necks; neither
shall ye go haughtily: [g]for this time *is* evil.
4 In that day shall *one* [h]take up a parable
against you, and [i]lament [k]with a doleful lamentation, *and* say, We be ut-
terly spoiled: [l]he hath changed
the portion of my people: how
hath he removed *it* from me!
[m]turning away he hath divided our fields.
5 Therefore thou shalt have none that shall
cast [n]a cord by lot in the congregation of the
LORD.
6 [o] [p]Prophesy [q]ye not, *say they to them that*
prophesy: they shall not prophesy to them,
that they shall not take shame.
7 O *thou that are* named the house of Jacob,
is the Spirit of the LORD [r]straitened? *are*
these his doings? do not my words do good
to him that walketh [s]uprightly?

A. M. cir. 3274
B. C. cir. 730
A. U. C. cir. 24
Romuli,
R. Roman.,
cir. annum 24

[a]Hos. vii. 6——[b]Psa. xxxvi. 4——[c]Gen. xxxi. 29——[d]Isa. v. 8——[e]Or, *defraud*——[f]Jer. viii. 3——[g]Amos v. 13; Eph. v. 16——[h]Hab. ii. 6——[i]2 Sam. i. 17——[k]Heb. *with a lamentation of lamentations*——[l]Ch. i. 15

[m]Or, *instead of restoring*——[n]Deut. xxxii. 8, 9——[o]Or, *Prophesy not* as *they prophesy*——[p]Heb. *drop, &c.*; Ezek. xxi. 2——[q]Isa. xxx. 10; Amos ii. 12; vii. 16——[r]Or, *shortened*——[s]Heb. *upright*

NOTES ON CHAP. II

Wo to them that devise iniquity] Who lay *schemes* and *plans* for transgressions; who make it their *study* to find out new modes of sinning; and make these things their *nocturnal* meditations, that, having fixed their plan, they may begin to execute it as soon as it is *light* in the *morning.*

Because it is in the power of their hand.] They think they *may* do whatever they have *power* and *opportunity* to do.

Verse 2. *They covet fields*] These are the rich and mighty in the land; and, like Ahab, they will take the vineyard or inheritance of any poor Naboth on which they may fix their covetous eye; so that they take away even the *heritage* of the poor.

Verse 3. *Against this family* (the Israelites) *do I devise an evil*] You have *devised* the evil of *plundering* the upright; I will devise the evil to you of *punishment* for your conduct; you shall have your *necks* brought under the yoke of servitude. Tiglath-pileser ruined this kingdom, and transported the people to Assyria, under the reign of Hezekiah, king of Judah; and Micah lived to see this catastrophe. See on ver. 9.

Verse 4. *Take up a parable against you*] Your wickedness and your punishment shall be subjects of common conversation; and a *funeral dirge* shall be composed and sung for you as for the *dead.* The *lamentation* is that which immediately follows: *We be utterly spoiled;* and ends, *Are these his doings?* ver. 7.

Verse 5. *None that shall cast a cord*] You will no more have your inheritance divided to you by lot, as it was to your fathers; ye shall neither have fields nor possessions of any kind.

Verse 6. *Prophesy ye not*] Do not predict any more evils—we have as many as we can bear. We are utterly ruined—shame and confusion cover our faces. The original is singular, and expressive of sorrow and sobbing. Literally, "Do not cause it to rain; they will cause it to rain; they cannot make it rain sooner than this; confusion shall not depart from us." To *rain,* often means to *preach,* to *prephesy;* Ezek. xx. 46, xxi. 2; Amos vii. 16; Deut. xxxii. 2; Job xxix. 22; Prov. v. 3, &c.

The last line Bp. *Newcome* translates, "*For* he shall not remove *from himself* reproaches;" and paraphrases, "The true prophet will subject himself to public disgrace by exercising his office."

Verse 7. *Is the Spirit of the Lord straitened?*] This is the complaint of the Israelites, and a part of the lamentation. Doth it not speak by other persons as well as by Micah? Doth it communicate to us such influences as it did formerly? Is it true that these evils are threatened by that Spirit? Are these his doings? To which Jehovah answers, "Do not my words do good to him that walketh uprightly?" No upright man need fear any word spoken by me: my words to such yield instruction and comfort; never dismay. Were ye upright, ye would not complain of the words of my prophets. The last clause may be translated, "Walking with him that is upright." The upright

A. M. cir. 3274
B. C. cir. 730
A. U. C. cir. 24
Romuli,
R. Roman.,
cir. annum 24

8 Even [t]of late my people is
risen up as an enemy: ye pull
off the robe [u]with the garment
from them that pass by securely
as men averse from war.
9 The [v]women of my people have ye cast
out from their pleasant houses; from their
children have ye taken away my glory for
ever.
10 Arise ye, and depart; for this *is* not *your*
[w]rest: because it is [x]polluted, it shall destroy
you, even with a sore destruction.
11 If a man [y]walking [z]in the spirit and
falsehood do lie, *saying,* I will prophesy unto
thee of wine and of strong
drink; he shall even be the prophet of this people.
12 [a]I will surely assemble, O
Jacob, all of thee; I will surely gather the
remnant of Israel; I will put them together
[b]as the sheep of Bozrah, as the flock in the
midst of their fold: they shall make great
noise by reason of *the multitude of* men.
13 The breaker is come up before them:
they have broken up, and have passed through
the gate, and are gone out by it: [c]and [d]their
king shall pass before them, [e]and the LORD
on the head of them.

A. M. cir. 3274
B. C. cir. 730
A. U. C. cir. 24
Romuli,
R. Roman.,
cir. annum 24

[t]Heb. *yesterday*——[u]Heb. *over against a garment*——[v]Or, *wives*——[w]Deut. xii. 9——[x]Lev. xviii. 25, 28; Jeremiah iii. 2

[y]Or, *walk with the wind, and lie falsely*——[z]Ezek. xiii. 3——[a]Chap. iv. 6, 7——[b]Jer. xxxi. 10——[c]Ezek. xxxvi 37——[d]Hos. iii. 5——[e]Isa. lii. 12

man walks *by* the word; and the word walks *with* him who walks *by* it.

Verse 8. *My people is risen up as an enemy*] Ye are not only opposed to me, but ye are enemies to each other. Ye rob and spoil each other. Ye plunder the peaceable passenger; depriving him both of his *upper* and *under* garment; *ye pull off the robe* from those who, far from being spoilers themselves, *are averse from war.*

Verse 9. *The women of my people*] Ye are the cause of the women and their children being carried into captivity—separated from their pleasant habitations, and from my temple and ordinances—and from the blessings of the covenant, which it is my *glory* to give, and theirs to receive. These two verses may probably relate to the war made on Ahaz by Rezin, king of Syria, and Pekah, king of Israel. They fell suddenly upon the Jews; killed in one day *one hundred and twenty thousand,* and took *two hundred thousand* captive; and carried away much spoil. Thus, they *rose up against them as enemies,* when there was peace between the two kingdoms; spoiled them of their goods, carried away *men, women,* and *children,* till, at the remonstrances of the prophet *Oded,* they were released. See 2 Chron. xxviii. 6, &c. Micah lived in the days of Ahaz, and might have seen the barbarities which he here describes.

Verse 10. *Arise ye, and depart*] Prepare for your captivity; ye shall have no *resting* place here: the very *land is polluted* by your iniquities, and shall vomit you out, and it shall be *destroyed;* and the *destruction* of it shall be great and *sore.*

Some think this is an exhortation to the *godly,* to leave a land that was to be destroyed so speedily.

Verse 11. *If a man walking in the spirit and falsehood*] The meaning is: If a man who professes to be *Divinely inspired* do *lie,* by prophesying of plenty, &c., then such a person shall be *received* as a *true prophet* by this people. It not unfrequently happens that the Christless worldling, who has got into the priest's office for a maintenance, and who leaves the people undisturbed in their unregenerate state, is better received than the faithful pastor, who proclaims the justice of the Lord, and the necessity of repentance and forsaking sin, in order to their being made partakers of that holiness without which no man shall see God.

Verse 12. *I will surely assemble*] This is a promise of the restoration of Israel from captivity. He compares them to a flock of sheep rushing together to their fold, the *hoofs* of which make a *wonderful noise* or *clatter.* So when *one hundred* sheep run, *eight hundred* toes or divisions of these *bifid* animals make a clattering noise. This appears to be the image.

Verse 13. *The breaker is come up*] He who is to give them *deliverance,* and lead them out on the way of their return. He who takes down the *hurdles,* or makes *a gap* in the *wall* or *hedge,* to permit them to pass through. This may apply to those *human agents* that shall permit and order their return. And *Jehovah* being *at their head,* may refer to their final restoration, when the Lord Jesus shall become their leader, they having returned unto him as the shepherd and bishop of their souls; and they and the Gentiles forming one fold under one shepherd, to go no more out into captivity for ever. Lord, hasten the time!

CHAPTER III

In this chapter the prophet inveighs with great boldness and spirit against the princes and prophets of Judah; and foretells the destruction of Jerusalem as the consequence of their iniquity, 1–12. *The last verse was fulfilled to a certain extent by Nebuchadnezzar; but most fully and literally by the Romans under Titus. See* **Josephus.**

A. M. cir. 3294
B. C. cir. 710
A. U. C. cir. 44
NumæPompilii,
R. Roman.,
cir. annum 6

AND I said, Hear, I pray you,
O heads of Jacob, and ye
princes of the house of Israel;
[a]*Is it* not for you to know judgment?
2 Who hate the good, and love the evil;
who pluck off their skin from off them, and
their flesh from off their bones;
3 Who also [b]eat the flesh of my people,
and flay their skin from off them, and they
break their bones, and chop them in pieces, as
for the pot, and [c]as flesh within the caldron.
4 Then [d]shall they cry unto the LORD, but
he will not hear them; he will even hide his
face from them at that time, as they have behaved themselves ill in their doings.
5 Thus saith the LORD [e]concerning the prophets that make my people err, that [f]bite with
their teeth, and cry, Peace; and [g]he that putteth not into their mouths, they
even prepare war against him:

A. M. cir. 3294
B. C. cir. 710
A. U. C. cir. 44
NumæPompilii,
R. Roman.,
cir. annum 6

6 [h]Therefore night *shall be*
unto you, [i]that ye shall not have
a vision; and it shall be dark unto you, [k]that
ye shall not divine; [l]and the sun shall go
down over the prophets, and the day shall be
dark over them.
7 Then shall the seers be ashamed, and the
diviners confounded: yea, they shall all cover
their [m]lips; [n]for *there is* no answer of God.
8 But truly I am full of power by the Spirit
of the LORD, and of Judgment, and of might,
[o]to declare unto Jacob his transgression, and
to Israel his sin.
9 Hear this, I pray you, ye heads of the house
of Jacob, and princes of the house of Israel,
that abhor judgment, and pervert all equity.
10 [p]They build up Zion with [q]blood,

---

[a]Jer. v. 4, 5——[b]Psa. xiv. 4——[c]Ezek. xi. 3, 7 [d]Psa. xviii. 41; Prov. i. 28; Isa. i. 15; Ezek. viii. 18; Zech. vii. 13——[e]Isa. lvi. 10, 11; Ezek. xiii. 10; xxii. 25——[f]Chap. ii. 11; Matt. xii. 15——[g]Ezek. xiii. 18, 19——[h]Isa. viii. 20, 22; Ezek. xiii. 23, 24; Zech. xiii. 4——[i]Heb. *from a vision*——[k]Heb. *from divining*——[l]Amos vii. 9——[m]Heb. *upper lip*——[n]Psa. lxxiv. 9; Amos viii. 11——[o]Isa. lviii. 1——[p]Jeremiah xxii. 13——[q]Ezekiel xxii. 27; Habakkuk ii. 12; Zeph. iii. 3

NOTES ON CHAP. III

Verse 1. *Hear—O heads of Jacob*] The metaphor of the *flock* is still carried on. The *chiefs of Jacob*, and the *princes of Israel*, instead of taking care of the *flocks*, defending them, and finding them pasture, oppressed them in various ways. They are like *wolves*, who *tear the skin of the sheep*, and the *flesh off their bones*. This applies to all unjust and oppressive rulers.

Suetonius tells us, in his Life of *Tiberius*, that when the governors of provinces wrote to the emperor, entreating him to increase the *tributes*, he wrote back: "It is the property of a good *shepherd* to *shear* his sheep, not to *skin* them." Præsidibus onerandas tributo provincias suadentibus rescripsit: BONI PASTORIS esse TONDERE pecus, non DEGLUBERE. This is a maxim which many rulers of the earth do not seem to understand.

Verse 4. *Then shall they cry*] When calamity comes upon these oppressors, they shall cry for deliverance: but *they shall not be heard;* because, in their unjust exactions upon the people, they went on ruthlessly, and would *not hear* the cry of the oppressed.

Verse 5. *That bite with their teeth*] That eat to the full; that are well provided for, and as long as they are so, prophesy smooth things, and cry, *Peace!* i. e., Ye shall have nothing but peace and prosperity. Whereas the true prophet, "who putteth not into their mouths," who makes no provision for their evil propensities, "they prepare war against him." קדשו עליו מלחמה *kiddeshu alaiv milchamah*, "They *sanctify a war* against him." They call on all to help them to put down a man who is speaking evil of the *Lord's people;* and predicting the destruction of *his temple*, and *Israel his inheritance*.

Verse 6. *Night* shall be *unto you*] Ye shall have no *spiritual light*, nor will God give you any revelation of his will.

The sun shall go down over the prophets] They prospered for a while, *causing the people to err;* but they shall also be carried into captivity, and then the sun of their prosperity shall go down for ever, and the very *day* that gives *light* and comfort to others, shall be *darkness* and calamity to them.

Verse 7. *Shall the seers be ashamed*] For the *false visions* of comfort and prosperity which they pretended to see.

And the diviners confounded] Who pretended to foretell future prosperity; for they themselves are now *thralled* in that very *captivity* which the true prophets foretold, and which the false prophets said should not happen.

Verse 8. *But—I am full of power*] Here is the character of the true prophet. *He is filled*, all his soul is occupied with *power*, כח *coach*, with heavenly energy; *by the Spirit of the Lord*, the fountain of all truth and might; *and of judgment*, which enables him to make a proper discernment between the precious and the vile; *and of might*, גבורה *geburah*, prevalent power, against which vice shall not be able to prevail, and before which iniquity shall not be able to stand: but all shall fall together, and be confounded.

Verse 9. *Hear this*] An appeal similar to that in ver. 1.

Verse 10. *They build up Zion with blood*] They might cry out loudly against that butchery practised by Pekah, king of Israel, and Pul coadjutor of Rezie, against the Jews. See on chap. ii. 9. But these were by no means clear themselves; for if they *strengthened the city*, or *decorated the temple*, it was by the produce of their *exactions* and *oppressions* of the people.

I do not know a text more applicable than

A. M. cir. 3294
B. C. cir. 710
A. U. C. cir. 44
NumæPompilii,
R. Roman.,
cir. annum 6

[r]and Jerusalem with iniquity.
11 [s]The heads thereof judge for reward, and [t]the priests thereof teach for hire, and the prophets thereof divine for money: [u]yet will they lean upon the LORD, [v]and say, *Is* not the LORD among us? none evil can come upon us.
12 Therefore shall Zion for your sake be [w]ploughed *as* a field; [x]and Jerusalem shall become heaps, and [y]the mountain of the house as the high places of the forest.

[r]Heb. *bloods*——[s]Isa. i. 23; Ezek. xxii. 12; Hos. iv. 18; chap. vii. 3——[t]Jer. vi. 13——[u]Isa. xlviii. 2; Jer. vii. 4; Rom. ii. 17——[v]Heb. *saying*——[w]Jer. xxvi. 18; chap. i. 6——[x]Psa. lxxix. 1——[y]Chap. iv. 2

this to *slave-dealers;* or to any who have *made their fortunes* by such *wrongs* as affect the *life* of man; especially the former, who by the gains of this diabolic traffic have *built houses*, &c.; for, following up the prophet's *metaphor*, the *timbers*, &c., are the *bones* of the hapless Africans; and the *mortar*, the blood of the defenceless progeny of Ham. What an account must all those who have any hand in or profit from this detestable, degrading, and inhuman traffic, give to Him who will shortly judge the quick and dead!

Verse 11. *The heads thereof judge for reward*] This does not apply to the *regular law officers*, who have their proper *salaries* for giving up their whole time and attention to the conscientious discharge of the duties of their office; but to those who take a *reward*, who take BRIBES, for the perversion of justice; who will decide in favour of those from whom they get the *greatest reward.*

The prophets—divine for money] These are evidently the false prophets; for none, professing to be sent by God, used any kind of *divination.*

Yet will they lean upon the Lord] They will prescribe fasts and public thanksgivings, while not one sin is repented of or forsaken, and not one public grievance is redressed.

Is *not the Lord among us?*] Here is his *temple*, here are his *ordinances*, and here are his *people*. Will he leave these? Yes, he will abandon the whole, because all are *polluted.*

Verse 12. *Therefore shall Zion—be ploughed* as *a field*] It shall undergo a variety of reverses and sackages, till at last *there shall not be one stone left on the top of another, that shall not be pulled down;* and then a *plough* shall be drawn along the site of the walls, to signify an irreparable and endless destruction. Of this ancient custom *Horace* speaks, *Odar.* lib. i., Od. 16, ver. 18.

Altis urbibus ultimæ
Stetere causæ cur perirent
Funditus, imprimeretque muris
Hostile aratrum exercitus insolens

"From hence proud cities date their utter falls;
When, insolent in ruin, o'er their walls
The wrathful soldier drags the hostile plough,
That haughty mark of total overthrow."
FRANCIS.

Thus did the *Romans* treat Jerusalem when it was taken by *Titus. Turnus Rufus*, or as he is called by St. Jerome, *Titus Arinius Rufus*, or *Terentius Rufus*, according to *Josephus*, caused a plough to be drawn over all the courts of the temple to signify that it should never be rebuilt, and the place only serve for *agricultural* purposes. See the note on Matt. xxiv. 2. Thus *Jerusalem became heaps*, an indiscriminate mass of ruins and rubbish; and *the mountain of the house*, Mount Moriah, on which the temple stood, became so much neglected after the total destruction of the temple, that it soon resembled the *high places of the forest.* What is said here may apply also, as before hinted, to the ruin of the temple by Nebuchadnezzar in the last year of the reign of Zedekiah, the last king of the Jews.

As the *Masoretes*, in their division of the Bible, reckon the *twelve minor prophets* but as *one book*, they mark this verse (*twelfth* of chap. iii.) the MIDDLE *verse* of these prophets.

CHAPTER IV

In the commencement of this chapter we have a glorious prophecy of the establishment and prosperity of the Messiah's kingdom; its peaceful character, increasing spiritual and political influence, ultimate universality, and everlasting duration, 1–4. *Then breaks in a chorus of his people declaring their peculiar happiness in being members of his kingdom,* 5. *The prophet resumes the subject; predicts the restoration and future prosperity of Israel,* 6–8; *and exhorts them not to be discouraged at their approaching captivity, as they should in due time not only be delivered from it, but likewise be victorious over all their enemies,* 9–13. *These last verses, which evidently contain a prediction of the final triumph of Christianity over every adversary, have been applied to the conquests of the Maccabees; but the character and beneficial results of their military exploits, as far as we have any account of them, correspond but in a very faint degree to the beautiful and highly wrought terms of the prophecy. The first* three *verses of this chapter are very similar to the commencement of the second chapter of* Isaiah; *and the* fourth, *for beauty of imagery and elegance of expression, is not unworthy of that prophet.*

A. M. cir. 3294
B. C. cir. 710
A. U. C. cir. 44
NumæPompilii,
R. Roman.,
cir. annum 6

BUT [a]in the last days it shall
come to pass, *that* the
mountain of the house of the
LORD shall be established in the
top of the mountains, and it shall be exalted
above the hills; and people shall flow unto it.
2 And many nations shall come, and say,
Come, and let us go up to the [b]mountain of
the LORD, and to the house of the God of
Jacob; and he will teach us of his ways, and
we will walk in his paths; for the law shall
go forth of Zion, and the word of the LORD
from Jerusalem.
3 And he shall judge among many people,
and rebuke strong nations afar off; and they
shall beat their swords into [c]ploughshares,
and their spears into [d]pruninghooks: nation
shall not lift up a sword against nation,
[e]neither shall they learn war any more.
4 [f]But they shall sit every man under his
vine and under his fig tree; and none shall
make *them* afraid: for the
mouth of the LORD of hosts hath
spoken *it*.
5 For [g]all people will walk
every one in the name of his god, and [h]we
will walk in the name of the LORD our God
for ever and ever.
6 In that day, saith the LORD, [i]will I assemble her that halteth, [k]and I will gather her that
is driven out, and her that I have afflicted;
7 And I will make her that halted [l]a remnant, and her that was cast far off a strong
nation: and the LORD [m]shall reign over them
in Mount Zion from henceforth, even for ever.
8 And thou, O tower of [n]the flock, the
stronghold of the daughter of Zion, unto thee
shall it come, even the first dominion; the
kingdom shall come to the daughter of Jerusalem.
9 Now why dost thou cry out aloud? [o]*is there*
no king in thee? is thy counsellor perished?

A. M. cir. 3294
B. C. cir. 710
A. U. C. cir. 44
NumæPompilii,
R. Roman.,
cir. annum 6

[a]Isa. ii. 2, &c.; Ezek. xvii. 22, 23——[b]Isa. xiv. 25——[c]Isa. ii. 4; Joel iii. 10——[d]Or, *scythes*——[e]Psa. lxxii. 7——[f]1 Kings iv. 25; Zech. iii. 10——[g]Jer. ii. 11——[h]Zech. x. 12——[i]Ezek. xxxiv. 16; Zeph. iii. 19

[k]Psa. cxlvii. 2; Ezek. xxxiv. 13; xxxvii. 21——[l]Chap. ii. 12; v. 3, 7, 8; vii. 18——[m]Isa. ix. 6; xxiv. 23; Dan. vii. 14, 27; Luke i. 33; Rev. xi. 15——[n]Or, *Edar;* Gen. xxxv. 21——[o]Jer. viii. 19

NOTES ON CHAP. IV

Verses 1-4. *But in the last days it shall come to pass*] These *four* verses contain, says Bp. *Newcome*, a prophecy that was to be fulfilled by the coming of the Messiah, when the Gentiles were to be admitted into covenant with God, and the apostles were to preach the Gospel, beginning at Jerusalem, Luke xxiv. 47; Acts ii. 14, &c.; when Christ was to be the spiritual Judge and King of many people, was to convince many nations of their errors and vices, and was to found a religion which had the strongest tendency to promote peace. Bp. *Lowth* thinks that "Micah took this passage from Isaiah;" or the Spirit may have inspired both prophets with this prediction; or both may have copied some *common original*, the words of a prophet well known at that time. The variations (few and of little importance) may be seen in the notes on the parallel passages, Isa. ii. 2, &c.; to which the reader is requested to refer.

Verse 4. *Under his vine and under his fig tree*] A proverbial expression, indicative of perfect peace, security, and rural comfort. See on Isa. ii. 1. This verse is an addition to the prophecy as it stands in Isaiah.

Verse 5. *Every one in the name of his god*] This shall be the state of the Gentile world; but after the captivity, the Jews walked in the name of Jehovah alone; and acknowledge no other object of religious worship to the present day.

Verse 6. *Will I assemble her that halteth—driven out—afflicted*] Under these epithets, the state of the Jews, who were to be gathered into the Christian Church, is pointed out. They *halted* between the true God and idols; they were *driven out* into captivity, because of this idolatry; and they were variously *afflicted*, because they would not return unto the Lord that bought them.

Verse 7. *Her that halted a remnant*] I will preserve them as a distinct people after their return from captivity, for the farther purposes of my grace and mercy.

And the Lord shall reign over them in Mount Zion] The *Chaldee* is remarkable here, and positively applies the words to the Messiah: "But thou, O Messiah, of Israel, who art hidden because of the sins of the congregation of Zion, the kingdom shall come unto thee."

Verse 8. *O tower of the flock*] I think the temple is meant, or Jerusalem; the place where the *flock*, the whole *congregation* of the people assembled to worship God. *Newcome* retains the Hebrew word עדר *eder*, a tower in or near *Beth-lehem*, Gen. xxxv. 21, or, as some think, a tower near the *sheep-gate* in Jerusalem. I believe Jerusalem, or the temple, or both, are meant; for these were considered *the stronghold of the daughter of Zion*, the fortress of the Jewish people.

Even the first dominion] What was this? The Divine *theocracy* under Jesus Christ; this former, this *first dominion*, was to be restored. Hence the angel called him *Immanuel*, God with us, ruling among us.

Verse 9. Is there *no king in thee?*] None. And why? Because thou hast rejected Jehovah thy king.

Is thy counsellor perished?] No: but thou hast rejected the words and advices of the prophets.

A. M. cir. 3294
B. C. cir. 710
A. U. C. cir. 44
NumæPompilii,
R. Roman.,
cir. annum 6

for [p]pangs have taken thee as a
woman in travail.
10 Be in pain, and labour to
bring forth, O daughter of Zion,
like a woman in travail: for now shalt thou go
forth out of the city, and thou shalt dwell in the
field, and thou shalt go *even* to Babylon; there
shalt thou be delivered; there the LORD shall
redeem thee from the hand of thine enemies.
11 [q]Now also many nations are gathered
against thee, that say, Let her be defiled, and
let our eye [r]look upon Zion.
12 But they know not [s]the
thoughts of the LORD, neither
understand they his counsel: for
he shall gather them [t]as the
sheaves into the floor.
13 [u]Arise and thresh, O daughter of Zion:
for I will make thine horn iron, and I will
make thy hoofs brass: and thou shalt [v]beat
in pieces many people: [w]and I will consecrate their gain unto the LORD, and their
substance unto [x]the LORD of the whole
earth.

A. M. cir. 3294
B. C. cir. 710
A. U. C. cir. 44
NumæPompilii,
R. Roman.,
cir. annum 6

[p]Isa. xiii. 8; xxi. 3; Jer. xxx. 6; l. 43——[q]Lam. ii. 16——[r]Obad. 12; chap. vii. 10——[s]Isa. lv. 8; Rom. xi. 33——[t]Isa. xxi. 10——[u]Isa. xli. 15, 16; Jer. li. 33——[v]Dan. ii. 44——[w]Isa. xviii. 7; xxiii. 18; lx. 6, 9——[x]Zech. iv. 14; vi. 5

Pangs have taken thee] He is speaking of the desolations that should take place when the Chaldeans should come against the city; and hence he says, "Thou shalt go to Babylon;" ye shall be cast out of your own land, and sent slaves to a foreign country. He represents the people under the notion of a *woman in travail*.

Verse 10. *There shalt thou be delivered*] There God shall meet thee; and by redeeming thee from thy captivity, bringing thee back to thine own land, and finally converting thee unto himself, shall deliver thee from the *burden* of grief and wo which thou now bearest, and under which thou dost groan.

Verse 11. *Many nations are gathered against thee*] The Chaldeans, who were composed of many nations. And, we may add, all the surrounding nations were their enemies; and rejoiced when the Chaldean army had overthrown Jerusalem, destroyed the temple, and led the people away captive.

Let her be defiled] This was their cry and their wish: Let Jerusalem be laid as *low* as she can be, like a thing *defiled* and *cast away* with abhorrence; that *their eyes might look upon Zion* with scorn, contempt, and exultation.

Verse 12. *But they know not the thoughts of the Lord*] These think that God has utterly rejected his people, and they shall have a troublesome neighbour no more: but this is not his design; he will afflict them for a time; but these, the enemies of his people, he will gather as *sheaves* into the *threshing-floor*, there to be trodden, and the wheel to go over them. This is the *counsel*, the *purpose of God*, which these do not understand. The persons here referred to are not only the *Chaldeans* which were threshed by the *Persians* and *Medes;* but the Idumeans, Ammonites, Moabites, and Philistines, which the Jews afterwards subdued.

Verse 13. *Arise and thresh, O daughter of Zion*] This refers to the subject of the preceding verse. When God shall have *gathered together* all thy enemies, as into the *threshing-floor*, he will give thee *commission* and *power* to get a complete victory over them, and reduce them to servitude. And that thou mayest be able to do this, he will be on thy side as a powerful helper; here signified by the metaphors, *iron horns*, and *brazen hoofs*. Thou shalt have *power*, *authority*, and *unconquerable strength;* for thine enemies shall be no more against thee than the *corn* against *oxen* shod with *brass*, or a puny animal against the horn of a fierce *bull* tipped with *iron*.

I will consecrate their gain unto the Lord] What they have taken from thee in the way of spoil shall be restored; and again consecrated unto the service of him who will show himself to be *the Lord*, the Supreme Governor of the *whole earth*. Was not this prediction fulfilled when Cyrus gave the Jews permission to return to their own land, and gave them back the sacred vessels of the temple which Nebuchadnezzar had carried away? The Maccabees and their successors recovered much of the booty of which the neighbouring nations had deprived the Jews; and the *treasure* taken was devoted to Jehovah. The *first* verse of the next chapter should conclude this.

CHAPTER V

This chapter begins, according to the opinion of some commentators, with a prophecy concerning the siege of Jerusalem by Nebuchadnezzar, and the great indignities which Zedekiah should suffer from the Babylonians, 1. *We have next a most famous prediction concerning the birthplace of the Messiah, "whose goings forth have been from* of old, *from* EVERLASTING," 2. *See* Matt. ii. 6. *The Jews obstinately persisting in their opposition to the Messiah, God will therefore give them up into the hands of their enemies till the times of the Gentiles be fulfilled: and then all the posterity of Jacob, both* Israel *and* Judah, *shall be converted to the faith of our Lord Jesus Christ, and, along with the Gentiles, be brought into the large and peaceful pastures of this Great Shepherd of the sheep,* 3, 4. *After this illustrious prophecy, the prophet goes on to foretell the downfall of the Assyrians, by whom are meant the enemies of the Church in general, the* type *being probably put for the* antitype; *the miraculous discomfiture of the great Assyrian army in the reign of Sennacherib strongly shadowing forth the glorious and no less miraculous triumphs of Christianity in the latter times,* 5, 6. *See* Isa. xi. 16. *Some understand this prophecy of Antiochus and the seven famous Maccabees, with their eight royal successors, from Aristobulus to Antigonus; and it is not impossible that these people may be also intended, for we have often had occasion to remark that a prophecy of the Old Testament Scriptures has frequently more than one aspect. The* seventh *verse was fulfilled by the Jews spreading the knowledge of the true God during their captivity, and so paving the way for the Gospel; but will be more signally fulfilled after their conversion and restoration. See* Rom. xi. 12–15. *The remaining verses contain a prophecy of the final overthrow of all the enemies of pure and undefiled religion, and of the thorough purification of the Church of God from the corruptions of Antichrist,* 9–15.

A. M. cir. 3294 B. C. cir. 710 A. U. C. cir. 44 NumæPompilii, R. Roman., cir. annum 6

NOW gather thyself in troops,
O daughter of troops: he
hath laid siege against us: they
shall [a]smite the judge of Israel,
with a rod upon the cheek.
2 But thou, [b]Beth-lehem Ephratah, *though*
thou be little [c]among the [d]thousands of Judah,
yet out of thee shall he come forth unto me
that is to be [e]Ruler in Israel; [f]whose goings forth *have been* from of old, from
[g]everlasting.
3 Therefore will he give them
up, until the time *that* [h]she
which travaileth hath brought
forth: then [i]the remnant of his
brethren shall return unto the children of
Israel.
4 And he shall stand and [k]feed [l]in the
strength of the LORD, in the majesty of the
name of the LORD his God; and they shall
abide: for now [m]shall he be great unto the
ends of the earth.

A. M. cir. 3294 B. C. cir. 710 A. U. C. cir. 44 NumæPompilii, R. Roman., cir. annum 6

[a]Lam. iii. 30; Matt. v. 39; xxvii. 30——[b]Matt. ii. 6; John vii. 42——[c]1 Sam. xxiii. 23——[d]Exod. xviii. 25 [e]Gen. xlix. 10; Isa. ix. 6——[f]Psa. xc. 2; Prov. viii. 22, 23; John i. 1

[g]Heb. *the days of eternity*——[h]Chap. iv. 10——[i]Chap. iv. 7——[k]Or, *rule*——[l]Isa. xl. 11; xlix. 10; Ezek. xxxiv. 23; chap. vii. 14——[m]Psa. lxxii. 8; Isa. lii. 13; Zech. ix. 10; Luke i. 32

NOTES ON CHAP. V

Verse 1. *O daughter of troops*] The Chaldeans, whose armies were composed of *troops* from various nations.

He (Nebuchadnezzar) *hath laid siege against us;* (Jerusalem;) *they shall smite the judge of Israel* (Zedekiah) *with a rod upon the cheek.*] They shall offer him the greatest *indignity.* They slew his sons before his face; and then put out his eyes, loaded him with chains, and carried him captive to Babylon.

Verse 2. *But thou, Beth-lehem Ephratah*] I have considered this subject in great detail in the *notes* on Matt. ii. 6, to which the reader will be pleased to refer. This verse should begin this chapter; the *first* verse belongs to the preceding chapter.

Beth-lehem Ephratah, to distinguish it from another Beth-lehem, which was in the tribe of *Zebulun,* Josh. xix. 15.

Thousands of Judah] The tribes were divided into small portions called *thousands;* as in our country certain divisions of counties are called *hundreds.*

Whose goings forth have been *from of old*] In every age, from the foundation of the world, there has been some manifestation of the Messiah. He was the hope, as he was the salvation, of the world, from the promise to Adam in paradise, to his manifestation in the flesh *four thousand* years after.

From everlasting] מימי עולם *miyemey olam,* "From the days of all time;" from time as it came out of eternity. That is, there was *no time* in which he has not been *going forth*—*coming* in various ways to save men. And he that *came forth* the moment that time had its birth, was *before that time* in which he began to *come forth* to save the souls that he had *created.* He was *before* all things. As he is the *Creator* of all things, so he is the *Eternal,* and *no part* of what was *created.* All *being* but God has been *created.* Whatever has *not been created* is God. But Jesus is the *Creator* of all things; therefore he is God; for he cannot be a *part* of his *own work.*

Verse 3. *Therefore will he give them up*] Jesus Christ shall give up the disobedient and rebellious Jews into the hands of all the nations of the earth, till *she who travaileth hath brought forth;* that is, till the Christian Church, represented Rev. xii. 1, under the notion of a *woman in travail,* shall have had the fulness of the Gentiles brought in. *Then the remnant of his brethren shall return;* the Jews also shall be converted unto the Lord; and thus *all Israel shall be saved,* according to Rom. xi. 26.

Unto the children of Israel.] Taking in *both families,* that of *Judah* and that of *Israel.* The remnant of the *ten tribes,* wherever they are, shall be brought in under Christ; and though now *lost* among the nations of the earth, they will then not only be brought in among the *fulness of the Gentiles,* but most probably be *distinguished* as *Jews.*

On this verse Abp. *Newcome* says, "The sense is, God will not fully vindicate and exalt his people, till the virgin mother shall have brought forth her Son; and till Judah and Israel, and all the true sons of Abraham among their brethren the Gentiles, be converted to Christianity.

Verse 4. *He shall stand and feed*] The *Messiah* shall *remain* with his followers, supporting and *governing them in the strength and majesty of the Lord,* with all the miraculous interferences of his power, and all the glories of his grace.

And they shall abide] After this the Jews shall no more go astray, but shall remain one people with the Gentiles, under the one Shepherd and Bishop of all souls.

Newcome translates, "They shall be converted," for instead of וישבו *veyashebu,* he reads וישובו *veyashubu,* which gives him the translation above. This is the reading of *three* MSS. of *Kennicott's* and *De Rossi's,* with the *Syriac, Chaldee,* and *Vulgate.*

For now shall he be great] The Messiah shall be *great,* as bringing salvation to the *ends*

A. M. cir. 3294
B. C. cir. 710
A. U. C. cir. 44
NumæPompilii.
R. Roman.,
cir. annum 6

5 And this *man* [n]shall be the peace, when the Assyrian shall come into our land: and when he shall tread in our palaces, then shall we raise against him seven shepherds, and eight [o]principal men.

6 And they shall [p]waste the land of Assyria with the sword, and the land of [q]Nimrod [r]in the entrances thereof: thus shall he [s]deliver *us* from the Assyrian, when he cometh into our land, and when he treadeth within our borders.

7 And [t]the remnant of Jacob shall be in the midst of many people [u]as the dew from the LORD, as the showers upon the grass, that tarrieth not for man, nor waiteth for the sons of men.

A. M. cir. 3294
B. C. cir. 710
A. U. C. cir. 44
NumæPompilii,
R. Roman.,
cir. annum 6

8 And the remnant of Jacob shall be among the Gentiles in the midst of many people as a lion among the beasts of the forest, as a young lion among the flocks of [v]sheep: who, if he go through, both treadeth down, and teareth in pieces, and none can deliver.

9 Thine hand shall be lifted up upon thine adversaries, and all thine enemies shall be cut off.

10 [w]And it shall come to pass in that day, saith the LORD, that I will cut off thy horses out of the midst of thee, and I will destroy thy chariots:

11 And I will cut off the cities of thy land, and throw down all thy strongholds:

---

[n]Psa. lxxii. 7; Isa. ix. 6; Zech. ix. 10; Luke ii. 14; Eph. ii. 14——[o]Heb. *princes of men*——[p]Heb. *eat up* [q]Gen. x. 8, 10, 11

[r]Or, *with her own naked swords*——[s]Luke i. 71 [t]Ver. 3——[u]Deut. xxxii. 2; Psa. lxxii. 6; cx. 3——[v]Or, *goats*——[w]Zech. ix. 10

---

of the earth. All nations shall receive his religion, and he shall be universal King.

Verse 5. *And this* man *shall be the peace*] This clause should be joined to the preceding verse, as it finishes the prophecy concerning our blessed Lord, who is the *Author* and *Prince of Israel;* and shall finally give *peace* to all nations, by bringing them under his yoke.

When the Assyrian shall come] This is a new prophecy, and relates to the subversion of the Assyrian empire.

Then shall we raise against him seven shepherds] Supposed to mean the *seven Maccabees*, *Mattathias*, and his *five* sons, and *Hyrcanus*, the son of *Simon*.

Eight principal men.] Eight princes, the *Asmonean* race; beginning with *Aristobulus*, and ending with *Herod*, who was married to *Mariamne.—Sharpe*. Perhaps *seven* and *eight* are a definite for an indefinite number, as Eccl. xi. 2; Job v. 19. The prophet means the chiefs of the Medes and Babylonians, the prefects of different provinces who took Nineveh, whose number may have been what is here specified.—*Newcome.*

Calmet considers this as referring to the invasion of Judea by *Cambyses*, when the Lord raised up against him the *seven magi.* He of them who passed for king of the Persians was the *Smerdis* of *Herodotus*, the *Oropastes* of Trogus, and the *Artaxerxes* of Ezra. These magi were put to death by *seven Persian chiefs;* who, having delivered the empire from them, set one of themselves, *Darius*, the son of Hystaspes, upon the throne.

Verse 6. *The land of Nimrod*] Assyria, and Nineveh its capital; and Babylon, which was also built by Nimrod, who was its *first* king, Gen. x. 11, 12, in the *margin.*

In the entrances thereof] At its *posts* or *watergates;* for it was by rendering themselves masters of the Euphrates that the Medes and Persians took the city, according to the prediction of Jeremiah, chap. li. 32, 36.

Calmet thinks that this refers to the deliverance of the land from *Cambyses* by his death, and the insurrection of the *eight princes* mentioned above, who made themselves masters of the whole Babylonian empire, &c. Perhaps it is best to refer it to the invasion of Judea by *Nebuchadnezzar;* and the final destruction of the *Babylonish* empire by *Cyrus*, who took Babylon, slew Belshazzar, and possessed himself of the kingdom.

Verse 7. *The remnant of Jacob*] From the reign of *Darius Hystaspes* (*Ahasuerus*, husband of *Esther*) the Jews were greatly favoured. Those who continued in Persia and Chaldea were greatly honoured under the protection of *Mordecai* and *Esther.—Calmet.* But others consider this as applying to the *Maccabees.*

As a dew from the Lord] Even during their captivity many of the Jews were the means of *spreading the knowledge of the one true God;* see Dan. ii. 47; iii. 29; iv. 34; vi. 26. This may be *the dew from the Lord* mentioned here. When the Messiah appeared, the Gospel was preached by *them;* and it shall again be propagated by their future glorious restoration, Rom. xi. 12, 25.

The grass, that tarrieth not for man] Which *grass* springs up without the attention and culture of man; לאיש *leish*, even the *best* and *most skilful* of men.

Nor waiteth for the sons of men.] לבני אדם *libney adam*, for the *sons of Adam*, the first transgressor. The *dew* and the *showers* descend on the earth and water it, in order to render it fruitful; and the *grass* springs up independently either of the *worth* or *wickedness* of man. All comes through *God's bounty*, who causes his *sun* to shine on the *just* and the *unjust*, and his *rain* to descend on the *evil* and the *good.*

Verse 8. *As a lion*] In this and the following verse the victories of the Maccabees are supposed to be foretold.

Verse 9. *All thine enemies shall be cut off.*] The *Assyrians*, who had destroyed *Israel;* and the *Babylonians*, who had ruined *Judah.*

Verse 10. *I will cut off thy horses*] Thou shalt have no need of *cavalry* in thine armies; God will fight for you.

Verse 11. *I will—throw down all thy strong-*

A. M. cir. 3294
B. C. cir. 710
A. U. C. cir. 44
NumæPompilii,
R. Roman.,
cir. annum 6

12 And I will cut off witchcrafts out of thine hand; and thou shalt have no *more* [x]soothsayers.

13 [y]Thy graven images also will I cut off, and thy [z]standing images out of the midst of thee; and thou shalt [a]no more worship the work of thine hands.

14 And I will pluck up thy groves out of the midst of thee: so will I destroy thy [b]cities.

15 And I will [c]execute vengeance in anger and fury upon the heathen, such as they have not heard.

[x]Isa. ii. 6——[y]Zech. xiii. 2——[z]Or, *statues*——[a]Isa. ii. 8——[b]Or, *enemies*——[c]Psa. cxlix. 7; ver. 8; 2 Thess. i. 8

holds] Thou shalt have no need of *fortified cities;* I will be thy defence.

Verse 12. *I will cut off witchcrafts*] Thou shalt seek help only in Jehovah thy God. They have had neither soothsayers, images, groves, nor high places, from the captivity to the present day.

Verse 13. *Thy graven images also will I cut off*] Thou shalt be no more an idolatrous people.

Verse 15. *I will execute vengeance—upon the heathen*] And he did so; for the empires of the *Assyrians*, *Chaldeans*, and others, the sworn enemies of the Jews, have long since been utterly destroyed.

CHAPTER VI

This chapter reproves and threatens. The manner of raising the attention by calling on man to urge his plea in the face of all nature, and on the inanimate creation to hear the expostulation of Jehovah with his people, is awakening and sublime. The words of Jehovah follow, 3–5. *And God's mercies having been set forth to his people, one of them is introduced, in a beautiful dramatic form, asking what his duty is towards a God so gracious,* 6, 7. *The answer follows in the words of the prophet,* 8; *who goes on to upbraid the people of his charge with their injustice and idolatry, to which he ascribes want of success in their lawful undertakings, and those heavy calamities which are now impending,* 9–15.

A. M. cir. 3294
B. C. cir. 710
A. U. C. cir. 44
NumæPompilii,
R. Roman.,
cir. annum 6

HEAR ye now what the LORD saith; Arise, contend thou [a]before the mountains, and let the hills hear thy voice.

2 [b]Hear ye, O mountains, [c]the LORD's controversy, and ye strong foundations of the earth: for [d]the LORD hath a controversy with his people, and he will plead with Israel.

3 O my people, [e]what have I done unto thee? and wherein have I wearied thee? testify against me.

4 [f]For I brought thee up out of the land of Egypt, and redeemed thee out of the house of servants; and I sent before thee Moses, Aaron, and Miriam.

[a]Or, *with*——[b]Deut. xxxii. 1; Psalm l. 1, 4; Isa. i. 2——[c]Hos. xii. 2——[d]Isa. i. 18; v. 3, 4; xliii. 26; Hos. iv. 1——[e]Jer. ii. 5, 31——[f]Exod. xii. 51; xiv. 30; xx. 2; Deut. iv. 20; Amos ii. 10

NOTES ON CHAP. VI

Verse 1. *Arise, contend thou*] This chapter is a sort of *dialogue* between God and the people. GOD speaks the *five* first verses, and convicts the people of sin, righteousness, and judgment. The PEOPLE, convinced of their iniquity, deprecate God's judgments, in the *sixth* and *seventh* verses. In the *eighth* verse God prescribes the *way* in which they are to be *saved;* and then the *prophet*, by the command of God, goes on to remonstrate from the *ninth* verse to the end of the chapter.

Verse 2. *Hear ye, O mountains*] Micah, as God's advocate, summons this people into judgment, and makes an appeal to inanimate creation against them. He had spoken to the priests, to the princes, to the people. He had done every thing that was necessary to make them wise, and holy, and happy; they had uniformly disobeyed, and were ever ungrateful. It was not consistent with either the justice or mercy of God to permit them to go on without reprehension and punishment. He now calls them into judgment; and such was the nature of their crimes that, to heighten the effect, and show what reason he had to punish such a people, he appeals to *inanimate creation.* Their ingratitude and rebellion are sufficient to make the *mountains*, the *hills*, and the *strong foundations of the earth* to hear, tremble, and give judgment against them. This, then, is the *Lord's controversy* with his people, and thus he will plead with Israel.

Verse 3. *O my people, what have I done unto thee?*] They are called to show why God should not pronounce sentence upon them. This condescension is truly astonishing! God appears to humble himself to his creatures. You have acted basely, treacherously, and ungratefully to me; this had already been proved by the prophets. What *cause* have I given you for such conduct? I have required a *religious service* from you; but have I wearied you by a fatiguing round of difficult duties? If I have, now testify against me; and you shall be first heard, and your plea received, if it be reasonable and good. They are silent; and God proceeds, and states what he has done for them.

Verse 4. *I brought thee up out of the land*

A. M. cir. 3294 B. C. cir. 710 A. U. C. cir. 44 NumæPompilii, R. Roman., cir. annum 6

5 O my people, remember now
what [g]Balak king of Moab consulted, and what Balaam the son
of Beor answered him from
[h]Shittim unto Gilgal; that ye may know
[i]the righteousness of the LORD.

6 Wherewith shall I come before the LORD,
and bow myself before the high God? shall
I come before him with burnt-offerings, with
calves [k]of a year old?

7 [l]Will the LORD be pleased
with thousands of rams, *or* with
ten thousands of [m]rivers of oil?
[n]shall I give my first-born *for*
my transgression, the fruit of my [o]body *for*
the sin of my soul?

A. M. cir. 3294 B. C. cir. 710 A. U. C. cir. 44 NumæPompilii, R. Roman., cir. annum 6

8 He hath [p]showed thee, O man, what
is good; and what doth the LORD require of
thee, but [q]to do justly, and to love mercy, and
to [r]walk humbly with thy God?

[g]Num. xxii. 5; xxiii. 7; xxiv. 10, 11; Deut. xxiii. 4, 5; Josh. xxiv. 9, 10; Rev. ii. 14——[h]Num. xxv. 1; xxxiii. 49; Josh. iv. 19; v. 10——[i]Judg. v. 11——[k]Heb. *sons of a year?*——[l]Psa. l. 9; li. 16; Isa. i. 11——[m]Job xxix. 6

[n]2 Kings xvi. 3; xxi. 6; xxiii. 10; Jer. vii. 31; xix. 5; Ezek. xxiii. 37——[o]Heb. *belly*——[p]Deut. x. 12; 1 Sam. xv. 22; Hos. vi. 6; xii. 6——[q]Gen. xviii. 19; Isa. i. 17 [r]Heb. *humble* thyself *to walk*

of Egypt] Where you were *slaves*, and grievously oppressed; from all this I *redeemed* you. Was this a small benefit? *I sent before thee* MOSES, my chosen servant, and instructed him that he might be your *leader* and *lawgiver. I sent with* him AARON, that he might be your *priest*, and transact all spiritual matters between myself and you, in offerings, sacrifices, and atonements. I *sent* MIRIAM, to whom I gave the spirit of *prophecy*, that she might tell you things to come, and be the director of your *females.* To this sense the *Chaldee*, "I have sent *three* prophets before you; Moses, that he might teach you the tradition of judgments; Aaron, that he might make atonement for the people; and Miriam, that she might instruct the females."

Verse 5. *Remember now what Balak king of Moab consulted*] He sent for Balaam to *curse* your fathers; but by my influence he was obliged to *bless them.* See Num. xxii. and xxiii., and the notes there, where this subject is largely considered.

From Shittim unto Gilgal] From the encampment at Shittim, Num. xxv. 1, on the way to that of Gilgal, Josh. iv. 19. Balaam gave different answers in the interval between these places. We may suppose that the encampments of Israel advanced slowly to that part of Jordan which was opposite to Gilgal. The *Chaldee* has, "Were there not wonderful things done in your behalf from the valley of Shittim to the house of Gilgal?" See Josh. iii. 1; iv. 20. Thus there will be a reference to the miraculous passage over Jordan. See *Newcome.*

That ye may know the righteousness] The just, equitable, and merciful dealing of the Most High. Recollect *those* things, that ye may have a proper impression of *this.* There are many interpretations given of this rather obscure clause; what I have proposed seems to me the most *simple.*

This is the sum of the address; and here the case of the plaintiff terminates, the prisoners being called to show why the sentence of the law should not be pronounced. I make no apology for using any *forensic* terms, as the passages before us refer to a *case* brought into a *court* to be *judged*, and the terms in the original are all such as are proper for a *court of justice;* and the thing itself is called the *Lord's controversy*, ריב יהוה *rib Yehovah, Jehovah's suit at law.* And hence it is said, *He will plead*, litigate, *with Israel.*

Verse 6. *Wherewith shall I come before the Lord*] Now the people, as defendants, appear; but instead of vindicating themselves, or attempting to dispute what has been alleged against them, they seem at once to *plead guilty;* and now anxiously inquire how they shall appease the wrath of the Judge, how they shall make atonement for the sins already committed.

Bow myself before the high God] They wish to pray, and to make supplication to their Judge; but how shall they come before him? They have no right to come into his presence. Some *offering* must be brought; but of what *kind*, or of what *value?* Their sin is unprecedented, and usual methods of access will not avail. They are distracted in their minds, and make a variety of proposals to themselves, some *rational*, some *absurd* and *impossible*, and some even *sinful.*

Shall I come before him with burnt-offerings] This is *resonable*, and according to the *law;* but this will be insufficient.

Verse 7. *Will the Lord be pleased with thousands of rams*] These might be *procured*, though with difficulty; but conscience says, neither will these do.

With ten thousands of rivers of oil] This is *absurd* and *impossible;* but could even these be procured, could they all make atonement for such *guilt*, and *ingratitude*, and *rebellion?*

Shall I give my first-born for *my transgression*] This was *sinful and wicked;* but such offerings had been made by the *Phœnicians*, and their successors the *Carthaginians;* and this very custom was copied by the corrupt Israelites. See some cases of such offerings, 2 Kings iii. 27; Lev. xx. 27.

The fruit of my body for *the sin of my soul?*] This clause is an explanation of the former. Shall I make the first-born, the best and goodliest of my children, חטאת *chattath*, a SIN-OFFERING *for my soul?* And thus the original is used in a multitude of places.

When they had put all these questions to their reason and conscience, they found no satisfaction; their distraction is increased, and despair is about to take place, when Jehovah, the plaintiff, in his mercy interposes:

Verse 8. *He hath showed thee, O man, what is good*] All the modes of expiation which ye have proposed are, in the sight of God, unavailable; they cannot do away the *evil*, nor purify from the *guilt* of sin. He himself has shown thee what is *good;* that which is *profitable* to *thee*, and *pleasing* to himself. And what is *that?* Answer. Thou art—

A. M. cir. 3294
B. C. cir. 710
A. U. C. cir. 44
NumæPompilii,
R. Roman.,
cir. annum 6

9 The [s]LORD's voice crieth unto
the city, and [t]*the man of* wisdom
shall see thy name: hear ye the
rod, and who hath appointed it.
10 [u]Are there yet the treasures of wickedness in the house of the wicked, and the
[v]scant measure [w]*that is* abominable?
11 [x]Shall I count *them* pure
with the [y]wicked balances, and
with the bag of deceitful weights?
12 For the rich men thereof are full of vio-

A. M. cir. 3294
B. C. cir. 710
A. U. C. cir. 44
NumæPompilii,
R. Roman.,
cir. annum 6

[s]Deut. xv. 5; xxvi. 17; xxviii. 1, 2; xxx. 10——[t]Or, *thy name shall see that which is*——[u]Or, Is there *yet unto every man a house of the wicked*, &c.——[v]Hebrew, *measure of leanness;* Amos viii. 5——[w]Deuteronomy xxv. 13–16; Proverbs xi. 1; xx. 10, 23——[x]Or, *Shall I be pure with*, &c.——[y]Hos. xii. 7

I. *To do justly;* to give to all their due.

1. To *God* his due; thy *heart*, thy *body, soul*, and *spirit;* thy *wisdom, understanding, judgment.* "To love him with all thy heart, soul, mind, and strength, and thy neighbour as thyself." This is God's *due* and *right* from every man.

2. Thou art to give thy *neighbour* his due; to do to him as thou wouldst that he should do to thee, never working ill to him.

3. Thou art to give to *thyself* thy due; not to deprive thy soul of what God has provided for it; to keep thy body in temperance, sobriety, and chastity; avoiding all excesses, both in *action* and *passion.*

II. *Thou art to love mercy;* not only to do what *justice* requires, but also what *mercy, kindness, benevolence*, and *charity* require.

III. But how art thou to do this? Thou art to *walk humbly with thy God;* הצנע *hatsnea*, to *humble thyself* to walk. This implies to acknowledge thy iniquity, and submit to be saved by his free mercy, as thou hast already found that no kind of *offering* or *sacrifice* can avail. Without this humiliation of soul there never was, there never can be, any *walking with God;* for without his mercy no soul can be saved; and he must be THY *God* before thou canst *walk with him.* Many, when they hear the nature of sin pointed out, and the way of salvation made plain through the blood of the Lamb, have shut their eyes both against sin and the proper sacrifice for it, and parried all exhortation, threatening, &c., with this text: "God requires nothing of us but to do justly, love mercy, and walk humbly with him." Now I ask any man, Art thou willing to *stand* or *fall* by *this text?* And it would cost me neither much time nor much pains to show that on this ground no soul of man can be saved. Nor does God say that this *doing justly*, &c., shall *merit* eternal glory. No. He shows that in *this way* all men *should walk;* that this is *the duty of* EVERY *rational being:* but he well knows that no *fallen soul* can act thus without especial assistance from him, and that it is only the *regenerate man*, the man who has found redemption through the blood of the cross, and has God for HIS God, that can *thus act* and *walk. Salvation is of the mere mercy of God alone;* for by the *works of the law shall no flesh be justified.*

The manner of raising attention, says Bp. *Newcome*, on ver. 1, 2, by calling on man to urge his plea in the face of all nature, and on the inanimate creation to hear the expostulation of Jehovah with his people, is truly awakening and magnificent. The words of Jehovah follow in ver. 3, 4, 5. And God's mercies having been set before the people, one of them is introduced in a beautiful dramatic form; asking what his duty is towards so gracious a God, ver. 6, 7. The answer follows in the words of the prophet, ver. 8. Some think we have a sort of dialogue between *Balak* and *Balaam*, represented to us in the prophetical way. The *king of Moab* speaks, ver. 6. *Balaam* replies by another question in the two first hemistichs of ver. 7. The *king of Moab* rejoins in the remaining part of the verse; and *Balaam* replies, ver. 8. Bps. *Butler* and *Lowth* favour this. I cannot agree.

Verse 9. *The Lord's voice crieth unto the city*] No man is found to hear; but the *man of wisdom* will hear, תושיה *tushiyah;* a word frequent in the writings of Solomon and Job, signifying wisdom, wealth, substance, reason, essence, happiness; any thing that is complete; or that which is substantial, in opposition to vanity, emptiness, mere show, unsubstantiality. When God speaks, the *man of common sense*, who has any knowledge of God or his own soul, will *see* thy *name;* but instead of יראה *yireh, will see*, the *Septuagint, Syriac, Vulgate*, and *Arabic*, with *twelve* of *Kennicott's* and *De Rossi's* MSS., have read יראי *yirey, they that* FEAR. The *Vulgate* reads:—

Et salus erit timentibus nomen tuum.

"And thou shalt be salvation to them that fear thy name."

The *Septuagint*—Και σωσει φοβουμενους το ονομα αυτου.

And he shall save those who fear his name.—This the *Arabic* copies.

The *Targum* has, "And the teachers shall fear the name." That is, יהוה *Yehovah.*

The *French Bible* is very strange:—

Car ton nom voit comme il va de tout.

"For thy name sees how every thing goes."

The word תושיה *tushiyah*, mentioned above, which occasions all the difficulty, has been read with an ע *ain* by the *Vulgate* and *Septuagint*, as coming from the root ישע *yasha, to be saved;* and it is very likely that this was the *original* reading. The two last letters in the word, יה, might have been easily mistaken in the MS. for the letter ע, where I may suppose the word stood thus, תושע, *shall be saved;* and as several MSS. read יראי *yirey*, they who *fear*, instead of יראה *yireh*, he shall *see*, the whole clause might have been just what it appears in the *Vulgate* and *Septuagint.* It is also necessary to remark that the word in dispute has various forms in some MSS., which is a strong presumption against its authenticity. See *Kennicott* and *De Rossi.*

Verse 10. *Are there yet the treasures of wickedness*] Such as false balances and deceitful weights. See on Hos. xii. 7. This shows that they were not DOING JUSTLY. They did not *give to each his due.*

A. M. cir. 3294
B. C. cir. 710
A. U. C. cir. 44
NumæPompilii,
R. Roman.,
cir. annum 6

lence, and the inhabitants thereof have spoken lies, and [z]their tongue *is* deceitful in their mouth.

13 Therefore also will I [a]make *thee* sick in smiting thee, in making *thee* desolate because of thy sins.

14 [b]Thou shalt eat, but not be satisfied; and thy casting down *shall be* in the midst of thee; and thou shalt take hold, but shalt not deliver; and *that* which thou deliverest will I give up to the sword.

15 Thou shalt [c]sow, but thou shalt not reap; thou shalt tread the olives, but thou shalt not anoint thee with oil; and sweet wine, but shalt not drink wine.

A. M. cir. 3294
B. C. cir. 710
A. U. C. cir. 44
NumæPompilii,
R. Roman.,
cir. annum 6

16 For [d]the statutes of [e]Omri are [f]kept, and all the works of the house of [g]Ahab, and ye walk in their counsels; that I should make thee [h]a [i]desolation, and the inhabitants thereof a hissing: therefore ye shall bear the [k]reproach of my people.

---

[z]Jer. ix. 3, 5, 6, 8——[a]Lev. xxvi. 16; Psa. cvii. 17, 18 [b]Lev. xxvi. 26; Hos. iv. 10——[c]Deut. xxviii. 38, 39, 40; Amos v. 11; Zeph. i. 13; Hag. i. 6——[d]Or, *he doth much keep the*, &c.

[e]1 Kings xvi. 25, 26——[f]Hos. v. 11——[g]1 Kings xvi. 30, &c.; xxi. 25, 26; 2 Kings xxi. 3——[h]1 Kings ix. 8; Jer. xix. 8——[i]Or, *astonishment*——[k]Isa. xxv. 8; Jer. li. 51; Lam. v. 1

Verse 12. *For the rich men thereof are full of violence*] This shows that they did not *love mercy.*

The inhabitants thereof have spoken lies] This shows that they did not *humble themselves to walk with God.*

Verse 13. *Will I make* thee *sick in smiting thee*] Perhaps better, "I also am weary with smiting thee, in making thee desolate for thy sins." They were corrected, but to no purpose; they had stroke upon stroke, but were not amended.

Verse 14. *Thou shalt eat, but not be satisfied*] All thy possessions are cursed, because of thy sins; and thou hast no *real good* in all thy enjoyments.

And thy casting down] For וישחך *veyeshchacha*, "thy casting down," *Newcome*, by transposing the ח and ש, reads ויחשך *veyechshach*, "and it shall be dark;" and this is probably the true reading. The *Arabic* and *Septuagint* have read the same. "There shall be calamity in the midst of thee." It shall have its *seat* and *throne* among you.

Verse 15. *Thou shalt sow, but thou shalt not reap*] Thou shalt labour to amass property, but thou shalt not have God's blessing; and whatever thou collectest, thy enemies shall carry away. And at last carry thyself into captivity.

Verse 16. *The statutes of Omri are kept*] *Omri*, king of Israel, the father of Ahab, was one of the worst kings the Israelites ever had; and *Ahab* followed in his wicked father's steps. The *statutes* of those kings were the very grossest *idolatry. Jezebel*, wife of the latter, and daughter of *Ithobaal*, king of Tyre, had no fellow on earth. From her Shakespeare seems to have drawn the character of *Lady Macbeth;* a woman, like her prototype, mixed up of *tigress* and *fiend*, without *addition.* Omri, Ahab, and Jezebel, were the *models* followed by the Israelites in the days of this prophet.

The inhabitants thereof a hissing] לשרקה *lishrekah*, "for a *shriek;*" because those who should see them should be both *astonished* and *affrighted* at them.

There are few chapters in the prophets, or in the Bible, superior to this for genuine worth and importance. The structure is as elegant as it is impressive; and it is every way worthy of the Spirit of God.

CHAPTER VII

The prophet begins this chapter with lamenting the decay of piety and the growth of ungodliness, using a beautiful allegory to imply (as explained in verse 2) *that the good man is as seldom to be met with as the early fig of best quality in the advanced season, or the cluster after the vintage*, 1, 2. *He then reproves and threatens in terms so expressive of great calamities as to be applied in the New Testament to times of the hottest persecution.* 3–6. *See* Matt. x. 35, 36. *Notwithstanding which a Jew is immediately introduced declaring, in the name of his captive people, the strongest faith in the mercy of God the most submissive resignation to his will, and the firmest hope in his favour in future times, when they should triumph over their enemies*, 7–10. *The prophet upon this resumes the discourse, and predicts their great prosperity and increase*, 11, 12; *although the whole land of Israel must first be desolated on account of the great wickedness of its inhabitants*, 13. *The prophet intercedes in behalf of his people*, 14. *After which God is introduced promising, in very ample terms, their future restoration and prosperity*, 15–17. *And then, to conclude, a chorus of Jews is introduced, singing a beautiful hymn of thanksgiving, suggested by the gracious promises which precede*, 18–20.

A. M. cir. 3294
B. C. cir. 710
A. U. C. cir. 44
NumæPompilii,
R. Roman.,
cir. annum 6

WO is me! for I am as
[a]when they have gathered
the summer fruits, as [b]the grape-
gleanings of the vintage: *there
is* no cluster to eat: [c]my soul desireth the
first-ripe fruit.
2 The [d]good [e]*man* is perished out
of the earth: and *there is* none upright
among men: they all lie in wait for blood;
[f]they hunt every man his brother with a
net.
3 That they may do evil with both hands
earnestly, [g]the prince asketh,
[h]and the judge *asketh* for a reward; and the great *man*, he
uttereth [i]his mischievous desire:
so they wrap it up.
4 The best of them [k]*is* as a brier: the most
upright *is sharper* than a thorn hedge: the
day of thy watchmen *and* thy visitation cometh; now shall be their perplexity.
5 [l]Trust ye not in a friend, put ye not confidence in a guide: keep the doors of thy
mouth from her that lieth in thy bosom.

A. M. cir. 3294
B. C. cir. 710
A. U. C. cir. 44
NumæPompilii,
R. Roman.,
cir. annum 6

[a]Heb. *the gatherings of summer*——[b]Isa. xvii. 6; xxiv. 13——[c]Isa. xxviii. 4; Hos. ix. 10——[d]Psa. xii. 1; xiv. 1, 3; Isa. lvii. 1——[e]Or, *godly*, or *merciful*

[f]Hab. i. 15——[g]Hos. iv. 18——[h]Isa. i. 23; chap. iii. 11——[i]Heb. *the mischief of his soul*——[k]2 Sam. xxiii. 6, 7; Ezek. ii. 6; see Isa. lv. 13——[l]Jer. ix. 4

NOTES ON CHAP. VII

Verse 1. *Wo is me!* This is a continuation of the preceding discourse. And here the prophet points out the *small number* of the upright to be found in the land. He himself seemed to be the only person who was on God's side; and he considers himself as a *solitary grape*, which had escaped the general gathering. The word קיץ *kayits*, which is sometimes used for *summer*, and *summer fruits* in general, is here translated *late figs;* and may here, says Bishop *Newcome*, be opposed to the *early ripe fig* of superior quality. See on Hos. ix. 10, and Amos viii. 1, 2. He desired to see the *first-ripe fruit*—distinguished and eminent piety; but he found nothing but a very imperfect or spurious kind of godliness.

Verse 2. *The good* man *is perished out of the earth*] A similar sentiment may be found, Psa. xii. 1; Isa. lvii. 1. As the *early fig* of excellent flavour cannot be found in the advanced season of summer, or a *choice cluster of grapes* after vintage, so neither can the good and upright man be discovered by searching in Israel. This comparison, says Bp. *Newcome*, is beautifully implied.

They hunt every man his brother with a net.] This appears to be an allusion to the ancient mode of duel between the *retiarius* and *secutor*. The former had a *casting net*, which he endeavoured to throw over the head of his antagonist, that he might then despatch him with his short sword. The other parried the cast; and when the *retiarius* missed, he was obliged to *run* about the field to get time to *set his net in right order* for another throw. While he ran, the other *followed*, that he might despatch him before he should be able to recover the proper position of his net; and hence the latter was called *secutor*, the *pursuer*, as the other was called *retiarius*, or the *net man*. I have explained this before on Job, and other places; but because it is rarely noticed by commentators, I explain the allusion here once more. Abp. *Newcome*, by not attending to this, has translated איש את אחיהו יצודו חרם *ish eth achihu yatsudu cherem*, "They hunt every man his brother for his destruction;" though he put *net* in the *margin*.

Verse 3. *That they may do evil with both hands*] That is, earnestly, greedily, to the uttermost of their power. The *Vulgate* translates: Malum manuum suarum dicunt bonum; "The evil of their hands they call good."

The prince asketh] A bribe, to forward claims in his court.

The judge asketh *for a reward*] That he may decide the cause in favour of him who gives most money, whether the cause be *good* or *evil*. This was notoriously the case in our own country before the giving of *Magna Charta;* and hence that provision, Nulli vendemus justitiam aut rectum: "We will not sell justice to any man." And *this* was not the only *country* in which justice and judgment were put to sale.

The great man, *he uttereth his mischievous desire*] Such consider themselves *above law*, and they make no secret of their unjust determinations. *And so they wrap it up*—they all conjoin in doing evil in their several offices, and oppressing the poor; so our translators have interpreted the original ויעבתוה *vayeabtuha*, which the *versions* translate variously. *Newcome* has, "And they do abominably."

Verse 4. *The best of them* is *as a brier*] They are useless in themselves, and cannot be touched without *wounding* him that comes in contact with them. He alludes to the *thick thorn hedges*, still frequent in Palestine.

The day of thy watchmen] The day of vengeance, which the prophets have foreseen and proclaimed, is at hand. *Now shall be their perplexity;* no more *wrapping up*, all shall be *unfolded*. In that day every man will wish that he were different from what he is found to be; but he shall be judged for what he *is*, and for the deeds he *has done*.

Verse 5. *Trust ye not in a friend*] These times will be so evil, and the people so wicked, that all *bonds* will be *dissolved;* and even the most intimate will betray each other, when they can hope to serve themselves by it.

On this passage, in the year 1798, I find I have written as follows:—

"*Trust ye not in a friend.*—Several of those whom I have delighted to call by that name have deceived me.

"*Put ye not confidence in a guide.*—Had I followed some of these I should have gone to perdition.

"*Keep the door of thy mouth from her that lieth in thy bosom.*—My wife alone never deceived me."

It is now *twenty-seven* years since, and I find no cause to alter what I then wrote.

A. M. cir. 3294 B. C. cir. 710 A. U. C. cir. 44 NumæPompilii, R. Roman., cir. annum 6

6 For [m]the son dishonoureth
the father, the daughter riseth up
against her mother, the daughter-
in-law against her mother-in-
law; a man's enemies *are* the men of his own
house.
7 Therefore [n]I will look unto the LORD: I
will wait for the God of my salvation: my
God will hear me.
8 [o]Rejoice not against me, O mine enemy:
[p]when I fall, I shall arise; when I sit in darkness, [q]the LORD *shall be* a light unto me.
9 [r]I will bear the indignation of the LORD,
because I have sinned against him, until he
plead my cause, and execute judgment for
me: [s]he will bring me forth to the light, *and*
I shall behold his righteousness.
10 [t]Then *she that is* mine
enemy shall see *it*, and [u]shame
shall cover her which said unto
me, [v]Where is the LORD thy
God? [w]mine eyes shall behold her: now [x]shall
she be trodden down [y]as the mire of the
streets.
11 *In* the day that thy [z]walls are to be built,
in that day shall the decree be far removed.
12 *In* that day *also* [a]he shall come even to
thee from Assyria, [b]and *from* the fortified
cities, and from the fortress even to the river,
and from sea to sea, and *from* mountain to
mountain.
13 [c]Notwithstanding the land shall be desolate because of them that dwell therein,
[d]for the fruit of their doings.

---

[m]Ezek. xxii. 7; Matt. x. 21, 35, 36; Luke xii. 53; xxi. 16; 2 Tim. iii. 2, 3——[n]Isa. viii. 17——[o]Prov. xxiv. 17; Lam. iv. 21——[p]Psa. xxxvii. 24; Prov. xxiv. 16——[q]Psa. xxvii. 1——[r]Lam. iii. 39——[s]Psa. xxxvii. 6——[t]Or, *And thou wilt see her that is mine enemy, and cover her with shame*——[u]Psa. xxxv. 26——[v]Psa. xlii. 3, 10; lxxix. 10; cxv. 2; Joel ii. 17——[w]Chap. iv. 11——[x]Heb. *she shall be for a treading down*——[y]2 Sam. xxii. 43; Zech. x. 5——[z]Amos ix. 11, &c.——[a]Isa. xi. 16; xix. 23, &c.; xxvii. 13; Hos. xi. 11——[b]Or, *even to*——[c]Or, *After that it hath been*——[d]Jeremiah xxi. 14; chap. iii. 12

Verse 6. *For the son dishonoureth the father*] See the use our Lord has made of these words, where he quotes them, Matt. x. 21, 25, 36, and the notes there.

Verse 7. *Therefore I will look unto the Lord*] Because things are so, I will *trust* in the Lord more firmly, *wait* for him more patiently, and more *confidently* expect to be supported, defended, and saved.

Verse 8. *Rejoice not against me, O mine enemy*] The captive Israelites are introduced as speaking here and in the preceding verse. The *enemy* are the *Assyrians* and *Chaldeans;* the *fall* is their *idolatry* and consequent *captivity;* the *darkness*, the *calamities* they suffered in that captivity; their *rise* and *light*, their *restoration* and consequent *blessedness.*

To *rejoice over the fall or miseries of any man*, betrays a malignant spirit. I have known several instances where people professing to *hold a very pure and Christian creed*, having become unfaithful and fallen into sin, their opponents, who held a very impure and unchristian creed, have exulted with "Ha, ha! so would we have it!" and have shown their malignity more fully, by giving all possible *publicity* and *circulation* to such *accounts.* Perhaps in the sight of God this was worse than the poor wretch's *fall*, in which they exulted as having taken place in one who held a creed different from their own. But these *arose again* from their fall, while those *jesters at holiness* continued in the *gall of bitterness* and *bonds of inward corruption.*

Verse 9. *I will bear the indignation of the Lord*] The words of the penitent captives, acknowledging their sins and praying for mercy.

Until he plead my cause] And wo to the *slanderers*, when God undertakes to plead for the *fallen* who have *returned* to him with *deep compunction of heart*, seeking redemption in the blood of the cross.

Verse 10. *Then* she that is *mine enemy*] This may refer particularly to the *city of Babylon.*

Shall she be trodden down] Literally fulfilled in the sackage of that city by the Persians, and its consequent total ruin. It became as *mire;* its walls, formed of brick *kneaded with straw* and *baked in the sun*, becoming exposed to the *wet*, dissolved, so that a vestige of the city remains not, except a few bricks digged from under the rubbish, several pieces of which now lie before me, and show the perishing materials of which the *head* of this proud empire was composed.

Verse 11. In *the day that thy walls are to be built*] This refers to *Jerusalem;* the *decree*, to the purpose of God to deliver the people into captivity. "This shall be far removed." God having *purposed* their return, I cannot think, with some commentators, that this verse contains *threatenings* against Jerusalem, and not *promises.* See the *first* chapter of Haggai, where the subject is similar; and the restoration of Jerusalem is certainly what the prophet describes.

Verse 12. In *that day* also *he shall come*] Bp. *Newcome* translates:—

"And in that day they shall come unto thee
From Assyria and the fenced cities;
And from Egypt even unto the river."

Calmet translates:—

"They shall come to thee from Assyria even unto Egypt;
And from Egypt even to the river; (Euphrates;)
And from one sea to another, and from one mountain to another."

This, says he, gives an easy sense; whereas we cannot tell where to find those *fortified cities* spoken of by other *translators.* The

A. M. cir. 3294
B. C. cir. 710
A. U. C. cir. 44
NumæPompilii,
R. Roman.,
cir. annum 6

14 [e]Feed thy people with thy rod, the flock of thine heritage, which dwell solitarily *in* [f]the wood, in the midst of Carmel: let them feed *in* Bashan and Gilead, as in the days of old.

15 [g]According to the days of thy coming out of the land of Egypt will I show unto him marvellous *things.*

16 The nations [h]shall see and be confounded at all their might: [i]they shall lay *their* hand upon *their* mouth, their ears shall be deaf.

17 They shall lick the [k]dust like a serpent, [l]they shall move out of their holes like [m]worms of the earth: [n]they shall be afraid of the LORD our God, and shall fear because of thee.

A. M. cir. 3294
B. C. cir. 710
A. U. C. cir. 44
NumæPompilii,
R. Roman.,
cir. annum 6

18 [o]Who *is* a God like unto thee, that [p]pardoneth iniquity, and passeth by the transgression of [q]the remnant of his heritage? [r]he retaineth not his anger for ever, because he delighteth *in* mercy.

19 He will turn again, he will have compassion upon us; he will subdue our iniquities; and thou wilt cast all their sins into the depths of the sea.

20 [s]Thou wilt perform the truth to Jacob, *and* the mercy to Abraham, [t]which thou hast sworn unto our fathers from the days of old.

---

[e]Or, *Rule;* Psalm xxviii. 9; chap. v. 4——[f]Isaiah xxxvii. 24——[g]Psalm lxviii. 22; lxxviii. 12——[h]Isa. xxvi. 11——[i]Job xxi. 5; xxix. 9——[k]Psalm lxxii. 9; Isa. xlix. 23——[l]Psa. xviii. 45——[m]Or, *creeping things*

[n]Jeremiah xxxiii. 9——[o]Exodus xv. 11——[p]Exodus xxxiv. 6, 7; Jeremiah l. 20——[q]Chap. iv. 7; v. 3, 7, 8 [r]Psalm ciii. 9; Isa. lvii. 10; Jer. iii. 5——[s]Luke i. 72, 73 [t]Psalm cv. 9, 10

Israelites were to return from their captivity, and re-occupy their ancient country from Assyria to Egypt; that is, from the *river Euphrates* to the *river Nile;* and from the *Mediterranean Sea* to the *Ocean;* and from *Mount Libanus* to the *mountains of Arabia Petræa,* or Mount *Seir.* See Amos viii. 12. This prediction was literally fulfilled under the *Asmoneans.* The Jewish nation was greatly extended and very powerful under Herod, at the time that our Lord was born. See *Calmet.*

Verse 13. *Notwithstanding the land shall be desolate*] This should be translated in the preter tense, "Though the land HAD been desolate;" that is, the land of Israel had been desolate during the captivity, which captivity was the "fruit of the evil doings of them that had dwelt therein."

Verse 14. *Feed thy people with thy rod*] בשבטך *beshibtecha,* "with thy crook." The shepherd's crook is most certainly designed, as the word *flock* immediately following shows. No *rod* of *correction* or *affliction* is here intended; nor does the word mean such.

Solitarily] They have been long without a shepherd or spiritual governor.

In the midst of Carmel] Very fruitful in vines.

Bashan and Gilead] Proverbially fruitful in pasturages.

Verse 15. *According to the days*] This is the answer to the prophet's prayer; and God says he will protect, save, defend, and *work miracles for them* in their restoration, such as he wrought for their fathers in their return from Egypt to the promised land.

Verse 16. *The nations shall see and be confounded*] Whether the words in these verses (15, 16, and 17) be applied to the return from the Babylonish captivity, or to the prosperity of the Jews under the Maccabees, they may be understood as ultimately applicable to the final restoration of this people, and their lasting prosperity under the Gospel.

Verse 18. *Who is a God like unto thee, &c.*] Here is a challenge to all idol worshippers, and to all those who take false views of the true God, to show his like. See his characters; they are immediately subjoined.

1. *He pardoneth iniquity.* This is the prerogative of God alone; of that Being who alone has power to *save* or to *destroy.*

2. *He passeth by transgression.* He can heal *backsliding,* and restore them that are fallen.

3. *He retaineth not his anger for ever.* Though, justly displeased because of sin, he pours out his judgments upon the wicked; yet when they return to him, he shows "that he retaineth not his anger forever," but is indescribably ready to save them.

4. *He delighteth in mercy.* Judgment is his strange work: he is ever more ready *to save* than to *destroy.* Nothing can *please him better* than having the opportunity, from the return and repentance of the sinner, to show him that mercy without which he must perish everlastingly.

5. Because he is such a God—1. "He will turn again." His face has been long turned from us, because of our sins. 2. "He will have compassion upon us," pity our state, and feel for our sorrows. 3. "He will subdue our iniquities." Though they have been mighty, he will bring them down, and bruise them under our feet. 4. "He will cast all their sins into the depths of the sea." Will fully pardon them, and never more remember them against us. Instead of חטאתם *chattotham,* THEIR *sins,* five MSS. of *Kennicott's* and *De Rossi's,* with the *Septuagint, Syriac, Vulgate,* and *Arabic,* read חטאתינו *chattotheynu,* OUR *sins.* He will plunge them into eternal oblivion, never more to come into sight or remembrance; like a stone dropped into the "depths of the sea."

Verse 20. *Thou wilt perform the truth to Jacob*] The *promises* which he has made to Jacob and his posterity. Not one of them can ever fall to the ground. "And the mercy to Abraham, which thou hast sworn;" viz., that "in his Seed all the families of the earth should be blessed;" that the *Messiah* should come from ABRAHAM, *through* his son ISAAC, *by* JACOB and

DAVID; be a light to lighten the Gentiles, and the glory of his people Israel. And this *promise*, and this *oath*, God has most signally fulfilled by the *incarnation of Christ*, who was sent to bless us by turning away every one of us from his iniquities; and for this purpose he was delivered for our offences, and rose again for our justification; and repentance and remission of sins are preached in his name to all nations. The proclamation was *first* made at Jerusalem; and that the prophet refers to *this*, is evident from the use made of these words by Zacharias, the father of John the Baptist, when, under the *full afflatus of the Spirit of God*, he quoted this phophecy of Micah, as fulfilled in the *incarnation of Christ*, Luke i. 72, 73. The *Chaldee* paraphrases this last verse with spirit and propriety: "Thou wilt give the truth to Jacob his son, as thou hast promised by oath to him in Beth-el. And the mercy to Abraham and to his seed after him, as thou didst swear to him amidst the divisions. Thou wilt be mindful of us on account of the binding of Isaac, who was bound upon the altar before thee. And thou wilt do us that good, which, from the most ancient days, thou hast promised to our fathers by an oath." *Between the divisions*, refers to the covenant made between God and Abraham, Gen. xv. 9, 10, 11, 17, 18. Well might the prophet exult in his challenge to earth and hell. WHO IS A GOD LIKE UNTO THEE! Hell is speechless, earth is dumb. Infidels dare not open their mouths!!! Hallelujah! מי אל כמוך *mi El camocha!* JESUS is the mighty God and Saviour, pardoning iniquity, transgression, and sin, and saving to the uttermost all that come unto God through him. Blessed be God! Reader, lay this to heart.

INTRODUCTION TO THE BOOK

OF THE

PROPHET NAHUM

NAHUM, the *seventh* of the *twelve* minor prophets, was a native of Elkoshai, a little village of Galilee, whose ruins were still in being in the time of St. Jerome. However there are some who think that Elkoshai is rather the name of his father, and that the place of his birth was Bethabor, or Bethabara, beyond Jordan. They used to show the tomb of the prophet at a village called Beth-gabre, now called Gibbin, near Emmaus. The Chaldee calls him Nahum of Beth-koshi, or of Beth-kitsi; but the situation of this place is as much unknown as that of Elkoshai.

The particular circumstances of the life of Nahum are altogether unknown. His prophecy consists of *three* chapters, which make up but *one* discourse, wherein he foretells the destruction of Nineveh. He describes it in so lovely and pathetic a manner, that he seems to have been upon the spot to declare to the Ninevites the destruction of their city.

Opinions are divided as to the time in which he prophesied. Josephus will have it that he foretold the fall of Nineveh *one hundred and fifteen* years before it happened, which will bring the time of Nahum to that of King Ahaz. The Jews say that he prophesied under Manasseh. We are inclined to be of St. Jerome's opinion, that he foretold the destruction of Nineveh in the time of Hezekiah, and after the war of Sennacherib in Egypt, mentioned by Berosus. Nahum speaks plainly of the taking of No-Ammon, a city of Egypt; of the haughtiness of Rabshakeh; of the defeat of Sennacherib; and he speaks of them as things that were past. He supposes that the Jews were still in their own country, and that they there celebrated their festivals. He speaks of the captivity, and of the dispersion of the *ten* tribes. All these evidences convince us that Nahum cannot be placed before the *fifteenth* year of Hezekiah, since the expedition of Sennacherib against this prince was in the *fourteenth* year of his reign.

This prophet gives us a fine description of the destruction of Nineveh. He says that this city should be ruined by a deluge of waters, which should overflow it and demolish its walls.

Diodorus Siculus and *Athenæus* relate, that during the time this city was besieged by Belesis and by Arbaces, under Sardanapalus, the river Tigris swelled so as to overthrow twenty furlongs of the walls of Nineveh. But as the siege mentioned by Nahum was long after the taking of Nineveh under Sardanapalus, it must needs be that the same thing happened to Nineveh at the second and last siege, under Nebuchadnezzar and Astyages. Probably the besiegers at this second siege determined the course of the waters, and brought on the same fate to the city by the same means as at the first siege. And as the walls of those ancient cities were generally formed of *brick kneaded with straw* and *baked in the sun*, a *flood* of *waters* could easily effect their dissolution. *Babylon* was built in the same manner; and this is the reason why scarcely any vestiges of those cities are to be found. See on chap. iii. 14.

The time of the prophet's death is not known. The Greek meneologies and the Latin martyrologies place his festival on the first of December. *Petrus Natalis* places it on the twenty-fourth of the same month, which he says was the day of his death, without acquainting us whence he had learned this circumstance.

The conduct and imagery of this prophetical poem are truly admirable.

The exordium sets forth with grandeur the justice and power of God, tempered by lenity and goodness, chap. i. 1–8.

A sudden address to the Assyrians follows; and a prediction of their perplexity and overthrow, as devisers of evil against the true God, ver. 9–11. Jehovah himself then proclaims freedom to his people from the Assyrian yoke, and the destruction of the Assyrian idols, ver. 12–14. Upon which the prophet, in a most lively manner, turns the attention of Judah to the approach of the messenger who brings such glad tidings, and bids her celebrate her festivals and offer her thank-offerings, without fear of so powerful an adversary, ver. 15.

Chap. ii. In the next place Nineveh is called on to prepare for the approach of her enemies, as instruments in the hands of Jehovah; and the military array and muster of the Medes and Babylonians, their rapid approach to the city, the process of the siege, the capture of the place, the captivity, lamentation, and flight of the inhabitants, the sacking of the wealthy city, and the consequent desolation and terror, are described in the true spirit of Eastern poetry, and with many pathetic, vivid, and sublime images, ver. 1–10. A grand and animated allegory succeeds this description, ver. 11, 12; which is explained and applied to the city of Nineveh in ver. 13.

Chap. iii. The prophet denounces a wo against Nineveh for her perfidy and violence, and strongly places before our eyes the number of her chariots and cavalry, her burnished arms, and the great and unrelenting slaughter which she spread around her, ver. 1–3.

He assigns her idolatries as one cause of her ignominious and unpitied fall, ver. 4–7.

He foretells that No-Ammon, (the Diospolis in the Delta,) her rival in populousness, confederacies, and situation, should share a like fate with herself, ver. 8–11; and beautifully illustrates the ease with which her strong holds should be taken, ver. 12, and her pusillanimity during the siege, ver. 13.

He pronounces that all her preparations, ver. 14, 15, her numbers, her opulence, her multitude of chief men, would be of no avail, ver. 15–17.

He foretells that her tributaries would desert her, ver. 18.

He concludes with a proper epiphonema; the topics of which are, the greatness and incurableness of her wound, and the just triumph of others over her on account of her extensive oppressions, ver. 19.

To sum up all with the decisive judgment of an eminent critic: "Not one of the minor prophets equals the sublimity, genius, and spirit of Nahum. Besides, his prophecy is a perfect poem. The *exordium* is exceedingly majestic. The *apparatus* for the destruction of Nineveh, and the description of that catastrophe, are painted in the most glowing colours, and are admirably clear and powerful." *Lowth*, Prælect. Heb. xxi., p. 282.

It must be farther observed, that this prophecy was highly interesting to the Jews; as the Assyrians had often ravaged their country, and I suppose had recently destroyed the kingdom of Israel. See *Calmet.*

THE BOOK
OF THE
PROPHET NAHUM

Chronological Notes relative to this Book, upon the supposition that it was written about seven hundred and thirteen *years before the commencement of the Christian era*

Year from the Creation, according to Archbishop Usher, 3291.—Year of the Julian Period, 4001.—Year since the Flood, 1635.—Year from the vocation of Abram, 1208.—Year since the first celebration of the Olympic games in Elis by the Idæi Dactyli, 741.—Year from the destruction of Troy, according to the general computation of chronologers, 471.—Year since the commencement of the kingdom of Israel, by the Divine appointment of Saul to the regal dignity, 383.—Year from the foundation of Solomon's temple, 299.—Year since the division of Solomon's monarchy into the kingdoms of Israel and Judah, 263.—Year since the restoration of the Olympic games at Elis by Lycurgus, Iphitus, and Cleosthenes, 172.—Year from the foundation of the kingdom of Macedon by Caranus, 102.—Year from the commencement of the reign of Ardysus over Lydia, 84.—Year since the conquest of Corœbus at Olympia, usually called the first Olympiad, 64.—Fourth year of the *sixteenth* Olympiad.—Year from the building of Rome, according to the Varronian computation, 41.—Year from the building of Rome, according to Cato and the Fasti Consulares, 40.—Year from the building of Rome, according to Polybius the historian, 39.—Year from the building of Rome, according to Fabius Pictor, 35.—Year of the era of Nabonassar, 35.—Year since the destruction of the kingdom of Israel by Shalmaneser, king of Assyria, 9.—Year before the birth of Christ, 709.—Year before the vulgar era of Christ's nativity, 713.—Cycle of the Sun, 25.—Cycle of the Moon, 11.—Eleventh year of Zeuxidamus, king of Lacedæmon, of the family of the Proclidæ.—Twelfth year of Eurycrates, king of Lacedæmon, of the family of the Eurysthenidæ.—Sixth year of Gyges, king of Lydia.—Tenth year of Hippomenes, decennial archon of the Athenians.—Second year of Cordiccas, governor of the Medes, according to some chronologers.—Seventeenth year of Perdiccas, king of Macedon.—Third year of Numa Pompilius, the second king of Rome.—Fourteenth year of Hezekiah, king of Judah.

CHAPTER I

This chapter opens the prophecy against the Assyrians and their metropolis with a very magnificent description of the infinite justice, tender compassion, and uncontrollable power of God, 1–8. *To this succeeds an address to the Assyrians; with a lively picture of their sudden overthrow, because of their evil device against Jerusalem,* 9–11. *Then appears Jehovah himself, proclaiming deliverance to his people from the Assyrian yoke, and the destruction of the Assyrian idols,* 12–14; *upon which the prophet, with great emphasis, directs the attention of Judah to the approach of the messenger who brings such glad tidings; and exultingly bids his people to celebrate their solemn feasts, and perform their vows, as a merciful Providence would not suffer these enemies of the Jewish state to prevail against them,* 15.

A. M. cir. 3291
B. C. cir. 713
Ol. cir. XVI. 4
NumæPompilii,
R. Roman.,
cir. annum 3

THE burden of [a]Nineveh. The book of the vision of Nahum the Elkoshite.
2 [b]God *is* [c]jealous, and [d]the
LORD revengeth; the LORD revengeth, and [e]*is* furious; the LORD will take vengeance on his adversaries, and he

A. M. cir. 3291
B. C. cir. 713
Ol. cir. XVI. 4
NumæPompilii,
R. Roman.,
cir. annum 3

[a]Zech. ii. 13——[b]Or, *The LORD* is *a jealous God, and a Revenger*, &c.——[c]Exod. xx. 5; xxxiv. 14; Deut. iv. 24; Josh. xxiv. 19——[d]Deut. xxxii. 35; Psa. xciv. 1; Isa. lix. 11——[e]Heb. *that hath fury*

NOTES ON CHAP. I

Verse 1. *The burden of Nineveh.*] משא *massa* not only signifies a *burden*, but also a thing *lifted up*, *pronounced*, or *proclaimed;* also a *message.* It is used by the prophets to signify the *revelation* which they have received from God to deliver to any particular people: the *oracle*—the *prophecy.* Here it signifies the *declaration* from God relative to the overthrow

A. M. cir. 3291
B. C. cir. 713
Ol. cir. XVI. 4
NumæPompilii,
R. Roman.,
cir. annum 3

reserveth *wrath* for his enemies.
3 The LORD *is* [f]slow to anger,
and [g]great in power, and will
not at all acquit *the wicked;* [h]the LORD
hath his way in the whirlwind and in the
storm, and the clouds *are* the dust of his
feet.
4 [i]He rebuketh the sea, and maketh it dry,
and drieth up all the rivers: [k]Bashan languisheth,
and Carmel, and the flower of Lebanon
languisheth.
5 [l]The mountains quake at him, and [m]the
hills melt, and [n]the earth is burned at his
presence; yea, the world, and
all that dwell therein.
6 Who can stand before his
indignation? and [o]who can [p]abide
in the fierceness of his anger? [q]his fury is
poured out like fire, and the rocks are thrown
down by him.
7 [r]The LORD *is* good, a [s]strong hold in the
day of trouble; and [t]he knoweth them that
trust in him.
8 [u]But with an overrunning flood he will
make an utter end of the place thereof, and
darkness shall pursue his enemies.
9 [v]What do ye imagine against the LORD?

---

[f]Exod. xxxiv. 6, 7; Neh. ix. 17; Psa. ciii. 8; Jonah iv. 2——[g]Job ix. 4——[h]Psa. xviii. 7, &c.; xcvii. 2; Hab. iii. 5, 11, 12——[i]Psa. cvi. 9; Isa. l. 2; Matt. viii. 26——[k]Isa. xxxiii. 9——[l]Psa. lxviii. 8——[m]Judg. v. 5; Psa. xcvii. 5; Mic. i. 4——[n]2 Pet. iii. 10——[o]Mal. iii. 2——[p]Heb. *stand up*——[q]Rev. xvi. 1——[r]1 Chron. xvi. 34; Psa. c. 5; Jer. xxxiii. 11; Lam. iii. 25——[s]Or, *strength*——[t]Psa. i. 6; 2 Tim. ii. 19——[u]Dan. ix. 26; xi. 10, 22, 40——[v]Psa. ii. 1

---

of Nineveh, and the *commission* of the prophet to deliver it.

As the Assyrians under Pul, Tiglath-pileser, and Shalmaneser, three of their kings, had been employed by a just God for the chastisement of his disobedient people; the end being now accomplished by them, God is about to *burn the rod* wherewith he corrected Israel; and Nineveh, the capital of the Assyrian empire, is to be destroyed. This prediction appears to have been accomplished a short time after this by Nebuchadnezzar and Cyaxares, the Ahasuerus of Scripture.

Nahum, נחום *Nachum,* signifies *comforter.* The name was very suitable, as he was sent to *comfort* the people, by showing them that God was about to destroy their adversaries.

Verse 2. *God* is *jealous*] For his own glory.

And—revengeth] His justice; by the destruction of his enemies.

And is *furious*] So powerful in the manifestations of his judgments, that nothing can stand before him.

He reserveth wrath] Though they seem to prosper for a time, and God appears to have passed by their crimes without notice, yet he *reserveth—treasureth* up—*wrath* for them, which shall burst forth in due time.

Verse 3. *The Lord* is *slow to anger*] He exercises much longsuffering towards his enemies, that this may lead them to repentance. And it is because of this longsuffering that vengeance is not speedily executed on every evil work.

Great in power] Able at all times to *save* or to *destroy.*

The Lord hath *his way in the whirlwind and in the storm*] These are the *effects* of his *power;* and when they appear unusual, they may be considered as the *immediate* effects of his power: and although he be *in them* to punish and destroy, he is in them to *direct* their *course,* to determine their *operations,* and to defend his followers from being injured by their violence. The pestilential wind which slew *one hundred and eighty-five thousand* of the Assyrians did not injure *one* Israelite. See 2 Kings xix. 35.

The clouds are *the dust of his feet.*] This is spoken in allusion to a *chariot and horses* going on with *extreme rapidity:* they are all *enveloped in a cloud of dust.* So Jehovah is represented as coming through the circuit of the heavens as rapidly as lightning; the *clouds* surrounding him as the *dust* does the chariot and horses.

Verse 4. *He rebuketh the sea*] The Red Sea, and the rivers: probably an allusion to the passage of the *Red Sea* and *Jordan.*

The description of the coming of Jehovah, from the third to the sixth verse, is dreadfully majestic. He is represented as controlling *universal nature.* The *sea* and the *rivers* are dried up; the *mountains* tremble, the *hills* melt, and the *earth* is burnt at his presence. *Bashan, Carmel,* and *Lebanon* are withered and languish: streams of *fire* are poured out, and the *rocks* are cast down to make him a passage. If, then, the *seas,* the *rivers,* the *mountains,* the *hills,* the *rocks,* and the *earth* itself, fail before Jehovah, or flee from his presence, how shall *Nineveh* and the *Assyrian empire* stand before him?

Verse 7. *The Lord* is *good*] In the midst of judgment he remembers mercy; and among the most dreadful denunciations of wrath he mingles promises of mercy. None that trust in him need be alarmed at these dreadful threatenings; they shall be discriminated in the day of wrath, for the *Lord knoweth them that trust in him.*

Verse 8. *But with an overrunning flood*] Bishop *Newcome* thinks this may refer to the manner in which Nineveh was taken. The *Euphrates* overflowed its banks, deluged a part of the city, and overturned *twenty* stadia of the wall; in consequence of which the desponding king burnt himself, and his palace, with his treasures.—*Diodor. Sic.,* Edit. Wessel., p. 140, lib. ii., s. 27.

Darkness shall pursue] Calamity. All kinds of calamity shall pursue them till they are destroyed.

Verse 9. *Affliction shall not rise up the second time.*] There shall be no need to *repeat the judgment;* with *one blow* God will make a full end of the business.

A. M. cir. 3291
B. C. cir. 713
Ol. cir. XVI. 4
NumæPompilii,
R. Roman.,
cir. annum 3

[w]he will make an utter end:
affliction shall not rise up the
second time.
10 For while *they be* folden
together [x]*as* thorns, [y]and while they are
drunken *as* drunkards, [z]they shall be devoured as stubble fully dry.
11 There is *one* come out of thee, [a]that
imagineth evil against the LORD, [b]a wicked
counsellor.
12 Thus saith the LORD; [c]Though *they be*
quiet, and likewise many, yet thus [d]shall they
be [e]cut down, when he shall [f]pass through.
Though I have afflicted thee, I will afflict thee
no more.

[w]1 Sam. iii. 12——[x]2 Sam. xxiii. 6, 7——[y]Chap. iii. 11——[z]Mal. iv. 1——[a]2 Kings xix. 22, 23——[b]Heb. *a counsellor of Belial*——[c]Or, *If* they would have been *at peace, so* should they have been *many, and so should they have been shorn, and he should have passed away*

A. M. cir. 3291
B. C. cir. 713
Ol. cir. XVI. 4
NumæPompilii,
R. Roman.,
cir. annum 3

13 For now will I [g]break his
yoke from off thee, and will
burst thy bonds in sunder.
14 And the LORD hath given
a commandment concerning thee, *that* no
more of thy name be sown: out of the house
of thy gods will I cut off the graven image
and the molten image: [h]I will make thy
grave; for thou art vile.
15 Behold [i]upon the mountains the feet of
him that bringeth good tidings, that publisheth peace! O Judah, [k]keep thy solemn
feasts, perform thy vows: for [l]the [m]wicked
shall no more pass through thee; [n]he is
utterly cut off.

[d]2 Kings xix. 35, 37——[e]Hebrew, *shorn*——[f]Isaiah viii. 8; Daniel xi. 10——[g]Jeremiah ii. 20; xxx. 8——[h]2 Kings xix. 37——[i]Isaiah lii. 7; Romans x. 15——[k]Hebrew, *feast*——[l]Hebrew, *Belial*——[m]Ver. 11, 12——[n]Ver. 14

Verse 10. *While* they be *folden together*] However united their counsels may be, they shall be as *drunken men*—perplexed and unsteady in all their resolutions; and before God's judgments they shall be as *dry thorns* before a devouring fire.

Verse 11. *Imagineth evil against the Lord*] Such were *Pul*, 2 Kings xv. 10; *Tiglath-pileser*, 2 Kings xv. 29; *Shalmaneser*, 2 Kings xvii. 6; and *Sennacherib*, 2 Kings xviii. 17, and xix. 23.

A wicked counsellor.] *Sennacherib* and *Rabshakeh.*

Verse 12. *Though* they be—*many*] *Sennacherib* invaded Judea with an army of nearly *two hundred thousand* men.

Thus shall they be cut down] The angel of the Lord (a suffocating wind) slew of them in one night *one hundred and eighty-five thousand,* 2 Kings xix. 35.

Verse 13. *Now will I break his yoke from off thee*] This refers to the *tribute* which the Jews were obliged to pay to the Assyrians, 2 Kings xvii. 14.

Verse 14. *No more of thy name be sown*] No more of you shall be carried away into *captivity.*

I will make thy grave; for thou art vile] I think this is an address to the Assyrians, and especially to *Sennacherib.* The text is no obscure intimation of the fact. The *house of his gods is to be his grave:* and we know that while he was worshipping in the house of his god *Nisroch,* his two sons, *Adrammelech* and *Sharezer,* smote him there that he died, 2 Kings xix. 37.

Verse 15. *Behold upon the mountains*] Borrowed probably from Isa. lii. 7, but applied here to the *messengers* who brought the *good tidings* of the *destruction of Nineveh.* Judah might then *keep her solemn feasts,* for the wicked Assyrian should *pass through the land no more;* being entirely cut off, and the imperial city razed to its foundations.

CHAPTER II

Nineveh is now called upon to prepare for the approach of her enemies, the instruments of Jehovah's vengeance, 1; *and the military array and muster, the very arms and dress, of the Medes and Babylonians in the reigns of Cyaxares and Nabopolassar; their rapid approach to the city; the process of the siege, and the inundation of the river; the capture of the place; the captivity, lamentation, and flight of the inhabitants; the sacking of this immense, wealthy, and exceedingly populous city; and the consequent desolation and terror, are all described in the pathetic, vivid, and sublime imagery of Hebrew poetry,* 2–10. *This description is succeeded by a very beautiful and expressive allegory,* 11–12; *which is immediately explained, and applied to the city of Nineveh,* 13. *It is thought by some commentators that the metropolitan city of the Assyrian empire is also intended by the tender and beautiful simile, in the* seventh verse, *of a great princess led captive, with her maids of honour attending her, bewailing her and their own condition, by beating their breasts, and by other expressions of sorrow.*

A. M. cir. 3291
B. C. cir. 713
Ol. cir. XVI. 4
NumæPompilii,
R. Roman.,
cir. annum 3

HE [a]that [b]dasheth in pieces is come up before thy face: [c]keep the munition, watch the way, make *thy* loins strong, fortify *thy* power mightily.

2 [d]For the LORD hath turned away [e]the excellency of Jacob, as the excellency of Israel: for [f]the emptiers have emptied them out, and marred their vine branches.

3 The shield of his mighty men is made [g]red, the valiant men *are* [h]in scarlet: the chariots *shall be* with [i]flaming torches in the day of his preparation, and the fir trees shall be terribly shaken.

4 The chariots shall rage in the streets, they shall jostle one against another in the broad ways: [k]they shall seem like torches, they shall run like the lightnings.

5 He shall recount his [l]worthies: they shall stumble in their walk; they shall make haste to the wall thereof, and the [m]defence shall be prepared.

6 The gates of the rivers shall be opened, and the palace shall be [n]dissolved.

7 And [o]Huzzab shall be [p]led away captive, she shall be brought up, and her maids shall lead *her* as with the voice of [q]doves, tabering upon their breasts.

8 But Nineveh *is* [r]of old like a pool of water: yet they shall flee away. Stand, stand, *shall they cry;* but none shall [s]look back.

[a]Or, *The disperser*, or *hammer*——[b]Jer. l. 23——[c]Jer. li. 11, 12; chap. iii. 14——[d]Isa. x. 12; Jer. xxxv. 29——[e]Or, *the pride of Jacob as the pride of Israel*——[f]Psa. lxxx. 12; Hos. x. 1——[g]Isa. lxiii. 2, 3——[h]Or, *dyed scarlet*——[i]Or, *fiery torches*

[k]Heb. *their show*——[l]Or, *gallants*——[m]Heb. *covering*, or *coverer*——[n]Or, *molten*——[o]Or, *that which was established*, or *there was a stand made*——[p]Or, *discovered*——[q]Isa. xxxviii. 14; lix. 11——[r]Or, *from the days* that *she* hath been——[s]Or, *cause* them *to turn*

NOTES ON CHAP. II

Verse 1. *He that dasheth in pieces*] **Or** *scattereth.* The Chaldeans and Medes.

Keep the munition] Guard the fenced places. From this to the end of the fifth verse, the *preparations* made at Nineveh to repel their enemies are described. The description is exceedingly picturesque.

Watch the way] By which the enemy is most likely to approach.

Make thy *loins strong*] Take *courage.*

Fortify thy *power*] Muster thy troops; call in all thy allies.

Verse 2. *For the Lord hath turned away*] Bishop *Newcome* reads, *for the Lord restoreth,* by a slight alteration in the text. I do not see that we gain much by this. The Lord *has* been opposed to Jacob, and the enemy has prevailed against him.

Emptied them out] Brought them from their own land into captivity. This was the *emptying!*

Verse 3. *The shield of his mighty men is made red*] These things may refer to the warlike preparations made by the Ninevites: they had *red shields*, and *scarlet* or *purple clothing;* their chariots were finely *decorated*, and proceeded with amazing rapidity.

The fir trees shall be terribly shaken.] This may refer to the *darts, arrows*, and *javelins*, flung with destructive power.

Verse 4. *The chariots shall rage*] Those of the *besiegers* and the *besieged*, meeting in the streets, producing universal confusion and carnage.

Verse 5. *He shall recount his worthies*] Muster up his most renowned warriors and heroes.

Shall make haste to the wall] Where they see the enemies making their most powerful attacks, in order to get possession of the city.

Verse 6. *The gates of the rivers shall be opened*] I have already referred to this, see the note on chap. i. 8; but it will be necessary to be *more particular.* The account given by *Diodorus Siculus*, lib. ii., is very surprising. He begins thus: Ην δ' αυτῳ λογιον παραδεδομενον εκ προγονων, κ. τ. λ.—"There was a prophecy received from their forefathers, that Nineveh should not be taken *till the river first became an enemy to the city.* It happened in the *third* year of the siege, that the Euphrates [query, *Tigris*] being swollen with continued rains, overflowed part of the city, and threw down *twenty* stadia of the wall. The king then imagining that the oracle was accomplished, and that *the river was now manifestly become an enemy to the city,* casting aside all hope of safety, and lest he should fall into the hands of the enemy, built a large funeral pyre in the palace, (εν τοις βασιλειοις,) and having collected all his gold and silver and royal vestments, together with his concubines and eunuchs, placed himself with them in a little apartment built in the pyre; burnt them, himself, and the palace together. When the death of the king (*Sardanapalus*) was announced by certain deserters, the enemy entered in by the breach which the waters had made, and took the city."

Thus the prophecy of Nahum was literally fulfilled: "the gates of the river were opened, and the palace dissolved," i. e., *burnt.*

Verse 7. *And Huzzab shall be led away captive*] Perhaps *Huzzab* means the *queen of Nineveh*, who had escaped the burning mentioned above by Diodorus. As there is no account of the *queen* being burnt, but only of the king, the concubines, and the eunuchs, we may, therefore, naturally conclude that the queen escaped; and is represented here as *brought up* and delivered to the conqueror; her maids at the same time bewailing her lot. Some think Huzzab signifies Nineveh itself.

Verse 8. *But Nineveh* is *of old like a pool of water*] מימי *mimey*, from days. Bp. *Newcome* translates the line thus: "And the waters of Nineveh are a pool of waters." There may be reference here to the fact given in the preceding note, the *overflowing of the river* by which the city was primarily destroyed.

Stand, stand] Consternation shall be at its utmost height, the people shall flee in all directions; and though *quarter* is offered, and they

A. M. cir. 3291
B. C. cir. 713
Ol. cir. XVI. 4
NumæPompilii,
R. Roman.,
cir. annum 3

9 Take ye the spoil of silver,
take the spoil of gold: [t]for
there is none end of the store
and glory out of all the [u]pleasant
furniture.

10 She is empty, and void, and waste: and
the [v]heart melteth, and [w]the knees smite together, [x]and much pain *is* in all loins, and
[y]the faces of them all gather blackness.

11 Where *is* the dwelling of [z]the lions, and
the feeding place of the young lions, where
the lion, *even* the old lion, walked, *and* the
lions' whelp, and none made
them afraid?

12 The lion did tear in pieces
enough for his whelps, and
strangled for his lionesses, and filled his holes
with prey, and his dens with ravin.

13 [a]Behold, I *am* against thee, saith the
LORD of hosts, and I will burn her chariots
in the smoke, and the sword shall devour thy
young lions: and I will cut off thy prey from
the earth, and the voice of [b]thy messengers
shall no more be heard.

---

[t]Or, *and* their *infinite store*, &c.——[u]Heb. *vessels of desire*——[v]Isa. xiii. 7, 8——[w]Dan. v. 6——[x]Jer. xxx. 9——[y]Joel ii. 6

[z]Job iv. 10, 11; Ezek. xix. 2–7——[a]Ezek. xxix. 3; xxxviii. 3; xxxix. 1; chap. iii. 5——[b]2 Kings xviii. 17, 19; xix. 9, 23

---

are assured of safety if they remain, yet not *one looketh back.*

Verse 9. *Take ye the spoil*] Though the king burnt his treasures, vestments, &c., he could not totally *destroy* the *silver* and the *gold.* Nor did he burn the *riches of the city;* these fell a prey to the conquerors; and there was *no end of the store* of *glorious* garments, and the most costly *vessels* and *furniture.*

Verse 10. *She is empty, and void, and waste*] The original is strongly emphatic: the words are of the *same sound;* and increase in their *length* as they point out *great, greater,* and *greatest* desolation.

בוקה ומבוקה ומבלקה

Bukah, umebukah, umebullakah.

She is *void, empty,* and *desolate.*

The faces of them all gather blackness.] This marks the diseased state into which the people had been brought by reason of *famine,* &c.; for, as Mr. *Ward* justly remarks, "*sickness* makes a great change in the countenance of the Hindoos; so that a person who was rather *fair* when in *health,* becomes nearly *black* by *sickness.*" This was a general case with the Asiatics.

Verse 11. *Where* is *the dwelling of the lions*] *Nineveh,* the habitation of *bold, strong,* and *ferocious* men.

The feeding place of the young lions] Whither her victorious and rapacious generals frequently *returned* to *consume* the produce of their success. Here they *walked* at large, and *none made them afraid.* Wheresoever they turned their arms they were victors; and all nations were afraid of them.

Verse 12. *The lion did tear*] This verse gives us a striking picture of the manner in which the Assyrian conquests and depredations were carried on. How many people were spoiled to enrich his *whelps*—his sons, princes, and *nobles!* How *many women* were *stripped* and *slain,* whose spoils went to decorate his *lionesses*—his *queen concubines* and *mistresses.* And they had even more than they could assume; *their holes and dens*—treasure-houses, palaces, and *wardrobes*—were filled *with ravin,* the riches which they got by the plunder of *towns, families,* and *individuals.* This is a very fine allegory, and admirably well supported.

Verse 13. *Behold, I* am *against thee*] Assyria, and Nineveh its capital. I will deal with you as you have dealt with others

The voice of thy messengers] Announcing thy splendid victories, and the vast spoils taken—*shall no more be heard*—thou and thy riches, and ill-got spoils, shall perish together.

CHAPTER III

The prophet denounces a wo against Nineveh for her perfidy and violence. He musters up before our eyes the number of her chariots and cavalry; points to her burnished arms, and to the great and unrelenting slaughter which she spreads around her, 1–3. *Because Nineveh is a city wholly given up to the grossest superstition, and is an instructress of other nations in her abominable rites, therefore she shall come to a most ignominious and unpitied end,* 3–7. *Her final ruin shall be similar to that of No, a famous city of Egypt,* 8–11. *The prophet then beautifully describes the great ease with which the strong holds of Nineveh should be taken,* 12, *and her judicial pusillanimity during the siege,* 13; *declares that all her preparation, her numbers, opulence, and chieftains, would be of no avail in the day of the Lord's vengeance,* 14–17; *and that her tributaries would desert her,* 18. *The whole concludes with stating the incurableness of her malady, and the dreadful destruction consequently awaiting her; and with introducing the nations which she had oppressed as exulting at her fall,* 19.

A. M. cir. 3291
B. C. cir. 713
Ol. cir. XVI. 4
NumæPompilii,
R. Roman.,
cir. annum 3

WO to the [a]bloody [b]city!
it *is* all full of lies *and*
robbery; the prey departeth not;
2 The noise of a whip, and [c]the
noise of the rattling of the wheels, and of the
prancing horses, and of the jumping chariots.
3 The horsemen lifteth up both [d]the bright
sword and the glittering spear: and *there is*
a multitude of slain, and a great number
of carcasses; and *there is* none end of
their corpses; they stumble upon their
corpses:
4 Because of the multitude of the whoredoms of the well-favoured harlot, [e]the mistress of witchcrafts, that selleth nations
through her whoredoms, and families through
her witchcrafts.
5 [f]Behold, I *am* against thee, saith the LORD
of hosts; and [g]I will discover thy skirts upon
thy face, [h]and I will show the nations thy
nakedness, and the kingdoms thy shame.

[a]Heb. *city of bloods*——[b]Ezek. xxii. 2, 3; xxiv. 6, 9; Hab. ii. 12——[c]Jer. xlvii. 3——[d]Heb. *the flame of the sword, and the lightning of the spear*——[e]Isa. xlvii. 9, 12; Rev. xviii. 2, 3——[f]Chap. ii. 13——[g]Isa. xlvii. 2, 3; Jer. xiii. 22, 26; Ezek. xvi. 37; Mic. i. 11——[h]Hab. ii. 16

6 And I will cast abominable
filth upon thee, and [i]make thee
vile, and will set thee as [k]a gazing-stock.

A. M. cir. 3291
B. C. cir. 713
Ol. cir. XVI. 4
NumæPompilii,
R. Roman.,
cir. annum 3

7 And it shall come to pass, *that* all they
that look upon thee [l]shall flee from thee, and
say, Nineveh is laid waste: [m]who will bemoan her? whence shall I seek comforters for
thee?
8 [n]Art thou better than [o]populous[p] [q]No,
that was situate among the rivers, *that*
had the waters round about it, whose rampart *was* the sea, *and* her wall *was* from the
sea?
9 Ethiopia and Egypt *were* her strength,
and *it was* infinite; Put and Lubim were [r]thy
helpers.
10 Yet *was* she carried away, she went into
captivity: [s]her young children also were dashed in pieces [t]at the top of all the streets: and
they [u]cast lots for her honourable men, and

[i]Mal. ii. 9——[k]Heb. x. 33——[l]Rev. xviii. 10——[m]Jer. xv. 5——[n]Amos vi. 2——[o]Or, *nourishing*——[p]Heb. *No Amon*——[q]Jer. xlvi. 25, 26; Ezek. xxx. 14–16——[r]Heb. *in thy help*——[s]Psa. cxxxvii. 9; Isa. xiii. 16; Hos. xiii. 16——[t]Lam. ii. 19——[u]Joel iii. 3; Obad. 11

NOTES ON CHAP. III

Verse 1. *Wo to the bloody city!*] Nineveh: the threatenings against which are continued in a strain of invective, astonishing for its richness, variety, and energy. One may hear and see the *whip crack*, the *horses prancing*, the *wheels rumbling*, the *chariots bounding* after the *galloping steeds;* the *reflection* from the *drawn* and highly *polished swords;* and the *hurled spears*, like *flashes* of *lightning*, dazzling the eyes; the *slain* lying in *heaps*, and *horses* and *chariots* stumbling over them! O what a picture, and a *true representation* of a battle, when one side is broken, and all the *cavalry* of the conqueror fall in upon them, *hewing* them down with their swords, and trampling them to pieces under the hoofs of their horses! O! infernal war! Yet sometimes thou art the scourge of the Lord.

Verse 4. *Because of the multitude of the whoredoms*] Above, the Ninevites were represented under the emblem of a *lion tearing all to pieces;* here they are represented under the emblem of a *beautiful harlot* or public *prostitute*, enticing all men to her, inducing the nations to become idolatrous; and, by thus perverting them, rendering them also objects of the Divine wrath.

Mistress of witchcrafts, that selleth nations through her whoredoms] Using every means to excite to idolatry; and being, by *menace* or *wiles*, successful in all.

Verse 5. *I will discover thy skirts upon thy face*] It was an ancient, though not a laudable custom, to strip prostitutes naked, or throw their clothes over their heads, and expose them to public view, and public execration. This verse alludes to such a custom.

Verse 6. *I will cast abominable filth upon thee*] I will set thee as a *gazing-stock*. This was a punishment precisely like our *pillory*. They put such women in the pillory as a *gazing-stock;* and then, *children* and *others* threw *mud, dirt*, and *filth* of all kinds at them.

Verse 7. *Who will bemoan her?*] In such cases, who pities the delinquent? She has been the occasion of ruin to multitudes, and now she is deservedly exposed and punished. And so it should be thought concerning Nineveh.

Verse 8. *Art thou better than populous No*] No-Ammon, or *Diospolis*, in the *Delta*, on one branch of the Nile. This is supposed to be the city mentioned by *Nahum;* and which had been lately destroyed, probably by the Chaldeans.

The waters round about it] Being situated in the *Delta*, it had the *fork* of two branches of the Nile to defend it by land; and its barrier or *wall* was the *sea*, the Mediterranean, into which these branches emptied themselves: so that this city, and the place it stood on, were wholly surrounded by the waters.

Verse 9. *Ethiopia and Egypt* were *her strength*] The land of *Cush*, not far from *Diospolis;* for it was in Arabia, on the *Red Sea*.

Put and Lubim] A part of Africa and Libya, which were all within reach of forming alliances with *No-Ammon* or *Diospolis*.

Verse 10. *They cast lots for her honourable men*] This refers still to the city called *populous No*. And the custom of *casting lots* among the commanders, for the prisoners which they had taken, is here referred to.

A. M. cir. 3291
B. C. cir. 713
Ol. cir. XVI. 4
NumæPompilii,
R. Roman.,
cir. annum 3

all her great men were bound
in chains.
11 Thou also shalt be [v]drunk-
en: thou shalt be hid, thou
also shalt seek strength because of the
enemy.
12 All thy strong holds *shall be like* [w]fig
trees with the first-ripe figs: if they be shaken,
they shall even fall into the mouth of the
eater.
13 Behold, [x]thy people in the midst of thee
are women: the gates of thy land shall be
set wide open unto thine enemies: the fire
shall devour thy [y]bars.
14 Draw thee waters for the siege, [z]fortify
thy strong holds: go into clay, and tread the
mortar, make strong the brick-kiln.
15 There shall the fire devour thee; the
sword shall cut thee off, it shall eat thee up
like [a]the cankerworm: make thyself many as
the cankerworm, make thyself
many as the locusts.
16 Thou hast multiplied thy
merchants above the stars of
heaven: the cankerworm [b]spoileth, and fleeth
away.
17 [c]Thy crowned *are* as the locusts, and
thy captains as the great grasshoppers, which
camp in the hedges in the cold day, *but* when
the sun ariseth they flee away, and their place
is not known where they *are.*
18 [d]Thy shepherds slumber, O [e]king of
Assyria: thy [f]nobles shall dwell *in the dust:*
thy people is [g]scattered upon the mountains,
and no man gathereth *them.*
19 *There is* no [h]healing of thy bruise; [i]thy
wound is grievous: [k]all that hear the bruit
of thee shall clap the hands over thee: for
upon whom hath not thy wickedness passed
continually?

A. M. cir. 3291
B. C. cir. 713
Ol. cir. XVI. 4
NumæPompilii,
R. Roman.,
cir. annum 3

---

[v]Jer. xxv. 17, 27; chap. i. 10——[w]Rev. vi. 13——[x]Jer. l. 37; li. 30——[y]Psa. cxlvii. 13; Jer. li. 30——[z]Chap. ii. 1——[a]Joel i. 4——[b]Or, *spreadeth himself*——[c]Revelation ix. 7

[d]Exod. xv. 16; Psa. lxxvii. 6——[e]Jer. l. 18; Ezek. xxxi. 3, &c.——[f]Or, *valiant ones*——[g]1 Kings xxii. 17 [h]Heb. *wrinkling*——[i]Mic. i. 9——[k]Lam. ii. 15; Zeph. ii. 15; see Isa. xiv. 8, &c.

Great men were bound in chains] These were reserved to grace the *triumph* of the victor.

Verse 12. *Thy strong holds*] The effects of the consternation into which the Ninevites were cast by the assault on their city are here pointed out by a very expressive metaphor; the *first-ripe figs*, when at *full maturity*, fell from the tree with the *least shake;* and so, at the first *shake* or *consternation*, all the *fortresses* of Nineveh were abandoned; and the king, in despair, burnt himself and household in his own palace.

Verse 13. *Thy people*—are *women*] They lost all courage, and made no resistance. O verè Phrygiæ, neque enim Phryges: "Verily, ye are Phrygian women, not Phrygian men." So said *Numanus* to the *Trojans. Virg., Æn.* ix.

Verse 14. *Draw thee waters for the siege*] The Tigris ran near to Nineveh, and here they are exhorted to lay in plenty of fresh water, lest the siege should last long, and lest the enemy should cut off this supply.

Go into clay, and tread the mortar] This refers to the manner of forming bricks anciently in those countries; they digged up the clay, kneaded it properly by *treading*, mixed it with straw or *coarse grass*, moulded the bricks, and dried them in the sun. I have now some of the identical bricks, that were brought from this country, lying before me, and they show all these appearances. They are compact and very hard, but wholly soluble in water. There were however others without *straw*, that seem to have been *burnt in a kiln* as ours are. I have also some fragments or *bats* of these from Babylon.

Verse 15. *Make thyself many as the cankerworm*] On the *locusts*, and their operations in their various *states*, see the notes on Joel ii. The multitudes, successive swarms, and devastation occasioned by locusts, is one of the most expressive similes that could be used to point out the successive armies and all-destroying influences of the enemies of Nineveh. The account of these destroyers from Dr. *Shaw*, inserted Joel ii., will fully illustrate the verses where allusion is made to locusts.

Verse 16. *Thou hast multiplied thy merchants*] Like Tyre, this city was a famous resort for merchants; but the multitudes which were there previously to the siege, like the locusts, took the alarm, and fled away.

Verse 17. *Thy crowned* are *as the locusts*] Thou hast numerous *princes* and numerous *commanders.*

Which camp in the hedges in the cold day] The locusts are said to *lie in shelter* about the *hedges* of fertile spots when the weather is *cold*, or during the *night;* but as soon as the *sun* shines out and is hot, they come out to their forage, or take to their wings.

Verse 18. *Thy shepherds slumber*] That is, the rulers and tributary princes, who, as *Herodotus* informs us, deserted Nineveh in the day of her distress, and came not forward to her succour.

Diodorus Siculus says, lib. ii., when the enemy shut up the king in the city, many nations revolted, each going over to the besiegers, for the sake of their liberty; that the king despatched messengers to all his subjects, requiring power from them to succour him; and that he thought himself able to endure the siege, and remained in expectation of armies which were to be raised throughout his empire, relying on the *oracle* that *the city would* not be taken *till the river became its enemy.* See the note on chap. ii. 6.

Verse 19. There is *no healing of thy bruise*] Thou shalt never be rebuilt.

All that hear the bruit of thee] The report or account.

Shall clap the hands] Shall exult in thy downfall.

For upon whom hath not thy wickedness passed] Thou hast been a *universal oppressor*, and therefore all nations rejoice at thy fall and utter desolation.

Bp. *Newton* makes some good remarks on the fall and total ruin of Nineveh.

"What probability was there that the capital city of a great kingdom, a city which was *sixty* miles in compass, a city which contained so many *thousand* inhabitants, a city which had walls a *hundred* feet high, and so thick that *three* chariots could go abreast upon them, and which had *one thousand five hundred* towers, of *two hundred* feet in height; what probability was there that such a city should ever be totally destroyed? And yet so totally was it destroyed that the place is hardly known where it was situated. What we may suppose helped to complete its ruin and devastation, was Nebuchadnezzar's enlarging and beautifying Babylon, soon after Nineveh was taken. From that time no mention is made of Nineveh by any of the sacred writers; and the most ancient of the heathen authors, who have occasion to say any thing about it, speak of it as a city that was once great and flourishing, but now destroyed and desolate. Great as it was formerly, so little of it is remaining, that authors are not agreed even about its situation. From the general suffrage of ancient historians and geographers, it appears to have been situated upon the Tigris, though others represent it as placed upon the Euphrates. *Bochart* has shown that *Herodotus*, *Diodorus Siculus*, and *Ammianus Marcellinus*, all *three* speak differently of it; sometimes as if situated on the Euphrates, sometimes as if on the Tigris; to reconcile whom he supposes that there were *two* Ninevehs; and Sir *John Marsham*, that there were *three;* the Syrian upon the Euphrates, the Assyrian on the Tigris, and a *third* built afterwards upon the Tigris by the Persians, who succeeded the Parthians in the empire of the East, in the *third* century, and were subdued by the Saracens in the *seventh* century after Christ. But whether this latter was built in the same place as the old Nineveh, is a question that cannot be decided.

"There is a city at this time called Mosul, situate upon the western side of the Tigris; and on the opposite eastern shore are ruins of great extent, which are said to be those of Nineveh.

"Dr. *Prideaux*, following *Thevenot*, observes that Mosul is situated on the west side of the Tigris, where was anciently only a suburb of the old Nineveh; for the city itself stood on the east side of the river, where are to be seen some of its ruins of great extent even to this day. Even the ruins of old Nineveh, as we may say, have been long ago ruined and destroyed; such an utter end hath been made of it, and such is the truth of the Divine predictions!

"These extraordinary circumstances may strike the reader more strongly by supposing only a parallel instance. Let us then suppose that a person should come in the name of a prophet, preaching repentance to the people of this kingdom, or otherwise denouncing the destruction of the capital city within a few years. 'With an overflowing flood will God make an utter end of the place thereof; he will make an utter end: its place may be sought, but it shall never be found.' I presume we should look upon such a prophet as a madman, and show no farther attention to his message than to deride and despise it. And yet such an event would not be more strange and incredible than the destruction and devastation of Nineveh; for Nineveh was much the larger, stronger, and older city of the two. And the Assyrian empire had subsisted and flourished more ages than any form of government in this country; so there is no objecting the instability of Eastern monarchies in this case. Let us then, since this event would not be more improbable and extraordinary than the other, suppose again, that things should succeed according to the prediction; that the floods should arise, and the enemies should come; the city should be overthrown and broken down, be taken and pillaged, and destroyed so totally that even the learned could not agree about the place where it was situated. What would be said or thought in such a case? Whoever of posterity should read and compare the prophecy and event together, must they not, by such an illustrious instance, be thoroughly convinced of the providence of God, and of the truth of his prophet, and be ready to acknowledge, 'Verily, this is the word which the Lord hath spoken; verily, there is a God who judgeth the earth?' "—See Bp. *Newton*, vol. i., dissert. 9.

THE BOOK

OF THE

PROPHET HABAKKUK

Chronological Notes relative to this Book, upon the supposition that it was written a little before the destruction of Jerusalem, about six hundred *years before the commencement of the Christian era.*

Year from the Creation, according to Archbishop Usher, 3404.—Year of the Julian Period, 4114.—Year since the Flood, 1748.—Year since the vocation of Abram, 1321.—Year from the foundation of Solomon's temple, 412.—Year since the division of Solomon's monarchy into the kingdoms of Israel and Judah, 376.—First year of the *forty-fifth* Olympiad.—Year since the destruction of the kingdom of Israel by Shalmaneser, king of Assyria, 121.—Year before the birth of Jesus Christ, 596.—Year before the vulgar era of Christ's nativity, 600.—Cycle of the Sun, 26.—Cycle of the Moon, 10.—Third year of Æropas, king of Macedon.—Twentieth year of Alyattes II., king of Lydia.—Twenty-sixth year of Cyaxares or Cyaraxes, king of Media.—Sixth year of Agasicles, king of Lacedæmon, of the family of the Proclidæ.—Eighth year of Leon, king of Lacedæmon, of the family of the Eurysthenidæ.—Seventh year of Nebuchadnezzar, king of Babylon.—Seventeenth year of Tarquinius Priscus, king of the Romans.—Eleventh year of Jehoiakim, king of Judah.

CHAPTER I

The prophet enters very abruptly on his subject, his spirit being greatly indignant at the rapid progress of vice and impiety, 1–4. *Upon which God is introduced threatening very awful and sudden judgments to be inflicted by the ministry of the Chaldeans,* 5–10. *The Babylonians attribute their wonderful successes to their idols,* 11. *The prophet then, making a sudden transition, expostulates with God (probably personating the Jews) for permitting a nation much more wicked than themselves, as they supposed, to oppress and devour them, as fishers and foulers do their prey,* 12–17.

A. M. cir. 3404
B. C. cir. 600
Ol. XLV. 1
TarquiniiPrisci,
R. Roman.,
cir. annum 17

THE [a]burden which Habakkuk the prophet did see.
2 O LORD, how long shall I
cry, [b]and thou wilt not hear!
even cry out unto thee *of* violence, and thou wilt not save!
3 Why dost thou show me
iniquity, and cause *me* to behold

[a]Zech. ix. 1; xii. 1; Mal. i. 1

[b]Lam. iii. 8

We know little of this prophet; for what we find in the *ancients* concerning him is evidently fabulous, as well as that which appears in the *Apocrypha*. He was probably of the tribe of *Simeon*, and a native of *Beth-zacar*. It is very likely that he lived after the destruction of Nineveh, as he speaks of the *Chaldeans*, but makes no mention of the *Assyrians*. And he appears also to have prophesied *before* the Jewish captivity, see chap. i. 5; ii. 1; iii. 2, 16-19; and therefore Abp. *Newcome* thinks he may be placed in the reign of Jehoiakim, between the years 606 B. C. and 598 B. C.

As a *poet*, Habakkuk holds a high rank among the Hebrew prophets. The beautiful connection between the parts of his prophecy, its diction, imagery, spirit, and sublimity, cannot be too much admired; and his hymn, chap. iii., is allowed by the best judges to be a masterpiece of its kind. See *Lowth's* Prælect. xxi., xxviii.

NOTES ON CHAP. I

Verse 1. *The burden*] המשא *hammassa* signifies not only the *burdensome* prophecy, but the prophecy or *revelation* itself which God presented to the *mind* of Habakkuk, and which he *saw*—clearly perceived, in the light of prophecy, and then faithfully declared, as this book shows. The word signifies an *oracle* or *revelation* in general; but chiefly, one relative to *future calamities*.

Verse 2. *O Lord, how long shall I cry*] The prophet feels himself strongly excited against the vices which he beheld; and which, it appears from this verse, he had often declaimed

A. M. cir. 3404
B. C. cir. 600
Ol. XLV. 1
TarquiniiPrisci,
R. Roman.,
cir. annum 17

grievance? for spoiling and violence *are* before me: and there are *that* raise up strife and contention.

4 Therefore the law is slacked, and judgment doth never go forth: for the [c]wicked doth compass about the righteous; therefore [d]wrong judgment proceedeth.

5 [e]Behold ye among the heathen, and regard, and wonder marvellously: for *I* will work a work in your days, *which* ye will not believe, though it be told *you*.

6 For, lo, [f]I [g]raise up the Chaldeans, *that* bitter and hasty nation, which shall march through the [h]breadth of the land, to possess the dwellingplaces *that are* not theirs.

7 They *are* terrible and dreadful: [i]their judgment and their dignity shall proceed of themselves.

8 Their horses also are swifter than the leopards, and are more [k]fierce than the [l]evening wolves: and their horsemen shall spread themselves, and their horsemen shall come from far; [m]they shall fly as the eagle *that* hasteth to eat.

9 They shall come all for violence: [n]their[o] faces shall sup up *as* the east wind, and they

[c]Job xxi. 7; Psa. xciv. 3, &c.; Jer. xii. 1——[d]Or, *wrested*——[e]Isa. xxix. 14; Acts xiii. 41——[f]Deut. xxviii. 49, 50; Jer. v. 15——[g]Fulfilled 2 Chron. xxxvi. 6 [h]Heb. *breadths*——[i]Or, *from them shall proceed the judgment of these, and the captivity of these*——[k]Heb. *sharp*——[l]Ezekiel xxii. 27; Jeremiah v. 6; Zephaniah iii. 3——[m]Jeremiah iv. 13——[n]Or, *the supping up of their faces*, &c., or *their faces shall look toward the east*——[o]Hebrew, *the opposition of their faces toward the east*

against, but in vain; the people continued in their vices, and God in his longsuffering.

Habakkuk begins his prophecy under a similar *feeling*, and nearly in similar *words*, as *Juvenal* did his Satires:—

Semper ego auditor tantum? Nunquamne reponam?
Vexatus toties rauci Theseide Codri?
Sat. i. 1.

"Shall I always be a hearer only? Shall I never reply? So often vexed?"

Of *violence*] The most unlawful and outrageous acts.

Verse 3. *And cause* me *to behold grievance*] עמל *amal*, labour, toil, distress, misery, &c., the common fruits of sin.

Verse 4. *The law is slacked*] They pay no attention to it; it has lost all its vigour, its restraining and correcting power; it is not executed; right *judgment* is never *pronounced;* and the *poor righteous man* complains in vain that he is grievously oppressed by the *wicked*, and by those in power and authority. That the utmost depravity prevailed in the land of Judah is evident from these verses; and can we wonder, then, that God poured out such signal judgments upon them? When *judgment doth not proceed* from the seat of judgment upon earth, it will infallibly *go forth* from the throne of judgment in heaven.

Verse 5. *Behold ye among the heathen*] Instead of בגוים *baggoyim*, among the *nations* or *heathen*, some critics think we should read בגדים *bogedim*, *transgressors;* and to the same purpose the *Septuagint*, *Syriac*, and *Arabic* have read; and thus it is quoted by St. *Paul*, Acts xiii. 41. But neither this, nor any tantamount reading, is found in any of the MSS. yet collated. *Newcome* translates, "See, ye transgressors, and behold a wonder, and perish."

I *will work a work in your days*] As he is speaking of the desolation that should be produced by the *Chaldeans*, it follows, as Bp. *Newcome* has justly observed, that the Chaldeans invaded Judah *whilst* those were living whom the prophet addressed.

Which *ye will not believe*] Nor did they, after all the declarations of various prophets. They still supposed that God would not give them up into the hands of their enemies, though they continued in their abominations!

It is evident that St. Paul, in the above place, *accommodates* this prediction to his own purpose. And possibly this sense might have been the intention of the Divine Spirit when he first spoke the words to the prophet; for, as God *works* in reference to *eternity*, so he *speaks* in reference to the same; and therefore there is an infinity of meaning in his WORD. These appear to be the words of God in answer to the prophet, in which he declares he will entirely ruin this wicked people by means of the Chaldeans.

Verse 6. That *bitter and hasty nation*] Cruel and oppressive in their disposition; and prompt and speedy in their assaults and conquests.

Verse 7. *Their judgment—shall proceed of themselves.*] By revolting from the Assyrians, they have become a great nation. Thus, their judgment and excellence were the result of their own valour. Other meanings are given to this passage.

Verse 8. *Their horses also are swifter than the leopards*] The Chaldean cavalry are proverbial for swiftness, courage, &c. In Jeremiah, chap. iv. 13, it is said, speaking of Nebuchadnezzar, "His chariots are as a whirlwind; his horses are swifter than eagles."

Oppian, speaking of the horses bred about the Euphrates, says, "They are by nature warhorses, and so intrepid that neither the sight nor the roaring of the lion appals them; and, besides, they are astonishingly fleet."

The *leopard*, of all quadrupeds, is allowed to be the *swiftest*.

The evening wolves] The wolf is remarkable for his quick sight. *Ælian* says, Οξυωτεστατον εστι ζωον, και μεντοι, και νυκτος και σεληνης ουκ ουσης ὁδε ὁρᾳ; "The wolf is a very fleet animal; and, besides, it can see by night, even when there is no moonlight." Some think the *hyæna* is meant: it is a swift, cruel, and untameable animal. The other prophets speak of the Chaldeans in the same way. See Deut. xxviii. 49; Jer. xlviii. 40; xlix. 22; Ezek. xvii. 5; Lam. iv. 19.

Verse 9. *Their faces shall sup up* as *the east*

A. M. cir. 3404
B. C. cir. 600
Ol. XLV. 1
TarquiniiPrisci,
R. Roman.,
cir. annum 17

shall gather the captivity as the sand.

10 And they shall scoff at the kings, and the princes shall be a scorn unto them: they shall deride every strong hold; for they shall heap dust, and take it.

11 Then shall *his* mind change, and he shall pass over, and offend, [p]*imputing* this his power unto his god.

12 [q]*Art* thou not from everlasting, O LORD my God, mine Holy One? we shall not die. O LORD, [r]thou hast ordained them for judgment; and, O [s]mighty God, thou hast [t]established them for correction.

13 [u]*Thou art* of purer eyes than to behold evil, and canst not look on [v]iniquity: [w]wherefore lookest thou upon them that deal treacherously, *and* holdest thy tongue when the wicked devoureth *the man that is* more righteous than he?

A. M. cir. 3404
B. C. cir. 600
Ol. XLV. 1
TarquiniiPrisci,
R. Roman.,
cir. annum 17

14 And makest men as the fishes of the sea, as the [x]creeping things, *that have* no ruler over them?

15 They [y]take up all of them with the angle, they catch them in their net, and gather them in their [z]drag: therefore they rejoice and are glad.

16 Therefore [a]they sacrifice unto their net, and burn incense unto their drag; because by them their portion *is* fat, and their meat, [b]plenteous.[c]

17 Shall they therefore empty their net, and not spare continually to slay the nations?

[p]Dan. v. 4——[q]Psa. xc. 2; xciii. 2; Lam. v. 19——[r]2 Kings xix. 25; Psa. xvii. 13; Isa. x. 5, 6, 7; Ezek. xxx. 25——[s]Heb. *rock;* Deut. xxxii. 4——[t]Heb. *founded*——[u]Psa. v. 5

[v]Or, *grievance*——[w]Jer. xii. 1——[x]Or, *moving*——[y]Jer. xvi. 16; Amos iv. 2——[z]Or, *flue net*——[a]Deut. viii. 17; Isa. x. 13; xxxvii. 24, 25——[b]Or, *dainty*——[c]Heb. *fat*

wind] This may be an allusion to those *electrical winds* which prevail in that country. Mr. *Jackson*, in his overland journey from India, mentions his having bathed in the *Tigris*. On his coming out of the river one of those winds passed over him, and, in a moment, carried off every particle of *water* that was on his body and in his bathing dress. So, the Chaldeans shall leave no substance behind them; their *faces*, their bare *appearance*, is the proof that nothing good shall be left.

Shall gather the captivity as the sand.] They shall carry off innumerable captives.

Verse 10. *They shall scoff at the kings*] No power shall be able to stand before them. It will be only as *pastime* to them to take the strongest places. They will have no need to build formidable ramparts: by sweeping the *dust* together they shall make mounts sufficient to pass over the walls and take the city.

Verse 11. *Then shall* his *mind change*] This is thought to relate to the change which took place in Nebuchadnezzar, when "a beast's heart was given to him," and he was "driven from the dwellings of men." And this was because of his *offending*—his pride and arrogance; and his attributing all his success, &c., to his *idols.*

Verse 12. Art *thou not from everlasting*] The idols change, and their worshippers change and fail: but thou, Jehovah, art *eternal;* thou canst not change, and they who trust in thee are safe. Thou art infinite in thy mercy; therefore, "we shall not die," shall not be totally exterminated.

Thou hast ordained them for judgment] Thou hast raised up the Chaldeans to correct and punish us; but thou hast not given them a commission to destroy us totally.

Instead of לא נמות *lo namuth,* "we shall not die," *Houbigant* and other critics, with a little transposition of letters, read אל אמת *El emeth,* "God of truth;" and then the verse will stand thus: "Art thou not from everlasting, O Jehovah, my God, my Holy One? O Jehovah, GOD OF TRUTH, thou hast appointed them for judgment." But this emendation, however elegant, is not supported by any MS.; nor, indeed, by any of the ancient *versions*, though the *Chaldee* has something like it. The common reading makes a very good sense.

Verse 13. Thou art *of purer eyes*] Seeing thou art so pure, and canst not look on iniquity—it is so abominable—how canst thou bear with them who "deal treacherously, and hold thy tongue when the wicked devour the righteous?" All such questions are easily solved by a consideration of God's ineffable mercy, which leads him to *suffer long* and be kind. He has no pleasure in the death of a sinner.

Verse 14. *Makest men as the fishes of the sea*] Easily are we taken and destroyed. We have no *leader* to guide us, and no *power* to defend ourselves. Nebuchadnezzar is here represented as a fisherman, who is constantly casting his nets into the sea, and enclosing multitudes of fishes; and, being always successful, he sacrifices to his own net—attributes all his conquests to his own power and prudence; not considering that he is only like a *net* that, after having been used for a while, shall at last be thrown by as useless, or burnt in the fire.

Verse 16. *They sacrifice unto their net*] He had no God; he cared for none; and worshipped only his *armour* and *himself.* King *Mezentius*, one of the worst characters in the *Æneid* of *Virgil*, is represented as invoking his own *right hand* and his *spear* in battle. *Æn.* x. 773.

Dextra mihi Deus, et telum quod missile libro,
Nunc adsint.

"My strong right hand and sword, assert my stroke.
Those only gods Mezentius will invoke."

DRYDEN.

And *Capaneus*, in *Statius*, gives us a more decisive proof of this *self-idolatry*. *Thebaid*, lib. x.

Ades, O mihi dextera tantum
Tu præses belli, et inevitabile Numen,
Te voco, te solum Superum contemptor adoro.

"Only thou, my right hand, be my aid; I contemn the gods, and adore thee as the chief in battle, and the irresistible deity." The poet tells us that, for his impiety, Jupiter slew him with thunder.

This was an ancient idolatry in this country, and has existed till within about a century. There are relics of it in different parts of Europe; for when military men *bind themselves* to accomplish any particular purpose, it is usual to *lay their hand* upon their sword: but formerly they *kissed* it, when swearing by it. With most heroes, the *sword* is both their *Bible* and their *God*. To the present day it is a custom among the *Hindoos* annually to *worship* the implements of their *trades*. See WARD.

Verse 17. *And not spare continually to slay the nations?*] They are running from conquest to conquest; burning, slaying, sacking, and slaughtering. Like the fishermen, who throw cast after cast while any fish are to be caught, so Nebuchadnezzar is destroying one nation after another. This last sentence explains the allegory of the *net*.

CHAPTER II

The prophet, waiting for a return to his expostulation, is answered by God that the time for the destruction of the Jewish polity by the Chaldeans is not only fixed in the Divine counsel, but is awfully near; and he is therefore commanded to write down the vision relative to this appalling subject in the most legible characters, and in the plainest language, that all who read it with attention (those just persons who exercise an unwavering faith in the declaration of God respecting the violent irruption of the merciless Babylonians) may flee from the impending vengeance, 1–4. *The fall of the Chaldeans, and of their ambitious monarch is then predicted,* 5–10; *and, by a strong and bold personification, the very stone and wood of those magnificent buildings, which the Babylonish king had raised by oppression and bloodshed, pronounce his wo, and in responsive taunts upbraid him,* 11, 12. *The prophet then beautifully sets forth the absolute impotence of every effort, however well conducted, which is not in concert with the Divine counsel: for though the wicked rage, and threaten the utter extermination of the people of God; yet when the* SET time *to favour Zion is come, the destroyers of God's heritage shall themselves be destroyed, and "the earth shall be filled with the knowledge of the glory of God, as the waters cover the sea,"* 13, 14. *See* Psa. cii. 13–16. *For the cup of idolatry which Babylon has given to many nations, she will receive of the Lord's hand the cup of fury by the insurrection of mighty enemies (the Medes and Persians) rushing like wild beasts to destroy her,* 15. *In the midst of this distress the prophet very opportunely asks in what the Babylonians had profited by their idols, exposes the absurdity of trusting in them, and calls upon the whole world to stand in awe of the everlasting Jehovah,* 16–19.

A. M. cir. 3404 B. C. cir. 600 Ol. cir. XLV. 1 TarquiniiPrisci, R. Roman., cir. annum 17

I WILL [a]stand upon my watch,
and set me upon the [b]tower,
[c]and will watch to see what he
will say [d]unto me, and what I
shall answer [e]when [f]I am
reproved.
2 And the LORD answered me,
and said, [g]Write the vision, and

A. M. cir. 3404 B. C. cir. 600 Ol. cir. XLV. 1 TarquiniiPrisci, R. Roman., cir. annum 17

[a]Isa. xxi. 8, 11——[b]Heb. *fenced place*——[c]Psa. lxxxv. 8——[d]Or, *in me*——[e]Or, *when I am argued with*——[f]Heb. *upon my reproof, or arguing*——[g]Isa. viii. 1; xxx. 8

NOTES ON CHAP. II

Verse 1. *I will stand upon my watch*] The prophets are always represented as *watchmen*, watching constantly for the comfort, safety, and welfare of the people; and watching also to receive information from the Lord: for the prophetic influence was not *always* with them, but was granted only at particular times, according to the will of God. When, in doubtful cases, they wished to know what God was about to do with the country, they retired from society and gave themselves to meditation and prayer, waiting thus upon God *to hear what he would say* IN *them*.

What he will say unto me] בי *bi*, IN *me*—in my understanding and heart.

And what I shall answer when I am reproved.] What I shall say to God *in behalf* of the people; and what the Lord shall command me to say *to the people*. Some translate, "And what he will answer for my conviction." Or, "what shall be answered to my pleading."

Verse 2. *Write the vision*] Carefully take down all that I shall say.

Make it *plain upon tables*] Write it in a full, plain, legible hand.

That he may run that readeth it.] That he who attentively peruses it may speed to save his life from the irruption of the Chaldeans, by which so many shall be cut off. The prophet does not mean that the words are to be made so plain, that a man *running by* may easily read them, and catch their meaning. This interpretation has been frequently given; and it has been incautiously applied to the whole of the Bible: "God's book is so plain, that he that runs may read;" but it is very foolish: God

A. M. cir. 3404
B. C. cir. 600
Ol. cir. XLV. 1
TarquiniiPrisci, R. Roman., cir. annum 17

make *it* plain upon tables, that
he may run that readeth it.
3 For [h]the vision *is* yet for
an appointed time, but at the
end it shall speak, and not lie: though it
tarry, wait for it; because it will [i]surely come,
it will not tarry.
4 Behold, his soul *which* is lifted up is not
upright in him: but the [k]just shall live by
his faith.
5 [l]Yea also, because he transgresseth by
wine, *he is* a proud man, neither keepeth at
home, who enlargeth his desire [m]as hell, and *is*
as death, and cannot be satisfied, but gathereth unto him all nations, and
heapeth unto him all people:
6 Shall not all these [n]take up a
parable against him, and a
taunting proverb against him, and say, [o]Wo
to him that increaseth *that which is* not his!
how long? and to him that ladeth himself
with thick clay!
7 Shall they not rise up suddenly that shall
bite thee, and awake that shall vex thee, and
thou shalt be for booties unto them?
8 [p]Because thou hast spoiled many nations,
all the remnant of the people shall spoil thee;
[q]because of men's [r]blood, and *for* the violence

[h]Dan. x. 14; xi. 27, 35——[i]Heb. x. 37——[k]John iii. 36; Rom. i. 17; Gal. iii. 11; Heb. x. 38——[l]Or, *How much more*

[m]Prov. xxvii. 20; xxx. 16——[n]Mic. ii. 4——[o]Or, *Ho, he*——[p]Isaiah xxxiii. 1——[q]Ver. 17——[r]Hebrew, *bloods*

never intends that his words shall be understood by the *careless*. He that *reads, studies, meditates*, and *prays*, shall understand every portion of this sacred book that relates immediately to his own salvation. But no *trifler* can understand it. If the contents of a *play-bill* were to be read as many read the *Bible*, they would know just as much of the *one* as they do of the *other*.

Verse 3. *The vision* is *yet for an appointed time*] The Chaldeans, who are to ruin Judea, shall *afterwards* be ruined themselves: but they must do this work *before* they receive their wages; therefore the vision is for an *appointed time. But at the end it shall speak.* When his work of devastation is done, his day of retribution shall take place.

Though it tarry] Though it appear to be long, do not be impatient; *it will surely come; it will not tarry* longer than the prescribed time, and this time is not far distant. Wait for it.

Verse 4. *Behold, his soul* which *is lifted up*] He that presumes on his safety without any special warrant from God, is a *proud man;* and whatever he may profess, or think of himself, his *mind is not upright in him.* But he that is *just by faith shall live*—he that *believes* what God hath said relative to the Chaldeans besieging Jerusalem, shall make his escape from the place, and consequently shall *save his life.* The words in the *New Testament* are accommodated to the *salvation* which *believers in Christ* shall possess. Indeed, the just—the true Christians, who believed in Jesus Christ's words relative to the destruction of Jerusalem, when they found the Romans coming against it, left the city, and escaped to *Pella* in Cœlesyria, and did *live*—their lives were saved: while the unbelieving Jews, to a man, either *perished* or were made *slaves.* One good sense is, He that believes the promises of God, and has found life through believing, shall live by his faith.

Verse 5. *Because he transgresseth by wine*] From the present translation, it is not easy to see either reason or meaning in the first clause of this verse. *Newcome* translates, "Moreover, as a mighty man transgresseth through wine, he is proud, and remaineth not at rest." *Houbigant* thus: "For he, though he be a despiser, and powerful, and proud, yet shall he not have rest."

Nebuchadnezzar is here represented in his usual character, *proud, haughty*, and *ambitious;* inebriated with his successes, and determined on more extensive conquests; and, like the *grave*, can never have enough: yet, after the subjugation of many peoples and nations, he shall be brought down, and become so despicable that he shall be a *proverb* of *reproach*, and be taunted and scorned by all those whom he had before enslaved.

And cannot be satisfied] When he has obtained all that is within his reach, he wishes for more; and becomes miserable, because any limits are opposed to his insatiable ambition. It is said of *Alexander:*—

Unus Pellæo juveni non sufficit orbis;
Æstuat infelix angusto limite mundi.
Juv. Sat. x. 168.

One world sufficed not Alexander's mind;
Coop'd up, he seem'd on earth and seas confined.

And the poet justly ridicules him, because at last the sarcophagus was found *too large* for his body!

Verse 6. *Shall not all these take up a parable against him*] His ambition, derangement, and the final destruction of his mighty empire by the Persians, shall form the foundation of many *sententious sayings* among the people. "He who towered so high, behold how *low* he is fallen!" "He made himself a god; behold, he herds with the *beasts* of the field!" "The disturber of the peace of the world is now a *handful of dust!*"

Verse 7. *Shall they not rise up suddenly*] Does not this refer to the *sudden* and *unexpected taking of Babylon by Cyrus*, whose troops entered into the city through the bed of the Euphrates, whose waters they had diverted by another channel; so that the Babylonians *knew nothing of the matter* till they *saw* the Persian soldiers *rise up as in a moment*, in the very heart of their city?

Verse 8. For *the violence of the land*] Or, *for the violence* done *to the land* of Judea, *and to the city* of Jerusalem.

A. M. cir. 3404
B. C. cir. 600
Ol. cir. XLV. 1
TarquiniiPrisci,
R. Roman.,
cir. annum 17

of the land, of the city, and of
all that dwell therein.
9 Wo to him that [s]coveteth [t]an
evil covetousness to his house,
that he may [u]set his nest on high, that he
may be delivered from the [v]power of evil!
10 Thou hast consulted shame to thy house
by cutting off many people, and hast sinned
against thy soul.
11 For the stone shall cry out of the wall,
and the [w]beam out of the timber shall [x]an-
swer it.
12 Wo to him that buildeth a town with
[y]blood, [z]and stablisheth a city by iniquity!
13 Behold, *is it* not of the LORD of hosts
[a]that the people shall labour in the very fire,
and the people shall weary themselves [b]for
very vanity?

14 For the earth shall be filled
[c]with the [d]knowledge of the
glory of the LORD, as the waters
cover the sea.

A. M. cir. 3404
B. C. cir. 600
Ol. cir. XLV. 1
TarquiniiPrisci,
R. Roman.,
cir. annum 17

15 Wo unto him that giveth his neighbour
drink, that puttest thy [e]bottle to *him,* and
makest *him* drunken also, that thou mayest
[f]look on their nakedness!
16 Thou art filled [g]with shame for glory:
[h]drink thou also and let thy foreskin be uncovered: the cup of the LORD's right hand
shall be turned unto thee, and shameful spew-
ing *shall be* on thy glory.
17 For the violence of Lebanon shall cover
thee, and the spoil of beasts, *which* made them
afraid, [i]because of men's blood, and for the
violence of the land, of the city, and of all
that dwell therein.

---

[s]Jer. xxii. 13——[t]Or, *gaineth an evil gain*——[u]Jer. xlix. 16; Obad. 4——[v]Heb. *palm of the hand*——[w]Or, *piece*, or *fastening*——[x]Or, *witness against it*——[y]Jer. xxii. 13; Ezek. xxiv. 9; Mic. iii. 10; Nah. iii. 1

[z]Heb. *bloods*——[a]Jer. li. 58——[b]Or, *in vain*——[c]Or, *by knowing the glory of the LORD*——[d]Isa. xi. 9——[e]Hos. vii. 5——[f]Gen. ix. 22——[g]Or, *more with shame than with glory*——[h]Jer. xxv. 26, 27; li. 57——[i]Ver. 8

Verse 9. *An evil covetousness to his house*] Nebuchadnezzar wished to aggrandize his *family*, and make his *empire* permanent: but both *family* and *empire* were soon cut off by the death of his son Belshazzar, and the consequent destruction of the Chaldean empire.

Verse 10. *Hast sinned* against *thy soul.*] Thy *life* is forfeited by thy crimes.

Verse 11. *The stone shall cry out of the wall, and the beam out of the timber shall answer it.*] This appears to refer to the ancient mode of building walls; *two* or *three courses* of *stone*, and then *one course* of *timber*. See 1 Kings vi. 36: thus was the palace of Solomon built. The splendid and costly buildings of Babylon have been universally celebrated. But how were these buildings erected? By the *spoils* of conquered nations, and the expense of the *blood* of multitudes; therefore the *stones* and the *timber* are represented as calling out for vengeance against this ruthless conqueror.

Verse 12. *Wo to him that buildeth a town with blood*] At the expense of much slaughter. This is the answer of the *beam* to the *stone.* And these things will refer to the vast fortunes gained, and the buildings erected, by means of the *slave-trade;* where, to a considerate and humane mind, the *walls* appear as if composed of the *bones* of *negroes*, and *cemented* by their *blood!* But the towns or houses *established* by this *iniquity* soon come to ruin; and the fortunes made have, in most cases, become as chaff and dust before the whirlwind of God's indignation. But where are the dealers in the souls and bodies of men? Ask *him* who has them in his keeping. He can tell.

Verse 13. *The people shall labour in the very fire*] All these superb buildings shall be burnt down. See the parallel passage, Jer. li. 58, and the note there.

Shall weary themselves for very vanity?] For the gratification of the wishes of ambition, and in buildings which shall be brought to naught.

Verse 14. *For the earth shall be filled*] This is a singular and important verse. It may be *first* applied to *Babylon.* God's power and providence shall be widely displayed in the destruction of this city and empire, in the humiliation of Nebuchadnezzar, Dan. iv. 37, and in the captivity and restoration of his people. See *Newcome*, and see Isa. xi. 9.

Secondly. It may be applied to the *glorious days* of the *Messiah.* The *land of Judea* should by his preaching, and that of his disciples, be *filled with the knowledge of God.* God's great design fully discovered, and the scheme of salvation amply explained.

Thirdly. It may be applied to the *universal spread of the Gospel* over the habitable globe; when the fulness of the Gentiles should be brought in, and the Jews gathered in with that fulness. The *earth* cannot perish till every continent, island, and inhabitant, is illuminated with the light of the Gospel.

Verse 15. *Wo unto him that giveth his neighbour drink*] This has been considered as applying to *Pharaoh-hophra*, king of Egypt, who enticed his neighbours Jehoiachin and Zedekiah to rebel against Nebuchadnezzar, whereby the nakedness and imbecility of the poor Jews was soon discovered; for the Chaldeans soon took Jerusalem, and carried its kings, princes, and people, into captivity.

Verse 16. *The cup of the Lord's right hand*] Among the ancients, all drank out of the same cup; was passed from hand to hand, and each drank as much as he chose. The Chaldeans gave to the neighbouring nations *the cup of idolatry* and of *deceitful alliance;* and in return they received from the Lord the *cup of his fury.* So *Grotius.*

Verse 17. *For the violence of Lebanon*] Or, the violence done to *Lebanon;* to *men*, to *cattle*, to *Judea*, and to *Jerusalem.* See the note on the parallel place, ver. 8. This may be a threatening against *Egypt*, as the former was against *Chaldea.*

A. M. cir. 3404
B. C. cir. 600
Ol. cir. XLV. 1
Tarquinii Prisci,
R. Roman.,
cir. annum 17

18 [k]What profiteth the graven
image that the maker thereof
hath graven it; the molten image,
and a [l]teacher of lies,
that [m]the maker of his work trusteth therein,
to make [n]dumb idols?
19 Wo unto him that saith to the wood,
Awake; to the dumb stone,
Arise, it shall teach! Behold, it
is laid over with gold and
silver, [o]and *there is* no breath
at all in the midst of it.
20 But [p]the LORD *is* in his holy temple:
[q]let [r]all the earth keep silence before him.

A. M. cir. 3404
B. C. cir. 600
Ol. cir. XLV. 1
Tarquinii Prisci,
R. Roman.,
cir. annum 17

---

[k]Isa. xliv. 9, 10; xlvi. 2——[l]Jer. x. 8, 14; Zech. x. 2——[m]Heb. *the fashioner of his fashion*——[n]Psa. cxv. 5; 1 Cor. xii 2——[o]Psa. cxxxv. 17——[p]Psa. xi. 4——[q]Heb. *be silent all the earth before him*——[r]Zeph. i. 7; Zech. ii. 13

Verse 18. *What profiteth the graven image*] This is against idolatry in general, and every species of it, as well as against those princes, priests, and people who practise it, and encourage others to do the same. See on the parallel passages in the margin.

Dumb idols?] אלילים אלמים *elilim illemim*, "dumb nothings." This is exactly agreeable to St. Paul, 1 Cor. viii. 4, who says, "An idol is nothing in the world." What signify the idols worshipped by the Chaldeans, Tyrians, and Egyptians? They have not been able to save their worshippers.

Verse 19. *Wo unto him*] How foolish and contemptible to worship a thing *formed by the hand of man* out of *wood, stone, gold*, or *silver!* The meanest *brute* is superior to them all; it *breathes* and *lives*, but they have *no breath* in them. However, they are said above to be *teachers of lies;* that is, they appeared to give out *oracles:* but these were *lies;* and were not given by the *statue, but by the priest.*

Verse 20. *The Lord* is *in his holy temple*] Jehovah has his *temple*, the *place* where he is to be *worshipped;* but *there* there is no *image. Oracles*, however, are given forth; and every word of them is *truth*, and is fulfilled in its season. And this temple and its worship are *holy;* no *abomination* can be practised there, and every thing in it leads to *holiness* of heart and life.

Let all the earth keep silence before him.] Let all be dumb. Let none of them dare to open their mouths in the presence of Jehovah. He alone is Sovereign. He alone is the arbiter of life and death. Let all hear his commands with the deepest respect, obey them with the promptest diligence, and worship him with the most profound reverence. When an Asiatic sovereign goes to the mosque on any of the eastern festivals, such as the *Bairham*, the deepest *silence* reigns among all his retinue, viziers, foreign ambassadors, &c. They all bow respectfully before him; but no word is spoken, no sound uttered. It is to this species of reverence that the prophet alludes, and with this he concludes the *prophetic* part of this book. What God has threatened or promised, that he will fulfil. Let every soul bow before him, and submit to his authority.

CHAPTER III

The prophet, being apprized of the calamities which were to be brought on his country by the ministry of the Chaldeans, and the punishments which awaited the Chaldeans themselves, partly struck with terror, and partly revived with hope and confidence in the Divine mercy, beseeches God to hasten the redemption of his people, 1, 2. *Such a petition would naturally lead his thoughts to the astonishing deliverance which God vouchsafed to the same people of old; and the inference from it was obvious, that he could with the same ease deliver their posterity now. But, hurried on by the fire and impetuosity of his spirit, he disdains to wait the process of connecting these ideas, and bounds at once into the midst of his subject: "God came from Teman,"* &c., 3. *He goes on to describe the majesty and might which God displayed in conducting his people to the land of promise; selecting the most remarkable circumstances, and clothing them in the most lofty language. As he goes along, his fancy becomes more glowing, till at length he is transported to the scene of action, and becomes an eyewitness of the wonders he describes. "I beheld the tents of Cushan in affliction,"* 4–6. *After having touched on the principal circumstances of that deliverance which he celebrates, he returns to what passed before them in Egypt; his enthusiasm having led him to begin in the midst of his subject,* 7–15. *And at last he ends the hymn as he began it, with expressing his awe of the Divine judgments, and his firm trust in the mercy and goodness of God while under them; and that in terms of such singular beauty, elegance, and sublimity, as to form a very proper conclusion to this admirable piece of Divinely inspired composition,* 16–19. *It would seem from the title, and the note appended at the end, that it was set to music, and sung in the service of the temple.*

A. M. cir. 3404
B. C. cir. 600
Ol. cir. XLV. 1
Tarquinii Prisci,
R. Roman.,
cir. annum 17

A PRAYER of Habakkuk the prophet [a]upon [b]Shigionoth.

2 O LORD, I have heard [c]thy speech, *and* was afraid: O LORD, [d]revive[e] thy work in the midst of the years, in the midst of the years make known: in wrath remember mercy.

3 God came from [f]Teman, [g]and the Holy One from Mount Paran. Selah. His glory covered the heavens, and the earth was full of his praise.

4 And *his* brightness was as the light; he had horns *coming* out of his hand: and there *was* the hiding of his power.

5 [i]Before him went the pestilence, and [k]burning [l]coals went forth at his feet.

A. M. cir. 3404
B. C. cir. 600
Ol. cir. XLV. 1
Tarquinii Prisci,
R. Roman.,
cir. annum 17

[a]Psalm vii. title——[b]Or, *according to variable songs,* or *tunes,* called in Hebrew, *Shigionoth*——[c]Hebrew, *thy report,* or *thy hearing*——[d]Or, *preserve alive*——[e]Psa. lxxxv. 6——[f]Or, *the south*——[g]Deuteronomy xxiii. 2; Judges v. 4; Psalm lxviii. 7——[h]Or, *bright beams out of his side*——[i]Nah. i. 3——[k]Or, *burning diseases;* Deuteronomy xxxii. 24——[l]Psa. xviii. 8, 12; Isa. vi. 6; xlvii. 14

NOTES ON CHAP. III

Verse 1. *A prayer of Habakkuk—upon Shigionoth.*] See the note on the *title* of Psa. vii., where the meaning of *Shiggaion* is given. The *Vulgate* has, *pro ignorantiis, for ignorances,* or sins committed in ignorance; and so it is understood by the *Chaldee.* The *Syriac* has nothing but merely, *A prayer of Habakkuk.* And the *septuagint,* instead of *Shigionoth,* have *μετα ῳδης, with a hymn,* which is copied by the *Arabic.*

I suspect that the *title* here given is of a *posterior* date to the prophecy. It appears to interrupt the connection between this and the termination of the preceding verse. See them together:—

Chap ii 20: "But the Lord is in his holy temple:
Be silent before him, all the earth.
iii. 1: O Lord, I have heard thy speech:
I have feared, O Lord, thy work.
As the years approach thou hast shown;
As the years approach thou makest known.
In wrath thou rememberest mercy."

The prophet may here refer to the *speech* which God had communicated to him, chap. i. 5-11, ii. 4-20, and the terror with which he was struck, because of the judgments denounced against Jerusalem. I have followed the version of Apb. *Newcome* in this *first* verse. The critical reader may consult his notes, and the *various readings* of *Kennicott* and *De Rossi.*

Verse 2. *In the midst of the years*] בקרב שנים *bekereb shanim,* "As the years approach." The nearer the time, the clearer and fuller is the prediction; and the signs of the times show that the complete fulfilment *is at hand.* But as the judgments will be heavy, (and they are not greater than we deserve,) yet, *Lord, in the midst of wrath*—infliction of punishment—*remember mercy,* and spare the souls that return unto thee with humiliation and prayer.

Verse 3. *God came from Teman*] Bp. *Lowth* observes: "This is a sudden burst of poetry, in the true spirit of the ode; the concealed connection being that God, who had formerly displayed such power in delivering the Israelites from Egyptian slavery, might succour their posterity in a like wonderful manner." Hence the prophet selects the most striking facts of that first deliverance; and to decorate and render them impressive, brings forth all the powers of his genius, in all the strength and elegance of his language. "What crowns the sublimity of this piece," says Bp. *Lowth,* "is the singular elegance of the close; and were it not that antiquity has here and there thrown its veil of obscurity over it, there could not be conceived a more perfect and masterly poem of its kind." See, for more particulars, his *twenty-eighth* Prelection.

I shall endeavour to show the *facts* in the *deliverance from Egypt,* to which the prophet refers.

Teman] This was a city, the capital of a province of Idumea, to the south of the land of Canaan. Num. xx. 21; Jer. xlix. 7.

Paran] Was a city which gave its name to a province in Arabia Petræa. Gen. xxi. 21; Deut. xxxiii. 2.

Selah] This word is not well known; probably it means a pause or alteration in the music. See it in the Psalms, and its explanation there.

His glory covered the heavens] His glory when he descended on Mount Sinai, and in the pillar of fire by night.

The earth was full of his praise.] All the land was astonished at the magnificence of his works in behalf of his people. Instead of *praise,* some translate *splendour.* The whole land was illuminated by his glory.

Verse 4. *He had horns* coming *out of his hand*] קרנים *karnayim, rays.* His *hand*—his *power*—was manifested in a particular place, by the sudden issuing out of pencils of rays, which diverged in coruscations of light, so as to illuminate the whole hemisphere. Yet "there was the hiding of his power." His Majesty could not be seen, nor any kind of image, because of the insufferable splendour. This may either refer to the *lightnings* on Mount *Sinai;* or to the *brightness* which occasionally proceeded from the *shechinah* or glory of God between the cherubim, over the mercy-seat. See *Capellus* and *Newcome.* If *lightnings* are intended, the *dense cloud* from which they proceeded may be meant by the "hiding of his power;" for when the lightnings burst forth, his power and energy became manifest.

Probably from this the *Jupiter Keraunos* or *Jupiter Brontes* of the heathens was borrowed; who is always represented with forked or zigzag lightnings in his hand.

Verse 5. *Before him went the pestilence*] This plague was several times inflicted on the disobedient Israelites in the wilderness; see Num. xi. 33, xiv. 37, xvi. 46; and was always the proof that the *just God* was then manifesting his *power among them.*

A. M. cir. 3404
B. C. cir. 600
Ol. cir. XLV. 1
Tarquinii Prisci,
R. Roman.,
cir. annum 17

6 He stood, and measured the
earth: he beheld, and drove
asunder the nations; [m]and the
[n]everlasting mountains were
scattered, the perpetual hills did bow: his
ways are [o]everlasting.
7 I saw the tents of [p]Cushan [q]in affliction:
and the curtains of the land of Midian did
tremble.
8 Was the LORD displeased against the
rivers? *was* thine anger
against the rivers? *was* thy
wrath against the sea, [r]that
thou didst ride upon thine
horses *and* [s]thy chariots of salvation?
9 Thy bow was made quite naked, *according*
to the oaths of the tribes, *even thy* word.
Selah. [t]Thou [u]didst cleave the earth with
rivers.

A. M. cir. 3404
B. C. cir. 600
Ol. cir. XLV. 1
Tarquinii Prisci,
R. Roman.,
cir. annum 17

[m]Nah. i. 5——[n]Gen. xliv. 26——[o]Psa. cxxxix. 24
[p]Or, *Æthiopia*——[q]Or, *under affliction*, or *vanity*
[r]Deut. xxxiii. 26, 27; Psa. lxviii. 4; civ. 3; ver. 15

[s]Or, *thy chariots* were *salvation*——[t]Or, *Thou didst cleave the rivers of the earth*——[u]Psalm lxxviii. 15, 16; cv. 41

Burning coals went forth at his feet.] *Newcome* translates, "And flashes of fire went forth after him." The disobedient Israelities were consumed by a *fire* that went out from Jehovah; see Lev. x. 2; Num. xi. 1, xvi. 35. And the burnt-offering was consumed by a fire which came out from before Jehovah, Lev. xi. 24.

Verse 6. *He stood, and measured the earth*] ארץ *erets, the land;* he divided the promised land among the *twelve tribes*. This is the allusion; and this the prophet had in his eye. God not only made a *general assignment* of the land to the Hebrews; but he even *divided it* into *such portions* as the different families required. Here were both *power* and *condescension*. When a conqueror had subdued a country, he divided it among his soldiers. Among the Romans, those among whom the conquered lands were divided were termed *beneficiarii;* and the lands *beneficia*, as being held on the beneficence of the sovereign.

He beheld, and drove asunder the nations] The nations of *Canaan*, the *Hittites, Hivites, Jebusites*, &c., and all who opposed his people. Even his *look* dispersed them.

The everlasting mountains were scattered] Or, *broken asunder*. This may refer to the *convulsions* on Mount Sinai; and to the earthquake which announced the descent of the Most High. See Exod. xix. 18. "God occupied the summit of the eternal Mount Sinai; and led his people over the eternal mountains of Arabia Petræa; and this sense is preferable to the figurative one, that his ways or doings are predetermined from everlasting."—*Newcome*. The epithets עד *ad*, and עולם *olam, eternal*, and *everlasting*, are applied to mountains and immense rocks, because no other parts of nature are less subject to *decay* or *change*, than these immense masses of earth and stone, and that almost indestructible stone, *granite*, out of which *Sinai* appears to be formed. A piece of the beautiful granite of this mountain now lies before me. This is a figurative description of the passage of the Israelites through the deserts of Arabia, over mountains, rocks, and through the trackless wilderness; *over* and *through* which God, by his power and providence, gave them a safe passage.

The following beautiful piece from the Fragments of Æschylus will illustrate the preceding description, and please the learned reader.

Χωριζε θνητων τον Θεον, και μη δοκει
Ομοιον αυτῳ σαρκινον καθεσταναι·
Ουκ οισθα δ' αυτον· ποτε μεν ὡς πυρ φαινεται
Απλαστον ὁρμῃ· ποτε δ' ὑδωρ, ποτε δε γνοφος.
Και θηρσιν αυτος γινεται παρεμφερης,
Ανεμῳ, νεφει τε, κᾳστραπῃ, βροντῃ, βροχῃ.
Ὑπηρετει δ' αυτῳ θαλασσα, και πετραι,
Και πασα πηγη, χ' ὑδατος συστηματα·
Τρεμει δ' ορη και γαια και πελωριος
Βυθος θαλασσης, κωρεων ὑψος μεγα,
Οταν επιβλεψῃ γοργον ομμα δεσποτου.

ÆSCHYLI *Fragm.*

Confound not God with man; nor madly deem
His form is mortal, and of flesh like thine.
Thou know'st him not. Sometimes like *fire* he glows
In wrath severe; sometimes as *water* flows;
In brooding *darkness* now his power conceals
And then in *brutes* that mighty power reveals.
In *clouds* tempestuous we the Godhead find;
He mounts the *storm*, and rides the winged *wind;*
In vivid *lightnings* flashes from on high;
In rattling *thunders* rends the lowering sky;
Fountains and *rivers, seas* and *floods* obey,
And *ocean's* deep abyss yields to his sway;
The *mountains* tremble, and the *hills* sink down,
Crumbled to dust by the Almighty's frown.
When God unfolds the terrors of his eye,
All things with horror quake, and in confusion lie.

J. B. B. CLARKE.

Verse 7. *I saw the tents of Cushan in affliction*] *Cush* is Arabia. The Arabians dwelt in *tents*, hence they were called *Scenitæ*. When the Lord appeared on *Mount Sinai*, the *Arabs* of the Red Sea abandoned their tents, being terror-struck; and the *Midianites* also were seized with fear. See the desolation wrought among this people by Phinehas, Num. xxxi. 1, &c., on account of their having enticed the Israelites to idolatry, Num. xxv. 1, &c. Either *Cush* and *Midian* lay contiguous to each other; or, these names are poetically used to express the *same place*.

Verse 8. *Was the Lord displeased against the rivers?*] *Floods;* here is a reference to the passage of the Red Sea. The Lord is represented as heading his troops, riding in his chariot, and commanding the sea to divide, that a free passage might be left for his army to pass over.

Verse 9. *Thy bow was made quite naked*] That is, it was *drawn out of its case;* as the *arrows* had their *quiver*, so the *bows* had their *cases*. A fine *oriental bow* and *bow-case*, with *quiver* and *arrows*, are now before me; they show with what propriety Jehovah is represented as taking his bow out of its case, in

A. M. cir. 3404
B. C. cir. 600
Ol. cir. XLV. 1
Tarquinii Prisci,
R. Roman.,
cir. annum 17

10 [v]The mountains saw thee,
and they trembled: the overflowing of the water passed
by: the deep uttered his voice,
and [w]lifted up his hands on high.
11 [x]The sun *and* moon stood still in their
habitations; [y]at the light of thine [z]arrows they
went, *and* at the shining of thy glittering spear.
12 Thou didst march through the land in
indignation, [a]thou didst thresh
the heathen in anger.
13 Thou wentest forth for the
salvation of thy people, *even* for
salvation with thine anointed; [b]thou woundedst the head out of the house of the wicked,
[c]by discovering the foundation unto the neck.
Selah.
14 Thou didst strike through with his staves

[v]Exod. xix. 16, 18; Judg. v. 4, 5; Psa. lxviii. 8; lxxvii. 18; cxiv. 4——[w]Exod. xiv. 22; Josh. iii. 16——[x]Josh. x. 12, 13——[y]Or, *thine arrows walked in the light,* &c.

[z]Josh. x. 11; Psa. xviii. 14; lxxvii. 17, 18——[a]Jer. li. 33; Amos i. 3; Mic. iv. 13——[b]Josh. x. 24; xi. 8, 12; Psa. lxviii. 21——[c]Heb *making naked*

order to set his arrow upon the cord, to shoot at his enemies. It is not the *drawing out*, or *making bare* the *arrow*, that is mentioned here; but the taking the *bow out of its case* to prepare to shoot.

This verse appears to be an answer to the questions in the preceding: "Was the Lord displeased," &c. The answer is, All this was done "according to the oaths of the tribes;" the covenant of God, frequently repeated and renewed, which he made with the tribes, to give them the land of the Canaanites for their inheritance.

Thou didst cleave the earth with rivers.] Or, "Thou didst cleave the streams of the land." Or, "Thou cleavedst the dry land into rivers." This may be a reference to the passage of Jordan, and transactions at *Arnon* and the brook *Jabbok*. See Num. xxi. 13-15.

In this verse we have *Selah* again, which, as before, may signify a *pause*, or some alteration in the *music*.

Verse 10. *The mountains saw thee*] This is the continued answer to the questions in ver. 8. These are figures highly poetic, to show with what ease God accomplished the most arduous tasks in behalf of his people. As soon as the *mountains* saw him, they trembled, they were in *pangs*. When he appeared, the *sea* fled to right and left, to give him a passage. "It uttered its voice." The separation of the waters occasioned a terrible noise. "And it lifted up its hands on high." Its waters, being separated, stood in *heaps* on the right hand and left. These heaps or waves are poetically represented here as the *hands* of the *sea*.

Verse 11. *The sun* and *moon stood still*] This was at the prayer of Joshua, when he fought against the Amorites. See Josh. x. 11, 12, and the notes there.

At the light of thine arrows they went] I think we should translate,—

By *their* light, thine arrows went abroad;
By *their* brightness, the lightning of thy spear.

Calvin very justly remarks that the *arrows* and *spears* of the Israelites are called those *of God*, under whose auspices the people fought: the meaning is, that by the *continuation* of the *light of the sun and moon*, then stayed in their course, the Israelites *saw* how to continue the battle, till their enemies were all defeated.

Verse 12. *Thou didst march through the land*] This refers to the conquest of Canaan. God is represented as going at the head of his people as general-in-chief; and leading them on from conquest to conquest—which was the fact.

Thou didst thresh the heathen in anger.] Thou didst *tread them down*, as the oxen do the sheaves on the threshing-floor.

Verse 13. *Thou wentest forth for the salvation of thy people*] Their deliverance would not have been effected but through thy interference.

For salvation with thine anointed] That is, with *Joshua*, whom God had *anointed*, or solemnly *appointed* to fill the place of Moses, and lead the people into the promised land. If we read, with the common text, משיחך *meshichecha*, "thy anointed," the singular number, Joshua is undoubtedly meant, who was God's instrument to put the people in possession of Canaan: but if, with several MSS. and some copies of the *Septuagint*, we read משיחיך *meshicheycha*, "thy anointed ones," the *Israelites* must be intended. They are frequently called *God's anointed*, or *God's saints*. The sense is very far-fetched when applied to *Jesus Christ*.

Thou woundedst the head out of the house of the wicked] This alludes to the slaying of the *first-born* through all the land of Egypt. These were the *heads* of the *houses* or *families*.

By discovering the foundation unto the neck.] The general meaning of this clause is sufficiently plain: the government of these lands should be utterly subverted; the very foundations of it should be *razed*. But what means *unto the neck*, עד צואר *ad tsavvar?* Several critics read עד צור *ad tsur*, "Unto the ROCK," that on which the house is founded: and this very intelligible reading is obtained by the *omission* of a *single letter*, א *aleph*, from the word צוער. This conjecture has been adopted by *Newcome*, though unsupported either by *MS.* or *version*. But is the conjecture necessary? I think not: read the verse as it ought to be read, and all will be plain. "Thou hast wounded the head even unto the neck, in the house of the wicked, by laying bare the foundation." The whole head, neck, and all are cut off. There was no hope left to the Egyptians, because the *first-born* of every family was *cut off*, so that the very *foundation* was *laid bare*, no first-born being left to continue the *heirship* of families.

Verse 14. *Thou didst strike through*] The Hebrew will bear this sense: "Thou hast pierced amidst their tribes the head of their troops," referring to Pharaoh and his generals, who came like a *whirlwind* to fall upon the poor Israelites, when they appeared to be hemmed in by sea, and no place for their escape. If we follow the common reading, it seems to intimate that the troops of Pharaoh, in their confusion (for God shone out upon them from the cloud) fell foul of each other; and with

A. M. cir. 3404 B. C. cir. 600 Ol. cir. XLV. 1 Tarquinii Prisci, R. Roman., cir. annum 17

the head of his villages: they [d]came out as a whirlwind to scatter me: their rejoicing *was* as to devour the poor secretly.

15 [e]Thou didst walk through the sea with thine horses, *through* the [f]heap of great waters.

16 When I heard, [g]my belly trembled; my lips quivered at the voice; rottenness entered into my bones, and I trembled in myself, that I might rest in the day of trouble: when he cometh up unto the people, he will [h]invade them with his troops.

17 Although the fig tree shall not blossom, neither *shall* fruit *be* in the vines; the labour of the olive shall [i]fail, and the fields shall yield no meat; the flock shall be cut off from the fold, and *there shall be* no herd in the stalls:

18 [k]Yet I will [l]rejoice in the LORD, I will joy in the God of my salvation.

19 The Lord GOD *is* [m]my strength, and he will make my feet [n]like hinds' *feet,* and he will make me to [o]walk upon mine high places. To the chief singer on my [p]stringed instruments.

[d]Heb. *were tempestuous*——[e]Ver. 8; Psa. lxxvii. 19——[f]Or, *mud*——[g]Psa. cxix. 120; Jer. xxiii. 9——[h]Or, *cut them in pieces*——[i]Heb. *lie*——[k]Job xiii. 15

[l]Isa. xli. 16; lxi. 10——[m]Psa. xxvii. 1——[n]2 Sam. xxii. 34; Psa. xviii. 33——[o]Deut. xxxii. 13; xxxiii. 29——[p]Heb. *neginoth;* Psa. iv. title

their staves, or weapons, slew one another: but the *head of the villages* or *towns*, i. e., *Pharaoh*, was drowned with his army in the Red Sea.

Verse 15. *Thou didst walk through the sea*] There was no occasion to *hurry* across; all was safe, for God had divided the waters: and his *terrible cloud* had removed from *before*, and stood *behind* them, so that it was between them and the Egyptians. See Exod. xiv. 19, 20.

Verse 16. *When I heard, my belly trembled*] The prophet, having finished his account of the wonders done by Jehovah, in bringing their fathers from Egypt into the promised land, now returns to the desolate state of his countrymen, who are shortly to be led into captivity, and suffer the most grievous afflictions; and although he had a *sure word of prophecy* that they should be ultimately *delivered*, yet the thoughts of the evils they must previously endure filled his soul with terror and dismay; so that he wishes to be removed from earth before this tribulation should come, that his eyes might not behold the desolations of his country. *When he* (Nebuchadnezzar) *cometh up unto the people,* (the Jews,) *he will invade them* (overpower and carry them away captive) *with his troops.*

Verse 17. *Although the fig tree shall not blossom*] תפרח *tiphrach*, "shall not flourish," shall *not put forth its young figs*, for the fig tree does *not blossom.* The *young figs appear* as soon as the *old ones* are *ripe*, as I have often had occasion to observe.

This verse most nervously paints the desolate state of the land of Judea during the captivity. In its hemistich form, it may be translated thus:—

For the fig tree shall not flourish,
And there shall be no fruit on the vines;
The fruit of the olive shall fail,
And the fields shall supply no food:
The flocks shall be cut off from the fold,
And no herds shall be found in the stalls:
Yet in Jehovah will I exult;
I will joy in the God of my salvation.

The *Vulgate* has:—

Yet I in the Lord will rejoice,
And will exult in Jesus my God.

The *Targum* countenances this version:— ואנא במימרא דיי אבוע *veana bemeimra dayai abua*, "But in the WORD of the Lord will I rejoice," i. e., the *personal, substantial* Word of Jehovah.

These two verses give the finest display of *resignation* and *confidence* that I have ever met with. He saw that evil was at hand, and *unavoidable;* he *submitted* to the dispensation of God, whose Spirit enabled him to paint it in all its calamitous circumstances. He knew that God was merciful and gracious. He trusted to his promise, though all appearances were against its fulfilment; for he knew that the word of Jehovah could not fail, and therefore his confidence is unshaken.

No paraphrase can add any thing to this hymn, which is full of inexpressible *dignity* and *elegance*, leaving even its unparalleled *piety* out of the question.

Verse 19. *The Lord God* is *my strength*] This is an imitation, if not a quotation, from Psa. xviii. 32, 33, where see the notes.

Will make me to walk upon mine high places] This last verse is spoken in the person of the people, who seem to anticipate their restoration; and that they shall once more rejoice in the hills and mountains of Judea.

To the chief singer on my stringed instruments.] This line, which is evidently a *superscription*, leads me to suppose that when the prophet had completed his short ode, he folded it up, with the *above direction* to the master singer, or leader of the choir, to be sung in the temple service. Many of the *Psalms* are directed in the same way. "To the master singer;" or, "chief musician;" to be sung, according to their nature, on *different kinds* of instruments, or with particular *airs* or *tunes.*

Neginoth, נגינות which we translate *stringed instruments*, means such as were struck with a *plectrum*, or *excited* by some kind of *friction* or *pulsation;* as *violins* and *cymbals*, or *tambarines* are. I do not think that the line makes any part of the prophecy, but merely the *superscription* or *direction* of the work when it was finished. The ending will appear much more dignified, this line being separated from it.

THE BOOK

OF THE

PROPHET ZEPHANIAH

Chronological Notes relative to this Book, upon the supposition that it was written in the twelfth year of the reign of Josiah, king of Judah

Year from the Creation, according to Archbishop Usher, 3374.—Year of the Julian Period, 4084.—Year since the Flood, 1718.—Year from the vocation of Abram, 1291.—Year from the foundation of Solomon's temple, 382.—Year since the division of Solomon's monarchy into the kingdoms of Israel and Judah, 346.—Year since the conquest of Corœbus at Olympia, usually called the first Olympiad, 147.—Third year of the *thirty-seventh* Olympiad.—Year from the building of Rome, according to the Varronian computation, 124.—Year of the era of Nabonassar, 118.—Year since the destruction of the kingdom of Israel by Shalmaneser, king of Assyria, 92.—Year before the birth of Christ, 626.—Year before the vulgar era of Christ's nativity, 630.—Cycle of the Sun, 24.—Cycle of the Moon, 18.—Eighteenth year of Phraortes, king of Media. This monarch is supposed by some to have been the same with the Arphaxad of the Apocrypha.—Eleventh year of Philip I., king of Macedon.—Twenty-second year of Archidamus, king of Lacedæmon, of the family of the Proclidæ.—Fifteenth year of Eurycrates II., king of Lacedæmon, of the family of the Eurysthenidæ.—Twenty-ninth year of Cypselus, who had seized upon the government of Corinth.—Forty-second year of Psammitichus, king of Egypt, according to Helvicus.—Tenth year of Kiniladachus, king of Babylon, according to the same chronologer. This monarch was the immediate predecessor of Nabopolassar, the father of Nebuchadnezzar.—Second year of Sadyattes, king of Lydia.—Eleventh year of Ancus Martius, the fifth king of the Romans.—Twelfth year of Josiah, king of Judah.

CHAPTER I

This chapter begins with denouncing God's judgments against Judah and Jerusalem, 1–3. Idolaters, and sinners of several other denominations, are then particularly threatened; and their approaching visitation enlarged on, by the enumeration of several circumstances which tend greatly to heighten its terrors, 4–18.

A. M. cir. 3374
B. C. cir. 630
Olymp.
cir. XXXVII. 3
A. U. C. cir.
124

THE word of the LORD
which came unto Zephaniah the son of Cushi, the
son of Gedaliah, the son of
Amariah, the son of Hizkiah,
in the days of Josiah the son
of Amon, king of Judah.
2 [a]I will utterly consume all

[a]Heb. *By taking away I will make an end*

NOTES ON CHAP. I

Verse 1. *The word of the Lord which came unto Zephaniah*] Though this prophet has given us so large a list of his ancestors, yet little concerning him is known, because we know nothing certain relative to the persons of the family whose names are here introduced. We have one *chronological note* which is of more value for the correct understanding of his prophecy than the other could have been, how circumstantially soever it had been delivered; viz., that he prophesied *in the days of Josiah, son of Amon, king of Judah;* and from the description which he gives of the *disorders* which prevailed in Judea in his time, it is evident that he must have prophesied *before* the reformation made by Josiah, which was in the *eighteenth* year of his reign. And as he predicts the *destruction of Nineveh*, chap. ii. 13, which, as *Calmet* remarks, could not have taken place before the *sixteenth* of Josiah, allowing with *Berosus twenty-one* years for the reign of Nabopolassar over the Chaldeans; we must, therefore, place this prophecy about the beginning of the reign of Josiah, or from B. C. 640 to B. C. 609. But see the chronological notes.

Verse 2. *I will utterly consume all things*]

A. M. cir. 3374
B. C. cir. 630
Olymp.
cir. XXXVII. 3
A. U. C. cir.
124

things from off [b]the land, saith
the LORD.
3 [c]I will consume man and
beast, I will consume the fowls
of the heaven, and the fishes of the sea, and
[d]the [e]Stumbling-blocks with the wicked; and
I will cut off man from off the land, saith the
LORD.
4 I will also stretch out mine hand upon
Judah, and upon all the inhabitants of Jerusalem; and [f]I will cut off the remnant of Baal
from this place, *and* the name of [g]the Chemarims with the priests;
5 And them [h]that worship the host of heaven upon the housetops: [i]and them that worship *and* [k]that swear [l]by the LORD, and that
swear [m]by Malcham:
6 And [n]them that are turned
back from the LORD; and *those*
that [o]have not sought the
LORD, nor inquired for him.
7 [p]Hold thy peace at the presence of the
Lord GOD: [q]for the day of the LORD *is* at
hand: for [r]the LORD hath prepared a sacrifice, he hath [s]bid his guests.
8 And it shall come to pass in the day of
the LORD's sacrifice, that I will [t]punish [u]the
princes, and the king's children, and all such
as are clothed with strange apparel.
9 In the same day also will I punish all
those that leap on the threshold, which fill
their masters' houses with violence and deceit.
10 And it shall come to pass in that day,
saith the LORD, *that there shall be* the noise

A. M. cir. 3374
B. C. cir. 630
Olymp.
cir. XXXVII. 3
A. U. C. cir.
124

---

[b]Heb. *the face of the land*——[c]Hos. iv. 3——[d]Ezek. vii. 19; xiv. 3, 4, 7; Matt. xiii. 41——[e]Or, *idols*——[f]Fulfilled, cir. 624; 2 Kings xxiii. 4, 5——[g]Hos. x. 5——[h]2 Kings xxiii. 12; Jer. xix. 13——[i]1 Kings xviii. 21; 2 Kings xvii. 33, 41——[k]Isa. xlviii. 1; Hos. iv. 15

[l]Or, *to the LORD*——[m]Josh. xxiii. 7; 1 Kings xi. 33——[n]Isa. i. 4; Jer. ii. 13, 17; xv. 6——[o]Hos. vii. 7——[p]Hab. ii. 20; Zech. ii. 13——[q]Isa. xiii. 6——[r]Isa. xxxiv. 6; Jer. lvi. 10; Ezek. xxxix. 17; Rev. xix. 17——[s]Heb. *sanctified*, or *prepared*——[t]Heb. *visit upon*——[u]Jer. xxxix. 6

All being now ripe for destruction, I will shortly bring a universal scourge upon the land. He speaks particularly of the idolaters.

Verse 3. *I will consume man and beast*] By *war*, and by *pestilence*. Even the *waters* shall be infected, and the *fish* destroyed; the *air* become contaminated, and the *fowls* die.

Verse 4. *I will cut off the remnant of Baal*] I think he refers here, partly at least, to the reformation which Josiah was to bring about. See the account, 2 Kings xxiii. 5.

The Chemarims] The *black-robed* priests of different idols. See the note on 2 Kings xxiii. 5. These were put down by Josiah.

Verse 5. *The host of heaven*] Sun, moon, planets, and stars. This worship was one of the most ancient and the most common of all species of idolatry; and it had a greater semblance of reason to recommend it. See 2 Kings xxiii. 5, 12; Jer. xix. 13, xxxii. 29.

That swear by the Lord, and that swear by Malcham] Associating the name of an *idol* with that of the Most High. For *Malcham*, see on Hos. iv. 15, and Amos v. 26.

Verse 6. *Them that are turned back*] Who have forsaken the true God, and become idolaters.

Nor inquired for him] Have not desired to know his will.

Verse 7. *Hold thy peace at the presence of the Lord God*] הס *has*, the same as *hush, hist*, among us. Remonstrances are *now* useless. You had time to acquaint yourselves with God; you would not: you cry now in vain; destruction is at the door.

The Lord hath prepared a sacrifice] A slaughter of the people.

He hath bid his guests] The Babylonians, to whom he has given a commission to destroy you. In all festivals sacrifices, 1. The victims were offered to God, and their blood poured out before the altar. 2. The people who were invited feasted upon the sacrifice. See on Isa. xxxiv. 6.

Verse 8. *I will punish the princes, and the king's children*] After the death of Josiah the kingdom of Judah saw no prosperity, and every reign terminated miserably; until at last King Zedekiah and the *king's children* were cruelly massacred at Riblah, when Nebuchadnezzar had taken Jerusalem.

Strange apparel] I really think this refers more to their embracing idolatrous customs and heathen usages, than to their *changing their dress*. They acquired *new habits*, as we would say; *customs*, that they used as they did their *clothing*—at all times, and in every thing.

Verse 9. *That leap on the threshold*] Or, *that leap over the threshold*. It is most probable that the *Philistines* are here meant. After the time that Dagon fell before the ark, and his hands were broken off on the threshold of his temple, his worshippers would no more set a foot upon the threshold, but stepped or leaped over it, when they entered into his temple. The *Chaldee* understands this of the Philistines, without giving this reason for it. Some understand it of haughtiness and pride: others think that *leaping on the threshold* refers to the customs of the Arabs, who used to ride into people's houses, and take away whatever they could carry; and that this is the reason why, in several parts of the East, they have their doors made very low, to prevent those depredators from entering. In this manner, we learn the *Persians* have frequently oppressed the poor *Armenians*, going on horseback into their houses, and taking whatever they thought proper. Mr. *Harmer* understands it in this way.

Verse 10. *A cry from the fish-gate*] This gate, which is mentioned Neh. iii. 3, was opposite to Joppa; and perhaps the way in which the news came of the irruption of the Chaldean army, the *great crashing from the hills*.

The second] Or *second* city, may here mean a part of Jerusalem, mentioned 2 Kings xxii. 14, 2 Chron. xxxiv. 22.

A. M. cir. 3374 B. C. cir. 630 Olymp. cir. XXXVII. 3 A. U. C. cir. 124

of a cry from [v]the fish-gate, and a howling from the second, and a great crashing from the hills.

11 [w]Howl, ye inhabitants of Maktesh, for all the merchant people are cut down; all they that bear silver are cut off.

12 And it shall come to pass at that time, *that* I will search Jerusalem with candles, and punish the men that are [x]settled [y]on their lees: [z]that say in their heart, The LORD will not do good, neither will he do evil.

13 Therefore their goods shall become a booty, and their houses a desolation: they shall also build houses, but [a]not inhabit *them*; and they shall plant vineyards, but [b]not drink the wine thereof.

14 [c]The great day of the LORD *is* near, *it is* near, and hasteth greatly, *even* the voice of the day of the LORD: the mighty man shall cry there bitterly.

A. M. cir. 3374 B. C. cir. 630 Olymp. cir. XXXVII. 3 A. U. C. cir. 124

15 [d]That day *is* a day of wrath, a day of trouble and distress, a day of wasteness and desolation, a day of darkness and gloominess, a day of clouds and thick darkness.

16 A day of [e]the trumpet and alarm against the fenced cities, and against the high towers.

17 And I will bring distress upon men, that they shall [f]walk like blind men, because they have sinned against the LORD: and [g]their blood shall be poured out as dust, and their flesh [h]as the dung.

18 [i]Neither their silver nor their gold shall be able to deliver them in the day of the LORD's wrath; but the whole land shall be [k]devoured by the fire of his jealousy: for [l]he shall make even a speedy riddance of all them that dwell in the land.

---

[v]2 Chron. xxxiii. 14——[w]James v. 1——[x]Heb. *curded*, or *thickened*——[y]Jer. xlviii. 11; Amos vi. 1 [z]Psa. xciv. 7——[a]Deut. xxviii. 30, 39; Amos v. 11 [b]Mic. vi. 15——[c]Joel ii. 1, 11

[d]Isa. xxii. 5; Jer. xxx. 7; Joel ii. 2, 11; Amos v. 18; ver. 18——[e]Jer. iv. 19——[f]Deut. xxviii. 29; Isa. lix. 10 [g]Psa. lxxix. 3——[h]Psa. lxxxiii. 10; Jer. ix. 22; xvi. 4 [i]Prov. xi. 4; Ezek. vii. 19——[k]Ch. iii. 8——[l]Ver. 2, 3

Verse 11. *Maktesh*] *Calmet* says this signifies a *mortar*, or a *rock in form of a mortar*, and was the name of a quarter of Jerusalem where they hulled rice, corn, &c., according to St. Jerome. Some think the city of Jerusalem is meant, where the inhabitants should be beat and pounded to death as grain is pounded in a mortar.

Newcome translates it, the *lower* city, and considers it the *valley* in Jerusalem, which divided the *upper* from the *lower* city.

They that bear silver] The merchants, money-changers, usurers, rich men.

Verse 12. *I will search Jerusalem with candles*] I will make a universal and thorough search.

That are settled on their lees] Those who are *careless*, satisfied with the goods of this life; who trust in their riches, and are completely irreligious; who, while they acknowledge that there is a God, think, like the *Aristotelians*, that he is so supremely happy in the contemplation of his own excellences, that he feels it beneath his dignity to concern himself with the affairs of mortals.

Verse 13. *Their goods* (in which they trust) *shall become a booty*] To the Chaldeans. They shall have no profit of all their labours. *The houses they have built they shall not inhabit;* of the wine of the *vineyards they have planted,* they shall not drink. See Amos v. 11, where we find the same evils threatened.

Verse 14. *The great day of the Lord* is *near*] It commenced with the death of the good king Josiah, who was slain by Pharaoh-necho at Megiddo, and continued to the destruction of Jerusalem by Nebuchadnezzar.

Verse 15. *That day* is *a day of wrath*] See the parallel passages in the *margin*, and the notes there. From the *fourteenth* to the *sixteenth* verse inclusive there is a most beautiful amplification of the disasters that were coming on Jerusalem; the *invasion*, *incursion*, *attack*, *carnage*, *confusion*, *horrible din* occasioned by the *sound* of the *trumpet*, the *cries* of the *people*, and the *shrieks* and *groans* of the *dying*, are pointed out with great force and mighty effect.

Verse 17. *They shall walk like blind men*] Be in the most perplexing *doubt* and *uncertainty;* and while in this state, have their blood poured out by the sword of their enemies, and their flesh trodden under foot.

Verse 18. *Their silver nor their gold*] In which they trusted, and from which they expected happiness; these shall not profit them in this awful day. And God will bring this about speedily; and a *speedy riddance*—a universal desolation, shall in a short time take place in every part of the land.

CHAPTER II

The prophet, having declared the judgments which were ready to fall on his people, earnestly exhorts them to repentance, that these judgments may be averted, 1–3. He then foretells the fate of other neighbouring and hostile nations: the Philistines, 4–7; Moabites and Ammonites, 8–11; Ethiopians, 12; and Assyrians, 13. In the close of the chapter we have a prophecy against Nineveh. These predictions were accomplished chiefly by the conquests of Nebuchadnezzar.

A. M. cir. 3374
B. C. cir. 630
Olymp. cir. XXXVII. 3
A. U. C. cir. 124

GATHER [a]yourselves to-
gether, yea, gather to-
gether, O nation [b]not desired;
2 Before the decree bring
forth, *before* the day pass [c]as the chaff, before
[d]the fierce anger of the LORD come upon you,
before the day of the LORD's anger come upon
you.
3 [e]Seek ye the LORD, [f]all ye meek of the
earth, which have wrought his judgment, seek
righteousness, seek meekness: [g]it may be ye
shall be hid in the day of the LORD's anger.
4 For [h]Gaza shall be forsaken, and Ashkelon a desolation: they shall drive out Ashdod
[i]at the noonday, and Ekron shall be rooted up.
5 Wo unto the inhabitants of [k]the sea-
coasts, the nation of the Cherethites; the
word of the LORD *is* against you; O [l]Canaan,
the land of the Philistines, I will even destroy
thee, that there shall be no inhabitant.
6 And the sea-coasts shall be
dwellings *and* cottages for
shepherds, [m]and folds for flocks.
7 And the coast shall be for [n]the remnant of
the house of Judah; they shall feed thereupon:
in the houses of Ashkelon shall they lie down
in the evening: [o]for the LORD their God shall
[p]visit them, and [q]turn away their captivity.
8 [r]I have heard the reproach of Moab, and
[s]the revilings of the children of Ammon,
whereby they have reproached my people, and
[t]magnified *themselves* against their border.
9 Therefore *as* I live, saith the LORD of
hosts, the God of Israel, Surely [u]Moab shall
be as Sodom, and [v]the children of Ammon as
Gomorrah, [w]*even* the breeding of nettles, and
salt-pits, and a perpetual desolation: [x]the

A. M. cir. 3374
B. C. cir. 630
Olymp. cir. XXXVII. 3
A. U. C. cir. 124

[a]Joel ii. 16——[b]Or, *not desirous*——[c]Job xxi. 18; Psa. i. 4; Isa. xvii. 13; Hos. xiii. 3——[d]2 Kings xxiii. 26——[e]Psa. cv. 4; Amos v. 6——[f]Psa. lxxvi. 9——[g]Joel ii. 14; Amos v. 15; Jonah iii. 9——[h]Jer. xlvii. 4, 5; Ezek. xxv. 15; Amos i. 6, 7, 8; Zech. ix. 5, 6——[i]Jer. vi. 4; xv. 8——[k]Ezek. xxv. 16——[l]Josh. xiii. 3——[m]See Isa. xvii. 2 ver. 14

[n]Isa. xi. 11; Mic. iv. 7; v. 7, 8; Hag. i. 12; ii. 2; verse 9——[o]Or, *when*, &c.——[p]Exod. iv. 31; Luke i. 68——[q]Psa. cxxvi. 1; Jer. xxix. 14; chap. iii. 20——[r]Jer. xlviii. 27; Ezek. xxv. 8——[s]Ezek. xxv. 3, 6——[t]Jer. xlix. 1——[u]Isa. xv.; Jer. xlviii.; Ezek. xxv. 9; Amos ii. 1——[v]Amos i. 13——[w]Gen. xix. 25; Deut. xxix. 23; Isa. xiii. 19; xxxiv. 13; Jer. xlix. 18; l. 40——[x]Ver. 7

NOTES ON CHAP. II

Verse 1. *Gather yourselves*] Others, *sift yourselves. Separate* the *chaff* from the wheat, before the judgments of God fall upon you. *O nation not desired—unlovely*, not delighted in; hated because of your sin. The Israelites are addressed.

Verse 3. *Ye meek of the earth*] ענוי *anavey*, ye *oppressed* and *humbled* of the land.

It may be ye shall be hid] The sword has not a commission against you. Ask God, and he will be a refuge to you from the storm and from the tempest.

Verse 4. *Gaza shall be forsaken*] This prophecy is against the *Philistines*. They had been greatly harassed by the kings of Egypt; but were completely ruined by Nebuchadnezzar, who took all Phœnicia from the Egyptians; and about the time of his taking Tyre, devastated all the seignories of the Philistines. This ruin we have seen foretold by the other prophets, and have already remarked its exact fulfilment.

Verse 5. *The sea-coasts, the nation of the Cherethites*] The *sea-coasts* mean all the country lying on the Mediterranean coast from Egypt to Joppa and Gaza. The *Cherethites*—the *Cretans*, who were probably a colony of the Phœnicians. See on 1 Sam. xxx. 14, and Amos ix. 7.

Verse 6. *And the sea-coasts shall be dwellings*] *Newcome* considers רת *keroth* as a proper name, not *cottages* or *folds*. The *Septuagint* have Κρητη, *Crete*, and so has the *Syriac*. Abp. *Secker* notes, *Alibi non extat* כרת, *et forte notat patriam* των כרתים. "The word כרת is not found elsewhere, and probably it is the name of the country of the Cherethim."

Verse 7. *The coast shall be for the remnant*] Several devastations fell on the Philistines. Gaza was ruined by the army of Alexander the Great, and the *Maccabees* finally accomplished all that was predicted by the prophets against this invariably wicked people. They lost their polity, and were at last obliged to receive circumcision.

Verse 8. *I have heard the reproach of Moab*] God punished them for the cruel part they had taken in the persecutions of the Jews; for when they lay under the displeasure of God, these nations insulted them in the most provoking manner. See on Amos i. 13, and the parallel texts in the *margin*.

Verse 9. *The breeding of nettles*] That is, their land shall become desolate, and be a place for nettles, thorns, &c., to flourish in, for want of cultivation.

A. M. cir. 3374
B. C. cir. 630
Olymp.
cir. XXXVII. 3
A. U. C. cir.
124

residue of my people shall
spoil them, and the remnant of
my people shall possess them.
10 This shall they have [y]for
their pride, because they have reproached and
magnified *themselves* against the people of the
LORD of hosts.
11 The LORD *will be* terrible unto them: for
he will [z]famish all the gods of the earth;
[a]and *men* shall worship him, every one from
his place, *even* all [b]the isles of the heathen.
12 [c]Ye Ethiopians also, ye *shall be* slain by
[d]my sword.
13 And he will stretch out his hand against
the north, and [e]destroy Assyria; and will make
Nineveh a desolation, *and* dry
like a wilderness.
14 And [f]flocks shall lie down
in the midst of her, all [g]the
beasts of the nations: both the [h]cormorant
[i]and the bittern shall lodge in the [k]upper
lintels of it; *their* voice shall sing in the
windows; desolation *shall be* in the thresholds: [l]for he shall uncover the [m]cedar work.
15 This *is* the rejoicing city [n]that dwelt
carelessly, [o]that said in her heart, I *am,* and
there is none beside me: how is she become
a desolation, a place for beasts to lie down in!
every one that passeth by her [p]shall hiss *and*
[q]wag his hand.

A. M. cir. 3374
B. C. cir. 630
Olymp.
cir. XXXVII. 3
A. U. C. cir.
124

---

[y]Isa. xvi. 6; Jer. xlviii. 29——[z]Heb. *make lean*——[a]Mal. i. 11; John iv. 21——[b]Gen. x. 5——[c]Isa. xviii. 1. xx. 4; Jer. xlvi. 9; Ezek. xxx. 9——[d]Psa. xvii. 13——[e]Isa. x. 12; Ezek. xxxi. 3; Nah. i. 2; ii. 10; iii. 15, 18——[f]Ver. 6

[g]Isa. xiii. 21, 22——[h]Or, *pelican*——[i]Isa. xxxiv. 11, 14——[k]Or, *knops,* or *chapiters*——[l]Or, *when he hath uncovered*——[m]Jer. xxii. 14——[n]Isa. xlvii. 8——[o]Rev. xviii. 7——[p]Job xxvii. 23; Lam. ii. 15; Ezek. xxvii. 36——[q]Nah. iii. 19

Verse 10. *Because they have reproached*] See on ver. 8.

Verse 11. *He will famish all the gods of the earth*] They shall have no more *sacrifices;* their worship shall be entirely destroyed. Idolaters supposed that their gods actually *fed* on the *fumes* and *spirituous* exhalations that arose from the burnt-offerings which they made unto their idols. It is in reference to this opinion that the Lord says, "He will famish all the gods of the land."

Verse 12. *Ye Ethiopians also*] Nebuchadnezzar subdued these. See Jer. xlvi. 2, 9; Ezek. xxx. 4, 10. See also on Amos ix. 17.

Verse 13. *He will—destroy Assyria*] He will overthrow the empire, and *Nineveh,* their metropolitan city. See on Jonah and Nahum.

Verse 14. *And flocks shall lie down in the midst of her*] Nineveh was so completely destroyed, that its situation is not at present even known. The present city of *Mossoul* is supposed to be in the *vicinity* of the place where this ancient city stood.

The cormorant קאת *kaath; and the bittern,* קפד *kippod.* These *Newcome* translates, "The pelican and the porcupine."

Their voice shall sing in the windows] The windows shall be all demolished; wild fowl shall build their nests in them, and shall be seen coming from their sills; and the fine *cedar* ceilings shall be exposed to the weather, and by and by crumble to dust. See the note on Isa. xxxiv. 11, 14, where nearly the same terms are used.

I have in another place introduced a remarkable couplet quoted by Sir *W. Jones* from a Persian poet, which speaks of desolation in nearly the same terms.

پرده داري ميكند در قصر قيصر عنكبوت
بومي نوبت ميزند بر كنبد افراسياب

"The spider holds the veil in the palace of Cæsar:
The owl stands sentinel in the watchtower of Afrasiab."

Verse 15. *This is the rejoicing city*] The city in which mirth, jocularity, and pleasure, reigned without interruption.

And *wag his hand*] Will point her out as a mark and monument of Divine displeasure.

CHAPTER III

The prophet reproves Jerusalem, and all her guides and rulers, for their obstinate perseverance in impiety, notwithstanding all the warnings and corrections which they had received from God, 1–7. They are encouraged, however, after they shall have been chastised for their idolatry, and cured of it, to look for mercy and restoration, 8–13; and excited to hymns of joy at the glorious prospect, 14–17. After which the prophet concludes with large promises of favour and prosperity in the days of the Messiah, 18–20. We take this extensive view of the concluding verses of this chapter, because an apostle has expressly assured us that in EVERY *prophetical book of the Old Testament Scriptures are contained predictions relative to the Gospel dispensation.* See Acts iii. 24.

A. M. cir. 3374
B. C. cir. 630
Olymp.
cir. XXXVII. 3
A. U. C. cir.
124

WO to [a]her [b]that is filthy and
polluted, to the oppressing
city!
2 She [c]obeyed not the voice;
she [d]received not [e]correction; she trusted not
in the LORD; she drew not near to her God.
3 [f]Her princes within her *are* roaring lions;
her judges *are* [g]evening wolves; they gnaw
not the bones till the morrow.
4 Her [h]prophets *are* light *and* treacherous persons: her priests have polluted the
sanctuary, they have done [i]violence to the
law.
5 [k]The just LORD [l]*is* in the midst thereof;
he will not do iniquity: [m]every morning doth
he bring his judgment to light, he faileth not:
but [n]the unjust knoweth no shame.
6 I have cut off the nations: their [o]towers
are desolate; I made their streets
waste, that none passeth by:
their cities are destroyed, so that
there is no man, that there is
none inhabitant.
7 [p]I said, Surely thou wilt fear me, thou
wilt receive instruction; so their dwelling
should not be cut off, howsoever I punished
them; but they rose early, *and* [q]corrupted all
their doings.
8 Therefore [r]wait ye upon me, saith the
LORD, until the day that I rise up to the prey:
for my determination *is* to [s]gather the nations,
that I may assemble the kingdoms, to pour
upon them mine indignation, *even* all my
fierce anger: for all the earth [t]shall be devoured with the fire of my jealousy.
9 For then will I turn to the people [u]a pure

A. M. cir. 3374
B. C. cir. 630
Olymp.
cir. XXXVII. 3
A. U. C. cir.
124

[a]Or, *gluttonous*——[b]Heb. *craw*——[c]Jer. xxii. 21——[d]Jer. v. 3——[e]Or, *instruction*——[f]Ezek. xxii. 27; Mic. iii. 9, 10, 11——[g]Hab. i. 8——[h]Jer. xxiii. 11, 32; Lam. ii. 14; Hos. ix. 7——[i]Ezek. xxii. 26——[k]Deut. xxxii. 4

[l]Ver. 15, 17; see Mic. iii. 11——[m]Heb. *morning by morning*——[n]Jer. iii. 3; vi. 15; viii. 12——[o]Or, *corners*——[p]So Jer. viii. 6——[q]Gen. vi. 12——[r]Psa. xxvii. 14; xxxvii. 34; Prov. xx. 22——[s]Joel iii. 2——[t]Chap. i. 18——[u]Isa. xix. 18

NOTES ON CHAP. III

Verse 1. *Wo to her that is filthy*] This is a denunciation of Divine judgment against Jerusalem.

Verse 2. *She obeyed not the voice*] Of conscience, of God, and of his prophets.

She received not correction] Did not profit by his chastisements; was uneasy and ill-tempered under her afflictions, and derived no manner of good from these chastisements.

She trusted not in the Lord] Did not consider him as the *Fountain* whence all help and salvation should come; and rather sought for support from *man* and *herself*, than from God.

She drew not near to her God.] Did not worship him; did not walk in his ways; did not make *prayer* and supplication to him.

Verse 3. *Her princes*—are *roaring lions*] Tearing all to pieces without shadow of law, except their own despotic power.

Her judges are *evening wolves*] Being a little afraid of the lion-like princes, they practise their unjust dealings from evening to morning, and take the *day* to find their rest.

They gnaw not the bones till the morrow.] They devour the flesh in the night, and gnaw the bones and extract the marrow afterwards. They use all violence and predatory oppression, like wild beasts; they shun the light, and turn day into night by their revellings.

Verse 4. *Her prophets* are *light* and *treacherous persons*] They have no *seriousness*, no *deep conviction* of the awful nature of their *office*, no *concern* for the *immortal souls* of the people. *Treacherous persons*—they betray the souls of the people for the sake of worldly *honour*, *pleasure*, and *profit*. Even in our own enlightened country we find prophets who prefer *hunting* the *hare* or the *fox*, and pursuing the *partridge* and *phesant*, to *visiting the sick*, and *going* after the *strayed*, *lost sheep* of the *house of Israel*. Poor souls! They know neither God nor themselves; and if they did visit the sick, they could not speak to them to exhortation, edification, or comfort. God never called them to his work; therefore they know nothing of it. But O, what an account have these *pleasure-taking false prophets* to render to the Shepherd of souls!

They have done violence to the law.] They have forced wrong constructions on it in order to excuse themselves, and lull the people into spiritual slumber. So we find that it was an ancient practice for men to wrest the Scriptures to their own destruction.

Verse 5. *The just Lord* is *in the midst thereof*] He sees, marks down, and will punish all these wickednesses.

Every morning doth he bring his judgment to light] The sense is, says Bp. *Newcome*, "Not a day passes but we see instances of his goodness to righteous men, and of his vengeance on the wicked."

Verse 6. *I have cut off the nations*] Syria, Israel, and those referred to, Isa. xxxvi. 18, 20. —*Newcome.*

Verse 7. *Surely thou wilt fear me*] After so many displays of my sovereign power and judgments.

But they rose early] And instead of returning to God, they practised every abomination. They were diligent to find out times and places for their iniquity. This is the worst state of man.

Verse 8. *Wait ye upon me*] Expect the fulfilment of all my promises and threatenings: I am God, and change not.

For all the earth] All the land of Judah.

Verse 9. *Will I turn to the people*] This promise must refer to the conversion of the Jews under the Gospel.

That they may all call] That the whole nation may invoke God by Christ, and serve him with *one consent;* not one unbeliever being found among them.

The *pure language*, שפה ברורה *saphah beru-*

A. M. cir. 3374 B. C. cir. 630 Olymp. cir. XXXVII. 3 A. U. C. cir. 124

[v]language, that they may all
call upon the name of the LORD,
to serve him with one [w]consent.
10 [x]From beyond the rivers of
Ethiopia my suppliants, *even* the daughter of
my dispersed, shall bring mine offering.
11 In that day shall thou not be ashamed for
all thy doings, wherein thou hast transgressed
against me: for then I will take away out of
the midst of thee them that [y]rejoice in thy
pride, and thou shalt no more be haughty [z]because
of my holy mountain.
12 I will also leave in the midst of thee [a]an
afflicted and poor people, and they shall trust
in the name of the LORD.
13 [b]The remnant of Israel [c]shall not do
iniquity, [d]nor speak lies; neither
shall a deceitful tongue be
found in their mouth: for [e]they
shall feed and lie down, and none
shall make *them* afraid.
14 [f]Sing, O daughter of Zion: shout, O
Israel; be glad and rejoice with all the heart,
O daughter of Jerusalem.
15 The LORD hath taken away thy judgments,
he hath cast out thine enemy: [g]the King of
Israel, *even* the LORD, [h]*is* in the midst of thee:
thou shalt not see evil any more.
16 In that day [i]it shall be said to Jerusalem,
Fear thou not: *and to* Zion, [k]Let not thine
hand be [l]slack.
17 The LORD thy God [m]in the midst of thee

---

[v]Heb. *lip*——[w]Heb. *shoulder*——[x]Psa. lxviii. 31; Isa. xviii. 1, 7; lx. 4, &c.; Mal. i. 11; Acts viii. 27——[y]Jer. vii. 4; Mic. iii. 11; Matt. iii. 9——[z]Heb. *in my holy*——[a]Isa. xiv. 32; Zech. xi. 11; Matt. v. 3; 1 Cor. i. 27, 28; James ii. 5——[b]Mic. iv. 7; chap. ii. 7

[c]Isa. lx. 21——[d]Isa. lxiii. 8; Rev. xiv. 5——[e]Ezek. xxxiv. 28; Mic. iv. 4; vii. 14——[f]Isa. xii. 6; liv. 1; Zech. ii. 10; ix. 9——[g]John i. 49——[h]Ver. 5, 17; Ezek. xlviii. 35; Rev. vii. 15; xxi. 3, 4——[i]Isa. xxxv. 3, 4——[k]Heb. xii. 12——[l]Or, *faint*——[m]Ver. 15

---

rah, may here mean the *form of religious worship*. They had been before *idolaters:* now God promises to restore his *pure worship* among them. The word has certainly this meaning in Psa. lxxxi. 6; where, as God is the speaker, the words should not be rendered, "I heard a language which I understood not;" but, "I heard a religious confession, which I approved not." See Isa. xix. 18; Hos. xiv. 3; and see Joel ii. 28, where a similar promise is found.

Verse 10. *From beyond the rivers of Ethiopia*] This may denote both *Africa* and the southern *Arabia*. *Bochart* thinks that *Arabia Chusœr* is meant; and that the rivers are *Besor*, which flows into the *Mediterranean; Rhinocorura*, which flows into the Lake *Sirbonis; Trajanus Amnis*, which flows into the *Red Sea;* and the river *Corys*. *Calmet* thinks that these *rivers* mean the *Nile*, which by *seven mouths* falls into the Mediterranean. The Nile comes from *Ethiopia*, properly so called; and runs through all Egypt, and falls into the sea at that part of Arabia which the Scripture calls *Cush* or *Ethiopia*.

My dispersed] The Jews, scattered through different parts of the world. *Shall bring mine offering*. Shall acknowledge my mercy in sending them the *Messiah* to bless them, by turning every one of them away from their iniquities.

Verse 11. *Shalt thou not be ashamed*] Thy punishment shall cease, for God shall pardon thy sin.

For then I will take away out of the midst of thee] The wicked Jewish priests and scribes who blasphemed Christ, and would not come under his yoke.

Because of my holy mountain.] Thou wilt no more *boast in my temple*, but become *meek* and *lowly* in following him who is meek and lowly in heart, that ye may obtain rest to your souls.

Verse 12. *An afflicted and poor people*] In such a state will the Jews be found when they shall hear the universal call, and believe in Christ Jesus. Indeed, this is the *general state* of the Jews in the *present day;* except a *few* that are *called Jews*, who are *very rich;* and who believe just as much in the *God of Jacob*, as they do in *Jesus Christ*.

Verse 13. *The remnant of Israel shall not do iniquity*] O what a change! And then, how different shall they be from their *present selves!* Iniquity, lying, and deceit shall not be found among them! A Jew once said to me, "Tere are shome of you Christians who are making wonderful efforts to convert the Tshews (Jews.) *Ah, dere ish none but Gott Almighty dat can convert a Tshew.*" Truly I believe him. Only God can convert any man; and if there be a *peculiar difficulty* to convert any soul, that difficulty must lie in the *conversion* of the *Jew*.

Verse 14. *Sing, O daughter of Zion*] Here is not only a gracious prophetic promise of their restoration from captivity, but of their conversion to God through Christ.

Verse 15. *The King of Israel*, even *the Lord*, is *in the midst of thee*] They have never had a *king* since the death of Zedekiah, and never shall have one till they have the *King Messiah* to reign among them; and this promise refers to that event.

Verse 16. *Fear thou not*] Thou shalt have no more captivities nor national afflictions.

Let not thine hands be slack.] This may refer, *first*, to the rebuilding of the temple of God, after the return from Babylon; and, *secondly*, to their diligence and zeal in the Christian Church.

Verse 17. *The Lord thy God*] יהוה אלהיך *Yehovah Eloheycha*, "The self-existent and eternal Being, who is in covenant with you;" the character of God in reference to the Jews when standing in the nearest relation to them.

Is *mighty*] גבור *gibbor*, is the *prevailing One*, the *all-conquering Hero*. The character which is given to Christ, Isa. ix. 6: "His name shall be called אל גבור *El gibbor*, the prevailing Almighty God."

He will save] *Deliver* thee from all the

A. M. cir. 3374 B. C. cir. 630 Olymp. cir. XXXVII. 3 A. U. C. cir. 124

is mighty; he will save, [n]he will
rejoice over thee with joy; [o]he
will rest in his love, he will joy
over thee with singing.
18 I will gather *them that* [p]*are* sorrowful
for the solemn assembly, *who* are of thee, *to*
whom [q]the reproach of it *was* a burden.
19 Behold, at that time I will undo all that
afflict thee: and I will save her that [r]halteth,
and gather her that was driven
out; and [s]I will get them praise
and fame in every land [t]where
they have been put to shame.
20 At that time [u]will I bring you *again,*
even in the time that I gather you: for I will
make you a name and a praise among all people of the earth, when I turn back your captivity before your eyes, saith the LORD.

[n]Deut. xxx. 9; Isa. lxii. 5; lxv. 19; Jer. xxxii. 41 — [o]Heb. *he will be silent* — [p]Lam. ii. 6 — [q]Heb. *the burden upon it* was *reproach* — [r]Ezek. xxxiv. 16; Mic. iv. 6, 7 — [s]Heb. *I will set them for a praise* — [t]Heb. *of their shame* — [u]Isa. xi. 12; xxvii. 12; lvi. 8; Ezek. xxviii. 25; xxxiv. 13; xxxvii. 21; Amos ix. 14

power from all the *guilt*, and from all the *pollution* of thy sins; and when thus *saved*, "he will rejoice over thee with joy," with peculiar gladness. "He will rest in his love,"—he will renew his love. He will show the same love to you that he did of old to *Abraham, Isaac,* and *Jacob.*

He will joy over thee with singing.] The conversion of the Jews will be a subject of peculiar delight and exultation to God himself! There will be a *more* than *ordinary joy* in heaven, when the Jews return to God through Christ. This event cannot be at a great distance; they are as *wretched* and as *ungodly* as they can well be. The *arms of Christians* are open to receive them; and *all things are now ready!*

Verse 18. *I will gather—sorrowful*] This may refer to those who, during the captivity, *mourned* for their former religious assemblies; and who were *reproached* by their enemies, because they could not enjoy their religious solemnities. See Psa. cxxxvii.: "By the rivers of Babylon, there we sat down; yea, we wept, when we remembered Zion. For there they that carried us away captive required of us a song," &c. This very circumstance may be the reference here.

Verse 19. *I will undo all that afflict thee*] They who have persecuted you shall be punished for it. It shows much malignity and baseness of mind, to afflict or reproach those who are lying under the chastising hand of God. This was the conduct of the Edomites, Moabites, and Ammonites, when the Jews were in adversity; and how severely did the Lord punish them for it! And he gave this as the *reason* for the severity of the punishment.

The first clause here is translated thus by Abp. *Newcome:* "Behold I will work with thee for thy sake at that time." The original is obscure; and it may bear the above sense.

I will save her that halteth] See Micah iv. 6, where there is a parallel place.

And gather her that was driven out] By captivity. The reference may be to renewing the covenant with the Jews, who were considered as an unfaithful spouse divorced by her husband. I will bring her back to my house.

I will get them praise and fame in every land] They shall become a great, a good, and a useful people. And as they are now a proverb of reproach, full of base wiles and degrading selfishness, they shall lose this character, and be totally changed; and they shall be as eminent for excellence, as they were before for baseness, in those countries where they had sojourned.

Verse 20. *At that time*] *First,* when the *seventy* years of the Babylonish captivity shall terminate. "I will bring you again" to your own land; and this restoration shall be a type of their redemption from sin and iniquity; and *at this time,* and at this only, will they have a *name* and *praise* among *all* the *people* of the *earth*, not only among the Jews, but the Gentiles.

Before your eyes] Some read *before* THEIR *eyes;* that is, the eyes of all people. On their conversion to Christianity, they shall become as eminent as they ever were in the most illustrious days of their history, Lord, hasten the conversion of Israel! Amen.

THE BOOK

OF THE

PROPHET HAGGAI

Chronological Notes relative to this book

Year from the Creation, according to Archbishop Usher, 3484.—Year of the Julian Period, 4194.—Year since the Flood, 1828.—Year from the vocation of Abram, 1301.—Year since the first celebration of the Olympic games in Elis by the Idæi Dactyli, 934.—Year since the foundation of the monarchy of the Israelites by the Divine appointment of Saul to the regal dignity, 576.—Year from the foundation of the temple, 492.—Year from the division of Solomon's monarchy into the kingdoms of Israel and Judah, 456.—Year since the re-establishment of the Olympic games at Elis by Lycurgus, Iphitus, and Cleosthenes, 365.—Year since the conquest of Corœbus at Olympia, usually called the first Olympiad, 257.—First year of the *sixty-fifth* Olympiad.—Year from the building of Rome, according to the Varronian or generally received computation, 234.—Year from the building of Rome, according to Cato and the Fasti Consulares, 233.—Year from the building of Rome, according to Polybius the historian, 232.—Year from the building of Rome, according to Fabius Pictor, 228.—Year of the era of Nabonassar, 228.—Year since the destruction of the kingdom of Israel by Shalmaneser, king of Assyria, 202.—Year since the destruction of the kingdom of Judah by Nebuchadnezzar, king of Babylon, 68.—Year since the destruction of the Chaldean empire by the Persians, 18.—Year before the birth of Christ, 516.—Year before the vulgar era of Christ's nativity, 520.—Cycle of the Sun, 22.—Cycle of the Moon, 14.—Second year of Darius I., king of Persia.—Twenty-eighth year of Amyntas, king of Macedon.—Seventh year of Demaratus, king of Lacedæmon, of the family of the Proclidæ.—Eleventh year of Cleomenes, king of Lacedæmon, of the family of the Eurysthenidæ.—Fifteenth year of Tarquinius Superbus, the last king of the Romans.—This was about twelve years before the abolition of the regal government of the Romans by the expulsion of the Tarquins.—Confucius, the celebrated Chinese philosopher, is supposed to have flourished about this time.

CHAPTER I

The prophet reproves the people, and particularly their ruler and high priest, for negligence and delay in rebuilding the temple; and tells them that their neglect was the cause of their having been visited with unfruitful seasons, and other marks of the Divine displeasure, 1–11. *He encourages them to set about the work, and on their doing so, promises that God will be with them,* 12–15.

A. M. 3484
B. C. 520
Ol. LXV. 1
Anno Tarquinii Superbi, R. Roman., 15

IN [a]the second year of Darius the king, in the sixth month, in the first day of the month, came the word of the LORD [b]by Haggai the prophet unto [c]Zerubbabel the son of Shealtiel, [d]gov-

[a]Ezra iv. 24; v. 1; Zechariah i. 1——[b]Hebrew *by the hand of Haggai*——[c]1 Chronicles iii. 17, 19; Ezra iii. 2; Matthew i. 12; Luke iii. 27——[d]Or, *captain*

We know nothing of the parentage of *Haggai.* He was probably born in Babylon during the captivity, and appears to have been the first prophet sent to the Jews after their return to their own land. He was sent particularly to encourage the Jews to proceed with the building of the temple, which had been interrupted for about *fourteen* years. *Cyrus,* who had published an edict empowering the Jews to return to Jerusalem and rebuild their city and temple, revoked this edict in the second year of his reign, through the evil advice of his courtiers and other enemies of the Jews. After his death *Cambyses* renewed the prohibition; but after the death of Cambyses, *Darius,* the son of *Hystaspes,* renewed the *permission;* and Haggai was sent to encourage his countrymen to proceed with the work. Darius came to the throne

A. M. 3484 B. C. 520 Ol. LXV. 1 Anno Tarquinii Superbi, R. Roman., 15

ernor of Judah, and to [e]Joshua
the son of Josedech, [f]the high
priest, saying,
2 Thus speaketh the LORD of
hosts, saying, This people say, The time is not
come, the time that the LORD's house should
be built.
3 Then came the word of the LORD [g]by
Haggai the prophet, saying,
4 [h]*Is it* time for you, O ye, to dwell in your
ceiled houses, and this house *lie* waste?
5 Now therefore thus saith the LORD of
hosts; [i]Consider [k]your ways.
6 Ye have [l]sown much, and bring in little;
ye eat, but ye have not enough; ye drink, but
ye are not filled with drink; ye clothe you,
but there is none warm; and [m]he that earneth wages, earneth wages *to put it* into a bag
[n]with holes.

7 Thus saith the LORD of
hosts; Consider your ways.
8 Go up to the mountain, and
bring wood, and build the house;
and I will take pleasure in it, and I will be
glorified, saith the LORD.
9 [o]Ye looked for much, and, lo, *it came*
to little; and when ye brought *it* home, [p]I
did [q]blow upon it. Why? saith the LORD
of hosts. Because of mine house that *is*
waste, and ye run every man unto his own
house.
10 Therefore [r]the heaven over you is stayed
from dew, and the earth is stayed *from* her
fruit.
11 And I [s]called for a drought upon the land,
and upon the mountains, and upon the corn,
and upon the new wine, and upon the oil, and
upon *that* which the ground bringeth forth,

A. M. 3484 B. C. 520 Ol. LXV. 1 Anno Tarquinii Superbi, R. Roman., 15

[e]Ezra iii. 2; v. 2——[f]1 Chron. vi. 15——[g]Ezra v. 1 [h]2 Sam. vii. 2; Psa. cxxxii. 3, &c.——[i]*Set your heart on your ways*——[k]Lam. iii. 40; ver. 7——[l]Deut. xxviii. 38; Hos. iv. 10; Mic. vi. 14, 15; chap. ii. 16

[m]Zech. viii. 10——[n]Heb. *pierced through*——[o]Chap. ii. 16——[p]Chap. ii. 17——[q]Or, *blow it away*——[r]Lev. xxvi. 19; Deut. xxviii. 23; 1 Kings viii. 35——[s]1 Kings xvii. 1; 2 Kings viii. 1

about the year B. C. 521, and published his edict of permission for the Jews to rebuild the city and temple in the second year of his reign, which was the *sixteenth* of their return from Babylon.

NOTES ON CHAP. I

Verse 1. *In the sixth month*] Called *Elul* by the Hebrews. It was the *sixth* month of the ecclesiastical year, and the *last* of the *civil* year, and answered to a part of our *September*.

Zerubbabel the son of Shealtiel] Who was son of *Jeconiah*, king of Judah, and of the family of David, and exercised the post of a governor *among* the people, but not *over* them, for both he and they were under the Persian government; but they were permitted to have *Zerubbabel* for their own governor, and *Joshua* for their high priest; and these regulated all matters relative to their peculiar political and ecclesiastical government. But it appears from Ezra, v. 3, that *Tatnai*, the governor on this side the river, had them under his cognizance. None of their own governors was absolute. The Persians permitted them to live under their own laws and civil regulations; but they always considered them as a colony, over which they had a continual superintendence.

Joshua the son of Josedech] And son of Seraiah, who was high priest in the time of Zedekiah, and was carried into captivity by Nebuchadnezzar, 1 Chron. vi. 15. But Seraiah was slain at Riblah, by order of Nebuchadnezzar, 2 Kings xxv. 18-21.

Verse 2. *The time is not come*] They thought that the *seventy years* spoken of by Jeremiah were not yet completed, and it would be useless to attempt to rebuild until that period had arrived. But Abp. *Usher* has shown that from the commencement of the last siege of Jerusalem unto this time, precisely *sixty-nine* years had been completed.

Verse 4. Is it *time for you*] If the *time be not come* to rebuild the *temple*, it cannot be come for you to *build yourselves comfortable houses:* but ye are rebuilding your houses; why then do ye not rebuild the house of the Lord? The foundation of the temple had been laid *fourteen* years before, and some considerable progress made in the building; and it had been *lying waste* in that unfinished state to the present time.

Verse 5. *Consider your ways*] Is it fit that you should be building yourselves *elegant houses*, and neglect a *place* for the *worship* of that God who has restored you from captivity?

Verse 6. *Ye have sown much*] God will not bless you in any labour of your hands, unless you rebuild his temple and restore his worship. This verse contains a series of *proverbs;* no less than *five* in the compass of a few lines.

Verse 8. *Go up to the mountain, and bring wood*] Go to Lebanon, and get timber. In the second year of the return from the captivity, they had procured cedar trees from Lebanon, and brought them to Joppa, and had hired masons and carpenters from the Tyrians and Sidonians; but that labour had been nearly lost by the long suspension of the building. Ezra iii. 7.

Verse 9. *Ye looked for much*] Ye made great pretensions at first; but they are come to nothing. Ye did a little in the beginning; but so scantily and unwillingly that I could not but reject it.

Ye run every man unto his own house.] To rebuild and adorn it; and God's house is neglected!

Verse 10. *Therefore the heaven over you is stayed from dew*] It appears from the following verse that God had sent a drought upon the

A. M. 3484
B. C. 520
Ol. LXV. 1
Anno Tarquinii Superbi,
R. Roman., 15

and upon men, and upon cattle,
and [t]upon all the labour of the
hands.
12 [u]Then Zerubbabel the son
of Shealtiel, and Joshua the son of Josedech,
the high priest, with all the remnant of the
people, obeyed the voice of the LORD their God,
and the words of Haggai the prophet, as the
LORD their God had sent him, and the people
did fear before the LORD.
13 Then spake Haggai the LORD's messenger in the LORD's message unto the people,
saying, [v]I *am* with you, saith
the LORD.
14 And [w]the LORD stirred up
the spirit of Zerubbabel the son
of Shealtiel, [x]governor of Judah, and the
spirit of Joshua the son of Josedech, the high
priest, and the spirit of all the remnant of
the people: [y]and they came and did work in
the house of the LORD of hosts, their God.
15 In the four and twentieth day of the
sixth month, in the second year of Darius the
king.

A. M. 3484
B. C. 520
Ol. LXV. 1
Anno Tarquinii Superbi,
R. Roman., 15

---

[t]Chap. ii. 17——[u]Ezra v. 2——[v]Matt. xxviii. 20; Romans viii. 31——[w]2 Chron. xxxvi. 22; Ezra i. 1——[x]Chap. ii. 21——[y]Ezra v. 2, 8

---

land, which threatened them with scarcity and famine.

Verse 12. *Then Zerubbabel*] The threatening of Haggai had its proper effect. The civil governor, the high priest, and the whole of the people, united together to do the work. When the authority of God is acknowledged, his words will be carefully obeyed.

Verse 13. *Then spake Haggai*] He was the *Lord's messenger*, and he came with the *Lord's message*, and consequently he came with *authority*. He is called מלאך יהוה *malach Yehovah, the angel of Jehovah*, just as the *pastors* of the seven Asiatic Churches are called ANGELS *of the Churches*, Rev. i. 2.

I am with you, saith the Lord.] Here was high encouragement. What may not a man do when God is his helper?

Verse 14. *And the Lord stirred up the spirit*] It is not only necessary that the *judgment* should be enlightened, but the *soul* must be *invigorated* by the Spirit of God, before any good work can be effectually done.

Verse 15. *In the four and twentieth day*] Haggai received his commission on the *first* day of this month and by the *twenty-fourth* day he had so completely succeeded that he had the satisfaction to see the whole people engaged heartily in the Lord's work; they left their own houses to build that of the Lord. Here was a *faithful reprover*, and he found *obedient ears;* and the Lord's work was done, for *the people had a mind to work.*

CHAPTER II

When this prophecy was uttered, about four *years before the temple was finished, and* sixty-eight *after the former one was destroyed, it appears that some old men among the Jews were greatly dispirited on account of its being so much inferior in magnificence to that of Solomon. Compare* Ezra iii. 12. *To raise the spirits of the people, and encourage them to proceed with the work, the prophet assures them that the glory of the second temple should be greater than that of the first, alluding perhaps to the glorious doctrines which should be preached in it by Jesus Christ and his apostles,* 1–9. *He then shows the people that the oblations brought by their priests could not sanctify them while they were unclean by their neglect of the temple; and to convince them that the difficult times they had experienced during that neglect proceeded from this cause, he promises fruitful seasons from that day forward,* 10–19. *The concluding verses contain a prediction of the mighty revolutions that should take place by the setting up of the kingdom of Christ under the type of Zerubbabel,* 20–23. *As the time which elapsed between the date of the prophecy and the dreadful concussion of nations is termed in verse* 6, A LITTLE WHILE, *the words may likewise have reference to some temporal revolutions then near, such as the commotions of Babylon in the reign of Darius, the Macedonian conquests in Persia, and the wars between the successors of Alexander; but the aspect of the prophecy is more directly to the amazing victories of the Romans, who, in the time of Haggai and Zechariah, were on the* VERY EVE *of their successful career, and in the lapse of a few centuries subjugated the whole habitable globe; and therefore, in a very good sense, God may be said by these people to have shaken "the heavens, and the earth, and the sea, and the dry land;" and thus to have prepared the way for the opening of the Gospel dispensation. See* Heb. xii. 25–29. *Others have referred this prophecy to the period of our Lord's second advent, to which there is no doubt it is also applicable; and when it will be in the most signal manner fulfilled. That the convulsion of the nations introducing this most stupendous event will be very great and terrible, is sufficiently plain from* Isaiah xxxiv., xxxv., *as well as from many other passages of holy writ.*

A. M. 3484
B. C. 520
Ol. LXV. 1
Anno Tarquinii Superbi,
R. Roman., 15

IN the seventh *month,* in the
one and twentieth *day* of
the month, came the word of the
LORD [a]by the prophet Haggai,
saying,
2 Speak now to Zerubbabel the son of Shealtiel, governor of Judah, and to Joshua the
son of Josedech, the high priest, and to the
residue of the people, saying,
3 [b]Who *is* left among you that saw this
house in her first glory and how do ye see
it now? [c]*is it* not in your eyes in comparison
of it as nothing?
4 Yet now, [d]be strong, O Zerubbabel, saith
the LORD; and be strong, O Joshua, son of
Josedech, the high priest; and be
strong, all ye people of the land,
saith the LORD, and work: for I
am with you, saith the LORD of
hosts:
5 [e]*According to* the word that I covenanted
with you when ye came out of Egypt, so [f]my
Spirit remaineth among you: [g]fear ye not.
6 For thus saith the LORD of hosts: [h]Yet
once, it *is* a little while, and [i]I will shake the
heavens, and the earth, and the sea, and the
dry *land;*
7 And I will shake all nations, [k]and the
Desire of all nations shall come; and I will fill
this house with glory, saith the LORD of hosts.

[a]Heb. *by the hand of*——[b]Ezra iii. 12——[c]Zech. iv. 10
[d]Zech. viii. 9——[e]Exod. xxix. 45, 46

[f]Neh. ix. 20; Isa. lxiii. 11——[g]Isa. vii. 4——[h]Ver. 21; Heb. xii. 26——[i]Joel iii. 16——[k]Gen. xlix. 10; Mal. iii. 1

NOTES ON CHAP. II

Verse 1. *In the seventh* month] This was a *new* message, and intended to prevent discouragement, and excite them to greater diligence in their work.

Verse 3. *Who is left among you that saw this house in her first glory?*] Who of you has seen the *temple* built by *Solomon?* The foundation of the present house had been laid about *fifty-three* years after the destruction of the temple built by Solomon and though this prophecy was uttered *fifteen* years after the foundation of this second temple, yet there might still survive some of those who had seen the temple of Solomon.

Is it *not in your eyes*] Most certainly the Jews at this time had neither *men* nor *means* to make any such splendid building as that erected by Solomon. The *present* was as nothing when compared with the *former.*

Verse 4. *Yet now be strong*] Do not let this discourage you. The chief glory of the temple is not its splendid building, but my *presence;* and as *I covenanted to be with you* when ye came out of Egypt, so I will fulfil my covenant; for *my Spirit remaineth among you, fear not;* ver. 5. What is the most splendid cathedral, if God be not in it, influencing all by his presence and Spirit? But he will not be in it unless there be a messenger of the Lord there, and unless he deliver the Lord's message.

Verse 6. *Yet once, it is a little while, and I will shake the heavens*] When the law was given on Mount Sinai, there was an earthquake that shook the whole mountain, Exod. xix. 18. "The political or religious revolutions which were to be effected in the world, or both, are here," says Abp. *Newcome,* "referred to; compare ver. 21, 22; Matt. xxiv. 29; Heb. xii. 26-28. The political ones began in the overthrow of the Persian monarchy by Alexander, within two centuries after this prediction; and if the Messiah's kingdom be meant, which is my opinion, this was erected in somewhat more than five centuries after the second year of Darius; a short period of time when compared with that which elapsed from the creation to the giving of the law, or from the giving of the law to the coming of the Messiah's kingdom. It must be understood that the word אחת *achath, once,* has a clear sense, if understood of the *evangelical age;* for *many* political revolutions succeeded, as the conquest of Darius Codomanus, and the various fortunes of Alexander's successors; but only one great and final *religious revolution.*"—*Newcome.*

Verse 7. *And the Desire of all nations shall come*] The present Hebrew text is as follows: ובאו חמדת כל הגוים. This is a difficult place if understood of a *person:* but חמדת *chemdath, desire,* cannot well agree with באו *bau, they shall come.* It is true that some learned men suppose that חמדות *chemdoth, desirable things,* may have been the original reading: but this is supported by no MS., nor is באו found in the *singular* number in any. It is generally understood of the *desirable* or *valuable things* which the different nations should bring into the temple; and it is certain that many rich presents were brought into this temple. All are puzzled with it. But the principal difficulty lies in the verb ובאו *ubau, they shall come.* If we found ובאה חמדת *ubaa chemdath* in the singular, then it would read as in our text, *And the Desire of all nations shall come:* but no such reading appears in any MS.; nor is it *fairly* acknowledged, except by the *Vulgate,* which reads, Et veniet desideratus cunctis gentibus, "And that which is desired," or the desired Person, "shall come to all nations." In ver. 7 God says *he will shake* or stir up *all nations;* that these nations shall *bring their desirable things;* that the house shall be *filled with God's glory;* that the *silver* and *gold,* which these nations are represented as bringing by way of gifts, are *the Lord's;* and that the glory of this latter house shall exceed the former. Bp. *Chandler* labours to vindicate the present translation; but he makes rash assertions, and is abandoned by the Hebrew text. The בא *ba, to come,* is often used in the sense of *bring,* and that חמדת *chemdath, desire,* may be considered as the *plural* for חמדות, having the point *holem* instead of the ו *vau,* and thus mean *desirable things,* will not be denied by those who are acquainted with the

A. M. 3484
B. C. 520
Ol. LXV. 1
Anno Tarquinii
Superbi,
R. Roman., 15

8 The silver *is* mine, and the
gold *is* mine, saith the LORD of
hosts.
9 [l]The glory of this latter
house shall be greater than of the former,
saith the LORD of hosts: and in this place
will I give [m]peace, saith the LORD of hosts.
10 In the four and twentieth *day* of the
ninth *month,* in the second year of Darius,
came the word of the Lord by Haggai the
prophet, saying,
11 Thus saith the LORD of hosts; [n]Ask
now the priests *concerning* the law, saying,
12 If one bear holy flesh in the skirt of his
garment, and with his skirt do touch bread, or
pottage, or wine, or oil, or any meat, shall
it be holy: And the priests answered and said,
No.
13 Then said Haggai, If *one that is* [o]unclean
by a dead body touch any of these, shall it be
unclean? And the priests an-
swered and said, It shall be
unclean.
14 Then answered Haggai, and
said, [p]So *is* this people, and so *is* this nation
before me, saith the LORD; and so *is* every
work of their hands; and that which they
offer there *is* unclean.
15 And now, I pray you, [q]consider from
this day and upward, from before a stone was
laid upon a stone in the temple of the LORD:
16 Since those *days* were, [r]when *one* came
to a heap of twenty *measures,* there were *but*
ten: when *one* came to the press-fat for to
draw out fifty *vessels* out of the press, there
were *but* twenty.
17 [s]I smote you with blasting and with mildew and with hail [t]in all the labours of your
hands; [u]yet ye *turned* not to me, saith the
LORD.

[l]John i. 14——[m]Psa. lxxxv. 8, 9; Luke ii. 14; Eph. ii. 14——[n]Lev. x. 10, 11; Deut. xxxiii. 10; Mal. ii. 7——[o]Num. xix. 11——[p]Titus i. 15

[q]Chap. i. 5——[r]Chap. i. 6, 9; Zech. viii. 10——[s]Deut. xxviii. 22; 1 Kings viii. 37; chap. i. 9; Amos iv. 9——[t]Chap. i. 11——[u]Jer. v. 3; Amos iv. 6, 8, 9, 10, 11

genius and construction of the Hebrew language. Bp. *Chandler* thinks that בא, *he came*, cannot be used of *things*, but of *persons* only. Here he is widely mistaken, for it is used of *days* perpetually; and of the *ark*, 2 Sam. vi. 9; and of *mounts coming* against Jerusalem, Jer. xxxii. 24; and of *trees coming* to adorn the temple, Isa. lx. 13; and of *silver* and *gold coming* into the temple, Josh. vi. 19; and Jer. vi. 20, Why doth *incense come* to me? See Abp. *Secker's* notes. I cannot see how the words can apply to Jesus Christ, even if the construction were less embarrassed than it is; because I cannot see how he could be called THE DESIRE OF ALL NATIONS. The whole seems to be a metaphorical description of the *Church of Christ*, and of his filling it with all the excellences of the Gentile world, when the fulness of the Gentiles shall be brought in.

Verse 9. *And in this place will I give peace*] שלום *shalom, a peace-offering*, as well as *peace* itself; or *Jesus Christ*, who is called the *Prince of peace*, through whom *peace* is proclaimed between God and man, between man and his fellows; and through whom *peace* is established in the *disconsolate soul*. And at this temple this *peace* was first promulgated and proclaimed.

But it is said that *the glory of this latter house shall be greater than of the former*. Now this cannot be said because Jesus Christ made his *personal* appearance in that temple, or rather in that built by Herod; for, though we allow that Jesus Christ is *equal* with God, we do not grant that he is *greater*. Now the *first temple* was the *dwelling-place of God:* here he manifested his glory between the cherubim, and it was his *constant residence* for more than *four hundred* years. But the *glory of this latter house was greater* because under it the grand scheme of human salvation was exhibited, and the redemption price paid down for a lost world. As all probably applies to the *Christian Church*, the *real house of God*, its glory was most certainly *greater* than any glory which was ever possessed by that of the Jews. See on ver. 22, 23.

Verse 10. *In the four and twentieth* day *of the ninth* month] Three months after they had begun to rebuild the temple, Haggai is ordered to go and put *two questions* to the priests. 1. If one bear holy flesh in the skirt of his garment, and he touch any thing with his skirt, is that thing made holy? The priests answered, No! ver. 12. 2. If one has touched a *dead body*, and thereby become unclean, does he communicate his uncleanness to whatever he may *touch?* And the priests answered, YES! ver. 13.

Verse 14. *Then answered Haggai—So is this people*] As an *unclean* man communicates his uncleanness to every thing he touches, so are ye unclean; and whatever ye have hitherto done is polluted in the sight of God. For your neglect of my temple has made you unclean, as if you had contracted legal pollution by touching a dead body.

Verse 16. *Since those* days *were*] I have shown my displeasure against you, by sending *blasting* and *mildew;* and so poor have been your *crops* that a heap of corn which should have produced *twenty measures* produced only *ten;* and that quantity of *grapes* which in other years would have produced *fifty* measures, through their poverty, smallness, &c., produced only *twenty*. And this has been the case ever since the *first stone was laid in this temple;* for your hearts were not right with me, and therefore I blasted you in all the labours of your hands; and *yet ye have not* turned *to me*, ver. 17.

A. M. 3484
B. C. 520
Ol. LXV. 1
Anno Tarquinii
Superbi,
R. Roman., 15

18 Consider now from this
day and upward, from the four
and twentieth day of the ninth
month, even from [v]the day that
the foundation of the LORD's temple was laid,
consider *it*.
19 [w]Is the seed yet in the barn? yea, as
yet the vine, and the fig tree, and the pomegranate, and the olive tree, hath not brought
forth: from this day will I bless *you*.
20 And again the word of the LORD came
unto Haggai, in the four and twentieth day
of the month, saying,
21 Speak to Zerubbabel, [x]governor of Judah,
saying, [y]I will shake the heavens
and the earth;
22 And [z]I will overthrow the
throne of kingdoms, and I will
destroy the strength of the kingdoms of the
heathen; and [a]I will overthrow the chariots,
and those that ride in them; and the horses
and their riders shall come down, every one
by the sword of his brother.
23 In that day, saith the LORD of hosts,
will I take thee, O Zerubbabel, my servant,
the son of Shealtiel, saith the LORD, [b]and
will make thee as a signet: for [c]I have chosen
thee, saith the LORD of hosts.

[v]Ezek. viii. 9——[w]Zech. viii. 12——[x]Ch. i. 14——[y]Ver. 6, 7; Heb. xii. 26——[z]Dan. ii. 44; Matt. xxiv. 7

[a]Mic. v. 10; Zech. iv. 6; ix. 10——[b]Cant. viii. 6; Jer. xxii. 24; Ecclus. xlix. 11——[c]Isa. xlii. 1; xliii. 10

Verse 18. *Consider now from this day*] I will now change my conduct towards you: *from this day* that ye have begun heartily to rebuild my temple, and restore my worship, *I will bless you.* Whatever you *sow*, whatever you *plant*, shall be blessed; your land shall be fruitful, and ye shall have abundant crops of all sorts.

Verse 20. *Again the word of the Lord came*] This was a *second* communication in the same day.

Verse 21. *I will shake the heavens and the earth*] *Calmet* supposes that the invasion of *Cambyses*, and his death, are what the prophet has in view by this *shaking of the heavens and the earth:* but this invasion and defeat happened *three years before* they had begun to work at the temple; and how could it be made a matter of *interest* to Zerubbabel? *Calmet* answers this, by translating the words in the *past tense;* and shows that the fact was recalled to Zerubbabel's attention, to fix his confidence in God, &c. Bp. *Newcome* says we may well understand this and the *twenty-second* verse of the calamity undergone by Babylon in the reign of Darius; of the Macedonian conquests in Persia; and of the wars which the successors of Alexander waged against each other: others understand it of the Romans.

Verse 23. *In that day, saith the Lord*] Some think, says this same learned writer, that *Zerubbabel* is put here for his *people* and *posterity:* but it may well be said that the commotions foretold began in the rebellion of Babylon, which Darius besieged and took; and exercised great cruelties upon its inhabitants.—*Herod.* lib. iii., sec. 220. *Justin.* i. 10. *Prideaux* places this event in the *fifth* year of Darius; others, with more probability, in the *eighth* year. Compare Zech. ii. 9.

And will make thee as a signet] I will exalt thee to high dignity, power, and trust, of which the *seal* was the instrument or sign in those days. Thou shalt be under my peculiar care, and shalt be to me very precious. See Jer. xxii. 24; Cant. viii. 6; and see the notes on these two places.

For I have chosen thee] He had an important and difficult work to do, and it was necessary that he should be assured of God's especial care and protection during the whole.

ON the *three* last verses of this prophecy a sensible and pious correspondent sends me the following illustration, which I cheerfully insert. Though in many respects different from that given above, yet I believe that the kingdom of Christ is particularly designed in this prophecy.

"I think there is an apparent difficulty in this passage, because the wars of the Persians and Babylonians were not so interesting to the rising commonwealth of the Jews as many subsequent events of *less* note in the world, but which were more directly levelled at their own national prosperity; and yet neither the one nor the other could be termed 'a shaking of the heavens and the earth, and an overthrow of the throne of kingdoms.'

"I know not if the following view may be admitted as an explanation of this difficult passage. I take 'the shaking of the heavens and earth' here (as in ver. 6) to have a more distant and comprehensive meaning than can belong to Zerubbabel's time, or to his immediate posterity; and that it extends not only to the overthrow of kingdoms *then* existing, but of the future great monarchies of the world; and not excepting even the civil and ecclesiastical establishments of the Jews themselves. For I take 'the heavens,' in the prophetic language, uniformly to denote the true Church, and never the superstitions and idols of the nations.

"What, then, are we to understand by the *promise* made to Zerubbabel, 'I will make thee as a signet?' In the first place, the *restitution* of the religious and civil polity of the people of Israel, conformably to the promises afterwards given in the *four* first chapters of Zechariah. And, secondly, as the royal signet is the instrument by which kings give validity to laws, and thereby unity and consistence to their empire; so Jehovah, the God and King of Israel, condescends to promise he will employ *Zerubbabel* as his instrument of gathering and uniting the people again as a distinguished nation; and that such should be the *permanency* of their political existence, that, whilst other nations and mighty empires should be overthrown, and their very *name* blotted out under heaven, the Jews should ever remain a distinct people, even in the wreck of their own government, and the

loss of all which rendered their religion splendid and attractive.

"In confirmation of this interpretation, I would refer to the threatening denounced against Jeconiah, (called Coniah, Jer. xxii.,) the *last* reigning king of Judah, and the progenitor of Zerubbabel. I apprehend I may be authorized to read Jer. xxii. 24 *thus:* 'As I live, saith the Lord, though Coniah, the son of Jehoiakim, king of Judah, *be the signet* upon my right hand, yet will I pluck thee thence, and I will give thee into the hand of them that seek thy life,' &c.

"If it be considered that the kings of Judah were in an *especial* and peculiar manner the delegates of Jehovah, governing in his name and by his authority, a peculiar propriety will appear in their being resembled to *signets*, or royal seals contained in rings. Compare Gen. xli. 42; Esth. iii. 10, 12, viii. 2, 8; Dan. vi. 7. And the promise to Zerubbabel will be equivalent to those which clearly predict the preservation of the Jewish people by the Divine command. see Zech. ii.; and the faithfulness of God to his covenant concerning the Messiah, who should be born of the seed of Abraham, and in the family of David, of whose throne he was the rightful Proprietor.

"According to this view, by the promise, 'In that day—I will make thee as a signet,' &c., must be understood, that the preservation of the Jews as a distinct people, *when all the great empires of the heathen were overthrown*, would *manifest* the honour now conferred on Zerubbabel as *the instrument of their restoration* after the Babylonish captivity. Thus the promise to Abraham, Gen. xii., 'I will make of thee a great nation—and in thee shall all families of the earth be blessed,' evidently referred to a very distant future period and the honour connected with it could not be enjoyed by Abraham during his mortal life."

M. A. B.

I think, however, that we have lived to see the spirit of this prophecy fulfilled. The earth *has been* shaken; another shaking, and time shall be swallowed up in eternity.

INTRODUCTION TO THE BOOK

OF THE

PROPHET ZECHARIAH

ZECHARIAH, the eleventh of the twelve minor prophets, was son of Berechiah, and grandson of Iddo. He returned from Babylon with Zerubbabel: and began to prophesy in the second year of the reign of Darius, son of Hystaspes, in the year of the world 3484; before Christ, 516; before the vulgar era, 520; in the eighth month of the holy year; and two months after Haggai had begun to prophesy.

These two prophets, with united zeal, encouraged at the same time the people to go on with the work of the temple, which had been discontinued for some years.

The time and place of the birth of Zechariah are unknown. Some will have him to have been born at Babylon, during the captivity; others think he was born at Jerusalem, before the tribes of Judah and Benjamin were carried away. Some maintain that he was a priest; but others affirm that he was no priest. Many say he was the immediate son of Iddo; others believe, with much more reason, that he was son of Berechiah, and grandson of Iddo.

He has been confounded with one Zechariah, the son of Barachiah, who lived in the time of Isaiah; and with Zechariah, the father of John the Baptist; which opinion is plainly incongruous. Lastly, he has been thought to be Zechariah the son of Barachiah, whom our Saviour mentions, and says he was killed between the temple and the altar; though no such thing is anywhere said of our prophet. A tomb is shown to this day at the foot of the Mount of Olives, which, it is pretended, belongs to the prophet Zechariah. *Dorotheus* maintains that he was buried in a place called Bethariah, one hundred and fifty furlongs from Jerusalem.

Zechariah is the longest and the most obscure of all the twelve minor prophets. His style is interrupted, and without connection. His prophecies concerning the Messiah are more particular and express than those of the other prophets. Some modern critics, as *Mede* and *Hammond*, have been of opinion that the *ninth*, *tenth*, and *eleventh* chapters of this prophet were written by Jeremiah; because in Matthew, chap. xxvii. 9, 10, under the name of Jeremiah, we find quoted Zechariah; (chap. xi. 12;) and as the aforesaid chapters make but one continued discourse, they concluded from thence that all three belonged to Jeremiah. But it is much more natural to suppose that, by some unlucky mistake, the name of Jeremiah has slipped into the text of St. Matthew instead of that of Zechariah.

The prophet Zechariah exactly foretold the siege of Babylon by Darius, son of Hystaspes. This prince laid siege to that rebellious city at the beginning of the *fifth* year of his reign, and reduced it at the end of *twenty* months. The prophets Isaiah and Jeremiah had foretold this calamity, and had admonished the Jews, that inhabited there to make their escape when they perceived the time draw nigh. Isaiah says to them, "Go ye forth to Babylon, flee from the Chaldeans; with a voice of singing declare ye, tell this, utter it even to the end of the earth; say ye, The Lord hath redeemed his servant Jacob." And Jeremiah says, "Remove out of the midst of Babylon, and go forth out of the land of the Chaldeans, and be as the he-goats before the flocks." And elsewhere, "Flee out of the midst of Babylon, and deliver every man his soul; be not cut off in her iniquity: for this is the time of the Lord's vengeance, He will render unto her a recompense." Lastly, Zechariah, a little before the time of her fall, writes thus to the Jews that were still in this city: "Ho, ho, come forth, and flee from the land of the north, saith the Lord; for I have spread you abroad as the four winds of heaven, saith the Lord. Deliver thyself, O Zion, that dwellest with the daughter of Babylon. For thus saith the Lord of hosts, after the glory hath he sent me unto the nations which spoiled you, for he that toucheth you, toucheth the apple of his eye. For, behold, I will shake mine hand upon them, and they shall be a spoil to their servants; and ye shall know that the Lord of hosts hath sent me."

It is probable that the Jews took advantage of these admonitions, and returned from Babylon into their country; or, at least, withdrew into a place of more security till the city was taken. We do not hear, either from the history or the prophecies, that they suffered any thing by this siege, or that Darius, son of Hystaspes, bore them any grudge for the revolt of Babylon; which seems to indicate that they had no part in it.

The Mohammedans do not distinguish between the prophet Zechariah, and Zachariah the father of John the Baptist. Some of them make him to be descended from David; and others, from Levi. By an anachronism that is still more insupportable, these confound Mary, the mother of Jesus Christ, with Mary or Miriam, the sister of Moses, which they derive even from the Koran itself.

The author of Tarik Montekhib relates that, when Jesus Christ was born of the virgin, the prophet Zechariah could not believe that a child could be born without a father; and that, declaring his sentiments upon this point, the Jews entertained a suspicion of him, and obliged him to betake himself to flight. He withdrew; and hid himself in a hollow oak, which the Jews sawed in two.

Such is the ignorance of the Mussulmans as regards the history both of the Old and New Testaments.

THE BOOK
OF THE
PROPHET ZECHARIAH

Chronological Notes relative to this Book

Year from the Creation, according to Archbishop Usher, 3484.—Year of the Julian Period, 4194.—Year of the Jewish era of the world, 3241.—Year from the Flood, 1828.—Year from the vocation of Abram, 1401.—Year since the first celebration of the Olympic games in Elis, by the Idæi Dactyli, 934.—Year since the destruction of Troy, according to the general account, 664.—Year since the foundation of the monarchy of the Israelites by the Divine appointment of Saul to the regal dignity, 576.—Year from the foundation of Solomon's temple, 492.—Year from the division of Solomon's monarchy into the kingdoms of Israel and Judah, 456.—Year since the re-establishment of the Olympic games in Elis by Lycurgus, Iphitus, and Cleosthenes, 365.—Year since the conquest of Corœbus at Olympia, usually called the first Olympiad, 257.—First year of the *sixty-fifth* Olympiad.—Year from the building of Rome, according to the Varronian or generally received computation, 234.—Year from the building of Rome, according to Cato and the Fasti Consulares, 233.—Year from the building of Rome, according to Polybius the historian, 232.—Year from the building of Rome, according to Fabius Pictor, 228.—Year of the era of Nabonassar, 228.—Year since the destruction of the kingdom of Israel by Shalmaneser, king of Assyria, 202.—Year since the destruction of the kingdom of Judah by Nebuchadnezzar, king of Babylon, 68.—Year since the destruction of the Chaldean empire by the Persians, 18.—Year before the birth of Christ, 516.—Year before the vulgar era of Christ's nativity, 520.—Cycle of the Sun, 22.—Cycle of the Moon, 14.—Second year of Darius I., king of Persia.—Twenty-eighth year of Amyntas, king of Macedon.—Seventh year of Demaratus, king of Lacedæmon, of the family of the Proclidæ.—Eleventh year of Cleomenes, king of Lacedæmon, of the family of the Eurysthenidæ.—Fifteenth year of Tarquinius Superbus, the last king of the Romans.—This was about twelve years before the commencement of the consular government. According to some chronologers this was the age of Confucius.

CHAPTER I

The prophet earnestly exhorts the people to repentance, that they may escape such punishments as had been inflicted on their fathers, 1–6. *The vision of the* horses, *with the signification,* 7–11. *The angel of the Lord successfully intercedes in behalf of Jerusalem,* 12–17. *The vision of the* four horns, *and of the* four carpenters, 18–21.

A. M. 3484
B. C. 520
Ol. LXV. 1
Anno Tarquinii Superbi,
R. Roman., 15

IN the eighth month, [a]in the second year of Darius, came the word of the LORD [b]unto Zechariah, the son of Berechiah, the son of Iddo the prophet, saying,

2 The LORD hath been [c]sore displeased with your fathers.

3 Therefore say thou unto them, Thus saith the LORD of hosts; Turn [d]ye unto me, saith the LORD of

A. M. 3484
B. C. 520
Ol. LXV. 1
Anno Tarquinii Superbi,
R. Roman., 15

---

[a]Ezra iv. 24; Hag. i. 1——[b]Ezra v. 1; Matt. xxiii. 35
[c]Heb. *with displeasure*

[d]Jer. xxv. 5; xxxv. 15; Mic. vii. 19; Mal. iii. 7; Luke xv. 20; James iv. 8

NOTES ON CHAP. I

Verse 1. *In the eighth month, in the second year of Darius*] This was *Darius Hystaspes;* and from this date we find that Zechariah began to prophecy just *two months* after *Haggai.*

Son of Iddo] There are a number of various readings on this name, עדו *Iddo*, and עדוא *Iddo*, both in MSS. and in editions; but they are only different ways of writing the same name.

Verse 2. *The Lord hath been sore displeased with your fathers.*] For their ingratitude, idolatry, iniquity, and general rebellion.

Verse 3. *Turn ye unto me*] This shows that they had *power* to return, if they would but *use* it.

A. M. 3484
B. C. 520
Ol. LXV. 1
Anno Tarquinii Superbi, R. Roman., 15

hosts, and I will turn unto you, saith the LORD of hosts.

4 Be ye not as your fathers, [e]unto whom the former prophets have cried, saying, Thus saith the LORD of hosts; [f]Turn ye now from your evil ways, and *from* your evil doings: but they did not hear, nor hearken unto me, saith the LORD.

5 Your fathers, where *are* they? and the prophets, do they live for ever?

6 But [g]my words and my statutes, which I commanded my servants the prophets, did they not [h]take hold of your fathers? and they returned and said, [i]Like as the LORD of hosts thought to do unto us, according to our ways, and according to our doings, so hath he dealt with us.

7 Upon the four and twentieth day of the eleventh month, which *is* the month Sebat, in the second year of Darius, came the word of the LORD unto Zechariah, the son of Berechiah, the son of Iddo the prophet, saying,

8 I saw by night, and behold [k]a man riding upon a red horse, and he stood among the myrtle trees that *were* in the bottom; and behind him *were there* [l]red horses, [m]speckled, and white.

A. M. 3484
B. C. 520
Ol. LXV. 1
Anno Tarquinii Superbi, R. Roman., 15

9 Then said I, O my lord, what *are* these? And the angel that talked with me said unto me, I will show thee what these *be*.

10 And the man that stood among the myrtle trees, answered and said, [n]These *are they* whom the LORD hath sent to walk to and fro through the earth.

11 [o]And they answered the angel of the LORD that stood among the myrtle trees, and said, We have walked to and fro through the earth, and, behold, all the earth sitteth still, and is at rest.

12 Then the angel of the LORD answered and said, [p]O LORD of hosts, how long wilt thou not have mercy on Jerusalem, and on the cities of Judah, against which thou hast had indignation [q]these threescore and ten years?

[e]2 Chron. xxxvi. 15, 16——[f]Isa. xxxi. 6; Jer. iii. 12; xviii. 11; Ezek. xviii. 30; Hos. xiv. 1——[g]Isa. lv. 1——[h]Or, *overtake*——[i]Lam. i. 18; ii. 17

[k]Josh. v. 13; Rev. vi. 4——[l]Chap. vi. 2–7——[m]Or, *bay*——[n]Heb. i. 14——[o]Psa. ciii. 20, 21——[p]Psa. cii. 13; Rev. vi. 10——[q]Jer. xxv. 11, 12; Dan. ix. 2; ch. vii. 5

And I will turn unto you] I will show you mercy and grant you salvation, if you will *use the grace I have already given you.* Men are *lost*, because they *turn not* unto God; but no man is lost because he had not *power* to return. God gives this, and he will require it.

Verse 5. *Your fathers, where* are *they?*] *Israel* has been destroyed and ruined in the bloody wars with the *Assyrians;* and *Judah*, in those with the *Chaldeans.*

The prophets, do they live for ever?] They also, who spoke unto your fathers, are dead; but their *predictions* remain; and the *events*, which have taken place according to those predictions, prove that God sent them.

Verse 6. *Did they not take hold of your fathers?*] Every thing happened according to the predictions, and they were obliged to acknowledge this; and yet they would not turn from their evil way.

Verse 7. *Upon the four and twentieth day of the eleventh month*] This revelation was given about *three months* after the former, and *two months* after they had recommenced the building of the temple.

Sebat] Answers to a part of our February. See Hag. ii. 18.

Verse 8. *I saw by night*] The time was emblematical of the affliction under which the Jews groaned.

A man] An angel in the form of a man: supposed to have been the *Lord Jesus;* who seems to have appeared often in this way, as a prelude to his incarnation; see Josh. v. 13; Ezek. i. 26; Dan. vii. 13, and x. 5. The same, probably, that appeared to Joshua with a drawn sword, as the *captain of the Lord's host.* Josh. v. 13-15.

A red horse] An emblem of war and bloodshed.

Among the myrtle trees] This tree was an emblem of *peace;* intimating that all war was shortly to end. But some think these trees are emblematical of the true followers of Christ.

And behind him were there *red horses*] Probably pointing out the *different orders* of angels in the heavenly host, which are employed by Christ in the defence of his Church. The different *colours* may point out the *gradations* in power, authority, and excellence, of the angelic natures which are employed between Christ and men.

Verse 9. *O my lord, what* are *these*] The angel here mentioned was distinct from those mentioned in the *eighth* verse; he who talked with the prophet, ver. 13.

Verse 10. *The man that stood among the myrtle trees*] The angel of the Covenant, as above, ver. 11.

Whom the Lord hath sent] Who are constituted guardians of the land.

Verse 11. *All the earth sitteth still, and is at rest.*] There is general *peace* through the Persian empire, and other states connected with Judea; but the Jews are still in *affliction;* their city is not yet restored, nor their temple built.

Verse 12. *Then the angel of the Lord*] He who was among the myrtles—the Lord Jesus.

O Lord of hosts, how long] Jesus Christ was not only the "Lamb slain from the foundation of the world," but was always the sole *Mediator* and *intercessor* between God and man.

These threescore and ten years?] This cannot mean the duration of the captivity for that was nearly twenty years past. It must mean simply the time that had elapsed from the de-

A. M. 3484
B. C. 520
Ol. LXV. 1
Anno Tarquinii Superbi,
R. Roman., 15

13 And the LORD answered the angel that talked with me *with* [r]good words, *and* comfortable words.

14 So the angel that communed with me said unto me, Cry thou, saying, Thus saith the LORD of hosts; I am [s]jealous for Jerusalem and for Zion with a great jealousy.

15 And I am very sore displeased with the heathen *that are* at ease: for [t]I was but a little displeased, and they helped forward the affliction.

16 Therefore thus saith the LORD; [u]I am returned to Jerusalem with mercies: my house shall be built in it, saith the LORD of hosts, and [v]a line shall be stretched forth upon Jerusalem.

17 Cry yet, saying, Thus saith the Lord of hosts; My cities through [w]prosperity shall yet be spread abroad; [x]and the LORD shall yet comfort Zion, and [y]shall yet choose Jerusalem.

A. M. 3484
B. C. 520
Ol. LXV. 1
Anno Tarquinii Superbi,
R. Roman., 15

18 Then lifted I up mine eyes, and saw, and behold four horns.

19 And I said unto the angel that talked with me, What *be* these: And he answered me, [z]These *are* the horns which have scattered Judah, Israel, and Jerusalem.

20 And the LORD showed me four carpenters.

21 Then said I, What come these to do? And he spake, saying, These *are* the horns which have scattered Judah, so that no man did lift up his head: but these are come to fray them, to cast out the horns of the Gentiles, which [a]lifted up *their* horn over the land of Judah to scatter it.

[r]Jer. xxix. 10——[s]Joel viii. 18; ch. viii. 2——[t]Isa. xlvii. 6——[u]Isa. xii. 1; ch. ii. 10; viii. 3——[v]Ch. ii. 1, 2

[w]Heb. *good*——[x]Isa. li. 3——[y]Isa. xiv. 1; ch. ii. 12; iii. 2——[z]Ezra iv. 1, 4, 7; v. 3——[a]Psa. lxxv. 4, 5

struction of the temple to the time in which the angel spoke. As the temple was destroyed in the *nineteenth* year of Nebuchadnezzar, and this vision took place in the *second* year of Darius, the term of *seventy* years was completed, or nearly so, between these two periods.

Verse 13. *The Lord answered the angel*] And the angel told the prophet that the answer was gracious and comfortable. This answer is given in the next verse.

Verse 14. *I am jealous for Jerusalem*] I have for them a strong affection; and indignation against their enemies.

Verse 15. *I was but a little displeased*] I was justly displeased with my people, and I gave their enemies a commission against them; but they carried this far beyond my design by oppression and cruelty; and now they shall suffer in their turn.

Verse 16. *I am returned to Jerusalem with mercies*] Before, he came to them in *judgments;* and the principal mercy is, the house of the Lord shall be rebuilt, and the ordinances of the Lord re-established.

And a line shall be stretched forth] The circuit shall be determined, and the city built according to the *line* marked out.

Verse 17. *My cities—shall yet be spread abroad*] The whole land of Judea shall be inhabited, and the ruined cities restored.

Verse 18. *And behold four horns.*] Denoting *four powers* by which the Jews had been oppressed; the *Assyrians*, *Persians*, *Chaldeans*, and *Egyptians*. Or these enemies may be termed *four*, in reference to the *four cardinal points of the heavens*, whence they came:—

1. NORTH. The Assyrians and Babylonians.
2. EAST. The Moabites and Ammonites.
3. SOUTH. The Egyptians.
4. WEST. The Philistines. See *Martin*.

Verse 20. *Four carpenters.*] Four other *powers*, who should defeat the powers intended by the *horns*. These are the same as the *four chariots* mentioned chap. vi. 1, 2, 3, 6, 7. The *first* was NABOPOLASSAR, father of Nebuchadnezzar, who overturned the empire of the *Assyrians*. The *second* was CYRUS, who destroyed the empire of the *Chaldeans*. The *third* was ALEXANDER *the Great*, who destroyed the empire of the *Persians*. And the *fourth* was PTOLEMY, who rendered himself master of *Egypt*. Some of these had already been cast down; the rest were to follow. *Calmet* gives this interpretation, and vindicates it at length.

Verse 21. *These are come to fray them*] To break, pound, and reduce them to powder. *Fray*, from the French, *frayer*, to *rub*. חרשים *charashim* signifies either *carpenters* or *smiths;* probably the latter are here intended, who came with *hammers*, *files*, and such like, to destroy these *horns*, which no doubt seemed to be of *iron*.

From a sensible correspondent I have received the following note:—

"The word we translate *carpenters*, חרשים *charashim*, is a root which, according to Mr. *Parkhurst*, denotes *silent thought* or *attention;* and in *kal* and *hiphil*, to *contrive*, *devise secretly*, or *in silence;* hence applied as a noun to an *artificer* of any kind, and to any work which disposes to silent attention. Thus, to *potters' ware*, Lev. vi. 28; Job ii. 8; and in many other places. So also to *ploughing*, Deut. xxii. 10; Prov. xx. 4, which requires constant attention to make 'the right-lined furrow.' Let it be remembered that in ancient times *such works* were more esteemed than the useless ones we have learned to admire. So again, in Gen. xxiv. 21, and elsewhere, it implies *to be silent*, as in deep thought or great attention.

"Now it is evident that the purport of this vision is the same with the gracious declarations which precede it, viz., to express the return of the protecting mercies of God to his people, delivering them from their enemies. I should therefore be inclined to render חרשים

charashim here, *watchers* or *inspectors*, in the sense which our translators have rendered the *Chaldee* עיר *ir, a watcher*, in the *fourth* chapter of Daniel, ver. 13; understanding thereby 'spirits of the heavens, which go forth from standing before the Lord of all the earth,' Zech. vi. 5, and are described in the first vision as 'sent to walk to and fro through the earth.' This gives to the whole narrative a sublime and important sense, affording us some glimpse of the Divine government by the ministration of angels, such as Jacob was favoured with in his vision at Beth-el, and which our Saviour himself informed Nathanael constituted part of the glory of his mediatorial kingdom."

M. A. B.

CHAPTER II

The vision with which this chapter opens, portended great increase and prosperity to Jerusalem. Accordingly Josephus tells us, (Wars v. iv. 2,) *that "the city, overflowing with inhabitants, extended beyond its walls," as predicted in the* fourth *verse, and acquired much glory during the time of the Maccabees; although these promises, and particularly the sublime image in the* fifth *verse, has certainly a still more pointed reference to the glory and prosperity of the Christian Church in the latter days,* 1–5. *See* Rev. xxi., xxii. *In consequence of these promises, the Jews, still inhabiting Babylon and the regions round about, are called upon to hasten home, that they might not be involved in the fate of their enemies, who were destined to fall a prey to the nations which they had formerly subdued; God's great love and zeal for his people moving him to glorify them by humbling all their adversaries,* 6–9. *The most gracious promises of God's presence with his Church, and her consequent increase and prosperity, set forth in the remaining verses,* 10–13, *were to a certain extent fulfilled in the great number of proselytes made to Judaism after the return from the captivity; but shall be more fully accomplished after the restoration of the Jews to the favour of God under the Gospel. "For if the casting away of the natural Israel be the reconciling of the world, what shall the receiving of them be but life from the dead?"*

A. M. cir. 3485
B. C. cir. 519
Ol. cir. LXV. 2
Tarquinii Superbi, R. Rom., cir. annum 16

I LIFTED up mine eyes again,
and looked, and behold [a]a
man with a measuring-line in his
hand.
2 Then said I, Whither goest thou? And
he said unto me, [b]To measure Jerusalem, to
see what *is* the breadth thereof, and what *is*
the length thereof.
3 And, behold, the angel that talked with me
went forth, and another angel went out to
meet him,
4 And said unto him, Run, speak to this
young man, saying, [c]Jerusalem shall be inhabited *as* towns without walls for the
multitude of men and cattle
therein:
5 For I, saith the LORD, will
be unto her [d]a wall of fire
round about, [e]and will be the glory in the
midst of her.
6 Ho, ho, *come forth,* and flee [f]from the
land of the north, saith the LORD: for I have
[g]spread you abroad as the four winds of the
heaven, saith the LORD.
7 [h]Deliver thyself, O Zion, that dwellest
with the daughter of Babylon.
8 For thus saith the LORD of hosts; after
the glory hath he sent me unto the nations

A. M. cir. 3485
B. C. cir. 519
Ol. cir. LXV. 2
Tarquinii Superbi, R. Rom., cir. annum 16

---

[a]Ezekiel xl. 3——[b]Revelation xi. 1; xxi. 15, 16——[c]Jeremiah xxxi. 27; Ezekiel xxxvi. 10, 11——[d]Isaiah xxvi. 1; chap. ix. 8——[e]Isaiah lx. 19; Rev. xxi. 23

[f]Isaiah xlviii. 20; lii. 11; Jeremiah i. 14; l. 8; li. 6, 45——[g]Deuteronomy xxviii. 64; Ezekiel xvii. 21——[h]Revelation xviii. 4

NOTES ON CHAP II

Verse 1. *A man with a measuring-line in his hand.*] Probably a representation of *Nehemiah*, who got a commission from *Artaxerxes Longimanus* to build up the walls of Jerusalem; for hitherto it had remained without being enclosed.

Verse 4. *Run, speak to this young man*] Nehemiah must have been a *young man* when he was ساقي *sakee*, or cup-bearer, to Artaxerxes.

As *towns without walls*] It shall be so numerously inhabited as not to be contained within its ancient limits. *Josephus*, speaking of this time, says, WARS v. iv. 2, "The city, overflowing with inhabitants, by degrees extended itself beyond its walls."

Verse 5. *I—will be unto her a wall of fire*] Her safety shall consist in my defence. I shall be as *fire* round about her. No adversary shall be permitted to touch her. Much of this must refer to the *New Jerusalem.*

Verse 6. *Flee from the land of the north*] From Chaldee, Persia, and Babylon, where several of the Jews still remained. See ver. 7.

Verse 8. *After the glory*] After your *glorious deliverance* from the different places of your dispersion; *He hath sent me unto the nations which spoiled you*, that *they* may fall under grievous calamities, and be punished in their turn. On *Babylon* a great calamity fell, when besieged and taken by the *Persians.*

The following note I received from a sensible and pious correspondent:—

5. "For I, saith the Lord, will be unto her a wall of fire round about, and will be the glory in the midst of her.

8. "For thus saith the Lord of hosts, who hath sent *me, the future glory* (or the glory

A. M. cir. 3485
B. C. cir. 519
Ol. cir. LXV. 2
Tarquinii Superbi, R. Rom., cir. annum 16

which spoiled you: for he that
[l]toucheth you toucheth the apple
of his eye.
9 For behold, I will [k]shake
mine hand upon them, and they shall be a
spoil to their servants: and [l]ye shall know
that the LORD of hosts hath sent me.
10 [m]Sing and rejoice, O daughter of Zion:
for lo, I come, and I [n]will dwell in the midst
of thee, saith the LORD.
11 [o]And many nations shall be joined to
the LORD [p]in that day, and shall
be [q]my people: and I will dwell
in the midst of thee, and [r]thou
shalt know that the LORD of
hosts hath sent me unto thee.
12 And the LORD shall [s]inherit Judah his
portion in the holy land, and [t]shall choose
Jerusalem again.
13 [u]Be silent, O all flesh, before the LORD:
for he is raised up [v]out of [w]his holy habitation.

[i]Deut. xxxii. 10; Psa. xvii. 8; 2 Thess. i. 6——[k]Isa. xi. 15; xix. 16——[l]Chap. iv. 9——[m]Isa. xii. 6; liv. 1; Zeph. iii. 14——[n]Lev. xxvi. 12; Ezek. xxxvii. 27; chap. viii. 3; John i. 14; 2 Cor. vi. 16——[o]Isa. ii. 2, 3; xlix. 22; lx. 3, &c.; chap. viii. 22, 23

[p]Chap. iii. 10——[q]Exod. xii. 49——[r]Ezek. xxxiii. 33; ver. 9——[s]Deut. xxxii. 9——[t]Chap. i. 17——[u]Hab. ii. 20; Zeph. i. 7——[v]Psa. lxviii. 5; Isa. lvii. 15——[w]Heb. *the habitation of his holiness;* Deuteronomy xxvi. 15; Isa. lxiii. 15

which is to come) unto the nations which spoiled you; for he that toucheth you toucheth the apple of his eye. Behold, I will shake mine hand upon them, and they shall be a spoil to their servants; and ye shall know that the Lord of hosts hath sent *me.* Sing and rejoice, O daughter of Zion; for lo, *I come,* and I will dwell in the midst of thee, saith the Lord. And *many* nations shall be joined to the Lord in that day, and shall be *my* people; and I will dwell in the midst of thee, and thou shalt know that the Lord of hosts hath *sent me* unto thee. And the Lord shall inherit Judah his portion in the holy land, and shall choose Jerusalem again.

"*If* in the *eighth* verse אחר כבוד may be rendered the *future,* or the *glory that is to come,* it will harmonize with the context as a prophecy of the Messiah, whereas in our English translation the words *after the glory* are unintelligible. And so the *Seventy.*

"It is evident the person speaking is distinguished from the Lord of hosts, as being *sent by him;* yet this person sent is also called Jehovah; and the nations who shall be joined to Jehovah in that day are called *his people;* and *he* (the person sent) will dwell in the midst of *thee,* (i. e., Zion,) and shall inherit Judah his portion, &c.

"In confirmation of my view of the *eighth* verse, I think Exod. xxxiii. may be compared with it. Moses besought God that he would show him *his glory;* upon which it was said to him, "Whilst my glory passeth by,' I will put thee in a cleft of the rock, and will cover thee with my hand *whilst I pass by;* and I will take away my hand, and thou shalt see my אחר *achar.* Now as this was a fulfilment of Moses's request, who entreated to behold the glory, it follows that this אחר was the Divine glory, which *alone he was capable of seeing.*

"'No man hath seen God at any time, the only begotten Son, (the Lord Jesus Christ,) which is in the bosom of the Father, *he hath declared him.'"*

M. A. B.

Toucheth the apple of his eye.] בבבת עינו *bebabath eyno, the babet of his eye.* This is a remarkable expression. Any person, by looking into the eye of another, will see his own image perfectly expressed, though in extreme minature, in the pupil. Does our English word *babbet* or *baby* come from this? And does not the expression mean that the eye of God is ever *on* his follower, and that his person is ever impressed on the eye, the notice, attention, providence, and mercy of God?

Verse 9. *I will shake mine hand upon them*] I will *threaten* first, and then stretch out my hand of *judgment* against them.

A spoil to their servants] To those whom they had formerly *subjected* to their sway. As the *Babylonians* to the Medes and Persians; and so of the rest in the subversion of empires.

Verse 10. *I will dwell in the midst of thee, saith the Lord*] This must chiefly refer to the *Christian church,* in which God ever dwells by the power of his Spirit, as he *had* done by the symbol of his presence in the first Jewish temple.

Verse 11. *Many nations shall be joined to the Lord*] This most certainly belongs to the *Christian church.* No *nation* or *people* ever became converts to the Jewish religion; but *whole nations* have embraced the faith of our Lord Jesus Christ.

Verse 12. *The Lord shall inherit Judah his portion in the holy land*] This is a promise of the final restoration of the Jews, and that they should be God's portion in their *own land.*

Verse 13. *Be silent, O all flesh*] Let all the nations of the world be astonished at this. God will *arise,* and deliver this ancient people, and bring them into the glorious liberty of the sons of God.

CHAPTER III

While the Jews were rebuilding their temple, their adversaries endeavoured to stop the work, Ezra v. *This vision is therefore calculated to give them the strongest encouragement that God, after plucking them as brands out of the fire (or captivity of Babylon,) would not now give them up, but would continue to prosper and favour them; and that notwithstanding the interruptions they should meet with, the work should be finished under the gracious superintendence of Providence; and their high priest, clothed in his pontifical robes, would soon officiate in the holy of holies,* 1–7. *The subject is then, by an easy transition, applied to a much greater future deliverance and restoration, of which Joshua and his companions, delivered now, are declared to be figures or types; for that the Messiah or Branch, the great high priest typified by Joshua, would be manifested; and, like the principal stone represented in the vision, become the chief corner stone of his Church; that the all-seeing eye of God would constantly guard it; and that by his atonement he would procure for it peace and pardon,* 8–10.

A. M. cir. 3485
B. C. cir. 519
Ol. cir. LXV. 2
Tarquinii Superbi, R. Rom., cir. annum 16

AND he showed me [a]Joshua
the high priest standing before the angel of the LORD, and
[b]Satan [c]standing at his right
hand [d]to resist him.
2 And the LORD said unto Satan, [e]The
LORD rebuke thee, O Satan; even the LORD
that [f]hath chosen Jerusalem rebuke thee: [g]*is*
not this a brand plucked out of the fire?
3 Now Joshua was clothed with [h]filthy garments, and stood before the angel.
4 And he answered and spake unto those
that stood before him, saying,
Take away the filthy garments
from him. And unto him he
said, Behold, I have caused thine
iniquity to pass from thee, [i]and I will clothe
thee with change of raiment.
5 And I said, Let them set a fair [k]mitre upon
his head. So they set a fair mitre upon his
head, and clothed him with garments. And
the angel of the LORD stood by.
6 And the angel of the LORD protested unto
Joshua, saying,

A. M. cir. 3485
B. C. cir. 519
Ol. cir. LXV. 2
Tarquinii Superbi, R. Rom., cir. annum 16

[a]Hag. i. 1——[b]Psa. cix. 6; Rev. xii. 10——[c]That is, *an adversary*——[d]Heb. *to be his adversary*——[e]Jude 9——[f]Chap. i. 17; Rom. viii. 33

[g]Amos iv. 11; Rom. xi. 5; Jude 23——[h]Isa. lxiv. 6——[i]Isa. lxi. 10; Rev. xix. 8; Luke xv. 22——[k]Exod. xxix. 6; chap. vi. 11

NOTES ON CHAP. III

Verse 1. *And he showed me Joshua the high priest*] The Angel of the Lord is the *Messiah*, as we have seen before; Joshua, the high priest, may here represent the *whole Jewish people;* and *Satan*, the grand *accuser* of the brethren. What the subject of dispute was, we perhaps learn from Jude 9. Michael and Satan disputed *about the body of Moses.* This could not refer to the *natural body* of the Jewish lawgiver, which had been dead about *one thousand* years; it must therefore refer to that *body of laws* given to the Jews by Moses, for the breach of which Satan, who was their *tempter* to disobedience, now comes forward as their *accuser;* that, exciting the justice of God against them, they may be all brought to perdition. There is a *paronomasia* here:—

Satan standing at his right hand to resist him.] שטן Satan signifies an *adversary.* לשטנו *lesiteno*, to be his adversary, or accuser.

Verse 2. Is *not this a brand plucked out of the fire?*] The Jews were *nearly destroyed* because of their sins; a remnant of them is yet left, and God is determined to preserve them. He has had mercy upon them, and forgiven them their sins. Wouldst thou have them destroyed? It is God that hath justified them; who art *thou* that condemnest them? *The Lord rebuke thee!* God confound thee for what thou hast done, and for what thou desirest farther to do! It is evident that Jude 9 relates to this circumstance—the very same *phraseology* which occurs here. See the notes on Jude 9, where the subject is largely considered. With difficulty has this remnant escaped, and God will not permit fresh evils to fall upon them, by which they might be totally consumed. This was Satan's design, who accuses the followers of God day and night. See Rev. xii. 10.

Verse 3. *Joshua was clothed with filthy garments*] The Jewish people were in a most forlorn, destitute, and to all human appearance despicable, condition; and besides all, they were sinful, and the priesthood defiled by idolatry; and nothing but the mercy of God could save them.

Verse 4. *Take away the filthy garments*] The Jews wore *sackcloth* in times of public calamity; probably the *filthy garments* refer to this. Let their clothing be changed. I have turned again their captivity; I will fully restore them, and blot out all their iniquities.

Verse 5. *A fair mitre upon his head*] To signify that he had renewed to him the office of the *high priesthood*, which had been defiled and profaned before. The *mitre* was the *bonnet* which the high priest put on his head when he entered into the sanctuary, Exod. xxviii. 4, &c.

Clothed him with garments] Referring to the vestments of the high priest. The true high priest, who is over the house of God, will establish his office among them, when they shall acknowledge him as their *Messiah*, and seek redemption in the blood of the sacrifice which he has offered for their sins; and not for theirs only, but for the sins of the whole world.

A. M. cir. 3485
B. C. cir. 519
Ol. cir. LXV. 2
Tarquinii Superbi, R. Rom., cir. annum 16

7 Thus saith the LORD of hosts; If thou wilt walk in my ways, and if thou wilt [l]keep my [m]charge, then thou shalt also [n]judge my house, and shalt also keep my courts, and I will give thee [o]places to walk among these that [p]stand by.

8 Hear now, O Joshua the high priest, thou and thy fellows that sit before thee: for they *are* [q]men [r]wondered at: for behold, I will bring forth [s]my servant The [t]BRANCH.

9 For behold the stone that I have laid before Joshua; [u]upon one stone *shall be* [v]seven eyes: behold, I will engrave the graving thereof, saith the LORD of hosts, and [w]I will remove the iniquity of that land in one day.

10 [x]In that day, saith the LORD of hosts, shall ye call every man his neighbour [y]under the vine and under the fig tree.

[l]Lev. viii. 35; 1 Kings ii. 3; Ezek. xliv. 16——[m]Or, *ordinance*——[n]Deut. xvii. 9; Mal. ii. 7——[o]Heb. *walks* ——[p]Chap. iv. 14; vi. 5——[q]Psa. lxxi. 7; Isa. viii. 18; xx. 3 ——[r]Heb. *men of wonder*, or *sign*, as Ezek. xii. 11; xxiv. 24 ——[s]Isa. xlii. 1; xlix. 3, 5; lii. 13; liii. 11; Ezek. xxxiv. 23, 24 ——[t]Isa. iv. 2; xi. 1; Jer. xxiii. 5; xxxiii. 15; chap. vi. 12; Luke i. 78——[u]Psa. cxviii. 22; Isa. xxviii. 16——[v]Chap. iv. 10; Rev. v. 6——[w]Jer. xxxi. 34; l. 20; Mic. vii. 18, 19; chap. xiii. 1——[x]Chap. ii. 11; Isa. ii. 11; xxvi. 1; xxix. 28; lii. 6——[y]1 Kings iv. 25; Isa. xxxvi. 16; Mic. iv. 4

Verse 7. *If thou wilt walk in my ways*] If ye, Israelites, priests and people, now restored to your own land, will walk in my ways, &c., ye shall be a part of my family; and have *places*—mansions—in eternal glory, with all them that are sanctified.

Verse 8. *O Joshua—thou, and thy fellows*] Thy *countrymen*, who have now returned from your captivity, in a very *wonderful* manner. אנשי מופת *anshey mopheth, figurative men*, men whose office and ministration *prefigured* the Lord Jesus Christ; and therefore it is immediately added, "I will bring forth my servant The BRANCH." Abp. *Newcome* thinks this means *Zerubbabel*, so called because he was the grandson of Jehoiakim, or Jeconiah, king of Judah, Matt. i. 12, and heir to the throne of Judah. The *Chaldee* has, "My servant the Messiah." See the note on Isa. iv. 2. I think the word cannot apply to Zerubbabel, except as a *type* of Christ; in that sense it may be understood of him. See chap. vi. 11, 12.

Verse 9. *For behold the stone that I have laid*] Alluding no doubt to the *foundation stone* of the temple: but this represented *Christ Jesus:* "Behold, I lay in Zion for a foundation a STONE, a tried stone, a precious CORNER STONE, a SURE FOUNDATION," Isa. xxviii. 16. This means Christ, and none other; on him his whole Church rests, as a building does on its foundation.

Upon one stone shall be *seven eyes*] This is supposed to mean the *providence* of God, as under it all the work should be completed. There may be an allusion to the *seven counsellors*, which stood always about the persons of the Asiatics sovereigns; and those who were the governors of provinces were termed the *eyes of the king*. To this there is an allusion in Rev. i. 4. In Christ there is a plentitude of *wisdom, power, goodness, mercy, truth, love*, and *compassion*, to *direct, protect, save, uphold, purify, govern*, and *preserve* all the souls that trust in him.

I will engrave the graving thereof] This is an allusion to *engraving precious stones*, in which the ancients greatly excelled. *Heads, animals*, and *various devices* were the subjects of those engravings. But what was *this* engraving? Was it not the following words? I will remove the iniquity of that land in one day;" and was not this when Jesus Christ *expired upon the cross?* This was the grand, the only atonement, satisfaction, and sacrifice for the sins of the whole world. Does not our Lord refer to this place, John vi. 27? *Him hath God the Father sealed;* and on the inscription there was, "This is my beloved Son, in whom I am well pleased." See the note on the above passage.

Verse 10. *Shall ye call every man his neighbour*] See on Isa. xxxvi. 16. Every one shall be inviting and encouraging another to believe on the Lord Jesus Christ; and thus taste and see that God is good. See on Isaiah ii. 2, 3. And there shall be the utmost liberty to preach, believe on, and profess the faith of our Lord Jesus Christ.

CHAPTER IV

The prophet, overpowered by his last vision, is roused by the angel to behold another, 1; *intended also to assure the Jews of the success of Joshua and Zerubbabel in building the temple, and surmounting every obstacle in the way; till at length, by the good providence of God, it should be finished, amidst the joyful acclamations of the spectators*, 2–10. *The angel's explanation of the* golden candlestick, and *of the* two olive trees, 11–14.

A. M. cir. 3485
B. C. cir. 519
Ol. cir. LXV. 2
Tarquinii Superbi, R. Rom.,
cir. annum 16

AND [a]the angel that talked
with me came again, and
waked me, [b]as a man that is
wakened out of his sleep,
2 And said unto me, What seest thou? And
I said, I have looked, and behold [c]a candlestick all *of* gold, [d]with a bowl upon the top
of it, [e]and his seven lamps thereon, and
[f]seven pipes to the seven lamps, which *are*
upon the top thereof.
3 [g]And two olive trees by it, one upon the
right *side* of the bowl, and the other upon the
left *side* thereof.
4 So I answered and spake to the angel that
talked with me, saying, What *are* these, my
lord?
5 Then the angel that talked with me answered and said unto me, Knowest thou not
what these be? And I said, No,
my lord.
6 Then he answered and spake
unto me, saying, This *is* the word
of the LORD unto Zerubbabel, saying, [h]Not
by [i]might, nor by power, but by my Spirit,
saith the LORD of hosts.
7 Who *art* thou, [k]O great mountain? before
Zerubbabel *thou shalt become* a plain: and
he shall bring forth [l]the headstone *thereof*
[m]*with* shoutings, *crying,* Grace, grace, unto it.
8 Moreover, the word of the LORD came
unto me, saying,
9 The hands of Zerubbabel [n]have laid the
foundation of this house; his hands [o]shall also
finish it; and [p]thou shalt know that the
[q]LORD of hosts hath sent me unto you.
10 For who hath despised the day of [r]small

A. M. cir. 3485
B. C. cir. 519
Ol. cir. LXV. 2
Tarquinii Superbi, R. Rom.,
cir. annum 16

[a]Chap. ii. 3——[b]Dan. viii. 18——[c]Exod. xxv. 31; Rev. i. 12——[d]Heb. *with her bowl*——[e]Exod. xxv. 37; Rev. iv. 5——[f]Or, *seven several pipes to the lamps*, &c. [g]Ver. 11, 12; Rev. xi. 4

[h]Hos. i. 7——[i]Or, *army*——[k]Jer. li. 25; Matt. xxi. 21 [l]Psa. cxviii. 22——[m]Ezra iii. 11, 13——[n]Ezra iii. 10 [o]Ezra vi. 15——[p]Chap. ii. 9, 11; vi. 15——[q]Isa. xlviii. 15; chap. ii. 8——[r]Hag. ii. 3

NOTES ON CHAP. IV

Verse 1. *The angel—came again, and waked me*] Abp. *Newcome* considers this vision as represented on the same night, chap. i. 8, with the preceding ones. See the latter part of ver. 10, compared with chap. iii. 9. After some interval the prophet, overpowered with the vision which had been presented to him, was awakened from his prophetic trance as from a sleep.

Verse 2. *A candlestick all* of *gold*] This candlestick is formed in some measure after that of the *sanctuary*, Exod. xxv. 31, 32: but in that of the sanctuary there was no *bowl*, nor *seven pipes*, nor *seven lamps*, nor the *two olive trees*. The *two olive trees* were to supply the *bowl* with *oil;* the *bowl* was to communicate the oil to the *seven pipes;* and the *seven pipes* were to supply the *seven lamps*. In general, the *candlestick*, its *bowl*, *pipes*, *lamps*, and *olive trees*, are emblems of the pure service of God, and the grace and salvation to be enjoyed by his true worshippers. The *candlestick* may, however, represent the whole *Jewish state, ecclesiastical* and *civil;* the *oil*, producing the *light*, the *grace* and *mercy* of God; and the *two olive trees*, the source of *infinite* love, whence that grace proceeds. The *pipes* may signify all *means of grace;* and the *seven lamps*, the perfection and abundance of the *light* and salvation provided. Some may take them in the following way:—1. The *olive trees*, the Divine goodness, yield the *oil* from the *olive berry*, which is its fruit. 2. From each comes a pipe to convey the oil to the bowl. 3. This *oil* is collected in the *bowl*, which is supposed to represent Jesus, the great Mediator, through whom alone all grace and mercy descend to man. 4. The *seven pipes*, the various means of grace—reading, hearing, prayer, sacraments, &c.—through which Christ dispenses his grace and blessing to his followers. 5. The *seven lamps*—the Spirit of God in its plentitude of graces, gifts, and light, dispensed to the Christian Church.

Verse 6. *This* is *the word of the Lord unto Zerubbabel*] This prince was in a trying situation, and he needed especial encouragement from God; and here it is:

Not by might, (of thy own,) *nor by power*, (authority from others,) *but by my Spirit*—the providence, authority, power, and energy of the Most High. In this way shall my temple be built; in this way shall my Church be raised and preserved. No secular arm, no human prudence, no earthly policy, no suits at law, shall ever be used for the founding, extension, and preservation of my Church. But the spirit of the world says, "These are all *means* to which we must have recourse; otherwise the cause of God may be ruined." Satan, thou liest!

Verse 7. *O great mountain?*] The hinderances which were thrown in the way; the regal prohibition to discontinue the building of the temple.

Before Zerubbabel—a plain] The sovereign power of God shall remove them. March on, Zerubbabel; all shall be made plain and smooth before thee. I have given thee the work to do, and I will remove all hinderances out of thy way.

He shall bring forth the headstone] As he has laid the *foundation stone*, so shall he put on the headstone: as he has *begun* the building, so shall he *finish* it!

With *shoutings*] The universal acclamation of the people.

Grace, grace unto it.] How beautiful is this structure! May the favour of God ever rest upon it, and be manifested in it!

Verse 10. *Who hath despised the day of small things?*] The poverty, weakness, and un-

A. M. cir. 3485
B. C. cir. 519
Ol. cir. LXV. 2
Tarquinii Superbi, R. Rom., cir. annum 16

things? [s]for they shall rejoice, and
shall see the [t]plummet in the hand
of Zerubbabel *with* those seven;
[u]they *are* the eyes of the LORD,
which run to and fro through the whole earth.
11 Then answered I, and said unto him,
What *are* these [v]two olive trees upon the
right *side* of the candlestick, and upon the left
side thereof?
12 And I answered again, and said unto him,
What *be these* two olive branches
which, [w]through the two golden
pipes, [x]empty [y]the golden *oil* out
of themselves?
13 And he answered me and said, Knowest
thou not what these *be?* And I said, No, my
lord.
14 Then said he, [z]These *are* the two
[a]anointed ones, [b]that stand by [c]the LORD of
the whole earth.

[s]Or, *since the seven eyes of the LORD shall rejoice*——[t]Heb. *stone of tin*——[u]2 Chron. xvi. 9; Prov. xv. 3; chap. iii. 9——[v]Ver. 3——[w]Heb. *by the hand*——[x]Or, *empty out of themselves* oil into *the gold*——[y]Heb. *the gold*——[z]Rev. xi. 4——[a]Heb. *sons of oil*——[b]Chap. iii. 7; Luke i. 19; [c]See Josh. iii. 11, 13; chap. vi. 5

befriended state of the Jews. It was said, "What do these feeble Jews?" "Will they build," &c.? No. But God will build by them, and perfect his building too.

And shall see the plummet in the hand of Zerubbabel] He is *master builder* under God, the *grand architect.*

Those seven—are *the eyes of the Lord*] Either referring to his particular and especial *providence;* or to those *ministering spirits,* whom he has employed in behalf of the Jews, to dispense the blessings of that providence. See the reading in the *margin.*

Verse 11. *What* are *these two olive trees*] See on ver. 2.

Verse 12. *What* be *these two olive branches*] That is, two *boughs* laden with *branches of olive berries.*

Verse 14. *These* are *the two anointed ones*] Joshua, the high priest; and Zerubbabel the governor. These are *anointed*—appointed by the Lord; and *stand by him,* the one to minister in the *ecclesiastical,* the other in the *civil* state.

Probably we may not be able to comprehend the whole of this hieroglyphical vision; for even the interpreting angel does not choose to answer the questions relative to this, which were put to him by the prophet. See ver. 4 and 11. But though the *particulars* are hard to be understood; yet the general meaning has, I hope, been given.

CHAPTER V

The vision of the large flying roll, with the angel's explanation, 1–4. *The vision of the ephah, and of the woman sitting on it, with the signification,* 5–11.

A. M. cir. 3485
B. C. cir. 519
Ol. cir. LXV. 2
Tarquinii Superbi, R. Rom., cir. annum 16

THEN I turned, and lifted up
mine eyes, and looked, and
behold a flying [a]roll.
2 And he said unto me, What
seest thou? And I answered, I see a flying
roll; the length thereof *is* twenty cubits, and
the breadth thereof ten cubits.
3 Then said he unto me, This *is* the [b]curse
that goeth forth over the face of the whole
earth: for [c]every one that stealeth shall be
cut off *as* on this side, according
it; and every one that sweareth
shall be cut off *as* on that side,
according to it.
4 I will bring it forth, saith the LORD of
hosts, and it shall enter into the house of the
thief, and into the house of [d]him that sweareth
falsely by my name: and it shall remain in the
midst of his house, and [e]shall consume it, with
the timber thereof, and the stones thereof.

[a]Ezek. ii. 9——[b]Mal. iv. 6——[c]Or, *every one of this* people *that stealeth holdeth* himself *guiltless, as it* doth——[d]Lev. xix. 12; chapter viii. 17; Mal. iii. 5——[e]See Lev. xiv. 45

NOTES ON CHAP. V

Verse 1. *Behold a flying roll.*] This was *twenty cubits long,* and *ten cubits broad;* the prophet saw it expanded, and *flying.* Itself was the catalogue of the crimes of the people, and the punishment threatened by the Lord. Some think the crimes were those of the *Jews;* others, those of the *Chaldeans.* The *roll* is mentioned in allusion to those large rolls on which the Jews write the *Pentateuch.* One now lying before me is one hundred and fifty-three feet long, by twenty-one inches wide, written on fine brown Basle goat-skin; some time since brought from Jerusalem, supposed to be four hundred years old.

Verse 3. *Every one that stealeth—and every one that sweareth*] It seems that the roll was written both on the front and back: *stealing* and *swearing* are supposed to be two general heads of crimes; the former, comprising sins against men; the latter, sins against God. It is supposed that the roll contained the sins and punishments of the Chaldeans.

Verse 4. *Into the house of him*] Babylon, the house or city of Nebuchadnezzar, who was

A. M. cir. 3485 B. C. cir. 519 Ol. cir. LXV. 2 Tarquinii Superbi, R. Rom., cir. annum 16

5 Then the angel that talked
with me went forth, and said unto
me, Lift up now thine eyes, and
see what *is* this that goeth forth.
6 And I said, What *is* it? And he said,
This *is* an ephah that goeth forth. He said
moreover, This *is* their resemblance through
all the earth.
7 And, behold, there was lifted up a [f]talent
of lead; and this *is* a woman that sitteth in
the midst of the ephah.
8 And he said, This *is* wickedness. And
he cast it into the midst of the ephah; and he
cast the weight of lead upon the
mouth thereof.
9 Then lifted I up mine eyes,
and looked, and, behold, there
came out two women, and the wind *was* in
their wings; for they had wings like the wings
of a stork: and they lifted up the ephah between the earth and the heaven.
10 Then said I to the angel that talked with
me, Whither do these bear the ephah?
11 And he said unto me, [g]To build it a
house in [h]the land of Shinar: and it shall be
established, and set there upon her own base.

[f]Or, *weighty piece*

[g]Jer. xxix. 5, 28——[h]Gen. x. 10

a public *plunderer*, and a most glaring *idolater*.

Verse 6. *This* is *an ephah that goeth forth.*] This, among the Jews, was the ordinary measure of grain. The *woman* in the *ephah* is supposed to represent *Judea*, which shall be visited for its sins; the *talent of lead* on the *ephah*, within which the woman was enclosed, the *wrath* of God, bending down this culprit nation, in the measure of its sins; for the angel said, "This is wickedness;" that is, the *woman* represents the *mass of iniquity* of this nation.

Verse 9. *There came out two women*] As the *one woman* represented the *impiety* of the Jewish nation; so these *two* women who were to *carry the ephah*, in which the woman INIQUITY was shut up, under the *weight* of a *talent of lead*, may mean the desperate UNBELIEF of the Jews in rejecting the Messiah; and that IMPIETY, or universal *corruption* of manners, which was the consequence of their *unbelief*, and brought down the wrath of God upon them. The strong *wings*, like those of *a stork*, may point out the *power* and *swiftness* with which Judea was carried on to fill up the *measure* of her iniquity, and to meet the punishment which she deserved.

Between the earth and the heaven.] Sins against GOD and MAN; sins which *heaven* and *earth* contemplated with *horror*.

Or the *Babylonians* and *Romans* may be intended by the *two women* who carried the Jewish ephah to its final punishment. The *Chaldeans* ruined Judea *before* the advent of our Lord; the *Romans*, shortly *after*.

Verse 11. *To build it a house in the land of Shinar*] The land of *Shinar* means *Babylon*; and *Babylon* means *Rome*, in the Apocalypse. The *building the house* for the woman imprisoned in the ephah may signify, that there should be a *long captivity* under the *Romans*, as there was under that of *Shinar* or *Babylon*, by which *Rome* may here be represented. That *house* remains to the present day: the *Jewish woman* is still in the *ephah; it* is *set on its own base*—continues still as a *distinct nation;* and the *talent of lead*—God's displeasure—is still on the top. O Lord, save thy people, the remnant of Israel!

CHAPTER VI

The vision of the four chariots drawn by several sorts of horses, 1–8. *The other vision in this chapter may refer in its primary sense to the establishment of the civil and religious polity of the Jews under Joshua and Zerubbabel; but relates, in a fuller sense, to the Messiah, and to that spiritual kingdom of which he was to be both king and high priest. In him all these types and figures were verified; in him all the promises are* yea and amen, 9–15.

A. M. cir. 3485 B. C. cir. 519 Ol. cir. LXV. 2 Tarquinii Superbi, R. Rom., cir. annum 16

AND I turned, and lifted up
mine eyes, and looked, and
behold, there came four chariots
out from between two mountains;
and the mountains *were* mountains of brass.
2 In the first chariot *were* [a]red
horses; and in the second chariot
[b]black horses;
3 And in the third cha-
riot [c]white horses; and in the fourth

[a]Chap. i. 8; Rev. vi. 4

[b]Rev. vi. 5——[c]Rev. vi. 2

NOTES ON CHAP. VI

Verse 1. *There came four chariots*] Four monarchies or empires. This is supposed to mean the same with the vision of the *four horns*, in chap. i.

Mountains of brass.] The strong barriers of God's purposes, which restrained those powers within the times and limits appointed by Jehovah.

Verse 2. *In the first chariot* were *red horses*] The empire of the Chaldeans, which overthrew the empire of the *Assyrians.*

A. M. cir. 3485
B. C. cir. 519
Ol. cir. LXV. 2
Tarquinii Superbi, R. Rom., cir. annum 16

chariot grisled and [d]bay horses.
4 Then I answered [e]and said
unto the angel that talked with
me, What *are* these, my lord?
5 And the angel answered and said unto me,
[f]These *are* the four [g]spirits of the heavens,
which go forth from [h]standing before the
LORD of all the earth.
6 The black horses which *are* therein go
forth into [i]the north country; and the white
go forth after them; and the grisled go forth
toward the south country.
7 And the bay went forth, and sought to go,
that they might [k]walk to and fro through the
earth: and he said, Get you hence, walk
to and fro through the earth. So they
walked to and fro through the
earth.
8 Then cried he upon me, and
spake unto me, saying, Behold,
these that go toward the north country have
quieted my [l]spirit in the north country.
9 And the word of the LORD came unto me,
saying,
10 Take of *them of* the captivity, *even* of
Heldai, of Tobijah, and of Jedaiah, which are
come from Babylon, and come thou the same
day, and go into the house of Josiah the son
of Zephaniah;
11 Then take silver and gold, and make
[m]crowns, and set *them* upon the head
of Joshua the son of Josedech, the high
priest;

A. M. cir. 3485
B. C. cir. 519
Ol. cir. LXV. 2
Tarquinii Superbi, R. Rom., cir. annum 16

[d]Or, *strong*——[e]Chap. v. 10——[f]Psa. civ. 4; Heb. i. 7, 14——[g]Or, *winds*——[h]1 Kings xxii. 19; Dan. vii. 10; chap iv. 14; Luke i. 19

[i]Jer. i. 14——[k]Gen. xiii. 17; chap. i. 10——[l]Judg. viii. 3; Eccles. x. 4——[m]Exod. xxiii. 36; xxix. 6; Lev. viii. 9; chap. iii. 5

The second chariot black horses] The empire of the *Persians*, founded by *Cyrus*, which destroyed the empire of the *Chaldeans.*

Verse 3. *The third chariot white horses*] The empire of the *Greeks*, founded by *Alexander the Great*, which destroyed the empire of the *Persians.*

The fourth chariot grisled and bay horses.] That is *party-coloured horses;* or with horses, some *grisled* and some *bay*. The empire of the Romans or of the Greeks. The Greeks *divided* after the death of Alexander; one part pointing out the *Lagidæ*, who attacked and subdued *Egypt;* and the other, the *seleucidæ*, who subdued Syria under Seleucus.

Verse 5. *The four spirits of the heavens*] Ministers of God's wrath against the sinful nations of the world.

Verse 6. *The black horses*] This refers to the *second chariot;* of the *first* the angel makes no mention, because the empire designed by it had ceased to exist. *This had red horses*, to show the *cruelty* of the Chaldeans towards the Jews, and the *carnage* they committed in the land of Judea.

The black] *Cyrus*, at the head of the *Persians* and *Medes*, bringing devastation and death among the Chaldeans, called the *north* in many parts of Scripture.

The white] *Alexander*, who was *splendid* in his victories, and *mild* towards all that he conquered

The grisled] The *Lagidæ* or *Ptolemies*, who founded an empire in Egypt; of these some were *good*, some *bad*, some *despotic*, some *moderate*, some *cruel*, and some *mild;* represented by the *party-coloured horses.*

Verse 7. *And the bay went forth*] The *Seleucidæ*, who conquered Syria and the upper provinces, and who wished to extend their conquests, and "sought to go, that they might walk to and fro throughout the earth," were of unbounded ambition, and sought *universal empire;* such as *Antiochus the Great.* "So they walked to and fro," did extend their conquests; and harassed many countries by their vexatious and almost continual wars. Some think the *Romans* are meant, who carried their conquests hither and thither, just as the Divine providence permitted them.

Verse 8. *Have quieted my spirit in the north country.*] They have fulfilled my judgments on *Assyria* and *Chaldea*. Nabopolassar and Cyrus first, against the Assyrians and Chaldeans; and Alexander next, against the Persians. On this vision Abp. *Newcome* remarks:—

The *black horses* seem to denote the *Persian* empire; which, by subduing the *Chaldeans*, and being about to inflict a second heavy chastisement on *Babylon, quieted God's spirit* with respect to *Chaldea;* a country always spoken of as lying to the *north* of the Jews.

The *white horses* seem to be the Macedonian empire; which, like the Persian, overcame *Chaldea.*

The *spotted bay horses* seem to be the *Roman* empire. This description suits it because it was governed by *kings, consuls, dictators*, and *emperors.* It penetrated *southward* to Egypt and Africa. The Roman empire is mentioned twice, ver. 6, 7, under each epithet given it, ver. 3.

Verse 10. *Take of* them of *the captivity*] The names that follow were probably those to whom the silver and golden vessels of the temple were intrusted; and who might have had *bullion* of silver and gold, for particular purposes, about the ornaments of the temple.

The house of Josiah] Probably an artificer in silver, gold, &c.

Verse 11. *Make crowns*] עטרות *ataroth;* but *seven* MSS. of *Kennicott's* and *De Rossi's*, and *one* ancient of my own, with the *Syriac* and *Chaldee*, have עטרת *atereth*, a *crown*, or *tiara.* And as *Joshua* the high priest is *alone* concerned here, I think *one crown* only is intended.

A. M. cir. 3485 B. C. cir. 519 Ol. cir. LXV. 2 Tarquinii Superbi, R. Rom., cir. annum 16

12 And speak unto him, saying, Thus speaketh the LORD of hosts, saying, Behold [n]the man whose name *is* The [o]BRANCH; and he shall [p]grow up out of his place, [q]and he shall build the temple of the LORD.

13 Even he shall build the temple of the LORD; and he [r]shall bear the glory, and shall sit and rule upon his throne; and [s]he shall be a priest upon his throne: and the counsel of peace shall be between them both.

14 And the crowns shall be to Helen, and to Tobijah, and to Jedaiah, and to Hen the son of Zephaniah, [t]for a memorial in the temple of the LORD.

15 And [u]they *that are* far off shall come and build in the temple of the LORD, and [v]ye shall know that the LORD of hosts hath sent me unto you. And *this* shall come to pass, if ye will diligently obey the voice of the LORD your God.

[n]See Luke i. 78; John i. 45——[o]Chap. iii. 8——[p]Or, *branch up from under him*——[q]Chap. iv. 9; Matt. xvi. 18; Eph. ii. 20, 21, 22; Heb. iii. 3

[r]Isa. xxii. 24——[s]Psa. cx. 4; Heb. iii. 1——[t]Exod. xii. 14; Mark xiv. 9——[u]Isa. lvii. 19; lx. 10; Eph. ii. 13, 19——[v]Chap. ii. 9; iv. 9

Verse 12. *Behold the man whose name* is *The BRANCH!*] I cannot think that *Zerubbabel* is here intended; indeed, he is not so much as mentioned in chap. iii. 8. *Joshua and his companions* are called אנשי מופת *anshey mopheth*, *figurative* or *typical men;* the crowning therefore of Joshua in this place, and calling him the BRANCH, was most probably in reference to that glorious person, the *Messiah*, of whom he was the *type* or *figure.* The *Chaldee* has, "whose name is my MESSIAH," or CHRIST.

And he shall grow up out of his place] That is, out of David's root, tribe, and family.

And he shall build the temple of the Lord.] This cannot refer to the building of the temple then in hand, for Zerubbabel was its builder: but to that temple, the Christian Church, that was typified by it; for Zerubbabel is not named here, and only *Joshua* or *Jesus* (the name is the same) is the person who is to be *crowned* and *to build this spiritual temple.*

Verse 13. *Even he shall build the temple*] *Joshua*, not *Zerubbabel.*

He shall bear the glory] Have all the honour of it; for none can do this but himself. The *Messiah* is still intended.

And shall sit and rule upon his throne] For the government of the Church shall be upon his shoulder.

And he shall be a priest upon his throne] He shall, as the great *high priest*, offer the only *available offering* and *atonement;* and so he shall be both *king* and *priest*, a *royal king* and a *royal priest;* for even the *priest* is here stated to *sit upon his throne.*

And the counsel of peace shall be between them both.] Whom? Zerubbabel and Joshua? Certainly not Zerubbabel, for he is not mentioned in all this prediction; but, as the *Messiah* is intended, the *counsel of peace*—the *purpose to establish peace* between heaven and earth, must be between the *Father* and the *Son.*

Verse 14. *And the crowns shall be*] One of my MSS. has אטרות *ataroth, crowns*, corrected into עטרת *atereth, crown;* and so the *Septuagint, Syriac*, and *Arabic.* The *Chaldee* has, "And praise shall be," &c. The meaning appears to be this, that the *crown* made for *Joshua* should be delivered to the persons mentioned here and in ver. 10, to be laid up in the temple of the Lord, as a *memorial* of this typical transaction.

Verse 15. *And they* that are *far off shall come*] The Gentiles shall come to the Saviour of the world; and *build*—become a part of this new temple; for they, as *living stones*, shall become a holy temple, a habitation of God through the Spirit.

Ye shall know that the Lord of hosts hath sent me] These predictions, relative to the *regal* and *sacerdotal offices* of the Messiah, shall be so circumstantially fulfilled, that ye, Jews, shall be obliged to acknowledge that the Lord of hosts hath sent me with this message.

And this *shall come to pass*] Your own temple shall be rebuilt, and God shall dwell among you now, *if ye will diligently obey the voice of Jehovah your God.*

CHAPTER VII

Some Jews being sent from those who remained at Babylon to inquire of the priests and prophets at Jerusalem whether they were still bound to observe those fasts which had been appointed on occasion of the destruction of Jerusalem, and kept during the captivity, the prophet is commanded to take this opportunity of enforcing upon them the weightier matters of the law, judgment *and* mercy, *that they might not incur such calamities as befell their fathers. He also intimates that in their former fasts they had regarded themselves more than God; and that they had rested too much on the performance of external rites, although the former prophets had largely insisted on the superior excellence of moral duties,* 1–14.

A. M. 3486
B. C. 518
Ol. LXV. 3
Anno Tarquinii Superbi,
R. Roman., 17

AND it came to pass in the fourth year of king Darius, *that* the word of the LORD came unto Zechariah in the fourth *day* of the ninth month, *even in* Chisleu;

2 When they had sent unto the house of God Sherezer and Regem-melech, and their men, [a]to pray before the LORD,

3 *And* to [b]speak unto the priest which *were* in the house of the LORD of hosts, and to the prophets, saying, Should I weep in [c]the fifth month, separating myself, as I have done these so many years?

4 Then came the word of the LORD of hosts unto me, saying,

5 Speak unto all the people of the land, and to the priests, saying, When ye [d]fasted and mourned in the fifth [e]and seventh *month*, [f]even those seventy years, did ye at all fast [g]unto me, *even* to me?

6 And when ye did eat, and when ye did drink, [h]did not ye eat *for yourselves*, and drink *for yourselves?*

7 [i]*Should ye* not *hear* the words which the LORD hath cried [k]by the former prophets, when Jerusalem was inhabited and in prosperity, and the cities thereof round about her, when *men* inhabited [l]the south and the plain?

A. M. 3486
B. C. 518
Ol. LXV. 3
Anno Tarquinii Superbi,
R. Roman., 17

8 And the word of the LORD came unto Zechariah, saying,

9 Thus speaketh the LORD of hosts, saying, [m]Execute [n]true judgment, and show mercy and compassions every man to his brother:

10 And [o]oppress not the widow, nor the fatherless, the stranger, nor the poor, [p]and let none of you imagine evil against his brother in your heart.

11 But they refused to hearken, and [q]pulled [r]away the shoulder, and [s]stopped [t]their ears, that they should not hear.

12 Yea, they made their [u]hearts *as* an adamant stone, [v]lest they should hear the law, and the words which the LORD of hosts hath sent in his [w]Spirit by the former prophets:

[a]Heb. *to entreat the face of the LORD;* 1 Sam. xiii. 12; chap. viii. 21——[b]Deut. xvii. 9, 10, 11; xxxiii. 10; Mal. ii. 7——[c]Jer. lii. 12; chap. viii. 19——[d]Isa. lviii. 5——[e]Jer. iv. 1; chap. viii. 19——[f]Chap. i. 12 [g]See Rom. xiv. 6——[h]Or, be *not ye they that*, &c. [i]Or, Are *not* these *the words*——[k]Heb. *by the hand of*, &c.——[l]Jer. xvii. 26——[m]Isa. lviii. 6, 7; Jer. vii. 23; Mic. vi. 8; chap. viii. 16; Matt. xxiii. 23 [n]Heb *Judge judgment of truth*——[o]Exod. xxii. 21, 22; Deut. xxiv. 17; Isa. i. 17; Jer. v. 28——[p]Psa. xxxvi. 4; Mic. ii. 1; chap. viii. 17——[q]Neh. ix. 29; Jer. vii. 24; Hos. iv. 16——[r]Heb. *they gave a backsliding shoulder* [s]Heb. *made heavy*——[t]Acts vii. 57——[u]Ezek. xi. 19; xxxvi. 26——[v]Neh. ix. 29, 30——[w]Heb. *by the hand of*

NOTES ON CHAP. VII

Verse 1. *The fourth year of King Darius*] Two years after they began to rebuild the temple, see chap. i. 1, A. M. 3486.

The ninth month, even *in Chisleu*] This answers to a part of our *November* and *December*. The names of the month appear only under and after the captivity.

Verse 2. *When they had sent—Sherezer and Regem-melech*] To inquire whether the fasts should be continued, which they had hitherto observed on account of their ruined temple; and the reason why they inquired was, that they were rebuilding that temple, and were likely to bring it to a joyful issue.

Verse 5. *When ye fasted and mourned in the fifth*—month] This they did in the remembrance of the *burning of the temple*, on the *tenth* day of that month; and on the *seventh month*, on the *third* of which month they observed a fast for the murder of Gedaliah, and the dispersion of the remnant of the people which were with him. See Jer. xli. 1, and 2 Kings xxv. 25.

Verse 6. *And when ye did eat*] They had not observed those fasts as they should have done. They deplored the loss of their temple, and its riches, &c.; but they did not *humble themselves* because of those iniquities which had brought the *displeasure* of God upon them, their temple, and their city.

Verse 7. *The words which the Lord hath cried by the former prophets*] נביאים הראשנים *nebiim harishonim*, is the title which the Jews give to *Joshua*, *Judges*, the two books of *Samuel*, and the two books of *Kings*.

The *latter prophets*, נביאים אחרונים *nebiim acharonim*, are *Isaiah*, *Jeremiah*, *Ezekiel*, and the *twelve minor prophets*.

The *hagiographa*, כתובים *kethubim*, holy writings, are the *Psalms*, *Proverbs*, *Job*. *Canticles*, *Ruth*, *Lamentations*, *Ecclesiastes*, *Esther*, *Daniel*, *Ezra*, *Nehemiah*, and the two books of *Chronicles*. But the above words, *the former prophets*, seem to apply to *Isaiah*, *Jeremiah*, and *Ezekiel*.

The south and the plain?] From Eleutheropolis to the sea, Obad. 19. The *south* was the wilderness and mountainous parts of Judea: and the *plain*, the plains of Jericho.

Verse 9. *Execute true judgment*] See the parallel texts in the margin.

Verse 10. *Evil against his brother in your heart.*] Do not indulge an *unfavourable opinion* of another: do not *envy* him; do not *harbour* an *unbrotherly feeling* towards him.

Verse 11. *Pulled away the shoulder*] From under the yoke of the law, like an unbroken or restive bullock in the plough.

Verse 12. *Made their hearts* as *an adamant stone*] שמיר *shamir* may mean the *granite*. This is the hardest stone with which the common people could be acquainted. Perhaps the *cor-*

A. M. 3486
B. C. 518
Ol. LXV. 3
Anno Tarquinii Superbi, R. Roman., 17

[x]therefore came a great wrath
from the LORD of hosts.
13 Therefore it is come to
pass, *that* as he cried, and they
would not hear; so [y]they cried, and I would
not hear, saith the LORD of hosts.
14 But [z]I scattered them with
a whirlwind among all the nations
[a]whom they knew not. Thus
[b]the land was desolate after
them, that no man passed through nor returned:
for they laid [c]the [d]pleasant land desolate.

[x]2 Chron. xxxvi. 16; Dan. ix. 11——[y]Prov. i. 24–28; Isa. i. 15; Jer. xi. 11; xiv. 12; Mic. iii. 4——[z]Deut. iv. 27; xxviii. 64; Ezek. xxxvi. 19; ch. ii. 6——[a]Deut. xxviii. 33——[b]Lev. xxvi. 22——[c]Dan. viii. 9——[d]Heb. *land of desire*

undum, of which *emery* is a species, may be intended. *Bochart* thinks it means a stone used in *polishing* others. The same name, in Hebrew, applies to different stones.

Verse 14. *I scattered them with a whirlwind*] This refers to the swift victories and cruel conduct of the Chaldeans towards the Jews; they came upon them like a *whirlwind;* they were tossed to and fro, and up and down, everywhere scattered and confounded.

CHAPTER VIII

In this chapter God promises the continuance of his favour to those who are returned from the captivity; so that, upon the removal of his judgments, the fasts they had observed during the captivity may now be converted to so many occasions of rejoicing. He likewise promises in due time a general restoration of his people, and the enlargement of the Church by the accession of the Gentiles, 1–20. The conclusion of the chapter intimates farther that the Jews, after their restoration, will be instrumental in converting many other nations, 21–23. Compare Rom. xi. 15, 16.

A. M. 3486
B. C. 518
Ol. LXV. 3
Anno Tarquinii Superbi, R. Roman., 17

AGAIN the word of the LORD
of hosts came *to me,* saying,
2 Thus saith the LORD of hosts;
[a]I was jealous for Zion with
great jealousy, and I was jealous for her with
great fury.
3 Thus saith the LORD; [b]I am returned
unto Zion, and [c]will dwell in the midst of Jerusalem: and Jerusalem [d]shall be called A city
of truth: and [e]the mountain of the LORD of
hosts, [f]The holy mountain.
4 Thus saith the LORD of hosts; [g]There
shall yet old men and old women dwell in the
streets of Jerusalem, and every
man with his staff in his hand
[h]for very age.
5 And the streets of the city
shall be full of boys and girls playing in the
streets thereof.
6 Thus saith the LORD of hosts; If it be
[i]marvellous in the eyes of the remnant of this
people in these days, [k]should it also be marvellous in mine eyes? saith the LORD of hosts.
7 Thus saith the LORD of hosts; Behold, [l]I
will save my people from the east country, and
from [m]the west country;

[a]Neh. i. 2; chap. i. 14——[b]Chap. i. 16——[c]Chap. ii. 10——[d]Isa. i. 21, 26——[e]Isa. ii. 2, 3——[f]Jer. xxxi. 23——[g]See 1 Sam. ii. 31; Isa. lxv. 20, 22; Lam. ii. 20, &c.; v. 11–14——[h]Heb. *for multitude of days*——[i]Or, *hard,* or *difficult*——[k]Gen. xviii. 14; Luke i. 37; xviii. 27; Rom. iv. 21——[l]Isa. xi. 11, 12; xliii. 5, 6; Ezek. xxxvii. 21; Amos ix. 14, 15——[m]Heb. *the country of the going down of the sun;* See Psa. l. 1; cxiii. 3; Mal. i. 11

NOTES ON CHAP. VIII

Verse 2. *I was jealous*] Some refer this to the *Jews* themselves. They were as the *spouse* of Jehovah: but they were *unfaithful*, and God punished them as an *injured husband* might be expected to punish an unfaithful wife. Others apply it to the *enemies of the Jews.* Though I gave them a commission to afflict you, yet they exceeded their commission: I will therefore deal with them in *fury*—in *vindictive justice.*

Verse 3. *I am returned unto Zion*] I have restored her from her captivity. I will dwell among them. The temple shall be rebuilt, and so shall Jerusalem; and instead of being false, unholy, and profligate, it shall be *the city of truth,* and *my holy mountain.* TRUTH *shall dwell in it.*

Verse 4. *There shall yet old men and old women*] In those happy times the followers of God shall live out all their days, and the *hoary head* be always found in the way of righteousness.

Verse 5. *The streets of the city shall be full of boys and girls*] The progeny shall be *numerous, healthy,* and *happy.* Their innocent gambols and useful exercises shall be a means of *health*, and a proof of *happiness.* To be healthy, children must have exercise. But they cannot take exercise, except in the way of play and diversion: *ergo*, such playfulness cannot be sinful. Let them be kept from evil words, lying, swearing, and scurrility; and all the rest may be innocent.

Verse 6. *If it be marvellous*] You may think that this is impossible, considering your present low condition: but suppose it be impossible in *your eyes*, should it be *so* in *mine? saith the Lord of hosts.*

Verse 7. *I will save my people from the east*

A. M. 3486
B. C. 518
Ol. LXV. 3
Anno Tarquinii
Superbi,
R. Roman., 17

8 And I will bring them, and they shall dwell in the midst of Jerusalem: [n]and they shall be my people, and I will be their God, [o]in truth and in righteousness.

9 Thus saith the LORD of hosts; [p]Let your hands be strong, ye that hear in these days these words by the mouth of [q]the prophets, which *were* in [r]the day *that* the foundation of the house of the LORD of hosts was laid, that the temple might be built.

10 For before these days [s]there was no [t]hire for man, nor any hire for beasts; [u]neither *was there any* peace to him that went out or came in because of the affliction: for I set all men every one against his neighbour.

11 But now I *will* not *be* unto the residue of this people as in the former days, saith the LORD of hosts.

12 [v]For the seed *shall be* [w]prosperous; the vine shall give her fruit, and [x]the ground shall give her increase, and [y]the heavens shall give their dew; and I will cause the remnant of this people to possess all these *things*.

13 And it shall come to pass, *that* as ye were [z]a curse among the heathen, O house of Judah, and house of Israel; so will I save you, and [a]ye shall be a blessing: fear not, *but* [b]let your hands be strong.

A. M. 3486
B. C. 518
Ol. LXV. 3
Anno Tarquinii
Superbi,
R. Roman., 17

14 For thus saith the LORD of hosts; [c]As I thought to punish you, when your fathers provoked me to wrath, saith the LORD of hosts, [d]and I repented not:

15 So again have I thought in these days to do well unto Jerusalem and to the house of Judah: fear ye not.

16 These *are* the things that ye shall do; [e]Speak ye every man the truth to his neighbour; [f]execute the judgment of truth and peace in your gates:

17 [g]And let none of you imagine evil in your hearts against his neighbour; and [h]love no false oath: for all these *are things* that I hate, saith the LORD.

18 And the word of the LORD of hosts came unto me, saying,

19 Thus saith the LORD of hosts; [i]The fast of the fourth *month*, [k]and the fast of the fifth, [l]and the fast of the seventh, [m]and the fast of the tenth, shall be to the house of Judah [n]joy and gladness, and cheerful [o]feasts; [p]therefore love the truth and peace.

20 Thus saith the LORD of hosts; *It shall*

---

[n]Jer. xxx. 22; xxxi. 1, 33; ch. xiii. 9——[o]Jer. iv. 2——[p]Hag. ii. 4; ver. 18——[q]Ezra v. 1, 2——[r]Hag. ii. 18——[s]Or, *the hire of man became nothing*, &c.——[t]Hag. i. 6, 9, 10; ii. 16——[u]2 Chron. xv. 5——[v]Hos. ii. 21, 22; Joel ii. 22; Hag. ii. 19——[w]Heb. *of peace*——[x]Psa. lxvii. 6——[y]See Hag. i. 10——[z]Jer. xlii. 18——[a]Gen. xii. 2; Ruth iv. 11, 12; Isa. xix. 24, 25; Zeph. ii. 20; Hag. ii. 19

[b]Ver. 9——[c]Jer. xxxi. 28——[d]2 Chron. xxxvi. 16: chap. i. 6——[e]Chap. vii. 9; ver. 19; Eph. iv. 25——[f]Heb. *judge truth and the judgment of peace*——[g]Prov. iii. 29; chap. vii. 10——[h]Chap. v. 3, 4——[i]Jer. lii. 6, 7——[k]Jer. lii. 12, 13; chapter vii. 3, 5——[l]2 Kings xxv. 25; Jer. xli. 1, 2——[m]Jer. lii. 4——[n]Esth. viii. 17; Isa. xxxv. 10——[o]Or, *solemn*, or *set times*——[p]Ver. 16

---

country, and from the west] From every land in which any of them may be found. But these promises principally regard the Christian Church, or the bringing in the Jews with the fulness of the Gentiles.

Verse 9. *By the mouth of the prophets*] The day or time of the foundation was about *two years* before, as this discourse of the prophet was in the *fourth* year of Darius. After this God raised up prophets among them.

Verse 10. *For before these days there was no hire for man*] Previously to this, ye had no prosperity; ye had nothing but civil divisions and domestic broils. I abandoned you to your own *spirits*, and to your own *ways*.

Verse 12. *For the seed* shall be *prosperous*] Ye shall be a holy and peaceable people; and God will pour down his blessing on yourselves, your fields, and your vineyards.

Verse 13. *As ye were a curse*] Instead of being execrated among the people, ye shall be blessed; instead of being reproached, ye shall be commended. Ye shall be a *blessing* to all the nations round about. All these promises we may expect to be completely fulfilled when the Jews acknowledge their Messiah.

O house of Judah, and house of Israel] The restoration shall be complete, when both *Israel* and *Judah* are brought back.

Verse 16. *Speak ye every man the truth*] See chap. vii. 9, 10.

Verse 19. *The fast of the fourth* month] To commemorate the *taking of Jerusalem;* 2 Kings xxv. 3; Jer. xxxix. 2, and lii. 6, 7.

The fast of the fifth] In memory of the *ruin of the temple*, 2 Kings xxv. 8; Jer. lii. 12, 13.

The fast of the seventh] For the *murder of Gedaliah*, Jer. xli. 1-17.

The fast of the tenth] In commemoration of the *siege of Jerusalem*, which began on the *tenth* day of the *tenth* month; 2 Kings xxv. 1; Jer. lii. 4; Ezek. xxiv. 1, 2; and see on chap. vii. 3, 5.

Cheerful feasts] Ye shall find all your evils so completely redressed, that these *mournful fasts* shall be turned into *joyful feasts*.

Verse 20. *There shall come people*] Similar promises to those in Isa. ii. 3, and in Mic. iv. 1, 2. Many *Gentiles*, as well as *Jews*, will then be found devoting themselves to the Lord.

A. M. 3486
B. C. 518
Ol. LXV. 3
Anno Tarquinii Superbi,
R. Roman., 17

yet *come to pass,* that there shall
come people, and the inhabitants
of many cities:
21 And the inhabitants of one
city shall go to another, saying, [q]Let us [r]go
[s]speedily [t]to pray before the LORD, and to
seek the LORD of hosts: I will go also.
22 Yea, [u]many people and strong nations
shall come to seek the LORD of hosts in Jerusalem, and to pray before the
LORD.
23 Thus saith the LORD of
hosts; In those days *it shall*
come to pass, that ten men shall [v]take hold
out of all languages of the nations, even shall
take hold of the skirt of him that is a Jew,
saying, We will go with you: for we have
heard [w]*that* God *is* with you.

A. M. 3486
B. C. 518
Ol. LXV. 3
Anno Tarquinii Superbi,
R. Roman., 17

[q]Isa. ii. 3; Mic. iv. 1, 2——[r]Or, *continually*——[s]Hebrew, *going*——[t]Heb. *to entreat the face of the LORD;* chapter vii. 2——[u]Isaiah lx. 3, &c.; lxvi. 23——[v]Isaiah iii. 6; iv. 1——[w]1 Cor. xiv. 25

Verse 21. *I will go also.*] This is the answer of the person *invited.* It is a good work. We must have God for our friend. We cannot expect this unless we *seek* him: and as we know not what an hour may bring forth, let us go *speedily.*

Verse 22. *And strong nations*] This may refer to the conversion of the *Mohammedan* tribes; especially to those in the vicinity of Palestine. Perhaps even the *Egyptians,* inhabitants of *Arabia Petræa,* of *Syria,* &c.

Verse 23. *Ten men—shall take hold of the skirt of him that is a Jew*] The converts from among the Gentiles shall be to the Jews as *ten* to *one.* But *ten* may here signify a great number, without comparison. And from this scripture it appears as if the Jews, converted to God, should be the instruments of converting many *Gentiles.* See on Isa. iii. 6. *Catching hold of the skirt* is a gesture naturally used to entreat assistance and protection. This and the three foregoing verses, says Abp. *Newcome,* refer to the great accession of converts which the Jewish Church received between the captivity and the coming of Christ; to the number of *Christian* disciples which the Jewish preachers made, and to the future conversions of which the restoration of the Jews will be an eminent cause.

CHAPTER IX

Syria, Phœnicia, and Palestine, were conquered by Nebuchadnezzar, and afterwards by Alexander. Some apply the beginning of this chapter (1–7) *to the one event, and some to the other. The close of the* seventh *verse relates to the number of Philistines that should become proselytes to Judaism; (see* Joseph. *Antiq.* xiv. 15, 4;) *and the* eighth, *to the watchful providence of God over his temple in those troublesome times. From this the prophet passes on to that most eminent instance of God's goodness to his Church and people, the sending of the Messiah, with an account of the peaceable tendency and great extent of his kingdom,* 9, 10. *God then declares that he has ratified his covenant with his people, delivered them from their captivity, and restored them to favour,* 11, 12. *In consequence of this, victory over their enemies is promised them in large and lofty terms, with every other kind of prosperity,* 13–17. *Judas Maccabeus gained several advantages over the troops of Antiochus, who was of Grecian or Macedonian descent. But without excluding these events, it must be allowed that the terms of this prophecy are much too strong to be confined to them; their ultimate fulfilment must therefore be referred to Gospel times.*

A. M. cir. 3417
B. C. cir. 587
Ol. XLVIII. 2
TarquiniiPrisci,
R. Roman.,
cir. annum 30

THE [a]burden of the word of
the LORD in the land of Hadrach, and [b]Damascus *shall be*
the rest thereof: when [c]the eyes
of man, as of all the tribes of
Israel, *shall be* toward the LORD.
2 And [d]Hamath also shall
border thereby; [e]Tyrus, and

A. M. cir. 3417
B. C. cir. 587
Ol. XLVIII. 2
TarquiniiPrisci,
R. Roman.,
cir. annum 30

[a]Jer. xxiii. 33——[b]Amos i. 3——[c]2 Chron. xx. 12; Psa. cxlv. 15——[d]Jer. xlix. 23——[e]Isa. xxiii.; Ezek. xxvi., xxvii., xxviii.; Amos i. 9

NOTES ON CHAP IX

Verse 1. *The burden of the word of the Lord*] The *oracle* contained in the word which Jehovah now speaks.

This is a prophecy against Syria, the Philistines, Tyre, and Sidon, which were to be subdued by Alexander the Great. After this the prophet speaks gloriously concerning the coming of Christ, and redemption by him.

Most learned men are of opinion that this and the succeeding chapters are not the work of *Zechariah,* but rather of *Jeremiah, Hosea,* or some one before the captivity. It is certain that chap. xi. 12, 13, is quoted Matt. xxvii. 9, 10, as the language of *Jeremiah* the prophet. The *first eight* chapters appear by the introductory parts to be the prophecies of *Zechariah:* they stand in connection with each other, are pertinent to the time when they were delivered, are uniform in style and manner, and constitute a regular whole; but the *six last* chapters are not expressly assigned to Zechariah, and are unconnected with those that precede:—the *three* first of them are unsuitable in many parts to the time when Zechariah lived; all of them

A. M. cir. 3417 B. C. cir. 587 Ol. XLVIII. 2 TarquiniiPrisci, R. Roman., cir. annum 30

[f]Zidon, though it be very
[g]wise.
3 And Tyrus did build herself
a strong hold, and [h]heaped up
silver as the dust, and fine gold as the mire of
the streets.
4 Behold, [i]the LORD will cast her out, and
he will smite [k]her power in the sea; and she
shall be devoured with fire.
5 [l]Ashkelon shall see *it,* and fear; Gaza
also *shall see it,* and be very sorrowful, and
Ekron; for her expectation shall be ashamed;
and the king shall perish from
Gaza, and Ashkelon shall not be
inhabited.
6 And a bastard shall dwell
[m]in Ashdod, and I will cut off the pride of
the Philistines.
7 And I will take away his [n]blood out of
his mouth, and his abominations from between
his teeth: but he that remaineth, even he
shall be for our God, and he shall be as a
governor in Judah, and Ekron as a Jebusite.
8 And [o]I will encamp about mine house

---

[f]1 Kings xvii. 9; Ezekiel xxviii. 21; Obadiah 20 — [g]Ezekiel xxviii. 3, &c. — [h]Job xvii. 16; Ezekiel xxviii. 4, 5 — [i]Isaiah xxiii. 1 — [k]Ezekiel xxvi. 1, 7

[l]Jeremiah xlvii. 1, 5; Zephaniah ii. 4 — [m]Amos i. 8 — [n]Hebrew, *bloods* — [o]Psalm xxxiv. 7; chapter ii. 5

---

have a more adorned and poetical turn of composition than the eight first chapters, and they manifestly break the unity of the prophetical book.

I conclude, from internal marks, that these three chapters, (ix., x., xi.,) were written much *earlier* than the time of Jeremiah, and before the captivity of the *ten tribes.* They seem to suit *Hosea's* age and manner; but whoever wrote them, their Divine authority is established by the two *quotations* from them, chap. ix. 9, and xi. 12, 13. See below.

The *twelfth, thirteenth,* and *fourteenth* chapters form a distinct prophecy, and were *written after the death of Josiah,* chap. xii. 11; but whether before or after the captivity, and by *what prophet,* is uncertain, although I incline to think that the author lived *before* the destruction of Jerusalem by the Babylonians. See on chap. xiii. 2-6. They are *twice* quoted in the New Testament, chap. xii. 10, and xiii. 7.—*Newcome.*

My own opinion is, that these chapters form not only a distinct *work,* but belong to a *different author.* If they do not belong to *Jeremiah,* they form a *thirteenth* book in the *minor prophets,* but the inspired writer is unknown.

The land of Hadrach] The valley of Damascus, or a place near to Damascus. Alexander the Great gained possession of Damascus, and took all its treasures; but it was without blood; the city was betrayed to him.

Damascus shall be *the rest thereof*] The principal part of this calamity shall fall on this city. God's anger *rests* on those whom he *punishes,* Ezek. v. 13, xvi. 42, xxiv. 13. And his rod, or his *arm, rests* upon his enemies, Psa. cxxv. 3; Isai. xxx. 23. See *Newcome.*

When the eye of man] *Newcome* translates thus:

"For the eye of Jehovah is *over* man,
And over all the tribes of Israel."

This is an easy sense, and is followed by the *versions.*

Verse 2. *And Hamath also shall border thereby*] *Hamath* on the river Orontes; and *Tyre* and *Sidon,* notwithstanding their political wisdom, address, and cunning, shall have a part in the punishment.

These prophecies are more suitable to the days of *Jeremiah* than to those of *Zechariah;* for there is no evidence—although Alexander did take Damascus, but *without bloodshed*—that it was destroyed from the times of Zechariah to the advent of our Lord. And as *Tyre* and *Sidon* were lately destroyed by Nebuchadnezzar, it is not likely that they could soon undergo another devastation.

Verse 3. *And Tyrus did build herself*] The rock on which Tyre was built was strongly *fortified;* and that she had abundance of *riches* has been already seen, Ezek. xxviii. 1, &c.

Verse 4. *Will smite her power in the sea*] See Ezek. xxvi. 17. Though Alexander did take Tyre, Sidon, Gaza, &c.; yet it seems that the prediction relative to their destruction was fulfilled by *Nebuchadnezzar.* See Amos i. 6-8; Zeph. ii. 4, 7.

Verse 5. *Ashkelon shall see* it, *and fear*] All these prophecies seem to have been fulfilled before the days of Zechariah; another evidence that these last chapters were not written by him.

Her expectation shall be ashamed] The expectation of being succoured by Tyre.

Verse 6. *A bastard shall dwell in Ashdod*] This character would suit Alexander very well, who most certainly was a *bastard;* for his mother Olympia said that Jupiter Ammon entered her apartment in the shape of a dragon, and begat Alexander! Could her husband Philip believe this? The word signifies a *stranger.*

Verse 7. *I will take away his blood out of his mouth*] The Philistines, when incorporated with the Israelites, shall abstain from *blood,* and every thing that is abominable.

And Ekron as a Jebusite.] As an inhabitant of Jerusalem. Many of the Philistines became proselytes to Judiasm; and particularly the cities of Gaza, and *Ashdod.* See *Joseph.* Antiq. lib. xiii., c. 15, s. 4.

Verse 8. *I will encamp about mine house*] This may apply to the conquests in Palestine by *Alexander,* who, coming with great wrath against Jerusalem, was met by *Jaddua* the high priest and his fellows in their sacred robes, who made intercession for the city and the temple; and, in consequence, Alexander spared *both,* which he had previously purposed to destroy. He showed the Jews also much favour, and remitted the tax every *seventh year,* be-

A. M. cir. 3417
B. C. cir. 587
Ol. XLVIII. 2
TarquiniiPrisci,
R. Roman.,
cir. annum 30

because of the army, because of
him that passeth by, and because
of him that returneth: and [p]no
oppressor shall pass through
them any more: for now [q]have I seen with
mine eyes.

9 [r]Rejoice greatly, O daughter of Zion;
shout, O daughter of Jerusalem: behold, [s]thy
King cometh unto thee: he *is* just, and
[t]having salvation; lowly, and riding upon an
ass, and upon a colt the foal of an ass.

10 And I [u]will cut off the chariot from
Ephraim, and the horse from Jerusalem, and
the battle bow shall be cut off: and he shall
speak [v]peace unto the heathen: and his dominion *shall be* [w]from sea *even*
to sea, and from the river *even*
to the ends of the earth.

A. M. cir. 3417
B. C. cir. 587
Ol. XLVIII. 2
TarquiniiPrisci,
R. Roman.,
cir. annum 30

11 As for thee also, [x]by the
blood of thy covenant I have sent forth thy
[y]prisoners out of the pit wherein *is* no water.

12 Turn you to the strong hold, [z]ye prisoners of hope: even to-day do I declare *that*
[a]I will render double unto thee;

13 When I have bent Judah for me, filled
the bow with Ephraim, and raised up thy sons,
O Zion, against thy sons, O Greece, and made
thee as the sword of a mighty man.

14 And the LORD shall be seen over them,
and [b]his arrow shall go forth as the lightning:

---

[p]Isa. lx. 18; Ezek. xxviii. 24——[q]Exod. iii. 7——[r]Isa. lxii. 11; ch. ii. 10; Matt. xxi. 5; John xii. 15——[s]Jer. xxiii. 5; xxx. 9; John i. 49; Luke xix. 38——[t]Or, *saving himself*——[u]Hos. i. 7; ii. 18; Mic. v. 10; Hag. ii. 22

[v]Eph. ii. 14, 17——[w]Psa. lxxii. 8——[x]Or, *whose covenant is by blood;* Exod. xxiv. 8; Heb. x. 29; xiii. 20——[y]Isa. xlii. 7; li. 14; lxi. 1——[z]Isa. xlix. 9——[a]Isa. lxi. 7——[b]Psa. xviii. 14; lxxvii. 17; cxliv. 6

---

cause the *law* on that year forbade them to *cultivate* their ground. See this extraordinary account in *Joseph.* Antiq. lib. xi., c. 8, s. 5. Bishop *Newcome* translates: "I will encamp about my house with an army, so that none shall pass through or return."

Verse 9. *Rejoice greatly, O daughter of Zion*] See this prophecy explained on Matt. xxi. 5.

Behold, thy King cometh] Not *Zerubbabel*, for he was never *king;* nor have they had a *king*, except Jesus the Christ, from the days of Zedekiah to the present time.

He is just] The righteous One, and the Fountain of righteousness.

Having salvation] He alone can *save* from *sin, Satan, death*, and *hell.*

Lowly] Without *worldly pomp* or *splendour;* for neither his kingdom, nor that of his followers, is of *this world.*

Riding upon an ass] God had commanded the kings of Israel not to multiply *horses.* The kings who broke this command were miserable themselves, and scourgers to their people. Jesus came to *fulfil the law.* Had he in his title of *king* rode upon a *horse*, it would have been a *breach* of a positive command of God; therefore, he rode upon an *ass*, and thus fulfilled the *prophecy*, and kept the *precept* unbroken. Hence it is immediately added—

Verse 10. *I will cut off the chariot from Ephraim, and the horse from Jerusalem*] No wars shall be employed to spread the kingdom of the Messiah; for it shall be founded and established, "not by might nor by power, but by the Spirit of the Lord of hosts," chap. iv. 6.

Verse 11. *As for thee also* (Jerusalem) *by the blood of thy covenant*] The covenant made with Abraham, Isaac, Jacob, and the Israelites in general, and ratified by the *blood* of many victims; until the time should come in which the *Messiah* should shed his blood, as typified by the ancient sacrifices.

I have sent forth thy prisoners] Those who were under the arrest of God's judgments; the *human race*, fast bound in sin and misery, and who by the pitifulness of his tender mercy were loosed, he dying in their stead.

Verse 12. *Turn you to the strong hold*] Ye who *feel* your *sins*, and are *shut up* under a sense of your guilt, look up to him who was delivered for your offences, and rose again for your justification. Ye have *hope;* let that hope lead you to *faith*, and that faith to the *blood of the covenant;* and, through that *blood*, to GOD, the Father of all.

I will render double unto thee] Give thee an *abundance* of peace and salvation.

Verse 13. *When I have bent Judah*] Judah is the *bow*, and Ephraim is the *arrows;* and these are to be shot against the *Greeks.* I am inclined, with Bp. *Newcome*, to consider that the language of this prophecy is too strong to point out the only trifling advantage which the *Maccabees* gained over *Antiochus*, who was of *Macedonian descent;* and it is probable that these prophecies remain to be fulfilled against the present possessors of *Javan* or *Greece, Macedonia*, and a part of *Asia Minor.*

Verse 14. *The Lord shall be seen over them*] Shadowing and refreshing them, as the cloud did the camp in the wilderness.

His arrow shall go forth as the lightning] They shall be conquered in a way that will show that God fights for his followers.

The description here is very sublime; we have a good imitation of it in Nonnus:—

Και τοτε γαιαν ἁπασαν επεκλυσεν ὑετιος Ζευς,
Πυκνωσας νεφεεσσιν ὁλον πολον· ουρανιη γαρ
Βρονταιοις παταγοισι Διος μυκησατο σαλπιγξ.
NONN. DIONYS., lib. 6. ver. 229.

"When heaven's dread *trumpet*, sounding from on high,
Breaks forth in thunders through the darken'd sky;
The pregnant clouds to floods of rain give birth.
And stormy Jove o'erwhelms the solid earth."
J. B. B. C.

In these two verses there is a fine *image*, and an *allusion* to a particular fact, which have escaped the notice of every commentator. I

A. M. cir. 3417
B. C. cir. 587
Ol. XLVIII. 2
TarquiniiPrisci,
R. Roman.,
cir. annum 30

and the Lord God shall blow the trumpet, and shall go [c]with whirlwinds of the south.
15 The Lord of hosts shall
defend them; and they shall devour, and [d]subdue with sling-stones; and they shall drink, *and* make a noise as through wine; and they [e]shall be filled like bowls, *and* as [f]the corners of the altar.

16 And the Lord their God
shall save them in that day as the flock of his people: for [g]*they shall be as* the stones of a crown, [h]lifted up as an ensign upon his land.
17 For [i]how great *is* his goodness, and how great *is* his beauty! [k]corn shall make the young men [l]cheerful, and new wine the maids.

---

[c]Isa. xxi. 1——[d]Or, *subdue the stones of the sling*——[e]Or, *shall fill both the bowls, &c.*——[f]Lev. iv. 18, 24; Deut. xii. 27

[g]Isa. lxii. 3; Mal. iii. 17——[h]Isa. xi.1 2——[i]Psa. xxxi. 19——[k]Joel iii. 18; Amos ix. 14——[l]Or, *grow*, or *speak*

---

must repeat the verses: 13: When I have *bent* Judah for me, *filled the bow* with Ephraim, and raised up thy sons, O Zion, against thy sons, O Greece, and made thee as the sword of a mighty man. 14: And the Lord shall be seen over them, and *his arrows shall go forth like lightning*. The reader will consult what is said on Hos. vii. 16, relative to the *oriental bow*, which resembles a ◯ in its quiescent state, and must be *recurved* in order to be strung. Here, *Judah* is represented as the *recurved bow; Ephraim*, as an *arrow* placed on the *string*, and then discharged against the Javanites or Greeks with the momentum of *lightning;* the *arrow kindling* in its course through the air, and thus becoming the bolt of death to them against whom it was directed.

Volat illud, et incandescit eundo,
Et quos non habuit, sub nubibus invenit ignes.

"It flies apace; and, *heating*, mounts on high,
Glows in its course, and *burns* along the sky."

Verse 15. *The Lord of hosts shall defend them*] He alone is the sure trust of his Church.

Subdue with sling-stones] This was an ancient and powerful *instrument* in the hands of the Hebrews. See the note on Judg. xx. 16.

They shall drink] After the victory gained as above, thy people shall hold a *feast*, and *drink and be filled with wine*. There is no intimation here that they shall *drink the blood of their enemies*, as some barbarous nations were accustomed to do. When they have gained the victory, they shall banquet abundantly on the spoils taken from the enemy.

As the corners of the altar.] They shall pour out libations of wine at the foot of the altar, as the priests were accustomed to pour out the blood of the victims.

Verse 16. *Shall save them in that day*] They are his *flock*, and he is their *Shepherd;* and, as his own, he shall save and defend them.

As *the stones of a crown*] אבני נזר מתנוססות *abney nezer mithnosesoth*, "crowned stones erecting themselves;" i. e., being *set up by themselves*, as *monuments* of some deliverance, they seem to be *lifting themselves up;* offering themselves to the *attention* of every passenger. It may however refer to *stones anointed with oil;* a sort of temporary *altars* set up to the Lord for a victory gained. The same word is used, Lev. xxi. 12: "Because the crown, נזר *nezer*, of the anointing oil of his God is upon him." Perhaps most of those *upright stones*, standing in *circles*, which pass for *druidical monuments*, were erected to commemorate victories, or to grace the tomb of an illustrious chief. These verses may refer to some final victory over the enemies of God's people.

Verse 17. *How great* is *his goodness*] In *himself* and towards *them.*

And how great is *his beauty!*] His *comeliness*, *holiness*, and *purity*, put *in* and upon them.

Corn shall make the young men cheerful] They shall be gladdened and strengthened by plenty of food; and they shall *speak aloud* of God's mercies in their *harvest home.*

And new wine the maids.] Who shall prepare the wine from an abundant vintage.

CHAPTER X

The promise of prosperity and plenty in the close of the preceding chapter leads the prophet to suggest, next, the means of obtaining them; supplication to Jehovah, and not to idols, whose worship had already proved a fertile source of calamities, 1–3. The rest of the chapter (like the preceding) promises to the Jews a restoration to their own land under rulers and governors, victory over their enemies, and much increase and prosperity; and this in a manner so miraculous that it is described, 4–12, by allusions to the deliverance from Egypt.

A. M. cir. 3417
B. C. cir. 587
Ol. XLVIII. 2
TarquiniiPrisci,
R. Roman.,
cir. annum 30

ASK ye [a]of the LORD [b]rain
[c]in the time of the latter
rain; *so* the LORD shall make
[d]bright clouds, and give them
showers of rain, to every one grass in the field.
2 For the [e]idols[f] have spoken vanity, and
the diviners have seen a lie, and have told
false dreams; they [g]comfort in vain: therefore they went their way as a flock, they [h]were
troubled, [i]because *there was* no shepherd.
3 Mine anger was kindled against the shepherds, [k]and I [l]punished the goats: for the
LORD of hosts [m]hath visited his flock the house
of Judah, and [n]hath made them as his goodly
horse in the battle.
4 Out of him came forth [o]the corner, out of
him [p]the nail, out of him the battle-bow, out
of him every oppressor together.
5 And they shall be as mighty *men,* which
[q]tread down *their enemies* in the mire of the
streets in the battle: and they
shall fight, because the LORD *is*
with them, and [r]the riders on
horses shall be confounded.

A. M. cir. 3417
B. C. cir. 587
Ol. XLVIII. 2
TarquiniiPrisci,
R. Roman.,
cir. annum 30

6 And I will strengthen the house of Judah,
and I will save the house of Joseph, and [s]I
will bring them again to place them; for I
[t]have mercy upon them: and they shall be
as though I had not cast them off: for I *am*
the LORD their God, and [u]will hear them.
7 And *they of* Ephraim shall be like a
mighty *man,* and their [v]heart shall rejoice as
through wine: yea, their children shall see
it, and be glad; their heart shall rejoice in
the LORD.
8 I will [w]hiss for them, and gather them;
for I have redeemed them: [x]and they shall
increase as they have increased.
9 And [y]I will sow them among the people: and they shall [z]remember me in far

[a]Jer. xiv. 22——[b]Deut. xi. 14——[c]Job. xxix. 23; Joel ii. 23——[d]Or, *lightnings;* Jer. x. 13——[e]Jer. x. 8; Heb. ii. 18——[f]Heb. *teraphim;* Judg. xvii. 5——[g]Job xiii. 4——[h]Or, *answered that,* &c.——[i]Ezek. xxxiv. 5 [k]Ezek. xxxiv. 16——[l]Heb. *visited upon*——[m]Luke i. 68 [n]Cant. i. 9

[o]Num. xxiv. 17; 1 Sam. xiv. 38; Isa. xix. 13——[p]Isa. xxii. 23——[q]Psa. xviii. 42——[r]Or, *they shall make the riders on horses ashamed*——[s]Jer. iii. 18; Ezek. xxxvii. 21 [t]Hos. i. 7——[u]Chap. xiii. 9——[v]Psa. civ. 15; chap. ix. 15——[w]Isa. v. 26——[x]Isa. xlix. 19; Ezek. xxxvi. 37 [y]Hos. ii. 23——[z]Deut. xxx. 1

NOTES ON CHAP. X

Verse 1. *Ask ye of the Lord rain*] Rain in the due seasons—1. To *impregnate* the *seed* when sown; and 2. To *fill the ear* near the time of *harvest*—was so essential to the fertility of the land, and the well-being of the people, that it stands well among the chief of God's mercies; and the promise of it here shows that God designs to ensure the prosperity promised, by using those means by which it was promoted.

Verse 2. *The idols have spoken vanity*] This is spoken of the *Jews,* and must refer to their idolatry practised before the captivity, for there were no *idols after.*

Therefore they went their way] They were like a *flock* that had no *shepherd,* shifting from place to place, and wandering about in the wilderness, seeking for pasture, wherever they might find it. Some think that the *idols* and *diviners* were those of the *Seleucidæ Greeks,* who excited their masters with promises of success against the Maccabees. Others think that the Babylonish captivity is foretold; for a *determined future* event is frequently spoken of by the prophets as *past.*

Verse 3. *Mine anger was kindled against the shepherds*] Bad kings and bad priests. *I will punish the goats;* these were the wicked *priests,* who were *shepherds* by their *office,* and *goats* by the *impurity* of their *lives.*

As his goodly horse in the battle.] The honourable *war horse,* or the *horse* that carried the general's equipage. In the unaccountable variation of interpreters on these chapters, this, among other things, is thought to be spoken of *Matthias,* and *Judas Maccabeus,* who assembled the people from all quarters, as a shepherd gathers his sheep together; and led them against the *sons of Greece,* the *Seleucidæ Greeks.* Others refer every thing here to times before the *captivity.*

Verse 4. *Out of him came forth the corner*] This is spoken of the tribe of Judah: all strength, counsel, and excellence came from that tribe. The *corner stone,* the *ornament* and *completion* of the building; *the nail,* by which the tents were fastened, and on which they hung their clothes, armour, &c.; *the battlebow,* the choicest archers.

Every oppressor together.] Those heroes and generals, by whom, under God, their foes should be totally routed. *Newcome* translates, "Every ruler together." Perhaps all this is spoken of the *Messiah.*

Verse 5. *They shall be as mighty* men] The Maccabees and their successors.

Riders on horses] The Macedonians, who opposed the Maccabees, and had much cavalry; whereas the Jews had none, and even few weapons of war; yet they overcame these horsemen.

Verse 6. *I will strengthen the house of Judah*] I doubt whether the *sixth, seventh, eighth,* and *ninth* verses are not to be understood of the future ingathering of the Jews in the times of the Gospel. See Jer. iii. 14; xxiii. 6; Hosea i. 2; vi. 11.

Verse 7. *Ephraim shall be like a mighty* man] This tribe was always distinguished for its valour.

Verse 8. *I will hiss for them*] אשרקה *eshrekah,* "I will shriek for them;" call them with such a *shrill strong voice,* that they shall *hear* me, and find that it is the voice of their redemption.

Verse 9. *I will sow them among the people*]

A. M. cir. 3417
B. C. cir. 587
Ol. XLVIII. 2
TarquiniiPrisci,
R. Roman.,
cir. annum 30

countries; and they shall live
with their children, and turn
again.
10 [a]I will bring them again also
out of the land of Egypt, and gather them out
of Assyria; and I will bring them into the land
of Gilead and Lebanon; and [b]*place* shall
not be found for them.
11 [c]And he shall pass through the sea with
affliction, and shall smite the
waves in the sea, and all the deeps
of the river shall dry up: and
[d]the pride of Assyria shall be
brought down, and [e]the sceptre of Egypt
shall depart away.
12 And I will strengthen them in the LORD:
and [f]they shall walk up and down in his name,
saith the LORD.

[a]Isa. xi. 11, 16; Hos. xi. 11——[b]Isa. xlix. 20——[c]Isa. xi. 15, 16——[d]Isa. xiv. 25——[e]Ezek. xxx. 13——[f]Mic. iv. 5

Wherever they have been dispersed, my voice in the preaching of the Gospel shall reach them. *And they shall remember me*, and they and their children *shall turn again to the Lord*, through Messiah their King.

Verse 10. *Out of the land of Egypt*] I will bring them out of all the countries where they have been dispersed, and bring them back to their own land; and they shall be so numerous that they shall scarcely find there, in all its length and breadth, a sufficiency of room. If all the Jews that are now scattered over the face of the earth were gathered together, they would make a *mighty nation*. And God will gather them together. As a wonderful providence has preserved them in every place, so a wondrous providence will collect them from every place of their dispersion. When the *great call* comes, no one soul of them shall be left behind.

Verse 11. *And he shall pass through the sea*] Here is an allusion to the passage of the *Red Sea*, on their coming *out of Egypt*, and to their *crossing Jordan*, when they went into the *promised land;* the *waves* or waters of both were *dried up*, thrown from side to side, till all the people passed safely through. When they shall return from the various countries in which they now sojourn, God will work, if necessary, similar miracles to those which he formerly worked for their forefathers; and the people shall be glad to let them go, however much they may be profited by their operations in the state. Those that oppose, as *Assyria* and *Egypt* formerly did, shall be *brought down*, and their *sceptre broken*.

Verse 12. *I will strengthen them in the Lord*] I, the God of Israel, will strengthen them in the Lord—Jesus, *the Messiah;* and thus indeed the *Chaldee: I will strengthen them*, בימרא דיי *bemeymre dayai, in* or *by the* WORD *of Jehovah*, the same *personal Word* which we so often meet with in the *Chaldee* paraphrases or *Targum*.

They shall walk up and down in his name] In the name of the Messiah. *Saith the Lord*—GOD speaks here, not of himself, but concerning his *Christ*. The Jews shall have complete liberty; they shall appear everywhere as a part of the flock of Christ, and no difference be made between them and the converted Gentiles. They shall be all *one fold* under *one Shepherd* and Bishop of all souls.

CHAPTER XI

The commencement of this chapter relates to the destruction of Jerusalem and the Jewish polity, probably by the Babylonians; at least in the first instance, as the fourth *verse speaks of the people thus threatened as the prophet's charge, 1–6. The prophet then gives an account of the manner in which he discharged his office, and the little value that was put on his labours. And this he does by symbolical actions, a common mode of instruction with the ancient prophets, 7–14. After the prophet, on account of the unsuccessfulness of his labours, had broken the two crooks which were the true badges of his pastoral office, (to denote the annulling of God's covenant with them, and their consequent divisions and dispersions,) he is directed to take instruments calculated to hurt and destroy, perhaps an iron crook, scrip, and stones, to express by these symbols the judgments which God was about to inflict on them by wicked rulers and guides, who should first destroy the flock, and in the end be destroyed themselves, 15–17. Let us now view this prophecy in another light, as we are authorized to do by Scripture,* Matt. xxvii. 7. *In this view the prophet, in the person of the Messiah, sets forth the ungrateful returns made to him by the Jews, when he undertook the office of shepherd in guiding and governing them; how they rejected him, and valued him and his labours at the mean and contemptible price of thirty pieces of silver, the paltry sum for which Judas betrayed him. Upon which he threatens to destroy their city and temple; and to give them up to the hands of such guides and governors as should have no regard to their welfare.*

A. M. cir. 3417
B. C. cir. 587
Ol. XLVIII. 2
TarquiniiPrisci,
R. Roman.,
cir. annum 30

OPEN [a]thy doors, O Lebanon,
that the fire may devour thy
cedars.
2 Howl, fir tree; for the cedar
is fallen; because the [b]mighty is spoiled:
howl, O ye oaks of Bashan; [c]for [d]the forest
of the vintage is come down.
3 *There is* a voice of the howling of the
shepherds; for their glory is spoiled; a voice
of the roaring of young lions; for the pride of
Jordan is spoiled.
4 Thus saith the LORD my God; [e]feed the
flock of the slaughter;
5 Whose possessors slay them, and [f]hold
themselves not guilty: and they that sell
them [g]say, Blessed *be* the LORD; for I am
rich: and their own shepherds pity them
not.
6 For I will no more pity the inhabitants of
the land, saith the LORD: but lo,
I will [h]deliver the men every
one into his neighbour's hand,
and into the hand of his king:
and they shall smite the land, and out of their
hand I will not deliver *them.*
7 And I will [i]feed the flock of slaughter,
[k]*even* you, [l]O poor of the flock. And I took
unto me two staves; the one I called Beauty,
and the other I called [m]Bands; and I fed the
flock.
8 Three shepherds also I cut off [n]in one
month; and my soul [o]loathed them, and their
soul also abhorred me.
9 Then said I, I will not feed you: [p]that
that dieth, let it die: and that that is to be cut
off, let it be cut off; and let the rest eat
everyone the flesh [q]of another.
10 And I took my staff, *even* Beauty, and

A. M. cir. 3417
B. C. cir. 587
Ol. XLVIII. 2
TarquiniiPrisci,
R. Roman.,
cir. annum 30

[a]Chap. x. 10——[b]Or, *gallants*——[c]Isa. xxxii. 12
[d]Or, *the defenced forest*——[e]Ver. 7——[f]Jer. ii. 3; l. 7
[g]Deut. xxix. 19; Hos. xii. 8——[h]Heb. *make to be found*
[i]Ver. 4

[k]Or, *verily the poor*——[l]Zeph. iii. 12; Matt. xi. 5
[m]Or, *Binders*——[n]Hos. v. 7——[o]Heb. *was straitened for them*——[p]Jer. xv. 2; xliii. 11——[q]Heb. *of his fellow*, or *neighbour*

NOTES ON CHAP. XI

Verse 1. *Open thy doors, O Lebanon*] I will give Mr. *Joseph Mede's* note upon this verse:—

"That which moveth me more than the rest, is in chap. xi., which contains a prophecy of the destruction of Jerusalem, and a description of the wickedness of the inhabitants, for which God would give them to the sword, and have no more pity upon them. It is expounded of the destruction by *Titus;* but methinks such a prophecy was nothing seasonable for Zachary's time, (when the city yet for a great part lay in her ruins, and the temple had not yet recovered hers,) nor agreeable to the scope. *Zachary's* commission, who, together with his colleague *Haggai,* was sent to encourage the people, *lately returned* from captivity, to build their temple, and to instaurate their commonwealth. Was this a fit time to foretell the destruction of both, while they were yet but *a-building?* And by Zachary too, who was to encourage them? Would not this better befit the desolation by Nebuchadnezzar?" I really think so. See Mr. *J. Mede's* lxi. Epistle.

Lebanon signifies the temple, because built of materials principally brought from that place.

Verse 2. *Howl, fir tree*] This seems to point out the fall and destruction of all the mighty men.

Verse 3. *Young lions*] Princes and rulers. By *shepherds, kings* or *priests* may be intended.

Verse 4. *Feed the flock of the slaughter*] This people resemble a flock of sheep *fattened* for the shambles; *feed,* instruct, this people who are about to be *slaughtered.*

Verse 5. *Whose possessors*] Governors and false prophets, *slay them,* by leading them to those things that will bring them to destruction.

And they that sell them] Give them up to idolatry; and bless God, strange to tell, that they get *secular advantage* by the establishment of this *false religion.*

Verse 6. *For I will no more pity*] I have determined to deliver them into the hands of the Chaldeans.

Verse 7. *And I will feed the flock of slaughter*] I showed them what God had revealed to me relative to the evils coming upon the land; and I did this the more especially for the sake of *the poor of the flock.*

Two staves] Two *shepherd's crooks.* One I called *Beauty*—that probably by which they marked the sheep; dipping the end into *vermilion,* or some red liquid. And this was done when they were to *mark* every *tenth* sheep, as it came out of the field, when the *tithe* was to be set apart for the Lord.

The other I called Bands] Probably that with the *hook* or *crook* at the head of it, by which the shepherd was wont to catch the sheep by the horns or legs when he wished to bring any to hand.

And I fed the flock.] These two rods show the *beauty* and *union* of the people, while under God as their Shepherd. It was the *delight* of God to see them in a state of *peace* and *harmony.*

Verse 8. *Three shepherds also I cut off in one month*] Taking this *literally,* some think the *three shepherds* mean the *three* Maccabees, *Judas, Jonathan,* and *Simon;* others, the *three* wicked high priests, *Jason, Alcimus,* and *Menelaus;* others, the *three* last princes of the Asmonean race, *Alexander, Hyrcanus,* and *Antigonus.*

Perhaps *three orders* may be intended: 1. The *priesthood.* 2. The *dictatorship,* including the Scribes, Pharisees, &c. 3. The *magistracy,* the great sanhedrin, and the smaller councils. These were all annihilated by the Roman conquest.

Verse 9. *I will not feed you*] I shall instruct

A. M. cir. 3417 B. C. cir. 587 Ol. XLVIII. 2 TarquiniiPrisci, R. Roman., cir. annum 30

cut it asunder, that I might break my covenant which I had made with all the people.

11 And it was broken in that day: and [r]so [s]the poor of the flock that waited upon me knew that it *was* the word of the LORD.

12 And I said unto them, [t]If ye think good, give *me* my price, and if not, forbear. So they [u]weighed for my price thirty *pieces* of silver.

13 And the LORD said unto me, Cast it unto the [v]potter: a goodly price that I was prized at of them. And I took the thirty *pieces* of silver, and cast them to the potter in the house of the LORD.

14 Then I cut asunder mine other staff, *even* [w]Bands, that I might break the brotherhood between Judah and Israel.

15 And the LORD said unto me, [x]Take unto thee yet the instruments of a foolish shepherd.

16 For lo, I will raise up a shepherd in the land, *which* shall not visit those that be [y]cut off, neither shall seek the young one, nor heal that that is broken, nor [z]feed that that standeth still: but he shall eat the flesh of the fat, and tear their claws in pieces.

17 [a]Wo to the idol shepherd that leaveth the flock! the sword *shall be* upon his arm, and upon his right eye: his [b]arm shall be clean dried up, and his right eye shall be utterly darkened.

[r]Or, *the poor of the flock*, &c., *certainly knew*——[s]Zeph. iii. 12; ver. 7——[t]*If* it be *good in your eyes*——[u]Matt. xxvi. 15; see Exod. xxi. 32

[v]Matt. xxvii. 9, 12——[w]Or, *Binders*——[x]Ezek. xxxiv. 2, 3, 4——[y]Or, *hidden*——[z]Or, *bear*——[a]Jer. xxiii. 1; Ezek. xxxiv. 2; John x. 12, 13——[b]Psa. x. 5

you no longer: some of you are appointed to death by *famine;* others, to be *cut off* by the *sword;* and others of you, to such *desparation* that ye shall *destroy one another.*

Verse 10. *I took my staff—Beauty, and cut it asunder*] And thus I showed that I determined no longer to preserve them in their *free* and *glorious* state. And thus I *brake my covenant with them,* which they had broken on their part already.

Verse 11. *So the poor of the flock*] The pious, who attended to my teaching, saw that this was the *word*—the *design*, of God.

Verse 12. *If ye think good, give* me *my price*] "Give me my hire." And we find they rated it contemptuously; *thirty* pieces of silver being the price of a slave, Exod. xxi. 32.

Verse 13. *And the Lord said unto me, Cast it unto the potter*] Jehovah calls the price of his prophet *his own price;* and commands that it should not be accepted, but given to a potter, to foreshadow the transaction related Matt. xxvii. 7.

"Earthen vessels were used in the temple; and we may suppose that some Levites were employed within the sacred precincts to furnish them. To these, the humblest of his ministers in the temple, God commands that the *degrading price* should be cast." This is the substance of the notes on these two verses, given by Abp. *Newcome.*

We may look at it in another light, *Give me my price!* הבו שכרי *habu sichri, bring my price,* or *give* him *my price;* that is, Give the money to Judas which you have agreed to give him; for he can neither betray me nor you crucify me, but my own permission. *But if not, forbear;* take time to consider this bloody business, and in time *forbear.* For though I *permit* you to do it, yet remember that the *permission* does not *necessitate* you to do it; and the salvation of the world may be effected without this *treachery* and *murder.*

See my notes on this place, Matt. xxvii. 9, where I have examined the evidence for the reading of "Zechariah the prophet," instead of "Jeremiah."

Verse 14. *That I might break the brotherhood*] I cannot, says *Newcome*, explain this passage, without supposing that the kingdom of Israel *subsisted* when the prophet wrote it; and that either the wars between Judah and Israel are referred to, (see 2 Kings xvi. 5,) or the captivity of the ten tribes, when the *brotherly connection* between these kingdoms ceased.

Verse 15. *The instruments of a foolish shepherd.*] Such as a *bag without bread*, a *scrip without measure*, and a *staff without a hook*, &c.; things that were needless or of no use; to point out to the Jewish pastors, who took no care of the flock, but devoured them, or ruled them with force and with cruelty.

Verse 16. *I will raise up a shepherd in the land*] Some wicked king; and *Newcome* supposes *Hoshea* may be meant. See 2 Kings xvii. 1, 2, and to such an abominable sovereign the prophecy may well apply.

Verse 17. *Wo to the idol shepherd*] רעי האליל *roi haelil*, "the worthless," or "good for nothing shepherd." The shepherd in name and office, but not performing the *work* of one. See John x. 11.

The sword shall be *upon his arm*] Punishment shall be executed upon the wicked Jews, and especially their wicked kings and priests. See ver. 16.

Arm—the secular power; *right eye*—the ecclesiastical state.

His arm shall be clean dried up] The secular power shall be broken, and become utterly inefficient.

His right eye shall be utterly darkened] Prophecy shall be restrained; and the whole state, ecclesiastical and civil, shall be so completely *eclipsed*, that none of their functions shall be performed. This may refer to the worthless and wicked governor mentioned in the preceding verse.

There are several things in this chapter that are very *obscure*, and we can hardly say what opinion is right; nor is it at all clear whether they refer to a very early or late period of the Jewish history.

CHAPTER XII

The first part of this chapter, with several passages in chap. xiv., *relates to an invasion that shall be made on the inhabitants of Judea and Jerusalem in the latter ages of the world, some time after the restoration and settlement of the Jews in their own land. It also describes, in very magnificent terms, the signal interposition of God in their favour. From this the prophet proceeds in the latter part of the chapter,* 10–14, *to describe the spiritual mercies of God in converting his people; and gives a very pathetic and affecting account of the deep sorrow of that people, when brought to a sense of their great sin in crucifying the Messiah, comparing it to the sorrow of a parent for his first-born and only son, or to the lamentations made for Josiah in the valley of Megiddon,* 2 Chron. xxxv. 24, 25. *A deep, retired sorrow, which will render the mourners for a season insensible to all the comforts and enjoyments of the most endearing society.*

A. M. cir. 3417
B. C. cir. 587
Ol. XLVIII. 2
TarquiniiPrisci,
R. Roman.,
cir. annum 30

THE burden of the word of
the LORD for Israel, saith
the LORD, [a]which stretcheth
forth the heavens, and layeth the
foundation of the earth, and [b]formeth the
spirit of man within him.
2 Behold, I will make Jerusalem [c]a cup of
[d]trembling unto all the people round about,
[e]when they shall be in the siege both against
Judah *and* against Jerusalem.
3 [f]And in that day will I make Jerusalem
[g]a burdensome stone for all people: all that
burden themselves with it shall be cut in
pieces, though all the people of the earth be
gathered together against it.
4 In that day, saith the LORD, [h]I will smite
every horse with astonishment, and his rider
with madness: and I will open mine eyes upon
the house of Judah, and will smite every
horse of the people with blindness.
5 And the governors of Judah
shall say in their heart, [i]The
inhabitants of Jerusalem *shall be* my strength
in the LORD of hosts their God.
6 In that day will I make the governors of
Judah [k]like a hearth of fire among the wood,
and like a torch of fire in a sheaf; and they
shall devour all the people round about, on the
right hand and on the left: and Jerusalem shall
be inhabited again in her own place, *even* in
Jerusalem.
7 The LORD also shall save the tents of
Judah first, that the glory of the house of
David and the glory of the inhabitants of
Jerusalem do not magnify *themselves* against
Judah.
8 In that day shall the LORD defend the

[a]Isa. xlii. 5; xliv. 24; xlv. 12, 18; xlviii. 13——[b]Num. xvi. 22; Eccles. xii. 7; Isa. lvii. 16; Heb. xii. 9——[c]Isa. li. 17, 22, 23——[d]Or, *slumber*, or *poison*——[e]Or, *and also against Judah* shall he be *which shall be in siege against Jerusalem*——[f]Ver. 4, 6, 8, 9, 11; chap. xiii. 1; xiv. 4, 6, 8, 9, 13——[g]Matt. xxi. 44——[h]Psa. lxxvi. 6; Ezek. xxxviii. 4——[i]Or, There is *strength to me* and *to the inhabitants*, &c.; Joel iii. 16——[k]Obad. 18

NOTES ON CHAP. XII

Verse 1. *The burden of the word of the Lord*] This is a new prophecy. It is directed both to *Israel* and *Judah*, though *Israel* alone is mentioned in this verse.

Which stretcheth forth the heavens] See on Isa. xlii. 5.

Formeth the spirit of man within him.] Then it is not the *same substance* with his body. It is a SPIRIT within HIM.

Verse 2. *Jerusalem a cup of trembling*] The Babylonians, who captivated and ruined the Jews, shall in their turn be ruined.

I incline to think that what is spoken in this chapter about the *Jews* and *Jerusalem*, belongs to the "glory of the latter times."

Shall be in the siege] This may refer to some war against the Church of Christ, such as that mentioned Rev. xx. 9.

Verse 3. *A burdensome stone*] Probably referring to that *stone* which was thrown on the breast of a *culprit* adjudged to lose his life by *stoning*, by which the whole region of the thorax, *heart, lungs, liver*, &c., was broken to pieces.

Verse 4. *I will smite every horse*] Some apply this to the *wars* of the *Maccabees* with the *Syrians;* but it is more likely to be a prophecy not yet accomplished. The terms are too strong for such petty and evanescent victories as those of the Maccabees.

Verse 5. *The governors of Judah*] This supposes a *union* between the two kingdoms of Israel and Judah.

Verse 6. *Jerusalem shall be inhabited again*] This seems to refer to the future conversion of the Jews, and their "return to their own land."

Verse 7. *The Lord also shall save the tents of Judah first*] This, I suppose, refers to the same thing. The Gospel of Christ shall go from the *least* to the *greatest. Eminent men* are not the *first* that are called; the *poor* have the Gospel preached to them. And this is done in the wise providence of God, that the "glory of the house of David," &c., that secular influence may appear to have no hand in the matter; and that God does not send his Gospel to a *great man*, because he is *such*.

Verse 8. *He that is feeble among them—shall be as David*] Here is a marked *difference* between *Judaism* and *Christianity*. So clear, full, and efficient shall be the salvation of believers under the *Gospel*, that the *feeblest* among them

A. M. cir. 3417
B. C. cir. 587
Ol. XLVIII. 2
TarquiniiPrisci,
R. Roman.,
cir. annum 30

inhabitants of Jerusalem; and [l]he that is [m]feeble [n]among them at that day shall be as David; and the house of David *shall be* as God, as the angel of the LORD before them.

9 And it shall come to pass in that day, *that* I will seek to [o]destroy all the nations that come against Jerusalem.

10 [p]And I will pour upon the house of David, and upon the inhabitants of Jerusalem, the spirit of grace and supplications: and they shall [q]look upon me whom they have pierced, and they shall mourn for him, [r]as one mourneth for *his* only *son,* and shall be in bitterness for him, as one that is in bitterness for *his* first-born.

A. M. cir. 3417
B. C. cir. 587
Ol. XLVIII. 2
TarquiniiPrisci,
R. Roman.,
cir. annum 30

11 In that day shall there be a great [s]mourning in Jerusalem, [t]as the mourning of Hadadrimmon in the valley of Megiddon.

12 [u]And the land shall mourn, [v]every family apart; the family of the house of David apart, and their wives apart; the family of the house of [w]Nathan apart, and their wives apart;

13 The family of the house of Levi apart, and their wives apart; the family [x]of Shimei apart, and their wives apart;

14 All the families that remain, every family apart, and their wives apart.

[l]Joel iii. 10——[m]Or, *abject*——[n]Heb. *fallen*——[o]Hag. ii. 22; ver. 3——[p]Jer. xxxi. 9; l. 4; Ezek. xxxix. 29; Joel ii. 28——[q]John xix. 34, 37; Rev. i. 7——[r]Jer. vi. 26; Amos viii. 10

[s]Acts ii. 37——[t]2 Kings xxiii. 29; 2 Chron. xxxv. 24——[u]Matthew xxiv. 30; Revelation i. 7——[v]Hebrew, *families, families*——[w]2 Sam. v. 14; Luke iii. 31——[x]Or, *of Simeon*, as LXX.

shall be as strong, as full of courage, and as successful as David when he went against Goliath. The least in the kingdom of heaven was greater than John the Baptist.

And the house of David—as the angel of the Lord] The *family*, the *Church* of the *true David*, the *Lord Jesus*, shall be as the *angel* of the Lord; shall *stand in the Divine presence* like *Gabriel;* for Christ hath said, "Blessed are the pure in heart, for they shall see God." So "we all, with open face beholding as in a glass the glory of the Lord, are changed from glory into glory, as by the Spirit of the Lord." Thus the house of David, the *true Christians*, shall here walk *with*, *after*, and *before* God.

Verse 9. *I will seek to destroy all the nations*] When this time shall arrive, all nations that "will not receive the faith of our Lord Jesus" shall be destroyed, when the longsuffering of God shall no longer wait upon them. This seems to belong to a period yet very remote.

Verse 10. *I will pour upon the house of David*] This is the *way* in which the *Jews* themselves shall be brought into the *Christian Church*. 1. "They shall have the spirit of grace;" God will show them that he yet bears *favour* to them. 2. They shall be excited to *fervent* and continual *prayer* for the restoration of the Divine favour. 3. Christ shall be preached unto them; and they shall *look upon* and believe in him *whom they pierced*, whom they crucified at Jerusalem. 4. This shall produce deep and sincere repentance; they shall *mourn*, and be in bitterness of soul, to think that they had crucified the Lord of life and glory, and so long continued to contradict and blaspheme, since that time.

Verse 11. *A great mourning*] A universal repentance.

As the mourning of Hadadrimmon] They shall mourn as deeply for the crucified Christ as their forefathers did for the death of Josiah, who was slain at Hadadrimmon in the valley of Megiddon. See 2 Chron. xxxv. 24, 25.

Verse 12. *Every family apart*] The meaning of the word *apart*, which recurs here so often, may be this: Their sorrow shall be so deep and distressing, that every one will endeavour to avoid another, and vent his grief and distress of soul in *private*. And even *husbands* and *wives* shall separate from each other in this general mourning, as they were obliged to do by law in certain circumstances. See 1 Cor. vii. 5, and the note there.

CHAPTER XIII

After the humiliation and conversion of the Jews, foretold in the preceding chapter, they are here promised the full pardon of their sins, and a deliverance from idolatry and false prophets, 1–6. *Prophecy concerning the death of the Messiah, and the persecution of his disciples,* 7. *The remaining verses may refer to those Jewish converts to Christianity who survived the calamities which their country suffered from the Romans,* 8, 9.

A. M. cir. 3417
B. C. cir. 587
Ol. XLVIII. 2
TarquiniiPrisci,
R. Roman.,
cir. annum 30

IN [a]that day there shall be [b]a fountain opened to the house of David and to the inhabitants of Jerusalem for sin and for [c]uncleanness.

2 And it shall come to pass in that day, saith the LORD of hosts, *that* I will [d]cut off the names of the idols out of the land, and they shall no more be remembered: and also I will cause [e]the prophets and the unclean spirit to pass out of the land.

3 And it shall come to pass, *that* when any shall yet prophesy, then his father and his mother that begat him shall say unto him, Thou shalt not live; for thou speakest lies in the name of the LORD: and his father and his mother that begat him [f]shall thrust him through when he prophesieth.

A. M. cir. 3417
B. C. cir. 587
Ol. XLVIII. 2
TarquiniiPrisci,
R. Roman.,
cir. annum 30

4 And it shall come to pass in that day, *that* [g]the prophets shall be ashamed every one of his vision, when he hath prophesied; neither shall they wear [h]a [i]rough garment [k]to deceive:

5 [l]But he shall say, I *am* no prophet, I *am* a husbandman; for man taught me to keep cattle from my youth.

6 And *one* shall say unto him, What *are* these wounds in thine hands? Then he shall answer, *Those* with which I was wounded *in* the house of my friends.

7 Awake, O sword, against [m]my Shepherd, and against the man [n]*that is* my Fellow,

[a]Chap. xii. 3——[b]Heb. ix. 14; 1 Pet. i. 19; Rev. i. 5——[c]Heb. *separation for uncleanness*——[d]Exod. xxiii. 13; Josh. xxiii. 7; Psa. xvi. 4; Ezek. xxx. 13; Hos. ii. 17; Mic. v. 12, 13——[e]2 Pet. ii. 1

[f]Deut. xiii. 6, 8; xviii. 20——[g]Mic. iii. 6, 7——[h]2 Kings i. 8; Isa. xx. 2; Matt. iii. 4——[i]Heb. *a garment of hair*——[k]Heb. *to lie*——[l]Amos vii. 14——[m]Isa. xl. 11; Ezek. xxxiv. 23——[n]John x. 30; xiv. 10, 11; Phil. ii. 6

NOTES ON CHAP. XIII

Verse 1. *In that day there shall be a fountain opened*] This chapter is a *continuation* of the preceding, and should not have been separated from it.

A fountain] The source of mercy in Christ Jesus; perhaps referring to the death he should die, and the *piercing* of *his side*, when *blood and water issued out*.

To the house of David] To David's family, and *such like persons* as it included. See the history of David and his sons, and then learn *for whom* Christ shed his blood.

Inhabitants of Jerusalem] Such like persons as the Jews were in *every part of their history*, and in their *last* times, when they clamoured for the blood of Christ, and pursued him unto death! Learn from this also *for whom* Christ died! These were the *worst* of the human race; and if he died for *them*, none need *despair*. They *rejected*, *betrayed*, *crucified*, *slew*, and *blasphemed* Christ, and afterwards persecuted his followers. For these he died! Yes: and he tasted death for EVERY MAN.

For sin and for uncleanness.] For the removal of the *guilt* of sin, and for the *purification* of the soul from the uncleanness or pollution of sin.

Verse 2. *I will cut off the names of the idols*] There shall not only be no *idolatry*, but the very *names* of the *idols* shall be forgotten, or be held in such abhorrence that no person shall *mention* them. This prophecy seems to be ancient, and to have been delivered while idolatry had prevalence in Israel and Judah.

I will cause the prophets] All false teachers.

And the unclean spirit] That which leads to impurity, the spirit of *divination;* the lust of the flesh, and of the eye, and the pride of life. Satan shall have neither a *being in*, nor *power over*, the hearts of sincere believers in Christ.

Verse 3. *When any shall yet prophesy*] Falsely; such shall be the horror of such an evil, that there shall be no toleration of it. Itself, and they who practise it, shall be everywhere destroyed.

Verse 4. *Neither shall they wear a rough garment*] A *rough garment* made of *goats'* hair, *coarse* wool, or the *course pile* of the *camel*, was the ordinary garb of God's prophets. And the false prophets wore the same; for they pretended to the same gifts, and the same spirit, and therefore they wore the same kind of *garments*. John Baptist had a garment of this kind.

Verse 5. *But he shall say, I* am *no prophet*] This must be the case of a *false prophet* or diviner, who had been obliged to give up his infamous practice, and become even a *labourer* in the land. But having been known to be such, he is questioned by the people to see if he still were addicted in heart to the same practices. He declares he is *no prophet*, neither true nor false; that he is now a *husbandman*, and was brought up a *herdsman*.

Verse 6. *What are these wounds in thine hands?*] *Marks* which he had received in honour of his idols. But he shall excuse himself by stating that he had received these marks in his *own family;* when, most probably, they had been dedicated to some of those idols. See the note on Isa. xliv. 5. I do not think that these words are spoken at all concerning Jesus Christ. I have heard them quoted in this way; but I cannot hear such an application of them without horror. In quoting from the Old Testament in reference to the New, we cannot be too cautious. We may wound the truth instead of honouring it.

Verse 7. *Awake, O sword, against my Shepherd*] This is generally understood of Jesus Christ. The *sword* is that of Divine justice, which seemed to have been long *asleep*, and should long ago have struck either MAN, or his SUBSTITUTE, the *Messiah*. Jesus is here called God's *Shepherd*, because he had appointed him to *feed* and *govern*, as well as to *save*, the whole lost world. This is a prosopopœia, and

A. M. cir. 3417
B. C. cir. 587
Ol. XLVIII. 2
TarquiniiPrisci,
R. Roman.,
cir. annum 30

saith the LORD of hosts: [o]smite
the Shepherd, and the sheep shall
be scattered: and I will turn
mine hand upon [p]the little ones.
8 And it shall come to pass, *that* in all the
land, saith the LORD, two parts therein shall
be cut off *and* die; [q]but the third shall be
left therein.

[o]Matt. xxvi. 31; Mark xiv. 27——[p]Matt. xviii. 10, 14; Luke xii. 32——[q]Rom. xi. 5——[r]Isa. xlviii. 10——[s]1 Pet. i. 6, 7

the address to the sword is very poetic. There is a fine passage in *Æschylus* to the same effect:—

> Ξενος δε κληροις επινωμᾳ,
> Χαλυβος Σκυθων αποικος,
> Κτεανων χρηματοδαιτας
> Πικρος, ωμοφρων σιδαρος,
> Χθονα ναιειν διαπηλας
> Ὁποσαν αν και φθιμενοισι κατεχειν,
> Των μεγαλων πεδιων αμοιροις,
> ÆSCHYL. *Sept. cont. Theb.* 733.

> "The rude barbarian, from the mines
> Of Scythia, o'er the lots presides;
> Ruthless to each his share assigns,
> And the contested realm divides:
> To each allots no wider a domain
> Than, on the cold earth as they lie,
> Their breathless bodies occupy,
> Regardless of an ampler reign:
> Such narrow compass does the *sword*—
> A cruel umpire—their high claims afford."
> POTTER.

The man that is *my Fellow*] ועל גבר עמיתי *veal geber amithi*, "upon the strong man," or, "the hero that is *with* ME;" my neighbour. "The WORD was God, and the WORD was WITH God;" John i. 1. "I and my Father are ONE;" John x. 30.

Smite the Shepherd, and the sheep shall be scattered] This is quoted by our Lord, Matt. xxvi. 31, in relation to his disciples, who should be scattered on his crucifixion: and they were so; for every one, giving up all for lost, *went to his own house.*

And I will turn mine hand upon the little ones.] I will take care of the *little flock*, and preserve them from Jewish malice and Gentile persecution. And so this little flock was most wondrously preserved, and has been increasing from year to year from that time to the present day.

Verse 8. *Two parts therein shall be cut off*] In the war with the Romans.

But the third shall be left] Those who believe on the Lord Jesus Christ shall be preserved alive; and not one of these perished in the siege, or afterwards, by those wars.

Verse 9. *I will bring the third part through the fire*] The *Christian Church* shall endure a great fight of afflictions, by which they shall be refined—not consumed.

They shall call on my name] In this way shall they offer all their prayers and supplications to God.

I will say, It is *my people*] The Church that I have chosen in the place of the Jews who have filled up the measure of their iniquity.

And they shall say, The Lord is *my God*] And thus *communion* shall be established between me and them for ever. Thus there shall be a general restoration.

9 And I will bring the third
part [r]through the fire, and
will [s]refine them as silver is
refined, and will try them as
gold is tried: [t]they shall call on my name,
and I will hear them: [u]I will say, It *is* my
people; and they shall say, The LORD *is* my
God.

A. M. cir. 3417
B. C. cir. 587
Ol. XLVIII. 2
TarquiniiPrisci,
R. Roman.,
cir. annum 30

[t]Psa. l. 15; xci. 15; chap. x. 6——[u]Psalm cxliv. 15; Jeremiah xxx. 22; Ezekiel xi. 20; Hosea ii. 23; chap. viii. 3

CHAPTER XIV

The commencement of this chapter relates to the destruction of Jerusalem by the Romans, and to the calamities consequent on that event. From this great Jewish tragedy the prophet immediately passes to the utter extermination of the enemies of Christianity in the latter days. God will display his power in behalf of his people in a manner so astonishing and miraculous, that even they themselves, and much more their enemies, shall be struck with terror, 4, 5. *The national prosperity of the Jews shall then be permanent and unmixed,* 6, 7; *and these people shall be made the instruments of converting many to the faith of the Messiah,* 8, 9. *The great increase and prosperity of the Christian Church, the New Jerusalem, is then described in terms accommodated to Jewish ideas; and the most signal vengeance denounced against all her enemies,* 10–19. *From that happy period God's name will be honoured in every thing, and his worship every where most reverently observe,* 20, 21.

A. M. cir. 3417
B. C. cir. 587
Ol. XLVIII. 2
TarquiniiPrisci,
R. Roman.,
cir. annum 30

BEHOLD, [a]the day of the
LORD cometh, and thy spoil
shall be divided in the midst of
thee.
2 For [b]I will gather all nations against
Jerusalem to battle; and the city shall be
taken, and [c]the houses rifled, and the women
ravished; and half of the city shall go forth
into captivity, and the residue of the people
shall not be cut off from the city.
3 Then shall the LORD go forth, and fight
against those nations, as when he fought in
the day of battle.
4 And his feet shall stand in that day [d]upon
the mount of Olives, which *is* before Jerusalem on the east, and the mount of Olives shall
cleave in the midst thereof toward the east and
toward the west, [e]*and there shall be* a very
great valley; and half of the
mountain shall remove toward
the north, and half of it toward
the south.

A. M. cir. 3417
B. C. cir. 587
Ol. XLVIII. 2
TarquiniiPrisci,
R. Roman.,
cir. annum 30

5 And ye shall flee *to* the valley of [f]the
mountains; [g]for the valley of the mountains
shall reach unto Azal: yea, ye shall flee like as
ye fled from before the [h]earthquake in the days
of Uzziah king of Judah: [i]and the LORD my
God shall come, *and* [k]all the saints with thee.
6 And it shall come to pass in that day, [l]*that*
the light shall not be [m]clear, *nor* [n]dark:
7 But [o]it shall be [p]one day [q]which shall
be known to the LORD, not day, nor night: but
it shall come to pass, *that* at [r]evening time it
shall be light.
8 And it shall be in that day, *that* living
[s]waters shall go out from Jerusalem: half of

[a]Isaiah xiii. 9; Joel ii. 31; Acts ii. 20——[b]Joel iii. 2——[c]Isa. xiii. 16——[d]See Ezek. xi. 23——[e]Joel iii. 12, 14——[f]Or, *my mountains*——[g]Or, *when he shall touch the valley of the mountains to the place he separated*——[h]Amos i. 1——[i]Matt. xvi. 27; xxiv. 30, 31; xxv. 31; Jude 14

[k]Joel iii. 11——[l]That is, it shall not be clear in some places, and dark in other places of the world——[m]Heb. *precious*——[n]Heb. *thickness*——[o]Or, *the days hall be one*——[p]Rev. xxii. 5——[q]Matt. xxiv. 36——[r]Isa. xxx. 26; lx. 19, 20; Rev. xxi. 23——[s]Ezek. xlvii. 1; Joel iii. 18; Rev. xxii. 1

NOTES ON CHAP. XIV

Verse 1. *Behold, the day of the Lord cometh*] This appears to be a prediction of that war in which Jerusalem was finally destroyed, and the Jews scattered all over *the face of the earth;* and of the effects produced by it.

Verse 2. *I will gather all nations*] The *Romans*, whose armies were composed of all the nations of the world. In this verse there is a pitiful account given of the *horrible outrages* which should be committed during the siege of Jerusalem, and at its capture.

The residue of the people shall not be cut off] Many were preserved for *slaves*, and for *exhibition* in the provincial theatres.

Verse 3. *Then shall the Lord go forth, and fight against those nations*] Against the Romans, by means of the northern nations; who shall destroy the whole empire of this once mistress of the world. But this is an obscure place.

Verse 4. *And his feet shall stand*] He shall appear in full possession of the place, as a mighty conqueror.

And the mount of Olives shall cleave] God shall display his miraculous power as fully in the final restoration of the Jews, as he did when he divided the Red Sea that their forefathers might pass through dry-shod. Some refer this to the *destruction of the city by the Romans.* It was on the mount of Olives that *Titus* posted his army to batter Jerusalem. Here the *tenth* legion that came to him from Jericho was placed. JOSEPH. *De Bello*, lib. vi. c. 3. It was from *this mountain* that our Lord beheld Jerusalem, and predicted its future destruction, Luke xix. 41, with Matt. xxiv. 23; and it was from this mountain that he ascended to heaven, (Acts i. 12,) utterly leaving an ungrateful and condemned city.

And half of the mountain shall remove] I really think that these words refer to the *lines* of *circumvallation*, to intrenchments, redoubts, &c., which the Romans made while carrying on the siege of this city; and particularly the *lines* or *trenches* which the army made on Mount *Olivet* itself.

Verse 5. *Ye shall flee to the valley*] Some think this refers to the valley through which *Zedekiah* and others endeavoured to escape when Nebuchadnezzar pressed the siege of Jerusalem: but it appears to speak only of the *Jewish wars* of the *Romans.*

Azal] This, as a *place*, is not known. If a *place*, it was most probably *near* to Jerusalem; and had its *name* from that circumstance.

Verse 6. *The light shall not be clear*, nor *dark*] Metaphorically, there will be a *mixture* of *justice* and *mercy* in all this; or a *bright light and darkness. Mercy* shall triumph over *judgment.* There shall be *darkness*—distress, &c.; but there shall be more *light*—joy and prosperity—than *darkness.*

Verse 7. *At evening time it shall be light.*] At the *close* of this awful visitation, there shall be *light.* The light of the glorious Gospel shall go forth from Jerusalem; and next, from the Roman empire to every part of the earth.

Verse 8. *Living waters shall go out*] There shall be a wide diffusion of Divine knowledge, and of the plan of human salvation, which shall go out by apostles and preachers, first from Jerusalem, then to Syria, Asia Minor, Greece, Italy, the isles of the sea, Britain, &c.

The former sea, and—the hinder sea] The *Dead Sea* and the *Mediterranean;* see on Joel ii. 20. These are *metaphors.*

In summer] In time of *drought;* or in the countries where there was *no knowledge of God*, there shall these *waters* flow. The stream shall never cease; it shall run in *summer* as

A. M. cir. 3417
B. C. cir. 587
Ol. XLVIII. 2
TarquiniiPrisci,
R. Roman.,
cir. annum 30

them toward the [t]former sea, and half of them toward the hinder sea: in summer and in winter shall it be.

9 And the LORD shall be [u]King over all the earth: in that day shall there be [v]one LORD, and his name one.

10 All the land shall be [w]turned [x]as a plain from Geba to Rimmon south of Jerusalem; and it shall be lifted up, and [y]inhabited [z]in her place, from Benjamin's gate unto the place of the first gate, unto the corner gate, [a]and *from* the tower of Hananeel, unto the king's winepresses.

11 And *men* shall dwell in it, and there shall be [b]no more utter destruction; [c]but Jerusalem [d]shall be safely inhabited.

12 And this shall be the plague wherewith the LORD will smite all the people that have fought against Jerusalem; Their flesh shall consume away while they stand upon their feet, and their eyes shall consume away in their holes, and their tongue shall consume away in their mouth.

A. M. cir. 3417
B. C. cir. 587
Ol. XLVIII. 2
TarquiniiPrisci,
R. Roman.,
cir annum 30

13 And it shall come to pass in that day, *that* [e]a great tumult from the LORD shall be among them; and they shall lay hold every one on the hand of his neighbour, and [f]his hand shall rise up against the hand of his neighbour.

14 And [g]Judah also shall fight [h]at Jerusalem; [i]and the wealth of all the heathen round about shall be gathered together, gold, and silver, and apparel, in great abundance.

15 And [k]so shall be the plague of the horse, of the mule, of the camel, and of the ass, and of all the beasts that shall be in these tents, as this plague.

16 And it shall come to pass, *that* every one that is left of all the nations which came against Jerusalem shall even [l]go up from year to year

[t]Or, *eastern*, Joel ii. 20——[u]Dan. ii. 44; Rev. xi. 15——[v]Eph. iv. 5, 6——[w]Or, *compassed*——[x]Isa. xl. 4——[y]Chap. xii. 6——[z]Or, *shall abide*——[a]Neh. iii. 1; xii. 30; Jer. xxxi. 38——[b]Jer. xxxi. 40——[c]Jer. xxiii. 6——[d]Or, *shall abide*——[e]1 Sam. xiv. 15, 20——[f]Judg. vii. 22; 2 Chron. xx. 23; Ezek. xxxviii. 21——[g]Or, *thou also, O Judah, shalt*——[h]Or, *against*——[i]Ezek. xxxix. 10, 17, &c.——[k]Ver. 12——[l]Isa. lx. 6, 7, 9; lxvi. 23

well as *winter*. These are living waters—*perennial, incessant;* and waters that shall *preserve life*. See John vii. 37.

Verse 9. *And the Lord shall be King*] When this universal diffusion of Divine knowledge shall take place. Wherever it goes, the *laws of God* shall be *acknowledged;* and, consequently, he shall be King over the whole earth.

One Lord, and his name one.] There shall be in those blessed days, only *one religion*, and one *form of religion*. There shall not be *gods many*, and *lords many*. All *mankind* shall be of *one religion*, the essence of which is, "Thou shalt love the *Lord thy God* with all thy heart, soul, mind, and strength; and thy NEIGHBOUR as thyself."

Verse 10. *All the land shall be turned as a plain*] Or rather, "He shall encompass the whole land as a plain." He shall cast his defence all around it; from *Geba*, in Benjamin, north of Jerusalem, (Josh. xxi. 17,) to *Rimmon* in Judah, to the *south of Jerusalem*, Josh. xv. 32.

It shall be lifted up] The city shall be exhalted.

And inhabited in her place] Jerusalem, shall be rebuilt *in the very place* in which it originally stood. From *Benjamin's gate*, which was probably on the *north* side of Jerusalem, unto the *place of the first gate*, supposed to be that called the *old gate*, Neh. iii. 6, xii. 39, placed by *Lightfoot* towards the *southwest*.

Unto the corner gate] See 2 Kings xiv. 13.

The tower of Hananeel] This *tower* and the *corner gate* seem to be placed as *two extremities* of the city.

Unto the king's wine-presses] Near to the *king's gardens, southward.*—See *Newcome*.

Verse 11. *There shall be no more utter destruction*] After this final restoration of Jerusalem it shall never more be destroyed; but as this was the *first city* of the living God upon earth, so shall it be *the last;* it shall be *safely inhabited*. It shall see war no more.

Verse 12. *And this shall be the plague*] All her enemies shall be destroyed.

Their flesh shall consume away] These are the effects of *famine* which are described in this verse.

Verse 13. *A great tumult from the Lord*] Among those enemies of his Church, who shall engage and destroy each other.

Verse 14. *And Judah also shall fight*] They shall have little else to do than take the spoil, *the wealth of all the heathen round about;* gold, silver, and apparel.

Verse 15. *So shall be the plague of the horse, and the mule*] There shall be plagues on the *substance* of the enemies of the Church, as there were on the *cattle* and *goods* of the *Egyptians*.

Verse 16. *Shall even go up from year to year*] The Jews had *three* grand original festivals, which characterized different epochs in their history, viz.:—

1. The *feast* of the *passover*, in commemoration of their departure from Egypt.
2. The *feast* of *pentecost*, in commemoration of the giving of the law upon Mount Sinai.
3. The *feast* of *tabernacles*, in commemoration of their wandering forty years in the wilderness.

This last feast is very properly brought in here to point out the final restoration of the Jews, and their *establishment* in the light and liberty of the Gospel of Christ, after their *long wandering* in vice and error.

A. M. cir. 3417 B. C. cir. 587 Ol. XLVIII. 2 TarquiniiPrisci, R. Roman., cir. annum 30

to worship the King, the LORD of hosts, and to keep [m]the feast of tabernacles.

17 [n]And it shall be, *that* whoso will not come up of *all* the families of the earth unto Jerusalem to worship the King, the LORD of hosts, even upon them shall be no rain.

18 And if the family of Egypt go not up, and come not, [o]that [p]*have* no *rain,* there shall be the plague wherewith the LORD will smite the heathen that come not up to keep the feast of tabernacles.

19 This shall be the [q]punishment of Egypt, and the punishment of all nations that come not up to keep the feast of tabernacles.

20 In that day shall there be upon the [r]bells of the horses, [s]HOLINESS UNTO THE LORD; and the pots in the LORD's house shall be like the bowls before the altar.

21 Yea, every pot in Jerusalem and in Judah shall be holiness unto the LORD of hosts: and all they that sacrifice shall come and take of them, and seethe therein: and in that day there shall be no more the [t]Canaanite in [u]the house of the LORD of hosts.

[m]Lev. xxiii. 34, 43; Deut. xvi. 13, 16; Neh. viii. 14; Hos. xii. 9; John vii. 2——[n]Isa. lx. 12——[o]Heb. *upon whom* there is *not*

[p]Deut. xi. 10——[q]Or, *sin*——[r]Or, *bridles*——[s]Isa. xxiii. 18——[t]Isa. xxxv. 8; Job iii. 17; Rev. xxi. 27; xxii. 15——[u]Eph. ii. 19, 20, 21, 22

Verse 17. *Upon them shall be no rain.*] Those who do not worship God shall not have his blessing; and those who do not attend *Divine ordinances* cannot have the graces and blessings which God usually dispenses by them. On such slothful, idle Christians, *there shall be no rain!*

Verse 18. *If the family of Egypt*] This may allude to those Jews who, flying from the persecution of *Antiochus Epiphanes*, settled in Egypt, and built a temple at *Heliopolis*, under the direction of *Onias*, son of the high priest. *Joseph.* Antiq. lib. xiii., c. 6, and WAR, lib. vii., c. 36. If these do not rejoin their brethren, *they shall have no rain*, no interest in the favour of God.

Verse 19. *This shall be the punishment—of all nations that come not up*] God will have his public worship *established* everywhere, and those who do not worship him shall lie under his curse.

Verse 20. *Upon the bells of the horses*] They appear, formerly, to have had bells on horses, camels, &c., as we have now, to amuse the animals, and encourage them in their work. In some very fine Asiatic paintings now before me, I see *bells* both on *horses, mules*, and *camels;* little bells tied to their *legs*, and *larger* ones about their *necks*, particularly in the representation of a *caravan* passing through the valley of serpents, in the island of *Serendib*, now *Ceylon*. The margin reads *bridles*.

HOLINESS UNTO THE LORD] As the Gospel is a *holy* system, preaching *holiness* and producing *holiness* in those who believe, so all *without*, as well as *within*, shall bear this *impress;* and even a man's *labour* shall be begun and continued, and ended in the Lord; yea, and the *animals* he uses, and the *instruments* he works with, shall be all consecrated to God through Christ.

The pots] "The meanest utensil in the house of God, Neh. x. 29, shall be as the vessels of silver, and gold used in solemn sacrifice; they shall be *like the bowls before the altar.*"—See *Newcome.*

Verse 21. *Yea, every pot in Jerusalem*] "The utensils of the Jews shall be treated as *holy*, and the worshippers shall use them reverently. The idea of *preparing food* in them (*they that—seethe therein*) is taken from the custom of feasting after sacrifice. And no *trafficker* (see Ezek. xviii. 4) shall pollute the house of God, as was the custom when our blessed Lord cleansed the temple."—See *Newcome.* This is what is called the *Canaanite in the house of God.* The *Canaanite* is the *merchant;* and where such are tolerated in a place dedicated to Divine worship, *that* is not the house of the *Lord of hosts.* In *churches* and *chapels, collections* may be made for the *simple purpose* of *supporting* and *extending* the worship of Jehovah; but for no other purpose, especially on the Lord's day. *Amen.*

THE BOOK

OF THE

PROPHET MALACHI

Chronological Notes relative to this Book

Year from the Creation, according to Archbishop Usher, 3607.—Year from the vocation of Abram, 1524.—Year since the destruction of Troy, 787.—Year since the commencement of the kingdom of Israel by the Divine appointment of Saul to the regal dignity, 698.—Year from the division of Solomon's monarchy into the kingdoms of Israel and Judah, 578.—Fourth year of the *ninety-fifth* Olympiad.—Year from the building of Rome, according to the Varronian computation, 356.—Year before the vulgar era of Christ's nativity, 397.—Cycle of the Sun, 5.—Cycle of the Moon, 4.

CHAPTER I

This chapter begins with showing the great and free favour which God had manifested to the Israelites, above what he had done to the Edomites, who are threatened with farther marks of the Divine displeasure; alluding, perhaps, to the calamities which they suffered from Judas Maccabeus and John Hyrcanus, (see 1 Macc. v. 65, *and Joseph.* Antiq. xiii. 9,) 1–5. *God then reproaches his people, and especially their priests, for their ungrateful returns to his distinguished goodness,* 6. *They are particularly charged with sacrificing the refuse of beasts,* 7–9, *for which God threatens to reject them,* 10, *and choose other nations who will show more reverence to his name and worship,* 11–14.

A. M. cir. 3607
B. C. cir. 397
Ol. cir. XCV. 4
Urbis Conditæ
cir. annum
356

THE burden of the word of the
LORD to Israel [a]by Malachi.
2 [b]I have loved you, saith the
LORD. Yet ye say, Wherein
hast thou loved us? *Was* not Esau Jacob's
brother? saith the LORD: yet
[c]I loved Jacob,
3 And I hated Esau, and [d]laid
his mountains and his heritage
waste for the dragons of the wilderness.

[a]Heb. *by the hand of Malachi*——[b]Deut. vii. 8; x. 15——[c]Rom. ix. 13——[d]Jer. xlix. 18; Ezek. xxxv. 3, 4, 7, 9, 14, 15; Obadiah 10, &c.

NOTES ON CHAP. I

Verse 1. *The burden of the word of the Lord to Israel by Malachi.*] This prophet is undoubtedly the *last* of the Jewish prophets. He lived after Zechariah and Haggai; for we find that the *temple*, which was begun in their time, was standing complete in his. See chap. iii. 10. Some have thought that he was contemporary with Nehemiah; indeed, several have supposed that *Malachi*, is no other than *Ezra* under the feigned name of *angel of the Lord*, or *my angel*. John the Baptist was the link that connected Malachi with Christ. According to Abp. *Usher* he flourished B. C. 416; but the authorized version, which we have followed in the margin, states this event to have happened *nineteen* years later. Both the Hebrew language and poetry had declined in his days.

Israel.—Here means the Jewish people in general.

Verse 2. Was *not Esau Jacob's brother?*] Have I not shown a greater *partiality* to the *Israelites* than I have to the *Edomites?*

I loved Jacob] My *love to Jacob* has been proved by giving him greater privileges and a better inheritance than what I have given to *Esau.*

Verse 3. *And I hated Esau*] I have shown him *less love;* Gen. xxix. 30, 31. I comparatively *hated* him by giving him an inferior lot. And now, I have not only laid waste the dwelling-place of the Edomites, by the incursions of their enemies; but (ver. 4) they shall remain the perpetual monuments of my vengeance. On the subject of *loving Jacob* and *hating Esau*, see the notes on Gen. xxvii., and Rom. ix. 13. Let it be remembered, 1. That there is not a word spoken here concerning the *eternal state* of either Jacob or Esau. 2. That what is spoken concerns merely their *earthly possessions.* And, 3. That it does not concern the *two brothers* at all, but the *posterity* of each.

A. M. cir. 3607
B. C. cir. 397
Ol. cir. XCV. 4
Urbis Conditæ
cir. annum
356

4 Whereas Edom saith, We are impoverished, but we will return and build the desolate places; thus saith the LORD of hosts, They shall build, but I will throw down; and they shall call them, The border of wickedness, and, The people against whom the LORD hath indignation for ever.

5 And your eyes shall see, and ye shall say, [e]The LORD will be magnified [f]from [g]the border of Israel.

6 A son [h]honoureth *his* father, and a servant his master: [i]if then I *be* a father, where *is* mine honour? and if I *be* a master, where *is* my fear? saith the LORD of hosts unto you, O priests, that despise my name. [k]And ye say, Wherein have we despised thy name?

7 [l]Ye offer [m]polluted bread upon mine altar; and ye say, Wherein have we polluted thee? In that ye say, [n]The table of the LORD *is* contemptible.

8 And [o]if ye offer the blind [p]for sacrifice, *is it* not evil? and if ye offer the lame and sick, *is it* not evil? offer it now unto thy governor; will he be pleased with thee, or [q]accept thy person? saith the LORD of hosts.

9 And now, I pray you, Beseech [r]God that he will be gracious unto us: [s]this hath been [t]by your means: will he regard your persons? saith the LORD of hosts.

A. M. cir. 3607
B. C. cir. 397
Ol. cir. XCV. 4
Urbis Conditæ
cir. annum
356

10 Who *is there* even among you that would shut the doors *for naught?* [u]neither do ye kindle *fire* on mine altar for naught. I have no pleasure in you, saith the LORD of hosts, [v]neither will I accept an offering at your hand.

11 For [w]from the rising of the sun even unto the going down of the same my name *shall be* great [x]among the Gentiles; [y]and in every place [z]incense *shall be* offered unto my name, and a pure offering; [a]for my name *shall be* great among the heathen, saith the LORD of hosts.

12 But ye have profaned it, in that ye say, [b]The table of the LORD *is* polluted; and the fruit thereof, *even* his meat, *is* contemptible.

13 Ye said also, Behold, what a weariness *is it!* [c]and ye have snuffed at it, saith the LORD of hosts; and ye brought *that which was* torn, and the lame, and the sick; thus ye brought an offering: [d]should I accept this of your hand? saith the LORD.

14 But cursed *be* [e]the deceiver, [f]which hath in his flock a male, and voweth, and sacrificeth unto the LORD a corrupt thing: for [g]I *am* a great King, saith the LORD of hosts, and my name *is* dreadful among the heathen.

---

[e]Psa. xxxv. 27——[f]Or, *upon*——[g]Heb. *from upon* [h]Exod. xx. 12——[i]Luke vi. 46——[k]Chap. ii. 14, 17; iii. 7, 8, 13——[l]Or, *Bring unto*, &c.——[m]Deut. xv. 21 [n]Ezek. xli. 22; ver. 12——[o]Lev. xxii. 22; Deut. xv. 21; ver. 14——[p]Heb. *to sacrifice*——[q]Job xlii. 8——[r]Heb. *the face of God*——[s]Hos. xiii. 9——[t]Heb. *from your hand*

[u]1 Cor. ix. 13——[v]Isa. i. 11; Jer. vi. 20; Amos v. 21 [w]Psa. cxiii. 3; Isa. lix. 19——[x]Isa. lx. 3, 5——[y]John iv. 21, 23; 1 Tim. ii. 8——[z]Rev. viii. 3——[a]Isaiah lxvi. 19, 20——[b]Ver. 7——[c]Or, *whereas ye might have blown it away*——[d]Lev. xxii. 20, &c.——[e]Ver. 8——[f]Or, *in whose flock is*——[g]Psa. xlvii. 2; 1 Tim. vi. 15

Verse 4. *They shall build, but I will throw down*] We have already seen enough of the wickedness of the *Edomites* to justify the utmost severity of Divine justice against them. The *pulling down* predicted here was by Judas Maccabeus· see 1 Mac. v. 65; and by John Hyrcanus; see *Joseph.* Antiq., lib. xiii. c. 9. s. 1.

They shall call them, The border of wickedness] A wicked land. Among this people scarcely any trace of good could ever be noted.

Verse 5. *Your eyes*] Ye Israelites *shall see*, in your succeeding generations, that—

The Lord will be magnified] By his kindness *in* Israel, and his judgments *beyond.*

Verse 6. *A son honoureth* his *father*] I am your *Father*—where, then, is my honour? Where your filial obedience?

If I be *a master, where* is *my fear?*] The respect due to me.

Verse 7. *Ye offer polluted bread*] The priests, probably to ingratiate themselves with the people, took the refuse beasts, &c., and offered them to God; and thus the sacrificial ordinances were rendered *contemptible.*

Verse 8. *Offer it now unto thy governor*] פחת *pechath*, a word signifying a *lieutenant*, or *viceroy*, among the Chaldeans, Syrians, and Persians; for neither at this time, nor ever after, was there a *king* in Israel.

Verse 9. *Beseech God*] There were evident marks of God's displeasure in the land, and it was occasioned by these pollutions through the priests. And now he exhorts *them* to pray to God that they may be pardoned: for, if this practice be persisted in, God will not accept any offering made by them.

Verse 10. *Who* is—*among you*] From this we learn that there was not one sincere or honest priest among them. They were selfish and worldly; and so basely so, that not one of them would even kindle a fire on the hearth of the altar unless he were paid for it.

Verse 11. *From the rising of the sun*] The total abolition of the Mosaic sacrifices, and the establishment of a *spiritual* worship over the whole earth, is here foretold. The *incense* of praise, and the *pure offering* of the *Lamb without spot*, and through him a holy, loving heart, shall be presented everywhere *among the Gentiles;* and the Jews and their mock offerings shall be rejected.

Verse 12. *Ye have profaned it*] Ye have desecrated God's worship; is it any wonder that God should cast you off, and follow you with his judgments?

Verse 13. *Ye have snuffed at it*] A metaphor taken from cattle which do not like their *fodder.* They *blow strongly* through their nose upon it; and after this neither *they* nor *any other cattle* will eat it.

Ye brought that which was *torn, and the lame, and the sick*] There had never been such abominations in the Divine worship before. What was of no worth in itself, and what could not be used by its owner, was brought to God's altar, and offered for sacrifice! Was not the punishment of these wretches less than their crimes?

Verse 14. *Cursed* be *the deceiver*] Those who act thus, as they cannot elude God's *notice,* so neither shall they escape his *curse.*

And voweth, and sacrificeth—a corrupt thing] The history of Ananias and Sapphira, Acts v. 1, &c., is a complete comment on this. It was high time to break up this corrupt service; and after this time God does not appear to have paid any regard to it, for he sent them no other prophet.

CHAPTER II

The priests reproved for their unfaithfulness in their office, for which they are threatened to be deprived of their share of the sacrifice, (the shoulder,) and rewarded only with ignominy and ordure, 1–3. *The degeneracy of the order is then complained of, and they are again threatened,* 4–9. *The rest of the chapter reproves the people for marrying strange and idolatrous women; and multiplying divorces, with all their consequent distress, in order to make way for such illicit alliances,* 10–17. *See* Neh. x. 30, *and* xiii. 33, *&c.*

A. M. cir. 3607 B. C. cir. 397 Ol. cir. XCV. 4 Urbis Conditæ cir. annum 356

AND now, O ye priests, this
commandment *is* for you.
2 [a]If ye will not hear, and if
ye will not lay *it* to heart, to
give glory unto my name, saith the LORD of
hosts, I will even send a curse upon you, and
I will curse your blessings: yea, I have
[b]cursed them already, because ye do not lay
it to heart.

3 Behold, I will [c]corrupt your
seed, and [d]spread dung upon
your faces, *even* the dung of
your solemn feasts; and [e]*one*
shall [f]take you away with it.
4 And ye shall know that I have sent this
commandment unto you, that my covenant
might be with Levi, saith the LORD of hosts.
5 [g]My covenant was with him of life and

A. M. cir. 3607 B. C. cir. 397 Ol. cir. XCV. 4 Urbis Conditæ cir. annum 356

[a]Lev. xxvi. 14, &c.; Deut. xxviii. 15, &c.——[b]2 Pet. ii. 14——[c]Or, *reprove*——[d]Heb. *scatter*

[e]Or, *it shall take you away to it*——[f]1 Kings xiv. 10 [g]Num. xxv. 12; Ezek. xxxiv. 25; xxxvii. 26

NOTES ON CHAP. II

Verse 2. *If ye will not hear*] What I have spoken, *lay it to heart,* and let it sink down into your souls.

Give glory unto my name] That *honour* that is due to me as a *Father,* and that *fear* that belongs to me as a *Master,* chap. i. 6.

I will even send a curse upon you] I will dispense no more good.

I will curse your blessings] Even that which *ye have* already shall not profit you. When temporal blessings are not the means of leading us to God and heaven, they will infallibly lead us to hell. In speaking of the abuse of temporal blessings, one of our old poets, in his homely phrase, expresses himself thus,—

Thus God's best gifts, usurped by wicked ones,
To poison turn by their con-ta-gi-ons.

Yea, I have cursed them already] This may refer, generally, to *unfruitful seasons;* or, particularly, to a *dearth* that appears to have happened about this time. See Haggai i. 6-11.

Verse 3. *Behold, I will corrupt your seed*] So as to render it unfruitful. *Newcome* translates,—"I will take away from you the shoulder." This was the part that belonged to the priest, Lev. vii. 32; Deut. xviii. 3.

Spread dung upon your faces] Instead of *receiving* a sacrifice at your hands, I will throw your offerings back into your faces. Here God shows his *contempt* for *them* and their offerings.

Verse 4. *This commandment*] That in the *first* verse; to drive such priests from his presence and his service.

That my covenant might be with Levi] I gave the priesthood and the service of my altar to that tribe.

Verse 5. *My covenant was with him of life and peace*] These are the *two* grand blessings given to men by the NEW *Covenant,* which was shadowed by the OLD. To man, excluded from the favour of God, and sentenced to death because of sin, God gave ברית *berith,* a *covenant sacrifice,* and this secured *life*—exemption from the death deserved by transgressors; communication of that *inward spiritual life* given by Christ, and issuing in that *eternal life* promised to all his faithful disciples. And, as it secured *life,* so it gave *peace,* prosperity, and happiness; *peace* between God and man, between man and man, and between man and his own conscience.

A. M. cir. 3607
B. C. cir. 397
Ol. cir. XCV. 4
Urbis Conditæ
cir. annum
356

peace; and I gave them to him
[h]for the fear wherewith he feared
me, and was afraid before my
name.

6 [i]The law of truth was in his mouth, and
iniquity was not found in his lips: he walked
with me in peace and equity, and did [k]turn
many away from iniquity.

7 [l]For the priest's lips should keep knowledge, and they should seek the law at his
mouth: [m]for he *is* the messenger of the LORD
of hosts.

8 But ye are departed out of the way; ye
[n]have caused many to [o]stumble at the law;
[p]ye have corrupted the covenant of Levi, saith
the LORD of hosts.

9 Therefore [q]have I also made you contemptible and base before all the people, according as ye have not kept my ways, but [r]have
[s]been partial in the law.

10 [t]Have we not all one Father? [u]hath not
one God created us? why do we
deal treacherously every man
against his brother, by profaning
the covenant of our fathers?

A. M. cir. 3607
B. C. cir. 397
Ol. cir. XCV. 4
Urbis Conditæ
cir. annum
356

11 Judah hath dealt treacherously, and an
abomination is committed in Israel and in
Jerusalem; for Judah hath profaned the holiness of the LORD which he [v]loved, [w]and hath
married the daughter of a strange god.

12 The LORD will cut off the man that doeth
this, [x]the master and the scholar, out of the
tabernacles of Jacob, [y]and him that offereth
an offering unto the LORD of hosts.

13 And this have ye done again, covering
the altar of the LORD with tears, with weeping, and with crying out, insomuch that he
regardeth not the offering any more, or receiveth *it* with good will at your hand.

14 Yet ye say, Wherefore? Because the
LORD hath been witness between thee and
[z]the wife of thy youth, against whom thou hast

---

[h]Deut. xxxiii. 8, 9——[i]Deut. xxxiii. 10——[k]Jer. xxiii. 22; James v 20——[l]Deut. xvii. 9, 10; xxiv. 8; Lev. x. 11; Ezra vii. 10; Jer. xviii. 18; Hag. ii. 11, 12 [m]Gal. iv. 14——[n]1 Sam. ii. 17; Jer. xviii. 15——[o]Or, *fall in the law*——[p]Neh. xiii. 29——[q]1 Sam. ii. 30

[r]Or, *lifted up the face against*——[s]Heb. *accepted faces* [t]1 Cor. viii. 6; Eph. iv. 6——[u]Gen. i. 27; Deut. iv. 32; Job xxxi. 15——[v]Or, *ought to love*——[w]Ezra ix. 1; x. 2; Neh. xiii. 23——[x]Or, *him that waketh and him that answereth*——[y]Neh. xiii. 28, 29——[z]Prov. v. 18

Verse 6. *The law of truth was in his mouth*] See the qualifications of Levi: 1. "He feared me;" he was my sincere worshipper. 2. "He was afraid;" he acted as in the presence of a *just* and holy God, and acted *conscientiously* in all that he did. 3. "My law of truth was ever in his mouth;" by this he directed his own conduct and that of others. 4. "No iniquity;" nothing contrary to justice and equity ever proceeded "from his lips." 5. "He walked with me in peace;" he lived in such a way as to keep up union with me. 6. "He did turn many away from iniquity;" by his upright administration, faithful exhortations, and pious walk, he became the instrument of converting many sinners. This character suits every genuine minister of God. And as the priest's *lips* should preserve knowledge, so the *people* should seek "the law at his mouth;" for he is the messenger of the Lord of hosts, ver. 7.

Verse 8. *But ye are departed out of the way*] Ye are become impure yourselves, and ye have led others into iniquity.

Verse 9. *Therefore have I also made you contemptible*] The people despised you because they saw that you acted contrary to your functions. This has happened repeatedly since, to several *classes of priests.* Not maintaining, by *purity of life* and *soundness of doctrine*, the dignity of the ministerial function, they became contemptible before the people; their meager preaching was disregarded, and their persons at last cast out as a general loathing to the universe! See what happened to the truly abominable priesthood of France and Rome, 1796-8. They were the *sole cause* of that *infidelity* that brought about the *revolution.* They are now partially restored; and are endeavouring to supply by *grimace, paltry superstition,* and *jesuitical cunning,* what they want in purity of morals, soundness of doctrine, and unction from God. They must mend, or look for another revolution. Mankind will no longer put up with the *chaff* of puerile and fanatical ceremonies in place of the *wheat* of God's word and worship.

Verse 10. *Have we not all one Father?*] From this to ver. 16 the prophet censures the *marriages* of *Israelites* with *strange women*, which the law had forbidden, Deut. vii. 3. And also *divorces*, which seem to have been multiplied for the purpose of contracting these prohibited marriages.—*Newcome.*

Why do we deal treacherously] Gain the affections of the daughter of a brother *Jew*, and then *profane the covenant* of *marriage*, held sacred among *our fathers*, by putting away this same wife and daughter! How wicked, cruel, and inhuman!

Verse 11. *Daughter of a strange god.*] Of a man who worships an idol.

Verse 12. *The master and the scholar*] He who teachers such doctrine, and he who follows this teaching, the Lord will cut off both the one and the other.

Verse 13. *Covering the altar of the Lord with tears*] Of the poor women who, being *divorced* by cruel husbands, come to the priests, and make an appeal to God at the altar; and ye do not speak against this glaring injustice.

Verse 14. *Ye say, Wherefore?*] Is the Lord angry with us? Because ye have been *witness* of the *contract* made between the parties; and

A. M. cir. 3607
B. C. cir. 397
Ol. cir. XCV. 4
Uebis Conditæ
cir. annum
356

dealt treacherously: [a]yet *is* she
thy companion, and the wife of
thy covenant.
15 And [b]did not he make one?
Yet had he the [c]residue of the Spirit. And
wherefore one? That he might seek [d]a [e]godly
seed. Therefore take heed to your spirit, and
let none deal [f]treacherously against the wife of
his youth.
16 For [g]the LORD, the God of Israel, saith
[h]that he hateth [i]putting away: for *one* covereth violence with his garment,
saith the LORD of hosts: therefore take heed to your spirit,
that ye deal not treacherously.
17 [k]Ye have wearied the LORD with your
words. Yet ye say, Wherein have we wearied
him? When ye say, Every one that doeth
evil *is* good in the sight of the LORD, and he
delighteth in them; or, Where *is* the God of
judgment?

A. M. cir. 3607
B. C. cir. 397
Ol. cir. XCV. 4
Urbis Conditæ
cir. annum
356

[a]Prov. ii. 17——[b]Matt. xix. 4, 5——[c]Or, *excellency*——[d]Heb. *a seed of God*——[e]Ezra ix. 2; 1 Cor. vii. 14——[f]Or, *unfaithfully*

[g]Deut. xxiv. 1; Matt. v. 32; xix. 8——[h]Or, *if he hate her, put her away*——[i]Heb. *to put away*——[k]Isa. xliii. 24; Amos ii. 13; chap. iii. 13, 14, 15

when the lawless husband divorced *his wife, the wife of his youth, his companion,* and the *wife of his covenant,* ye did not execute on him the discipline of the law. They kept their wives till they had *passed their youth,* and then put them away, that they might get *young ones* in their place.

Verse 15. *And did not he make one?*] ONE of *each kind,* Adam and Eve. *Yet had he the residue of the Spirit;* he could have made millions of pairs, and inspired them all with *living souls.* Then *wherefore one?* He made one pair from whom all the rest might proceed, that he might have a *holy offspring;* that children being a marked property of *one man* and *one woman,* proper care might be taken that they should be brought up in the discipline of the Lord. Perhaps the *holy* or *godly seed,* זרע אלהים *zera Elohim, a seed of God,* may refer to the MESSIAH. God would have the *whole human race* to spring from *one pair,* that Christ, springing from the *same family,* might in his sufferings taste death for every *man;* because he had that nature that was common to the *whole human race.* Had there been *several heads of families* in the beginning, Jesus must have been incarnated *from each of those heads,* else his death could have availed for those only who belonged to the *family* of which he was incarnated.

Take heed to your spirit] Scrutinize the motives which induce you to put away your wives.

Verse 16. *For the Lord—hateth putting away*] He abominates all such divorces, and *him* that makes them.

Covereth violence with his garment] And he also *notes* those who frame idle excuses to *cover* the *violence* they have done to the wives of their youth, by putting them away, and taking others in their place, whom they *now* happen to like better, when their own wives have been worn down in domestic services.

Verse 17. *Ye have wearied the Lord*] He has borne with you so long, and has been provoked so often, that he will bear it no longer. It is not fit that he should.

Every one that doeth evil] Ye say that it is *right* in the sight of the Lord to put away a wife, because she has no longer found favour in the sight of her husband. And because it has not been signally punished hitherto, ye blaspheme and cry out, "Where is the God of judgment?" Were he such as he is represented, would he not speak out? All these things show that this people were horribly corrupt. The priests were bad; the prophets were bad; the Levites were bad; and no wonder that the people were irreligious, profane, profligate, and cruel.

CHAPTER III

In allusion to the custom of sending pioneers to prepare the way for the march of an eastern monarch, the coming of Christ's forerunner is described, and then the coming of Christ himself, 1; *with the terrible judgments which were to accompany that event, in order to refine and purify his people and his priests,* 2–6. *The following verses reprehend them for withholding the legal tithes and offerings, with large promises in case of their repentance and amendments,* 7–12. *The prophet expostulates with the people for their hard and profane speeches against the conduct of Providence, and declares God will one day make a fearful and final distinction between the righteous and the wicked, whose different characters are in the mean time carefully recorded,* 13–18.

A. M. cir. 3607
B. C. cir. 397
Ol. cir. XCV. 4
Urbis Conditæ
cir. annum
356

BEHOLD, [a]I will send my messenger, and he shall [b]prepare the way before me: and the LORD, whom ye seek, shall suddenly come to his temple, [c]even the Messenger of the covenant, whom ye delight in: behold, [d]he shall come, saith the LORD of hosts.

2 But who may abide [e]the day of his coming? and [f]who shall stand when he appeareth? for [g]he *is* like a refiner's fire, and like fuller's soap.

3 And [h]he shall sit *as* a refiner and purifier of silver; and he shall purify the sons of Levi, and purge them as gold and silver, that they may [i]offer unto the LORD an offering in righteousness.

4 Then [k]shall the offering of Judah and Jerusalem be pleasant unto the LORD, as in the days of old, and as in [l]former years.

5 And I will come near to you to judgment; and I will be a swift witness against the sorcerers, and against the adulterers, [m]and against false swearers, and against those that [n]oppress the hireling in *his* wages, the widow, and the fatherless, and that turn aside the stranger *from his right,* and fear not me, saith the LORD of hosts.

A. M. cir. 3607
B. C. cir. 397
Ol. cir. XCV. 4
Urbis Conditæ
cir. annum
356

6 For I *am* the Lord, [o]I change not; [p]therefore ye sons of Jacob are not consumed.

7 Even from the days of [q]your fathers ye are gone away from mine ordinances, and have not kept *them.* [r]Return unto me, and I will return unto you, saith the LORD of hosts. [s]But ye said, Wherein shall we return?

8 Will a man rob God? Yet ye have robbed me. But ye say, Wherein have we robbed thee? [t]In tithes and offerings.

9 Ye *are* cursed with a curse: for ye have robbed me, *even* this whole nation.

[a]Matt. xi. 10; Mark i 2; Luke i. 76; vii. 27——[b]Isa. xl. 3——[c]Isa. lxiii 9——[d]Hag. ii. 7——[e]Chap. iv. 1 [f]Rev. vi. 17——[g]See Isa. iv. 4; Matt. iii. 10, 11, 12 [h]Isa. i. 25; Zech. xiii. 9——[i]1 Pet. ii. 5

[k]Chap. i. 11——[l]Or, *ancient*——[m]Zech. v. 4; James v. 4, 12——[n]Or, *defraud*——[o]Num. xxiii. 19; Rom. xi. 29; James i. 17——[p]Lam. iii. 22——[q]Acts vii. 51——[r]Zech. i. 3——[s]Chap. i. 6——[t]Neh. xiii. 10, 12

NOTES ON CHAP. III

Verse 1. *Behold, I will send my messenger*] מלאכי *Malachi*, the very name of the *prophet.* But this speaks of John the Baptist. I, the Messiah, the *Seed of God*, mentioned above, *will send my messenger*, John the Baptist.

He shall prepare the way] Be as a pioneer before me; a corrector of civil abuses, and a preacher of righteousness.

And the Lord, whom ye seek] The *Messiah*, whom ye expect, from the account given by the prophet Daniel, in his *seventy weeks*, chap. ix. 24.

Shall suddenly come to his temple] Shall soon be presented before the Lord in his temple; cleanse it from its defilement, and fill it with his teaching and his glory.

The Messenger of the covenant] He that comes to fulfil the great design, in reference to the covenant made with Abram, that *in his seed all the families of the earth should be blessed.* See the *parallel* texts in the margin, and the *notes* on them.

Verse 2. *But who may abide the day of his coming?*] Only they who shall believe on his name; for they that *will* not, shall be blinded, and the unbelieving nations shall be destroyed by the Romans.

Like fuller's soap] כברית *keborith*, from ברר *barar*, to *cleanse*, any thing that deterges. *Kali*, or *fern ashes*, or such things. I doubt whether the *composition* which we call *soap*, was known in ancient times.

Verse 3. *He shall sit as a refiner*] Alluding to the case of a refiner of metals, *sitting* at his fire; increasing it when he sees necessary, and watching the process of his work.

The sons of Levi] Those who minister in their stead under the NEW *covenant*, for the OLD Levitical institutions shall be abolished; yet, under the preaching of our Lord, a *great number of the priests became obedient to the faith*, Acts vi. 7; and, as to the others that did not believe, this great Refiner threw them as *dross* into the Roman fire, that consumed both Jerusalem and the temple.

Verse 5. *I will come near to you to judgment*] And what fearful *cases* does he get to judge! *Sorcerers, adulterers, false swearers, defrauders of the wages* of the *hireling, oppressors* of *widows* and *orphans*, and *perverters* of the *stranger* and such as *do not fear the Lord:* a horrible crew; and the land at that time was full of them. Several were converted under the preaching of Christ and his apostles, and the rest the Romans *destroyed* or carried into *captivity.*

Verse 6. *I am the Lord, I change not*] The new dispensation of grace and goodness, which is *now* about to be introduced, is not the effect of any *change* in my *counsels;* it is, on the contrary, the fulfilment of my everlasting purposes; as is also the throwing aside of the Mosaic ritual, which was only intended to *introduce* the great and glorious Gospel of my Son.

And because of this ancient covenant, ye Jews are not *totally consumed;* but ye are now, and shall be still, preserved as a distinct people—monuments both of my justice and mercy.

Verse 7. *Gone away from mine ordinances*] Never acting according to their spirit and design.

Return unto me] There is still space to repent.

Wherein shall we return?] Their consciences were *seared*, and they knew not that they were *sinners.*

Verse 8. *Will a man rob God?*] Here is one point on which ye are guilty; ye withhold the *tithes* and *offerings* from the temple of God, so that the Divine worship is neglected.

A. M. cir. 3607
B. C. cir. 397
Ol. cir. XCV. 4
Urbis Conditæ
cir. annum
356

10 [u]Bring ye all the tithes into [v]the storehouse, that there may be meat in mine house, and prove me now herewith, saith the LORD of hosts, if I will not open you the [w]windows of heaven, and [x]pour [y]you out a blessing, that *there shall* not *be room* enough *to receive it.*

11 And I will rebuke [z]the devourer for your sakes, and he shall not [a]destroy the fruits of your ground; neither shall your vine cast her fruit before the time in the field, saith the LORD of hosts.

12 And all nations shall call you blessed: for ye shall be [b]a delightsome land, saith the LORD of hosts.

13 [c]Your words have been stout against me, saith the LORD. Yet ye say, What have we spoken *so much* against thee?

14 [d]Ye have said, It *is* vain to serve God: and what profit *is it* that we have kept [e]his ordinance, and that we have walked [f]mournfully before the LORD of hosts?

A. M. cir. 3607
B. C. cir. 397
Ol. cir. XCV. 4
Urbis Conditæ
cir. annum
356

15 And now [g]we call the proud happy; yea, they that work wickedness [h]are set up; yea, *they that* [i]tempt God are even delivered.

16 Then they [k]that feared the LORD [l]spake often one to another: and the LORD hearkened, and heard *it,* and [m]a book of remembrance was written before him for them that feared the LORD, and that thought upon his name.

17 And [n]they shall be mine, saith the LORD of hosts, in that day when I make up my [o]jewels;[p] and [q]I will spare them, as a man spareth his own son that serveth him.

18 [r]Then shall ye return, and discern between the righteous and the wicked, between him that serveth God and him that serveth him not.

---

[u]Prov. iii. 9, 10——[v]1 Chron. xxxvi. 20; 2 Chron. xxxi. 11; Neh. x. 38; xvi. 12——[w]Gen. vii. 11; 2 Kings vii. 2——[x]Heb. *empty out*——[y]2 Chron. xxxi. 10 [z]Amos iv. 9——[a]Heb. *corrupt*——[b]Dan. viii. 9——[c]Ch. ii. 17——[d]Job xxi. 14, 15; xxii. 17; Psa. lxxiii. 12; Zeph. i. 12——[e]Heb. *his observation*——[f]Heb. *in black*

[g]Psa. lxxiii. 12; chap. ii. 17——[h]Heb. *are built* [i]Psa. xcv. 9——[k]Psa. lxvi. 16; chap. iv. 2——[l]Hebrews iii. 13——[m]Psa. lvi. 8; Isa. lxv. 6; Rev. xx. 12——[n]Exodus xix. 5; Deut. vii. 6; Psa. cxxxv. 4; Tit. ii. 14; 1 Peter ii. 9——[o]Or, *special treasure*——[p]Isa. lxii. 3 [q]Psalm ciii. 13——[r]Psa. lviii. 11

Verse 9. *Ye are cursed with a curse*] The whole nation is under my displeasure. The curse of God is upon you.

Verse 10. *Bring ye all the tithes*] They had so withheld these that the priests had not food enough to support life, and the sacred service was interrupted. See Neh. xiii. 10.

And prove me now herewith] What ye give to God shall never lessen your store. Give as ye *should,* and see whether I will not so increase your store by *opening the windows of heaven*—giving you *rain* and *fruitful seasons* —that your *barns* and *granaries* shall not be able to contain the abundance of your *harvests* and *vintage.*

Verse 11. *I will rebuke the devourer*] The *locusts,* &c., shall not come on your crops; and those that are in the country I will disperse and destroy.

Neither shall your vine cast her fruit] Every *blossom* shall bear *fruit,* and every *bunch of grapes* come to *maturity.*

Verse 12. *All nations shall call you blessed*] They shall see that a peculiar blessing of God rests upon you, and your *land shall be delightsome;* like *Paradise,* the *garden of the Lord.*

Verse 13. *Your words have been stout against me*] He speaks here to *open infidels* and *revilers.*

What have we spoken] They are ready either to deny the whole, or impudently to maintain and defend what they had spoken!

Verse 14. *Ye have said, It* is *vain to serve God*] They strove to destroy the Divine worship; they asserted that it was *vanity;* that, if they performed acts of worship, they should be nothing the better; and if they abstained, they should be nothing the worse. This was their teaching to the people.

Walked mournfully] Even *repentance* they have declared to be useless. This was a high pitch of ungodliness; but see what follows; behold the general *conclusions* of these reprobates—

Verse 15. *And now we call the proud happy*] Proud and insolent men are the only happy people, for they domineer everywhere, and none dares to resist them.

They that work wickedness are set up] The *humble* and *holy* are depressed and miserable; the *proud* and *wicked* are in places of *trust* and *profit.* Too often it is so.

They that *tempt God are even delivered.*] Even those who *despise* God, and *insult* his justice and providence, are preserved in and from dangers; while the *righteous* fall by them.

Verse 16. *They that feared the Lord*] There were a few godly in the land, who, hearing the language and seeing the profligacy of the rebels above, concluded that some signal mark of God's vengeance must fall upon them; they, therefore, as the corruption increased, cleaved the closer to their Maker. There are *three characteristics* given of this people, viz.:—

1. *They feared the Lord.* They had that reverence for Jehovah that caused them to depart from evil, and to keep his ordinances.

2. *They spake often one to another.* They kept up the communion of saints. By mutual exhortation they strengthened each other's hands in the Lord.

3. *They thought on his name.* His name was sacred to them; it was a fruitful source of profound and edifying *meditation.* The *name of God* is *God himself* in the plenitude of his power, omniscience, justice, goodness, mercy, and truth. What a source for thinking and contemplation! See how God treats such per-

sons: *The Lord hearkened* to their conversation, *heard* the meditations of their hearts; and so *approved* of the whole that *a book of remembrance was written before the Lord*—all their *names* were carefully *registered* in heaven. Here is an allusion to *records* kept by kings, Esth. vi. 1, of such as had performed signal services, and who should be the first to be rewarded.

Verse 17. *They shall be mine*] I will acknowledge them as *my subjects and followers;* in *the day*, especially, when I come to punish the wicked and reward the righteous.

When I make up my jewels] סגלה *segullah*, my *peculium*, my *proper treasure;* that which is *a man's own*, and *most prized* by him. Not *jewels;* for in no part of the Bible does the word *mean* a *gem* or *precious stone* of any kind. The interpretations frequently given of the word in this verse, comparing *saints* to *jewels*, are *forced* and *false.*

I will spare them] When I come to visit the wicked, I will take care of them. I will act towards them as a *tender father* would act towards his most *loving* and *obedient son.*

Verse 18. *Then shall ye return*] To your *senses*, when perhaps *too late;* and *discern*—see the difference which God makes, *between the righteous and the wicked*, which will be most *marked* and *awful.*

Between him that serveth God] Your obedience to whom, ye said, would be unprofitable to you.

And him that serveth him not.] Of whom ye said, his disobedience would be no prejudice to him. You will find the former received into the kingdom of glory; and the latter, with yourselves, thrust down into the bitter pains of an eternal death. Reader, ponder these things.

In the great day of the Lord, at least, if not long before, it will be fully discovered who have been the truly wise people; those who took up their cross and followed Christ; or those who satisfied the flesh, with its affections and desires, following a multitude to do evil.

CHAPTER IV

God's awful judgments on the wicked, 1. *Great blessedness of the righteous*, 2, 3. *The prophet then, with a solemnity becoming the last of the prophets, closes the Sacred Canon with enjoining the strict observance of the law till the forerunner already promised should appear, in the spirit of Elijah, to introduce the Messiah, and begin a new and everlasting dispensation*, 4–6.

A. M. cir. 3607 FOR behold, [a]the day cometh,
B. C. cir. 397 that shall burn as an oven;
Ol. cir. XCV. 4 and all [b]the proud, yea, and all
Urbis Conditæ cir. annum 356 that do wickedly, shall be [c]stub-
ble: and the day that cometh shall burn them
up, saith the LORD of hosts, that it shall [d]leave
them neither root nor branch.

2 But unto you that [e]fear my A. M. cir. 3607
name shall the [f]Sun of right- B. C. cir. 397
eousness arise with healing in his Ol. cir. XCV. 4
wings; and ye shall go forth, and Urbis Conditæ cir. annum 356
grow up as calves of the stall.
3 [g]And ye shall tread down the wicked; for
they shall be ashes under the soles of your

[a]Joel ii. 31; ch. iii. 2; 2 Pet. iii. 7——[b]Chap. iii. 18 [c]Obad. 18——[d]Amos ii. 9——[e]Chap. iii. 16

[f]Luke i. 78; Eph. v. 14; 2 Pet. i. 19; Rev. ii. 28——[g]2 Sam. xxviii. 43; Mic. vii. 10; Zech. x. 5

NOTES ON CHAP. IV

Verse 1. *Behold, the day cometh, that shall burn as an oven*] The destruction of Jerusalem by the Romans.

And all the proud] This is in reference to ver. 15 of the preceding chapter.

The day that cometh shall burn them up] Either by famine, by sword, or by captivity. All those rebels shall be destroyed.

It shall leave them neither root nor branch.] A proverbial expression for total destruction. Neither *man* nor *child* shall escape.

Verse 2. *You that fear my name*] The persons mentioned in the *sixteenth* verse of the preceding chapter; ye that look for redemption through the Messiah.

The Sun of righteousness] The Lord Jesus, the promised Messiah; the Hope of Israel.

With healing in his wings] As the *sun*, by the rays of *light* and *heat*, revives, cheers, and fructifies the whole creation, giving, through God, *light* and *life* everywhere; so Jesus Christ, by the influences of his *grace* and *Spirit*, shall quicken, awaken, enlighten, warm, invigorate, heal, purify, and refine every soul that believes in him; and, by his *wings* or *rays*, diffuse these blessings from one end of heaven to another; everywhere invigorating the *seeds* of *righteousness*, and *withering* and *drying up* the *seeds of sin.* The *rays* of this *Sun* are the *truths* of his *Gospel*, and the *influences* of his *Spirit.* And at present these are universally diffused.

And ye shall go forth] Ye who believe on his name shall go forth out of Jerusalem when the Romans shall come up against it. After Cestius Gallus had blockaded the city for some days, he suddenly raised the siege. The Christians who were then in it, knowing, by seeing Jerusalem encompassed with armies, that the day of its destruction was come, when their Lord commanded them to flee into the mountains, took this opportunity to escape from Jerusalem, and go to Pella, in Cœlesyria; so that no Christian life fell in the siege and destruction of this city.

But these words are of more general application and meaning; "ye shall go forth" in all the occupations of life, but particularly in the means of grace; and—

Grow up as calves of the stall] Full of health, of life, and spirits; satisfied and happy.

Verse 3. *Ye shall tread down*] This may be the commission given to the Romans: Tread down the wicked people, tread down the wicked place; set it on fire, and let the *ashes* be trodden down under your feet.

A. M. cir. 3607
B. C. cir. 397
Ol. cir. XCV. 4
Urbis Conditæ
cir. annum
356

feet in the day that I shall do
this, saith the LORD of hosts.
4 Remember ye the [h]law of
Moses my servant, which I com-
manded unto him [i]in Horeb for all Israel, *with*
[k]the statutes and judgments.
5 Behold, I will send you [l]Elijah the prophet [m]before the coming of the
great and dreadful day of the
LORD:
6 And [n]he shall turn the heart
of the fathers to the children, and the heart of
the children to their fathers, lest I come and
[o]smite the earth with [p]a curse.

[h]Exod. xx. 3, &c.——[i]Deut. iv. 10——[k]Psa. cxlvii. 19
[l]Matt. xi. 14; xvii. 11; Mark ix. 11; Luke i. 17
[m]Joel ii. 31——[n]Ecclus. xlviii. 10——[o]Zech. xiv. 12
[p]Zech. v. 3

Verse 4. *Remember ye the law of Moses*] Where all these things are predicted. The *Septuagint, Arabic,* and *Coptic,* place this verse the last.

Verse 5. *Behold, I will send you Elijah the prophet*] This is meant alone of John the Baptist, as we learn from Luke i. 17, (where see the note,) in whose spirit and power he came.

Verse 6. *And he shall turn* (convert) *the heart of the fathers* (על *al,* WITH) *the children*] Or, together with the children; both old and young. *Lest I come, and,* finding them unconverted, *smite the land with a curse,* חרם *cherem, utter extinction.* So we find that, had the Jews turned to God, and received the Messiah at the preaching of John the Baptist and that of Christ and his apostles, the awful חרם *cherem* of final excision and execration would not have been executed upon them. However, they filled up the cup of their iniquity, and were *reprobated,* and the Gentiles *elected* in their stead. Thus, the last was first, and the first was last. Glory to God for his unspeakable gift!

There are *three* remarkable *predictions* in this chapter:—1. The advent of John Baptist, in the spirit and authority of Elijah. 2. The manifestation of Christ in the flesh, under the emblem of the Sun of righteousness. 3. The final destruction of Jerusalem, represented under the emblem of a burning oven, consuming every thing cast into it. These three prophecies, relating to the most important facts that have ever taken place in the history of the world, announced here nearly *four hundred* years before their occurrence, have been most circumstantially fulfilled.

In most of the Masoretic Bibles the *fifth* verse is repeated after the *sixth*—"Behold, I send unto you Elijah the prophet, before the great and terrible day of Jehovah come;" for the Jews do not like to let their sacred book end with a *curse;* and hence, in reading, they immediately subjoin the above verse, or else the *fourth*—"Remembering ye the law of Moses my servant."

In one of my oldest MSS. the *fifth* verse is *repeated,* and written at full length: "Behold, I send you Elijah the prophet, before the coming of the great and dreadful day of the Lord." In another, only these words are added: "Behold, I will send you Elijah." It is on this ground that the Jews expect the reappearance of Elijah the prophet; and at their marriage-feast always set a chair and knife and fork for this prophet, whom they suppose to be invisibly present. But we have already seen that John the Baptist, the forerunner of our Lord, was the person designed; for he came in the spirit and power of Elijah, (see on chap. iii. 1,) and has fulfilled this prophetic promise. John is come, and the Lord Jesus has come also; he has shed his blood for the salvation of a lost world; he has ascended on high; he has sent forth his Holy Spirit; he has commissioned his ministers to proclaim to all mankind redemption in his blood; and he is ever present with them, and is filling the earth with righteousness and true holiness. Hallelujah! The kingdoms of this world are about to become the kingdoms of God and our Lord Jesus! And now, having just arrived at the end of my race in this work, and seeing the wonderful extension of the work of God in the earth, my heart prays:—

O Jesus, ride on, till all are subdued,
Thy mercy make known, and sprinkle thy blood;
Display thy salvation, and teach the new song,
To every nation, and people, and tongue!

In most MSS. and *printed Masoretic Bibles* there are only *three* chapters in this prophet, the *fourth* being joined to the *third,* making it *twenty-four* verses.

In the Jewish reckonings the *Twelve Minor Prophets* make but one book; hence there is no Masoretic note found at the end of any of the preceding prophets, with accounts of its *verses, sections,* &c.; but, at the end of *Malachi* we find the following table, which, though it gives the number of verses in each prophet, yet gives the *total sum, middle verse,* and *sections,* at the end of Malachi, thereby showing that they consider the whole *twelve* as constituting but *one book.*

MASORETIC NOTES

On the Twelve Minor Prophets

Hosea has - - - - - -	197 verses.
Joel- - - - - - - - -	73
Amos - - - - - - - -	146
Obadiah - - - - - - -	21
Jonah - - - - - - -	48
Micah - - - - - - -	105
Nahum - - - - - - -	57
Zephaniah - - - - - -	53
Habakkuk - - - - - -	56
Haggai - - - - - - -	38
Zechariah - - - - - -	211
Malachi - - - - - - -	55

The sum of all the verses of the Twelve Minor Prophets is 1060

The middle verse is Micah, chap. iii. ver. 12.

Number of Sections, 21.

TO GOD THE FATHER, SON, AND HOLY GHOST, BE ETERNAL PRAISES. AMEN.

I have this day completed this Commentary, on which I have laboured *above thirty* years; and which, when I began, I never expected to live long enough to finish. May it be a means of securing glory to God in the highest, and peace and good will among men upon earth! Amen, Amen. ADAM CLARKE.

Heydon Hall, Middlesex,
Monday, March 28, A. D. 1825.

AN

EPITOME OF THE JEWISH HISTORY

FROM THE

TIME OF NEHEMIAH AND MALACHI TO THE BIRTH OF CHRIST

FILLING UP THE CHASM BETWEEN

THE OLD AND NEW TESTAMENTS

As many have wished to see an epitome of the Jewish history, from the days of the prophet Malachi to the advent of Christ, in order to connect the history of the Old and New Testaments, I have prepared the following, which, in such a work as this, is as much as should be expected.

On all hands *Malachi* is allowed to have been the *last* prophet under the Old Testament; and he flourished about *four hundred and nine* years before the coming of Christ, according to the commonly received chronology; and *Nehemiah*, who was contemporary with him, was the last of those civil governors appointed by God himself. His last act of reformation is fixed by Prideaux, B. C. 409; soon after which it is supposed that he died, as at this time he could not be less than *seventy* years of age. For the administration of affairs in his times and in those of Ezra, whom he succeeded in the government of Judea, the reader is referred to the notes on Ezra, Nehemiah, and Daniel.

We have seen, in the book of Nehemiah, that, on the return of the Jews from the Chaldean captivity, many of them brought strange wives and a spurious offspring with them, and refusing to put them away, were banished by Nehemiah, and went and settled in Samaria. Among those exiles there was a son of Jehoiada, the high priest, named *Manasseh*, who had married the daughter of Sanballat the Horonite, and put himself under the protection of his father-in-law, who was governor of the place. After the death of Nehemiah, Sanballat obtained a grant from Darius to build a temple on Mount *Gerizim*, near Samaria, of which he made *Manasseh*, his son-in-law, high priest. This temple was begun to be built B. C. 408.

From the building of this temple, *Samaria* became the refuge of all refractory Jews: and though by this means the old superstition of the land was reformed to the worship of the God of *Israel*, they of *Jerusalem* would never consider the *Samaritan Jews* otherwise than *apostates*. On the other hand, the *Samaritans* maintained that Mount *Gerizim* was the only proper place for the worship of God. This people rejected all traditions, and adhered only to the written word contained in the five books of *Moses*.

Nehemiah's death was also attended with a change of the *Jewish* government at *Jerusalem*. *Judea* had no longer a governor of its own. It was united to the *prefecture* of *Syria;* the rulers of which committed the administration of both *civil* and *ecclesiastical* affairs to the high priest for the time being.

By this means the high priesthood became an office under the *heathen;* and towards the latter end of *Artaxerxes Mnemon's* reign, B. C. 405, who succeeded his father *Darius Nothus*, B. C. 423, the office was conferred by the governor of *Syria* and *Phœnicia*. For *Bagoses*, the governor, took upon himself to displace *Johanan* the high priest, in favour of the said priest's brother *Joshua;* which nomination, though it did not take place, (for *Johanan* slew his brother *Joshua* in the inner court of the temple, as he endeavoured by force to usurp the high-priest's office by virtue of the governor's commission, B. C. 366,) was attended with this bad consequence—that *Bagoses*, hearing of the murder, came in great wrath to *Jerusalem*, and laid a heavy fine upon the nation, which lasted *seven* years, or during the whole of his government.

Artaxerxes Mnemon died B. C. 359, with grief at the brutality of his son *Ochus*, who had so terrified his eldest brother *Ariaspes*, that he poisoned himself, and had his younger brother *Harpates* assassinated. So that *Ochus* succeeded to the dignity and empire of his father.

In the third year of *Ochus*, about 356 before *Christ*, *Alexander the Great* was born at *Pella* in *Macedonia*. *Ochus*, having reigned *twenty-one* years, was poisoned by his favourite *Bagoas*, in hopes of getting the whole government into his own hands, and to put the crown on the head of *Arses*, his youngest son, whom he also poisoned soon after, and raised *Codomannus*, a distant relation of the late king, to the throne. This new king took the name of *Darius;* and when *Bagoas* had also prepared a poisonous draught for *him*, he obliged *Bagoas* to drink it himself; by which means he saved his own life, and punished the traitor.

It was about the year B. C. 336 that *Alexander the Great* succeeded to the kingdom of *Macedon*, on the death of his father *Philip*, who was slain by the noble Macedonian *Pausanias*, as he celebrated the marriage of his daughter with *Alexander*, king of *Epirus*, before he set out upon the *Grecian* expedition against *Persia*, being chosen *captain-general* of the united forces of *Greece*.

Alexander also succeeded to that command by a new election. In one campaign he overran all *Asia Minor;* vanquished *Darius* in two battles; took his mother, wife, and children prisoners; and subdued all *Syria* as far as *Tyre*, B. C. 332.

During the siege of *Tyre*, he demanded the submission of the neighbouring provinces of *Galilee*, *Samaria*, and *Judea*. The two former submitted to him; but *Judea* would not renounce their allegiance to *Darius* so long as he lived. This brought upon them the wrath of the conqueror; who, having taken *Tyre*, by carrying a bank from the continent through the sea to the island on which the city stood, and burned it down to the ground, destroyed and slew all the inhabitants in a barbarous manner, both in the sackage of the town, and afterwards in cold blood; and then marched to Jerusalem to wreak his vengeance upon the Jews. Upon his approach, and the report of his having crucified *two thousand* of the *Tyrian* prisoners, the high priest *Jaddua* and all the city were under dreadful apprehensions. They had nothing but God's protection to depend upon. They fasted and prayed: and God in a vision directed the high priest to go in his pontifical robes, attended by the high priests in their proper habits, and all the people in white garments, and meet *Alexander* out of the city.

As soon as *Alexander* saw this procession moving towards him, and the high priest in the front, he was overawed, drew near, bowed down, and saluted him in a religious manner; alleging that he did so in regard to that God whose priest he was; adding, moreover, that the high priest so habited had appeared to him in a dream at *Dio* in *Macedonia*, assuring him of success against the *Persians*.

Jaddua conducted him into the city; and, having offered sacrifices in the temple, showed him the prophecies of *Daniel*, concerning the overthrow of the *Persian* empire by a *Grecian* king.

Alexander was well satisfied with his reception at *Jerusalem;* and at his departure granted the *Jews* a *toleration* of their religion, and an exemption from tribute every *seventh* year. And the *Jews* were so well pleased with the conqueror's behaviour, that, upon his signifying that he would receive as many of them as would enlist into his service, great multitudes entered under his banner, and followed him in his other expeditions.

The *Samaritans* met him with great pomp and parade, as he left *Jerusalem*, and invited him to their city. But *Alexander* deferred both the invitation, and petition for certain privileges, till his return from *Egypt;* and left his favourite *Andromachus* governor of *Syria* and *Palestine*.

Andromachus, coming some time after to *Samaria* upon business, was burned to death in his house, as it was thought on purpose, by the *Samaritans*, in revenge of the slight which they apprehended *Alexander* had shown them. But as soon as *Alexander* heard it, he caused those to be put to death who had acted any part in the murder, banished all the other inhabitants from *Samaria*, planted therein a colony of *Macedonians*, and gave the residue to the *Jews*.

Upon the ruin of the *Persians*, *Alexander* had erected the *Grecian* or *Macedonian* monarchy. But coming to *Babylon*, after the conquest of the most part of the then known world, he gave himself up so much to drunkenness and gluttony, that he soon put an end to his life, B. C. 323.

Here it cannot be amiss to observe, that *Alexander* was of a bold and enterprising spirit; but more full of fire than discretion. His actions, though successful, were furious and extravagantly rash. His few virtues were obscured with more and greater vices. *Vainglory* was his predominant passion; and the fables of the ancient *Greek* heroes were the only *charts* by which he steered his conduct. His dragging *Balis* round *Gaza*, his expedition into *India*, his drunken procession through *Caramania*, and taking to himself the name of the son of *Jupiter*, are so many vouchers of this assertion. And, were all his actions duly considered and estimated, he would be properly characterized the great *cut-throat* of the age in which he lived; as all they are who delight in bloodshed, and will forfeit ALL to obtain *universal monarchy;* whereas those only are the true *heroes* who most benefit the world, by promoting the peace and welfare of mankind. In a righteous cause, or a just defence of a man's country, all actions of valour are worthy of praise; but in *all other* cases *victory* and *conquest* are no more than *murder* and *robbery*. Therefore *Alexander's* heroism is to be avoided, and not to be followed, as the surest way to honour and glory.

Alexander was no sooner dead, than *Ptolemy Soter* seized upon *Egypt;* and having in vain endeavoured to gain *Syria*, *Phœnicia*, and *Judea* from *Laomedon*, whom *Alexander* had appointed governor instead of *Andromachus*, who was burnt, invaded them by sea and land, took *Laomedon* prisoner, and got possession of those provinces also, except *Judea;* which, upon the account of their allegiance to the surviving governor, refusing to yield, felt the severity of the conqueror; for, understanding that the *Jews* would not so much as defend themselves on the *Sabbath day*, he stormed *Jerusalem*, took it without resistance on that day, and carried above *one hundred thousand* of them captives into *Egypt*.

From this time we may date the *Jews'* subjection to the kings of *Egypt*. And it was in the *fifth* year of this *Ptolemy's* reign that *Onias* the *Jewish* high priest died, and was succeeded by his son *Simon the Just*, on whom an eulogium may be found in Ecclus. l. 1, &c., B. C. 292.

Simon the Just was high priest *nine* years, and is supposed to have completed the canon of the Old Testament by adding the books of *Ezra*, *Nehemiah*, *Esther*, *Malachi*, and the two books of *Chronicles*, with the aid and assistance of the great synagogue. He was succeeded by his brother *Eleazar*, his son *Onias* being a minor, B. C. 291.

Ptolemy Soter was succeeded by his son *Ptolemy Philadelphus*, B. C. 285, who completed the college or *museum* of learned men, and the famous library at *Alexandria* in *Egypt*, which was begun by his father, and contained *seven hundred thousand* volumes, and placed in that library an authentic translation of the book of the *law*. This translation was finished under the inspection of *Eleazar* the high priest, and is called the *Septuagint*, on account of the joint labour of *seventy-two* translators employed in it, B. C. 254.

Ptolemy Philadelphus died in the *thirty-ninth* year of his reign, and in the *sixty-third* of his age, B. C. 247. He was a learned prince, and a great patron of learning; so that men of learning flocked to his court from all parts, and partook of his favour and bounty. Among these were the poets *Theocritus*, *Callimachus*, *Lycophron*, and *Aratus*, and *Manetho*, the *Egyptian* historian.

B. C. 247, *Ptolemy Euergetes* succeeded his father *Ptolemy* in *Egypt*. He found *Onias*, the son of *Simon the Just*, in the *pontificate* at *Jerusalem*, who was very old, weak, inconsiderate, and covetous. And *Euergetes*, perceiving that the high priest had for many years kept back the annual tribute, sent one *Athenion*, an officer at court, to *Jerusalem*, to demand it, being a very large sum, with threats of sending an army to dispossess them of the country upon refusal.

This demand and threatening threw the whole nation into great confusion; and one *Joseph*, the high priest's nephew by his sister's side, rebuked his uncle sharply for his injustice and ill management of the public interest, proposed *Onias's* journey to *Alexandria*, as the best expedient, and, upon his uncle's refusal, offered to go in person to pacify the king's wrath, which was accepted by the high priest, and approved by the people, B. C. 226.

Joseph all this time had entertained *Athenion* in a most elegant manner at his own house, and at his departure loaded him with such valuable gifts, that when he arrived at *Alexandria*, he found the king prepared much in his favour to receive him, and made himself more acceptable by informing him concerning the revenues of *Cœlesyria* and *Phœnicia*, whose value he had inquired more perfectly from their *farmers*, with whom he had traveled to court part of the way; and was thereupon admitted the king's *receiver general* of *Cœlesyria*, *Phœnicia*, *Judea*, and *Samaria*. He immediately satisfied the king for his uncle's arrears with *five hundred* talents he borrowed at *Alexandria* on the credit of his new office, which he enjoyed *twenty-two* years, though he met with great opposition at his first collecting, till he had brought some of the ringleaders to exemplary punishment.

B. C. 221. All things were again composed at *Jerusalem;* and *Philopater* having succeeded his father *Ptolemy Euergetes* in *Egypt*, and defeated the army of *Antiochus the Great*, he in the *fifth* year of his reign took the tour of *Jerusalem* while he visited his conquests. But this was very unfortunate for the *Jews*. For *Philopater* being led by a vain curiosity to enter into the *sanctuary* and the *holy of holies* on the great day of *expiation*, B. C. 217, where no one but the high priest was allowed to enter, he was opposed by the deprecations and lamentations of the people; and when he would still advance beyond the inner *court*, he was seized with such a terror and consternation, that he was obliged to be carried back in a manner half dead. He recovered; but when he left the city, he vowed revenge. And accordingly, he was no sooner returned to *Alexandria* than he deprived the *Jews* of all their rights and privileges; ordered them to be stigmatized with a burn representing an *ivy leaf*, under pain of death, in honour of his god *Bacchus;* and excluded all persons from his presence that would not sacrifice to the god he worshipped. Then he commanded as many *Jews* as he could seize in *Egypt* to be brought and shut up in the *Hippodrome*, or place for horse-races, at *Alexandria*, to be destroyed by *elephants*. But God turned the wild beasts upon those that came to see the dreadful massacre, by which numbers of the spectators were slain; and so terrified the king and his subjects with other tokens of his displeasure and power, that *Philopater* immediately not only released the *Jews* from the *Hippodrome*, but restored the whole nation to their privileges, reversed every decree against them, and put those *Jews* to death who for fear of persecution had apostatized from their religion.

Ptolemy Philopater was succeeded, B. C. 204, by his son *Ptolemy Epiphanes*, then only five years old. This minority gave *Antiochus the Great* an opportunity to regain *Cœlesyria* and *Palestine:* in which expedition the *Jews* had shown so much favour to *Antiochus*, that he granted them many favours, a liberty to live according to their own laws and religion, a prohibition to strangers to enter within the *sept* of the temple, &c. But as soon as *Ptolemy* was marriageable, he made peace with him, and gave him his daughter, with *Cœlesyria* and *Palestine* for her portion. On this occasion *Joseph*, who had been *Ptolemy's* receiver general in those provinces, and displaced by *Antiochus*, was restored.

Ptolemy in a short time had a son; and it being customary on such occasions for all the great officers of state to congratulate the king and queen, and to carry them presents, *Joseph*, whose age would not permit him to take so long a journey, sent his son *Hyrcanus*, B. C. 187, who, upon an unlimited credit given him by his father, when he was arrived at *Alexandria*, borrowed a *thousand talents*, or *two hundred thousand pounds* sterling, with which, buying a hundred beautiful boys for the king, and as many beautiful young maids for the queen, at the price of a talent per head, and presenting them each with a talent in their hands, and disposing of the remaining sum among the courtiers and great officers, he so obliged the king and queen, and all the court, that he found it easy to supplant his father, and obtained the king's commission for collecting the royal revenues in all the country beyond *Jordan*.

Hyrcanus, having thus abused his trust, went with a strong guard to execute his office; and being met by his brothers, killed two of them. He came to *Jerusalem;* but his father would not admit him to his presence, and he was shunned by every body. Upon the death of his father, which happened soon after, he endeavoured by force of arms to oust his brethren from the *paternal* estate. This disturbed the peace of Jerusalem for a while; till at last his brothers, being assisted by the high priest and the generality of the people, drove him over *Jordan*, where he lived in a strong castle, till he fell upon his own sword and killed himself to avoid the punishment with which *Antiochus Epiphanes*, upon his succeeding to the throne of *Syria*, threatened him. B. C. 175.

Antiochus the Great being slain by the inhabitants of *Elymais*, as he attempted by night to plunder the temple of *Jupiter Belus*, thereby to pay the *Romans* according to his agreement, his son *Seleucus Philopater* succeeded him in the provinces of *Syria*, *Judea*, &c., and resided at *Antioch*.

Seleucus, at his first advancement to the dominion of these provinces, continued his father's favours to the *Jews;* but being afterwards informed by one *Simon* a *Benjamite* that there was great treasure in the temple, he sent one *Heliodorus* to seize it, and to bring all the riches he could find therein to *Antioch*. *Heliodorus* attempted to execute this commission; but he was so terrified at the sight of an armed host of angels that appeared to defend the entrance of the sacred treasury, that he fell speechless to the ground; nor did he recover till the high priest interceded to God for him.

This same *Heliodorus* poisoned his sovereign *Seleucus*, hoping to obtain the kingdom; but his design was frustrated by *Eumenes*, king of *Pergamus*, and his brother *Attalus*, who set *Antiochus Epiphanes*, another son of *Antiochus the Great*, on the throne of *Syria*.

Epiphanes, at his accession to the throne, finding himself hard pressed by the *Romans*, endeavoured to raise their heavy tribute by all manner of exactions. Amongst other means he deposed the good and pious high priest, *Onias*, and sold the pontificate to his brother *Jason* for the yearly sum of *three hundred and sixty* talents; and afterwards he deposed *Jason*, and sold it to his brother *Menelaus* for *three hundred* talents more, B. C. 174.

Menelaus, having invaded the pontificate by these unjust means, and finding himself straitened to raise the annual payment according to contract, by the means of *Lysimachus*, another of his brothers, he robbed the temple of many gold vessels, which, being turned into money, he paid to the king; and bribed *Andronicus*, the governor of *Antioch*, to murder his brother *Onias*, lest at any time he should stand in his way. It is true that at the instance of the people *Andronicus* was seized and executed for his villany and murder, and *Lysimachus* was put to death by the mob at *Jerusalem;* yet *Menelaus* found means by bribery, not only to acquit himself, but to obtain sentence against, and even the execution of, the *three* delegates that went from *Jerusalem* to prosecute him in the name of the *sanhedrin*.

But while *Antiochus* was engaged in the *Egyptian* war, *Jason* on a false report that the king was dead, marched with a thousand men, surprised the city of *Jerusalem*, drove *Menelaus* into the castle, and cruelly put to the sword and to other kinds of death all those that he thought were his adversaries.

Immediately the news of this revolution and massacre reached *Antiochus*, he hastened to reduce the *Jews* to their obedience; and in his way, being informed that the inhabitants of *Jerusalem* had made great rejoicings at the report of his death, he was so provoked, that, taking the city by storm, B. C. 170, he slew *forty thousand* persons, and sold as many more for slaves to the neighbouring nations. He entered the *holy of holies*, sacrificed a sow upon the altar of burnt-offerings, and caused the broth or liquor thereof to be sprinkled all over the temple. He plundered the temple of as much gold and furniture as amounted to *eight hundred* talents of gold. Then, returning to *Antioch*, he made one *Philip*, a most barbarous and cruel man, governor of *Judea; Andronicus*, as bad a man, governor of *Samaria;* and continued *Menelaus*, the worst of all, in the pontificate. And, as if this was not sufficient to satisfy his rage, he not long after sent an army of *two and twenty thousand* men, under *Apollonius* his general, with commission to put all the men of *Jerusalem* to the sword, and to make slaves of the women and children; which was rigorously executed on a Sabbath day, so that none escaped but such as could hide themselves in caves, or reach the mountains by flight.

This cruelty soon after pursued the *Jews*, wherever dispersed: for by a *general* decree to oblige all people in his dominions to conform to the religion of the king, one *Athenæus*, a *Grecian* idolater, was pitched upon to receive and instruct all the *Jews* that would turn idolaters, and to punish with the most cruel deaths those who refused. It was at this time that the temple was dedicated to *Jupiter Olympius;* the books of the law were burned; and women, accused of having their children circumcised, were led about the streets with these children tied about their necks, and then both together cast headlong over the steepest part of the wall, B. C. 167; for many of them chose rather to die than to renounce their God; as the holy zeal and religious fortitude of the very aged and pious *Eleazar*, a chief doctor of the law, and of the heroine *Salomona* and her seven sons, do testify; whom neither the instruments of death could terrify, nor the allurements of the tyrant could persuade, to forfeit their interest with the Almighty, either by idolatry or dissimulation.

Matthias, great grandson of *Asmonæus*, and a priest of the first course, retired with his five sons, *John*, *Simon*, *Judas*, *Eleazar*, and *Jonathan*, from the persecution at *Jerusalem*, to a little place called *Modin*, in the tribe of *Dan*. But as soon as they were discovered, *Antiochus* sent one *Appelles* to that place, to oblige all the inhabitants, on pain of death, to turn idolaters. This officer delivered his commission by endeavouring to persuade *Matthias* to embrace idolatry, tendering to him the king's favour, and promising him great riches; which the good priest not only scornfully rejected, but slew the first *Jew* that dared to approach the idolatrous altar; and then, turning upon the king's commissioner, he despatched him and all his attendants, with the assistance of his sons and those that were with them. After this he put himself at the head of as many *Jews* as he could collect; and, having broken down the idols and the altars of the heathens, retired with them into the mountains. Here, as he took measures for their defence, he was joined by a numerous party of *Assidæans;* a valiant people, who practised great hardships and mortifications, and were resolved to lay down their lives for the recovery of the temple. By these, and the accession of great numbers of other *Jews*, *Matthias* found himself in a capacity to take the field; but as their mistaken notion about resting on the *Sabbath day* had been one great cause of their being surprised by their enemies, and brought many great misfortunes upon them, because they would not defend themselves on that day from their enemies, he caused it to be unanimously agreed and decreed, that it was lawful, and that they might defend themselves, and repel force by force, on the Sabbath day, should they be attacked.

After this decree had passed, with the approbation of the priests and elders, *Matthias* left his lurking-places, marched round the cities of *Judah*, pulled down the *heathen* altars, restored the true worship and circumcision, and cut off both the apostates and persecutors that fell in his way, till death summoned him to immortality, in the *hundred and forty-seventh* year of his age.

When he found death approaching, he exhorted his five sons to persevere in the cause of God, as he had begun; and he appointed his son *Judas* his successor in the command of the army; and *Simon* to be their counsellor, B. C. 166. He was buried at *Modin* with great lamentation of all *Israel*.

Judas, who had signalized himself on former occasions for his great valour, was distinguished by the title *Maccabeus;* and having taken the command of his people upon him, he prosecuted the good work of reformation begun by his father, and took all the measures he was able, by fortifying towns, building castles, and placing strong garrisons, to maintain the liberty and religion of his country against all opposition.

Apollonius was sent by *Antiochus* to march an army of *Samaritans* against him; but he was killed, and his troops defeated and entirely routed, after a great slaughter, by our young general, who, finding *Apollonius's* sword among the spoils, took it for his own use, and generally fought with it ever after.

This news having reached *Cœlosyria*, *Seron*, deputy-governor of that province, marched with all the forces he could collect to revenge the death of *Apollonius;* but he met with the same fate.

Antiochus was so enraged at these defeats, that he immediately ordered *forty thousand* foot, *seven thousand* horse, and a great number of auxiliaries, made up of the neighbouring nations and apostate *Jews*, to march against *Judea*, under the command of *Ptolemy Macron*, *Nicanor*, and *Gorgias*, *three* eminent commanders, B. C. 162.

Upon their advancing as far as *Emmaus*, about *seven* miles from *Jerusalem*, *Judas*, who may be suppoesd at that time besieging or at least blocking up *Jerusalem*, then in the hands of the heathen, retired to *Mizpeh*. Here the whole army addressed themselves to God. *Judas* exhorted them most pathetically to fight for their *religion*, *laws*, and *liberties;* but at last, giving those leave to withdraw from his army that had built houses, or betrothed wives within the year, or that were in any degree fearful, he presently found himself at the head of no more than *three thousand* men.

However, he was resolved to give the enemy battle. In the mean time God ordained him an easy victory; for while *Gorgias* was detached with *five thousand* foot and *one thousand* horse to surprise his little army by night, *Judas*, being informed of the design, marched by another way, fell upon the camp in the absence of *Gorgias*, killed *three thousand* men, put the rest to flight, and seized the camp. *Gorgias*, not finding the *Jews* in their camp, proceeded to the mountains, supposing they were fled thither for safety. But not meeting with them there, he was much surprised in his return at what had happened in his absence; and his army, hearing that *Judas* waited to give them a warm reception in the plains, flung down their arms and fled. *Judas* in the pursuit killed *six thousand* more, and wounded and maimed most of the rest. This victory opened to him the gates of *Jerusalem*, where he and his army celebrated the next day, which was a *Sabbath*, with great devotion and thanksgiving.

Timotheus and *Bacchides*, governors or lieutenants under *Antiochus*, marched immediately to the assistance of *Gorgias;* but they fell a sacrifice to the valour and conduct of *Judas*, who, by the spoils taken from the enemy, was enabled the better to carry on the war.

This defeat was succeeded by another of *Lysias*, the governor of all the country beyond the *Euphrates*. He had penetrated as far as *Bethzura*, a strong fortress about *twenty* miles from *Jerusalem*, threatening to destroy the country with an army of *sixty thousand* foot and *five thousand* horse. But he was defeated also by *Judas* with *ten thousand* men only.

This victory gave him some respite; and accordingly he restored the temple to the true worship of God, removed all the profanations, built an altar of *unhewn stones*, and replaced the furniture that *Antiochus* had carried away, out of the gold and other rich spoils taken in this war. Thus he dedicated the temple again, and ordained that a feast of *dedication* should be kept *annually*, in commemoration thereof for ever, about the 20th of *November*.

His next care was to subdue the fortress on Mount *Acra*, which *Apollonius* had erected to command the temple; and being yet in the power of the heathens, gave them great opportunities to annoy the *Jews* that went to worship in the temple. But not having men enough to spare to form a blockade, he silenced it by another fortification, which he erected on the mountain of the temple.

When this revolt and success of the *Jews* reached *Antiochus*, in his expedition into *Persia*, he threatened utterly to destroy the whole nation, and to make *Jerusalem* the common place of burial to all the *Jews*. But God visited him with a sudden and sore disease. He at first was afflicted with grievous torments in his bowels; his *privy parts* were ulcerated and filled with an innumerable quantity of vermin; and the *smell* was so offensive that he became nauseous to himself and all about him. Then his mind was so tormented with direful spectres and apparitions of evil spirits, and the remorse of his wicked life and profanations gnawed him so grievously, that he at last acknowledged the justice of God in his punishment, and offered up many vows and promises of a full reparation in case he recovered. But God would not hear him; therefore, when his body was almost half consumed with abominable ulcers, he died under the most horrid torments of body and mind, in the twelfth year of his reign.

Judas Maccabeus began now to consider how the government should be fixed, and therefore, in a general assembly held at *Maspha*, he revived the ancient order, and appointed rulers over thousands, hundreds, fifties, and tens. And it is also probable that he constituted the high court of *sanhedrin*, in which was a settled *Nasi*, president or prince, who was the high priest for the time being; an *Abbethdin*, or father of the house of judgment, who was the president's *deputy;* and a *Chacan*, or *the wise man*, who was *sub-deputy*. The other members were called *elders* or *senators*, men of untainted birth, good learning, and profound knowledge in the law, both priests and laymen. And they in particular were empowered to decide all *private* difficult controversies, all *religious* affairs, and all important matters of *state*.

This was properly the senate or great council of the nation, which grew into great power under the administration of the *Asmonean* princes, and was in great authority in the days of our Saviour's ministry.

Lysias, who had been so shamefully routed by *Judas*, having the care of *Antiochus's* son, who was called *Antiochus Eupater*, and only *nine* years old, set him on the throne, and seized the government and tuition of the young king into his own hands, and immediately combined with the neighbouring *Idumeans* and other nations, enemies to *Judah*, to unite in an attempt utterly to destroy and extirpate the whole race of *Israel*.

When *Judas* was informed of this confederacy, he resolved to prevent their intentions, and to carry the war into *Idumea*. Thus he entered their country by *Acrabatene*, a canton of *Judea*, near the southern extremity of the *Dead Sea*, and slew there *twenty thousand* of them. Then falling upon the children of *Bean*, another tribe of the *Idumeans*, he killed *twenty thousand* more, routed their army, and took their strong holds. Hence passing over *Jordan* into the land of the *Ammonites*, he defeated them in several engagements, slew great numbers of them, and took the city *Jahazah*, at the foot of Mount *Gilead*, near the brook *Jazah;* and so returned home.

After his return into *Judea*, one *Timotheus*, a governor in those parts, pretended to follow him with a numerous army. But *Judas* fell upon him; and having overthrown him with a very great slaughter, pursued him to the city *Gazara*, in the tribe of *Ephraim*, which he took; and he slew both *Timotheus* and his brother *Chereas*, governor of that city, and *Apollophanes*, another great captain of the *Syrian* forces.

This success stirred up the jealousy of the heathen nations about *Gilead*, who fell upon the *Jews* in the land of *Tob;* and, having slain *one thousand*, took their goods, carried their wives and children captives, and drove the residue to seek for refuge and security in the strong fortress *Dathema*, in *Gilead*. But *Timotheus*, the son of him slain at *Gazara*, shut them up with a great army, and besieged them, while the inhabitants of *Tyre*, *Sidon*, and *Ptolemais*, were contriving to cut off all the *Jews* that lived in *Galilee*.

Judas, in this critical juncture, by the advice of the *sanhedrin*, dividing his army into *three* parts, he and his brother *Jonathan* marched with *eight thousand* men to the relief of the *Gileadites;* his brother marched with *three thousand* into *Galilee;* and his brother *Joseph* was left with the command of the remainder to protect *Jerusalem* and the country round, and to remain wholly on the *defensive*, till *Judas* and *Simon* should return.

In their march to *Gilead*, *Judas* and *Jonathan* attacked *Bossora*, a town of the *Edomites*, slew all the males, plundered it, released a great number of *Jews* reserved to be put to death as soon as *Dathema* should be taken, and burned the city. When they arrived before *Dathema*, which was by a forced march in the night, the brothers gave *Timotheus* so sudden and violent an assault, that they put his army to flight, and slew *eight thousand* in the pursuit. And wherever he came and found any *Jews* oppressed or imprisoned, he released them in the same manner as he did at *Bossora*.

At the same time *Simon* defeated the enemy several times in *Galilee*, drove them out of the country, and pursued them with very great slaughter to the gates of *Ptolemais*. But *Joseph*, contrary to his orders, *leaving Jerusalem*, was put to flight by *Gorgias*, governor of *Syria*, and lost *two thousand* men in that ill-projected expedition, against *Jamnia*, a seaport on the *Mediterranean*.

Lysias by this time had assembled an army of *eight hundred thousand* men, *eighty* elephants, and all the horse of the kingdom, and marched in person against the *Hebrew* conqueror. *Judas* met him at the siege of *Bethzuna*, gave him battle, slew *eleven thousand* foot, *one thousand six hundred* horse, and put the rest to flight.

This victory was happily attended with a peace between *Judas* and *Lysias*, in the name of the young king; by which the heathen decree of uniformity made by *Epiphanes* was rescinded, and the *Jews* permitted to live according to their own laws.

However, this peace was soon broke by the people of *Joppa* and *Jamnia;* but *Judas* was no sooner informed that they had cruelly treated and murdered the *Jews* that lived amongst them, but he fell upon *Joppa* by night, burned their shipping, and put all to the sword that had escaped the fire; and he set fire to the haven of *Jamnia*, and burned all the ships in it.

Timotheus also, who had fled before this conqueror, was discontented with the peace, and gathered an army of *one hundred and twenty thousand* foot, and *two thousand five hundred* horse, in order to oppress the *Jews* in *Gilead*. But when the news of this armament reached *Judas*, he marched against him; and after he had defeated a strong party of wandering *Arabs*, and made peace with them; taken the city *Caspis*, which was *Heshbon* in the tribe of *Reuben;* slain the inhabitants; destroyed the place; taken *Caraca* also, and put its garrison of *ten thousand* men to the sword, he came up with *Timotheus* near *Raphon* on the river *Jabbok*, gave him battle, slew *thirty thousand* of his men, took him prisoner, pursued the remainder of his army to *Carnion* in *Arabia;* took that city also, and slew *twenty-five thousand* more of *Timotheus's* forces; but gave him his life and liberty, on the promise that he would release all the *Jewish* captives throughout his dominions.

As he returned to *Jerusalem* he stormed the strong city of *Ephron*, well garrisoned by *Lysias*, put *twenty-five thousand* people to the sword; plundered it, and razed it to the ground; because the people refused to grant him a passage through it. This campaign was concluded with a day of thanksgiving in the temple at *Jerusalem*.

Thus *Judas*, finding himself disengaged from the treaty of peace by these hostilities, carried the war into the south of *Idumea;* dismantled *Hebron*, the metropolis thereof; passed into the land of the *Philistines*, took *Azotus* or *Ashdod*, destroyed their idols, plundered their country, and returned to *Judea*, to reduce the fortress of *Acra*, which was still in the hands of the king of *Syria*, and was very troublesome in time of war to those that resorted to the temple.

Judas prepared for a regular siege; but *Antiochus*, being informed of its distress, marched to its relief with an army of *one hundred and ten thousand* foot, *twenty thousand* horse, *thirty-two* elephants with castles on their backs full of archers, and *three hundred* armed chariots of war. In his way through *Idumea*, he laid siege to *Bethzura*, which at last was forced to surrender, after *Judas*, who had marched to its relief, had killed *four thousand* of the enemy by surprise in the night; lost his brother *Eleazar* in battle, crushed to death by an elephant that he had stabbed; and was forced to retreat and shut himself and his friends up in the temple.

The king and *Lysias* were both present in this army of the *Syrians;* and would have compelled *Judas* to surrender, had not *Philip*, whom *Epiphanes* had upon his death-bed appointed guardian of his son, taken this opportunity of their absence to seize upon *Antioch*, and to take upon him the government of the *Syrian* empire.

Upon this news *Lysias* struck up a peace immediately with *Judas*, upon honourable and advantageous terms to the *Jewish* nation. But though it was ratified by oath, *Eupater* ordered the fortifications of the temple to be demolished.

It was in this war that *Menelaus*, the wicked high priest, fell into disgrace with *Lysias*, while he was prompting the heathen barbarity to destroy his own people: for being accused and convicted of being the author and fomentor of this *Jewish* expedition, *Lysias* ordered him to be carried to *Berrhœa*, a town in *Syria;* and there to be cast into a high tower of *ashes*, in which there was a wheel which continually stirred up and raised the ashes about the criminal, till he was suffocated, and died. This was a punishment among the *Persians* for criminals in high life. This wicked high priest was succeeded at the promotion of *Antiochus Eupater*, by one *Alcimus*, a man altogether as wicked as his immediate predecessor.

Eupater returned home, and by an easy battle killed the usurper *Philip*, and quelled the insurrection in his favour. But it was not so with *Demetrius*, the son of *Seleucus Philopater*, who, being now come to maturity, claimed the kingdom in right of his father, elder brother to *Epiphanes*.

Demetrius had been sent to *Rome*, as a hostage, in exchange for his uncle *Antiochus Epiphanes*, in the very year that his father died. *Antiochus*, returning in the very nick of time, was declared king, in prejudice to the right of *Demetrius*. And though *Demetrius* had often solicited the assistance of the *Roman* senate, under whom he was educated, to restore him to his kingdom, reasons of state swayed with them rather to confirm *Eupater*, a *minor*, in the government, than to assert the right of one of a mature understanding. Yet, though he failed in this application, *Demetrius* resolved to throw himself upon Providence. To which end, leaving *Rome incog.*, *Demetrius* got safe to *Tripolis*, in *Syria;* where he gave out that he was sent, and would be supported by the *Romans*, to take possession of his father's kingdom. This stratagem had its desired effect; every one deserted from *Eupater* to *Demetrius;* and the very soldiers seized on *Eupater* and *Lysias*, and would have delivered them into his hands. But *Demetrius* thought it more politic not to see them; and having ordered them to be put to death, was presently settled in the possession of the whole kingdom.

During this interval the *Jews* enjoyed a profound peace, but having refused to acknowledge *Alcimus* their high priest because he had *apostatized* in the time of the persecution, *Alcimus* addressed the new king, *Demetrius*, implored his protection against *Judas Maccabeus*, and so exasperated him against the whole body of his party by false representations, that *Demetrius* ordered *Bacchides* to march an army into *Judea*, and to confirm *Alcimus* in the pontificate.

Alcimus was also commissioned with *Bacchides* to carry on the war in *Judea*, who upon the promise of a safe conduct, having got the scribes and doctors of the law into their power, put *sixty* of them to death in one day. *Bacchides* left him in possession with some forces for his support; with which he committed many murders, and did much mischief; and at last obtained another army from *Demetrius*, under the command of *Nicanor*, to destroy *Judas;* to disperse his followers, and the more effectually to support the said *Alcimus* in his post of high priest.

Nicanor, who had experienced the valour of *Judas*, proposed a compromise: but *Alcimus*, expecting more advantage to himself by a war, beat the king off it; so that *Nicanor* was obliged to execute the first order. The war was carried on with various success, till *Nicanor* was slain in a pitched battle near a village called *Bethoron;* and his whole army of *thirty-five thousand* men, casting down their arms, were to a man cut off in the flight.

This victory was followed with a day of thanksgiving, which was established to be continued every year under the name of the *anniversary* day of solemn thanksgiving.

Judas, observing that the *Syrians* paid no regard to any treaties, thought that, by making a league with the *Romans*, his nation would be much better secured against such a perfidious people. Therefore he sent *Jason* and *Eupolemus* to *Rome*, who soon obtained the ratification of a league of mutual defence between them, and a letter to *Demetrius*, requiring him, upon the peril of having war denounced against him, to desist from giving the Jews any more uneasiness and trouble.

This, however, proved of no service. For while this league was negotiating, *Demetrius* sent *Bacchides* and *Alcimus* a second time into *Judea* with a numerous army to revenge the defeat and death of *Nicanor*. At this time *Judas* had no more than *three thousand* men to oppose them; and of these all but *eight hundred* deserted their general, at the report of the number and strength of their enemies. Yet *Judas* refused to yield up the cause of God; and being followed by that handful of brave men, he charged and broke the right wing, where *Bacchides* commanded in person, and pursued them as far as the mountains of *Azotus;* and must have gained a complete victory, had not his little army been followed and encompassed by the *left* wing. But being surrounded with an exceeding great force, the *Jews* sold their lives at a dear rate; *Judas* was killed, and then such as survived him were forced to flee away.

His body was carried off by his brothers *Simon* and *Jonathan*, and buried in the sepulchres of his ancestors, at *Modin*, with great funeral honour, as he deserved.

Bacchides, after his success, seized on the whole country, and used the adherents of the *Maccabees* so inhumanly, that *Jonathan* was necessitated to retire at the head of his distressed countrymen to the Wilderness of *Tekoa*. This little army encamped with a morass on one side, and the river *Jordan* on the other. *Bacchides* pursued them; secured the pass of their encampment; and, though he attacked them on the *Sabbath day*, he lost a *thousand* men in the assault, before the *Maccabees* broke; and then, being overpowered by numbers, they threw themselves into the river, and escaped by swimming to the other side, without being pursued.

About this time (B. C. 160) *Alcimus*, the wicked pontiff, died suddenly of a palsy; and *Demetrius*, having received the *senatorian* letter from *Rome*, commanding him to desist from vexing the *Jews*, recalled *Bacchides;* so that *Jonathan* found himself in a condition to bring his affairs into better order. But this state of rest lasted only for two years; for the malcontents invited *Bacchides* to return with his army, under a promise to support his enterprise, and to seize *Jonathan*. But before this association could take place, *Jonathan* had information of it, took *fifty* of the principal conspirators, and put them to death. And when *Bacchides* arrived with his great army, *Jonathan* and his brother *Simon* gave him such uneasiness, and so artfully distressed and harassed his army, without giving him any pitched battle, that *Bacchides* grew weary of his undertaking, put several of those that invited him to that expedition to death, and at last made peace with the *Maccabees*, restored all his prisoners, and swore never more to *molest* the *Jews*, B. C. 158.

When *Jonathan* found himself in quiet possession of *Judea*, and that there was no more to fear from *Bacchides*, he punished the apostate *Jews* with death, reformed the Church and state, and rebuilt the walls about the temple and city of *Jerusalem*. And soon after, the high priesthood having been vacant seven years, he put on the *pontifical* robe, at the nomination of *Alexander*, who, by the assistance of the *Roman* senate, and the management of one *Heraclides*, claimed the crown of *Syria* in right of his pretended father *Antiochus Epiphanes*.

Jonathan, though *Demetrius* made him more advantageous offers, suspected that these promises were not real, but only to serve the present purpose, and accepted *Alexander's* proposals; which was so acceptable to the new king, that when he had beaten and slain *Demetrius*, and made himself master of the whole *Syrian* monarchy, he invited *Jonathan* to his marriage with *Cleopatra*, daughter of *Ptolemy*, king of *Egypt;* and, besides great personal honours, conferred on him the post of *general* of all his forces in *Judea*, and chief sewer of his household, B. C. 153.

However, this prosperity was soon disturbed by *Apollonius*, governor of *Cœlosyria*, who, taking part with *Demetrius*, the son of *Demetrius* the late king, who had concealed himself with his brother *Antiochus* in *Crete*, during the late troubles, was now landed in *Cilicia* with an army of mercenaries, and had marched with an army as far as *Jamnia*, challenging *Jonathan* to give him battle. *Jonathan* marched out with a body of *ten thousand* men; took *Joppa* in sight of the enemy; gave *Apollonius* battle, beat him, and pursued his broken forces to *Azotus*, where he destroyed *eight thousand* men, the temple of *Dagon*, and the city, with fire and sword, which engaged *Alexander's* affections so much, that he gave him the golden *buckle*, (a distinguished mark of the royal family of *Persia*,) and the city and *territories* of *Ecron*.

After this succeeded a surprising revolution in *Syria*. *Alex-*

ander had called to his assistance his father-in-law *Ptolemy Philometer*, who, suspecting that his son *Alexander* had conspired his death, carried off his daughter *Cleopatra;* gave her to *Demetrius*, *Alexander's* competitor; then, turning his arms upon *Alexander*, settled *Demetrius* upon the throne of his ancestors; and, after gaining a complete victory, forced him to flee into *Arabia*, where *Zabdiel*, the king of the country, cut off his head, and sent it to *Ptolemy*, B. C. 146.

This *Demetrius* took the style of *Nicanor*, or Conqueror; and though he summoned *Jonathan* to appear before him to answer certain accusations, the high priest found means to gain his favour; and not only a confirmation of former, but a grant of additional privileges; which, with the promise to withdraw the heathen garrison from *Acra*, so recommended him to *Jonathan*, that, when *Demetrius* was in danger of being murdered by the inhabitants of *Antioch*, he marched *three thousand* men to the king's assistance, burned a great part of the city, slew *one hundred thousand* of the inhabitants with fire and sword, and obliged the rest to throw themselves upon the king's mercy. Yet this service, and his promise also, was presently forgot by *Demetrius*, when he thought the storm was blown over; and, he would, on the contrary, have certainly obliged him, under pain of military execution, to pay the usual taxes and tribute paid by his predecessors, had he not been prevented by the treason of a discontented courtier, whose name was *Tryphon*.

Tryphon (B. C. 144) at first declared for, and set *Antiochus Theos*, the son of the late *Alexander*, on the throne of *Syria*, after he had vanquished *Demetrius*, and forced him to retire into *Seleucia*. *Jonathan*, for his own interest, declared for the new king; by which he obtained a confirmation of the pontificate, &c., and his brother *Simon* was made commander of all his forces from *Tyre* to *Egypt*.

As soon as *Demetrius* heard of *Jonathan's* revolt, he marched to chastise him for it; but it turned to his loss; for he was repulsed twice, and lost *Gaza*, with all the country as far as *Damascus*, and *Joppa* in the land of the *Philistines*.

Tryphon intended now to pull off the mask; but not daring to attempt so foul a crime till *Jonathan* could be removed, prevailed with him to disband his army, and to accompany him with *one thousand* men only to *Ptolemais;* where he was no sooner entered, but his men were put to the sword, and *Jonathan* put under an arrest. Then, marching his army into *Judea*, he proposed to restore him, on condition of *one hundred* talents; and that his two sons should be given for hostages of their father's fidelity. *Jonathan* was persuaded to comply with this demand: but the villain not only caused them and their father to be put to death, but having also murdered *Antiochus* privately, he assumed the title of king of *Syria*.

Simon (B. C. 143,) hearing that his brother was murdered, and buried at *Bascama*, in *Gilead*, sent and brought him thence, and buried him under a curious monument of white wrought and polished marble, at *Modin*. And after he was admitted governor in his stead, he offered his service to *Demetrius*, then at *Laodicea;* who, on condition that the *Jews* would assist him in the recovery of his crown, conceded to him the high priesthood and principality, and granted the people many privileges.

But *Demetrius* being about this time persuaded to head the *Elymæan*, *Parthian*, and *Bactrian* revolters against *Mithridates*, king of *Parthia*, *Simon* applied himself to fortifying his cities; and reduced the fortress of *Acra;* which he not only took, but even levelled the mount on which it was built.

Mithridates (B. C. 141) vanquished *Demetrius;* and after he had taken him prisoner, gave him his daughter *Rhodaguna* in marriage; which so exasperated his wife *Cleopatra*, then shut up in *Seleucia*, that she offered herself and the kingdom to *Antiochus*, his brother, B. C. 139, then in *Crete*. *Antiochus* accepted the proposal; and upon his landing in *Syria* with an army of mercenaries, he was so strengthened with deserters from *Tryphon's* forces, that he drove him into *Apamea*, near the mouth of the *Orontes*, and took him and put him to death.

Thus *Antiochus* became possessed of his father's throne; though not without the assistance of *Simon*, whom he had promised to reward with many new privileges. But he no sooner found himself delivered from all opposition, than he forgot his promises; and, on the contrary, demanded the restoring of *Joppa* and *Gazara*, &c., or a *thousand* talents in lieu of them.

Simon refused to comply; and *Antiochus* sent *Cendebeus* with an army to force him. *Simon*, now very old, attended by his sons *Judas* and *John Hyrcanus*, put him to flight at the first onset, and killed a great number of the enemy in the pursuit. After this, *Simon*, and his sons *Judas* and *Mattathias*, B. C. 135, being perfidiously murdered by *Ptolemy*, *Simon's* son-in-law, whom he had made governor of the *plains of Jericho*, at an entertainment prepared for them in the castle of *Jericho*, with a design to usurp the government of *Judea* to himself, sent a party to *Gazara* to seize *John Hyrcanus* also. But he was informed, and so prepared to receive them, that he despatched the intended murderers; and hastening to *Jerusalem*, secured both the city and the temple, where he was declared his father's successor in the pontificate and principality of the *Jews*.

Antiochus thought to serve himself of these distractions and accordingly marched a large army into *Judea;* and after he had driven *Hyrcanus* into *Jerusalem*, obliged him to accept of a peace upon the hard terms of delivering up their arms, dismantling *Jerusalem*, paying a tribute for *Joppa*, &c., held by the *Jews* out of *Judea*, and *five hundred* talents to buy off the rebuilding of *Acra*.

Hyrcanus accompanied *Antiochus* to the *Parthian* war, in which he signalized himself with great renown. He returned home at the end of the year. But *Antiochus*, who chose to winter in the *East*, was with his whole army destroyed in one night by the natives, who, taking the advantage of their separate quarters all over the country, rose on them, and cut their throats in cold blood: so that *Antiochus* himself was slain, and out of *four hundred thousand* persons, of which his army consisted, scarce a man escaped to carry home the news of this massacre.

Phraortes, the king of *Parthia*, having suffered much by this invasion of *Antiochus*, endeavoured to get quit of him by sending his prisoner *Demetrius Nicanor* into *Syria*, to recover his own kingdom; so that when the news came of *Antiochus's* death, he was without more delay reinstated on the throne. But his tyrannical proceedings presently raised him up a new pretender to the crown, (B. C. 127,) one *Alexander Zabina*, the pretended son of *Alexander Balas*, who, by the assistance of *Ptolemy Physcon*, king of *Egypt*, defeated him in the field; and, taking him prisoner in *Tyre*, put him to death.

Zabina being raised to the throne of *Syria* by the king of *Egypt*, *Ptolemy* expected that he should hold it in homage from him; and, upon his refusal, gave his daughter *Tryphæna* to *Antiochus Gryphus*, the son of *Nicanor*, whom he made king of *Syria*, and pursued *Zabina* till he got him into his hands, and put him to death.

Hyrcanus, in the midst of these revolutions, shook off the *Syrian* yoke. He built the famous tower of *Baris* upon a steep rock. He took several cities on the borders of *Judea*, amongst which was *Shechem*, the chief seat of the *Samaritans*, (B. C. 130,) and destroyed the temple on Mount *Gerizim*. He extended his conquests over the *Idumeans*, (B. C. 129,) who were prevailed on to embrace the *Jewish* religion; so that from this time they exchanged the name of *Idumeans* or *Edomites* for that of *Jews*. He renewed the alliance with the senate of *Rome*, and obtained greater privileges and advantages than his nation ever had before; and concluded his military operations with the siege and utter destruction of *Samaria*, under the conduct of his sons *Aristobulus* and *Antigonus*.

After these great actions, *Hyrcanus* enjoyed full quiet from all foreign wars; and had nothing to trouble him at home, but the false insinuations of the Pharisee *Eleazar*, who declared that his mother was a captive taken in the wars, and that, therefore, he was incapable of holding the high priesthood. *Hyrcanus* had been educated in this sect: but one *Jonathan*, an intimate friend of his, and a *Sadducee*, took this opportunity to draw him over to his own sect; which he effected so sincerely, that *Hyrcanus* renounced the Pharisees for ever, abrogated their traditional constitutions, and made it penal for any one to observe them. Yet he was an excellent governor; and, dying in the *thirtieth* year of his administration, left *five* sons: but the high priesthood and sovereignty he left to *Judas Aristobulus*, his eldest son, B. C. 107.

Aristobulus (B. C. 107) was the first since the captivity that put on the diadem, and assumed the title of *king:* but he was of that suspicious and cruel disposition, that he cast his own mother into prison, and starved her to death, imprisoned all his brethren except *Antigonus*, whom at last he ordered to be murdered in a fit of jealousy, B. C. 106: of which, however, he repented, and gave up the ghost in great anxiety of mind, after a reign of no more than *one* year; though in that time *Antigonus* had reduced the *Itureans* to his *obedience*, and forced them to conform to the religion of the *Jews*. At this time *Pompey* and *Cicero* were born.

Alexander Jannæus, his *third* brother, was released from his confinement by *Salome*, *Aristobulus's* widow. The like favour was also extended to his two other brothers. But as soon as *Jannæus* was settled on the throne, he put one of them to death under a suspicion of treason, and he took *Absalom* the younger into his favour.

This *Alexander* (B. C. 105) attempted to extend his dominions by new conquests. But in his attempts against *Ptolemais* and *Ptolemy Lathyrus*, who came to the assistance of *Zoilus* and the *Gazæans*, he lost a fine army, and was reduced to sue for protection from *Cleopatra*, who had seized upon *Egypt*, and obliged her son *Lathyrus* to be contented with the island of *Crete*.

Cleopatra, at first, was inclined to take advantage of *Alexander's* misfortunes, and to seize upon him and his dominions; but *Ananias*, one of her generals, by birth a *Jew*, and a relation to *Alexander*, dissuaded her from so unjust a design, and obtained her protection for him.

Nevertheless *Alexander's* martial spirit sought out new employments. His country being clear of foreign forces, he attacked and took *Gadara* and *Amathus* in *Syria*. But being followed by *Theodorus*, prince of *Philadelphia*, who had laid up his treasure at *Amathus*, he lost his plunder, *ten thousand* men, and all his baggage, B. C. 101.

This did not deter him from attempting the reduction of *Gaza;* which, however, he could not have taken, had it not been treacherously surrendered to him by *Lysimachus*, the governor's brother. Here *Alexander*, ordering his soldiers to kill, plunder, and destroy, was the author of a sad scene of barbarity, and reduced that ancient and famous city to ruin and desolation.

After his return from this carnage, he was grossly insulted by a mob at home, while he was offering the usual sacrifices on the *feast of tabernacles*. But he made the people pay dearly for it; for he fell upon them with his soldiers, and slew *six thousand*. And from this time he took into his pay *six thousand* mercenaries from *Pisidia* and *Cilicia*, who always attended his person, and kept off the people while he officiated.

B. C. 101. All being again quieted at home, *Alexander* marched against the *Moabites* and *Ammonites*, and made them tributaries. In his return he took possession of *Amathus*, which *Theodorus* had evacuated; but he lost most of his army, and was very near losing his own life in an ambuscade which *Thedus*, an *Arabian* king, had laid for him near *Gadara*. This raised fresh discontents among his subjects, and new troubles at home, which were attended with the most unheard-of barbarities. They were not able to overpower him; but his wickedness had so provoked them that nothing but his blood could satisfy them; and at length, being assisted by *Demetrius Euchærus*, king of *Damascus*, they entirely routed him, so that he was forced to consult his own safety by fleeing to the mountains.

His misfortune was the cause of *six thousand* of his rebel subjects deserting him; which, when *Demetrius* perceived, he withdrew, and left the revolters to fight their own battle. After this separation *Alexander* gained several advantages; and at last, having cut the major part off in a decisive battle, he took *eight hundred* of the rebels in *Bethome*, whom he carried to *Jerusalem;* and having first killed their wives and children before their faces, he ordered them all to be crucified in one day, before him and his wives and concubines, whom he had invited to a feast at the place of execution. Then, resolving to revenge himself on the king of *Damascus*, he made war on him for three years successively, and took several places; when, returning home, he was received with great respect by his subjects.

His next expedition was against the castle of *Ragaba*, in the country of the *Gerasens*, where he was seized with a quartan ague, which proved his death, B. C. 79. His queen *Alexandra*, by his own advice, concealed it till the castle was taken; and then, carrying him to *Jerusalem*, she gave his body to the leaders of the Pharisees, to be disposed of as they should think proper; and told them, as her husband had appointed her regent during the minority of her children, she would do nothing in the administration without their advice and help.

This address to the Pharisees so much gained their esteem that they not only settled the queen dowager in the government, but were very lavish in their encomiums on her deceased husband, whom they honoured with more than ordinary pomp and solemnity at his funeral.

The Pharisees having now the management of the queen regent, and of *Hyrcanus* and *Aristobulus*, her sons by *Alexander*, had all the laws against Pharisaism repealed and abolished, recalled all the exiles, and demanded justice against those that had advised the crucifixion of the *eight hundred rebels*.

The queen made her eldest son, *Hyrcanus*, high priest. But *Aristobulus* was not contented to live a private life; and therefore, as soon as his mother seemed to decline, he meditated in what manner he might usurp the sovereignty from his brother, at her decease; and he had taken such measures beforehand, that upon the death of his mother he found himself strong enough to attempt the crown, though *Alexandra* had declared *Hyrcanus* her successor. The two armies met in the plains of *Jericho;* but *Hyrcanus*, being deserted by most of his forces, was obliged to resign his crown and pontificate to *Aristobulus*, and promise to live peaceably upon his private fortune.

This resignation was a subject of great discontent to some of *Hyrcanus's* courtiers, among whom was *Antipater*, father to *Herod the Great*, who persuaded *Hyrcanus* to fly to *Aretas*, king of *Arabia*, who, on certain conditions, supplied him with *fifty thousand* men, with which *Hyrcanus* entered *Judea*, and gained a complete victory over *Aristobulus*. But while he besieged him in the temple, *Aristobulus*, with the promise of a large sum of money, engaged *Pompey*, the general of the *Roman* army, then before *Damascus*, to oblige *Aretas* to withdraw his forces; but *Aristobulus*, though he was for the present delivered from his brother's rage, prevaricated so with *Pompey*, that he at last confined *Aristobulus* in chains, took *Jerusalem* sword in hand, retrenched the dignity and power of the principality, destroyed the fortifications, ordered an annual tribute to be paid to the *Romans*, and restored *Hyrcanus* to the pontificate, and made him prince of the country, but would not permit him to wear the diadem.

Pompey, having thus settled the government of *Judea*, returned in his way to *Rome* with *Aristobulus*, his sons *Alexander* and *Antigonus*, and two of his daughters, to adorn his triumph.

Alexander found means to escape, by the way, and about three years after arrived in *Judea*, and raised some disturbance; but he was defeated in all his attempts by *Gabinius*, the *Roman* governor in *Syria*, who, after this, coming to *Jerusalem*, confirmed *Hyrcanus* in the high priesthood, but removed the civil administration from the *sanhedrin* into five courts of justice of his own erecting, according to the number of five provinces, into which he had divided the whole land.

When *Aristobulus* had lain five years prisoner at *Rome*, he with his son escaped into *Judea*, and endeavoured to raise fresh trouble; but Gabinius soon took them again; and being remanded to *Rome*, the father was kept close confined, but the children were released.

It was about this time, B. C. 48, that the civil war between *Pompey* and *Cæsar* broke out; and when *Aristobulus* was on the point of setting out, by *Cæsar's* interest, to take the command of an army in order to secure *Judea* from *Pompey's* attempts, he was poisoned by some of *Pompey's* party.

When *Cæsar* was returned from the *Alexandrian* war, he was much solicited to depose *Hyrcanus* in favour of *Antigonus*, the surviving son of *Aristobulus;* but *Cæsar* not only confirmed *Hyrcanus* in the high priesthood and principality of Judea, and to his family in a perpetual succession, but he abolished the form of government lately set up by *Gabinius*, restored it to its ancient form, and appointed *Antipater* procurator of *Judea* under him.

Antipater, who was a man of great penetration, made his son *Phasael* governor of the country about *Jerusalem*, and his son *Herod* governor of *Galilee*.

Soon after this appointment, *Herod*, who was of a very boisterous temper, having seized upon one *Hezekiah*, a ringleader of a gang of thieves, and some of his men that infested his territories, he put them to death. This was presently looked upon as a breach of duty to the *sanhedrin*, before whom he was summoned to appear. But lest the sentence of that court should pass upon him, he fled to *Sextus Cæsar*, the *Roman* prefect of *Syria* at *Damascus;* and, with a large sum of money, obtained of him the government of *Cælesyria*. He afterwards raised an army, marched into *Judea*, and would have revenged the indignity which he said the *sanhedrin* and high priest had cast upon him, had not his father and brother prevailed with him to retire for the present.

While *Julius Cæsar* lived, the *Jews* enjoyed great privileges; but his untimely death, B. C. 44, by the villanous and ungrateful hand of *Brutus*, *Cassius*, &c., in the senate house, as he was preparing for an expedition against the *Parthians* to revenge his country's wrong, delivered them up as a prey to every hungry general of *Rome*. *Cassius* immediately seized upon *Syria*, and exacted above *seven hundred* talents of silver from the *Jews;* and the envy and villany of *Malicus*, who was a *natural Jew*, and the next in office under *Antipater*, an *Idumean*, rent the state into horrid factions. *Malicus* bribed the high priest's butler to poison his friend *Antipater*, to make way for himself to be the next in person to *Hyrcanus*. *Herod*, making sure of *Cassius*, by obtaining his leave and assistance to revenge his father's death, took the first opportunity to have him murdered by the *Roman* garrison at *Tyre*.

The friends of *Malicus*, having engaged the high priest and *Felix* the *Roman* general at *Jerusalem* on their side, resolved to revenge his death on the sons of *Antipater*. All *Jerusalem* was in an uproar; *Herod* was sick at *Damascus;* so that the whole power and fury of the assailants fell upon *Phasael*, who defended himself very strenuously, and drove the tumultuous party out of the city. As soon as *Herod* was able, the two brothers presently quelled the faction; and had not *Hyrcanus* made his peace by giving *Herod* his granddaughter *Mariamne* in marriage, they certainly would have shown their resentment of the priest's behaviour with more severity.

Again, this faction was not so totally extinguished but that several principal persons of the Jewish nation, upon the defeat of *Brutus* and *Cassius*, accused *Phasael* and *Herod* to the conqueror, *Mark Anthony*, of usurping the government from *Hyrcanus*. But the brothers had so much interest with the conqueror that he rejected the complaints of the deputies, made them both tetrarchs, and committed all the affairs of Judea to their administration; and to oblige the *Jews* to obey his decision in this affair, he retained fifteen of the deputies as hostages for the people's fidelity, and would have put them to death had not *Herod* begged their lives.

The *Jews*, however, when *Anthony* arrived at *Tyre*, sent *one thousand* deputies with the like accusations, which he, looking upon as a daring insult, ordered his soldiers to fall upon them, so that some were killed and many wounded. But upon *Herod's* going to *Jerusalem* the citizens revenged this affront in the same manner upon his retinue; the news whereof so enraged *Anthony*, that he ordered the fifteen hostages to be immediately put to death, and threatened severe revenge against the whole faction. But after that *Mark Anthony* was returned to *Rome*, the *Parthians*, at the solicitation of *Antigonus*, the son of *Aristobulus*, who had promised them a reward of a thousand talents and eight hundred of the most beautiful women in the country, to set him on the throne of Judea, entered that country, and being joined by the factious and discontented Jews, (B. C. 37,) took *Jerusalem* without resistance, took *Phasael* and *Hyrcanus*, and put them in chains; but *Herod* escaped under the cover of night and deposited his mother, sister, wife, and his wife's mother, with several other relations and friends, in the impregnable fortress *Massada*, near the lake *Asphaltites*, under the care of his brother *Joseph*, who was obliged to go to *Rome* to seek protection and relief.

In the mean time *Antigonus* remained in possession of all the country, and was declared king of *Judea*. The *Parthians* delivered *Hyrcanus* and *Phasael* to *Antigonus;* upon which *Phasael*, being so closely handcuffed and ironed that he foresaw his ignominious death approaching, dashed his own brains out against the wall of the prison. *Antigonus* cut off the ears of *Hyrcanus*, to incapacitate him from the high priesthood, and returned him again to the *Parthians*, who left him at *Seleucia*, in their return to the East.

Herod on this occasion served himself so well on the friendship which had been between his father and himself with the *Roman* general, *Mark Anthony*, and the promise of a round sum of money, that he in seven days' time obtained a senatorial decree, constituting him king of *Judea*, and declaring *Antigonus* an enemy to the *Roman* state. He immediately left *Rome*, landed at *Ptolemais*, raised forces, and being aided with *Roman* auxiliaries, by order of the senate, he reduced the greater part of the country, took *Joppa*, relieved *Massada*, stormed the castle of *Ressa*, and must have taken *Jerusalem* also, had not the *Roman* commanders who were directed to assist him been bribed by *Antigonus*, and treacherously obstructed his success. But when *Herod* perceived their collusion, he, for the present, satisfied himself with the reduction of *Galilee;* and hearing of *Anthony's* besieging *Samosata* on the *Euphrates*, went in person to him to represent the ill treatment he had met with from the generals, *Ventidius* and *Silo*, whom he had commanded to serve him.

Upon his departure, *Herod* left the command of his forces to his brother *Joseph*, with charge to remain upon the defensive. But Joseph, contrary to orders, attempting to reduce *Jericho*, was slain, and most of his men were cut to pieces. And thus *Herod* again lost *Galilee* and *Idumea*.

Mark Anthony granted all he requested; and though at first the army which *Anthony* had spared him was roughly handled, and he himself wounded as he approached *Jerusalem* to revenge his brother's death, he afterwards slew *Pappus*, *Antigonus's* general, and entirely defeated his army; and in the next campaign, after a siege of several months, *Herod*, assisted by *Socius*, the *Roman* general, took it by storm. The soldiers expecting the spoils of the city as their due, and being exasperated by the long resistance of the citizens, spared neither men, women, nor children, and would certainly have utterly destroyed every thing and person with rapine and devastation, death and slaughter, had not *Herod* redeemed them with a large sum of money.

Antigonus surrendered himself to *Socius*, who carried him in chains to *Anthony;* and he for a good sum of money was bribed to put him to death, that in him the *Asmonœan* family, which had lasted *one hundred and twenty-nine* years, might be extinct.

By this event *Herod* found himself once more in full power, and at liberty to revenge himself upon his enemies. He began his reign with the execution of all the members of the great *Sanhedrin* except *Pollio* and *Sameas*, who are also called *Hillel* and *Shammai*. Then he raised one *Ananel*, born of the pontifical family at *Babylon*, to the place of *high priest;* but *Mark Anthony*, at the intercession of *Cleopatra*, queen of Egypt, who was solicited thereto by *Alexandra*, *Mariamne's* mother, and the entreaties of his own beloved *Mariamne* in behalf of her young brother, prevailed with him to annul this nomination, and to prefer *Aristobulus* to the pontificate. But as *Hyrcanus* was yet alive, and the *Jews*, in the place of his exile, paid him all the honours and reverence due to their king and high priest, *Herod*, under a pretence of gratitude and friendship to that author of all his fortunes, prevailed with the old prince to desire it, and with *Phraortes*, king of *Parthia*, to permit his return to *Jerusalem*, with an intention to cut him off at a proper opportunity; which he soon after did on a pretence of his holding treasonable correspondence with *Malchus*, king of *Arabia*. But in the mean time *Alexandra*, valuing herself upon the interest she had with *Cleopatra*, laid a scheme to obtain the regal dignity for her son *Aristobulus*, by the same means that she had got him the pontificate. But this intrigue ended in the death of *Aristobulus*, and her own close confinement at first, and afterwards in her own and her daughter *Mariamne's* death; though this tragic scene was at several times acted under disguise. *Aristobulus* was drowned at *Jericho*, as it were accidentally, B. C. 29, in a fit of jealousy; *Mariamne* was adjudged to die, and *Alexandra* was ordered for execution, B. C. 28, on a supposition that she wished his death; which unjust sentence pursued his very innocent children *Alexander* and *Aristobulus*, for expressing their dislike of their father's cruelty to their mother *Mariamne*. But it is very probable that he himself had fallen a sacrifice to *Octavius* after the battle, and the total loss of *Mark Anthony* at *Actium*, (fought B. C. 31,) had he not hastened to the conqueror at *Rhodes*, and in an artful speech appeased him, and with a promise to support his faction in those parts, obtained from him a confirmation of his royal dignity.

The cruelties, however, which he exercised to his own flesh and blood filled his mind with agonies of remorse, which brought him into a languishing condition; and what helped to increase his disorder was the conspiracy of *Antipater*, his eldest son by *Doris*, born to him whilst he was a private man. But *Herod* having discovered the plot, accused him thereof before *Quintilius Varus*, the *Roman* governor of *Syria*, and put him to death also; which occasioned that remarkable exclamation of the Emperor *Octavius*, that "it was better to be *Herod's* hog than his son."

The great pleasure that *Herod* took (B. C. 25) in obliging his protector *Octavianus*, and the dread he had of being dethroned for his cruelties, prompted him to compliment him with the names of two new cities, the one to be built on the spot where *Samaria* stood before *Hyrcanus* destroyed it, (B. C. 22,) which he called *Sebaste*, the Greek word for *Augustus*, the other was *Cæsarea*, once called the *Tower of Straton*, on the sea-coast of *Phœnicia*. After this he built a theatre and amphitheatre in the very city of *Jerusalem*, to celebrate games and exhibit shows in honour of *Augustus;* set up an image of an eagle, the *Roman* ensign, over one of the gates of the temple; and at last carried his flattery so far as idolatrously to build a temple of white marble in memory of the favours he had received from *Octavianus Augustus*.

These advances to idolatry were the foundation of a conspiracy of ten men, who bound themselves with an oath to assassinate him in the very theatre. But being informed thereof in time, *Herod* seized the conspirators, and put them to death with the most exquisite torments; and to ingratiate himself with the *Jews*, he formed a design to rebuild the temple, (B. C. 17,) which now, after it had stood five hundred years, and suffered much from its enemies, was fallen much into decay. He was two years in providing materials; and it was so far advanced that Divine service was performed in it nine years and a half more, though a great number of labourers and artificers were continued to finish the outworks till several years after our Saviour's ascension; for when *Gessius Florus* was appointed governor of *Judea*, he discharged *eighteen thousand* workmen from the temple at one time. And here it should be observed that these, for want of employment, began those mutinies and seditions which at last drew on the destruction both of the temple and *Jerusalem*, in A. D. 70.

Thus I have finished that brief connection of the affairs of the *Jews* from the death of *Nehemiah* and conclusion of the Old Testament, to the coming of *Christ*, where the New Testament begins, which from the creation of the world, according to the most exact computation, is the year 4000.

The general state of the heathen world was in profound peace under the *Roman* emperor, *Augustus*, to whom all the known parts of the earth were in subjection when Christ was born. This glorious event took place in the year of the Julian Period 4709, and the fifth before the vulgar era of Christ commonly noted A. D., Anno Domini, or the year of our Lord. See the learned *Dr. Prideaux's* connected History of the Old and New Testaments.

I need not add here the years from the birth of Christ to the end of the New Testament History, as these are regularly brought down in a *Table of Remarkable Eras*, immediately succeeding the Acts of the Apostles, and terminating at A. D. 100.

For the desolation that took place when the temple was taken and destroyed, see the notes on Matt. xxiv. 31.

The general history of the Jews, especially from the destruction of their temple, A. D. 70, to the end of the *sixteenth* century, has been written by Mr. *Basnage*, entitled, "Histoire des Juifs, depuis Jesus Christ, jusqu à present; pour servir de continuation à l'Histoire de Joseph;" the *best edition* of which was printed at the Hague, 1716, 12mo., in *fifteen* vols. The *first* edition was translated into English by T. Taylor, A. M., Lond. 1708, fol.; but the author has greatly enlarged and corrected his work in the Hague edition above mentioned. The *learning* and *research* manifested in this work are amazing; and on the subject nothing better, nothing more accurate and satisfactory, can be well expected. This work I heartily recommend to all my readers.

For the *state* of the Jews in different nations of the earth, the Itinerary of *Rabbi Benjamin*, a native of Tudela, in the kingdom of Navarre, has been referred to; first translated from *Hebrew* into *Latin* by *B. A. Montanus*, and printed at Antwerp, in 1575, and much better by *Constantine L'Empereur*, and printed at Leyden, 12mo., with the Hebrew text and notes, 1633. This work has gone through *many* editions among the Jews, in Hebrew and in German. It has also been translated into *French* by *Baratier*, with many learned notes, Amsterdam, 1734.

But all the preceding translations have been totally eclipsed by that of the Rev. *B. Gerrans*, lecturer of St. Catherine Coleman, and second master of Queen Elizabeth's free grammar school, St. Olave, Southwark, with a Dissertation and Notes, 12mo., Lond. 1784. If we can believe *Rab. Benjamin*, (who it appears flourished in A. D. 1160,) he travelled over the whole world, and found the Jews in general in a most *flourishing* state, and living under their own laws in many places. But the work is a wretched imposition, too hastily credited by some learned men; written with a view of keeping up the credit of the Jewish people, and with the tacit design to show that *the Messiah is not yet come*, and that the *sceptre has not departed from Judah, nor a lawgiver from between his feet;* but he is at such variance with himself, and with the whole geography of the globe, that, as Mr. *Gerrans* properly observes, no *map* could possibly be made of his travels. "Reduce," says he, "the universe to its primeval chaos; confound Asia with Africa; north with south, and heat with cold; make cities provinces, and provinces cities; people uncultivated deserts with free and independent Jews, and depopulate the most flourishing kingdoms; make rivers run when and where you please, and call them by any names but the right one; take Arabia upon your back, and carry it to the north of Babylon; turn the north pole south, or any other way you please; make a new ecliptic line, and place it in the most whimsical and eccentric position which the most hobby-horsical imagination can possibly conceive or describe; and such a *map* will best suit such an *author*." What therefore this author says of his travels and discoveries is worthy of no regard; and it is a doubt with me (if this person ever existed) whether he ever travelled beyond the limits of the kingdom of Navarre, or passed the boundaries of the city of Tudela. I mention these works, the *first* in the way of strong recommendation; the *second*, to put the reader on his guard against imposition; at the same time recommending these *outcasts of Israel* to his most earnest commiseration and prayers, that the God of all grace may speedily call them to eternal glory by Christ Jesus, that all Israel may be saved; and that through all their dispersions they may be soon found singing the song of Moses and the Lamb! Amen, Amen.

CONCLUSION

In my *general preface* prefixed to the book of *Genesis*, I gave a succinct account of the *plan* I pursued in preparing this work for the press; but as this plan became necessarily *extended*, and led to much farther reading, examination, and discussion, I judge it necessary, now that the work is concluded, to give my readers a general *summary* of the whole, that they may be in possession of my mode of proceeding, and be enabled more fully to comprehend the *reasons* why the work has been *so long* in passing through the press. [This refers only to the *first* edition.]

My education and habits from early youth led me to read and study the Bible, not as a *text-book* to confirm the articles of a *preconceived creed*, but as a *revelation from God to man*, (of his will and purposes in reference to the origin and designation of his human offspring,) which it was the duty of all the inhabitants of the earth deeply to study, and earnestly to endeavour to understand, as it concerned their peace and happiness, and the perfection of their being in reference to both worlds.

Conscious that translators in general must have had a *particular creed*, in reference to which they would naturally consider every text, and this reference, however honestly intended, might lead them to glosses not always fairly deducible from the original words, I sat down with a heart as free from bias and sectarian feeling as possible, and carefully read over, cautiously weighed, and literally translated every word, *Hebrew* and *Chaldee*, in the Old Testament. And as I saw that it was possible, even while assisted by the best *translations* and best *lexicographers*, to mistake the import of a Hebrew term, and considering that the *cognate Asiatic languages* would be helps of great importance in such an inquiry, I collated every verse where I was apprehensive of any difficulty with the *Chaldee*, *Syriac*, *Arabic*, and *Persian*, and the *Æthiopic* in the Polyglot *translation*, as far as the sacred writings are extant in these languages; and I did this with a constant reference to the *various readings* collected by *Houbigant*, *H. Michaelis*, *Kennicott*, and *De Rossi*, and to the best editions of the *Septuagint* and *Vulgate*, which are the earliest translations of the Hebrew text that have reached our times.

Nor have I been satisfied with these collections of various readings; I have examined and collated several ancient *Hebrew* MSS., which preceding scholars had never seen, with many ancient MSS. of the *Vulgate* equally unknown to Biblical critics. This work required much time and great pains, and necessarily occasioned much delay; and no wonder, when I have often, on my plan, been obliged to employ as much time in visiting many sources and sailing down their streams, in order to ascertain a genuine reading, or fix the sense of a disputed verse, as would have been sufficient for some of my contemporaries to pass whole sheets of their work through the press. Had I not followed this method, which to me appeared absolutely necessary, I should have completed my work, such as it would have been, in less than one half of the time.

These previous readings, collations, and translations, produced an immense number of notes and observations on all parts of the Old Testament, which, by the advice and entreaty of several learned and judicious friends, I was induced to extend in the form of a *perpetual comment* on every book in the Bible. This being ultimately revised and completed as far as the book of *Judges*, which formed, in my purpose, the boundary of my proceedings on the Hebrew Scriptures, I was induced to commit it to press.

Though my friends in general wished me to go forward with the *Old Testament*, yet, as several of them were apprehensive, from the infirm state of my health at that time, that I might not live long enough to finish the whole, they advised me strongly to omit for the present the Old Testament, and begin with the New. This was in conformity with my own feelings on the subject; having wished simply to add the *four Gospels* and *Acts of the Apostles* to the *five books of Moses* and the books of *Joshua* and *Judges;* as these two parcels of Divine revelation, carefully illustrated, would give a full view of the *origin* and *final settlement* of the *Church* of the *Old Covenant*, and the commencement and completion of *that* of the *New*. And thus I proceeded:—

After having literally translated every word of the *New Testament*, that last best gift of God to man; comparing the whole with all the *ancient versions*, and the most important of the *modern;* collating all with the *various readings* collected by *Stephens*, *Courcel*, *Fell*, *Gherard of Maestricht*, *Bengel*, *Mill*, *Wetstein*, and *Griesbach;* actually examining many MSS., either cursorily or not at all examined by *them;* illustrating the whole by quotations from ancient authors, *rabbinical*,

Grecian, Roman, and *Asiatic;* I exceeded my previous design, and brought down the work to the end of the *Apocalypse;* and passed the whole through the press.

I should mention here a *previous* work, (without which any man must be ill qualified to undertake the illustration of the New Testament,) viz., a careful examination of the *Septuagint.* In *this* the phraseology of the New Testament is contained, and from this the import of that phraseology is alone to be derived. This I read carefully over to the end of the book of Psalms, in the edition of Dr. *Grabe,* from the *Codex Alexandrinus;* collating it occasionally with editions taken from the *Vatican* MS., and particularly that printed by *Field,* at Cambridge, 1665, 18mo., with the Parænetic preface of the learned Bishop Pearson. Without this previous work, who did ever yet properly comprehend the *idiom* and *phraseology* of the Greek Testament? Now, all these are parts of my labour which common readers cannot conceive; and which none can properly appreciate, as to the pains, difficulty, and time which must be expended, who have not themselves trodden this almost unfrequented path.

When the New Testament was thus prepared and finished at press, I was induced, though with great reluctance, to recommence the Old. I was already nearly worn down by my previous work, connected with other works and duties which I could not omit; and though I had gone through the most important parts of the sacred records, yet I could easily foresee that I had an ocean of difficulties to wade through in those parts that remained. The *Historical Books* alone, in their *chronology, arrangement of facts, concise* and often *obscure phraseology,* presented not a few; the books of *Solomon,* and those of the *major* and *minor prophets,* a *multitude.* Notwithstanding all these, I hope I may say that, having obtained help of God, I am come with some success to the conclusion; having aimed at nothing, throughout the whole, but the *glory of God* and the *good of men.*

But still something remains to be said concerning the *modus operandi,* or *particular plan of proceeding.* In prosecuting this work I was led to attend, in the *first* instance, more to *words* than to *things,* in order to find their true ideal meaning; together with those different shades of *acceptation* to which they became subject, either in the circumstances of the speakers and those who were addressed, or in their application to matters which use, peculiarity of place and situation, and the lapse of time, had produced. It was my invariable plan to ascertain first, the *literal meaning* of every word and phrase; and where there was a *spiritual* meaning, or reference, to see how it was founded on the literal sense. He who assumes his spiritual meanings first, is never likely to interpret the words of God either to his own credit or to the profit of his readers; but in this track commentator has followed commentator, so that, in many cases, instead of a careful display of *God's words* and the *objects* of his providence and mercy, we have tissues of *strange doctrines, human creeds,* and *confessions of faith.* As I have said in another place, I speak not against *compilations* of this kind; but let them be founded on the words of God, first properly understood.

As I proceeded in my work I met with other difficulties. I soon perceived an almost continual reference to the *literature, arts,* and *sciences* of the *Ancient World,* and of the *Asiatic* nations in particular; and was therefore obliged to make these my particular study, having found a thousand passages which I could neither illustrate nor explain, without some general knowledge at least of their *jurisprudence, astronomy, architecture, chemistry, chirurgery, medicine, metallurgy, pneumatics,* &c., with their *military tactics,* and the *arts* and *trades* (as well *ornamental* as *necessary*) which are carried on in common life.

In the course of all this labour I have also paid particular attention to those *facts* mentioned in the sacred writings which have been the subjects of *animadversion* or *ridicule* by *free-thinkers* and *infidels* of all classes and in all times: and I hope I may say that no such passage is either designedly *passed by* or *superficially* considered; that the strongest objections are fairly produced and met; that all such parts of these Divine writings are, in consequence, exhibited in their own lustre; and that the truth of the doctrine of our salvation has had as many *triumphs* as it has had *attacks* from the rudest and most formidable of its antagonists; and on all such disputed points I humbly hope that the reader will never consult these volumes in vain. And if those grand doctrines which constitute what by some is called *orthodoxy;* that prove that God is loving to every man; that from his innate, infinite, and eternal goodness, he *wills* and has made *provision* for the salvation of *every human soul;* be found to be those which alone have stood the rigid test of all the above sifting and examination; it was not because these were sought for beyond all others, and the Scriptures *bent* in that way in order to favour them; but because these doctrines are essentially contained in, and established by, the ORACLES OF GOD.

I may add, that these doctrines and all those connected with them, (such as the defection and sinfulness of man; the incarnation and sacrificial death of Christ; his infinite, unoriginated, and eternal Deity; justification by faith in his blood; and the complete sanctification of the soul by the inspiration of the Holy Spirit,) have not only been shown to be *the doctrines* of the sacred records, but have also been subjected to the strongest test of logical examination; and, in the notes, are supported by arguments, many of them new, applied in such a way as has not been done before in any similar or theological work.

In this arduous labour I have had no assistants; not even a single week's help from an *amanuensis;* no person to look for common-places, or refer to an ancient author; to find out the place and transcribe a passage of Greek, Latin, or any other language, which my memory had generally recalled, or to verify a quotation; the help excepted which I received in the *chronological* department from my nephew. I have laboured *alone* for nearly *twenty-five years previously* to the work being sent to press; and *fifteen* years have been employed in bringing it through the press to the public; and thus about *forty years* of my life have been consumed; and from this the reader will at once perceive that the work, *well* or *ill* executed, has not been done in a *careless* or *precipitate* manner; nor have any means within my reach been neglected to make it in every respect, as far as possible, what the title-page promises,—A HELP TO A BETTER UNDERSTANDING OF THE SACRED WRITINGS.

Thus, through the merciful help of God, my labour in this field terminates; a labour, which were it yet to commence, with the knowledge I now have of its difficulty, and my, in many respects, *inadequate means,* millions, even of the gold of Ophir, and all the honours that can come from man, could not induce me to undertake. Now that it is finished, I regret not the labour; I have had the testimony of many learned, pious, and judicious friends relative to the execution and usefulness of the work. It has been admitted into the very *highest ranks* of society, and has lodged in the cottages of the poor. It has been the means of doing good to the *simple of heart;* and the *wise man* and the *scribe,* the *learned* and the *philosopher,* according to their own generous acknowledgments, have not consulted its pages in vain.

For these, and all his other mercies to the writer and reader, may God, the Fountain of all good, be eternally praised!

ADAM CLARKE.

Eastcott, April 17, 1826.

A TABLE

Of the several places of the Old Testament *cited in the* New, *which are taken from the Hebrew or Septuagint, from both, or from neither*

In this Table, O stands for the *Old Testament;* H, for *Hebrew;* G, for the *Greek* version or *Septuagint;* and N, for *neither*, or *doubtful*.

MATTHEW

Chap.	Ver.		
i.	23.	from Isa. vii. 14.	O
ii.	6.	from Mic. v. 2.	N
	15.	from Hos. xi. 1.	H
	18.	from Jer. xxxi. 15.	H
	23.	from Judg. xiii. 5.	N
iii.	3.	from Isa. xl. 3.	G
iv.	4.	from Deut. viii. 3.	G
	6.	from Psa. xci. 11, 12.	N
	7.	from Deut. vi. 16.	G
	10.	from Deut. vi. 13.	N
	15, 16.	from Isa. ix. 1, 2.	N
v.	21.	from Exod. xx. 13; Lev. xxiv. 21.	N
	31.	from Deut. xxiv. 1.	O
	33.	from Num. xxx. 2.	N
	38.	from Exod. xxi. 24.	O
	43.	from Lev. xix. 18.	N
viii.	17.	from Isa. liii. 4.	H
ix.	13.	from Hos. vi. 6.	H
xi.	10.	from Mal. iii. 1.	H and N
	14.	from Mal. iv. 5.	H
xii.	4.	from 1 Sam. xxi. 6.	O
	5.	from Num. xxviii. 9.	O
	18,	&c., from Isa. xlii. 1.	G and N
xiii.	14.	from Isa. vi. 9, 20.	G
	35.	from Psa. lxxviii. 2.	G and N
xv.	4.	from Exod. xx. 12, xxi. 17.	O
	8, 9.	from Isa. xxix. 13.	G
xix.	4.	from Gen. i. 27.	O
	5.	from Gen. ii. 24.	O
	7.	from Deut. xxiv. 1.	O
xxi.	5.	from Zech. ix. 9.	N
	9.	from Psa. cxviii. 25, 26.	O
	13.	from Isa. lvi. 7, partim. }	N
		from Jer. vii. 11, partim. }	
	16.	from Psa. viii. 2.	O
	42.	from Psa. cxviii. 22, 23.	O
xxii.	24.	from Deut. xxv. 5.	O
	32.	from Exod. iii. 6.	O
	37.	from Deut. vi. 5.	N
	39.	from Lev. xix. 18.	O
	44.	from Psa. cx. 1.	O
xxiv.	15.	from Dan. xii. 11.	G
	29.	from Isa. xiii. 10.	N
xxvii.	9, 10.	from Zech. xi. 13.	O and N
	35.	from Psa. xxii. 18.	O
	46.	from Psa. xxii. 1.	O

MARK

Chap.	Ver.		
i.	2.	from Mal. iii. 1.	O
	3.	from Isa. xl. 3.	O
ii.	26.	from 1 Sam. xxii. 6.	N
iv.	12.	from Isa. vi. 9.	O
vii.	6.	from Isa. xxix. 13.	O
x.	8.	from Gen. ii. 24.	O
xi.	9, 10.	from Psa. cxviii. 22, 23.	O
	17.	from Isa. lvi. 7: Jer. vii. 11.	O
xii.	10, 11.	from Psa. cxviii. 22, 23	O
	19.	from Deut. xxv. 5.	O
xii.	26.	from Exod. iii. 6.	O
	29, 30.	from Deut. vi. 4, 5.	O
	31.	from Lev. xix. 18.	O
	36.	from Psa. cx. 1.	O
xiii.	14.	from Dan. xii. 11.	O
xiv.	27.	from Zech. xiii. 7.	H and N
xv.	28.	from Isa. liii. 12.	O
	34.	from Psa. xxii. 1.	O

LUKE

Chap.	Ver.		
ii.	23.	from Exod. xiii. 2; Num. viii. 17.	N
	24.	from Lev. xii. 8.	O
	34.	from Isa. viii. 14.	N
iv.	4.	from Deut. viii. 3.	O
	8.	from Deut. vi. 13.	O
	10, 11.	from Psa. xci. 11, 12.	O
	12.	from Deut. vi. 16.	O
	18, 19.	from Isa. lxi. 1, 2.	G and N
vi.	4.	from 1 Sam. xxi. 6.	O
vii.	27.	from Mal. iii. 1.	O
x.	27.	from Deut. vi. 5; Lev. xix. 18.	O
xix.	46.	from Isa. lvi. 7; Jer. vii. 11.	O
xx.	17.	from Psa. cxviii. 22.	O
	37.	from Exod. iii. 6.	O
	42, 43.	from Psa. cx. 1.	O
xxii.	37.	from Isa. liii. 12.	O

JOHN

Chap.	Ver.		
i.	23.	from Isa. xl. 3.	O
ii.	17.	from Psa. lxix. 9.	O
vii.	42.	partim from Mic. v. 2, partim.	O
		from 1 Sam. xvi. 1, partim.	O
viii.	5.	from Lev. xx. 10.	O
	17.	from Deut. xvii. 6.	O
x.	34.	from Psa. lxxxii. 6.	O
xii.	15.	from Zech. ix. 9.	O
	38.	from Psa. liii. 1.	C
	40.	from Isa. vi. 10.	N
xiii.	18.	from Psa. xli. 9.	N
xix.	24.	from Psa. xxii. 18.	O
	28, 29.	from Psa. lxix. 21.	O
	36.	from Exod. xii. 46.	N
	37.	from Zech. xii. 10.	H

ACTS

Chap.	Ver.		
i.	20.	partim from Psa. lxix. 26, partim.	N
		from Psa. cix. 8, partim.	N
ii.	17,	&c. from Joel ii. 28, &c.	G
	25,	&c. from Psa. xvi. 8, &c.	G
	34, 35.	from Psa. cx. 1.	O
iii.	22.	from Deut. xviii. 15, 18, 19.	N
	25.	from Gen. xxii. 18.	N
iv.	25, 26.	from Psa. ii. 1, 2.	O

Chap.	Ver.		
vii.	42, 43.	from Amos v. 25, 26, 27.	N
	49, 50.	from Isa. lxvi. 1, 2.	O
viii.	32, 33.	from Isa. liii. 7, 8.	G
xiii.	33.	from Psa. ii. 7.	O
	34.	from Isa. lv. 3.	O
xiii.	35.	from Psa. xvi. 10.	O
	41.	from Hab. i. 5.	G
	47.	from Isa. xlix. 6.	O
xv.	16, 17.	from Amos ix. 11, 12.	G
xxiii.	5.	from Exod. ii. 28.	O
xxviii.	26, 27.	from Isa. vi. 9, 10.	O

ROMANS

Chap.	Ver.		
i.	17.	from Hab. ii. 4.	O
iii.	4.	from Psa. li. 4.	G
	10, 11, 12.	from Psa. xiv. 1, 2, 3.	N
	13.	from Psa. v. 10; Psa. cxl. 4.	
	14.	from Psa. x. 7.	
	15.	from Prov. i. 16.	from Psa. xiv. 1, 2, 3, juxta, lxx. G
	16, 17.	from Isa. lix. 7, 8.	
	18.	from Psa. xxxvi. 12.	
iv.	3.	from Gen. xv. 6.	O
	17.	from Gen. xvii. 5.	O
	18.	from Gen. xv. 5.	O
viii.	36.	from Psa. xliv. 23.	O
ix.	9.	from Gen. xviii. 10.	O
	12.	from Gen. xxv. 23.	O
	13.	from Matt. i. 2.	O
	15.	from Exod. xxxiii. 9.	O
	17.	from Exod. ix. 16.	H
	25.	from Hos. ii. 23.	O
	26.	from Hos. i. 10.	O
	27, 28.	from Isa. x. 22, 23.	O
	29.	from Isa. i. 9.	O
	33.	from Isa. viii. 14, and xxviii. 16	H
	5.	from Lev. xviii. 5.	O
	6.	from Deut. xxx. 12.	O
	8.	from Deut. xxx. 14.	O
	11.	from Isa. xxviii. 16.	G
	13.	from Joel ii. 32.	O
	15.	from Isa. lii. 7.	H
	16.	from Isa. liii. 1.	O
	18.	from Psa. xix. 5.	O
	19.	from Deut. xxxii. 21.	O
x.	20, 21.	from Isa. lxv. 1, 2.	O
xi.	3.	from 1 Kings xix. 10.	O
	4.	from 1 Kings xix. 18.	H
	8.	from Isa. xxix. 9, vi. 9.	N
	9, 10.	from Psa. lxix. 23, 24.	G
	26.	from Isa. lix. 20.	N
	27.	from Isa. xxvii. 9.	O
	34.	from Isa. xl. 13.	H
	35.	from Job xli. 2 or 10.	H
xii.	19.	from Deut. xxxii. 35.	O
	20.	from Prov. xxv. 21, 22.	N
xiv.	11.	from Isa. xlv. 23.	O
xv.	3.	from Psa. lxix. 10.	O
	9.	from Psa. xviii. 50.	O
	10.	from Deut. xxxii. 43.	O
	11.	from Psa. cxvii. 1.	O
	12.	from Isa. xi. 10.	O
	21.	from Isa. lii. 15.	O

1 CORINTHIANS

Chap.	Ver.		
i.	19.	from Isa. xxix. 14.	G and N
	31.	from Jer. ix. 24.	O
ii.	9.	from Isa. lxiv. 4.	N
	16.	from Isa. xl. 13.	O
iii.	19.	from Job v. 13.	H
	20.	from Psa. xciv. 11.	N
vi.	16.	from Gen. ii. 24.	O
ix.	9.	from Deut. xxv. 4.	O
x.	7.	from Exod. xxxii. 6.	O
	26.	from Psa. xxiv. 1.	O
xiv.	21.	from Isa. xxviii. 11, 12.	N
xv.	45.	from Gen. ii. 7.	O
	54.	from Isa. xxv. 8.	H

2 CORINTHIANS

Chap.	Ver.		
iv.	13.	from Psa. cxvi. 10.	O
vi.	2.	from Isa. xlix. 8.	O
	16.	from Lev. xxvi. 11, 12; Ezek. xxxvii. 27.	O
vi.	17.	from Isa. lii. 11.	O
	18.	from Jer. xxxi. 1, 9.	O
viii.	15.	from Exod. xvi. 18.	O
ix.	9.	from Psa. cxii. 9.	O
xiii.	1.	from Deut. xvii. 6.	O

GALATIANS

Chap.	Ver.		
iii.	8.	from Gen. xii. 3, xviii. 18.	O
	10.	from Deut. xxvii. 26	O
	11.	from Hab. ii. 4.	O
	12.	from Lev. xviii. 5.	O
	13.	from Deut. xxi. 23.	O
	16.	from Gen. xvii. 7.	O
iv.	22.	from Gen. xvi. 15, 21.	O
	27.	from Isa. liv. 1.	O
	30.	from Gen. xxi. 10.	O

EPHESIANS

Chap.	Ver.		
iv.	8.	from Psa. lxviii. 19.	N
v.	31.	from Gen. ii. 24.	O
vi.	2, 3.	from Exod. xx. 12; Deut. v. 16.	G

1 TIMOTHY

Chap.	Ver.		
v.	18.	from Deut. xxv. 4.	O

HEBREWS

Chap.	Ver.		
i.	5.	from Psa. ii. 7; 2 Sam. vii. 14.	O
	6.	from Psa. xcvii. 7.	G
	7.	from Psa. civ. 4.	O
	8, 9.	from Psa. xlv. 6, 7.	O
	10–12.	from Psa. cii. 25–27.	O
	13.	from Psa. cx. 1.	O
ii.	6–8.	from Psa. viii. 4–6.	O
	12.	from Psa. xxii. 22.	O
	13.	from 2 Sam. xxii. 3, and Isa. viii. 18.	O
iii.	7–11.	from Psa. xcv. 7–11.	O
iv.	4.	from Gen. ii. 2.	O
v.	5.	from Psa. ii. 7.	O
	6.	from Psa. cx. 4.	O
vi.	14.	from Gen. xxii. 17.	O
vii.	1.	from Gen. xiv. 18.	O
	17.	from Psa. cx. 4.	O
viii.	5.	from Exod. xxv. 40.	O
	8–12.	from Jer. xxxi. 31–34.	N
ix.	20.	from Exod. xxiv. 8.	O
x.	5–7.	from Psa. xl. 6–8.	G
	16, 17.	from Jer. xxxi. 32, 34.	O
	30.	from Deut. xxxii. 35, 36.	O
	37, 38.	from Hab. ii. 3, 4.	G and N
xi.	5.	from Gen. v. 24.	G
	18.	from Gen. xxi. 12.	O
	22.	from Gen. xlvii. 31.	G
xii.	5, 6.	from Prov. iii. 11, 12.	O
	16.	from Gen. xxv. 33.	O
	18.	from Exod. xix. 16.	O
	20.	from Exod. xix. 19.	O
	26.	from Hag. ii. 6.	O
	29.	from Deut. iv. 24.	O
xii.	5.	from Deut. xxxi. 6, 8, and Josh. i. 5.	O
	6.	from Psa. cxviii. 6.	O

JAMES

Chap.	Ver.		
i.	12.	from Job v. 17.	N
ii.	8.	from Lev. xix. 18.	O
	23.	partim from Gen. xv. 16, partim.	O
		from 2 Chron. xx. 7, partim.	O

Chap.	Ver.		
iv.	5.	from Gen. vi. 3, 5.	N
	6.	from Prov. iii. 34.	G

1 PETER

Chap.	Ver.		
i.	16.	from Lev. xi. 44.	O
	25.	from Isa. xl. 6, 7.	G
ii.	6.	from Isa. xxviii. 16.	O
	7.	from Psa. cxviii. 22; Isa. viii. 14.	O
	22.	from Isa. liii. 9.	O
ii.	24, 25.	from Isa. liii. 5, 6.	O
iii.	6.	from Gen. xviii. 12.	O
	10–12.	from Psa. xxxiv. 12–16.	O
iv.	18.	from Prov. xi. 31.	N
v.	5.	from Prov. iii. 34.	O

2 PETER

Chap.	Ver.		
ii.	22.	from Prov. xxvi. 11.	O
iii.	8.	from Psa. xc. 4.	O
	9.	from Ezek. xxxiii. 11.	O

JUDE

Chap.	Ver.		
	9.	from Zech. iii. 2.	H

APOCALYPSE

Chap.	Ver.		
i.	7.	from Zech. xii. 10.	H
ii.	23.	from Psa. vii. 10.	O
	27.	from Psa. ii. 10.	O
iii.	7.	from Isa. xxii. 22.	O
	19.	from Prov. iii. 12.	O
iv.	8.	from Isa. vi. 3.	O
v.	5.	from Gen. xlix. 9.	O
	11.	from Dan. vii. 10.	O
vi.	14.	from Isa. xxxiv. 4.	O
	16.	from Isa. ii. 19; Hos. x. 8.	O
vii.	3.	from Ezek. ix. 4.	O
vii.	17.	from Isa. xxv. 8.	O
x.	5.	from Dan. xii. 7.	O
	9.	from Ezek. iii. 3.	O
xi.	4.	from Zech. iv. 3.	O
xii.	5.	from Psa. ii. 9.	O
xiii.	10.	from Gen. ix. 6.	O
xiv.	5.	from Psa. xxxii. 2.	O
	8.	from Psa. xxi. 9.	O
	10.	from Psa. lxxv. 8.	O
xv.	4.	from Jer. x. 7.	O
	8.	from Exod. xl. 34.	O
xviii.	2.	from Isa. xiii. 21, 22.	O
	4.	from Isa. xlviii. 20; Jer. l. 8.	O
	6.	from Psa. cxxxvii. 8.	O
	7.	from Isa. xlvii. 7, 8.	O
	11.	from Ezek. xxvii. 35, 36.	O
	17, &c.	from Ezek. xxix. 29, &c.	O
	21.	from Jer. li. 64.	O
	23.	from Jer. xxv. 10.	O
xix.	13.	from Isa. lxiii. 2, 3.	O
xx.	8.	from Ezek. xxxviii. 2; xxxix. 1.	O
xxi.	1.	from Isa. lxv. 17.	O
	4.	from Isa. xxv. 8.	O
	15.	from Ezek. xl. 3.	O
	23.	from Isa. lx. 19.	O
	25.	from Isa. lx. 20.	O
	27.	from Isa. xxxv. 8.	O
xxii.	5.	from Isa. lx. 19, 20.	O

18 H. 27 G. 47 N. Plerumque O.; i. e., 200, aut eo circiter.

The above table was printed by Mr. E. Leigh, for his *Critica Sacra*. I have made a few corrections and additions.—A. C.

TABLE I

Of passages collected from the Old Testament, *as a testimony to the* New; *not indeed in the same words, but having the same meaning*

Chap. Ver.

GENESIS

i. 1. By faith we know that the worlds were made. Heb. xi. 3.
The heavens were of old. 2 Pet. iii. 5.
27. Adam was first formed. 1 Tim. ii. 13.
ii. 22. But the man is not of the woman. 1 Cor. xi. 8.
iii. 4. But the serpent deceived Eve by his subtilty. 2 Cor. xi. 3.
6. Adam was not deceived. 1 Tim. ii. 14.
iv. 4. By faith Abel offered unto God a more excellent sacrifice than Cain. Heb. xi. 4.
8. From the blood of righteous Abel. Matt. xxiii. 35.
Not as Cain, who was of that wicked one. 1 John iii. 12.
Wo to them, for they have gone in the way of Cain. Jude 12.
v. 24. By faith Enoch was translated. Heb. xi. 5.
vi. 12. When once the longsuffering of God waited. 1 Pet. iii. 20.
13. By faith Noah was warned. Heb. xi. 7.
22. Noah, the eighth person, a preacher of righteousness. 2 Pet. ii. 5.
vii. 4. For as the days that were before the flood. Matt. xxiv. 32.
ix. 6. All they that take the sword shall perish by the sword. Matt. xxvi. 52; Rev. xiii. 10.
xii. 4. By faith Abraham, when he was called. Heb. xi. 8.
xiv. 18. For this Melchisedek. Heb. vii. 1.
xvi. 15. Abraham had two sons, the one by a bondmaid. Gal. iv. 22.
xvii. 11. And gave him the covenant of circumcision. Acts vii. 8; Rom. iv. 11.
xviii. 10. By faith Sarah herself received strength. Heb. xi. 11.
12. As Sarah obeyed Abraham. 1 Pet. iii. 6.
xix. 25. And the cities of Sodom and Gomorrah. 2 Pet. ii. 6.
As Sodom and Gomorrah. Jude 7.
26. Remember Lot's wife. Luke xvii. 32.
For as it was in the days of Lot, they ate, they drank, they bought. Luke xvii. 27.
xxi. 1. Abraham had a son by the free-woman. Gal. iv. 22.
xxii. 1. By faith, Abraham, when he was tried. Heb. xi. 17.
9. Abraham offered his son upon the altar. James ii. 21.
xxii. 16. As he spoke unto our fathers. Luke i. 55.

Chap. Ver.

xxv. 22. Rebecca also conceived by one, our father Isaac. Rom. ix. 10.

31. Lest there be a fornicator or profane person, as was Esau, who for one mess of pottage sold his birthright. Heb. xii. 16.

xxvii. 28. By faith he blessed them concerning things to come. Heb. xi. 20.

xlviii. 15. By faith, Jacob when he was dying. Heb. xi. 21.

xlix. 10. Of whom Moses wrote in the law. John i. 45.

l. 24. By faith, Joseph, when he died. Heb. xi. 22.

EXODUS

ii. 2. By faith, Moses, when he was born. Heb. xi. 23.

11. By faith, Moses, when he was come to years. Heb. xi. 24.

Moses, seeing one of them suffering wrong. Acts vii. 24.

iii. 2. And when forty years were expired. Acts vii. 30.

xii. 11. Through faith he kept the passover. Heb. xi. 28.

xix. 22. They were baptized unto Moses in the cloud. 1 Cor. x. 2.

By faith they passed through the Red Sea. Heb. xi. 29.

xvi. 15. Our fathers ate manna in the wilderness. John vi. 49.

He gave them bread from heaven. John vi. 31.

They did all eat that spiritual meat. 1 Cor. x. 3.

xvii. 6. For they drank of that spiritual rock which followed them. 1 Cor. x. 4.

xix. 6. A holy nation, a peculiar people. 1 Pet. ii. 9.

12. And if a beast touch the mountain. Heb. xii. 20.

16. Ye are not come unto the mountain. Heb. xii. 18.

xxiv. 8. When Moses had spoken every precept. Heb. ix. 19.

xxvi. 1. For there was a tabernacle made, the first. Heb. ix. 2.

xxxii. 6. Be not ye idolaters, as were some of them. 1 Cor. x. 7.

xl. 4. Wherein was the candlestick. Heb. ix. 2.

LEVITICUS

xii. 3. Ye on the Sabbath circumcise a man. John vii. 22.

When eight days were fulfilled. Luke ii. 21.

4. When the days of their purification. Luke ii. 22.

6. And to offer a sacrifice according to the law. Luke ii. 24.

xiv. 4. Bring the gift which Moses hath commanded. Matt. viii. 4; Mark i. 44.

xvi. 14. If the blood of bulls and goats. Heb. ix. 13.

17. The whole multitude of the people were without worshipping. Luke i. 10.

xix. 15. Not with respect to persons. James ii. 1.

17. If thy brother sin against thee. Matt. xviii. 15; Luke xvii. 3.

xx. 10. Moses in the law commanded such to be stoned. John viii. 5.

Chap. Ver.

NUMBERS

viii. 16. Every male that openeth the womb. Luke ii. 23.

ix. 18. All our fathers were under the cloud. 1 Cor. x. 1.

xi. 7. He gave them bread from heaven to eat. John vi. 31.

xii. 7. Moses was faithful in all his house. Heb. iii. 2.

xiv. 37. Whose carcasses fell in the wilderness. Heb. iii. 17.

xvi. 1. They have perished in the gainsaying of Korah. Jude 11.

xix. 3. For the bodies of the beasts whose blood is brought. Heb. xiii. 12.

xx. 10. They drank of that spiritual rock that followed them. 1 Cor. x. 4.

xxi. 5. Neither let us tempt Christ. 1 Cor. x. 9.

9. As Moses lifted up the serpent in the wilderness. John iii. 14.

xxii. 23. The dumb ass speaking with a man's voice. 2 Pet. ii. 16.

39. Following the way of Balaam. 2 Pet. ii. 15; Jude 11.

xxiv. 14. They hold the doctrine of Balaam, who taught Balak. Rev. ii. 14.

xxv. 6. Let us not commit adultery as some of them. 1 Cor. x. 8.

xxvi. 64. Whose bodies fell in the wilderness. 1 Cor. x. 5.

xxviii. 8. The priests profane the Sabbath in the temple. Matt. xii. 5.

DEUTERONOMY

i. 16, 17. Have not respect of persons. James ii. 1, 9.

x. 17. For there is no respect of persons with God. Rom. ii. 11; Acts x. 34; Col. iii. 25; Ephes. vi. 9.

xvii. 6. He that despised Moses' law. Heb. x. 28.

xviii. 1. Do ye not know that they who minister in holy things. 1 Cor. ix. 13.

xxiv. 1. Whosoever shall put away his wife. Matt. v. 31, xix. 7; Mark x. 4.

JOSHUA

ii. 1. Likewise Rahab the harlot. James ii. 25.

vi. 20. By faith the walls of Jericho fell down. Heb. xi. 30.

By faith, Rahab the harlot. Heb. xi. 31.

1 SAMUEL

xxi. 6. Do ye not know what David did when he was hungry. Matt. xii. 3; Mark ii. 25; Luke vi. 4.

1 KINGS

ii. 10. Let me speak freely concerning the patriarch David. Acts ii. 29, xiii. 36.

x. 1. The queen of the south. Matt. xii. 42; Luke xi. 31.

xvii. 1. The heavens were shut for the space of three years. Luke iv. 25.

Elijah was a man of like passions with us. James v. 17.

2 KINGS

iv. 29. Salute no man by the way. Luke x. 4.

v. 13. Many lepers were in Israel. Luke iv. 27.

Chap.	Ver.	
		1 CHRONICLES
xxiii.	13.	But no man receiveth this honour to himself, but he that was called, as was Aaron. Heb. v. 4.
		JOB
i.	21.	For we brought nothing into this world. 1 Tim. vi. 7.
v.	17.	Blessed is the man that endureth temptation. James i. 12.
xxxiv.	19.	For God is no respecter of persons. Acts x. 34.
		PSALMS
xli.	10.	But the Son of man goeth. Matt. xxvi. 24; Mark xiv. 21; Luke xxii. 22.
cxxxii.	5.	David desired to find a tabernacle for the God of Jacob. Acts vii. 46.
		PROVERBS
xi.	31.	If the righteous scarcely be saved. 1 Pet. iv. 18.
xvii.	27.	Let every one be swift to hear. James i. 19.
xx.	9.	If we say we have no sin. 1 John i. 8.
xxiv.	13.	Have not the faith, with respect of persons. James ii. 1.
xxv.	6.	Sit not down in the chief seat. Luke xiv. 8.
		ISAIAH
viii.	14.	Behold this is set for the fall and rising again. Luke ii. 34.
xiii.	10.	After the tribulation of those days, the sun shall be darkened. Matt. xxiv. 29; Mark xiii. 24.
xli.	8.	He hath holpen his servant Israel. Luke i. 54.
liv.	1.	Blessed are the barren. Luke xxiii. 29.
lviii.	7.	I was hungry and ye gave me meat. Matt. xxv. 35.
lxiii.	2.	Clothed with a garment dipped in blood. Rev. xix. 13.
		JEREMIAH
ii.	21.	A man that was a householder. Matt. xxi. 33; Mark xii. 1; Luke xx. 9.
xviii.	6.	Shall the thing formed say to him who formeth it. Rom. ix. 20.
		EZEKIEL
xii.	21.	Where is the promise of his coming. 2 Pet. iii. 4.
xviii.	7.	I was hungry and ye gave me meat. Matt. xxv. 35.
xxxix.	2.	And when the thousand years shall be finished. Rev. xx. 7.
		DANIEL
vii.	10.	And thousands of thousands. Rev. v. 11.
xii.	7.	And the angel which I saw standing on the sea. Rev. x. 5.
		JOEL
iii.	15.	The sun shall be darkened. Matt. xxiv. 29; Mark xiii. 24.
		MICAH
ii.	10.	Here we have no continuing city. Heb. xiii. 14.
iv.	7.	He shall reign over the house of Jacob. Luke i. 33.

TABLE II

Of passages collected from the Old Testament, *as a testimony to the* New; *not indeed in the same words, but having the same meaning*

Chap	Ver.	
		GENESIS
i.	27.	He made them male and female. Matt. xix. 4.
ii.	2.	And God rested the seventh day. Heb. iv. 4.
	7.	And the first man Adam was. 1 Cor. xv. 47.
	24.	Therefore shall a man leave father and mother. Matt. xix. 5; Mark x. 7; 1 Cor. vi. 16; Eph. v. 31.
		And they two shall be one flesh. Matt. xix. 5; Mark x. 7; 1 Cor. vi. 16; Eph. v. 31.
xii.	1, 5, 6.	Go out of thy country. Acts vii. 3.
		In thy seed shall all the kindreds of the earth be blessed. Acts iii. 25.
xv.	5.	So shall be thy seed. Rom. iv. 18.
	6.	And Abraham believed. Rom. iv. 18; James ii. 23; Gal. iii. 6.
	13, 16.	Thy seed shall sojourn. Acts vii. 6.
xvii.	4.	Thou shalt be a father of many nations. Rom. iv. 17.
xviii.	10.	I will return, according to the time of life. Rom. ix. 9.
xxi.	10.	Cast out the bondwoman and her son. Gal. iv. 30.
		In Isaac shall thy seed be called. Rom. ix. 7.
xxii.	17.	In blessing will I bless thee. Heb. vi. 14.
	18.	In thy seed shall all nations of the earth be blessed. Gal. iii. 8; Acts iii. 25.
xxv.	23.	The elder shall serve the younger. Rom. ix. 12.
		EXODUS
iii.	6.	I am the God of Abraham. Matt. xxii. 32; Mark xii. 26; Luke xx. 37; Acts vii. 32.
ix.	16.	For this cause have I raised thee up. Rom. ix. 17.
xii.	46.	A bone of him shall not be broken. John xix. 36.
xiii.	2.	Every male that openeth the womb. Luke ii. 23.
xvi.	18.	He that gathered much had nothing over. 2 Cor. viii. 15.
xx.	12.	Honour thy father and mother. Matt. xv. 4; Eph. vi. 2.
	13.	Thou shalt not kill. Matt. v. 21.
	14.	Thou shalt not commit adultery. Matt. v. 27.
	15.	Thou shalt not steal, &c. Rom. xiii. 9.
	17.	Thou shalt not covet. Rom. vii. 7.

Chap. Ver.

xxi. 17. He that curseth his father or mother. Matt. xv. 4; Mark vii. 10.

24. Eye for eye, tooth for tooth. Matt. v. 38.

xxii. 28. Thou shalt not speak evil of the ruler of thy people. Acts xxiii. 5.

xxiv. 8. Behold the blood of the covenant. Heb. ix. 20; xiii. 20; 1 Pet. i. 2.

xxv. 40. Look that thou make all after the pattern. Heb. viii. 5; Acts vii. 44.

xxxii. 1. Make us gods that may go before us. Acts vii. 40.

xxxiii. 19. I will be gracious to whom I will be gracious. Rom. ix. 15.

xxxiv. 33. Moses put a veil on his face. 2 Cor. iii. 13.

LEVITICUS

xi. 44. Ye shall be holy, for I am holy. 1 Thess. iv. 7; 1 Pet. i. 15, 16.

xviii. 5. Which if a man do, he shall live in them. Luke x. 28; Rom. x. 5.

xix. 12. Ye shall not swear by my name falsely. Matt. v. 33; James v. 12.

18. Thou shalt love thy neighbour as thyself. Matt. v. 43; xxii. 39; Gal. v. 14; James ii. 8.

xx. 9. Every one that curseth father or mother. Matt. xv. 4.

xxiv. 20. Eye for eye, tooth for tooth. Matt. v. 38.

xxvi. 11. I will dwell among you. 2 Cor. vi. 16.

NUMBERS

ix. 12. Nor break any bone of it. John xix. 36.

DEUTERONOMY

iv. 24. The Lord thy God is a consuming fire. Heb. xii. 29.

v. 16. Honour thy father and thy mother. Matt. xv. 4; Mark vii. 13; Eph. vi. 2.

17. Thou shalt not kill. Matt. v. 21.

18. Thou shalt not commit adultery. Luke xviii. 20.

19. Thou shalt not steal. Luke xviii. 20; Rom. xiii. 9.

20. Thou shalt not bear false witness. Luke xviii. 20; Rom. xiii. 9.

21. Thou shalt not covet. Rom. vii. 7.

vi. 4. Hear, O Israel, the Lord our God is one Lord. Mark xii. 29.

5. Thou shalt love the Lord. Matt. xxii. 37; Mark xii. 30; Luke x. 27.

13. Thou shalt fear the Lord thy God, and serve him. Matt. iv. 10; Luke iv. 8.

16. Ye shall not tempt the Lord your God. Matt. iv. 7; Luke iv. 12.

viii. 3. Man doth not live by bread only. Matt. iv. 4; Luke iv. 4.

x. 17. God accepteth not persons. Acts x. 34; Rom. ii. 11; Gal. ii. 6; Eph. vi. 9; 1 Pet. i. 17.

xviii. 15. A prophet shall the Lord raise up unto thee. John i. 45; Acts iii. 22, vii. 37.

xix. 15. At the mouth of two witnesses. Matt. xviii. 16; John viii. 17; 2 Cor. xiii. 1; 1 Tim. v. 19; Heb. x. 28.

21. An eye for an eye, tooth for tooth, hand for hand. Matt. v. 38.

xxi. 23. He that is hanged is accursed. Gal. iii. 13.

xxv. 4. Thou shalt not muzzle the ox. 1 Cor. ix. 9; 1 Tim. v. 18.

5. If a man's brother die. Matt. xxii. 24; Mark xii. 19; Luke xx. 28.

Chap. Ver.

xxvii. 26. Cursed is he who confirmeth not all the words of this law. Gal. iii. 10.

xxx. 12. Who shall go up for us to heaven. Rom. x. 6, &c.

14. But the word is very nigh unto thee. Rom. x. 6, &c.

xxxii. 21. I will move them to jealousy. Rom. x. 19.

35. To me belong vengeance and recompense. Rom. xii. 19; Heb. x. 30.

JOSHUA

i. 5. I will not fail thee. Heb. xiii. 5.

2 SAMUEL

vii. 14. I will be his father. Heb. i. 5.

1 KINGS

xix. 10. They have slain thy prophets. Rom. xi. 3.

18. I have left me seven thousand in Israel. Rom. xi. 4.

JOB

v. 13. He taketh the wise in their own craftiness. 1 Cor. iii. 19.

PSALMS

ii. 1. Why do the heathen rage. Acts iv. 25.

7. Thou art my Son, this day have I begotten thee. Acts xiii. 33; Heb. i. 5; v. 3.

9. Thou shalt break them with a rod of iron. Rev. ii. 27, xii. 5, xix. 15.

iv. 4. Stand in awe and sin not. Eph. iv. 26.

v. 9. Their throat is an open sepulchre. Luke xi. 44; Rom. iii. 13.

vi. 8. Depart from me, ye workers of iniquity. Matt. vii. 23, xxv. 41; Luke xiii. 27.

viii. 2. Out of the mouths of babes and sucklings. Matt. xi. 25, xxi. 16; 1 Cor. i. 27.

4. What is man that thou art mindful of him. Heb. ii. 6.

6. Thou hast put all things under his feet. 1 Cor. xv. 27; Heb. ii. 8.

x. 7. His mouth is full of cursing. Rom. iii. 14.

xiv. 3. There is none that doeth good. Rom. iii. 10.

xvi. 8. I have set the Lord always before me. Acts ii. 25.

10. Thou wilt not suffer thy holy one to see corruption. Acts ii. 31, xiii. 35.

xviii. 2. My God, in whom I will trust. Heb. ii. 13.

49. I will give thanks unto thee among the heathen. Rom. xv. 9.

xix. 4. Their line is gone out through all the earth. Rom. x. 18.

xxi. 1. My God, my God, why hast thou forsaken me? Matt. xxvii. 46; Mark xv. 34.

18. They part my garments among them. Luke xxiii. 34; John xix. 23, 24.

22. I will declare thy name to my brethren. Heb. ii. 12.

xxiv. 1. The earth is the Lord's. 1 Cor. x. 26, 28.

xxxi. 5. Into thy hand I commit my spirit. Luke xxiii. 46; Acts vii. 59.

xxxiv. 12. What man is he that desireth life. 1 Pet. iii. 10.

Chap.	Ver.	
xxxv.	19.	They hated me without a cause. John xv. 25.
xl.	6.	Sacrifice and offering thou didst not desire. Matt. xii. 7; Heb. x. 5.
xli.	9.	He who did eat of my bread. John xiii. 18.
xliv.	22.	For thy sake are we killed all the day. Rom. viii. 36.
xlv.	6.	Thy throne, O God, is for ever and ever. Heb. i. 8.
li.	4.	That thou mightest be justified when thou speakest. Rom. iii. 4.
lv.	22.	Cast thy burden upon the Lord. 1 Pet. v. 7.
lxii.	12.	Thou renderest to every man according. Matt. xvi. 27; Rom. ii. 6; 1 Cor. iii. 8.
lxviii.	18.	Thou hast ascended on high, and led captivity captive. Eph. iv. 8.
lxix.	9.	The zeal of thy house hath eaten me up. John ii. 17.
		The reproaches of them that reproach thee. Rom. xv. 3.
	22.	Let their table become a snare. Rom. xi. 9, 10.
	25.	Let their habitation be desolate. Acts i. 20.
lxxviii.	2.	I will open my mouth in parables. Matt. xiii. 35.
	24.	He gave them bread from heaven. John vi. 31; 1 Cor. x. 3.
lxxxii.	6.	I have said, Ye are gods. John x. 34.
lxxxix.	20.	I have found David my servant. Acts xiii. 22.
xci.	11.	He will give his angels charge concerning thee. Matt. iv. 6; Luke iv. 10.
xciv.	11.	The Lord knoweth the thoughts of man. 1 Cor. iii. 20.
xcv.	7.	To-day, if ye will hear his voice. Heb. iii. 7, iv. 7.
	11.	Unto whom I sware in my wrath. Heb. iv. 3.
cii.	25.	Thou, Lord, in the beginning hast laid. Heb. i. 10.
civ.	4.	Who maketh his angels spirits. Heb. i. 7.
cix.	8.	His bishopric let another take. Acts. i. 20.
cx.	1.	The Lord said unto my lord. Matt. xxii. 44; Mark xii. 42; Acts ii. 34; 1 Cor. xv. 25.
		Until I make thine enemies thy footstool. 1 Cor. xv. 25.
	4.	Thou art a priest for ever. Heb. v. 6, vii. 17. 21.
		The Lord hath sworn, and will not repent. Heb. vii. 17.
cxii.	9.	He hath dispersed abroad. 2 Cor. ix. 9.
cxvi.	10.	I believed; therefore have I spoken. 2 Cor. iv. 13.
	11.	I said in my haste, All men are liars. Rom. iii. 4.
cxvii.	1.	Praise the Lord, all ye nations. Rom. xv. 11.
cxviii.	6.	The Lord is on my side. Heb. xiii. 6.
	22.	The stone which the builders rejected. Matt. xxi. 42; Mark xii. 10; Luke xx. 17; Acts iv. 11; 1 Pet. ii. 4, 7.
	25, 26.	Save now, I beseech thee,—Blessed is he that cometh. Matt. xxi. 9.
cxxxii.	11.	Of the fruit of thy body. Luke i. 69; Acts ii. 30.
cxl.	3.	Adder's poison is under their lips. Rom. iii. 13.

PROVERBS

Chap.	Ver.	
iii.	7.	Be not wise in thine own eyes. Rom. xii. 16.
	11.	My son, despise not the chastening of the Lord. Heb. xii. 5.
	12.	For whom the Lord loveth he chasteneth. Rev. iii. 19.
x.	12.	Love covereth all sins. 1 Pet. iv. 8.
xvii.	15.	Whoso rewardeth evil for good. 1 Thess. v. 15; 1 Pet. iii. 9.
xx.	20.	Whoso curseth his father. Matt. xv. 4.
xxv.	21.	If thine enemy be hungry, give him bread. Matt. v. 44; Rom. xii. 20.
xxvi.	11.	As a dog returneth to his vomit. 2 Pet. ii. 22.

ISAIAH

Chap.	Ver.	
i.	9.	Except the Lord had left us a very small remnant. Rom. ix. 29.
v.	1, &c.	My well beloved hath a vineyard. Matt. xxi. 33; Mark xii. 1; Luke xx. 9.
vi.	3.	Holy, holy, holy. Rev. iv. 8.
	9.	Hear ye indeed, but understand not. Matt. xiii. 14; Mark iv. 12; Luke viii. 10; John xii. 40; Acts xxviii. 26; Rom. xi. 8.
vii.	14.	Behold, a virgin shall conceive. Matt. i. 23; Luke i. 31.
viii.	18.	Behold, I and the children. Heb. ii. 13.
ix.	1.	The land of Zebulun and the land of Naphtali. Matt. iv. 16.
x.	22.	Yet a remnant of them shall return. Rom. ix. 27.
xi.	4.	With the breath of his lips shall he slay the wicked. 2 Thess. ii. 8; Rev. i. 16.
xxi.	9.	Babylon is fallen, is fallen. Rev. xiv. 8, xviii. 2.
xxii.	13.	Let us eat and drink, for to-morrow we die. 1 Cor. xv. 32.
	22.	He shall open, and none shall shut. Rev. iii. 7.
xxv.	8.	The Lord will wipe away tears from all faces. Rev. vii. 17.
xxviii.	11.	For with stammering lips and another tongue. 1 Cor. xiv. 21.
	16.	Behold, I lay in Zion for a foundation. Matt. xxi. 42; Acts iv. 11; Rom. ix. 33; Eph. ii. 20; 1 Pet. ii. 6–8.
xxix.	13.	This people draw near me with their mouth. Matt. xv. 8, 9; Mark vii. 6.
	14.	The wisdom of their wise shall perish. 1 Cor. i. 19.
xxxiii.	18.	Where is the wise, where is the receiver? 1 Cor. i. 20.
xl.	3.	The voice of him that crieth in the wilderness. Matt. iii. 3; Mark i. 3; Luke iii. 4; John i. 23.
	6.	All flesh is grass. James i. 10; 1 Pet. i. 24.
	13.	Who hath directed the Spirit of the Lord. Rom. xi. 34; 1 Cor. ii. 16.
xli.	4.	I the Lord the first, and with the last. Rev. i. 17.
xlii.	1.	Behold my servant whom I uphold Matt. xii. 18.
xliii.	19.	Behold, I will do a new thing. 2 Cor. v. 17; Rev. xxi. 5.
xliv.	6.	I am the first, and I am the last. Rev. xxii. 13.
xlv.	9.	Shall the clay say to him that fashioneth it. Rom. ix. 20.
	23.	Unto me every knee shall bow. Rom. xiv. 11; Phil. ii. 10.
xlix.	6.	I will give thee for a light to the Gentiles. Luke ii. 32; Acts xiii. 47, xxvi. 8.

Chap. Ver.

8. In an acceptable time have I heard thee. 2 Cor. vi. 2.
10. They shall not hunger nor thirst. Rev. vii. 16.
l. 6. I hid not my face from shame and spitting. Matt. xxvi. 67, xxvii. 26.
lii. 7. How beautiful upon the mountains. Rom. x. 15.
5. My name continually every day is blasphemed. Rom. ii. 24.
11. Depart ye, depart ye, touch no unclean thing. 2 Cor. vi. 17; Rev. xviii. 4.
15. For that which had not been told them. Rom. xv. 21.
liii. 1. Who hath believed our report? John xii. 38; Rom. x. 16.
4. Surely he hath borne our griefs. Matt. viii. 17.
5. He was bruised for our iniquities. Rom. iv. 25; 1 Cor. xv. 3; 1 Pet. ii. 24.
7. He is brought as a lamb to the slaughter. Acts viii. 32.
9. He did no violence, neither was deceit found in his mouth. 1 Pet. ii. 22.
12. He was numbered with the transgressors. Mark xv. 28; Luke xxii. 37.
liv. 1. Sing, O barren, thou that didst not bear. Gal. iv. 27.
13. All thy children shall be taught of the Lord. John vi. 45; 1 Cor. ii. 10.
lv. 1. Ho, every one that thirsteth. John iv. 14, vii. 37; Rev. xxi. 6, xxii. 17.
3. I will give you the sure mercies of David. Acts xiii. 34.
lvi. 7. For my house shall be called a house of prayer. Matt. xxi. 13; Mark xi. 17; Luke xix. 46.
lix. 7. Wasting and destruction are in their paths. Rom. iii. 15.
17. He put on righteousness as a breastplate. Eph. vi. 14, 17; 1 Thess. v. 8.
20. The Redeemer shall come to Zion. Rom. xi. 26.
lx. 11. Thy gates shall be open continually. Rev. xxi. 25.
19. The sun shall be no more thy light. Rev. xxi. 23, xxii. 5.
lxi. 1. The Spirit of the Lord is upon me. Luke iv. 18.
lxii. 11. Say ye to the daughter of Zion. Matt. xxi. 5; John xii. 15.
lxiv. 4. Men have not seen nor perceived by the ear. 1 Cor. ii. 9.
lxv. 1. I am sought of them that asked not for me. Rom. ix. 24–26, x. 20; Eph. ii. 13.
2. I have spread out my hands all the day. Rom. x. 21.
17. I create new heavens and a new earth. 2 Pet. iii. 13; Rev. xxi. 1.
lxvi. 1. Heaven is my throne. Acts vii. 48, 49, xvii. 24.
24. Their worm shall not die, neither shall their fire. Mark ix. 44–48.

JEREMIAH

vii. 11. Is this house become a den of robbers. Matt. xxi. 13; Luke xix. 46.
ix. 24. But let him that glorieth glory in this. 1 Cor. i. 31; 2 Cor. x. 17.
x. 7. Who would not fear thee, O king of nations! Rev. xv. 4.
xvii. 10. I the Lord search the heart and try the reins. Rom. viii. 27; Rev. ii. 23.
xxxi. 9. I will be a father to Israel. 2 Cor. vi. 18; Rev. xxi. 7.
15. A voice was heard in Ramah. Matt. ii. 17, 18.
31. Behold, the days come—that I will make a new covenant. Heb. viii. 8, x. 10.
li. 8. Babylon is suddenly fallen. Rev. xiv. 8, xviii. 2.

EZEKIEL

iii. 1–3. Eat this roll. Rev. x. 9.
xx. 11, 13, 21. Which if a man do he shall even live in them. Rom. x. 5; Gal. iii. 12.
xxxii. 8. All the bright lights of heaven will I make dark. Matt. xxiv. 29.
xxxvi. 23. I will sanctify my great name which was profaned. Rom. ii. 24.

DANIEL

ix. 27. The overspreading of abominations. Matt. xxiv. 15; Mark xiii. 14; Luke xxi. 20.

HOSEA

i. 10. In the place where it was said unto them. Rom. ix. 26.
ii. 23. I will say unto them that were not my people. Rom. ix. 25; 1 Pet. ii. 10.
vi. 6. For I desired mercy, and not sacrifice. Matt. ix. 13; xii. 7.
x. 8. They shall say unto the mountains, Cover us. Luke xxiii. 30; Rev. vi. 16, ix. 6.
xi. 1. I called my son out of Egypt. Matt. ii. 15.
xiii. 14. O death, I will be thy plagues. 1 Cor. xv. 54, 55.

JOEL

ii. 28. It shall come to pass in the last days. Acts ii. 17.
32. Whosoever shall call on the name of the Lord. Rom. x. 13.

AMOS

v. 25. Have ye offered to me sacrifices. Acts vii. 42.
vi. 1. Wo to them that are at ease in Zion. Luke vi. 24.
ix. 11. I will raise up the tabernacle of David. Acts xv. 16, 17.

JONAH

i. 17. Jonah was in the belly of the fish three days and three nights. Matt. xii. 40, xvi. 4; Luke xi. 30.
iii. 4–9. The people of Nineveh repented. Matt. xii. 41; Luke xi. 32.

MICAH

v. 2. Thou, Beth-lehem Ephratah. Matt. ii. 6; John vii. 42.
vii. 6. The son dishonoureth his father. Matt. x. 21, 35, 36; Luke xii. 53, xxi. 16.

NAHUM

i. 15. Behold upon the mountains the feet. Rom. x. 15.

HABAKKUK

i. 5. Behold ye among the heathen—and wonder. Acts xiii. 41.

Chap. Ver.

ii. 4. But the just shall live by faith. John iii. 36; Rom. i. 17; Gal. iii. 11; Heb. x. 38.

HAGGAI

ii. 6. I will shake the heavens and the earth. Heb. xii. 26.

ZECHARIAH

viii. 16. Speak every man truth to his neighbour. Eph. iv. 25.

ix. 9. Behold thy King cometh. Matt. xxi. 5; John xii. 15.

xi. 11, 12. So they weighed for my price thirty pieces of silver. Matt. xxvi. 15, xxvii. 9, 10.

Chap. Ver.

xii. 10. They shall look upon me whom they have pierced. John xix. 34, 37; Rev. i. 7.

xiii. 7. I will smite the Shepherd. Matt. xxvi. 31; Mark xiv. 27.

MALACHI

i. 2, 3. I loved Jacob, and hated Esau. Rom. ix. 13.

iii. 1. Behold, I send my messenger. Matt. xi. 10; Mark i. 2; Luke i. 76, vii. 27.

iv. 5. Behold, I will send you Elijah the prophet. Matt. xi. 14, xvii. 11; Mark ix. 11; Luke i. 17.

6. He shall turn the hearts of the fathers to the children. Luke i. 17.

GENERAL INDEX

TO THE

NOTES ON THE OLD TESTAMENT

N. B. *In principio* refers to the observations at the *beginning*, and *in fine* to those at the *end*, of the chapter.

A

Index to the Old Testament

B

Baal, what this term imports, Judg. ii. 11.
Baal-bek, the ancient Aven or Heliopolis, Amos i. 5.
Baal-hatturim, (*Rabbi Jacob*) account of this commentator, General Preface, p. 2.
Baal-peor, probably the Priapus of the Moabites, and worshipped with the same obscene and abominable rites, Num. xxiii. 28; Deut. iii. 29.
Baal-zebub, the god of Ekron, why so named, Exod. iii. 24; 2 Kings i. 2.
Baal-zephon, probably an idol temple, Exod. xiv. 2.
Babel, derivation and import of this name, Gen. xi. 9.
Babel, tower of, heathen testimonies concerning, Gen. xi. 4. Various conjectures relative to the purpose for which this tower was built, Gen. xi. 9.
Babet or *Baby*, conjecture respecting the origin of this word, Zech. ii. 8.
Babylon, its great naval power before the time of Cyrus, Isa. xliii. 14. Semiramis, the foundress of this part of the Babylonian greatness, *ibid.* Manner of the taking of Babylon by Cyrus, Isa. xxi. 1, xliv. 27, xlv. 2; Jer. l. 24. Policy of the Persian monarchs in destroying the naval importance of Babylon, Isa. xliii. 14. Some particulars of the greatness of Babylon, Isa. xiii. 19, xlv. 2. Notation of the several steps by which the remarkable prophecies against this great city were ultimately accomplished in its total ruin, *ibid.* The annihilation of its walls accounted for, *ibid.* Deliverance from Babylon a frequent figure in the prophetical writings for the deliverance of the people of God from the power of evil under the Gospel dispensation, Isa. xl. 6–8.
Babylonian embassy to Hezekiah, observations on the, 2 Kings xxi., *in fine.*
Babylonians, singular custom among these people of selling all their marriageable virgins by public auction, Gen. xxix. 20. In what the dress of this people consisted, according to Herodotus, Dan. iii. 21.
Babylonish robes, some account of the, Josh. vii. 21.
Bacchus, some portions of the fable concerning, very similar to what is related of Moses, Exod. iv. 17. This idol worshipped under the form of a goat by the ancient Egyptians, Exod. viii. 26.
Backbite and *Backbiter*, words of Anglo-Saxon origin, Psa. xv. 3. Intended to convey the treble sense of *knavishness, cowardice*, and *brutality, ibid.*
Bacon's (*Friar*) method of restoring and strengthening the natural heat, 1 Kings i., *in fine.*
Badad, בדד, import of this word when employed by the Jews as a memorial symbol, Masoretic notes at the end of Numbers.
Badgers' skins, the Hebrew words so translated of very uncertain import, Exod. xxv. 5.
Baeshah, באשה, various conjectures respecting the meaning of this word, Job xxxi. 40.
Ba gad, בא גד, import of this phrase when employed by the Jews as a memorial symbol, Masoretic Notes at the end of Leviticus.
Baking in the East, manner of, with an account of the instruments employed in the process, Lev. ii. 7.
Balaam, character of this prophet of the Most High God, Num. xxiv., *in fine.* Observations on his famous prophecy concerning a star to spring out of Jacob, Num. xxiv. 6.
Balance, trial by the, a species of ordeal among the Hindoos, Num. v., *in fine.*
Banditti, hordes of, frequent in Arabia to the present day, Job i. 15.
Banner, giving the, very ingenious illustration of, by Mr. Harmer, Psa. lx. 4, *et in fine.*
Barach, ברך, generally rendered *to bless*, very extensive import of the original word, Gen. ii. 3; 1 Kings xxi. 9.
Barbary, Dr. Shaw's account of the chocolate-coloured pottage made by the inhabitants of, Gen. xxv. 29.
Bards, among the ancient Druids, who, Num. xxi. 27.
Barley harvest, time of its commencement in Palestine, Ruth i. 22.
Barrady, Maundrell's account of this river, 2 Kings v. 12.
Barrows or *Tumuli*, in England, what, 2 Sam. xviii. 17.
Bars of the pit, what probably meant by this phrase among the ancients, Job xvii. 16.
Batanim, בטנים, its import uncertain, Gen. xliii. 11.
Bath, some account of this Hebrew measure of capacity, Exod. xvi. 16; Ezra vii. 22.
Battering-ram, description of the, Ezek. v. 2. This machine unknown in the time of Homer, *ibid.*
Battle, trial by, when and where supposed to have had its origin, Num. v., *in fine.*
Baxter, (*Richard*) a commentator on the New Testament, General Preface, p. 7.
Beards, held in high respect in the East, the possessor considering it his greatest ornament, often swearing by it, and in matters of great importance pledging it, 2 Sam. x. 4; Song v. 13; Isa. vii. 20. Never cut off but in mourning or as a mark of slavery, *ibid.*; Jer. xli. 5. Considered by the Turks a great affront to take a man by his beard, unless it be to kiss it, Isa. vii. 20. Beards of the Macedonians ordered by Alexander to be shaved off, and the singular reason given by this king for the mandate, 2 Sam. ii. 16.
Bedaui or *Beduui*, a people of Arabia, Isa. xlii. 11.
Bede, account of this commentator, General Preface, p. 4.
Bedolach, בדלח, translated *bdellium*, Bochart's opinion respecting the meaning of this word, Gen. ii. 12.
Bedouin, Volney's description of the, Job v. 5.
Beds of ivory, what, Amos vi. 4.
Beech tree, juice of the, used for drink in the northern parts of Europe, Job xxx. 4.
Bees, Homer's very nervous description of a great swarm of, Psa. cxviii. 12.
Behemah, בהמה, translated *cattle*, import of the term, Gen. i. 24.
Behemoth, various conjectures respecting the animal intended by this name in Scripture, Job xl. 15. Reasons for supposing it to have been a species now extinct, perhaps the mammoth, *ibid.*
Belial, its derivation and import, Deut. xiii. 13, xv. 9.
Belibbo, בלבו, import of this memorial symbol of the rabbins, Masoretic Notes at the end of Exodus.
Bellerophon, son of Glaucus, king of Ephyra, story of, supposed to be a fabulous formation from the Scripture account of David's adultery with Bathsheba, and his murder of Uriah, 2 Sam. xi. 14.
Bells on horses, camels, &c., account of the, Zech. xiv. 20.
Belt, the chief ornament of a soldier, and highly prized in all ancient nations, 2 Sam. xviii. 11. Considered a rich present from one chieftain to another, *ibid.*
Ben, בן, *a son*, whence derived, Ruth iv. 11; Psalm cxxvii. 1.
Beneficiarii, among the Romans, who, Hab. iii. 6.
Bene-jaakan, the twenty-seventh station of the Israelites in the wilderness, Num. xxxiii. 31.
Beney adam, בני אדם, and *beney ish*, בני איש, very remarkable distinction between, Psa. lxii. 9.
Bengel, (*John Albert*) author of an edition of the Greek Testament, with various readings and critical notes, General Preface, p. 10.
Benjamin, why so named, Gen. xxxv. 18. Remarks upon the provisions set before this patriarch by Joseph being much greater than what were set before each of his brethren, Gen. xliii. 34.
Benjamite messenger, remarks upon his very laconic relation of the discomfiture of the Israelites by the Philistines, and of the taking of the ark of God, 1 Sam. iv. 17.
Benson, (*Dr.*) a commentator on different portions of the New Testament, General Preface, p. 8.
Bereshith, the first book of the Hebrew Scriptures, whence so named, Preface to the Book of Genesis.
Berith, ברית, rendered *covenant*, what it imports, Gen. vi. 18; Lev. xxvi. 15.
Beryl, account of this precious stone, Exod. xxviii. 17; Ezek. x. 9.
Bethany, why so named, Isa. x. 30.
Beth-el, meaning of this name, Gen. xxviii. 19.
Beth-jesimoth, the forty-second and last station of the Israelites in the wilderness, where situated, Num. xxxiii. 49.
Bethron, why probably so named, Song ii. 17.
Beth-shean, the same that was afterwards called *Scythopolis*, Josh. xvii. 11.
Beth-shemesh, various conjectures concerning the number of the inhabitants of, who were smitten for looking into the ark, 1 Sam. vi. 19. The words חמשים אלף איש *chameshim, elaph ish, fifty thousand men*, which stand in our present Hebrew copies, most probably an interpolation, *ibid.*
Bethyllia or *consecrated stones*, remarks upon the, Gen. xxviii. 18; Job xxxi. 1; Isa. lvii. 6.
Bey of Tunis, his manner of living, as mentioned by Pococke, Neh. iv. 18.
Beza, (*Theodore*) account of this commentator, General Preface. p 8.
Bezer, one of the cities of refuge, import of the name, Josh. xx. 7.
Bibliotheca Magna Rabbinica of Bartolocci, account of this great work, General Preface, p. 3.
Bildad, the Shuhite, who, Job ii. 11.
Bipens, a military weapon of the ancients, Eph. vi. 13.
Birds, thoughts on the wonderful structure of their wings and feathers, Gen. i. 22.
Birth-days, keeping of, a custom of very remote antiquity, Gen. xl. 20.

D

E

H

J

Judges, book of, very uncertain by whom written, Preface to Judges. Chronological table of this book, according to Archbishop Usher, *ibid.* Chronology of this book, according to Sir John Marsham, *ibid.*

Judgment, great variety of acceptations of the Hebrew word so translated, Isa. xlii. 1.

Juggernaut, a Hindoo temple, where human victims are frequently offered to Cali, a goddess of the Hindoos, Deut. xii. 31.

Juju, a serpent-god worshipped by the inhabitants of Bonny in Africa, Deut. xx. 5; to whom they dedicate an apartment of their dwellings, *ibid.*

Julius Cæsar, his letter to the Roman senate, communicating the total defeat of Pharnaces, king of Pontus, 1 Sam. iv. 17. Great mourning for the death of Julius Cæsar as described by Virgil, Jonah iii. 8.

Juniper, roots of, formerly used for food among the Goths, according to the testimony of one of their prelates, Job xxx. 4. Charcoal made of this wood the most durable of all others, *ibid.*

Juno, distance from the sun and earth, diameter, and relative surface and volume, of this primary planet, Gen. i. 1.

Juno, worshipped under the form of a heifer by the ancient Egyptians, Exod. viii. 26.

Jupiter, periodic and sidereal revolutions, mean distance from the sun, perigeal and apogeal distances, diameter in English miles, relative volume, time of rotation, inclination of axis to orbit, mass or quantity of matter, and mean hourly orbitical motion, of this primary planet, Gen. i. 1.

Jupiter, worshipped by the ancient Egyptians under the form of a ram, Exod. viii. 26. The infant Jupiter, according to Callimachus, tenderly nursed with goat's milk and honey, Isa. vii. 15.

Jupiter and Semele, fable of, whence it originated, Exod. xxxiii. 20.

Jupiter Brontes, or *Jupiter Keraunos*, always represented with forked or zigzag lightnings in his hand, Hab. iii. 4.

Juror, among the Jews, lifted up his right hand to heaven, Ezek. xx. 5.

Justification by faith, without any merit of works, shown to be a doctrine of Scripture, Gen. xv. 6, xxviii. 4, xlviii. 14; Job ix. 3; Mic. vi. 8.

Justus, bishop of Orgelitanum, account of this commentator, General Preface, p. 4.

Juvenal, excellent advice of, with respect to putting confidence in the Divinity, Psa. xxxvii. 7. Remarkable passages from this Roman poet, in which is described the miserable condition of the Jews after the destruction of their polity by the Romans, Psa. cix. 11.

K

Kab, some account of this Hebrew measure of capacity, Exod. xvi. 16; 2 Kings vi. 25.

Kadim, or *the east-wind*, a very stormy wind in the Levant, supposed to be the same with that called by the Greeks Euroclydon, Job xv. 2.

Karkor, קרקר, rendered in our version as the name of a place, signifies more probably *rest*, Judg. viii. 10.

Kasheth, or *The Song of the Bow*, exquisite excellences of the, pointed out, 2 Sam. i., *in fine.* Dr. Kennicott's Latin version of this song, *ibid.*

Kadesh, one of the cities of refuge, import of the name, Josh. xx. 7.

Kedeshah, קדשה, rendered *harlot* in our version, inquiry into its precise import, Gen. xxxviii. 21.

Keeumras, the first king of the Peeshdadian dynasty, according to the Persian historians, Gen. xiv. 1. Possibly the same with the Chedorlaomer of Scripture, *ibid.*

Kehelathah, the eighteenth station of the Israelites in the wilderness, Num. xxxiii. 22.

Keimah, כימה, rendered *the Pleiades*, of very uncertain import, Job ix., *in fine.*

Kennicott, (*Dr.*) his account of the great differences in the Hebrew and Samaritan copies with respect to the history of the first seven Egyptian plagues, Exod. xi., *in fine.* Observations of this great Biblical critic upon the four hundred and thirty years' sojourning of the children of Israel, Exod. xii. 40. His removal of some difficulties in the book of Numbers, chap. xxi., *in fine.* Reasons advanced by him to show that from the *twelfth* to the *thirty-first* verse (both inclusive) of the seventeenth chapter of the first book of Samuel is an interpolation of some rabbin, 1 Sam. xvii., *in fine.* His translation of that portion of the sacred history which gives an account of David's taking from the Jebusites the strong hold of Zion, 2 Sam. v. 6–8. His remarks upon the catalogue of David's mighty men of valour, as given in two different portions of Scripture, 1 Chron. xi. 11. His reasons for the supposition that the first fourteen verses of the *fortieth* chapter of Job are transposed, Job xl., *in fine.*

Kepler, curious notion of, relative to the *animation* of the whole material universe, Neh. ix. 6.

Kerchief, derivation and import of this word, Ezek. xiii. 18.

Kermez oak, a shrub growing in Provence and Languedoc, why so named, Isa. i. 18.

Kermez, or *summer fig*, some account of the, by Dr. Shaw, Isa. xxviii. 4.

Kernaw, the ancient name for Cornwall, Isa. v. 1. Its import in the ancient British and Phœnician languages, *ibid.*

Kerub, כרב or כרוב, translated *cherub*, derivation and import of the word, Gen. iii. 24.

Kesil, כסיל, rendered *Orion*, of very uncertain import, Job ix., *in fine.*

Kesitah, a word of doubtful signification, Gen. xxxiii. 19.

Kethem, כתם, its derivation and import, Job xxviii. 16.

Kethubim, same as *Hagiographa*, see Zech. vii. 7.

Kets, קץ, beautiful paronomasia on this word, Ezek. vii. 6. *Hakets*, הקץ, *the end*, personified, *ibid.*

Keys of the ancients, description of the, Isa. xxii. 2. When borne on the shoulder, a mark of office, *ibid.*

Khondemir's fabulous relation respecting Job, Preface to Job.

Khosroo, a verse in this Persian poet very similar to a passage in Job. See Job xiv. 10. Citation of a very beautiful passage, in which the poet deplores the loss of all his friends, Psa. lxxxviii. 18.

Kibroth-hattaavah, the twelfth station of the Israelites in the wilderness, some account of, Num. xxxiii. 16.

Kidneys of wheat, inquiry into the meaning of this phrase, Deut. xxxii. 14.

Kikayon, קיקיון, rendered *gourd*, probably the *ricinus*, or *palma Christi*, Jonah iv. 6.

Kimchi, (*Rabbi David*) account of this commentator, General Preface, p. 3.

King, manner of the, which God commanded Samuel to show to the Israelites, Puffendorf's excellent observations concerning the, 1 Sam. viii. 9.

King can do no wrong, on what ground this political maxim in our laws is formed, 2 Sam. xix. 43.

King of terrors, an epithet given to death (either literally or substantially) by the ancient Greeks and Romans, Job xviii. 14. The words so rendered in the book of Job shown not to contain the sense of the original, *ibid.*

King's mowings, what to be understood by this expression, Amos vii. 1.

Kings, books of the, this portion of holy writ generally supposed to have been compiled by Ezra, Preface to 1 Kings.

Kings, folly of, to have foreigners for their valets and most confidential servants, 2 Chron. xxiv. 26.

Kings of Israel, how the ceremonies of their proclamation and anointing were probably performed, 1 Kings i. 35.

Kings of Israel and Judah, years of the reigns of the, synchronically arranged, from the commencement of the reigns of Rehoboam and Jeroboam to the destruction of the kingdom of Israel by Shalmaneser, 2 Chron., *in fine.*

Kinnor, כנור, rendered *harp*, what it imports, Gen. iv. 21; 1 Sam. x. 5; Job xxi. 12; Psa. lxxxi. 2. The testudo, or lyre with three strings, according to Calmet, Psa. xxxiii. 2.

Kir, thought to be the same with the country of Cyrene, Amos i. 5.

Kir-haraseth, the royal city of the Moabites, 2 Kings iii. 25; Isa. xvi. 7, 11.

Kirjath-arba, or *City of the Four*, conjectures why so named, Gen. xxiii. 2; Josh. xv. 15.

Kishon, some account of this brook, Judg. iv. 6.

Kissing the beard, the neck, and the shoulders, in use among the Asiatics to the present day, Gen. xlv. 14.

Kissing the hand often practised by idolaters in honour of their divinities, 1 Kings xix. 18. How this ceremony was performed, *ibid.* *Kissing the hand* shown to be derived from and synonymous with *adoration*, *ibid.*

Knave, ancient and modern imports of this word, Psa. lxxxvi. 16, cxiii. 1.

Kneading troughs of the Arabs, description of the, Exod. xii. 34.

Kneeling ever considered to be the proper posture of supplication, Exod. ix. 29; 1 Kings viii. 22. If the person to whom the supplication was addressed was within reach, the supplicant caught him by the knees, *ibid.*

Knight, great stature of two brothers of this name, who were born in the same township with the author, 1 Sam. xvii., *in fine.*

M

O

P

Philo Judæus, account of this Jewish commentator, General Preface, p. 2.

Philosopher, anecdote of a, Jer. v. 1. Remarkable saying of a philosopher when at sea in a violent storm, Jonah i. 7.

Φιλοσοφος, probable origin of this word, Gen. xli. 8.

Phlegon, one of the horses of the sun, according to the pagan mythology, what the name signifies, 2 Kings ii. 11.

Phoceans, remarkable imprecation of the, when resolved to leave their country, and never to revisit it, Jer. li. 64.

Phocylides, citation of a very remarkable passage from this poet, Jer. ix. 24.

Phosphorescence of the sea in certain states of the weather, Job xli. 32.

Phrygians, Bochart's conjecture concerning their origin, Gen. x. 2.

Phut, a people of Africa, Ezek. xxvii. 10.

Phylacteries, particular account of the, Exod. xiii. 9.

Pibeseth, probably the same with Bubastum, or Bubaste, Ezek. xxx. 17.

Pihahiroth, the third station of the Israelites in the wilderness, what supposed to be its present appellation, Num. xxxiii. 7.

Pikudim, פקדים, its derivation and import, Lev. xxvi. 15.

Pilgash, פלגש, rendered *concubine*, inquiry into its import, Gen. xxii. 24, xxxiv. 31.

Pilgrim, a word of French or Latin origin, Gen. xlvii. 9.

Pilkington's reasons for the supposition that from the 12th to the 31st verse of the first book of Samuel is an interpolation of some rabbin, 1 Sam. xvii., *in fine*.

Pillar of a cloud in the wilderness, observations concerning the, Exod. xiii. 21, xiv. 20.

Pillar of salt into which Lot's wife was changed, various opinions and legends concerning the, Gen. xix. 26.

Pillars of heaven, what intended by this strongly figurative expression, Job xxvi. 11.

Pindar's elegant ridicule of the work of the statuary, when set in competition with his own poetry, Isa. xlvi. 3.

Pinna magna, a species of muscle found on the shores of the Mediterrenean, 1 Chron. xv. 27; Prov. xxxi. 22. Description of a pair of gloves which the author has seen made of this very rich stuff, *ibid*.

Piscator, (*John*) author of a comment on the whole Scriptures, General Preface, p. 6.

Pitcher broken at the fountain, what meant by this phrase, Eccles. xii. 6.

Pitfall or *fovea*, among the ancients, what, Psa. vii. 15, lvii. 6; Isa. xxiv. 17, 18; Ezek. xix. 4.

Plagues of Egypt, times of their happening, according to Archbishop Usher, Exod. vii. 17. Critical observations on these Divine judgments, Exod. vii., *et seq*. Seven of these plagues more largely described in the Samaritan copies than in the Hebrew, Exod. xi., *in fine*. Translation of the *eleventh* chapter of Exodus from the Samaritan text ranged in collateral columns with that in our common version, to show the great additions in the former, *ibid*. General observations on the ten plagues of Egypt, Exod. xii., *in fine*.

Plane tree, conjectures why this tree was so named, Gen. xxv. 37.

Planets, primary and secondary, tables of their revolutions, distances, &c., Gen. i. 1. To prevent mistake, it will be proper to observe that the least and greatest distances of the planets and satellites from the earth, contained in these tables, are their perigeal and apogeal distances when the radii vectores of the planets are equal to the semimajor axes of their orbits, the earth being in every case assumed to be at its mean distance from the sun. But on account of the eccentricities of the planetary orbits, the distances of the planets from the earth, when in *perigee* and *apogee*, are very variable. The nearest possible approaches of the inferior planets Mercury and Venus to the earth (viz., when the inferior conjunction of each takes place in the higher apsis) are, respectively, 52,376,602 and 27,339,176 English miles. The greatest possible distances of these planets from the earth (viz., when the superior conjunction of each is made in the aphelion) are, respectively, 138,620,495 and 163,667,549 English miles. The perigeal distances of Mars, Jupiter, Saturn, and Herschel (when the opposition of each to the sun takes place in the lower apsis or perihelion) are respectively, 35,357,826, 376,944,330, 766,223,200, and 1,642,663,450 English miles. The greatest possible apogeal distances of these planets (viz., when the conjunction of each with the sun is in the higher apsis) are, respectively, 255,709,508, 616,586,248, 1,056,059,684 and 2,002,487,006 English miles. In these calculations the eccentricities of the orbits of the planets, in English miles, have been assumed as follows:—that of Mercury, 7,598,601; Venus, 471,320; the Earth, 1,604,800; Mars, 13,665,466; Jupiter, 24,346,964; Saturn, 50,988,386; and Herschel, 85,035,892.

Plant of renown, observations on the Hebrew words thus rendered, Ezek. xxxiv. 29.

Platforms common on the houses of the East, Judg. iii. 20.

Plato, republic of, thoughts concerning the, Deut. xxxiv., *in fine*.

Pledge of the beard, in the East, the most secure of all pledges, which the owner will redeem at the hazard of his life, 2 Sam. x. 4.

Pleiades, Hebrew word so translated of very uncertain import, Job ix. 9, xxxviii. 31.

Ploughing the foundations of cities, a custom among ancient conquerors to signify an *irreparable and total destruction*, Mic. iii. 12.

Ploughing with one's heifer, or *ploughing in another man's ground*, what meant by this phrase among the ancient Jews, Greeks, and Romans, Judg. xiv. 18.

Ploughing iniquity and reaping the same, a proverbial mode of expression, illustrated by quotations from sacred and profane writers, Job iv. 8.

Plutarch's account of a man who, aiming a blow at his enemy's life, cut open an imposthume, which, by a salutary discharge, saved his life, Prov. xxvii. 5.

Poetic compositions, titles of, among the Asiatics, frequently bore no resemblance to the subjects, Psa. xxii., *in principio*. Many examples produced, *ibid*.

Poetry in use among all nations from the remotest antiquity, Exod. xv. 1. Its advantages pointed out, *ibid.;* Deut. xxxi. 19. Character of the Hebrew poetry; and its great superiority, in many respects, over that of any other nation, Isa. ii. 13–16.

Poison, trial by, a species of ordeal among the Hindoos, Num. v., *in fine*.

Poison of serpents supposed by the ancients to consist in their gall, which is thought to be copiously exuded when these animals are enraged, Job xx. 16.

Polygamy tolerated under the Mosaic dispensation, 2 Sam. v. 13. Shown to be unnatural, and what could not have entered into the original design of God, *ibid.;* Mal. ii. 14, 15.

Polytheism, in some of its branches, so utterly contemptible, that it became an object of ridicule among the more serious heathens, Psa. cxv. 4. Quotation of a remarkable passage from Juvenal to this effect, *ibid*.

Poole, (*Matthew*) account of this commentator, General Preface, pp. 7, 11.

Pools, Maundrell's description of the supposed remains of those made by Solomon for the reception and preservation of the waters of a spring, Isa. i. 30.

Popilius, remarkable anecdote concerning this Roman legate, Dan. xi. 30.

Porte, the, why the Ottoman court was probably so named, Isa. xxix. 21.

Postdiluvian patriarchs, table of the great discrepances in the Hebrew, Samaritan, and Septuagint copies, with respect to the times they are stated to have lived before their sons' birth, Gen. v. 3.

Potters' wheel, description of the, Jer. xviii. 3.

Præster, terrible effects of the bite of the, as described by Lucan, Num. xxi. 6.

Prayer, observations on, Psa. lxxxviii. 2. Citation of a very remarkable passage from the Iliad upon this subject, *ibid*.

Prayers to angels and departed saints, examination of a passage in the Psalms which the Romanists allege in favour of, Psa. cxxxviii. 1.

Preaching from a text, probable origin of, Neh. viii., *in fine*.

Precession of the equinoxes, quantity of the, in 4138 years, Job ix., *in fine*. The precession caused by a very slow revolution of the celestial poles around the poles of the ecliptic, Psa. xix. 5. See *Equinoctial points, precession of the*.

Predestination, unconditional, to eternal life and to eternal death, cannot be supported by the example of God's dealings with Jacob and Esau, or their posterity, Gen. xxv. 23, xxvii. 28–40, *et in fine;* xxix. 31; Mal. i. 3.

Presents to the great indispensable in Eastern countries, Isa. lvii. 9. When accepted by the superior, a certain pledge of favour, Gen. xxxiii. 10. Offered with very great ceremony, Judg. iii. 18. Numerous examples in Homer and other ancient writers of presents of arms and clothing made by warriors to each other in token of friendship, 1 Sam. xviii. 4.

Prevent, acceptation of this term among our English ancestors, Psa. xxi. 3. Whence derived, *ibid*.

Pride ever makes its possessor unhappy, Esth. v. 13. Examples produced, *ibid*.

Prideaux's account of the monies of different nations, Exod. xxxix. 24.

Priesthood, Jewish and pagan, none eligible to the, that had any sort of blemish, Lev. xxi. 17–21.

Q

R

Raiment, shaking of the, what it imported among the ancient Jews, Neh. v. 13.

Rain, how produced, Gen. ii. 6; Exod. ix. 27; Job xxxvi. 27; Eccles. i. 7. Rain, according to St. Jerome, never falls in Judea in the time of harvest, 1 Sam. xii. 17. Times of the *former* and *latter* rain, Jer. iii. 3, v. 24.

Rainbow, origin and nature of the, Gen. ix. 13. Reasons for believing that this phenomenon was of as frequent occurrence *before* as *after* the flood, *ibid.* Quotations from Homer and Virgil to show that both the Greeks and Romans considered the rainbow as a Divine token or portent, Gen. ix. 17.

Rakesh, רקש, rendered *dromedaries,* probably means *post-horse,* 1 Kings iv. 28.

Rakia, רקיע, translated *firmament,* proper meaning of the term, Gen. i. 6.

Ram, a sacred animal among the Egyptians, Exod. viii. 26. Eusebius's reasons for this, *ibid.* Rams with *red* or *violet-coloured* fleeces often mentioned by ancient writers, Exod. xxv. 5.

Rameses, the same with *Goshen,* Gen. xlvi. 28, 34, xlvii. 23.

Ramoth, one of the cities of refuge, import of the name, Josh. xx. 7.

Ranges for pots, description of an Arabian custom to which this expression has an allusion, Lev. xi. 35.

Rape of the Sabine women, substance of Livy's account of the, Judg. xxi., *in fine.*

Raphelius, (*G.*) an eminent Biblical critic, General Preface, p. 12.

Rash judgments, doubly pernicious, 2 Sam. vi. 22.

Rashim, ראשים, a degree of civil distinction among the Hebrews, Josh. xxiii. 2.

Ravens, arguments to show that Elijah was not fed by these birds, as stated in our English version, but that the Hebrew word ערבים *orbim,* is probably the name of a people that lived in or near Arabia, 1 Kings xvii., *in fine.*

Rebellion against the state, act of, defined, Judg. iii., *in fine;* Ezra iv. 19.

Rechabites, short sketch of their history, Jer. xxxv. 2.

Red heifer, remarks upon several curious particulars respecting the ordinance of the, Num. xix. 2.

Red Sea, conjecture why so named, Exod. x. 19; Num. xxiii. 10. Description of its two gulfs, *ibid.* Observations upon the miraculous separation of its waters in the time of Moses, Exod. xiv. 21, *et in fine.* The sixth station of the Israelites in the wilderness was in the vicinity of this sea, Num. xxxiii. 10. Manifest allusion, in the book of Job, to the miraculous passage of the Israelites through the Red Sea, Job xxvi. 12.

Redeemer of blood, who, among the Jews, Num. xxxv. 19.

Redemption of the first-born, a rite still practised among the Jews, Num. xviii. 16. How performed, according to Leo of Modena, *ibid.*

Refraction, observations on the nature of, 2 Kings xx., *in fine.* Extraordinary refraction of the rays of light in Nova Zembla in the year 1596, *ibid.*

Rehoboam, Houbigant's conjecture relative to the age of this prince at the commencement of his reign over Judah, 2 Chron. xii. 13.

Religion, in its pure state, the strongest bulwark of the state, 1 Chron. xxvi., *in fine.* Definition of true religion, Gen. ix. 20; Prov. i. 7.

Remes, רמש, translated *creeping thing,* inquiry into its import, Gen. i. 24.

Remigius of Auxerre, a commentator on the twelve minor prophets, General Preface, p. 4.

Rending the clothes, a mark of deep affliction and distress among the ancients, Josh. vii. 6; 1 Sam. iv. 12; Ezra ix. 3; Job i. 20, ii. 12; Jer. xvi. 6.

Renominatus, derivation and import of this Latin term, Gen. vi. 4.

Rephaim, valley of, celebrated for its plentiful harvest, Isa. xvii. 5. Used poetically for any fruitful country, *ibid.*

Rephidim, the tenth station of the Israelites in the wilderness, Num. xxxiii. 14.

Reprobation, unconditional, doctrine of, demonstrated to be a lie against all the attributes of Deity, Psa. cxlv. 9; Jer. xviii. 6.

Responsive songs, frequent among the ancient Jews, Isa. vi. 3, xxvii. 2, xl. 9.

Restitution, doctrine of, Gen. xlii., *in fine.*

Resurrection of the dead, doctrine of the, a popular and common doctrine among the Jews long before the advent of our Lord, Isa. xxvi. 19, xlv. 8.

Retiarius, among the Romans, who, Job xix. 6; Mic. vii. 2.

Reuben, import of the name, Gen. xxix. 32.

Revelation of God, particular explanation of the various terms employed to point out different properties of the, Lev. xxvi. 15; Psa. cxix., *in principio.*

Reverend, and *most reverend,* observations on these ecclesiastical titles, Psa. cxi. 9.

Revolutions, periodic and *sidereal,* of the sun, moon, and planets, Gen. i. 1. Periodic and synodic revolutions of the satellites of Jupiter, Saturn, and the Georgium Sidus, *ibid.*

Riblah, where this ancient city was situated, Jer. xxxix. 5.

Rice, method practised by the ancients of sowing this grain, Eccles. xi. 1; Isa. xxxii. 20.

Rice, trial by, a species of ordeal among the Hindoos, Num. v., *in fine.*

Riches, instances of immense, possessed by some of the ancients, Esth. iii. 9.

Ricinus or *Palma Christi,* account of the, as given by Celsus, Jonah iv. 6.

Ricknild or *Icknild-street,* where situated, Job xxiii. 11.

Riddles or *enigmas,* customary among the ancient Greeks to propose such at entertainments, and to give a recompense to those who found them out, Judg. xiv. 14. Examples of Greek enigmas, with their solutions, *ibid.* From what the English word *riddle* is derived, Ezek. xvii. 2.

Ridorus, (*C. Cæcilius*) immense wealth of this individual, Esth. iii. 9.

Righteous and *righteousness,* true etymology of these words, Psa. xii. 8. Their import, *ibid.*

Rimmon, a Syrian idol, possibly the same with the Remphan of the New Testament, 2 Kings v. 26. Supposed by Selden to be the same with Elion, a god of the Phœnicians, *ibid.* Other suppositions, *ibid.*

Rimmon-parez, the fifteenth station of the Israelites in the wilderness, Num. xxxiii. 19.

Ring of Saturn, its perigeal and apogeal distances, diameter, time of rotation, and inclination of axis to the orbit of the planet, Gen. i. 1.

Rings of gold, ensigns of civil power among the ancients, Psa. lxxiii. 6.

Rissah, the seventeenth station of the Israelites in the wilderness, Num. xxxiii. 21.

Rithmah, the fourteenth station of the Israelites in the wilderness, where situated, and why so named, Num. xxxiii. 18.

River of the pool, see *Pallacopas.*

Robe of the Jewish high priest, description of the, Exod. xxviii. 4, 31.

Rock in Horeb, some account of the, Exod. xvii. 6; Psa. cv. 41. Its present appearance, *ibid.*

Rock of a sword, meaning of this phrase, Deut. viii. 8.

Rolls of the Jews, how made, and in what manner written upon, Jer. xxxvi. 2; Ezek. ii. 9, 10.

Roman moneys, table of the, Exod. xxxviii. 24.

Rome, Ovid's account of the ceremonies used in laying the foundations of the walls of the city of, Neh. xii. 27.

Ropes of great strength made in Ireland of the fibres of bog-wood, or the larger roots of the fir, Judg. xvi. 7. Ropes made of the leaves of the flag by the Egyptians, Job viii. 11.

Rotations of the sun, moon, and planets, in what times performed, Gen. i. 1.

Rough garments of the ancient prophets, some account of the, Zech. xiii. 4.

Royal river, see *Naharmalca.*

Ruach, רוח, various opinions concerning the meaning of this word, Gen. i. 2; Eccles. iii. 21.

Ruby, some account of the oriental, Job xxviii. 18. Its component parts, Job xxxviii. 38.

Rushn Achter's extraordinary fortune as expressed in a Persian couplet, Eccles. iv. 15.

Ruth, book of, uncertain by whom written, Preface to Ruth. Sum of its history, *ibid.*

Rutty, (*Dr. John*) extract from his Spiritual Diary, Introduction to the Psalms.

S

Saady, beautiful couplet in this poet, in which the work of total desolation is most forcibly expressed, Job xviii. 15.

Saba, reservoir of, description of this stupendous work of antiquity, Isa. i. 30. By whom supposed to have been constructed, *ibid.*

Sabbath, observations on the institution of the, Gen. ii. 3. Rigorous observances of this day by the ancient Jews, Exod. xvi. 29.

Sabbatus, Houbigant's excellent observations on the remarkable fulfilment of the prophecy that the land of Israel should enjoy her Sabbaths in a state of desolation which the Israelites had profaned in the time of their prosperity, Lev. xxvi. 34.

Shophetim, שפטים, a degree of civil distinction among the Hebrews, Josh. xxiii. 2. See also the Preface to the book of Judges.

Shoshabin or *Paranymph*, see *Paranymph*.

Shoshanim, ששנים, import of this term, Psa. xlv., *in principio*.

Shoterim, שטרים, a degree of civil distinction among the Hebrews, Josh. xxiii. 2. In what the *Shoterim* differed from the *Shophetim*, Deut. xvi. 18; Josh. i. 10.

Shrub we krub, a beautiful rill of water that runs into a basin of Roman workmanship, Judg. v. 11. Why so named, *ibid.*

Shual, שועל, rendered *fox*, inquiry into the precise import of the original term, Judg. xv. 4. Dr. Kennicott's arguments to show that Samson's destruction of the standing corn of the Philistines was not effected by three hundred foxes with one hundred and fifty firebrands, but by three hundred handfuls or sheaves of corn, and one hundred and fifty firebrands, *ibid.* Reasons for rejecting the doctor's hypothesis, *ibid.*

Shuner, (*Agnes*) extraordinary longevity of this woman, Psa. xc., *in fine*.

Shushan-eduth, import of this term, Psa. lx., *in principio*.

Sibbah, סבה, inquiry into the import of this term, 1 Kings xii. 15.

Sibyl, Cumean, Virgil's description of the seat of the, Isa. xlv. 17.

Sidon, סדון, whence supposed to be derived, and its import, Prov. xxxi. 24. The mother city of Tyre, Isa. xxiii. 4.

Sikera, Σικερα, the same with the date or palm wine, according to Theodoret and Chrysostom, Isa. v. 11. See *Sakar*.

Silence, a species of reverence paid by the retinue, viziers, foreign ambassadors, &c., of an Asiatic sovereign when he goes to the mosque on any of the great festivals, Hab. ii. 20.

Siloah, brook of, where situated, Isa. viii. 6, 7.

Silver, account of the purification of, by the cupel. See *Cupel*.

Silver cord, what to be understood by this phrase, Eccles. xii. 6.

Simeon, import of this name, Gen. xxix. 33. The tribe of Simeon generally believed among the Jews to have been schoolmasters to the other tribes, Gen. xlix. 7.

Simoom, or *smoom*, account of this very destructive Eastern wind, Gen. xli. 6; Deut. xxviii. 22.

Simple, whence this word is derived, Prov. i. 4. Striking contrast between its ancient and modern acceptation, *ibid.*

Sin, import of this word, Judg. xx. 16; 1 Sam. xvii. 49; Job v. 24. Doctrine that there is no total deliverance from sin in this life stated and refuted, 1 Kings viii. 46.

Sin, wilderness of, the seventh station of the Israelites in the wilderness, where situated, Num. xxxiii. 11.

Sinai, whence this name is probably derived, Exod. iii. 1.

Sinai, wilderness of, the eleventh station of the Israelites in the wilderness, where probably situated, Num. xxxiii. 15.

Sincere, derivation and import of the term, Gen. xvii. 1; Phil. i. 10.

Sistrum of Egypt, description of the, Isa. xviii. 1. This musical instrument given in a medal of Adrian as the proper attribute of Egypt, *ibid.* In shape somewhat like the ancient lyre, *ibid.*

Sitting, common manner of, in Eastern countries, Isa. lii. 2. Account of the Asiatic mode of *sitting in state*, *ibid.*

Sitting on the ground, a token of sorrow among the ancients, Gen. xxxiii. 3; Job i. 20, ii. 13; Isa. iii. 26.

Skins of the sacrifices appertained to the priests among both Jews and Gentiles, Lev. vii. 8. The heathen priests lay upon them in their temples in hope to have future things revealed to them in their dreams, *ibid.* This superstition prevails to the present day in the Highlands of Scotland, *ibid.*

Slaves employed in the Brazils to search for particles of gold and diamonds; and by a law of the state, he who finds a diamond of a given number of carats obtains his liberty, Prov. i. 4.

Slave trade, remarks on this odious traffic, Lev. xxii. 10; Hab. ii. 12.

Sleep of the soul, from the moment of the death of the body till the resurrection, a doctrine which cannot be legitimately deduced from the sacred oracles, Job xiv. 12.

Sling, a very ancient warlike instrument, Judg. xx. 16. The inhabitants of Majorca and Minorca the most famous slingers of antiquity, *ibid.* Observations respecting the *velocity* of the ball projected from the sling, *ibid.* From what distance, according to Vegetius, expert slingers could in general hit the mark, *ibid.* Description of the sling that was in use among the Greeks and Hebrews, 1 Sam. xvii. 40. Quotation from Diodorus Siculus to show the great destructiveness of the missiles discharged by skilful hands from the slings, 1 Sam. xvii. 49.

Slot or *track* of the hart, observations on the, Psa. xvii., *in fine*.

Sloth, passage from the celebrated fable of, by Prodicus, describing the transparent garments of the ancients, Isa. iii. 23.

Sluggard, remarks on Solomon's very beautiful and instructive parable of the, Prov. xxiv. 30, *et seq.*

Smiting upon the thigh, a usual sign of deep affliction, Jer. xxxi. 19. Two quotations from the Iliad in illustration of this, *ibid.*; Ezek. xxi. 12.

Smoom, see *Simoom*.

Snare or *toils*, account of the, among the ancients, Isa. xxiv. 17, 18.

Snow, general definition of, Job xxxvii. 6. Mode of its formation, *ibid.* Appearance of a flake of snow, as seen through a magnifying glass, *ibid.* To what the *whiteness* and *lightness* of snow are owing, *ibid.* The immediate cause of the formation of snow not well understood, *ibid.* Snow an especial blessing of Providence in northern countries, *ibid.*

Snow houses in use in the East, Prov. xxv. 13.

Snow water, supposed by the ancients to have a more detergent quality than common water, Job ix. 30.

Soap, what known at present by this name probably unknown to the ancients, Mal. iii. 2.

Sofas of the Asiatics, account of the, Isa. lii. 2.

Solar light, how much it exceeds that of the full moon, Gen. i. 14. Dr. Herschel's very probable hypothesis that the solar light, abstractedly considered, is not the cause of heat, but that *heat* is the result of the action of the rays of light upon the atmosphere, Gen. i. 16.

Solar system, general view of the, Gen. i. 1; Psa. viii. 3.

Solomon, son of David, the commencement of the reign of this monarch inauspicious, 1 Kings iii. 1. His marriage of Pharaoh's daughter shown to have been a direct violation of the law of God, *ibid.* His decision of the case brought before him by the two tavern-keepers a proof of his sound wisdom, penetration, and acquaintance with human nature, 1 Kings iii. 25. Great extent of Solomon's kingdom, 1 Kings iv. 21. In what the great wisdom of Solomon consisted, 1 Kings iv. 29–33. Reasons advanced to show that this king was probably the writer of the book of Job, Preface to Job. The Iliad of Homer supposed by some to have been the work of Solomon, *ibid.* Solomon's dreadful apostacy, 1 Kings xi. 1, &c. Sketch of his reign and character, 1 Kings xi., *in fine*.

Solomon's throne, curious account of the, extracted from a Persian manuscript, 2 Chron. x., *in fine*.

Solon, law of, excluding natural children from the paternal inheritance, Gen. xxv. 6. His law respecting lost property, Lev. vi. 3.

Somerhill, (*Mrs.*) remarkable longevity of this woman, Psa. xc., *in fine*.

Son, among the Jews, was the title of a *disciple* or *scholar*, Prov. i. 8.

Son of man, import of this phrase when applied to a created being, Ezek. i. 3; when applied to our Lord Jesus Christ, *ibid.*

Song of Deborah and Barak, Kennicott's and Hales' observations on the, Judg. v., *in fine*. Their versions of it in collateral columns, *ibid.*

Song of Moses, celebrating the discomfiture of the Egyptian host, and the miraculous passage of the Israelites through the Red Sea, the earliest specimen of epic poetry extant, Exod. xv. 1. Observations on the song which Moses composed a short time before his death, Deut. xxii., *in fine*.

Song of Solomon, various opinions respecting this composition, Introduction to Solomon's Song. Harmer's view of the design of the Canticles, *ibid.* Considered by some as a regular drama, *ibid.* Dr. Mason Good considered the Canticles as a collection of sacred idyls, twelve in number, *ibid.* Scheme of the idyls, according to this celebrated critic, *ibid.* See *Canticles*.

Songs, sacred and *profane*, in great repute from very remote antiquity, Exod. xv. 1; Deut. xxxi. 19. The record of things of great importance, and of common concern, whether in verse or prose, generally sung by the ancients, Deut. xxxi. 19.

Sophocles, passage in the Antigone of, very similar to one in the book of Psalms, Psa. cxxi. 4.

Sophonites, a people mentioned by Ptolemy, whence they probably had their name, Deut. i. 1.

Sophronia, anecdote concerning, as given by Tasso in the Gerusalemme Liberata, Josh. ii., *in fine*.

Sorek, valley of, where situated, Isa. v. 2. The vine of Sorek known to the Israelites, *ibid.*

U

V

W

X

Y

Z